W9-AZB-005

THE RANDOM HOUSE ENCYCLOPEDIA

THE RANDOM
ENCYCL

HOUSE
OPEDIA

JAMES MITCHELL, EDITOR IN CHIEF

JESS STEIN, EDITORIAL DIRECTOR

RANDOM HOUSE NEW YORK

Published in New York by Random House, Inc., and simultaneously in Canada by Random House of Canada, Ltd.

a.rr/hh

Library of Congress Cataloging in Publication Data

Main entry under title:

The Random House encyclopedia.

Bibliography: pp. 2698ff.
Includes index.
1. Encyclopedias and dictionaries. I. Mitchell, James, 1939–
AG5.R25 031 77-3447
ISBN 0-394-40730-X

Manufactured in the United States of America

CONTENTS

PREFACE

The Random House Encyclopedia has been conceived as a "family bible" of knowledge for our times. Like other encyclopedias, its function is to provide access to information and to be a guide to general knowledge.

The Random House Encyclopedia is a *general* encyclopedia, a book giving basic information on all major areas of knowledge. Moreover, it has been created for ordinary people, not specialists. There are many specialist works for those requiring specialist information; our object has been to provide knowledge for everyman. It is our hope that this volume will become accepted and trusted by all who use it.

Use of an encyclopedia

An encyclopedia has to be many things to many users. For each type of use there is an ideal reference work, which, being ideal for one purpose, is of less value for other purposes.

All encyclopedias are, therefore, the result of a compromise of one sort or another: an attempt to satisfy several conflicting requirements, with varying degrees of success, or an attempt to satisfy just one requirement in an acceptable way.

The history of these works has shown that there are two principal concepts of an encyclopedia. The first is that of a comprehensive fact-book for easy quick-reference use. The second is the complete library—a collection of treatises on all subjects. In planning *The Random House Encyclopedia,* we examined these two approaches, considering the advantages and disadvantages of each type. The solution we reached—which was to take the two traditions and marry them—was made primarily with the user in mind.

The Random House Encyclopedia consists of two elements: an A–Z section that provides brief answers to factual questions and a thematic section that gives longer, illustrated expositions of more important subjects. We consider that this arrangement renders the encyclopedia more useful to the reader than if we had opted for either an alphabetical or a thematic structure alone. Moreover, the simple system of cross-reference between and within the two sections ensures that the user can quickly find his way. We have called the A–Z section the *Alphapedia* and the thematic section the *Colorpedia*. These words started as nicknames inside the publishing house, and, as nicknames will, they have stuck. I particularly apologize to classicists and etymologists about the latter; I am fully aware that, properly, the word ought to be *Chromatopedia* (teaching through color) in respect to the Greek language. No disrespect is intended. Nor, indeed, is disrespect intended to the editors of the great new *Encyclopaedia Britannica* with its *Propaedia, Micropaedia,* and *Macropaedia:* we are all in the "pedia" business, and everyone has his own solutions to the best organization of knowledge.

Level of readership

The level for which we have created *The Random House Encyclopedia* is intended to be almost a universal one. Some aspects of knowledge are more complicated than others, and so readers will find the level varies in different parts of the encyclopedia. This is quite deliberate. It is an encyclopedia for all the family.

Some younger people should be able to enjoy and to absorb the pages on the animal world, for example, from as young as ten or eleven—but the level has been set primarily for teenagers and adults.

Illustrations and text

It is not new for encyclopedias to have pictures. Early editions of the *Encyclopaedia Britannica* 200 years ago included diagrams not unlike those which appear, in color, in *The Random House Encyclopedia*. But the special emphasis given to illustrations—and particularly to explanatory diagrams—in this book will, we hope, mark something of a development in the history of encyclopedias.

The diagrams and pictures in this encyclopedia—there are more than 13,800 of them—took six years to research and make, and the information that they provide is intended to be more concise, simpler, and easier to learn from than that contained in traditional works. For a new generation brought up with television, words alone are no longer enough, and so in our *Colorpedia* section we have tried to make a new type of compact pictorial encyclopedia for a visually oriented age.

However beautiful and carefully drawn they may be, pictures on their own are still only part of the story. A strong, clear text plays an equal part in the well-balanced provision of information. The authors of the text of this encyclopedia are experts in their fields. Each word of the encyclopedia has also been read by independent academic advisers to ensure the highest possible accuracy and objectivity of content.

Simplicity

The great and the best-selling popular encyclopedias of the past have always had one thing in common—simplicity. The ability to make even complicated subjects clear, to distill, to extract the principles from behind the complicated formulas, the gift of getting to the heart of things: these are the elements that make popular encyclopedias really useful to the people who read them. We have done our best to follow these principles.

In an age of specialization there will be those who, I suppose, may be suspicious of a work that seems to paint a simplified picture of man and his knowledge. And there are, of course, always dangers in compression and selection. But there are also advantages in being able to see the forest for the trees. And of what use is knowledge if it has forever to be out of reach of ordinary people?

Perhaps the issue is really one of scale. A great multivolume encyclopedia in tens of thousands of pages is a whole universe of knowledge: it is so great and daunting that it cannot all be taken in—one can only stand in awe and study portions of the whole. But a concise work like this, massive though it may still be in some ways, is nonetheless a small enough universe for most of us to comprehend at least roughly in outline. It is in a human scale, and that is somehow reassuring.

Ideologies

The most controversial areas of any 20th-century encyclopedia are surely those that cover the study of man himself—his psychology, his social behavior (including politics), and, related to these, his interpretation of history. These are the danger areas. We have done our best to be as balanced as we can: where there is controversy we have tried to present both sides of a case; where there is uncertainty our contributors have been encouraged to say so; where there are questions we have asked them.

If a view of man does emerge from these pages, and if it sometimes seems to have a rounded look to it, that will not be because I—or the editors of or contributors to this work—have any particular ax to grind. Quite the reverse: we are much more in the traditional mold of observers who describe what they see and wonder at it and want to pass on the excitement they have learned in discovery.

Perhaps, then, there will be a value in these pages if, through the information and knowledge that they make available, they deepen the insight and respect we have for one another as persons free from the shackles of dogmatism old or new. That, if anything, is our editorial philosophy: openness, with a profound, though not sectarian, humanism in the best sense. So it was that, in planning this book, we resolved that it should not only record the incredible marvels of history and technology, but also promote a proper human balance to help its readers gain self-knowledge as well as knowledge: to help the reader use the inner as well as the outer eye.

International cooperation

We were also enormously helped by another, more practical discipline that is, perhaps, not usual in traditional publishing. The creative costs of the project we planned were, we found, going to be so high that it was immediately clear that it would be possible to make the book only on the premise that the encyclopedia's readership would be the combined reading public of all major countries of the world. And, of course, those readers would have to have a reference work that treated their own interests and preoccupations and did so in their own language. Our encyclopedia had to be international in scope and approach. Thus we decided to make an encyclopedia for the world, not just for individual nations.

We had already achieved the first part of our aim before publication—this encyclopedia is, or will be, on sale in most major countries in each country's national language. Its balance and contents have been deeply influenced by the editors of leading publishing houses all over the world, and it would be fair to say that without their contribution the encyclopedia would never have been born and could certainly never have achieved the global perspective we feel it has as a result.

The joy of knowledge

Finally, to the reader, may I say this: Please *enjoy* the book. We have had a very enjoyable time planning, writing, editing, and illustrating it. We want you to enjoy it, too.

JAMES MITCHELL
Editor In Chief

STAFF, CONTRIBUTORS, AND CONSULTANTS

Editor in Chief	James Mitchell
Editorial Director	Jess Stein
Consulting Editor	Philip W. Goetz
Executive Editors	Frank Wallis
	Stanley Schindler
	Stephen P. Elliott
Creative Director	Ed Day
Project Directors	Peter Mollman
	Harold Bull
Editorial and Graphics Advisor	Paul Anbinder

Publishing Director	Anthony Schulte

Special Contributors (Introductory Essays)

Sir Bernard Lovell
Professor of Radio Astronomy
Univesity of Manchester

Loren Eiseley
Benjamin Franklin Professor of Anthropology
University of Pennsylvania

William A. Nierenberg
Director, Scripps Institution of Oceanography
University of California

Christopher Hill
Master, Balliol College
Oxford University

Salvador E. Luria
Institute Professor of Biology
Massachusetts Institute of Technology

I. Bernard Cohen
Professor of the History of Science
Harvard University

William O. Baker
President
Bell Laboratories

Editorial Staff

Senior Editors — Erik Abranson; Ruth Binney; John Clark; Lawrence Clarke; Roger Hearn; Jane Kenrick; Ernest Kohlmetz; Max Monsarrat; Patrick Moore; John Tusa

Production Editor — Helen Yeomans; P. Martha Carlson

Project Associate — Graham Darlow

Associate Editors — Don Binney; Arthur Butterfield; Carol C. Dudley; Susan Carter Elliott; Marya Holcombe; Donald Wayne Hunt; Charyn Jones; Lesley Krauss; Albert F. May; Jenny Mulherin; Shiva Naipaul; Peter O'Connell; Nancy T. Peterson; Kathleen Roberts; David Sharpe; Jack Tresidder

Research Adviser — Jeremy Weston

Research Assistants — Dougal Dixon; Peter Furtado; Malcolm Hart; Peter Kilkenny; Ann Kramer; Lloyd Lindo, Heather Maisner; Valerie Nicholson; Elizabeth Peadon; John Smallwood; Jim Somerville

Senior Picture Researchers — Jenny Golden; Kate Parish

Picture Researchers — Roberta Guerette; Diane Hamilton; Phyllida Holbeach; Philippa Lewis; Caroline Lucas; Ann Usborne

Project Assistants — Sandra Creese; Judy Garlick

Editorial Assistants — Dianne Burch; Joyce Evison; Miranda Grinling; Jeff Groman; Gwendolyn Gunn; Susan Hannah; Elaine D. Hess; Anthony Livsey; Rebecca Lyon; Jane K. Mollman; Deborah Olderman

Design and Production Staff

Production Managers — Patricia W. Ehresmann; Howard Goldstein

Art Director — Rod Stribley

Jacket Art Director — Robert Scudellari

Design Director — Bernard Klein

Associate Art Directors — Anthony Cobb; Ted McCausland

Senior Designer — Sally Smallwood

Designers — Roasmund Briggs; Mike Brown; Lynn Cawley; Nigel Chapman; Pauline Faulks; Nicole Fothergill; Juanita Grout; Ingrid Jacob; Carole Johnson; Anne Lian; Chrissie Lloyd; Aean Pinheiro; Andrew Sutterby

Production Controllers — Jeremy Albutt; Anthony Bonsels; Jerry Grundish; Dorothy Hays; Richard Koser; John Olive

Production Assistants — Nick Rochez; John Swan

Administrative Staff

International Coordinator — Averil Macintyre

Administrative Supervisor — Diane Bell Surprenant

Administrative Assistants — Suzanne Burke; Bert Kinne; Katherine Rae; Roslyn Schindler; Carolyn Westberg

Major Contributors and Consultants

Fabian Acker, *Electrical Review;* Steven Adkins; Nancy Ahlstrom; Sidney Ahlstrom, Yale University; H. C. Allen, University of East Anglia; Derek Allinson; Leonard Amey; Robert S. Anderson; Rose Mary Anderson; Neil Ardley; Joseph J. Arnold, University of New Haven; H. R. V. Arnstein, University of London; Russell Ash; Norman Ashford, University of Loughborough; Robert Ashton, University of East Anglia; B. W. Atkinson, University of London; Anthony Atmore, Polytechnic of Central London; Philip S. Bagwell; Robert Balay, Yale University; Lynne M. Baldwin; Peter Ball; Edwin Banks, London College of Printing; Michael Banton, University of Bristol; Dulan Barber; Celia Barlow; Harry Barrett, *Fishing News;* J. P. Barron, University of London; Sergio Barzanti, Fairleigh Dickinson University; Barry Batorsky; Loring W. Batten III; W. G. Beasley, University of London; Alan Bender, General Electric Company; Lionel Bender; Eric Bergeraud; Israel Berkovitch; Howard R. Bernstein; David Berry, University College, Cardiff; M. L. Bierbrier, British Museum; A. T. E. Binsted; David Black; Maurice E. F. Block, London School of Economics; Malcolm Bochner; James Boling; Marsha Boling; Richard H. Bomback; Basil Booth, Imperial College of Science and Technology; J. Harry Bowen, University of Swansea; Charles Boyle; Bill Braddock, *The New York Times;* Tim Brennan; Mary Briggs; Robert L. Brite, University of New Orleans; John Brodrick; J. M. Bruce, Royal Air Museum; D. A. Bullough, University of St. Andrew; Sheila Butterworth; Tony Buzan; Alan R. Cane; George Carson; J. G. de Casparis, University of London; Jeremy Catto, Oxford University; Denis Chamberlain; E. W. Chanter; Barbara Charton; John Terry Chase; Colin Cherry,

Imperial College of Science and Technology; Anne C. Chittenden; A. H. Christie, University of London; Anthony W. Clare, University of London; Jeffrey G. Clarke, Center of Military History; Marsha Cochran; Katherine Cole; Sonia Cole; Mimsie G. Coleman; Jacquelin Collins; John R. Collis; Gordon Connell-Smith, University of Hull; A. H. Cook, Cambridge University; B. K. Cooper, *Railway World;* Mel Cooper; Jean Corcoran; Penelope J. Corfield, University of London; Robin Cormack, Courtauld Institute; Nona Coxhead; Patricia Crone, Warburg Institute; Geoffrey P. Crow, Imperial College of Science and Technology; J. G. Crowther; Judith G. Cuddihy; William B. Cummings; R. B. Cundall, University of Salford; Noel Currer-Briggs; Christopher Cviic, *The Economist;* John Daintith; Gordon Daniels, University of Sheffield; George Darby; G. J. Darwin, University of Reading; William Day; David Delvin; Robin Denselow; Jordan A. Deutsch; Bernard L. Diamond, University of California, Berkeley; John Dickson; Alan Dingle; Paul Dinnage; M. L. Dockrill, University of London; Frederick J. Dockstader, formerly, Museum of the American Indian; Patricia Dodd; James Dowdall; Anne Dowson; Peter M. Driver; C. W. Dugmore, University of London; Herbert L. Edlin; Pamela Egan; Robert Elia; S. R. Elliot; Gail Ernsting; H. J. Eysenck, University of London; Peter Fenwick; Francine Failkoff; Jim Flegg; Andrew M. Fleming; Antony Flew, University of Reading; Florence Fogelin; Wyn K. Ford; Paul Freeman; Kenneth Furie, *High Fidelity;* G. E. Fussell; Sue Gaisford; Kenneth W. Gatland, *Spaceflight;* Norman Gelb; John Gilbert; A. C. Gimson, University College, London; Gleb Glinka; John Glaves-Smith, Courtauld Institute; David Glen, *Fish Farming International;* S. J. Goldsack, Imperial College of Science and Technology; Richard Gombrich, Oxford University; A. F. Gomm; A. Goodwin, University of Manchester; William Gould; Robert Grant; J. R. Gray, University of London; Christopher Green, Courtauld Institute; Annette Greenbaum; Francesca Greenoak; Richard L. Gregory, University of Bristol; Bernice Grohskopf; Donna L. Groth; John M. Gunn; Bill Gunston; A. Rupert Hall, Imperial College of Science and Technology; Richard Halsey; Lynette K. Hamblin; Norman Hammond, Cambridge University; Patrick Hanks; Thomas G. Harding, University of California, Santa Barbara; Richard Harris; Randall P. Harrison, University of California, San Francisco; Cyril Hart; Jean L. Hart; Robert E. Hart; Anthony P. Harvey, British Museum; Leonore C. Hauck; Nigel Hawkes; Sarah Hayes; F. P. Heath; Peter Hebblethwaite; Frances Mary Heidensohn; Alan Hill; Robert Hillenbrand, University of Edinburgh; F. H. Hinsley; Richard Hitchcock, University of Exeter; Walter Holden; Marcia Holly; Dorothy Hollingsworth; H. P. Hope, *Farmers Weekly;* Antony Hopkins; Brian Hook, University of Leeds; Helen Houpert; Peter Howell, University of London; Kenneth Huff; Walter W. Hunsinger; K. Hunt, International Institute for Strategic Studies; Peter Hurst; Anthony Hyman; R. S. Illingworth, University of Sheffield; Oliver Impey, Ashmolean Museum; D. E. G. Irvine, British Museum; L. M. Irvine, British Museum, Alan Isaacs; Jane F. Jackson; Joseph H. Jackson; Jay Jacobs; Mary James; Anne Jamieson; Michael A. Janson; P. A. Jewell, University of London; David Johnson; Hugh Johnson; Virginia Johnson; I. E. Johnston; I. P. Jolliffe, University of London; D. E. H. Jones, University of Newcastle-upon-Tyne; Peter D'A. Jones, University of Illinois, Chicago Circle; R. H. Jones, University of Nottingham; Stephen Jones; Bernice Kaczynski; Rena Kalna; Kenneth Katzner; Hugh Kay; Martin S. Kay; Roberta S. Kay; Janet Kear; Sam Keen; Geraldine R. Keith; Eleanor Kelman; D. R. C. Kempe, British Museum; Alan Kendall; Raymond Kennedy; Michael Kenward, *The New Scientist;* John C. Keogh; John R. King, Imperial College of Science and Technology; D. G. King-Hele; Donald Kinsman, University of Connecticut; J. F. Kirkaldy, University of London; Malcolm Kitch, University of Sussex; Michael Kitson, Courtauld Institute; George C. Kohn; Henry I. Kurtz; B. C. Lamb, Imperial College of Science and Technology; Nick Landon, *Pulse;* Suzanne La Prade; J. C. Larminie; Peter Lasko, Courtauld Institute; Diana Leat; Daniel R. Lesnick; Erwin Levine, Skidmore College; Roger Lewin, *The New Scientist;* J. D. Liddell-King; Mada Liebman; Judith K. R. Linscott; Harold K. Lipset; Normal Longmate; Eric Lowenkron; John Lowry, Victoria and Albert Museum; Kenneth E. Lowther; Diana Lucas; Keith Lye; Heather S. Lyon; Peter Lyon, University of London; Nancy Macomber; Jean Macqueen; William Baird MacQuitty; Sarah Magee; Gerald A. Main; Elizabeth Martin; Jonathan Martin, Cranfield Institute of Technology; E. L. Mascall, King's College; Helen Matthews; Charles May; Christopher Maynard; Joseph Mazurkiewicz; Judith Mazurkiewicz; Martin McCauley, University of London; Sean McConville, University of Sussex; Mary McFarland; Molly McGrath; D. F. M. McGregor, University of London; Jill A. McGuire; David J. McQuade; A. J. Meadows, University of Leicester; Marcia Mermelstein; Judy Merriam; J. S. G. Miller, University of Bristol; Alarie Millington, University of London; Philip Mitchell; John Modlenhauer; Peter L. Moldon; Patrick Moore; Robin Mowat, Oxford Polytechnic; J. Michael Mullin, British Museum; Alistair Munroe; Martin Murphy; Harry E. Neal; Jacob Needleman, San Francisco State University; Donald M. Nicol, University of London; Gerald Norris; Caroline E. Oakman, University of London; S. O'Connell, University of Surrey; Michael Overman; Di Owen; A. R. D. Pagden, Oxford University; E. J. Pagel, Royal Greenwich Observatory; Carol Parker; Derek Parker; Julia Parker; Stanley Parker; Colin Murray Parkes; Geoffrey Parrinder, University of London; Moira Paterson; Walter C. Patterson; Bennett Paul; John H. Peel; D. J. Penn, Imperial War Museum; Basil Peters; D. L. Phillips; B. T. Pickering, University of Bristol; John Picton, British Museum; Susan Pinkus; C. S. Pitcher; Valerie Pitt; Alfred Plaut; A. S. Playfair; Antony Polonsky, London School of Economics; Joyce Pope, British Museum; David Porteus; Gail Porteus; B. L. Potter; Lois Powell; Steven Powell; Paulette Pratt; Antony Preston; Joanne Proctor; Frank J. Pycroft; Margaret Quass; K. Anne Ranson; D. C. Reams, Jr., University of New Haven; John Reckless; Loree Reed; Walter Reed, University of Texas at Austin; Roberta Reeder; Trevor Reese; Derek A. Reid, Royal Botanic Gardens; Robert Reinstein; Clyde Reynolds; Carol Rice; John Rivers, Zoological Society of London; Peter Roberts; Colin A. Ronan; Richard Rose, University of Strathclyde; Dean C. Rosener; Harold Rosenthal; T. G. Rosenthal; Anne Ross; William D. Routt, La Trobe University; Georgina Russell, Courtauld Institute; Charles Rycroft; Susan Saunders, University of London; Robert Schell; Michael Scherk; Leonard G. Schifrin, College of William and Mary; Robert Schindler; Judith Scott; Anil Seal, Cambridge University; Mary P. Seamen; Michael Sedgwick; Martin Seymour-Smith; Aaron Shatzman, Washington University; John Shearman, Courtauld Institute; Martin Sherwood; Roland Siiter, Montclair State College; John F. Sims, United Press International; A. C. Simpson; Christine J. Sirois; Nigel Sitwell, *Wildlife;*

Alan Sked, London School of Economics; Julie Slavin; Kenneth Slavin; Alec Xavier Snobel; Terry Snow; Margaret Sobotka; Sharon Solomon; Alexis N. Sommers, University of New Haven; Justine F. Sorrentino; Jennifer Speake; Alan H. Squires; Pamela Staples; Carolyn Stapleton; Rodney Steel, British Museum; Stella Stiegeler; Charles S. Steinger; Geoffrey Stern, London School of Economics; Maryanne Stevens, Courtauld Institute; John Stevenson, Oxford University; J. Stidworthy, British Museum; D. Michael Stoddart, University of London; Bernard Stonehouse, University of Bradford; Anthony Storr; Richard Storry, Oxford University; Anne M. Storz; P. Y. Su; Della Summers; William H. Taft, University of Missouri; Colin Taylor; John Taylor, University of London; John W. R. Taylor; R. B. Taylor; Barbara Tchabovsky; Georgette Thabault; Glynn Thomas; J. David Thomas; Harvey Tilker; Don Tills, British Museum; Jon Tinker, *New Scientist;* Gerald Tolchin, Southern Connecticut State College; M. Tregear, Ashmolean Museum; R. W. Trender, London School of Journalism; David Trump; M. F. Tuke; Christopher Tunney; Kathleen Turek; Karen Tweedy-Holmes; Sara Tykol; William D. Wagoner, University of New Orleans; Richard L. Walker, University of South Carolina; Lance Wallace; Betty C. Wallerstein; Gail Walsh; Louellen Walsh; Sally Walters; Christopher Wardle; James Wargo; D. Washbrook, University of Warwick; David Watkins; George Watkins; University of Bath; J. W. N. Watkins, London School of Economics; Anthony J. Watts; Geoff Watts, *World Medicine;* Kenneth P. Werrell; Richard G. West; Melvyn Westlake; Anthony White; P. J. S. Whitmore; G. R. Wilkinson, University of London; Eileen Williams; H. A. Williams; Bruce H. Wilson; Christopher Wilson, Courtauld Institute; Christopher Kent Wilson, Yale University; David M. Wilson, University College, London; Gwendolyn Wilson; John B. Wilson, Institute of Oceanographic Sciences; Joseph W. Wilton, formerly, University of New Haven; Philip Windsor, London School of Economics; M. J. Wise, London University; Dinah B. Witchel; Roy Wolfe, University of London; Rita S. Woodhull; David Wooding; Bernard Yallop, Royal Greenwich Observatory; Virginia Yans-McLaughlin, City University of New York; John Yudkin, University of London; Georg Zappler, formerly, Staten Island Zoo

Special Acknowledgement

The Editor in Chief wishes particularly to thank the following for all their support: Nicolas Bentley; Bill Borchard; Adrianne Bowles; Yves Boisseau; Irv Braun; Theo Bremer; *the late* Dr Jacob Bronowski; Sir Humphrey Browne; Barry and Helen Cayne; Peter Chubb; William Clark; Sanford and Dorothy Cobb; Alex and Jane Comfort; Jack and Sharlie Davison; Manfred Denneler; Stephen Feldman; Orsola Fenghi; Dr Leo van Grunsven; Jan van Gulden; Graham Hearn; *the late* Raimund von Hofmansthal; Dr Antonio Houaiss; *the late* Sir Julian Huxley; Alan Isaacs; Julie Lansdowne; Andrew Leithead; Richard Levin; Oscar Lewenstein; The Rt Hon Selwyn Lloyd; Simon macLachlan; George Manina; Stuart Marks; Bruce Marshall; Francis Mildner; Bill and Christine Mitchell; Janice Mitchell; Patrick Moore; Mari Pijnenborg; *the late* Donna Dorita de Sa Putch; Tony Ruth; Dr Jonas Salk; Guy Schoeller; Dr E. F. Schumacher; Christopher Scott; Anthony Storr; Hannu Tarmio; Ludovico Terzi; Ion Trewin; Egil Tveteras; Russ Voisin; Nat Wartels; Hiroshi Watanabe; Adrian Webster; Jeremy Westwood; Harry Williams.

ORGANIZATION OF THE ENCYCLOPEDIA

The Random House Encyclopedia is arranged in two main complementary sections—the *Colorpedia* and the *Alphapedia*. Other sections include the *Time Chart* and the *Bibliography*. The function of the *Colorpedia* section is to provide general knowledge; the function of the *Alphapedia* section is to provide brief answers to factual questions.

Many people consult an encyclopedia for quick-reference purposes—to find out facts about people, places, animals, events, etc—and, for this type of use, A–Z organization of information is by far the best. The *Alphapedia* section consists of more than 25,000 mostly short, and always concise, entries packed with comprehensive information. The reader wanting to know who won the battle of Waterloo, for example, simply looks up *Waterloo, Battle of,* in the *Alphapedia*.

For treatment of more complex topics—technological, historical, scientific—alphabetical organization is a drawback. General knowledge of this sort is best imparted by drawing together facts and presenting them in proper perspective by subject area. This is how the *Colorpedia* is organized. Within seven main subject areas—*The Universe; The Earth; Life on Earth; Man; History and Culture; Man and Science;* and *Man and Machines*—nearly 900 longer articles, each arranged over two facing pages with color diagrams and pictures, tell the unfolding story of knowledge rather like chapters in a book.

The encyclopedia can be entered in numerous ways, each of which leads the reader to related materials. Particular attention has been given to the user's need for rapid access to specific information as well as for an overview that places interrelated information in perspective. The comprehensive Table of Contents displays the subject matter in the *Colorpedia*. Almost every *Colorpedia* spread has a list of "Connections" that direct the reader to spreads with related information. The *Alphapedia* has a network of references to the *Colorpedia* as well as thousands of internal cross references.

All important *Alphapedia* entries are indexed to the *Colorpedia* pages. The index references to the *Colorpedia* are at the end of *Alphapedia* articles and are clearly indicated by a triangle (△) followed by a page reference. And every important person, place, or thing mentioned on a *Colorpedia* page has an *Alphapedia* entry. Abraham Lincoln's name, for example, is mentioned in the *Colorpedia* spread on the American Civil War—a spread whose function it is to tell the reader about the events and significance of the war. The *Colorpedia* story is not, however, interrupted to give Lincoln's biography; that would be confusing. Instead, the reader wanting to know more about him can look him up quickly in the *Alphapedia* and find all his basic biographical facts. At the end of the Lincoln article is a triangle (△) and a page reference that sends the reader to the *Colorpedia* spread on the American Civil War. The golden rule is: if in doubt, look it up in the *Alphapedia* first. That is the best place to start.

Maps

The *Colorpedia* contains 22 pages of physical maps, covering the land masses and the ocean floors. Colors used on the maps of the continents reflect those of the land areas if observed from space during the growing season, disregarding the fact that growing seasons occur at different times in different areas. On the maps of the ocean floors the colors thought to exist on the seabed are shown.

The last section of the encyclopedia is an *Atlas* of 80 pages of political maps followed by a 48-page atlas index, which contains the names and map coordinates of more than 21,000 cities and physical features. The editors have chosen a limited number of map scales to permit comparison of areas throughout the world. The coverage of the coterminous United States is all in a single scale.

Names of countries and major features extending across international boundaries are given in English, but the emphasis for all other names is on the local form. English alternates are shown where possible. For names in languages not normally written in the Roman alphabet the local official transliteration system has been used. Where no such system exists, transliteration follows closely that adopted by the United States Board of Geographic Names. Terrain characteristics are shown by use of hill shading, and political units are delineated by colored boundary markings.

The Alphapedia

The *Alphapedia* consists of more than 25,000 articles, most of them carrying cross references to other articles in the *Alphapedia,* or to the *Colorpedia,* or to both. To distinguish between cross references to articles in the *Alphapedia* and those to articles in the *Colorpedia,* references to the *Colorpedia* are preceded by the symbol △. Thus a typical *Alphapedia* article may end "*See also* Lincoln, Abraham. △ 1276," the first reference being to an *Alphapedia* article on Lincoln and the second to the *Colorpedia* spread on the American Civil War.

Articles in the *Alphapedia* are arranged on the basis of the letter-by-letter system. Strict alphabetical order is followed no matter how many words a title contains, and that system continues up to the punctuation mark. Thus *Confederate States of America* precedes *Confederation,* which in turn precedes *Confederation, Articles of.* Words in parentheses are not taken into account. Names beginning with *Mc, St,* or *SS* are alphabetized as if they were spelled out (ie, *Mac, Saint,* or *Saints*).

Titled persons with the same name are listed in the order of saints, popes, emperors, kings; untitled persons with the same surname and given names are listed chronologically by birth date. Where persons, places, and things have the same name, they are listed in that order. Places with the same name are listed by the alphabetical position of their countries; thus Athens, Greece, precedes Athens, Georgia (United States). Cities of the same name in the United States are alphabetized by states; thus Columbus, Mississippi, precedes Columbus, Ohio.

Both the *Alphapedia* and the *Colorpedia* include the equivalent metric weights and measures in parentheses.

The Colorpedia

Each *Colorpedia* section opens with a general introduction, followed by facing two-page articles on specific topics. Although these articles are in turn self-contained, they are arranged within most sections so that, read in sequence, they build to complete coverage of the subject of the section. The way in which each section is arranged is described later in this guide.

Cross references

The single most important feature of the *Colorpedia*—and, indeed, of the whole encyclopedia—is its system of cross reference. Almost every *Colorpedia* article contains a list of cross references entitled "Connections." These cross references are divided into two categories: "Read First" and "See Also." In those few *Colorpedia* articles that depend on preceding articles for complete understanding, the "Read First" entries direct the reader to the relevant preceding articles. The "See Also" entries direct him or her to related articles, in order of importance.

The text in *Colorpedia* articles carries numbers and the word "Key" in square brackets. These are direct references to the numbered illustrations and captions accompanying the main text article. "Key" is explained in the next paragraph.

Illustrations

Illustrations in the *Colorpedia* follow a logical or chronological sequence within each article. The illustration marked "Key," set in the top right-hand corner of the right-hand page, usually reflects the main theme of the article. The numbered illustrations run left to right, top to bottom on the left-hand page and then in the same way across and down the right-hand page. Many illustrations carry annotation, which is explained in the accompanying caption.

Captions

It is important to note that captions and illustrations supplement, not merely complement, the main text. The articles have been so written that there is little overlap of information between text and captions; thus, if the reader finds a necessary fact missing in the text, he or she should find that fact in the appropriate caption below.

How the Sections are Arranged

The Universe

The *Universe* section is primarily concerned with the extent of modern astronomical observations and the hypothetical analysis of systems within and beyond them. Like any scientific discipline, astronomy has its own language and tools. Fundamental ways of describing dimensions are outlined in the section's opening articles, together with a brief historical background to the development of astronomy from the ancients to the Copernican revolution.

The articles that follow discuss optical telescopes and equipment that explores the universe through invisible wavelengths such as radio and X ray.

The section then deals with the Solar System, beginning with the closest observable object, the Moon. It discusses the inner and outer planets and finally places the Sun in perspective as one of many millions of stars. The Sun's position in the stellar evolutionary sequence provides comparisons with stars of varying types from newborn nebulae to dying pulsars.

Discussion of the coherent systems of stars or galaxies extends the scope of the section to the observable limits. Beyond the galaxies are quasars, possibly 6,000 light-years away and shining as brightly as 200 complete galaxies. Their nature leads directly to speculations on the origin of the universe itself.

The section's concluding articles are concerned with attempts to place man's observational platform beyond the limiting effects of the Earth's atmosphere. Following a brief historical outline of space achievements to date, eight articles discuss the future of man's exploration of the universe.

The Earth

The *Earth* section falls broadly into two parts. The first deals with the physical nature of the Earth; the second, with man's utilization—and exploitation—of it. A consideration of the gross structure of our planet—its interior and its crust—leads to articles on global tectonics, earthquakes and volcanoes, and then to an article on the shape of the Earth. The eight physical maps that follow are interspersed with satellite pictures of the Earth's surface.

From a consideration of the atmosphere, the source of weather and climate, the section proceeds to nine articles on chemical, physical, and geological oceanography.

The part of the Earth of most immediate importance to man—the solid surface—is dealt with next. Crystallography, mineralogy, and petrology are described, together with the formation of mountains and highlands and their weathering by waters, ice, and winds. Deserts and coastlines find their place here, too.

After four articles that enable the reader to understand how geologists unravel the history of the Earth by "reading the rocks," the section deals with economic geology: the prospecting for and exploitation of ores, fuels, and other energy sources. The effect of economic geology on the environment is dealt with in five articles.

An article on land uses serves as a link to the second subsection on agrarian sciences. This subsection is put into perspective with an opening article on world food resources. The history of agriculture, soil science, irrigation, and the use of fertilizers and of pesticides are covered before the focus is directed to food crops, herbs and spices, and crops for industry.

A discussion of stock breeding, farm animals and their products, fisheries, fish farming, and edible fish and seafoods concludes with an article on the way food is preserved. Finally, the section deals with the future of food, the projection into the future of the problems with which the discussion of agriculture opened.

Life on Earth

The *Life on Earth* section begins with a brief review of the origin of life. This is followed by descriptions of the structure and functions of the cell and the forces of evolution and genetics that have molded cells into the living organisms that inhabit the Earth.

The clearest way to study animals and plants is to review systematically the major groups into which they are classified, beginning with the simplest organisms, the bacteria and viruses. The plant kingdom is treated next because plants preceded animals in evolutionary history.

The articles on animals begin with descriptions of animal classification, anatomy, and behavior. These are followed by reviews of single-celled animals and of such varied creatures as worms, jellyfish, snails, and sea urchins, all of which are invertebrates, or animals without backbones. Animals with backbones, the vertebrates, of which man himself is one, conclude the articles on classification. The anatomy and behavior of fish, amphibians, reptiles, birds, and mammals are explained here.

The section then discusses the detailed evolution of the main groups of plants and animals from the simplest to the most complex, through panoramic reconstructions of the Earth's landscape as it probably appeared millions of years ago.

Although it is convenient to "partition" plants and animals into groups for simple description, each is adapted for life in a particular environment. In the second half of the section, the Earth's main environmental regions are examined. The survey of life on Earth ends with a review of man's influence on the organisms with which, for both ill and good, he shares the planet.

Man

As man is a distinct species, this section opens with the story of his evolution. The physical make-up of humans is explored next, system by system, organ by organ, and then the various human diseases, and their cures, are considered.

But humans are much more than physical machines; their minds too are subject to disorders, so the major mental illnesses are examined, with their symptoms, effects, and cures.

The various branches of psychology have many answers to the question "What is man?" First the development of the individual from newborn baby to adolescent is explored. Then the social, psychological, and practical problems and challenges that face the individual are dealt with. Finally, there is a short composite portrait of man drawn from many thinkers and viewpoints that includes such topics as consciousness, predestination, and free will.

The exploration of the individual finishes with the distinctive answers of mythology, religion, and philosophy.

The second part of the section explores man the social creature, since it is impossible to understand human beings without looking at their interrelationships. Anthropology, or the study of primitive man, has shed an enormous amount of light on the many different social institutions that have evolved, and this part of the section attempts to show how the relationships and conflicting needs of any group of people are channeled so as to minimize tension and maximize cooperation. Man's political and legal systems are also covered here.

Finally, man at work and play is examined from the psychological, social, and economic points of view.

History and Culture

History depends on records and primarily on written ones. The section therefore begins by considering the earliest civilizations of which written records exist.

Greece and Rome are given considerable prominence because of their direct influences on a large part of the modern world; there is a series of articles on contemporary affairs in Asia; then the rise of Europe is traced to the point where, through the efforts of its explorers, it became involved with the rest of the world. At that point the opportunity is taken to consider the areas Europeans set out to explore. The European thread is picked up again with articles on the roots of our contemporary patterns of social and economic organization.

As trade expanded and the world was more fully explored because the technology of sea travel made it possible for greater quantities of men and goods to be moved more swiftly from one country to another, the world gradually took on a much more international aspect. That theme is traced through to the 19th century.

When the 20th century is reached, the strong common international elements of different countries are grouped and treated collectively, but the largest countries and those outside the orbit of the advanced industrial nations still receive special consideration, as do specific circumstances (such as the wars of Indochina). The section concludes with twenty spreads on the American experience.

Articles on the history of the arts fall adjacent to those on the history of the civilizations that bore the most significant artistic fruit. To give a full picture of any given age, nation, or trend, works of art have also often been used to illustrate history.

Man and Science

Traditionally, science can be divided into various disciplines, and this division sometimes suggests that the different subject areas are self-contained. The aim of the *Man and Science* section of the encyclopedia is to show how, in fact, the various branches of science interrelate, and at the same time to organize the subject into a series of coherent sections.

After an introductory account of the history of science, a series of articles on mathematics emphasizes the uses to which mathematics is put in the modern world. The rules concerning numbers and their theory lead through basic arithmetic to measurement and algebra. Graphs, logarithms, and the "modern math" of sets and groups is followed by an account of calculus. Plane geometry, trigonometry, and solid geometry serve to introduce the ideas of symmetry, topology, and mathematical mapping. The subsection concludes with articles on statistics and probability.

After discussing atomic physics, the section continues by considering the way forces act on stationary and moving objects. Sound is a form of energy; articles on sound relate it to forces and vibrations.

The states of matter—gas, liquid, and solid—are dealt with at the atomic level and related to heat and temperature, which are measures of atomic activity. Light, color, and the way light behaves in reflection and refraction introduce a basic concept of modern physics: relativity. The theories of electricity and magnetism lead to articles on semiconductors and electronics.

The chemistry subsection begins with a definition of the subject and a review of the chemical elements. The idea of chemical combination is then developed, with accounts of the overlap between electricity and chemistry and the modern methods of chemical analysis. The section concludes with the basic principles of organic chemistry and biochemistry—the chemistry of living things.

Man and Machines

The *Man and Machines* section begins with the Stone Age and proceeds to describe man's technological development up to the age of steel. Articles on the extracting and shaping of the metals used today lead to a discussion of building techniques, both simple and complex. This part of the section also deals with other materials, such as rubber, plastics, cloth, and paper.

After a description of the basic types of engines, the section goes on to deal with steam, oil, gas, wind, flowing water, nuclear fuels, and coal and electricity as sources of power and discusses ways in which they can be most economically used.

Machines—even the most complicated ones—use only a few basic principles, and these are dealt with next. Four articles on electronic machines—including computers—conclude the subsection.

Transportation technology is traced from ships, hydrofoils, hovercraft, and submarines through such land vehicles as carriages, bicycles, motorcycles, cars, and buses to the railroads of the future. Air travel begins with the balloon and culminates with spacecraft.

It is an important, if disagreeable, fact that much of the progress made in technology has come as a result of war. The *Man and Machines* section recognizes this by devoting almost a dozen articles to the development of weapons, concluding with a discussion of nuclear, chemical, and biological warfare.

Civil engineering—roads, airports, tunnels, bridges, harbors, canals, dams, water supply, and sewage treatment—as well as communications and chemical engineering are discussed before the section concludes with an account of the construction and workings of various everyday machines and mechanisms, from zippers to washing machines.

The Time Chart

The chart opens at 4000 BC and covers milestones in politics, religion and philosophy, music, literature, art and architecture, and science and technology. A special section covers American history. The chart may be used in three ways. First, readers who wish to get the flavor of a period may do so by reading the introductory paragraphs to each subject. These paragraphs, which are set in bold type, sum up the events covered on each two-page spread of the chart. Second, the chart may be used to follow the development of a particular discipline, such as philosophy, through the ages. Third, the chart may be used to discover what progress was being made in other fields at the time a particular discovery was made or a particular event took place. Thus the reader who finds, say, a reference to the invention of the steam engine in a *Colorpedia* article may turn to the *Time Chart* and discover against what political, philosophical, artistic, and scientific background the discovery was set.

The periods of time covered by each two-page spread of the *Time Chart* shorten as the present is approached, so that proportionately more space is given to recent events.

Illustrations seek to give an impression of some of the most important events and developments in the period covered by each two-page spread. Wherever possible, contemporaneous material is used.

Because the illustrations are of different widths they do not necessarily fall precisely into the dated columns into which each page is divided. In the earlier periods, in which dating is less certain than it is in modern times and material less available, the editors have chosen to set the illustrations in the order that best characterizes the events covered by the spreads.

From the rise of Greece onward (that is, from the spread entitled "The birth of philosophy" through to the present), illustrations are set in precise chronological order. Specific dates are included in captions to the illustrations only where there is no such specific reference to the illustration in the text itself.

The Bibliography

The *Bibliography* of approximately 1,500 citations follows the *Alphapedia* and is organized topically in the same sequence as the seven sections of the *Colorpedia*. Each section begins with a list of the significant periodicals that report on events in the field. The sections are divided into major-category subsections so the reader can pursue specialized interests if he wishes. Citations in each category are listed alphabetically by author.

COLORPEDIA: CONTENTS

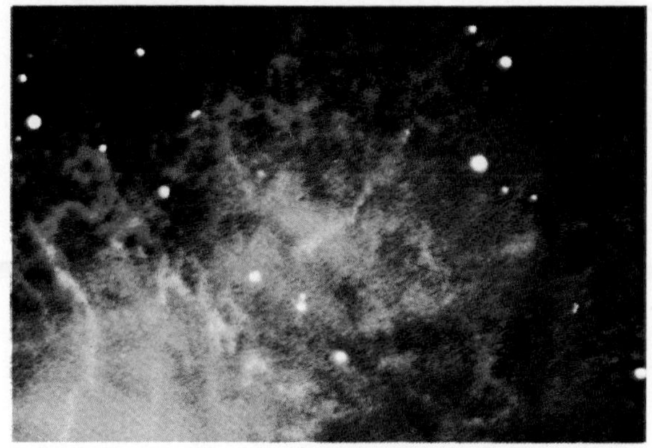

THE UNIVERSE

THE EARTH

LIFE ON EARTH

MAN

HIC HAROLD MARE NAV

HISTORY AND CULTURE

MAN AND SCIENCE

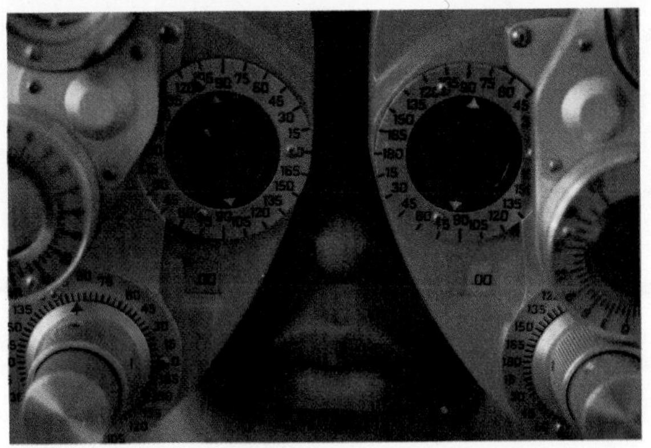

MAN AND MACHINES

TIME CHART: CONTENTS

CIRCIVS
VEL TRESIIAS

ATLAS: CONTENTS

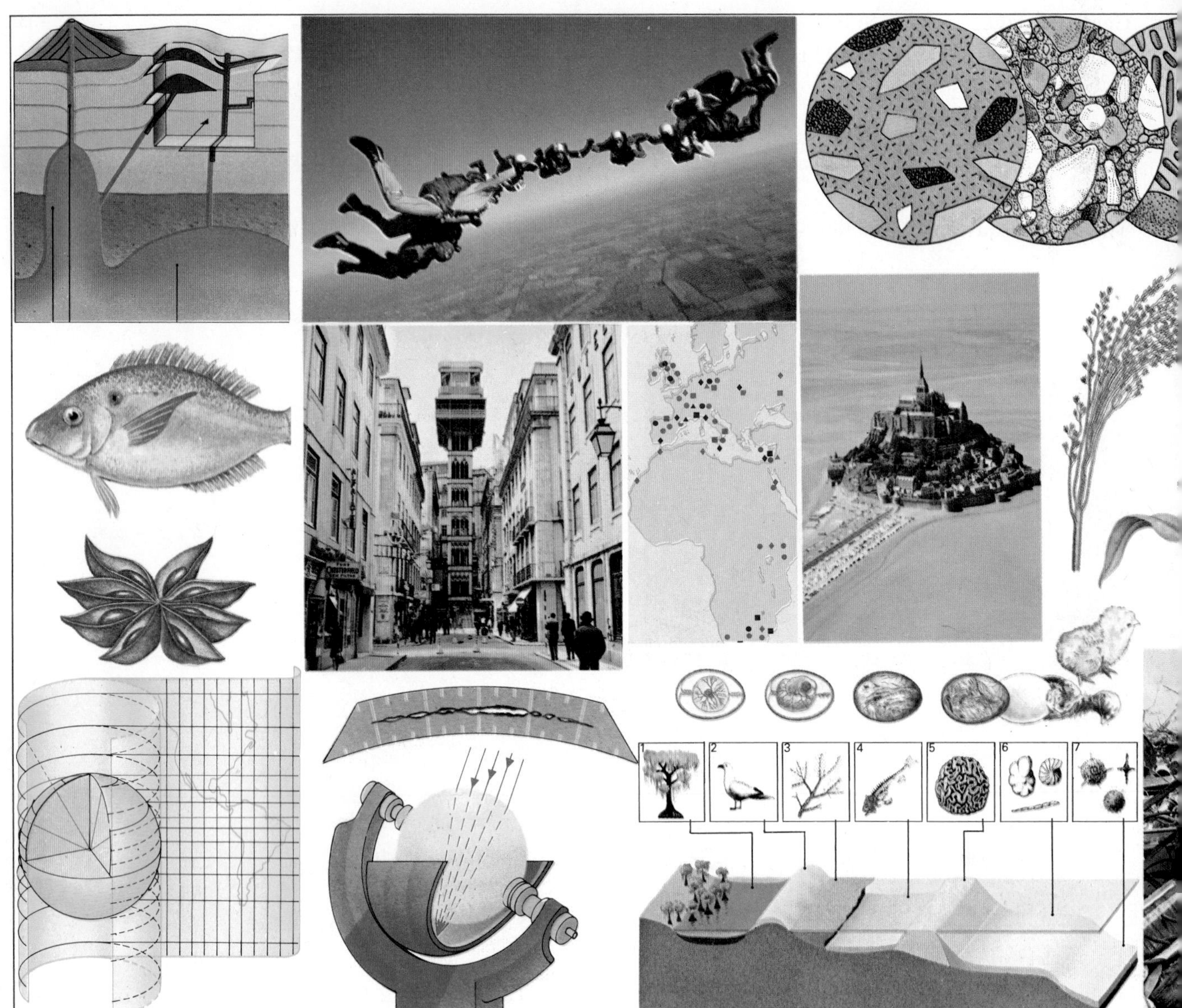

UV
IR

COLORPEDIA

THE UNIVERSE

THE UNIVERSE

by Sir Bernard Lovell

Throughout the ages astronomical discovery has stretched the imagination of the human mind. The transference from the belief in a flat Earth to a globe that could be circumnavigated must have been exceedingly difficult. (Indeed, the direct visual and photographic evidence of the sphericity of the Earth awaited the high-flying aircraft and Earth satellites of our own age.) In the 16th and 17th centuries the recognition that the Earth is not fixed at the center of the universe created immense turmoil in the human mind. The comprehensive models developed by Aristotle in the 4th century BC and by Ptolemy in the 2nd century AD provided explanations of the motions of the heavenly bodies on the assumption that the Earth is fixed at the center of the system of heavenly bodies. In the Ptolemaic system each planet moved in a small circle whose center was carried around the Earth in a larger orbit; for 14 centuries astronomers used this as the basis for calculation of the planetary positions.

The Sun appears to rise in the east in the morning, moving across the sky and setting in the west in the evening. The concept that this movement of the Sun might be a phenomenon associated with the rotation of the Earth seemed to defy common sense. When the proposition was made by Copernicus about 500 years ago, Luther declared, "The fool will turn the whole science of astronomy upside down." But, as Holy Writ declares, it was the Sun—and not the Earth—which Joshua commanded to "stand still." In 1508, Copernicus wrote an astronomical commentary in which he said, "What appears to us as motions of the Sun arises not from its motion but from the motion of the Earth," and his heliocentric theory, published in the famous *De Revolutionibus Orbium Coelestium* in 1543, the year of his death, marks a vital stage in the development of human thought.

The Copernican theory dethroned the Earth from its hierarchical static position at the center of the Solar System, and, with the invention of the telescope and its gradual improvement over the next few centuries, man's interest turned to the stars. It is curious that, for nearly another four centuries after the acceptance of the Copernican theory, the Sun and the Solar System were believed to be at the center of the stellar universe. The decade following 1918 was the critical epoch during which astronomical measurements finally eroded man's fundamental egocentric concept of his place in the universe. These years mark a period of revolutionary progress in our understanding of the structure of the Milky Way and of the larger-scale organization of the cosmos. This emergence of a new understanding followed the discovery of a means for measuring the distances of stars far removed from the Solar System. For the past century it had been possible to measure the distance of the nearer stars by the straightforward trigonometric method of measuring their displacement against the background of faint stars when the Earth is at opposite points of its orbit around the Sun. The first measurement of this type was made by Friedrich Bessel (1784–1846) in 1838. Even with the advent of photographic techniques this trigonometric method had been extended only to distances of about 100 light-years by the end of the century, by which time the distance of a few thousand stars had been determined. The discovery in 1908 by Henrietta Leavitt (1868–1921) of the relationship between the period of variability and the apparent magnitude of the Cepheid variables—pulsating stars that fluctuate regularly in brightness—and the calibration by Harlow Shapley (1885–1972) in terms of absolute magnitude instantly led to the possibility of a great extension in the distance measurements. Immediately there was a revolution in our understanding of the larger-scale structure of the universe.

Shapley studied the Cepheid variables in the globular clusters—areas in our Galaxy that contain dense concentrations of stars. By 1918 he had measured the distances of 25 of the 100 known objects of this type and found that they are at great distances from the Sun—15,000 to 100,000 light-years. The clusters are unevenly distributed over the sky—a third are concentrated in the neighborhood of the Sagittarius star cloud—and Shapley concluded that the Sun is far removed from the center of the Milky Way system of stars. His work marked the final destruction of the age-old egocentric

Professor of Radio Astronomy, University of Manchester (England); Director of the Nuffield Radio Astronomy Laboratories, Jodrell Bank (England); Fellow of the Royal Society; Honorary Member of the American Academy of Arts and Sciences; Honorary Member of the New York Academy; author of *Man's Relation to the Universe; Discovering the Universe; The Origins and International Economics of Space Exploration; The Story of Jodrell Bank; Out of the Zenith; The Individual and the Universe,* etc.

concept of man's place in the universe. The 100 billion stars of the Milky Way are not arranged symmetrically with ourselves at the center. They lie in a flattened disk that extends for 100,000 light-years, with the Sun lying 33,000 light-years from the central region. The structure of this star system is complex and no astronomer today can give a wholly agreed-upon account of its evolution.

The contemporary achievements of the radio astronomers who have been able to study the neutral hydrogen gas in the Milky Way soon led to a definitive picture of the spiral structure of the Galaxy, but these measurements have also raised many new difficulties. It is accepted that the Galaxy is rotating with its arms trailing like a viscous fluid. At our distance from the center we rotate once in 230 million years, whereas at a tenth of this distance the rotation rate is once in 28 million years. We know that of the total mass of the Galaxy, equivalent to about two trillion Suns, only about 2 percent is in the form of dust and gas, most of which (nearly 99 percent) is in the form of hydrogen gas. The irregular distribution of this gas and the recent discovery of small amounts of other complex molecules (including water) raise challenging problems.

One of the remarkable features in the structure of the Galaxy is that in the central regions the mass is composed of old red stars—within 2,000 light-years the gas contributes only about 1 percent of the total mass. On the other hand, in the spiral arms, where the Sun is situated, the ratio is markedly different—the stars are predominantly young blue stars and the gas represents about 20 percent of the mass. We do not know why these differences occur. At least it can no longer be assumed that the central regions and the spiral arms formed simultaneously—indeed, one view is that the arms were ejected from the nucleus of the Galaxy at a late stage in its formation.

We believe that the contemporary observations of the gas clouds in the spiral arms provide good evidence that new stars are forming in these clouds. The results obtained by radio astronomers, using radio telescopes working at very short wavelengths to study these gas clouds, have therefore been of special significance. Neutral hydrogen emits a spectral line at a wavelength of 21cm. Similarly, other molecules have characteristic spectral-line features, but until recently no one envisaged the possibility of finding evidence for them in the interstellar medium. In 1963 the hydroxyl radical (OH) was detected, and in the three years following 1969 the spectral lines characteristic of another 25 radicals were found. Since that time the number of molecules known to exist in space has steadily increased. The subject of astrochemistry has arisen, and a scientific basis has now been established for the speculation that organic evolution may have occurred elsewhere in space.

Shapley's measurements on the globular clusters in 1918, which so quickly led to a radically new understanding about the Milky Way and also to a host of formidable unsolved problems, was one of two major discoveries during the years immediately following World War I. The 100-inch telescope on Mt. Wilson had just been commissioned, and with this instrument Edwin Hubble (1889–1953) obtained the first definitive evidence that the Milky Way Galaxy did not comprise the whole universe. There had been speculations for a century that some of the nebulous objects seen in the heavens might be separate stellar systems outside the Milky Way. Once more the ability to measure distances using the Cepheid variables provided the answer. In 1926, Hubble published the results on 400 nebulae in which he had measured the light variation of Cepheid variables. He found that they were at great distances from the Milky Way. Hubble's proof of the extragalactic nature of these star systems was a major event in the history of astronomy. So, too, were the observations he published a few years later on the relation between the distance of these nebulae and the shift toward the red end of the spectrum of their spectral line. Interpreting the Red Shift as a Doppler effect (that is, the observed shift of the light from a star toward a lower wavelength as the distance between the light source and the observer increases), he found that the speed of recession increased linearly with the distance of the nebulae and thereby established the observational foundation for the belief in the large-scale expansion of the universe.

When Hubble published these results, he estimated that with the sensitivity of the 100-inch Mt Wilson telescope it was possible to penetrate 140 million light-years into space, which encompassed two million extragalactic nebulae, and that the speed of recession at these limits of penetration was about 2,000 miles per second. Results published in 1975, obtained with the new Anglo-Australian telescope at Siding Spring in Australia, refer to nebulae at least five magnitudes fainter than the faintest objects observable by Hubble. The number of observable extragalactic objects is estimated to be 100 million, but at these limits the number is still increasing at the rate of about two or three times per magnitude. Some of these objects are immensely far away—billions of light-years—and receding at more than half the velocity of light.

The great extension of our knowledge about the distant regions of space and time during the last half-century has also been accompanied by a radical revision of our ideas about the nature of the extragalactic system. Hubble found that the extragalactic nebulae were primarily of two types. The spherical and elliptical galaxies exhibiting little or no structure comprised about one-fifth of the nebulae he measured. Apart from a small percentage of irregular objects, he classed the remainder as spiral galaxies, and he believed that there is an evolutionary progression from the ellipticals to the spirals. Doubts about this evolutionary sequence arose with the discovery that the stars in the elliptical galaxies were mostly old, whereas the young stars were in the arms of the spiral galaxies. It was the discoveries made with the radio telescopes after 1950, however, that finally shattered belief in any such straightforward ordered sequence.

This new and confusing era began in 1951, when a strong radio source in Cygnus was identified with a peculiar image on a photograph taken with the 200-inch telescope on Mt Palomar. The Red Shift measurements on this faint object established the distance as 700 million light-years, and the double nature of the image led to the impression that this was a case of two galaxies in collision. With the rapid discovery of more objects of this type, soon to be known as radio galaxies, and the realization that extremely large amounts of energy were involved, the idea of collisions was abandoned. Additionally, more detailed radio studies revealed that many of the radio galaxies consisted of two strong centers of emission straddling the optical image, and the view that some violent disruptive event has occurred in the nuclei of the galaxies has gained favor. The strength of the radio signals from these radio galaxies encouraged the optical identification of more and more distant objects. In 1959 an important stage was reached with the radio and optical identification of a galaxy in Boötes with a Red Shift implying a recessional velocity of 40 percent of the velocity of light and a distance of 4½ billion light-years.

The attempt to find even more distant objects led to a surprising discovery. Objects, which from their radio properties were believed to be even more distant, were

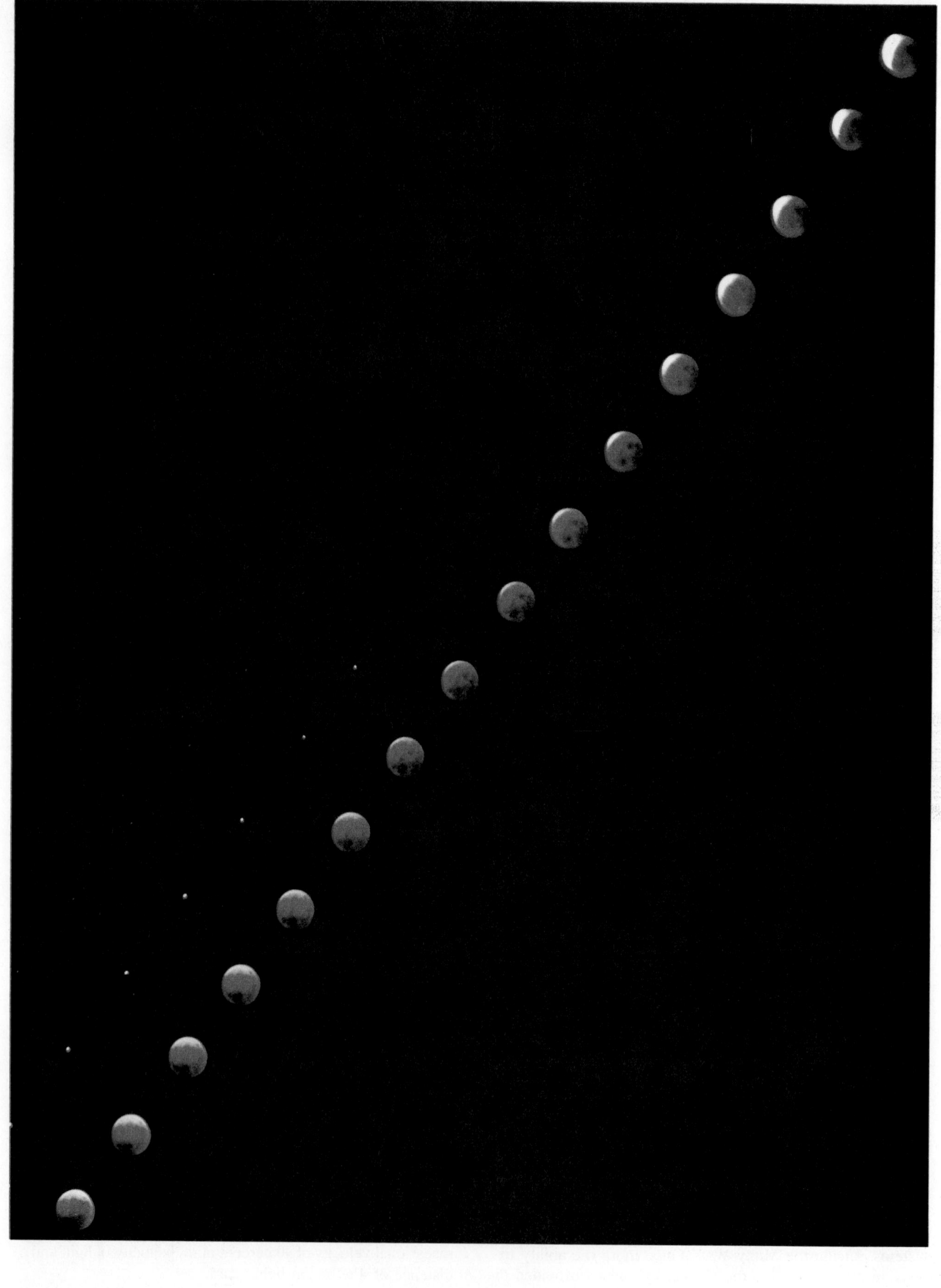

identified in 1960 with photographic images having a starlike appearance. They were characterized by their unusual intensity in the blue region of the spectrum and for several years were thought to be a new type of star in the Milky Way. Then, in the spring of 1963, Maarten Schmidt at Mt Palomar succeeded in the attempt to identify the spectral features of one of these objects. In fact, they were not local to the Milky Way but, on the contrary, possessed the largest Red Shifts of any objects known. They soon became known as quasars, and since that time about 500 have been identified. Most of them have Red Shifts indicating recessional velocities of more than half the velocity of light, and a few are known in which the implied recessional velocities are of the order of 80 percent of the velocity of light. Their distances depend on the cosmological model adopted for the universe, but, on the assumption that the Red Shifts are wholly associated with the cosmological expansion of the universe (and it must be said that there is still no unanimous agreement on this point), these high Red Shift quasars are probably about 7 billion light-years distant.

The difficulty of finding an explanation for these phenomena in the remote regions of the universe is very great. For example, we do not understand how the quasars generate their vast output of energy—especially since in many cases the energy appears to be generated in volumes of space that are exceedingly small by astronomical standards. There has been much theoretical speculation about the problem of gravitational collapse and the existence of super-dense matter in the nuclei of the quasars. It is remarkable that radio galaxies and quasars, which were beyond imagination when Hubble established the existence of extragalactic objects, should now play such a vital role in our attempts to understand the universe.

At least the avenue by the discovery of radio galaxies and quasars led to an optimistic assessment that we might soon obtain a decisive answer to a major cosmological problem. The observed rate of expansion of the universe seemed to imply that the primeval material must have existed 10 billion years ago in a highly condensed state. In that case the possibility of studying quasars with a "look-back" time of more than three-quarters of the time since the beginning of the expansion offered hope that the early history of the universe would be revealed. The attempts to interpret these observations within a cosmological framework led to great dispute—especially between the adherents of the steady-state and evolutionary cosmologies. Important and probably decisive evidence came unexpectedly from an entirely different source. In 1965, scientists at the Bell Telephone Laboratories in New Jersey devised equipment designed for communication tests using US balloon satellites. They found that the signals from the sky exceeded by 100 times the noise level they had anticipated and furthermore that those signals were uniform from all parts of the sky. Their initial claim that the signals were the relic radiation from the initial hot and dense state of the universe 10 billion years ago has subsequently received substantial confirmation from many other measurements by radio telescopes and by equipment carried in rockets and balloons to high altitude.

One of the most remarkable features of contemporary science is that we now appear to have this direct evidence of the state of the universe only seconds after the beginning of the expansion, when the temperature of the primeval material was billions of degrees. The possibility that the universe evolved from a dense initial condition was embraced by Einstein's general theory of relativity in 1917, but the contemporary observational evidence in favor of such an initial state poses a severe problem. The singularity in the solution of the equations implying that at zero time the universe was of infinitesimal dimensions and of infinite density has often been regarded as a mathematical difficulty arising from the assumption that the universe is uniform. But the measurements of the relic radiation now indicate that the universe does possess a high degree of uniformity. Within the framework of the contemporary laws of physics it seems possible to envisage a physical state where the entire primeval material existed within a universe of dimensions 10^{-33} cms—a condition predicted to exist 10^{-43} seconds after the beginning of the expansion. In the approach to a physical description of the beginning of time we reach a barrier in contemporary theory at this point. The problem as to whether or not this really is a fundamental barrier to a scientific description of the initial state of the universe, and the associated conceptual difficulties in the consideration of a single entity at the beginning of time, are questions of outstanding importance in modern thought.

Whereas we can observe the past history of the universe for many billions of years, we can only speculate about its future history. Will the universe continue to expand forever, or will it eventually collapse upon itself to another state of high density? There are clear observational tests to be applied in the attempt to answer this question—tests, for example, to determine whether the strictly linear relation between Red Shift and distance breaks down at great distances, and whether the density of the universe is greater or less than 2×10^{-29} grams per cubic centimeter. If it is greater, the gravitational forces will eventually overcome the forces of expansion, and the universe will collapse. These types of measurements are fraught with difficulties that have not yet been surmounted, and we do not know the answer.

The immense advances in our knowledge of the universe have been related to our ability to study the universe over a wide range of the spectrum. The first great advance came immediately after World War II, when the new techniques of radio astronomy emerged. Then, with the launching of Sputnik 1 in 1957, another era opened because it became possible to dispatch scientific instruments into space and so evade the problems posed by the Earth's atmosphere. The entire spectrum embracing gamma rays, X-rays, and the long-wave radio waves has now been thrown open for investigation. Even from the earliest results it is evident that only one prediction is safe: Our future description of the universe and all its component parts will change continuously, as it has done for centuries past.

The restless sky

Astronomy is the oldest of all the sciences. It was a natural and long-held assumption that the Earth must be flat and lie at rest in the center of the universe, with the entire sky revolving around it once every 24 hours; but at an early stage it was also clear that many of the celestial bodies had relative motions of their own.

Movements in our sky

The Moon was seen to shift quickly in position against the starry background, and the Sun, of course, had its own motion. Then there were occasional spectacular phenomena; sometimes the Sun was blotted out during a solar eclipse and sometimes the Moon became strangely dim when full. It was not then known that a solar eclipse occurs when the Moon passes between the Sun and Earth, casting a shadow on the Earth, or that a lunar eclipse occurs when the Sun, Earth, and Moon are in line and the Moon enters Earth's shadow. But it has been suggested, with good evidence, that some of the old stone circles were primitive eclipse computers [Key].

The Greeks recognized that the five bright planets—Mercury, Venus, Mars, Jupiter, and Saturn—moved against the stars and were thus fundamentally different from them. The constellation patterns remained unchanged over long periods, leading to the thought that the stars were fixed on a sphere revolving around the Earth.

The planets were regarded as being closer to the Earth, and it was thought that they, like the Sun and Moon, moved around the Earth between the Earth's surface and the sphere of the so-called "fixed stars." The old system was perfected by Ptolemy (*c.* AD 90–168). In the Ptolemaic system [1], all celestial orbits were assumed to be perfectly circular. Since the observed movements of the planets did not conform to the idea of circular motion at uniform velocity, however, it was necessary to introduce complications such as the epicycle, which described the movement of a planet as a small circle the center of which (the deferent) moved around the Earth in a circle.

A few of the earlier Greek philosophers, notably Aristarchus (310–230 BC), had believed that the Earth moved around the Sun, but the Sun-centered, or heliocentric, theory was generally rejected until the work of Copernicus (1473–1543), a Polish canon, made its impact in the sixteenth century. Copernicus took the drastic step of removing the Earth from its proud central position and put the Sun there instead [2]. He retained, however, perfectly circular orbits and was even compelled to retain epicycles. The modern phase of astronomy dates from the publication of his great book *De Revolutionibus Orbium Coelestium* in 1543.

Revolutionary outlooks

Inevitably, the Copernican system was strongly opposed. Tycho Brahe (1546–1601), the Danish astronomer who was the most thorough observer of pre-telescopic times, believed the planets to move around the Sun while the Sun and Moon moved around the Earth [3]. When Tycho died his observations of the positions of the stars and the movements of the planets came into the possession of his last assistant, Johannes Kepler (1571–1630), who used them

CONNECTIONS

See also
40 Measuring the rest less sky
1442 Alchemy and the a of reason
1444 Mathematics and civilization
1006 Greek science
1160 Science and techn ogy 1500–1700
1206 China from 1368 t *c.* 1800
850 Religion and the plight of modern m

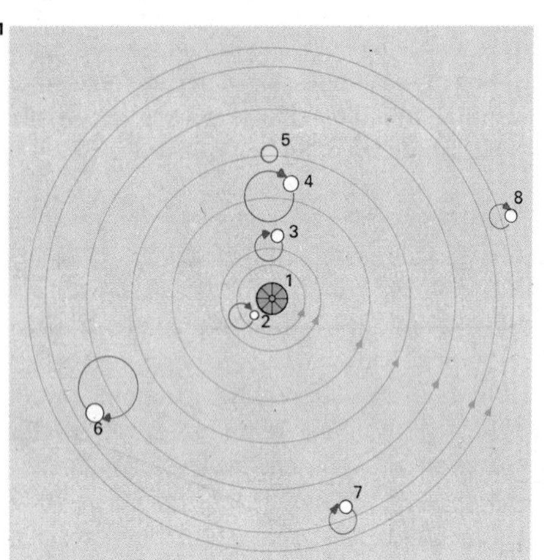

1
2
3
4
5
6
7
8

1 In the Ptolemaic system, the Earth [1] lies at rest in the center of the universe. Around it move the Moon [2], Mercury [3], Venus [4], the Sun [5], Mars [6], Jupiter [7], and Saturn [8], each body moving in a small epicycle.

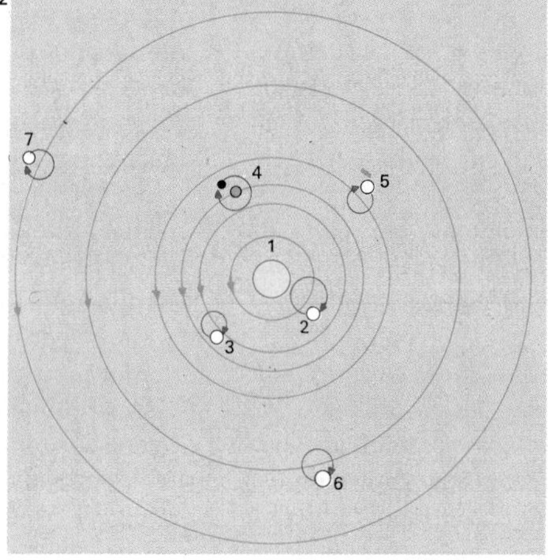

1
2
3
4
5
6
7

2 The Copernican theory places the Sun [1] in the center of the Solar System, orbited by Mercury [2], Venus [3], the Earth [4], Mars [5], Jupiter [6], and Saturn [7]. Copernicus's book was published in 1543. His theory met strong opposition from the Church. Copernicus retained both circular orbits and epicycles in his heliocentric theory.

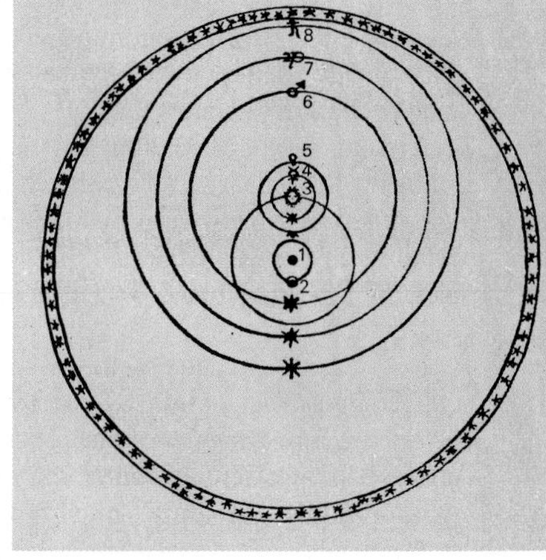

1
2
3
4
5
6
7
8

3 Tycho Brahe believed that the Earth [1] was the center of the Solar System, orbited by the Moon [2] and the Sun [3]. The planets Mercury [4], Venus [5], Mars [6], Jupiter [7], and Saturn [8] moved around the Sun with the stars beyond.

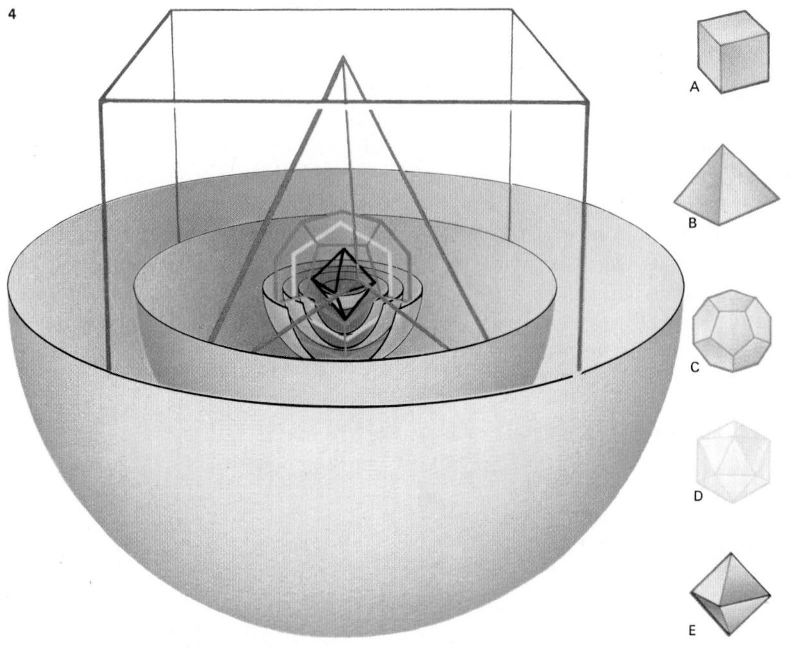

4
A
B
C
D
E

4 Kepler's theories derived from the work of the ancient Greeks, Copernicus, and Tycho Brahe. He believed that Euclid's "five regular solids" – the cube [A], tetrahedron [B], dodecahedron [C], icosahedron [D], and octahedron [E] – could be fitted inside the orbits of the planets, reasoning incorrectly that there were only five such solids and five spaces between the six known planets: Mercury, Venus, Earth, Mars, Jupiter, and Saturn. It was, however, Kepler's brilliant elaboration of Copernicus's heliocentric theory, based upon observations made by Tycho Brahe, that led him to his three principles of planetary motion. Kepler was both a mathematical genius and a mystic.

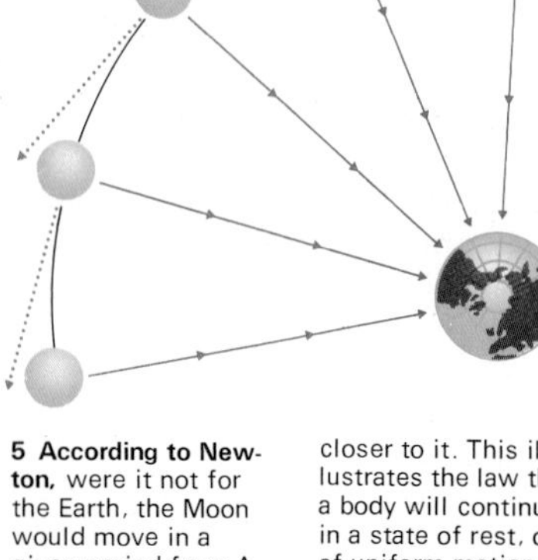

5
A1
A
A2

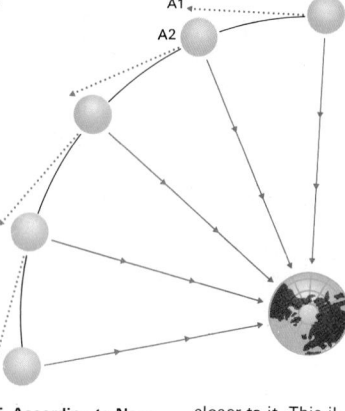

5 According to Newton, were it not for the Earth, the Moon would move in a given period from A to A1, but because of Earth's pull, the actual movement is from A to A2. The Moon keeps "falling" toward the Earth, although it comes no closer to it. This illustrates the law that a body will continue in a state of rest, or of uniform motion in a straight line, unless acted upon by an outside force. This law was laid down in Newton's *Philosophiae naturalis principia mathematica.*

well. After years of work Kepler realized that the planets move around the Sun not in circles but in ellipses; and between 1609 and 1618 he published his three fundamental laws of planetary motion. The first law states that the orbit of a planet is an ellipse, with the Sun at one of the foci. The second law states that a planet moves at its fastest when it is closest to the Sun. The third law provides a definite relationship between a planet's sidereal period (that is, the time taken for the planet to complete one journey around the Sun) and its distance from the Sun. Using Kepler's laws it became possible to draw a scale map of the Solar System.

The revolution in outlook was completed by Isaac Newton (1642–1727), whose book—usually called the *Principia* [5], published in 1687—laid the foundations of all subsequent work. By then the distance of the Sun from the Earth was known with reasonable accuracy and it had become clear that the Solar System was a very small part of the universe as a whole. The stars were known to be suns in their own right and to be so far away that their apparent individual (or "proper") motions were actually very slight.

Edmund Halley (1656–1742) used ancient observations to show that a few of the bright stars had shown relative shifts over the centuries, so that even constellation patterns could change gradually with time.

The scale of the universe

The scale of the universe was established much later, when distances to stars began to be measured. In 1838 Friedrich Bessel (1784–1846) first measured such a distance to a nearby star (in Cygnus) and found it to be about 60 trillion miles (96 trillion kilometers) away. Since light takes about 11 years to cover this distance, the star is said to be 11 light-years away. Most stars are much more remote than this, but modern techniques enable astronomers to measure their proper motions from year to year. The old name of "fixed stars" is misleading; all the stars are moving at high velocities relative to each other. In our own century it has been shown that our star-system, or Galaxy, is one of millions of galaxies.

KEY

A

B

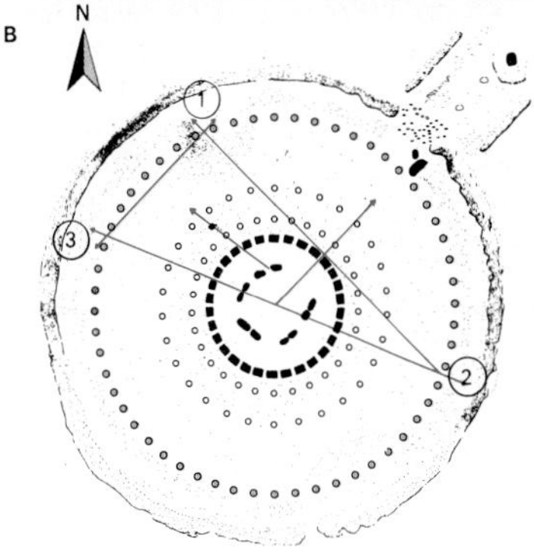

N
1
2
3

Stonehenge [A], the famous megalithic "stone circle" in Wiltshire, England, is made of standing stones with alignments that may have astronomical significance. Many of the alignments among the concentric rings [B] point to spots on the horizon where the Moon and Sun rise and set. For example, stone 1 as viewed from stone 2 marks the point where the Moon sets in its most northerly position in midwinter. Viewed from stone 3, stone 1 marks the midsummer sunrise. Stonehenge may have been an early primitive computer predicting eclipses for religious reasons or, more practically, for fixing the solstices, which were important in the agricultural calendar.

6 A

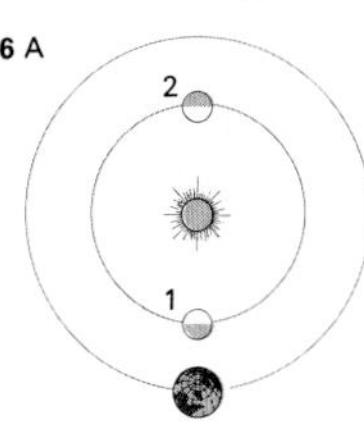

2
1

B

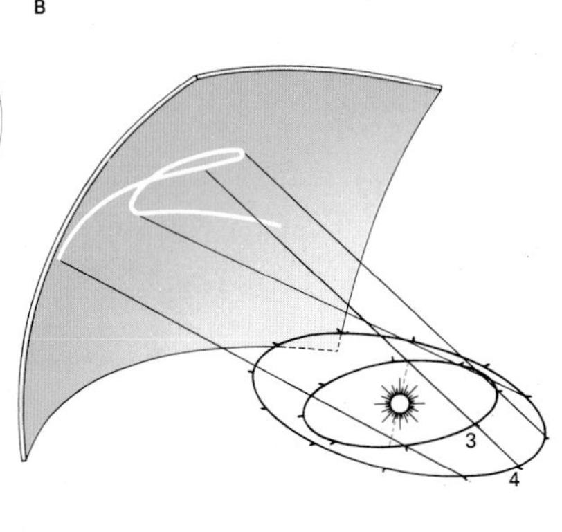

3
4

6 The two planets whose orbits lie within that of the Earth—Mercury and Venus—show lunar-type phases and remain in the same area of the sky as the Sun [A]. An inner planet is at inferior conjunction [1], its dark side is turned toward Earth so it appears "new." When on the far side of the Sun [2], it is full. The synodical period, or mean interval between successive inferior conjunctions, is 115.9 days for Mercury and 583.9 days for Venus. The orbits [B] of the Earth [4] and Venus [3] are shown; the white line indicates the apparent motion of Venus in the sky. Mercury behaves in a similar way.

7 A

2

1

B

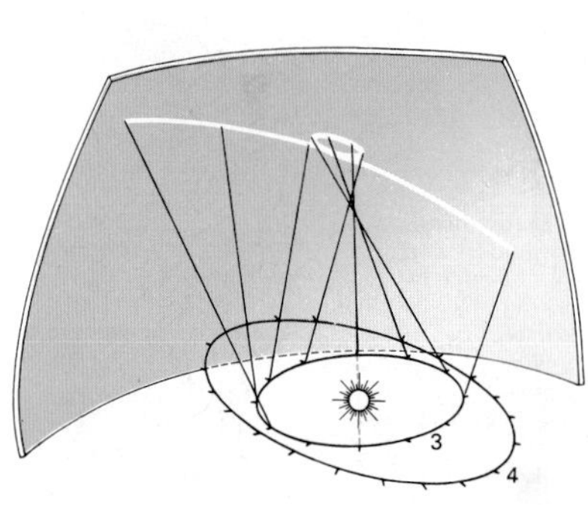

3
4

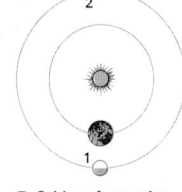

7 Orbits of superior planets [A], beyond Earth's orbit, reach opposition [1] and conjunction [2]. Apparent motion [B] of a superior planet [4] in relation to Earth [3] appears temporarily retrograde.

8

4

3

1

Aldebaran

2

8 Astronomers visualize the stars, for the sake of convenience, as lying on the inside of a sphere centered on the Earth. To an observer on Earth [1], the horizon becomes a circle [2] when projected onto this celestial sphere. As the Earth rotates west to east, the sky seems to move east to west, taking the stars, such as Aldebaran in Taurus, with it. The north pole of the sky [3], which is indicated approximately by Polaris, is stationary to an observer in the Earth's Northern Hemisphere. Stars in the mauve area [4], drawn for an observer at latitude 50°N, remain permanently above the horizon and are called circumpolar stars. The circumpolar area depends on the observer's latitude.

9 A

B

C

10 A

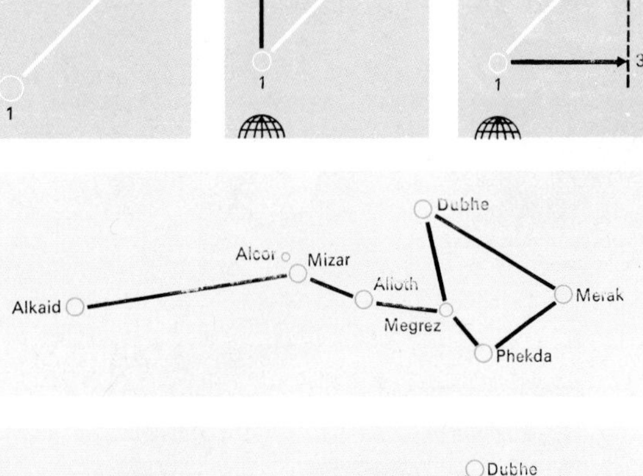

2
1
3
2
1
2
3
1
Dubhe
Alcor
Mizar
Alioth
Merak
Alkaid
Megrez
Phekda

9 The real movement of a star in space includes actual motion [A], where the star moves from 1 to 2 in a given period. Radial motion [B] is when the star moves from 1 to 3 if receding (positive radial motion), or 3 to 1 if approaching (negative radial motion). Proper motion [C] is the term used for the transverse movement (1 to 3) against the background of more distant stars. [A] combines [B] and [C].

B

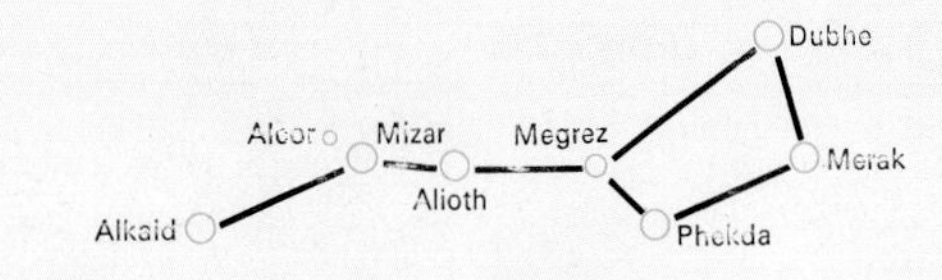

Dubhe
Alcor
Mizar
Megrez
Merak
Alioth
Alkaid
Phekda

C

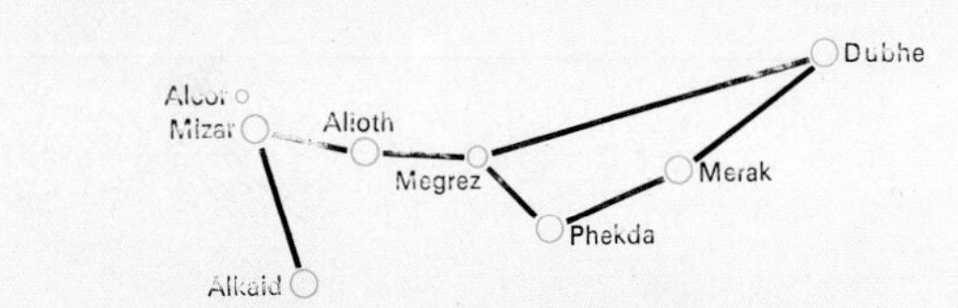

Dubhe
Alcor
Mizar
Alioth
Merak
Megrez
Phekda
Alkaid

10 To the naked eye constellations appear unchanged over thousands of years, but over a sufficiently long period the proper motions show up. The seven main stars of Ursa Major, including the double star Mizar, are shown as they were 100,000 years ago [A], as they are today [B], and as they will appear 100,000 years from now [C]. It is evident that Dubhe and Alkaid are moving in an almost opposite direction to that of the other five stars in the Dipper.

Measuring the restless sky

The size of the universe is almost unimaginable. It is easy to comprehend the distance from New York to London, or from San Francisco to Australia, and the Moon does not seem impossibly remote, because its distance is only ten times greater than that of a journey around the Earth. But any attempt to visualize what is meant by "a million miles" is doomed to failure—and a million miles is a very short distance on the cosmic scale.

Early estimates of distance

The ancients had no idea of scale (it was once thought that the diameter of the Sun was only 27 inches [70cm]), but they were able to measure the size of the Earth itself with remarkable accuracy [1]. As soon as the old concept of an Earth-centered universe was abandoned, distance estimates became much more realistic. Giovanni Cassini (1625–1712) gave the distance between the Earth and the Sun as 86 million miles (138 million kilometers), which approaches the true figure. Astronomers then decided that the Earth-Sun distance was to be *the* astronomical unit, and measuring it became a major task [Key].

The basis of any method of computing this distance was Kepler's third law, which established a definite relationship between the revolution period of a planet and its distance from the Sun. The revolution period of the Earth was known to be 365.25 days and the periods of the other planets could be found from observation—687 days for Mars, and so on—with the result that a complete scale model of the Solar System could be drawn up. Thus, if it were possible to obtain the distance from Earth to any planet (Mars or Venus, for example), Kepler's third law would give the distance of the Earth from the Sun [4].

The parallax principle

The obvious way to calculate the distance from the Earth to one of the planets was to use parallax [2], a method also used by surveyors. If a not-too-distant object is observed against a background of more remote objects, its position will seem to alter according to the position of the observer. If the distance between the two observation points is known, and the respective angles formed by the object with the line connecting the points are measured, one can calculate by trigonometry the height of the triangle thus formed, that is, the distance to the object.

Edmund Halley (1656–1742), the second British astronomer royal, proposed to make use of transits of Venus—the rare occasions when Venus passes in front of the Sun as seen from Earth and appears as a black spot against the solar disc—to determine the planet's absolute distance. Attempts made during the transits of 1761 and 1769 were only partly successful. (Captain Cook's voyage to the South Seas in the latter year was for the express purpose of observing the transit.) The next transits were in 1874 and 1882; all measurements agreed and it was determined that the astronomical unit is about 93 million miles (150 million kilometers).

When Venus passed across the face of the Sun, however, it seemed to draw a strip of blackness after it, distorting its shape.

CONNECTIONS

Read first
38 The restless sky

See also
1478 The scale of the universe

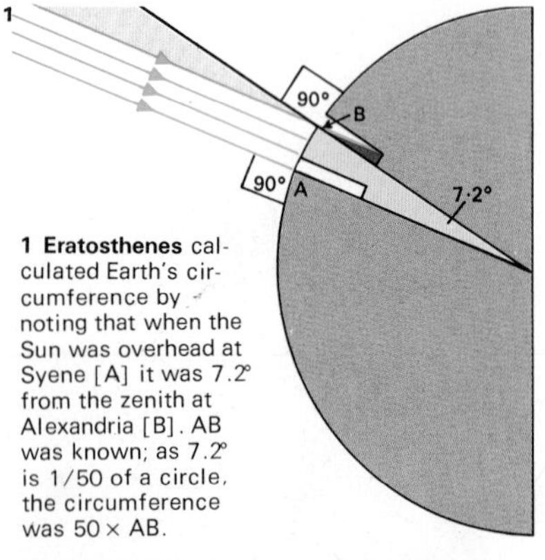
1
90°
B
90°
A
7.2°

1 Eratosthenes calculated Earth's circumference by noting that when the Sun was overhead at Syene [A] it was 7.2° from the zenith at Alexandria [B]. AB was known; as 7.2° is 1/50 of a circle, the circumference was 50 × AB.

2 Apparent parallaxes of stars are illustrated in these diagrams. The parallaxes are measured for the apparent movements of relatively nearby stars against a background of more remote stars, which are too distant for any detectable motion. With a star (open circle) lying in the direction of the axis Y of the Earth's orbit, the parallactic motion over a year will be circular [A]. If a star is coplanar with the ecliptic [B], the parallactic motion will take the form of a to-and-fro straight line. P is the angle of parallax and from this the distance of the star can be measured. The main difficulty is that the angle P is always very small. With modern photography and other techniques we can now "see" out to at least 200 light-years, but at greater distances the extremely small parallax shifts are swamped by observational errors.

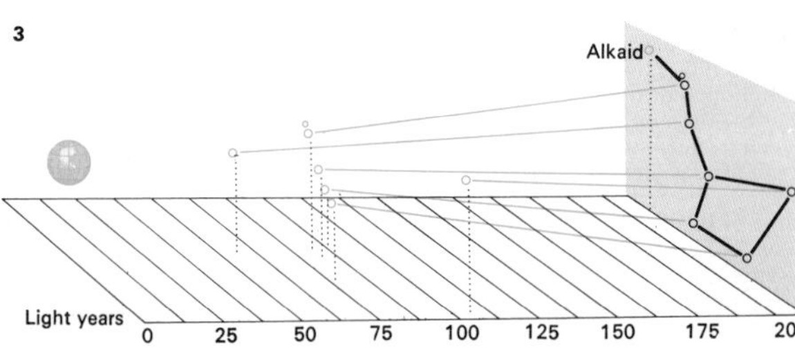
3
Alkaid
Light years
0
25
50
75
100
125
150
175
200

3 Stars in Ursa Major seem to the casual observer to be the same distance from the Earth; there is no "three-dimensional" effect. In fact the stars in any particular constellation are not necessarily associated. The diagram shows the relative distances of the seven main stars in the Big Dipper; Alkaid (210 light-years) is easily the most remote. Mizar, lying next to it in the sky, is only 88 light-years away.

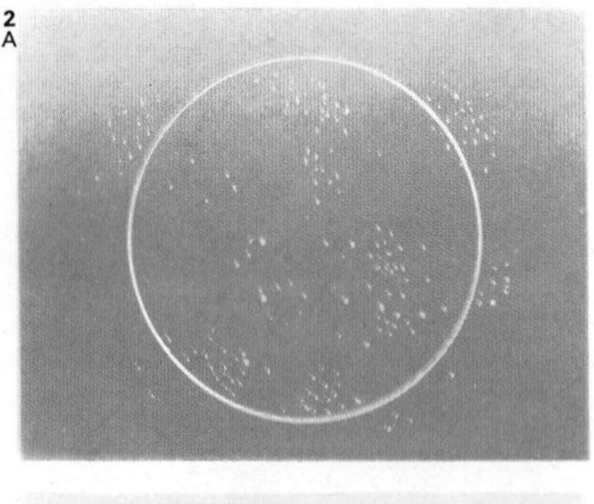
2
A

B

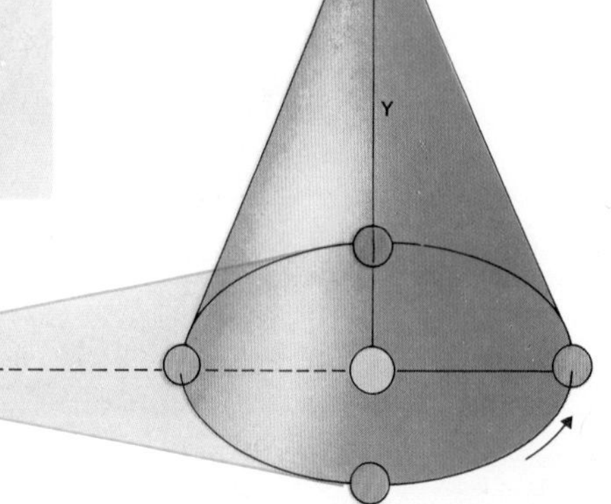
A
P
Y
B
P

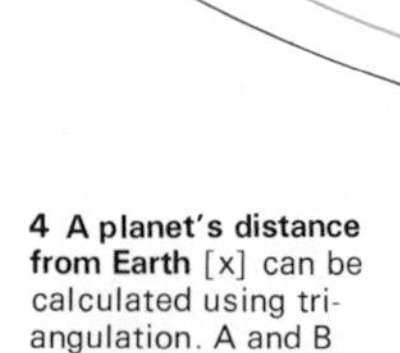
4
W1
W2
x
A
B
1
2
M2
M1
T1
T2

4 A planet's distance from Earth [x] can be calculated using triangulation. A and B are the distances of Earth [1] and the planet [2] from the Sun. M1 and M2 are the planet's apparent positions as seen from W1 and W2 on Earth. The ratio of the angles at M1 and M2 is the same as the ratio of the distances W1-W2 and x. Using Kepler's third law $(T1/T2)^2 = (A/B)^3$, where T is the period of orbit, A and B can be found.

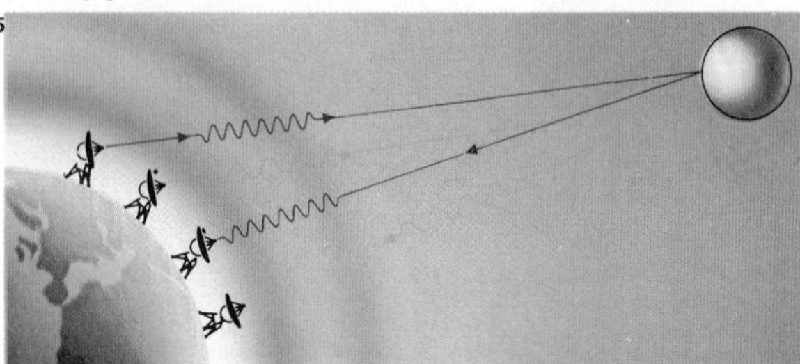
5

5 The distance of Venus can be measured by radar. Once this is known, Kepler's third law can be used to find the distance of the Earth from the Sun. Radar pulses of differing wavelengths are reflected from Venus to the receivers on Earth. The time lag between transmitting and receiving echoes gives the distance traveled, provided allowances have been made for delaying of echoes by the ionosphere.

When this so-called "black drop" vanished, the transit had already begun, which meant that the measurements were subject to considerable error.

New methods involve the use of radar. Radar transmits a pulse of energy to a remote object and receives an echo from it. Radio waves travel with the speed of light and, because this speed is constant, the time lapse between the transmission and the arrival of the echo enables the distance of the object to be calculated. The planet Venus can be contacted by radar [5]. The new method gives the length of the astronomical units as 92,957,000 miles (149,600,000 kilometers).

The problem of mapping the stars

Star distance presented different problems, and here again parallax was used. If a nearby star is observed over a six-month interval, it will show a parallax shift against the background stars because during the interim the Earth will have moved from one side of its orbit to the other, giving a "baseline" of 186 million miles (300 million kilometers). This method was first applied in 1838, when Friedrich Bessel (1784–1846) showed that a faint star in Cygnus lay at a distance of 11 light-years. One light-year is the distance traveled by light in one year; that is, 5,880,000,000,000 miles (9,460,000,000,000 kilometers).

The parallax methods work well for the nearer stars, but beyond a few hundred light-years the shifts become too fine to be measured and less direct methods must be used. Spectroscopic methods reveal the real luminosity of a star, and this compared with its apparent brightness (or visual magnitude) gives the distance. It is now known that the diameter of our Galaxy is about 100,000 light-years.

But our Galaxy is not the only one. The hazy patches known as nebulae are of two kinds: some can be resolved into many distant stars, others are only nearby gas and dust. In 1845 Lord Rosse (1800–67) discovered that many of the starry nebulae are spirals, and it has now been found that spirals and other forms are external galaxies of stars millions of light-years away.

KEY

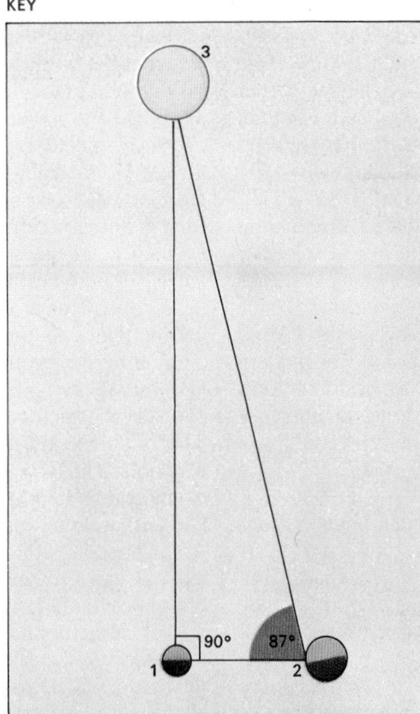
3
90°
87°
1
2

Aristarchus, a Greek astronomer of the 3rd century BC, is said to have been the first man to propose a heliocentric theory of the universe. He was also able to measure the relative distances of the Sun and Moon. When the Moon is at first quarter [1], the angle it makes with the Sun [3] is near 90°. By measuring the angle at the Earth [2] Aristarchus could determine from the triangle the relative distances from Earth. He found the angle to be 87°, instead of the true value of 80°52′; but even such a small error can lead to a large discrepancy in the ratio of the distances of the Sun and Moon respectively from the Earth. Aristarchus' ratio was 19 to 1; the true ratio is 390 to 1.

6

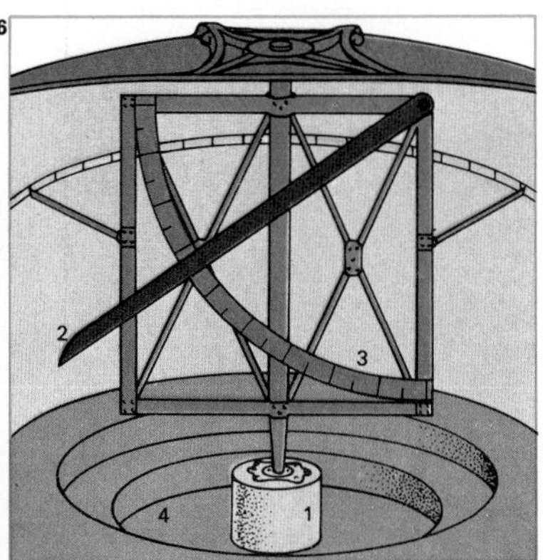
2
3
4
1

6 Tycho Brahe's quadrant was one of the early instruments used for measuring star positions. This quadrant, used between 1576 and 1596, was mounted on a central pillar [1]; a pointer [2] with sights moved along a graduated metal circle [3]. The well [4] accommodated the observer at various levels determined by the position of the pointer. Modern work depends on basics like those established by Tycho.

7 Ancient astrolabes [A] had simple pointers and scales to measure the altitudes of stars and other objects in the sky. In the modern astrolabe [B] the light strikes a prism [1] and a mercury surface [2], forming a double image along the collimation line [3]. The images separate when the object moves, and this separation is measured by the azimuth scale [4], giving the altitude of a moving celestial body.

7

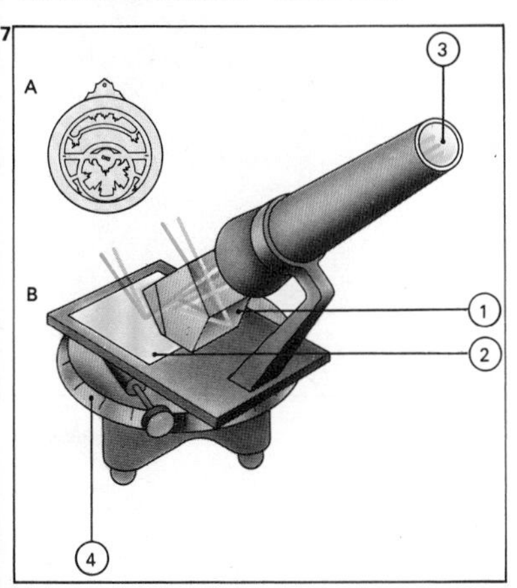
A
B
1
2
3
4

8

JANUARY
FEBRUARY
MARCH
APRIL
MAY
JUNE
JULY
AUGUST
SEPTEMBER
PLANETS
THE SOLAR SYSTEM
Gemini
Cancer
Leo
Virgo
Libra
Scorpio
Sagittarius
Aquarius
Pisces

8 An orrery made in 1790 is shown here. The name originates from the Earl of Cork and Orrery, for whom an elaborate instrument was made. Orreries indicate the movements of the planets around the Sun. In the elaborate orrery shown here, the Sun is represented by a brass ball in the center. Around it move the three innermost planets, Mercury, Venus, and Earth. An ingenious system of gears makes the planets move around the Sun in the correct relative periods, even though on a scale of this kind it is impossible to give the correct relative distances. The lands and seas of Earth are shown, as is the Moon in its orbit, which is inclined at the correct angle to the Earth. When the mechanism is moved by turning a handle, the planets revolve around the Sun and the Moon revolves around the Earth. More recent orreries are driven by clockwork, and in some of them the more distant planets are also shown Forerunners of the planetarium, orreries are useful in explaining celestial mechanics.

Telescopes

The telescope is the main research instrument of astronomy. Without it knowledge of the cosmos would be very limited. Other instruments—such as those based upon the principle of the spectroscope—depend upon telescopes to collect light that is to be analyzed. George Ellery Hale (1868–1938), who was largely responsible for the building of the 200-in (508-cm) reflector at Palomar, in California, which was for many years the most powerful telescope in the world, once said that his call was always for "More light!" This is still true today, for modern astronomers are doing their best to investigate very faint objects lying at immense distances from the Earth.

How refractors work

Telescopes are of two main kinds: refractors and reflectors [Key]. Each type has its own advantages and its own drawbacks. Refractors, developed during the first decade of the seventeenth century, were the first used and were employed by pioneers such as Galileo (1564–1642). In a refractor the light from the object to be studied passes through a specially shaped lens known as an object glass, or objective, which brings the rays of light to focus; the resulting image is magnified by a second lens known as an eyepiece, or ocular. The larger the objective the greater the light-gathering power of the telescope. Thus a 6-in (15.2-cm) refractor (that is to say, a refractor with an objective six inches across) is twice as powerful as a small 3-in (7.6-cm) refractor.

The only function of the objective is to collect light; all the actual magnification is done by the eyepiece. Every astronomical telescope is equipped with several eyepieces, which can be used as desired. The limit depends upon the amount of light available. Thus if, say, an eyepiece giving a magnification of 500 were used with a 3-in (7.6-cm) refractor, the resulting image would be so faint that it would be useless; to make use of a magnification of 500 a larger objective would be needed.

All refractors have one defect in common: they produce false color. This is due to the nature of light itself, which is a blend of all the colors of the spectrum [1]. As the ray of light passes through the objective it is bent, or refracted, in order to be brought to focus; but the longer wavelengths are bent less sharply than the shorter ones. Thus the red part of the beam is bent less than the blue and so is brought to focus in a different place.

The result is that a bright object such as a star is associated with false color that may look beautiful but which, to the astronomer, is unwelcome. This can be partly remedied by using compound objectives with one lens of crown glass and the other of flint glass; these have different refractive properties, and the false color is reduced. It could be almost entirely removed by adding more lenses but that would reduce the amount of light reaching the observer, a fundamental consideration in astronomy. [2].

Reflecting telescopes

The reflecting telescope, of which the first working example was made by Isaac Newton (1642–1727) in about 1671, works on an entirely different principle. On the Newto-

CONNECTIONS

See also
44 Great observatories
1518 Mirrors and lenses
1520 Light waves

1 When white light, which contains all wavelengths of the visible spectrum, is passed through a glass prism, the beam is split up [A], because the colors bend unequally, into a spectrum ranging from the longest wavelength (red) to the shortest (violet). When one color is passed through a hole and a second prism, there is no further splitting [B]. Inverting the second prism recombines the colors [C].

2 The cause of the irritating false color that is always present when a refractor is used is shown here. The light from the object passes through the objective lens and is split to some extent so that the red rays are brought together farther away from the lens than the blue rays [A]. The same is true if a different kind of lens is used [B]. The solution is to use a compound objective [C] made up of two lenses combined; the errors then tend to cancel each other out and the false color is appreciably reduced, although for color correction a refractor is always inferior to the results obtained with a reflector.

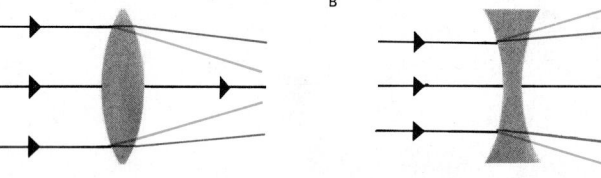

3 Reflectors are of various types. In the Newtonian pattern the light is collected by a parabolic mirror and sent onto a flat mirror at an angle of 45 degrees; the light is sent into the side of the tube, where the image is formed and magnified. To avoid the admittedly small light loss due to the flat mirror, William Herschel tilted the main mirror and dispensed with the flat. This design is unsatisfactory, however. In the Cassegrain the secondary is concave and the light is reflected back down through a hole in the main mirror. In some designs the returning light is diverted by a second flat mirror into the side of the tube, which avoids making a hole in the main mirror.

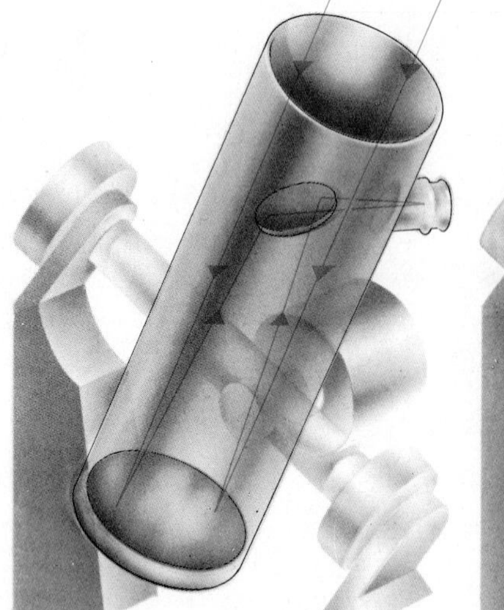

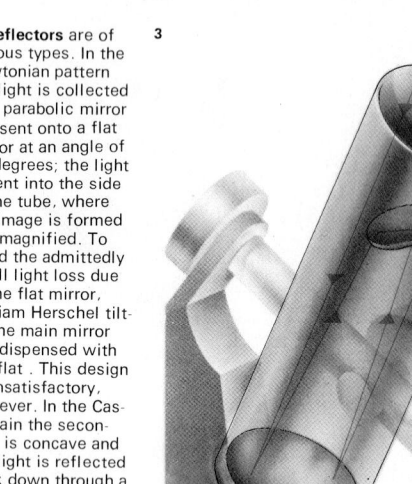

Newtonian reflector

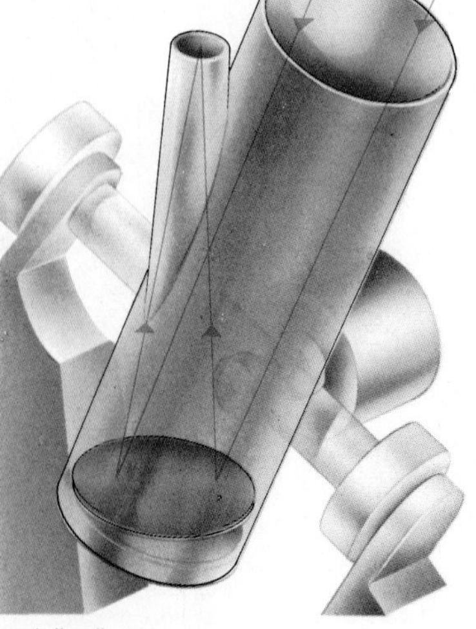

Herschel's reflector

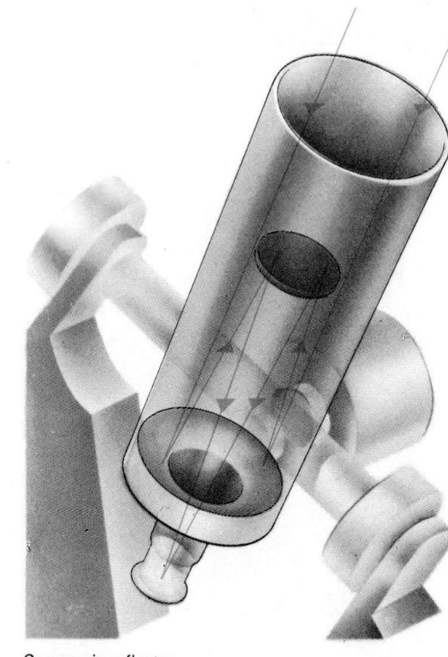

Cassegrain reflector

ian pattern [3] the light passes down an open tube until it hits a mirror at the far end. This mirror is curved; the shape is that of a paraboloid and the light is reflected back up the tube onto a second, flat mirror placed at an angle of 45 degrees. The light is then directed into the side of the tube, where it is brought to focus, and the image is magnified by an eyepiece as in the refractor. The presence of the flat mirror in the tube cuts out some of the light but the loss is not serious and with the Newtonian pattern there is no way of avoiding it.

Because a mirror reflects all colors equally there is no chromatic aberration, although a certain amount of false color may be produced in the eyepiece. Modern mirrors are ceramic and are coated with a thin layer of some highly reflective substance such as aluminum or silver.

The Newtonian is not the only form of reflector. In the Cassegrain, or Gregorian, type [3] the second mirror is also curved and the light is reflected back through a hole in the main mirror. In the Herschelian type of reflector the main mirror is tilted and the secondary mirror is dispensed with altogether, but this involves distortions and Herschelian telescopes are now considered to be obsolete.

Advantages and disadvantages

Aperture for aperture a refractor is more effective than a reflector, but it is also more expensive because large lenses are harder to make than large mirrors. For this and other reasons all the world's largest telescopes are reflectors [5]. For amateur use the minimum useful aperture is about 3in (7.6cm) for a refractor and 6in (15.2cm) for a reflector.

The question of a mount is all-important. If the mounting is unsteady the telescope will be useless. It is highly desirable to use an equatorial stand in which the telescope is attached to an axis that is parallel to the axis of the Earth. With a driving mechanism added, the telescope can be driven in a way that compensates for the Earth's rotation and keeps an object fixed in the field of view, which is essential for accurate photography.

KEY

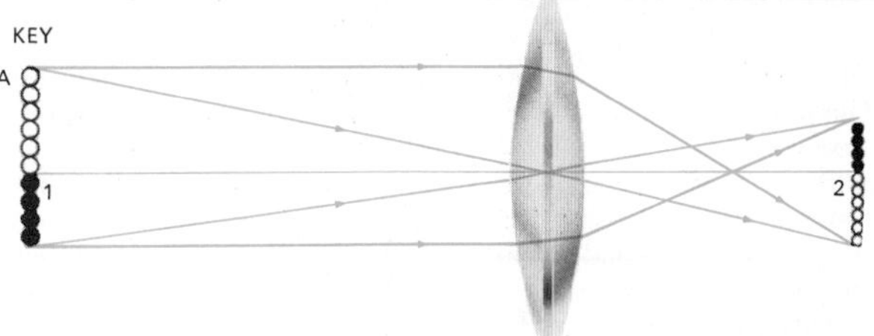

A
1
2

In a refractor [A] light from the object [1] passes through the lens to form an image [2]. The distance between the lens and the focal point is known as the focal length. Unless an extra lens system is used, the image is inverted.

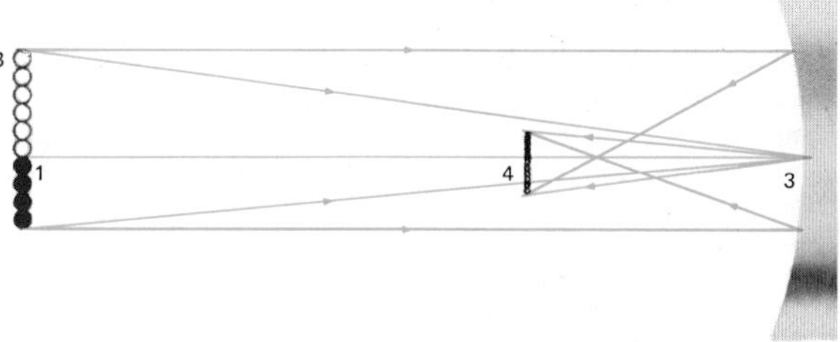

B
1
4
3

In a reflector [B] light from the object [1] is collected by a curved mirror [3] and is brought to focus, forming an image [4].

4 A more modern type of reflector is the Coudé, which has a secondary mirror and an extra, rotatable mirror on the polar axis of the telescope. Since the light rays are reflected in a constant direction the image formed is stationary and the observer need not move as the telescope rotates. This has the great advantage that heavy and delicate equipment need not be moved. Most modern reflectors allow for a Coudé focus and can be used according to several optical systems, which permits great versatility; in some telescopes the change to a Coudé system can be made very quickly. It can also be used with refractors.

4

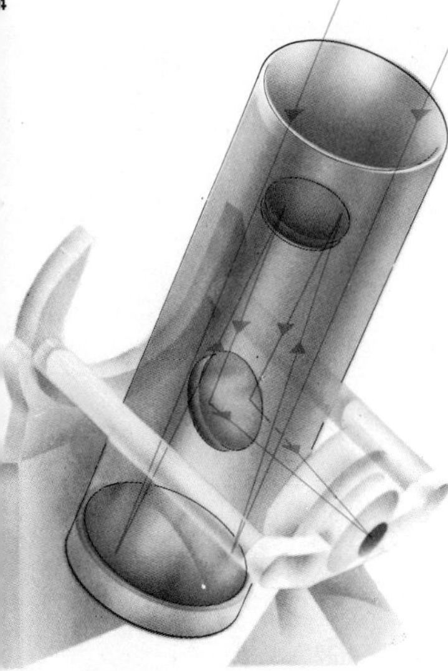

Coudé telescope

5 The 200-in (508-cm) Hale reflector was for many years the world's largest and was unrivaled in its light-collecting power. The diagram shows the primary mirror [1]; observer's cage [2]; Cassegrain focus [3]; the Coudé focus [4]; the southern end of the polar axis [5]; the Cassegrain and Coudé secondary mirror [6]; the right-ascension drive [7]; the declination axis [8]; the dome shutter, with an opening of 30ft (9m) [9]; the 137-ft (42-m) dome [10]; the primary focus, 54ft (16.5m) [11]; the northern pillar [12]; the southern pillar [13]; and the control panel [14], from which the telescope can be made to point to any part of the sky.

5

1
2
3
4
5
6
7
8
9
10
11
12
13
14

6 The cage for the observer can be set up within the tube itself in a telescope that is as large as the Hale reflector. This means that photographs can be taken at the prime focus. This is an obvious advantage because no secondary mirror is needed—and every reflection from a mirror inevitably involves some loss of light. It is obvious, too, that the observer's cage blocks a considerable amount of light but this shortcoming is tolerated because of the cage's benefits

6

7 One of the observers at Palomar loads a plate at the 200-in (508-cm) reflector, which was here being used at the Coude focus. To change from one optical system to another takes a certain amount of time, but it is routine.

7

Great observatories

It is often thought that an astronomical observatory consists simply of a dome-shaped building containing a telescope. This is certainly true of some amateur observatories, but professional observatories are extremely elaborate and contain equipment of many kinds. Great care has to be taken in selecting a site for an observatory because a dark sky with no interference from artificial light and a clear, transparent atmosphere are absolutely necessary.

Today little optical astronomical work is carried out visually—that is to say, by an observer sitting at the eye-end of a telescope. Virtually all optical research is carried out by means of photography and the world's largest telescopes are used as giant cameras.

Observatory sites and equipment

To photograph a very faint object such as a remote galaxy it is necessary to make a time exposure, which may last many hours. Consequently, stray light is probably the astronomer's worst enemy. Today, with the spread of cities and the resulting marked increase in light pollution, it is becoming more and more difficult to find sites that combine darkness with a high percentage of clear, cloudless nights. In addition, the Earth's atmosphere is subject to turbulence and also absorbs light, so that it is desirable to set major telescopes upon mountains, above the densest atmospheric layers. This means that an observatory must be virtually self-contained, with accommodations for the observers as well as workshops, photographic laboratories, and lecture halls. Even so, the usual procedure is for the observer to spend a limited time at the observatory itself and then return to his office with the photographic results of his work.

Observatories built during the late nineteenth century were equipped with large refractors [6]. The largest is the 40-inch (102-cm) refractor at the Yerkes Observatory in Williams Bay, Wis. It is not likely that any larger refractor will be built, because a lens has to be supported around its edge and above a certain limiting size (about 40 inches) the lens starts to distort under its own weight. This does not apply to a mirror, which is supported by its back. Large lenses are also subject to severe chromatic and spherical aberrations that distort the image; these aberrations can be avoided by mirrors. For these reasons most modern telescopes are reflectors.

The Hale Observatories

The most famous planner of giant telescopes was George Ellery Hale (1868–1938), who designed observatories and persuaded interested millionaires to finance them. At Mt Wilson, north of Pasadena, Calif., Hale was responsible for the erection first of a 60-inch (152-cm) reflector and then a 100-inch (254-cm). The latter, completed in 1918, remained the largest telescope in the world for more than 30 years and was effective in making fundamental advances in astronomy. It was then surpassed by the 200-inch (508-cm) reflector installed in 1948 at Palomar, Calif., and also masterminded by Hale, who unfortunately died before the telescope was completed. Fittingly, Mt Wilson and Palomar are now administered jointly under the name of the Hale Obser-

CONNECTIONS

See also
42 Telescopes
46 Invisible astronon
1160 Science and Technology 1500-1700

1 The world's larges optical telescope is the 235-inch (600-cm) reflecting instrument in Zelenchukskaya, USSR. Its technical advantage over the Hale 200-inch (508-cm) at Palomar is considerable, although observing conditions in the Caucasus are not as good as in California. Its altazimuth mounting, allowing movement in both vertical and horizontal planes has a more complicated drive mechanism than the usual equatorial mount. The dome is made on the conventional pattern. The telescope was developed to study remote star systems, exploiting its immense light-gathering power.

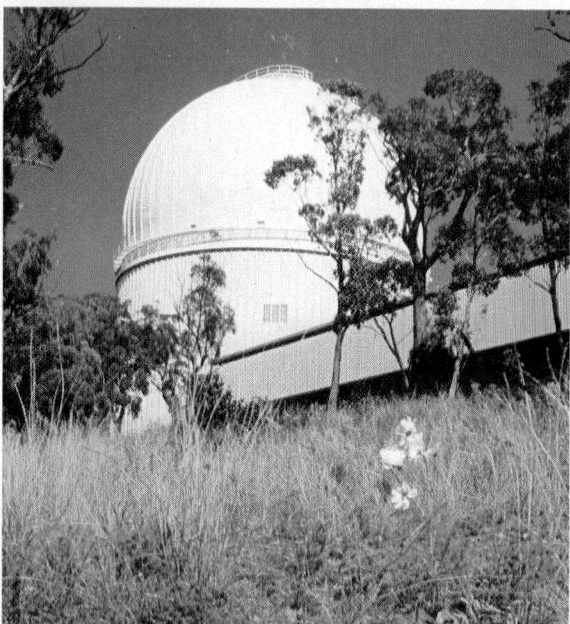

2 The Anglo-Australian telescope at Siding Spring Mountain, New South Wales, is a 153-inch (389-cm) reflector. Four different optical systems can be used: prime focus, *f*/8 or *f*/15 Cassegrain, and *f*/36 Coudé. The total mass of the telescope is 358 tons. It is similar to the 150-inch Kitt Peak Telescope.

3 Lick Observatory in California was founded after a donation from James Lick in 1874–75, and came under the direction of the University of California in 1888. The principal instrument is the 120in (305cm) reflecting telescope, shown here, that went into operation in 1959. Design features are similar to the 200in at Palomar.

vatories. The 200-inch (508-cm) telescope can be used on three optical systems—prime focus, Cassegrain, and Coudé—and is so large that the observer's cage can be placed inside the tube—in the position occupied by the 45-degree flat mirror of an amateur Newtonian telescope. The 48-inch (122-cm) Schmidt [4] telescope at Palomar is used purely photographically and incorporates a spherical mirror together with a complicated correcting plate. The advantage of a Schmidt telescope is that it can photograph wide areas of the sky with a single exposure, whereas the field of a telescope such as the 200-inch is necessarily very small.

The world's largest telescopes

The 200-inch Palomar telescope is no longer the largest optical telescope in the world, since the Soviet Union completed a 235-inch (600-cm) and set it up in the Caucasus, [1]. There are also various telescopes of the 100–160-inch (254–406-cm) range. Major observatories have been set up in the Southern Hemisphere, where the skies are clear and the important objects of the far south, such as the Magellanic Clouds, are accessible. There are sites in Australia [2], South America, and South Africa where observing conditions are particularly good.

The largest telescope in Britain is a 98-inch (249-cm) reflector, known as the INT, or Isaac Newton Telescope, at Herstmonceux, Sussex. During the 1950s the instruments at the famous observatory at Greenwich [Key] were moved to Sussex, but even there difficulties arose with clouds and scattered light and it was decided that the 98-inch (249-cm) telescope would be moved to a new site in the Canary Islands, where there would also be a new 160-inch (406-cm) reflector.

Some observatories have special roles; for instance at Kitt Peak, near Tucson, Ariz., there is elaborate equipment for studying the Sun, while the Lowell Observatory [5], near Flagstaff, specializes in planetary work. New observatories are being planned and several artificial satellites have been equipped with telescopes, including Skylab and Soyuz.

KEY

Flamsteed House, in Greenwich Park, London, designed by Christopher Wren (1632–1723), is the site of the old Royal Observatory, set up in 1675. The Greenwich meridian passes through the old observatory, now a museum.

4 A

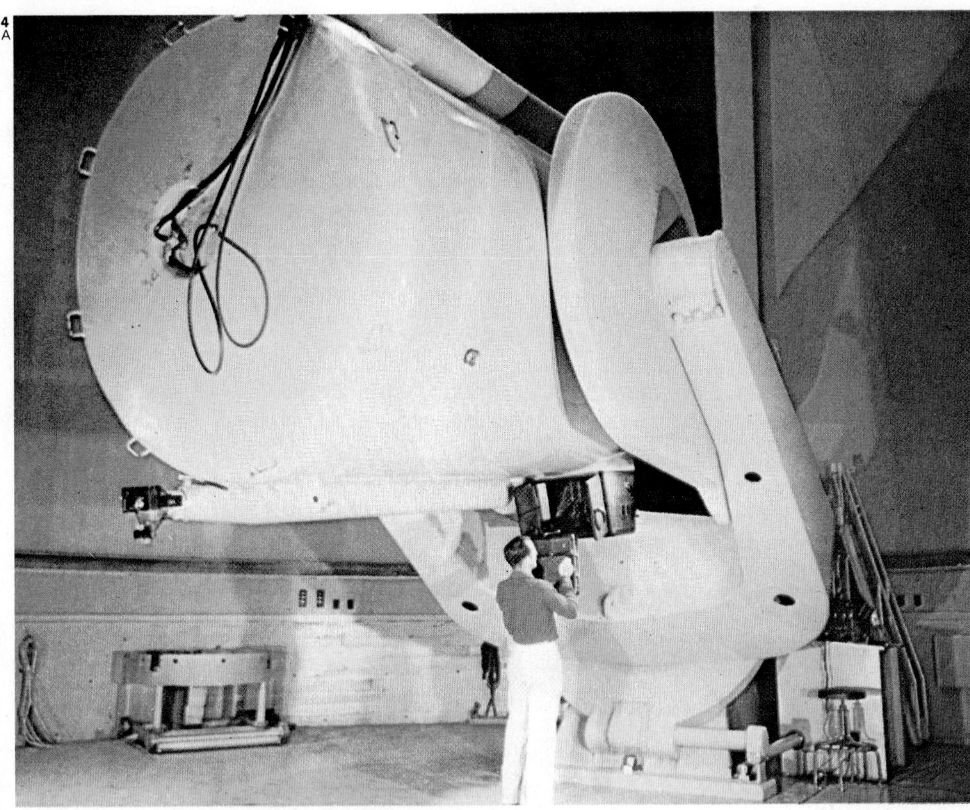

B

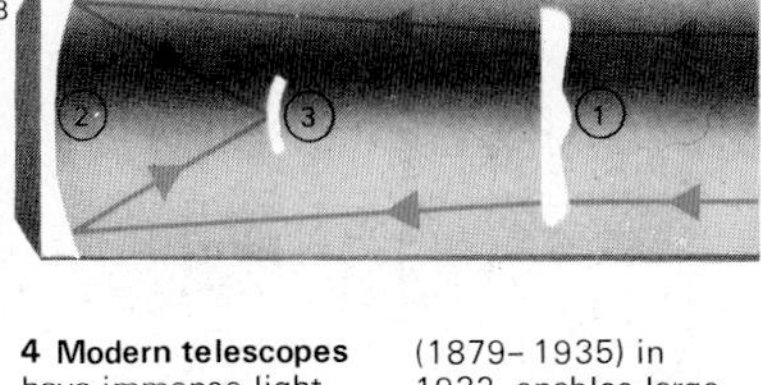
2
3
1

4 Modern telescopes have immense light-gathering power. The conventional telescope, however, is only able to cover a small area of sky with one photographic exposure. For studying individual objects, such as galaxies, this does not matter, but it means that to compile a photographic map of the whole sky would take too long. The principle of the Schmidt telescope [B], developed by Estonian optician Bernhard Schmidt (1879–1935) in 1932, enables large areas to be photographed with each exposure. There is a spherical mirror and a glass correcting plate over the end of the tube to compensate for optical distortion. The light passes through the plate [1] to the mirror [2] and is reflected onto a curved photographic plate [3] in the tube. The Schmidt telescope at Palomar [A] has a 48-inch (122-cm) correcting plate and a 72-inch (183-cm) mirror.

5

5 The Lowell Observatory at Flagstaff, Ariz., was set up by Percival Lowell (1855–1916) in 1895. The observatory has always been known for its planetary work, although much equipment, including a large reflector, has been added since Lowell's time. The photograph shows the dome of the 24-inch (61-cm) refractor that Lowell used for his Martian studies from 1895 to 1916. The fine-quality optics are as good as when new.

6

6 The 26-inch (66-cm) telescope at the US Naval Observatory in Washington, DC, is one of the earliest of the great refractors. It was installed in 1862 and with it Alvan Clark (1832–97), who ground the object glass, found the White Dwarf companion of Sirius. Asaph Hall (1829–1907) used it to discover the two satellites of Mars, in 1877. The photograph shows it as it is today with the telescope balanced by a counterweight.

Invisible astronomy

Up to the 1920s, astronomers had to depend entirely upon the visible light coming from objects in space. This was a severe limitation, because visible light makes up only a small part of the range of wavelengths or "electromagnetic spectrum."

Light may be regarded as a wave motion and the color of the light depends on its wavelength [1]. The usual unit of wavelength is the ångström, which is equal to one hundred-millionth of a centimeter. Visible light extends from about 4,000Å for violet light up to 7,200 Å for red. If the wavelength lies outside these limits the "light" does not affect our eyes. Below the violet end of the visible spectrum come ultraviolet, X rays, and the very short, penetrating gamma rays; beyond the red end there are infrared, microwaves, and finally radio waves, whose wavelengths may amount to many miles.

Radio waves from space

The discovery of radio waves from space was made by Karl Jansky (1905–50) in the United States in 1931. The discovery was fortuitous. Jansky, a radio engineer, was investigating the nature of static when he found that he was picking up emissions from the sky [Key]. He tracked them to the Milky Way. He published a few papers, but never followed the subject through. Before World War II, an American, G. Reber, set up a dish-shaped radio telescope and made the first radio map of the Milky Way. During the war a British team led by J. S. Hey found that radar equipment was being jammed, not by transmissions from Germany, as was originally thought, but by radio waves from the Sun.

Subsequently, radio telescopes were set up [2, 3] and a new branch of science was under way. It was found that the Sun is a radio source, but by cosmic standards not a powerful one; it is obstrusive only because it is so close to the Earth. Jupiter is also known to be a source of radio waves. But most radio sources lie far beyond the Solar System. Those in our Galaxy include many supernova remnants, of which the Crab Nebula is the most celebrated example. At greater distances still are the radio galaxies, which are extremely powerful at long wavelengths, although the reason for this is still not definitely known.

Radio astronomy has added tremendously to our knowledge of the universe. Without it little would be known about pulsars, which are neutron stars, or quasars, which are extragalactic and may well be the most powerful objects known. Moreover, radio waves have been studied from greater distances than visible light waves, so that our information about the most distant regions of the universe is derived entirely from radio work.

Infrared radiations

Beyond the longwave end of the visible range is the infrared region of the electromagnetic spectrum [1]. Most infrared radiations are absorbed by the upper atmosphere and these are studied by means of equipment carried by satellites. There are, however, a few "windows" through which infrared radiations penetrate the atmosphere, and these can be studied from the ground. This branch of research has pro-

CONNECTIONS

See also
108 Pulsars and black holes
124 Radio galaxies and quasars

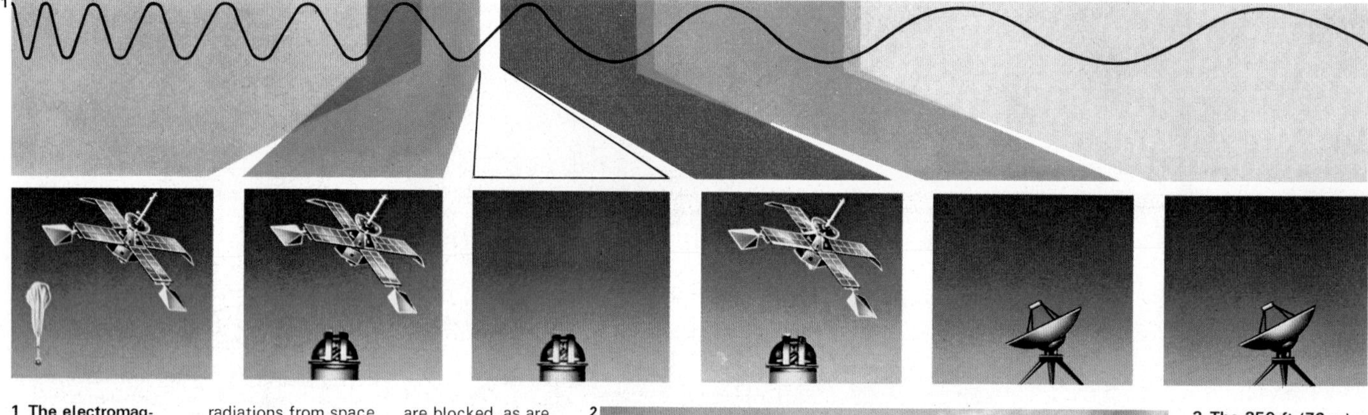

1 The electromagnetic spectrum shows the restricted "windows" in which radiations from space can reach the Earth's surface. Many of the longest wavelengths are blocked, as are all the shortest. (The illustration is not drawn to scale.)

2 The 250-ft (76-m) paraboloid at Jodrell Bank, in England, was for many years the world's largest fully steerable radio telescope. It was planned by Bernard Lovell (1913) and has been responsible for fundamental advances in our knowledge. At first it was used in tracking artificial satellites and space probes, but it is now used exclusively for research into the stars and the galaxies.

3 The Arecibo radio telescope, in Puerto Rico, has been built in a natural bowl. It is 1000ft (300m) in diameter. Although this radio telescope is not steerable, some degree of direction can be obtained by moving the receiving antenna.

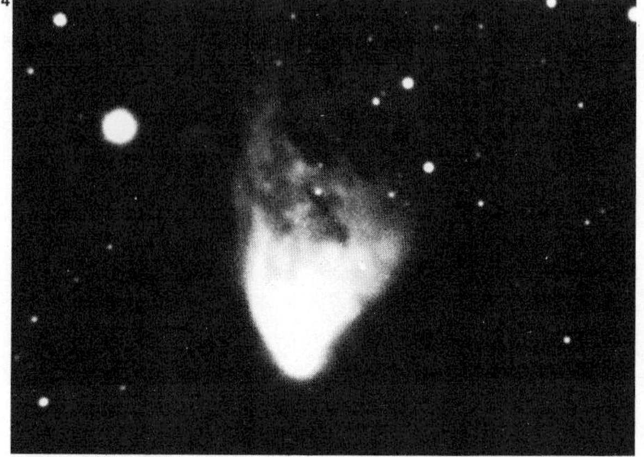

4 Hubble's variable nebula in Monoceros is 6,500 light-years away and is associated with a variable star, R Monocerotis. The infrared radiation, of which it is a source, also varies periodically.

vided a great deal of information about tellar evolution. For instance, there are extremely young stars, such as the variable V1057 in Cygnus, which seem to be surrounded by dust clouds, so that the dust heated by the star contained in the cloud sends out excess infrared. There are even some objects that are detectable only by infrared techniques, for example Becklin's Object inside the Orion Nebula. It may well be an immensely powerful star, perhaps a million times as luminous as the Sun, but it can never be seen because it is concealed by the nebulosity and only its infrared radiation can pass through. The secondary component of the eclipsing binary Epsilon Aurigae is also detectable only in the infrared, either because it is a very young star, not yet hot enough to shine in the visible range, or because it is a black hole and the radiations we receive come from dust just above.

Ultraviolet, gamma, and X rays

Ultraviolet radiation, X rays, and gamma rays lie beyond the shortwave end of the visible band of the electromagnetic spectrum. For high-energy ultraviolet, X-rays, and gamma-ray studies (that is, radiations below 2,900Å), equipment carried by rockets or satellites has to be used since these radiations are absorbed by the upper atmosphere [1]. There are many X-ray sources and there is a concentration at the main plane of the Milky Way [5], indicating that these sources are inside our own Galaxy—although X radiations come from more distant sources as well. The celebrated galaxy M87 in Virgo, already known as a radio source, is also an emitter of X rays.

The Crab Nebula [7], in our galaxy at a distance of 4,000 light-years from Earth, contains a pulsar, an X-ray source. X-ray "binaries," are also known, each made up of an X-ray star orbiting a normal giant, and short-lived X-ray sources that may become obtrusive for a few weeks before fading.

Gamma rays must also be studied from rocket-born equipment, and gamma-ray astronomy, although still in its infancy, has great potential. "Invisible astronomy" has caused a scientific revolution and is now a vital part of astronomical research.

KEY

An improvised antenna was set up by Karl Jansky in 1931. He intended to study static on behalf of the Bell Telephone Company, and in the process discovered radio waves from the Milky Way, which led to the science of radio astronomy.

5 About 160 locations of X-ray sources (red circles) along the main plane of the Milky Way have been identified, and their distribution indicates that they belong to our Galaxy. More sources are found each year. Not all are permanent; the British Ariel satellite found a highly energetic source in Taurus (near, but not associated with, the Crab Nebula) that lasted for some months in 1975.

6 This radio plot of emissions near the center of the Galaxy also shows X-ray emissions superimposed as numbers. The higher the number the greater the emission. The highest (9) is in the galactic center.

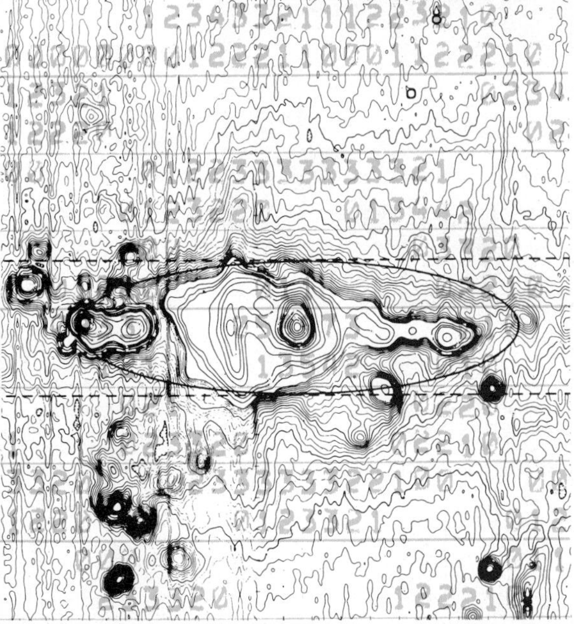

7 The Crab Nebula, in Taurus, is the wreck of the brilliant supernova seen by Chinese and Japanese astronomers in 1054. Today it is a cloud of expanding gas in which lies a pulsar—the only pulsar so far optically identified. The Crab is 4,000 light-years away, so that the actual supernova outburst occurred in prehistoric times. As well as being a source of radio waves, the Crab also sends out radiation at virtually all wavelengths, so that it has been of the utmost value to astronomers. As far as we know there is nothing else quite like it. With a small telescope it may be seen as a dim, misty patch near the 3rd magnitude Star Zeta Tauri.

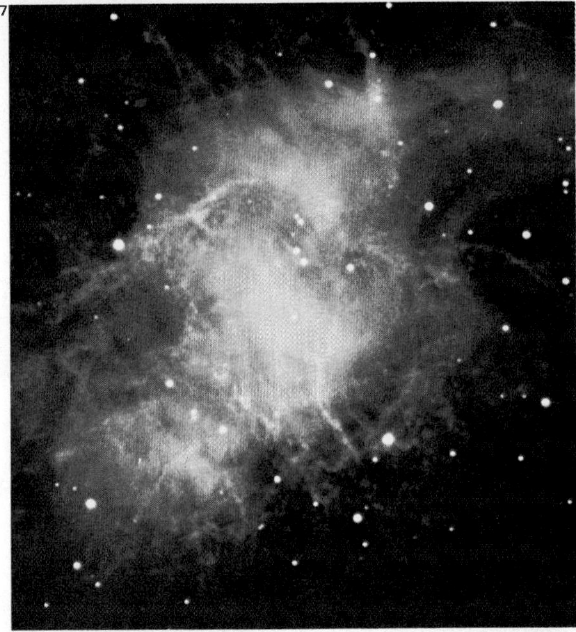

Evolution of the solar system

The question of how the Earth came into existence is one that has long intrigued mankind. It was not until comparatively recently that plausible theories were advanced and even today it is impossible to be sure that the main problems have been solved, but at least some concrete facts exist.

The concept of a central Earth, with the Sun moving around it, was abandoned during what is often called the "Copernican revolution." This began in 1543 with the publication of Copernicus's book *De Revolutionibus Orbium Caelestium* and was finally completed by the work of Newton in the latter part of the seventeenth century. With the Earth no longer central, it could be assumed that it must have been formed in the same way as the other planets.

The age of the Solar System

Several centuries ago Archbishop Ussher of Armagh maintained, on religious grounds, that the world had come into existence at a definite moment in 4004 BC. Geological evidence soon disproved this, but it was not until much more recently that any reliable estimates could be made. The modern estimate of the age of the Earth is between 4.5 and 4.7 billion years.

Further confirmation of the Earth's age has been obtained from analyses of the rocks brought back from the Moon by the Apollo missions and from the Soviet probes. It is now known that the Moon and the Earth are about the same age and it is likely that the same is true of the other planets. The Sun must be at least as old as the planets and probably somewhat older.

The first scientific theories

The first serious attempt to explain the origin of the Solar System scientifically was made by the French mathematician Pierre Laplace (1749–1827) in 1796 (although earlier ideas, less scientific, had been proposed by Thomas Wright in England and Immanuel Kant in Germany). According to Laplace, whose "nebular hypothesis" [Key] elaborated an idea proposed by René Descartes (1596–1650) in 1644, the planets were formed from a rotating gas cloud that shrank under the influence of gravitation. As it contracted, the cloud shed various rings, each of which condensed into a planet. The theory would mean that the outermost planets were the oldest and the innermost planets the youngest, with the Sun itself representing the remaining part of the original gas cloud.

The nebular hypothesis was accepted for many years, but it was then found to have fatal mathematical weaknesses and was abandoned. Next, a number of tidal theories were proposed, including the ideas put forward in the United States by Thomas Chamberlin and Forest Moulton, who revived George de Buffon's original idea (1745), further developed by James Jeans (1877–1946) in England [19]. It was assumed that the planets were formed by the action of a passing star, which came close to the Sun and pulled off a vast tongue of material. As the star receded, the tongue of matter was left whirling around the Sun and broke up into drops, each drop becoming a planet. This theory was in agreement with the sizes of the planets, since the giants Jupiter and Saturn lie in the middle part of

CONNECTIONS

See also
50 Members of the Sc System
276 Earth's time scale
406 Life and its origins
1490 Attraction and repsion
1494 Circular and vibrat motion
1514 Extremes of pressu
834 Myths of spring

1 According to modern theory, the Solar System began as a mass of gas without any definite form. There was no true Sun and no production of nuclear energy. Most of the gas was hydrogen.

2 As time passed this cloud, which may be referred to as a solar nebula, began to assume a regular shape; and there was a certain increase in temperature, though the Sun was not yet recognizable.

3 The gas cloud continued to contract under the influence of gravitation and the densest part of it was at the center. This was the site of the Sun, which now began to radiate and became a "star."

4 As the Sun increased in luminosity, the gas cloud became less uniform. Condensations appeared in it, and were able to draw in surrounding material, thus making up protoplanets.

5 As the protoplanets increased in size and in mass, their gravitational pulls became stronger and they were able to pull in more and more material from the surrounding regions of the nebula.

6 As the solar nebula shrank, more and more material from it was absorbed into the protoplanets, while the radiation from the Sun continued to increase. The Solar System was not yet recognizable

7 The main protoplanets continued to grow and to draw in more material by means of their own gravitational effects so that the number of protoplanets became steadily less and less.

8 As the protoplanets grew, their form became spherical and the Solar System began to assume its familiar form. The Sun was now radiating energy from thermonuclear reactions.

9 During this long period of protoplanet formation, the Sun had completed its main contraction and had settled down to its stable period on the main sequence, which would last for 10 billion years.

10 By about 5 billion years ago, the Solar System had assumed its present form, with a stable central Sun surrounded by planets and their satellites.

11 In perhaps 5 billion years from now the Sun will have exhausted its supply of available hydrogen and its structure will change. The core will shrink and the surface will expand considerably, with a lower surface temperature.

12 The next stage of solar evolution will be expansion to the red giant stage, with luminosity increased by 100 times. The size of the globe will increase with the overall increase in energy outputs and the inner planets be destroyed.

13 With a further rise in core temperature, the Sun will begin to burn its helium, with a rapid rise in temperature and increase in size. The Earth cannot survive this phase of evolution as the Sun expands to more than 50 times its size.

14 By now the Sun will be at its most unstable, with an intensely hot core and a rarefied atmosphere. The helium will begin to burn giving the so-called helium flash. After a temporary contraction it will be 400 times its present size.

15 Different kinds of reactions inside the Sun will lead to an even further increase of core temperature. The system of planets will no longer exist in the form we know today, and the supply of nuclear energy will be almost exhausted.

16 When all the nuclear energy is used up, the Sun will collapse, very rapidly on the cosmic scale, into a very small, very dense, and very feeble white dwarf. It will continue to shine, because it will still be contracting gravitationally.

17 The final stage of the Sun will be that of a black dwarf, devoid of any light or heat, still circled by its surviving but now dead planets. Black dwarfs may be common, but because they emit no radiation they cannot be detected.

the System, where the thickest part of the cigar-shaped tongue would have been.

This theory too has serious mathematical objections. Also, it is very doubtful whether a tongue of matter could break up into drops as Jeans believed. A modification by Harold Jeffreys (1891–), according to which the intruding star actually struck the Sun a glancing blow, also has marked weaknesses and few modern astronomers support any form of tidal theory for the evolution of the Solar System.

It was also proposed, by Fred Hoyle (1915–), that the Sun was once a binary star [18] and that the companion exploded as a supernova, producing scattered debris that formed the planets before the companion itself moved off into space by a kind of recoil action. This has met with little support among other astronomers.

The future of the Solar System

Modern theories assume the existence of what may be termed a solar nebula, which contained the material that gradually built up into the planets by an accretion process. The exact details are a matter for debate, but in essence the theories are supportable. If they prove valid, the Sun and planets have a common origin and are composed of essentially the same kind of material.

The Sun is believed to be a stable main sequence star, but it will not remain so indefinitely. In the far future—perhaps in some 5 billion years—its structure will have to change, since the supply of available hydrogen "fuel" will be exhausted. The Sun will then expand into a red giant star and for a period it will send out about 100 times as much energy as it does at present.

The effects of this expansion on the inner planets will be disastrous; even if they are not destroyed they will be stripped of their atmospheres and will become intolerably hot. Subsequently the Sun will collapse into a very small, feeble, white dwarf star, still surrounded by the surviving members of its planetary system. The exact time scale cannot be determined, but it is certain that life on Earth will not continue indefinitely and that the Solar System in its present form must have a limited existence.

KEY

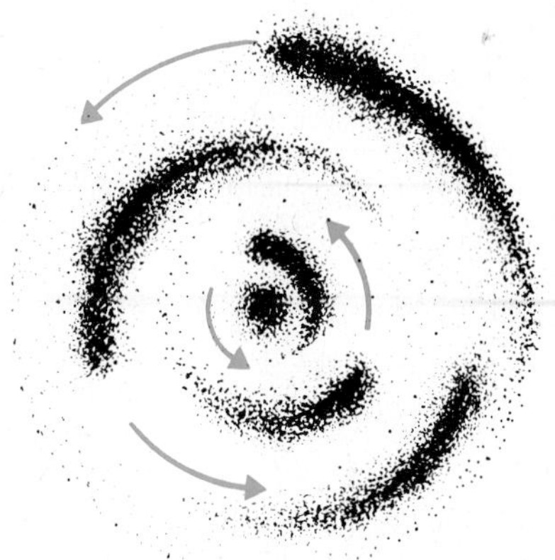

The nebular hypothesis, proposed by Laplace, assumed that before the birth of the planets the Solar System consisted of a gas cloud that shrank because of gravitational forces. This resulted in an increase in the speed of rotation and a ring separated from the nebula. The ring slowly condensed into a planet. Further rings were then thrown off, each producing a planet. The theory is mathematically weak.

18

A

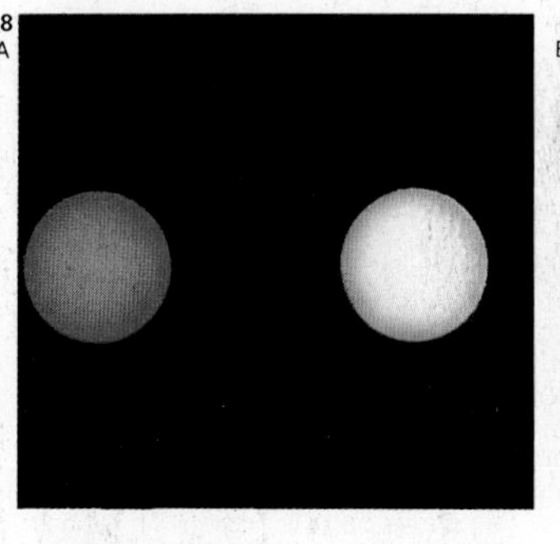

B

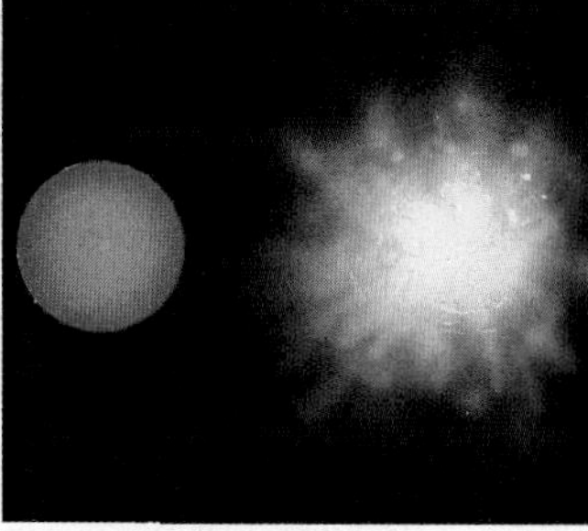

C

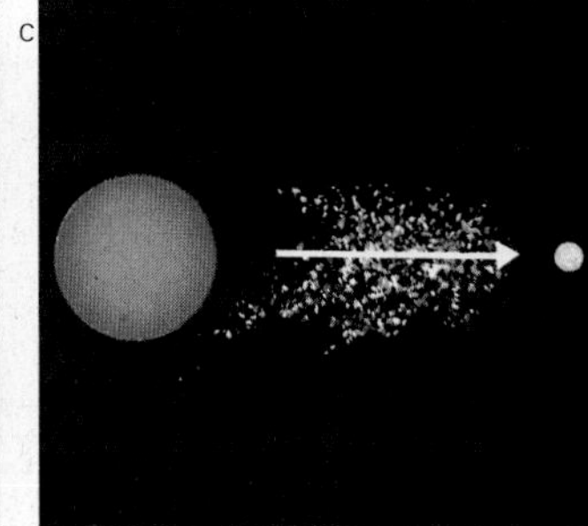

D

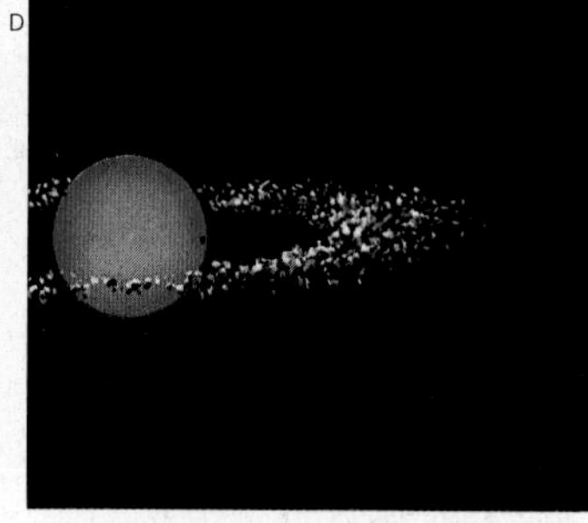

18 The binary theory of the origin of the Solar System was proposed by Fred Hoyle. He argued that the Sun once had a binary companion [A] that exploded as a supernova [B] and was blown off, leaving a cloud of fragments [C] in orbit around the Sun. These fragments collected together by the process of accretion to form the planets [D], while the remnant of the supernova companion moved away into space and cannot now be identified. This theory is very difficult to substantiate and is not now generally favored. If valid, it would mean that planetary systems would be uncommon although in modern solar cloud theories they are likely to be very common in our Galaxy.

19 A

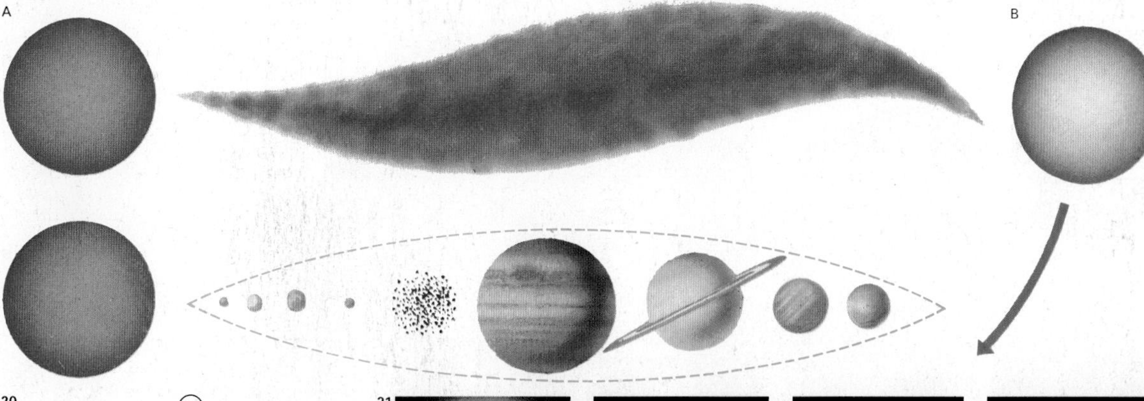

B

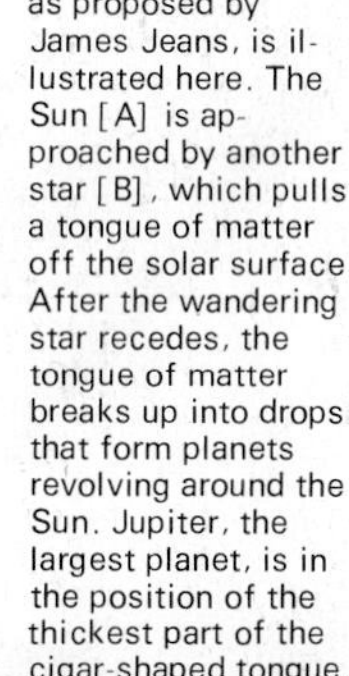

19 The tidal theory, as proposed by James Jeans, is illustrated here. The Sun [A] is approached by another star [B], which pulls a tongue of matter off the solar surface. After the wandering star recedes, the tongue of matter breaks up into drops that form planets revolving around the Sun. Jupiter, the largest planet, is in the position of the thickest part of the cigar-shaped tongue.

20

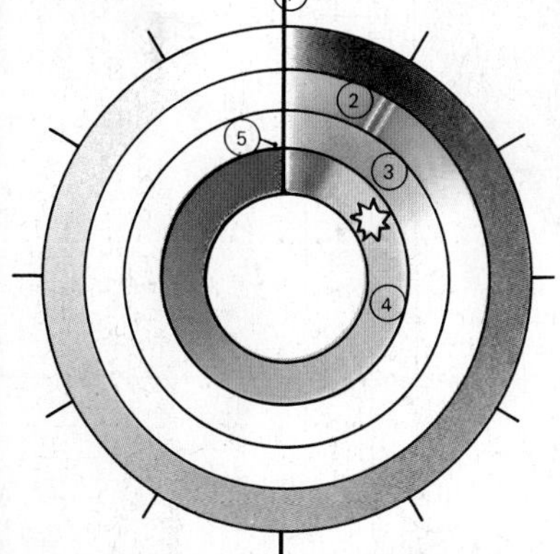

1
2
3
4
5

21

A

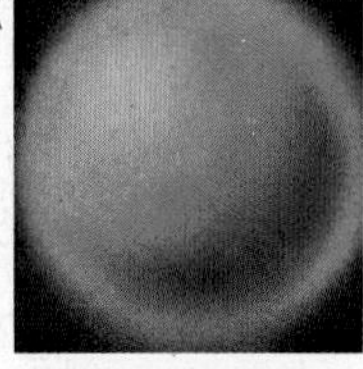

B

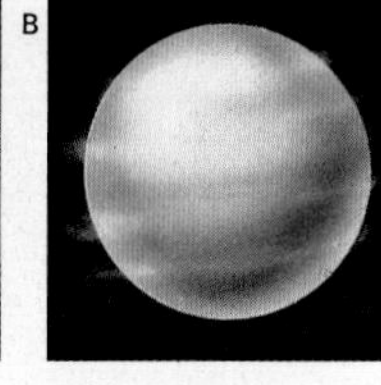

C

D

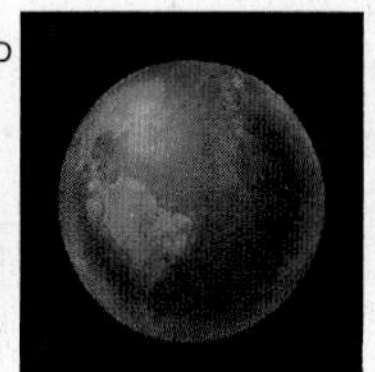

E

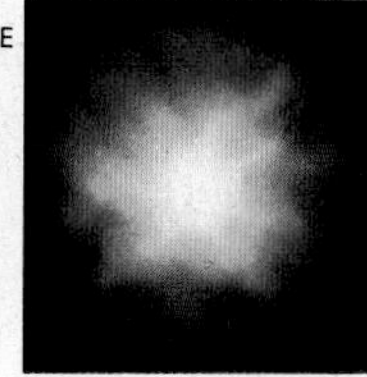

20 The time scale of the Solar System can be represented on a 12-hour clock. From the inner circle outward the life span of the Sun, inner planets, Earth, and outer planets are traced respectively. At the 12 O'clock position [1] the Solar System was created. After 4 billion years conditions on Earth are favorable for life [2]. As a red giant the Sun engulfs the inner planets [3] to collapse as a white dwarf [4] and end as a black dwarf [5].

21 The Earth had its origin in the material of the solar nebula [A], which at first had no regular form. When Earth reached its present size [B] the original hydrogen atmosphere had already been lost and had been replaced by a new one, caused by gases sent out from the interior. Life could begin and today the Earth is moving in a stable orbit around a stable star, so that it is habitable [C]. This state will not persist indefinitely. When the Sun enters the red giant stage, the Earth will be heated, so that the oceans will boil and the atmosphere will be driven off [D]; finally the Earth will be destroyed [E].

Members of the Solar System

The Solar System is made up of one star—the Sun—nine principal planets, and various bodies of lesser importance, such as the satellites that attend some of the planets and the asteroids. It is entirely dependent on the Sun, which is by far the most massive body and the only one to be self-luminous. The remaining members of the Solar System shine by reflected sunlight and appear so brilliant in our skies that it is difficult to accept that in the universe as a whole they are not nearly as important as they look to us here on Earth.

The inner planets

The planets are divided into two well-marked groups. First come four relatively small planets: Mercury, Venus, the Earth, and Mars, with diameters ranging from 7,926 miles (12,756km) for the Earth to only 3,032 miles (4,880km) for Mercury. These planets have various factors in common. All, for example, have solid surfaces and are presumably made up of similar materials, although the Earth and Mercury are more dense than Mars and Venus. Their orbits do not in general depart much from the circular, although the paths of Mercury and Mars are considerably more eccentric than those of Earth and Venus. Mercury and Venus are known as the "inferior planets" because their orbits lie inside that of the Earth. They show lunar-type phases from new to full and remain in the same region of the sky as the Sun. Mercury and Venus are unattended by any satellites. The Earth has one satellite (our familiar Moon), while Mars has two, Phobos and Deimos, both of which are very small and different in nature from the Moon.

Asteroids and giant planets

Beyond Mars comes a wide gap, in which move thousands of small worlds known as the asteroids, planetoids, or minor planets. Even Ceres, the largest, is only about 600–750 miles (1,000–1,200km) in diameter. This is much larger than was once thought, but is still small by planetary standards. It is not therefore surprising that the asteroids remained undiscovered until relatively recent times; Ceres was found in 1801. Only one asteroid, Vesta, is ever visible to the naked eye. Far beyond the main asteroid zone come the four giant planets: Jupiter, Saturn, Uranus, and Neptune. These worlds are quite different from the terrestrial planets: they are fluid (that is, gas or liquid) rather than solid bodies, with very dense atmospheres. Their masses are so great that they have retained much of their original hydrogen; the escape velocity of Jupiter, for instance, is 37 miles (60km) per second as against only 7 miles (11.2km) per second for Earth. Their mean distances from the Sun range from 483 million miles (778 million km) for Jupiter out to 2,794 million miles (4,497 million km) for Neptune. Conventional diagrams of the Solar System tend to be misleading as far as scale is concerned: for example, Saturn and Uranus are often depicted near each other when in fact the distance of Uranus from the Earth's orbit is about twice that of Saturn.

The giant planets have various points in common, but differ markedly in detail. Their densities are comparatively low; Saturn's density is actually less than that of

CONNECTIONS

See also
48 Evolution of the Solar System
52 The Moon
62 The planet Mercury
64 The planet Venus
66 The planet Earth
68 The planet Mars
78 Minor planets
80 The planet Jupiter
84 The planet Saturn
88 The outer planets
90 Comets
92 Meteors and meteorites
94 The Sun and the solar spectrum

1

1 Shown here in cross-section, the Sun has an equatorial diameter 109 times that of Earth, or 865,000 miles (1,392,000 km). Despite the fact that its volume is more than a million times the Earth's, the Sun's mass is only 333,000 times the Earth's, as the density is lower. (The mean solar specific gravity, on a scale where water = 1, is only 1.4.)

2 The planets of the Solar System are shown at the same scale. On the right is a segment of the Sun [1]; from its surface rises a huge prominence [2], made up of glowing gas. Then come the inner planets: Mercury [3], Venus [4], the Earth [5] with its Moon [6], and Mars [7]. Mars has two dwarf satellites, Phobos [8] and Deimos [9], which are exaggerated here. If shown to scale, they would be microscopic. Beyond Mars are the asteroids, or minor planets [10], of which even the largest is only about 600–750 miles (1,000–1,200km) in diameter. And beyond lie the giant planets: Jupiter [11] with its four large satellites Io [12], Europa [13], Ganymede [14], and Callisto [15] and its nine small satellites; Saturn [16] with its retinue of satellites, of which the largest is Titan [17]; Uranus [18] with five satellites; Neptune [19] with Triton [20]; and Pluto [21].

2

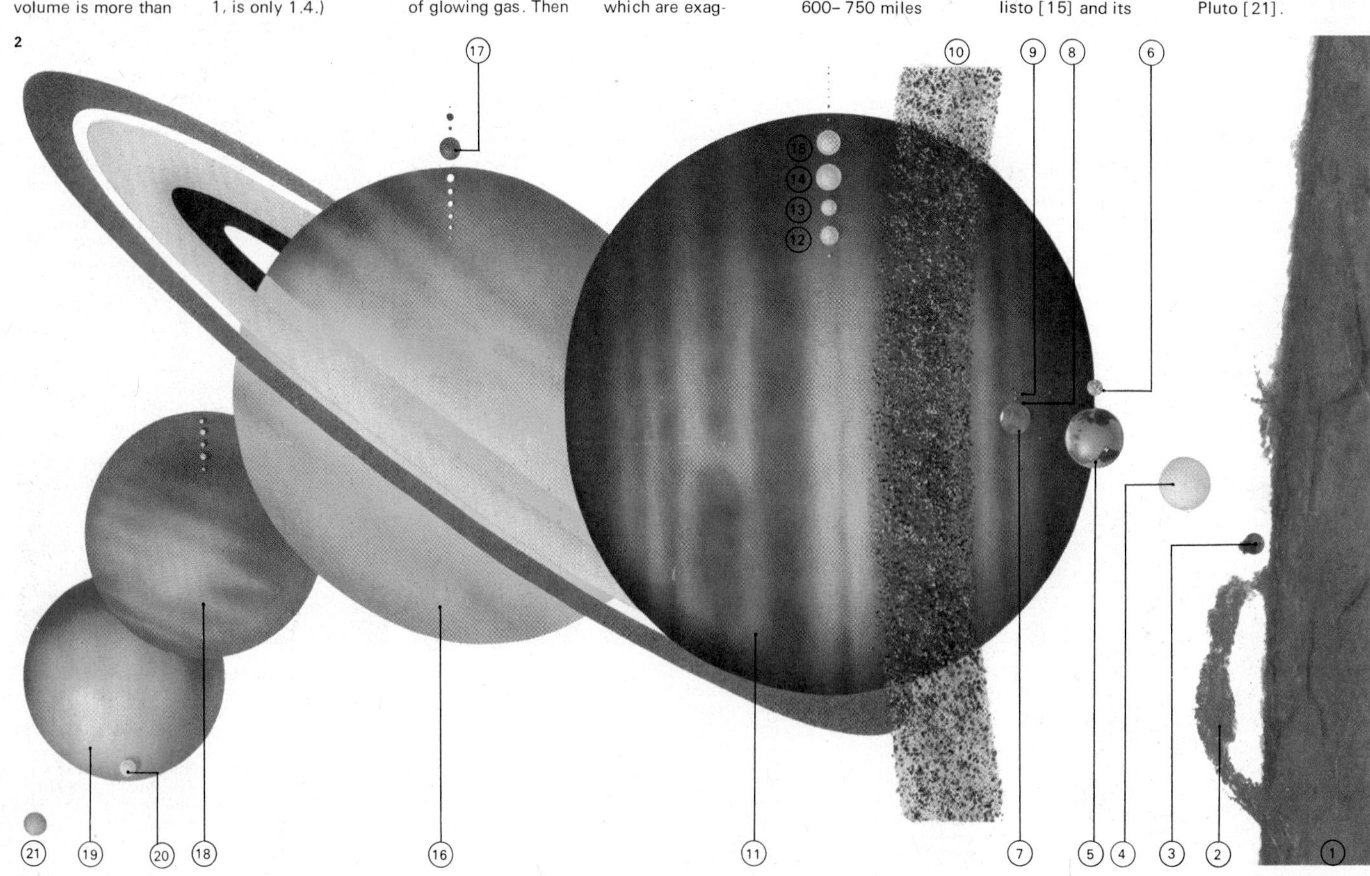

17
10
9
8
6
15
14
13
12
21
19
20
18
16
11
7
5
4
3
2
1

water. Although Jupiter is seen solely by reflected sunlight, the planet does generate some heat of its own. The core temperature must be high; however, it is not nearly high enough for nuclear reactions to begin, so that Jupiter cannot be compared to a star like the Sun.

The outer planets

Five of the planets—Mercury, Venus, Mars, Jupiter, and Saturn—have been known from ancient times, since all are prominent naked-eye objects. Uranus, which is just visible with the naked eye, was discovered by chance in 1781 by William Herschel (1738–1822), and Neptune was added to the list of known planets in 1846 as a result of mathematical investigations of the movements of Uranus. All the giants are attended by satellites [2]: Jupiter has thirteen attendants, Saturn ten, Uranus five and Neptune two. Of these, several are of planetary size, with diameters at least equal to that of Mercury.

The outermost known planet is Pluto, discovered in 1930 by Clyde Tombaugh at the Lowell Observatory, Flagstaff, Arizona. It is not a giant, being smaller than the Earth, and is usually ranked as a terrestrial-type planet, even though little is known about it. Whereas most of the planets have orbital inclinations similar to that of the Earth (the difference is 7 degrees for Mercury, much less for the remainder), the orbit of Pluto is tilted at the relatively steep angle of 17 degrees and the orbit is so eccentric that at perihelion, or closest approach to the Sun, Pluto will, in the near future, come closer than Neptune. Pluto seems, in fact, to be in a class of its own and it may be a former satellite of Neptune that has achieved independence. Whether or not some more distant planets exist remains to be seen.

Comets are also members of the Solar System. They contain both dust particles and volatile material together with tenuous gas. Most of them have very eccentric orbits. Finally there are meteoroids, which may be regarded as the debris of the Solar System; some meteors are associated with comets.

KEY

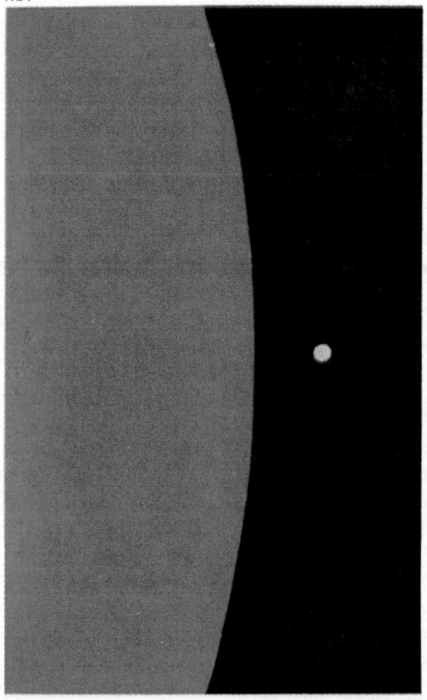

The Sun is an ordinary main-sequence star with a magnitude of +5. It is the body on which the Solar System depends, and its volume is more than a million times greater than that of the Earth. It is, in fact, far more massive than all the planets combined. When compared with a giant star, however, the Sun is small. The diagram shows the Sun alongside a segment of the giant red star Betelgeuse, which marks Orion's right shoulder. Betelgeuse is of spectral Class M2—a very cool star—but has an absolute magnitude of −5.5. Its diameter is 300–400 times that of the Sun and its circumference is large enough to contain the orbit of the Earth.

3

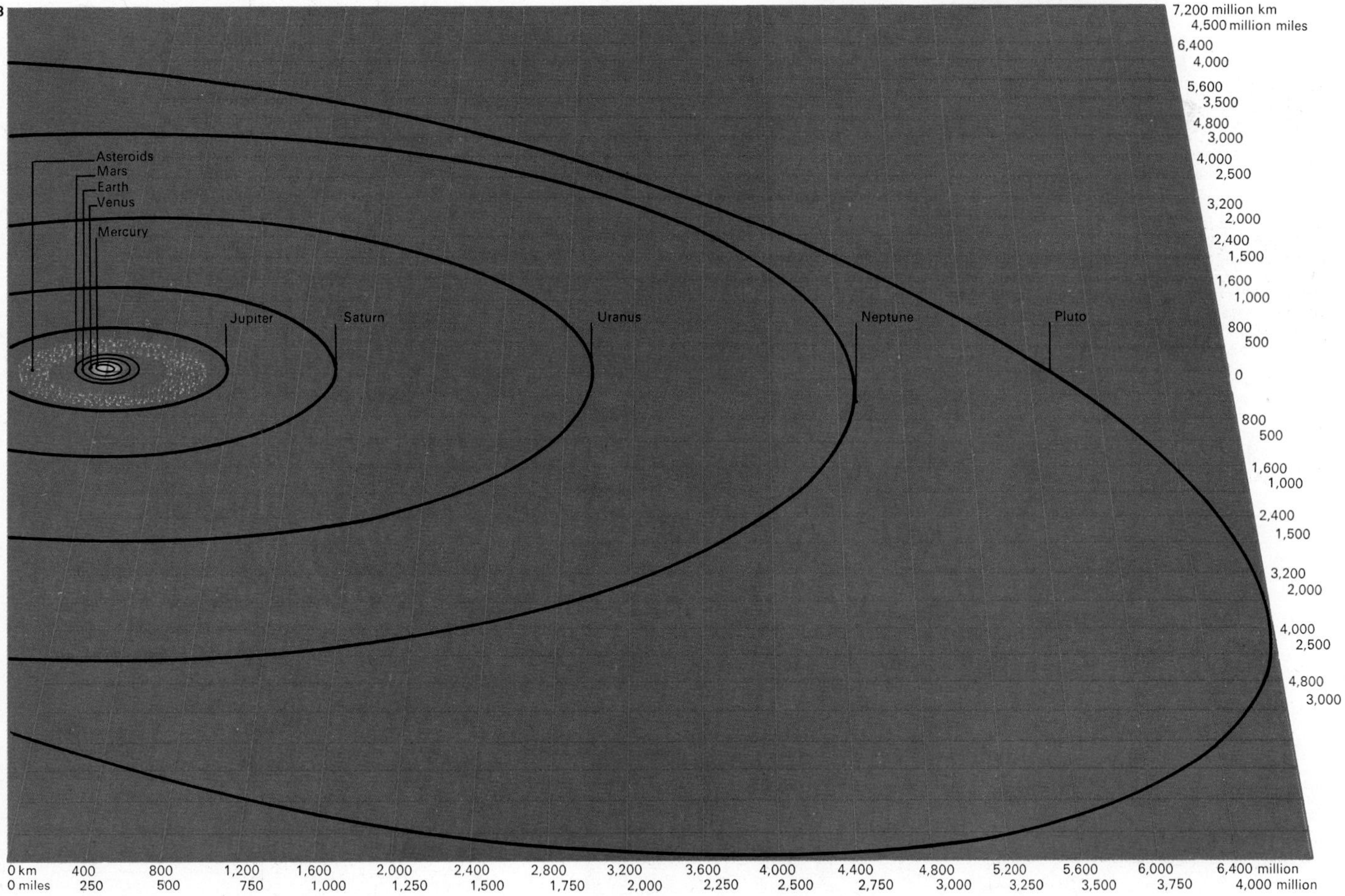

Asteroids
Mars
Earth
Venus
Mercury
Jupiter
Saturn
Uranus
Neptune
Pluto
7,200 million km
4,500 million miles
6,400
4,000
5,600
3,500
4,800
3,000
4,000
2,500
3,200
2,000
2,400
1,500
1,600
1,000
800
500
0
800
500
1,600
1,000
2,400
1,500
3,200
2,000
4,000
2,500
4,800
3,000
0 km 400 800 1,200 1,600 2,000 2,400 2,800 3,200 3,600 4,000 4,400 4,800 5,200 5,600 6,000 6,400 million
0 miles 250 500 750 1,000 1,250 1,500 1,750 2,000 2,250 2,500 2,750 3,000 3,250 3,500 3,750 4,000 million

3 The map of the Solar System shows the approximate solar orbit of each of the nine planets against a grid giving distances in miles and kilometers. The following measurements for diameter and rotation period refer to each planet's equator. The sidereal period is the time taken by each planet to orbit the Sun once.

Mercury
Distance from Sun, mean 58 million km (36 million miles)
Diameter, 4,880km (3,032 miles)
Rotation period, 58·7 Earth-days
Mass, 0·05 Earth.
Surface gravity, 0·37 Earth.
Escape velocity, 4·2km (2·6 miles) per second.
Sidereal period, 88 Earth-days.

Venus
Distance from Sun, mean 108,200,000km (67,200,000 miles)
Diameter, 12,100km (7,500 miles)
Rotation period, 243 Earth-days.
Mass, 0·82 Earth.
Surface gravity, 0·90 Earth.
Escape velocity, 10·36km (6·4 miles) per second.
Sidereal period, 224·7 Earth-days.

Earth
Distance from Sun, mean 149,596,000km (92,750,000 miles)
Diameter (equatorial), 12,755km (7,908 miles), Polar 12,714km (7,883 miles).
Rotation period, 23hr 56min.
Escape velocity, 11·2km (7 miles) per second.
Sidereal period, 365·2 days.
Axial inclination: 23·5°.

Mars
Distance from Sun, mean 227,940,000km (141,323,000 miles)
Diameter, 6,790km (4,220 miles)
Rotation period, 24hr 37min. 23sec.
Mass, 0·11 Earth.
Surface gravity, 0·4 Earth.
Escape velocity, 5km (3·1 miles) per second.
Sidereal period, 686·96 Earth-days.

Jupiter
Distance from Sun, mean 778,300,000km (483,600,000 miles)
Diameter (equatorial) 143,000km (89,000 miles)
Rotation period (equatorial), 9hr 51min.
Mass, 318 Earth.
Surface gravity, 2·64 Earth.
Escape velocity, 60·22km (37·4 miles) per second.
Sidereal period, 11·86 Earth-years.

Saturn
Distance from Sun, mean 1,427 million km (887 million miles)
Diameter (equatorial), 120,000km (75,000 miles)
Rotation period (equatorial), 10hr 14min.
Mass, 95 Earth.
Surface gravity, 1·16 Earth.
Escape velocity, 36km (22 miles) per second.
Sidereal period, 29·46 Earth-years.

Uranus
Distance from Sun, mean 2,869,600,000km (1,780 million miles).
Sidereal period, 84 years.

Neptune
Distance from Sun, mean 4,497 million km (2,794 million miles)
Sidereal period, 164·8 years.

Pluto
Distance from Sun, mean 5,900 million km (3,658 million miles).
Sidereal period, 248·5 years.

The Moon

The Moon is the closest natural body to Earth in the sky. Its distance from the Earth averages only 239,000 miles (384,000km), which is about equal to ten times the distance around the Earth's equator. It is a small world [1] with a diameter of 2,160 miles (3,426km); its mass is only 1/81 that of the Earth and the escape velocity is 1.5 miles (2.4km) per second, which is too low to enable the Moon to retain an appreciable atmosphere.

Movements of the Moon

It is not entirely correct to say that the Moon revolves around the Earth. More properly, the Earth and Moon revolve around the "barycenter," or center of gravity of the system. But because of the discrepancy between the masses of the two bodies, the barycenter lies well inside the terrestrial globe, so that the simple statement that "the Moon goes around the Earth" is good enough for most purposes. The period of revolution around the Earth is 27.3 days and this is also the time taken for the Moon to rotate once on its axis. As a result, the same hemisphere is always turned toward Earth.

The Moon's path is not quite circular, so the apparent diameter of the disk varies within narrow limits. The familiar phases occur because the Moon does not always turn its daylight side toward Earth [2]. Before the flight of the circumlunar probe Luna 3, in 1959, nothing was definitely known about the Moon's far side. Effects known as librations [3]—irregularities in the Moon's movement—extend the visible area to a total of 59 percent of the whole surface (although never more than 50 percent at any one time).

Theories of origin

Although the Moon is formally listed as the Earth's satellite, it seems disturbingly large to be a truly secondary body. There are other satellites in the Solar System that are larger than the Moon (three members of Jupiter's family, one of Saturn's, and one of Neptune's), but all of these move around giant planets. Thus Triton, the senior attendant of Neptune, has only 1/750 of the mass of its primary, although it is possibly larger than the planet Mercury and certainly larger than the Moon.

Thus, the Earth-Moon system should perhaps be regarded as a double planet, which leads to the problem of the Moon's origin. The tidal theory proposed by George Darwin (1845–1912) in the nineteenth century was popular for many years. According to this hypothesis, the Earth and Moon were once a single body, rotating rapidly and therefore becoming unstable. Eventually the globe became so distorted that part of it broke away and moved off to form the Moon.

There are, however, mathematical objections to this theory that are so serious that few astronomers now support it in any form. It is much more likely that the Moon and the Earth were formed in the same way, from the solar nebula, either close together in space or else independently—in which case the Moon would have been "captured" by the Earth later on. On the whole, the former alternative seems to be the more plausible.

CONNECTIONS

See also
54 Moon missions
56 The Moon's structure
58 Moon maps
60 Moon panorama
146 Colonizing the Moon
66 The planet Earth
226 Waves and tides
246 The rock cycle and igneous rocks

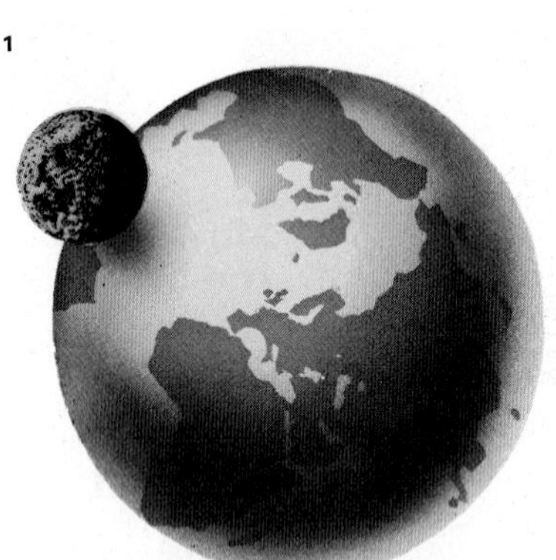

1 The Moon is a small world compared with the Earth. Its mass is much less and its specific gravity is lower. But the discrepancy between Earth and Moon is much less marked than with the satellites of other planets. With Neptune, for instance, the mass of its largest satellite, Triton, is only 1/750 of that of the planet. This is one reason why the Earth-Moon system may be regarded as a double planet.

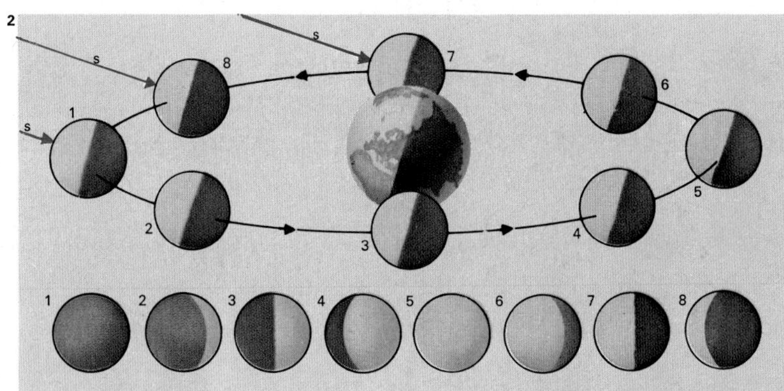

s
1
2
3
4
5
6
7
8

2 The phases of the Moon occur because the Moon has no light of its own. The daylight side reflects the Sun; the night side reflects "Earthshine." In the illustration, sunlight comes in from the upper left. In [1], the Moon's dark side is turned Earthward (new) and the Moon cannot be seen—unless it passes directly in front of the Sun, producing a solar eclipse. Between [1] and [3] the Moon is crescent; at [3], half (first quarter); at [4], gibbous; and at [5], full. The Moon then wanes, through gibbous [6] to half, or last quarter [7], crescent in the morning sky [8], and back to new.

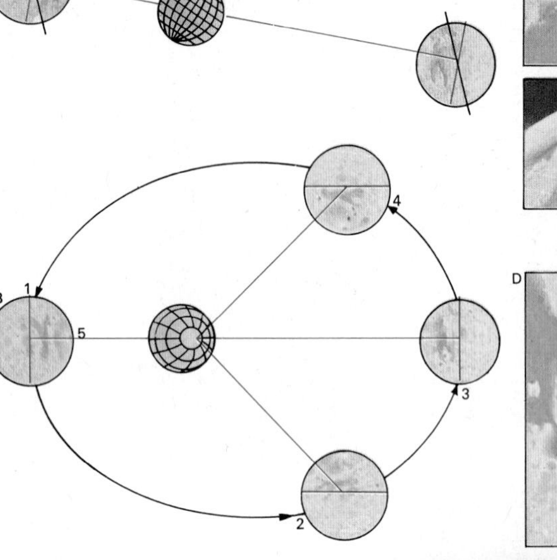

3A
B
1
2
3
4
5

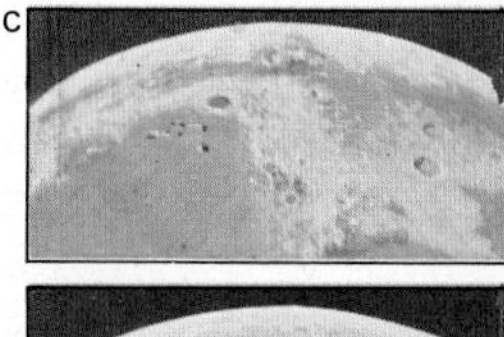

C

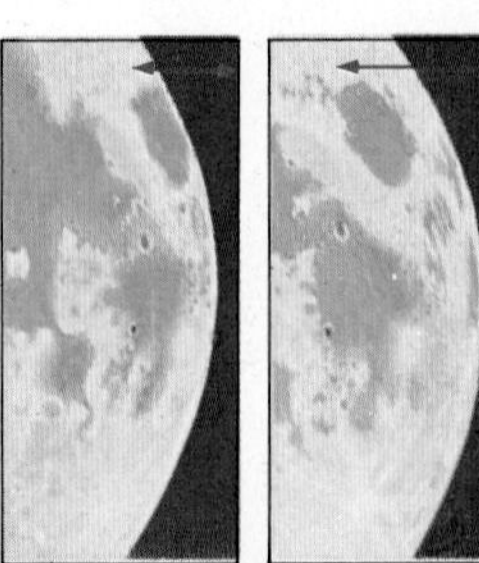

D

3 Librations are irregularities in the Moon's movement. Libration in latitude [A] occurs because the Moon's axis is tilted to its orbital plane, thus allowing views over the north [C] and south poles. Libration in longitude [B] occurs when the Moon's speed of revolution changes slightly—it moves fastest at perigee [1] and slowest at apogee [3]. The effect can be seen by tracing point 5 through its orbit from 1 to 4. This allows a view around each limb (edge) [D].

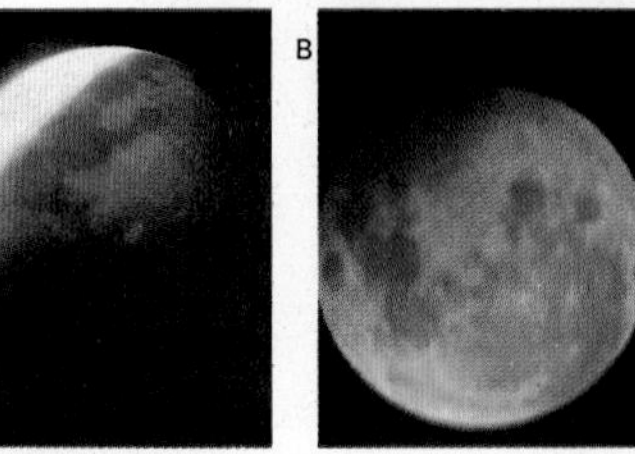

4
A
B

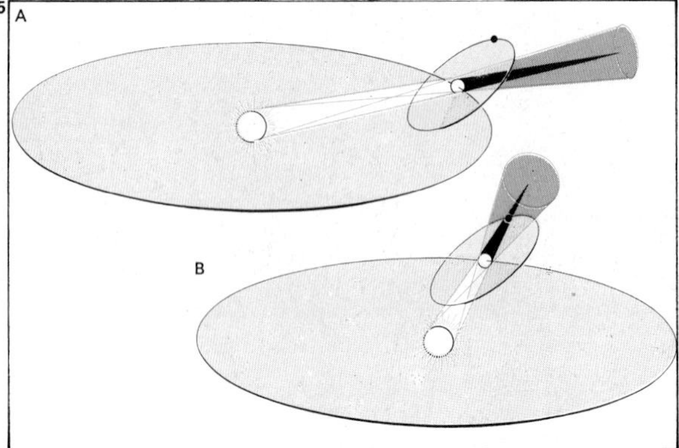

5
A
B

4 During a total eclipse [A] the Moon does not vanish completely because a certain amount of light is refracted onto its surface by way of the Earth's atmosphere. The boundary between light and dark is never sharp. Partial eclipses [B] also occur. When the Moon passes through the area of "penumbra" that lies on either side of the main shadow cone, the visible effect is less striking.

5 Eclipses do not occur at every full Moon because the Moon's orbit is inclined at 5° to that of the Earth. At most full Moons, the Moon passes either above or below the shadow [A]. A lunar eclipse [B] is produced when the Moon passes into the shadow cast by the Earth.

Surface features: seas and craters

The first telescopic maps of the Moon were drawn in 1609. The English mathematician Thomas Harriot (1560–1621) drew a chart that shows many features in recognizable form. A longer and more systematic study was carried out from 1610 by Galileo, who described the mountains, the craters, and the gray plains in some detail. The gray areas were named "seas" and the nomenclature has not been altered, although for centuries it has been known that there is no water in them. The names are usually given in Latin; thus the Sea of Clouds is Mare Nubium and the Ocean of Storms is Oceanus Procellarum.

The walled structures commonly known as craters dominate the entire lunar scene. In size, they range from vast enclosures more than 150 miles (240km) in diameter to tiny pits too small to be seen from Earth. In a typical crater there is a rampart that rises to only a modest height above the outer terrain, the floor is sunken, and there may be a central mountain or mountain group. In some the wall may be more than 10,000ft (3,000m) above the deepest part of the floor. There have been endless arguments about the origin of the craters. The main controversy centers on whether the craters were produced by external forces (meteoritic impact) or by internal ones (vulcanism). No doubt both types of craters exist on the Moon, as on Earth.

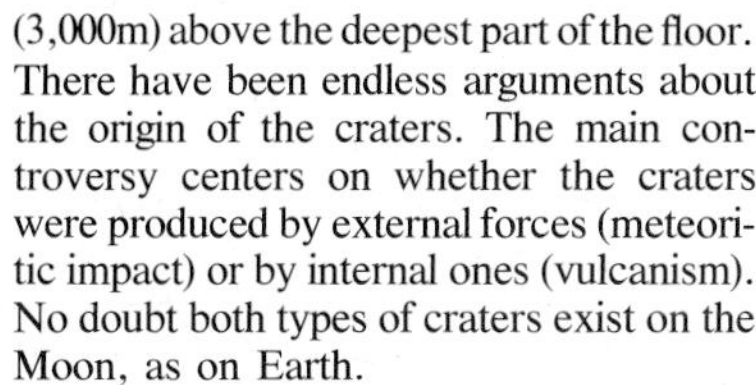

Some of the waterless seas, like the regular craters, are more or less circular with mountainous borders. The huge Mare Imbrium, or Sea of Showers, for example, is bounded by the lunar Apennines, Carpathians, and Alps, although the mountain boundary is not continuous and there are wide gaps. The Apennines [7] are the most spectacular of the ranges; their loftiest peaks reach more than 15,000ft (4,570m).

Other lunar features include hills; domes, with gentle slopes and often a craterlet or craterlets on the summit; occasional faults; and many cracklike features called clefts or rills. Any small telescope will reveal these details clearly; but even to the naked eye various markings can be identified.

KEY

The dark "seas" and bright uplands of the full Moon are seen here. The crater Tycho dominates the southern hemisphere.

6 The Sinus Medii, or Central Bay, photographed from Apollo 10, is one of the relatively smooth mare areas.

7 The lunar Apennines are here photographed with a 12in (30cm) reflector. The highest mountains rise to 15,000ft (4,570m) above the plains. They are by far the most spectacular lunar peaks.

8 The great crater Langrenus has massive terraced walls and a complicated central mountain.

9 This crater on the far side of the Moon was photographed by Apollo 10.

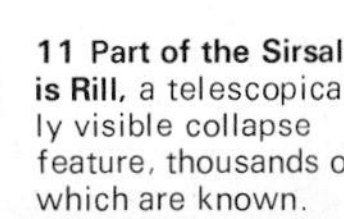

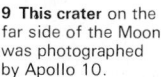

10 Clavius, photographed from Earth, is a walled plain 144 miles (230km) wide with superimposed craters.

11 Part of the Sirsalis Rill, a telescopically visible collapse feature, thousands of which are known.

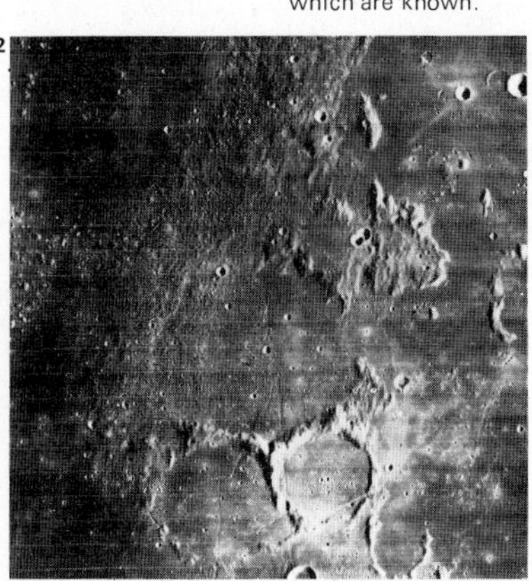

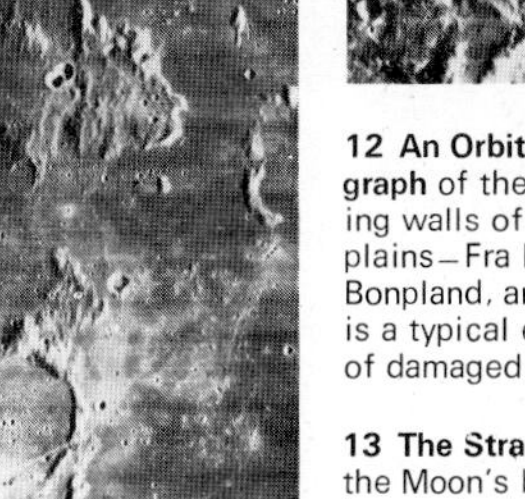

12 An Orbiter photograph of the connecting walls of three plains – Fra Mauro, Bonpland, and Parry – is a typical example of damaged walls.

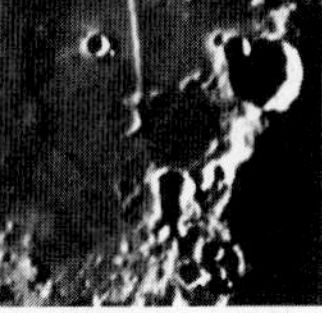

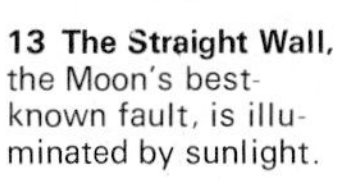

13 The Straight Wall, the Moon's best-known fault, is illuminated by sunlight.

Moon missions

Flight to the Moon became a practical possibility after the opening of the Space Age in October 1957, when the Soviet Union launched Sputnik 1, a satellite that circled the Earth. Two years later three Soviet vehicles were sent on lunar missions. The first of these (Luna, or Lunik 1) bypassed the Moon and sent back useful information, notably that there was no appreciable magnetic field. Luna 2 crash-landed on the Mare Imbrium in September 1959 and in October Luna 3 [1] went on a round trip, sending back the first photographs of the Moon's far side. This proved to be just as mountainous, crater-scarred, and sterile as the side seen from Earth, but there were no comparable seas.

Early unmanned explorations

The American Ranger program [2] introduced a new phase in man's knowledge of the Moon. The Rangers were designed to send back close-range photographs before crashing onto the Moon. Ranger 7, in 1964, was the first successful probe of this kind. Two more followed; the last of them came down in the prominent crater Alphonsus, near the center of the Moon's disk as seen from Earth. In January 1966 the Soviet Union achieved a major triumph by soft-landing an automatic probe, Luna 9, on the surface of the Moon. Its cameras showed a landscape that looked remarkably like a lava plain, with hummocks and crater pits everywhere. Luna 9 was of special importance because it finally disproved a curious theory that the lunar seas were filled with soft, treacherous dust to a depth of several hundred feet. The landing showed that the Moon's surface layer, or regolith, can support the weight of a spacecraft [12].

Lunar mapping was more or less completed during the two years following August 1966. Five US Orbiters [4] moved around the Moon in closed paths, sending back amazingly detailed pictures. The United States also soft-landed several vehicles—the Surveyors. On January 10, 1968, Surveyor 7 came down near the crater Tycho, in the southern uplands, and sent back high-quality pictures of the outer slopes of the wall.

The Soviet Union continued its program of unmanned exploration into the 1970s. It achieved a major triumph with Luna 16 [6] in 1970, which landed in the Mare Foecunditatis and then returned, bringing samples of lunar rocks. Later in the same year Luna 17 landed in the Mare Imbrium. From it emerged Lunokhod 1 [7], an eight-wheeled craft powered by solar batteries and guided from Earth. After extensive exploration it ceased to function on October 4, 1971. Lunokhod 2 followed in 1973.

Men on the Moon

From the mid 1960s onward the United States had been concentrating on the Apollo program of sending men to the Moon. This culminated in July 1969, when Neil Armstrong (1930–) and Edwin Aldrin (1930–) left Eagle [5], the lunar module of Apollo 11 [8], and made the historic "one small step" onto the lunar surface. After collecting samples of lunar material [14] and leaving recording instruments behind [12], the two astronauts returned to their module and rejoined the third member of the exped-

CONNECTIONS

See also
52 The Moon
56 The Moon's structure
58 Moon maps
60 Moon panorama
146 Colonizing the Moon
142 A history of space achievements

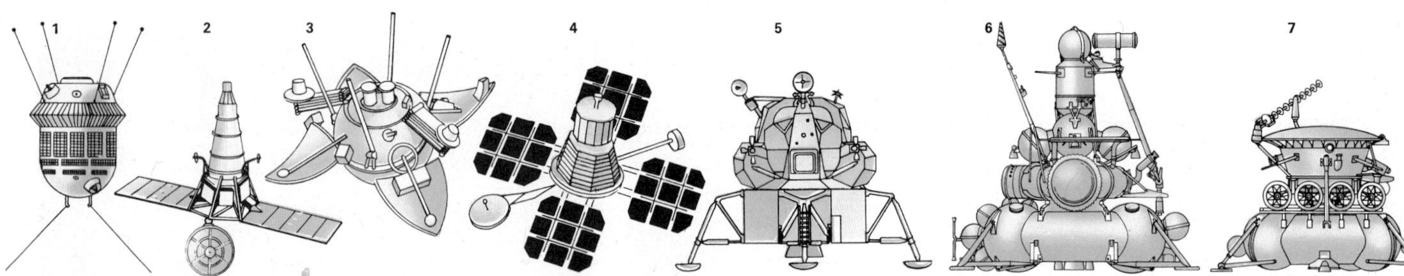

1
2
3
4
5
6
7

1 Luna 3 was the probe that made the first circumlunar flight (October 1959). It sent back pictures of the far side.

2 Ranger 8 (1965) crash-landed near the crater Delambre but sent back excellent pictures before impact.

3 Luna 13, launched December 21, 1966 made the first successful lunar soft landing and sent back pictures.

4 Orbiter 5, last of the series of Orbiters, completed (1968) full photographic coverage of the lunar surface.

5 Eagle (1969), the lunar module of Apollo 11, took Armstrong and Aldrin to Tranquility Base on the Moon.

6 Luna 16 (1970) landed in the Mare Foecunditatis and collected samples of lunar material to bring back.

7 Lunokhod 1 landed with Luna 17 in November 1970, took photographs, and crawled about collecting data.

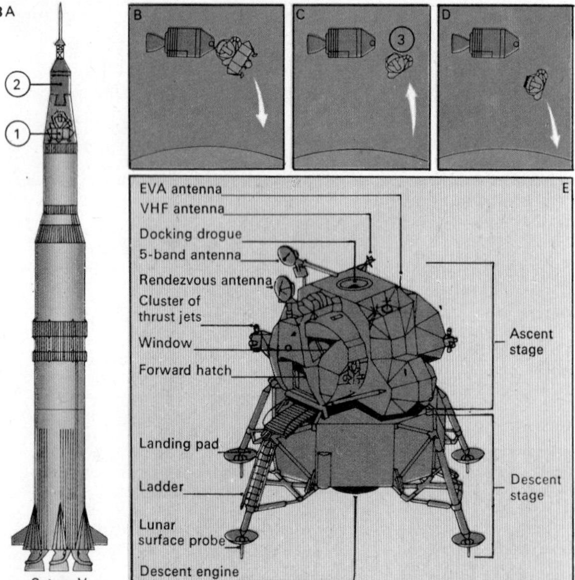

8A
B
C
D
E
2
1
3
Saturn V
EVA antenna
VHF antenna
Docking drogue
S-band antenna
Rendezvous antenna
Cluster of thrust jets
Window
Forward hatch
Landing pad
Ladder
Lunar surface probe
Descent engine
Ascent stage
Descent stage

8 The Apollo Moon program used a Saturn rocket [A] to carry the lunar module [1] and the command and service modules [2]. The lunar module, holding two astronauts, descended to the Moon [B]. Its upper part [3] later left, blasting off from the descent stage back into orbit [C] to rendezvous with the third member of the team, still in orbit around the Moon. The module was then jettisoned [D] and crashed onto the Moon. The lunar module is shown in detail [E].

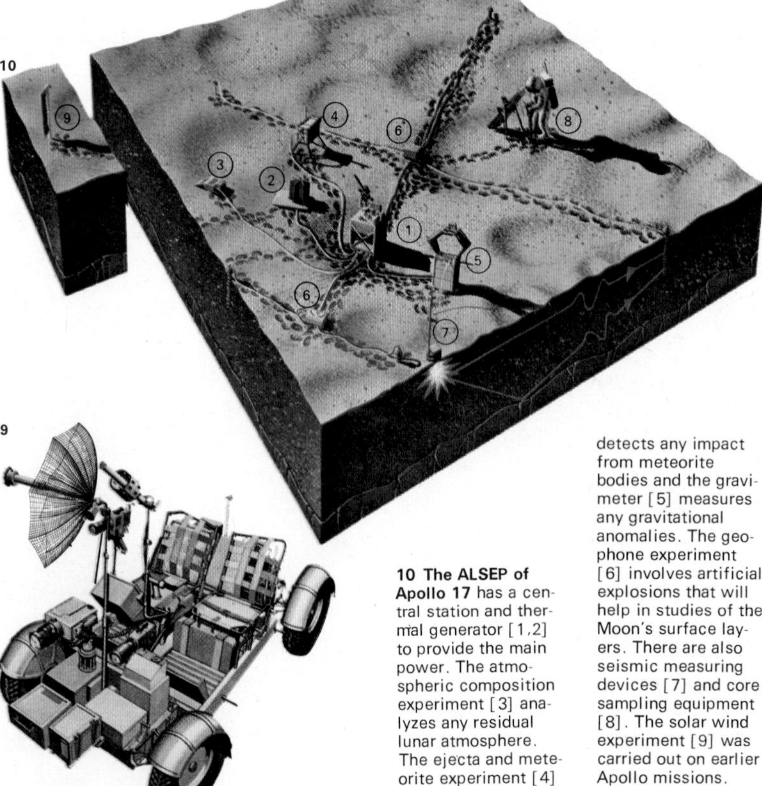

10
9
1
2
3
4
5
6
7
8
9

9 The Lunar Roving Vehicle (LRV) was carried by the last three Apollos (15, 16, and 17) and was used by the astronauts to drive across the Moon's surface for considerable distances. It had a maximum speed of 8 mph (13 km/h).

10 The ALSEP of Apollo 17 has a central station and thermal generator [1,2] to provide the main power. The atmospheric composition experiment [3] analyzes any residual lunar atmosphere. The ejecta and meteorite experiment [4] detects any impact from meteorite bodies and the gravimeter [5] measures any gravitational anomalies. The geophone experiment [6] involves artificial explosions that will help in studies of the Moon's surface layers. There are also seismic measuring devices [7] and core sampling equipment [8]. The solar wind experiment [9] was carried out on earlier Apollo missions.

ition, Michael Collins (1930–), who was orbiting the Moon in the command module of Apollo 11.

Apollo 12 followed later in 1969. The explorers, astronauts Charles Conrad (1930–) and Alan Bean (1932–), landed near a previous automatic probe, Surveyor 3, and were able to bring parts of it home. With the next mission, Apollo 13, came the first real failure. An explosion in the service module of the spacecraft during the outward journey put the main power supplies out of action. The lunar landing was canceled and it was only by a combination of courage, skill, and luck on the part of the astronauts and the operators at mission control that tragedy was averted. Since then there have been four more Apollo landings. The series ended in 1972 with Apollo 17, which landed in the Taurus-Littrow region, manned by Eugene Cernan (1934–) and Harrison Schmitt (1935–).

Each successful mission deployed what is called an Apollo Lunar Surface Experiments Package (ALSEP) [10]. Various investigations have been carried out and knowledge of the Moon has improved immensely, even though astronomers still argue about the origin of the main craters. At the beginning of 1974 all the ALSEPs, apart from that of Apollo 11, were still transmitting information back to Earth.

Lunar landscape

Conditions on the Moon are unfamiliar. An astronaut has only one-sixth of his normal weight (although his mass is unaltered). There is virtually no local surface color and the lunar sky is black even when the Sun is above the horizon. The lunar day is long because the Moon spins slowly. So far, all the landings have been made in the early morning on a selected region of the Moon.

The Moon is not a welcoming world. The temperatures range between about 195°F (90°C) at noon on the equator down to well below −200°F (−130°C) at night. There is no air or water and it is now believed that there has never been any life. Yet the Moon is of tremendous importance. Before the year 2000 a lunar base may be established there for scientific research.

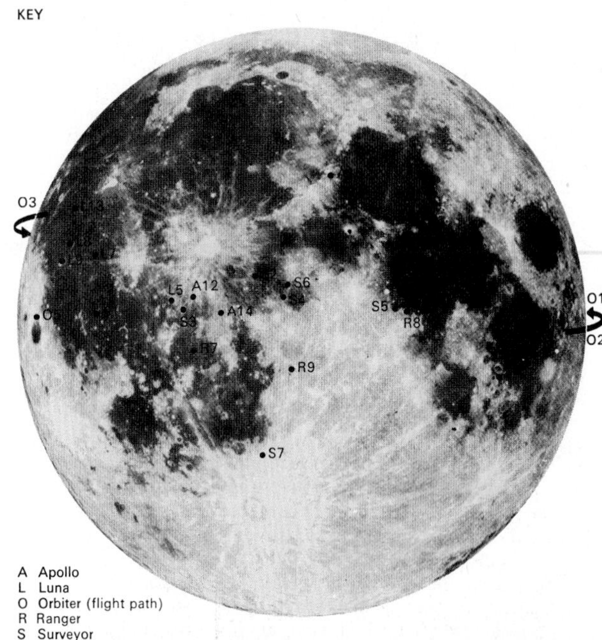
KEY
O3
L5
A12
S6
S5
O1
R8
O2
A14
S3
R7
R9
S7
A Apollo
L Luna
O Orbiter (flight path)
R Ranger
S Surveyor

11 This lunar landscape photograph, taken on the Apollo 11 mission, illustrates several surface details encountered by the astronauts, although the area shown is smooth by lunar standards.

12 During the Apollo 11 mission Armstrong and Aldrin set up a lunar seismometer to measure ground tremors. The seismometer is similar to instruments used on Earth but can be more sensitive as the Moon is seismically "quiet." This particular one failed after a short period but similar instruments left on the Moon by later Apollos have shown that minor tremors do occur frequently.

13 Edwin Aldrin's footprint on the surface of the Moon had a depth of penetration less than 1 in (2.5cm).

14 Rock samples brought back from the Moon by Apollo 11 included this one, of basaltic type. It shows virtually no evidence of any hydrated material. Samples brought back from the later Apollo and Luna missions show that there are numerous types of lunar rock; most of the minerals of which they are composed have been identified on Earth.

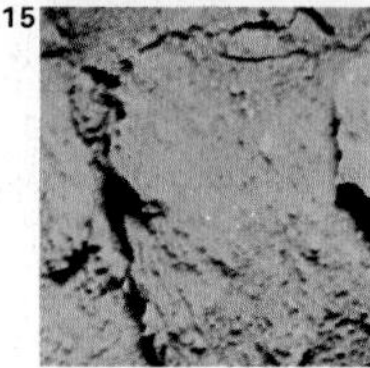

15 A section of the rock in illustration 14 is enlarged here; the fine structure is clearly shown. This was one of the first rocks to be analyzed.

16 Microstructure photographs [A–E] of samples brought back by Armstrong and Aldrin from the Mare Tranquillitatis are shown here. Substances identified include plagioclase, ilmenite, pyroxene, and microscopic rubies. There are many "glass marbles," shown in [E]. These particles are small; the largest of them is only 0.02in (0.5mm) in diameter.

16 A

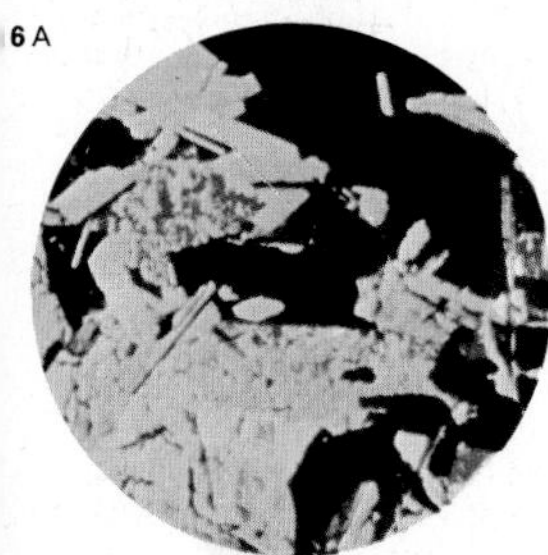

B

C

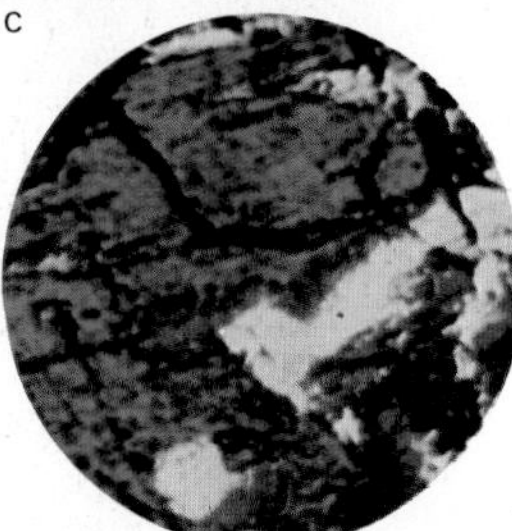

D

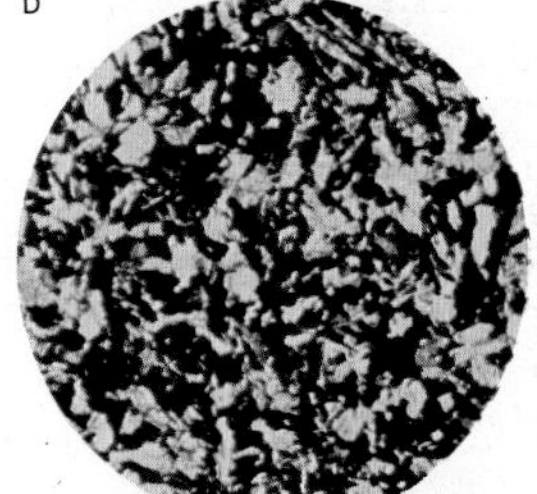

E

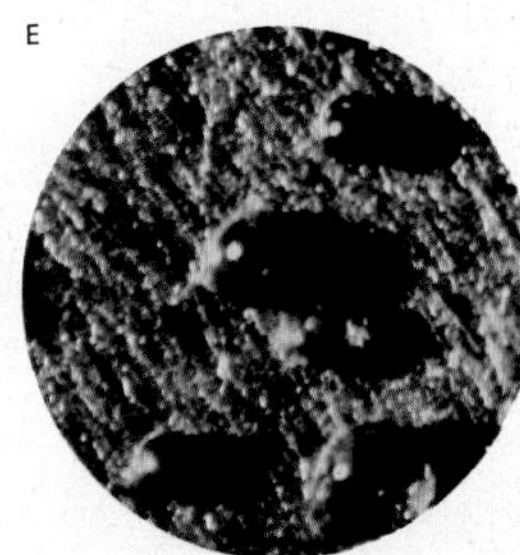

The Moon's structure

Analysis of the samples brought back from the Moon by the US Apollo missions and the Soviet unmanned probes have established that the Earth and the Moon are about the same age (between 4.5 and 4.7 billion years). But because the masses of the Earth and the Moon are so different they have undergone different evolutionary sequences [1].

The surface of the moon

The nature of the Moon's surface is intimately bound up with the problems of the origin of its craters and other features, and this has led to endless arguments that have not been resolved even by the Apollo results. Some strange theories of crater origin have been advanced (ranging from coral atolls to atomic bombs), but the whole problem centers on whether the craters were formed by internal action or by external bombardment. These rival theories are generally called the "meteoric," or "impact," theory [2] and the "volcanic" theory [3].

Both processes must, in fact, have operated to some extent, for both kinds of craters occur on Earth and no doubt do so on the Moon as well. What must be decided is which of the two processes played the more important role. Opinion is sharply divided, although some of the features, such as the small chain craters, are undeniably "volcanic" in the broad sense.

Internal origin theory

Many efforts have been made to link the main lunar craters with terrestrial impact craters such as the Barringer Crater in Arizona, although the scales are different; if transferred to the Moon, this crater would appear insignificant. On the other hand, supporters of the volcanic theory point out that the distribution of the Moon's craters is not random [4]; for instance, the great crater plains tend to appear in distinct lines. When one crater formation breaks into another the smaller crater almost always intrudes into the larger. This is easier to explain with a theory of internal origin than with one of impact. Furthermore, the lunar rock samples are essentially volcanic, and meteoritic material is relatively scarce.

It is also questionable whether the circular maria, or lunar "seas," are essentially similar to the large craters in origin. At least there is some reliable information about their age and it seems probable that the chief maria (Imbrium, Serenitatis, Crisium, and the rest) were formed about 4 billion years ago. The Mare Orientale is probably the youngest of them, with an age of perhaps 3.8 billion years.

Most experts agree that when the mare basins were formed they did not contain lava; the question of whether they were created by internal (endogenic) or external (exogenic) factors does not affect this conclusion. Between 3.8 and 3.2 billion years ago, the mare basins began to be filled by lava that poured out from beneath the crust and finally produced the aspect that is seen today. Because the eruptions occurred over a period of almost a million years, the mare surfaces, although apparently simple, are in fact a complicated patchwork of overlapping lava flows [7].

A certain amount of cratering occurred during this period. The ray-craters such as

CONNECTIONS

Read first
52 The Moon

See also
54 Moon missions
58 Moon maps
60 Moon panorama
174 Earthquakes
176 Volcanoes
246 The rock cycle and igneous rocks

1 The mare basins were formed, either by internal accretion or by impact, at an early stage in the history of the development of the Moon and Earth surfaces (4 billion years ago). The general aspect of the Moon then must not have been dissimilar to that of today, although the basins were not filled. Little is known about surface details on Earth at this time. The surface of both the Earth and the Moon then remained the same for a considerable period of time. Two billion years ago the basins on the Moon were filled in. A billion years after that lunar activity was at an end. Geological techniques permit us to partially reconstruct the appearance of the Earth at that same period of time.

Present day
1,000 million years

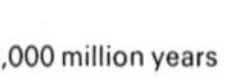

2,000 million years
3,000 million years
4,000 million years

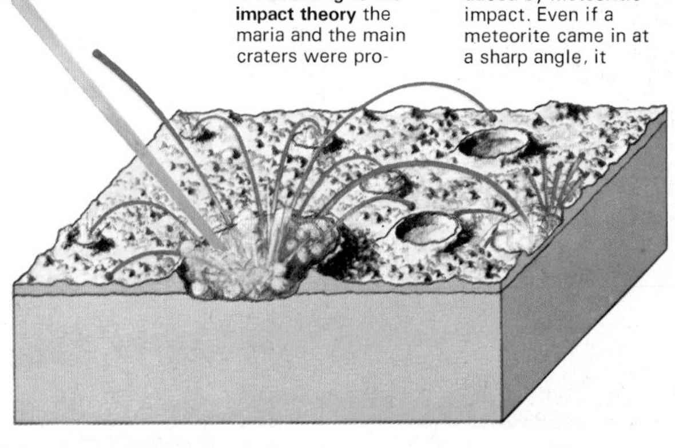

2 According to the impact theory the maria and the main craters were produced by meteoritic impact. Even if a meteorite came in at a sharp angle, it would still produce a circular formation. This theory is a popular one today.

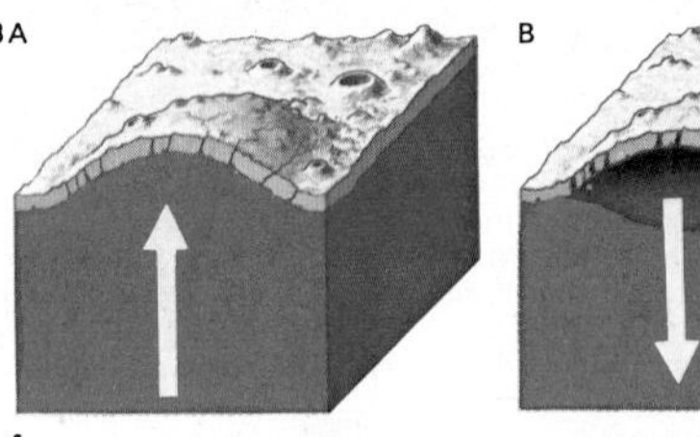

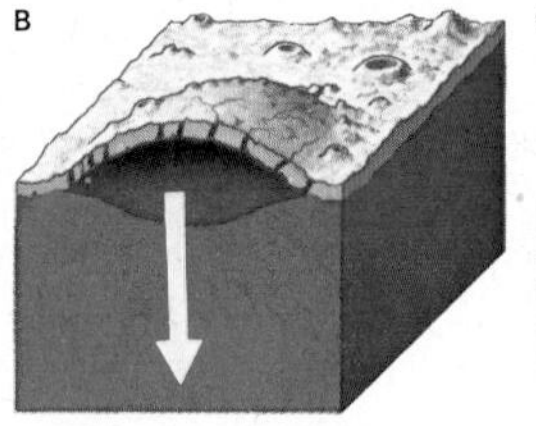

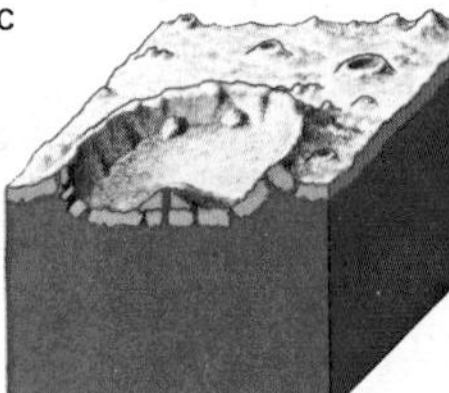

3 The rival volcanic theory states that when the lunar surface was hot and plastic [A], domes were produced—by magmatic convection, for example. On cooling, the underlying material sank [B], leaving a void. The surface layer collapsed, forming a crater [C]. Peaks are caused by penetration of magma.

4 The distribution of the lunar craters and walled formations is clearly crucial to any considerations of their origin. The small features tend to line up in chains and many of the so-called rills are in part crater chains; these must be of internal origin. On the Earth-turned hemisphere the major formations also tend to line up. There are important chains, such as those including Vendelinus and Petavius (and also the Mare Crisium) in the east and the Grimaldi chain in the west. It has been argued that the important features formed along lines of crustal weakness produced by the gravitational influence of the Earth on the Moon.

Tycho and Copernicus are probably the youngest of the major features, and the age of Copernicus may be even less than a billion years. Subsequently the main activity ceased and only small (mainly impact) craters have been formed since.

Evolution of the Moon

Curiously, more information exists about the geological evolution of the Moon than that of the Earth. Unlike the Earth, which has a long history of continual erosion, the Moon has not suffered erosion for a long time. Two billion years ago the Moon may have looked much the same as it does today, whereas the Earth would perhaps have been unrecognizable.

The Apollo seismometers have been able to record "moonquakes" [6] and there is now no doubt that a certain amount of volcanic activity lingers on [5]. Some of the moonquakes occur close to the crust, but others are deep-seated—up to halfway to the Moon's core [6]. It has also been established that the Moon may have a hot core, so that the old idea of a globe that is cold throughout may be incorrect [Key]. Studies of moonquake records indicate that if a molten core exists it must be smaller than that of the Earth, both relatively and absolutely. Above this [6] is the so-called asthenosphere, or zone of partial melting of the mantle; above that the lithosphere, the solid rocky part of the mantle, topped by the crust and rubbly regolith. There is virtually no general lunar magnetic field now, although some areas are locally magnetized. It seems that in the remote past the Moon had an appreciable general field that has now disappeared.

Earth-based lunar observers have recorded various minor "events" that may indicate the emission of gas from below the crust. These are known commonly as TLP, or Transient Lunar Phenomena [8]. They are thought to be commonest near perigee, when the Moon is at its closest to the Earth. The Earth's gravitational pull then produces the greatest strain on the lunar rocks and there may be a connection between this force and the positions of the epicenters of moonquakes.

KEY

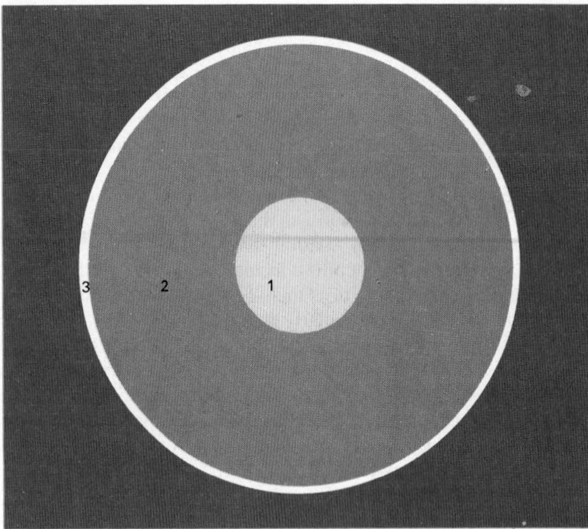
3
2
1

The core of the Moon [1] is believed to be much smaller than that of the Earth, both relatively and absolutely, and it is probably extremely rich in iron. Surrounding it is the lunar mantle [2]. This is overlaid by the crust [3], which is covered by a rocky "topsoil" known as the regolith.

5

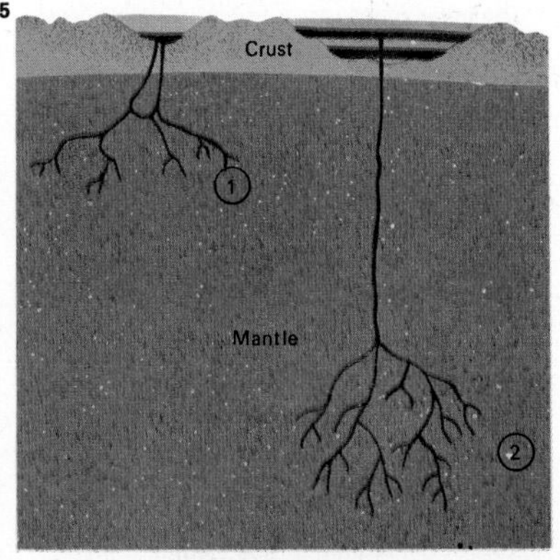
Crust
1
Mantle
2

5 The lunar maria were formed when floods of lava erupted onto the Moon's surface, filling in basins previously excavated by planetesimal impact. They did not erupt in one burst of volcanic activity but over a period of one billion years. The oldest basalts are thought to have been produced at a depth of 95 miles (150km) [1]. The more recent rocks were generated later at a depth of about 150 miles (240 km) [2].

6

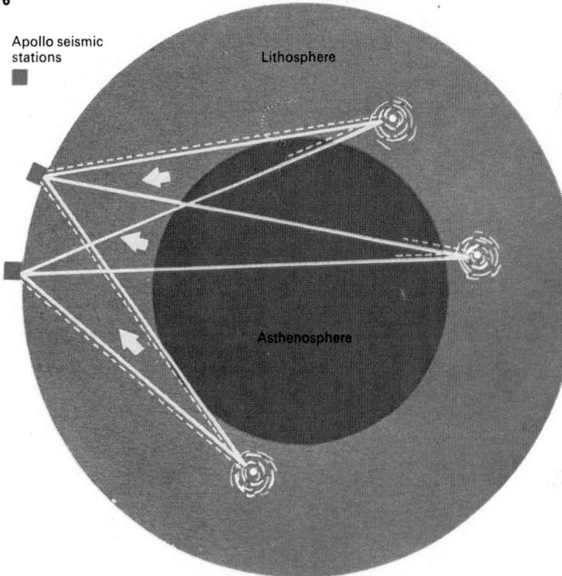
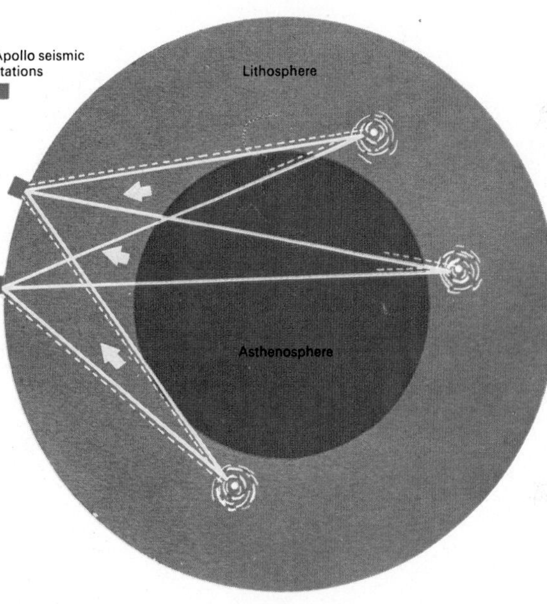
Apollo seismic stations
Lithosphere
Asthenosphere

6 During the Apollo program seismometers were set up on the Moon's surface and studies were made of moonquake waves. The force of even a major moonquake is slight by terrestrial standards, but valuable information about the structure of the Moon has been obtained from studies of the quakes, of which there are two types. Some occur just below the surface, but others have been recorded at a depth halfway between the Moon's surface and core. Shear waves [broken lines] are weakened when passing through a nonrigid medium. Compressional waves [solid lines] can pass through all material. The lunar lithosphere is solid; the asthenosphere is a near-melting zone.

7 A

B

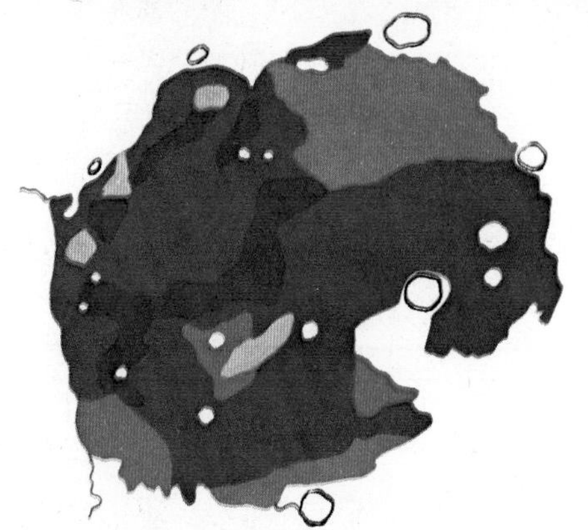

7 In the Mare Imbrium [A] the darkest red coloration on the map [B] represents the youngest of the lava flows, least affected by cratering. The lightest red represents the oldest flow. The most extensive flow dates back approximately 3.3 billion years.

8

8 Transient Lunar Phenomena (TLP) do exist on the Moon, as has been established in recent years. The TLP-prone sites [solid circles] tend to congregate around the borders of the circular maria and in regions rich in rills. The most active lunar area is that around the crater Aristarchus. TLP seem to occur most often near perigee, when the Moon is closest to Earth.

Moon maps

Even with the naked eye the Moon can be seen in considerable detail, and binoculars or any telescope provide the observer with a seemingly inexhaustible panorama. Obviously the view depends on the angle of sunlight over the area being studied. A crater is at its most prominent when near the terminator (the boundary between the day and night hemispheres of the Moon), so that its floor is wholly or partially shadow-filled. Even a major crater may become difficult to identify under a high angle of illumination, unless its floor is either particularly dark or particularly brilliant. In general, the lunar surface has a low reflecting power, or albedo, of about seven percent—that is, it reflects only about seven percent of the sunlight falling on it—but the brightest craters possess walls and central peaks that have albedos of more than 15 percent.

The northern hemisphere

The northern hemisphere of the Earth-turned side of the Moon is dominated by two great seas, the Mare Imbrium (Sea of Showers) and the Mare Serenitatis (Sea of Serenity), both of which are approximately circular, although foreshortening makes them appear somewhat elliptical. The Mare Imbrium has mountainous borders for much of its outline, including the majestic Apennines with peaks rising to some 15,000ft (4,575m). Between the Apennines and the rather lower Caucasus Mountains there is a gap linking the Mare Imbrium to the Mare Serenitatis. The 60mi (96km) dark-floored crater Plato lies in the region of the Alps and also in this range is the remarkable Alpine Valley, 80mi (129km) long.

On the floor of the Mare Imbrium there are several major craters, including the 50mi (80km) Archimedes and its two smaller but deeper companions called Aristillus and Autolycus. The Mare Serenitatis includes no crater of this size; the largest, Bessel, is only 24mi (39km) across.

The Mare Tranquillitatis (Sea of Tranquility), adjoining the Mare Serenitatis to the south, is less regular in form and is presumably older. It was in this sea that the astronauts of Apollo 11 made the pioneer lunar landing in July 1969.

The Mare Crisium (Sea of Crises), not far from the limb, is smaller but well marked and is easily visible with the naked eye. Of the other seas in this hemisphere the largest is the Oceanus Procellarum (Ocean of Storms), separated from the Mare Imbrium by the relatively modest Carpathian Mountains. Aristarchus, on the Oceanus Procellarum, is generally regarded as the brightest crater on the Moon and can often be seen shining prominently even when on the dark side of the terminator, lit only by light reflected from the Earth. The crater Copernicus, south of the Carpathian Mountains, is the center of a bright ray system.

Another interesting feature in the northern hemisphere is a great bay, the Sinus Iridum (Bay of Rainbows), which leads off the Mare Imbrium. When the Sun is rising over it, illuminating the mountainous border, the effect is comparable to a jeweled handle.

The southern hemisphere

Slightly south of the equator are the great plains of which Ptolemaeus is the senior

CONNECTIONS

See also
52 The Moon
54 Moon missions
56 The Moon's structure
60 Moon panorama

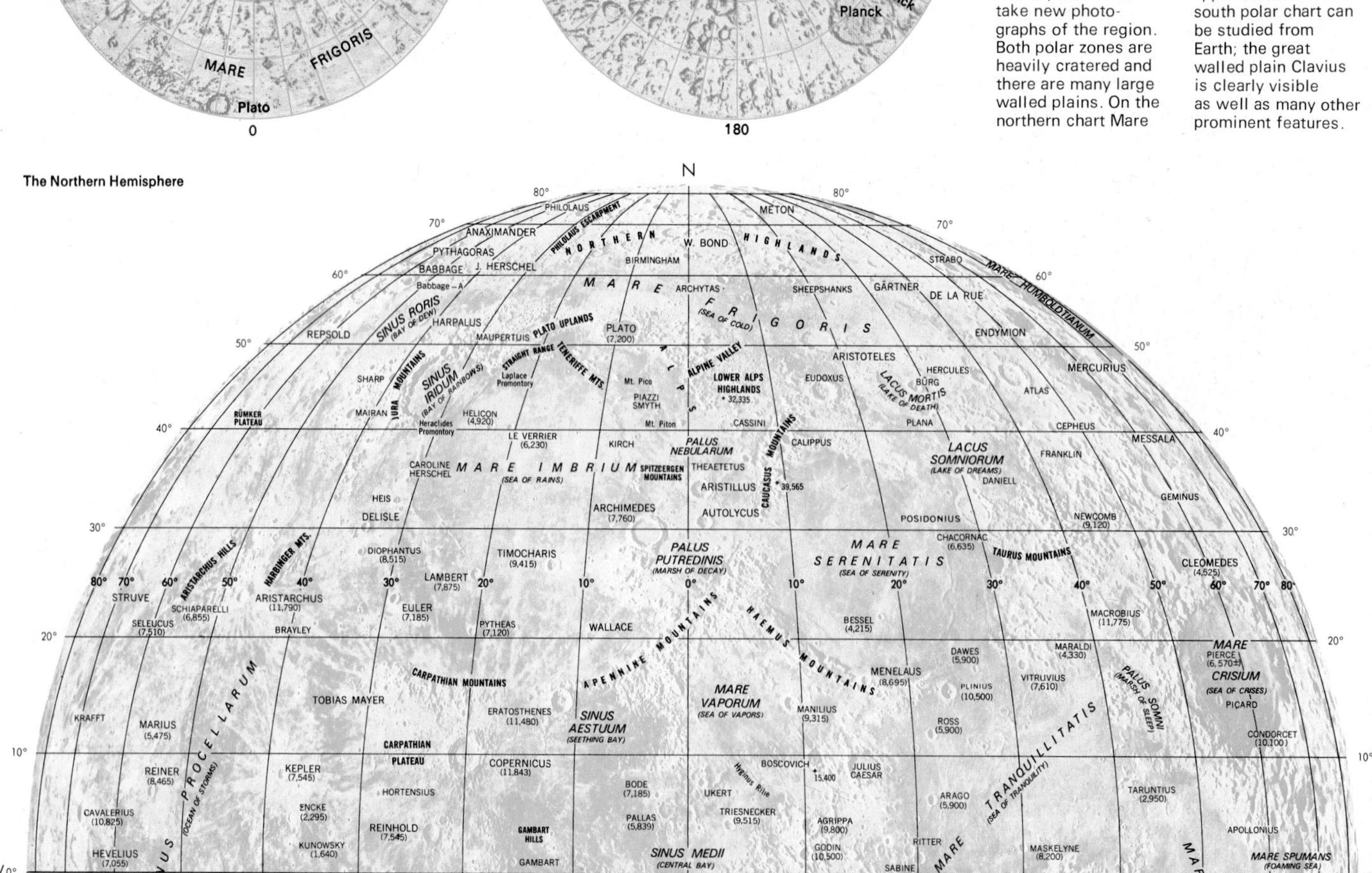

1
180
90
N
MARE
FRIGORIS
Plato
0
Clavius
S
Schrödinger
Rima Planck
Planck
The Northern Hemisphere
N
PHILOLAUS
METON
ANAXIMANDER
PYTHAGORAS
BABBAGE
J. HERSCHEL
NORTHERN HIGHLANDS
W. BOND
BIRMINGHAM
STRABO
MARE HUMBOLDTIANUM
MARE FRIGORIS
ARCHYTAS
SHEEPSHANKS
GÄRTNER
DE LA RUE
SINUS RORIS
HARPALUS
PLATO UPLANDS
PLATO (7,200)
MAUPERTUIS
REPSOLD
ENDYMION
ALPINE VALLEY
ARISTOTELES
SINUS IRIDUM
SHARP
Laplace Promontory
Mt. Pico
LOWER ALPS HIGHLANDS
EUDOXUS
LACUS MORTIS
HERCULES
BÜRG
MERCURIUS
ATLAS
RÜMKER PLATEAU
MAIRAN
HELICON (4,920)
Heraclides Promontory
PIAZZI SMYTH
Mt. Piton
CASSINI
PLANA
CEPHEUS
LE VERRIER (6,230)
KIRCH
PALUS NEBULARUM
CALIPPUS
LACUS SOMNIORUM
FRANKLIN
MESSALA
CAROLINE HERSCHEL
MARE IMBRIUM (SEA OF RAINS)
SPITZBERGEN MOUNTAINS
THEAETETUS
ARISTILLUS
CAUCASUS MOUNTAINS
DANIELL
HEIS
DELISLE
ARCHIMEDES (7,760)
AUTOLYCUS
POSIDONIUS
GEMINUS
NEWCOMB (9,120)
DIOPHANTUS (8,515)
TIMOCHARIS (9,415)
PALUS PUTREDINIS (MARSH OF DECAY)
MARE SERENITATIS (SEA OF SERENITY)
CHACORNAC (6,635)
TAURUS MOUNTAINS
CLEOMEDES (4,525)
ARISTARCHUS HILLS
HARBINGER MTS.
STRUVE
ARISTARCHUS (11,790)
LAMBERT (7,875)
SCHIAPARELLI (6,855)
SELEUCUS (7,510)
BRAYLEY
EULER (7,185)
PYTHEAS (7,120)
WALLACE
BESSEL (4,215)
MACROBIUS (11,775)
APENNINE MOUNTAINS
HAEMUS MOUNTAINS
DAWES (5,900)
MARALDI (4,330)
MARE CRISIUM (SEA OF CRISES)
PIERCE
PICARD
CARPATHIAN MOUNTAINS
OCEANUS PROCELLARUM (OCEAN OF STORMS)
TOBIAS MAYER
ERATOSTHENES (11,480)
SINUS AESTUUM (SEETHING BAY)
MARE VAPORUM (SEA OF VAPORS)
MENELAUS (8,695)
PLINIUS (10,500)
VITRUVIUS (7,610)
PALUS SOMNI (MARSH OF SLEEP)
KRAFFT
MARIUS (5,475)
MANILIUS (9,315)
ROSS (5,900)
CONDORCET (10,100)
CARPATHIAN PLATEAU
COPERNICUS (11,843)
BOSCOVICH
JULIUS CAESAR
MARE TRANQUILLITATIS (SEA OF TRANQUILITY)
REINER (8,465)
KEPLER (7,545)
HORTENSIUS
BODE (7,185)
Hyginus Rille
UKERT
ARAGO (5,900)
TARUNTIUS (2,950)
CAVALERIUS (10,825)
ENCKE (2,295)
REINHOLD (7,545)
GAMBART HILLS
PALLAS (5,839)
TRIESNECKER (9,515)
AGRIPPA (9,800)
APOLLONIUS
HEVELIUS (7,055)
KUNOWSKY (1,640)
SINUS MEDII (CENTRAL BAY)
GODIN (10,500)
RITTER
MASKELYNE (8,200)
MARE SPUMANS (FOAMING SEA)
GAMBART
SABINE
W 0°
0°

1 The polar zones of the Moon are difficult to study from Earth because of extreme foreshortening. Some of the areas in these maps cannot be seen at all and our knowledge of them is derived mainly from photographs sent back by the five highly successful Orbiters. Mapping of part of the south polar region is not quite complete, although future probes will take new photographs of the region. Both polar zones are heavily cratered and there are many large walled plains. On the northern chart Mare Frigoris, visible from Earth, is shown; Plato appears near the bottom of the map. One of the interesting features in the south polar map is the large walled plain Schrödinger on the far hemisphere, together with a similar structure Planck. Associated with these two features is a long rill, the Rima Planck (also called the Shrödinger Valley). The area in the upper section of the south polar chart can be studied from Earth; the great walled plain Clavius is clearly visible as well as many other prominent features.

member, Ptolemaeus is almost 100mi (160km) in diameter, with a relatively level, darkish floor. Adjoining it is the rather smaller Alphonsus, with a central mountain group and a system of rills on its floor. It was here in 1958, that the Russian astronomer N. A. Kozyrev recorded a reddish glow—one of the best authenticated examples of a Transient Lunar Phenomenon (TLP). This, he believed, indicated a certain amount of surface or subsurface activity, which he interpreted as being of volcanic origin. The third member of the Ptolemaeus chain, Arzachel, is smaller than Alphonsus, but deeper, with a higher central peak.

The southern part of the Moon consists largely of rugged upland, although there are some sea areas—the Mare Nubium (Sea of Clouds) and the smaller Mare Humorum (Sea of Moisture). On the former, not far from Arzachel, is the Rupes Recta (Straight Wall), which is a major fault in the surface, with a length of 80mi (128km) and with a height of 800ft (244m).

Among other major walled plains are the dark-floored Schickard and the 144 mile (232km) Clavius, which has a chain of craters inside it. North of the Southern Highlands is the crater Tycho, called the "metropolitan crater" of the Moon because of its system of bright rays, which are brilliant and extensive. Near full Moon, as seen from Earth they dominate the entire southern hemisphere and render virtually invisible even larger walled plains in the vicinity. Tycho is 54mi (87km) in diameter, with massive walls, and even under low illumination when the rays are not visible, it remains one of the most prominent craters on the Moon.

The far side of the Moon

The libration regions of the Moon were not well mapped until the age of space probes. Today we also have full information about the Moon's far side, although it has been seen "direct" only by the Apollo astronauts who have been around the Moon. Here there are no major maria, but there are walled structures of all kinds; of special interest is Tsiolkovskii, which has a very dark floor and was identifiable on the photographs sent back by Luna 3 in October 1959.

KEY

This Apollo 16 photograph shows parts of both the Earth-turned hemisphere and the far side of the Moon not seen from Earth.

2

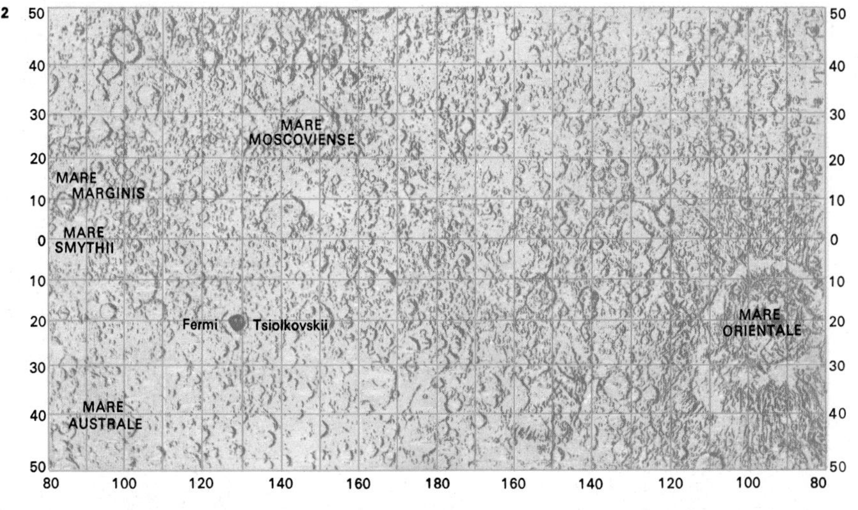
MARE MOSCOVIENSE
MARE MARGINIS
MARE SMYTHII
Fermi
Tsiolkovskii
MARE ORIENTALE
MARE AUSTRALE
50
40
30
20
10
0
10
20
30
40
50
80
100
120
140
160
180
160
140
120
100
80

2 A map of the far side of the Moon shows no major maria similar to those on the familiar side of the Moon. The Mare Orientale is visible from Earth, although very foreshortened. On the far side there are craters of all kinds and the whole surface is crowded uplands. The most striking feature is the dark-floored Tsiolkovskii, first seen on the Luna 3 photographs in 1959. It abuts another structure, Fermi, which has a light floor. On the Luna 3 photographs a bright streak showed up, thought to be a major mountain chain; the Russians named it the "Soviet Range," but subsequently it was found to be nothing more than a bright ray. The Mare Moscoviense (Moscow Sea) was also identified on the Luna 3 pictures. The question of naming the features on the far side caused some controversy. The nomenclature given here is that now officially adopted by a special committee set up by the International Astronomical Union. The Mare Marginis, Mare Smythii and Mare Australe may also be seen from the Earth.

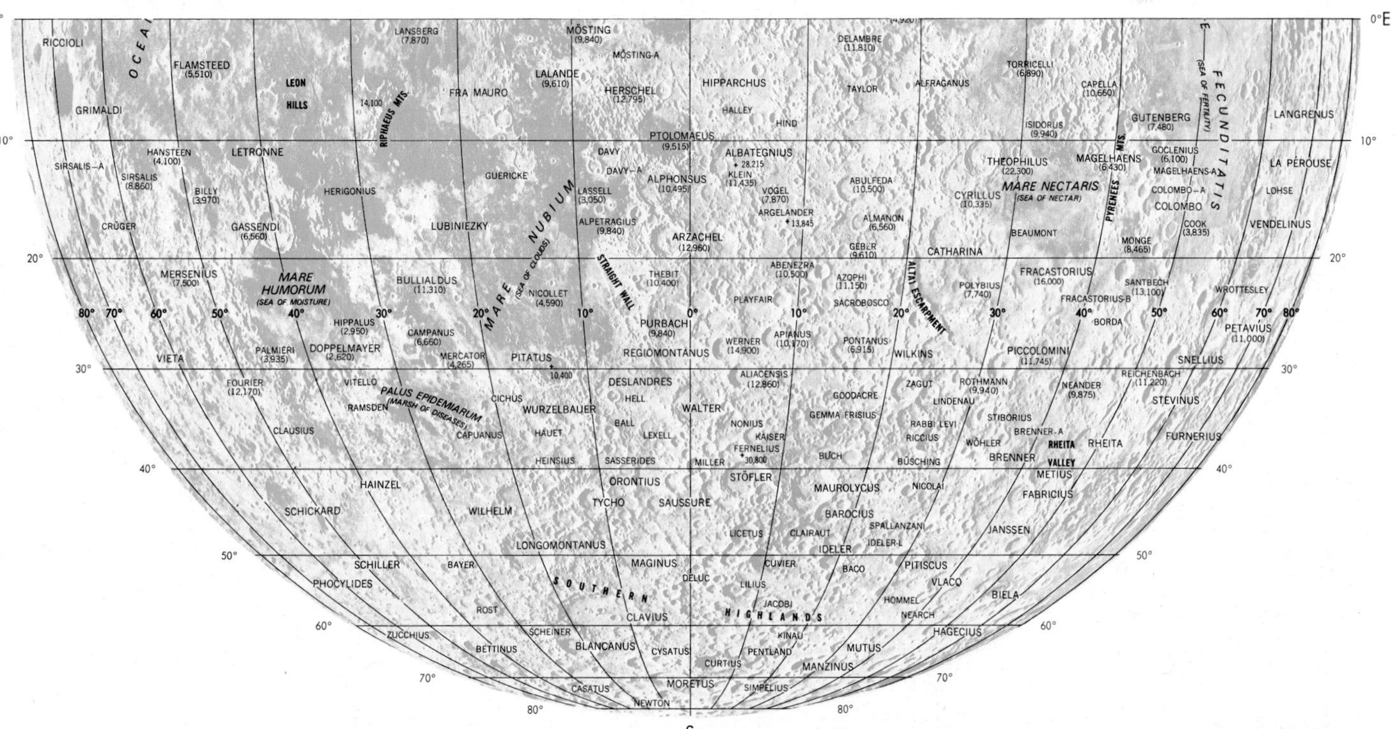
RICCIOLI
OCEAN
FLAMSTEED (5,510)
LEON HILLS
LANSBERG (7,870)
RIPHAEUS MTS
MÖSTING (9,840)
MÖSTING-A
LALANDE (9,610)
FRA MAURO
HERSCHEL (12,795)
HIPPARCHUS
HALLEY
HIND
DELAMBRE (11,810)
TAYLOR
ALFRAGANUS
TORRICELLI (6,890)
CAPELLA (10,660)
ISIDORUS (9,940)
GUTENBERG (7,480)
SEA OF FERTILITY
FECUNDITATIS
LANGRENUS
GRIMALDI
PTOLOMAEUS (9,515)
ALBATEGNIUS
KLEIN (11,435)
HANSTEEN (4,100)
LETRONNE
SIRSALIS-A
SIRSALIS (8,860)
BILLY (3,970)
HERIGONIUS
GUERICKE
DAVY
DAVY-A
ALPHONSUS (10,495)
LASSELL (3,050)
VOGEL (7,870)
ABULFEDA (10,500)
THEOPHILUS (22,300)
MAGELHAENS (6,430)
GOCLENIUS (6,100)
MAGELHAENS-A
LA PÉROUSE
MARE NECTARIS
SEA OF NECTAR
CYRILLUS (10,335)
COLOMBO-A
COLOMBO
LOHSE
PYRENEES MTS.
CRÜGER
GASSENDI (6,560)
LUBINIEZKY
MARE NUBIUM
SEA OF CLOUDS
ALPETRAGIUS (9,840)
ARGELANDER
ALMANON (6,560)
ARZACHEL (12,960)
BEAUMONT
COOK (3,835)
VENDELINUS
MONGE (8,465)
GEBER (9,610)
CATHARINA
MERSENIUS (7,500)
MARE HUMORUM
SEA OF MOISTURE
BULLIALDUS (11,310)
STRAIGHT WALL
THEBIT (10,400)
ABENEZRA (10,500)
AZOPHI (11,150)
ALTAI ESCARPMENT
FRACASTORIUS (16,000)
POLYBIUS (7,740)
FRACASTORIUS-B
SANTBECH (13,100)
WROTTESLEY
NICOLLET (4,590)
PLAYFAIR
SACROBOSCO
BORDA
PETAVIUS (11,000)
HIPPALUS (2,950)
CAMPANUS (6,660)
PURBACH (9,840)
WERNER (14,900)
APIANUS (10,770)
PONTANUS (6,915)
WILKINS
PICCOLOMINI (11,745)
SNELLIUS
VIETA
PALMIERI (3,935)
DOPPELMAYER (2,620)
MERCATOR (4,265)
PITATUS
REGIOMONTANUS
ALIACENSIS (12,860)
ZAGUT
ROTHMANN (9,940)
NEANDER (9,875)
REICHENBACH (11,220)
FOURIER (12,170)
VITELLO
PALUS EPIDEMIARUM
MARSH OF DISEASES
DESLANDRES
HELL
GOODACRE
LINDENAU
STEVINUS
RAMSDEN
CICHUS
WURZELBAUER
WALTER
GEMMA FRISIUS
RABBI LEVI
STIBORIUS
CLAUSIUS
CAPUANUS
HAINZEL
BALL
LEXELL
NONIUS
KAISER
RICCIUS
BRENNER-A
FURNERIUS
HEINSIUS
SASSERIDES
FERNELIUS
WÖHLER
RHEITA VALLEY
RHEITA
MILLER
BUCH
BÜSCHING
BRENNER
METIUS
ORONTIUS
STÖFLER
MAUROLYCUS
NICOLAI
FABRICIUS
SCHICKARD
WILHELM
TYCHO
SAUSSURE
BAROCIUS
SPALLANZANI
JANSSEN
LICETUS
CLAIRAUT
IDELER
LONGOMONTANUS
SCHILLER
BAYER
MAGINUS
CUVIER
BACO
PITISCUS
PHOCYLIDES
DELUC
LILIUS
VLACQ
BIELA
SOUTHERN HIGHLANDS
ROST
JACOBI
HOMMEL
NEARCH
CLAVIUS
ZUCCHIUS
SCHEINER
BLANCANUS
KINAU
HAGECIUS
BETTINUS
CYSATUS
PENTLAND
MUTUS
CURTIUS
MANZINUS
CASATUS
MORETUS
SIMPELIUS
NEWTON
S
0°E
10°
20°
30°
40°
50°
60°
70°
80°

The Southern Hemisphere

Moon panorama

The Moon is a world of considerable variety. In addition to the marked differences between the Earth-turned and the far hemispheres, there are also obvious changes of scenery on the familiar face of the Moon. The southwestern quadrant, for example, is dominated by rough uplands, with large craters and walled plains clustering thickly, while the northeastern quadrant contains vast stretches of mare surface.

In particular there is the region of Aristarchus [3], the brightest crater on the Moon, which is of special interest because so much of the local area is dark, as reported by Earth-based observers. Sir William Herschel (1738–1822), one of the greatest practical observers, on several occasions mistook Aristarchus for a volcano in eruption when he saw it shining conspicuously from that part of the Moon illuminated only by Earthshine.

Aristarchus is not the only feature in or near which activity has been suspected. Another is the walled plain Alphonsus [1], in the great Ptolemaeus chain near the center of the Earth-turned hemisphere. Although Alphonsus and Aristarchus are so different, they do have one thing in common: they lie in areas that are rich in rills or clefts. The same is true of most other regions where mild activity has been reported.

The Moon before Orbiter

Before the space probe era knowledge of the Moon was bound to be limited, despite the fact that the lack of a lunar atmosphere makes surface details more distinct. Measurements of the positions on the disk of various lunar features were possible and although work undertaken by S. A. Saunder and J. A. Hardcastle in 1907–09 was of value (the Saunder-Hardcastle measures are still referred to today), certain areas could still not be resolved. In particular, little was known about the limb regions, which are quite foreshortened as seen from the Earth. When a crater is seen under such conditions it may be impossible to distinguish it from a ridge. Nor could there be any positive information about the Moon's far side. By "plotting back" the lunar rays that were seen to come from the far side it was possible to fix the positions of a few ray-centers with reasonable accuracy, but the distribution of the features on the far side remained unknown. It was, however, significant that none of the major maria on the Earth-turned side extends onto the far side—apart from the Mare Orientale, whose nature was not then realized.

Photographic missions

The original photographs sent back by the Soviet probe Luna 3 were of immense value, but they were blurred and indistinct and thus widely misinterpreted [Key]. In particular, a long feature seen stretching across the disk was taken to be a major mountain range and was titled the Soviet Mountains; later photographs showed it to be nothing more than a bright ray. It was therefore not until the advent of the Orbiters that lunar research made its greatest stride forward, although the three successful Rangers, which crash-landed but managed to send back many thousands of useful pictures during the last minutes of their flights, also played a part.

CONNECTIONS

See also
52 The Moon
54 Moon missions
56 The Moon's structure
58 Moon maps

1

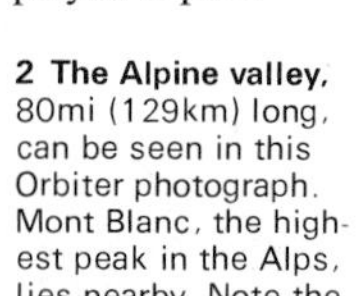

1 Alphonsus, the walled plain in which Ranger 9 landed and in which mild activity has been reported, is a member of the Ptolemaeus chain, Ptolemaeus itself is to the north [above] and Arzachel to the south.

2 The Alpine valley, 80mi (129km) long, can be seen in this Orbiter photograph. Mont Blanc, the highest peak in the Alps, lies nearby. Note the delicate rill running along the valley floor.

2

3

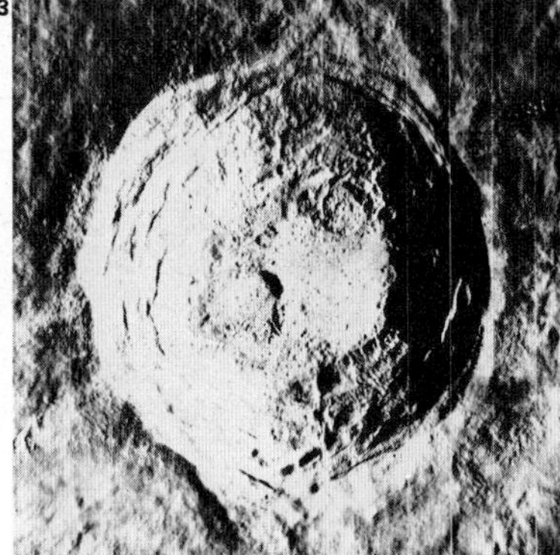

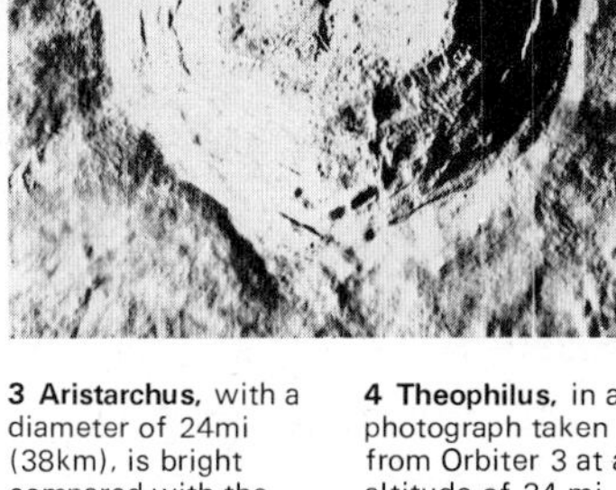

3 Aristarchus, with a diameter of 24mi (38km), is bright compared with the surrounding region. The walls are heavily terraced and the floor contains a central mountain of considerable height.

4 Theophilus, in a photograph taken from Orbiter 3 at an altitude of 34 mi (55km), shows the ramparts and the central mountain mass. Above and to the right can be seen the walls of Cyrillus.

4

Despite the comprehensive coverage of the Orbiter project, involving thousands of photographs—many of which still await complete analysis—there were still a number of outstanding questions. The Apollo program to a large extent supplemented the work of the Orbiters, particularly with more detailed coverage of future landing sites (for example, Apollo 10, the last pre-landing probe, photographed the Mare Tranquillitatis—the site selected for Apollo 11). The curtailment of the program, however, has meant that some areas still remain to be studied and some questions still have not been answered.

Ray craters

The ray craters, and the processes by which they were produced, also wait examination. They seem to be the youngest of the major features of the Moon; the estimated age of Copernicus and Tycho, for example, is no more than one billion years, but because samples have not been collected and analyzed from those regions it is dangerous to be too definite. The last Surveyor landed on the outer wall-slopes of Tycho [5] and confirmed that the surface is extremely rough. This had been expected because it was already known from infrared studies (carried out mainly by the US astronomers J. Saari and R. W. Shorthill) that Tycho cools down less rapidly during a lunar eclipse, or during a lunar night, than its surrounding areas. This implied a difference in surface covering or texture. Other ray craters behave in the same way and have been called, rather misleadingly, "hot spots." This does not imply any internal source of heat; all it means is that during periods of darkness the "hot spots" have a higher temperature than other parts of the Moon—although they warm up less slowly after sunrise.

It has been suggested that ray craters were formed in a different way from other types of craters, but this seems unlikely. For instance, there is no real difference in form between Tycho, which is the center of the greatest ray system on the Moon, and Theophilus [4], which is not associated with a comparable system of rays.

KEY

In 1959 the Soviet Luna 3 sent back the first close-range photographs of the Moon. Here Mare Moscoviense is seen.

5 Tycho, the great lunar ray crater, was photographed from Orbiter 5. The terraced walls, the central elevations, and the roughness of the floor are clearly shown. There is no evidence of lava flows of mare material. Tycho lies in the uplands and is probably one of the youngest of major craters.

6 The Hyginus Rill is one of the best known on the Moon. It is not, properly speaking, a rill, or cleft; it is basically a crater chain, as is shown in this view of it taken from Orbiter 3. Hyginus itself, in the midposition in the rill, is 4mi (6km) across.

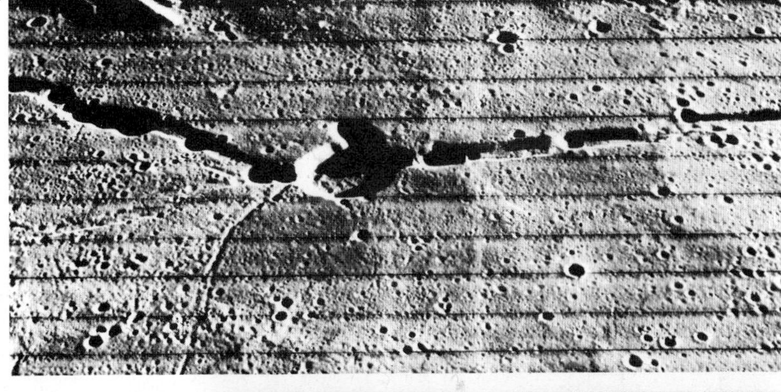

7 This photograph of the Mare Australe was taken from Orbiter 4 at a height of 2,175 mi (3,500km) above the Moon. The craters are flooded with mare material, but Australe is not a regular structure.

8 The Mare Orientale, photographed from Orbiter 4, is a complex structure with multiple ring-walls. To the right is seen dark-floored Grimaldi, which is flooded with mare material.

The planet Mercury

Mercury can sometimes be seen with the naked eye but is much harder to sight than the other four planets that were known in ancient times—Venus, Mars, Jupiter, and Saturn. It is the closest planet to the Sun and takes only 88 Earth-days to travel around it at a mean distance from it of about 36 million miles (58 million km). In size and mass, Mercury is more like the Moon than the Earth [1]. Its diameter is 3,032mi (4,880km). The escape velocity of only 2.7mi (4.3km) per second suggests that it can have little atmosphere.

Observation difficulties

The chief difficulty in observing Mercury is that it is never seen against a completely dark background because it remains in the same part of the sky as the Sun. Although quite bright, it is never conspicuous to the naked eye. An observer without a telescope sees it only on favorable occasions, either low in the west after sunset or low in the east before sunrise. To make matters worse, the phase (illuminated surface) decreases as Mercury gets nearer to the Earth [3]. At its closest Mercury is at inferior conjunction and cannot be seen at all (except in a rare transit across the Sun) because its dark, or night, hemisphere is turned Earthward.

Mapping the planet

The first serious attempts to map Mercury were made in Milan during the latter part of the nineteenth century by Giovanni Schiaparelli (1835–1910). Rather than study the planet at night when he could see it with the naked eye, Schiaparelli worked in broad daylight, with Mercury high above the horizon. He was able to see some dark shadings and brighter areas, but his chart was rough. Later, between 1924 and 1933, a long study was carried out by E. M. Antoniadi. Antoniadi, who used the 33-in (84-cm) refractor at the Observatory of Meudon, France, also made his observations in broad daylight and his chart [Key] remained the best—although it too was inaccurate—until the fly-bys of Mariner 10 in 1974.

Antoniadi, like Schiaparelli, believed that the rotation period of Mercury was captured, or synchronous. If that were so, then both the revolution period and the axial spin would be 88 Earth-days and, as a result, part of the planet would be permanently illuminated by the Sun while another part would be in everlasting night. Because the Mercurian orbit is decidedly eccentric, there would be an intermediate "twilight zone" between these two extremes over which the Sun would rise and set, always keeping close to the horizon. The effects would be analogous to the oscillations of the Moon. It is now known that Antoniadi was wrong. Radar measurements carried out since 1962 show that the true rotation period is 58.7 Earth days, so that all regions of the planet receive sunlight at some time [5]. Because of a curious relationship, Mercury presents the same hemisphere to the Earth every time it is best placed for study; this is what misled the earlier observers.

Antoniadi believed that he had observed local darkening or "clouds" on Mercury, which sometimes veiled the surface features. This was puzzling because it was obvious that the atmosphere must be extremely rarefied by terrestrial standards. It

CONNECTIONS

See also
150 Exploring the inner planets
142 A history of space achievements
1524 The idea of relativit
50 Members of the Sol System

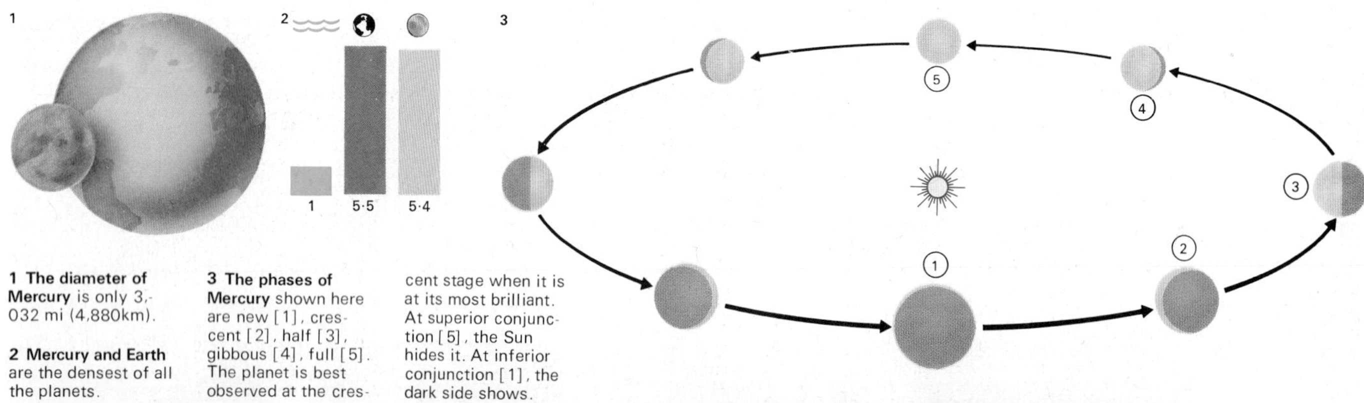
1
2
1
5·5
5·4
3

1 The diameter of Mercury is only 3,032 mi (4,880km).

2 Mercury and Earth are the densest of all the planets.

3 The phases of Mercury shown here are new [1], crescent [2], half [3], gibbous [4], full [5]. The planet is best observed at the crescent stage when it is at its most brilliant. At superior conjunction [5], the Sun hides it. At inferior conjunction [1], the dark side shows.

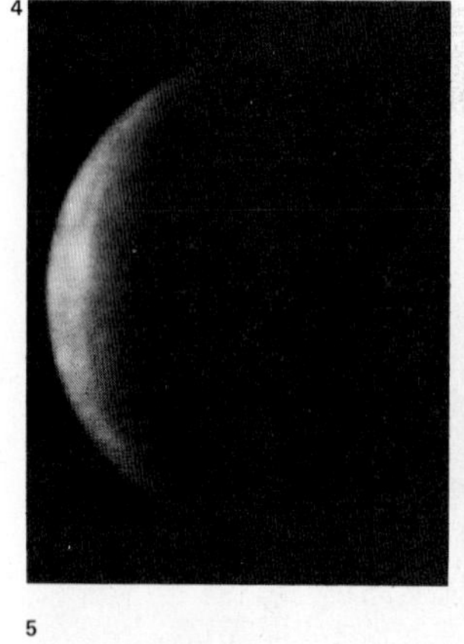

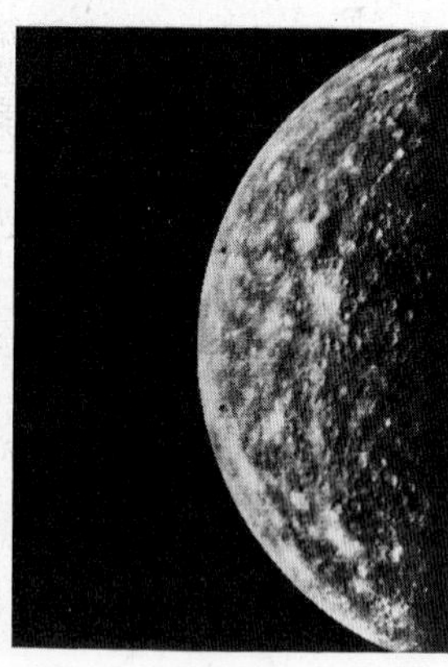

4 Four photographs taken from Mariner 10, in March 1974, show Mercury in different phases. Surface features became clearer as Mariner approached. The resolution on the last picture is 12.4mi (20km)—the size of the smallest discernible object. The probe was then 591,900 mi from the planet. Craters show up best when close to the Mercurian terminator, the boundary between light and dark.

5 Daylight on Mercury lasts about as long as the planet takes to orbit the Sun—88 days. The marker shows the rotation of a fixed point on the planet during this period.

6 Transits of Mercury (its passages across the Sun as seen from Earth) are plotted from 1960 to 2016. Not all are of equal duration; that of 2016 will last much longer than that of 2003. During a transit Mercury shows a small, well-defined black disk, invisible to the naked eye.

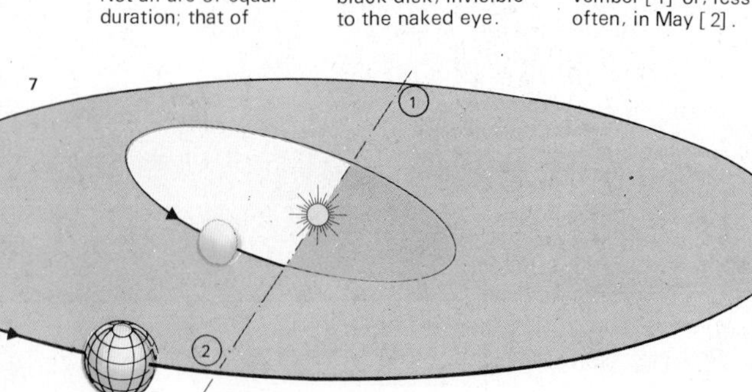
7
1
2

7 Transits are rare as Mercury's orbital angle is different from the Earth's. They usually occur in November [1] or, less often, in May [2].

is now known that the atmosphere is much too thin to support clouds of any kind. Because of Mercury's closeness to the Sun, its surface is extremely hot during daylight and a thermometer would register a temperature of more than 700°F (370°C), at maximum, but because of the virtual lack of atmosphere the nights are bitterly cold. No known form of life can survive on Mercury.

Mariner 10 probe

The first close-range information about Mercury's surface was received in 1974 from the flight of Mariner 10, the first "two-planet" probe. In February 1974 it by-passed Venus, sending back pictures, and then swung inward toward a rendezvous with Mercury during the following month. The photographs revealed a landscape that was strikingly like that of the Moon [4]. Craters, mountains, ridges, and valleys showed everywhere, although there were fewer broad dark plains like the lunar Mare Imbrium. On Mercury, the chief plain, a mountain-rimmed basin, has been named the Caloris Basin [9].

In September 1974, after orbiting the Sun, Mariner 10 made a second rendezvous with Mercury and took more high-quality pictures. The third encounter took place in March 1975. Despite the incompleteness of the pictures, they revealed the same types of craters and mountains. Much of Mercury has now been mapped and there is now reliable information on what this strange world is really like.

One discovery of great interest was the detection of a magnetic field. This field is weak compared with that of the Earth—the maximum field strength is 700 gammas compared with about 30,000 gammas for the Earth—but it produces a true magnetosphere. As expected, the atmosphere is negligible.

Further probes to Mercury are being planned, but the chances of manned expeditions there are slight, at least in the foreseeable future. Mercury is much more like the Moon [12] than the Earth and overwhelmingly hostile, although from the scientific point of view it is considered to be of exceptional interest.

KEY

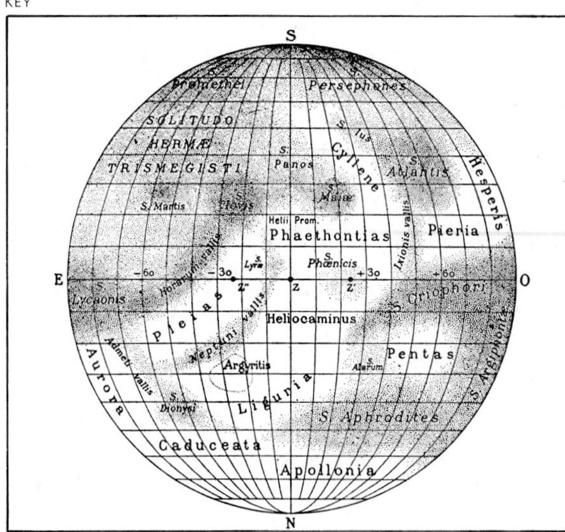
S
Promethei
Persephones
SOLITUDO
HERMAE
TRISMEGISTI
Panos
Cyllene
Atlantis
Hesperis
Phaethontias
Pieria
Phoenicis
Heliocaminus
Lycaonis
Argyritis
Pentas
Aurora
Liguria
S. Aphrodites
Caduceata
Apollonia
E
O
N

This map of Mercury was drawn between 1924 and 1933 by Antoniadi, who named the main features. There is poor correlation between the dark areas shown and the results from Mariner 10, and some renaming will be needed.

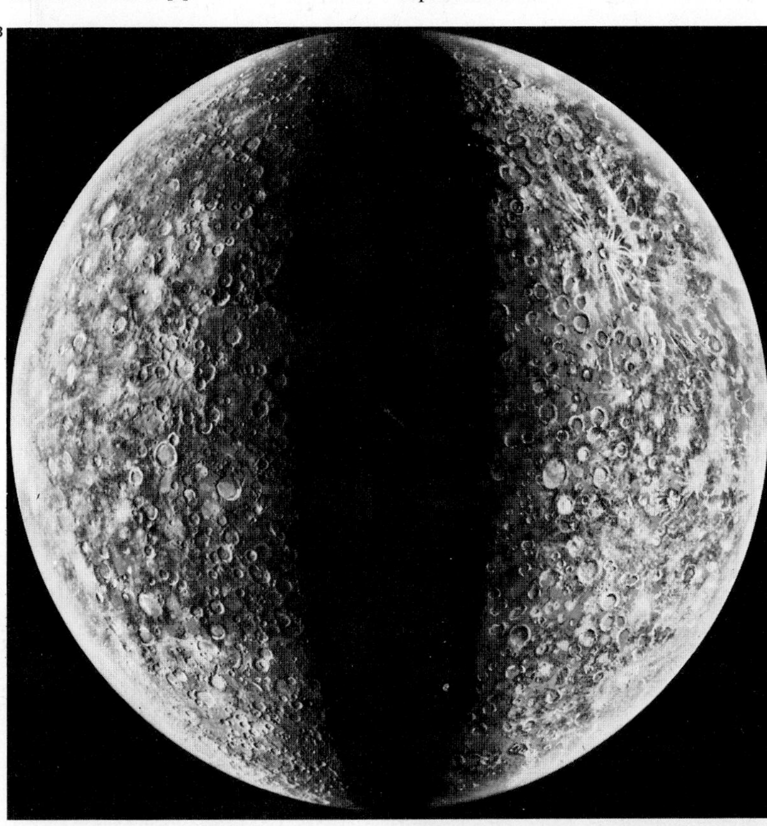

8 The whole surface of Mercury shown in this mosaic of Mariner 10 photographs is extensively cratered and distinctly lunar in appearance. There are also bright ray systems (upper right) like those of the Moon. The Mariner photographs were highly informative.

9 This mosaic of the Caloris Basin from Mariner 10 shows what is probably the most distinctive plain on Mercury. The mountain rim around the basin can be clearly seen and the interior is different from the surrounding region. The origin of the basin is still unknown.

10 Hills and ridges cut across many of the craters in the region shown here, which is unique to the planet. Their origin is obscure. They may be the result of shock waves caused by the formation of the 800-mi (1,300-km) Caloris Basin, which lies diametrically opposite.

11 Another region of Mercury shows an area crowded with craters and craterlets. One interesting feature is the crater valley to the upper left, which resembles many of the crater chains on the surface of Earth's satellite, the Moon.

12 The similarity of Mercury to the Moon is clear in this Mariner 10 photograph. Some craters have centered peaks and all the well-marked craters are basically circular, although here they appear elliptical because of foreshortening.

The planet Venus

Venus, the second planet in order of distance from the Sun, is almost as large as the Earth and has more than 80 percent of the terrestrial mass [1, 2]. Instead of being devoid of atmosphere, it has a deep, dense, and cloudy blanket that hides the true surface of the planet.

The mean distance of Venus from the Sun is 67.2 million miles (108.2 million km) and its orbit is more nearly circular than that of any other planet. The revolution period is 224.7 days. Before the age of space probes and powerful radar, the rotation period of Venus was unknown; there are no markings on the disk persistent enough to be used for rotation measurements, as with Mars or Mercury. All that can be seen from Earth is the upper layer of cloud and the shadings and bright regions on the disk are always vague and transitory.

Observing Venus from Earth

To the naked eye Venus is a splendid object, far brighter than any other celestial body except for the Sun and the Moon, which may be why it was named after the goddess of beauty. Telescopically, however, Venus is a disappointment and until recent years it was often called the "planet of mystery" [4].

In the 1930s some positive information emerged. It was established that the atmosphere of Venus is made up largely of carbon dioxide, which tends to act as a blanket that shuts in the Sun's heat. Two theories of the planet were current. In one, the surface was covered mainly with water, in which primitive life forms might have developed just as happened on the Earth billions of years ago. In the other Venus was a scorching-hot, arid dust-desert.

Information from early probes

The probe era began in 1962, when the US probe Mariner 2 by-passed Venus and sent back information that confirmed that the surface is extremely hot. It was also found that the axial rotation period is slow—about 243 Earth-days, which is longer than the revolution period of 224.7 days; therefore on Venus the "day" is longer than the "year," giving rise to a peculiar calendar.

It has been established that Venus rotates in a retrograde direction: east to west, instead of west to east as with the Earth and most of the other planets. To an observer on the surface of Venus, the Sun would appear to rise in the west and set in the east—although, in fact, the cloud-laden atmosphere would hide the sky completely.

Following Mariner 2, the USSR soft-landed various automatic probes on the surface of Venus, bringing them down by parachute through the dense atmosphere. A temperature of about 900°F (485°C) was recorded, with a ground pressure about 100 times that of the Earth's air at sea level.

Mariner 10 by-passed Venus in February 1974 and sent back the first pictures of the top of the cloud layer. Mariner 10 made only one pass of Venus; its main target was the innermost planet, Mercury. The pictures were of high quality, however, and showed the banded appearance of the clouds [9]. They also confirmed that the cloud tops have a rotation period of only four days, so that the atmospheric structure is unlike that of the Earth [5].

CONNECTIONS

See also

150 Exploring the inner planets
142 A history of space achievements
50 Members of the Solar System

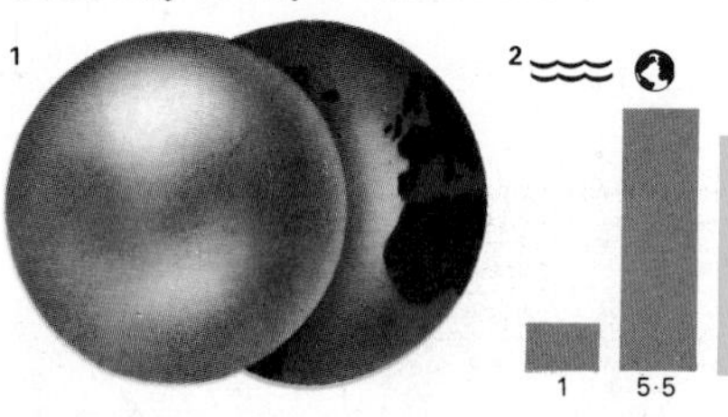

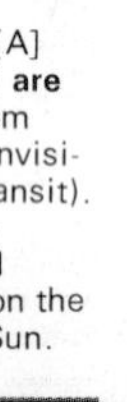

1
5·5
5·2

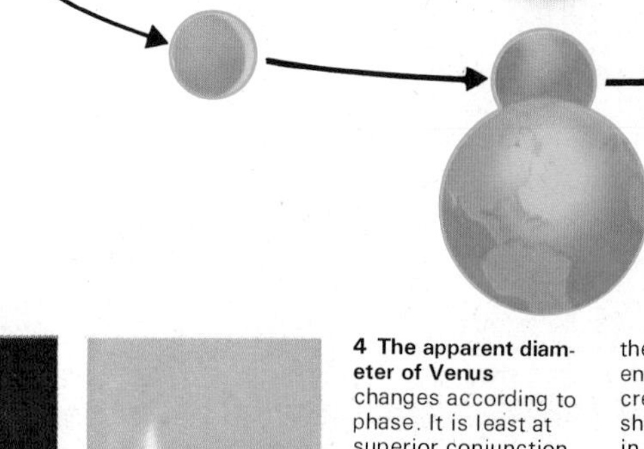

1 Venus and the Earth are almost equal in size, mass, and surface gravity.

2 The density of Venus is less than Earth's, although there may be a heavy core.

3 When Venus [A] **and Mercury** [B] **are new** as seen from Earth, they are invisible (except at transit). At superior conjunction and full phase they are on the far side of the Sun.

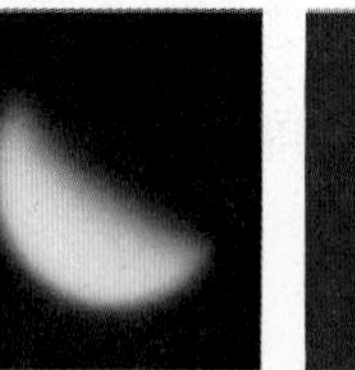

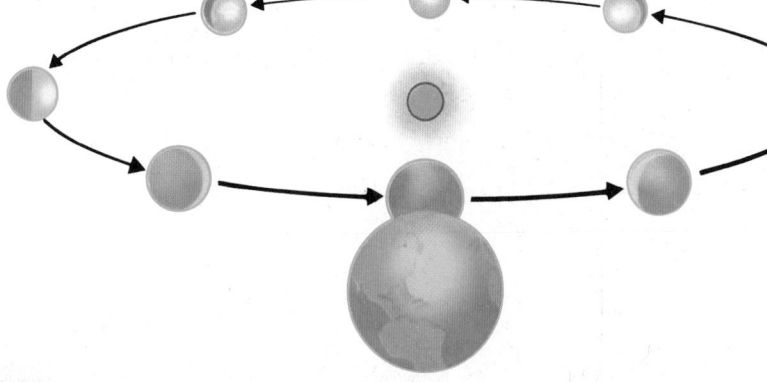

4 The apparent diameter of Venus changes according to phase. It is least at superior conjunction, when Venus is full, because the planet is then on the far side of the Sun and is at its most remote from the Earth. The apparent diameter increases as the phase shrinks, as is shown in these photographs, which were taken with a 12-in (30-cm) reflecting telescope. To the naked eye it is a brilliant object.

5 Mariner 10 provided the first really conclusive optical evidence of the 4-day rotation period of the upper clouds of Venus, although this phenomenon had been suspected from observations made from Earth. In these three photographs taken in February 1974 the cloud patterns are clearly shown (the arrow indicates the same area of Venus). The photographs were taken on February 2 at intervals of 7 hours (note the movement of the arrowed marking). The axis of Venus is almost perpendicular to the plane of the orbit, but the rotation is retrograde in direction, that is, the planet rotates from east to west.

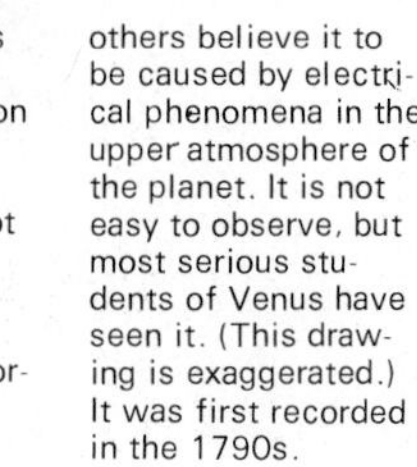

9-XII-1874
3-VI-1769
6-VI-2012
6-VI-1761
6-XII-1882
8-VI-2004

6 Transits of Venus (its passage across the Sun as seen from Earth) occur in pairs with an interval of 8 years, each pair separated by more than a century. The diagram shows the transit paths of Venus for 1761–69, 1874–82, and 2004–12.

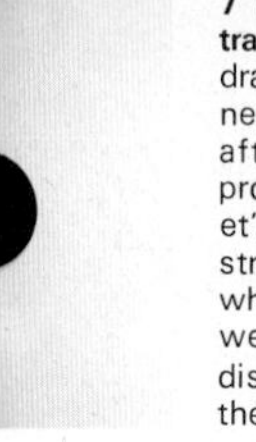

7 When Venus enters transit, it seems to draw a strip of blackness ("black drop") after it, an effect produced by the planet's atmosphere. The strip disappears only when the planet is well onto the Sun's disk, making timing the entry difficult.

8 The ashen light is a faintly luminous patch that appears on the night side of Venus when it is in crescent. This is not the same as Earthshine on our Moon, and its cause is uncertain. Some authorities regard it as a contrast effect; others believe it to be caused by electrical phenomena in the upper atmosphere of the planet. It is not easy to observe, but most serious students of Venus have seen it. (This drawing is exaggerated.) It was first recorded in the 1790s.

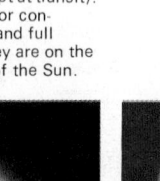

Meanwhile, US radar studies had shown that the surface contains large, shallow craters [11]. The origins of the craters are not known, but there must be intense erosion in so dense an atmosphere, so that by "geological" standards they cannot be very old. Volcanic action may be the cause of the cratering and the idea that volcanism is in progress on Venus has not been ruled out. It was also found that the clouds contain a great deal of sulfuric acid (perhaps even fluorosulfuric acid). As this leads to a corrosive "rain," Venus is clearly hostile.

The transmission of pictures

The next major step came in October 1975, when two Soviet probes, Veneras 9 and 10, made controlled landings on the surface and transmitted pictures back. The pictures were relayed by the orbiting sections of the probes, which remained circling Venus at a height of about 900mi (1,500km). It was a great accomplishment for the Soviet scientists—although neither Venera 9 nor 10 could transmit for more than about one hour before being put permanently out of action by the extreme temperature and pressure.

Surprisingly, the surface of Venus proved to be strewn with smooth rocks, many of which were about 3.5ft (1m) in diameter [12]. There was plenty of light—in the Soviet description, about as much as at noon in Moscow on a cloudy summer day—and the probes did not use their floodlights. Neither was the atmosphere super-refractive, as had been expected, and all the details of the landscape were clear. A temperature of 900°F (485°C) was recorded and pressure was found to be 90 times that on Earth. It was also determined that the cloud layer ends at a height of some 19mi (30km). Below this is what may be called a region of super-hot corrosive smog.

Venus is far from being the friendly world that was once thought. With its carbon dioxide atmosphere, its sulfuric acid clouds, and intense heat, it is wholly hostile to man. This knowledge has altered some goals; less than twenty years ago, Venus was widely regarded as a more promising space target than Mars.

KEY

This drawing of Venus made by A. Dollfus at the Pic-du-Midi Observatory in France reveals more than any photograph taken from Earth, but the surface detail is obscure and hard to draw accurately; also the cloud patterns change quickly.

9 Venus as photographed from Mariner 10. The light and dark zones of the cloud system, which is responsible for Venus's brilliance, are distinctly shown.

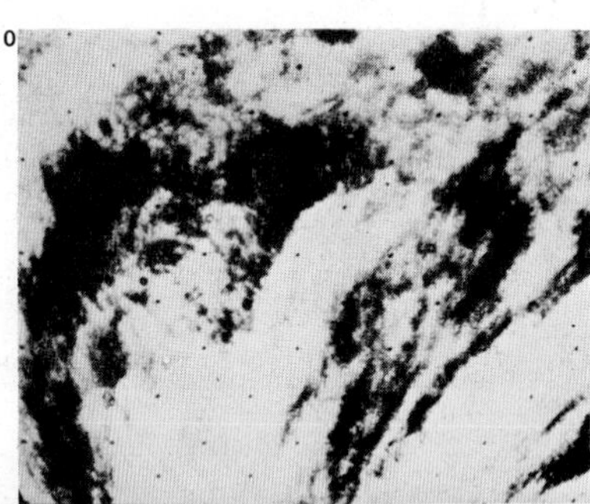

10 In the equatorial zone of the planet the atmospheric conditions on Venus differ from those at the poles. This photograph was taken from Mariner 10.

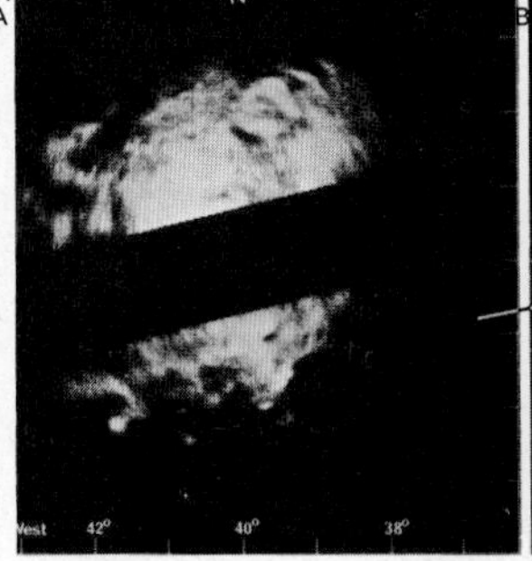
N
42°
40°
38°

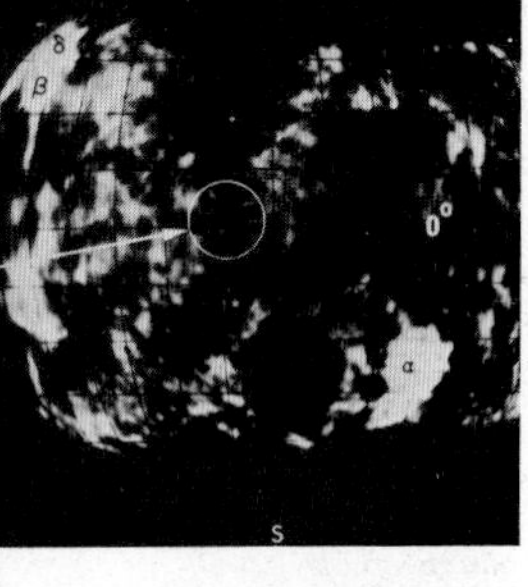
N
W
S

11 Craters on Venus can be detected only by radar. The planet's dense layers of brilliant cloud makes telescopic observation of surface features impossible. Only a small part of the planet has so far been studied in detail, as shown here (the black strip has not been analyzed). Various features detected by means of radar are revealed in this picture [A], which covers an area in the equatorial zone of the planet, indicated in the circle [B]. The craters are of particular interest. They appear to be much shallower than those on Mars or Mercury, although details are blurred in comparison with those obtained from other planets.

12 In October 1975 the Soviet probe Venera 9 soft-landed on Venus and transmitted this picture back to Earth, showing a rock-strewn landscape. Part of the probe device is seen at the bottom. The vertical lines are transmission errors.

The planet Earth

The Earth is the largest member of the group of inner planets and is also the most massive. The difference in size and mass between the Earth and Venus is slight (the ratio for mass is 1 to 0.82), but Mars is much smaller, and Mercury is more comparable with the Moon than with the Earth.

When the Earth is compared with its planetary neighbors, marked similarities as well as marked differences are found. Of course, what singles the Earth out from any other planet is the fact that it has an oxygen-rich atmosphere and a temperature that makes it suitable for life of the kind we can understand. Were the Earth slightly closer to the Sun, or slightly farther away, life here might not have developed.

The ecosphere

What is termed the "ecosphere" [4], or the region in which solar radiation will produce tolerable conditions for terrestrial-type life, extends from just inside the orbit of Venus out to that of Mars. Until about 1960 it was commonly thought that such life might exist throughout the whole region. Although this possibility was far more remote for Mars, with a significantly lower mass than that of Earth, and hence a very tenuous atmosphere, Venus was looked upon as the Earth's twin. Approximately equal in density as well as size and mass, Venus also absorbs about the same amount of solar energy as Earth due to the high reflecting power of its dense cloud. It was not until 1967 when the surface temperature of Venus was shown to be up to 900°F (485°C) that it was universally accepted that advanced terrestrial life could develop only within a very limited zone.

Another essential need for life is an atmosphere that will not only enable living creatures to breathe, but will also protect the planet from lethal short-wave radiations coming from space. On the surface of the Earth there is no danger, because the radiations are blocked out by layers in the upper atmosphere; but the Moon is unprotected, and so too is Mercury. Had the Earth been more massive, it might have been able to retain at least some of its original hydrogen (as Jupiter and Saturn have done) and the resulting atmosphere might have been unsuitable for life. A lower mass might have led to the escape not only of the hydrogen but also of all other gases, so that a fortunate combination of circumstances has produced terrestrial life.

There is also the question of temperature, which depends not only upon the distance of the planet from the Sun or upon the composition of its atmosphere, but upon the axial rotation period as well. The Earth spins round once in approximately 24 hours, and the rotation period of Mars is only 37 minutes longer. But the situation with Mercury and Venus is very different—the periods are 58.7 days and 243 days respectively—leading to very peculiar "calendars." Were the Earth a slow spinner, the climatic conditions would be both unfamiliar and hostile.

The Earth's magnetic field

The Earth's heavy, iron-rich core is associated with the magnetic field, and here too comparisons may be made with other planets. Venus, with its comparable size

CONNECTIONS

See also
48 Evolution of the Solar System
50 Members of the Solar System
276 Earth's time scale
212 The atmosphere

1A

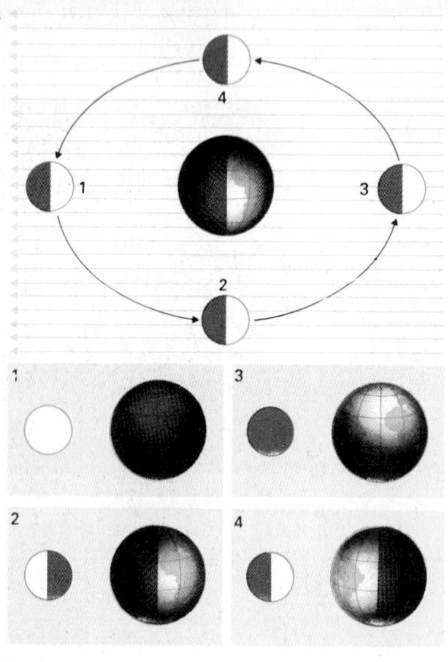
B
4
1
3
2
1
3
2
4

1 From space Earth shows phases, just as the Moon does. The five photographs shown [A] were taken from a satellite over a period of 12 hours. [B] shows the phases of the Earth as they are seen from the Moon. For this purpose it can be assumed that the Earth is stationary, with the Moon moving around it in a period of 27.3 days. When the Moon is full from Earth [1] a lunar observer will have "new earth"; at our new moon [3] a lunar observer will see full earth. Below the main diagram, the different phases of the Moon [left] and Earth are shown [1–4].

2

A
B
C

2 Relative sizes of Jupiter [A], the Earth [B], and Mercury [C]. Jupiter is the largest planet, Mercury the smallest; Earth is intermediate in size, but much more nearly comparable with Mercury. Earth is in fact the largest of the so-called terrestrial planets (Mercury, Venus, Earth, Mars, Pluto) but far inferior to the smallest of the giants (Uranus).

3

3 Apollo 10 sent back these pictures in May 1969; it was the second vehicle to take men around the Moon. The pictures show the Earth coming into view as the spacecraft comes from behind the far side of the Moon, from which the Earth can never be seen. In the first photograph the sharpness of the lunar horizon is particularly notable; there is no lunar atmosphere to cause the slightest blurring or distortion. Note the changing Earth phase.

and mass, should have the same kind of core and hence an appreciable magnetic field; but space probes have so far failed to detect any magnetism, and it is now certain that even if a magnetic field exists it is very weak. The same may be true of Mars, but Mercury has a perceptible field and even a magnetosphere. It is probably significant that Mercury and the Earth are the densest of all the planets, with specific gravities of about 5.5 (that is, their masses are 5.5 times greater than that of equal volumes of water).

The watery planet

The Earth is again unique in having a surface that is largely covered with water; thus, although it is the largest of the four inner planets, its land surface is much less than that of Venus and equal to that of Mars. There can be no oceans or even lakes on Mars, because of the low atmospheric pressure, and of course none on the Moon or Mercury, which are essentially without atmosphere. On Venus the surface temperature is certainly too high for liquid water to exist, so that the old, intriguing picture of a "Carboniferous" Venus, with luxuriant vegetation flourishing in a swampy and very moist environment, has been given up.

Because the Earth is so exceptional, there have been suggestions that it was formed in a manner different from that of the other planets; but this is certainly not so. The age of the Earth, as measured by radioactive methods, is of the order of 4 billion years and studies of the lunar rocks show that the age of the Moon is the same. There is no reason to doubt that the Earth and all other members of the Solar System originated by the same process, and at about the same time, from the primeval solar nebula. It is often said that Mars is more advanced in its evolution than the Earth, but the absolute ages of the two worlds are probably the same, though Mars has "aged" more quickly.

The Earth's position in the middle of the ecosphere, and the particular size and mass that led to its own kind of atmosphere, single it out. There is no other planet in the Solar System upon which men could survive except under artificial conditions.

KEY

23.5°

The Earth's axis is inclined at 23.5° to the perpendicular to the orbital plane. This causes the seasons; the varying distance of the Earth from the Sun has only a minor effect.

4

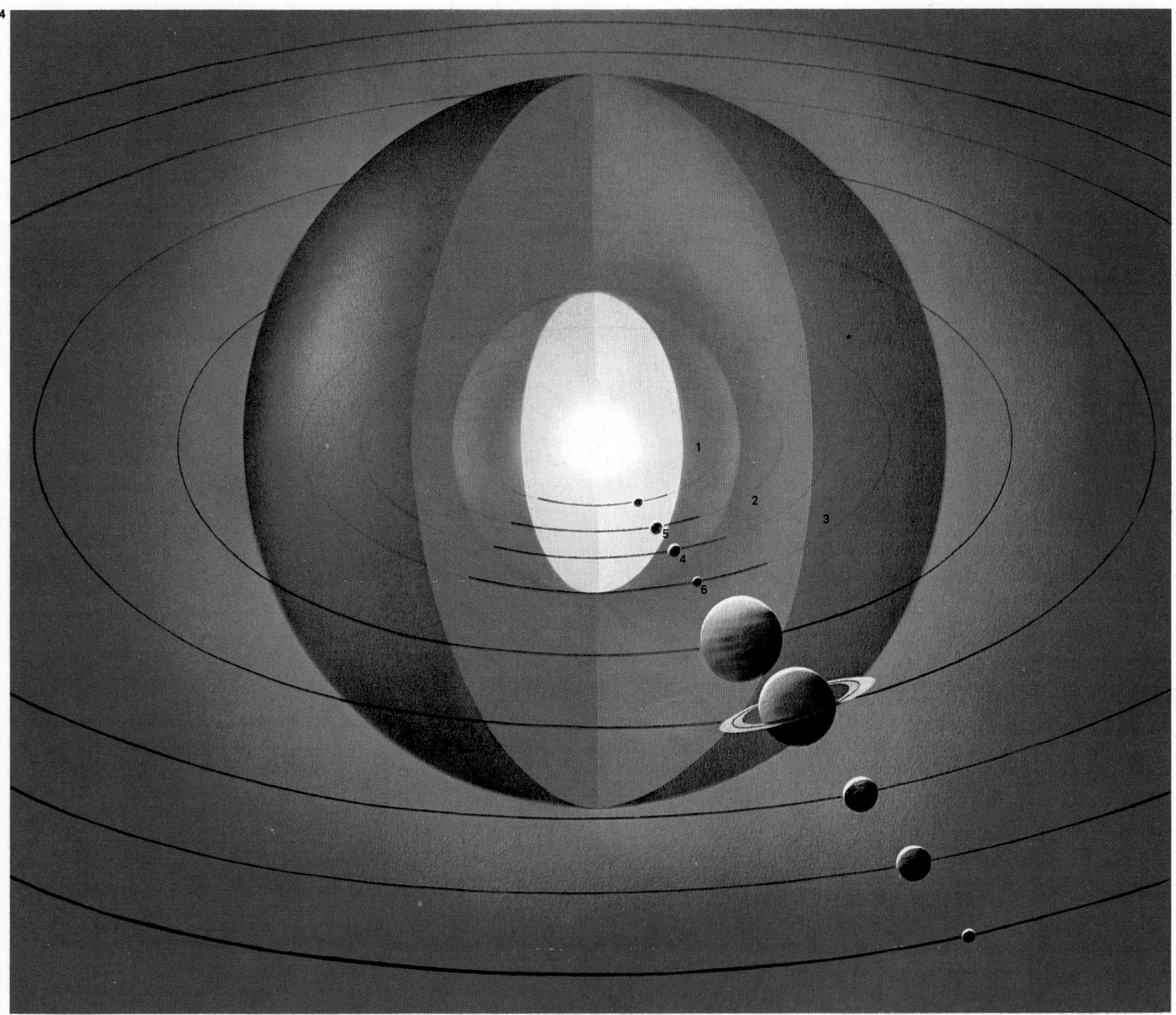
1
2
3
5
4
6

4 This diagram shows the ecosphere, or the region around the Sun in which a planet will be at a suitable temperature for life to exist—assuming that the planet is of Earth type. The inner yellow zone [1] is too hot. Beyond is the ecosphere [2] [orange], and beyond this [3] temperatures will be too low. The Earth [4] lies in the middle of the ecosphere; Venus [5] is at the inner limit and Mars [6] at the outer.

The planet Mars

Mars, the first planet beyond the Earth in the Solar System, is of special interest. In the earlier part of this century many astronomers believed implicitly in the existence of an advanced civilization on Mars. This belief has been shattered. There are no Martians and it seems that the most advanced life the planet could support would be very primitive. Despite this, Mars is still more Earthlike than any other known world and it must surely be the first target for manned space exploration after the Moon.

Through a telescope, Mars shows a red disk with white caps at the poles and prominent dark markings that are essentially permanent [Key]. Its mean distance from the Sun is 141.5 million miles (228 million km).

The Martian year is equal to 687 Earth-days and a day is equal to 24hr 37min. Moreover, the axial tilt is only slightly greater than the Earth's, so that the seasons are of the same basic type, although much longer. As with the Earth, the south pole is tilted sunward at perihelion (the point in orbit when a planet is nearest the Sun). The effect of this upon the climate of Mars is greater than its effect on Earth's climate because the orbit of Mars is more eccentric. The climates in the planet's southern hemisphere are more extreme than those in the northern; the summers are shorter and hotter and the winters longer and colder. The noon temperature on the Martian equator at midsummer may rise to more than 60°F (16°C). The nights are bitterly cold, because the thin atmosphere is inefficient in retaining warmth.

The Martian atmosphere

Because Mars is not only less dense than the Earth but much smaller—the diameter is only 4,220 miles (6,790km)—the escape velocity (the speed an object must reach to overcome gravity) is low: 3.1 miles (5km) per second, which explains the tenuous atmosphere [4]. The main constituent is now known to be carbon dioxide (95%) and the barometric pressure at ground level is less than 10 millibars. It follows that no advanced creatures of terrestrial type can survive there.

There is no free water on the Martian surface. It now seems that the white polar caps are made up chiefly of water ice with some solid carbon dioxide also present. The size of the caps varies according to the Martian season; at their greatest extent they are conspicuous and can be seen with a small telescope [7].

Features shown on early maps

The first drawing to show any markings on the surface of Mars was made by the Dutch astronomer Christiaan Huygens (1629–95) in 1659 [1A]. It shows the V-shaped region now called the Syrtis Major Planitia, although in somewhat exaggerated form. Later observers, using more powerful telescopes, produced drawings that showed more detail. The first reasonably reliable maps date from the second half of the nineteenth century. What may be called the "modern" period of telescopic research was initiated by Giovanni Schiaparelli (1835–1910) in 1877, when Mars was simultaneously at perihelion and opposition and was excellently placed for observation.

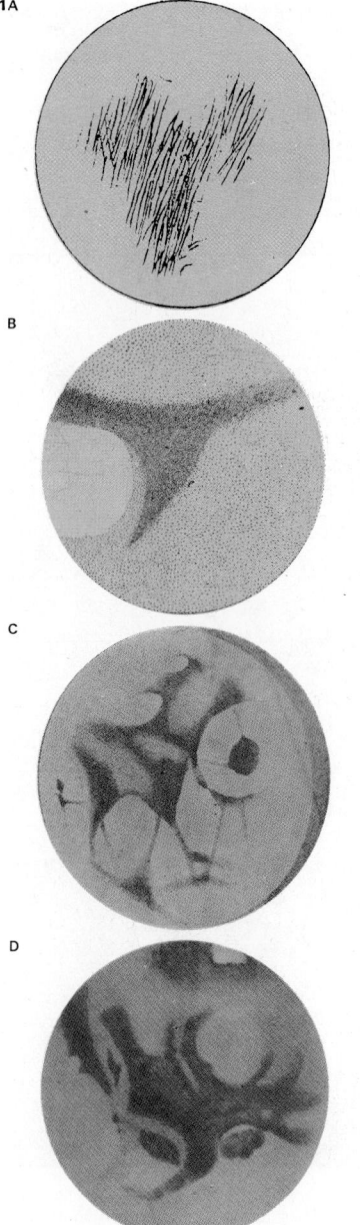

CONNECTIONS

See also
70 Mars missions
72 Mars maps
74 Mars panorama
76 The moons of Mars
148 The Martian base
50 Members of the Solar System

1A

B

C

D

E

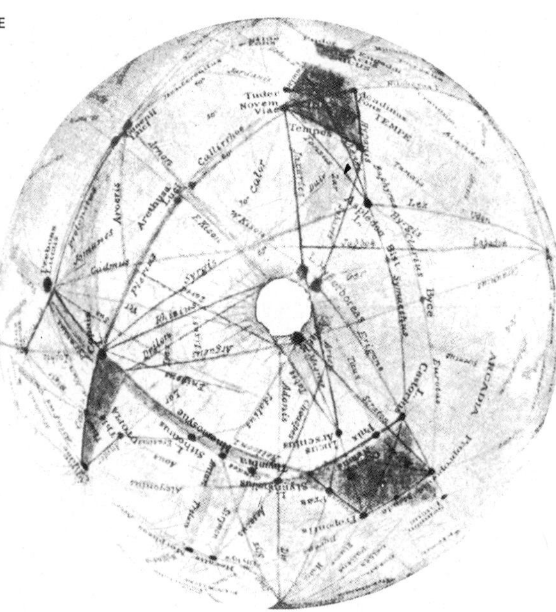

1 Different stages in the telescopic exploration of Mars are shown in these five drawings. The first, [A], made in 1659 by Christiaan Huygens, shows only the Syrtis Major. In drawing [B], made by Johann Schröter (1745–1816) in 1800, the Syrtis Major is again shown, comparatively accurately. The famous canal network appears in Schiaparelli's drawing [C] made in 1877. E. M. Antoniadi, who used the 33in (83cm) Meudon refractor from 1900-30, had no faith in the canals, and his drawing [D] was remarkably accurate. The drawing by Percival Lowell [E] shows the illusory canal network.

2

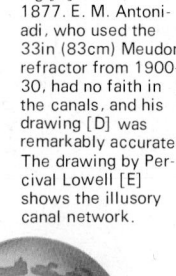

2 The surface area of Mars is 28% that of the Earth. Its diameter of about 4,220 miles (6,790km) is a little more than half that of the Earth and approximately twice that of the Moon. It has only one-tenth of the Earth's mass. The color is generally red.

3 The density of Mars is appreciably less than the Earth's with a specific gravity of only 3.94, resulting in a fairly low escape velocity. The Martian surface gravity is 0.38 that of the Earth's. There is no detectable magnetic field and so presumably no heavy core.

3

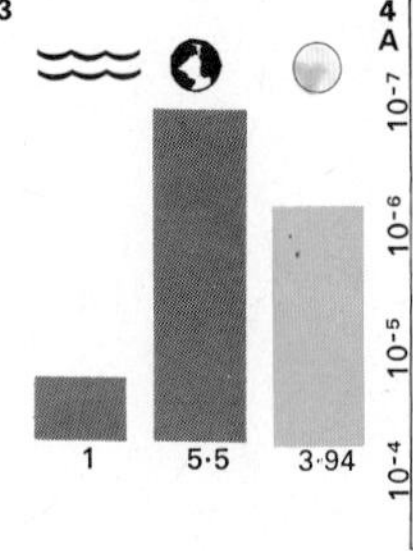

1
5·5
3·94

4 Temperature and wind speed on the Martian surface were monitored by Viking 1 in the area of Chryse Planitia. Despite a diurnal range of more than 70°C [A], the maximum temperature recorded during a Martian day was still below freezing point. Chryse is, however, well to the north of the Martian equator. The speed (meters per second) and direction of winds were also recorded throughout the Martian day [B]: wind direction is indicated by the arrows. The pattern was repeated day after day, the winds remaining gentle, never attaining as much as 15 mph (24kph) throughout the period of study.

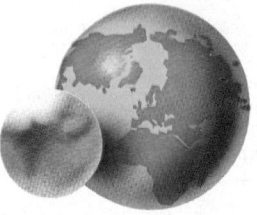

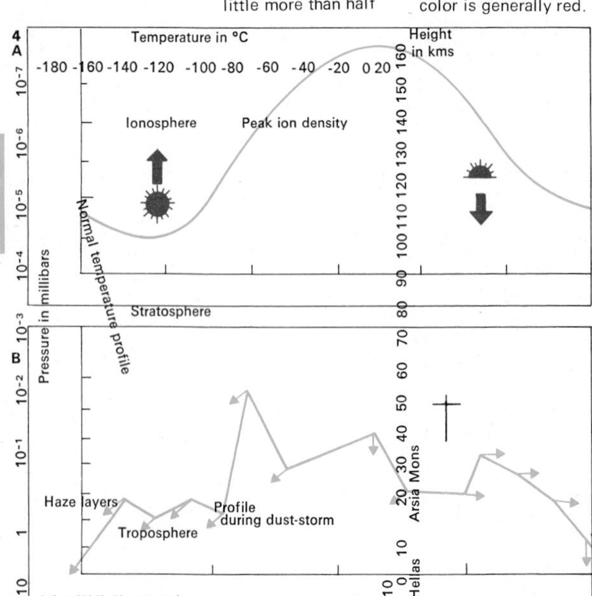

4
A
Temperature in °C
-180 -160 -140 -120 -100 -80 -60 -40 -20 0 20
Height in kms
Ionosphere
Peak ion density
Normal temperature profile
Stratosphere
Pressure in millibars
B
Haze layers
Profile during dust-storm
Troposphere
Arsia Mons
Hellas
(after W.K. Hartmann)

Schiaparelli, observing from Milan, drew a map that was superior to any of its predecessors [1C]. On it he showed straight, artificial-looking features that he called *canali* or channels but which afterward became known as the Martian canals. Inevitably, it was suggested that these features were artificial waterways constructed by the planet's inhabitants to form a vast irrigation system. According to this intriguing theory, water would be drawn from the ice-covered polar caps and pumped to the arid regions closer to the equator. Where canals crossed each other, they did so with the formation of small patches called "oases," which were regarded as centers of population. Schiaparelli himself kept a reasonably open mind. But the American astronomer Percival Lowell (1855–1916), the founder of the Lowell Observatory at Flagstaff, Arizona, believed that Mars supported a highly developed civilization.

The Martian surface

After it became obvious that the dark patches on the surface of Mars could not be seas, it was generally believed that they must be tracts of vegetation growing in depressions. This was still thought to be true until the first successful space probe to Mars, Mariner 4, flew by Mars in 1965. It was found that the dark regions are not depressions; some of them, including the Syrtis Major, are lofty plateaus sloping off on all sides. Evidently their coloring arises from some difference in surface texture and not from any vegetation.

Most of the Martian surface is reddish-ochre; these areas are generally called deserts, which may be an appropriate name, although there is no strict analogy with terrestrial deserts such as the Sahara. Dust storms are not uncommon, and there are winds in the atmosphere of the planet [6].

While the Martian "canals" do not exist, Viking spacecraft have given the clearest evidence yet that water once flowed on Mars in abundance. In the Chryse region cleanly cut channels meander and intertwine like dried river beds, and "islands" of ancient rock, presumably shaped by water, have tails extending downstream.

KEY

Martian volcanoes, three in the Tharsis Mountains and Olympus Mons; the largest were photographed by Viking 1 from 348,000 miles. Also seen is the impact basin Argyre.

5 A

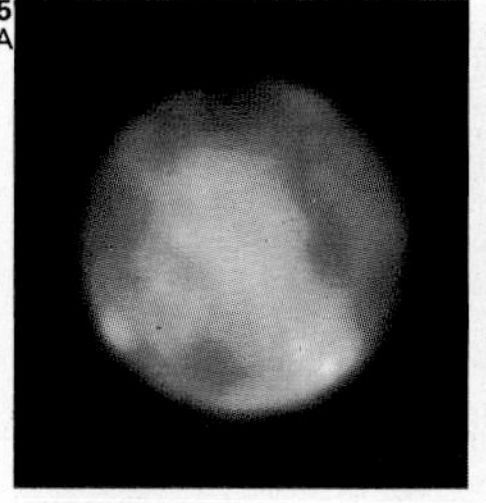

B

C

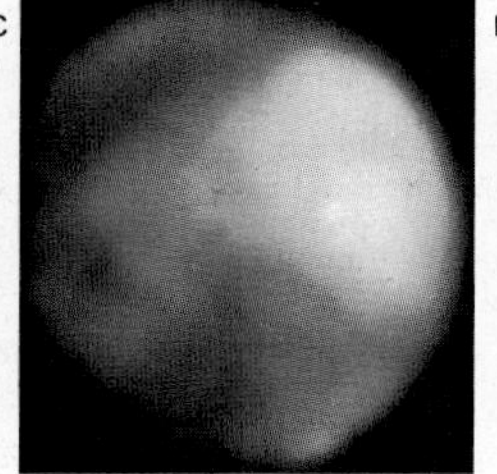

D

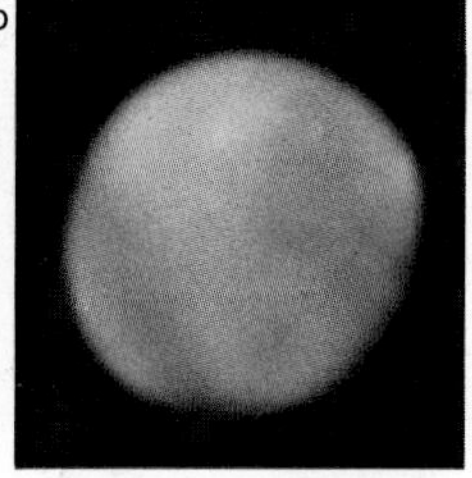

5 Martian clouds consist of high-altitude "white" clouds and much less common but more extensive dust clouds. These four views show Mars taken through different colored filters. The area of cloud that forms every summer over the Syrtis Major is shown in [A]. [B, C and D] show the Syrtis Major to the left, covered by the same cloud. The bright area to the right is Elysium.

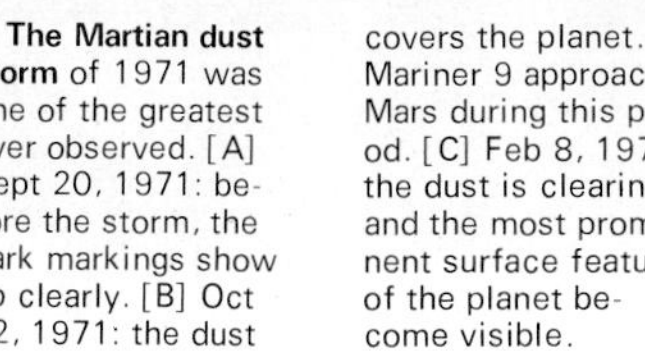

6 The Martian dust storm of 1971 was one of the greatest ever observed. [A] Sept 20, 1971: before the storm, the dark markings show up clearly. [B] Oct 12, 1971: the dust covers the planet. Mariner 9 approached Mars during this period. [C] Feb 8, 1972: the dust is clearing and the most prominent surface features of the planet become visible.

7 Observations of Mars made in 1972 show a dark peripheral band well defined in [A] at the edge of shrinking polar caps [B to F]. Gerard de Vaucouleurs in 1939 attributed the shrinking to release of water vapor, which might support vegetation. But it is known that the caps are largely water ice with some solid carbon dioxide (dry ice) also present.

7 A

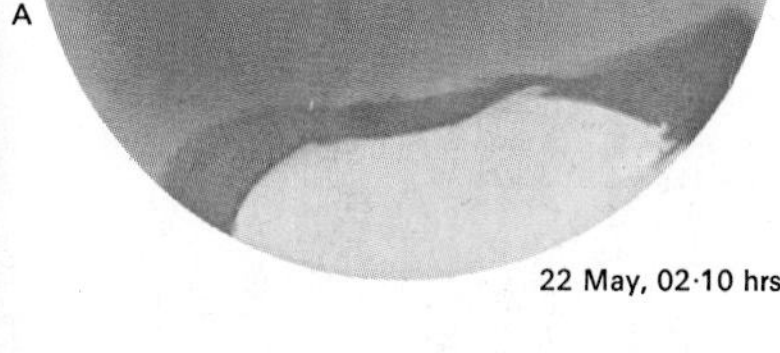

22 May, 02·10 hrs

B

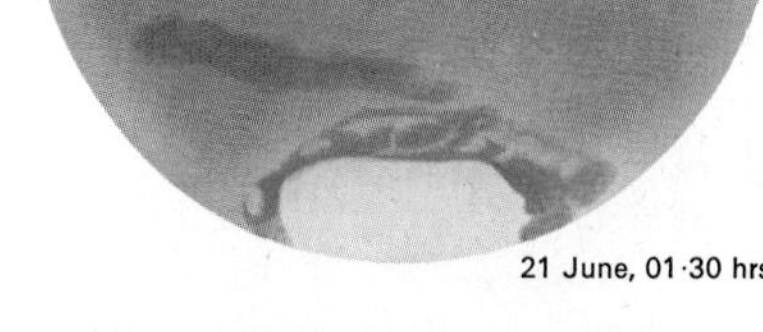

21 June, 01·30 hrs

C

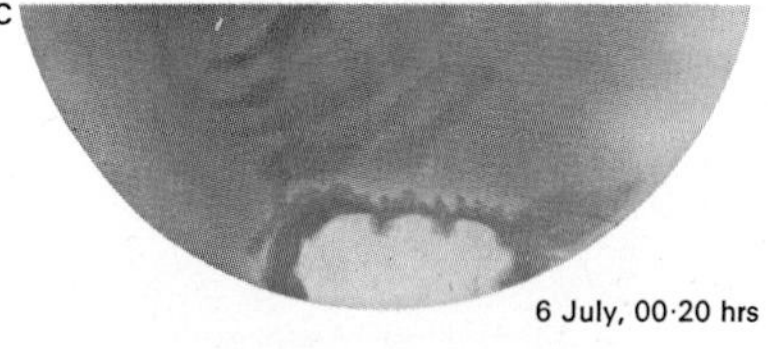

6 July, 00·20 hrs

D

16 August, 22·00 hrs

E

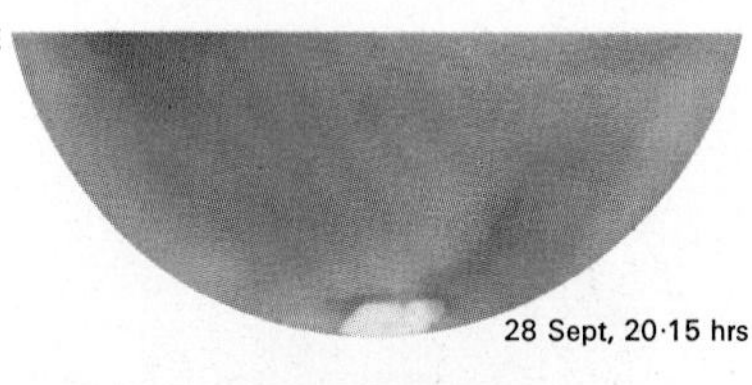

28 Sept, 20·15 hrs

F

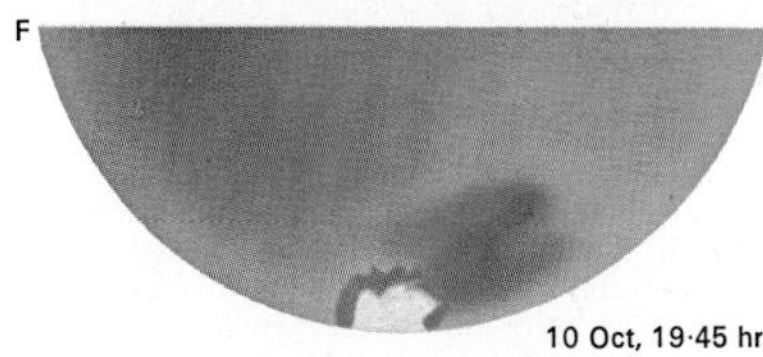

10 Oct, 19·45 hrs

6

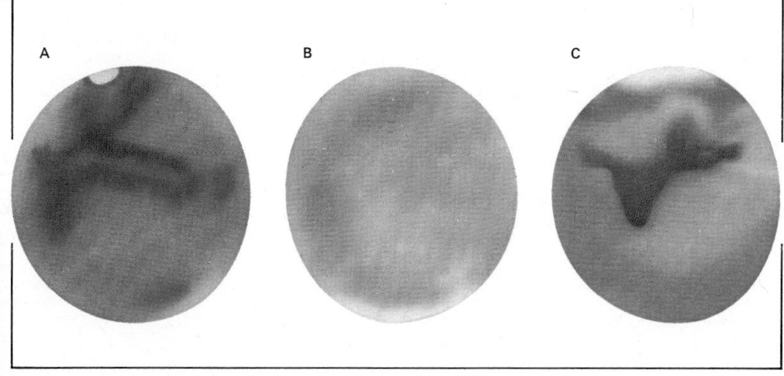
A
B
C

8 A

B

C

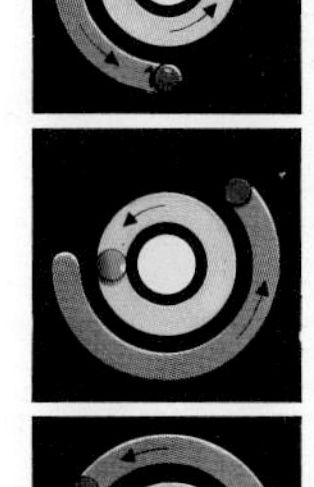

D

8E

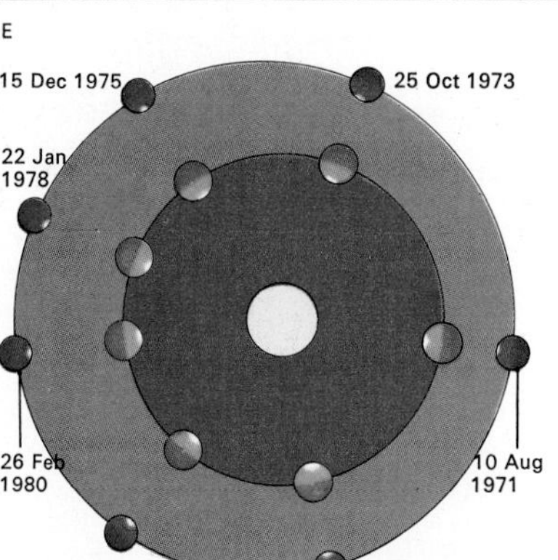
15 Dec 1975
25 Oct 1973
22 Jan 1978
26 Feb 1980
10 Aug 1971
15 April 1967
31 May 1969

8 The "opposition of Mars" describes the lining up in sequence of the Sun, Earth, and Mars. Mars takes 687 Earth days to complete one revolution around the Sun and this means that it comes to opposition once in approximately 780 days. As shown in [E], oppositions occurred in 1967, 1969, 1971, 1973, and 1975; the next will be in Jan 1978 and Feb 1980. The series of drawings [A to D] begins with Earth and Mars in opposition; by the time Mars has reached position 1 [A], the Earth will have moved to position 2. By the time the Earth has completed one full circuit [B], Mars has made only a little more than half a revolution. When the Earth has made 1.5 circuits [C], Mars has made almost one and after 780 days the two planets are again in opposition [D].

Mars missions

Mars is a fairly small world and can be properly observed from Earth for only a few months in every alternate year (the average interval between successive oppositions is 780 days). Before the Space Age man's knowledge of Mars was bound to be incomplete; then in 1962 the U.S.S.R. made a preliminary attempt to send a space probe past it [1]. This failed because contact with the vehicle was lost at a relatively early stage and was never regained. But in July 1965 the U.S. probe Mariner 4 [2] bypassed Mars at close range and sent back the first detailed information about the planet.

What the Mariner program revealed

The Martian atmosphere proved to be as thin as had been expected in that instead of being made up of nitrogen, with a ground pressure of 85 millibars, it was found to be composed mainly of carbon dioxide, with a pressure of less than 10 millibars—which at once reduced the possibility of any advanced life forms. But the most spectacular discovery was of craters, superficially similar to those of the Moon. The craters were large and some of them had lunar-type central peaks.

This came as a major surprise because scientists had expected that Mars would have a smooth landscape with no lofty mountains or deep valleys. Indeed, it seemed that Mars was less like Earth and more like the Moon than anticipated.

The next American probes, Mariners 6 [3] and 7, followed in the summer of 1969, only a few days after Neil Armstrong and Edwin Aldrin, in Apollo 11, made their landing on the Moon. Both the Mariners were successful, and both sent back excellent pictures. They again showed craters, together with mountainous regions. When measurements were taken there were some more surprises. For instance, the circular white patch known as Hellas, just south of the V-shaped Syrtis Major, proved to be a depression instead of a raised plateau. Hellas is in fact the most depressed area on Mars and it seems to be almost devoid of craters or other important features.

The first three Mariners were fly-by probes, making one pass of Mars and then moving on to solar orbit. Mariners 8 and 9, launched in 1971, were different. They were intended to orbit Mars in order to send back data—including photographs—over a period of months instead of only a few days. Mariner 8 failed immediately after blast-off and fell into the sea, but Mariner 9 [4] was a success, giving us a wealth of new data, including 7,329 photographs.

The craft went into orbit around Mars on November 14, 1971, when almost the whole of the planet was surrounded by dust and little could be seen. When the dust cleared, the spacecraft's cameras discovered volcanoes, similar in form to the terrestrial volcanoes of Hawaii, but much larger. For instance, Olympus Mons reaches up to about 15.5 miles (25km) above the general level of the surface. There were deep rift valleys, and features that looked like dried river beds.

Viking's search for life

But did some kind of life await discovery somewhere on this cold, harsh landscape? The United States sent the Vikings to find

CONNECTIONS

See also

68 The planet Mars
72 Mars maps
74 Mars panorama
76 The moons of Mars
148 The Martian base
142 A history of space achievements

1 Launched by the USSR on November 1, 1962, Mars 1 went into the right orbit, but contact with it was lost early in its flight.

2 The first successful Mars probe, the US Mariner 4, was launched in 1964. It sent back the first pictures of Martian craters in 1965.

3 Mariner 6 bypassed Mars in July 1969 and sent back detailed information. Mariner 7 made its pass 5 days later. Mariner 6 studied the equatorial regions, while Mariner 7's coverage included the south pole. There was extensive photographic coverage and both made improved studies of the atmosphere.

4 Mariner 9, a very successful Mars probe, was a complicated vehicle. The cameras could be controlled from the Earth and their working life exceeded the planned life of the probe. Control was lost only in October 1972, when the gas controlling the craft's attitude jets was exhausted. Mariner 9 measured temperature, analyzed the Martian atmosphere, and sent back spectacular pictures that enabled astronomers to prepare accurate maps in preparation for the Viking landings to come in 1975. Both Martian satellites were also photographed.

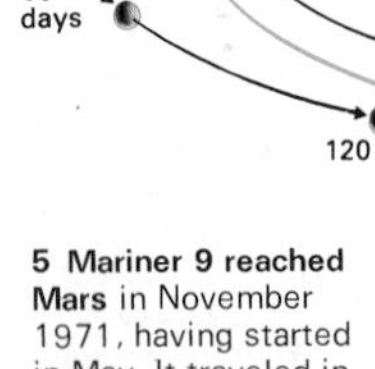

5 Mariner 9 reached Mars in November 1971, having started in May. It traveled in a transfer orbit using the Sun's gravity. The probe was accelerated from the Earth and swung outward in order to rendezvous with its target planet.

6 As Mariner 9 approached Mars, it passed and photographed the two tiny Martian satellites, Deimos (far left) and Phobos (left). The probe entered an elliptical orbit of Mars after it had joined a closed path around the planet.

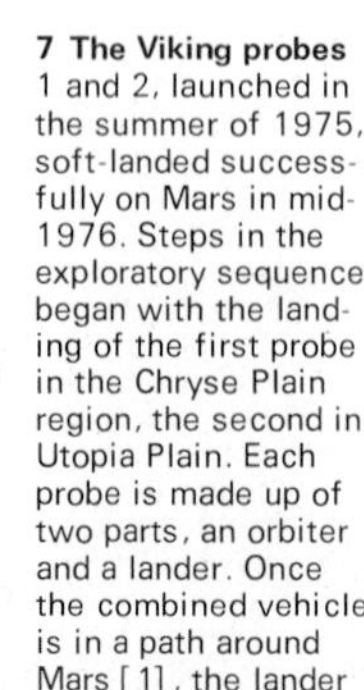

Solid rocket separation
Launch

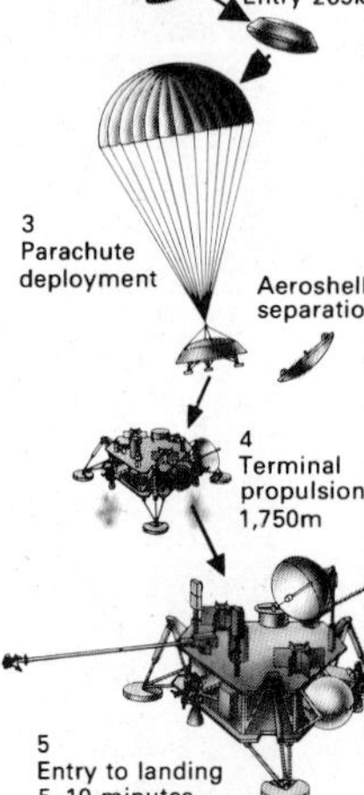

3
Parachute deployment
4
Terminal propulsion 1,750m
5
Entry to landing 5–10 minutes

7 The Viking probes 1 and 2, launched in the summer of 1975, soft-landed successfully on Mars in mid-1976. Steps in the exploratory sequence began with the landing of the first probe in the Chryse Plain region, the second in Utopia Plain. Each probe is made up of two parts, an orbiter and a lander. Once the combined vehicle is in a path around Mars [1], the lander separates from the orbiter [2], enters the planet's atmosphere and begins its descent to the surface. At a comparatively low level, the main parachute opens [3]. Next, the lander separates from the parachute [4] and completes the descent to the surface under its own power. This turns off at about 50ft (15m) above the surface, and the lander falls gently on to its chosen site [5]. During the descent analyses are made of the nature of the Martian atmosphere. The orbiter meanwhile remains in a closed path around Mars, acting as a relay link for the lander, which, once it has grounded, begins to carry out numerous experiments. The principal objective of the probes was to study the surface geology and chemistry and test its soil for signs of life.

out. The first swung into orbit on June 19, 1976, the second on August 7, 1976. After a period of photoreconnaissance to establish suitable landing sites, both released landers. That of Viking 1 touched down on the broad Chryse basin in Mars' northern middle latitudes on July 20. The other landed on September 3 on Utopia Planitia roughly 4,600 miles (7,400km) from Viking 1 and 870 miles (1,400km) nearer the north pole.

Spectacular photographs received from the landers showed rock-strewn terrain in both places with an overlying reddish soil. The sky was pink from light scattered by red dust particles in the air. Major elements in the soil, as detected by Viking 1's X-ray fluorescence spectrometer, were silicon, iron, calcium, aluminum, and titanium.

Both spacecraft dug into the soil to deliver samples for analysis to the biology laboratories, with results that both surprised and tantalized. The experiments had been designed on the basis that any life-forms in the soil must use and excrete certain basic chemicals. The initial "gas exchange" experiment rapidly detected 15 times as much oxygen as had been expected. All terrestrial life-forms with which science is familiar take time to grow and reproduce, and the findings from this experiment seemed to be the result of a chemical reaction in the iron-rich soil.

The results of the "labeled release" experiment also at first looked interesting. If microbes were present, they were expected to take up carbon-14 and give off radioactive wastes such as carbon dioxide and carbon monoxide. A generous amount of carbon dioxide was detected but again the cause seemed to be chemistry. The "pyrolytic" experiment indicated that something was taking carbon dioxide out of the air in the test chamber and incorporating it into other compounds within the soil.

What worried scientists most was the absence of organic molecules. All three biology experiments showed many signs that could be interpreted as the result of living organisms, only if organic compounds were also present. This disappointment, however, did not detract from the overwhelming success of Viking.

KEY

The sampler scoop of Viking 1 is seen poised over the red-orange soil of Chryse Planitia. Some of the rocks are dark and coarse-grained, while others have a lighter, mottled appearance and may have come from lava flows or stream deposits.

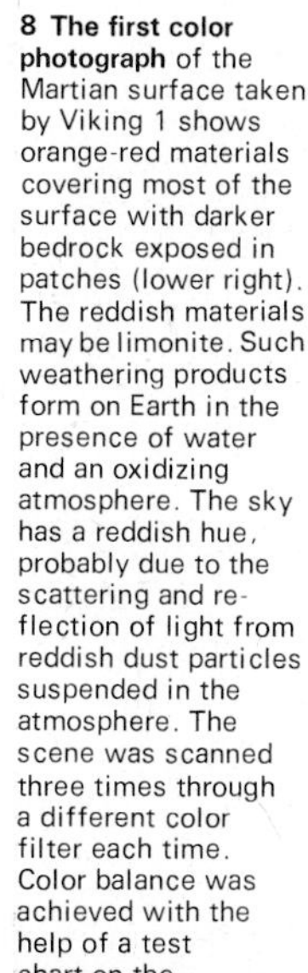

8 The first color photograph of the Martian surface taken by Viking 1 shows orange-red materials covering most of the surface with darker bedrock exposed in patches (lower right). The reddish materials may be limonite. Such weathering products form on Earth in the presence of water and an oxidizing atmosphere. The sky has a reddish hue, probably due to the scattering and reflection of light from reddish dust particles suspended in the atmosphere. The scene was scanned three times through a different color filter each time. Color balance was achieved with the help of a test chart on the spacecraft.

8

9

9 A panoramic view from Viking 2 shows the scene on Utopia Planitia in a composite of three shots. The surface is strewn with rocks out to the horizon ranging in size up to several yards. Some may have come from the nearby impact crater Mie, which is about 0.62 mile (1km) across. The picture has been electronically rectified to remove the effect of the spacecraft's 8 degree tilt.

10 This spectacular sunset over Chryse Planitia was photographed by Viking 1. The camera began scanning the scene from the left about 4 minutes after the sun had dipped below the horizon, and continued for 10 minutes. The sun had set nearly 3 degrees below the horizon by the time the picture was completed. The surface appears black and the horizon line is very sharp.

10

Mars maps

Most of the Martian features were renamed by Giovanni Schiaparelli (1835–1910) after 1877. His system replaced the older nomenclature; for instance, the "Kaiser Sea" or "Hour Glass Sea" was renamed the Syrtis Major. Further revisions by the International Astronomical Union following the Mariner 9 results have assigned Latin qualifications to those of Schiaparelli. These are given to topographical features as opposed to those features associated with the reflecting power (albedo) of the planet. The new Latin names have been used on the maps below.

The western hemisphere

The western hemisphere (below left) includes most of the Acidalium Planitia. To most observers it is the more interesting of the two hemispheres because it also contains some of the greatest of the volcanoes, notably Olympus Mons, which can be seen as a tiny patch from Earth and is surrounded by an extensive, roughly circular area comparatively free of major craters. This area includes Amazonis Planitia to the west, Arcadia Planitia to the northwest and Tharsis Montes to the southeast of these. The relatively few small craters here were probably produced by meteoritic impact and are not the result of the extensive Martian volcanism that took place in past ages. Of special significance in volcanic areas are the lava flows, which are particularly well marked around Olympus Mons. Ascraeus Mons, Pavonis Mons, and Arsia Mons are also lofty volcanic cones that together make up the Tharsis Montes. During the great dust storm of late 1971, when Mariner 9 reached Mars, these three peaks were among the few features that could be identified because their summits protruded through the top of the dust cloud.

The Vastitas Borealis extends around the north polar region and its southern border is seen across the top of the first map. During the northern winter the white deposits of the polar cap may extend as far south as Tempe Dorsum.

Two areas on this map, Chryse Planitia and Utopia Planitia, were the landing sites for the first two Viking probes in the summer of 1976. About 5° south of the equator and on longitude zero lies the Sinus Meridianii, used to mark the zero for Martian longitudes, and at a point 20° west and 20° south of that is the dark patch of Margaritifer Sinus. These names did not survive the IAU revisions (and are not on the map) because the markings do not correspond with any obvious topographical features.

The hemisphere is dominated by the tremendous system of rift valleys extending eastward from the Tharsis Montes through Tithonius Chasma, Melas Chasma, and Coprates Chasma through Simud Vallis. Immediately south of Tithonius Chasma lies Solis Planum, one of the most variable areas on Mars. Observers since 1877 have noted pronounced changes of shape and shade. Such variations were easy to explain with the old vegetation hypothesis, but now that the dark areas are believed to be inorganic the changes are more puzzling.

The prominent dark patches around the furrows of Sirenum Dorsum and the serpentine Nirgal Vallis are two of the classical maria ("seas") that have disappeared in the

CONNECTIONS

See also
68 The planet Mars
70 Mars missions
74 Mars panorama
76 The moons of Mars

1

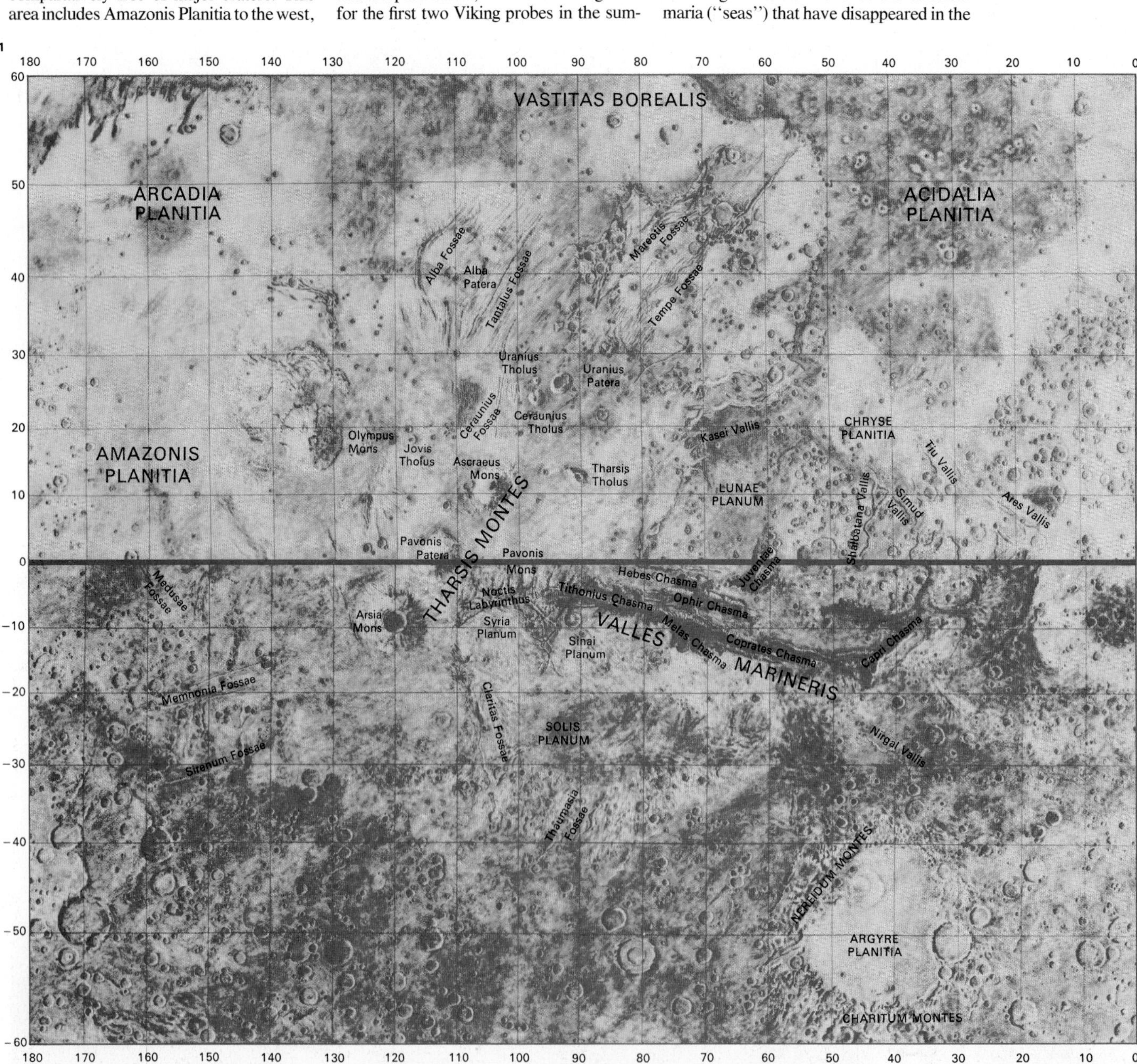

180 170 160 150 140 130 120 110 100 90 80 70 60 50 40 30 20 10 0
60 50 40 30 20 10 0 −10 −20 −30 −40 −50 −60
VASTITAS BOREALIS
ARCADIA PLANITIA
ACIDALIA PLANITIA
Alba Fossae
Alba Patera
Tantalus Fossae
Mareotis Fossae
Tempe Fossae
Uranius Tholus
Uranius Patera
Ceraunius Fossae
Ceraunius Tholus
Olympus Mons
Jovis Tholus
Ascraeus Mons
Tharsis Tholus
AMAZONIS PLANITIA
Kasei Vallis
CHRYSE PLANITIA
Tiu Vallis
LUNAE PLANUM
Shalbatana Vallis
Simud Vallis
Ares Vallis
Pavonis Patera
THARSIS MONTES
Pavonis Mons
Medusae Fossae
Hebes Chasma
Juventae Chasma
Noctis Labyrinthus
Tithonius Chasma
Ophir Chasma
Arsia Mons
Syria Planum
VALLES
Melas Chasma
Coprates Chasma
Capri Chasma
Sinai Planum
MARINERIS
Memnonia Fossae
Claritas Fossae
SOLIS PLANUM
Nirgal Vallis
Sirenum Fossae
Thaumasia Fossae
NEREIDUM MONTES
ARGYRE PLANITIA
CHARITUM MONTES

new nomenclature. Both are heavily cratered. The Soviet Mars 3 probe landed south of Sirenum Dorsum in December 1971, but it transmitted for only 20 seconds after arrival and nothing was learned from it.

The eastern hemisphere

The main feature in the eastern hemisphere (below right) is the Syrtis Planitia, which was recorded by Christiaan Huygens (1629–95) in 1659 and is the most prominent dark marking on Mars. Mariner 9 showed it to be a relatively smooth plateau sloping eastward toward the basin of Isidis Planitia and not, as had been believed, a sunken sea bed. Surprisingly, there is little, apart from its color, to distinguish it from the lighter Isidis Planitia and therefore the conclusion can be drawn that its prominence is caused by the low albedo of its rocks.

Elysium Planitia to the east of the map is a volcanic province of intermediate geological age. It contains two large volcanic craters (calderas) as well as a clearly marked dome. The dark region north of latitude 55° is the other half of Vastitas Borealis. It may be partly responsible for the dark peripheral region of the polar cap formerly attributed to the visible effects of melting ice. The southern portion of this hemisphere is dominated by Hellas Planitia, which may appear extremely brilliant from Earth and can sometimes be mistaken for an extra polar cap. East of Hellas lie the two prominent dark features of Mare Tyrrhenum and Mare Cimmerium, omitted from the new names.

The polar caps

In the north polar region [Key] the white cap never vanishes completely. Part of the Acidalium Planitia is shown; this is the most prominent of the dark features in the northern hemisphere of the planet.

In the south polar zone [Key] the area within 10° of the actual south pole is seen to be smooth and laminated, with the summer remnant of the polar cap offset at longitude 45°. The dark surrounding areas are heavily cratered, with a prominent ridge, Argyre Dorsum. During the southern winter the polar deposit covers almost the whole area.

KEY

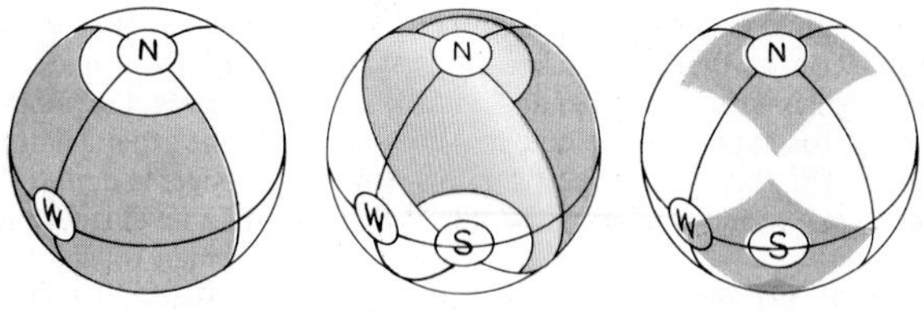

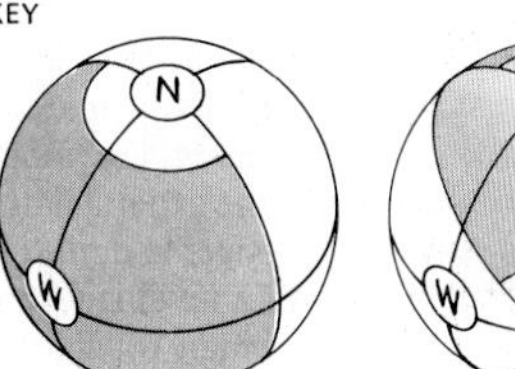

N
W
S

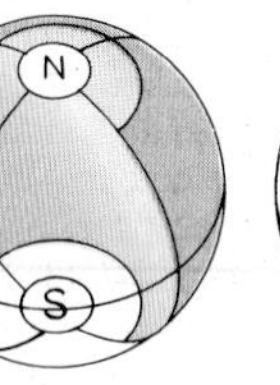

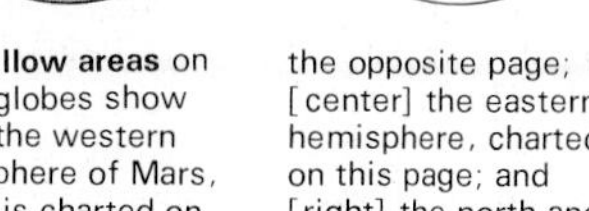

The yellow areas on these globes show [left] the western hemisphere of Mars, which is charted on the opposite page; [center] the eastern hemisphere, charted on this page; and [right] the north and south poles of the planet, which are charted on the two small maps immediately below.

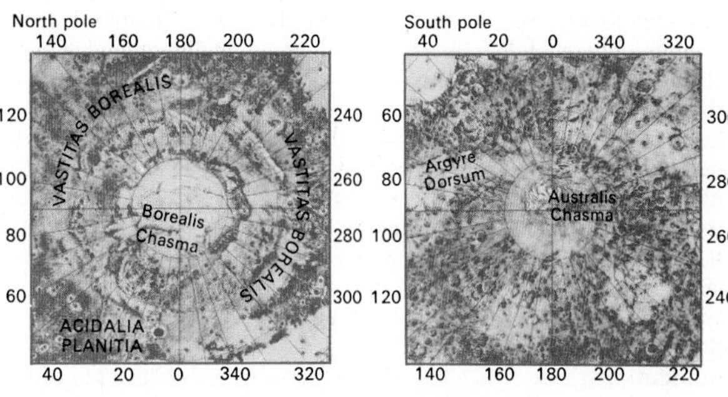

North pole
VASTITAS BOREALIS
Borealis Chasma
ACIDALIA PLANITIA
South pole
Argyre Dorsum
Australis Chasma

2

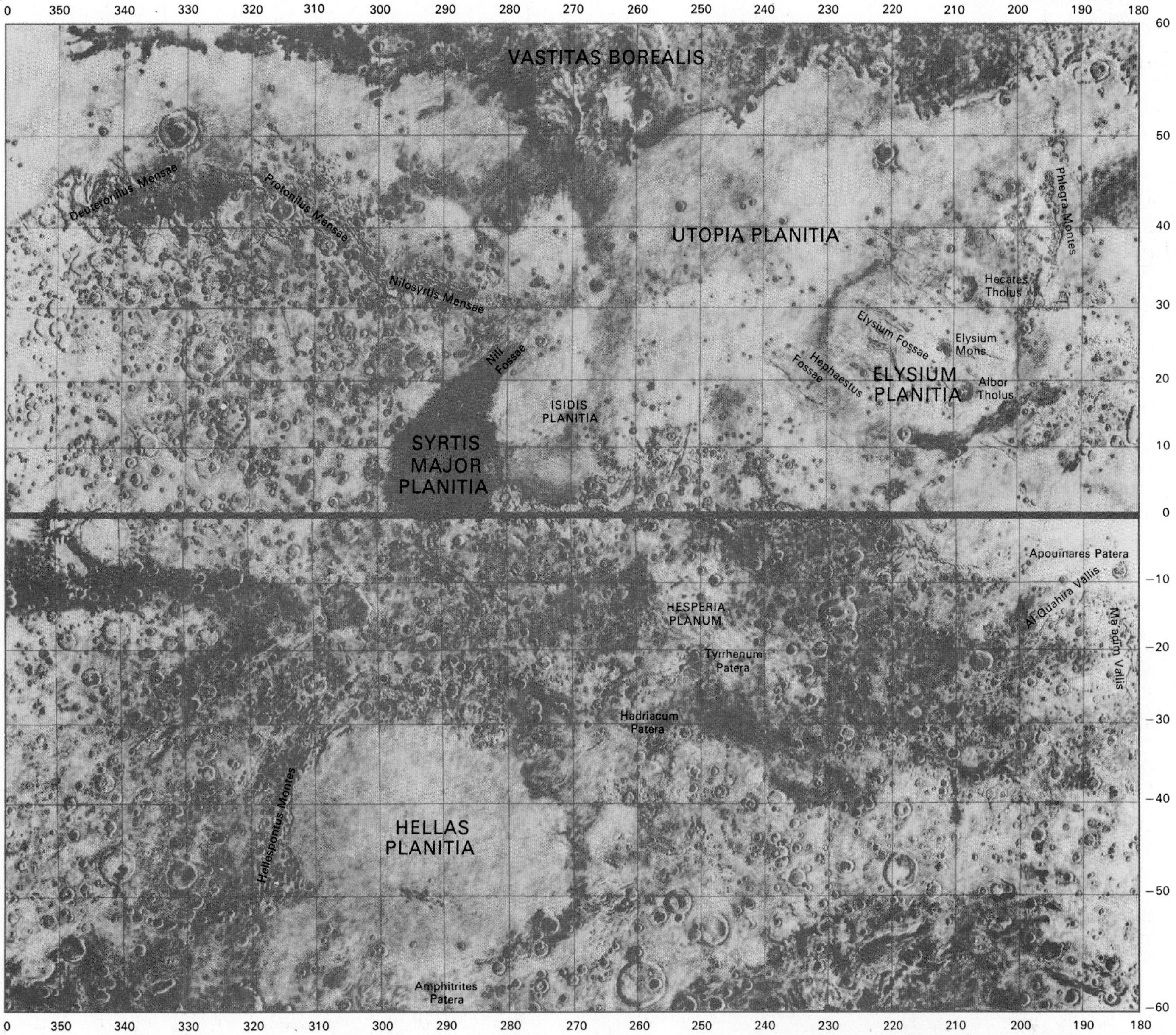

VASTITAS BOREALIS
Deuteronilus Mensae
Protonilus Mensae
Nilosyrtis Mensae
Nili Fossae
UTOPIA PLANITIA
Phlegra Montes
Hecates Tholus
Elysium Fossae
Elysium Mons
Hephaestus Fossae
ELYSIUM PLANITIA
Albor Tholus
ISIDIS PLANITIA
SYRTIS MAJOR PLANITIA
Apollinares Patera
Al-Qahira Vallis
Ma'adim Vallis
HESPERIA PLANUM
Tyrrhenum Patera
Hadriacum Patera
Hellespontus Montes
HELLAS PLANITIA
Amphitrites Patera

Mars panorama

Although Mars is almost certainly about the same age as the Earth (about 4.7 billion years), it is so much smaller and less massive that it has evolved more quickly. This fact suggested that the surface features were likely to be more worn and eroded.

Theories old and new

It is interesting to look back at what astronomers thought about Mars before 1965, when the first successful probe, Mariner 4, sent back data from close range. It was believed that the dark areas were depressions, probably old sea beds, while bright regions such as Hellas Planitia and Argyre Planitia were plateaus. Also the surface was thought to be gentle in relief, with no lofty mountains or deep valleys anywhere. Recent volcanic activity was regarded as unlikely, and it was tacitly assumed that Mars must have an iron core smaller than that of the Earth, so that there would be no appreciable magnetic field.

Few of these conclusions have been confirmed—apart from the weakness of the Martian magnetic field. The first pictures sent back from Mariner 4 showed signs of craters [Key] and, as the probe approached the planet, the photographs became clearer and the general nature of the landscape was no longer in doubt. Instead of being a world with a level landscape, Mars proved to be extremely rough. Yet even from the Mariner 4 evidence it was clear that there were marked differences over various areas and that the surface of Mars was likely to be much more variegated than that of the Moon. Mariner 4 also showed that the atmosphere of the planet was much more tenuous than had been previously supposed and the theory of vegetation-filled sea beds began to look less plausible.

Mariners 6 and 7, in 1969, produced a similar picture of Mars and it seemed that there were cratered areas and others that were described as "chaotic," with no particular pattern. Because of technical improvements, pictures were far clearer than those from Mariner 4; much had been learned during the intervening four years. But there was a time, following the publication of the Mariner 6 and 7 results, when interest in the planet began to wane because the possibility of finding life on Mars continued to recede. The chances of finding life were diminishing largely by the nature of the Martian surface.

Mariner 9 and the Vikings

Striking discoveries of Mars came in 1971 from Mariner 9, which proved to be a tremendous success—the more so because it also had to compensate for the failure of its predecessor, Mariner 8. After it had approached the planet and photographed the two Martian satellites, Mariner 9 had to wait for dust storms to subside. It appeared that the dust extended almost to the top of Olympus Mons and Arsia Mons, the highest known points on Mars, with altitudes of more than 12 miles (20km). When the atmosphere became clear, these towering volcanoes were revealed—and ideas about the nature of Mars changed yet again. Few astronomers had expected to find volcanoes of a terrestrial type, yet the similarity between Olympus Mons and Arsia Mons on the one hand, and the Earth's Hawaiian

CONNECTIONS

See also
68 The planet Mars
70 Mars missions
72 Mars maps
76 The moons of Mars

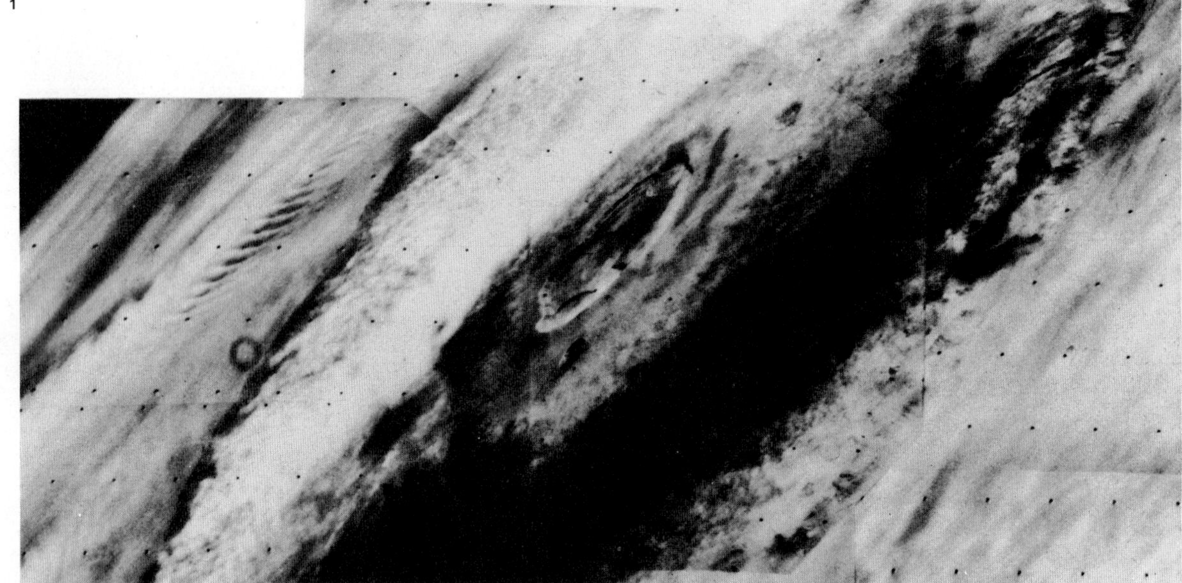

1 The Great Martian volcano Olympus Mons was photographed by Viking 1 from a distance of 5,000 miles (8,000 km). The 15.5-mile (25km) high mountain is seen in mid-morning, wreathed in clouds that rise to an altitude of about 12 miles (19km). The multiringed caldera, some 43 miles (70km) across, extends into the stratosphere. A cloud train stretches several hundred miles behind the mountain.

2 This oblique view across Argyre Planitia extends toward the horizon some 12,000 miles (19,000km) away. Argyre–surrounded by heavily cratered terrain–is the plain at left center.

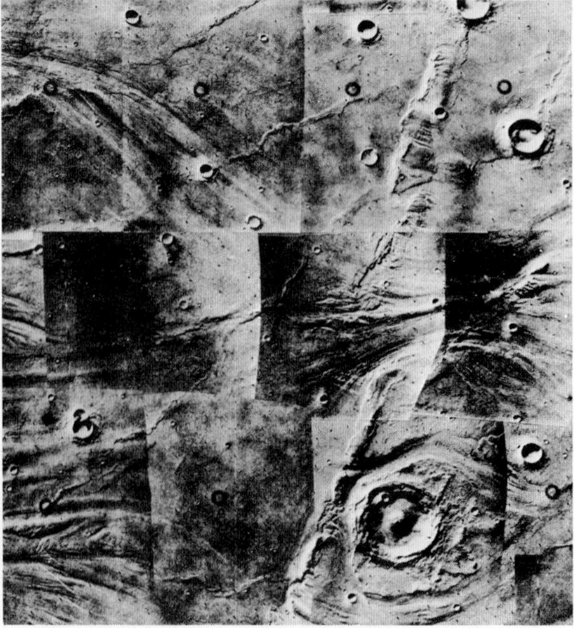

3 Eroded channels were photographed near the Viking 1 landing site in Chryse Planitia. They may be the remains of ancient stream beds that fade out near the landing ellipse, suggesting that the area is a sediment basin. The picture is a mosaic of 15 photographs taken by Viking Orbiter 1 from a distance of 1,040 miles (1,680km) and covers an area of about 155 by 120 miles (250 by 200km). The lava flows are broken by faults that form ridges and are peppered by meteorite impact craters. A small stream flowed northward (toward upper right) from Lunae Planum, crossed the area, and descended toward the east.

volcanoes on the other, was unmistakable. The main discrepancy was in scale; the Martian volcanoes are about three times as high as their Hawaiian counterparts. The caldera on Olympus Mons has a diameter of 40 miles (65km).

On July 20, 1976, exactly seven years after man first walked on the Moon, Viking 1 touched down on the Martian plain known as Chryse Planitia about 20° north of its equator. It transmitted brilliantly clear pictures of the rust-colored terrain and the salmon-pink sky (although first interpretations mistakenly indicated that the sky color ranged from gray to blue). The surface cover appeared to be a thin veneer over darker bedrock exposed in patches; the red color of the sky is probably caused by scattering and reflection from sediment suspended in the lower atmosphere. On September 3, Viking 2 landed on the more northerly Utopia Planitia on the opposite side of Mars. Photographs revealed a region quite similar to the one Viking 1 had surveyed—relatively flat and strewn with porous rocks, but cut by a shallow channel.

Each Viking lander was equipped with a miniaturized biology laboratory designed to detect life processes on Mars. A robot arm with a scoop sampled the Martian soil and dropped it into the minilab. Results, even from Viking 2, which was in a potentially more fertile area, were inconclusive.

Photographic coverage

Thousands of pictures were sent back by Mariner 9 and the Vikings and a full analysis will take years; virtually the whole of the surface was covered so that maps of Mars may now be regarded as reliable. The most striking aspect is the diversity of the features in different areas. Regions that are thickly cratered are succeeded by relatively level areas; there are great volcanoes, with drainage canyons, and deep basins, of which Hellas and Argyre are the best examples. It has not yet been established whether Mars is seismically active, but it will certainly be a geologist's paradise. Despite inconclusive evidence from Vikings 1 and 2, the existence of primitive life cannot be ruled out.

KEY

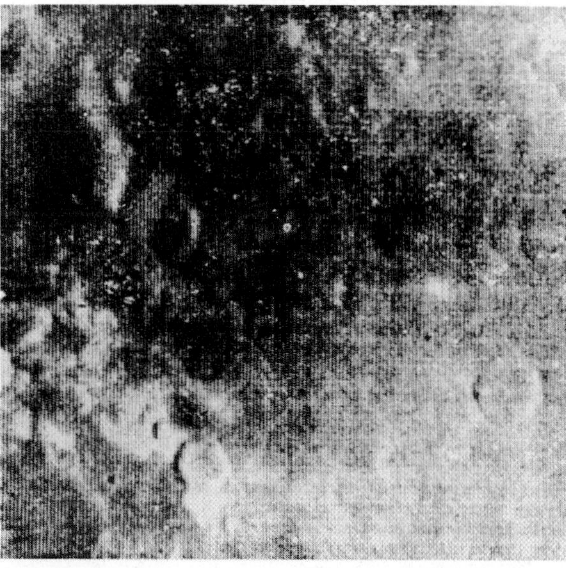

In 1965 Mariner 4 sent back the first close-range photographs of Mars. This picture took 8hr 35 min to transmit.

4

4 Large amounts of water still exist on Mars locked up in the north polar cap. In these overlapping pictures taken by Viking Orbiter 2 from 2,480 miles (4,000km), the northern cap has receded to its smallest size as midsummer approaches. The solid white area toward the top (north) is ice—mainly water ice with most of the frozen CO_2 evaporated off. The dark bands are regions devoid of ice.

5

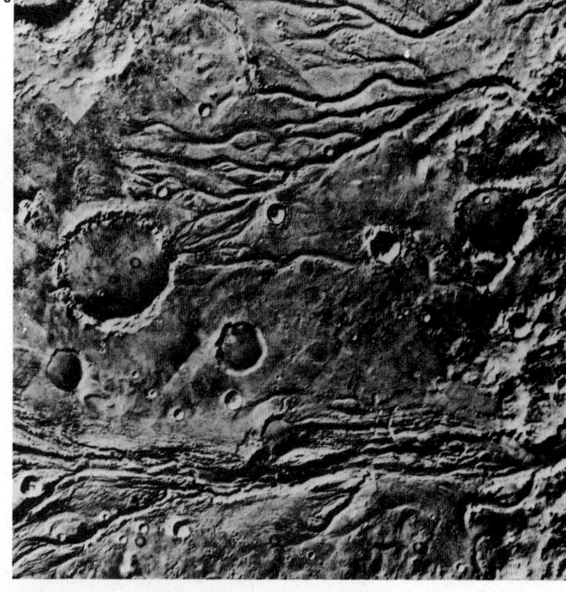

5 The terrain in this Viking Orbiter 1 picture slopes from west to east with a drop of about 1.8 miles (3km). The channels are a continuation of those to the west of the Viking 1 landing site in Chryse Planitia. They are suggestive of a massive flood of waters from Lunae Planum, across this intervening cratered region, and into the general region from which Viking 1 took its soil samples.

6

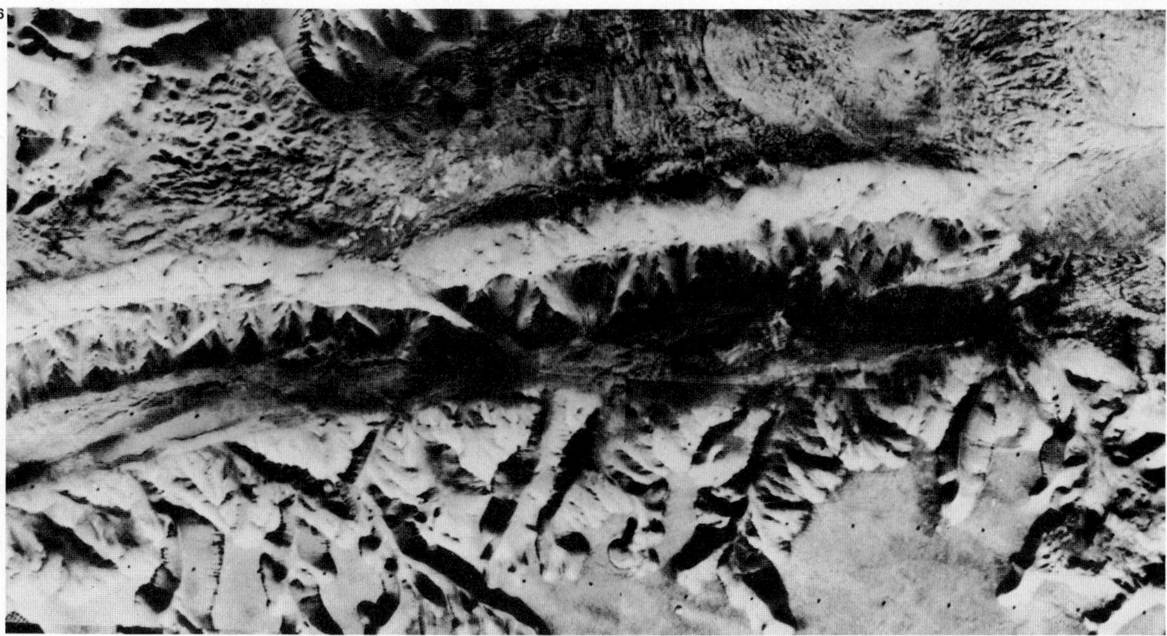

6 Valles Marineris is an enormous equatorial canyon that stretches nearly a third of the way around Mars. The far wall shows several large landslides that probably took place in series and perhaps were triggered by Marsquakes. Along the near wall another widening process seems to have occurred; a series of branch channels cuts into the plateau at the bottom. These may have been formed by slow erosion by ground water, or by mass wasting processes in which rock debris moves downhill as ground ice freezes and thaws. The photomosaic was made from pictures taken by Viking Orbiter 1 from a distance of 2,600 miles (4,200km).

The moons of Mars

In 1877 Asaph Hall (1829–1907), using the 26-inch (66-cm) Naval Observatory refractor in Washington, D.C., discovered two satellites of Mars; they were subsequently named Phobos and Deimos. Both are extremely small and are in no way comparable with the Moon. They had not been found before 1877, despite periodic searches, because they are too faint.

Phobos and Deimos before Mariner

Telescopically, Phobos and Deimos appear as small, starlike points, but they caused a great deal of interest in the pre-Space Age period because of their unusual orbits [1]. Phobos moves around Mars at a mean distance of only 5,800 miles (9,350km) from the center of the planet, so that the distance between Phobos and the Martian surface is about the same as that between New York City and Nome, Alaska. The revolution period is only 7 hours 39 minutes; and since the rotation period of Mars is 24 hours 37 minutes, the "month," reckoning by Phobos, is shorter than the Martian day. In relation to Mars, Phobos rises in a westerly direction and sets toward the east; it is above the horizon for only 4.5 hours at a time, during which it goes through more than half its cycle of phases, and the interval between successive risings is a little more than 11 hours. The apparent diameter never exceeds 12.3 degrees, less than half that of the Moon as seen from Earth, and the amount of light sent down to the Martian surface is about the same as the amount Venus sends to Earth. Phobos transits the Martian view of the Sun 1,300 times each year [2], taking 19 seconds or so to pass across the solar disk.

Even when above the Martian horizon, Phobos remains eclipsed by the shadow of the planet for long periods, and from Martian latitudes greater than 69 degrees it never rises at all. The orbit is practically circular and the inclination of the orbit to the equatorial plane of Mars is only a little more than one degree.

Deimos, smaller than Phobos and 14,600 miles (23,500km) from the center of Mars, has a revolution period of 30 hours 14 minutes; it remains above the Martian horizon for 2.5 days consecutively, but it sends less light to Mars than the star Sirius sends to Earth. To an observer on Mars its phases would be almost imperceptible. Its maximum diameter is only about 7.5 miles (12km), approximately half that of Phobos.

The nature of the two satellites is a matter for debate. They could be former asteroids that were captured from the minor planet zone. Some years ago it was suggested that Phobos was spiraling slowly down toward Mars and would collide with the planet in the foreseeable future. This led to a suggestion that it was being "braked" by the very tenuous Martian atmosphere. As its mass would have to be almost negligible for that to happen, one researcher reached the remarkable conclusion that Phobos was a hollow space station built by the Martians! The idea came from Joseph Shklovsky (1916–), an eminent Soviet astronomer, but it received little support.

Mariner 9 discoveries

The first positive information about the satellites came from Mariner 9, which ap-

CONNECTIONS

See also
68 The planet Mars
70 Mars missions
72 Mars maps
74 Mars panorama

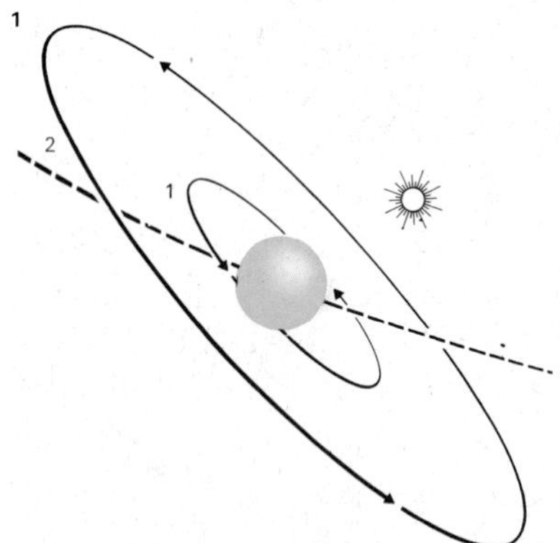
1
2

1 Both of the satellites of Mars move in orbits that are practically circular and in the plane of the planet's equator. Phobos [1] is remarkably close to Mars and may approach to within 3,600 miles (5,800 km). It is the only known natural satellite with a revolution period shorter than the rotation period of its primary. Deimos [2] is farther out, with a period of 30 hours 14 minutes.

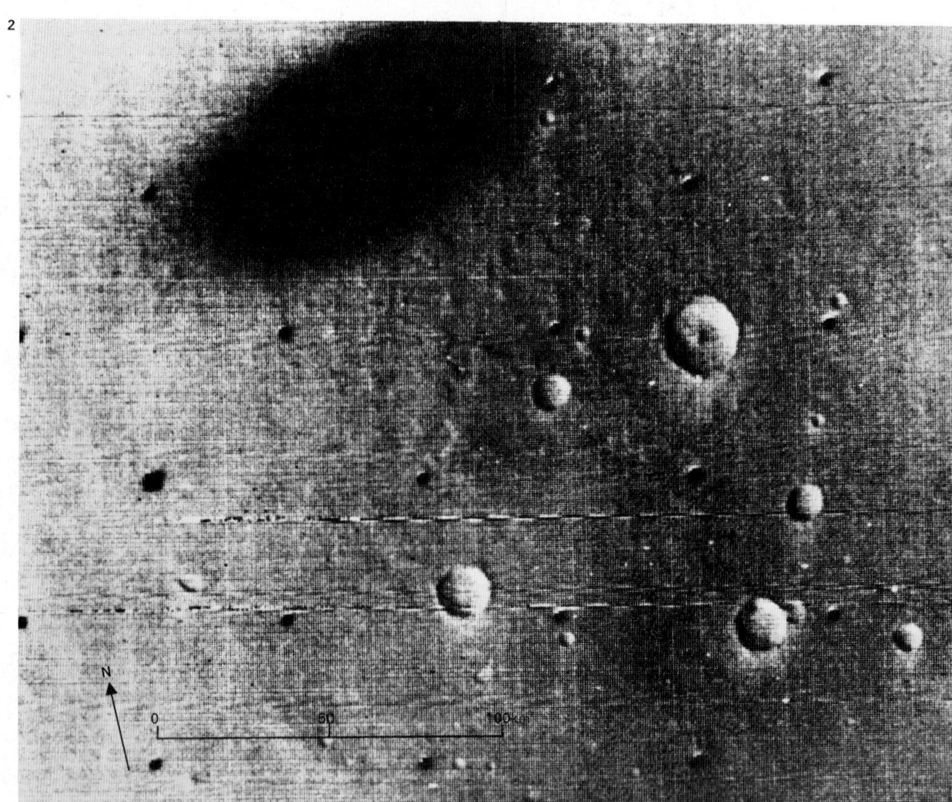
N
0
50
100km

2 The Aethiopis region on Mars (lat. 14°N, long. 235°) is shown in detail in this Mariner photograph. The elliptical dark patch is the shadow of Phobos, measuring 80 miles (130km) by 175 miles (280km), so that an observer standing in the shadowed area would see a transit of Phobos across the Sun's disk. Since Phobos seems so much smaller than the Sun, it cannot produce a total eclipse.

3 A

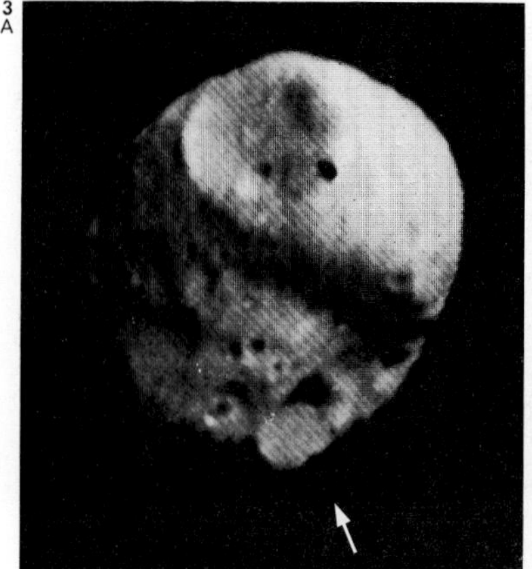

B

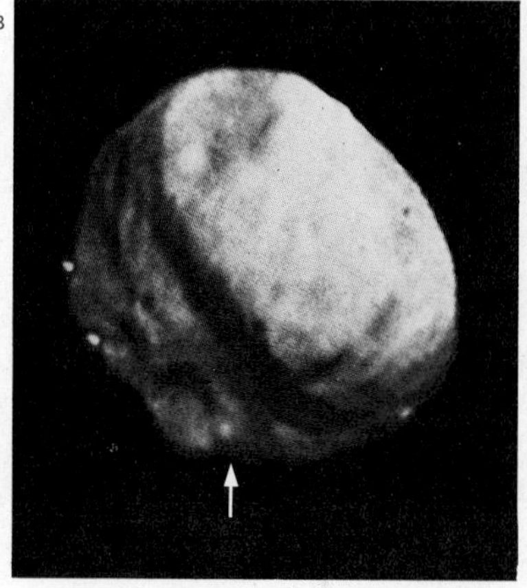

C

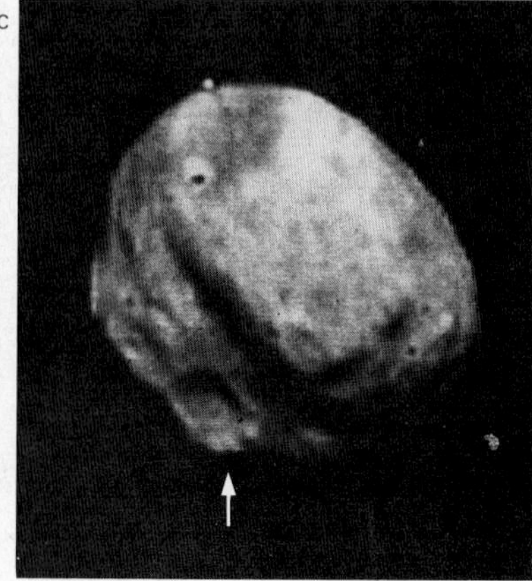

3 This series of photographs of Phobos was taken by Mariner 9 in late 1971. The approximate position of the south pole of the satellite is indicated by the arrow in each photograph. There is a pronounced surface bulge toward the top; this "synchronous" bulge is permanently turned toward Mars, because the rotation period of Phobos is exactly the same as the time that it takes for it to complete one revolution.

proached Mars in late 1971 and entered an orbit around the planet. During its approach, Mariner photographed both Phobos and Deimos and showed that both are irregular in form. Phobos [3] proved to be shaped rather like a potato, with a longest diameter of 17 miles (28km) and a shortest diameter of 12 miles (20km). Its surface is pitted with craters, of which the largest formation (since named Stickney) has a diameter of 4 miles (6.5km) [4]. More than 50 features have been charted [5], of which seven have been given official names; Roche, Wendell, Todd, Sharpless, D'Arrest, Stickney, and the Kepler Ridge. Variations in surface height amount to as much as 20 percent of the satellite's radius. The rotation is synchronous, so that Phobos always keeps the same face to Mars; the longest axis points to the planet.

The origin of the craters on Phobos is not definitely known. Meteoritic impact has been suggested. Japanese astronomer S. Miyamoto theorized that the craters are of the blowhole variety, produced during the cooling period of the satellite. If impact is the cause, it appears that Phobos has been severely battered; the diameter of Stickney is about one quarter that of Phobos itself.

Viking discoveries

When Viking Orbiter 2 swung within 545 miles (880km) of Phobos in September 1976, it was able to photograph objects on the surface only 130ft (40m) across. The features observed indicated that Phobos has the structural strength of solid rock; the main material is probably basalt. The escape velocity is very low, only 12 miles (20km) per hour, so that there can be no trace of atmosphere. The tiny moon was seen to be heavily cratered, as expected, but also showed striations (grooves) and chains of small craters. Similar crater chains appear on Earth's Moon.

Deimos is of the same general type as Phobos, although smaller. It too is cratered, and the two main formations have been named Swift and Voltaire [7], after two writers who predicted in the eighteenth century that Mars would be found to have two satellites.

KEY

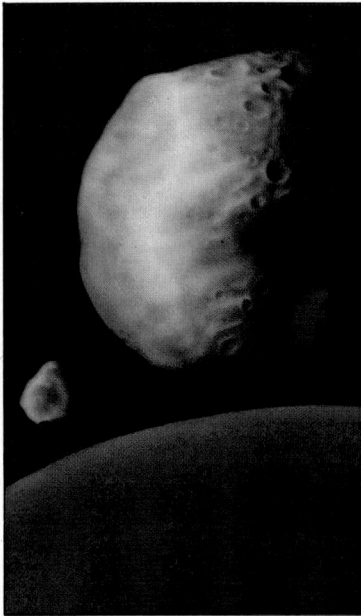

Phobos and Deimos, the satellites of Mars, are much smaller than the Moon. Here they are shown as seen from the Martian equator while the Moon is shown as seen from Earth; all three are drawn to scale. The nature of the satellites remains uncertain, but the Mariner 9 photographs suggest that both Phobos and Deimos are solid rock. They are quite different from our own Moon; it is possible that they are captured asteroids. Neither provides as much illumination as the Moon at night. Phobos gives about as much light to Mars as Venus does to Earth, while Deimos is still more faint. The surface of both satellites is dark.

4 A

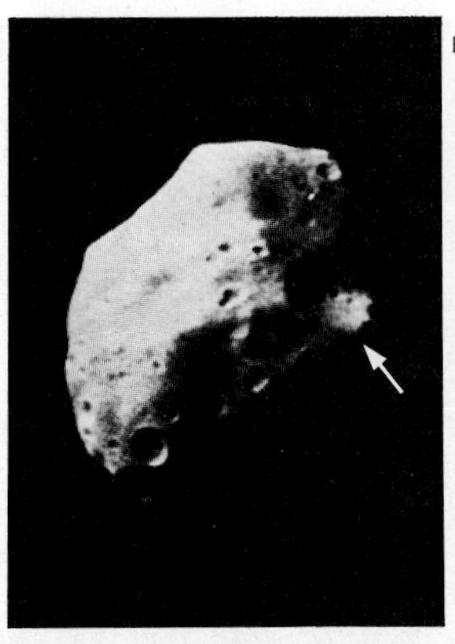

B

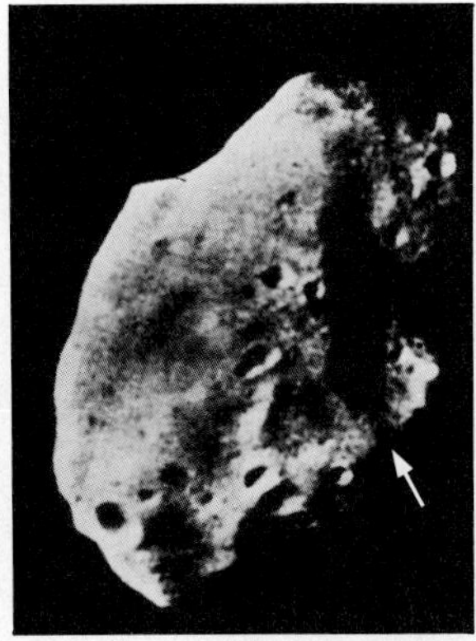

C

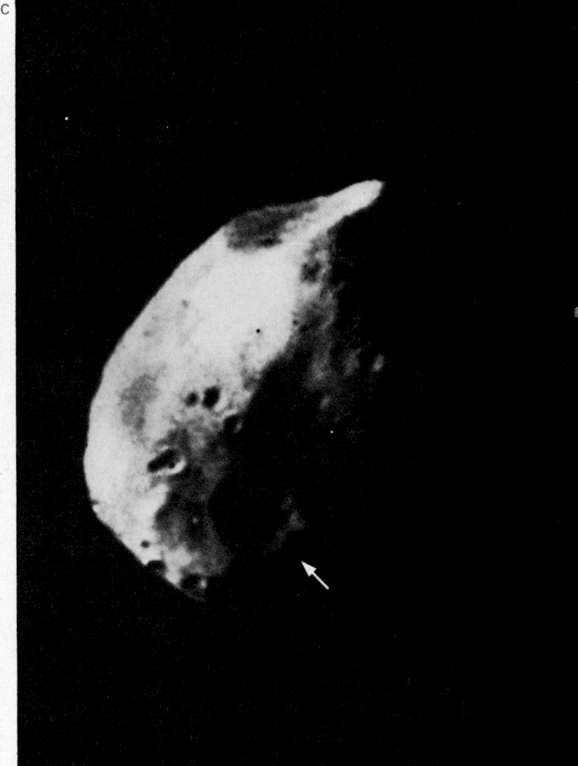

4 These photographs of Phobos were taken by Mariner 9. The approximate position of the south pole is indicated by the arrow in each photograph. The largest crater, 4 miles (6.5km) in diameter, is Stickney. The apparent indentation (upper right) in the first two pictures shows up as a crater in the third. The satellite is not even approximately spherical; its form is quite irregular, similar to a potato.

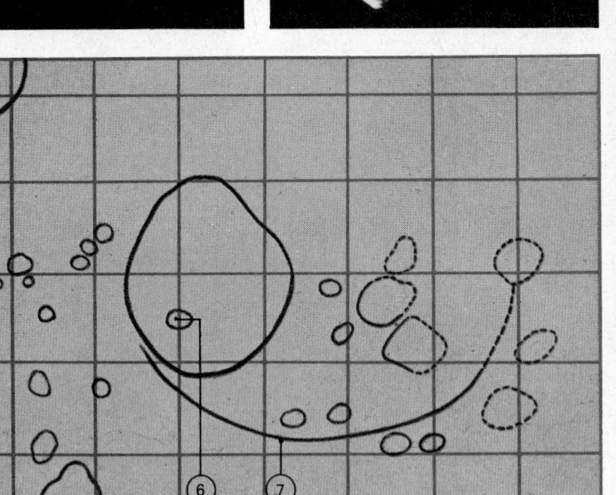
1
2
3
4
5
6
7

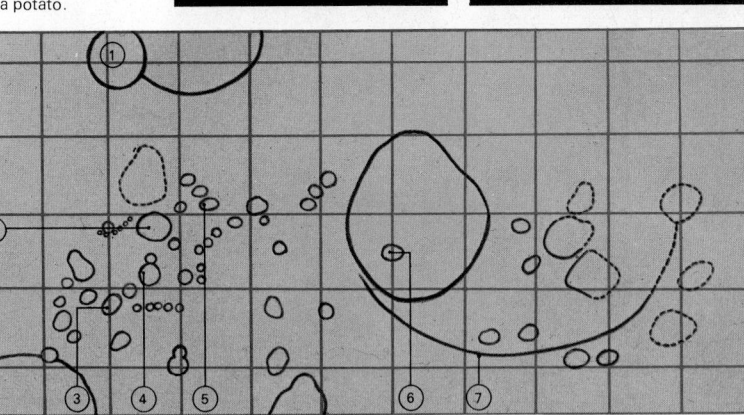

5 This Phobos map was compiled from the Mariner 9 photographs. Fifty craters have been charted, of which six have been given official names: Roche [1], Todd [2], D'Arrest [3], Sharpless [4], Wendell [5], and Stickney [6]. The ridge [7] has been named the Kepler Ridge. The whole surface of Phobos is heavily cratered and fractured, which is probably the result of large meteroid impacts, although this theory has not yet been proven.

6

6 This closest ever view of Phobos may help to resolve the question of how the tiny moons of Mars originated. Clues seen in the photo are a crater with a central peak, crater chains running parallel to the equator, and striations (grooves) covering more than half the surface. One theory supposed that the grooves were caused by Phobos passing through a swarm of smaller bodies. The smallest visible object is 130ft (40m) in diameter.

7

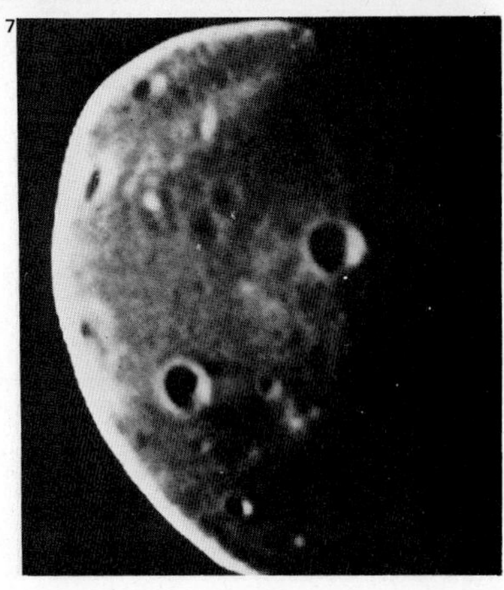

7 Deimos was viewed by Viking Orbiter 1 from a distance of 2,050 miles (3,300 km); Mars is to the left. About half the side facing the camera is illuminated and the lighted portion measures about 7.5 by 5 miles (12 by 8km). While Mariner 9 photographs taken from greater distances showed only a few large craters, at least a dozen are prominent here; the largest have diameters of 0.8 miles (1.3km) and 0.62 miles (1km). A linear feature appears near the top.

Minor planets

The Solar System is divided into two main parts by a wide gap between the outermost of the inner planets, Mars, and the first of the giants, Jupiter. A numerical relationship known as Bode's law, discovered by Titius of Wittenberg (1729–96), but popularized by Johann Bode (1747–1826) in 1772, led astronomers to suppose that there might be an extra planet there.

At the end of the eighteenth century, a group of astronomers headed by Johann Schröter (1746–1826) and Baron von Zach (1754–1832) organized with the intention of searching for the new planet, and became known as "the celestial police."

New discoveries: the minor planets

In fact, they were forestalled on January 1, 1801, by Giuseppe Piazzi (1746–1826) at Palermo in Sicily. He discovered a starlike body that moved perceptibly from night to night and that proved to be a planet moving in the gap between Mars and Jupiter. It was named Ceres, in honor of the patron goddess of Sicily. During the next few years the "celestial police" found three more planets: Pallas, Juno, and Vesta [Key, 2]. Together with Ceres, these bodies became known as the minor planets, asteroids, or planetoids. All are small and, apart from Ceres, less than 300 miles (500km) in diameter. Only Vesta is ever visible to the naked eye.

No more asteroids were evident and the "police" disbanded, but in 1845 a German amateur, Karl Hencke (1793–1866), discovered a fifth asteroid, Astraea. Since 1850 no year has passed without the discovery of several asteroids and to date the orbits of several thousands have been computed [4]. Doubtless many more await discovery; the number of asteroids may exceed 50,000.

The diameters of some asteroids have recently been remeasured and in general earlier measurements are shown to have underestimated them [Key]. Ceres is now thought to have a diameter of 600–750 miles (1,000–1,200km), while the rest are smaller.

Irregular orbiters

Not all the asteroids keep strictly to their main zone [4]. In 1898 Carl Witt at Copenhagen discovered number 433, Eros, which can move well inside the orbit of Mars and occasionally approaches to within 15 million miles (24 million km) of the earth. That happened in 1931 and again in 1975. In 1931, Eros was extensively studied because exact calculation of its orbit can help in measuring the length of the astronomical unit, or Earth-Sun distance. In shape Eros is elongated, with a long diameter of about 17 miles (27km) and a short diameter of less than 10 miles (16km) [Key B]. Although small, Eros is larger than other so-called "Earth-grazers" [5]. For example, Hermes has a diameter of only 0.6 mile (1km), and brushed past the Earth in 1937 at a distance of 485,000 miles (780,000km), less than twice the distance to the Moon. It is of course possible that the Earth will be hit by an asteroid of this kind and considerable devastation would result. Fortunately the chances of a direct collision are slight.

One asteroid, Icarus [3], actually approaches the Sun closer than does the planet Mercury. It must undergo some of the most extreme temperature changes in the Solar System. At the closest point in its

CONNECTIONS

See also
150 Exploring the inner planets
92 Meteors and meteorites
50 Members of the Sola System

1 This photograph taken by Max Wolf (1863–1932) shows a star field and two streaks representing asteroid trails. The photograph is a time exposure; while it was being taken the driving mechanism of the telescope was adjusted to follow the stars (to compensate for the rotation of the Earth). The stars remained in the same relative positions while the asteroids shifted perceptibly against the background. Wolf was the great pioneer of this method of asteroid discovery. Previously the method had been to chart the same area of the sky for several consecutive nights, so that any starlike object that moved could be identified as an asteroid. Wolf's photographic method was far quicker and more efficient. Discovering asteroids is now much easier but keeping track of them and computing their orbits is time-consuming.

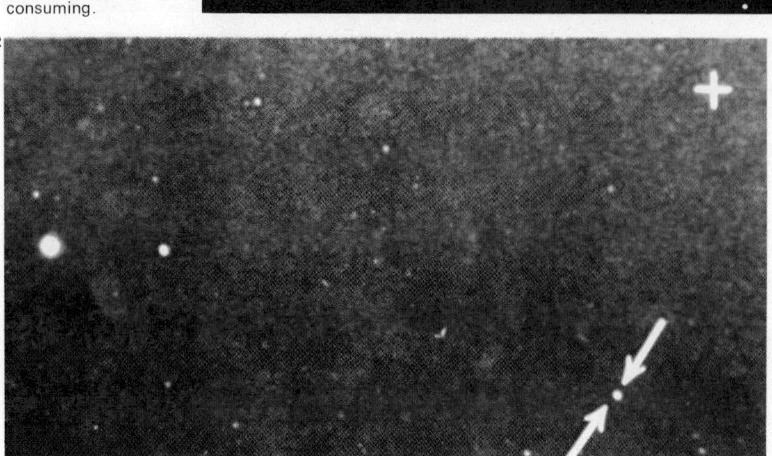

2 Vesta, discovered in the early nineteenth century and shown here between the arrows, is the brightest but not the largest of the minor planets. It looks exactly like a star, although its night-to-night movements betray its true nature. The cross at the upper right shows Vesta's position 24 hours later. Photographs do not show surface detail – asteroids are too small. Their rotation periods can be determined by variations in brilliancy.

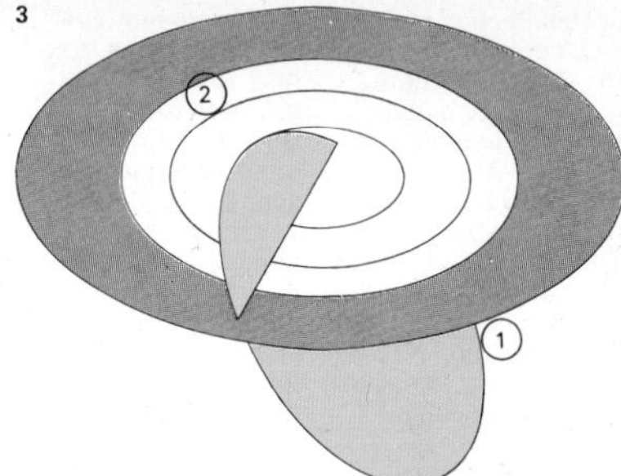
2
1

3 Icarus, about 1 mile (1km) in diameter, was discovered by Walter Baade (1893–1960) in 1949. Its orbit [1] is highly inclined at 23° to the ecliptic plane [2]. It is the only asteroid with a perihelion inside the orbit of Mercury.

orbit, only 17 million miles (28 million km) from the Sun, the surface temperature on Icarus must be more than 500°C (932°F). At its aphelion (farthest point), only 200 days later, it has moved out to a distance of 183 million miles (295 million km)—well beyond the farthest orbital point of Mars.

On the other hand, number 944, Hidalgo, has an eccentric path that takes it out almost as far as the orbit of Saturn, while the members of the Trojan group move in the same path as Jupiter. One group keeps approximately 60 degrees ahead of Jupiter and the other group 60 degrees behind; there is no danger of a collision.

Through a telescope, asteroids look exactly like stars, and the only way to identify them is by checking their movements from night to night. Modern discoveries are made photographically. During a time exposure, an asteroid will often move enough to show up as a trail on the plate rather than as a point of light [1]. Because of this, asteroids can be a nuisance to astronomers. Photographic plates exposed for quite different reasons are often found to be dotted with asteroids and each must be identified, which is quite time-consuming. The composition of asteroids is not yet known, but Mariner 9 photographs of the two dwarf satellites of Mars, Phobos and Deimos—which may be captured asteroids—suggest that the surfaces of many may be pitted with craters. Some of the smaller satellites of the giant planets—the outer members of Jupiter's family, Phoebe in Saturn's, Nereid in Neptune's—may be captured asteroids.

Origin of asteroids

The origin of the asteroids is still uncertain. According to one theory, they represent the debris of a former planet (or planets) that orbited the Sun beyond the path of Mars and met with some disaster in the remote past. But on the whole it seems more likely that they were never part of a larger body. The immensely powerful gravitational effect of Jupiter could prevent a large planet from forming in the region of the asteroid zone. It is also worth noting that all the asteroids combined would still not make up one body as massive as the Moon.

KEY

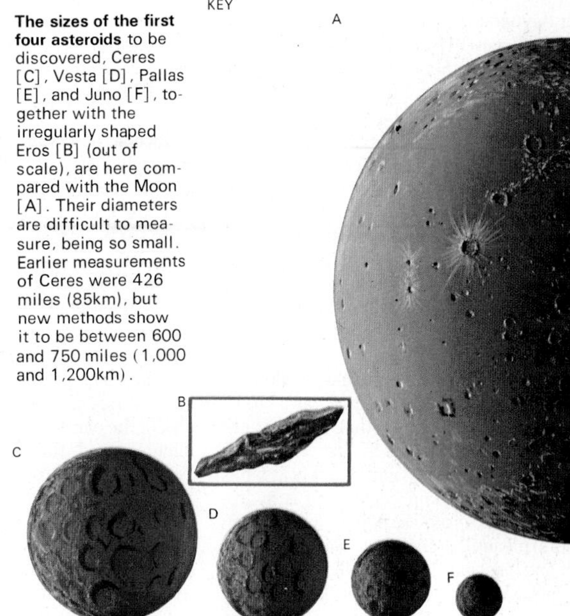
A
B
C
D
E
F

The sizes of the first four asteroids to be discovered, Ceres [C], Vesta [D], Pallas [E], and Juno [F], together with the irregularly shaped Eros [B] (out of scale), are here compared with the Moon [A]. Their diameters are difficult to measure, being so small. Earlier measurements of Ceres were 426 miles (85km), but new methods show it to be between 600 and 750 miles (1,000 and 1,200km).

4

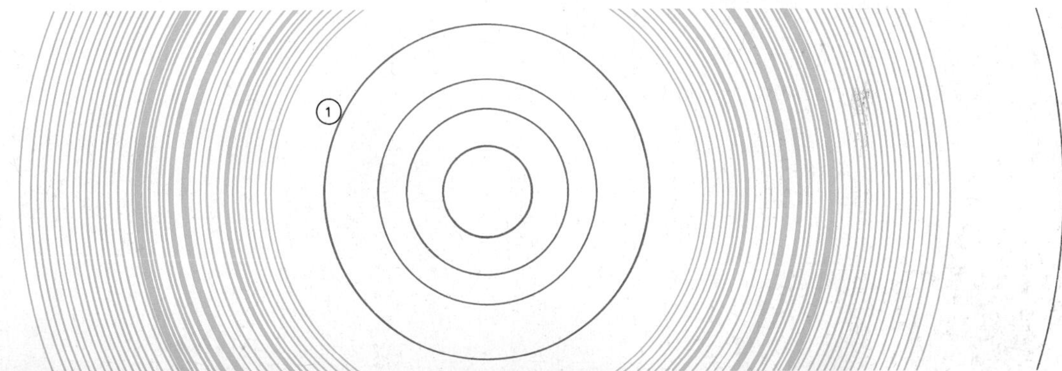
2
1

4 Most of the orbits of the minor planets lie well beyond the orbit of Mars [1] and well inside that of Jupiter [2]. Within this distribution there are certain regions, known as Kirkwood gaps, in which there are very few minor planets. These gaps lie at particular orbital distances from the Sun where Jupiter's gravitational field has forced the asteroids into different orbits.

5

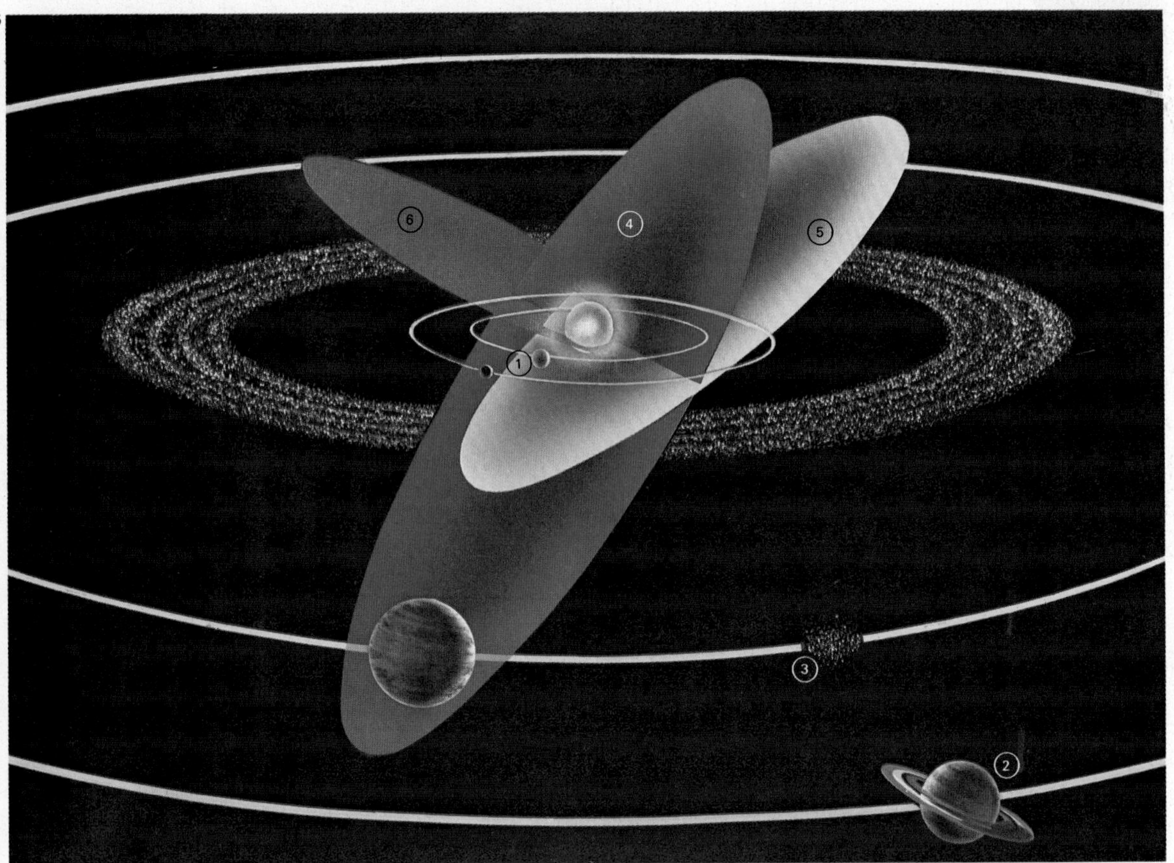
6
4
5
1
3
2

5 The orbits of the planets are shown from Earth [1] out to Saturn [2], with those of some asteroids which are of particular interest (the illustration is not to scale). Most of the asteroids move in the region between the orbits of Mars and Jupiter. The Trojan asteroids [3] move in the same orbit as Jupiter but keep their distance and collisions are unlikely to occur. One group moves 60° ahead of the planet and the other 60° behind, although they do move for some distance to either side of their mean positions. Hidalgo [4] has a path that is highly inclined and so eccentric—much like a comet—that its aphelion is not far from the orbit of Saturn. Amor [5] and Apollo [6] belong to the so-called "Earth-grazing" asteroid group. All the Earth-grazers are very small. Amor has a diameter of 5 miles (8km) and Apollo has a diameter of about 1.25 miles (2km).

The planet Jupiter

Far beyond the main asteroid belt lies Jupiter, the largest of the planets. It has a greater mass than the other planets combined and it has been said that "the Solar System is made up of the Sun, Jupiter, and assorted debris." The mean distance of Jupiter from the Sun is 483,600,000 miles (778,300,000km), the revolution period is 11.86 years, and the synodic period (that is, the mean interval between successive oppositions) is 399 days. Thus Jupiter is well placed for observation for several months each year and it is always a brilliant object. It is surpassed only by Venus and, on rare occasions, by Mars.

Jupiter's huge globe could swallow up 1,300 bodies of the volume of Earth but its mass is only 318 times that of the Earth because Jupiter is much less dense [1]. From the outer layers and possibly as far as the center, the main constituent is hydrogen. The quick rotation period (less than ten hours) means that the equator tends to bulge out and a casual glance through a telescope is enough to show that the planet is very much flattened at the poles. Jupiter's equatorial diameter is 89,000 miles (143,000km), while the polar diameter of the planet is less than 84,000 miles (135,000km).

Telescopic observations

Through a telescope, the yellow disk of Jupiter is seen to be crossed by dark streaks that are known as cloud belts. Normally there are two prominent belts, one on either side of the equator, while others may also become conspicuous. With high magnifications, the details are complicated—and they are always changing, because Jupiter is a highly active world.

The quick rotation means that the various features can be seen to shift across the disk of the planet even over periods of a few minutes, and the rotation periods have been deduced from observations of this kind. When a feature reaches the central meridian as seen from Earth it is said to be in transit; and successive transit timings provide all the information needed for working out the period of axial rotation. Jupiter does not spin in the way that a solid body would; different regions of latitude have different periods. Thus the mean period in System I (between the two equatorial belts) is five minutes shorter than that of the rest of the planet, referred to as System II. Moreover, various definite surface features have periods of their own and so drift in longitude.

Jupiter and the Great Red Spot

Spots are often seen on Jupiter but most of them are short-lived. The exception is the Great Red Spot, which has been under observation for more than 300 years; it sometimes disappears for a while, but always returns. This spot became prominent in 1878 when it developed into a brick-red elliptical patch 30,000mi (48,000km) long by 7,000mi (11,000km) wide, so that its surface area was greater than that of the Earth. It has been prominent again since the mid-1960s.

For many years it was believed that the Red Spot might be a kind of "island" floating in Jupiter's outer gas; variations in level could cause its occasional disappearances,

CONNECTIONS

See also
82 Jupiter panorama
86 The moons of Jupiter and Saturn
152 Exploring Jupiter and Saturn
50 Members of the Solar System

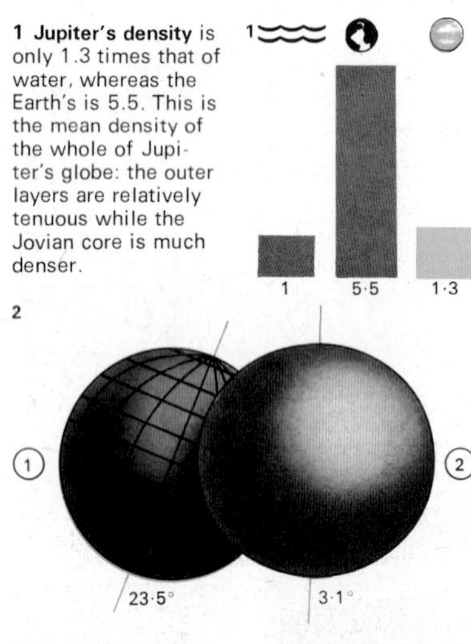

1
1
5·5
1·3
2
1
2
23·5°
3·1°

1 Jupiter's density is only 1.3 times that of water, whereas the Earth's is 5.5. This is the mean density of the whole of Jupiter's globe: the outer layers are relatively tenuous while the Jovian core is much denser.

2 The Earth's axis is tilted at an angle of 23.5 degrees from the perpendicular to the plane of the orbit [1]. In the case of Jupiter [2] the tilt is only 3.1 degrees and Jupiter is practically "upright." Of the other principal planets, only Mercury's axial inclination is like this.

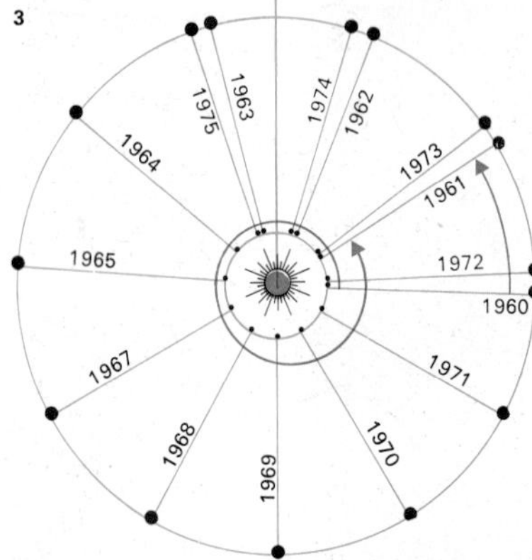

3
1963
1975
1974
1962
1964
1973
1961
1965
1972
1960
1967
1971
1968
1969
1970

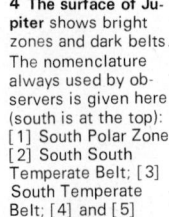

3 Jupiter comes to opposition at mean intervals of 399 days, so that it is always well placed for observation for several months each year. The diagram shows the opposition positions between 1960 and 1975. Because Jupiter's orbit is notably eccentric, the opposition distance ranges from 366–416 million miles (589–669 million km). In 1975 Jupiter was at its closest to Earth.

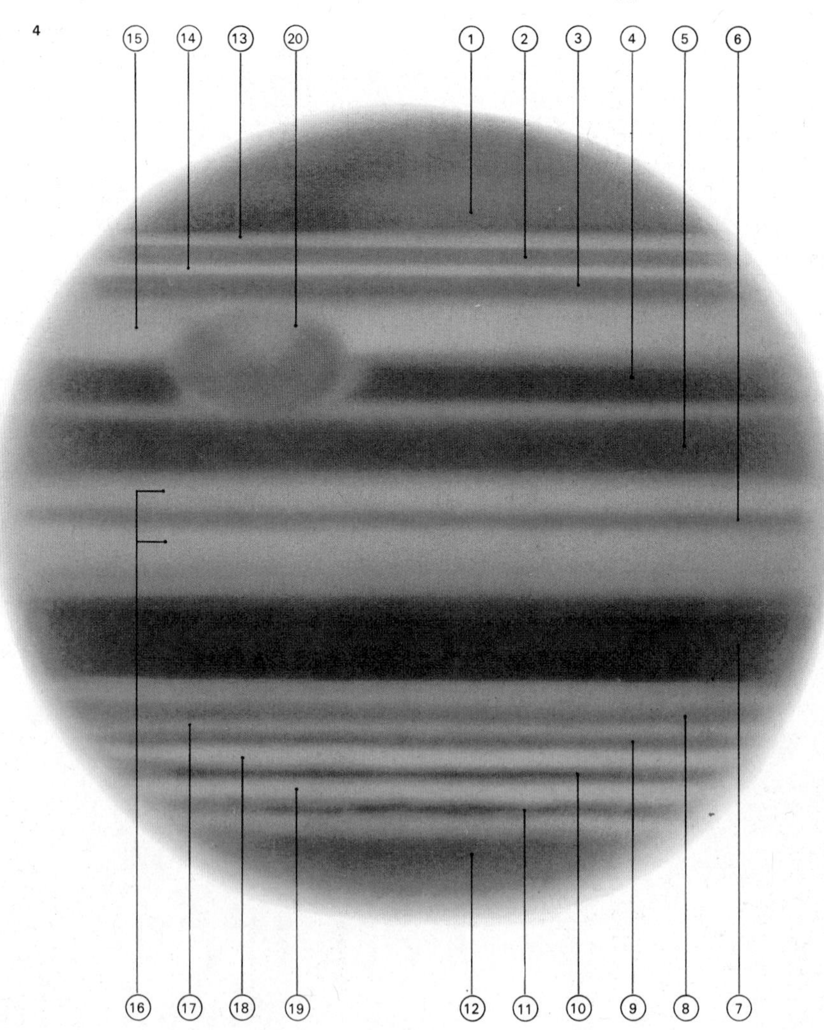

4
15
14
13
20
1
2
3
4
5
6
16
17
18
19
12
11
10
9
8
7

4 The surface of Jupiter shows bright zones and dark belts. The nomenclature always used by observers is given here (south is at the top): [1] South Polar Zone; [2] South South Temperate Belt; [3] South Temperate Belt; [4] and [5] South Equatorial Belt, frequently seen to be divided into two well marked components; [6] Equatorial Band; [7] and [8] North Equatorial Belt, also frequently divided into two components; [9] North Temperate Belt; [10] North North Temperate Belt; [11] North North North Temperate Belt; [12] North Polar Zone; [13] South South Temperate Zone; [14] South Temperate Zone; [15] South Tropical Zone; [16] Equatorial Zone; [17] North Tropical Zone; [18] North Temperate Zone; [19] North North Temperate Zone; [20] the Great Red Spot, together with its associated Hollow. The region between the south edge of the North Equatorial Belt and the north edge of the South Equatorial Belt is System I; the rest of the planet (System II) has a rotation period that averages five minutes longer. The belts show marked variations in intensity; for example the normally narrower South Equatorial Belt is sometimes as broad and dark as the North Equatorial.

so that when it sank it would be covered up. Alternatively it was attributed to a "Taylor column," that is, the top of a column of stagnant gas produced by the interruption of the atmospheric circulation by some large topographical feature on the surface of Jupiter. But results from the US Pioneer probes indicate that the spot is a huge whirling storm. The reason for its color remains unknown.

Jupiter's structure

The internal constitution of Jupiter has been investigated theoretically. One theory that was popular for many years suggested that there was a rocky core overlaid by a thick layer of ice, which was in turn overlaid by the atmosphere, but this idea has now fallen into disfavor. Spectroscopic work has shown that the outer gases are rich in hydrogen (together with hydrogen compounds, such as ammonia and methane) and hydrogen, possibly in a liquid state is believed to be the main constituent throughout Jupiter because of its low mean density. Near the core, however, where pressures and temperatures are high, the hydrogen would start to assume some of the characteristics of a metal.

The temperature at the center of Jupiter may reach several thousand degrees—very much higher than that of the Earth, although there is no doubt that Jupiter must be regarded as a true planet and not a small star; the core temperature is much too low for nuclear reactions to begin. Yet Jupiter does seem to send out more energy than it would if it depended entirely upon the Sun and this may be due to a very slight, steady contraction (too small to be observable) that would release an appropriate amount of gravitational energy. Jupiter is also characterized by a powerful magnetic field and strong radio emissions; but astronomers have as yet been unable to explain their origins.

Jupiter has a gaseous or possibly liquid surface and as a result no landing can take place there. Some people believe that life may exist below the outer clouds, where all the necessary ingredients are found and the temperatures may be tolerable, but this idea is highly speculative.

KEY

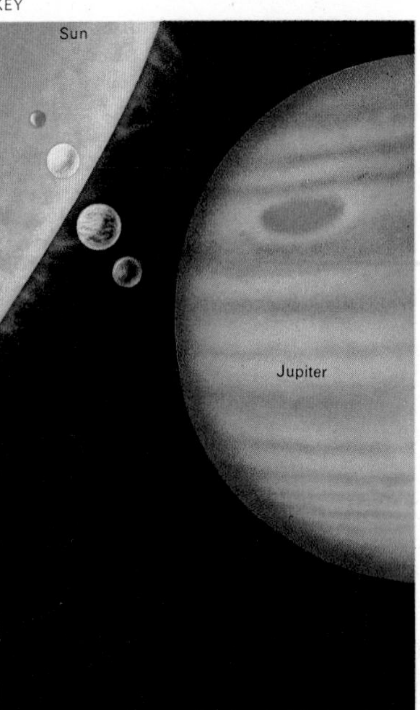

Sun
Jupiter

Jupiter was aptly named after the chief of the Roman gods by the ancient astronomers, although they had no idea at the time of the planet's dimensions or the number of its satellites. It is larger than all the other planets combined, although it has a diameter about one-tenth of that of the Sun. Two of Jupiter's satellites are approximately the same size as the smallest of the principal planets, Mercury, and it has more satellites (13) than any other planet. This drawing shows the comparative sizes of the four inner planets together with segments of the Sun and Jupiter. Despite its great distance, Jupiter is a brilliant object in the sky.

6 A

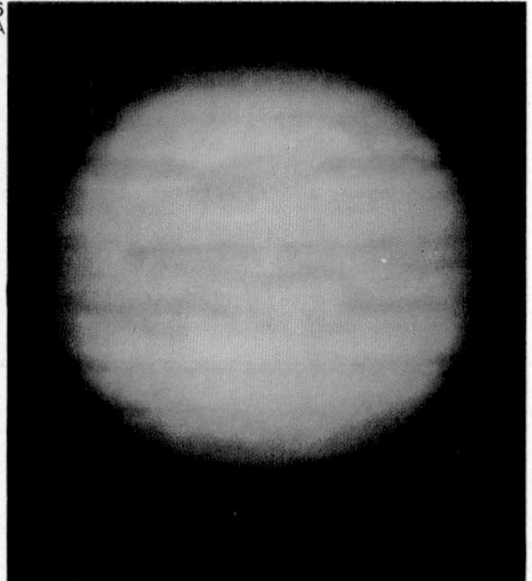

B

C

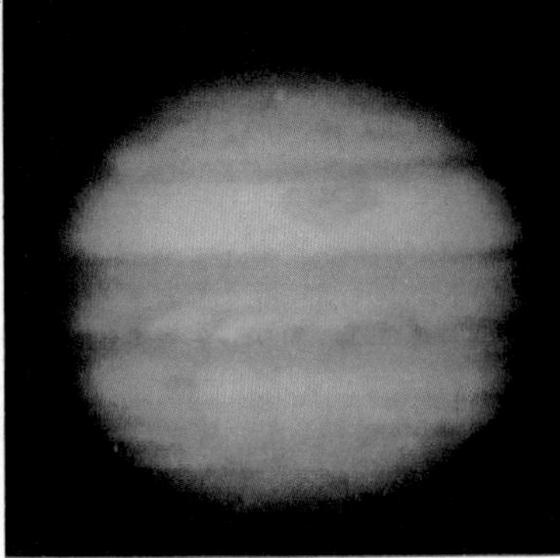

5 One of the best color photographs of Jupiter ever taken from the Earth was secured by G. P. Kuiper with the 61-in (155-cm) reflector at the McDonald Observatory, Texas. South is at the top. At this time the Great Red Spot was very prominent and above it was a well marked white spot. The structure of the belts is very complex, although through a small telescope the belts give the impression of being straight and uniform. Ganymede's shadow is also shown.

6 This series of Jupiter photographs was taken from the Lowell Observatory at Flagstaff, Arizona, on June 4, 1972 [A and B] and July 25, 1973 [C]. They were made possible by combining images, originally recorded at the telescope on black and white film, through color filters. At that time the whole of System I, between the two equatorial belts, was an unusual orange hue, although the effect had lessened by the middle of 1973 when the last photograph was taken. The Great Red Spot is not shown in the middle picture because it was then on the far side of the globe. There is, however, a comparatively good view of one of the shorter-lived bright white spots that appear in the South Temperate Zone (south at top).

Jupiter panorama

To send a spacecraft to the Moon takes a few days. To reach Mars or Venus takes a few months. Jupiter, however, is so remote that a journey to it would take more than a year. The difficulties of guidance are increased enormously by distance and there is also the problem of receiving the information sent out from on-board transmitters: an extremely small amount of energy reaches Earth from a probe at the distance of Jupiter, 390 million miles (629 million km).

The first Jupiter vehicle

Pioneer 10, the first Jupiter vehicle, was launched in March 1972 and it was not until December 1973 that it reached its target. Its main task was to study the conditions in the region around Jupiter and to take photographs. Radio emissions from Jupiter (which had been picked up by accident in 1955 by B. F. Burke and W. Franklin in the United States) had indicated the presence of a powerful magnetic field. It was thought likely that there would also be zones of intense radiation of the same basic type as the Van Allen belts encircling the Earth. Scientists were apprehensive about the effects of Jovian radiation upon the instruments carried in the spacecraft, particularly since Pioneer 10 was scheduled to pass over Jupiter's equatorial regions, where the intensity of radiation would be greater than at the poles.

In fact, Pioneer 10 functioned excellently. It passed within 82,000 miles (132,000km) of Jupiter and sent back data about the magnetic field—which proved to be powerful yet different in structure from that of the Earth—and also about the radiation zones. The instruments were almost saturated; had Pioneer 10 approached much closer, the radiation would have put the equipment out of action altogether. After its rendezvous, Pioneer 10 moved away from Jupiter and began a never-ending journey into space. It will escape from the Solar System in the 1980s and for many millions of years to come it will continue to travel silently in the space between the stars.

Pioneer 11 followed a year later. It was launched in April 1973 and reached Jupiter in December 1974. This time the approach was from the pole of the planet and the spacecraft passed relatively quickly across the equatorial regions in a successful attempt to avoid the worst of the radiation. Further data were obtained, confirming the results from Pioneer 10. Subsequently, Pioneer 11 was put into an orbit aimed at taking it to a rendezvous with Saturn in 1979.

The achievements of two Pioneers

The two Pioneer probes have answered some of the questions about Jupiter, although many puzzles remain to be solved. First, there is the question of the Red Spot, which is unique both because of its size and color and because it is so long-lived. The "floating island" theory has proved to be wrong; the spot is not a semi-solid body floating in Jupiter's outer atmosphere. The Red Spot must be classed as a phenomenon of Jovian meteorology. Definite structure in it is shown on some of the Pioneer pictures [1, 4].

The bright zones on the surface of the planet are at a higher level than the dark

CONNECTIONS

See also
80 The planet Jupiter
86 The moons of Jupit[er] and Saturn
152 Exploring Jupiter a[nd] Saturn
142 A history of space achievements
50 Members of the So[lar] System

1 This photograph of Jupiter was taken on December 1, 1973, as the space probe Pioneer 10 neared the planet; the distance was then about 1.55 million miles (2.5 million km). The Red Spot is well shown, with indications of structure; it lies in a bright zone. The irregular outline of the belts is also obvious. The black disk is the shadow of Io, the innermost of the large satellites, which moves in the outer part of Jupiter's magnetosphere; it is larger than our Moon.

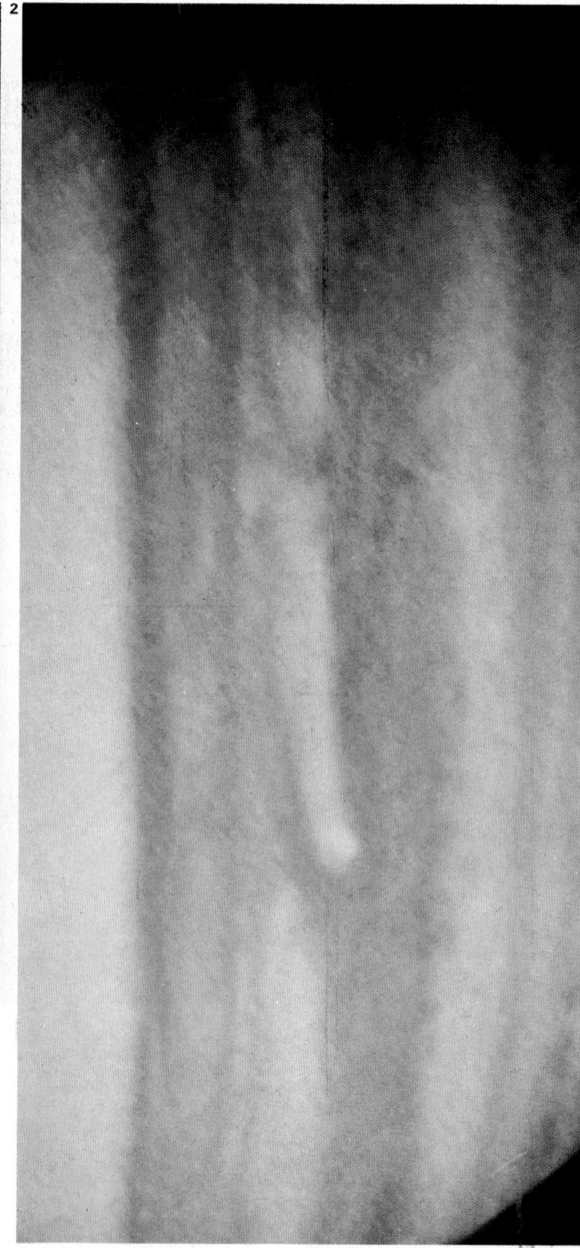

2 This part of the surface of Jupiter was photographed from Pioneer 10 at 1,121,000 miles (1,804,000km). The section shown here provides a view of one of the notable "plumes." It is thought that near the nucleus of the plume, cloud particles are forming from below and are then spreading into the nucleus. The "tail" of the plume is more than 40,000 miles (64,000km) long. The plume itself is higher than the surrounding clouds.

belts and they are also colder by several degrees. That was to be expected, but it has also been found that the surface temperature at the poles is the same as at the equator. If Jupiter depended upon heat received only from the Sun, the poles would be the coldest regions; there seems no doubt that there must be an internal source of heat. If this internal heat is more effective at high latitudes on Jupiter there should be a noticeable effect upon the structure of the gaseous layers, with the setting up of turbulence and convection currents. Pioneer pictures of the poles show that that is precisely what happens; the change in appearance is conspicuous.

Further discoveries

Investigations of the precise structure of the layers had not previously been possible because from Earth it is hopeless to try to see details as delicate as those revealed by photographs taken from comparatively close range. The stable belt/zone structure breaks up at about 45 degrees Jovian latitude and increasingly toward the poles the regions are more unstable, with many eddies detectable [5].

Among other interesting features are so-called 'plumes,'' which have a superficially cometary appearance [2]. Pioneer 10 recorded one plume that was still in existence when Pioneer 11 flew past a year later. Records of Jupiter made by Earth-based observers (mainly amateurs) show that this particular plume has existed since 1964, so that it has lasted for virtually one Jovian year (12 Earth years). Other plumes may have lasted longer but have not been recorded as continuous; from 1963 to 1975 the equatorial zone of the planet was unusually dark and thus the plume could easily be seen rising much higher than the clouds surrounding Jupiter.

Experiences with the first two Pioneers will be applied to future probes. Spacecraft sent out to the more remote planets will, in general, pass by Jupiter to make use of the strong gravitational field of the planet in speeding them on their way and they will provide opportunities for carrying out further studies of Jupiter itself.

KEY

A comparison of this photograph of Jupiter taken from Earth (1964) with any of the Pioneer photographs vividly illustrates how much significant detail can be picked up by a probe.

3 The two Pioneers by-passed Jupiter at an interval of one year (Pioneer 10 in December 1973, Pioneer 11 in December 1974) and it was obviously important to note any major changes in the surface structure in the interim period. This photograph was taken on December 6, 1974, by Pioneer 11 and the equatorial plume may be compared with the view as shown in illustration 2. The white plume is still easily recognizable and is in fact a long-lived feature; observational records of it from Earth go back for a Jovian year and it has altered little.

4 This Pioneer 11 photograph was taken on December 6, 1974, at a distance from the planet of 683,000 miles (1,100,000km). The Great Red Spot is prominently displayed and close inspection shows that there is definite inner structure—it has even been compared with a "Cyclopean eye." There now seems no doubt that it is a kind of whirling storm, although whether or not it will gradually decay remains to be seen. Certainly it is as conspicuous now as it was in the 17th century, when it was first observed. Note particularly the very marked phase of Jupiter.

3

5

5 Taken on December 12, 1974, when Pioneer 11 was 750,000 miles (1,207,000km) from Jupiter, this photo shows the north pole, from a latitude of about 50°. The pole itself is roughly on the line of the terminator (shadow line) across the top of the planet. This is one of the most significant views obtained, as it shows the obvious difference in surface structure between the polar regions and the equatorial zone. The convection cell structure at the pole is well displayed and the atmospheric circulation is different in high latitude. There is a bluish cast to the pole (noted by observers on Earth).

The planet Saturn

Saturn, the outermost of the planets known in ancient times, is a conspicuous naked-eye object, although in pre-telescopic times there was no means of distinguishing its rings, which are one of the most beautiful sights in the entire sky.

Saturn's mean distance from the Sun is 887 million miles (1,427 million km) and its revolution period is 29.46 years. It comes to opposition once in approximately 378 days, so that it is well placed for observation for several months in every year.

Physical characteristics

Saturn is the second largest of the planets [1]. Its equatorial diameter is 75,000 miles (120,000km), but the polar diameter is considerably less, because the planet is strongly flattened. This is partly because of its low density [2] (less than that of water, making it unique among the principal planets) and partly because of its rapid axial rotation. The rotation period at the equator is 10 hours 45 minutes and at the pole about 26 minutes longer, but precise measurements of Saturn are less easy to make than of Jupiter; the surface markings are less complex and, on the whole, less distinct. Saturn is a gas-giant whose main constituent is hydrogen. There is more detectable methane and less ammonia than in Jupiter, because a lower temperature has frozen more of the ammonia out of the planet's atmosphere. Although Saturn's mass is 95 times that of Earth, scientists believe that its surface gravity is only slightly greater than Earth's. Near the core, the temperature is probably high, the pressure considerable, and the hydrogen metallic. As yet there is no evidence for the existence of a magnetic field, but final conclusions must wait for the fly-by of the first Saturn probe, which will not take place until the year 1979 at the earliest.

Observed through a medium-powered telescope, Saturn shows a yellowish disk, crossed by cloud belts that are basically the same as those of Jupiter but considerably less active. Spots are relatively rare, but they do occur occasionally—the best modern example was that discovered in 1933 by the English amateur astronomer Will Hay. Hay's white spot [10] became conspicuous for a short period, but soon spread out and disappeared. It was undoubtedly due to the upflow of gaseous material from beneath the visible surface. Saturn shows no spots comparable with the famous Great Red Spot on Jupiter. Apart from the belts, all Saturn's surface features are comparatively short-lived and changeable.

Saturn's bright ring system

The main glory of Saturn is its ring system [5]. There are two bright rings, A and B, separated by the wide gap known as Cassini's Division in honor of its discoverer, Giovanni Cassini (1625–1712). Closer to the planet there is a fainter semitransparent ring discovered in 1850 by William Bond (1789–1859) at Harvard and known generally as the Crêpe, or Dusky, ring. Other faint rings have been reported from time to time; in 1909 French astronomers reported an extra dusky ring outside ring A (the outermost ring). It was known as ring D. Some astronomers, however, are doubtful about these extra rings, whose existence has yet

CONNECTIONS

See also
86 The moons of Jupite and Saturn
152 Exploring Jupiter and Saturn
50 Members of the Solar System

Saturn

Earth to same scale

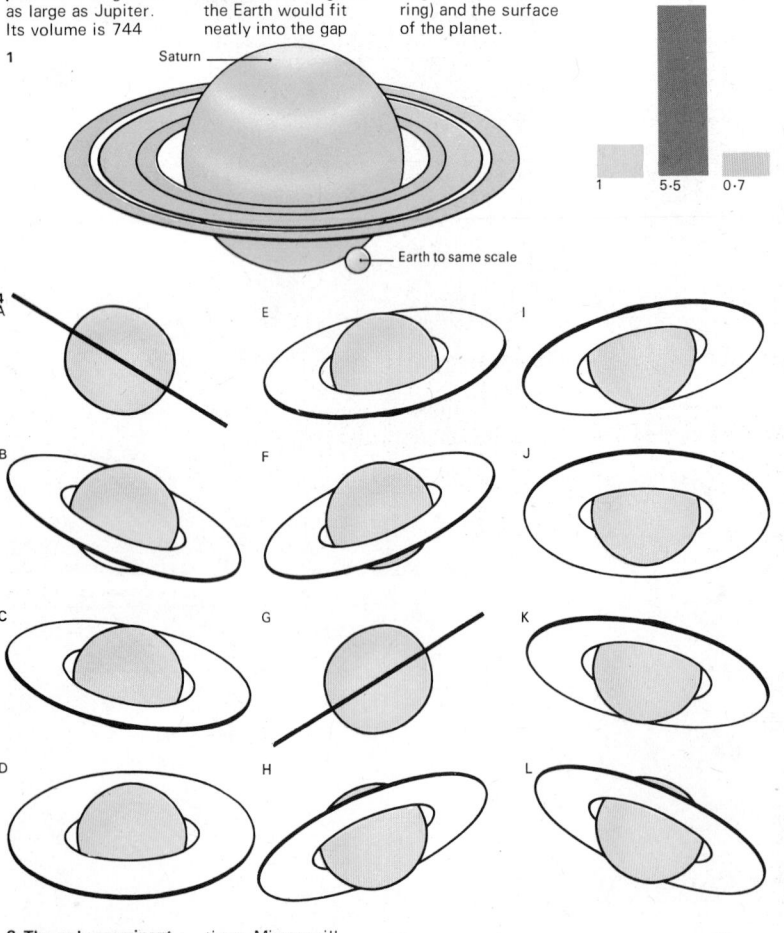

1 Saturn is a giant planet, although not as large as Jupiter. Its volume is 744 times that of Earth. In this scale diagram the Earth would fit neatly into the gap between the Crêpe ring (the innermost ring) and the surface of the planet.

1 5·5 0·7

2 The mean density of Saturn's globe is only 0.7 that of water. This is much less than that of any other principal planet. It has been said that if Saturn were dropped into an ocean, it would float. The low density is due to the preponderance of the very light elements, hydrogen and helium. The columns show the mean densities of the Earth and Saturn respectively compared with the density of water (which is one).

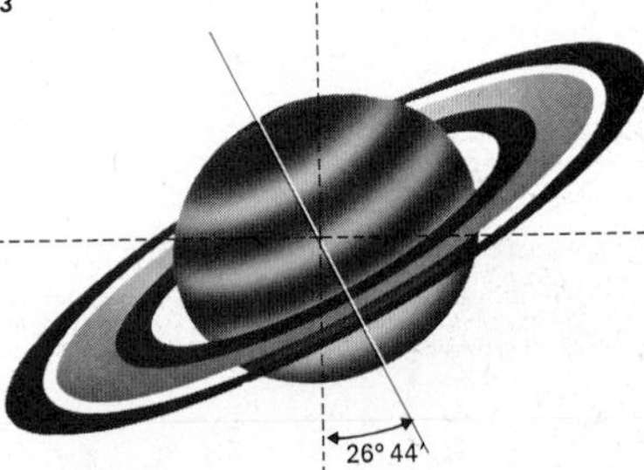
26° 44'

3 The inclination of Saturn's axis to the plane of the orbit is 26°44', only slightly greater than that of the Earth. The rings lie exactly in the plane of the planet's equator and are made up of small particles.

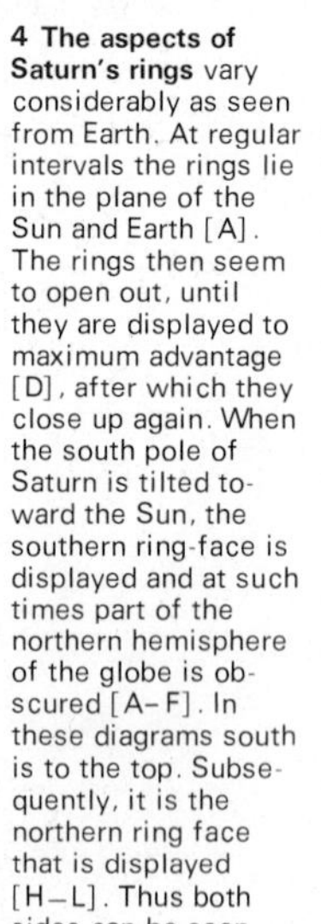

4 The aspects of Saturn's rings vary considerably as seen from Earth. At regular intervals the rings lie in the plane of the Sun and Earth [A]. The rings then seem to open out, until they are displayed to maximum advantage [D], after which they close up again. When the south pole of Saturn is tilted toward the Sun, the southern ring-face is displayed and at such times part of the northern hemisphere of the globe is obscured [A–F]. In these diagrams south is to the top. Subsequently, it is the northern ring face that is displayed [H–L]. Thus both sides can be seen.

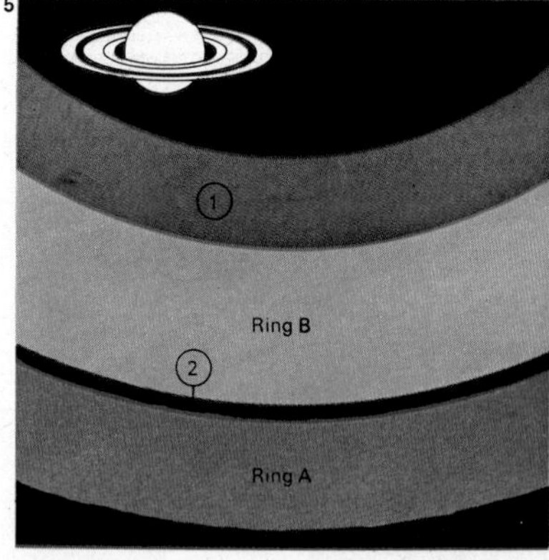

1
Ring B
2
Ring A

5 There are three principal rings. The outermost, ring A, is 10,000 miles (16,000km) wide, ring B is brighter and is 17,000 miles (27,000km) wide. Between it and the planet is the Crêpe ring [1]. Rings A and B are separated by a wide gap known as Cassini's Division [2].

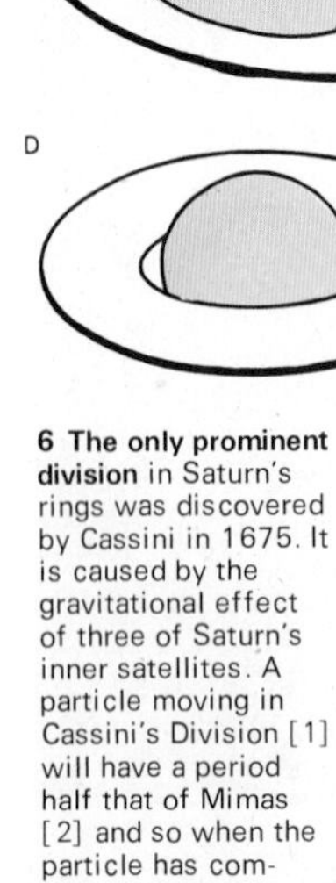

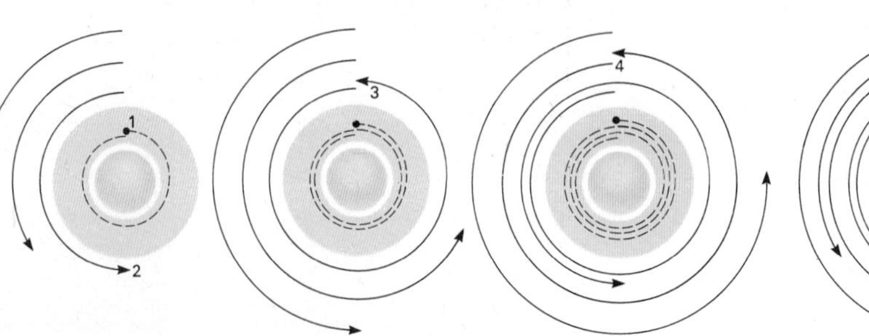

6 The only prominent division in Saturn's rings was discovered by Cassini in 1675. It is caused by the gravitational effect of three of Saturn's inner satellites. A particle moving in Cassini's Division [1] will have a period half that of Mimas [2] and so when the particle has completed two revolutions, Mimas will have completed one [3]. When the particle has completed three revolutions, Enceladus will have completed one [4] and for four revolutions, Tethys will have completed one [5]. These consistent perturbations will move the particle out of the division.

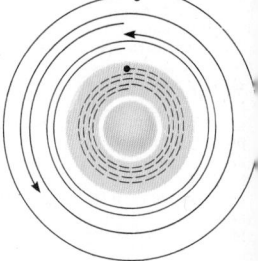

to be confirmed. There is also the problem of the extra ring divisions, of which Encke's Division is the best known. It may be that Encke's and other reported minor divisions are merely "ripples" in the ring structure rather than true gaps such as Cassini's Division. Edouard Roche (1820–83) gave his name to the distance between the center of a planet and its satellite, within which the satellite cannot approach without being broken up. Saturn's rings lie inside the planet's Roche limit and cannot therefore be solid or liquid sheets. The rings are made up of relatively small particles, icy or ice-covered, with each particle moving around Saturn in its own independent orbit, like a dwarf satellite. Cassini's Division is the result of the gravitational effects of Saturn's inner satellites [6], which may be said to keep the area of the division clear of ring particles.

The ring system is easily seen through a small telescope. The rings lie in the plane of the planet's equator, so that they can often be seen at a suitable angle [4]. When edge-on to Earth, as happened in 1966 and will happen again in 1980, they appear as a thin line of light and can be traced only with powerful telescopes. This shows that although the ring system measures 169,000 miles (272,000km) from one side to the other, it is also extremely thin, with a thickness of not more than a mile or two. If Saturn were represented as being the size of a tennis ball, the rings would be thinner than a sheet of tissue paper.

Information from space probes

Because Saturn is so far from Earth, a space probe will take years to reach it. The first Saturn probe was Pioneer 11, which by-passed Jupiter in December 1974, sending back excellent pictures as well as miscellaneous information; it was then sent on for a rendezvous with Saturn, scheduled for 1979. It is hoped that Pioneer will pass through the ring system. Whether the instruments on board will be operational afterward is uncertain, but in the foreseeable future some really detailed, close-range information about the ringed planet may be acquired.

KEY

A
B

The southern hemisphere of Saturn is displayed in this photograph. Part of the northern hemisphere is covered by the rings. There is a marked difference in brightness between ring A and ring B: the latter is much more brilliant.

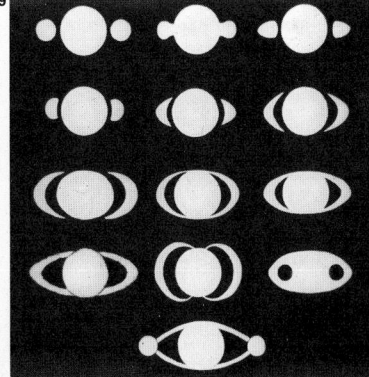

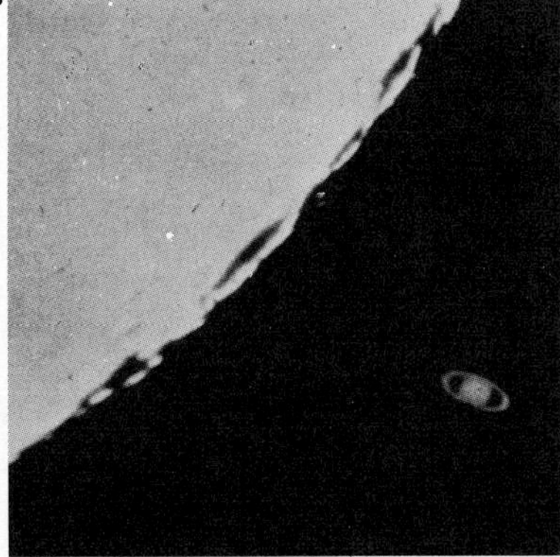

9 To early telescopic observers, Saturn was an observational enigma. The first recorded drawings seem to have been made by Galileo (1564–1642), whose feeble telescope was not strong enough to show the ring system in its true guise. He believed Saturn to be a triple planet and after two years' observation he lost sight of the rings altogether because during that time they had turned edge-on to the Earth.

7 Although Saturn is bright to the naked eye, it is impossible to detect any trace of its intricate ring system without a telescope. The only way to distinguish Saturn from the stars is by its slow movement from one night to the next. The planet Saturn is seen against its star field in this photograph.

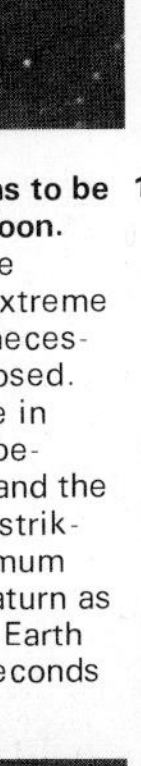

8 Saturn seems to be close to the Moon. The limb of the Moon, to the extreme upper left, is necessarily overexposed. The difference in apparent size between Saturn and the Moon is quite striking. The maximum diameter of Saturn as seen from the Earth is only 20.9 seconds of arc.

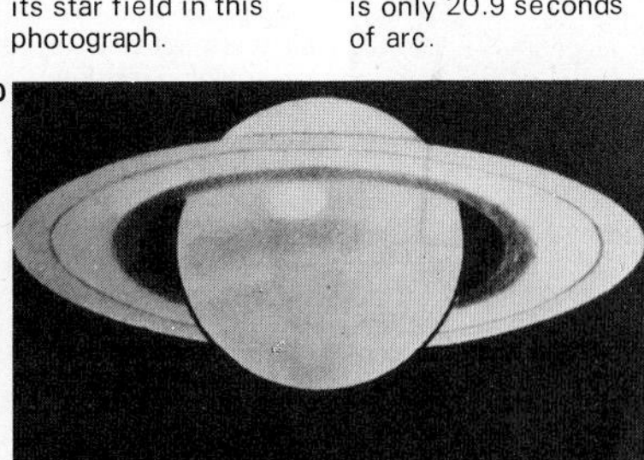

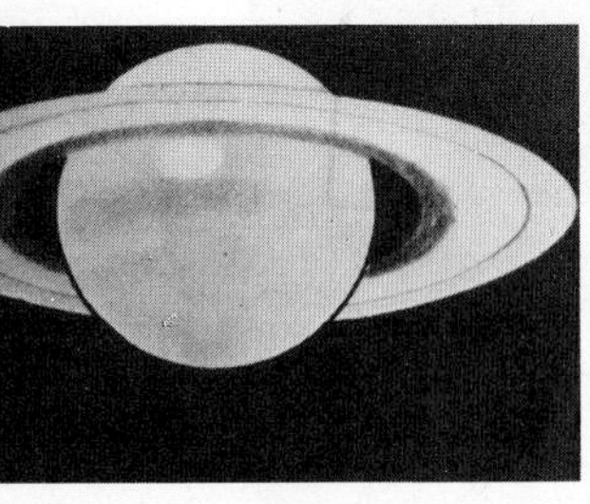

10 This drawing of Saturn was made in August 1933 by Will Hay, a British amateur astronomer. It dimly shows the white spot that suddenly appeared in the equatorial region of the planet and that became prominent for a few weeks. The spot gradually lengthened and the portion of the disk following it darkened. Subsequently the forward edge of the spot was no longer identifiable because it had been obscured by a mass of matter thrown up from below the visible surface. Other spots of the same basic type have also been seen and, like Hay's white spot, these features have been short-lived.

11 One of the best photographs of Saturn ever taken was by Gerard Kuiper (1905–) at the McDonald Observatory in Texas with a 61-in (155-cm) reflector. The rings were opening out (edgewise presentation had occurred earlier). It is clear that ring B (inner) is much brighter than ring A and indications of the so-called Encke's Division can be seen in ring A itself. Kuiper stated that Encke's Division was a ring irregularity rather than a true gap—viewed visually with the Palomar 200-in (508-cm) reflector. The shadow of the ring on the disk is prominent. There is a bright region at the planet's equator and the polar zones appear rather dusky in the photograph.

The moons of Jupiter and Saturn

Both of the giant planets have extensive satellite families. Jupiter has 13 known attendants, Saturn 10. They seem to fall into distinct categories: not all are large, but four—Io, Ganymede, and Callisto in Jupiter's system, and Titan in Saturn's—are bigger than our Moon [2].

The Jovian satellites

The four bright Jovian satellites were discovered by Galileo (1564–1642) in the winter of 1609–10 with one of his first telescopes. All would be visible to the naked eye were they not overpowered by the brilliance of Jupiter itself. They were seen at about the same time by Simon Marius (1570–1624), and there was a dispute between Marius and Galileo over priority—which may be the reason Marius' names for them—Io, Europa, Ganymede, Callisto—were not generally accepted until quite recently.

Even a small telescope will pick up the "Galilean" satellites. Since their orbits lie virtually in the plane of Jupiter's equator, they are often seen in a line, and their phenomena are easy to observe. A satellite may pass in transit across Jupiter's disk; it may pass behind the planet and be occulted; or it may be eclipsed by Jupiter's shadow [5]. Shadow transits are also seen [4]. All the Galileans show perceptible disks and large telescopes can pick up surface details. Io and Ganymede were photographed from the Pioneer probes of 1973 and 1974.

Ganymede is the largest and brightest of the Galileans; its diameter is about 3,100 miles (5,000km) according to recent measurements, which makes it larger than the planet Mercury. Callisto is nearly as big, but much less massive, so that its density is lower. Io and Europa are more like the Moon in size and density; Io was found by Pioneer 10 to have a tenuous atmosphere and also an ionosphere that affects the radio emissions from Jupiter, since it moves through the outer part of the Jovian magnetosphere.

The remaining satellites are much smaller. No 5, discovered by Edward Barnard (1857–1923) in 1892, is the closest to the planet, with an orbit inside that of Io. Its mean distance from the center of Jupiter is only 112,000 miles (181,000km) and it has a period of only 11 hours 57 minutes. The estimated diameter is 124 miles (200km), so that it is not visible with small telescopes. No 5 has been named Amalthea, although this name is still unofficial. All the other small, asteroidal satellites are farther out than Callisto. Four of them move around Jupiter in a retrograde direction, which tends to support the idea that they have been captured from the minor planet zone. Moreover, they are so far from Jupiter—out to almost 15 million miles (24 million km)—that they are strongly perturbed by the Sun, and their orbits are not even approximately circular.

Titan: the unique satellite

The satellite family of Saturn is somewhat different from that of Jupiter. It contains only one satellite that is of planetary size (Titan) and only one that is definitely asteroidal in nature (Phoebe); the rest are of intermediate type.

Titan was discovered by the Dutch astronomer Christian Huygens (1629–95) in

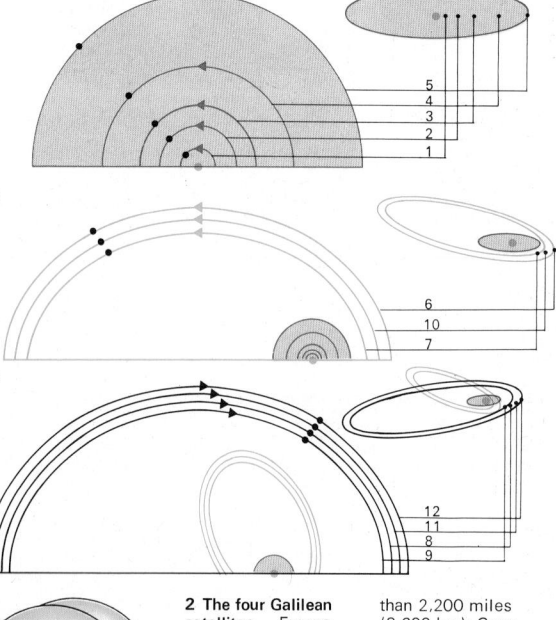

CONNECTIONS

See also
80 The planet Jupiter
82 Jupiter panorama
84 The planet Saturn
152 Exploring Jupiter and Saturn

1 The satellites of Jupiter fall into several well-defined groups. In the first group [A], the satellite Amathea [1] seems to be in a class of its own; the diameter is only 124 miles (200km). Then come the four satellites discovered by Galileo from 1609–10—Io [2], Europa [3], Ganymede [4], and Callisto [5]—with mean distances from Jupiter ranging between 262,000 miles (422,000km) for Io to 1,170,000 miles (1,880,000 km) for Callisto. The next group [B] consists of three satellites [6, 10, 7] plus a 13th, recently discovered and the third group [C] has four retrograde satellites [12, 11, 8, 9].

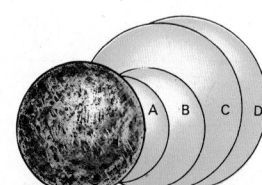

2 The four Galilean satellites – Europa [A], Io [B], Ganymede [C], and Callisto [D] – are compared in size with the Moon. Europa is smaller, while Io is larger, with a diameter of more than 2,200 miles (3,600 km); Ganymede and Callisto are comparable to Mercury – Ganymede's diameter is 3,100 miles (5,000 km) while Mercury's is 3,032 miles (4,880km).

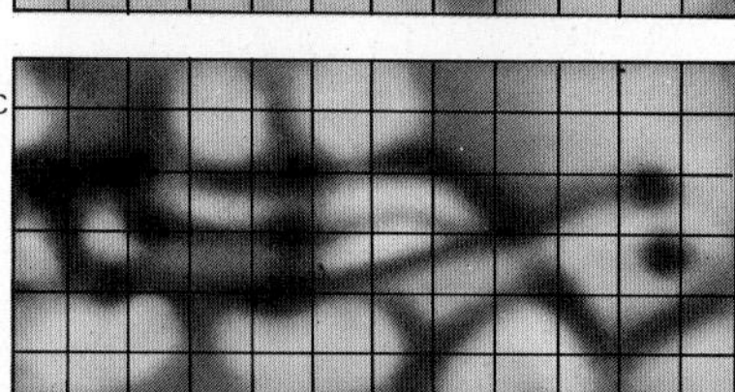

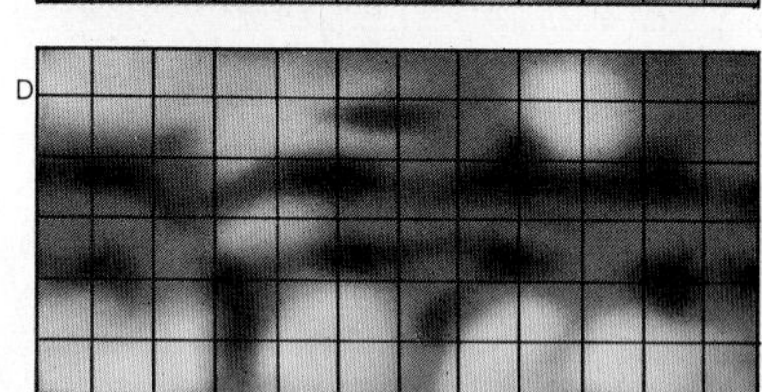

3 Surface details on the Galilean satellites may be discerned with very large telescopes. Io [A], orange in color, has a bright equatorial region and darker poles. This has been confirmed by the Pioneer probes. Europa [B] has the brightest surface of the four main satellites. Unlike Io, Europa apparently has a dark equatorial region and brighter poles. The surface may well be ice covered. Ganymede [C] is the easiest of the Galilean satellites to study, and it has been photographed by the Pioneer probes. Bright areas are visible; as are some darker areas that may be compared with the "seas" of Earth's Moon. Callisto [D] has a relatively low reflecting power, and details are not easy to make out. This drawing, like the others, was made by Dollfus from observations with the Pic-du-Midi 24-inch refractor.

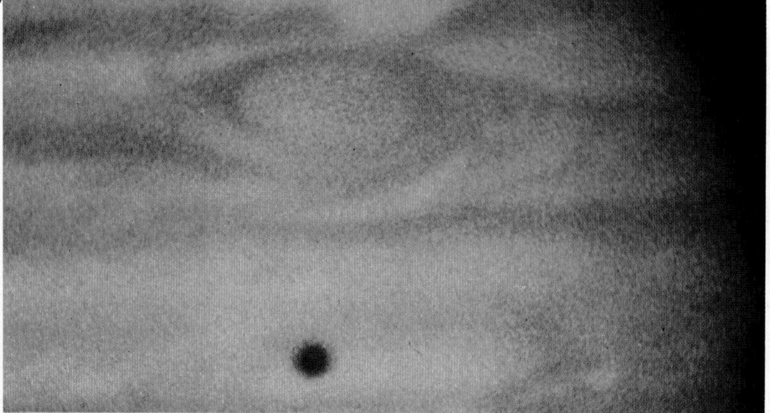

4 When a satellite passes in transit across Jupiter it may be seen as a bright spot. The two inner large satellites (Io and Europa) are easier to see in transit than are Ganymede or Callisto because of their higher albedos, or reflecting powers. Shadow transits are more striking. In this photograph, which was taken with the 61-inch (155-cm) reflector at the Catalina Observatory in Texas, the shadow of Ganymede can be seen as a prominent black spot.

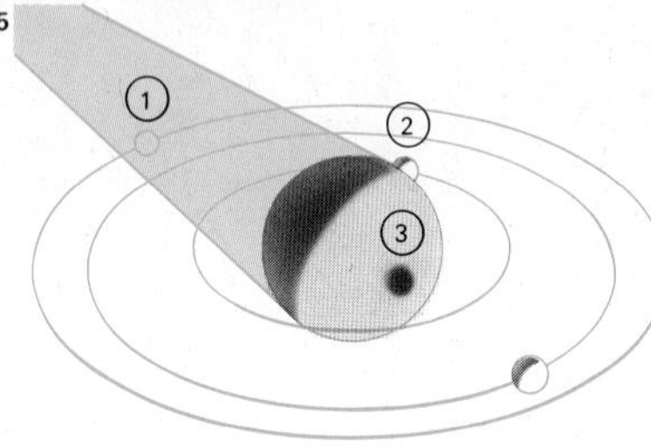
1
2
3

5 The Galilean satellites' orbits make them easy to observe. They may be eclipsed by the planet [1]; they may be occulted [2]; or their shadows may be seen in transit across the planet [3]. Observations of Callisto, the outermost of the large satellites, are less common because of its greater distance from Jupiter.

1655 and is easily viewed with a small telescope. It moves around Saturn at a distance of 760,000 miles (1,220,000km) in a circular orbit at half a degree of inclination from the plane of the rings. It has a period of 15 days 22.5 hours. The diameter is estimated as being between 2,700 miles (4,300km) and 3,000 miles (4,800km). Thus Titan is considerably larger than the Moon.

Titan is unique in being the only satellite known to have an appreciable atmosphere, composed primarily of methane. The ground pressure is about 100 millibars, which is 10 times that on the surface of Mars. The atmosphere, however, undergoes cyclic changes; its molecules escape continuously, although at a relatively slow rate in the extremely cold surface temperatures. The gravity of Saturn keeps the escaped molecules within Titan's orbit, however, enabling the satellite to pick them up again and keeping the overall atmospheric density almost constant.

Since this satellite is of such interest to astronomers, a special probe to Titan is being considered, and the Mariners that are due to fly past Saturn within the next few years should be able to photograph it.

The other satellites of Saturn

Saturn's other satellites are much smaller than Titan. The inner four (Janus, Mimas, Enceladus, and Tethys) are of low density and have been described as large ice balls; only Tethys is as much as 600 miles (1,000km) in diameter. Janus, the closest, was discovered by Audouin Dollfus (1924–   ) in 1966 and is visible only when the rings are edge-on. The fifth and sixth satellites, Dione and Rhea, are denser and more massive, although still smaller than the Moon. Next in order is Titan, followed by a very small satellite, Hyperion, and then by Iapetus, which exhibits strong variations in brilliancy and is much brighter when to the west of Saturn than when to the east. Presumably it has a synchronous rotation and it must either be irregular in shape or else have a surface of unequal reflecting power. Phoebe, up to 8 million miles (13 million km) from Saturn, is probably a captured asteroid.

KEY

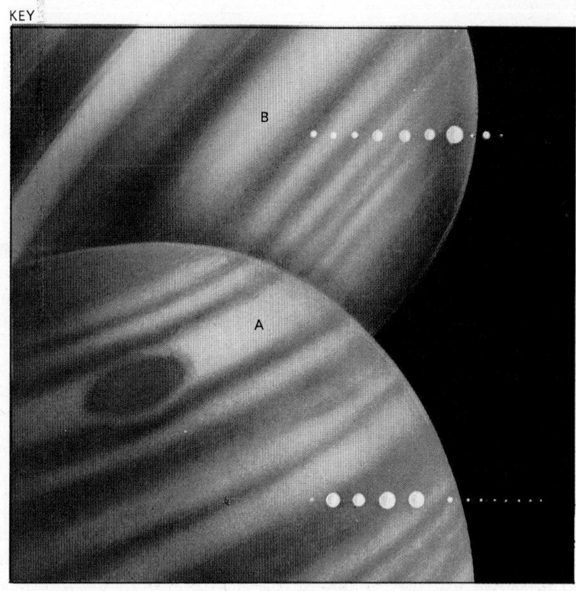
B
A

Jupiter [A] and Saturn [B] have 13 and 10 satellites respectively. Four of Jupiter's and one of Saturn's are large.

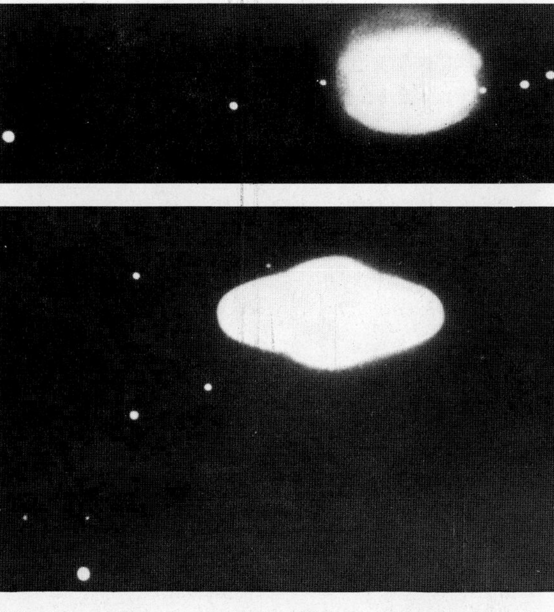

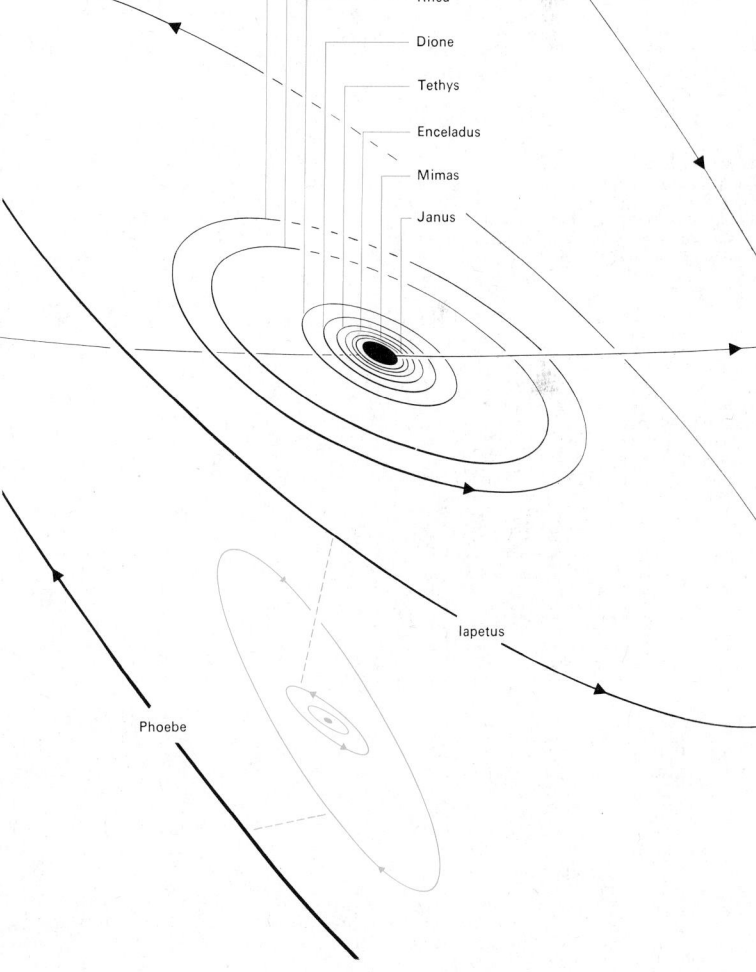

6 The inner satellites of Saturn shown [A] from right to left are Dione, Tethys, Mimas, Enceladus, Rhea, and Titan. The image of Saturn is necessarily overexposed since otherwise the faint inner satellites would be lost. The same satellites were photographed on March 24, 1948 [B]. At that time the ring-system was fairly wide open. The two faint objects just above Titan are background stars.

7 Janus [arrow] is visible only when the ring system is edge-on. The discoverer of Janus, Dollfus, took this photograph at Pic-du-Midi. The brighter satellite to the left of Saturn is Mimas.

8

Hyperion
Titan
Rhea
Dione
Tethys
Enceladus
Mimas
Janus
Iapetus
Phoebe

8 The orbits of Saturn's satellites, shown to scale, are varied. The orbits from Janus to Hyperion are almost circular; they move practically in the plane of the planet's equator, which is also the plane of the ring system. Iapetus, the outer member of the main satellite family, has an orbit that is more sharply inclined. Phoebe is shown to the lower left, together with Hyperion and Iapetus; it has retrograde motion, and may be a captured asteroid. In 1905 William Pickering (1858–1938) reported another satellite between the orbits of Titan and Hyperion, but it has not been seen since; he probably mistook a star for a satellite.

The outer planets

In ancient times Saturn was the outermost of the planets known to man. There were seven main bodies in the Solar System (the five planets visible to the naked eye, plus the Sun and the Moon) and because seven was the mystical number of the astrologers no more planets were expected. Then in 1781 William Herschel (1738–1822), while mapping stars in the constellation of Gemini, came upon an object that showed a disk and that moved perceptibly from night to night. Herschel thought that it must be a comet, but when its orbit was worked out he found that it was a planet much more remote than Saturn. The planet was named Uranus.

Uranus and its strange tilt

Uranus is only dimly visible to the naked eye, and it is not surprising that it was overlooked until Herschel's fortuitous discovery. The planet is classed as a giant, with a diameter of 32,200 miles (51,800km), but this is less than half that of Saturn. Its outer layers, at least, are gaseous and the surface temperature is extremely low. When seen through a telescope, Uranus shows a decidedly greenish disk; bright and dark zones may be made out with difficulty.

Uranus has a mean distance from the Sun of 1,783,000,000 miles (2,869,600,000 km) and a revolution period of 84 years. The axial rotation period is about 11 hours [2]. The axial tilt is very strange: it amounts to 98 degrees, which is more than a right angle, so that from Earth Uranus is sometimes seen pole-on and sometimes with the equator crossing the center of the disk. The reason for this peculiar inclination is unknown.

Our knowledge of Uranus is not at all complete and, unfortunately, with the cancellation of the 1979 flyby mission to Jupiter, Uranus, and Neptune, there are no plans to send a probe to the major planets in the immediate future. Uranus has five satellites [3], all of which are smaller than our Moon and all of which revolve in the plane of the planet's equator, so that their movements are technically retrograde. There is some disagreement about the sizes of the satellites, but Miranda, the smallest, is about 340mi (550km) in diameter; Umbriel about 620mi (1,000km); and Ariel about 930mi (1,500km). The two largest, Oberon and Titania, have diameters of approximately 995mi (1,600km) and 1,120mi (1,800km), respectively.

The discovery of Neptune

With the discovery of Uranus the Solar System seemed to be complete, but after a few years a strange problem arose. Uranus did not move as expected—it persistently wandered away from its calculated path. The only logical solution was that the action of a more distant, still unknown planet was pulling Uranus out of position. This idea was proposed in 1834 and was communicated to George Biddell Airy (1801–92), who became astronomer royal at Greenwich the following year, but he showed little interest. John Couch Adams (1819–92), working at Cambridge in 1843, resolved to tackle the problem. He thought that by using the perturbations of Uranus it would be possible to find the position of the unknown planet and after some months of

CONNECTIONS

See also

154 Exploring the outer planets

50 Members of the Sola System

1

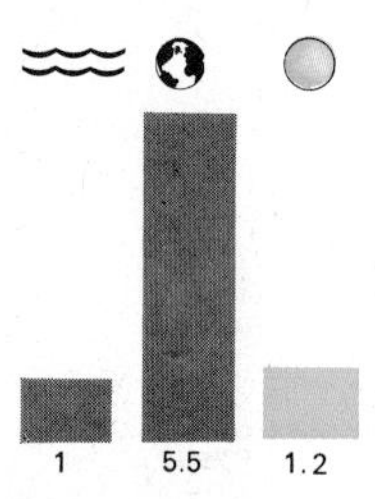
1
5.5
1.2

1 Uranus has a density of 1.2 times that of water – rather less than that of Jupiter and much more than that of Saturn, although less than that of Earth (5.5).

2

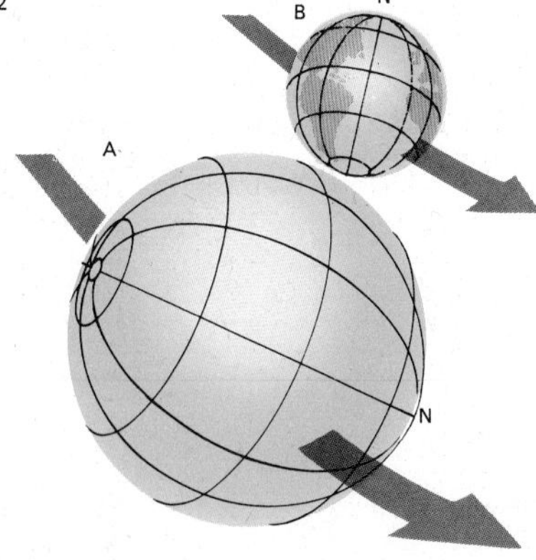
B
N
A
N

2 Uranus [A] has an axial rotation of about 11 hours at its equator, although the rotation in the polar zones is slightly longer. The tilt of the axis as compared to the Earth [B] is 98 degrees – unique in the Solar System. Because this is more than a right angle the rotation is technically retrograde (although not usually reckoned as such). All five satellites of Uranus move almost in the plane of the planet's equator.

3

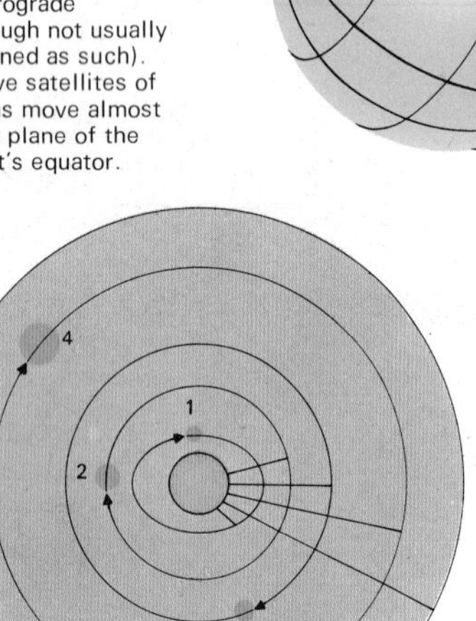
4
1
2
3
5

3 Orbits of the five satellites of Uranus are shown in this diagram as they would be seen looking down on the planet's pole: Miranda [1], Ariel [2], Umbriel [3], Titania [4] and Oberon [5]. When the planet is seen pole-on from Earth the orbits appear circular. But when Uranus is seen equator-on, as occurred in 1945, the orbits appear almost linear. Miranda is the smallest and most recently discovered.

4

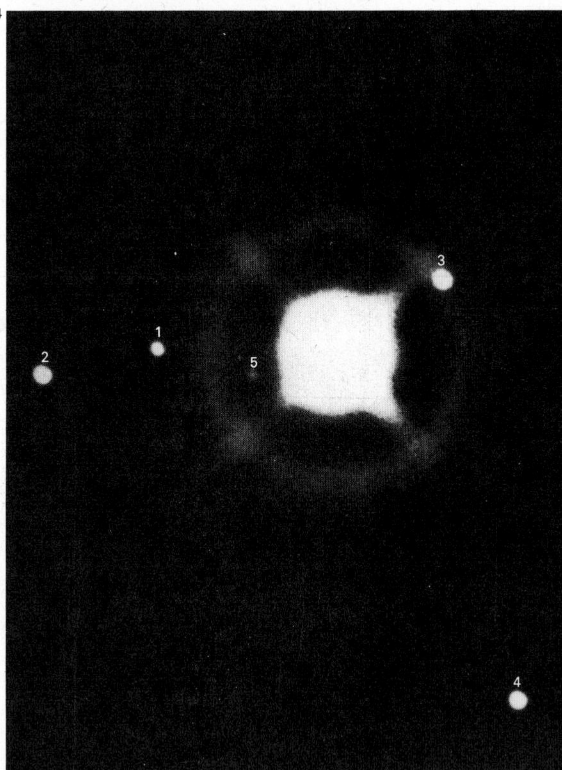
3
1
2
5
4

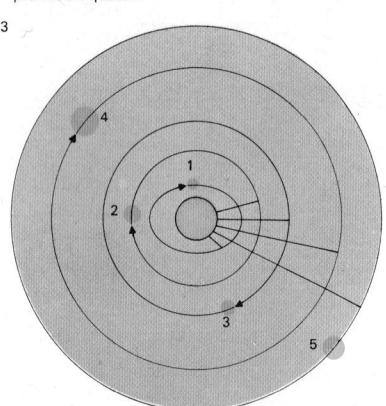

4 Uranus was photographed with all five of its satellites by G. P. Kuiper, with the 82-in(208-cm) reflector at the McDonald Observatory, Texas, in 1948. That was the year in which Kuiper discovered Miranda, innermost and faintest of the satellites. Shown here are Ariel [1], Umbriel [2], Titania [3], Oberon [4] and Miranda [5]. The image of Uranus is overexposed and the ring is a photographic effect.

5

1 5.5 1.67

5 Uranus and Neptune are similar in size. Neptune is decidedly the more massive (17 Earth masses, as against only 15 for Uranus) and until recently it was thought to be larger, 30,250mi (48,400km) compared with 29,440mi (47,100km). The occultation of a star by Neptune in 1968 gave a value of 30,760mi (49,500km) and in 1970 an experiment with a balloon-borne telescope at Princeton University gave a new value for Uranus of 32,200mi (51,800km). The density of Neptune (1.67) is greater than that of Uranus, and in fact it is the densest of the outer planets with the exception of the ninth planet Pluto.

6 A

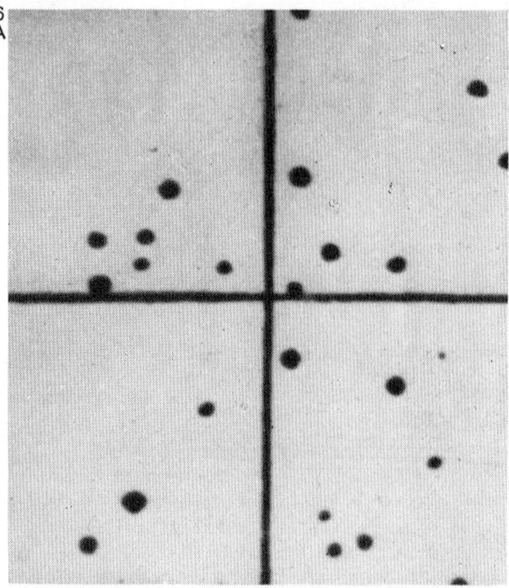

B

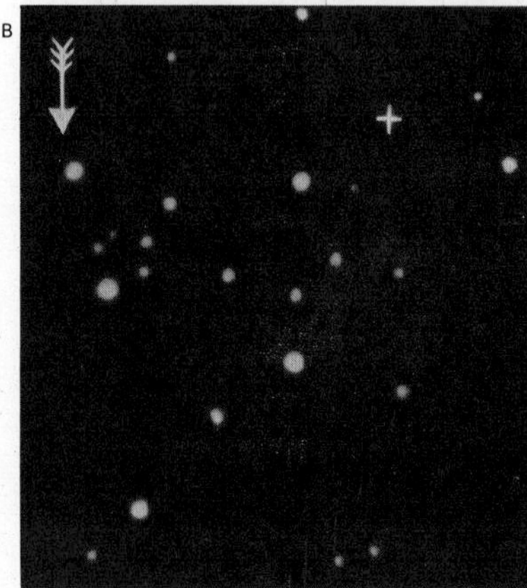

6 When Galle and d'Arrest set out to look for Neptune in 1846, using the calculations of Leverrier, they were able to make use of a new star map of the area, a corner of which is shown in diagram [A]. Challis, searching at Cambridge, had no such map and his task was thus much more laborious. [B] shows the corresponding portion of the sky; Leverrier's estimated position for Neptune is shown by a cross and the arrow indicates the actual position.

hard work he felt that he had fixed the position accurately. He too contacted Airy, but again the astronomer royal took no action (although, to be fair, this was partly due to a series of misunderstandings). In the meantime, similar calculations made by the French mathematician Urbain Leverrier (1811–77) were sent to the Berlin Observatory where two observers, Johann Galle (1812–1910) and Heinrich d'Arrest (1822–75) quickly located the planet in almost exactly the position indicated by Leverrier. The discovery was made in 1846 [6]. Very shortly afterward James Challis (1803–82), working at Cambridge on the basis of Adams's work, independently located the planet. The planet was named Neptune.

Neptune is almost a twin of Uranus. It is slightly smaller, with a diameter of 30,760mi (49,500km), and more massive; it does not have Uranus's remarkable axial tilt. The revolution period is 164.8 years and the mean distance from the Sun is 2,794,000,000 miles (4,497,000,000km). No telescope will show definite surface details on Neptune; all that can be seen is a pale bluish disk. Of the two satellites [8], Triton is larger than our Moon and has a circular orbit, but moves round Neptune in a retrograde direction. The other satellite, Nereid, is very small and has an eccentric orbit.

The enigma of Pluto

Even with the discovery of Neptune there were still discrepancies in the movements of the outer giants and Percival Lowell (1855–1916) undertook new calculations with the aim of finding yet another planet. In 1930, at the Lowell Observatory in Arizona, the planet was located [9].

Pluto, as the new planet was named, has posed astronomers problem after problem. It is apparently smaller than the Earth and perhaps even smaller than Mars; it has an eccentric, inclined orbit that can bring it closer to the Sun than Neptune [10]; and its lack of mass means that it cannot produce marked perturbations in the motions of Uranus or Neptune—yet it was precisely because of such perturbations that Pluto was detected. The revolution period is 247.7 years and the rotation period 6.4 Earth days.

KEY

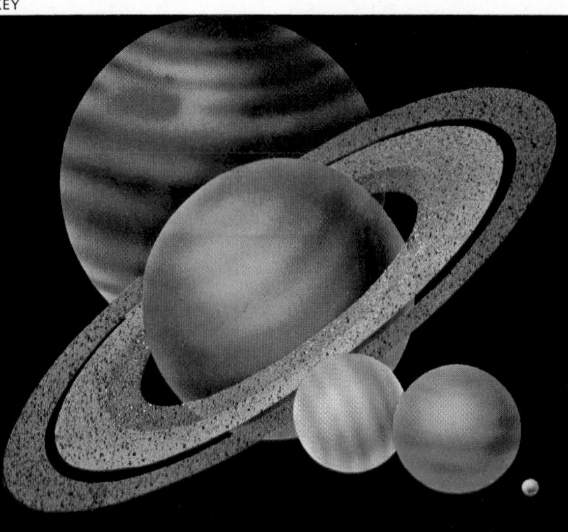

The sizes of the outermost planets are compared here with Jupiter and Saturn. Uranus and Neptune are giants with gaseous surfaces; Pluto is smaller than the Earth, and is classed as a "terrestrial" planet although its nature is uncertain.

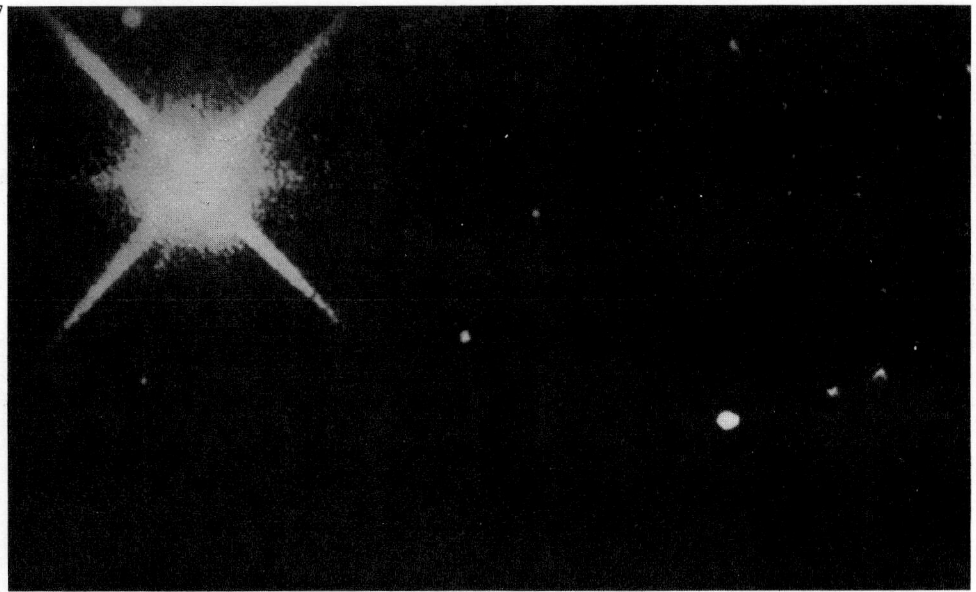

7 This photograph shows Neptune together with its satellite Triton. The brighter of Neptune's two satellites, Triton appears as the rounded bump at the rim of the overexposed image of Neptune, and was discovered by the British astronomer William Lassell only a few weeks after the discovery of Neptune. Nereid is very faint and does not appear.

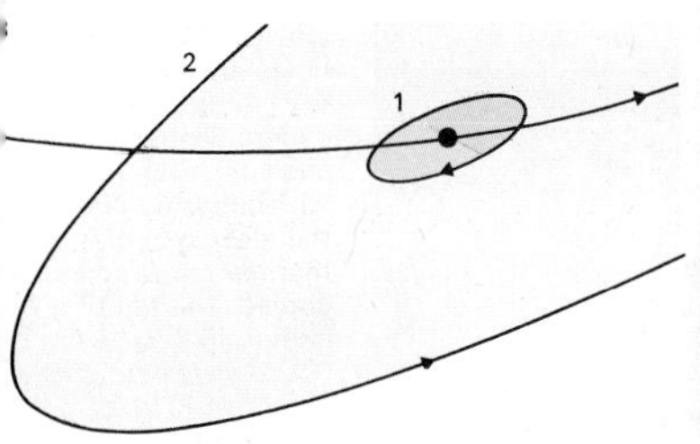
2
1

8 Orbits of Triton [1] and Nereid [2], Neptune's satellites, are quite different. Triton's is almost circular but it has retrograde motion; it is the only large satellite in the Solar System to behave in this way. Nereid has direct motion but an eccentric orbit like that of a comet.

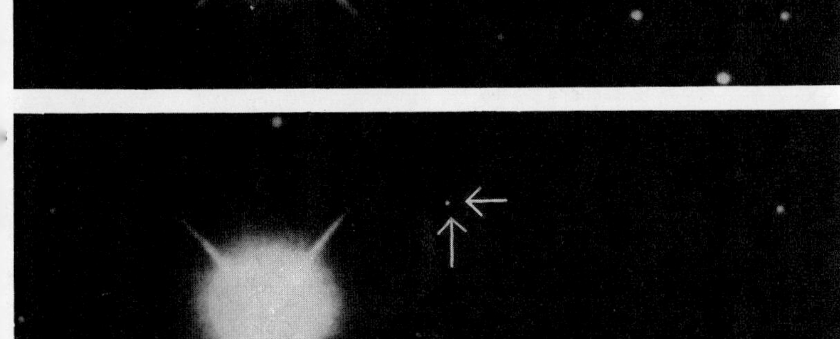

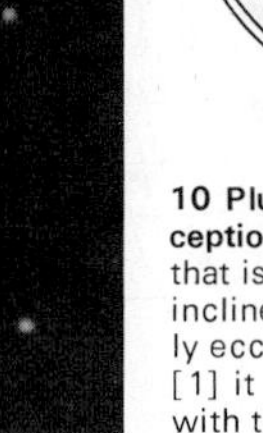

9 These photographs show the discovery of Pluto in 1930 by Clyde Tombaugh at the Lowell Observatory on the basis of Percival Lowell's calculations–[A] on March 2; [B] on March 5. The shift of Pluto, indicated by the arrows, is very noticeable. The overexposed image is that of the third-magnitude star Delta Geminorum. Pluto is now of about magnitude 14 and may thus be seen with moderate-size telescopes.

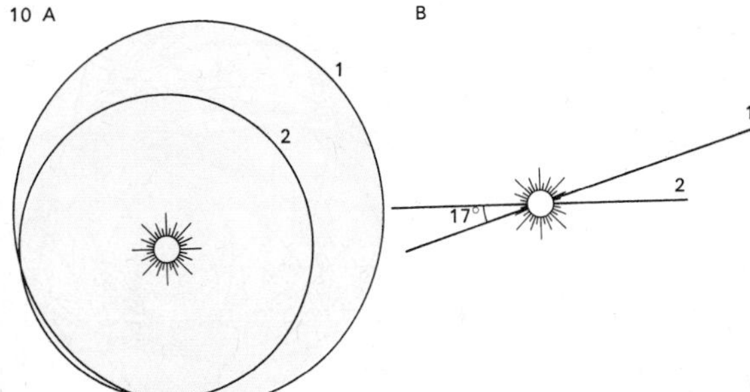
10 A
B
1
2
1
2
17°

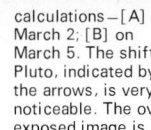

10 Pluto has an exceptional orbit [A] that is both relatively inclined and decidedly eccentric. Here [1] it is compared with that of Neptune [2]. At perihelion Pluto may come within Neptune's path but [B] Pluto's inclination of 70° [1] to the ecliptic [2] means that there can be no collision. The next perihelion passage is due in 1989. Its peculiar orbit has raised doubts whether Pluto is a true planet.

Comets

A great comet, with a brilliant head and a tail stretching half-way across the sky, is a spectacular object—and it is easy to understand why comets of this kind caused such terror in ancient times. Comets have always been regarded as unlucky and fear of them is still not dead in some of the world's primitive societies.

Yet a comet is not nearly as important as it may look. It is made up of small particles (mainly icy) and tenuous gas. On several occasions the Earth has been known to pass through a comet's tail without suffering the slightest damage.

A comet's anatomy

A large comet is made up of three principal parts: a nucleus (containing most of the mass); a coma, or head; and a tail [2]. The coma and tail appear only when the comet approaches the Sun and solar radiation vaporizes part of the icy nucleus. As the comet recedes the tail disappears. Small comets, however, are often devoid of tails and look like small patches of faintly luminous cotton balls in the sky.

The tails of comets are of two main kinds: dust and gas. Generally the gas tail is relatively straight, while the dust tail is curved—because it lags behind as the comet moves forward. One remarkable feature of tails is that they always point more or less away from the Sun, so that when a comet is receding it travels tail-first. The causes of this are not known for certain, but it is thought that the tiny particles in the tail are repelled by the so-called "solar wind," a stream of electrified, low-energy particles constantly flowing outward from the Sun.

Comets are members of the Solar System but their paths, in most cases, differ from those of the planets in that they are much more eccentric. Dozens of comets with short-period orbits are known; the period of Encke's comet, for instance, is only 3.3 years, so that it is seen regularly and has been observed at more than 50 returns to perihelion (the point in its orbit when it is closest to the Sun—aphelion is the point farthest from the Sun) since it was first sighted in the eighteenth century. Comets are not visible through the emission of light of their own, but through the reflection of the Sun's radiation, which causes the cometary material to fluoresce. Thus most comets cannot be followed throughout their orbits and can only be seen when relatively close to the Earth and the Sun.

Short- and long-period comets

All the short-period comets are faint and many of them are difficult objects to view telescopically. A few (notably Schwassmann-Wachmann I and the more recent Gunn's comet) have more circular paths [3] and can be followed throughout their orbits.

Other comets take decades to travel once around the Sun. The most famous of these is Halley's comet [5], which is a bright naked-eye object and is seen every 76 years or so (the period of a comet is not constant, because of the perturbations caused by the planets). Halley's comet last returned to perihelion in 1910 and is due back once more in 1986.

Other great comets have much longer periods—so long that they have not been

CONNECTIONS

See also
92 Meteors and meteorites
154 Exploring the outer planets
50 Members of the Sola System

1
C
B
1
2
A

1 There are three main classes of comets. Short-period comets [A] often have their aphelia at approximately the distance of Jupiter's orbit [1]. Their periods amount to a few years, and all short-period comets are faint. Long-period comets [B] have aphelia near or beyond Neptune's orbit [2] – Halley's is the only conspicuous member of the class. Comets with very long periods [C] have such great orbital eccentricities that the paths are almost parabolic. Because only a short arc can be measured, it is impossible to calculate the periods of these comets accurately. All the really brilliant comets, apart from Halley's comet, are in the very long-period category.

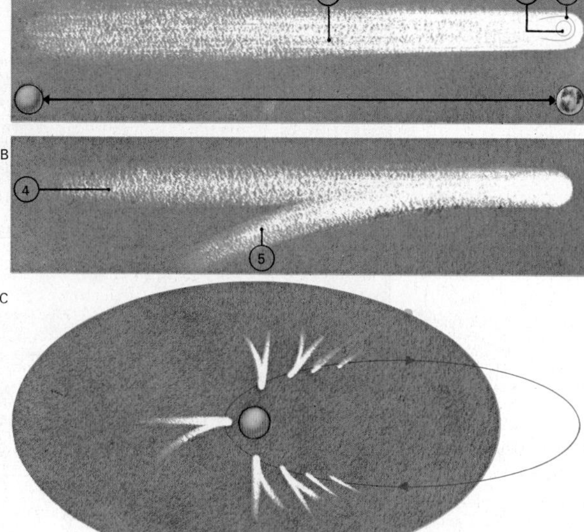
2 A
3
1
2
B
4
5
C

2 The anatomy of a large comet [A] contains the nucleus [1], which may or may not be a conglomerate; [2] the coma, made up of small particles and tenuous gas; and [3] the tail, extending away from the coma. The two types of tail shown in (B) are a gaseous tail [4], which is generally straight, and a dust tail [5], which lags behind the moving comet, so that the tail appears curved. The tail of a comet, like Halley's (C), always points approximately away from the Sun whatever its orbital position. A comet develops a tail only as it nears perihelion and particles and gases are driven off, losing it as it recedes from the Sun.

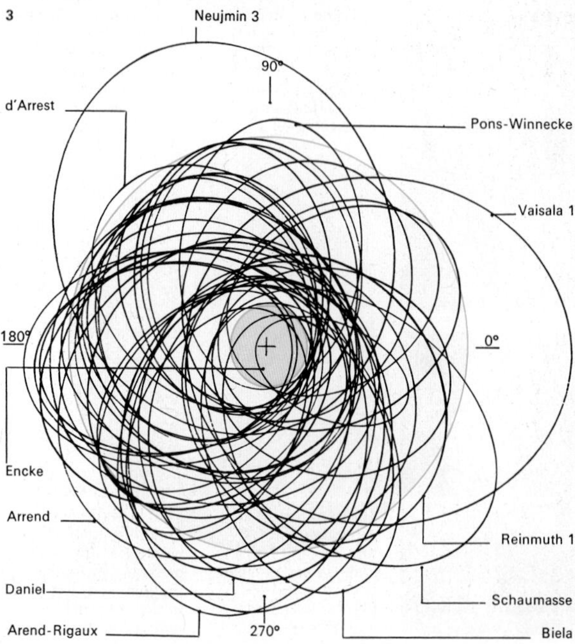
3
Neujmin 3
90°
d'Arrest
Pons-Winnecke
Vaisala 1
180°
0°
Encke
Arrend
Reinmuth 1
Daniel
Schaumasse
Arend-Rigaux
270°
Biela

3 The orbits of some short-period comets are shown. Their aphelia lie near Jupiter's orbit and they are said to belong to Jupiter's family. Encke's comet has the shortest period (3.3 years); that of Schaumasse's comet is over eight years. It used to be thought that comets came from interstellar space and were "captured" by the planets, particularly Jupiter, but this theory has been generally rejected by modern astronomers.

4 Donati's comet of 1858 was generally considered the most beautiful ever observed. It was a brilliant naked-eye object and had tails of both gas and dust. This picture of the comet is taken from an old woodcut.

measured accurately. Thus comets of this kind cannot be predicted and are always apt to arrive unexpectedly. Such was the great comet of 1843, whose coma was larger than the Sun, even though its mass was, by astronomical standards, negligible. Other great comets appeared in 1811, 1882, and 1910. The Daylight comet of 1910 (not to be confused with Halley's) was probably the brightest to have been seen during the present century. Kohoutek's comet of 1973 was expected to be brilliant but proved a great disappointment [9].

Short-lived comets

Some great comets approach the Sun very closely and are termed "sun-grazers." As the comet passes perihelion the tail swings around, and it often happens that the original tail is destroyed and a new one forms. The tails of comets are produced by evaporation from the nucleus and there must be a steady wastage of material, so that by cosmic standards comets are short-lived. We even know of comets that have disappeared. Westphal's comet of 1913, which had a period of 62 years, faded out as it approached perihelion and was never seen again. Biela's periodic comet, which took 6.75 years to complete one orbit, split in two in 1846; the "twins" were seen again in 1852 but that was their last appearance as comets. In 1872, when they were due to return, a bright meteor shower was seen in the region from which they should have come. This emphasizes the close connection between comets and meteors. Meteors may be regarded as cometary debris.

There is considerable uncertainty about the origin of comets. According to J. H. Oort, a Dutch astronomer, there is a vast "comet cloud" at a great distance from the Sun; sometimes a comet will swing inward toward the Sun, at which time it can be observed.

Although professional astronomers are engaged in comet-hunting, many discoveries are made by amateurs. G. E. D. Alcock, an English schoolmaster, discovered four, while the bright comet of 1970 was found by a South African, J. Bennett, also an amateur.

KEY

This brilliant comet is Bennett's comet, photographed on March 12, 1970. The tail is quite long and its fine, gaseous nature is clearly seen. The nucleus is not shown because of the overexposure of the coma, or head, in order to bring out the structure of the tail. The coma is made up of material from the nucleus that is vaporized by solar radiation as the comet approaches the Sun, when its temperature may rise to several thousand degrees. A comet's emission spectrum reveals the presence of such elements as iron, calcium, sodium, potassium, copper, chromium, nickel, and traces of several other metals.

5

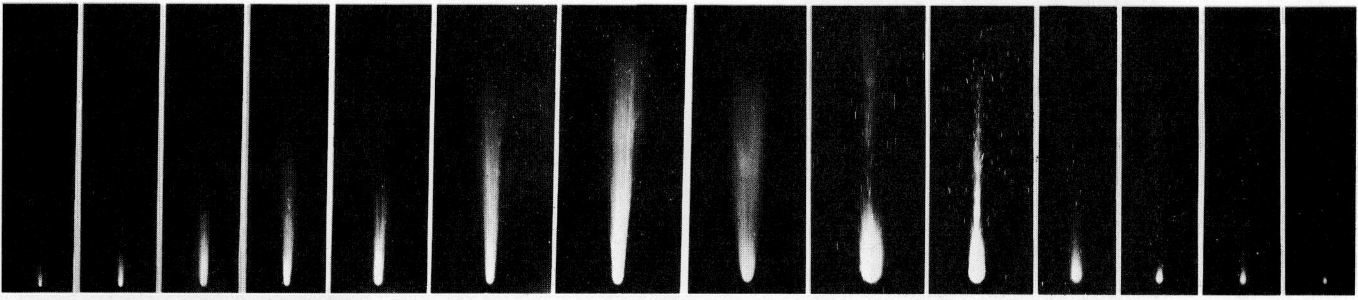

6

5 Halley's comet last returned to perihelion in 1910. Although not as bright as the great "nonperiodic" comets, the increase and decline of the tail is clearly shown in this sequence. As it approached perihelion the tail developed enormously. After the closest approach to the Sun the tail contracted, so that when the comet was last seen the tail had disappeared. The seventh picture shows the tail shortly before perihelion passage. Halley's comet is due back at perihelion in 1986.

6 Morehouse's comet of 1908 had a complex tail, the structure of which changed rapidly. Great disturbances must have been taking place, but the comet was not bright enough for the details of these changes to be seen.

7 Comet Arend-Roland of 1957 was one of the most interesting comets of recent times. The apparent "forward spike" is not an extra tail but is illuminated meteoritic debris lying along the comet's orbit.

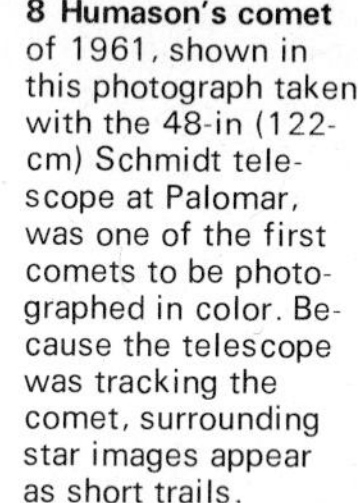

8 Humason's comet of 1961, shown in this photograph taken with the 48-in (122-cm) Schmidt telescope at Palomar, was one of the first comets to be photographed in color. Because the telescope was tracking the comet, surrounding star images appear as short trails.

9 Kohoutek's comet of 1973 was not as spectacular as was hoped. There will be no opportunity to see it again since it will not return to perihelion for 75,000 years.

7

8

9

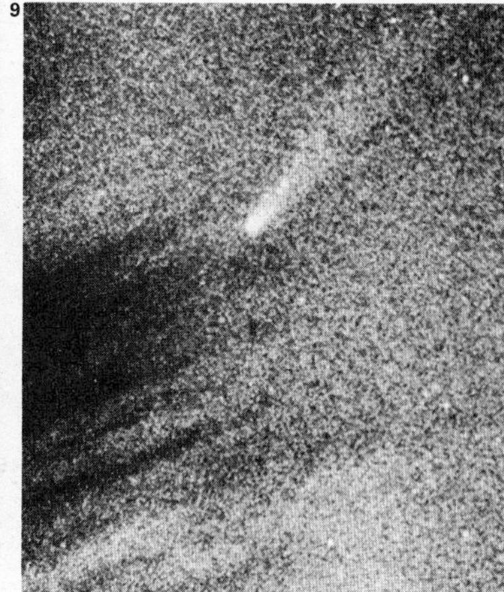

Meteors and meteorites

Meteors, or shooting stars, can usually be seen on clear August nights in the Northern Hemisphere. They are rapidly moving points of light, often with luminous tails, caused by objects traveling quickly across the sky. Such shooting stars have been known since antiquity, but not until the beginning of the nineteenth century was their nature understood.

Meteorites, which fall to earth, are not as numerous as meteors and are an entirely different kind of heavenly body. They are not merely large meteors, nor are they related to comets, which they resemble visually as streaks in the sky. Rather they are more closely associated with the asteroids.

High-velocity particles

A meteor is a tiny particle, usually smaller than a grain of sand, moving around the Sun. It is so small that it can be seen only when it enters the Earth's upper atmosphere. With a velocity of entry possibly as high as 45 miles (72km) per second, the meteor sets up friction with the air molecules, which causes it to destroy itself well before it reaches the ground. The resulting luminous streak in the sky, characteristic of the shooting star, is not produced by the meteor itself but by its effect on the atmosphere [Key].

Meteors are of two main kinds: sporadic and shower. Sporadic meteors may appear from any direction at any time. Shower meteors, on the other hand, are associated with comets. The famous Leonid shower meteors of November, for example [3, 4], are linked with the faint periodic Tempel's comet and move in the same orbit as the comet itself. It has been said that meteors are cometary debris. This may be an oversimplification, but it is certainly true that one periodic comet, Biela's, was seen to divide and has now been replaced by a meteor shower [1, 2]. Moreover, there is no doubt that as a comet moves along it "sheds" meteoric material.

The richness of a meteor shower is measured by its so-called Zenithal Hourly Rate (ZHR). This is a measure of the number of meteors per hour that would be seen by a watcher observing under ideal conditions with the shower radiant at the zenith. The most reliable annual shower, that of the Perseids, has a ZHR of about 70. Meteors below naked-eye visibility are not included, so that in fact there are many more meteors than might be thought. Those that are too small to produce any luminous effects are known as micrometeors.

Because the meteors in a shower are traveling through space in parallel paths, they seem to radiate from one particular point in the sky, which is known as the radiant. The principle is analogous with the view from a bridge overlooking a highway. The parallel lanes of the highway will seem to meet at a point near the horizon, which may be termed the apparent "radiant" of the lanes. Thus, on the same principle, the November Leonids have their radiant in the constellation Leo, the August Perseids in Perseus, and so on.

Regular annual showers

Showers of meteors occur regularly on an annual basis. These include the Quadrantids (January 1–6, maximum January 3–4);

CONNECTIONS

See also
90 Comets
78 Minor planets
50 Members of the Solar System

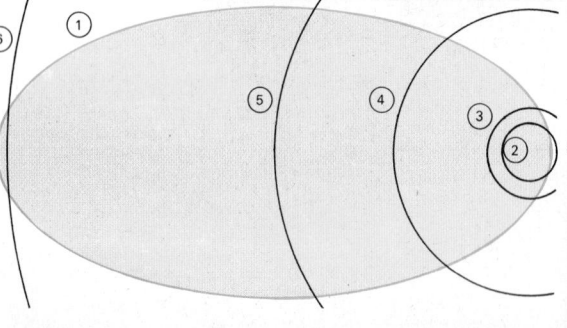

1 Biela's comet once had a period of 6.75 years. In 1846, as shown in a contemporary drawing by Angelo Secchi (1818–78), it divided into a pair of comets. The division may have been caused initially by a close approach to Jupiter in 1842, with the pull of the Sun accounting for the rest of the change. The two comets, separated by over 1.25 million miles (2 million km), returned in 1852. Because of their unfavorable positions they were not seen in 1858 and did not appear in 1866. They have not been seen again.

2 A brilliant meteor shower [red] from a radiant in Andromeda [blue] where Biela's comet should have been was seen in 1872. It was probably the comet's debris. The shower is now extremely feeble.

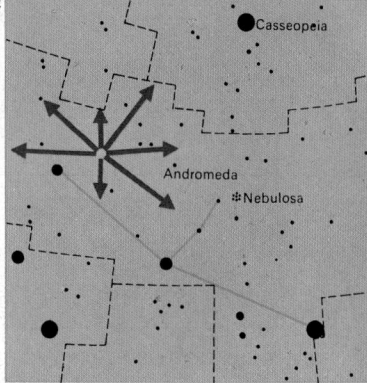

3 The orbit of the Leonid meteor stream [1] intersects the orbits of the Earth [2], Mars [3], Jupiter [4], Saturn [5], and Uranus [6]. Because the meteors are not distributed evenly, major meteor showers appear only occasionally. The average interval was once just over 33 years, but the expected showers of 1899 and 1933 were missed because the shower orbit had experienced perturbations.

4 A splendid Leonid meteor shower was photographed from Arizona on November 17, 1966. The shower was not visible from Europe.

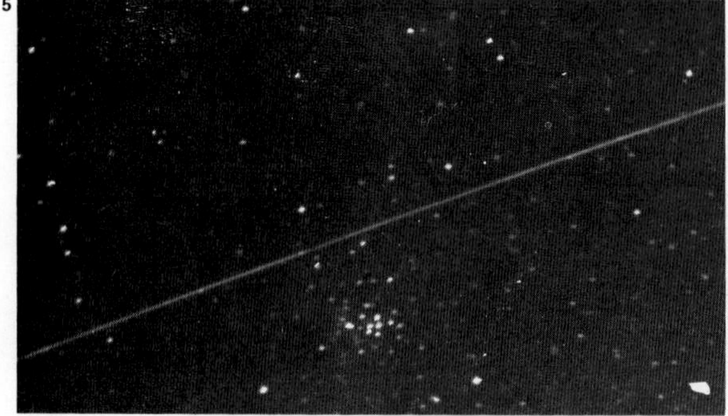

5 A meteor trail is seen here near the cluster Praesepe. The meteor was of about 2nd magnitude and lasted 1.5 sec.

Lyrids (April 19–24); Eta Aquarids (May 1–8, associated with the famous Halley's comet); Perseids (July 25–August 18); Orionids (October 16–26); Taurids (October 20–November 30); the far southern Phoenicids (December 4–5); the Geminids (December 7–15); and the Ursids (December 17–24). The Leonids, which are at their peak on November 17, are less reliable because the meteors are clustered rather than spread along the cometary orbit. Therefore a major shower cannot be seen until the Earth passes through the main swarm. This happened in 1799, 1833, 1866, and in 1966 [4], so that there could possibly be another display in 1999. In the years between these major showers the Leonids are decidedly sparse.

The history of meteorites

A larger body encountering the Earth's atmosphere may survive the journey to the ground without being destroyed. These meteorites may be of several kinds. Aerolites [10] are mainly of stone while siderites [12] have a high percentage of iron. There are various intermediate types. Etching a meteorite with acid will show the characteristic forms, known as the Widmanstätten patterns, and this is one sure way of telling whether a piece of material is of meteoritic origin or not.

Meteorites have been known for many centuries, but for a long time their cosmic origin was doubted. In 1795, when a 56-lb (25-kg) meteorite fell in Yorkshire, England, it was suggested that the object was a stone from the Icelandic volcano Hekla.

In 1803, however, a meteorite group fell at L'Aigle in France and the famous astronomer Jean-Baptiste Biot (1774–1862) was able to demonstrate that the objects definitely came from the sky. Most museums have meteorite collections; the largest meteorite on display, at the Hayden Planetarium in New York City, weighs about 34 tons. Fortunately, major meteorite falls are rare. The best examples of craters produced by large meteorites are the Meteor (Diablo) Crater near Winslow, Arizona [6, 7] and the Wolf Creek Crater in Australia.

KEY

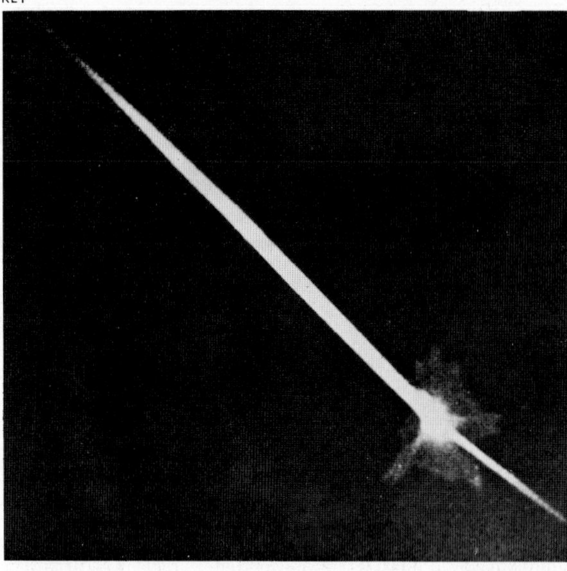

The exploding Andromedid meteor was photographed on November 23, 1895. This is one of the finest meteor photos.

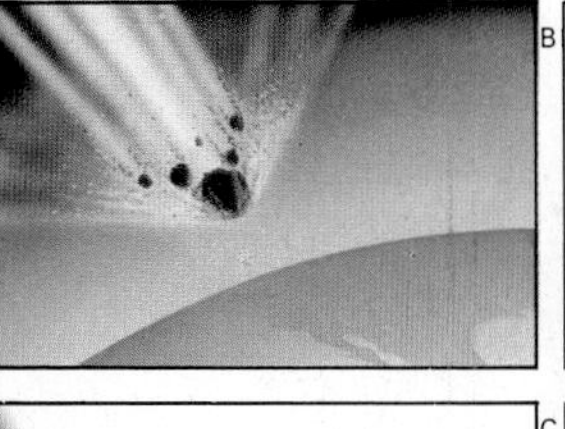

B

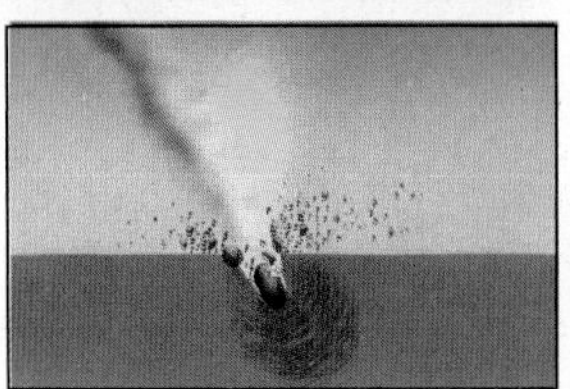

C

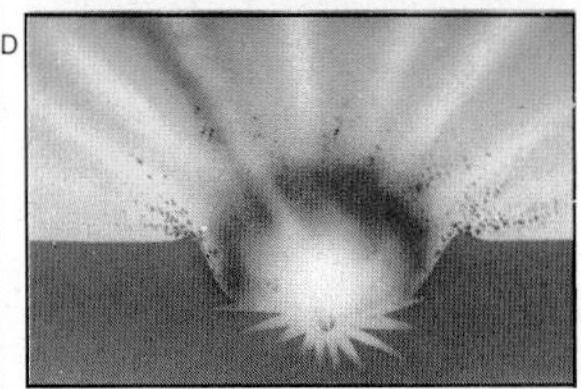

D
Wind direction

6 The Arizona meteorite crater was formed by several nickel-iron meteorites. Burning up as they plunged through the atmosphere [A], they shattered the Earth's outer layer of rock on impact [B]. Because of their high speed they burrowed, causing friction, heat, compression, and shock waves [C], culminating in a violent explosion [D] that left a crater. Areas of meteorite fragments [E] show those that were unaltered by heat [blue], small heat-affected fragments [yellow], heavy heat-altered boulders [black], and metallic spheroids formed by condensation [red].

7

7 The impact crater near Winslow, Arizona, is about 0.75 mile (1.2 km) in diameter. It may be over 10,000 years old. Many meteorite fragments have been found in the area of the crater.

8

8 The Hoba West meteorite, near Grootfontein in Namibia (South West Africa), is the largest known meteorite. It weighs over 66 tons and its weight before entering the Earth's atmosphere may have been 22 tons more. The meteorite still lies where it fell in prehistoric times. No crater was produced. A meteorite of this kind could be very destructive but fortunately major falls are extremely rare.

9

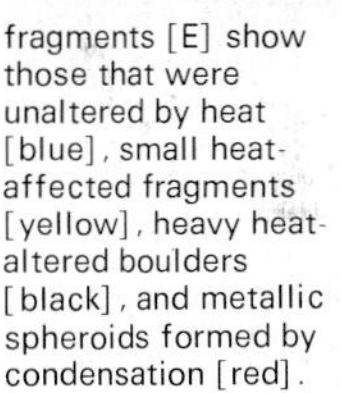

10

9 The Orgueil meteorite of 1864 contains organic compounds.

10 The Norton-Furnas aerolite of 1948 is the heaviest (1 ton) of its type of stony meteorite.

11

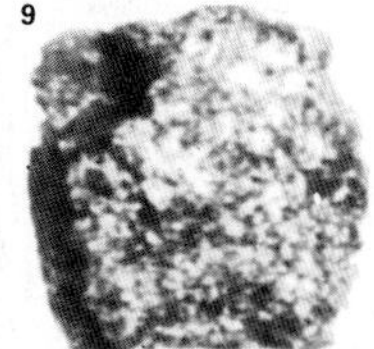

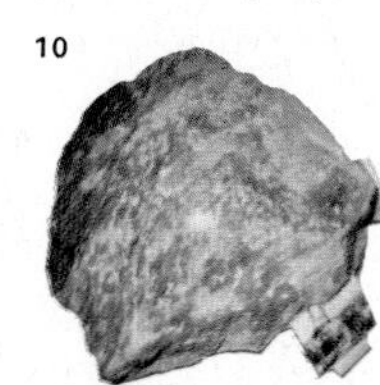

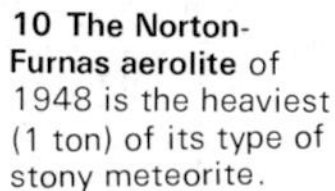

11 The most destructive fall of modern times was that of 1908 in the Tunguska region of Siberia. A meteorite came down in forested country, flattening pine trees for several miles.

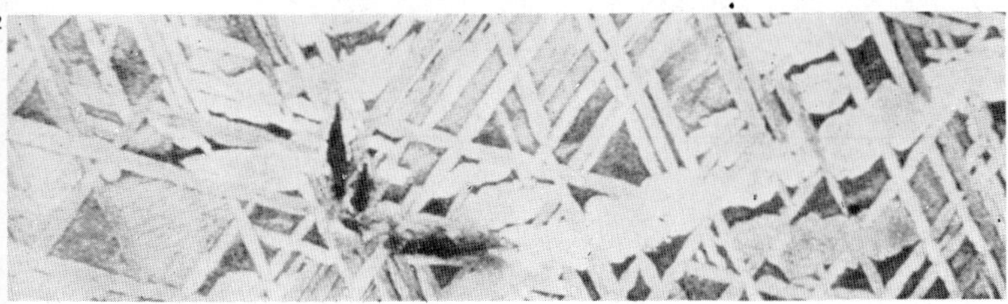

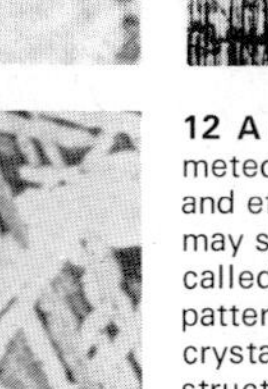

12 A siderite (iron meteorite), when cut and etched with acid, may show what are called Widmanstätten patterns, due to a crystalline metallic structure that requires unusual conditions for formation. Such crystals are unique to meteorites.

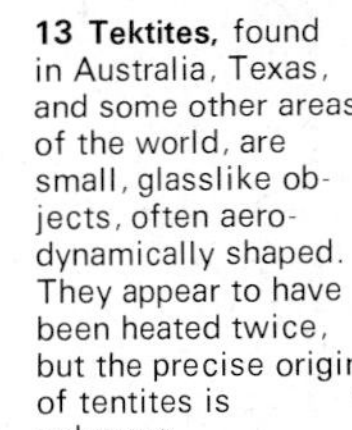

13 Tektites, found in Australia, Texas, and some other areas of the world, are small, glasslike objects, often aerodynamically shaped. They appear to have been heated twice, but the precise origin of tentites is unknown.

13

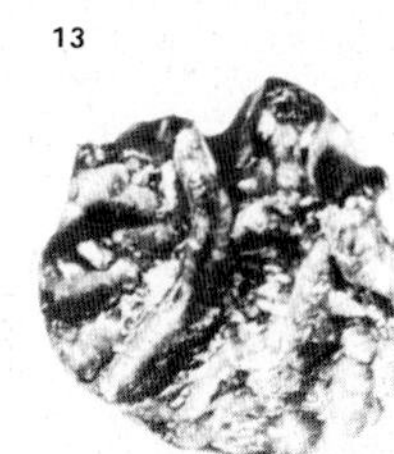

The Sun and the solar spectrum

The Sun is a star, one of 100 billion stars in our Galaxy. In the universe as a whole it is insignificant and is classed as a yellow dwarf star with a spectrum of type G, but in our planetary system—"the Solar System"—it is the all-important controlling body.

Immensely larger than the Earth, the Sun is made principally of hydrogen and helium and has a diameter of 864,950 miles (1,392,000km). Although it is big enough to contain more than a million bodies the volume of the Earth, its mass is only 4.39×10^{30} pounds (1.99×10^{30}kg)—that is, approximately 333,000 times that of the Earth. The reason it is not as massive as might be expected is that its density is lower than that of an Earth-type planet. The mean value for the specific gravity is 1.409 (that is, 1.409 times that of an equal volume of water) but it is not homogeneous and the density increases rapidly beneath the bright surface.

The Sun lies some 32,000 light-years from the center of our Galaxy and takes approximately 225,000,000 years to complete one journey around the galactic nucleus. It has an axial rotation period of 25.4 days at the equator, but the period is considerably longer near the solar poles, being about 35 days.

The photosphere

The bright outer surface of the Sun is known as the photosphere and has a temperature of 9,930°F (5,500°C). On it may be seen darker patches, which are known as sunspots [Key]. These are not truly black, but appear so by contrast. If a spot could be seen shining on its own its surface brilliancy would be greater than that of an arc-lamp.

To look at the Sun through any telescope or binoculars will almost certainly blind an observer permanently and dark filters are unreliable safeguards. The only sensible method is that of projection—using a telescope to throw the solar image onto a screen held or fastened behind the eyepiece. The Sun is not as generally smooth and featureless as might be thought; granules exist on it, each of which is about 1,000mi (1,500km) in diameter. Convection currents occur below the Sun's outer layer and the rising gas columns they generate cause the granules, whose dark edges show cooler gases dropping downward [7].

A typical large sunspot consists of a central dark umbra surrounded by a lighter area of penumbra, although the shapes are usually very irregular and spots tend to occur in groups—generally with two main spots, one "leader" and one "follower" [3]. Some groups may be immensely complex and of tremendous area, but they are not long-lived. Even a large group will generally persist for only a few months at most, while smaller spots may last for only a few hours. As the Sun rotates, the spots may be seen to be carried slowly across the disk from one side to the other. It takes about two weeks for a spot to make the full crossing.

Regular cycles

The 11-year cycle of solar activity has been fairly regular in recent centuries; thus there were maxima in 1957–58 and again in 1969–70 when groups were plentiful [4B]. At the intervening spot-minima the disk may be featureless for many consecutive days.

CONNECTIONS

See also
96 The Sun's atmosphere and radiation
98 Solar eclipses
100 Star types
50 Members of the Solar System

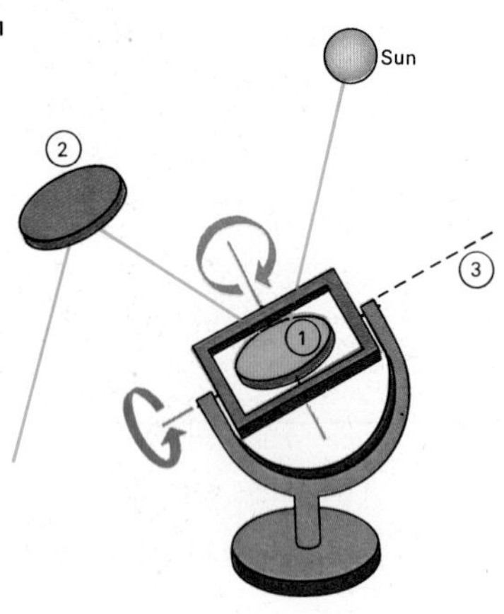

1
Sun
2
3
1

1 The coelostat, used to observe the Sun, overcomes the problem of maneuvering large telescope mounts by using a movable mirror [1] that rotates with the Sun while another is stationary [2]. One axis [3] of the rotating mirror points to the celestial pole and the other is adjustable.

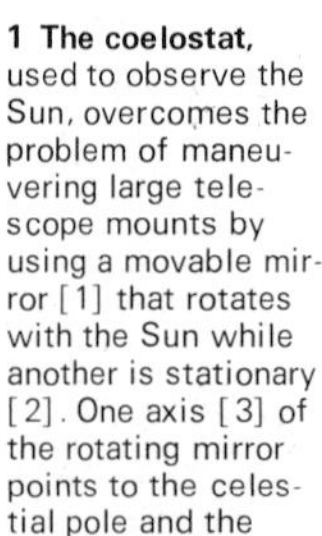

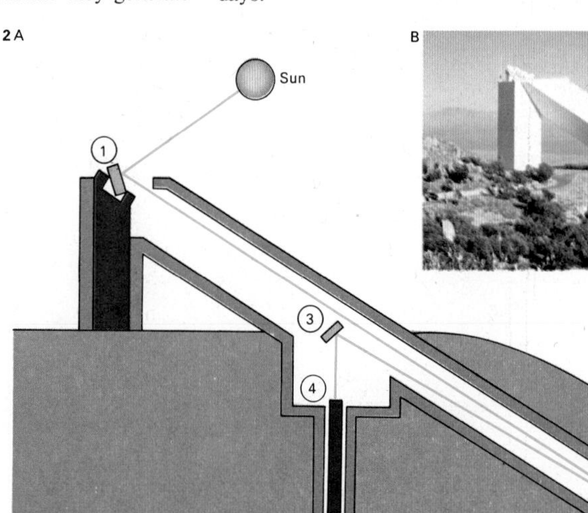

2A
Sun
1
3
4
2
B

2 The heliostat [A], an elaborate version of the coelostat, is installed in the 500-ft (152.4-m) telescope at Kitt Peak, Arizona [B], to track the Sun. Sunlight falls on a rotating mirror [1]. It reflects down a tube to a concave mirror [2], focuses on a plane mirror [3], and passes through a spectrograph [4] to be analyzed.

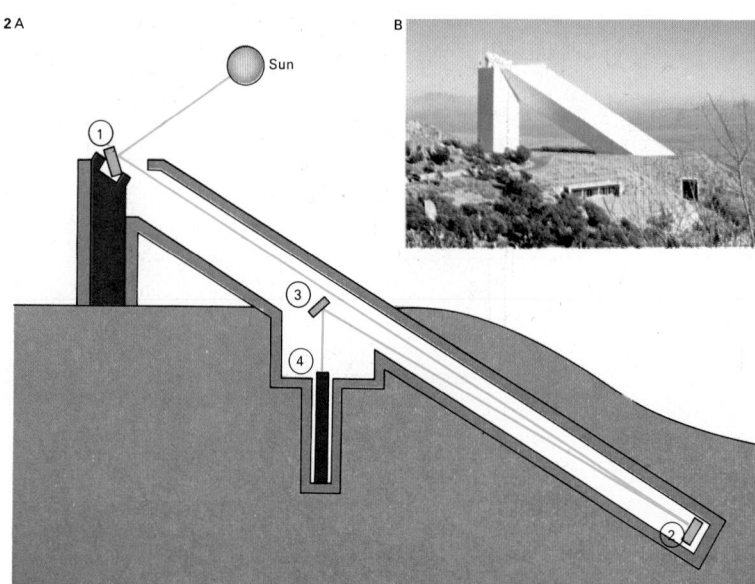

3 The sunspot observations of 1947 show that on February 11 [A] the identities of the leader and follower were still in doubt. But as the lines indicate the magnetic polarities were clear. From March 9 [B] to April 7 [C] the leader [1] and follower [2] are distinct. By May 5 [D] activity has ceased.

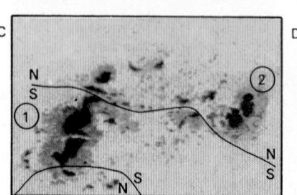

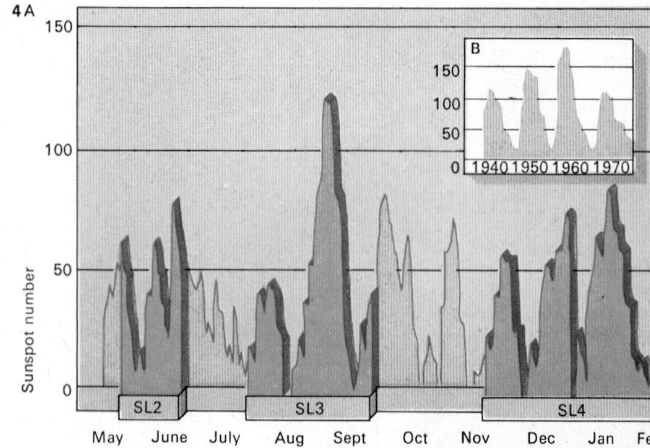

4A
150
100
50
0
Sunspot number
B
150
100
50
0
1940 1950 1960 1970
SL2
SL3
SL4
May June July Aug Sept Oct Nov Dec Jan Feb

4 Sunspot numbers fluctuated widely [A] during the Skylab mission between May 14, 1973, and February 8, 1974. The periods when the Skylab was manned (28, 59, and 84 days respectively for the three crews) are shown in orange on the large graph; [SL2, SL3, and SL4]. The inset graph [B] charts the sunspot cycle from 1935 to 1973. The 1969–70 maximum was much less intense than that of 1957–58.

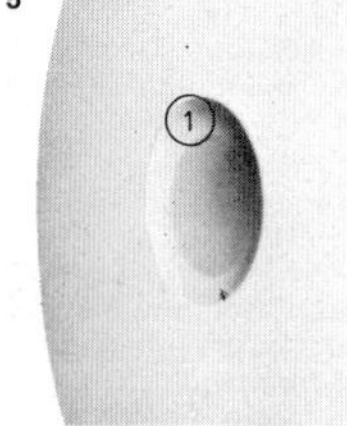

1

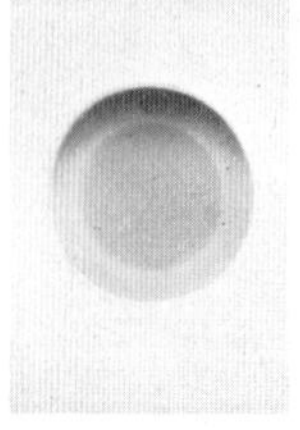

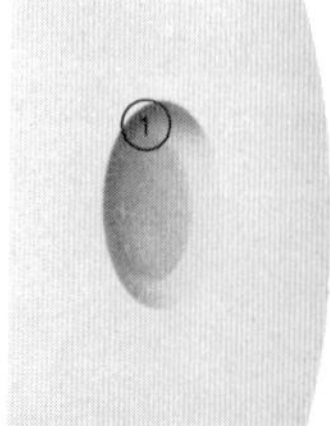

1

5 The penumbra of sunspots [1] near the Sun's rim (the limb) seems to narrow on the side nearest the center of the disk, indicating that the spots are depressions in the photosphere. This effect was first noted by A. Wilson in 1769.

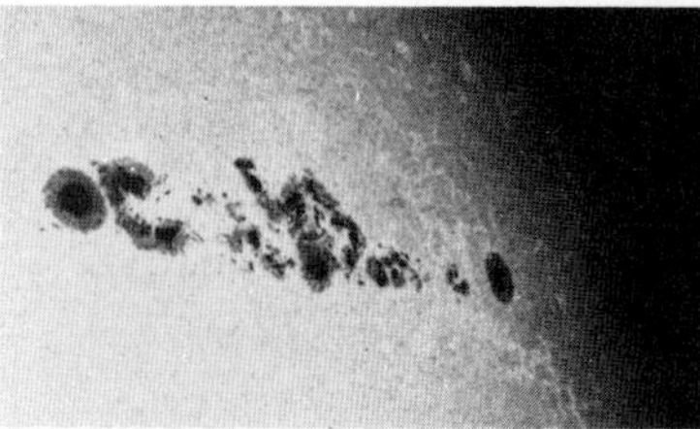

6 A sunspot near the limb illustrates the Wilson effect. A narrowing of the penumbra toward the center of the Sun's disk is clear. The bright streaks are called faculae and are usually associated with major sunspot groups.

Sunspots are associated with very strong magnetic fields and this has led to the modern theory of spot formation laid down by Harold Babcock (1882–1968) in 1962. The Sun has an overall magnetic field and it may be assumed that the lines of magnetic force run from one pole to the other below the bright surface. Owing to the difference in rotation period between the equatorial and the polar zones, the magnetic lines become distorted over an interval of some years and are "pulled out" along the equator, while the polar magnetic field is reinforced and becomes unstable. Eventually a loop of magnetic energy breaks through the surface producing two spots, one with north polarity and the other with south. Because of the magnetic linking, the polarities for the leading and following spots are opposite in the two hemispheres of the Sun. After about 11 years the "knots" in the lines break and the Sun reverts abruptly to its original state. But for the following cycle the polarities of spots are reversed.

Visual studies of the Sun's photosphere give us only limited information to draw on and most of our knowledge comes from instruments based on the principle of the spectroscope. According to the laws of spectroscopy as laid down by G. Kirchhoff (1824–87) in 1859, an incandescent solid, liquid, or high-pressure gas will produce a continuous, or rainbow, spectrum, while a low-pressure gas will yield an emission spectrum consisting of isolated bright lines.

New elements found

Gaseous elements in the Sun's atmosphere absorb light at specific frequencies from the continuous spectrum emitted by the photosphere, producing gaps or dark lines on the spectrum. These dark lines are called, in the case of the Sun, Fraunhofer lines. The elements present in the Sun's atmosphere can be identified from the positions (that is, the frequencies) and intensities of the lines on the spectrum.

In this way more than 60 elements have already been found in the Sun. One of them—helium—was even identified in the Sun before it was found on our own planet Earth.

KEY

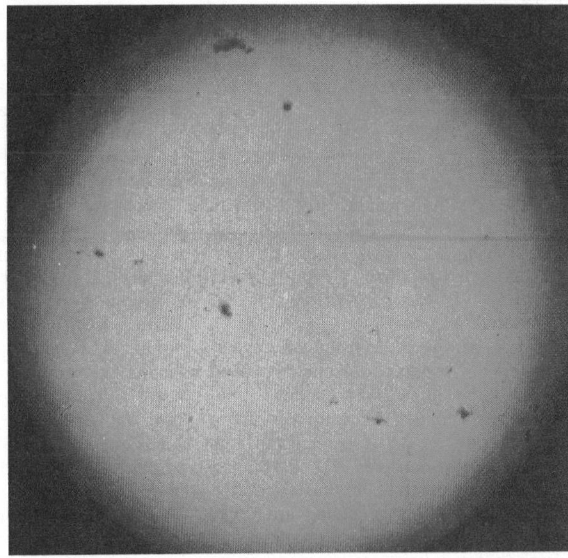

The solar maximum of 1958 was the most energetic ever recorded. The photograph shows a heavily spotted disk.

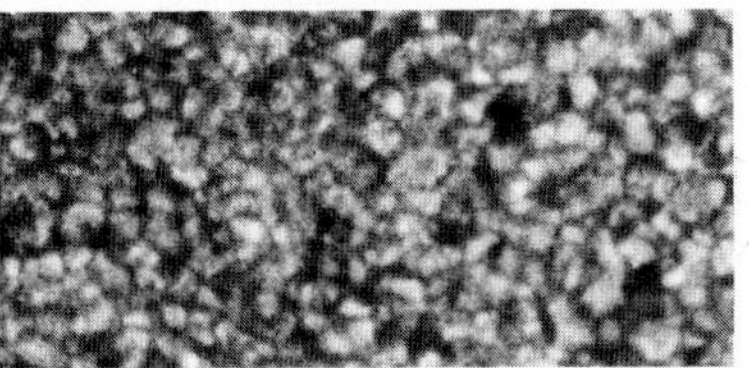

7 Solar granulation is due to convection effects. These gaseous columns occur all over the Sun's disk. Their diameter averages 1,000mi (1,500 km), but their size range is fairly wide.

8 Large and complex sunspot groups were still common when the Sun was well past the peak of its 1947 cycle of activity. This group was photographed at Mount Wilson on May 17, 1951.

8

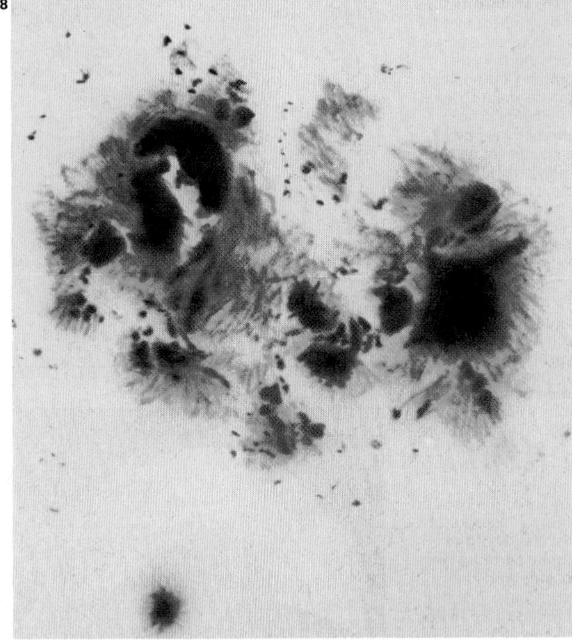

9

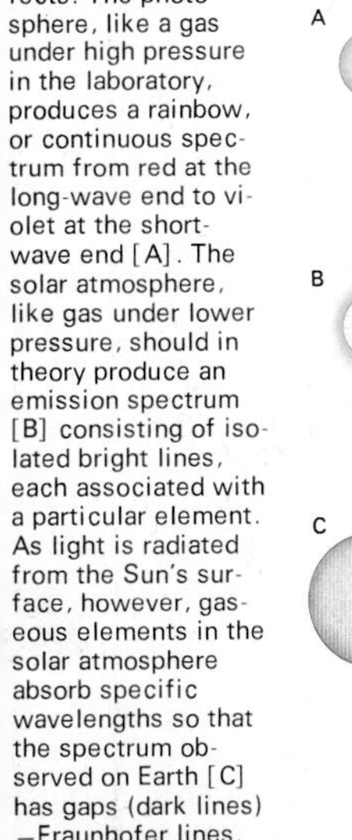

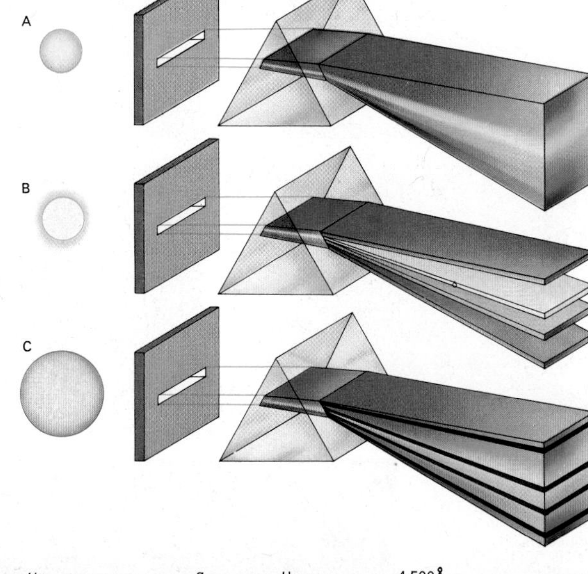
A
B
C

9 The solar spectrum combines two effects. The photosphere, like a gas under high pressure in the laboratory, produces a rainbow, or continuous spectrum from red at the long-wave end to violet at the short-wave end [A]. The solar atmosphere, like gas under lower pressure, should in theory produce an emission spectrum [B] consisting of isolated bright lines, each associated with a particular element. As light is radiated from the Sun's surface, however, gaseous elements in the solar atmosphere absorb specific wavelengths so that the spectrum observed on Earth [C] has gaps (dark lines) —Fraunhofer lines.

10 Lines in the solar spectrum can be accurately mapped with the 13-ft (4-m) spectrograph at the Mount Wilson observatory. The range illustrated is from 3,900 to 6,900 angströms, ie from violet through to red. (One angström equals one hundred millionth of a centimeter.) Each line can be identified; thus the D lines in the center of the spectrum are due to sodium, the H-Alpha line to hydrogen, and so on.

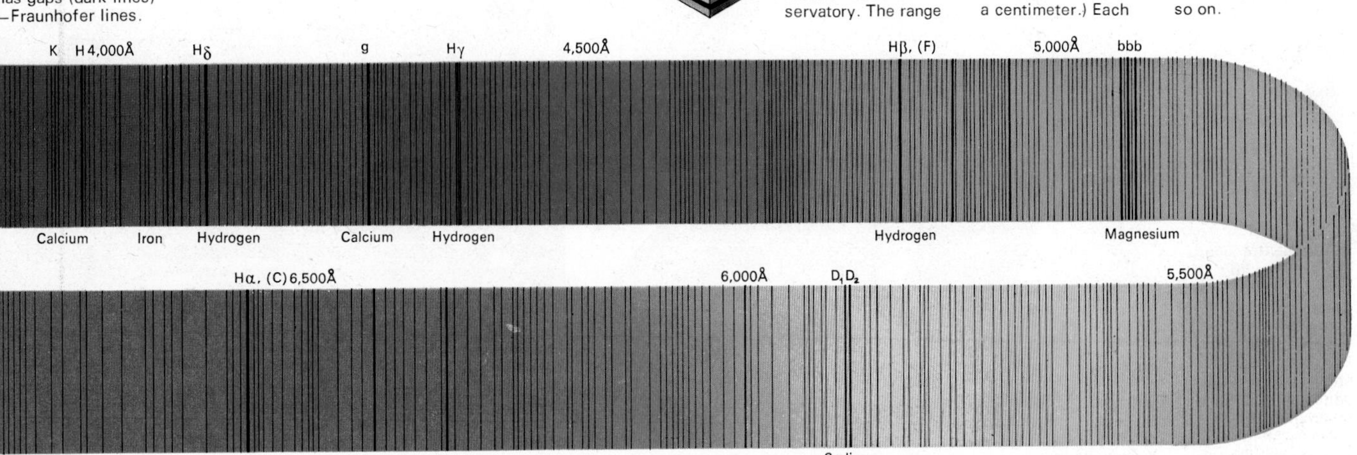
K H 4,000Å
Hδ
g
Hγ
4,500Å
Hβ, (F)
5,000Å
bbb
Calcium
Iron
Hydrogen
Calcium
Hydrogen
Hydrogen
Magnesium
Hα, (C) 6,500Å
6,000Å
D_1D_2
5,500Å
Hydrogen
Sodium

The Sun's atmosphere and radiation

Ordinary telescopes show only the bright surface, or photosphere, of the Sun and features such as the spots, the granulation, and the bright faculae (temporary patches on the Sun's surface) that lie above the photosphere itself. More complicated methods are needed to study the solar atmosphere because the Sun's surroundings can be seen with the naked eye (or with an ordinary telescope) only during the rare intervals when the Moon covers the Sun completely and produces a total eclipse.

Prominences and flares

The part of the solar atmosphere immediately above the photosphere is called the chromosphere ("color sphere") because it has a characteristically reddish appearance. This is also the region of the large and brilliant prominences. To observe the prominences, instruments based on the principle of the spectroscope are used. There are two main types of prominences, eruptive [2] and quiescent [Key]. Eruptive prominences are in violent motion and have been observed extending to more than 310,000 miles (500,000km) above the Sun's surface. Quiescent prominences are much more stable and may hang in the chromosphere for days before breaking up. Both are most common near the peak of the solar cycle of activity.

Prominences are often associated with major spot groups. Active groups also produce "flares," which are not usually visible, although a few have been seen. The flares are short-lived and emit streams of particles as well as short-wave radiation. These emissions have marked effects upon the Earth, producing magnetic storms or disturbances of the Earth's magnetic field affecting radio communications and compass needles. They also produce the beautiful polar lights, or aurorae [3, 4]. The Sun also sends out a constant stream of low-energy particles in all directions, making up what is now known as the solar wind. It is this emission that has a strong effect upon the tails of comets, forcing them to point away from the Sun.

In addition to sending out light, the Sun is an important source of infrared (heat) and ultraviolet radiation, as well as radio waves, X rays, and gamma rays. Studies are difficult to carry out from Earth because of the screening effect of the atmosphere, but knowledge has been greatly increased as a result of work carried out by satellites and by the Skylab astronauts in 1973–74. It was fortunate that the Sun was reasonably active [5, 6] while the astronauts were in orbit, since many of the results could not possibly have been duplicated in ground-based observations.

The powerhouse

Although astronomers cannot prove most of their theories about the nature of the Sun, they have a good idea of its composition. The temperature increases toward the core, until at the center it reaches about 18 million degrees F (10 million degrees C). Here, in what can be called the Sun's "powerhouse," the energy is being generated.

It is erroneous to suppose that the Sun is burning in the same way that a fire burns. A sun made up entirely of coal, and radiating as fiercely as the real Sun does, would not

CONNECTIONS

Read first
94 The Sun and the sola
spectrum

See also
98 Solar eclipses
100 Star types
50 Members of the Sola
System

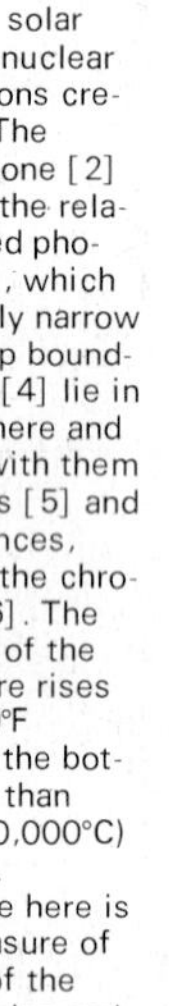
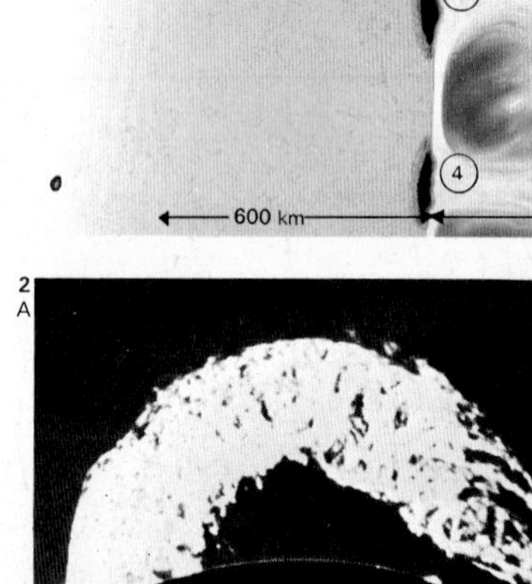
600 km
14,500 km

1 The main structure of the Sun cannot be drawn to an accurate scale. In the solar interior [1], nuclear transformations create energy. The convective zone [2] leads out to the relatively rarefied photosphere [3], which is surprisingly narrow and has sharp boundaries. Spots [4] lie in the photosphere and associated with them are the flares [5] and the prominences, which lie in the chromosphere [6]. The temperature of the chromosphere rises from 11,000°F (6,000°C) at the bottom to more than 90,000°F (50,000°C) near the top. (Temperature here is purely a measure of the speeds of the atomic particles and does not indicate extra "heat.") In the chromosphere there are spicules [7] – masses of high-temperature gases shooting up rapidly into the immensely rarefied corona [8]. The corona is large and streamers [9] issue from it.

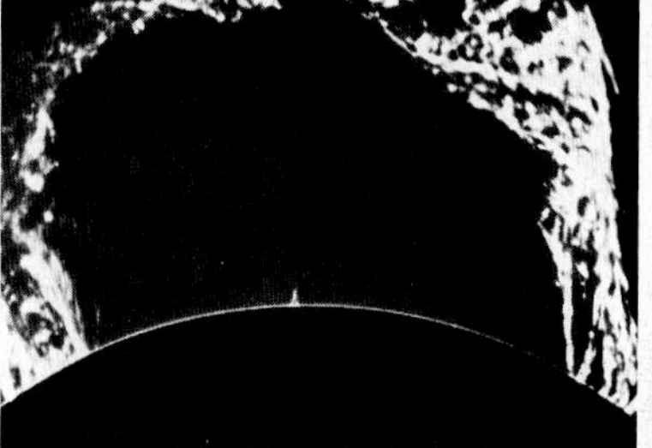
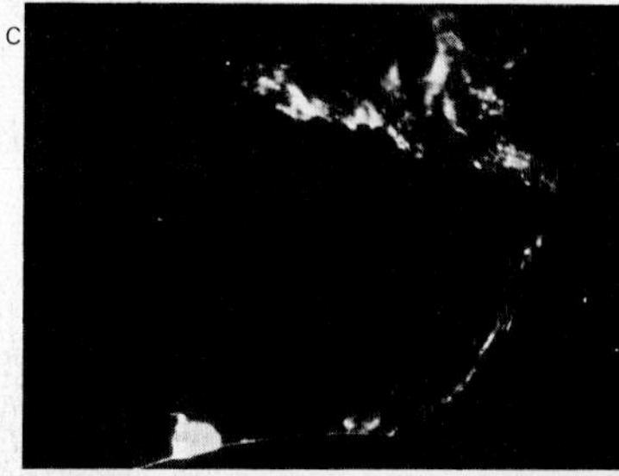

2 A large eruptive prominence occurred on June 4, 1946, at 16.03 hours [A]. It took the form of an arch. By 17.03 hours [B], it had been blown to 200,000 miles (322,000km) above the Sun's surface. Little remained of the great arch by 17.23 hours [C]; the prominence is shown dispersing.

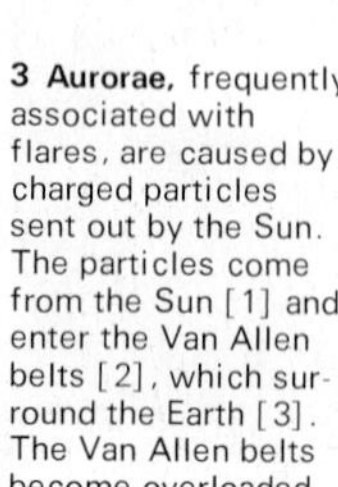
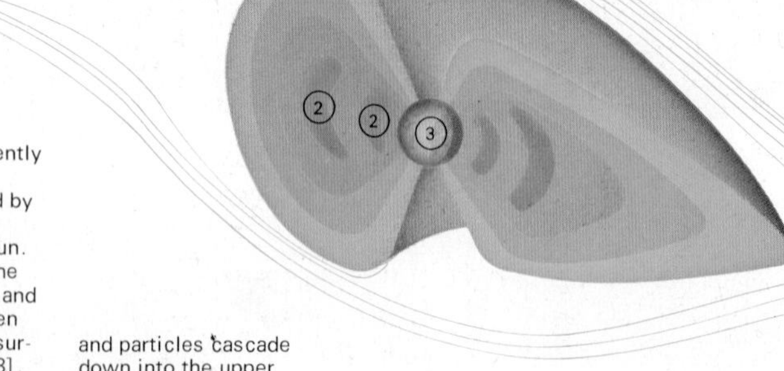

3 Aurorae, frequently associated with flares, are caused by charged particles sent out by the Sun. The particles come from the Sun [1] and enter the Van Allen belts [2], which surround the Earth [3]. The Van Allen belts become overloaded and particles cascade down into the upper air, producing the auroral glows.

4 Aurorae may take many forms, such as curtains, arches, and draperies, all with varied and lovely colors. They are aptly called "flaming surges." The electrified particles tend to spiral toward the Earth's magnetic poles, which is why aurorae are best seen from high latitudes; in low latitudes they are rare. Aurorae are most common when the Sun is active, near the maximum of its 11-year sunspot cycle.

last long on the cosmic scale and astronomers believe that the Sun is at least 5 billion years old. (It is certainly older than the Earth, which has an age of about 4.6 billion years.) The source of solar energy is to be found in nuclear transformations. Hydrogen is the main constituent and near the core, where the temperatures and pressures are so extreme, the second lightest element, helium, is formed from hydrogen nuclei by nuclear fusion. It takes four hydrogen nuclei to make one nucleus of helium; in the process a little mass is lost, being converted into a large amount of energy. The energy produced keeps the Sun radiating; the loss of mass amounts to four million tons per second. This is negligible compared with the total mass of the Sun; there is enough hydrogen available to keep the Sun shining in its present form for at least another 5 billion years, perhaps considerably longer.

Eventually the hydrogen will become exhausted and the Sun will change its structure drastically. According to present theory, it will pass through a red giant stage when it will have a luminosity at least 100 times as great as today; it will then collapse into a small dense star of the type known as a white dwarf. The Earth also has a limited life-span. It cannot survive the red giant stage; along with the other inner planets it will certainly be destroyed.

Solar research

Knowledge of the Sun has been drawn from many different areas of research. Radio astronomy is of special importance. This is a method of studying astronomy in the long-wavelength region of the electromagnetic spectrum. The Sun is a strong radio source, a fact known since the early days of radio astronomy. The study of X rays and gamma rays from the Sun is much more recent because it depends upon instruments operating above Earth's atmosphere.

There has been much discussion about the extent of the solar atmosphere. Beyond the chromosphere lies the corona, which is immensely rarefied and has no definite boundary. It merely thins out to become the solar wind. The Sun is a complicated and varied body, but it is probably a typical star.

KEY

The most spectacular of solar features are the streams of hot gas called prominences. Quiescent prominences may hang in the chromosphere for days or weeks, bulging out from the surface about 20,000 miles (32,000km). This example was photographed with a red filter on a 4-in (10-cm) refractor. Eruptive prominences, the other main type of prominence, are thin flames of gas often reaching heights of 310,000 miles (500,000km); they are formed more frequently in those areas containing sunspots. The invention of the coronagraph in 1930 enabled continuous photography of prominences, which were only seen before during a total eclipse.

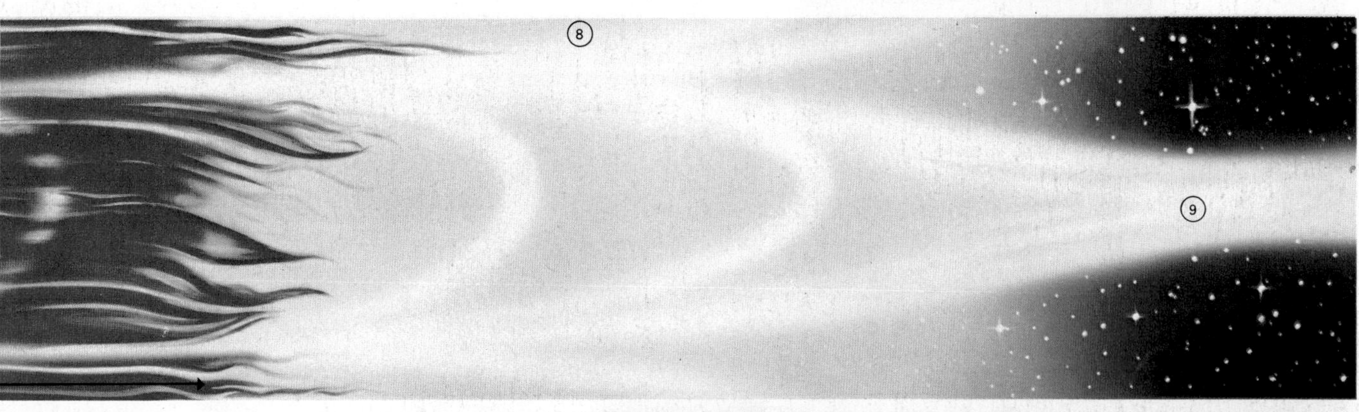
8
9

5 This solar prominence was photographed by the astronauts on board Skylab. The colors in this extreme ultraviolet shot are false. They represent the degree of radiation intensity from red, through yellow and blue, to purple and white where the activity is most intense. This picture could only be taken with equipment carried above the layers of the Earth's atmosphere.

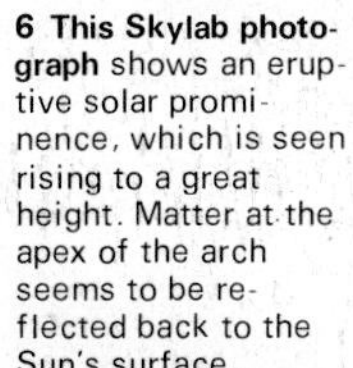

6 This Skylab photograph shows an eruptive solar prominence, which is seen rising to a great height. Matter at the apex of the arch seems to be reflected back to the Sun's surface.

5

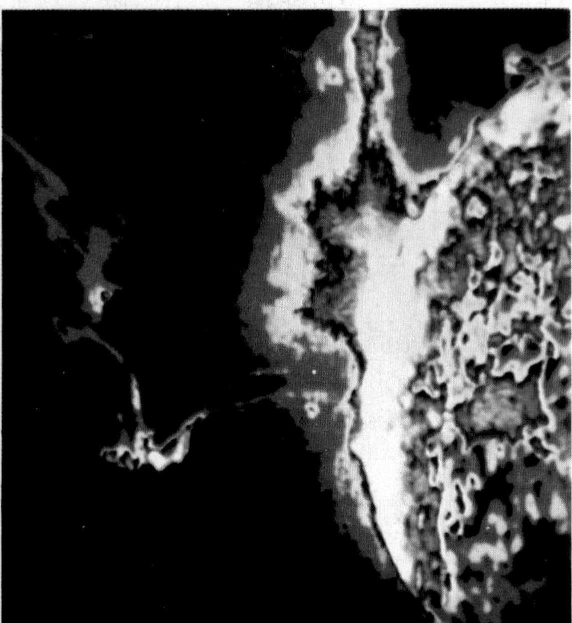

6

Solar eclipses

The Skylab missions in 1973 and 1974 considerably improved man's knowledge of the Sun because they made possible extended observations of features not visible from Earth's surface. Before these missions the best views of those features had been obtained during total eclipses.

The Moon is so much closer to the Earth than the Sun is that despite its small size it appears just as large in our sky. The coincidence is fortunate; it means that when the three bodies are exactly lined up, the Moon can just blot out the Sun's brilliant photosphere, leaving the chromosphere and the corona to shine out unhindered [1B]. The spectacle is always brief, however, because the Moon's shadow only just touches the Earth [1A]. The track of totality can never be more than 167 miles (269km) wide, and the maximum duration in any one spot is less than eight minutes.

Eclipse types

Because the Moon has an orbit that is not circular, its apparent size varies. At apogee (the point of greatest distance from the Earth), the full moon appears 10 percent smaller than the full moon at perigee (the point nearest the Earth). The apparent diameter of the Sun also changes, being greatest in December and least in June because of the Earth's varying distance from the Sun. If the Moon appears smaller than the Sun, it is unable to cover the photosphere completely and the result is an annular (ring-shaped) eclipse, leaving a ring of sunlight showing around the dark mass of the Moon [1D]. There are also partial eclipses [1C], when not all of the Sun is hidden. Annular and partial eclipses are relatively unimportant because the Sun's chromosphere and corona do not come into view.

Eclipse records date back many centuries; there are records of an eclipse seen from China as long ago as 2136 BC. Eclipses do not occur at every new Moon because the lunar orbit is appreciably inclined to that of the Earth [1F]. Any eclipse, however, may be followed by another similar eclipse (total or partial) 18 years 10.3 days (or 11.3 days with five leap years) later when the Sun, Moon, and Earth then return to almost the same relative positions. This period is known as the Saros (although there will be other eclipses in the intervening period). The Saros [Key] is not exact, but it is useful for predictions and the ancients made use of it. From about 600 BC eclipse records are reasonably complete.

Observing the corona

The glory of a total eclipse lies in the view of the corona [5, 6]. It has been found that the shape of the corona varies according to the state of the solar cycle. Near sunspot-minimum the corona is fairly symmetrical, whereas near sunspot-maximum there are long streamers. The sky is dark enough for planets and bright stars to be seen and on several occasions unexpected comets have been found close to the hidden Sun. Unfortunately, total eclipses are rare in any particular place on Earth. The next total eclipse over North America, on February 26, 1979, will cross northwestern United States and central Canada and scientists will again be able to easily observe the corona.

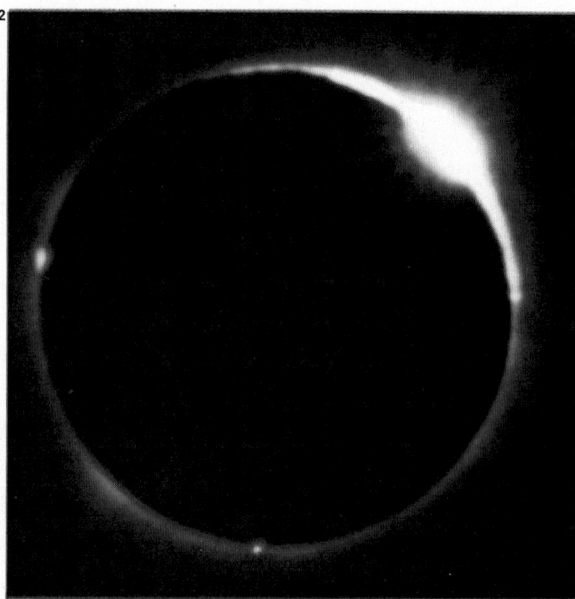

CONNECTIONS

See also
94 The Sun and the sola
spectrum
96 The Sun's atmosphe
and radiation
142 A history of space achievements
144 Stations in space
838 Myths of autumn

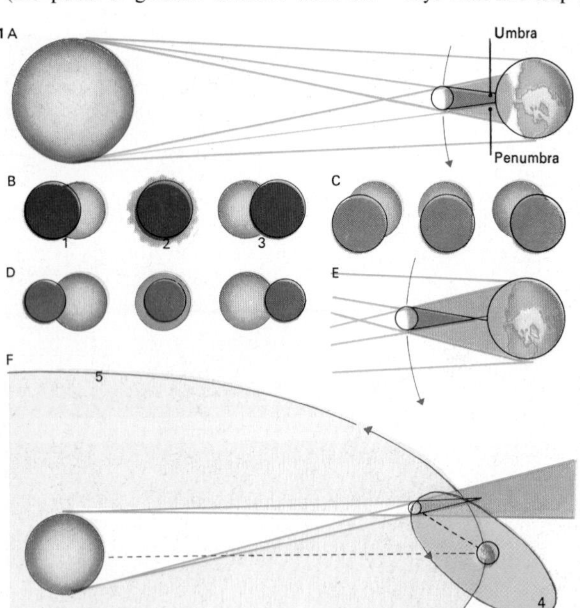
1A
Umbra
Penumbra
B
1
2
3
C
D
E
F
5
4

1 In a total eclipse [A] the main cone of shadow, or umbra, reaches the Earth's surface while to either side of it, in the partial shadow, or penumbra, a partial eclipse is seen. The Moon and Sun [B] approach totality [1], arrive at totality [2], and leave totality [3]. C shows a partial eclipse that is not total anywhere on Earth. An annular eclipse [D] occurs when the umbra stops short of the Earth [E]. F shows how the tilt of the Moon's orbit [4] to the plane of the Earth's orbit [5] prevents the conditions for an eclipse from occurring in every lunar month of the year.

2 As the Sun's disk reappears from behind the Moon after totality, there is a glorious "diamond ring" effect, as occurred in the total eclipse of Nov 12, 1966.

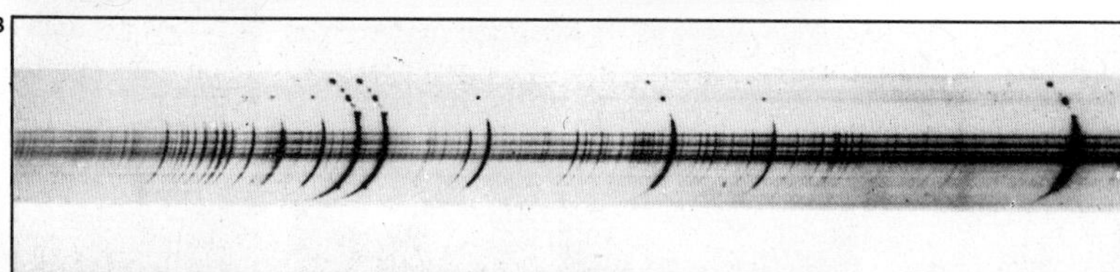

3 Just before totality begins, or just after it ends, at the moment of the "diamond ring" effect, the Sun's atmosphere is seen without the background photosphere. The dark absorption lines become suddenly bright emission lines, producing the "flash spectrum," a negative of which is shown here. The effect is brief, but it has been photographed many times, providing information about the solar atmosphere.

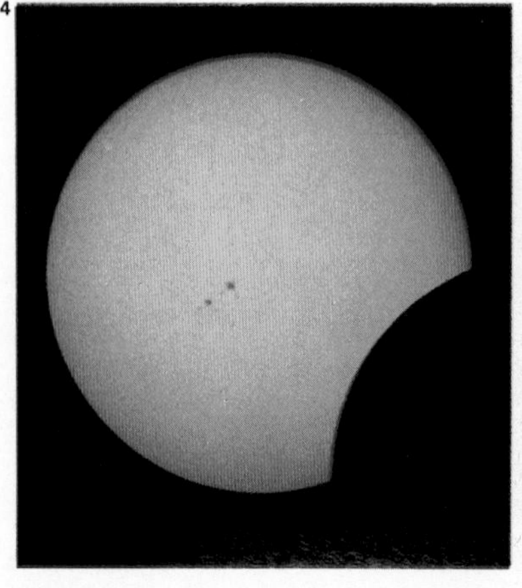

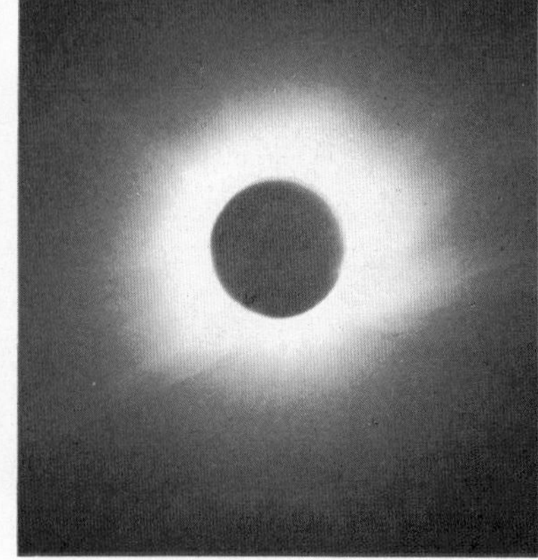

4 View of the Sun partly covered on Nov 12, 1966 reveals several sunspots.

5 Photographing an eclipse from an airplane has advantages—there are no clouds and the airplane can follow the Moon's shadow. Here the chromosphere and inner corona are clear.

6 The 1961 eclipse, taken with a long exposure, shows more of the outer corona. The inner corona and prominences are overexposed.

With the development of spectroscopy as a research method, it became possible to study the chromosphere and the prominences at any time. The corona, however, is a more difficult feature to investigate because even its inner part is much fainter than the chromosphere. The French astronomer Bernard Lyot (1897–1952) developed a device known as a coronagraph, which can be used from high-altitude observatories to observe the inner corona. From Earth, the outer part remains unobservable except during totality. Attempts to increase our knowledge of the Sun have been hampered by the fact that certain electromagnetic radiations, including x-rays, cannot penetrate to the surface of the Earth. In the past, various methods have been worked out to overcome the screening effects of the Earth's atmosphere. For instance, balloons have been used, although they cannot fly as high as astronomers would like. An effective solution to the problem was achieved when sophisticated equipment for studying solar radiation was taken up in Skylab in 1973 and used to good effect [7]. The corona was examined at all wavelengths, and it may be said that future total eclipses will be less important than those of the past. The first Skylab crew returned with film of the corona representing more hours of observations than had been acquired in the millennia of man's observations during natural eclipses.

Future studies of the Sun

Despite the newly acquired knowledge, many problems remain. A more complex coronal structure than was previously known has been revealed through Skylab ultraviolet experiments. X-ray pictures have also revealed low-density coronal regions, or coronal holes, which could be the source of disturbance in the solar wind.

Undoubtedly the future of the study of the Sun's outer surroundings lies in space-research methods. Skylab has shown the way and future orbiting stations, as well as equipment operated from the surface of the Moon, will tell man much more about his own particular star than he can claim to know at present.

KEY

The 12 solar eclipses whose tracks of totality are shown here [A] belong to the same Saros family. The eclipse of 1991 will be total over Central America, but the next one in the cycle will only be partial there – that is, the "returns" are not exact. The eclipse of March 7, 1970 [B] was total over Mexico and Florida and partial over most of North America. This made observation convenient.

A

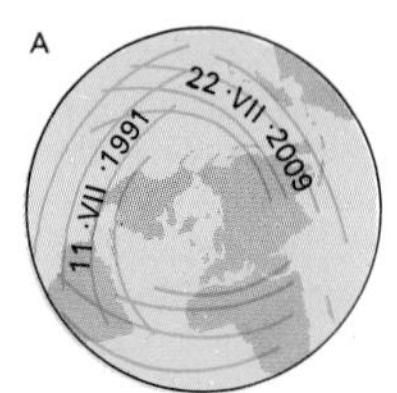
22·VII·2009
11·VII·1991

B

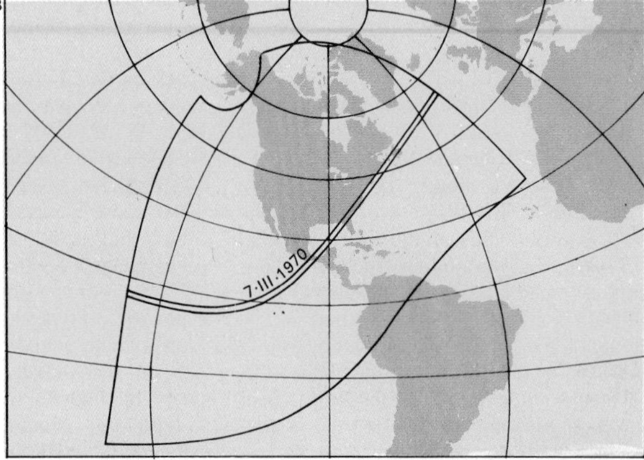
7·III·1970

7

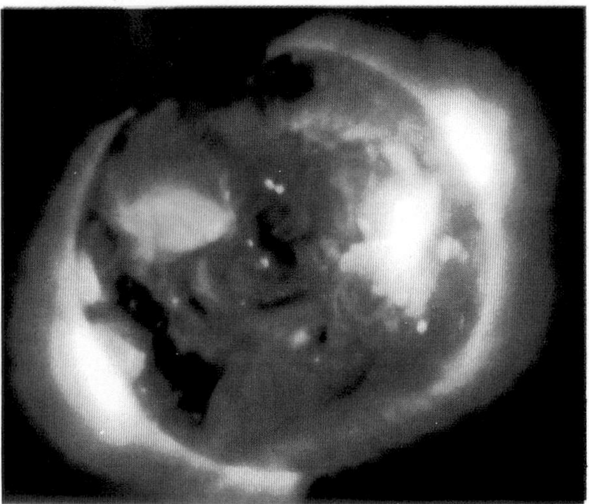

7 This X-ray image of the Sun's corona was taken by Skylab at the total eclipse of June 30, 1973. The Sun was near the minimum of its cycle of activity, and the corona was fairly symmetrical. The dark lane at the top is a "coronal hole."

8

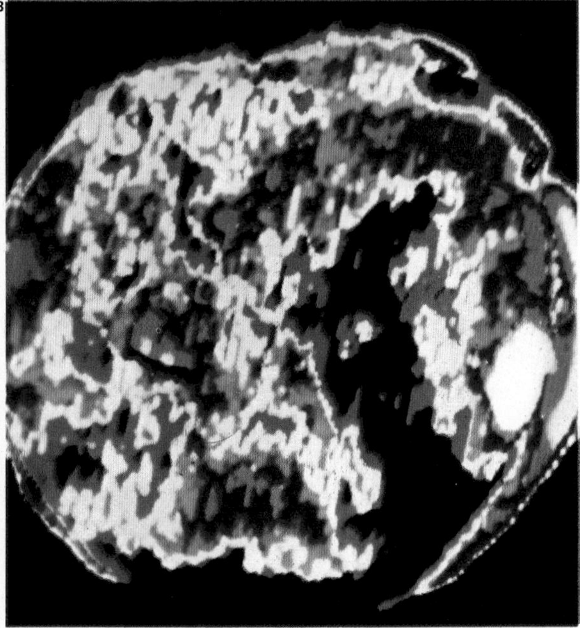

9

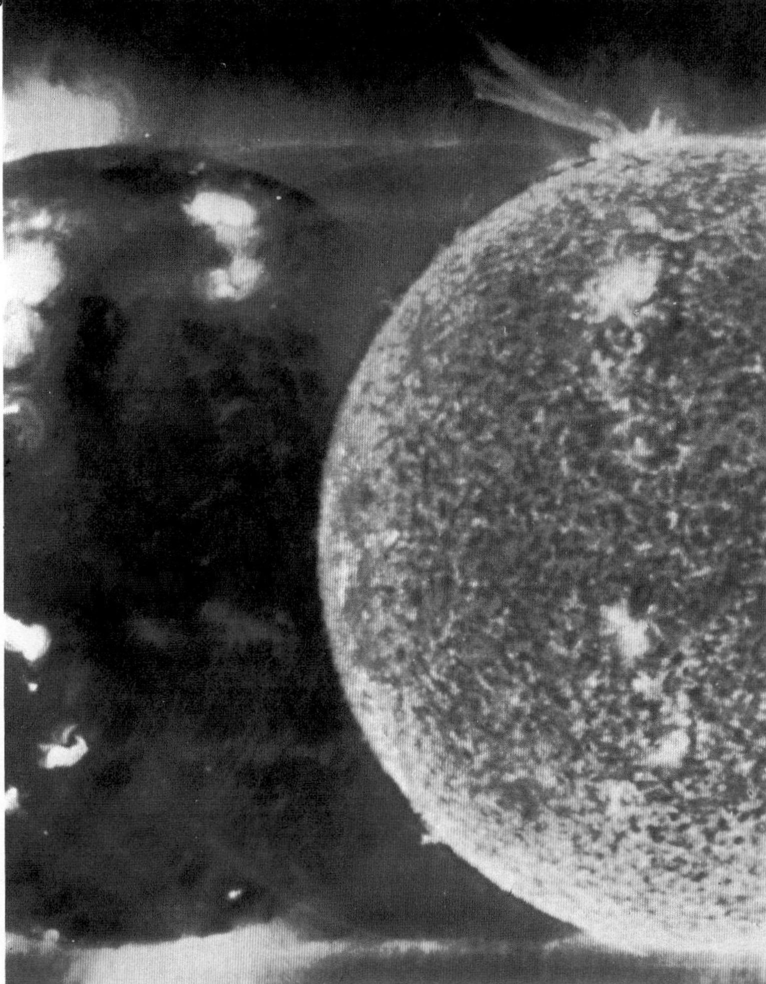

8 A large coronal hole is indicated by the dark stream in this extreme ultraviolet picture of the Sun taken from Skylab. It illustrates that the structure of the corona itself is far from being perfectly uniform and the shape varies.

9 One of the most impressive events recorded during the studies of the Sun carried out from Skylab is shown in this picture. Film taken on June 10, 1973 showed a huge "blob" of tenuous material. This appears around the prominence that produced it (top, right) and in an image with another filter (top, left). It was moving outward through the corona at a velocity approaching 250 miles (400km) per second. During the mission more than 40 similar events were studied. Although the sizes of the "blobs" were great, the actual amount of material involved was relatively slight because the material was so rarefied. It was the first time this type of solar phenomenon had been observed.

Star types

No star, apart from the Sun, is close enough to Earth to appear as anything but a point of light; studies of the Sun are therefore all-important in stellar astronomy. Moreover, the value of the telescope on its own is limited. Astrophysics mainly relies on instruments based on the principle of the spectroscope, which splits up light and gives information about the substances present in the light source.

Stellar spectra

The spectrum of the Sun was first studied by Isaac Newton (1642–1727) in 1666, but real progress was not made until the early nineteenth century, mainly by Joseph von Fraunhofer (1787–1826), who mapped the dark absorption lines in the solar spectrum, still often called Fraunhofer lines. The lines were correctly interpreted by Gustav Kirchhoff (1824–87) and Robert Bunsen (1811–99) in 1859. Stellar spectroscopy, however, is a much more difficult matter, because so little light is available and spectroscopic equipment must be used in conjunction with powerful telescopes.

Pioneer work, carried out largely by Angelo Secchi (1818–78) in Italy and William Huggins (1824–1910) in England, established that the stars may be divided into several reasonably well-defined spectral types. The system now adopted [3] is that drawn up at the Harvard College Observatory under the direction of Edward Pickering (1846–1919). The spectral types are assigned letters of the alphabet. In order of decreasing surface temperature the six main types are B,A,F,G,K, and M; the complete sequence includes five more groups of rarer type, W, O, R, N, and S, which denote somewhat different spectral characteristics. The sequence is alphabetically chaotic because there were several major revisions during the research period; types C and D, for instance, were found to be unnecessary.

The color of a star is a key to its spectral type. Stars of types O, B, and A are white or bluish-white; F and G, yellow; K, orange; and the rest orange-red. Subdivisions are given by figures; thus G0 is the hottest G-type star, G5 is midway in the sequence between G and K, and G9 is only slightly hotter than K0 (the spectral class of the Sun is G2). Stars at the beginning of the sequence are conventionally referred to as "early" type stars and those near the end (types K, M, R, N, and S) as "late" type, although the Harvard sequence is no longer thought to be truly evolutionary. The situation is far more complicated than once thought.

The Hertzsprung-Russell classification

In 1908 the Danish astronomer Ejnar Hertzsprung (1873–1967) drew up a diagram in which he plotted the stars according to their luminosities and their spectral types. Research of similar kind was being carried out in the United States by Henry Russell (1877–1957) and the diagrams produced are now known as Hertzsprung-Russell, or H–R, diagrams [6]. They have proved to be immensely informative. A casual glance at an H–R diagram shows that the stars are not randomly distributed all over it, although the H–R diagram does not, as was once supposed, mark a strict evolutionary sequence. Most of the stars lie in a well-defined belt extending from the upper left to the

CONNECTIONS

See also
102 Stellar evolution
94 The Sun and the solar spectrum
104 Galactic nebulae
106 Nebulae and Pulsars
108 Pulsars and black holes

1

1 If a camera is pointed at the night sky and a time exposure made without the camera being moved, stars will appear as trails because of the rotation of the Earth. The longer the exposure, the longer the trail. By making long exposures, such as the one illustrated, the different colors of the stars are more easily resolved. The hotter stars will be blue or white, cooler stars yellow and still cooler stars red.

2

2 The famous constellation Crux (the Southern Cross) was photographed from Rhodesia. The camera was attached to a driven telescope, so that the stars are shown as hard points and not as trails. Of the four main stars of the Cross, three are hot and white, but the fourth—Gamma Crucis—is a red giant and its color is clearly shown here. The colors can be seen well through binoculars.

3

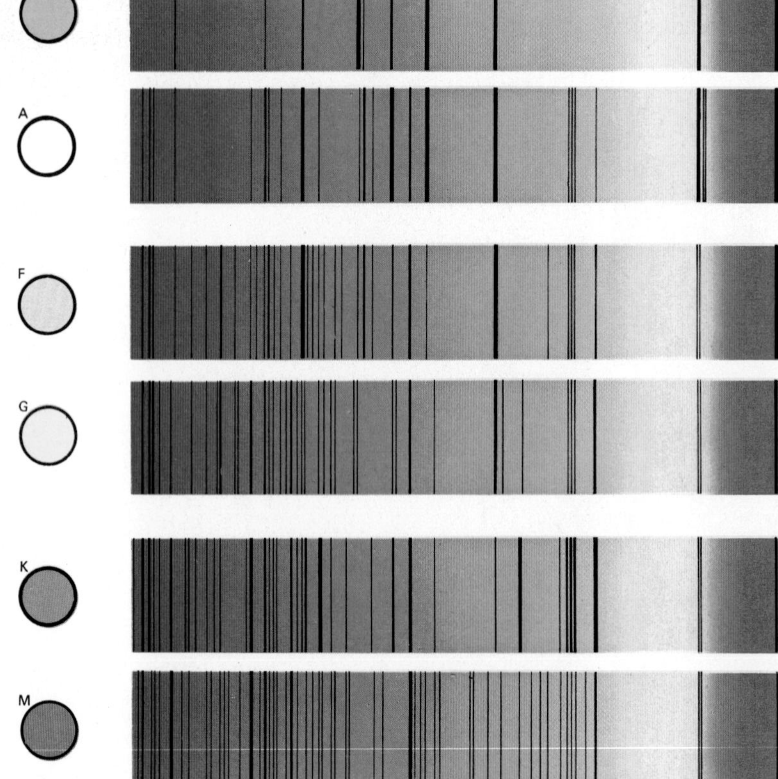

B
A
F
G
K
M

3 The Harvard classification of spectral type is illustrated for the six principal classes of stars: B, A, F, G, K, and M. The spectrum for each is shown with the color symbol that is repeated on the diagram [opposite]. An example of a star in each class is given. B-type stars (Rigel): helium lines are prominent; 25,000°C surface temperature. A-type stars (Sirius): hydrogen lines are prominent, 10,000°C surface temperature. F-type stars (Polaris): calcium lines are prominent, 7,500°C. Giant and dwarf division is appearing. G-type stars (the Sun): 5,700°C (giants) and 6,400°C (dwarfs) surface temperatures. The giant and dwarf division is very clear. K-type stars (Arcturus): 4,100°C (giants) and 5,100°C (dwarfs). M-type stars (Betelgeuse): 3,100°C (giants) and 3,500°C (dwarfs) surface temperatures; many are variable and advanced in evolution.

4

4 Magnesium lines in the green region of the Sun's spectrum were photographed by H. R. Hatfield with his spectrohelioscope. These magnesium lines lie at a wave-length of 5,170 Ångstroms.

5

5 The double D line of sodium, also in the solar spectrum, was photographed by H. R. Hatfield. These are among the most prominent of all spectral lines and are well shown in many stellar spectra.

lower right; this belt has become known as the main sequence; the Sun is a typical main sequence star.

It is also obvious that with the red and orange stars, and to a lesser extent with the yellow—that is, from types G to the end of the sequence—there is a sharp division into giants and dwarfs. Consider, for instance, two stars of type M: Betelgeuse in Orion and our nearest stellar neighbor, Proxima Centauri. The surface temperatures are much the same, but this is the only point of similarity. Betelgeuse has a variable diameter of 260–350 million miles (420–560 million km)—large enough to hold the entire orbit of the Earth—and a luminosity more than 10,000 times that of the Sun. The diameter of Proxima is about 620,000 miles (1 million km) and it has only one ten-thousandth of the Sun's luminosity [Key]. M-type stars with luminosities about the same as that of the Sun do not exist, as the H–R diagram shows. The discrepancy between giant and dwarf is less with "earlier" spectral types and beyond type F it is more difficult to distinguish. (The white dwarfs, located in the lower left of the H–R diagram, fall into an entirely different category.)

The rarer classifications

Most of the stars lie in that part of the Harvard sequence from B to M. Stars of type W have high surface temperatures, of the order of 80,000°C, and their spectra show bright emission lines, produced in the star's gaseous atmosphere. W-stars, also known as Wolf-Rayet stars, are rare; about 150 are known in our Galaxy and another 50 in the Large Magellanic Cloud. Allied to them are the O-type stars, with lower surface temperatures (about 35,000°C) and both bright and dark spectral lines. Zeta Orionis, or Alnitak, for example, in Orion's belt, is of type O9.

At the other end of the sequence are stars of types R, N, and S. All of them are remote, so that they appear faint, and almost all are variable. They are often called carbon stars because lines due to molecules containing carbon are prominent in their spectra. The reddest are of type S.

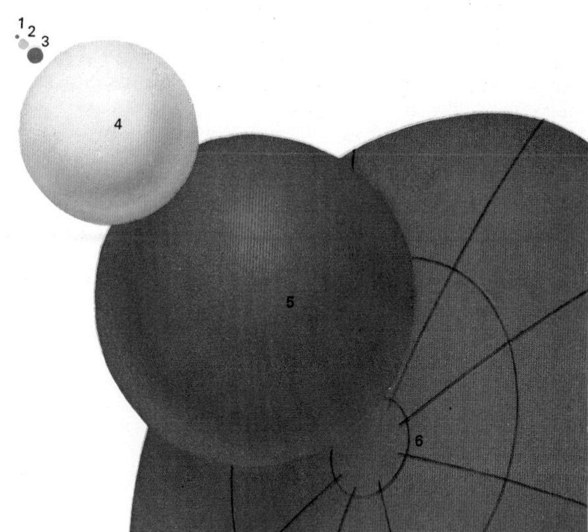

KEY
1
2
3
4
5
6

Stars vary in size, temperature, and luminosity. Wolf 359 [1] is a faint red dwarf and Epsilon Eridani [2] is smaller and cooler than the Sun [3], while Rigel [4] is 50,000 times brighter. Aldebaran [5] and Antares [6] are red giants.

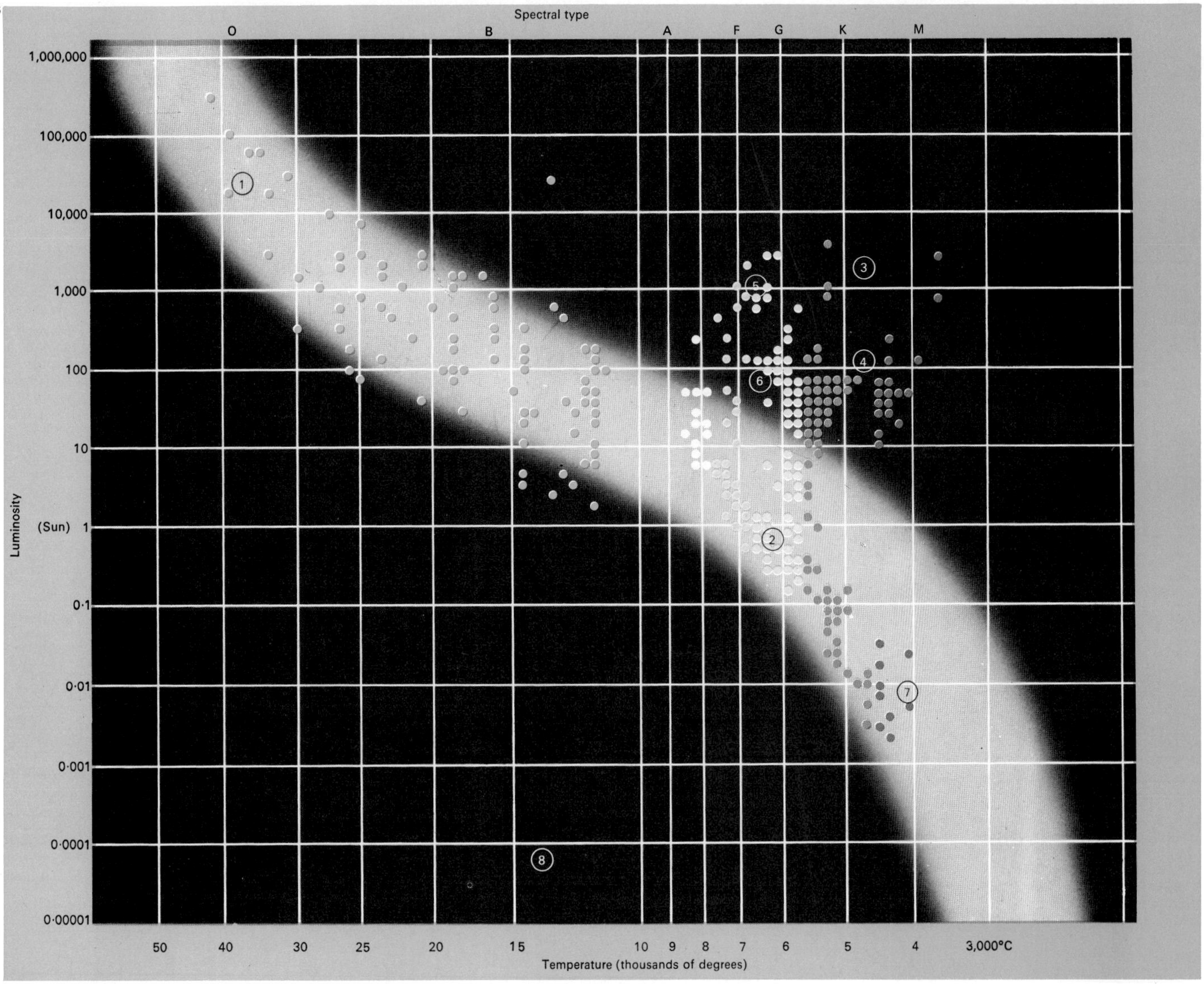

6 The Hertzsprung-Russell, or H-R, diagram is of fundamental importance. The stars are plotted on the graph according to their luminosities relative to that of the Sun, their spectral types, and their surface temperatures. Most of the stars lie along the well-defined belt known as the main sequence. The main sequence extends from the upper left, with very hot O-type stars [1], through G-type stars [2] such as the Sun, and the red dwarfs of type M [7] of low luminosity. To the upper right lie the red supergiants [3] and the giant branch [4]. Also shown are the Cepheid variables [5] and the RR Lyrae variables [6]. To the lower left of the diagram are the white dwarfs [8]. Stars of types K and M are divided into giant and dwarf groups which can be clearly seen. The H-R was first drawn up in 1908.

Stellar evolution

In the early years of the twentieth century, many astronomers assumed that stars evolved strictly along the course plotted on a Hertzsprung-Russell diagram [Key], starting as very luminous white stars and ending as dim red ones. According to this theory, a star would begin by condensing out of interstellar dust and gas. Gravitational forces would shrink it so that the interior would heat up. The star would start shining as a large, diffuse red giant of type M1. It would continue to contract and heat up until it joined the top of the main sequence, moving down the main sequence until it became a faint M-type red dwarf. Finally it would turn into a cold, dead globe.

Evolution of a star of solar mass

That plausible sequence of stellar evolution is now known to be completely wrong. A red giant such as Betelgeuse is not young. It is very old, has used up most of its energy reserves, and is in an advanced stage of evolution. The stars are now known to shine because of nuclear reactions taking place inside them and the course of stellar evolution is known to depend largely upon the initial mass of a star when it is formed from the nebular material—a massive star evolves very differently from a star of much lesser mass. The only common factor is that all stars begin their careers in gaseous nebulae, of which the Orion Nebula M42 is the best-known example.

As an embryo star shrinks it heats up, but if the mass is extremely low no nuclear reactions are able to start and the star never joins the main sequence. Instead it radiates feebly until its energy has been dissipated. In the case of a star with a mass about that of the Sun [3] a stage is reached as the gravitational shrinkage continues, when heat is carried from the interior to the surface by convection. In a very short time (perhaps only a century or so) the star becomes from 100 to 1,000 times as luminous as the Sun is today. After this initial burst of glory it continues to shrink and also becomes fainter—it is approaching the main sequence. Then, when the core temperature has risen sufficiently, nuclear reactions begin. Hydrogen nuclei combine to form helium nuclei, resulting in a loss of mass and the release of energy, and the star settles down on the main sequence to a long period of stable existence, lasting perhaps as long as 10 billion years. The Sun, which may be about 5 billion years old, is thus halfway along its main sequence career.

Eventually the supply of available hydrogen fuel begins to run low and the star has to rearrange itself. The helium core contracts rapidly and is heated up once more, enabling hydrogen nuclei to "burn" in a shell surrounding the core, while the outer layers expand and cool. The star swells to become a red giant. The central temperature rises to about 180 million degrees F (100 million degrees C), although the outer layers are cool and extremely rarefied.

White and black dwarfs

Further types of reactions follow, but at last there is no nuclear energy left and the star collapses into a very small, dense white dwarf. Because the component atoms are crushed and broken they can be tightly packed, and the star's density may reach

CONNECTIONS

Read first
100 Star types

See also
104 Galactic nebulae
106 Nebulae and pulsars
108 Pulsars and black holes

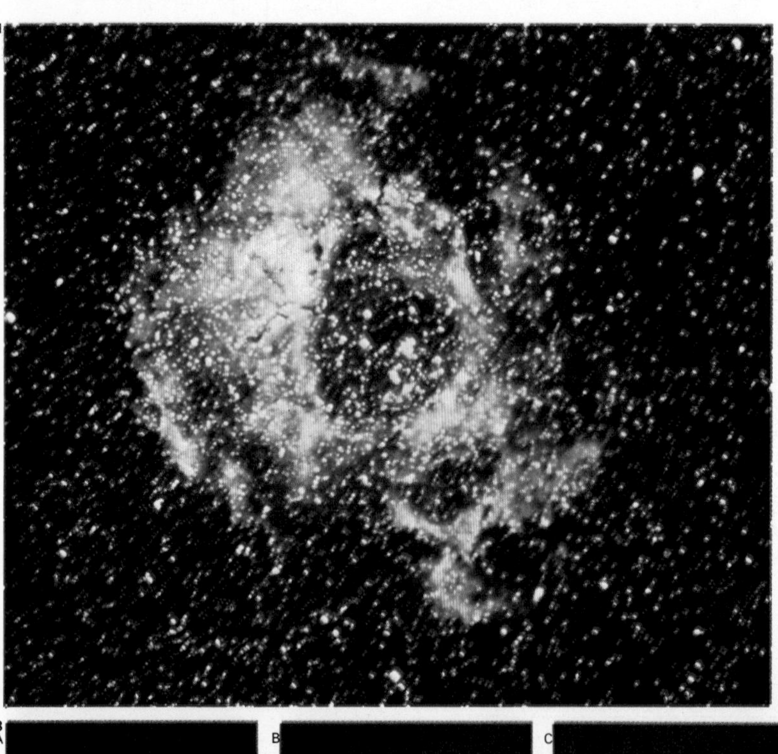

1 The Rosette Nebula, NGC 2237, is shown here in a photograph taken with the 48-in (122-cm) Schmidt telescope at Palomar, Calif. The nebula lies in the constellation of Monoceros but is not a bright object. It is a typical emission nebula; the brightest star in it has a spectral type of O9. There is no doubt that the nebula represents a region where fresh stars are being formed. Although the gas is prominent, it is extremely rarefied and the formation of new stars within the region is by no means rapid.

2 Stars are of many types, some of them far more luminous than the Sun. Rigel [A], type B8, for example, a massive luminous star at the upper left of the main sequence, is 49,000 times as powerful as the Sun; the supergiant Antares [B], of type M, in the giant branch, has a diameter of about 260 million miles (420 million km) and its luminosity is 3,400 times that of the Sun. Aldebaran [C], type K, 90 times more luminous than the Sun, is a less extreme red giant, diameter 40 million miles (67 million km).

3 The evolution of a solar-type star is shown in this series of graphs. The star contracts out of the interstellar material [A]. It then joins the main sequence [B]. After perhaps 10 billion years it leaves the main sequence and moves into the giant branch [C], increasing in luminosity to 1,500 times that of the Sun and expanding in diameter to 50 times that of the Sun. It then becomes unstable and ejects matter [D]. The star collapses into a white dwarf [E]. The red line follows the star's evolutionary track.

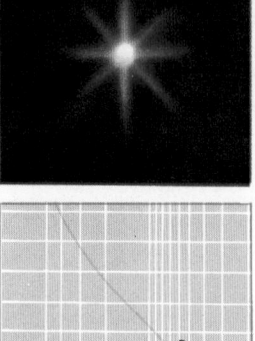

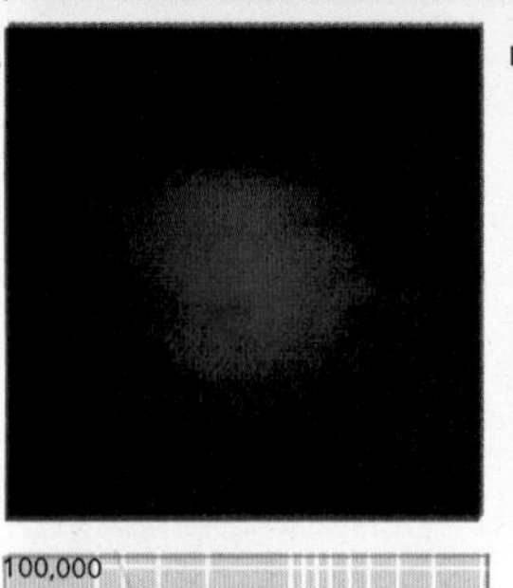

A
100,000
10,000
1,000
100
10
1
0·1
0·01
°C 50,000 20 10 5 4 3 2

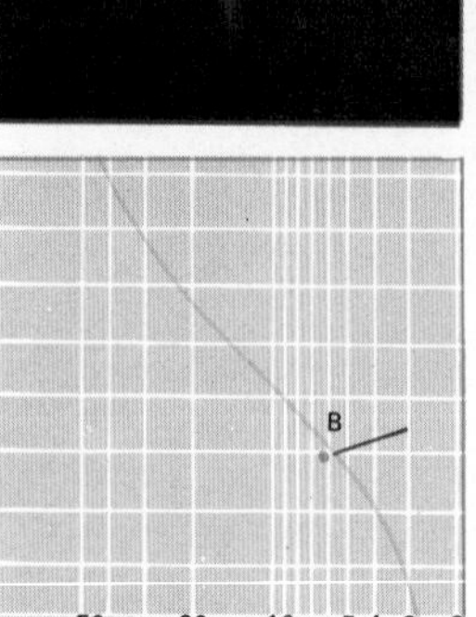

B
50 20 10 5 4 3 2

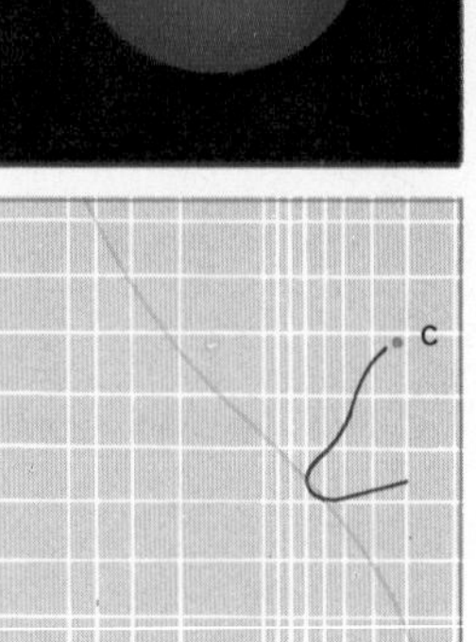

C
50 20 10 5 4 3 2

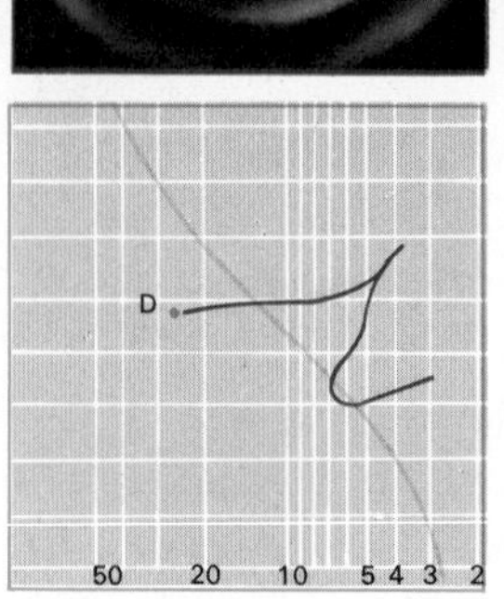

D
50 20 10 5 4 3 2

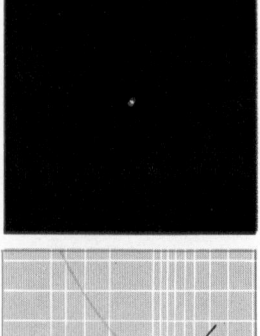

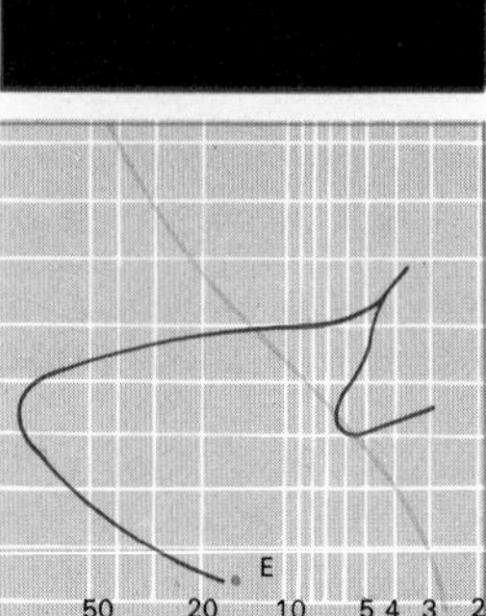

E
50 20 10 5 4 3 2

more than 100,000 times that of water. After another long period all light and heat leave the star and it becomes a dead black dwarf.

There is no positive information about black dwarfs, which send out no detectable radiation, and one can only guess about their numbers. White dwarfs, however, are known to be common. The first to be identified (by Walter Adams [1876–1956] in 1916) was the companion of Sirius, which had been discovered by Alvan Clark (1832–97) more than half a century earlier, but had always been assumed to be cool and red. The surface temperature of the companion is greater than that of the Sun, but its diameter is only three times that of the Earth, so that an immense amount of matter—almost as much as is contained in the Sun—is packed into a relatively small globe. Other white dwarfs since found are even more dense.

Evolution of a massive star

A star with a mass much greater than the Sun's [6] evolves more rapidly. The very luminous S Doradus in the Large Magellanic Cloud, for example, cannot go on pouring forth energy at its present rate for much longer than a million years, whereas the Sun will not leave the main sequence for at least another 5 billion years; stars of lower mass change even more slowly. Very massive stars do not merely collapse into white dwarfs. When the core temperature has reached about 9 billion degrees F (5 billion degrees C) there is a catastrophic change in structure; the core collapses and the outer layers of the star, in which nuclear reactions are still going on, are abruptly heated to about 540 million degrees F (300 million degrees C). The result is a supernova outburst in which the star emits as much energy in a few seconds as the Sun does in millions of years. Material is ejected and when the convulsions are over all that remains is a cloud of expanding gas together with a neutron star or pulsar, even smaller and denser than a white dwarf. The Crab Nebula is a supernova remnant; the outburst was seen in China in 1054. The Rosette [1] represents a stellar birthplace while the Crab [4] shows the death of a star.

KEY

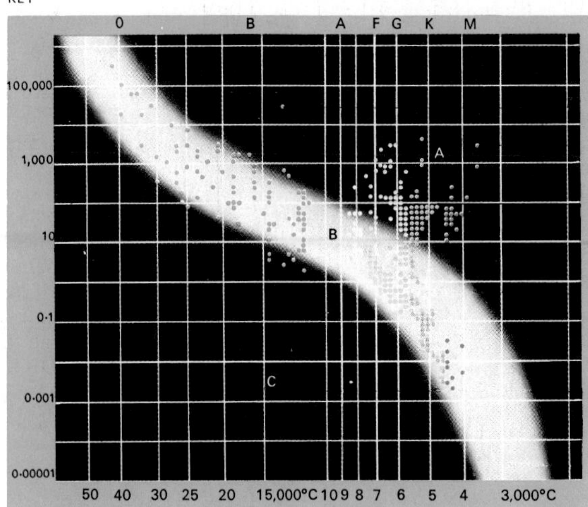
0
B
A
F
G
K
M
100,000
1,000
10
0·1
0·001
0·00001
A
B
C
50 40 30 25 20 15,000°C 10 9 8 7 6 5 4 3,000°C

This Hertzsprung-Russell diagram in simplified form shows the main classes into which stars are grouped during their evolution. Typical stars in the giant class [A] have evolved out of the main sequence [B]. At the lower left [C] are white dwarfs. Luminosity is measured vertically on the diagram and spectral type across the top.

4

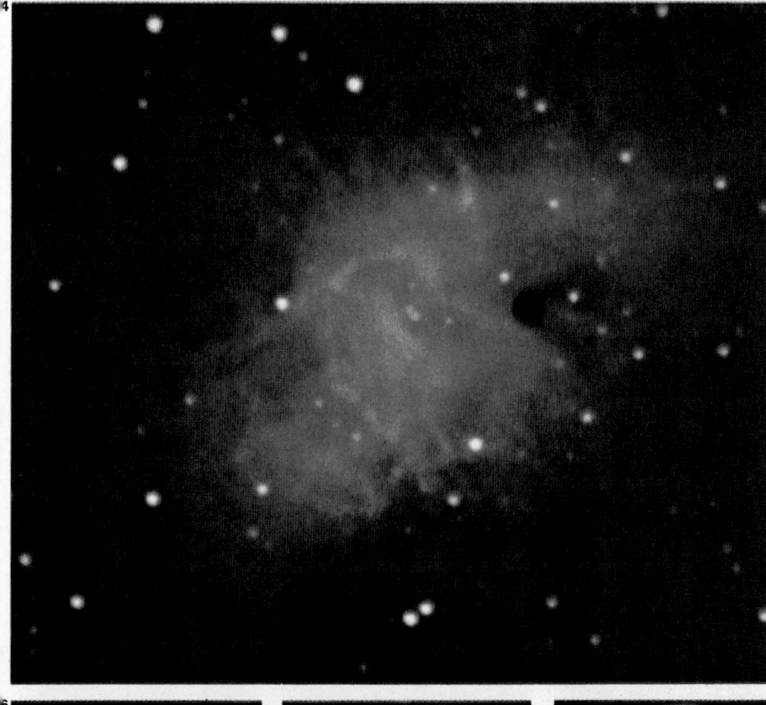

4 The Crab Nebula in Taurus is an exceptional object. The supernova that appeared in 1054 became so bright that it could be seen in daylight with the naked eye, but after it faded below the sixth magnitude it was inevitably lost. The association between the supernova of 1054 and the modern Crab Nebula has been questioned, but no longer seems to be in doubt. The Crab Nebula contains the only pulsar to have been identified with an optical object; the pulsar has been termed the Crab's "powerhouse."

5 A B

C

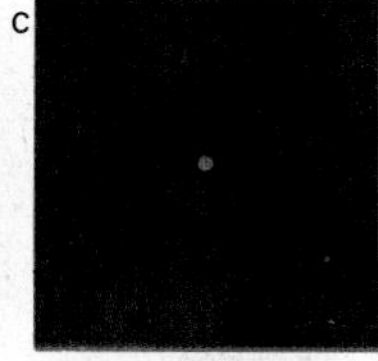

5 Stars on the main sequence, such as the Sun, are classed as dwarfs to distinguish them from members of the giant branch. The Sun [A] is a typical G-type main sequence dwarf. Capella is also of type G, but on the giant branch, with a luminosity 150 times that of the Sun. It is quite different from a white dwarf such as the companion of Sirius [B], which has collapsed, presumably from the giant stage, or a red dwarf such as Wolf 359 [C], one of the feeblest stars, with a luminosity 0.00002 times the Sun's.

6 The evolution of a massive star—that is, one with an initial mass more than three times that of the Sun—is shown. The star contracts out of the interstellar material [A] and joins the main sequence [B]. After a period that is much shorter than for a solar-type star, it moves into the giant region of the H-R diagram [C], "burning" first helium and then heavier elements. Eventually it experiences a supernova explosion [D] and sends most of its material outward, leaving a small, extremely dense neutron star or pulsar [E].

6 A

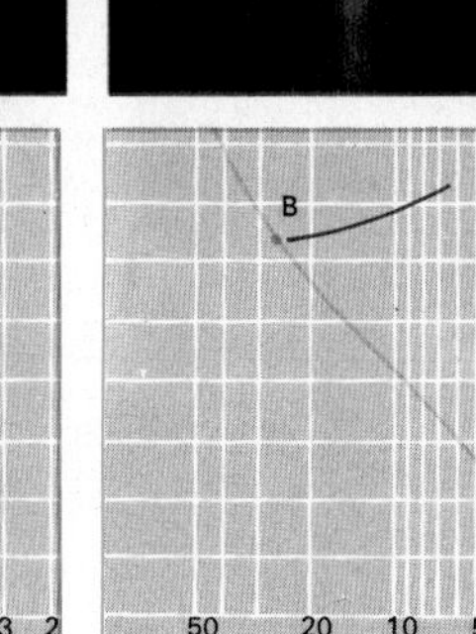
100,000
10,000
1,000
100
10
1
0·1
0·01
°C 50,000 20 10 5 4 3 2
A
B
50 20 10 5 4 3 2

C

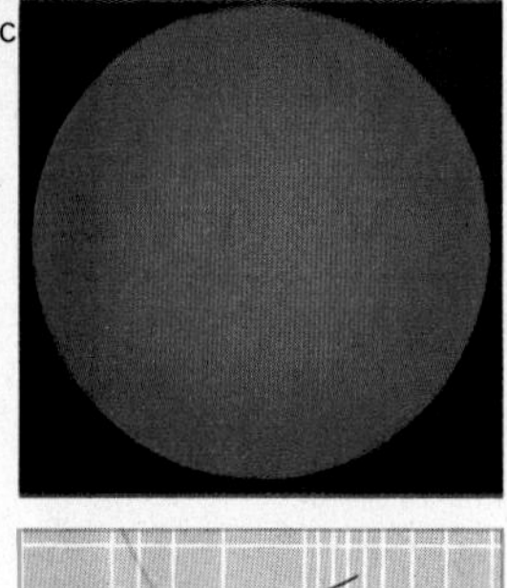

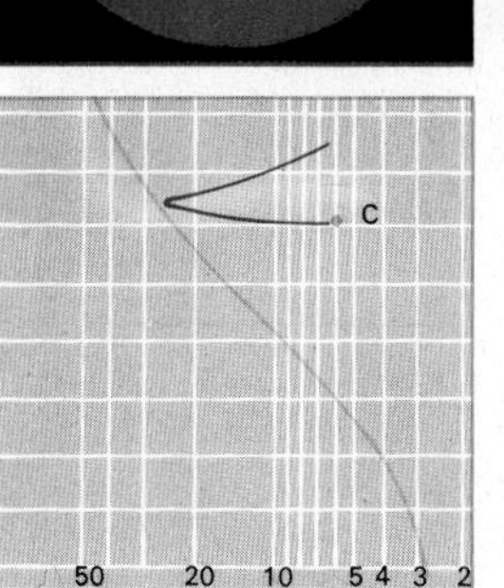
C
50 20 10 5 4 3 2

D

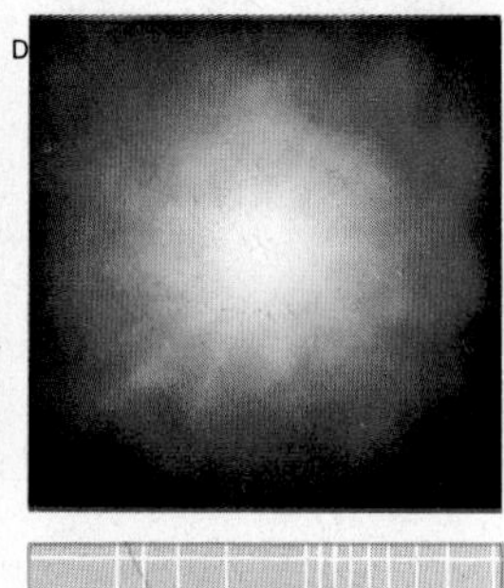

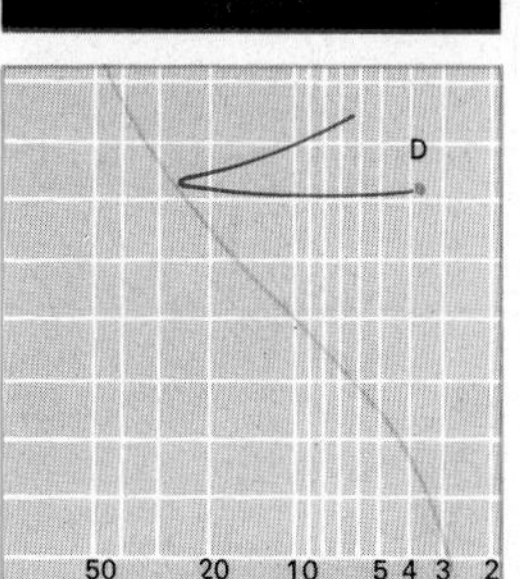
D
50 20 10 5 4 3 2

E

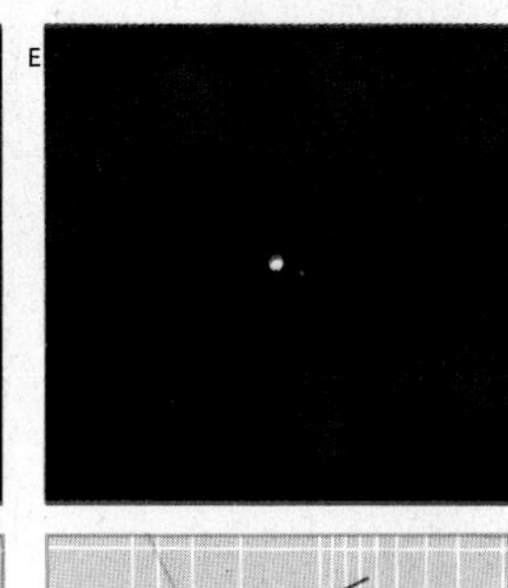
E
50 20 10 5 4 3 2

Galactic nebulae

Nebulae (clouds) are of various kinds and have proved to be of the utmost importance in modern astronomical theory. They appear in several parts of the sky as luminous patches that look like shining mist.

Several catalogs of nebulae have been drawn up by astronomers over the years. One of the most famous is that published by the French astronomer Charles Messier (1730–1817) in 1781. It contains more than 100 objects. Ironically, Messier was not in the least interested in nebulae; he was a comet-hunter who compiled his catalog of nebular objects in order to avoid confusing them with possible new comets. In the late nineteenth century an extensive catalog based on the observations of William Herschel (1738–1822) and his son John Herschel (1792–1871), was compiled by the Danish astronomer Johan Dreyer (1852–1926). It is known as the New General Catalog (NGC). Today the NGC numbers and Messier's "M" numbers are still used.

Two kinds of nebulae

Messier cataloged all the nebulous objects, from star clusters to gaseous nebulae and to the systems such as the Andromeda Spiral, M31, that we now know to be galaxies. Astronomers have now agreed that the term "nebula" should be confined exclusively to clouds of gas or dust in order to avoid confusion.

Galactic nebulae are of two main kinds: emission and reflection. Both types occur not only in our own Galaxy, but in others. The so-called Tarantula Nebula lies in the Large Cloud of Magellan—30 Doradûs (listed by Dreyer as NGC 2070)—and is much larger than the Orion Nebula, M42 [Key, 8], which is the most famous nebula in our Galaxy. The main constituent of all nebulae is hydrogen, which is the most abundant substance in the entire universe, but there is also a great deal of dust and it is this that absorbs starlight. Inside some of the nebulae are objects that cannot be seen, but that can be detected by infrared photography; Becklin's Object in the Orion Nebula is an excellent example. It may well be a star of tremendous luminosity, but it is permanently concealed from view.

Vast though they are, the nebulae are made up of extremely tenuous material. The gas is many millions of times less dense than the air we breathe.

Luminosity of nebulae

A nebula depends for its luminosity upon the presence of stars that are either very close to it or are contained in it. If the stars are extremely hot, the hydrogen in the nebula is ionized and emits a certain amount of light of its own [Key, 2, 3, 8]. (Certain spectral lines in nebulae were once thought to indicate the presence of an unknown element, but it was subsequently found that the lines are due to familiar elements, such as oxygen, produced under unfamiliar conditions.) If the stars are less hot, the nebula shines only by reflection [5, 6]. If there are no suitable stars, the nebula does not shine at all; it remains dark and can be detected only because it blots out the light of stars beyond [5, 7].

There are various galactic nebulae within the range of small telescopes, although the vivid colors of the photographs

CONNECTIONS

Read first
100 Star types

See also
102 Stellar evolution
106 Nebulae and pulsar
108 Pulsars and black holes

1

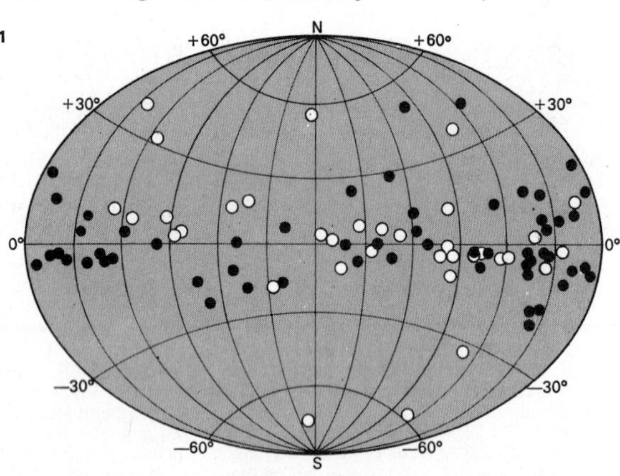

N
+60°
+60°
+30°
+30°
0°
0°
−30°
−30°
−60°
−60°
S

1 Gaseous nebulae are not distributed equally all over the sky. They occur in Population I regions. In galaxies these regions are located in the main plane or spiral arms of the galaxy. Population II regions occur in the nucleus of the galaxy. Seen from the Earth the galactic plane is identified by the Milky Way—the area of the sky where most nebulae are found. The diagram shows the Milky Way region (galactic latitude 0 degrees) with the nebulae indicated by circles—black for reflection nebulae and white for emission ones. Only a relatively few nebulae are shown, but the distributions are clear.

2

Nebula

star

2 An emission nebula emits light characteristic of the substance from which it is made, if the nebulosity is illuminated by a suitably placed star. A star of type W, O, or B can cause ionization of the hydrogen atoms out to about 500 light-years, which is known as an H-II region. If the temperatures of the associated stars are too low there will be no emission from the nebula and the nebula will shine only by reflection.

3

3 A famous emission nebula is the Trifid in Sagittarius, M20 (NGC 6514), shown in this Palomar photograph. Visible in a small telescope, it is 30 light-years across and more than 3,000 light-years away.

4

4 The main galactic nebula in Sagittarius is M8 (NGC 6523), known as the Lagoon Nebula. Described by John Flamsteed (1646–1719) in 1680, it is easy to view telescopically because the integrated magnitude is 6.0. M8 is a dense nebula with 16,000 to 160,000 atoms per cubic inch (1,000 to 10,000 atoms per cc) in the central region. It is 4,850 light-years from Earth. Associated with it is the galactic star cluster NGC 6530. M8 contains a number of T Tauri variables and also some dark globules that may eventually start to shine. Each globule has a diameter of about one light-year. Flare stars in M8 are also known. M8 is also a source of radio emission.

below cannot be seen visually. The colors themselves are genuine, but are too faint to be detected by the eye.

According to a classification produced by Walter Baade (1893–1960), there are two kinds of regions in our Galaxy (and in other galaxies): Population I and Population II. In Population I areas [1] there is a great deal of interstellar material and the brightest stars are hot and white. In Population II areas the interstellar material has largely been used up in star formation and the brightest stars are red giants. Since these stars are well advanced in their evolution, Population II regions seem to be relatively old. Gaseous nebulae occur in Population I areas, so their stars are young by cosmic standards.

The formation of stars

The most important feature of Population I areas from the theoretical point of view is that they are apparently regions in which star formation is in progress. According to current ideas, a star begins by condensing out of interstellar material. Nebulae are obvious sites for such activity because the material in other regions of space between the stars is much too tenuous. On the average, interstellar space contains 16 atoms of matter per cubic inch (1 atom per cc); nebulae, although rarefied, are more condensed than this. Objects such as the Orion Nebula, the Lagoon Nebula [4], and the Trifid Nebula [3] are in fact stellar birthplaces. The same is true of galactic nebulae in other systems, such as the Large Cloud of Magellan and the nebulae observable in the Andromeda Spiral. Dark patches in nebulae, known as globules, may be embryo stars.

Nebulae also contain many stars that are variable in light and are unstable. These are known as T Tauri variables and are thought to be stars at a very early stage in their careers that are still contracting toward the main sequence. Some stars have even been seen to increase in luminosity over a period of years, presumably because they have blown away their original dust clouds. One of these is FU Orionis, in the Orion Nebula, which became brighter in 1936 and must be one of the youngest stars known.

KEY

In the Sword of Orion is the most spectacular of the gaseous nebulae (M42). Within this Orion Nebula the famous multiple star, the Trapezium, responsible for the nebula's luminosity, is clearly visible. The brightest star is Theta Orionis.

5 A

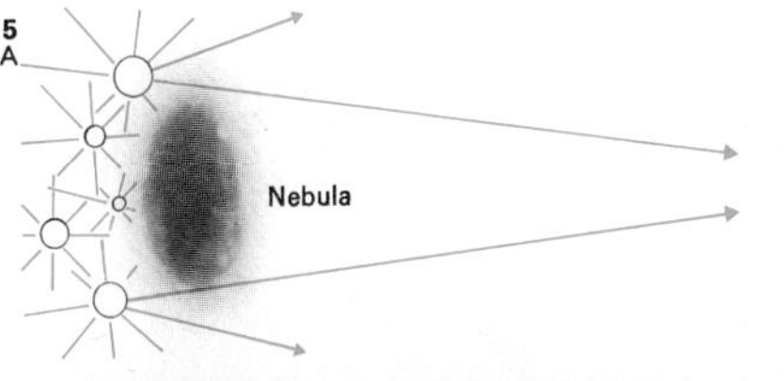
Nebula

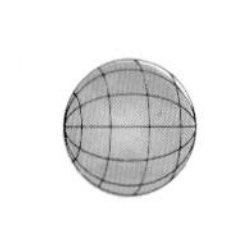

B

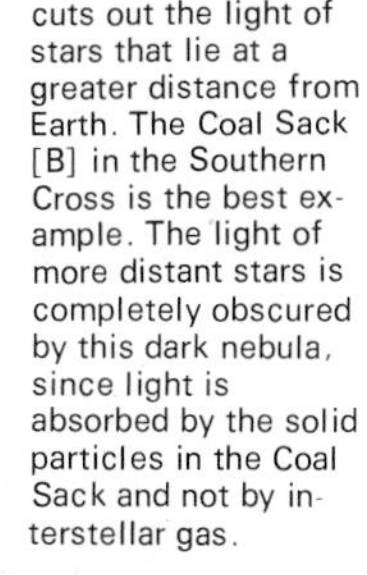

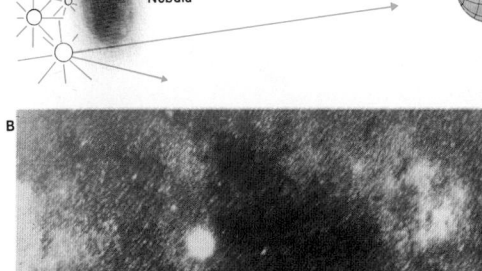

5 A dark nebula [A] cuts out the light of stars that lie at a greater distance from Earth. The Coal Sack [B] in the Southern Cross is the best example. The light of more distant stars is completely obscured by this dark nebula, since light is absorbed by the solid particles in the Coal Sack and not by interstellar gas.

6 A

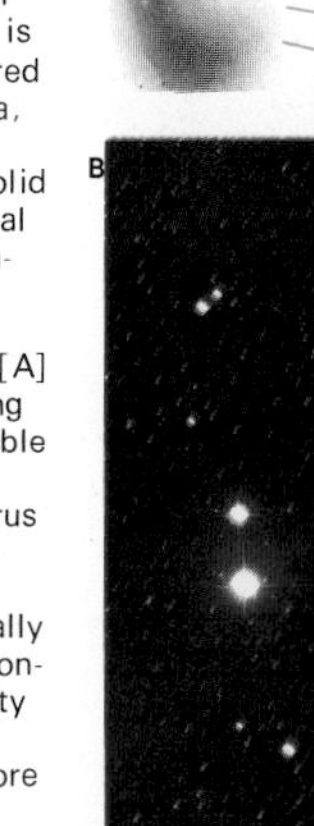
star
Nebula

B

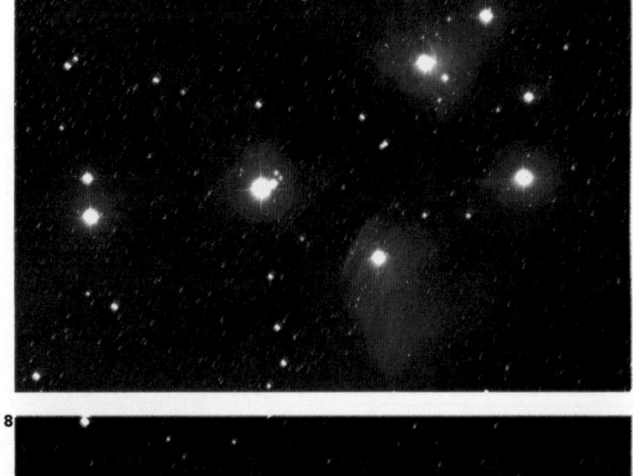

6 A bright nebula [A] shines by reflecting the light of a suitable star. The Pleiades cluster [B] in Taurus is an example of a reflection nebula. Such nebulae usually have a high dust content. The nebulosity in the Pleiades is faint and is therefore best examined by using long-exposure photographs.

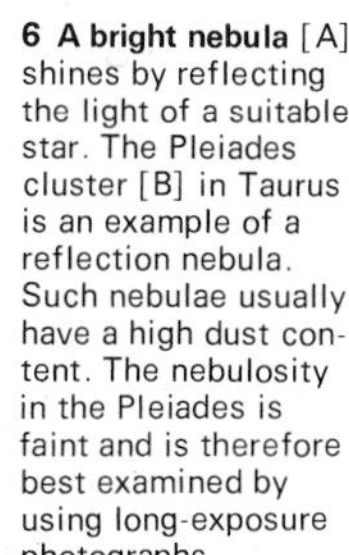

7

7 The "Horsehead" Nebula in Orion lies close to Zeta Orionis, the most southerly star of the Belt. This dark nebula, shaped like the head of a knight in chess, is No 2024 in the New General Catalog. It can be seen with a small telescope, although it is best studied in photographs, such as this Mt Palomar picture.

8

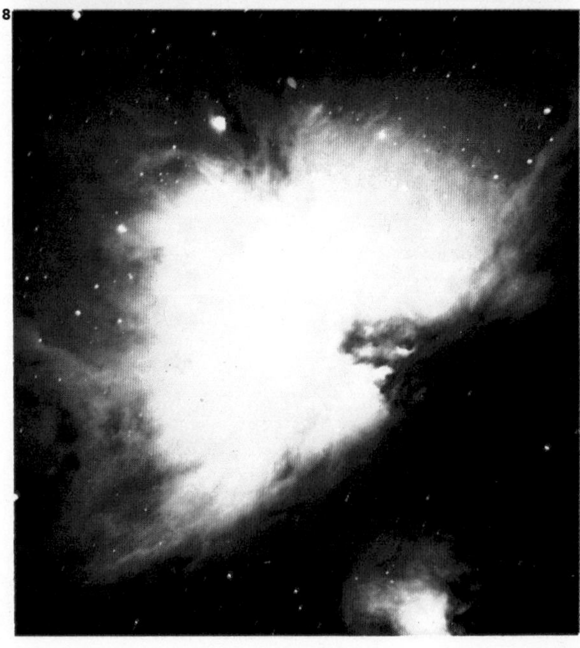

8 The bright Orion Nebula to the south of the Belt in the "Hunter's Sword" can easily be seen with the naked eye. Its luminosity is due chiefly to the multiple star, Theta Orionis, on the side of the nebula turned to the Earth. If this star did not exist, the nebula would be just as dark as the "Horsehead" Nebula.

Nebulae and pulsars

Until fairly recent times it was not generally realized how different the various types of nebulae are. Looking at the Omega Nebula in Sagittarius and then the Crab Nebula in Taurus, for example, leads to the conclusion that they are much the same. In fact they represent diametrically opposite ends of the stellar evolutionary sequence. In Omega—a diffuse nebula—stars are being forced out of the interstellar material; the Crab represents the debris of a supernova explosion at the center of which is a pulsar—a collapsed dense star.

Nebulae: the early stages

One interesting nebula is associated with the young star T Tauri, which is irregularly variable and is still contracting toward the main sequence. The nebula was discovered in 1852 by J. R. Hind, an English amateur who was using a 7in (17.8cm) refractor to hunt for asteroids. Nine years later it had disappeared. It has since been seen again and is within range of large telescopes, but it is not nearly as prominent as it was when Hind discovered it. Moreover, T Tauri itself is not hot enough to excite the nebular material to self-luminosity; it is, however, an infrared source and there is no doubt that it is associated with the nebulous material around it from which it has been formed. There are other variable nebulae similarly associated with young stars, for example, R Monocerotis in the Orion area and R Coronae Australis in the southern sky.

These, then, are nebulae involved in stellar birth. So are the familiar gaseous or galactic nebulae, such as M42 in Orion. Deep inside M42, permanently hidden from Earth by the nebular material, is an infrared source known as Becklin's Object. It may be a very young star or else an extremely powerful object at least a million times as luminous as the Sun. There is, however, no way of knowing because it is possible to study only its infrared radiation, which can pass through the nebula and reach the Earth. In any case, star formation is in progress in the Orion cloud.

A. Blaauw and W. W. Morgan, in the United States, studied an O-type star, AE Aurigae, which has the high velocity of about 80mi (130km) per second. It looks faint only because it is remote; it is in fact a very luminous young star. Tracing its path "backward," indicates that about two and a half million years ago it was in the region of the Orion Nebula [1]. Moving in the opposite direction is another O-type star, Mu Columbae, which has similar velocity and is about equally far from the nebula. It has been suggested that a colossal disturbance hurled these two stars violently outward from their place of birth.

Planetary nebulae

Other nebulae represent later stages in the evolution of a star; in particular there are the planetaries, which look like small, feebly luminous disks or rings, not unlike those of planets. The planetaries like the diffuse nebulae, are gaseous, but they are neither planets nor nebulae so their popular name could hardly be less apt. The best known is the Ring Nebula, M57 Lyrae [4], discovered in 1779. It is made up of a central star surrounded by a spherical gaseous shell. Looking at it, more is seen of the glowing material

CONNECTIONS

Read first
100 Star types

See also
102 Stellar evolution
104 Galactic nebulae
108 Pulsars and black holes

1 The Orion Nebula, a stellar birthplace, is the most famous of all gaseous nebulae. This photograph was taken with the 200in (508cm) Hale reflector at Palomar, Calif. The "hollow" in the border to the right-hand side is due to the presence of the multiple star Theta Orionis, which lies close to the Earth-turned edge of the nebula. There is no doubt that fresh stars are condensing out of the nebula.

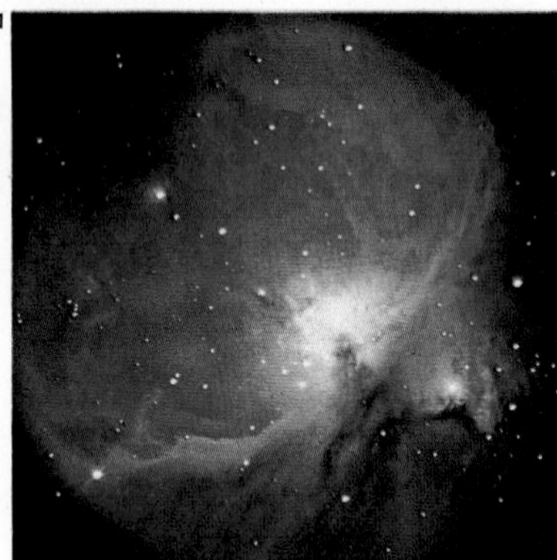

2 The gaseous nebula M16 (NGC 6611) lies in Serpens near its boundary with the small constellation of Scutum, which adjoins the "tail" of Aquila. M16 has an integrated magnitude of 6.4, so that it is visible with binoculars; the distance from Earth is 5,900 light-years. Seen through a foreground of stars the nebula, photographed in red light, shows both bright and dark nebulosity.

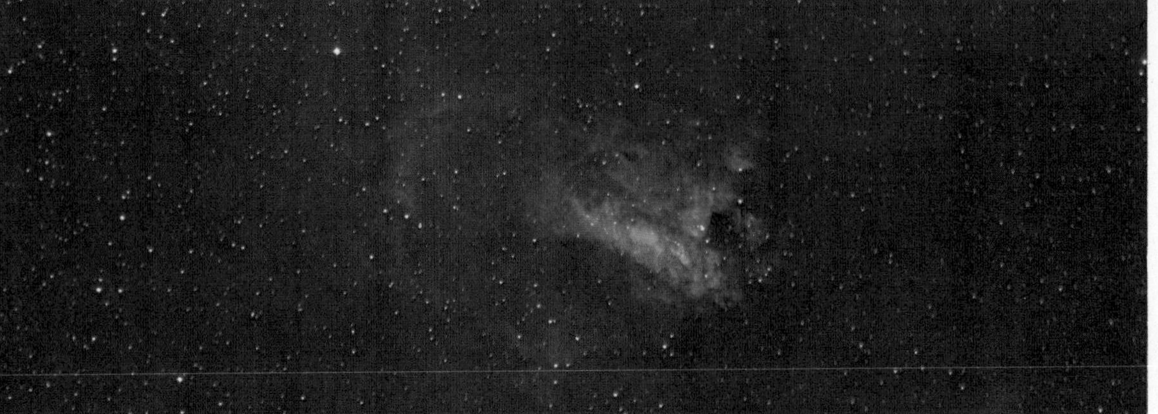

3 The Omega Nebula M17 (NGC 6618), sometimes known as the Horseshoe Nebula, was discovered by the French astronomer L. de Chèseaux in 1746. It is an easy binocular object, 1.5° S and 2° E of the 5th-magnitude star Gamma Scuti. It is more massive than the Orion Nebula; like so many other diffuse nebulae it has bright areas as well as signs of dark obscuring material. M17 lies where the constellations Serpens, Sagittarius, and Scutum meet.

at the edge than at the center, so that the nebula resembles a ring. The diameter of M57 is almost one light-year but the gaseous envelope is immensely rarefied, millions of times less dense than the Earth's air at sea level. Some planetary nebulae are larger; NGC 7293 Aquarii [5] is twice the size of M57. Other planetaries are asymmetrical, such as the Owl Nebula, M97 Ursae Majoris, and the Dumbbell Nebula, M27 in Vulpecula.

All planetaries are expanding and their age can hardly be more than a few tens of thousands of years. It has been estimated that if the gaseous shell is ejected from an old star, the material cannot continue to shine for more than 100,000 years. According to one theory, a planetary is produced by a red giant star "puffing off" its outer layers, so that the central stars in planetary nebulae represent the cores of old giants. These stars have high surface temperatures, of about 90,000°F (50,000°C) and have completed their main nuclear burning; they are well on the way to becoming white dwarfs. The "puffing out" theory fits in with the proposed evolutionary sequence, although it is not certain that every normal star becomes a planetary nebula at a late stage in its career. Over 400 such planetaries have been discovered. They have been found at distances ranging from 3,000 to 30,000 light-years from Earth.

Supernovae and pulsars

Finally, there are nebulae that represent the end products of stellar evolution. Although the Crab Nebula is the best known example, there are others but almost all are much older than the Crab and so their forms are not as well marked. (In any case, the Crab, with its unusual central pulsar, seems to be an exceptional object.) With the Veil Nebula [6], in Cygnus, the arched shape of the luminous material is very plain and all the evidence indicates that it is the debris of a prehistoric supernova outburst. The present rate of expansion is 75mi (120km) per second. There is thus a full sequence of nebulae, from those of the T Tauri type associated with stellar birth through to the stellar remnants of supernovae explosions.

KEY

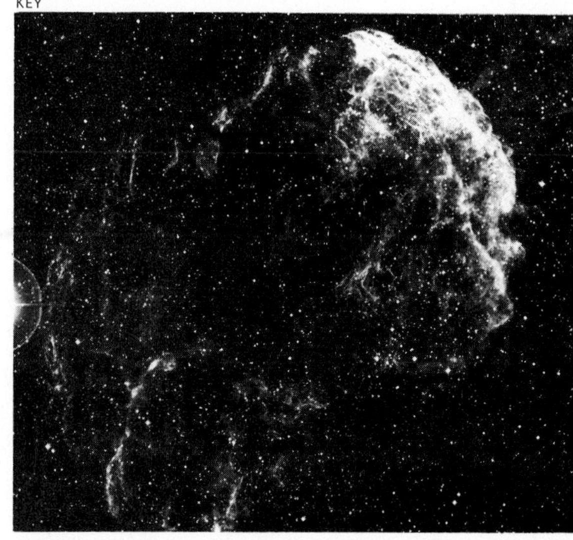

This gaseous nebula in Gemini is probably associated with the death of a star; it gives every impression of being the remnant of a supernova outburst. Other types of nebulae are considered by astronomers to be the birthplaces of stars.

4

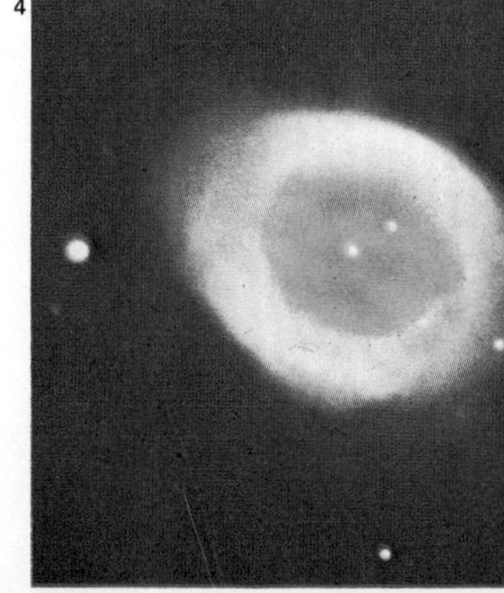

4 M57 (NGC 6720), the Ring Nebula in Lyra—the most famous of the planetaries—lies midway between the two naked-eye stars Beta and Gamma Lyrae. The variation in colors is caused by temperature differences. The integrated magnitude is 9.3 and the distance from Earth 1,400 light-years. The central star, although clearly shown, is by no means bright; the second star beside it is in the foreground.

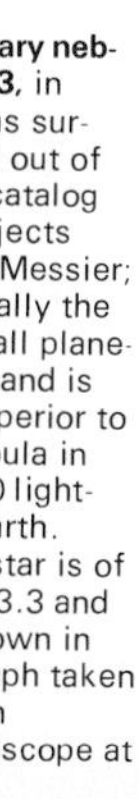

5 The planetary nebula NGC 7293, in Aquarius, was surprisingly left out of the famous catalog of nebula objects drawn up by Messier; yet it is actually the brightest of all planetary nebulae and is definitely superior to the Ring Nebula in Lyra. It is 600 light-years from Earth. The central star is of magnitude 13.3 and is clearly shown in this photograph taken with the 48in (122cm) telescope at Palomar.

5

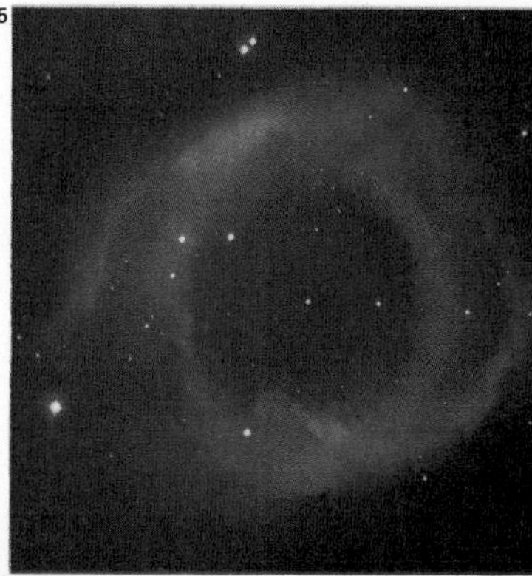

6 The Veil Nebula in Cygnus, NGC 6992—sometimes called the Cirrus Nebula—may be a supernova remnant. This photograph with the 48in (122cm) Schmidt telescope, Palomar, shows its arched shape. The Nebula is 2,500 light-years away and from motions in the gas it has been calculated that the supernova outburst occurred 50,000 years ago. In 25,000 years it will cease to be luminous.

6

Pulsars and black holes

To explain the nature of a black hole, it is necessary to examine stellar evolution [1]. A star such as the Sun contracts toward the main sequence. When the core temperature has risen sufficiently, nuclear processes begin. After the supply of available "fuel" has run low, the star swells to become a red giant, after which it collapses to the white dwarf condition.

A more massive star will behave differently, and, when its nuclear reserves fail, it will explode as a supernova, ending its luminous career as a neutron star, or pulsar, together with a cloud of expanding gas.

White dwarfs and black holes

In a white dwarf the atoms are crushed, broken, and packed together so tightly that there is little remaining space. In a neutron star the gravitational field is so intense that the protons and electrons are forced to combine with each other to form neutrons; the density of neutron star material far exceeds that of a white dwarf. There is now little doubt that the radio sources known as pulsars are really neutron stars, although only one—the pulsar in the Crab Nebula—has been identified with an optical object [Key, 3].

If a massive star collapses, it can pass through densities that correspond to the white dwarf and neutron star stages and still continue to contract, becoming steadily smaller and denser, it is hypothesized, and entering a state of gravitational collapse that no known physical process could halt. Light would find it more difficult to escape and soon the body would contract within a critical (Schwarzschild) radius at which point its gravitational field would become so strong that not even light would be able to move away from it. The star would then be surrounded by what might be termed a "forbidden zone" from which nothing can escape. This is termed a black hole—a region that acts as a center of gravitational attraction.

Inside a black hole, all the normal laws of physics would break down. There have been highly speculative suggestions that the collapsed star may eventually be crushed out of existence altogether. And there have been sensational predictions that black holes may extend until they swallow everything in the universe, including Earth.

In search of black holes

The most promising place to look for a black hole is in a binary system, where the effects of an invisible body on a visible one may be detected. Close by the brilliant yellow star Capella is a small triangle of stars known as the Haedi, or Kids. At the apex of the triangle is Epsilon Aurigae, which is always visible to the naked eye. In 1821 it was discovered to be variable, with a magnitude range of 3.3 to 4.2. Later it was found that Epsilon Aurigae is an eclipsing binary of unusual type, for the eclipses take place only once in 27 years and last for more than 700 days.

The brighter member of the pair is a highly luminous yellow supergiant, 60,000 times as powerful as the Sun. The fainter component, which causes the eclipses, has never been seen; it radiates only in the infrared and until recently it was generally thought to be a large, cool star, still shrink-

CONNECTIONS

See also
100 Star types
102 Stellar evolution
104 Galactic nebulae
106 Nebulae and pulsars

1 The relative sizes of a giant, the Sun, a white dwarf, a neutron star, and a black hole are shown. The ratios are given for each diagram; thus the diameter of the Sun is approximately 100 times that of a white dwarf. The neutron star has the same mass as that of the Sun but is extremely dense.

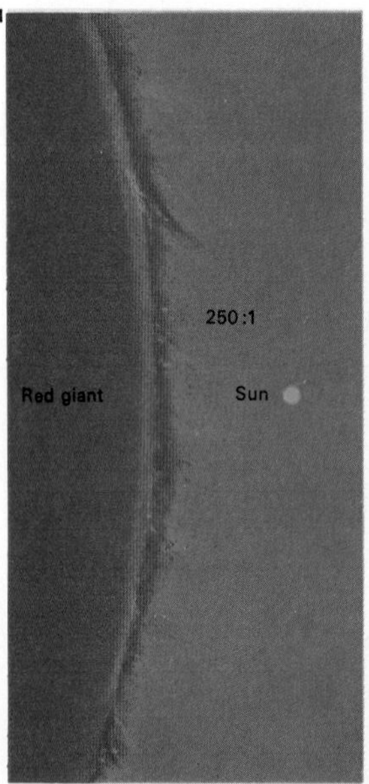

250:1
Red giant
Sun

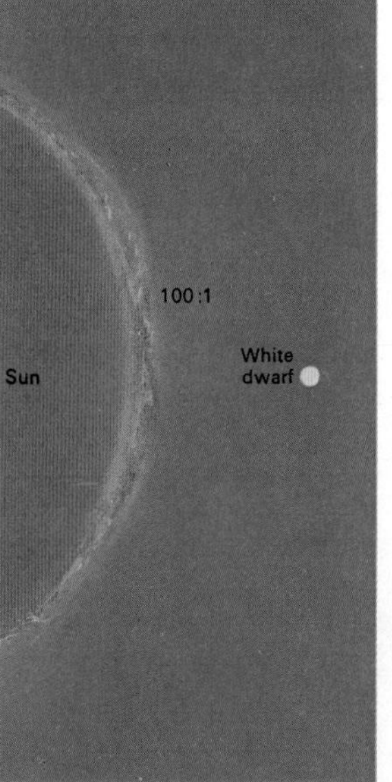

100:1
Sun
White dwarf

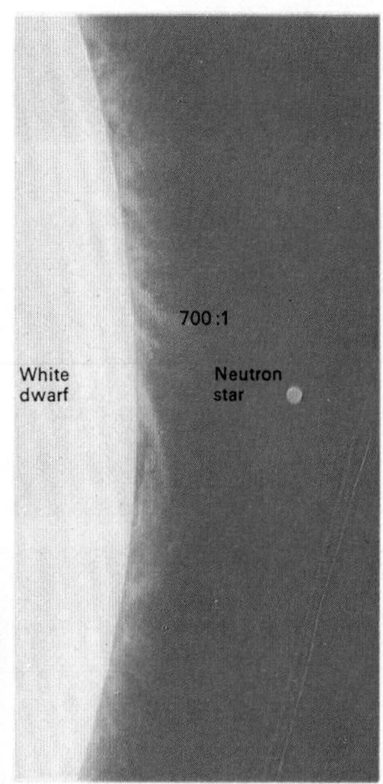

700:1
White dwarf
Neutron star

3:1
Neutron star
Black hole

2 A pulsar's radiation varies. The red on the diagram indicates the ends of the magnetic axis of a pulsar. As the pulsar rotates, the signal strength varies according to the position of the axis. When one end faces Earth [1], the intensity is at its maximum. When the other end faces Earth [2], intensity is at its minimum.

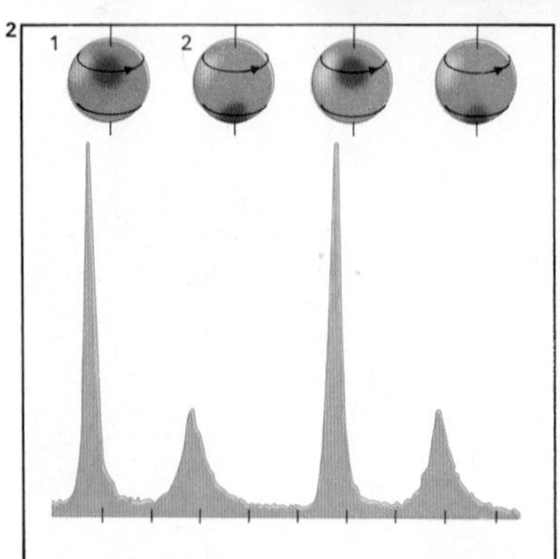

1
2

3 The Crab Nebula pulsar is of great importance to astronomers, for so far it is the only one to have been identified with an optical instrument. These photographs were taken at the Lick Observatory, California, with its 120-in (305-cm) reflector. The pulsar is easily identifiable in A, but in B it is almost completely invisible. The whole pulse cycle amounts to only 33 milliseconds. There is now little doubt that pulsars are, in fact, identical with neutron stars.

4 Radiation at all wavelengths is emitted by the Crab pulsar. The pulse cycle at a wavelength of 200MHz in the radio range is shown [A] and at 400 MHz [B]; in the optical range [C] and in the X ray range [D]. The beam of radiation has similar characteristics across the electromagnetic spectrum.

ing after its condensation from interstellar material, but not hot enough to shine by nuclear power. Now, however, there are suggestions that the infrared member of the Epsilon Aurigae system may be a black hole.

This infrared component seems to have a mass 23 times that of the Sun, which by stellar standards is very high. It should therefore be luminous, but it is not. The US astronomers A. G. W. Cameron and R. Stothers suggest that it may be a black hole, surrounded by a cloud of solid particles that are spiraling around the critical boundary [7] and sending out the infrared radiation detected from Earth. Over the course of time the particles would cross the event horizon and enter the black hole, from which they could never emerge.

X ray sources

Another possible black hole is the companion of a supergiant star in Cygnus, known by its catalog number, HDE 226868 [6]. The companion is a source of X rays and it has been suggested that these are produced by material falling in toward the black hole and being accelerated to high velocities.

X ray astronomy is a recent development, because it involves sending equipment above the shielding layers of the atmosphere. Many X ray sources have been found, one of which is the Crab Nebula [Key, 4]. Apparently most galactic X ray sources are members of binary systems and are neutron stars associated with giants. There are also X ray novae, which flare up, last for a few weeks or months, and then fade.

Most of the X ray sources are members of our Galaxy and lie reasonably near the main plane of the Milky Way, but some other galaxies also emit X rays, notably the massive system in Virgo known as Messier 87. It is also a source of radio emissions.

Progress in astronomy has been amazingly rapid during the past few decades. In 1960 quasars and pulsars had not been detected and black holes were only of theoretical interest; X ray studies had scarcely begun and even radio astronomy was primitive by current standards.

KEY

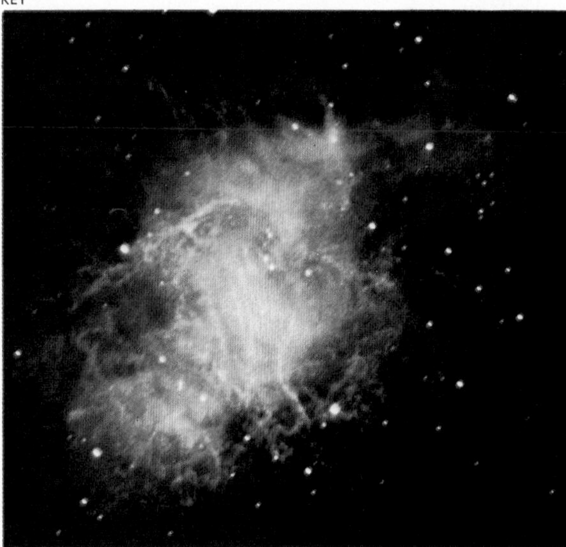

The Crab Nebula (M1, NGC 1952) is the remnant of a supernova in 1054. It contains a pulsar, said to be the "powerhouse" of the Crab, which is 6,000 light-years distant.

5

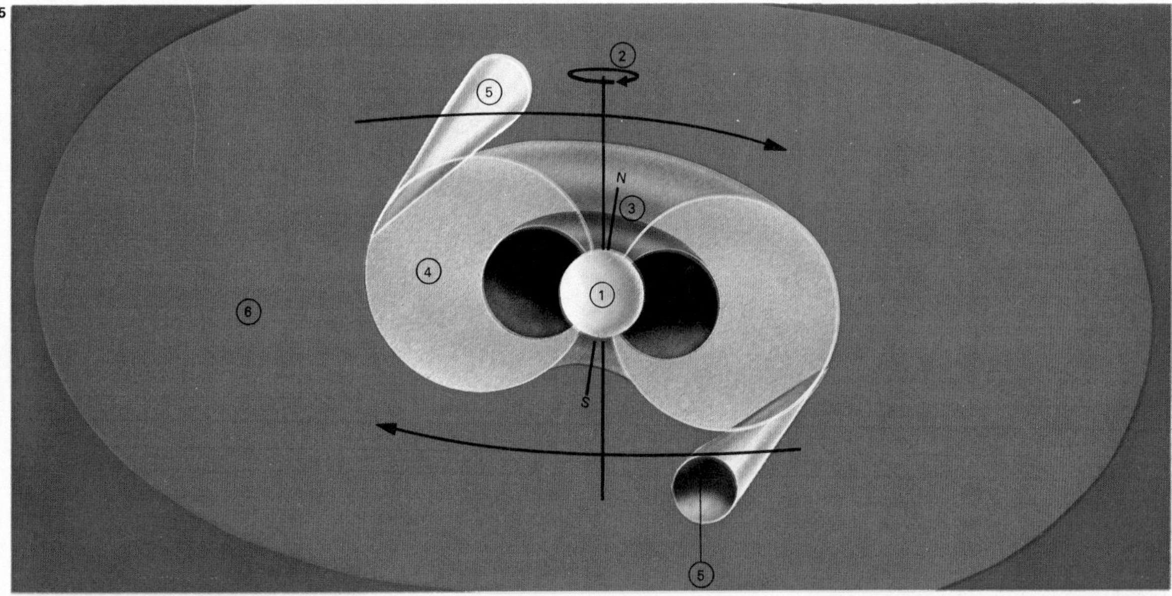
1
2
3
4
5
6
N
S

5 When pulsars were discovered, it was thought that the signals might come from rotating white dwarf stars. Now it is certain that a pulsar is a rotating neutron star [1], whose axis of rotation [2] does not coincide with the magnetic axis [3]. Near the star the plasma rotates [4], sending out radio waves in beams [5]. Beyond this the plasma is stationary [6]. It is now agreed that it is the magnetic field of the rotating neutron star that generates the pulses as it turns over and over. The mechanism is related to the region some distance from the star where the magnetic field would have to travel at the speed of light to pace the rotation.

6

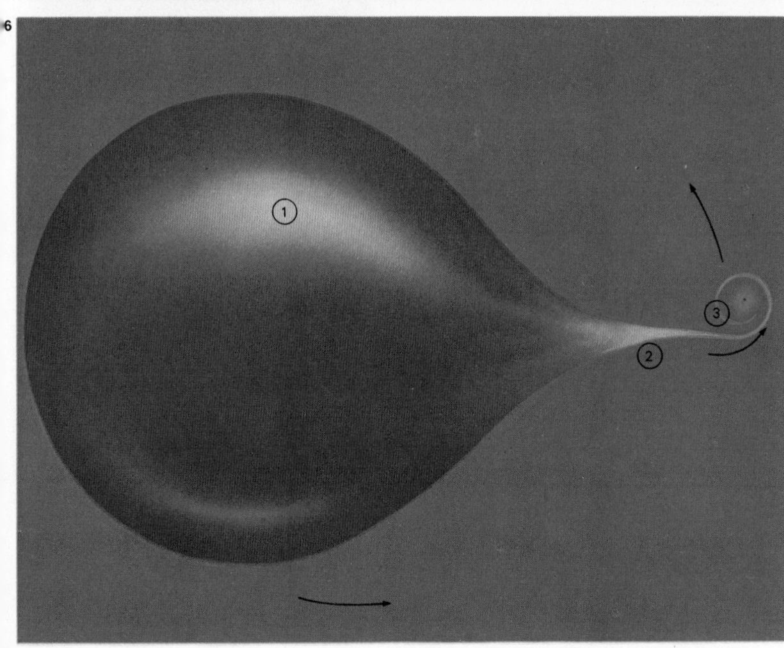
1
2
3

7

6 The blue supergiant [1], it is believed, has material pulled away from it in a jet [2] by the black hole [3], which is so small it can be regarded as a point mass. Because of its small size, material can be funneled into the black hole only slowly, before which it is compressed and subjected to intense heat, so emitting powerful X rays. The invisible companion of HDE 226868 in Cygnus may be a black hole with a diameter of 60 mi; the supergiant's is 300,000 times that.

7 The "event horizon" is the critical boundary of a black hole [black area]. The origins of some light sources are shown with locations of each light a moment later [white circles], depicting how gravity effectively bends light.

Double stars

The Solar System is centered on a single star, the Sun, but the universe contains many stars that appear to be close pairs or even members of complicated systems.

These double stars are surprisingly common, but are not always exactly what they seem. Some are indeed binary, or physically associated systems; the association of others is an illusion, the result of a mere line-of-sight effect. If two stars, as seen from Earth, happen to lie in much the same direction, they will appear to be side by side in the sky, even though there is no real connection between them. An example is Vega, the brilliant blue star in Lyra. It has a 12th-magnitude companion that is much farther away, although, from a terrestrial point of view it appears close.

Binary stars and their structure

It was originally thought that all double stars must be the result of a line-of-sight effect. Not until 1793, and the observations of William Herschel (1738–1822), were true binary pairs discovered. In a binary system, the two components move around a common center of gravity. For some pairs, the period of revolution is short—in extreme cases, less than 20 minutes—while for others it is very long.

Gamma Virginis, not far from Spica, is made up of two equal components with a revolution period of 180 years. The angular separation is now less than it was earlier in this century because the two stars are moving closer to the same line of sight. The pair used to be separable with any small telescope, but by the year 2016, Gamma Virginis will appear to be single, except in giant telescopes.

Mizar [Key], and its companion Alcor, in Ursa Major, is a particularly easy binary to spot—it was the first double star discovered by telescope. Like Alpha Centauri, it has two rather unequal components, one of magnitude 2.4, the other of 3.9.

Some pairs, such as Gamma Arietis, have the same spectral type for both components, but others are distinguished by their beautifully contrasting colors. Antares, the brilliant red star in the Scorpion, has a faint green companion; the same is true of the red giant star Alpha Herculis [3, 4]. Perhaps the best example is Beta Cygni [8, 9], or Albireo, which has a golden-yellow primary and a blue companion.

Spectroscopic and eclipsing binaries

If the separation between the components is slight, the binary will appear single. The revolution of the two components around their common center, however, will show up in a spectroscope [10]. The brighter component of the Mizar pair is a spectroscopic binary.

There are also systems made up of more than two stars. Alpha Centauri [1, 2], for instance, the closest of all the bright stars, is made up of two rather unequal components (of magnitudes 0.0 and 1.7) and has a revolution period of 80 years. Closely associated with it is Proxima Centauri, making Alpha into a triple star. Proxima is the nearest star to Earth, but it much less bright than Alpha. Epsilon Lyrae [13], near Vega, is an example of a wide pair, each component of which is again double. Castor, in Gemini, is a six-fold system, in which four of the compo-

CONNECTIONS

Read first
100 Star types

See also
130 Star guide: northern sky I
132 Star guide: northern sky II
134 Star guide: southern sky I
136 Star guide: southern sky II
138 Seasonal star maps: northern
140 Seasonal star maps: southern

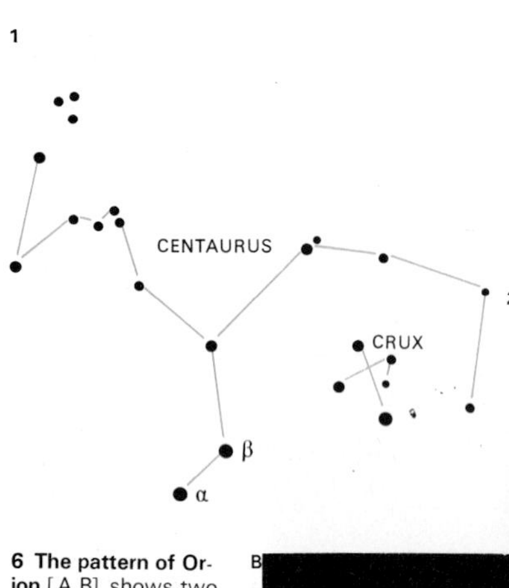

1
CENTAURUS
CRUX
β
α

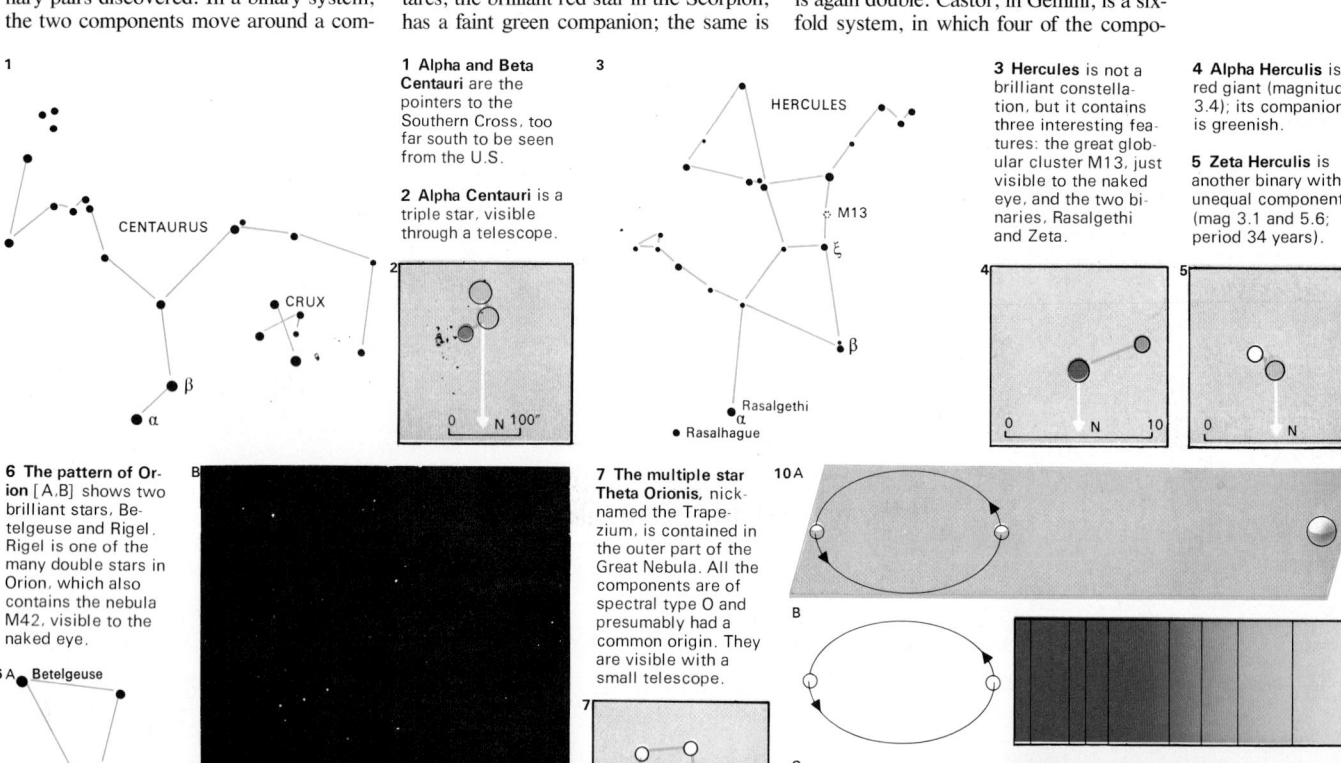

1 Alpha and Beta Centauri are the pointers to the Southern Cross, too far south to be seen from the U.S.

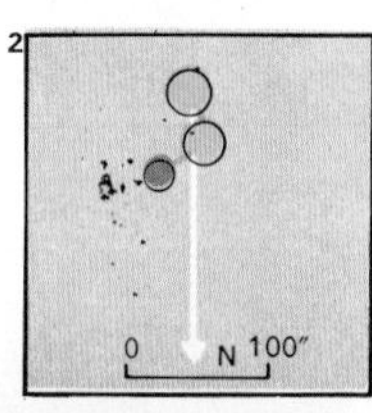

2
0
N 100″

2 Alpha Centauri is a triple star, visible through a telescope.

3 HERCULES M13 ξ β Rasalgethi α Rasalhague

3 Hercules is not a brilliant constellation, but it contains three interesting features: the great globular cluster M13, just visible to the naked eye, and the two binaries, Rasalgethi and Zeta.

4 Alpha Herculis is a red giant (magnitude 3.4); its companion is greenish.

5 Zeta Herculis is another binary with unequal components (mag 3.1 and 5.6; period 34 years).

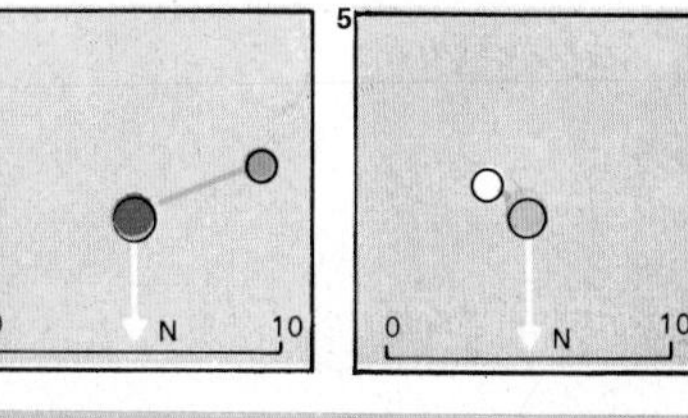

4
0
N
10
5
0
N
10″

6 The pattern of Orion [A,B] shows two brilliant stars, Betelgeuse and Rigel. Rigel is one of the many double stars in Orion, which also contains the nebula M42, visible to the naked eye.

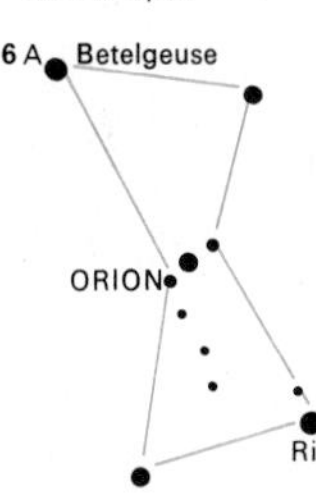

6A
Betelgeuse
ORION
Rigel

7 The multiple star Theta Orionis, nicknamed the Trapezium, is contained in the outer part of the Great Nebula. All the components are of spectral type O and presumably had a common origin. They are visible with a small telescope.

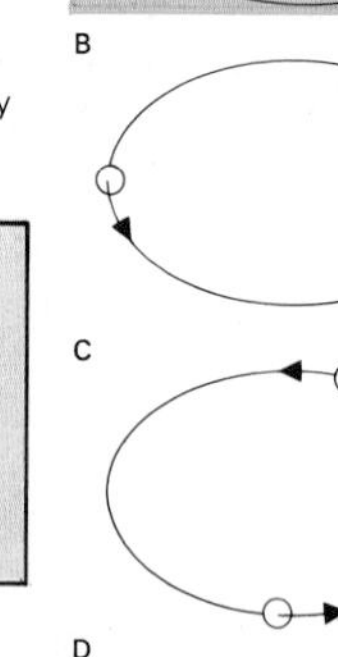

7
N

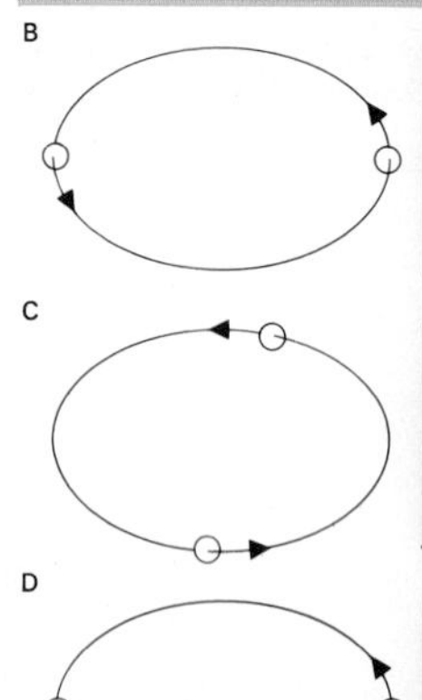

10A
B
C
D
E

8 Cygnus is one of the richest of all constellations because it lies in the Milky Way. Its leading star, Deneb, is a highly luminous giant. The constellation takes the form of a cross, but the symmetry is spoiled by Albireo (Beta Cygni), a double with a yellow primary and also a green companion.

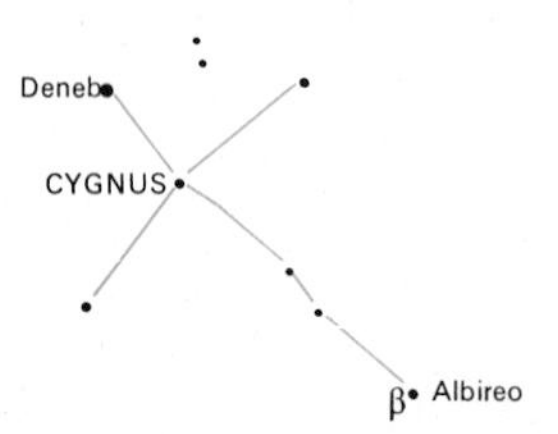

8
Deneb
CYGNUS
β Albireo

9 The golden-yellow primary of Beta Cygni is of type K, with an absolute magnitude of −2.2. Its companion is of magnitude 5.4. Despite their great separation these are still binary stars.

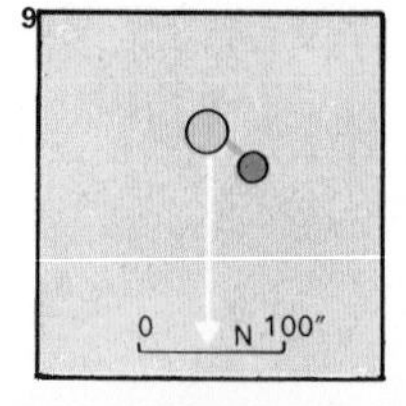

9
0
N 100″

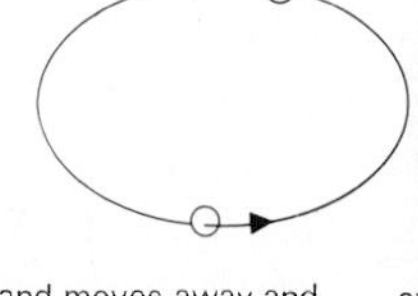

10 Analysis of a spectroscopic binary assumes that the stars are equal in mass, thus moving in circular orbit around their common center of gravity [A]. The Earth, many light-years away, lies in the plane of their orbit. The stars move transversely to the line of sight from Earth [B]. Then the lower star moves toward the Earth and its spectral lines shift to the blue (or violet); the upper star shows a red shift and moves away and the lines in the combined spectrum appear double [C]. The stars again move transversely and the lines merge [D]. The sets of lines again shift in opposite directions [E]. Periodic doubling indicates a binary.

nents are bright and the other two are dim red dwarfs; it comprises two spectroscopic binaries and a third much fainter companion that is also a binary.

During the revolution of the two stars of a binary system, one component may pass behind the other, either totally or partially. When this happens, the light visible from Earth will be reduced and the star will seem to give a long, slow "wink." The prototype of these eclipsing binaries is Algol (Beta Persei) [11, 12], in which eclipses occur every 2.87 days and the magnitude drops from 2.2 to 3.5. Minimum magnitude lasts for 20 minutes and each fade—and recovery—takes five hours. Many stars of the Algol type are known. With Beta Lyrae [13, 14], near Vega, the components are close and less unequal. As a result there are two well-marked minima during the total period, which amounts to 12.9 days. Some eclipsing binaries have short periods—Delta Librae's, for example, is only 2.3 days. Others have long periods—972 days for Zeta Aurigae, near Capella, and as much as 27 years for Epsilon Aurigae, which lie in the same region of the sky [15, 16], but which are not genuinely associated.

It is evident that there is no essential difference between an eclipsing binary and an ordinary system; everything depends on the angle from which observations are made. Seen from a different angle, Algol would not show eclipses at all.

The importance of binary stars

Binary pairs were formerly thought to be the result of the fission or breaking up of a single star that rotated so quickly as to become unstable. It is now thought that the components of the binary stars are formed separately in the same region of space and at the same time.

Binary stars are more readily analyzed than most other stars. Measuring the mass of a single star is difficult, but observation of the components' orbital movements enables astronomers to estimate the combined mass of binary systems. Eclipsing binaries provide further opportunities for collecting data; study of their light-curves gives insights into the diameters of the components.

KEY

The 7 stars of Ursa Major [A] – the star pattern called the Big Dipper – include Mizar, magnitude 2.4, or Zeta Ursae Majoris, in the handle of the dipper. Naked-eye observation on a clear night reveals Alcor, magnitude 3.9, apparently close beside Mizar. Through a telescope the binary system is seen clearly. There is an obvious difference between the primary and secondary components [B]. The system is further complicated – as the results of spectroscopic research show – for Mizar itself is another binary. Alcor is a true member of the system, but is so far from Mizar that orbital revolution takes millions of years.

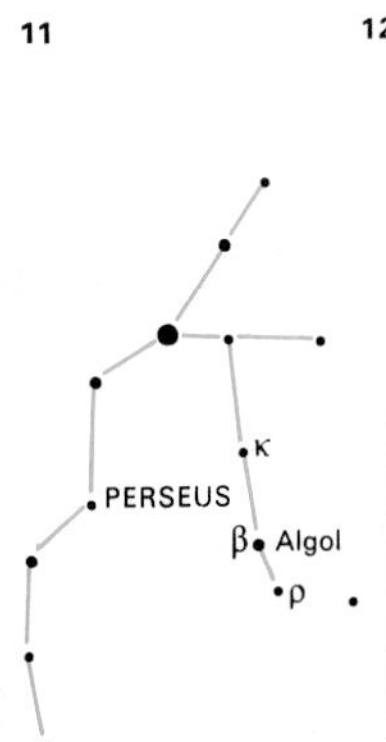

κ
PERSEUS
β
Algol
ρ

11 Perseus contains some fairly bright stars and is a distinctive shape. Algol lies in the southern part of the constellation and has much fainter stars (Kappa and Rho) on either side of it.

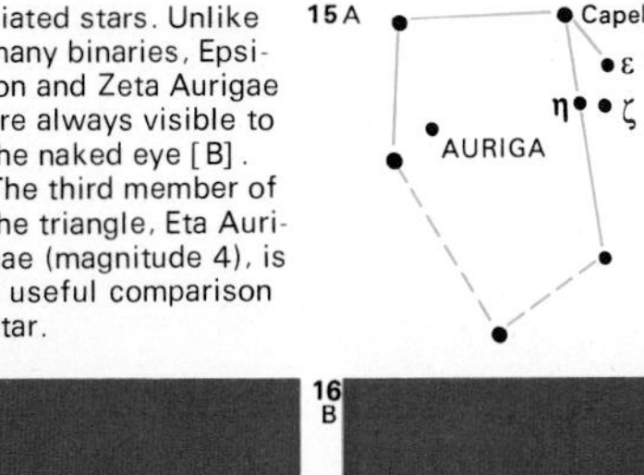

hours
5 0·3 5
68·8
5 0·3 5

12 The Algol Binary System has a small, bright star of type B8 (yellow) and a large, fainter star of type K (orange). When the brighter star passes in front of the fainter one [1], the total light received drops imperceptibly. When the two stars shine together [2], the light is constant. The main minimum occurs when the fainter star passes in front of the brighter one [3], its size blocking much of the light.

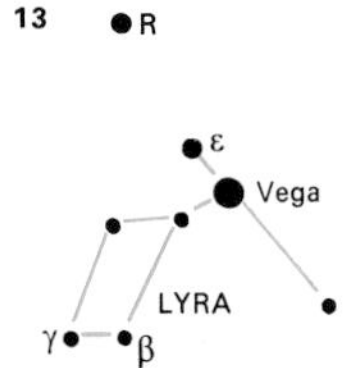

R
ε
Vega
LYRA
γ
β

13 The brilliant blue star Vega, 26 light-years away, lies in the small constellation of Lyra. Fifty times as luminous as the Sun, Vega dominates the whole region. Close by is the quadruple star Epsilon Lyrae (composed of a wide pair, each double) and a red, semi-variable, R. Lyrae. Beta Lyrae (or Sheliak), the eclipsing binary, makes up a pair with its neighbor, the third-magnitude Gamma Lyrae.

14 The components of Beta Lyrae are so close that they almost touch. Although they cannot be seen separately and are surrounded by complicated gas clouds, it is known that they must be egg-shaped due to their close proximity. Unlike Algol, Beta Lyrae is always varying – there are two minima, one of magnitude 3.8 and the other 4.3, taking place alternately. The maximum magnitude is 3.4; the period is 12.9 days.

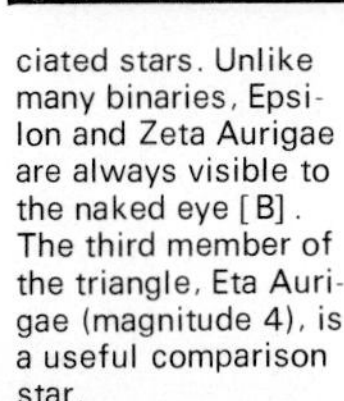

Capella
ε
η
ζ
AURIGA

15 The pattern of Auriga [A] is dominated by the bright yellow Capella. The two eclipsing binaries Epsilon and Zeta Aurigae lie in the small triangle close by Capella, but are not genuinely associated stars. Unlike many binaries, Epsilon and Zeta Aurigae are always visible to the naked eye [B]. The third member of the triangle, Eta Aurigae (magnitude 4), is a useful comparison star.

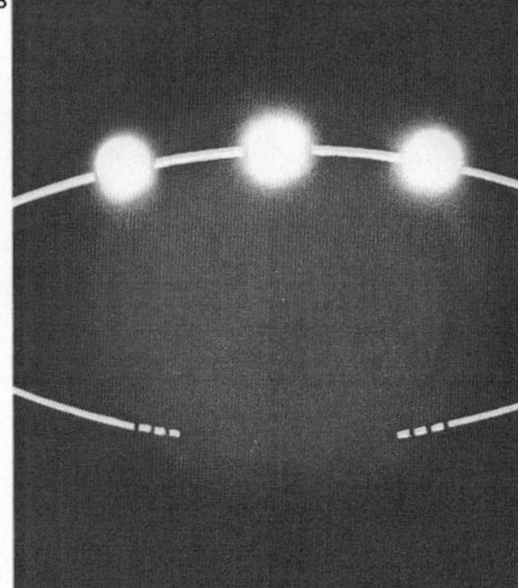

16 Zeta Aurigae is made up of an orange supergiant star type K9, diameter 180 million miles (290 million km) and a hot white star type B7, diameter 2.5 million miles (4 million km). When the bright star is eclipsed [A] (every 972 days), it shines for three weeks through the supergiant's tenuous outer layers, with informative spectral changes. When the bright star passes in front of the supergiant [B] there is no marked decrease in light.

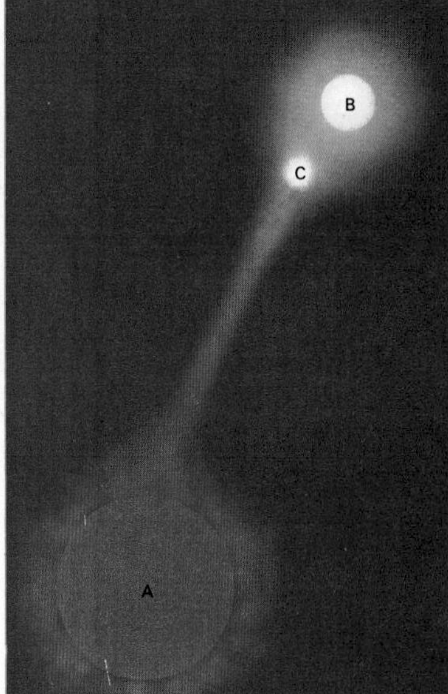

B
C
A

17 Dwarf nova binaries (or U Geminorum stars) are close binaries, in which one star is a member of the main sequence and the other is a white dwarf. Material is pulled off the larger star [A] across to the white dwarf [B] in a jet, striking the gaseous envelope and producing a spot [C] brighter than the stars themselves. Variations in this jet produce rapid flickerings in the light, detectable only with electronic equipment. Periodic outbursts come from the white dwarf.

Pulsating stars

Pulsating stars are variables whose brightness wanes with time because of cycles of expansion and contraction. The variations may be regular or irregular, varying from a few minutes to many centuries. Astronomers have been continually engaged in monitoring and searching for new variables [2, 3]. A notable observer, John Goodricke (1764–86), was the first to realize that the curious "winking" behavior of Algol, in Perseus, is caused by the periodic eclipse of the bright star by a darker companion; he also discovered the variability of Delta Cephei, which has proved to be one of the really important members of the Galaxy as far as theoretical research is concerned.

Delta Cephei [5], in the far north of the sky, has a fairly small magnitude range of 3.6 to 4.3, so that it is never conspicuous and yet never becomes so dim that it is hard to see with the naked eye. Its period—the time between one maximum and the next—is 5.3 days and absolutely regular, so that the brightness for any particular moment can always be predicted. Subsequently, other stars of the same kind were discovered: Eta Aquilae in the Eagle, with a period of 7.17 days; Zeta Geminorum in the Twins, 10.2 days; and Kappa Pavonis [6B] in the southern constellation of the Peacock, 9.1 days. With modern methods many thousands of similar variables have been found and they have become classified as Cepheids, after the first member of the class.

The period-luminosity law

Cepheids are giant stars of high luminosity. Being well advanced in their careers, they have become unstable. They are quite unlike the explosive stars, however, whose behavior cannot be predicted. But the Cepheids are of vital importance for one main reason: their changes in output provide a key to their real luminosities and hence to their distances.

That key was discovered in 1912 by Henrietta Leavitt, who was working on photographs of the external system known as the Small Magellanic Cloud [Key, 2]. The Cloud contains Cepheids, and Leavitt found that the stars of longer period looked brighter than those of shorter period. For practical purposes the stars in the Cloud can be regarded as equally distant from Earth—just as, for practical purposes, two men, one standing in Times Square and the other by the Statue of Liberty, are equally distant from London or Paris—and so it followed that the brighter Cepheids were genuinely the more luminous. If a star's real power and apparent brightness are known, then its distance can be determined. Naturally, many corrections had to be made (notably for the absorption of light in space), but the principle was clear and the Cepheid period-luminosity law has provided the main method of gauging distance in the Galaxy.

Beyond the Galaxy

In 1923 Edwin Hubble (1889–1953), at Mount Wilson, found Cepheids in some of the "starry nebulae," including M31 in Andromeda. As soon as he had found their periods, he could obtain their distances. He realized that the Cepheids—and hence the spirals themselves—lay far beyond the

CONNECTIONS

Read first
100 Star types

See also
114 Irregular stars
130 Star guide: northern sky I
132 Star guide: northern sky II
134 Star guide: southern sky I
136 Star guide: southern sky II
138 Seasonal star maps: northern
140 Seasonal star maps: southern

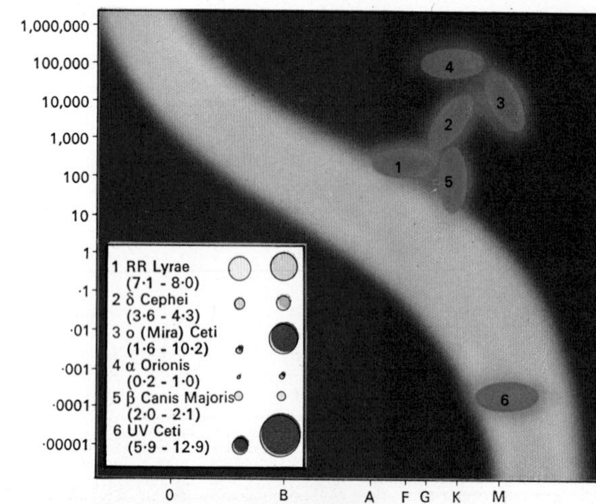
1
1,000,000
100,000
10,000
1,000
100
10
1
·1
·01
·001
·0001
·00001
1 RR Lyrae
(7·1 - 8·0)
2 δ Cephei
(3·6 - 4·3)
3 o (Mira) Ceti
(1·6 - 10·2)
4 α Orionis
(0·2 - 1·0)
5 β Canis Majoris
(2·0 - 2·1)
6 UV Ceti
(5·9 - 12·9)
O B A F G K M

1 The Hertzsprung-Russell diagram shows a star's luminosity (or absolute magnitude) against its spectral type. Here the main classes of pulsating stars are plotted—RR Lyrae stars [1], Cepheids [2], the long-period Mira stars [3], red variables [4], Beta Canis Majoris variables [5], and flare stars [6]. The inset gives the variation in magnitude from minimum to maximum of the principal members of each class. The Cepheids are of early spectral type, in a stage through which many stars are thought to pass.

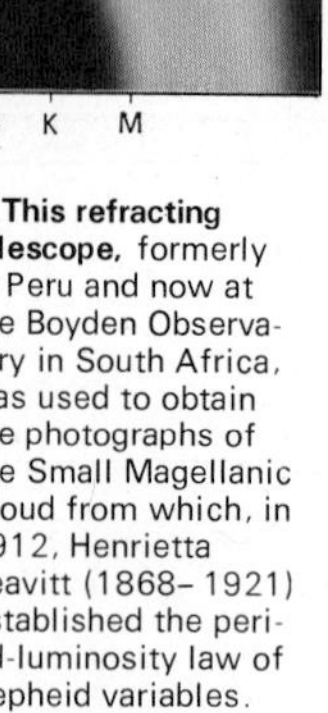

2 This refracting telescope, formerly in Peru and now at the Boyden Observatory in South Africa, was used to obtain the photographs of the Small Magellanic Cloud from which, in 1912, Henrietta Leavitt (1868–1921) established the period-luminosity law of Cepheid variables.

3 The 100-in (254-cm) Hooker reflector at Mount Wilson was completed in 1918. For 30 years the most powerful telescope in the world, it was used by Hubble in studies of short-period variables in external galaxies. At that time, the 1920s, no other instrument was powerful enough for research of this kind. The 100-inch is still in full operation. The mounting is of the English type, so that the telescope can never be pointed towards the celestial pole. The driving mechanism is run by falling weights.

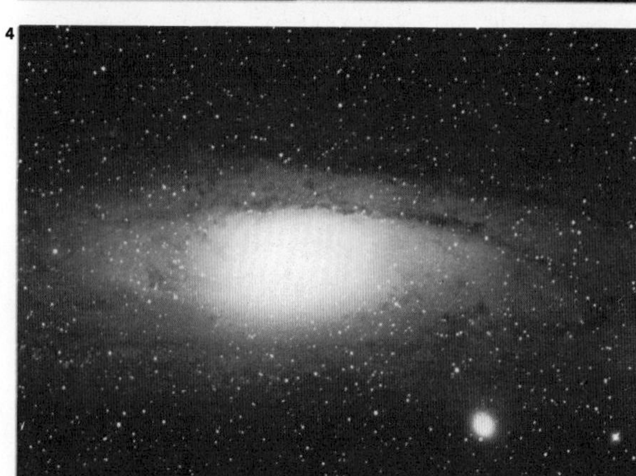

4 Trying to find short-period variables in external galaxies, Hubble concentrated on the Andromeda Spiral—not then known to be beyond our Galaxy. As the most impressive of the spirals, it seemed likely to be relatively near by cosmic standards. Hubble failed to find RR Lyrae variables in it, but he was able to locate Cepheids, and as soon as he had observed their periods he was able to use the period-luminosity law to show that the Cepheids—and hence the Spiral itself—must be beyond the Milky Way. His estimate was 750,000 light-years but the real value is 2.2 million light-years.

limits of our own Galaxy. Without Hubble's discovery of those convenient Cepheids, proof would have been difficult to obtain. His original estimates, however, were too low because of an error in the Cepheid scale that was not corrected until 1952. Hubble believed the Andromeda Spiral to be 750,000 light-years away; the distance turned out to be 2.2 million light-years [4].

Because Cepheids are so powerful, they can be seen over immense distances and even at about 40 million light-years are still detectable. There are also some associated variables of shorter period (less than a day), all of which appear to be of about the same luminosity, roughly 90 times that of the Sun. Once called cluster-Cepheids, they are now known as RR Lyrae stars after the best-known member of the class.

Long-period stars

Cepheids and RR Lyrae variables [7] are pulsating stars, alternately swelling and shrinking. There are also stars that pulsate in much longer periods, of from a few weeks up to a year or more. These are the long-period variables, often called Mira stars after Mira [10, 11, 12], the "Wonderful Star" in Cetus, the Whale. Virtually all stars of this kind are old red giants of tremendous size and high luminosity; they have used up their available hydrogen "fuel" and are unstable. Mira stars follow no Cepheid-type period-luminosity law and indeed the periods and the amplitudes are not constant. Mira itself has a period of 331 days, which may vary by a week or so either way from one cycle to another. At some maxima Mira may become as bright as the Pole Star (magnitude 2), while at other maxima it is no brighter than the fourth magnitude. When at its faintest the magnitude is about 10, so that ordinary binoculars will not show it. Another Mira star is Chi Cygni, in the Swan, which ranges between magnitudes 3.3 and 14.2.

There are also semiregular variables, such as Betelgeuse in Orion, with small amplitudes and periods that are very irregular. Most are red giants and they too swell and shrink, changing their output of energy as they do so.

KEY

The Small Magellanic Cloud is in the southern sky, inaccessible from the great northern observatories. Photographs taken from Peru established that it contains Cepheids, on which the period-luminosity law was based.

5

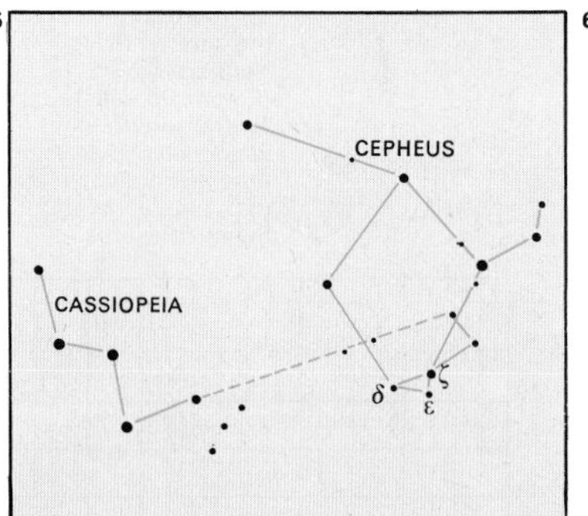
CEPHEUS
CASSIOPEIA
δ
ζ
ε

5 Delta Cephei lies in the far north of the sky. It forms a triangle with Epsilon and Zeta Cephei, which act as convenient comparison stars. The fluctuations of Delta are obvious.

7 The periods of RR Lyrae stars, formerly called cluster-Cepheids, are much shorter than those of the classical Cepheids. They are all of about the same luminosity.

6 A

B

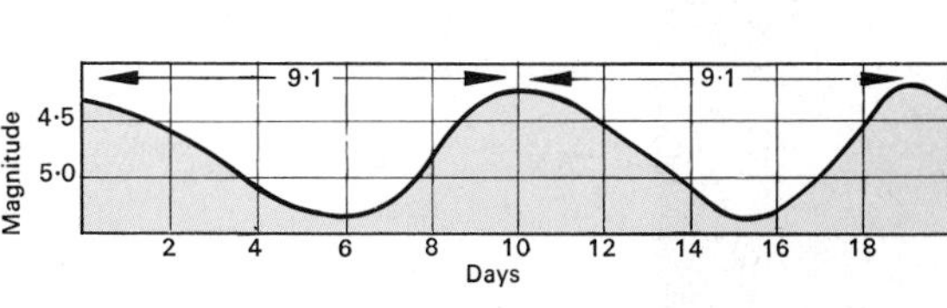
9·1
9·1
Magnitude
4·5
5·0
2
4
6
8
10
12
14
16
18
Days

6 Cepheid variables are notable for their regularity. Delta Cephei itself has a period of 5.3 days [A]; in comparison the light curve of the southern Cepheid variable Kappa Pavonis has a period of 9.1 days [B]. The shapes of the curves are not identical. Kappa Pavonis, with a longer period, is the more luminous. Other famous Cepheids are Zeta Geminorum (10.2 days) and Eta Aquilae (7.17 days).

7

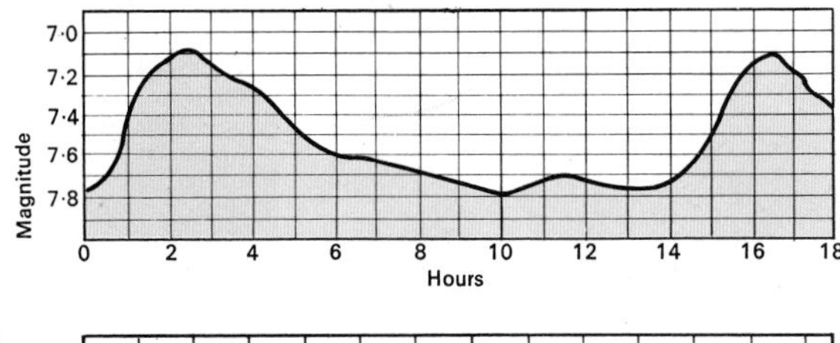
7·0
7·2
7·4
7·6
7·8
Magnitude
0
2
4
6
8
10
12
14
16
18
Hours

8 Eta Geminorum is a semiregular variable with a small magnitude range; neither the period nor the amplitude is constant from one period to another but the fluctuations are relatively slight.

8

9

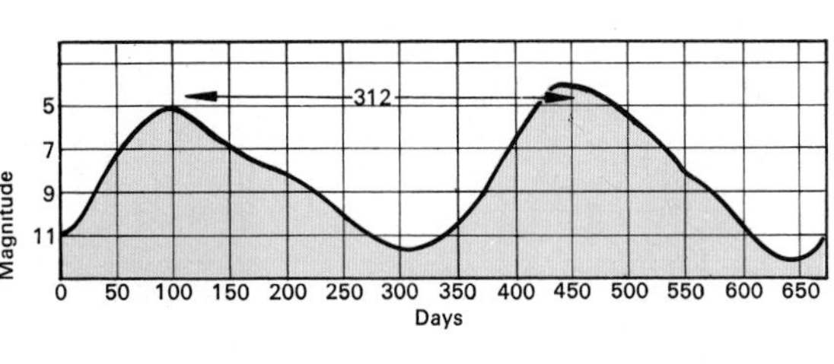
312
5
7
9
11
Magnitude
0
50
100
150
200
250
300
350
400
450
500
550
600
650
Days

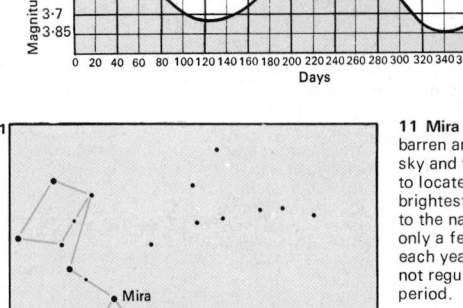

9 The light curve of R Leonis is a typical long-period variable of the Mira type. As with all Mira stars, both period and amplitude are subject to fluctuation. At its brightest, R Leonis is a naked-eye object.

10

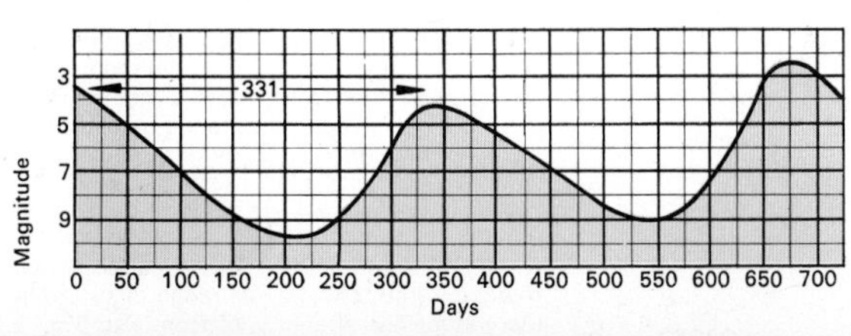
331
3
5
7
9
Magnitude
0
50
100
150
200
250
300
350
400
450
500
550
600
650
700
Days

10 Mira Ceti is another long-period variable that is visible to the naked eye. The average period is 331 days; the magnitude ranges from 1.7 to 4 at maximum and down to 10 at minimum.

11

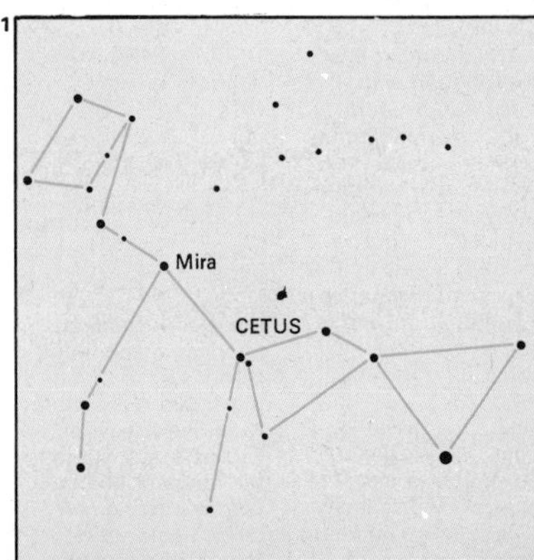
Mira
CETUS

11 Mira Ceti lies in a barren area of the sky and thus is easy to locate when at its brightest. It is visible to the naked eye for only a few weeks each year, although not regularly in each period.

12 The size of Mira is here compared with the Sun; it has a diameter, like all red giants, of more than 100 million miles (160 million km). The diameter changes as the star's output of energy varies.

12

Irregular stars

Not all variable stars are predictable. Like the regular pulsating stars, the many irregular variables are categorized into groups of similar type. For instance, all semiregular stars, such as Betelgeuse, have only approximate periods—the time elapsed between a star's magnitude at maximum and minimum. R Coronae stars [2] remain normally at maximum and suffer sudden, unpredictable drops to minimum. U Geminorum stars [3, 4], or "dwarf novae," are normally at minimum, but increase abruptly to maximum before fading away again. RV Tauri stars [5, 6] are G- to K-type giants and have alternate deep and shallow minimums, upon which are superimposed periods of total irregularity. Flare stars [Key], for example the M-type giant UV Ceti, show sudden increases over periods of minutes and remain at maximum only briefly, so that their changes can actually be watched. Recurrent novae show sudden, violent outbursts over periods of years; thus T Coronae exploded in 1866 and again in 1946. Normal novae [7–10] show one outburst only and then return to their former obscurity. The exceptional star Eta Carinae [11, 12] is classed as a pseudo-nova.

It is customary to draw light curves of irregular variable stars and novae in the same way as those for regular pulsating stars, relating apparent magnitude to time. (Apparent, or visual, magnitude is the apparent brightness of a celestial body as seen with the eye. The brighter the object, the smaller the numerical value of the magnitude.) It must be emphasized that the apparent magnitude of a star is its brilliancy as seen from Earth; it is not a reliable guide to a star's real luminosity. Only the variable stars and novae show short-term changes in apparent magnitude.

Semiregular and irregular stars

Most of the semiregular stars are red giants. They are regarded as unstable because they swell and shrink. Betelgeuse in Orion is one such star. Sometimes it almost equals Rigel in brilliance; its mean magnitude (0.85) is comparable to that of Aldebaran. It has an approximate period of five to six years between maximum and minimum, but the irregularities are very marked. Rasalgethi, or Alpha Herculis, is another semiregular variable that is easily visible to the naked eye. Semiregular stars that can be detected only by telescope are also common. Generally the variations in magnitude are not great.

Most irregular variables are telescopic objects. Gamma Cassiopeiae [1], however, can rise to almost the brilliance of Castor in the Twins—as it did in 1936. From the spectral changes it appeared that the star was throwing off a shell of material.

Probably the most erratic variable in the sky is Eta Carinae, in the southern hemisphere. During the middle of the nineteenth century it shone more brightly than any star in the sky except Sirius, but since 1867 it has been too faint to be seen with the naked eye. When seen through a telescope it appears orange-red and surrounded by nebulosity. Very luminous and remote, it may provide a link between variable stars and novae.

R Coronae and U Geminorum stars

R Coronae Borealis [2], in the Northern Crown, is the prototype of a class of stars of

CONNECTIONS

Read first
100 Star types

See also
112 Pulsating stars
130 Star guide: northern sky I
132 Star guide: northern sky II
134 Star guide: southern sky I
136 Star guide: southern sky II
138 Seasonal star maps: northern
140 Seasonal star maps: southern

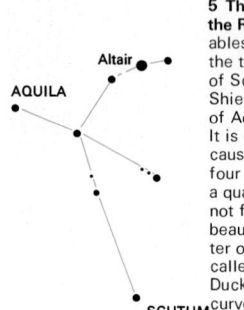

1 The W of Cassiopeia contains the irregular variable star Gamma [1]. Alpha Cassiopeiae, or Shedir [2] (spectral type K), is also suspected of slight variability, although with a small range of magnitude.

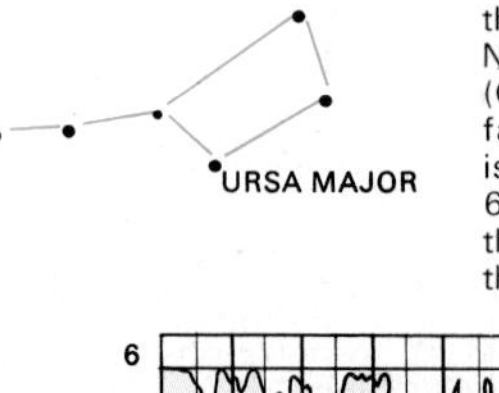
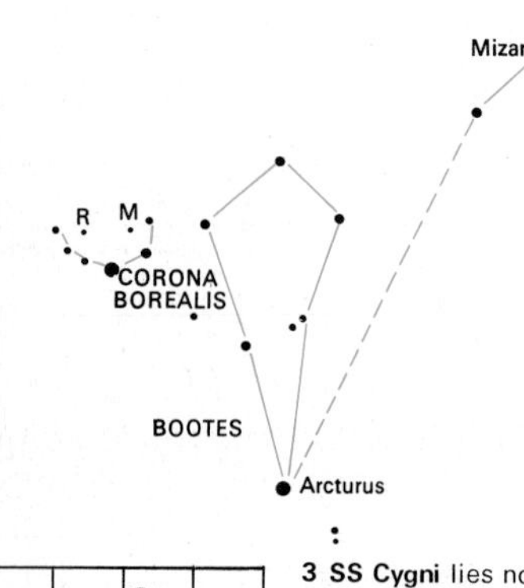

Mizar
URSA MAJOR
R
M
CORONA BOREALIS
BOOTES
Arcturus

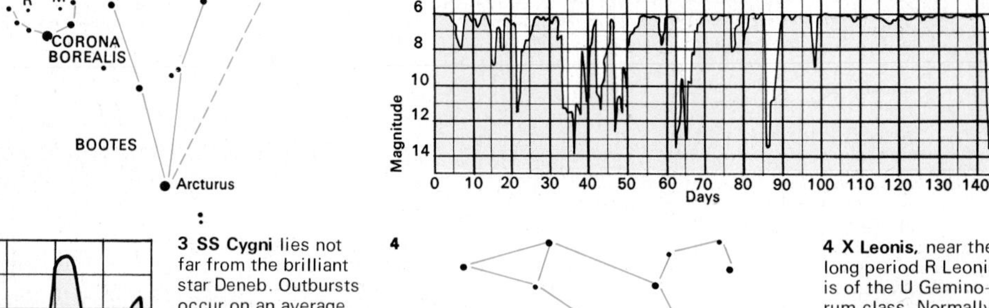

Magnitude
Days

2 R Coronae lies in the bowl of the Northern Crown (Corona Borealis) not far from Arcturus. It is normally about the 6th magnitude, so that, together with the most useful comparison star [M] with a magnitude of 6.6, it can be seen clearly with binoculars. At some minimums R Coronae drops to 15 and cannot be seen through small telescopes.

3 SS Cygni lies not far from the brilliant star Deneb. Outbursts occur on an average of every six weeks (from magnitude 12 to 8.25), but this may show wide fluctuation. SS Cygni is the brightest U Geminorum variable.

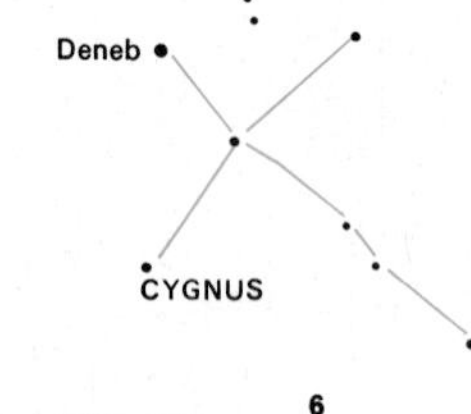

Deneb
CYGNUS

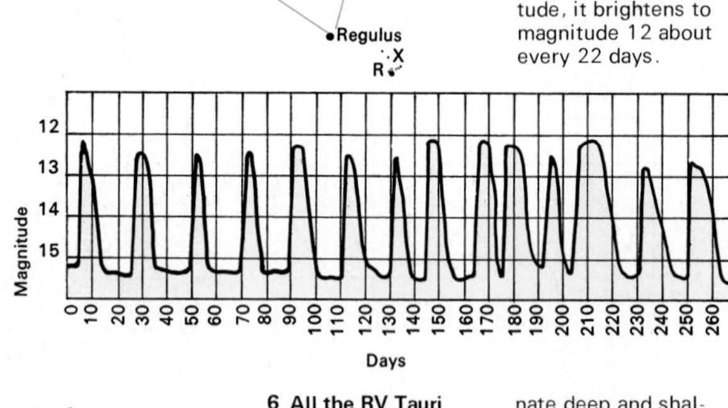

LEO
Regulus
X
R
Magnitude
Days

4 X Leonis, near the long period R Leonis, is of the U Geminorum class. Normally of the 15th magnitude, it brightens to magnitude 12 about every 22 days.

5 The brightest of the RV Tauri variables is R Scuti in the tiny constellation of Scutum, the Shield, near the tail of Aquila, the Eagle. It is easy to find because it is one of four stars making up a quadrilateral and is not far from the beautiful open cluster of M11, which is called the "Wild Duck." The light curve shows magnitude plotted against time; but the curve is only an average, since all RV Tauri stars are erratic in their behavior. The range of R Scuti is between magnitudes 5 and 8.6, so that at maximum it is visible to the naked eye. It always stays within the range of binoculars, appearing reddish in color. It is therefore a favorite object for amateur astronomers with small telescopes.

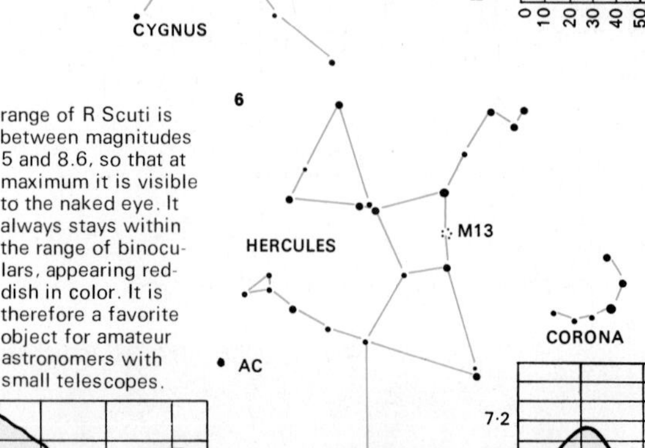

HERCULES
M13
AC
CORONA
Rasalgethi
α
Rasalhague

6 All the RV Tauri stars are highly luminous and are among the most massive variables known; some are at least 25 times as massive as the Sun. Unfortunately, all are remote and few are within binocular range. The alternate deep and shallow minimums may sometimes be replaced by periods of total irregularity. AC Herculis, whose light curve is shown here, is a case in point; it has a magnitude with a range of variation of from 7 to 8.5.

which less than 50 members are known. R Coronae stars stay at their brightest for most of the time but suffer sudden, unpredictable falls to minimum. They are poor in hydrogen but rich in carbon and it has been suggested that the minimums may be caused by the accumulation of carbon particles in the star's outer atmosphere, which causes the radiation from the star itself to be temporarily shut in. R Coronae at maximum is on the fringe of naked-eye visibility.

The U Geminorum, or SS Cygni, stars normally stay at minimum, but undergo periodic outbursts. The average interval between outbursts of SS Cygni [3] is about six weeks. It is now known that all U Geminorum stars are close binaries, with one white dwarf component together with a red dwarf.

Normal and recurrent novae

A nova is not a new star; it is a formerly obscure star that has suddenly increased in brilliancy. Some novae have been very brilliant; both Nova Persei (1901) [7] and Nova Aquilae (1918) [8] exceeded the first magnitude at maximum. Once a nova has passed its peak it fades back to its original brightness, although it may take years to do so. It is thought that the outburst affects only the star's outer layers—whereas in a supernova explosion the star in its old form is destroyed. Many, perhaps all, novae are spectroscopic binaries.

One of the most interesting novae of modern times, HR Delphini [10], was discovered in July 1967. It never became brighter than magnitude 3.6, but it was very slow to fade and remained a naked-eye object for a year. By 1975 it had fallen to below magnitude 11, but it may not fade much further. It is one of the few novae whose pre-outburst magnitude (12) is well known. Since it is about 30,000 light-years away, we are watching the results of an explosion that happened 30,000 years ago.

A few stars have been known to experience more than one outburst: T Coronae blazed up from magnitude 9 to 2 in 1866 and from magnitude 10 to above 3 in 1946. Such stars are known as recurrent novae, but not many of them are recorded.

KEY

1.00am 1.15 1.30 1.45

Radio intensity

Flare stars, such as UV Ceti, are nearby dwarfs and, alone among variable stars, change in brilliancy so quickly that they can be watched as their luminosity increases over a period of minutes. The sudden increases are due to flare activity.

7

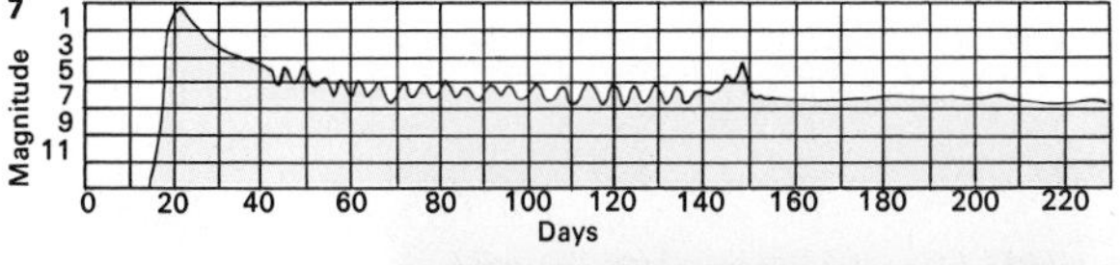
Magnitude
1
3
5
7
9
11
0 20 40 60 80 100 120 140 160 180 200 220
Days

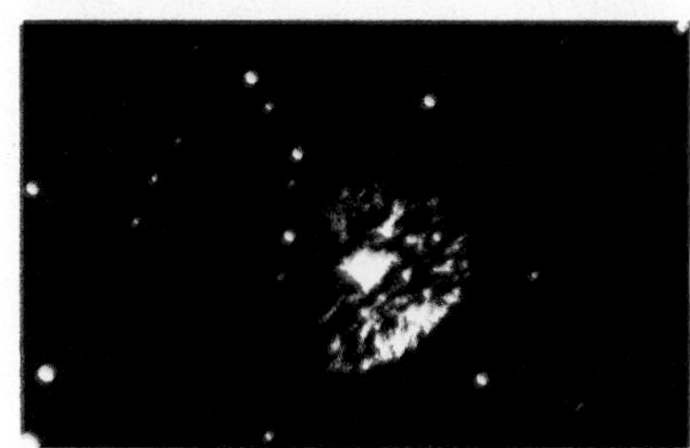

7 Nova Persei (1901) became very brilliant but declined rapidly. The decrease was attended by marked fluctuations. Nebulosity around the star was illuminated, giving the false impression of an expanding cloud. Today Nova Persei is a faint object in the sky.

8

Magnitude 0 5 10

0 50 100 150 200 250 300 350 400 450 500 550 600

Days

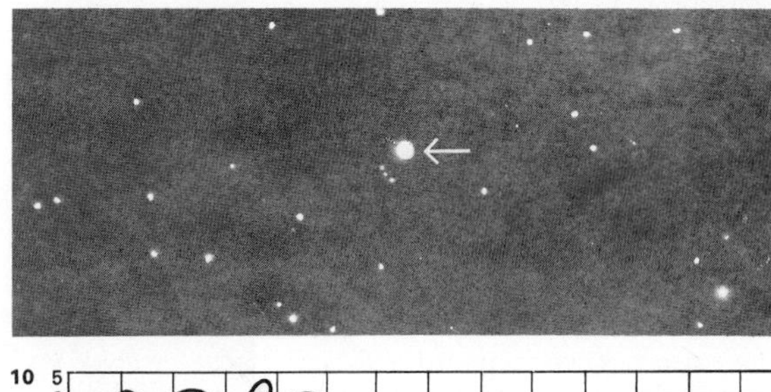

8 Nova Aquilae (1918) appeared with dramatic suddenness. At its maximum, on June 9, its magnitude was −1.4, equal to Sirius. It soon faded, but remained visible to the naked eye until November 1918. A nebulous cloud around it steadily expanded and became dimmer, finally disappearing from view in 1940. The old nova is still visible, although extremely faint. It was the brightest nova of modern times.

9

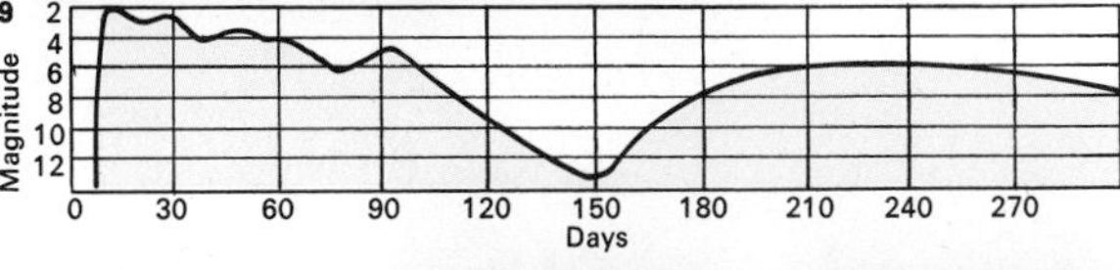
Magnitude
2
4
6
8
10
12
0 30 60 90 120 150 180 210 240 270
Days

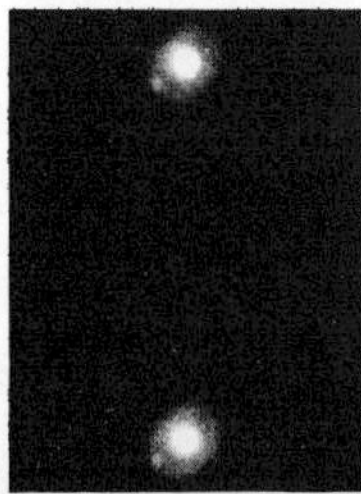

9 Nova (DQ) Hercúlis (1934) exceeded the 2nd magnitude and was unusual because it showed a temporary recovery after its drop from maximum. These photographs taken in 1951 show that the nova is a close binary with associated nebulosity. It is classed as a "slow nova."

10

Magnitude 5 6 7 8 9

1 2 3 4 5 6 7 8 9 10 11 12 13 14

Months

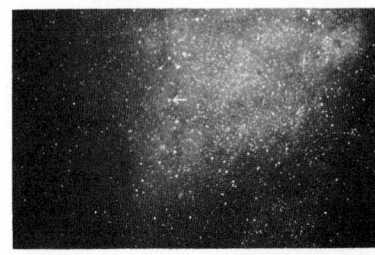

10 HR Delphini (1967) has the distinction of being the slowest true nova on record. The maximum lasted for six months, although with definite fluctuations, and the subsequent fall was gradual. HR Delphini can be observed through a small telescope.

11 Eta Carinae is not a normal nova. It is intensely luminous and is associated with complex nebulosity. The fluctuations may be due in part to variations in density of the nebulosity, but the star itself must also be intrinsically variable. In the telescope it is very strongly red and is much less well defined than a normal star because of the nebulosity.

11

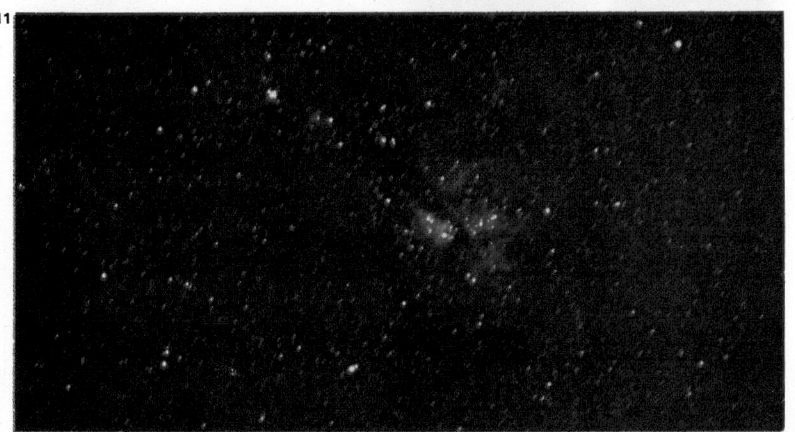

12

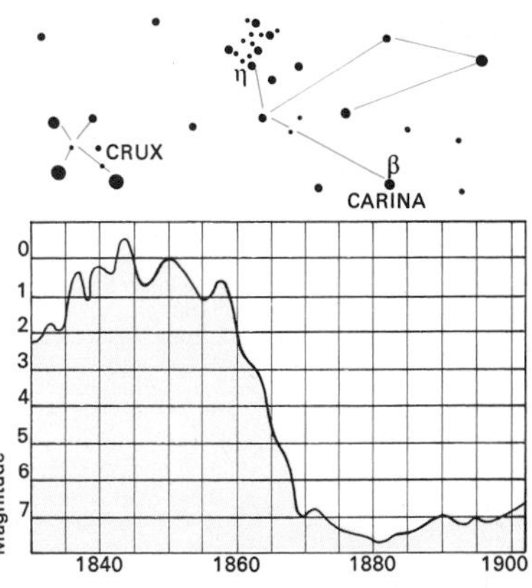
η
CRUX
β
CARINA
Magnitude
0
1
2
3
4
5
6
7
1840 1860 1880 1900

12 In the Keel of the Ship, near the Southern Cross and the 2nd-magnitude star Beta Carinae, lies Eta Carinae. It is the most erratic of all variables. It reached its maximum brightness in the 1840s when it was exceeded only by Sirius; it then declined and since about 1867 has not been visible to the naked eye, although binoculars will show it. It is surrounded by nebulosity and is in every way an exceptional object of high luminosity.

Stellar clusters

The Earth is in a part of the Galaxy in which the density distribution of the stars in space is about average. Its nearest neighbor, Proxima Centauri, is more than four light-years away and there are not many stars within a radius of ten light-years from the Sun. Here and there in the Galaxy, however, are groups of stars making up genuine clusters. The best-known example is the cluster of the Pleiades, or Seven Sisters [5], in Taurus; several others are easily visible to the naked eye and the number of known clusters visible through a telescope is very great.

Open clusters

Clusters are essentially of two kinds: open and globular. The open, or loose, clusters are found in the spiral arms of our Galaxy and are irregular in shape; they may be rich with thousands of members or poor with only a dozen or two. They are not due merely to line-of-sight effects.

There are wide differences between the various open clusters. In the Pleiades cluster the brightest stars are hot and white and there is a large reflection nebula indicating the presence of a great deal of interstellar material; by cosmic standards the group is extremely young. Several of its chief stars are known to be in rapid rotation, and one of them, Pleione, is so unstable that it periodically sheds some of its material, producing a shell or gaseous ring around its equator. This can be studied only by spectroscopic methods.

In the second of the Taurus clusters, the Hyades [3] (around Aldebaran), the star density is smaller; the principal members are not so energetic and the amount of material spread between the stars is less. The Hyades are not as spectacular as the Pleiades because they are largely overpowered by the brilliant orange light of Aldebaran. Yet Aldebaran is not a true member of the cluster at all and here a line-of-sight effect is found: Aldebaran lies midway between Hyades and ourselves.

Other naked-eye clusters are Praesepe, the "Beehive" [4], in Cancer and the lovely southern cluster around Kappa Crucis, known as the "Jewel Box" because it contains stars of varied colors. In Perseus, not far from the W of Cassiopeia, is the "Sword Handle" [2], made up of two rich clusters in the same telescopic field.

Open clusters are not stable associations and must eventually be disrupted by the gravitational pulls of field stars in the Galaxy. It has been estimated that most of them have life spans of no more than 1 billion years before being scattered to the extent of losing their separate identity. One of the oldest clusters known, M67 in Cancer, which is easily visible with binoculars near the star Alpha Cancri, may be more than 4 billion years old, but it lies well away from the galactic plane and so is less liable to disruption.

Globular clusters

Globular clusters are of an entirely different type. Only about 120 are known to exist in our Galaxy. They are symmetrical and may contain hundreds of thousands of stars. As seen from Earth they are so condensed toward their centers that they are difficult to resolve into individual stars. Even so, the danger of stellar collisions occurring re-

CONNECTIONS

Read first
100 Star types

See also
130 Star guide: northern sky I
132 Star guide: northern sky II
134 Star guide: southern sky I
136 Star guide: southern sky II

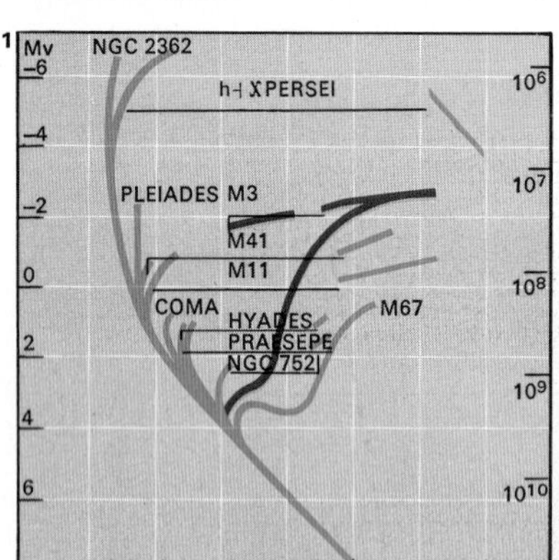

Mv
NGC 2362
h-χ PERSEI
PLEIADES M3
M41
M11
COMA
HYADES
PRAESEPE
NGC 752
M67
-6
-4
-2
0
2
4
6
10⁶
10⁷
10⁸
10⁹
10¹⁰
-0·4
0
0·4
0·8
1·2
1·6
2·0 B-V

1 The color-magnitude graph of open clusters shows absolute magnitude (Mv) against color index (B–V=photographic magnitude minus visual magnitude). The age (years) is given on the right.

2 The twin clusters in Perseus were cataloged by Dreyer as NGC 869 and 884; they are also known as h and Chi Persei. Each cluster is 75 light-years across and contains about 350 stars.

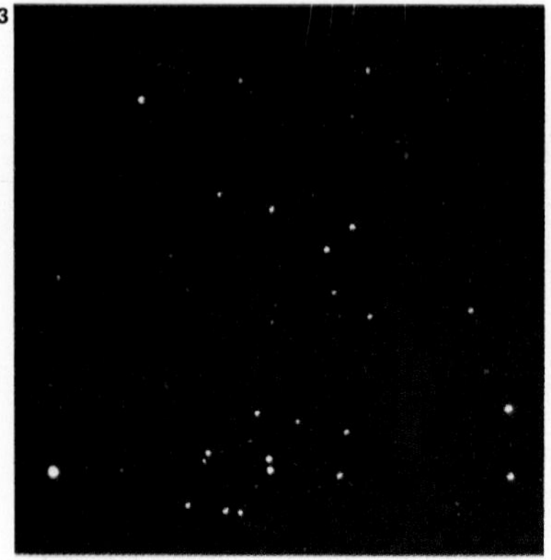

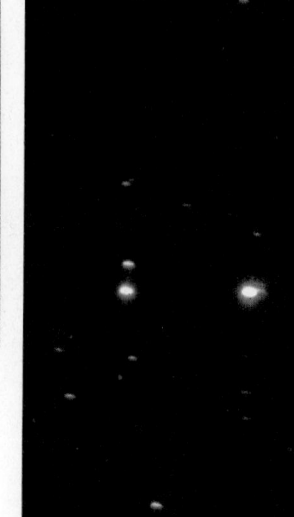

3 The Hyades, around Aldebaran (lower left, not itself a cluster member) are visible to the naked eye. The group extends in a V formation away from Aldebaran. The stars are easy to make out and one of them, Theta Tauri, is a naked-eye double. The Hyades are so scattered that the group is not nearly so spectacular as the Pleiades. The best view is obtained with binoculars or with a telescope of low magnification and a wide field that will include all the stars.

4 Praesepe, in Cancer, is an example of an open cluster visible to the naked eye. It is 525 light-years away and has been known since early times. It is not a condensed cluster, and lies well away from the galactic plane.

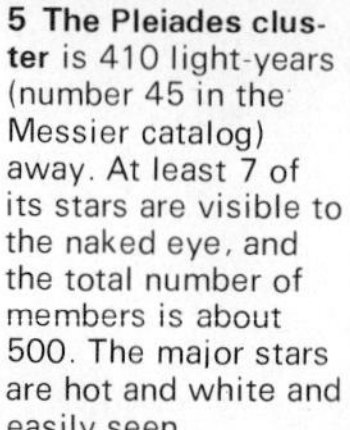
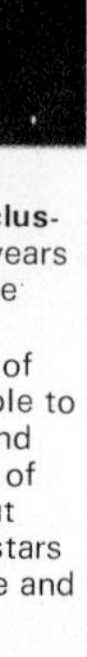

5 The Pleiades cluster is 410 light-years (number 45 in the Messier catalog) away. At least 7 of its stars are visible to the naked eye, and the total number of members is about 500. The major stars are hot and white and easily seen.

mains slight; but to an inhabitant of a planet that was moving around a star in such a region, the night sky would be scattered with thousands of stars that would be shining more brightly than Sirius or even the full Moon as it appears to us.

The distribution of the globular clusters is not uniform over the whole sky; they surround the galactic center, so that from Earth they are only seen in the direction of the center. The distances of globular clusters have been measured by using the RR Lyrae variables contained in them. Because all RR Lyrae stars have similar periods and luminosity, their distances can be calculated more easily, enabling effective measurements of the globular clusters themselves. It was by this method that Harlow Shapley, more than 60 years ago, was able to work out the size of our Galaxy from his studies of globular clusters. Because of their considerable remoteness they form an "outer framework" to the main galactic system [Key].

The brightest globular clusters, Omega Centauri and 47 Tucanae, lie too far south in the sky to be seen from most of North America. Both are easily visible with the naked eye, and Omega Centauri in particular is a superb sight through a telescope; it is resolvable to its center. In the north, the best example is M13 in Hercules [9], which lies at a distance of 26,700 light-years and is about 100 light-years in diameter. It is just visible to the naked eye and binoculars show it well.

Globular clusters belong to the galactic halo and move around the nucleus in highly inclined, eccentric orbits. They are stable and are not subject to disruption in the same way as open clusters. They are made up of Population II objects, so that their brightest stars are, in general, of late spectral type.

Moving clusters

In addition to the open and globular clusters, there are the so-called moving clusters, whose members are widely separate but move through space in the same direction and with the same velocity. Hot, luminous O and B type stars form "stellar associations," of which nearly 100 are now known.

KEY

A

+30° +60° N +60° +30°

0° 0°

−30° −60° S −60° −30°

B

S

Two main types of stellar clusters are found in and around our Galaxy. Open, or loose clusters [A], are composed of Population I stars and they lie near the main plane of the Galaxy, although there are a few exceptional clusters that are well away from it, an example being the old cluster M67. The open clusters are therefore a part of the general rotation of the Galaxy around its nucleus. Globular clusters [B], which are made up of Population II stars, are distributed throughout the galactic halo. The position of the Sun [S] is indicated by the small open circle at the left of the Galaxy.

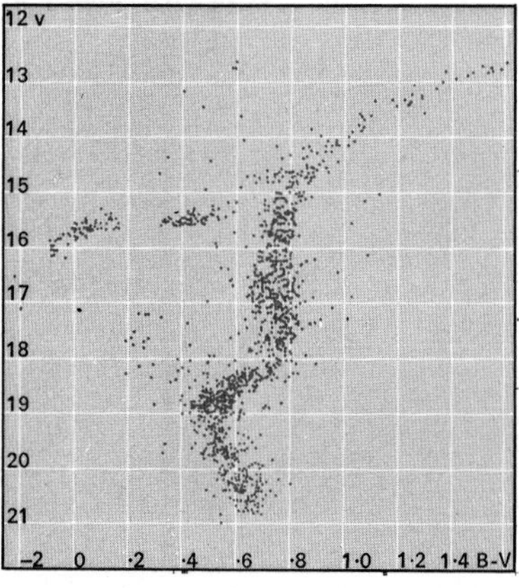

12 V
13
14
15
16
17
18
19
20
21
−2 0 ·2 ·4 ·6 ·8 1·0 1·2 1·4 B-V

6 The globular cluster M3 in Canes Venatici (the Hunting Dogs) is 48,500 light-years from us. In this color-magnitude diagram apparent magnitude, V, is plotted against the color index (B-V). The RR Lyrae variables, used to measure the distance of the cluster, lie at V=15.7—the gap in the horizontal branch.

7 The globular cluster M3 in Canes Venatici contains more than 44,000 stars of magnitude 22.5 or brighter within an 8′ radius of the center. It is typical of its kind and quite symmetrical.

8 The globular cluster M5 in Serpens was discovered in 1702 and is a bright telescopic object. It is exceptionally rich in RR Lyrae variables and more than 100 have been discovered in it.

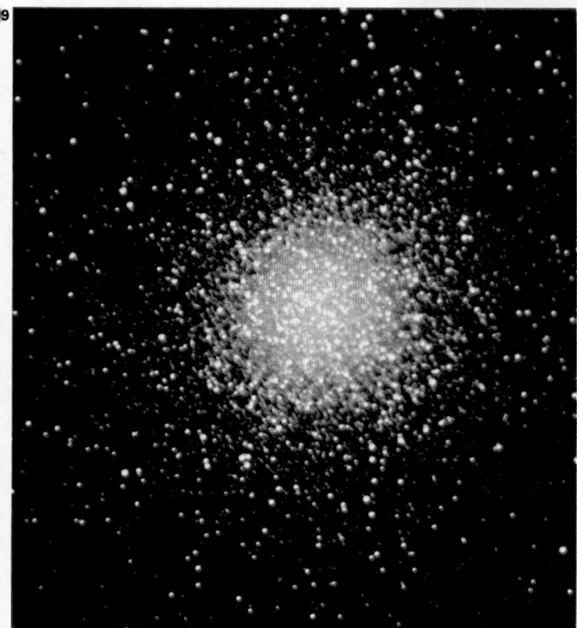

9 M13 in Hercules is the finest globular cluster in the northern sky and is found between the stars Zeta and Eta Herculish. It is 26,700 light-years away from Earth. Surprisingly, it is poor in RR Lyrae variables and less than 20 have been discovered, as against over 100 in other clusters.

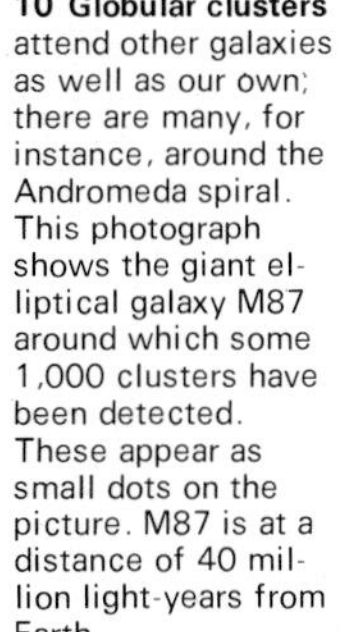

10 Globular clusters attend other galaxies as well as our own; there are many, for instance, around the Andromeda spiral. This photograph shows the giant elliptical galaxy M87 around which some 1,000 clusters have been detected. These appear as small dots on the picture. M87 is at a distance of 40 million light-years from Earth.

Our Galaxy

The Solar System, with the Sun at its center, is an insignificant part of a local system of about 100 billion suns called the Galaxy. In relation to those other stars, the Sun is neither exceptionally luminous nor exceptionally dim.

The Sun is almost certainly older than the Earth and its age cannot be less than 5 billion years. The Galaxy itself is presumably much older, although we do not have any clear knowledge of its early history. The Galaxy is a flattened system [1] and when we look along its main plane we see many stars in almost the same line of sight. That is why the stars in the Milky Way seem so closely crowded together that they appear almost to touch [Key, 6, 7].

Early observations

The Milky Way is a dominant feature of the night sky. One of the earliest and best descriptions of it was written about AD 150 by Ptolemy of Alexandria, the last great astronomer of classical times. "The Milky Way," he wrote, "is not a circle but a zone, which is everywhere as white as milk and this has given it the name it bears. Now this zone is neither equal nor regular anywhere, but varies as much in width as in shade or color, as well as in the number of stars in its parts and in the diversity of positions; also in some places it is divided into two branches, as is easy to see if we examine it with a little attention."

Most countries have legends about the Milky Way, but its nature was not known until Galileo (1564–1642) first examined it with a telescope in the winter of 1609–10. He found it to be made up of "a mass of innumerable stars," an observation that may be checked even with binoculars. The first to record the approximate shape of our Galaxy was William Herschel (1738–1822), who compared it to "a cloven grindstone." Herschel is best remembered for his discovery of the planet Uranus in 1781, although his major contributions were in the field of stellar astronomy. In particular he considered whether the starry, or resolvable, nebulae, such as those in the constellation of Andromeda, might be separate star systems well beyond our own. He was to be proved wrong, however, in his belief that the Sun lay at the center of the galactic plane.

We can never see the center of the Galaxy because of the obscuring effect of the interstellar material. Present knowledge is derived mainly from radio astronomy, by which the center can be located. It lies beyond the glorious star clouds in Sagittarius, where the Milky Way is particularly thick with stars [4]. It has been suggested that there may be a quasar there or even a black hole, but these speculations rest on uncertain evidence. Certainly radio waves come from the galactic center and it was the source of the first radio waves from the sky ever to be detected—by Karl Jansky (1905–50), founder of radio astronomy, in the early 1930s.

The form of our Galaxy

During World War I, Harlow Shapley (1885–1972) in the United States measured the size of our Galaxy from his studies of RR Lyrae variable stars in globular clusters and his estimates were very close to the

CONNECTIONS

See also
120 The local group of galaxies
122 Types of galaxies
130 Star guide:northern sky I
132 Star guide: northern sky II
134 Star guide: southern sky I
136 Star guide: southern sky II

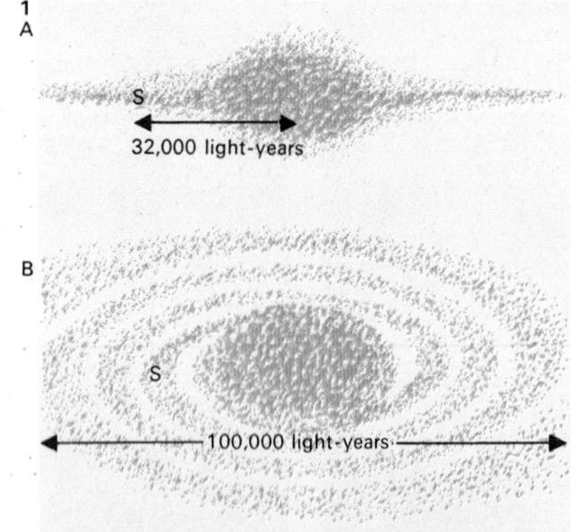

A
S
32,000 light-years
B
S
100,000 light-years

1 The shape of the Galaxy would appear different if viewed from separate vantage points well out in space. In an edge-on view [A] the shape is flattened, with a pronounced nucleus. S indicates the position of the Sun. As seen from an angle [B], the general form of the Galaxy remains clear, but the spiral arms are now displayed. The Galaxy is a rather loose spiral, but the arms can be clearly seen.

2

BD12° 4523
Munich 15040
ε Indi
Alpha Centauri
Proxima Centauri
61 Cygni
Σ2398
OA (N) 17415
Krüger 60
Ross 248
Groombridge 34
4
8
12
16 light-years
Corboda Vh 243
Sirius
Lalande 8760
ε Eridani
Procyon
BD 51° 658

2 Stars within a radius of ten light-years from the Sun make up only a small area of the Milky Way. The two ellipses around the Sun indicate the possible maximum distances of orbiting comets. Most of the nearby stars are faint red dwarfs; there are also some white dwarfs (such as the companion of Sirius). The only stars more luminous than the Sun are Sirius, Procyon, and Alpha Centauri.

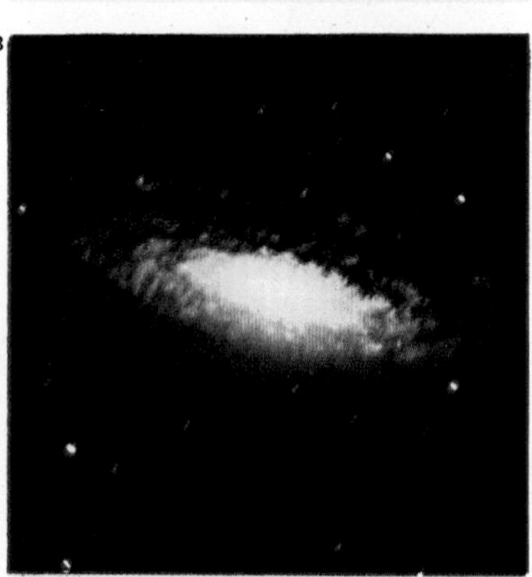

3 Galaxy NGC 7331 in Pegasus is very similar in size and mass to our own, although its spiral arms are wound more tightly. It contains some 100 billion stars. Only when the existence of galaxies outside our own was established could a true idea of the status of our Galaxy be worked out; even in 1920 it was believed that our Galaxy was unique and that the other spiral galaxies were contained inside it.

4 The center of the Galaxy lies beyond the star clouds in Sagittarius, which are seen in this photograph taken with the 48-in (122-cm) Schmidt telescope at Palomar. In addition to the star clouds, the photograph shows a considerable amount of dark nebulosity, stellar matter that betrays its presence by blotting out the light of stars beyond. This is the richest part of the entire Milky Way area.

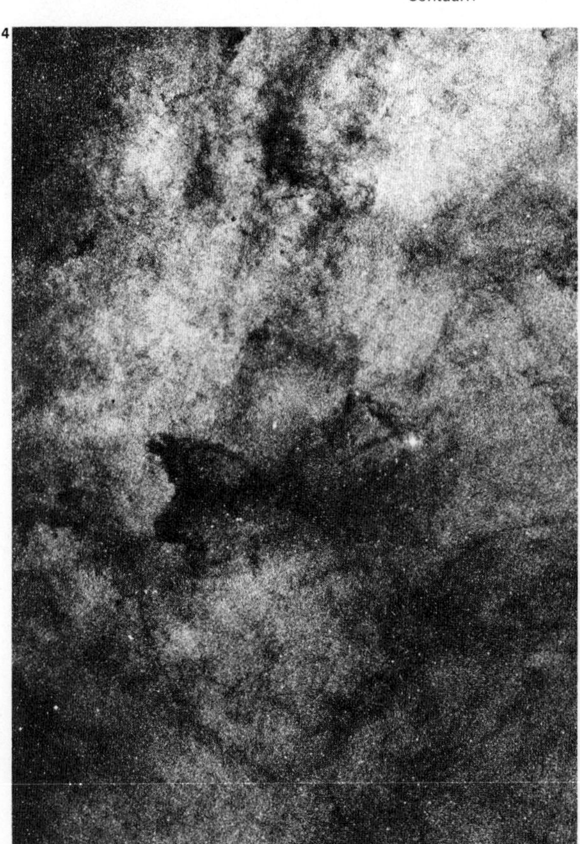

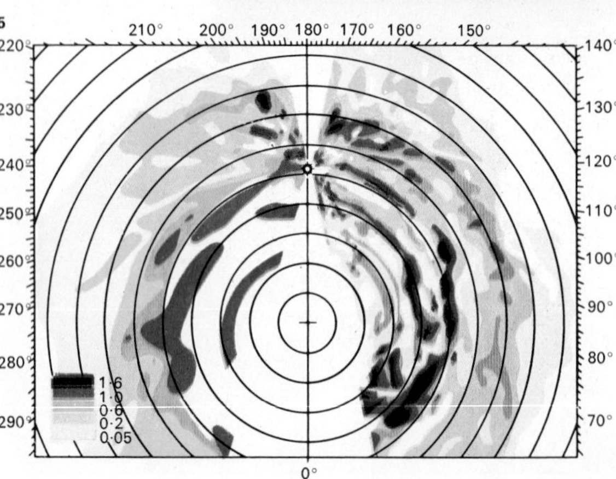

210°
200°
190°
180°
170°
160°
150°
220°
230°
240°
250°
260°
270°
280°
290°
140°
130°
120°
110°
100°
90°
80°
70°
0°
1·6
1·0
0·6
0·2
0·05

5 Radio maps like this one have been drawn to show the distribution of the clouds of cold, rarefied hydrogen in the plane of the Galaxy. The clouds are indicated in blue and contours have been drawn in accordance with a density scale giving the average number of atoms per cubic centimeter. The map is incomplete, but the indications of spiral structure are unmistakable. These regions have a high proportion of Population I stars.

truth. He also proved that the Sun, together with the Earth and the other members of the Solar System, lies well away from the center; the modern estimate of its distance from the galactic nucleus is 32,000 light-years. The comparative size and structure of the Galaxy was uncertain, however, and became clear only with the work of Edwin Hubble (1889–1953), who showed in the 1920s that the spiral galaxies [3] are external systems, of the same basic type as our own.

If so, then there seemed no reason to doubt that our own Galaxy must also be spiral (although since the Earth is situated inside it, the spiral effect is naturally lost). The final proof came from radio astronomy. During World War II Hendrik van de Hulst (1918–) and his colleagues in the Netherlands calculated that the clouds of cold hydrogen spread through the Galaxy should radiate at a wavelength of 21cm and in 1951 E. Purcell and H. Ewen, in the United States, showed that this is what does happen. When the positions and the movements of these hydrogen clouds were worked out, an unmistakable spiral structure was found [5]. It has also been established that the Galaxy is rotating, not as a solid body, at one rate, but showing differential rotation. In the neighborhood of the Sun, the revolution period is of the order of 225 million years—known unofficially as the cosmic year. One cosmic year ago, the Earth was at the beginning of the Triassic period, when reptiles were replacing amphibians as the dominant life form.

The relative size of the Galaxy

Our Galaxy is above average in size but some other known systems are decidedly bigger, including the Andromeda Spiral, M31, in our local group.

Today the term "Galaxy" is taken to refer to the star system and Ptolemy's "Milky Way" to the luminous aspect in the sky. In appearance, the Milky Way is extremely beautiful; it is particularly rich in areas such as in Crux, in Cygnus (where there are dark obscuring rifts of nonluminous matter), and in Scorpio-Sagittarius.

KEY

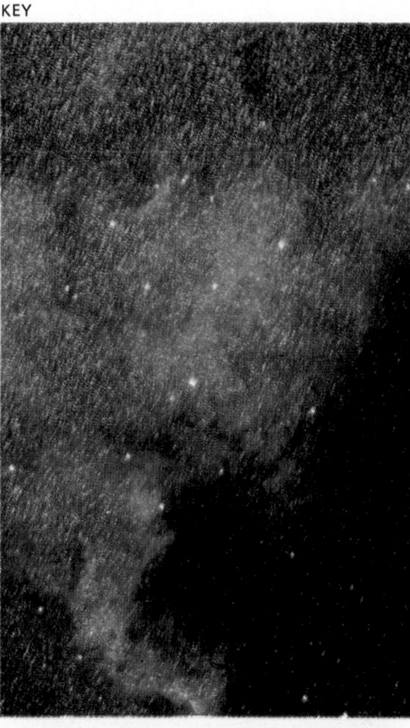

NGC 7000 has been given the unofficial title of the "North America Nebula" because of its striking resemblance to the continent. It is in the constellation of Cygnus, 1,000 light-years away from Earth. This photograph was taken with the 48-in (122-cm) Schmidt telescope at Palomar. The nebula is associated with the exceptionally luminous supergiant Deneb, or Alpha Cygni. The comparatively dark areas seen in the photograph are caused by an intervening cloud of opaque dust, which cuts out the light of the nebula as well as that of the background stars. The nebula is one of the richest areas of the Milky Way.

6

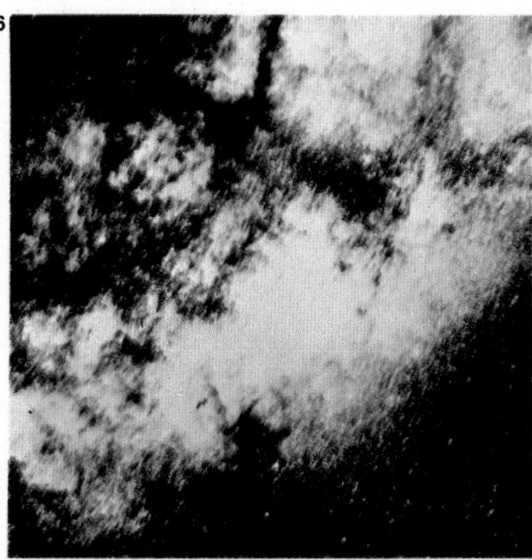

6 Myriads of stars can be seen in this photograph taken at Palomar, although it covers only a small part of the Milky Way. Many of the stars are much more luminous than our Sun.

7

7 These star fields in the Milky Way were photographed at the Naval Observatory, Flagstaff, Arizona. The trail of the balloon satellite Echo I can be seen as it crossed the field during the exposure.

8 The Milky Way, as mapped by Martin and Tatiana Keskula at the Lund Observatory in Sweden, has coordinates referring to galactic latitude and longtitude measured from the galactic plane. The zero point for longitude is the intersection between the galactic plane and the celestial equator near the borders of Aquila and Serpens. The north Galactic pole is in Coma Berenices, the south Galactic pole is in Sculptor.

8

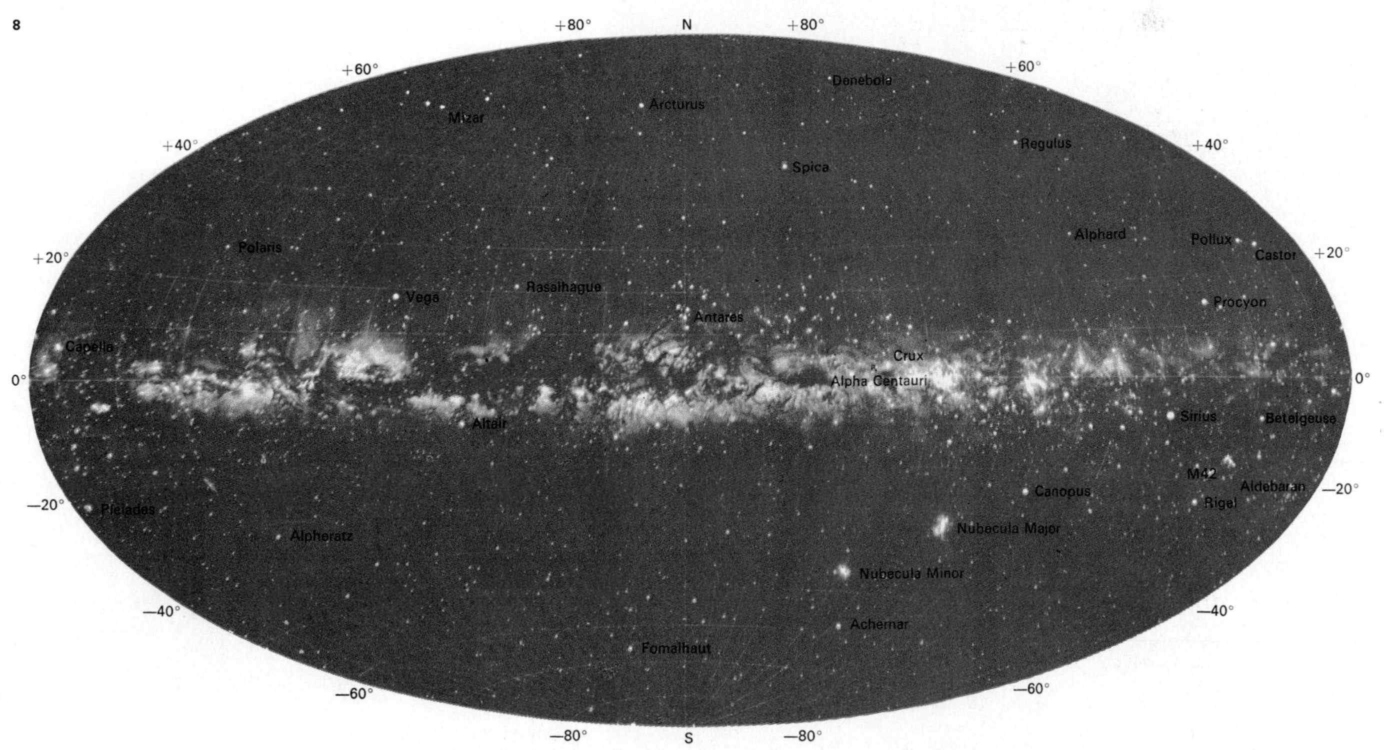
+80°
N
+80°
+60°
Denebola
+60°
Mizar
Arcturus
+40°
Regulus
+40°
Spica
Alphard
Pollux
Castor
+20°
Polaris
+20°
Vega
Rasalhague
Procyon
Antares
Capella
Crux
0°
Alpha Centauri
0°
Altair
Sirius
Betelgeuse
M42
Aldebaran
–20°
Canopus
Rigel
–20°
Pleiades
Nubecula Major
Alpheratz
Nubecula Minor
–40°
–40°
Achernar
Fomalhaut
–60°
–60°
–80°
S
–80°

The local group of galaxies

Galaxies tend to occur in groups usually termed clusters. These should not be confused with the open and globular clusters of stars that occur in our own Galaxy and others. Many clusters of galaxies are known, some of which include hundreds of members. It is therefore not surprising to find that our Galaxy is a member of such a system, known generally as the local group.

The local group [Key] includes our Galaxy, the Andromeda Spiral, the Triangulum Spiral (M33), the two Magellanic Clouds (Nubecula Major and Minor), and more than two dozen smaller systems that are classed as dwarf galaxies. There may also be two large extra members, known as Maffei 1 and Maffei 2 in honor of their Italian discoverer Paolo Maffei, but neither of these systems can be seen properly because they lie inconveniently close to the plane of the Milky Way and are obscured by dust.

A stable system

It is generally agreed that the universe is expanding and that all the galaxies outside the local group are receding at various rates. The members of the local group, however, are not moving away from our own Galaxy. Indeed, the Andromeda Spiral actually shows a movement of approach, although for the most part this is due to the Sun's own motion around the galactic center. The local group makes up a stable system.

In attempting to determine the membership of the group, theorists faced a serious initial difficulty. The distance of the Andromeda Spiral [1, 2] was originally estimated as being 750,000 light-years. But this estimate produced a number of anomalies; the globular clusters surrounding the spiral were calculated, at that distance, to be different in size from similar globular structures in our own Galaxy. Equally puzzling, RR Lyrae stars could not be found inside the Andromeda Spiral. Although RR Lyrae stars are less luminous than Cepheid variable stars, they should still have shown up quite well had the spiral been only 750,000 light-years away. Even a subsequent increase in the estimated distance of the Andromeda Spiral to 900,000 light-years did not resolve these anomalies.

The distances of the galaxies had been calculated by reference to the period and luminosity of the Cepheid variables. In 1952, Walter Baade (1893–1960) announced that the accepted Cepheid scale was inaccurate. There are, in fact, two kinds of Cepheids, one much brighter than the other. The Cepheids in the Andromeda Spiral had been taken as being less luminous but they were really members of the highly luminous class, which meant that they were much more remote than had been believed. Today the Spiral is estimated to lie at a distance of 2.2 million light-years.

Distance and relative size

The Andromeda Spiral is the largest member of the local group, with our own Galaxy a poor second. Next comes the Triangulum Spiral [4] and then the two Magellanic Clouds or Nebeculae, which are too far south to be visible from the United States or Europe. The remaining galaxies in the local group are much smaller.

The Magellanic Clouds [5, 6] look like detached portions of the Milky Way, but

CONNECTIONS

See also
118 Our Galaxy
122 Types of galaxies
126 The expanding universe

1

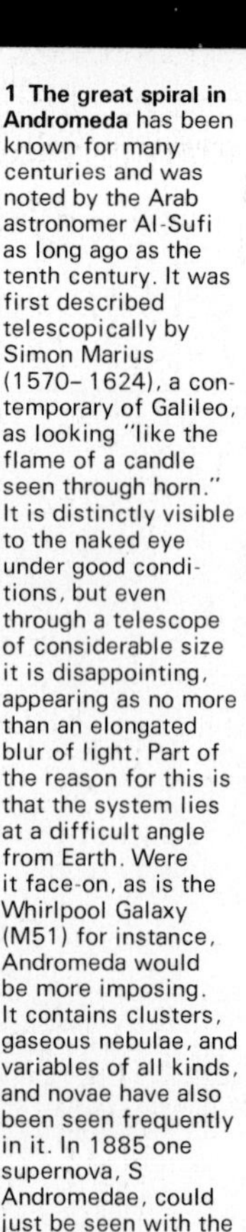

1 The great spiral in Andromeda has been known for many centuries and was noted by the Arab astronomer Al-Sufi as long ago as the tenth century. It was first described telescopically by Simon Marius (1570–1624), a contemporary of Galileo, as looking "like the flame of a candle seen through horn." It is distinctly visible to the naked eye under good conditions, but even through a telescope of considerable size it is disappointing, appearing as no more than an elongated blur of light. Part of the reason for this is that the system lies at a difficult angle from Earth. Were it face-on, as is the Whirlpool Galaxy (M51) for instance, Andromeda would be more imposing. It contains clusters, gaseous nebulae, and variables of all kinds, and novae have also been seen frequently in it. In 1885 one supernova, S Andromedae, could just be seen with the naked eye.

2
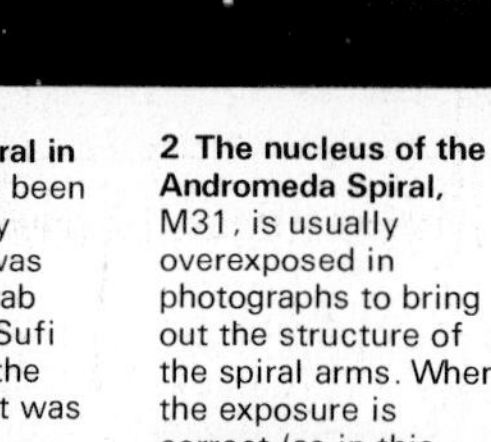

2 The nucleus of the Andromeda Spiral, M31, is usually overexposed in photographs to bring out the structure of the spiral arms. When the exposure is correct (as in this picture) the arms do not show. The scattered stars are members of our own Galaxy and simply happen to lie in the foreground. The nucleus of M31 contains mostly Population II stars, as do many galactic nuclei.

3
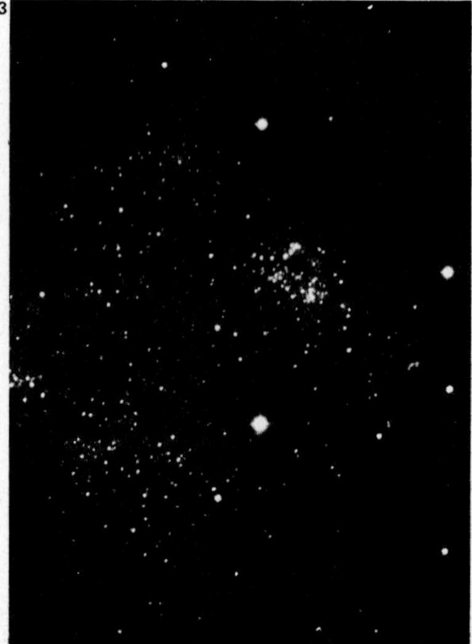

3 The dwarf galaxy in Sextans [center] in the local group has relatively few stars. The bright star below it is a foreground star in our Galaxy, the Milky Way.

each lies about 150,000 light-years from Earth. They are irregular in form and have been regarded as satellite galaxies of our own, although whether they are moving around our Galaxy is problematical. The richer Large Cloud is about 40,000 light-years in diameter and the Small Cloud 20,000 light-years, so that both are very much smaller than our Galaxy. The distance between their centers is 75,000 light-years and both seem to be contained in a common envelope of rarefied hydrogen. Population I stellar characteristics are evident; novae and huge gaseous nebulae have been seen in them. Both contain Cepheid variables.

The Andromeda Spiral also has two companion galaxies, M32 (NGC 221) and NGC 205. Both are dwarf elliptical systems, made up of Population II stars. They are visible in small telescopes, but do not seem to be of the same class as the Magellanic Clouds. It had been thought that the Magellanic Clouds, the spirals in Andromeda and Triangulum, and the companions to the Andromeda Spiral were the only members of the local group, but many smaller systems have been discovered.

Sparsely populated systems

All these smaller systems are of relatively low mass; the two dwarf systems in Sculptor and Fornax make up a total of only about one percent of the mass of our Galaxy. These and similar systems are so sparsely populated that they are not immediately recognizable as distinct galaxies. They are made up of Population II stars, so their leading stars are old red giants. There is little or no interstellar material prominent enough to be detected, which suggests that star formation in them has ceased.

There seems to be no real difference between the local group and many other groups of galaxies known to us. The local group is much easier to study, however, because it is in our own part of the universe. The really small galaxies, such as those in Sculptor and Fornax, would not be detectable at all if they lay at distances of millions of light-years, and it is likely that more remain to be identified in the local group.

KEY

Leo II
Leo I
Our Galaxy
Nubecula Major
NGC 185
M33
NGC 147
Sculptor
Nubecula Minor
Fornax
M31
M 32
NGC 205
NGC 6822
IC 1613
Wolf-Lundmark

The local group of galaxies is small, with less than 30 known members. Only the Andromeda Spiral (M31) and the Magellanic Clouds (Nubecula) are naked-eye objects.

4 The Triangulum Spiral, M33, is the third largest member of the local group and the loose spiral form is well shown. At 2,350,000 light-years, it is slightly more remote than M31.

5 The Small Magellanic Cloud lies in the far southern constellation of Tucana. It is an easy naked-eye object in a dark, clear sky. It contains many variable, short-period stars.

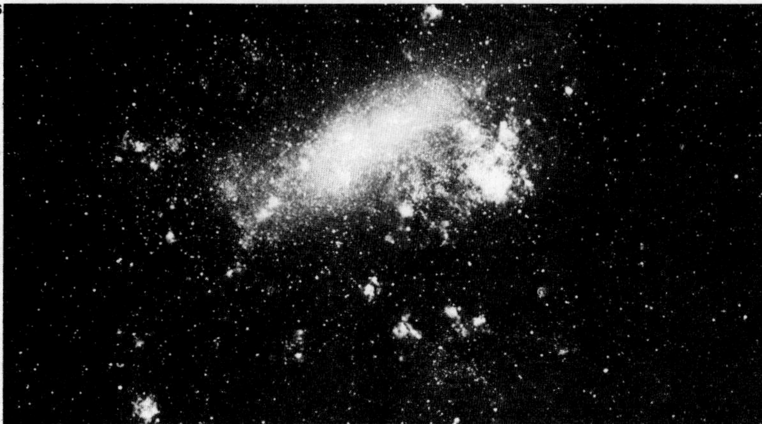

6 The Large Magellanic Cloud is characteristic in shape and contains many stars. Part of it lies in the constellation of Dorado, part in Mensa. It is a bright naked-eye object.

7 In the Large Cloud lies the Great Looped Nebula surrounding the star 30 Doradus. The star is variable and is the most luminous star known—about a million times as powerful as the Sun—but it cannot be seen without optical aid.

Types of galaxies

Galaxies assume various forms [Key]. There are galaxies that show a spiral pattern, some of them loose, some tightly coiled. Among these are the barred spirals, in which the arms seem to protrude from the ends of a "bar" apparently through the center of the system. Other galaxies appear elliptical, ranging from extremely long, narrow systems to shapes that are almost circular as seen from Earth. There are also irregular galaxies, with no definite shape at all. Most of the dwarfs belong to this category, but there are larger irregular systems, such as M82, a radio source in Ursa Major, the Big Dipper.

The Hubble classification

The study of galaxies entered its modern phase in the early 1920s, when work carried out by Edwin Hubble (1889–1953), using the 100-in (254-cm) Hooker reflector telescope at Mount Wilson in California, definitely confirmed the existence of external systems that were not outlying parts of our own Galaxy. Hubble established a method of classification that has served as the basis of subsequent, more complicated, classifications [1]. He distinguished three basic types of galaxies: the spirals, the ellipticals, and the barred spirals. The irregular galaxies were not classified separately although they were recognized. It was clearly tempting to regard the Hubble classification as an evolutionary sequence. It is, however, purely a classification intended to recognize increasing degrees of flattening; the elliptical systems are in fact spheroidal—they look elliptical only in projection. Present knowledge is so limited that most astronomers regard any overall evolutionary sequence with skepticism.

There is still little idea of how spiral arms are formed, although it has definitely been established that the stars in the disk of a spiral galaxy mostly revolve about the center in approximately circular paths in the same direction. The spiral pattern appears to revolve also in the same direction with the arms "trailing." There is uncertainty about whether or not the spiral arms—apparently some sort of wave moving through the stars and gas—are long-lasting on the cosmic scale. Spirals, with their numerous hot Population I stars and their interstellar matter, appear to be less advanced in their evolution than the elliptical galaxies, where the leading stars are red giants of late spectral type and where there is comparatively little nebular material. In the Seyfert galaxies—first noted by Carl Seyfert (1911–60) in 1943—the nuclei are almost stellar in appearance and the spiral arms are relatively obscure and tightly wound. Seyfert galaxies emit radio waves, and great disturbances may well be in progress there. A particularly good example of a Seyfert galaxy is M77 in Cetus, which has a total mass estimated at about 800 billion times that of the Sun.

The Hubble constant

Even before Hubble's researches had proved that the galaxies lie well beyond our own system, it had been found that the 40-odd galaxies for which suitable spectra had been obtained were apparently receding. This was established by the Doppler shift [11]. If a galaxy is receding, the lines in

CONNECTIONS

See also
118 Our Galaxy
120 The local group of galaxies
124 Radio galaxies and quasars
130 Star guide: northern sky I
132 Star guide: northern sky II
134 Star guide: southern sky I
136 Star guide: southern sky II

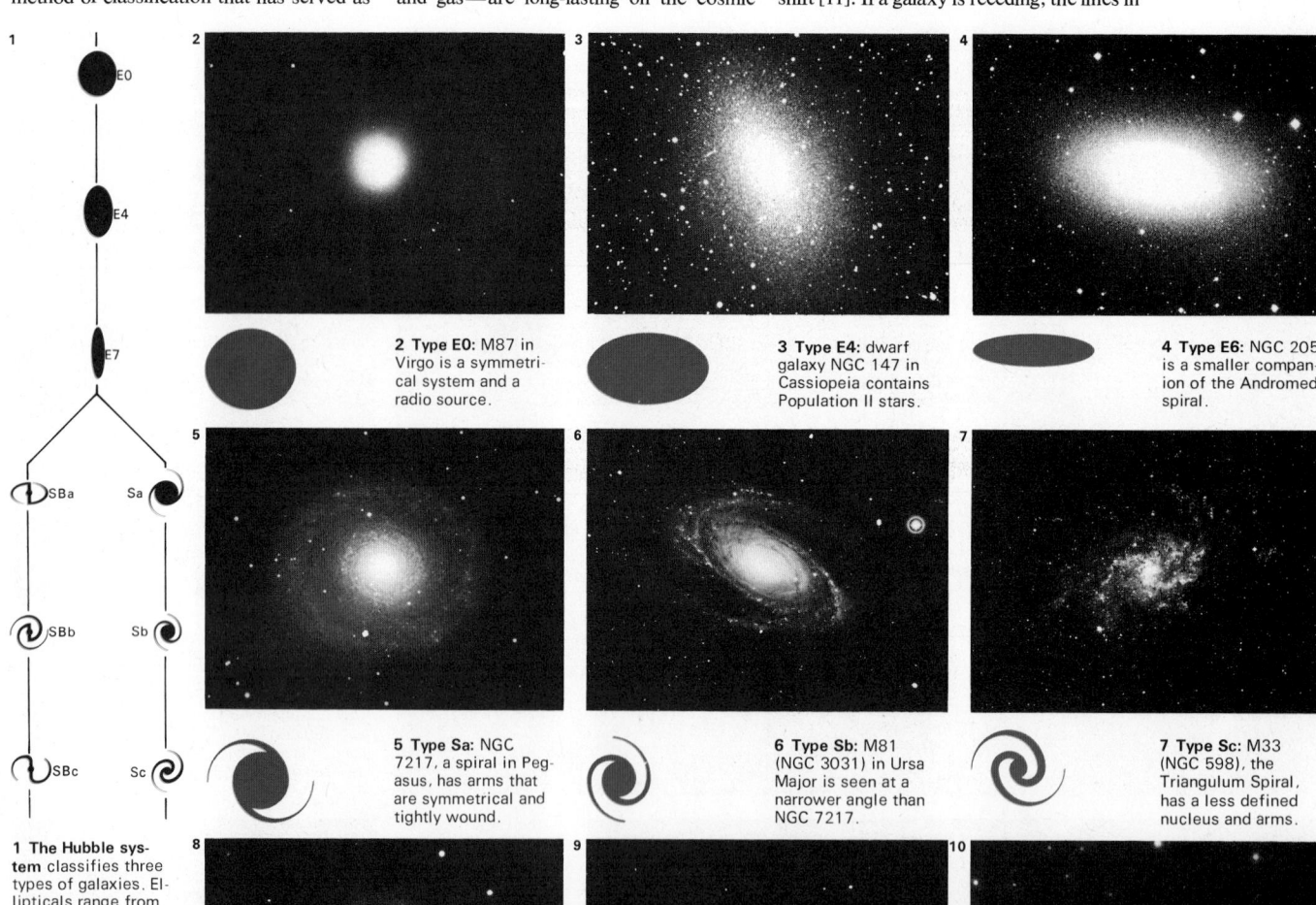

1 The Hubble system classifies three types of galaxies. Ellipticals range from E0 to E7. Those of E0 appear spherical and, as a result, look misleadingly like globular clusters; those of E7 are decidedly elliptical. Spirals are of types Sa, with large nucleus and tightly wound arms; Sb, with smaller nucleus, looser arms; and Sc, with small nucleus, very loose arms. Barred spirals are divided into SBa, SBb, SBc.

2 Type E0: M87 in Virgo is a symmetrical system and a radio source.

3 Type E4: dwarf galaxy NGC 147 in Cassiopeia contains Population II stars.

4 Type E6: NGC 205, is a smaller companion of the Andromeda spiral.

5 Type Sa: NGC 7217, a spiral in Pegasus, has arms that are symmetrical and tightly wound.

6 Type Sb: M81 (NGC 3031) in Ursa Major is seen at a narrower angle than NGC 7217.

7 Type Sc: M33 (NGC 598), the Triangulum Spiral, has a less defined nucleus and arms.

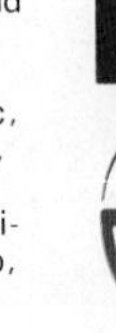

8 Type SBa: NGC 3504 in Leo Minor has spiral arms extending from the ends of a bar.

9 Type SBb: NGC 7479 in Pegasus has a pronounced bar with arms extending from its ends.

10 Type SBc in the Hercules cluster has a dominant bar and the arms are small extensions.

its spectrum are shifted toward the red, or long-wave, end. The farther away a galaxy lies, the greater the speed at which it is receding. Hubble established that there is a definite empirical relationship between distance and the speed of recession. In essence the speed of recession is proportional to the distance; the factor of proportionality is known as Hubble's constant and its value is about 10 percent of the speed of light for each billion light-years of separation between galaxies.

Measuring distances

Measurement of the distances of galaxies cannot be precise. For nearby systems—those of the local group, and even beyond—the period/luminosity relation for Cepheid variables can be used. This method for establishing the distance of Cepheids, which can then be used as "standard candles" for other stellar distance measurements, seems to be reliable now that the difference between types of variable stars has been clarified. Cepheids are powerful stars that can be observed at distances of several millions of light-years. Supergiant stars, however, are more powerful than the Cepheids and it seems plausible that the brightest supergiants in our Galaxy are more or less equal to the supergiants in other galaxies, so that they too can be used as indicators. This method works for distances up to about 40 million light-years. Beyond this, in clusters of galaxies, like the Virgo cluster, galaxies of all kinds are found, including spirals [Key]. Having calculated their sizes, it is possible to use them in the same way as the Cepheids and the supergiants, although accuracy is less. Supernovae can also be used when they appear in remote systems. For the extremely distant galaxies there is as yet no means of measuring a distance independently of the red shift, but if the red shift can be measured the distance may be inferred (assuming that Hubble's law is valid).

Galaxies that lie beyond the local group yield little detail even when viewed with large telescopes. Only detailed photography can reveal the diverse and fascinating nature of more distant star systems.

KEY

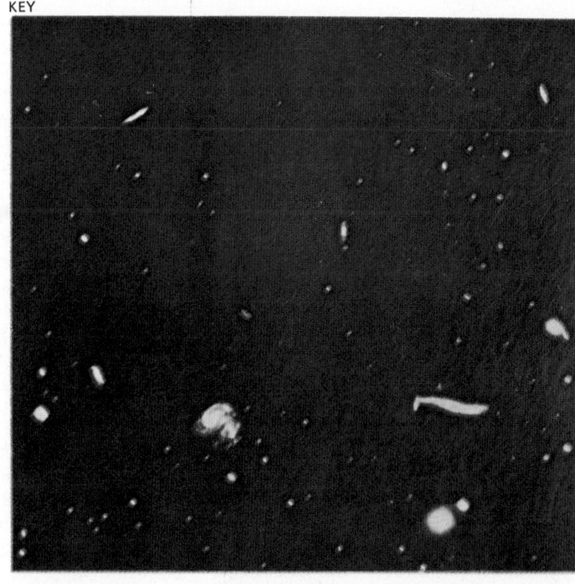

These galaxies in Hercules include spirals, barred spirals, and elliptical systems. They form a genuine cluster.

11 The Doppler shift occurs when, from an approaching light source [A], more waves per second enter the eye than would enter from a source without relative motion [B], and the wavelength [A] shifts toward the short-wave, violet end of the spectrum. Without relative motion [B], the light is unaffected. Recessional velocity [C] produces an apparent increase in wavelength.

11

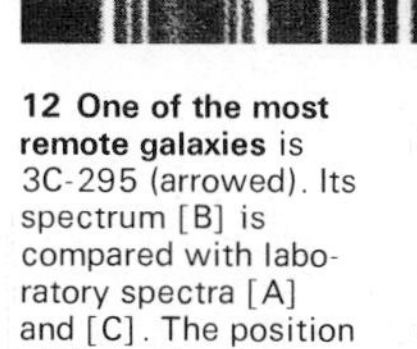
A
B
C

12

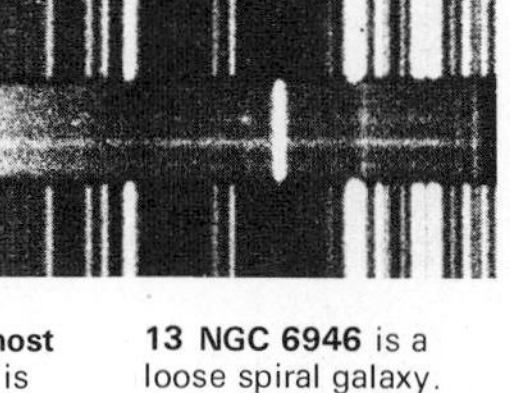
A
B
C

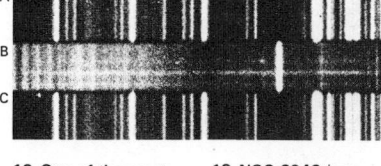

12 One of the most remote galaxies is 3C-295 (arrowed). Its spectrum [B] is compared with laboratory spectra [A] and [C]. The position of the white line shows that 3C-295 is red-shifted.

13

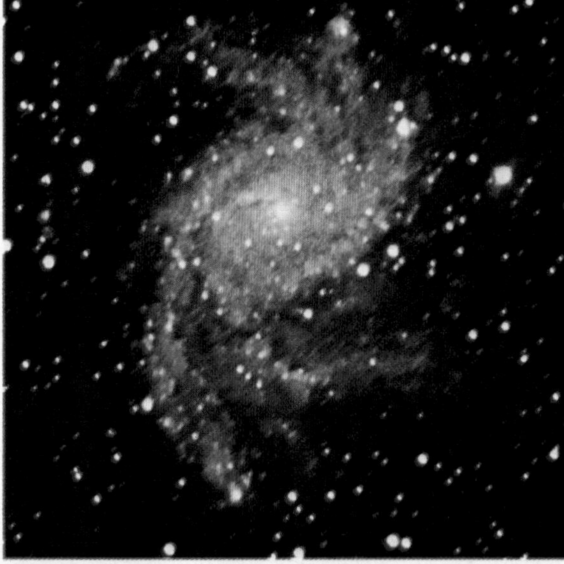

13 NGC 6946 is a loose spiral galaxy. The nucleus is well marked but not large compared with the spiral arms, which are much less pronounced and tightly wound than those of galaxies classed Sa.

14

15

16

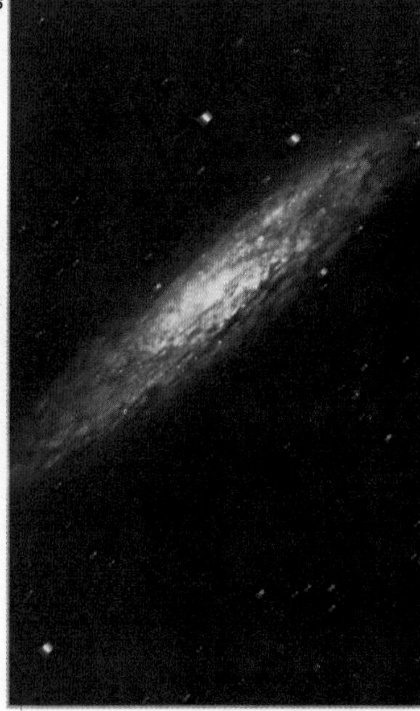

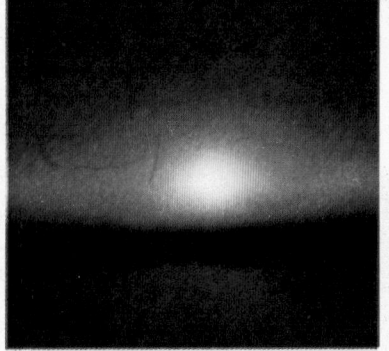

14 The Whirlpool galaxy, M51 in Canes Venatici, is 37 million light-years away. It is face-on to us and therefore is excellently displayed. This was the first spiral galaxy to be recognized (by the Earl of Rosse in 1845).

15 The Sombrero Hat galaxy, M104, part of the Virgo cluster, is at a distance of 41 million light-years.

16 Spiral galaxy NGC 253, in Sculptor, is almost edge-on to Earth. As a result, the spiral form is not well displayed.

Radio galaxies and quasars

CONNECTIONS

See also
122 Types of galaxies
46 Invisible astronomy
126 The expanding universe

Some galaxies are powerful sources of radio waves as well as of light. These are known as "radio galaxies." No doubt all galaxies send out long-wavelength radiations because of the supernova remnants and other discrete radio sources inside them, but the energy of radio galaxies is of an entirely different order of magnitude.

Problems of radio galaxies

A typical galaxy with a strong radio source is M87 in the famous Virgo cluster, approximately 60 million light-years from Earth. A curious jet issues from it that looks as though it may be composed of material being ejected at high velocity. M87 sends out about 10,000 times as much energy at radio wavelengths as it might be expected to do. Some other radio galaxies are much more remote; for instance Cygnus A, the first radio galaxy identified optically (in 1954), is 700 million light-years distant, assuming a Hubble constant of 50km/sec/megaparsec (a parsec is the distance at which a star would show a parallax of one second of arc. It is equal to 3.26 light-years).

Many theories have been proposed to explain the radio emissions from these exceptional galaxies. Originally it was thought that there might be not one galaxy, but two—in fact, two separate systems passing through each other in opposite directions. If so the individual stars would seldom collide, but the interstellar matter would be in collision throughout the encounter and would—it was suggested—produce the radio emission that is recorded. Certainly radio galaxies such as Centaurus A give the impression of being compound. Cygnus A, like many other radio galaxies, has two powerful centers of radio emission straddling the optical image, with a weak radar source coinciding with the optical object.

Further research showed that collisions could not produce nearly enough energy to explain the observations, and the theory of colliding galaxies was abandoned. It now seems that the radio emissions are the result of tremendous explosions inside the galaxies themselves. One excellent example of this is M82, an irregular galaxy in Ursa Major [3]. It has been found that there are huge, intricate gas structures inside the galaxy, moving about at speeds of up to 100 miles (160km) per second. From the present movements it seems that an outburst took place near the center of M82 about one and a half million years ago (although since the distance of the galaxy is 10.5 million light-years, the explosion occurred 12 million years ago in our time frame). The radio emission from objects like M82 is believed to be generated by the synchroton process, that is, energy radiated by the acceleration of high-energy electrons in a strong magnetic field. The cause of these outbursts in radio galaxies is not yet understood.

New objects in the sky: quasars

In 1960 the search for distant objects in the universe led to a surprising sequence of events. A few objects, which from their radio properties were believed to be distant, were identified with blue starlike objects on photographs obtained with the Palomar telescope. Until 1963 they were believed to be a hitherto unidentified type of star in the Milky Way. In March of that year Maarten

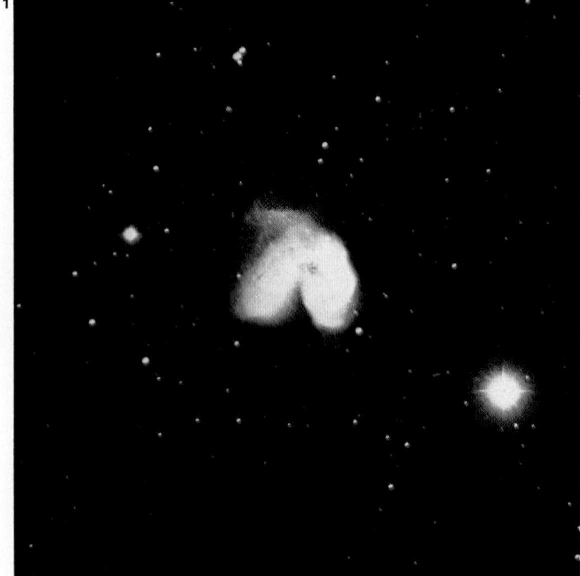

1 Galaxies NGC4038 and 4039 in Corvus are classified Sc because each galaxy is a loose spiral. Each is also a radio source. There is no doubt that the two systems are genuinely associated and that they lie at the same distance from the Earth. They give the appearance of being interlocked and it was this particular aspect that led to the theory that radio emissions from galaxies are due to collisions. If this theory had been valid, NGC 4038 and 4039 would have been spectacular examples. It is now known that the theory of colliding galaxies is wrong, however. The star to the lower right is in our own Galaxy and hence shows up in the foreground.

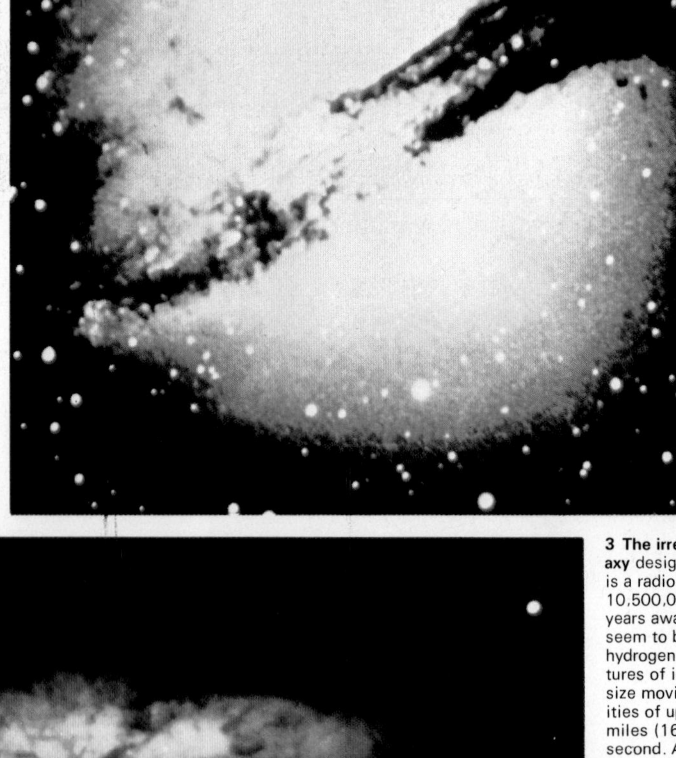

2 The radio galaxy Centaurus A (NGC 5128) is now thought to be a single system, although it was once believed to be a collision of two galaxies. At its distance of 12 million light-years, it is one of the closest of the radio galaxies and seems to contain an unusual amount of diffused dusty material. The radio sources do not coincide with the center of the optical object, but lie on either side.

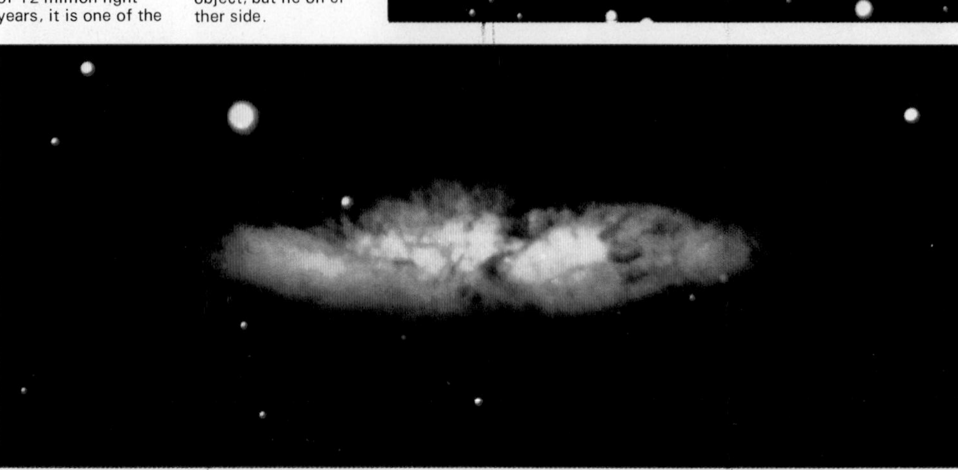

3 The irregular galaxy designated M82 is a radio source 10,500,000 light-years away. There seem to be intricate hydrogen gas structures of immense size moving at velocities of up to 100 miles (160km) per second. All the indications are that a tremendous explosion took place inside the nucleus of the system 1.5 million years before our present view of it. M82 is therefore the best-known example of an exploding galaxy.

Schmidt, working with the 200-in telescope, succeeded in identifying the spectrum of the radio object known as 3C 273 (that is, the 273rd object in the third Cambridge catalog of radio sources) [4] and at the same time Jesse L. Greenstein published his red shift measurements on another blue object—3C 48. The red shifts were extremely large, and as more objects of this type were identified it became clear that a new class of object had been discovered, more remote than any hitherto recognized and in many cases receding with velocity greater than half the velocity of light.

Problems associated with quasars

These distant objects, known as quasars—a contraction of their original name, quasi-stellar objects—have presented astronomers with a series of baffling problems. Assuming that the estimates of their distances are correct, a powerful quasar may far outshine a whole galaxy such as our own—and it is difficult to know how a relatively small object can emit so much energy. Radio measurements of the angular diameters of quasars and the rapidity of the light variations found in some of these objects imply that the main output of energy may arise from a region of space only a few light-years across.

None of the processes of energy production encountered in normal stars or galaxies seems adequate to account for these phenomena and many theories about quasars have been put forward in recent years. It has been suggested that a quasar might be produced by many supernovas exploding in quick succession, but there seems no reason why such an event should happen; and theories involving antimatter or black holes are entirely speculative. It is possible that quasars and certain types of radio galaxies (notably the Seyfert systems—those having bright central nuclei with emission-line spectra) are different stages of evolution of the same class of object, but there is still no reliable information. More recently two American astronomers, J. Oke and J. Gunn, found that the peculiar object known as BL Lacertae [8] may be a quasar embedded in a normal galaxy.

KEY

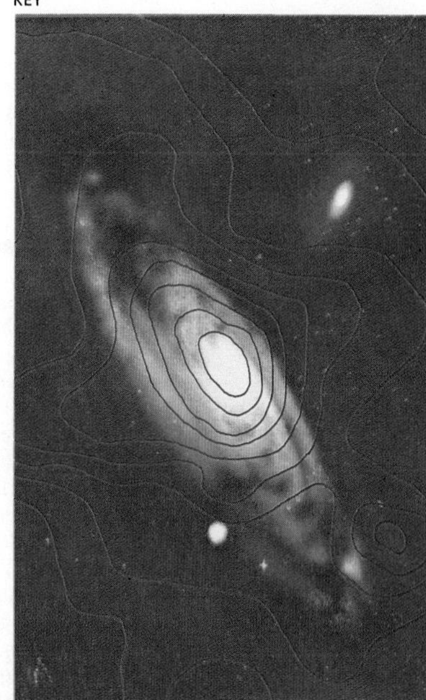

Optical telescopes reveal objects in the heavens that emit light, whereas radio telescopes detect the longer wavelength radiation emitted by them. Each technique can highlight a different feature of the same object. Here the radio map of the Andromeda galaxy [red lines] is superimposed on its optical image. The galaxy is a weak radio emitter, but the map reveals radio sources that are invisible because they emit no light, such as the one near the lower right corner. The wavelengths detected by radio telescopes range from about 30m down to 1cm, below which any incoming radio waves from space are blocked by Earth's atmosphere.

4 The quasar 3C 273, photographed with the 200-in Palomar reflector, lies in Virgo and with a magnitude of 13 is visually the brightest of the quasars. It was one of the earliest to be identified (1963).

5 Quasar 3C 147 has been photographed from Palomar with the 200-in reflector. The quasar [arrowed] looks remarkably like the object just below it, which is an ordinary star in our Galaxy.

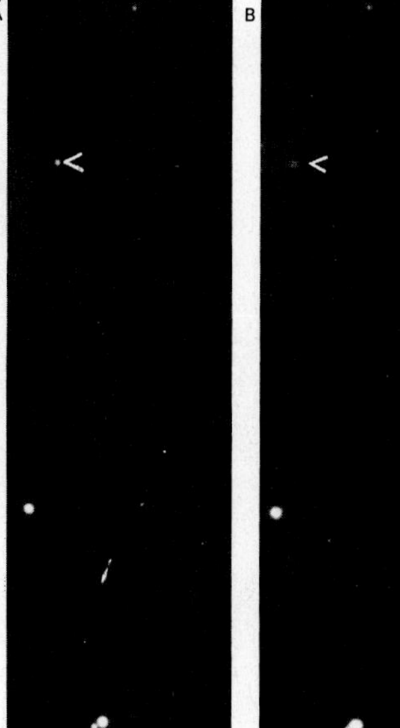

6 These two photographs of the quasar 3C 345 were taken at the Royal Greenwich Observatory in August 1966 [A] and in September 1971 [B]. The quasar is arrowed and the decrease in brightness compared with the other stars can be seen quite easily. Quasars show fluctuations over short periods and this is evidence that they must be extremely small compared with galaxies.

GAL A

390.3

GAL B

7 The galaxy marked Gal A is the closest of the three radio galaxies in this photograph and may be associated with the elliptical galaxy to the upper left. 3C 390.3 and Gal B are also radio sources identified optically in this photograph.

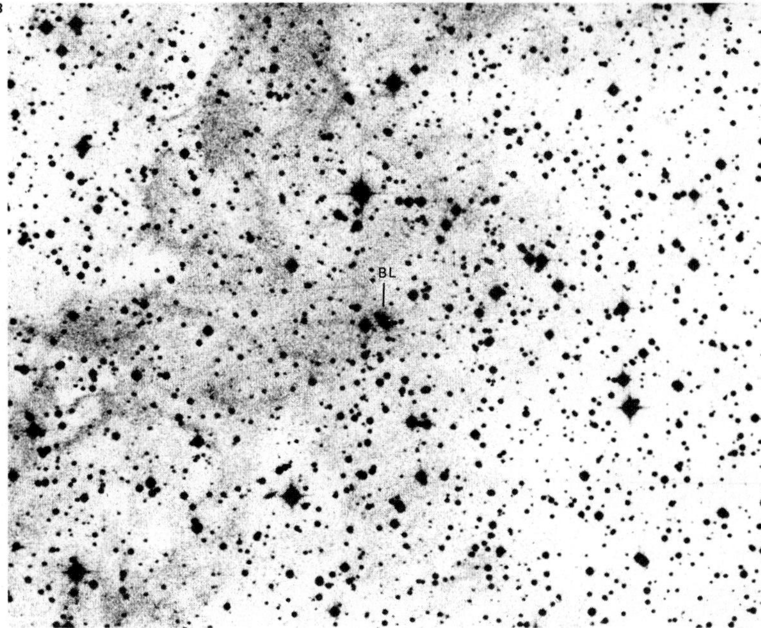
BL

8 The extraordinary object BL Lacertae, which superficially looks like a star, is variable, and near minimum a slight fuzziness is recorded around it. The spectrum is quite featureless, with no bright or dark lines. It has been found that the outer "fuzz" shows a spectrum resembling that of an elliptical galaxy. BL Lacertae is not a star; it is very remote and luminous—possibly intermediate in luminosity between a galaxy and a quasar. There is a strong infrared emission.

The expanding universe

Of all the questions facing mankind, that of the origin of the universe is one of the most fascinating—and certainly one of the most difficult to answer.

The Doppler significance

The movement of a luminous body toward or away from us can be found from its spectrum. If the body is approaching, the wavelength of the light appears slightly shortened and the body appears "too blue." If it is receding, the apparent wavelength is lengthened and the body appears "too red." This is known as the Doppler effect after Christian Doppler (1803–53), the Austrian physicist who first drew attention to it in 1842. The Doppler effect shows up in the spectrum of any body that is self-luminous. If the spectral lines are shifted toward the red or long-wavelength end, then the body is receding.

The spectrum of an external galaxy is made up of the combined spectra of millions of stars, but the main lines are identifiable and it has been found that apart from the members of our local group of galaxies [1], all the shifts are to the red. If these shifts are Doppler effects, it follows that the whole universe is in a state of expansion. It has also been found that the farther away a galaxy lies, the greater is its red shift—and thus the greater its recessional velocity. This was shown by the work of Edwin Hubble (1889–1953) at Mount Wilson during the years following 1923 when he first showed conclusively that certain nebulae were in fact external galactic systems rather than objects in our Milky Way system.

Theories of the universe

Several years before Hubble discovered the observational evidence for the expansion of the universe, a Dutch astronomer, Willem de Sitter (1872–1934), found a solution to the cosmological theory published by Albert Einstein (1879–1955) in 1917. Then the Russian scientist A. Friedmann discovered a whole range of solutions to the Einstein equations in which the radius and mean density of the universe varied with time. By adjusting the parameters in the equations, the theoretical models predicted either a universe expanding indefinitely as time advanced or one that would eventually collapse. Many distinguished theorists such as Arthur Eddington (1882–1944) and George Lemaître (1894–1966) developed variations of the models of the expanding universe. All had in common an initial "beginning" in time when the primeval material was compressed into an infinitely small space. In 1946 George Gamow (1904–68) developed the idea (popularized as the "big bang theory") that this initial state was at an extremely high temperature, resulting in a primordial explosion. He also proposed that the common elements were formed from the primeval hydrogen in the first minutes after the beginning of the expansion.

The difficult conceptions involved in a "beginning of time" (and a comparison of the predicted age of the universe and that of the Earth) led Fred Hoyle and Thomas Gold to propose in 1948 that the universe never had a beginning, but was in a steady state of continuous creation. That is, hydrogen atoms were being continually created and forming into stars and galaxies at a sufficient

CONNECTIONS

See also
124 Radio galaxies and quasars
1478 The scale of the u verse
1522 The speed of light
1524 The idea of relativi
840 Myths of winter

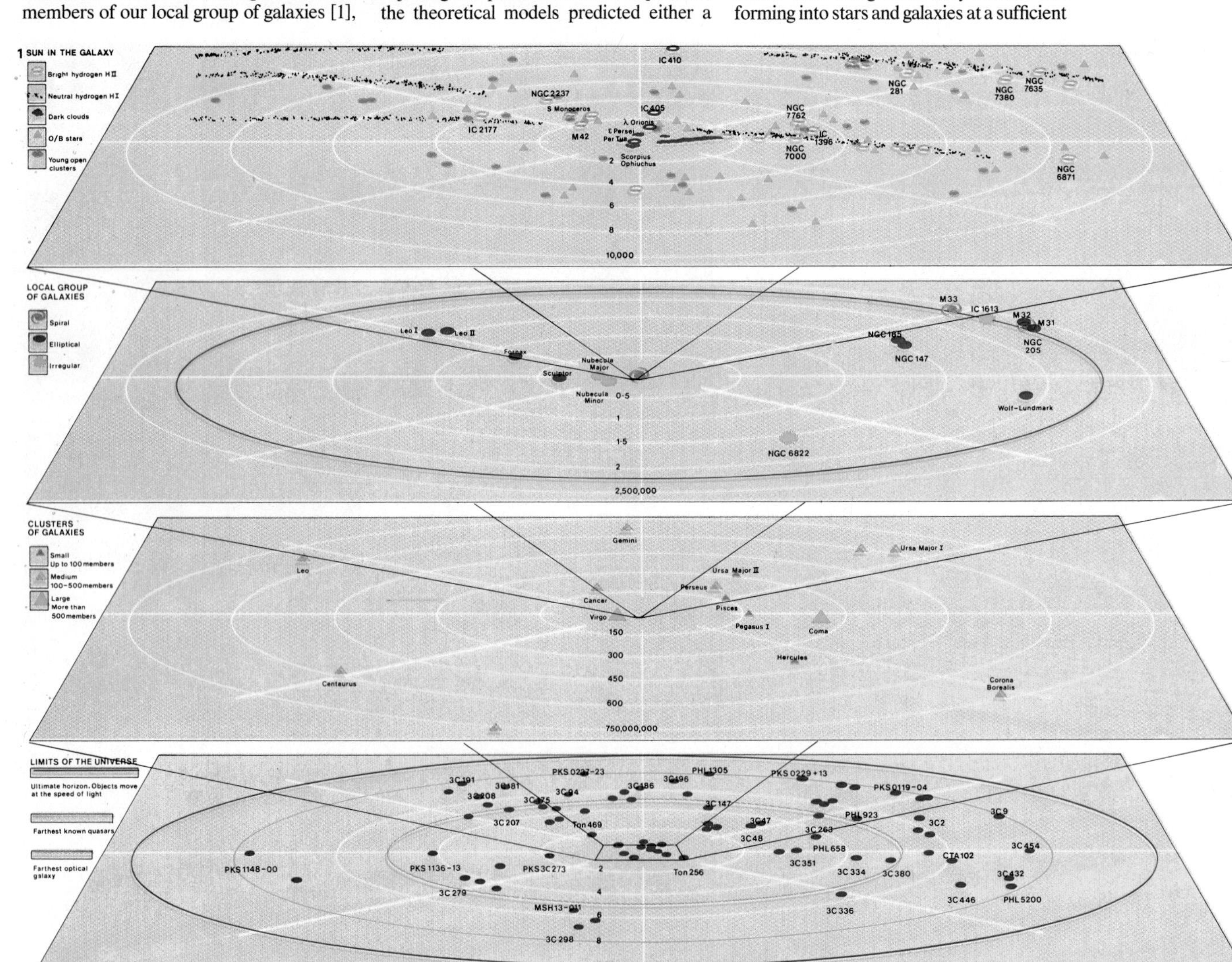

1 SUN IN THE GALAXY
Bright hydrogen HII
Neutral hydrogen HI
Dark clouds
O/B stars
Young open clusters
IC 410
NGC 2237
S Monoceros
IC 405
λ Orionis
ξ Persei
M42
IC 2177
Scorpius Ophiuchus
NGC 7762
IC 1396
NGC 7000
NGC 281
NGC 7380
NGC 7635
NGC 6871
2
4
6
8
10,000
LOCAL GROUP OF GALAXIES
Spiral
Elliptical
Irregular
Leo I
Leo II
Fornax
Sculptor
Nubecula Major
Nubecula Minor
0·5
1
1·5
2
2,500,000
M33
IC 1613
M32
M31
NGC 185
NGC 147
NGC 205
Wolf-Lundmark
NGC 6822
CLUSTERS OF GALAXIES
Small Up to 100 members
Medium 100–500 members
Large More than 500 members
Gemini
Leo
Ursa Major I
Ursa Major II
Perseus
Cancer
Virgo
Pisces
Pegasus I
Coma
Hercules
Centaurus
Corona Borealis
150
300
450
600
750,000,000
LIMITS OF THE UNIVERSE
Ultimate horizon. Objects move at the speed of light
Farthest known quasars
Farthest optical galaxy
PKS 0237-23
PHL 1305
PKS 0229+13
PKS 0119-04
3C 191
3C 181
3C 208
3C 175
3C 94
3C 186
3C 196
3C 147
3C 207
Ton 469
3C 47
3C 48
PHL 923
3C 263
3C 2
3C 9
PHL 658
3C 351
CTA 102
3C 454
PKS 1148-00
PKS 1136-13
PKS 3C 273
Ton 256
3C 334
3C 380
3C 432
3C 279
3C 446
PHL 5200
MSH 13-011
3C 336
3C 298
2
4
6
8
10,000,000,000

1 The immense scale of the universe is shown in these diagrams. The region of our Galaxy that can be examined optically is shown in the top diagram (Sun at center). On this scale the entire Solar System would be a microscopic dot. In addition to the visible stars there are clusters, stellar associations, and gaseous nebulae such as the Rosette Nebula NGC 2237 and the Orion Nebula M42. Distances are given in thousands of light-years, so that the outermost white line represents a distance of 10,000 light-years from the Sun. The local group of galaxies contains over 24 members, of which the largest are the spiral galaxy M31 in Andromeda, our own galaxy, the Triangulum Spiral M33, and the large and small Magellanic Clouds, the companions of our galaxy; the other members such as Leo I and Leo II are dwarf galaxies. Distances are given in millions of light-years. Two recently discovered galaxies Maffei 1 and 2 may be members of the local group but are so heavily obscured by dust in the plane of our Galaxy that they are hard to study. The galaxies in the local group are not receding from us. The area out to 750 million light-years contains many clusters of galaxies—such as the rich Virgo cluster. The region out beyond 8 to 10 billion light-years is still beyond the limits of either optical methods (yellow line) or the newer radio methods (blue line).

rate to replace the galaxies that were moving out of the field of view through the expansion of the universe. Great arguments then arose about whether measurements from radio investigations of the distant parts of the universe supported the steady state or evolutionary models of the universe.

In 1965 scientists at the Bell Telephone Laboratories in New Jersey discovered by accident a radiation from the sky with maximum intensity at a wavelength of 7cm distributed uniformly over the heavens. In subsequent years measurements of the spectrum of this microwave radiation seemed to confirm their initial claim that this is "relic" radiation from the initial high temperature-high density phase of the universe envisaged by Gamow.

Questions about evolution

Since the discovery of the relic microwave radiation the concept that the universe is in an evolutionary, as distinct from a steady, state has been widely accepted. Major problems remain, however. One concerns the future behavior of the universe. Is there enough material in the universe to overcome by gravitational attraction the forces of expansion? The critical density is 2×10^{-29} grams per cubic centimeter, but it is unlikely that measurements of this density can settle the problem because of uncertainty about how much unobservable material exists in space. It seems more probable that the issue will be settled by observations of the properties of the remote objects in the universe such as quasars; for example, how do their recessional velocities vary with distance? At present the results are too scattered to permit any conclusions.

A more imponderable problem concerns the state of the universe at the beginning of time. The theories propose a singular condition of infinite density at time zero. The microwave measurements probably refer to a time only a minute or so after the beginning of the expansion. Present physical theories can envisage a much earlier phase only a fraction of a second after the beginning of the expansion, and with continued research a more definite theory of the beginning of the universe will be developed.

KEY

M101 in Ursa Major is a typical spiral galaxy. This is one of the systems that is close enough to be studied in detail.

2

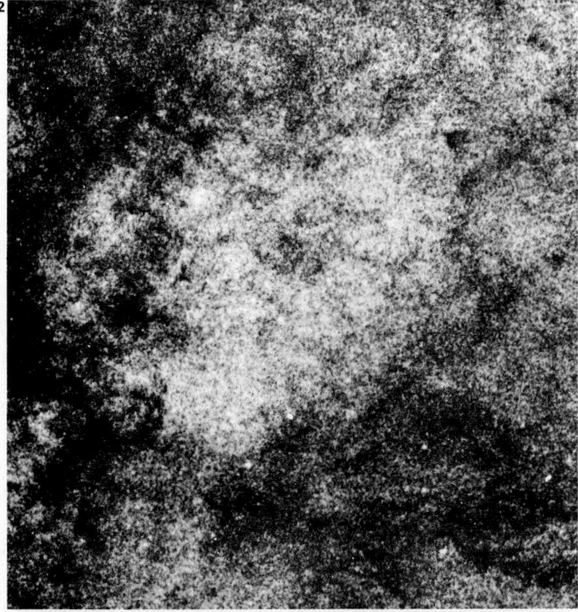

2 Star clouds in the Galaxy, shown here in the region of Sagittarius and photographed with the Schmidt telescope, indicate the direction of the center of our Galaxy (illustration 1A). All galaxies beyond the local group are receding from our Galaxy, which, apart from the Andromeda system, is the largest member of the local group.

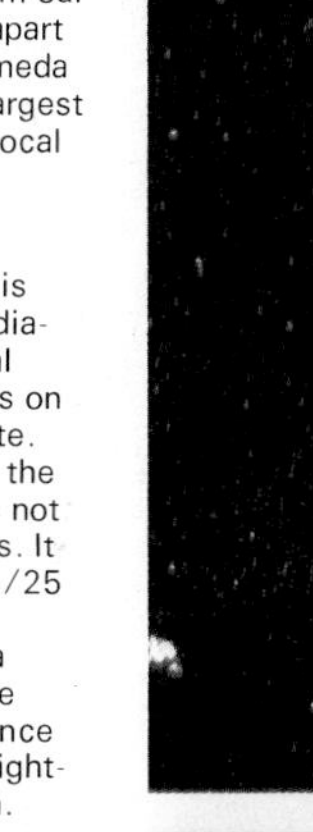

3 M33, the Triangulum Spiral, is included in the diagram of the local group of galaxies on the page opposite. As a member of the local group, it is not receding from us. It has only about 1/25 the mass of our Galaxy. M33 is a normal open type spiral. The distance is 2.35 million light-years from Earth.

3

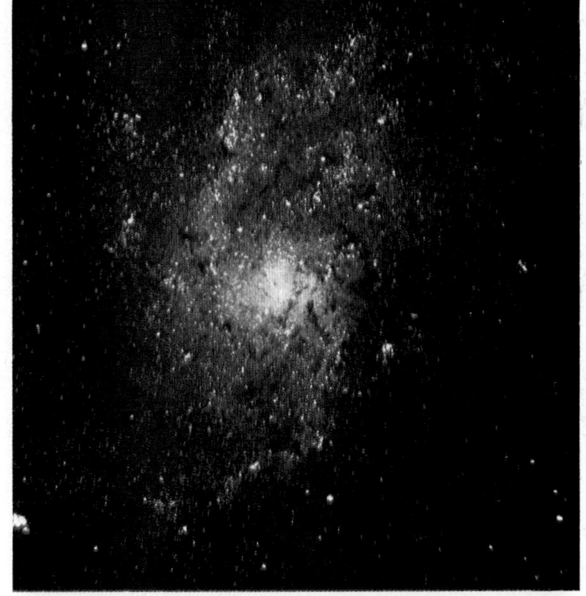

4

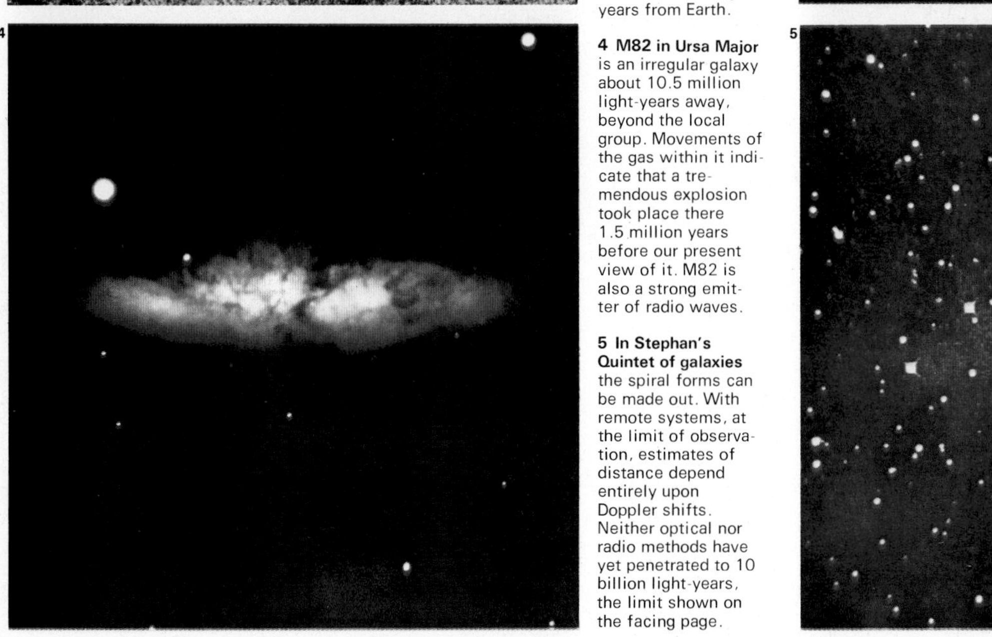

4 M82 in Ursa Major is an irregular galaxy about 10.5 million light-years away, beyond the local group. Movements of the gas within it indicate that a tremendous explosion took place there 1.5 million years before our present view of it. M82 is also a strong emitter of radio waves.

5 In Stephan's Quintet of galaxies the spiral forms can be made out. With remote systems, at the limit of observation, estimates of distance depend entirely upon Doppler shifts. Neither optical nor radio methods have yet penetrated to 10 billion light-years, the limit shown on the facing page.

5

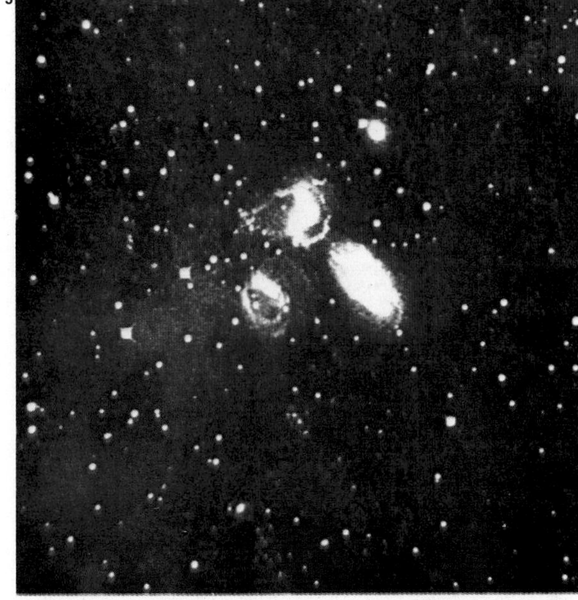

Mapping constellations

It requires only a little imagination to make patterns out of the stars in the sky. There are some groups that beg for treatment: for instance the seven stars making up the Big Dipper and those within the pattern of Orion. In the far south the four stars of the Southern Cross are equally distinctive.

At a very early stage in history the stars were divided into constellations and named. It is, however, important to remember that these visual categories are created simply by line-of-sight and that the stars in any particular constellation are not necessarily associated. Thus in the handle of the Big Dipper, the "end" star, Alkaid, is more than twice as far away from Earth as the second star, the binary Mizar. Nor are the constellations permanent; patterns change with time as the stars move relative to each other.

Early star maps

Ancient star-gazers, who had no idea of the construction of the universe, believed the stars to be equally distant. If they were, the constellation patterns would presumably be of real importance. The zodiacal constellations are probably the oldest: the Babylonians traced the Zodiac and divided it into 12 constellations [1], which led to our present division of the year into 12 months. The ancient Chinese [6] and the Egyptians [4] drew up maps of the sky, showing named constellations; and so did the Greeks. It is the Greek system that has survived.

Naming the constellations

About 150 BC Hipparchus, one of the greatest astronomers of the Classical period, compiled a star catalog. It was this catalog that was used by Ptolemy of Alexandria as a basis for his own work, undertaken around AD 150. Ptolemy gave a list of 48 constellations, all of which are still found on astronomical maps even though their boundaries have been modified. Ptolemy also divided the stars into magnitudes, or grades of apparent brilliancy, from 1 (very bright) to 6 (the faintest stars normally visible with the naked eye on a clear night). The "Ptolemaic" constellations were named after mythological figures, living creatures, and, in a few cases, inanimate objects. The list included virtually all the famous constellations that can be seen from the latitude of Alexandria where Ptolemy spent his life. His Latin names are still used: Ursa Major (the Great Bear), Aries (the Ram), and Aquarius (the Waterbearer), and those of mythological characters such as Perseus, Cepheus, Cassiopeia, and Andromeda.

The sky may be viewed as a picture book[1] in which the classical legends are illustrated and preserved. There is, for example, the tale of how tactless boasting by a proud queen, Cassiopeia, about the beauty of her daughter Andromeda led to the princess being chained to a rock on the seashore, there to await the coming of a monster sent by the sea god. This is one of the legends that has a happy ending. Andromeda was rescued by the gallant hero Perseus, who was returning from an expedition during which he had killed a hideous creature named Medusa, the Gorgon, who had snakes instead of hair and whose glance would turn an onlooker to stone. All the

CONNECTIONS

See also
40 Measuring the restless sky
130 Star guide: northern sky I
132 Star guide: northern sky II
134 Star guide: southern sky I
136 Star guide: southern sky II
826 Astrology

1

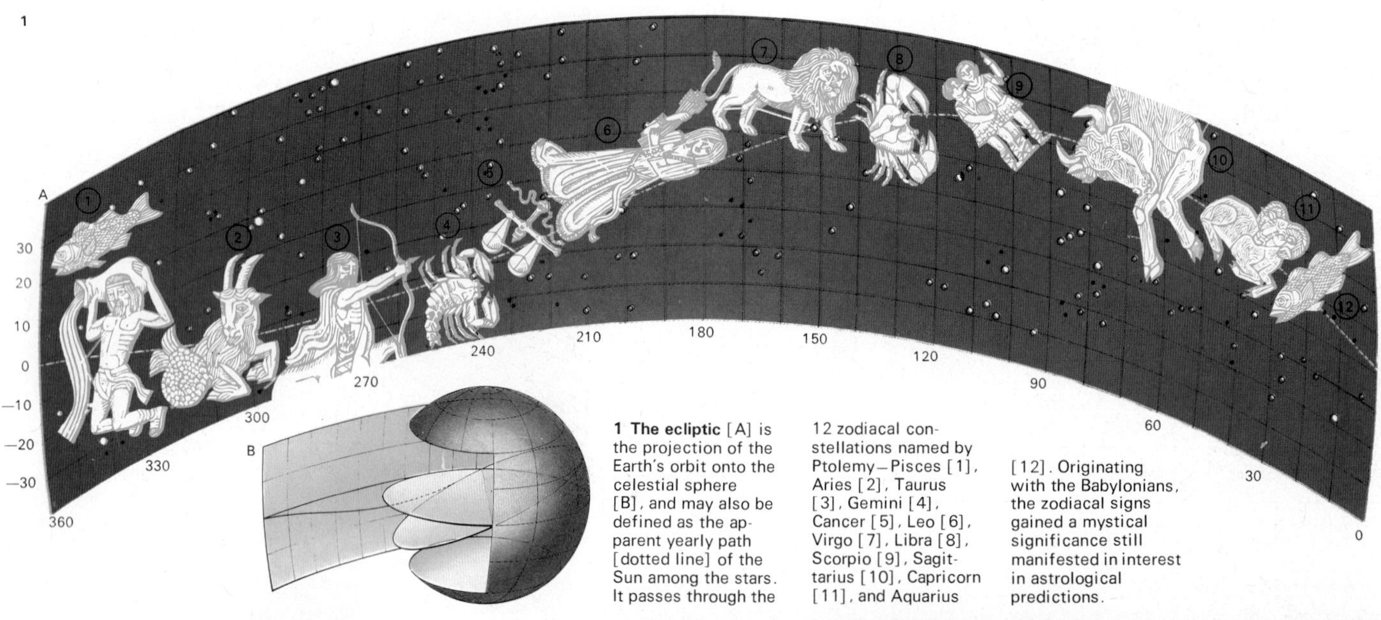

A
B
30
20
10
0
–10
–20
–30
360
330
300
270
240
210
180
150
120
90
60
30
0

1 The ecliptic [A] is the projection of the Earth's orbit onto the celestial sphere [B], and may also be defined as the apparent yearly path [dotted line] of the Sun among the stars. It passes through the 12 zodiacal constellations named by Ptolemy–Pisces [1], Aries [2], Taurus [3], Gemini [4], Cancer [5], Leo [6], Virgo [7], Libra [8], Scorpio [9], Sagittarius [10], Capricorn [11], and Aquarius [12]. Originating with the Babylonians, the zodiacal signs gained a mystical significance still manifested in interest in astrological predictions.

2

3

3 Indian constellation patterns included Makara [A], the Sea Monster, and Kumbha [B], the Water Pot, containing an elixir that the gods took to heaven–an occasion celebrated by an Indian festival.

2 This early Arab water clock is surrounded by an Arab Zodiac, with the constellation figures clearly represented. The Arab star catalogs were more accurate than any previously made.

4

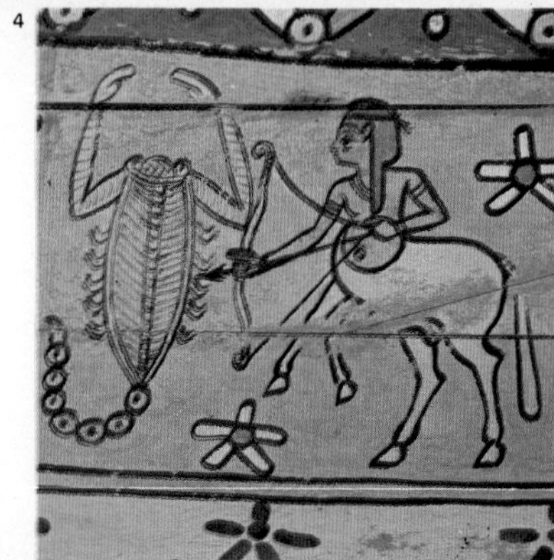

4 The impact of Greek astrology on the Egyptians can be clearly seen in these two zodiacal figures (Scorpio and Sagittarius), found inside an Egyptian mummy case of the 2nd century AD.

main characters in the story can be seen in the Northern Hemisphere: Andromeda, her parents Cassiopeia and Cepheus, the sea-monster (Cetus), and of course Perseus himself, with the Gorgon's head marked by the "demon star," the eclipsing binary Algol. Another legend concerns Orion, the great hunter. A scorpion was sent by Apollo who wished to protect his sister Artemis from Orion. Orion escaped from the scorpion but was killed by one of Artemis' arrows, she being unaware of whom she had shot. In remorse, Artemis placed Orion among the stars, but as far as possible from the Scorpion.

Extending Ptolemy's list

Few of the constellation patterns bear any resemblance to the objects for which they are named; Scorpio is one of the exceptions. The system, however, has been followed for so long that it will perhaps never be altered.

Ptolemy's list did not include all the stars visible from Alexandria and he could know nothing about the stars to be seen from places farther south. Later astronomers extended his list, even to the extent of borrowing stars from the original 48 groups. At times it appeared that each astronomer felt obligated to make at least one addition to the constellations in an already crowded sky. The climax came with the maps by the German astronomer J. E. Bode in the late eighteenth century. These included groups with such names as Sceptrum Brandenburgicum (the Sceptre of Brandenburg), Lochium Funis (the Log Line), and Officina Typographica (the Printing Press). Subsequently the list was reduced to a more manageable 88 groups and the boundaries were rigidly defined by a commission of the International Astronomical Union in 1934.

The constellations are unequal in size and in importance. One (Argo Navis, the Ship Argo) was so huge that it has been split up into several parts; the largest constellation now recognized is Hydra (the Watersnake), which sprawls its way across the sky but has only one bright star. The famous Southern Cross, Crux, is the smallest constellation; it was named in 1679.

KEY

I II IV V VII VIII X XI

The 12 constellations of the Zodiac are shown in relation to the Sun during its apparent movement along the ecliptic – a result of the orbital motion of the Earth. A line from the Earth through the Sun passes through Aries in March, but the constellation is only above the horizon during daylight.

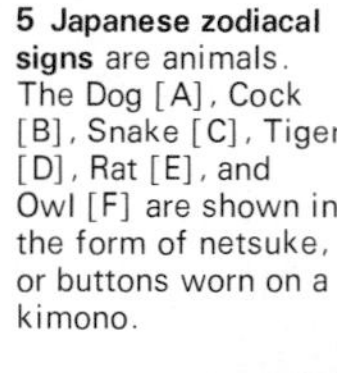

5 Japanese zodiacal signs are animals. The Dog [A], Cock [B], Snake [C], Tiger [D], Rat [E], and Owl [F] are shown in the form of netsuke, or buttons worn on a kimono.

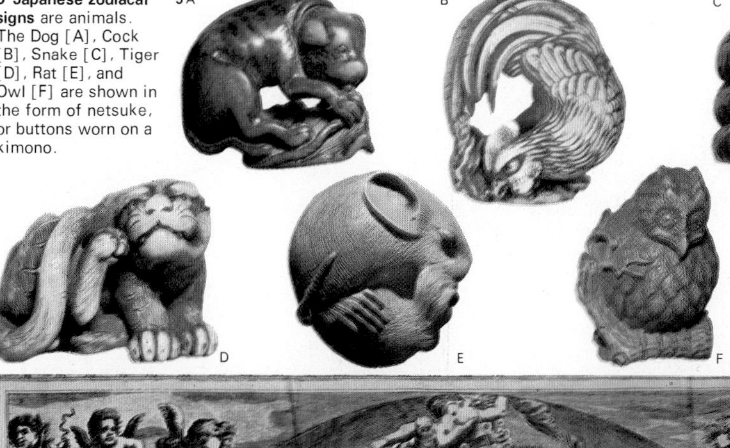

6 Chinese zodiacal signs are also animals, some of which are depicted here on a vase [A] of the 5th or 6th century AD. This Chinese horoscope [B] has an intricate layout.

HEMISPHE
ALIS COELI

7 The main constellation patterns listed by Ptolemy are shown in this map drawn by Joannes Janssonius in 1660. The map is oriented to the pole of the ecliptic. The confusion of the intricate patterns led the 18th-century astronomer William Herschel to comment that they were created to "cause as much inconvenience as possible." The patterns were subsequently modified and fixed by the International Astronomical Union in 1934.

Star guide: northern sky I

The far northern sky is dominated by the constellation of Ursa Major, the Great Bear, probably the most famous constellation in the sky. Its seven bright stars make up the pattern that is commonly known as the Big Dipper.

Ursa Major—the key constellation

The shape of the Dipper is so distinctive that it cannot be overlooked. Six of the stars are of about the second magnitude, but the seventh, Delta Ursae Majoris, or Megrez, is below the third. Its relative faintness cannot be missed—and yet astronomers of ancient times ranked it equal with its companions, so that if their descriptions are accurate, Megrez has faded appreciably. Alpha, or Dubhe, the brighter of the Pointers to the Pole Star, is orange; the rest of the stars are white or bluish-white. Mizar, or Zeta Ursae Majoris, has a fainter star, Alcor, close beside it. Through a telescope, Mizar can be seen to be a fine double.

From the northernmost part of the United States, Ursa Major is circumpolar—that is, it never sets; and it is extremely useful as a guide for locating other stars and constellations. Ursa Minor, the Little Bear, is easily found [Key]. It resembles a faint and distorted version of the Great Bear, but it has two stars of the second magnitude—Polaris itself and the orange Beta, or Kocab, sometimes nicknamed the Guardian of the Pole. Between the Bears there sprawls the long, dim constellation of Draco, the Dragon, whose brightest star, Gamma, or Etamin, is of about the second magnitude. Alpha Draconis, or Thuban, between Kocab and Alkaid in the Dipper, was the pole star in ancient times.

Left map—from Hercules to Virgo

In the large but rather ill-formed Hercules the brightest star, Beta, is above the third magnitude. Alpha, or Rasalgethi, is a semiregular variable, with a range of between magnitudes 3 and 4; it is a huge red giant star with a small greenish companion visible in small telescopes. Close by it is the 2nd magnitude Rasalhague, the brightest star in another large, rather dim group, Ophiuchus. The most interesting objects in Hercules, however, are the globular clusters M13 (NGC 6205) and M92 (NGC 6341). M13, the finer, is just visible with the naked eye and a small telescope will resolve its outer portions into stars. Following around the "tail" of the Great Bear leads to Arcturus, the brilliant orange star in Boötes, the Herdsman. Arcturus is the brightest star in the northern hemisphere of the sky. Its magnitude is −0.06 and it is light orange in color, with a K-type spectrum. It is 36 light-years from Earth and 100 times more luminous than the Sun. The rest of Boötes is not notable, although Epsilon (Izar) is a beautiful double star. Close to Boötes is the conspicuous little semicircle of stars making up Corona Borealis, the Northern Crown, which contains the celebrated variable star R Coronae. This is normally of about the sixth magnitude, but experiences sudden, unpredictable drops to minimum. R Coronae is the prototype star of its class and is much the brightest example. Also in this constellation is T Coronae. It is normally of the 10th magnitude, but flared up to naked-eye visibility in 1866 and again in 1946.

CONNECTIONS

See also
132 Star guide: northern sky II
134 Star guide: southern sky I
136 Star guide: southern sky II
138 Seasonal star maps: northern
140 Seasonal star maps: southern
128 Mapping the constellations
100 Star types

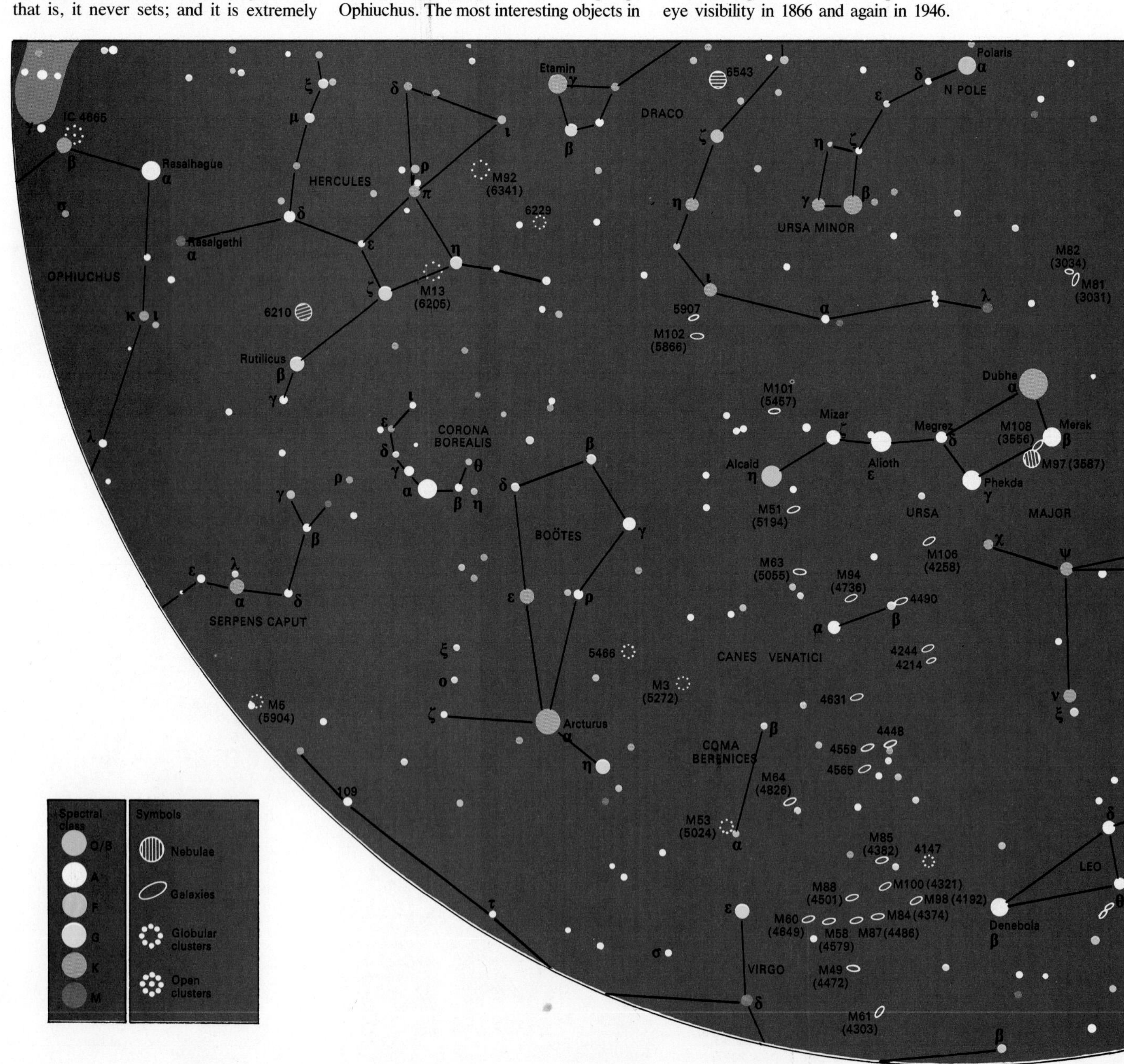
Polaris
N POLE
URSA MINOR
DRACO
Etamin
6543
HERCULES
M92
(6341)
6229
M13
(6205)
IC 4665
Rasalhague
Rasalgethi
OPHIUCHUS
6210
Rutilicus
5907
M102
(5866)
M82
(3034)
M81
(3031)
Dubhe
Merak
M108
(3556)
M97 (3587)
Phekda
Megrez
Mizar
Alioth
Alcaid
M101
(5457)
M51
(5194)
URSA
MAJOR
M106
(4258)
M63
(5055)
M94
(4736)
4490
CORONA
BOREALIS
BOÖTES
SERPENS CAPUT
CANES VENATICI
5466
M3
(5272)
4244
4214
4631
M5
(5904)
Arcturus
COMA
BERENICES
4448
4559
4565
M64
(4826)
109
M53
(5024)
M85
(4382)
4147
LEO
M88
(4501)
M100 (4321)
M98 (4192)
Denebola
M60
(4649)
M58
(4579)
M84 (4374)
M87 (4486)
VIRGO
M49
(4472)
M61
(4303)
Spectral class
O/B
A
F
G
K
M
Symbols
Nebulae
Galaxies
Globular clusters
Open clusters

Part of Virgo is also shown, although its leading star, Spica, is in the southern hemisphere. This region is particularly rich in faint galaxies, and between Virgo and Ursa Major lies the constellation Coma Berenices, which looks like a large, dim cluster. Canes Venatici, the Hunting Dogs, has only one star as bright as the 2nd magnitude.

Right map—from Leo to Canis Minor
Leo, the Lion, is the most easily visible of the constellations during spring in the Northern Hemisphere. Its leading star, Regulus, lies at one end of a curved line making up the pattern known as the Sickle and is of magnitude 1. Gamma, or Algeiba, is a fine double star with rather unequal components. Beta, or Denebola, on the other side of Leo, is now of the second magnitude, but in ancient times it was ranked as being of the first and there is a chance that it, too, has faded appreciably. Adjoining Leo is Cancer, the Crab, which contains the famous open clusters M44 (NGC 2632), or Praesepe, easily visible with the naked eye on a dark night, and M67 (NGC 2682), visible with binoculars and thought to be one of the oldest of the loose clusters.

The brilliant constellation of Orion is cut in half by the celestial equator, so that part of it is shown on this map; the leader is the orange-red Betelgeuse. Not far from Orion are the Twins, Castor and Pollux, in the constellation of Gemini. Pollux is of the first magnitude and Castor between the first and the second—another possible case of fading. Pollux has a K-type spectrum and is clearly orange; Castor is a multiple star, made up of two main components, each of which is a very close binary, together with a fainter companion that is also a binary. The other bright star in Gemini is Gamma, or Alhena (magnitude 2). Adjoining Gemini is Canis Minor, the Little Dog, with one brilliant first-magnitude star, Procyon, which is one of our nearest stellar neighbors; it has a white dwarf companion. The Milky Way flows through Gemini and its neighbor Auriga, the Charioteer, resulting in many rich starfields. Auriga includes several bright open clusters within it.

KEY

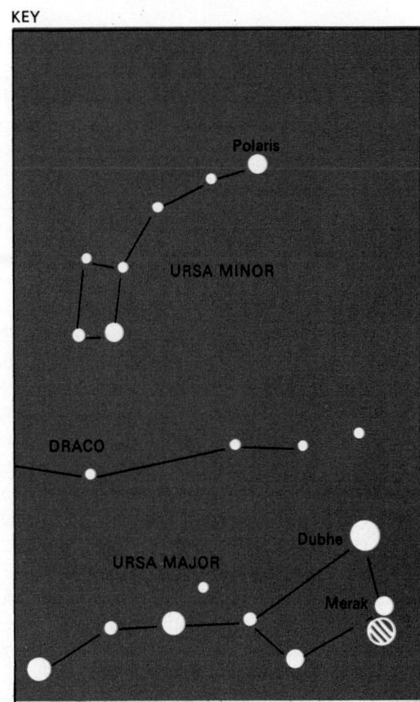
Polaris
URSA MINOR
DRACO
Dubhe
URSA MAJOR
Merak

The north celestial pole is easy to locate, since Polaris lies within one degree of it. Polaris can be found by following the line of the Pointers, Merak and Dubhe, in the Great Bear. As the Earth rotates, the celestial pole remains stationary while all other objects appear to circle it slowly. Depending on the position of the observer, the pole star will be in a different area of the sky; only at the North Pole is it seen directly overhead. As the celestial pole is thus an extension of the Earth's axis, so also is the celestial equator a projection of the Earth's Equator. A star at the celestial equator will rise in the east and set in the west 12 hours later.

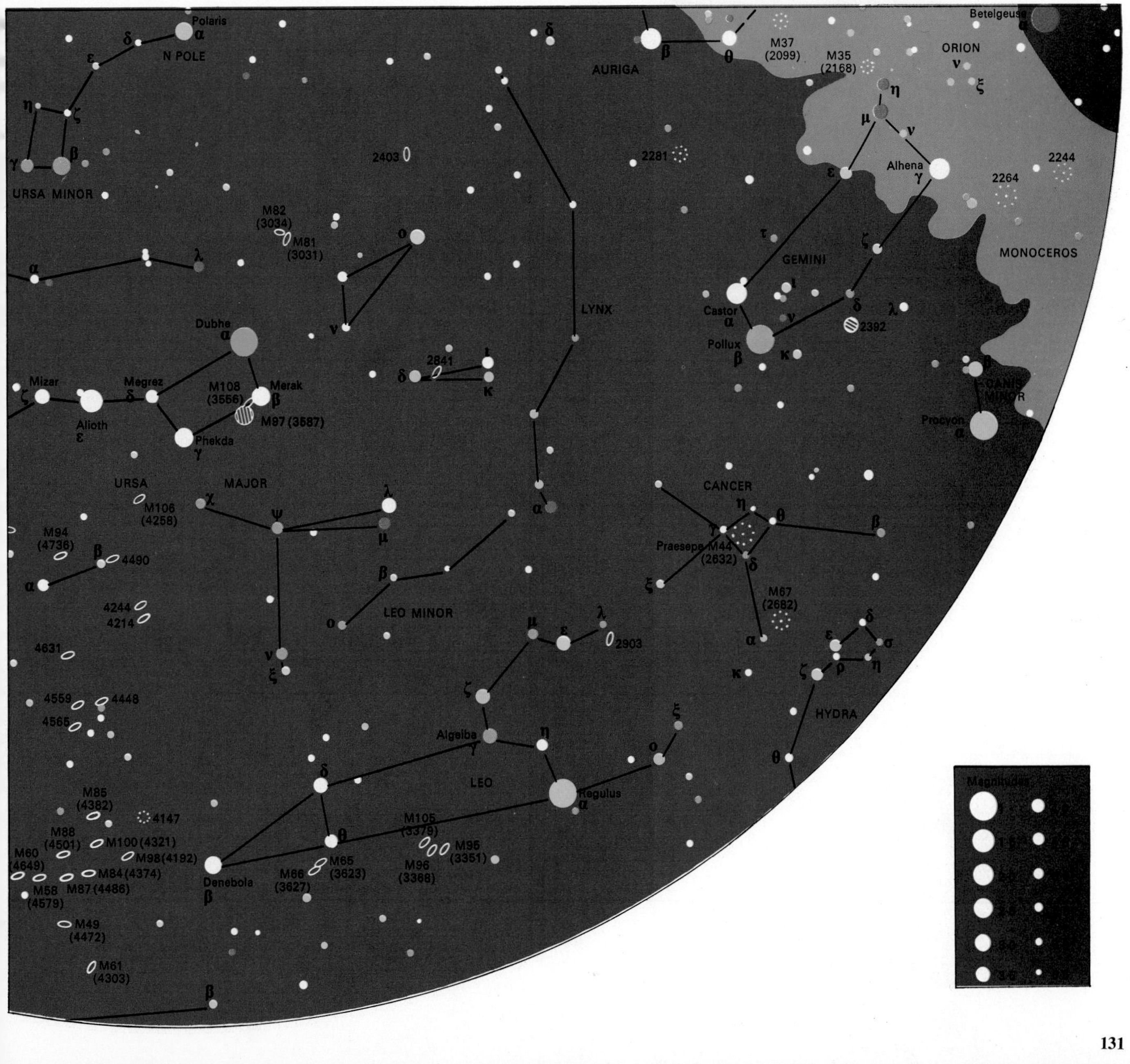

Star guide: northern sky II

Cassiopeia, whose leading stars make up a well-marked W or M form, is second in importance only to Ursa Major among the constellations of the far north.

Cassiopeia—the key constellation
Like Ursa Major, Cassiopeia is circumpolar over northern United States. The best way to find it is to extend a line from Mizar, the second star in the tail of the Great Bear, through Polaris and along a line for an equal distance in the opposite direction. Gamma Cassiopeiae, the middle star of the W, is an irregular variable. It is usually just below the second magnitude, but sometimes it can flare up to 1.6, as it did in 1936. Its spectrum is peculiar and it is a highly unstable star. Alpha, or Shedir, is of type K and is suspected of slight variability; Beta is invariable at magnitude 2.3. Tycho Brahe's supernova of 1572 flared out in Cassiopeia and is still a radio source.

Two of the stars in the W point to Perseus, which has one second-magnitude star, Alpha, or Mirfak, as well as the celebrated eclipsing binary Algo (Beta), which has a magnitude range of 2.2 to 3.5. Perhaps the most notable object in Perseus is the Sword Handle, Chi-h (known officially as H.Vi.33–4), which consists of two beautiful open clusters in the same telescopic field, making a glorious spectacle. Each cluster has a diameter of 75 light-years and lies at a distance of 7,000 light-years from Earth.

Left map—from Auriga to Triangulum
The Milky Way flows through Cassiopeia and Perseus and into Auriga, where the leading star is Capella—almost exactly equal in brilliancy to Vega and on the opposite side of the celestial pole. Capella is 45 light-years away and has the same spectral type as the Sun, though it is a giant star and much more luminous. The small triangle beside it makes up the Haedi, or Kids. Epsilon Aurigae, the apex of the triangle, is a remarkable object; it is an eclipsing binary and the secondary is either a very young star or perhaps a black hole. Zeta Aurigae, close beside it, is also an eclipsing binary of long period (972 days). Auriga itself is made up of a quadrilateral of stars.

Taurus, the Bull, adjoins Auriga. Aldebaran, orange and of the first magnitude, lies in line with the three stars of Orion's belt, which are just in the Southern Hemisphere. Taurus contains the two most famous open clusters in the sky, the Pleiades and the Hyades, as well as the Crab Nebula, M1, near third-magnitude Zeta Tauri.

Cassiopeia can also be used to locate the Square of Pegasus, which is prominent during autumn evenings in the Northern Hemisphere. Of the four leaders, Beta, or Scheat, is semiregular, with a period of about 35 days; it is visible as a huge, red giant. The line of stars leading off from Pegasus makes up Andromeda—celebrated because of the presence of the spiral galaxy M31. Alpheratz, or Alpha Andromedae, is included in the Square of Pegasus. Of the other second-magnitude leaders of Andromeda, Beta is orange-red and Gamma, orange, is a fine binary easily separable with a small telescope. Pegasus contains one bright star away from the Square, Epsilon, or Enif. Adjoining the Square is the dim zodiacal constellation of Pisces, and in this

CONNECTIONS

See also
128 Mapping the conste lations
130 Star guide: norther sky I
134 Star guide: souther sky I
136 Star guide: souther sky II
138 Seasonal star maps northern
140 Seasonal star maps southern
100 Star types

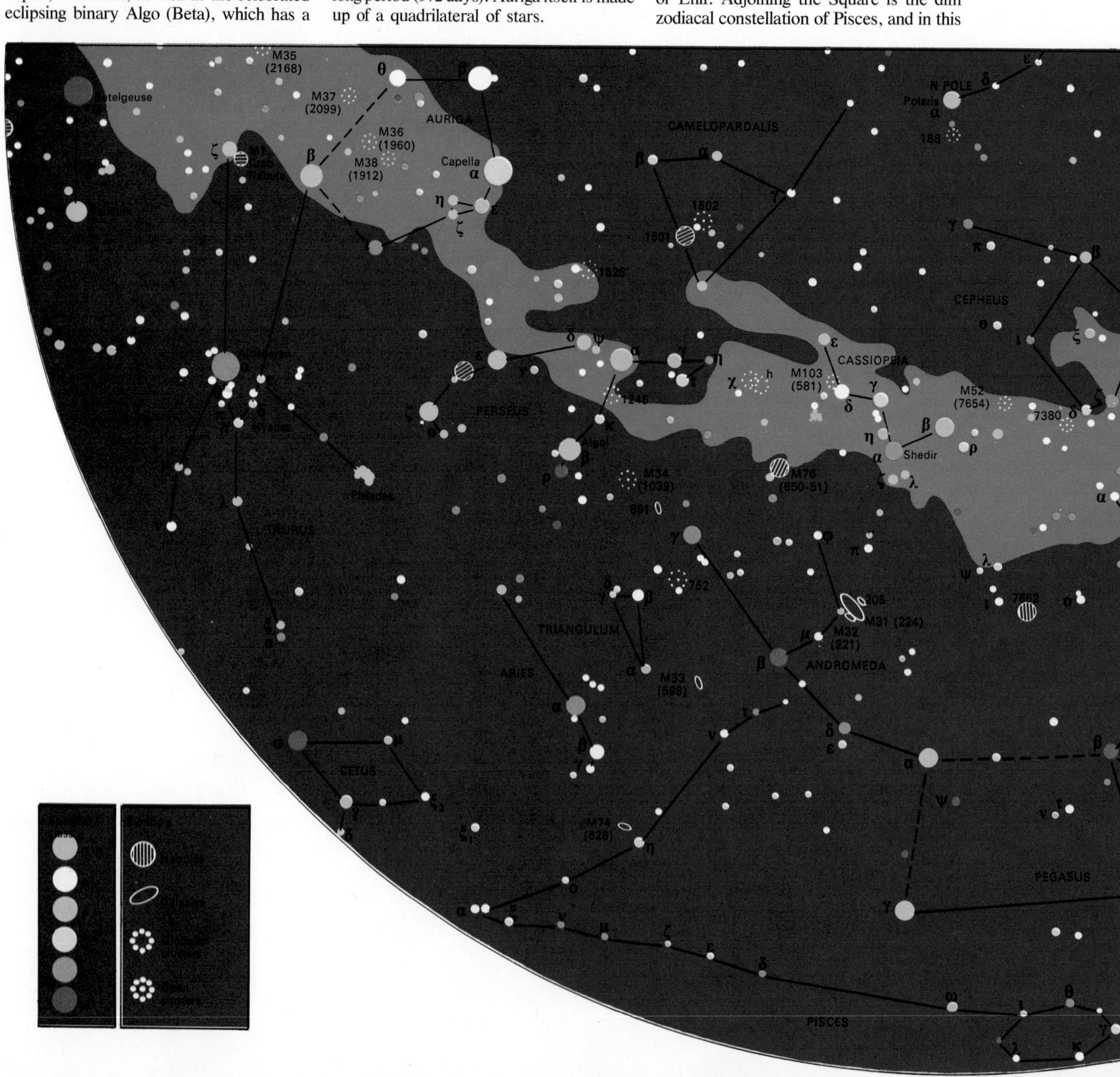

M35 (2168)
M37 (2099)
AURIGA
M36 (1960)
M38 (1912)
Capella
CAMELOPARDALIS
N POLE
Polaris
188
1502
1501
1528
CEPHEUS
CASSIOPEIA
M103 (581)
M52 (7654)
7380
Shedir
1245
PERSEUS
Algol
Pleiades
Hyades
TAURUS
M34 (1039)
891
M76 (650-51)
752
205
M31 (224)
M32 (221)
ANDROMEDA
TRIANGULUM
ARIES
M33 (598)
CETUS
M74 (628)
PEGASUS
PISCES
7662

region also lie Aries, with the second-magnitude Hamal (Alpha), and Triangulum. Triangulum contains the loose spiral galaxy M33, a member of our local group of galaxies, and visible with binoculars.

Right map—from Lyra to Delphinus

Vega, in Lyra, is one of three brilliant stars making up what is informally called the Summer Triangle. Vega is the fifth brightest star in the sky and is easy to identify. From the northern United States it is almost overhead during summer evenings. Lyra is a small constellation, but contains a great many interesting objects. Epsilon Lyrae is a quadruple star, while Beta is the famous eclipsing variable. M57 (NGC 6720) is the most famous of the so-called planetary nebulae, which are surrounded by huge gaseous shells; it lies between Beta Lyrae and the 3rd-magnitude Gamma.

The other two members of the Summer Triangle are Deneb in Cygnus and Altair in Aquila. Cygnus is a superb group. It is shaped like a cross and among its many interesting objects are the beautiful double Beta, or Albireo, in which the primary is golden-yellow (magnitude 5) and the companion blue (magnitude 3), and the long-period variable Chi, between Albireo and the center of the cross, which has a very large magnitude range (3.3–14.2) and a period of 407 days. Like most of its type, it is very red and at maximum is easy to locate. The Milky Way is particularly rich in this area, so that Cygnus is well worth looking at through binoculars.

Altair, in Aquila, is recognizable, partly because of its brightness and partly because it has a fainter star to either side of it. Close to it is a line of stars, of which the central member, Eta Aquilae, is a typical Cepheid, with a period of 7.17 days; it is always easily visible with the naked eye.

In the general area of Cygnus and Aquila there are some small but quite distinctive constellations—notably Delphinus, the Dolphin, which looks at first glance like a very open cluster. It was here that the famous slow nova, HR Delphini, appeared in 1967; it rose to magnitude 3.6 and is still visible with a small telescope.

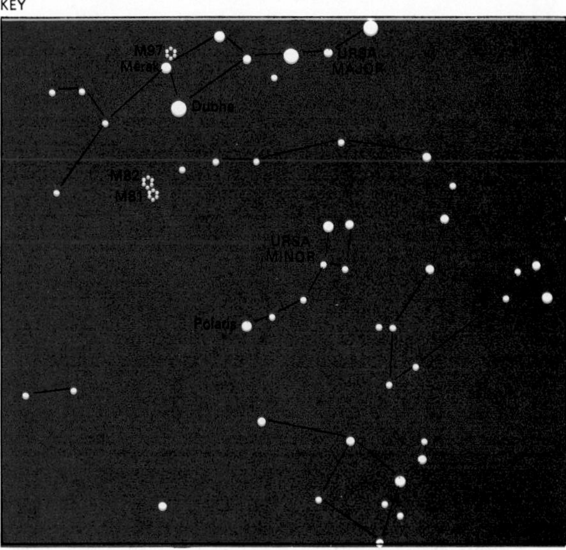
KEY
M97
Merak
URSA MAJOR
Dubhe
M82
M81
URSA MINOR
Polaris

The area of the North Pole is marked by Polaris, with Ursa Major to one side and the rather formless Cepheus to the other. A star in Draco was nearest to the pole 5,000 years ago.

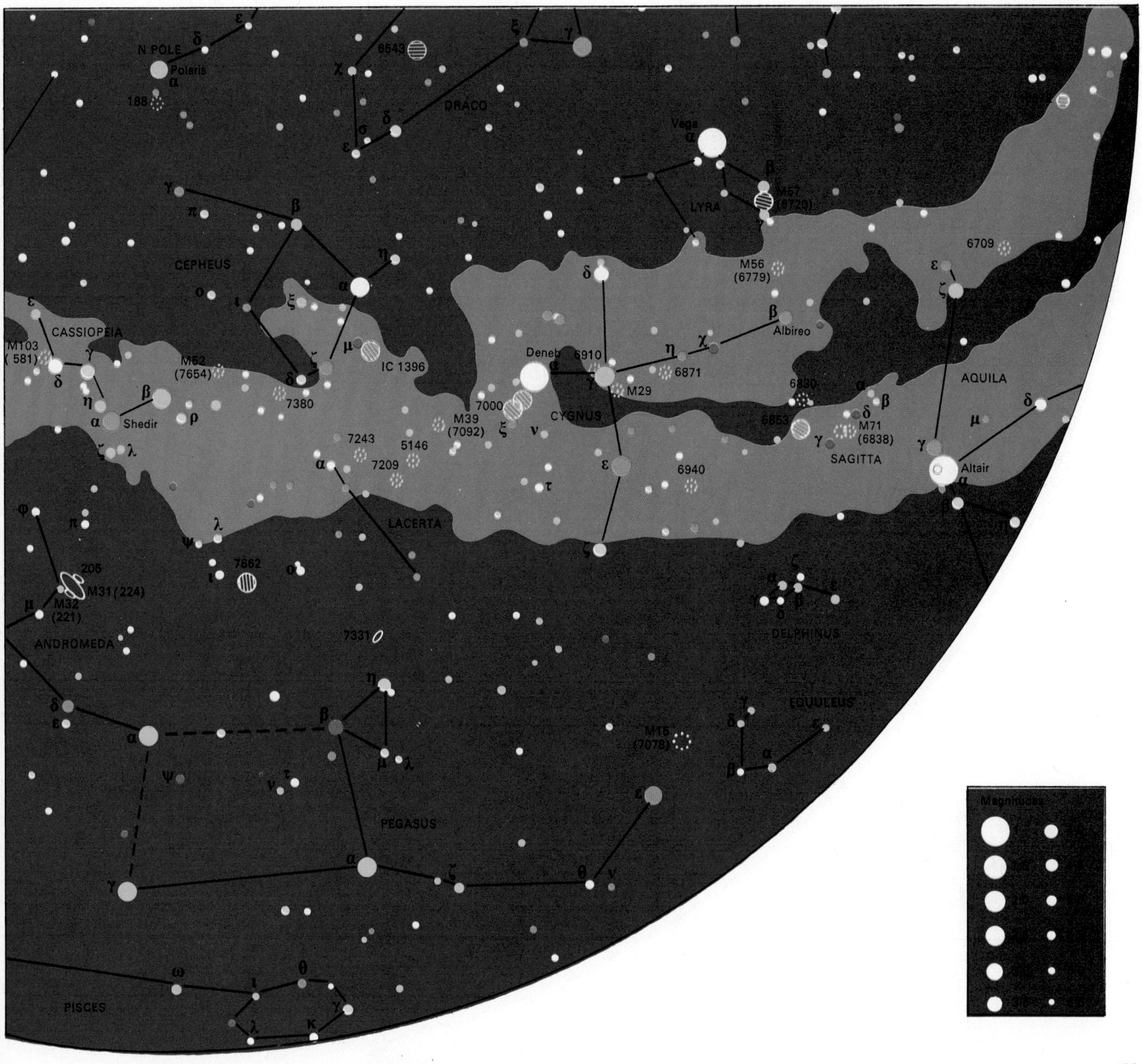

Star guide: southern sky I

There can be little doubt that the stars of the far south are more splendid than those of the far north. Brilliant constellations such as Centaurus, Carina, and above all Crux are not visible from most of the United States or Europe, and the same is true of the bright external systems known as the Magellanic Clouds, or Nubeculae. Other stars, such as Sirius, which are visible from the Northern Hemisphere, are much brighter seen from south of the Equator.

Crux—the key constellation
Crux, the Southern Cross, is the most famous of all the far southern groups and is, incidentally, the smallest of all the recognized constellations. Since it is not at all visible from the Northern Hemisphere it is not one of the ancient constellations, and it was not added to star maps until the seventeenth century. It is not like a cross because there is no central star to make up the X as there is with Cygnus in the northern sky; Crux more nearly resembles a kite, but it is so compact that it cannot be mistaken. Acrux, or Alpha Crucis, the leader, is a fine binary 270 light-years from Earth. The magnitudes of the components are 1.6 and 2.1, giving a combined naked-eye magnitude of 0.8. The pair may be seen well with a small telescope. Beta Crucis (magnitude 1.3) is a very luminous B-type star, and Gamma Crucis (magnitude 1.6) is a red giant. The fourth star of the pattern is much fainter at magnitude 3 and thus spoils the symmetry. Crux also includes the Jewel Box cluster, Kappa Crucis (NGC4755), and the dark nebula that is usually termed the Coalsack—a mass of dust and gas cutting out the light of stars beyond.

Left map—from Carina to Hydra
Carina is part of the old constellation of Argo Navis, in mythology, the ship that carried Jason and his companions in search of the Golden Fleece—but Argo was so large that it was cut up into a Keel, a Poop, and Sails (Carina, Puppis, and Vela). Carina contains many bright stars, including Canopus, an F-type supergiant of magnitude −0.7, and also the extraordinary object Eta Carinae, which is wreathed in nebulosity and is variable. For a period between 1834 and 1844 it ranked as one of the brightest stars in the sky at magnitude −0.7, but for almost a century now it has been below naked-eye visibility at magnitude 7.7.

The so-called False Cross is made up of two stars in Carina and two in Vela, all of about the second magnitude. It is often confused with Crux, but it is larger and not so bright. The Milky Way flows through the Ship and the region abounds with clusters and rich starfields. By contrast, Canis Major is relatively barren of interesting telescopic objects, although it contains several bright stars in addition to Sirius. Although it is at least 20 times more luminous than the Sun, Sirius owes its apparent eminence to its closeness (8.7 light-years from Earth) rather than its power, and it is feeble compared with Canopus, which appears fainter but is farther away and extremely luminous.

Right map—from Hydra to Scorpio
Hydra, the Watersnake, is a barren area of the sky. It does contain, however, the red-

CONNECTIONS

See also
128 Mapping the conste lations
130 Star guide: northern sky I
132 Star guide: northern sky II
136 Star guide: southern sky II
138 Seasonal star maps: northern
140 Seasonal star maps: southern
100 Star types

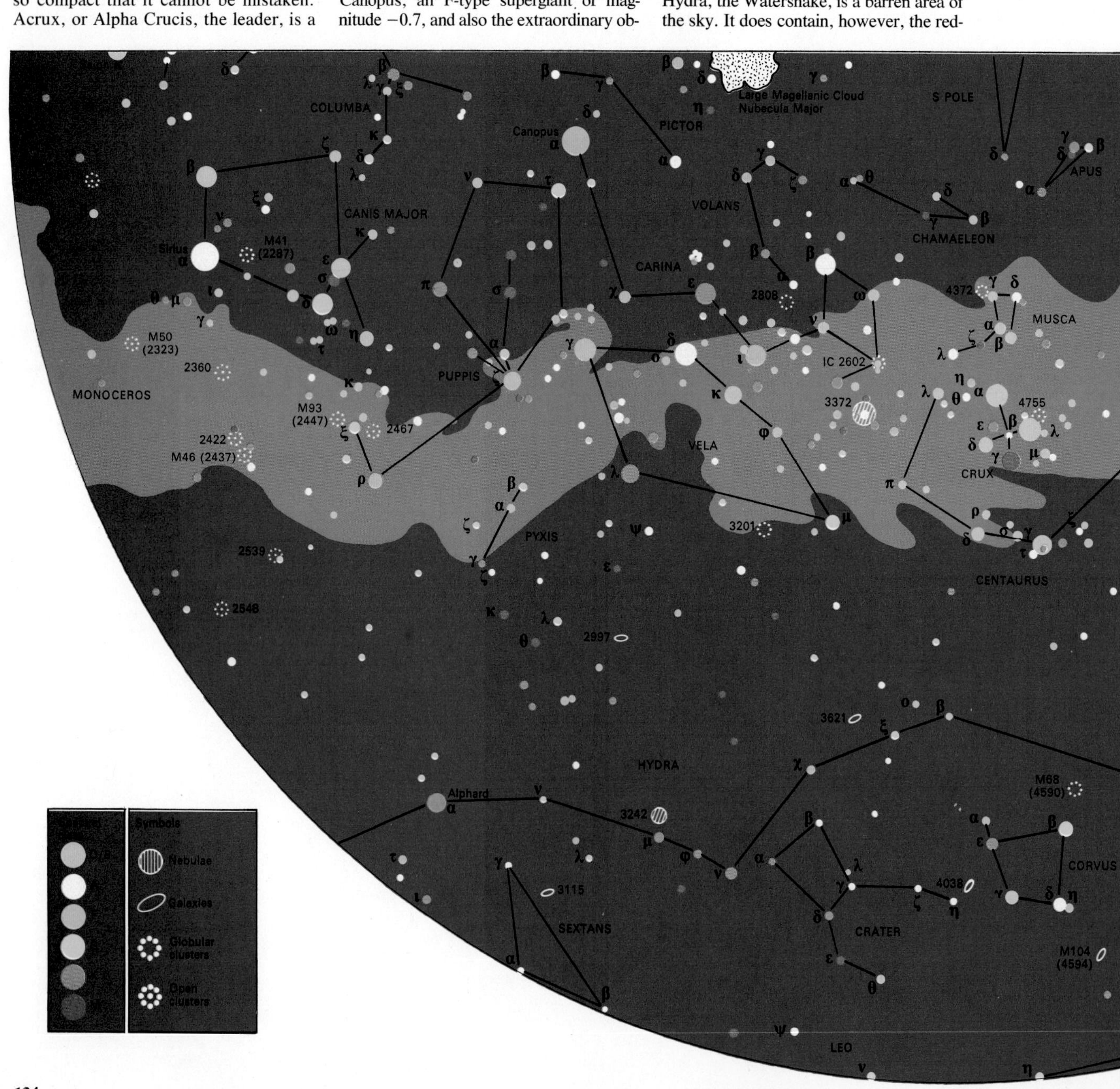

COLUMBA
Canopus
PICTOR
Large Magellanic Cloud
Nubecula Major
S POLE
APUS
VOLANS
CHAMAELEON
CANIS MAJOR
Sirius
M41 (2287)
CARINA
2808
4372
MUSCA
M50 (2323)
2360
MONOCEROS
PUPPIS
IC 2602
M93 (2447)
2467
3372
4755
2422
M46 (2437)
VELA
CRUX
3201
PYXIS
2539
2548
CENTAURUS
2997
3621
HYDRA
Alphard
M68 (4590)
3242
CORVUS
3115
SEXTANS
4038
CRATER
M104 (4594)
LEO
Symbols
Nebulae
Galaxies
Globular clusters
Open clusters

dish 2nd-magnitude star Alphard, the solitary one, which appears distinct against its isolated background. The conspicuous quadrilateral of Corvus, the Crow, is also shown, and part of Virgo, including the 1st-magnitude Spica. Gamma Virginis, or Arich, is a fine binary with a period of 180 years.

Crux is more or less surrounded by Centaurus, which is yet another magnificent group with many brilliant stars. Alpha Centauri, sometimes called Rigil Kent, or Toliman, is a binary with a period of 80 years; any small telescope will separate its components of types G and K. At its distance of 4.3 light-years it is the nearest of all the bright stars, and its faint red dwarf companion Proxima, the nearest star to Earth, is only slightly closer. Adjoining Alpha is the very remote Beta Centauri; at magnitude −4.3 it is more than 4,000 times as luminous as the Sun and bluish-white in color. Also in Centaurus lies Omega (NGC 5139), the finest of all the globular clusters—conspicuous to the naked eye as a hazy patch and resolvable with a small telescope.

Adjoining Centaurus are Lupus, the Wolf, and Triangulum Australe, the Southern Triangle. Lupus is rather formless, but the Triangle is distinctive. Its leader, Alpha, is strongly orange in hue and is of magnitude 1.9. The other two members of the Triangle, Beta and Gamma, are of the 3rd magnitude.

Also shown on this map is Scorpius, or Scorpio (the Scorpion), which is one of the most distinctive of the zodiacal constellations and one of the few that slightly resembles its namesake, as it consists of a long line of stars, many of them bright. Its brightest star, Antares, is a vast red giant, with a diameter of about 260 million miles (420 million km); it is about 400 light-years away and its luminosity is almost 5,000 times that of the Sun. It has an apparent magnitude of 1.

Next to Scorpius is the obscure zodiacal constellation of Libra. The brightest star, Beta Librae, is of magnitude 2.7. Delta Librae is an eclipsing binary, with a magnitude range from 4.8 to 5.9. It is of Algol type and bright enough to be seen throughout its period with a pair of binoculars.

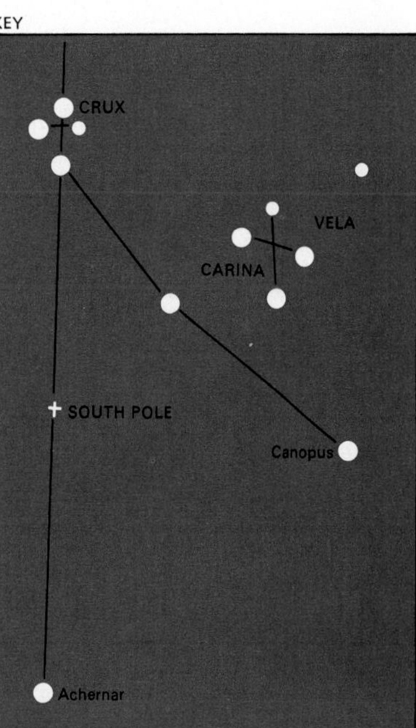
KEY
CRUX
VELA
CARINA
SOUTH POLE
Canopus
Achernar

The south celestial pole is, compared with its counterpart in the north, more difficult to locate. The north celestial pole is conveniently marked by a bright star, Polaris, in the constellation of Ursa Minor, which lies within one degree of the polar point. Unfortunately there is no convenient south polar star; the pole lies in a barren region made up of the faint constellation of Octans. The best way to locate the pole is to follow the longer axis of Crux to the point about midway between Crux and the bright star Achernar in the constellation of Eridanus. The nearest naked-eye star to the pole is the 5th-magnitude Sigma Octantis.

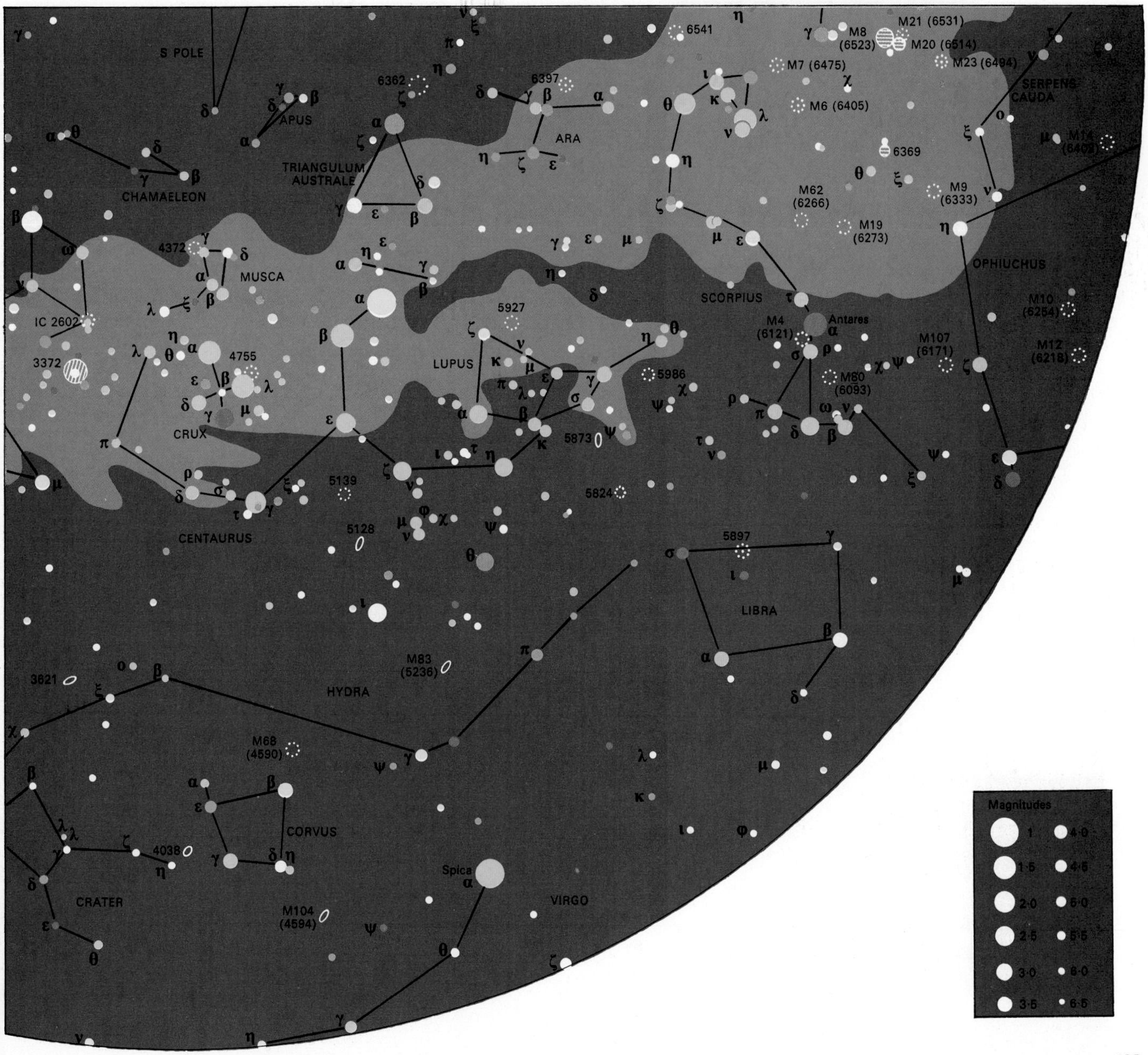

Star guide: southern sky II

Because of the great quantities of dust that lie in the main plane of the Galaxy, it is impossible to see through to the galactic center, but its position is known. It lies beyond the star clouds of Sagittarius, at a distance of about 33,000 light-years from Earth; thus Sagittarius is immersed in the richest part of the Milky Way.

Sagittarius—the key constellation

The constellation of Sagittarius (the Archer) is not hard to identify; it contains several reasonably bright stars, although there are no stars of the first magnitude. In shape Sagittarius is rather hard to define; some people with vivid imaginations have compared it to a teapot. It adjoins the Sting of Scorpius and between the Sting and the leader of Sagittarius (Epsilon Sagittarii, or Kaus Australis) there are two bright open clusters, M6 and M7. Sagittarius is also rich in globular clusters.

Strangely enough the star cataloged as Alpha Sagittarii is obscure; the Greek letters are not necessarily in sequence. Near Alpha is the circle of stars marking Corona Australis, the Southern Crown, which is not nearly as prominent as the Northern Crown, but easier to identify. If Sagittarius is an especially rich region, the south pole of the sky is particularly barren. There is no bright south polar star; the nearest naked-eye object is Sigma Octantis, which is only of the 5th magnitude—a poor substitute for the northern Polaris.

Left map—from Grus to Capricornus

The four "Southern Birds" are shown: Grus (the Crane), Pavo (the Peacock), Tucana (the Toucan), and Phoenix (the Phoenix). This is a confusing area because only Grus has a distinctive form; it really does give the impression of a flying crane. The leaders, Alpha (Alnair, magnitude 2.1) and Beta (magnitude 2.2) are very different. Alnair is bluish-white, while Beta is orange, and the difference is striking when the stars are seen through binoculars or any telescope. Adjoining Grus is Piscis Austrinus, the Southern Fish, which has as its leader the 1st-magnitude Fomalhaut, which is 23 light-years distant and about 15 times as luminous as the Sun. Tucana is the most obscure of the four birds, but it contains a fine double, Beta, and 47 Tucanae, a fine globular cluster.

Finally there are two obscure constellations of the zodiac, Aquarius and Capricornus. There are a few interesting objects in Aquarius, notably the bright globular cluster M2, while in Capricornus there is the naked-eye double Alpha, or Al Giedi; Beta Capricorni is also a very wide, easily seen double, separable with binoculars.

Right map—from Cetus to Orion

Close to Phoenix lies Achernar, the "End of the River" and the only really bright star in the long constellation of Eridanus, which winds its way from near the south pole as far as the boundaries of Orion. Achernar (magnitude −1.3) is 75 light-years from Earth and has a luminosity 256 times that of the Sun. Farther along the line of Eridanus is Theta, or Acamar, which is a fine double, and—like Castor in Gemini and Megrez in the Great Bear—is suspected of having faded during historic times, because ancient

CONNECTIONS

See also

130 Star guide: northern sky I
132 Star guide: northern sky II
134 Star guide: southern sky I
138 Seasonal star maps: northern
140 Seasonal star maps: southern
128 Mapping the constellations
100 Star types

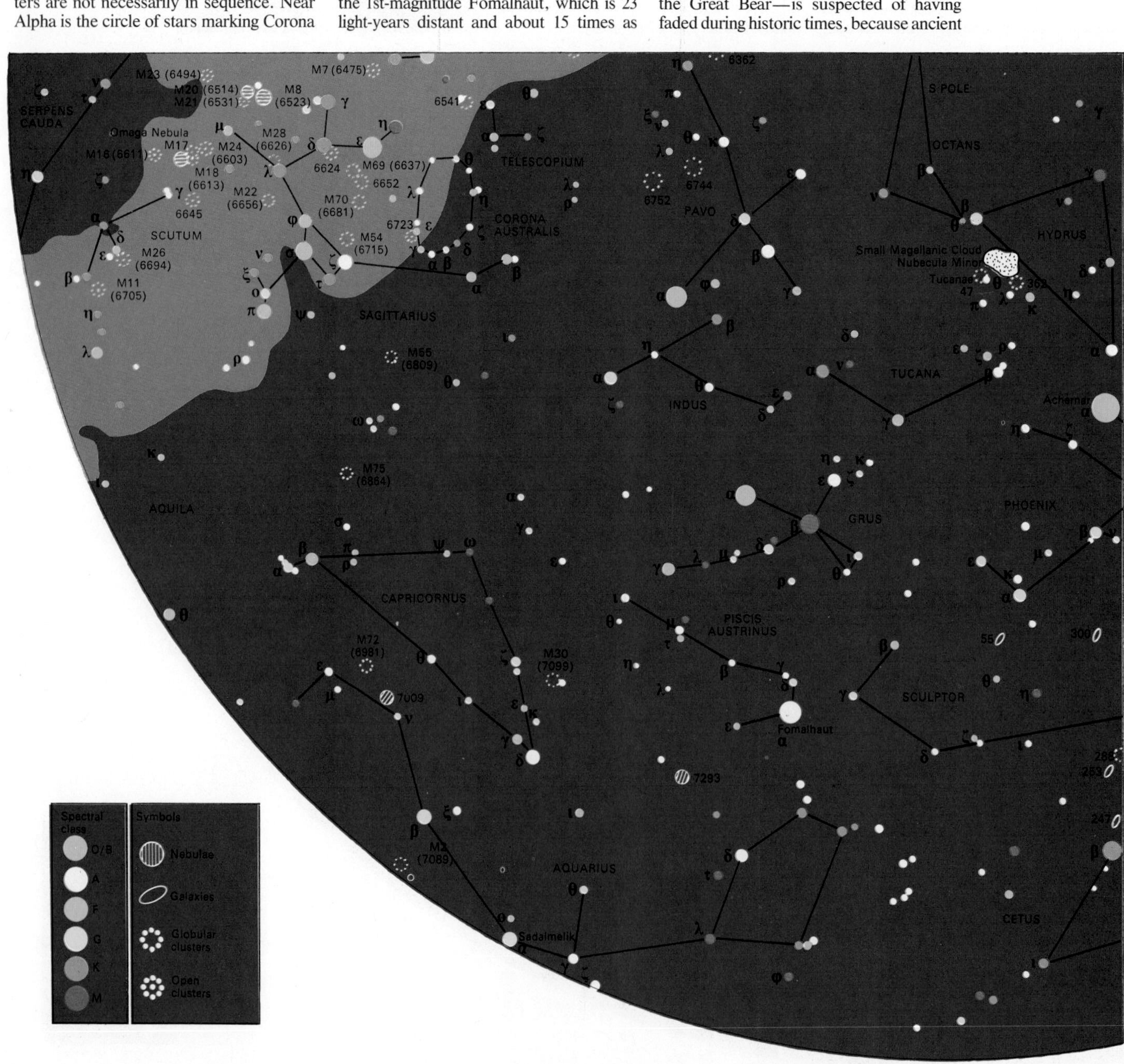

SERPENS CAUDA
M23 (6494)
M20 (6514)
M21 (6531)
M8 (6523)
M7 (6475)
Omega Nebula
M17
M16 (6611)
M28 (6626)
M24 (6603)
M18 (6613)
M22 (6656)
6624
M69 (6637)
6652
M70 (6681)
6723
M54 (6715)
6541
6645
SCUTUM
M26 (6694)
M11 (6705)
TELESCOPIUM
CORONA AUSTRALIS
SAGITTARIUS
M55 (6809)
M75 (6864)
AQUILA
CAPRICORNUS
M72 (6981)
M30 (7099)
7009
M2 (7089)
AQUARIUS
Sadalmelik
6362
6744
6752
PAVO
INDUS
S POLE
OCTANS
HYDRUS
Small Magellanic Cloud
Nubecula Minor
Tucanae 47
TUCANA
Achernar
GRUS
PHOENIX
PISCIS AUSTRINUS
Fomalhaut
SCULPTOR
7293
CETUS
Spectral class
O/B
A
F
G
K
M
Symbols
Nebulae
Galaxies
Globular clusters
Open clusters

astronomers ranked it of the 1st magnitude and it is now below the third.

Cetus, the Whale, or Sea-monster, is a long, rather faint constellation, most of which lies in the Southern Hemisphere, although the head is just north of the equator. It has one 2nd-magnitude star, Beta, or Diphda, which is suspected of variability. Here too is Omicron Ceti, or Mira, the most celebrated long-period variable in the sky. It has a mean period of 331.6 days and at maximum it has been known to exceed the second magnitude; at minimum it descends to the tenth. Its variability was recognized as long ago as 1638. For much of the year, however, it is below naked-eye visibility. Mira is a red giant and its color is very noticeable, particularly near maximum.

Not far from the south pole the two remarkable Magellanic Clouds can be seen. Unfortunately they can never be seen by observers in the United States or Europe. The clouds are external systems, even though they look at first glance like detached portions of the Milky Way. They are about 150,000 light-years away from the Earth and are therefore the most remote objects clearly visible with the naked eye apart from the spiral galaxy M31 in Andromeda. The Large Cloud is so bright that even moonlight will not hide it. Binoculars bring out its form well and telescopic research has shown that it contains objects of all kinds, including globular clusters and gaseous nebulae. One star, S Doradus, is thought to be a million times more luminous than the Sun, and yet without optical aid it cannot be seen at all. The Large Cloud also contains the Great Looped Nebula, which is visible to the naked eye.

Orion, divided by the equator of the sky, is visible from every inhabited part of the world. The equator passes near Delta, or Mintaka, in the Belt, so that the brilliant Rigel lies well in the Southern Hemisphere. Rigel (magnitude −7.0) is a highly luminous star, thought to be about 49,000 times as powerful as the Sun; it lies at a distance of 850 light-years from Earth. Also in the southern part of Orion lies the Great Nebula, M42, which contains the multiple star Theta Orionis, the Trapezium.

KEY

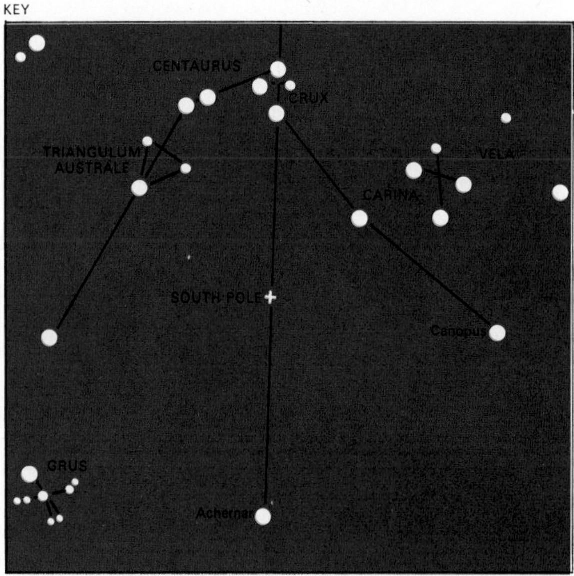
CENTAURUS
CRUX
TRIANGULUM AUSTRALE
VELA
CARINA
SOUTH POLE
Canopus
GRUS
Achernar

The south polar area contains no bright star, but it is surrounded by brilliant constellations like Crux and Centaurus.

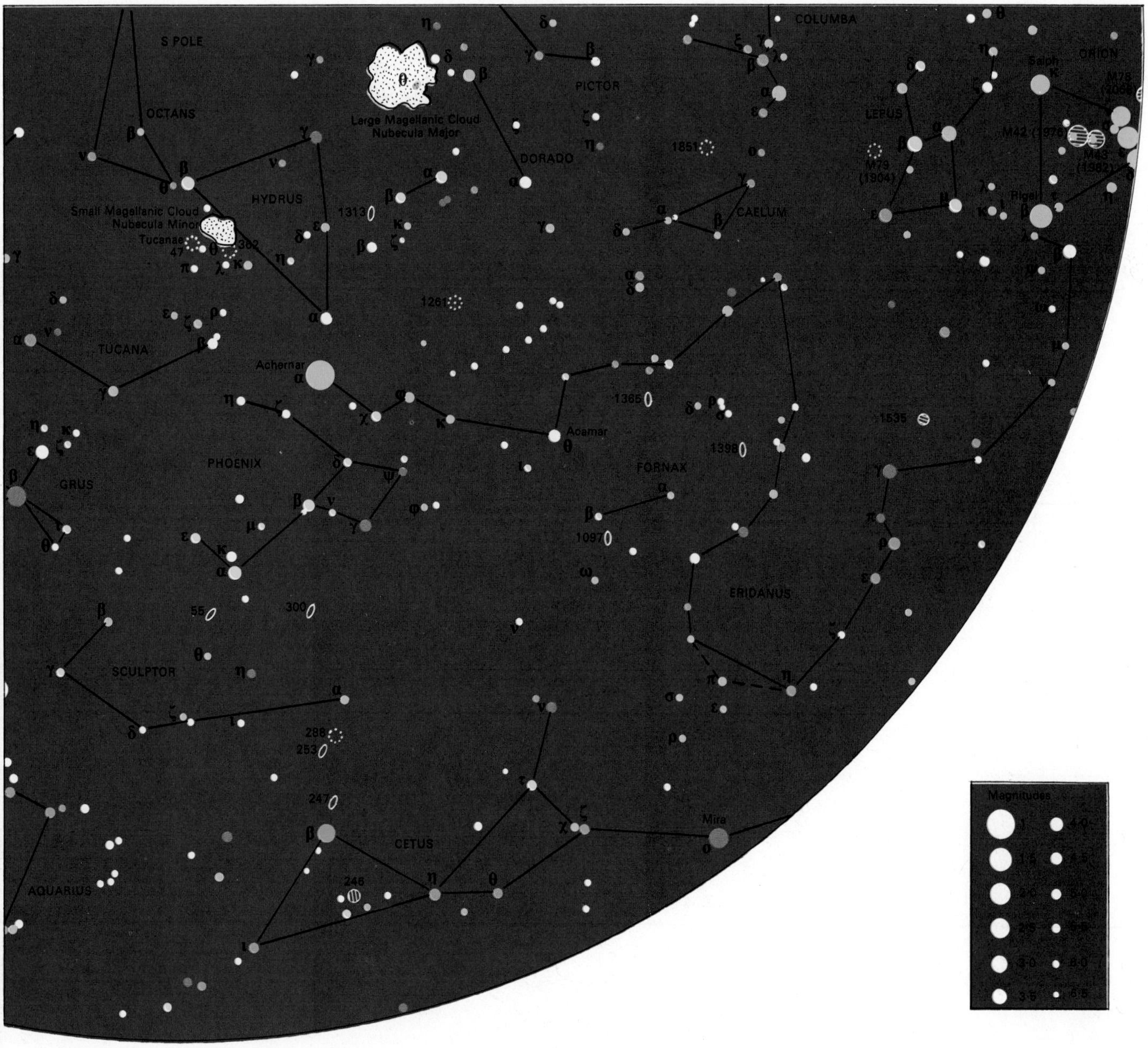

Seasonal star maps: northern

All the stars of the northern sky are visible to an observer in the Northern Hemisphere in the course of a year. The charts on these two pages are suitable for observers living between latitudes 30° and 50°N [Key]. The horizon is shown by the latitude marks near the bottom of the charts. Thus for an observer who lives at latitude 30°N, the northern horizon on Chart 1 [N] will pass just above Deneb and Deneb will be invisible.

Limits of Visibility

A star rises earlier, on the average, by two hours each month; thus the stars for 11:00 pm on January 1 will be the same as those for 9:00 pm on February 1, 7:00 pm on March 1, and so on. All the times given in the charts are in standard time.

A star that never sets is said to be circumpolar; thus Cassiopeia is circumpolar from the northern United States, while Arcturus is not. Limits on the visibility of a star for an observer at any latitude can be worked out from its declination (that is, the star's angular distance north or south of the celestial equator). To an observer in the Northern Hemisphere, a star is at its lowest point when it is below the pole and therefore due north. The circumpolar region of the sky can be found by subtracting the observer's latitude from 90°. Suppose, for example, that an observer lives at latitude 42°N. Subtracting 42 from 90 gives 48; a star that is north of declination +48° will never set, while a star south of declination −48° will never rise. Thus, from latitude 42°N, which is about the latitude of Boston or Chicago, the star Mirfak (declination +50° in Perseus) will be circumpolar, while Arcturus (declination +19°) will be well seen but will not be circumpolar. Canopus (declination −53°) will remain permanently below the horizon from this latitude.

Alkaid or Eta Ursae Majoris, the star at the end of the handle of the Big Dipper, has a declination of approximately +50°. It will therefore be circumpolar from latitudes north of 40°N (since 90 − 50 = 40) and it will be invisible from latitudes south of 40°S.

The charts show the southern [S] and the northern [N] aspects of the sky from the viewpoint of an observer in northern latitudes. The descriptions that follow are for the late evening (when the sky appears the same as it did three months previously).

Stars of chart 1

In winter, the southern aspect is dominated by the constellation Orion and its retinue. Capella is almost at the zenith, or overhead point, and Sirius is at its clearest—although as seen from the United States or the northern part of Europe, Sirius is always rather low down and so the effects of the Earth's atmosphere make it twinkle strongly. Other stars in the general region of Orion are Aldebaran, Castor and Pollux, and Procyon, while Orion itself has two brilliant leaders, the blue-white Rigel and the orange-red Betelgeuse. Apart from its beauty, Orion is invaluable as a guide to other groups; for instance, Aldebaran can be found by following the upward direction of the three stars in Orion's belt.

The sickle forming the head of Leo is prominent in the east (as shown here it is cut by the two maps). In the northeast lies Ursa Major, the Great Bear (including the Big

CONNECTIONS

See also

130 Star guide: northern sky I
132 Star guide: northern sky II
134 Star guide: southern sky I
136 Star guide: southern sky II
40 Measuring the restless sky

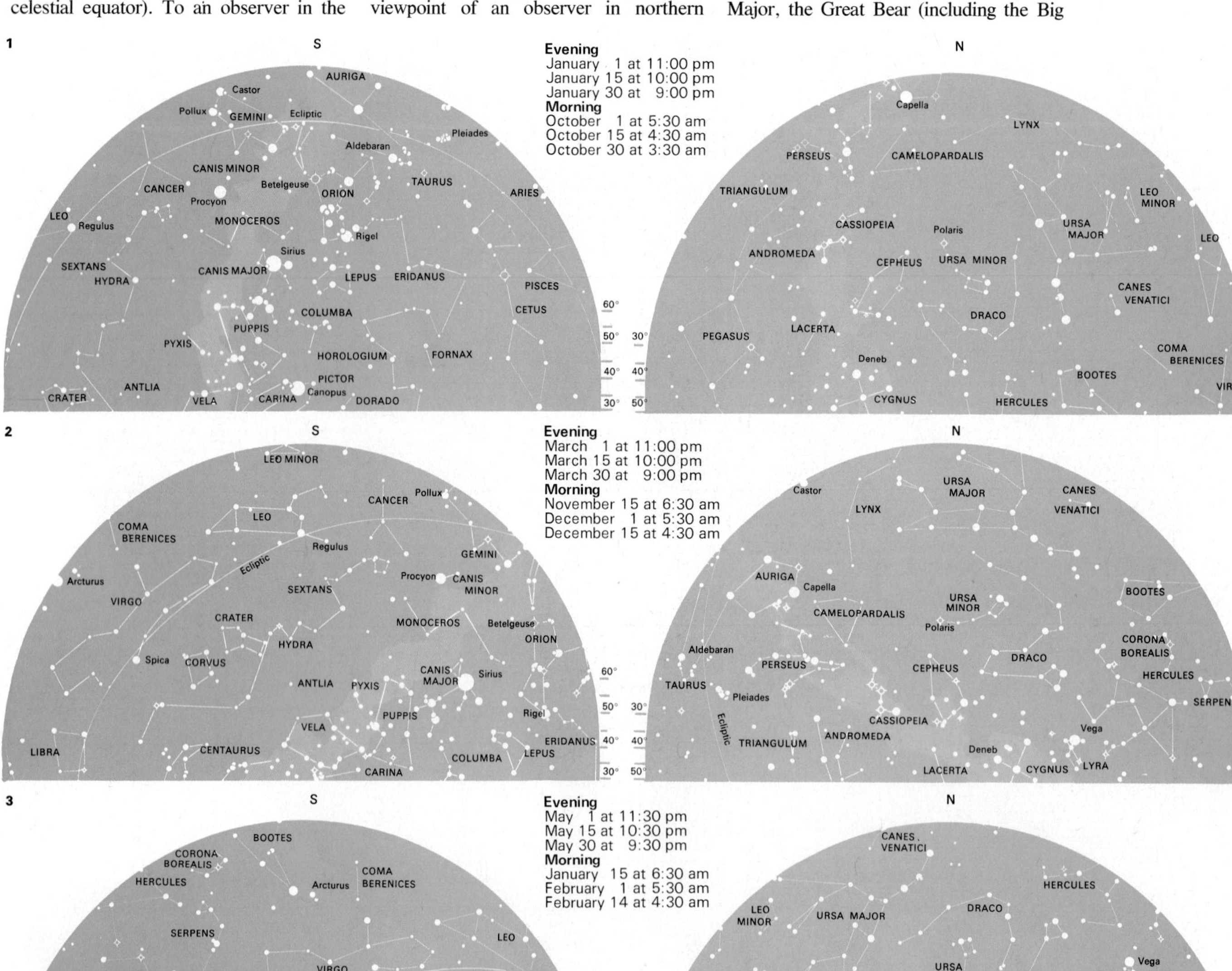

1
S
AURIGA
Castor
Pollux
GEMINI
Ecliptic
Pleiades
Aldebaran
CANIS MINOR
TAURUS
CANCER
Betelgeuse
ORION
ARIES
Procyon
LEO
Regulus
MONOCEROS
Rigel
Sirius
SEXTANS
HYDRA
CANIS MAJOR
LEPUS
ERIDANUS
PISCES
COLUMBA
CETUS
PUPPIS
PYXIS
HOROLOGIUM
FORNAX
PICTOR
ANTLIA
Canopus
CRATER
VELA
CARINA
DORADO
Evening
January 1 at 11:00 pm
January 15 at 10:00 pm
January 30 at 9:00 pm
Morning
October 1 at 5:30 am
October 15 at 4:30 am
October 30 at 3:30 am
60° 50° 40° 30°
30° 40° 50°
N
Capella
LYNX
PERSEUS
CAMELOPARDALIS
TRIANGULUM
LEO MINOR
CASSIOPEIA
Polaris
URSA MAJOR
LEO
ANDROMEDA
CEPHEUS
URSA MINOR
CANES VENATICI
DRACO
LACERTA
PEGASUS
COMA BERENICES
Deneb
BOOTES
VIRGO
CYGNUS
HERCULES
2
S
LEO MINOR
Pollux
CANCER
LEO
COMA BERENICES
Regulus
GEMINI
Ecliptic
Arcturus
Procyon
CANIS MINOR
SEXTANS
VIRGO
CRATER
MONOCEROS
Betelgeuse
ORION
HYDRA
Spica
CORVUS
CANIS MAJOR
Sirius
ANTLIA
PYXIS
PUPPIS
Rigel
VELA
ERIDANUS
LIBRA
CENTAURUS
LEPUS
COLUMBA
CARINA
Evening
March 1 at 11:00 pm
March 15 at 10:00 pm
March 30 at 9:00 pm
Morning
November 15 at 6:30 am
December 1 at 5:30 am
December 15 at 4:30 am
N
URSA MAJOR
Castor
CANES VENATICI
LYNX
AURIGA
Capella
BOOTES
URSA MINOR
CAMELOPARDALIS
Polaris
CORONA BOREALIS
Aldebaran
DRACO
PERSEUS
CEPHEUS
HERCULES
TAURUS
Pleiades
SERPENS
CASSIOPEIA
Ecliptic
Vega
TRIANGULUM
ANDROMEDA
Deneb
LACERTA
CYGNUS
LYRA
3
S
BOOTES
CORONA BOREALIS
COMA BERENICES
HERCULES
Arcturus
SERPENS
LEO
OPHIUCHUS
VIRGO
Regulus
LIBRA
Spica
Ecliptic
CRATER
SEXTANS
CORVUS
SCUTUM
Antares
SCORPIUS
AQUILA
CENTAURUS
HYDRA
SAGITTARIUS
LUPUS
ANTLIA
NORMA
CRUX
Evening
May 1 at 11:30 pm
May 15 at 10:30 pm
May 30 at 9:30 pm
Morning
January 15 at 6:30 am
February 1 at 5:30 am
February 14 at 4:30 am
N
CANES VENATICI
HERCULES
DRACO
LEO MINOR
URSA MAJOR
URSA MINOR
Vega
LYRA
Polaris
CYGNUS
LYNX
CANCER
CEPHEUS
Deneb
VULPECULA
Pollux
Castor
CAMELOPARDALIS
CASSIOPEIA
GEMINI
LACERTA
Altair
Capella
CANIS MINOR
AURIGA
PERSEUS
DELPHINUS
Procyon
ANDROMEDA

Dipper), invaluable also in recognizing other constellations. The two Pointers at the end of the Dipper show the way to Polaris, the North, or Pole, Star, which is of the second magnitude. It lies less than one degree away from the celestial north pole, so that its declination exceeds +89°. Vega is at its lowest and is not shown on the first chart; it is not circumpolar from the New York area, and is barely so from England. Vega, Polaris, and Capella lie approximately in a line. Thus when Capella is almost at the zenith, Vega is at the horizon (on winter evenings) and when Vega occupies the zenith, Capella is at the horizon (on summer evenings).

Stars of charts 2–6

During spring evenings [chart 2] Orion is still above the horizon; Leo is high up with Virgo to the east; Capella is descending in the northwest and Vega rising in the northeast. In the west, Aldebaran and the Pleiades are still visible.

By early summer [chart 3] Orion has disappeared, although Castor and Pollux remain in view. Vega has risen, Capella is descending, and Ursa Major is not far from the zenith. This is the best time for evening viewing of Arcturus, which is of a beautiful light-orange hue and is actually the brightest star in the Northern Hemisphere (fractionally superior to Vega or Capella). To observers near latitude 30°N, part of Centaurus can be seen very low in the south.

During summer evenings [chart 4] Vega occupies the zenith and its brilliance and distinct bluish color make it unmistakable. An excellent view is afforded of the so-called "summer triangle" (Vega in Lyra, Deneb in Cygnus, and Altair in Aquila) and, in the south, of the brilliant Antares in the Scorpion and the star clouds of Sagittarius in the direction of the center of our Galaxy.

In autumn [chart 5] the Square of Pegasus is high, the summer triangle is still apparent, and Ursa Major is at its lowest.

By early winter [chart 6] Pegasus is still high and Vega and its companions are sinking, but Orion has returned once again and will dominate the evening sky until well into the following year.

KEY

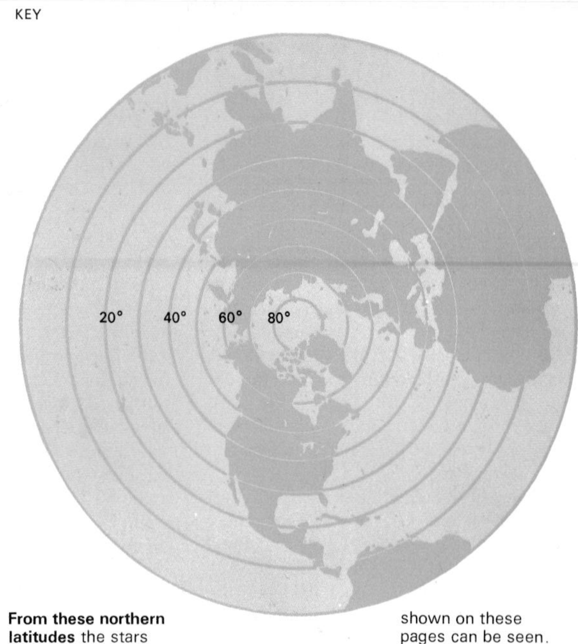
20°
40°
60°
80°

From these northern latitudes the stars shown on these pages can be seen.

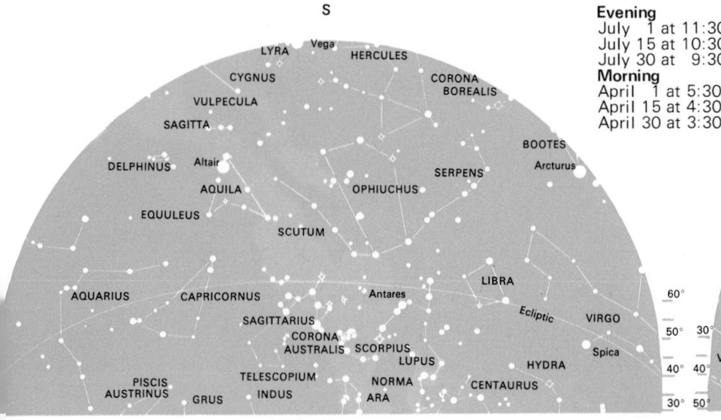

Evening
July 1 at 11:30 pm
July 15 at 10:30 pm
July 30 at 9:30 pm
Morning
April 1 at 5:30 am
April 15 at 4:30 am
April 30 at 3:30 am

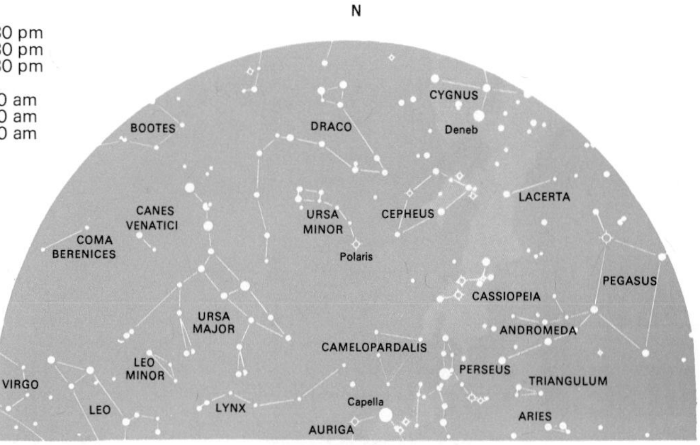

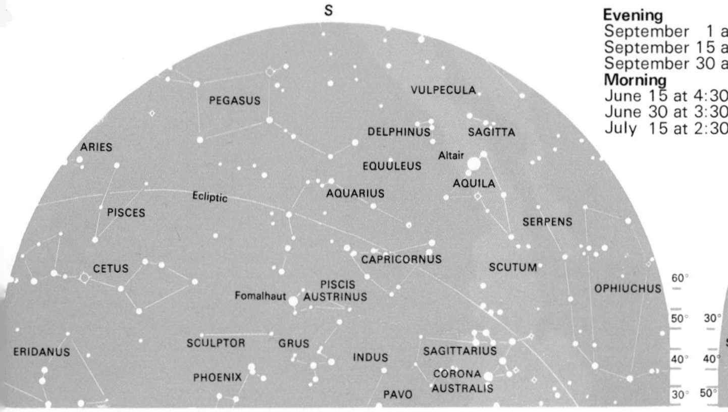

Evening
September 1 at 11:30 pm
September 15 at 10:30 pm
September 30 at 9:30 pm
Morning
June 15 at 4:30 am
June 30 at 3:30 am
July 15 at 2:30 am

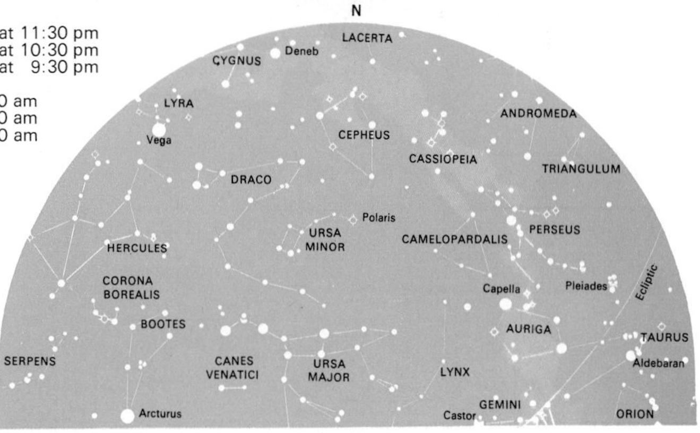

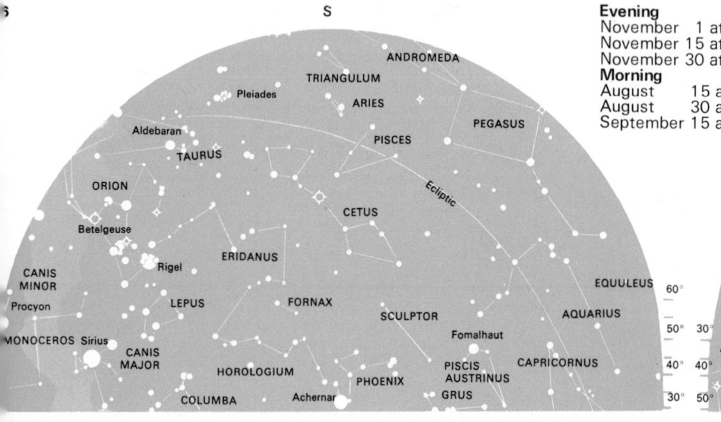

Evening
November 1 at 11:30 pm
November 15 at 10:30 pm
November 30 at 9:30 pm
Morning
August 15 at 4:30 am
August 30 at 3:30 am
September 15 at 2:30 am

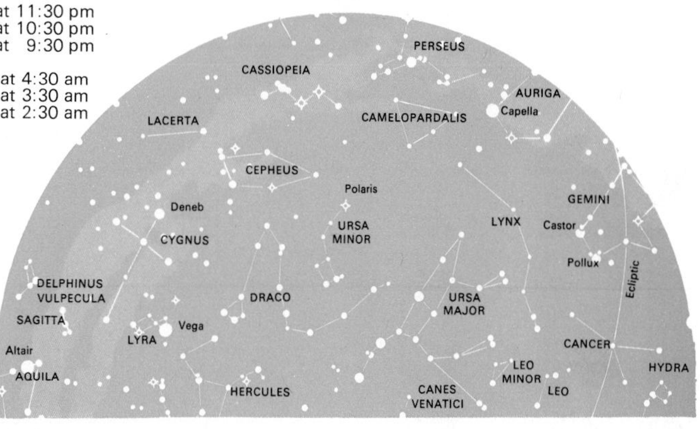

Seasonal star maps: southern

The far southern skies are much superior to those of the Northern Hemisphere for astronomical observation. They contain a number of brilliant groups that are not seen from most of the United States or Europe.

Northern observers lack both the Southern Cross and the two Clouds of Magellan, which are of special importance astronomically. Other objects of the far south include Alpha Centauri, nearest of the bright stars; the globular clusters Omega Centauri and 47 Tucanae; and the remarkable irregular variable, Eta Carinae. The Milky Way is very rich in its southernmost portions and in the Southern Cross there is the so-called "Coal Sack"—the best example of a dark nebula—together with the glorious open cluster that is nicknamed the "Jewel Box."

There is no bright star in the south polar region, however. This area is remarkably barren and is covered by some ill-defined constellations with modern names such as Octans (the Octant), which includes the pole. The nearest star visible with the naked eye is Sigma Octantis, of the fifth magnitude—a poor substitute for the northern Polaris.

The six pairs of charts shown on these two pages are arranged with the left-hand chart looking toward the northern horizon and the right-hand chart looking toward the southern. They are valid for observers living in South Africa, Australia, New Zealand, and most of South America, and calculations can be made by reference to a star's declination.

Stars of chart 1

In the evenings during January, the southern summer, Orion is high up; from the Southern Hemisphere Rigel is higher than Betelgeuse, while the Belt stars point "up" toward Sirius and "down" toward Aldebaran. The whole of the Ship (Argo) is displayed. This huge constellation was regarded by astronomers as an unwieldy section for observation and was divided, the principal sections now recognized being Carina (the Keel), Vela (the Sails) and Puppis (the Stern). Carina contains Canopus, the second brightest star in the sky, which is very high during January evenings. It does not appear as brilliant as Sirius (its apparent magnitude is −0.7, as against −1.47 for Sirius) but in reality it is much more luminous and lies at a distance of hundreds of light-years from Earth.

Crux is rising in the southeast in chart 1. Strictly speaking it is shaped more like a kite than a cross; it is the smallest of the 88 constellations in the sky, but is very compact. Two of its stars (Acrux, or Alpha Crucis, and Beta) are ranked as being of the first magnitude. The third (Gamma Crucis) is ranked just below this, while the fourth star of the kite pattern is much more faint. Even a casual glance shows that of the four main stars, Gamma is orange-red (spectrum M) and the others white. The two Pointers to the Cross are Alpha and Beta Centauri; Alpha is the brightest star in the sky apart from Sirius and Canopus and lies at a distance of only 4.3 light-years. It is a clear binary, separable with a small telescope.

Achernar in Eridanus (the River) is to the southwest. Probably the best way to locate the region of the south celestial pole

CONNECTIONS

See also
130 Star guide: northe sky I
132 Star guide: northe sky II
134 Star guide: southe sky I
136 Star guide: southe sky II
40 Measuring the rest less sky

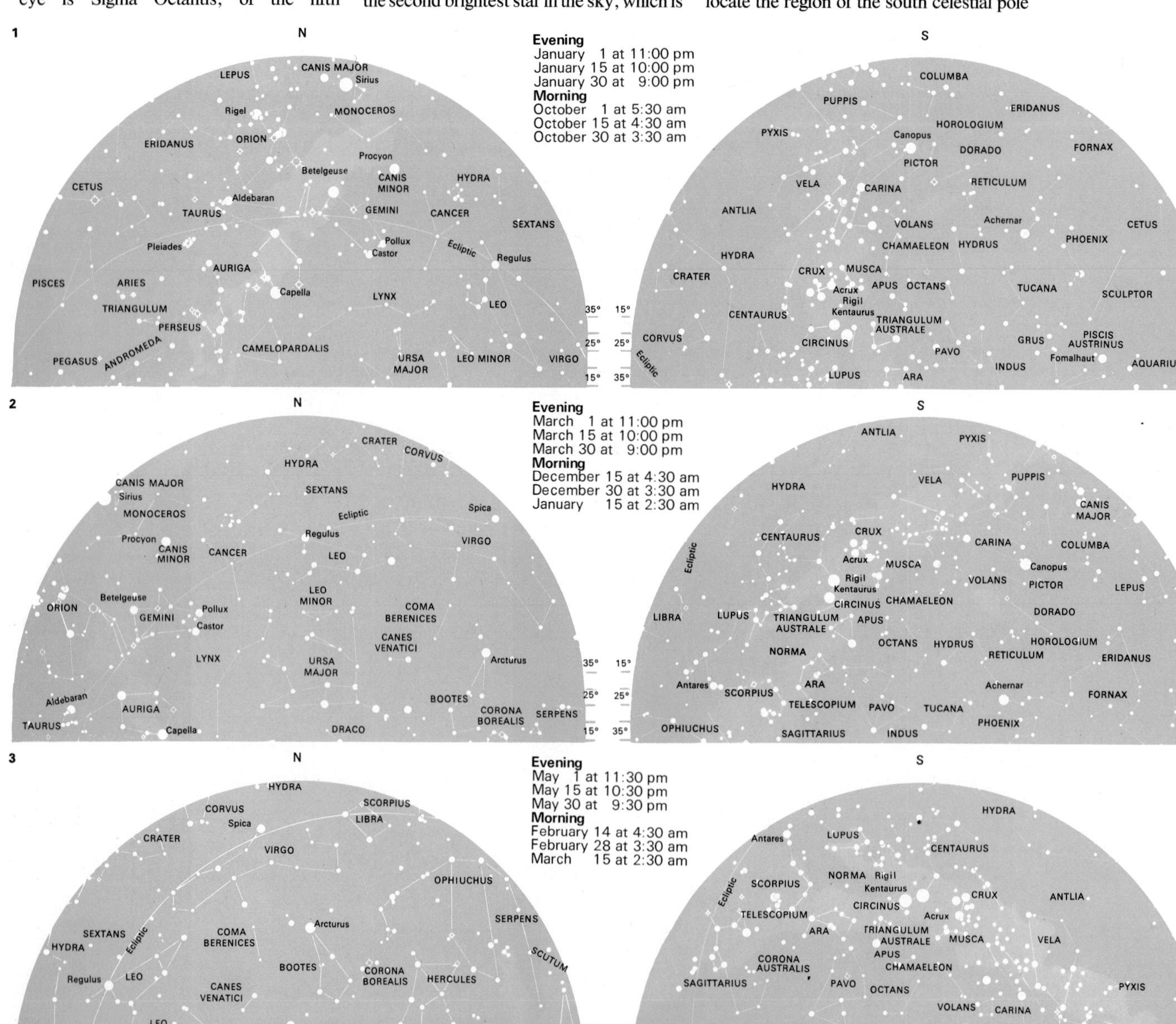

1
N
S
Evening
January 1 at 11:00 pm
January 15 at 10:00 pm
January 30 at 9:00 pm
Morning
October 1 at 5:30 am
October 15 at 4:30 am
October 30 at 3:30 am
LEPUS
CANIS MAJOR
Sirius
Rigel
MONOCEROS
ORION
ERIDANUS
Procyon
Betelgeuse
CANIS MINOR
HYDRA
CETUS
Aldebaran
TAURUS
GEMINI
CANCER
SEXTANS
Pleiades
Pollux
Castor
Ecliptic
Regulus
AURIGA
PISCES
ARIES
Capella
LYNX
LEO
TRIANGULUM
PERSEUS
ANDROMEDA
CAMELOPARDALIS
PEGASUS
URSA MAJOR
LEO MINOR
VIRGO
35°
25°
15°
COLUMBA
PUPPIS
ERIDANUS
HOROLOGIUM
PYXIS
Canopus
DORADO
FORNAX
PICTOR
VELA
CARINA
RETICULUM
ANTLIA
VOLANS
Achernar
CETUS
PHOENIX
CHAMAELEON
HYDRUS
HYDRA
CRATER
CRUX
MUSCA
Acrux
APUS
OCTANS
TUCANA
Rigil Kentaurus
SCULPTOR
CENTAURUS
TRIANGULUM AUSTRALE
CORVUS
CIRCINUS
GRUS
PISCIS AUSTRINUS
PAVO
Ecliptic
INDUS
Fomalhaut
AQUARIUS
LUPUS
ARA
2
Evening
March 1 at 11:00 pm
March 15 at 10:00 pm
March 30 at 9:00 pm
Morning
December 15 at 4:30 am
December 30 at 3:30 am
January 15 at 2:30 am
CRATER
CORVUS
HYDRA
CANIS MAJOR
Sirius
SEXTANS
MONOCEROS
Ecliptic
Spica
Regulus
Procyon
CANIS MINOR
CANCER
LEO
VIRGO
Betelgeuse
LEO MINOR
ORION
GEMINI
Pollux
Castor
COMA BERENICES
CANES VENATICI
LYNX
URSA MAJOR
Arcturus
Aldebaran
AURIGA
BOOTES
CORONA BOREALIS
SERPENS
TAURUS
Capella
DRACO
ANTLIA
PYXIS
VELA
PUPPIS
HYDRA
CANIS MAJOR
CENTAURUS
CRUX
CARINA
COLUMBA
Acrux
MUSCA
Canopus
Rigil Kentaurus
VOLANS
PICTOR
LEPUS
CIRCINUS
CHAMAELEON
LIBRA
LUPUS
TRIANGULUM AUSTRALE
APUS
DORADO
OCTANS
HYDRUS
HOROLOGIUM
NORMA
RETICULUM
ERIDANUS
Antares
ARA
Achernar
SCORPIUS
TELESCOPIUM
PAVO
TUCANA
FORNAX
PHOENIX
OPHIUCHUS
SAGITTARIUS
INDUS
3
Evening
May 1 at 11:30 pm
May 15 at 10:30 pm
May 30 at 9:30 pm
Morning
February 14 at 4:30 am
February 28 at 3:30 am
March 15 at 2:30 am
HYDRA
CORVUS
SCORPIUS
Spica
LIBRA
CRATER
VIRGO
OPHIUCHUS
SERPENS
SEXTANS
Arcturus
HYDRA
COMA BERENICES
SCUTUM
Regulus
LEO
BOOTES
CORONA BOREALIS
HERCULES
CANES VENATICI
LEO MINOR
AQUILA
URSA MAJOR
CANCER
Vega
LYRA
Altair
LYNX
DRACO
SAGITTA
HYDRA
Antares
LUPUS
CENTAURUS
NORMA
Rigil Kentaurus
SCORPIUS
CRUX
ANTLIA
CIRCINUS
TELESCOPIUM
Acrux
ARA
TRIANGULUM AUSTRALE
MUSCA
VELA
APUS
CORONA AUSTRALIS
CHAMAELEON
SAGITTARIUS
PAVO
OCTANS
PYXIS
VOLANS
CARINA
INDUS
PICTOR
PUPPIS
HYDRUS
CAPRICORNUS
TUCANA
Canopus
AQUARIUS
PISCIS AUSTRINUS
GRUS
Achernar
RETICULUM
DORADO
COLUMBA
CANIS MAJOR

is to look midway between Achernar and Crux, but there are no really bright stars to help in identification of the pole itself.

Stars of charts 2 and 3

By March evenings [chart 2] Canopus is descending in the southwest and Crux is rising to its greatest altitude; together with the Pointers they comprise a beautiful group. Not far from it is the magnificent globular cluster Omega Centauri, much the finest of its type in the entire sky. The Milky Way is extremely rich in this whole area and even binoculars will give a good view of the Coal Sack, which conveys the impression of being a virtually starless area. Scorpius (or Scorpio) is coming into prominence in the southeast and Orion is dropping.

March is the best time of year for seeing Ursa Major, although the constellation never rises to observers in the southernmost parts of the latitudes for which the maps have been drawn. (From New Zealand, for instance, the seven main stars of Ursa Major never rise, but from Bolivia they can attain considerable altitude.) May evenings show Alpha and Beta Centauri very high up, with Crux; Canopus is visible in the southwest, but Orion and Sirius have set. Arcturus is prominent in the north, with Spica and Virgo not far from the zenith. Scorpius (the Scorpion) is now dominant.

The Scorpion group is a splendid one, with a long chain of stars that cannot be mistaken. Adjoining the Scorpion is Sagittarius (the Archer), where the Milky Way is at its richest.

Stars of charts 4, 5 and 6

The Scorpion is near the zenith in chart 4 while Crux and Centaurus remain prominent in the southern aspect of the sky. The brilliant northern stars Vega, Altair, Deneb, and Arcturus are all visible, but Canopus is at its lowest.

Pegasus is high in the north in chart 5; Vega, Altair, and Deneb can still be seen, and Fomalhaut is almost overhead. The Scorpion is sinking in the southwest and Crux is almost out of view.

Orion has returned in chart 6 and with it Sirius, Canopus, and other adjacent stars.

KEY

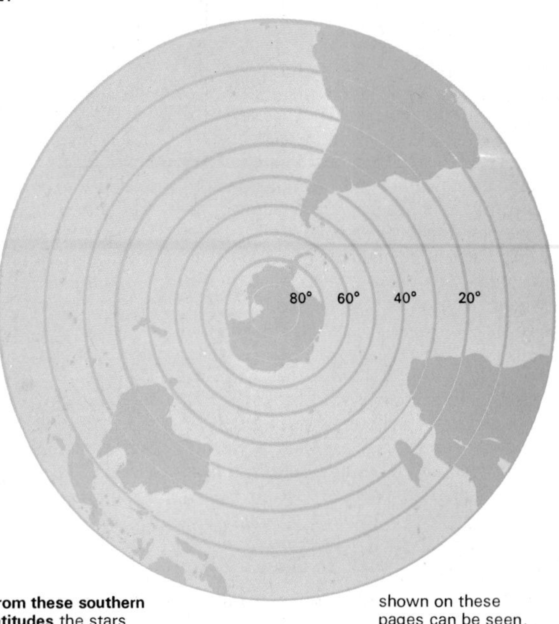
80°
60°
40°
20°

From these southern latitudes the stars shown on these pages can be seen.

4

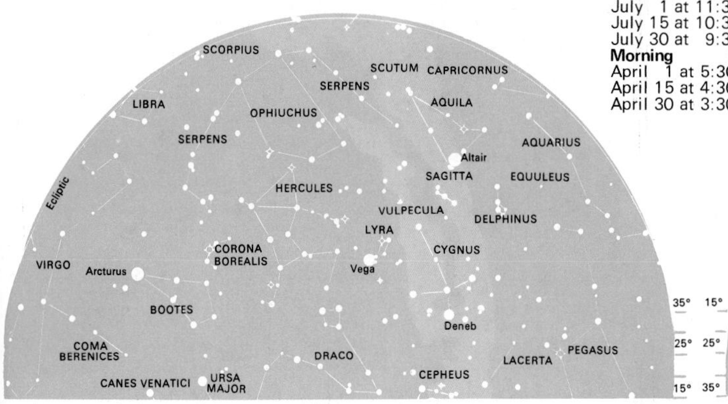

Evening
July 1 at 11:30 pm
July 15 at 10:30 pm
July 30 at 9:30 pm
Morning
April 1 at 5:30 am
April 15 at 4:30 am
April 30 at 3:30 am

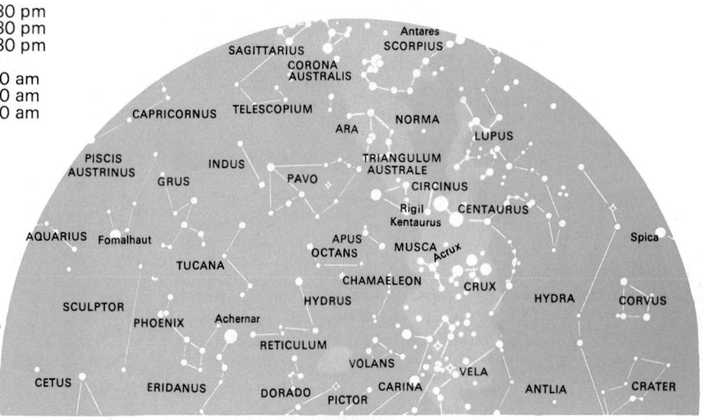

5

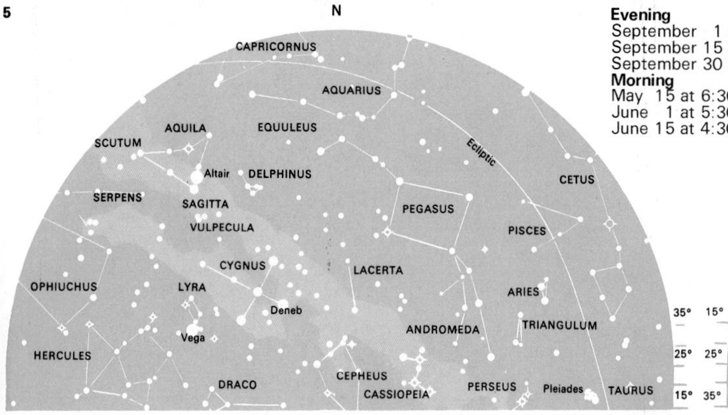

Evening
September 1 at 11:30 pm
September 15 at 10:30 pm
September 30 at 9:30 pm
Morning
May 15 at 6:30 am
June 1 at 5:30 am
June 15 at 4:30 am

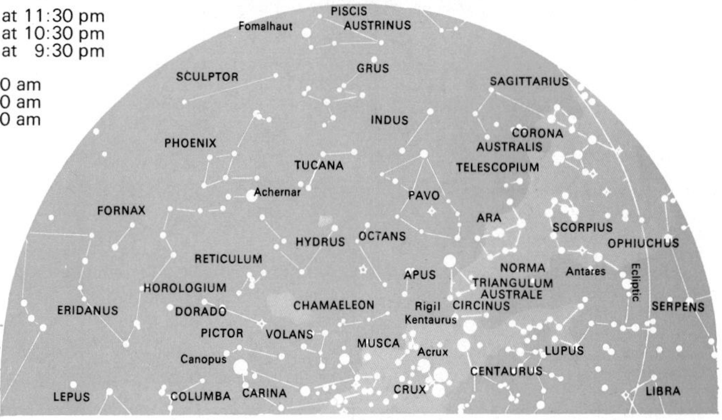

6

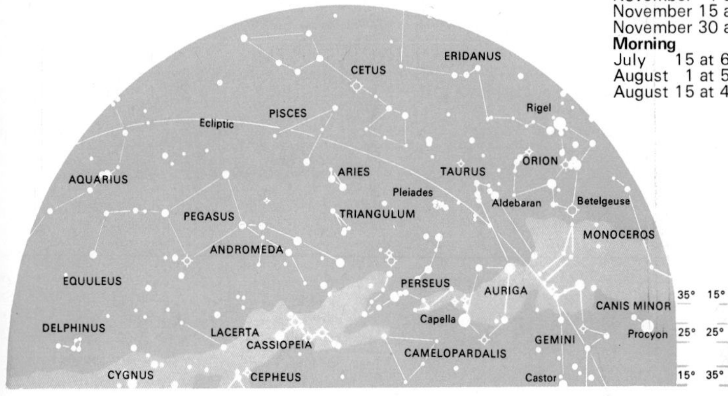

Evening
November 1 at 11:30 pm
November 15 at 10:30 pm
November 30 at 9:30 pm
Morning
July 15 at 6:30 am
August 1 at 5:30 am
August 15 at 4:30 am

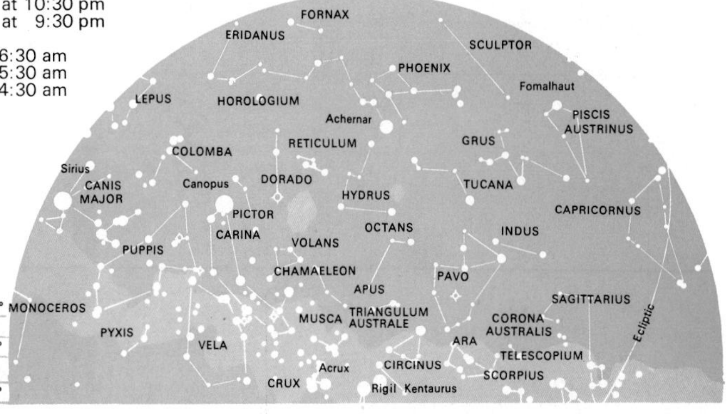

A history of space achievements

The idea of reaching other worlds is far from new [Key]. As long ago as the second century AD a Greek satirist, Lucian of Samosata, wrote a story about a journey to the Moon, although he did not intend it to be taken seriously. As he commented, his *True History* was made up of nothing but lies from beginning to end. Another famous space-travel story, by the German astronomer Johannes Kepler (1571–1630), was published posthumously in 1634. This time the "astronaut" was taken to the Moon by an obliging demon.

Early space rockets

It is only in modern times that space research has become a practical possibility. In the Earth's atmosphere winged aircraft can use conventional engines, such as gas turbines, which need a supply of air to burn their fuel. The atmosphere does not extend upward for very far on a cosmic scale; therefore, in space a vehicle needs an engine that does not "use" air, that is, a rocket motor. In a rocket, a stream of gas emitted from the exhaust of the vehicle provides the propulsive power needed. It has been said that a rocket "kicks against itself" and the presence of a resisting atmosphere is actually a hindrance.

The great theoretical pioneer of astronautics was a Russian, K. E. Tsiolkovsky [1], whose first papers on the subject appeared in 1903, although at the time they aroused little comment. Tsiolkovsky realized that solid fuels, such as gunpowder, are inadequate for space flight and he proposed the use of a liquid-propellant rocket motor. The first rocket to have an engine of this type was fired by R. H. Goddard (1882–1945) [2], in the United States in 1926. Although it achieved a maximum speed of only 60mph (97kph) in its brief flight, it proved the principle to be valid. Subsequently, a German team, including Wernher von Braun (1912–), developed liquid-propellant rockets with some success. The team was then taken over by the Nazi government for military purposes and transferred to the island of Peenemünde in the Baltic, where the V2 weapon was developed in time to be used in the last stages of World War II. The V2 was the direct ancestor of the space probes of today, as after the end of the war most of the German researchers went to the United States, where progress continued steadily. In 1949 a compound rocket [3] reached an altitude of 244 miles (393km).

From Earth satellites to Moon landing

By the early 1950s, scientific rockets were proving useful in studying the upper atmosphere and what may be called "near space," but it was realized that an artificial satellite would achieve the same purpose much more efficiently. A scientific vehicle set in a stable orbit around the Earth will behave in the same way as a natural astronomical body, provided it is clear of the resisting atmosphere. The first artificial satellite [4] was launched by the USSR on October 4, 1957, marking the real start of the Space Age. The vehicle, Sputnik 1, was only about the size of a football and carried little apart from a radio transmitter, but it paved the way for all future research. Other Soviet satellites followed and in 1958 the

CONNECTIONS

See also
- **54** Moon missions
- **62** The planet Mercury
- **64** The planet Venus
- **70** Mars missions
- **82** Jupiter panorama
- **144** Stations in space
- **1722** Space vehicles
- **1724** Man in space
- **1598** Aluminum and its us

1 1903: Konstantin Tsiolkovsky (1857–1935) founded astronautics when he published a series of papers in Russia that laid down the fundamental principles with remarkable foresight.

limit of atmosphere

2 1926: Robert H. Goddard launched the first liquid propellant rocket in the United States. Although his rocket was small, his experimental work was of immense significance.

3 1949: The first step rocket was launched from White Sands, N.M. It consisted of a V2 carrying a WAC Corporal rocket and reached an altitude of 244 miles (393km), a record height.

4 1957: Sputnik 1, the first artificial satellite, was launched by Russia.

5 1959: Luna 1 was the first successful lunar probe, by-passing the moon at 3,728 miles (6,000km)

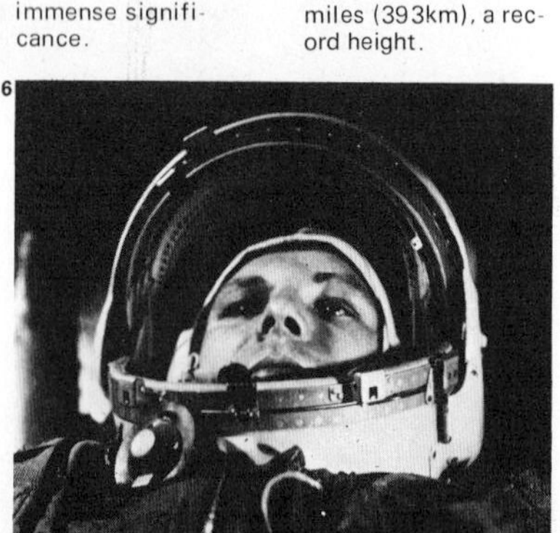

6 1961: Yuri Gagarin of the USSR became the first man in space. Launched on April 12, his craft, Vostok 1, made a complete circuit of the Earth at a height ranging from 112 miles (180km) to 187 miles (301km). His flight of 1 hr 29 min showed that man could enter space and return safely to a predetermined location. Gagarin made only one space flight. With tragic irony, he was killed in 1968 in an airplane crash.

7 1961: Alan Shepard was the first American space traveler, making a 15-minute suborbital "hop" on May 5. A decade later, he commanded the Apollo 14 Moon flight.

8 1962: Telstar, the first active communications satellite, provided a transatlantic television relay. Only 34.5in (88cm) in diameter, it ceased functioning in 1963 but remained in orbit.

9 1965: Two US space vehicles launched on December 4 and 15, Gemini 7 and 6, were brought to within 12in (30cm) of each other in a rehearsal of the docking procedure essential to the success of the Apollo Moon landing.

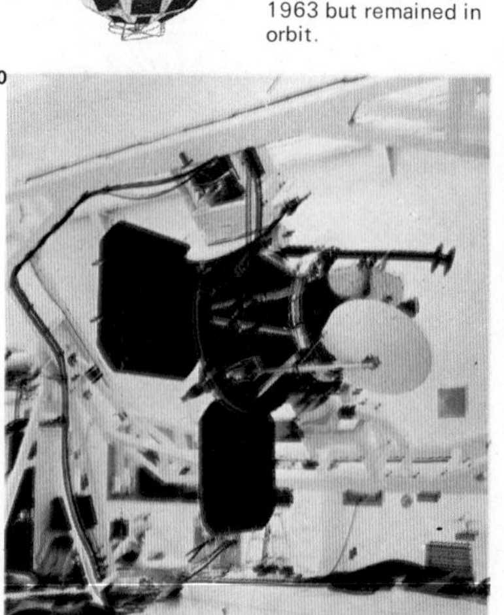

10 1966–67: Orbiters 1 to 5 were put into closed orbits around the Moon. All these space vehicles were operated successfully; they sent back thousands of photographs covering the lunar surface.

11 1968: US astronauts Frank Borman, James Lovell, and William Anders made the first manned flight around the Moon in Apollo 8 from December 21 to 27. This was an essential preliminary to the actual Moon landing in 1969. Having reached the vicinity of the Moon, Apollo 8 was put into a closed path and completed 10 circuits before returning to Earth transfer orbit.

United States launched its first satellite, Explorer 1. It provided the first information about the radiation zones that surround the Earth, now known as the Van Allen belts after James Van Allen, who formulated the present concept.

In January 1959 Luna 1 [5] by-passed the Moon and later in the year another Soviet satellite circled the Moon, sending back photographs of its far side. In 1961 came the first manned satellite, Vostok 1, in which Yuri Gagarin (1934–68) [6] made a full circuit of the Earth. By this time the whole concept of space research was being taken very seriously, although less than a decade earlier it had been widely ridiculed.

During the early 1960s earth satellites were developed that were able to send back detailed photographs of the Earth, as well as providing miscellaneous information. They were also used for communication purposes. In 1962 Telstar [8], the first television relay satellite, was launched. Manned vehicles became capable of sending up two or three men instead of only one and space-docking [9] maneuvers were carried out. Meanwhile, the US Apollo program to land a man on the Moon was being developed. It culminated with the Apollo 11 flight in July 1969, when Neil Armstrong (1930–) and Edwin Aldrin (1930–) made the first Moon walk [12].

Exploring the Solar System

The first successful planetary probe was Mariner 2, which by-passed Venus in 1962 and sent back the first reliable information about that peculiar world. Mars was contacted in 1965 by Mariner 4 and in 1971 Mariner 9 [14] entered a closed orbit around Mars. In 1973 the first Jupiter probe, Pioneer 10 [15], reached its target, and in 1974 the US Mariner 10 by-passed both Venus and Mercury. By 1975 Pioneer 11 was on its way to Saturn. In the same year the Soviet Veneras 9 and 10 sent back photographs from the surface of Venus that showed surface details to be markedly different from those anticipated. In 1976 the US Vikings 1 and 2 [18] landed on Mars in a program of direct scientific observation of the planet.

KEY

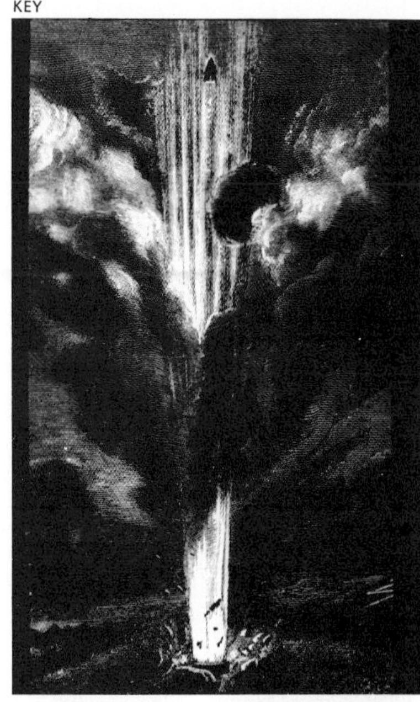

In his science-fiction story *From The Earth To The Moon* (1865), the French novelist Jules Verne (1828–1905) suggested that voyagers could be sent to the Moon in a projectile fired from a huge cannon he called "Columbiad." The principle is not practical and in his story Verne had to invent a second natural satellite to swing the projectile back to its starting point, Earth. But Verne's use of scientific detail to give an air of realism to fanciful adventures prompted others, including H. G. Wells (1866–1946), to write of space travel. Their fantasies were only a few generations away from the actuality of the first Moon landing.

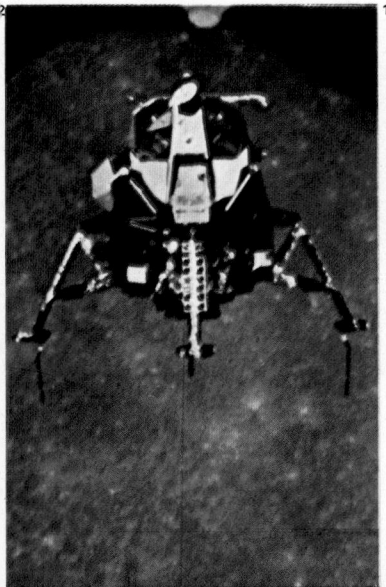

12

13

12 1969: Neil Armstrong and Edwin Aldrin made the first lunar landing during the Apollo 11 mission, with Michael Collins piloting the command module. They landed in Mare Tranquillitatis.

13 1970: Lunokhod 1, a Soviet "crawler," moved around the lunar surface sending back valuable information. Carried by Luna 16, launched in September, it operated until October 1971.

14

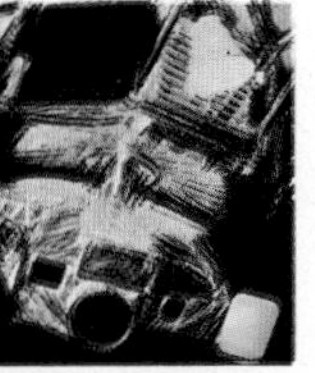

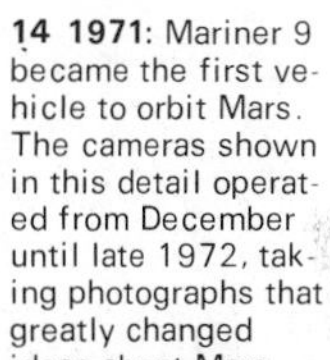

14 1971: Mariner 9 became the first vehicle to orbit Mars. The cameras shown in this detail operated from December until late 1972, taking photographs that greatly changed ideas about Mars.

15

15 1972: Pioneer 10, the first Jupiter probe, by-passed the planet in December 1973 at a distance of about 82,000 miles (131,400km), sending back information and pictures of the planet.

16

16 1973: Skylab, the first American space station, was manned by three successive crews, the last spending 84 days in space. Owen Garriott of the second crew is seen here at the telescope console.

17

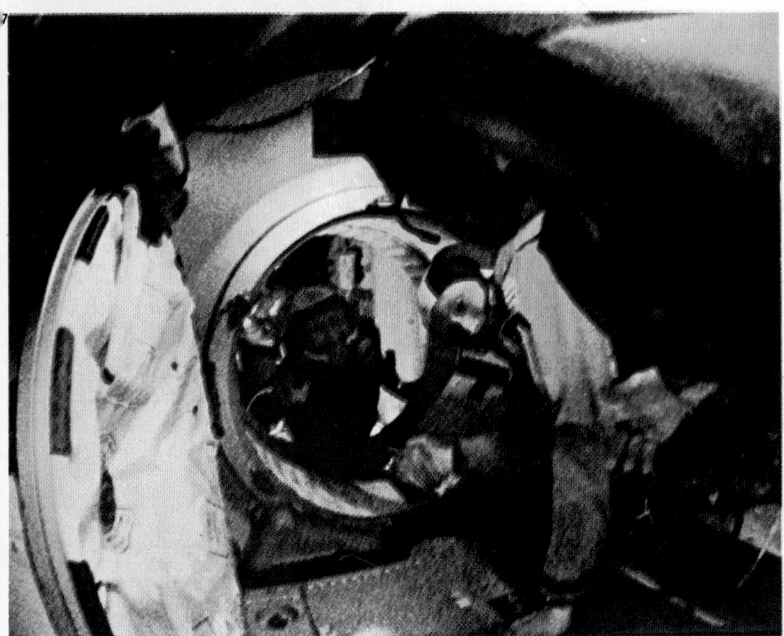

18

17 1975: Apollo-Soyuz, the first joint US–USSR space project, enabled the crews of the Soyuz Soviet craft and a modified Apollo capsule to enter each other's vehicles after docking in space. The US commander was Gen. Thomas Stafford, with Vance Brand and Donald Slayton. The USSR craft was commanded by Alexei Leonov. It was a valuable exercise in joint scientific research.

18 1976: Vikings 1 and 2, US probes (this is a drawing), softlanded on Mars carrying instruments for direct observation. Each photographed the rock-strewn surface and tested soil samples.

Stations in space

The idea of a space station or artificial manned satellite permanently circling the Earth outside its atmosphere was discussed by a Russian scientist Konstantin E. Tsiolkovsky (1857–1935) around the turn of the century, although at that time the idea was regarded as little more than a fantasy. He looked on the space station both as a stepping-stone refueling base for spaceships visiting other planets and as a laboratory in which scientists could carry out experiments that would be impossible on Earth. He even proposed growing plants in space stations to provide their crews with food and oxygen.

The problem of gravity

The effect that weightlessness would have on space travelers was unknown. In orbit—where gravitational attraction is opposed by equal and opposite inertial forces—a body experiences no mechanical stress and astronauts and any loose objects float weightless. The same is true of an unpowered spaceship moving in frictionless space toward or away from the Earth.

It was widely believed that even short periods of weightlessness (or zero gravity) would have ill effects on space travelers and thoughts turned to creating artificial gravity. One of Tsiolkovsky's first designs showed a huge cylindrical space station that spun on its central axis. The crew had their feet firmly planted on the inside walls, with their heads pointed at the spin axis, by action of centrifugal force. Vegetation in a "cosmic garden" grew inward toward the center of the station.

As late as 1952 Wernher von Braun (1912–), who worked on the V-2 at Peenemünde and who was mainly responsible for the rockets that launched America's first artificial satellite and the Apollo mooncraft, proposed a space station that had the form of a huge rotating wheel [2]. The crew quarters were in the rim of the wheel, docking ports for visiting spacecraft were in the central hub and tubular "spokes" allowed people to move from one part of the space station to the other.

Yuri Gagarin's flight in Vostok 1 in 1961 showed that weightlessness is not uncomfortable and since then men have remained in orbit under conditions of zero gravity for nearly three months. It is still uncertain whether, after spending much longer periods in space, the human body can adjust to normal gravity conditions without ill effects and we may yet see attempts to create artificial gravity in large vehicles intended for extended periods in space.

Present and future space stations

True orbital stations were first launched during the early 1970s after experience had been gained with the Soviet Soyuz and American Apollo spacecraft that carried a variety of scientific instruments.

Although there was considerable trouble with the first of the 21-ton Salyut stations, the Soviet Union did fly a number of highly successful missions. The United States had problems, too. Skylab was damaged when it was launched and had to be repaired in orbit before space teams could begin their experiments. It was manned by three successive crews who spent 28, 59, and 84 days in space [Key, 1].

CONNECTIONS

See also
142 A history of space achievements
98 Solar eclipses
1724 Man in space

1

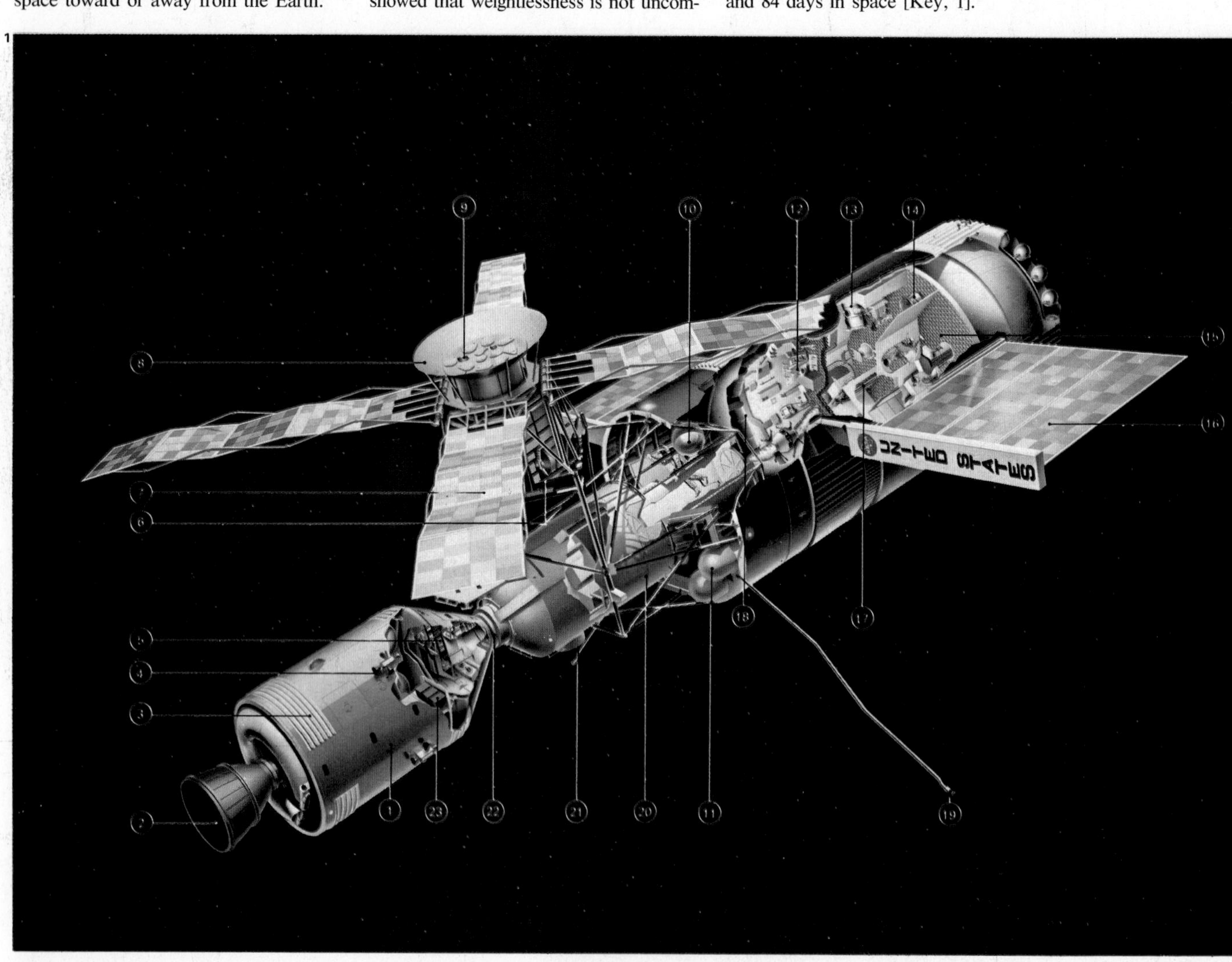
9
10
12
13
14
15
8
16
7
6
5
4
3
2
1
23
22
21
20
11
19
18
17

1 Skylab, the first American space station, was launched on May 14, 1973 and was manned by three successive crews for a total of 171 days. Its weight was about 82 tons and it measured 82 ft (25 m) in length and 22 ft (6.7 m) across the workshop section. While in orbit, the instruments and systems were powered by solar cells mounted on the wing panels. The various components are indicated by the following key: [1] modified Apollo spacecraft (command module plus service module) used to take crews to the space station; [2] service propulsion system engine, with a thrust of 20,000 lb (9,100 kg); [3] radiators; [4] attitude control jets used in docking, each nozzle with a thrust of 100 lb (45 kg); [5] crew station in command module; [6] Apollo telescope mount; [7] solar cells, converting sunlight to electricity to power the Apollo telescope mount; [8] sun shield (this gave trouble initially but was later rectified); [9] telescope apertures; [10] oxygen tank and [11] nitrogen tank for the two-gas atmosphere inside Skylab; [12] foot-controlled maneuvering unit; [13] lower body negative pressure device; [14] gravity substitute workbench; [15] food provisions; [16] the solar cells; [17] sleep restraints; [18] water containers; [19] antenna; [20] multiple docking adapter; [21] alternative docking port; [22] atmosphere interchange duct; and [23] descent battery packs.

The first ferry craft to bring crew and cargo to space stations were versions of existing spacecraft launched by expendable rockets. To reduce the cost of space operations the United States has developed the reusable "space shuttle," which can take off vertically like a rocket, launch satellites or visit a space station, and fly back to Earth like an aircraft [3]. The winged orbiter is designed to be reused at least 100 times. When not used for other purposes, the shuttle can become a miniature space station in its own right. Within its cargo bay (60 × 15 ft or 18.3 × 4.6m) will fit a space laboratory in which four scientists can work without spacesuits for up to 30 days as the spaceplane swings around the Earth. After a mission the laboratory can be exchanged for another cargo ready for another flight.

The uses of orbiting stations

Orbiting stations are able to carry out work that cannot be done efficiently by unmanned satellites. The first space stations were used for research in biology, chemistry, and physics; for observations of the Earth's natural resources; and for studies of the Sun and other stars.

Skylab and the Apollo spacecraft that took part in the "space handshake" with Soyuz in 1975 both carried small electric furnaces to melt various metal samples under weightless conditions. In the future it may be possible to make ultra-lightweight foamed steels with many of the properties of solid steel, to combine dissimilar materials like steel and glass, and to grow crystals of great purity for the electronics industry. The gravity-free environment should also be ideal for isolating biological materials for the treatment of certain diseases and to purify vaccines.

Future space stations will be assembled from modules (units) ferried into orbit by the shuttle. Eventually, it may be possible to build orbiting power stations that have immense solar-cell collectors generating electricity from sunlight. The energy would be beamed to Earth by microwave antennas for use in factories and homes, and would provide a limitless supply of power to replace Earth's diminishing energy sources.

KEY

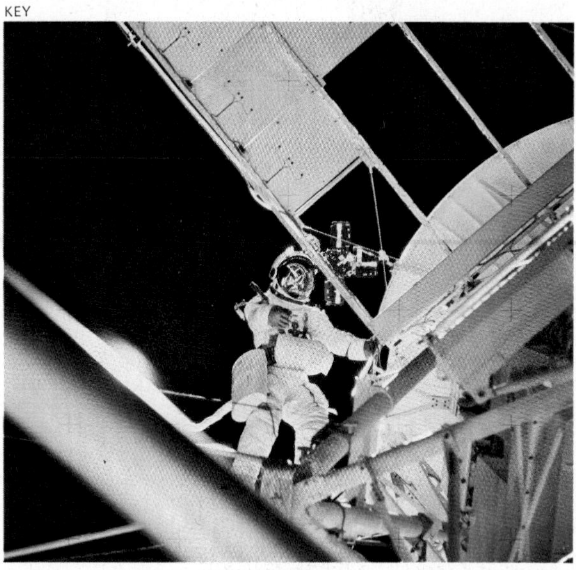

Owen K. Garriott scientist-astronaut on the Skylab 3 mission, performs extravehicular activity (EVA). He has just deployed one of the many experiments on board the orbiting station.

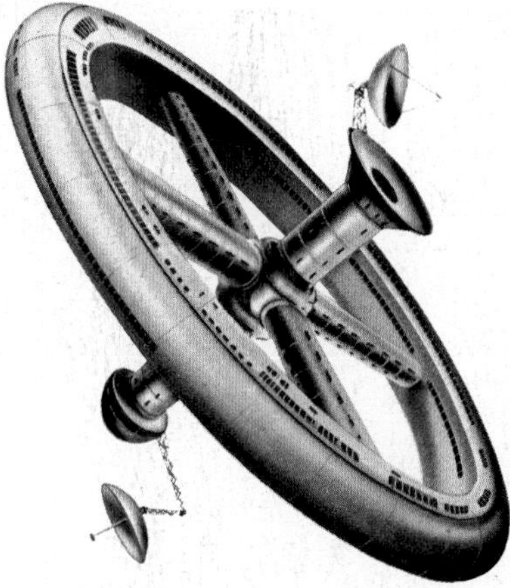

2 Early space-station design took the form of a wheel with the power supplies in the hub and the crew quarters arranged around the rim. This design was originally worked out to provide "substitute gravity" by rotation of the wheel. It was believed that zero gravity might be harmful to astronauts even over short periods, but after Yuri Gagarin's flight and subsequent experiences with Skylab and the Soviet Salyut stations this was disproved.

1
2
3
4
5
6

3 The NASA Space Shuttle has a winged Orbiter that lifts off [1] with a large external tank containing the ascent propellants and two solid rocket boosters that separate [2] when the craft has climbed 28 miles (45km). The tank is discarded [3] just before the Orbiter goes into orbit. Typical payloads are a space laboratory, space probes for release in orbit [4], or modules for assembly into a space station. The Orbiter uses its maneuvering engines as retrorockets to reenter the atmosphere [5], where it endures high temperatures. It lands back at base [6] like an aircraft.

4 Future orbiting space stations will be different from the neat wheel design of pioneer days. A station, assembled in space, is designed to move around the Earth at a height of about 300 miles (500 km) and will accommodate a crew of up to 100 members. This picture shows a space shuttle that has just delivered a propellant module for a spaceship bound for Mars. The nearer shuttle has just fired its retrorockets to start its journey back to Earth. Below, the surface of the Earth itself is largely covered with cloud. Various service vehicles are shown in the black sky around the space station.

Colonizing the Moon

The Apollo missions to the Moon were essentially reconnaissances [Key]. All that Apollo could hope to do was to take three men to the neighborhood of the Moon, land two of them on the surface for a brief period and then bring all members of the crew home safely. There was no provision for rescue in the event of a failure of the lunar module during the surface expedition and the available time was very limited. Yet Apollo was an essential part of the main program of lunar colonization and it showed that there is no reason why research bases could not be set up on the Moon using present technology.

Problems encountered on the Moon

There is no possibility of turning the Moon into a kind of second Earth. The main problem is the lack of atmosphere. The Moon is an airless world and there is not the slightest chance of providing it with a breathable atmosphere; the low escape velocity makes it incapable of retaining a dense atmosphere similar to that of the Earth. Lack of atmosphere means a total lack of water and it now seems that—contrary to earlier expectation—it will not be possible to extract water from the lunar rocks for the simple reason that there is none to extract. Neither is there any hope of finding underground supplies of ice. The colonists of the future will have to take everything with them or will have to receive a continuous stream of supplies from Earth. It will be a long time before a lunar station can hope to become self-supporting.

The development of lunar bases

By about 1990 nuclear or other space propulsion systems will have been developed with capabilities far beyond the chemically-propelled vehicles of Apollo. By then, too, the space-station projects should be well under way and it will be practicable to consider going back to the Moon. Possibly the first step will be to send supplies to the surface, setting them down at a prearranged location to await the arrival of the explorers, so that when the astronauts land they will find supplies ready for use. The lunar modules themselves may be used as the first bases, but this pioneer phase would not last long and more elaborate designs would be developed quite quickly. One pattern, dating from the 1930s, is that of a series of domes, each kept inflated by the pressure of air inside it and equipped with a system of airlocks for the exit and entry of the crew members. This kind of design might be developed. Fortunately, it is now known that there is little danger from meteoritic bombardment, so that the relative fragility of the domes should not be a problem. Underground shelters would be needed only for shielding during periods of intense radiation from solar flares.

Even when space shuttles have been perfected, the expense of traveling between the Earth and the Moon will still be considerable and every possible method will have to be used to cut supply journeys to a minimum. Everything (including human waste products) will have to be "recycled," particularly the atmosphere. The colonists will spend long periods on the Moon and the conditions must be made as comfortable as possible. Inside the base it will be essential

CONNECTIONS

See also
52 The Moon

1 Science-fiction writers have always been attracted by the Moon. Jules Verne (1828–1905) described a circumlunar voyage more than 100 years ago and H. G. Wells (1866–1946) a fantastic world peopled by insectlike beings. In 1902 came the first famous Moon-voyage film, produced by George Méliès (1861–1938). This frame from the film shows the arrival of the rocket (to the distress of the Moon), after which the space travelers went for a walk on the surface, not forgetting to put up their umbrellas to shield themselves from the strong rays of sunlight.

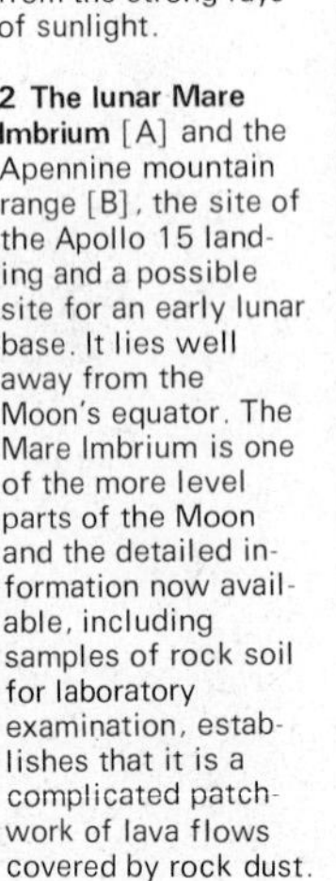

2 The lunar Mare Imbrium [A] and the Apennine mountain range [B], the site of the Apollo 15 landing and a possible site for an early lunar base. It lies well away from the Moon's equator. The Mare Imbrium is one of the more level parts of the Moon and the detailed information now available, including samples of rock soil for laboratory examination, establishes that it is a complicated patchwork of lava flows covered by rock dust.

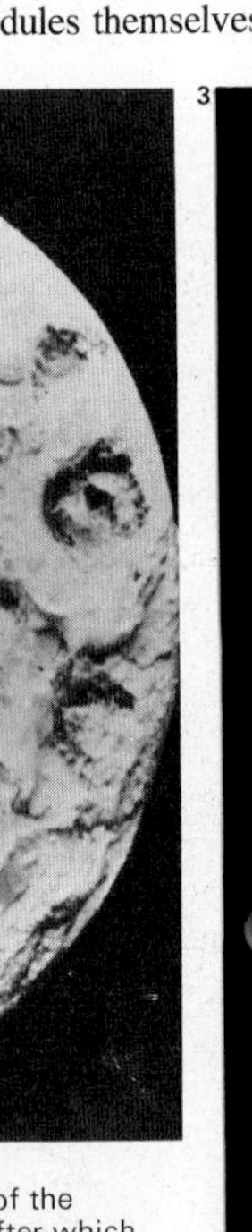

3 The first lunar base is unlikely to be at all like the final elaborate stations. Here is shown a scene after a pioneer expedition has established itself. In the foreground is the basic space-station module which will serve as the center of the future station. It can accommodate a crew of up to a dozen members and it can also provide all that is needed for a prolonged stay. In an emergency the expedition can be halted and the crew returned to Earth by means of ferry vehicles. Also shown is a lunar rover, similar to the vehicles used by the last three Apollo expeditions, which proved to be so successful; a cargo-landing craft with a separate cargo module; and a lunar drill on the right.

for the colonist to be able to take off his or her spacesuit and behave as naturally as is possible under conditions where gravity is only 7 percent of the Earth's. There is also the question of recreation, which will be important in view of the relatively long tours of duty that are to be expected. Books, films, and musical recordings present no problems; but no doubt various new athletic activities suited to conditions of low gravity will be developed to ensure the continued physical fitness of the inhabitants of the lunar base.

Essential supplies of food

To bring all food supplies from the Earth will be impractical and efforts will be made to grow edible plants on the Moon. This cannot be done in the open, but inside the domes the principle of hydroponic farming, whereby plants can be grown without soil, may be used. The plants are suspended in netting inside a tank and are fed liquid nutrients circulated beneath them. The principle has been tested and found to be practical and there seems no reason why it should not work on the Moon even in the relatively low-gravity environment.

The early lunar bases may be staffed entirely by scientists. There may be physicists, anxious to take advantage of the low gravity, the limitless hard vacuum, and the chance to study all the radiations coming in from space; astronomers, thankful to escape from the restrictions imposed by the screening layers in the atmosphere of the Earth; chemists, biologists, medical men—in fact, scientists of all disciplines. The lunar base should add appreciably to the sum total of man's knowledge of the universe.

As the colony becomes more and more self-supporting, it may be able to take in nonscientists as well, at least for brief visits. The idea of "vacations on the Moon" may not be too fantastic a hundred years from now. By then there may be children born on the Moon who regard it and not the Earth as their home world. Before the end of the twenty-first century the Moon may support not one base, but many used for a variety of purposes.

KEY

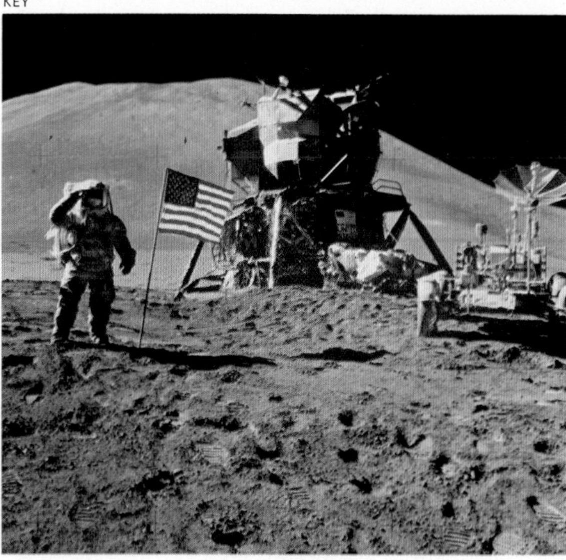

Astronaut James Irwin of the Apollo 15 mission is standing in the Hadley-Apennines region—possible site for the first lunar base. The peak of Hadley Delta is seen beyond.

4

4 A permanent lunar base will probably be set up in the far north of the Moon in order to avoid the intense daytime heat of lower latitudes. (The night temperature is virtually the same at all points on the surface.) The relatively low altitude of the Earth in the sky indicates the high altitude of the site. At the limb of the Earth-turned hemisphere, an observer on the Moon would see the Earth at the horizon (with slight variations due to the irregular orbit of the Moon), while from the Moon's far side the Earth would never rise at all. In this illustration the Earth is shown as full, with its surface details masked by cloud. It has just passed through the Milky Way into the constellation of Gemini, the Twins. The red star to the right is the semi-regular variable, Eta Geminorum. The Moon base is made up of several domes, each with its separate system of airlocks. It will be essential to conserve atmosphere to the greatest possible extent and individual airlocks are necessary to guard against the sudden failure of pressure in one of the domes. Radio antennas and various kinds of instruments are also shown. The illumination is purely by earthlight (because the Earth is full and the Sun is below the horizon). To a terrestrial observer, the Moon is new when in this position.

The Martian base

In the early part of the twentieth century it was generally supposed that Mars might be able to support terrestrial life, and that the planet might even be inhabited. In 1877 the Italian astronomer Giovanni Schiaparelli (1835–1910) had set the world talking about intelligent beings on Mars who had constructed a vast network of canals to irrigate their dying planet. "All the vast extent of the Continent," he wrote, "is furrowed upon every side by a network of numerous lines of a more less pronounced color . . . Some of the shorter ones do not attain 300 miles; others extend for many thousands." It did not seem to matter that, at the distance of Mars, such features would have to be tens of miles across to be seen at all.

Life on Mars

The myths were shattered when the first space probes reached Mars in the 1960s and 1970s. Instead of great Saharalike deserts and "canals," the orbiting cameras swept across scenes of natural splendor—thousands of Moonlike craters, huge volcanoes and immense canyons, and features that appear like the dried-out beds of ancient rivers. Whatever water existed on Mars in the past is very scarce today; some may be locked up beneath the surface in the form of ice and permafrost. The glistening white polar caps, however, do appear to be composed mainly of water ice. The climate is cold and extremely hostile to terrestrial life and the thin, mainly carbon dioxide atmosphere (less than one percent the density of Earth's) does not allow water to exist in a free state.

The space probes solved another mystery. The so-called "dark areas" on Mars, which some astronomers had linked with the growth and decay of vegetation, seemed to be caused by wind storms, which redistributed light-colored dust over a darker surface. In 1975 two Viking spacecraft, each carrying an automatic laboratory, were sent to analyze the atmosphere and to see if the soil contained evidence of life.

Exploration: problems and plans

The main problems in sending people to Mars are time and distance. Whereas astronauts can land on the Moon and return in less than two weeks, a Mars ship must leave the Earth-Moon system and embark on an immense journey that takes it around the Sun. Before such a project can even begin it is necessary to build a space station in Earth-orbit that can be used as an assembly and refueling depot. Such a station will take up to two years to build.

Opportunities to launch to Mars occur at intervals of about 25 to 26 months when Mars is at opposition. One US plan, shelved for the time being because of the enormous cost, involved a possible expedition this century. Two atomic-powered ships each 270 feet (82.3m) long were each to carry six explorers. Work had already started on Nerva rocket engines that used nuclear heat to expand liquid hydrogen fuel into a powerful propelling jet. The journey was to take the explorers around the Sun to a point in space where Mars would be nine months after leaving. For most of the flight the two ships would be docked together nose-to-nose, separating before they arrived. They were to orbit Mars for 80 days while three

CONNECTIONS

See also
68 The planet Mars
76 The moons of Mars

1 **The engineering replica** (simulator) of the Viking lander at the Jet Propulsion Laboratory (JPL) at Pasadena, California, was used by scientists to solve problems with the actual spacecraft on Mars. They were thus able, for example, to free a locking pin on the Viking 1 soil scoop that had failed to eject. JPL commanded the scoop arm to shake out the pin after working out a series of movements with the simulator. The "repair" was effected across more than 212 million miles (340 million km) of space. The sampler scoop, cameras (upper left and center), and meteorology beam (upper right) can be seen clearly.

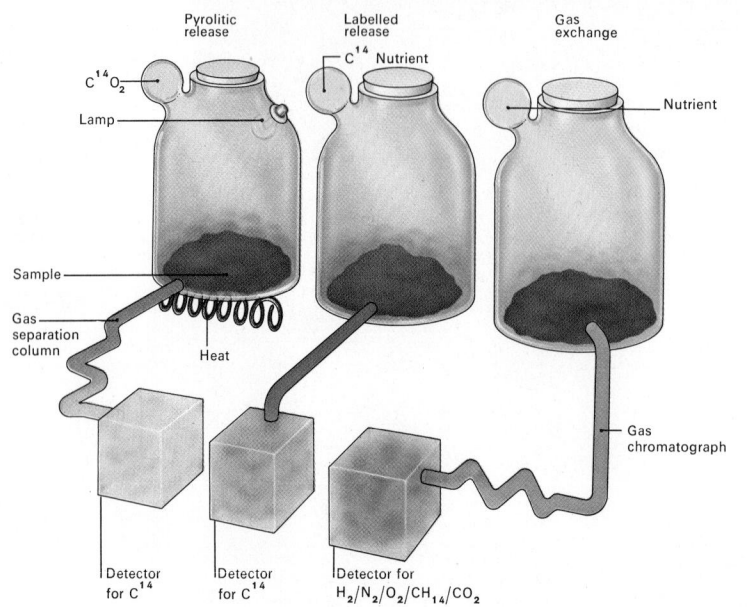

2

Pyrolitic release
Labelled release
Gas exchange
$C^{14}O_2$
C^{14} Nutrient
Nutrient
Lamp
Sample
Gas separation column
Heat
Gas chromatograph
Detector for C^{14}
Detector for C^{14}
Detector for $H_2/N_2/O_2/CH_{14}/CO_2$

2 The search for life was an important task for Viking. Each lander has a laboratory to which soil samples were delivered by a mechanical scoop in three experiments: Pyrolytic Release was designed to detect any microorganisms that live by photosynthesis, taking CO_2 and using it to make organic matter in artificial sunlight (lamp). Labelled Release looked for evidence that organisms in the soil were maintaining and reproducing themselves. Gas Exchange looked for any exchange of gases between microbes in the soil and atmosphere of the chamber.

3

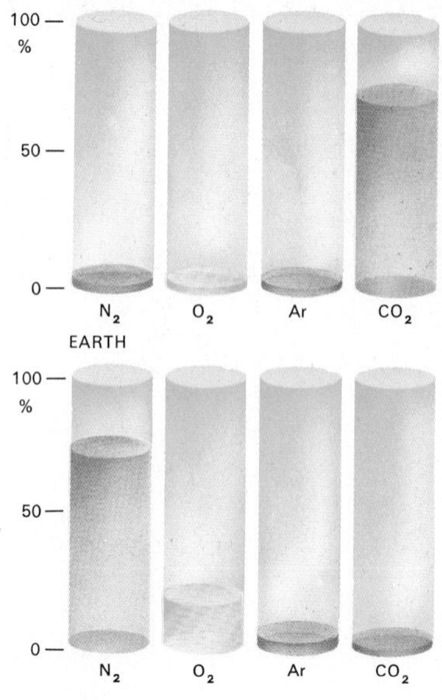
MARS
100
%
50
0
N2
O2
Ar
CO2
EARTH
100
%
50
0
N2
O2
Ar
CO2

3 The main constituents of the Martian atmosphere are here compared with those of Earth's atmosphere.

explorers from each ship descended to the surface in landing craft.

Inside their pressurized, temperature-controlled landers, the astronauts would enjoy a "shirtsleeve" environment. They would have to don spacesuits before leaving the ship in order to set up their instruments, take samples, and make excursions in a Mars roving vehicle. When the time came to leave they would stow their samples and blast off from Mars, leaving the lower section of the landing craft behind, to rendezvous and dock with their orbiting motherships. At a pre-calculated time, the ships were to blast out of Mars orbit, and continue their long journey around the Sun flying close to Venus and, using its gravity to slow down, arrive back at the Earth station after a round trip of 21 months. The enormous cost and complexity of such a mission makes it unlikely that human beings will land on Mars this century.

Intelligent machines

A scientific base on Mars would need an even larger investment, and its value must be weighed against the ability of intelligent machines to gather scientific information. For example, computer-controlled roving vehicles have been devised to avoid the time-lag in radio-communications (up to 23 minutes in the case of Mars) that rules out direct radio-control steering from Earth. The USSR has experimented with a six-legged vehicle with a computer "brain" and a laser "eye." The laser probes ahead for obstacles and the computer works out an avoidance path.

It is likely that unmanned spacecraft can be made to land on Mars, release an automatic rover, and obtain soil and rock samples at different sites. After the samples have been placed into a return rocket, at the appropriate time it would be launched back to Earth.

Any specimens taken from Mars must be kept in isolation lest they spread some unknown disease, the best place being a space laboratory in Earth orbit. This underlines the many unknowns that face any expedition, manned or otherwise, to other members of the Solar System.

KEY

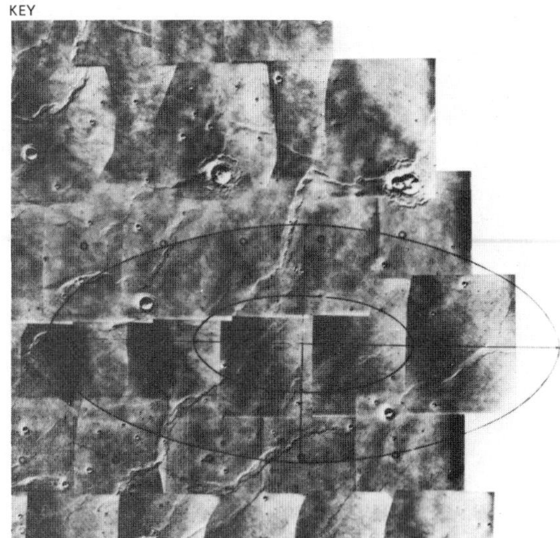

The Viking 1 landing site in Chryse Planitia—a channelled lowland below Mars' mean "sea level"—lies northeast of the great Martian volcanoes. The craft landed near the center of the target ellipse in the picture.

4 The procedure for establishing a base on Mars will differ from that on the Moon. It will be necessary to construct a complete base immediately, since Earth is too far away in case of an emergency. In this illustration a Mars Excursion Module (MEM), similar to the type needed to carry astronauts to the surface of the planet, has just arrived. Its cargo includes an inflatable pressure dome like the one already set up in the background. Another MEM is about to land a roving laboratory, which the astronauts will use to explore the ground. The landing technique follows the practice of Viking. After being released from the orbiting mother craft, the MEM fires a braking rocket to descend. It enters the Martian atmosphere at about, 10,000 mph (16,000 kph) to be slowed first by aerodynamic drag on the blunt heat shield, then by parachutes. About a mile up, the parachutes are discarded and retro-rockets cushion the touchdown. Equipment landed on Mars must take into account climatic conditions. The pressure domes must be double-walled to protect the people inside from the cold. Radar dishes are mounted in radomes mainly for protection from wind-blown dust. Other supplies landed include nuclear generators for power supply, reserves of oxygen for life-support systems, and food and water. Sources of water and oxygen on Mars must be established to make the base less dependent on Earth. The search will already have begun with projectilelike probes launched from orbit that penetrate deep into the soil. Where likely places are found, astronauts will drive out to make a thorough study.

Exploring the inner planets

Although Venus approaches the Earth more closely than any other planet, it took a long time to discover the true nature of its surface because it is perpetually shrouded by a cloudy white atmosphere. Only slightly smaller than the Earth, Venus orbits some 26 million miles (42 million km) nearer the Sun and intercepts about twice as much heat and light. These simple facts led astronomers to some quite bizarre theories. The Swedish Nobel prizewinner Svante Arrhenius in 1918 imagined the planet was covered in seas, swamps, and steamy jungles and was populated, perhaps, by primeval monsters.

Astronomers of the 1930s and 1940s had different ideas. With the spectroscope they had discovered that the chief constituent of the atmosphere was the heavy gas carbon dioxide. This suggested that radiation from the Sun would be trapped by a "greenhouse" effect creating high temperatures, which, some believed, might attain the boiling point of water. One theory was that Venus was in the throes of extensive volcanic activity and that its thick atmosphere was volcanic dust suspended in a perpetually warm fog. The American astronomers F. L. Whipple and D. H. Menzel, on the other hand, thought it possible that the planet was entirely covered by ocean. Others anticipated a hot, windy desert.

Venus: a hostile environment

Radar signals bounced off the planet from Earth in the 1960s indicated a rugged surface and possibly large craters. By finding a fixed point of reference these radar soundings showed that Venus turned on its axis—in a reverse direction to Earth, east to west—once in 243 days. Space probes—beginning with the flyby of the US Mariner 2 in 1962 and continuing with the Soviet Venera capsules that entered the atmosphere—produced clear evidence of surface temperatures far above the melting point of lead and atmospheric pressures that would crush any normal spacecraft.

In 1975 Veneras 9 and 10 swung into orbit around Venus after releasing camera-equipped capsules that landed some 1,370 miles (2,200km) apart. Ruggedly built to withstand extremely high pressures, their descent was slowed by parachutes and a circular air brake. The first capsule—transmitting to Earth via its orbiting mother craft—worked for 53 minutes. It sent a panoramic picture of its surroundings showing a scattering of sharp-edged rocks 12 to 16in (30 to 40cm) across, which appeared to be little affected by heat or wind erosion. The rocks seemed to be comparatively young and of a kind that may have been produced by subsidence or a meteorite impact. Instruments showed the pressure of the atmosphere was 90 times that on Earth, the temperature 900°F (485°C). The second capsule, which transmitted for 65 minutes, showed a different landscape, one typical of old mountain formations. The rocks resembled huge pancakes with sections of cooled lava or the debris of weathered rocks in between . Here the pressure was 92 atmospheres, suggesting that the capsule had come down in a valley.

The Veneras 9 and 10 mother craft, continuing the survey, built up a detailed pic-

CONNECTIONS

See also
62 The planet Mercury
64 The planet Venus
78 Minor planets

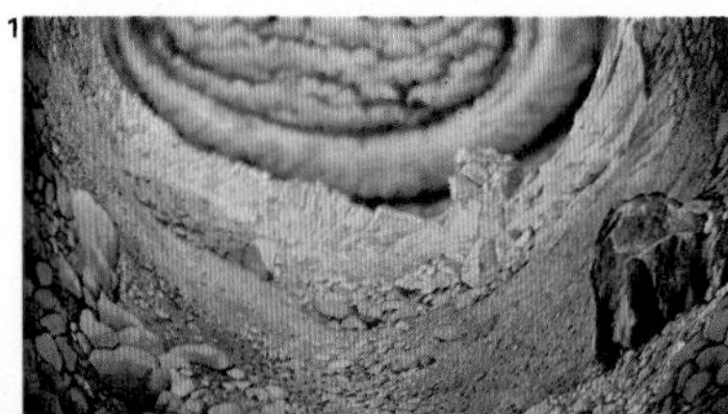

1 The dense atmosphere of Venus led scientists to believe that it must be "super-refractive"; that is, the rays of light would be bent to such an extent that an observer on the planet's surface would have the impression of being in a vast bowl, with the horizon curving upward around him. The Veneras 9 and 10 pictures showed that this is not the case. The atmosphere of Venus does not show the super-refraction characteristic that had been anticipated.

2 Venus has proved to be a world very different from anything that had been expected. The pictures from Veneras 9 and 10 reveal what the Russians have called a "stony desert," shown in this artist's impression. The rocks are relatively smooth, and it is thought that the erosion on Venus is less than on the Earth or even Mercury. The open sky can never be seen through the dense, corrosive clouds of acidic vapor that surround the planet, making Venus a gloomy, hostile world. As a site for a potential colony, Venus has proved to be a disappointment. The surface features are almost certainly volcanic in origin. It is not known if volcanic activity is continuing.

ture of the planet's cloud cover, adding to information received from Mariner 10 in 1974. Clouds tending to spiral around the planet reached a height of 40 miles (65km) with atmospheric gases moving at different speeds at different heights. Near the surface, wind speed was low, increasing with altitude until at the cloud tops it was 60 times that of the planet's own very slow rotation.

Russian and US specialists agreed that the brilliant white clouds might be laden with sulfuric acid and possibly small amounts of other acids. From the evidence of the surface cameras, the atmosphere was dust-free and a remarkable amount of light penetrated to the surface.

Mercury: solar observation point

Mercury, the nearest planet to the Sun, takes nearly 88 days to make one revolution at an average distance of 36 million miles (58 million km). A little less than half Earth's diameter, the planet turns slowly on its axis, completing a day in 58.5 Earth days. As a result its surface is alternately baked by the great heat of the Sun and frozen by the cold of outer space.

Mariner 10—which flew past Mercury in 1974 after skirting Venus—discovered a Moonlike world with craters, mountains, and valleys. There was barely a trace of atmosphere and instruments could not detect a magnetic field.

Although it has been suggested that this tiny sun-baked planet could be a useful scientific outpost for studying the Sun, space probes have already swung closer to the Sun than Mercury—and robots are far cheaper and less trouble to send than men and all the equipment to keep them alive.

The asteroids: beacons in space

Mercury and Venus are the only planets closer to the Sun than is the Earth. Farther out, Mars is our nearest neighbor and then comes the main zone of asteroids or minor planets [Key]. The largest of these bodies, Ceres, is about 600–750 miles (1,000–1,200km) across, but most are so small that contacts with them would be more in the nature of docking operations than landings.

KEY

The asteroids or minor planets may one day be the object of an exploratory mission. In this artist's impression the astronauts have docked with Eros and are setting up an inflatable, semi-transparent dome; they are preparing to make a geological survey of the asteroid. Eros is about 17 miles (27km) in diameter, and it is irregular in shape, like most of the asteroids, so that its horizon slope seems strange. The orbit of Eros takes it away from the main belt of the minor planets and it may approach to within 15 million miles (24 million km) of Earth. Its surface is pitted with craters resulting from collisions with debris.

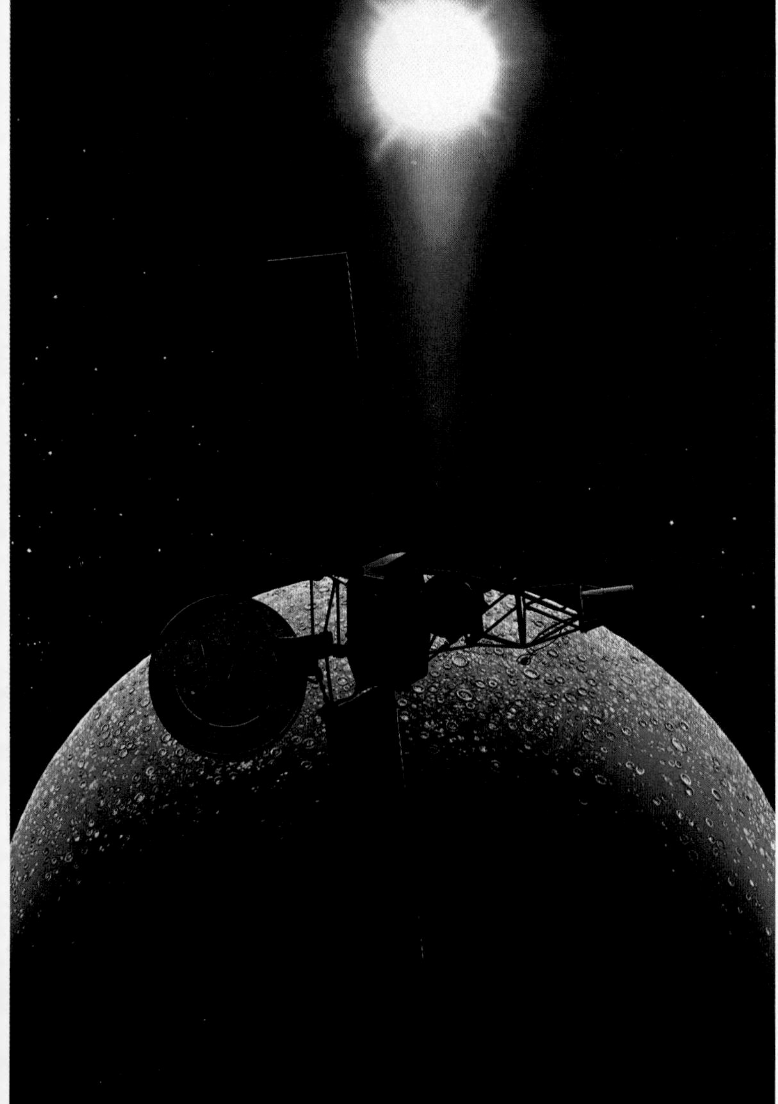

3 Mariner 10 approached Mercury in March 1974, 7 weeks after Venus, and sent back the first close-range pictures, showing that Mercury, like the Moon, is cratered. In this drawing Mariner 10's two "paddles" spanning nearly 29.5ft (9m) are seen; these provide the solar power for the various on-board systems. The dish antenna transmits information to Earth, and there are devices to measure magnetic fields, charged particles, and ultraviolet and infrared radiation. Mariner passed Mercury three times and on each occasion produced valuable data. It will continue to orbit the Sun indefinitely, although its "useful" life was over after it passed Mercury in the spring of 1975.

4

4 The planet Mercury has virtually no atmosphere and it is just as hostile as the Moon. In this drawing the Sun is hidden behind a plug of lava from a volcanic eruption millions of years previously, since worn down by alternate expansion and contraction as a result of Mercury's great diurnal temperature range. Craters are seen on the surface, and what appears as a bright star in the upper right is the Earth-Moon pair. Mercurian days and nights are long because the planet rotates so slowly on its axis, and it is a desolate, lifeless world.

Exploring Jupiter and Saturn

Chemically-propelled vehicles have taken men to the Moon. Whether such vehicles will suffice for manned journeys to Mars is problematic and they will certainly be inadequate for manned missions to Jupiter. The transfer orbit, at present the only means of making an extended journey, allows a probe to utilize the gravitational pull of a planet to accelerate and direct the probe on its way to the target planet. When a probe is moving in a transfer orbit almost all the journey is carried out in free fall, so that no propellant is expended. Using this technique a probe would take more than two years merely to reach the neighborhood of Jupiter. Such a long journey is technically impractical. For missions to the giant planets we must await the development of efficient nuclear rocket motors and dispense with the idea of extended transfer orbits.

Jupiter and its satellites

Jupiter, the closest of the giants, has no solid surface and is surrounded by zones of intense radiation that would be lethal to any astronaut incautious enough to come within range. There is, too, the high escape velocity—37.4 miles (60.22km) per second —which would make maneuvering almost impossible. The only alternative, then, would be to land on one of the Jovian satellites.

Ganymede would probably be the first choice. It is of planetary size (slightly larger than Mercury, though not so massive) and it is reasonably far out, with a mean distance from Jupiter of 621,000 miles (1,000,000km). From Ganymede the view would be spectacular: the giant planet would seem to spin rapidly, showing the panorama of its belts, its zones, and its Great Red Spot. Like all large satellites, Ganymede has a captured, or synchronous, rotation. It takes about 7.15 days to complete one revolution around Jupiter and its axial rotation period is the same, so that one side of Ganymede constantly faces Jupiter and from it the appearance of the planet constantly changes as it rotates.

Like Ganymede, the smaller but denser satellite Europa has almost no atmosphere. It may be ice covered and the view of Jupiter from its surface must be imposing. The innermost large satellite, Io [1] is the smallest known body with an atmosphere (possibly of ammonia) and Amalthea [2] is a dwarf moon whirling around Jupiter at a distance of only 112,000 miles (181,000km) in a period of almost 12 hours. To an observer on Amalthea, Jupiter would fill a quarter of the sky and its surface features would seem to change much more slowly than from Ganymede or Europa because Amalthea has a rotation period only two hours longer than that of Jupiter itself.

It is tempting to picture an observatory on Amalthea, ideally placed to study events on Jupiter, but this may never be possible simply because Amalthea lies inside the zone of Jovian radiation, which may make it a very dangerous location.

The problems of Saturn

If manned expeditions go out to Jupiter within the next 200 years, then Saturn [3] would be the next target. Here the problems are somewhat different. The distance in-

CONNECTIONS

See also
80 The planet Jupiter
84 The planet Saturn
86 The moons of Jupiter and Saturn

1

1 Jupiter would dominate the sky to an observer standing on Io, one of its four large satellites. He would clearly see the dark belts, the bright zones, and the Great Red Spot. Io lies 262,000 miles (422,000km) from the center of Jupiter, which is somewhat more than the distance of the Moon from the center of the Earth. But the revolution period of Io is only one day 18.5 hours because Jupiter's powerful gravitational pull causes it to move much faster in its orbit. Io moves in the Jovian magnetosphere and affects radio emissions from the planet. Parts of Io may be ice coated.

2

2 Jupiter, as seen from Amalthea, would look magnificent, with the shadows of Io and Europa clearly visible. Officially known as Satellite 5, Amalthea is the innermost member of the Jovian family, lying only about 70,000 miles (110,000km) from the planet's surface. It moves at a mean distance of 112,000 miles (181,000km) from Jupiter's center. Amalthea is only 124 miles (200km) in diameter and is possibly distorted in shape by the intensely powerful pull of gravity from the planet. Expeditions to Amalthea could prove highly dangerous because it lies within the radiation zone of Jupiter.

volved is greater, but in compensation Saturn seems to lack the lethal radiation zones that characterize Jupiter. Of the numerous satellites of Saturn, Titan is far more interesting and important than any member of the Jovian family.

From the inner satellites Saturn would look magnificent, despite the edge-on presentation of the rings. The passage of a vehicle through the ring-system itself would be extremely hazardous. The danger would come not from radiation, but from solid particles of matter. Presumably the exploration of the regions in and near the ring-system would be left to automatic probes.

Saturn, like Jupiter, lacks any solid surface, so that landings would have to be restricted to its satellites. All the inner members of the family move practically in the plane of the rings and, as a result, the rings appear edge-on. But this does not apply to Iapetus, which moves at a mean distance of 2.2 million miles (3.6 million km) from Saturn. It completes one revolution in 79.33 days and is about 700 miles (1,100km) in diameter—about half the size of the Moon. Because its orbit is appreciably inclined to the ring-plane, Iapetus would provide the best base for studying Saturn itself.

The lure of Titan

It is Titan that really captures the imagination. Here is a world of planetary size, 760,000 miles (1,200,000km) from Saturn, with an atmosphere that may contain clouds and with a density ten times greater than that of Mars at the surface. Unfortunately Titan's atmosphere is composed mostly of methane, which will not support life as it is known on Earth, and some hydrogen, but the satellite is regarded with special interest and there is even discussion of sending a probe specifically to study it.

If a base were to be built on Titan, it could be on the same lines as those proposed for Mars. Everything would have to be made self-supporting, and there could be no chance of a prompt rescue in an emergency. The close-range view of Saturn from Titan would exceed by far in splendor and interest anything else in the inner part of the Solar System.

KEY

Saturn, surrounded by a host of stars, appears to the naked eye as a particularly bright star. Although remote, it is far closer than any star and lies within probe range.

3

3 Saturn, seen from Rhea, would display four of its inner satellites: Dione, Tethys, Enceladus, and Mimas. With the Sun below the horizon, Saturn's strong yellow light would cast a bright glow over Rhea's surface. Rhea is the sixth farthest satellite from Saturn and moves around the planet at a distance of 327,000 miles (527,000km) from its center, the distance from Rhea to Saturn's surface being about 290,000 miles (467,000km). Rhea takes 4 days 12.5 hours to complete one journey around Saturn. It is much smaller than the Moon and nothing positive is known about its surface except that it lacks an atmosphere and the temperature is extremely low. Like the other inner satellites (and indeed all of Saturn's attendants, apart from the two outermost members, Iapetus and Pheobe) Rhea moves virtually in the plane of Saturn's equator, which is also in the plane of the rings. Therefore, from Rhea, the rings would appear as a thin line of light and would always be seen edge-on. An observer on Rhea would not be able to see the Cassini Division in the ring system of the planet.

Exploring the outer planets

In the mid-1970s Jupiter was the most remote world to have been contacted by a space probe, although by 1979 the Pioneer 11 probe is expected to have reached Saturn. Plans are being made to send vehicles out to the next giant planet, Uranus, which has features of special interest, but the journey will take much longer—a point that is not always easy to appreciate from a casual glance at a map of the Solar System (Uranus is 1,690 million miles [2,720 million km] from the Earth). A spacecraft traveling traveling to Uranus will have reached only the halfway mark when it crosses the orbit of Saturn.

Uranus and its satellites

It is too early to speculate about when the first manned expedition will venture as far as Uranus. Vehicles much more sophisticated than those planned at the moment will be needed; even so, landing on the planet's surface would be impossible. Uranus, like Jupiter and Saturn, has a surface of gas, although the constitution of the planet differs in various important details. There is no evidence so far to indicate the existence of dangerous radiation zones like those of Jupiter.

Of the five satellites, Miranda is the closest to the planet, only 80,000 miles (130,000km) out, but it is likely that the first landing will be made on one of the larger satellites, such as Ariel [1]. Because of its pronounced axial tilt Uranus sometimes appears as a crescent with its horns extending from one side of the equator to the other rather than from pole to pole—a case unique in the Solar System. The strange greenish light of Uranus upon the rocks of one of its satellites will make an eerie picture, and one of emptiness and desolation.

Neptune and Triton

Beyond Uranus lies Neptune—but again, the distances involved are immense; the distance of Neptune from Earth is 1.5 times that of Uranus [2]. But at least there is a more promising satellite, Triton, which is much larger than any of the attendants of Uranus and may possibly have the same kind of atmosphere as Titan (Saturn's largest satellite), although no proof of this has yet been obtained. Triton is unique among large satellites, in that it moves around its primary in a retrograde direction. Neptune has a rotation period of 15 hours 48 minutes, while Triton has a revolution period of only 5 days 21 hours. Because of these relative movements, the drift of surface markings on Neptune will be rapid from the viewpoint of a Tritonian observer, providing a fascinating view of Neptune.

If an outpost is to be established in these desolate regions of the Solar System it is most likely to be upon Triton. The other satellite of Neptune, Nereid, is extremely small—less than 185 miles (300km) in diameter—and with its highly eccentric orbit it would offer few advantages as an observation base. Even from Triton the other planets would not be seen to advantage; only Uranus would seem brighter than it does from Earth and it would be an inferior planet, keeping in the same area of the sky as the shrunken but still intensely brilliant Sun. Moreover, when Uranus and Neptune lie on opposite sides of the Sun an observer

CONNECTIONS

See also
88 The outer planets
90 Comets

1

1 Uranus is seen from its satellite Ariel in this artist's impression. A probe visiting Uranus from Earth would be launched to the neighborhood of Jupiter and the powerful Jovian gravity would be then used to pull the probe along and accelerate it out beyond Jupiter and on toward Uranus. The gaseous nature of Uranus clearly prohibits any landing. Landing may be possible upon some of its five satellites, however. Of these the closest to Uranus, Miranda, is very small. The innermost of the main satellites is Ariel, which moves around Uranus at a distance of 119,000 miles (192,000km) from the center of the planet in a period of 2 days 12 hours 29 minutes. Nothing is known about the surface of Ariel, but its size seems to be considerably smaller than the Moon—about 930 miles (1,500km) in diameter. Ariel, like the other satellites, moves in the plane of Uranus's equator. In this view Uranus looks like a crescent, but the horns extend from one side of the equator to the other. With its remarkable inclination of 98°, in 1985 one pole of Uranus will face the Sun (so that there will be a "polar day" lasting 21 Earth years) and from Ariel or any other satellite Uranus will appear as a half disk. The changing surface will be displayed, although the greenish disk of Uranus is less active than Jupiter or Saturn.

on Triton would find Uranus very difficult to see over a period of years. Saturn would be even more elusive because the distance between Neptune and Saturn is much greater than that between Saturn and Earth and the inner planets would be virtually out of view. Yet from Triton there would be no interference from brilliant solar radiation and because of this useful observations outside the Solar System could be made from a base there.

Pluto and beyond

Little is known about Pluto, the outermost planet [3]. It may not be much larger than Triton and all that is known about its surface is that it contains methane ice, which forms at 50 degrees above absolute zero. At perihelion, or closest point to the Sun, it comes within the orbit of Neptune; the next perihelion passage is due in 1989. At aphelion, the farthest point from the Sun, Pluto recedes to more than 4.5 billion miles (7.3 billion km) from the Sun.

Information sent back to Earth from a future space probe to Pluto would be of great interest. The mass of Pluto is still not accurately known, but the effect it has upon a flyby probe would enable scientists to calculate its value. If astronauts ever land there, they will find that the Sun looks no larger than Jupiter does as seen from Earth, although it will still shed light over the bleak Plutonian surface.

Communications with Earth will be slow. A radio wave would take about five hours to cross the space from Pluto to Earth—so that if a message is transmitted from Earth, it will be ten hours before any response can be received.

Although Pluto is the outermost known planet, there may well be opportunities for studying material from even farther out in the Solar System. Comets [Key], those beautiful and insubstantial objects, mostly have very eccentric orbits and there is a real possibility of sending a probe through a comet that has come from the region beyond the orbits of Neptune and Pluto. This may be attempted in the near future—perhaps even with Halley's comet at its next return in 1985.

KEY

Comets, the erratic wanderers of the Solar System, can travel farther than the known outermost planet, Pluto. Shown here is a probe approaching a comet on its journey; the Earth and Moon appear in the upper right. Unlike a planet a comet is not a solid, massive body; it is composed of relatively small particles, mainly icy in nature, together with extremely tenuous gas. There is no reason why a probe should not be able to pass right through it. The tail is particularly tenuous, thus the background stars can be seen through it virtually undimmed. Some comets travel a distance 1.3 times Pluto's distance from the Sun.

2

2 Neptune, unlike Uranus, has a "normal" axial inclination of 29°—less than 6° greater than that of the Earth. Surface details on its bluish disk are very hard to make out, but there seems little doubt that Neptune and Uranus are similar. The illustration shows a view as it would appear from Nereid, the smaller of Neptune's two satellites, which has an eccentric orbit. At its closest to the planet Nereid approaches to within 870,000 miles (1,400,000km) and this is depicted in the illustration. Nereid takes almost one Earth year to complete a full revolution.

3

3 Pluto will come within the path of Neptune because of its relatively eccentric orbit. The next perihelion is due in 1989; for some years on either side of that date Pluto will no longer be the outermost known planet. At aphelion it recedes to more than 4.5 billion miles (7.3 billion km) from the Sun. The temperature of Pluto is estimated to be as low as −230°C (−382°F). So far no atmosphere has been detected—only frozen methane on Pluto's surface. The methane might be frozen in "lakes." The bright star seen through the cave opening on Pluto is the Sun.

Beyond the Sun's family

Exploration of the Solar System is progressing and, at the present rate of progress, all the planets will have been contacted by unmanned probes within the next 50 years—probably well before—while manned expeditions will have been sent to those worlds like Mars that are not overwhelmingly hostile and are within reasonable range. Yet even when man has finished his exploration of the Solar System, he will hardly have begun to explore the universe.

Problems of interstellar travel

The Solar System is only a small part of the universe. If the distance between the Earth and the Sun were represented by 1 inch (2.5cm), the nearest star would be almost 4.3 miles (7km) away. Stellar distances are so great that man's present technology cannot bridge them in any meaningful way except perhaps by radio messages. Although two interstellar probes have been dispatched—Pioneer 10, which flew by Jupiter in December 1973, and Pioneer 11, which did so about a year later—neither will approach a star for many thousands of years. They are gambles, launched into space in the hope that they may reach a world of advanced beings who can communicate with Earth—and in the hope that when that happens mankind will have advanced sufficiently to be able to understand that communication.

Even if it traveled at the speed of light, a probe would take more than four years to reach Proxima Centauri—the nearest star, and one that is sufficiently like the Sun to have a family of planets moving round it. According to the theory of relativity, it is impossible for any material body to travel at the speed of light; any spacecraft that can be planned in the present state of technology is, by comparison, very slow indeed.

Journeys to other solar systems will have to be made by methods that are as yet unknown and will probably be more technologically advanced than television would have been in the days of Julius Caesar. All kinds of suggestions have been made. A favorite science-fiction idea is that of the space-ark in which those who set out are succeeded by their descendants, who ultimately finish the journey. Alternatively, it has been suggested that the travelers could be put into a state of suspended animation and conveniently awakened just before arrival at a suitable planet. Other ideas involve telepathy and teleportation—transporting matter through space in much the same way as television transmits pictures. They are all intriguing, but at present beyond man's powers to implement; however, a spectacular breakthrough may come eventually and it is always conceivable that some alien beings may communicate with or visit the Earth before man has learned how to contact them.

Finding new planets

What are the prospects of finding planets orbiting other stars? The Sun is a normal G-type dwarf and there is no reason to regard it as exceptional in any way. Moreover, G-type dwarfs are common and it seems likely that planetary systems are abundant in the Galaxy. Other kinds of stars are less promising. For instance, a red giant star that has left the main sequence and has

CONNECTIONS

See also
50 Members of the Solar System
100 Star types

1

1 The Moon can be reached from Earth in a few days and sending a rocket to Mars or Venus involves a journey of only a few months. But interstellar travel presents quite a different picture and poses many problems. The distances involved are millions of millions of miles and even light, moving at a speed of 186,000 miles (300,000km) a second, takes more than four years to reach the nearest star. Rockets powered by chemical fuels of the type in use today would be hopelessly inadequate for flight to any star. Much research has gone into the possibility of building what is termed a photon rocket, in which the gases emitted from the exhaust of a chemical rocket are replaced by a stream of photons, that is, a beam of light. The thrust produced would be very low, but it could be maintained indefinitely. Over a period of years the acceleration would build until the velocity of the vehicle approached that of light. (According to relativity theory, the precise velocity of light can never be reached by a material body, since it would involve infinite mass.) In principle, the photon rocket can be compared to a gigantic searchlight that is driven forward by the light emitted. One possible design is shown here. The rocket would be more than 6 miles (9.5km) long with a crew of 300-500. Our Galaxy is in the background. In the inset, lower right, our Galaxy is shown first face-on and edge-on, with the position of the Solar System indicated by a red circle. Even at the velocity of light, it would take a probe 100,000 years to pass from one side of the Galaxy to the other.

swelled to many times its original size will have swallowed up any planets it may once have had [2], while a very hot, massive blue or white star will have run through the earlier part of its evolution so quickly that Earthlike planets will hardly have had time to develop.

Then there are the faint red stars, so feeble that they have never joined the main sequence and are on their way to extinction. Barnard's Star, at a distance of only a little more than five light-years from Earth, is one of these. As it moves through space it wobbles slightly and there have been suggestions that it is being pulled out of position by an orbiting planet or planets.

An alien environment

By Earth standards, a planet associated with a star like Barnard's would be a dreary world. Its only light would come from a dim red sun and it would therefore be cold. Any life there would have to contend with an environment that man would find intolerable. Yet it would be unwise to dismiss such planets as possible colonies.

Barnard's Star is not very active by stellar standards. Stars that are much more violent become unstable as they use up their nuclear energy and some produce novalike outbursts [3]. The effects of these upon any orbiting planets would be catastrophic. If our Sun became a nova, all life on Earth would be destroyed in a matter of hours. Fortunately, the Sun is a stable star and will not significantly change its structure for at least 5 billion years. There must, however, have been planetary systems that were engulfed by their dying central stars.

There would have been a period of warning in which the inhabitants of a threatened planet, if they were sufficiently advanced technologically, could have taken steps to save themselves. The obvious step would be into space—abandonment of the world about to die in favor of a new start on a new world, however difficult that might prove. That, too, is a favorite speculation of science-fiction writers. The wildest speculation is that it has already happened—and that the new world the lifeboats landed on was Earth.

KEY

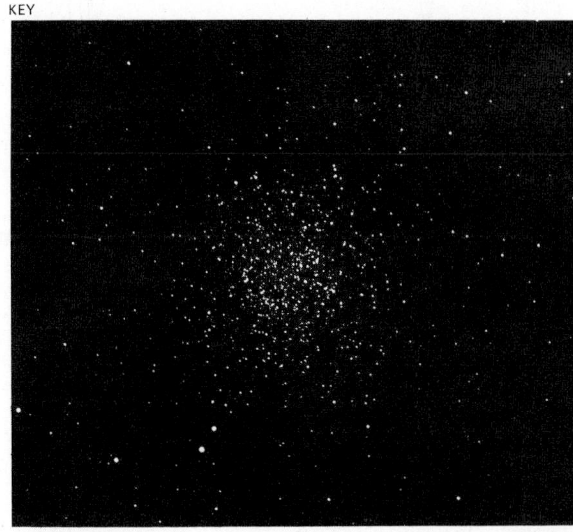

In this cluster of stars, NGC 5897 in Libra, photographed with the 200-in reflector at Palomar, each star is a sun in its own right. Many may have associated planet-families, but there is no direct optical proof; no telescope yet built or planned can show a planet of another star.

2 Zeta Aurigae is a binary system made up of a vast red supergiant together with a much smaller white star. The red supergiant is an old star that has left the main sequence and has swelled out to a diameter greater than that of the orbit of the Earth around the Sun. Since it has become very luminous, it will have raised the temperatures of its planets to intolerable levels and any inner planets of its original system will have been destroyed. No life can be expected in a system of this kind. The illustration shows a view of the two stars from a hypothetical planet.

2

3

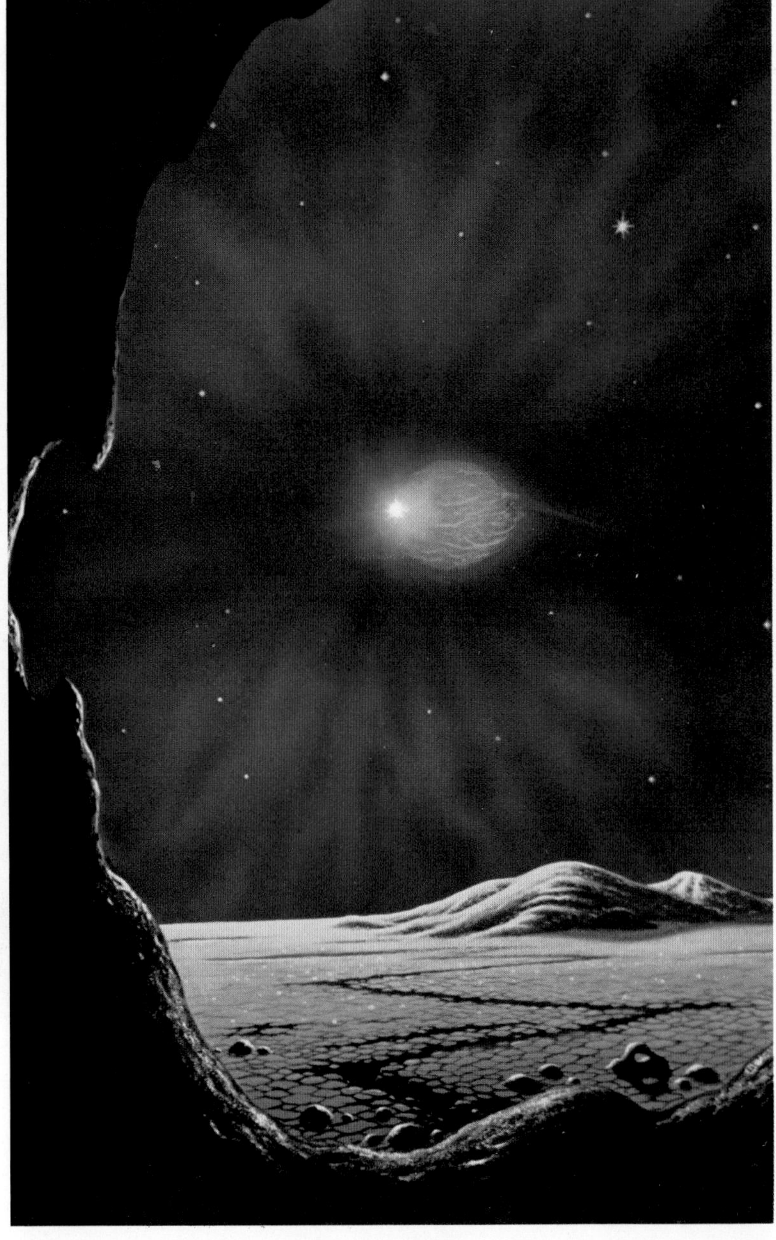

3 This barren, dead planet is on the outskirts of a hypothetical planetary system – the "Pluto" of the system. The central star, a binary system, has flared up as a nova, resulting in a tremendous, although temporary, increase in luminosity. The planet's surface has been scorched by the tremendous radiation; its water has evaporated and even its atmosphere has been driven away so that no life can possibly survive. The inner planets of the system have been completely destroyed. The sky is enriched by an auroralike display, caused by a shell of gases released by the star as its outer layers expand. When the nova outburst is over, the planet will remain, cold and sterile, circling the feeble remnant of its once glorious sun.

Worlds of many kinds

Life on Earth has developed along its familiar lines because the conditions are suitable for it. If the Earth were smaller, colder, or less massive, then life would have taken on different forms; and if the conditions were unsuitable, no living organisms would have developed at all. Life, wherever it is found, is suited to its environment. If a star like the Sun were attended by a planet the size and mass of the Earth orbiting it at a distance of 93 million miles (150 million kilometers), then Earth-type life might reasonably be expected. In 1972 Pioneer 10 was launched to probe beyond the Solar System. It carried a plaque [Key] to communicate with any intelligent life that might encounter it.

Alien life forms?

This does not mean that all forms of life must correspond with the terrestrial pattern. There is nothing, in theory, against an intelligent astronomer having six legs and two heads. If he were made up of the same materials as ourselves he would not, despite his appearance, qualify as one of those interesting creatures science-fiction writers call "bug-eyed monsters." This term is reserved for entirely alien creatures, breathing pure methane, say, and able to survive in temperatures of −250°F (157°C) or below. It cannot be said definitely that alien life does not exist; all that can really be done is to take the available facts and then put the most reasonable interpretation upon them. When this is done, bug-eyed monsters appear improbable.

Rational discussion of life on other planets must be confined to "life as we know it." Any extension to include alien life forms means that speculation becomes not only endless, but also pointless.

An Earth-type planet may be expected to produce Earth-type life, essentially similar to our own and no doubt subject to the same weaknesses. For instance, the star Delta Pavonis, at a distance of 19 light-years from the Earth, is strikingly similar to the Sun; we have no idea whether or not it has a planetary system, but there seems no reason why it should not be attended by a world similar to the Earth, in which case its inhabitants may at this very moment be speculating about the possibility of intelligence upon a planet orbiting a fourth-magnitude yellow star in their own sky. If this hypothetical planet lay farther from Delta Pavonis than the Earth does from the Sun, the colder climate would produce life forms more akin to those in our polar zones; if it lay closer, life would be more equatorial. Of course, this can be no more than speculation because nobody knows whether a planet capable of supporting life will actually produce it.

Different perspectives

Many stars in the Galaxy are members of binary systems and it is fascinating to picture a planet lit by two suns—perhaps of different colors, one yellow and one blue, giving strange, spectacular color effects. Then there are the variable stars, some of which are completely regular while others are violently explosive. It is hard to see how a variable star could be attended by a life-bearing planet because there would be extreme fluctuations in climate; but most variable stars are well advanced in their evolu-

CONNECTIONS

See also
126 The expanding universe

1 A planet of Proxima Centauri, the nearest star to the Earth, may exist, according to recent investigations. This picture of its surface is thus founded on something more than sheer imagination. Proxima Centauri is a dim red dwarf that has never joined the main sequence nor passed through the giant stage of evolution. Proxima does not cast as much light as the Sun on its attendants. The planet thought to be moving around it is assumed to have an orbital period of between 10 and 12 days. The outer edge, or limb, of Proxima is not sharp, like that of our Sun, but is diffuse, since the density of the outer layers is very low. It is also assumed that the planet retains a tenuous atmosphere. Since Proxima is a flare star, the climate of an inner planet will be very unstable and the landscape extremely desolate. No life can be expected there. But water, shown in the picture as a lake fringed by glittering crystals of ice, may survive. The black disk represents a possible satellite as it would be seen in silhouette against the red disk of Proxima. In the sky is seen a familiar constellation pattern: the W of Cassiopeia, all of whose stars are very remote and will therefore look much the same from the planet of Proxima as it does from our own planet. To the left of the W of Cassiopeia is another star—our own Sun—which will be easily visible with the naked eye to an observer.

tion, so that life on any of their surviving planets may have died out.

The Sun lies in a relatively sparsely-populated region of the Galaxy, at the edge of one of the spiral arms (from which it emerged perhaps 5 billion years ago). If the Sun lay in one of the rich globular clusters the sky would be ablaze; there would be many stars shining more brilliantly than Venus does to us and since globular clusters are "old" by stellar standards there would be many red stars that would have left the main sequence. There is no reason why stars inside globular clusters should not be attended by planetary systems. Astronomers there would be at something of a disadvantage, because it would be difficult for them to see clearly beyond the confines of their own dense cluster and they could know little about the universe beyond.

Interstellar communication

The only means of achieving communication with other planetary systems, using existing techniques, is by radio. Radio waves move at the same velocity as light and would take years to reach even the nearest star; nevertheless, the reception of a signal-pattern rhythmical enough to be classed as artificial would be of unparalleled significance. Attempts have already been made to distinguish such a pattern.

In 1960 radio astronomers at Green Bank, West Virginia, began an ambitious program known officially as Project Ozma. With powerful equipment they concentrated upon the two nearest stars that are reasonably like the Sun—Tau Ceti and Epsilon Eridani, both of which are slightly smaller and cooler than the Sun and are more than ten light-years away. A wavelength of 21.1cm (8in) was selected because this is the wavelength of the radio signals emitted by the clouds of cold hydrogen spread throughout the Galaxy. It is logical to believe that other astronomers, wherever they may be, are also devoting their attention to this particular wavelength. The earliest that a return signal from an alien world might be received by astronomers on Earth is 1980, but it probably will be many years after that before contact is made.

KEY

This plaque is carried on Pioneer 10 (launched in 1972, it will be the first vehicle to leave the Solar System). The radiating lines represent 14 pulsars; the binary notation gives their frequencies relative to the universal constant—the hydrogen atom (upper left). The regular decrease in the pulsars' frequencies will give the time elapsed since launch. The Earth's position with Pioneer's path (bottom) and the male and female in proportion to Pioneer are shown.

2 Communication with alien civilizations could be achieved by means of mathematics—a system man discovered rather than invented. One suggested method is the transmission of two signals of different kinds (say dots and dashes). 209 signals are sent as 0's and 1's. A listener could represent the 0's by black squares and the 1's by white squares (or vice versa). 209 has only two factors: 11 and 19. Accordingly, a receiver has the choice of dividing the signals into 11 groups of 19 or 19 groups of 11. The second alternative gives the correct intelligible picture—that of a biped.

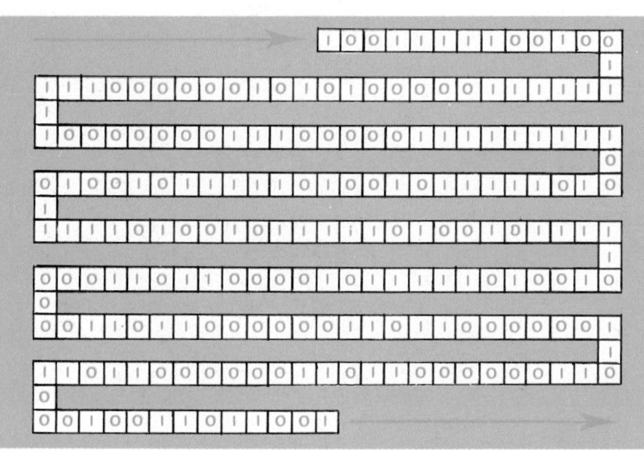

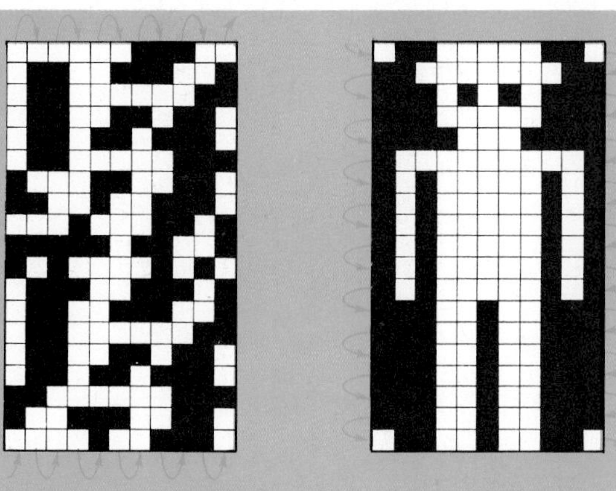

3 A radio telescope of the kind pictured here may well exist on a planet far away in the Galaxy and could be used to transmit codes. The parent star (bottom left) is like the Sun, and the planet itself is like the Earth, which means that any forms of life found there would be expected to be similar to those now on Earth. A large nearby satellite is shown. The radio telescope is constructed along essentially the same lines as those already set up on Earth and it could establish contact with an instrument such as the Haystack radio telescope at the Massachusetts Institute of Technology.

EARTH

EARTH

by Professor William A. Nierenberg

Until 1960 geology had, in a sense, no coherent history. It was simply a large collection of facts about the surface and near-surface of the Earth. The ten years between 1960 and 1970, however, saw the transformation of geology into a true science. At the heart of that transformation lay the hypothesis of sea-floor spreading and the theory of continental drift.

Historically, there were earlier concepts that were used as tools in geological thought—for example, neptunism, plutonism, catastrophism, and uniformitarianism. Of these, only the last two have survived as useful ideas.

Catastrophism arose from the observation that at particular times in the Earth's history dramatic changes have occurred. Largely unexplained in origin, they have given rise to interesting speculations. For example, there have been theories that the Cambrian revolution occurred at a time of closest approach of the Moon to the Earth—raising giant tides and causing great alterations in the ocean and the atmosphere. Fluctuations in the energy output of the Sun—due either to internal variations or to periodic passage through absorbing cosmic-dust clouds—are hypotheses put forward to explain climate changes and the massive disappearance of species. Other theories have been based on periodic increases in convection under the Earth's mantle caused by excess heat generated by radioactivity. It now appears likely, however, that the "new geology" of sea-floor spreading and continental drift may provide a demonstrable basis for many of these changes.

Uniformitarianism has survived the new geology very well. It is the concept that the geological forces we see operating about us today—erosion by stream, wind, and wave; volcanism; sedimentation, and so on (except for the catastrophic events)—have operated as continuously in the geological past as they do today.

The transformation of geology between 1960 and 1970 need not have taken so long. Observations had been made that could have led more quickly to the sea-floor spreading hypothesis and the theory of continental drift. It was thought that erosion of the continents should, in a ten-million-year period, supply enough sediment to fill the oceans of the world—but manifestly it has not. Subtler evidence in support of the theories came from the field of paleomagnetism, which is concerned with the magnetic properties of rocks and with the history of the Earth's magnetic field. But the concept of continental drift, which derived from sea-floor spreading, had to wait for the new science of marine geology. The probable reason for the delay was that, when geology was confined to observations on land, the tremendous complexity of the twisting, warping, erosion, and cutting that occurs offered so much information that it obscured the ultimate simple truth, whereas the mechanics of the study of land underlying the oceans was (and is still) so complex and difficult that only the larger and simpler features could be observed.

Marine geology was accelerated by antisubmarine techniques developed during World War II, and from the outset the results were exciting. The study of underwater sedimentation, seismology, heat flow, and magnetism combined to create a hypothesis that was handsomely verified by the first voyages of the *Glomar Challenger,* the best-equipped oceanographic vessel in the world. That story is told in detail in this section of the encyclopedia. The sea floor is analogous to a magnetic recording on an endless cassette. The tape can be reversed—and, when it is, the present-day continents coalesce very nicely into a single continent about 200,000,000 years ago. In particular, the South American and African plates join neatly, proving that the early theorists, like Francis Bacon (1561–1626), were right.

In a sense the new geology provides a dynamic picture. Corresponding questions can now be posed. What happens at the active continental margins where thick sediments pile up at the base of the continents and are transformed by temperature, pressure, and erosion to what is observed at or near the surface? What is the origin and description of the circulation in the Earth's upper mantle that gives the observed extrusions along the crests of the midocean ridges? Will the new theory help to locate useful thermal beds for the extraction of geothermal energy? Perhaps new light can be shed on the old question of the source of the Earth's magnetism and its

---

Director of the Scripps Institution of Oceanography, University of California; Senior Consultant to the White House Office of Science and Technology Policy; former Chairman and Member of the National Advisory Committee on Oceans and Atmosphere; Fellow of the American Academy of Arts and Sciences; Member of the National Academy of Sciences.

aperiodic reversals. These and other important questions can be dealt with in greater confidence given the framework provided by the new geology.

The oceans and oceanography

Scientists can explain very little of what they observe of the oceans. There is a tradition that Aristotle was so frustrated by his inability to account theoretically for the tides he observed that he cast himself into the sea and drowned. We know that his knowledge of the oceans derived from observations of the Mediterranean—a very poor place to study tidal action because the restrictive effect of the Strait of Gibraltar reduces the tidal variation to only a few inches in many areas.

Oceanography is now divided into a number of differently defined disciplines. The first is physical oceanography. It is concerned with the variations in temperature, salinity, and density among the different waters and includes the behavior of the visible ocean currents of the world. It also involves the study of the much slower motions of the bulk masses, including those near the bottom. Despite many years of work and measurement there is no thoroughly satisfactory explanation for most of the observed motions—so many factors are involved. In this sense oceanography is akin to meteorology, which deals with another geophysical field and in which the science continually improves but will never be in a state of total understanding.

Another major field is biological oceanography. In today's meaning it could readopt its original name of "ecology" because the first serious attempts to describe an ecological model dealt with the food chain in the ocean. Protein in the form of fish from the sea has always been important; it now reaches nearly 80,000,000 tons a year—close to the maximum expected yield—from the world's oceans. It is vital that the best possible understanding be reached of the interactions of oceanic life and the oceans. Unfortunately, the continental borders of the oceans, where the major fisheries lie, are also close to the densest concentrations of the world's population. The intentional discharge of waters in the form of sewage and chemical wastes and such unintentional discharge as the runoff of DDT and other pesticides pose threats to the fisheries that are becoming as critical as those of overfishing.

One branch of physical oceanography that seems to be emerging as a separate discipline is the air-sea interaction, the meeting ground of the meteorologist and oceanographer. The Earth has a continual history of severe climate changes, the best-known and most recent being the Ice Ages. It is now clear, however, that the oceans play a fundamental role in the shorter-range climate changes that have severely affected man's life on this planet in the last 2,000 years.

Man's commercial exploitation of the sea is at odds with his use of it for pleasure. The most violent conflict is between offshore oil production and onshore building, on the one hand, and the desire, on the other hand, to preserve scenic beauty and to encourage such activities as swimming, sport fishing, and boating. Some of man's most valuable assets are beaches, and they are disappearing in many places of the world at an alarming rate. The principal reason is the damming of rivers for power, irrigation, and flood control. The rivers are the principal source of replenishment for the sand lost from beaches in the complex activity that takes place in the near-shore region of the oceans.

Other important resources that can be obtained from the oceans are more speculative. The most interesting is tidal power, but it is inadequate when measured against global needs. More attractive as a long-term source is the energy available in the temperature difference between the upper 650 to 1,000 feet (200–300 m) of the Earth's oceans and the cold waters of the depths. This difference is about 27°F (15°C) for much of the world's oceans. With modern technology, proposals to tap that energy seem feasible, and it has been estimated that this source could supply all the world's needs to beyond the beginning of the 21st century. Another attractive supply of energy resides in ocean waves. An idea of the magnitude of this source can be obtained from the fact that waves from an average sea, the width of a typical freighter, carry ten times more power than is needed to drive the ship.

The science of agriculture

Agriculture as a human activity is only about 10,000 years old. It is a miracle of modern times. For many years predictions of calamity based on worldwide food shortages have been made, but the combined efforts of farmers, scientists, industry, and government have averted crisis after crisis by achieving new levels of production at each epoch.

Once man had found that it was more convenient to remain in one place and deliberately choose certain plants to cultivate, he then slowly improved the original choices be selective breeding of his plants and animals. Even the first crude agriculture must have been economically more profitable than nomadic hunting and was the takeoff point for man's rapid development. Storage of agricultural products smoothed the fluctuations in food supply, and the economy of effort yielded extra time for development of other activities that could enrich man's life materially and spiritually.

A successfully developing agriculture depends on four factors: selection and development of appropriate crops; land and fertilizers; water; climate. In time man has learned how to manage the first three. The last is still elusive—and potentially more dangerous because of the success with the first three. By genetic engineering, biologists are able to supply strains resistant to new pests and are capable of increasing yields in terms of both acreage and effort. Equally important in modern times has been the success in increasing the nutrient value of the crops, particularly the value of the protein in terms of the quantity and balance of their amino acids.

From the very beginning the availability of water was a major factor in determining the type and quality of local agriculture. In many areas irrigation had to be practiced from the beginning. Coupled with the problem of irrigation were the nature and suitability of the soil. Man soon learned that intensive cultivation exhausted the soil and this reduced the value of irrigation. Except for some particularly favorable areas such as the Nile valley, where the seasonal flooding and silting brought both water and nutrients, exhaustion of the soil resulted in wholesale displacement of populations—as happened with the Mayas. But in many regions man learned the practice of crop rotation and the enriching effect of certain nitrogen-fixing plants. Many cultures introduced the systematic recycling of nutrients back to the soil. Man was able to cope using such simple methods because population was limited by disease. The great advances in medicine in the 19th century led to rapidly increasing populations demanding more and more food. The answer to this problem is the expansion of cultivation, the development of newer and better strains of plants—the so-called "green revolution"—and the introduction of more productive animals. Yet for the breeding program and the green revolution to work, large quantities of artificial fertilizers are required. Furthermore, for fullest efficiency only the optimum variety is used covering vast areas—hundreds of square

miles in extent. This is the state of modern agriculture and is described as "monoculture." In this state it is capable of feeding the world for generations to come. Arable land can be doubled. Water can be used more efficiently. More important, the protein supplement can displace the need for animal protein, yielding a many-fold increase in available grain. The technology can be applied to the underproducing nations if their political systems will allow it.

These advances are marginal at each stage. Even though modern agriculture is able to match the growing population, the methods open up new vulnerabilities. The first is the dependence on the gene pool of wild plants for the development of new strains. The monoculture technique makes the total harvest vulnerable to new pests—even a single one can cause havoc, spreading without the natural barriers of a heterogeneous culture. If these pests cannot be chemically or biologically controlled, new strains of plants must be developed. As the remaining wild areas of the Earth are being converted to modern agriculture—particularly in the tropics—the danger of losing the wild species and the corresponding gene pool for developing new varieties looms ever larger.

The one overriding concern today is the climate, in the understanding of which little progress has been made. Short-term climate changes can produce important changes in the world's food supply, and, given the always marginal difference between need and production (a few months of reserve at best), genuine crises in food can be expected. In a sense, nothing has changed. In 10,000 years, despite the extraordinary changes in the technology of agriculture, we, like the Mayas, live with the threat of food shortages—only the nature of the threat is different.

Anatomy of the Earth

The Earth is made up of several concentric shells, like the bulb of an onion. Each shell has its own particular chemical composition and physical properties. The outermost shell is called the crust, and it surrounds the mantle; the innermost shell is the core.

The solid crust on which we live is no thicker in relation to the Earth than an egg shell, accounting for only one-and-a-half percent of its volume. Scientists have been able to learn about the uppermost part of the crust by direct observation. Their knowledge of the Earth's interior comes from the study of earthquake wave paths.

Earthquake waves are bent when they traverse rock boundaries with different densities. If the waves hit the boundary at a low angle, they are reflected instead. Waves from distant earthquakes emerge steeply through the crust while those from earthquakes nearby emerge at shallow angles. By knowing these angles, the velocities at which the waves emerge, their times of arrival and distances traveled, geophysicists have been able to compute the positions and densities of the Earth's shells.

Observing the Earth's crust

The chemical composition of the crust [Key] and upper mantle is known from direct observation of rocks at or near the Earth's surface [2]. Below the upper mantle little is certain, although it has been suggested that similarities exist between iron and stony meteorites and the composition of the Earth's deep interior. The upper crust over continental areas is granitic in composition and is known as "sial" (from the first two letters of its most abundant elements, silicon and aluminum). Over oceanic areas, and underlying the continental sial, is the basaltic crust called "sima" (from silicon and magnesium, two abundant elements found in it) [Key]. The sial has a density of 2.7g/cm^3; it is lighter than the sima (density 2.9g/cm^3), and lies above it to form the continents. The oceanic crust is made of sima with a thin veneer of sediments and lavas.

The crust is separated from the mantle by a sudden change of density (2.9 to 3.3 g/cm^3), which shows up as a good reflecting plane for earthquake waves. This plane is known as the Mohorovičić discontinuity (Moho for short) [2], after the Croatian who discovered it in 1909, and is taken to represent the base of the crust. The Moho is at an average depth of 20 miles (35km) under the continents and 6 miles (10km) below sea level under the seas.

Beneath the crust

The upper mantle [1] consists of a thin rigid top layer extending from below the Moho to a depth of about 40–60 miles (60–100km), a pasty layer, or asthenosphere, down to about 120 miles (200km), and a thick bottom layer between 120 and 430 miles (200–700km). The uppermost layer together with the overlying crust forms the rigid lithosphere, which is divided laterally into plates. These plates drift on the asthenosphere where pressure and temperature almost reach melting point, leading to near-fluidity. The upper mantle is separated from the lower mantle by another discontinuity, where the rock density again increases (3.3 to 4.3g/cm^3). Here, the composition is thought to be chiefly peridotite, plus miner-

CONNECTIONS

See also
174 Earthquakes
178 Gravity and the shape of the Earth
170 Global tectonics
48 Evolution of the Solar System
56 The Moon's structure

1 The Earth's crust varies in thickness from 25 miles (40km) to 3 miles (5km) under the sea floor. With the uppermost mantle it forms the rigid lithosphere [1], which overlays a plastic layer, the asthenosphere [2], on which it may drift sideways. The upper mantle [3] extends down to 430 miles (700km), where it overlays the lower mantle [4]. The mantle is thought to be made of peridotite that is near melting point in the asthenosphere. This would explain the slowing-down of seismic waves at those depths and it fits the plate tectonics theory. The increase of density in the lower mantle is thought to be caused by increased pressure and packing of the atoms, without a change of chemical composition. The mantle is separated from the outer core [6] by another seismic wave discontinuity, the Gutenberg discontinuity [5]. P wave velocity drops from 9 miles (14km) to 5 miles (8km) per second and S waves are not transmitted inside the outer core. These observations indicate that the outer core is in a liquid state. The density jumps from 5.5g/cm^3 for the lower mantle to 10g/cm^3 for the outer core where it increases downward to 12 or 13 g/cm^3. Although the core is only 16% of the Earth by volume, it represents 32% of its mass. The core is thought to consist of iron and nickel, an hypothesis that fits the data and is inspired by iron-nickel meteorites, which are thought to be the remnants of another planet. P waves show another discontinuity [7] and increase their speed in the center of the Earth or inner core [8], which is solid.

1

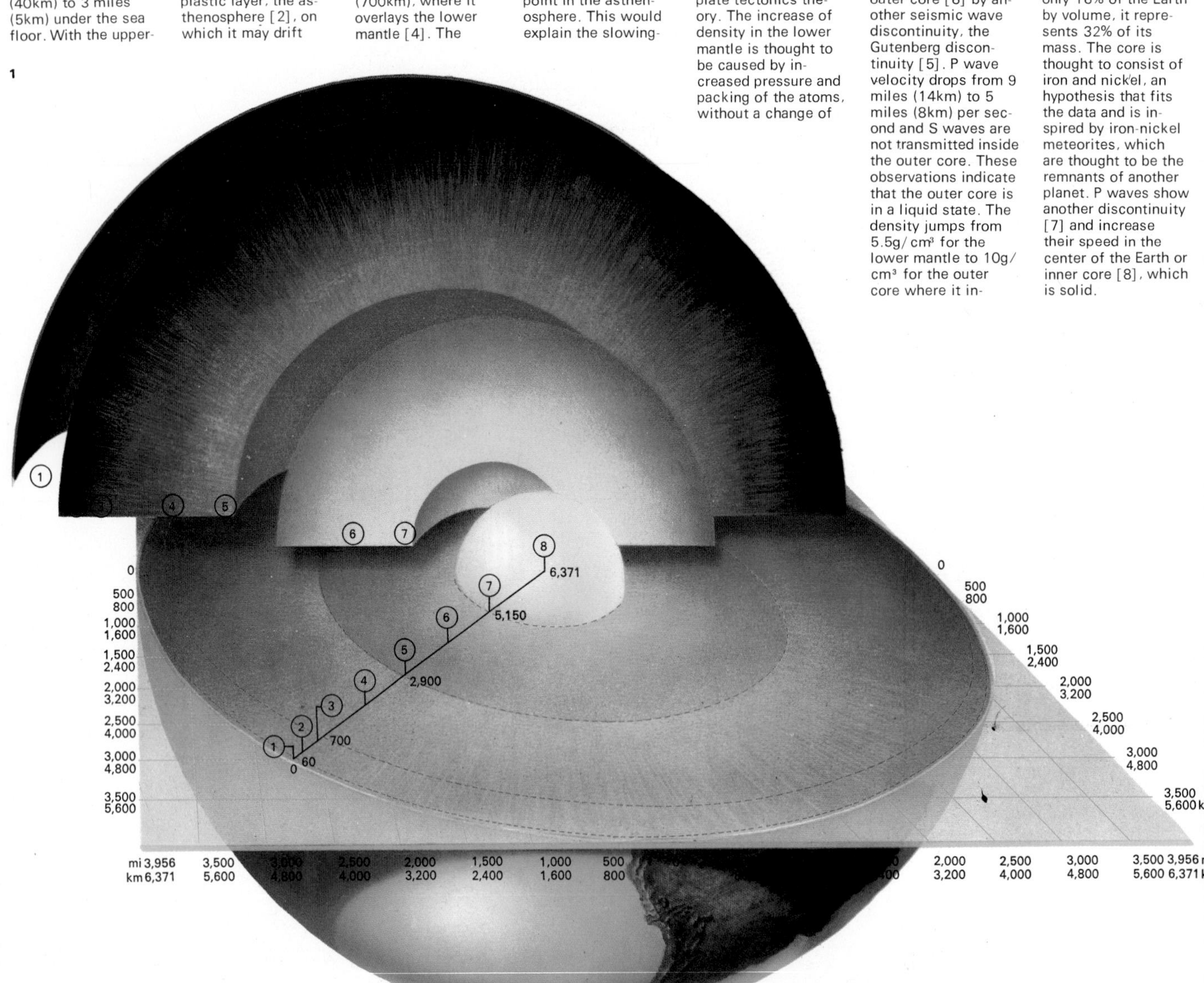

1
4
5
6
7
8
0
60
700
2,900
5,150
6,371
500 800
1,000 1,600
1,500 2,400
2,000 3,200
2,500 4,000
3,000 4,800
3,500 5,600
mi 3,956 km 6,371

als of higher density, the latter formed as a result of the pressure of the rocks above.

Between the lower mantle and the core lies a further discontinuity at a depth of 1,800 miles (2,900km), at which the density increases from 5.5 to 10.0g/cm^3. This is the Gutenberg discontinuity, discovered in 1914. The core itself is divided at a depth of 3,200 miles (5,150km) into an outer and an inner zone thought to be composed of iron-nickel alloy. The outer zone is believed to be liquid because it stops S waves (shearing earthquake waves), while the inner zone is believed to be solid because P (compressional) waves travel slightly faster there. The density changes from 12.3 to about 13.3g/cm^3 at the boundary of outer and inner cores and increases to about 13.6g/cm^3 at the center of the Earth, 3,956 miles (6,371km) down.

Meteorites reaching the Earth's surface provide clues to its composition. Such meteorites are made either of stone or are made predominantly of iron. The proportion of stony to iron meteorites is more or less equal to the proportion of the mass of the mantle to the core of the Earth. The inference to be drawn is that meteorites may represent the remains of another planet whose structure was similar to Earth's [1].

Heat behavior

The amount of heat reaching the surface from within the Earth can be represented on a heat flow profile [2]. From the Earth's surface, the temperature rises to about 710°F (375°C), increasing in the upper mantle to 1,480°F (800°C) at 32 miles (50km) and 3,300°F (1,800°C) at 625 miles (1,000km). The estimated temperature for the lower mantle is 5,430°F (3000°C) at a depth of 1,250 miles (2,000km) and 6,330°F (3,500°C) at the mantle-core boundary—a depth of 1,800 miles (2,900km). The temperature at the center of the Earth is probably about 7,230°F (4,000°C). In the solid layers heat is probably transferred to the surface by conduction; in the liquid layers by convection. Convection in the outer core is believed to be responsible for the Earth's magnetic field and convection within the mantle for the processes of plate tectonics.

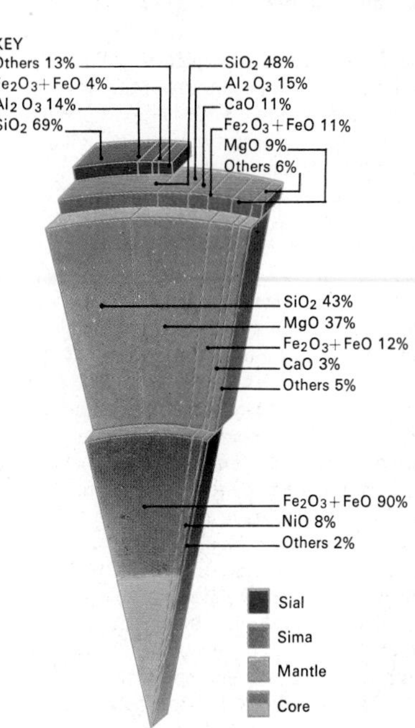

KEY
Others 13%
Fe_2O_3+ FeO 4%
Al_2O_3 14%
SiO_2 69%
SiO_2 48%
Al_2O_3 15%
CaO 11%
Fe_2O_3+FeO 11%
MgO 9%
Others 6%
SiO_2 43%
MgO 37%
Fe_2O_3+FeO 12%
CaO 3%
Others 5%
Fe_2O_3+FeO 90%
NiO 8%
Others 2%
Sial
Sima
Mantle
Core

The Earth is composed of three main layers—the crust, mantle, and core. The crust is subdivided into continental and oceanic material. The upper continental crust is essentially granite, rich in silicon and aluminum (*si*licon and *al*uminum = *sial*). The oceanic crust is essentially basalt, rich in silicon and magnesium (*si*licon and *ma*gnesium = *sima*); sima also underlies continental sial. The sial continents, being of a lighter material than the sima, tend to float upon it like icebergs in the sea. The mantle consists of rock, rich in magnesium and iron silicates; and the dense core probably consists mainly of iron and nickel oxides, partially molten.

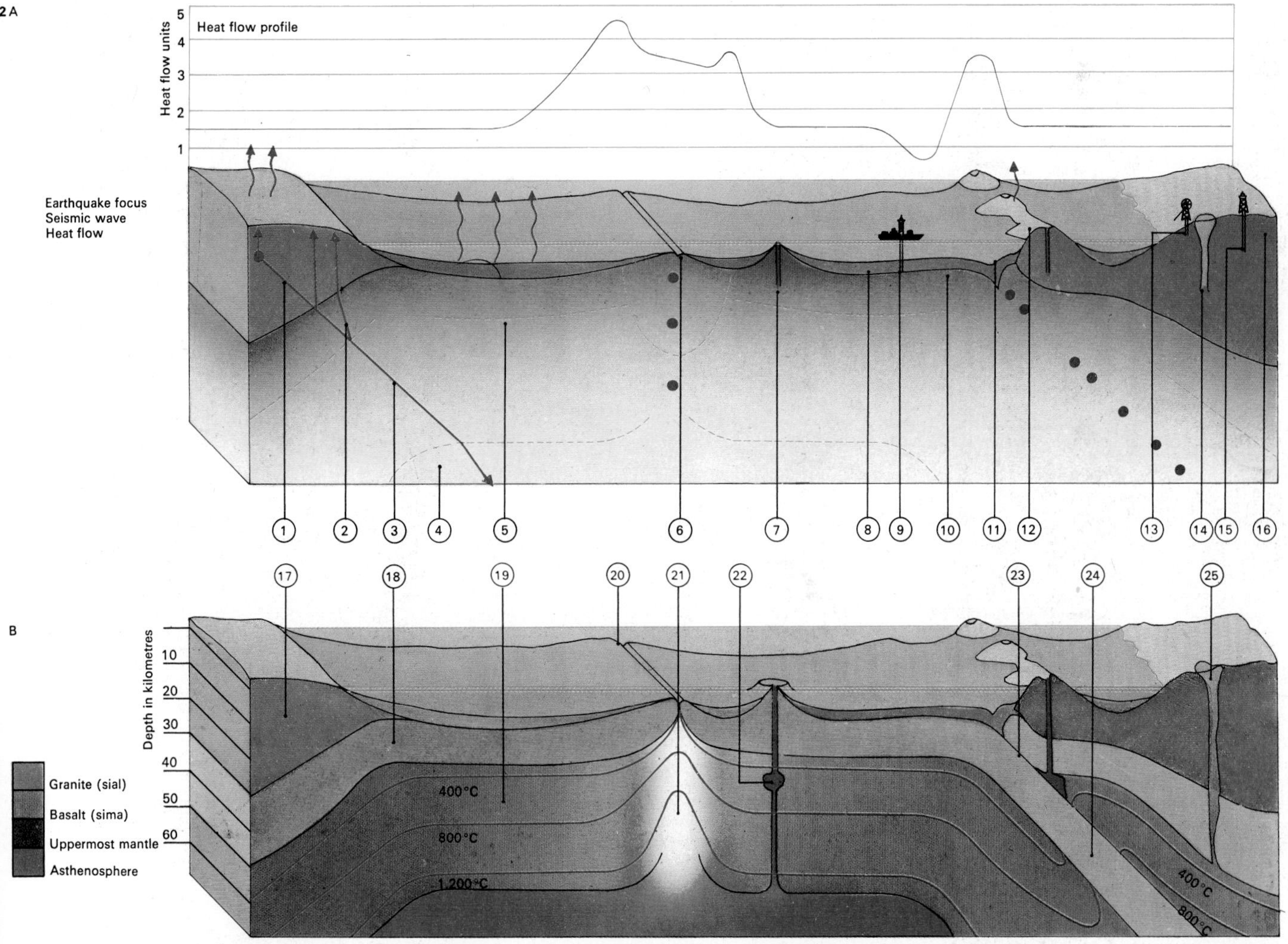

2 A

Heat flow profile

Heat flow units 1 2 3 4 5

Earthquake focus
Seismic wave
Heat flow

1 2 3 4 5 6 7 8 9 10 11 12 13 14 15 16

17 18 19 20 21 22 23 24 25

B

Depth in kilometres 10 20 30 40 50 60

400°C
800°C
1,200°C

Granite (sial)
Basalt (sima)
Uppermost mantle
Asthenosphere

2 The mantle and crust are studied by various means [A]. Heat flow from the Earth's interior is high over volcanic areas [7], island arcs, [12] and along ocean ridges [6], and low along ocean trenches [11]. The zone of direct observation reaches its limits at [9] the deepest marine drill-hole, 4,265ft (1,300m) below the sea bottom, at [13] the deepest mine, 12,600ft (3,840m), and [15] the deepest land borehole, 31,441 ft (9,583m). Earthquake foci occur in particular planes. Earthquake shocks generate seismic waves that travel faster the deeper they go through the crust [1,2] Beyond the Mohorovičić discontinuity [5] lies the mantle, where the seismic waves enter a high-velocity zone [3], later slowing down in the underlying low-velocity zone [4]. Marine sediments [8] accumulate on the ocean floor above the oceanic crust [10]. The continental crust [16] lies above the latter. At [14] is a peridotite massif, rich in iron and magnesium, intruded from the Earth's interior. All these data are interpreted in [B]. The sea-floor crust [18] is composed of basalt, and the continental one [17] of granite overlying the basaltic layer. The mantle [19] is made of peridotite. High heat flow and low-intensity seismic waves are associated with oceanic ridges [20], up which magma ascends from the mantle [21]. Sometimes magma is temporarily stored in a magma chamber [22] before eruption. At [24] the cold lithospheric plate is subducted along the Benioff shear zone [23], diving into the mantle. Peridotitic intrusions [25] have risen through deep crustal cracks to the Earth's surface.

The Earth as a magnet

The Earth has a strong magnetic field [Key]. A bar magnet suspended by a thread eventually comes to rest with one end pointing toward the Earth's north magnetic pole, the other toward the south magnetic pole. It behaves as though another bar magnet, or large coil of wire with electricity flowing through it, had been brought near.

Origin of the Earth's magnetic field

As the Earth spins on its axis the fluid layer of the outer core allows the mantle and solid crust to rotate relatively faster than the inner core. As a result, electrons in the core move relative to those in the mantle and crust. It is this electron movement that constitutes a natural generator and creates a magnetic field, similar to that of an electric coil [1].

The magnetic axis of the Earth is inclined slightly to the Earth's geographical axis [Key] by about 11 degrees, and the magnetic poles do not coincide with the geographic north and south poles. The Earth's magnetic axis is continually changing its angle in relation to the geographic axis, but over tens of thousands of years an average relative position is established.

A compass needle points to a position some distance away from the geographical north and south poles. The difference, known as the declination [3], varies from one geographical location to the next. Small-scale variations in the Earth's magnetism are probably caused by minor eddies in the outer core at the junction between the core and the mantle. Large bodies of magnetized rock and ore in the crust can have a similar effect.

The Earth's magnetic field is distorted by electrically charged particles from the Sun [5]. These particles flow in the upper atmosphere and create small variations of the magnetic field at ground level. Some variations are regular—such as the diurnal (night and day) variation—and some are occasional, such as magnetic storms, some of which are related to Sun spot eruptions.

The Earth's magnetic field in ancient times

The study of the magnetic field of the geological past is called paleomagnetism. It relies on the fact that rocks may pick up a permanent magnetization when they are formed, or when they remelt and cool at some later date. When rocks are heated they lose their magnetization, as an ordinary bar magnet does when heated. Rocks are remagnetized by the Earth's field when they cool. This natural remnent magnetization, as it is called, lies parallel to the lines of the Earth's magnetic field at the time of rock formation. Rocks magnetized in this way therefore carry a permanent record of past fields, and can thus be used to study the history of the Earth's magnetic field.

There are several ways in which magnetic "clues" to the Earth's history can be deposited in the rocks. The technique of paleomagnetic investigation is to drill out a cylinder (core) of rock and then measure its natural remnent magnetism. This gives the paleomagnetic coordinates of the specimen, which allows its original position to be plotted. Magnetic coordinates, expressed in magnetic latitudes [4], are similar to geographical latitudes (but the pole considered is the magnetic pole instead of the rotation

CONNECTIONS

Read first
166 Anatomy of the Earth

See also
170 Global tectonics
172 Continents adrift
1534 Magnets and magnetism
1540 Transformers, motors and generators

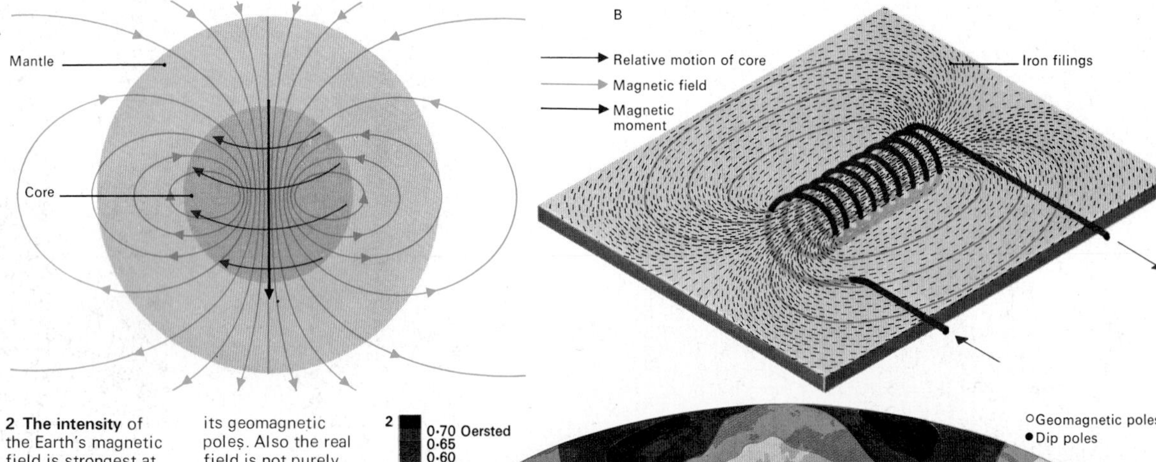

1
A
Mantle
Core
B
Relative motion of core
Magnetic field
Magnetic moment
Iron filings

1 The magnetic field originating inside the Earth makes up about 90 percent of the field observed at ground level. The remainder is caused by currents of charged particles coming from the Sun and by the magnetism of rocks in the crust. The difference in rotation speed between the liquid outer core and the mantle creates a generator effect [A], which produces a field similar to that of a coil [B]. In reality the situation is more complex, for it involves interaction between two types of magnetic fields, and small variations may change the polarity of the Earth's field. Irregularities in the magnetic field at the Earth's surface are caused by minor eddies of the core liquid. Their displacement in time results in long-term variations of the geomagnetic field, causing gradual changes of direction for magnetic north in given locations.

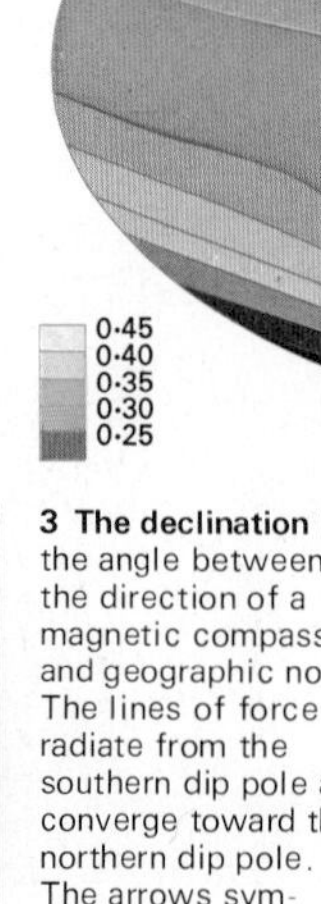

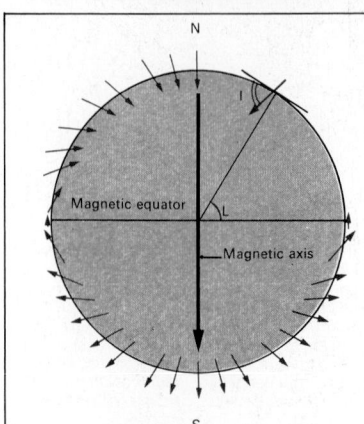

2
0·70 Oersted
0·65
0·60
0·55
0·50
0·45
0·45
0·40
0·35
0·30
0·25
○Geomagnetic poles
●Dip poles

2 The intensity of the Earth's magnetic field is strongest at the poles and weakest in the equatorial regions. If the field were purely that of a bar magnet in the center of the earth and parallel to the spin axis, the lines of equal intensity would follow the lines of latitude and the magnetic poles would coincide with the geographic poles. In reality the "bar magnet" field is inclined at about 11° to the spin axis and so are its geomagnetic poles. Also the real field is not purely that of a bar magnet. The "dip poles," where the field direction is vertical (downward at the north dip pole and upward at the south dip pole), are themselves offset in respect to the geomagnetic poles—each by a different amount so that the S dip pole is not exactly opposite the N dip pole. The poles and the configuration of the field change slowly with time.

3

3 The declination is the angle between the direction of a magnetic compass and geographic north. The lines of force radiate from the southern dip pole and converge toward the northern dip pole. The arrows symbolize the direction of the magnetic north in 1955. Declination exists because the Earth's field is not exactly like that of a bar magnet lined up along the axis of the Earth. Account of this significant declination must be taken in navigation.

4
N
I
Magnetic equator
L
Magnetic axis
S

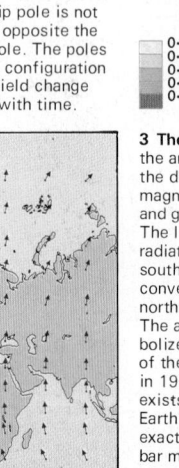

4 The dip, or inclination [1], of the magnetic field at the surface of the Earth is related to the magnetic latitude [L], measured relative to the magnetic axis. Assuming that the Earth's field averages out like a bar magnet aligned along the geographical axis, this allows the calculation of ancient latitudes of a land using paleomagnetic data. The inclination is measured with a special compass with a horizontal pivot but does not pose a navigation problem.

pole). Paleomagnetic coordinates are respective to the apparent magnetic pole at the time the rock was magnetized. Evidence from this type of work reveals that the magnetic poles were not always in the position that they now occupy and have "wandered" over the years.

Polar wandering differs from continent to continent. But the poles for a specific time in geological history can be aligned through the various continents by envisaging the continents in different positions from those they now occupy. It is in this way that the progress of continental drift can be plotted. The results of this technique agree fairly well with other drift indicators such as sea-floor spreading and evidence of ancient climates shown by rocks and their fossils.

Some rocks formed over short time intervals show fossil magnetic polarities 180 degrees apart. This cannot be explained by a 180-degrees rotation of a continent because there was not enough time for that. Thus the Earth's field must have undergone a switching of its magnetic polarity, as when the direction of the current in a coil is reversed [6]. This switching is known as a "reversal." Reversals mark the boundaries of periods varying in length throughout geological time when the magnetic field was of constant polarity. The dating of reversals (by studying the decay of radioactive isotopes in the rocks) provides the geologist with a paleomagnetic time scale. This can, in turn, be used to date other rocks by analyzing their remanent magnetization. It was the comparison of this paleomagnetic time scale with the "magnetic anomalies" on the sea floor that supported the sea-floor spreading hypothesis.

Magnetic and electrical prospecting

Many ore bodies and rocks rich in magnetic minerals have a strong local magnetic field [7]. This is utilized by prospectors using sensitive instruments to detect minerals of economic value. Another method utilizes natural electrical currents that are set up between the surface and an ore body by percolating ground water. Its interaction with the magnetic field can be measured and used to locate useful deposits.

KEY

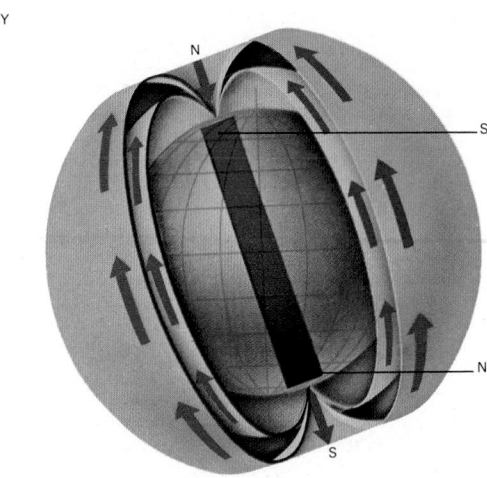

The Earth's magnetic field is like that of a giant natural bar magnet placed inside the Earth with its magnetic axis inclined at a small angle to the geographical axis. The poles of a compass needle are attracted by the magnetic poles of the Earth and swing so that one end points to the north magnetic pole and the other to the south.

5

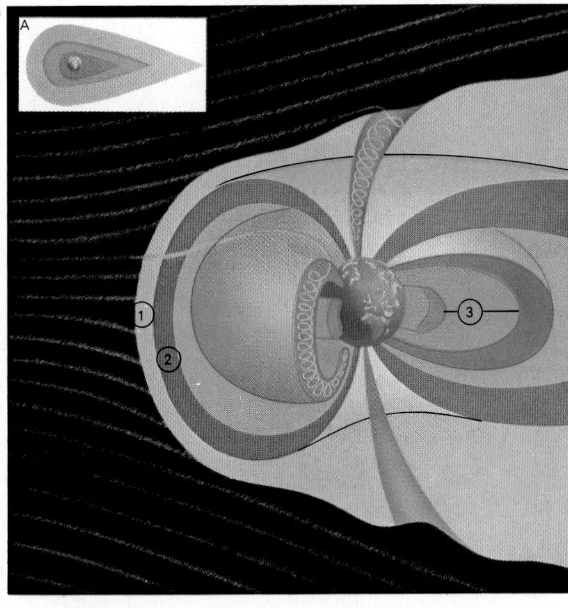

A
1
2
3

5 The magnetosphere is the region in which the Earth's magnetic field can be detected. It would be symmetrical were it not for electrically charged particles streaming from the Sun [A], which distort it to a teardrop shape. The particles meet the Earth's magnetic field at the shock front [1]. Behind this is a region of turbulence and inside the turbulent region is the magnetopause [2], the boundary of the magnetic field. The Van Allen belts [3] are two zones of high radiation in the magnetopause. The inner belt consists of trapped high-energy particles produced by cosmic rays and the outer belt of solar electrons.

6

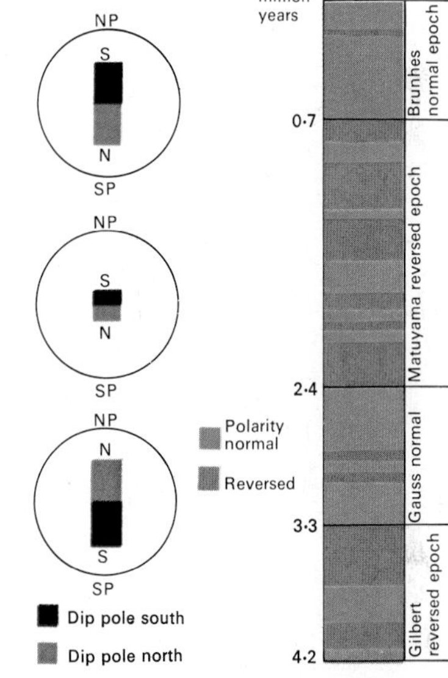

A
NP
S
N
SP
NP
S
N
SP
NP
N
S
SP
Dip pole south
Dip pole north
B
million years
0·7
2·4
3·3
4·2
Brunhes normal epoch
Matuyama reversed epoch
Gauss normal
Gilbert reversed epoch
Polarity normal
Reversed

6 Field reversals are the changes of polarity (north becoming south and vice versa) that occurred many times during geological history. The polarity of the Earth's magnetic field does not flip over; its magnetic strength decreases to zero then slowly increases in the opposite direction [A]. Rocks "fossilize" the magnetic field when they are formed. If a sufficient number of rocks of different ages are dated, and their polarity measured, a world-wide magnetic time scale featured here [B] shows the significant changes in magnetic polarity over the last 4.2 million years.

7

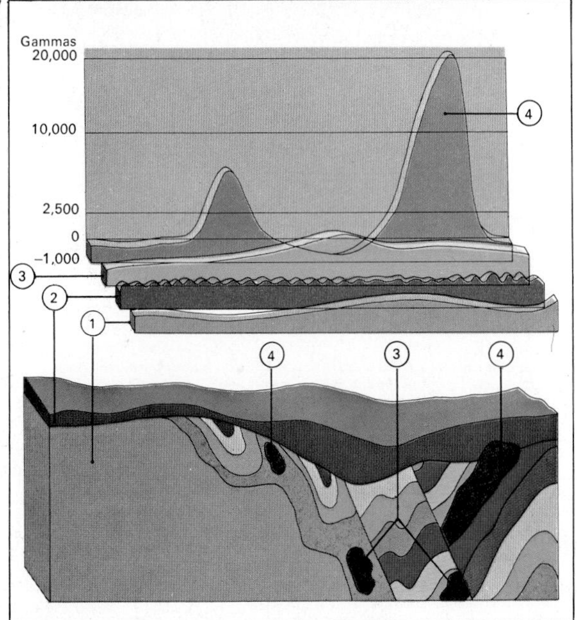

Gammas
20,000
10,000
2,500
0
−1,000
4
3
2
1
4
3
4

7 In mineral prospecting magnetometers can be used to detect variations in the Earth's magnetic field due to ores: [1] regional magnetism of the country rocks; [2] background magnetism due to topsoils; [3] effects of deep-seated ore bodies; [4] effects from near surface ores.

8

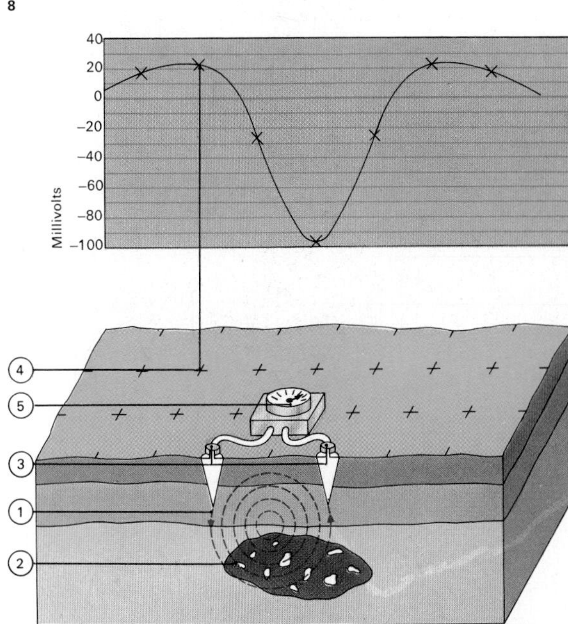

40
20
0
−20
−40
−60
−80
−100
Millivolts
4
5
3
1
2

8 Electrical prospecting for minerals makes use of natural ground currents [1] related to the magnetic field and influenced by ore bodies [2]. Two electrodes [3], placed in the ground at staked points [4], are connected to a millivoltmeter [5] and the voltages at the points are measured. Variations may indicate the presence of mineral ores.

Global tectonics

The theory of plate tectonics was advanced in the late 1960s and has had a revolutionary effect on the earth sciences. It is a unifying theory, offering an explanation of many of the Earth's varied structural and geophysical phenomena from mountain building to earthquakes and continental drift.

Crustal plates

The theory envisages the crust of the Earth together with the upper part of the mantle, which form the lithosphere, as consisting of rigid slabs, or plates, that are continuously moving their position in relation to each other [1]. Below the lithosphere is the asthenosphere, which is thought to be plastic.

The plates are bounded by oceanic ridges, trenches, and transform faults [1]. Oceanic ridges occur where two plates are moving apart leaving a gap that is continuously filled by magma (molten rock) rising from the asthenosphere. As the magma cools, new crust is created and becomes part of the moving plates. This is the phenomenon of sea-floor spreading. Spreading rates, though slow, are not negligible. The Atlantic is opening up by 0.75in (2cm) a year. The fastest rate is found at the East Pacific Rise, which creates 4in (10cm) of new crust every year—that is 620 miles (1,000km) in ten million years.

Trenches are formed where plates converge. One of the plates slides steeply under the other [6] and enters the mantle. Thus trenches are areas where plate edges are destroyed. Since the volume of the Earth does not change, the amount of crust created at the ridges is balanced by that destroyed at the trenches.

The leading edges of the colliding plates may be oceanic crust, such as in the Tonga-Kermadec trench north of New Zealand; or one may be oceanic (and will be the sinking plate) while the other is continental, such as at the Peru-Chile trench; or both plates may be continental, such as those of northern India and Tibet. In the last two instances the thick sedimentary covers are crumpled and injected with material melted by the heat generated by the collision, and mountains such as the Andes and the Himalayas are created [7].

Transform faults form where two plates slide past one another [1, 8]. They offset oceanic ridges and their continuation scars can be followed in places for thousands of miles [5]. They sometimes slice through continents, as does the famous San Andreas fault, which runs from the Gulf of California through San Francisco.

The cause of plate movements

As early as 1927 British geologist Arthur Holmes suggested that convection currents in the mantle could explain the continental drift theory. Convection currents are generated by heat differences—they can be observed in a pan of water placed over a fire. Global tectonics theory proposes that convection currents exist in the asthenosphere and perhaps in the lower mantle. They form convection cells that rise under ridges and descend under trenches. This theory is supported by measurements of heat radiated from the Earth which show high values along ridges and low values along trenches.

The amazing world pattern of ridges, trenches, and faults was discovered in the

CONNECTIONS

See also
172 Continents adrift
168 The Earth as a magnet
174 Earthquakes
176 Volcanoes
252 Life and death of mountains

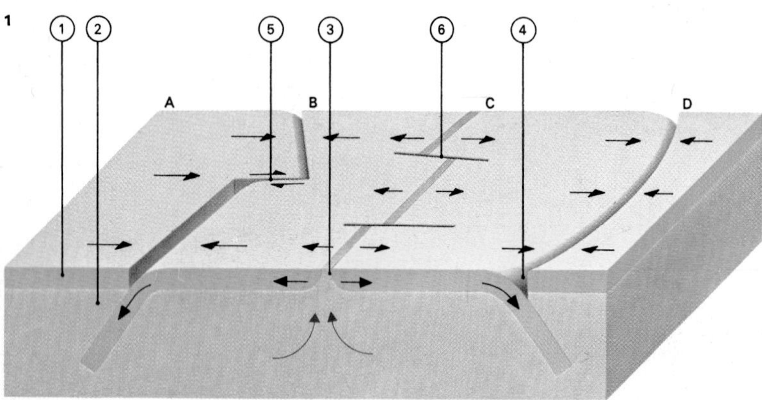

1
A
B
C
D

1 The plate tectonics theory envisages the Earth's lithosphere [1] as a series of rigid, but mobile, slabs called plates [A, B, C, D]. The lithosphere floats on a plastic layer called the asthenosphere [2]. There are three types of boundaries possible. At the oceanic ridges [3], upwelling of mantle material occurs and new sea floor is formed. A trench [4] is formed where one plate of oceanic crust slides beneath the other, which may be oceanic or continental. The third type of boundary is where two plates slide past one another, creating a transform fault [5,6]. Transform faults link two segments of the same ridge [6], two trenches [5], or a ridge to a trench. Plates move from ridges and travel like conveyor belts toward trenches, where they sink into the asthenosphere.

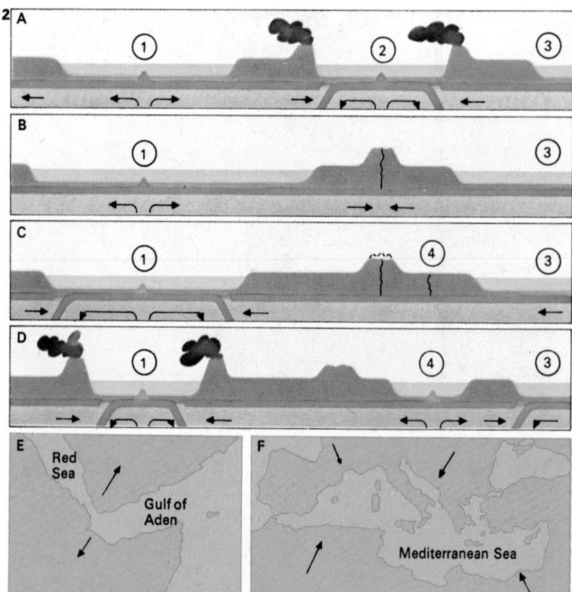

2
A
B
C
D
E
Red Sea
Gulf of Aden
F
Mediterranean Sea

2 The birth and death of oceans is a continuous process. [A] Ocean 1 is growing by sea-floor spreading from a mid-ocean ridge while Ocean 2 is closing because of the continents forcing the ocean floor down at the trenches. Ocean 3 is young and growing. In [B] Ocean 1 has reached maturity, Ocean 3 is still growing and Ocean 2 has disappeared with the joining of the continental masses. In [C] Oceans 1 and 3 are declining while a new crack appears at 4. [D] shows Ocean 1 still declining and Ocean 4 growing. [E] shows widening of the Red Sea Gulf of Aden while [F] indicates that the Mediterranean has been shrinking.

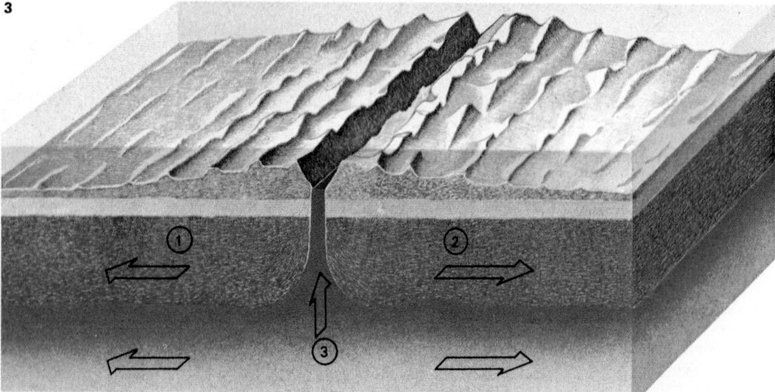

3

3 Oceanic ridges are found where two plates [1,2] are moving away from each other. Magma from the mantle [3] continuously wells up from below. As the magma cools, it becomes part of the plates and it is in turn injected by fresh magna. The ridges are thus the newest part of the Earth's crust, while the oldest oceanic crust is found where it plunges into the trenches. The dating of cores from the drilling ship *Glomar Challenger* supports the theory.

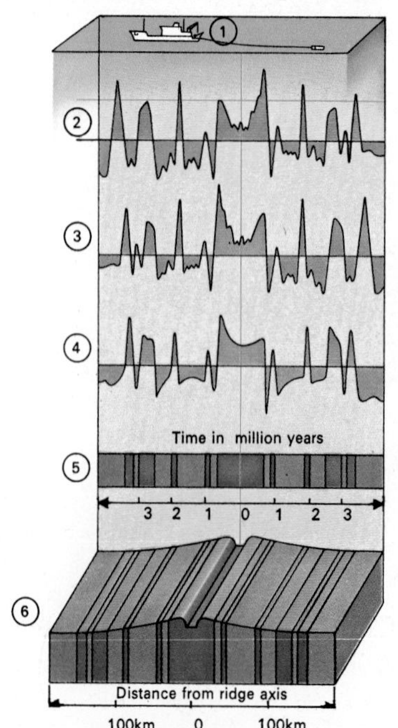

4
Time in million years
3 2 1 0 1 2 3
Distance from ridge axis
100km 0 100km

4 A magnetic survey from a research ship [1] sailing back and forth over a mid-oceanic ridge gives readings [2,3,4] that indicate that the magnetism of the rocks points alternately north and south in a series of bands parallel to the ridge [6]. The pattern of bands is identical at each side of the axis and correponds to the pattern of reversals in the Earth's magnetic field over the last few million years [5]. The rocks carry a record of the Earth's magnetic field.

1940s and 1950s. Their distribution was seen to fit that of earthquakes and volcanoes. In 1962 US geologist Harry Hess suggested that these features, as well as continental drift, could be explained by sea-floor spreading, but could not prove his point. Mysterious zebra patterns of magnetic anomalies had also been mapped on the ocean floor.

The proof of a theory

In 1963 two Cambridge University graduate students, Frederick Vine and Drummond Matthews, explained these magnetic anomalies in a way that strongly supported sea-floor spreading. They suggested that material welling up from the mantle along a ridge acquires a remnant magnetization as it cools that is parallel to the then prevailing magnetic field of the earth. The earth's magnetic field is known to have reversed its polarity many times during geological history. Assuming that the newly forming crust at oceanic ridges picked up the prevailing polarity signal of the earth's magnetic field, the result over a long period of time would be strips of ocean floor that were alternatively normally and reversely magnetized. The correspondence between the symmetrical zebra patterns on the ocean floor and the known history of the Earth's magnetic field is remarkable [4].

By 1966 the hypothesis of sea-floor spreading had been further established by independent oceanographic data involving microfossils, sediment thickness (thicker on older crust where sediments had more time to accumulate), measures of heat flow from the Earth's interior, and paleomagnetic and seismological studies. The expression "global tectonics" came into use in 1968, to explain the links between spreading ridges, transform faults, sinking trenches, drifting continents, and mountain building.

Also in 1968 the United States commissioned the deep-sea drilling ship *Glomar Challenger* [Key] for a major program of oceanographic exploration. Drilled cores have been collected from all the oceans and seas and the sea floor has been directly dated, proving the validity of the global tectonics theory.

KEY

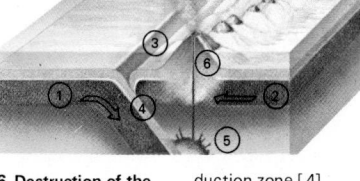

The Glomar Challenger is a US research vessel built for the Deep Sea Drilling Project (DSDP). The vessel is equipped to drill and retrieve cores from the floors of the deep oceans.

5

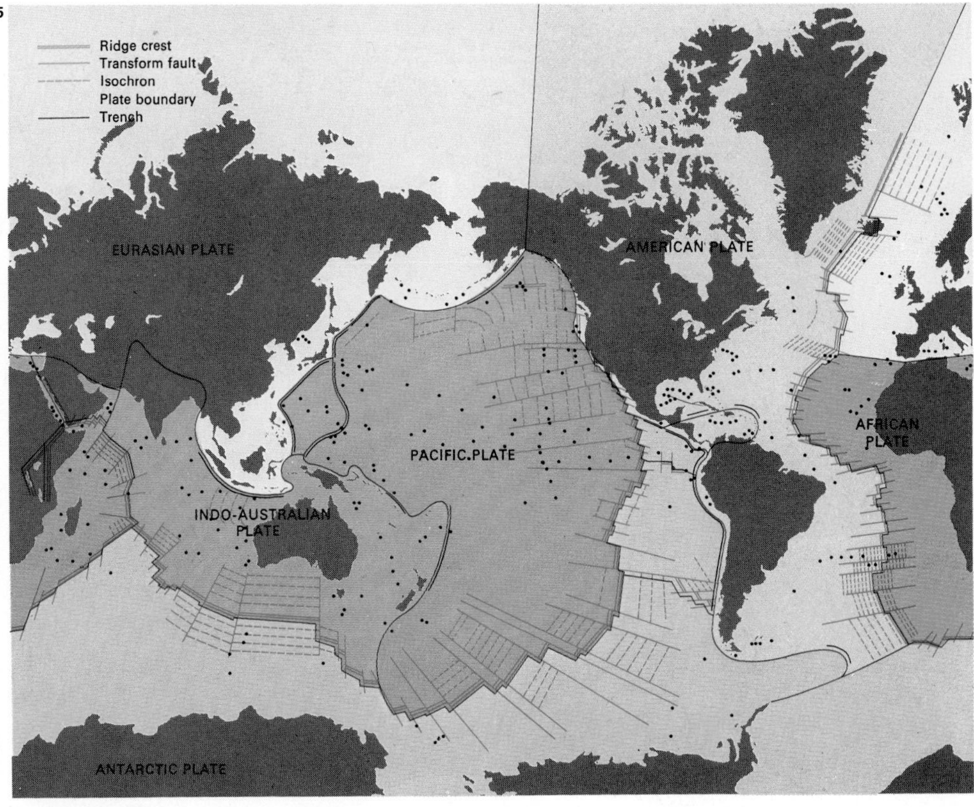
Ridge crest
Transform fault
Isochron
Plate boundary
Trench
EURASIAN PLATE
AMERICAN PLATE
AFRICAN PLATE
PACIFIC PLATE
INDO-AUSTRALIAN PLATE
ANTARCTIC PLATE

5 The Earth's outer shell is formed of six major mobile plates (the American, Eurasian, African, Indo-Australian, Pacific, and Antarctic plates) separated by ridges, transform faults, and trenches. These plates contain some smaller plates such as the Arabian and West Indian plates that "absorb" the geometrical discrepancies between the major plates by creating or destroying compensating amounts of crust. The dotted lines parallel to the ridges are lines of equal age (isochrons) based on magnetic anomalies. The lines closest to the ridges are 10 million years old; each successive line is 10 million years older than its immediate neighbor toward the ridge. Fast rates of spreading are shown by widely spaced isochrons. The age of the crust has been directly verified at most of the DSDP drilling sites [black dots]. The African plate has no trenches on its border; it is therefore growing in area. Its east-west growth is being compensated for by crust disappearing in the Tonga-Kermadec and Peru-Chile trenches, two and three plates away. Similarly the Antarctic plate is growing northward, the compensation taking place in the Indonesian, North Pacific, and Middle America trenches. Despite spreading along one of their margins, the Pacific and Indo-Australian plates are shrinking overall.

6

7
3
6
1
4
2
5

6 Destruction of the oceanic crust takes place where one plate [1] sinks beneath the other [2], forming a trench [3], while the dipping plane forms the subduction zone [4]. Friction along this zone creates localized melting [5] and lava rises to the surface creating volcanoes [6] forming islands arcs [7].

7

7 Collision zones are where two plates each carrying a continental mass meet. When, in this zone, one of the plates is forced beneath the other the buoyant continental material is thrust upward in a series of high overthrusts and folds, producing great mountain ranges. The Himalayas are the result of such forces.

8

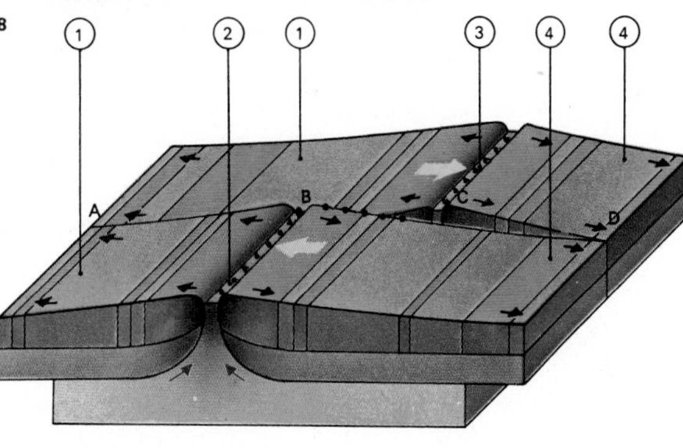
1
2
1
3
4
4
A
B
C
D

8 Transform faults separate two crustal plates [1,4] where they move apart from one another. A transform fault links two segments of a ridge [2,3] and the ridge offset gives an apparent motion [blue arrows] opposite to the real movement [black]. The transform fault is active only between the ridge crests [BC] where opposite crustal spreadings occur; it is only a dead scar along [AB] and [CD] where both sides move together at the same rate.

Continents adrift

The idea that the continents were once joined together is not a new one: it was held by Francis Bacon in 1620 and in 1658 R. P. Placet published a book in French whose title, in translation, means "the corruption of the great and little world, where it is shown that before the deluge, America was not separated from the other parts of the world." The first map showing the fit of the continents was published in 1858 by A. Snider-Pelligrini who based his theory on the similarity of the fossil plants that had been found in Europe and North America.

Alfred Wegener's hypothesis

The man most closely associated with the theory of continental drift is Alfred Wegener (1880–1930) [2], a German meteorologist. An American, F. B. Taylor, had independently put forward the same ideas a few years before Wegener's first lectures on the subject in 1912. Like others before him, Wegener had been attracted to the idea of drifting continents because of the appearance of the land masses on the world map. He brought geological, geodetic, geophysical, paleontological, and paleoclimatic evidence into his discussions.

It was geologists in the Southern Hemisphere who collected evidence that strongly supported Wegener's own theories. Glaciation during Permo-Carboniferous times was more intense and widespread than that of the more recent Pleistocene ice age. Geological fieldwork revealed evidence of it in South America, Africa, Australia, India, Antarctica, and Madagascar [4]. Geologists examining deposits of till (sediment carried and deposited by a glacier) and fossil plants were able to correlate them between the continents. If these land masses had always been fixed in their present positions, it would mean that the ice stretched from the polar regions to the Equator—clearly a preposterous idea. Joining the areas together not only reconciles the geological facts but also provides evidence of the land mass wandering over the South Pole. This, in turn, allows for an explanation of the other known climatic belts of the world during this period: for example, tropical conditions experienced in northern Europe during the Carboniferous period.

Corresponding structures and fossils

Work in India and in Australia has proved the existence of links between these continents; for example, the basins of Permian age in northwest Australia can be correlated with those of India, and the structural features of eastern Australia can be matched with those of Antarctica.

The close links between the geology of West Africa and Brazil provide further proof of their former contact. There is a clear boundary between the 2 billion-year-old rocks of West Africa and the much younger geological province (about 350 million years old) to the east. The boundary between these two is near Accra in Ghana and it heads out into the Atlantic Ocean in a southwesterly direction. A geological expedition was mounted to seek the continuation of this boundary in Brazil; it was found, exactly as predicted, at São Luis.

The drawing together of the now widely separated northern lands (North America,

CONNECTIONS

Read first
276 Earth's time scale

See also
168 The Earth as a magr
170 Global tectonics
264 Ice caps and ice age
578 Regions of the Earth zoogeography

1 A
135 million years ago

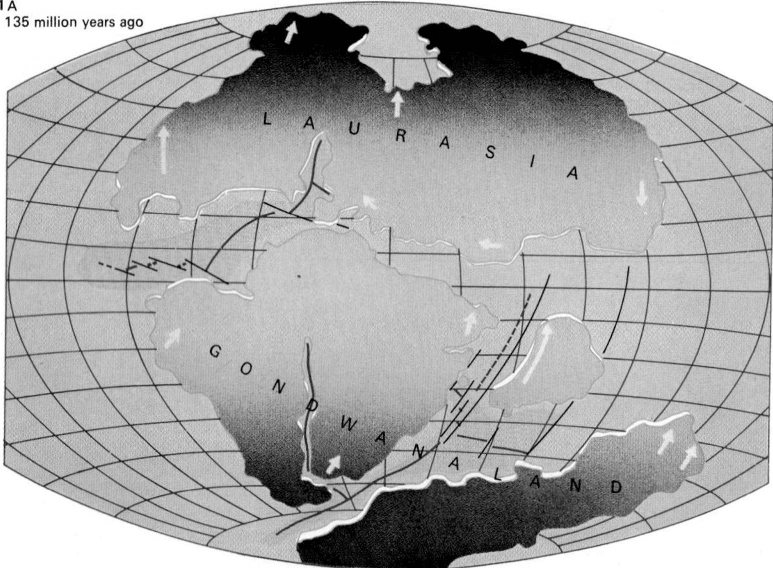
L A U R A S I A
G O N D W A N A L A N D

B
65 million years ago

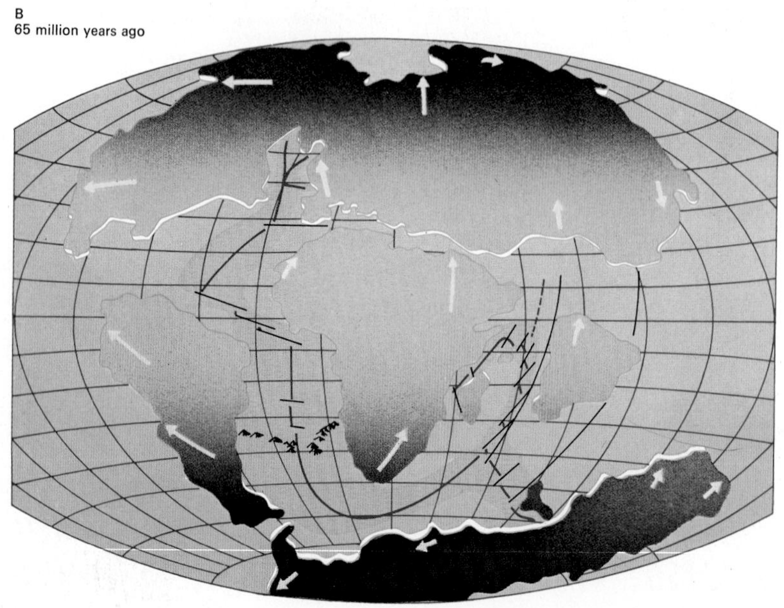

1 A map of Pangaea cannot be accurately constructed. The most suitable fit of the land masses is obtained by matching points midway down the continental slope, at a depth of about 6,560ft (2,000m). In reconstructing the appearance of the giant continent, many investigators have used computers. The easiest areas to fit together are Africa and the South American continent. Whereas the fit of the northern lands is possible with a certain degree of accuracy, much remains to be learned of the complex fit of India, Antarctica, and Australia with Africa and South America. The breakup of Pangaea began about 200 million years ago. By the end of the Jurassic period, about 135 million years ago [A], the North Atlantic and Indian Oceans had become firmly established. The Tethys Sea was being diminished by the Asian land mass rotating in counterclockwise direction. South America had begun to move away from Africa. By the end of the Cretaceous, about 65 million years ago [B], the South Atlantic had grown, Madagascar had parted from Africa, and India continued northward. Antarctica was moving away from the central mass, while linked with Australia. The North Atlantic rift forked at the north, thus forming Greenland. North and South America, separated since the Pangaea era, began to drift closer.

2

2 Alfred Wegener was born in 1880. Trained as an astronomer, he became interested in meteorology and geophysics. He lectured on continental drift in 1912 and his first paper on the subject was published later the same year. In 1915, his classic exposition, *The Origin of Continents and Oceans*, appeared in print. He died while leading an expedition over the ice cap of Greenland in 1930.

3

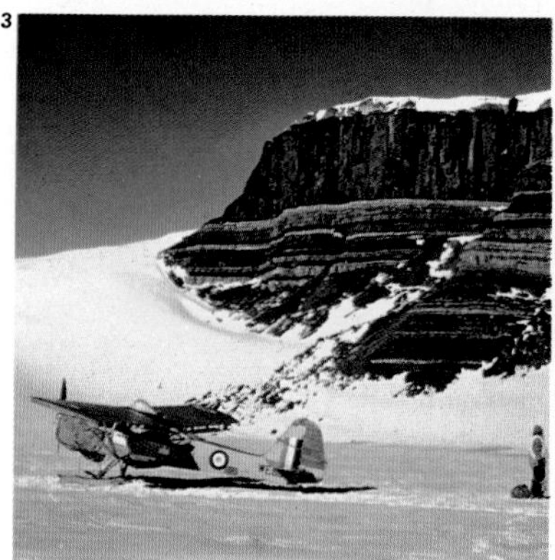

3 Antarctica's tropical past is shown by the existence of coal seams up to 13ft (4m) thick. The study of changes of climate provides evidence confirming continental drift. In the Southern Hemisphere, rocks between 350 million and 180 million years old show marked similarities over now widely separated continents. Plant fossils in coal seams and layering of glacial deposits in one place match those of another, thus providing evidence for the theory.

Europe and Asia) has been a little more difficult, but there now exists overwhelming evidence for their once having formed part of a single continent, Laurasia [1]. Geologists have shown that the now widely separated Norwegian, Caledonian, Appalachian, and East Greenland mountains were formed as a single chain.

Wegener paid considerable attention to the distribution of fossils. When his theory was first put forward, paleontologists were still postulating land bridges to account for the distribution of some plants and animals in the fossil record. In many cases the land bridges would have to have covered an area equal to that of the continents they joined. It was long assumed that the land bridges disappeared by subsidence. The detailed study of the ocean floors in recent years has ruled out this idea. If, however, the idea of Gondwanaland—the old grouping of Africa, South America, Antarctica, India, and Australia—is accepted [4], it becomes much easier to explain the distribution of many animals and plants. For example, remains of the 300 million-year-old reptile *Mesosaurus* have been discovered only in western South Africa and in Brazil. This small reptile would have been incapable of swimming an ocean.

New developments

Recent investigations, especially the study of paleomagnetism (the history of the earth's changing magnetic field [6]), have provided data that not only support continental drift but also locate the positions of the various land masses during past geological time. Perhaps the most important impetus to the theory of continental drift has come from the twin theories of sea-floor spreading and plate tectonics which have been so rapidly developed since the 1960s. One of the weakest points in Wegener's original arguments centered on the tremendous forces necessary to drive the continents apart. These new theories, which have been substantially proven, provide an explanation of the necessary forces, although there is still much to be learned about the break-up of Pangaea, the original single continent [Key].

KEY

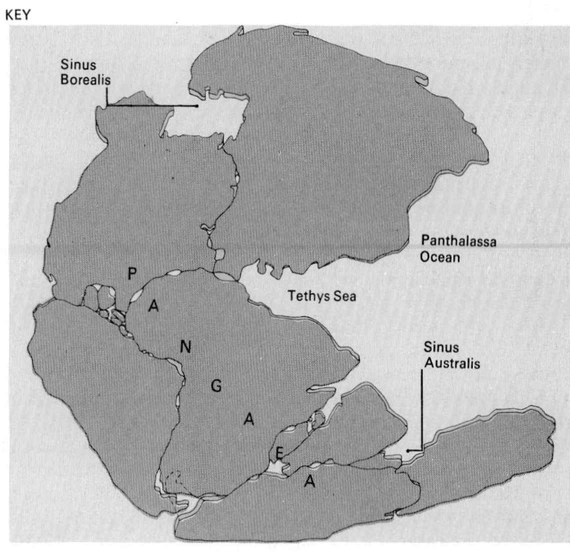

Sinus Borealis
Panthalassa Ocean
P
A
N
G
A
E
A
Tethys Sea
Sinus Australis

The theory of continental drift proposes a period when all the continents formed one land mass, called Pangaea. The initial break-up made a northern mass, Laurasia, and a southern one, Gondwanaland, named after a province in India.

4

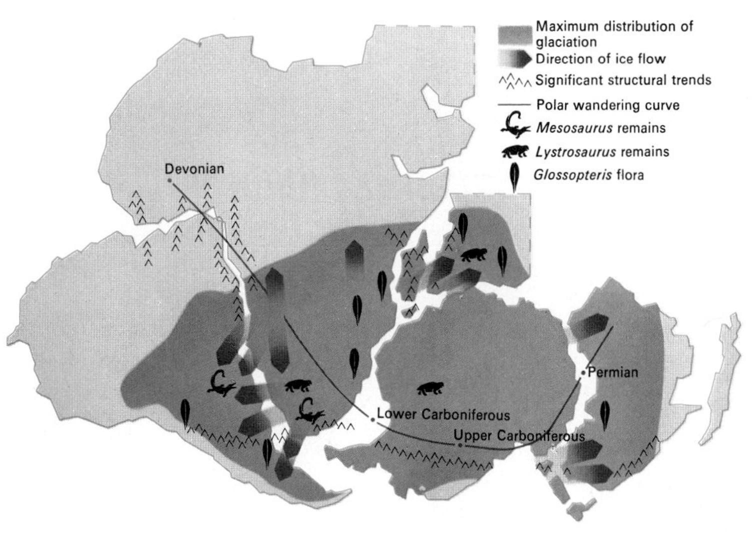

Maximum distribution of glaciation
Direction of ice flow
Significant structural trends
Polar wandering curve
Mesosaurus remains
Lystrosaurus remains
Glossopteris flora
Devonian
Lower Carboniferous
Upper Carboniferous
Permian

4 The existence of Gondwanaland is confirmed in many different ways. Constant directions of iceflow in Permo-Carboniferous glaciations; structural trends traced and matched from continent to continent; and fossil distribution form part of the evidence. The distribution of *Mesosaurus*, *Lystrosaurus*, and the fossil fern *Glossopteris* suggest the presence of a single land mass in Permian times. Paleomagnetic techniques—which locate the magnetic pole of any stage in the past—give consistent results on each continent only when the continents are placed in the estimated configuration that represents Gondwanaland.

5

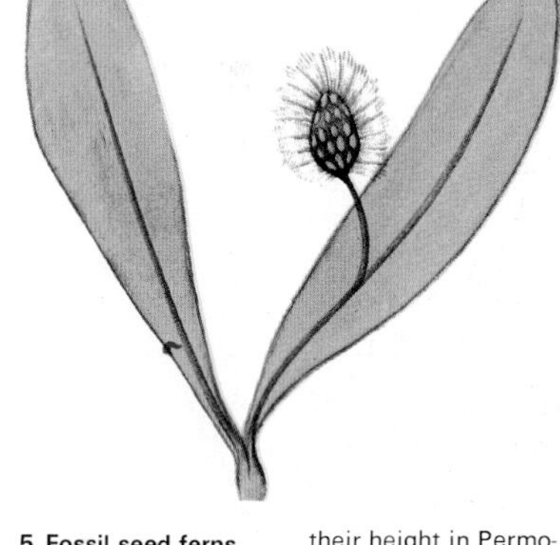

5 Fossil seed ferns (especially the tonguelike *Glossopteris* and *Ganganopteris*) in rocks of the Gondwana series in the southern continents lend support for continental drift theory. They reached their height in Permo-Carboniferous times and the complex nature of their species distribution can best be explained if the now widely separated locations had been in one land mass.

6

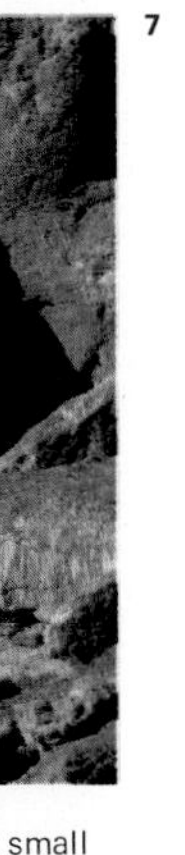

6 Paleomagnetism—the study of the magnetization of rocks—has developed since the 1950s into a powerful tool for continental drift studies. Rocks record the earth's magnetic field at the time of their formation. Portable drills cut small cylindrical rock cores which are oriented relative to the present north and in a vertical position. In the laboratory a magnetometer determines their original north direction and their original latitude for comparison.

7 50 million years ahead

7 The continents are still drifting, and there is no reason to expect them to stop. The map shows how the world may look 50 million years from now if drift is maintained as predicted. The most striking change in the "new world" is the area of new land in the Caribbean, the splitting away from North America of Baja, California and the San Andreas fault line, the northward drift of Africa almost eliminating the Mediterranean, and the breaking away of that part of the African continent east of the present-day rift valley. Australia has continued its journey northward, but Antarctica remains in its present southerly position. North America and Eurasia change little in latitude.

Earthquakes

An earthquake at the Earth's surface is the sudden release of energy in the form of vibrations and tremors caused by compressed or stretched rock snapping along a fault in the Earth's surface. Rising lava under a volcano can also produce small tremors. It has been estimated that about a million earthquakes occur each year, but most of these are so minor that they pass unnoticed. The cause of deep earthquakes —those as much as 450 miles (700km) below the surface—is not known.

Waves and their measurement

Slippage along a fault is initially prevented by friction along the fault plane. This causes energy, which generates movement, to be stored up as elastic strain; a similar effect is created when a bow is drawn. Eventually the strain reaches a critical point, the friction is overcome, and the rocks snap past each other, releasing the stored energy in the form of earthquakes by vibrating back and forth. Earthquakes can also occur when rock folds that can no longer support the elastic strain break to form a fault. The point on the Earth's surface immediately above the source of the original disturbance is known as the epicenter [5], while the actual point of fracture within the Earth is known as the focus.

Seismic (earthquake) waves spread outward in all directions from the focus—much as sound waves do when a gun is fired [Key, 4]. There are two main types of seismic waves: the compressional wave and the shear wave [2]. Compressional waves cause the rock particles through which they pass to shake back and forth in the direction of the wave. Shear waves make the particles vibrate at right angles to the direction of their passage. Neither type of seismic wave physically moves the particles; instead it merely travels through them.

Compressional waves, which travel 1.7 times faster than shear waves, are the first to be noticed at an earthquake recording station [3]. Consequently seismologists refer to them as primary (P) waves and to the shear waves as secondary (S) waves. A third wave type is recognized by seismologists—the long (L), or surface, wave. L waves produce the most violent shocks. Intensity, the degree of shaking at a particular location, is expressed in the 12-degree Mercalli scale [6], each degree representing a rating based on observed effects. Magnitude is measured with the formal Richter scale, based on instrument readings.

Tsunamis—giant sea waves

Earthquakes are best known for the havoc they can wreak [1, 9]. The destruction may be the result of ground vibrations or giant waves *(tsunamis)* generated by seismic disturbances on the sea floor. At sea *tsunamis* have wavelengths—the distance between one crest and the next—as great as 500 miles (800km). They can travel at speeds of 500mph (800kph). When they reach a gently sloping shore they slow down and gather height. As the *tsunami* approaches, the sea withdraws, then rushes back in a series of giant waves that may travel far inland.

In 1755 the city of Lisbon was reduced to rubble in six minutes during one of the most devastating earthquakes ever re-

CONNECTIONS

Read first
166 Anatomy of the Earth

See also
250 Folds and faults
176 Volcanoes

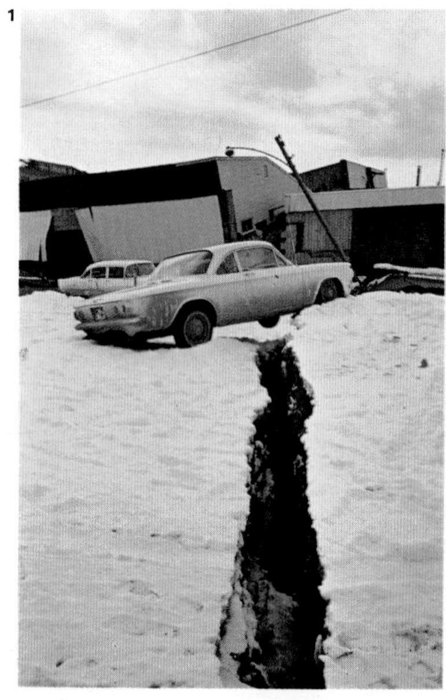

1 Severe surface disturbance ripped apart a road during the 1964 earthquake in Anchorage, Alaska, and minor subsidence left a crack 20in (50cm) wide. Ground waves, such as those responsible for the break-up of this highway, can disrupt underground services in cities and start fires. Broken water mains may hamper fire fighting and encourage the spread of epidemics. The Alaskan quake affected only a sparsely populated area and 114 lives were lost—a small number considering the magnitude of the shock, which caused a permanent tilting of the land mass along the southern coast of Alaska.

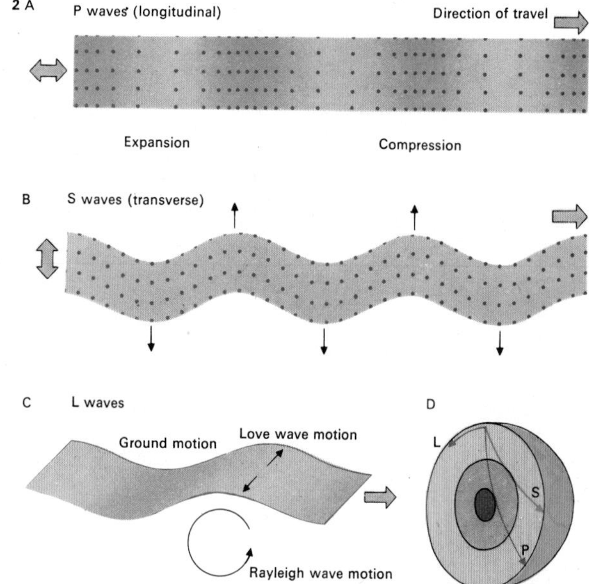

2 A
P waves (longitudinal)
Direction of travel
Expansion
Compression
B
S waves (transverse)
C
L waves
Ground motion
Love wave motion
Rayleigh wave motion
D
L
S
P

2 Seismic waves are basically of two kinds. Primary (P) waves [A] are compressional and cause the particles of rock to vibrate backwards and forwards like a coil spring. Secondary (S), or shear, waves [B] cause the particles to oscillate at right angles to the wave direction like a vibrating guitar string. When P and S waves reach the surface they are converted into long (L) waves [C] which either travel along the surface vibrating horizontally at right angles to the wave direction (known as Love waves) or travel like sea waves (Rayleigh waves). Some of the paths followed are shown in [D].

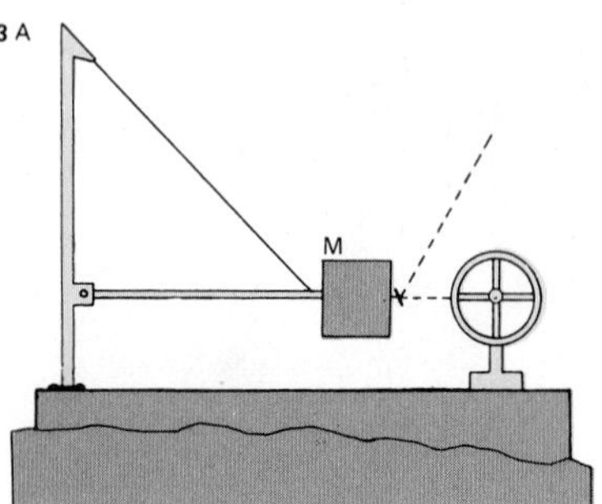

3 A
M

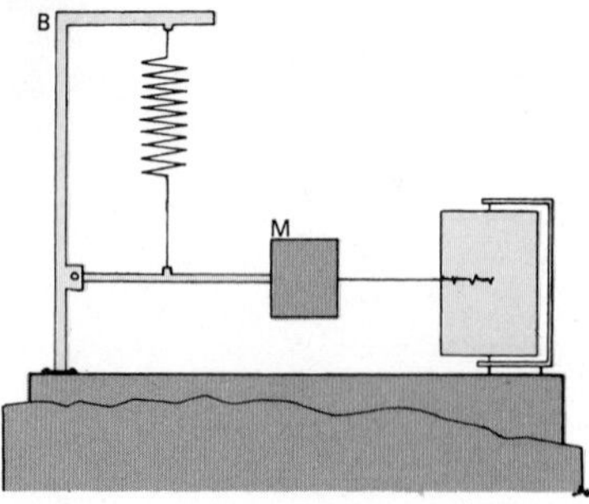

B
M

C P S L

3 Seismographs are instruments that detect and record seismic waves of three types (the P, S, and L). Most seismographs contain a sprung mass (M) that, when an earthquake passes, stays still while the rest of the instrument moves. Some seismographs detect horizontal motion [A] while others detect vertical motion [B]. The trace of the waves is recorded by a vibrating pen on a traveling strip of paper [C]. The time interval between the arrival of the P and S waves can be calculated and this interval, applied to a graph [5B], gives the distance between stations and epicenter.

4 Seismic wavepaths vary with the density of the rock, forming curving patterns as they move away from the focus [1]. Primary (P) waves can pass through gases, liquids, and solids. The primary waves travel fastest, increasing their velocity as they pass through the mantle [2], but decreasing in the outer core [3], only to increase again in the inner core [4] due to varying densities and pressures. Secondary (S) waves travel through solids only and do not penetrate into the dense molten outer core. As the waves travel down they meet concentric layers of increasing density that bend, or refract, the waves toward the surface along curved paths. The region between [5] and [6] does not receive any direct waves. This area is known to seismologists as the wave shadow zone. Seismic wave propagation has given scientists invaluable information about the interior of the Earth.

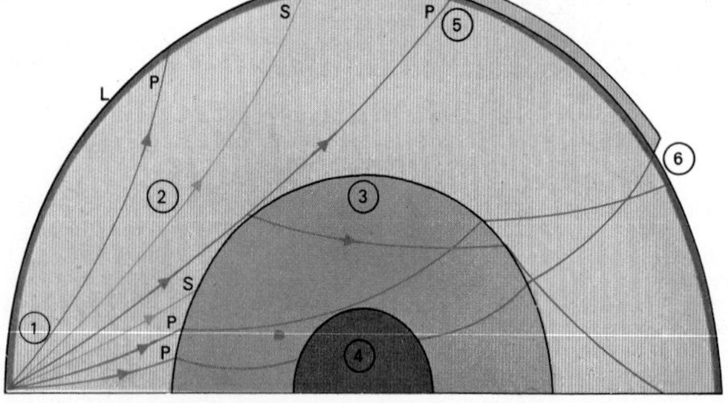

4
S
P
5
L
P
6
2
3
S
1
P
P
4

corded. The sea withdrew from the harbor and rushed back as a 55-ft (17-m) high *tsunami*, drowning hundreds. Smaller aftershocks caused landslides, fires broke out, and by nightfall 60,000 people were dead.

Despite the innate destructive capacity of earthquakes, it is possible in some circumstances to take precautions that minimize the hazards. Tall buildings can be constructed on reinforced concrete rafts that literally float during the passage of earthquake waves. Careful planning can ensure that streets are wide in relation to the height of buildings (many of the deaths caused during earthquakes are due to the collapse of tall buildings into narrow streets).

Control and prediction

In the mid-1960s, the dumping of water-based waste into a well in Denver, Colorado, set up a series of small earthquakes. Thus the idea was born that by drilling deep holes along a fault, and then pumping water down, it might be possible to relieve strains in a series of small, nondestructive earthquakes instead of allowing them to build up over a period of time until a major earthquake occurs [8].

Just before an earthquake the ground on either side of a fault suffers elastic deformation that can be measured by triangulation with a theodolite or laser beam. Tiltmeters can also be used to discover how much warping of the ground has taken place. Monitoring of large areas has now been introduced. Using artificial satellites, information is transmitted from devices placed in the vicinity of major faults and radioed back to centers where it can be analyzed. It is now possible to detect very small movements on the Earth's surface and locate areas where strain is building up.

Another recently discovered method involves measuring the amount of water the rocks contain. Under strain, the pores in the rock enlarge, allowing more water to enter. Because of the importance of ground water in producing earthquakes, knowledge of the water level in wells in earthquake-prone areas is very valuable.

KEY

An earthquake takes place when two parts of the Earth's surface move suddenly in relation to each other along a crack called a fault [1]. The point from which this movement originates is called the focus [2] and the point on the surface directly above this is called the epicenter [3]. Shock waves [4] travel outward from the focus decreasing in intensity the farther they go. These shock waves travel more quickly as they pass through denser material at great depths and so the direction of their travel [5] is curved as shown. On the surface the pattern of waves is similar to that of the isoseismal lines connecting points feeling equal shocks.

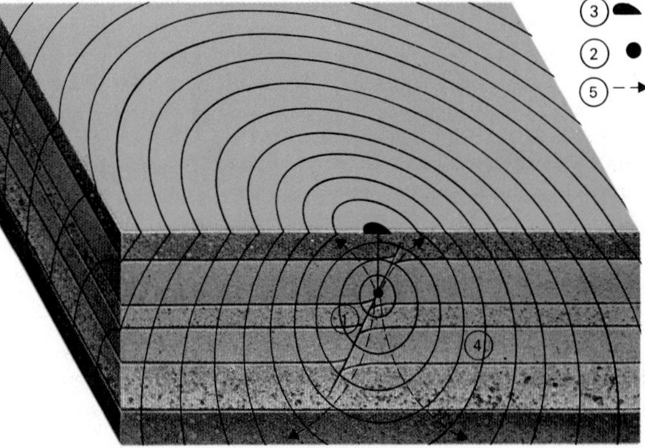

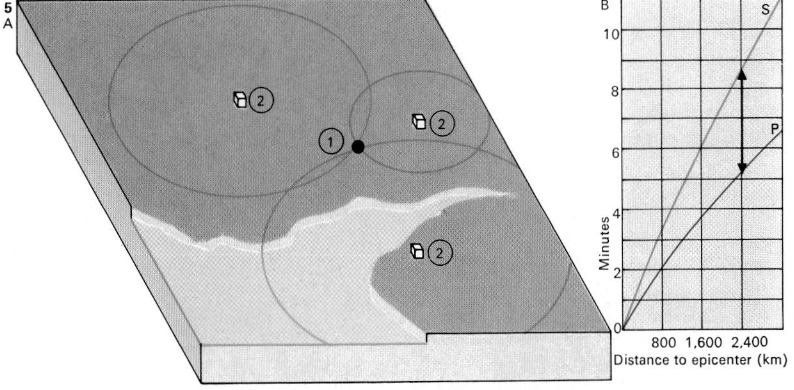
5
A
B
S
P
10
8
6
4
2
0
Minutes
800 1,600 2,400
Distance to epicenter (km)

5 The location of an epicenter [1] is found by plotting its distance from three recording stations [2]. Each station notes the different arrival times of P and S waves and uses a graph [B] that allows the distance from the epicenter to be measured. The distance is then used as the radius of a circle around each station [A]. The epicenter of the earthquake is located at the intersection of these three circles.

6 Earthquake ground-shaking intensity is based on a measure of the damage caused in populated areas. The most common intensity scale used is the Wood-Neumann, or modified Mercalli.

6 Modified Mercalli scale

1 Earthquake not felt, except by few.

2 Felt on upper floors by few at rest. Swinging of suspended objects.

3 Quite noticeable indoors, especially on upper floors. Standing automobiles may sway.

4 Felt indoors. Dishes and windows rattle, standing cars rock. Like heavy truck hitting building.

5 Felt by nearly all, many wakened. Fragile objects broken, plaster cracked, trees and poles disturbed.

6 Felt by all, many run outdoors. Slight damage, heavy furniture moved, some fallen plaster.

7 People run outdoors. Average homes slightly damaged, substandard ones badly damaged. Noticed by car drivers.

8 Well-built structures slightly damaged, others badly damaged. Chimneys and monuments collapse. Car drivers disturbed.

9 Well-designed buildings badly damaged, substantial ones greatly damaged, shifted off foundations. Conspicuous ground cracks.

10 Well-built wood structures destroyed, masonry structures destroyed. Rails bent, ground cracked, landslides. Rivers overflow.

11 Few masonry structures left standing. Bridges and underground pipes destroyed. Broad cracks in ground. Earth slumps.

12 Damage total. Ground waves seem like sea waves. Line of sight disturbed. Objects thrown upwards in the air.

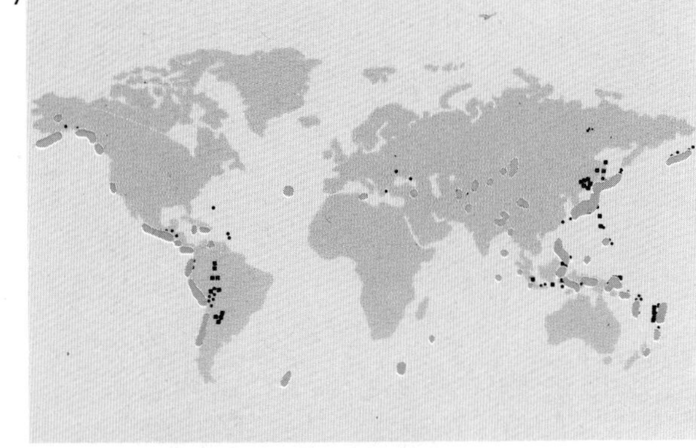

7 Earthquakes occur in geologically active areas such as mid-oceanic ridges and mountain-building regions. They can be classified according to the depth of their foci, deep-focus earthquakes (black squares) occurring at depths of between 185 and 400miles (300–650km), intermediate focus (black dots) 35 to 150 miles(55–240km), and shallow focus (grey areas) from the surface down to 35 miles (55km).

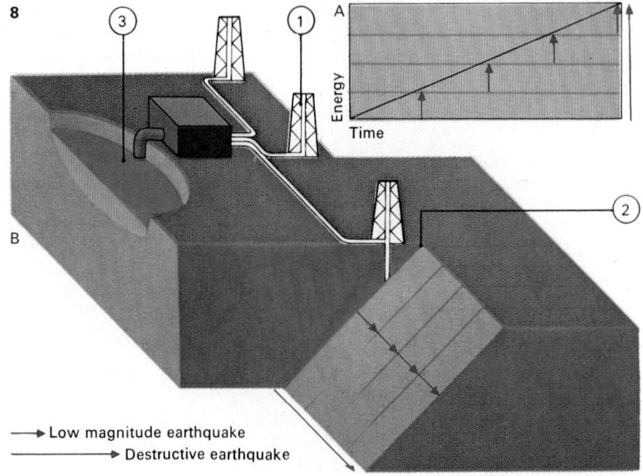
8
A
Energy
Time
B
Low magnitude earthquake
Destructive earthquake

8 Release of the pressure that could cause a severe earthquake may be achieved by deliberately causing a number of small quakes in the fault area. Researchers are investigating the possibility of minimizing the destructive effects of earthquakes by regulating their occurrence. Many small earthquakes, for instance, may release as much energy as a single devastating one by lessening the strain built up over a period of time [A]. One method of achieving this may be to pump water to act as a lubricant [B]. A number of wells [1] may be set up along a fault line [2] in which stress has been detected. Large quantities of water from a reservoir [3] would then be pumped into the wells to lessen friction between rocks in the fault and allow them to slip smoothly in a series of gentle tremors. Another method of triggering off small "quakes" may be to explode nuclear devices along a fault plane in the earth.

9 The Guatemala earthquake of 1976 completely destroyed many buildings and villages. Dazed survivors picked their way through piles of shattered masonry. Falling masonry is the greatest hazard during an earthquake and most injuries are caused outside rather than inside buildings. Disease often spreads among survivors after the breakdown of essential services. There were more than 16,000 deaths in the Guatemala quake. Other disastrous earthquakes since 1965 have been in Peru in 1970 (66,794 deaths), in northeastern Iran in 1968 (11,588 deaths), and in China in 1976 (total unknown).

Volcanoes

Volcanoes, the Earth's most spectacular displays of energy, are responsible for forming large parts of the Earth's crust. They give clues to the Earth's history and evolution, and to the nature of the Earth's interior. Soils formed by the weathering of volcanic rocks are exceptionally fertile so that, despite the danger, large numbers of people often live near them—a cause, all too often, of major disasters. The Earth's upper mantle, under the outer shell, is nearly molten. A slight drop in pressure caused, say, by crustal plates drifting apart, completes the melting process. The molten rock (magma), being lighter than the surrounding rocks, rises slowly to the surface, often along faults. A small increase in heat, such as that generated by overriding plates, will also melt the rock and it is believed that pockets of radioactive elements generate enough heat to form magma.

Along the mid-ocean ridges, where the crustal plates drifting apart create a drop of pressure, magma rises more or less continuously and cools to form new crust. Elsewhere it forms underground reservoirs, which, if they do not cool, can become unstable and produce eruptions. When this happens the flow is speeded up as the drop of pressure allows the gas dissolved in the magma to form bubbles [2]. Many of the gases, such as hydrogen sulfide and carbon monoxide, burn as they reach the air; this increases the temperature at the vent, making the lava even more fluid. If the lava is viscous, trapping the gases, they may escape explosively. The force of such eruptions is increased when water seeps down to the magma and turns into steam.

The volcanoes formed by escaping magma are characterized by their vent, or crater, at the summit. They often have side vents as well. Sometimes such large amounts of magma bubble out during an eruption that the chamber below the volcano is more or less emptied. The volcano then collapses into the void, forming a large, steep-sided depression known as a caldera.

Location of volcanoes

Volcanoes are found along the big tensional cracks of the Earth's surface—the mid-ocean ridges and their continental continuations—and along the collision edges of crustal plates. The famous "ring of fire" encircling the Pacific is the boundary of the plate that forms the Pacific.

The largest number of volcanoes is under the sea floor, forming the abyssal hills. Most are probably extinct. They exist because the oceanic crust is relatively thin and easily pierced by the underlying magma. The Pacific alone is thought to have more than 10,000 volcanoes of above 3,300ft (1,000m) in height. The Hawaiian volcanoes are thought to be caused by fixed "plumes," or "hot spots," in the mantle, that give rise to a string of volcanoes as the plate drifts slowly over them. A few volcanoes that exist on land away from the plate boundaries are perhaps the result of localized heating by radioactivity or of a hot spot in the mantle.

Apart from the uncounted abyssal volcanoes, there are about 500 active volcanoes, of which perhaps 20 or 30 erupt in any given year. Between eruptions a volcano is said to be dormant. An active vol-

CONNECTIONS

Read first
166 Anatomy of the Earth

See also
246 The rock cycle and igneous rocks
170 Global tectonics
286 Energy supplies
288 Energy for the future
964 Minoan civilization 2500–1400 BC

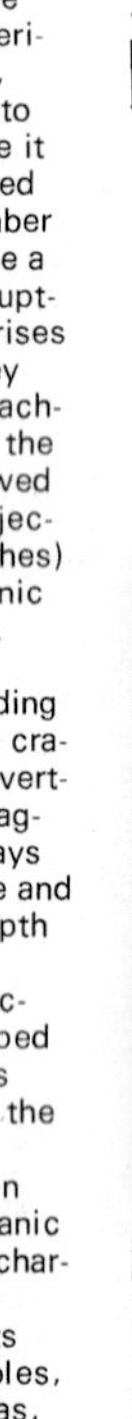

1 Rainwater seeps down, is heated by the magma and surfaces as hot springs and geysers, often loaded with dissolved minerals
Fissure eruptions do not form volcanoes but release flows of very fluid lava that can cover areas up to 500km² (200 square miles)
A magma chamber of fluid rock underlies many volcanoes. This is released as ash and lava during eruptions
Lava flows can be released from side vents and gases can issue from crevices in the loose flanks of the volcano
Stratified layers of volcanic rocks build up the main cone. Each eruption adds at least one layer
Pressure in the main vent encourages the opening of side vents as alternative paths to the surface
Geysers are intermittent fountains of water and steam created by the vaporizing of ground waters. They operate like giant safety valves
Active or recent cones often form inside explosion craters or crater-shaped calderas due to the collapse of an empty magma chamber
A laccolith is a giant, lens-shaped intrusion that pushes up the strata above. It is fed from the magma chamber

1 Volcanoes are fed by hot molten rock that rises from the mantle. This material, called magma, may rise directly to the surface where it erupts, or be stored in a magma chamber that swells up like a balloon before erupting. The magma rises through a chimney and eventually reaches the surface at the vent. Matter spewed forth as lava or ejecta (bombs and ashes) builds up a volcanic cone, or volcano. Vent explosions caused by expanding gases often form craters shaped as inverted cones. The magma does not always reach the surface and often cools at depth forming plutons (large bodies), laccoliths (lens-shaped structures), dikes (that cut through the strata) and sills (injected between two strata). Volcanic regions are also characterized by hot springs, gas vents known as fumaroles, and, in some areas, by geysers.

2 As the pressure in rising magma falls, dissolved gases are forced out of the melt; these form expanding bubbles and drive the magma out of the volcano.

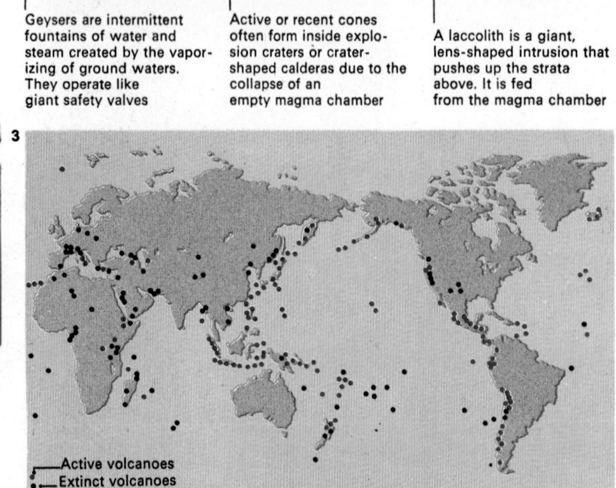

Active volcanoes
Extinct volcanoes

3 Active volcanoes mostly occur at crustal plate boundaries. The principal zone of activity is found along a great arc around the Pacific, from Chile to the East Indies.

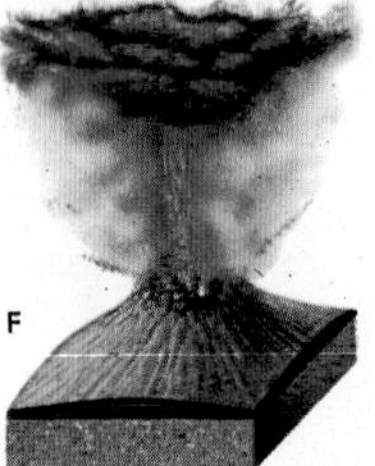

4 Volcanic eruptions take various forms. Fissure eruptions [A] release the most basic and runny lava. In Hawaiian eruptions [B] the lava is less fluid and produces a low cone. The Vulcanian type [C] is more violent and ejects solid lava. Strombolian eruptions [D] blow out incandescent material. In the Peléean type [E] a blocked vent is cleared explosively. A Plinian eruption [F] is a continuous gas blast that ejects pumice.

cano is one that has erupted in historic times. Volcanoes can, however, be dormant for periods longer than historic times and "extinct" volcanoes sometimes come back to life, as Helgafell in Heimaey, Iceland, did in 1973 [8]. The best-known new volcano on land is Paricutin, in Mexico, which appeared in a field in 1943. The map [3] shows active volcanoes and recent extinct volcanoes, many of which were seen erupting by prehistoric man.

Volcanic products and eruption types

Volcanoes emit gases, liquids, and solids. The gases are mainly nitrogen, carbon dioxide, hydrogen chloride, water vapor, carbon monoxide, and hydrogen sulfide. Liquid emissions, known as lavas, are either ropy *pahoehoe* [10] or clinker-like *aa* [9], depending on the temperature.

Fluid lava allows calm eruptions; more viscous lava, by preventing the escape of gas, thus causing it to reach high pressure, is accompanied by explosions; very viscous magma is thrown out as ash and rubble in huge explosions. Craters at rest are often filled by a lake; an eruption often creates a mud flow, which is as destructive as, and even more lethal (owing to its speed), than a lava flow.

Catastrophic eruptions

Volcanoes are in a sense safety valves in the Earth's crust; the tighter the valve the greater the eruption will be. The 1815 eruption of Tambora in Indonesia ranks as the greatest volcanic disaster in history. Ten thousand people were killed outright during the eruption and 82,000 died later of disease and starvation. Again in Indonesia, the uninhabited island of Krakatoa was blown to pieces [Key] in 1883, creating a tidal wave that killed 3,000 people. Evidence on the island of Thera [11], near Crete, suggests that an even larger explosion occurred there around 1470 BC.

Eruptions cannot be prevented, but they may be predicted by monitoring the small earthquakes created by rising magma, measuring the swelling of the ground with tiltmeters, and watching variations in the output of gas and steam vents.

KEY

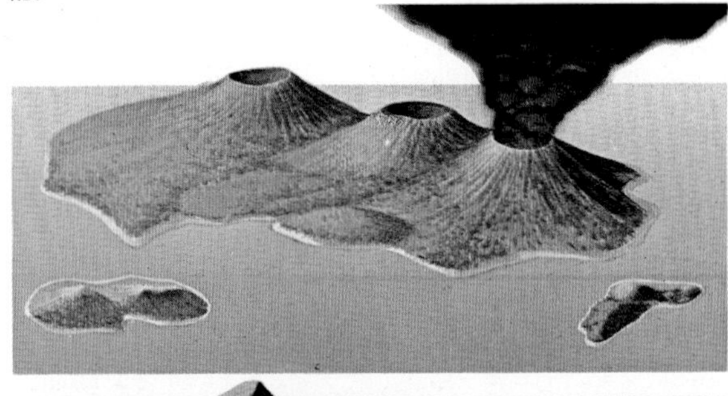

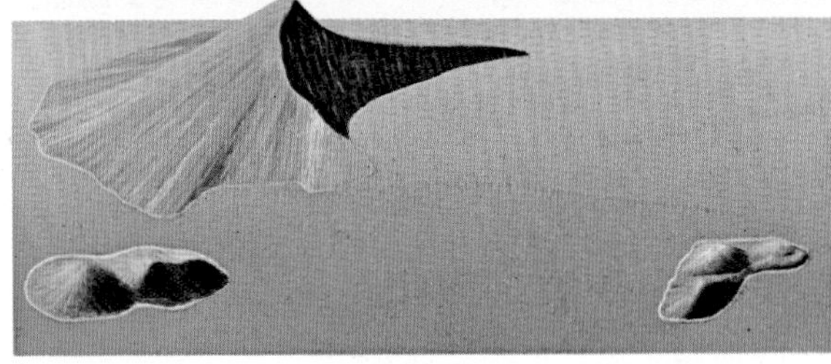

Krakatoa was a small volcanic island in the Sunda Strait of Indonesia that had been inactive since 1680. Two thirds of the island was destroyed in an eruption in August 1883.

5 Hawaiian-type eruptions are characterized by lava flows consisting of basalt and they are often accompanied by fiery lava fountains which can sometimes be as tall as the Eiffel tower—1,000ft (300m). The Hawaiian eruption pictured here shows how the incandescent lava from the fountain has filled the crater and has overflown to form a lava flow partially chilled on its surface. Such flows can travel far.

6

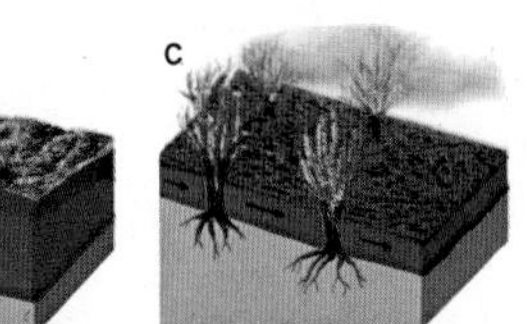

A
C

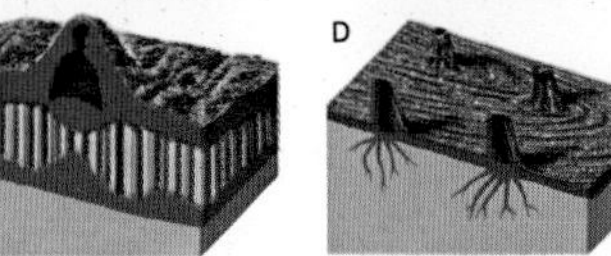

B
D

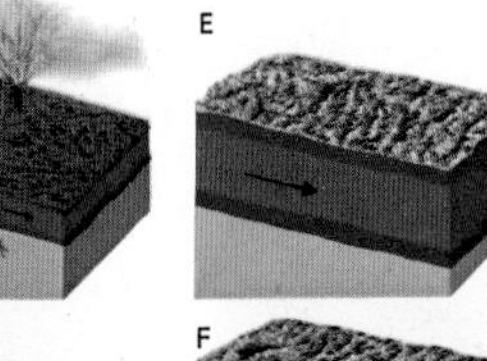

E

F

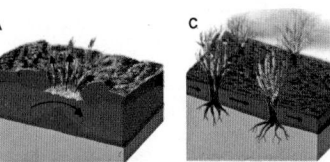

6 Lava formations include hornitos, or spatter cones, small bursts [A] that form miniature volcanoes on lava flows [B]. Tree molds [C] form where trees have burned away beneath the cooled lava [D]. Lava tubes occur when the surface flow cools [E] and the hot interior drains away [F].

8

8 Ash falls can cause more damage to property and agricultural land than lava flows because they cover greater areas. Volcanic ash is made of fine ejecta of less than 4mm (0.15in) diameter and is forced out by the cubic mile. Most is deposited within 6 miles (10km) of the volcano. The picture shows some houses of Heimaey, Iceland, buried by ash from the Helgafell eruption of 1973.

7

7 Spindle bombs are the product of molten rock pulling apart after ejection. Larger blobs twist in flight and their drawn-out ends curl and give the bomb its characteristic lozenge shape.

9

9 The texture of a lava flow depends on the temperature and the velocity of the flow during the eruption and on the composition of the lava. Geologists have borrowed two words from the Hawaiian language, *aa* and *pahoehoe*, to describe two typical surfaces. *Aa* lava has a very rough and clinkerlike aspect and is formed by slowly moving or relatively cool outpourings. Several years after the solidification of this flow, vegetation returns.

10

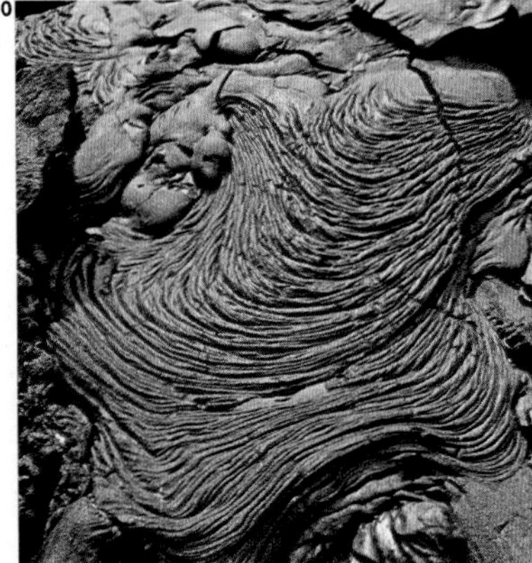

10 Pahoehoe, or ropy lava, has a smooth but twisted surface. It is formed by fast-flowing fluid lava, which develops a plastic skin on its surface, by cooling. The skin is dragged into picturesque folds by the still liquid lava beneath it.

11

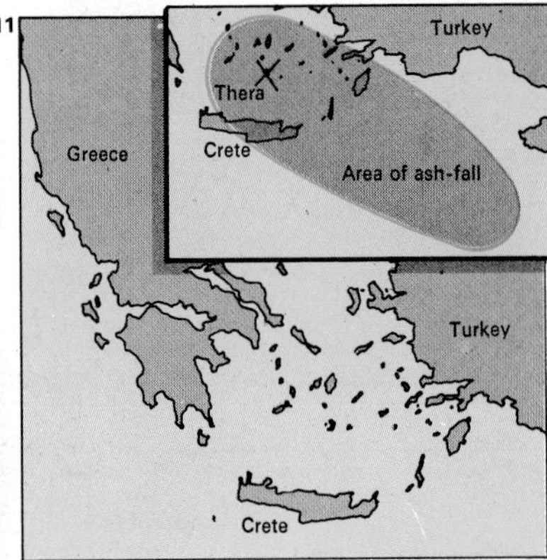

Turkey
Thera
Greece
Crete
Area of ash-fall
Turkey
Crete

11 In the late Bronze Age the island of Thera experienced an eruption that had a catastrophic effect on the people of Crete and may have been responsible for the fall of the Minoan civilization and the creation of the Atlantis legend.

Gravity and the shape of the Earth

CONNECTIONS

See also
166 Anatomy of the Earth

Gravity is the mutual attraction of two bodies; its strength depends on the mass of the bodies and their distance apart. The strength of the Earth's gravitational field is therefore proportional to the Earth's mass and decreases as the distance from the surface increases.

Gravity is responsible for nearly all the major erosion that takes place. Rain falls under gravity; streams, rivers, and glaciers move and sediments compact under gravity.

Rotation, shape, and sea level

The Earth's rotation creates a centrifugal force that is greater at the equator than elsewhere, causing the Earth to bulge out slightly at the equator and to flatten at the poles [1]. This makes the Earth's diameter at the equator greater than that through the poles by about 25 miles (41km).

Mean sea level is the average sea level between tides and is taken as the base level when measuring altitudes. It is always perpendicular to the force of gravity. Mean sea level taken all over the Earth is known as the "geoid," which is what the Earth's true shape is called [2]. The surface of the geoid is irregular because the gravity field varies locally and depends on the type of rocks in the crust. A large ore body or mountain chain will deflect a nearby plumb line away from the center of the Earth and thus the geoid's shape is obtained by directly measuring gravity on land [3] or its variation at sea, where wave motion precludes direct measurement. Perturbations of artificial satellite orbits are now extensively used for broad-scale geoid studies. The shape of the geoid is defined by its departure from a "reference ellipsoid" that fits most closely to the shape of the Earth. In this case, the average level of the land and sea is taken as the norm. Mountains are then higher and sea floors lower than the surface of this ellipsoid.

The Trigonometrical Survey of India

During the Trigonometrical Survey of India, in the nineteenth century, it was found that some stations, whose positions were determined by astronomical surveying methods, did not coincide with those determined by triangulation, which allowed for the extra sideways attraction of the Himalayas to the north. The Himalayas were exerting a smaller gravitational pull on the plumb line than expected and introducing discrepancies as large as 300ft (91.5m). As a result, both J. H. Pratt and G. B. Airy (1801–92) proposed that the continents consisted of lighter material floating on a denser substratum [5]. Pratt believed that the different heights of mountains were caused by blocks of different densities floating at the same base level, while Airy thought the heights were caused by blocks of different thickness but of the same density floating at different depths. Today, Airy's hypothesis is generally accepted.

Another way of stating Airy's hypothesis is that lighter continental crustal materials "float" in equilibrium on the denser but slightly plastic underlying basaltic crust like a cork floating on water. This is called isostatic equilibrium, or isostasis. If such a cork were given an extra load (such as a coin) it would sink a little until the extra im-

1

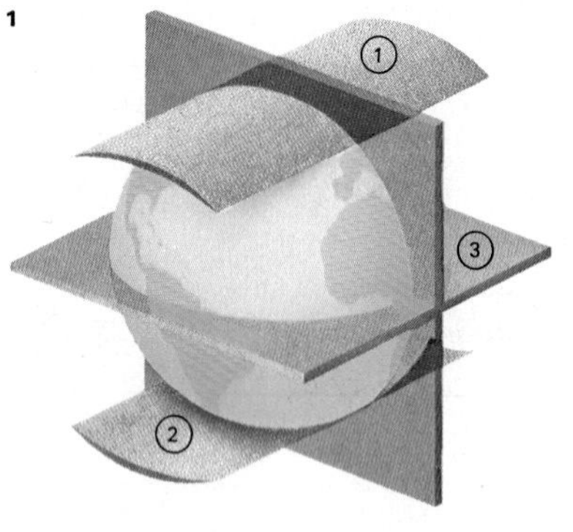

1 The Earth's surface is not a true sphere but approximates an ellipsoid whose equatorial diameter exceeds its polar diameter. The difference is about 25 miles (41km) and may be illustrated by forcing hypothetical wedges [1, 2] through the spaces over the poles; this would not be possible at the equator [3]. The equatorial bulge is caused by the effect of centrifugal force as the Earth rotates.

2

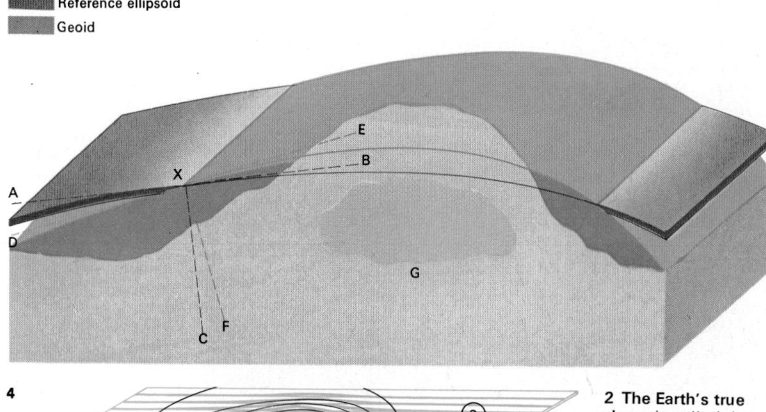
Reference ellipsoid
Geoid
A
B
C
D
E
F
G
X

2 The Earth's true shape is called the geoid. Because gravity varies locally, the geoid is irregular. Large rock masses in mountains [G] attract a plumb line and the assumed direction of the center of gravity [XC] for the ellipsoid is deflected to the local direction of the center of gravity [XF]. As [XF] is perpendicular to the true level [DE] based on the geoid, [AB] is only the assumed level based on the ellipsoid.

3

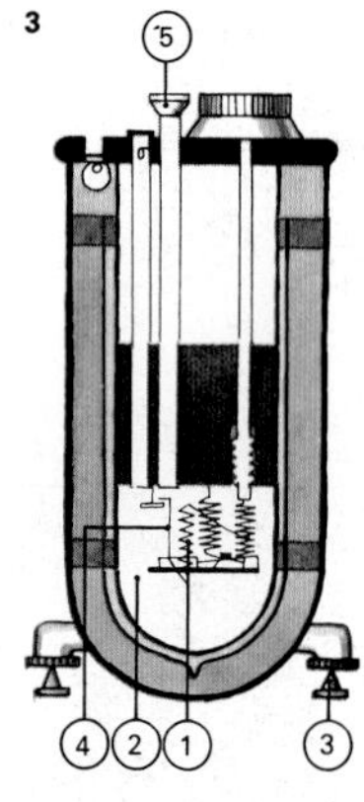

3 A gravimeter is a device used for measuring gravity at a point on the Earth's surface by observing the extension of a weighted spring. A quartz spring [1] is housed in a partially evacuated chamber [2] that protects it from pressure changes. Leveling screws [3] keep the meter vertical and the movement of the spring is indicated by the position of the pointer [4] observed through an eyepiece [5].

4

4 A negative gravity anomaly—a lower gravity reading than normal—is found over an intrusion of light rock near the surface. A less dense salt dome [1] rises through denser crustal rocks [2] disturbing the local gravitational field. Readings taken on the surface can be plotted on a map [3] and these will show an area of low gravity above the dome. A dense metallic ore body would show a positive anomaly.

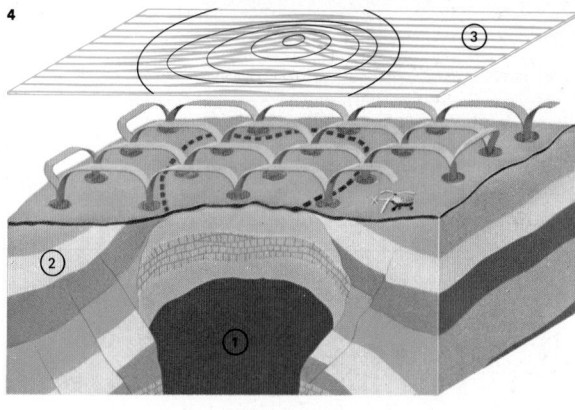

5A B

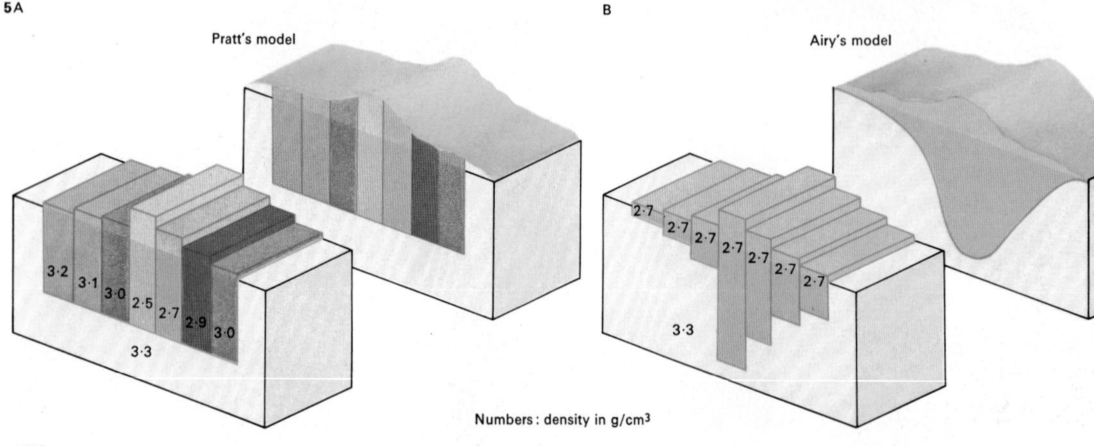
Pratt's model
3·2
3·1
3·0
2·5
2·7
2·9
3·0
3·3
Airy's model
2·7
2·7
2·7
2·7
2·7
2·7
2·7
3·3
Numbers: density in g/cm3

5 In the 1850s Pratt and Airy proposed that the continents consisted of light material floating on a denser substratum. Whereas Pratt suggested that the different heights of mountains were caused by blocks of different densities floating at the same base level [A], Airy believed that they were caused by blocks of different heights of the same density floating at different depths [B]. Research has shown Airy's view to be the more likely.

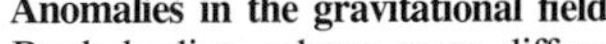

mersed volume created enough buoyancy to compensate for the load. This is what is observed for the Earth's crust; extra loads cause downwarping of the continental crust [7]. When the load disappears, for example by the melting of ice at the end of an ice age or by erosion, the crust bobs up, regaining new isostatic equilibrium.

Parts of Norway and Sweden are still rising, following the melting of the thick Pleistocene ice caps 10,000 years ago, and it is estimated that the crust there must rise a further 700ft (213m) before equilibrium is restored. As Scandinavia rises, however, the coastlines of the Netherlands and parts of Denmark are sinking [8] because lithosphere material flowing up under Scandinavia is drawn from beneath the Netherlands and parts of Denmark. Isostatic equilibrium is maintained by variation in the depth of the Earth's crust, and scientists have shown that every mountain chain in the upper layer of the crust floats on a deep root in the basaltic layer. Conversely, below the oceans only a thin basaltic layer of crust is found.

Anomalies in the gravitational field

Rock bodies, whose mass differs greatly from that of the surrounding area, cause small variations, or anomalies, in the local gravitational field, making it possible to detect them with sensitive gravity meters [Key]. Gravity meters work on the principle that gravity changes will cause minute variations in a very fine quartz spring [3].

Gravity surveys reveal that large salt domes near the surface (often associated with oil and gas) will show up as a negative anomaly (that is, as a mass deficit, because salt is lighter than other rocks) [4], while a dense ore body will show up as a positive gravity anomaly (mass excess). Geologists exploring the terrain carry out surveys of the Earth's gravity field and the observed values are corrected to eliminate the influence of latitude, height, and the mass of material between the observation point and sea level or the lowest level obtainable. This allowance is called the Bouguer correction. A Bouguer anomaly map can be used to determine the possible positions and sizes of economic ores and oil reserves.

KEY

Underground rock formations can be detected by measuring the local variations in the pull of gravity on a delicate spring balance called a gravimeter. The lighter the material, the weaker the pull.

1 Normal gravity reading **2** Heavy igneous material near surface giving gravity high **3** Anticline giving gravity high **4** Rift valley where lighter surface material continues to a greater depth giving gravity low **5** Salt dome or upward emplacement of light material giving gravity low **6** Oceanic trough where lighter crustal material deep in mantle gives gravity low.

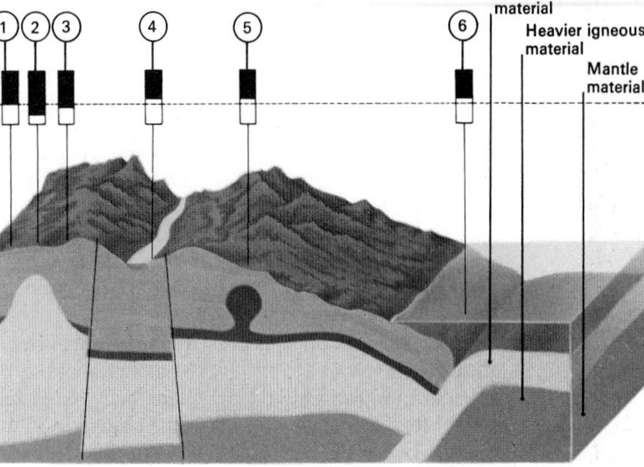

1
2
3
4
5
6
Lighter igneous material
Heavier igneous material
Mantle material

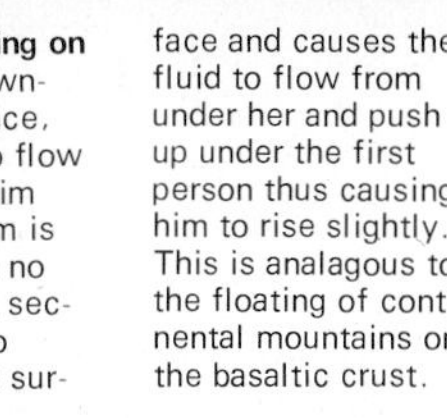

6 A person sitting on a water bed downwarps the surface, causing fluid to flow from beneath him until equilibrium is reached and he no longer sinks. A second person also downwarps the surface and causes the fluid to flow from under her and push up under the first person thus causing him to rise slightly. This is analagous to the floating of continental mountains on the basaltic crust.

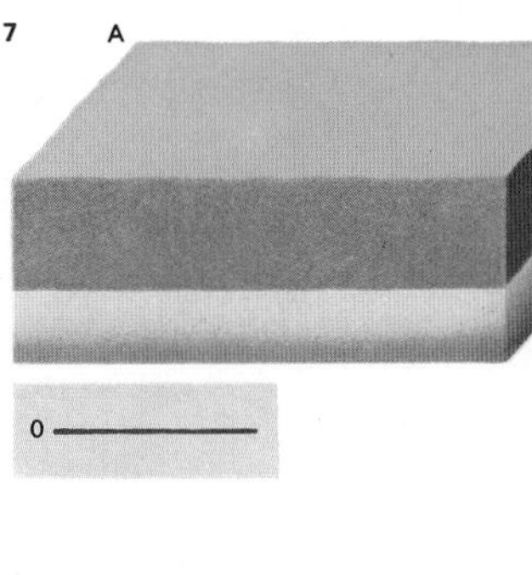

A
0

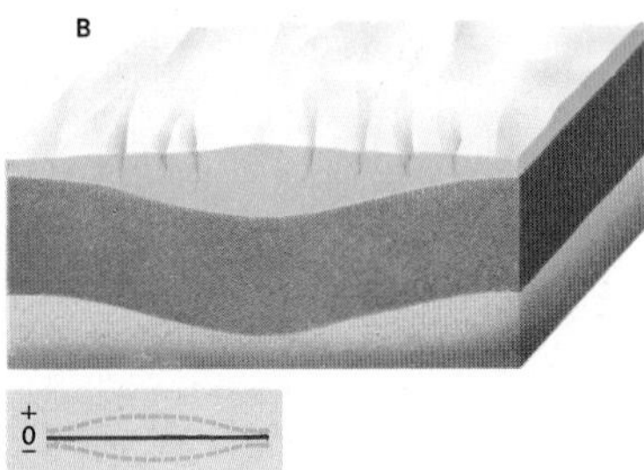

B
+
0
−

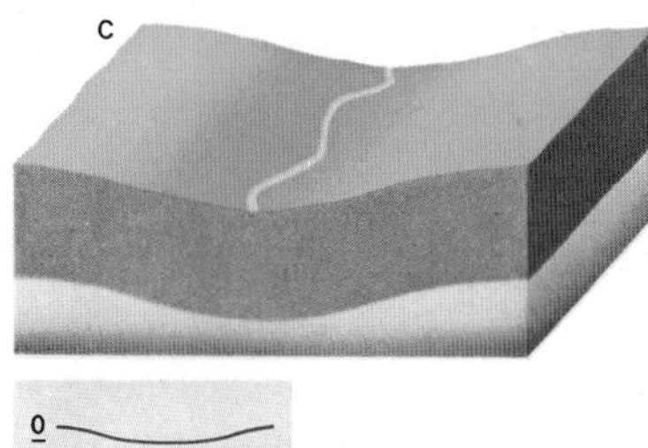

C
0

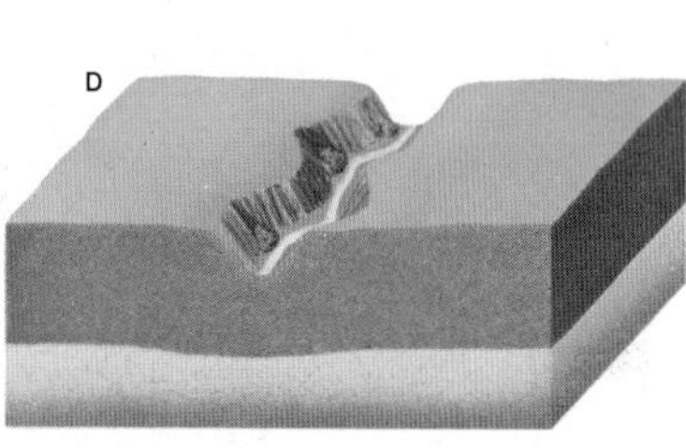

D
0

7 When the Earth's surface acquires a heavy load, the lithosphere (crust and uppermost mantle) downwarps into the lower part of the mantle, the asthenosphere. In [A] the lithosphere is in equilibrium with the asthenosphere. An ice sheet [B] produces a positive gravity anomaly. To compensate, the lithosphere downwarps, giving a deficiency in mass and a negative anomaly. The positive and negative anomalies cancel and the lithosphere remains in equilibrium. When the ice melts [C] the load is removed leaving a negative anomaly. To restore equilibrium [D] the land rises and rivers rejuvenate.

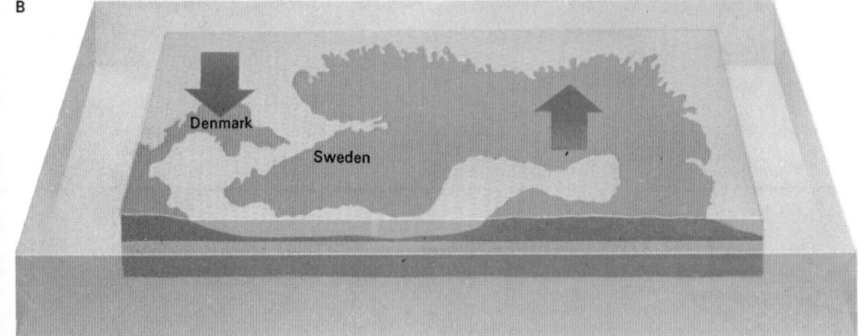

Denmark
Sweden

8 Glacial rebound is an example of isostatic activity. During the last ice age Scandinavia was weighed down by ice, causing the north of Europe to tilt [A]. After the ice melted the continent returned to its original attitude [B], buoyed up on asthenosphere material flowing from under the sinking areas.

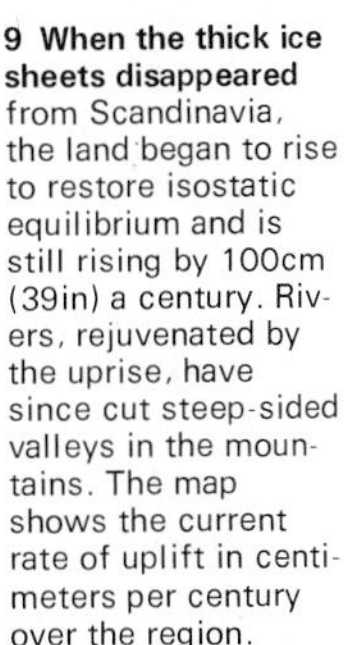

9 When the thick ice sheets disappeared from Scandinavia, the land began to rise to restore isostatic equilibrium and is still rising by 100cm (39in) a century. Rivers, rejuvenated by the uprise, have since cut steep-sided valleys in the mountains. The map shows the current rate of uplift in centimeters per century over the region.

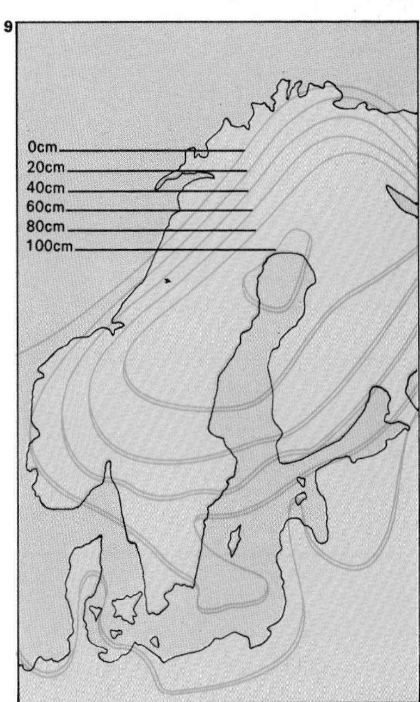

0cm
20cm
40cm
60cm
80cm
100cm

Mapping the Earth

Throughout history man has recorded, analyzed, and communicated information in map form. The oldest map in existence is engraved on a Babylonian clay tablet dating from 3000 BC and, like many surviving examples of early mapping, it records land tenure. It was not until the fifth century BC, however, that Greek philosophy stimulated attempts to create a map of the world. Unfortunately these were based on philosophical theories rather than the geographical knowledge of the day. Nevertheless, in the following 600 years Greek scholars did develop a more scientific approach to cartography.

Early attempts at cartography

At the end of the first century AD Ptolemy of Alexandria compiled his *Geographia*. In it he discussed the problem of representing the spherical shape of the Earth on a plane surface and also introduced the concepts of longitude and latitude [4].

After Ptolemy, cartography entered a period of decline until the Crusades and an expansion of trade revived interest. A cartographic renaissance came in the fifteenth century with the discovery and publication of Ptolemy's work, voyages of exploration like those of Vasco da Gama (*c.* 1469–1525) and Christopher Columbus (1451–1506), and the invention of printing and engraving. In the sixteenth century the work of map publishing houses in Holland and France, and particularly that of Gerhardus Mercator (1512–94), laid the foundations of modern map making.

By the middle of the eighteenth century the French had initiated the first topographic survey. Many special-purpose, or thematic, maps have been produced since the nineteenth century. Their variety reflects the increasingly specialized demands of modern life, which require such aids as land-use maps, geological maps, pilot charts, and road maps.

Modern surveying

Small areas of the Earth can be mapped by plane surveying, but larger areas must be done by geodesy, which takes into account the Earth's curvature. A variety of instruments and techniques is used to determine position, height, and extent of features. Instruments such as graduated metal rods, chains, tapes, and portable radar or radio transmitters are used for measuring distances; the theodolite [Key] is used for measuring angles. By using measured distances and angles further distances and angles are calculated by a process called triangulation [1]. Heights are determined in a similar fashion [2].

Perhaps the most dramatic changes in cartography have come with the development of aerial survey techniques. Photographs from satellites or aircraft are used together with data from ground surveys to map accurately large areas of the earth. This technique, called photogrammetry, is particularly useful for mapping remote areas [3], and also for mapping the Earth's natural resources. Almost all topographic mapping today is done from aerial photographs.

Map projections

It is impossible to represent accurately the surface of a sphere on a flat plane without

CONNECTIONS

See also
178 Gravity and the shape of the Earth
182 The face of the Earth
300 Land uses
1472 Mathematics and mapping

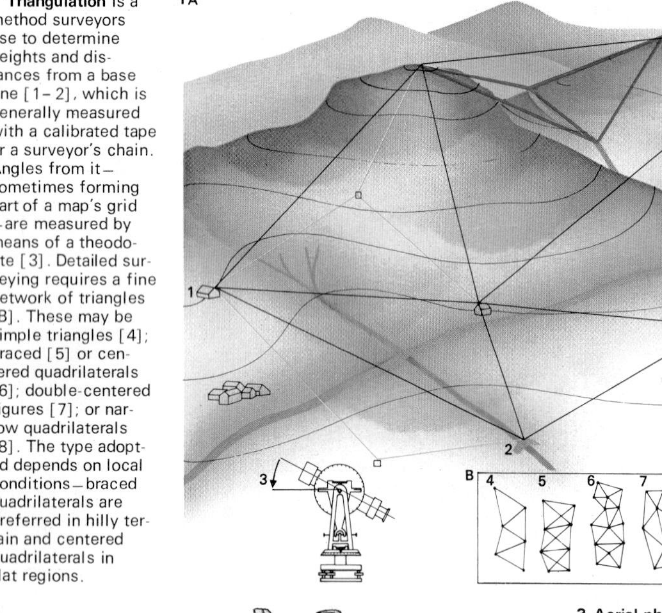

1A
1
2
3
B
4
5
6
7
8

1 Triangulation is a method surveyors use to determine heights and distances from a base line [1–2], which is generally measured with a calibrated tape or a surveyor's chain. Angles from it—sometimes forming part of a map's grid—are measured by means of a theodolite [3]. Detailed surveying requires a fine network of triangles [B]. These may be simple triangles [4]; braced [5] or centered quadrilaterals [6]; double-centered figures [7]; or narrow quadrilaterals [8]. The type adopted depends on local conditions—braced quadrilaterals are preferred in hilly terrain and centered quadrilaterals in flat regions.

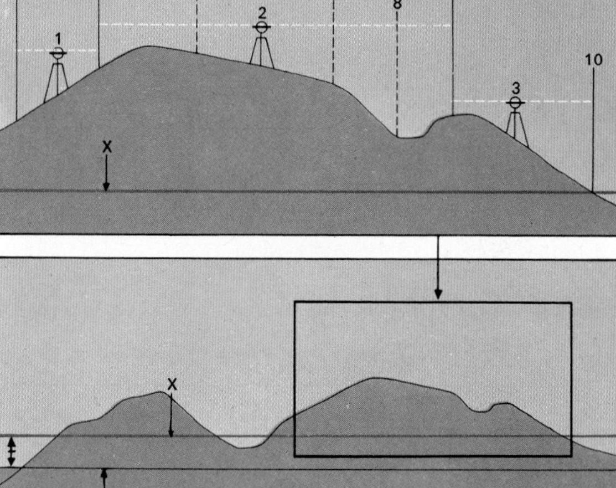

2
1
2
3
4
5
6
7
8
9
10
X
Y

2 Height above sea level is usually determined by means of a leveling instrument [1, 2, 3] and a measuring rod [4–10] with reference to a known height or bench mark [X]. Level 1 sights on the rod at 4 and then at 5. The instrument is moved to 2 to begin the second stage, sighting first on 5 and then on 6. Finally 10 will be reached using stage 3. Intermediate heights are determined by placing the rod at 8. The heights of the points 4–10 are related to sea level [Y] because the height above sea level of the bench mark [X] is known from previous authoritative surveys of the area.

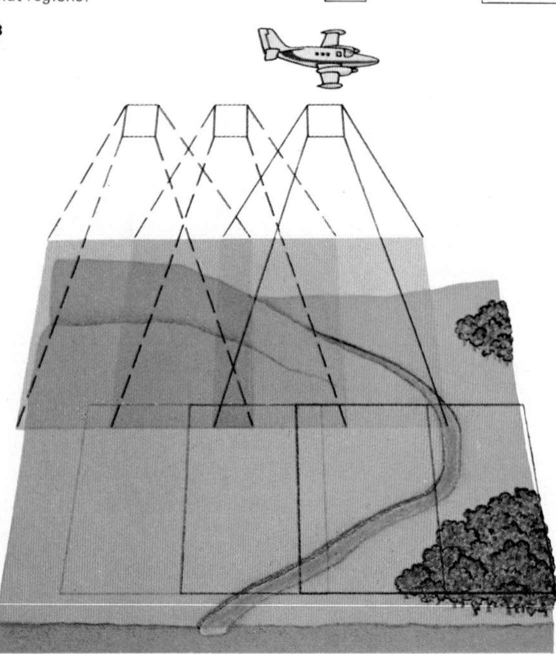

3

3 Aerial photography is one of the modern techniques that have helped the work of the cartographer. An aircraft flies over the area to be mapped, taking a continuous series of photographs. The area covered by each photograph overlaps by 60% the area of the previous one and so, after processing, any adjacent pair of photographs can be examined stereoscopically and the relief of the area studied directly in three dimensions. By means of an optical instrument the positions of corresponding points on each photograph can be compared and the height of that point calculated. Each "run" of photographs overlaps by 10% the previous run, ensuring total coverage.

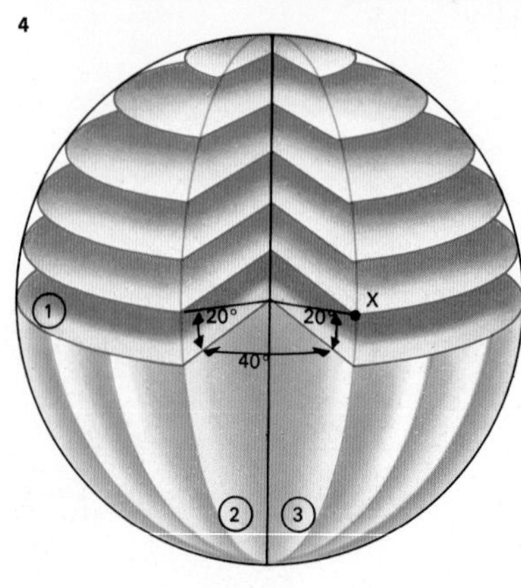

4
1
20°
20°
X
40°
2
3

4 Any point on the surface of the Earth can be located in terms of longitude and latitude—that is, in degrees, minutes, and seconds east or west of a prime meridian or line of longitude, and north or south of the equator. The latitude of X (the angle between X, the center of the Earth and the plane of the equator [1]) equals 20° while its longitude (the angle between the plane of the prime meridian [2] and that passing through X [3] and the poles) equals 40°

distorting the relationships among features on that surface. A map projection is a device used to plot the Earth's features with a minimum of such distortion. There are a number of different types of projection and the choice depends on the purpose of the particular map.

If the map is to show relatively small areas of the world, as in a national topographic series that will be used by planners, engineers, and the general public, then a projection must be selected that shows distance, angle, and shape with accuracy. For this reason conformal projections are chosen. If on the other hand the map is to show distribution of, say, cultivated land throughout the world, then a projection that shows those areas at their correct relative size must be selected. Such projections are called equivalent projections, or equal area projections.

Conformal projections are not used for world maps except in special circumstances because they exaggerate polar regions to an enormous extent. The Mercator projection, the best known example, is, however, invaluable to navigators as it shows all lines of constant direction as straight lines.

The first essential in making any map is to establish its purpose. The necessary data must then be assembled—this may be in the form of survey data, aerial photography, existing maps, and written material—analyzed, evaluated, and edited before any drafting can begin. Many factors influence the presentation of information in map form, from the size of paper that can be handled in a cockpit or automobile to the visual preconceptions of the probable user. The cartographer has all the techniques of graphic communication at his disposal and he must consider the possibilities they offer when designing the map. Various symbols, lines, and shading may be used. Contours are widely used to represent relief [8]; however, they give little visual impression of the appearance of the landscape. Cartographers often use layer-coloring for greater clarity and spot heights are marked where an accurate assessment of height or depth is desired, or when a particular crest or low point falls between contours.

KEY

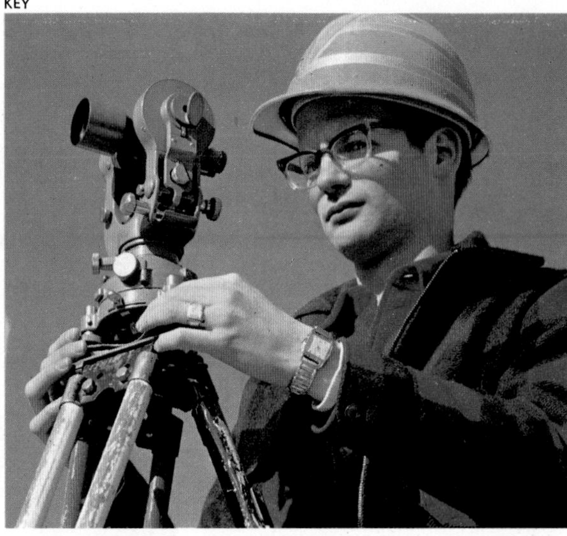

A theodolite is essentially a tripod-mounted telescope on a base plate that is marked in degrees, minutes, and seconds to allow the surveyor to measure horizontal angles. He makes vertical readings from an upright plate at the side.

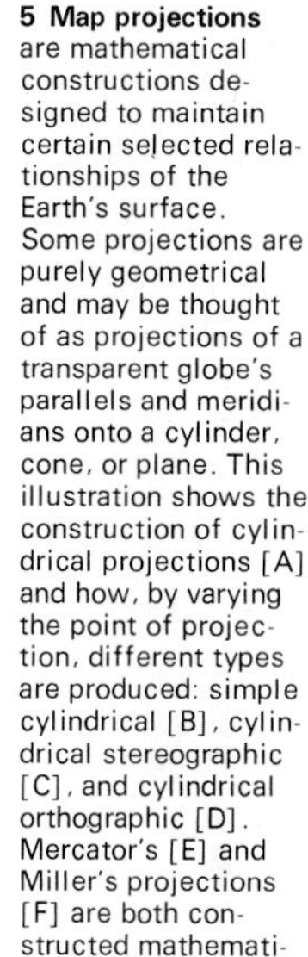

5 Map projections are mathematical constructions designed to maintain certain selected relationships of the Earth's surface. Some projections are purely geometrical and may be thought of as projections of a transparent globe's parallels and meridians onto a cylinder, cone, or plane. This illustration shows the construction of cylindrical projections [A] and how, by varying the point of projection, different types are produced: simple cylindrical [B], cylindrical stereographic [C], and cylindrical orthographic [D]. Mercator's [E] and Miller's projections [F] are both constructed mathematically.

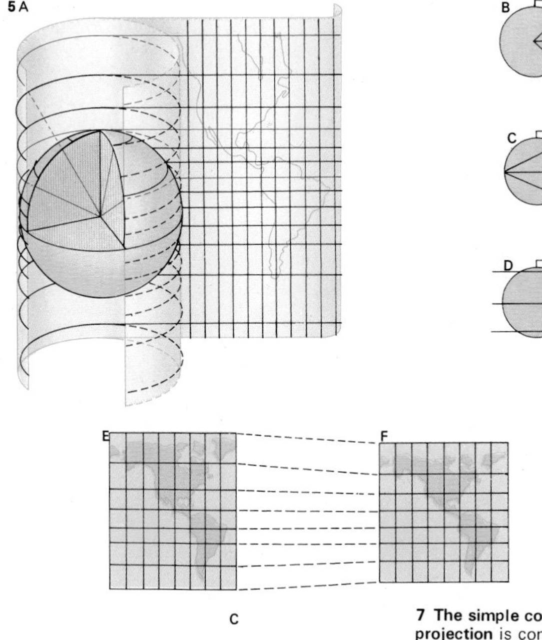
5 A
B
C
D
E
F

6 Azimuthal or zenithal projections are those produced on plane surfaces [A]. Angles measured from the center (the point of contact with the globe) are correct; however, distortion of shape and area increases with distance from the center. The gnomonic projection [B] shows all great circles (circumferences of planes through the center of the Earth) as straight lines. As these are the shortest distances between two points this projection is of importance in navigation. Lambert's projection [C] combines usefully the properties of azimuthal and equal-area projections.

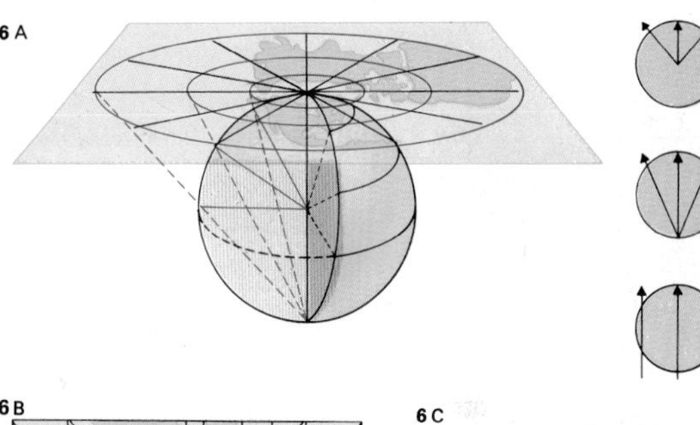
6 A

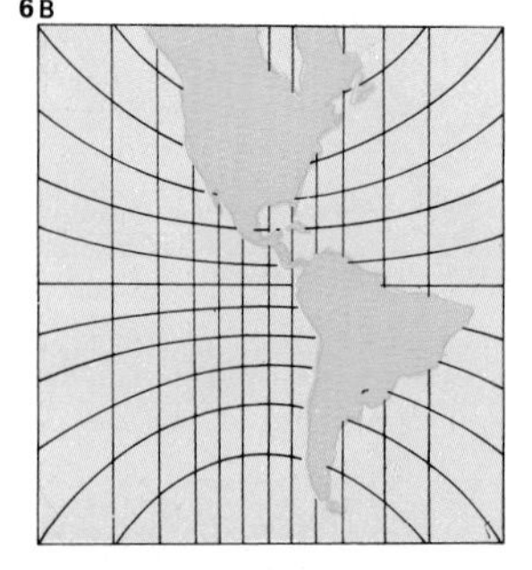
6 B

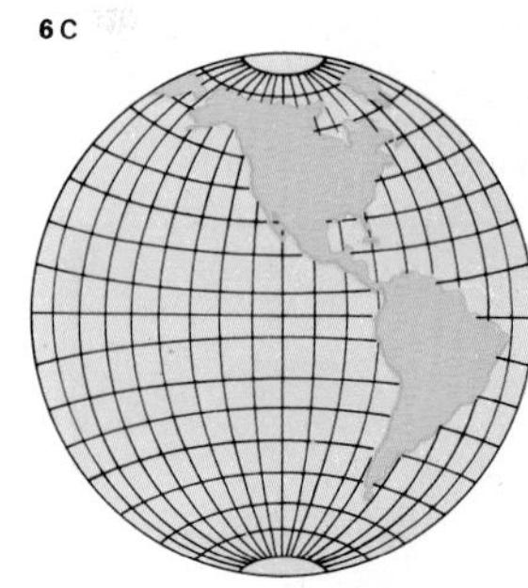
6 C

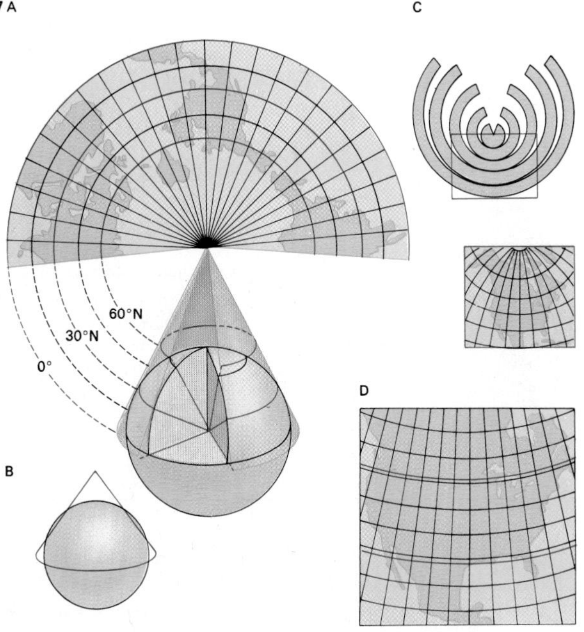
7 A
C
60°N
30°N
0°
B
D

7 The simple conic projection is constructed from a cone tangential to the globe [A]. Only the scale along the parallel in contact with the globe—the standard parallel—is correct. Projections constructed from a secant cone [B] have two standard parallels and because scale error increases away from them more of the projection is nearer the correct scale. The polyconic projection [C], mathematically constructed to have all parallels standard, is very accurate over small areas and is therefore used for topographic series. Alber's equal area projection (D) is a modification of the conic projection with two standard parallels, but with further corrections.

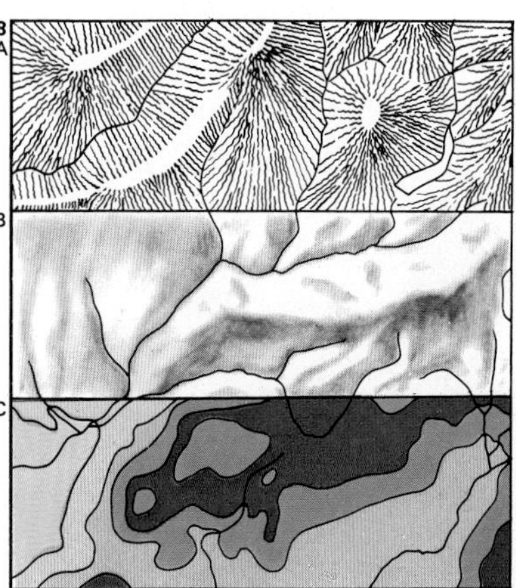
8 A
B
C

8 Height and slope can be represented on a map in many ways, including hatching [A], in which fine lines follow the direction of greatest slope. This method can give an excellent impression of the landscape but may obscure other information. Hill shading [B], the representation of a landscape illuminated from one direction, can be used alone or with colors. Contours [C] can be separated by colored areas, and intermediate heights given.

The face of the Earth

The Earth is the third planet from the Sun. It is the heaviest of the stony planets (the gas giants such as Jupiter are heavier), and the densest of all planets. Its orbit 93 million miles (150 million kilometers) away from the Sun ensures that the planet is neither scorching nor freezing and the presence of water and an atmosphere allowed the evolution of life.

From a distance the Earth appears to be one of the most interesting objects in the solar system. This is largely the result of the variable cloud cover that permits a distant observer to see the lands and oceans on the surface. Astronaut Neil Armstrong (1930–) said, during the Apollo II flight in 1969, that the Earth "looks like a beautiful jewel in space." The Earth is much brighter than the Moon, reflecting about 40 percent of the light falling on it, compared with the Moon's 7 percent. From Mercury, Venus, and Mars the Earth would look to the naked eye like a brilliant bluish star but from Jupiter and the more distant planets the Earth would be hidden from easy view by the glare of the Sun.

1

1 This sunset seen from space shows the diffraction of sunlight by the Earth's atmosphere. Only the lower 17 miles (30km) of atmosphere are dense enough to produce this effect.

2 A "full Earth" was a spectacle unseen by man before the Apollo flights. North and South America and Africa are shown here but the cloud cover tends to obscure the shapes of the continents.

3 These spectacular cloud vortices, photographed from Skylab in 1973, are the result of air being drawn into the pronounced low pressure area in the lee of Guadalupe Island, off the coast of Baja California, Mexico.

2

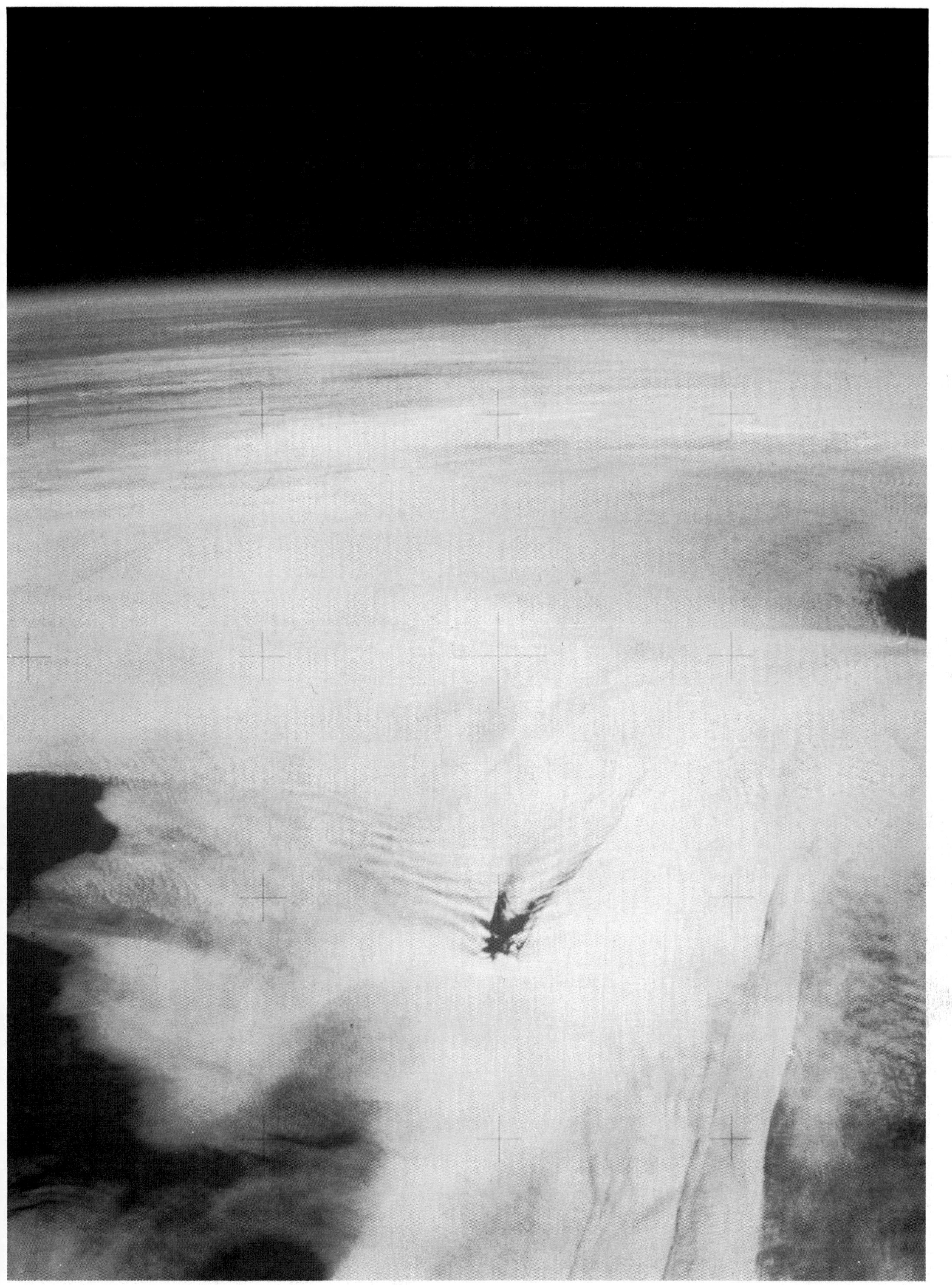

The World

Land Features

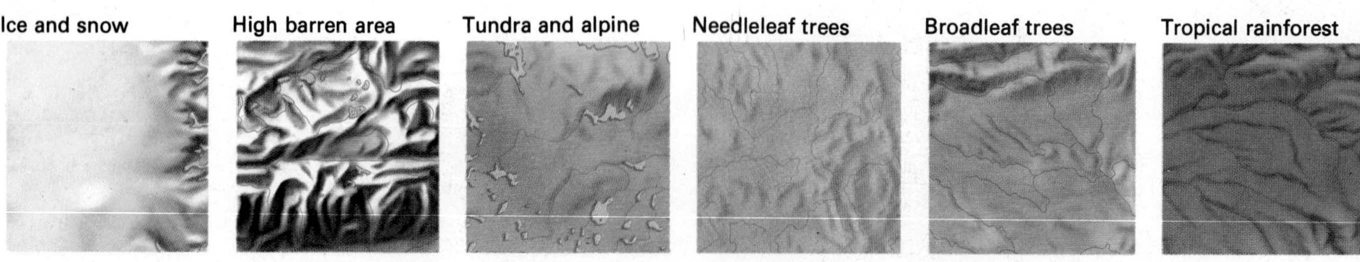
Ice and snow
High barren area
Tundra and alpine
Needleleaf trees
Broadleaf trees
Tropical rainforest

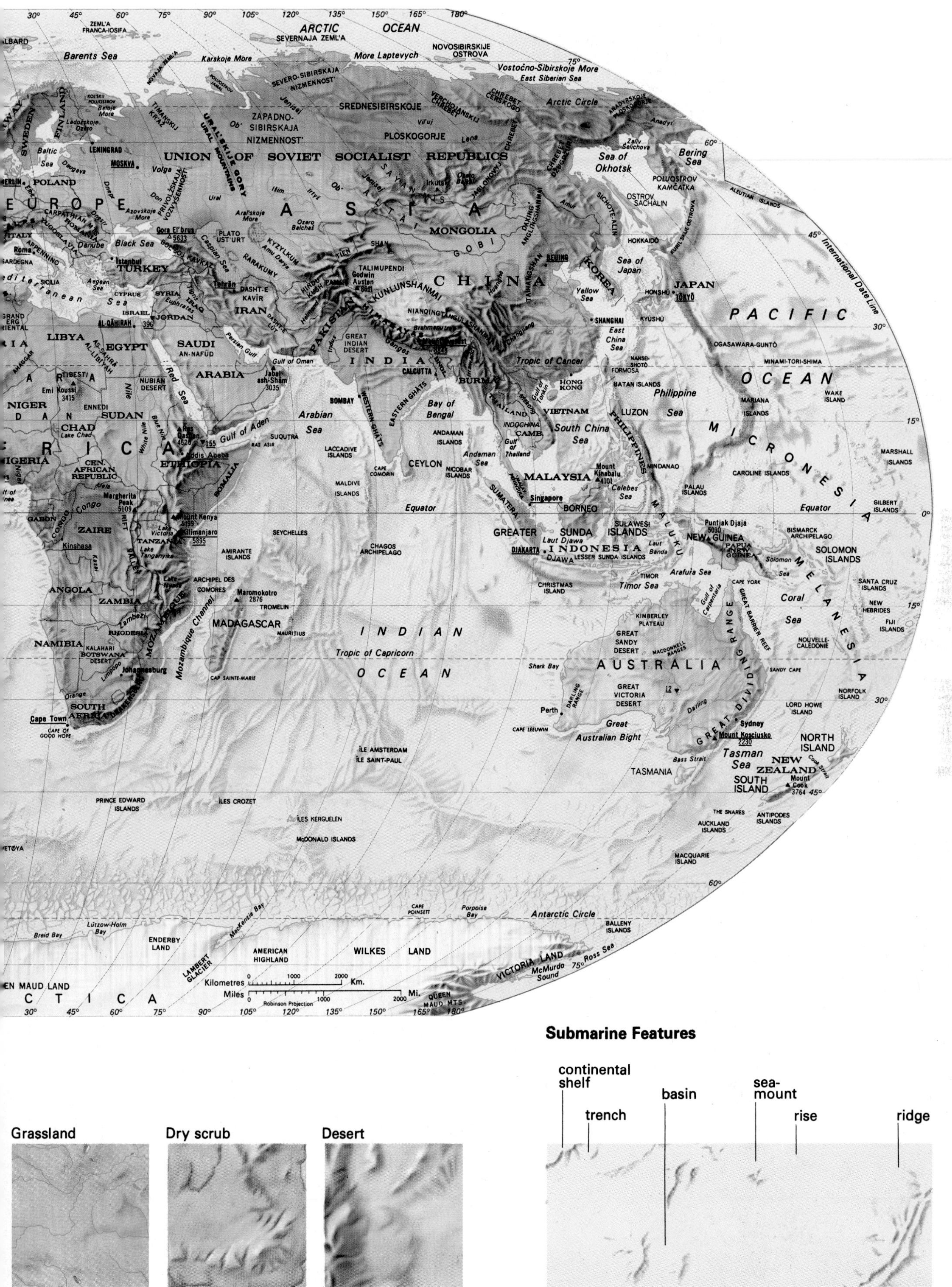
ARCTIC OCEAN
SEVERNAJA ZEML'A
ZEML'A FRANCA-IOSIFA
Barents Sea
Karskoje More
More Laptevych
NOVOSIBIRSKIJE OSTROVA
Vostočno-Sibirskoje More
East Siberian Sea
Arctic Circle
SEVERO-SIBIRSKAJA NIZMENNOST'
SREDNESIBIRSKOJE PLOSKOGORJE
ZAPADNO-SIBIRSKAJA NIZMENNOST'
FINLAND
SWEDEN
LENINGRAD
MOSKVA
Baltic Sea
POLAND
UNION OF SOVIET SOCIALIST REPUBLICS
Sea of Okhotsk
Bering Sea
POLUOSTROV KAMČATKA
OSTROV SACHALIN
EUROPE
ASIA
MONGOLIA
GOBI
Black Sea
Caspian Sea
Gora El'brus 5633
Aral'skoje More
TURKEY
Istanbul
Roma
ITALY
Aegean Sea
CYPRUS
SYRIA
IRAQ
ISRAEL
JORDAN
IRAN
Tehrān
DASHT-E KAVĪR
AL-QĀHIRAH
EGYPT
LIBYA
SAUDI ARABIA
Persian Gulf
Gulf of Oman
Red Sea
Gulf of Aden
TALIMUPENDI
Godwin Austen 8611
KUNLUNSHANMAI
CHINA
BEIJING
KOREA
Sea of Japan
JAPAN
TŌKYŌ
HONSHŪ
HOKKAIDŌ
KYŪSHŪ
Yellow Sea
SHANGHAI
East China Sea
PACIFIC
OCEAN
Tropic of Cancer
PAKISTAN
HIMALAYA
INDIA
GREAT INDIAN DESERT
CALCUTTA
BOMBAY
Arabian Sea
Bay of Bengal
BURMA
HONG KONG
FORMOSA
VIETNAM
THAILAND
LUZON
PHILIPPINES
Philippine Sea
South China Sea
MINDANAO
MARIANA ISLANDS
MICRONESIA
CEYLON
ANDAMAN ISLANDS
Andaman Sea
NICOBAR ISLANDS
LACCADIVE ISLANDS
MALDIVE ISLANDS
MALAYSIA
Singapore
SUMATERA
BORNEO
Mount Kinabalu 4101
Celebes Sea
SULAWESI ISLANDS
GREATER SUNDA ISLANDS
DJAKARTA
INDONESIA
DJAWA
LESSER SUNDA ISLANDS
Laut Djawa
Laut Banda
MALUKU
NEW GUINEA
PAPUA NEW GUINEA
Puntjak Djaja 5030
BISMARCK ARCHIPELAGO
SOLOMON ISLANDS
Equator
MARSHALL ISLANDS
CAROLINE ISLANDS
GILBERT ISLANDS
MELANESIA
Arafura Sea
Timor Sea
TIMOR
CHRISTMAS ISLAND
Coral Sea
SANTA CRUZ ISLANDS
NEW HEBRIDES
FIJI ISLANDS
NOUVELLE-CALEDONIE
CAPE YORK
Gulf of Carpentaria
GREAT BARRIER REEF
KIMBERLEY PLATEAU
GREAT SANDY DESERT
AUSTRALIA
GREAT VICTORIA DESERT
GREAT DIVIDING RANGE
Perth
Shark Bay
CAPE LEEUWIN
Great Australian Bight
Sydney
Mount Kosciusko 2230
Bass Strait
TASMANIA
Tasman Sea
NORFOLK ISLAND
LORD HOWE ISLAND
NEW ZEALAND
NORTH ISLAND
SOUTH ISLAND
Mount Cook 3764
THE SNARES
AUCKLAND ISLANDS
ANTIPODES ISLANDS
MACQUARIE ISLAND
International Date Line
NUBIAN DESERT
SUDAN
CHAD
Lake Chad
NIGER
ETHIOPIA
Addis Abeba
SOMALIA
SUQUTRĀ
CEN. AFRICAN REPUBLIC
Congo
GABON
ZAIRE
Kinshasa
Mount Kenya 5199
Kilimanjaro 5895
Lake Victoria
TANZANIA
Lake Tanganyika
ANGOLA
ZAMBIA
RHODESIA
MOZAMBIQUE
Mozambique Channel
MADAGASCAR
Maromokotro 2876
NAMIBIA
KALAHARI
BOTSWANA
Johannesburg
SOUTH AFRICA
Cape Town
CAPE OF GOOD HOPE
SEYCHELLES
CHAGOS ARCHIPELAGO
AMIRANTE ISLANDS
ARCHIPEL DES COMORES
TROMELIN
MAURITIUS
INDIAN OCEAN
Tropic of Capricorn
ÎLE AMSTERDAM
ÎLE SAINT-PAUL
PRINCE EDWARD ISLANDS
ÎLES CROZET
ÎLES KERGUELEN
McDONALD ISLANDS
Antarctic Circle
BALLENY ISLANDS
ENDERBY LAND
AMERICAN HIGHLAND
WILKES LAND
LAMBERT GLACIER
VICTORIA LAND
McMurdo Sound
Ross Sea
Lützow-Holm Bay
Breid Bay
Mackenzie Bay
Porpoise Bay
CAPE POINSETT
QUEEN MAUD MTS.
Kilometres 0 1000 2000 Km.
Miles 0 1000 2000 Mi.
Robinson Projection
Submarine Features
continental shelf
trench
basin
sea-mount
rise
ridge
Grassland
Dry scrub
Desert

Europe and North Africa

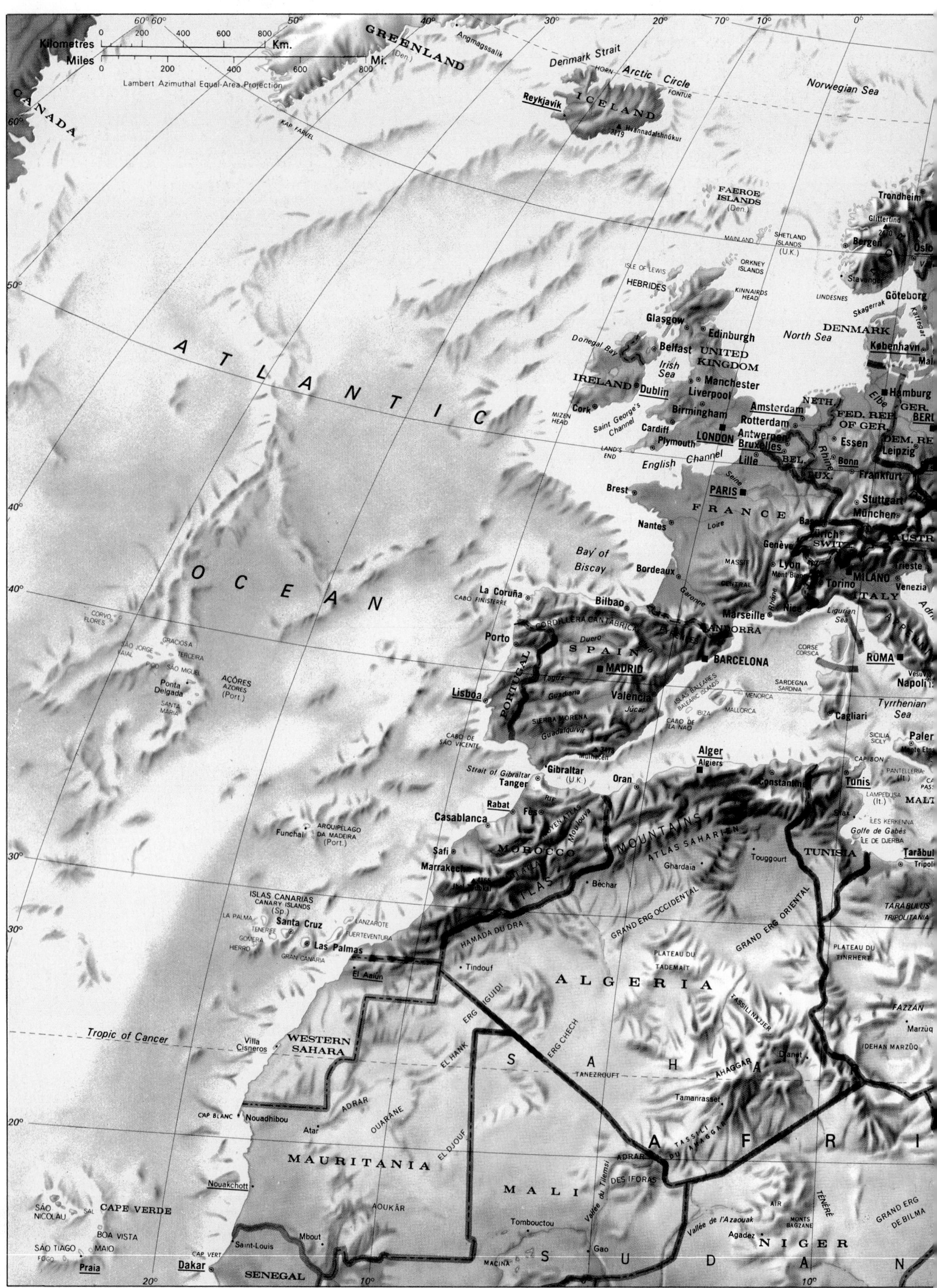
Kilometres
0 200 400 600 800 Km.
Miles
0 200 400 600 800 Mi.
Lambert Azimuthal Equal-Area Projection
CANADA
GREENLAND
(Den.)
Angmagssalik
KAP FARVEL
Denmark Strait
Arctic Circle
HORN
FONTUR
Reykjavík
ICELAND
Norwegian Sea
FAEROE ISLANDS
(Den.)
Trondheim
Glittertind
MAINLAND
SHETLAND ISLANDS
(U.K.)
Bergen
Oslo
ISLE OF LEWIS
HEBRIDES
ORKNEY ISLANDS
KINNAIRDS HEAD
Stavanger
LINDESNES
Göteborg
Skagerrak
Kattegat
Glasgow
Edinburgh
DENMARK
North Sea
København
Donegal Bay
Belfast
UNITED KINGDOM
Irish Sea
IRELAND
Dublin
Manchester
Liverpool
Cork
MIZEN HEAD
Saint George's Channel
Birmingham
Amsterdam
NETH.
Elbe
Hamburg
GER.
Rotterdam
FED. REP. OF GER.
Cardiff
Plymouth
LONDON
Antwerpen
Bruxelles
Essen
Rhine
DEM. RE
Leipzig
LAND'S END
English Channel
Lille
BEL.
Bonn
LUX.
Frankfurt
ATLANTIC
OCEAN
Brest
Seine
PARIS
FRANCE
Stuttgart
München
Nantes
Loire
Genève
SWITZ.
Bay of Biscay
Bordeaux
MASSIF CENTRAL
Lyon
Mont Blanc
Trieste
Venezia
Torino
MILANO
La Coruña
CABO FINISTERRE
Bilbao
Garonne
Rhône
Nice
Marseille
ITALY
CORVO
FLORES
CORDILLERA CANTABRICA
PYRENEES
ANDORRA
Ligurian Sea
Porto
Duero
SPAIN
GRACIOSA
SÃO JORGE
FAIAL
TERCEIRA
PICO
SÃO MIGUEL
Ponta Delgada
SANTA MARIA
AÇÔRES
AZORES
(Port.)
PORTUGAL
MADRID
BARCELONA
CORSE
CORSICA
ROMA
Tagus
Guadiana
Valencia
Júcar
ISLAS BALEARES
BALEARIC ISLANDS
MENORCA
MALLORCA
IBIZA
SARDEGNA
SARDINIA
Napoli
Lisboa
SIERRA MORENA
Guadalquivir
CABO DE LA NAO
Tyrrhenian Sea
Cagliari
CABO DE SÃO VICENTE
Mulhacén
Alger
Algiers
SICILIA
SICILY
Strait of Gibraltar
Gibraltar
(U.K.)
Tanger
Oran
CAP BON
Constantine
Tunis
PANTELLERIA
(It.)
Rabat
LAMPEDUSA
(It.)
MALT
Casablanca
Fès
Moulouya
MOUNTAINS
ATLAS SAHARIEN
ÎLES KERKENNA
Golfe de Gabès
ÎLE DE DJERBA
Funchal
ARQUIPÉLAGO DA MADEIRA
(Port.)
Safi
MOROCCO
Touggourt
TUNISIA
Ghardaïa
Tarābul
Tripoli
Marrakech
ATLAS
Béchar
ISLAS CANARIAS
CANARY ISLANDS
(Sp.)
LA PALMA
TENERIFE
GOMERA
HIERRO
Santa Cruz
Las Palmas
GRAN CANARIA
LANZAROTE
FUERTEVENTURA
HAMADA DU DRA
GRAND ERG OCCIDENTAL
GRAND ERG ORIENTAL
TARABULUS
TRIPOLITANIA
PLATEAU DU TINRHERT
PLATEAU DU TADEMAÏT
El Aaiún
Tindouf
ALGERIA
ERG IGUIDI
TASSILI N'AJJER
FAZZAN
Marzūq
IDEHAN MARZŪQ
Tropic of Cancer
Villa Cisneros
WESTERN SAHARA
EL HANK
ERG CHECH
SAHARA
Djanet
AHAGGAR
TANEZROUFT
Tamanrasset
ADRAR
CAP BLANC
Nouadhibou
Atar
OUARÂNE
EL DJOUF
TASSILI DU HOGGAR
AFRICA
MAURITANIA
ADRAR DES IFORAS
MALI
Vallée du Tilemsi
TÉNÉRÉ
Nouakchott
SÃO NICOLAU
SAL
CAPE VERDE
BOA VISTA
AOUKÂR
Tombouctou
AIR
MONTS BAGZANE
Vallée de l'Azaouak
GRAND ERG DE BILMA
Mbout
Agadez
NIGER
SÃO TIAGO
MAIO
FOGO
Praia
Saint-Louis
CAP VERT
Dakar
Gao
MACINA
SUDAN
SENEGAL

NORDKAPP
Hammerfest
OSTROV KOLGUJEV
MYS KANIN NOS
Murmansk
KOL'SKIJ POLUOSTROV
KOLA PENINSULA
Kiruna
Arctic Circle
Narjan-Mar
Pečora
Usa
Vorkuta
Obskaja Guba
Salechard
A S I A
Jenisej
Pur
Taz
Beloje More
White Sea
Archangel'sk
Mezen'
TIMANSKIJ KR'AŽ
Ižma
Gora Narodnaja
1894
URAL'SKIJE GORY
URAL MOUNTAINS
Kazym
Ob'
ZAPADNO- SIBIRSKAJA
NIZMENNOST'
Chanty-Mansijsk
Konda
Oulu
FINLAND
Gulf of Bothnia
Umeälven
Severnaja Dvina
Onežskoje Ozero
Kotlas
SEVERNYJE UVALY
Kama
Tavda
Tobol'sk
Irtyš
Om'
Ladožskoje Ozero
Lake Ladoga
Helsinki
Gulf of Finland
Suchona
Vologda
Rybinskoje Vodochranilišče
Kamskoje Vdchr.
Nižnij Tagil
Tura
SVERDLOVSK
T'umen'
LENINGRAD
Kirov
Perm'
Omsk
Stockholm
Tallinn
Čudskoje Ozero
Ozero Il'men'
Jaroslavl'
Gor'kovskoje Vodochranilišče
V'atka
Tobol
GOTLAND
Rižskij Zaliv
Rīga
Velikaja
Volga
Gor'kij
Kazan'
Ufa
Čel'abinsk
S O V I E T
Kalinin
ÖLAND
Klaipėda
Daugava
Lovat'
MOSKVA
MOSCOW
Oka
Kujbyševskoje Vodochranilišče
O F
Magnitogorsk
Išim
Baltic Sea
Nemunas
U N I O N
Kujbyšev
Celinograd
Vilnius
Smolensk
Sura
PRIVOLŽSKAJA VOZVYŠENNOST'
TURGAJSKAJA
Gdańsk
Desna
Tula
Penza
Orsk
R E P U B L I C S
Ozero Tengiz
POLAND
Minsk
SREDNERUSSKAJA VOZVYŠENNOST'
Orenburg
Warszawa
Dnepr
P
E
Saratov
Warta
Bug
R
O
Gomel'
Kursk
Voronež
S O C I A L I S T
STOLOVAJA STRANA
Wisła
Kijev
Don
Volgogradskoje Vodochranilišče
Ural
Katowice
Kraków
Char'kov
L'vov
VOLGOGRAD
Emba
Južnyj Bug
Dnepropetrovsk
Doneck
Cimľanskoje Vodochranilišče
Volga
PRIKASPIJSKAJA NIZMENNOST'
Novokazalinsk
Zaporožje
Dnestr
Aral'skoje More
Aral Sea
Syrdarja
BUDAPEST
Kišin'ov
Rostov-na-Donu
Astrachan'
HUNGARY
Cluj
Prut
ODESSA
Azovskoje More
Krasnodar
K Y Z Y L K U M
PLATO UST' URT
Sevastopol'
Nukus
Beograd
Bucuresti
Gora El'brus
Groznyj
Caspian Sea
Amudarja
Danube
Varna
B l a c k S e a
Batumi
Zaliv Kara-Bogaz-Gol
BULGARIA
TBILISI
BAKU
Krasnovodsk
K A R A K U M Y
Tiranë
ALBANIA
ISTANBUL
Samsun
Jerevan
Thessaloníki
Marmara Denizi
Kizil Irmak
Euphrates
Aschabad
GREECE
Eskişehir
Sakarya
Ankara
T U R K E Y
5165
3916
Olimbos
Aegean Sea
EVVOIA
Tuz Gölü
Van Gölü
Tabriz
Daryācheh-ye Rezā'īyeh
Rasht
Mashhad
İzmir
Tigris
Athínai
KIKLADHES
A S I A   M I N O R
Ionian Sea
Adana
Al-Mawṣil
TEHRAN
Hamadān
DODHEKÁNISOS
RODHOS
TOROS DAĞLARI
Ḥalab
İskenderun Körfezi
Levkosia
AFG.
Iráklion
KRITI
CRETE
CYPRUS
LEBANON
Bayrūt
ŞYRIA
BĀDIYAT ASH-SHĀM
Dimashq
MESOPOTAMIA
Baghdād
DASHT-E KAVĪR
Daryācheh-ye Namak
ISRAEL
I R A Q
Tigris
Eṣfahān
Yazd
DASHT-E LŪT
M e d i t e r r a n e a n   S e a
'Ammān
Yerushalayim
Dead Sea
396
Euphrates
Al-Baṣrah
Banghāzī
Bengasi
Tubruq
Al-Iskandarīyah
Alexandria
Tel Aviv-Yafo
Bur Sa'īd
Ghazzah
AL-WIDYĀN
Ābādān
Kermān
Khalīj Surt
BARQAH
CYRENAICA
Qanāt as-Suways
JORDAN
AL-HAMĀD
Al-Kuwayt
KUWAIT
Shīrāz
42
133
AL-QĀHIRAH
CAIRO
SHIBH JAZĪRAT SĪNĀ'
Jabal al-Lawz
2580
NEUTRAL ZONE
Persian Gulf
Bandar 'Abbās
QESHM
Strait of Hormuz
AṢ-ṢAḤRĀ'
Gulf of Aqaba
Khalīj as-Suways
AL-GHARBĪYAH
AN-NAFŪD
Al-Manāmah
BAHRAIN
OMAN
Asyūṭ
Nile
QATAR
Gulf of Oman
E G Y P T
JABAL TUWAYQ
AD-DAHNĀ
Al-Hufūf
SARĪR NERASTRO
AL-HIJĀZ
Al-Madīnah
Ar-Riyāḍ
UNITED ARAB EMIRATES
AL-KUFRAH
HADABAT AL-JILF
Aswān
Tropic of Cancer
A R A B I A N
Jabal ash-Shām
3035
Lake Nasser
Red Sea
S A U D I
NAFŪD AD-DAHY
Jabal al-'Uwaynāt
1934
Juddah
Makkah
A R A B I A
NUBIAN DESERT
AR-RAB' AL-KHĀLĪ
Būr Sūdān
S U D A N
P E N I N S U L A
Nile
'Atbarah
Wādī al-Malik
Atbarah
DAHLAK ARCHIPELAGO
Arabian Sea
Ghubbat al-Qamar
Umm Durmān
P.D.R. OF YEMEN
Al-Khurṭum
Khartoum
ETHIOPIA
Asmera
Mesewa
YEMEN
Ṣan'ā'
RA'S FARTAK

Southern Africa

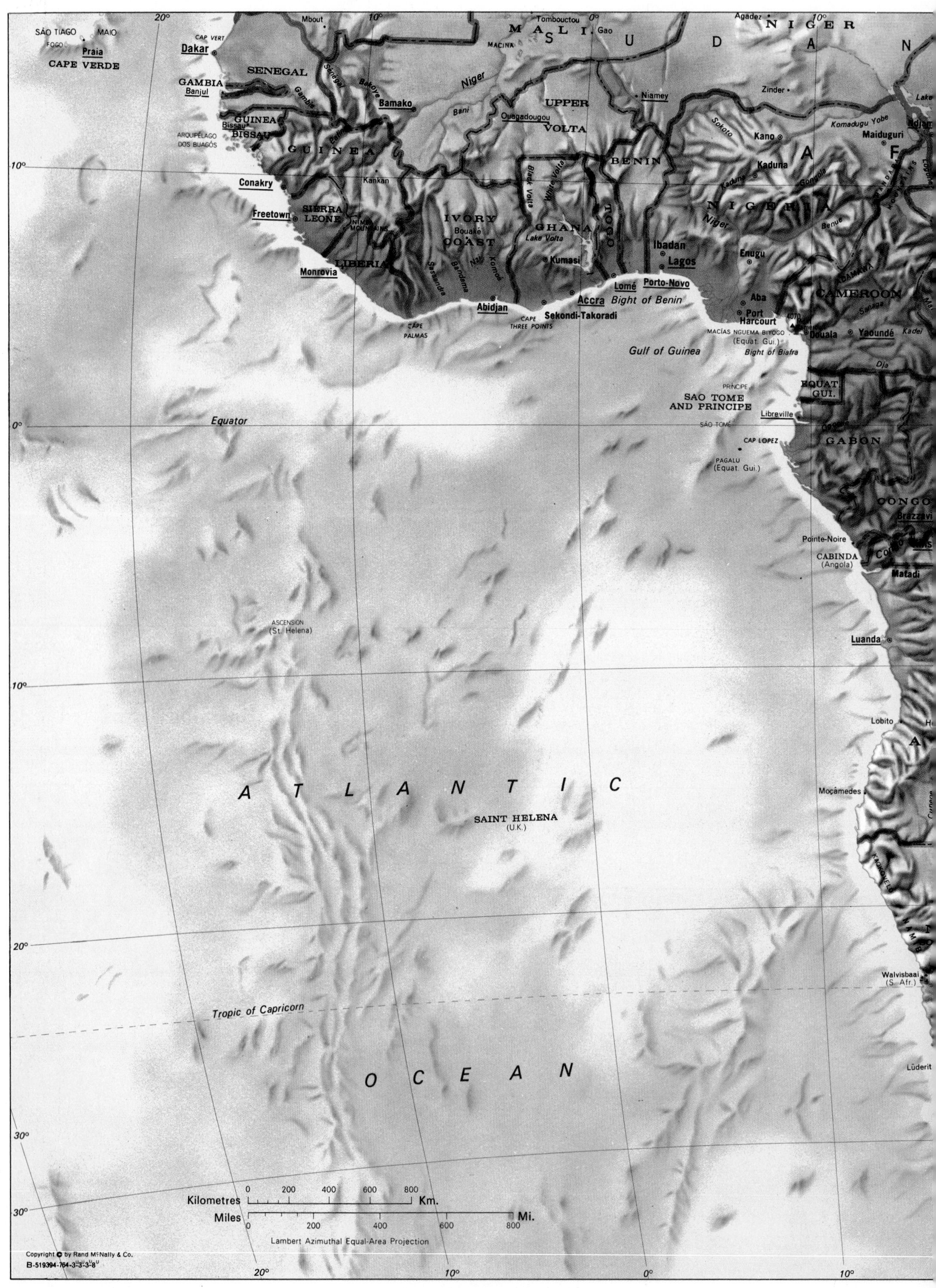

SÃO TIAGO
MAIO
FOGO
Praia
CAPE VERDE
CAP VERT
Dakar
SENEGAL
GAMBIA
Banjul
Gambia
Sénégal
Bakoye
Mbout
Bamako
Niger
Bani
MALI
Tombouctou
Gao
MACINA
SUDAN
Agadez
NIGER
Zinder
Niamey
UPPER VOLTA
Ouagadougou
GUINEA-BISSAU
Bissau
ARQUIPÉLAGO DOS BIJAGÓS
GUINEA
Kankan
Conakry
Freetown
SIERRA LEONE
NIMBA MOUNTAINS
Monrovia
LIBERIA
IVORY COAST
Bouaké
Sassandra
Bandama
Nzi
Komoé
Abidjan
CAPE PALMAS
GHANA
Black Volta
White Volta
Lake Volta
Kumasi
CAPE THREE POINTS
Sekondi-Takoradi
Accra
TOGO
Lomé
BENIN
Porto-Novo
Bight of Benin
Ibadan
Lagos
NIGERIA
Sokoto
Kano
Kaduna
Komadugu Yobe
Maiduguri
Gongola
Benue
Enugu
Aba
Port Harcourt
ADAMAWA
CAMEROON
Sanaga
Douala
Yaoundé
Kadei
MACÍAS NGUEMA BIYOGO (Equat. Gui.)
Bight of Biafra
Gulf of Guinea
PRINCIPE
SAO TOME AND PRINCIPE
SÃO TOMÉ
EQUAT. GUI.
Libreville
CAP LOPEZ
PAGALU (Equat. Gui.)
GABON
CONGO
Brazzaville
Pointe-Noire
CABINDA (Angola)
Matadi
Luanda
Lobito
Moçâmedes
Walvisbaai (S. Afr.)
Lüderit
Equator
ASCENSION (St. Helena)
ATLANTIC
SAINT HELENA (U.K.)
Tropic of Capricorn
OCEAN
Kilometres 0 200 400 600 800 Km.
Miles 0 200 400 600 800 Mi.
Lambert Azimuthal Equal-Area Projection
Copyright © by Rand McNally & Co.
B-519394-764-3-3-3-8

SUDAN
Umm Durmān
Al-Khurtum
Khartoum
Al-Fāshir
Al-Ubayyid
Abéché
JABAL MARRAH
White Nile
Blue Nile
Atbarah
Wādī al-Malik
Asmera
Mesewa
DAHLAK ARCHIPELAGO
Tekeze
Ras Dashen
Gonder
Lake Tana
YEMEN
San'ā'
P.D.R. OF YEMEN
Ghubbat al-Qamar
RA'S FARTAK
Al-Mukallā
Arabian Sea
Aden
Gulf of Aden
Bab el-Mandeb
AFARS AND ISSAS (Fr.)
Djibouti
Berbera
'Alula
'ABD AL-KŪRĪ
SUQUTRA (P.D.R. of Yem.)
RAS ASIR CAPE GUARDAFUI
RAS HAFUN
Hargeysa
Dire Dawa
Awash
Addis Abeba
ETHIOPIA
Bahr al-'Arab
Bahr al-Ghazāl
Sobat
Boro
Jur
Sarh
Bahr Aouk
CENTRAL AFRICAN REPUBLIC
Kotto
Chinko
Mbari
Mbomou
Bomu
Mountain Nile
Jūbā
Bangui
Uele
Congo
Aruwimi
CONGO
Kisangani
Tshuapa
STANLEY FALLS
MURCHISON FALLS
Lake Albert
UGANDA
Lake Kyoga
Margherita Peak
5109
4321
Mount Elgon
Kampala
KENYA
Lake Edward
Lake Victoria
Nairobi
5199
Lake Rudolf
Lake Abaya
Genale
Dawa
Shebelle
SOMALIA
Mogadisho
Juba
Tana
Athi
Equator
Lac Tumba
BASIN
ZAIRE
Lac Kivu
RWANDA
Kigali
BURUNDI
Bujumbura
Lac Mai-Ndombe
Lukenie
Kasai
Kwilu
Kwenge
Kananga
Lomami
Lualaba
Lake Natron
SERENGETI PLAIN
Mwanza
Kilimanjaro
Lake Eyasi
Pangani
Mombasa
MASAI STEPPE
PEMBA ISLAND
Zanzibar
ZANZIBAR
INDIAN
OCEAN
AMIRANTE ISLANDS (Sey.)
SEYCHELLES
Lake Tanganyika
TANZANIA
Dar-es-Salaam
MAFIA ISLAND
Lake Rukwa
Great Ruaha
Luwegu
RIFT VALLEY
Loange
Chicapa
Chiumbe
Cassai
Lubilash
Lulua
Luvua
Lake Mweru
KATANGA PLATEAU
Lubumbashi
Lake Bangweulu
Ruvuma
Mtwara
ALDABRA ISLANDS (Sey.)
ASSUMPTION ISLAND
COSMOLEDO GROUP (Sey.)
FARQUHAR GROUP (Sey.)
GRANDE COMORE
COMORO ISLANDS
ANJOUAN
MOHELI
MAYOTTE (Fr.)
Channel
CAP D'AMBRE
Diego-Suarez
2876
Maromokotro
Lungué-Bungo
OLA
Ndola
Kabompo
MUCHINGA MOUNTAINS
Luangwa
Lake Malawi
Lugenda
M'Salu
Lurio
ZAMBIA
Zambezi
Kwando
Lusaka
Kafue
Lilongwe
Lake Chilwa
Zomba
Blantyre
MOZAMBIQUE
Moçambique
Mozambique
CAP SAINT-ANDRÉ
Baie d'Antongil
TROMELIN (Fr.)
Cubango
Cuito
Lake Kariba
Livingstone
VICTORIA FALLS
Okavango
Salisbury
RHODESIA
Betsiboka
Tamatave
Tananarive
Tsumeb
KAUKAUVELD
Bulawayo
Beira
MADAGASCAR
MASCARENE ISLANDS
MAURITIUS
REUNION (Fr.)
BOTSWANA
BASSAS DA INDIA (Fr.)
ÎLE EUROPA (Fr.)
Mangoky
CAP SAINT-VINCENT
Tuléar
Tropic of Capricorn
Limpopo
PONTA SÃO SEBASTIÃO
PONTA DA BARRA FALSA
KALAHARI
DESERT
Nossob
Gaborone
Olifants
Changane
Pretoria
Maputo
Mbabane
JOHANNESBURG
SWAZILAND
KAAP PLATO
Vaal
Fort-Dauphin
CAP SAINTE-MARIE
SOUTH AFRICA
Orange
Maseru
Thabana Ntlenyana
3482
Bloemfontein
LESOTHO
Durban
DRAKENSBERG
GREAT KARROO
East London
Port Elizabeth
CAPE AGULHAS
10°
0°
20°
30°
40°
50°
60°

Earth panorama: Europe

Europe is the second smallest continent. It is bounded by the Arctic Ocean to the north, the Atlantic Ocean to the west, and the Mediterranean and Black Seas to the south. It merges into Asia to the east, and the conventional boundary follows the Caucasus mountains, the Caspian Sea, and the Ural mountains.

A line following the northern edge of the Pyrenees mountains, the Rhône valley, and the northern edge of the Alps and Carpathian mountains separates northern from southern Europe. Northern Europe thus consists of large sedimentary plains, a Precambrian shield, and worn-down Paleozoic highlands. Southern Europe is characterized by Cenozoic mountains (Alps, Pyrenees, Carpathians) surrounding restricted basins.

Apart from a small subarctic fringe in the extreme north, most of Europe is in the temperate zone. The distance from the Atlantic and the situation of the mountains create a climatic subdivision of Europe into marine areas to the west, Mediterranean to the south, and continental to the east.

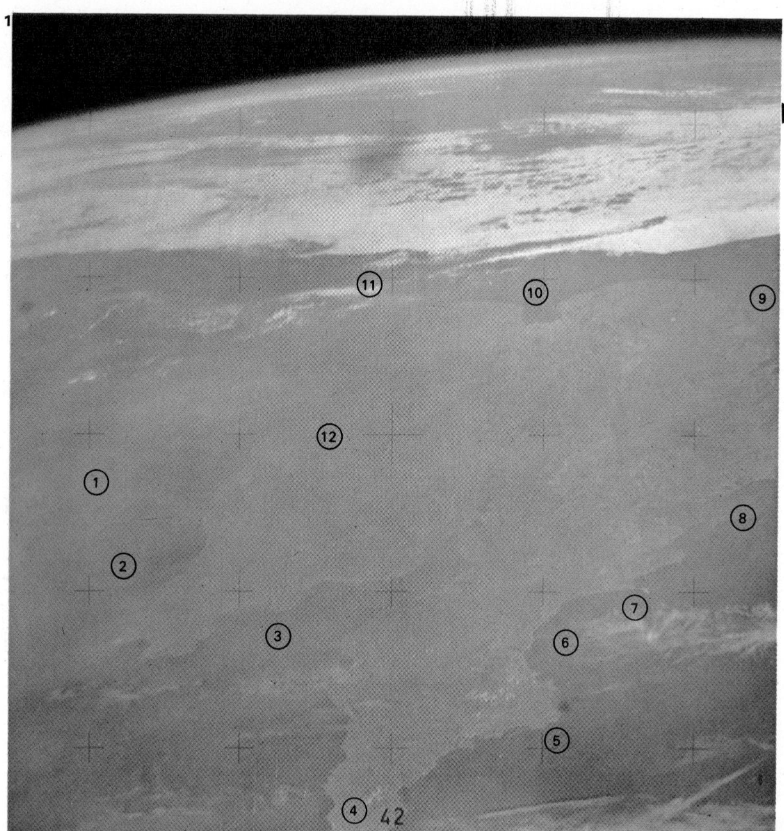
1
11
10
9
12
1
8
2
7
3
6
5
4
42

Eire
UK

1 Great Britain and Ireland are islands of the European continental shelf; they were part of the mainland during the recent Ice Age. The Irish seashore is indistinct north of Anglesey [1], but Cardigan Bay [2], the Bristol Channel [3], Cornwall [4], and Start Point [5] are clearly visible. All of this part of Britain consists of ancient Precambrian and Paleozoic rocks. East of a line from Lyme Bay [6] to Grimsby [11], the rocks are Mesozoic and Cenozoic. North of Derby [12] the rocks are again Paleozoic. Other features include Portland Bill [7], the Isle of Wight [8], Orford Ness [9], and the Wash [10], a 20-mile (32-km) long, shallow inlet of the North Sea.

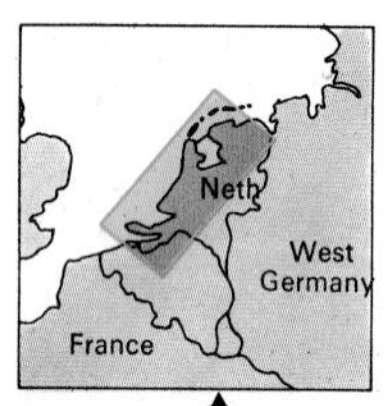
Neth
West
Germany
France

2 The Dutch coast, from the Schelde and Rhine estuaries [1] to the Frisian islands [2], is seen here, including the cities of the Hague [3], Rotterdam [4], and Amsterdam [5] and the IJsselmeer [6].

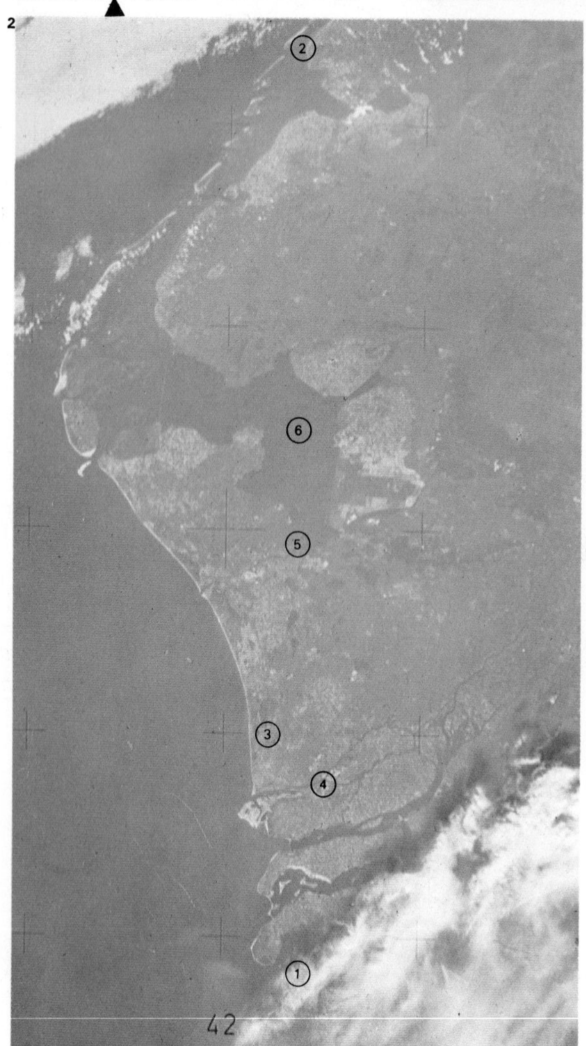
2
2
6
5
3
4
1
42

3
7
5
6
2
3
1
4

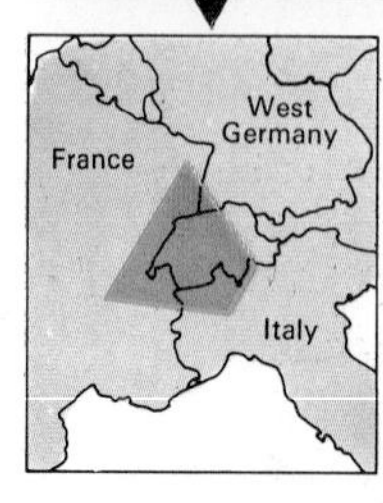
West
Germany
France
Italy

3 The Alps are the highest mountains in eastern Europe, extending 620 miles (1000km) from the Mediterranean to Vienna. They are the western limb of a much larger system of mountains that extends to Indonesia through the Balkans and the Himalayas. The highest summit is Mont Blanc [1] at 15,771ft (4,807m). It is part of the inner granite core, which has been thrust up in places and uncovered by erosion. Lake Geneva [2], which divides the upper Rhône valley [3] from the lower [4], is in a depression between the Alps and the Jura mountains [5], which were folded, but less severely, as a consequence of the Alpine upheaval. The lakes of Neuchâtel [6] and Thun [7] can also be seen.

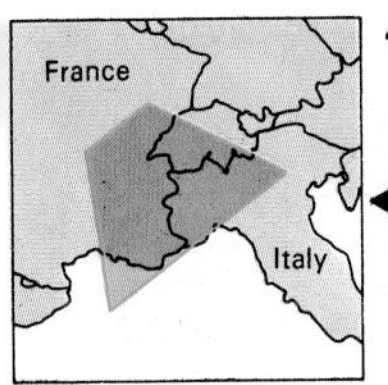
France
Italy

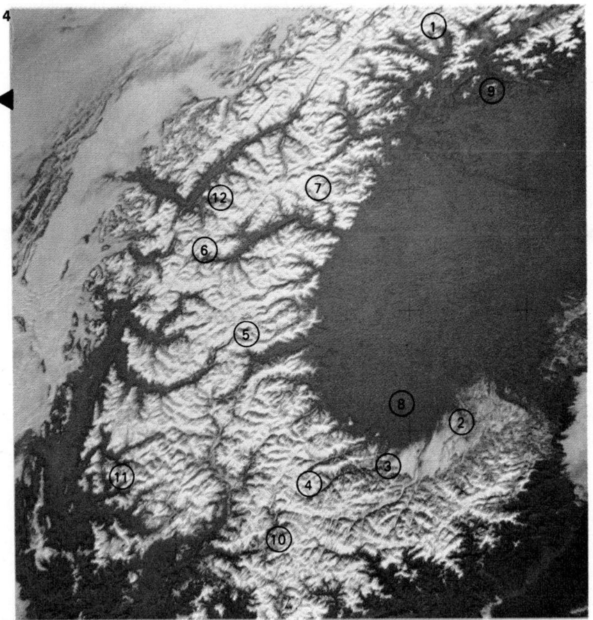
4

4 The Western Alps extend from the Mediterranean coast (lower right) to the Adula massif [1]. They enclose the Po valley. The following massifs can be seen here: Argentera [2], Monte Viso [3], Mont Pelvoux [4], Vanoise [5], Mont Blanc [6], and Monte Rosa [7]. The major rivers on the Italian side are the Po [8] and the Adda [9], draining through Lake Como; and the Durance [10], Isère [11], and Rhône [12] on the French side.

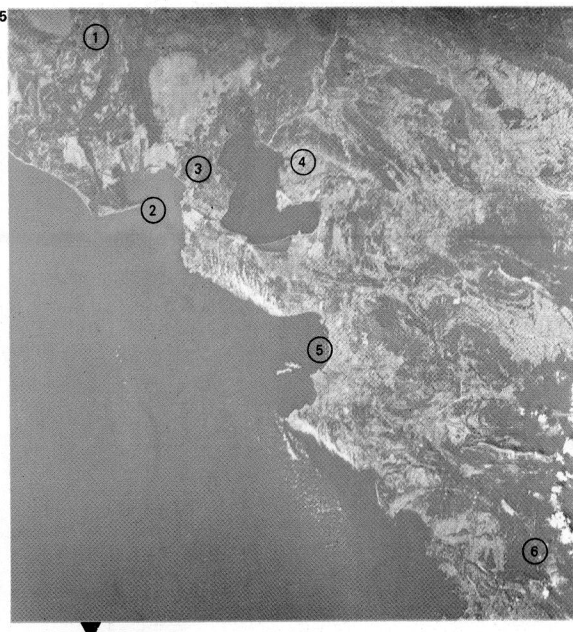
5

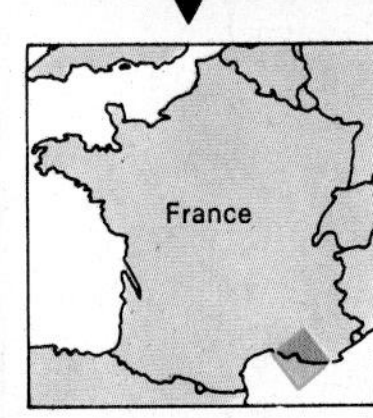
France

5 Part of the south coast of France from the Vaccares marshes [1] to Toulon [6] is shown here. The main Rhône outlet [2] is seen near the huge docks of the modern harbor of Fos-sur-Mer [3]. Port-de-Bouc docks on the sea side of the canal link the Berre lake [4] with the Mediterranean. The artificial breakwater [5] of the New Harbor of Marseille can also be seen in this view.

6 A

6 B

Austria
Hungary
Italy
Yugoslavia
A
B

6 The famous boot-shape of southern Italy [A] appears far more squat here because of the camera angle. The western side of the peninsula right down to the "toe" of Calabria has a pronounced relief due to the Apennine range. The Bay of Naples [1] is limited to the north by the island of Ischia and to the south by Capri. Just inland of the bottom of the bay the volcano Mt Vesuvius can be seen, as can Botte Donato mountain [2]. The "arch" between the toe and the heel is the Gulf of Taranto; the heel is terminated by Cape Santa Maria di Leuca. Between the heel and the spur of Gargano (which has some lakes on its north side) is a dry limestone area, Puglia. The eastern coast of Sicily [B] is seen in this infrared photograph. Mt Etna, the highest volcano in Europe, is still active as is evidenced by the thin plume of smoke rising from its crater. The mountain's height of 10,960ft (3,340m) is approximate, because it changes at each eruption. Recent lava flows at the crest appear dark in contrast to the older red ones. The numerous small "warts" on the flank of the volcano are cinder cones created by side vents. The town of Catania nestles at the foot of Mt Etna by the sea. Beyond it is a cultivated plain with fields of various colors and a meandering river. The town of Augusta, enclosed by a breakwater, is located at the bottom edge.

Earth panorama: Africa

Africa is the third largest continent and is devoid of any peripheral island arcs. It is entirely surrounded by mid-oceanic ridges (one of them, in the Red Sea, coming right up to its shores) except to the north where it abuts the Mediterranean and the Alpine system. The Maghreb (Morocco, Algeria, and Tunisia) is the only geologically recent province, and it is separated from the Precambrian basement and shield forming the rest of the continent by a big fault running from Agadir to Gabes.

The rolling basement to the south of this fault line forms great basins (Niger, Chad, Congo, Kalahari) surrounded by highlands that dominate the coasts. More than half of the continent lacks drainage toward the sea, and the large rivers (Nile, Congo, Niger, and Zambezi) have long paths to the sea.

The climate is zoned, with a central equatorial band grading the north and the south into tropical lands with a marked dry season, the length of which increases poleward until the desert areas. South Africa has a warm maritime climate, but its northern fringe has a dry Mediterranean climate.

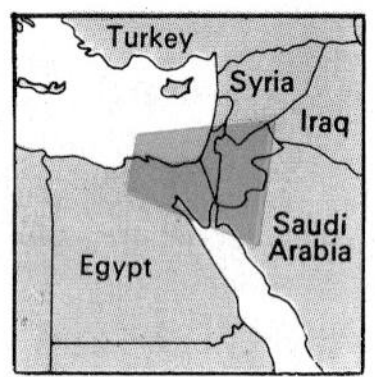

Turkey
Syria
Iraq
Saudi Arabia
Egypt

1

1 Where the Nile flows, the land is lush and green; where its waters do not reach there is desert. The ribbon oasis along the Nile valley to the south (right) of Cairo [1] spreads out into a rich alluvial delta. The river branches into two, the Rosetta Nile [2] and the Damietta Nile [3]. The front of the delta is marked by large lagoons and infertile desert sand. Between Alexandria [4] and Cairo there are large fields and modern irrigation projects. The Suez Canal runs from Port Said [5] to Suez [6]. A narrow strip of vegetation links the Nile with Ismailia [7] the halfway station on the Suez Canal.

2

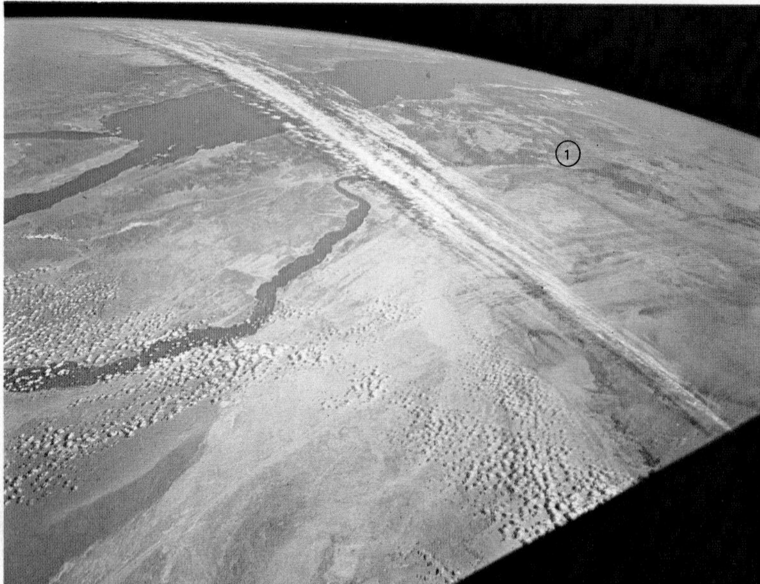

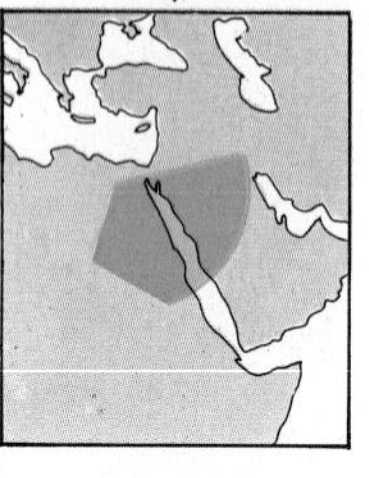

2 The ribbon oasis of the Nile divides the Libyan desert in the foreground from the Arabian desert in the background, beyond which the Red Sea, the gulfs of Suez and Aqaba, and the Sinai peninsula can be seen. The Nile's yearly flood used to bring about 55 million tons of new fertile silt, but much of this is now stopped by the Aswan Dam [1], and it is silting up the artificial reservoir, Lake Nasser. The lake loses water through evaporation, a situation aggravated by the presence of water hyacinths. The reduced flow has increased the salinity of the eastern Mediterranean and seriously affected its plankton population. The local sardine fishing industry has suffered as a result of this ecological imbalance.

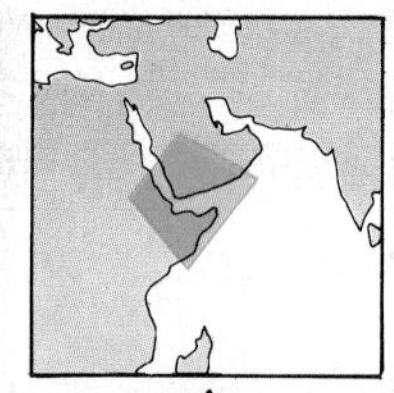

3 The Arabian peninsula [1] has moved and rotated away from Africa, opening up the Gulf of Aden [2] and the Red Sea [3]. The Bab el Mandeb strait [4] is a triple junction of three spreading axes: the Gulf of Aden, which links up with the Carlsberg Ridge in the Indian Ocean; the Red Sea axis, which extends to the Dead Sea; and the Afar Triangle [5] linking up with the East African Rift.

3

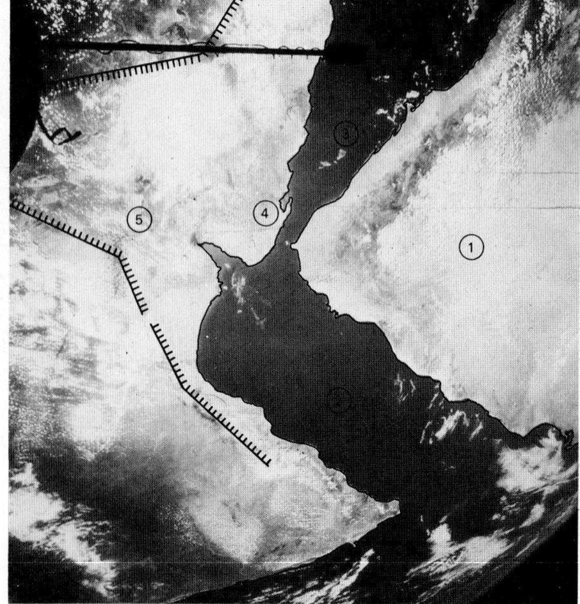

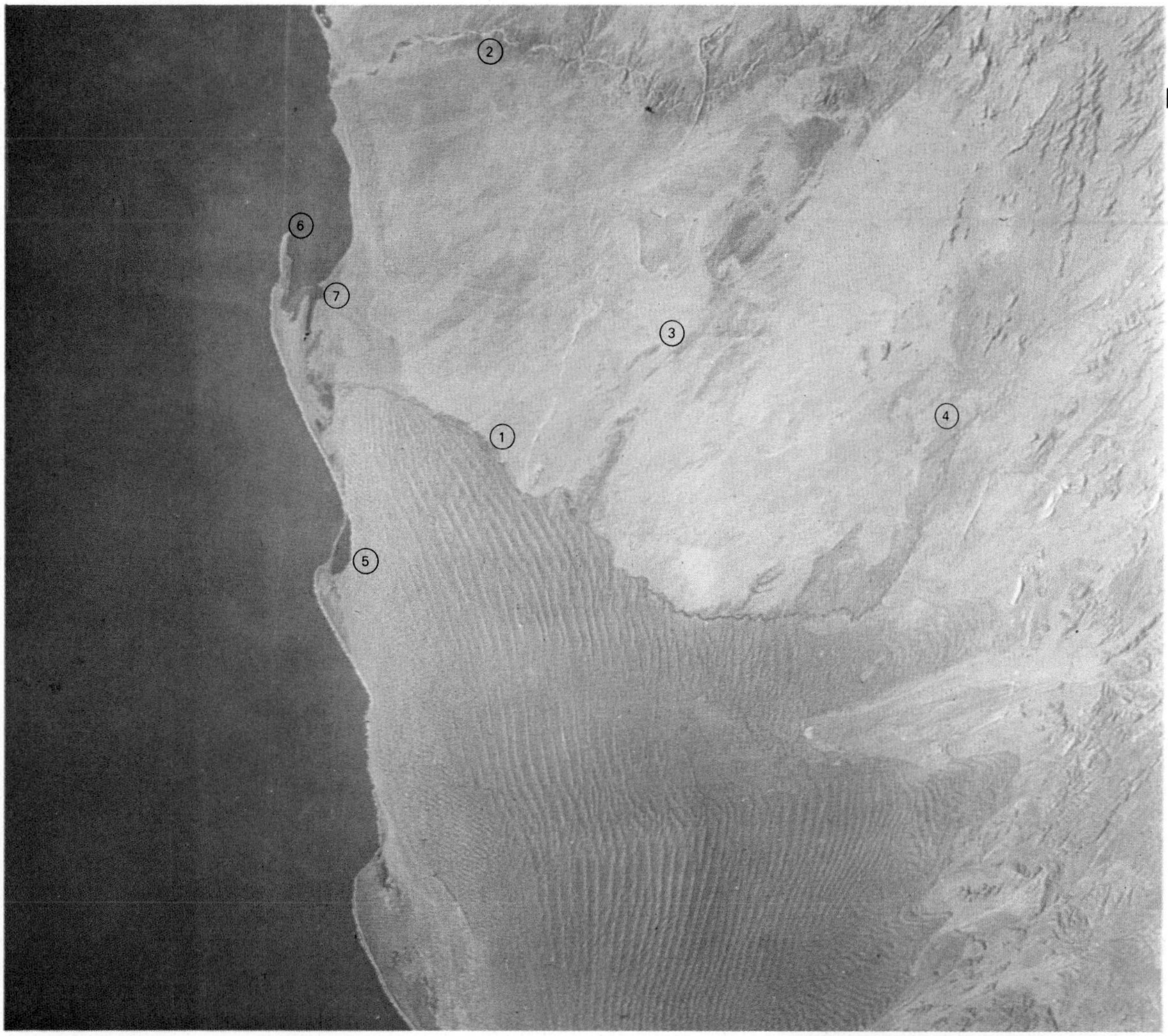

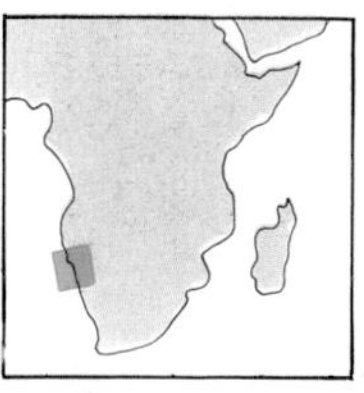

4 The Namib Desert in Namibia (South-West Africa) is rocky to the north and sandy to the south. The sand sea, or erg, is limited to the north by the Kuiseb River [1]. The Swakop River [2] can also be seen. The rocky area is a peneplain exposing the roots of an old Precambrian mountain range; the lineations of the folds can easily be followed. These rocks and folds have a southwesterly trend, and they are cut off by the continental shelf. The missing continuation is found in South America, a clear proof of continental drift. The rocks are granite, gneiss, and marble, which forms white ridges [3]. A sill of basic rock also shows up [4]; both the sill and marble are rich in minerals. The longshore drift toward the north forms sandspits, often enclosing lagoons [5]. A big sandspit encloses Walvis Bay [6]; Walvis Bay town [7] appears blue.

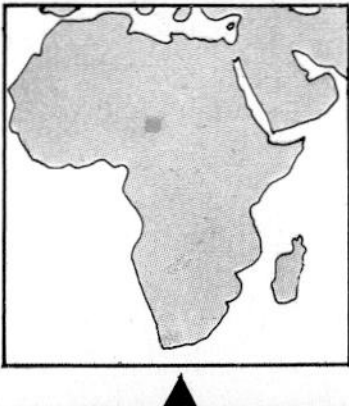

5 Lake Chad lies across the borders of Chad, Niger, Nigeria, and Cameroon. It is the center for an inland drainage system and has no outlet to the sea. Its main tributary is the 750-mile (1200-km) Chari, flowing from the south. The intermittent wadi Bahr el Ghazal drains the rare rains from the Saharan north. Because of the high evaporation and the marked seasonal variation of the inflow, the area of the lake varies, and therefore precise contours are rarely shown on maps. It is a shallow lake whose average level is dropping at a rate of 0.5in (1.25cm) a year. It is rarely more than 25ft (7.6m) deep.

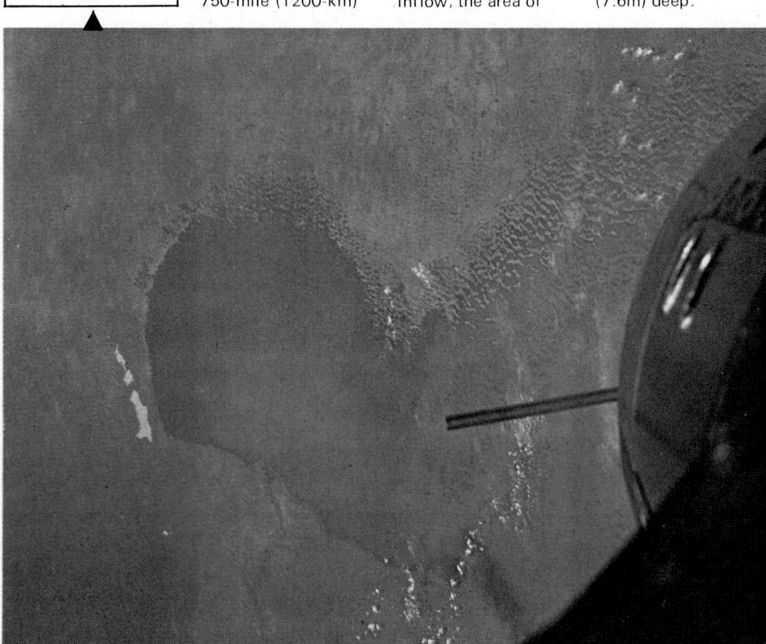

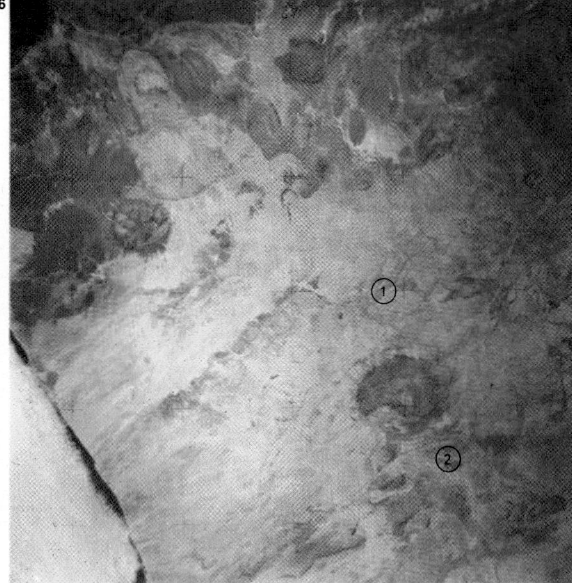
1
2

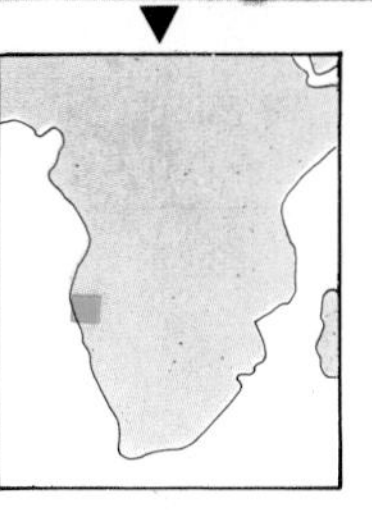

6 This is the bare African shield in southwest Africa – the roots of Precambrian mountains that have been worn down to a peneplain. The area consists mainly of gneiss. The conspicuous circular patches are plugs of granite known as inselbergs. Two main intermittent wadis can be seen. The coastline is underlined by a narrow strip of blue sea; the rest of the sea is clouded over because of the cold Benguela current, which promotes cloud formation.

Northern Asia

Kilometres 0 200 400 600 Km.
Miles 0 200 400 600 Mi.
Lambert Azimuthal Equal-Area Projection
GREENLAND
(Den.)
KAP MORRIS JESUP
NORDOST-RUNDINGEN
KAP BREWSTER
Reykjavík
HORN
ICELAND
2119 Hvannadalshnúkur
FONTUR
Denmark Strait
Greenland Sea
JAN MAYEN
(Nor.)
ARCTIC
ATLANTIC OCEAN
SPITSBERGEN
SVALBARD
(Nor.)
NORDAUSTLANDET
FAEROE ISLANDS
(Den.)
HEBRIDES
ORKNEY ISLANDS
SHETLAND ISLANDS
KINNAIRDS HEAD
Norwegian Sea
Arctic Circle
ZEML'A FRANCA-IOSIFA
FRANZ JOSEPH LAND
Barents Sea
IRELAND
Dublin
Irish Sea
Glasgow
Edinburgh
Manchester
Cardiff
Birmingham
LONDON
UNITED KINGDOM
North Sea
Stavanger
Bergen
Glittertind 2470
Trondheim
NORWAY
Vestfjorden
Narvik
Kiruna
NORDKAPP
Hammerfest
LINDESNES
Skagerrak
Oslo
SWEDEN
Lulealven
Umealven
Indalsalven
Vänern
Vättern
Göteborg
Kattegat
DENMARK
København
Malmö
Gulf of Bothnia
Oulu
FINLAND
Stockholm
ÖLAND
GOTLAND
BELGIUM
Bruxelles
Amsterdam
NETHERLANDS
LUX.
FRANCE
Rhine
Köln
Bonn
Essen
FED. REP. OF GER.
Elbe
Hamburg
GER. DEM. REP.
BERLIN
Stuttgart
Frankfurt
Leipzig
MÜNCHEN
SWITZ.
ALPS
Baltic Sea
Gdańsk
Kaliningrad
Klaipėda
Riga
Rižskij Zaliv
Tallinn
Gulf of Finland
Helsinki
Čudskoje Ozero
LENINGRAD
Ladožskoje Ozero
Lake Ladoga
Onežskoje Ozero
Murmansk
KOL'SKIJ POLUOSTROV
KOLA PENINSULA
Beloje More
White Sea
MYS KANIN NOS
Archangel'sk
Mezen'
Severnaja Dvina
TIMANSKIJ KR'AŽ
Pečora
Izma
OSTROV KOLGUJEV
Narjan-Mar
NOVAJA ZEML'A
Kara Sea
OSTROV BELYJ
OSTROV VAJGAČ
POLUOSTROV JAMAL
Obskaja Guba
Vorkuta
Usa
1894 Gora Narodnaja
Salechard
Ob'
Pur
Kazym
PRAHA
CZECHOSLOVAKIA
POLAND
Oder
Warta
Bug
Wisła
Katowice
Kraków
Warszawa
Nemunas
Vilnius
Daugava
Velikaja
Lovat'
Ozero Il'men'
Minsk
Smolensk
Dnepr
Kalinin
Volga
Rybinskoje Vodochranilišče
Vologda
Suchona
Kotlas
UNION
EUROPE
AUSTRIA
WIEN
VIENNA
Graz
BUDAPEST
HUNGARY
Gerlachovský štít 2655
CARPATHIAN MOUNTAINS
L'vov
Tisza
Beograd
YUGOSLAVIA
Adriatic Sea
Drava
Cluj
ROMANIA
CARPAŢII MERIDIONALI
Dnestr
Siret
Prut
Olt
Danube
Bucureşti
Sofija
STARA PLANINA
BULGARIA
Kišin'ov
ODESSA
Južnyj Bug
Kijev
Gomel'
Desna
Kursk
SREDNERUSSKAJA VOZVYŠENNOST'
Voronež
Char'kov
Jaroslavl'
MOSKVA
MOSCOW
Tula
Oka
Gor'kovskoje Vodochranilišče
Gor'kij
SEVERNYJE UVALY
Kirov
Perm'
Kama
Kazan'
Penza
Kujbyševskoje Vodochranilišče
Kujbyšev
VOZVYŠENNOST'
PRIVOLŽSKAJA
Saratov
Ufa
URAL'SKIJ MOUNTAINS
URAL'SKIJE GORY
Nižnij Tagil
SVERDLOVSK
Čel'abinsk
Magnitogorsk
Ural
Orenburg
Orsk
Tavda
Tura
Tobol
Tobol'sk
T'umen'
Irtyš
Išim
Omsk
Om'
Novosibi
ZAPADNO
SIBIRSKAJA
NIZMENNOST'
OF SO
Chanty-Mansijsk
Konda
Vach
Ozero Čany
Dnepropetrovsk
Don
Zaporožje
Doneck
Azovskoje More
Rostov-na-Donu
Volgogradskoje Vodochranilišče
VOLGOGRAD
Cimľanskoje Vodochranilišče
Krasnodar
Sevastopol'
Black Sea
Varna
GREECE
ISTANBUL
Marmara Denizi
Sakarya
Aegean Sea
Eskişehir
İzmir
Kızıl Irmak
Samsun
Ankara
Tuz Gölü
TURKEY
ASIA MINOR
3916 Erciyeş Daği
ZIGANA DAĞLARI
TOROS DAĞLARI
Adana
İskenderun Körfezi
CYPRUS
Lefkoşa
Mediterranean Sea
Ḥalab
Bayrūt
LEBANON
ISRAEL
Tel Aviv-Yafo
SYRIA
Dimashq
'Ammān
Yerushalayim
Dead Sea
EGYPT
JORDAN
Gulf of Aqaba
Red Sea
Jabal al-Lawz 2580
SAUDI ARABIA
BĀDIYAT ASH-SHĀM
AL-ḤAMĀD
AL-WIDYĀN
MESOPOTAMIA
Baghdād
IRAQ
Tigris
Euphrates
Hawr al-Hammār
Al-Mawṣil
Al-Başrah
BOL'ŠOJ KAVKAZ
CAUCASUS
5633 El'brus
Batumi
Groznyj
TBILISI
5165 Büyük Ağrı Dağı
Jerevan
Murat
Van Gölü
Tabrīz
Daryācheh-ye Reẕā'īyeh
Rasht
TEHRĀN
RESHTEH-YE KŪHHĀ-YE ALBORZ
5604 Qolleh-ye Damāvand
Hamadān
Daryācheh-ye Namak
DASHT-E KAVĪR
Esfahān
IRAN
PRIKASPIJSKAJA NIZMENNOST'
Astrachan'
Volga
Caspian Sea
BAKU
Zaliv Kara-Bogaz-Gol
Krasnovodsk
KARAKUMY
KOPPEH DAGH
Aschabad
Mashhad
PLATO UST'URT
Emba
TURGAJSKAJA STOLOVAJA STRANA
Ozero Tengiz
Aral'skoje More
Aral Sea
Nukus
Novokazalinsk
Syrdarja
Amudarja
KYZYLKUM
Celinograd
KAZACHSKIJ MELKOSOPOČNIK
Karaganda
Džezkazgan
Balchaš
Ozero Balchaš
Ozero Alakol'
Semipala
Ust'-Kamenogorsk
Frunze
Ozero Issyk-Kul'
Alma-Ata
7439 Pik Pobedy
TIEN
Taškent
Fergana
Samarkand
Pik Kommunizma 7495
Dušanbe
PAMIR
Kashi
Fayzābād
HINDU KUSH
TALIMUPE
TAKLA MAK
Souche
Copyright © by Rand McNally & Co.
B-515200-764-1-1-2-8

UNITED STATES
Bering Strait
Chukchi Sea
OSTROV VRANGEL'A
OCEAN
North Pole
Proliv Longa
Vostočno-Sibirskoje More
East Siberian Sea
NOVOSIBIRSKIJE OSTROVA
NEW SIBERIAN ISLANDS
SEVERNAJA ZEML'A
NORTH LAND
More Laptevych
Laptev Sea
ČUKOTSKIJ POLUOSTROV
Anadyrskij Zaliv
ANADYRSKOJE PLOSKOGORJE
Arctic Circle
Bering Sea
ALEUTIAN ISLANDS
Unalaska
POLUOSTROV KAMČATKA
KAMCHATKA PENINSULA
POLUOSTROV TAJMYR
CHREBET ČERSKOGO
VERCHOJANSKIJ CHREBET
REPUBLICS
SOCIALIST
Sea of Okhotsk
Magadan
Petropavlovsk-Kamčatskij
SREDNESIBIRSKOJE PLOSKOGORJE
Noril'sk
Jakutsk
KURIL'SKIJE OSTROVA
KURIL ISLANDS
OSTROV SACHALIN
SAKHALIN
ALDANSKOJE NAGORJE
STANOVOJ CHREBET
Tatarskij Proliv
La Perouse Strait
SICHOTE-ALIN'
Komsomol'sk-na-Amure
Chabarovsk
Amur
Heilongjiang
HOKKAIDO
Asahikawa
Sapporo
Hakodate
Aomori
Krasnojarsk
Kemerovo
Novokuzneck
Irkutsk
Ozero Bajkal
Ulan-Ude
Čita
SAJAN MOUNTAINS
Chövsgöl Nuur
Ulaanbaatar
MONGOLIA
DAXINGANLINGSHANMAI
Qiqihaer
Haerbin
Vladivostok
Changchun
Sea of Japan
HONSHU
Sendai
TOKYO
JAPAN
Nagoya
Kyōto
ŌSAKA
SHENYANG
MUKDEN
Fushun
NORTH KOREA
Andong
P'yŏngyang
SŎUL
SOUTH KOREA
Taegu
Pusan
Hiroshima
Fukuoka
KYUSHU
Kagoshima
GOBI
ASIA
Wulumuqi
SHAN
ALTAI
Zhangjiakou
BEIJING
PEKING
TIANJIN
TIENTSIN
Huhehaote
Luda
Dairen
Bohai
Huanghe
Taiyuan
Ji'nan
Qingdao
Tsingtao
Yellow Sea
Korea Strait
Yinchuan
CHINA
Lanzhou
Zhengzhou
Nanjing
SHANGHAI
EAST CHINA SEA

Southern Asia

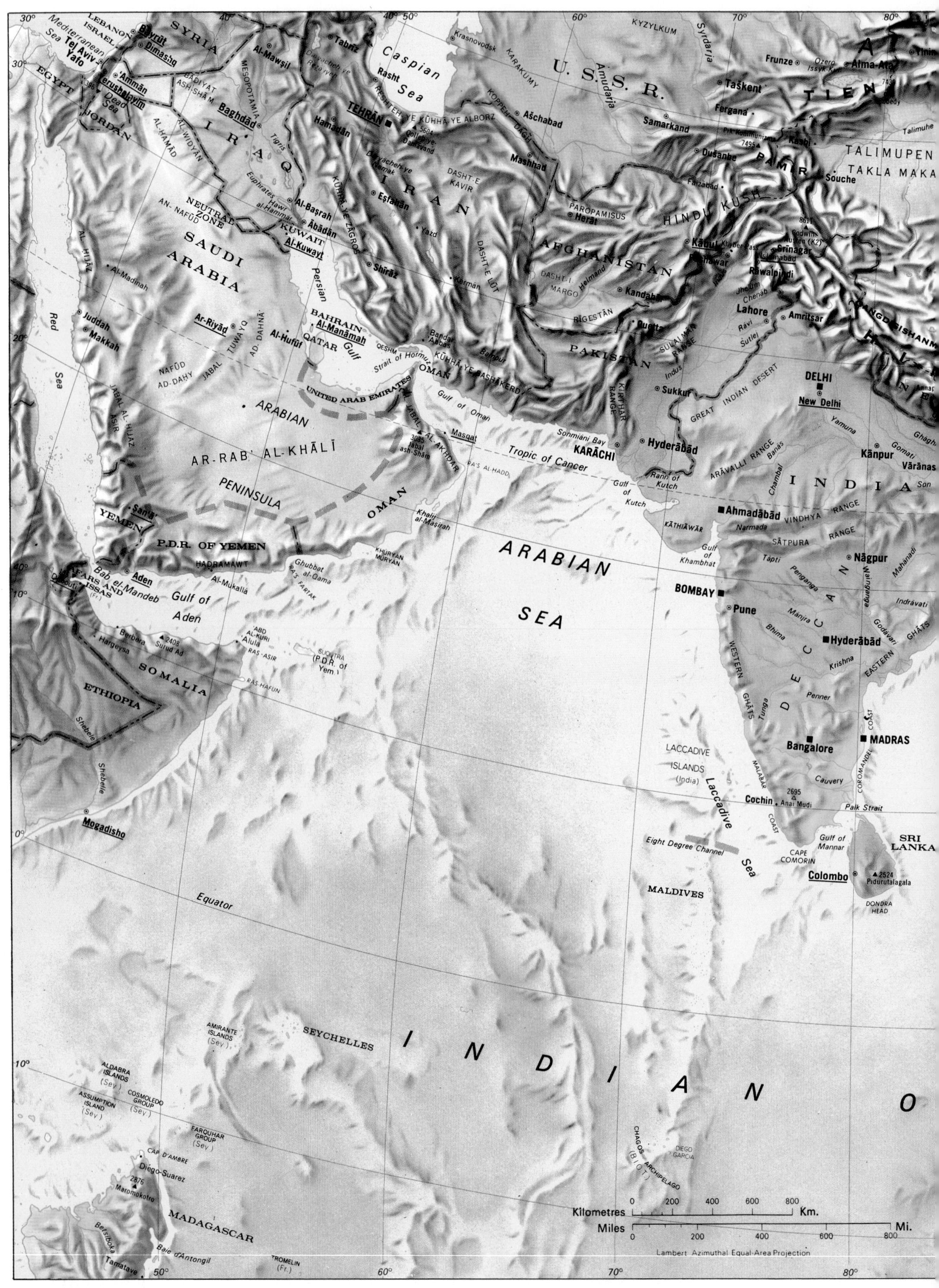

Kilometres 0 200 400 600 800 Km.
Miles 0 200 400 600 800 Mi.
Lambert Azimuthal Equal-Area Projection

Wulumuqi
GOBI
Zhangjiakou
BEIJING
PEKING
Huhehaote
Huanghe
TIANJIN
TIENTSIN
Taiyuan
Luda
Dairen
Korea Bay
Bohai
SOUL
SOUTH KOREA
Taegu
Pusan
Hiroshima
JAPAN
SHIKOKU
Bungo-suido
KYUSHU
Fukuoka
Korea Strait
Mokp'o
Qingdao
Tsingtao
Ji'nan
Yellow Sea
CHEJU DO (S. Kor.)
Kagoshima
Luobubo
Lop Nor
Yinchuan
Ruoshui
TAIHANGSHAN
Liaodongwan
QILIANSHANMAI
ERJINSHANMAI
CHAIDAMUPENDI
Qinghai
Lanzhou
Grand Canal
Yunhe
Hongzehu
Zhengzhou
Yinghe
Xi'an
QINLINGSHANMAI
Nanjing
SHANGHAI
EAST CHINA SEA
AMAMI-O-SHIMA
TOKUNO-SHIMA
OKINO-ERABU-SHIMA
KUNLUNSHANMAI
DABASHAN
WUHAN
Hangzhou
Ningbo
NANSEI-SHOTO
RYUKYU ISLANDS
OKINAWA-JIMA
OKINO-DAITO-JIMA
Naha
MINAMI-DAITO-JIMA
Tropic of Cancer
TANGGULASHANMAI
Changjiang
Poyanghu
Nanchang
Wenzhou
MIYAKO-JIMA
Salween
Mekong
Chengdu
CHONGQING
Changsha
Minjiang
Fuzhou
Formosa Strait
T'aipei
IRIOMOTE-JIMA
ISHIGAKI-SHIMA
TAIWAN
Namuhu
NIANQINGTANGGULASHANMAI
Lasa
Brahmaputra
8848 Mount Everest
Changjiang
Guiyang
Xiangjiang
Xiamen
Amoy
3997 Hsinkao Shan
FORMOSA
BHUTAN
Liuzhou
GUANGZHOU
CANTON
Bashi Channel
Luzon Strait
BATAN ISLANDS
Kunming
Xijiang
Macau (Port.)
VICTORIA
HONG KONG (U.K.)
Balintang Channel
BABUYAN ISLANDS
ESCARPADA POINT
Philippine Sea
Patna
Ganges
Jamuna
Chindwin
Irrawaddy
Youjiang
Nanning
Red
Black
NORTH VIETNAM
CAPE BOJEADOR
LUZON
SIERRA MADRE
BANGLADESH
Dacca
CALCUTTA
Chittagong
Mandalay
BURMA
Hai-phong
Ha-noi
Gulf of Tonkin
Haikou
1879 Wuzhishan
HAINANDAO
Lingayen Gulf
POLILLO ISLANDS
Louang Prabang
Sittwe
Quezon City
MANILA
CATANDUANES
PHILIPPINES
CHEDUBA ISLAND
Salween
Chiang Mai
Vientiane
Udon Thani
Mekong
LAOS
Huê
Da-nang
SOUTH CHINA SEA
MINDORO
TABLAS
MASBATE
SAMAR
Sibuyan Sea
LEYTE
PANAY
CEBU
CALAMIAN GROUP
Moulmein
Gulf of Martaban
Rangoon
THAILAND
BOHOL
Mindanao Sea
NEGROS
Bay of Bengal
PREPARIS ISLAND
COCO ISLANDS
KRUNG THEP
BANGKOK
INDOCHINA
CAMBODIA
Tônlé Sab
SOUTH VIETNAM
MINDANAO
Davao
2954 Mount Apo
PALAWAN
Sulu Sea
Moro Gulf
BASILAN ISLAND
ANDAMAN ISLANDS (India)
Andaman Sea
Phnum Pénh
SAI-GON
SPRATLY ISLAND
BALABAC ISLAND
Balabac Strait
JOLO ISLAND
Gulf of Thailand
ISTHMUS OF KRA
MUI BAI BUNG
TAWITAWI ISLAND
Celebes Sea
Ten Degree Channel
4101 Mount Kinabalu
Darvel Bay
BRUNEI (U.K.)
Bandar Seri Begawan
NICOBAR ISLANDS (India)
NATUNA BESAR
MALAYSIA
IRAN MOUNTAINS
Kajan
Pinang
MALAY PENINSULA
LUMUT
MALAYSIA
Teluk Tomini
Rajang
TANDJUNG MANGKALIHAT
Selat Makasar
KEPULAUAN TOGIAN
Medan
Kuala Lumpur
KEPULAUAN ANAMBAS
Kuching
PEGUNUNGAN MULLER
BORNEO
Teluk Tolo
Strait of Malacca
SINGAPORE
SINGAPORE
Equator
Kapuas
2278 Bukit Raja
PEGUNUNGAN SCHWANER
Balikpapan
SULAWESI
CELEBES
PULAU SIMEULUE
SUMATERA
SUMATRA
Kampar
KEPULAUAN LINGGA
PULAU SINGKEP
Kahajan
Barito
Teluk Bone
PULAU BUTUNG
PULAU NIAS
KEPULAUAN BATU
Bandjarmasin
Selat Karimata
PULAU LAUT
Udjung Pandang
KEPAULAN MENTAWAI
PULAU SIBERUT
BANGKA
TANDJUNG PUTING
TANDJUNG SELATAN
3800 Gunung Kerintji
Palembang
BELITUNG
PULAU SELAJAR
PULAU KALAOTOA
PULAU LOMBLEN
INDONESIA
Laut Djawa
Java Sea
KEPULAUAN KANGEAN
Laut Flores
EAN
Selat Sunda
DJAKARTA
MADURA
Laut Bali
SUMBAWA
FLORES
Savu Sea
TIMOR
PULAU ENGGANO
Surabaja
3676 G. Semeru
BALI
LOMBOK
SUMBA
Bandung
DJAWA
JAVA
LESSER SUNDA ISLANDS
PULAU SAWU
PULAU ROTI
CHRISTMAS ISLAND (Austl)
AUSTRALIA
COCOS ISLANDS (Austl)
Copyright © by Rand McNally & Co.
CAPE LATOUCHE TREVILLE
Broome
90°
100°
110°
120°
130°
40°
30°
20°
10°
0°

Earth panorama: Asia

Asia is the largest of the seven continents. The eastern and southeastern parts of the continent are fringed by a series of island arcs, which have frequent earthquakes and many volcanoes: Indonesia, the Philippines, Ryukyu, Japan, and the Kurils.

The Himalayas are the seam welding India and Asia proper. Also, the Arabian peninsula is geologically part of Africa, not of Asia. The recent mountains (Caucasus, Zagros, Himalayas, Tien Shan, Altai) sometimes enclose highland plateaus such as Anatolia, the Iranian plateau, and Tibet. These mountains surround the geological heartland of Asia—the Siberian shield.

Asia has four broad climatic domains—Mediterranean, desert, continental, and monsoon. The Mediterranean zone is limited to a narrow fringe in Turkey and the Middle East. The continental zone comprises Siberia, Mongolia, and Tibet and is characterized by very harsh winters. The desert climate is found from Arabia to Pakistan. Monsoon Asia, where 90 percent of the Asiatic population lives, extends from India to Japan.

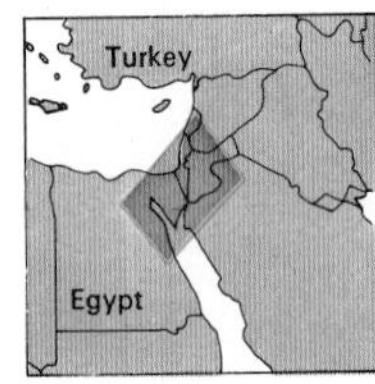

Turkey
Egypt

5
4
3
2
1

1 The Red Sea [1] is a giant rift in the earth's surface that separates Asia from Africa. It is a cleft formed by sea-floor spreading. To the north it is split in two. The Gulf of Suez [2] follows the same line, and at its inner end the Suez Canal and the Great Bitter Lake can be seen. The Gulf of Aqaba [3] is the southern end of another big rift that can be followed through the Dead Sea [4] and Lake Tiberias [5]. The Sinai is the peninsula between the gulfs of Suez and Aqaba. The dark mountains in the south are Precambrian terrains that can be traced southward into Egypt and the Arabian Peninsula.

W
6
Y
2
Z
1
3
5

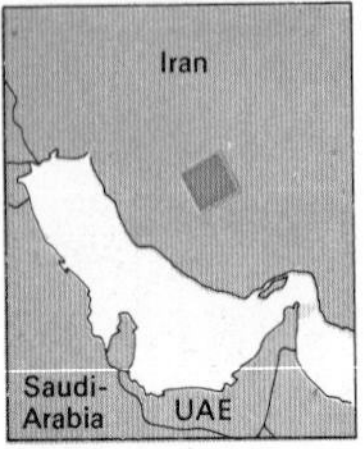

Iran
Saudi-Arabia
UAE

2 Lakes Bakhtegan [1] **and Teshk** [2] in the Zagros Mountains of Iran are normally dry except following rare rainfalls or the spring thaw in the mountains. The lakes are fed by the Kur River [3]. The thick salt deposits are conspicuous. The terrains to the top of the picture have been pushed over those to the bottom in a thrust line [WX], while to the left there is an ordinary fault [YZ]. An eroded anticline [4] and a dome [5] are visible. The dark patches [6] are extinct volcanoes.

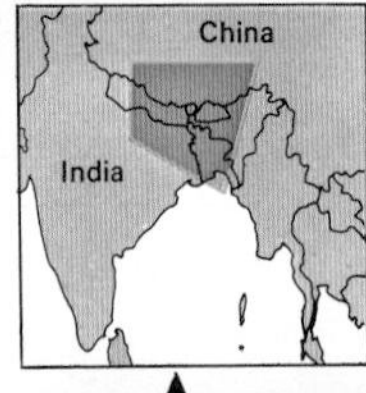

China
India

3 The high mountain ranges of the Himalayas rise above the Indo-Gangetic plain [1]. Katmandu [2] is the capital of Nepal. Annapurna, 26,503ft (8,078m), is visible [3] above the deep valley of the Gandaki River. The border with Tibet passes at the head of the valley along the narrow snowy "connection." The big central valley in Tibet is that of the upper Brahmaputra. This river runs across to the horizon on the left and then crosses the Himalayas to join the Indo-Gangetic plain. Lhasa is at [4]. Mt Everest [5] is the highest mountain in the world, reaching a height of 29,030ft (8,848m).

4
5
1
3
2

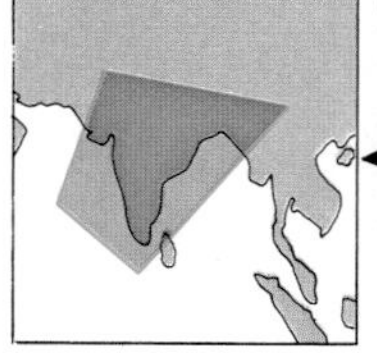

4

4 This Gemini 9 picture of the Indian subcontinent, taken from an altitude of 460 miles (740km) has a peculiar perspective caused by the wide-angle lens. The indentation at the north end of the west coast is the Gulf of Cambay. The Western Ghats are to the left, and the Deccan plateau basalts are the dark areas to the upper left. The shallowness of the strait separating Sri Lanka from the mainland is apparent. The conspicuous river and delta just to the north is the Coleroon, and to the north of the Bay of Bengal, the huge delta of the Ganges River can be seen. The high ranges of the Himalayas are hidden on the horizon by clouds.

5

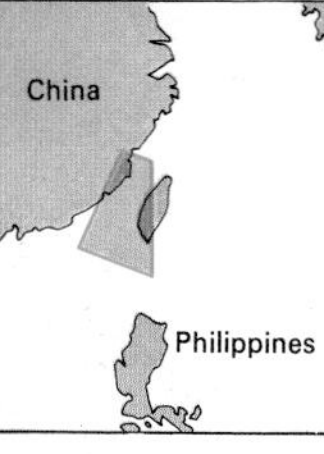
China
Philippines

5 The complicated coastline of southeast China is due to the flooding of a worn-down peneplain by the sea, following subsidence of the land in the last few million years. The remaining knolls are predominantly made of granite and lavas. Particularly conspicuous is the island of Hainan (lower left); the land mass to the right is Taiwan. The current flowing north through the strait is an arm of the "black current" or Kuroshio, which warms local climates in the South China Sea.

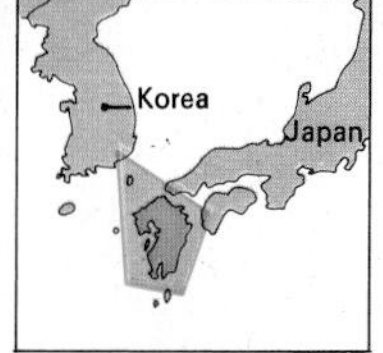
Korea
Japan

6 Japan is an archipelago bounding the shallow epicontinental Sea of Japan on its eastern side. On Japan's Pacific coast the sea bed plunges down to the Ryukyu and Japan trenches, part of the major Pacific trench system; thus the Japanese islands are part of the same tectonic system as other island arcs such as the West Indies and Indonesia. In this photograph of the island of Kyushu evidence of tectonic activity can be seen in the plume of smoke rising from the volcano on Sakura Jima in Kagoshima Bay [1]. Aso-san [2], in the center of the island, is the world's largest active volcanic crater.

6

2
1

Australia and Antarctica

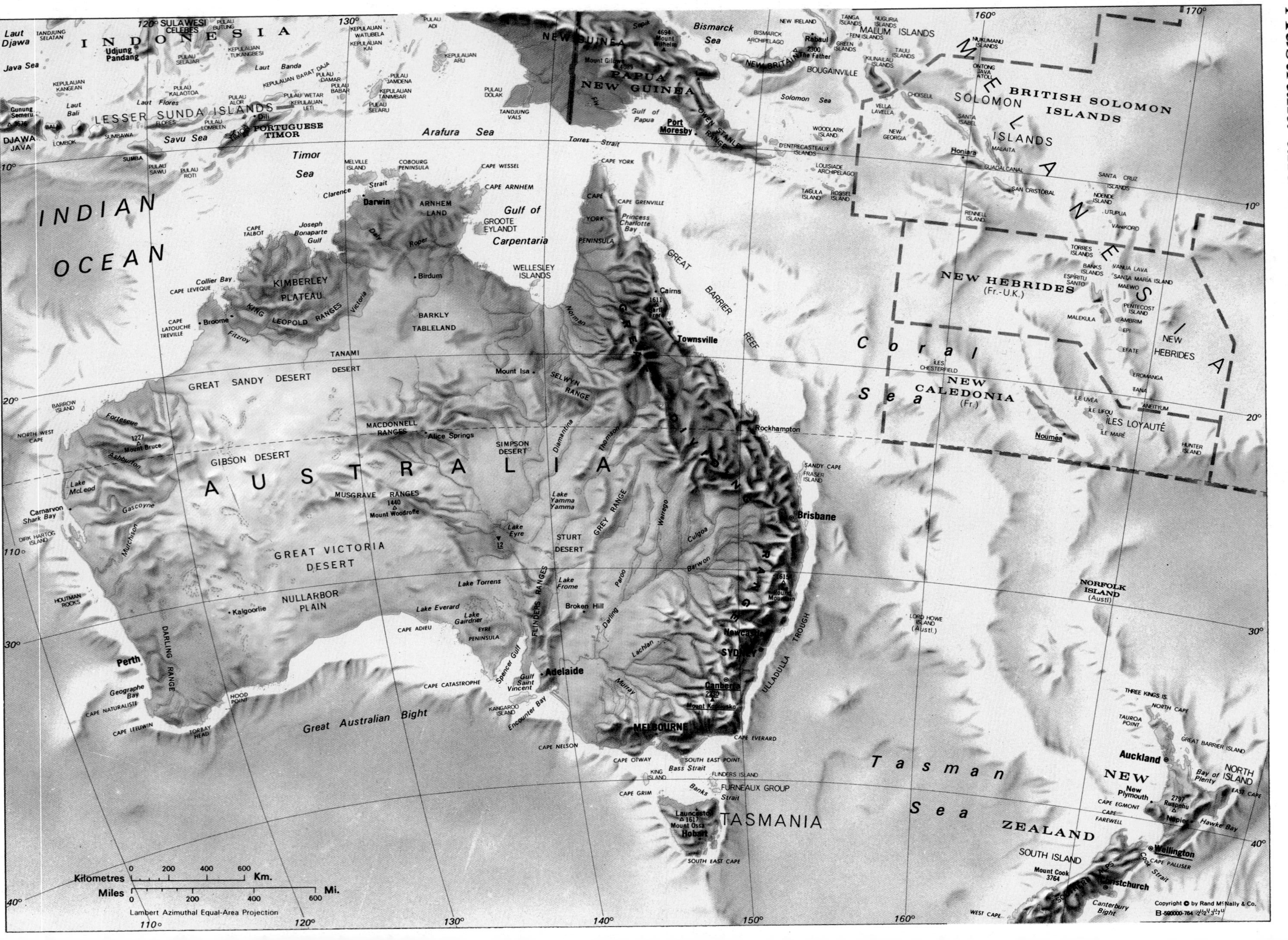

INDIAN OCEAN
AUSTRALIA
INDONESIA
PAPUA NEW GUINEA
NEW GUINEA
BRITISH SOLOMON ISLANDS
SOLOMON ISLANDS
MELANESIA
NEW HEBRIDES (Fr.-U.K.)
NEW CALEDONIA (Fr.)
ÎLES LOYAUTÉ
NEW ZEALAND
NORTH ISLAND
SOUTH ISLAND
TASMANIA
NORFOLK ISLAND (Austl.)
LORD HOWE ISLAND (Austl.)
PORTUGUESE TIMOR
LESSER SUNDA ISLANDS
Coral Sea
Tasman Sea
Arafura Sea
Timor Sea
Savu Sea
Java Sea
Solomon Sea
Bismarck Sea
Gulf of Carpentaria
Great Australian Bight
Torres Strait
Bass Strait
Cook Strait
GREAT BARRIER REEF
GREAT SANDY DESERT
GIBSON DESERT
GREAT VICTORIA DESERT
NULLARBOR PLAIN
SIMPSON DESERT
STURT DESERT
TANAMI DESERT
KIMBERLEY PLATEAU
BARKLY TABLELAND
ARNHEM LAND
CAPE YORK PENINSULA
MACDONNELL RANGES
MUSGRAVE RANGES
FLINDERS RANGES
GREY RANGE
DARLING RANGE
SELWYN RANGE
KING LEOPOLD RANGES
OWEN STANLEY RANGE
Lake Eyre
Lake Torrens
Lake Gairdner
Lake Frome
Lake Everard
Perth
Adelaide
MELBOURNE
SYDNEY
Canberra
Brisbane
Darwin
Townsville
Cairns
Rockhampton
Alice Springs
Mount Isa
Kalgoorlie
Broken Hill
Broome
Carnarvon
Hobart
Launceston
Port Moresby
Honiara
Nouméa
Auckland
Wellington
Christchurch
Rabaul
Darling
Murray
Lachlan
Kilometres
Miles
Lambert Azimuthal Equal-Area Projection
Copyright © by Rand McNally & Co.

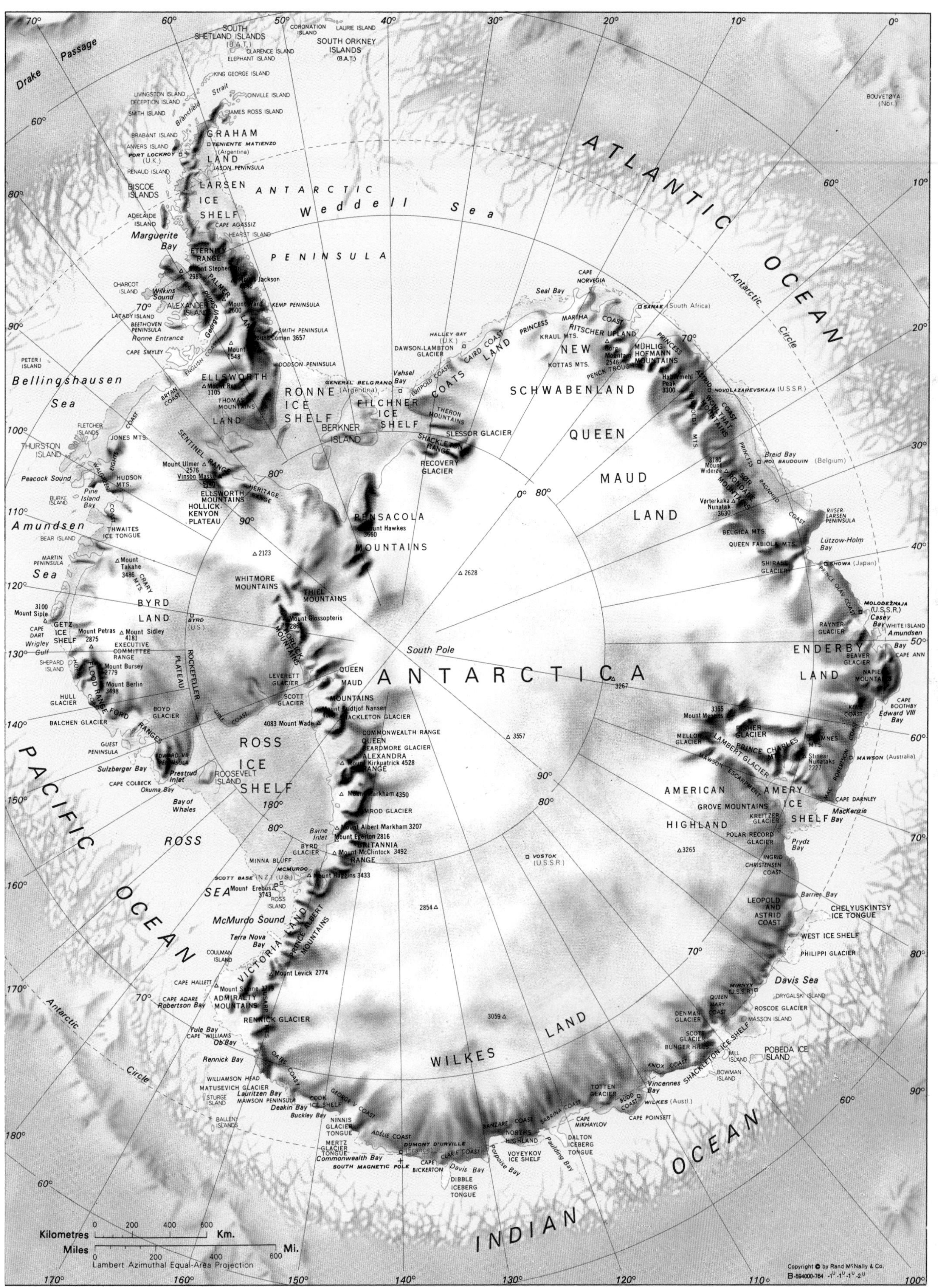
Drake Passage
SOUTH SHETLAND ISLANDS (B.A.T.)
CORONATION ISLAND
LAURIE ISLAND
SOUTH ORKNEY ISLANDS (B.A.T.)
CLARENCE ISLAND
ELEPHANT ISLAND
KING GEORGE ISLAND
LIVINGSTON ISLAND
DECEPTION ISLAND
JOINVILLE ISLAND
SMITH ISLAND
JAMES ROSS ISLAND
Bransfield Strait
BRABANT ISLAND
ANVERS ISLAND
GRAHAM LAND
TENIENTE MATIENZO (Argentina)
PORT LOCKROY (U.K.)
JASON PENINSULA
RENAUD ISLAND
BISCOE ISLANDS
LARSEN ICE SHELF
ANTARCTIC
Weddell Sea
ADELAIDE ISLAND
CAPE AGASSIZ
Marguerite Bay
HEARST ISLAND
ETERNITY RANGE
PENINSULA
Mount Stephenson 2987
Mount Jackson
CHARCOT ISLAND
Wilkins Sound
ALEXANDER ISLAND
KEMP PENINSULA
LATADY ISLAND
BEETHOVEN PENINSULA
SMITH PENINSULA
Ronne Entrance
Mount Coman 3657
CAPE SMYLEY
ENGLISH COAST
Mount 1548
PETER I ISLAND
DODSON PENINSULA
Bellingshausen Sea
ELLSWORTH LAND
Mount Rex 1105
BRYAN COAST
THOMAS MOUNTAINS
RONNE ICE SHELF
GENERAL BELGRANO (Argentina)
Vahsel Bay
FILCHNER ICE SHELF
BERKNER ISLAND
FLETCHER ISLANDS
JONES MTS.
THURSTON ISLAND
SENTINEL RANGE
Mount Ulmer 2576
Vinson Massif 5140
Peacock Sound
HUDSON MTS.
ELLSWORTH MOUNTAINS
HERITAGE RANGE
HOLLICK-KENYON PLATEAU
Pine Island Bay
BURKE ISLAND
Amundsen
THWAITES ICE TONGUE
BEAR ISLAND
Mount Takahe 3486
CRARY MTS.
MARTIN PENINSULA
Sea
WHITMORE MOUNTAINS
BYRD LAND
Mount Siple 3100
CAPE DART
GETZ ICE SHELF
Wrigley Gulf
Mount Petras 2875
Mount Sidley 4181
EXECUTIVE COMMITTEE RANGE
BYRD (U.S.)
SHEPARD ISLAND
Mount Bursey 2779
Mount Berlin 3498
HULL GLACIER
BALCHEN GLACIER
FORD RANGES
BOYD GLACIER
ROCKEFELLER PLATEAU
GUEST PENINSULA
EDWARD VII PENINSULA
Sulzberger Bay
Prestrud Inlet
CAPE COLBECK
Okuma Bay
ROOSEVELT ISLAND
ROSS ICE SHELF
Bay of Whales
PACIFIC OCEAN
ROSS SEA
MINNA BLUFF
MCMURDO (U.S.)
SCOTT BASE (N.Z.)
Mount Erebus 3743
ROSS ISLAND
McMurdo Sound
Terra Nova Bay
COULMAN ISLAND
VICTORIA LAND
PRINCE ALBERT MOUNTAINS
Mount Levick 2774
CAPE HALLETT
CAPE ADARE
Robertson Bay
ADMIRALTY MOUNTAINS
RENNICK GLACIER
Yule Bay
CAPE WILLIAMS
Ob' Bay
Rennick Bay
WILLIAMSON HEAD
MATUSEVICH GLACIER
Lauritzen Bay
MAWSON PENINSULA
STURGE ISLAND
Deakin Bay
Buckley Bay
BALLENY ISLANDS
OATES COAST
Antarctic Circle
PENSACOLA MOUNTAINS
Mount Hawkes 3660
THIEL MOUNTAINS
Mount Glossopteris 2865
HORLICK MOUNTAINS
LEVERETT GLACIER
SCOTT GLACIER
QUEEN MAUD MOUNTAINS
Mount Fridtjof Nansen 4068
SHACKLETON GLACIER
4083 Mount Wade
COMMONWEALTH RANGE
QUEEN ALEXANDRA RANGE
BEARDMORE GLACIER
Mount Kirkpatrick 4528
Mount Markham 4350
NIMROD GLACIER
Barne Inlet
Mount Albert Markham 3207
Mount Egerton 2816
BYRD GLACIER
BRITANNIA RANGE
Mount McClintock 3492
Mount Huggins 3433
South Pole
ANTARCTICA
RECOVERY GLACIER
SHACKLETON RANGE
SLESSOR GLACIER
THERON MOUNTAINS
LUITPOLD COAST
COATS LAND
CAIRD COAST
HALLEY BAY (U.K.)
DAWSON-LAMBTON GLACIER
Seal Bay
CAPE NORVEGIA
SANAE (South Africa)
PRINCESS MARTHA COAST
RITSCHER UPLAND
KRAUL MTS.
NEW SCHWABENLAND
MÜHLIG-HOFMANN MOUNTAINS
KOTTAS MTS.
PENCK TROUGH
Habermehl Peak 3300
PRINCESS ASTRID COAST
NOVOLAZAREVSKAJA (U.S.S.R.)
WOHLTHAT MOUNTAINS
QUEEN MAUD LAND
Breid Bay
ROI BAUDOUIN (Belgium)
PRINCESS RAGNHILD COAST
SØR RONDANE MOUNTAINS
Vørterkaka Nunatak 3630
BELGICA MTS.
QUEEN FABIOLA MTS.
RIISER-LARSEN PENINSULA
Lützow-Holm Bay
SHOWA (Japan)
SHIRASE GLACIER
PRINCE OLAV COAST
MOLODEŽNAJA (U.S.S.R.)
Casey Bay
RAYNER GLACIER
WHITE ISLAND
Amundsen Bay
ENDERBY LAND
BEAVER GLACIER
CAPE ANN
NAPIER MOUNTAINS
CAPE BOOTHBY
Edward VIII Bay
KEMP COAST
Mount Menzies 3355
MELLOR GLACIER
FISHER GLACIER
LAMBERT GLACIER
PRINCE CHARLES MTS.
FRAMNES MTS.
Stinear Nunataks 2227
MAWSON (Australia)
MAWSON ESCARPMENT
MAC. ROBERTSON COAST
AMERICAN HIGHLAND
GROVE MOUNTAINS
AMERY ICE SHELF
CAPE DARNLEY
MacKenzie Bay
KREITZER GLACIER
POLAR RECORD GLACIER
Prydz Bay
INGRID CHRISTENSEN COAST
VOSTOK (U.S.S.R.)
Barrier Bay
LEOPOLD AND ASTRID COAST
CHELYUSKINTSY ICE TONGUE
WEST ICE SHELF
PHILIPPI GLACIER
Davis Sea
MIRNYY (U.S.S.R.)
QUEEN MARY COAST
DRYGALSKI ISLAND
ROSCOE GLACIER
MASSON ISLAND
DENMAN GLACIER
SCOTT GLACIER
BUNGER HILLS
SHACKLETON ICE SHELF
MILL ISLAND
POBEDA ICE ISLAND
KNOX COAST
BOWMAN ISLAND
WILKES LAND
Vincennes Bay
WILKES (Austl.)
TOTTEN GLACIER
BUDD COAST
CAPE POINSETT
SABRINA COAST
CAPE MIKHAYLOV
BANZARE COAST
NORTHS HIGHLAND
DALTON ICEBERG TONGUE
VOYEYKOV ICE SHELF
Paulding Bay
Porpoise Bay
GEORGE V COAST
COOK ICE SHELF
NINNIS GLACIER TONGUE
ADÉLIE COAST
MERTZ GLACIER TONGUE
Commonwealth Bay
SOUTH MAGNETIC POLE
DUMONT D'URVILLE (France)
CLARIE COAST
CAPE BICKERTON
Davis Bay
DIBBLE ICEBERG TONGUE
INDIAN OCEAN
ATLANTIC OCEAN
BOUVETØYA (Nor.)
Kilometres 0 200 400 600 Km.
Miles 0 200 400 600 Mi.
Lambert Azimuthal Equal-Area Projection
Copyright © by Rand McNally & Co.
B-594000-764

Earth panorama: the Pacific

The Pacific is the largest of all the oceans and has an area of 64 million square miles (165 million square km). It is roughly circular and is bounded on three sides by Australia, Asia, and the Americas. It is open to the south toward Antarctica and has a wide contact south of Australia with the Indian Ocean, a limited contact with the same ocean through the Indonesian archipelago, and a smaller contact with the Atlantic Ocean through Drake Passage.

The hydrography of the Pacific is relatively simple. In the Northern Hemisphere there is a clockwise-current loop, driven by the northeast trade winds toward the Philippines and curving up toward Japan before carrying on toward Alaska and looping down past California back to its departure in the North Equatorial Current. The new sea floor created by sea-floor spreading is compensated by sea-floor "sinking" into the trenches that extend from New Zealand around to Alaska and from Central America to Chile. Active volcanoes are associated with these trenches and form a fiery circle around the Pacific.

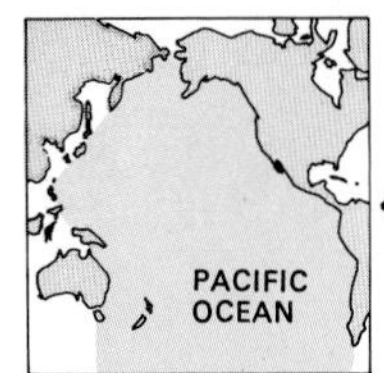

PACIFIC OCEAN

1 **The oceanic hemisphere** could well be another name for the expanse of the Pacific Ocean. Despite its many islands, such as New Zealand, Papua and New Guinea, Borneo, Sakhalin, and Japan, the proportion of dry land within the area is extremely small. The Pacific is the still-shrinking remains of the original world ocean Panthalassa that surrounded the dry land before it broke up into the continents known today.

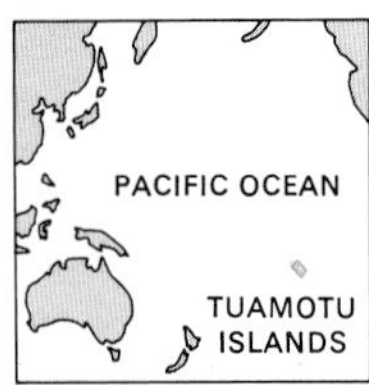

PACIFIC OCEAN
TUAMOTU ISLANDS

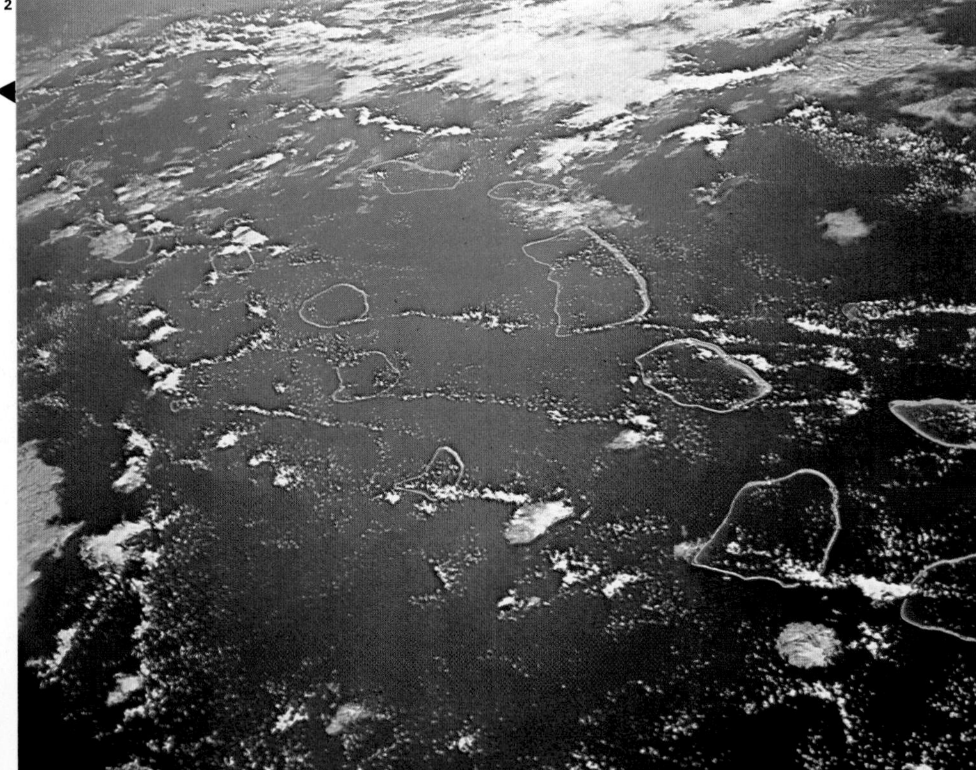

2 **Many of the tropical Pacific Islands,** for instance the Tuamotus, are coral atolls—ring-shaped islands surrounding a shallow lagoon. The atolls rise from great depths, yet the corals that built them cannot grow in depths of more than 150ft (45m). The early mariners thought that atolls were created by divine providence as convenient shelters for seafarers. Some naturalists believed that they were founded on shallow crater rims. In 1837, Charles Darwin proposed that they were once volcanic islands that sank by subsidence of the sea floor as coral growth toward the surface kept pace creating coral atolls.

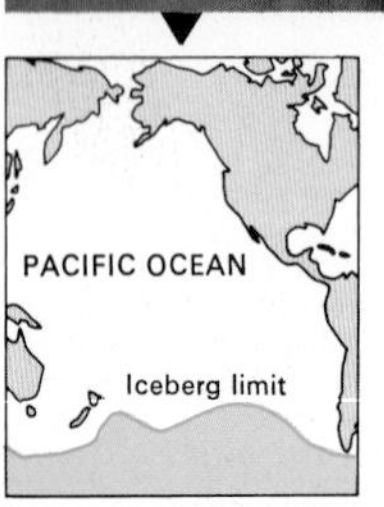

PACIFIC OCEAN
Iceberg limit

3 **Icebergs** shed from the huge Antarctic ice sheet drift in a northeasterly direction and are a danger to shipping. In the Pacific they can drift as far north as 41°S before they melt away. Some of them can be 2,000ft (600m) thick.

3
2
1
5
4

NSW
VICTORIA

4 **This section of the south coast** of the state of Victoria, Australia, extends from Geelong [1] to Wilson's Promontory [5]. Bass Strait [4] separates mainland Australia from Tasmania. Melbourne [3] is at the head of Port Phillip Bay [2].

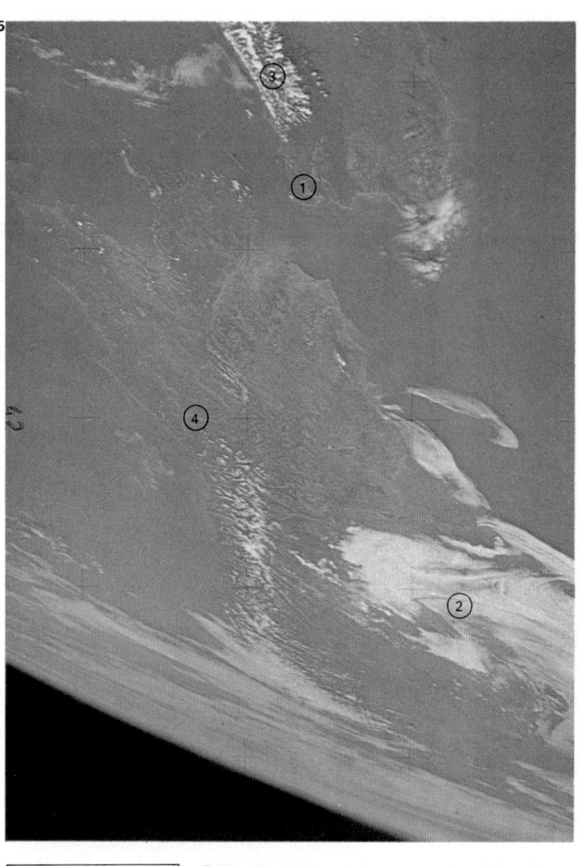

NEW ZEALAND
5
6

5 Cook Strait, named after the explorer James Cook, separates the North and South Islands of New Zealand. Wellington, the capital, can be seen [1] and also Christchurch [2]. The Tararua Range [3] and the Southern Alps [4] are covered with snow. The Earth's curvature is visible.

6 The South Island of New Zealand consists primarily of a Cenozoic folded mountain range, the Southern Alps, which was uplifted by the collision of the Pacific crustal plate to the east [top] and the Australian plate to the west. This Skylab 4 photograph was taken over Cook Strait [1] looking south, with the city of Christchurch [2] visible.

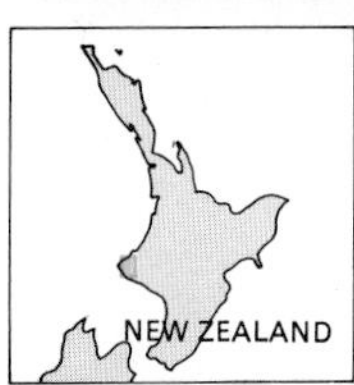
NEW ZEALAND

7 The North Island of New Zealand is a volcanic area. Mount Egmont at 8,260ft (2,520m) is a symmetrical volcano, although it carries several secondary cones on its flanks. Water erosion has carved several radial gullies around the craters. The border between the volcanic scoriae and rock forming the volcano and the agricultural plain that surrounds it is distinct. Mount Egmont is an extinct volcano.

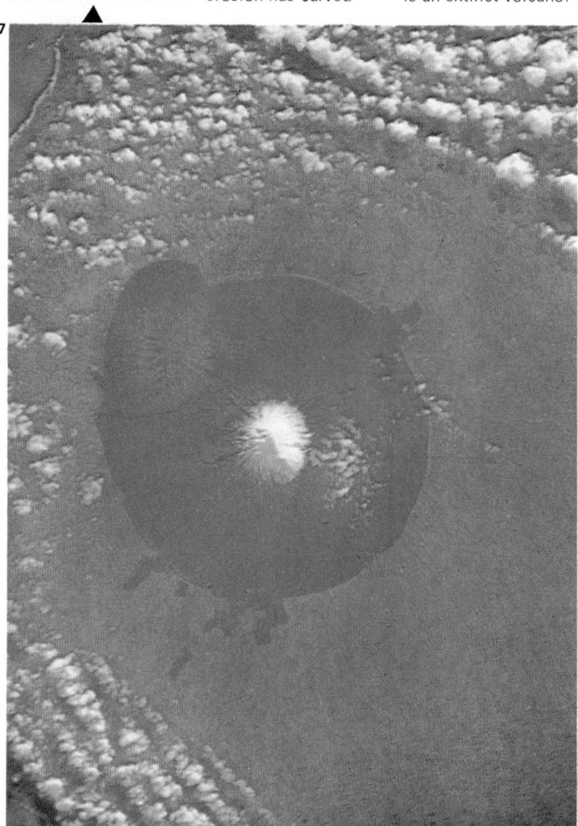

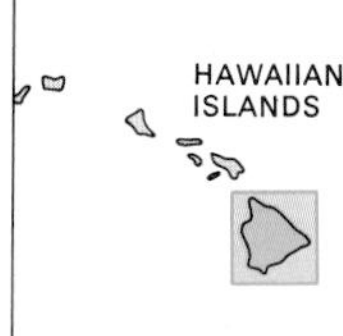
HAWAIIAN ISLANDS

8 Hawaii is the largest island in the Hawaiian archipelago. It was formed by the coalescence of two large volcanoes – Mauna Kea [1], 13,796ft (4,200m), and Mauna Loa [2], 13,680ft (4,160m). With its foot resting on the sea floor 18,000ft (5,500m) below sea level, Mauna Kea has a greater base-to-summit difference than even Mt Everest. It is a dormant, perhaps extinct, volcano, but Mauna Loa is one of the most active volcanoes in the world. Its most active vent, Kilauea [3], is on its southeast flank. The rim of the Kilauea caldera (collapse crater) is 8 miles (13km) in circumference. The caldera floor has an inner crater named Halemaumau. The level of the lava is 740ft (230m) below the rim.

North America

ARCTIC
OCEAN
North Pole
ATLANTIC
OCEAN
GREENLAND
(Den.)
ICELAND
Reykjavík
Norwegian Sea
Greenland Sea
SVALBARD
(Nor.)
SPITSBERGEN
JAN MAYEN
(Nor.)
Denmark Strait
Labrador Sea
Davis Strait
Baffin Bay
BAFFIN ISLAND
Foxe Basin
Hudson Strait
Hudson Bay
James Bay
SOUTHAMPTON ISLAND
COATS ISLAND
ELLESMERE ISLAND
DEVON ISLAND
Lancaster Sound
QUEEN ELIZABETH ISLANDS
VICTORIA ISLAND
BANKS ISLAND
MELVILLE ISLAND
Viscount Melville Sound
Beaufort Sea
Amundsen Gulf
Gulf of Boothia
Arctic Circle
CANADA
NORTH AMERICA
UNITED STATES
U.S.S.R.
Chukchi Sea
Vostočno-Sibirskoje More
East Siberian Sea
BERING SEA
Bering Strait
Gulf of Alaska
BROOKS RANGE
ALASKA RANGE
MACKENZIE MOUNTAINS
SELWYN MOUNTAINS
OGILVIE MOUNTAINS
PELLY MOUNTAINS
COAST MOUNTAINS
ROCKY
CARIBOO MTS.
Great Bear Lake
Great Slave Lake
Lake Athabasca
Lake Winnipeg
Yukon
Mackenzie
Saskatchewan
Churchill
Nelson
Anchorage
Fairbanks
Nome
Barrow
Inuvik
Yellowknife
Edmonton
Calgary
Saskatoon
Regina
Winnipeg
Vancouver
Victoria
Seattle
Churchill
Moosonee
Fort George
Goose Bay
St. John's
NEWFOUNDLAND
Gulf of Saint Lawrence
Strait of Belle Isle
Cabot Strait
PRINCE EDWARD
QUEEN CHARLOTTE ISLANDS
VANCOUVER ISLAND
KODIAK ISLAND
SAINT LAWRENCE ISLAND
NUNIVAK ISLAND
ALASKA PENINSULA
SWEDEN
NORWAY
Narvik
70°
80°
90°
120°
150°
180°
160°
170°
60°
50°
140°
40°
30°
20°
10°
0°

ATLANTIC
OCEAN
PACIFIC
OCEAN
GULF OF
MEXICO
CARIBBEAN
SEA
UNITED STATES
GREAT PLAINS
ROCKY MOUNTAINS
APPALACHIAN MOUNTAINS
MEXICO
SOUTH AMERICA
COLOMBIA
VENEZUELA
LLANOS
BERMUDA (U.K.)
BAHAMAS
WEST INDIES
CUBA
JAMAICA
HAITI
HISPANIOLA
DOMINICAN REPUBLIC
PUERTO RICO (U.S.)
NETHERLANDS ANTILLES
GREATER ANTILLES
CAYMAN ISLANDS (U.K.)
BELIZE (U.K.)
GUATEMALA
HONDURAS
EL SALVADOR
NICARAGUA
COSTA RICA
PANAMA
CANAL ZONE (U.S.)
Tropic of Cancer
Straits of Florida
Yucatan Channel
Gulf of Honduras
Bahía de Campeche
Golfo de Tehuantepec
Golfo de California
BAJA CALIFORNIA
YUCATAN PENINSULA
SIERRA MADRE ORIENTAL
SIERRA MADRE OCCIDENTAL
SIERRA MADRE DEL SUR
SIERRA NEVADA
COAST RANGES
GREAT BASIN
EDWARDS PLATEAU
OZARK PLATEAU
CORDILLERA OCCIDENTAL
CORD. ORIENTAL
Mississippi
Missouri
Rio Grande
Río Bravo del Norte
Colorado
Lake Michigan
Lake Huron
Lake Erie
Lake Ontario
Sault Sainte Marie
Sudbury
Ottawa
TORONTO
Buffalo
Albany
Portland
BOSTON
Providence
Hartford
NEW YORK
PHILADELPHIA
Baltimore
WASHINGTON
Richmond
Norfolk
Raleigh
Charlotte
Columbia
Charleston
Savannah
Jacksonville
Tampa
Miami
Pittsburgh
CLEVELAND
DETROIT
Lansing
CHICAGO
Milwaukee
Madison
Indianapolis
Cincinnati
Louisville
Nashville
Chattanooga
Atlanta
Birmingham
Montgomery
Mobile
New Orleans
Jackson
Memphis
Little Rock
Shreveport
ST. LOUIS
Kansas City
Des Moines
Minneapolis
Saint Paul
Duluth
Fargo
Bismarck
Pierre
Omaha
Cheyenne
Wichita
Oklahoma City
Dallas
Fort Worth
San Antonio
Laredo
Brownsville
Matamoros
Monterrey
Denver
Albuquerque
Santa Fe
El Paso
Phoenix
Salt Lake City
Boise
Reno
Las Vegas
Sacramento
SAN FRANCISCO
LOS ANGELES
San Diego
Hermosillo
Chihuahua
Torreón
La Paz
Mazatlán
Guadalajara
CIUDAD DE MÉXICO
MEXICO CITY
Puebla
Veracruz
Tampico
Oaxaca
Acapulco
Mérida
Villahermosa
Belize
Belmopan
Guatemala
San Salvador
Tegucigalpa
Managua
Bluefields
San José
Panamá
Colón
La Habana
Havana
Guantánamo
Santiago de Cuba
Kingston
Port-au-Prince
Santo Domingo
San Juan
Nassau
Maracaibo
CARACAS
Barquisimeto
Barranquilla
Cartagena
Cúcuta
San Cristóbal
Bucaramanga
Medellín
Manizales
BOGOTÁ
Cali
Buenaventura
Tumaco
Puerto Ayacucho
Kilometres 0 200 400 600 800 Km.
Miles 0 200 400 600 800 Mi.
Lambert Azimuthal Equal-Area Projection
Copyright © by Rand McNally & Co.

Earth panorama: North America

North America extends from 15° to 83° latitude north, from the Isthmus of Tehuantepec in Mexico to the Arctic. Nearly all types of climate are found in this great geographical region, from the polar climate in the north, through the subarctic tundra and conifer forest climates, the temperate climates, the high-altitude climates of the Rockies and Sierras, the tropical deserts of Arizona, New Mexico, and northern Mexico, to the humid tropical climates of Florida, much of the Gulf Coast, and the southern lowlands of Mexico.

The core of the continent consists of a Precambrian basement of granite and gneiss. This is overlaid by a horizontal sedimentary cover in the Middle West Plains and reaches the surface north of the Great Lakes and the St Lawrence to form the Canadian Shield. To the west of this basement, geologically recent foldings have uplifted the Rocky Mountains. West of these lie even more recent ranges, still the site of faulting, folding, and volcanic eruptions. To the east of the basement is an ancient range, the Appalachians.

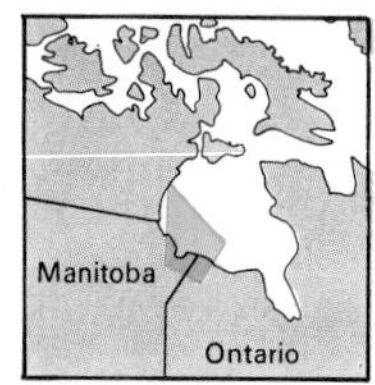

Manitoba
Ontario

1 Hudson Bay is a large inland sea of 475,000 sq miles (1,230,250 sq km), which is open to navigation for only three months a year because of the ice. The area shown here is the Ontario and Manitoba shoreline. Hudson Bay is a shallow sea underlaid by the North American continental shield. Like the Baltic, this sea has filled a depression made by the weight of the Ice Age ice sheet, and the sea bed is now slowly rising.

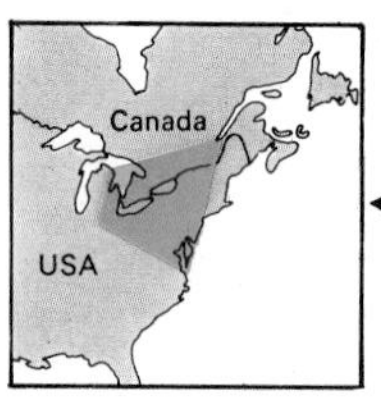

Canada
USA

2 The Great Lakes, the largest body of fresh water in the world, occupy depressions carved by the Quaternary ice sheet. The St Lawrence waterway allows large ships to reach Duluth, Minn.

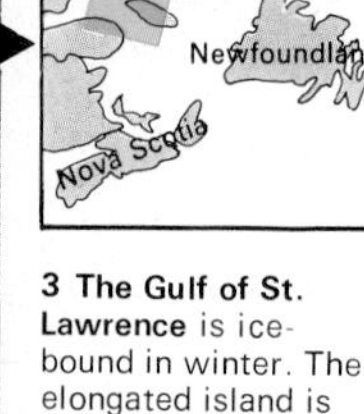

Quebec
Newfoundland
Nova Scotia

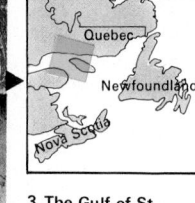

3 The Gulf of St. Lawrence is icebound in winter. The elongated island is Anticosti. To the north is the mainland of Quebec, and the rounded coastline to the south is the Gaspé peninsula.

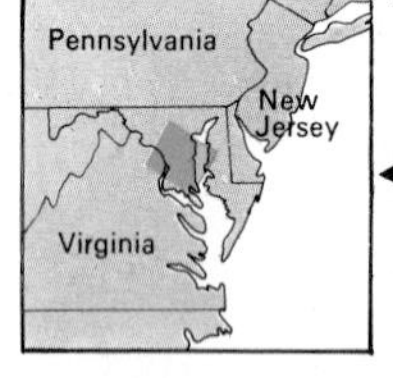

Pennsylvania
New Jersey
Virginia

4 This Skylab view of Chesapeake Bay shows the cities of Washington [below] and Baltimore [above]. The Potomac River flowing between Washington and Alexandria (on the south) can be seen at the bottom. The beltways around Washington and Baltimore and the Interstate 95 highway joining the two cities are conspicuous, as is the bridge of US Route 50 across Chesapeake Bay. The US Naval Academy at Annapolis is to the south of the bridge's Washington side. The tunnel across Baltimore's harbor can be guessed from its aerial accessway. The bay's sedimentation and circulation, which combine in murky patterns, are the subject of study by scientists.

5

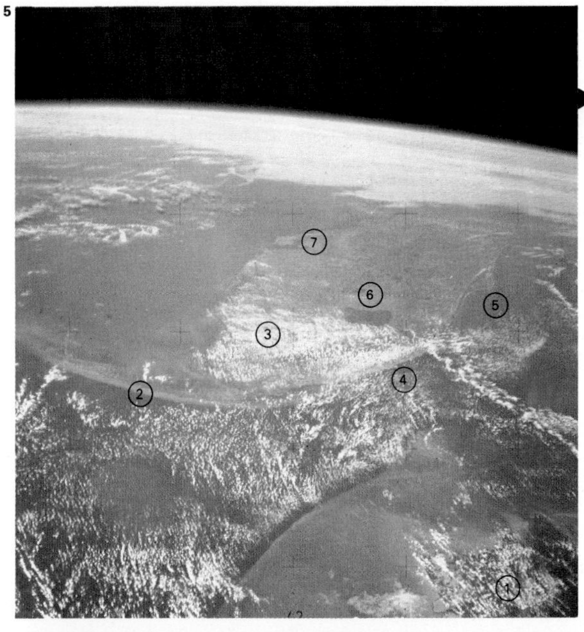

5 The Straits of Florida, through which the Gulf Stream flows, appear as a dark blue zone between the Bahama bank (bottom right) and the Florida peninsula. The Bahamas, of which only Andros [1] can be seen here, and the Florida Keys [2] are built of coral and algal reefs. The Everglades [3], Miami [4], Cape Canaveral and the John F. Kennedy Space Center [5], Lake Okeechobee [6], and Tampa Bay [7] can also be seen.

6

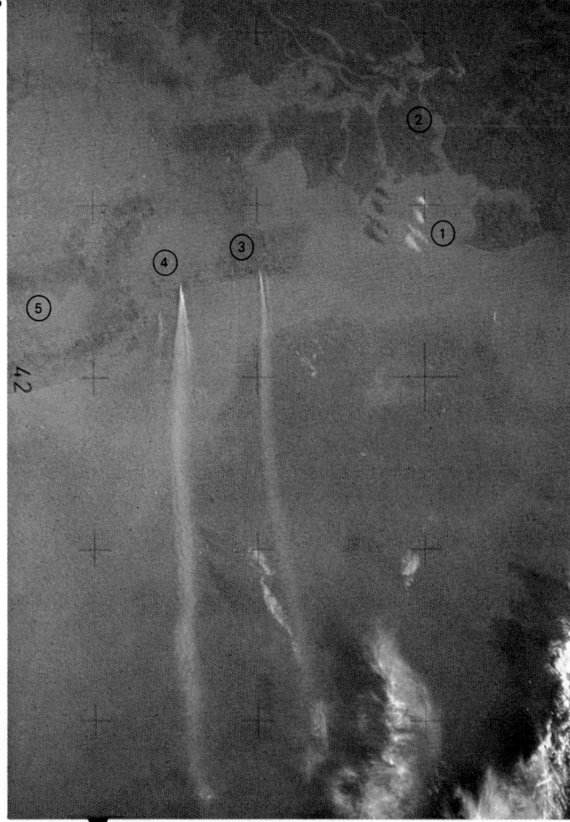

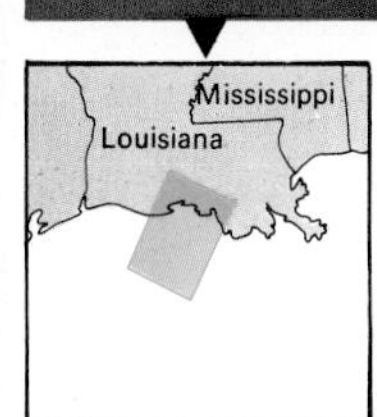
Mississippi
Louisiana

6 This swampy coast of Louisana consists of Atchafalaya Bay [1], Atchafalaya River [2], which is a secondary effluent of the Mississippi, small muddy islands off the delta such as Isles Dernieres, and Marsh Island [3] in front of Vermillion Bay [4]. White Lake [5] is another conspicuous feature. The two smoke plumes are oil well fires. The wells extend 200mi (320km) into the Gulf.

7

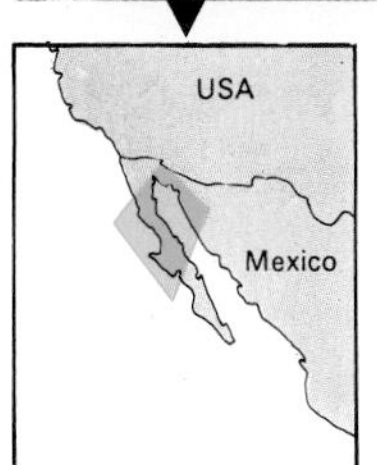
USA
Mexico

7 Baja California peninsula was part of the Mexican mainland before it drifted 300miles (480km) in a northwesterly direction, opening up the Gulf of California. This sliding motion is also shearing California along the San Andreas Fault, which starts near the mouth of the Colorado River [1] and continues northward about 600mi (965 km). The large amount of sediment carried by this river is shown by the discoloration of the water. The islands of Angel de la Guarda [2] and Tiburón [3] are clearly seen and so is that of Cedros [4] off Sebastián Vizcaino Bay. At the head of this bay are two lagoons, the larger of which is Scammon's Lagoon [5], to which the California gray whale migrates each year.

8

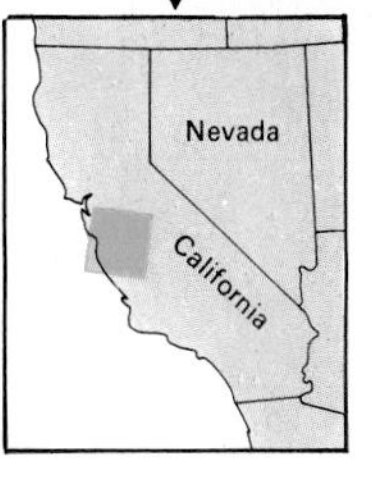
Nevada
California

8 The San Andreas Fault is a huge break in the earth's crust running 600mi (965 km) from the top of the Gulf of California to a point north of San Francisco. Its movement caused the 1906 San Francisco earthquake. It can be seen [XY] in this Skylab picture running parallel and to the east of the cultivated Salinas River valley. To the west Monterey Bay can be clearly seen. The large mottled expanse to the east is the Central Valley, California's largest agricultural belt.

South America

ATLANTIC OCEAN
CARIBBEAN SEA
Tropic of Cancer
Equator
Yucatan Channel
WEST INDIES
GREATER ANTILLES
LESSER ANTILLES
BAHAMAS
CUBA
La Habana
Havana
Santiago de Cuba
Guantánamo
JAMAICA
Kingston
HAITI
Port-au-Prince
DOMINICAN REPUBLIC
Santo Domingo
HISPANIOLA
PUERTO RICO
San Juan
VIRGIN ISLANDS (U.K. and U.S.)
ANTIGUA (U.K.)
GUADELOUPE (Fr.)
DOMINICA (U.K.)
MARTINIQUE (Fr.)
SAINT LUCIA (U.K.)
BARBADOS
SAINT VINCENT (U.K.)
GRENADA
TRINIDAD AND TOBAGO
Port of Spain
NETHERLANDS ANTILLES
CAYMAN ISLANDS (U.K.)
HONDURAS
NICARAGUA
COSTA RICA
San José
PANAMA
Panamá
CANAL ZONE (U.S.)
VENEZUELA
CARACAS
Maracaibo
Barquisimeto
Ciudad Bolívar
Ciudad Guayana
COLOMBIA
BOGOTÁ
Medellín
Cali
Barranquilla
Cartagena
Cúcuta
Bucaramanga
GUYANA
Georgetown
SURINAM
Paramaribo
FRENCH GUIANA
Cayenne
ECUADOR
Quito
Guayaquil
PERU
LIMA
Iquitos
BRAZIL
SOUTH AMERICA
Manaus
Belém
São Luís
Fortaleza
Natal
João Pessoa
Recife
Maceió
Salvador
Brasília
Teresina
Campina Grande
Santarém
Pôrto Velho
Rio Branco
BOLIVIA
La Paz
Amazon
Orinoco
Negro
Madeira
Purus
Juruá
Tocantins
Xingu
Tapajós
São Francisco
SELVAS
LLANOS
PLANALTO DO MATO
CORDILLERA OCCIDENTAL
CORDILLERA ORIENTAL

PACIFIC
OCEAN
ATLANTIC
OCEAN
Scotia Sea
Drake Passage
Tropic of Capricorn
PARAGUAY
URUGUAY
PAMPAS
PATAGONIA
ARGENTINA
CHILE
ANDES
GRAN CHACO
BUENOS AIRES
Montevideo
SANTIAGO
Asunción
SÃO PAULO
RIO DE JANEIRO
Belo Horizonte
Porto Alegre
Curitiba
Santos
Florianópolis
Pelotas
Rio Grande
Lagoa dos Patos
Lagoa Mirim
Rosario
Córdoba
Santa Fe
Corrientes
Posadas
Concepción
Villarrica
San Miguel de Tucumán
Santiago del Estero
Salta
Tarija
Mendoza
San Juan
Valparaíso
Concepción
Valdivia
Osorno
Puerto Montt
Coquimbo
Antofagasta
Iquique
Mar del Plata
La Plata
Rocha
Salto
Paysandú
Rivera
Santa Maria
Bahía Blanca
Neuquén
Viedma
Rawson
Comodoro Rivadavia
Golfo San Jorge
Golfo San Matías
Golfo de Penas
Río Gallegos
Punta Arenas
Ushuaia
Stanley
FALKLAND ISLANDS (U.K.)
WEST FALKLAND
EAST FALKLAND
SOUTH GEORGIA (Falk. Is.)
SOUTH SANDWICH ISLANDS (Falk. Is.)
ISLA GRANDE DE TIERRA DEL FUEGO
Estrecho de Magallanes
Strait of Magellan
Estrecho de le Maire
ISLA DE LOS ESTADOS
ISLA NAVARINO
ISLA HOSTE
CABO DE HORNOS
CAPE HORN
ISLA DE CHILOÉ
ARCHIPIÉLAGO DE LOS CHONOS
ISLA MAGDALENA
ISLA CAMPANA
ISLA WELLINGTON
ISLA MADRE DE DIOS
ARCHIPIÉLAGO REINA ADELAIDA
ISLA DESOLACIÓN
ISLA SANTA INÉS
MESETA DE LAS VIZCACHAS
PAMPA DEL CASTILLO
ISLAS JUAN FERNÁNDEZ (Chile)
ISLA ROBINSON CRUSOE
ISLA ALEJANDRO SELKIRK
ISLA SAN FÉLIX (Chile)
ISLA SAN AMBROSIO (Chile)
DESIERTO DE ATACAMA
Salar de Uyuni
Salar de Atacama
Cerro Aconcagua
Cerro Tres Picos 1243
Cerro Champaquí 2884
Paso de Bermejo 3798
Monte Sarmiento 2300
Volcán Corcovado 2300
SERRA DE MARACAJU
SERRA DO MAR
SA. DA MANTIQUEIRA
SA. DA CANASTRA
Paraná
Uruguay
Paraguay
Iguaçu
Pilcomayo
Bermejo
Salado
Colorado
Negro
Chubut
Chico
Río de la Plata
PENÍNSULA VALDÉS
Kilometres 0 200 400 600 800 Km.
Miles 0 200 400 600 800 Mi.
Lambert Azimuthal Equal-Area Projection

Earth panorama: South America

The structure of South America is in many ways comparable to that of North America. High recent mountains—the Andes—follow the Pacific coast, and old and worn highlands are found to the east: the Guiana Highlands and the Brazilian plateau. The Andes and the eastern highlands define vast alluvial basins that are drained by large rivers such as the Orinoco, Amazon, Tocantins, São Francisco, Uruguay, and Paraná. More than 90 percent of the continent's drainage is toward the Atlantic Ocean; in terms of water flow the imbalance is even higher because the Andean coast receives very little rain between 5° and 35° south.

The Andes are a young and still extremely active chain of mountains. Their geological crumpling is the result of the Andes area being squeezed between the American and the East Pacific (Antarctic) plates, which move toward each other.

The climate is equatorial in the north and in the Amazon basin. It is tropical south of the Amazon basin and temperate south of southern Brazil. The Andean mountains south of Ecuador have a dry, cold climate.

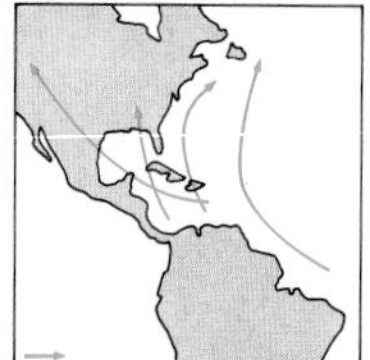

1 Hurricanes are prominent weather features when seen from space, as in this Apollo photograph. The Caribbean island arc experiences about a dozen hurricanes a year (the word may be derived from the name of the native Mayan god of the big wind, Hunraken). Hurricanes are tropical depressions with extremely steep pressure gradients. They often originate in the Atlantic and travel westward toward the American coast.

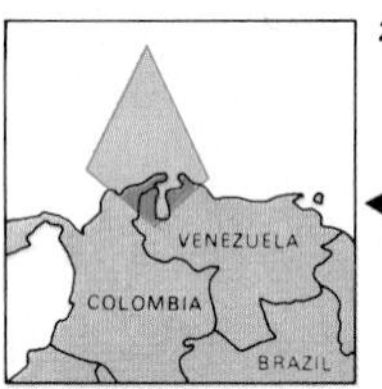
VENEZUELA
COLOMBIA
BRAZIL

1
2
3

2 The Gulf of Venezuela lies between the peninsulas of Guajira [1] and Paraguaná [2]. The town of Maracaibo is on the channel leading from the gulf to Lake Maracaibo [3], South America's largest.

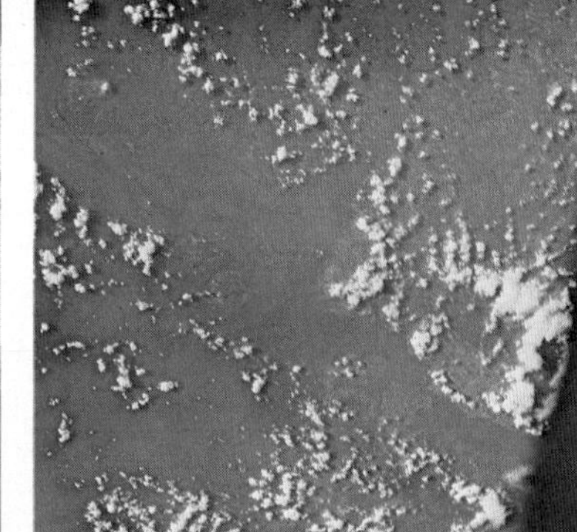

VENEZUELA
BRAZIL

3 The Orinoco is the largest river in Venezuela. It meanders its way to the coast. Not far from its spring it links up with the Río Negro by a natural canal, the 100-mile (160-km) long Canal Casiquiare.

URUGUAY
ARGENTINA

4 The large body of reddish water is the Río de la Plata, between Uruguay and Argentina, which flows into the deep blue South Atlantic. The red plume is probably sediment moving seaward from the river mouth. Montevideo is the lighter area surrounding the deep bay where the coastline changes direction. To the west, the River Santa Lucia enters the Río de la Plata, and it is the major drainage for the area. The small island at its mouth is Isla del Tigre. The white beaches and sand dunes are visible along the coast. Major thoroughfares and residential areas are seen. Green and gray rectangular patterns are fields and show local types of agriculture.

5

BRAZIL
PERU
BOLIVIA
ARGENTINA

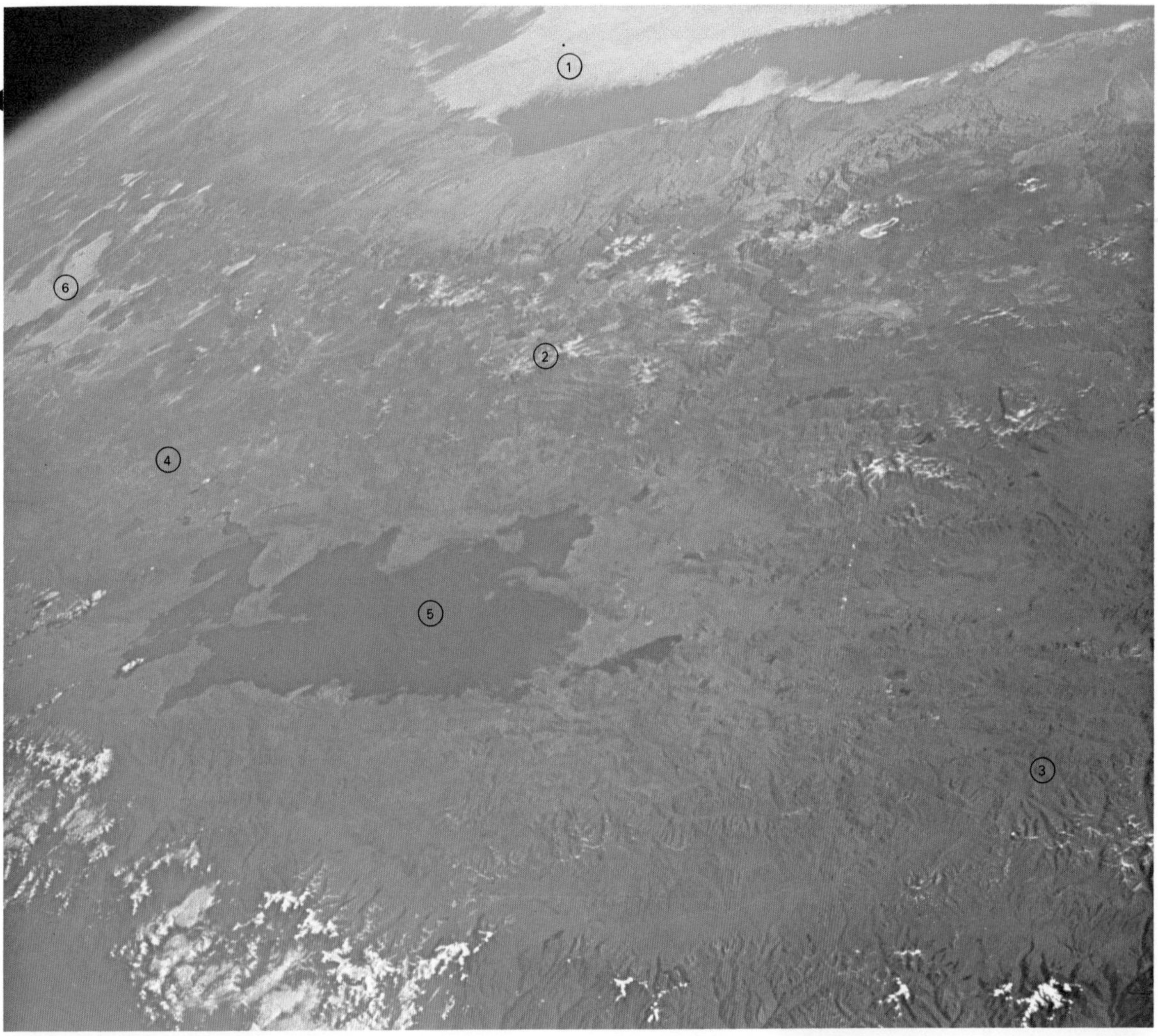

5 Taken high over the Andes, looking south, this photograph reveals their basic shape and structure. The Pacific Ocean [1] washes the base of the Cordillera Occidental [2], some summits of which are snow-covered. This chain is made up of Mesozoic sediments and has numerous volcanoes, some of them active, located along fault lines that run parallel to the axis. East of the Cordillera Occidental is a central zone. To the north are some high folded mountains, the Cordillera Central [3]. To the south they dip under a debris-filled highland plain, the Altiplano [4], which is a graben (depression bounded by faults). Lake Titicaca [5] drains into the salt lake Poopó (not shown), which in turn drains into the salt pans of Coipasa and Uyuni [6]. The divide between the waters draining into the Altiplano and into the Amazon basin is distinct.

6

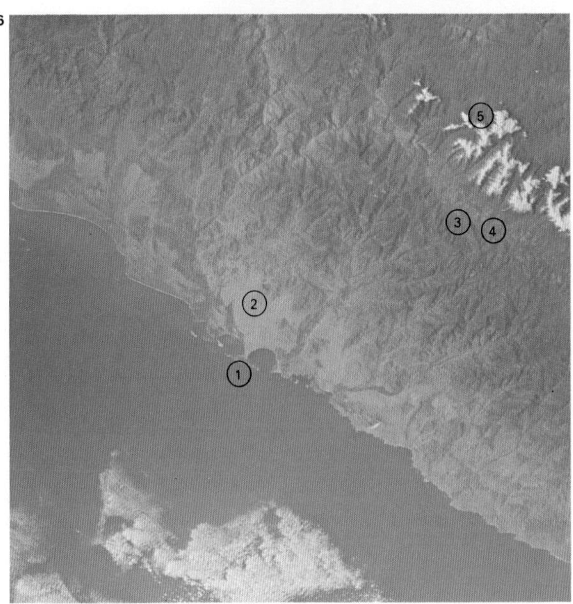

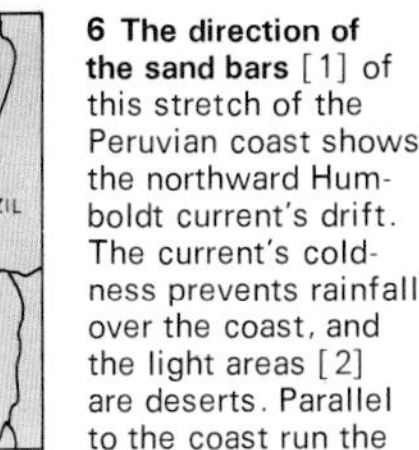
ECUADOR
PERU
BRAZIL

6 The direction of the sand bars [1] of this stretch of the Peruvian coast shows the northward Humboldt current's drift. The current's coldness prevents rainfall over the coast, and the light areas [2] are deserts. Parallel to the coast run the Cordillera Negra [3], of volcanic origin, and the snow-covered Cordillera Blanca [5]. The town of Yungay [4], in the Río Santa valley, was wiped out in 1970 by a landslide triggered by an earthquake; about 25,000 people were killed.

CHILE
ARGENTINA

7 An interesting pattern of valleys is displayed in this area of the Andes between Chile and Argentina. They were carved by glaciers that left the valley floors covered with moraine debris when they melted.

7

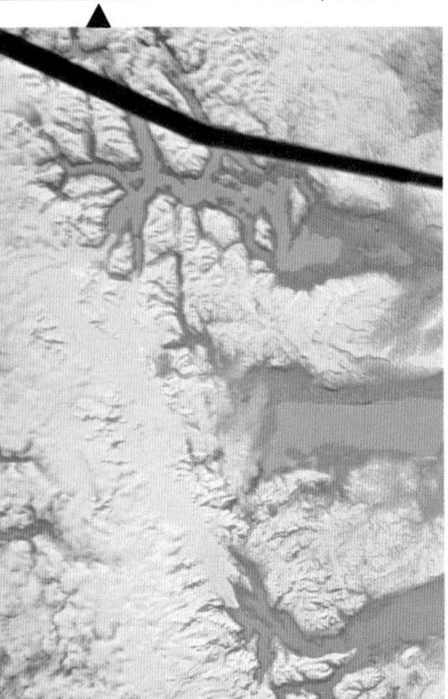

8

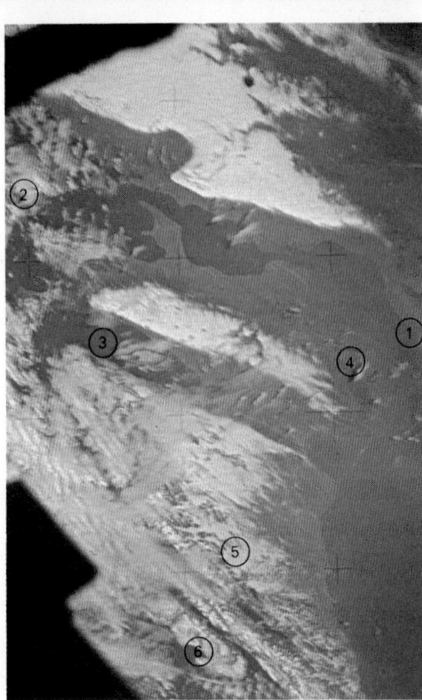

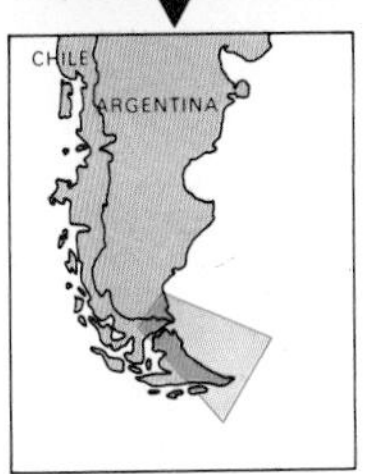
CHILE
ARGENTINA

8 The eastern half of the Magellan Strait extends from Cape Virgenes [1] past the town of Punta Arenas [2] and Useless Bay [3] to Punta Catalina [4]. Tierra del Fuego [5] is separated from Navarino Island [6] by Beagle Channel.

The atmosphere

The origin of the atmosphere was no doubt closely associated with the origin of the Earth. When the earth was still a molten ball, it was probably surrounded by a large atmosphere of cosmic gases, including hydrogen, that were gradually lost into space. As the Earth began to develop a solid crust over a molten core, gases such as carbon dioxide, nitrogen, and water vapor were slowly released to form an atmosphere with a composition not unlike the present emanations from volcanoes. Further cooling probably led to massive precipitation of water vapor, so that today it occupies less than four percent by volume of the atmosphere. The advent at a much later stage of the all-important oxygen content of the atmosphere was caused by green plants releasing oxygen as a result of combining water and carbon dioxide to form carbohydrates [Key].

Heated from below

Up to a height of about 31 miles (50km) the composition of the atmosphere [1] is remarkably homogeneous, comprising a mixture of gases each with its own physical properties. Carbon dioxide, water vapor, and ozone, although only small constituents of the atmosphere, play vital roles in absorption of solar and terrestrial radiation, thus allowing life on Earth. Because of the action of gravity, this homogeneous mixture of gases is compressed [2], giving the highest values of density and pressure near the Earth's surface; average surface density is 1.2kg/m^3 and average surface pressure is 1,013 millibars (mb) (roughly 1 kg/cm^2 or 14.7lb per square inch). At a height of 9 miles (16km), pressure falls to 100mb and the density is less than 11 percent of the density at sea level.

The constituent gases of the atmosphere largely allow the Sun's radiation to pass without interception. Fortunately, the small amount of ozone, concentrated most strongly at 15 miles (24km) height, but in significant amounts up to 31 miles (50km), filters out most of the ultraviolet rays harmful to life on Earth. If all the ozone were brought down to sea level, it would form a layer only 0.1in (0.25cm) thick. After scattering, reflection, and some absorption in the lower, denser layers of the atmosphere, only about 46 percent of the solar radiation reaching the upper atmosphere is absorbed by the solid Earth's surface as heat. This input of energy raises the Earth's surface to a mean temperature of 57°F (14°C). Because this is lower than the 10,290°F (5,700°C) of the Sun's surface, the Earth radiates energy of much longer wavelengths (infrared or heat rays) than solar radiation and these longer waves are absorbed by the carbon dioxide, water vapor, and clouds in the lower atmosphere.

This means that the atmosphere is directly heated from below, not from above. Just as the Earth radiates heat, so does the atmosphere—upward to be lost to space and downward to be reabsorbed by the Earth. The net effect of these exchanges [3] is that as much heat is lost to space as is gained from solar radiation.

Temperature distribution

In the bottom 80 percent (in mass) of the atmosphere, temperature falls with height, in accord with the heating from below [4].

CONNECTIONS

See also
96 The Sun's atmosphere and radiation
214 Winds and weather systems
216 Weather
218 Forecasting
292 Pollution of the air

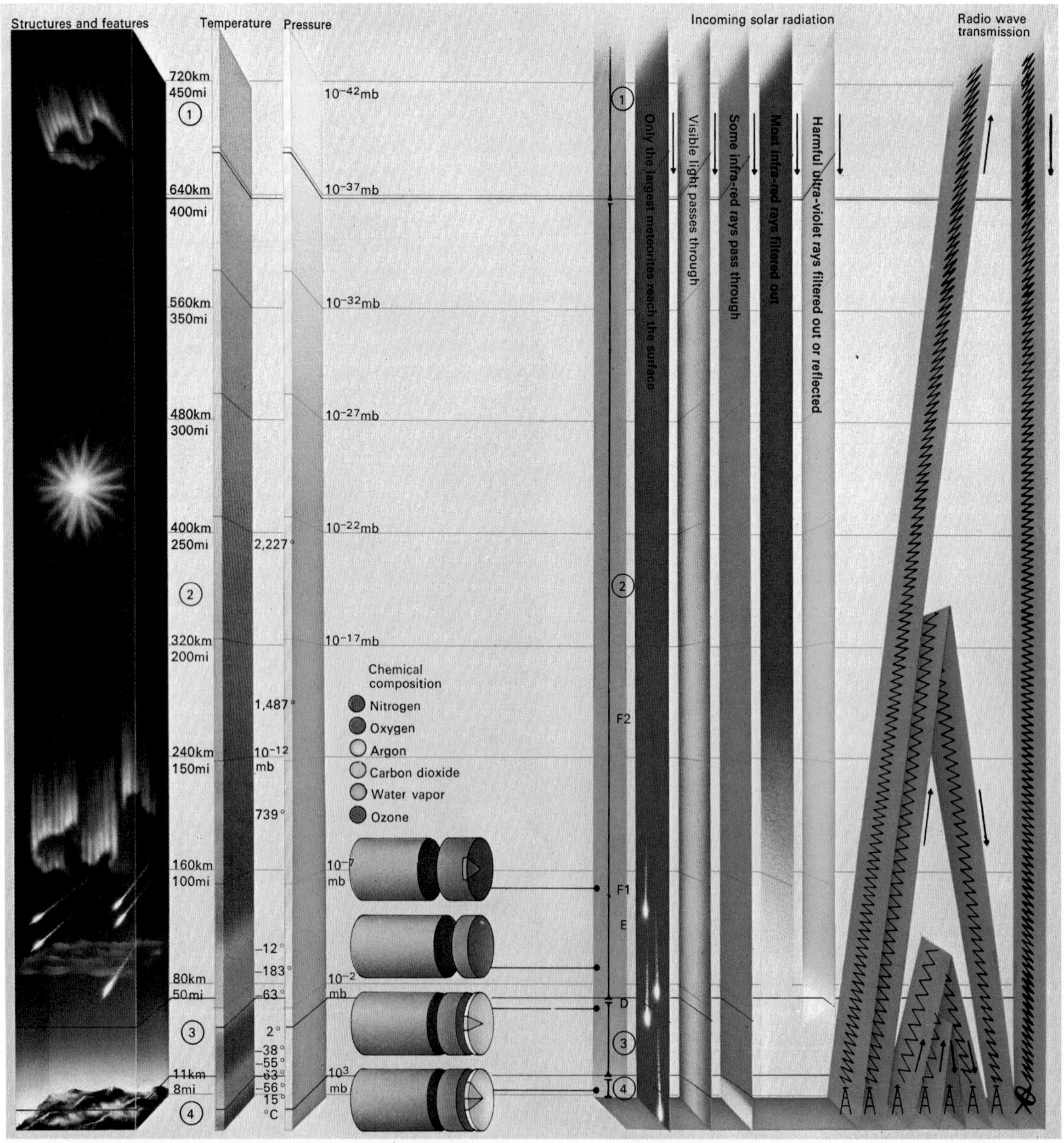

1

Structures and features
Temperature
Pressure
Incoming solar radiation
Radio wave transmission
720km 450mi
640km 400mi
560km 350mi
480km 300mi
400km 250mi
320km 200mi
240km 150mi
160km 100mi
80km 50mi
11km 8mi
10^{-42}mb
10^{-37}mb
10^{-32}mb
10^{-27}mb
10^{-22}mb
10^{-17}mb
10^{-12} mb
10^{-7} mb
10^{-2} mb
10^{3} mb
2,227°
1,487°
739°
-12°
-183°
-63°
2°
-38°
-55°
-63°
-56°
15°
°C
Chemical composition
Nitrogen
Oxygen
Argon
Carbon dioxide
Water vapor
Ozone
Only the largest meteorites reach the surface
Visible light passes through
Some infra-red rays pass through
Most infra-red rays filtered out
Harmful ultra-violet rays filtered out or reflected
F2
F1
E
D

1 The atmosphere shows a surprising variety of characteristics on a vertical scale. Gravity means that air density and associated pressure increase near the surface. Pressure of about 1,000 millibars (mb) at sea level falls to virtually nothing at a height of 447 miles (720km). Temperature also varies with height, falling and rising in several layers, ultimately increasing toward outer space. Even the mixture of gases shows variations, with water vapor being added at low levels. Four broad atmospheric layers can be identified. The exosphere [1] is a rarefied region above 250 miles (400km) with differing proportions of oxygen, helium, and hydrogen. The highest auroras are found in this region. The ionosphere [2], where charged particles (ions and electrons) occur, makes up a deep layer comprising the meso- and thermospheres, subdivided into four minor layers (F2, F1, E, and D). Their ion density has a marked effect on radio waves—very high frequency waves penetrate but shortwave transmissions are reflected. The stratosphere [3] contains small but vital amounts of ozone filtering out harmful solar radiation. The troposphere [4] contains the bulk of the atmosphere and all its weather. With the outer layers it acts as a particle and radiation shield. Temperatures decrease to its upper boundary.

This layer of the atmosphere 5 miles (8km) deep in polar regions and about 11 miles (18km) deep over the equatorial regions, is known as the troposphere. It is characterized by wind speeds increasing with height, considerable moisture at low levels, and appreciable vertical air movement, and it is generally the source of "weather." The tropopause marks the boundary between the troposphere and the stratosphere.

The temperature is virtually constant throughout the lower stratosphere, but this layer has strong air circulation patterns and high wind speeds in the jet streams that are used by airliners. In the upper stratosphere, above about 15 miles (25km), temperature gradually increases with height to a broad maximum at the stratopause. Above the stratopause, in the mesosphere, the temperature begins to decline sharply with increasing height, to a minimum at about 52 miles (85km). Above this mesopause is the thermosphere, where temperature is believed to increase to the thermopause at 250 miles (400km). Beyond, in the exosphere, the pressure drops to virtually a vacuum.

Within the troposphere another type of heat balance operates. More radiant heat is received than lost in tropical latitudes and the converse is true in polar latitudes. This broad temperature gradient from equator to pole generates a pressure gradient in the same direction; warm air moves down the gradient, reducing temperature extremes by cooling the tropics and warming the polar areas [3C].

Humidity of the atmosphere

The water content of the atmosphere is primarily in vapor form. Humidity decreases with height [5] because water enters the atmosphere by evaporation from the Earth's surface. The driest parts of the lower atmosphere are over the subtropical deserts; the wettest are over the equatorial and summer monsoon regions, especially ocean surfaces. Water is constantly being cycled between the Earth and the atmosphere. The amount in the atmosphere at any one time is only a fraction of one percent of the total water in the planet, but it provides enough rainfall to sustain life.

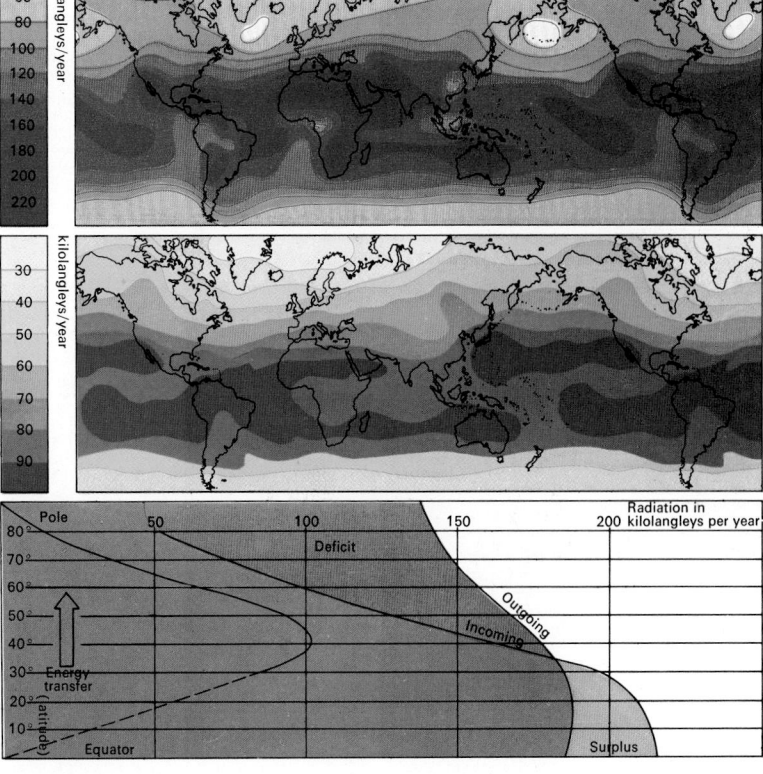

KEY
Methane and hydrogen
Ammonia
Water vapor
Nitrogen
Carbon dioxide
Oxygen

5,000 4,000 3,000 2,000 1,000
Million years before present

Important changes have occurred in the Earth's atmosphere since it formed 4.6 billion years ago as hydrogen, methane, and ammonia. Most of the primitive hydrogen was lost to outer space and large quantities of steam and other gases were produced. This led to an atmosphere consisting mainly of nitrogen, water, sulfur dioxide, and carbon dioxide. Photosynthesizing algae appeared 3.5 billion years ago to produce free oxygen and the resulting ozone made up an ultraviolet shield, permitting life to spread on land.

2 Air is easily compressed, so the atmosphere becomes "squashed" by the effect of gravity. This results in the bulk (80%) of the atmosphere being in the troposphere, occupying a volume of about 1.4 × 10^9 cubic miles. As air density decreases with altitude, the smaller amounts of air in the stratosphere (19%) and the ionosphere and above (1%) occupy a greater volume.

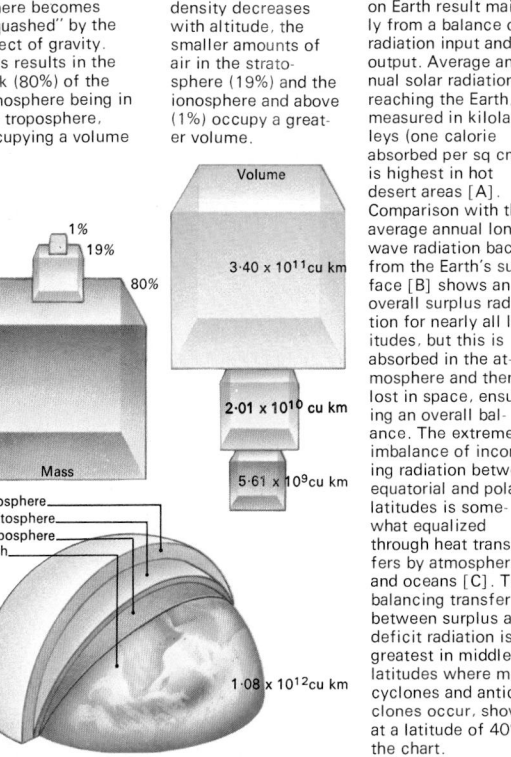

2

1%
19%
80%
Mass
Volume
3·40 x 10^{11}cu km
2·01 x 10^{10} cu km
5·61 x 10^9cu km
1·08 x 10^{12}cu km
Ionosphere
Stratosphere
Troposphere
Earth

3 Temperatures in the atmosphere and on Earth result mainly from a balance of radiation input and output. Average annual solar radiation reaching the Earth, measured in kilolangleys (one calorie absorbed per sq cm) is highest in hot desert areas [A]. Comparison with the average annual long-wave radiation back from the Earth's surface [B] shows an overall surplus radiation for nearly all latitudes, but this is absorbed in the atmosphere and then lost in space, ensuring an overall balance. The extreme imbalance of incoming radiation between equatorial and polar latitudes is somewhat equalized through heat transfers by atmosphere and oceans [C]. This balancing transfer between surplus and deficit radiation is greatest in middle latitudes where most cyclones and anticyclones occur, shown at a latitude of 40° on the chart.

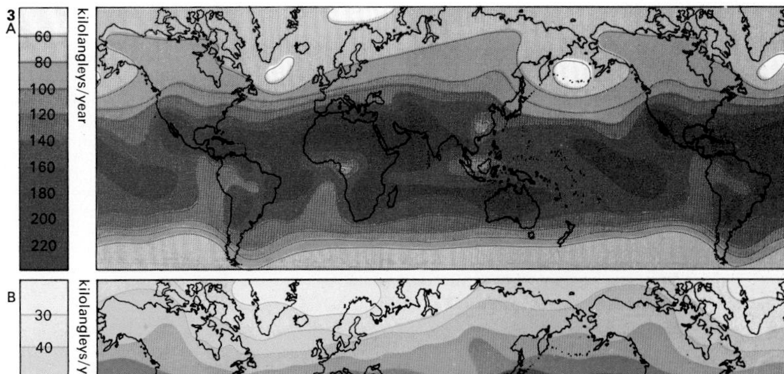

3
A
kilolangleys/year
60
80
100
120
140
160
180
200
220
B
kilolangleys/year
30
40
50
60
70
80
90

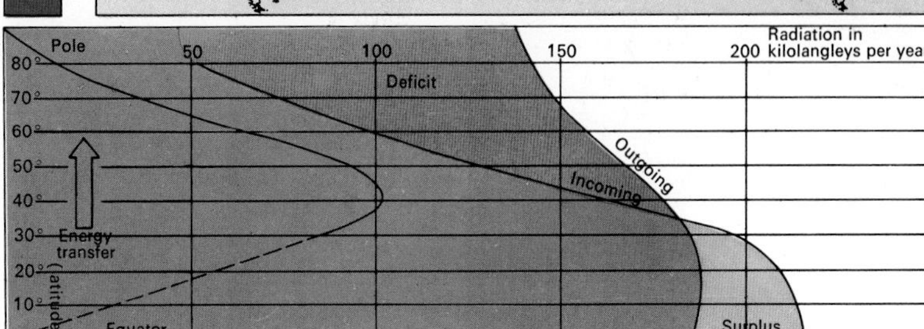

C
Pole
50
100
150
200
Radiation in kilolangleys per year
Deficit
Outgoing
Incoming
Energy transfer
Surplus
Equator
(latitude)
80°
70°
60°
50°
40°
30°
20°
10°

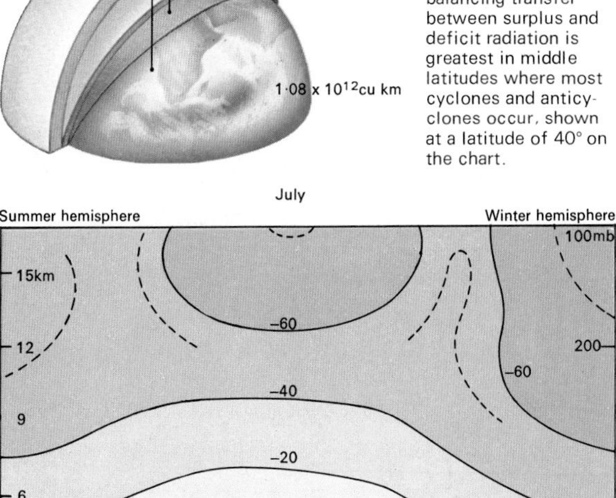

4
July
Summer hemisphere
Winter hemisphere
15km
12
9
6
3
100mb
200
500
1,000
-60
-40
-20
0
20
0
-60
90°N
60°
30°
0
30°
60°
90°S

4 Atmospheric temperatures tend to decrease evenly with increase in height and latitude up to a level called the tropopause at a height of about 5.5 miles (9km) at the poles rising to 11 miles in the tropics.

5 Humidity falls with height in the troposphere. Warm air can hold more water vapor than cold air and therefore the warmer mid-latitude atmosphere holds more water vapor than the colder air over the Antarctic.

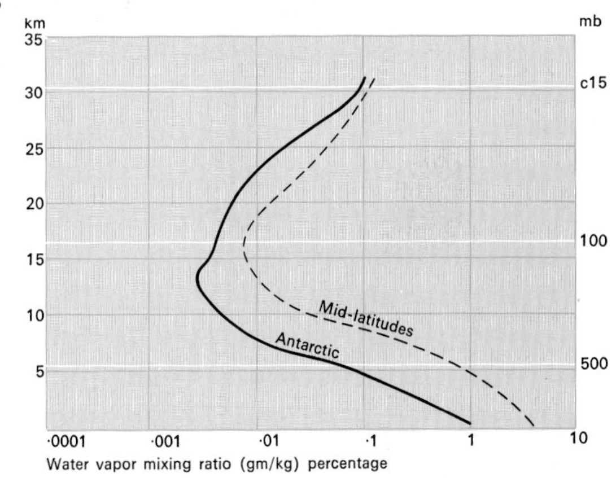

5
km
35
30
25
20
15
10
5
mb
c15
100
500
Mid-latitudes
Antarctic
·0001
·001
·01
·1
1
10
Water vapor mixing ratio (gm/kg) percentage

Winds and weather systems

Wind is the movement of air, and large-scale air movements, both horizontal and vertical, are important in shaping weather and climate. The chief forces affecting horizontal air movements are pressure gradients, the Coriolis effect, and friction.

Pressure gradients are caused by the unequal heating of the atmosphere by the Sun [1]. Warm equatorial air is lighter and, therefore, has a lower pressure than cold, dense, polar air. The strength of air movement from high to low pressure areas—known as the pressure gradient—is proportional to the difference in pressure.

The Coriolis effect, caused by the Earth's rotation, deflects winds to the right in the Northern Hemisphere [3] and to the left in the Southern. As a result, winds do not flow directly from the point of highest pressure to the lowest. Instead, winds approaching a low-pressure system are deflected around it rather than flowing directly into it. This creates air systems, with high or low pressure, in which winds circulate around the center. Horizontal air movements are important around cyclonic (low pressure) and anticyclonic (high pressure) systems. Horizontal and vertical movements combine to create a pattern of prevailing winds.

Along the Equator is a region called the doldrums, where the Sun warms the rising air. This air eventually flows north and south away from the Equator. It finally sinks at about 30°N and 30°S, creating subtropical high pressure belts, from which trade winds flow back toward the Equator and westerlies toward the mid-latitudes.

Cyclones and anticyclones

Along the polar front in the Northern Hemisphere, the warm air of the westerlies meets the polar easterlies. Waves, or bulges, develop along the polar front, some of which grow quickly in size [4]. Warm air flows into the bulge and cold air flows in behind it.

The warm, light air rises above the cold air along the warm front. Behind, the cold air forces its way under the warm air along the cold front. Gradually, the cold front catches up to the warm front and the warm air is pushed above the cold in an occlusion. In cyclones in the Northern Hemisphere, the air circulates in a counterclockwise direction (clockwise in the Southern). Along the warm front, a broad belt of cloud forms, bringing rain and sometimes thunderstorms. The cold front usually has a much narrower belt of clouds. Clouds and rain normally persist for some time along occluded fronts.

Air circulation in anticyclones is the reverse of cyclones, being clockwise in the Northern Hemisphere and counterclockwise in the Southern. Many anticyclones are formed in subtropical regions by sinking air. In winter anticyclones form over continental interiors in temperate latitudes by the cooling of air.

How monsoons occur

Monsoons [2] are seasonal reversals of wind directions. The most celebrated monsoon occurs in India, where the generally northerly winds of winter are replaced by generally southerly winds in summer. The summer winds contain much water vapor.

CONNECTIONS

See also
212 The atmosphere
216 Weather
218 Forecasting
220 Climates

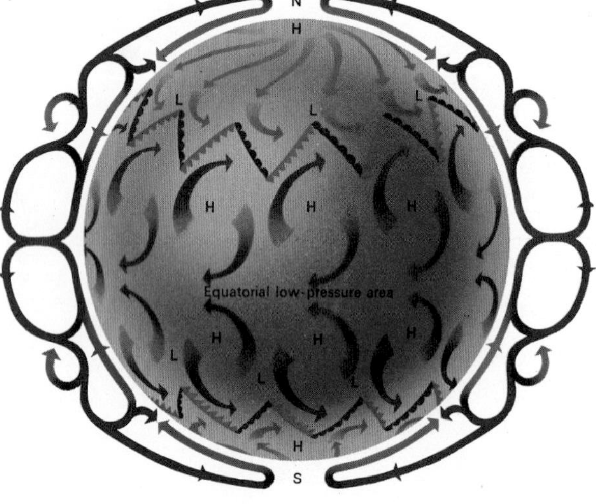

1
N
H
L
H
Equatorial low-pressure area
S
Warm air
Cool air
Cold air
Warm front
Cold front
H=High pressure
L=Low pressure

1 The Earth's atmosphere acts as a giant heat engine. The temperature differences between the poles and the Equator provide the thermal energy to drive atmospheric circulation, both horizontal and vertical. In general, warm air at the Equator rises and moves toward the poles at high levels and cold polar air moves toward the Equator at low levels to replace it. The pattern of prevailing winds is complicated by the rotation of the Earth which causes the Coriolis effect by cells of high pressure and low pressure systems (depressions), and by the distribution of land and sea.

2 World winds in July and January form a pattern. Patterns at a low level are influenced by cells of low pressure, into which air flows, and high-pressure cells from which air flows outward. If the Earth did not rotate, winds would blow directly from high-pressure cells to low-pressure cells. But the Coriolis effect causes winds to be deflected to the right in the Northern Hemisphere and to the left in the Southern Hemisphere. Wind patterns are remarkably constant between summer and winter west of Africa. But, in the east, variations are caused by monsoons (reversals of wind flows). Monsoons arise from the unequal heating of land and sea. For example, dry winds blow outward in winter across India from the cold high pressure system over southern Siberia. In summer, the land heats quickly and a low pressure system develops over northwestern India. Moist, southeasterly trade winds are drawn into this system.

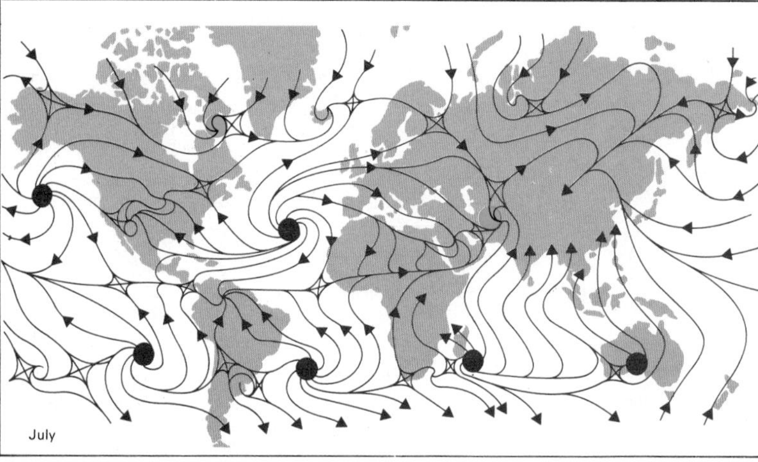

2
July
Low-pressure areas
High-pressure areas

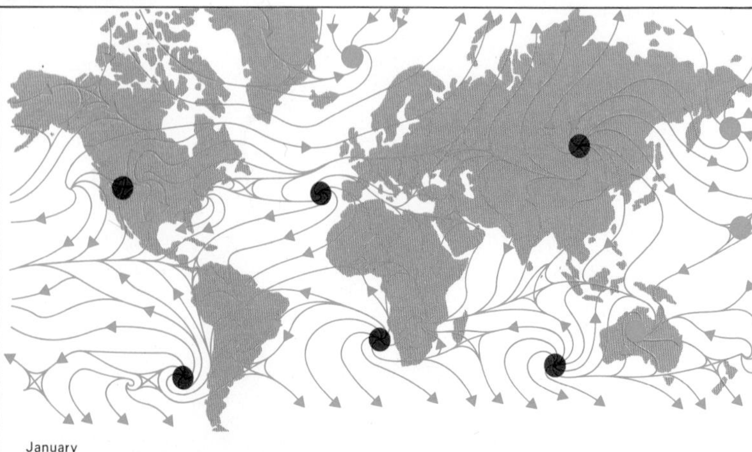

January

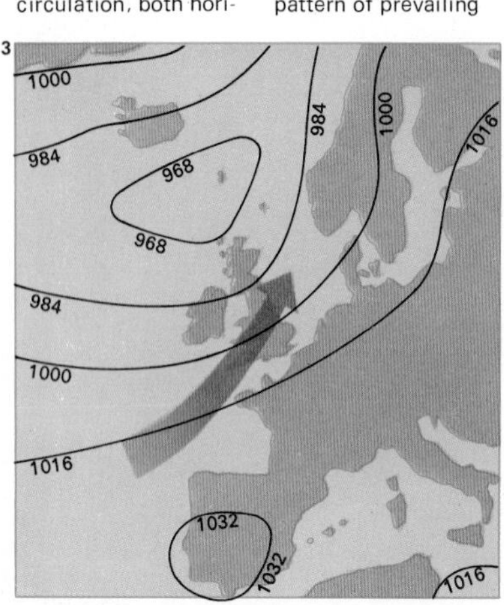

3
1000
984
968
968
984
1000
1016
1032
1032
984
1000
1016
1016

3 A weather chart shows a "low" or depression to the south of Iceland and a "high" or anticyclone over southern Portugal and Spain. The isobars join points with equal atmospheric pressure. The values of the isobars are in millibars (1,000 millibars is the equivalent of about 750.1mm [29.53in] of mercury). Because winds are deflected, they circulate in a counterclockwise direction around a "low" and clockwise around a "high".

Another reversal of winds on a local scale occurs with land and sea breezes. Sea breezes spring up on warm days along sea and lake coasts when a pressure gradient is established between the rapidly heating land and the less rapidly heating water. As a result, winds blow onto land. At night, the land cools faster than the water, so a reverse gradient makes winds blow from the land onto the water.

Thunderstorms, hurricanes, and tornadoes
The most common storms are thunderstorms [6]. About 45,000 occur every day in both temperate and tropical regions, and prerequisites for their formation are strong, rising air currents. As the air rises, it is cooled and latent heat is released as condensation occurs. The release of heat provides energy that intensifies the upsurgence of air and the development of the storm. The condensation causes cumulonimbus clouds to rise sometimes more than 15,000ft (4,570m) from base to top. These clouds bring rain and hail and, sometimes, thunder and lightning.

Hurricanes [5]—also called typhoons or tropical cyclones—form over warm oceans. They have fast spiraling winds that may reach 150–200mph (240–320kph). The calm center, or eye, contains warm subsiding air. The eye may be 4 to 30 miles (6.5–48km) across. The hurricane itself may have a diameter of 300 miles (480km). The warmth of the air in the eye contributes to low air pressure at the surface. Warm, moist air spirals upward around the eye. Condensation creates cumulonimbus clouds and releases latent heat, which further increases the upward spiral of air. Hurricanes are especially destructive along coastlines where storm waves and rain cause flooding.

Tornadoes [Key] are violent whirlwinds, but they cover a far smaller area than hurricanes. A tornado forms when a downward growth starts from a cumulonimbus cloud. When the funnel-shaped extension of the cloud reaches the ground, it may be between 165–1,650ft (50–500m) wide. It crosses land at speeds of 20–40mph (32–65kph) and usually dies out after 20 miles (32km) but may travel up to 300 miles (480km).

KEY

Hundreds of tornadoes strike the United States each year, especially in the Midwest. They may last for several hours, traveling up to 300 miles (480km) and causing great damage. At the center winds may reach 400mph (644kph).

4

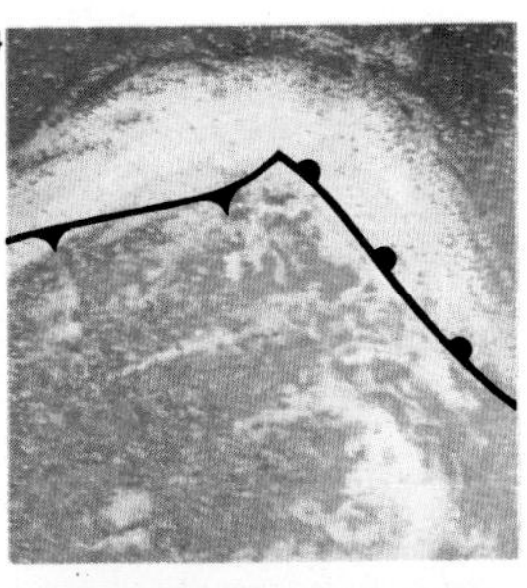

Fronts form in temperate latitudes where a cold air mass meets a warm air mass.

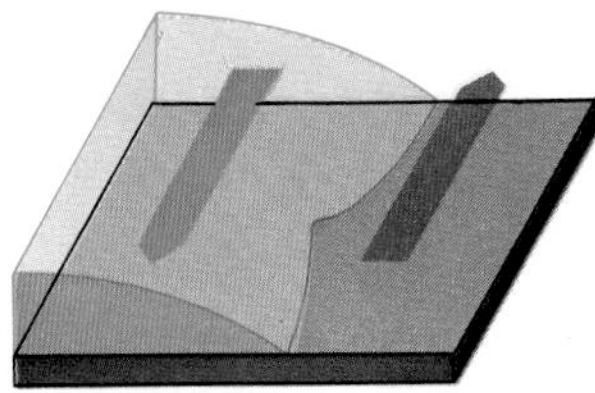

The air masses spiral round a bulge causing cold and warm fronts to develop.

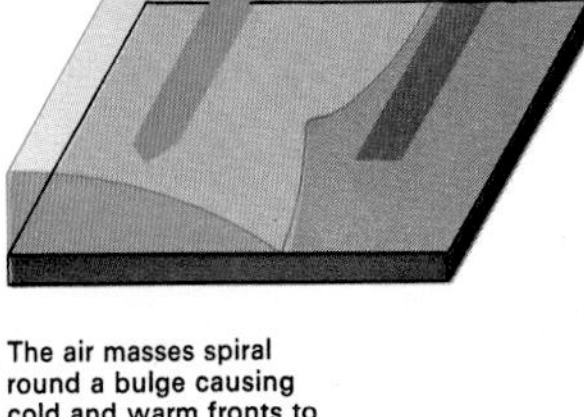

The warm air rises above the cold front and the cold air slides underneath the warm.

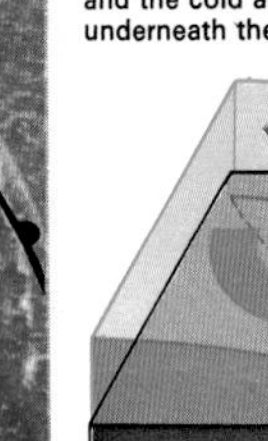

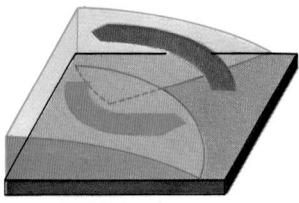

Eventually, the cold air areas merge, and the warm air is lifted up or occluded.

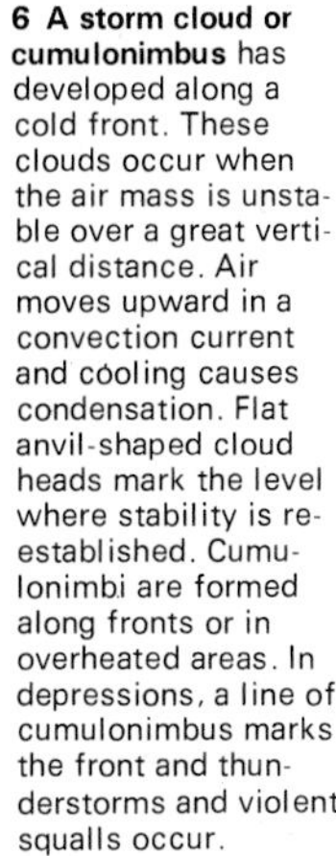

4 A front is a narrow band of changing weather lying between two air masses of different temperature and humidity. When the two air masses meet, each pushes against the other to form a cold, warm, or occluded front.

5

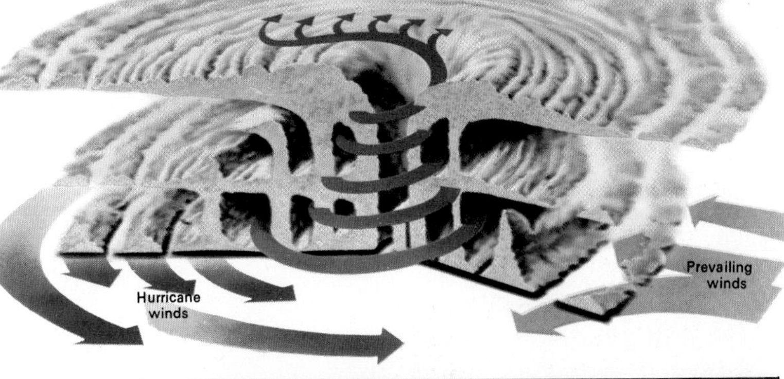

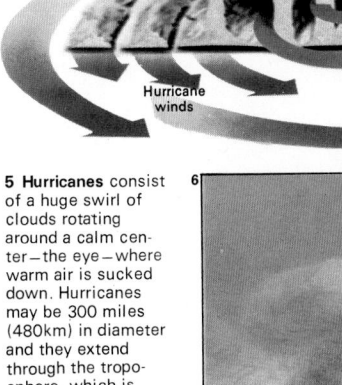

Hurricane winds
Prevailing winds

5 Hurricanes consist of a huge swirl of clouds rotating around a calm center—the eye—where warm air is sucked down. Hurricanes may be 300 miles (480km) in diameter and they extend through the troposphere, which is about 9 to 12 miles (15–20km) thick. Clouds, mainly cumulonimbus, are arranged in bands around the eye, the tallest forming the wall of the eye.

6

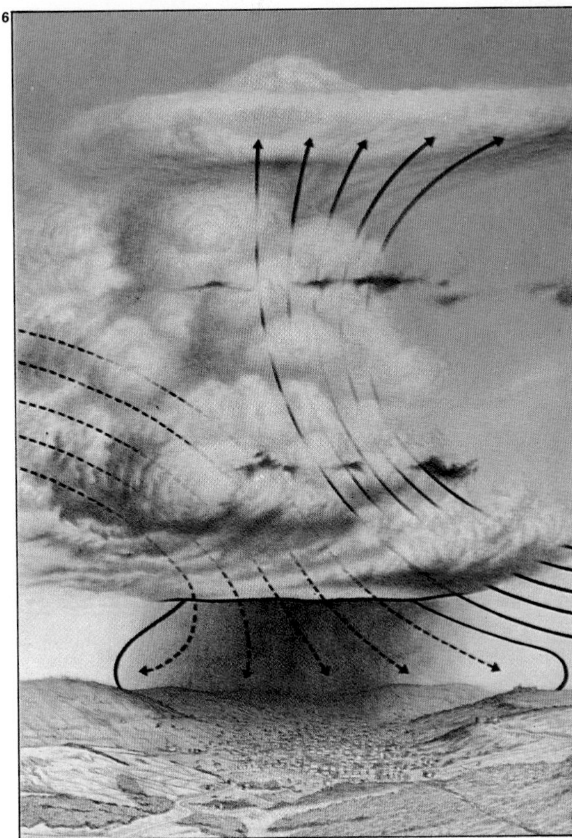

6 A storm cloud or cumulonimbus has developed along a cold front. These clouds occur when the air mass is unstable over a great vertical distance. Air moves upward in a convection current and cooling causes condensation. Flat anvil-shaped cloud heads mark the level where stability is re-established. Cumulonimbi are formed along fronts or in overheated areas. In depressions, a line of cumulonimbus marks the front and thunderstorms and violent squalls occur.

Weather

"Weather" in any language means rain and sunshine, heat and cold, clouds and wind. Humidity and visibility might be added to the list. In fact, if not in terminology, this layman's catalog comprises the six elements that, for the meteorologist, make weather: air temperature, barometric pressure, wind velocity, humidity, clouds, and precipitation.

Cloud formation

Clouds are made up of millions of very small drops of liquid water or ice crystals that are too light to fall out of the atmosphere. The cloud particles form from air that contains water vapor when the temperature falls to a critical level called the dewpoint. These liquid cloud droplets may then freeze into an ice crystal. But before either water or ice particles can form, two things must happen. First, the moist air must rise, reducing its pressure and giving up its heat to the surrounding atmosphere. Second, dust particles must already be present on which the cooled vapor can condense to form droplets or ice crystals. These tiny particles are called, respectively, condensation nuclei and ice nuclei.

The formation of a cloud does not necessarily mean that it will precipitate. Condensation cannot create droplets or crystals that would survive the fall to the ground. They would evaporate even if they were large enough to overcome the force of the rising air. Two other mechanisms, the Bergeron, or ice-crystal, process and the coalescence process, account for precipitation-sized particles. In clouds that contain both ice crystals and droplets of supercooled water (water at a temperature less than 0°C), the droplets evaporate and the vapor condenses onto the ice crystal. Thus the crystals grow at the expense of the droplets until they are large enough to fall out of the cloud. If they melt on the way down, rainfall is observed. If the cloud contains no ice crystals, precipitation particles grow by the coalescence of different sized droplets as they fall through the cloud. The larger a drop becomes, the more efficient it is at collecting smaller ones and the greater its chance of reaching the ground.

The two basic shapes of clouds—in layers or in heaps—are caused by the two different ways in which air can move upward. When air rises slowly over large areas at rates of a few inches a second, layer or stratified clouds are formed. This frequently occurs in cyclones, particularly in warm sectors and at warm fronts. Rapidly rising air (several feet per second) occurs in convection currents which are usually only a few hundred feet across near the ground. These currents widen with altitude but the resultant heaped or cumuliform clouds are rarely more than a mile or two across. If the atmosphere is unstable they may grow into very large cumulonimbus clouds.

The easiest way to identify a cloud [1] is by its shape and height above the ground. This was recognized by Luke Howard, a London chemist, as early as 1833, when he presented his first cloud classification. This still forms the basis of the World Meteorological Organization's International Classification of ten cloud types, which fall into three families according to their height. The highest clouds—about 5–6

CONNECTIONS

Read first
214 Winds and weather systems

See also
212 The atmosphere
218 Forecasting
220 Climates

1

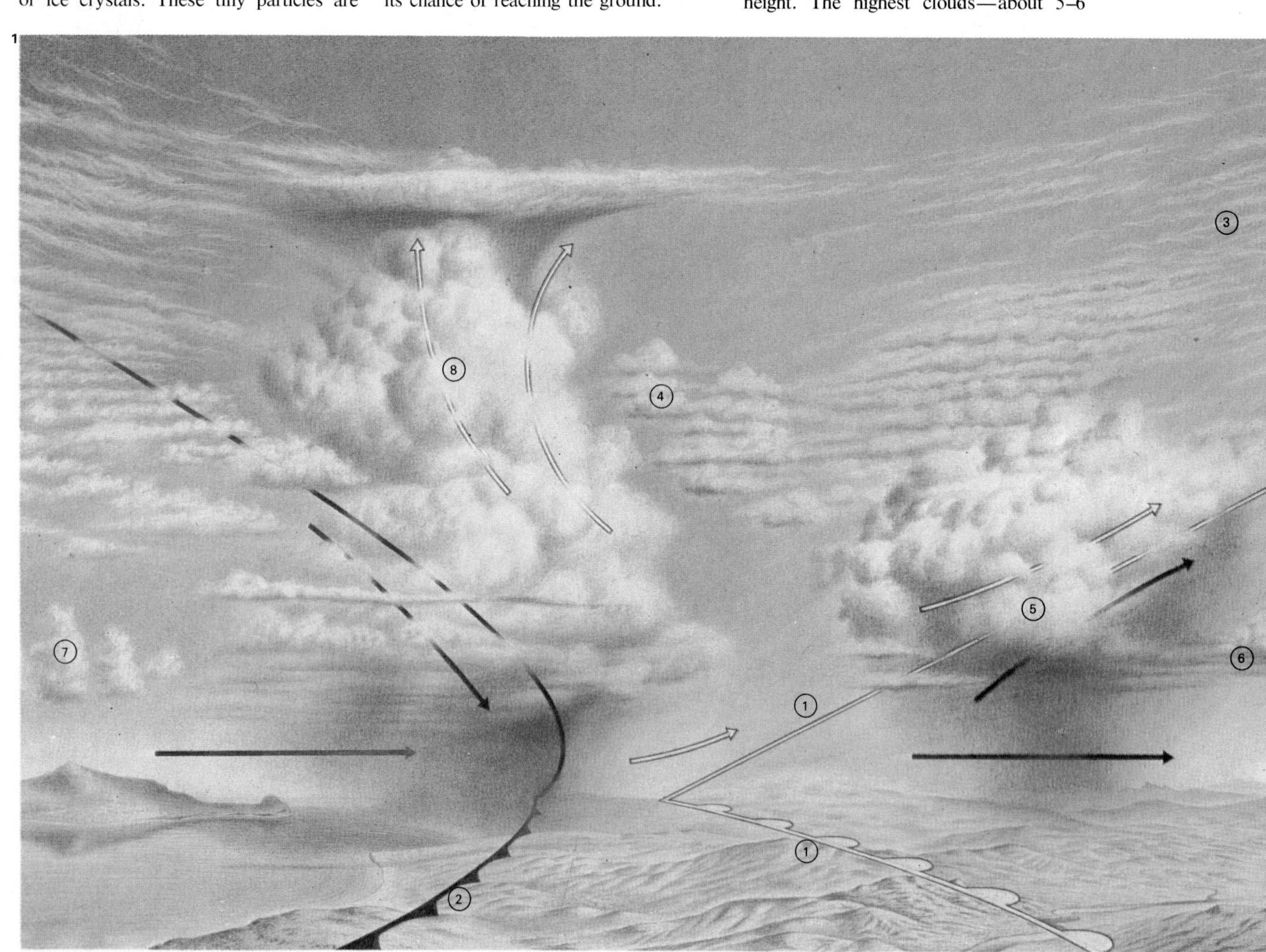
8
4
3
5
6
7
1
1
2

1 The different cloud types are best illustrated within the context of the familiar mid-latitude frontal depression. Most of the major types occur within such cyclones. Here a schematic, generalized Northern Hemisphere depression is viewed from the south as it moves from west [left] to east [right]. It is in a mature state, prior to the occlusion stage, and both warm [1] and cold [2] fronts are clearly visible. Over the warm front, which may have a slope ranging from 1/100 to 1/350, the air rises massively and slowly over the great depth of the atmosphere. This results in a fairly complete range of layer-type clouds ranging from cirrus [3] and altocumulus [4] to nimbostratus [5]. The precipitation area often associated with such cloud types, and especially with nimbostratus, usually lies ahead of the surface warm front and roughly parallel to it [6]. Turbulence may cause some clouds to rise and produce heavy convective rainfall, as well as the generally lighter and more widespread classical warm front rainfall. Stratus often occupies the warm sector, but a marked change occurs at the cold front. Here the wind veers (blowing in more clockwise direction) and cumulus clouds [7] are often found in the cold air behind the front. At the front itself, the atmosphere is often quite unstable and cumulus clouds grow into cumulonimbus formations [8]. The canopy of cirrus clouds—of all types—may extend over the whole depression and is often juxtaposed with the anvil shape of the nimbus. These cloud changes are accompanied by pressure, wind temperature, and humidity changes as the fronts pass the observer.

miles (8–10km)—made of ice, are called cirrus, cirrostratus and cirrocumulus; the middle clouds—2–5 miles (3–8km)—of water and ice, are called altocumulus and altostratus; and the low clouds—below 2 miles (3km)—usually of water, are called stratus, stratocumulus and nimbostratus. The two remaining types are cumulus and cumulonimbus. There are, however, many variations on these ten types. Clouds of different types may occur together.

Sun, wind and humidity

Long periods of sunshine are, of course, marked by clear skies, which usually result from sinking air in anticyclones. The longest periods of sunshine occur in the polar summer when the Sun never sets, but the highest intensities and temperatures occur in the main deserts of the world, which lie roughly at the latitudes 30°N and S. The daily maximum temperature in these areas may be more than 95°F (35°C), falling to below freezing at night.

Wind speed and direction at low levels are affected by friction between the air and the ground and by local topography. Friction means the wind speeds near the ground are generally less than at high levels and it also accounts for the generally higher speeds over water as compared with the rougher land surface. Air flow is often channeled in both valleys and urban areas.

There are several ways of expressing the humidity of the air, but relative humidity is the most widely used. This is the percentage of water vapor actually held in a given volume of air relative to the amount that the air could hold if saturated at the same temperature. In middle latitudes the daily values usually lie between 60 and 80 percent, but they can range from 8 to 100 percent.

Fog is a modern menace

Visibility has assumed a great importance in the modern world. Fog [3], which is cloudy air at ground level, presents dangers to aircraft, ships, and motor vehicles alike. It can also affect the man in the street; if fog becomes contaminated with smoke and other pollutants it may become dangerous smog and a health hazard.

KEY

The structure of a hurricane may be difficult to discern at ground level but from a satellite in orbit around the Earth the pattern of air movements involved can be seen clearly.

2

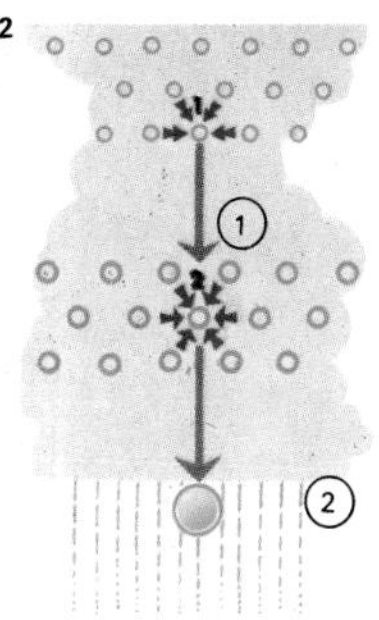
1
2

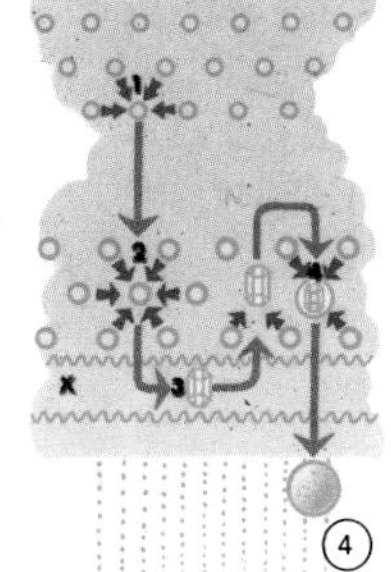
3
4

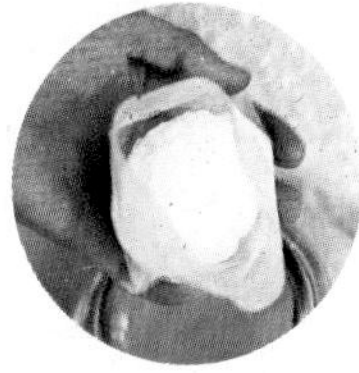

2 Repeated coalescence of droplets [1] forms drops [2] too large to float on air currents. Ice crystals collect in hexagonal patterns [3] then agglomerate into snowflakes. Water can freeze around an ice embryo [4] to form hail.

3

3 Advection fog is caused by warm, damp air blowing over cold land or cold water. The wavy red arrows show the direction of transfer of heat between the air and water. Straight blue arrows show the cooling of air. When the temperature reaches dew point, fog forms. This type of fog occurs at the Newfoundland banks.

4

4 Radiation fog occurs when air is cooled to its dew point by contact with land that has itself been cooled by longwave radiation loss [long red arrows]. As the ground cools, surrounding air transfers heat by conduction [short red arrows]. The cooling of the air is shown by the blue arrows.

5

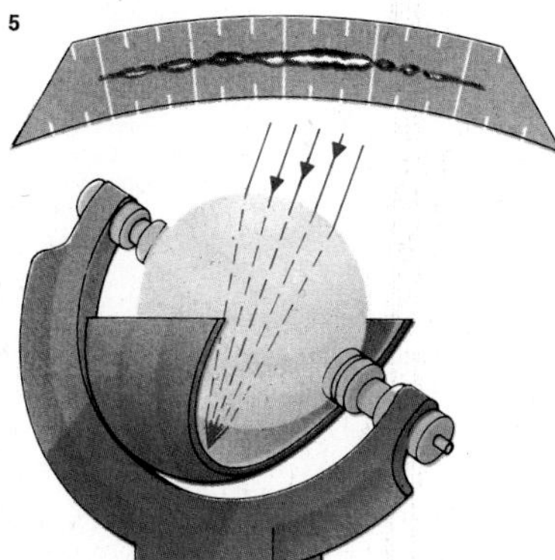

5 A Campbell-Stokes recorder registers the duration of sunshine. A glass ball focuses the sun's rays onto a specially prepared piece of card on which a trace is burned as long as the sun shines brightly. The instrument must be oriented to the noonday Sun at an angle determined from the declination of the Sun. Three sets of grooves in the bowl behind the glass sphere will accommodate the different cards that are used for summer, winter, and the equinoxes.

6

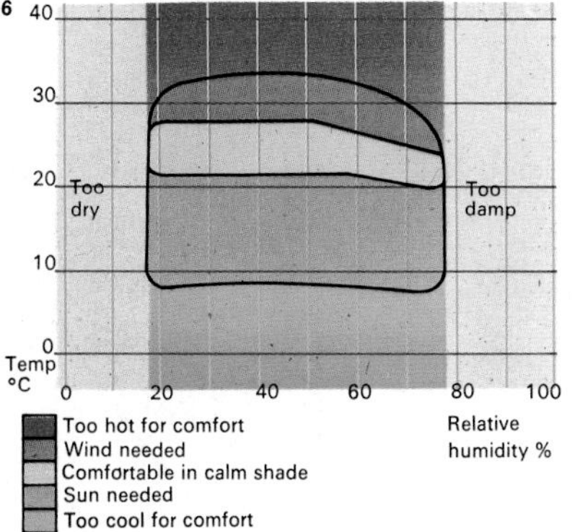
40
30
20
10
0
Temp °C
Too dry
Too damp
0
20
40
60
80
100
Relative humidity %
Too hot for comfort
Wind needed
Comfortable in calm shade
Sun needed
Too cool for comfort

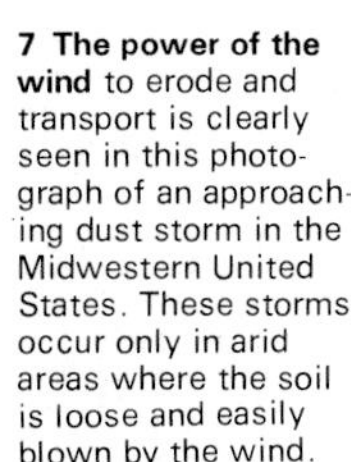

6 Human beings can tolerate only certain ranges of temperature and humidity, and within those ranges other elements like Sun and wind are needed to produce comfortable conditions in which people can live and work.

7

7 The power of the wind to erode and transport is clearly seen in this photograph of an approaching dust storm in the Midwestern United States. These storms occur only in arid areas where the soil is loose and easily blown by the wind.

Forecasting

Day-to-day weather depends on the movements of huge air masses, which take their characteristics of temperature and humidity from the land or water surface beneath them and shift slowly over the surface of the Earth. Some are virtually static, providing steady weather conditions for days or weeks in their area of origin. These produce, for example, the constant, predictable weather of tropical deserts and oceans and the heartlands of the great continents. Other air masses are affected by the Earth's rotation and move and swirl rapidly, interacting in different ways with neighboring masses. These provide the changeable weather of temperate latitudes, which is much more difficult to predict accurately and presents a constant challenge to the weather forecaster.

Factors that influence the weather

To predict the weather over a particular area, the forecaster must first know the pattern of air masses that overlies it at any given time. Then he must try to predict how the pattern will change during the period of forecast—usually the next few hours or days—drawing on his experience of how similar patterns have changed in the past.

Weather forecasting originated in the observations of farmers and sailors, whose special interest caused them to watch the weather closely and discover the patterns underlying it. Even in temperate regions this is not as difficult as it may seem at first. For example, much of North America's weather depends on a west-to-east procession of cyclones, or depressions, and the passage of "fronts"—planes of contact between neighboring air masses of differing temperature and humidity. Fronts that bring the worst weather lie generally in the southern half of the depressions. An observer who sees the barometer falling and notices a change of wind (often accompanied by a thickening and lowering of cloud), is keeping track of the movement of a depression and warm front. He can predict fairly accurately the sequence of weather that will arise from it, and even the speed with which the changes will take place. Similarly, a rising or high and steady barometer, with clear skies and light breezes, usually means that an anticyclone has formed. This often brings clear, steady weather for several days until the next depression moves in to replace it.

The forecaster at work

The professional forecaster begins his work by preparing a synoptic chart [3], that is, an accurate map of the weather prevailing at the time over a large area surrounding his position. In this he is helped by observations from many surface stations, which come to him in encoded form over teleprinter and radio networks. There are more than 8,000 surface stations providing this service around the world. They include mountain outposts, ships at sea, polar bases, and automatic (unmanned) units that record the weather and send information out at regular intervals.

In his synoptic chart the forecaster plots pressure, wind, temperature, cloud types, humidities, and pressure tendency, and notes past and present weather. This enables him to draw in isobars (lines connecting

CONNECTIONS

Read first

214 Winds and weather systems
216 Weather

See also

212 The atmosphere
220 Climates

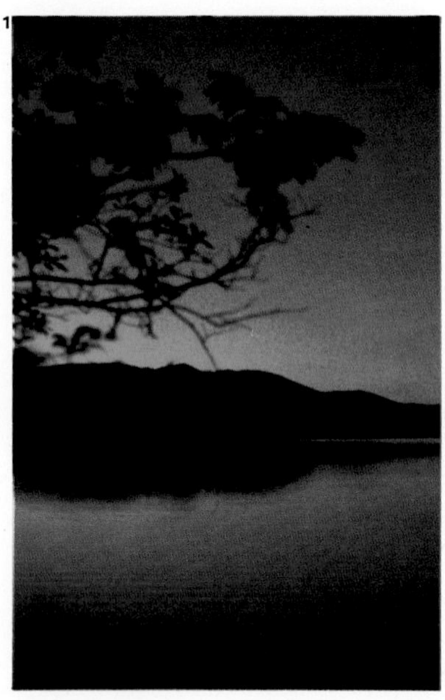

1 Red skies at night, as shepherds have long known, usually indicate good weather for the next day, while red skies at dawn may mean foul weather before the day is out. These observations are not infallible but often make meteorological sense. Red skies in the evening are caused by the scattering of light by dust particles in the atmosphere and are found in anticyclonic conditions of calm, stable weather. Dust tends to settle during the night and so a red sky in the morning is more likely to be caused by scattering of light from water droplets in a damp atmosphere at low levels. Moist conditions indicate a depression is forming.

Wind
Sunshine
Rainfall
Pressure
Humidity
Temperature

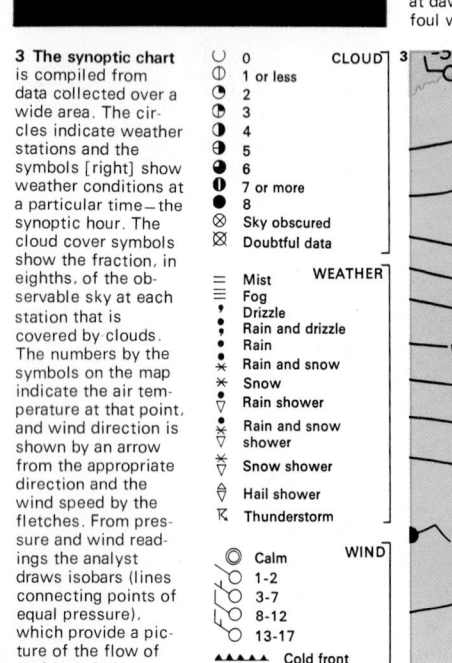

2 Analysis and forecasting require simultaneous, standard, and regular observations at many stations. The internationally standard weather station includes a variety of equipment. The Stevenson screen [1] is a box that shelters thermometers and other instruments from sunlight; it contains wet- and dry-bulb thermometers and recording instruments. Open land [2] allows the state of the ground to be assessed. A minimum thermometer [3] records the lowest ground temperature during the past 24 hours. The anemometer and vane [4] show wind speed and direction. The Campbell-Stokes sunshine recorder or radiometer [5] records hours of sunshine. Radiosonde balloon [6] and theodolite [7] show wind speed and direction, and other data from high altitude. A rain gauge [8] records the amount of precipitation. The weather office also has a barometer and barograph, to record atmospheric pressure.

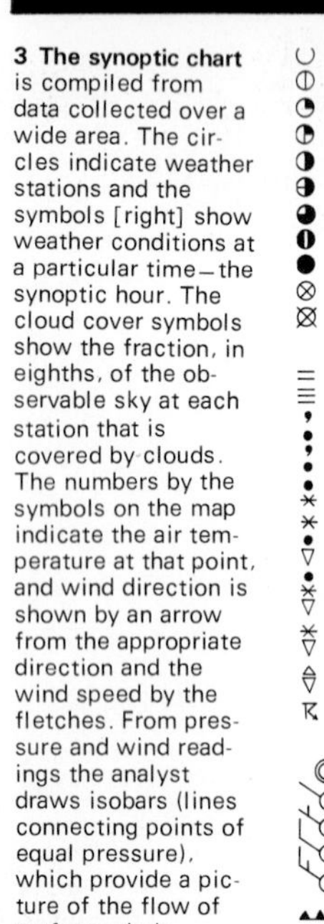

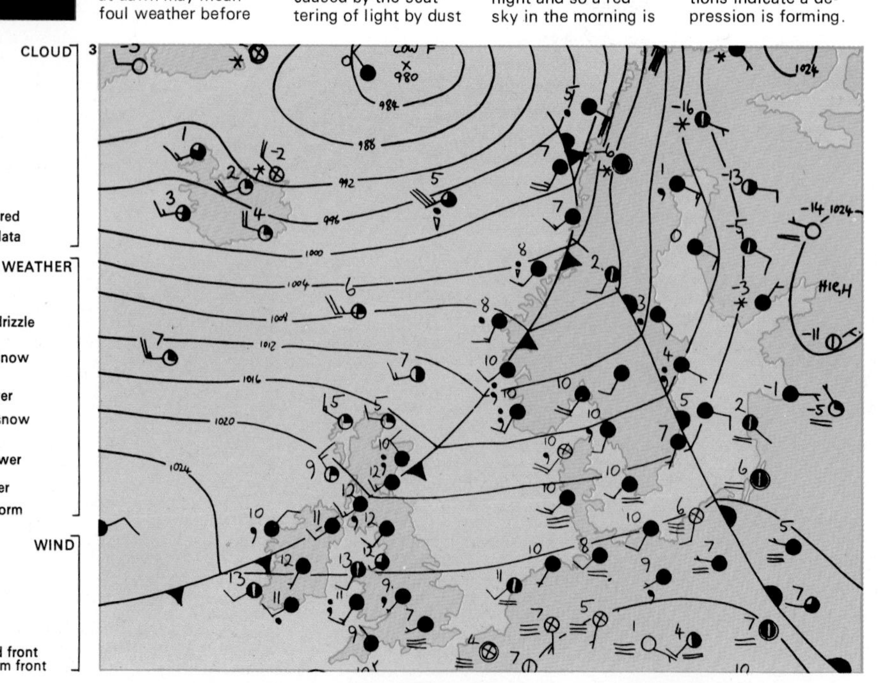

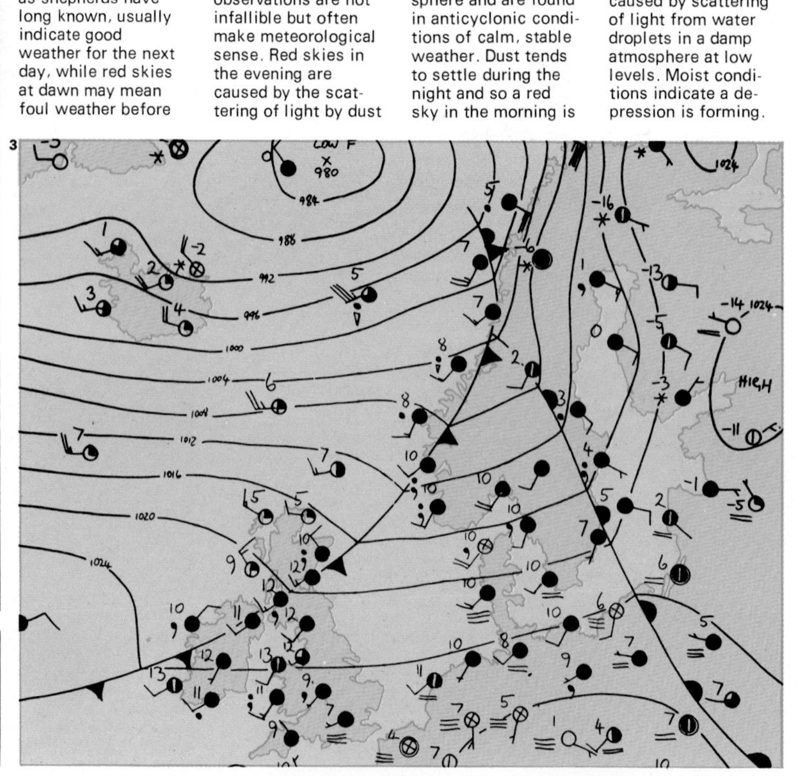

CLOUD
0
1 or less
2
3
4
5
6
7 or more
8
Sky obscured
Doubtful data
WEATHER
Mist
Fog
Drizzle
Rain and drizzle
Rain
Rain and snow
Snow
Rain shower
Rain and snow shower
Snow shower
Hail shower
Thunderstorm
WIND
Calm
1-2
3-7
8-12
13-17
Cold front
Warm front
LOW
HIGH

3 The synoptic chart is compiled from data collected over a wide area. The circles indicate weather stations and the symbols [right] show weather conditions at a particular time—the synoptic hour. The cloud cover symbols show the fraction, in eighths, of the observable sky at each station that is covered by clouds. The numbers by the symbols on the map indicate the air temperature at that point, and wind direction is shown by an arrow from the appropriate direction and the wind speed by the fletches. From pressure and wind readings the analyst draws isobars (lines connecting points of equal pressure), which provide a picture of the flow of surface winds.

points of equal atmospheric pressure) and the position of fronts. Knowing the weather picture, and the rate at which it is changing, he is then able to predict what the weather will be like at any point on his map in the near future. His work is made easier by upper-air observations (taken by weather balloons with radiosonde attachment) and photographs from weather satellites [6] that give him an astronaut's view of patterns. Much of the forecaster's work of plotting and analysis has been automated and mathematical analysis plays an increasing role in forecasting as more accurate data from all levels of the atmosphere become available.

Short- and long-term forecasting

Short-term forecasting is of great importance to farmers and sailors, and the safety of many millions of airline passengers depends on it each year. There is also an increasing demand for long-term forecasting, covering periods of from five days to six months ahead. Different techniques of analysis are required for this kind of forecasting.

In areas of the world where the climate varies little from one year to another, comparatively simple statistical methods are used to relate the character of one season to the next as a basis for prediction. More variable climates demand more sophisticated methods and detailed research into the nature, origins, and movements of air masses. Recently, analysis of relationships between the atmosphere and the ocean have been of great value to long-range forecasters, particularly in predominantly maritime climates that depend on air masses that have passed over the ocean.

The first attempt to coordinate meteorological observations on an international basis was not made until 1853, when the major maritime nations formulated a system of weather observations over the oceans to help navigation. In 1878 the International Meteorological Organization (IMO) was set up to keep a constant watch on the weather, and in 1951 the IMO was reorganized to become the World Meteorological Organization (WMO), which was recognized by the United Nations.

KEY

Television brings the daily weather forecast into viewers' homes. From internationally collected data, the presenter prepares a simplified synoptic chart. On this he explains the pressure situation, discusses the position and movement of fronts, and predicts the weather for the next few days.

4

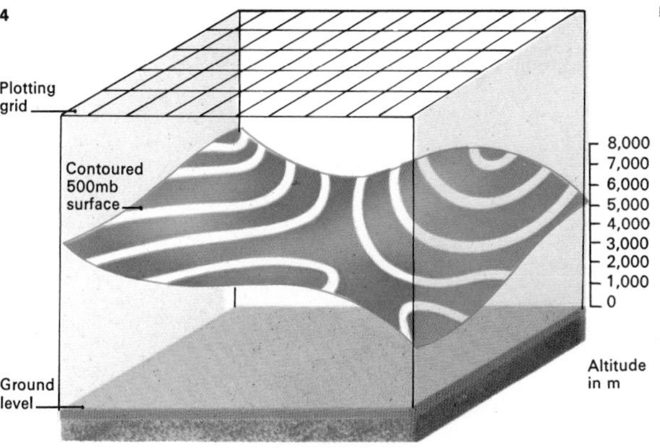

Plotting grid
Contoured 500mb surface
Ground level
8,000
7,000
6,000
5,000
4,000
3,000
2,000
1,000
0
Altitude in m

4 Basic mathematical models are designed to forecast the altitude of a pressure surface, usually the 500-mb or 600-mb level. From them, air flow at that level can be defined and the future position of cyclones and anticyclones plotted. Pressure surfaces are contoured in the same way as ground maps: surface heights are plotted by calculation over a grid. This method is suitable for large-scale forecasting usually on a 155-mile (250-km) grid. A two-level model may be used, on which two pressure surfaces—eg, the 500-mb and 1000-mb surfaces—are plotted on the same grid.

5

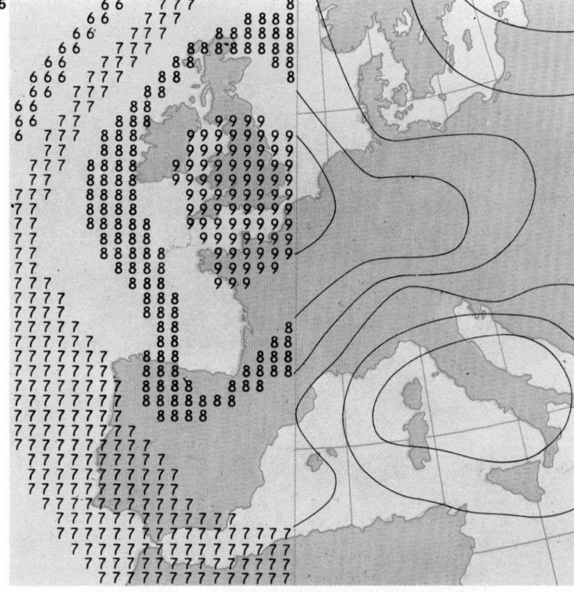

5 Accurate weather forecasting involves the processing of large quantities of data that flow into the weather centers several times each day. The introduction of computers and plotting machines allows forecasters to handle the data more rapidly. Recent developments in plotting machinery display processed data in map form using a line printer or plotting table. Here both types of output are shown; isobars can be interpolated from the pattern of figures [left], or the isobars can be computed and drawn in automatically [right]. These techniques can produce maps like this one in seconds rather than hours.

6

7

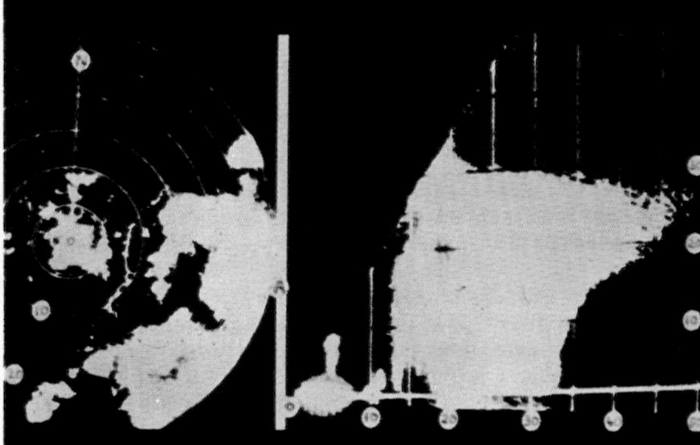

PPI

RHI

6 Weather satellites have provided photographs of clouds since 1960, with steady improvement in photographic quality and coverage. A sequence of photographs showing developing cloud patterns greatly helps the forecaster.

7 Radar helps to locate rain clouds. Signals are reflected by raindrops and ice particles, registering on the Plan Position Indicator (PPI) showing the pattern over an area, or on the Range Height Indicator (RHI) showing the vertical distribution. The brightness of the echo shows the intensity of precipitation. Rangemarkers (radiating from the center of the PPI and bottom left of the RHI) are in miles while heights (on the right of the RHI) are shown in thousands of feet.

Climate

The climate of an area is its characteristic weather over a long period. Climate depends first on latitude, which determines whether an area is hot or cold and how strongly marked are its seasons. It depends also on the moving air masses that prevail in the area. These may be purely local in origin or they may have moved into the area from several hundred miles away, bringing cooler or warmer, wetter or drier conditions with them. Climate is also influenced by the relative distribution of land and sea, high ground and low, and the presence nearby of such major features as forests, lakes, valleys, and glaciers.

On a world scale, macroclimate is defined primarily in terms of temperature and rainfall, and the world can be divided into large climatic zones on this basis. On a smaller scale, humidity, wind strength, orientation to the Sun, and other local features determine local climate. On an even smaller scale, microclimate refers to the conditions in a particular woodland, under a particular stone, or even surrounding a particular large building.

The range of climates can be broadly grouped under three headings according to latitude. Tropical climates are hot and dominated by equatorial air masses throughout the year. Temperate climates of the mid-latitude zone are variable, dominated alternately by subtropical and subpolar air masses, and usually seasonal. Polar climates of high latitudes are uniformly cold, under the continuous control of subpolar and polar air masses.

Characteristics of tropical climates

Because of constant daily sunshine, equatorial and tropical regions are warm throughout the year and the moving air masses that affect them are also warm [6, 7]. The wettest regions lie in a belt of shallow depressions and convection formed where the trade winds meet. This belt shifts north and south seasonally on either side of the Equator, but temperatures vary only slightly and rainfall is steady throughout the year. Monsoon climates of India, Southeast Asia, and China occur where seasonal winds blow from almost opposite directions; warm, moist winds alternate with warm, dry ones, giving cloudy, wet "summers" and drier "winters." Dry, tropical climates occur in broad zones on either side of the Equator between latitudes 15° and 30°. These are anticyclonic areas of warm, dry air.

Temperate climates and their features

The middle latitudes of both hemispheres are battlegrounds where warm subtropical and cool subpolar air masses jostle for position. The day-to-day battle lines are the warm and cold fronts of the weather charts, which tend to occur along broad frontal zones. On the equatorial side of these zones warm air is present most of the time. The zones shift north and south with the seasons so that an area such as the south of France may bask reliably in subtropical air throughout the summer but suffer occasional onslaughts of cold subpolar air in winter. On western flanks of the continents in the warmer zone the air tends to be dry, bringing hot, dry summers and mild, damper winters—the "Mediterranean" climate of California and of the eastern

CONNECTIONS

Read first
216 Weather

See also
214 Winds and weather systems
218 Forecasting
224 Ocean currents
312 The living soil

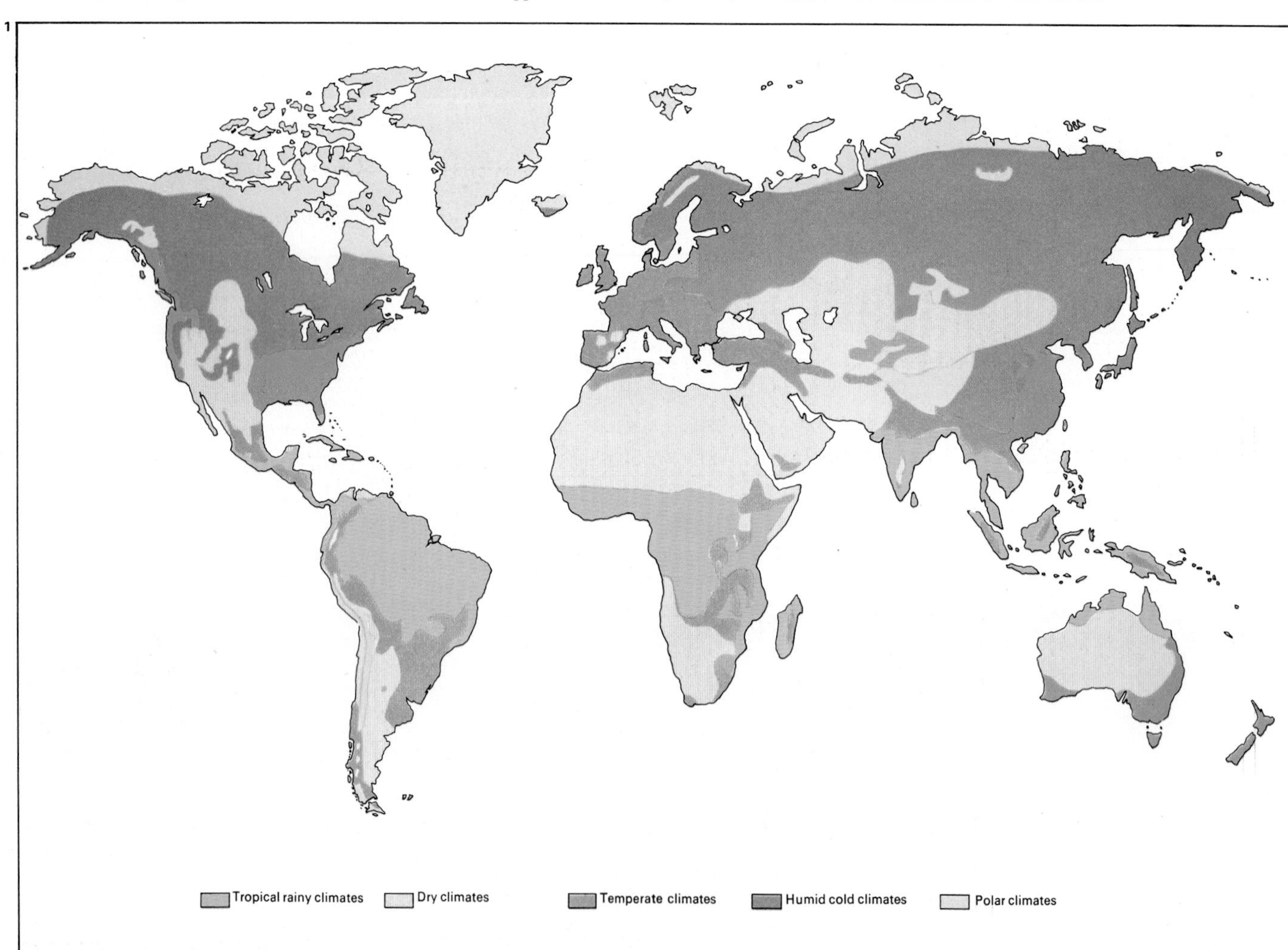

Tropical rainy climates
Dry climates
Temperate climates
Humid cold climates
Polar climates

1 Climate on a global scale presents a bewildering variety and has provided would-be classifiers with a challenge for more than a century. The most generally accepted classifications reflect the close links that exist between vegetation and climate. A system in wide use today is that of W. Köppen (1846–1940), a German biologist who devoted most of his life to climatic problems and modified his own system many times before he was satisfied with it. The Köppen system of classification recognizes five major climatic categories, each quite distinct. These are (A) equatorial and tropical rain climates, (B) dry climates, (C) temperate climates of the (mainly) broadleaf forest zone, (D) colder temperate climates, and (E) polar climates. Each category is defined in terms of temperature and some in terms of rainfall, too. Köppen also devised additional symbols for times of year in which most rain falls and for other climatic qualities that affect the growth of vegetation. The map locates the hot, wet tropical rain forests of South America, Africa, and the Far East. Farther away from the Equator the world's great deserts, dominated by the Sahara, straddle subtropical latitudes and the edges of the tropics, as a result of the stable high pressures there. The deserts are more evident in the Northern than in the Southern Hemisphere, mainly because of the extensive southern oceans. Nearer the poles, a mosaic pattern of mid-latitude climates occurs. This is less complex over the huge continental areas of Siberia and North America, particularly in tundra and boreal regions. Extreme polar and highland climates occupy smaller areas.

Mediterranean itself. Eastern flanks of the continents draw moist, unstable air from over the sea; they tend to be warm throughout the year.

In higher latitudes, farther from tropical influences, cool subpolar air masses prevail. A procession of cyclones or depressions, swinging eastward around the Earth, brings moist maritime air to the western flanks of North America and Europe. Great Britain and western Canada stand in prevailing south westerlies, creating mild, cloudy, and damp conditions in winter and summer alike. Alternating air masses from the eastern continents bring cold, clear winter and hot, dry summer weather, and air from the north is usually cold and crisp. Central and eastern regions of the continents tend to be drier, with colder winters and hotter summers.

The cold, dry polar climates

Nearer the poles are climatic regions controlled by polar air masses [2]. Despite brief, sunny summers, they tend to be cold and dry throughout the year. The broad boreal zone is forested; the tundra zone supports shrubs, rough grassland, and mosses. The true polar climate, which covers the northern fringes of Canada, Europe, and Asia and the whole of the Antarctic continent, is generally too cold and dry to support any but the most hardy vegetation. The coldest regions of the Northern Hemisphere lie in the heartlands of northern Canada and northeastern Siberia, where winter temperatures fall well below −22°F (−30°C). On the high polar plateau of Antarctica summer temperatures hover around −22°F (−30°C), while winter temperatures average −94°F (−70°C) or lower.

Geological evidence suggests that the modern situation in which different parts of the globe have certain well-defined climatic patterns is unusual. In past ages climates tended to be fairly even over most of the Earth's surface. For example, the Permian period (280 million years ago) was characterized by extensive desert over most of the continents. The present pattern may be due, in part, to the fact that the Earth is still recovering from the last Ice Age.

KEY

21 March

22 June

22 December

23 September

The seasons are primarily controlled by the rotation of the Earth around the Sun and the inclination of the Earth's axis to the plane of rotation. Inclination of 23.5° means that the Sun is directly over the Tropic of Cancer (23.5°N) on June 22 and over the Tropic of Capricorn (23.5°S) on December 22. At the equinoxes, March 21 and September 23, the Sun is over the Equator. The Sun's apparent movement is accompanied by a similar shift in belts of pressure and wind.

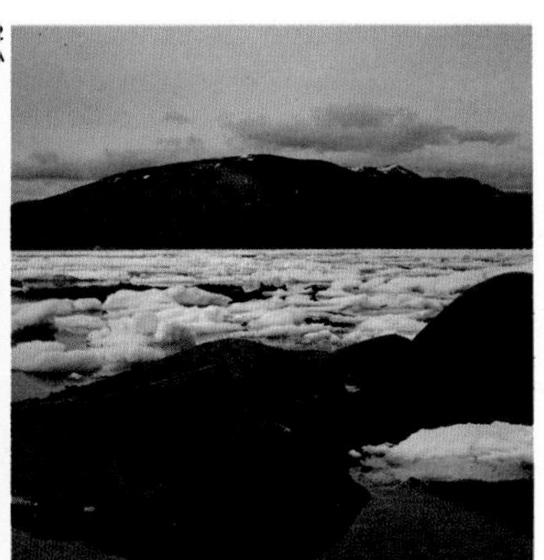

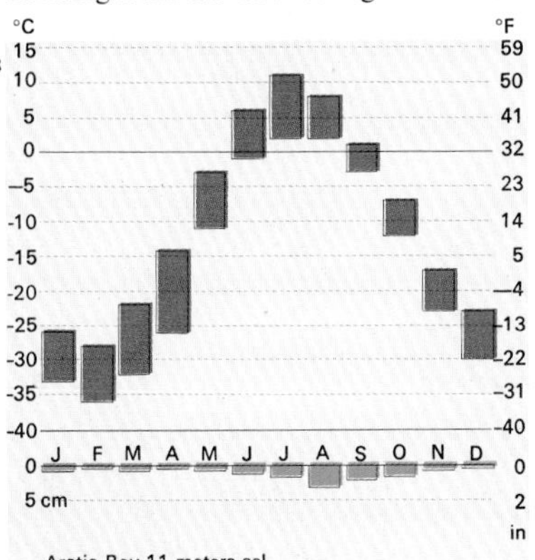
B
°C
°F
J F M A M J J A S O N D
5 cm
in
Arctic Bay 11 meters asl

2 Polar climates, as in Canada's Arctic Bay [A], are very cold and dry. Only three months of summer are frost-free [B]. There is little precipitation but much surface water due to poor drainage.

3 A continental climate is found in Calgary, Alberta. Temperatures there are high in summer and low in winter; annual precipitation is low. This type of climate supports grasslands and cereal crops.

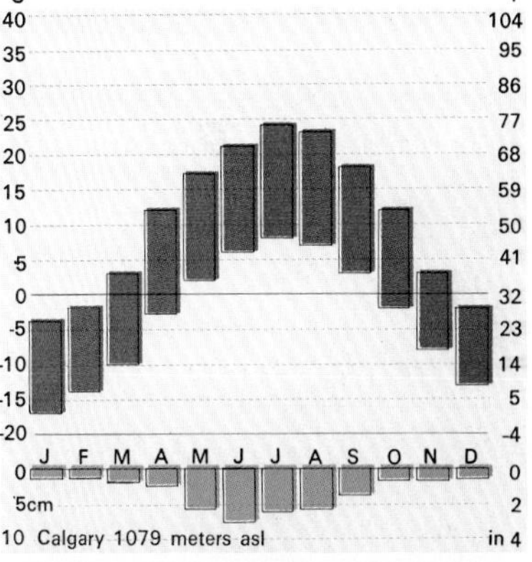
3
°C
°F
J F M A M J J A S O N D
5cm
10 Calgary 1079 meters asl
in 4

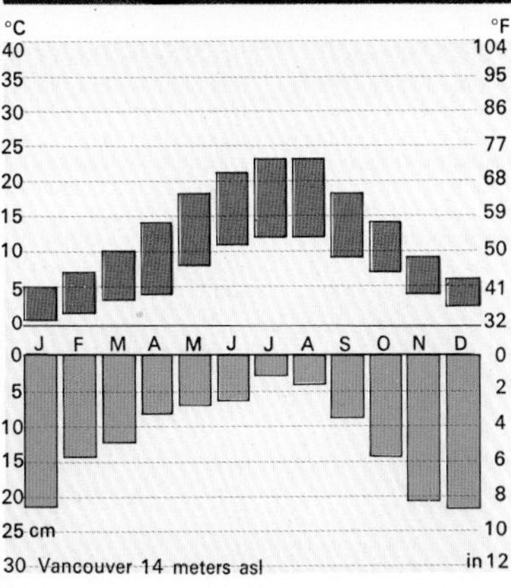
°C
°F
J F M A M J J A S O N D
25 cm
30 Vancouver 14 meters asl
in 12

4 The Canadian city of Vancouver has a mid-latitude maritime climate, with warm summers and mild winters. Monthly temperature ranges are greatest in summer, precipitation is highest in winter.

5 A Mediterranean climate is typified by Rome [B] and its environs [A], with hot, dry summers and warm, moist winters. Similar latitudes of western United States enjoy similar climates.

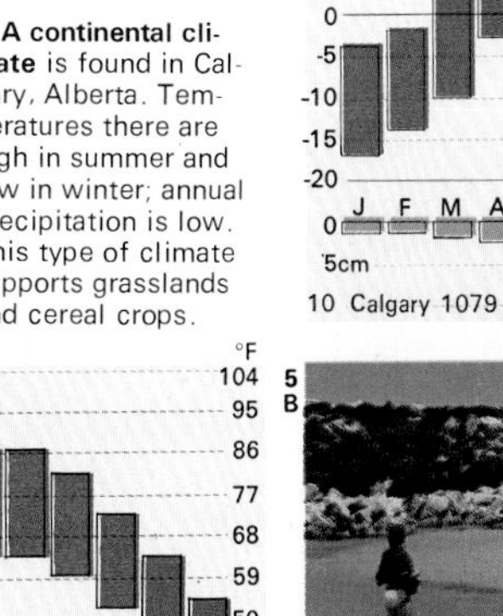
5
A
°C
°F
J F M A M J J A S O N D
10 cm
in
Rome 115 meters asl

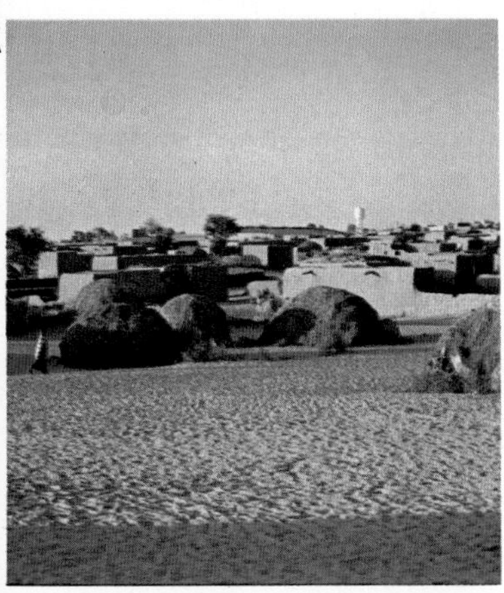

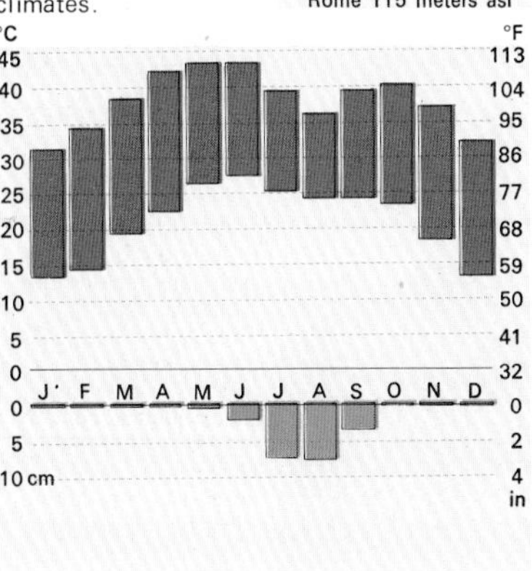
B
°C
°F
J F M A M J J A S O N D
10 cm
in
Timbuktu 301 meters asl

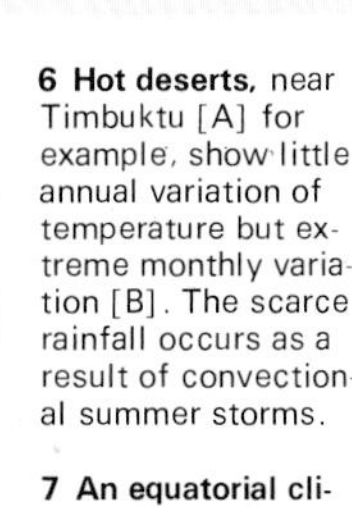

6 Hot deserts, near Timbuktu [A] for example, show little annual variation of temperature but extreme monthly variation [B]. The scarce rainfall occurs as a result of convectional summer storms.

7 An equatorial climate, that of Manaus in central Amazonia for example, is typified by high, constant temperature throughout the year and very heavy rainfall. There is no dry season, although the level of rainfall may vary at times.

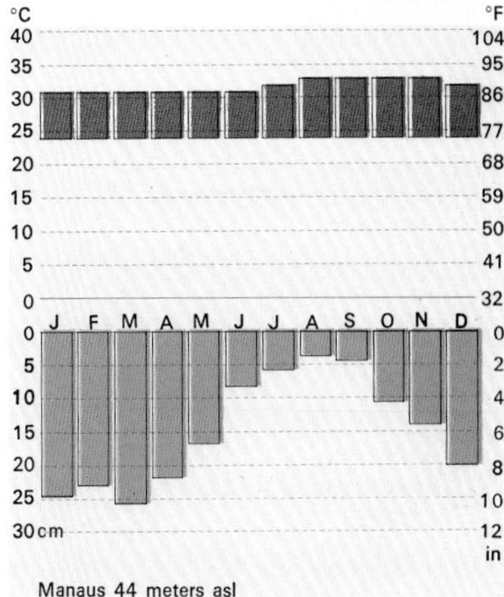
7
°C
°F
J F M A M J J A S O N D
30cm
in
Manaus 44 meters asl

The sea and seawater

Photographs of the Earth from space suggest that "Ocean" would be a more suitable name for our planet, because the oceans cover 70.8 percent of the Earth's surface [Key]. There are three major oceans, the Pacific, the Atlantic, and the Indian, but the waters of the Arctic and Antarctic are also described as oceans. These five oceans are not separate areas of water but form one continuous oceanic mass. The boundaries between them are arbitrary.

The study of oceanography

The vast areas of interconnected oceans contain 97.2 percent of the world's total water supply. The study of oceans, including their biology, chemistry, geology, and physics has become a matter of urgency, because man's future on Earth may depend on his knowledge of the ocean's potential resources of food, minerals, and power.

The most obvious resource of the oceans is the water itself. But seawater is salty, containing sodium chloride (common salt), which makes it unsuitable for drinking or farming. One kilogram (2.2lb) of seawater contains about 35g (1.2oz) of dissolved material, of which chlorine and sodium together make up nearly 85 percent.

Seawater is a highly complex substance in which 73 of the 93 natural chemical elements are present in measurable or detectable amounts [1]. Apart from chlorine and sodium, seawater contains appreciable amounts of sulfate, magnesium, potassium, and calcium, which together add up to over 13 percent of the total. The remainder, less than one percent, is made up of bicarbonate, bromine, boric acid, strontium, fluorine, silicon and trace elements. Because the volume of the oceans is so great, there are substantial amounts of some trace elements. Seawater contains more gold, for example, than there is on land, despite its low concentration [3].

Also present in seawater are dissolved gases from the atmosphere, including nitrogen, oxygen, and carbon dioxide. Of these, oxygen is vital to marine organisms. The amount of oxygen in seawater varies according to temperature. Cold water can contain more oxygen than warm water. But cold water in the ocean deeps, which has been out of contact with the atmosphere for a long period, usually contains less oxygen than surface water.

Other chemicals in seawater that are important to marine life include calcium, silicon, and phosphates, all of which are used by marine creatures to form shells and skeletons. For cell and tissue building, marine organisms extract such chemicals as phosphates, certain nitrogen compounds, iron, and silicon. The chief constituents of seawater—namely chlorine, sodium, magnesium, and sulfur—are not used to any great extent by marine organisms.

The salinity of the oceans

The volume of dissolved salts in seawater is called the salinity of the sample. The average salinity of seawater ranges between 33 and 37 parts of dissolved material per 1,000 parts of water. Oceanographers usually express these figures as 33 parts per thousand (33‰) to 37‰. The salinity of ocean water varies with local conditions [6]. Large

CONNECTIONS

See also
236 Oceanographic exploration
280 Mineral resources of the sea
298 Pollution of the sea
224 Ocean currents
226 Waves and tides
624 Life in the oceans

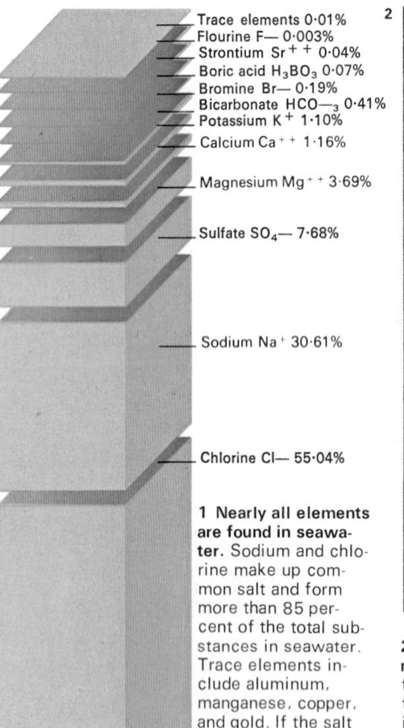

Trace elements 0·01%
Flourine F— 0·003%
Strontium Sr^{++} 0·04%
Boric acid H_3BO_3 0·07%
Bromine Br— 0·19%
Bicarbonate HCO_3— 0·41%
Potassium K^+ 1·10%
Calcium Ca^{++} 1·16%
Magnesium Mg^{++} 3·69%
Sulfate SO_4— 7·68%
Sodium Na^+ 30·61%
Chlorine Cl— 55·04%

1 Nearly all elements are found in seawater. Sodium and chlorine make up common salt and form more than 85 percent of the total substances in seawater. Trace elements include aluminum, manganese, copper, and gold. If the salt in the oceans were precipitated, it would cover the earth's land areas with a layer 520ft (153m) thick.

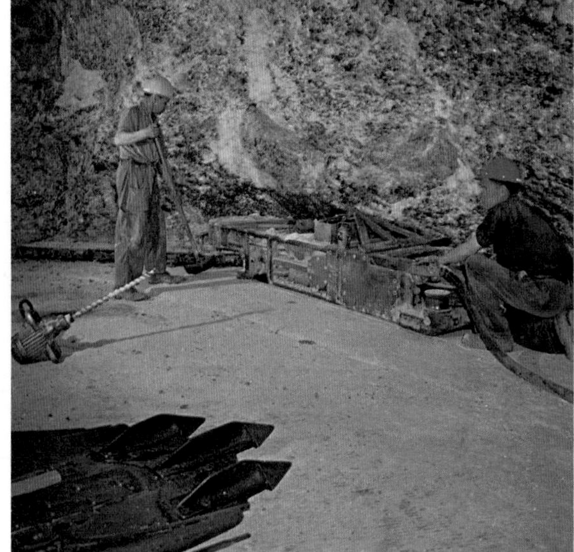

2 The salt in salt mines was formed from ocean water or from saline water in inland seas. The salt layers accumulated over extremely long periods in basins where evaporation caused the salt to precipitate from the water. The salt mines of Wieliczka, Poland, contain a layer of salt 1,200ft (366m) thick, while those of Texas are up to 12,000ft (3,658m) thick. A column of seawater about 1,000ft (305m) high would precipitate only about 15ft (4.6m), so very thick salt deposits are difficult to explain. Illustration 4 depicts the way that layers of salt may have accumulated.

3 One of the elements in seawater is gold. Although gold forms only 0.000004 parts per million, the total amount of gold in ocean water, represented by the large cube, is about 13.2 billion pounds (6 billion kg), about 100 times more than all the gold in man's possession represented by the small cube. Germany once tried to extract oceanic gold to pay war debts, but it was too expensive.

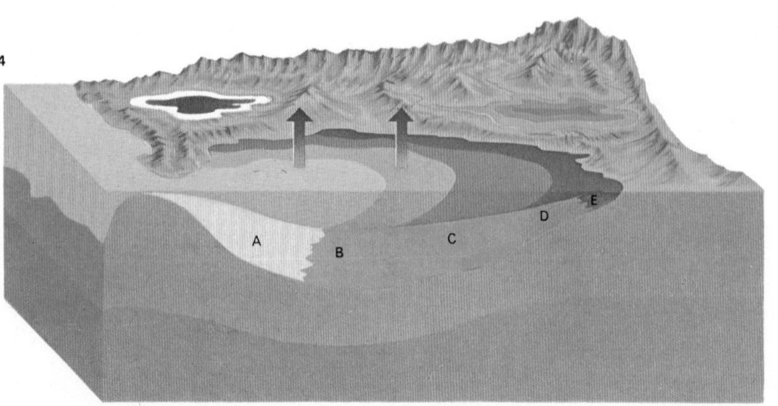

A
B
C
D
E

4 The formation of saline rocks takes place in dry, arid regions. Seawater flows into the gulfs where it tends to evaporate, concentrating the dissolved salts and making the water very saline. Finally, the salts are precipitated out when the solution becomes too concentrated to hold them. When subsidence occurs at the same time as the precipitation of the salts very thick deposits are formed. The sequence [A–E] is explained in figure 5.

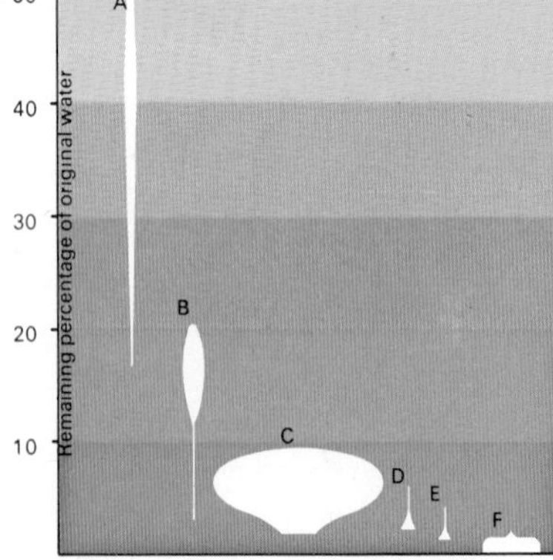

50
40
30
20
10
Remaining percentage of original water
A
B
C
D
E
F

5 When half a seawater sample has evaporated, calcium and magnesium carbonates [A] precipitate out. They are completely removed from the brine when it is 15% of its original volume. At about 20% calcium sulfate [B] starts precipitating followed by common salt [C], other sulfates [D], rare salts of magnesium, potassium, sodium, and borates and fluorides [E]. Finally magnesium and potassium chloride precipitate [F]. White areas show amounts of salts.

rivers or melting ice reduce salinity, for example, whereas it is increased in areas with little rainfall and high evaporation. The Baltic Sea, which receives large quantities of fresh water from rjvers and melting snow, has a low salinity of 7.2‰. The highest salinity of any seawater is found in the Red Sea, where it reaches 41‰.

To produce fresh water from seawater the dissolved salts must be separated out. This desalination can be carried out by electrical, chemical, and change-of-phase processes. Change-of-phase processes involve changing the water into steam and distilling it, or changing it into ice, a process that also expels the salt. Eskimos have used sea ice as a source of fresh water for hundreds of years [8] and primitive coastal tribes still take salt from the sea by damming water in holes and letting it evaporate in the sun.

Density, light, and sound

The density of seawater is an important factor in causing ocean currents and is related to the interaction of salinity and temperature [7]. The temperature of surface water varies between −2°C and 29°C (28°F and 85°F). Ice will form if the temperature drops below −2°C (28°F).

The properties of light passing through seawater determine the color of the oceans. Radiation at the red, or longwave, end of the visible spectrum is absorbed near the surface [9] while the shorter wavelengths (blue) are scattered, giving the sea its blue color. The depth to which light can penetrate is important to marine life. In clear water light may penetrate to 360ft (110m); in muddy coastal waters it may penetrate to a depth of only 50ft (15m).

Water is a good conductor of sound. Sound travels at about 4,954ft (1,507m) per second through seawater, compared with 1,092ft (333m) per second through air. Echosounding is based on measurement of the time taken for sound to travel from a ship to the sea floor and back again. Temperature and pressure both affect the speed of sound, however, causing the speed to vary by about 328ft (100m) per second and creating phenomena such as sound "shadow" zones and slow velocity zones [10].

KEY

60°N
30°
0°
30°
60°S
Pacific 165,063,000km²
Atlantic 84,133,000km²
Indian 65,522,000km²
Antarctic 32,248,000km²
Arctic 14,090,000 km²
Land 148,900,000km²

The oceans cover about 70 percent of the Earth's surface. No other planet in the solar system has as much water. The five oceans are all connected and can be thought of as one large oceanic mass. Oceanography is the study of this great area of water.

6 Salinity ‰

6. In an isohaline map of the Atlantic Ocean the lines join the places of equal salinity. The range of salinity in most of the ocean is between 33 and 37 parts per thousand. The map shows that salinity in the tropics, where evaporation is considerable, is relatively high. In the almost enclosed Mediterranean Sea it is higher still. In the Arctic Ocean, however, the salinity is lowered by melting ice and rainfall. In Hudson Bay the salinity falls considerably below the normal ocean values because of the inflow of fresh water from rivers. In the tropics, large rivers, such as the Amazon and the Congo reduce the salinity locally.

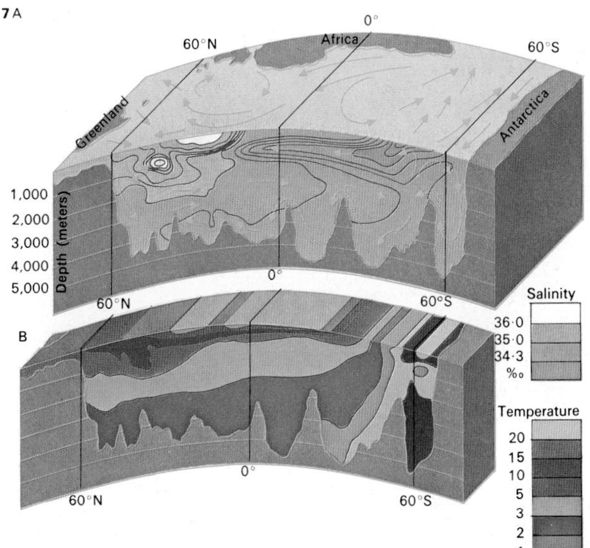
7A
0°
60°N
Africa
60°S
Greenland
Antarctica
1,000
2,000
3,000
4,000
5,000
Depth (meters)
B
Salinity
36·0
35·0
34·3
‰
Temperature
20
15
10
5
3
2
1
0
°C

7 The physical properties of seawater, including the salinity [A] and temperature [B], are relatively constant at great depths compared with the variations produced at the surface. The surface salinity varies greatly with inflows of fresh water and variations in the rate of evaporation but it remains quite constant in deep water as mixing of water by deep currents is very slow. The same is true of the temperature, which remains fairly constant at depth despite the climatic variation at the surface. In the Atlantic a larger body of cold water exists at the south than the north and this has some effect on the surface temperature range.

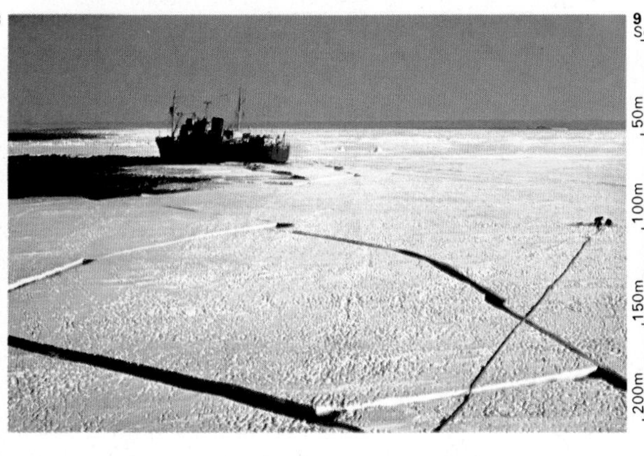

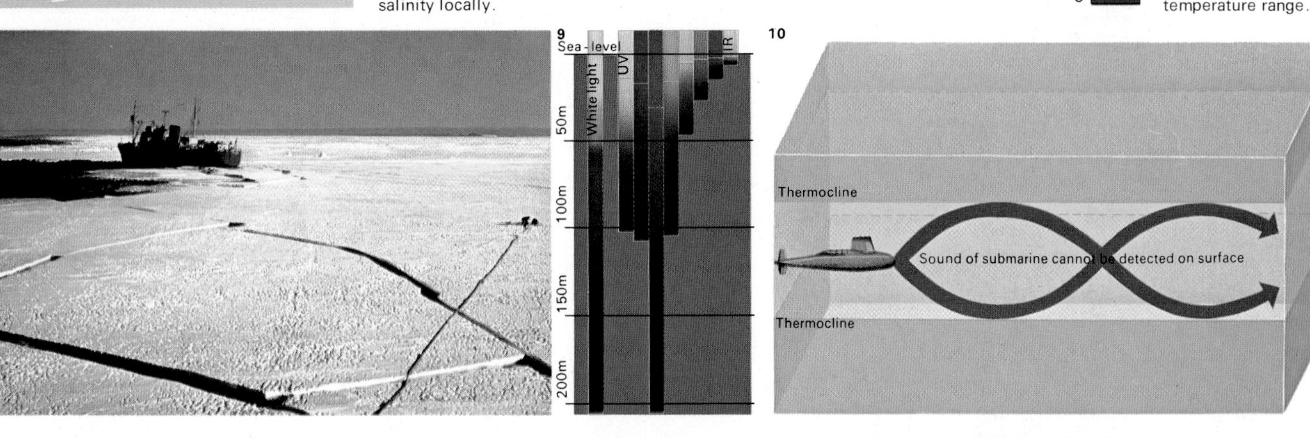
Sea-level
White light
UV
IR
50m
100m
150m
200m
Thermocline
Sound of submarine cannot be detected on surface
Thermocline

8 One of the ways of removing salt from seawater is the direct freezing method. This happens naturally when the temperature of seawater with a salinity of 35 parts per 1,000 falls below −2°C (28°F). This freezing results in the formation of surface ice that contains little if any salt. Eskimos and other peoples living in polar climates have long used sea ice as a source of fresh water. Such freezing leads to an increase in the salinity of the water beneath the ice.

9 Seawater reduces the intensity of sunlight (attenuates it) selectively according to its wavelength. Attenuation is minimum for blue and maximum for red and infrared (IR). It is caused by absorption and the scattering of light in all directions. The blue wavelengths (UV), being less absorbed, are more scattered. As a result clear seawater looks blue. Impurities in seawater, such as organic life and silt, especially around coastlines, greatly increase the attenuation. The diagram shows the attenuation for different wavelengths of light in pure seawater, the bottom of each column being the point at which only one percent of the light intensity at the surface remains, showing maximum penetration of blue.

10 The velocity of sound in seawater is more than 45 times as great as in air but it varies with pressure, salinity, and temperature. Sound waves passing through water in which these vary are refracted, or bent. Refraction can take place at a thermocline – the boundary between warm surface water and cold water at depth, which may be up to 1,000ft (305m) thick. Submarines can make use of this layer to hide the sound of their passage from an enemy.

Ocean currents

No part of the ocean is completely still, although in the ocean depths the movement of water is often extremely slow. Exploration of the deeper parts of the oceans, however, has revealed the existence of marine life. If the water were not in motion, the oxygen—upon which life depends—would soon be used up and life would be impossible. The discovery that all ocean water moves is of great significance. It was once thought that dangerous radioactive wastes could be dumped in sealed containers in the ocean depths. If the containers were to corrode, the radioactive substances would be released into the water and gradually circulate around the globe, poisoning marine life.

Causes of ocean currents

Surface currents in the oceans have been recorded since ancient times and were used by early navigators. In 1947 Thor Heyerdahl sailed on his raft, the *Kon-Tiki,* from Peru to the Tuamotu Islands east of Tahiti in 101 days. This journey of nearly 4,300 miles (7,000km) was powered mainly by the Peru and South Equatorial currents.

Prevailing winds sweep surface water along to form drift currents. These surface currents do not conform precisely with the direction of the prevailing wind because of the Coriolis effect [Key] caused by the rotation of the Earth. This effect, which increases away from the Equator, makes currents in the Northern Hemisphere veer to the right of the wind direction and currents in the Southern Hemisphere veer to the left. The result is a general clockwise circulation of water in the Northern Hemisphere and a counterclockwise circulation in the Southern Hemisphere [5].

Other factors affecting currents are the configuration of the ocean bed and the shapes of land masses. For example, in the Atlantic Ocean, the North Equatorial Current flows toward the West Indies. Most of this current is channeled into the Gulf of Mexico where it veers northeastward, flowing into the Atlantic as the Gulf Stream. (The term "stream" is used for currents with fairly clear boundaries.) This current, known as the North Atlantic Drift once it leaves the American coast, then flows at four to five knots in a northeasterly direction. Even this marked current is confined to waters near the surface. At a depth of about 1,150ft (350m), its effect is hardly noticeable. But in the late 1950s a large current was discovered flowing under the Gulf Stream in the opposite direction.

Variations in density

The causes of currents that are now powered by winds are related to the density of ocean water, which varies according to temperature and salinity. Heating at the Equator causes the water to become less dense. Cooling around the poles has the opposite effect. Salinity is affected by the inflow of fresh water from rivers, melting ice, and rainfall and by evaporation. For example, a high rate of evaporation in the Mediterranean Sea increases the salinity and therefore the density of the water [2]. As a result, currents of less dense (less saline) water flow into the Mediterranean from the Atlantic and the Black Sea. Smaller counter-currents with a higher density flow outward beneath these currents so that

CONNECTIONS

See also
236 Oceanographic exploration
226 Waves and tides
222 The sea and seawater

1 A

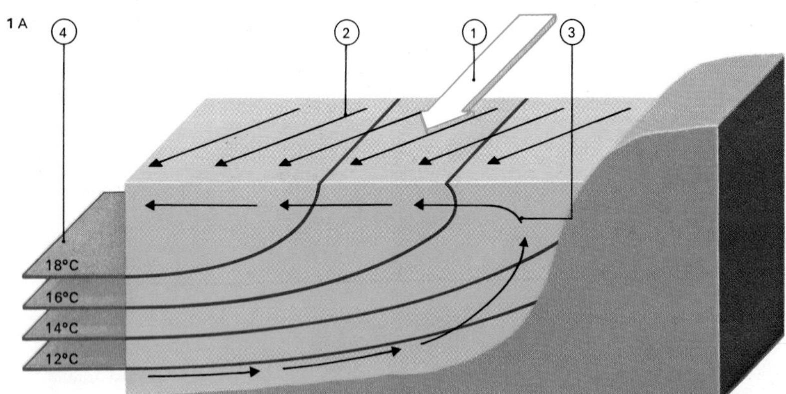
4
2
1
3
18°C
16°C
14°C
12°C

1 Upwelling [A] occurs when a longshore wind [1] pushes surface water away from a coast at an angle [2] allowing subsurface water to rise [3]. This slow motion can best be seen as temperature gradients [4] where the deeper water is colder. Subsurface water often contains many nutrients. Thus areas where upwelling occurs are often rich fishing grounds, such as off the west coast of South America [B].

B

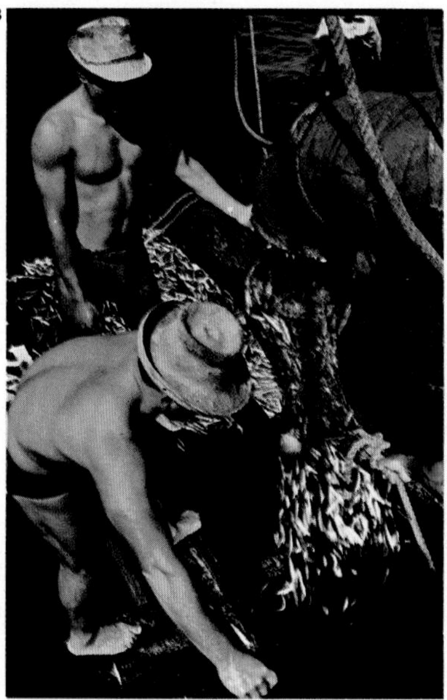

2

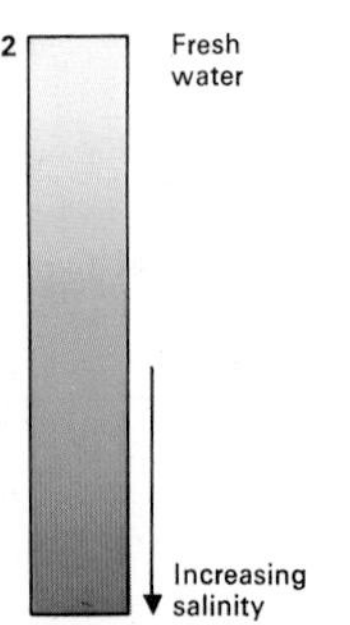
Fresh water
Increasing salinity

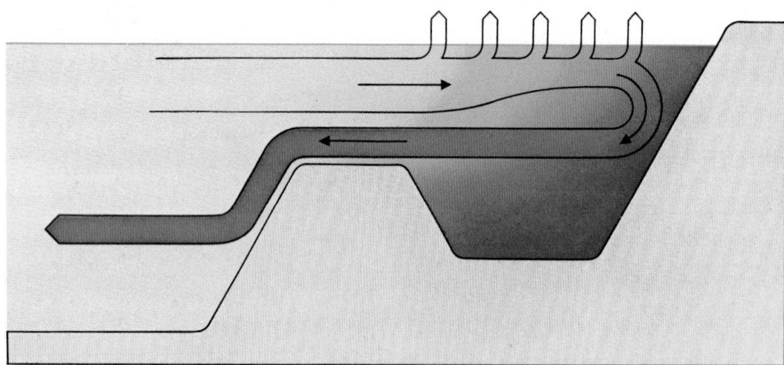

2 The water of the Mediterranean is constantly evaporating at its surface causing its salinity to increase. A current of normal salinity flows in and the excess salt is carried out by a deep-water current.

3

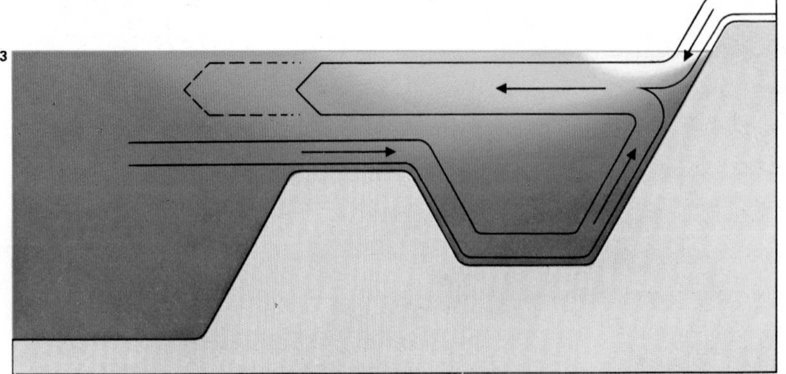

3 In the Baltic, a surface current of low salinity flows outward. The overall salinity of the Baltic is maintained by a small undercurrent bringing in as much salt as the amount that is carried away by the outflow.

4

4 Current meters are the most accurate instruments used to measure and record the direction and rate of flow of ocean currents. The meters are sometimes attached to buoys or they may be anchored to the sea bed and left to measure the current over a period of time. They usually contain some kind of propeller that is turned by the moving water and a vane connected to a compass, which orients the meter so that it always faces the current.

the salt content of the basin remains constant.

One of the simplest ways of measuring the speed and direction of surface currents is to record the movement of floating objects such as icebergs or wreckage. Ships record the flow of currents, sometimes by trailing a drift buoy and noting its movements. Current meters [4] of many kinds are also used.

Effects of ocean currents

One of the most important effects of ocean currents is that they mix ocean water and so affect directly the fertility of the sea. Mixing is especially important when subsurface is mixed with surface water. The upwelling [1] of subsurface water may be caused by strong coastal winds that push the surface water offshore, allowing subsurface water to rise. Such upwelling occurs off the coasts of Peru, California, and Mauritania. Subsurface water rich in nutrients rises to the surface, stimulating the growth of plankton, which provides food for great shoals of fish, such as Peruvian anchovies. But the anchovies are adversely affected by another current: when the winds fail, disaster occurs in the form of a warm current called El Niño, which flows into the area about the end of December, killing the cold-water plants and animals.

Water has a high heat capacity and can retain heat two and a half times as readily as land. The heat of the Sun absorbed by water around the Equator is transported north and south by currents. Part of the North Atlantic Drift flows past Norway warming offshore winds and giving northwest Europe a winter temperature 20°F (11°C) above the average for those latitudes [6]. The northward-flowing Peru and Benguela currents have a reverse effect, bringing cooler weather to the western coasts of South America and southern Africa. In such ways, currents have a profound effect on climate. Currents from polar regions can also create hazards for shipping. The Labrador and East Greenland currents carry icebergs and pack ice into shipping lanes, and fog often occurs where cold and warm currents meet.

KEY

Wind direction

Surface current

Net water mass transport

Depth of frictional resistance

Surface currents are caused largely by prevailing winds. The Coriolis effect results in the deflection of currents to the right of the wind direction in the Northern Hemisphere. In the same manner, the surface motion drives the subsurface layer at an angle to it, and so on. Each layer moves at a slower speed than the one above it and at a greater angle from the wind. The Ekman spiral shown here depicts the way in which the water mass moves above the depth of frictional resistance at an angle of about 90° to the wind.

5

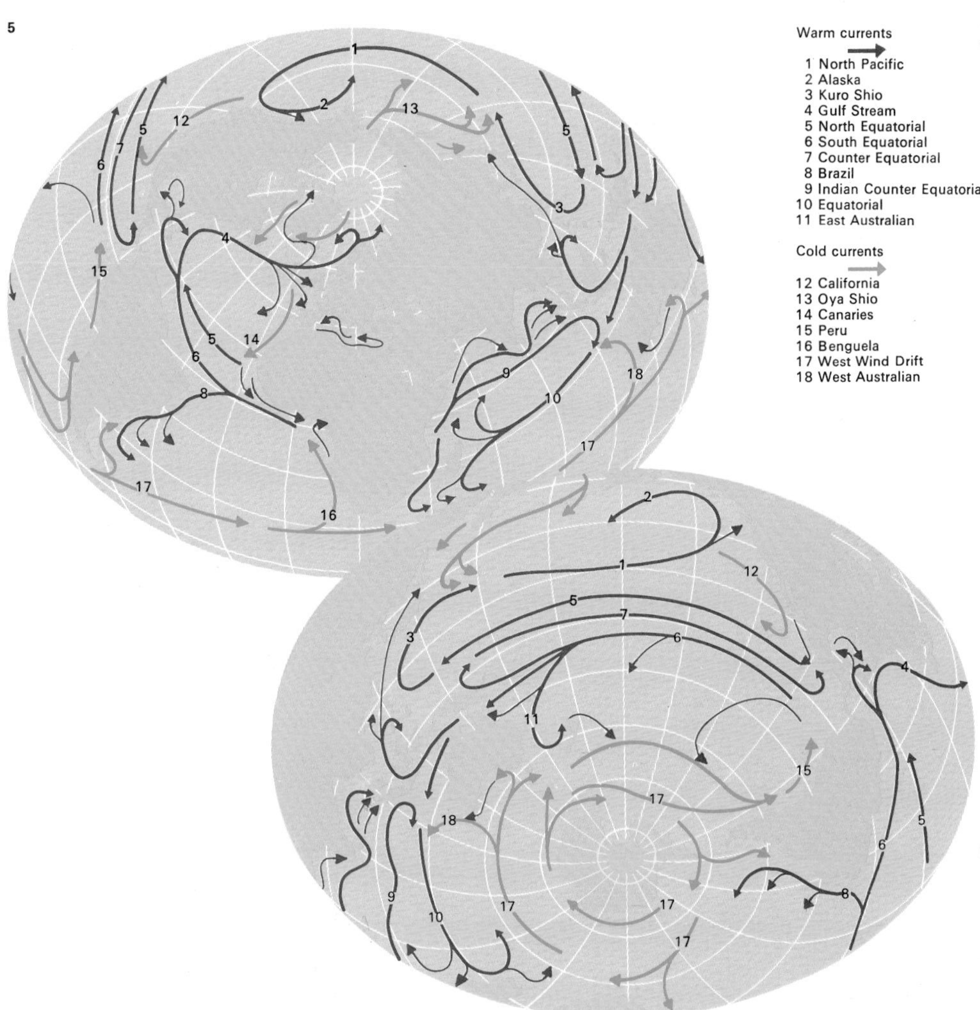

Warm currents

1 North Pacific
2 Alaska
3 Kuro Shio
4 Gulf Stream
5 North Equatorial
6 South Equatorial
7 Counter Equatorial
8 Brazil
9 Indian Counter Equatorial
10 Equatorial
11 East Australian

Cold currents

12 California
13 Oya Shio
14 Canaries
15 Peru
16 Benguela
17 West Wind Drift
18 West Australian

5 The surface currents of the world circulate in a clockwise direction in the Northern Hemisphere and in a counterclockwise direction in the Southern Hemisphere. These circulatory systems are called gyres. There are two large clockwise gyres in the Northern Hemisphere (in the North Atlantic and in the North Pacific) and three counterclockwise gyres in the Southern Hemisphere (in the South Atlantic, the South Pacific, and the Indian Ocean). Beneath the surface are undercurrents whose direction may be opposite to those at the surface. Beneath the northeastward flowing Gulf Stream off eastern United States lies a large cold current flowing south from the Arctic. The Gulf Stream finally splits in the North Atlantic, branching past eastern Greenland, northern Europe and southern Europe, while part of the current returns southward to complete the gyre. Surface cold currents in the Northern Hemisphere generally flow southward. In the Southern Hemisphere, cold water circulates around Antarctica, while offshoots flow northward. The warm currents are very strong in tropical and subtropical regions. They include the Equatorial and Indian currents.

6 A

6 Climate is profoundly affected by ocean currents. Where winds blow off the warm sea rather than the cold land the North Atlantic Drift can bring mild weather to some European coasts. New York City [A] lies at a latitude only 100 miles (160 km) north of Lisbon, Portugal [B]. But New York has an average January temperature of 31°F (−1°C), while Lisbon averages 50°F (10°C).

B

Waves and tides

Waves and tides are the most familiar features of oceans and seas. Sometimes the energies of waves, tides, and high winds combine with devastating effect. In January 1953, a high spring tide, storm waves, and winds of 115mph (185kph) combined to raise the usual level of the North Sea by 10ft (3m). The main force of this surge in the sea was directed against the Netherlands, where 4.3 percent of the entire country was inundated. About 30,000 houses were destroyed or damaged and 1,800 people died.

Waves and wave movements

Some wave motion occurs at great depth along the boundary of two opposing currents, but most waves are caused by the wind blowing over an open stretch of water. This area where the wind blows is known as the "fetch." As waves move beyond the fetch, they combine into more orderly waves to form a swell that can travel for great distances. Waves are movements of oscillation—that is, the shape of the wave moves across the water, but the water particles rotate in a circular orbit with hardly any lateral movement [Key]. As a result, if there is no wind or current, a bottle bobs up and down in the waves, but stays in more or less the same spot.

Waves have two basic dimensions [1]. Wave height is the vertical distance between the crest and the trough. Wave length is the distance between two crests. At sea, waves seldom exceed 39ft (12m) in height, although a wave 112ft (34m) high was observed in the Pacific [3] in 1933. Such a wave requires a long fetch and high-speed winds. Wave motion continues for some distance beneath the surface, but the rotating orbits diminish in diameter and become negligible at a depth of about half the wave length.

Waves that break along a seashore may have been generated by storms in mid-ocean or by local winds. As waves approach shallow water [1] (defined as a depth of half a wave length), their character changes. As waves "feel" the bottom, they gradually slow down and the crests tend to crowd together. When the water in front of a wave is insufficient to fill the wave form, the rotating orbit, and hence the wave, breaks. There are two main kinds of breakers. Spilling breakers occur on gently sloping beaches, where the crests spill over to form a mass of surf. Plunging breakers develop on more steeply inclined slopes.

Tsunamis

Tsunamis [4], sometimes called tidal waves, have no connection with tides. Tsunamis are caused mainly by earthquakes, and also by submarine landslides and volcanic eruptions. At sea, they pass unnoticed by ships, because the height of the wave is seldom more than 2–3ft (60–90cm), but the wave length may be hundreds of miles long. Tsunamis travel at hundreds of miles per hour because of their long wave length. For example, an earthquake in the Aleutian Trench in the far north of the Pacific in 1946 triggered a tsunami that devastated Honolulu. The tsunami took 4 hours 34 minutes to reach Honolulu, a distance of more than 2,000 miles (3,220km); it had a speed of about 438mph (700kph). Waves more than 50ft (15m) high struck Honolulu, killing 173

CONNECTIONS

See also
236 Oceanographic exploration
224 Ocean currents
286 Energy supplies
288 Energy for the future
222 The sea and sea water

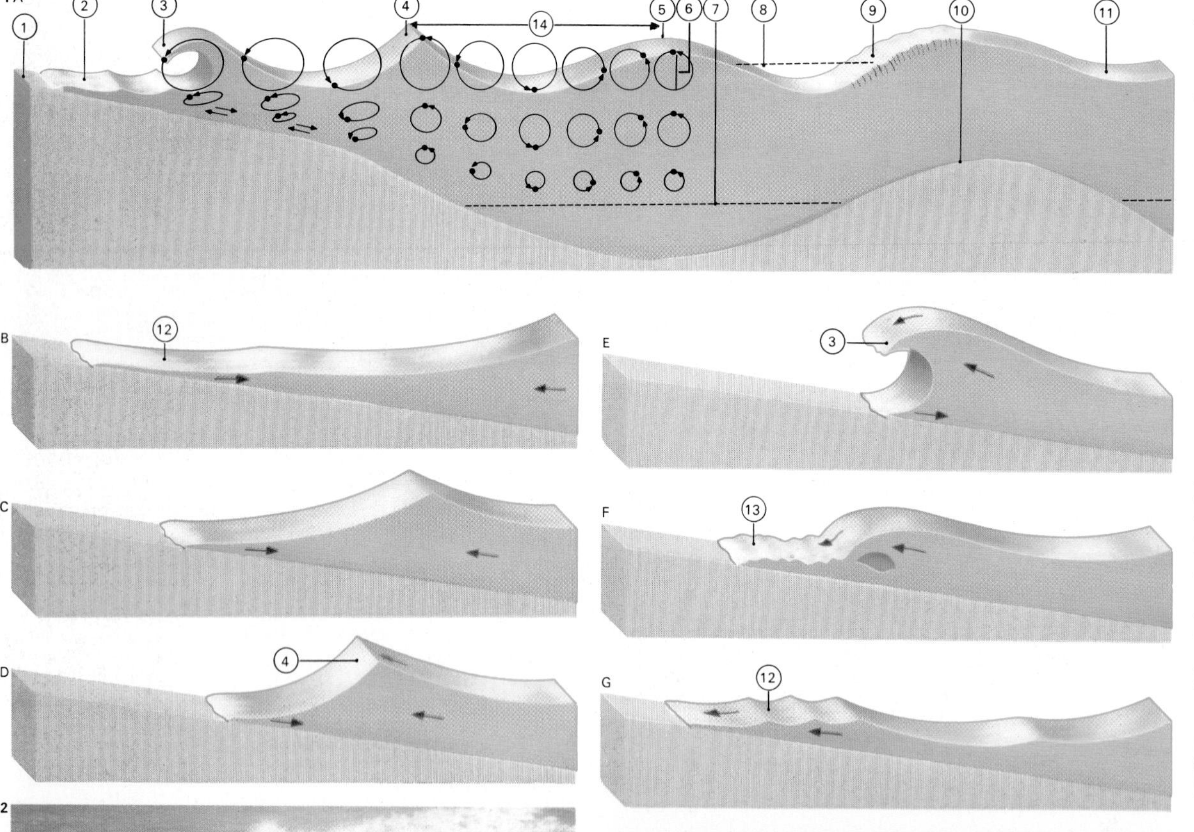

1A
1
2
3
4
14
5
6
7
8
9
10
11
B
12
C
D
4
E
3
F
13
G
12

1 Waves have length and height [A]. The wave length [14] is the distance between one crest [5] and another, in this case, a peaking wave [4]. Between crests is a trough [11]. The wave height [6] is the distance between the crest and the trough. If wave action ceased, the water would settle at the "still water level" [8]. Wave action extends to the wave base [7]. Wave distortion is caused by frictional drag on the bottom. If waves pass over a sand bar [10], a spilling breaker [9] may form. Sometimes, waves in shallow water move the whole body of the water forward in translation waves [2] toward the shore [1]. In the development of a breaking wave, B shows backwash [12]. C shows the advance of the next wave, which peaks [4] in D and then becomes a plunging breaker [3] in E. F and G show swash [13] rushing up after the wave breaks.

2 Surfing is a popular sport. Surf forms as the crest of a wave breaks. The force of the wave pushes the surfboard ahead of it.

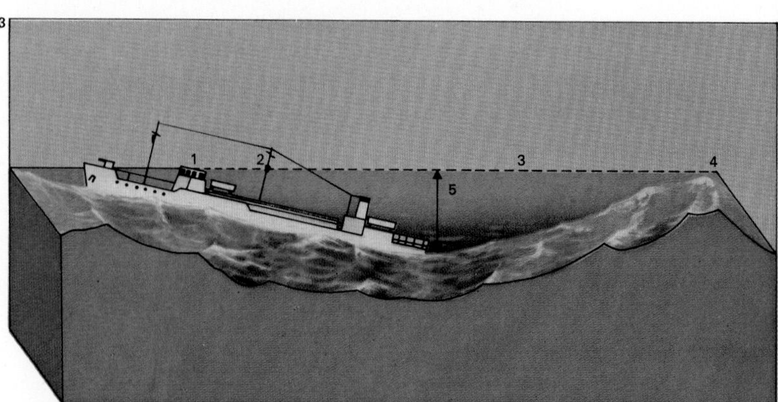

3
1
2
3
4
5

3 The tallest recorded wave in open sea was 112ft (34m) high. An officer on the USS *Ramapo's* bridge [1] in the Pacific in 1933 saw the crest of a wave [4] in line with horizon [3] and crow's nest [2], enabling him to work out height [5] people. Although the height of the crest is low at sea, tsunamis have immense energy, which, as they lose speed in shallower water, is converted into an increase in height. The waves may be 125ft (38m) or more high on reaching the shore.

Most destructive tsunamis occur in the Pacific [5], but they have been recorded in the Atlantic. A tsunami battered Lisbon shortly after the earthquake of 1755. It was later felt in the West Indies in the form of a destructive 13–20ft (4–6m) high wave. Other tsunamis can be caused by the surge of water when the barometric pressure is very low, as in a hurricane.

Tides and their causes

Tides are the alternate rise and fall of the sea's surface, caused chiefly by the gravitation pull of the Moon and the Sun [6]. The tidal effect of the Sun is only 46.6 percent that of the Moon. Tides are also affected by the shapes of ocean basins and land masses. The Moon's gravitational pull makes the waters of the Earth bulge outward when the Moon is overhead at any meridian. Another bulge occurs on the opposite side of the Earth at the same time because of centrifugal force. Since the Moon orbits the Earth once every 24 hours 50 minutes, it causes two high tides and two low tides in that period.

Spring tides [7] occur when the Earth, Moon, and Sun are in a straight line. The combined gravitational attraction makes high tides higher and low tides lower, giving a large tidal range. Neap tides [7], which have the smallest tidal range, occur when the Sun, Earth, and Moon form a right angle.

In the open sea, the tidal range is no more than a few feet and in enclosed basins, such as the Mediterranean, it is little more than 12in (30cm). In shallow seas, however, it may be more than 20ft (6m) and in tidal estuaries 40–50ft (12–15m). In some estuaries, including the Bay of Fundy in eastern Canada and the Severn in England, tidal bores occur. Bores are bodies of water with a wall-like front that surge up rivers. They form because estuaries act as funnels, the narrowing effect leading to a rise in the height of the water as it flows upstream.

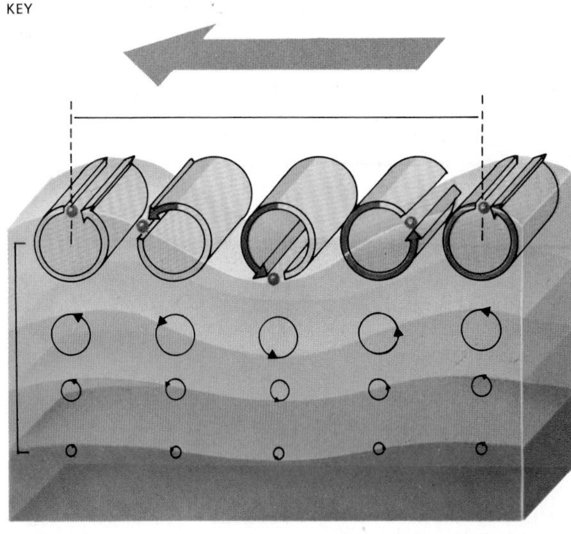
KEY

Most waves are generated by the wind. As a wave travels through water, however, the water particles do not move up and down but rotate in circular orbits. As depth increases, the rotations of the water particles diminish rapidly. This is why submarines escape the effects of severe storms.

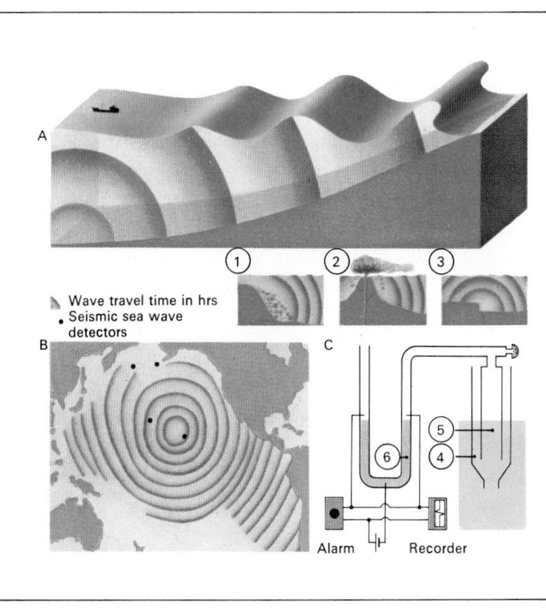
A
1
2
3
Wave travel time in hrs
Seismic sea wave detectors
B
C
5
6
4
Alarm
Recorder

4 Tsunamis [A] caused by landslides [1], volcanoes [2], or earthquakes [3], reach great heights near land. Pacific warning stations [B] use detectors [C]. A container [4], half in seawater, has air in a tube [5]. When a wave increases the pressure, mercury is forced around [6], closing a circuit and giving an alarm.

5 Tremendous damage is caused by tsunamis. They occur mainly in the Pacific.

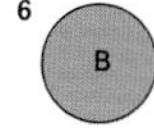
B

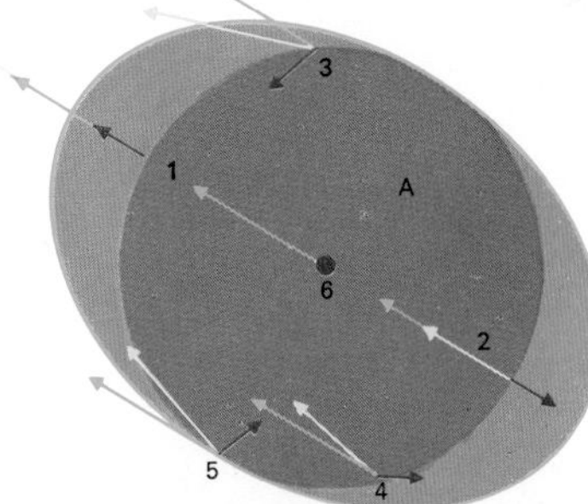
Average gravitational pull
Actual gravitational pull
Tide generating force
1
2
3
4
5
6
A

6 Water on the Earth [A] is attracted to the Moon [B] on the near side but pushed away on the far side. This causes tidal bulges at the nearest [1] and farthest [2] points, tidal flows at [3] and [4], and low tides at median points [5]. The force at work [red arrows] is the difference between the Moon's actual gravitational pull and its average pull at the Earth's center [6], where it is exactly balanced by centrifugal force.

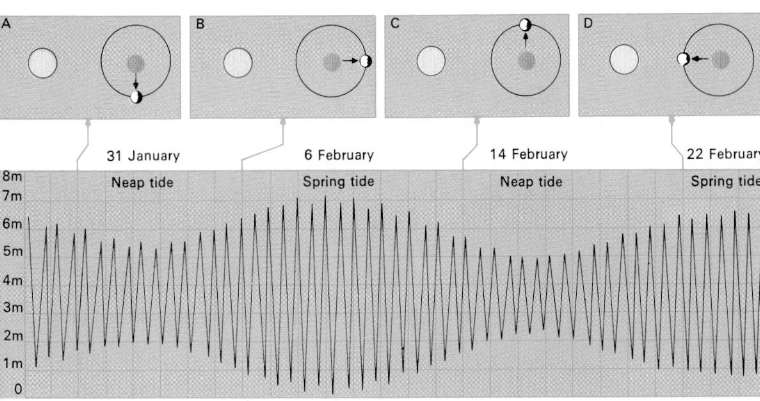
A
B
C
D
31 January
6 February
14 February
22 February
Neap tide
Spring tide
Neap tide
Spring tide
8m
7m
6m
5m
4m
3m
2m
1m
0

7 The height of tides varies according to the positions of the Sun and Moon in relation to the Earth. When the Moon is in its first quarter [A], and again when it is in its last quarter [C], the Moon, Earth and Sun form a right angle. The gravitational forces are therefore opposed, causing only a small difference between high and low tide. Such tides are called neap tides. The Moon, Earth, and Sun form a straight line at full Moon [B] and at new Moon [D]. The high tides then become higher and the low tides lower. These are called spring tides. Because of friction and inertia, both spring and neap tides come about two days after the Moon's phases. The graph shows the tidal range over a lunar month.

8 At low tide [A] the sea recedes from Mont St Michel, off the northern coast of France, and it becomes part of the mainland. At high tide [B], the sea surrounds it, creating an island. A causeway connects it to the mainland.

The sea bed

The floor of the deep ocean has always fascinated man. Plato's legendary lost continent of Atlantis, "beyond the Pillars of Hercules," has never lost its hold on the imagination, although there is no geological evidence to support the most common belief that it lay south of the Azores, on the Mid-Atlantic Ridge.

Early knowledge of the sea floor was restricted to depth soundings, taken by lead and line in the areas around the known islands. Magellan tried—and, of course, failed—to reach the bottom of the Pacific with 1,200ft (366m) of rope. The first true oceanic sounding was made by James Clark Ross in 1840 when he reached a depth of nearly 12,140ft (3,700m) with a hemp line.

Probing the sea floor

The epic voyage of *HMS Challenger*—the first true oceanic depth survey—was made between 1872 and 1876. The *Challenger* expedition used soundings weights with tubelike cups to obtain a sample of the material forming the sea floor. Thus, at the time when Jules Verne (1828–1905) was writing of the wonders of the sea in *Twenty Thousand Leagues Under the Sea* (1870), man first developed a systematic knowledge of the deep sediments. Their classification, which was developed by the *Challenger* expedition's geologist John Murray (1841–1916) and others who studied the samples after the ship's return, has been improved but never discarded.

Even so, the widely prevalent idea that the ocean floor consisted of a sandy waste extending for thousands of miles, dotted with only a few islands and occupied by exotic fish, was only slowly discarded. The early samples of sediment obtained by *Challenger,* and the soundings obtained in the mid-Atlantic which actually mapped the Mid-Atlantic Ridge, did not lead to full understanding of the variation in the extent and thickness of the sediments. They did not supply any scientific reasons for this variation nor was it appreciated that mid-ocean ridges ran through all the world's major oceans. In this century improved coring devices greatly enlarged the collective knowledge of oceanic sediments.

The actual topography of the deep ocean has been revealed by echo-sounding equipment using sonic or ultrasonic signals. Scientists can calculate the depth of the water by noting how much time passes between sending the signals and receiving the echo. Since the 1940s seismic methods have also been used. These have shown that the ocean floor is made up of hills, volcanic mountains, and island arcs [1]—of which the islands are only the visible tips of huge and complex submarine mountain chains.

The continental shelf

If one walks down a pebbly beach, the pebbles usually give way to sand, which continues out to sea. This is the continental shelf [1, 2], which may be covered by relatively coarse sediments or muds and silts. It is inhabited by seaweeds of many kinds, as well as numerous animals: corals, sea anemones, and other coelenterates; many species of burrowing worms and minute colonial rock-encrusting animals (Bryozoa); and clams, mussels, oysters, scallops, and other mollusks. There are also sea urchins,

CONNECTIONS

See also
236 Oceanographic exploration
230 The Atlantic Ocean
232 The Pacific Ocean
234 The Indian Ocean and the polar seas
170 Global tectonics
238 Man under the sea
280 Mineral resources of the sea
268 Coastlines
506 Invertebrate oddities

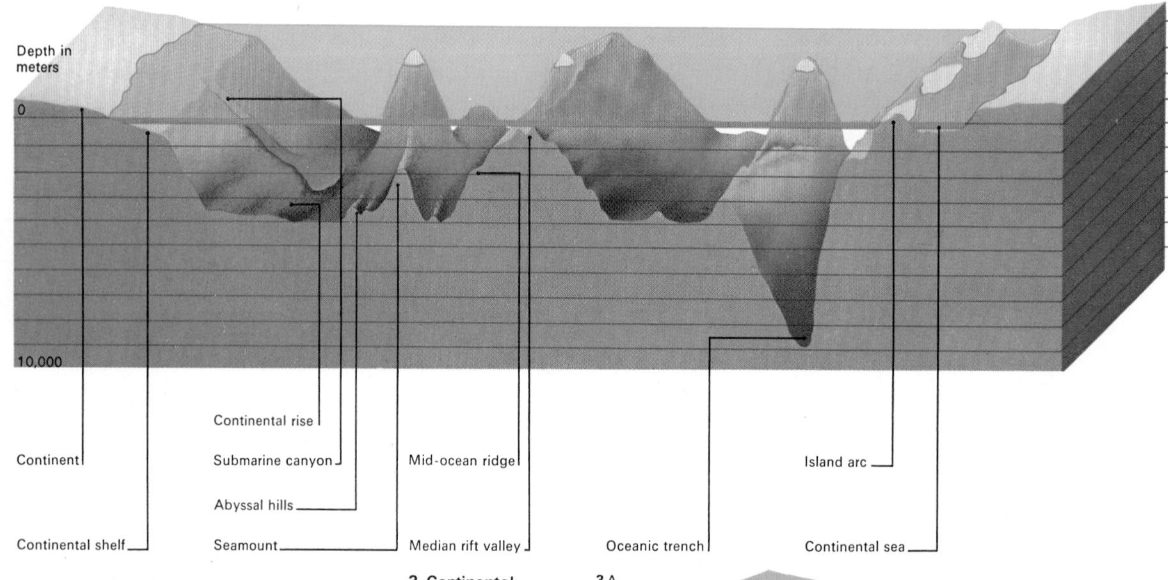

1
Depth in meters
0
10,000
Continent
Continental shelf
Continental rise
Submarine canyon
Abyssal hills
Seamount
Mid-ocean ridge
Median rift valley
Oceanic trench
Island arc
Continental sea

1 The sea bed consists of different zones, the shallowest of which is the continental shelf, which lies between the coast and the 650 ft (200m) depth contour. The shelf occupies 7.5% of the sea floor and corresponds to the submerged portion of the continental crust. Farther out, the sea floor slopes to form the continental slope, which occupies some 8.5% of the sea floor. This area may be dissected by submarine canyons. The continental slope meets the abyssal basins at a more gentle slope called the continental rise. The basins lie at depths of 2.5 miles (4,000m) and show many mountain ranges and hills.

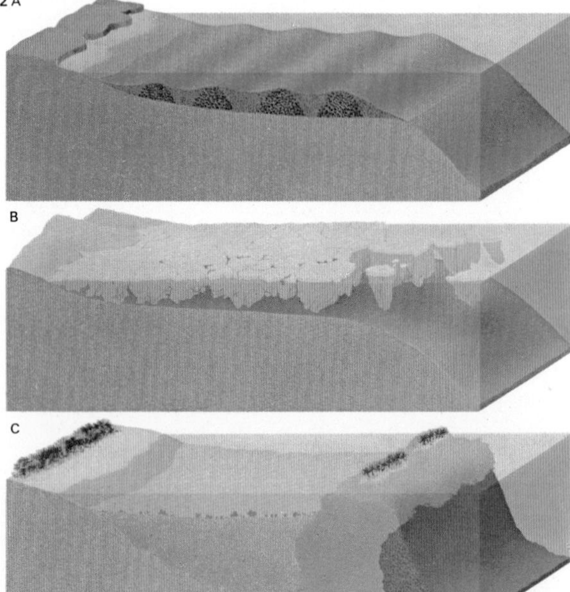

2 A
B
C

2 Continental shelves are the regions immediately off the land masses. There are several different sorts. Off Europe and North America the shelf [A] has a gentle relief, often with sandy ridges and barriers. In high latitudes, floating ice wears the shelf smooth [B] and in clear tropical seas a smooth shelf may be rimmed with a coral barrier like the Great Barrier Reef off eastern Australia [C], leaving an inner lagoonal area "dammed" by the reef.

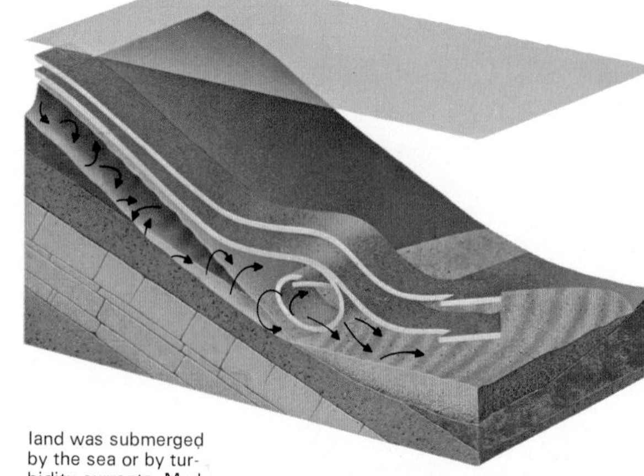

3 A

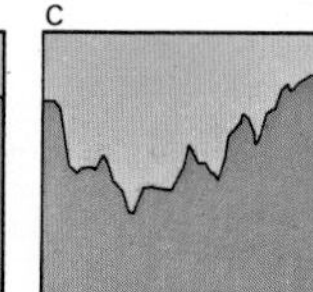

B
C

3 Submarine canyons like the 5,000 ft (1,525m) deep gorge off Monterey, California [B], are found on the continental slopes [A]. They can be caused by river erosion before the land was submerged by the sea or by turbidity currents. Mud and sediment-laden water often pour out of major estuaries, scouring gorges out of slope rock and sediment. These canyons may be deeper than the Grand Canyon [C].

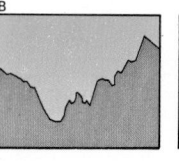

starfish, brittle stars, sea cucumbers, and sponges, as well as bottom-dwelling fish.

This is the region of sand banks and sand waves (underwater dunes). In the North Sea, sand waves form when masses of loose sand, propelled by currents, move around like sand dunes in the desert. Vast oil and gas reservoirs, sometimes associated with salt domes, as in the Gulf of Mexico, have been found in the rocks beneath the surface sand of the shelf.

At the edge of continental shelf, at about 650ft (200m) depth, the sea floor begins to dip markedly down; this is the upper boundary of the continental slope. It is dissected in places by submarine canyons [1, 3] in which underwater avalanches, known as turbidity currents, carry mud, pebbles, and sand far out to sea and deposit them at the foot of the slope, on the continental rise [1], at depths of about 6,560ft (2,000m). Life is much more scarce on the continental slope and rise. Large free-swimming mollusks—octopuses, cuttlefish, and large squid—brittle stars, worms, and strange fish are the most common forms.

The continental rise leads to the abyssal plains—vast empty basins occupied by fewer even stranger fish, worms, brittle stars, and deep-sea free-swimming mollusks, with little plant life. From these plains rise huge mountain ranges, the mid-ocean ridges [1], from 13,200ft (4,000m) deep to some 3,300ft (1,000m) below the surface with occasional peaks reaching the surface as islands. Seamounts [5] also rise from the abyssal plains, sometimes as part of island chains like the Hawaii-Emperor chain in the Pacific, but often as isolated peaks. They are nearly all volcanic and may be crowned with coral.

Sea-bed maps

On the six pages following, the floors of the five oceans are mapped. The projections used were chosen to give maximum coverage to sea areas relative to land and the colors reflect those thought to exist on the sea floor. Continental shelves are shown in the grayish-green of the terrigenous oozes, while the calcareous oozes of the deeper areas are shown in pale grays and tan.

KEY

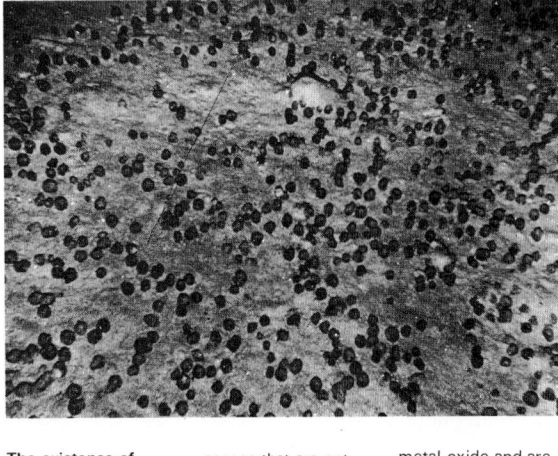

The existence of manganese nodules on the deep ocean floor was discovered by the *Challenger* expedition. These potato-shaped nodules form on the ocean floor by processes that are not fully understood, although a great deal of research is going on to find out how they grow. They consist of a rock nucleus surrounded by concentric layers of metal oxide and are of potential economic importance because they contain enough copper, cobalt, and nickel as well as manganese, to last the world for thousands of years.

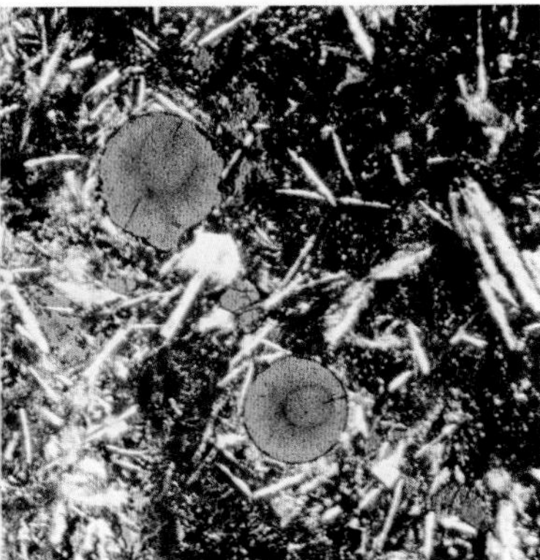

4 Basalt is the rock most commonly found on the sea floor. It is a lava that forms the bulk of the seamounts and ocean ridges and it underlies the marine sediments in the abyssal plains. Submarine eruptions produce lumps of basalt "frozen" into pillow shapes (pillow lavas). The submarine basalt shown here is seen through a microscope. It shows small crystals, glassy patches, and mica-filled gas bubbles.

5

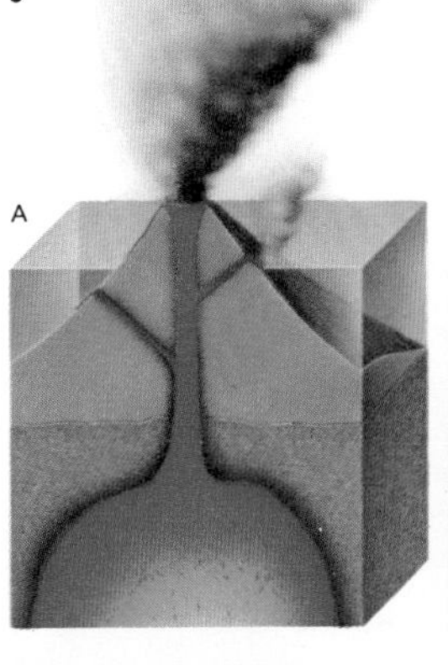

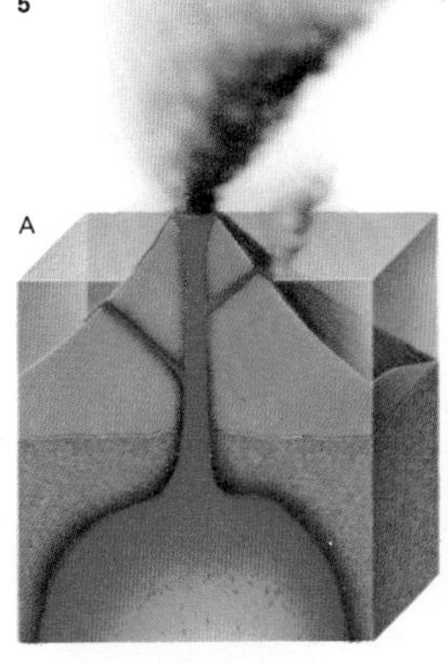

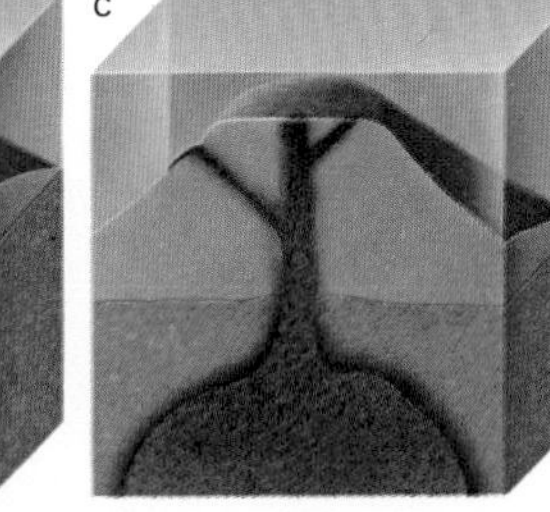

A
B
C

5 Seamounts are submarine mountains rising at least 3,300 ft (1,000m) above their surroundings; they are nearly always volcanoes. Some seamounts, called tablemounts or guyots, have flat tops at depths down to 1.5 miles (2,500m). These tops are often too large to be explained as ancient craters filled to the rim by sediments. Thus it has been proposed that guyots were volcanoes built above sea level [A], which were worn flat by waves [B] and which then sank as the sea level rose or as the sea bed subsided [C]. The idea has been supported by the dredging of beach pebbles.

7

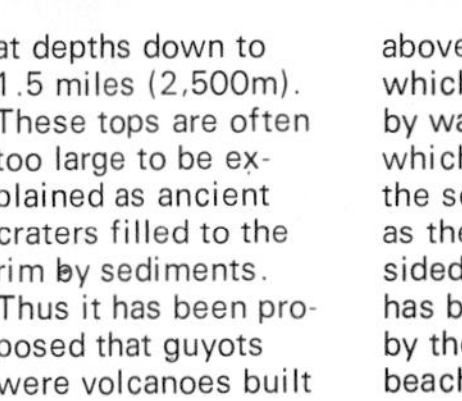

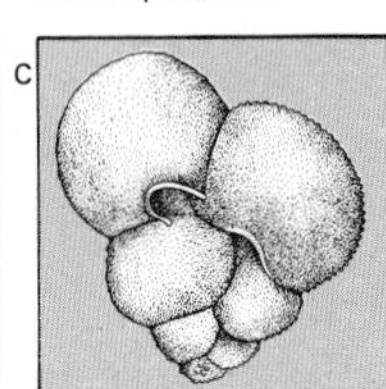

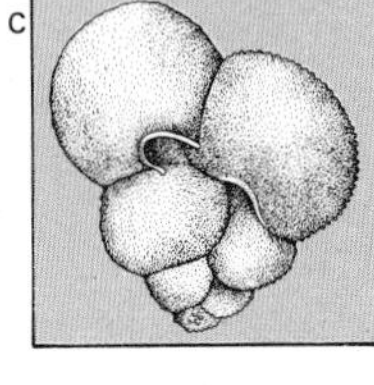

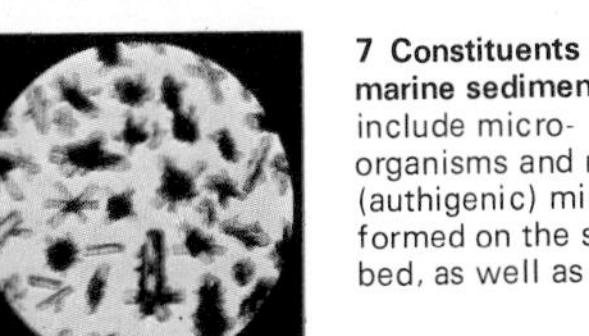

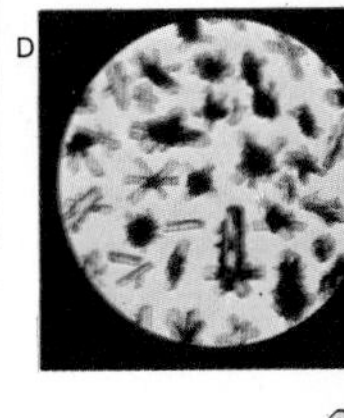

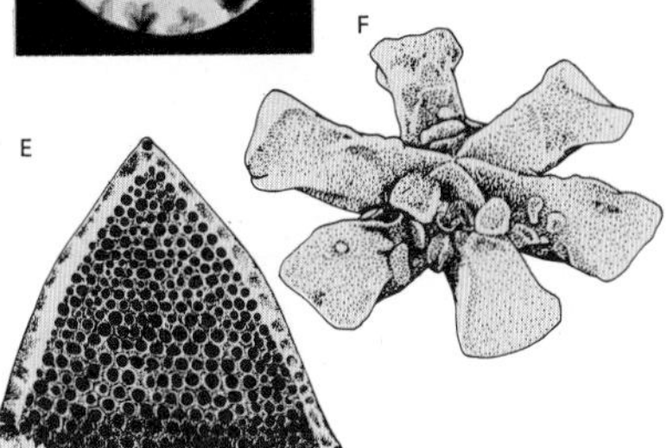

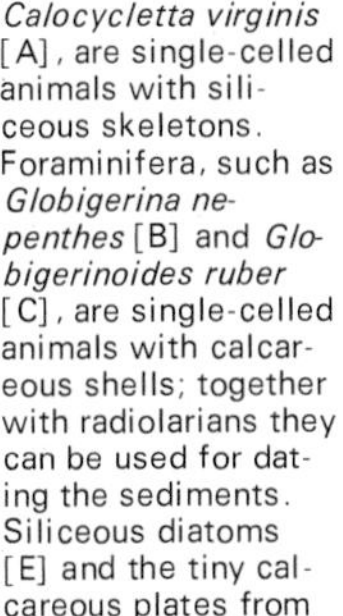

A
B
C
D
E
F

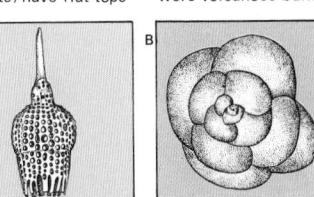

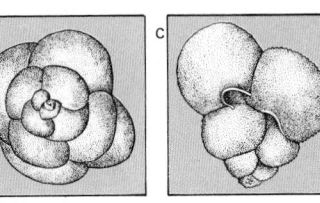

7 Constituents of marine sediments include micro-organisms and new (authigenic) minerals formed on the sea bed, as well as clays. Radiolarians, such as *Calocycletta virginis* [A], are single-celled animals with siliceous skeletons. Foraminifera, such as *Globigerina nepenthes* [B] and *Globigerinoides ruber* [C], are single-celled animals with calcareous shells; together with radiolarians they can be used for dating the sediments. Siliceous diatoms [E] and the tiny calcareous plates from flagellates known as coccoliths [F] are also common. Philipsite [D] is a typical authigenic mineral.

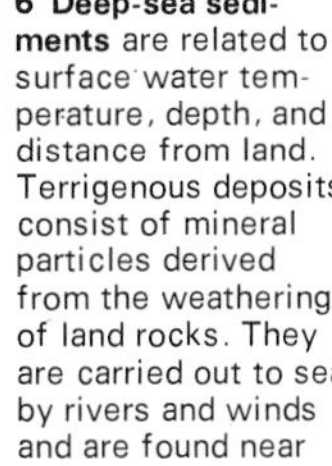

Terrigenous deposits
Red clay
Globigerina ooze
Pteropod ooze
Diatom ooze
Radiolarian ooze

6 Deep-sea sediments are related to surface water temperature, depth, and distance from land. Terrigenous deposits consist of mineral particles derived from the weathering of land rocks. They are carried out to sea by rivers and winds and are found near the coasts. The deep-sea floor is often blanketed by ooze that is formed by the endless "snowfall" of the shells or skeletons of countless tiny planktonic animals and algae. Globigerina and radiolarian ooze are made from the remains of single-celled animals with calcareous and siliceous skeletons, respectively. Occasionally the shells of pteropods—small swimming mollusks—form deposits of pteropod ooze. In cold seas, silica-shelled microscopic algae, the diatoms, thrive and form diatom ooze. In very deep areas, atmospheric dust settles very slowly to become abyssal red clays.

The Atlantic Ocean

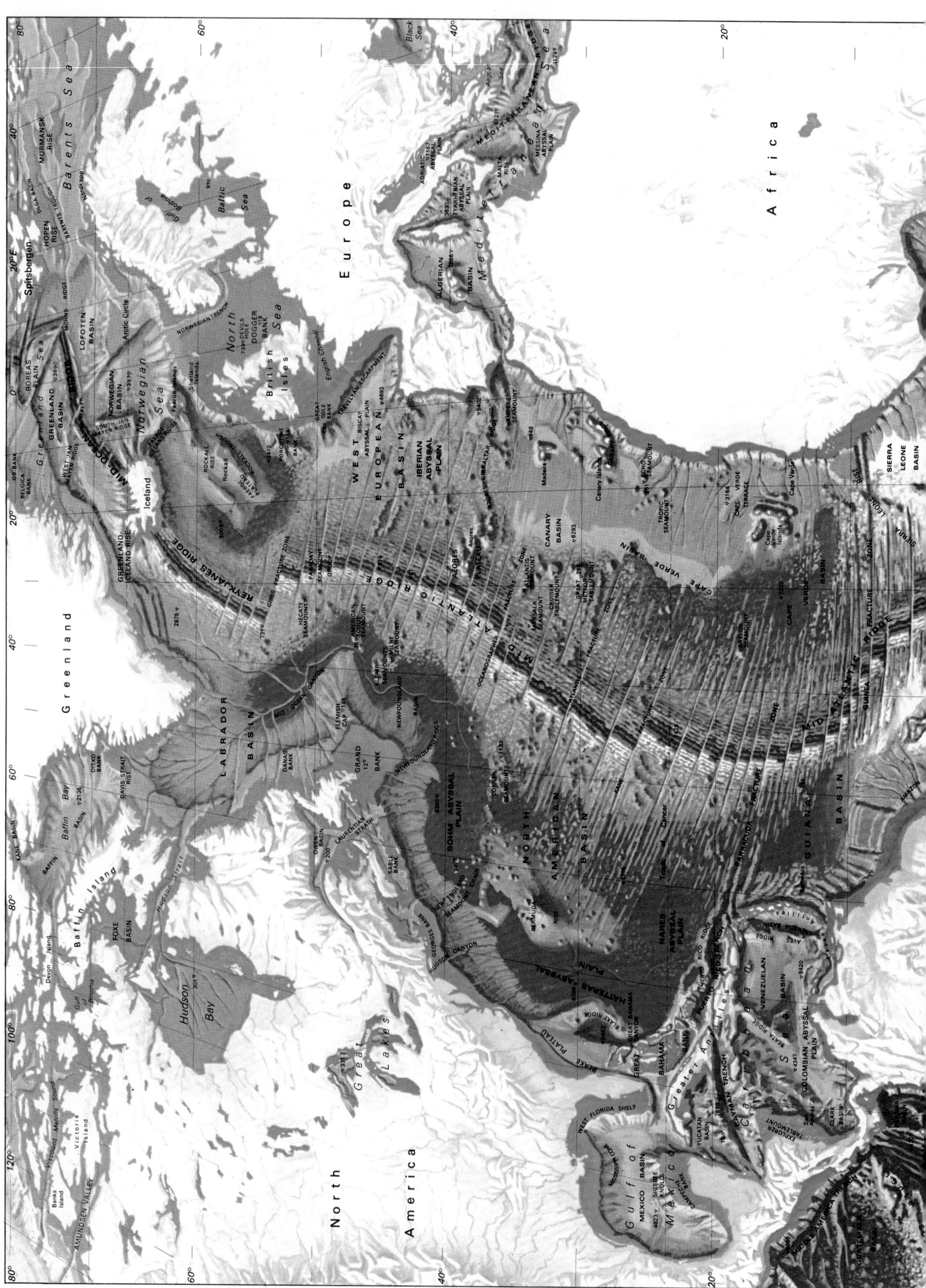

Europe
Africa
Greenland
North America
Barents Sea
Baltic Sea
North Sea
Norwegian Sea
Greenland Sea
Mediterranean Sea
Black Sea
British Isles
Iceland
Spitsbergen
Hudson Bay
Baffin Bay
Baffin Island
Great Lakes
Gulf of Mexico
Caribbean Sea
LABRADOR BASIN
REYKJANES RIDGE
MID-ATLANTIC RIDGE
WEST EUROPEAN BASIN
IBERIAN ABYSSAL PLAIN
CANARY BASIN
CAPE VERDE BASIN
NORTH AMERICAN BASIN
SOHM ABYSSAL PLAIN
HATTERAS ABYSSAL PLAIN
NARES ABYSSAL PLAIN
GUIANA BASIN
VENEZUELAN BASIN
COLOMBIAN ABYSSAL PLAIN
MEXICO BASIN
GRAND BANK
NEWFOUNDLAND BASIN
BERMUDA RISE
AZORES
Tropic of Cancer

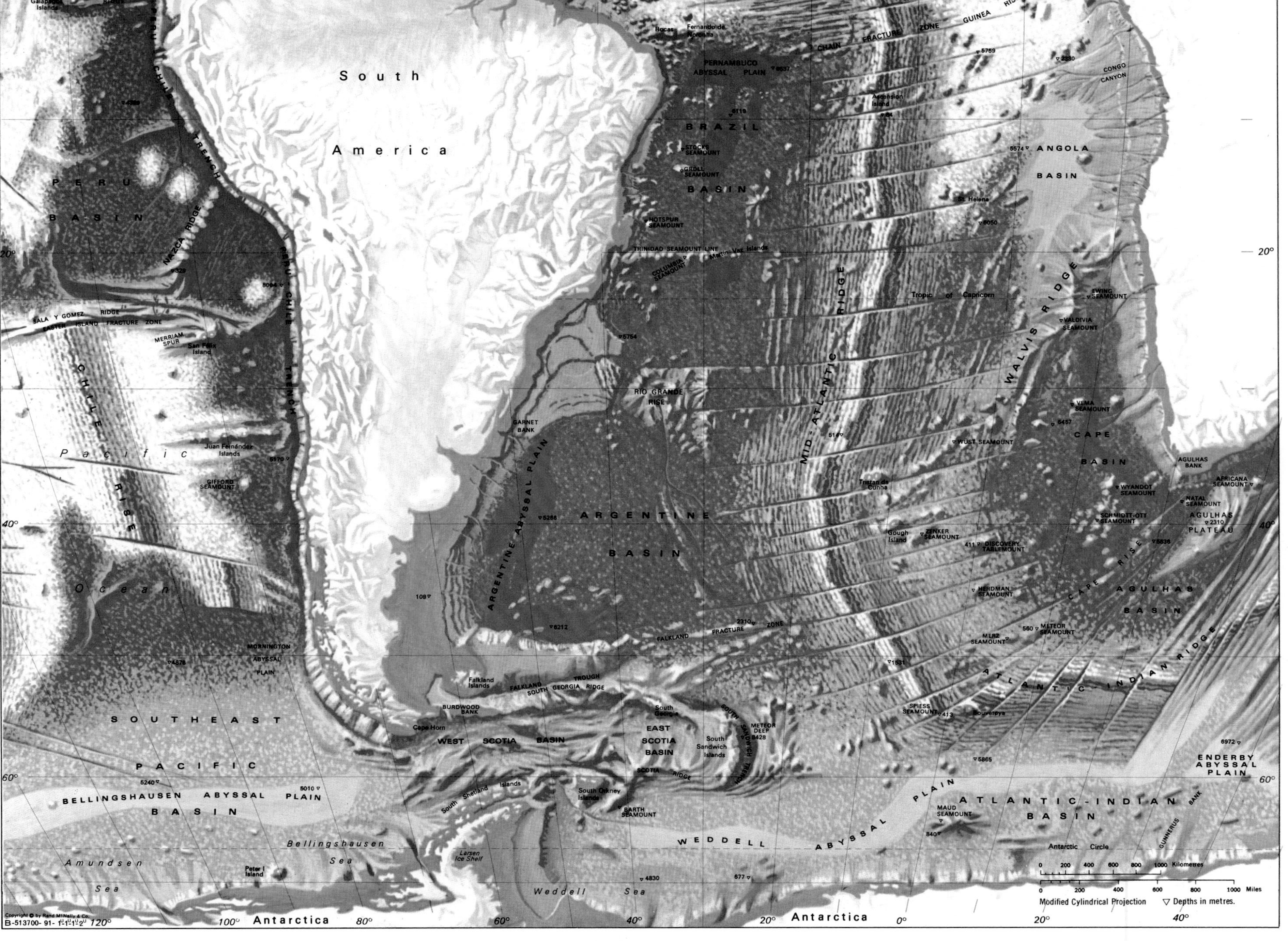
South America
Pacific Ocean
Antarctica
PERU BASIN
PERU-CHILE TRENCH
NAZCA RIDGE
CHILE RISE
BRAZIL BASIN
PERNAMBUCO ABYSSAL PLAIN
ANGOLA BASIN
CAPE BASIN
WALVIS RIDGE
MID-ATLANTIC RIDGE
RIO GRANDE RISE
ARGENTINE BASIN
ARGENTINE ABYSSAL PLAIN
AGULHAS BASIN
AGULHAS PLATEAU
ATLANTIC-INDIAN RIDGE
ATLANTIC-INDIAN BASIN
ENDERBY ABYSSAL PLAIN
SOUTHEAST PACIFIC BASIN
BELLINGSHAUSEN ABYSSAL PLAIN
WEST SCOTIA BASIN
EAST SCOTIA BASIN
WEDDELL ABYSSAL PLAIN
Weddell Sea
Bellingshausen Sea
Amundsen Sea
Tropic of Capricorn
Antarctic Circle
Modified Cylindrical Projection
▽ Depths in metres.
Copyright © by Rand McNally & Co.

The Pacific Ocean

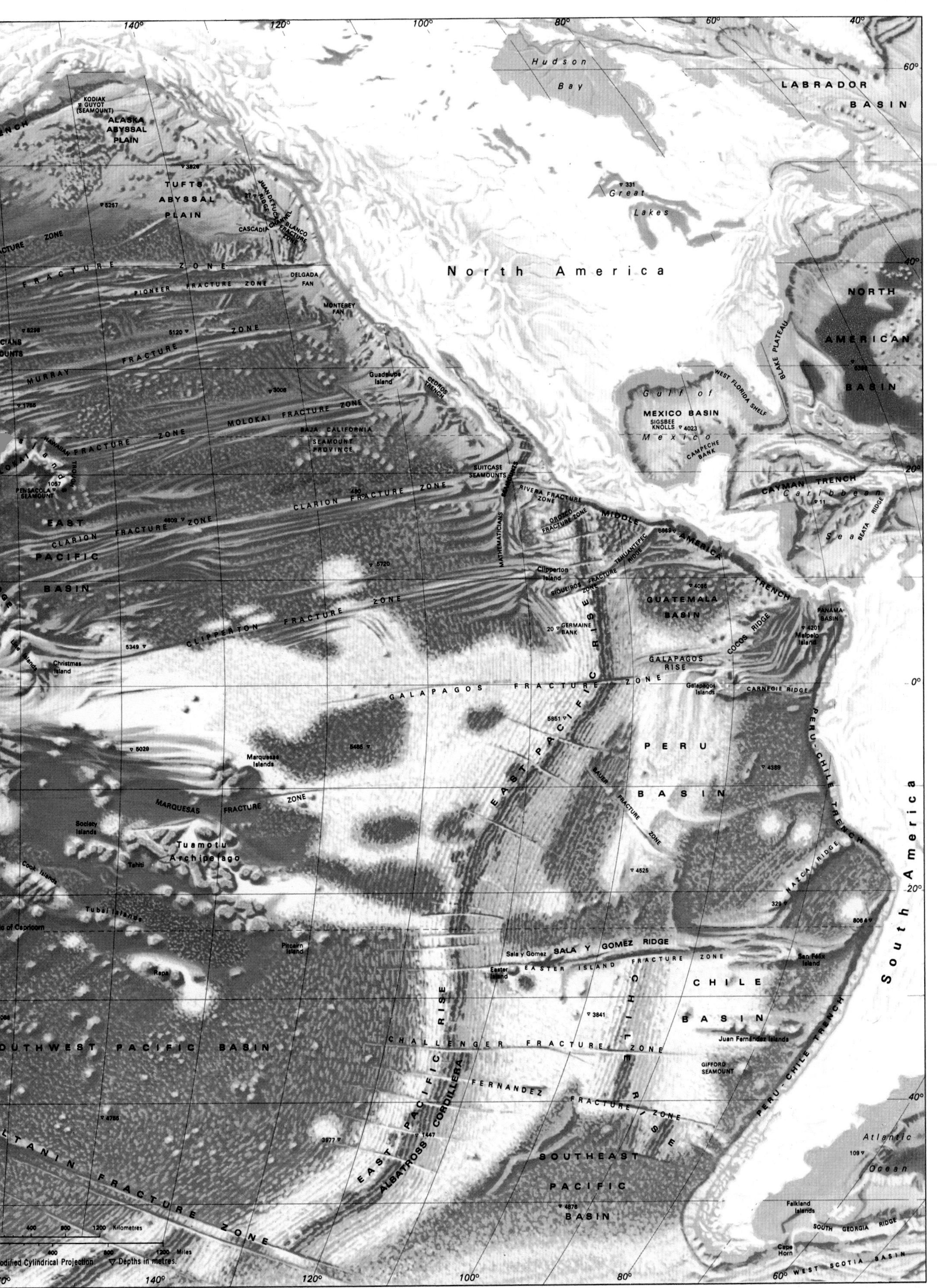
140°
120°
100°
80°
60°
40°
60°
40°
20°
0°
20°
40°
Hudson Bay
LABRADOR BASIN
KODIAK GUYOT (SEAMOUNT)
ALASKA ABYSSAL PLAIN
TUFTS ABYSSAL PLAIN
JUAN DE FUCA RIDGE
CASCADIA CHANNEL
BLANCO FRACTURE ZONE
Great Lakes
North America
FRACTURE ZONE
PIONEER FRACTURE ZONE
DELGADA FAN
MONTEREY FAN
NORTH AMERICAN BASIN
BLAKE PLATEAU
MURRAY FRACTURE ZONE
Guadalupe Island
CEDROS TRENCH
WEST FLORIDA SHELF
Gulf of Mexico
MEXICO BASIN
SIGSBEE KNOLLS
CAMPECHE BANK
MOLOKAI FRACTURE ZONE
BAJA CALIFORNIA SEAMOUNT PROVINCE
PENSACOLA SEAMOUNT
SUITCASE SEAMOUNTS
CLARION FRACTURE ZONE
RIVERA FRACTURE ZONE
OROZCO FRACTURE ZONE
MIDDLE AMERICA TRENCH
CAYMAN TRENCH
Caribbean Sea
BEATA RIDGE
EAST PACIFIC BASIN
MATHEMATICIANS
TEHUANTEPEC RIDGE
Clipperton Island
SIQUEIROS FRACTURE ZONE
GUATEMALA BASIN
PANAMA BASIN
CLIPPERTON FRACTURE ZONE
GERMAINE BANK
COCOS RIDGE
Malpelo Island
Christmas Island
GALAPAGOS RISE
GALAPAGOS FRACTURE ZONE
Galapagos Islands
CARNEGIE RIDGE
EAST PACIFIC RISE
PERU BASIN
PERU-CHILE TRENCH
Marquesas Islands
MARQUESAS FRACTURE ZONE
BAUER FRACTURE ZONE
Society Islands
Tuamotu Archipelago
Tahiti
Cook Islands
Tubai Islands
NAZCA RIDGE
South America
Pitcairn Island
Sala y Gomez
SALA Y GOMEZ RIDGE
San Félix Island
Easter Island
EASTER ISLAND FRACTURE ZONE
Rapa
CHILE BASIN
CHILE RISE
SOUTHWEST PACIFIC BASIN
CHALLENGER FRACTURE ZONE
Juan Fernández Islands
GIFFORD SEAMOUNT
FERNANDEZ FRACTURE ZONE
ALBATROSS CORDILLERA
ELTANIN FRACTURE ZONE
SOUTHEAST PACIFIC BASIN
Atlantic Ocean
Falkland Islands
SOUTH GEORGIA RIDGE
Cape Horn
WEST SCOTIA BASIN
400 800 1200 Kilometres
400 800 1200 Miles
Modified Cylindrical Projection
Depths in metres.

The Indian Ocean and the polar seas

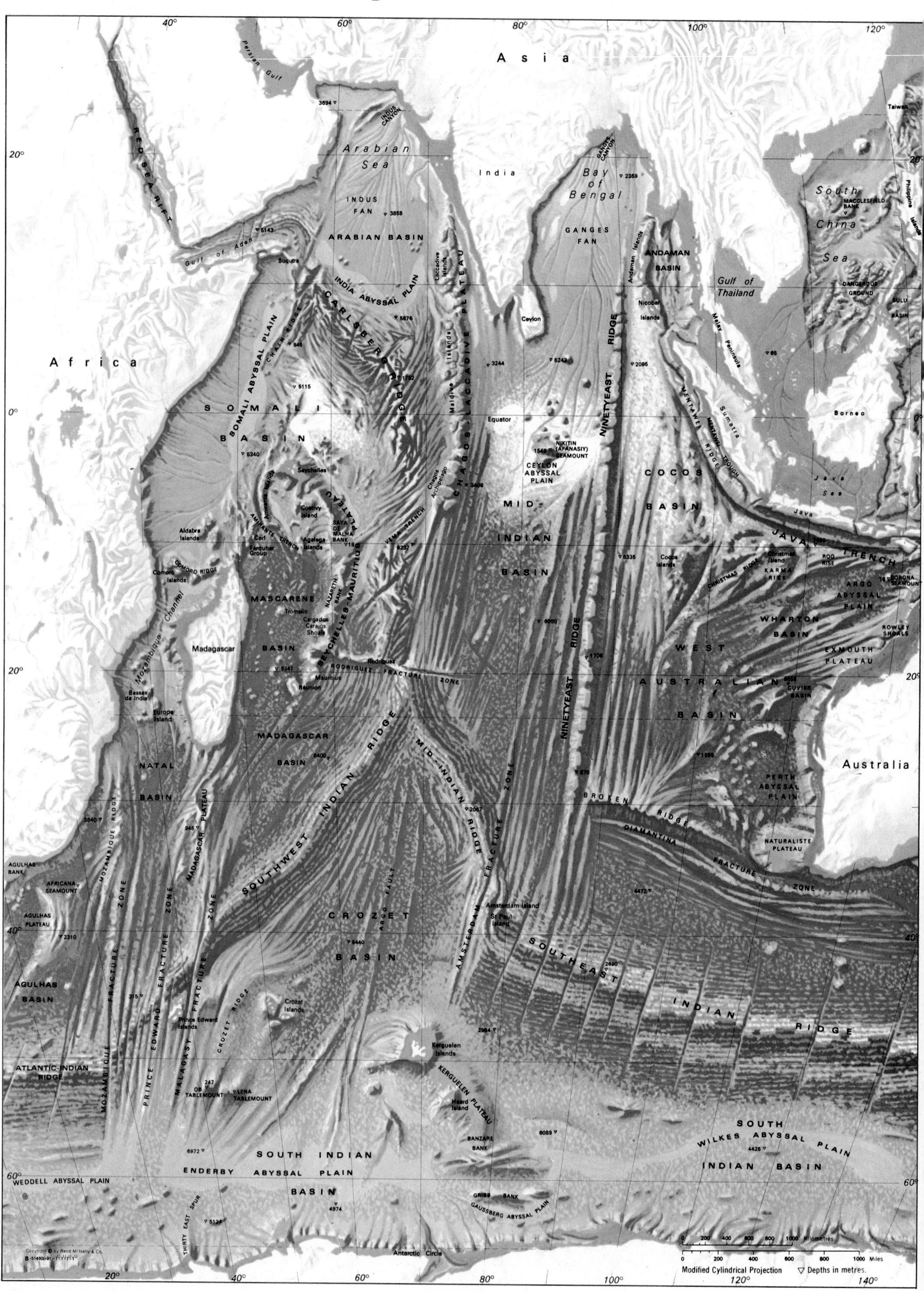

Asia
Africa
India
Arabian Sea
Bay of Bengal
South China Sea
Gulf of Thailand
Persian Gulf
Gulf of Aden
RED SEA RIFT
INDUS FAN
ARABIAN BASIN
GANGES FAN
ANDAMAN BASIN
CARLSBERG RIDGE
SOMALI BASIN
SOMALI ABYSSAL PLAIN
CHAGOS-LACCADIVE PLATEAU
NINETYEAST RIDGE
CEYLON ABYSSAL PLAIN
MID-INDIAN BASIN
COCOS BASIN
JAVA TRENCH
MASCARENE BASIN
MADAGASCAR BASIN
NATAL BASIN
WEST AUSTRALIAN BASIN
WHARTON BASIN
PERTH ABYSSAL PLAIN
BROKEN RIDGE
DIAMANTINA FRACTURE ZONE
SOUTHWEST INDIAN RIDGE
MID-INDIAN RIDGE
SOUTHEAST INDIAN RIDGE
CROZET BASIN
KERGUELEN PLATEAU
AGULHAS BASIN
ATLANTIC-INDIAN RIDGE
SOUTH INDIAN BASIN
ENDERBY ABYSSAL PLAIN
WEDDELL ABYSSAL PLAIN
SOUTH INDIAN BASIN
WILKES ABYSSAL PLAIN
Madagascar
Australia
Antarctic Circle
Modified Cylindrical Projection
▽ Depths in metres.
Copyright © by Rand McNally & Co.

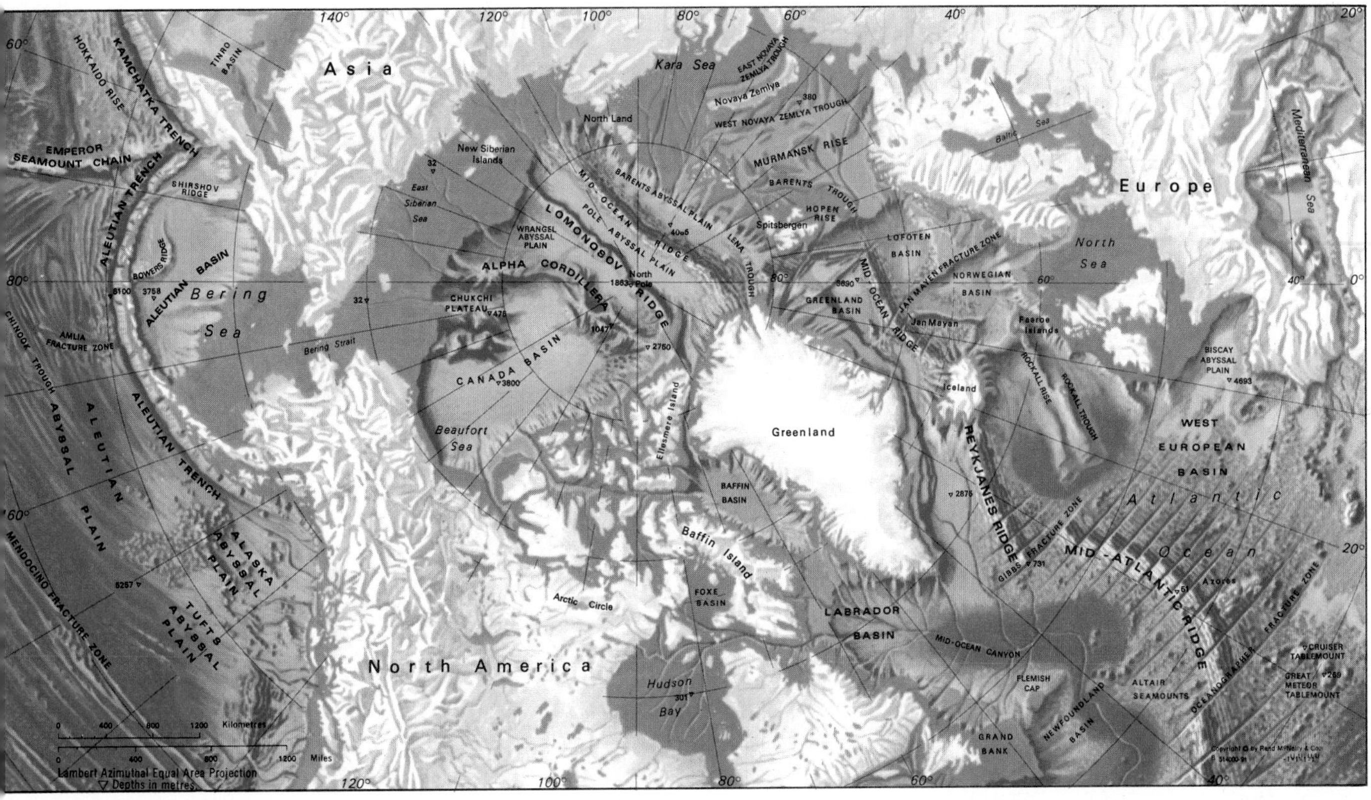

Asia
Kara Sea
EAST NOVAYA ZEMLYA TROUGH
Novaya Zemlya
WEST NOVAYA ZEMLYA TROUGH
North Land
New Siberian Islands
East Siberian Sea
KAMCHATKA TRENCH
HOKKAIDO RISE
TINRO BASIN
EMPEROR SEAMOUNT CHAIN
ALEUTIAN TRENCH
SHIRSHOV RIDGE
BOWERS RIDGE
ALEUTIAN BASIN
Bering Sea
AMLIA FRACTURE ZONE
CHINOOK TROUGH
ALEUTIAN ABYSSAL PLAIN
MENDOCINO FRACTURE ZONE
ALASKA ABYSSAL PLAIN
TUFTS ABYSSAL PLAIN
MURMANSK RISE
BARENTS ABYSSAL PLAIN
BARENTS TROUGH
HOPEN RISE
Spitsbergen
MID-OCEAN RIDGE
LOMONOSOV RIDGE
POLE ABYSSAL PLAIN
WRANGEL ABYSSAL PLAIN
ALPHA CORDILLERA
CHUKCHI PLATEAU
North Pole
LENA TROUGH
Bering Strait
CANADA BASIN
Beaufort Sea
Ellesmere Island
Greenland
LOFOTEN BASIN
JAN MAYEN FRACTURE ZONE
NORWEGIAN BASIN
GREENLAND BASIN
MID-OCEAN RIDGE
Jan Mayen
Iceland
Faeroe Islands
North Sea
Baltic Sea
Europe
Mediterranean Sea
BISCAY ABYSSAL PLAIN
ROCKALL RISE
ROCKALL TROUGH
REYKJANES RIDGE
WEST EUROPEAN BASIN
Atlantic Ocean
GIBBS FRACTURE ZONE
MID-ATLANTIC RIDGE
Azores
OCEANOGRAPHER FRACTURE ZONE
CRUISER TABLEMOUNT
GREAT METEOR TABLEMOUNT
ALTAIR SEAMOUNTS
BAFFIN BASIN
Baffin Island
FOXE BASIN
LABRADOR BASIN
MID-OCEAN CANYON
FLEMISH CAP
NEWFOUNDLAND BASIN
GRAND BANK
Arctic Circle
North America
Hudson Bay
Lambert Azimuthal Equal Area Projection
▽ Depths in metres

SOUTHWEST PACIFIC BASIN
Pacific Ocean
ELTANIN FRACTURE ZONE
PACIFIC-ANTARCTIC RIDGE
SOUTHEAST PACIFIC BASIN
BELLINGSHAUSEN ABYSSAL PLAIN
Bellingshausen Sea
Peter I Island
Amundsen Sea
Alexander Island
South America
Falkland Islands
FALKLAND TROUGH
SCOTIA RIDGE
WEST SCOTIA BASIN
EAST SCOTIA BASIN
South Shetland Islands
South Orkney Islands
South Georgia
BARTH SEAMOUNT
South Sandwich Islands
SOUTH SANDWICH TRENCH
ARGENTINE BASIN
Atlantic Ocean
FALKLAND FRACTURE ZONE
MID-ATLANTIC RIDGE
Tristan da Cunha
Gough Island
Weddell Sea
Berkner Island
WEDDELL ABYSSAL PLAIN
Chatham Island
CHATHAM RISE
Bounty Islands
Scott Island
PENNELL BANK
Ross Sea
South Pole
MAUD SEAMOUNT
SPEISS SEAMOUNT
DISCOVERY TABLEMOUNT
MERZ SEAMOUNT
METEOR SEAMOUNT
CAPE BASIN
SCHMIDTT-OTT SEAMOUNT
CAPE RISE
CAMPBELL PLATEAU
New Zealand
Campbell Island
Auckland Islands
BALLENY BASIN
Balleny Islands
EMERALD BASIN
MACQUARIE RIDGE
Macquarie Island
HJORT BASIN
Antarctica
ATLANTIC-INDIAN BASIN
Antarctic Circle
TASMAN BASIN
TASMAN RISE
Tasmania
Australia
SOUTHEAST INDIAN RIDGE
SOUTH INDIAN BASIN
WILKES ABYSSAL PLAIN
GAUSSBERG ABYSSAL PLAIN
GRIBB BANK
KERGUELEN PLATEAU
Heard Island
Kerguelen Islands
ENDERBY ABYSSAL PLAIN
LENA TABLEMOUNT
OB TABLEMOUNT
Crozet Islands
Prince Edward Islands
PRINCE EDWARD FRACTURE ZONE
MALAGASY FRACTURE ZONE
MOZAMBIQUE FRACTURE ZONE
AGULHAS PLATEAU
AFRICANA SEAMOUNT
Indian Ocean
Africa
Lambert Azimuthal Equal Area Projection
▽ Depths in metres

Oceanographic exploration

The topography of the ocean floor is hardly better known than the farside of the Moon. Much remains to be discovered about the oceanic two-thirds of our planet and oceanographic research is not just a matter of scientific curiosity—man is beginning to depend increasingly on the largely untapped food, mineral, and energy resources of the sea.

Early observations

The earliest scientific observations of the sea were recorded by Aristotle (384–322 BC), who described 180 marine animal species. Little further progress was made until the age of discovery during the fifteenth and sixteenth centuries when knowledge of the seas, their currents, and geography was enlarged. Later, in 1670, Robert Boyle (1627–91) published his *Observations and Experiments on the Saltiness of the Sea* in which he correctly deduced that the salt is derived from weathering of the land. He introduced the silver nitrate test to measure the chloride content of seawater, a method still in use today.

The Italian count Luigi Marsigli (1658–1730), a contemporary of Boyle, deserves to be called the first oceanographer because he studied the whole realm of the sea, from its flora and fauna to its currents. He invented the propeller current meter and discovered the deep counter-current in the Bosporus, correctly attributing it to differences in salinity between the Black Sea and the Mediterranean. (The Black Sea receives more water from rivers than it loses through evaporation, hence the main surface current flows toward the Mediterranean.)

In the eighteenth century Benjamin Franklin (1706–90) published a chart of the Gulf Stream that was used by navigators to shorten the passage time of the mail packets between North America and England. James Cook (1728–79), during his famous Pacific voyages from 1768 to 1779, finally exploded the geographical myth of a great southern continent in the South Pacific.

At the very beginning of the nineteenth century Alexander von Humboldt (1769–1859) described the cold current that flows up the Andean coast to the Galapagos Islands. In 1835 Charles Darwin (1809–82) visited these islands during his round-the-world voyage on *HMS Beagle*. Darwin made many sea-related observations, including some on plankton (the microscopic life forms of the sea). He also proposed a theory about the origins of coral reefs which after more than a century of heated debate was finally proved correct by well-drilling on Eniwetok atoll in 1952. In the middle of the nineteenth century, Lieutenant Matthew Fontaine Maury (1806–73) of the US Navy published *Wind and Current Charts*, the first pilot charts, compiled from the data in ship's log books.

The *Challenger* expedition

The findings of the early scientists and the many unanswered questions posed induced the British government in 1872 to finance a circumnavigating expedition for which the Royal Navy provided a ship, *HMS Challenger*.

Challenger, under the scientific direction of Charles Wyville Thomson (1830–82), sailed 69,000 nautical miles between

CONNECTIONS

See also
238 Man under the se
230 The Atlantic Ocea
232 The Pacific Ocear
234 The Indian Ocean the polar seas
222 The sea and seaw
224 Ocean currents
226 Waves and tides
228 The sea bed
170 Global tectonics
1802 Radar and sonar

1 The natural history laboratory aboard *HMS Challenger* was fitted for the study of marine, bird, and island life. The first true oceanographic ship, *Challenger* was a converted man-of-war and this laboratory was installed on her gun deck and lit naturally by light from a gunport.

2 Dredging on the *Challenger* expedition was a slow tedious operation and was nicknamed drudging by the crew who failed to share the enthusiasm of the scientists. The dredge was streamed out at the end of a warp and was made to sink by a sliding weight.

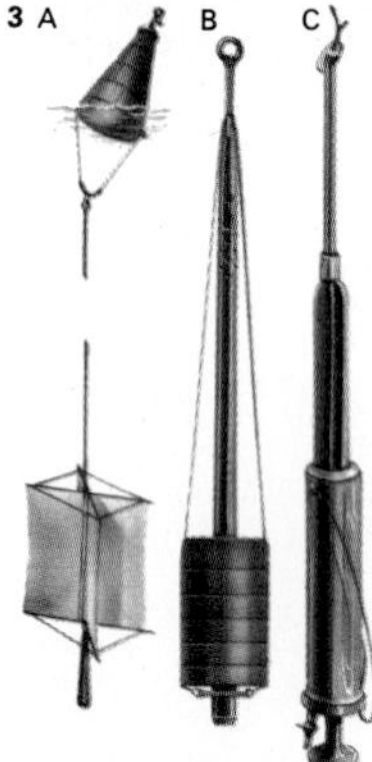
A
B
C

3 Instruments used on the *Challenger* included a current drag [A], which was lowered to a predetermined depth, the drift being shown at the surface by a buoy. The Baillie sounding machine [B] measured depth and collected samples of sediment. The slip water bottle [C] was used for sampling the bottom water for analysis.

4 This dredge was used on the *Challenger* for collecting biological specimens from the sea floor.

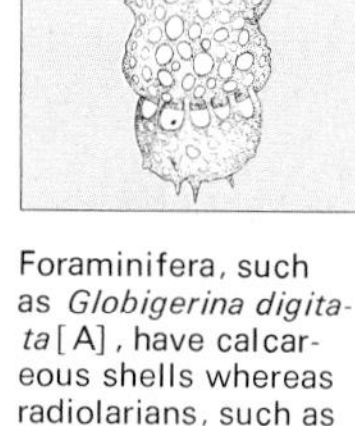

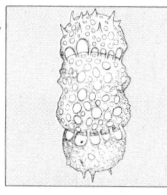

5 The first world map of marine sediments was provided by the *Challenger* expedition. Vast areas of the sea floor were found to consist of dead shells of single-celled animals (mainly foraminiferans and radiolarians) and algae (diatoms). Foraminifera, such as *Globigerina digitata* [A], have calcareous shells whereas radiolarians, such as *Panartus tetrathalamus* [B], have siliceous shells. The *Challenger* discovered 3,508 new species of radiolarians on the voyage.

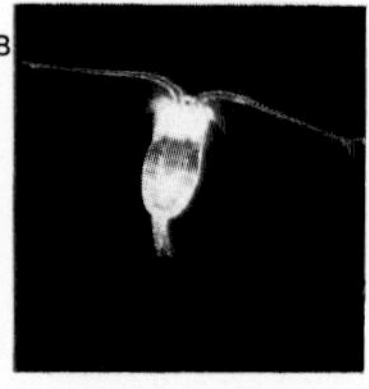

6 The Challenger expedition also studied the species and individuals forming plankton, such as the comb jelly [A], a ctenophore, and the copepod [B], a crustacean, both food for marine life.

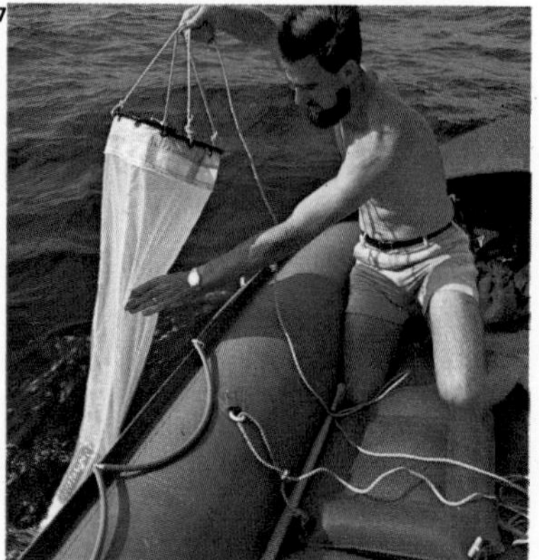

7 A plankton net is a cone of fine muslin kept open by a hoop and weighted by a sinker on its bridle. The small end is tied to the neck of a jar in which the plankton is collected for onboard examination.

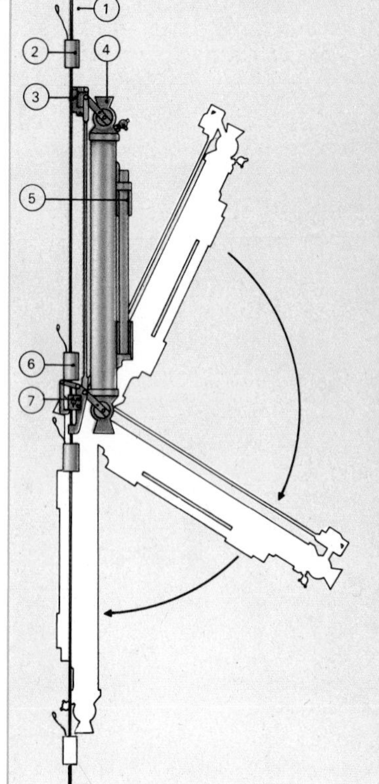
1
2
3
4
5
6
7

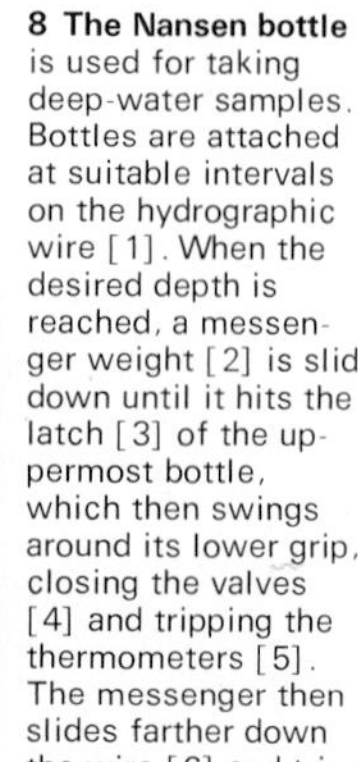

8 The Nansen bottle is used for taking deep-water samples. Bottles are attached at suitable intervals on the hydrographic wire [1]. When the desired depth is reached, a messenger weight [2] is slid down until it hits the latch [3] of the uppermost bottle, which then swings around its lower grip, closing the valves [4] and tripping the thermometers [5]. The messenger then slides farther down the wire [6] and trips the lever [7], releasing a new messenger to operate the next bottle down.

1872 and 1876. Among other observations, ocean depths and surface currents were measured, water samples taken for analysis [3], and sea life was dredged or trawled [2, 4[. The ship was also fitted with laboratories [1]. The *Challenger* expedition outlined the broad features of the sea floor and the nature of its sediments and discovered some 4,417 new species of animals and plants. It also showed that life existed in the extreme depths. Thus modern oceanography began.

Modern oceanography

Many expeditions were to follow using improved techniques and instruments. The Norwegian polar explorer Fridtjof Nansen (1861–1930) invented the deep-water sampling bottle [8] that bears his name. It can carry thermometers for determining the temperature at depth [9]. Plankton nets [7] were perfected and many ingenious instruments, such as the bathythermograph [10], were invented. A breakthrough came with the discovery of echo-sounding [13] just before World War I, but it was only perfected for use at great depths after World War II.

A new era in marine geosciences was introduced in 1961 by the Mohole project using the US drilling ship *CUSS I* (from the initials of the participating oil companies). The aim, to drill down to the Earth's mantle, was not achieved, but the accumulated experience was put to use in the US Deep Sea Drilling Project that started in 1968. This project confirmed the sea-floor spreading theory, which states that new sea floor is generated along both sides of the mid-oceanic ridges.

The emphasis in oceanography has changed since the early days when the main object was to collect samples of sediment, water, and marine life. While this is still part of the research, the aims are increasingly to find new food and physical resources (minerals and energy), to control pollution, and to conserve the biological resources of the sea. Oceanography has become a high-powered science involving satellite navigation, expensive ships [Key] with on-board computers and laboratories and backed up by sophisticated shore facilities for comprehensive study of the Earth's oceans.

KEY

Modern research vessels such as the *David Starr Jordan* of the Scripps Institution of Oceanography are designed for various scientific tasks. This ship is 254 ft(80m) long and carries four laboratories. She has two winches and two cranes for lowering scientific gear. A central well through the hull allows further use as a drilling platform. Propulsion is provided by two cycloidal propellers, which give total maneuverability in all directions. The ship has an automatic satellite navigation system that provides a digital display of both the latitude and longitude, essential for pinpointing sites.

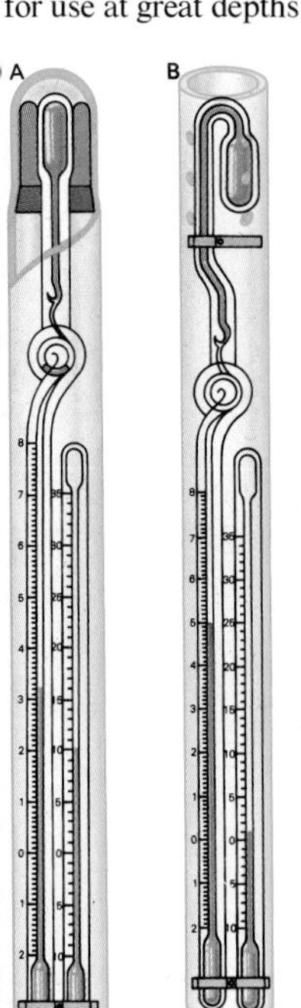
A
B

9 Deep-sea reversing thermometers (DSRT) are fixed on Nansen bottles. The protected thermometer [A] is insulated from pressure and records the temperature when the bottle is tripped. The unprotected thermometer [B] is similar but the hydrostatic pressure squeezes the reservoir so that the reading is a function of both temperature and depth. The small auxiliary thermometers indicate the temperature at the time of the reading and this must be introduced as a correction.

10 The bathythermograph simultaneously records temperature and depth down to 1,000 ft(300m), but it lacks the precision and the depth range of the DSRT.

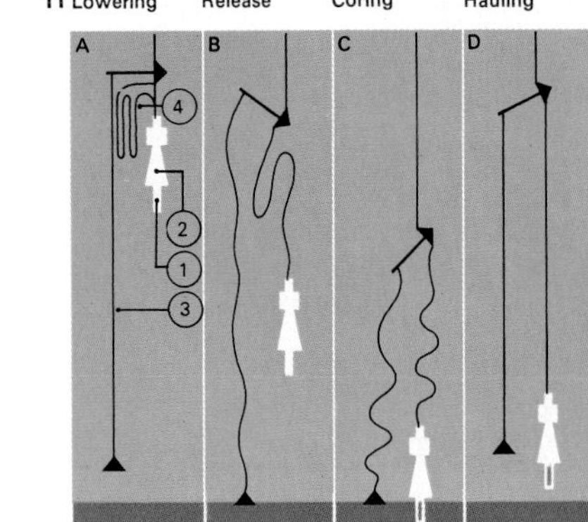
11 Lowering
Release
Coring
Hauling
A
B
C
D
4
2
1
3

11 The gravity corer, which takes samples of the sea floor sediments, consists of a metal tube [1] with a lead weight [2], and a tripping device [3]. The instrument is lowered in the sea [A] with the lower part of the wire coiled [4]. When the tripping device touches the bottom [B], the coil is released and the core barrel falls and punches into the sediments [C]. It is then brought back to the surface [D].

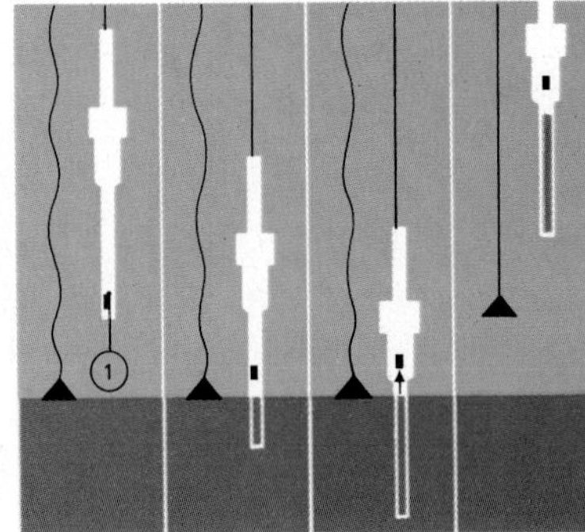
12 Free fall
Partial penetration
Full penetration
Hauling
1

12 The piston corer is an improvement on the gravity corer. Its penetration is increased by an internal piston [1] which sucks the corer deeper into the sediment. Piston cores can exceed 60 ft(18m) in length, whereas gravity cores seldom exceed 6 ft(1.8m).

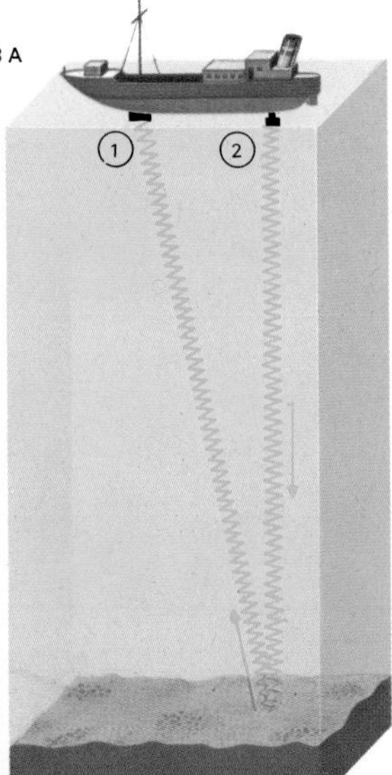
13 A
1
2

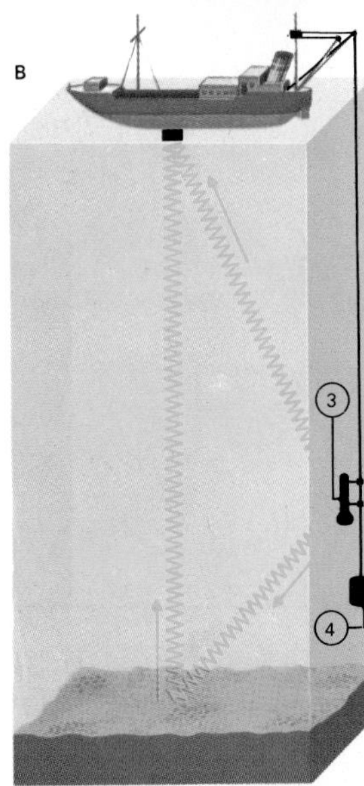
B
3
4

13 Echo-sounding is a method of measuring depth using the speed of sound in seawater and timing the lapse between the sending of a sound signal and the receiving of its echo bouncing off the bottom. In A both the receiver [1] and the transmitter [2] are on the ship, and the water depth is measured. In B the height of an instrument [4] above the bottom is found by mounting the sound source [3] near the instrument.

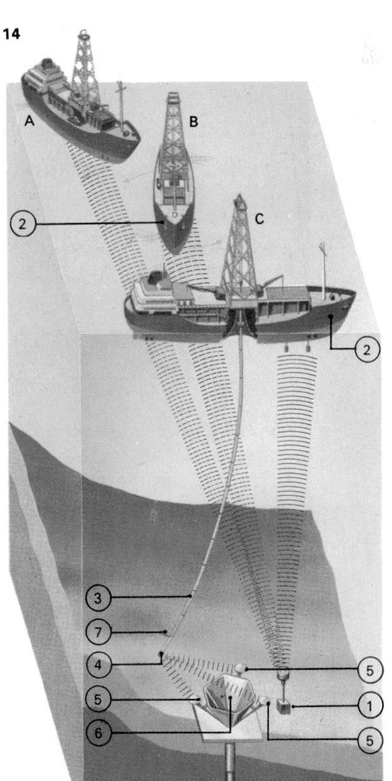
14
A
B
C
2
2
3
7
4
5
6
5
1
5

14 The US deep-sea drilling vessel *Glomar Challenger* maintains its station by dynamic positioning; the drift of the ship is computed relative to a sonar beacon [1] and is automatically corrected [A, B, C] by side thrusters [2] and the main propeller. After a worn drill bit at the end of the drill string [3] is renewed, the string is guided back to the hole by fitting the core barrel with a sonar device [4], which determines its position relative to three sonar reflectors [5] placed around the re-entry funnel [6]. The drill is then guided into the funnel by a sideways jet [7].

Man under the sea

For centuries man has striven to conquer the world beneath the sea. Even in the fourth century BC Alexander the Great (356–323 BC) was lowered into the sea in a large glass barrel, and he used divers in military operations such as the seige of Tyre (334 BC).

Early diving apparatus

The earliest reliable diving bells, which were open at the base and supplied with air by a hose from the surface, date from the sixteenth century. In 1663 one such bell was used to recover 53 cannons from the Swedish galleon *Vasa*. The first practical bell holding more than one diver was built by Edmond Halley (1656–1742) [1] in 1690, and bells are still used for harbor construction and salvage. The familiar "hard hat" diving suit [2] introduced by Augustus Siebe in 1837 is still used extensively in underwater engineering down to a depth of 200ft (61m), but it is the aqualung [3], developed by Jacques Cousteau and Emile Gagnan in 1943, that gives the greatest mobility.

The air supplied to divers, whether from a pump or from aqualung tanks, must be at the same pressure as the surrounding water so that the diver's body is not crushed. At a depth of less than 33ft (10m) water pressure equals that of the atmosphere—14.7lb/in^2 (1.03kg/cm^2); each 33ft from the surface increases pressure by one atmosphere. The result of breathing air at higher than normal pressure is that nitrogen (which forms 80 percent of air) becomes highly concentrated in the blood and tissue fluids. This dissolved nitrogen can turn back into a gas in the organs and blood stream if pressure is lowered too suddenly, leading to decompression sickness, usually called "the bends." If a diver rises from below 45ft (14m) too quickly, the nitrogen in his blood is not expelled in the normal way through his lungs, and the bubbles formed in his system prevent proper circulation of his blood. To avoid the bends, divers are raised in stages, stopping for a set period at predetermined depths as they ascend. If for any reason this has not been possible, the diver can be put into a decompression chamber [5]. This subjects him to the same pressure at which he was working under water and then slowly returns him to normal atmospheric pressure.

At depths greater than 130ft (40m) dissolved nitrogen can produce narcosis, a state in which a diver becomes so confused or euphoric that he may even remove his air supply. Narcosis can be avoided by using a mixture of oxygen and helium, but the mixture alters the diver's voice, making his speech almost unintelligible, and causes him to lose body heat rapidly—a hazard in cold water unless he wears a heated suit.

The deepest dive made at sea to date using Self-Contained Underwater Breathing Apparatus (SCUBA) [3] was 437ft (133m), accomplished in 1968. Deep dives have been simulated in compression chambers. In 1970 two British Royal Navy divers went to an equivalent of 1,500ft (457m) for ten hours. The "dive" and subsequent decompression took 15 days to complete.

Saturation diving

The disadvantages of the need for decompression after each dive are being overcome by saturation diving techniques. Twenty-four hours' exposure to nitrogen-free arti-

CONNECTIONS

See also

236 Oceanographic exploration

1 Edmond Halley's diving bell was 8ft (2.4m) high and 5ft (1.5m) wide at the base. It was wooden with glass portholes and was weighted with lead. Air was supplied from one of two lead-lined barrels. When one barrel was exhausted it was pulled back to the surface to be refilled.

2 The standard diving suit consists of a heavy metal helmet with breastplate, tough watertight diving dress, heavily weighted boots, and a flexible tube carrying air pumped from the surface.

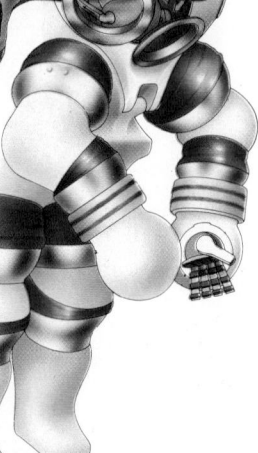

3 The aqualung (or SCUBA) diver wears a rubber suit. Compressed air carried in tanks is delivered at ambient water pressure (equal to that of the surrounding water) via a demand valve.

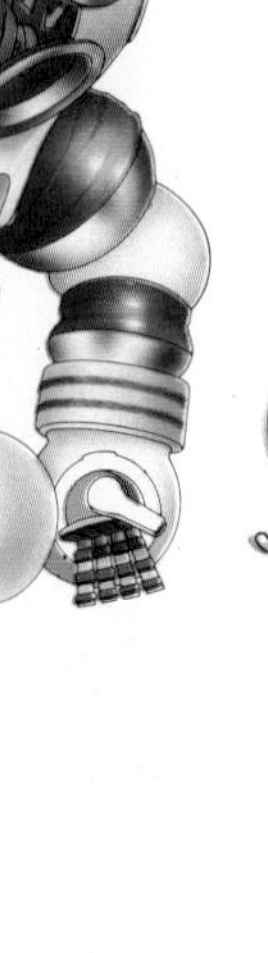

4 This atmospheric diving suit, dubbed "Jim," has a working depth to 1,000ft (300m). The articulated arms and legs permit only limited movement; tools are gripped by manipulators. The diver works at surface rather than ambient pressure, which avoids decompression. Soda lime filters remove exhaled CO_2, and oxygen is replenished from two cylinders.

5 A submerged decompression chamber can be used to treat an injured diver or one who is suffering from the bends. He can be admitted to the main chamber through an airlock from a portable pressure vessel [left], which has its own bottled air supply. The rate of decompression can then be carefully controlled.

ficial air (such as a mixture of oxygen and helium) under pressure causes a diver to become "saturated" at that pressure. He can remain under pressure for several weeks, greatly increasing his working capacity, after which only one decompression is necessary. Divers working under saturation conditions live in a large decompression chamber on deck. They then transfer under pressure into a smaller chamber from which they can swim out to work. On their return the transfer is reversed.

Underwater habitats such as Conshelf, Tektite [6], and Sealab, are variations on the saturation diving system. The living chamber lies on the sea floor, and divers enter and leave through an entry unit. These habitats are used mainly for scientific research in depths down to 328ft (100m).

Submersibles for industry and research

Cornelius van Drebble built one of the earliest submersibles in 1620. Powered by 12 oarsmen, it traveled 16ft (5m) below the surface of the Thames. Subsequent development of small submarines was largely directed toward military objectives. Only in the 1960s was much attention paid to the development of submersibles for scientific research [Key]. Since 1960 more than 50 submersibles have been built with depth ranges from 300 to 6,500ft (92–200m) and displacements of 5 to 100 tons.

The present generation of working submersibles, used in biological and geological research, are mostly in the 10 to 20 ton range and carry a pilot and one or two observers who enter the submersible on the mother ship. The interior is at atmospheric pressure throughout the dive.

Since 1973 submersibles have been used increasingly by the offshore oil and natural gas industry for pipeline inspection, repairs, and platform site surveys. The serious quest to probe great depths began in 1930 when Otis Barton and William Beebe descended to 1,400ft (425m) off Bermuda in a steel pressure sphere, or bathysphere, lowered on a cable from a ship. On January 23, 1960, Jacques Piccard and Donald Walsh descended 35,820ft (10,917m) to the bottom of the Challenger Deep in the Mariana Trench.

KEY

Submersibles are used in both research and engineering. They carry hydraulic arms for handling equipment, TV, and photographic cameras. The maximum operational depths of some research submersibles are shown in this diagram.

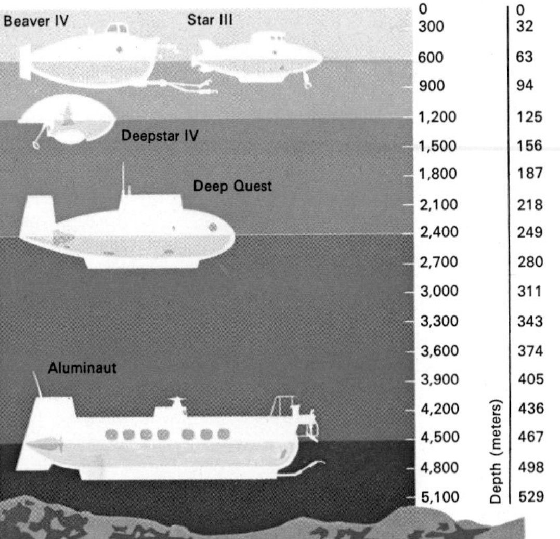

Beaver IV
Star III
Deepstar IV
Deep Quest
Aluminaut
Depth (meters)
0
300
600
900
1,200
1,500
1,800
2,100
2,400
2,700
3,000
3,300
3,600
3,900
4,200
4,500
4,800
5,100
Pressure (kg/cm²)
0
32
63
94
125
156
187
218
249
280
311
343
374
405
436
467
498
529

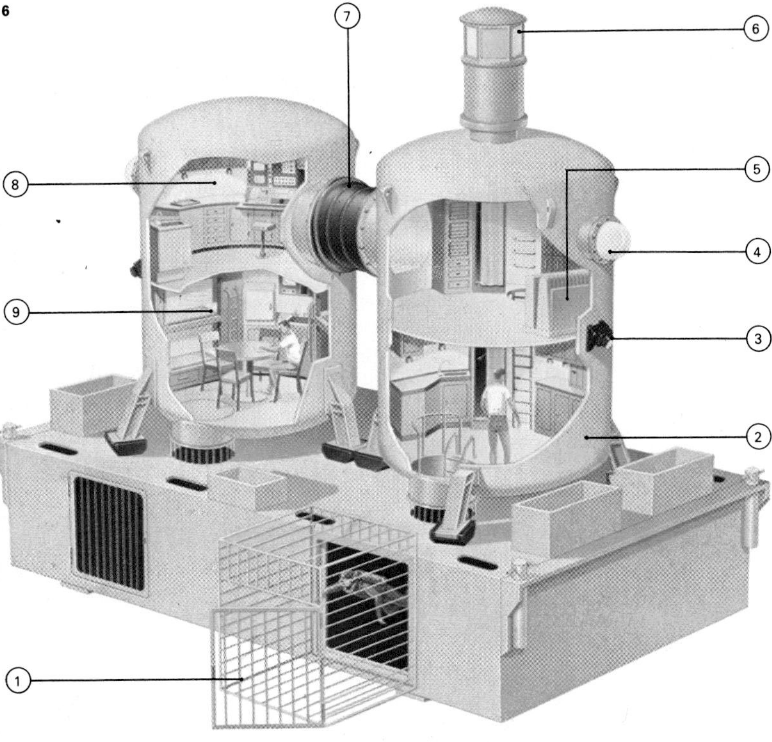

6
1
2
3
4
5
6
7
8
9

1 Shark cage protecting the entrance
2 Wet room
3 External light
4 Observation port
5 Air conditioning and purification equipment
6 Beacon light
7 Connecting passage
8 Control and communication room
9 Living quarters

6 Tektite was designed to study the reactions of scientists working underwater for long periods under saturated diving conditions. It has four chambers and accommodates four to five persons.

7 The submersible Pisces III is 19ft (5.8m) long, weighs 11 tons, and has a maximum operating depth of 3,600ft (1,100m). It is launched from an A-frame at the stern of the mother ship.

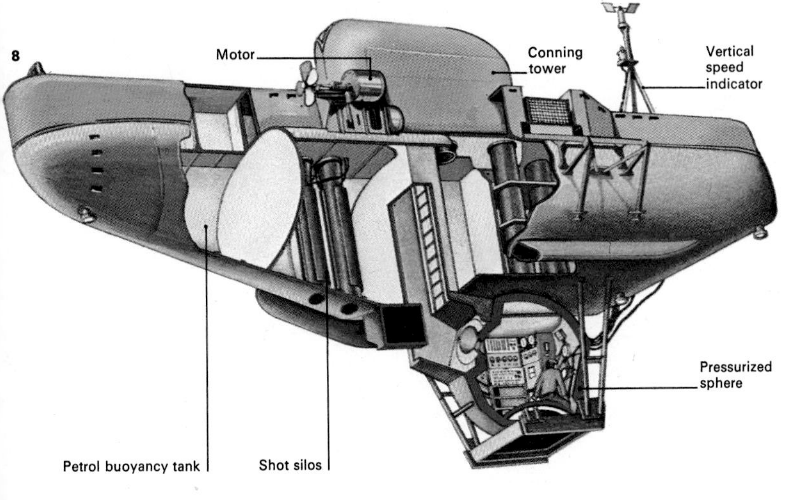

8
Motor
Conning tower
Vertical speed indicator
Pressurized sphere
Petrol buoyancy tank
Shot silos

8 The bathyscaphe FRNS 3 consists of a pressure sphere fitted with an entrance hatch and a conical Plexiglas window. Entry is through an airlock. The buoyancy tanks are in compartments built of light sheet metal and filled with gasoline for buoyancy. To descend, the remaining tanks and airlock are flooded. Electric motors provide lateral movement at depth and lead shot ballast is jettisoned for ascent.

9
Diver transferred to decompression chamber on board ship

9 The submersible VOL L-1 operates down to 1,200ft (365m). The pilot, diving supervisor, and observer travel in the forward compartment at atmospheric pressure while the two divers in the chamber are pressurized to the working depth.

Shapes and structures of crystals

Crystals are solids that have their atoms, ions, or molecules arranged in mathematically regular patterns. Because most solid matter is crystalline, this ordered construction gives such substances important properties that are not possessed by liquids or gases. Ordinary table salt and sugar are perhaps the most obviously crystalline substances in common use, but even substances like clay and steel are crystalline. It is often difficult to recognize a single crystal in nature because the basic regularity of its true form is usually hidden by the aggregation of several small crystals.

The science of crystallography began with the study of "well-formed" crystals. The Danish physician Nicolaus Steno (1638–86) discovered in 1669 that the angles between the faces of different quartz crystals were constant. In 1783 the Frenchman Jean-Baptiste Romé de l'Isle (1736–90) established that the angles between a crystal's faces were characteristic of the substance of which it is formed. Another Frenchman, the abbot René Just Häuy (1743–1822), explained the constancy of the angles between the faces by the stacking of tiny unit blocks known today as unit cells. He also described the seven basic crystalline systems [2–8] and the principles of their symmetry. What transformed crystallography from a side branch of mineralogy into an essential branch of physics was the discovery in 1912 of the internal structure of crystals through the phenomenon of X-ray diffraction [9].

Crystal lattices and crystalline systems

The rows of particles (atoms, ions, or molecules) in a crystal form a lattice. The simplest three-dimensional particulate structure that can re-create the crystal by repetition is the unit cell. The unit cell is represented by a geometrical solid, the corners of which are centered on particles. These corner particles must all be the same type; the other types (if they exist) are contained within the cell. For example, the unit cell of a crystal of halite (common salt or sodium chloride) can be considered as a cube with eight chlorine (C1) ions at the corners [1B]. This cube contains one sodium (Na) ion at its center. Each of the corner C1 ions, being also shared by seven other contiguous cubes, has only one-eighth of its volume within the unit cell under consideration, so that the unit cell has one Na ion and the equivalent of one C1 ion, which together equal the compound's formula, NaCl.

The external shape of well-developed crystals reflects precisely the symmetry of the unit cell. The unit cell of sodium chloride is a cube; the crystal shape of halite is therefore also a cube or another geometric shape closely related to the cubic form, such as an octahedron.

The elements of symmetry that can be found in crystals are axes, planes, and centers. A symmetry axis is such that an object (including a crystal) rotated around it by a given angle will produce a configuration identical to the original one. The number of such rotations to obtain a full 360° turn is the order of the axis. Crystals can have two-, three-, four-, and six-fold (order) axes. Planes of symmetry are like mirrors; a center of symmetry is such that any feature

CONNECTIONS

See also

1506 States of matter: solids
1468 Shape and symmetry
242 Earth's minerals
244 Gems and semiprecious stones
278 Mineral resources of the land
422 Bacteria and viruses

1 A

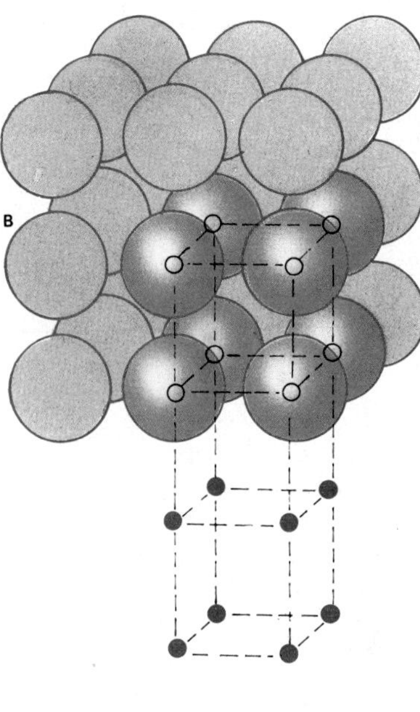

B

1 Crystals are formed by the regular stacking of particles, which can be atoms, ions (electrically charged atoms), or molecules (assemblages of atoms). The particles stand in rows that define many families of parallel lines that form the crystal lattices. The pictures show how the smallest possible volume, the unit cell, is defined as that which will reproduce the crystal by repetition. The lattice lines forming the edges of the unit cell define the directions of the reference axes of the crystal. They are such that they are often parallel to the symmetry axes (when these exist).

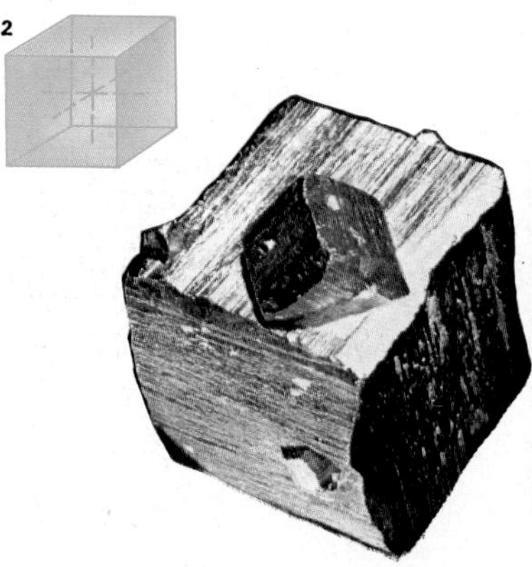

2 Pyrite (iron sulfide) crystallizes in the cubic system. The unit cell is such that all the axes are of equal length and the angles between them are 90°. Of the crystalline systems, only the cubic one does not polarize light passing through it. Cubic crystals sometimes exhibit the related octahedron and dodecahedron shapes. Garnet, halite, and fluorite also crystallize in the cubic system.

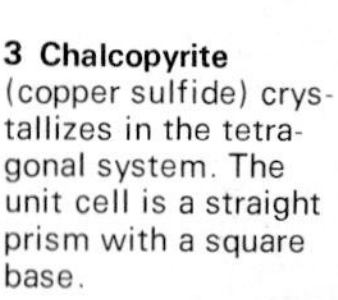

3 Chalcopyrite (copper sulfide) crystallizes in the tetragonal system. The unit cell is a straight prism with a square base.

4 Calcite (calcium carbonate) crystallizes in the trigonal system. The unit cell is like a cube that has been stretched along one diagonal.

5 Beryl (beryllium silicate) belongs to the hexagonal system. The basic unit is a hexagonal prism.

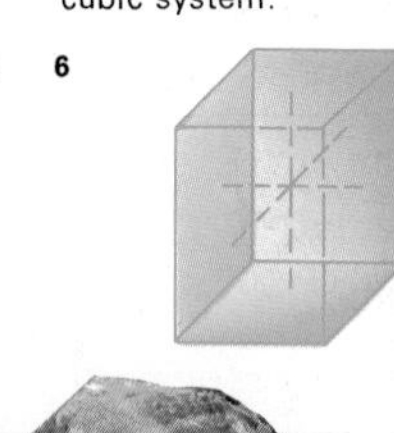

6 Topaz (fluorine and aluminum silicate) crystallizes in the orthorhombic system, which has a straight prism with a rectangular base as unit cell.

7 Augite, a calcium, iron, and magnesium silicate of the pyroxene group, crystallizes in the monoclinic system, in which the unit cell resembles a bottomless and lidless rectangular crate that has been pushed sideways. Opposite sides are parallel.

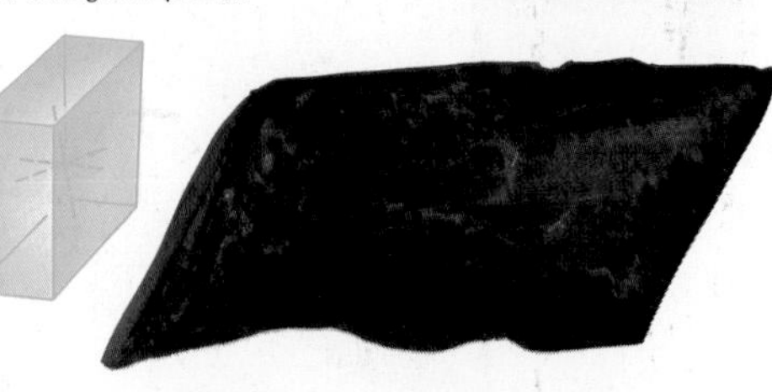

8 Chalcanthite, a form of the deep-blue, water-soluble substance copper sulfate, belongs to the triclinic system, which has a unit cell with no right angles.

is repeated upside down at an equal distance from the center and on the opposite side of it. Thirty-two combinations of symmetry elements are found in crystals; these 32 classes are grouped into seven systems [2–8].

X-raying crystal lattices

The shape and size of the unit cells, and the positions of the particles within them, are determined by using X rays. These rays have a very short wavelength that is about the same as the spacings between the lattice planes of crystals. They are consequently diffracted by these planes. Bragg's law relates the X-ray wavelength, the spacing between a given set of parallel lattice planes, and the angle of incidence [9B]. Thus by using X rays of known wavelength and measuring angles of incidence where diffraction occurs it is possible to calculate the distance between the lattice planes. Since atoms, ions, or molecules are assumed to touch each another, these distances can also yield the effective diameters of the particles.

X-ray diffraction methods can use either a single rotating crystal [9] or powdered crystals. The diffracted rays expose a photographic film or are measured by a scintillation counter.

The properties of crystals

The size and configuration of crystals in a metal affect its mechanical properties: stress behavior, fatigue, and resistance depend on the crystal structuring. Impurities, in concentrations of only a few parts per billion, account for the semiconducting properties of elements such as silicon and germanium; the magnetic properties of many materials are influenced by the internal disposition and shapes of crystals. Some crystals respond to vibrations by generating electricity (piezoelectricity), and this is the principle behind record-player needles. The converse is used in ultrasonic transducers and radio- or clock-tuning crystals. Transparent crystals of all systems except the cubic rotate the plane of polarization of polarized light [12]. Polaroid polarizing sheets or glasses contain small crystals.

KEY

Crystal shapes, when apparent, are related to the underlying lattice forming them, but the same lattice can produce different shapes. The dogtooth calcite shown here has the same lattice as the Iceland-spar calcite shown in illustration 4. Both types of crystals have the same internal symmetry.

9

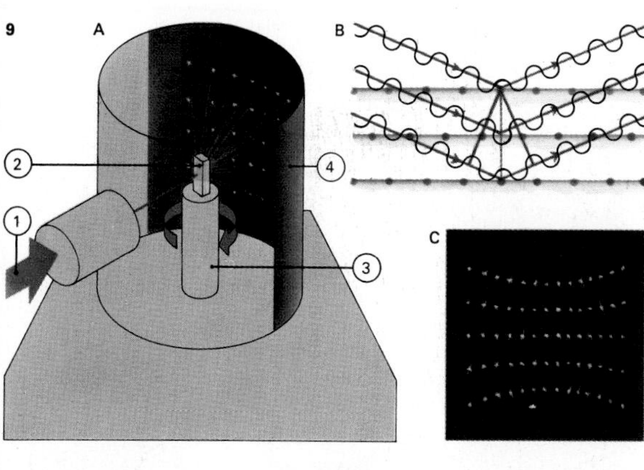
A
B
1
2
3
4

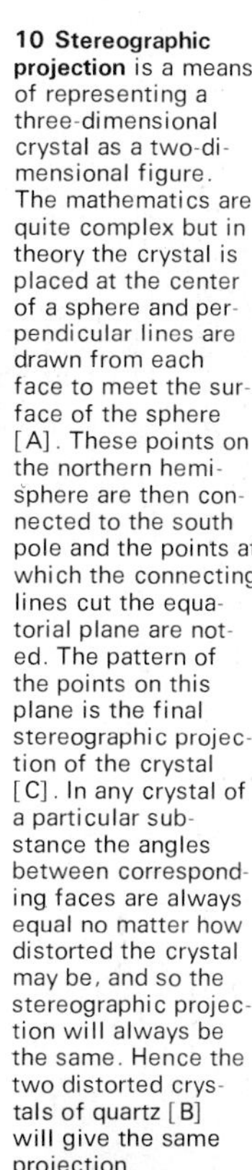
C

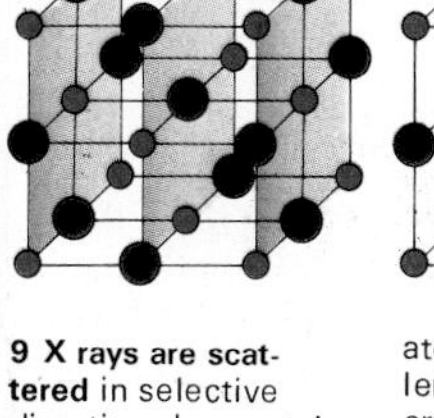
D

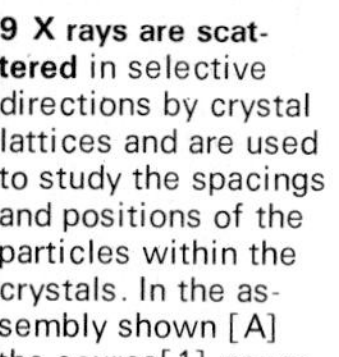

9 X rays are scattered in selective directions by crystal lattices and are used to study the spacings and positions of the particles within the crystals. In the assembly shown [A] the source [1] generates single wavelength X rays to hit a crystal [2] on a revolving axis [3]. Diffraction occurs, in accordance with Bragg's law, when X rays reflected by parallel lattice planes are in phase [B]. Diffracted beams expose rows of spots on a cylindrical photographic plate [4] or curved lines of spots on a flat plate [C]. Different potential reflecting planes [D] may occur within the same crystal.

10 Stereographic projection is a means of representing a three-dimensional crystal as a two-dimensional figure. The mathematics are quite complex but in theory the crystal is placed at the center of a sphere and perpendicular lines are drawn from each face to meet the surface of the sphere [A]. These points on the northern hemisphere are then connected to the south pole and the points at which the connecting lines cut the equatorial plane are noted. The pattern of the points on this plane is the final stereographic projection of the crystal [C]. In any crystal of a particular substance the angles between corresponding faces are always equal no matter how distorted the crystal may be, and so the stereographic projection will always be the same. Hence the two distorted crystals of quartz [B] will give the same projection.

10

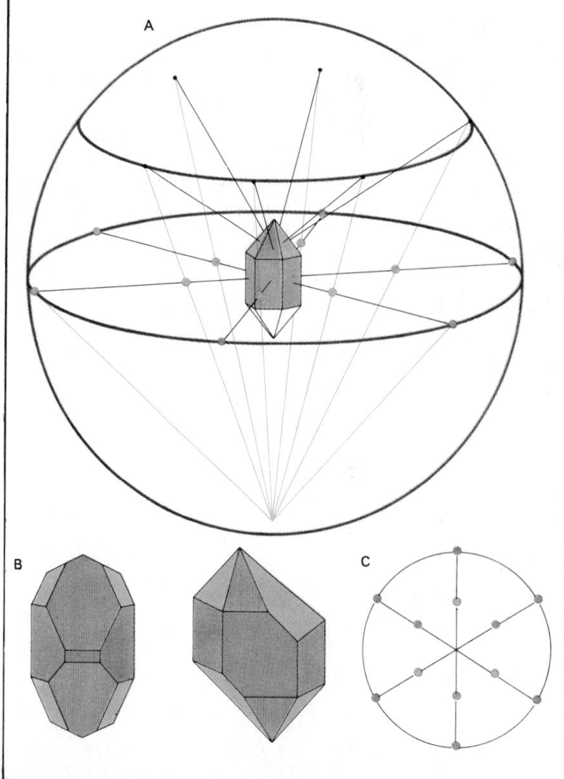
A
B
C

11

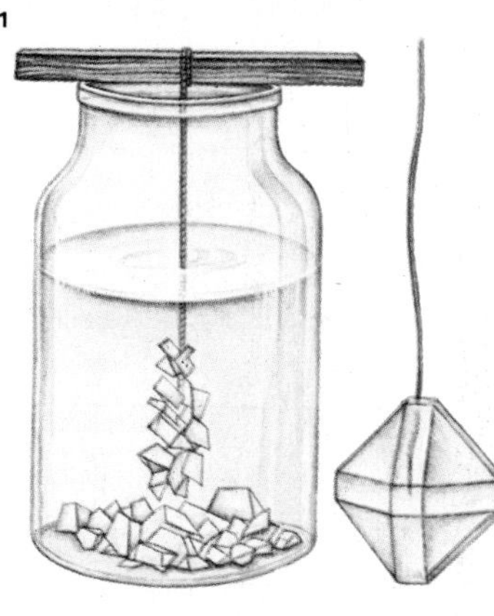

11 Crystals grow by precipitation out of a solution or a cooling melt. The atoms or ions coalesce into tiny "seeds" around which further particles build up the lattice layers. If alum powder is dissolved in hot water with a drop or two of sulfuric acid and placed in a jar as shown, alum crystals will grow as the solution cools. Slower cooling gives larger crystals. A similar experiment can be done by melting and then cooling powdered sulfur to grow crystals.

12

12 The colors of mineral crystals in a thin section of rock viewed through a polarizing microscope can help to identify the constituent minerals. Polarized light (light vibrating in one plane) passing through the microscope and through the thin section is distorted by the internal structure of the crystals and these distortions give rise to the colors observed. In this example, the yellow crystals are pyroxine while the small grey ones are feldspar.

Earth's minerals

A rock is generally not a homogeneous mass of material with a constant chemical composition throughout its bulk. Most rocks when examined closely are seen to be made of many components, each different from the others and usually forming discrete crystals. These are the minerals.

The economic minerals such as precious stones and the ores of useful metals are those that usually come to mind when minerals are mentioned, but these actually represent a small part of the mineral kingdom. The largest components are the rock-forming minerals, the building blocks from which the Earth's crust and all its rocks are constructed. These can be so attractive, with their great variety of crystal shapes and range of colors, that finding and collecting minerals has long been a popular hobby.

The constituents of the rocks

Minerals are defined as naturally occurring inorganic substances made up of one or more elements. Most have a constant chemical composition and are usually crystalline [1]. There are exceptions to this, however. Some minerals, such as opal [1E], are non-crystalline and in others the chemical composition varies. In olivines and pyroxenes, for example, the proportions of magnesium and iron atoms are not constant.

The quantities of the Earth's elements are reflected in their relative abundances in minerals. The element oxygen is most abundant, thus a large number of minerals contain oxygen. Hematite [7] is an oxide of iron. Silicon is the next most abundant, so silica, the oxide of silicon, plays a large part in the composition of minerals. Quartz [2, 3] can be pure silica and is an extremely common mineral, but the silica is more often found in combination with other elements to produce the numerous rock-forming minerals known as silicates. Olivine, for instance, is a common silicate mineral in igneous rocks where no pure quartz is present and consists of silica combined with varying amounts of iron and magnesium. Other groups of minerals found are compounds of sulfur such as anhydrite, gypsum [13] and galena [9] and carbonates such as calcite and malachite [10, 12]. Occasionally, as with native copper and gold [8], a mineral has only one element.

Many minerals crystallize from the molten state. The overall composition of magma, the molten material from which igneous rocks are formed, is fairly constant but when it starts to solidify the minerals that crystallize out vary greatly from place to place. The resulting rock has a character and composition very different from those of another rock formed elsewhere from the same magma.

The formation of minerals

Olivines have a high melting point so they tend to crystallize first from a cooling magma. Once crystallized they may sink to the bottom of the magma chamber and leave the rest of the liquid deficient in iron and magnesium. Other minerals, such as feldspar [3, 14B], in which sodium, calcium, and aluminum combine with what silica is left then crystallize out, leaving a cooling magma with yet another composition that solidifies into even more minerals. Some minerals are formed in sedimentary envi-

CONNECTIONS

Read first
240 Shapes and structure of crystals

See also
244 Gems and semiprecious stones
246 The rock cycle and igneous rocks
248 Sedimentary and metamorphic rocks
278 Mineral resources of the land
280 Mineral resources of the sea

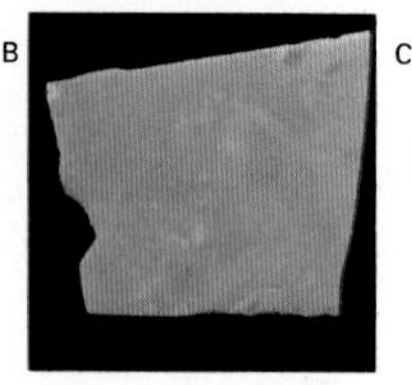
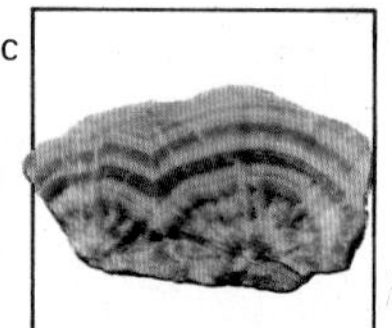

1 A crystal is a solid in which the molecules, atoms, or ions are arranged along regular and repetitive lattices, its external shape reflecting its internal symmetry. Not all crystals are minerals – sugar [A] is a crystalline organic substance. Opal [B] is an "amorphous" mineral without a crystalline internal structure. Calcite [C] (calcium carbonate), like most minerals, is crystalline.

2 Where a mineral such as quartz grows unimpeded it shows its typical "automorphic" shape, with plane faces reflecting the internal lattice structure. Quartz crystallizes in the trigonal system.

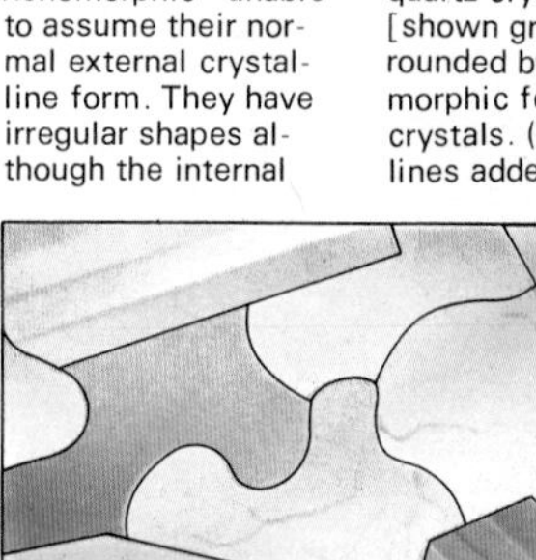

3 The last minerals to crystallize in a rock are crowded by the others and are xenomorphic – unable to assume their normal external crystalline form. They have irregular shapes although the internal crystalline lattice is retained. This section of granite contains xenomorphic quartz crystals [shown grey] surrounded by automorphic feldspar crystals. (Black outlines added.)

Fluorite
Quartz
Fluorite
Quartz

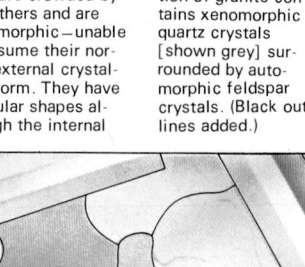

4 Pseudomorphism is the replacement of one mineral with an external crystal shape by another that is in every way identical in shape and volume, but not in internal crystalline lattice. The quartz shown is forming a pseudomorph of a fluorite crystal that was dissolved. The quartz would normally form a six-sided prism but instead has filled the octahedral shape of the fluorite crystal.

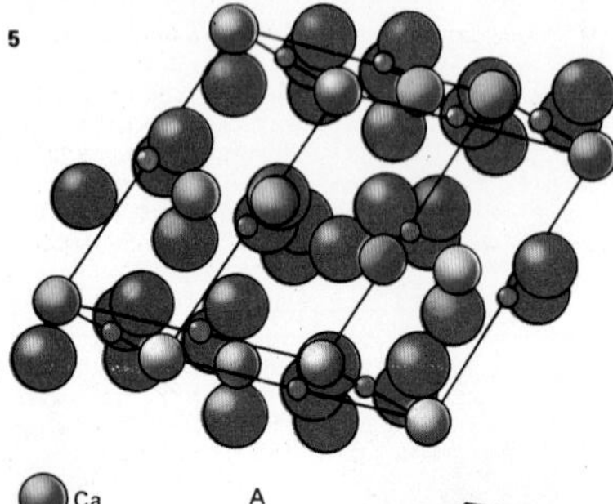

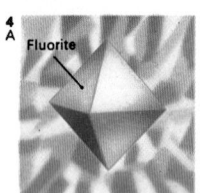

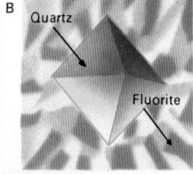

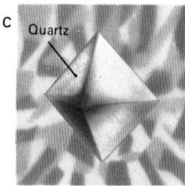

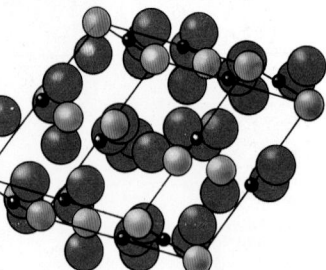

Ca
O
C
A
Na
O
N
B

5 Minerals of different chemical composition may possess identical lattice structures and will have similarly shaped crystal faces under normal circumstances. This is called isomorphism and is shown for calcite (calcium carbonate) [A] and sodaniter (sodium nitrate) [B] crystals. Because of a near similarity in size, the ions of isomorphic minerals can readily substitute for each other in the structure of a crystal if they are also chemically similar.

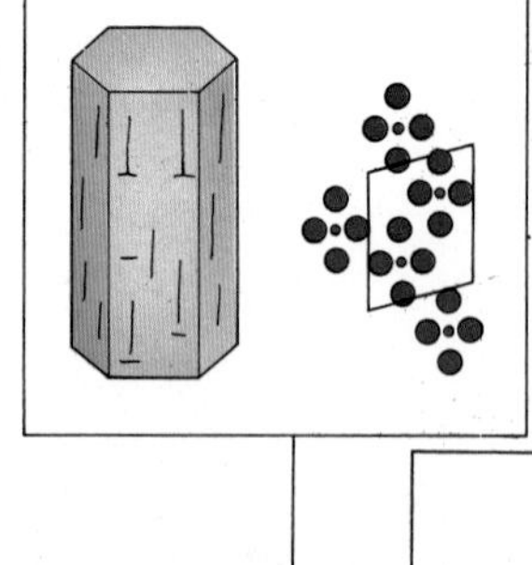
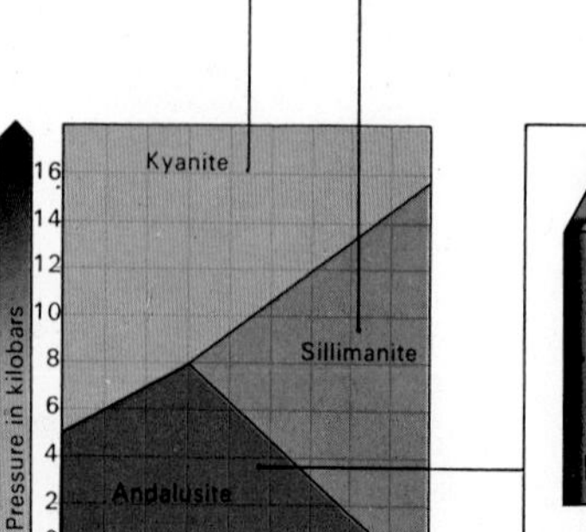

Kyanite
Sillimanite
Andalusite
Pressure in kilobars
16
14
12
10
8
6
4
2
0
200
400
600
800
Temperature °C

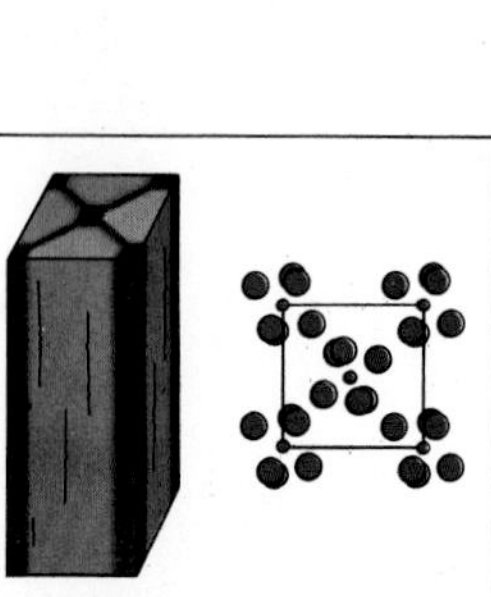

Oxygen
Aluminium

6 Compounds that can assume more than one crystalline structure are said to be polymorphous and they form different kinds of minerals. The type of crystal lattice in which the compound will crystallize is determined by the pressure and temperature that the compound experiences at the time of formation. Kyanite, sillimanite, and andalusite are three quite different crystal types and minerals of a single silicate compound that is common in metamorphic rocks.

ronments. When seawater evaporates in restricted basins the salts dissolved in it are crystallized out and form sedimentary rocks consisting of minerals such as halite (sodium chloride) and gypsum (hydrated calcium sulfate).

Other minerals form under metamorphic conditions where the minerals of rocks already formed are altered by heat or pressure to produce new minerals. Kyanite (an aluminum silicate) is found in schists formed under great pressure, while andalusite (which has the same chemical composition) is formed when rocks are altered under moderate heat and low pressure [6].

Related to the metamorphic minerals are those formed by metasomatism—the movement of hot fluids from igneous bodies through rocks already present. Quartz is often formed in this way [2], as well as by the more usual process of direct crystallization from a molten magma [3].

Mineral identification

There are many ways in which minerals can be recognized and identified. The crystal shape is the best clue, but it is rarely well-defined because the minerals usually suffer effects of weather, or lack definite shapes, having been formed too close to other growing crystals [3]. Akin to this is the way a mineral breaks, the cleavage planes being related to the crystal lattice.

The hardness of a mineral is significant in identification and can be determined by the mineralogist. He finds out whether the mineral can be scratched by a number of different substances whose hardnesses are known. The color is not usually definitive because impurities almost invariably creep into the mineral as it formed and discolor it. But when a mineral is scratched against a white surface it leaves a streak of color that is usually distinctive. The luster—the way in which the light is reflected from the surface—is different in different minerals. Quartz has a glassy luster while mica [14] can be pearly or metallic. These diagnostic features are used to make tentative identifications. It is only when the specimen is back in the laboratory that its chemical composition can be investigated.

KEY

An open-pit copper mine in Montana produces ore in the form of the sulfide minerals of copper. Where an exploitable mineral occurs near the surface it can be extracted in this way. Once the overburden of soil and rock is removed the exposed ore is blasted loose or, if soft enough, scooped up by machines with enormous buckets. Minerals such as bauxite, iron, and gypsum are mined in this fashion.

7 Mineral identification seldom needs the complexities of a laboratory and is in fact an easy and fascinating hobby. Hematite, an iron ore, is identified by its color, hardness, and density. Rubbed against a piece of unglazed china, it leaves a dark red streak. It scratches glass but is not scratched by a knife. It is heavy. In further tests, powdered and heated in a blue (reducing) flame it becomes magnetite and will be picked up by a magnet after cooling. Heated in concentrated hydrochloric acid it will dissolve and color the acid rust. Cut into thin sections in laboratory tests it will be shown to be black or red in transmitted light, but bright and metallic when exposed to reflected light.

8 Gold—like silver, copper and sulfur—is a naturally occurring native element found in igneous formations but at such low concentrations that it can hardly be said to be an ore.

9 Galena is lead sulfide; sulfides are formed by the combination of one or more metals with sulfur and provide many commercially valuable ores. Galena is widely used in electronics.

10 Oxygen combined with one or more metals forms the oxide minerals. Cassiterite (SnO_2), a reddish-brown mineral with a distinctive, pyramid-ended structure, is tin oxide.

11 Rock salt, or halite, is sodium chloride, a mineral found in thick deposits precipitated during the evaporation of shallow seas and lakes, such as those in Utah.

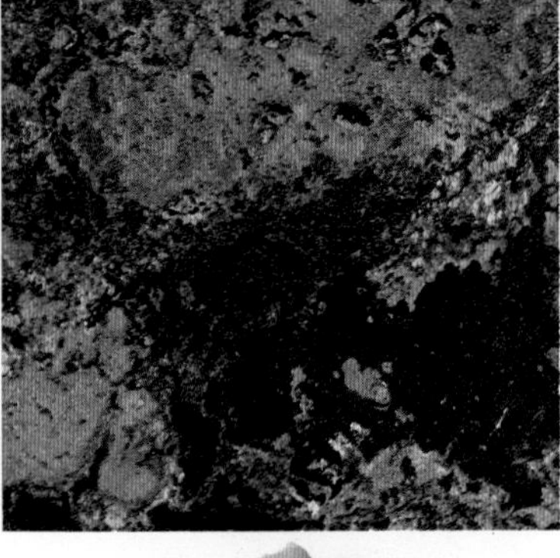

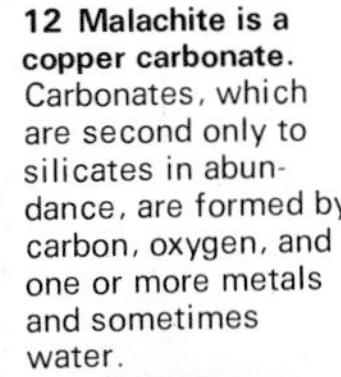

12 Malachite is a copper carbonate. Carbonates, which are second only to silicates in abundance, are formed by carbon, oxygen, and one or more metals and sometimes water.

13 Sulfates are made of a sulfur oxide combined with a metal; gypsum, which also contains water, is the most common. Barite can assume shapes like the "desert rose" shown here.

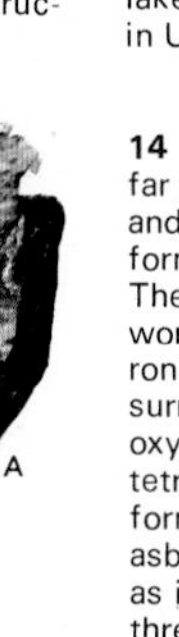

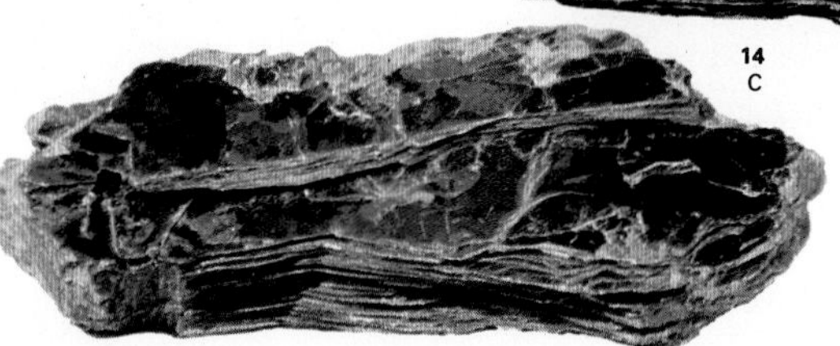

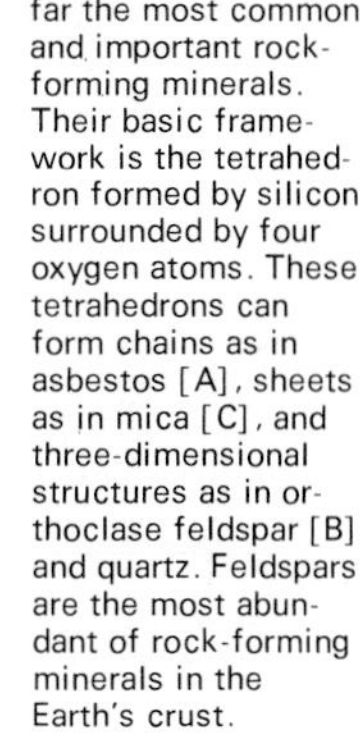

14 Silicates are by far the most common and important rock-forming minerals. Their basic framework is the tetrahedron formed by silicon surrounded by four oxygen atoms. These tetrahedrons can form chains as in asbestos [A], sheets as in mica [C], and three-dimensional structures as in orthoclase feldspar [B] and quartz. Feldspars are the most abundant of rock-forming minerals in the Earth's crust.

Gems and semiprecious stones

Gems are valued by man for their beauty, rarity, and durability. The most precious gems are naturally occurring minerals such as diamonds, emeralds, sapphires, and rubies. Some organic substances are also considered to be gems; amber is a fossil resin, coral is made by tiny sea creatures, and pearls are formed from nacre, the iridescent substance forming the inner layer of many seashells, especially the oyster. Fashion often determines the popularity of gems. Jet, a hard shiny black fossilized wood, was widely used in jewelry after Queen Victoria was widowed in 1861.

Formation of gems

Gems that are of inorganic origin and occur as natural minerals are formed in several different ways. Many gems are found in igneous rock, that is, rock formed directly from magma that has welled up from the Earth's interior and solidified beneath the surface. As magma cools, the elements tend to separate into distinct regions where they form different minerals. Pockets of gases and superheated water often dissolve many elements; these finally cool and combine to form precious or semiprecious minerals. Pegmatites—light-colored, coarsegrained igneous rocks—are formed by superheated gas and water and they often contain stocks of gems including beryl, quartz, tourmaline, and feldspars. Gases and solutions in the cooling pegmatites help form minerals such as the fluorine-bearing topaz and boron-containing tourmaline [6].

Other gems are formed when heat, pressure, or chemical action alters the structure of existing rocks, causing them to re-crystallize or re-form in different ways as metamorphic rocks. Olivine [14], emerald, and garnet [7] are found in metamorphic rocks. Great heat and pressure were probably responsible for formation of diamond from carbon in kimberlite [3]. Many gem materials, including diamond, are found as crystals or rolled pebbles in alluvial gravels (stream deposits).

Properties of gems

Gem minerals can be identified by a number of qualities such as the shape of the uncut crystals, their color, hardness, refractive index and specific gravity (density). A gem's value is established by rarity, luster, purity, color, and hardness. Demand also determines the value of a gem; diamonds are in constant demand for industrial use in cutting instruments as well as for jewelry.

One of the main factors that determines the beauty of a gem is how light is reflected, refracted (bent), and dispersed (split up) into the spectrum by the gem. Each stone has its own refractive index. This index is measured by dividing the sine of the angle of incidence (the angle between the ray of light and a line drawn perpendicular to the surface) by the sine of the angle of refraction. Of all natural gems, diamond has the highest index of refraction. This gives the stone its characteristic brilliance. Its ability to disperse white light gives the diamond its special fire.

The colors of diamonds are generally caused by a lattice defect in the crystal and rarely by trace elements. Most other gemstones are colored by metal oxides that are either impurities or components. The

CONNECTIONS

See also
278 Mineral resources of the land
280 Mineral resources of the sea
240 Shapes and structures of crystals
242 Earth's minerals
826 Astrology

1 ◆ Diamond
● Ruby
▲ Sapphire
■ Emerald
● Turquoise
▲ Pegmatite gems
■ Malachite
◆ Zircon
▲ Lapis lazuli
● Amber

◆ Rhodochrosite
■ Garnet
○ Cordierite
□ Quartz
◇ Opal
△ Chalcedony
○ Jade
△ Amethyst
□ Peridot

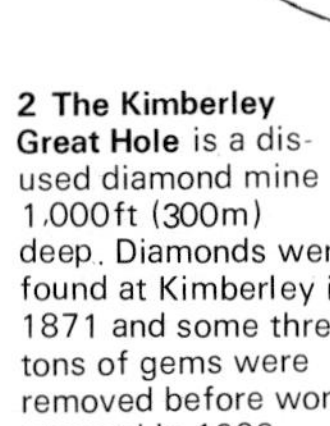

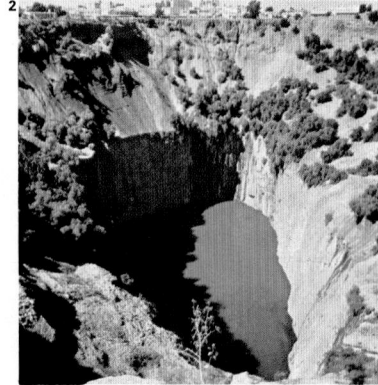

1 The gem-producing regions of the world are shown on the map. The diamond, ruby, sapphire, and emerald are classed as precious stones; all the other gems are classed as semi-precious stones.

2 The Kimberley Great Hole is a disused diamond mine 1,000ft (300m) deep. Diamonds were found at Kimberley in 1871 and some three tons of gems were removed before work stopped in 1909.

3 Diamonds are made by intense heat and pressures in volcanic plugs, or kimberlite pipes, deep below the Earth's crust [A]. As pressure increases gas collects in fissures and explodes, forming a hollow in the Earth's surface [B]. Diamond-bearing kimberlite wells up the fissures [C] to fill the cavity [D]. The kimberlite may rise above the surface [E]. Shafts are sunk for access [F].

4 A rough diamond is cut to shape along the cleavage planes [A]. These are first grooved [B] and then cleaved with a blade [C] until a workable shape [D] is obtained. Cutting is done first with a coarse [E] and then a fine [F] saw to give the final shape [G,H,I,J,]. Polishing is done on a lap [K], covered in diamond powder, producing the facets [L,M] that reflect light from the interior [N].

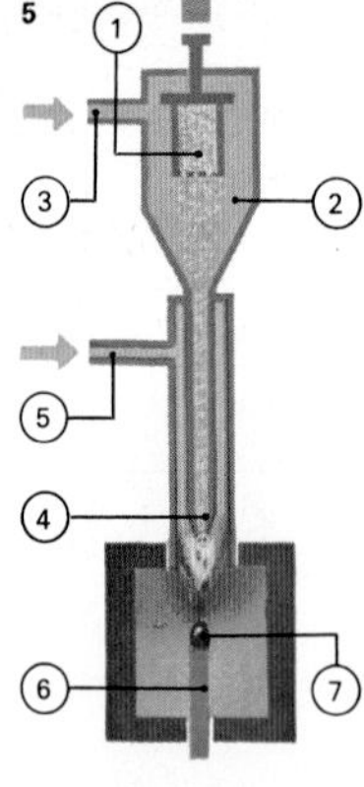

5
1
2
3
5
4
6
7

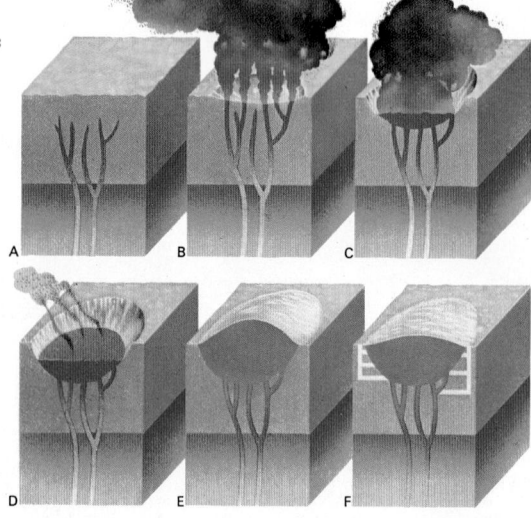

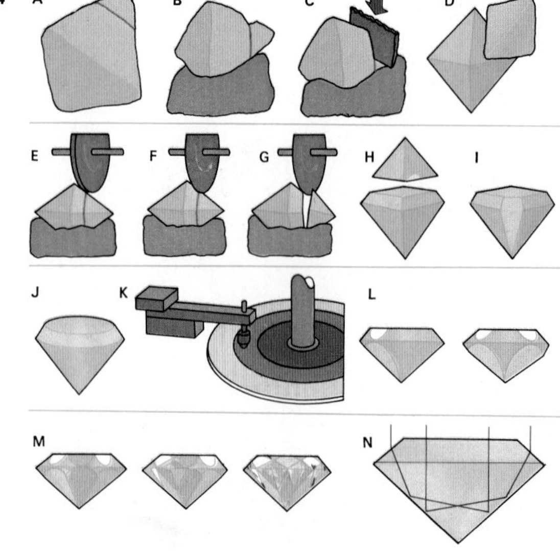

4
A
B
C
D
E
F
G
H
I
J
K
L
M
N

5 Synthetic gems are produced by a flame-fusion process, known as Verneuil's method. Alumina powder in the container [1] falls into the chamber [2]. Oxygen [3] mixes with the alumina and carries it to the tip of the torch [4], where it burns with hydrogen entering through the tube [5]. In the intense heat produced, the fine alumina particles fuse into gem droplets and fall onto a support [6] on which the body of the gem is being formed [7].

transparent red ruby [13] and the blue sapphire [15] (both of which are forms of a normally dull, grey or colorless mineral called corundum), the green emerald, a form of the mineral beryl, and the yellow topaz are all admired because of their pure tints. Opaque or cloudy gems such as opals depend entirely upon their color to make them attractive.

Specific gravity is the weight of the mineral compared with the weight of an equal amount of pure water. Diamond, for example, has a specific gravity of 3.52, which means that it weighs 3.52 times an equal amount of pure water, whereas amber has a specific gravity of 1.07. The weight of a diamond is usually expressed in carats—one carat is equivalent to 200 milligrams (0.007oz).

Hardness ensures durability, and accordingly the most valuable gems are stones that wear for a long time. Hardness is measured on the Moh's scale, which consists of numbers from 1 to 10, indicating the relative hardness of substances. The diamond has a hardness of 10 on this scale and is by far the hardest of all natural substances. It is about 90 times harder than corundum, which rates as 9 on the scale. Some gems are quite soft and are valued for other properties.

Polishing and cutting of gems

The beauty of gems is greatly enhanced by skilful cutting and polishing [4], for this removes the surface flaws and heightens the color or brilliance of a stone. The oldest form in which gems were cut was a rounded shape called *cabochon*, a French word for "head." The *cabochon* is used for stones that have properties of chatoyancy (cat's-eyes) and asterism (star-stones), which are caused by reflections from inclusions.

Faceting—first started by Indian cutters polishing small facets on diamonds—soon became applied to other stones. Thus evolved the brilliant, step, and mixed cuts, which depend on various facets being ground and polished in symmetrical arrangements on the stones. The facets on a diamond are cut and polished in one operation, but other precious stones have their facets first ground and then polished.

KEY

The largest cut diamond in the world is the Star of Africa, weighing a little over 530 carats. It came from the biggest diamond ever found, the Cullinan. This stone, found in 1905 in the Premier mine of South Africa, was named after Thomas Cullinan, chairman of the mining company. It weighed 3,106 metric carats (1.3 lb, or 0.60kg) but was cut into two large stones, seven medium, and 96 smaller stones. The largest of these, the Star of Africa, is now among the British Crown Jewels in the Tower of London. Another diamond in this collection is the Indian diamond Koh-i-noor, which was given to Queen Victoria in 1850 by the East India Company.

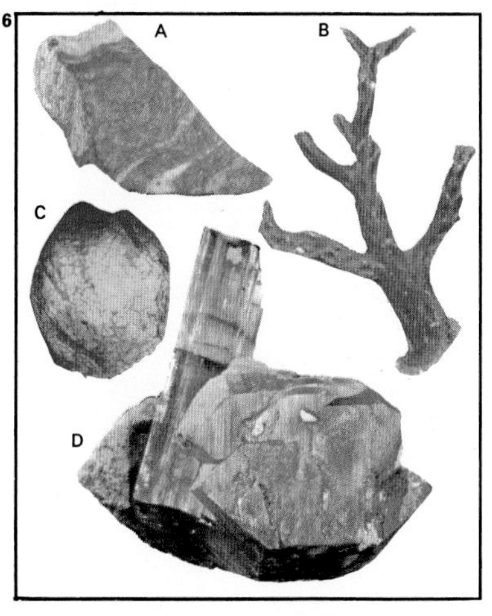

6
A
B
C
D

6 Most gems are minerals. Lapis lazuli [A] is the name given to a rock rich in lazurite. Tourmaline [D] is a complex borosilicate. Organic gems include coral [B] (the skeletons of coral polyps) and amber [C] which is a fossil resin.

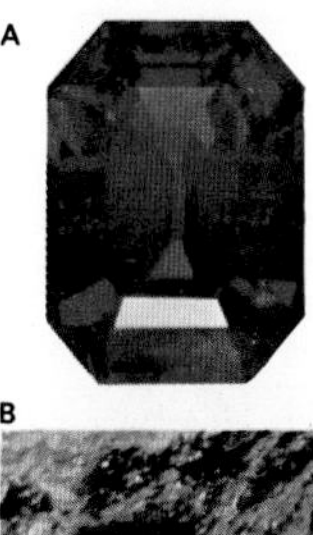

7 Garnet [A], the birthstone for January, symbolizes faithfulness. Garnets are formed from silica and two metals [B]. Those with aluminum and magnesium are the prized ruby-red pyrope.

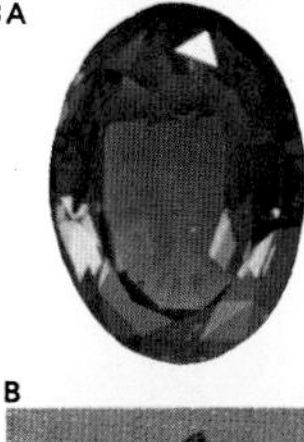

8 Amethyst [A], the birthstone for February, symbolizes sincerity. Amethysts are a form of transparent quartz [B], with a violet or purple color. They are mined in USSR and South America.

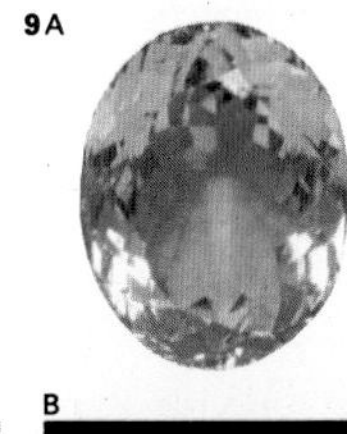

9 Aquamarine [A], one of the March birthstones, symbolizes courage. Aquamarines are a blue or blue-green variety of the mineral beryl [B]. The best are mined in Brazil and the Urals.

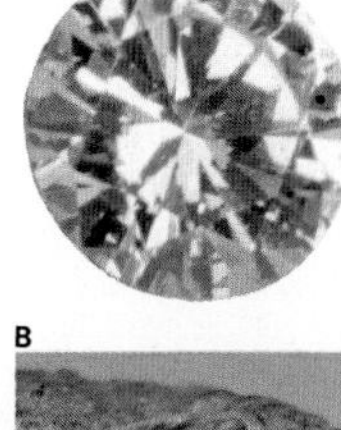

10 Diamond [A], the April birthstone, symbolizes innocence. Diamonds are pure crystallized carbon [B], the hardest natural substance. South Africa is the main source of diamonds.

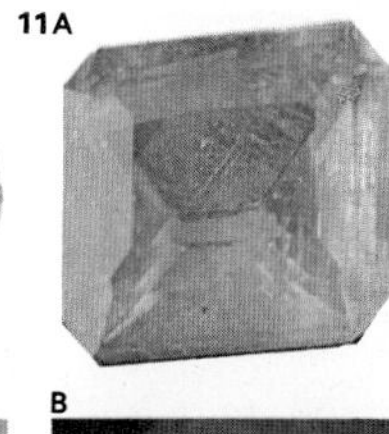

11 Emerald [A], the birthstone for May, represents love. Emerald is a gem-quality, rare green variety of the mineral beryl [B]. The best emeralds occur in Colombia in South America.

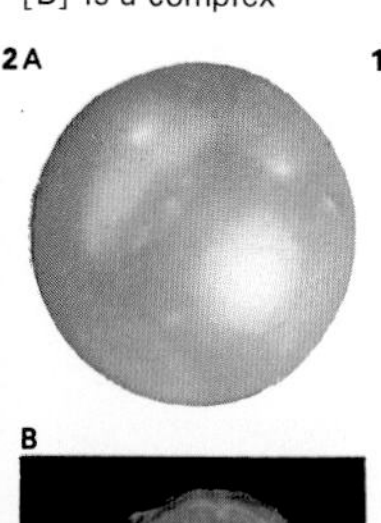

12 Pearl [A], one of the June birthstones symbolizes health. Pearls are organic gems produced mainly by oysters [B] from nacre, the iridescent substance forming the inner layer of the shell. Pearls are prized for their luster.

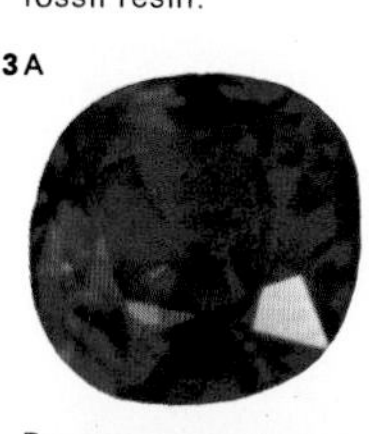
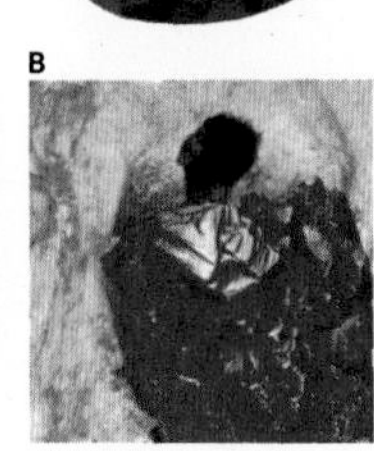

13 Ruby [A], the July birthstone, represents contentment. Ruby is a red variety of the hard grey or colorless aluminum oxide mineral corundum [B]. The finest rubies, from Burma, are colored a deep red by a chromium impurity.

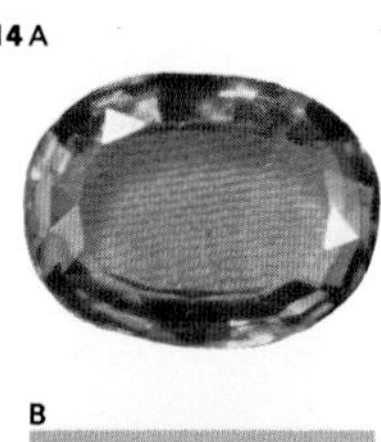

14 Peridot [A] is one of the birthstones for August. It symbolizes married happiness. Peridots are a transparent green variety of the mineral olivine [B], which is a magnesium-iron silicate, a common rock-forming mineral.

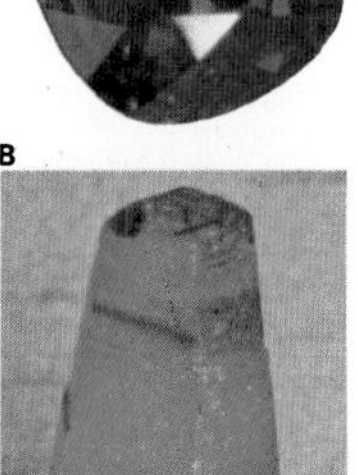

15 Sapphire [A], the September birthstone, represents clear thinking. Sapphire, like ruby, is a variety of the mineral corundum [B]. It occurs in many colors but the most valued are blue. The best come from Burma and Thailand.

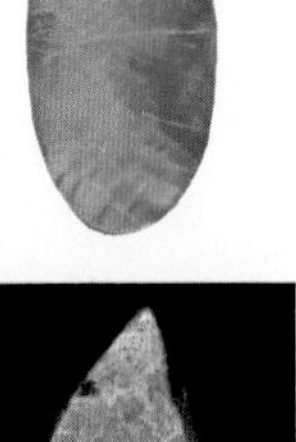

16 Opal [A] is the October birthstone. It symbolizes hope. Opals are a form of noncrystalline quartz [B]. The most prized specimens are the so-called black opals found in Australia, which show flashes of several iridescent colors.

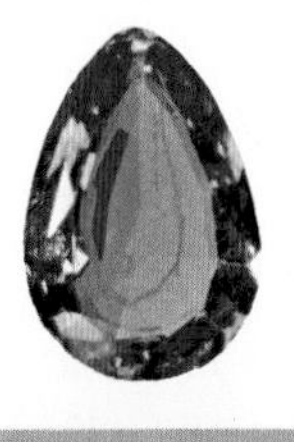

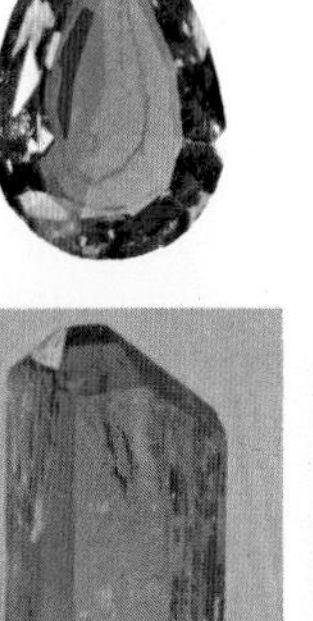

17 Topaz [A], the birthstone for November, symbolizes fidelity. The most prized varieties are yellow. Topaz is a mineral compound of aluminum, silica, and fluorine [B]. It is found mainly in Brazil, USSR and the United States.

18 Turquoise [A], the birthstone for December, represents prosperity. Turquoise is a hydrous copper-aluminum phosphate [B] sometimes containing iron. The most prized color is sky blue and comes from Iran.

The rock cycle and igneous rocks

The rocks on the Earth's surface can be divided into three kinds: igneous, metamorphic, and sedimentary. Igneous rocks have formed by the cooling of molten magma [3]. Metamorphic rocks have formed by the baking or the compression of older rocks. New crystals have grown in these rocks under pressure and are generally aligned because they tend to grow in only one direction. Sedimentary rocks are composed of the weathered or eroded fragments of older rocks or of the remains of living organisms.

Each of these three classes formed under very different conditions from the others. Sedimentary rocks formed on the surface of the Earth under extremely low pressures, metamorphic rocks formed below the surface where both the temperature and pressure are high, and intrusive igneous rocks formed where the temperatures are even higher.

Rock cycle

The rock cycle [2] describes the relationship between these three types of rocks. The first part of the rock cycle takes place on the Earth's surface. This is the erosion and weathering of older rocks to soil and sand and the transportation of the resulting sediment by rivers down to the sea. Nearly all the sediment produced, whether on the land or along the coast, is eventually transported to deep basins under the sea. In these areas great thicknesses of sediment accumulate. For instance, the Mississippi has been pouring sediment into the Gulf of Mexico at the rate of about 500 million tons a year for the last 150 million years. The pile of sediment is now 7 miles (12km) thick.

Formation of rocks from sediments

The water circulating through the sand deposits iron oxide, silica, clay, or lime between the grains and this cements the loose sand into sandstone. Mud is squeezed by the weight of the sediment above until it becomes shale. This process of changing sediment into rock is called lithification.

Most great thicknesses of sedimentary rocks accumulate in long, narrow trenches on the sea floor called geosynclines. These depressions are caused by descending convection currents in the lower mantle. These carry the oceanic crust down into the Earth's interior where both the pressure and temperature are high. The sedimentary rock in the depression is carried down with the crust. It is folded and squeezed and heated up to between 392°F (200°C) and 932°F (500°C). This changes the sedimentary rock to a metamorphic rock.

The movement of the Earth's crust may carry the rock as much as 454 miles (700km) below the surface. Here the temperature and pressure will be even higher, rising to 3,600°F (2,000°C), and the rock will begin to melt. Molten rock is lighter than solid rock and it will begin to rise up through the overlying rock toward the surface. If it reaches the surface as a lava flow it will begin to weather and erode and start a new cycle. More often the molten rock solidifies underground and then all the rock above it must be eroded away before it is available to begin the cycle again.

Although the complete cycle is from sedimentary to metamorphic to igneous,

CONNECTIONS

See also
248 Sedimentary and metamorphic rocks
176 Volcanoes
242 Earth's minerals
54 Moon missions

1

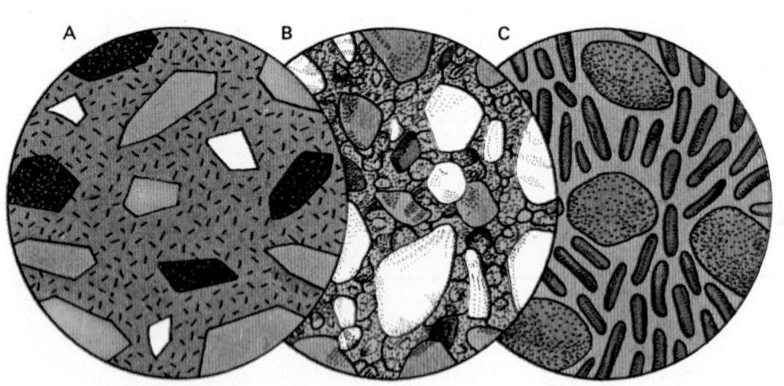

A
B
C

1 Textures can be used to identify rock types. Igneous rocks [A] show well-developed crystals, sedimentary [B] contain older pieces, and metamorphic [C] show the stresses of their formation.

2

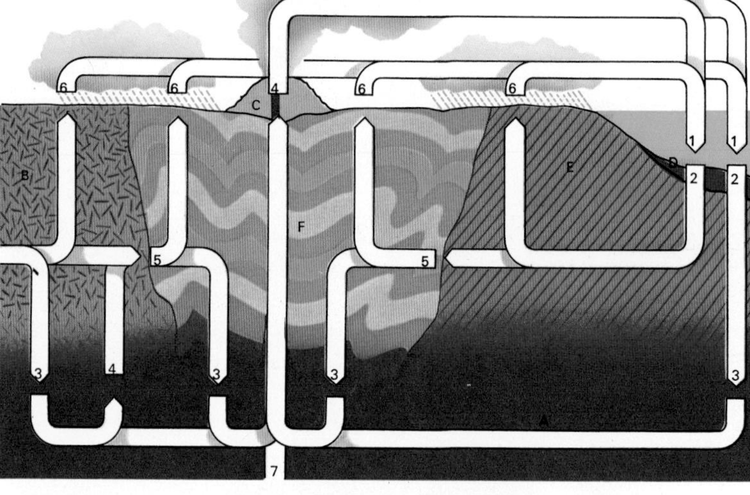

2 The rock cycle is the slow change from one rock type to another. Erosion produces sediments that harden to form sedimentary rocks. If these are deeply buried the temperature and pressure turn them into metamorphic rocks. Intense heat at great depths melts metamorphic rocks. This rock may be pushed up closer to the surface, forming igneous rocks. Erosion begins the cycle again.

A Molten matter
B Intrusive igneous rocks
C Extrusive igneous rocks
D Sediments
E Sedimentary rocks
F Metamorphic rocks

1 Deposition
2 Lithification
3 Fusion
4 Solidification
5 Metamorphism
6 Erosion
7 Emplacement of new material from earth's interior

3

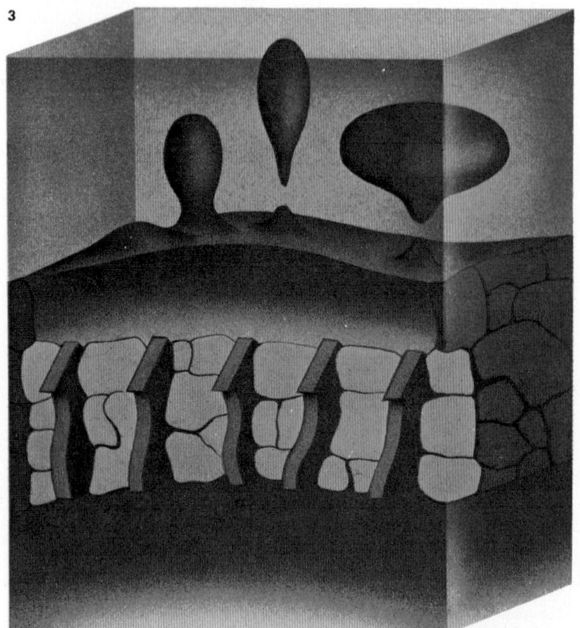

3 Granite is the most abundant igneous rock. It is formed by the partial melting of older deeply buried rocks. Initially, the molten liquid stays between the remaining grains but later it migrates to form small pods, which in turn collect together into layers. Because the liquid is lighter than the surrounding rock it rises upward and intrudes the rock above, forming large masses called batholiths.

4

Granite: 70·8%, 14·6%, 1·6%, 1·8%, 0·9%, 0·4%, 2·0%, 3·5%, 4·2%

Basalt: 49·0%, 18·2%, 3·2%, 6·0%, 7·6%, 1·0%, 11·2%, 2·6%, 0·9%

Silica
Alumina
Ferric Oxide
Ferrous oxide
Magnesia
Titanium oxide
Calcium oxide
Sodium oxide
Potassium oxide

4 Basalt and granite are the two rocks most abundant on the Earth's surface. Both rocks are composed mostly of the elements silicon and oxygen. These are combined with minor amounts of other elements into natural chemical compounds called minerals. Basalts occur either as lava flows or dikes, while granites occur as batholiths.

many rocks short-cut the cycle, usually by missing the igneous or metamorphic stages.

Igneous rocks

Igneous rocks [5] are divided into extrusive and intrusive rocks. Extrusive rocks are those that were ejected by volcanoes and cooled as lavas on the surface of the Earth. Intrusive rocks are those that solidified beneath the Earth's surface. The grain, or crystal size, of a rock depends on how fast it cooled; coarse-grained rocks are the result of slow cooling, which has given crystals time to grow to sizes greater than two millimeters in length. Rocks cool slowly when deep in the Earth's crust and coarseness is characteristic of intrusive rocks. Fine-grained rocks have cooled rapidly either on or near the Earth's surface. Most extrusive rocks are fine grained, although some are cooled so rapidly that no crystals have time to grow and a glassy material called obsidian is formed.

Igneous rocks [6] are classified by the amount of silica they contain and the size of the grains. The chemical composition [4] and the silica content in particular depend on the origin of the magma from which the rock was made. The magma may have resulted from the partial melting of the rocks beneath the Earth's crust or from the melting of the crust itself as part of the rock cycle. Magma from the crust contains more silica than that from below it and generally gives rise to light colored rocks, whereas deep-seated magma yields dark rocks rich in iron and magnesium.

The partial melting of the rocks beneath the Earth's crust produces basalts (fine-grained extrusive lavas), dolerite (medium-grained intrusive rock), and gabbros (coarse-grained intrusive rock) [7]. Basalts form the floors of the oceans and occur extensively in Iceland and in some continental areas. Dolerites are found in thin extensive sheets called dikes and sills [5] injected in or between the sedimentary rock layers.

The melting of rocks that were once sediments on the crust produces granites [3] and andesites. Granites occur in very large intrusions called batholiths [5].

KEY

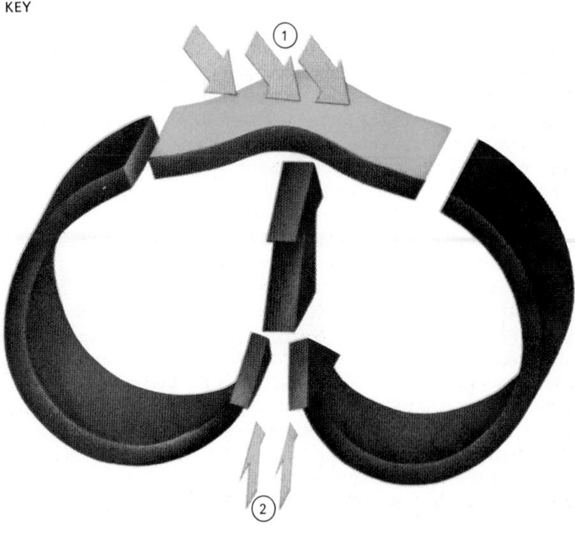
1
2

The energy to power the rock cycle is derived from the heat of the Sun [1], which indirectly breaks down existing rocks to sediments, and the heat from the Earth's interior [2], which melts existing material to yield igneous rocks and also causes the movements of the Earth's outer shell.

5

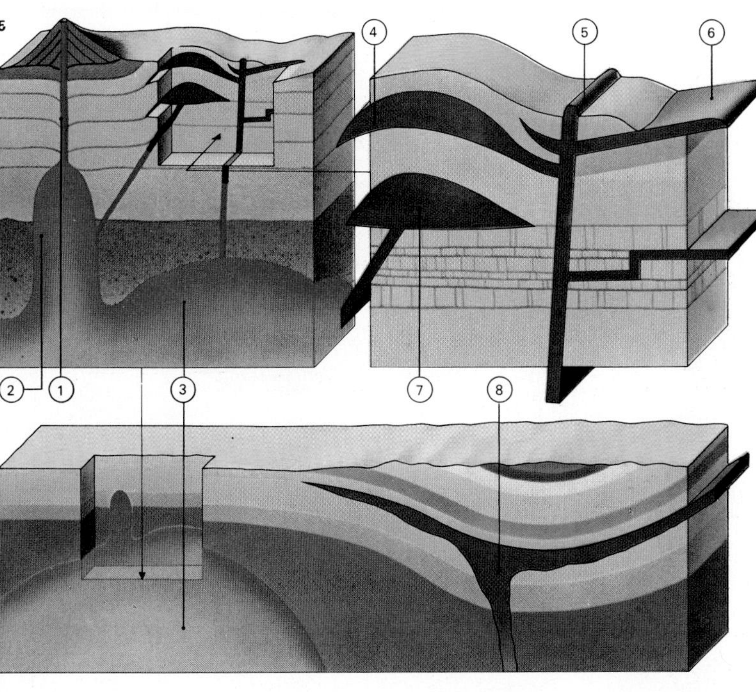
4
5
6
2
1
3
7
8

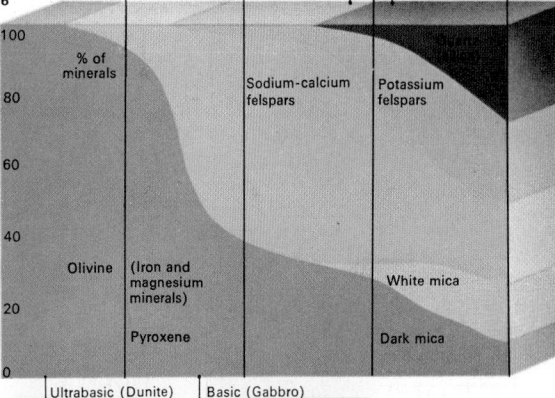

5 Many different shapes of igneous rocks exist. A neck [1] is a circular vertical feed channel of a volcano. A stock [2] is a large mass of rock that solidified at great depth. A batholith [3] is a large body of granite with no detectable bottom. A laccolith [4, 7] is a dome-shaped mass that has arched up the rock above. A dike [5] is a vertical sheetlike mass of rock, and a sill [6] is a horizontal sheet-shaped body of rock. A lopolith [8] is a saucer-shaped mass of rock.

6 Igneous rocks are comprised of varying amounts of minerals in which the quantity of silica (SiO_2) determines the acidity of the rock and thus its classification. This proportion of silica determines the type and proportion of the minerals present. Thin rock sections examined by polarized light reveal the individual minerals in distinctive colors, helping to identify them and to classify the rock.

Intermediate (Diorite)

Acidic (Granite)

6

% of minerals

100 80 60 40 20 0

Olivine | (Iron and magnesium minerals) | Pyroxene | Sodium-calcium felspars | Potassium felspars | White mica | Dark mica

Ultrabasic (Dunite)

Basic (Gabbro)

B

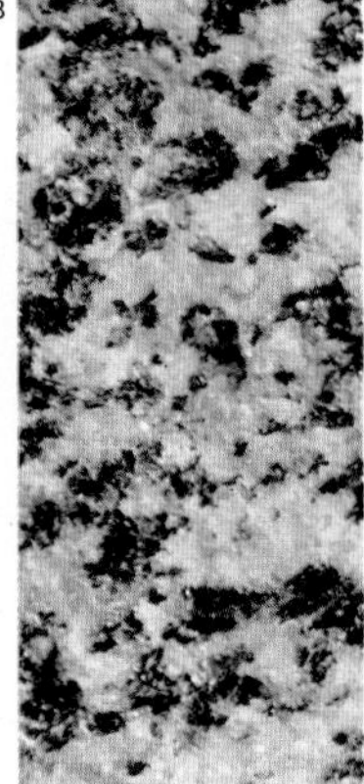

C

D

7 Intrusive rocks can often be identified with the naked eye. Granite [A] contains a great deal of free silica in the form of quartz, giving the rock a light color. Diorite [B] is darker, having less quartz and a quantity of dark minerals. These dark minerals, such as olivine and pyroxene, are more common in gabbro [C]. Here the light colored minerals are feldspars. Ultrabasic rocks such as dunite [D] consist almost entirely of dark ferromagnesian minerals.

Sedimentary and metamorphic rocks

The rocks of the Earth's surface are of three sorts: igneous (formed from molten magma), sedimentary, and metamorphic [Key]. Sedimentary rocks are formed from chemicals, organic materials, and fragments produced by the weathering and erosion of older rocks. Metamorphic rocks are formed by the heating under pressure of older rocks.

Sedimentary rocks are divided into three types [1]. The first, called clastic, is formed by fragments of older rocks; the second is organic, composed of the remains of animals or plants; and the third is chemical, produced by the precipitation of minerals and salts from water. Streams, moving ice, and waves break up older rocks into fragments, some large, like stones or boulders, some about 1mm (0.04in) across, like sand, and some too fine to see, which form mud. Most of these are carried down to the sea by rivers and deposited in deltas or farther out on the sea floor. Stones too large to be moved by the water remain near the heads of streams or on beaches and are eventually cemented together to form a rock known as conglomerate. Sand is deposited near the coast or on the continental shelf and eventually forms sandstone. Sands are also deposited by wind in desert environments. Mud is often carried far from the shore to become clay or shale.

Plant and animal origins

Organic sedimentary rocks may be made of plant remains, like coal, or from the hard parts of animals. Many limestones are made of fossil shells and corals which have extracted lime from seawater to make their skeletons and, dying, have left their remains on the sea floor. In time the movement of the sea wears the shells into fragments. Over a period of millions of years, the fragments are compacted by weight and cemented to one another by various processes [2] to give limestone. This is called lithification. Accumulation of lime is at present taking place in the Bahamas and the Persian Gulf, but in the past warm seas were much more extensive and limestone was produced over large areas. Chalk is made of countless small shells so minute that they can only be seen with a microscope. Seawater contains large amounts of salts and, if it is evaporated, they are precipitated out. In tropical areas where hot, dry winds blow over shallow seas, much of the water is evaporated and lime forms on the sea floor, hardening to a fine-grained limestone [4]. If there is a partially enclosed basin, then not only lime but salts such as gypsum (calcium sulfate) will be precipitated.

Sedimentary rocks are important because they provide oil, natural gas, coal, and building stone. They are of great interest, too, because they were formed at the Earth's surface and provide much evidence of its nature many millions of years ago. Fine red sandstone [3], for example, indicates the former presence of deserts. The study of ancient environments through the examination of present-day rocks is called stratigraphy.

New rocks from old

Metamorphic rocks are usually much harder than sedimentary rocks. Some are formed by deep burial, others by the heat of

CONNECTIONS

Read first
246 The rock cycle and igneous rocks

See also
282 Energy resources: coal
284 Energy resources: oil and gas
242 Earth's minerals
312 The living soil
270 The record in the rocks
272 Clues to the past
560 Fossils: the life of the past

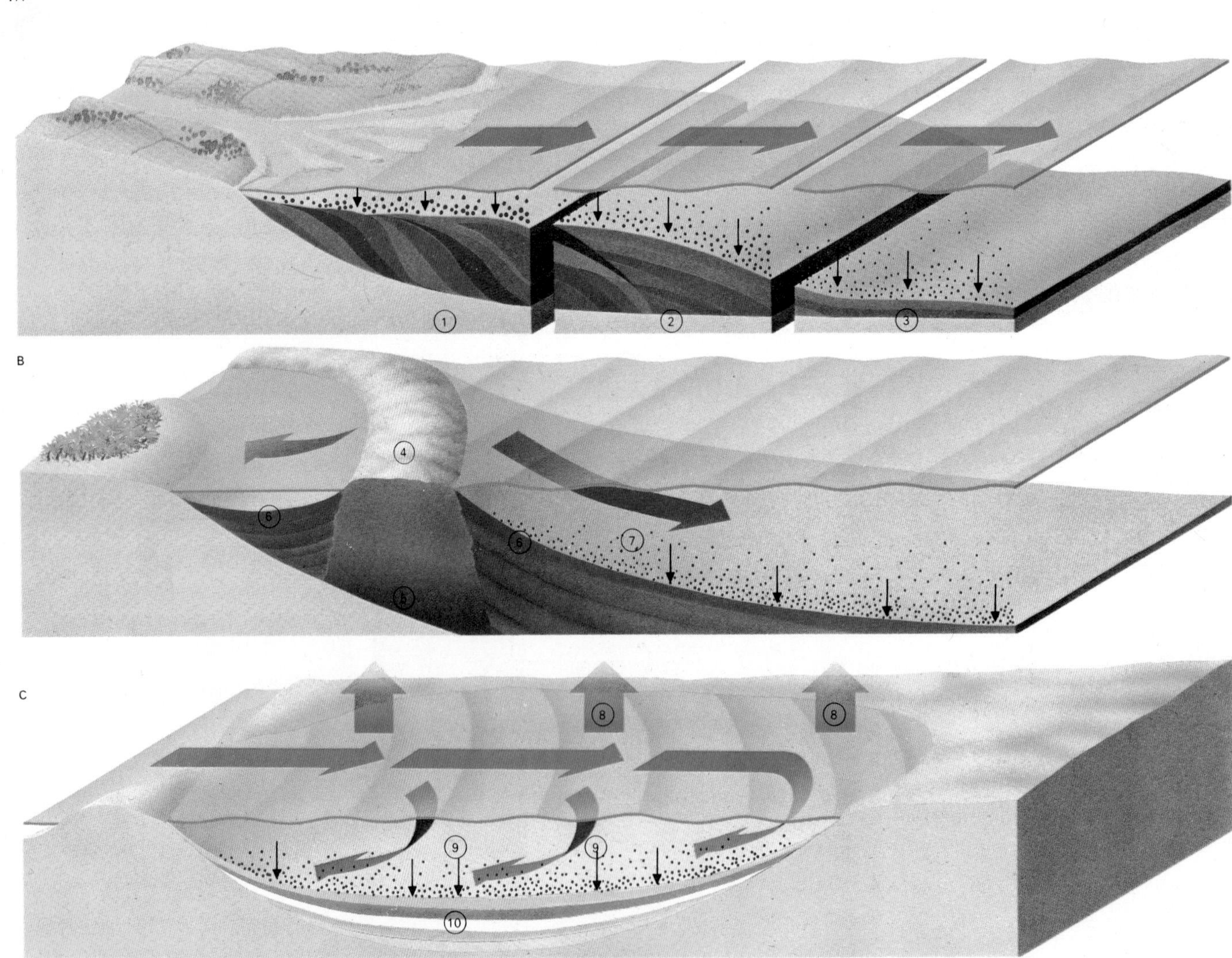
1 A
1
2
3
B
4
5
6
7
C
8
9
10

1 The three types of sedimentary rocks are clastic [A], produced by erosion from older rocks; organic [B], formed by the decomposition of living matter; and chemical [C], formed from salts deposited by evaporation. [A] Erosion produces sand and mud, which are brought down to the sea by rivers, deposited in deltas [1] and on the sea floor where they harden into rock [2]. Large grains are deposited inshore, fine mud [3] farther away – a common origin for clastic rocks. [B] On a coral reef, living coral [4] is found only near the surface. It rests on hundreds of feet of dead coral [5] and on both sides are piles of broken pieces of coral eroded by the waves [6]. The shells of other organisms also accumulate on the sea floor [7]. All will form reef limestone, a typical organic rock. [C] Where a partially enclosed basin is found in the tropics the seawater is evaporated [8] and the salts in it deposited [9], eventually forming chemical rocks [10].

igneous intrusions. Their grains are all interlocking crystals and many, such as slates, schists, and gneisses, split easily along certain planes. Others like hornfels, quartzite, and marble, are compact rocks that break in any direction.

When sedimentary rocks are intruded by a molten mass of magma they are altered. This process is a form of metamorphism known as thermal, or contact, metamorphism. Small intrusions such as dikes and sills merely bake a thin skin of rock and make it harder; large intrusions alter the rock for several miles around. A large intrusion may heat the rock to 1,290°F (700°C) and take more than a million years to cool, giving time for new minerals to grow.

The rocks surrounding an igneous intrusion can be divided into zones, depending on how much they have been altered. Shales will have been changed to slates on the outside, and near the intrusion new minerals, such as andalusite, will occur in the slate. Next to the intrusion a hard rock, hornfels, will form.

Alteration of large areas

Regional (or dynamic) metamorphism [5] occurs where large areas of rock have been buried sufficiently deep for the increase in temperature and pressure to alter the rocks. The pressure increase is caused by the weight of rocks above and the increase in temperature by the Earth's interior heat. Slates are formed by both regional and thermal metamorphism, but schists and gneisses are found only in regional metamorphism. Regionally metamorphosed rocks outcrop over a large part of the Earth's surface, where old mountain ranges have been eroded away, exposing rocks that were once deeply buried.

A third, more rare type of metamorphism is dislocation metamorphism, caused by large areas of rock moving past one another. The pressure shatters the rock and the friction is so great that the rock is partially melted, producing a rock called mylonite. It occurs only in narrow strips. Unlike sedimentary rocks, metamorphic rocks are of no great use to mankind, containing no oil and few useful minerals.

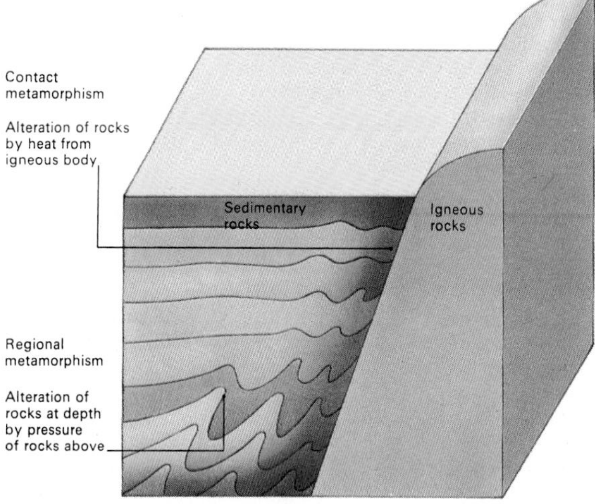
KEY
Contact metamorphism
Alteration of rocks by heat from igneous body
Regional metamorphism
Alteration of rocks at depth by pressure of rocks above
Sedimentary rocks
Igneous rocks

The three groups of rock are igneous, sedimentary, and metamorphic. They are seen together where igneous rock has intruded sedimentary rocks. Its heat has caused the sedimentary rock to be thermally metamorphosed. Deeply buried sedimentary rock is regionally metamorphosed.

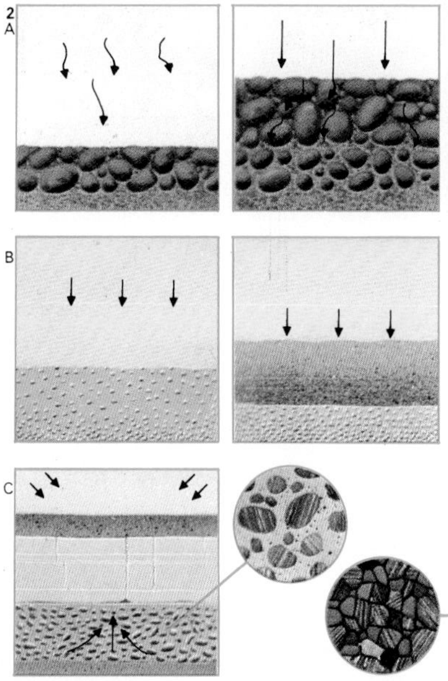

2 Three processes turn loose sediment into rock. Cementation [A] occurs where water percolates between grains, depositing thin layers of iron oxide, calcium carbonate, or silica around grains. Grains are cemented together, becoming sandstone. Compaction [B] occurs where water between grains of sediment is squeezed out by the weight of more sediment. By this means, clay becomes mudstone. The third process occurs during mountain building [C], when large forces cause the minerals of rocks to recrystallize in a solid mass, leaving no spaces. This is common in marbles.

Sandstone

3 Grains of quartz sand cemented together with lime, iron oxide, or silica make up sandstone and each grain can easily be seen. Sandstones are usually red, cream, or brown, but are sometimes green.

Limestone

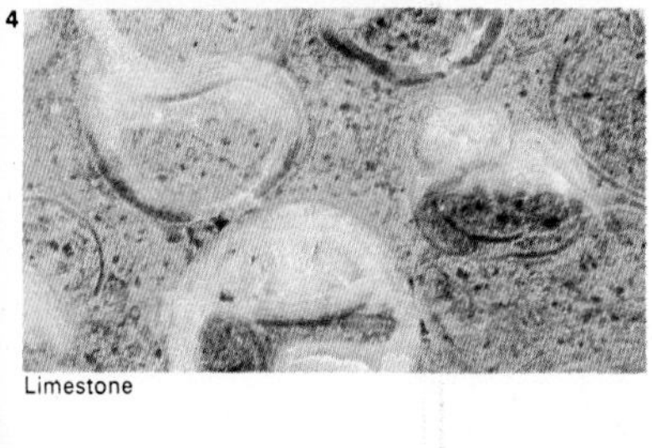

4 Limestone is white, grey, or cream-colored rock, often containing many fossils. Limestones are made of calcium carbonate and are formed by the evaporation of seawater or from shells, often preserved as fossils.

Clay

Shale

Slate

Schist

Gneiss

Hornfels

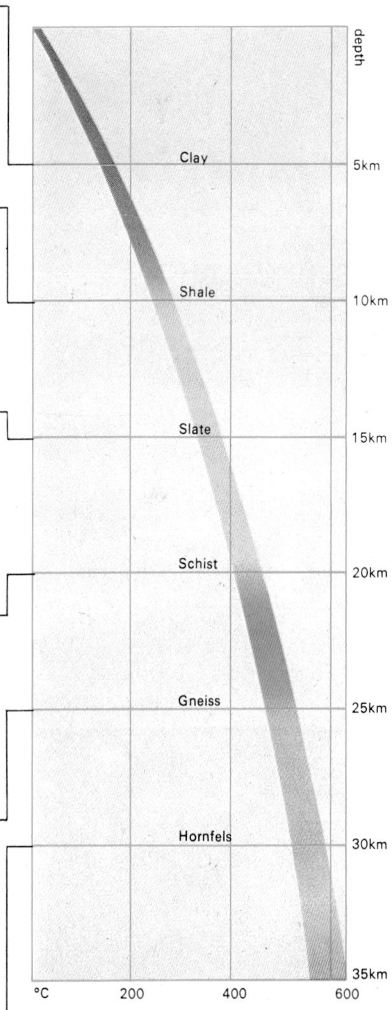

depth

Clay 5km
Shale 10km
Slate 15km
Schist 20km
Gneiss 25km
Hornfels 30km
35km

°C 200 400 600

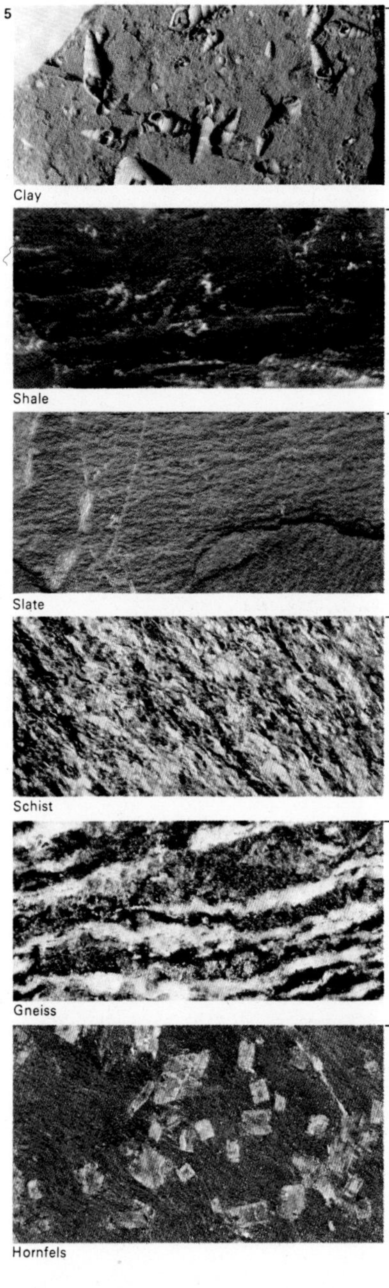

5 Pressure and heat on old, deeply buried rocks produces regional metamorphism. The temperature and pressure increase with depth of burial, causing new minerals to grow in the rock, and the size of the mineral crystals increases with depth. Clay is made of very small crystals, but gneiss has crystals 0.75 in(2cm) long. Minerals tend to grow in the direction of least pressure. They are often aligned and will split easily one way. Hornfels does not show lineations.

Folds and faults

The Earth's mountains and valleys are formed by folds and faults in its ceaselessly changing crust. Folds are rock waves and faults are cracks, and both are caused by the intense pressures of continental drift. They are of major significance to industrial geologists because they often form traps for valuable minerals.

Folds and faults are usually well developed in sedimentary and volcanic rocks. They may also form in intrusive igneous rocks such as granite and gabbro. Correct interpretation of their structure is essential in mining. Recumbent folding and reverse faulting can cause beds of coal, for example, to be repeated vertically, while normal faulting can cause a horizontal gap. A coal seam may thus be passed through several times in drilling or missed altogether.

Faults that develop above an intrusive granite allow mineralizing fluids to pass into the overlying rocks and there deposit minerals such as lead, tin, zinc, and copper ores. Similarly, faults that do not reach the surface may form channels up which oil and gas can rise. In downward folds, where porous sandbeds overlie impermeable clays and shale, collections of water can produce artesian springs.

How folds and faults form

Movement of the massive plates of rock that compose the Earth's outer shell (lithosphere) produces intense pressure at the margins of the plates. Where two plates converge, these sometimes throw the rocks up into highly folded and faulted mountain chains. At other plate edges, stretching pulls the rocks apart and forms long depressions bounded by faults, like the rift valleys of East Africa.

Folds vary greatly in size, from fractions of an inch to hundreds of miles across. Downward or basin-shaped folds are called synclines and upward folds are called anticlines [Key]. Synclinoria and anticlinoria are large synclines or anticlines that have smaller folds on their limbs.

Folds that form at the same time as deposition are known as supratenuous folds. These occur when material that compacts at different rates is deposited at the same time in the same area, as when sand is deposited around coral. Domes are folds in which the beds dip outward on all sides, whereas when the beds dip inward they are called basins [3].

Classification of folds

There are three main kinds of folds. First true, or flexure, folding forms by the compression of competent (strong) rocks. This may grade into the second type, flow folding, in areas where incompetent (weak) rocks occur [4]. The incompetent rocks behave like a thick paste; they cannot easily transmit pressure and many minor folds usually form. Third, shear folding [5] may occur in brittle rocks by the formation of minute cleavagelike fractures in which thin slices of rock are able to move in relation to each other like a pack of cards pushed in from the side. Except where cut by a fault, all folds eventually die out by closure, the shape of the fold becoming like that of a half basin or dome.

Simple folds usually occur in young rocks like those of the Tertiary and Quater-

CONNECTIONS

See also
252 Life and death of mountains
174 Earthquakes

1

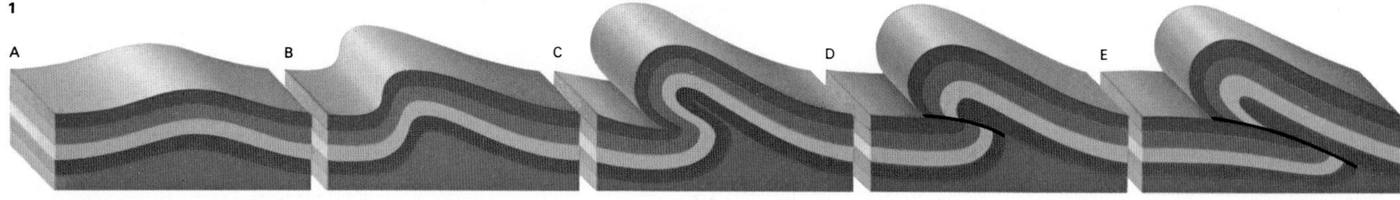

A
B
C
D
E

1 Compression creates folds in the Earth's crust. First, a simple fold may be created, probably a symmetric anticline [A]. But if there is a continuation of pressure, the fold may become uneven and develop into an asymmetric anticline [B]. At a later stage, a recumbent fold may develop [C]. The anticline is then lying on top of the syncline and the layers of rock on one side of the anticline are inverted. If pressure continues to be exerted, these layers will thin and eventually break to produce an overthrust (or thrust) fold [D]. When these layers disappear due to stretching and fracture, a nappe is formed [E]. Over a long period this nappe may be pushed out many miles from its original position.

2 A symmetric anticline [1] and syncline [2] have limbs that dip at similar angles on either side of the axial plane of the fold. The position of the axial plane of an asymmetric anticline [3] and syncline [4] may be more difficult to establish. Where compression produces a reverse fault [5] one side of the fault (in this case the left) overrides the horizontal strata on the other side. In the case of a monocline fold [6], rock strata lying at two distinct levels may be separated from each other by a limb that may be shallow or relatively steep.

2

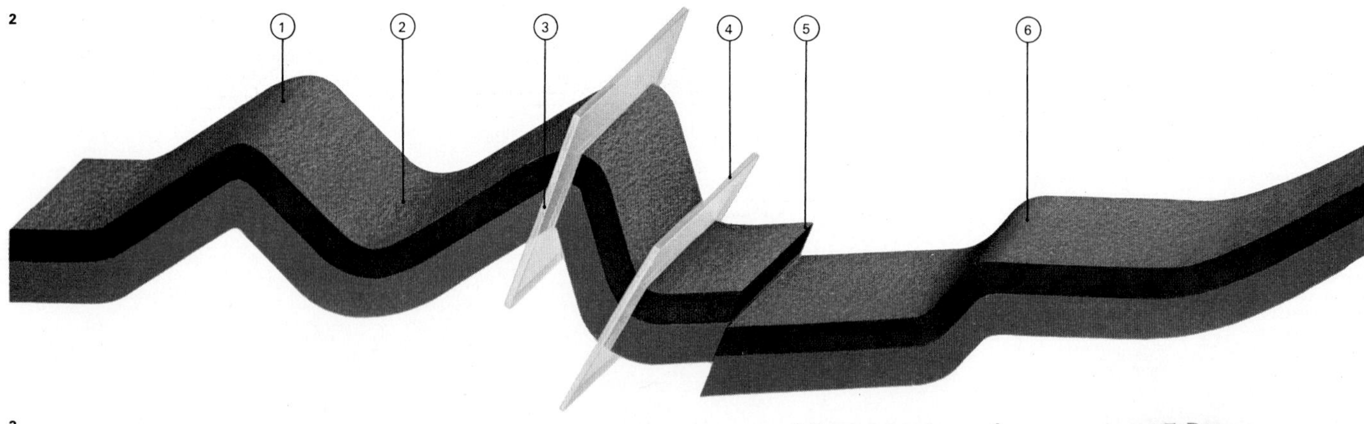

1
2
3
4
5
6

3

3 Domes and basins are folds that are about as wide as they are long. They are caused by complex compressions of the crust. Isolated domes can be the result of a subterranean rise of magma or rock salt.

4

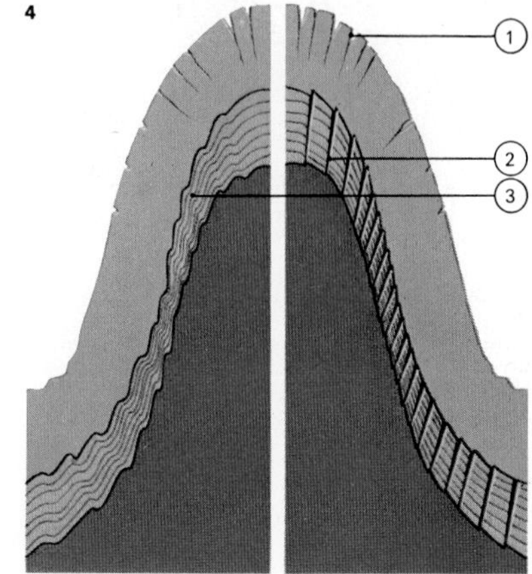

1
2
3

4 Beds can be competent or incompetent according to their reaction to folding. Competent beds bend and crack [1] without much flowage, while incompetent beds shear [2] or form shearing microfolds [3] that alter the thickness.

nary eras. Complex folds are found in older rocks that have been exposed to Earth movements for a longer period and that have often been deeply buried within the Earth's crust. Very old rocks, such as the Precambrian of Norway, have been refolded many times, with the development of structures such as boudinage, mullion, and cleavage [6, 7]. These ancient rocks have also been considerably altered by heat and pressure from igneous intrusions and deep burial. Platy minerals, such as micas, then develop parallel to each other and the rock tends to split easily along thin planes. Rocks with this property are known as schists.

With increasing distance from the source of pressure that causes folding, the folds gradually die out both in horizontal and vertical directions. This is well displayed in the Alps.

Faults and refaulting

When rocks can no longer bend under pressure they crack and a fault is formed [Key]. If the rocks are pulled apart a normal fault forms [10A], while if they are compressed reverse and thrust faults form [10B]. Movement along the fault plane causes grooves and scratches to be ground out on adjacent walls. These scratches allow geologists to measure the relative lateral and vertical movements of faults, and tell, for example, whether the movement was linear or rotational. Faults, which are often associated with earthquakes, are well expressed at the surface as fault scarps and rift valleys (e.g., the San Andreas fault and the Rhine rift valley).

As they are produced by the same pressures, faults are frequently associated with folded areas. Sometimes the surface strata may crack into a complex mosaic of blocks by renewed movement along an existing buried fault. Reactivation of such a buried fault is believed to have been responsible for the disastrous 1966 Tashkent (USSR) earthquake. Refaulting occurs in many areas where new and different stress fields are superposed upon ancient ones. Some regions have been refaulted and refolded several times, as in the complex Precambrian areas of Finland and Canada.

KEY

Fold structures include:
[1] Trace of the axial plane of a syncline
[2] Trace of the axial plane of an anticline.
[3] Crest of the fold
[4] Limb of the fold
[5] Anticline
[6] Dip of the rock strata
[7] Trough between folds
[8] Syncline

Fault structures include:
[1] Downthrown block
[2] Angle of dip
[3] Fault plane
[4] Net slip
[5] Hade
[6] Upthrown block
[7] Hanging wall
[8] Foot wall
[9] Horizontal dip slip (known as heave)
[10] Vertical slip (throw)

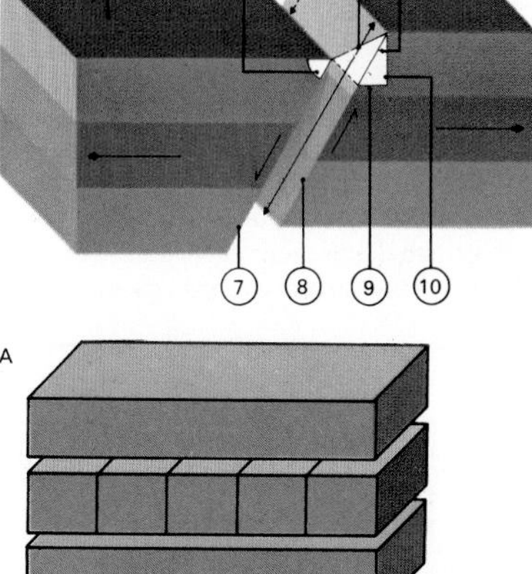

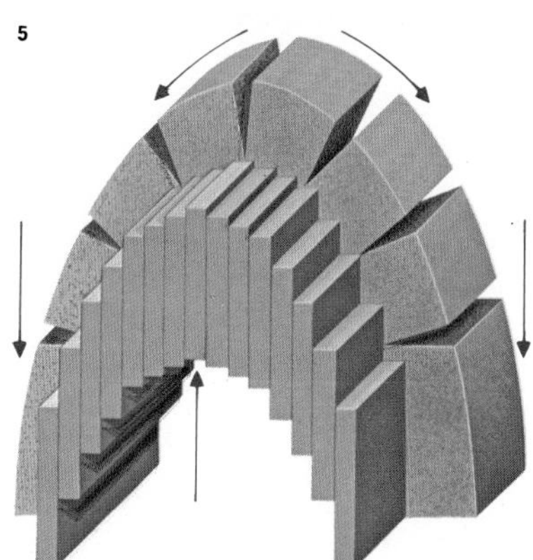

5 Rocks can break instead of bending. Coarse-grained rocks cleave on planes perpendicular to bedding. When the space between fractures exceeds an inch or two, they are called joints. Fractures form at the tops of anticlines where weak beds are pulled apart during folding. Finer-grained rocks split by close-spaced faults into slices that are parallel to the direction of pressure.

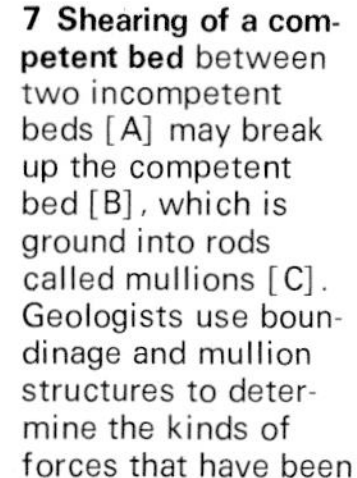

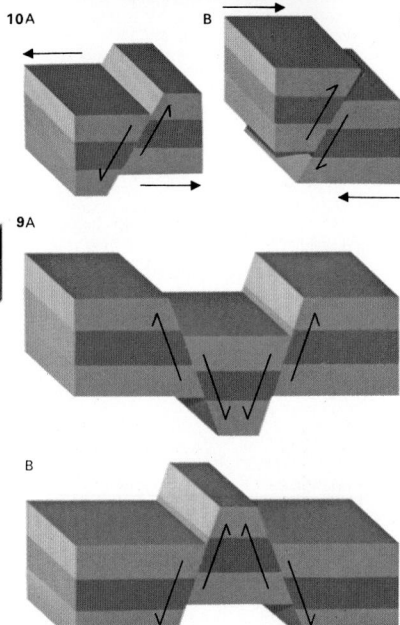

6 Strong rock in a competent bed between two incompetent beds [A] is sometimes subjected to stretching force [B]. The competent bed then deforms and breaks up into flattened rods, which are called boudins [C]. The incompetent beds on either side flow into the spaces between the boudins.

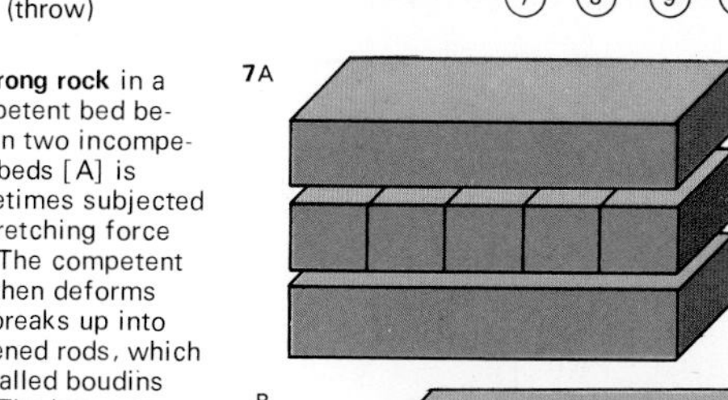

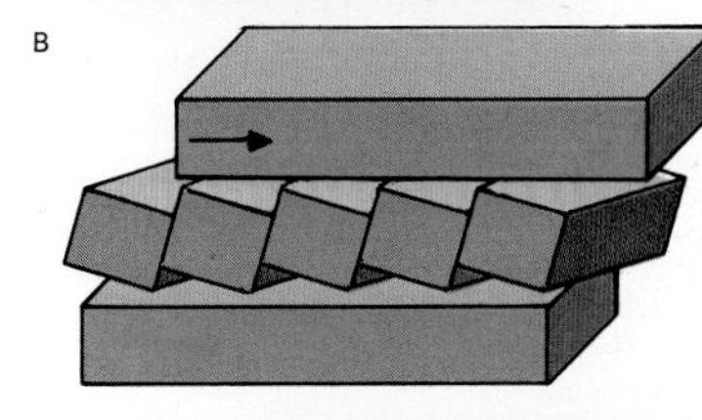

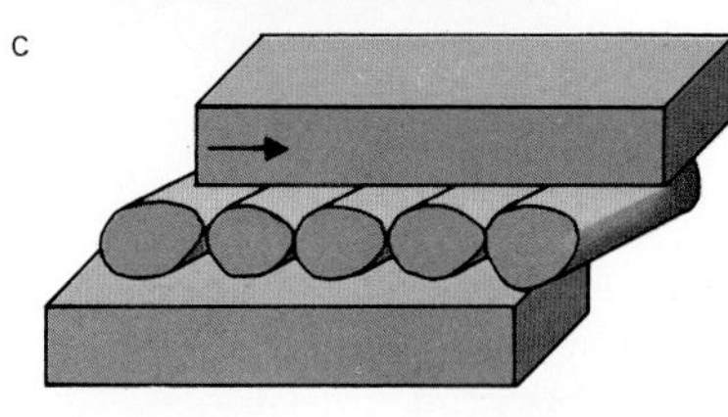

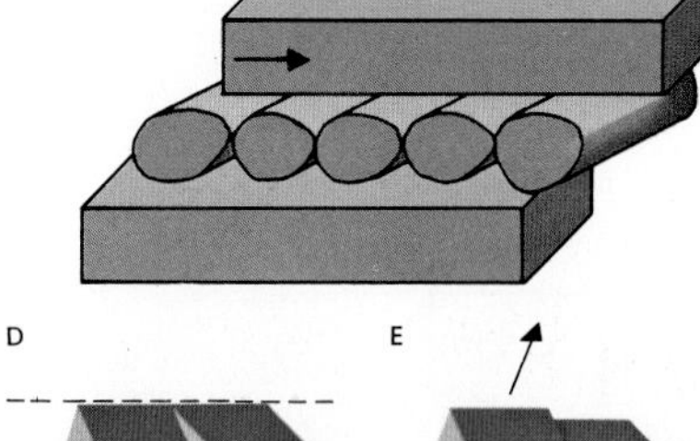

7 Shearing of a competent bed between two incompetent beds [A] may break up the competent bed [B], which is ground into rods called mullions [C]. Geologists use boundinage and mullion structures to determine the kinds of forces that have been at work and in what directions they acted.

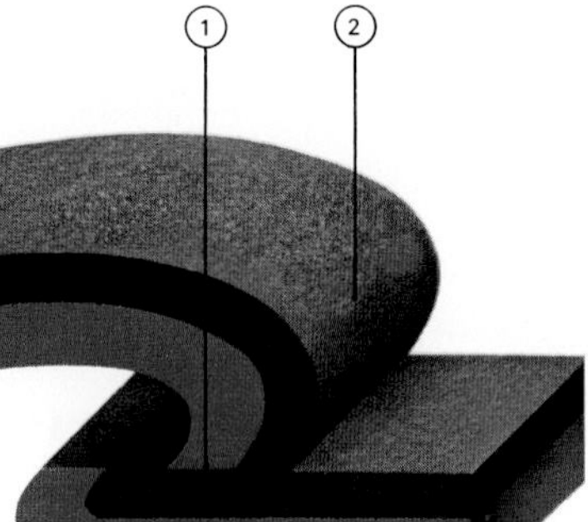

8 Lateral pressure, when applied to a recumbent fold, can produce a low-angle crack [1] along which the overturned limb of the fold [2] may slide. This type of crack in a rock structure is called a thrust fault.

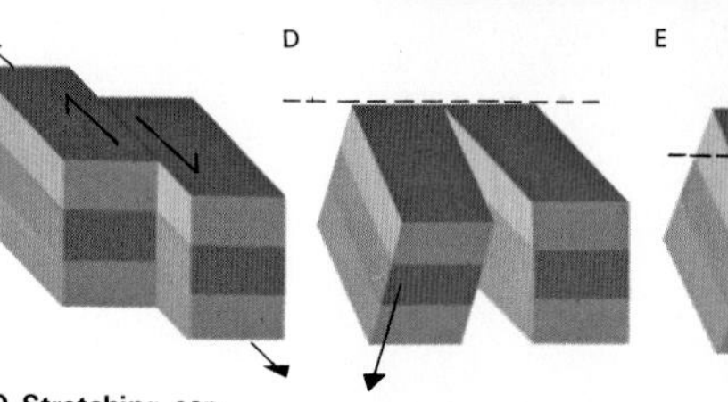

10 Stretching can produce a normal fault [A], compression a reversed fault [B], shearing a strike-slip fault [C], slumping a hinge fault [D], and twisting a rotational fault [E].

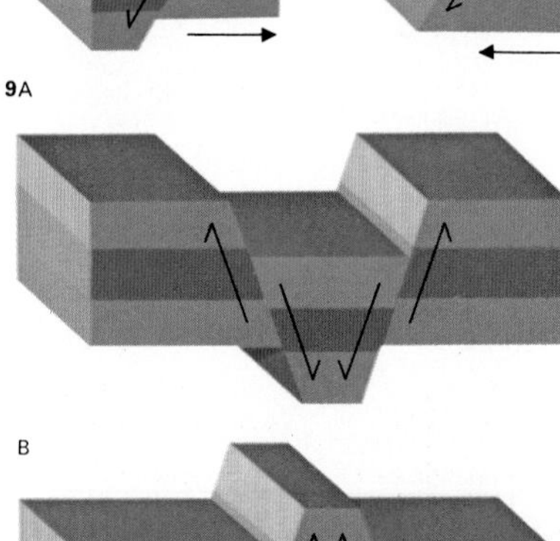

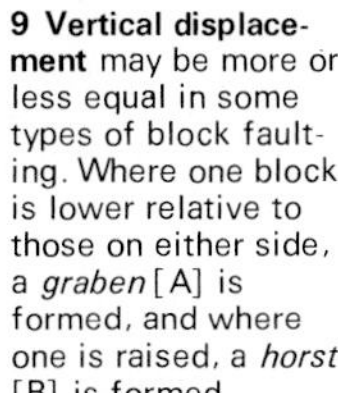

9 Vertical displacement may be more or less equal in some types of block faulting. Where one block is lower relative to those on either side, a *graben* [A] is formed, and where one is raised, a *horst* [B] is formed.

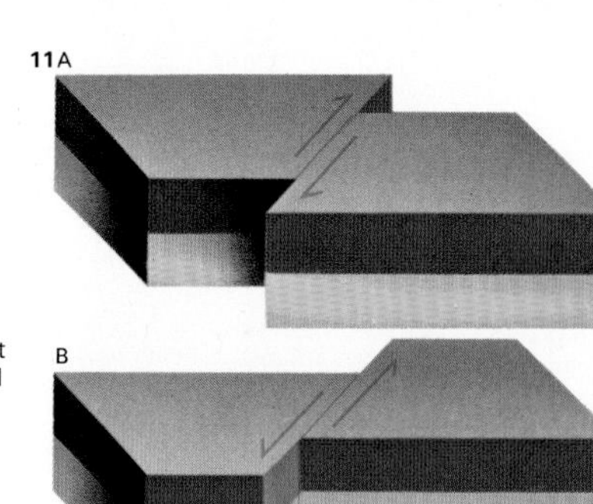

11 Strike-slip faults that move to the right [A] are called dextral faults, while movement to the left [B] produces sinistral faults. Transform faults are a special kind of strike-slip fault linking major Earth structures.

Life and death of mountains

A true mountain is more than a piece of high ground. It has underneath it specific geological formations, such as strongly folded and faulted rocks, ancient volcanic piles, or large igneous masses. Conversely, layers of sedimentary rocks that barely rise from the horizontal are not usually described as mountains, however high above sea level they are.

Types of mountains

There are four main types of mountains: fold, block, dome, and volcanic. Fold mountains vary widely in complexity but conform to the basic type. The Alps [10], Carpathians, and Himalayas form the world's largest fold-mountain chain. The rocks have been compressed and crumpled in extremely complex ways, with intrusions of molten rock, widespread metamorphism (changes in the rocks), and faulting.

Block mountains are large-scale faulted structures. Internally a block mountain is highly folded and faulted and may have been created either by a deep fault or by an exceptionally large block or raised strata (horst), which was then shaped by erosion. Many block mountains—for example, in the Basin and Range province of Nevada—rise abruptly above the surrounding lowland.

Domes are formed by the lifting of strata, as when granitic magma is intruded. As the lifting increases the surface is worn away by erosion and the underlying granite is exposed. When such domes are large and high they constitute true dome mountains. A good example of these are the Black Hills of Dakota.

Volcanic mountains differ from others in that they grow visibly during eruptions [4]. As more eruptions take place on the same site, the successive outflows of ash and lava increase the height of the volcano. Volcanic mountains in continental interiors are comparatively rare. They are mostly submarine or island features and can form island arcs of more than a thousand miles; one such arc is the Aleutian Island chain extending westward from Alaska.

Fold mountains are by far the most important because they form very large ranges thousands of miles long. Fold mountains are often associated with block-faulted mountains and with volcanic mountains because the forces causing the folding of the rocks are the same that produce faulting and promote vulcanism. The mechanism of the large horizontal compressions leading to the crumpling and folding of the sedimentary cover of the Earth's crust was poorly understood before the plate tectonics theory.

According to the plate tectonics theory, fold mountains are formed by the movements and collisions of large plates that make up the Earth's crust. These plates may underlie and carry whole continents. When two plates collide, one may slide beneath the other, squeezing upward the sediment deposited in the geosyncline [6], or trough, between them. The great folds formed in the compressed sediment eventually break out above the surrounding region as mountains.

A continental plate thrust under another tends to maintain an upward pressure, like a submerged cork trying to regain the surface: in time the stationary plate is levered up-

CONNECTIONS

See also
250 Folds and faults
170 Global tectonics
260 Land sculptured by water
262 Rivers of ice
176 Volcanoes

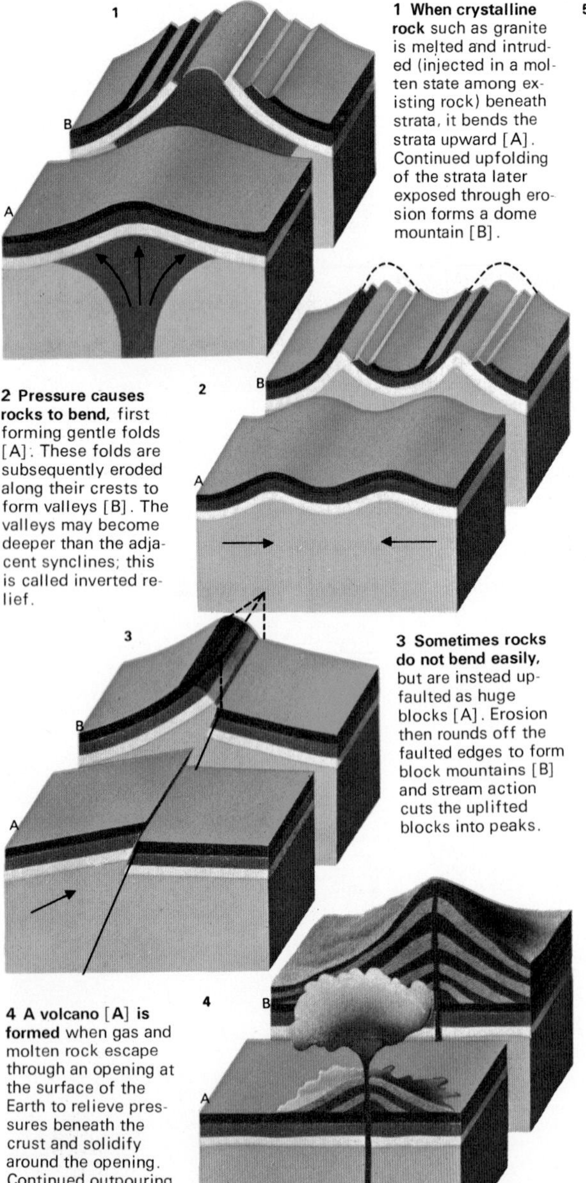

1
A
B
2
A
B
3
A
B
4
A
B

1 When crystalline rock such as granite is melted and intruded (injected in a molten state among existing rock) beneath strata, it bends the strata upward [A]. Continued upfolding of the strata later exposed through erosion forms a dome mountain [B].

2 Pressure causes rocks to bend, first forming gentle folds [A]. These folds are subsequently eroded along their crests to form valleys [B]. The valleys may become deeper than the adjacent synclines; this is called inverted relief.

3 Sometimes rocks do not bend easily, but are instead upfaulted as huge blocks [A]. Erosion then rounds off the faulted edges to form block mountains [B] and stream action cuts the uplifted blocks into peaks.

4 A volcano [A] is formed when gas and molten rock escape through an opening at the surface of the Earth to relieve pressures beneath the crust and solidify around the opening. Continued outpouring of ash and lava may build up a mountain [B].

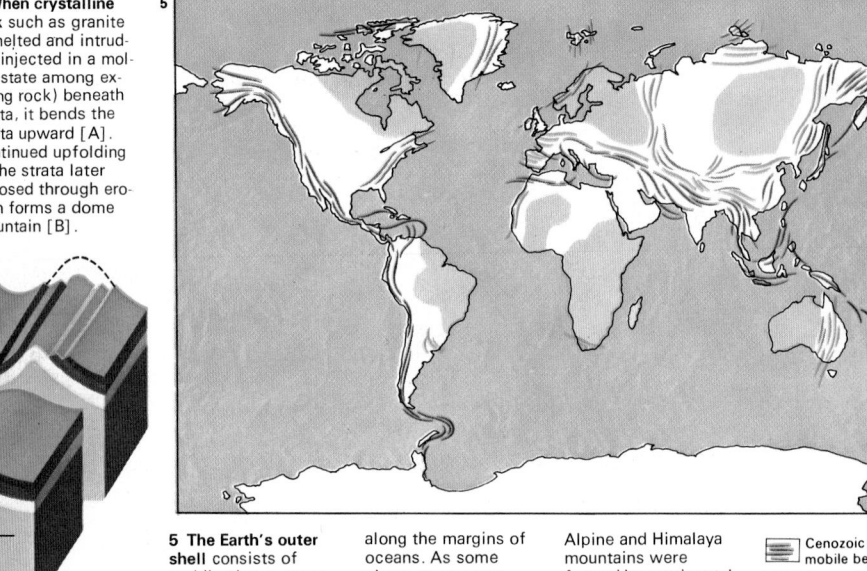

5 The Earth's outer shell consists of mobile plates, some of which carry continents made up of older nuclei or shields and more recent materials deposited in troughs along the margins of oceans. As some plates move apart and collide with continental plates, the material surrounding the shields gets crushed up into mountain chains. The Alpine and Himalaya mountains were formed by continental plate collisions, while the American cordillera was formed by collision between a continental and an oceanic plate.

Cenozoic mobile belts
Mesozoic mobile belts
Upper Palaeozoic mobile belts
Lower Palaeozoic mobile belts
Precambrian shield areas

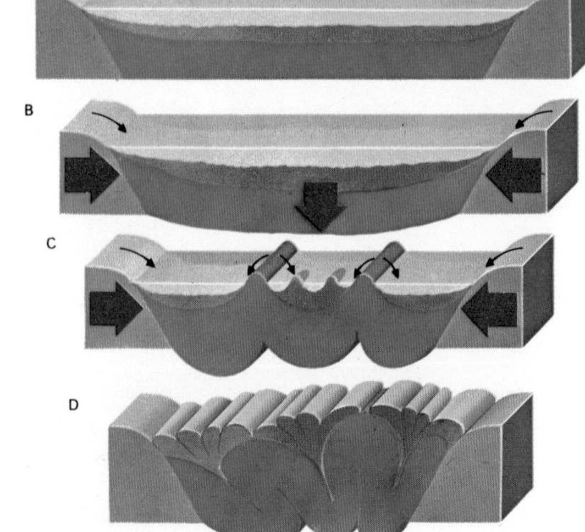

6 A
B
C
D

6 Geosynclines are the birthplaces of mountains. They are large troughs where thick layers of sediments can accumulate [A]. Where geosynclines develop between two colliding outer shell plates [B], the sediments can be squeezed up as broad ridges known as geanticlines [C]. Further compression creates mountain ranges [D]. The whole process is usually accompanied by pressure-induced recrystallization or melting, then forms metamorphic, plutonic, and volcanic rocks. Examples of each of these are gneisses, granites, and rhyolites.

ward and the attached fold mountains move with the plate. The Himalayas were formed when the northern edge of the Indian continental plate collided with and slid under the Asian plate; the Asian plate was then forced upward.

Death of mountains

Mountains are sculptured and destroyed by frost, water, and wind. Frost may shatter and break up rocks to form screes (masses of debris at a cliff base), and snow and glaciers gouge out rock debris and transport it down the mountainside, leaving the debris as elongated moraines at the tip and sides of the glacier. Lower down, rivers cut into the mountainside and form zigzag valleys with interlocking spurs. These spurs may in turn be sliced off by glaciers making their way to lower levels down the mountain. In short, the erosion of mountains is the continuing story of the breakup of rocks and their gradual descent to lower levels under the influence of gravity.

In time, weathering and erosion destroy mountains by lowering them so much that they are eventually transformed into broad plains cut by slowly meandering rivers. In arid climates wind erosion may finish the work by sand-blasting the remaining hills into a bare desert, leaving a surface known as a peneplain [Key]—that is, almost a plain. This stage is rarely reached however; more commonly, renewed Earth movements uplift the area again, and it enters a new geological phase.

The study of mountains

Mountains are important to geologists seeking to unravel the complexities of plate structures and to learn more about how rocks behave when they are compressed by moving continents. Mountains also mark the positions of ancient plate boundaries in, for example, Mesozoic-Cenozoic times when great ranges such as the Himalayas were being formed. Similarly, the study of ancient mountain ranges also reveals the sites of ancient oceans, enabling scientists to reconstruct segments of the planet as it must have looked many hundreds of millions of years ago.

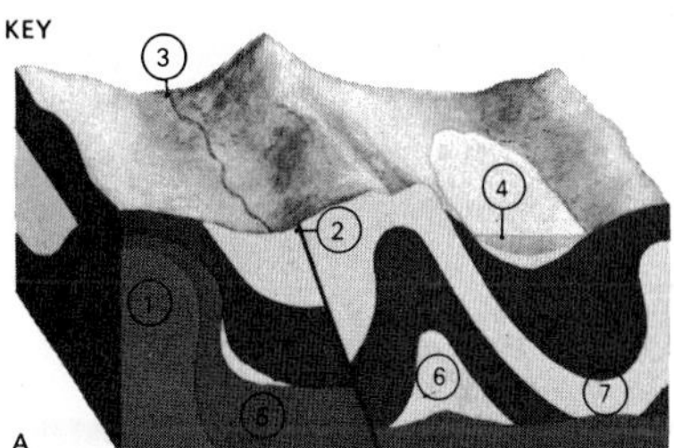
KEY
3
4
2
1
6
5
7
A

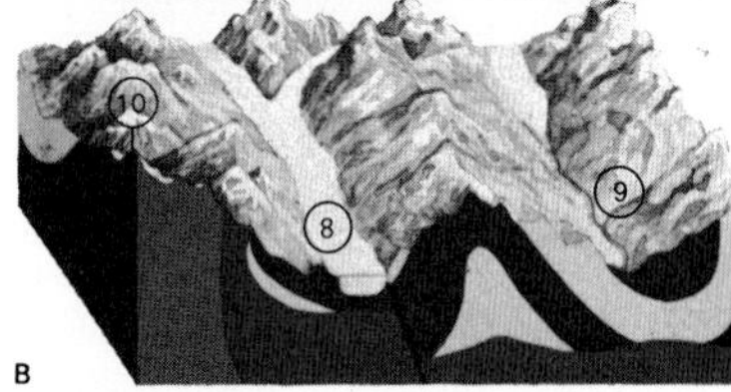
10
8
9
B

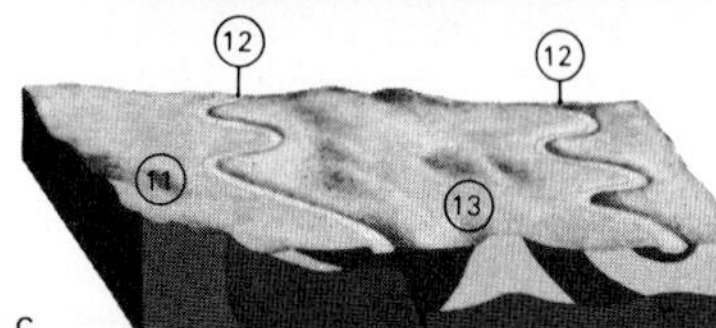
12
12
11
13
C

Three stages in the life of a mountain are shown here. [A] Idealized young complex mountain: [1] granite batholith; [2] major fault offsetting strata; [3] formation of a young stream; [4] sea level; [5] metamorphic rocks; [6] anticline of upfolded strata; [7] syncline of downfolded strata. [B] Mature complex mountain: [8] glacier scouring U-shaped valley; [9] glacial meltwater forming active stream; [10] erosional "horn"—a toothlike peak—top of granite batholith exposed by erosion. [C] Peneplain of old complex mountain: [11] peneplain due to total erosion of mountains; [12] rivers reworking sediments; [13] remnant of eroded mountain.

7

8

7 The Mont Blanc massif, a lofty mountain range in the French Alps, is typical of the popular conception of mountains. The cold climate caused by the high altitude allows frost to split the rocks, and glaciers carve the mountains into serrated ranges of jagged peaks called arêtes.

8 This peneplain in the Northern Territory of Australia was formed when a mountain range was eroded to an almost flat surface. Monadnocks jut up from the plain and reveal the former positions of peaks or hard rocks. The surface is scoured by wind and this forms a sandy desert.

9

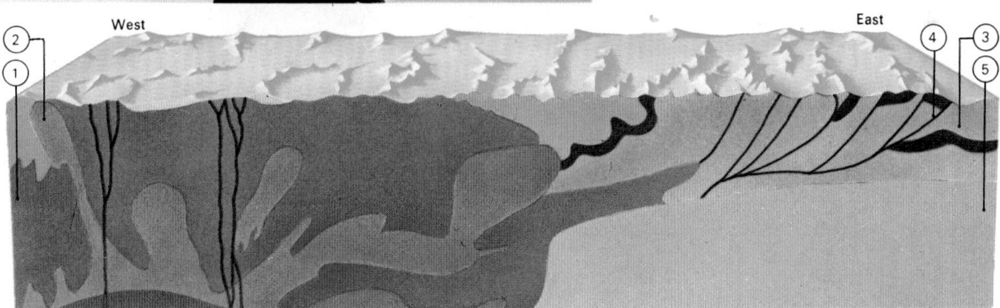
West
East
2
1
4
3
5

9 The Canadian Rockies, in their western part, consist of intensely metamorphosed strata [1]. High pressures caused granites to melt. These granites, expanding with heat, became lighter than the overlying rocks and rose up through them as intrusions [2]. The uplift sheared the Paleozoic strata [3] to the east along low-angle faults [4], which also separate these strata from the underlying crystalline basement [5]. The piling up of these slabs by thrust-faulting finally led to the development of a considerable thickness of sedimentary rocks.

10

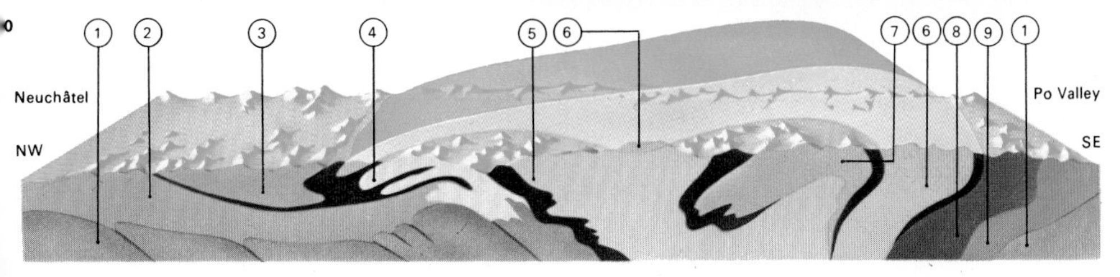
1
2
3
4
5
6
7
6
8
9
1
Neuchâtel
NW
Po Valley
SE

10 The highly folded strata of the western Alps have not only been crumpled and folded but also shoved great distances northward by Earth movements as nappes. Where pressure and heat were sufficient, the strata were transformed into metamorphic rocks, such as gneiss and schist [5, 6, 7, 8]. The areas shown here are [1] basement; [2] flysch zone; [3] Pre-Alps; [4] Helvetic nappes; [6] Dent Blanche nappe; [7] Mont Rosa nappe; [8] Iyree zone; and [9] Dinaric Alps.

Earth's water supply

Water is essential to all life on Earth. The study of the Earth's water supply, called hydrology, investigates the distribution of water, how it is used by man, and how it circulates from the oceans to land areas and back again in the hydrologic cycle.

The water cycle—from oceans to land
About 97 percent of the world's available water is in the oceans [Key]. Oceanic water is unsuitable for drinking or for farming. In some desert regions, where fresh water is in short supply, seawater is desalinated to make fresh water. But most of the world is supplied with fresh water by the natural process of the water cycle [1] which relies on two factors: the Sun's heat and gravity.

Over the oceans, which cover about 71 percent of the Earth's surface, the Sun's heat causes evaporation. Water vapor, an invisible gas, rises on air currents and winds. Some of it condenses and returns directly to the oceans as rain. But because of the circulation of the atmosphere, air bearing large amounts of water vapor is carried over land where it falls as rain and snow.

Much of this precipitation is quickly reevaporated by the Sun. Some soaks into the soil, where it is absorbed by plants and partly returned to the air through transpiration. Some water flows over the land surface as run-off, which collects into rills and flows into streams and rivers. Some rain and melted snow seeps through the soil into the rocks beneath to form ground water.

In polar and high mountainous regions most precipitation is in the form of snow. There it is compacted into ice, forming ice sheets and glaciers. The force of gravity causes these bodies of ice to move downward and outward and they may eventually return to the oceans, where chunks of ice break off at the coastline to form icebergs. Thus all the water that does not return directly to the atmosphere gradually returns to the sea to complete the water cycle. This continual movement of water and ice plays a major part in the erosion of land areas.

Of the total water on land, more than 75 percent is frozen in ice sheets and glaciers, as in Greenland and Antarctica [Key]. Most of the rest (about 22 percent) is water collected below the Earth's surface and is called ground water. Comparatively small quantities are in lakes, rivers, and in the soil. Water that is held in the soil and that nourishes plant growth is retained in the upper few feet by molecular attraction between the water and soil particles.

Ground water and the water table
Ground water [4] enters permeable rocks through what is called the zone of intermittent saturation. This layer may retain ground water after continued rain but soon dries up. Beneath this lies a rock zone where the pores or crevices are filled with water. It is called the zone of saturation and usually begins within 100ft (30m) of the surface, extending downward until it reaches impermeable rock, through which water cannot percolate. This impermeable rock layer, lying below the water-holding layer, or aquifer, is called a ground-water dam, or aquiclude. The top of the saturated zone is called the water table; it varies in level during the year, depending on the amount of rainfall.

CONNECTIONS

See also
258 Rivers and lakes
256 Caves and underground water
314 Water and irrigation

1

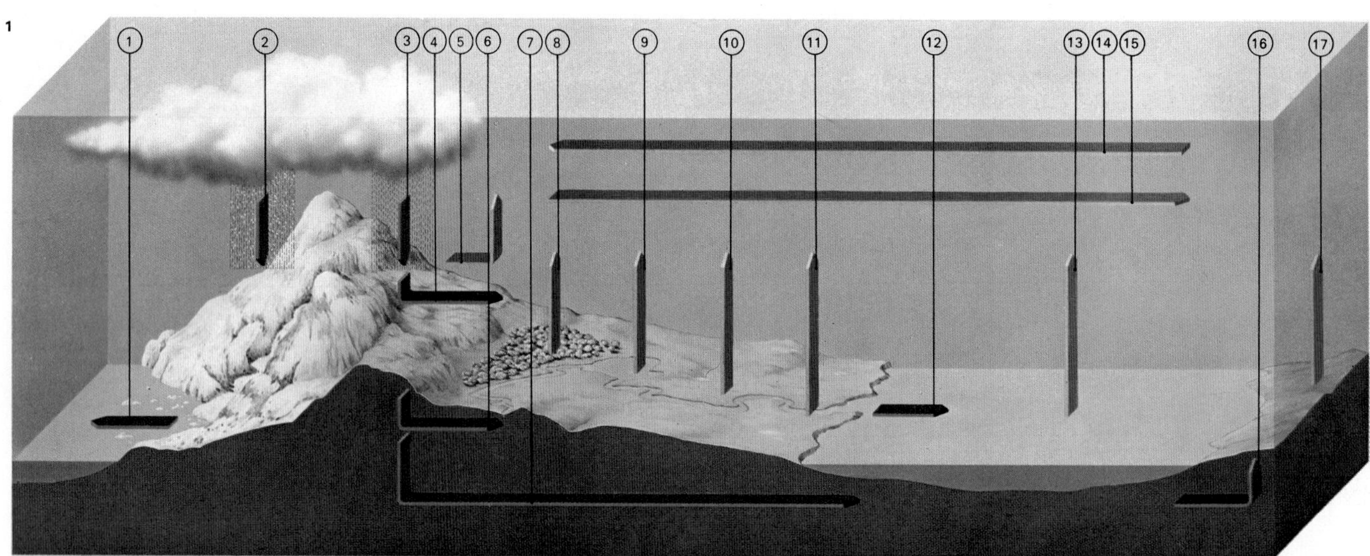
1 2 3 4 5 6 7 8 9 10 11 12 13 14 15 16 17

1 The hydrological, or water, cycle is the process whereby water, in some form, circulates from the oceans to land areas and back again. Fresh water is present on the Earth as water vapor in the atmosphere, as ice, and as liquid water. The elements of the cycle are precipitation as rain [3]; surface run-off [4]; evaporation of rain in falling [5]; ground water flow to rivers and streams [6]; ground water flow to the ocean [7]; transpiration from plants [8]; evaporation from lakes and ponds [9]; evaporation from the soil [10]; evaporation from rivers and streams [11]; evaporation from the oceans [13]; flow of rivers and streams to the oceans [12]; ground water flow from the ocean to arid land [16]; intense evaporation from arid land [17]; movement of moist air from the oceans [14] and to them [15]; precipitation as snow [2]; ice flow from the land into the sea [1].

2

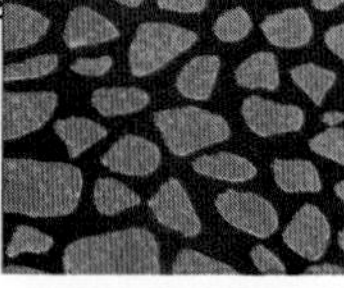

2 Sandstone (shown here in a cross-section) is a highly porous rock through which water percolates easily.

3

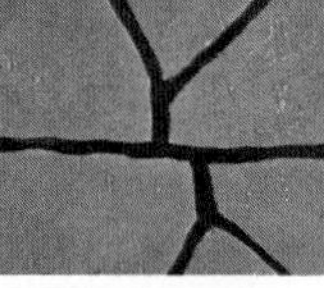

3 Limestone is a permeable but non-porous rock. Water can only percolate through the joints and the fissures.

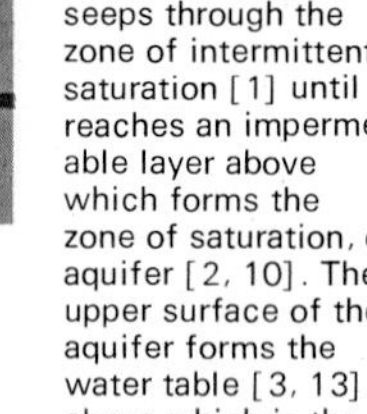

4 Ground water seeps through the zone of intermittent saturation [1] until it reaches an impermeable layer above which forms the zone of saturation, or aquifer [2, 10]. The upper surface of the aquifer forms the water table [3, 13], above which is the capillary fringe [6]. Wells [7] must be sunk to the water table because the capillary fringe is not saturated. Impermeable dikes [8] block the flow of ground water. In uniform material the water follows paths [4] that curve down and up again toward the nearest stream. If an aquifer is part of a series of strata including several impermeable layers [11] a perched water table [12] may result. If it lies between two impermeable strata it is said to be confined [14]. Its recharge area [15] is where water enters the confined aquifer. A stream below the water table is called a gaining stream [5] while a stream flowing above it is known as a losing stream [9] because it loses water by seepage.

4

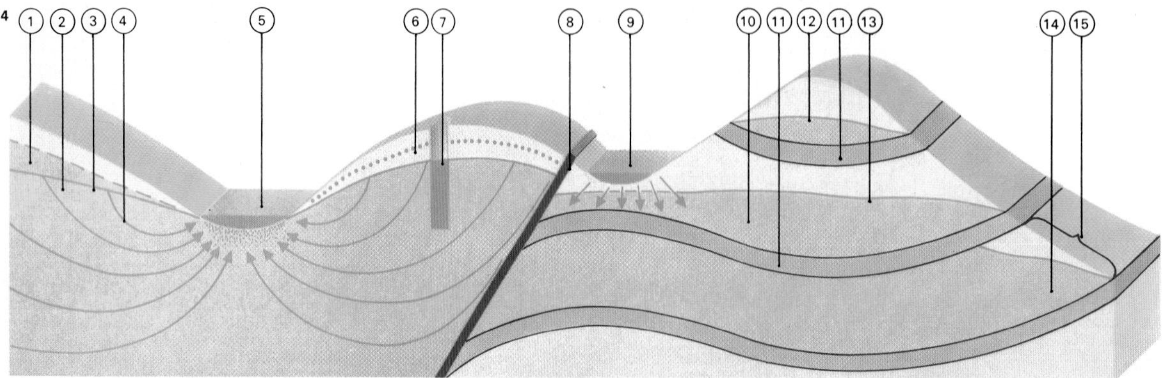
1 2 3 4 5 6 7 8 9 10 11 12 11 13 14 15

In some places the water table intersects the surface, forming such features as oases [6] in desert hollows, swamps, lakes, and springs. Springs [5] are gushes or seepages of water that may occur along the base of a hillside or in a valley in the hills. They are found where the water table appears at the surface because of the slope of the ground or because the aquifer is blocked by an impermeable rock, such as a volcanic dike. Spring water is usually fresh and clean because it passes through the fine pores of rocks such as sandstones [2], where impurities are filtered out.

Limestone is not a porous rock but it is permeable—that is, ground water can seep through the maze of fissures, joints, and caves in the rock [3]. These apertures are enlarged by rainwater containing dissolved carbon dioxide—a weak, carbonic acid that dissolves limestone. In limestone, ground water is not filtered in the same way as in porous rocks. In the late 1800s epidemics of cholera and typhoid often occurred in France in areas where springs emerged from limestone areas. It was finally established that the spring water had been contaminated miles away by garbage thrown into pot holes.

Some springs contain so much mineral substances in solution that their water is used for medicinal purposes. Spa towns have grown up around such mineral springs. Some of these springs are thermal, the water being heated by underground pockets of molten rock or magma.

Water from artesian wells

The lowest level of the water table, reached at the driest time of year, is called the permanent water table. Wells must be drilled to this level if they are to supply water throughout the year. In artesian wells [7] water is forced to the surface by hydrostatic pressure—this results from the rim of the well being below the level of the water table in the catchment area. Artesian water is obtained from porous sandstone aquifers that underlie the Great Artesian Basin of Australia. These aquifers are supplied with water from the rain that falls on the Eastern Highlands.

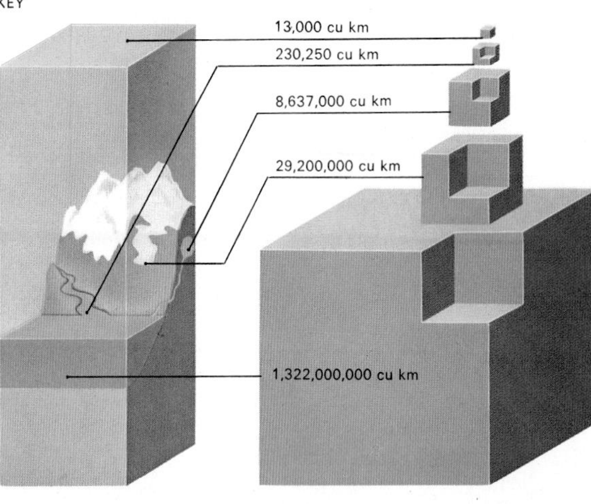

KEY
13,000 cu km
230,250 cu km
8,637,000 cu km
29,200,000 cu km
1,322,000,000 cu km

The total water supply of the world is estimated to be about 326.5 million cubic miles (1.36 billion cu km). The oceans contain 97.2 percent of it. Of the remainder, 2.15 percent is frozen in ice caps and glaciers, and most of the rest is in rivers and lakes (0.0171 per cent) or under land areas as ground water (0.625 percent). Water vapor represents only 0.001 percent, but without it there would be no life on land. Water vapor is carried over land and falls as rain or snow.

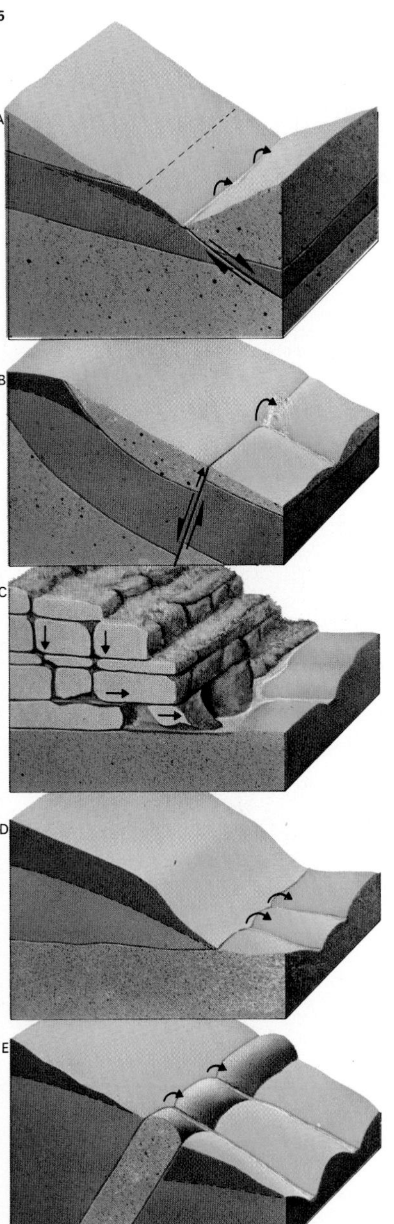

5
A
B
C
D
E

5 Springs appear where the water table meets the surface. [A] Springs may occur where a fault brings an aquifer into contact with an impermeable layer. [B] Water pressure creates artesian springs at points of weakness. [C] Water seeps through jointed limestone until it emerges above an impermeable layer. [D] Springs form where permeable strata overlay impermeable rock. [E] An impermeable barrier may lead to the formation of a spring line.

6

6 An oasis is an area in a desert that is made fertile by the presence of water. Some oases are found along rivers crossing the deserts, such as the Nile. Others owe their moisture to underground waters reaching the surface or near-surface. Wadis are intermittent streams that only flow after heavy rainfall but they often have a hidden flow under their beds which can reach the surface to create oases. Aquifers with recharge areas outside the desert can "pipe" water to oases under long stretches of arid desert. These recharge areas are usually mountains suitably sited for catching rain. The natural flow can be increased by pumping the ground water but if the rate of pumping exceeds the water flow into the aquifer the wells will dry up and not fill again until the aquifer is recharged.

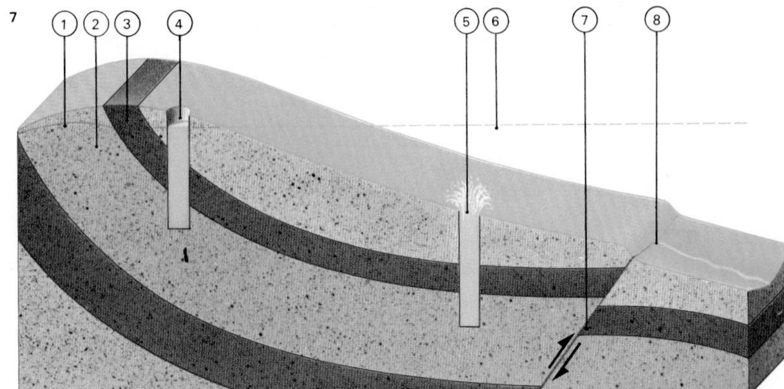

7
1
2
3
4
5
6
7
8

7 Artesian springs and wells are found where ground water is under pressure. The water table [1] in the confined aquifer [2] lies near the top of the dipping layers. A well [4] drilled through the top impervious layer [3] is not an artesian well because the head of hydrostatic pressure [6] is not sufficient to force water to the surface. In such wells the water must be pumped or drawn to the surface. The top of an artesian well [5] lies below the level of the head of hydrostatic pressure and so water gushes to the surface. Artesian springs [8] may occur along joints or faults [7] where the head of hydrostatic pressure is sufficient to force the water up along the fault. Areas with artesian wells are called artesian basins. In the London and Paris artesian basins the water has been so heavily tapped that the water level has dropped below the level of the well heads.

Caves and underground water

Most of the Earth's surface has been mapped, but in many areas vast networks of caves, largely unexplored, lie beneath the ground. There are several kinds of caves, including coastal caves, ice caves, and lava caves. The largest cave systems occur in carbonate rocks (limestone and dolomite), most of them forming in massive layers of limestone.

Formation of caves

Limestone is a fairly hard rock formed from calcium carbonate. Although insoluble in pure water, limestone is dissolved by rainwater containing carbon dioxide from the air and from the soil. Rainwater reacts chemically with limestone and converts it to soluble calcium bicarbonate. Limestone is riven by joints (vertical cracks) and bedding planes, which are usually horizontal. When limestone is exposed on the surface, rainwater widens the joints, dividing the limestone into blocks. This broken pavement surface is a feature of karst landscape, named after the limestone Karst district of the Dinaric Alps in Yugoslavia.

Some authorities believe that limestone caves are formed when rainwater slowly enlarges the joints and bedding planes as it seeps down to the water table. Eventually, streams flow into the enlarged joints, which form sink holes. Such streams may flow underground for many miles, dissolving vertical chimneys and horizontal galleries.

Other authorities do not believe that this explanation accounts for cave networks that have underground chambers with high roofs. Such caves, they argue, must have been formed when the land surface was far higher than it is now and when the limestone was below the water table and completely saturated with ground water [1]. They believe that the ground water seeped through the rock, dissolving much of it in the process. Eventually, the forces of erosion planed down the land surface, the water table dropped, and air entered the dissolved caves. Sink holes might have been formed when the roofs of these underground caves finally collapsed.

Mammoth Cave National Park in Kentucky [Key] is the site of the world's most extensive cave network, with a total mapped passageway of 144miles (231km), linking it with the Flint Ridge cave system. One of the deepest-known caves is the Gouffre de la Pierre St Martin in the western Pyrenees in France, which drops 3,850ft (1,174m). The largest underground chamber is the Big Room in Carlsbad Caverns, New Mexico. At a depth of 1,320ft (400m), the Big Room is 4,270ft (1,300m) long, 328ft (100m) high and 656ft (200m) wide.

Features of caves

Limestone caves contain many features formed from deposits of calcium carbonate, including iciclelike stalactites [6] and pillarlike stalagmites [5]. Stalactites develop when water that is highly charged with dissolved calcium bicarbonate seeps through holes in the roofs of caves. Drops of water that hang on the roof are partly evaporated and a tiny quantity of calcium carbonate is precipitated and sticks to the roof. Another drop of water deposits a second film of calcium carbonate in the same place and, in this way, stalactites slowly develop. Drops

CONNECTIONS

See also
254 Earth's water supply
248 Sedimentary and metamorphic rocks
652 From ancient to modern man

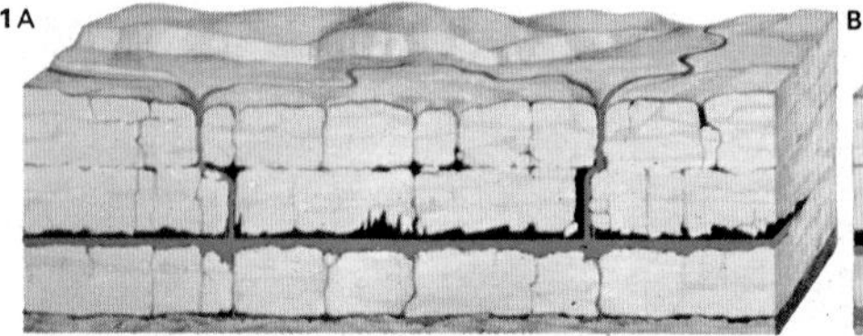

1A

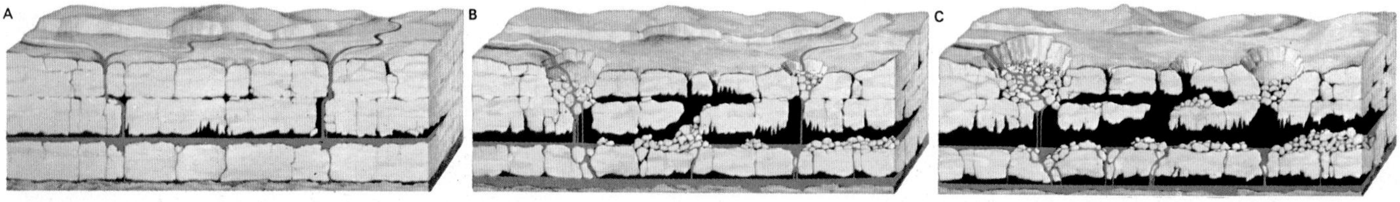

B

C

1 As rain falls, it dissolves carbon dioxide from the atmosphere and becomes a weak carbonic acid that attacks carbonate rock (limestone and dolomite) by transforming it into the soluble bicarbonate. Carbonate rocks are criss-crossed by vertical cracks and horizontal breaks [A]. Caves may have been formed when the rock was below the water table and saturated by water. Or they may have formed gradually above the water table by solution [B] into a major network [C].

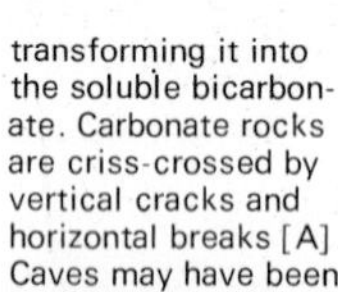

2 Limestone surfaces are often eroded into blocks called clints [1]. Surface streams flow into dissolved sink holes [2] that lead to a deep chimney [3]. Pot holes [7] are dry chimneys. Gours [4] are ridges formed as carbonate is precipitated from turbulent water. Streams flow at the lowest level of the galleries [17]. Abandoned galleries [13] are common. A siphon [12] occurs where the roof is below water level. Streams reappear at resurgences [20]. Abandoned resurgences [19] may provide entrances to caves. Stalactites [5] include macaroni stalactites [6]; curtain stalactites, or drapes [11]; and eccentric stalactites [16]. Stalagmites [14] sometimes have a pine cone shape [15] caused by splashing, or resemble stacked plates [8]. Stalactites and stalagmites may form columns [10]. Signs of ancient man [18] have been found and the specialized fauna includes blind salamanders [9].

2

of water that fall to the floor may also be partly evaporated, leaving small deposits of calcium carbonate that grow upward into stalagmites. Stalactites and stalagmites sometimes meet to form a column [6] extending from roof to floor.

The growth of stalactites and stalagmites is usually extremely slow. Some take 4,000 years to increase by only 1in (2.5cm) in length; however, stalactites in Ingleborough Cave, Yorkshire, England, have been known to increase by 3in (7.6cm) in ten years.

Another deposit, caused by water seeping through a long crack in the roof of a cave, is a wavy band of calcium carbonate that grows across the ceiling like a fringed curtain. Water flowing down a wall or across a floor of a cave may build up a flowstone. Delicate threadlike or fingerlike formations called helictites sometimes jut out from a stalactite. Their origin is disputed. On the roofs of some caves are anthodites, which are branching, flowerlike formations. In its pure state, calcium carbonate is transparent or white, but these and other cave features are often colored by impurities.

Life in caves

Caves harbor a variety of animal life especially adapted to the dark environment, including blind, colorless, almost transparent crustaceans, worms, mites, insects, and sightless salamanders as well as blind cave fish. These creatures live permanently in caves. Bats, also common in cave systems, have weak eyes and depend mainly on their sonar systems to guide them through the dark tunnels. Every night hundreds of thousands of bats emerge from Carlsbad Caverns. Within 15 minutes' flight of the caverns is the Pecos valley, where the bats feed on insects, returning to the caves shortly before dawn.

In prehistoric times the most important inhabitant of caves was man. Archeologists have found many traces of man's occupation—tools, bones, hearths, and, usually well inside the cave entrances, rock paintings that may have had ritual or magical significance.

KEY

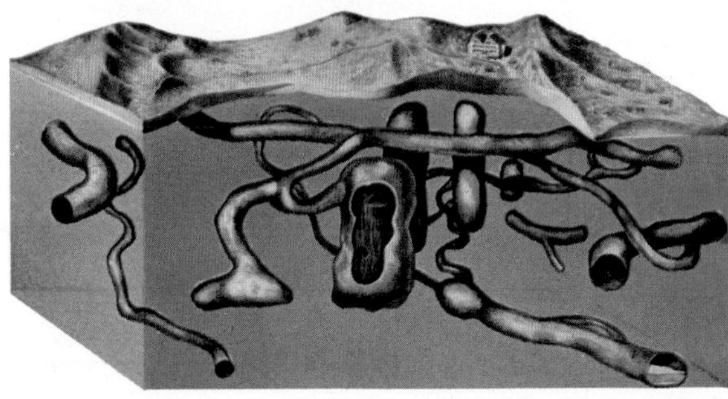

Mammoth Caves in Kentucky comprise the world's largest underground cave network. Mammoth Cave National Park consists of a limestone plateau whose surface is pitted by more than 60,000 sink holes. Surface water drains into the sink holes that link the caves to the surface. Some sink holes are connected to the caves by vertical chimneys. The underground caves are interlinked by a maze of passages. The Great Mammoth Cave has more than 30 miles (48km) of continuous passages. In the caves, water seeping through the limestock rock collects into rivers, which finally emerge into the open at the base of the plateau, in the Echo River valley. This system is typical of the arrangement of galleries, caverns, and sink holes found in many limestone areas where acidic water has seeped into the rock and dissolved it.

3 Gours are formed when carbonate-rich waters flow over an irregular surface. The turbulence deposits calcite on the irregularities, which grow into a series of ridges perpetuating the process.

4

4 Balcony stalactites are formed by water dripping from the side of a cave wall. They are called stalactites because they grow downward, but ordinary stalactites hang from the roof of a cave.

5

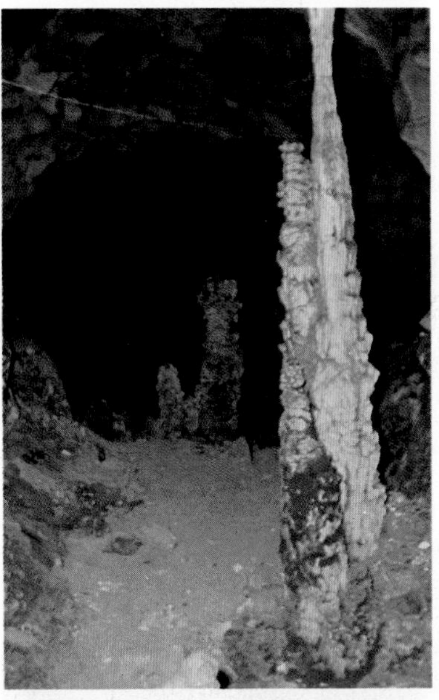

5 Stalagmites build upward from the floor of a cave. They are generally shorter and thicker than stalactites. The tallest stalagmite is 95ft (29m) high, in the Aven Armand Cave, in Lozère, France.

6

6 Stalactites, stalagmites, and columns of calcium carbonate are present in this cave. The columns are formed when stalactites and stalagmites meet. Stalactites are fragile structures and, as they easily break off, do not usually grow to great lengths. The longest known stalactite is supported by a wall in the Cueva de Nerja, near Málaga in Spain. It is 195ft (59cm) long and extends from the roof down to the floor.

7

7 A cave explorer climbs down a wire ladder into a cave. He wears a protective helmet with a carbide lamp. All his equipment must be collapsible to enable him to carry it through the confined spaces that he will encounter.

Rivers and lakes

When rain falls on the ground it is either absorbed in the soil or runs downhill over the surface in small temporary gullies called rills. These unite to form a stream. Other streams start from springs, where water that has sunk into the ground comes to the surface, or from melting glaciers. Streams and rivers usually begin in mountains or hills and the downward pull of gravity gives them energy to cut away the land and form valleys.

Erosion and transportation

The stones and sand formed by erosion of the rock are transported downstream and are finally deposited at the mouth of the river. Erosion, transportation, and deposition are the main work of a river and most rivers can be divided into three sections: an upper course in which erosion dominates; a middle one where transportation occurs; and a lower one where deposition takes place [1].

Stream water erodes in two ways: chemically and mechanically. Weak acids, such as carbonic acid, in the water help decompose limestone and other rocks. The ability of a stream to erode mechanically is closely related to its speed. During normal flow little mechanical erosion takes place, but during flood the movement of water becomes turbulent and this causes eddies that in turn cause rapid changes in the pressure on the rocks. Sometimes the pressure is so low that a partial vacuum is formed on a small part of the stream bed; as the eddy changes, this vacuum implodes (collapses inward). Much of the babble of a brook is the sound of implosions. Repeated implosions cause part of the rock to be sucked into the stream and carried away. Erosion mainly takes place at this stage by stones banging into the stream bed and sides.

The faster the stream flows the larger the fragments it can carry. It can also carry more of them. This is why most erosion and transportation occur during floods. The finest particles are carried in suspension, kept up by the turbulent motion of the water. Eddies bounce the sand from the bottom and it is carried downstream a small distance by the current before it falls to the bottom again. Coarser material is rolled along the stream bed.

Deposition of sediment

As the river enters more gentle slopes, some of its sediment is dropped. Where there is a sudden change in gradient and therefore water speed, as when a river leaves the mountains and runs out onto a plain, nearly all the sediment will be dropped, forming an alluvial fan [2]. More usually the material is deposited *en route* as the river current slows.

During a flood, however, river water moves at different speeds. In the river channel the current is fast moving, but where the river spreads over its banks onto the surrounding land (the flood plain) the current slows and mud and very fine sand are deposited as the water leaves its channel. This forms a ridge, or natural levee, along each bank.

The long profile of a river [Key]—the plot of the elevation of the river against distance traveled (exaggerated vertically to show significant features)—is theoretically a part of a hyperbola, being steepest at the

CONNECTIONS

Read first
254 Earth's water supply

See also
260 Land sculptured by water
256 Caves and underground water
296 Pollution of rivers and lakes

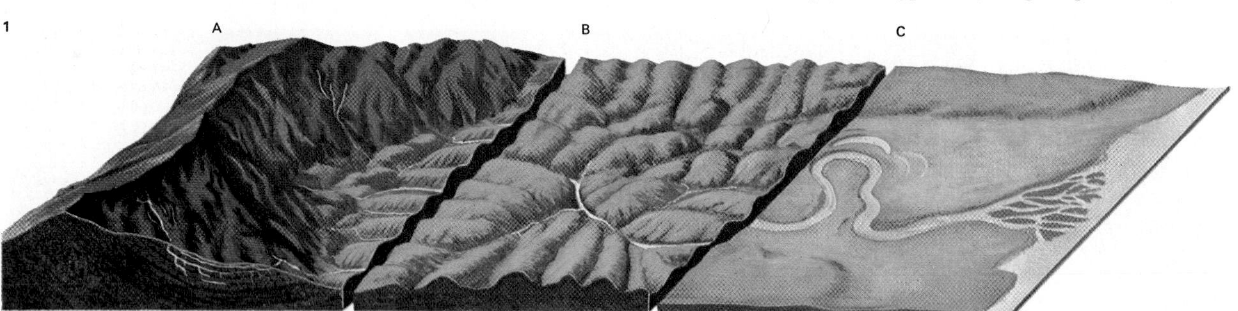

1
A
B
C

1 A river changes from a small stream in the mountains to a slow meandering river near the sea. The course of the river is divided into three stages. In its upper course [A] the river is fast flowing and able to wear away the rocks. In its middle section [B] it flows slowly and carries sediment to the lower section [C].

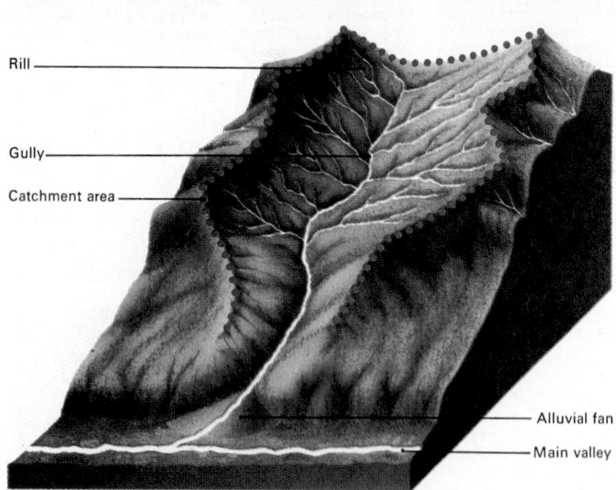

2
Rill
Gully
Catchment area
Alluvial fan
Main valley

2 Mountain streams are fed by rills meeting in catchment areas to form gullies that carry fast-flowing water to the main valley. Here velocity decreases and sediment is deposited as an alluvial fan at the foot of the mountains.

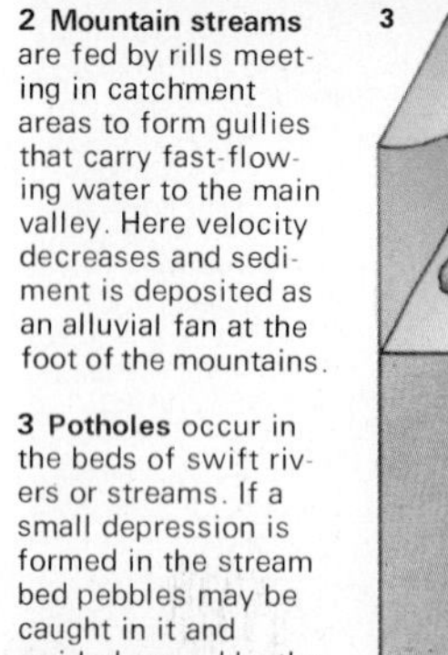

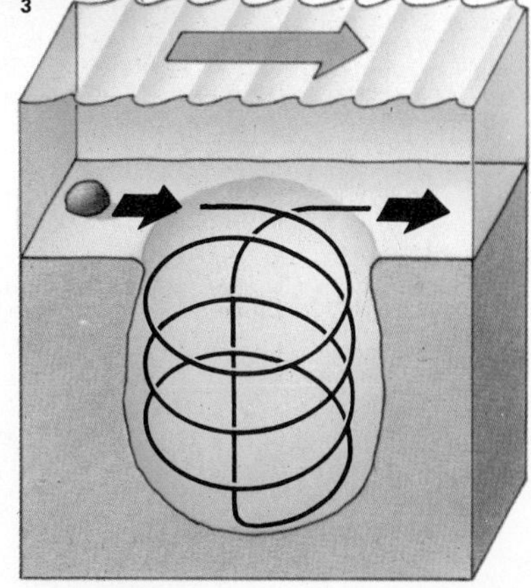

3

3 Potholes occur in the beds of swift rivers or streams. If a small depression is formed in the stream bed pebbles may be caught in it and swirled around by the water, enlarging the depression into a circular pothole.

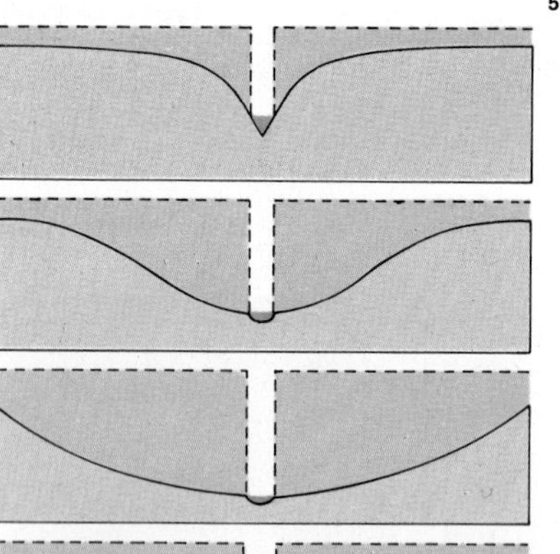

4
A
B
C
D
E

4 A valley is formed by two processes: down-cutting by the stream combined with mass movement of the valley walls. In [A] a young river flows in a v-shaped valley. Weathering widens the valley by changing the rocks forming the sides to soil [B]. As the velocity of water decreases, lateral erosion widens the valley floor [C, D]. In its advanced stage [E] the river flows slowly through a flat plain with deposited material forming levees.

5 San Juan River, Utah 1941
9 September
Normal
15 September
Surface raised 3m

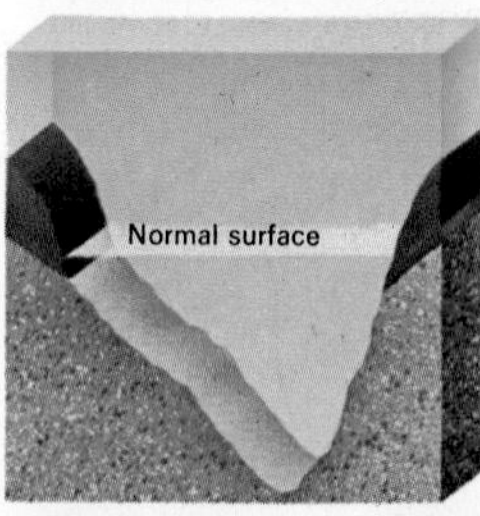

14 October
Surface raised 4·5m
Normal surface
Bed scoured and lowered 1m

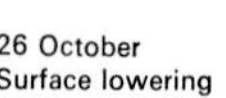

26 October
Surface lowering
Bed filling

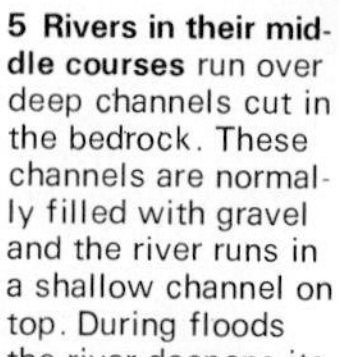

5 Rivers in their middle courses run over deep channels cut in the bedrock. These channels are normally filled with gravel and the river runs in a shallow channel on top. During floods the river deepens its channel by moving the sand below it. Only during the largest flood is the river able to scour the rock bottom. In a large flood the river may be 10 times deeper and carry 100 times more water.

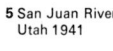

source and flattening at the mouth. This is an equilibrium curve toward which the stream tends to adjust its gradient, digging into its bed and removing material from the upper course and depositing it as the speed drops in the lower. In practice any number of factors can affect it—differences in rock types in the river bed and the addition of water from tributaries, for example, may produce irregularities in the profile.

The course of a river

Stream beds in their upper section are often bare rock patchily covered by pebbles. Here the stream has greatest capacity to erode and transport downstream all but the largest stones. The valley in the upper course has a v-shaped cross-section and most pools, rapids, waterfalls [6], and potholes [3] occur here, caused by the stream wearing away softer rock more quickly than hard rock. This results in rapids like the cataracts of the Nile. Where a river flows from a hard bed of rock to a soft one the latter will be eroded away and a waterfall will form.

In the middle section most of the irregularities have been worn away allowing the river to flow freely in a fairly flat channel. The current is just strong enough to carry most of the sediment supplied to it from higher up. It does not erode downward and most of the time runs on its own sediment.

In the lower section the river has a very low gradient, often less than 2 inches per mile (10cm per km). It flows across a broad flood plain. Where the river is flowing slowly, it cannot move stones, even in flood, but because it is large it is able to move a huge amount of fine material. The Mississippi carries approximately 500 million tons of very fine sand and mud past New Orleans each year. The river in this section meanders over a layer of its own sediment and does not touch bedrock [7].

When the river reaches the sea the sediment it is carrying is deposited. In some areas tidal currents remove it, and the river ends in an estuary. Where more sediment is brought down than can be removed by the sea a delta is formed [10].

KEY

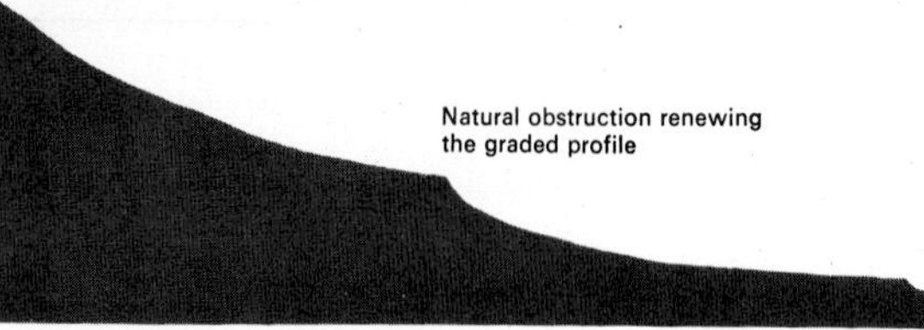
Natural obstruction renewing
the graded profile

A river conforms approximately to a convex upward curve that is nearly flat near the sea and gets steeper and more curved inland. This shape is called a graded profile. Waterfalls, lakes, and deltas may vary the shape of the stream bed without fundamentally altering the profile.

6

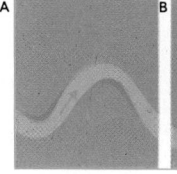

6 Pools and waterfalls are both caused by hard bands of rock spanning the river bed. The softer rocks below a pool have been eroded away leaving a hollow, and the hard rock stands up like a dam. Lakes are usually caused by landslides blocking the course of the river or by ice (during the Ice Age) scraping deep hollows. The lakes in the Great Lakes and in the English Lake District are hollows left by the ice. Other large lakes such as those of East Africa were caused by Earth movements. Water flowing over a hard bed erodes the softer beds below, causing a waterfall with a plunge pool beneath. Over time, erosion causes the face of the waterfall to retreat, leaving a gorge downstream. Niagara Falls is formed from a hard bed of nearly level rock and has a rubble-strewn gorge 6.5 miles (10.5km) long below it.

7

A
B
C
D
E

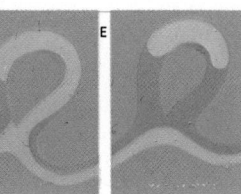

7 Meanders occur where the slope is shallow. In a river bend, the water flows more slowly along the inner bank, depositing sediments and building up the bank, and flows faster along the outer bank, eroding it. The meander becomes more pronounced [A, B, C], until the arms intersect, allowing the flow to take a shorter route [D]. The abandoned arm silts up [D], forming an oxbow lake [E].

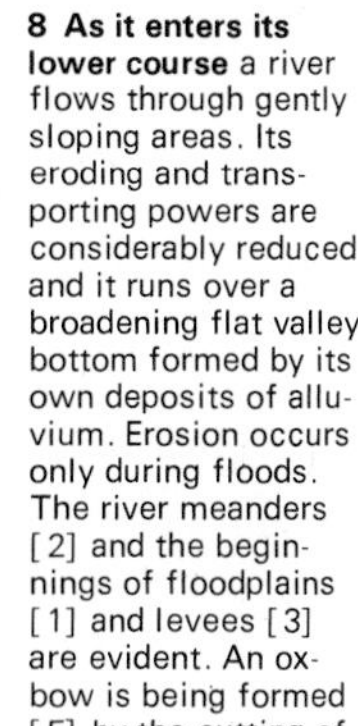

8 As it enters its lower course a river flows through gently sloping areas. Its eroding and transporting powers are considerably reduced and it runs over a broadening flat valley bottom formed by its own deposits of alluvium. Erosion occurs only during floods. The river meanders [2] and the beginnings of floodplains [1] and levees [3] are evident. An oxbow is being formed [5] by the cutting of a meander [4].

8

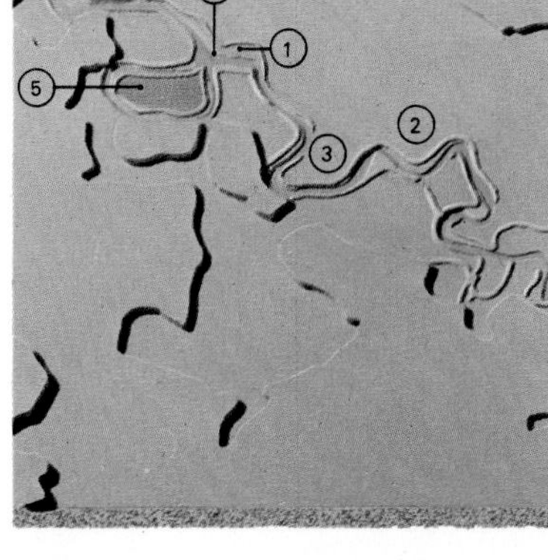
4
1
5
2
3

9

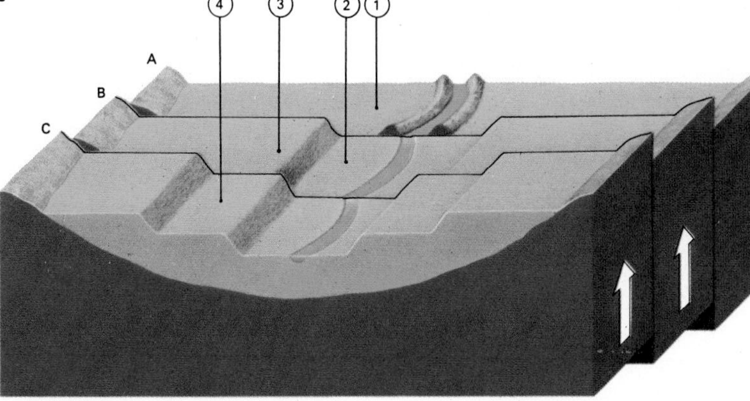
4
3
2
1
A
B
C

9 A terrace is a flat strip of land along the valley side just above the floodplain. A terrace is formed when the land is uplifted or the sea level drops [B] and the river begins to cut into its floodplain [1] and forms a new one [2] at a lower level. The old floodplain becomes a terrace [3]. Another uplift [C] would cause a new terrace [4]. [A] represents the river valley before uplift.

10

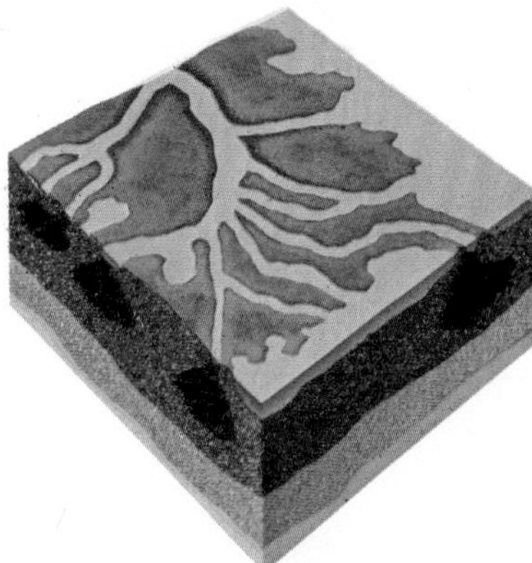

10 A delta is formed where a river enters the sea or a lake. Here all the sediment is dropped, forming a huge, gently sloping mound on the sea floor. This builds up, causing the river to flow over it to get to the sea. The river branches into separate streams, called distributaries. Deltas are found at the mouths of such rivers as the Nile, Mississippi, and Ganges. Other rivers have no deltas as sea currents carry away the rivers' sediments before they build up.

Land sculptured by water

Heavy and prolonged rain may make level ground waterlogged. But once the rain has stopped, the ground will dry out as the water sinks into it. In hot weather standing water will evaporate and plants will absorb water through their roots, transpiring it from their leaves. Sloping ground drains quickly, for the water that cannot sink into the ground flows downhill in rills, then in streams, and finally in rivers. That part of the rain that has percolated into the ground will emerge later at a lower level as a spring and flow away as a stream that may build to a river.

Erosion of the land

Water moving downhill will carry with it any particles that it can move. So moving water wears away—erodes—the ground over which it flows. In the course of time, streams and rivers sculpture deep gullies and valleys.

In some areas man's activities have greatly increased the erosive effects of rainfall. Too intensive cultivation of parts of the southwestern United States in the 1700s broke up the protective cover of vegetation. Heavy rains, falling on the cleared ground, ripped out rills that quickly widened and deepened into a mosaic of gullies, turning the land into man-made "badlands" such as are found naturally in arid regions [5], and destroying once productive land.

Landforms and drainage pattern

As soon as an area of the Earth's crust is uplifted above sea level, the process of erosion begins. The rain falling on it will develop a river system. The rivers will deepen and widen their valleys until the whole area is reduced to a low surface—assuming, that is, that there has been no further uplift to rejuvenate the drainage and start a new episode of vigorous downcutting. The inner gorge or canyon of the Colorado River, for example, was cut into a much wider, older valley. The drainage pattern and the landforms produced are determined by the nature and structure of the underlying rocks [10].

Rivers will quickly emphasize any differences in the hardness of the rocks over

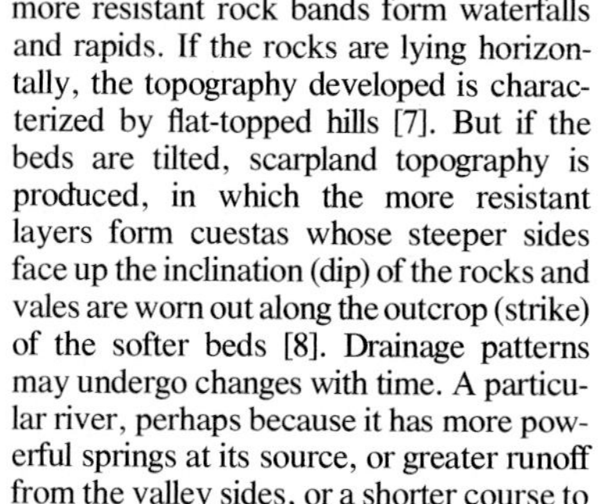

which they flow. In their upper reaches, the more resistant rock bands form waterfalls and rapids. If the rocks are lying horizontally, the topography developed is characterized by flat-topped hills [7]. But if the beds are tilted, scarpland topography is produced, in which the more resistant layers form cuestas whose steeper sides face up the inclination (dip) of the rocks and vales are worn out along the outcrop (strike) of the softer beds [8]. Drainage patterns may undergo changes with time. A particular river, perhaps because it has more powerful springs at its source, or greater runoff from the valley sides, or a shorter course to the sea, may cut down the level of its valley floor more quickly than its neighbor and eventually capture it [11].

In areas of gently folded rocks, inverted relief may develop, the river valleys being eroded along the line of the upfolds (anticlines), while downfolds (synclines) underlie the higher ground [19].

Where the beds are more tightly folded, or where near-vertical bodies of igneous rock have been intruded into gently dipping

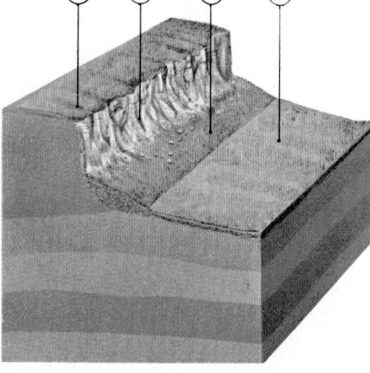

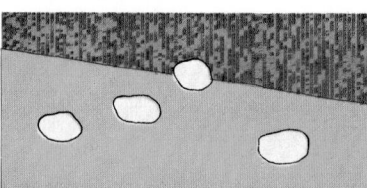

CONNECTIONS

Read first
254 Earth's water supply
258 Rivers and lakes

See also
256 Caves and underground water
262 Rivers of ice
266 Winds and deserts
616 Lakes and rivers

1 The rock formation of a hillside will be gradually broken down into stones and finally soil by water, wind, chemicals, and changing temperatures. This loose material will move downhill under the force of gravity. Slopes often show signs of such soil creep, the commonest indication being terracettes [1]. These look like countless little steps resembling sheep tracks. Other signs are walls tilting downslope [2], trees with curving trunks [3], a much higher level of soil on the uphill side of walls [4], and vertical strata curled over where they have been exposed [5].

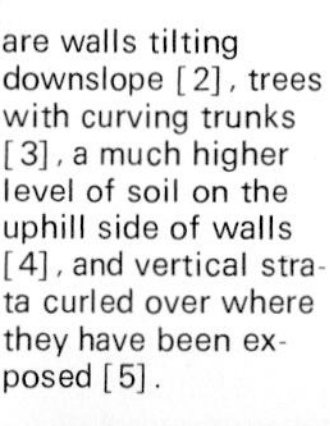

2 Many slopes have a characteristic shape after erosion. The top slope [1], the free face [2] where bare rock outcrops, the scree, or talus, slope [3] where debris is piled, and the waning slope [4].

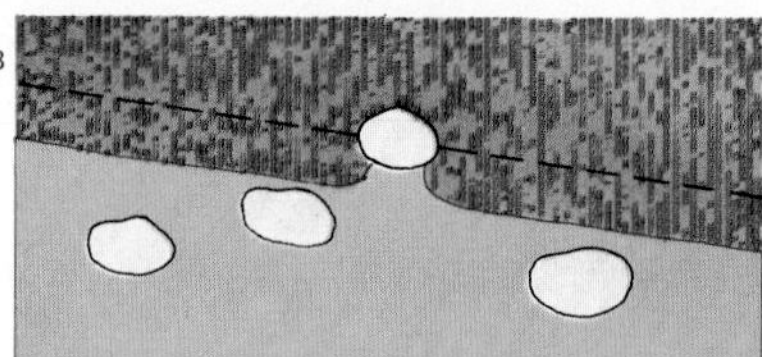

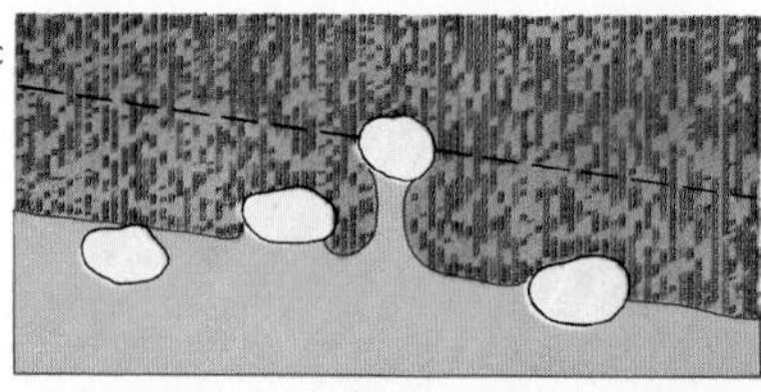

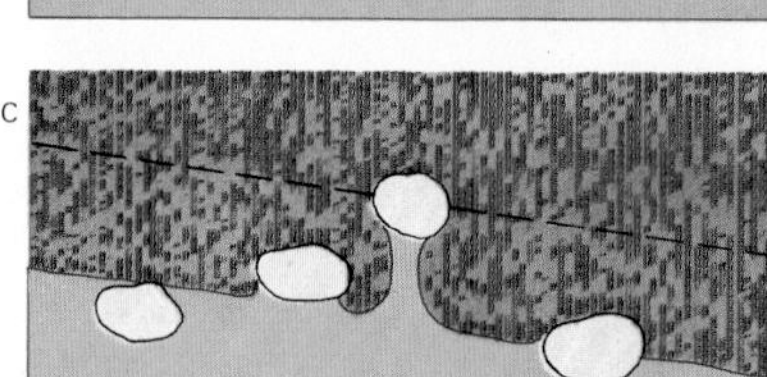

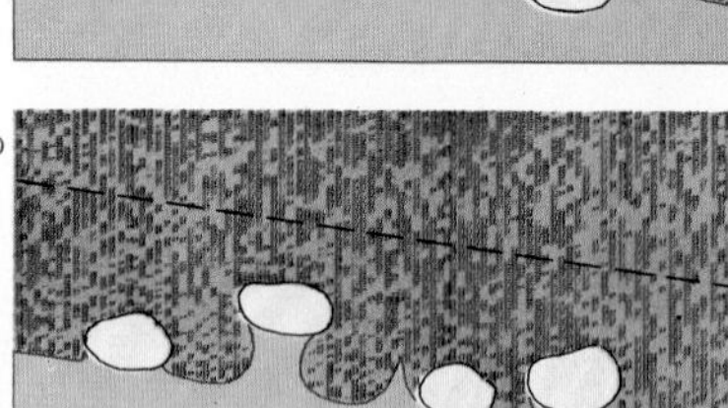

3 Earth pillars are formed where large rocks occur in the soil [A]. These shelter the underlying soil from erosion by rain and form pillars [B,C]. When the stone falls [D] the soil is washed away.

4 The river erosion of an area involves several stages. A newly raised plateau is usually quite flat; the rivers cut into it to form deep gorges. The picture shows the Blue Nile, which is cutting downward through the African plateau.

5 When rivers have deeply dissected a plateau, their valleys widen and the plateau areas between are reduced to isolated peaks. As this photograph of the South Dakota Badlands shows, the peaks tend to be the same height.

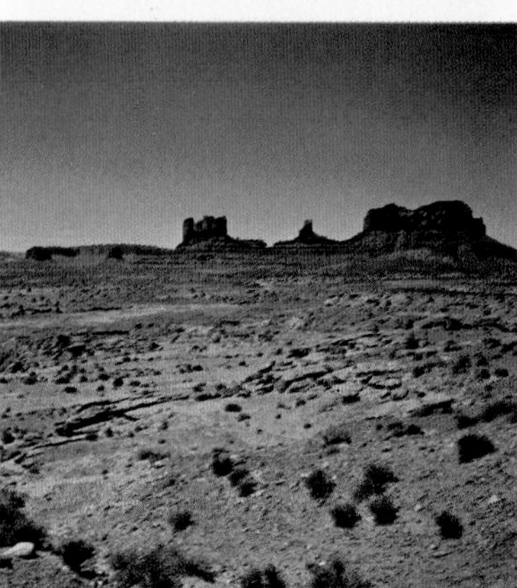

6 The ultimate stage in river erosion is the peneplain—a flat area of land from which almost all traces of the original plateau have disappeared. In the state of Utah, the wide desert floor is a good example of a well-eroded peneplain.

strata, hogback ridges, steep on both sides, will be produced, while the rivers will erode belts of weaker strata or the line of faults. The Great Glen cut through the Highlands of Scotland is such a fault-guided valley, but glacial erosion has greatly deepened the river-cut valley.

Superimposed drainage

Not all river systems are clearly related to the geological structure of the area across which they are now flowing. The drainage system of the English Lake District is clearly radial in plan, but the strike of the Lower Paleozoic rocks (570–395 million years old) runs southwest to northeast. Surrounding the Lake District is a ring of gently outwardly dipping Upper Paleozoic (395–225 million years old) strata. The present drainage system must have originated when these Upper Paleozoic rocks were uplifted to form a dome. Millions of years of erosion have removed all trace of these rocks and the drainage of the Lake District is now superimposed on the Lower Paleozoic rocks of different structure. In the future, the rivers will gradually adjust to this structure.

A more extreme case of superimposition, called "antecedent drainage," is found in India, where the Brahmaputra River has flowed from the Asian plateau to the Indian Ocean since early Tertiary times (about 60 million years ago), before the formation of the Himalayan mountain chains. But their rate of uplift was slow enough for the river to maintain its course across the rising mountains and now it flows through them in stupendous gorges.

In many limestone areas there is a complete valley system, but most of the valleys are now dry with no flowing streams in them. Limestone is a highly permeable rock, so that any rain quickly seeps into it to add to the ground water. In the past rainfall may have been much greater. The level of the ground water would then rise and springs would break out higher up the valley sides. During glacial episodes, rainfall or meltwater could not seep into the frozen ground, but must have flowed away, carving the valleys.

KEY

Landforms are the result of conflicting processes. Movement deep within the Earth may uplift areas of the crust, while weathering and erosion continually sculpture the surface of the land, wearing it down again. The shapes of individual features depend on the climate, the structure of the rock, and the rate of both the lateral and longitudinal erosion.

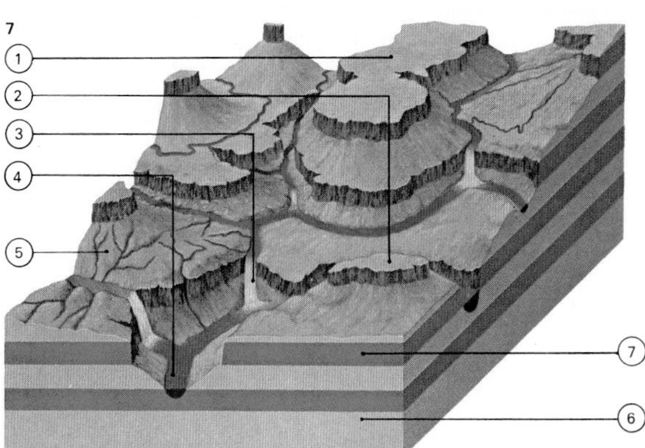

7 In an area underlain by horizontally bedded rocks, rivers follow a dendritic pattern. Their valleys are often steep sided but stepped where erosion has had greater effect on weak strata than on resistant beds. Mesas – isolated tablelands – may form, which may then be eroded to narrower buttes. Landscapes of horizontally bedded rocks are more distinctive in arid regions, where rain falls in sharp bursts and causes the rivers to swell. Features of such a landscape are: [1] mesa; [2] butte; [3] waterfall; [4] canyon; [5] badlands; [6] weak strata; and [7] more resistant strata.

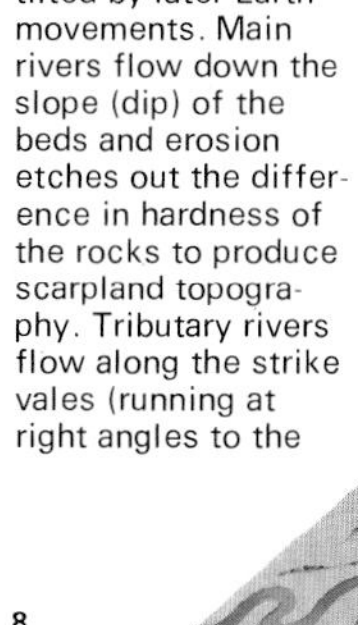

8 Sedimentary rocks laid down in horizontal layers are often tilted by later Earth movements. Main rivers flow down the slope (dip) of the beds and erosion etches out the difference in hardness of the rocks to produce scarpland topography. Tributary rivers flow along the strike vales (running at right angles to the dip of the rocks) on the outcrop of softer beds [1], while harder rocks [2] are weathered to form features called cuestas [3] with a steep scarp face and a gentle dip slope parallel to the dip of the beds. An intrusion of steeply dipping resistant rocks forms a hogback [4].

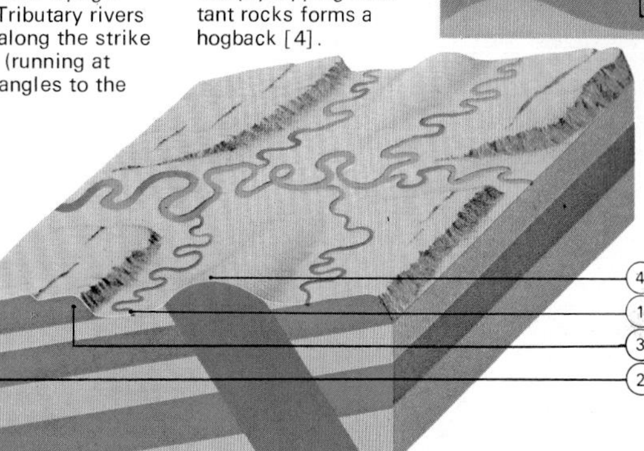

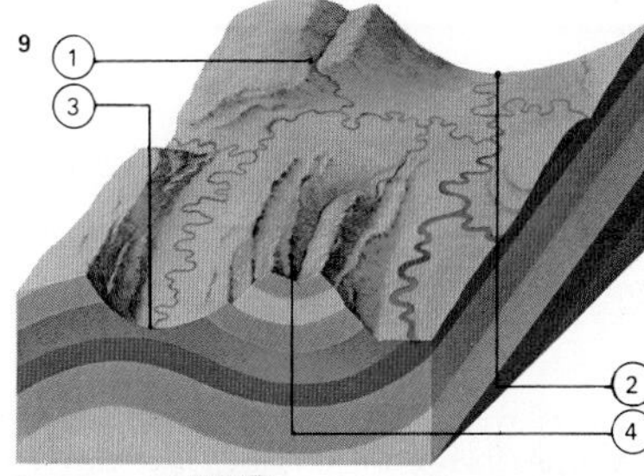

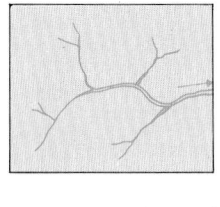

9 In folded rock areas erosion attacks the raised anticlines [1] more readily than the troughlike synclines [2] because anticlinal flexing of rocks tends to form cracks open to the weather. If this process goes far enough, the result is an inverted relief where the deeper valleys follow the anticlines [3] and the former troughs form the summits [4].

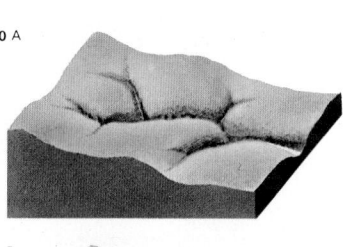

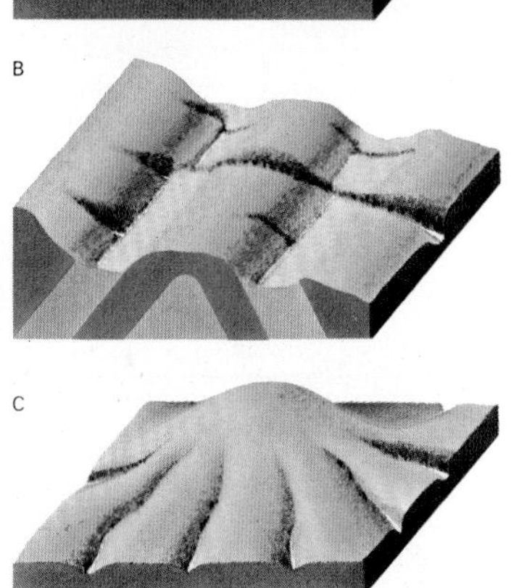

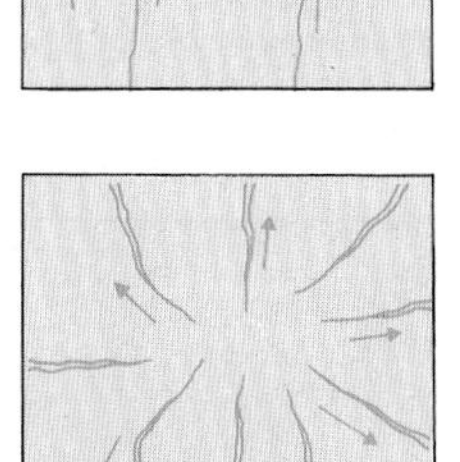

10 The pattern of a river and its tributaries is related to the rocks on which it formed or now flows. On rocks of equal resistance, a dendritic drainage pattern [A] develops. In areas of alternating hard and soft rock, the stream follows the soft rock, forming a trellis [B]. A radial river pattern forms on volcanoes and rock domes [C].

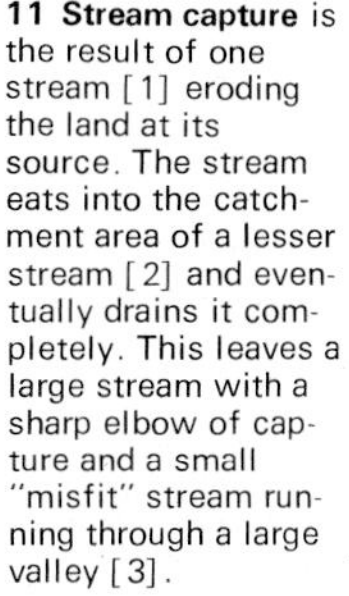

11 Stream capture is the result of one stream [1] eroding the land at its source. The stream eats into the catchment area of a lesser stream [2] and eventually drains it completely. This leaves a large stream with a sharp elbow of capture and a small "misfit" stream running through a large valley [3].

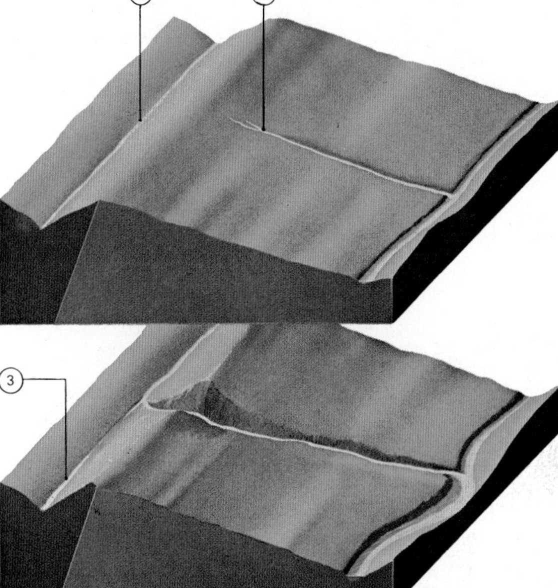

Rivers of ice

Ten percent of the Earth's land surface is covered by glaciers, the relentless and irresistible rivers of ice that are the sculptors of dramatic landscape—the peaks and valleys of the high mountains, the fiords and sea lochs of northwestern Europe, of Greenland, Canada, Chile, and New Zealand. Many existing landforms were created by the action of ice (which both destroys old features and creates new ones) during the ice ages of the Pleistocene, when as much as 30 percent of the land surface was glaciated.

Glaciers are formed wherever there is perpetual snow, in polar regions and on high mountains. As the snow accumulates year after year the older layers are compressed into a granular mass called névé, which later becomes firn when all air is expelled from it. Under the force of gravity this mass starts to move down the slope and becomes further compacted into clear glacier ice.

There are three main types of glaciers: the mountain or valley glaciers, which have their sources in the mountains above the snow line; the piedmont glaciers, formed by the joining of valley glaciers as they spread out at the foot of the mountains; and finally the ice caps, which spread over their source area.

The movement of mountain glaciers

In 1788 the Swiss physicist Horace de Saussure lost an iron ladder on an Alpine glacier. It was found 44 years later, 14,250ft (4,350m) lower down, thus demonstrating that glaciers move.

Ice is a crystalline solid, but it can deform and flow when subjected to a sustained pressure. In glaciers this occurs by slippage of the ice crystals, which are lubricated along their boundaries by a thin layer of liquid water melted by the pressure. The downward motion [2] of the glacier can be seen at its very top, where it is separated from the permanent snow by a deep crevasse known as the bergschrund. Lower down, the movement can be observed by taking sights from fixed points on the mountainside along rows of stakes planted across the glacier. These also show the differential movement of the ice, for a glacier moves faster in its center than it does along its edges, where it is slowed by friction. Along a vertical section the speed is fastest on the surface slab, which behaves in a rigid fashion (it breaks, forming crevasses [4]), and the speed decreases toward the bottom. Longitudinal crevasses appear in the surface slab owing to the increasing rate of flow toward the axis of the glacier tongue or owing to the widening of the glacier; transverse crevasses are formed where the slope suddenly increases. Where transverse and longitudinal crevasses intersect a spectacular ice topography of blocks or pinnacles of ice known as seracs is created.

The rate of movement of a glacier varies considerably and is dependent on the slope, thickness, cross-sectional area, roughness of the bottom, and the temperature. Rates can vary from an inch a day to several hundred feet.

A glacier can be divided into an upper section, where the temperature prevents melting and more ice is formed, and a lower section, where the temperature is higher and ice is lost through melting. A steady rate is achieved when the accretion of ice in the

CONNECTIONS

See also
264 Ice caps and ice ages
252 Life and death of mountains

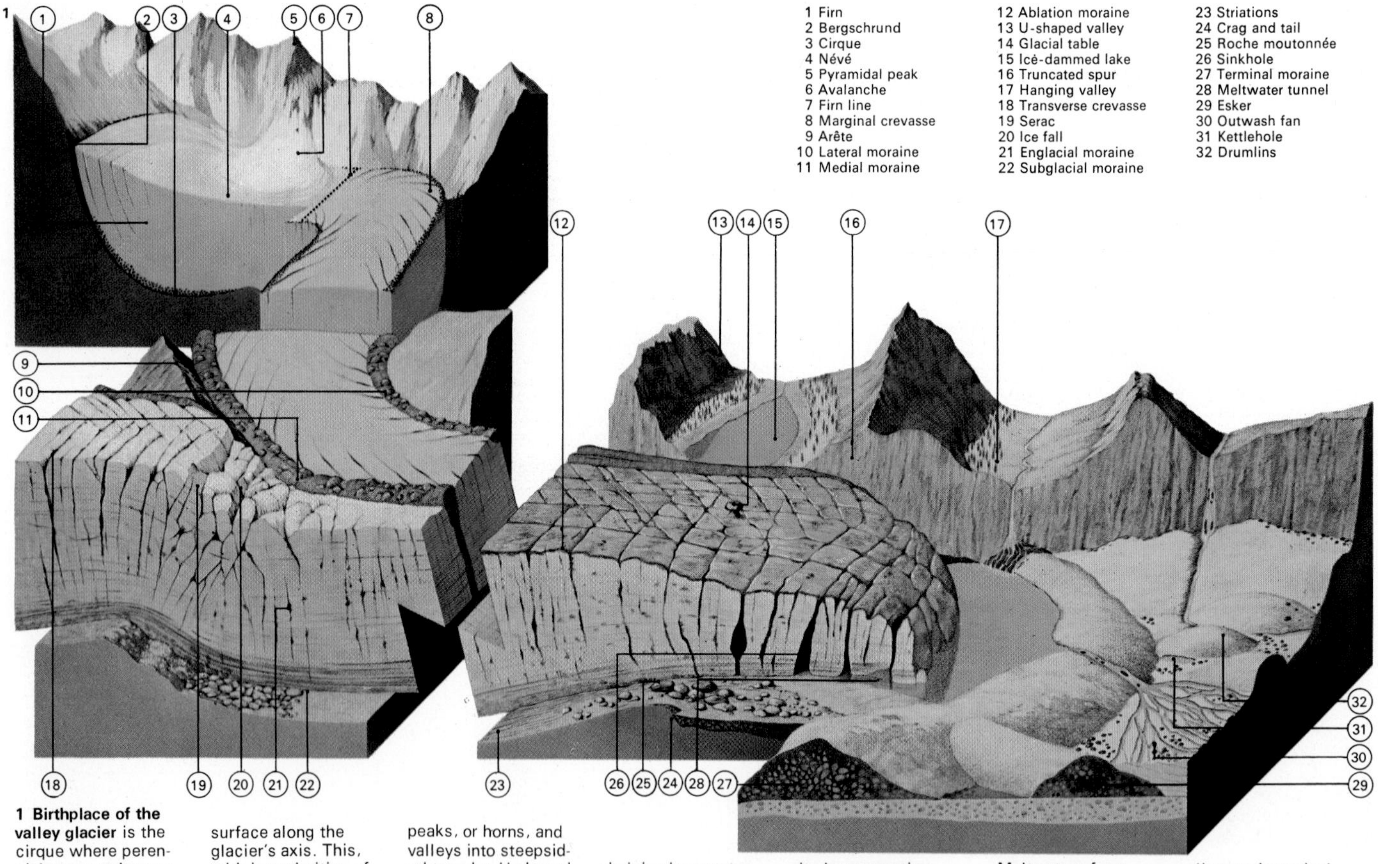

1 Firn
2 Bergschrund
3 Cirque
4 Névé
5 Pyramidal peak
6 Avalanche
7 Firn line
8 Marginal crevasse
9 Arête
10 Lateral moraine
11 Medial moraine
12 Ablation moraine
13 U-shaped valley
14 Glacial table
15 Ice-dammed lake
16 Truncated spur
17 Hanging valley
18 Transverse crevasse
19 Serac
20 Ice fall
21 Englacial moraine
22 Subglacial moraine
23 Striations
24 Crag and tail
25 Roche moutonnée
26 Sinkhole
27 Terminal moraine
28 Meltwater tunnel
29 Esker
30 Outwash fan
31 Kettlehole
32 Drumlins

1 Birthplace of the valley glacier is the cirque where perennial snow gathers as névé and is compressed. Pulling away from the valley head, the glacier forms a crevasse, the bergschrund. The ice flows fastest at the surface along the glacier's axis. This, with irregularities of the glacier bed, creates crevasses; where these intersect seracs are formed. Glaciers carve the mountains into ridges (arêtes), peaks, or horns, and valleys into steepsided troughs. U-shaped valleys, where glaciers once flowed, have floors that are deeper than those of tributary valleys, leaving the latter "hanging" and often draining by a waterfall. The load of moraine (rock debris) carried away by the glacier and deposited at its snout is called till. The glacier melts on the surface along its lower section. The amount of melting can be judged from the height of the glacier tables—unmelted ice pinnacles shaped by a moraine boulder. Meltwaters form subglacial streams that deposit long, winding piles of rubble called eskers under the snout. Other material under the ice forms drumlins, and terminal moraines are deposited by retreating glaciers while stationary.

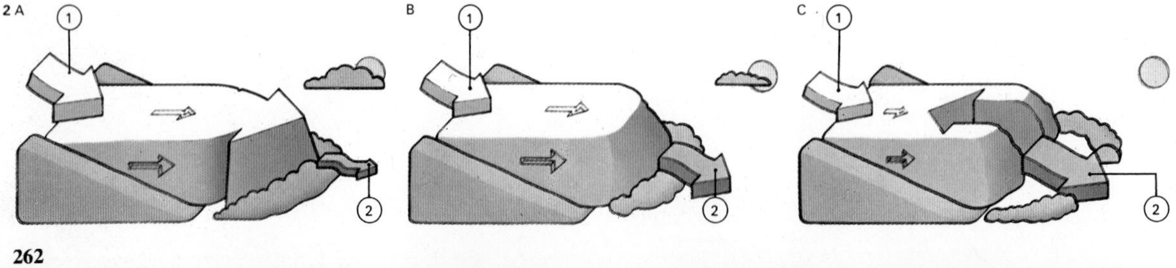

2 A

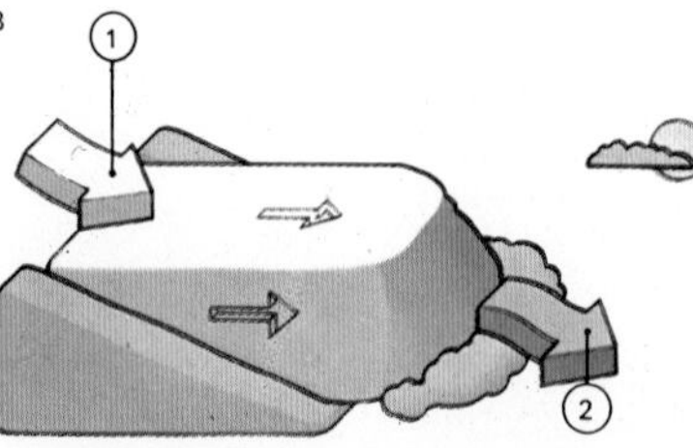

2 The material in a glacier moves constantly downhill. The position of the glacial snout, however, may move downhill [A], remain stationary [B], or move uphill [C], depending on the rate of melting of the ice [2] compared with the rate at which it accretes [1].

upper section roughly balances that lost lower down. In these conditions the foot of the glacier is stationary. If the climate becomes cooler the foot of the glacier advances until a new state of equilibrium is reached; under warmer conditions the foot of the glacier retreats.

Erosion and transport

A glacier is one of the most powerful agents of erosion. Its ice erodes by abrasion and by plucking away at the bedrock. Blocks embedded in the ice are scraped along the bottom, producing grooved (striated) rocks, and resistant rocks are polished into "roches moutonnées." The source area is enlarged into an amphitheater known as a cirque. Where two such cirques meet they are separated by a sharp ridge called an arête. Three cirques overlapping produce at their center a pyramidal peak or horn, of which a classic example is the Matterhorn [Key] on the Swiss-Italian border. Mountain glaciers carve their valleys into deep U-shaped troughs; bigger glaciers have deeper valleys than their smaller affluents giving rise to "hanging" valleys after the glaciers have disappeared.

Glaciers can carry huge loads of debris, or moraine [6]. Rocks falling from above onto the sides of a glacier form lateral moraines and where two glaciers converge the inner lateral moraines merge to form a medial moraine. Some debris falls into crevasses to form an englacial moraine and can work its way down to the rocks plucked off the bed and become part of the subglacial moraine.

Glacial deposits

The glacier's debris is eventually deposited at its foot, forming the terminal moraine, which is made of totally ungraded material ranging from clay to huge boulders. If the glacier retreats, the abandoned frontal moraine often makes a dam retaining a lake, and other lakes appear in the hard-rock depressions carved by the glacier. Rapidly retreating glaciers dump their loads as they go, leaving large rocks as clues to their former size; they also give information about former ice ages.

KEY

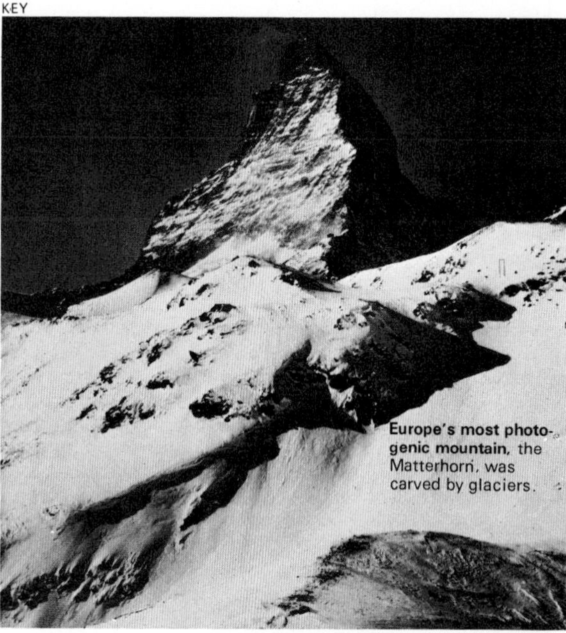

Europe's most photogenic mountain, the Matterhorn, was carved by glaciers.

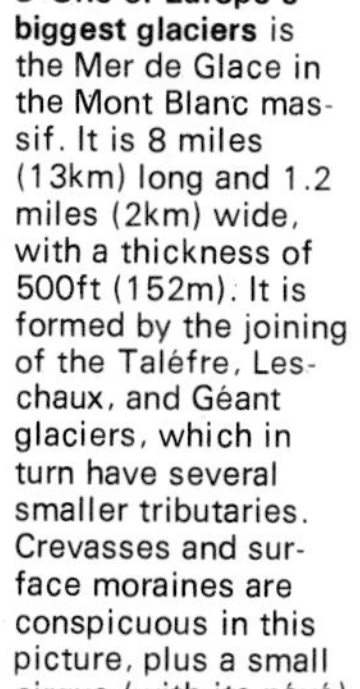

3 One of Europe's biggest glaciers is the Mer de Glace in the Mont Blanc massif. It is 8 miles (13km) long and 1.2 miles (2km) wide, with a thickness of 500ft (152m). It is formed by the joining of the Taléfre, Leschaux, and Géant glaciers, which in turn have several smaller tributaries. Crevasses and surface moraines are conspicuous in this picture, plus a small cirque (with its névé) in the background.

3

5 Ice caves in glaciers may be formed by incompletely closed crevasses, by the margins of the glacier when it skirts around an obstruction, or by meltwaters. Ice melting on the surface drains into crevasses. When a crevasse closes through ice movement, the drain hole is maintained by the water and forms a smoothsided well. Meltwaters running beneath the glacier can form a network of caves and tunnels.

5

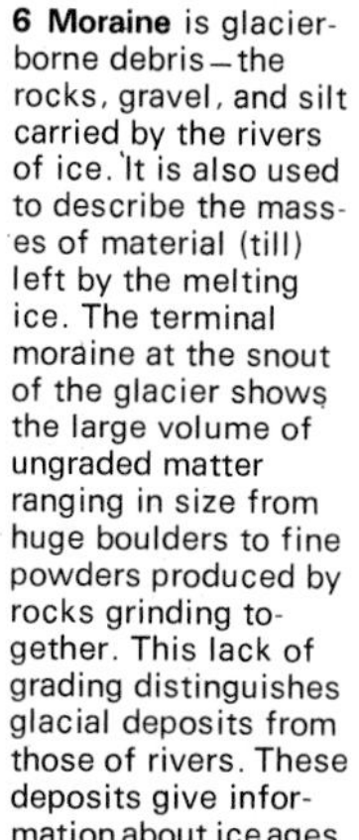

6 Moraine is glacier-borne debris—the rocks, gravel, and silt carried by the rivers of ice. It is also used to describe the masses of material (till) left by the melting ice. The terminal moraine at the snout of the glacier shows the large volume of ungraded matter ranging in size from huge boulders to fine powders produced by rocks grinding together. This lack of grading distinguishes glacial deposits from those of rivers. These deposits give information about ice ages.

6

4 The great mass of a glacier flows in a plastic manner, but its surface layers are always rigid and brittle. As a consequence, whenever a glacier flows around a corner or over a hump, or changes its speed, cracks called crevasses appear on the surface at points of tension and wrinkles or pressure ridges are seen at points of compression. The alignment of these depends on the direction in which the pressure acts; they appear in parallel swarms. Two different sets of pressures may produce intersecting swarms, leaving tall pinnacles of ice seracs between them.

4

7

7 Fiords are characteristic of recently glaciated coasts such as those of western Scotland, Norway, southern Chile, British Columbia, southern New Zealand, and Greenland. They are long and narrow inlets, steep-sided and often very deep. The deepest in the world is in Chile, with a depth of 4,225ft (1,288m); the Sogne fiord in Norway is the deepest in Europe, measuring 3,969ft (1,210m). Shown here is Hardanger fiord, also in Norway. The fiords were the sites of large valley glaciers during the Ice Age. The reason they have been gouged out to such great depths is that glaciers descended to the sea level, which was then very much lower because of the large amount of water locked into the ice.

Ice caps and ice ages

The polar ice caps hold just over 2 percent of the Earth's water; a small amount compared with the oceans (97.2 percent) but sufficient to raise the level of the oceans by some 130ft (40m) if they were to melt. Apart from their size, ice caps differ from mountain glaciers in that they flow outward in all directions from their centers. The largest ice caps are referred to as ice sheets; only two ice sheets exist, in Antarctica [2] and in Greenland.

The polar ice sheets

The Greenland ice sheet occupies 670,000 square miles (1,740,000sq km), 80 percent of the island's area, and has a volume of 672,000 cubic miles (2,800,000cu km). Its average thickness is 1 mile (1.6km) and it reaches 1.9 miles (3km) at the center.

The Antarctic ice sheet has an area about one and a half times as large as the United States—5 million square miles (13 million sq km), and it holds 119 times more ice than the Greenland ice sheet, 6 million cubic miles (25 million cu km). The ice thickness reaches up to 2.5 miles (4km). This mass flows north and reaches the sea through outlet glaciers and ice shelves that are floating extensions of the ice sheet. The shorelines of the shelves are constantly moving, shedding huge tabular icebergs that are sometimes known as ice islands.

Successive ages

The Greenland and Antarctic ice sheets are the last remnants of an ice age that ended, for the mid-latitudes, about 12,000 years ago. Features such as vast amounts of coarse sediments (now referred to as drift), erratic boulders, river terraces, and raised beaches had been noted by the early geologists but they were ascribed to the biblical Flood. It was not until the mid-nineteenth century that awareness of the Ice Age dawned.

During the past 2 to 2.5 million years there have been at least five episodes of major glacial advances and five of glacial retreats, the last of these being our present period, the Holocene [1].

Large ice sheets covered the northern continents: most of the British Isles, the North Sea, the Netherlands, northern Germany and Russia were part of an ice sheet centered on Scandinavia and the Baltic, while huge mountain glaciers descended from the Alps and the Pyrenees. Siberia and Kamchatka were glaciated, as well as the mountains to the south, and in America the sheet reached Montana, Illinois, and New Jersey, and the Rockies had extensive mountain glaciers. There was also an ice sheet covering Argentina up to a latitude of 40°S, large glaciers over the Andes, and an ice cap over New Zealand.

The chronology of the periods of glacial advance and retreat is established by the study of periglacial lake sediments (forming annual layers known as varves), of fossil pollens of plants (showing the climatic conditions), of fossil soils between two glacial layers, and of ancient beaches and river terraces, which reflect former sea levels. Other dating techniques involve radioisotopes and tree rings, while microfossils in deep-sea sediments and oxygen isotopic ratios from marine fossils provide clues to the then prevailing temperatures.

CONNECTIONS

Read first
262 Rivers of ice

See also
254 Earth's water supply
172 Continents adrift
610 Polar regions
654 Spread of man: 1

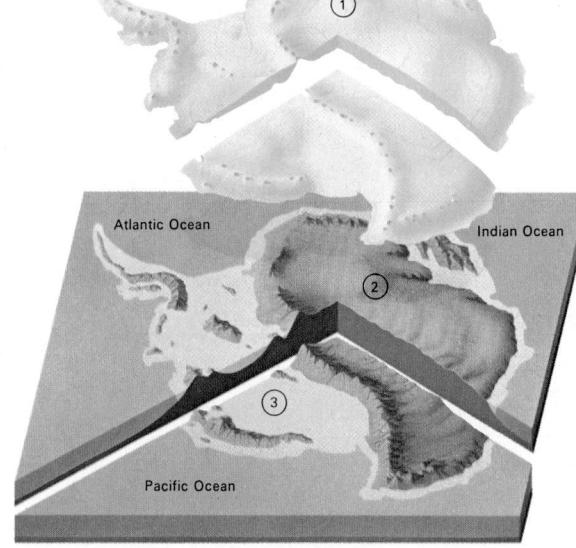

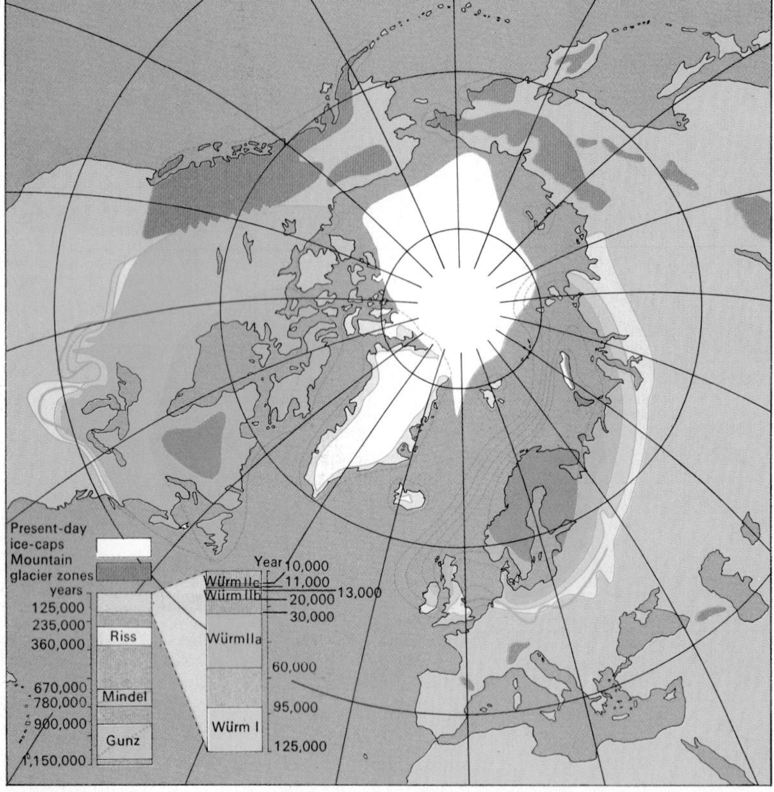

Present-day ice-caps
Mountain glacier zones
years
125,000
235,000
360,000
Riss
670,000
780,000
Mindel
900,000
Gunz
1,150,000
Year
10,000
Würm IIc
11,000
Würm IIb
20,000
13,000
30,000
Würm IIa
60,000
95,000
Würm I
125,000

1 The last ice age, the Pleistocene, consisted of several periods of glaciation separated by interglacial periods of mild climates. The earliest traces of the glacial advance have been found in Europe in sediments 2.5 million years old, and represent the Donau glacial stage. This was followed by the Günz (equivalent to the Nebraskan in the American system), the Mindel (Kansan), the Riss (Illinoian), and the four glacial stages of the Würm (Wisconsin).

2 Continental ice sheets are now found only in Antarctica and Greenland. In Antarctica the ice [1] covers not only the land [2] but also permanently frozen sea [3]. Beneath the ice the terrain is rugged and variable in height. Because of the weight of the ice, about 40% of the land is depressed below sea level. If the ice were to melt, there would be a gradual rising of the land, just as the Baltic area is now rising to compensate for the loss of its ice sheet some 12,000 years ago. Because of the meltwater, the sea would at first rise faster than the land, drowning much of Antarctica.

3 During the Ice Ages, much of northern Europe and North America looked like Antarctica today—a frozen and totally inhospitable world. Antarctica contains 90% of the world's ice and is the only continent without an indigenous human population. It is protected from land grabs both by its climate and by international treaties. The only human beings are found in scattered scientific stations provisioned and relieved from the outside.

Glacial deposits and ice-grooved and polished rock have also been identified in older geological formations, leading to the discovery of former ice ages. Three are known to have occurred during the late Precambrian (940, 770, and 615 million years ago), one during the Devonian (400 million years ago) and one during the Permo-Carboniferous (295 million years ago).

Origin of ice ages

Dozens of theories have been advanced to account for the origin of ice ages. Those based on purely terrestrial phenomena call for a predisposed position of the land masses such as the present positions of Antarctica and of the landlocked Arctic Sea, which prevent the temperature-evening effects of the sea from reaching the poles. Or else they presuppose changes in the atmosphere, such as a decrease in carbon dioxide content (allowing a faster rate of heat loss to outer space) or an increase in atmospheric dust due to paroxysmal volcanic eruptions.

Other hypotheses are astronomical. They propose variations in the Sun's output and changes in the Sun-Earth relationship. One such hypothesis relates the glaciations to the passage of the Solar System through the dust clouds of the two spiral arms of the galaxy: this implies an ice age lasting a few million years every 150 million years. Scientific evidence partially supports this theory, especially for the Precambrian and Permo-Carboniferous glaciations, but does not account for the appearance of the Devonian ice age or for the lack of one 150 million years ago.

According to the latter hypothesis, we should now be moving out of the last ice age, although there is currently much talk of an impending renewal of glaciation. This is based on a southward shift, over the last ten years or so, of the Northern Hemisphere's climatic belts, leading to less sunny summers in the temperate latitudes and to droughts in Ethiopia and Somalia. But the study of the climate over the past 10,000 years shows many such short-term fluctuations and the present state of knowledge about the origin of ice ages makes long term forecasting difficult.

KEY

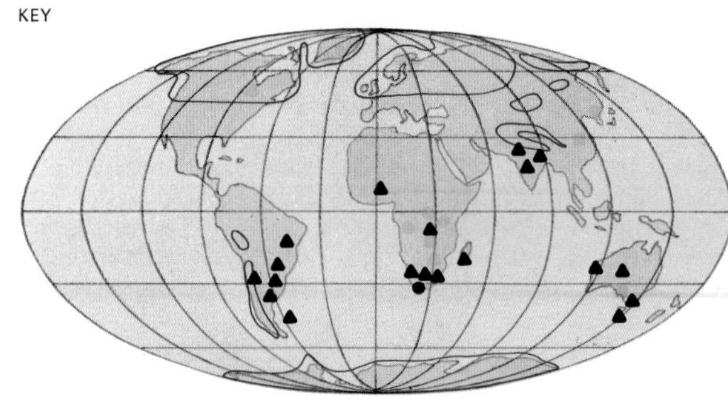

Area of Pleistocene glaciation

Devonian tillite

Precambrian 2 tillite (770 million years)

Permo-Carboniferous tillite

Precambrian 3 tillite (615 million years)

Precambrian 1 tillite (940 million years)

Ice ages have several times swept over various parts of the Earth and, although of short duration by geological standards, have left a durable impression on its crust. The map shows the limits reached by the ice sheets during the last ice age in the Pleistocene (two million to 12,000 years ago). Evidence for other ice ages comes from tillites, which are consolidated glacial deposits. Also shown are the main locations of Precambrian, Devonian, and Permo-Carboniferous tillites. These were laid down in high altitudes but have since been moved out of place by continental drift.

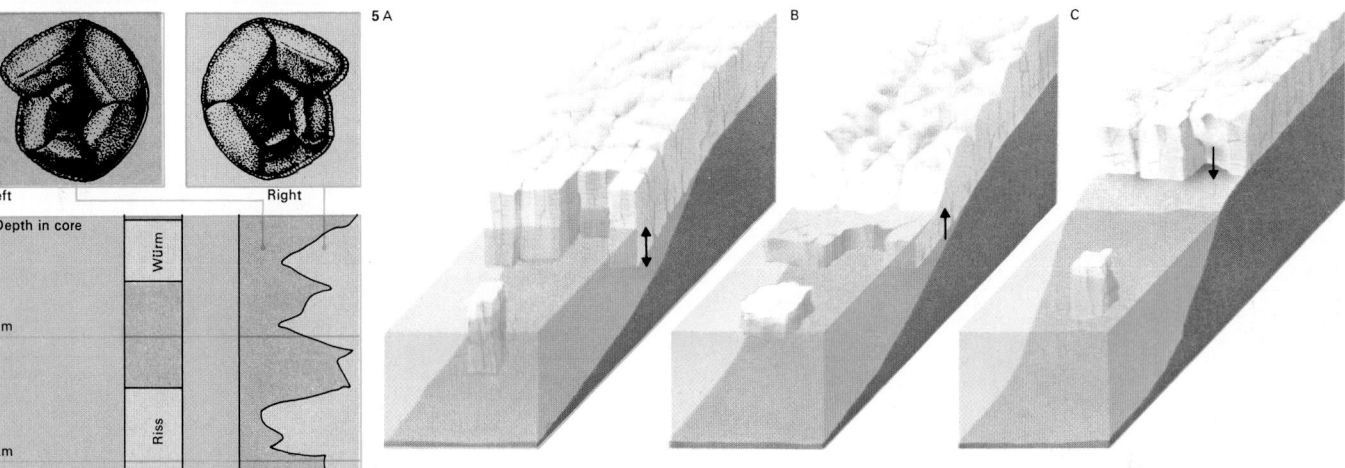

4

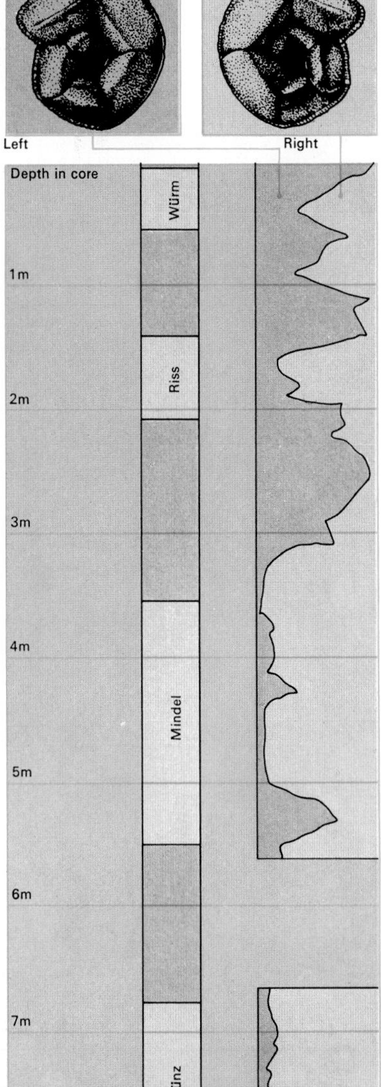

Left
Right
Depth in core
Würm
1m
Riss
2m
3m
4m
Mindel
5m
6m
7m
Günz
8m
Glacial periods
Coiling ratios

4 The sediments on the ocean floor accumulate slowly and a thickness of a few feet of sediment may represent millions of years. Microscopic fossils of such animals as foraminiferans can record changes of the climate. The coiling of *Globorotalia truncatulinoides* varies according to the temperature of the water, being predominantly to the left during cold periods and to the right under warm conditions. Analysis of specimens from many cores has provided a good indication of the changes in ocean temperatures. This method is often used with other investigations and particularly with studies on the abundance of other foraminifera such as *Globorotalia menardii* and *Globigerina pachyderma*, which are also sensitive to changes that affect the sea's temperature.

5 A

B

C

5 Icebergs form in several ways. When a glacier reaches the sea it floats away from the bed. The movement of waves and tides exerts pressures on this floating ice causing lumps to break away [A]. If the glacier is moving rapidly when it reaches the sea, a projecting shelf of ice forms under the water. The buoyancy of this shelf exerts an upward pressure, causing pieces to break off [B]. The snout of the glacier may be above the level of the sea and lumps may break off under the force of gravity and fall into the water [C]. The forming of new icebergs is known as "calving." Northern icebergs come from the Greenland ice sheet, but the largest ones originate in Antarctica. The largest iceberg ever seen was 208 miles (336km) long and 60 miles (97km) in width.

6

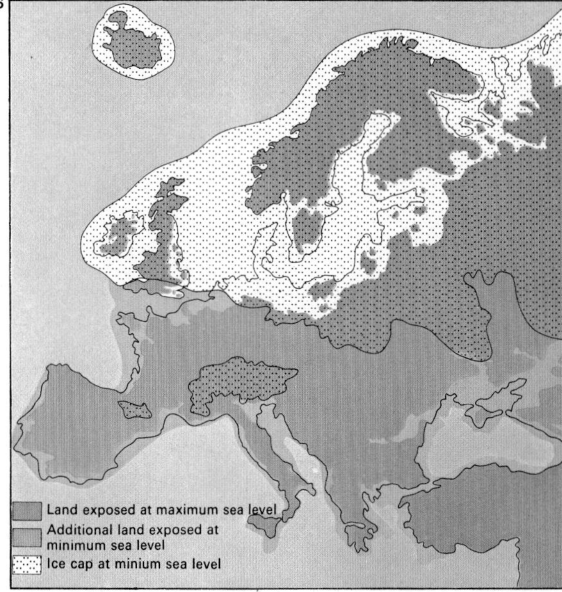

Land exposed at maximum sea level
Additional land exposed at minimum sea level
Ice cap at minium sea level

6 At periods of maximum glaciation, sea levels were 590ft (180m) lower than at the present time because of the large amount of water locked up in the ice. Many of today's islands were then joined to adjacent continental masses – the British Isles, for example, were part of Europe. Land bridges appeared, especially in such areas as the Bering Strait. These bridges helped man spread around the world.

Winds and deserts

The most obvious characteristic of the desert is its emptiness, for it is almost devoid of plants, animals, mankind, and water. Hot deserts are places where the heat of the Sun [3] is capable of evaporating all the water that falls as rain; most of them have less than 4in (10cm) of rain a year [2], which falls heavily and in rare showers. Many areas have no rain for years—then a sudden cloudburst causes temporary, fast-flowing streams called flash floods. This water usually drains into shallow lakes [4] that have no outlet, and there it soon evaporates.

The face of the desert

The hot desert is not all sand; in fact only about 20 percent is covered with sand. Much is bare rock, often cut by deep gullies (called wadis or dry washes) only intermittently filled with water [5] or carved into fantastic shapes by winds [1]. The landform of rock deserts is very angular. The rounded hill shapes of more humid lands are missing because there is no steady downwash. In many desert tracts the sand has been blown away, leaving a surface of boulders [6]. Rock or boulder desert may grade into sand desert [Key, 4]. At first there are dunes with no sand between them; these then pass into areas where the whole surface is sand-covered and is known as a sand sea.

The geographical locations of most deserts lie within the belts of high air pressure centered on the tropic of Cancer and Capricorn in which the air is always very dry [1]. The deserts of Asia and North America lie in the interior of those continents and are cut off from the rain-bearing winds by surrounding mountain ranges. The world's largest deserts stretch across Africa and great parts of Asia. Europe is the only continent with no large deserts. Deserts are usually thought of as being hot, but some areas, such as on high mountains and the cold tundra of the Arctic can also be considered deserts because of their extreme barrenness and low rainfall.

Weathering, the process by which rock is broken down, takes place very slowly in the hot desert compared with more humid lands. On many days the surface temperature of the rocks varies from about 40°F (4.4°C) at night to about 104°F (40°C) at midday. This results in a daily expansion and contraction of the rock surface, setting up strains that break it up into sand.

Water and wind effects

Water from occasional downpours drains rapidly into the gullies, carrying with it loose stones, sand, or mud. It rushes down as a flash flood and the stones it carries erode the sides of the ravines. At the end of the gully is a coneshaped pile of stones and sand called an alluvial fan [4]. The water sinks into this, leaving the coarse sediment it is carrying on top, and eventually drains out of the bottom, taking with it only the finest material, mostly mud and dissolved salts. It then runs into large, flat areas and forms temporary shallow lakes [4]. Within a few days the water evaporates, leaving a mixture of salt and mud in what are called salinas or playas.

The main effect of the wind in the desert is to move sand and dust. In humid areas vegetation protects the soil from the wind but in the desert there is no vegetation and

CONNECTIONS

See also
214 Winds and weather systems
604 Life in the desert
606 Desert birds and mammals

1 Deserts are formed in areas where the rate of water loss by evaporation is greater than the rate of water gain by precipitation. Temperature, as well as rainfall, is very important—forests grow in cool latitudes in rainfall that would only give scrub and semi-arid conditions in the tropics. Approximately 25 percent of the Earth's surface is characterized by dry climates, and deserts themselves cover a large proportion of the land between latitudes 10° and 35° north and south. On this map desert areas are red while regions of semi-arid climates are buff. Europe is the only continent with no major desert.

2 The rainfall in a desert area such as Cufra in Libya is vastly different from that in a wetter area such as Greenwich in England. Desert rainfall is usually less than 4in (10cm) a year and is irregular, with cloudbursts and long dry spells.

3 The daily temperature range in a desert is very great because of the lack of an insulating cloud layer. In higher-latitude deserts maximum temperature is lower but the temperature range is also less, since cloud cover contains the heat.

2

Cufra, Libya
Greenwich, England
8cms
6
4
2
Jan Feb Mar Apr May June July Aug Sept Oct Nov Dec

3

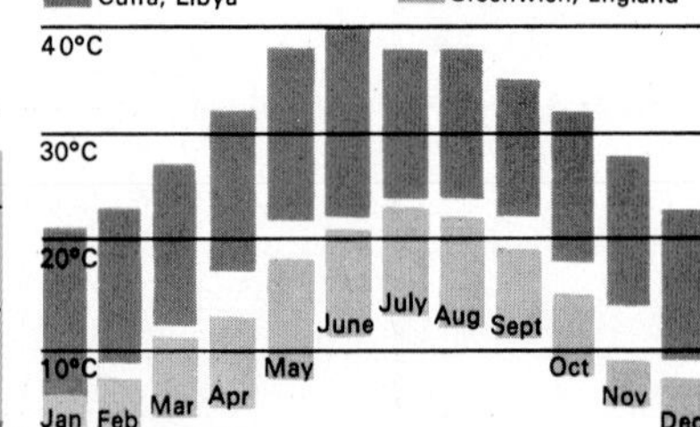

Cufra, Libya
Greenwich, England
40°C
30°C
20°C
10°C
Jan
Feb
Mar
Apr
May
June
July
Aug
Sept
Oct
Nov
Dec

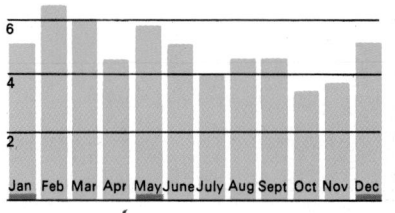

4 The topography of a desert is characterized by the relative absence of chemical weathering. Most erosion takes place mechanically through wind abrasion or the effect of heat. Mesas [1] are large flat-topped areas with steep sides. The butte [2] is a flat isolated hill also with steep sides. Yardangs [3] are wind-eroded features consisting of tabular masses of resistant rock resting on undercut pillars of softer material. They are elongated in the direction of the wind. Alluvial fans [5] are deltaic pebble-mounds deposited by flash floods, usually found at the end of gullies [4]. A salt pan [6] is a temporary lake of brackish water also formed by flash floods. An inselberg [7] is an isolated hill rising abruptly from the plain. A pediment [8] is a gently inclining rock surface.

4

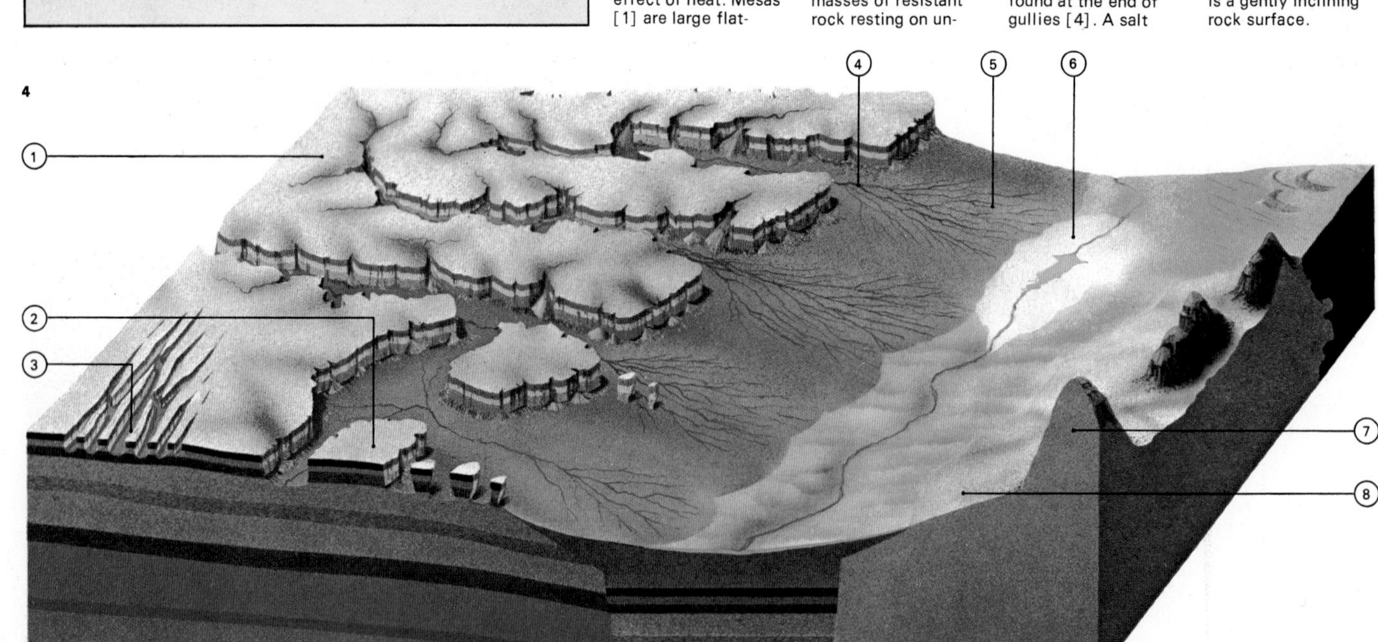

1
2
3
4
5
6
7
8

moreover the sand and dust are completely dry and easily moved. The wind takes the sand and dust from the surface of the alluvial fans, plus any sand produced by weathering, and blows it into dunes.

Sand grains are not carried far in the air, but the strongest wind causes the grains to move in series of bounces [10]. The windblown particles "sandblast" any rock or pebbles in their path and polish the surface of any pebble facing the wind. If the direction from which the wind comes varies, the pebble will acquire several flattened surfaces, giving it a pyramidal shape. Such a pebble is called a ventifact. The sand also erodes the solid rock, etching out any softer or weaker parts and leaving the harder rock standing in ridges called yardangs, or in pedestals [10].

How sand dunes are formed

There are two main types of sand dunes: barchan and seif dunes. Barchan dunes [9] are usually found on the edge of the desert where there is a relatively small amount of sand and often some scrub vegetation. These dunes are crescent shaped, with their points facing downwind, and between them there is only gravel or bare rock. The wind blows the sand up the gently sloping windward side of the dune and when the grains reach the top they roll down the steeper leeward side. Therefore the grains at the back of the dune are constantly being brought to the front; in this way the dune slowly advances. Large barchan dunes move extremely slowly, while small barchans may advance 50ft (15m) a year. Where there are many barchan dunes they may line up to form a transverse dune.

Seif, or longitudinal, dunes [8] cover a much larger area of the desert. They are long ridges of sand separated by strips of rock kept clean of sand by eddies of wind. Barchan and seif dunes merge into areas where all the desert floor is covered with sand and the dunes lose their shape and become part of a rolling sand surface.

The finest dust may be lifted thousands of feet into the air and carried for hundreds of miles and, if blown out of the desert, forms a very fertile soil called loess.

KEY

Deserts are extremely dry areas that support only a much reduced vegetation and a few nomadic tribes scattered in small encampments, such as the Saharan one shown here. A main geological agent in deserts is wind. Its effects are emphasized by the lack of vegetation and of moisture that holds fine-grained particles together. The wind sweeps some areas clean. Sand-laden winds sculpture the rocks and the sand is eventually deposited, forming dunes.

5

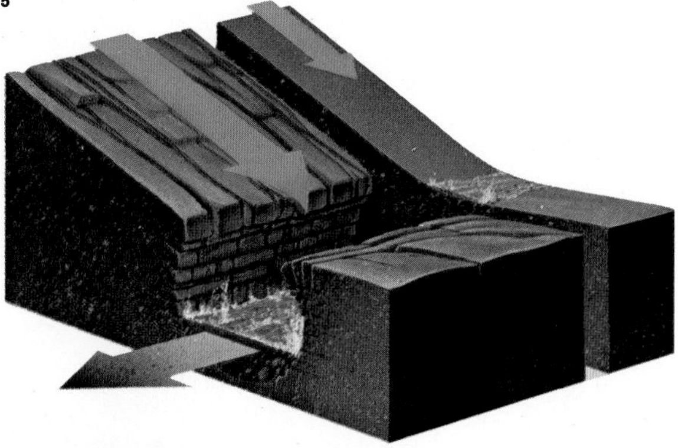

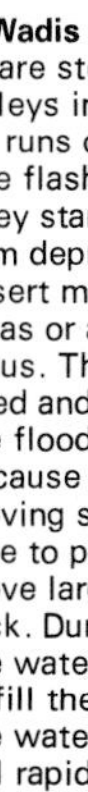

5 Wadis or dry washes are steep-sided valleys in which water runs only during rare flash floods. They start with random depressions in desert mountain areas or arid plateaus. They are deepened and widened by the floods, which, because the water is moving so fast, are able to pry away and move large slabs of rock. During a flood the water will entirely fill the wadi but the water level will fall rapidly.

6

6 Rocky surfaces are far more common in deserts than sand seas. When loose material containing pebbles or larger stones is exposed to wind, all the fine dust and sand particles are blown away, leaving a desert pavement, or reg. The surfaces of mesas and larger plateaus are scoured by the wind, and form rock deserts called hammadas showing wind-eroded features such as ridges and pedestals.

7 A

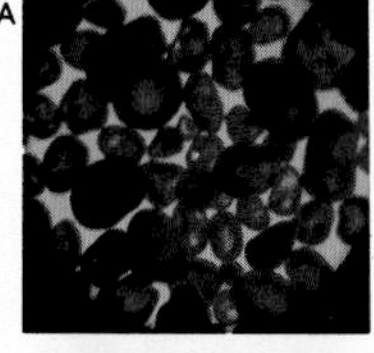

B

7 Grains of desert sand [A] are largely spherical and appear "frosted" because they have been rounded by countless collisions with other grains. River sand grains [B] are less polished, having suffered fewer collisions. River sand also contains many grains of soft minerals, such as mica, which would have been ground to dust in the desert. Desert sand is more uniform in size than river sand.

8

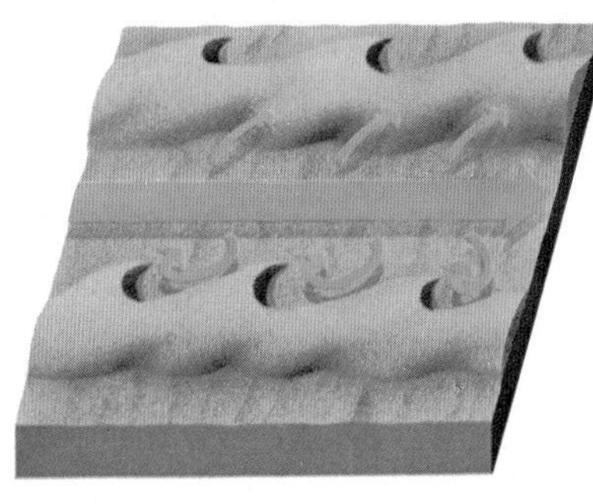

8 Seif dunes are long ridges of sand with bare rock between. Each dune may be up to 130ft (40m) high, 1,960ft (600m) wide, and 250 miles (400km) long. The wind blows parallel to the ridges.

9 Barchans are isolated and crescent-shaped dunes that slowly migrate downwind, horns forward. They occur only in areas such as Peru where the wind always blows from the same direction.

9

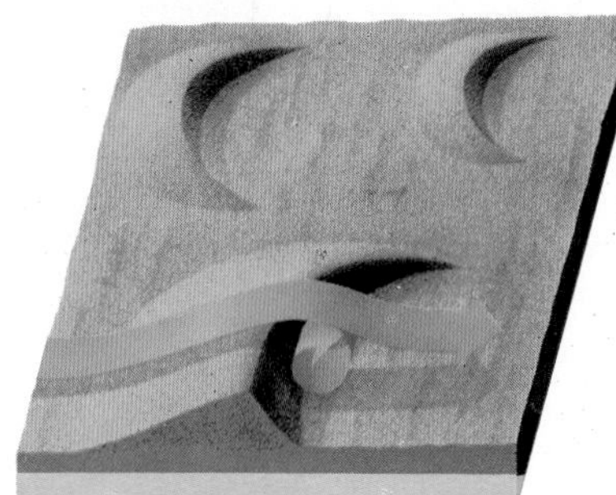

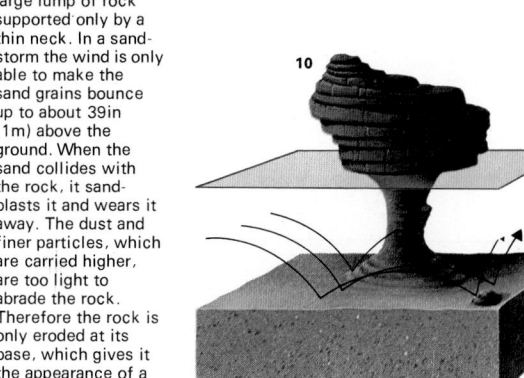

10 A pedestal is a large lump of rock supported only by a thin neck. In a sandstorm the wind is only able to make the sand grains bounce up to about 39in (1m) above the ground. When the sand collides with the rock, it sandblasts it and wears it away. The dust and finer particles, which are carried higher, are too light to abrade the rock. Therefore the rock is only eroded at its base, which gives it the appearance of a mushroom.

10

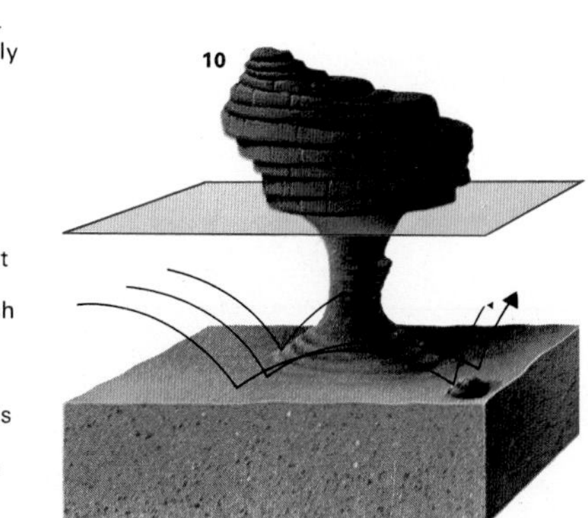

11 Rain falling on the Atlas Mountains drains into porous rocks underlying the Sahara. The water seeps through these rocks, which, wherever they come to the surface, give rise to oases.

11

12 In prehistoric times continuous rivers ran in the Sahara. Their former courses can still be seen from the air. But today it is much drier and habitation is restricted to a few oases.

12

Coastlines

Coasts are constantly changing [Key], sometimes at a dramatic rate. The rate of erosion, which is caused by waves [1], currents, and tides, depends on the nature of the rock. Tough outcrops of granite are much more resistant than, for example, the glacial boulder clays, gravels, and sands in Massachusetts where erosion of the cliffs of Martha's Vineyard island is taking place at a rate of 5.5ft (1.7m) per year.

The causes of coastal erosion

The force exerted by waves in the Atlantic has been estimated to be about 2,000lb per square foot (9,765kg per sq m) and this force may be three times as great during severe storms, when blocks of concrete weighing more than 1,000 tons have been dislodged. The hydraulic action of water is seen when high waves crash against a rock face. Air compressed by the water in cracks and crevices expands as it is released, sometimes with explosive force, enlarging cracks or shattering rock faces.

Another form of marine erosion is corrosion, when waves are armed with sand, pebbles, and, during storms, boulders. The waves lift up these materials and hurl them at the shore, bombarding and undercutting the bases of cliffs. Such action may hollow out sea caves within which erosion continues. Sometimes, the roof of a cave collapses to form a small opening, or blowhole. When waves pound through the cave, jets of spray spurt through the blowhole.

Because rocks differ in hardness, sea erosion may create a series of bays, cut in relatively soft rock, separated by headlands of fairly hard rock. The exposed headlands are battered from both sides. Sea caves forming on each side of the exposed headland may eventually meet in an arch. When the arch collapses, an offshore pillar of rock, called a stack [2], remains behind. In this way, even headlands of hard rock are finally worn away.

Another form of marine erosion, attrition, occurs when sand, pebbles, and rocks collide and are rubbed together by the moving water. Loose, jagged material is smoothed and ground down into finer and finer particles. The sea also erodes land by the solvent action of seawater, which dissolves some rock.

The movement of eroded material

Eroded material is transported along the coast mainly by wave action. Waves usually strike the shore obliquely. As they move forward, they sweep material diagonally up the beach. As the water recedes, the backwash pulls the loose fragments down the steepest slope at right angles to the shore. This zigzag movement, called beach drift [3], moves sand and pebbles along the coast. Currents and tides also contribute to the movement of eroded material.

Because of the importance of coastlines to man, attempts are often made to control beach drift and erosion. Common methods include the building of groins [5] (low walls usually at right angles to the shore) and sea walls to protect the coast against storm waves.

When material moved by beach drift meets an obstacle, such as a headland, or where the coast abruptly changes direction, the transport of material may slow down

CONNECTIONS

See also
260 Land sculptured by water
228 The sea bed
622 The seashore: life between the tides
468 Sea anemones, hydras, and corals

1

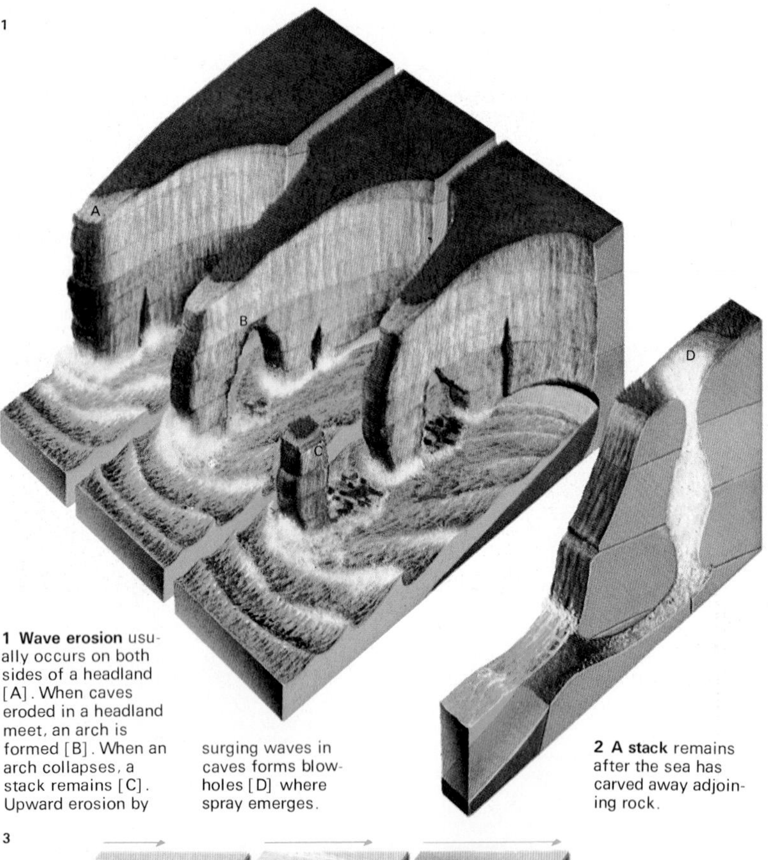
A
B
C
D

1 Wave erosion usually occurs on both sides of a headland [A]. When caves eroded in a headland meet, an arch is formed [B]. When an arch collapses, a stack remains [C]. Upward erosion by surging waves in caves forms blowholes [D] where spray emerges.

2

2 A stack remains after the sea has carved away adjoining rock.

3

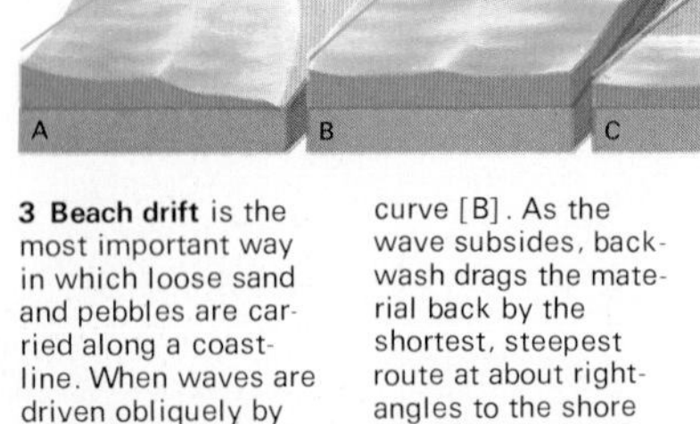
A
B
C

3 Beach drift is the most important way in which loose sand and pebbles are carried along a coastline. When waves are driven obliquely by wind and current against the shore [A], debris is swept up the beach in a forward sweeping curve [B]. As the wave subsides, backwash drags the material back by the shortest, steepest route at about right-angles to the shore [C]. Material is thus gradually carried along the coast in a zigzag path to be deposited elsewhere.

4

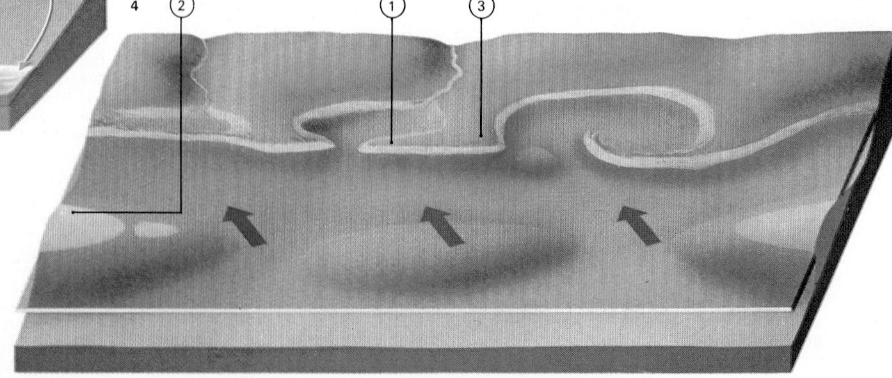
2
1
3

4 Sand spits [1] are ridges of material transported by beach drift. The material is dropped where waves meet an obstacle, such as a headland [3], or where the coastline suddenly changes direction. Bars [2] are offshore ridges of deposited material, generally parallel to shore. Bars accumulate on gently sloping beaches where backwash is not strong.

and it may pile up in narrow ridges called spits [4]. Spits often curve part of the way across bays and estuaries. Baymouth bars are spits that seal off a bay completely. Other bars, unlike spits, are not attached to land. They are formed in the sea and run roughly parallel to the coast. Similar features are tombolos—sand bridges joining an island to the mainland or linking one island to another.

Other characteristic coastlines

Since the end of the Pleistocene ice age, melted ice has increased the volume of the oceans and many coastlines have been flooded [7]. These coasts of submergence include flooded river valleys, called rias, and flooded glaciated valleys, called fiords. Other coasts have been raised up by Earth movements. Coasts of emergence can be identified by such features as raised beaches and former sea cliffs that are now inland.

Some coastlines have a special character related to the geological structure of the coast. The two main kinds of coastlines in this category are concordant, or longitudinal, coastlines and discordant, or transverse, coastlines. A concordant coastline occurs along the Oregon coast, where the geological structures parallel the coast. Following submergence, the sea has occupied former valleys while former mountain ranges have become offshore islands. Discordant coastlines occur where the coast cuts across the direction of the geological structures, as in the ria coastline of southwest Ireland.

A special feature of coastlines in tropical seas results from the growth of coral. Coral polyps live in warm water with plenty of sunlight and cannot grow in depths greater than 200ft (60m). Fringing coral reefs develop in shallow water near the shore. Barrier reefs lie some distance away from the shore. They may be built on a non-coral foundation or they may have increased in depth as the depth of the sea increased. The most intriguing coral features are atolls [8], circular or horseshoe-shaped groups of coral islands in mid-ocean. Some atolls consist of coral to depths of 5,250ft (1,600m).

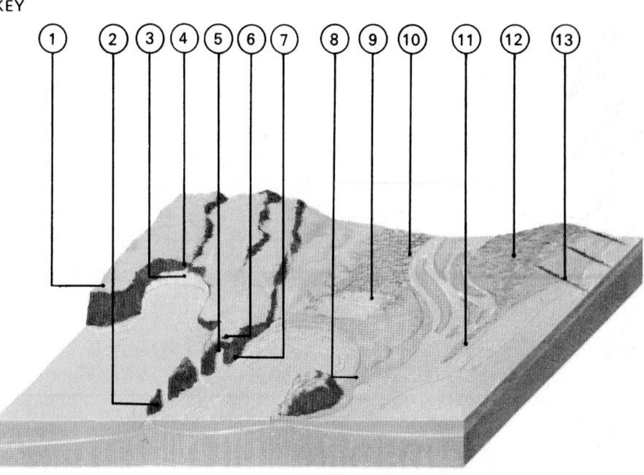
KEY
1
2
3
4
5
6
7
8
9
10
11
12
13

Coastlines are shaped by erosion and deposition, which are the result of wind, waves, currents, and tides interacting with the rocks and sediments of the land. Among common coastal features are headlands [1] of relatively hard rock, isolated rock pillars called stacks [2], cliffs [4], natural arches [5], caves [7], and blowholes [6] in the roofs of caves. Features resulting from deposition are beaches [3], tombolos [8], lagoons [9], salt marshes [10], spits, [11] and sand dunes [12]. To slow down the drift of eroded material along a coast, groins [13] are often built.

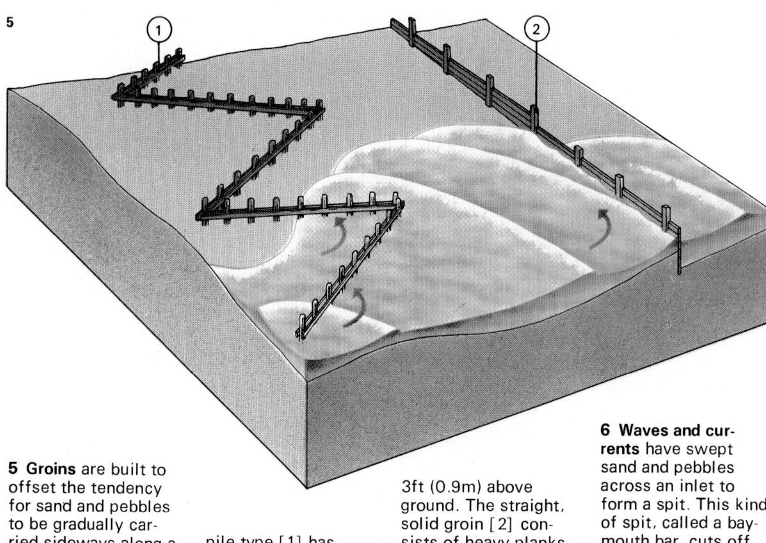
5
1
2

5 Groins are built to offset the tendency for sand and pebbles to be gradually carried sideways along a beach. There are two main kinds of groin. The zigzag timber pile type [1] has piles driven 6ft (1.8m) below the ground and standing 3ft (0.9m) above ground. The straight, solid groin [2] consists of heavy planks bolted to piles that are also sunk 6ft into the ground.

6 Waves and currents have swept sand and pebbles across an inlet to form a spit. This kind of spit, called a baymouth bar, cuts off the inlet from the sea, leaving behind it an enclosed lagoon.

7A

B

C

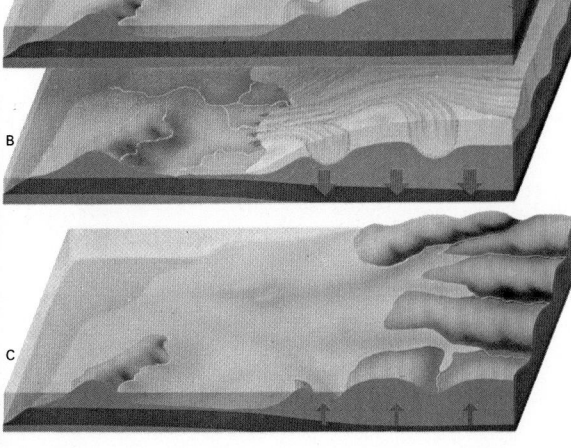

7 Changes in sea level caused by an increase in the volume of ocean water, or by Earth movements, determine the character of some coastlines. When a coastal area previously free of ice [A] is overtaken by an ice age, glaciers and ice caps form on the land [B]. The sea level drops and the weight of the ice eventually depresses coastal valleys. With the end of the ice age, melted ice returns to the sea. Even though the land begins to rise, recovery is not fast enough to offset a considerable rise in sea level [C]. Flooded river valleys or fiords (drowned glacial valleys) characterize such a coastline—a coast of submergence.

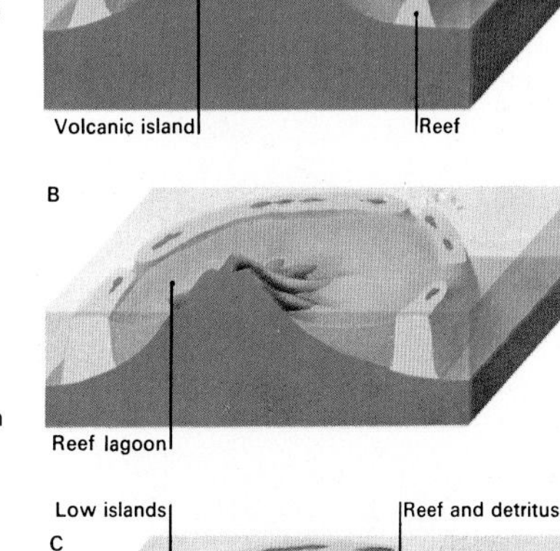
8A
Volcanic island
Reef
B
Reef lagoon
Low islands
Reef and detritus
C

8 Atolls and coral reefs are found only in tropical seas. The most striking coral feature is the atoll, a ring or horseshoe-shaped group of coral islands. Corals grow in warm, fairly shallow water to depths of about 200ft (60m). But the depth of coral skeletons in many atolls is much greater than this. One theory is that the coral began to form as a reef in the shallows of a volcanic island [A]. Then the sea level began to rise and the island slowly sank [B]. But coral growth kept pace with these changes, leaving an atoll of low islands [C]. In this way, depths of coral to as much as 5,250ft (1,600m) can be explained.

The record in the rocks

The Earth's rocks form a tattered and fragmented manuscript of our planet's past. Although sketchy in places, the historical record can be traced nearly 3.8 billion years back in time. This date corresponds to the age of the oldest known rocks. The sedimentary strata in particular are ideal signposts through the past, since their features identify the circumstances under which they were deposited and made into rocks.

The record of geological history, as preserved by sedimentary rocks [1], is known as the "stratigraphic column." It refers to the total succession of rocks, from the oldest to the most recent, that are found in the Earth. The study of its distinguishing features is the science of stratigraphy, which deals with the definition and interpretation of stratified sedimentary rocks.

Clues to the past

The science of geology was rescued from the futile perusal of biblical texts for clues to the Earth's past by the exposition of the principle of "uniformitarianism" by the Scottish geologist James Hutton (1726–97). This was propounded in Hutton's work, *Theory of the Earth* (1795), which maintained that the nature of present geological processes was fundamentally similar to that of the past and that rock folds and tilts revealed in strata were caused not by violent upheavals, but by gradual pressures within the Earth. Uniformitarianism implies that the characteristic features of erosion and the transportation and deposition of sediments produced by erosion are the same throughout history. Since these features can easily be recognized in sedimentary rock laid down millions of years ago, past events are best interpreted in the light of what is known about the present. In Hutton's words, "the present is the key to the past."

Superposition and correlation

The fundamental concept of stratigraphy is the law of "superposition," which states that in any horizontal, undisturbed sedimentary sequence, the lowest rocks are older than those lying above them. This law applies not only to the relative ages of different beds but also to the minerals and fossils found within a specific layer. Lower lying strata were deposited before those above them. Superposition is essential to establishing the comparative ages of the various beds in a sedimentary formation and is the single most important prerequisite of geological mapping. In archeology and paleontology the same principles apply. Artifacts and fossils found in deeper layers of Earth predate those found in layers above them.

Igneous rocks (formed from molten magma), unlike sedimentary ones, are not laid down in neat successive layers. They can only reach their positions by filtering up through existing formations while still in a molten state. These intrusive rocks, such as granite, gabbro, and diorite, are always younger than the rocks that surround them. When they reach the surface to form lavas—such as basalt, obsidian, and rhyolite (igneous rocks of very fine texture)—they are, as are sedimentary rocks, always younger than the rocks below them.

Since the complete stratigraphic column has never been discovered in any one site (it

CONNECTIONS

Read first
246 The rock cycle and igneous rocks
248 Sedimentary and metamorphic rocks

See also
276 Earth's time scale
272 Clues to the past
274 Geology in the field

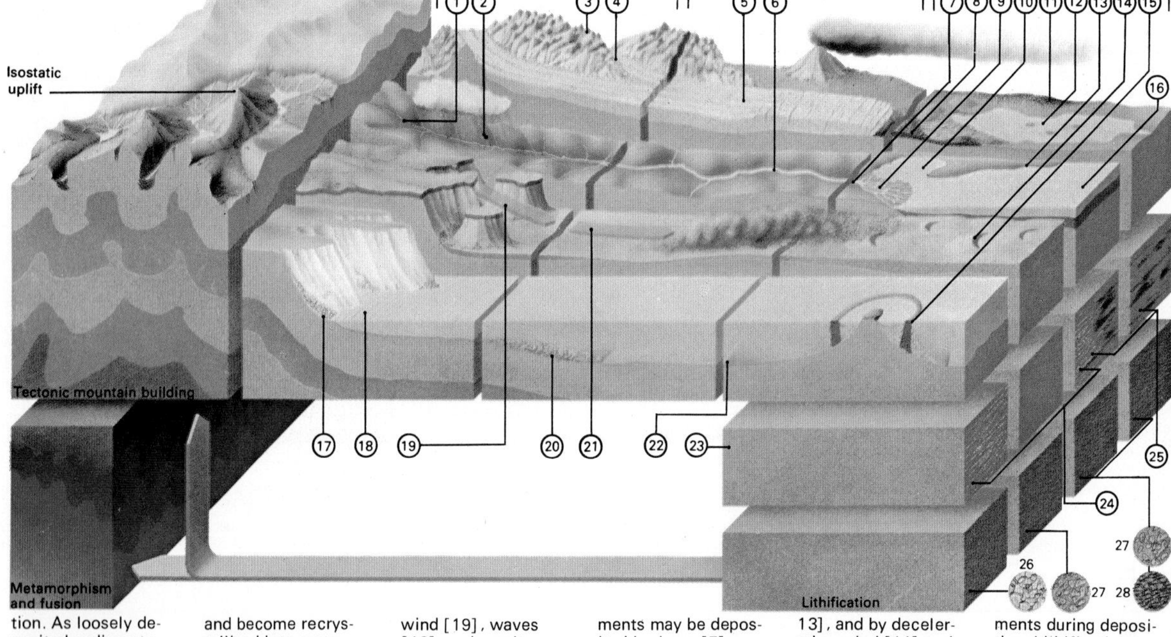

1
Erosion
Transportation
Deposition
Isostatic uplift
Tectonic mountain building
Metamorphism and fusion
Lithification
1 2 3 4 5 6 7 8 9 10 11 12 13 14 15 16
17 18 19 20 21 22 23 24 25 26 27 28

1 The sedimentary cycle begins when sedimentary, metamorphic, or igneous rocks are thrust toward the Earth's surface, at various times in their history by mountain building, folding, and faulting or the vertical uplift of land freed from the weight of glaciers after an ice age. Rock that becomes exposed to the chemical and mechanical agents of weathering and erosion will be rapidly worn down and deposited in new sites by various transporting mechanisms. Accumulating sediments possess characteristics that can identify the environment and the kind of rock found in their area of origin. They also acquire features that are clues to their environment of deposition, be it desert, swamp, lake bottom, or seashore. Thus, black shales derived from finely graded silt and mud can indicate a warm, humid climate and gentle conditions of deposition. As loosely deposited sediments build up they are transformed into rock. The newly formed rock may be subjected to further pressure and heat and become recrystallized into metamorphic rock or even fused into igneous rock. Agents of erosion include rivers [1], rain [2], frost [3], glaciers [4], wind [19], waves [18], and gravitational effects [17]. Transportation is performed by glaciers [5], rivers [6], wind [21], and ocean currents [20]. Sediments may be deposited in rivers [7], deltas [9], lagoons [10], lakes [12], deserts [14], coral reefs [15], shallow and deep seas [16, 22], along shorelines 13], and by decelerating wind [11] and melting glaciers [8]. Shells [24], plant debris [25] and remnants of other living organisms [23] may be added to sediments during deposition. Lithification (hardening process) occurs by compaction [28], cementation [27], and recrystallization of fragments [26].

2 The Grand Canyon of Arizona reveals a massive section of geological history of the Earth. Here, the swift-flowing Colorado River, laden with an estimated daily burden of some 500,000 tons of debris, has gouged a scar about 1 mile (1.6km) deep in the surrounding plateau. This erosive activity has been continuous since the Tertiary. The gradual but prolonged uplifting of the area caused the Colorado to cut a deep canyon in order to maintain its graded profile. In the canyon's plunging walls, hundreds of feet of sedimentary strata are exposed, consisting largely of marine limestones, fresh-water shales, and wind-deposited sandstones. The lowest Paleozoic rocks rest unconformably upon a basement of plutonic and metamorphic Precambrian rock. The granites and schists of this rock are the roots of ancient mountains, their tops long ago eroded away. Radiometric datings have established these rocks as being some 1.6 to 1.8 billion years old. Even a cursory inspection of the canyon is a good introduction to paleogeology. Here can be witnessed the successive ages when submergence, uplift, erosion, deposition, and folding and faulting have occurred in the plateau. The fossil record ranges from primitive algae and trilobites through dinosaurs, to the remains of early camels and horses. It is an invaluable source of information.

would have a thickness of many hundreds of miles), assembling its highly fragmented sections in correct order requires geological detective work to correlate widely scattered beds of rocks.

The most obvious tactic is to follow the layers of a specific outcrop as far as possible. This method is usually only possible over a limited area, since erosion, deposition, and folding or faulting will tend to interrupt or obliterate rock outcrops [3]. Another method of determining the extent of a formation is by searching for similarities in various rocks. Features of deposition, weathering, and mineralization all identify rocks that belong to the same formation. Correlations can also be established by comparing vertical sections of rock.

Using fossils as clocks

Fossils are an excellent tool for correlation [2]. The most useful are those that are widely distributed but limited in their vertical range, thus indicating that they flourished for relatively brief periods of time. These are known as index fossils.

As living organisms have always undergone continuous evolution, their fossil remains can be used to identify rocks of similar geological time. The fossil litter within sedimentary rocks enables paleontologists to recognize different strata of the same age. And it can be logically deduced from the law of superposition that the remains of earlier life forms occur in rocks lying beneath those containing more recent forms.

Most fossils are the remains of organisms that lived in approximately the same area and at the same time as the rock in which they are found was being deposited. They are excellent guides to the then existing environment. For instance, fossils of reef-building corals [5] are an indication of clear warm, shallow sea conditions.

One of the first attempts to relate fossils to the rocks in which they occur was made by the English surveyor William Smith in the late eighteenth century. He established the lateral, or horizontal, continuity that exists between scattered outcrops of rocks by identifying strata through their fossil content, texture, color, and position.

KEY

Towering buttes and mesas in Monument Valley, Arizona, reveal the character of the geological ages of the region. Individual beds within these outcrops can be traced throughout the area, although the rock in between is missing, thus demonstrating the use of lateral continuity. The scale of erosion in the Colorado Plateau is matched by few regions in the world. Several thousand feet of rock have been eroded, leaving only isolated, flat-capped outcrops dotted about the region. Not all these outcrops are sedimentary rock, for some are the solidified plugs of ancient volcanoes whose sloping flanks have long ago been worn away.

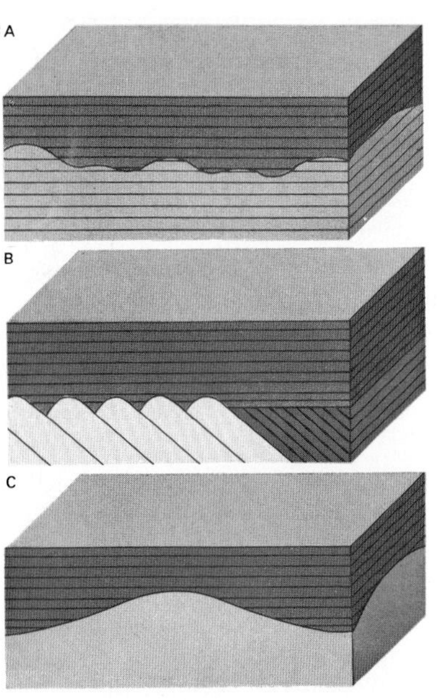
3 A
B
C

3 Unconformities occur when there is a break in sedimentation caused by erosion. This creates a gap in the geological record of the Earth's history. Unconformities are of three varieties. Disconformities [A] are recognizable because the older strata have not been tilted or in any way deformed before younger rock was deposited above them on the same horizontal plane. Angular unconformities [B] occur where the lower lying strata have been tilted, deformed, and eroded before the deposition of other rocks. Where bedded rock layers overlie a nonbedded igneous mass, a nonconformity [C] is said to occur.

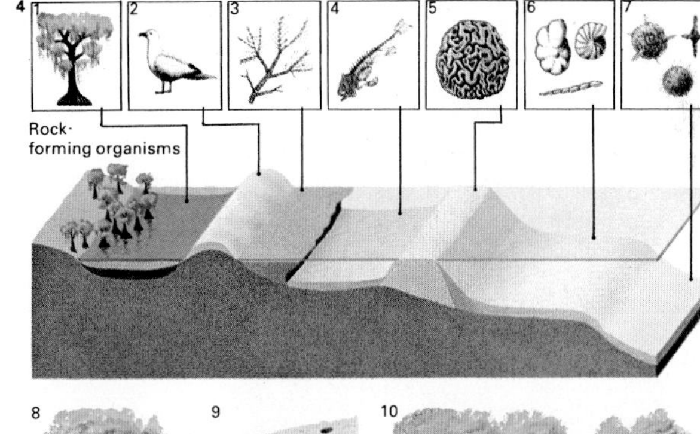
4
1
2
3
4
5
6
7
Rock-forming organisms

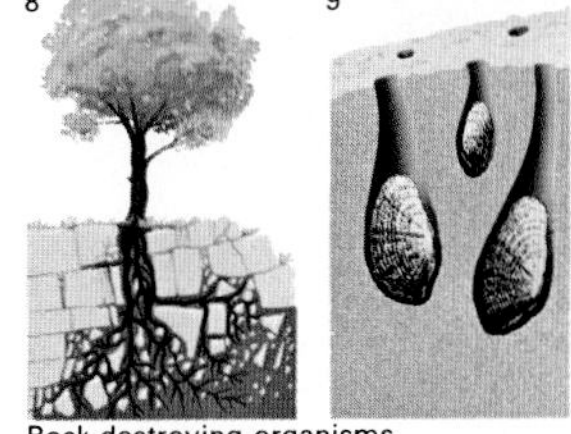
8
9
Rock-destroying organisms

10
11
Rock-accreting organisms

4 Living organisms may both create and destroy rocks. Some rocks are formed when decaying vegetation [1] becomes coal or when the droppings of bird colonies [2] accumulate as phosphate deposits. In marine environments calcareous algae [3] form limestone deposits while fish skeletons [4] may accumulate as beds of phosphate. Corals [5] and tiny foraminiferan skeletons [6] form limestone sediments while radiolarians [7], which build their hard parts with silica, create siliceous deposits. Tree roots [8] and rock-boring piddocks [9] hasten destruction. Mangrove [10] and dune grass [11] trap sediment that may harden.

5

5 Entire islands have been built by small organisms, corals and algae. The wreath-shaped reef and sheltered lagoon of a coral atoll is built upon the crown of a subsiding peak. The symbiotic relationship between certain algae and coral polyps is responsible for the formation of coral islands. Coral itself is too fragile to form a reef unless it is reinforced by the carbonate-producing algae *Zooxanthella*. Reef corals thrive in water no deeper than 200ft (60m) or colder than 68°F (20°C). Coral formations in a sedimentary sequence are excellent indicators of the prevailing climatic conditions at the time when the rock was laid down in the sea.

6

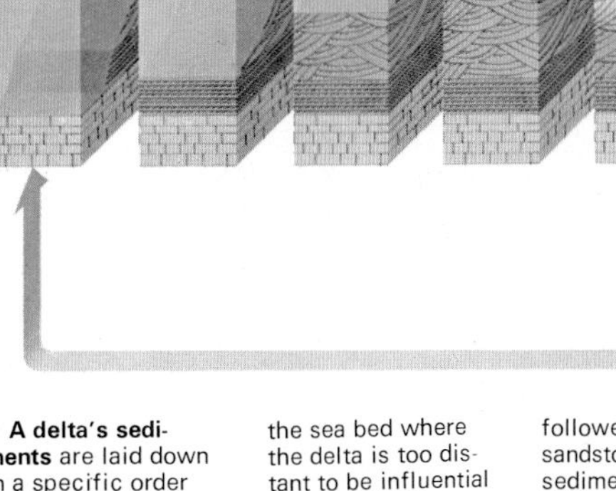
A
B
C
D
E
F
1
2
3
4

6 A delta's sediments are laid down in a specific order that may be endlessly repeated if the region of deposition is sinking. Limestone deposits [4] cover the sea bed where the delta is too distant to be influential [A]. As the delta encroaches [B], fine-grained muds that will become shale [3] are deposited, followed by coarser, sandstone-forming sediments [2] as the advance continues [C]. As the water becomes shallow, current bedding [D] indicates that sand is being deposited. Once the delta builds above water level [E] it can support swamp vegetation, which forms coal [1]. When the region sinks [F] the cycle restarts.

Clues to the past

The Earth's rocks are in a state of constant change. Mountains are worn away by wind, rain, and frost and the debris formed is transported by rivers, streams, glaciers, wind, and sea currents to be deposited on valley floors and sea beds. There the sediments are buried and subjected to processes that turn them into sedimentary rocks, later to be uplifted as mountains to start the process all over again. One of the tasks of a geologist is to determine the sequence of these events in particular areas; to do this he uses the telltale features preserved in the sedimentary rocks themselves. This study is known as stratigraphy.

The concept of facies

The term "facies" encompasses all the features of a particular rock or stratum of rock that indicate the conditions in which those rocks were formed. Such features include the mineral content, the shapes and sizes of the particles, the sedimentary structures, the fossils, the relationship to the beds above and below, the color, and even the smell of the rock.

The mineral content can show whether a sedimentary rock was precipitated out of salts dissolved in seawater or built up from material washed off already existing terrains, and can show the nature of these original landscapes. The presence of grains of garnet, for example, show that the original rocks were metamorphic, whereas olivine crystals indicate the existence of original rocks that were igneous. The shapes of the constituent particles indicate how far the material has been transported from the source—angular fragments have not traveled far but rounded grains have been carried long distances and have had their corners and edges broken off by the violence of their journey. If a rock consists of particles that are more or less the same size then it can be deduced that the particles have been moved (or sorted) by currents before coming to rest. A mixture of particle sizes denotes rapid transportation and dumping of material.

Sedimentary structures give a direct indication of the conditions under which the sediment was accumulated. Ripple marks [7] are formed under shallow water conditions; rain pits [13] and mud cracks show the drying out of shallow pools; small-scale cross-bedding shows the presence of currents whose direction can be determined by the attitude of the bedding.

Stories told by fossils

Animals and plants are selective about which environments they inhabit and a recognizable fossil in a rock can be the most important clue a geologist can have to deduce the environment under which the rock was formed [3, 9]. The modern bivalve mollusk *Scrobicularia,* for example, only lives buried in oxygen-deficient mud. When a fossil *Scrobicularia* is found in shale it can be inferred that the shale was laid down in an oxygen-poor environment. Such organisms are usually very sensitive to environment, and when they suddenly disappear in a geological succession it can be deduced that conditions have changed.

The condition of the fossils is also important. If the remains are broken up and the fragments are well sorted any deduc-

CONNECTIONS

See also
270 The record in the rocks
274 Geology in the field
276 Earth's time scale
246 The rock cycle and igneous rocks
248 Sedimentary and metamorphic rocks
560 Fossils: the life of the past
562 Plants of the past
564 Fossils without backbones
566 Fish and amphibians of the past
568 Toward life on land
570 Reptiles of the past
572 The age of reptiles
574 Mammals of the past
576 The age of mammals
410 The world before man

1 A cliff face gives a cross-section through the layers, or strata, of rocks that comprise part of the Earth's crust. If the rocks are sedimentary a geologist can use the cliff as the means to determine the history of that area. Most of the evidence is small-scale but a number of broad observations can be made by looking at the outcrop as a whole. First, since there is no evidence of major disturbance, the law of superposition may be invoked. This states that the oldest beds are at the bottom of the cliff. Next, since there are no unconformities (breaks in the sequence), it is evident that the beds were laid down continuously with no pauses in the sedimentation. Three major divisions are observed, corresponding to three different environments of deposition that succeeded one another during the history of this one area. Starting at the bottom of the sequence with the oldest rocks, there is a massive bed of limestone, the thickness of which is unknown as the base cannot be seen. This indicates a long period of marine deposition. It is followed by an alternating sequence of shales, sandstones, and coal suggesting a delta environment. A thick deposit of cross-bedded sandstone is found at the top, indicating a desert environment. Closer inspection of individual beds is needed before a detailed history of the sequence can be worked out.

11 The solid mosaic of the sandstone, when magnified, reveals the original rounded shapes of each grain within the crystals. This, and the red color and uniform size, suggests desert sand.

12 The conclusion that a desert existed when the sand was deposited is confirmed by the existence of large scale cross-bedding. This happens when sand dunes advance over one another, removing their tops and preserving the bedding on their downwind sides. The red color is due to the oxidation of iron—a reaction that takes place under very dry desert conditions.

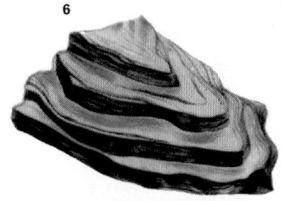

6 Shale, the lowest bed in the next division, is made up of fine mud particles showing that a river was emptying into the sea nearby. The finer debris was carried farther away from the shore.

7 Above the shale is found a bed of sandstone, which was formed as the river mouth encroached and deposited sand. Samples obtained from the cliff show ripple marks—typical structures of sands deposited in shallow waters—revealing that the sands were built up almost to sea level. The ripples are aligned at right angles to the current and so the direction of the river mouth is shown.

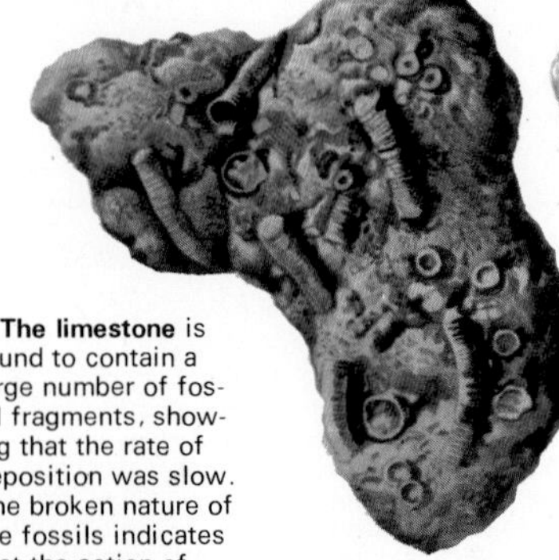

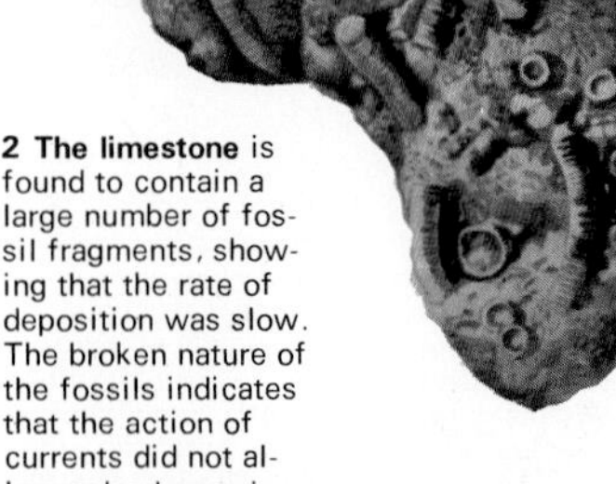

2 The limestone is found to contain a large number of fossil fragments, showing that the rate of deposition was slow. The broken nature of the fossils indicates that the action of currents did not allow a dead organism to settle for long.

3 Most of the fossils are of crinoids (sea lilies). These are relatives of starfish but are sessile, being anchored to the sea bed by a flexible stalk. Their presence indicates a shallow sea environment rich in floating organic food particles.

tions made from them are fairly suspect. It probably means that the dead bodies have been washed about by currents and in some cases they will have been brought into the area from a completely different environment. This is frequently the case. On the other hand, if the fossil is in its life position—for example a burrowing creature still in its burrow or a sedentary organism still attached to its substratum—then it is quite certain that this is the environment in which it lived.

Occasionally a derived fossil may be found. This is a fossil that has been eroded from an original rock and laid down with other rock debris to form the new deposit.

The evidence is put together

After analyzing the numerous features of sedimentary formations, a geologist must piece them together painstakingly to form a coherent whole. Some features are confusing and difficult to interpret; others speak for themselves. Thus a cross-section of rock grading from limestone to shale and sandstone [1] is a typical sequence indicating that the sea was encroached on by river sediments, eventually building the area up to above sea level. Similarly, periods of glaciation are typified by distinct striations or gouge marks in the rocks where ice sheets, carrying an enormous load of debris, have ground their way across the land. Another feature of glaciation is the random imbedding of irregularly shaped broken rock fragments in finer material. This occurs where the glacier deposits its load.

Paleogeography is the branch of historical geology that is concerned with the past distribution of land and sea. With the relevant data obtained from the study of sedimentary formations, a geologist can construct paleogeographic maps that give a picture of the geologic past. But such maps tend to be somewhat speculative. Information is often sparse and there are enormous difficulties in interpreting the relative ages of outcrops and thus plotting the ancient boundaries between the land and sea. What these maps do reveal with startling effect is the tremendous transformation that every region has experienced.

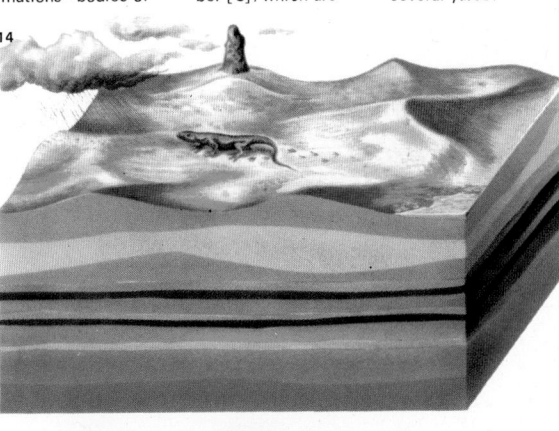

KEY

Rocks can be considered in terms of their stratigraphic units, of which the largest is the group. The Tonto Group of the Grand Canyon [A] is separated by distinct boundaries from the groups directly above and below. It in turn consists of three formations—bodies of rock that share certain common features. The Bright Angel Formation [B] consists mainly of shales distinct from the limestone and sandstone formations above and below it. Formations can be subdivided into members, such as the dolomite member [C], which are characterized by distinct structure and composition. The smallest stratigraphic units are beds. The lower dolomite bed [D] is readily identifiable by the division planes between it and its neighbors. A bed may range in thickness from a fraction of an inch to several yards.

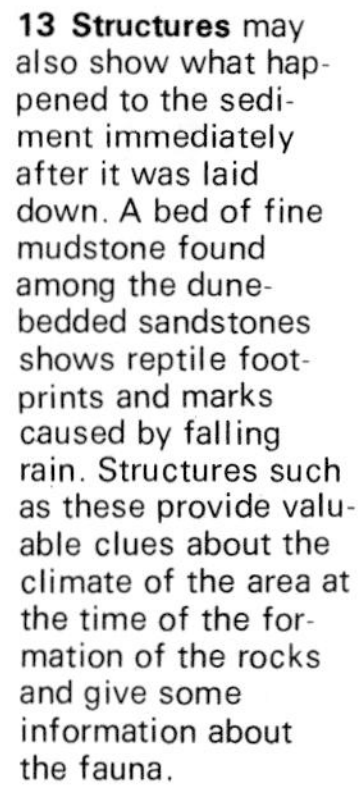

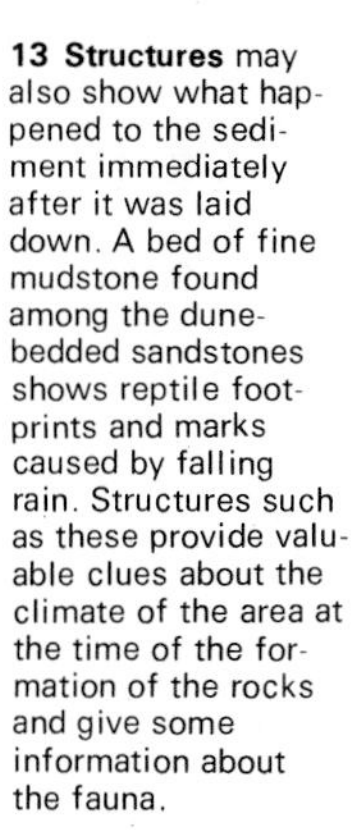

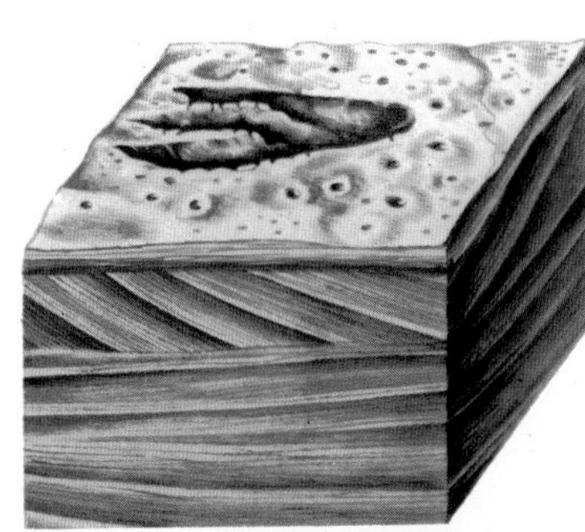

13 Structures may also show what happened to the sediment immediately after it was laid down. A bed of fine mudstone found among the dune-bedded sandstones shows reptile footprints and marks caused by falling rain. Structures such as these provide valuable clues about the climate of the area at the time of the formation of the rocks and give some information about the fauna.

14 A desert region was formed after the area was built up above sea level by the delta. Rainstorms occurred, causing local flooding. By now the volcano would have been eroded to a stump. Conditions such as these were common during the Permian and so the whole cliff face can be said to show a transition from marine to desert conditions between Upper Carboniferous and Permian times.

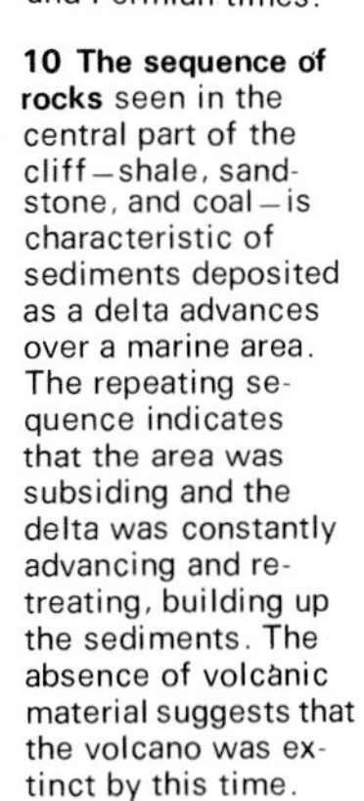

8 Coal, found above some of the beds of sandstone, indicates the presence of forested swamps in which vegetable matter accumulated. Boggy land had replaced the former shallow sea.

9 One of the most common fossils in coal deposits is that of a tree stump. The stump and roots retain their shape, being buried in the underlying sand; trunk and branches are turned to coal.

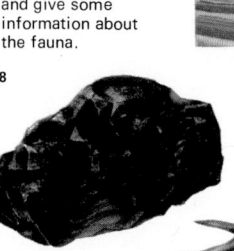

10 The sequence of rocks seen in the central part of the cliff—shale, sandstone, and coal—is characteristic of sediments deposited as a delta advances over a marine area. The repeating sequence indicates that the area was subsiding and the delta was constantly advancing and retreating, building up the sediments. The absence of volcanic material suggests that the volcano was extinct by this time.

4 A fossil ammonoid is also found in this limestone. This was a nautiluslike mollusk that carried most of its body inside the front part of a coiled shell. This shell was divided into chambers by zig-zag partitions that differed from species to species. Each species was free-swimming and common to the seas of the world at different times. Thus, whenever a recognizable species is found in a rock, that rock can be dated. This species is from the Upper Carboniferous.

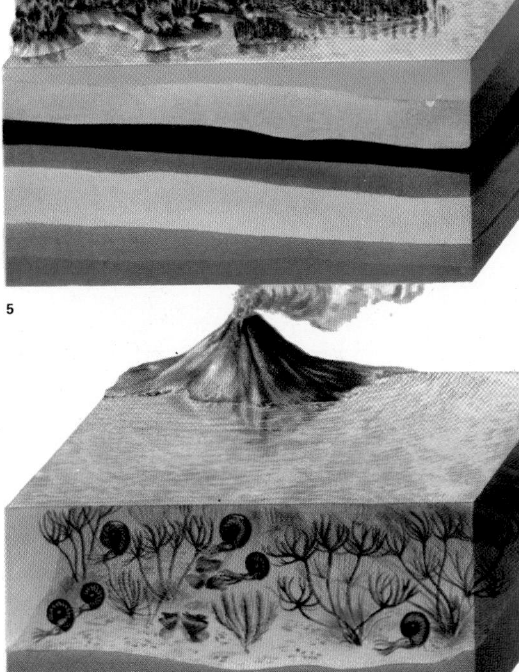

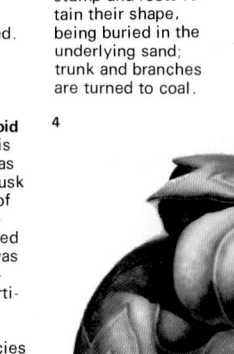

5 All the evidence indicates that the limestone at the base of the sequence was laid down during the Upper Carboniferous in a shallow, limy sea in which lived ammonoids and beds of crinoids. The crinoid fossils are called "facies fossils," since they indicate the nature of the environment, and the ammonoid is an "index fossil" giving a date to the bed. Microscopic investigation of the rock reveals volcanic ash indicating a nearby active volcano.

Geology in the field

The structure of rock formations is not always immediately apparent, especially where they are hidden beneath overlying layers of soil or are obscured by vegetation. One of the best ways of determining the relationships between rocks and the processes at work within the earth is by mapping. Geological maps are the key to understanding the geological history of any particular region.

The basis of geological maps

A geological map [2] shows the boundaries, or contacts, between various rock units, as if the topsoil and vegetation had been stripped off. Maps also reveal the size and extent of any rock formation.

Formations are the basic units of geological maps. They can be recognized by their well-defined contrast to surrounding layers and by the fact that they can be readily traced in the field. The basic criterion of a formation is that it must be a rock layer of sufficient importance and of sufficiently distinct an identity for geologists to agree about its characteristics.

Where formations have been partly obliterated by erosion, or obscured beneath overlying rock and soil, their shape must be pieced together from isolated and often widely scattered outcrops. A single outcrop is usually insufficient to reveal the complex interrelations of the various formations in a region. A geologist [6] must make detailed examinations of numerous rock exposures before he can draw a map that assembles his scattered findings into a coherent picture. Such a map reveals the disposition of the rocks and is the basis for understanding a region's structure and history.

The geologist will also draw up cross sections of the map, showing a vertical slice through the rocks. Canyon walls and coastal cliffs are natural cross sections of this kind. Because of their rarity, the geologist must construct his own interpretative section. Cross sections are derived from interpreting the contours and the orientation of surface outcrops and by making test borings. Such sections are essential for determining the commercial importance of ores and in preparing to dig tunnels and mines.

With the knowledge of the fundamental principles that apply to the formation of rocks, a geologist can set off into the field to decipher the structures of a specific region to determine their origins and possible commercial importance.

Techniques of mapping

There are many techniques for correlating rock formations but the best and most obvious method is to trace a continuous outcrop over a distance. Mostly, however, rocks are only sporadically revealed, so the geologist must look for similarities in the make-up of rocks, in outcrops. Rocks of the same formation are usually similar in color, mineral composition, and texture, although, because most strata change gradually over a distance, other means of identification are also used. Certain characteristics of deposition are especially helpful in identifying separate outcrops as belonging to the same formation. These include ripple marks, formed in sand under very shallow water and later preserved in stone; cross-bedding, which is characteristic of sand deposited in

CONNECTIONS

See also
270 The record in the rocks
272 Clues to the past
276 Earth's time scale

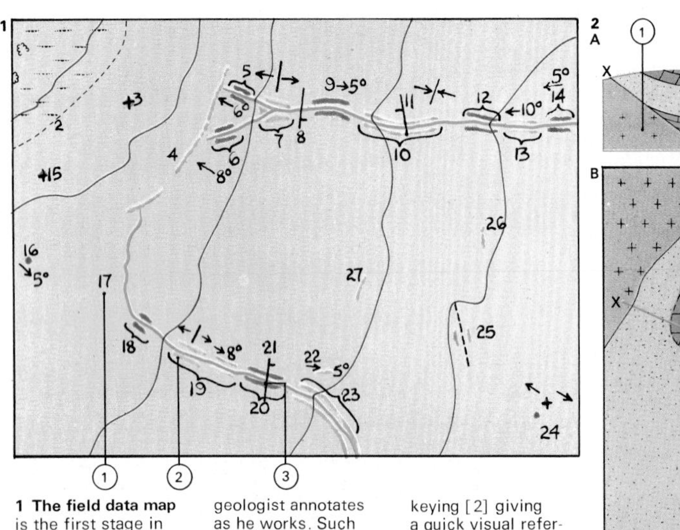
1
2
3
4
5
6
7
8
9→5°
10
12
13
14
+3
+15
16
17
18
19
20
21
22
23
24
25
26
27

1 The field data map is the first stage in the study of the area's geology and is usually a relief map of the area which the geologist annotates as he works. Such annotation may be numbers [1] referring to an entry in a notebook, color keying [2] giving a quick visual reference to the rock type, and symbols [3] that describe various structures.

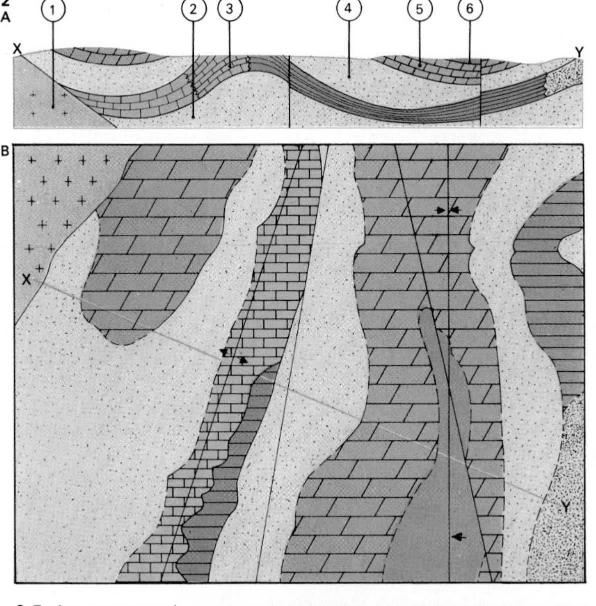
2
A
B
X
Y

2 Geological maps are interpreted from field maps. They show the surface disposition of the rocks as if the topsoil and the vegetation had been removed [B]. The same area is also shown in cross section [A]. Each rock formation is given a distinctive color. Fossils in a bed [3] identify a Carboniferous formation that grades laterally from limestone to shale and then sandstone. Much of this bed is buried by sandstone [4] with dolomite [5] and shale [6] completing the sequences. Two faults are shown by plain lines in [A]. In [B] a line with converging arrows is a syncline axis; with diverging arrows an anticline.

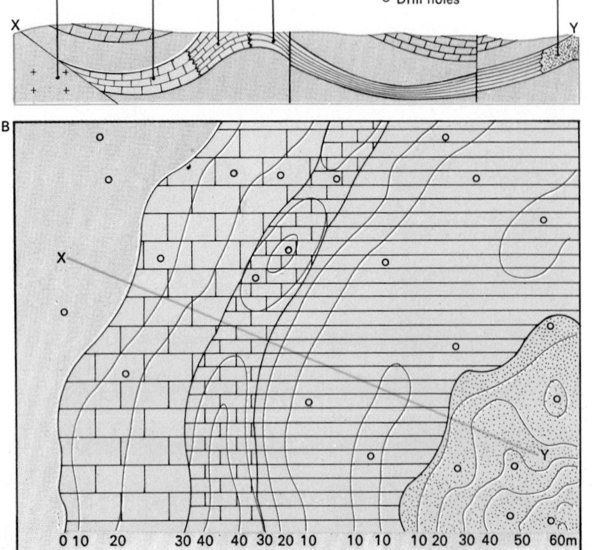
3
A
B
X
Y
Isopachs
o Drill holes
0 10 20 30 40 40 30 20 10 10 10 10 20 30 40 50 60m

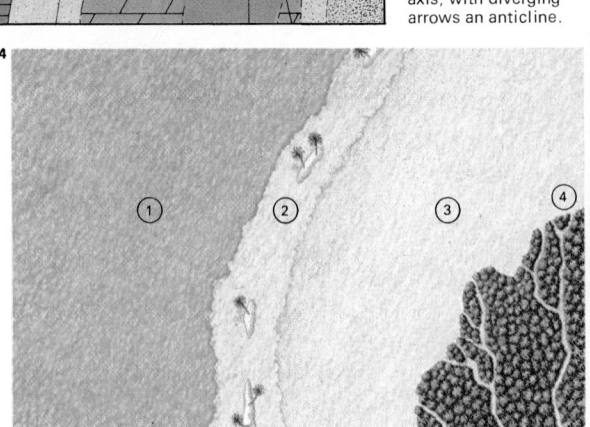

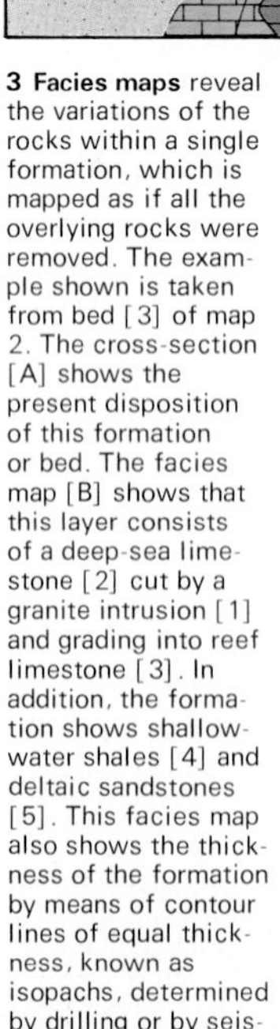

3 Facies maps reveal the variations of the rocks within a single formation, which is mapped as if all the overlying rocks were removed. The example shown is taken from bed [3] of map 2. The cross-section [A] shows the present disposition of this formation or bed. The facies map [B] shows that this layer consists of a deep-sea limestone [2] cut by a granite intrusion [1] and grading into reef limestone [3]. In addition, the formation shows shallow-water shales [4] and deltaic sandstones [5]. This facies map also shows the thickness of the formation by means of contour lines of equal thickness, known as isopachs, determined by drilling or by seismological methods.

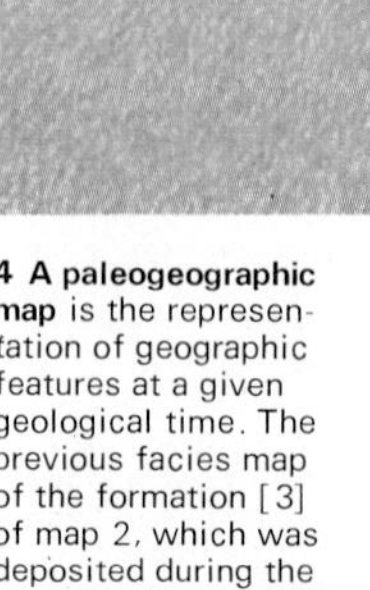

4 A paleogeographic map is the representation of geographic features at a given geological time. The previous facies map of the formation [3] of map 2, which was deposited during the Carboniferous, can be translated into this map. The shales and sandstone to the SE show the former existence of land in that direction and of a river flowing from it and building a delta [4] into a shallow sea [3]. Farther out to sea, in waters less than 150ft (4.5m) deep and more than 68°F (20°C) in temperature, corals and algae built barrier reefs and low-lying islands [2]. In the zone of open water [1] beyond the reef, calcareous plant and animal remains accumulated in deposits of limy mud, which in time became limestone.

a delta; and graded bedding, beds with coarse-material at the bottom and fine at the top.

A highly reliable technique of correlation is that of finding a similarity of sequence. The position of a layer between other readily identifiable layers is an ideal means of correlating scattered outcrops. The fossil contents of rocks are other excellent tools of correlation. Fossils can be characteristic of specific environments and of specific periods in history. They not only identify the formation in which they are found but also help to determine its age.

The structure of an area is important in determining the history of the rocks since their formation. Not all beds are horizontal. Many have been tilted, folded, and faulted into a variety of twisted positions. In the field, geologists may notice that the bedding planes of the strata in a particular outcrop slope diagonally into the ground. The acute angle between the plane of this rock and the horizontal surface of the earth is known as the "dip." The angle of dip is measured with a clinometer and is stated in degrees. The "strike" of a rock is the direction in which the face of its bedding plane lies—this is given as a compass direction. Strike and dip together measure the orientation, or attitude, of a formation. The attitude of rock beds is one of the best indications of the subsurface structure of a region.

Paleogeographic maps

By interpreting geological maps and examining rocks for clues about the environment in which they were originally deposited, it is possible to piece together knowledge about the earth's past. This information can be represented in paleogeographic maps, which portray the surface features of the Earth as it existed during any given era in history [4].

Maps can also be constructed so as to show the past distribution of climatic zones. The fossils of organisms that flourished only in specific environmental conditions are an important means of identifying climates, but more direct indicators of climate can be found—such as ice grooves in old erosion surfaces and rain pits in sandstone.

KEY

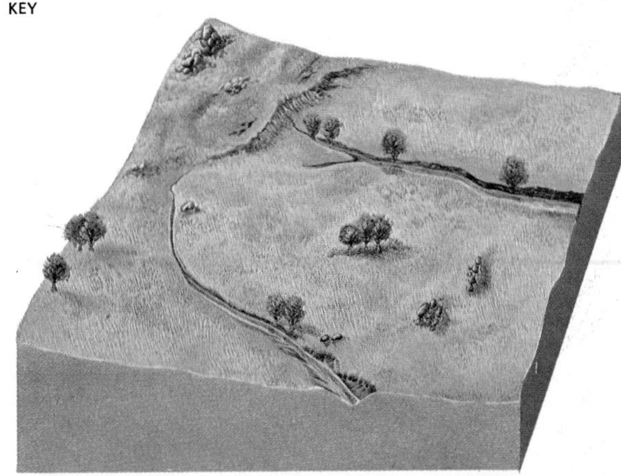

A geologist coming into an area for the first time is rarely faced with a completely exposed sequence of rocks as in the Grand Canyon. More often the rocks in his area of study are concealed beneath soil and vegetation and exposed only occasionally where the natural covering has been removed by the action of water or the weather. The geologist studies each outcrop and from his notes and the samples he has collected for further study he can reconstruct the area's geological history. The different steps in the study of the area shown are illustrated in maps 1 to 5.

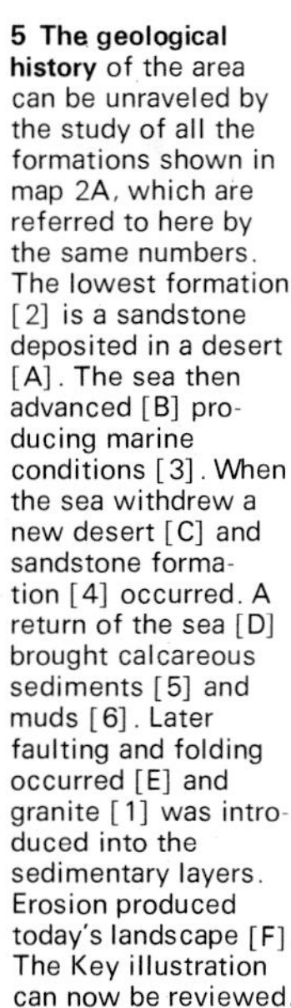

5 The geological history of the area can be unraveled by the study of all the formations shown in map 2A, which are referred to here by the same numbers. The lowest formation [2] is a sandstone deposited in a desert [A]. The sea then advanced [B] producing marine conditions [3]. When the sea withdrew a new desert [C] and sandstone formation [4] occurred. A return of the sea [D] brought calcareous sediments [5] and muds [6]. Later faulting and folding occurred [E] and granite [1] was introduced into the sedimentary layers. Erosion produced today's landscape [F]. The Key illustration can now be reviewed.

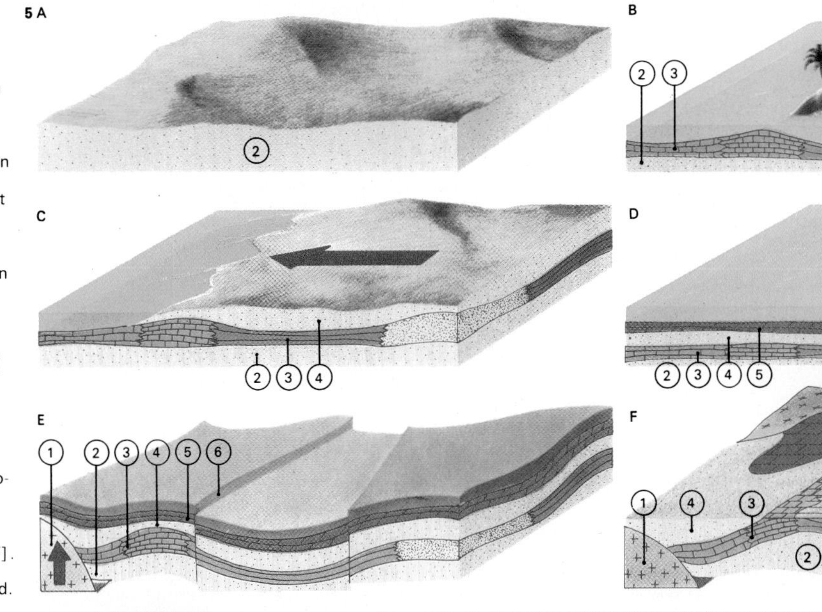

5 A
2
C
2 3 4
E
1 2 3 4 5 6

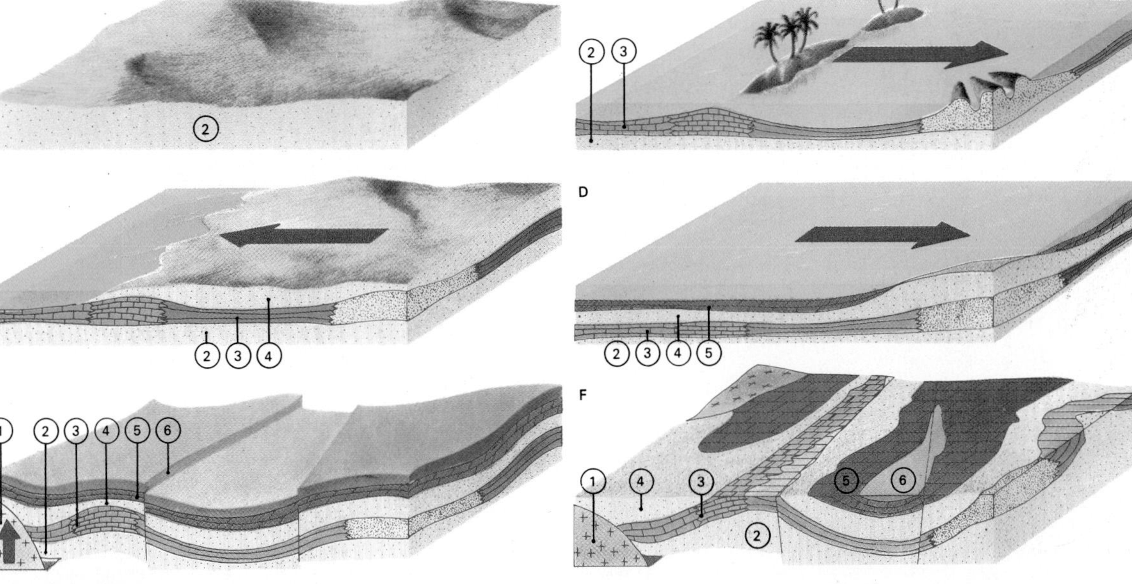

B
2 3
D
2 3 4 5
F
1 4 3
5 6
2

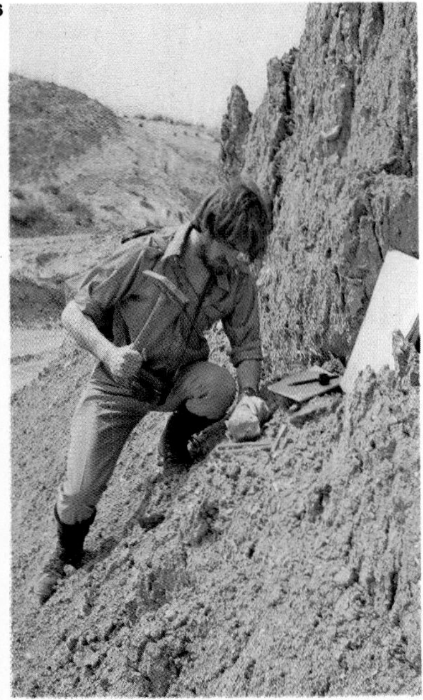

6 The geologist who sets out to do fieldwork must carry with him all the tools and measuring devices that he will need to make his observations. Typically, he will have a compass and clinometer to take the dips and bearings of bedding planes, faults, and other features. A hand lens is used to examine details in rocks and a camera is useful to record the orientation and structure of rock outcrops. A hammer is essential for breaking open rocks to examine their mineral composition and to chip off samples that are collected for the specimen bag. Most important is the pen and notebook in which all his observations, drawings, and maps are recorded.

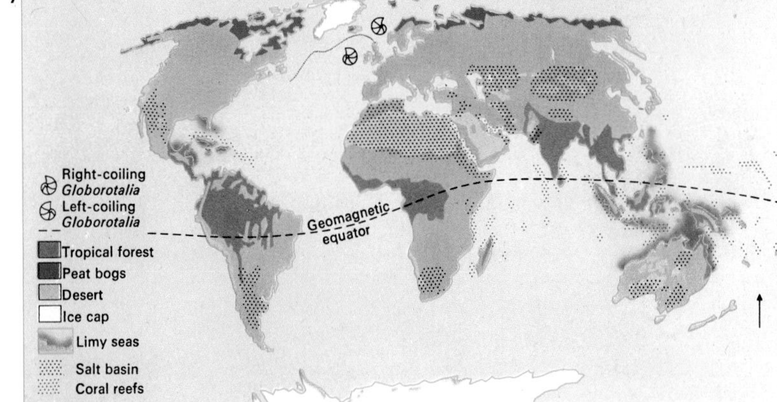

Right-coiling
Globorotalia
Left-coiling
Globorotalia
Geomagnetic equator
Tropical forest
Peat bogs
Desert
Ice cap
Limy seas
Salt basin
Coral reefs

7 Paleoclimatology is the study of ancient climates through traces left in contemporary rocks. The present-day formations of such preservable climate-related features are shown. The foraminiferan *Globorotalia* is an indicator of sea temperature. It coils right in warm waters and left in cold waters. Coral reefs and major carbonate deposits are both typical of warm, shallow seas. Common to desert environments are evaporite deposits (salt basins) and reddish-hued sandstones. The lush plant life of tropical forests and swamps is the raw material from which coal is formed. Ice sheets groove and scratch the face of rocks and leave characteristic deposits of glacial till, and peat bogs are typical of the tundra environment fringing the ice.

Earth's time scale

In the mid-seventeenth century, Archbishop James Usher (1581–1656) of Ireland reached the conclusion that the Earth was created at precisely 9am on October 23, 4004 BC. He arrived at his findings after diligent study of religious texts. Not until well into the nineteenth century did efforts to establish both absolute and relative techniques of geological dating meet with any real success. In 1897 the renowned British physicist, William Thomas Kelvin (1824–1907) attempted to deduce the Earth's age from the temperature difference between the young molten planet and its present state, assuming that the rate of heat loss was constant. His estimate of 20–40 million years was more than a hundred times too low. Radioactivity was then unknown, so Kelvin failed to take into account the copious heat generated by the decay of radioactive elements within the Earth.

The law of superposition

Although early efforts to find an absolute dating system repeatedly failed, a relative time scale proved far easier to develop. Such a system merely seeks to establish the order in which rocks were laid down [1]. It does not make any reference to fixed units of time. The entire sequence of rocks deposited since the beginning of time is known as the geological column. Once the law of superposition (which states that in strata that have remained undisturbed since deposition older rocks lie beneath younger ones) had been elucidated by William Smith (1769–1839) late in the eighteenth century, piecing together the geological column was simply a long, arduous task of identifying and correlating rocks and slotting them into their appropriate order in the stratigraphic sequence. The entire column was subdivided into units based on events that were taken to be natural breaks between one geological era and the next. The divisions, therefore, vary widely in length [5].

The correlation of rock strata was made easier by observing the fossils they contained. Organisms of a particular time in history possess distinct characteristics that can be used to identify the widely scattered rocks in which these fossils occur [3].

The search for absolute dating

The breakthrough to an absolute time scale was finally achieved with the discovery that radioactive decay proceeds at a constant rate. In 1907 a chemist at Yale University, Bertram Boltwood (1870–1927), found that the decay of radioactive minerals could be thought of as a convenient yardstick of time. He recognized the regular relationship that existed between decay products and their parent elements and that progressively older specimens possessed increasing amounts of stable end-products [8]. In this way, he was able to demonstrate the age of a sample of uranite crystal from Ceylon (Sri Lanka). It proved to be 2.2 billion years old, many times greater than any age proposed previously.

The most useful concept in radiological chronology is the notion of half-life. This is the time it takes for half a given amount of material to decompose, or decay, into a radiogenic product. The half-life of uranium 238, for example, is 4.5 billion years. After a lapse of this time, only half an original given quantity of uranium remains, the rest hav-

CONNECTIONS

See also
270 The record in the rocks
168 The Earth as a magne
172 Continents adrift
560 Fossils: the life of th past
562 Plants of the past
410 The world before ma

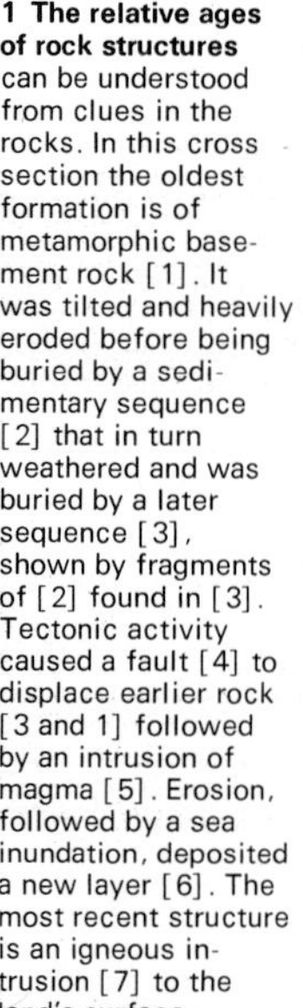

1
2
7
1
4
6
5
3

1 The relative ages of rock structures can be understood from clues in the rocks. In this cross section the oldest formation is of metamorphic basement rock [1]. It was tilted and heavily eroded before being buried by a sedimentary sequence [2] that in turn weathered and was buried by a later sequence [3], shown by fragments of [2] found in [3]. Tectonic activity caused a fault [4] to displace earlier rock [3 and 1] followed by an intrusion of magma [5]. Erosion, followed by a sea inundation, deposited a new layer [6]. The most recent structure is an igneous intrusion [7] to the land's surface.

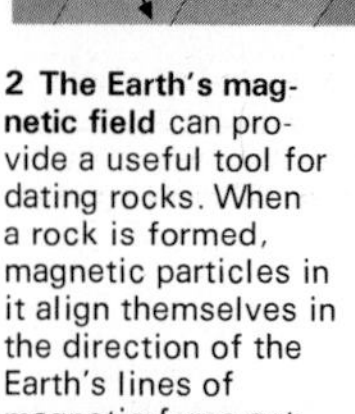

2

2 The Earth's magnetic field can provide a useful tool for dating rocks. When a rock is formed, magnetic particles in it align themselves in the direction of the Earth's lines of magnetic force acting at the time. If the changes in direction and position of the lines of force are established, the ages of the rocks of an undisturbed sequence can be determined by investigation of their magnetic alignment. If the rocks have been disturbed, as they have been in this quite complex example, the variations in their alignments indicate the nature of the movements involved.

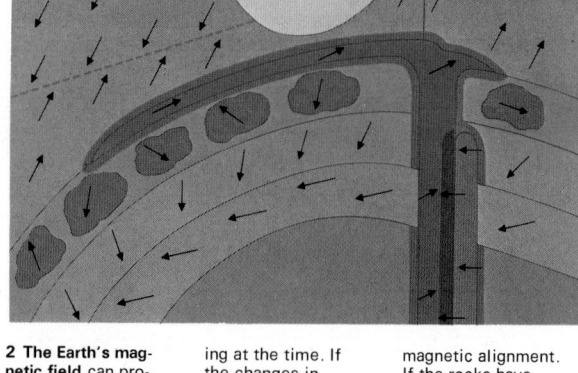

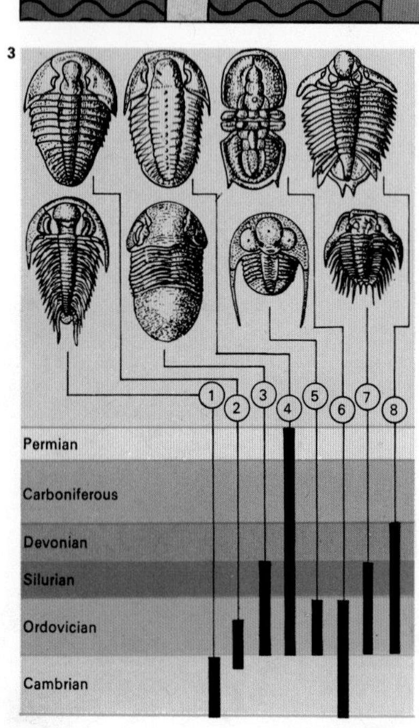

3
1
2
3
4
5
6
7
8
Permian
Carboniferous
Devonian
Silurian
Ordovician
Cambrian

3 Index fossils are useful for dating rocks. Age ranges of the various families of trilobites are known. If proetid [4] and agnostid [6] trilobites are found in the same rock, it is Ordovician in age.

1 Redlichiida
2 Asphidea
3 Ilanidae
4 Proetidae
5 Trinucleidae
6 Agnostida
7 Odontopleurida
8 Lichida

4

4 Orogeny is the process of mountain building by folding and thrusting. There were several major orogenic climaxes, which make ideal reference points as they form breaks in the stratigraphic column through changes in erosion and sedimentation patterns.

ing been transformed into a series of radioactive isotopes, eventually decaying to the lead isotope Pb-206.

The age of a rock specimen is determined by comparing the ratio of decay elements to the remaining amount of parent material. The known half-life of the element in question is then used to calculate the sample's age. This technique has only become reliable since the 1950s when mass spectrometers, instruments that can analyze and measure elements in quantities of only a few millionths of a gram, were developed.

The process of radioactive decay is extremely complex. The disintegration of unstable atoms is spontaneous and has never been shown to be affected by surrounding physical or chemical conditions. This is one of the few processes on Earth that can be assumed to have had a constant rate throughout time, making it an ideal standard for measuring absolute age.

Absolute dating establishes the age of a specimen from the time it crystallized into a mineral, not the age of the element itself. Once the mineral has been formed, chemical composition is fixed. The decay products that accumulate within it are entirely the result of the disintegration of a contained radioactive parent element.

Finding the age of the Earth

Uranium, and its close cousin thorium, are not the only elements that are suitable for absolute dating. Potassium 40, with a half-life of 1.3 billion years, occurs throughout the earth's crust in measurable quantities. It decays into argon 40, an inert gas found drifting in the atmosphere. A comparison of the ratio of these two elements in the crust and air yields a figure of some 4.6 billion years for the age of the Earth. The oldest rocks of the great Precambrian shields of North America, Greenland, Africa, and Australia yield dates of up to only 3.5 billion years. The discrepancy between the two figures is perfectly plausible since a long cooling period must be allowed for before any major rock systems could have formed a crust. Despite all these techniques, many rocks cannot be dated absolutely.

KEY

The colossal time span over which geological processes operate is emphasized if one compresses the 4.6 billion years of earth history into 12 hours on a clock face. The first 2 hours 52 minutes are obscure. The earliest rocks occur at about 2:52 but the planet remains a lifeless desert until 4:00, when bacterial and algal organisms appear. Eons drag by until just after 10:30 when there is an explosion of invertebrate life in the seas. Dinosaurs wander the land at 11:25 only to be replaced by birds and mammals 25 minutes later. Hominids arrive about half a minute before noon. The last tenth of a second covers the entire history of man's civilization on earth.

5

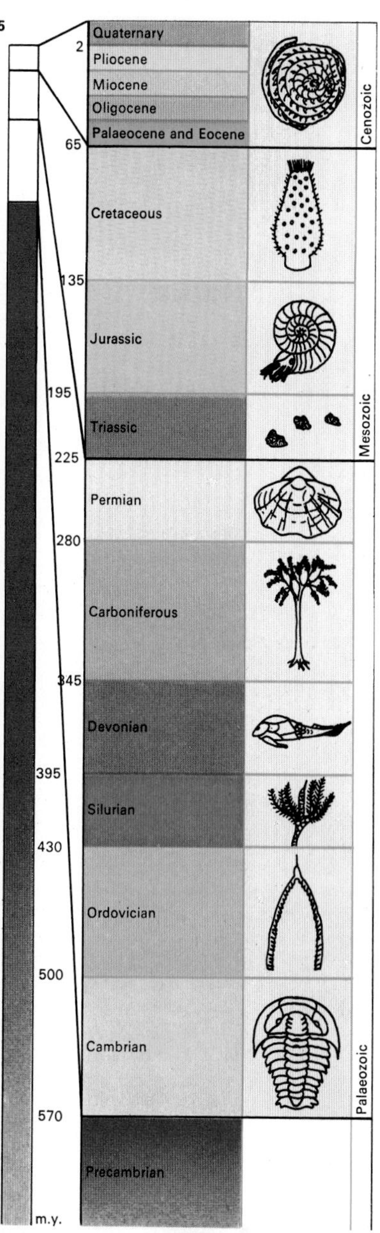

Quaternary
2
Pliocene
Miocene
Oligocene
Palaeocene and Eocene
65
Cenozoic
Cretaceous
135
Jurassic
195
Triassic
Mesozoic
225
Permian
280
Carboniferous
345
Devonian
395
Silurian
430
Ordovician
500
Cambrian
Palaeozoic
570
Precambrian
m.y.

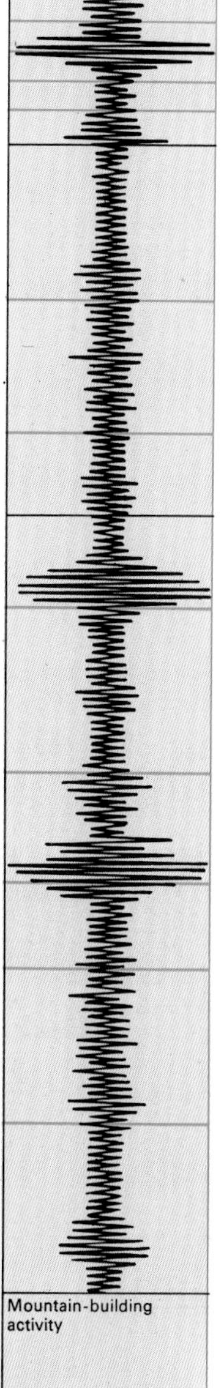

Mountain-building activity

6

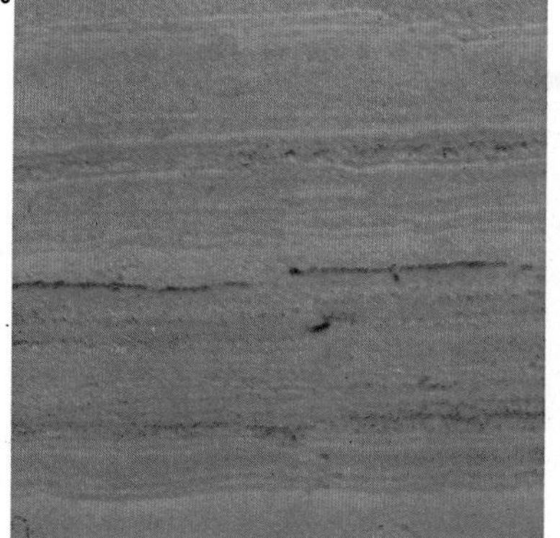

7

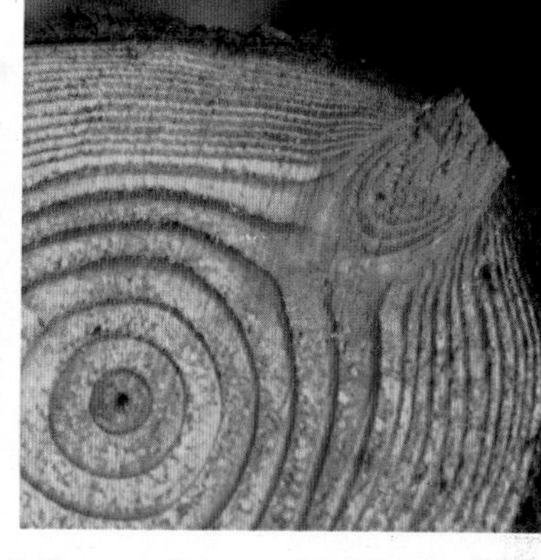

5 The age of the Earth is some 4.6 billion years, although only the last 570 million years show an abundance of plant and animal life. The most widely found fossil remains from any specific period are called index fossils and are used to correlate various rock formations of the same age. Mountain building took place mostly during specific periods in geological time.

6 Varves are thin bands of sand, clay, and silt deposited as easily recognized annual layers in glacier-fed lakes. Varves can be read to determine the dates of the retreat of the last ice age.

7 Dendrochronology is the use of annual growth rings of trees to measure time. The innermost rings of recent trees can be matched to the outer rings of older trees and a chronology can be set up.

8

N=neutron
P=proton
Normal carbon-12 atom
Nitrogen-14 atom
Carbon-14 atom
O_2
CO_2
Pulses in number of C-14 atoms
Time in years
5,570 years
11,460 years
0047
Carbon-14
Nitrogen-14
ß

8 Radiocarbon dating is typical of the techniques that use radioactive decay to estimate age. Carbon (C) possesses two isotopes, C-14 which is radioactive, formed by cosmic ray bombardment of nitrogen 14 (N-14), and C-12, which is not. The C-14 combines with oxygen to form carbon dioxide, which is absorbed by living organisms. A constant ratio of C-14 to C-12 is established in each organism during its life. After death no more carbon dioxide is absorbed and the C-14 decays steadily, by emitting beta particles, to N-14, falling to half its quantity every 5,570 years. Organic remains can be dated by comparing the ratio of C-14 to C-12.

Mineral resources of the land

CONNECTIONS

See also
280 Mineral resources o the sea
282 Energy resources: coal
284 Energy resources: o and gas
244 Gems and semiprecious stones
290 Earth's dwindling re sources
1596 Metals and their use
1598 Aluminum and its use
1608 Working with ceramics
1610 Materials for building

Minerals are the building blocks of rocks. A few rocks are made up of only one mineral, while most contain many of them. Only rarely do useful minerals occur in sufficient concentrations to make commercial exploitation worthwhile [Key]. Increasingly sophisticated technology means, however, that deposits that were uneconomic to work a few years ago can now be profitably exploited. New techniques have also made it possible to rework the waste heaps of some mines. Scarcity caused by increased demand or by depletion of richer reserves can also make the extraction of low-grade ore profitable without necessarily involving a change of the basic mining techniques.

The formation of ores

Concentrations of minerals that contain economic quantities of such metals as copper, tin, tungsten, lead, and others are called ores. These are formed in many different ways. Ores of the same metal can have dissimilar origins.

Magma [2], or molten rock, is the origin of many mineral deposits. Some deposits are formed within the cooled and consolidated igneous mass itself. The minerals become concentrated by magmatic segregation. Examples of deposits formed by this process are the chromite [5] deposits of South Africa, the famous iron ore deposits of Kiruna, Sweden, and the nickel sulfide of Sudbury, Ontario. Deposits formed at the same time as the surrounding rock are called syngenetic. A mineral deposit formed later is known as epigenetic.

During cooling of the magma, hot gases and liquids may be forced, under great pressure, into surrounding rocks. These mineral-rich solutions cool and are forced to drop their loads as pressure is reduced. Sometimes they find their way into small cracks to create veins, or a collection of veins (sometimes called a lode), containing both economically important minerals and worthless ones (gangue). Veins have no great thickness but may run for considerable distances and penetrate to great depths.

Deposits formed by gases are called pneumatolytic. The apatite (phosphatic mineral) deposits of Norway were formed in this way. Those that originate from hot aqueous solutions are known as hydrothermal deposits.

The heat of an igneous intrusion changes surrounding rocks, particularly those in direct contact with it. Where permeation of these by hot gaseous and mineral-rich solutions replaces some of the original rock the deposit is called pyrometasomatic and is often a source of copper, zinc, and lead.

Heat zones and weathering

Mineral-rich solutions sometimes replace only certain elements in the original rock; at other times the whole mass may be affected, forming large deposits such as the pyrite deposits of Rio Tinto in Spain and those of the Copper Belt of Zambia. The type of mineral deposit is determined by the temperature of the solution and associated gases. Specific minerals are associated with hotter and cooler areas. Tin, copper, lead, zinc, and iron are characteristically found in that order, working outward from the zone of most heat. Hydrothermal solutions

1
Iron
Tin
Copper
Zinc
Nickel
Chromium
Manganese
Magnesium
Aluminium
Lead
Gold
Silver

1 Reserves of important metals are widely distributed throughout the world. The map provides a guide to major ore-producing areas, but many other locations could be plotted if areas were shown in greater detail. (Placer deposits on coastal margins are not shown.) Information about reserves in communist countries is often withheld and it is likely, therefore, that reserves are greater than is indicated. The USSR is a leading producer of most metals. Except for Antarctica, major discoveries of minerals have been made in every continent since World War II. Some areas such as Australia and the Sahara have seen considerable mining development since the mid-1960s.

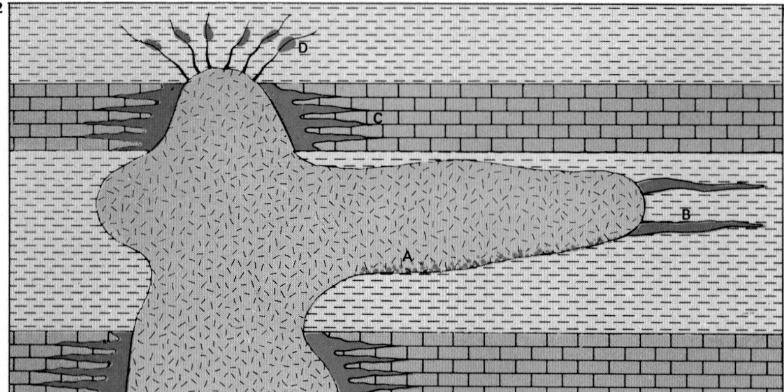
2
A
B
C
D

2 Magmatic ore bodies may result from several different causes: settling of denser minerals or elements to the lower part of a magma chamber during cooling [A]; injection of late-crystallizing magma components along fissures [B]; contact metamorphism, in which minerals of the wall rocks are replaced by other minerals derived from the magma [C]; and hydrothermal deposits filling the fissures with minerals derived from the magma and transported by hot watery solutions [D], as in the copper deposits of Butte, Montana.

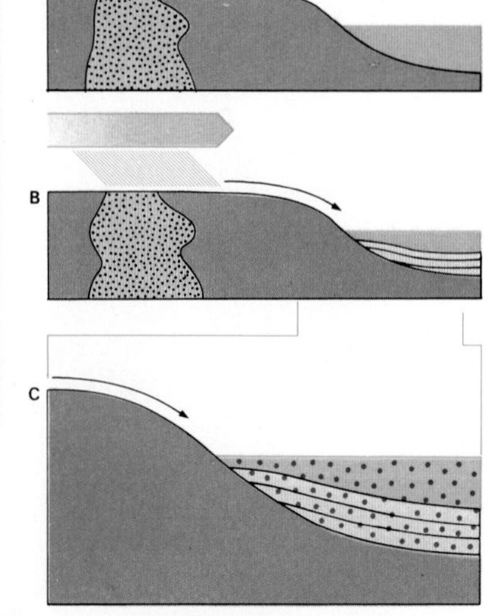
3 A
B
C

3 Sedimentary ore bodies are originally derived from metal-rich igneous rocks such as an iron-rich pluton [A]. On exposure to weather the igneous body is eroded and iron is dissolved away in the form of biçarbonate [B]. The solution of bicarbonate reaches a basin of deposition (a lake or the sea), where it becomes a hydrous oxide and is precipitated into the sediments [C]. Iron oxide rolled about by currents before settling may form small rounded aggregates. During consolidation of the sediment the water is squeezed out of the hydrous oxide yielding hematite.

sometimes reach the surface as hot springs to produce deposits of the mercury ore cinnabar, while sulfur deposits [7] are often found near volcanoes.

Rocks at the surface of the Earth are subjected to weathering. Downward percolation of ground water may leach some useful elements from upper layers and bring them to the water table level. Many valuable deposits of copper, for example, have been created from low-grade ores in this way. Below the layer of secondary enrichment the ore remains low grade. In tropical areas weathering may affect the top 250ft (76m) of the surface. Under such conditions aluminum silicate rocks are broken down to yield bauxite, the chief ore of aluminum. Some iron ores and some manganese deposits originated from weathering action.

Sedimentary rock deposits

When the rocks are broken down the particles are carried away by streams and rivers [3]. Minerals that are not easily changed and that are heavy may collect in workable quantities as placer deposits. Such deposits occur in streams and on beaches. Gold is one metal mined from placer deposits and finds of this sort led to the California gold rush of 1849. Most of the world's tin, which comes from Malaysia and Indonesia, is dredged from placer deposits.

Many other sedimentary rocks are important sources of minerals. Evaporation of seawater and inland lakes can give precipitation deposits of gypsum [Key, 8], anhydrite, halite (common salt), and potash [6]. Many of these are mined conventionally but some are exploited by solution mining—hot water is pumped into the deposit and the resulting brine forced to the surface. Important phosphate deposits are the result of vast accumulations of bird droppings called guano. Clays are sedimentary rock deposits important in brick manufacture and in pottery and ceramics. China clay, or kaolin, is a clay formed as a result of the action of hydrothermal solutions on the feldspars in granite. Marls are mixtures of clay and calcium carbonate and are quarried for the cement industry; limestone is exploited for building stones or for lime preparation.

KEY

Open-pit mining of gypsum produces the raw material known as plaster of paris. Where an exploitable mineral occurs near the surface it can be extracted in this way by removing the overburden of soil and rock to provide easy access to the mineral.

4 Garnierite, also known as noumeite, from Nouméa, New Caledonia, where it is found in veins, is a source of nickel. The New Caledonia deposits were once the most important in the world.

5 Chromite is found as a mineral in ultrabasic igneous rocks. In some areas, however, ore bodies have formed by segregation, as in New Caledonia, where this specimen was found, and in Rhodesia.

4

5

6

6 Potash salts are the last precipitates of an evaporating sea. Potash is used mainly as a fertilizer but also in the explosives industry and in various metallurgical processes.

7 Sulfur is often found in the native (pure) state around the vents of volcanoes; it is deposited by sulfurous gases. A major source of sulfur today results from the refining of crude oil.

8 Gypsum, like the potash salts, is an evaporite. It is found in Britain, Germany, and the United States and is used in plaster and cement and in paper and paint.

7

8

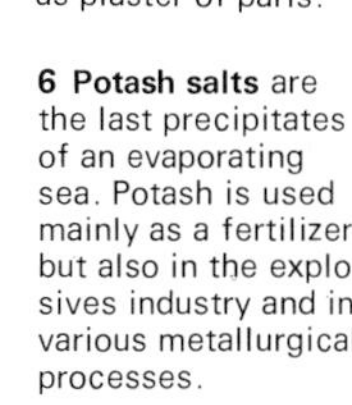

9

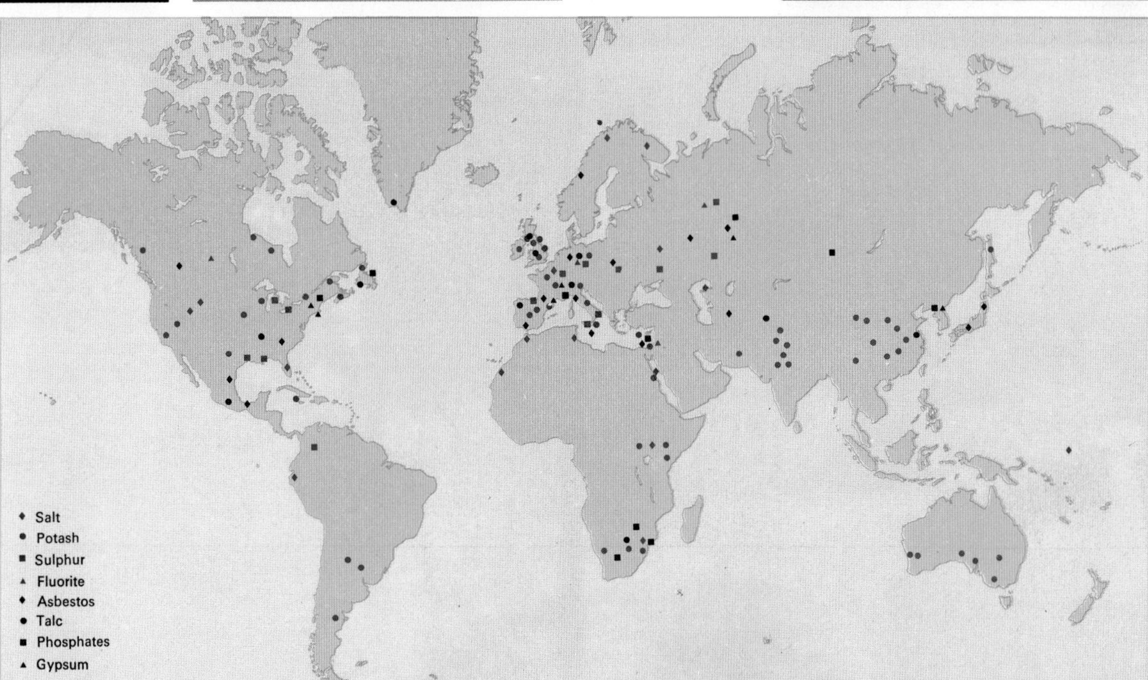
Salt
Potash
Sulphur
Fluorite
Asbestos
Talc
Phosphates
Gypsum

9 Reserves of non-metallic minerals of economic importance are distributed irregularly. This is partly due to lack of information about finds in certain areas and partly to the fact that some areas are inaccessible for exploration. It is likely that vast reserves will be discovered as new methods of exploration are developed. No country will ever have all the mineral resources it needs within its own boundaries. The "energy crisis" may be followed by a "mineral crisis," particularly if less developed nations advance rapidly along the road to full industrialization. They will then require their own resources rather than being able to export them for use by the big industrial nations.

Mineral resources of the sea

The oceans are vast storehouses of minerals [2]. Seawater itself contains almost all the elements, but many of them are present in such extremely low concentrations that the cost of extraction is high compared with the cost of mining them on land.

Chemicals from seawater

A few substances can be extracted economically from seawater—namely, common salt, magnesium, and bromine. Salt has been obtained from the sea since ancient times [3]. The traditional method is to flood coastal pans with seawater. As the water evaporates in the sun, some impurities are precipitated out. The concentrated brine is then passed to another pan where the salt is precipitated. Today about 33 percent of the world's salt output comes from ocean water.

Magnesium is an important metal in the lightweight alloys that are used to manufacture aircraft, missiles, and precision instruments. In World War II it was used in incendiary bombs. In the 1930s Germany produced nearly 66.6 percent of the world's output so American and British scientists began experiments to extract it from seawater. British efforts proved successful in 1939 with a process that removed the magnesium as a hydroxide after seawater had been mixed with lime. Today, magnesium from seawater accounts for 66.6 percent of the world's annual production.

Bromine, an important element in the photographic and pharmaceutical industries and in the production of high-octane gasoline, is also largely obtained from seawater. The prospects for extracting other elements from seawater are influenced by two main factors. First, there must be a shortage to justify the high investment required and, second, successful exploitation depends on technological developments.

The water of the oceans is a valuable resource in arid coastal areas [7]. Fresh water can be produced from seawater by evaporation and condensation—this is the natural derivation of rain and fresh waters on land. But the artificial speeding-up of the process in desalination plants uses large amounts of energy, and it is justified only where energy is cheap, as in Saudi Arabia.

Continental shelf resources

Apart from resources in seawater itself, exploitation of ocean floors is already yielding substantial supplies of many minerals. Most of these minerals are obtained around coastlines or in the shallow waters of continental shelves.

Sand, gravel, and limestone, which are used in building, are taken from beaches and coastal waters. Some beach deposits contain metals in quantities worth extracting. For example, the black sands along the Atlantic coast of the United States from New Jersey to Florida contain ilmenite and rutile, ores from which titanium is obtained, and monazite, a rare Earth mineral.

Mining materials on the sea floor in shallow water has also become important. Around Japan, underwater iron-bearing sands are piped ashore and, off the coast of southwest Africa, gravels containing diamonds have been mined since 1962.

Other minerals are extracted from rocks under the sea floor. Prospectors use methods similar to those used on land, aided by such techniques as underwater photog-

CONNECTIONS

See also
222 The sea and seawater
228 The sea bed
278 Mineral resources of the land
432 Algae and seaweeds

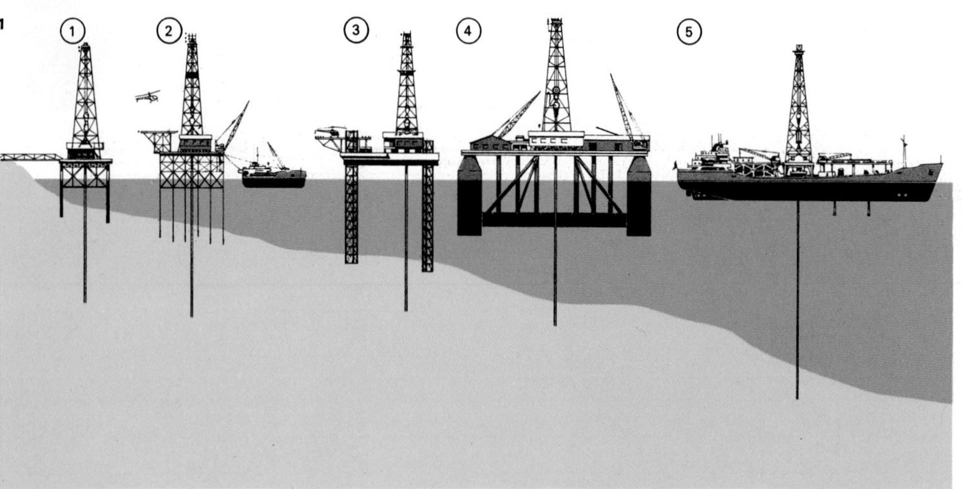
1
2
3
4
5

1 Early marine oil rigs [1] were essentially land rigs on wooden piles. Later designs [2] have multiple legs sunk into the sea floor. Jack-up rigs [3] have legs that are extended to the bottom. Large semi-submersible rigs [4] are supported by their buoyancy and tethers secure them to the bottom. Ships [5] are used in deep water. The drill is lowered through a hole in the hull.

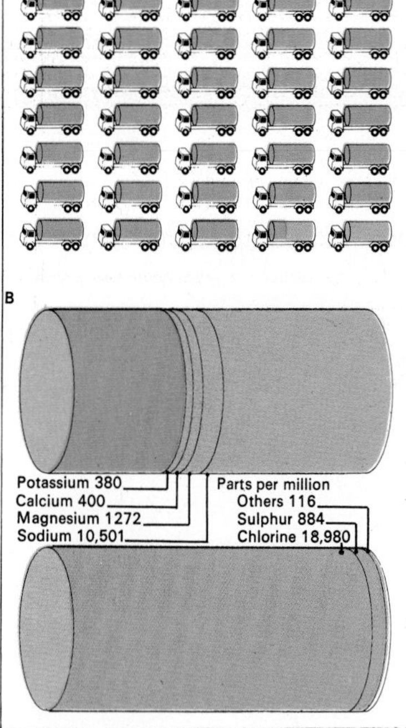
A
B
Potassium 380
Calcium 400
Magnesium 1272
Sodium 10,501
Parts per million
Others 116
Sulphur 884
Chlorine 18,980

2. Seventy three of the 93 natural elements are known to exist in seawater. The 50 tankers [A] represent 220,000 gals (1,000,000 liters) of seawater (each tanker contains 4,400 gals, or 20,000 liters). The last two tankers [B] contain the elements present in this volume and the proportions of each are indicated.

3 Salt has been extracted from seawater since the days of the Minoan civilization. Seawater is first trapped in coastal pans. As the water evaporates in the sun, the salt is precipitated.

4 The element iodine is present in seawater in very low concentration (0.006%). It is concentrated by seaweeds that, botanically, are the green, red, and brown algae. Iodine was first discovered in 1811 when it was extracted from the ashes of seaweed. Kelp, ribbonlike brown algae, was one of the earliest sources. Much iodine is now obtained from Chile saltpeter and from brine from oil wells, although seaweed remains a valuable source.

raphy. Today mining is effectively carried out in water up to 600ft (183m) deep. For example, about 20 percent of Japan's coal comes from submarine mines. Having located a coal bed, engineers build an artificial island and then drill down to the coal layers. In the Gulf of Mexico, sulfur is flushed out from beneath the sea bottom with superheated water.

The sulfur deposit in the Gulf of Mexico was discovered when prospectors were searching for oil. Currently, oil and natural gas are the most important minerals being extracted from under the sea [Key]. Oil rigs are located around the world [1], in such places as the Black Sea, the Gulf of Mexico, the Arctic Sea, off the coast of California, the North Sea, and the Sulu Sea in the Philippines. The setting-up of rigs in the sea has, however, met with many problems, involving risks for the operators. The rigs have to withstand severe storms and even the drift pressure of pack ice. But the technology of drilling in the sea floor has developed quickly. Today about 20 percent of the world's oil production comes from offshore operations and this proportion will increase as the land oilfields dry up.

Deep-sea deposits

Also present on the deep ocean floor are large numbers of so-called manganese nodules [5]. The presence of these potato-shaped nodules, which also contain cobalt, copper, iron, nickel, and other metals, has been known for 100 years [6]. In parts of the Pacific, the nodules are concentrated at more than 100lb per square yard (54kg per square meter), and they also occur in the Atlantic and Indian Oceans.

The origin of the nodules is unknown. Scientists believe that they must be formed by some biological process that is continuing to increase the number of nodules. Manganese, an important metal in steel-making, is unevenly distributed on land. But international control of deep-sea mining poses some problems. One proposal suggested that an international organization should collect royalties from deep-sea mining companies and use them to finance developing countries' mining operations.

KEY

Oil and natural gas are two of the most important mineral products being extracted from beneath the sea floor. The technology of drilling into the sea floor developed rapidly after 1945, and today about 20% of the world's total oil production originates from offshore oil wells.

5

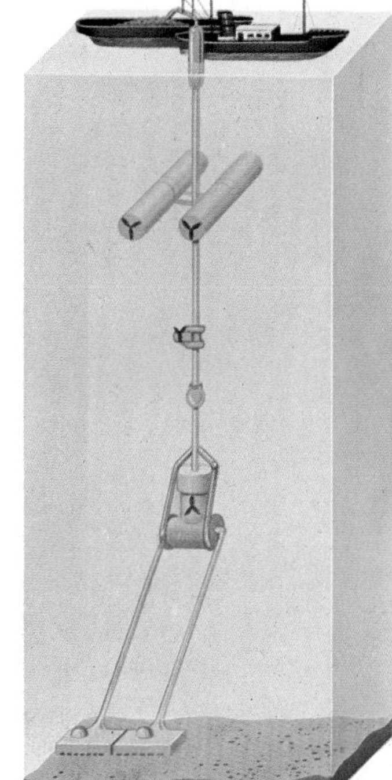

5 Ways of mining the rich deposits of manganese nodules in the deep waters of the ocean have been discussed for some time. The diagram shows one of the methods that has been proposed. This device employs the principle of the vacuum cleaner. It picks up the nodules and pumps them to the surface. On reaching the surface, the nodules are transferred to a barge. The device is driven by a series of propellers located between the surface and the bottom. Other proposed devices include self-propelled rigs with air-lift systems, and a bottom-crawling miner attached to a surface vessel by articulated arms. Such systems may incorporate closed-circuit television to aid in locating the nodules.

6 A

B

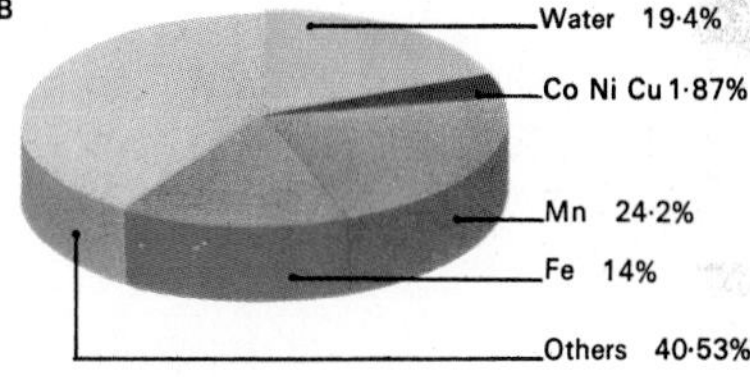

Water 19·4%
Co Ni Cu 1·87%
Mn 24·2%
Fe 14%
Others 40·53%

6 Manganese nodules [A] are potato-like lumps of minerals, possibly of plant or animal origin, found in great concentrations on parts of the ocean floor. The composition of the nodules varies to some extent. In addition to manganese (Mn), a valuable metal used in steel making, the nodules contain other metals [B], including cobalt (Co), copper (Cu), iron (Fe) and nickel (Ni).

7

7 One important oceanic resource is water. Desalination of seawater to obtain fresh water is achieved by electrical, chemical, and change-of-phase processes (by condensing steam from the water or by freezing it to remove the salt). All these processes require power and complicated machinery, which makes them expensive. Today desalination is carried out on a large scale only in areas where fresh water is desperately short, as in Israel. The profits from petroleum have made it possible for some Arab nations to do this in arid areas.

8

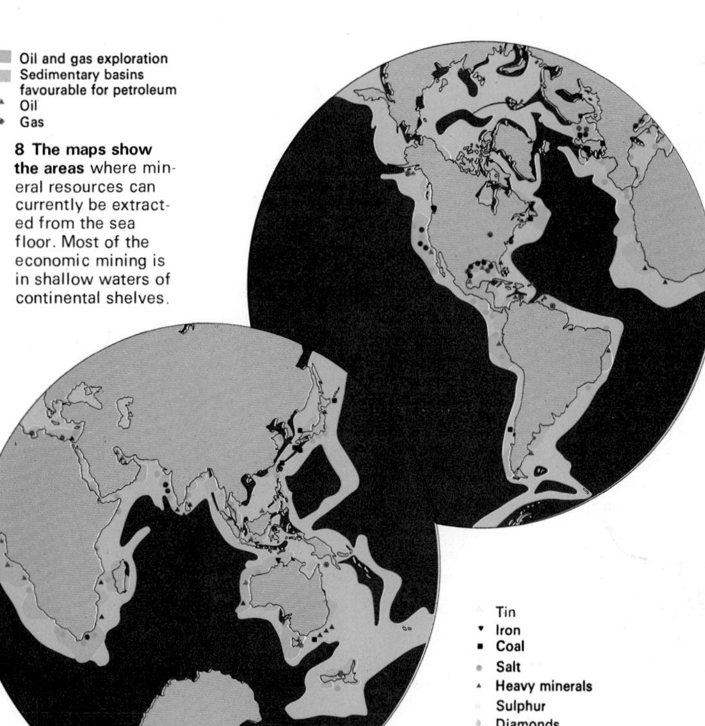

Oil and gas exploration
Sedimentary basins favourable for petroleum
Oil
Gas
Tin
Iron
Coal
Salt
Heavy minerals
Sulphur
Diamonds
Magnesium
Fresh water
Other minerals

8 The maps show the areas where mineral resources can currently be extracted from the sea floor. Most of the economic mining is in shallow waters of continental shelves.

Energy resources: coal

Coal was the first fossil fuel to be exploited on a large scale. It made possible the industrial revolution, which in turn benefited the coal industry by providing it with improved technology, thus enabling coal to be mined at even greater depths. Coal consumption has been declining for many years. In 1960 coal provided about half the world's energy; by 1970 its share had fallen to a third, oil and natural gas, the other two main fossils fuels, providing an ever-growing share of the world's needs. In the near future, however, the situation is likely to be reversed as oil and gas reserves are being depleted. There is estimated to be in excess of eight trillion metric tons of coal in world reserves, which is more than enough to last into the twenty-second century.

What is coal?

Like oil and natural gas, coal is organic material that has been slowly broken down by biological and geological processes, but whereas oil and gas are mainly derived from animal matter, such as plankton, coal consists of plant remains. The fossil fuels are a part of the carbon cycle [1] that is basic to life on Earth. There is probably about 50 times as much carbon locked up in fossil fuels as there is in all of the living matter, both plant and animal, on Earth.

Coal is a sedimentary rock consisting of carbon, water, and volatile gases, with small amounts of mineral impurities that produce ash when the coal is burned. Variation in the proportions of the constituents present produces the different types of coal and is responsible for their different calorific values. Lignite (brown coal) contains a high proportion of water (43 percent) and is therefore of lower calorific value than bituminous coal (ordinary household coal) which contains only 3 percent water. Anthracite, on the other hand, is almost all carbon (96 percent) and contains hardly any water or volatiles. It is of higher calorific value but less readily inflammable than bituminous coal, which has a high proportion of volatiles (32 percent). The mineral impurities present are mainly clays, chlorides, and sulfides. The latter in particular are troublesome on combustion, oxidizing to sulfur dioxide, a major cause of atmospheric pollution.

How coal is formed

The creation of coal is dependent upon abundant plant growth. This condition was fulfilled during the Carboniferous from 345 to 280 million years ago, when large areas of swamp forest covered low-lying regions [Key]. Most commercial deposits of coal date from this period, although there are deposits dating from most ages in the geological time scale.

Coal is formed when decaying plant material builds up faster than it can be destroyed by bacterial activity. The swamp environment is ideal for coal formation. The water tends to be stagnant and therefore deficient in oxygen, which inhibits bacterial activity, preventing the vegetable matter from being completely broken down. Once a certain stage is reached acids produced in the process prevent the bacteria from further activity. The initial product formed is peat. If it is then buried under other sedimentary material the peat becomes

CONNECTIONS

See also
1640 Coal: production and uses
286 Energy supplies
290 Earth's dwindling resources
172 Continents adrift
284 Energy resources: oil and gas
562 Plants of the past
568 Toward life on land
436 Mosses and liverworts
438 Ferns and horsetails

1

Sunrays | Photosynthesis | Carbon dioxide transfer | Carbonate transfer | Burial and rock formation

1 Coal and other fossil fuels are part of the complex carbon cycle that maintains life on Earth. Carbon dioxide (CO_2) is produced in the Earth's interior [1] and in rocks [2]; also, when animals breathe and when organic material—including fossil fuels—burns [3]. It is converted into living matter by the process of photosynthesis carried on by plants. Carbon dioxide exists in the atmosphere and in solution in seawater. It is exchanged between these two media when rain washes it out of the air [4]; it can also be dissolved by seawater [6]. Some of this dissolved gas is then deposited chemically [7] and organically [5] as carbonates.

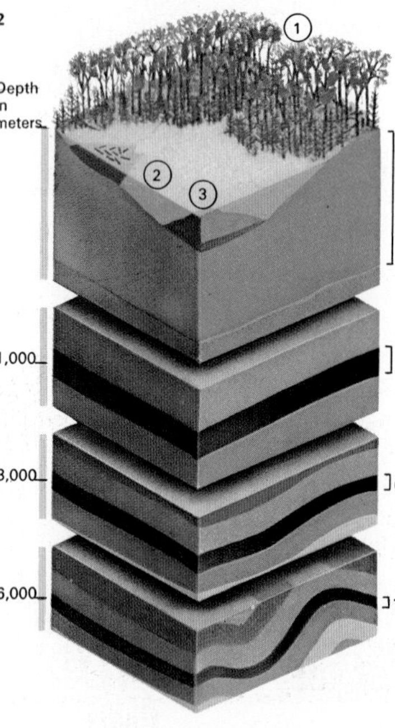

2
Depth in meters
1,000
3,000
6,000
1
2
3
4
5
6
7

2 The process of making coal starts with plant debris [1]. Dead vegetation lies in a swampy environment and forms peat [4], the first stage of coal formation. Underwater, bacteria remove some of the oxygen, nitrogen, and hydrogen from the organic material. Debris carried elsewhere and deposited by water forms a product called cannel coal [2]. Algal material collected underwater forms boghead coal [3]. If the dead organic material is buried by sediment, the weight on top of the peat, and higher temperature, will turn the peat into lignite [5]. With more heat and pressure, lignite becomes bituminous coal [6] and then anthracite [7].

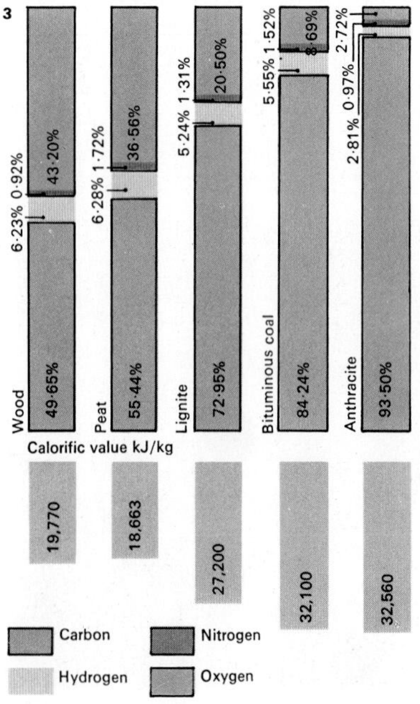

3
Wood 6·23% 0·92% 43·20% 49·65%
Peat 6·28% 1·72% 36·56% 55·44%
Lignite 5·24% 1·31% 20·50% 72·95%
Bituminous coal 5·55% 1·52% 8·69% 84·24%
Anthracite 2·81% 0·97% 2·72% 93·50%
Calorific value kJ/kg
19,770
18,663
27,200
32,100
32,560
Carbon
Nitrogen
Hydrogen
Oxygen

3 The economic value of a fuel is largely dependent on its energy content, that is, the amount of energy that can be recovered from burning a standard quantity of coal. This must be offset against cost of extraction and combustion. Shown here is a comparison of the energy content of the most commonly used kinds of coal. In fuel value alone anthracite appears to be the most attractive coal, but its disadvantage is that it is found deep underground and in thin seams. Lignite can be more attractive because it occurs in thick seams fairly close to the surface, and therefore can be retrieved by a strip mining process.

compressed, water and gases being squeezed from it, forming coal. If the sedimentary material is 0.6 miles (1km) deep a 66-ft (20-m) layer of peat yields a 13-ft (4-m) layer of lignite. If the material rests under 2 miles (3.2km) of Earth, the product is a 6.6ft (2m) layer of bituminous coal. If the depth is twice as great and the temperature higher, the 66-ft peat layer becomes a seam of anthracite 5ft (1.5m) thick. Anthracite is so hard and compacted that it is classed as a metamorphic rock.

The geology of coal is simpler than that of oil and gas and estimates of coal reserves are more reliable than those of oil and gas. Coal is found in seams of thickness from only a few inches to 100ft (30m) thick. Characteristically the seams are found interbedded with shales, sandstones, clays, and limestones of both marine and non-marine origin in a regular sequence. This phenomenon is known as cyclic sedimentation and indicates to the geologist that the coal was likely to have been laid down in a deltaic area. Many of the main coal deposits have been formed in this environment such as the Pennsylvanian (Upper Carboniferous) deposits of the United States and the Carboniferous coal deposits of the United Kingdom.

The prospects for coal

Although world reserves of coal are more than enough for our needs in the near future, only about half of the coal is exploitable. The rest must be left where it is to prevent adjacent coal mines from collapsing, or it is so inaccessable that mining would be a difficult and uneconomical operation. The Soviet Union is estimated to have the largest coal reserves, amounting to 68 percent of the remaining world resources; the United States has about 14 percent of world reserves. Of the Third World countries, India has the largest resources—one percent of world reserves—but large areas are yet to be properly surveyed, both in India and on the African continent. In Antarctica and Greenland large deposits of coal await improvements in mining technology and a rise in the economic value of coal to make their exploitation possible and profitable.

KEY

The Carboniferous period, 345 to 280 million years ago, was a time of extensive freshwater and coastal swamps covered in forests of ferns, horsetails, and other large treelike plants. The vegetation of these swamps produced most of today's coal. The coal seams resulted from compression of decaying vegetation by overlying sediment.

4

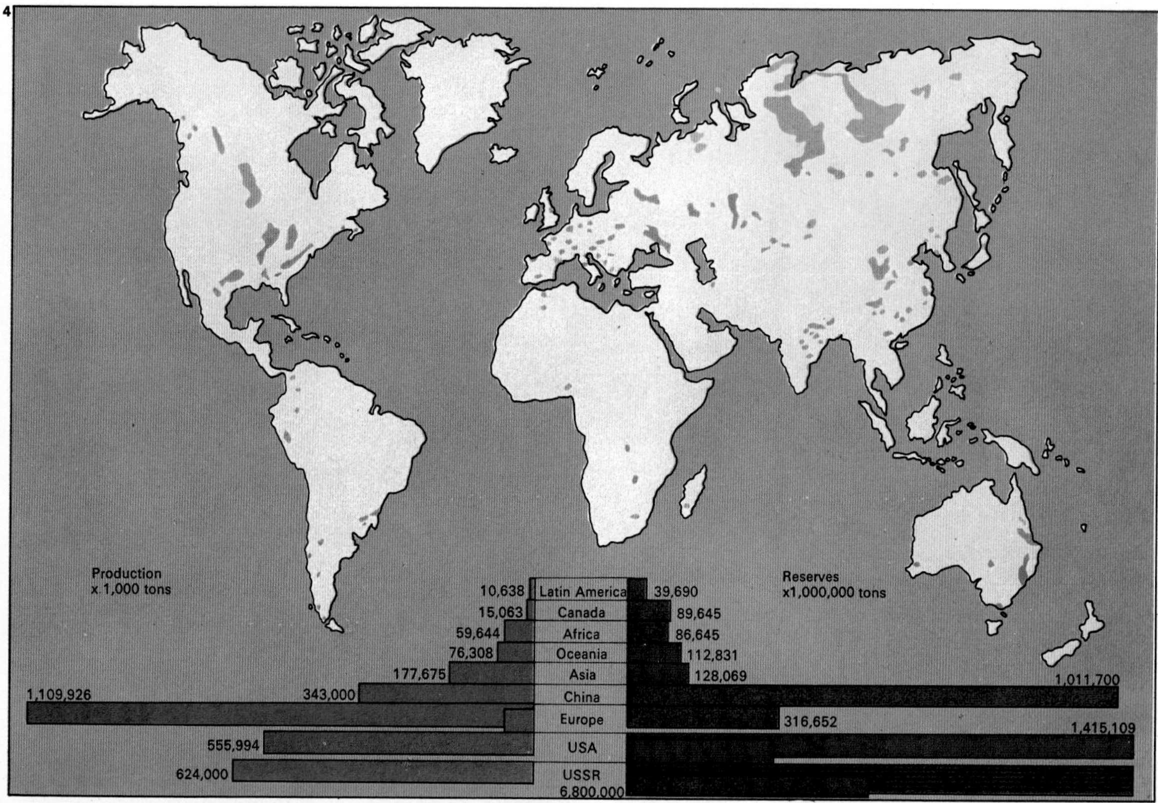
Production
x 1,000 tons
Reserves
x1,000,000 tons
10,638
Latin America
39,690
15,063
Canada
89,645
59,644
Africa
86,645
76,308
Oceania
112,831
177,675
Asia
128,069
343,000
China
1,011,700
1,109,926
Europe
316,652
555,994
USA
1,415,109
624,000
USSR
6,800,000

4 Coal was the major fossil fuel for two centuries until the rapid increase in oil production pushed it into second place. This has led to great changes in the coal industry during the last few decades. Europe and Japan have cut back much of their production, while other countries like the United States, China, and the USSR are still increasing their output. The figures shown indicate the known reserves of the world, but the actual reserves will be much greater since exploration is not yet complete. There is enough coal to last for at least another 200 years at present rates of consumption. Total reserves should not be confused with the recoverable reserves, which are often calculated as half the total. Advances in mining techniques and fluctuations in the economic value of coal mean that the recoverable fraction will become greater.

5

5 Underground coal seams may be thin and distorted and this makes mining hazardous and difficult. Today's sophisticated machinery is reducing the numbers of miners who have to work underground.

6

6 Strip-mining of coal and peat is relatively inexpensive. In some countries, notably Ireland, Finland, and the Soviet Union, peat digging is a useful source of fuel. Peat has to be dried before it can be burned.

Energy resources: oil and gas

Oil and gas provided 64 percent of all the energy used in the world in 1974: oil accounted for about 45 percent and natural gas for 19 percent of the total energy consumption. In 1962, by comparison, they accounted for just less than half the world's energy consumption.

Rise of oil power

In 1859 (the conventional date for the birth of the modern oil industry), Edwin L. Drake (1819–80) struck oil at Titusville, Pennsylvania, when drilling a well with a derrick. The contribution of oil and gas to world energy was, at that time, negligible. The speed and magnitude of the rise of oil as an energy source is staggering, and its consequences are even more spectacular. Modern civilization and technology and present-day population levels would be inconceivable without the cheap and plentiful energy provided by oil and gas. Petroleum is also the raw material for the petrochemical industries that produce plastics, synthetic fibers and hundreds of organic compounds used as drugs, pesticides, and detergents.

Drake's venture was not, however, the first use of petroleum. Noah is said to have used pitch (a form of asphalt, one of the petroleum products) to seal the seams of the Ark, a practice followed by boat builders to the present day. As early as 1000 BC the Chinese were using natural gas for fuel and the streets of Babylon were surfaced with processed asphalt in 600 BC.

The world's proven recoverable oil reserves are 666 million barrels—only 36 years' consumption at the 1972 production levels [4]. Even accounting for undiscovered fields and improved extraction, oil is a finite resource. It is therefore not surprising that oil, with its economic importance and with its declining reserves, has become a key issue in world politics.

How oil and gas are formed

Oil and gas are generally not considered "minerals," because although they occur in sedimentary rocks they are organic in origin. Collectively they are termed hydrocarbons because they are made of molecules consisting entirely or essentially of hydrogen and carbon. Petroleum or crude oil is a liquid ranging in color from yellow to black, including reds, browns, and dark greens. It is a mixture of many hydrocarbon compounds and its viscosity ranges from very fluid to highly viscous (as in natural asphalt). Natural gas contains smaller, lighter hydrocarbon molecules and is colorless.

Hydrocarbons are stored solar energy. Organic matter is synthesized by living plants using the Sun's energy converted by chlorophyll. One theory is that swarms of tiny plants and animals feeding on these plants lived in the seas and their dead bodies fell to the bottom. Under normal conditions, ordinary decay by aerobic bacteria (those breathing oxygen) would "burn up" the organic matter, producing carbon dioxide and water. But because oxygen was absent due to the conditions of burial, the process of decay was performed by anaerobic bacteria, and hydrocarbons and other organic compounds were produced [1].

Clays and silts were also deposited with the organic matter, and in time this sediment, rich in both carbon and hydrogen,

CONNECTIONS

See also

1642 Oil and natural gas
1644 Oil refining
280 Mineral resources of the sea
286 Energy supplies
288 Energy for the future
290 Earth's dwindling resources
282 Energy resources: coal

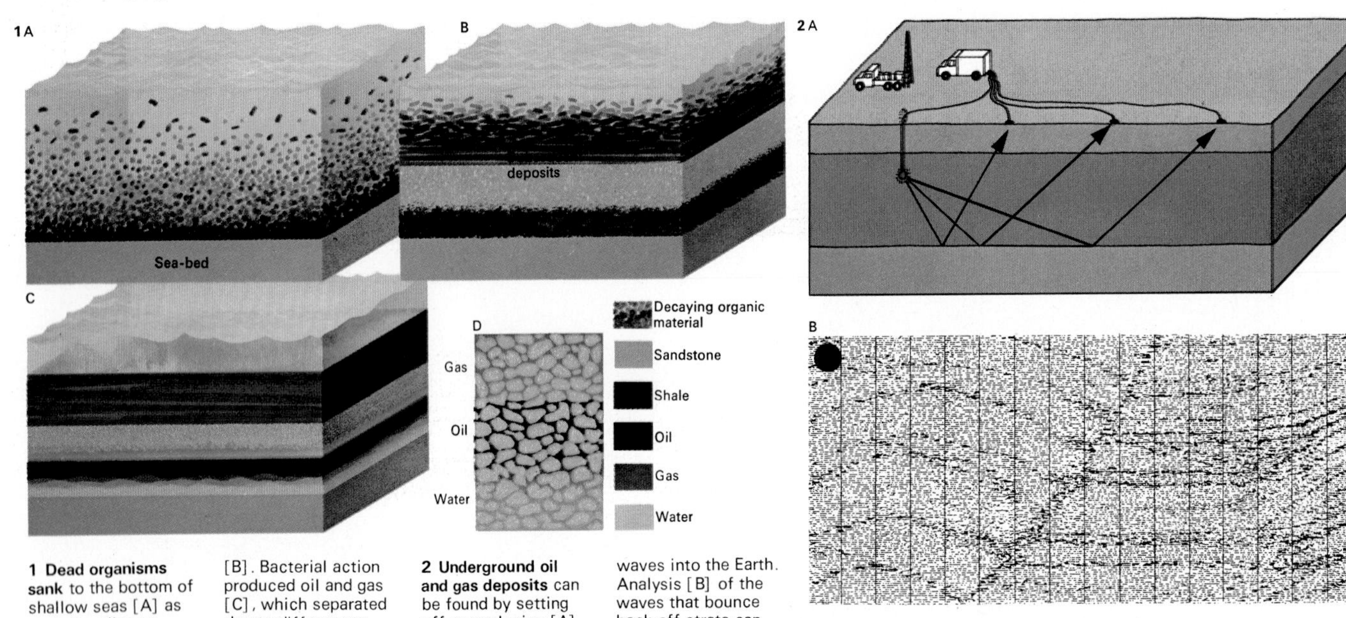

1A
Sea-bed
B
deposits
C
D
Gas
Oil
Water
Decaying organic material
Sandstone
Shale
Oil
Gas
Water
2A
B

1 Dead organisms sank to the bottom of shallow seas [A] as part of sediment compacted into shale [B]. Bacterial action produced oil and gas [C], which separated due to differences in densities [D].

2 Underground oil and gas deposits can be found by setting off an explosion [A] that sends sound waves into the Earth. Analysis [B] of the waves that bounce back off strata can locate deposits.

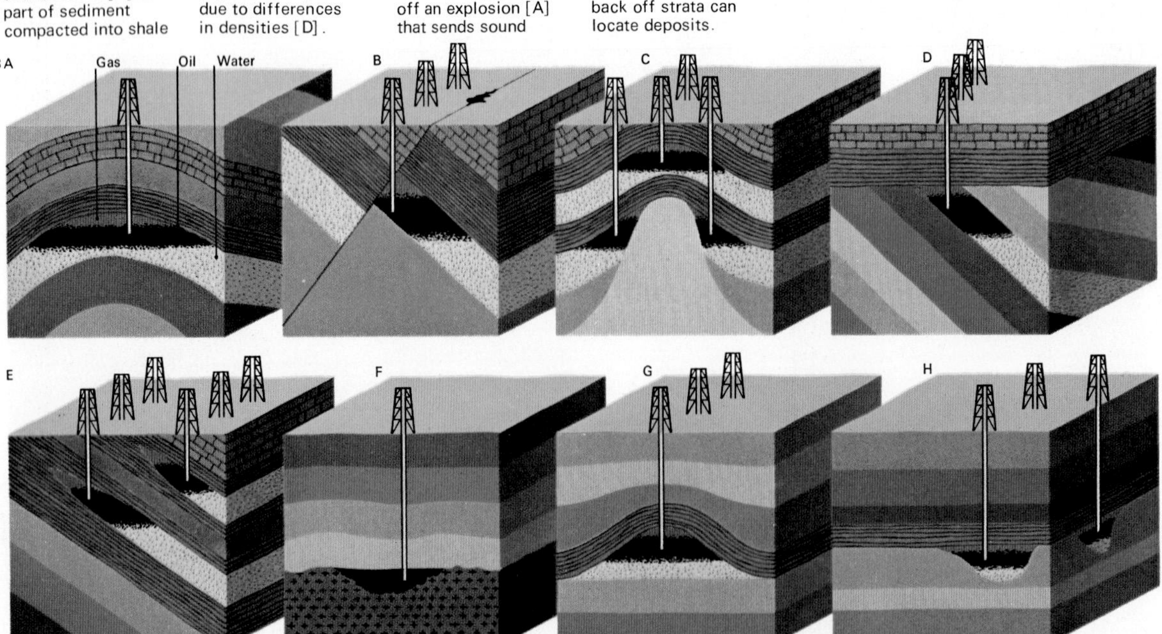

3A
Gas
Oil
Water
B
C
D
E
F
G
H

3 Oil and gas are found in reservoir rocks, but these are seldom the rocks in which they were formed. Reservoirs are capped by impervious rocks forming oil or gas traps. Anticlines possessing an impervious layer form traps [A], as do faults that bring an impervious rock in contact with a reservoir rock [B]. Salt domes [C] are similar to anticlines. Other traps are formed by impervious layers resting unconformably on tilted strata [D] and by reservoir rocks "pinching out" [E]. Where no water is present the oil may form pools in the hollows of a basement rock [F]. Fossil coral reefs [G] and fossil river beds [H] can form long and winding reservoirs.

was buried under newer layers and was compacted into shales. Pressure and heating caused by burial is thought to have completed the bacterial process that finally led to the formation of hydrocarbons.

Compaction and the eventual crustal movements often expelled oil and gas from their source rocks and an upward movement of the hydrocarbons occurred. If they reached the surface as a seep they were lost. Many seeps exist today, including the natural underwater oil seeps near Santa Barbara in California. Sometimes, however, the upward movement was stopped by an impermeable layer that formed a trap [3]. The hydrocarbons accumulated in the permeable rock under the trap, which is known as a reservoir rock. Reservoir rocks are usually sandstones and limestones.

Scarcity of oil and gas

Hydrocarbons were formed throughout the period of organic evolution and small quantities are still being formed today, but not sufficient to replenish current oil reserves. The conversion efficiency of solar energy into recoverable oil is exceedingly low. It took several millions of years to deposit the organic matter at any one place—because most of it was lost through decay—and several tens of millions of years to transform it into petroleum, most of which seeped away through the ground. Also, only about 30 percent of oil held in exploited reservoirs can actually be extracted by normal means.

Much thought is now being given to secondary recovery procedures to increase the yield of existing oilfields, to perhaps 70 percent. Secondary recovery procedures include pressurizing the reservoir rock (by pumping the gas back into it or by pumping water), fracturing it with explosives, attacking it with acid (in the case of limestones), heating it with pumped-in hot water, or pumping in chemicals that are effectively able to lower the viscosity of the crude oil.

Prospecting for oil consists first in determining those areas that have sedimentary rocks—the only rocks likely to contain oil [2]. Then the structures and successions of strata are studied to locate possible traps and reservoir rocks.

KEY

Offshore drilling is becoming a necessity if new oil and gas fields are to be found to replace the rapidly dwindling reserves from the land. It started in shallow and protected waters but the drilling industry is now moving to deep and stormy waters and the cost of offshore oil will be high.

4

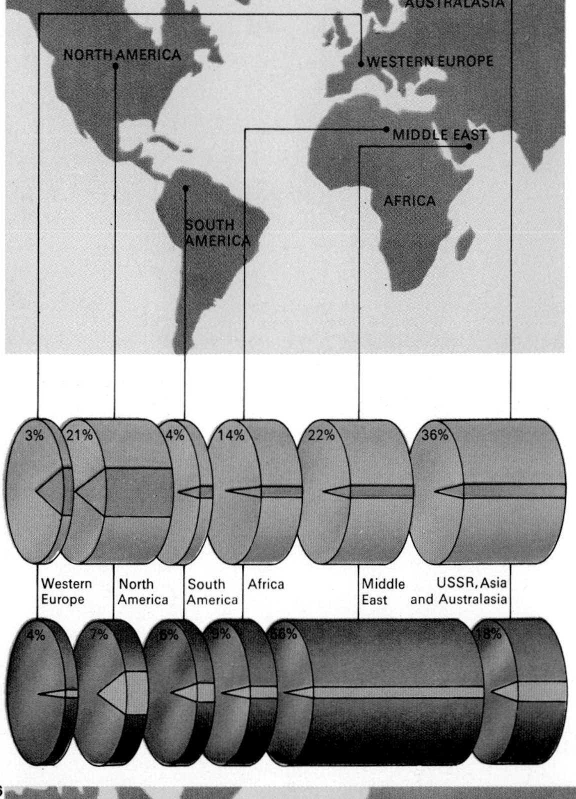
USSR, ASIA and AUSTRALASIA
NORTH AMERICA
WESTERN EUROPE
MIDDLE EAST
AFRICA
SOUTH AMERICA
3%
21%
4%
14%
22%
36%
Western Europe
North America
South America
Africa
Middle East
USSR, Asia and Australasia
4%
7%
6%
9%
66%
18%

4 "Proven" oil and gas reserves together with recent levels of oil consumption are shown here. It is reasonably certain that this much oil exists and more should be discovered. The true extent of the world's oil "crisis" is revealed by dividing the reserves by the annual consumption. This shows how long the known reserves will last at present consumption levels. One recent estimate suggested that the world's oil could last less than 40 years, and that does not allow for any growth in consumption. The United States has enough oil to last 13 years and gas for 12 years, while the Middle East and Asia have enough oil for 50 years and gas for 80 years at the levels of 1976.

Gas
% of world reserves
Annual consumption
Oil
% of world reserves
Annual consumption

5 The North Sea between Great Britain and Norway has been one of the most successful oil areas to be discovered in recent years. Natural gas was found first in 1965 and the gas fields were among the largest ever. The first oilfield was discovered off the southwest coast of Norway in November 1970. Soon after this British Petroleum found the first oil in the British sector of the North Sea—the huge Forties field. These discoveries have been followed by a steady flow of new finds of oil and gas in the North Sea. Production from these oilfields was well under way in 1976.

5

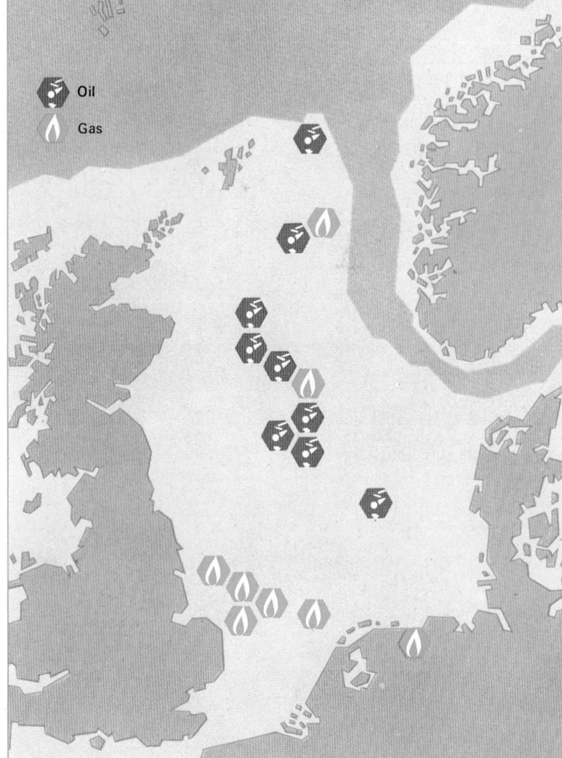
Oil
Gas

6

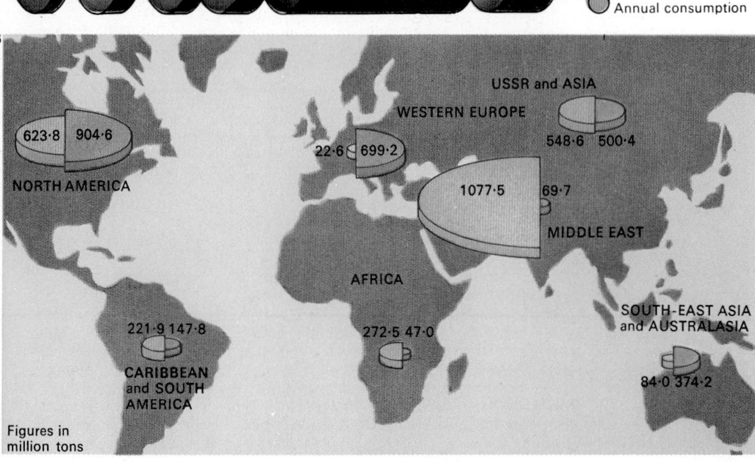
USSR and ASIA
WESTERN EUROPE
623·8
904·6
548·6
500·4
22·6
699·2
NORTH AMERICA
1077·5
69·7
MIDDLE EAST
AFRICA
SOUTH-EAST ASIA and AUSTRALASIA
221·9
147·8
272·5
47·0
CARIBBEAN and SOUTH AMERICA
84·0
374·2
Figures in million tons

6 Oil production and consumption in different regions are shown on this map. It reveals that oil production [yellow] and consumption [orange] are uneven. The Middle East produces a great deal of oil but consumes relatively little, while in Europe consumption is high and production is small but rising, from the discovery of oil in the North Sea. In 1974 the world's oil industry produced nearly 58 million barrels of oil a day, which added up to a total production of 2.8 billion metric tons of oil in the year (7.3 barrels of crude oil weigh a metric ton). The imbalance of production and consumption around the world means that there is a large and vulnerable international trade that can lead to energy crises.

Energy supplies

The energy resources being using up today took many millions of years to create [Key]. Coal, oil, and natural gas—the fossil fuels—store solar energy that reached the Earth perhaps 500 million years ago. They are produced from organic material that has been subjected to geological and biological processes lasting millions of years. There is little doubt that oil, gas, and coal will run out one day, and there is much debate about how much fossil energy is still available.

Energy from coal

Coal was the first of the fossil fuels to be exploited in quantity. The gradual industrialization of Western society was associated with the growth of coal mining. New technology made it possible to expand coal mining to greater depths underground and the availability of coal spurred the development of steam engines.

It is almost impossible to know exactly how much coal there is in the ground; but a reasonable estimate is that there are probably about 600 billion tons of coal that could be dug up using the mining techniques employed today. Some idea of how long that amount of coal might last can be gleaned from the fact that in the early 1970s the world's coal mining industry was digging up just over 2 billion tons of coal a year. About 25 percent of this was mined in the United States, while European coal production ran at about twice the US level. From these figures it is evident that the coal industry could survive, and even thrive, until well into the next century and perhaps longer. US coal reserves are among the world's largest. Other countries with large coal reserves include the Soviet Union and China.

The outlook for oil

Nearly half the world's energy is now supplied by oil, and a fifth of the energy comes from natural gas. The two together provide about 67 percent of our energy.

The long-term future of the oil and gas industries looks less certain than the future of the coal industry. In relation to demand oil reserves are much smaller than coal. A recent estimate put the world's oil reserves at about 100 billion tons. In 1973 annual production was running at about 3 billion tons. Clearly, if oil is used up as fast as it has been in the recent past, and if there are no new major discoveries of oil fields, the oil industry will be a thing of the past by the first quarter of the twenty-first century.

The situation is even more dramatic in the United States, which has something approaching 6 billion tons of known oil reserves (a figure that is the subject of heated argument) and which produced about 500 million tons in 1973. At this rate the United States could run out of oil well before the end of the twentieth century.

No one expects the oil industry to fail completely in its search for new oilfields, however. There is confidence that the offshore continental shelf will have some large underwater oilfields.

Other sources of energy

Hydroelectricity is an attractive energy source [5]. It is regularly renewed by rain and snow falls; thus, hydroelectric power stations do not depend on an exhaustible fuel supply. Unfortunately, most of the

CONNECTIONS

See also
288 Energy for the futu
282 Energy resources: coal
284 Energy resources: and gas
176 Volcanoes
226 Waves and tides
290 Earth's dwindling r sources
1634 Wind and water pow
1636 Power direct from th Sun and Earth
1638 Nuclear power
1648 Electricity generatic and distribution

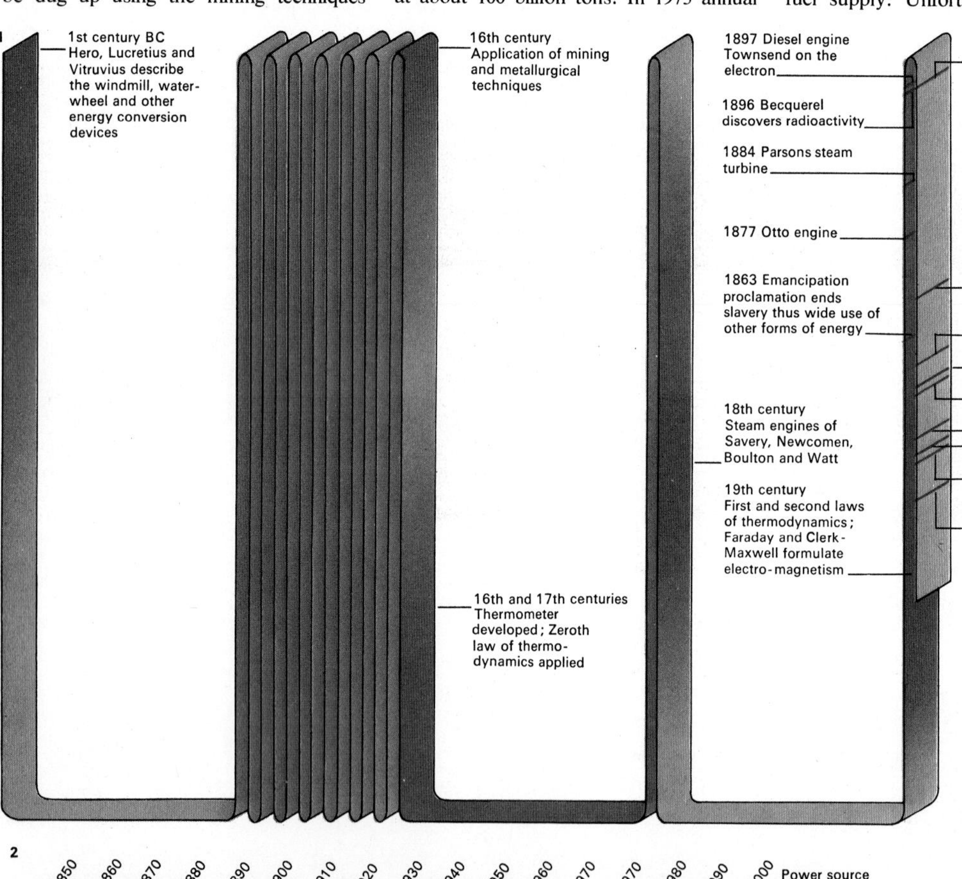

1
1st century BC Hero, Lucretius and Vitruvius describe the windmill, water-wheel and other energy conversion devices
16th century Application of mining and metallurgical techniques
16th and 17th centuries Thermometer developed; Zeroth law of thermo-dynamics applied
1897 Diesel engine Townsend on the electron
1896 Becquerel discovers radioactivity
1884 Parsons steam turbine
1877 Otto engine
1863 Emancipation proclamation ends slavery thus wide use of other forms of energy
18th century Steam engines of Savery, Newcomen, Boulton and Watt
19th century First and second laws of thermodynamics; Faraday and Clerk-Maxwell formulate electro-magnetism
1905 Einstein's theory of relativity
1933 Tennessee Valley Authority Act
1942 Fermi demonstrates self-sustaining nuclear chain reaction
1945 Hiroshima and Nagasaki
1946 Atomic Energy Commission established
1952 H-bomb at Eniwetok Atoll
1954 First civilian nuclear power plant in USSR
1955 Geneva conference on Peaceful Means of Uses of Atomic Energy
1960 Dresden plant; first privately-owned commercial nuclear power plant

1 The development of the world's energy system has been an accelerating series of scientific and technical discoveries. It took thousands of years to progress from muscle power and simple wood burning to sophisticated coal-fired power stations; but it did not take long to move from coal power stations to nuclear reactors. The selection of events here highlights various steps that have brought us to the present position. The early engineers built their coal-fired boilers without the help of science. The greatest advances have been made in the last four centuries with man's discoveries in science, particularly energetics, culminating in the use of atomic and nuclear energy.

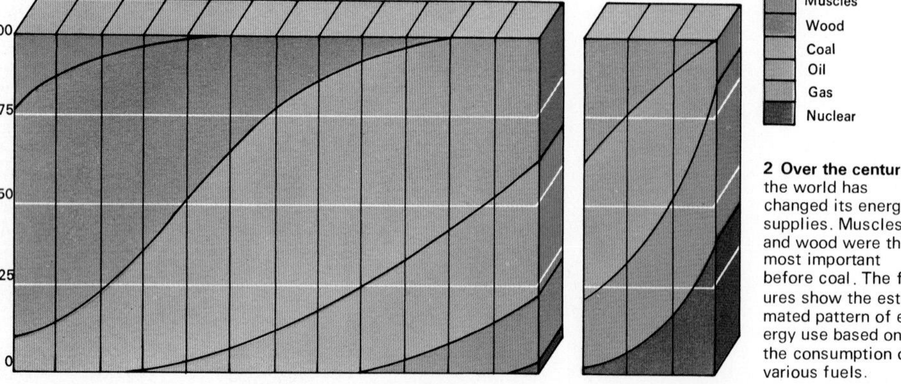

2
1850 1860 1870 1880 1890 1900 1910 1920 1930 1940 1950 1960 1970
1970 1980 1990 2000
100
75
50
25
0
Power source
Muscles
Wood
Coal
Oil
Gas
Nuclear

2 Over the centuries the world has changed its energy supplies. Muscles and wood were the most important before coal. The figures show the estimated pattern of energy use based on the consumption of various fuels.

3 2x10⁷ 4x10⁷ 6x10⁷ 8x10⁷ 10x10⁷ 12x10⁷ 14x10⁷

Hydrogen
Gasoline
Natural gas
Coal gas
Bituminous coal
Anthracite
Peat
Wood

Joules per kilogramme

3 Different fuels contain different amounts of energy. The graph shows how much energy is produced when a standard weight of fuel is burned. Hydrogen looks like the best fuel but it is a light gas that must be pumped through pipes. This means that to carry a quantity of energy through a pipe some energy must be used to power the pump, reducing the net energy transported.

promising hydroelectric sites that have yet to be developed are in remote parts of the world where the demand for power is not yet significant.

Around the world there are more than 60 hydroelectric projects with a power generating capacity of 1,000 MW (megawatts) or more, either in operation or planned for the near future. (One of the largest is the Grand Coulee Dam in Washington), with a capacity of nearly 10,000 MW). These projects will ease the pressure on fossil fuels, for the electricity from hydroelectric stations saves the equivalent of about 400 million tons of oil a year.

Today hydroelectric power stations produce more electricity than the world's nuclear power stations—which generated power equivalent to burning 65 million tons of oil in 1974. But nuclear power output is increasing each year and it may not be long before it overtakes hydroelectric power.

The amount of electricity that can be generated from the world's reserves of uranium [8] and other nuclear fuels depends very much upon the types of nuclear reactors that are built. One type of reactor—the fast breeder reactor—can produce about 60 times the energy that the same fuel would generate in a thermal reactor of the kind now being built. Without breeder reactors, which have yet to be developed to a commercial stage, the world could find itself short of uranium by the year 2000.

Geothermal energy from geysers and hot springs [7] is derived from the heat locked up in the Earth's core. Most of it was, and still is, produced by the slow decay of radioactive elements that occur naturally in rocks. The combined output of geothermal stations is about the same as the amount of power produced by one large nuclear reactor. Italy, Japan, New Zealand, the United States, and Mexico have the largest installed capacity for geothermal electricity generation. Geothermal energy can also be used to provide hot water. In New Zealand geothermal hot water is used in the paper-making industry, and the Icelandic capital of Reykjavik is almost entirely heated by a district heating system fed from a series of geothermal wells.

KEY

Oil 45%
Gas 19%
Coal 29%
Nuclear power 1%
Hydro-electricity 6%

The relative proportions of the diverse sources of energy used in the world in 1974 reflect their respective convenience, availability, and cost. By far the most important primary source of energy is oil, which in 1974 accounted for nearly half the world's energy consumption. Coal, the source that fueled the Industrial Revolution, was in 1974 only a poor second, although its long-term prospects are brighter than those for oil, as the reserves of coal are expected to last much longer than those of oil. Natural gas is a clean and popular source of energy but it might be the first of the fossil fuels to be exhausted. Hydroelectric power is most suited to mountainous areas and is a renewable source of energy. The most promising primary source is the 1% supplied by nuclear reactors. A similar graph for 1964 would not have shown this source at all.

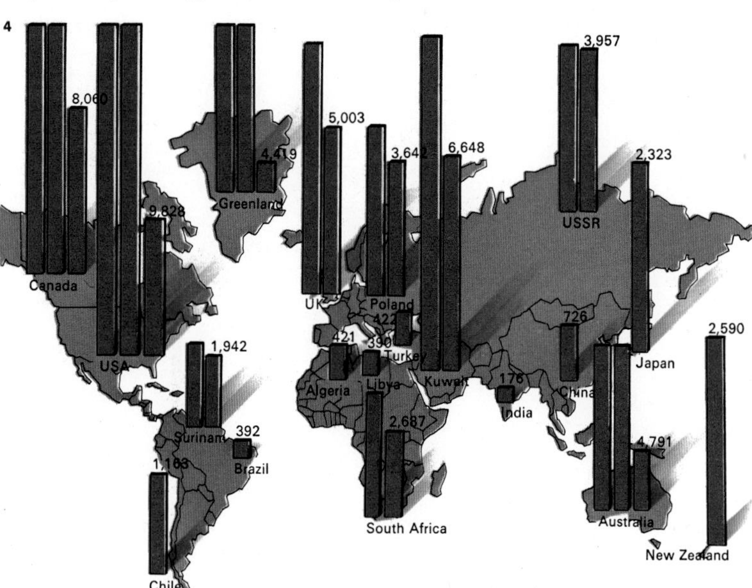
4
8,060
4,419
Greenland
9,828
Canada
USA
5,003
UK
Poland
3,642
6,648
3,957
USSR
2,323
726
China
Japan
2,590
421
390
Turkey
Algeria
Libya
Kuwait
176
India
2,687
South Africa
4,791
Australia
New Zealand
1,942
Surinam
392
Brazil
1,163
Chile
Energy consumption kilograms per capita

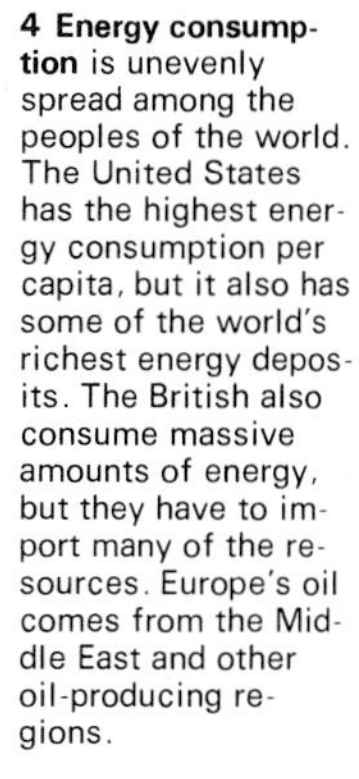
4 Energy consumption is unevenly spread among the peoples of the world. The United States has the highest energy consumption per capita, but it also has some of the world's richest energy deposits. The British also consume massive amounts of energy, but they have to import many of the resources. Europe's oil comes from the Middle East and other oil-producing regions.

5

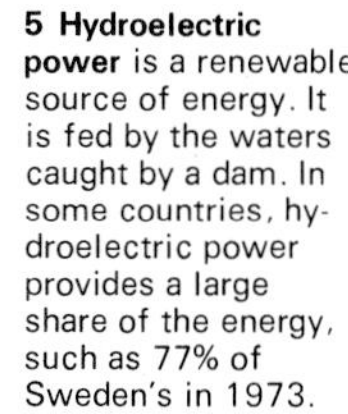
5 Hydroelectric power is a renewable source of energy. It is fed by the waters caught by a dam. In some countries, hydroelectric power provides a large share of the energy, such as 77% of Sweden's in 1973.

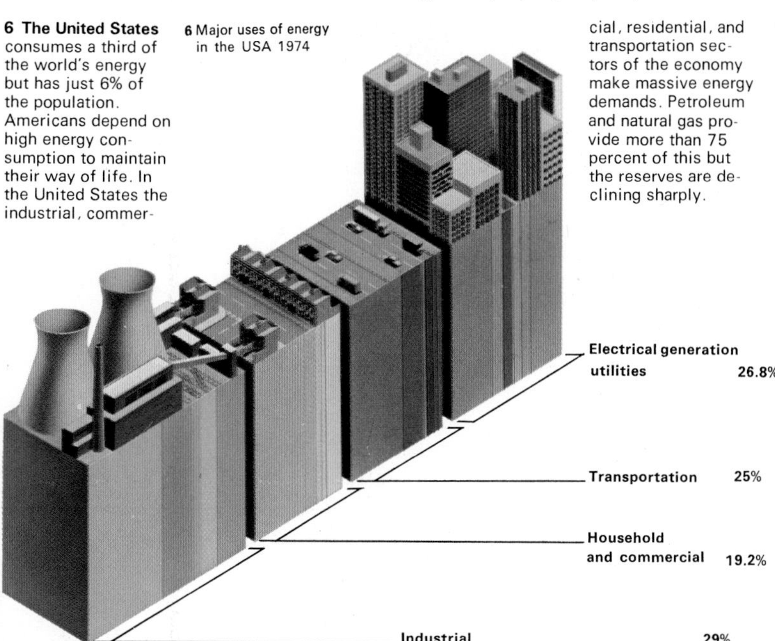
6 Major uses of energy in the USA 1974
Electrical generation utilities 26.8%
Transportation 25%
Household and commercial 19.2%
Industrial 29%

6 The United States consumes a third of the world's energy but has just 6% of the population. Americans depend on high energy consumption to maintain their way of life. In the United States the industrial, commercial, residential, and transportation sectors of the economy make massive energy demands. Petroleum and natural gas provide more than 75 percent of this but the reserves are declining sharply.

7

7 Geothermal energy from geysers and hot springs is derived from the Earth's internal heat. Steam and hot water are used to generate electricity in New Zealand, Italy, and Iceland.

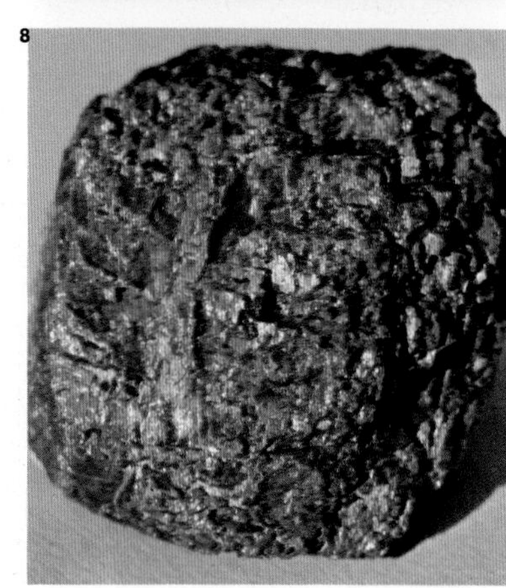
8

8 Most of the world's energy hopes rest on the use of nuclear fuels in power stations. Uranium is the major natural source of fuel. It occurs in most rocks—in only a few parts in a million—and there is even some uranium in seawater. But there are not many ore bodies rich enough in uranium to be worth exploiting. Uranium could be in short supply if new deposits are not found. Uraninite, here shown, is the major ore.

Energy for the future

Is there an energy crisis? In principle, no. The world's known reserves of energy are large enough to meet all foreseeable needs of mankind, if ways can be found of making use of all of them [1]. The oil shales of Colorado alone, for example, contain more oil than all the Middle East reserves added together. And the heat contained in a cube of rock with a 3 mile (5km) edge lying beneath the Jemez Plateau in New Mexico is as much heat as the whole world uses in an entire year.

Types of energy potentials

Potential sources of energy—oil shales, tar sands, solar and geothermal sources, waves, tides, winds, and nuclear fusion—could in principle provide far more energy than the world is ever likely to need. But many difficult problems have to be solved before any of these sources of energy can be tapped successfully.

Most untapped sources of energy are diffusely spread across the surface of the Earth, and not concentrated into neat packages as are coal, oil or natural gas. The sunlight falling on any country in the world would be more than enough to meet all power demands if it were not so thinly spread [6]. Short of covering very large areas of land with solar collectors, there is at present no way of using more than a minute fraction of the Sun's energy. Similarly, the energy of the waves [3] or the wind [4] is enormous, but so diffuse that huge structures or countless small ones would be needed to capture it. So far only one tidal power station exists, in northern France.

Diffusion and cost of alternative energy

Since most alternative energy sources are diffuse, it would be extremely costly to provide structures capable of concentrating them for use. The energy consumed in building these structures may well exceed, over their potential lifetime, the amounts of energy they would provide. Careful "energy analysis" is therefore needed in each case to make sure that the investment will be profitable in both financial and energy terms. Energy analysis of the rich oil shales of Colorado, for example, shows that the return in oil produced by mining and processing the shale would not exceed by a sufficient margin the amounts of oil that would be consumed by mechanical mining equipment, transportation of shale, process heat to extract the oil, and refinement to turn it into a useful form. Unless a less expensive technology can be found, therefore, oil shales are unlikely to provide a large source of oil, despite their theoretical value as reserves.

A third difficulty is what economists call a "rate and magnitude" problem. What matters, if the world is to avoid running out of energy, is not the potential amounts available but the rate at which they can be brought into use. Past energy sources—coal, oil, and natural gas—have been brought into use successively, each more quickly than the last. All alternative sources of energy are harder to bring into use, requiring bigger investments and producing smaller returns. In theory, an energy crisis could result simply because those resources could not be brought into use quickly enough to replace existing ones. If engineers

CONNECTIONS

Read first
286 Energy supplies

See also
282 Energy resources: coal
284 Energy resources: oil and gas
290 Earth's dwindling resources
1634 Wind and water power
1636 Power direct from the Sun and Earth
1638 Nuclear power
1648 Electricity generation and distribution
1646 Saving fuel and energy

1

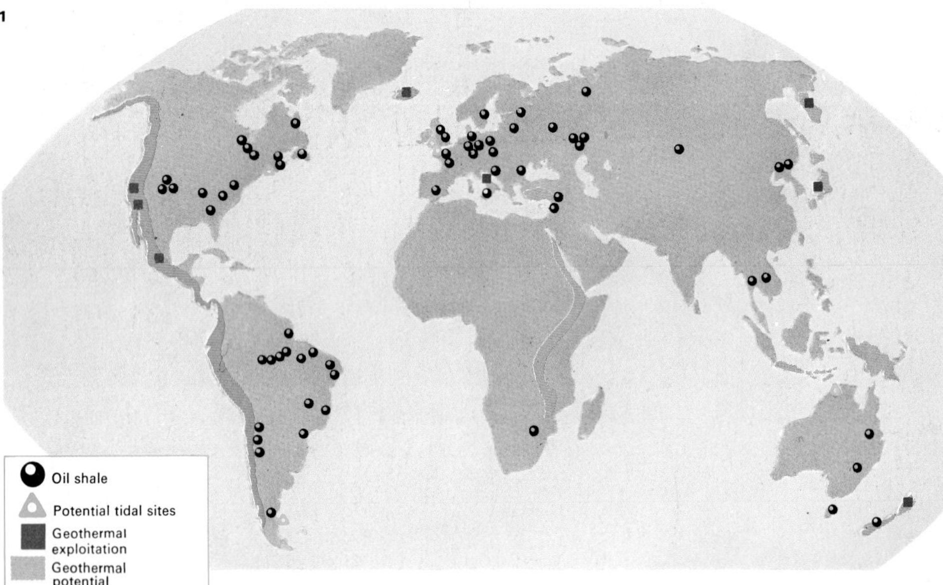

Oil shale
Potential tidal sites
Geothermal exploitation
Geothermal potential

1 Alternative energy sources are unevenly distributed through the world. The North American continent is best equipped, with large oil shale deposits in Colorado, tar sands in Alberta, good solar radiation and extensive geothermal potential in the geologically active western United States. Britain has one of the best tidal sites in the world in the Severn estuary, where the tide rises and falls more than 20 ft (6m) every day. Western Europe has good wave-power prospects, with the 3,000-mile (4,800km) "fetch" of the Atlantic driving waves on to the western coast. Alternative sources are likely to be exploited first where the source coincides with a large market. Many developing countries have good solar and geothermal prospects and their needs for energy are growing.

2

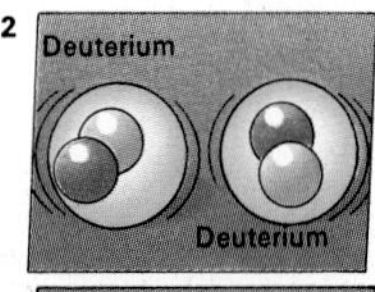

Deuterium
Deuterium

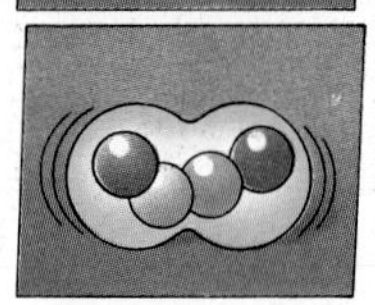

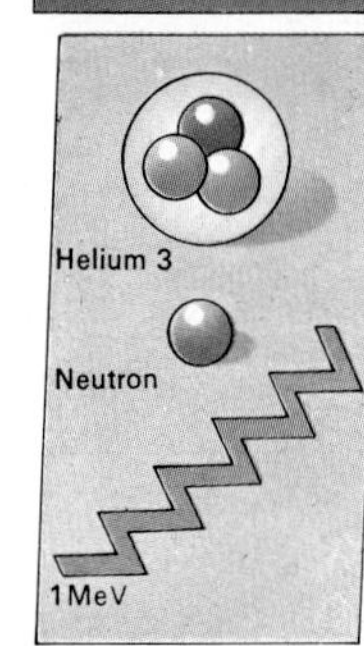

Helium 3
Neutron
1MeV

2 Fusion is a nuclear reaction that can take place between certain elements with low atomic numbers such as deuterium, the isotope of hydrogen. It involves a rearrangement of the nuclear particles and a release of energy. This would be a very attractive power source because of lack of radioactive waste products (the drawback in other nuclear reactions), the great quantities of energy released (it is the reaction that takes place in the Sun and stars), and availability of fuel. Shown are two deuterium nuclei yielding a helium 3 nucleus, a neutron, and 1 million electron volts (Mev) of energy.

3

3 Waves have enormous power, sufficient to destroy stone jetties weighing thousand of tons. They are strongest along the edge of great oceans, because their size depends both on the strength of the wind and on the distance it blows across the sea (the "fetch"). Waves grow and decline more slowly than wind, producing a power output with lower peaks. Thus they smooth out the rapid variations of strength and direction of the winds.

4

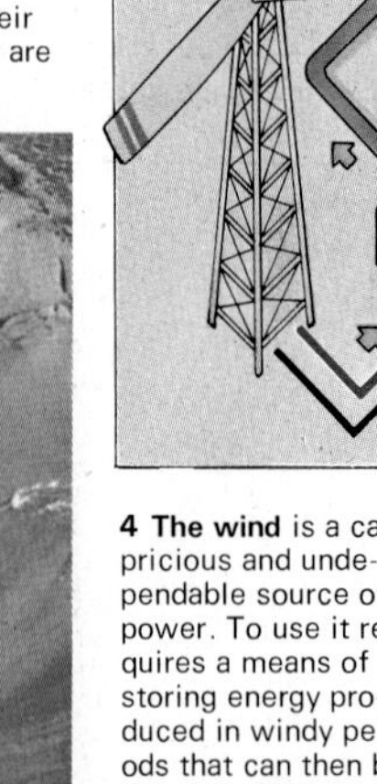

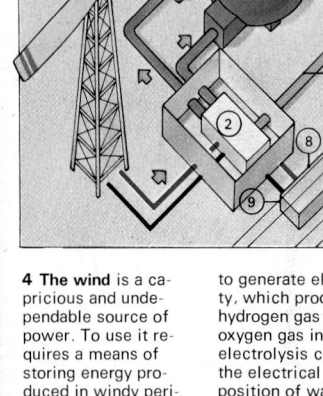

1 Wind generator
2 Electrolysis cell
3 Oxygen storage
4 Hydrogen storage
5 Fuel cell
6 Inverter
7 Recycled water
8 Pump back control
9 Rectifier

4 The wind is a capricious and undependable source of power. To use it requires a means of storing energy produced in windy periods that can then be used on calm days. This diagram shows one possibility. The wind turbine is used to generate electricity, which produces hydrogen gas and oxygen gas in the electrolysis cell by the electrical decomposition of water. The two gases are then combined in a fuel cell to produce electricity in the form of direct current, An inverter converts it into alternating current and feeds it to the grid. Power produced elsewhere could also be used to run the electrolysis cell when the wind is still. This would produce electricity on a continuous basis.

can overcome the "rate-and-magnitude" problem, alternative sources of energy could be brought into use.

Gravitational, solar, and nuclear sources

The major sources of unutilized energy fall into three categories: those derived from gravitation, those derived from the Sun, and those derived from nuclear processes. Only one potential source of energy, the tides, derives from gravitation. The pull of the Moon and the Sun on the world's oceans creates a potential for hydroelectric plants in places where the difference between high and low tide is greatest. So far only one tidal power station exists, on the Rance estuary in France. Solar energy sources include the familiar wood, coal, oil, and natural gas, all products of plant or animal life that could not exist without the Sun. Solar sources also include solar energy itself and, less obviously, wind [4], hydroelectric wave [3], and ocean thermal gradient [5] sources.

Nuclear processes provide three sources of energy; nuclear fission, which is already in use; nuclear fusion; and geothermal energy. Nuclear fusion would make use of the energy produced when two light elements fuse to produce a heavier one [2], a process that occurs only in the Sun and other stars and in the hydrogen bomb. Two approaches are being tried in the effort to tame fusion. The first is to bring light elements together in the form of a "plasma" at a very high temperature and prevent them from escaping by magnetic fields. The second is to force two light elements together by using an intense laser beam as a sledgehammer, pouring in energy so fast that the minute fuel pellet "implodes," producing a fusion reaction.

Geothermal energy uses the heat generated by nuclear processes deep in the Earth. It is in limited use already and has considerable future potential. Power plants worked from geothermal heat are usually driven by steam in hotspring areas such as in Iceland and New Zealand. More sophisticated schemes are being devised that would use hot water from the Earth to evaporate a low-boiling-point fluid and pass it through a turbine.

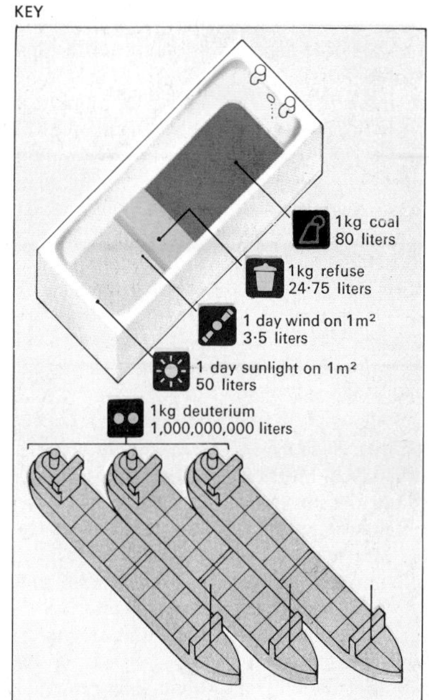
KEY
1kg coal
80 liters
1kg refuse
24·75 liters
1 day wind on 1m²
3·5 liters
1 day sunlight on 1m²
50 liters
1kg deuterium
1,000,000,000 liters

The light element deuterium, which would be used in a fusion power station, is the most concentrated of the alternative energy sources. Forty micrograms of deuterium are equivalent in energy content to a whole day's solar radiation at average intensity on a square yard of the Earth's surface. The diagram shows the volume of water boiled by comparable units of energy sources. In general, fuels of medium-energy concentration, such as coal, are the easiest to exploit. Diffuse sources of energy, such as wind and solar power, are difficult to exploit in a traditional central power station. It may be better to use small collectors suited to the local needs.

5

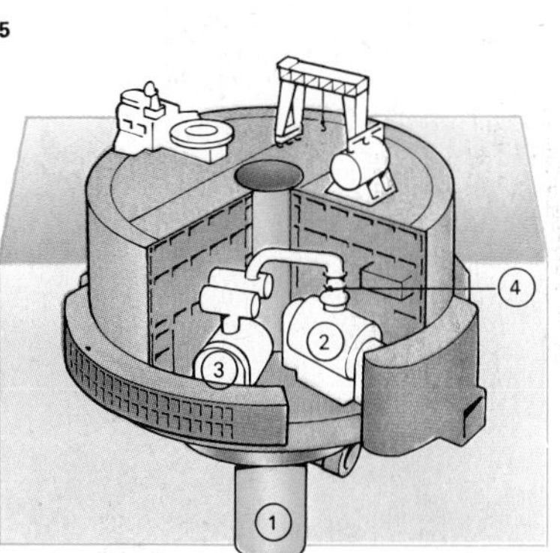
4
2
3
1

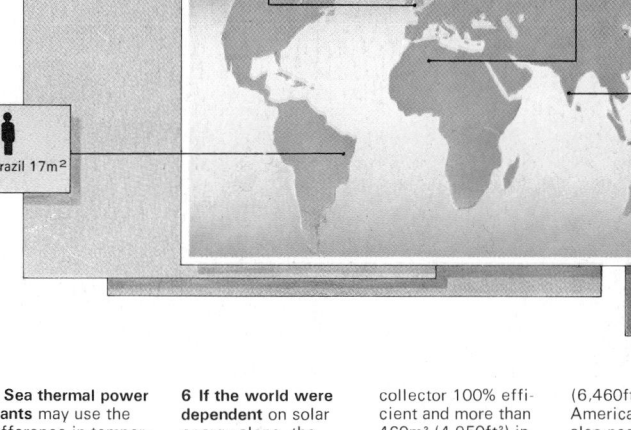

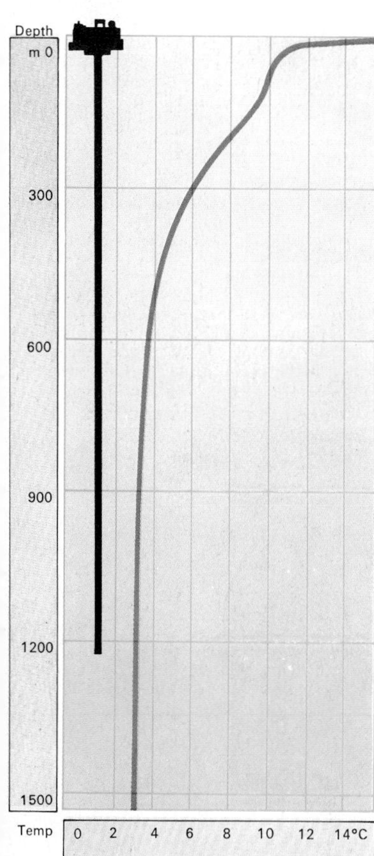
Depth
m 0
300
600
900
1200
1500
Temp
0
2
4
6
8
10
12
14°C

6

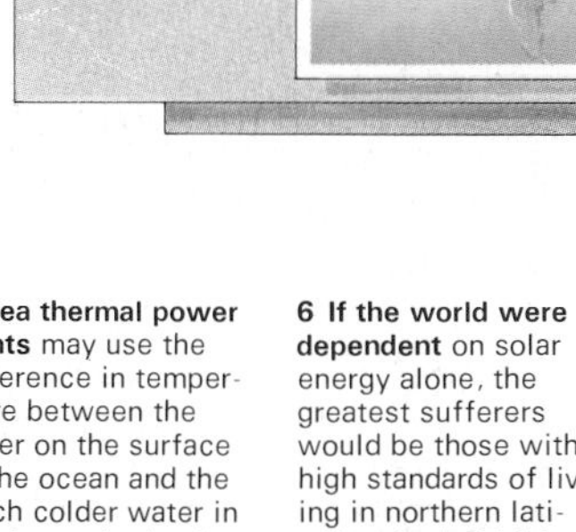
Greenland 600m²
United Kingdom 460m²
Algeria 20m²
Japan 212m²
India 8m²
Brazil 17m²
Australia 250m²

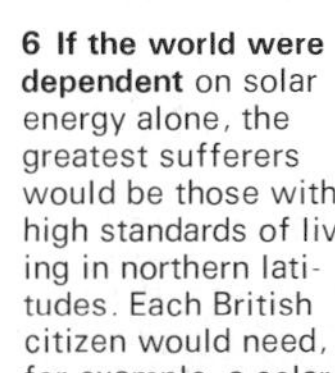

5 Sea thermal power plants may use the difference in temperature between the water on the surface of the ocean and the much colder water in the deeps. In the design shown, the power station floats on the surface with a 4,000ft (1,200m) pipe [1] descending into deep water. Cold water from the depths is pumped up and used to condense ammonia in a heat exchanger [2]. This liquid ammonia flows to a second heat exchanger [3] where it is evaporated by the heat of the surface water and passed back to the beginning of the cycle. As it flows around this closed system the ammonia drives a turbine [4]. It can work from fairly small temperature differences.

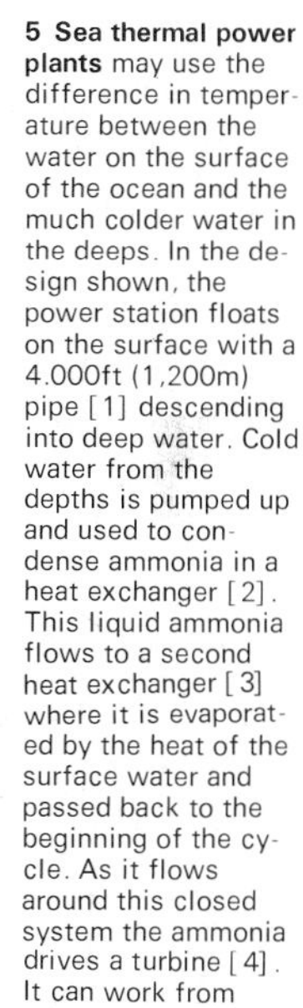

6 If the world were dependent on solar energy alone, the greatest sufferers would be those with high standards of living in northern latitudes. Each British citizen would need, for example, a solar collector 100% efficient and more than 460m² (4,950ft²) in surface area to capture as much energy from the Sun as he uses today. A Greenlander would need an even bigger collector, almost 600m² (6,460ft²). Most Americans would also need a large area because although solar radiation is high in many parts of the United States, consumption of energy is enormous. The developing countries such as India, could meet their present energy demands with comparatively small solar collectors. No solar collector, however, is efficient enough to collect 100% of the energy reaching it.

7

7 Every household in a developed country throws away energy every day as trash. The amount of paper thrown away by US households has increased by several factors since the end of World War II, while the amount of ash and cinders in the trash is far less than what it was then. Domestic trash and garbage can be burned to provide heat or generate electricity. Such programs serve to recover wasted energy.

Earth's dwindling resources

CONNECTIONS

Read first
278 Mineral resources of the land
280 Mineral resources of the sea

See also
286 Energy supplies
288 Energy for the future

The developed countries of the world are using up valuable resources at a rate unprecedented in human history. Fossil fuels, minerals, metals, water, timber, and even soils have been treated as if supplies were easily replenished. But most of the Earth's resources are not an income to be spent, but a stock of capital built up over billions of years before man evolved. If present rates of use continue, that capital will be exhausted in a few centuries.

How long will resources last?

Opinions differ about the rate at which the Earth's resources are being exhausted. Calculations of the "lifetime" of any given fuel or mineral resource [1] can vary widely depending on the assumptions used. Most experts, however, including organizations such as the US Geological Survey, estimate that present rates of fuel and mineral use can be sustained for only another generation or two. The timetable [1] depends both on the particular resource under consideration and on such imponderables as the future of the world economy, the possibility of finding new supplies, the geographical distributions of those supplies, and the extent to which the lifetime of any resource can be extended by more careful use [4, 5] or by recycling.

The consumption of most mineral resources was, until recently, increasing at an exponential rate. This rising curve of consumption meant that demand for crude oil, for example, doubled every decade. Other primary commodities showed a slower growth, with doubling times of between 10 and 20 years. The oil crisis and subsequent economic depression, which began late in 1973, slowed world demand for fuels and metals and stopped the steady increase in consumption for the first time in two decades. Most economists believe, however, that this is merely a pause in the growth of the world economy rather than a turning point toward zero growth.

Whether or not growth resumes is of crucial importance in assessing how long resources are going to last, for the effect of such growth on the demand for fuels and minerals is remarkable. In the case of crude oil, consumption for the decade from 1960 to 1970 was as much as in the entire century from the drilling of the first oil well in 1859 to 1960. The consequence of such a rapid growth rate is that discovery of new reserves must constantly expand to keep ahead of demand and that even a doubling of known world reserves of oil would add only 10 years to the lifetime of all oil resources.

Not all resources are in equal danger. Coal, for example, is more plentiful [2] than oil and natural gas; some metals, such as aluminum, iron, and magnesium, are relatively abundant. Others, including copper, vanadium, lead, and zinc, are less plentiful but not in imminent danger of running out. But a few, including mercury, silver, tin [3], tantalum, and platinum, are already becoming scarce.

Alarms about declining resources are not new, but so far the pessimists have been wrong. Improving technology, better methods of prospecting, and a bigger market and a better price have been enough to keep production ahead of demand.

1

Explosives

Hg Cu W Al Ag Mo Co Sn Zn Ni Pb Pt Mn Fe Au Cr P N

1981 1994 1986 2005 2005 1995 1985 1984 2015 1980 1980 2000 1984 2016 2045 2063

Hg Mercury
Cu Copper
W Tungsten
Al Aluminum
Ag Silver
Mo Molybdenum
Co Cobalt
Sn Tin
Zn Zinc
Ni Nickel
Pb Lead
Pt Platinum
Mr Manganese
Fe Iron
Au Gold
Cr Chromium
P Phosphates
N Nitrates

Environmental problems associated with specific recovery:
1 Waste disposal
2 Land reclamation
3 Aerial pollution
4 Water pollution
5 Poison control

1 Most of the Earth's mineral resources have taken millions of years to form and it has taken man but a minute proportion of this time to deplete seriously the known reserves of many of these. Some of the raw materials involved in the building and operation of a dump truck are shown on the picture with the date at which their reserves may be exhausted. Such dates are extrapolated from consumption trends and known reserves in the early 1970s. New finds, new extraction methods for lower grade ores, price increases leading to reduced demand, recycling, and the development of substitutes will push back the dates given.

2

2 World oil production is expected to peak after 1985 and then to decline about the end of the century, despite the development of the Alaskan North Slope and North Sea oil reserves. In the United States, coal is the most abundant fossil fuel but it ranks behind oil and natural gas in usage. US coal reserves are more than 700 times greater than present annual consumption, and it is expected that the use of coal will be expanded, particularly as it is converted to less polluting synthetic fuels.

3

3 Resources are wasted by tin cans and other packaging that cannot be recycled. Steel for cans is not in short supply but the tin to coat them is. Increases in tin prices have led to economies.

Reasons for pessimism

There are a number of reasons for believing that the pessimists cannot be wrong forever. The first is the fact that minerals are distributed unevenly over the Earth's surface. Because a rich ore is more profitable to exploit than a poor one, most of the best ones have already been mined out. Progressively thinner or less accessible ore deposits now have to be exploited, thus increasing costs and reducing returns. In the past geologists have argued that as the quality of an ore declines, its quantity increases; that there is 10 to 100 times as much of a low-grade ore to be extracted as there is of a high-grade ore. For some metals, including copper, this is true; but for others, it seems, there is either rich ore or unproductive rock—and nothing in between. For many metals the huge tonnages of low-grade ore once counted on to supplant the rich ores simply do not exist.

The second reason for pessimism is that mining is consuming ever-increasing quantities of energy to extract the same amounts of metal from ores of declining quality. Since energy is likely to be in short supply, it is unlikely that this process can continue. The same applies to extraction of metals and other minerals from seawater. Although the oceans contain huge resources of minerals, most occur in such small concentrations that the cost of extraction would be prohibitive. The energy needed to extract uranium, for example, from the sea, even using the most up-to-date technology, would exceed the energy the uranium would produce in a nuclear reactor.

Geographic and political factors

A final difficulty is related to the geography of resources. When ownership of a crucial resource is held in few hands its price can be manipulated to a level excessively above the cost of production. This has already happened to oil and could happen to a wide range of other resources in the future, including perhaps tungsten, of which China controls 75 percent of the known world deposits; chromium, of which South Africa controls 75 percent; or mercury, of which Spain controls 33 percent.

KEY

The automobile is a prime energy waster. Too heavy and too powerful, it converts only a fraction of fuel energy into motion. At full power the theoretical efficiency of an average combustion engine is about 25%—in practice it is 10%.

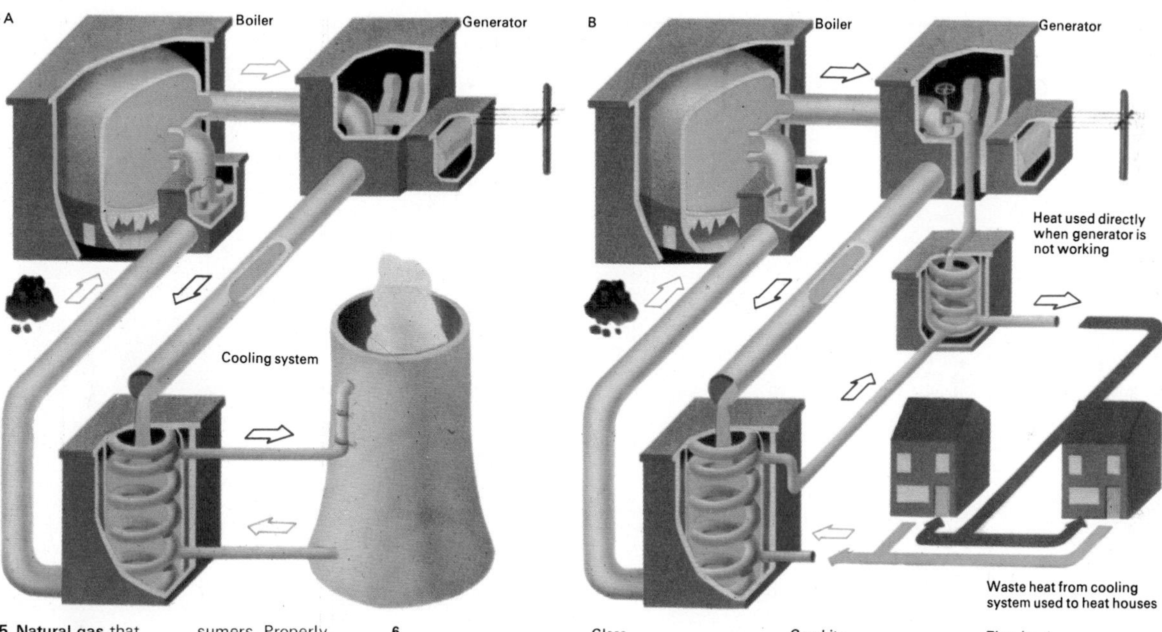
4 A
Boiler
Generator
Cooling system
B
Boiler
Generator
Heat used directly when generator is not working
Waste heat from cooling system used to heat houses

4 District heating plans can make much better use of diminishing fuel resources. In a conventional system [A] electricity is generated in a power station at an efficiency of 35 to 38%, distributed to houses with a further loss, and used for lighting and for heating at 55% efficiency. In a district heating plan [B] electricity and hot water or steam are generated at the power plant and distributed for domestic consumption, the electricity in the conventional way and the hot water or steam in insulated underground pipes. The overall efficiency can be as much as 80% to 85% if demands for heat and electricity coincide.

5 Natural gas that occurs in association with oil was formerly "burned off" as a waste product, because the price it brought was insufficient to justify its collection and distribution to consumers. Properly utilized, this gas is now an important source of heat for domestic and commercial purposes, for it has a higher heat-producing, or calorific, value than manufactured coal gas.

5

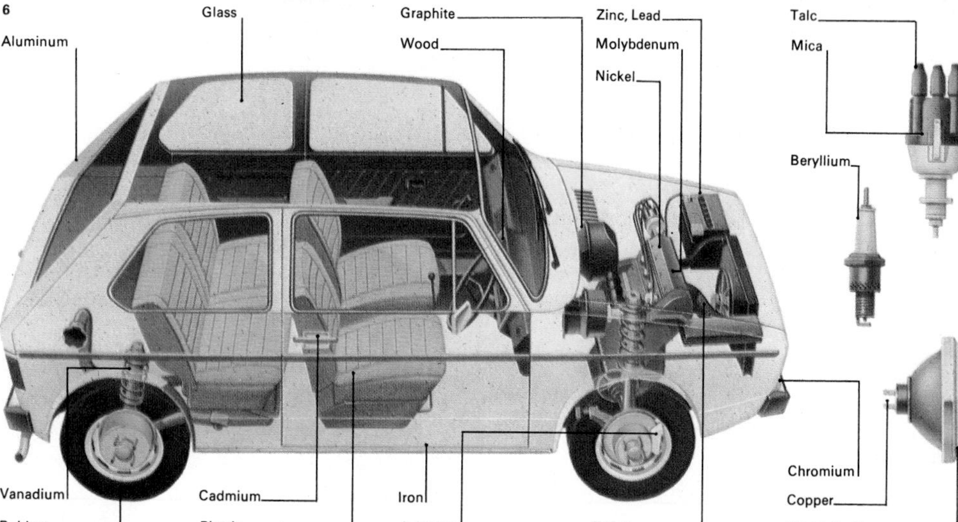
6
Aluminum
Glass
Graphite
Wood
Zinc, Lead
Molybdenum
Nickel
Talc
Mica
Beryllium
Vanadium
Rubber
Cadmium
Plastic
Iron
Asbestos
Tellurium
Chromium
Copper
Monazite, Tungsten

6 An everyday object like an automobile depends, for its manufacture, on a very large number of different minerals and raw materials. Some, such as iron and glass, have obvious structural applications while others, such as tellurium and talc, are used as fillers in rubber and paint. Such an intimate mixture of different materials makes their recycling difficult when the car's life is ended.

Pollution of the air

Clean, fresh air is a mixture of gases with tiny particles suspended in it. By volume it is made up of roughly 78 percent nitrogen and 21 percent oxygen, with much smaller amounts of carbon dioxide and argon, and traces of several other gases. Water vapor is present in varying amounts. The particles, which often help to make air visible and add color to the clouds and sky, include fine water droplets (forming mist, fog, and low clouds) and ice crystals (forming high clouds). Air that has blown over the sea may be loaded with tiny crystals of salt; wind from the land often contains dust that may include fine sand, pollen, plant spores, and a host of other substances both organic and inorganic. These gases and particles are not generally harmful to plants or animals, and humans can tolerate a wide range of atmospheric conditions.

How is the air polluted?

Air pollution is usually a result of man's activities [1]. Polluted air, of the kind found in cities and industrial areas, usually contains higher than normal concentrations of some of the "trace" gases and other gases that are not normally present in the atmosphere at all. It may also contain more particles, which darken the atmosphere and reduce visibility. Polluted air is often unpleasant to breathe and can be harmful to living creatures of all kinds. Man suffers from it directly, through deterioration of the environment and his health, and indirectly through damage to crops and property.

The chief cause of air pollution is the large-scale burning of fossil fuels. Coal burned in household furnaces, industrial furnaces, and railroad engines blackened the cities of Europe and North America during the eighteenth, nineteenth, and early twentieth centuries, and fumes of oil products—especially gasoline and diesel fuel—contribute heavily to the foul air of cities today.

Burning fuels, especially in furnaces or engines that are not properly maintained, produces a wide range of pollutants that affect the air in different ways. Prominent among pollutants is sulfur dioxide. This is an acrid gas that dissolves readily in water to form acid solutions that kill plants and damage buildings. In the high-temperature conditions of a furnace or engine cylinder, oxides of nitrogen may also be formed, again producing choking fumes that yield acid solutions. Nitrogen oxides and sunlight also react to form photochemical smog, which is particularly frequent in Los Angeles [4]. Unburned hydrocarbons and other particles enter the atmosphere in large quantities, forming soot and flash. These make greasy, black deposits on buildings and fabrics and also form nuclei on which water droplets condense, causing smoke haze and fog. "Smog" [4], a thick persistent fog that forms when polluted air over a city cannot rise because of a layer of warm air that traps cooler air below, combines these features and is a hazard to human life.

The role of the automobile

The gasoline used in most countries today contains lead compounds, which enter the atmosphere in enormous quantities from automobile exhausts [2]. Together with carbon monoxide, a poisonous gas pro-

CONNECTIONS

Read first
212 The atmosphere

See also
434 The lichens
294 Misuse of the land
296 Pollution of rivers and lakes
298 Pollution of the sea
420 Evolution in action
634 Destructive man
714 Diseases of breathing

1

51%
16%
15%
14%
4%

Transport
Domestic heating
Miscellaneous
Industrial pollution
Solid waste disposal

Carbon monoxide
Hydrocarbons
Solid particles
Sulphur dioxide
Nitrogen oxides

1 Some of the main sources and proportions of air pollution in an industrial region are shown in these diagrams. Gases and other products of transportation account for 51% of all atmospheric pollution. This is followed in decreasing proportions by pollution from domestic fires, forest and other open fires such as brush fires, industrial smoke, and the incineration of domestic waste.

2 The automobile is a major source of atmospheric pollution, producing oxides of nitrogen, unburned hydrocarbons, carbon monoxide, asbestos, and other poisons in the proportions shown.

2

Proportion of pollutants produced by various components

Gas tank
Exhaust
Carburetor
Crankcase

Carbon monoxide
Nitrogen oxides
Lead
Hydrocarbons
Solid particles

Pollution produced by a car in 20,000km (12,000 miles)

Lead	0·775kg
Nitrogen oxides	40·75kg
Hydrocarbons	234kg
Carbon monoxide	765kg

Idling / Acceleration / Cruising / Deceleration

Nitrogen oxides
Hydrocarbons
Carbon monoxide

3

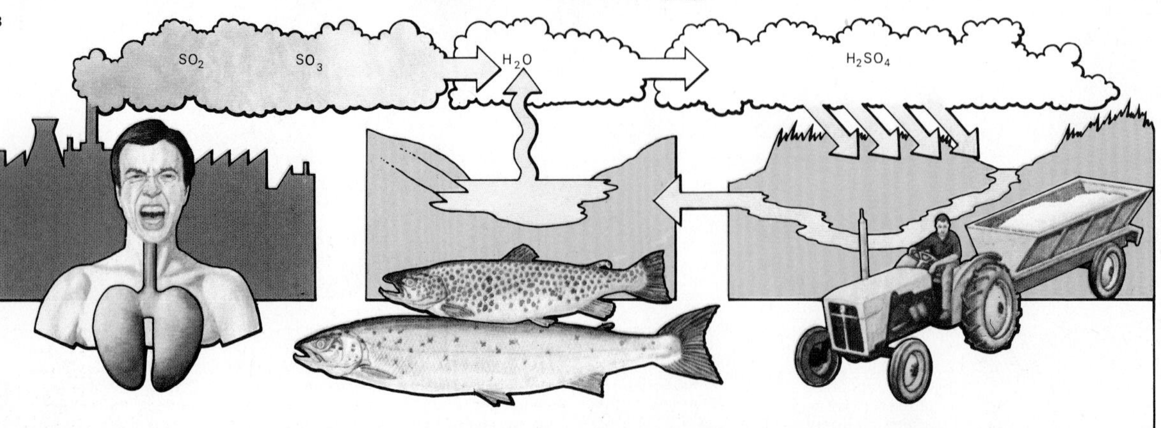

SO_2
SO_3
H_2O
H_2SO_4

3 Acid rain, believed to originate from industrial pollution in Western European countries, is damaging buildings, forests, and streams and affecting human health in Scandinavia. Sulfur dioxide, produced during the burning of coal and oil, is oxidized in the atmosphere to sulfur trioxide. These gases dissolve in water in the clouds, forming an acid rain that falls many miles downwind of the industrial areas from which the gases originated.

duced by burning hydrocarbon fuels, these compounds may reach intolerable concentrations.

The automobile produces other air pollutants, notably asbestos fibers from brake linings, which may enter the lungs and set up chronic irritation that may lead to cancer and other respiratory diseases. Asbestos fibers also enter the atmosphere from building materials. Many industrial chemical processes add to the atmosphere pollutant gases and particles, including ammonia and compounds of mercury, arsenic, and other poisonous substances.

Recent sources of atmospheric pollution

A small but growing source of atmospheric pollution is the release of radioactive particles, both from nuclear weapon testing and from peaceful uses of atomic energy [6]. Crop spraying with insecticides adds local concentrations of organic poisons to the air, sometimes to the detriment of plants and animals on neighboring land.

Many new organic chemicals released into the atmosphere have come under suspicion of causing long-term environmental damage. For example, the freons, used as refrigerants and aerosol propellants, may interfere with the protective ozone of the upper atmosphere and allow dangerous concentrations of ultraviolet light—which may harm the skin and body tissues—to reach the Earth's surface. Increased quantities of carbon dioxide, released into the atmosphere from burning fossil fuels, may be upsetting the heat balance of the Earth.

Legislation in the wealthier industrial countries has been effective in reducing smoke and smog pollution, keeping airborne effluent from factory chimneys under control, and generally improving the the quality of the atmosphere. New factories are better equipped to reduce pollution and ways are being sought to keep down the pollutants from automobile and aircraft engines. These remedies are costly; industrial man finds that he has to pay more to maintain and improve his standard of living. The developing countries, now on the brink of industrialization, still have the problem of air pollution in front of them.

KEY

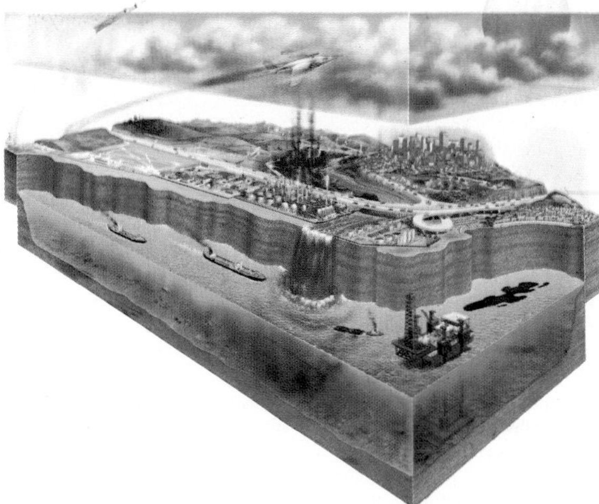

Pollution is a global problem affecting the land, rivers, the sea, and the atmosphere. It is especially acute in industrially developed countries, where for generations man has been dumping his waste without thought for the environment. The level of pollution now causes concern.

4

4 Smog caused 4,000 deaths in London in 1952 and is still a major hazard in Japan and the United States, particularly in Los Angeles, as this picture illustrates. In warm climates smog is caused by oxides of nitrogen and hydrocarbons from car exhausts undergoing chemical reactions influenced by sunlight. Photochemical smog is a poisonous mixture lethal to those with lung complaints.

5

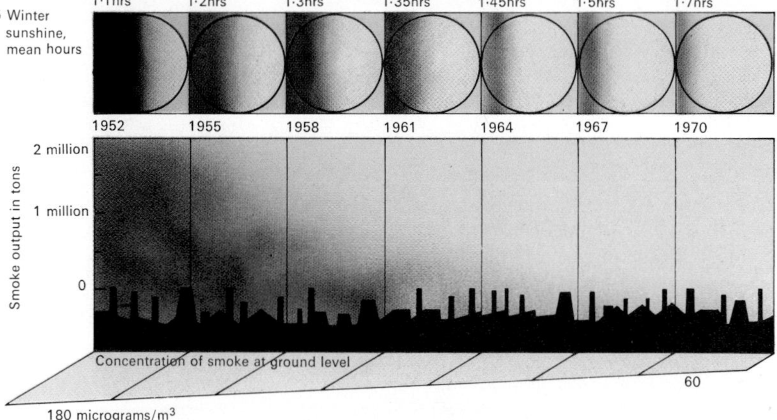

Winter sunshine, mean hours
1·1hrs
1·2hrs
1·3hrs
1·35hrs
1·45hrs
1·5hrs
1·7hrs
1952
1955
1958
1961
1964
1967
1970
Smoke output in tons
2 million
1 million
0
Concentration of smoke at ground level
60
180 micrograms/m³

5 Air was relatively pure until the Industrial Revolution. In the 18th and 19th centuries the coal that powered industry and provided domestic heat progressively blackened buildings and damaged vegetation and health. In England the lethal winter smogs of 1952 spurred government action and in 1956 clean-air legislation was enacted. This reduced the smoke output. Within a few years there was a distinct improvement in the quality of the air. Overall, the big clean-up attempts have been successful. London's last smog occurred in 1962 and, as the diagram shows, winter sunshine hours increased significantly. Air pollution in New York City (left) created potential health problems in the 1960s. In the 1970s legislation and pollution controls were introduced to attack air pollution.

6

6 Nuclear explosions have exposed man to damaging amounts of radiation. During the 1950s it was found that radioactive strontium-90, produced during the blasts, was being absorbed by vegetation. Grazing animals eat contaminated plants and thus human beings drink milk and eat meat containing strontium-90. This partly replaces calcium in bones and, by emitting beta particles, which interfere with blood cell production, can eventually cause leukemia.

Misuse of the land

Mark Twain, when asked for investment advice, replied: "Buy land. They've stopped making it." A century later it is clear that, far from being "made," land is being used in a manner that is often harmful to the interests of the Earth's population.

The dangers of industrial expansion

Land fulfills many roles, some of them mutually incompatible. Increasing disregard for the true value of land has been shown in recent assessments of agricultural and industrial requirements. The implications are ominous.

Failure to recognize priorities in the use of land has often made it more valuable as a support for concrete than as a support for food crops. Loss of agricultural land occurs every year in virtually every industrialized country. The cities of the world are spreading across the landscape, often encroaching upon all the open land in their path by the construction of houses, factories, and roads. Industrial expansion seeks open sites for new developments rather than rehabilitating old ones because the cost is less. The old sites are usually left to waste and are eyesores.

When farm land is taken over for industry the effects may be felt over an area much larger than that eventually occupied by the plant. The fallout from stack gases may blight the surrounding countryside for many miles around. Highways and their access routes cut through the rural landscape, and the traffic they carry emits exhaust fumes over a still wider area. They also carve wildlife habitats into smaller units that make life impossible for many of the larger species.

The effects of excavation and mining

To produce the materials for construction requires yet more land. The fill for foundations under buildings, roads, and dams is excavated from surrounding areas; hills are leveled to produce building materials. Even larger scars are left by open-pit mines for extracting valuable metals from rock and strip mines for extracting coal. An open-pit copper mine—such as that at Broken Hill in Australia or at Bougainville in New Guinea—may gouge into the ground for more than 0.6mi (1km) in width and almost as deep, involving earthmoving on a geological scale. Such mining practices lead to the leaching of metals by rainwater, which, as run-off, spreads its poisonous load in the surrounding region. Metal-poisoned soil is difficult to reclaim.

Strip-mining for coal does not go so deep but it can cover a vast area. With care, strip-mining [1] can be carried out without causing permanent damage. The topsoil can be set aside and replaced on leveled ground after the coal has been extracted from underneath, but the techniques are costly. Strip-mining that is not followed by refill and replanting produces an acidic water run-off (through leaching by rain) that blights the downslope vegetation. Mine operators concerned primarily with achieving high rates of production have, since the mid-1950s, created widespread devastation with strip-mining in the Appalachian region of the eastern United States. If the coal reserves of the western United States are brought into production by strip-mining, as presently

CONNECTIONS

See also
318 Protecting crops
292 Pollution of the air
296 Pollution of rivers and lakes
298 Pollution of the sea
628 Endangered mammals
634 Destructive man

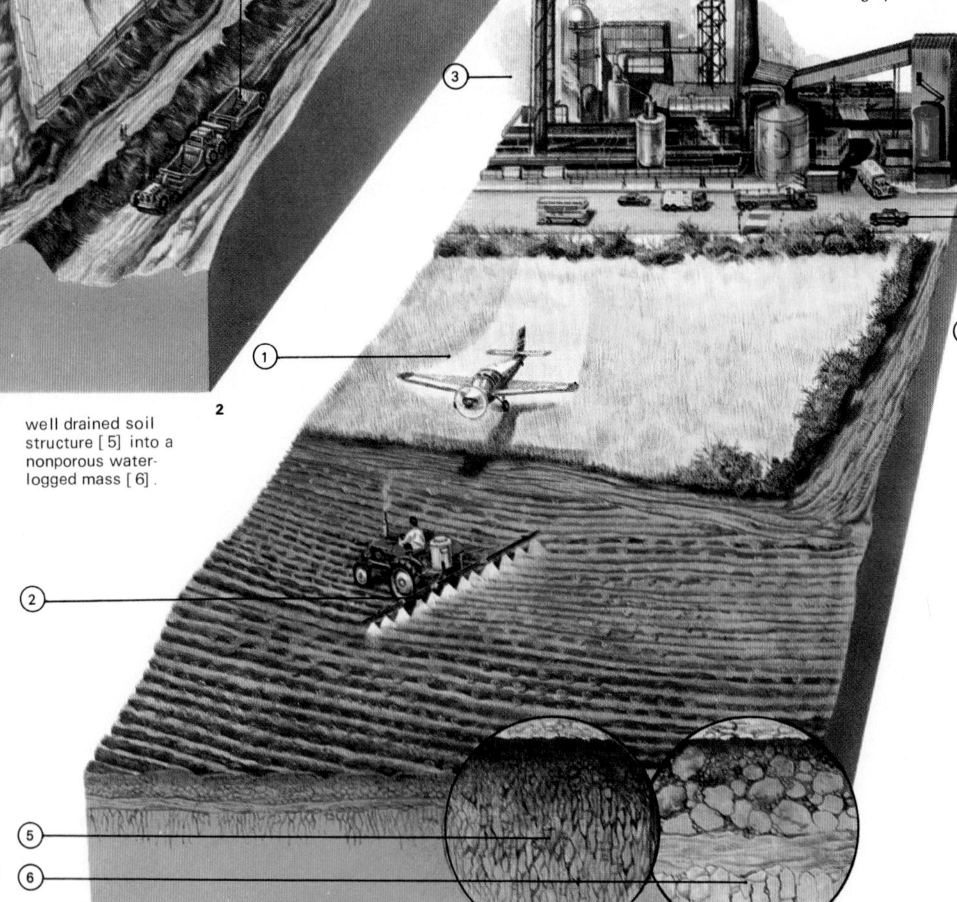

1 Mechanical interference with soil takes place in many ways. Road building [1] not only uses up land for the graded surface but also for the embankments where the soil is mechanically destroyed by heavy road-building machinery, furthermore the drainage pattern is often upset, with the run-off draining directly into streams instead of returning to the soil and the water table. Agricultural machinery [2] compacts the soil and affects its biological properties. Open-pit and strip-mining [3, 4] can create widespread land erosion, and exposed minerals can be leached away by rainwater, poisoning the land. The topsoil from pits and strips should be replaced over filled-in excavations after the end of mining operations.

2 Chemical degradation of the land can occur both by direct and indirect means. Substances applied directly to the soil in agricultural processes intended to produce beneficial results may have lethal side effects. Fertilizers and pesticides sprayed on crops [1] will pass into the soil and be distributed by ground water. This can alter the biochemical balance of the soil and kill off earthworms and other organisms that play a key role in maintaining soil porosity and aeration. Sewage sludge is often spread as a valuable organic fertilizer [2], but it is impossible to remove such metals as copper and zinc, which come from industrial effluent. These may build up and alter the chemistry of the soil. The soil can be polluted less directly by industrial processes when gases such as sulfur dioxide are released in the atmosphere by chimneys [3]. These are washed down in rain as acid, changing the acidity of the soil to the detriment of the plants and animals that feed on it. Unburned hydrocarbons, lead, and other noxious substances from motor vehicles [4] may build up in fields near roadways. Excessive use of heavy agricultural machinery can crush a well drained soil structure [5] into a nonporous waterlogged mass [6].

proposed, it will be necessary to enforce erosion-control measures and to prevent water pollution in order to rehabilitate the land for agricultural purposes. Otherwise the result will be a barren and eroded wasteland.

Land management and deforestation

Even when land is valued for its fertility, modern techniques of agriculture may have harmful effects. Excessive use of chemical pesticides [2] may kill the tiny organisms in the soil that help to maintain the soil's vitality. Chemical fertilizers make it possible to grow the same crop year after year, but the fine structure of the soil may break down if there is no organic matter in it. This breakdown may be accelerated by the repeated passage of heavy agricultural machinery [1], which compacts the soil.

In extreme cases under tropical conditions, delicate soil structures may be replaced by a solid, impenetrable mass called laterite or hardpan. In recent years some countries have proposed the opening up of tropical and subtropical regions to cultivation by clearing away rain forests, such as those of the Amazon basin in Brazil. The obliteration of the luxuriant but fragile vegetation of the rain forest, which plays a major part in maintaining the oxygen balance of the planet, might lead to an irreversible global catastrophe.

Plowing up the plains of North America to plant wheat resulted in the dust bowl of the 1930s. Many millions of tons of precious topsoil were swept away by the winds. A misjudged program of irrigation in Pakistan raised the salt level in hundreds of thousands of acres, making them useless for crops. The Sahara desert [4] is advancing southward about 300ft (92m) per year—partly because of careless, primitive agricultural and pastoral practices on the southern fringe.

On a local scale, city people have come to value land so little that gaping ugly garbage dumps [Key] are left suppurating in the neighborhood of countless communities. Though the need for useful land is increasing, mankind is destroying it on a geological scale through overpopulation.

KEY

The garbage dump is symbolic of man's use of natural resources. First, it shows the amount of raw materials used up and discarded. Second, it shows how valuable land can be lost in the creation of an unsightly dump. This land could be reclaimed but the problems are great.

3

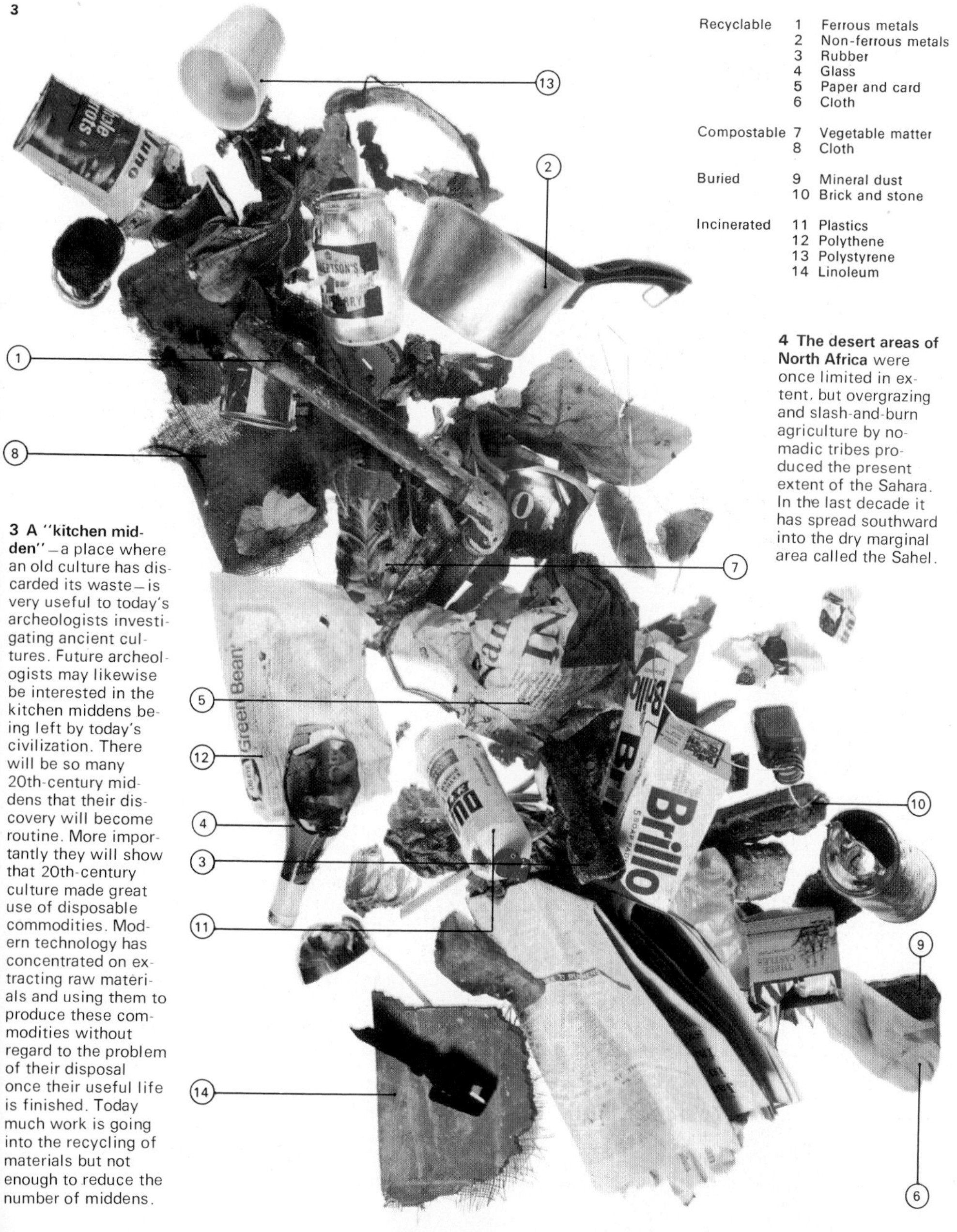

Recyclable	1	Ferrous metals
	2	Non-ferrous metals
	3	Rubber
	4	Glass
	5	Paper and card
	6	Cloth
Compostable	7	Vegetable matter
	8	Cloth
Buried	9	Mineral dust
	10	Brick and stone
Incinerated	11	Plastics
	12	Polythene
	13	Polystyrene
	14	Linoleum

3 A "kitchen midden"—a place where an old culture has discarded its waste—is very useful to today's archeologists investigating ancient cultures. Future archeologists may likewise be interested in the kitchen middens being left by today's civilization. There will be so many 20th-century middens that their discovery will become routine. More importantly they will show that 20th-century culture made great use of disposable commodities. Modern technology has concentrated on extracting raw materials and using them to produce these commodities without regard to the problem of their disposal once their useful life is finished. Today much work is going into the recycling of materials but not enough to reduce the number of middens.

4

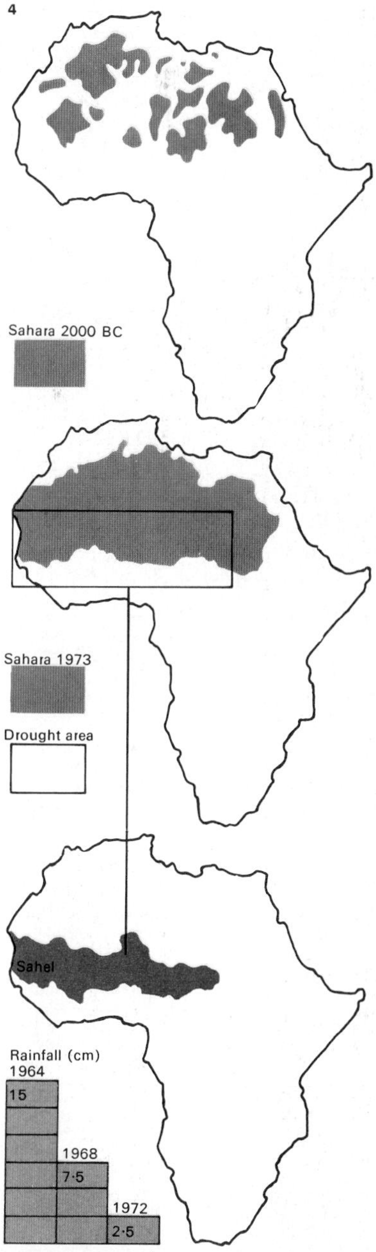

Sahara 2000 BC

Sahara 1973

Drought area

Sahel

Rainfall (cm)

1964: 15

1968: 7·5

1972: 2·5

4 The desert areas of North Africa were once limited in extent, but overgrazing and slash-and-burn agriculture by nomadic tribes produced the present extent of the Sahara. In the last decade it has spread southward into the dry marginal area called the Sahel.

Pollution of rivers and lakes

Water moves through a continuous cycle of evaporation, cloud formation, rainfall, collection in waterways, and then more evaporation. In doing so, the water is able to purify itself naturally of impurities: decaying organic matter, dissolved gases and minerals, and suspended solids.

Where people and animals are concentrated in large numbers, the self-purification capacity of fresh water can easily be overloaded, especially if water is used to collect and transport sewage wastes from settlements of any size. If sewage is deposited on soil in small quantities, soil organisms break it down, reuse the nutrient components and allow almost pure water to filter through into nearby waterways. But if the sewage is flushed directly into a waterway, its bacterial breakdown must take place in the water. A bacterial population explosion occurs that requires a tremendous supply of dissolved oxygen to oxidize the waste. The "biochemical oxygen demand" (BOD) thus imposed may severely lower the level of oxygen available to other organisms living in the water, especially fish and plants [1].

In extreme cases, the lack of oxygen may suffocate all the living organisms in the water. The water is then biologically dead, except for the anaerobic bacteria, which thrive in the absence of oxygen and produce noxious gases, such as hydrogen sulfide. The result may be a waterway both dead and foul smelling.

Life-giving oxygen

The same result can occur in water supplied with an excess of nutrient material, such as nitrate or phosphate, perhaps from the runoff of agricultural fertilizer or waste water containing detergent. The nutrients encourage the growth of organisms such as algae; but this growth also requires oxygen, and may exceed the capacity of the water to supply it. If this occurs, the algae die, and the decaying remains impose a further BOD, once again strangling the life of the waterway.

A lake may have a life span of some 20,000 years before it gradually silts up and disappears. But the effects of excess nutrients can accelerate the aging process, called "eutrophication," and reduce the lifespan of a lake, making it a much less welcome feature of the landscape [2].

The life-giving oxygen dissolved in waterways is less soluble at higher water temperatures. Some industries, notably the electricity generating industry, use enormous volumes of water for cooling purposes. The heated water is discharged back into waterways, further upsetting the biological balance of the aquatic system. The lower level of oxygen handicaps some species in favor of others; so does the higher mean temperature. Species that thrive in warmer water, however, may suffer disastrous consequences if a plant is shut down and its heated water flow interrupted [3].

Organic wastes, nutrients, and heat become major problems to freshwater ecological systems only when too abundant for the systems to handle. But in recent years the systems have had to deal with vast quantities of substances that are totally alien, and to which they may be acutely vulnerable. Pesticides from agricultural runoff, and metals and process chemicals from indus-

CONNECTIONS

See also
316 Improving crops
318 Protecting crops
292 Pollution of the air
294 Misuse of the land
298 Pollution of the sea
634 Destructive man
1808 Soaps and detergents

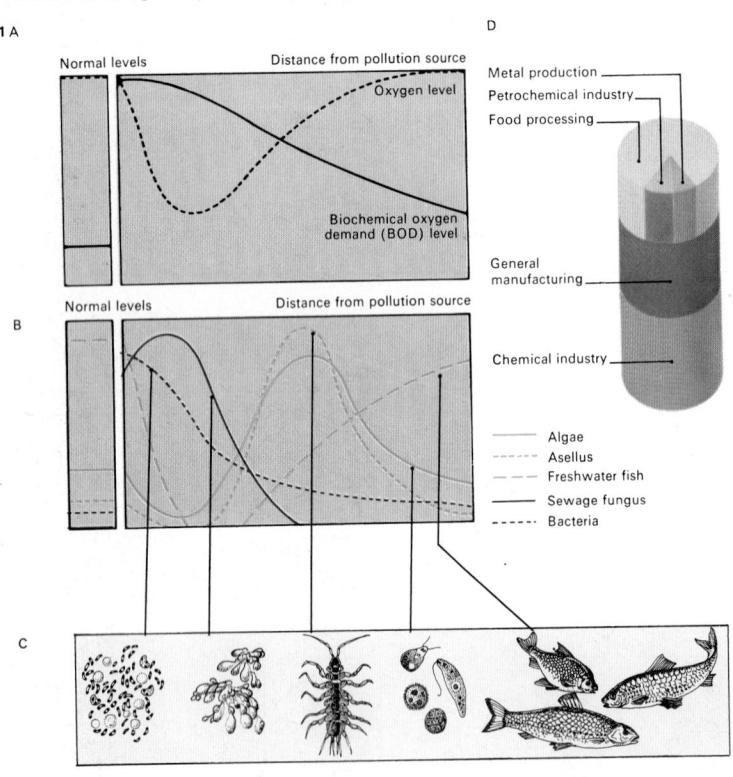

1 A
Normal levels
Distance from pollution source
Oxygen level
Biochemical oxygen demand (BOD) level

B
Normal levels
Distance from pollution source

C

D
Metal production
Petrochemical industry
Food processing
General manufacturing
Chemical industry

Algae
Asellus
Freshwater fish
Sewage fungus
Bacteria

1 Freshwater plants and animals almost all depend on oxygen dissolved in the water. Sewage also needs dissolved oxygen for its bacterial decay, thus competing with aquatic life. The pollutants cause the water's oxygen level to fall [A] by creating a biochemical oxygen demand (BOD) which is the amount of oxygen needed during the time it takes for the waste matter to be oxidized. Living organisms are directly affected by the wastes [B]. Some thrive on them, for example the so-called sewage fungus and other bacteria, while others, such as freshwater fish, may be suffocated. Some live algae and the isopod crustacean *Asellus*, flourish at medium levels of pollution. Some measure of the extent of pollution in freshwater can be gained by examining the peaks in populations of the plant and animal life [C] as the distance from the source of pollution increases. Industrial wastes discharged into waterways [D] are mostly responsible for causing pollution.

2 A

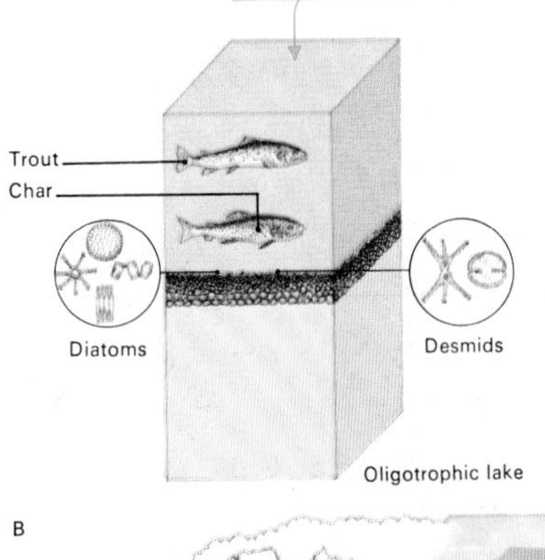

Trout
Char
Diatoms
Desmids
Oligotrophic lake

2 An oligotrophic lake is a young lake [A] having clear water and a low density of algae and plankton, in the form of diatoms and desmids. Typical fish are trout and char. As the lake ages, it becomes more fertile. Nutrients in the runoff water from the surrounding land [B] stimulate algae growth, especially green and blue-green algae. The water becomes muddy and the fish are mainly perch and bream.

B

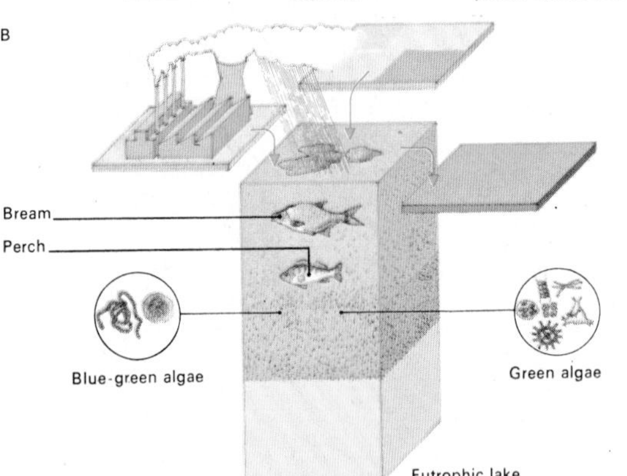

Bream
Perch
Blue-green algae
Green algae
Eutrophic lake

3 Waste hot water fed into rivers from the cooling systems of factories can kill indigenous fish, such as salmon [1] and trout [2] by raising the water temperature above toleration levels. They may be replaced by undesirable species, such as the guppy (*Lebistes reticulatus*) [3] and the cichlids *(Tilapia zilii)* [4]. Upstream water [A] with a temperature of 41°F (5°C) holds idigenous fish. The water enters a factory and emerges hot; the temperature rising to 70°F (21°C) [B], the indigenous fish die and undesirable fish thrive. [C] Downstream the water cools and the original species reappear.

3 A B C

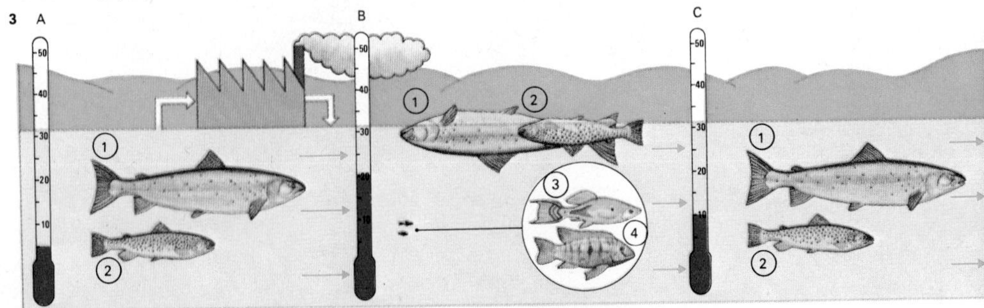

50
40
30
20
10
1
2
3
4

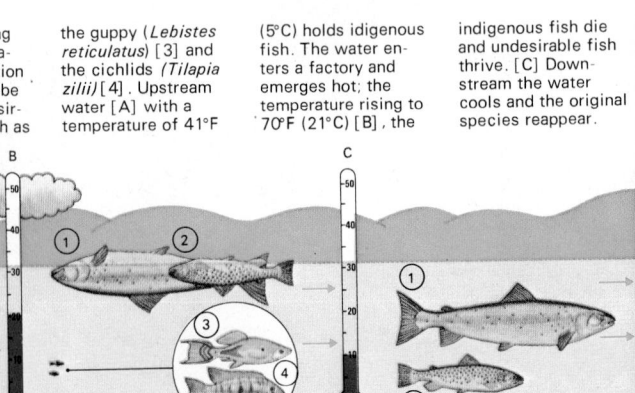

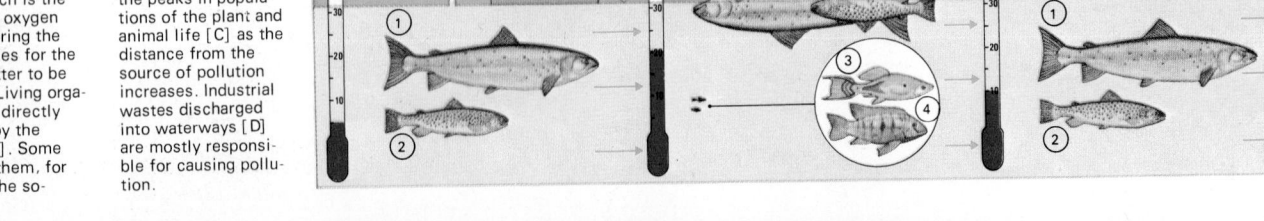

trial effluent, have managed to enter aquatic food chains, with unpredictable consequences. Species high up in the food chain may build up dangerous concentrations of such substances, making them yet more vulnerable to other environmental pressures [4].

Restoring water health

Polluted water can be cleansed. Even the natural water cycle will accomplish this, given the chance. But polluted basins—river beds, lake bottoms and such—may take much longer to recover their biological vitality once it is undermined. To allow natural systems a chance to restore themselves it is necessary to stop adding further burdens to waterways. Sewage plants can allow suspended solids to settle out to form sludge, reducing by half the BOD of waste water, and can even reduce the level of nutrients. But there is still the problem of industrial effluents poisoning sewage plants. Furthermore, the plants are costly to build, and their value in providing cleaner water is still not adequately recognized.

Urban settlements and industries find it convenient to dispose of their wastes into nearby waterways and are reluctant to stop, even when the wastes render the water useless or dangerous. Another problem arises in waterways that serve as regional boundaries, especially those between nations. The deterioration of the Great Lakes has been a diplomatic problem for many years [5].

Who is responsible?

Canada and the United States each find it difficult to justify effluent controls on their respective shores while the other still permits pollutants to enter the lakes. Even more desperate problems confront those attempting to prevent the biological death of the Rhine. Power stations, potash mines, and chemical industries line the river banks, loading it with a burden of heat and pollutants that seems bound to stifle it. But France, West Germany, the Netherlands, and Switzerland have been unable to agree on any collective form of control measures. All over the world, freshwater habitats are succumbing to the effect of pollution.

KEY

Water moves in an endless cycle, carrying with it a variety of dissolved or suspended substances, and purifying itself repeatedly by evaporation. Many of the substances in fresh water arise in nature, and reach waterways by natural means, such as rainfall or ground water runoff. Some man-made pollutants follow the same routes. Smoke, ash, and industrial gases can be brought down by rain; and chemicals and wastes spread on soil can be carried by ground water into waterways. Other wastes follow man-made routes, through drains and sewerage outlets. These wastes are usually noxious, but easier to control than those in natural pathways.

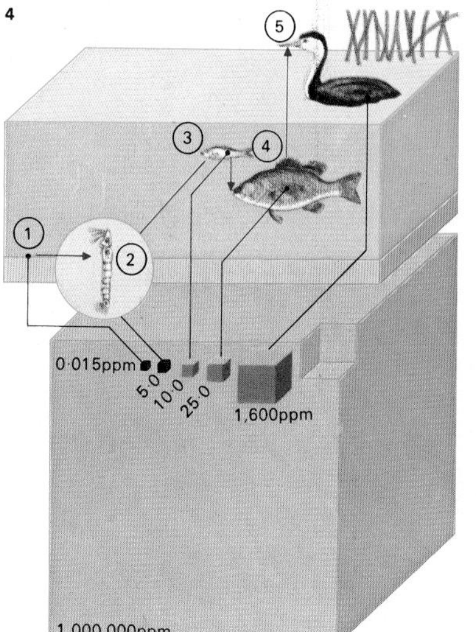
4
0·015ppm
5·0
10·0
25·0
1,600ppm
1,000,000ppm

4 Pesticides, even in small doses, are poisonous to many animals. The concentration of poison increases along the food chain, finally becoming lethal to animals at the end of the chain. A pesticide [1], such as DDT, is applied to water at 0.015 parts per million (ppm) to control midge larvae, but the plankton [2] accumulates 5ppm. The fish population [3,4] builds up still higher concentrations, and finally a grebe [5] that feeds on the fish accumulates as much as 1,600ppm of the pesticide in its body fat, which is enough to kill it.

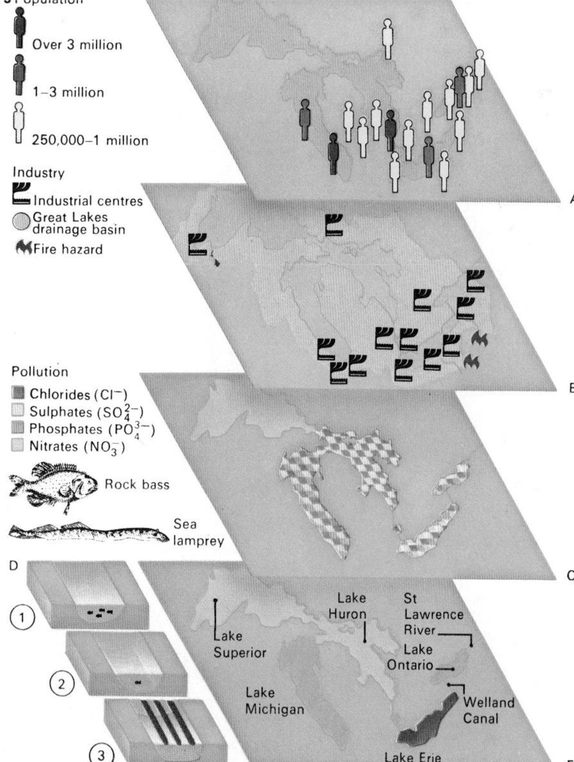
5 Population
Over 3 million
1–3 million
250,000–1 million
Industry
Industrial centres
Great Lakes drainage basin
Fire hazard
Pollution
Chlorides (Cl^-)
Sulphates (SO_4^{2-})
Phosphates (PO_4^{3-})
Nitrates (NO_3^-)
Rock bass
Sea lamprey
D
A
B
C
E
Lake Superior
Lake Huron
St Lawrence River
Lake Ontario
Lake Michigan
Welland Canal
Lake Erie

5 The Great Lakes are the largest fresh water lakes in the world, but their physical condition has deteriorated in the present century. Population increases [A] and industry [B] have been the main factors. Pollution from domestic and industrial wastes [C] has wrought changes in the chemical composition and fauna of the lakes. Local fish life has been devastated by the parasitic sea lamprey, which invaded the lakes via the Welland Canal, opened in 1932; and new species of fish, such as rock bass, are becoming dominant. Eutrophication [D, E], the natural aging process of all freshwater lakes, occurs in three stages, oligotrophic [1], mesotrophic [2] and eutrophic [3]. In the Great Lakes, the process has been artificially accelerated by human activity, and Lake Erie may have already entered its final eutrophic phase.

6 A

6 B

6 Natural waterways have been long regarded as obvious dumping grounds for man's wastes. In the modern technological society the wastes from industry have proved to be more than the waterways can handle. Instead of the water being able to break down the polluting substances naturally, these substances tend to accumulate and form poisonous suspensions or unsightly scum [A] in the water and kill off the animal and plant life [B].

Pollution of the sea

The world's oceans make up a vast expanse of water—the Pacific alone is greater in area than all the continents together. Man has accordingly looked upon them with awe—and then casually dumped into them every imaginable form of waste, solid, liquid, and gas. Ships and barges carry solid refuse and liquid effluent out of sight of land and unload them into the sea. Galley rubbish is tossed over the sides of ships, toilets are flushed directly into the sea. The world's rivers carry their burden of effluents, nutrients, and suspended solids into the coastal seas. The atmosphere wafts pesticides, lead compounds, and many other pollutants far out to sea where they add to the pollution of the oceans.

Accidental oil spills

Oil and water do not mix, but a staggering total of oil—millions of tons a year—is deposited in the ocean, by accident and by intent. Accidental oil spills are the most notorious. The wreck of the *Torrey Canyon* [4] in 1967 released nearly 100,000 tons of crude oil into the waters off Land's End, England, coating many miles of English and French coastlines with thick, black sludge, and killing thousands of sea birds, especially those, such as auks, that feed from the surface.

Every year adds to the toll of tanker wrecks. Sometimes these wrecks—such as those of the *Pacific Glory* and the *Allegro* in the English Channel in 1970—occur in crowded waterways. Others, such as that of the *Metula* in the Strait of Magellan in 1974, occur in remote waters. But all add to the patches of oil slowly spreading across the surface of the oceans. One of the worst oil spills came from a drilling platform not far off the California coast near Santa Barbara in 1969.

As tanker sizes increased, single accidents released greater deluges of oil into the oceans. But accidents do not release as much oil as do the irresponsible actions of a small minority of the world's tanker fleet operators. Tankers clean their tanks by flushing them with seawater. Reputable fleets have adopted a procedure called Load on Top (LOT) in which tanker washings are stored on board to be unloaded at special shore facilities. Overwhelmingly, however, the largest source of oil pollution at sea comes from the land—from industries and motor vehicles. Their oily residues are often discharged into the sea or carried there by rivers [2].

Death in the sea

The quantity of oil pollution is troublesome but at least oil is organic in origin and can in time be broken down by marine organisms. Heavy metals such as lead, cadmium, and mercury remain toxic indefinitely. Indeed, marine organisms may make them even more toxic. Mercury dumped into the coastal waters of Japan was thought to be of low toxicity. But there it was converted into methyl mercury, a vicious poison to the central nervous system. The poison was concentrated in fish and shellfish, producing an outbreak of what came to be known as Minamata disease [6], whose origins remained obscure for nearly a decade. Fishing will never be safe in Minamata Bay, which has 600 tons of mercury on its bottom, and

CONNECTIONS

See also
318 Protecting crops
292 Pollution of the air
294 Misuse of the land
296 Pollution of rivers and lakes
634 Destructive man

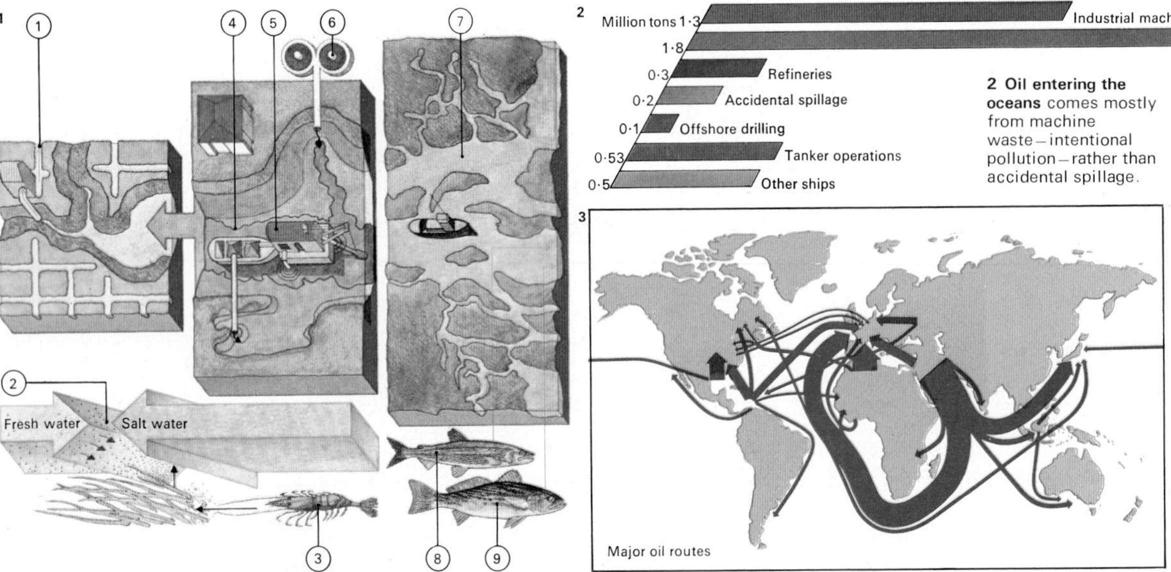

1
Fresh water
Salt water
2
Million tons 1·3
Industrial machine waste
1·8
Motor vehicle waste
0·3
Refineries
0·2
Accidental spillage
0·1
Offshore drilling
0·53
Tanker operations
0·5
Other ships
3
Major oil routes

1 Man's influence on the sea may begin upstream. He uses fresh water from an estuary to irrigate the land [1] and so alters the rate at which fresh water becomes salt at a river mouth [2] killing organisms like shrimp [3]. Reclamation of salt marshes or mud flats [4] destroys one of the most productive zones in the biosphere. Dredging [5] stirs up mud, reduces surface sunlight and oxygen levels. Raw sewage [6] overloads biological systems. An unspoiled estuary [7] is important to the fishing industry as species like menhaden [8] and spotted sea trout [9] return to fresh water to spawn. Sewage can hinder the ability of fish to "smell" their way to the breeding grounds or return to the sea.

2 Oil entering the oceans comes mostly from machine waste – intentional pollution – rather than accidental spillage.

3 Majors areas of potential oil pollution are found along the world's main shipping routes. Oil now outstrips all other commodities in international traffic and, as most exporting areas are thousands of miles from the areas of consumption, great fleets of tankers, some weighing half a million tons and carrying the same weight of crude oil, are constantly moving along the trade routes. Nearly three million tons of oil are seaborne every day and there are, on the average, two potentially serious collisions every week. The places that run the greatest risk of oil pollution are the major shipping bottlenecks, such as the English Channel, the Cape of Good Hope, and the Malay islands, but now that oil is being exploited in Arctic regions tanker fleets will soon be operating in areas where the hazards of navigation are magnified by ice and poor visibility for the greater part of the year and serious incidents can be expected. The escape of oil close to populated areas prompts most outcry but accidents elsewhere are just as dangerous to the local ecology. International organizations have taken some steps to reduce pollution by requiring the redesigning of tankers and by restricting dumping to certain specified areas.

4

4 Torrey Canyon, a supertanker carrying Kuwait crude oil, ran aground off Land's End, England, in 1967. Her back broken, she disgorged nearly 100,000 tons of oil. Emergency measures to combat the huge slick, including fire bombing, were unsuccessful. Sea birds were coated in oil and died by the thousands. The slick went ashore in quantities in southwest England and drifted to the south and east to coat the beaches of the Channel Islands and France. Spraying of detergent in an attempt to clean up proved even more deleterious to marine life than the oil. Species affected included flounder [1], edible crabs [2, 3], blenny [4], shrimp [5], lobster [6], and oysters [7].

some other Japanese bays where mercury still remains in the water.

The effects of marine dumping are still poorly understood. It took prolonged detective work to establish the cause of a notorious episode in the Irish Sea that involved the deaths of thousands of sea birds. The key factor was found eventually to be polychlorinated biphenyls (PCBs), organic chemicals in industrial effluent dumped in the estuary of the River Clyde. Some sea-borne organic chemicals travel much farther from their origins; birds and fish can carry DDT to remote parts of the globe, such as Antarctica. Photosynthesis in marine plant life, which makes an important contribution to the Earth's oxygen balance, can be inhibited by even quite low levels of DDT.

Closed systems

Some seas, such as the Mediterranean and the Baltic, are nearly closed systems having only limited interchange of water with the rest of the world's oceans. Such seas are already showing signs of serious biological breakdown [7]. But their plight is only a foretaste of what could happen in the entire marine environment.

In a very real sense the whole world of the oceans is a closed system, but the nations of the world have been unable to unite behind any effective measures to administer the oceans for the benefit of all. In the early 1970s the United Nations Inter-Governmental Maritime Consultative Organization (IMCO) drew up a convention for the control of maritime pollution by shipping, but a convention is only as strong as the steps taken to enforce it. The IMCO convention remains in essence a pious hope. The UN Conference on the Law of the Sea dragged on from 1958 in session after session, with very little real progress being made.

National interests are generally more jealously guarded than "the common heritage of all mankind" and until there is more internation cooperation the oceans will continue to be dumping grounds for sewage, pulp waste, radioactive wastes, and all the other refuse of civilization.

KEY

Waste returns to its originator. Smoke [1] and effluent [2], diluted or apparently dispersed in clouds [3], may return in concentrated form. Pollutants reach the sea in rain [4] and runoff from the land [5] and they are absorbed by marine organisms– first simple [6, 7], then larger species [8]. Fish [9] may be eaten by birds or by man [10] whose place at the apex of the food pyramid makes him especially vulnerable to the dangers of the waste that he creates.

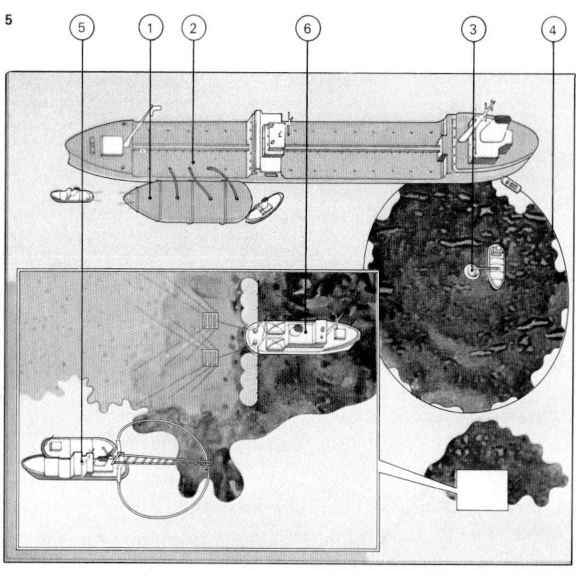

5 Tanker disasters of *Torrey Canyon* magnitude are hastening new techniques to minimize subsequent damage. A collapsible bladder [1] is towed alongside a stranded tanker [2] and used to store oil pumped from the ship. If any oil has been spilled a "skimmer" [3] collects the drifting oil, which has been confined by a floating boom [4]. The oil can be mopped up by a moving absorbent belt [5] also known as an "oil scrubber," or sprayed with a dispersant [6] to speed its breakdown by microorganisms. These techniques are not yet widely available.

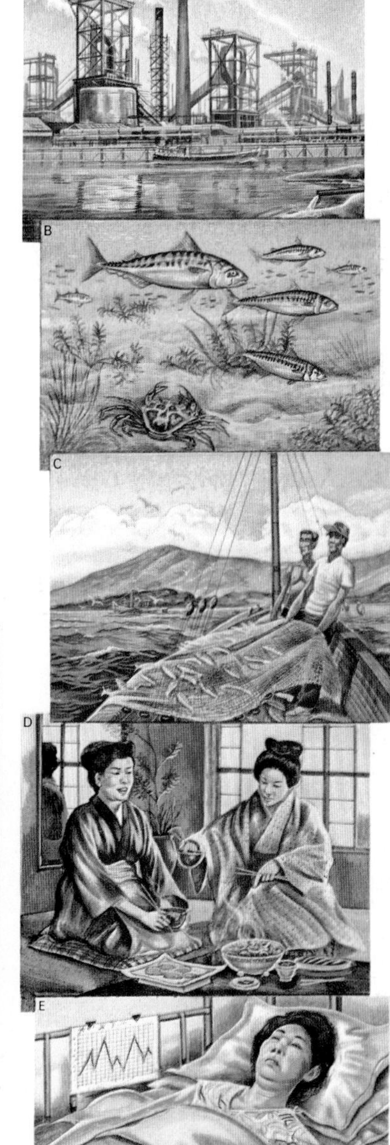

6 The effect of toxic pollution hit back at man himself on the shores of Minamata Bay, Japan, in the 1950s and 1960s. Inorganic mercury discharged into the bay as waste by industry [A] was converted by marine organisms into methyl mercury. This highly toxic substance accumulated in fish and shellfish [B], which were taken from the bay by local fishermen [C]. Fish is a staple diet [D] of the region. People became ill [E], died, or showed signs of brain disorder; children were born malformed. The plant has closed but fishing has not resumed in the bay.

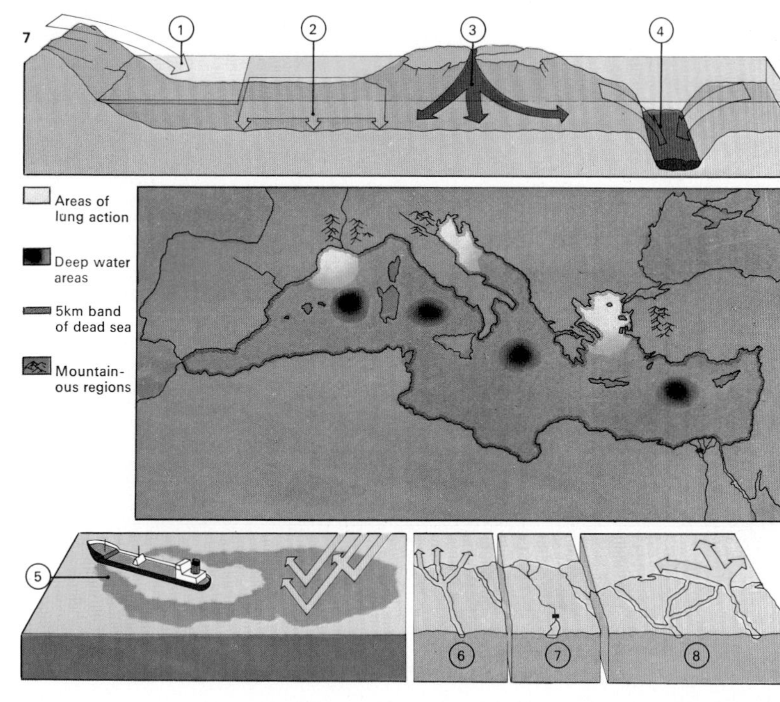
Areas of lung action
Deep water areas
5km band of dead sea
Mountainous regions

7 Life in some coastal waters of the Mediterranean is near death. This sea has three "lung basins" where cold air blown down from the mountains [1] forms a cold, oxygenated layer of water that sinks [2], releasing oxygen on the way. The basins are fed by effluent-poisoned rivers [3], the pollutants collecting in deep waters [4], where they have killed all life. Tanker waste [5] films the sea with oil, denying sunlight to phytoplankton. Man's work has killed sardine fishing off the Nile delta [6] by making the area unfavorable to the sardines. The Aswan dam [7] reduces the fresh water input and salinity is increased by a flow of water from the Red Sea via the Suez Canal [8]

Land uses

People are beginning, at last, to realize that if they are to continue to live on the planet Earth they must conserve its resources. For thousands of years human impact on the land was negligible. But since the middle of the eighteenth century, intensive agriculture, the search for minerals and energy sources, and the growth of population and transport systems have led to increasing interference with the balance of nature and to competition for available land in ways that are often destructive.

The eras of change

Until about 10,000 years ago people left little trace of their presence on the landscape. They hunted, fished, trapped, sheltered in caves, and searched for suitable materials for tools. Early mines were mere pits dug with picks made from the antlers of deer. But during the agricultural revolution of Neolithic times nomadic peoples settled down to cultivate fields, cut trees to build houses, and established a pattern of land use that altered the natural ecological balance. Despite this, communities were small, and even settled areas averaged perhaps 3 people per square mile. By the year AD 1000 world population had reached only about 350 million.

The growth of larger towns in medieval times, the spread of roads, and the quarrying of materials such as clay, stone, and iron gradually extended human impact on the landscape. Large areas of forest were cleared for grazing or cultivation of crops. The Industrial Revolution of the eighteenth century was a major turning point in land use.

The development of the steam engine led to the establishment of many new industries and to the rapid growth of towns to house an expanding population of factory workers. As the transport of manufactured goods became more important railroads, canals, and roads cut across the land. The world population almost doubled as it grew from about 900 million in 1800 to 1,650 million in 1900.

At the same time a second agricultural revolution began, bringing great changes in farming methods. Crops and livestock were improved and food and raw material production developed. Agriculture spread to newly discovered lands and farming techniques became steadily more mechanized. Throughout the nineteenth century disturbance of existing vegetation and wildlife, and pollution of the water and atmosphere, occurred with little awareness of the damage being done.

Man's adverse impact

Despite examples of the sensible conservation of land—such as reclamation in the Netherlands [3] and terrace cultivation in Asia—agricultural areas elsewhere were often mismanaged on a vast scale. Overuse of land in the western prairies of the United States broke up a stable ecosystem so that during a period of drought and high winds in the 1930's, the topsoil was removed and a dust bowl created. In other areas thoughtless removal of vegetation allowed heavy erosion of hilly areas. Rainwater then carved deep gullies and carried good topsoil into rivers, which denuded farming areas and caused further problems through silting.

CONNECTIONS

See also
294 Misuse of the land

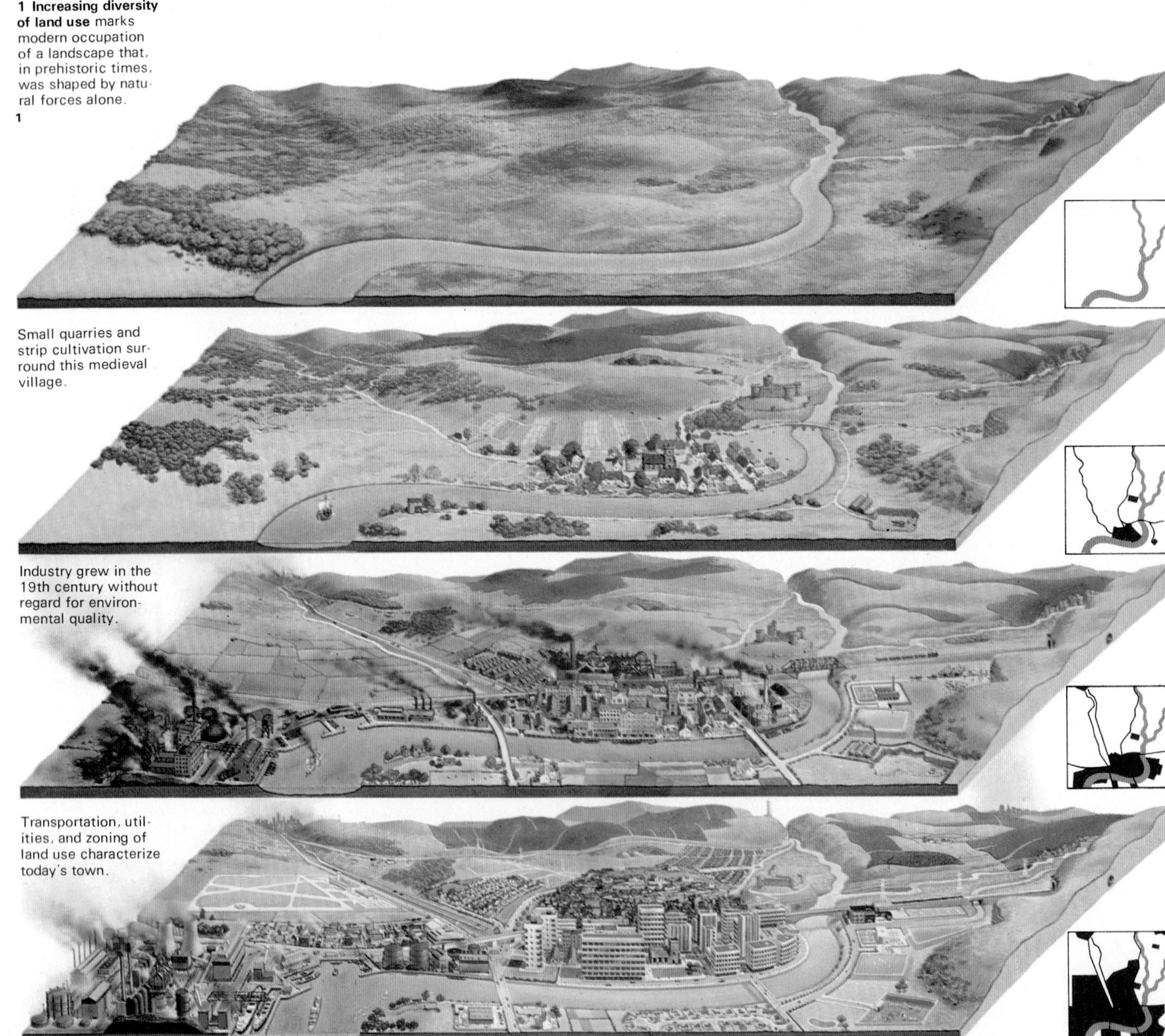

1 Increasing diversity of land use marks modern occupation of a landscape that, in prehistoric times, was shaped by natural forces alone.

Small quarries and strip cultivation surround this medieval village.

Industry grew in the 19th century without regard for environmental quality.

Transportation, utilities, and zoning of land use characterize today's town.

Relatively large areas of country on which people have had little or no impact remain, but the landscape in developed countries has become more and more formalized. With world population soaring to some 4 billion, cities continue to grow at the expense of the country. New roads sweep through previously impassable territory [Key] while in Europe and America extensive highway systems devour the land. Airports take good agricultural land near cities, and electric transmission lines stride over hills and valleys. The spread of technology has limited other possible land uses.

Human impact on rivers and lakes is already immense in terms of both construction and pollution, and still more spectacular interference may be expected in the future. The Soviet Union has begun to implement a policy to divert its northward flowing rivers to the south in order to make desert areas fertile. A recent survey of the North American continent has suggested the expenditure of $86 billion on 370 projects to divert rivers and prevent "loss" of water to the Arctic Ocean.

Such schemes involve the building of dams, an activity almost as old as terracing in agriculture. Although dams can control water flow, help irrigation, and generate electricity, they also have drawbacks. They may hold back valuable nutrients, drown vegetation in scenic areas, alter local climates, and even affect seismic activity.

New techniques of monitoring land resources are now being developed, the latest being satellite surveys by means of microwave, ultraviolet and infrared radiation [2]. These surveys [4] give a more detailed picture than does aerial photography [4] alone.

Conservation of land

With the recent emergence of strong political lobbies in favor of land conservation, more attention is being paid to the establishment of a balanced urban environment through replanting of trees and reclamation of previously waste areas. For example, old mine dumps have been leveled and landscaped, and abandoned canals have been cleaned and used for recreation.

KEY

Transcontinental roads such as the Pan-American highway, which will traverse America from north to south over a distance of nearly 5,000 miles (8,000km), have a great influence on land use. Apart from their immediate physical impact such roads open up new areas for settlement.

2

2 Accurate monitoring of the world's remaining resources of land is essential if the best possible use is to be made of them. Remote sensing by infrared photography provides pictures showing ground heat as shades of red and blue; it also "sees" through haze. Healthy vegetation appears red; harvested fields are purple, and ripe wheat fields are blue. Satellite surveys are now widely used. A National Aeronautics and Space Administration project in the United States orbited an Earth Resource Technology Satellite (ERTS) in 1972 to provide data of benefit the world over.

3 In areas of dense population people have attempted to increase land area by reclaiming it from the sea. The Dutch are the most famous makers of land, having perfected their methods over hundreds of years. Embankments, or dikes, are first built across inlets of the sea. The area enclosed is then drained and desalinated. Agricultural land is created and some freshwater lakes are left to provide fisheries and areas for recreation.

4

4 Land-use surveys are now being carried out on a national scale in many countries of the world. A map based on aerial photographs of the crowded coastline in the Kobe region of Japan shows clearly the confinement of the population to a narrow strip by the steep hills of the hinterland [buff]. Other obvious features include the residential area [red], heavy industries [pale blue], docks [pink], land fills reclaimed from the sea [deep yellow], large office buildings [purple] and wooded areas [green]. The first modern land-use survey was made by L. D. Stamp in Britain during the 1930's. Now the whole world is being surveyed in a series of maps being completed by the UN Food and Agriculture Organization.

World food resources

The average adult male needs between 2,300 and 2,700 calories and 1.3 to 2.2 ounces (37 to 62 grams) of protein each day to stay in good health. In addition, he needs adequate quantities of the appropriate micronutrients such as minerals and vitamins. The extent to which people receive this level of nutrition depends on how much food is produced. It also depends on how the food that is produced is distributed.

Early food resources

It is only in recent times that people have had control over their food resources. Originally hunters of wild animals and gatherers of nuts and berries, early people were occupied with the constant quest for food. Because they had no control over their sources of food, starvation posed a constant threat and tended to keep their numbers down.

Then about 10,000 years ago, people began to till the land for the first time. In the fertile flood plains of the Tigris and Euphrates, they planted crops and grew their own food. They also learned to domesticate and raise animals for food to supplement fresh and salt water fish.

In relying less on the bow and arrow than on furrow and seed, people gained a greater control over their food resources. By planting crops and raising livestock, they could be reasonably sure of having enough to eat the following year. And yet, they still found themselves at the mercy of elements over which they had no control. One year drought might wither the crops; another year locusts might destroy them; and yet another year, disease might decimate the herds. In years when natural disasters struck, starvation was a real threat.

People also found that certain constraints affected not only how much food they could grow, but also where they could grow it. Crops needed fairly flat and fertile land if they were to flourish. They also needed adequate rainfall and appropriately long growing seasons. Since the moisture requirements and growing seasons of various crops differed quite widely, certain crops grew better in particular regions of the world than in others. For example, rice grew better in the tropical regions with high temperatures and rainfall than in temperate regions with considerably lower temperature and rainfall. Nevertheless, limitations imposed by topography, soil fertility, rainfall, and temperature meant that at least 70 percent of the world's dry surface area was unsuited for farming.

Despite these constraints, people succeeded in greatly increasing their food production over the centuries. They were able to do this with the help of several major innovations which included (in roughly chronological order): the development of irrigation; the exchange of crops, such as wheat, barley, and corn [1], between the New World and the Old; the development of artificial fertilizers [9] and pesticides; the discovery of the laws controlling plant and animal genetics; and the substitution of the internal-combustion engine for human labor and animal power.

Feeding the population

While these innovations, along with many more minor ones, enabled people to grow

CONNECTIONS

See also
398 The future of food
940 International trade and finance

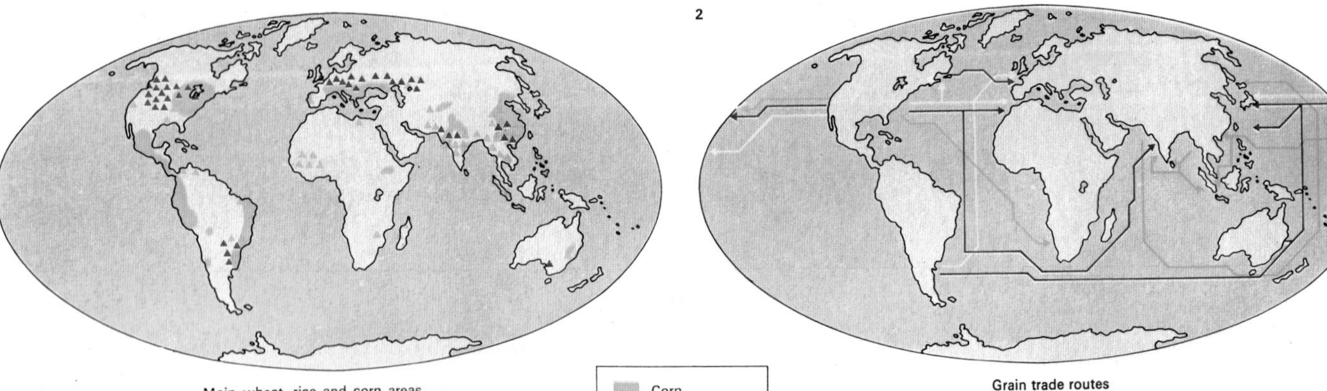

1
2

Main wheat, rice and corn areas

1 Wheat, rice, and corn are of vital importance because together they supply nearly half of the world's food energy. All the other grains, such as millet, sorghum, barley, and oats, supply only 10%. In addition, corn and, to a lesser extent, wheat are also important animal foodstuffs. The major grain-producing areas are those where oil conditions, topography, and climate favor the growing of these crops. Thus the river deltas in Asia favor the growing of rice, while on the cooler, drier plains of North America, wheat and corn flourish.

Corn
Wheat
Rice
Corn
Wheat
Rice

Grain trade routes

2 World grain trade patterns have changed radically since the 1930s. Before World War II, South America and North America were the two major exporters of grain. Since the war, the importance of South America as a grain exporter has declined as its population growth began to catch up with its ability to produce food. Today North America is the bread basket of the world. European nations are the main importers of grain. In recent years, developing nations, previously self-sufficient in grain, have begun to import more and more grain to meet their domestic requirements.

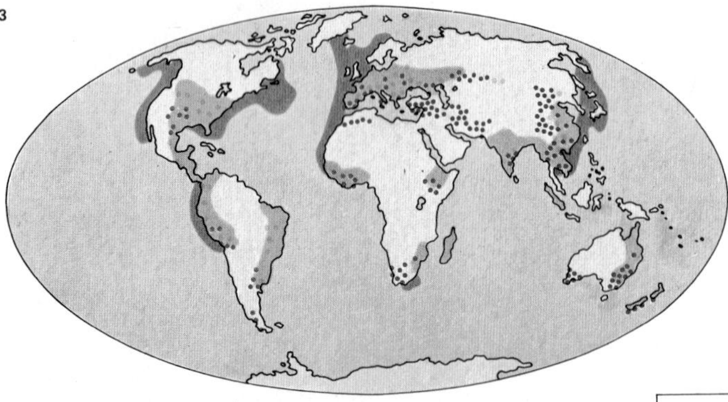

3

Meat, fish and dairy areas

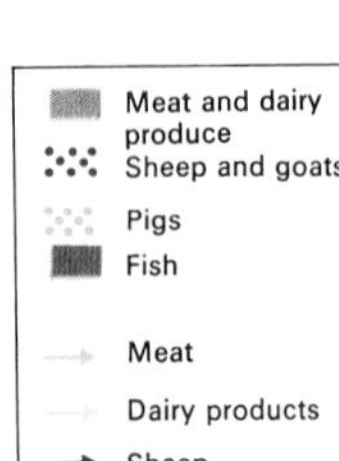

Meat and dairy produce
Sheep and goats
Pigs
Fish
Meat
Dairy products
Sheep
Pigs

4

Meat trade routes

3 Protein-rich foods of animal origin include meat, fish, eggs, and dairy products. Animal proteins cannot be entirely replaced by vegetable proteins in the diet; moreover their production is inefficient. Cattle require 20lb (9kg) of crude vegetable protein to produce 1lb (.05kg) of edible animal protein while broiler chicken requires 4.5lb (2kg). About one third of the world's grain production (400 million tons) is fed to livestock. This grain is enough to provide the energy needs of the populations of India and China. The major livestock regions are those where grain is abundant (the American Midwest) and where grassland is plentiful (Argentina).

4 Trade of livestock and animal proteins takes place primarily between countries of the developed world. In 1971, they accounted for over 90% of the world market economy's trade in meat. This reflects the fact that only more affluent nations can afford to buy animal products which are usually more expensive than other foods. Over the past century, there has been a growth in the consumption of meat in the developed countries. In Japan meat consumption has increased 4-fold since 1960. Since Japan does not possess the resources to grow sufficient food to satisfy her needs, she has had to increase her imports of meat as well as her imports of grain.

greater quantities of food, it seemed that the number of mouths that needed feeding grew almost as rapidly (and sometimes more rapidly) as their ability to grow more food. It is estimated that when people first began farming, the world's population numbered no more than ten million. By the time of Christ, this figure had grown to 250 million; by the mid-19th century, one billion; by 1900, one and a half billion; and by 1975, nearly four billion [1].

With population growing almost as rapidly as the ability to grow more food, famine and starvation continued to threaten major segments of the world's population.

Malnutrition: past and present

The threat of famine tended to be especially severe in years when natural disasters, such as floods or drought, caused sudden reductions in world food production. In the past, major famines included one in Italy in 436 BC and another in India in AD 1291, when large numbers of people died. In more recent years, the Irish famine of 1846, which was due to the failure of the Irish potato crop, forced 800,000 Irish people to migrate to the United States.

In recent years, famine has been reduced because world food production has tended to outstrip the growth in population and because certain nations have been able to build up reserves which they have distributed to other nations in times of disaster. Nevertheless, malnutrition remains widespread. The UN estimates that 460 million people do not receive an adequate amount of the right kinds of foods. The diet of these people is frequently lacking in calories, protein, and the essential micronutrients. Protein deficiency alone severely affects the development of many children.

The widespread incidence of malnutrition is not primarily due to inadequate world food production. Rather it is due to the inequitable distribution between (and for that matter, within) nations of the food that the world produces. Today, the affluent one-third of the world's population eats well over half the food that is produced. Is it surprising then that among the remaining two thirds malnutrition is rife?

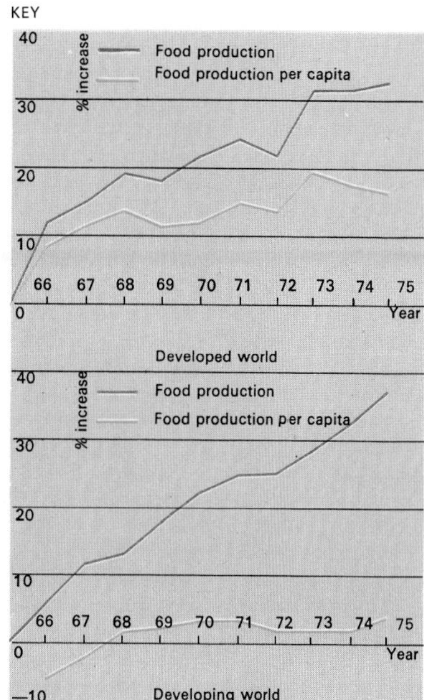

KEY
Food production
Food production per capita
% increase
40
30
20
10
0
66 67 68 69 70 71 72 73 74 75
Year
Developed world
Food production
Food production per capita
% increase
40
30
20
10
0
–10
66 67 68 69 70 71 72 73 74 75
Year
Developing world

The production of food has risen almost equally in the developed and developing nations in recent years. In the developed world, population growth has tended to lag behind the growth in food production, with the result that *per capita* food production has risen substantially. But in the developing world population has grown almost as rapidly as food production so that *per capita* food production has remained virtually unchanged. Because of population growth, attempts to improve diet and the level of nutrition have not been very successful. It is possible that *per capita* food production could even begin to fall in developing countries.

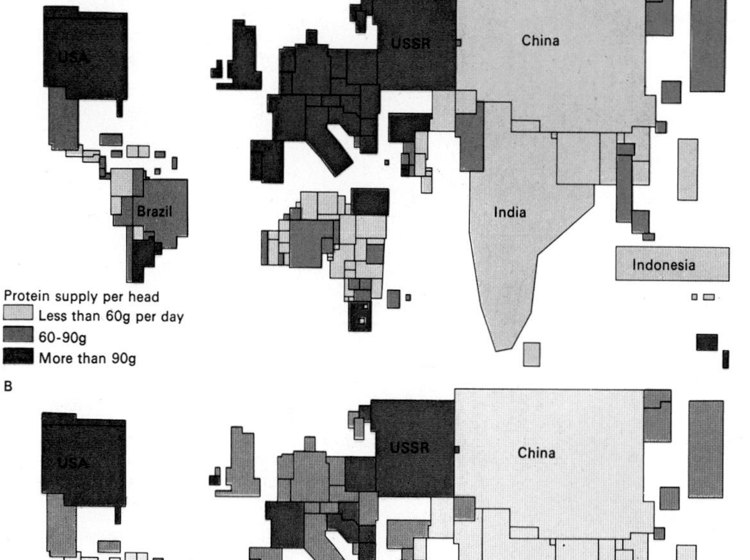

5A
USA
USSR
China
Brazil
India
Indonesia
Protein supply per head
Less than 60g per day
60-90g
More than 90g
B
USA
USSR
China
Brazil
India
Indonesia
Calorie supply per head
Less than 2,200 Calories per day
2,200-2,700 Calories
More than 2,700 Calories

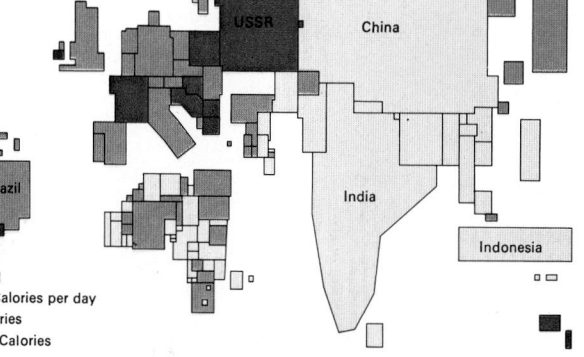

5 These maps of food supply represent each country by an area proportional to its population. They measure food supply in amount of protein per capita [A] and number of calories [B].

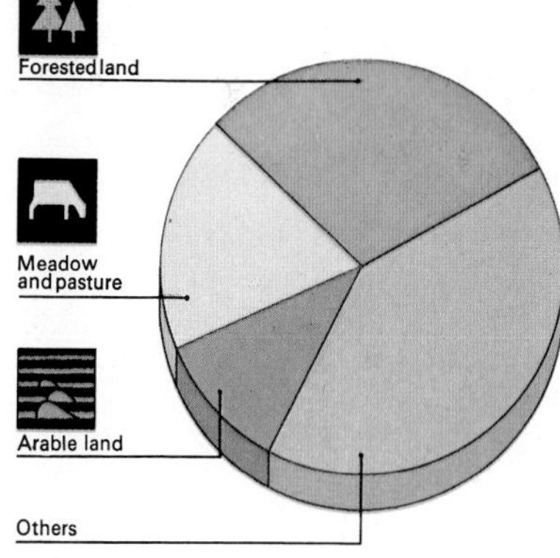

6
Forested land
Meadow and pasture
Arable land
Others

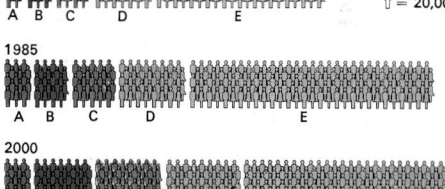

6 Arable land accounts for a small slice of the earth's total dryland surface area. Over 70% of the land area is unfit for agricultural purposes, which limits increases in food production.

7
1971
A B C D E
= 20,000,000
1985
A B C D E
2000
A B C D E
A North America
B Latin America
C Africa
D Europe and USSR
E Asia and Oceania

7 The world's population will number appoximately 6.5 billion by the year 2000. UN figures predict it is unlikely to stabilize before 2125, when the population may reach 12.3 billion.

8 Intensifying production could increase overall world food output. Unfortunately many of the more modern methods of food production which produce more food from a given area require large inputs of fuel energy for power and fertilizer production. It is estimated that if the whole world were to adopt the food production methods used in the United States, as well as its diet, the world's known oil reserves would be gone in 29 years.

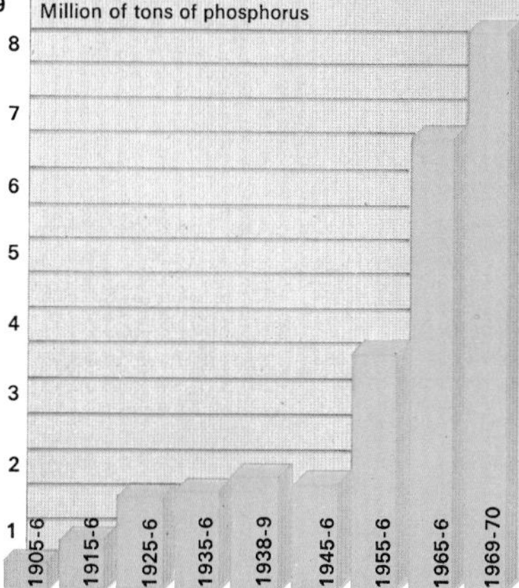

9
Million of tons of phosphorus
8
7
6
5
4
3
2
1
1905-6
1915-6
1925-6
1935-6
1938-9
1945-6
1955-6
1965-6
1969-70

9 Chemical fertilizers are being used in increasing quantities, as shown in this graph for phosphates expressed in millions of tons of phosphorus (the drop after 1938/39 was caused by World War II). Unfortunately the reserves of two of the three major plant nutrients, phosphorus and potassium, are limited and the processing of the third, nitrogen, requires large amounts of either natural gas or oil. Thus fertilizer shortages should grow increasingly worse.

History of agriculture

When *Homo sapiens* first evolved, he obtained food in the same ways as other animals, by gathering grain, fruits, roots, and nuts and by killing animals for meat. It was only about 10,000 years ago that people domesticated animals and discovered how to cultivate nutritious plants and harvest them.

Early farming methods

About 7000–9000 BC the invention of digging sticks and light plows for scratching the earth made it possible to cultivate light soils for crops. The basins of the Tigris and Euphrates rivers and the valley of the Nile became centers of great civilizations because farmers could produce enough food to supply urban populations. Similarly, farming evolved in northwest India, in north China, and in the Americas. Various plants were cultivated, such as rice in the East and corn and gourds in the Americas. Such primitive farming continues to this day in many undeveloped areas.

Ancient Greece and Rome imported grain from Egypt and Africa but also grew some grain of their own, as well as grapes, figs, and olives. The Greeks and the Romans plowed with scratch plows [3], and possibly used animal-drawn harrows. Sickles were used for harvesting the grain they cultivated (wheat and barley, not oats or rye). The system of farming was crop and fallow; that is, a crop was grown one year and the land left fallow the next to recover its fertility. Domesticated animals included horses, cattle, sheep, pigs, goats, poultry, and bees.

In northern Europe the forests were cleared from the land chosen for cultivation. Larger trees were felled, the brush cut, and the whole area burned. After a few crops the land was allowed to revert to scrub. This system, known as "slash and burn," is still practiced in parts of Central Africa and tropical America.

By the fall of the Roman Empire a new type of farming—the open field system [4]—was spreading all over western Europe. The tilled land was divided into three large fields cropped in a three-year rotation: wheat or rye in the first year; barley, oats, peas, and beans in the second; and then a year of fallow before beginning the rotation again. A new heavy, moldboard plow, hauled by two to eight oxen [5], was developed for plowing heavy soils.

When the Moors conquered most of Spain, they brought with them new crops—sugar cane, rice, and subtropical fruits—as well as Merino sheep, ancestors of the great flocks now bred in Australia. From Asia silkworms were brought into Italy and fed on mulberry leaves, and rice was grown in the south and the Piedmont.

New crops, methods, and machines

New crops and new foodstuffs, the most important of which was the potato, came to Europe from America and the Indies. Corn was rapidly adopted in Spain, southern France, and Italy, as was tobacco. Tomatoes and gourds were important novelties.

The most significant progress in farming techniques was made in Europe. By the fourteenth century farmers in the Low Countries began intensive cultivation by growing crops on the land formerly left fal-

CONNECTIONS

See also
306 The small farm
308 The farming corporation
310 Farm machinery and buildings
884 Origins of civilization
1090 Western European economy 1000–1250

1 Primitive agriculture involves the whole family in the task of providing enough food for subsistence. The field work is done mainly by women, after the men have completed the heavier work of clearing the land with oxen. While men tend the animals, women plant, harvest, and wage a constant battle against weeds. Work patterns of this sort persist in many peasant communities. The surplus of crop production over the subsistence level is often small; a year of crop failure from any cause may mean hunger and possibly even starvation in this inefficient system of agriculture.

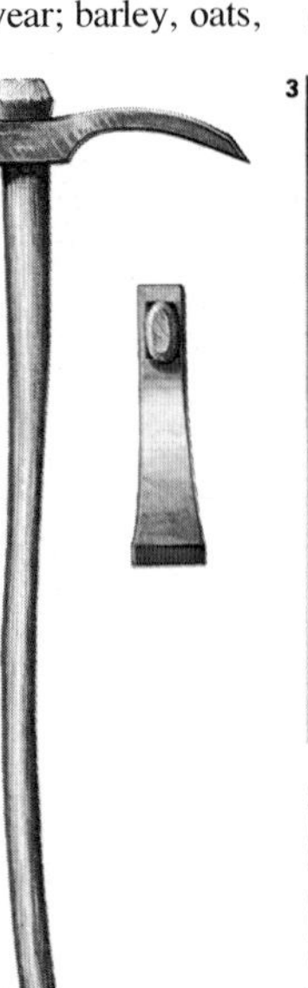

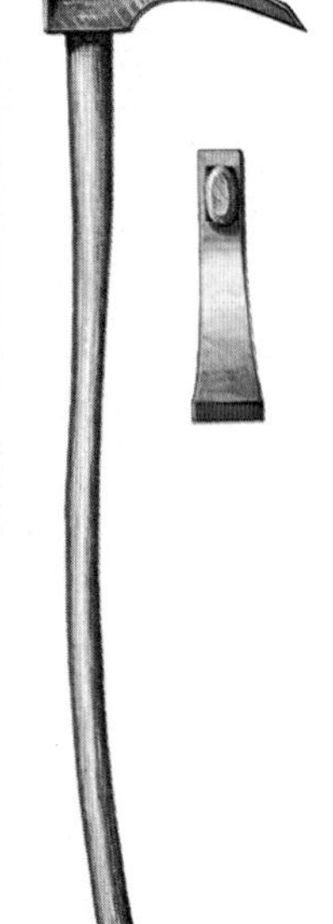

2 The mattock, or heavy hoe, was the basic and sometimes only tool used in early cultivation. It was used to break new ground or grub up roots and it served as a hoe when the crop was growing.

3 The scratch plow, still in use among peasant cultivators in some parts of the world, does not turn the soil over but breaks the surface for sowing. Originally dragged or pushed by men, it was later adapted for pulling by oxen, which doubled the area that a man could plow. Various methods of attachment were devised, usually with a rigid shoulder yoke pegged or strapped in place.

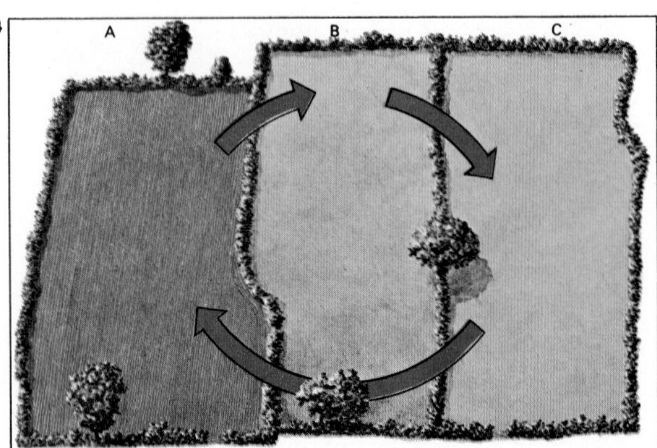

A
B
C

4 Medieval farming in Europe was based on a three-field rotation. One field [A] would be left fallow, the second [B] would grow wheat or rye, and the third [C] would contain barley, oats, beans, and peas. Unlike the modern example shown here, the medieval fields were vast, unfenced areas arranged around a village. Each field was divided into a large number of strips and each villager was allocated a number of strips befitting his status. As well as working his own land, the villager would also work that owned by the feudal lord of the manor. In spite of its use of crop rotation this system had many disadvantages, including the possibility of a badly farmed strip affecting adjacent strips.

5 Ox teams provided the basic power units of the farms of the Middle Ages in northern Europe. Sturdy moldboard plows extended farming to heavy soils that had defeated earlier cultivators. Cattle were still bred primarily as work animals, but their milk was sometimes made into butter and cheese, and the plow ox was fattened for slaughter when seven to nine years old. The working day of the oxen plow team was limited by the need for the animals to graze. The horses that replaced them could work longer hours and also could plow faster.

low. They planted chiefly grains, root crops, and fodder crops (clover, alfalfa, and rye grass) but also cultivated dye crops (madder, woad, and saffron). As mechanical skill developed, one of the foundations of modern mechanical farming—drilling seed by machine instead of broadcasting by hand—was invented.

The intensive cultivation of fodder crops made it necessary to abandon the open field system and to make fenced enclosures, both to protect the growing crops and to contain the grazing animals. A four-course rotation [6] replaced the earlier three-course rotation of open fields. This made for higher productivity, which in turn allowed more food for domestic animals. The animals were also being slowly improved by selective breeding.

The opening up of the American plains in the 19th century provided the real impetus for mechanization. The plains could grow millions of tons of wheat to feed the growing population of the industrial countries, but local labor was both scarce and expensive. By 1850 horse-drawn reaping machines were in use, and before long steam engines were used to power plowing, harvesting, and threshing.

Scientific farming and increased yields

The work once done by animals is today accomplished by tractors, while combine harvesters and other complex machines gather crops. An acre of wheat in AD 1200 might yield 5–6 bushels (420-530 liters per hectare); today an acre of wheat in Europe, America, Argentina, Australia, or Canada might yield 40–80 bushels (3,500–7,000 liters per hectare). In 1200 the yield of an acre was enough for perhaps two people for a year; today, in the advanced countries, an acre can supply 8 to 20 adults with bread for a year as well as seed for the next sowing.

Stock farming made unprecedented progress in the last hundred years. Farm animals have been improved by the production of more and better feeds and by selective breeding that uses the discoveries of genetics and such techniques as artificial insemination. They produce more meat, eggs, or milk in less time than before.

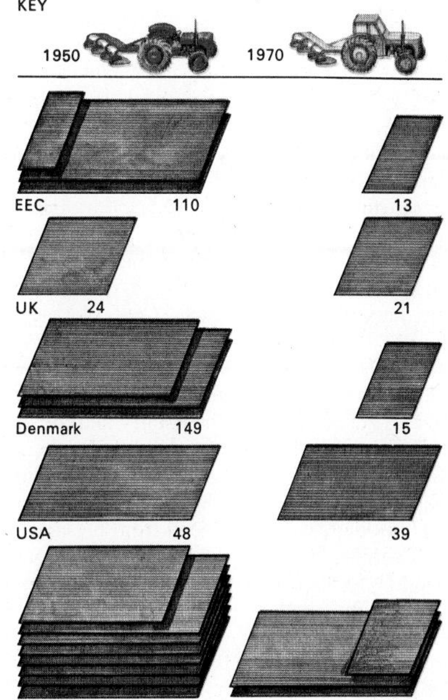
KEY
1950
1970
EEC
110
13
UK
24
21
Denmark
149
15
USA
48
39
USSR
390
117

A rapid replacement of human and animal muscle power by machines has taken place since World War II. This can easily be illustrated by dividing the area of farmed land by the number of tractors in developed countries to give the average number of hectares per tractor (1 hectare = 2.47 acres). In 1950 the USA and the UK were already mechanized, while parts of Europe were using horse-drawn machines and the USSR was recovering from war losses. By 1970 there were proportionately more tractors on the tiny farms of Western Europe, and large farms in the USA, and the USSR had switched to more powerful and versatile machines.

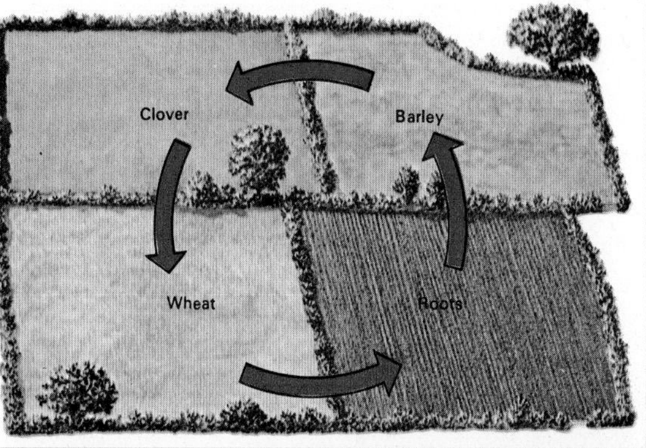
Clover
Barley
Wheat
Roots

6 By introducing new crops the four-field rotation eliminated the fallow year. Clover and turnips fed more stock and the manure from the stock helped in the growing of improved crops.

7 Stock breeders of the 18th and 19th centuries considerably improved beef cattle. The new breeds produced the large amounts of meat demanded by the growing population of northern Europe.

7

9

8 Modern farming is becoming increasingly specialized. The flat, fertile silts of South Lincolnshire, England, seen here from the air, carry no livestock. This is an area of cash crops: potatoes, sugar beets, field vegetables, and bulbs, with wheat as a break in the rotation. Most farms are large and use many tractors and other machines. In many areas huge investments in large-scale crop processing and marketing have transformed farming into "agribusiness."

9 Large numbers of beef cattle are kept throughout the year in open yards such as this US feed lot. Several thousand cattle many be assembled for fattening on a balanced diet of corn, silage, alfalfa hay, and mineral supplements. With mechanized feeding, labor requirements are small and each animal's growth is rapid. The capital required for such heavy production is large, and the owners are more likely to be corporate companies than traditional private farmers.

The small farm

Most of the world's farming is carried on in units that are small by the standards of North America or Australia. Land area is not the best measure of productivity in farming, however. On very fertile soil, with plenty of labor available, output can be high and special buildings and equipment can enable a livestock farmer or truck farmer to earn a good income by himself.

Traditional peasant farming

Much traditional peasant agriculture was carried on to keep the farmer's family alive rather than to earn a cash profit. The farmer often paid his rent in kind as a form of sharecropping. From the 17.3 acres (7 hectares) of a typical old-style Tuscan Italian farm [1], 47 percent of the produce went to the landlord and the remainder fed the eight adults and seven children working and living there, with only a small surplus for sale. This holding grew cereals, potatoes, beans, peas, other vegetables and greens for market, vines, olives, apples, pears, peaches, apricots, cherries, plums, and walnuts. It had four milking cows, two draft oxen, two pigs for meat, and a horse. Wine from the grapes and oil from olives were used on the farm and the main cash income was derived from the daily sale of vegetables in the local market. Such farms were still found in Italy until recently.

In northern Europe small farms of a different type developed during the nineteenth century as a result of increasing job opportunities outside farming and of a growing demand in the cities for meat and milk products. Areas of 25 to 125 acres (10–50 hectares) with dairy cows, pigs, and hens, were worked by a farmer and his son, or one hired man, the farmer's wife assisting with the poultry and the calves. In Scandinavia, a network of local cooperatives grew up to undertake the manufacture of butter, cheese, and other products from milk and of bacon from pigs. A somewhat similar pattern developed in parts of Ireland but was based mainly on grassland farming. Also using grass, small farms in the Netherlands and New Zealand could compete effectively in world markets for butter and cheese.

The majority of small farmers in Scandinavia [2], Ireland, and New Zealand were, or became, owners of their land. Government policies often encouraged the breakup of large holdings and provided loans on easy terms for small farmers to buy the land they worked. In countries where cereal growing was not protected by import duties, livestock farmers had the advantage of buying cheap feed from abroad , which enabled them to keep more animals than their land would support.

In some of these countries, and in many areas where agriculture was once run on traditional peasant lines, small farms have now been absorbed into larger units. Farm wages have risen continuously and the very small farmer finds it difficult to earn enough to pay a hired worker.

Help from the government

Voluntary amalgamations of small farms have been accelerated in some European countries (including France, the Netherlands. West Germany, and the United Kingdom) by official programs to provide

CONNECTIONS

See also
308 The farming corporation
310 Farm machinery and buildings

1 The buildings and yard of an Italian farm of 17.3 acres (7 hectares) near Florence had to serve a variety of needs and enterprises. The farm was divided into 20 small enclosures, some of them terraced on a steep slope. Much of the cropping was in the ground under fruit trees. The crops provided a meager living over the greater part of the year for the 15 people living on the farm. Tools and equipment were simple and the tenant's only capital was in the form of animals and growing crops. This situation was not unusual in the south of Europe, in areas where there was only small prospect of alternative employment. Attempts to rationalize farming in these areas have created political problems.

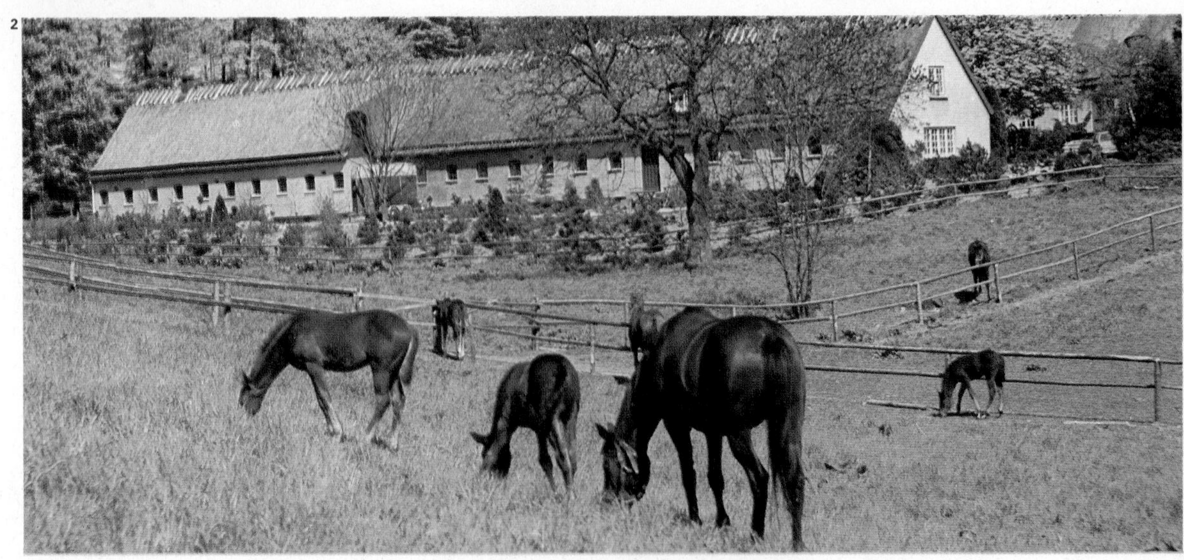

2 Scandinavian farms have been designed to be worked by at most two men, with family help at peak periods of the year. Severe winters call for substantial buildings to house the livestock, as on this horse farm. Animals are the main source of income and most of the tillable land is devoted to grain and forage to feed them. Milk from the cows goes to the creamery for butter making and the skim is returned; mixed with barley it feeds the best bacon pigs. This system is giving way to greater geographical specialization in Denmark. Other Scandinavian farmers often work in forestry in winter.

retirement pensions for older farmers and retrain younger men to work outside agriculture. The aim, not always successful in practice, is to bring the minimum reward of the full-time farmer up to that of an employed man. In assessing the viability of small farms and their qualification for government assistance United Kingdom economists use a unit that takes into account factors other than mere land area. Each enterprise on a farm is classified in terms of "standard man-days" [Key], based on average performance over the whole country; ten days are allotted per year for each milking cow, for instance, and five for each hectare of wheat or barley. If these add up to less than 275 the property is not considered to be a full-time farm. Standard man-days measure the farmer's capital investment in equipment, stock, and land.

Part-time small farms have been an important element in rural life over the centuries. They are still a common, though diminishing, feature of parts of Europe and the United States. Depending on geographic location, farming may be combined with fishing (in Scotland), with forestry (in Scandinavia), with small-scale mining or country crafts (in south Germany), or with part-time and seasonal work in nearby factories. Production from this form of agriculture may not be vital to the national economy, but for many people part-time farming satisfies a social need for an outdoor way of life and a certain independence [5].

Farming and the environment

Preservation of viable small farms, even if they are worked only part-time, is increasingly seen as important to tourism and to the wide enjoyment of the countryside. The traditional picture that many people have of farming and their knowledge of the countryside often come from small mixed farms on which they have stayed as summer guests. In the more difficult, if picturesque, environment of the mountains and uplands the disappearance of small farms could leave a depopulated wilderness. Year-round life is hard on such farms, and some countries have therefore introduced special programs of financial assistance.

KEY

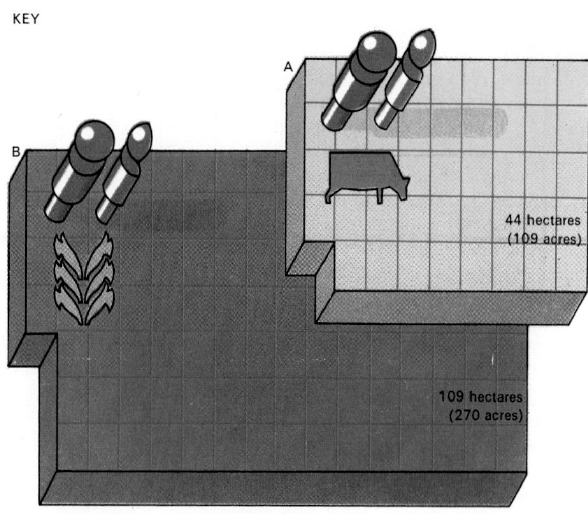
A
B
44 hectares
(109 acres)
109 hectares
(270 acres)

Two contrasting farm patterns both need the labor equivalent of a man and a half. The livestock farm [A] will have help from the farmer's wife and family at times, and possibly from a retired person or student. On the crop farm [B] the wife will not work but contractors will be used for some work and casual labor will be hired at busy periods.

3

1 Sugar beet
2 Fodder maize
3 Summer fallow
4 Milk tanker
5 Cattle in pasture
6 Barley
7 Oats
8 Glasshouse crops
9 Pigs
10 Silo
11 Wheat
12 Fowl
13 Ducks
14 Clover
15 Orchard
16 Farmhouse
17 Vegetables

3 A wide range of enterprises could be carried out on a small farm if they were all gathered together. In practice the number on a small mixed farm is not likely to total more than about half a dozen. In areas of high rainfall the emphasis will be on grazing livestock; where summers are dry crops will be of most importance.

4

4 Farming in Switzerland is restricted to a series of small farms. The high altitude of most of the agricultural land and the high rainfall prevent farming from being a major part of the Swiss economy; in recent years it has employed only about 20% of the population.

5

5 New England is one part of the United States where small mixed farms of an earlier traditional pattern survive. Many are now owned by city dwellers as places for relaxation and a change of scene, with caretaker workers in charge. This pattern is also spreading in Europe.

The farming corporation

Agriculture organized to provide the balanced food requirements of a community is probably as old as the first farms and towns in the Fertile Crescent of the ancient Near East. High production farming, or "agri-business," involving capital investment as well as scientific management and business techniques, is a response to the demands of the huge industrial populations of the Western world, and its benefits may be extended ultimately to countries that are now greatly undernourished. It is designed to stabilize if not increase profits in an area subject to the uncertainties of climate and of nature generally.

Surplus, not subsistence

The experience of English farming, notably in the southern and eastern counties in the eighteenth century, pointed the way by producing crops that were surplus to the needs of a simple subsistence economy (this still remains the occupation of farmers in the greater part of the world) in order to supply the burgeoning population of London and for export.

The Industrial Revolution provided an historic impetus toward the modern practice. In countries where the rapidly increasing urban population had led to a demand for food that could not be met by traditional farming methods, a market emerged for large-scale farming production and for imported food from developing production areas. Yet meat and dairy produce from far off regions could not be shipped in good condition to the urban markets. The answer to the problem was the introduction of mechanically refrigerated railroad cars, trucks, and ships. Modern techniques of refrigeration have developed to play a fundamental role in food distribution and in the organization of "agri business" with its huge output of deep-frozen, plastic-wrapped food for storage in domestic freezers.

Modern farming techniques

The modern farm may be one of a group of several operating under the control of a central organization, each larger in size than the national average. Economic studies have shown that farms of medium size tend to be more efficient than large ones. This is particularly true of dairying, in which there must be a close relationship between the milker and the cows he or she handles, and of farms with mixed cropping, in which timing calls for close supervision. Further limitations may be set on the size of some single livestock units to prevent the risk of disease and to aid the disposal of waste products.

Difficulties of supervision have been most successfully overcome with poultry, both for meat and egg production. In this area "factory farming" [1] has developed to its greatest extent. Birds bred specifically for a controlled environment and for rapid maturity spend their whole lives in buildings and are kept in very large numbers. The buildings are insulated against changes in outside temperature, with forced ventilation. For egg production, lighting simulates an even day length to eliminate the natural spring rise and autumn decline in laying that occurs out of doors. In this totally artificial environment birds are hatched, grown to maturity, and slaughtered in the hundreds

CONNECTIONS

See also
306 The small farm
310 Farm machinery and buildings

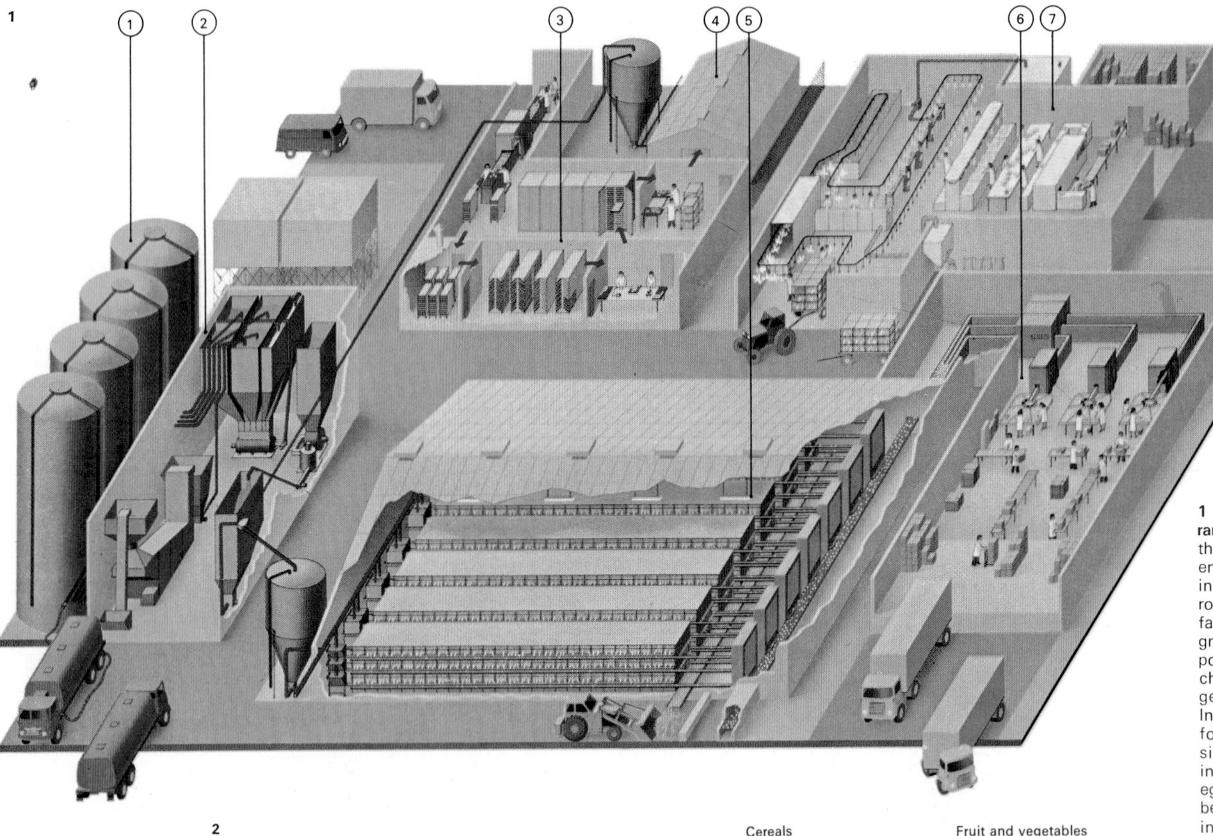
1
1
2
3
4
5
6
7

1 Far from the free-range life, tens of thousands of chickens spend their lives in an artificial environment. Factory farming has made its greatest strides in poultry breeding—chickens, ducks, geese, and turkeys. In a typical plant, food stored in grain silos [1] is milled into pellets [2]. The eggs, which have been checked for infertility, are incubated [3] and the chicks reared [4]. From there the young birds pass to the battery house [5] with its tiers of cages, automatic feeding and droppings disposal. The eggs are graded and dispatched [6], while birds destined for the table are transported to the broiler house [7], slaughtered and prepared before being deep-frozen and packed in plastic for dispatch to the chain stores and their customers' deep freezers.

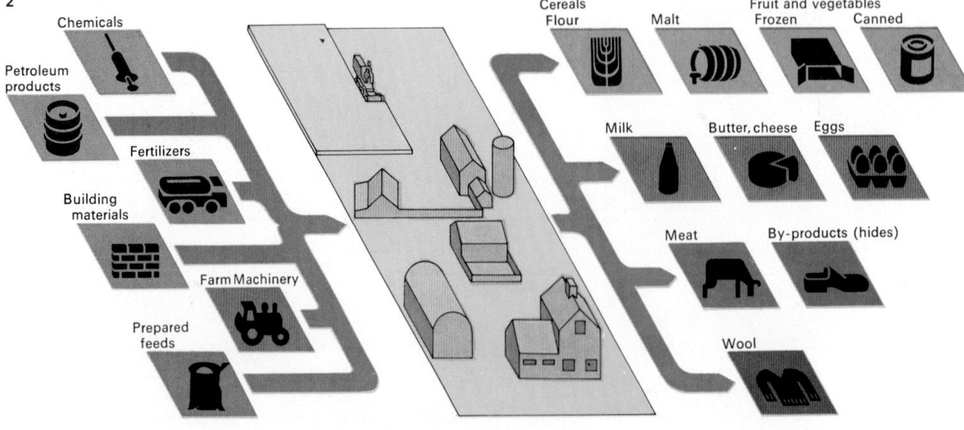
2
Chemicals
Petroleum products
Fertilizers
Building materials
Farm Machinery
Prepared feeds
Cereals Flour
Malt
Fruit and vegetables
Frozen
Canned
Milk
Butter, cheese
Eggs
Meat
By-products (hides)
Wool

2 Agriculture and industry in recent years have become highly interdependent. The farm, once self-sufficient, is now an important market for suppliers of petroleum products, crop dressings, synthetic fertilizers, machinery, and building materials. The farm in turn supplies food—cereals, fruit and various vegetables (fresh, frozen and canned), as well as dairy products, meat, and many kinds of animal by-products.

of thousands before being frozen to keep the plant's output steady throughout the year. This applies even to turkeys, where the market is seasonal, as at Thanksgiving and Christmas.

Production and processing

Pigs are also raised for slaughter in large numbers, but the breeding units are not on the scale of those used for poultry and are often in the hands of specialists rather than farmers. Slaughtering and processing are performed by outside commercial companies or by cooperatives, which may be wholly or only partly owned by farmers.

The integration of beef production and processing along similar lines is mainly confined to the United States, where the trend toward larger units for many types of livestock production was originally fostered by feed supply companies to increase their own sales. In Australia and New Zealand [3] much farming has always been on a large scale and geared to the requirements of export markets. This has led to highly developed methods of organization, often on a cooperative basis, with powerful producer boards and finance companies as well as firms specializing in the processing, packing, exporting, and marketing of food products.

Elsewhere the commodities most successfully produced by large units have been cereals, sugar, tropical industrial crops (tea, cotton, and rubber), vegetables (where there is a ready access to large markets) and salads (in the Netherlands, where land is at a premium, multistory greenhouses are in use), and orchard fruit.

Not all enterprises lend themselves to organization as large units—a fact discovered in places where agriculture has been nationalized or collectivized. In the Soviet Union much of the national supply of fresh meat and vegetables still comes from private plots worked by individual members of the collective.

The techniques of modern profitable farming call for large amounts of capital borrowed from banks or other outside investors, which enables more raw materials to be bought or products to be processed.

KEY

Harvest combines move across an enormous wheat field near Walla Walla, Washington.

3 New Zealand farming was for many years geared almost entirely to the export of dairy products, lamb, and wool. The climate of the islands favors grass growth for much of the year and large-scale farming is therefore almost all pastoral. Sheep farming, based partly on the experience of early Scottish settlers, utilizes three different environments. Mountain country in the South Island [A] is devoted almost completely to wool production from Merino [1] and Corriedale [2] sheep. The fertility of the high country has been greatly increased by using aircraft to spread lime and fertilizers, thus encouraging the growth of grasses and clover and improving their quality. The lower hill country [B] where conditions are less severe, is mainly stocked with Cheviot ewes [4], which, mated with Romney Marsh rams [3], produce crossbred ewes [6] that are hardy, productive and good milkers. The other main product of this zone is wool. When the crossbred ewes are moved down to the plains [C], where the stock density is greater, they are mated with a Southdown [5] or other Down breed rams and the offspring [7] are fattened for slaughter, as are the male crossbreds brought from the hills. This well-planned system makes possible the production of uniform carcasses, which are carefully graded for weight and "finish," and has given the product a high reputation in meat markets abroad. New Zealand is now developing new markets for sheep of a different kind. One of the most important customers for these is Japan, whose meat consumption has continued to increase in recent years.

3A

3B

3C

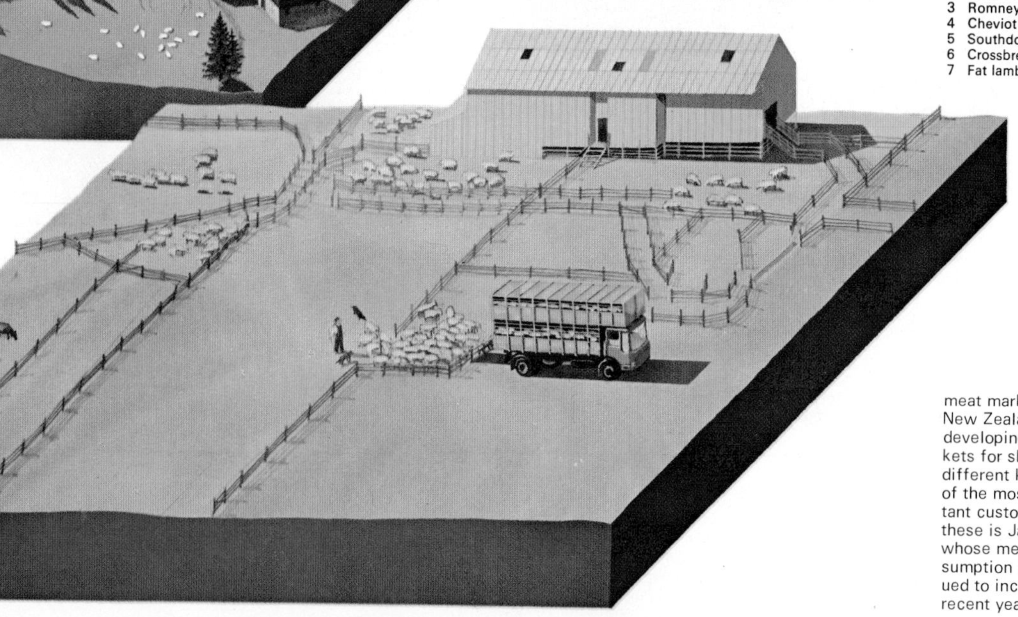

A High country farming
B Hill country farming
C Lowland farming
1 Merino
2 Corriedale
3 Romney ram
4 Cheviot ewe
5 Southdown ram
6 Crossbreed
7 Fat lamb

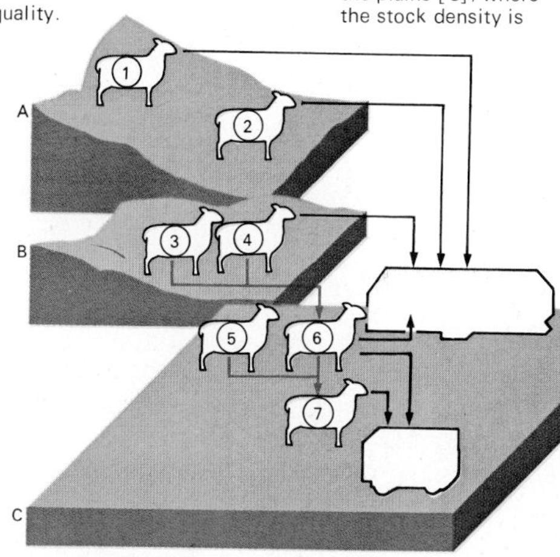

Farm machinery and buildings

Mobile farm machinery first came into general use during the nineteenth century. Before this a farmer with manual farming methods could grow little more than enough food for himself and his family. Some attempts had been made to mechanize such jobs as threshing, using a horse driven in a circle as the source of power. Before tractors, steam-powered plowing, although widely adopted on difficult soils, involved winching the implement from one side of the field to the other.

The most successful horse-drawn farm machine was the reaper invented by Cyrus McCormick in 1831, which cut grain crops and tied them into bundles. It made large-scale growing possible where labor was limited, as on the prairies of North America.

The rise of modern machinery

The development of the internal combustion engine replaced the horse teams with tractors [3]. At first these merely pulled trailed implements or replaced steam engines for stationary work when fitted with a belt-drive from the side. A hydraulic system, powered by a small rotary pump, enabled other implements to be attached directly at the front or rear; these were raised for transport and lowered for work.

Grain harvesting with a reaper-binder still involved manual work when assembling the cut and bound bundles for drying, carting, stacking, and handling for threshing. The combine harvester [2], controlled by one man, delivers the threshed grain in a single operation. As successive models have increased the work capacity, they have been fitted with their own power units, as have other large field machines.

Other types of farm machines include tillage machines, which break up the soil and prepare it for the seed. Various kinds of plows are the best known of this type and they do the heavy work. Rollers are used to flatten the larger clods of earth, and harrows make the soil surface fine and soft so that the seed can be easily buried. Sowing machines place the seed in the soil. Broadcasting machines sow seeds such as grass and clover at random, while drills that place seed in neat rows and at a given depth are used for crops such as wheat, barley, and root vegetables. Precision drills space the plants correctly and protect the seed from birds. Cultivators do the hoeing; they kill the weeds and keep fallow land from being overrun with weeds. The last main category comprises livestock machines. Milking machines, worked by vacuum pumps, have replaced the hand milker, and the milk is delivered by machine directly to the cooler. Animal feed is mixed and carried by air flow to the feeding point, and manure is also handled mechanically in the buildings and in the fields.

Development of farm buildings

Buildings have undergone radical changes in design and layout since 1940. The traditional European pattern [5] consisted of a group of structures around a yard or a number of yards, with solid outside walls for protection against bad weather and for the security of the stock. Typically, such an assembly would include a barn for storage of grain and forage, a shed for cows where the milking took place, a dairy, separate

CONNECTIONS

See also
306 The small farm
308 The farming corporation

1

1 Horse-drawn reaper-binders opened up the grain lands of the New World to large scale export production and had a far-reaching effect on world trade. Seasonal workers were still needed to assemble the bundles into piles for drying and to load them onto carts for transport back to the farm for threshing.

2

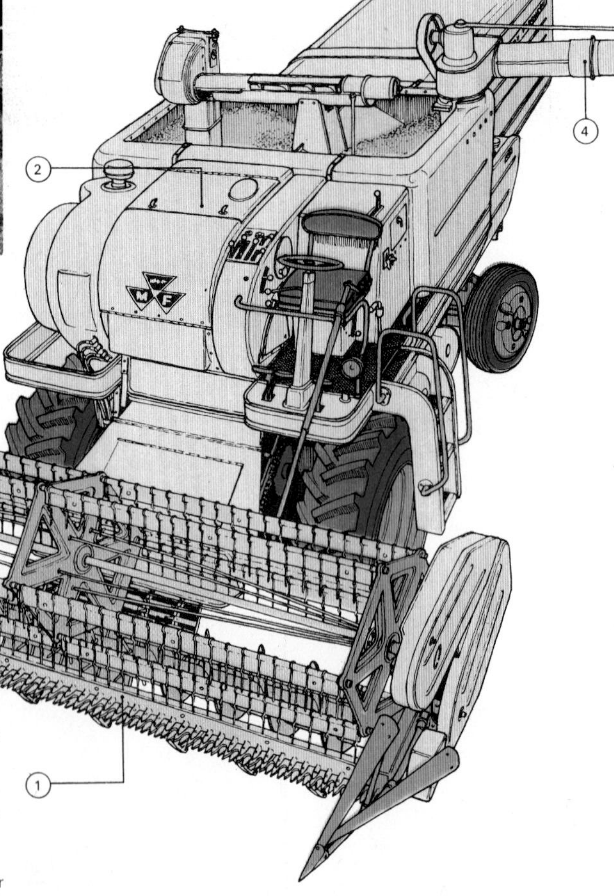

1
2
3
4

2 The combine harvester does its own threshing in the field, separating grain from straw, sieving out small weed seeds, and blowing away the chaff. Grain is collected in a bulk tank, then discharged into a servicing track. The main parts are: the cutter-bar assembly [1]; the threshing area [2] with beaters, sieves, and a fan to drive out the chaff; the straw walkers [3], where more grain is shaken out and the straw discharged; and the grain tank and discharge [4].

3

4

3 A modern high-power tractor can carry work implements both in front and at the rear. The bucket is carried on the hydraulic system and the operator, using a single lever, can manipulate it from his seat. The cab provides protection against overturning.

4 Most cultivating machinery is mounted on the 3-point linkage at the tractor's rear and connected to the power-takeoff shaft. It can be raised by the hydraulic system for transport and adjusted by it to control the depth or height of working. Implements such as this rotary cultivator can carry out several tasks at one pass of the field, reducing time and soil consolidation from the repeated passage of the tractor wheels.

stable boxes for horses, sties for pigs, and open-fronted shelter for the beef cattle, which trod straw into manure in the yards during the winter months.

Modern farm buildings are of two main types. The first and most usual was made possible by the development of wide-span metal, concrete, or laminated wood beams that carried lightweight roofing material without the need for an intermediate support. This meant that tractors and other machines could be driven anywhere in the building without obstruction. The basic "Dutch barn" [6] can be subdivided in any way that suits the farming system, given exterior cladding (for insulation) against the weather, and it can also be enlarged at the sides by adding lean-to extensions for purposes where height is not essential.

Parts of the covered area can be used for different purposes in the course of the year, for example for housing stock at one time and maintaining machinery at another. For dairy cows, the cow shed has been replaced by an open area with individual cubicles for lying down, a loafing area, and a bulk feeding area. Milking is done in a parlor adjoining the dairy to which the milk is piped, and concentrated rations may be automatically allocated to each individual cow by computer.

Controlled environment house

The second main type of building is the controlled environment house for intensive production [7] of pigs, broiler chickens, and eggs. This is normally a fairly low structure, with the hens housed in wire cages. The eggs roll onto the conveyor belts and are removed to a special egg-packing room. The interior is completely isolated from the outside world; the lighting is operated to make "days" and "nights" so that the hens lay eggs more often. There is also forced ventilation to control the temperature; except for piglets and young chicks, housed animals generate their own heating.

The closed yard has given way to a grid of all-weather concrete roads to carry the farm animals and materials, and to facilitate the delivery and dispatch of feed, fertilizer, and produce [Key].

KEY

Traffic around the buildings of a crop farm with livestock is considerable at any time of the year, particularly at harvest. A modern layout takes account of this. A hard surface around the buildings [1] not only allows free access for vehicles and machinery but also keeps animals clean (important for milking cows). Traffic concentration points include reception and loading areas [2] for grain and potatoes, the area where silage crops are unloaded from the field into towers [3], and points where livestock are handled [4]. Few farmers are able to start such an elaborate layout from scratch and therefore must make some compromises.

5

5 Traditional farm buildings and layouts are often very old and embody the needs and practices of different eras. This one belongs to the farming days of 19th-century Europe, with modern additions such as the Dutch barn [1]. There are storage buildings [2], an open-fronted shelter at the rear of the yard for steers to be fattened in the winter [3], a cowshed [4], a small range of pigsties [5], and stable boxes for horses [6]. These substantial and expensively constructed buildings are often difficult to adapt to modern mechanized agriculture.

6 Modern general purpose buildings consist of a light roof carried on wide beams high enough to admit fully laden vehicles and to allow for storage. The lean-to is an economical addition, needing only one set of uprights. The rest of the weight is taken by the original building. Cladding may be used to keep weather out and as temporary insulation. For bulk storage of potatoes, a layer of straw bales on the inside is provided. Cattle may be given access to concrete-floored yards for bulk feeding.

7

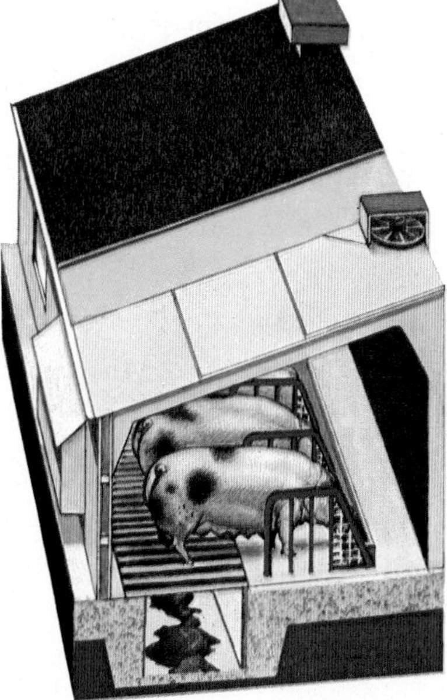

7 Intensive animal production calls for special housing to save on labor and the cost of feed. Ventilation and, sometimes, heating are needed to keep the animals at an optimum temperature; otherwise feeding is affected. With a high concentration of numbers in a small space there is an added risk of infectious diseases and a high standard of hygiene is essential. With hens, egg laying is related to day length; to maintain regularity, hours of artificial daylight are kept fairly constant. Buildings of this kind are normally low and have special arrangements for dealing with the large quantities of manure produced.

The living soil

All forms of life on land depend directly or indirectly on soil [Key]. Soil is a result of all the processes of physical and chemical weathering on the barren, underlying rock mass of the earth that it covers, and varies in depth from an inch or so to several yards. The depth of soil is measured either by the distance to which plants send down their roots or by the depth of soil directly influencing their systems. In some places only a very thin layer is necessary to support life.

Pedology [2], the study of soil and its unique biological, chemical, and physical properties, is a science that first came into its own at the close of the nineteenth century when the Russian geologist Vasilii Dokuchaev (1846–1903) identified the basic determining factors in the morphology—structure or form—of soils.

The organic content of soil

If soil is the outcome of time and weather at work upon rock it remains an unconsolidated mass of inorganic particles until it acquires a minimum organic content and plants take root and deposit their litter. As the organic matter accumulates, fine humus builds up in the upper soil horizons [1], enriching them chemically and providing an environment for a wide variety of life forms. In the course of time, plants, fungi, bacteria, worms, insects, and small burrowing animals reproduce in the soil and thrive in the ecosystem of a mature soil [3].

The formation of soil is the result of the interaction of five major elements—the parent rock, land relief, time, climate, and decay. The parent rock is the source of the vast bulk of all soil material. During weathering this rock is physically reduced to a mass of gravel, sand, silt, and clay. Soil is not always identical to its parent material because of the numerous chemical transformations and physical disturbances it may undergo during its formation.

Land relief is another factor influencing the creation of soils. On steep slopes only thin, dry layers accumulate because of the rapid water runoff. In level, high country, soil layers dense with clay tend to accumulate. Where organic decay is slow, in poorly drained regions, thick layers of dark organic soils build up. A hillside receiving direct sun will acquire a different soil from that hidden from direct exposure because of the differences in moisture content. Time is another passive agent in the formation of soils. Young soils have almost no distinct horizon markings, whereas mature ones acquire a well marked profile that undergoes only minimal changes with the passage of time.

Climate and soil composition

The single most important factor in the development of soil is climate [4, 5]. Water is essential to all chemical and biological change in soil; as it percolates through, it leaches the surface layers and deposits material in the subsoil. In areas of heavy rainfall the soil undergoes extreme leaching and is rendered relatively sterile. In contrast, excessive evaporation in arid climates results in the building up of salt deposits in the soil.

Temperature directly affects the rate of chemical and biological activity in the soil. In tropical climates where such activity is

CONNECTIONS

See also
316 Improving crops
474 Earthworms, clamworms, and roundworms
484 The joint-legged animals
488 Spiders and scorpions

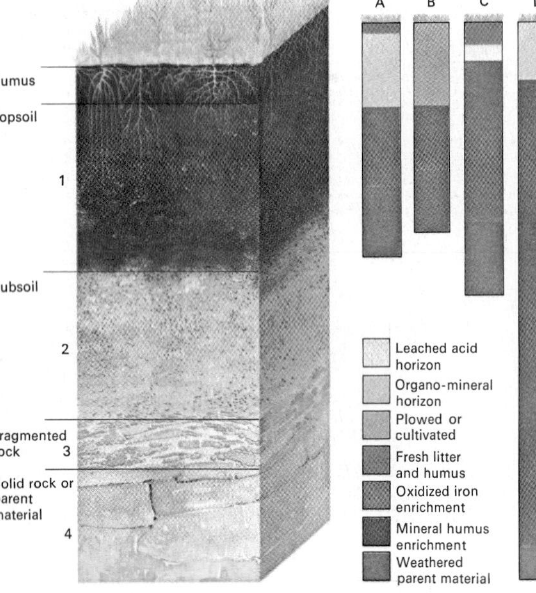

1
Humus
Topsoil
1
Subsoil
2
Fragmented rock 3
Solid rock or parent material
4
A
B
C
D
Leached acid horizon
Organo-mineral horizon
Plowed or cultivated
Fresh litter and humus
Oxidized iron enrichment
Mineral humus enrichment
Weathered parent material

1 The profile of the soil reaches down from the most recently deposited topsoil to the parent bedrock, revealing the various recognizable layers or horizons. Beneath a horizon of gray-black topsoil [1] and its upper layer of humus there lies the subsoil layer [2], which, while poorer in organic materials, is richer in accumulated minerals than both the topsoil and humus above it. Horizon [3] is made up of the partially weathered particles of the lifeless parent bedrock [4] at the bottom. Profile [A] is of acid brown earth found in temperate climates—this one on sandy rock—and [B] is a cultivated brown earth of the same climatic region. Gray leached podzol [C] is typical of wet, cool climates—for example, the taiga in the USSR—while oxisol [D], a thick red soil containing iron compounds, is found in humid, tropical lands where chemical and biological activities are both high.

2 The composition and color of a soil identifies it to a pedologist. This tundra soil [A] has a dark, peaty surface. Light-colored desert soil [B] is coarse and poor in organic matter. Chestnut-brown soil [C] and chernozem [D]—Russian for "black earth"—are humus-rich grassland soils typical of the steppes and prairies of North America. The reddish, leached latosol [E] of tropical savannas has a thin but rich humus layer. Podzolic soils are typical of northern climates where rainfall is heavy but evaporation is slow. They include the organically rich brown forest podzol [F] and the gray-brown podzol [H] and the gray stony podzol [I] that supports mixed growths of conifers and hardwoods. All are relatively acid. The red-yellow podzol [G] of pine forests is highly leached.

2 A B C D E F G H I

3 The soil is a complex ecosystem. A square yard of fertile soil teems with more than one billion individual forms of life, from microscopic organisms to insects, worms, and large animals such as burrowing rodents. In the steppes, for example, these include marmots, susliks, hamsters, and mole rats. All of these organisms, both simple and compex, play an important part in helping to aerate the soil and to accelerate the processes of decay and of humus formation.

3

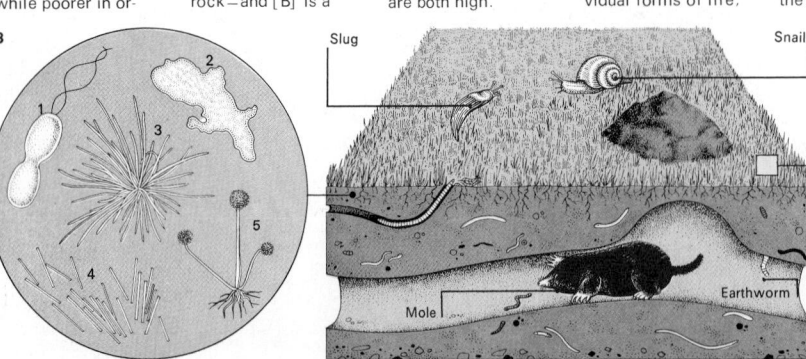

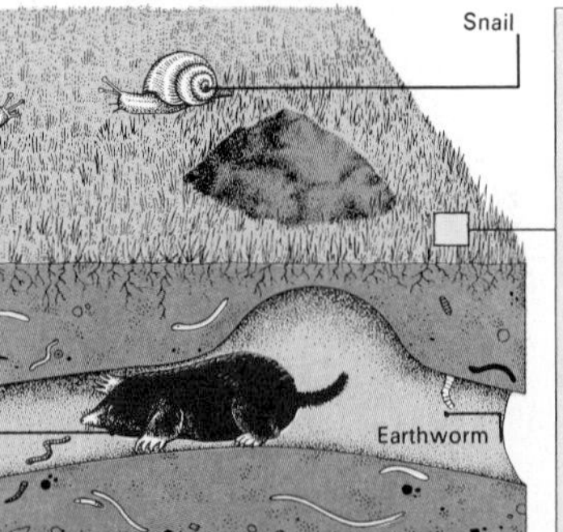

Slug
Snail
Mole
Earthworm

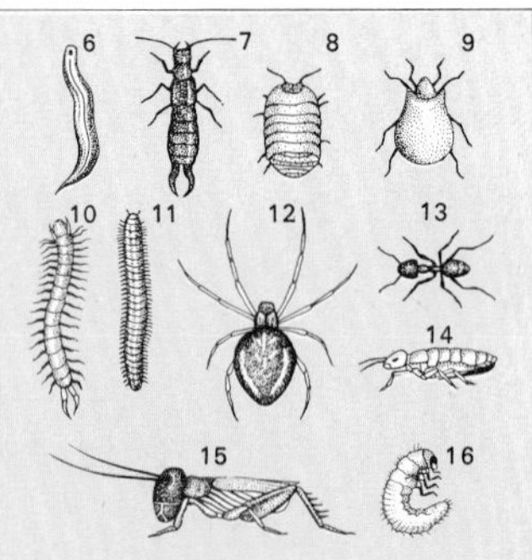

6
7
8
9
10
11
12
13
14
15
16

1 Bacterium
2 Protozoan
3 Alga
4 Virus
5 Fungus
6 Eelworm
7 Earwig
8 Woodlouse
9 Mite
10 Centipede
11 Millipede
12 Spider
13 Ant
14 Springtail
15 Cricket
16 Cockchafer larva

high, decay is rapid and the soils are poor in humus. In tundra regions, where the topsoil is frozen for more than half the year and the subsoil is permanently below the freezing point, the reverse holds true; organic matter accumulates in thick layers.

Lateritic soils are an excellent illustration of the effects of climate. In hot, wet environments such soils are highly leached, and contain little other than deposits of iron and aluminum oxides. If directly exposed to the tropical sun, these soils become a baked, bricklike mass known as laterite to which vegetation cannot return.

The importance of decay

A variety of biological factors influence soil formation. Plants stabilize the earth by reducing erosion and surface runoff. They also maintain soil fertility by concentrating organic material and nutrients back at the surface after they have been washed down. As they decay the plants also provide the fine organic humus litter vital to soil life.

The role of soil bacteria is crucial, for they not only fix nitrogen from the air in a form that plants can use but also promote the processes of decay. Animals whose homes are in the soil have a mechanical function in shifting and aerating the soil. It has been estimated that earthworms alone can turn over between 0.4 and 4 tons of soil per acre per year. As they eat and excrete the soil they also change its texture and composition.

Under normal conditions soils naturally replenish themselves. Yet where ruinous agricultural practices prevail, soils can easily deteriorate in fertility. A dramatic illustration of this is the dust bowl, a man-made desert from which the valuable topsoil has been removed by the wind in conditions of continuing drought. This is brought about by certain farming practices in regions with unsuitable climates. Soil conservation is the effort to avoid this destruction of the soil and to maintain it at the most productive level possible. This requires a combination of all the techniques of soil science in preparing the land, irrigating it, fertilizing it, and planting the right crops to stabilize the soil and prevent erosion.

KEY

The whole structure of life on earth, with the enormous diversity of plant and animal types—herbivores, carnivores, man himself—is dependent upon a thin, nutrient and moisture-rich mantle of soil.

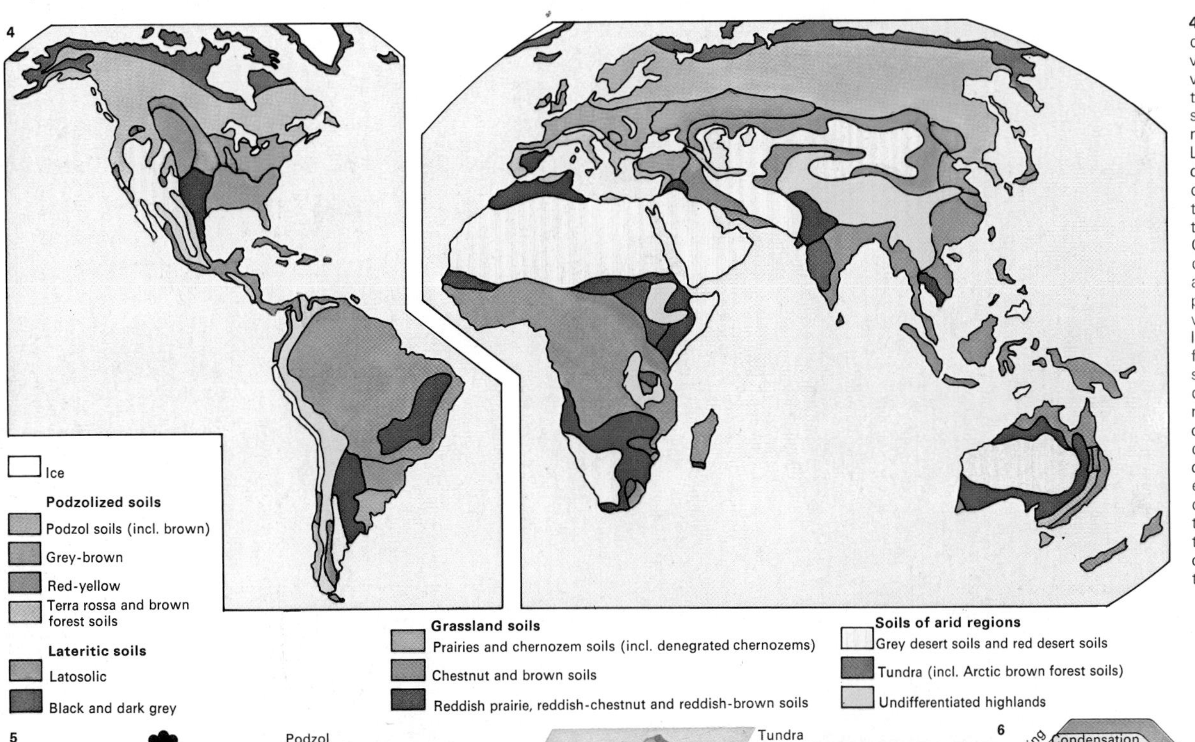
4
Ice
Podzolized soils
Podzol soils (incl. brown)
Grey-brown
Red-yellow
Terra rossa and brown forest soils
Lateritic soils
Latosolic
Black and dark grey
Grassland soils
Prairies and chernozem soils (incl. denegrated chernozems)
Chestnut and brown soils
Reddish prairie, reddish-chestnut and reddish-brown soils
Soils of arid regions
Grey desert soils and red desert soils
Tundra (incl. Arctic brown forest soils)
Undifferentiated highlands

4 Soil groups can be correlated with the various climatic and vegetation zones of the earth. Podzolic soils are found in moist, cool climates. Latosols and black or dark gray soils are common to the equatorial regions between the tropics of Cancer and Capricorn. In sub-humid and semi-arid temperate zones of the world, where the land is at its most fruitful, the prevalent soils are chernozem, chestnut, brown, and reddish prairie. Gray or red soils are typical of the near-barren desert regions of the earth while subpolar climates are characterized by the scanty tundra soils bearing only sparse vegetation.

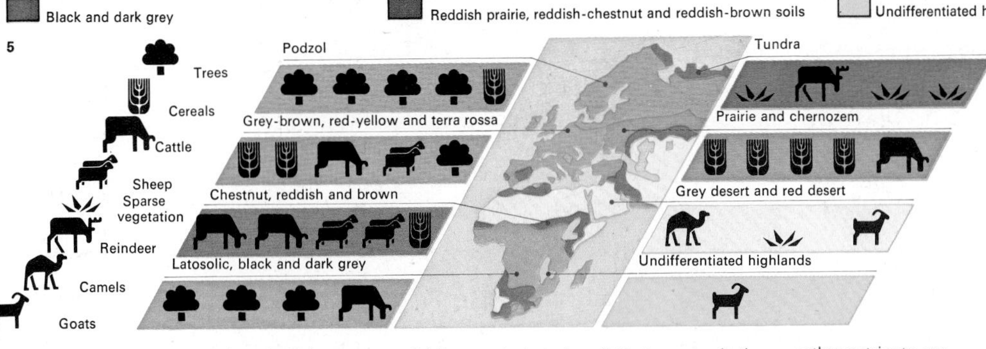
5
Trees
Cereals
Cattle
Sheep
Sparse vegetation
Reindeer
Camels
Goats
Podzol
Tundra
Grey-brown, red-yellow and terra rossa
Prairie and chernozem
Chestnut, reddish and brown
Grey desert and red desert
Latosolic, black and dark grey
Undifferentiated highlands

5 Climate exerts the strongest influence on the nature of the soil on which plant and animal life depends, and this, in turn, determines which species will flourish best in its particular area. Tundra regions, where the soil is frozen for at least half the year, and desert soils can support only a slender native plant and animal population, but ephemeral life—in the tundra, during its brief summer, or the desert regions after exceptional rainfall—will attract a considerable visiting population of animals. Other soil types, such as latosol, support a wide range of plants and animal—in the African savannas, for example, with their huge populations of vegetation-eating herbivores and attendant carnivorous predators.

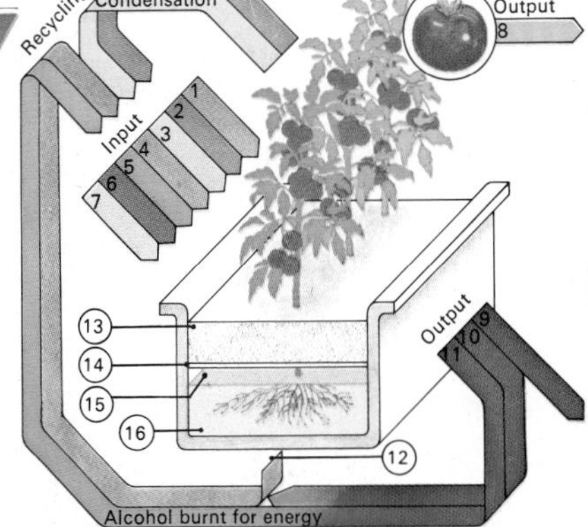
6
Recycling
Condensation
Output
8
Input
1
2
3
4
5
6
7
Output
9
10
11
13
14
15
16
12
Alcohol burnt for energy

6 Hydroponics is the science of making substitutes for soil and has been successful in growing plants in totally soilless conditions. In hydroponic agriculture all plant requirements including oxygen, light, water, mineral salts, and other nutrients, are artificially provided within the protected and temperature-controlled environments of a greenhouse. Under such conditions plants are freed from competition with weeds, and damage by pests is reduced.

1 Carbon dioxide
2 Oxygen
3 Water
4 Nutrients
5 Energy
6 Heat
7 Light
8 Harvest
9 Waste
10 Potash from burnt waste
11 Alcohol from waste
12 Recycled nutrients
13 Chemically inert support
14 Plastic mesh support
15 Air space
16 Water culture solution

Water and irrigation

Irrigation—the artificial watering of land—may be necessary for several reasons. Rainfall may be too sparse to raise any crops at all; it may be seasonal or erratic from year to year; or the natural supply of water may need to be supplemented in order to increase crop yields.

Systematic watering has been responsible for the transformation of vast expanses of arid, infertile land into highly-productive soil. Some 400 million acres (162 million hectares) of land are irrigated in the world today.

Ancient irrigation methods

Irrigation was crucial to the development of settled agriculture and the rise of the first great civilizations. More than 5,000 years ago, farmers along the banks of the Nile used its waters to irrigate their fields.

Ancient irrigation systems could be immense, even by modern standards. In Iraq, remnants of a canal 395ft (120m) wide and some 33ft (10m) deep have been traced for miles across the countryside. In Egypt, a channel some 12mi (19km) long connected the Nile to Lake Moeris, which was used as a reservoir for the river's regular and life-enriching flood-waters.

Ancient forms of irrigation ranged from simple networks of ditches that were filled from wells and rivers to elaborate systems of dams, reservoirs, and canals.

Traditional methods

Preindustrial civilizations possessed a wide variety of devices still used for lifting water to their fields. The Arabs, for example, use a simple contraption called the *shadoof,* which consists of a long, pivoted pole with a bucket at one end and a weight at the other that helps to counterbalance the weight of the water scooped up in the bucket.

The Archimedean screw, while still only a primitive form of water pump is, even so, a sophisticated irrigational device compared with the *shadoof.* It consists of a helical shaft housed in a long cylinder. One end of the assembly is dipped below the surface of the water, and when the shaft is turned water is lifted and disgorged from the other end of the cylinder onto the land.

Another ancient water-lifting device is the Persian wheel, consisting of an upright waterwheel linked by gears to a horizontal drive-wheel. A draft animal harnessed to the wheel walks in a circle to turn it.

Modern systems

Today, three main forms of irrigation are employed to provide the root systems of plants with a uniform supply of water.

The first is underground irrigation, a method that brings water to plants directly through the soil. This method is practical only where the terrain is level and where the soil is both highly permeable and situated over an impermeable layer that traps ground water and permits it to seep upward to the plants by capillary action. Underground irrigation minimizes water loss caused by evaporation. Unfortunately, it tends to deposit unwanted mineral salts at the surface. Such accumulations must be cleaned from the soil by occasional heavy rains or deliberate flooding.

The most common form of irrigation is surface irrigation. Land irrigated by this

CONNECTIONS

See also
254 Earth's water supply
294 Misuse of the land
984 The Persian Empire of the Achaemenids
1006 Greek science

1 Dry farming means growing crops without irrigation where the annual rainfall is below 20in (50cm). Olive trees are placed at the center of shallow earth basins that funnel rain water inward.

2 Drought-resistant sorghum is farmed in arid regions of Israel. Wide-spaced rows started under plastic sheets and well-filled, organically rich soil ensure the efficient use of the available natural water.

3 Irrigation systems, in arid areas, like the ancient Egyptian one shown here, presuppose stable, centralized societies. Without a stable society the complex of canals, ditches, dams, and reservoirs cannot be built or maintained. And without irrigation the civilization itself would collapse for lack of food. An 18th-century-BC Babylonian code gives elaborate irrigation regulations.

4A

4B 1900

1940

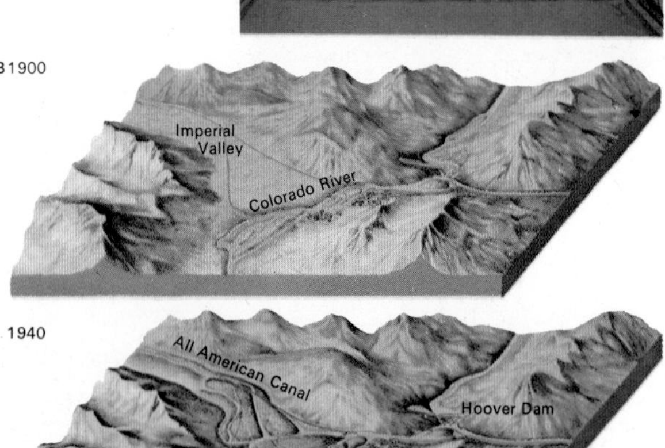

Imperial Valley
Colorado River
All American Canal
Hoover Dam

C

4 The Imperial Valley in California was transformed by large-scale irrigation engineering. It used to be arid [A], like the neighboring Great Basin region. It was impossible to grow commerical crops. Now it is an intensely farmed area. In 1905 and 1906 flooding of the Colorado River wrecked first attempts at irrigation. But with the construction of the Hoover Dam (1935), to control the Colorado, and the 80mi (130km) All American Canal (1940) the valley changed from parched desert to an agricultural garden. A 3,000mi (4,800km) irrigation network [B] is the area's mainstay; it waters half a million acres and Imperial Valley's productivity is immense [C]. One problem is that the valley is below sea-level so water cannot drain away. As the water evaporates, a growing residue of salt is left and this is a threat to the soil's future fertility.

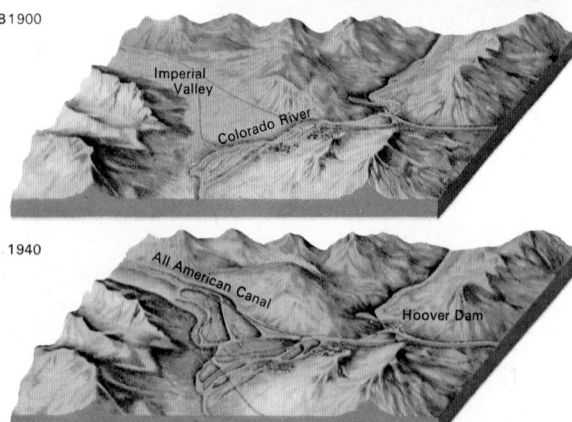

method is normally laid out in border strips, basins, or furrows.

The border strip technique entails dividing the land into long, rectangular sections fed by a common supply channel. Water flows as a broad sheet over the entire strip, the surplus draining off at the lower end. Border strips are most often used to grow small grains and forage crops.

In basic irrigation water is trapped by low retaining walls around the edge of the field until the earth becomes thoroughly soaked. Rice is the major crop irrigated in this way.

Furrow irrigation is most suitable for row crops such as corn and cotton. Furrows up to several hundred yards in length are plowed between the rows. They slope very gently away from the water source, so that water running along them does not cause excessive erosion but can soak in slowly.

The main drawback of surface irrigation is the difficulty of giving all parts of a field an equal amount of water. In making sure that all parts receive enough, many receive too much and valuable water is wasted.

The third watering method is overhead irrigation. Spray lines or sprinklers are used to simulate natural rainfall. Sprinklers can deliver water in a variety of concentrations from a fine mist to a heavy downpour. They are generally set up in rows and connected by pipes to a central pumping unit. The main advantages of sprinkler irrigation are that the land requires no special preparation and the application of water can be accurately controlled by the farmer.

A recent innovation has been the use of trickle systems. Water is brought directly to the base of a plant by narrow plastic tubing and steadily dripped from a nozzle. This method is highly efficient in its use of water and returns higher crop yields than any other approach. The high cost of installation is its main drawback.

Just one example is sufficient to indicate how enormously the amount of water needed varies with the climate and the nature of the soil. Grain crops that are able to flourish on about 18in (46cm) of water in one region may require nearly twice that amount elsewhere.

KEY

The waterwheel is one of the earliest devices known to have been used in irrigation. Like all the most basic irrigation implements, it was designed to lift water from wells, rivers, pools, and reservoirs and transfer it to ditches that carried it to the fields containing the crops to be irrigated.

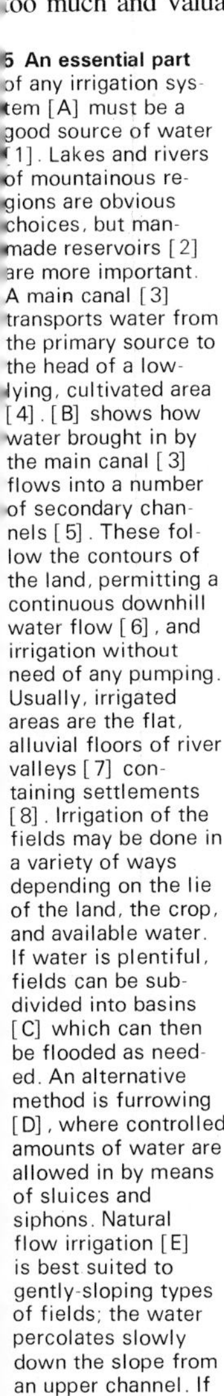

5 An essential part of any irrigation system [A] must be a good source of water [1]. Lakes and rivers of mountainous regions are obvious choices, but man-made reservoirs [2] are more important. A main canal [3] transports water from the primary source to the head of a low-lying, cultivated area [4]. [B] shows how water brought in by the main canal [3] flows into a number of secondary channels [5]. These follow the contours of the land, permitting a continuous downhill water flow [6], and irrigation without need of any pumping. Usually, irrigated areas are the flat, alluvial floors of river valleys [7] containing settlements [8]. Irrigation of the fields may be done in a variety of ways depending on the lie of the land, the crop, and available water. If water is plentiful, fields can be subdivided into basins [C] which can then be flooded as needed. An alternative method is furrowing [D], where controlled amounts of water are allowed in by means of sluices and siphons. Natural flow irrigation [E] is best suited to gently-sloping types of fields; the water percolates slowly down the slope from an upper channel. If the land slopes very sharply, then terraces can be cut into the hillside.

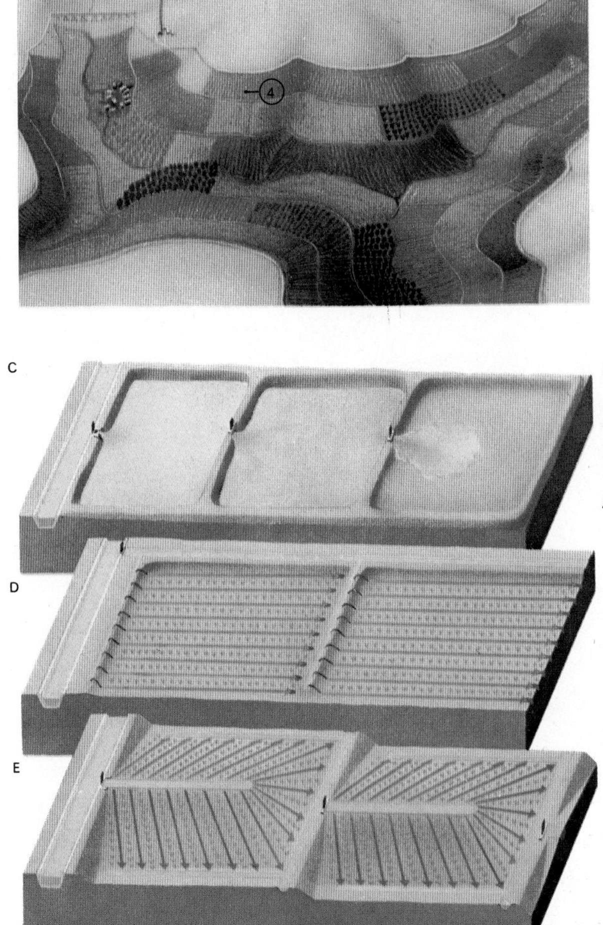
5
A
1
2
3
4
C
D
E

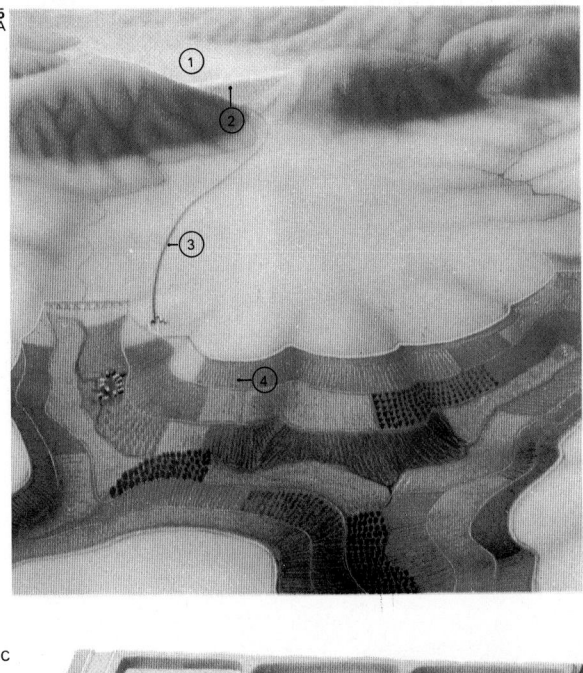

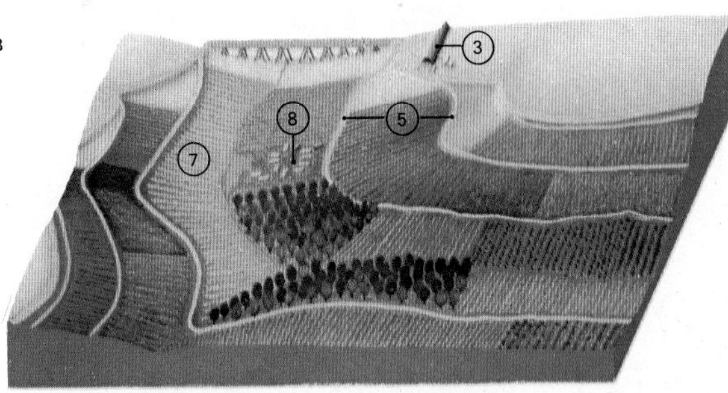
B
3
8
5
7

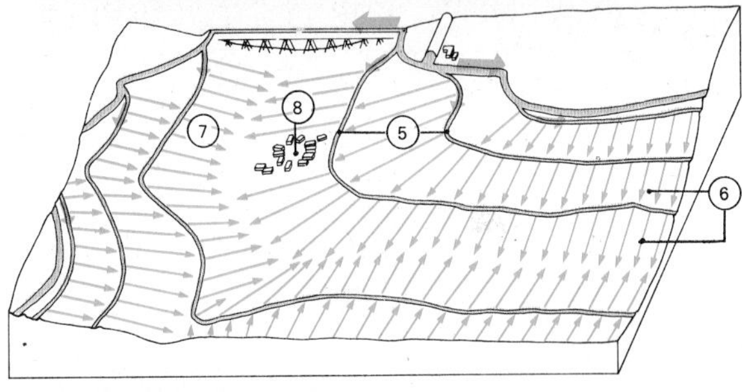
8
7
5
6

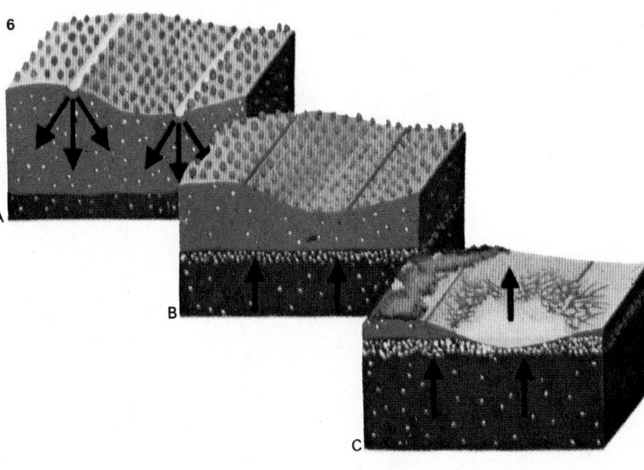
6
A
B
C

6 If poorly drained land [A] in a dry climate is irrigated, salts in the water used can seriously threaten crops and soil; water containing more than 700 parts per million of salt is directly harmful to plants but lower levels can also be disastrous. Poor drainage means that the water-table will eventually rise and bring dissolved salts back to the surface [B]. As the water evaporates, salt is deposited in the soil in ever-increasing amounts. Finally, the crops are killed and land once fertile becomes a desert [C]. Even so, the installation of a drainage system underground and new ditches will lower the water table once more. The salt can then be washed out of the soil by means of fresh water.

Improving crops

One of the most effective technical measures for increasing the productivity of crops and plants is the application of fertilizers [Key]. These are substances supplied to plants as nutrients. There are millions of living cells in a plant and to construct and maintain them the plant must obtain nutrients from air, water, and soil.

Where plant nutrients come from

Plants obtain carbon, hydrogen, and oxygen from air and water. They also need nitrogen (N) [1], phosphorus (P) [2] and potassium (K) [3] as primary nutrients, plus calcium (Ca), magnesium (Mg) and sulfur (S) as secondary nutrients. Plants also need an additional group of trace elements, sometimes called micronutrients because they are essential in minute quantities.

Some plant needs are met by the soil itself. But where the soil is naturally poor, or where the nutrients have been leached by heavy rain or removed by crops, fertilizers can be used to supply the necessary nourishment. Different crops have different needs, and the type and amount of fertilizer has to be related to the requirements of the crop as well as to the type of soil.

Some legume crops, such as clover, can obtain nitrogen from the air by the process known as "nitrogen fixation." But most plants need additional inorganic or organic nitrogen and this element is the one most widely used in fertilizers. In some form or other it accounts for almost half of the world consumption of fertilizers. Phosphorus makes up another 30 percent and potassium, the remaining primary nutrient, accounts for the balance. In recent years world consumption of fertilizers has totaled about 80 million tons, but it is very unevenly distributed. Only 15 percent is used in agricultural areas, such as China and India, which feed 70 percent of the world.

Natural and synthetic fertilizers

In the past farmyard manure was the basis of good farming and it is still an important fertilizer. Farmyard manure is the solid and liquid excreta of farm animals, usually left in heaps to allow it to rot. Its value lies both in its organic content and in the nitrogen, phosphorus, and potassium, (with small amounts of magnesium and trace elements), that it contains. The organic matter is beneficial to soil structure.

Synthetic fertilizer is most commonly supplied as a powder or in granules, but liquids or liquefied gases can also be used. Often it is supplied as a compound fertilizer (known as NPK) containing nitrogen, phosphorus, and potassium, in stated amounts. Many countries legally require that the composition be guaranteed.

Plants that are deficient in nutrients not only have smaller yields but also develop certain characteristic symptoms. Deficiency in nitrogen results in poor plant health: small plants; small, often yellowish-green leaves; and "scorched" lower leaves. Lack of phosphorus may reveal itself in stunted growth, leaves purplish or bronzed at the edges, and in slow-ripening, misshapen fruit. Similarly, leaves with whitish or brown spots, scorched or dead leaves, weak stems, and small fruit with cracks or injured spots indicate an inadequate supply of potassium. These are

CONNECTIONS

See also
278 Mineral resources the land
290 Earth's dwindling resources
292 Pollution of rivers a lakes
320 Organic farming

Nitrogen fixation
Nitrate utilization
Ammonification
Ammonia nitrification
Ammonia denitrification
Micro-organisms

1 Nitrogen, the most important fertilizer, undergoes a natural cycle. Together with its compounds it is involved in five basic processes: fixation of nitrogen from the air by micro-organisms and by plants of nitrates in the soil to make proteins; ammonium compound production in decaying plant and animal matter; nitrification of these to nitrites and then to nitrates; and denitrification of nitrogen compounds back to nitrogen gas. Nitrogen is removed from the cycle whenever humans consume animal or plant food but they replace it by adding nitrogenous fertilizers to the soil.

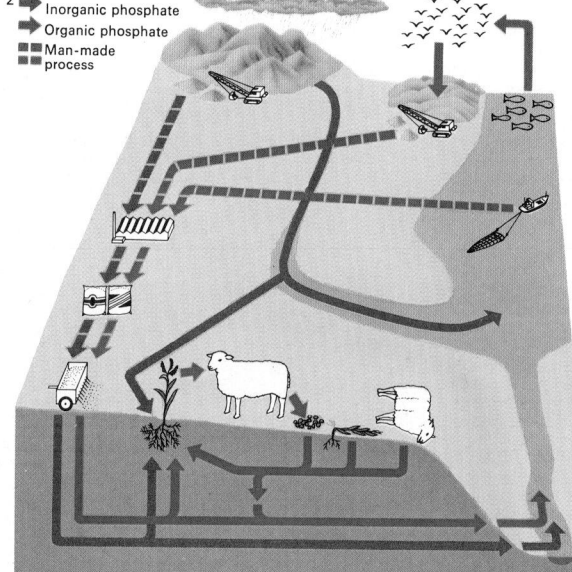

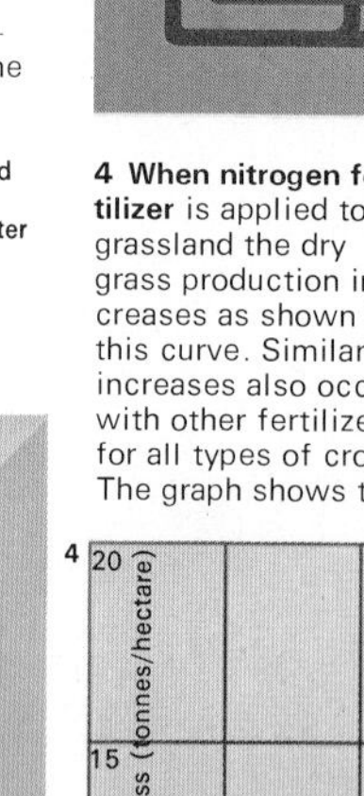
Inorganic phosphate
Organic phosphate
Man-made process

2 Most phosphate fertilizers, such as superphosphate and ammonium phosphate, are made from phosphate rock. Organic sources of phosphate include guano (bird droppings) and fish waste. Phosphates in the soil are taken up by plants, which may be eaten by animals. They return to the soil in dead plants, dead animals, and animal excretions. Much phosphate is supplied in compound fertilizer.

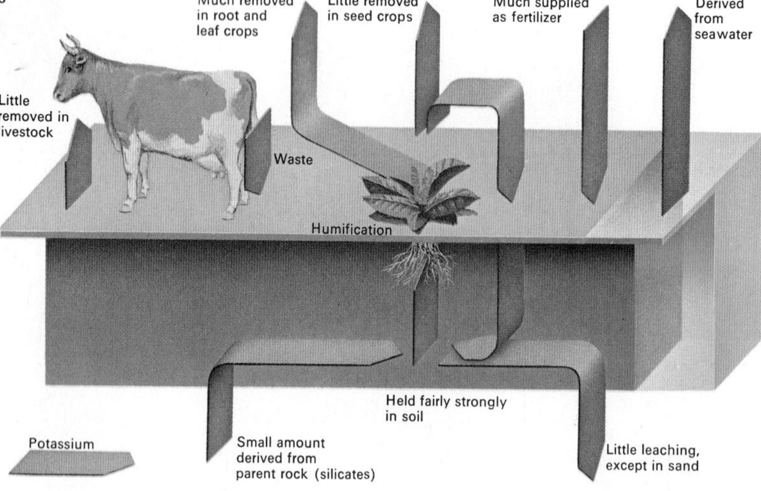
Much removed in root and leaf crops
Little removed in seed crops
Much supplied as fertilizer
Derived from seawater
Little removed in livestock
Waste
Humification
Held fairly strongly in soil
Potassium
Small amount derived from parent rock (silicates)
Little leaching, except in sand

3 Potassium is an essential plant nutrient. The quantity in circulation is more or less constant; losses are made up by inputs from rock erosion. But when plants are physically removed as crops their potassium is lost to the land and needs to be replaced by artificial means. A soil that is naturally deficient in potassium can be enriched by the application of fertilizer. The major sources of potassium fertilizer are deposits of potash salt (KCl).

4 When nitrogen fertilizer is applied to grassland the dry grass production increases as shown by this curve. Similar increases also occur with other fertilizers for all types of crops. The graph shows that a given quantity of fertilizer will produce a larger output increase on unfertilized or poorly fertilized land than on land already highly fertilized. This illustrates the law of diminishing returns. It follows that giving fertilizer to poor nations, which use little fertilizer, is better than giving them the grain grown with the same fertilizer on highly fertilized fields.

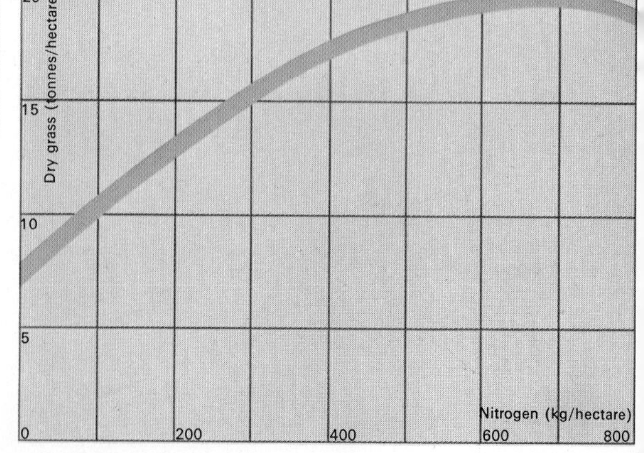
Dry grass (tonnes/hectare)
20
15
10
5
0
200
400
600
800
Nitrogen (kg/hectare)

only rough guides because many plants have complex metabolic systems in which there may be interactions between an excess of one nutrient and a deficiency of another. Physical conditions also play an important part in the growth of a plant and soil analysis is vital for correct assessment.

The United Nations Food and Agriculture Organization (FAO) publishes figures relating crop yield to the use of fertilizers. These are based on farm tests as well as on research carried out in scientific stations and include studies of the use of different sources of the same nutrient. In India, for example, the FAO has assessed the relative efficiencies of urea, ammonium sulfate, ammonium nitrate, and calcium ammonium nitrate as sources of nitrogen. Different phosphate materials also have been compared, as have other important factors such as plant varieties, plant populations, sowing time, and use of irrigation. These interact with fertilizer treatments and affect the response of crops. Overall, the FAO, after many years' research, reported an average increase of 58 percent for all crops using fertilizers and suggested that many crops could show even higher rises. Fertilizers also improve the yield per unit of water supplied—an important consideration in areas where water is in short supply.

In the humid tropics the soil tends to be acid. Where this is excessive, lime is added to reduce the acidity rather than to correct a nutritional deficiency. Ground limestone is one of the most effective and cheapest materials for this purpose.

Plant hormones and plant growth

The growth of plants can also be greatly influenced by applying materials known as plant hormones [7] or plant growth regulators. Used in very small amounts they promote, inhibit, or modify physiological processes within the plant. Plant hormones include auxins, kinins, gibberellins and abscisins. Compared with fertilizers they are relatively little used, although they are the subject of considerable research. They can all be produced artificially, and their main areas of application are to fruit, vegetables, flowers, and cereals.

KEY

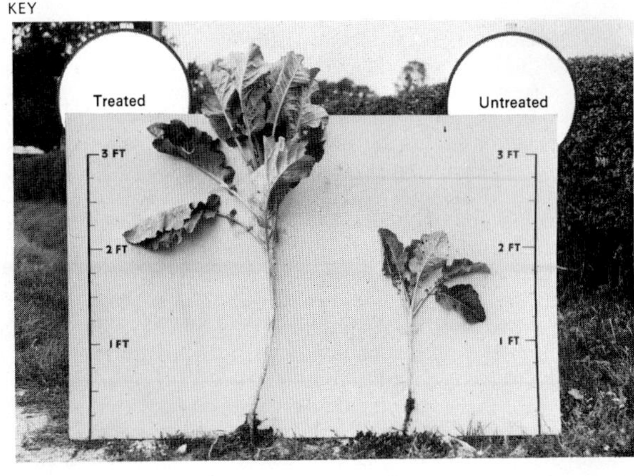

Treated
Untreated
3 FT
2 FT
1 FT
3 FT
2 FT
1 FT

The effect of fertilizer is evident in the growth rates of these kale plants. The one on the left has been treated with a nitrogen fertilizer. The other plant has stunted growth and discolored leaves common in plants lacking nitrogen. For healthy growth, plants need many elements as nutrients. Carbon, hydrogen, and oxygen are provided by air and water. Iron, magnesium, and sulfur are usually in the soil. Other important elements such as nitrogen, phosphorus, potassium, and calcium, may be in the soil—or may need to be added as fertilizer in the form of minerals, manure, or man-made chemicals.

5 An aircraft flies low to distribute fertilizer over New Zealand farmland. The use of aircraft in agriculture is especially advanced in New Zealand, where hilly pastures need fertilizer in order to produce more grass livestock. Aerial top-dressing is a quick and efficient method of spreading fertilizer over hilly or extensive areas where distribution in more conventional ways would be difficult and costly. The fertilizer is loaded mechanically into the plane's hoppers. The plane is then flown low over the distribution area and the pilot releases the fertilizer, which spreads evenly in controlled amounts.

6 The deposits of fertilizer minerals—phosphates [yellow], potash [blue], and sulfur [red] are unevenly distributed. The major phosphate producers are the US, the USSR, and Morocco. The major potash producers are again the US and the USSR, closely followed by West and East Germany and France. Natural nitrates have been superseded since 1914 by chemically produced nitrates that use atmospheric nitrogen. The process requires sulfuric acid and the latter's raw material is sulfur. The world's major sulfur producers are Canada, France, the US, the USSR, and Japan.

6

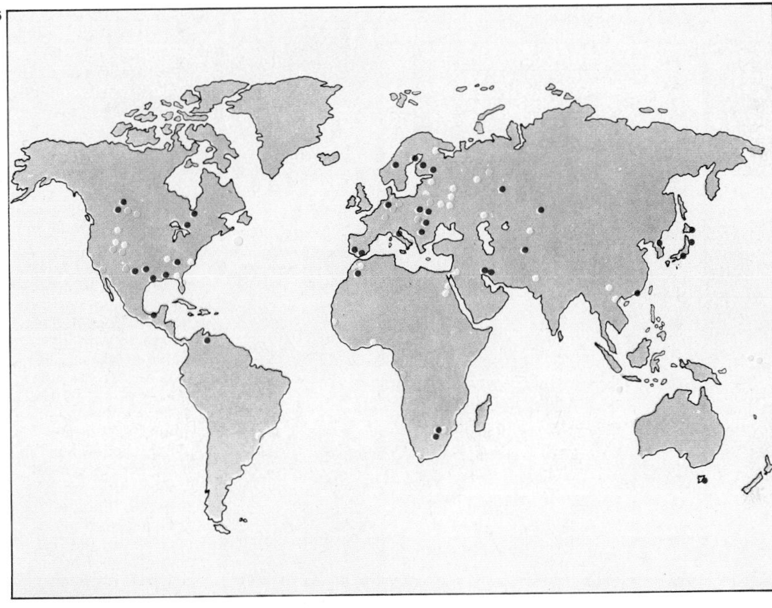

7 Plant hormones are chemicals that occur naturally in very small amounts in plants, where they control growth. They are used extensively in crop production. Their effect on plant cells and the uses to which they are put are shown here. Auxins [A] aid cell division and elongation and are used to stimulate fruiting. Ethylene [B] is a gas that acts as a hormone, ripening fruit by partial breakdown of cell walls. Gibberellins [C] promote cell elongation and are used to improve fruit quantity. Cytokinins [D] maintain nutrient levels in cells and help to preserve cut blooms. Chlorocholine chloride [E] inhibits cell elongation and causes dwarfism.

5

7

A
B
C
D
E

Protecting crops

Pests and diseases are estimated to destroy up to one third of the world's agricultural harvests each year. Crops can be ravaged at any stage during growth, harvest, and storage. The problem is most severe in the developing countries. For example, the Australian yield of rice is 2.87 tons per acre (6.44 T/ha), while in India the yield averages only about 0.77 tons per acre (1.62 T/ha). In some African countries the corresponding figure falls as low as 0.22 tons. Though there are many reasons for these substantial differences in yield, the major contributing factors are infestation of crops by insects, other pests, and diseases, and the competition for vital nutrients by weeds and useless grasses. Weather and good farming methods are also major contributing factors.

Increasing food production

In agriculture a pest is any organism that damages or destroys plants useful to man. Pests include animals such as harmful insects, mammals, and birds; disease-causing microorganisms; nematodes; and—last, but not least—weeds.

Pesticides include insecticides, fungicides, nematicides, and herbicides. Herbicides are chemicals used for weed control. In tropical and subtropical areas of the world the insecticides tend to be more important. In the United States, whose use of agricultural chemicals equals that of the rest of the world, herbicides are more widely applied than other pesticides. Pesticides are usually applied by spraying and dusting. Along with improvement in fertilizer use, farming techniques, and development of better crop varieties, pesticides have contributed to increasing food production and have been of benefit in food storage, forestry, and gardening.

Though chemical insecticides had been used earlier, it was the discovery of the insecticidal properties of DDT in 1939 that marked the dramatic growth of the use of synthetic organic pesticides. One of the most remarkable examples of the enormous gains in yield brought about by an intense and sustained campaign of pest control is provided by Japan. At the end of World War II Japanese rice output was a little over 0.7 tons per acre (1.6 T/ha). They succeeded in transforming rice cultivation into high yield, high quality production, which has resulted in an average output of almost 2.7 tons per acre (6 T/ha).

Harmful side effects

Chemical pesticides, despite their great benefits, have serious drawbacks. In some cases insecticides have become less potent because the insects developed resistance to their effects [2]. In other cases the insecticide has killed off the natural enemies of the harmful insects with the result that the insects have actually multiplied in number and become a greater crop threat.

A further possible harmful effect occurs when a long-lasting pesticide is eaten by a predator as it consumes its prey and then is eaten in turn by the animal preying on that predator. In this way the pesticide passes up the "food chain" [3] and may accumulate dangerously in the higher animals—including man. An example is a human becoming sick by eating meat from an animal that has eaten grain sprayed by pesticides.

CONNECTIONS

See also
294 Misuse of the land
496 Locusts, sucking bugs, and dragonflies
498 Advanced insects
422 Bacteria and viruses
426 Yeasts and molds
296 Pollution of rivers and lakes
298 Pollution of the sea
320 Organic farming

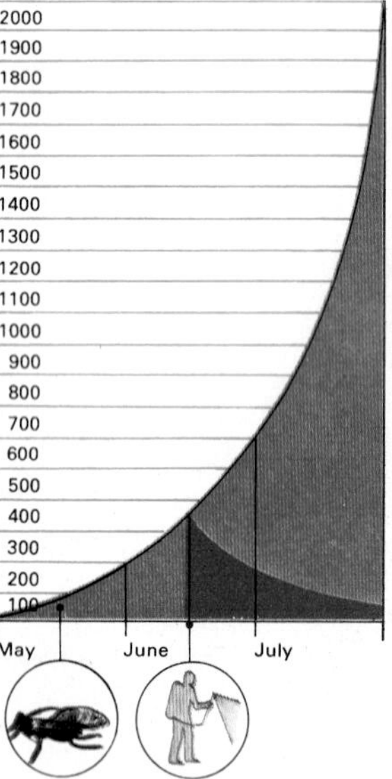

1 Aphids per bean stem
2000
1900
1800
1700
1600
1500
1400
1300
1200
1100
1000
900
800
700
600
500
400
300
200
100
May
June
July

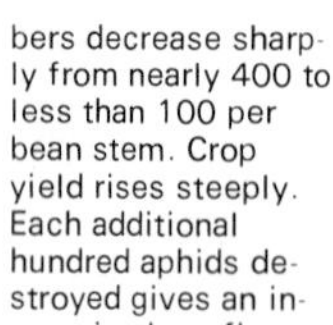

Crop yield Kg/4000m²
1500
1400
1300
1200
1100
1000
900
800
700
600
500
400
300
200
100
1500
1000
500
0
Aphids per bean stem

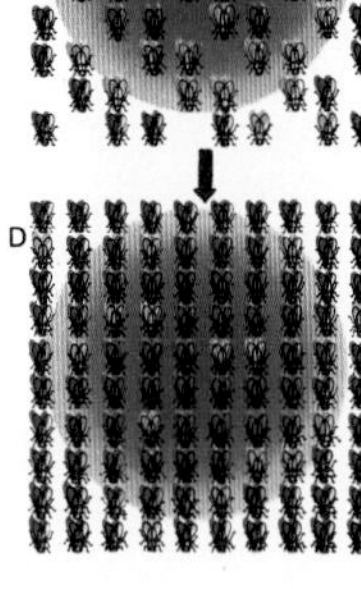

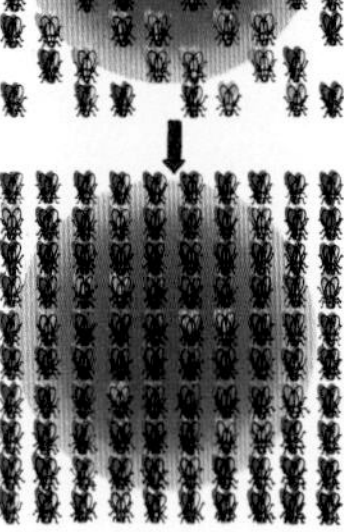

1 Productivity and yield of cultivated crops are reduced by insect pests. They lower plant vigor and may prove fatal. For example, if black bean aphids are left untreated on bean stems, they will multiply at an increasing rate during the summer months. The number on a stem may rise from about 200 early in June to 2,000 by the end of July. But if the aphids are treated in mid-June the numbers decrease sharply from nearly 400 to less than 100 per bean stem. Crop yield rises steeply. Each additional hundred aphids destroyed gives an increasing benefit.

Resistant flies
Susceptible flies
Killed flies
Insecticide

2 Resistance to insecticide may develop through several generations by natural selection. [A] If a house fly population is treated with insecticide, a few individuals may be resistant to normal concentrations and these will survive. [B] In the second generation there will be a much higher proportion of resistant flies descended from the survivors of the first application of insecticide [C,D]. Resistant and susceptible flies may reproduce with equal efficiency, but the proportion of resistant flies increases with each generation exposed to insecticide. Eventually an almost completely resistant population may be produced.

3 Long-lasting pesticides are concentrated up the food chain until they reach lethal doses for large predators. Hawks poisoned by DDT fail to reproduce. A possible pathway of DDT to hawks [D] occurs by way of aphids [A], ladybugs [B] and sparrows. [C] Dieldrin, used for protecting seeds, harms seed-eating birds [E,G] and their predators, including the badgers [F] and hawks [H].

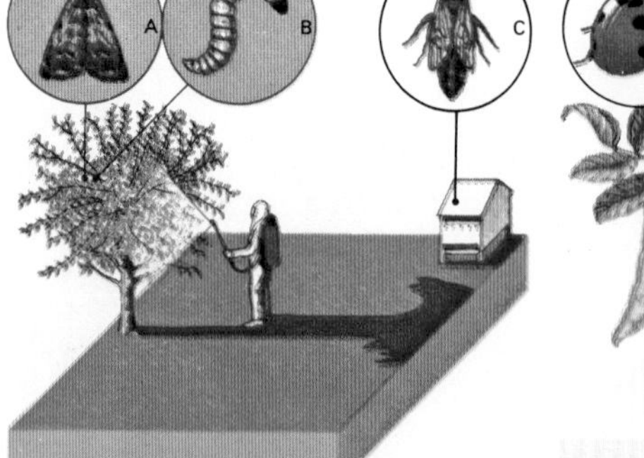

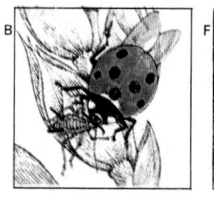

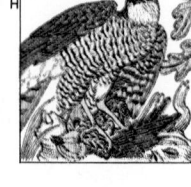

4 Spraying flowering crops during the day with contact poisons—which act, as their names indicates, by contact with susceptible insects—kills all insects, including the bees that pollinate the flowers. If the same poison is sprayed in the evening, when the bees [C] have returned to their hives, only the pests such as the codling moths [A] and caterpillars [B] are killed. The poison is a chemical that decomposes in a few hours.

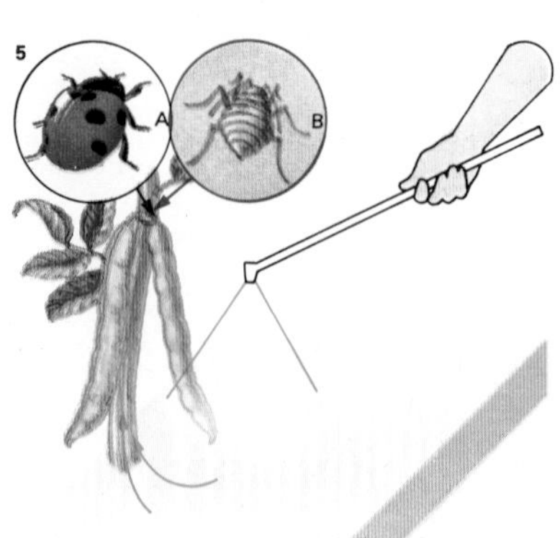

5 Systemic insecticides are chemicals that have the remarkable properties of being harmless to plants that absorb them, lethal to the herbivorous insects that feed on the plants, and harmless to their predators. When sprayed on leaves or soil, these insecticides are absorbed by plants, then act as stomach poisons to pests such as aphids [B], which are sap suckers, but leave ladybugs [A], which prey on aphids, unharmed.

Emphasis is now shifting from developing more effective methods of purely chemical control to so-called integrated approaches that attempt to combine profitable production with minimum disturbance of the environment. This environment is not, of course, the original ecological system but the system as altered to produce agricultural and forest crops (the "agro-eco-system") Government laboratories in many countries continually reappraise methods of pest control.

Biological controls

In the fight against insect pests there are now several methods that, unlike large-scale chemical spraying, lead to minimal environmental damage. These include biological control, sterilization, the use of pheromones, traps, and "antifeedants."

Biological control makes use of the pest's natural behavior to regulate its population density. For example, male insects are sterilized by radiation or by chemical treatment. When the sterilized males are released and mate with the females the resulting eggs are infertile. Pheromones are sex attractants produced by females to enable the males to locate them. When small amounts of certain specific pheromones are artificially released, the males may be disoriented—thus preventing the meeting of the sexes. Pheromones are also used to bait traps [6]. Other traps use light or other baits to lure the insects. Once trapped, they may simply starve or be killed by poisoning or irradiation. Antifeedants are synthetic chemicals that cause insects to remain on treated foliage without feeding. They eventually die from exposure, predation, or starvation. Vertebrate pests—rodents, foxes, rabbits, and birds—pose some of the most difficult problems. Poisons have been used extensively but they can be dangerous, expensive, and harmful to the environment. Killing off predatory pests brings its own problems, because some of them keep down other pests. In North America, for example, coyotes, although pests that are hunted by many farmers, help to keep down the population of mice and other small rodents.

KEY

Field tests are carried out to determine the value of proposed treatments in protecting crops against various kinds of pests. Pea vines on the left were treated with a selective weed-killer of the DNBP type to control wild mustard. Different selective weed-killers are used at various stages of the growth of the crop for best effects. For example, the triazine weed killers are applied before the peas are through the surface of the soil, while DNBP—which kills broad-leaved weeds—is used when the peas are 2-3in(5-8cm) tall.

6 Insect traps play an important role in pest control. One successful type uses a synthetic form of a sex attractant, or pheromone, which can be dispersed in a water-filled container covered with a film of oil. Attracted by the scent, which is the same as that produced by a female, males home in on the trap and are drowned. These traps have given excellent results in African rice fields.

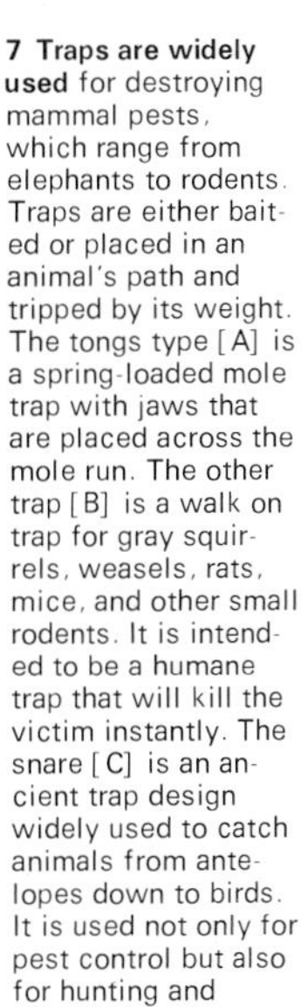

7 Traps are widely used for destroying mammal pests, which range from elephants to rodents. Traps are either baited or placed in an animal's path and tripped by its weight. The tongs type [A] is a spring-loaded mole trap with jaws that are placed across the mole run. The other trap [B] is a walk on trap for gray squirrels, weasels, rats, mice, and other small rodents. It is intended to be a humane trap that will kill the victim instantly. The snare [C] is an ancient trap design widely used to catch animals from antelopes down to birds. It is used not only for pest control but also for hunting and poaching.

8 A

B

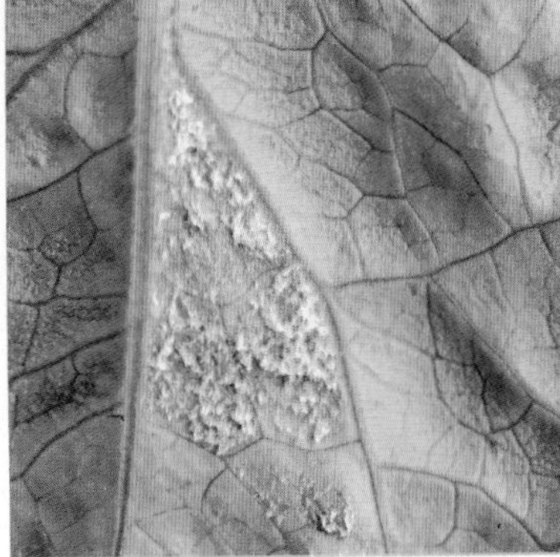

C

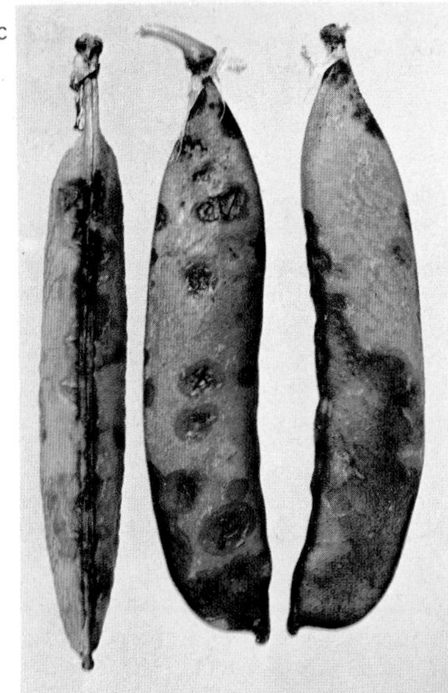

8 Crop diseases are produced by viruses, fungi, and bacteria which are often spread by insects, are the most difficult to treat. Preventive measures include destroying both the infected plants and the insect carriers. Tobacco mosaic virus (TMV) infects tomatoes [A], as well as tobacco. It also attacks leaves and fruit of many other plants and causes a drop in production. TMV is highly contagious and is carried on the fingers and clothes of growers. Bacterial and fungal diseases will respond to chemicals. Bacterial infections cause galls, wilts, spots and rot. Fungi are responsible for the greatest number of plant diseases. One, downy mildew, *(Bremia lactucae)* [B] is a common fungal disease of lettuces. It is controlled by regular applications of fungicide. The halo blight of beans and peas [C] is caused by a fungal infection that causes the pods to spot and rot.

9 A

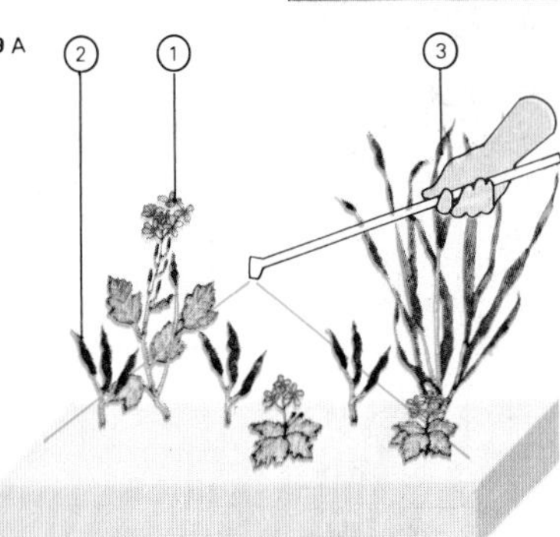

B

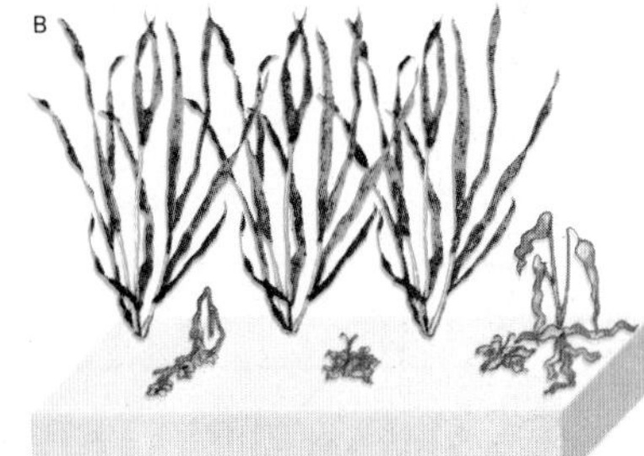

9 Physiological processes within plants can be affected by organic compounds other than nutrients. Some of these are herbicides akin to auxins, the so-called plant hormones. When these are used, they produce uncontrolled growth and eventual death. Their toxicity depends on how readily they are absorbed and also on the plant's stage of development. Broad-leaved plants absorb more readily than narrow-leaved cereals. [A] An auxin-type spray is applied to broad-leaved weeds [1] and to spring oats between the 3-leaf stage [2] and the beginning of jointing [3]. [B] The spraying program does not affect the spring oats, but the weeds die.

Organic farming

On an organic farm the farmer raises crops naturally, without using the inorganic fertilizers and chemical sprays that have revolutionized farming throughout the developed countries of the world. An organic farmer feeds the soil naturally to provide the nutrients necessary for plant life [5].

He uses, therefore, only manures that he is able to produce, while conventional farmers depend on limited resources of minerals and fuels for chemical fertilizers.

Conserving nature's balance

Organic farmers seek to avoid disturbing the balance of nature and they also fear the effects of pesticide residues in human food. Spraying against pests may be successful in the short term, but the practice has been known to upset the balance of insect life.

Farmers cannot be divided into two rigidly distinct camps—organic and conventional. While most organic farmers follow the same basic principles of rotation farming (crop growing and pastures in alternate periods), subsoiling and shallow cultivations, composting and a high level of self-sufficiency, some of them have adopted varying levels of modern chemical technology. Many use chemical weed killers to replace the hoe because farm labor is scarce. Manpower is one thing the organic farmer cannot do without. His manuring schedule demands more effort than spreading bags of chemical fertilizer.

The organic farm functions best if the farmer has a mixed system [1] with livestock grazing grass and other "break" crops (those that allow the soil a "break" or rest from growing grain) supplying manure [4] and slurry in place of bagged fertilizer. Stockless organic farming is possible, but the crop rotations [2] need skillful planning, making use of legume crops such as peas and beans.

Looking after the soil

A mixed farmer is more self-sufficient than a specialist. Unlike many pig and poultry producers, for example, he has a use for manure; he spreads it back on the land.

Care of the soil is the cornerstone of organic farming. Soil animals and microorganisms improve soil structure, release plant nutrients, and are claimed by some to combat soil-borne disease. To keep these soil workers active, the farmer supplies organic manures and cultivates carefully to maintain them in the top 4–8in (10–20cm) of soil where most fertility-building work is done. Deep-rooting pasture and clover crops bring up a broad spectrum of nutrients from the lower soil levels. They give nutritious food for stock and improve soil structure. When these crops are plowed up they provide large quantities of organic matter.

Lower crop yields are obtained on organic farms compared with those where chemical fertilizers are used, and some organic farmers purchase manure from outside to boost their productivity [3]. Arable crops (those that entail plowing and planting) favor the establishment of weeds, and the refusal to treat these with chemical weed-killers prevents the adoption of a crop rotation with a predominance of arable crops—another reason for the comparatively low production.

CONNECTIONS

See also
318 Protecting crops

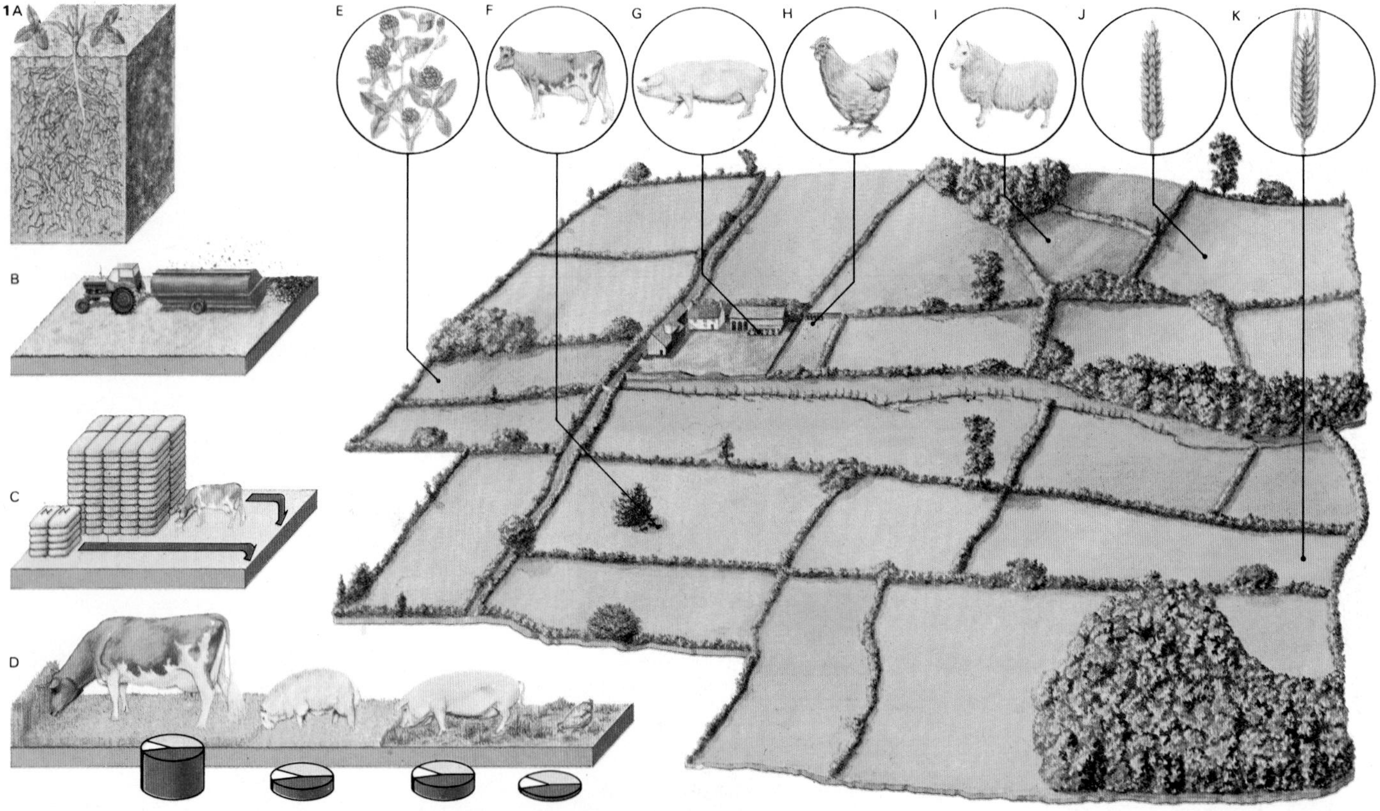

1 Soil fertility on an organic farm is maintained by rotation of crops. Legumes [A] fix soil nitrogen. Manure is spread on the stubble [B] after harvest. Microorganisms reduce this compost and turn it into topsoil. A ton of barley [C] fed to livestock can yield as much as 44lb (20kg) of nitrogen. Manure from livestock returns nutrients [D] extracted by growing crops. Manure typically contains a proportion of 38% nitrogen (blue) to 14% phosphorus (white) and 48% potassium (red), as shown. Organic farmers claim that when these chemicals are added inorganically the conventional farmer is oversimplifying nature. Clover planted in pastures [E] increases nitrogen in the soil. Cattle [F] graze on pastures and supply manure. Pigs [G], hens [H], and sheep [I] all contribute to the farm's self-sufficiency. Wheat [J] and barley [K] feed livestock in winter and provide grain for milling and for malting.

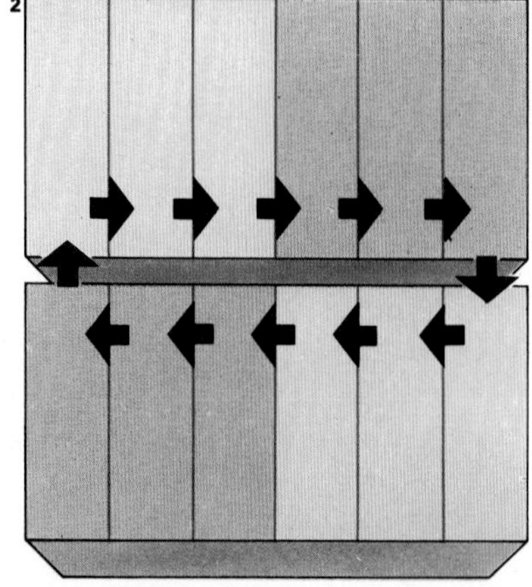

2 An organic farmer rotates his crops according to whether or not his farm is mixed and he adapts practices to the needs of the soil and to the weather conditions. Organic farming is best suited to a mixed farm system. Livestock manure is spread on the arable fields as natural organic fertilizer. In practice, to obtain reasonable yields the organic farmer usually has to buy extra manure. A rotation system is normally based on a three- or four-year deep-rooting perennial crops grazed by at least two kinds of livestock whose various grazing habits help build fertility. Such crops on an organic farm include a wide variety of grasses, clovers, and deep-rooting herbs such as chicory and yarrow. Often this is followed by two or three years of grain crops. Variations on this rotation may be a wheat, oats, and barley sequence with a break crop of a legume such as field beans. In the diagram the rotation is for a 6-year cycle that is then repeated. It may also use green manure crops such as rape and mustard and green crops grown between cereal crops. Before manufactured fertilizers were provided, farmers had to follow a rotation. In the Middle Ages, many followed a three-year rotation of autumn-sown cereal, spring-sown cereal or legume, and a year's fallow to allow the land time to recover its fertility.

Some crops are risky on organic farms. 'nsprayed potatoes may succumb to ight, sugar beets to virus yellows, and eans to aphids. But with cereals and fodder rops a healthy spontaneous ecological balnce may be obtained through "unforced" rowth and healthy soil microorganisms.

own on the organic farm

rganic farmers plan their holdings in varius ways [2]. A farmer with a mixed farm of 00 acres (80 hectares), for example, may mploy a team of five workers (three of iem part-time). The lower yields are comensated by the savings on machinery, ferlizers, and pesticides.

The farmer's milking herd of 30 Jersey ows gives first-rate milk and grazes rich astures containing clovers that "fix" atiospheric nitrogen. Following the cattle, 20 wes and their lambs graze the pastures and eplenish them with their droppings. The vestock includes 200 free-range hens and ome pigs.

On the farm there are 20 acres (9 hecares) of wheat, grown after beans. The beans, being legumes, enrich the soil with nitrogen. They yield about $1^1/_2$ tons per acre (3,200 to 3,800kg per hectare) and are fed to the cattle. The wheat yields about 2 tons per acre (4,800 to 5,000kg per hectare). Wheat is followed in rotation by oats, which are fed to the stock, and then barley for malting. The barley yields under 2 tons per acre (4,500kg per hectare).

The farm has 8 acres (3.2 hectares) of woodland, plus ponds, thickets, and hedges that harbor pest predators and pests, thus helping to provide a wider natural habitat for insects and wild plants. The farm also grows beets and hay and all stock feed is home grown; only salt blocks are brought in. The farm almost meets the organic farmer's ideal of self-sufficiency, and outside economic pressures are minimized.

With more research organic farming may hold the solutions for relieving the demand on the dwindling stocks of chemical fertilizer and raw materials (including energy) and for reducing the environmental problems created by many fertilizers and pesticides.

KEY

Manure spreading is a vital operation on most organic farms. Manure returns to the soil some of the nutrients extracted by crops. Soils must have sufficient nitrogen, phosphorus, and potassium, and have smaller amounts of calcium, magnesium, sulfur, and sodium, and traces of copper, zinc, and boron.

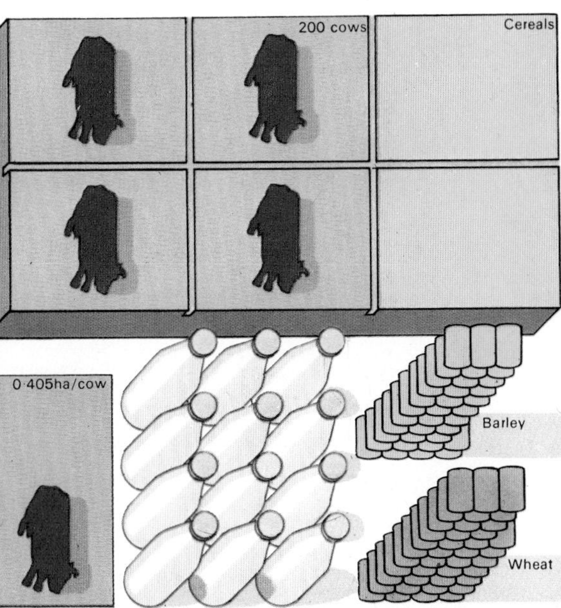
200 cows
Cereals
0·405ha/cow
Barley
Wheat

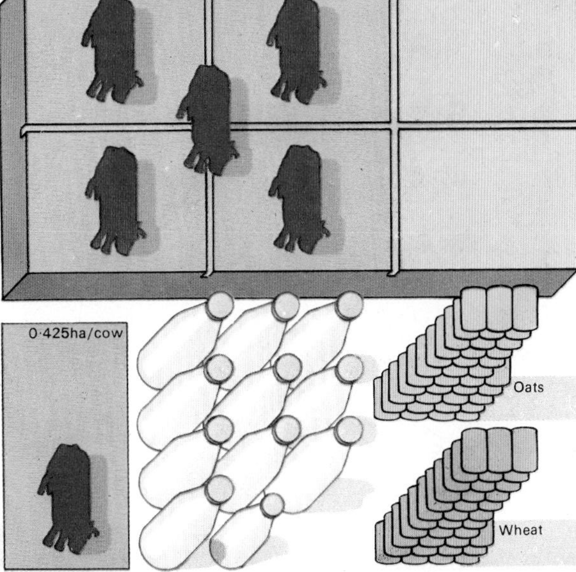
B
250 cows
Cereals
0·425ha/cow
Oats
Wheat

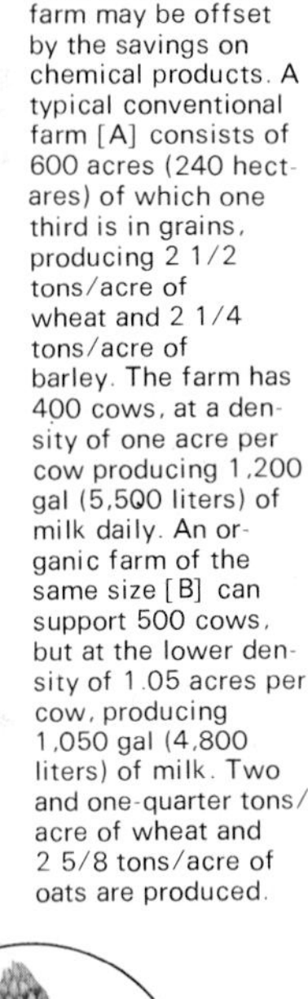

3 The lower productivity of an organic farm may be offset by the savings on chemical products. A typical conventional farm [A] consists of 600 acres (240 hectares) of which one third is in grains, producing 2 1/2 tons/acre of wheat and 2 1/4 tons/acre of barley. The farm has 400 cows, at a density of one acre per cow producing 1,200 gal (5,500 liters) of milk daily. An organic farm of the same size [B] can support 500 cows, but at the lower density of 1.05 acres per cow, producing 1,050 gal (4,800 liters) of milk. Two and one-quarter tons/acre of wheat and 2 5/8 tons/acre of oats are produced.

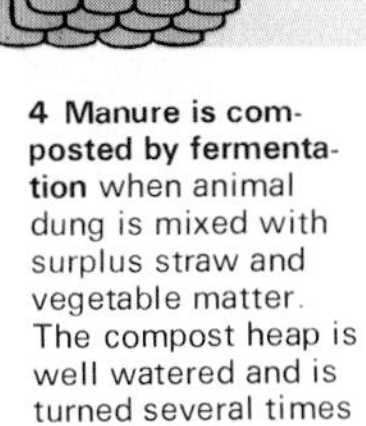

4 Manure is composted by fermentation when animal dung is mixed with surplus straw and vegetable matter. The compost heap is well watered and is turned several times to ensure mixing.

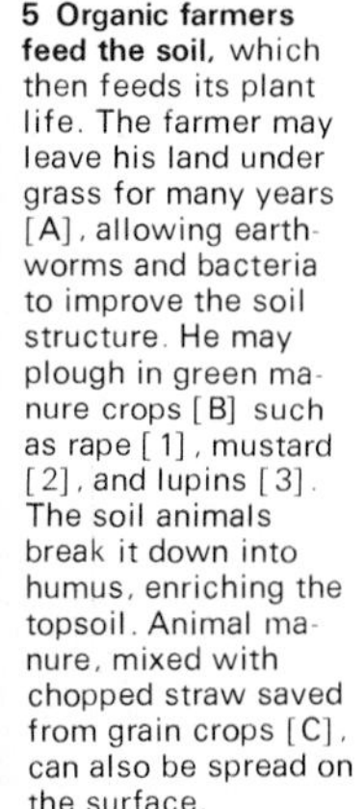

5 Organic farmers feed the soil, which then feeds its plant life. The farmer may leave his land under grass for many years [A], allowing earthworms and bacteria to improve the soil structure. He may plough in green manure crops [B] such as rape [1], mustard [2], and lupins [3]. The soil animals break it down into humus, enriching the topsoil. Animal manure, mixed with chopped straw saved from grain crops [C], can also be spread on the surface.

5

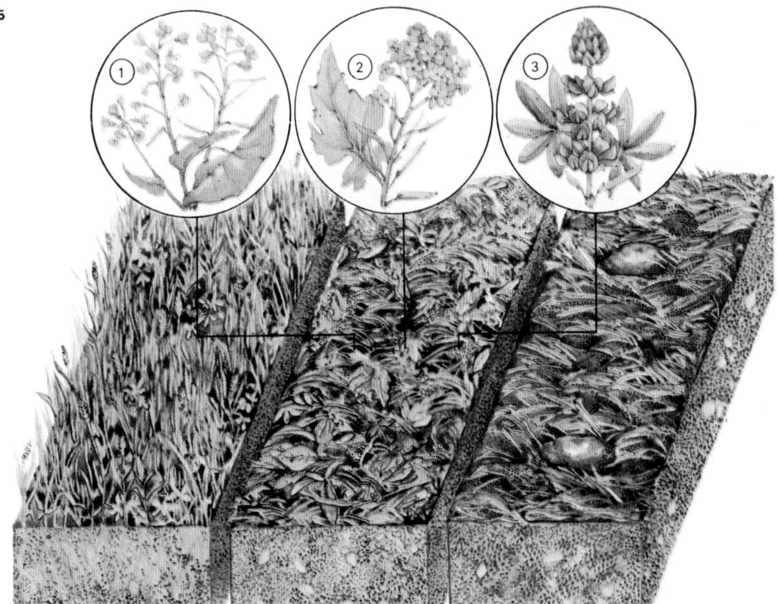
1
2
3
A
B
C

Plant genetic resources

Since the earliest days of agriculture people have tried to breed better food plants for themselves and for their domestic animals. For thousands of years they did this simply by saving seed from the best plants of the harvest. Only in the twentieth century has this method—mass selection—been supplemented with planned breeding.

Genes and their effects

The success of scientific plant breeding has depended largely on a knowledge of the inheritance of characteristics. The unit of inheritance is the gene. Every plant and animal cell possesses vast numbers of genes made of the chemical deoxyribonucleic acid (DNA), grouped together on chromosomes. It is on the plant's genetic makeup (genotype), and its environment, that its mature appearance depends.

There are so many genes in each plant that the potential variability in the characteristics conveyed from parents to offspring is enormous. The science of tapping this potential is still in its infancy, however. Success in using plant genetic resources to produce new varieties depends as much on agricultural practices as on the skill of the geneticist [2, 4].

The aims of modern plant-breeding programs almost invariably include an increase in yield. The plant breeder may also wish to improve such genetically determined characteristics as nutritional value, the time it takes the plant to mature, resistance to disease, and tolerance of unfavorable climates. Or he may aim to develop crops that grow to the same height and mature at the same time so they can be harvested mechanically [Key].

In nature plants usually change either through sudden alterations in genetic material, called mutations, or through the planned crossing or hybridization of different species or varieties [1]. Modern plant breeding is largely based on planned hybridization combined with rigorous selection to speed up the evolution of new varieties.

Plant-breeding programs

Experiments to evaluate the respective influences of genes and environment are usually the starting point of plant-breeding programs. The characteristics easiest to assess are those that are governed by one or a few major genes, such as the height of beans. Characteristics determined by the cumulative actions of many genes, especially those for yield, are harder to study and to control experimentally.

Individual plants selected for a program are used as parents in controlled hybridization. The design of the program depends on the way fertilization or pollination takes place. Wheat, rice, tomatoes, beans, peas, and many other important food plants are self-pollinated; that is, the pollen that fertilizes the ovule to give rise to seed comes from a flower on the same plant. In self-pollinating species the pollen and ovule share many common genes and their offspring are said to breed true. True-breeding plants are easy to control, and individuals in a crop are uniform in size and quality.

Cross-pollinated, or outbreeding, food plants, in which pollen and ovule are from different parents, include corn, clover, and cabbage. Although these plants rarely breed

CONNECTIONS

See also
416 Principles of hered
370 Farm stockbreedir and management

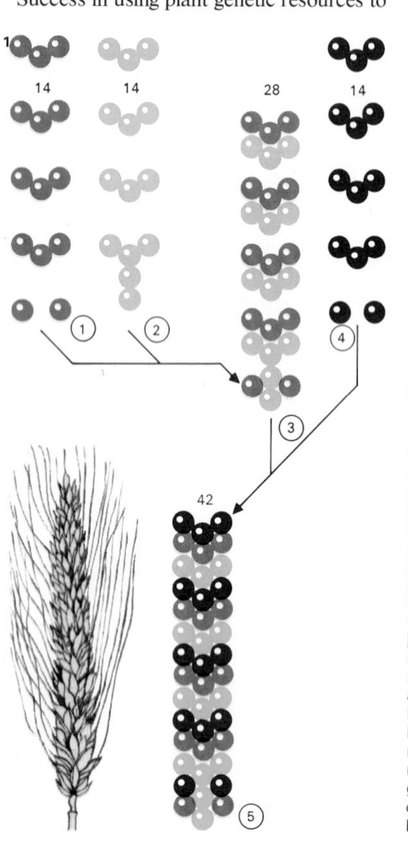

1
14
14
28
14
1
2
3
4
42
5

1 Man's daily bread is based on the accidental hybridization of wild grasses in the Near East more than 10,000 years ago. The wild wheat *(Triticum monococcum)* [1], and goat grass *(Aegilops speltoides)* [2], both with 14 chromosomes, had natural mechanisms that caused their light seeds to be scattered by the wind before they could be harvested. A hybrid between them, emmer *(T. dicoccum)* [3], found its way into cultivation although its seeds were easily scattered by wind. A second genetic accident, involving emmer and another goat grass *(A. squarrosa)*, [4], resulted in a full-eared bread wheat *(T. aestivum)* [5], with 42 chromosomes. The natural seed-dispersal mechanism of wheat was bred out of the new hybrid (from which modern wheats derive) to prevent the grain from dropping off the ears before harvesting.

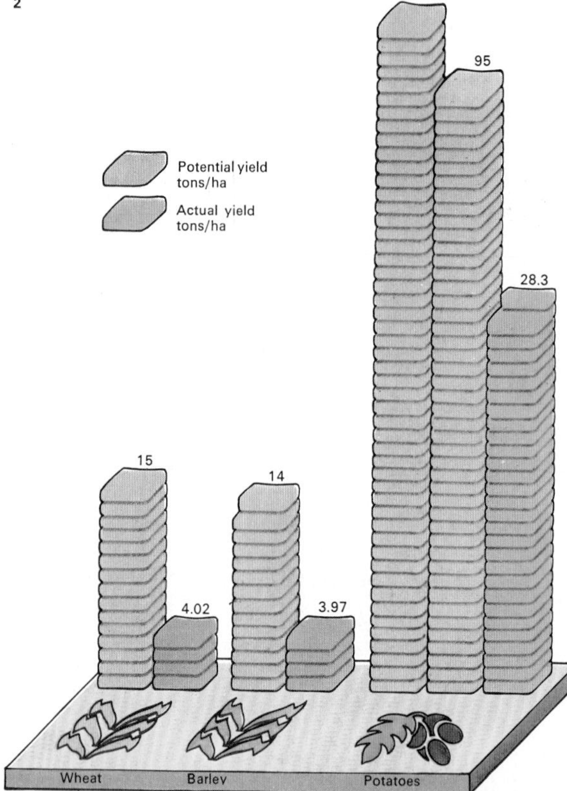

2
Potential yield tons/ha
Actual yield tons/ha
15
4.02
14
3.97
95
28.3
Wheat
Barley
Potatoes

2 Average farm yields still lag a long way behind the genetic potential of existing plant varieties, even in the most advanced agricultural areas. It has been calculated that in northwest Europe wheat could, under ideal conditions, yield up to 6.6 tons per acre, barley nearly 6 tons, and potatoes nearly 17 tons. (1 ton per acre= 2.25 metric tons per hectare.) The average yields for EEC countries in 1974 were: wheat 1.77 tons, barley 1.75 tons, and potatoes 12.5 tons. Under experimental plot conditions potato yields near the potential have been obtained, but the highest grain yields on a field scale are only two-thirds of the potential. Achievement of this ideal will depend on planting the best varieties, adequate and balanced provision of fertilizer, absence of disease and of competition from weeds, and the right balance of sun and moisture.

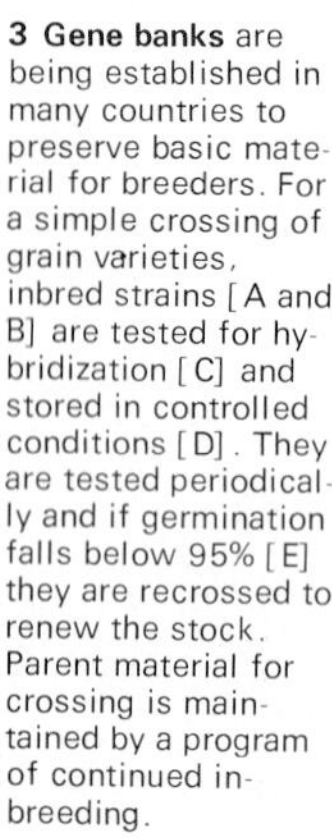

3 Gene banks are being established in many countries to preserve basic material for breeders. For a simple crossing of grain varieties, inbred strains [A and B] are tested for hybridization [C] and stored in controlled conditions [D]. They are tested periodically and if germination falls below 95% [E] they are recrossed to renew the stock. Parent material for crossing is maintained by a program of continued inbreeding.

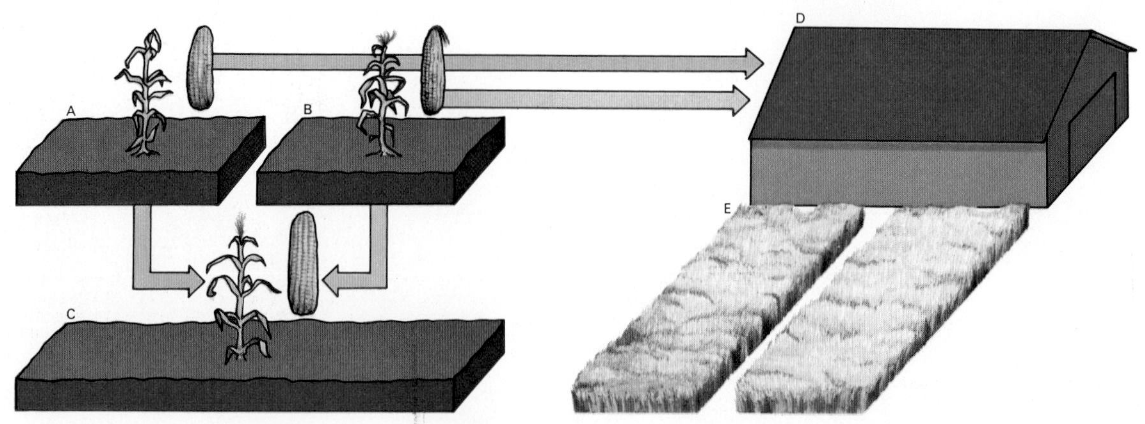

3
A
B
C
D
E

true, their first generation of offspring, known as F_1 hybrids, show particular vigor and uniformity. Increasing commercial use is being made of hybrid vigor, especially with corn, a plant in which hybridization is relatively easy to control because the male and female flowers are on different parts of the plant. In cross-pollinated species the production of hybrid varieties and mass selection are the two most important methods of plant breeding. Cross-pollination may also be used to hybridize different species whose genetic make-ups go well together, thus producing "synthetic" species.

In self-pollinated species mass selection has largely been replaced by pure-line selection and hybridization. In pure-line selection, used chiefly in the development of new crop species, plants with desirable characteristics are selected to produce offspring, and these progeny are allowed to self-pollinate for several generations.

The first step in hybridizing self-pollinating plants is to select the parent stock for cross-pollination. Each of the chosen parents usually possesses desirable characteristics lacked by the other. The progeny of the cross form the F_1 generation, and pairs of the best F_1 plants are then crossed to produce an F_2 generation. The plants of the F_2 and succeeding generations are generally allowed to self-pollinate and it may take many generations to produce really excellent plants.

Throughout a plant-breeding program meticulous records must be kept and plants must be tested in trials against other varieties in a wide range of conditions. For many thousands of crossings only one new line is likely to survive such testing.

Hopes for the future

Current research and breeding programs have many aims. One of the most important is the breeding of improved protein-rich soybeans, originally tropical plants, in temperate areas. Other research is directed toward development of a greater range of plants able to fix nitrogen from the air and incorporate it into proteins. Among crop plants only legumes to do this naturally.

KEY

Semidwarf wheat such as the Cambridge-bred Maris Fundin is the result of crossing high-yield dwarf wheats bred in Japan and Mexico with European varieties. The short stalks of these varieties help them withstand storms and make them easier to harvest mechanically.

4

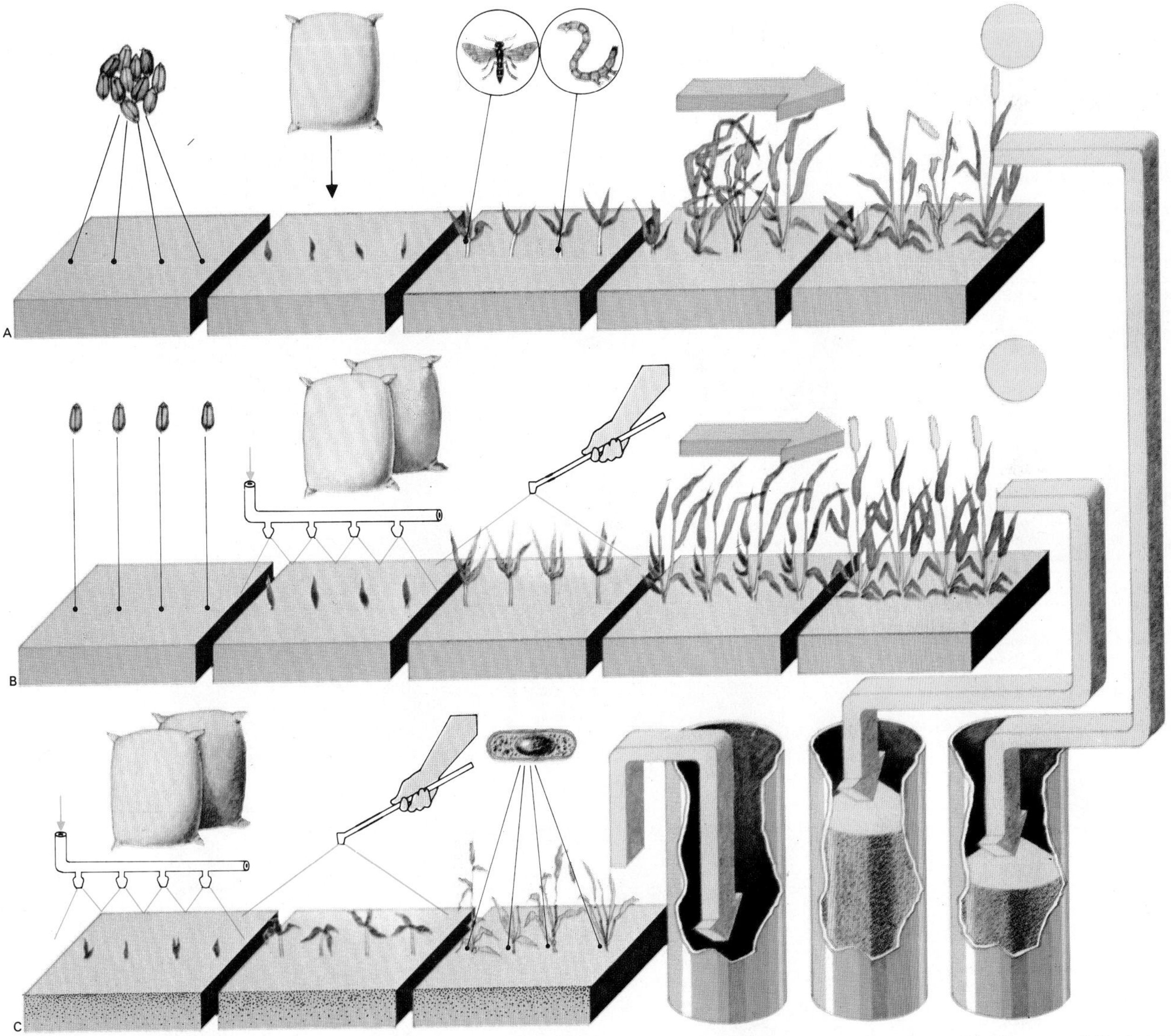

A

B

C

4 "Green revolutions" depend for success on more than simply introducing improved seed and farming techniques, as in this illustration. By traditional methods [A] diverse crop strains were sown and fertilizer used modestly; some crops were affected by disease and tall plants were sometimes blown over before harvest. Final yields were low. A new selected strain was planted in [B]. It was heavily fertilized and sprayed against pests and diseases. Low-growing plants stand up well for a full harvest. Yields are increased, but the continuation of this treatment [C] allows new strains of disease-producing organisms to flourish and kill the crop. Soil may also deteriorate as spray and fertilizer residues build up. Bad-weather yields drop well below the original average. Local trials are essential before new varieties become dominant. Even in advanced farming areas no one variety should be given more than one-third of the area of that crop.

Plant propagation

Flowering plants reproduce themselves by means of seeds and by vegetative means that bypass the normal sexual process. Given the appropriate stimulus, plant tissues that are apparently specialized by virtue of their position and function can change their character. Stem tissue or even leaves, for instance, may develop roots, and grow into a new plant if separated from the original plant. This adaptability has long been exploited for propagating plants. Even some wild species spread as much by vegetative means as by seed. Such troublesome weeds as quack grass (*Agropyron repens*) and goutweed (*Aegopodium podagraria*) form new plants at the joints of underground rhizomes. Tiger lilies (*Lilium tigrinum*) form bulbils in the axils of their leaves or—like some onions *(Allium)*—in place of a normal flower head.

Growing from clones

A group of plants that is grown vegetatively from a single specimen and is therefore genetically homogeneous is called a clone. Every named potato, apple, or rose represents a clone produced from an original plant that began as a hybrid seed. A hybrid may not be able to produce fertile seed; but even if it can, the resulting progeny are much more variable and unpredictable than are new plants produced by cloning. Also, grafted shrubs and trees can be brought to maturity more quickly than seedlings.

A potato tuber consists of a large mass of food storage cells, with cells adapted to growth just below the skin at the "eyes." Any small piece containing an "eye" is capable of developing into a new plant [5]. In fact botanists have produced new plants from microscopic cell material taken from the extreme point of a growing shoot. These cells are free from any virus that may be present in the rest of the plant and can be grown on to develop a virus-free clone. Many crops have been improved by this method.

Growing from stem and leaf cuttings

Stem cuttings are a convenient way of multiplying many ornamental species such as willows and poplars, timber trees, and shrubs [17]. The process of rooting is accelerated by the use of synthetic plant hormones, which encourage stem and leaf tissues to give rise to root tissues. Leaf cuttings are used to multiply species of gloxinia and of those begonias [21] grown for their decorative foliage. If the gardener removes the midrib of the leaf and fixes the leaf to a suitably moist soil, new plants develop at the inner ends of the cross ribs.

The rose family, to which many of our fruits belong, lends itself well to vegetative multiplication. Strawberries [8] send out runners from which new plants develop. In the genus *Rubus,* the raspberry *(R. idaeus)* spreads by way of underground rhizomes. The blackberry *(R. vitifolius)* and the loganberry (a hybrid between the raspberry and the blackberry) will root wherever a trailing stem touches the ground. The deliberate encouragement of this form of growth is known as layering [9].

Growing from grafts

Tree fruits of the rose family (apples, pears, plums, peaches, apricots, and cherries) de-

CONNECTIONS

See also
456 How flowering plants reproduce
322 Plant genetic resources

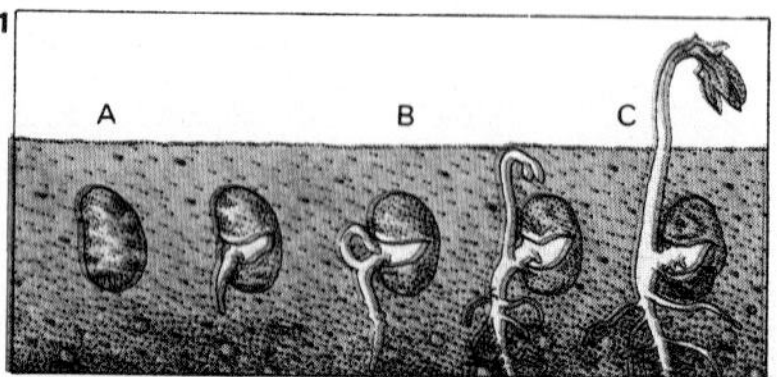
1
A
B
C

1 Dicotyledons, such as the bean [A], have two "seed leaves" as food stores for the embryo that lies at their junction. In the ground these cells divide, splitting the seed coat [B], and begin to differentiate into shoot and root. The shoot grows to the surface, carrying seed leaves with it, while the root grows down. At [C] the root has developed rootlets for anchorage and nourishment for continued growth.

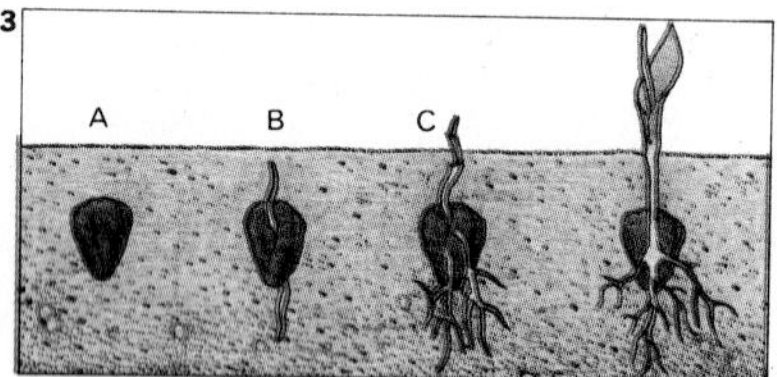
3
A
B
C

3 Monocotyledons such as corn [A] have only one internal food body from which the single cotyledon (seed leaf) feeds. A single shoot develops [B,C] and the cotyledon finally disintegrates.

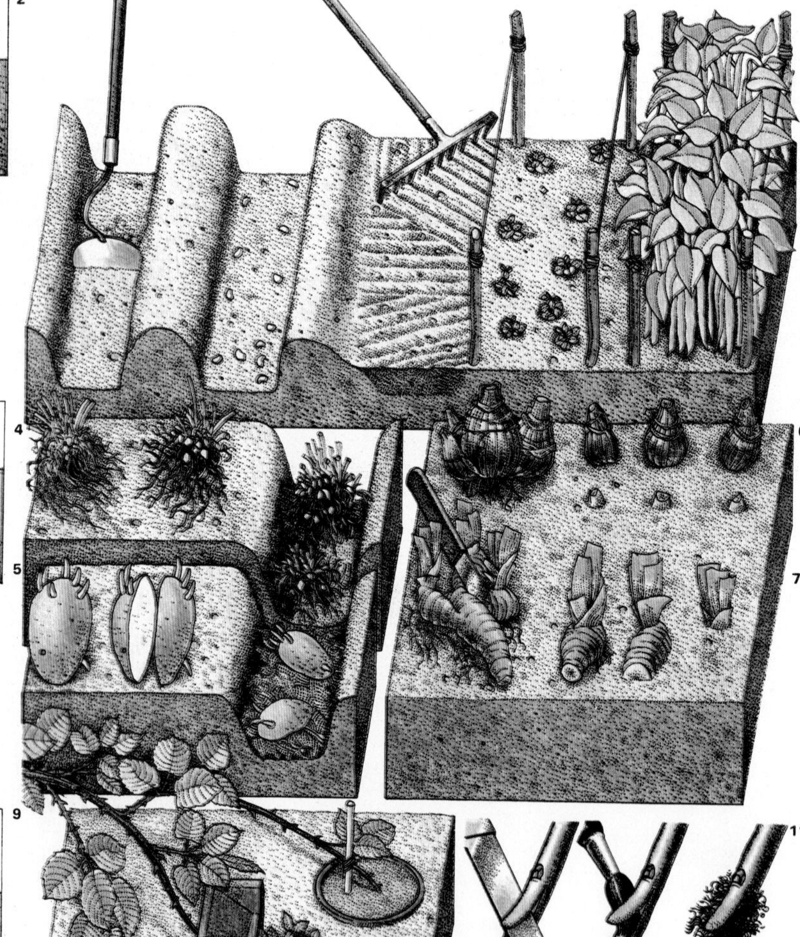
2
4
5
6
7
9
10
11
A
B
C
D
E
F

2 Bush beans growing in a garden are cultivated in stages. Shallow trenches are cut in the soil and bean seeds are sown in them at regular intervals. When the plants emerge, they are sometimes supported at the sides by cords tied between stakes, as on the right. Some beans are self-fertile, like peas; others are cross-pollinated naturally with the assistance of insects.

4 Fibrous rooted perennials, such as phlox, multiply when the roots are cut in two and replanted.

5 Seed potatoes, for planting, are cut into pieces that each contain at least one eye.

6 New bulbs of the daffodil *(Narcissus)* grow from the ball of an older bulb. They may be removed and planted separately. For commercial propagation they are lifted after two years in the field.

7 German irises form a mass of rhizomes near ground level. To grow them best these should be broken up after flowering and replanted singly. Some irises grow from bulbs instead of rhizomes.

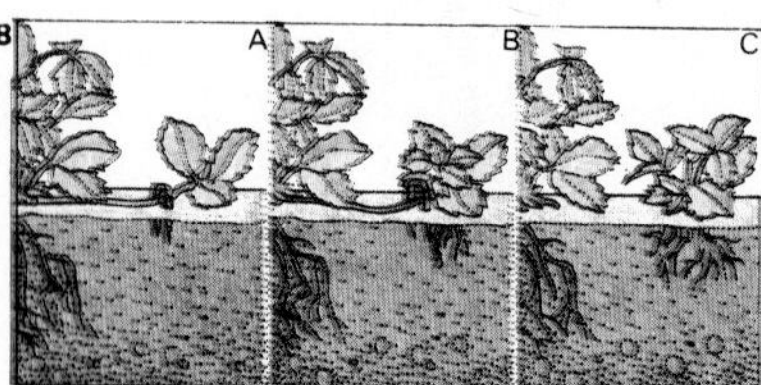
8
A
B
C

8 Strawberries and some related species spread and propagate mainly by runners (specialized stems that produce new plants at each of their nodes). Nourished at first by the parent plant, the new plants form roots of their own.

9 Blackberries will root naturally where trailing or damaged shoots touch the soil surface. Gardeners assist the process by weighting down the shoot or pegging its tip into a pot of prepared soil. Loganberries multiply the same way.

10 Strawberries may be multiplied simply by pegging their runners into peat pots sunk in soil. Well-grown young plants may be lifted when rooted and replanted without removal from the pots.

11 In one type of air-layering the plant's stem is slit [A] and the slit kept open [B]. After roots form [C] they are covered by moist peat [D-F] wrapped in plastic. When the roots have grown enough, the stem is cut off and planted.

velop quite freely from seed, but the seedlings vary in quality. Practically all those in cultivation are clones—often of a chance seedling, such as Northern Spy—produced by grafting cuttings onto rootstocks of the same or closely allied species. The type of stock used often affects the size of the mature tree or bush, while the scion determines fruit variety. In making a graft it is essential to align the cambium layer (a thin layer of tissue-forming cells under the bark) of the scion (the new plant material) with that of the stock (the host plant), since it is the active cambial tissue that fuses and that subsequently forms water- and nutrient-conducting tissues [16]. The scion is normally a short length of twig of the desired type, trimmed to fit into the prepared stock. Grafting dates back to classical times, when it was used especially for the propagation of grape vines.

Budding, as practiced with roses, is a type of grafting [12]. A bud of the desired clone, with a small spur of bark and cambium, is inserted under the bark on the stem of a young wild-rose rootstock. The rootstock most commonly used in the United States is *Rosa multiflora*. For a bush rose the bud is inserted at ground level on the stem of a two-year-old multiflora seedling. A standard (tree) rose is budded on young lateral shoots at the desired height, close to the main stem of the stock. After the bud begins growing, the gardener prunes the stock to concentrate the plant's whole activity into the developing scion. He may also graft stem cuttings onto the stock; this is the usual method for ramblers.

Much research has been carried out in recent years into the selection and breeding of stocks for grafting and budding and the range is now large. Horticulturists have paid particular attention to the production of dwarfing stocks for modern orchards. The dwarf trees permit closer planting with less labor for pruning and picking the fruit.

Root cuttings may be used for the propagation of some herbaceous plants [19]. Included among them are species of *Acanthus, Anchusa, Romneya,* and, in the kitchen garden, horseradish *(Armoracia rusticana)* and sea kale *(Crambe maritima)*.

Pollination is vital to the production of normal fruits. The process is usually left to insects, but they are not always to be relied upon in greenhouses. The family Cucurbitaceae—which includes squashes and melons—give problems in pollination because male and female organs are carried by separate flowers whose number may not balance. To ensure that the greatest number of female melon flowers are fertilized, gardeners sometimes resort to hand pollination [C]. Pollen from the male melon flower [B] is transferred by hand to the stigma of the female flower [A]. Hand pollination is also used with squashes but not with cucumbers.

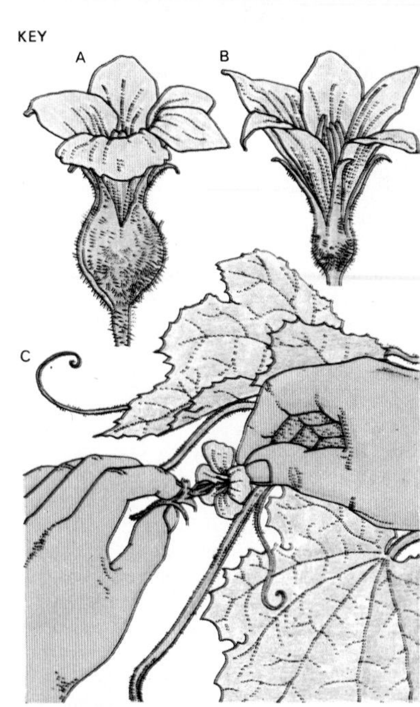
KEY
A
B
C

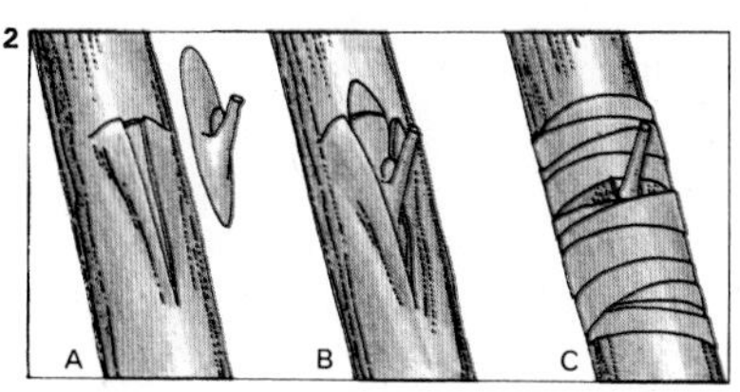
12
A
B
C

12 Budding, as used for roses, consists in taking a sliver from a leaf axil with a bud and inserting it into a T-shaped cut in the young skin of the stock [A,B] and secured with a rubber band [C]. Once established, the shoot into which it was put is severed above the join. This is a convenient way to propagate, because a healthy scion produces many buds. Stem cuttings may be grafted for ramblers.

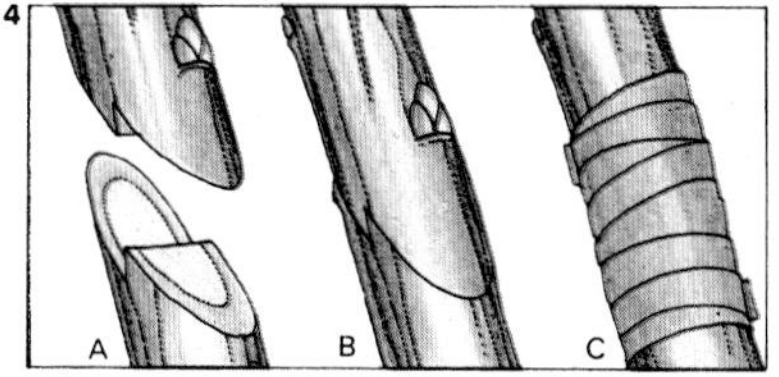
14
A
B
C

14 Whip and tongue grafts are usually carried out in the spring. Scion and stock [A] must match [B] and be at the same stage of development. The graft [C] is bound until it grows together with the stock.

15 Standard tree roses are budded high on a rootstock grown in the previous year. Bush roses are budded at ground level on younger stocks. Many roses will also grow from cuttings.

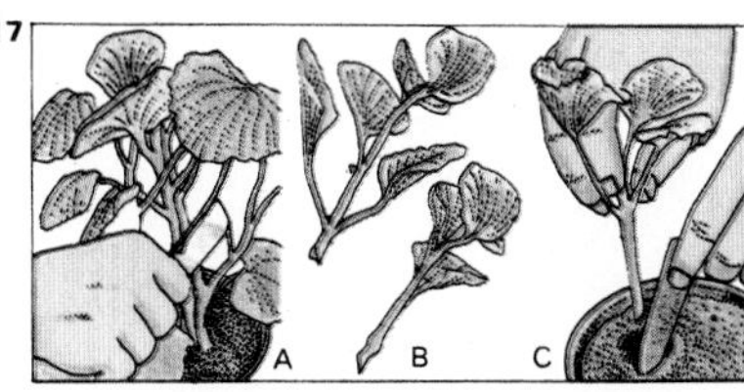
17
A
B
C

17 Stem cuttings [A] are taken of a variety of plants. They are trimmed just below a bud [B] and the leaves removed to adjust for depth of planting in a loose-textured compost [C]. Until roots form, the cuttings must be kept damp.

18 Camellias are normally propagated from leaf-bud cuttings. The leaf, with the bud in its axil, is cut off, together with a section of its bark. This is set with the exposed base of the bud on top of a compost-filled, protected pot.

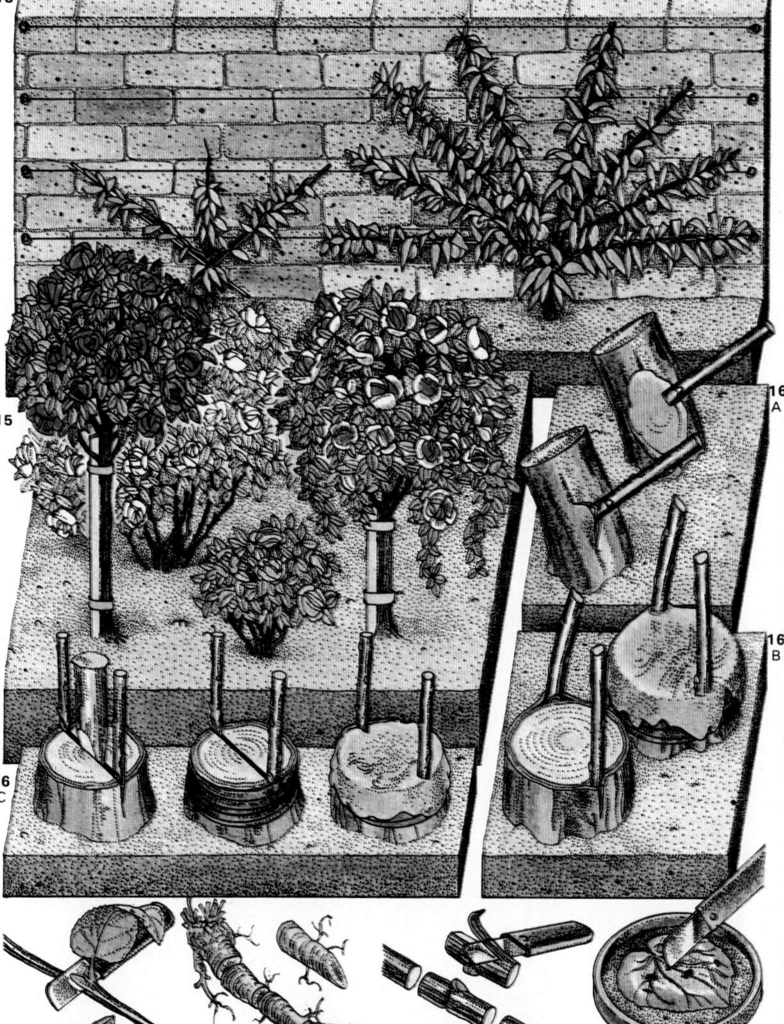
13
15
16 A
16 B
16 C
18
19
20
21

13 Trained fruit trees occupy less space than standards and take advantage of favorable positions, such as wall borders. Here, a peach is trained as a horizontal espalier. All but a few young branches are pruned away and two each year are tied to the wall. Often apples are restricted to one main stem grown on a diagonal, while peaches, apricots, and cherries are trained in a fan.

16 Grafting into old trees is commonly performed in orchard trees to change the variety without grubbing out the trees. A bark graft [A] is sealed in place with clay or grafting wax. The crown graft [B] is the most commonly adopted form. The cleft graft [C] requires the gardener to split the stock with a wedge so that he can insert the pointed twig of the scion. In all cases grafts must be tightly bound and sealed.

19 The hollyhock *(Althaea)* can be multiplied by root cuttings. This is useful for hybrids that do not seed readily.

20 Vines and vinestocks may be multiplied by bud cuttings. The bud, with its sliver of bark, is placed in a suitable rooting medium.

21 Begonia rex, grown for its foliage, forms new individuals at cuts in the main veins of its leaves when placed on moist, sandy compost.

Staple foods: grains

The history of civilization has always been closely paralleled by the development of cereals—mainly wheat and barley in the world's temperate zones and corn and rice in the tropics.

Wheat and barley

Wheat was perhaps the earliest cereal to be brought into cultivation, the oldest authenticated remains of wheat seeds being found in the excavated site of a seventh millennium BC village in the Tigris-Euphrates valley (now eastern Iraq). Grains there have been matched against wild wheats that still grow in the near East (*Triticum boeoticum* and *Triticum dicoccoides*).

Yields of these early wheats were small compared with those achieved by modern farmers who use more sophisticated varieties and intensive cultivation techniques to harvest up to 3 tons per acre (7 tons per hectare). The principal wheat-growing areas are the grassland zones [2], primarily the steppe regions of the Soviet Union and China, and the great prairies of the United States and Canada [Key]. Wheat cannot be grown in wet and humid tropical areas, as the grain is badly affected by disease.

Two major types of wheat are cultivated today—winter wheat and spring wheat. The former is sown in the autumn in regions where winters are comparatively mild. It grows strongly in the spring for harvest about ten months after sowing. Spring wheat is used in areas where severe winters would kill the plants of winter varieties. It is sown as soon as frost leaves the ground and is harvested in late summer—the same time as winter varieties. Winter wheats are higher yielding than spring wheats but produce a lower quality of flour.

Barley [10] originated in Abyssinia and has been cultivated in Egypt for at least 6,000 years. It grows mainly in the same areas as wheat, although plant breeding developments have extended barley growing into colder areas. It used to be grown mainly for human consumption as a parched grain or as a meal, but today it is used to feed animals and for making malt—which in turn is used for distilling or brewing into alcoholic drinks.

Two other cereals are important in temperate zones—oats and rye [10]. The common oat has been cultivated in western Asia and the Mediterranean countries for around 2,000 years. The main uses are for cattle fodder or for human consumption as a breakfast cereal. Most rye is grown in eastern Europe and the Soviet Union, as a forage crop for dairy cattle and for rye flour.

Corn and rice

Most important of the tropical cereals is corn, now second to wheat in international importance as a food grain [4, 5]. It was known in America before the Spaniards found the New World, and it was first domesticated in Central America. Today developments in plant breeding are extending the corn-growing areas farther into the temperate zones [6].

In general, however, corn requires a hot, humid climate and will not tolerate frost during the growing season. Its main use is as a fodder plant and for manufacturing purposes. The grains are used extensively in animal feeds and also for making starch

CONNECTIONS

See also

302 World food resources
398 The future of food
322 Plant genetic resources
328 Bread and pasta
350 Beer and brewing
452 Flowering plants: one seed leaf

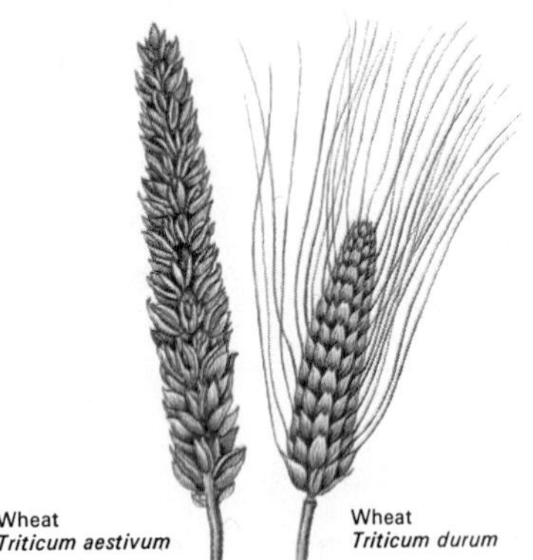

1
Wheat
Triticum aestivum
Wheat
Triticum durum

1 One of the common bread wheats grown extensively throughout the temperate lands is *Triticum aestivum*. It is a soft, mealy wheat used for flour and cracker manufacture. *Triticum durum*, however, is one of the hard wheats. This particular species of wheat is used primarily for grinding into a flour that is manufactured into pasta products, such as macaroni.

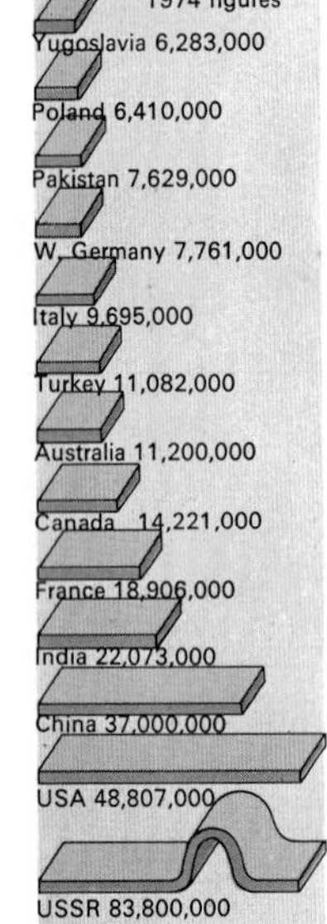

2 Wheat production in tons
1974 figures
Yugoslavia 6,283,000
Poland 6,410,000
Pakistan 7,629,000
W. Germany 7,761,000
Italy 9,695,000
Turkey 11,082,000
Australia 11,200,000
Canada 14,221,000
France 18,906,000
India 22,073,000
China 37,000,000
USA 48,807,000
USSR 83,800,000

2 Total world production of wheat is now more than 315 million tons. The wheat producing countries include those that are self-supporting or need to import to make up local deficiencies, such as India and most of Europe, and the exporters such as the United States, Canada, and Australia. The pattern of trade is for wheat to be exported from these countries to areas in the tropics.

3 Europe, excluding the Soviet Union, grows about a quarter of the total world wheat crop and the yields are the highest in the world. The Soviet wheat belt produces about one fifth of the world total. Key areas are the prairies of North America, India, China, the northern tip of Africa, the temperate zones of Australia, and the South American grain producers—Uruguay, Chile, and Argentina.

3 Wheat

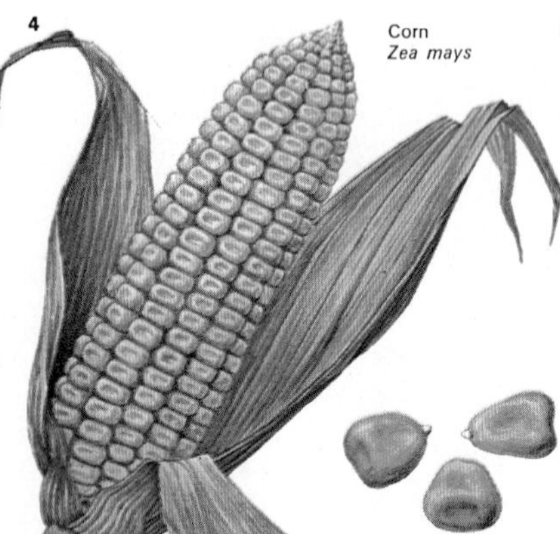

4
Corn
Zea mays

4 Corn *(Zea mays)* is the key cereal in the subtropical zones of the world. It can yield up to 2 tons per acre (5 tons per hectare). Modern techniques of harvesting and storage, and the fact that it is relatively free from most major cereal diseases (except blight and stem rot), have made it a favorite with farmers in developing countries. Hybridization techniques have resulted in many new varieties of corn with increased yield potential and a high degree of disease resistance.

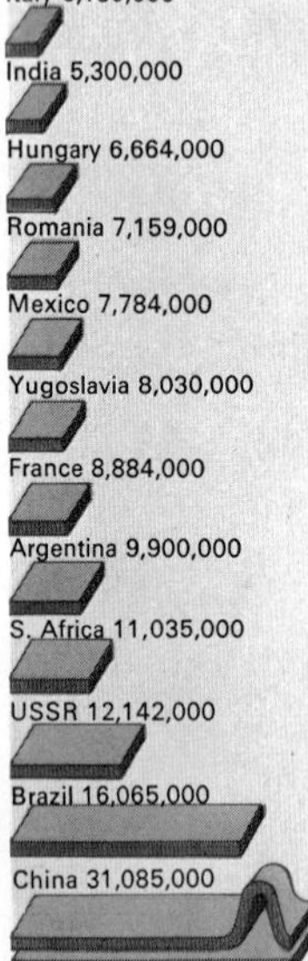

5 Corn production in tons
1974 figures
Italy 5,180,000
India 5,300,000
Hungary 6,664,000
Romania 7,159,000
Mexico 7,784,000
Yugoslavia 8,030,000
France 8,884,000
Argentina 9,900,000
S. Africa 11,035,000
USSR 12,142,000
Brazil 16,065,000
China 31,085,000
USA 118,144,000

5 World production of corn has almost trebled in the past 50 years, to 300 million tons. The United States is the major exporting country, although it now produces a lower proportion of the total world corn harvest than it did in the early part of the century. Small quantities are produced for export in Brazil, Argentina, and South Africa, most of it for animal feed used in northwestern Europe. Production in the Soviet Union is also high.

6 The US Corn Belt produces nearly half of the world's corn, although a decreasing proportion of this is exported. Most of it is used on farms and supports a vast cattle and pig producing industry. In Europe, corn is restricted to the warm, damper areas such as Romania, Yugoslavia, Hungary, and parts of Italy. It is the major cereal crop in Africa but of secondary importance to rice in most Asian countries. Mexico is also a major producer.

6 Corn

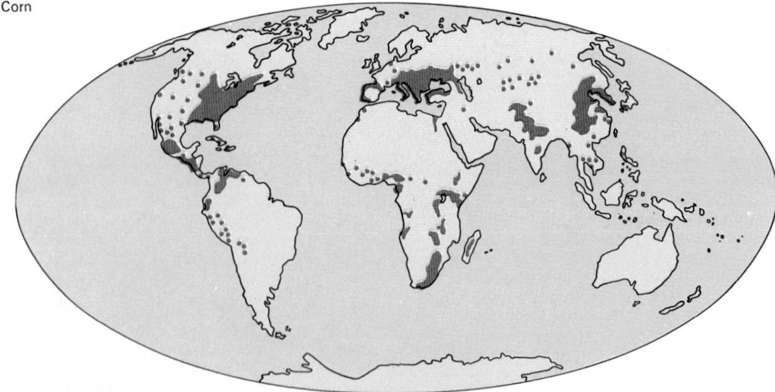

and for human consumption as corn meal and cornflakes.

The corn plant may grow to a height of 15ft (4.5m) and with its big, spreading leaves differs greatly from the grass-type cereals such as wheat and barley. In cooler, temperate countries it is now becoming an important forage crop for beef and dairy cattle. The whole corn plant is cut, wilted, and stored in a silo for winter feeding.

Although of less importance in world trading terms, rice is perhaps the most vital of cereals [7, 8]. It is said to provide food for more people than any other of the world's cereals. The plant can grow to a height of 5ft (1.5m) and is probably a native of India. It is an annual swamp plant [9]. Unlike the other major cereals, it is not sown directly into the field and left until harvest. Instead, the seeds are sown and when the young plants are big enough they are transplanted into flooded "paddy" fields. These fields are drained at harvest and the rice is then treated like the other small grains and, in developed farming areas, is harvested mechanically with a combine harvester.

The grains of the rice plant are high in starch. In some cases it is ground into a flour but mainly it is husked and eaten, boiled, in its original state. It is cultivated principally in southern and eastern Asia, the great river deltas and alluvial plains forming the main production areas. Some rice is still produced in hilly areas, where the slopes are terraced to allow flooding and draining.

The United States has become an important rice growing area, and research has shown that the laborious transplanting of the rice plant is unnecessary and the crop can be drilled directly into the field like other cereals. These techniques are cutting the cost of rice production and encouraging its spread and expansion.

Millet and sorghum

Another long-cultivated cereal, again native to China, is millet [10]. It grows to a height of around 40in (1m). Millet tolerates prolonged drought and is grown mainly in the rain-deficient tropical areas of Africa and Asia. Sorghum [10] is also vital to tropical Africa, where it is the main bread plant.

KEY

Huge wheat silos on the prairie skyline of midwest North America testify to this region's importance as a wheat producer. Known as "Kansas cathedrals," they could become bulwarks against global famine from population growth.

Rice
Oryza sativa

7 Rice *(Oryza sativa)* is the basic food grain in densely populated monsoon Asia. The husk of the grain has a high silicon content and is dangerous to animals. The outer skin and kernel contain the protein and vitamins. The rice plant is commonly known as paddy, thus "paddy fields," and only when it has been harvested and the husk removed does it technically become the rice that is sold.

8 Rice production in tons
1974 figures

USA	5,175,000
Port Timor	5,594,000
S. Korea	5,908,000
Brazil	6,817,000
Burma	8,446,000
Vietnam	11,400,000
Thailand	13,175,000
Japan	15,902,000
Bangladesh	17,222,000
Indonesia	22,800,000
India	61,500,000
China	115,275,000

8 In the early 1970s world production of rice totaled over 310 million tons, including an estimate for production in China. There is, however, little international trade. There was world overproduction of the grain in the early 1970s and developed countries were urged to curb production to avoid damaging the market for countries that relied on rice as a major source of their national income.

9 The river deltas and plains of China and southwest Asia are the main rice producing areas of the world and up to three or four crops a year are taken from many fields, although this practice soon depletes the soil. China produces an estimated 100 million tons, while India, Pakistan, and Bangladesh produce 60 million tons. Japan, Thailand, and Vietnam are other major producing areas.

9 Rice

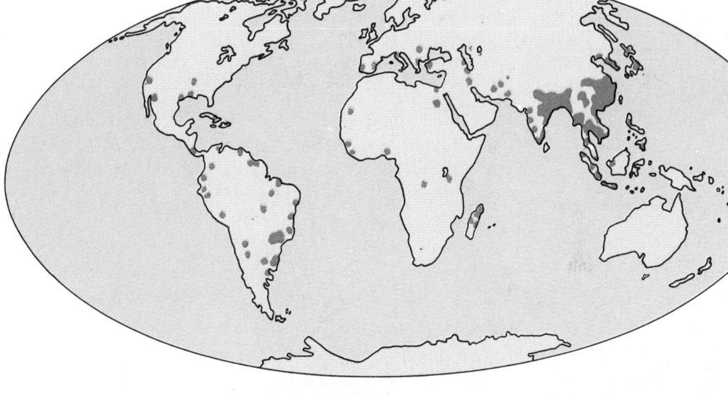

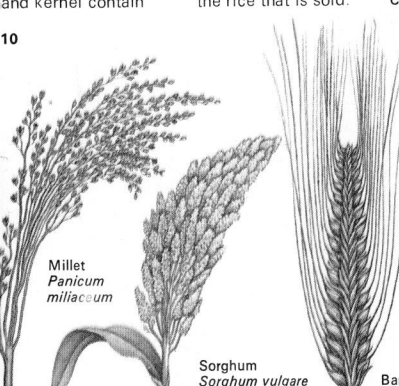

10

Millet *Panicum miliaceum*

Sorghum *Sorghum vulgare*

Barley *Hordeum vulgare*

Oats *Avena sativa*

Rye *Secale cereale*

10 One of the oldest cultivated small grains in the world is millet *(Panicum miliaceum)*, which is grown in tropical Africa. It tolerates prolonged drought and, when exported, is used largely in birdseed preparations. A grain of similar importance in Africa is sorghum *(Sorghum vulgare)*. It is used extensively in the manufacture of beer. Barley *(Hordeum vulgare)* is one of the principal cereals of temperate agriculture and is widely grown in Europe, America, and Australia. Most varieties are spring sown, as they will not tolerate frost during the growing season. Oats *(Avena sativa)* and rye *(Secale cereale)* are both thought to have been first noticed growing as weeds in early wheat cultivation. Both cereals are now extensively grown in many parts of Europe, rye proving particularly popular in the glacial soils of central Europe and the USSR. Rye grows well in poorer soils than those required for most cereal grains.

11

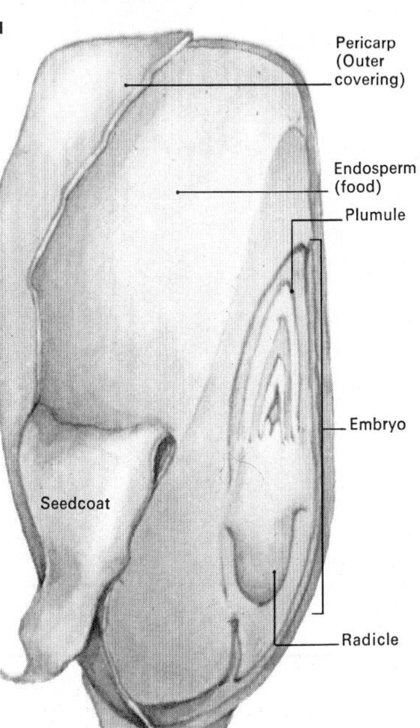
Pericarp
(Outer
covering)
Endosperm
(food)
Plumule
Embryo
Seedcoat
Radicle

11 A "seed" of corn *(Zea mays)* contains both the embryo of the future plant and also the food to nourish it while it germinates. The main food supply, as in all grain crops, is found in a single seed leaf since the plant is a monocotyledon (as opposed to a dicotyledon such as the bean, in which the food is contained in two leaves within the seed), and consists predominantly of carbohydrates. It is this food supply that makes the plant economically important. The embryo, consisting of the young shoot, the plumule, and the root, the radicle, contains much of the protein. Once lost through primitive winnowing techniques, today the embryo and its protein are saved.

Bread and pasta

Western man is capable of creating ever more complex and exotic gourmet dishes to tempt his palate. These invariably contain large amounts of protein, carbohydrate and fat but much of the world's population is concerned from day to day with ways in which to obtain staple, flour-based foods—mainly bread and pasta—that are the basic staff of life.

The first loaf of bread probably originated from the grass seeds that an ingenious prehistoric person, some 8,000 years ago, gathered, ground into flour, mixed with water, covered with hot ashes and baked on a hot stone. The ancient Hebrews, Chinese, and Egyptians all ate flat cakes made from flour and water, but the Egyptians were the first to discover that allowing the dough to ferment produced gases that made the resulting bread both lighter and softer.

Ancient recipes preserved

Despite the many variations that have developed [1], ranging from white bread and black bread to Alaskan sourdough bread and Irish soda bread, and despite modern production methods, in essence bread remains the same as when its Neolithic originator began making it. Bread is simply dough made from flour, moistened with water or milk, usually leavened with yeast or a similar fermenting agent, and then baked, or even steamed.

Bread flour is made from wheat, rye, barley, or oats. What makes a soft, spongy loaf is the nature of the wheat's protein (gluten). The different glutens in barley and rye make for heavy bread; corn and rice, having no gluten, cannot be made into leavened bread without combing them with gluten flours. Special gluten-free flour is produced, however, for people with certain digestive abnormalities. In the United States and Britain strong flour milled from hard wheat is preferred for its high gluten content, which helps the bread to keep fresh.

Despite the simplicity of using modern yeast [Key] many flat or unleavened breads, usually made from wheat, flour, salt, and water, remain popular for reasons of taste, tradition, religious practice, or climate. The Scandinavians favor a wide selection of crisp *flatbrods* and pliable *lefsers*. Among India's many flat-breads is the *poppadom*—a crisp, thin wafer that is sometimes crumbled over food. The Mexican *tortilla* is made with corn flour instead of wheat.

Nutritionally bread is a relatively inexpensive source of calories, protein, and vitamins. Modern wheat bread is made from flour fortified with small amounts of thiamin, nicotinic acid, iron, and calcium.

Pasta—pipes, shells, rings and bows

Although legend tells that Marco Polo returned from China to Venice more than 700 years ago with the pasta that became Italy's most distinctive national food, equipment for making *leganum* (pasta similar to *tagliatelli*) used by the Romans was found in the ruins of Pompeii. Whatever its origins, pasta has remained an Italian speciality, although it is popular in other countries also. Noodles still feature widely in Chinese and Southeast Asian cooking and with greater or lesser prominence in the cuisines of Japan, France, and the United States. In cen-

CONNECTIONS

See also
326 Staple foods: grai

1

1 Bread has always had a special meaning. Christians use it at Holy Communion to symbolize the body of Christ; the Arabic words for bread and life have the same origin. Festive breads such as Mexican fiesta bread, Russion kulich, and Jewish matzos have long been important in seasonal and religious celebrations.

1 Indian poppadum
2 Jewish matzos
3 Rye crispbread
4 Scandinavian crispbread
5 Pitta with sesame seeds
6 Pitta
7 Indian naan
8 Indian chapati
9 Dark rye
10 German rye
11 Pumpernickel
12 Russian black
13 Wholemeal loaf
14 Rye with caraway seeds
15 Danish rye
16 American sourdough
17 Irish soda
18 French petite baguette
19 American cornbread
20 French petit Parisien
21 French baguette
22 Scottish bap roll
23 English cottage
24 French pain Espagnol
25 Jewish challah
26 French épi de Charente
27 Croissant

tral Europe they are often served with meat instead of potatoes or rice. But the formidable assortment of Italian pasta and the many ways they are served are incomparable.

There are many more than 60 varieties of pasta [2] included in the three main categories—rod or tubular forms, like *spaghetti* and *macaroni;* flat sheets or strips like *lasagna* or *fettucini* (which may be flavored with spinach); and the small, grainlike soup pasta *(pastina).* Pasta is cooked by boiling or is boiled then baked and is always served with a sauce of some kind.

Food for more than half the world

Rice provides a staple diet for more than half the population of the world, for whom it provides 80 percent or more of their total diet. It is thought that altogether there are more than 7,000 cultivated varieties of rice, of which over 1,000 are grown in India alone [3]. Of the long-grained variety Patna and Basmati are among the most widely known. Although their names do not necessarily denote their origins, other varieties include Java or Spanish rice, with more oval shaped grains; Piedmont rice, which is short, round, and very white; and Carolina, another long-grained rice.

The rice plant grows best in paddy fields [4], although there is a variety that thrives on dry land [5]. Early records refer to Chinese irrigation systems for rice-growing in 770 BC, and in India and the Philippines terraces built 2,000 years ago still support rice cultivation. Today, as centuries ago, the rice plants are grown in water until they flower, then the field is slowly dried out as the grain ripens.

The grains are then hulled and undergo a polishing process that removes the germ and bran layers. In this process the rice is robbed of many of the proteins and vitamins it contains. In most lands where rice is the main food source only the husk is removed: the "brown rice" that remains retains its valuable nourishment.

While rice cannot be satisfactorily processed into bread, it is eaten extensively in many other ways—on its own, in soups, puddings, cakes, or accompanied by all kinds of vegetables and meat.

KEY

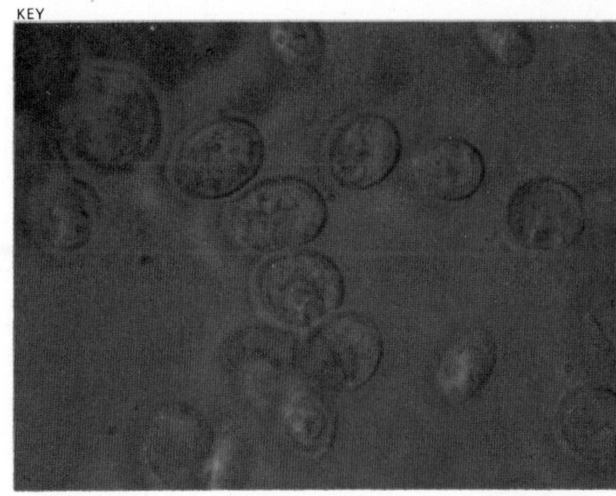

Baking yeast *(Saccharomyces cerevisiae)* is a microscopic form of life with remarkable powers. Combined with sugar and warmed, yeast ferments; an enzyme in it produces alcohol and the gas carbon dioxide from the sugar. It is the carbon dioxide that makes the yeast-leavened dough rise. Commercial yeast is available in two forms, compressed and granular. Billions of individual cells are contained in compressed yeast, each containing the enzyme responsible for the process of fermentation.

2

3

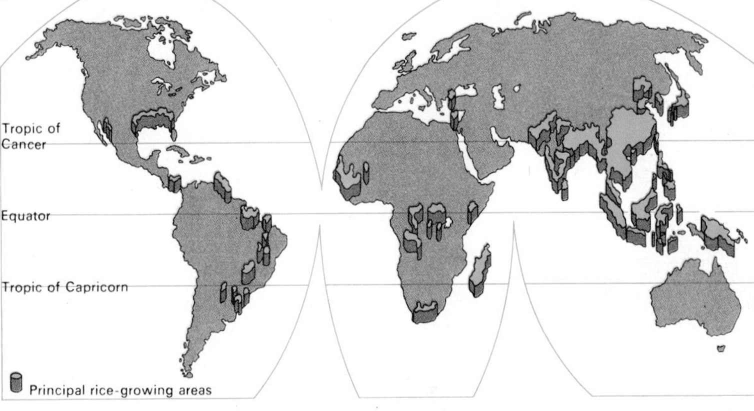

Tropic of Cancer
Equator
Tropic of Capricorn
Principal rice-growing areas

2 All pasta is made from the same ingredients following a basic method. A flour mixture is prepared from dried durum wheat. This is mixed with warm water and kneaded into a stiff dough. Dried or fresh eggs or spinach can be added, although most pasta is a simple flour and water combination. The dough is forced through perforated cylinders to be made into various shapes. Small pasta like *macaroni* is cut to size as it emerges from the presses while the longer noodles or *spaghetti* are produced to different lengths by machines. The cut pasta is then dried in ovens or on racks.

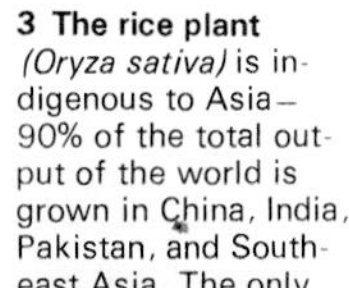

3 The rice plant *(Oryza sativa)* is indigenous to Asia—90% of the total output of the world is grown in China, India, Pakistan, and Southeast Asia. The only Asian countries to produce enough for export are Burma and Thailand. Cultivated rice was first referred to in China over 5,000 years ago. It was introduced to the Nile delta and thence to Spain and northern Italy in the fifteenth century from where its cultivation reached Brazil and North America in 1635.

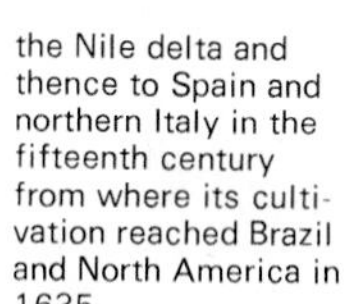

4

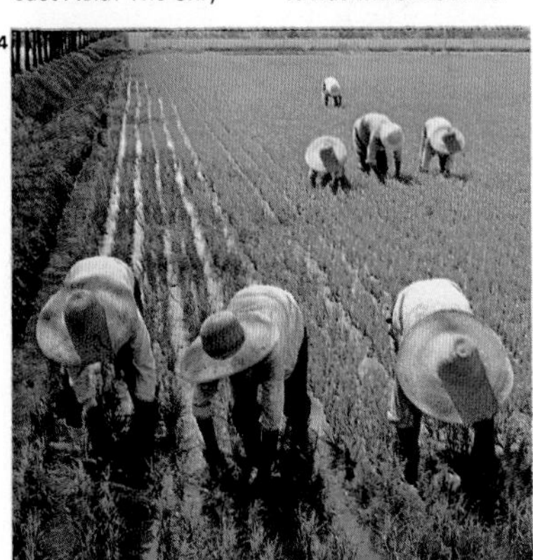

4 The staple diet of most people in the East, rice can be grown where there is sufficient water to flood the fields or paddies in which it is planted. Young plants are set out by hand in fertile mud, which is permanently flooded during the growing period and gradually drained as the rice grains ripen. The plants' nodding golden tassels are a familiar sight in temperate and tropical regions throughout the world.

5

5 The rice of the paddy fields is more common than any other variety. But about 10% of all rice is "upland rice." This grows on dry land and is cultivated in much the same way as any other cereal grain.

Staple foods: legumes

All commercially grown species of peas and beans are legumes, members of the family leguminosae. Generally, peas and beans can be eaten raw, but there is one major exception, the soybean [1].

Soybean production

Soybeans were first cultivated in China more than 4,000 years ago and today they are still one of the main sources of vegetable protein for people living in the Far East; elsewhere they are used mainly as food for animals. More than half of the world's annual crop of 50 million tons is now grown in the United States. But large areas of soybeans are still cultivated in China, Japan, and parts of the Soviet Union as well as in South America [4].

The importance of soybeans has now spread from the eastern countries to the West. In the United States the main production area is in the eastern and middle eastern states, where the crop is intensively cultivated by grain farmers, who can use the same harvesting and storage equipment for the crop as they use for wheat and barley. The crop is gradually being developed in more northerly latitudes as plant breeders introduce varieties that can resist cold climates. Parts of Europe, especially southern France, Italy, and Spain, now produce soybeans, and crops have been tried experimentally in Britain and Sweden. It is expected that varieties suitable for cultivation in northern Europe will be available by the 1980s.

Major livestock-producing nations use vast quantities of soybeans either ground or, more usually, crushed. Crushed soybeans yield large amounts of oil, which is used in the manufacture of margarine and cooking oils and, in a refined form, to make varnishes and other industrial products [3].

Recently soybeans have been used to make texturized vegetable proteins, also known as meat substitutes. Other legumes, such as field beans and field peas [6], can be used in a similar way. The protein content [7] is separated from a flour produced by milling beans or peas. This flour is then extruded into a thin silk-like thread that is woven mechanically to produce a solid form. The technology has become so advanced that imitations of meat, fish, and other natural foods can be manufactured. As animal proteins become more expensive to produce, such texturized vegetable substitutes will become relatively cheaper and may become part of the everyday diet in much of the world.

Peas and green beans

The most important legume grown in cool temperate zones is the pea [5]. Large areas are planted in Europe, the United States, and Canada, and in parts of the Southern Hemisphere with similar climates, such as New Zealand. The pea came originally from western Asia. It reached China from Persia about AD 400 and was introduced into the United States during the earlier years of colonization.

Peas have several uses. In most industrialized countries they are eaten either fresh or in some processed form—usually either canned or frozen. New techniques involving quick freezing of the crop within hours of harvest have widened its potential

CONNECTIONS

See also
362 Fiber and oil crops
302 World food resources
398 The future of food

1 Soybeans, grown throughout the world, are natives of China, where they were first cultivated some 4,000 years ago. They were introduced into North America in 1880. The plants can grow to about 24in (60 cm), but most varieties attain about 18in (45cm), carrying their pods quite near the ground.

Glycine max

2 The flowers of the soybean vary from white to light purple. The beans themselves are yellow, brown, or black, depending on the variety. The crop is now grown on a vast scale in the United States, but it is not high-yielding, producing less than a ton of dried beans to the acre. The soybean is today the largest single source of vegetable oil and protein meal in the United States.

3 The versatility of the soybean as a vegetable means it can be put to almost any use, ranging from direct consumption in less favored areas to sophisticated industrial uses in developed countries. Products made from it include bean curd [A]; vegetable oils [B], which are used in cooking and are refined for the manufacture of margarine; soy sauce [C], a fermented flavoring that is used in oriental cooking; and texturized vegetable protein [D]. The oil is also used in soap manufacture [E] and for inks, cosmetics, dyes, paints [F], varnishes [G], and glues. It is also processed into lacquers used in coloring floor coverings [H]. When the oil is crushed from the bean a high-protein meal remains. Once pressed, this can be fed directly to animals [I] or incorporated with cereals into livestock feeds [J].

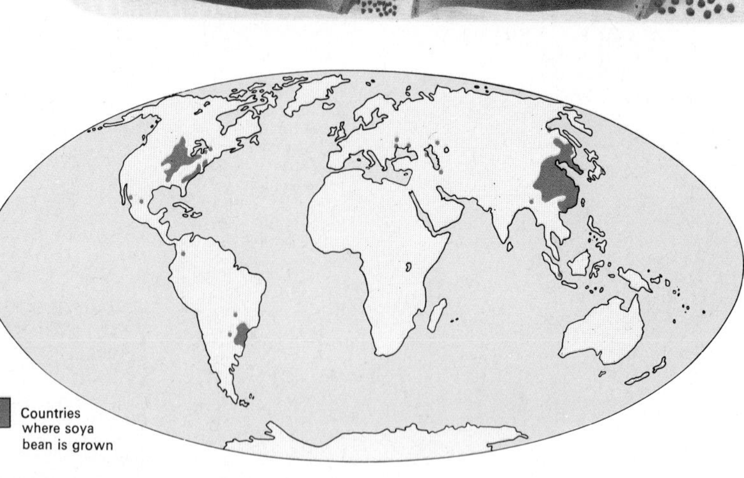
Countries where soya bean is grown

4 Cultivation of soybeans has spread in response to the increasing world demand for protein. The main areas are the United States, with more than half of world production, and the Far East, notably China, Japan, and Korea. The crop is spreading into parts of South America, especially Brazil, and into developing African states. As new varieties resistant to colder climates become available, more soybeans will be grown in Europe and northeast-ern Asia.

market and peas are now eaten all year round. Some varieties are not harvested in the fresh, immature state, but are left on the field to ripen and dry. They are then harvested with combine harvesters in much the same way as grain crops. They are dried further during storage and either sold dry, or soaked and canned as "processed" peas. Britain has traditionally imported Alaskan peas from North America for canning in this way, but now new varieties have been developed and the American trade has diminished.

Dwarf green beans are another important legume for the crop farmer and they are grown in the same areas as peas. The crop is also eaten either fresh or processed by canning or freezing.

Pea and bean crops are especially important to crop farmers because most do not need to have extra nitrates added to the soil to aid their growth. As leguminous plants, they have the ability to "fix" nitrogen from the air in small nitrate nodules that form on the roots of the plants (with the help of symbiotic bacteria). In this way they increase the fertility of the soil for the following crop. The dwarf green bean is an exception in that it needs the addition of inorganic nitrogen to give an economic yield.

Other edible pods and beans

Many other members of the bean family are common as garden plants grown for home consumption [6]. Scarlet runner beans, which are picked when immature and can be eaten fresh, frozen, or canned, broad beans, and various types of haricot beans belong to this category. Blackeyed peas and mung beans, however, form staple diets in the areas of the world in which they proliferate. One of the earliest cultivated legumes is the lentil, a native plant of Asia and a traditional source of vegetable protein in Middle Eastern countries.

One other bean that is widely grown in the United States and widely consumed is the navy bean, a variety of the same species as the dwarf green bean. It is shipped in the dry harvested state and is then processed and canned into the familiar baked bean, sometimes in a tomato-flavored sauce.

KEY

The soybean harvester is used when the crop is ready for harvesting. This is when the pod and stem dry out and the moisture content of the seed is about 13 percent. The low moisture level is essential for safe storage of the seed.

5

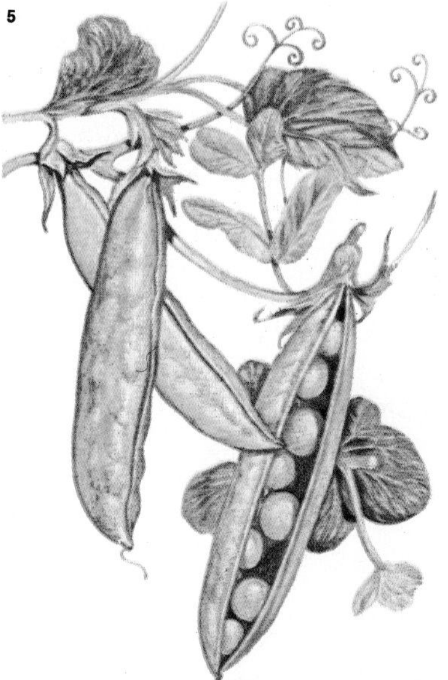

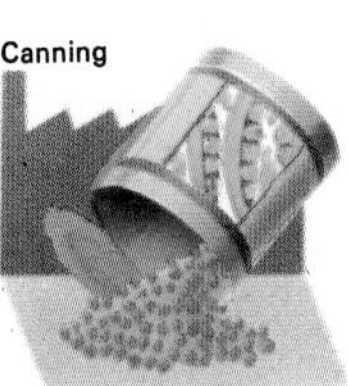
Canning

Freezing

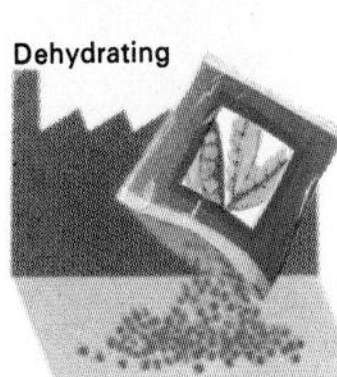

Dehydrating

5 The garden pea *(Pisum sativum)* is eaten all year round. The crop is grown on a field scale with planting dates staggered to allow steady harvesting for processing. For canning, freezing, and dehydrating the peas are taken into the factory within two or three hours of harvesting. For canning they are washed, sorted, and put into cans before cooking. For freezing, they are sorted, graded and blast-frozen. The whole process takes only about 20 minutes. The dehydration, or freeze-drying, technique is even quicker. All the water is extracted from the peas, which then have to be rehydrated by soaking before they are used as food.

6 Peas and beans are vital parts of the staple diet in many parts of the world, whether used for human consumption or as a prime feed protein for cattle. This international selection of peas and beans includes green gram, or mung, beans [A]; butter beans [B]; pea beans [C]; black gram beans [D]; pilab beans [F]; the traditional American blackeyed peas [G]; purple-coated kidney beans [H]; soybeans [I]; the brown and the white haricot bean [J,K], both varieties of the species *Phaseolus vulgaris;* scarlet runner beans [L]; and chick peas [M], also known as garbanzos.

6

A
B
C
D
E
F
G
H
I
J
K
L
M

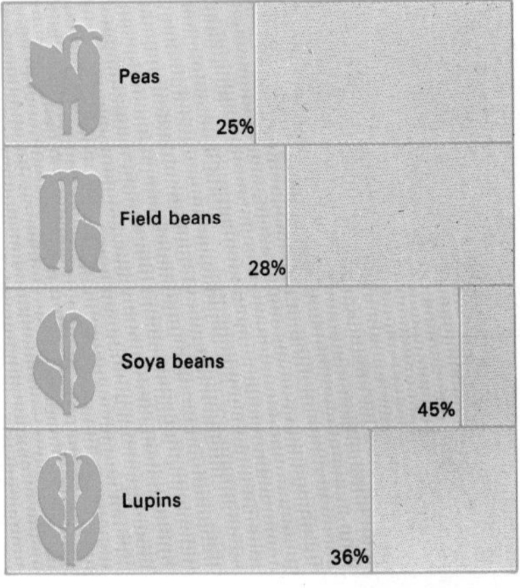
Peas
25%
Field beans
28%
Soya beans
45%
Lupins
36%

7 Most legumes contain protein in relatively large amount. The 25% protein content of peas is exploited through processing of the crop in Canada, where a high-protein flour is made for sale to countries short of protein. The horse bean is used mainly for animal feed. The soybean is useful for human or animal feed. Lupins are poisonous but can be treated to make animal feed.

8

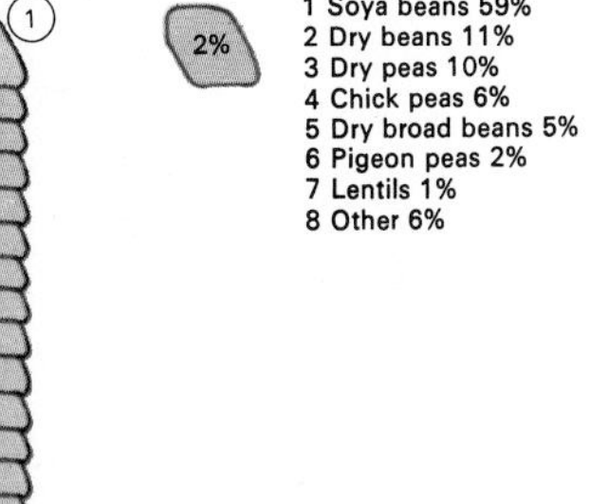
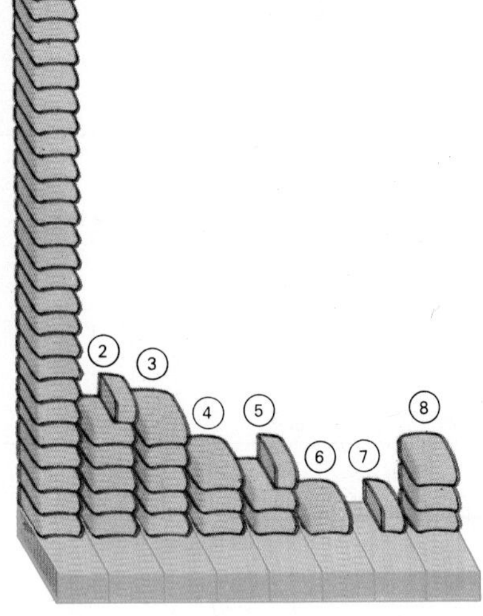
1
2%
2
3
4
5
6
7
8

1 Soya beans 59%
2 Dry beans 11%
3 Dry peas 10%
4 Chick peas 6%
5 Dry broad beans 5%
6 Pigeon peas 2%
7 Lentils 1%
8 Other 6%

8 World production of legumes should increase with the continued rise in the demand for both proteins and oils, in which most species are rich. Soybeans however, are likely to remain the most widely cultivated leguminous crop. Several types of pea crop could increase, especially if present North American breeding programs succeed in producing types higher in protein than those now available. The technique of extracting protein and starch separately from peas could have an effect on the areas cultivated. Horse beans, or faba beans, will also increase in popularity. Work in Europe on varieties with resistance to disease is well advanced in an attempt to find an alternative to the soybean.

Staple foods: tubers

Tubers are underground stems especially modified for the storage of plant food. Some plants have tuberous roots that serve the same function. They form part of the staple diet of almost all modern societies.

The most important tuber

To Western peoples, the most important tuber is the potato *(Solanum tuberosum)*. It was taken to Europe by the Spaniards after the middle of the sixteenth century from South America, where it had been a vital part of the diet of the Indians of the Andean Highlands from about AD 200.

Europe accepted the potato gradually. It appeared in the British Isles in the late 1580s and in Central Europe by the early seventeenth century. Russia, the world's major producer, started cultivating potatoes around 1750. English colonists in Virginia probably re-introduced potatoes to the New World. Sailors saw them as a partial defense against scurvy and spread them rapidly around the world.

The potato grows best in light, fertile soils but will survive cold and dampness better than many of the cereal grains. Today the Soviet Union and Poland produce 50 percent more than all the rest of Europe. Similarly, the development of the potato in the United States has been greatest in the north—Idaho, Washington, and Maine.

Modern agricultural techniques—the use of chemical fertilizers, mechanized planting and harvesting, insect control, and the development of disease-free seed potatoes and disease resistant varieties—have led to increased yields.

The potato crop

The potato crop is planted two weeks before the end of frost. Pieces of tubers with one or two eyes are placed at about 1ft (30cm) intervals in rows 2½-3ft (76-91cm) apart, well covered with soil. The plant shoots emerge within two or three weeks of planting and the tubers of early varieties are harvested [Key] about three months after planting [1]. The main part of the crop is taken in autumn. In the United States the fall crop accounts for 75–80 percent of the total production of the six seasonal crops (winter, early spring, late spring, early summer, late summer, and fall); Idaho produces about one-quarter of the total. The potato has traditionally been used as a fresh vegetable, but it is increasingly used as the raw material for the production of processed products [2]. Frozen french fries and potato chips [3], dehydrated potatoes for human consumption or for animal feed, and a variety of canned potato products are extending its use as a food. In the United States, where the trend toward processed and "convenience" foods has been most marked, up to 45 percent of the US potato crop has been eaten in this form. In England the proportion is about 15 percent, while in the Netherlands and Germany, processing potatoes into starch and alcohol is important.

The development of new uses for the potato and the need to adapt the plant to grow in many climates, and to mature earlier or later for specific markets, has led to the development of major plant-breeding programs. Some varieties have the characteristics of early maturity, high starch content, or a smaller proportion of water than usual.

CONNECTIONS

See also
324 Plant propagation
302 World food resources

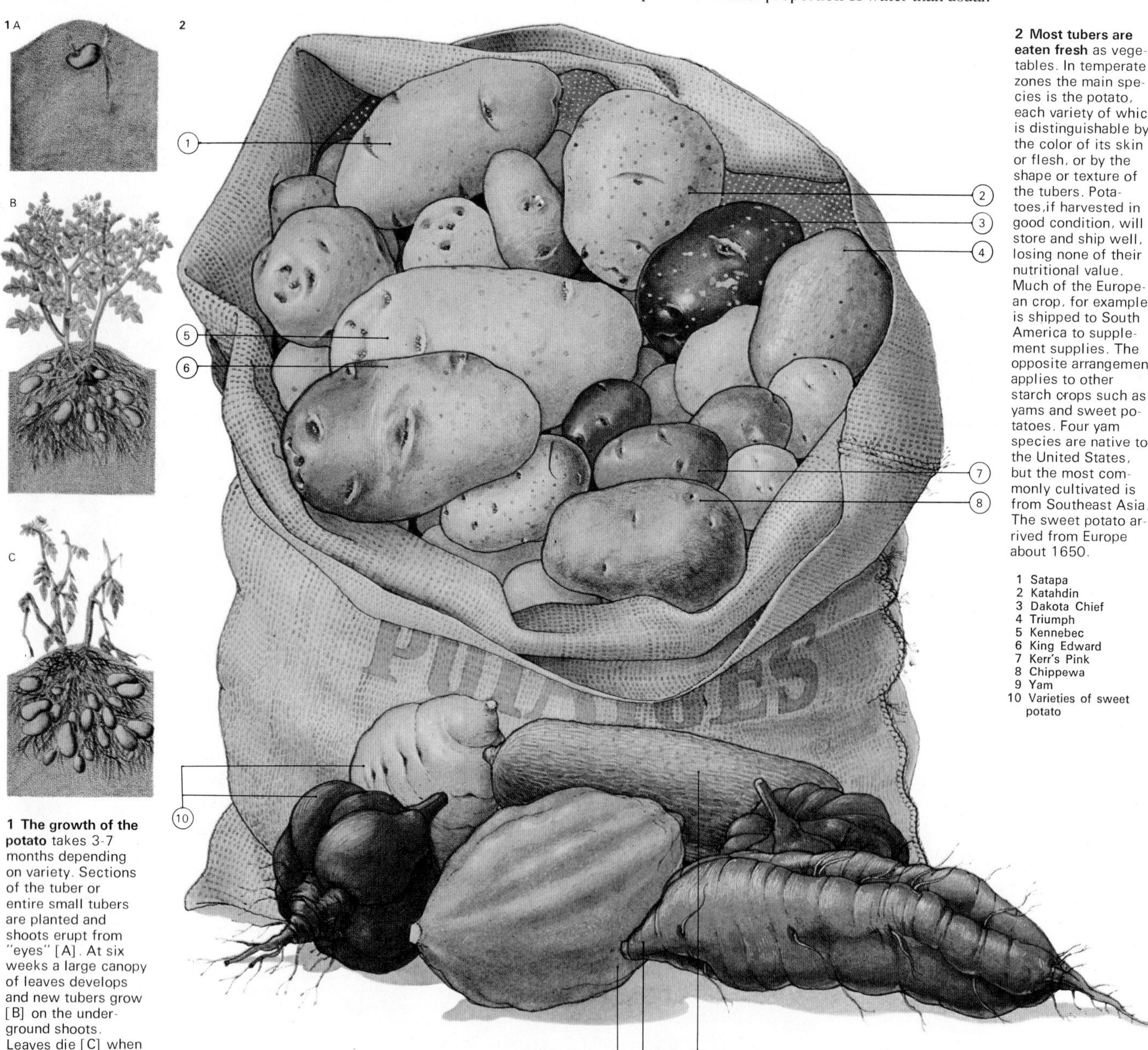
1 A
B
C
2
POTATOES

1 The growth of the potato takes 3-7 months depending on variety. Sections of the tuber or entire small tubers are planted and shoots erupt from "eyes" [A]. At six weeks a large canopy of leaves develops and new tubers grow [B] on the underground shoots. Leaves die [C] when a plant matures.

2 Most tubers are eaten fresh as vegetables. In temperate zones the main species is the potato, each variety of which is distinguishable by the color of its skin or flesh, or by the shape or texture of the tubers. Potatoes, if harvested in good condition, will store and ship well, losing none of their nutritional value. Much of the European crop, for example, is shipped to South America to supplement supplies. The opposite arrangement applies to other starch crops such as yams and sweet potatoes. Four yam species are native to the United States, but the most commonly cultivated is from Southeast Asia. The sweet potato arrived from Europe about 1650.

1 Satapa
2 Katahdin
3 Dakota Chief
4 Triumph
5 Kennebec
6 King Edward
7 Kerr's Pink
8 Chippewa
9 Yam
10 Varieties of sweet potato

Early-maturity varieties of potato have ɜcome vital to the economy of many less ɜveloped countries. In southern Europe ɪe varities harvested in early spring are exorted to northern Europe.

ess productive plants

ther starchy plants—mostly those in tropcal areas—have not yet benefited from ophisticated plant-breeding programs and re comparatively less productive. This ituation is likely to change, particularly ith cassava [6], a tall herb that originated n South and Central America. The two nost useful species are *Manihot dulcis*, the weet cassava, and *Manihot utilissima* (or *1. esculenta*), the manioc, or tapioca, lant.

The sweet cassava has a tuberous unerground stem that is eaten fresh as a vegtable or as a source of starch. By far the nost important species is manioc. When arvested it is bitter and poisonous, but vhen the poisonous juice is washed away he tuber is processed into tapicoa for uman consumption and into cassava meal for animal feed. The importance of the meal as a replacement for grain in animal feeding was highlighted during the world cereal shortage of 1973 and 1974. This shortage and the need to make tropical countries more self-sufficient in food, is leading to far-reaching plant-breeding programs for cassava, which will increase its importance.

Yam *(Dioscorea)* and taro *(Colocasia esculenta)* are tubers that are important in their respective geographic areas. Yams are native to tropical areas of both the Southern and Northern Hemispheres. Taro, which originated in southeastern Asia, has been an important staple food in the Pacific Islands, particularly Polynesia, where it forms the basis of the thick paste called poi.

The sweet potato *(Ipomoea batatas)* bears no relation to its more common namesake. It produces large, irregular roots and is widely cultivated as a vegetable in the southern United States, Central America, the warm Pacific Islands, Japan, and the Soviet Union. It is an annual that flourishes in light, sandy soils where there is a long growing season.

KEY

STANDEN
POTATO HARVESTER
TWF 81 H

Potatoes can be harvested mechanically or by hand. Hand picking of early crops may be done when mechanical lifting is stopped by bad weather, allowing the crop to reach the market when the price for early new potatoes is high.

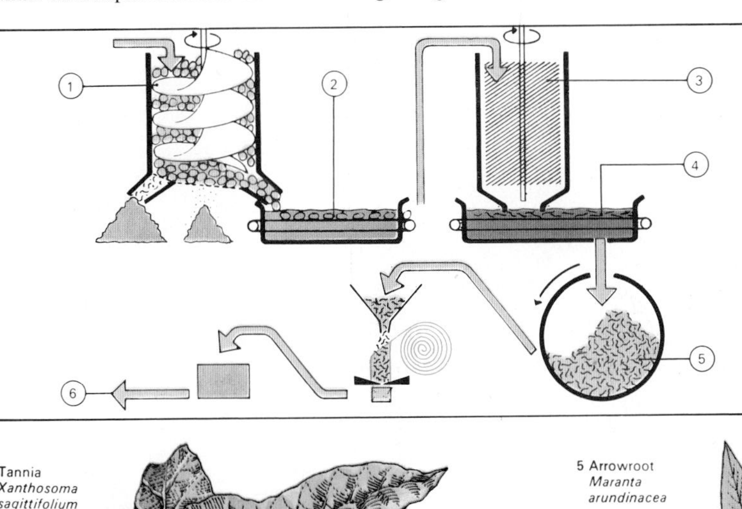
1
2
3
4
5
6

3 Potato chips are one of the chief forms of processed potato. The tuber must be high in dry matter and low in sugar content to be suitable. The potato is peeled [1] and washed [2] and blanched in boiling water before frying [4]. The chips are then dried and salted or flavored [5] before packaging in bags, boxes, or cans [6], ready for distribution. All this is done automatically.

4 Tannia *Xanthosoma sagittifolium*

5 Arrowroot *Maranta arundinacea*

6 Cassava *Manihot utilissima*

4 The rhizomes (tuberous stems) of the tropical tania plant are ground into meal. The plant grows to 3ft (91cm).

5 Arrowroot is cultivated in the West Indies, Southeast Asia, and South Africa. Its rhizomes produce a starchy powder used for thickening sauces.

6 The cassava is becoming one of the word's most important tubers because a processed form of meal, produced from its root, is used as a cereal substitute.

Vegetables

Vegetables are important to a healthy human diet even if the energy requirements of the body can be met by starches from cereals and by protein of animal origin. In addition to the starch and, in some cases, the protein that vegetables contain, they also provide vitamins (especially when fresh) that may be lacking in the diet. Furthermore, they provide bulk and add to the enjoyment of food. Seeds, pods, leaves, stems, and roots are used.

Pods and seeds

The young seeds or fleshy pods of immature legumes are widely eaten [1]. Peas *(Pisum)* and broad beans *(Vicia)* originated in the Old World. Green haricot and dwarf beans *(Phaseolus)* are from the New World. Most of these are eaten as pods, although some are allowed to mature or may be shelled like green peas.

Most versatile of all the vegetable groups are the brassicas, which include both leaf and root types, and others where the immature flower head is eaten. Many are subspecies of *Brassica oleracea,* whose area of origin is thought to be the Mediterranean region. They include cabbages, brussels sprouts, cauliflower, and broccoli [3]. The root species, in which the "root" is actually a modified stem, include kohlrabi *(B. caulorapa),* swede *(B. napobrassica),* and turnip *(B. rapa).*

Other leaf vegetables that are widely grown include spinach *(Spinacia oleracea)* and the Swiss chard *(Beta cicla),* lettuce *(Lactuca sativa),* endive *(Cichorium endivia),* and chicory *(C. intybus)* [4].

Less hardy because of their sensitivity to frost, but cultivated for many years in temperate as well as tropical climates, are the cucumbers *(Cucumis)* and several species of the genus *Cucurbita,* which includes zucchini, squash, and pumpkin. [8].

Fruiting species

A number of fruiting species botanically related to the potato came with it from America. Of these the most important today is the tomato *(Lycopersicum esculentum)* [6], although it was originally grown in Europe as a purely ornamental plant. Others in this group are the aubergine or eggplant *(Solanum melongena)* [6] and the sweet pepper *(Capsicum annuum)* [7]. The group figures increasingly in international trade.

Root vegetables, which cover a wide botanical range, have always been an important winter food, because many are biennials, whose roots carry the energy supply for the following year's flowering. Examples are the taprooted carrot *(Daucus carrota)* [5] and parsnip *(Pastanaca sativa),* whose wild forms are common all over Europe. The beet *(Beta sativa)* is one variety of a versatile species that includes the sugar beet and the mangold. Radishes *(Raphanus)* [5] have also been developed from common wild plants in Europe and Asia, where they are still weeds in tilled crops on some soils.

The genus *Allium* adds flavor to diets in many parts of the world. Vegetables of this genus include onions *(A. cepa)* [5] and their varieties, shallot *(A. ascalonicum),* leek *(A. porrum)* from the Mediterranean region, and garlic *(A. sativum)* from central Asia.

CONNECTIONS

See also
330 Staple foods: legumes
332 Staple foods: tubers
336 Green salads
696 A healthy diet
428 Mushrooms and toadstools

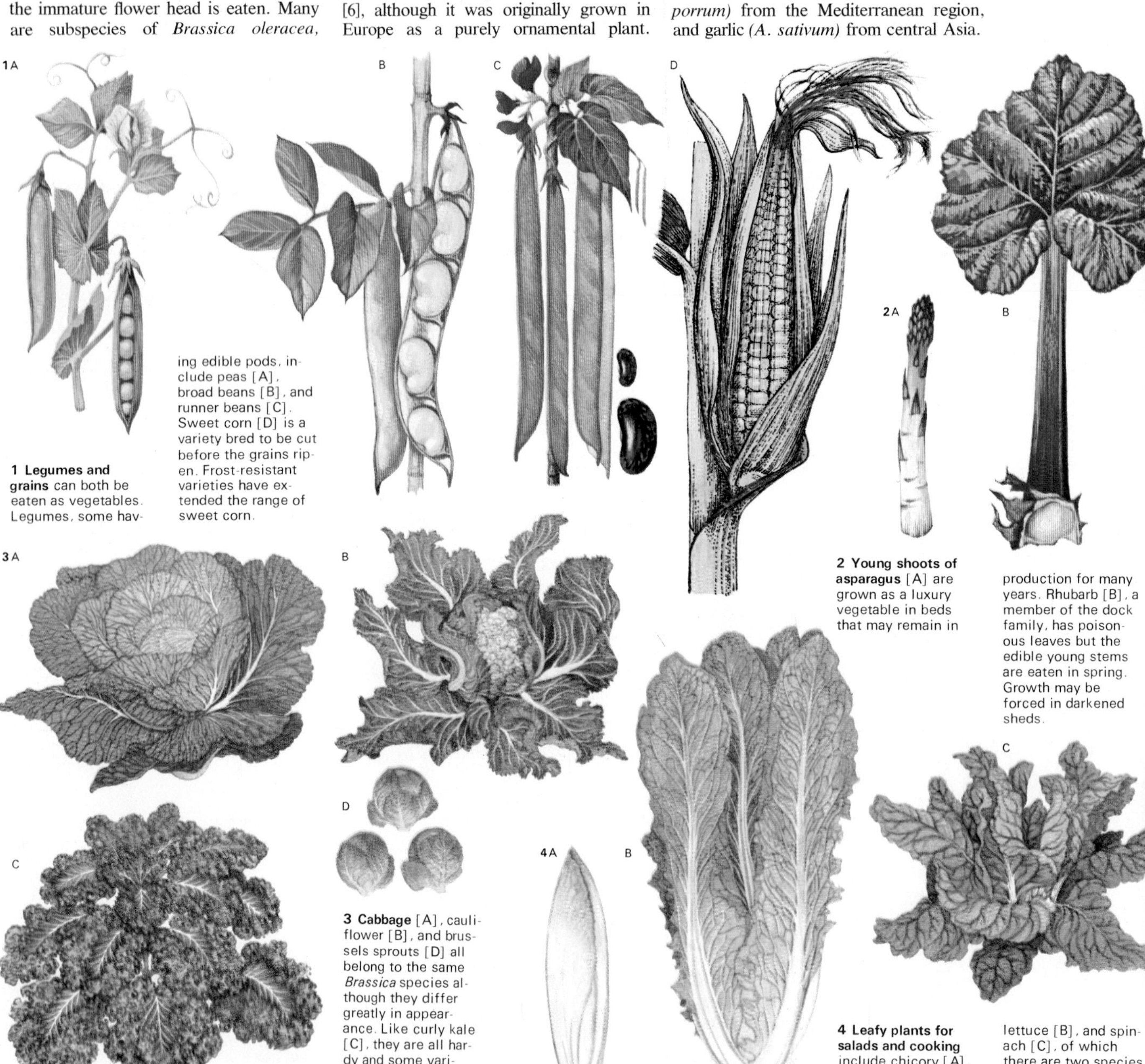
1A
B
C
D
2A
B
3A
B
C
D
4A
B
C

1 Legumes and grains can both be eaten as vegetables. Legumes, some having edible pods, include peas [A], broad beans [B], and runner beans [C]. Sweet corn [D] is a variety bred to be cut before the grains ripen. Frost-resistant varieties have extended the range of sweet corn.

2 Young shoots of asparagus [A] are grown as a luxury vegetable in beds that may remain in production for many years. Rhubarb [B], a member of the dock family, has poisonous leaves but the edible young stems are eaten in spring. Growth may be forced in darkened sheds.

3 Cabbage [A], cauliflower [B], and brussels sprouts [D] all belong to the same *Brassica* species although they differ greatly in appearance. Like curly kale [C], they are all hardy and some varieties can stand quite cold winters.

4 Leafy plants for salads and cooking include chicory [A], whose young shoots are forced in winter, lettuce [B], and spinach [C], of which there are two species to cover winter and summer cropping.

Plants such as celery *(Apium graveolens)* and sea-kale *(Crambe maritima)* are cultivated for their blanched stems. The young stems of *Asparagus officinalis* [2] are considered a particular delicacy. Rhubarb *(Rheum rhaponicum)* [2] is another stem vegetable of commercial importance in temperate countries. The globe artichoke *(Cynara scolymus)* is cultivated for its edible flower buds, as well as its decorative appearance.

The tropics support a wide variety of both root and leaf vegetables, most of which are mainly eaten locally. Two that have become more widely familiar are the green bananas or plantains, which are prominent in so much Creole cookery, and okra or gumbo *(Hibiscus esculentus)*, which is a close relation of cotton.

Cultivation and preservation

Vegetables lend themselves to small-scale cultivation in most parts of the world, by gardeners as well as professional cultivators; much of their production is still on small intensive holdings, largely run by family labor. With urbanization a larger proportion of the main species is grown on a field scale by general farmers or on big commercial holdings in areas such as California, where the weather is predictable, and irrigation combined with plentiful sun makes for quick growth and high yields.

Sophisticated handling and packing, with refrigerated transportation, make it possible to move even highly perishable vegetables to distant markets in a condition as good as that of produce grown on the outskirts of a city.

Large scale vegetable production has also been furthered by the technique of deep freezing. A crop with a comparatively short season, such as the green pea, can be made available to consumers all over the world throughout the year. It can also be produced to high standards of quality in the field and in the processing plant, while inferior grades are diverted to other forms of preservation, such as canning and drying. At the same time, the deep freeze has stimulated vegetable growing as a hobby, since it enables gardeners to store surplus.

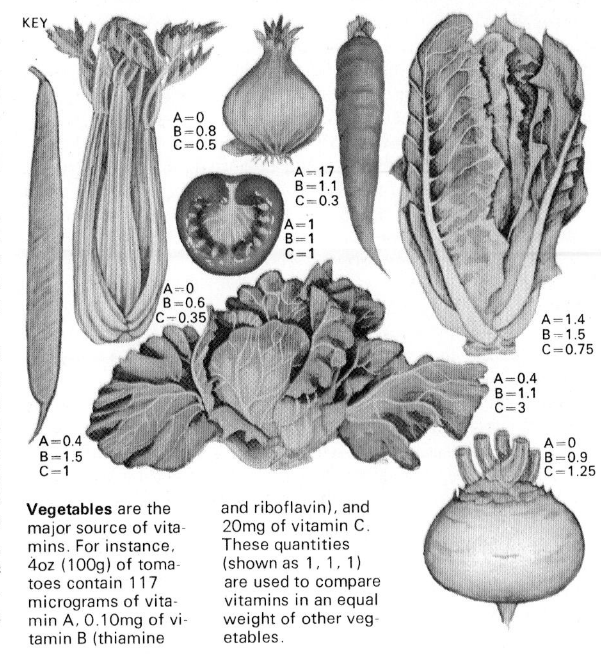
KEY
A=0
B=0.8
C=0.5
A=17
B=1.1
C=0.3
A=1
B=1
C=1
A=0
B=0.6
C=0.35
A=1.4
B=1.5
C=0.75
A=0.4
B=1.1
C=3
A=0.4
B=1.5
C=1
A=0
B=0.9
C=1.25

Vegetables are the major source of vitamins. For instance, 4oz (100g) of tomatoes contain 117 micrograms of vitamin A, 0.10mg of vitamin B (thiamine and riboflavin), and 20mg of vitamin C. These quantities (shown as 1, 1, 1) are used to compare vitamins in an equal weight of other vegetables.

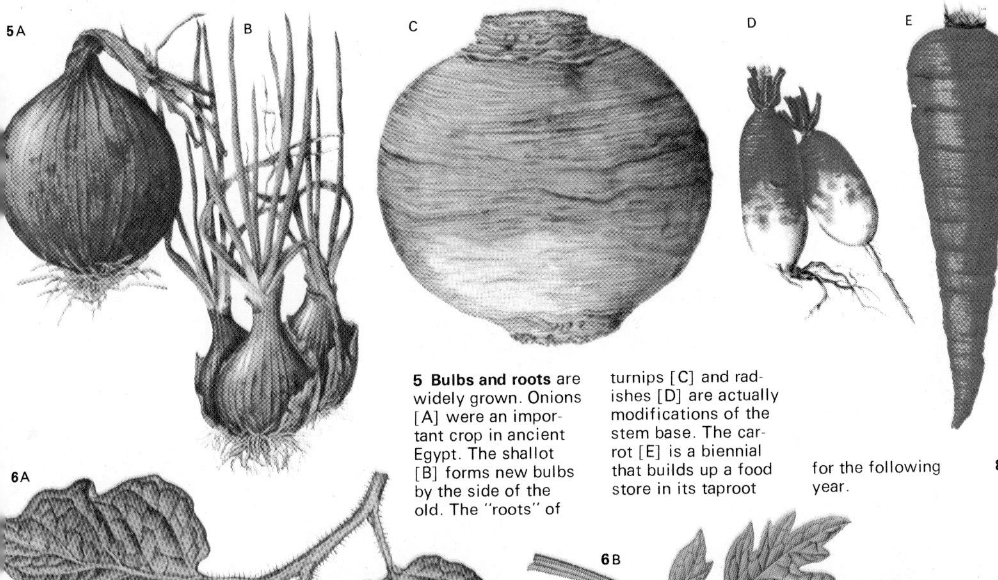

5 Bulbs and roots are widely grown. Onions [A] were an important crop in ancient Egypt. The shallot [B] forms new bulbs by the side of the old. The "roots" of turnips [C] and radishes [D] are actually modifications of the stem base. The carrot [E] is a biennial that builds up a food store in its taproot for the following year.

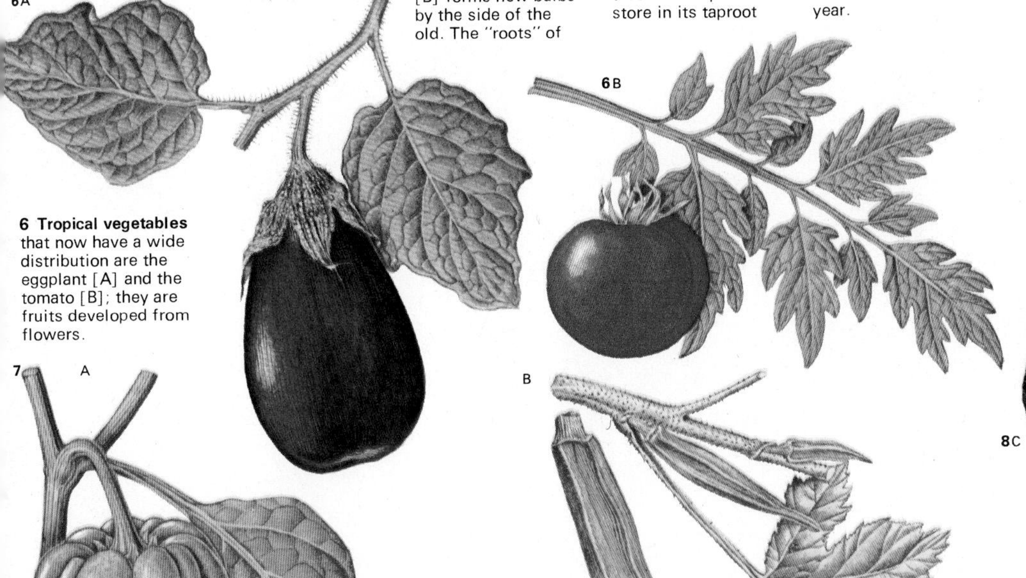

6 Tropical vegetables that now have a wide distribution are the eggplant [A] and the tomato [B]; they are fruits developed from flowers.

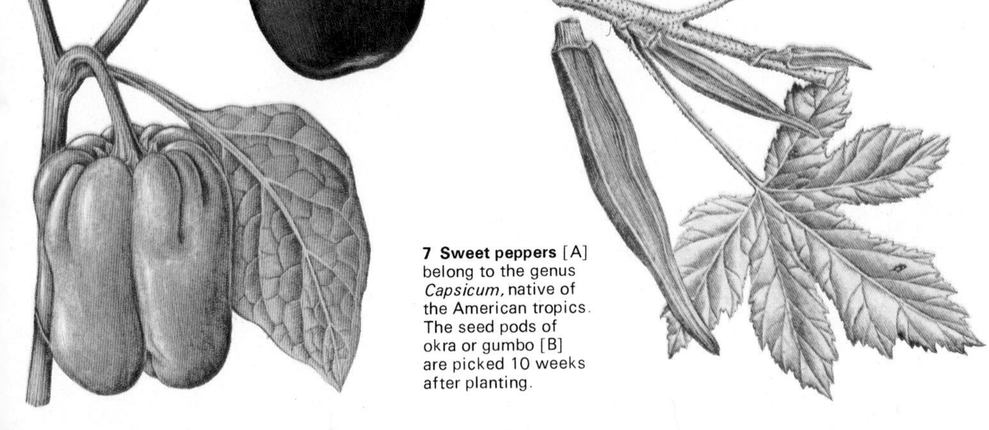

7 Sweet peppers [A] belong to the genus *Capsicum*, native of the American tropics. The seed pods of okra or gumbo [B] are picked 10 weeks after planting.

8 The fruits of the cucurbits are soft-fleshed with a high water content and include winter squash [A], pumpkin [B], summer squash [C], and its smaller versions, zucchini and cucumber [D]. The latter have been cultivated all over the world for centuries.

Green salads

The crispness and flavor of uncooked vegetables, together with their nutritional value and medicinal qualities, have been recognized for centuries. Lettuce was prepared for the kings of Persia in the sixth century BC, and early Greek doctors regarded lettuce as beneficial for the stomach.

Lettuce and other leaves

The leaves of salad vegetables were credited with other properties. The spicy flavored European garden rocket *(Eruca sativa)*, some varieties of which are grown for salads, was thought to be an aphrodisiac. Because of the milky juice characteristic of lettuce *(Lactuca sativa)* [1A], the vegetable was said to be good for nursing mothers. This belief belongs to the doctrine of plant signatures, which associated the physical form of the plant with the condition it was to aid; the word *lactuca* is derived from the Latin word for milk.

A prickly lettuce *(Lactuca serriola)*, native to Asia, is thought to have been the ancestor of *L. sativa*, but many varieties flourished in the East by the first century AD. During the Middle Ages lettuce spread to Europe and Christopher Columbus (1451–1506) may have taken it to the New World. Modern writers have noted that eating flowering lettuce in quantity induces a coma. In Beatrix Potter's animal tales the Flopsy Bunnies ate this type of lettuce and fell into so sound a sleep that they were oblivious to danger. Even so, lettuce has always been the basic salad ingredient. The Romans treated lettuce in brine, then in a salt water and vinegar mixture. A spicy vinaigrette (oil and vinegar) was used to dress fresh salads.

Embellishing a salad

The addition of other raw vegetables to the basic green salad lends it flavor and a crunchy quality. Blanched leaves of chicory *(Cichorium intybus)* (1E) are highly regarded by the French. The closely packed yellowish-white leaves of chicory were developed in 1850 by the head gardener of the Brussels Botanical Garden and introduced to the United States in the late nineteenth century. The related curly endive *(Cichorium endivia)* may have originated in Egypt, although it is said to have arrived in Europe from the East. There are many varieties, from the very curly—the most frequently grown as a tasty salad ingredient—to the slightly curled broad-leaved Batavian type, which is cooked. Another crisp addition is celery *(Apium graveolens)* [1L]. Or a lively embellishment is the distinct aniseed flavor of Florence fennel *(Foeniculum vulgare)* [1K].

Watercress *(Nasturtium officinale)* [1B], a wild aquatic plant belonging to the mustard family, is an ancient salad plant and it has a distinctive pungency. Purslane *(Portulaca oleracea)*, which grows in Iran, Africa, and Asia, and the leaves of the sorrel *(Rumex acetosa)* [3G], also add notable flavor. A wide selection of herbs, including basil [3I], tarragon, and parsley, is another addition. A dressing of oil and wine vinegar lends the salad a final piquancy.

An ancient Chinese art

The Chinese culinary art is one of skill and distinction. With infinite patience cooks

CONNECTIONS

See also
334 Vegetables

1

J
H
A
L
F
D
K
C
G
B
I
E

1 The salad bowl provides an endless variety of fresh vegetables. The cabbage lettuce [A], with its leaves folded into a neat crown, has a mild taste and pleasing texture. Forming a tall, loose head, leaves of the cos or Romaine lettuce [B] are stronger in flavor, while butterhead lettuce leaves [C] are thick and oily. Sea kale (not used as a salad vegetable) [D], chicory [E], and curly endive [F] are all rather bitter vegetables. When chicory is blanched the leaves add a suggestion of sharpness to a green salad. The white and seedy center of the cucumber *(Cucumis sativus)* [G] is another popular salad ingredient. Mustard greens [H] and watercress [I] are often used in salads as a garnish. The radish [J] adds a colorful finishing touch, and Florence fennel [K] and celery [L] a complementary crunchiness.

have evolved a style that preserves the natural textures and flavors of foods. The Chinese were among the first to understand and respect the value of partially cooked vegetables. They were using the cultivated lettuce as early as the fifth century BC, but *pe-tsai* or Chinese cabbage *(Brassica pekinensis)* is more commonly grown. Chinese cabbage has a long, sculptured heart, crisp as celery, and makes an excellent salad. The leaves are stir-fried, a classic method of Chinese cooking in which the thinly sliced food is turned quickly over and over in hot oil. *Bak choi (Brassica chinensis),* which is also Chinese cabbage, is looser and more floppy. In China cabbage is frequently used in soups. A hot leaf mustard, or mustard greens *(Brassica nigra),* is pickled in salt and vinegar.

The radish *(Raphanus sativus)* [1J], often used merely as a colorful garnish to the green salad, is an important vegetable in the East. An ingredient in many Japanese dishes is the *daikon,* a long, white radish of mild flavor. The radish is probably of Oriental origin and another large, firm winter root much grown in the East is known as Chinese radish. The delightful pale green *wasabi* is also used for seasoning. The flavor of this root, stronger than horseradish, can be preserved powdered in cans.

Chinese skill in the use of familiar vegetables is admirable, but their imaginative use of other plants is unique. Some of these, if seen in the West at all, serve only a decorative purpose. The tiger lily, for instance, is a plant prized in Europe for its beauty. In China its buds are dried into pale orange strips known as golden needles and several Chinese dishes are enriched by their aromatic properties. The lotus [20], sacred to Buddha and Kwan Yin, the goddess of mercy, is also eaten raw as a vegetable. The seeds of the lotus are preserved in syrup and its leaves are wrapped around spicy food for steaming. All over the Orient young shoots of the bamboo *(Bambusa)* [2C] are eaten raw. The water chestnut [2B] and the Chinese water chestnut [2F] are other crisp vegetables. Among the most beautiful water vegetables are the many kinds of seaweed, favored by the Japanese.

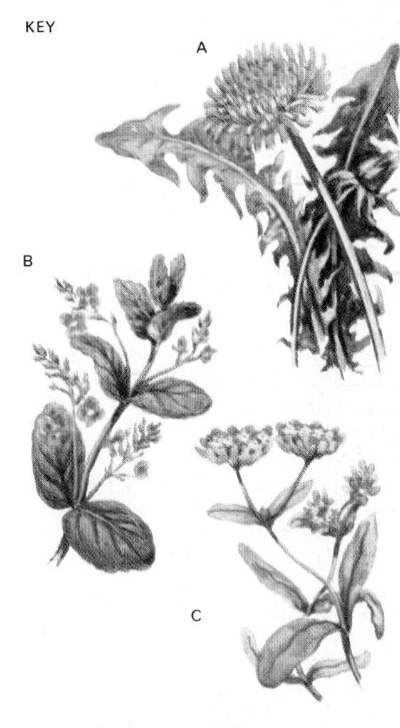
KEY
A
B
C

Three common, wild plants make pleasant tasting additions to a green salad. Young leaves of the dandelion *(Taraxacum)* [A] have a bitter taste. This persistent plant is especially common in grassland but can be found almost anywhere. Brooklime *(Veronica beccabunga)* [B] is found in slow-flowing streams and ditches. The leaves have a similar flavor to those of watercress. Cultivated fields and dunes are where corn salad *(Valerianella)* [C] grows. The leaves have a pungent taste. Other easily found wild salad plants are shown in illustration 3. Leaves are not the only edible part. The pignut *(Conopodium majus)* has edible tubers.

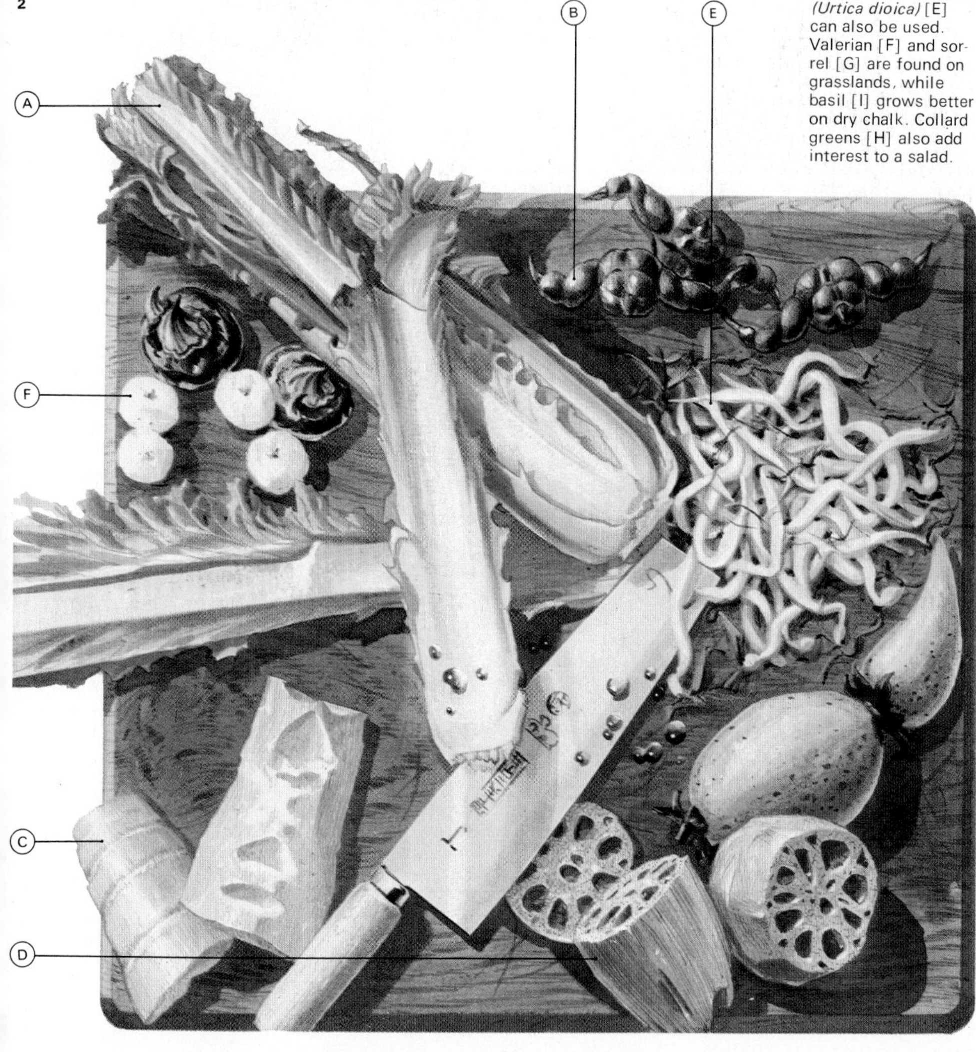
2
A
B
C
D
E
F

2 Unusual plants have been in use in China for centuries and the lively regard of the Chinese for texture and flavor is reflected in this array of vegetables commonly used in their cuisine. The *pe-tsai* [A] is a looseleafed cabbage that can be eaten raw. An important vegetable rich in starch, the tasty and crisp water chestnut [B] grows along the banks of the Yangtze River. Frequently used are delicately flavored bamboo shoots [C]. The perforated stem of the lotus [D], whole or sliced, is also used by the Chinese, as are Chinese water chestnuts [F] and various bean sprouts [E].

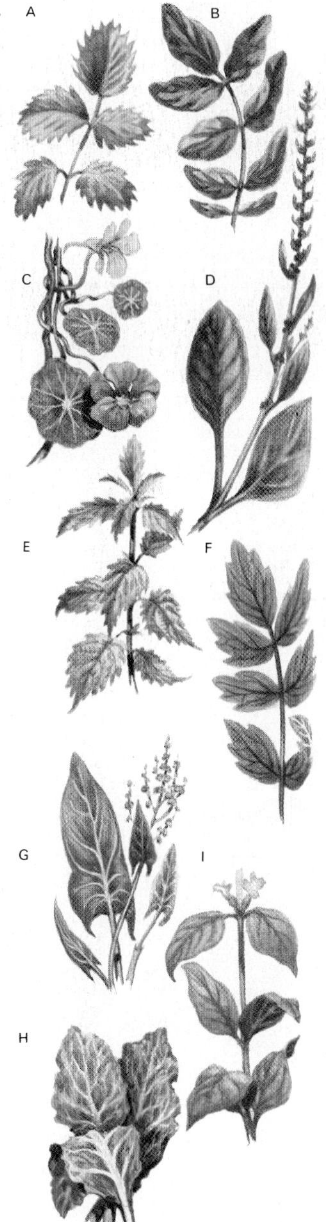
3
A
B
C
D
E
F
G
I
H

3 Crushed leaves of the salad burnet *(Poterium sanguisorba)* [A] make a more unusual salad than fennel, chicory, or watercress [B]. Flowers and leaves of nasturtium [C], sea beet (a variety of *Beta*) [D], and nettles *(Urtica dioica)* [E] can also be used. Valerian [F] and sorrel [G] are found on grasslands, while basil [I] grows better on dry chalk. Collard greens [H] also add interest to a salad.

Temperate fruits

Fruit is the botanical name given to the part of a flower that persists after the blossom dies and forms a vessel enclosing the seeds until they are ripe. The seed vessels of some plants have fleshy exteriors that form an attractive food for animals, which eat the flesh and the seeds. Most seeds pass unchanged through an animal's digestive tract and pass out in the feces. In this way, seeds are dispersed by animals.

Despite the botanical definition, a fruit-grower's use of the word "fruit" is limited to seed vessels that are juicy and edible by human beings [Key]. He also recognizes nuts as fruit. His chief concerns, therefore, are the quality and size of the edible part, whether he can grow it successfully in his particular area, and whether he can sell it at a profit. The fact that seeds are also produced is not relevant, although he knows that their presence is essential for the fleshy part he sells.

Fruits have always been an important part of the human diet. Initially, they were gathered directly from the wild, later trees and bushes were planted so that they grew conveniently near dwellings, and finally growers experimented by cross-fertilizing selected varieties to improve quality.

Citrus fruits

The orange, lemon, lime, grapefruit and tangerine are citrus fruits—an important group in which the "flesh" is formed by hairs radiating from the seeds. These hairs or pulp vesicles are swollen and juicy, giving fruit its characteristic texture. Citrus fruits have their origin in the East. Sweet oranges and lemons were first grown in China and limes in India, and sweet oranges did not appear in the West until the seventeenth century.

In most citrus fruits the fibrous flesh is eaten and the rind discarded, although in the citron and some others the fruit is gathered mainly for the rind. The rind of citrus fruits contains tiny reservoirs of oil. Orange and lemon rinds give body and flavor to marmalade, and they can be candied.

Lime juice was a valuable commodity in the eighteenth and nineteenth centuries when the voyages undertaken by sailing ships were so long that vegetables could not be kept fresh. Lime juice was drunk by the sailors to ward off scurvy, a disease caused by a lack of vitamin C, which fresh fruit and vegetables, particularly citrus fruits, contain.

Fruits of the rose family

A large number of fruits come from plants of the rose family (Rosaceae). These include the apple [3, 5], pear [5], cherry [4], peach [8], apricot [7], and plum [6]. Trees of this family are hardy and thrive in temperate regions. Apples and pears originated in Afghanistan, all varieties of apples being developed from the wild crab apple there. Today, apples represent the second most important fruit after the grape; the major producers are the United States, France, Germany, Switzerland, Italy, and the Balkan countries.

Larger trees, generally associated with apple orchards [1] planted after World War II, are becoming less economic because of the high cost of pruning and picking. For this reason most modern orchards have

CONNECTIONS

See also
340 Tropical fruits
696 A healthy diet
456 How flowering plants reproduce

1

1 Commercial apple orchards in the United States are found in 35 states, which produce 110 million bushels annually. Sixty-five percent of this crop is grown in New York, Washington, Michigan, Virginia, and California.

2

2 Fruit trees in gardens are grown on a smaller scale and can be trained against a wall espalier style, like this pear tree, so as to take up less space and not shade other plants.

3

3 The apple is one of the most important and widely cultivated fruits grown in temperate climates. Shown here is the Rhode Island Greening a popular apple for home cooking.

4

4 The cherry is a type of fruit known as a drupe, which takes the form of a single seed surrounded by fleshy fruit. Cherries date from Roman times and the one shown is the black Early Rivers.

5

1 Quince
2 Grapefruit
3 Ugli fruit
4 Crab apples
5 Newton apple
6 Red Richard apple
7 Conference pear
8 Cyprus lemon
9 Corinam pear
10 Sweet orange
11 Seville orange
12 Nectarine
13 Yellow plum
14 Clementine
15 Red plum
16 Rainbow-stripe cherry
17 Cyprus lime
18 Tangerine
19 Morello cherry
20 Starking cherries

5 Modern fruit is a result of thousands of years of selection of chance seedlings and mutations (sports) and, during the last 200 years, of controlled breeding. Large apples were developed from species such as the crab apple *(Malus sylvestris)*. Pears *(Pyrus sp)*, plums, and cherries *(Prunus sp)* were derived from wild European species. The quince *(Cydonia)* originated in the Middle East, and citrus fruits *(Citrus)* made their appearance in the Far East.

smaller trees planted close together so that work can be done from ground level. This has been made possible by the development of dwarfing and semi-dwarfing rootstocks.

Growers are also experimenting with mechanical pickers, but the techniques so far developed damage the fruit too much for it to be usable for high-quality sales or long-term storage. Some apples for cider, however, are shaken from the trees and picked up from the ground by machines.

Pears thrive in warmer temperate regions. In North America, Australia, and South Africa a large proportion of the crop is canned, but in Europe canning is less important. In France, Germany, Switzerland, and England some of the crop is made into a fermented drink called perry.

Fruits of the vine

Grapes are the world's most important perennial fruit and are grown for wine and dessert use. Related species are dried as currants and raisins. Nearly all European and Mediterranean grapes go into wine. In California, more than half of the crop is dried, one-third is used for wine, and the remainder is eaten fresh or canned. Each variety is grown for a specific purpose.

Most varieties of melon are derived from the musk melon *Cucumis melo* [10]; they include the cantaloupe melon, a dimpled and rough-skinned fruit grown in Italy in the fifteenth century from seed brought from Armenia, and the honeydew melon, which probably originated in Southeast Asia and was eaten by the ancient Egyptians and Persians. The watermelon is a variety of the species *Citrullus vulgaris* and probably originated in Africa.

Melons and grapes are susceptible to damage by frost so their open air cultivation is restricted mainly to warm-temperate and subtropical climates.

Temperate fruit trees are nearly all deciduous, passing the winter leafless. Most can resist temperatures of below 20°F (−7°C) during winter dormancy and many cannot grow in tropical or subtropical climates because prolonged exposure to low temperatures in the winter is necessary for normal development.

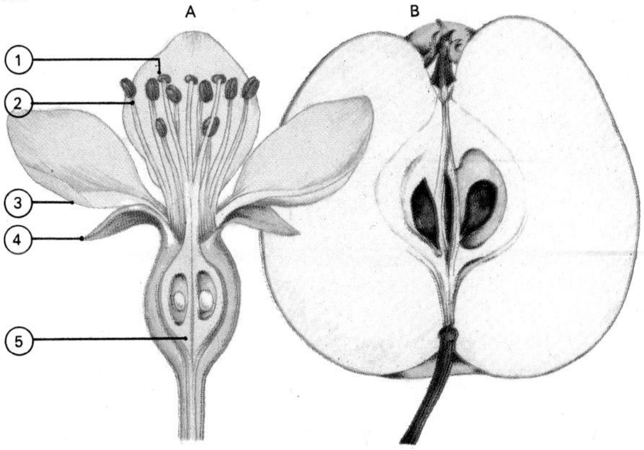

KEY

An apple blossom [A], when examined, shows the typical features of an angiosperm flower—stigmas [1], stamens [2], petals [3], sepals [4], and an inferior ovary [5] (one that lies below the other flower parts). After the ovaries have been fertilized (usually by bees carrying pollen), the flower parts fall away, leaving the receptacle (the "box" containing the ovaries) to become fleshy and swell and grow into the fruit. The flesh of the fruit [B] is formed from the receptacle wall, while the ovary wall remains as the leathery core. In other fruits different parts of the ovary structure may become the fleshy portions of the plant that are edible.

6

6 The plum *(Prunus domestica)* is a hybrid of two other fruits, the cherry plum and the sloe. The various varieties that have been derived from it are the mainstay of the plum and prune industries.

7

7 The apricot is also a member of the genus *Prunus* but is less hardy than the plum, requiring protection from frost and fungal diseases. The yellow and orange colored fruits are rich in sugar and contain iron and vitamin A.

8

8 The peach, like the apricot, originally came from China. Both fruits are marketed fresh, dried, or canned according to the variety. There are two types of peach—the freestone and the clingstone, which differ according to the ease with which the stone is removed from the flesh.

9

9 The persimmon is a tomato-shaped fruit grown extensively in China and Japan and introduced to southern Europe and the United States in the 19th century. In the US it is grown only on a small scale. The yellow-red fruit is rich in vitamins A and C and is astringent until it ripens.

10

10 Melons and grapes both need a great deal of sun and water. The fruits of the melon may need to be supported in nets while growing. Most grapes are grown for wine, but many fine varieties are grown as desserts or for drying.

1 Musk melon
2 Ogen melon
3 Winter melon
4 Cantaloupe melon
5 Balsam pear
6 Watermelon
7 White dessert grapes
8 Black dessert grapes

Tropical fruits

Palm-fringed tropical islands laden with exotic fruit must have seemed like paradise to early Western explorers. Their first impressions were justified, for the variety and luxuriance of plant life is unparalleled in the tropical regions of high annual rainfall and high temperatures.

Long inhabited, the tropics have provided fruits of great antiquity. The great oblong leaves of the banana plant [7], sometimes 20ft (6m) long, were said to have hidden the serpent in the Garden of Eden. The banana was known to the Arabs and the Roman scholar Pliny mentions that Alexander the Great saw it in India in 326 BC. The Islamic conquerors carried the banana to northern Egypt in AD 650 and later on to West Africa. Fifteenth-century slave traders took it to the Canary Islands and from there it was introduced to the Americas. The banana finally reached Mexico with the Spanish *conquistadores* in 1531. There are now more than 100 varieties of the cultivated banana. Besides the sweet dessert fruits there are the plantains for cooking and another form grown for making beer.

No tropical fruit, however, is as well-traveled as the coconut [2E], famed throughout the world as one of man's most bountiful providers. Growing along sandy coasts, the coconut palm's ripe nuts are swept by oceans to many tropical shores. The soft eye of the husk produces a plant which quickly takes root in new ground.

Staff of life

The coconut not only contains an edible kernel and a natural refreshing milk, but its fermented sap makes a heady toddy that can be distilled to make a potent spirit.

One of the most important oils is obtained from copra—the dried kernel or meat of the coconut. Coconut oil is used in the manufacture of soaps, detergents, margarines, and edible oils, and a host of other products. The husk itself yields coir, a tough fiber used in making ropes, mats, and baskets. The leaves are also utilized in basketry and thatching. The trunk of the coconut tree is used for constructing huts and fences.

The breadfruit [5A] is another invaluable tree that provides a staple food throughout the islands of Polynesia. The pulp of its fruit, roasted in its skin before it is fully ripe, tastes like freshly baked wheat bread. The first explorer to mention breadfruit was Captain William Dampier on his return from Guam in 1688. Captain William Bligh's mission in 1786 was to bring breadfruit plants from the Society Islands to the West Indies. The story of the mutiny on the *Bounty* is well known, but Captain Bligh's later voyage in 1791 was successful and the breadfruit is now cultivated from Florida to Brazil.

Symbol of fertility

One of the oldest Semitic representations of life and abundance was the multiseeded fruit of the pomegranate tree [4C]. King Solomon had an orchard of the fruit and the pillars of his temple were decorated with carvings of pomegranates. In Babylon it was served at wedding feasts and it played a similar role as a symbol of love and fertility in the Far East. The fat, ripe fruits were thrown on the floor of the bridal chamber so that the seeds burst from their smooth

CONNECTIONS
See also
338 Temperate fruits
696 A healthy diet
456 How flowering plants reproduce

1

1 The importance of fruit as a food in the tropics is evident from a glance at the stalls in any Indian market. Oranges and bananas are important crops in India. They are brought to market in carts by the growers at regular intervals and are displayed in an inviting manner to the passers-by. The growers judge the timing of their visits to fit in with fruit maturation and consumer demand.

2 A B C D E

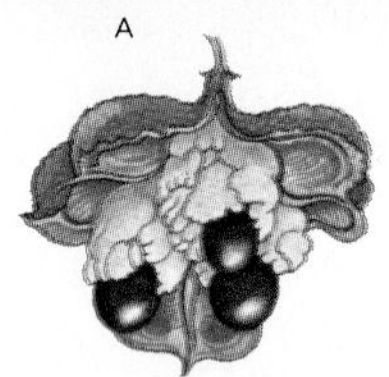

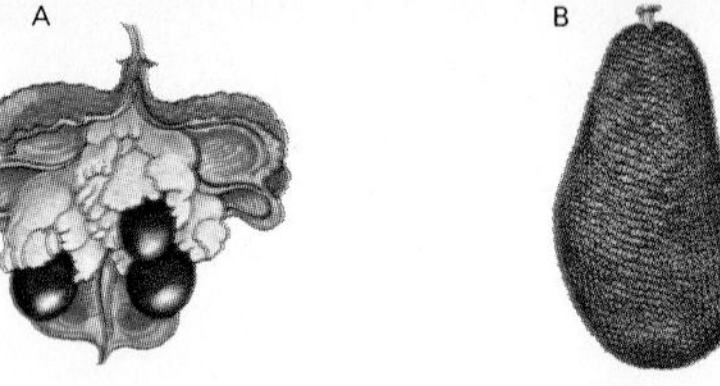

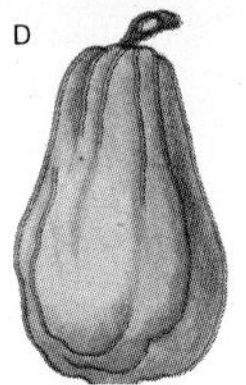

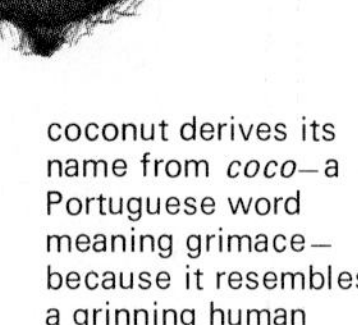

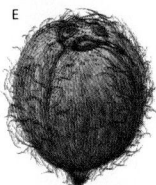

2 Astonishing variety characterizes the tropical fruits. Akee [A], although a fruit, is cooked as a vegetable and tastes like a fine omelet. When the fruit ripens it bursts open to reveal fleshy cream-colored arils, the edible parts of the akee. Jackfruit [B], a giant that can weigh up to 70lb(31kg), may be eaten raw or cooked. It has an unpleasant odor when cut, but the flavor of its creamy yellow pulp is more appealing. The sapodilla [C] is a Central American fruit with rough brown skin and a slightly grainy pulp. The sweet, khaki-colored flesh tastes like faintly astringent brown sugar. It is eaten when fully ripe. Papaya [D], sometimes sprinkled with lemon juice and sugar, is eaten for breakfast in the tropics. Its smooth skin ripens from green to yellow or orange and its succulent pulp encloses small black-brown seeds in the center. Papain, an enzyme contained in the leaves and unripe fruit, is used to tenderize meat. The coconut [E] has a hard, fibrous outer shell and a hollow center. Its flesh is most familiar in the West in its dried form. The soft translucent flesh of an immature coconut can be enjoyed only in the tropics. One of the world's most important crops, the coconut derives its name from *coco*—a Portuguese word meaning grimace—because it resembles a grinning human face.

3 A B C D E

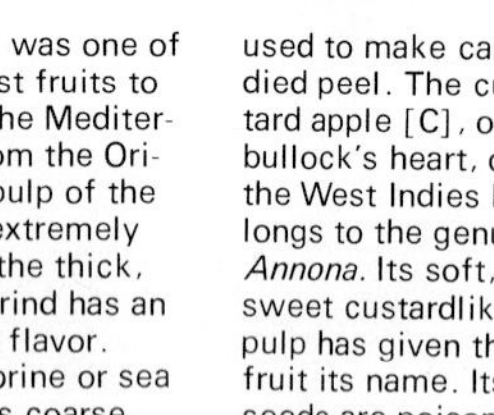

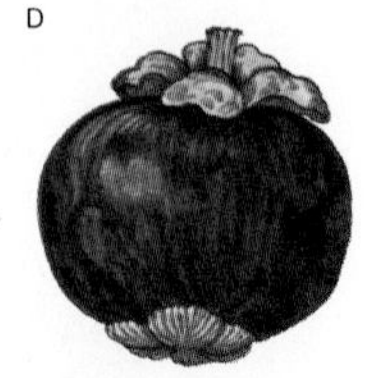

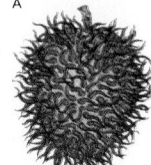

3 Native to Malaysia, the red fruit of the rambutan [A] is covered with soft spines. Its name comes from the Malay word for hair. It is a close relative of the litchee and resembles it in size. The fruit has a pleasant acid flavor. The citron [B] was one of the earliest fruits to arrive in the Mediterranean from the Orient. The pulp of the citron is extremely sour, but the thick, furrowed rind has an agreeable flavor. Cured in brine or sea water, this coarse outer covering is used to make candied peel. The custard apple [C], or bullock's heart, of the West Indies belongs to the genus *Annona*. Its soft, sweet custardlike pulp has given the fruit its name. Its seeds are poisonous and its dimpled skin resembles a quilted fabric. The sweetsop, indigenous to tropical America, is closely related to the custard apple. The snow-white flesh of the mangosteen [D] is delicate in texture and has a rather sweet-sour taste. The thick, dark purple rind surrounds a cavity in which the pulp lies in segments like those of a tangerine. Although the mangosteen has been highly valued in Indonesia and the Philippines since early times, the fruit has been cultivated only since the 19th century in the West Indies. The flower of the passion fruit [E] is said to have given this fruit its name because it symbolizes the passion of Christ. The corona resembles the crown of thorns and the five sepals and five petals have been interpreted as the ten apostles: Judas, who betrayed Christ, and Peter, who denied him, being left out. The passion fruit is a delicately flavored and highly aromatic fruit with a tough, purplish, often wrinkled skin.

skins. Centuries later the prophet Mohammed claimed another virtue for the pomegranate. He said that eating the fruit would banish envy and hatred. The pomegranate became the emblem of Granada, and Ibn-al-Awam, a thirteenth-century Moor, recorded some ten varieties of the fruit that flourished in southern Spain at the time. Spanish colonists probably took the plant to the New World, and today it is grown from the warmer areas of North America to Chile.

Fruits of hallowed legend

Throughout history the fig [4A] has played an important role in mythological tales. Adam and Eve covered their nakedness with fig leaves and it is thought that the Tree of Enlightenment that grew in Buddha's garden may have been the bo, or sacred fig. In Latin myth the fig was held sacred to Bacchus, god of wine, and was used in many religious ceremonies. It was also regarded by the Romans as a badge of prosperity because it grew over the wolf's cave where Romulus and Remus, Rome's legendary founders were found.

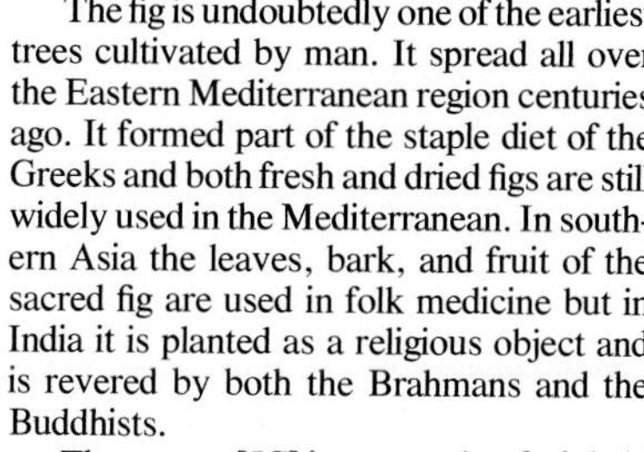

The fig is undoubtedly one of the earliest trees cultivated by man. It spread all over the Eastern Mediterranean region centuries ago. It formed part of the staple diet of the Greeks and both fresh and dried figs are still widely used in the Mediterranean. In southern Asia the leaves, bark, and fruit of the sacred fig are used in folk medicine but in India it is planted as a religious object and is revered by both the Brahmans and the Buddhists.

The mango [5C] is yet another fruit held in great esteem in India. Akbar, the Mogul emperor who ruled at Delhi in the 16th century, planted an orchard of 100,000 mango trees and one of the ancient names of the fruit stems from a Sanskrit word meaning food. Buddha also had a mango grove in which he found solitude for philosophical thought. The English name comes from *man-kay* or *man-gay*, a Tamil word adopted by the Portuguese in India. The tree did not appear in the Western hemisphere until about 1700, when it was planted in Brazil. The juicy mango varies in color from yellow to orange and has a spicy flavor.

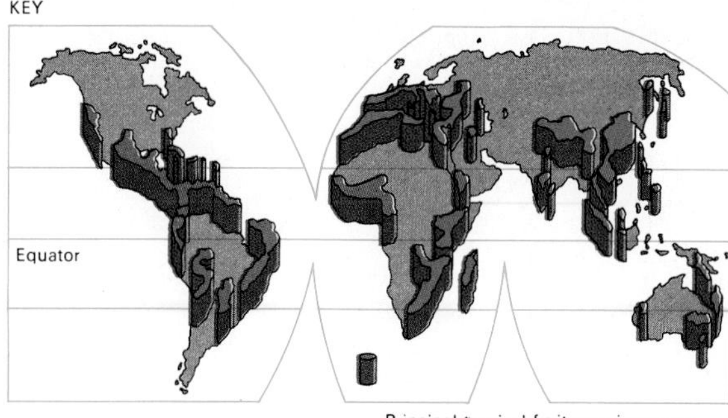

KEY
Equator

Principal tropical fruit growing areas

Tropical plantations producing exotic fruits for the world market are found in the tropical zones stretching between the Tropic of Cancer and the Tropic of Capricorn. About one quarter of the Earth's land surface lies within this region. Many of the crops characteristic of tropical agriculture are also cultivated in warmer parts of the temperate zones. The plantation system is very old in tropical areas. Coffee, tea, coconut palms, pineapples, bananas, and sugar cane are cultivated in this way. Tropical temperatures vary slightly from one month to the next and crops are grown year-round. The mango, citrus, and breadfruit trees are intensively cultivated in Southeast Asia, as are the guava and papaya trees in South America. Improved transportation has sent these luxuries to countries all over the world.

4 A B C D E

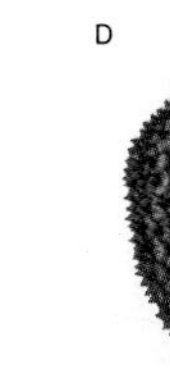

4 Heavily-seeded figs [A] belong to a family of more than 1,800 species. Pliny, the Roman scholar, mentions that slaves were given an inferior home-grown variety of figs, but Roman epicures ate a delicious sweet variety imported from Asia Minor. The fruit is indigenous to an area stretching from eastern Turkey to northern India. The durian [B], a favorite fruit in southeast Asia, has a repellent aroma. The delicate, creamy-white pulp of this large oval fruit has a soft, glutinous quality. But the fruit, despite its fetid smell, is sweet to the palate. The flesh of the pomegranate [C] is densely packed with seeds that scatter when the fruit is burst. This bursting action inspired the French to name military grenades after the pomegranate. Its refreshing flavor makes it popular in the arid areas where it grows. The litchee [D] is of Chinese origin and is the favorite fruit of the Cantonese. The skins are hard and scaly, turning from reddish-pink to brown. A white juicy pulp surrounds a single shiny brown seed. The litchee combines the subtle perfume of good quality grapes with a delectable flavor. The small, oval citruslike kumquat [E] was originally cultivated in China and Japan and is used there mainly as a candied fruit. The mild acid flavor is excellent for making marmalade and other preserves.

5 A B C

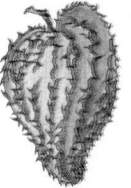

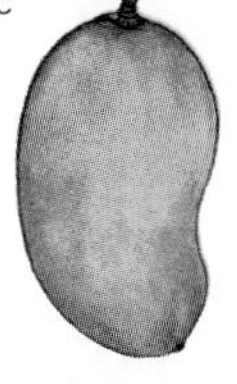

5 In prehistoric times the breadfruit [A], from a tree native to Malaysia, spread to the Pacific, where it became a staple food. The skin of the ripe fruit is brownish-green and the flesh white and rather fibrous. The fruit is baked or boiled, or sliced and fried like a potato. The inner bark of the tree is used to make cloth, and canoes are built from its wood. The soursop [B] is closely related to the custard apple. Its sour-sweet pulp is used to make soft drinks and sherbets. The heart-shaped, dark green fruit is covered with fleshy spines. The king of tropical fruits, the mango [C], is an oval or kidney-shaped fruit with a delicate fragrance. Its juicy flesh surrounds a single flat seed. The mango is grown as a garden plant throughout the tropical regions.

7

7 The banana was one of the first fruits to be cultivated by man and is believed to have originated in the Asian tropics. The "trunk" of the banana "tree" is really an elongated bundle of leaf bases with a single flowering stem emerging from the top. The bananas, growing in bunches called "hands" on the fruit stalk, are produced without pollination and so have no seeds. They require 75 to 150 days to mature and must be removed from the plant to ripen properly. After fruiting, the plant is cut down or collapses and a new one develops from buds on the underground stem. Several varieties are grown, each suitable for a different purpose. The Gros Michel variety has an excellent flavor but it is quite susceptible to disease and other varieties, such as the Cavendish, are now more important in the American tropics. Most bananas have yellow skins but some are red. These do not travel well and are eaten locally. Plantains are very large bananas that are rich in starch. They cannot be eaten raw and are used only for cooking. The Canary banana was introduced into those islands in the 15th century by slave traders and has now become a staple food in many other areas.

6 A B C

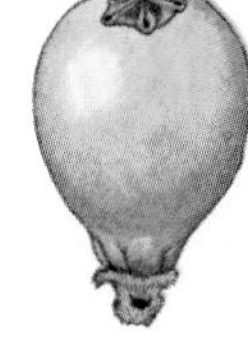

6 "Deliciousness itself" is how Mark Twain described the cherimoya [A]. Its texture and taste resemble a delicate ice cream flavored with pineapple and banana. Indigenous to the tropical highlands of Central and South America, it is related to the custard apple. The loquat [B] is a native to China and has been cultivated in Japan for centuries. It is often planted in parks and gardens. The fruit is borne in large, loose clusters and has an agreeably tart flavor. The flesh, whitish to orange in color, surrounds three or four large seeds from which the plant is frequently propagated. Borassus palm or palmyra palm grows wild in south India, Burma, and Sri Lanka. The immature nut [C] provides a refreshing drink and the soft kernel is edible. In India the fruit is used mainly for making sugar. A toddy is also made by fermenting a sweet juice collected from the palm.

Sugar and honey

Sugars are part of a group of chemicals known as carbohydrates and are found in a wide variety of foods. The most common forms are sucrose, glucose, and fructose. Less sweet sugars are lactose (found only in milk) and maltose, which is a by-product of grain germination. A well-balanced diet contains plenty of carbohydrates to provide energy and supplementary sugars are unnecessary.

Honey and its formation

The first concentrated source of sweetness available to early people probably was honey, which was prized both as a food and a medicine. The association of honey with health has lingered to the present day. As it is an almost immediate source of energy, its restorative reputation possibly has some slight basis in fact, but any other source of carbohydrate would do as well. Honey does have mildly antiseptic properties and can be used locally in the treatment of burns and cuts.

Honey is a sweet, viscous liquid that varies in color and taste according to the source of the nectar collected by the bee. Single-blossom honeys have quite distinct flavors; herbs produce a light, aromatic honey, while honey from pine cones is darker, with distinctly resinous overtones. The most common single-flower honey produced by commercial beekeepers is clover, which is pale amber and flavored. Heather honey is also common in some British country districts. Most honeys sold today are derived from a mixture of blossoms, since this involves less disturbance of the hive.

The honeybee *(Apis mellifera)* is a social insect with a rigidly organized life. There are three kinds of bees in each hive—the queen bee, which lays the eggs; male bees (drones), which fertilize them; and female worker bees. The small worker bees build the wax cells in which eggs are laid or honey is stored. They collect nectar from flowers in their honey sacs. The nectar is regurgitated and stored in the cells of the combs, where the honey forms by the conversion of sucrose to glucose and fructose and the evaporation of moisture.

Millions of flowers are needed to produce 1 pound (0.45kg) of honey, but thousands of tons of honey are produced annually. Honey extracted from the comb may crystallize or granulate, especially if it is held below 50°F (10°C). The honey can be cleared by gently warming the jar. Honey sold in the comb is regarded by many as a delicacy.

Honey-based beverages

Honey and sugar syrups have long been used in medicine to help disguise the bitterness of herbal remedies. This is still a common practice and mixtures containing honey and lemon are often taken to ease the symptoms of colds and influenza. Less common is the production of an alcoholic drink from honey. A mixture of fermented honey and water forms mead, once an important drink in northern countries where grape vines did not flourish. During the late Middle Ages beer was introduced and it eventually relegated mead to the home brewers' shelves. The name mead is derived from the Sanskrit word for honey,

CONNECTIONS

See also

1570 Toward the chemistry of life

498 Advanced insects

456 How flowering plants reproduce

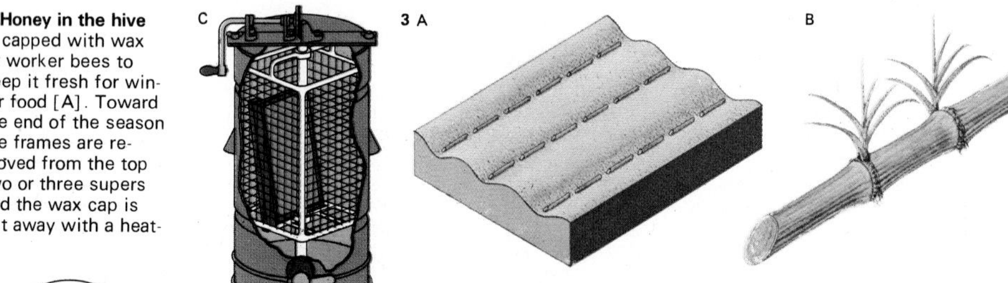

C
D
E
2 A
B
3 A
B

1 Commercial bee hives are divided into three or four sections called supers [2]. Worker bees [1] in each super use frames with man-made wax bases [3] as foundations for hexagonal cells in which eggs are laid and honey is stored. The queen bee is confined to a brood, or lower, chamber by means of a grid [4] through which only worker bees can pass. They enter the hives at the base [5].

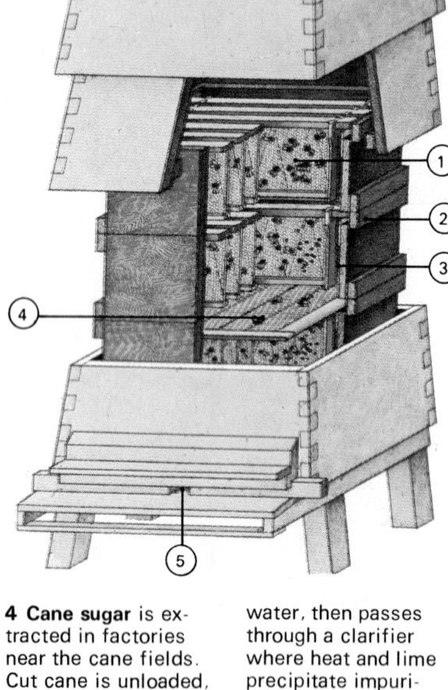

1
1
2
3
4
5

2 Honey in the hive is capped with wax by worker bees to keep it fresh for winter food [A]. Toward the end of the season the frames are removed from the top two or three supers and the wax cap is cut away with a heated knife [B]. Honey is extracted from the comb in a centrifugal machine [C] with a fine mesh basket that is rotated by a handle at high speed. The expelled honey drips into a reservoir. The honey passes through a straining mesh into a ripening tank [D], where it is left to stand. There air bubbles in the honey escape before the wax-free product is drawn into jars [E].

3 The sugarcane grown commercially is *Saccharum officinarum*, a giant tropical grass usually growing 10-15ft (3-4.5m) high. Sugarcane can be grown in most soil conditions but must have a constant temperature of about 80°F (30°C) during the main growing period. Although it is tolerant of drier conditions, it needs 3 to 5in (75-125mm) of rain a month if it is to grow to proper height and productivity. Usually the cane is propagated from sections of the main plant about 3ft (1m) long that are planted in furrows [A], where dormant buds send down roots and produce shoots [B]. Maturity is reached after one to two years, when moisture and sugar content are highest. Harvesting is by hand or by machine.

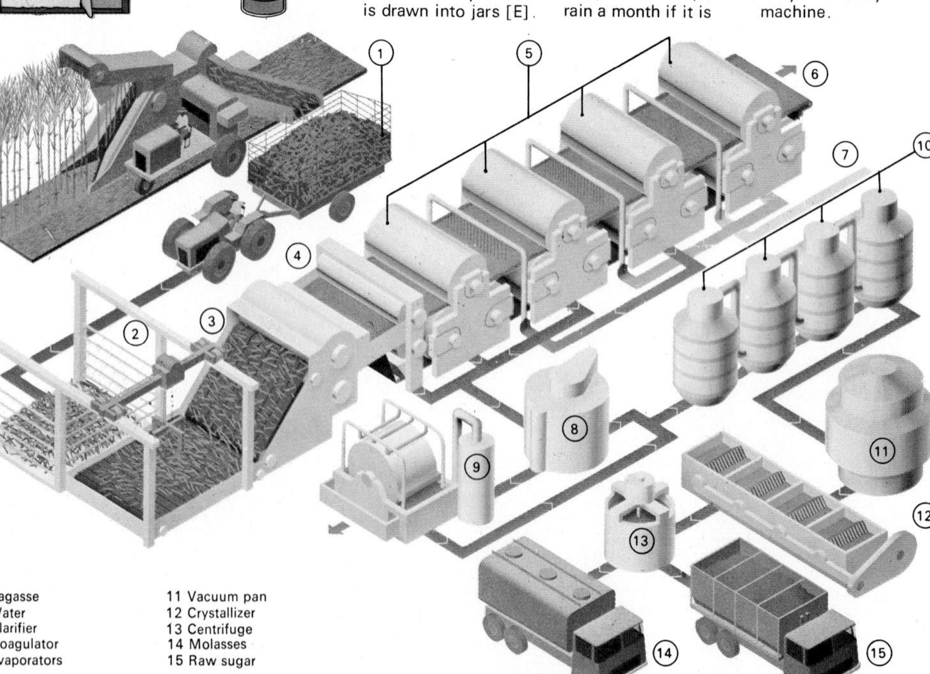

4
1
2
3
4
5
6
7
8
9
10
11
12
13
14
15

4 Cane sugar is extracted in factories near the cane fields. Cut cane is unloaded, washed, then passed through a shredder. Twin crushing rollers break up the cane and pass it through roller mills that exert pressures up to 3,875 tons per sq in (600 tons per sq cm). These press out the juice, leaving a crushed cane mixture known as bagasse, which is sprayed with water before passing to the last mill to aid final juice extraction. The juice, containing up to 90% water, then passes through a clarifier where heat and lime precipitate impurities. A series of evaporators and a vacuum pan reduce the juice to a syrup known as massecuite, which contains sugar crystals. Separation of the crystals in a centrifuge produces molasses and the raw sugar that is sent to refineries.

1 Cut cane
2 Washing bay
3 Shredding knives
4 Crushing roller
5 Mills
6 Bagasse
7 Water
8 Clarifier
9 Coagulator
10 Evaporators
11 Vacuum pan
12 Crystallizer
13 Centrifuge
14 Molasses
15 Raw sugar

mehdu, which may indicate that mead originated in the Middle East or Asia.

Sugar fads and facts

The sugar extracted from sugarcane and sugar beets [Key, 3, 4, 5] is sucrose. The juice can be refined until it is more than 99% pure to make white sugar, chemically one of the purest foods available. The brown sugar so highly prized as a health food contains a residue from the cane and beet crushing processes and is no more "natural" than white sugar [8]. Any form of sugar, including honey, can be harmful if taken in excess. Excess food is usually stored in the body as fat, which may contribute to heart disease.

The average daily consumption of sugar by the developed nations in 1975 would have been unthinkable even 200 years ago. High-yielding sugarcane was introduced into Europe during the 9th century, but cultivation was not successful. Supplies came instead from the Middle and Far East, where factories for refining sugar were established by Venetian merchants. These factories supplied Europe for several centuries. The expansion of world trade during the 14th and 15th centuries encouraged the development of plantations in the New World, particularly the West Indies. Some South American countries now produce a significant proportion of the world's sugar. In the mid-19th century, production from sugar beets became important in the Northern Hemisphere and about 40 percent of the world's sugar comes from this source [5, 6, 7]. Recent enzyme research has proved that sugar can be manufactured cheaply from corn, and this may prove to be an important source in the near future.

Maple syrup is the reduced sap of the maple tree and is expensive to produce [9]. The extraction and preparation of other natural syrups is equally costly and these have largely been replaced in the kitchen by syrups manufactured from cane and beet sugar or from corn. These include molasses and corn syrup, which are used to give both cohesion and taste to cakes, cookies, and candies, and as glazes. Such syrups are often artificially flavored and colored to make them similar to the natural syrups.

KEY

Sugar can be extracted from the stems of sugarcane or from the taproots of sugar beets. Sugar beets *(Beta vulgaris)* are biennials planted as seed in spring to mature the following autumn. Mechanical drilling and thinning yield 30,000 beets per acre. Well-drained loam, free of acid, is the ideal soil. Salt and chemical fertilizers are used to increase sugar content. Selective growth has produced a single taproot from which soil is easily removed after harvesting. Sugar beets now form part of crop rotations in most European countries, Canada, Japan, and the USSR. Sugar is extracted in much the same way as from sugarcane but the yield is lower.

Sugar beet
Sugar cane

5 Harvesting sugar beets extends over a three- to four-month period during which time the factory works 24 hours a day. Crops are timed and harvesting regulated to achieve an even flow of sugar beets to the factory. The harvester scoops up the roots and removes the tops, which are left in the field either to be plowed back or to provide fodder for cattle. After the beets are crushed, the juice goes through processes similar to those used in sugarcane processing, although it takes about 7 tons of beets to produce a ton of sugar. Beet pulp and molasses are fed to stock.

Equator
Main sugar beet areas
Main sugar cane areas

6 Sugarcane and sugar beets both produce sugar but they require completely different climatic conditions. Cane is grown as a single crop in areas between the tropics of Cancer and Capricorn. Sugar beets form part of regular crop rotation in Europe, the USSR, and North America. They are also a source of food for cattle. More recently beets have been grown in Japan and South America.

7 World production of sugar is led by the USSR with its vast sugar beet growing areas. But the most concentrated sugar output in the world is achieved in Cuba with fertile plantations of cane.

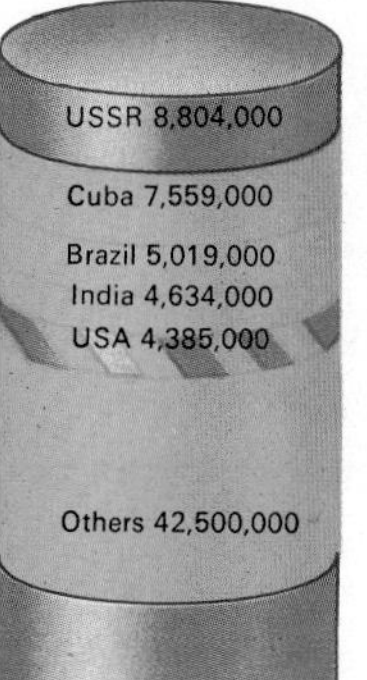
Cane in tons
Beet in tons
USSR 8,804,000
Cuba 7,559,000
Brazil 5,019,000
India 4,634,000
USA 4,385,000
Others 42,500,000

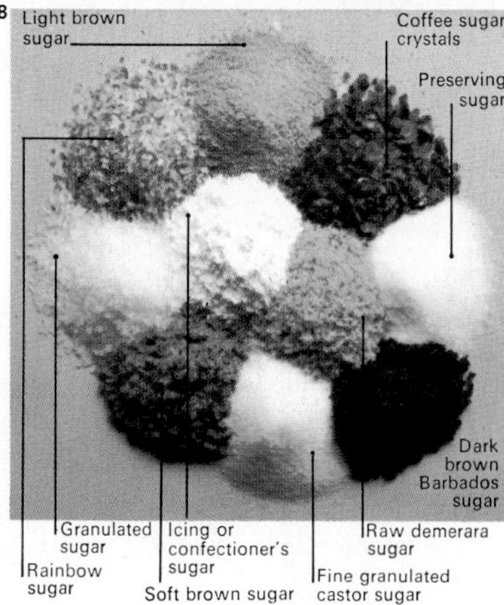
Light brown sugar
Coffee sugar crystals
Preserving sugar
Dark brown Barbados sugar
Granulated sugar
Icing or confectioner's sugar
Raw demerara sugar
Rainbow sugar
Soft brown sugar
Fine granulated castor sugar

8 Many varieties of refined sugar are produced for world trade. Of these the most popular in the United States are white granulated sugar, powdered or confectioners' sugar, and light and dark brown sugar. Special sugars are also made for use in candy and soft drinks. The darker sugars are taken out of the refining process earlier and contain impurities.

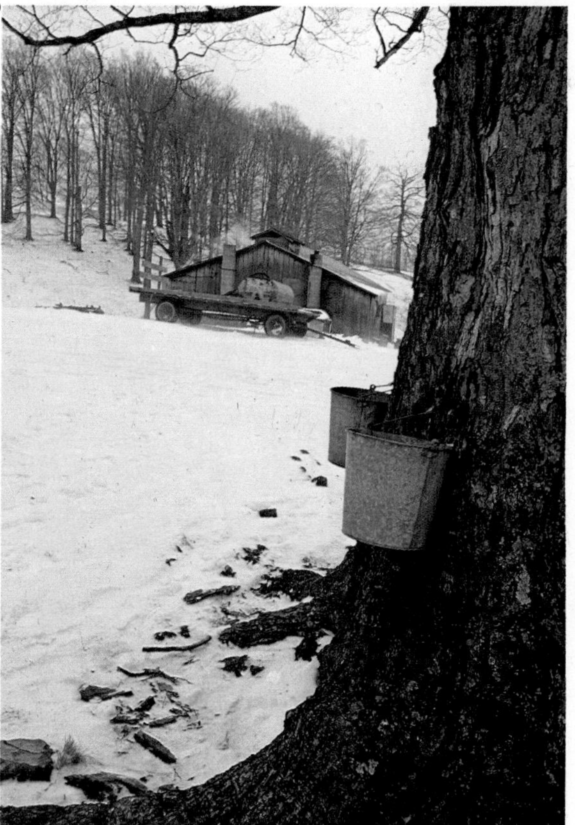

9 Syrups can be derived naturally from plants or produced artificially. A distinctively light and delicate syrup is collected from maples in Canada and the United States, particularly in New England. North American Indians used the sap of these trees to make a syrup long before the arrival of Europeans. In much the same way as latex is obtained, the sap is tapped as it rises in early spring. Maple syrup is considered to be a luxury because it requires about 40 gallons of sap to make a gallon of syrup. Other plants that yield syrup are corn, sorghum, and some date and palm trees. Molasses, a syrup that is produced during the refining of sugar, and corn syrup are widely used in cooking to give taste and cohesion to candies, glazes, and pastries. Artificial syrups, which are low in cost, consist mainly of sugar and water boiled until thick and sticky. Chemical flavorings are often added.

Origins of wine

The history of wine has marched hand in hand with the history of Western civilization. In the surviving artifacts and records of the ancient peoples of the Mediterranean—Egyptian [1], Phoenician, Minoan, Greek—the vine and its juice are always present in the evidence of daily life worship, myth, and poetry. The Mediterranean itself, a maritime marketplace crossed by traders, was Homer's "wine-dark sea."

Greek and Roman vineyards

The arrival of the vine in those European countries with which it is now principally associated probably coincided with the spread of Greek colonies during the millennium before Christ. It was then that the vine was first planted on sites where it was to settle so happily—Italy and southern France—and also throughout Asia Minor to the Black Sea. At that time vineyards were also first established in Spain and in North Africa. The Romans later introduced the grape to northern Europe.

The wines of Greece, praised and generously documented by its poets, might not have been admirable by modern standards since they were mixed, diluted with water, and often spiced and seasoned. Such wine might have tasted like *vin rosé* and honey, perhaps with a touch of muscat or with a taste of resin and possibly with concentrated flavorings.

The greatest Roman writers, including Virgil, wrote instructions to winegrowers. One sentence of Virgil's—"Vines love an open hill"—might be called the best single piece of advice that can be given to a winegrower. There has been much speculation about the quality of Roman wine. It apparently had extraordinary powers of keeping, which in itself suggests that it was very good. The great vintages were drunk and discussed for longer than seems possible. The famous Opimian—from the year of the consulship of Opimius, 121 BC—was being drunk even when it was 125 years old.

Wine follows the legions

The Romans had all that was necessary for aging wine. They were not limited to earthenware amphorae like the Greeks—although they did use these. They had barrels like modern barrels and bottles not unlike modern bottles. It is possible that the Italians of 2,000 years ago drank wines similar to those drunk by their descendants today; young, casually made, sharp or strong according to the summer weather. The Roman training of the vine up trees depicted in friezes on classical buildings is still practiced, particularly in the south of Italy and in northern Portugal.

In the first centuries after Christ, when the power of Rome was at its greatest in northwest Europe, the vine followed in the footsteps of the legions. By the time they withdrew in the 5th century they had laid the foundations for almost all the great vineyards of the modern world.

Starting in Provence, where vineyards had thrived for centuries (those of Marseilles were established by the Greeks), the planting of wine grapes spread up the valley of the Rhône and to Bordeaux in the first century. They arrived in Burgundy and the Loire [6] next and finally reached the valleys of the Rhine, Moselle, and Danube.

CONNECTIONS

See also
346 Vines and grapes
348 Wines of the world
426 Yeasts and molds
352 Spirits and distilling
350 Beer and brewing

1

1 The vine was cultivated in Egypt by about 3000 BC. On the wall of the tomb of Nakht, an official of Thebes who lived about 1,500 years before Christ, there is a mural showing a group of men treading grapes in a vine arbor. Wine was safer to drink than water.

2

2 Medieval workers are seen tying up vines and harvesting grapes in these woodcuts, which were used to illustrate the 1493 Speyer edition of Piero Crescentio's *Opus Ruralium Commodorum.* These crisp and expressive woodcuts have been reprinted repeatedly.

3 A

3 B

3 Wine played an important role in ancient life. The Romans used winemaking methods that have changed only little and had barrels and bottles similar to those used today. A 4th-century Roman mosaic [A] shows grapes being trampled in a trough. Earlier still, a Greek feast [B] is shown on a wine vase of about 480 BC that is now in the British Museum. Such scenes were a favorite motif of Greek vase painting. The guest on the left is playing the then fashionable after-dinner game of *kottabos.* This consisted of throwing the dregs of the wine in the cup at a target—a dish delicately balanced on a pole. The game was popular enough for partygoers to be coached in the finer points of "wine wasting" sessions. In ancient Greece only the most determined drunkards drank wine without diluting it with water or other beverages.

4

ET·HIC·EPISCOPVS·CIBV·E
POTV: BE NE DIC IT

4 In the Bayeux tapestry Bishop Odo of Bayeux, half-brother to William the Conqueror, blesses the wine before the departure from Normandy and the historic invasion of England in 1066.

All the early developments were in river valleys, natural lines of communication, which the Romans cleared of forest and cultivated. Wine is a heavy commodity to carry and boats provided an efficient means of transport. Of the great French wine regions, only Alsace and Champagne do not have Roman origins.

Spreading far and wide

The vineyards of France and of the Roman homeland survived the fall of the Roman Empire—and probably helped to mollify the invaders. The forays of the Viking raiders down the great rivers of western Europe—the Rhine, Seine, Loire, Gironde, and Rhône—led them not only to settlements but also to vineyards. The vineyards may have impressed them. Some historians believe that the Vinland of Norse sagas was a region of northeastern America in which Viking mariners found wild grapes at the end of the first millennium.

Throughout the Middle Ages vine growing flourished, most of it under the control of the powerful Church. Expanding religious orders cleared hillsides and planted fields of cuttings. Many winegrowers and proprietors bequeathed vineyards to the Church, which used them to support hospices, hospitals, and homes for the aged, which survive today. For centuries the Church owned many of the greatest vineyards of Europe. Wine was essential not only in ritual but also as a medicine, restorative, and disinfectant. By the sixteenth century wines were being made in Mexico, and in the seventeenth century they were produced in South Africa.

Until the seventeenth century, wine spent its life, as it had mostly done in Roman times, in casks. If bottles were used in the Middle Ages they were simply carafes for use at the table. The rediscovery of the cork some time in the seventeenth century, and the subsequent rediscovery that wine in a tightly corked bottle lasted much longer than wine kept in a barrel, brought about a wine revolution. The rise of the great estates and the evolution of modern wines dates, therefore, from the eighteenth century—the Age of Enlightenment.

KEY

The Romans interpreted the graceful Greek god of the vine, Dionysus, as a more fleshy creature, if not a bloated manikin. In a mosaic from Pompeii, now in the Museo Nazionale in Naples, he rides his traditional mount, a lion, and drinks from a brimming pot. The Romans called him Bacchus.

5

5 A late 15th-century tapestry in the Musée de Cluny in Paris shows the nobility taking an active interest in the work of the vintage as the crop of grapes is gathered and pressed on the banks of the Loire. The region is noted not only for the wine—red, white, and pink, still and sparkling—but also for some of the most magnificent of France's great châteaux. The valley of the Loire river is the longest in France—extending for more than 600mi (960km).

6 The long march west of the vine from its likely origin in the Caucasus of Mesopotamia [1]—the Fertile Crescent—began before 3000 BC, when it reached Phoenicia and Egypt [2] where it was planted. By 2000 BC it was to be found in Greece and Crete [3] and 1,000 years later it was growing in Italy, Sicily, and North Africa [4]. In 500 years it had reached Spain, Portugal, and the south of France [5], and later farther north [6].

6

7

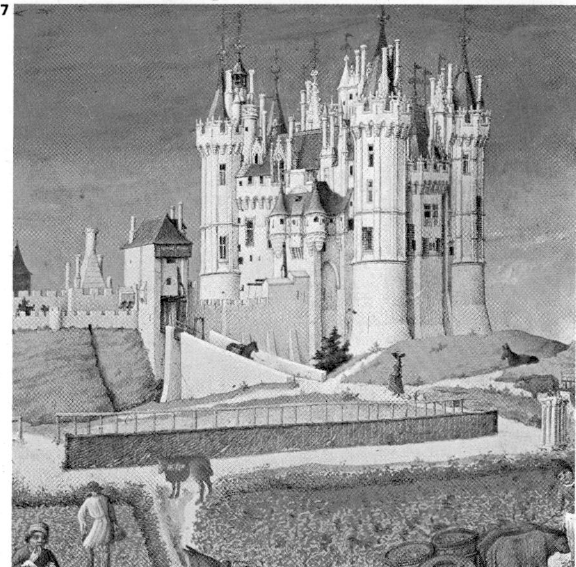

7 The most sumptuous of all the famous prayer books of the Middle Ages was the *Très Riches Heures*, with 39 illustrations painted by Pol Limburg and his brothers for Jean, Duc de Berri, about 1416, at the height of the 100 Years War. In this prayer book the month of September is represented by the first annual task at the time of the vintage: gathering grapes beneath the battlements of the fairytale castle of Saumur.

Vines and grapes

Wine is the fermented juice of the grape. The classical European wine-grape vine, *Vitis vinifera*, probably originated in Asia. Since earliest times varieties of grapes have been selected and propagated for various qualities, both for wine making and for eating. Today there are 5,000 or more named varieties. Of these perhaps 200, plus some varieties of native American vines (especially *Vitis labrusca*), are commonly used for wine. Variety, along with climate, soil, topography, and the maker's technique, determine the style and character of a wine.

Cultivation of the vine

Wild grapevines are climbing plants that use tendrils to grip and reach the tops of tall trees. Ancient winegrowers let the vine grow naturally; the Romans planted elm trees for its convenience. Such methods still survive in parts of Italy and Portugal.

A modern vineyard uses different techniques. The vine has become an industrial plant, pruned to put out a precise number of fruit-bearing canes each year. The grower thus limits production to the number of bunches of grapes that can ripen fully, given satisfactory weather. As a result, the exact desirable yield of each vine and each vineyard can be assessed. In many areas production quotas are legally enforced, and excess wine may have to be disposed of by distilling. As a result of these controls the average quality of wine in such areas is much higher than it would be if production were unregulated.

Propagation and growth

Vines, like most other plants, can reproduce from seed, but this method of propagation is impractical, since the seedlings produced usually differ markedly from their parents and from each other. Seeds (pips) are used for the production of new varieties by crossing existing varieties, but new vineyards are planted with cuttings. The cuttings may be grown on their own roots, but more often they are grafted to rooted cuttings of another species.

In traditional vineyards vines were planted about 3ft (1m) apart. Modern practice is to put them 6 to 9ft (2–3m) apart, because experiments have shown that the total wine yield of a vineyard remains the same with half as many vines exploiting the same volume of soil.

As the vine grows, its roots penetrate deeper into the earth. If manure is used too liberally, it can affect the taste of the wine, but more importantly for the health of the vine it may also encourage shallow root development. If the soil near the surface does not provide adequate nutrients and water, however, the vine will send its roots down to obtain them. This habit often results in the vine's finding valuable resources far from the surface [1].

Unfortunately vines are subject to many diseases. Some varieties are so susceptible to certain diseases, such as mildew, that they are gradually being abandoned. The best varieties combine hardiness with fine fruit, although rarely with high yield.

One insect pest nearly wiped out the wine industry. The vine louse, *Phylloxera vitifoliae*, lives on the root of the vine and kills it. In the 1870s it almost totally destroyed the vineyards of Europe and those

CONNECTIONS

See also
344 Origins of wine
348 Wines of the world
352 Spirits and distilling
350 Beer and brewing

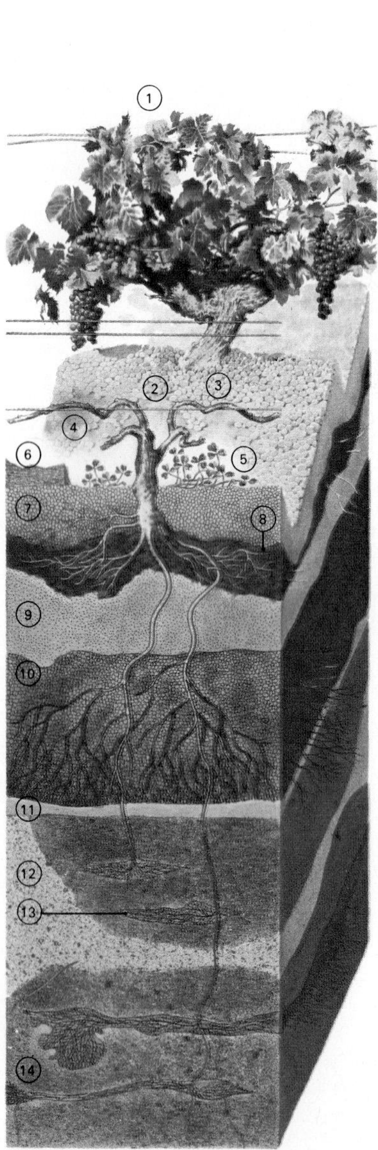

1
2
3
4
5
6
7
8
9
10
11
12
13
14

1 Poor soils grow some of the best wines. In poor soil the vine puts down deep roots to find moisture and nutrients, as shown in this cross-section of a Médoc vineyard. Gravel and sand are important for quality as they make the ground permeable to a great depth, let the rain run through and allow the vine to go deep. A 50-year-old Cabernet vine [1], trained on wires, bears fruit. A 10-year-old vine [2] in its winter state is pruned [3] and banked with earth around it for protection. Surface pebbles are stained with copper sulfate [4] sprayed on the vine to prevent infection and disease by fungi. Clover [5] is often plowed in as fertilizer. Pressed skins [6] are also spread on the ground. The top 12in (30cm) of soil [7] is pebbly and sandy with few roots. A layer of marl [8] brought from elsewhere was spread by hand years ago; roots and rootlets spread out in it. The next layer [9] is compacted sand and useless; main roots pass through it to another sand and gravel layer [10] that is organically richer. Roots flourish there but are checked by a compacted layer of sand at 4ft (1.2m) [11]. Below this, different types of sand [12, 13, 14] lie in clearly defined layers. The gray areas [13] are pockets of damp sand where the rootlets can spread out to obtain the necessary moisture for proper growth.

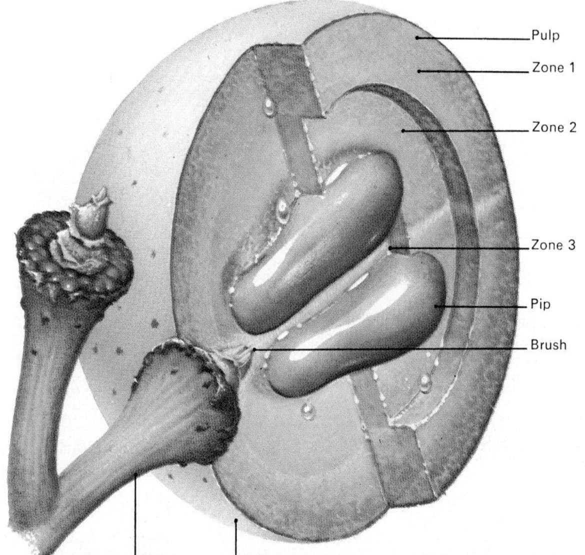

2
Pulp
Zone 1
Zone 2
Zone 3
Pip
Brush
Stalk
Skin

2 A Riesling grape is still green one month before the vintage. As it ripens, it becomes translucent gold, with distinctive dark speckles on its skin. The stems are now usually torn off before the grapes are pressed for wine. Formerly stems were left on, but they made the wine watery and sometimes bitter; in red wine they also absorbed valuable coloring matter. The pulp divides naturally into three zones. Zone 2 gives up its juice in the press first, before the zones between the pips and under the skin. The first juice makes the best wine.

3 A

B

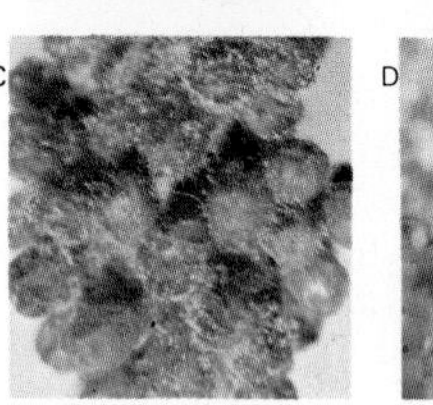

C

D

3 Vines are subject to many pests and diseases, among them the larva of the cochylis moth *(Clysia ambiguella)* [A] which eats flower buds. Another pest is a tiny red spider *(Tetranychus)* [B] that sucks sap from the undersides of leaves. Downy mildew [C] attacks anything green. Mildewed grapes never ripen properly. Powdery mildew [D] is often more serious. It rots the stalks, shrivels the leaves, and splits the grapes, ruining the juice and killing the vine.

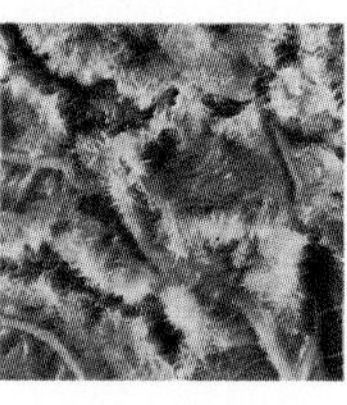

4 A

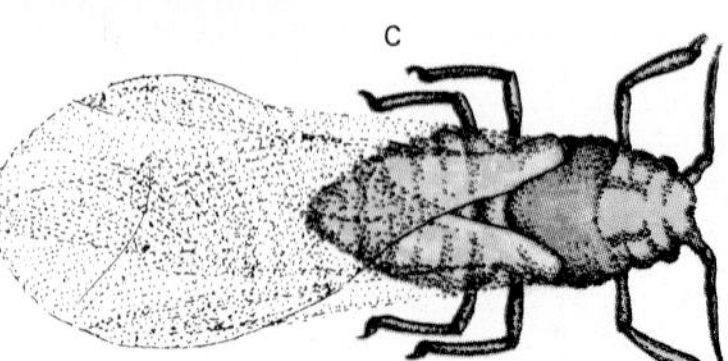

B
C

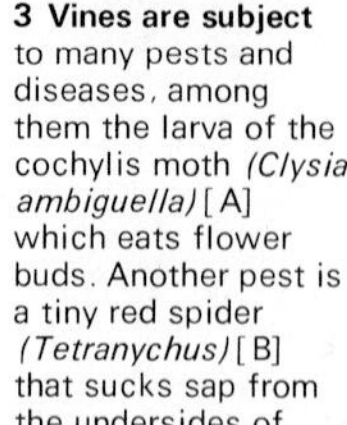

4 The deadliest enemy of the vine is the bug *Phylloxera vitifoliae*. The larvae [A] develop into a root-eating form, called "root louse" [B], which in the 1870s almost destroyed vineyards planted with European grapes, but the roots of several vines native to eastern North America were immune. Virtually every vine in Europe and California had to be pulled up and replaced with vines made by grafting European scions onto American rootstocks. [C] is the adult.

of California that had been planted with European varieties of *Vitis vinifera*. The insect came from eastern North America, and so did the cure. Because native American vines are immune to phylloxera, the disease was eventually controlled by grafting scions of European varieties onto rootstocks of American varieties, such as *Vitis rupestris* and *V. berlandieri*.

Selection of varieties

In the wine growing districts of the Old World, the selection of varieties that give the best quality combined with reasonable quantity and reasonable resistance to disease has taken place gradually over the centuries. In most areas no one grape provides exactly what is needed. Great vineyards grow and blend the varieties they use; lesser ones grow one or more varieties and either blend the resulting wines themselves or sell them to *négotiants*, or shippers, who do the blending.

In the main wine districts of Europe, the best wines are known by the vineyard in which they are grown rather than by the kinds of grapes that go into them. The choice of grape is often dictated by laws that make the use of traditional varieties a condition of using the traditional wine name. For example, the great white Burgundy wines must include specific proportions of Chardonnay grapes.

In the New World the choice of grapes is not a question of tradition but of judgment; a realistic balance of grape quality, productivity, and hardiness is sought. Hence the best wines of the New World use the grape name to specify the character of the wine, with the result that the name "Cabernet Sauvignon" may be more familiar to an average Californian than it would be to a Parisian wine connoisseur.

In an attempt to combine the hardiness, disease resistance, and productivity of certain American varieties with the winemaking qualities of European varieties, European viticulturists have developed many promising new wine-grape hybrids. None, however, has yet achieved the esteemed quality of the best of the old *vinifera* varieties.

KEY

Nurturing and protecting France's 3,000,000 acres of vines is increasingly difficult. Near Saumur, on the Loire, farmers spray their vineyards in midsummer with a copper sulfate solution and sulfur powder to prevent infection by fungus pests such as powdery and downy mildews.

5

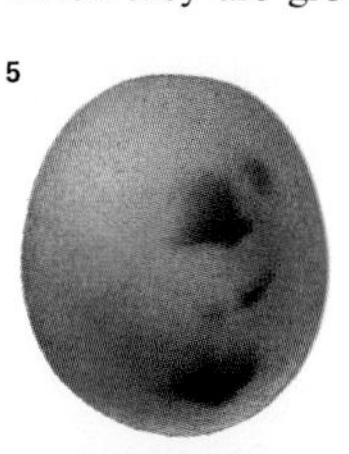

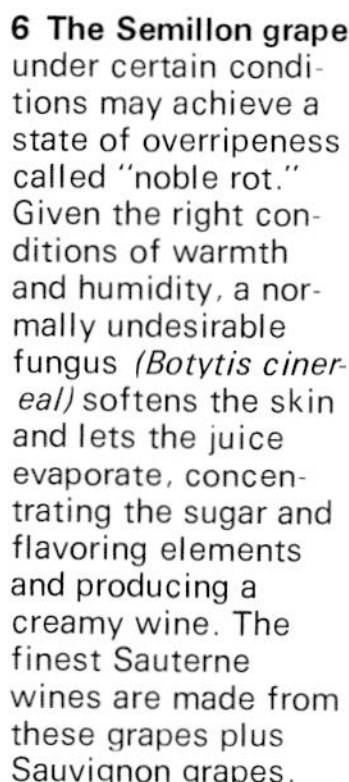

5 The Gamay grape makes first-class wine only on the granite hills of Beaujolais. In the rest of Burgundy it is an inferior variety and elsewhere it is dull, except in California where it is often excellent. At its best the Gamay Grape produces an incomparable wine that is light and fruity. At the present time it is often over-sugared; as a result, the wine tends to be too strong and dry to the palate.

6

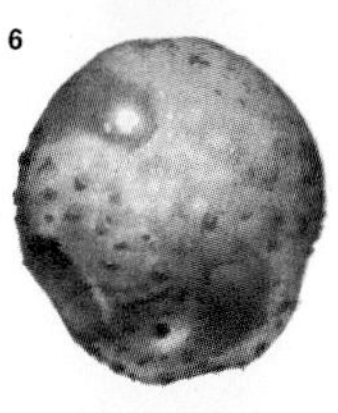

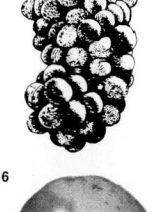

6 The Semillon grape under certain conditions may achieve a state of overripeness called "noble rot." Given the right conditions of warmth and humidity, a normally undesirable fungus *(Botytis cinereal)* softens the skin and lets the juice evaporate, concentrating the sugar and flavoring elements and producing a creamy wine. The finest Sauterne wines are made from these grapes plus Sauvignon grapes.

7

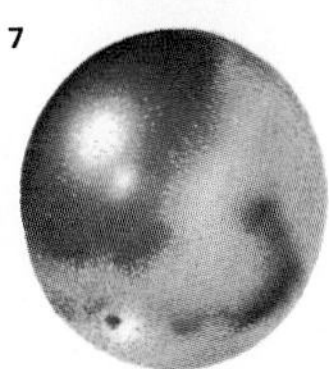

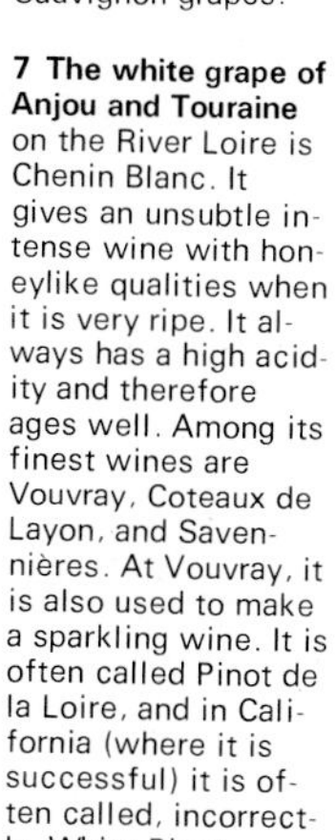

7 The white grape of Anjou and Touraine on the River Loire is Chenin Blanc. It gives an unsubtle intense wine with honeylike qualities when it is very ripe. It always has a high acidity and therefore ages well. Among its finest wines are Vouvray, Coteaux de Layon, and Savennières. At Vouvray, it is also used to make a sparkling wine. It is often called Pinot de la Loire, and in California (where it is successful) it is often called, incorrectly, White Pinot.

8

8 Chardonnay is the grape of white burgundy (Chablis, Montrachet, Meursault, and Pouilly Fuissé) and also of champagne. Chardonnay gives a firm, full, strong wine with scent and character, on chalky soils it can become almost luscious without being sweet. Its wine ages well and is produced in a number of regions, notably in northern California where it is a rival of classic white Burgundy.

9

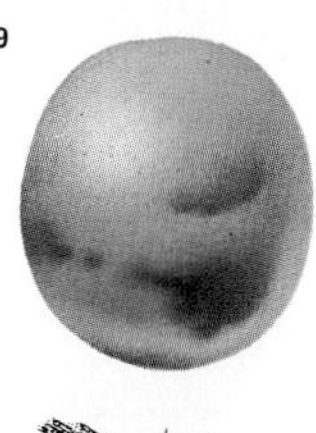

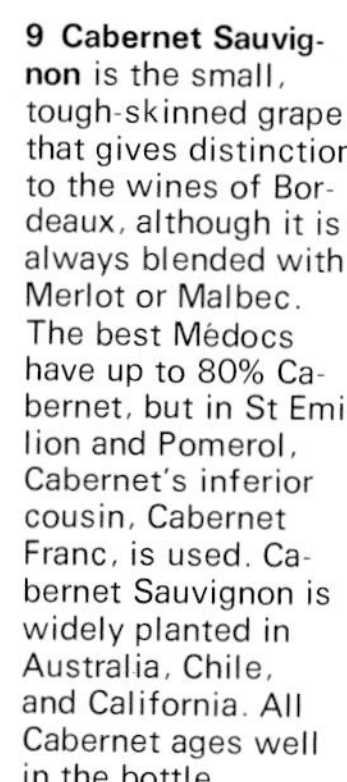

9 Cabernet Sauvignon is the small, tough-skinned grape that gives distinction to the wines of Bordeaux, although it is always blended with Merlot or Malbec. The best Médocs have up to 80% Cabernet, but in St Emilion and Pomerol, Cabernet's inferior cousin, Cabernet Franc, is used. Cabernet Sauvignon is widely planted in Australia, Chile, and California. All Cabernet ages well in the bottle.

10

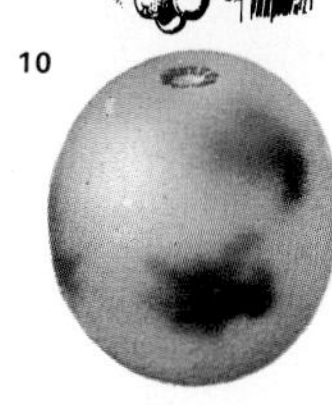

10 Pinot Noir is the great red grape of the Côte d'Or in Burgundy (Chambertin, Romanée, Corton, Beaune); it is the world's best wine grape in the right place. In Champagne it is pressed as soon as it is picked to make white wine, which becomes the greater part of the best champagnes. When it is good, its wines are a profound pleasure. As a rule it does not do so well outside France, but it is grown elsewhere in Europe and in California.

11

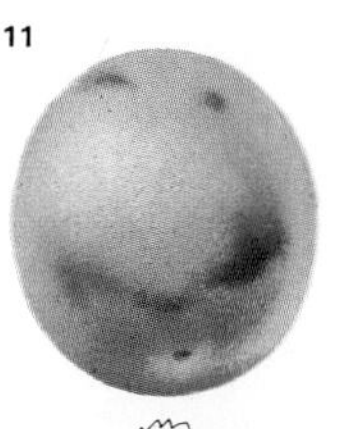

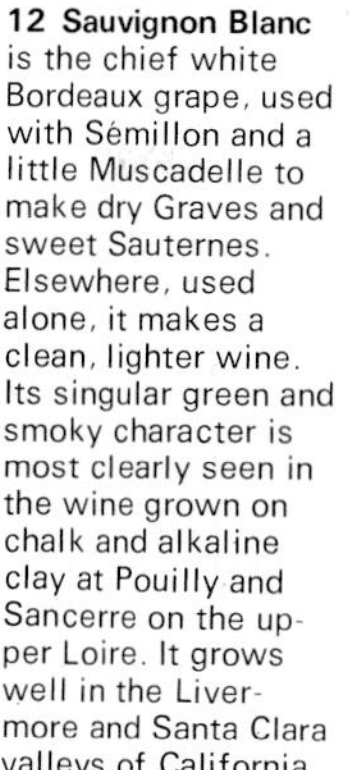

11 The Muscat grape can be black or white. Some of the first vineyards planted by the Greeks in France were Muscat. It also spread from the Aegean to the Crimea, Sicily, Italy, and to southern Spain. All Muscat wine, except that of Alsace and Bulgaria, is sweet. The best in France comes from Beaumes-de-Venise near Avignon. Muscat wines are made all over the world. Today Australia makes some of the best.

12

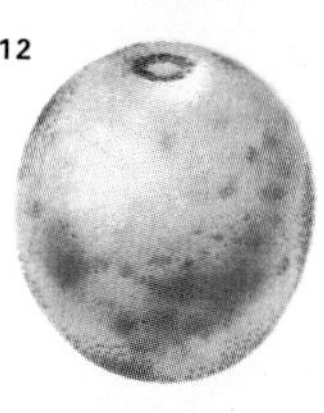

12 Sauvignon Blanc is the chief white Bordeaux grape, used with Sémillon and a little Muscadelle to make dry Graves and sweet Sauternes. Elsewhere, used alone, it makes a clean, lighter wine. Its singular green and smoky character is most clearly seen in the wine grown on chalk and alkaline clay at Pouilly and Sancerre on the upper Loire. It grows well in the Livermore and Santa Clara valleys of California.

13

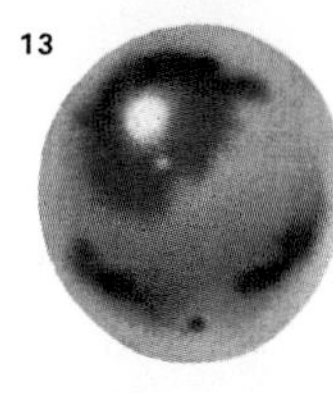

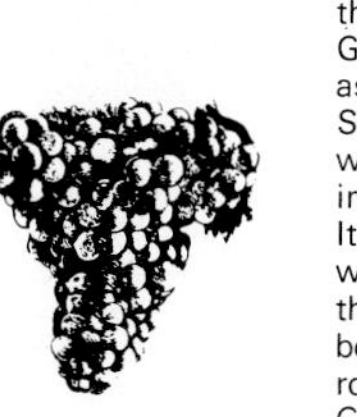

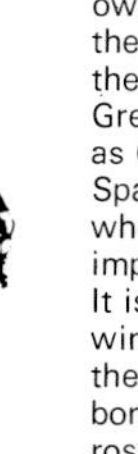

13 Grenache is a sweet grape with a character of its own but not a great deal of color. It is one of the varieties blended to make Châteauneuf du-Pape. On its own, it makes Tavel, the best rosé from the Rhône valley. Grenache is known as Garnacha to the Spanish of Rioja, where it is the most important red variety. It is used for dessert wines at Banyuls on the Franco-Spanish border and for light rosés – usually called Grenache rosé – in California.

14 A

B

C

D

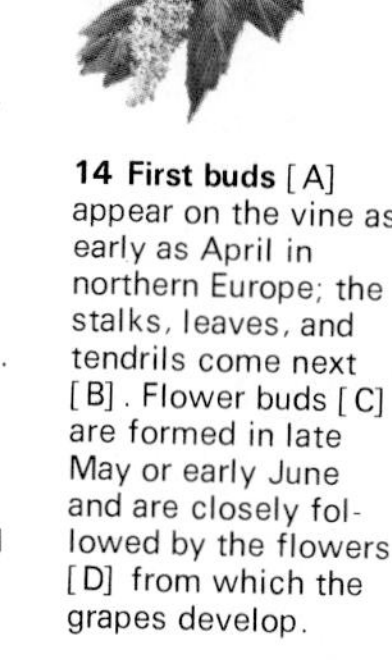

14 First buds [A] appear on the vine as early as April in northern Europe; the stalks, leaves, and tendrils come next [B]. Flower buds [C] are formed in late May or early June and are closely followed by the flowers [D] from which the grapes develop.

How wine is made

Crushed ripe grapes, left to themselves, ferment and make a wine of sorts. But fine wines are a product of man's knowledge, skill, and labor, as well as natural ingredients and favorable weather.

A modern winery is a factory where wine is made. It is in many ways the same as the traditional small property, which in Bordeaux, France, is usually called—often misleadingly—*château,* and in Burgundy and Germany *domain* or *domäne*. But a private estate normally makes only one or, at most, two types of wine, while a winery often makes a dozen. And a grower in Burgundy where properties are usually smaller than in Bordeaux, may make as few as 1,000 bottles of wine a year, while the vast E. & J. Gallo winery in Modesto, California, the world's largest, makes, bottles, and distributes about 300 million bottles a year.

What all growers have in common is the yearly round of duties divided between vineyard and cellar. These are described here as they occur in the life of a small and fairly traditional French winegrower who is conscientious about quality and sells most of his own wine to private clients—still a common practice in France.

A year's hard work

The year begins with pruning. Traditionally, this was started on St Vincent's Day, January 22, but nowadays it begins in December. Even if there is no snow, the ground is often frozen, but the sapless vines will survive temperatures down to about −1°F (−18°C). Indoors, the barrels of new wine from the September vintage must be kept full and their bungs wiped every other day with a disinfectant solution of sulfur dioxide. In fine dry weather the older wine can be bottled. The bottles are then labeled and packed for shipment.

Cutting and grafting

Pruning is finished in February, when cuttings are taken for grafting. They are grafted onto rootstocks, then placed in sand indoors. Chemical fungicides, such as Bordeaux mixture, are ordered for spraying later on in the year. In fine weather, when there is a new moon and a north wind (which are associated with high atmospheric pressure), the new wine is racked into clean barrels to clear it. The new wine may be blended to equalize the casks.

In mid-March, the vine begins to emerge from dormancy, the sap begins to rise, and the buds burst out of their protective sheaths. Any unfinished pruning is completed and tractors begin to move down the rows, turning over the soil to aerate it and to uncover the bases of the vines. The first racking of last year's wine is completed before the end of the month. With the coming of warmer weather the sap begins to rise in the vines and a second fermentation begins in the new wine. The casks are kept topped up and bottling of aged wine is finished.

Plowing comes to an end in April, the vineyard is cleaned up, and year-old cuttings are planted out from the nursery. Indoors, topping up of casks continues because 5 percent of the wine evaporates through the walls of the cask in a year and there must be no air space in the cask.

Frost danger is at its height in May. On clear nights, when frost is likely to strike,

CONNECTIONS

See also

344 Origins of wine
346 Vines and grapes
352 Spirits and distilling
350 Beer and brewing
730 Alcoholism and drug abuse

1
5
3
1
6
4
2
8
7
13
12
15
10
11
16
14
9

1 A typical small wine château in the Médoc, on which this drawing is broadly based, is a modest, specialized farm where the methods are up to date without being unusually modern. The château was probably built about 1830 and, like many in the Médoc region of Bordeaux, it has an air of importance above its station as an ordinary family house. Heavy silt land [1] beside a stream is useless for growing vines but the stream itself is useful for draining the vineyard. The bottle cellar [2] contains the château's recently bottled wines, which must mature at least two years in the bottle. The cellar also has examples of the château's wine and often that of its neighbors going back more than 50 years. Fodder and farm equipment, including the tall tractor used for straddling the vines, are kept in the barn [3]. In the second-year *chai*, or wine shed [4], barrels of wine are stored for a year before bottling. Some of the bottling is carried out at the château and some is done by *négociants*, or shippers, in nearby Bordeaux. The vineyard's full-time workman lives in a cottage on the premises [5]. Close by is the proprietor's office [6] where, on the wall, there are large-scale plans of the château and the vineyard, showing every barrel and vine. The wine château and its vineyards make up an industry that is integrated to an unusually high degree. It is as if a clothing factory bred its own sheep, sheared them, spun the yarn, wove the cloth, and made the cloth into garments. The ripe grapes are gathered by pickers, often students [7]. The grapes are collected from them by a horse-drawn cart. The *courtier*, or broker [8], arrives to hear news of the vintage and to form his first impressions of its likely quality. The *maître de chai*, or cellarmaster, measures the sugar content of the grape juice—and hence the future alcohol content of the wine—with a hydrometer [9]. Grapes go straight into a crusher-stemmer [10] to be crushed, destemmed, and pumped into a *cuve*, or a fermenting vat [12]. To eliminate vinegar bacteria, sulfur dioxide in powder or liquid form is sprinkled on the crushed grapes [11] at about 10 grams (0.35oz) for each 100 liters (21 gal). The vat is kept only 80% full to allow room for seething of the fermenting grapes. Twice a day the fermenting juice is pumped up and sprayed over the floating "cap" of skins [13]. This process is called *remontage*. In fine years the juice may be pumped via an open tub to help aeration. The hydraulic press [14] presses the pulp and skins to extract what remains after the free-run juice has been drawn off. The deeply colored *vin de presse* may be mixed with the rest of the wine. From the oak vats in which it has been made the wine may go to cement vats [15] for the winter. Many wines now go through a secondary fermentation that rids them of malic acid and makes them less harsh. In February the wine is pumped from cement vats into oak *barriques*, or barrels, in the first-year *chai*, or wine shed [16]. At some châteaux the wine goes directly from the fermenting vat to barrels. The barrels are stoppered with loose bungs and the wine then stays in the shed for a year, regularly topped up and occasionally racked into fresh wine barrels.

workers take small stoves out among the vines and stay up to keep them going. The soil is plowed again and the vines are sprayed against powdery and downy mildews. Suckers that drain the vine's energy are removed. As the vines begin to flower, the second racking of last year's wine begins indoors.

The vines flower at the start of June. Weather is critical at this time—the warmer and calmer, the better. After flowering, the shoots are thinned and the best ones tied to supporting wires. The second racking of new wine is completed.

The vines are sprayed with Bordeaux mixture again in July. The ground is cultivated again to keep down weeds. Long shoots are trimmed and vine growth slows down.

In August, the vintage is approaching. Grapes turn color. General upkeep, and the cleaning and preparation of the vats and casks to be used, keeps everyone busy. September is the vintage month. In about the third week the grapes are ripe and picking begins. The *cuves,* or vats, where the wine will be fermented, are scoured and are then filled with water, which swells the wood.

The vintage ends

The vintage continues for about two weeks into October. Once it is over, manure is spread on the ground and the land for new plantings is deep-plowed. The new wine is now fermenting, and the year-old wine is racked again. For the second year of aging the barrels are bunged tightly and put on their sides so that the bung stays wet and seals properly.

In November manuring is completed and the vineyard is plowed to throw soil over the bases of the vines to protect them from frost. The wine to be bottled is fined, or clarified, and given a final racking. December arrives again; if soil from the tops of slopes has been washed down, it must be carried back and redistributed. New casks must be checked and topped up frequently, and the aged wine can be bottled. Out in the vineyard pruning begins again and the cycle is renewed.

KEY

Chateau Langoa-Barton, in the Bordeaux region of western France, was built in 1758. Its wine is a typical Saint-Julien, the epitome of classical claret. The Bordeaux region has good drainage and an excellent climate for vines.

2

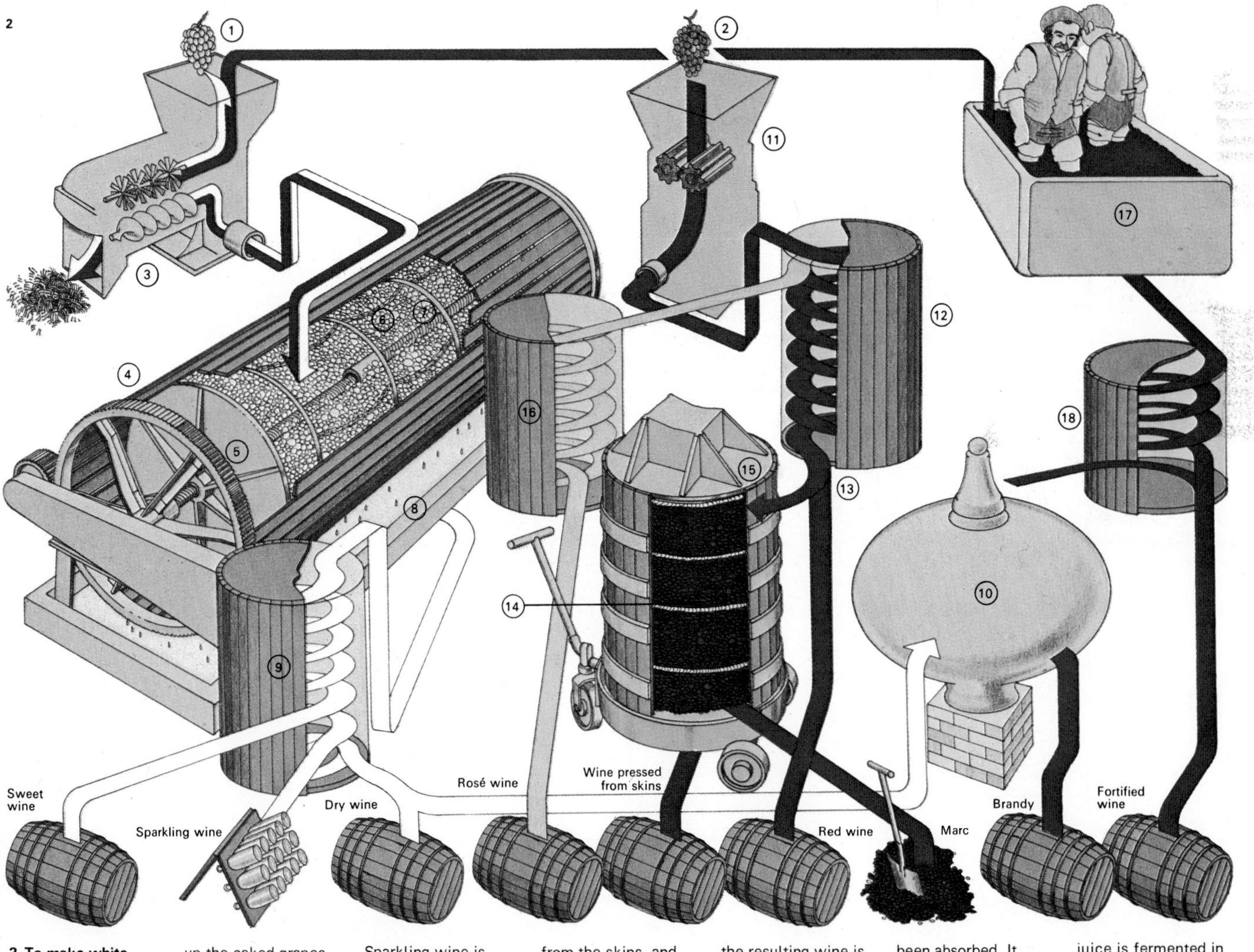

Sweet wine

Sparkling wine

Dry wine

Rosé wine

Wine pressed from skins

Red wine

Marc

Brandy

Fortified wine

2 To make white wine white [1] or red grapes are fed into a crusher-stemmer [3], which removes the stems and pumps the broken grapes into a horizontal press [4]. A screw brings the end plates [5] together and chains [6] and hoops [7] break up the caked grapes. The juice falls into a trough [8] and is pumped into a fermenting vat [9]. The juice is fermented completely to make dry wine. The fermentation may be halted before all the sugar is used up to make sweet wine. Sparkling wine is usually made by a secondary fermentation in the bottle. Wine may be distilled [10] to make brandy. For red wine, grapes [2] are crushed [11] and fermented with their skins in a vat [12]. Color and the tannin are absorbed from the skins, and when the fermentation is complete, the wine is drawn off [13]. For quicker-maturing wines the juice may be taken off the skins after a few days to finish fermenting separately. The skins [14] are pressed [15] and the resulting wine is usually mixed with that first drawn off. The cake of skins left in the press is called *marc* and can be used as fertilizer or distilled to make a cheap brandy. Rosé wine is drawn off the skins [12] when only a little color has been absorbed. It completes its fermentation in a second vat [16]. In making port and some other fortified wines, large amounts of color are extracted from the skins—traditionally by treading them in troughs [17]. In making port the juice is fermented in a vat [18] until the desired amount of sugar is converted to alcohol. Then brandy from a still [10] is added to stop fermentation and raise the alcohol level of the wine to over 16%.

Beer and brewing

Beer, rather than wine, is the traditional drink of those countries in which grapes cannot flourish. The making of beer and ales—brewing—has been known for many thousands of years. Some form of brewing was carried out in Babylon about 4000 BC [Key]. The ancient Egyptians were also familiar with brewing and passed on the knowledge to the Greeks, from whom the Romans learned it. Brewing, using a mixture of grain and honey, probably developed independently in northern Europe.

The composition of beers

The basic materials used in brewing are grain (the source of sugars), which is usually barley (but wheat, millet, rice, and corn are also used) and yeast, which breaks down the sugars by fermentation to form alcohol and carbon dioxide. The use of hops—introduced from Holland—as flavoring became widespread in England and Germany after the 16th century.

Today there are two main types of beer. Lagers are fermented with bottom-fermenting yeast, ales with top-fermenting yeast. Bottom-fermenting yeast moves to the bottom of the fermenting vessel toward the end of fermentation, top-fermenting yeast to the top.

Ale-type beers are the most common in the British Isles, Australia, and New Zealand. They include bitter or a pale ale, a highly hopped brew; draft mild ale; and bottled brown ale. The very dark stout and porter (which is a weak stout) are also top-fermented.

Lager-type beers are the most widespread. They have a longer maturation time than ales (up to six months as opposed to four weeks at the most for ales). The main types are Pilsener, which is light and medium-hopped, and the Munich and Bock beers (dark brown, full-bodied, and sweet).

The brewing process

Brewing begins with the production of barley malt. Grains of barley are soaked and allowed to germinate. During germination enzymes are produced that can convert starch within the grains to sugars. The germinated grains—the malt—are then dried and crushed in a grist mill. Just enough rupturing of the husk occurs to enable the grain, now called grist, to be infused with hot water in a process known as mashing. The object is to allow the conversion of the starch to fermentable sugars by enzyme action and to extract the sugars from the grist. Other crushed grains (wheat, corn, or rice) may be added at this stage to provide extra starch.

The mash is held in a vessel called the mash tun. The temperature and method of mashing define the type of beer to be produced. Most beers are produced by a three-mash process. Water at 38°C (100°F) is introduced and after two hours the temperature of the mash is raised to 65.5°C and then finally to 75.5°C. The liquid from the mash tun is known as "wort" and contains a mixture of sugars and other chemicals from the malt. The wort is run off from the mash tun through the bed of spent grain, which lies on perforated plates at the bottom of the mash tun. The wort is boiled, usually for about two hours, to destroy the enzymes and to sterilize and concentrate

CONNECTIONS

See also
326 Staple foods: grains
426 Yeasts and molds
352 Spirits and distilling

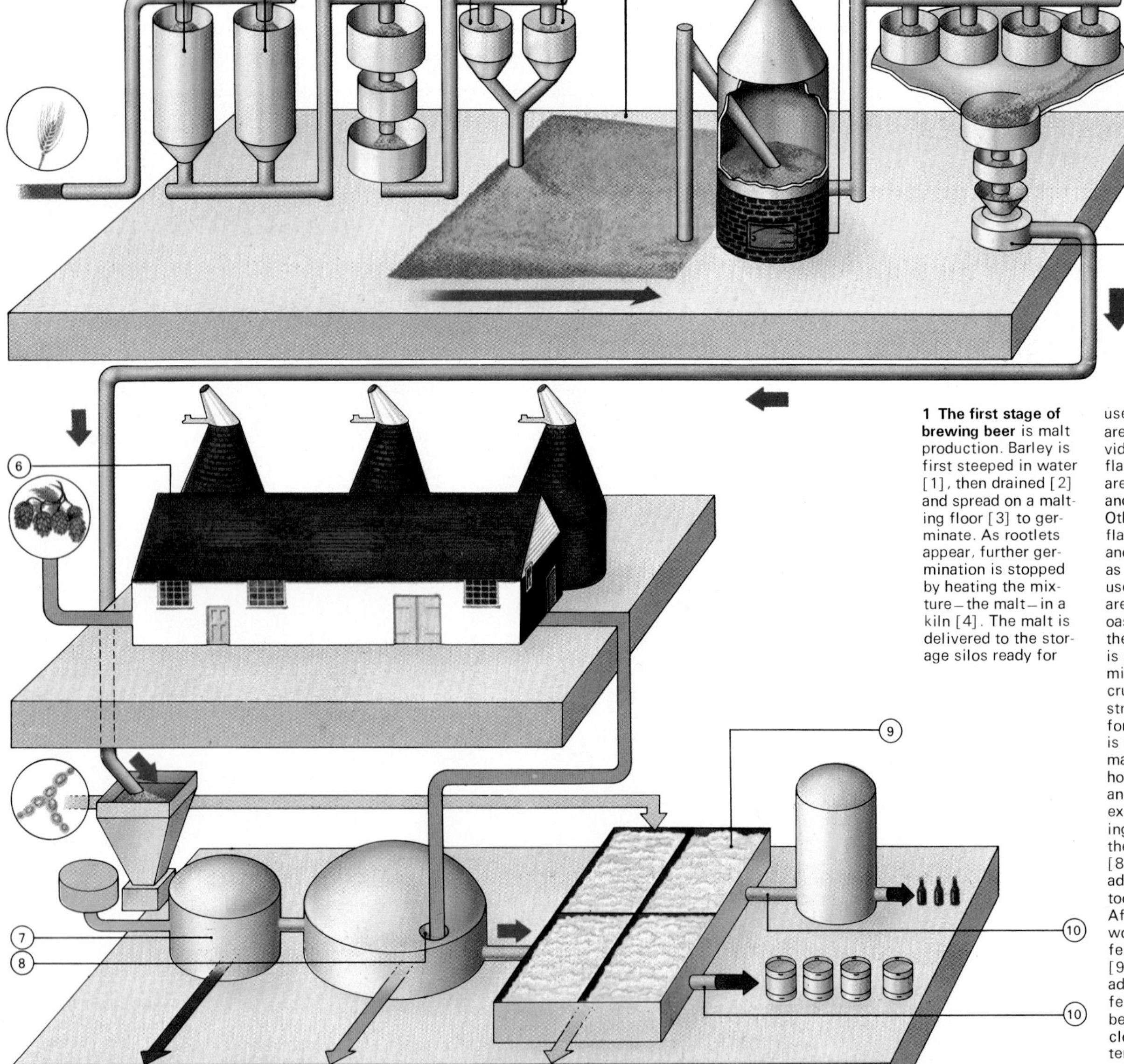
1
1
2
3
4
5
6
7
8
9
10
10
Spent grain used in cattle cake
Spent hops used in fertilizer
Surplus yeast used in food products

1 The first stage of brewing beer is malt production. Barley is first steeped in water [1], then drained [2] and spread on a malting floor [3] to germinate. As rootlets appear, further germination is stopped by heating the mixture—the malt—in a kiln [4]. The malt is delivered to the storage silos ready for use in brewing. Malts are blended to provide a continuity of flavor. Roasted malts are used for brown and stout beers. Other grains such as flaked wheat, rice, and corn can be used as adjuncts. Hops, used for flavoring, are dried in kilns or oast houses [6]. At the brewery, the malt is put in the malt mill, where it is crushed without destroying the husks to form grist [5]. This is then fed into a mash tun [7], where hot water is added and the goodness extracted. The resulting wort is boiled in the copper kettle [8], where hops are added, and sugar, too, if necessary. After cooling, the wort goes to the fermenting vessel [9], where yeast is added. The wort is fermented and the beer is matured in closed tanks and filtered. It is finally poured into casks, kegs, bottles, and cans [10].

the liquid. At this stage hops are added, to give the beer its bitter tang. Sugar may also be added during boiling. Any solid objects, including spent hops in the wort, are now filtered off. The liquid is cooled and transferred to the fermenting vessel. Living yeast *(Saccharomyces),* which is a type of fungus, is added at this stage. The character of the finished product depends in large measure on the purity and type of the yeast. Wild yeasts in a yeast culture cause the fermentation pattern to change and the whole character of the beer can be disturbed. The yeast culture, which is kept in aseptic, refrigerated storage, is checked frequently.

During fermentation stringent precautions are taken to ensure that no impurities invade the brew. The temperature of the fermenting wort is also carefully controlled. There is a tendency for the yeast to rise to the surface, or to fall to the bottom, depending on its type, and from time to time the contents of the fermenting vessel must be stirred or "roused."

After about eight days, when most of the sugar has been converted to alcohol, the beer is removed from the fermentation vessel and separated from the bulk of the yeast. The new or "green" beer is then stored in maturation tanks, so that it may develop flavor and character. At this stage a secondary fermentation occurs with lager beers and with some ale-type beers.

Basically, the brewing process is the same for both lager and ales, but in brewing lager the yeast is quite different and, because fermentation and maturation are carried out at a lower temperature, both processes take longer to complete.

Packaging the brew

After brewing comes packaging: filling casks or kegs for the draft beer trade or transferring the brew to a bottling room for packing into bottles or cans. Cask draft beer is filled through nozzles on simple gravity-feed machines. Kegs are sterilized and mounted on a filling head, which displaces air from the keg by means of CO_2. The CO_2 is in turn displaced by the in-flowing beer. Bottles and cans are filled in much the same way.

KEY

Brewing is an extremely ancient art. It probably originated some 6,000 years ago in Mesopotamia. This clay seal was made in the kingdom of Mitanni in northern Mesopotamia around 1500 BC. It depicts a hunting scene, mythological animals, and a man drinking beer through a straw. The art of brewing beer and ale spread westward to Europe through North Africa and eastward to China and Japan.

2

3 A

B

2 Barley may have come originally from central Asia. Eventually traders carried it as far north as Scandinavia and Britain. The art of brewing accompanied the geographical spread of the grain.

3 Hops are climbing vines. The common hop *(Humulus lupulus)* is grown in gardens [A] on inclined strings and wires. The female flower clusters [B] are used to impart a bitter flavor to beer.

4 The basic process of brewing, with variations in materials and detail of production, can give rise to many different types of beer. The flavor, sweetness, color, and gaseous content can all vary.

5 Home brewing, where it is permitted, can be practiced with little more than ordinary domestic equipment for mashing, boiling, fermenting, and bottling. Containers are of glass or stainless steel.

4

5

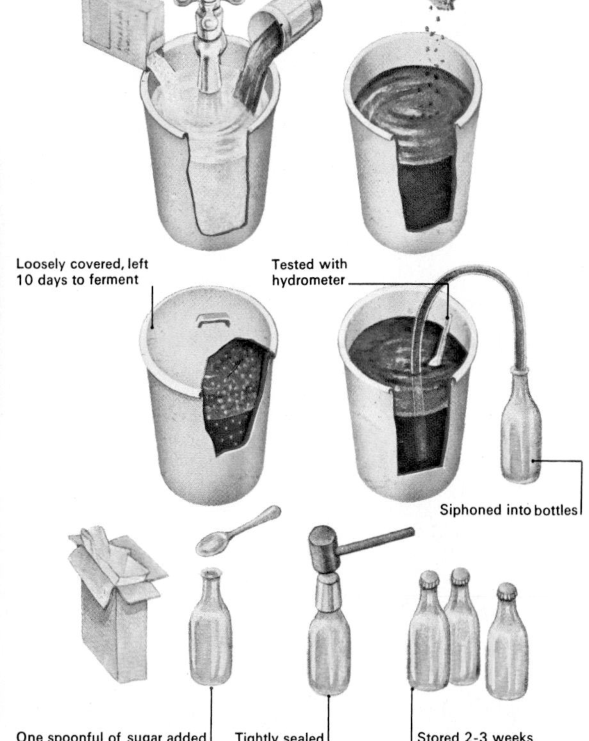

Sugar
Hot water (8 liters)
Hop and malt extracts
Yeast (sprinkled on when all has settled)
Loosely covered, left 10 days to ferment
Tested with hydrometer
Siphoned into bottles
One spoonful of sugar added
Tightly sealed
Stored 2-3 weeks

Spirits and distilling

Liquors, in common with all other alcoholic beverages, are produced basically by alcoholic fermentation (the decomposition of sugars into ethyl alcohol by yeasts) of sugar-rich liquids. The diversity of liquors and related alcoholic beverages is a reflection of the widely differing sources of fermentable sugar. This sugar is directly available in some raw materials (such as grapes and molasses), but in other raw materials (cereals, potatoes) starch must be converted into fermentable sugars by adding enzymes (biological catalysts). The traditional source of such enzymes is barley malt and the process of conversion is known as "mashing."

Distillation and maturation

Yeast fermentation leads to a maximum alcoholic content of about fifteen percent in beverages such as wine. But in the production of liquors, fermentation is followed by distillation, which concentrates alcohol in the distilled spirit. Distillation [Key, 1, 4, 6, 7] is the heating of alcohol-containing liquids, so that the alcohol boils off to be condensed, collected, and added as desired to increase strength. The degree of concentration and distillation of volatile flavoring substances or "congenerics" depends on the type of still and the way it is operated. Simple "pot" stills [6] distill alcohol at lower concentration to give a liquor with a characteristic flavor, whereas "continuous column" stills [7] are more efficient, yielding liquors of higher alcohol concentration but which have very little or even no congeneric flavor.

Newly distilled liquor is seldom suitable for immediate consumption. It is often stored in wooden casks [5] for a number of years to achieve a mellow and developed flavor such as that of whiskey or brandy. The quality of liquors is frequently related to the period of storage in wooden casks. For bottling, liquors are normally reduced with pure water to an alcohol content of about 40 percent by volume.

Malt and grain whiskeys

Scotch malt whiskey is made entirely from a mash of malted barley. The fermented mash produced in a mash tun [2] is first distilled into what are known as "low wines" in a mash still [4], and the low wines are redistilled in a similar pot still, the spirit still. In the second distillation "heads and tails" fractions (the first and last parts obtained in the distillation) are returned to the low wines. The middle fraction is the new whiskey. Malt whiskey is aged in reusable oak casks for eight, twelve, or more years before being sold as single malt whiskey—the product of an individual distillery.

Malt whiskey is blended with Scotch grain whiskey to produce blended Scotch whiskey. Grain whiskey is made from a mash of pre-cooked maize and a proportion of barley malt. The wash is distilled in a semicontinuous, two-column still. Scotch grain and malt whiskies are aged separately and blended shortly before bottling. Irish whiskey is made from unmalted cereals, including barley, wheat, and rye, which are mashed together with malted barley. Bourbon whiskey, named after Bourbon county, Kentucky, where it was first made, comes from a grain mash of at least 51 per-

CONNECTIONS

See also
344 Origins of wine
346 Vines and grapes
348 Wines of the world
350 Beer and brewing
730 Alcoholism and drug abuse

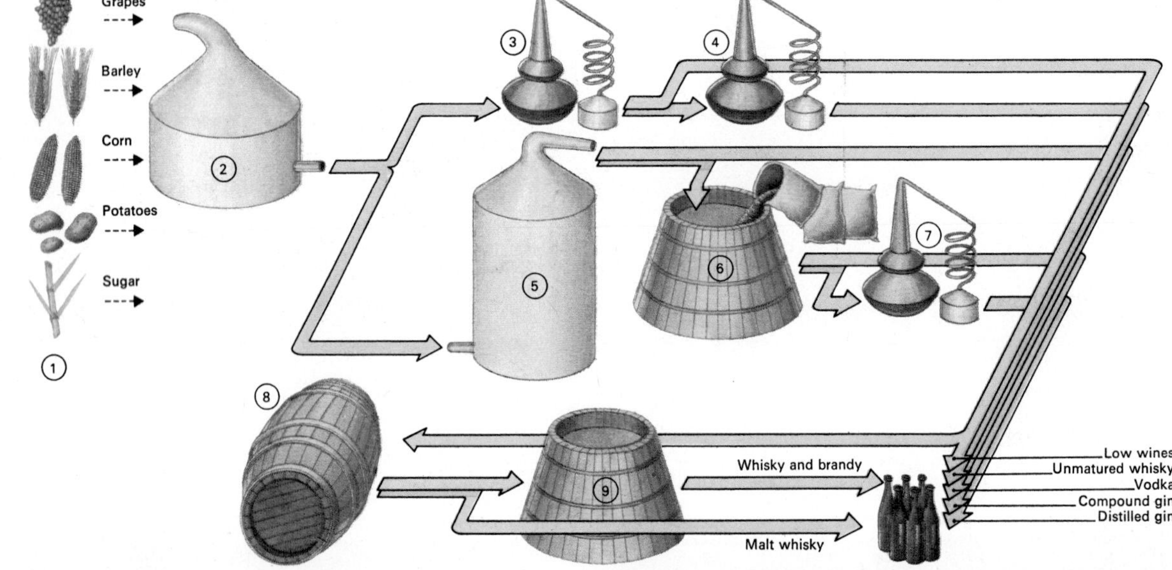

1
Grapes
Barley
Corn
Potatoes
Sugar
Whisky and brandy
Malt whisky
Low wines
Unmatured whisky
Vodka
Compound gin
Distilled gin

1 The distilling process varies according to the initial ingredients and the desired produce. The raw ingredients [1], crops that will supply the sugar for fermentation, are fermented in the mashing tun [2]. For whiskey and brandy the mash is distilled in a mash still [3] and the spirit produced redistilled in a spirit still [4]. It is then aged in oak casks [8] and may be blended [9] before bottling. Mash for other liquors may be distilled continuously in a distillation column [5], and the product usually has flavoring added [6]. The flavored liquor may be distilled again in a pot still [7]. Gin and vodka are made in this manner.

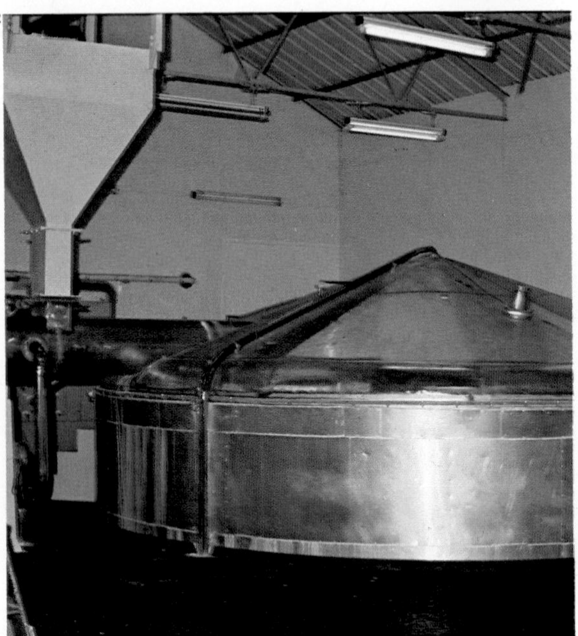

2 In Scotch malt whiskey distilleries mashing is carried out in a vessel called a "mash tun." This is filled with a mixture of milled barley malt and hot water. The liquid "worts" (infusions of malt before they are fermented), charged with soluble substances extracted from the malt, are drawn off through perforated plates in the base.

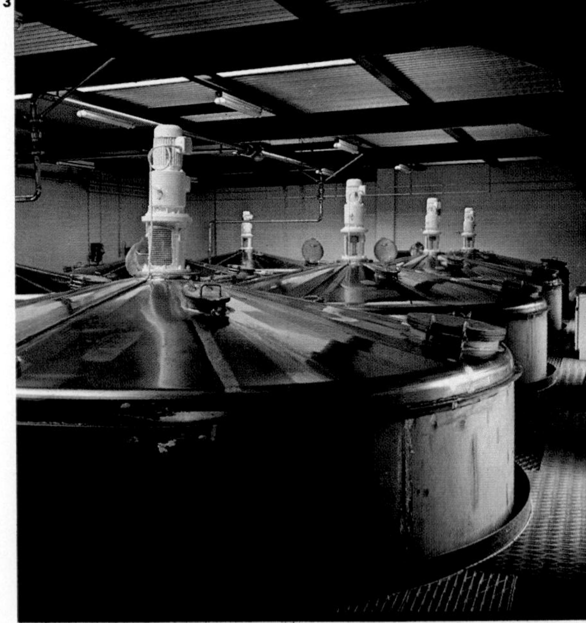

3 Worts from the mash tun are cooled and piped to the tun room for fermentation. The stainless-steel covered fermenters are filled with worts and yeast is added to start a vigorous fermentation. To prevent foam overflowing during fermentation, propellers are rotated inside.

cent corn. The distillate is generally matured for four years in new oak casks that are charred internally before filling. Kentucky is still the center of the bourbon industry. Canadian whiskey is a blend of a strongly flavored rye whiskey and a lighter corn-based whiskey. Blended whiskies are made by adding neutral spirits to the straight whiskey.

Other liquors

Brandy is the distillate of wine. Cognac, the best known brandy, is made from the wine of the Charente (a region in southwest France) by two successive distillations in characteristic pot stills. Cognac is matured in Limousin oak casks and the finer qualities age for ten, twenty, or even more years. The quality of Cognac depends on the soil and conditions of the particular vineyard from which the wine is produced around the town of Cognac. Armagnac, singly-distilled in a more efficient pot still, is made near Agen in southwestern France.

Rum is the distillate of fermented molasses, the mother liquor of crystallized cane sugar. Flavored rums, dark in color, are traditionally made by pot still distillation and aged in wood, but most white rums are distilled to a light flavor, which is modified by an additional treatment with charcoal. Other liquors are made from local sources of fermentable materials: arrack from palm juice, rice, or molasses; calvados and applejack from apples; kirschwasser from cherries; tequila from the Mexican agave or century plant. Vodka is a liquor that has no flavor apart from that of ethyl alcohol.

Liquors such as gin, ouzo, and liqueurs derive their flavor from added ingredients and are not, in general, from the cogenerics of the original spirit. They, like vodka, are made from a base liquor of relatively neutral and flavorless character, produced from a variety of materials, including grain, molasses, and potatoes. Gin is flavored by juniper berries [8] and spices. Ouzo is made by flavoring a base spirit with aniseed. Aquavit is a base liquor flavored with caraway. Liqueurs are liquors sweetened by the addition of sugar. Gin, vodka, and liqueurs do not generally require aging.

KEY

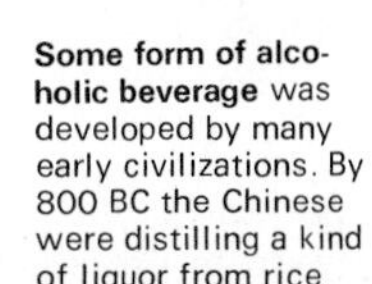

Some form of alcoholic beverage was developed by many early civilizations. By 800 BC the Chinese were distilling a kind of liquor from rice beer and the Romans also produced distilled beverages. Production in western Europe gained impetus after contact with the Arabs in the 8th century AD—the word "alcohol" is of Arabic derivation. This engraving of about 1480 from Salerno, Italy, is of a still.

4

4 Fermented mash is heated in a mash still until all the alcohol is distilled and collected as low wines. A similar but smaller liquor still is charged with a mixture of low wines and "feints" (impure liquors produced in the first and last stages of distillation), and the new whisky is selected as the middle portion of this distillation. The rest of the feints are collected separately and then returned for redistillation in the liquor still.

5

5 New whiskey is filled into oak butts, hogsheads, and barrels and stored on steel racks in warehouses until mature. After emptying, the casks are examined and repaired by coopers and refilled.

6 Copper pot stills charged with a batch of wash or wine are heated directly by a furnace or indirectly by steam. On boiling, the more volatile constituents vaporize and rise to the top of the still. The vapor that reaches the top of the column is then led over into the condenser, liquefied, and collected. Alcohol is progressively removed by distillation and the watery residue that remains is discharged.

6

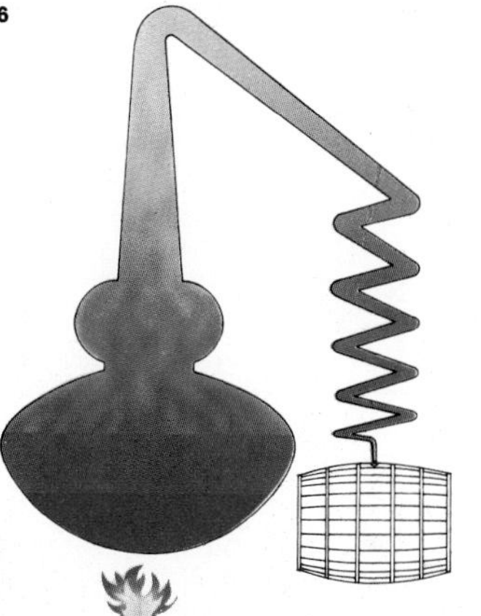

7

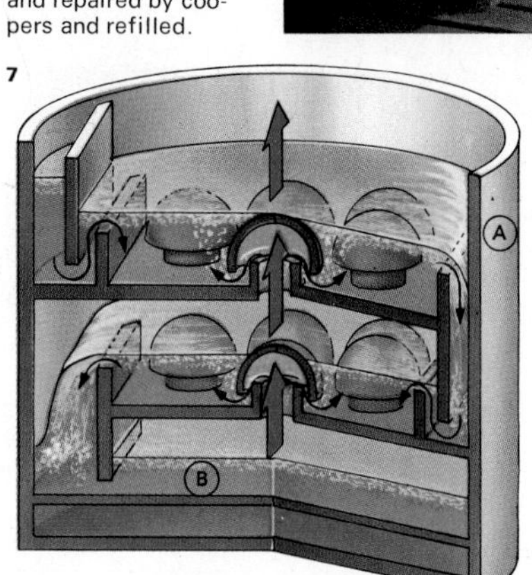
A
B

7 In a continuous still the columns are vertical copper cylinders [A] with horizontal, circular plates [B]. A "bubble cap" plate causes the mixing of the rising vapor with the falling liquid in the column, and this action promotes the separation of alcohol at the top and water at the bottom of the column. Through regulation of the steam supply and product feed, a dynamic balance is set up and liquor is drawn continuously from the top and waste water from the bottom.

8 Juniper berries are the principal flavoring of gin. In addition to other ingredients such as coriander seed, angelica root, cassia and cinnamon bark, orange peel, cardamom, licorice, nutmeg, and others, the juniper berries are distilled in a pot still with a charge of liquor. Dutch gin or "genever" is also redistilled with juniper and other flavorings, but the base liquor or "moutwyn" has a characteristic flavor. Liqueurs are brandies containing large proportions of sugar and alcohol and can be made from many fruits such as raspberries, cherries, and plums, or even tea, cocoa, and coffee.

8

Coffee, tea, and cocoa

Coffee, introduced to Europe by the Arabs in the sixteenth century, is the most widely drunk beverage in the world. It is enjoyed not only for its rich flavor and aroma, which come from an oil called caffeol produced in roasting, but also for the caffeine it contains, which has a stimulating effect on the nervous and blood systems. Leading coffee-drinking countries include the United States, West Germany, France, and Italy. Great coffee plantations are found in Latin America, southern Asia, and Africa.

Growing and processing coffee

The common coffee plants are *Coffea arabica* (now grown mostly in Latin America) [2, 3] and *C. robusta* (cultivated mainly in Africa). Coffee plants reach maturity after four years and remain productive for about 30 years more, but there is usually a drop in quality in about the 15th year, after which the trees are usually replaced.

After the ripe berries are picked, the coffee seeds, or beans, are extracted by machine and the residual pulpy mass left over is used for fertilizer. The seeds are cleaned and then sun- or machine-dried, after which they are hulled, sorted by quality and size, graded, and shipped to market.

Most coffee beans are roasted before being sold; this gives them a dry, brittle texture and a deep brown color. They also acquire their typically rich coffee aroma during roasting by undergoing a complex chemical change. The freshly roasted coffee is cooled and ground, although some customers prefer to grind and even roast the beans themselves. Instant coffee may be powdered or freeze-dried. Both types are made in two stages—brewing and moisture-removal. More than 100 different kinds of coffee beans are marketed, each with its own flavor. The differences arise mainly from the climate and soil types in the various growing regions.

The story of tea

Tea, like coffee, is stimulating because of its caffeine content. Tea remained unknown to the Western world until the sixteenth century, when European explorers who traveled to China and other Far Eastern countries returned with a host of new foods, spices, and beverages. Very soon a thriving commerce in China teas was established between Europe and the Far East. In 1826 the Dutch established plantations on Java, followed some ten years later by the British, who set up tea estates in India. The production of tea has since spread rapidly to regions in Sri Lanka, Bangladesh, Iran, Japan, the Soviet Union, and parts of Africa and South America.

Tea is made from the leaves of an evergreen tropical and subtropical plant, *Camellia sinensis* [5]. There are three major kinds of finished tea. Black tea, which makes up more than 90 percent of the tea trade, is produced by first allowing tea leaves to wither. The leaves are fed through rolling machines to release the juices. The rolled leaves are then placed in extremely humid rooms and left to ferment. Fermentation is stopped by drying the leaves over fires in pans, trays, or baskets, a process that also seals in their final flavor.

A second variety is oolong or semi-fermented tea which is prepared from a spe-

CONNECTIONS

See also
742 Origins of curative medicine
322 Plant genetic resources

1

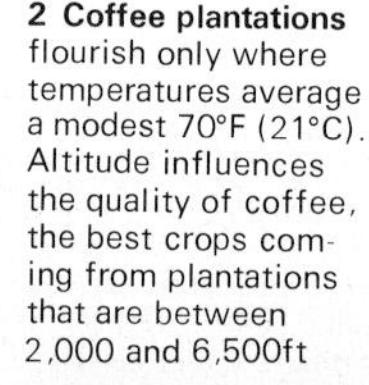

1 Coffee houses flourished in most large European towns in the 17th and 18th centuries and were the centers of much of the political, commercial, and literary activity of the time. The first one in London opened in 1652. The custom of drinking coffee spread westward from Arabia into Europe. Coffee itself is believed to have come originally from Ethiopia. According to legend a 9th-century goatherd noticed that his animals became livelier soon after eating some crimson coffee berries. He tasted some himself and experienced a feeling of exhilaration. The first reliable reference to coffee occurs in Arabian literature of the 10th century AD. But it was not until several hundred years later that the Arabs learned how to make a delicious drink from the roasted ground beans of the coffee berry.

2

2 Coffee plantations flourish only where temperatures average a modest 70°F (21°C). Altitude influences the quality of coffee, the best crops coming from plantations that are between 2,000 and 6,500ft (600 to 2,000m) above sea level. Coffee trees grow best in partial shade and for this reason are often planted on the east- or west-facing slopes of volcanic mountains, where they thrive in the well-drained, potash-rich soil. Once the berries have ripened they are harvested by hand. Each tree yields an average of about 1.5 pounds (0.7kg) of green beans each year.

3 Arabian coffee *Coffea arabica*

3 The coffee plant is a small evergreen tree with leaves some 3 to 6in (7.5–15cm) long. The Arabian species is the most common kind of coffee plant. Coffee trees are able to grow to 25ft (7.5m) high but are pruned to 10ft (3m) on plantations. The fragrant white blossoms are followed by tiny green berries, each holding two tough-skinned, greenish beans. The berries ripen to a deep red after six or seven months and are then picked.

cial kind of China tea plant. The leaves are heated before fermentation progresses very far, then they are rolled and dried.

Lastly, there are green or unfermented teas made by steaming or heating the leaves to sterilize them and kill the enzymes responsible for fermentation. The leaves are then rolled and roasted until they acquire a blue-green tint. Teas are graded for size, age, and quality, and classified according to leaf size such as orange pekoe, pekoe, and souchong.

Paraguay tea, or *maté,* which is widely drunk in South America, is made from the leaves of a species of holly *(Ilex paraguayensis).*

From cacao to chocolate

Cacao trees [6] had been cultivated in Central America for centuries before Columbus arrived there. The Spanish *conquistadores* were sufficiently impressed with *cacahuatl,* the bitter cocoa drink the Indians made from the seeds of the cacao tree [7], to take it back to the court of Spain. The secret of cocoa was jealously guarded by the Spaniards until the seventeenth century, when the rest of Europe was introduced to it. It became a highly fashionable drink virtually overnight. So great was the rage for cocoa that "chocolate houses" became popular.

The cacao tree is a pod-bearing evergreen, *Theobroma cacao*, which grows in tropical regions. The pods are cut down, split open with a heavy knife or mallet, and the pulp and seeds scooped out. The pulpy mass is left to ferment for a week, during which time the beans change from purple to reddish brown and acquire a pungent, chocolate aroma. When fermentation is complete, the beans are either sun- or kiln-dried, then cleaned and shipped to processing plants. The manufacture of cocoa continues with the roasting of the beans. Their shells are then cracked and removed and the nibs or kernels are finely ground to produce a liquid called chocolate liquor, which consists mainly of a fat called cocoa butter, Chocolate liquor is the raw substance from which cocoa powder and chocolate are produced.

KEY

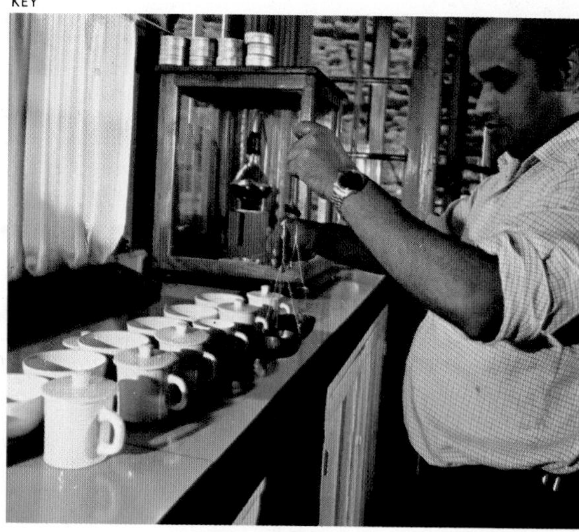

The world's tea crop is traded at great auctions such as one in London, through which the harvest of some 25 nations passes. Before the tea is bought for blending and packaging, tea-tasters examine the dry leaves and analyze the aroma, taste, and appearance of the actual brew.

4

4 Tea is cultivated mostly in monsoon areas of Asia – India, Sri Lanka, and China are the principal producers. Three original varieties of tea – China, Assam, and Cambodia – are the ancestors of the many hundreds of varieties grown today. Tea grows best in warm, well-watered climates where the soil is slightly acid, well-drained, and rich in organic compost. Like coffee, it seems to thrive at higher altitudes, and can be grown at a maximum height of 7,000ft (2,300m). Planters using hybrid plants and modern methods of agriculture can expect an annual yield of about 0.75 tons per acre (1.7 T/ha).

5

Tea
Thea sinensis

5 Tea is a small evergreen shrub that is kept pruned to a maximum height of 5ft (1.5m) on plantations. Its leathery, oblong leaves grow to a maximum of 10in (25cm) long. It takes roughly 40 days for a tea plant to produce a full "flush" of leaves ready for picking. From the top downward the leaves are named pekoe tip, orange pekoe, pekoe, first and second souchong, and first and second congou.

7

7 Aztec and Mixtec paintings show early American peoples drinking a beverage made from cocoa beans, which they cultivated, mixed with corn flour, spices, aromatic herbs, and water.

6

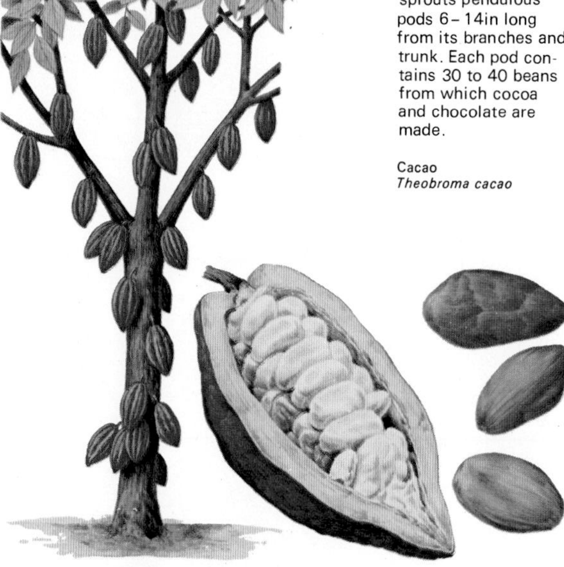

Cacao
Theobroma cacao

6 The cacao tree, a tropical plant, sprouts pendulous pods 6–14in long from its branches and trunk. Each pod contains 30 to 40 beans from which cocoa and chocolate are made.

8

Coffee
Cocoa
Tea

8 Coffee, tea, and cocoa are grown in tropical and subtropical areas. The coffee trade is valued at more than $6 billion a year and represents nearly 4.25 million tons of beans. The tea crop averages some 1.25 million tons, the largest producers being India and Sri Lanka. Nearly 70% of the world's cocoa, 1.36 million tons, comes from the African nations of Ghana, Nigeria, Ivory Coast, and the Cameroons.

Seeds and spices

Throughout the world the seeds, roots, leaves, and bark of certain herbs and trees have been sought out for use in flavoring food and drink. Their value as a means of varying the tastes of common staple foods such as beans, peas, rice, wheat, and root vegetables was widely appreciated in bibical times. In the course of centuries since then a great number have been cultivated all over the world.

Indigenous species still provide the dominant flavors in northern Europe, the Mediterranean, and the Middle East, but they are by no means confined by national or natural boundaries. Fenugreek seeds from the herb *Trigonella foenum-graecum,* a native of the Middle East and Asia, have a musky aromatic flavor and are used in vegetable dishes. In Egypt, Turkey, and Iran the seeds are used in candies, and in southern Asia they are used to flavor curries. The cumin seed *(Cuminum cyminum)* has similar origins and gives curry its characteristic pungency. Fresh aromatic cardamom seed *(Elettaria cardamonum)* is popular in Scandinavia. Cardamom seeds, which are encased in a parchment-colored pod, give a lift to coffee, cakes, and fruit, particularly simmered pears and quinces. Coriander *(Coriandrum sativum)* probably originated in the Mediterranean but now is grown all over the world. It is one of the oldest members of the parsley family, which provides many other seeds used for flavoring.

The prize of princes

Spices were products of Old World tropical climates. Until new sea routes broadened trade between Europe, Asia, and the Far East, such spices as pepper [Key], cloves [3G], and cinnamon [3C] were as rare as gold dust and just as valuable in Europe. During the sixteenth and seventeenth centuries wars were fought over footholds in Asia for a share in the wealth brought by the spices of the Orient. Perhaps the most prized spice was pepper. Now so common and cheap as to be taken for granted, a pound of pepper once cost the equivalent of several weeks' wages.

Spices such as nutmeg [3A], cinnamon, and turmeric [3H] were luxuries in the kitchens of Europe, used sparingly and on special occasions to add sweet aromas to mulled wines in the festive seasons and as ingredients for special cakes celebrating the end of Lent. They were not used freely even at the tables of princes. In the Middle East and Asia they were and still are used lavishly to make the staple diet of legumes and rice less monotonous and to disguise the fact that fresh meat, fish, and vegetables deteriorate rapidly without refrigeration.

Fashions in flavor

The uses of condiments and spices have varied with the passage of time and geographical location. Aniseed [1B], once commonly used in cakes, pastries, and bread throughout Europe, is now confined to sweets and the anise-flavored drinks for which the Mediterranean is famous. Aniseed flavors French *pastis,* Greek *ouzo,* and Turkish *raki*—all now internationally popular aperitifs. In the Middle East aniseed is used to flavor root vegetables and is very good with carrots.

CONNECTIONS

See also

358 Culinary and medicinal herbs

360 Berries, nuts, and olives

456 How flowering plants reproduce

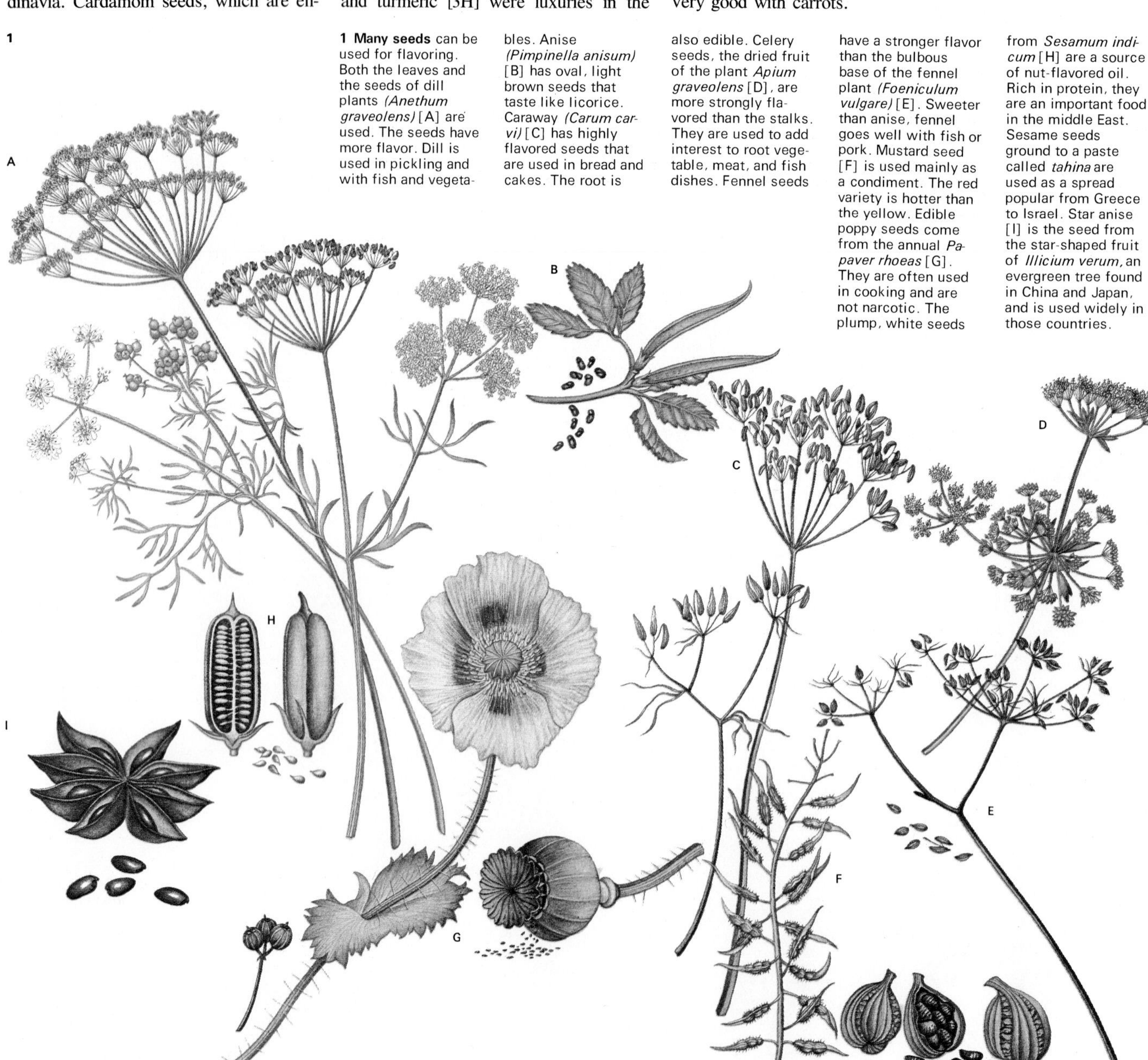

1
A
B
C
D
E
F
G
H
I

1 Many seeds can be used for flavoring. Both the leaves and the seeds of dill plants *(Anethum graveolens)* [A] are used. The seeds have more flavor. Dill is used in pickling and with fish and vegetables. Anise *(Pimpinella anisum)* [B] has oval, light brown seeds that taste like licorice. Caraway *(Carum carvi)* [C] has highly flavored seeds that are used in bread and cakes. The root is also edible. Celery seeds, the dried fruit of the plant *Apium graveolens* [D], are more strongly flavored than the stalks. They are used to add interest to root vegetable, meat, and fish dishes. Fennel seeds have a stronger flavor than the bulbous base of the fennel plant *(Foeniculum vulgare)* [E]. Sweeter than anise, fennel goes well with fish or pork. Mustard seed [F] is used mainly as a condiment. The red variety is hotter than the yellow. Edible poppy seeds come from the annual *Papaver rhoeas* [G]. They are often used in cooking and are not narcotic. The plump, white seeds from *Sesamum indicum* [H] are a source of nut-flavored oil. Rich in protein, they are an important food in the middle East. Sesame seeds ground to a paste called *tahina* are used as a spread popular from Greece to Israel. Star anise [I] is the seed from the star-shaped fruit of *Illicium verum,* an evergreen tree found in China and Japan, and is used widely in those countries.

In the East, fresh ginger [3D] is used as a spice for both fish and meat dishes. The sweet, rich root can provide a striking contrast of texture and taste in an otherwise bland dish. Dry, ground ginger is more often used in the West, usually in sweet foods. Almost every European country has a variety of gingerbread. Yet a dusting of ginger, nutmeg, and coriander turn buttered rice into a subtly different vegetable to serve with chicken or veal. Ginger was widely used in Roman times but is rarely found in modern Italian cuisine.

One fashion that has hardly changed in centuries is the Middle European use of poppy seeds [G] baked in or sprinkled on breads and cakes to flavor and decorate them. A stronger flavor is provided by the tang of caraway seeds in rye bread and pumpernickel. In the Middle East bread is often topped with sesame seeds [1H] before baking, so that they brown and impart a rich, nutty flavor to the bread. Small cakes of meal made from sesame mixed with lemon juice and honey are also popular. Middle Eastern meals are often accompanied by a paste made from chick peas, sesame-seed pulp *(tahina)*, lemon juice, and garlic. It is traditionally eaten with a flat, round, unleavened bread called pita.

Innovations and revivals

Sesame seeds are becoming more popular in Western cooking. They can be added to most sauces for poultry and meat dishes with impunity, creating a subtle difference without overpowering other flavors. Sesame-seed oil is a good addition to a French dressing for strong-flavored salad greens such as romaine, endive, or chicory. Nutmeg and mace were once much used as condiments for members of the cabbage family (which includes cauliflower and turnips) and can turn everyday cabbage into a much more interesting vegetable. Saffron [3E], the dried stamens from a crocus of Asia Minor, has always been the most expensive of spices, since the stamens are collected by hand and about 200,000 are needed to make up a pound of saffron. Saffron gives a deep yellow color and inimitable aroma to rice dishes such as paella.

KEY

Pepper is the dark round fruit of the native Indian vine *Piper nigrum*, now cultivated worldwide in the tropics. The fruit, when fresh and unripe, is green and pungent. It forms the basis of a popular French condiment. Black pepper is the whole dried fruit with an unmistakable aromatic taste. Freshly ground, it enhances the flavor of vegetables, meats, and fish, even fresh fruits. One famous meat dish that uses coarsely crushed peppercorns is steak *au poivre*. Long cooking can diminish the flavor of ground black pepper, so it is best to add it just before serving. White pepper is the seed obtained by removing the outer skin (pericarp) of the fruit.

2

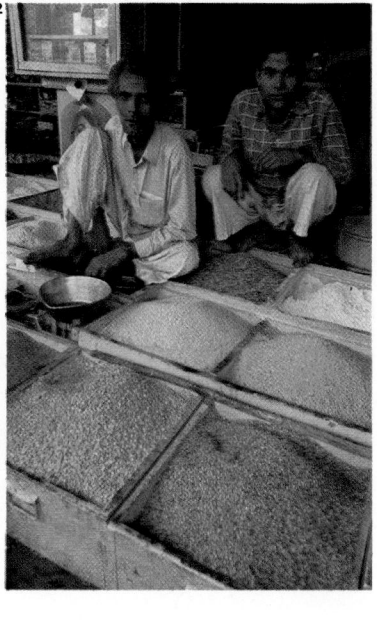

2 Indian merchants in a market sell unpackaged spices, carrying on an ancient tradition. Buyers will grind and blend the spices at home to make their own special seasonings for cooking.

3 The search for spices, a saga of triumph and bloodshed, covered every corner of the globe and their discovery brought great wealth. Nutmeg and mace [A] both come from the fruit of *Myristica fragrans*. The former is the kernel and the latter the netlike membrane, or aril, that surrounds it. Sassafras [B] is obtained from root bark of the tree *Sassafras albidum*. Cinnamon [C], the dried rolled bark of a small evergreen tree, *Cinnamomum zeylanicum*, is native to Sri Lanka, the Malabar coast of India, and Burma. Ginger [D] is the rhizome of the tropical plant *Zingiber officinale*. Saffron strands [E] are the dried stamens of *Crocus sativus*, from Asia Minor. Allspice [F] is the dried brown berry of *Pimenta dioica*, an evergreen tree that flourishes in Central and South America and the West Indies. Cloves [G], the dried flower buds of the tall evergreen tree *Eugenia aromatica*, nearly all come from Zanzibar. Turmeric [H] is obtained from the dried rhizome of a tropical plant, *Curcuma longa*.

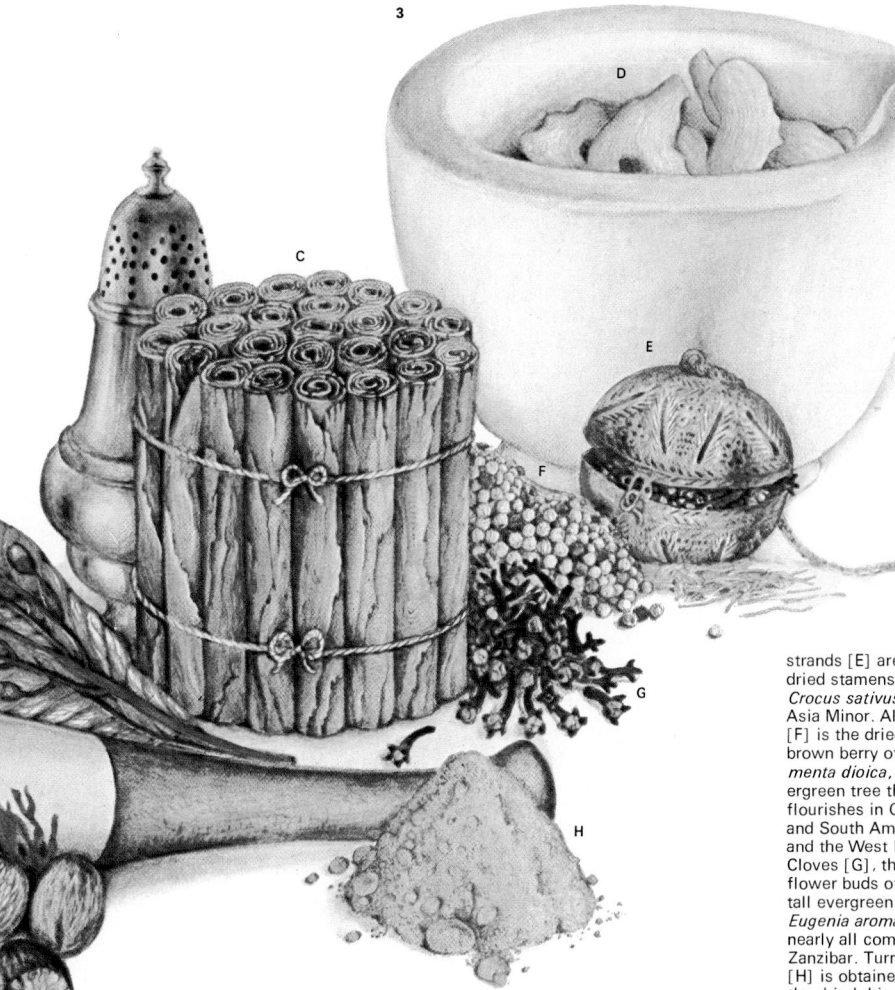

3

D
C
E
B
F
G
A
H

Culinary and medicinal herbs

Herbs have been used in the culinary arts, in medicine, and in making cosmetics since ancient times—so the excavations of sites in Greece, Italy, and the Mediterranean islands tell us. Hippocrates (of the 5th century BC), known as the "father of medicine," cultivated some 400 herbs and made herbal remedies and compounds to treat disease that continued in common use for centuries. Before his time, the Sumerians, Egyptians, and Chinese compiled herbals listing many medicinal plants.

Medicinal herbs

The medicinal use of herbs probably originated after people had discovered them for cooking purposes. Perhaps they first noticed the aromas when throwing plant waste onto their cooking fires. Thereafter they may deliberately have sought them out so that the scent and flavors would impart new zest to roast meat and fish. Later still, herbs were often used to disguise spoiled flavors in meat and game.

Herbs were introduced into most of Europe by the Romans, who in turn had adopted them from the Greeks. Many were thought to have mystical powers and they were used for ceremonial purposes. Triumphant Roman emperors are depicted wearing crowns of bay leaves [1C]; during the Middle Ages superstition held that hyssop and garlic would ward off witches, who themselves brewed concoctions of wild herbs and other plants. Peasants in some remote eastern European countries still protect their homes against evil spirits and vampires by hanging garlic wreaths over their front doors. Even in the late 20th century some civilized people persist in sowing parsley [1A] only by candlelight on Good Friday. Many still believe that transplanting parsley seedlings will bring bad luck.

The cultivation of herbs, as well as their use, became a specialty of the Christian monks and every monastery had its own extensive herb garden. The plants were widely grown for their medicinal qualities, and as late as the 18th century physicians still relied heavily on herbal medicines in the treatment of disease. The famous London herbalist John Gerard (1545–1612) published a huge volume in 1597 listing thousands of plants with healing properties. Herbs have dwindled in importance for the medical profession but many are still used in making perfumes, soaps, cosmetic creams, and skin lotions.

The heyday of the herb garden came in the 16th century, when wealthy landowners designed intricate herb gardens whose patterns were shaped with low hedges of lavender or box elder. An average herb garden of the famous Elizabethan knot garden type might include more than 50 different herbs—some grown for cooking, others for medicine and soothing balms and tonics.

The 19th century saw a decline in the use and growing of herbs, although nowhere as drastically as in Britain and North America, where cooks used few herbs besides parsley, sage [3B], thyme [3D], and mint [2E]. With the expansion of the tourist trade in the mid-20th century, many people gained a new appreciation of herbs as a result of eating foreign dishes.

The best flavor is obtained from fresh herbs. Dried herbs often have a stronger

CONNECTIONS

See also
356 Seeds and spices
360 Berries, nuts, and olives

1A
B
C
D
E

1 Parsley (*Petroselinum crispum*) [A] is the classic herb of European cooking. Plain and curly leaved varieties are available, both rich in vitamin C. The stalks have as much flavor as the leaves. Parsley is always used fresh in *bouquets garnis*. It is chopped to flavor sauces, salads, *fines herbes* and *maître d'hotel* butter, small fresh sprigs are used for garnishing a variety of dishes. Sweet basil (*Ocimum basilicum*) [B] is native to India and Iran. Young, sweetly clove-scented leaves have the best flavor and are used, chopped, in dishes containing tomatoes. Bay (*Laurus nobilis*) [C] is an evergreen tree from the Mediterranean. The aromatic leaves are used fresh or dried in *bouquets garnis* and to flavor meat and fish stews, pâtés, and soups. Chervil (*Anthriscus cerefolium*) [D] comes from eastern Europe. Its leaves have a slight resemblance to parsley but with a delicate anise flavor. It is used chopped in soups, sauces, and egg dishes. Coriander (*Coriandrum sativum*) [E] is sometimes known as Chinese or Japanese parsley because the feathery leaves are as popular in Eastern cooking as parsley is in Europe. It is one of the oldest herbs known and the seeds are an essential ingredient of *garam masala*, the spicy flavoring for Indian curries. In Europe and North America, the dried seeds of coriander are used for fish and meat dishes and bread and cakes.

2A
B
C
D
E

2 Dill *(Anethum graveolens)* [A] is a particularly popular herb in Scandinavian, German, Russian, and Balkan cookery. Both leaves and dried seeds are used to impart an anise flavor to sauces and vinegars, salads, and pickles. Fennel (*Foeniculum vulgare*) [B] comes from the Mediterranean and is much used in flavoring Provençal dishes. Stalks, leaves, and seeds have a licorice flavor that goes well with pork and veal. It is traditional with fish and as an addition to stuffings and sauces. Grilled sea bass and goatfish may be broiled over dried fennel stalks. Finely chopped leaves may also be used in small quantities to season soups, salads, mayonnaise, and *sauce vinaigrette*. Oregano (*Origanum vulgare*) [C] is a pungent flavored herb much used in Mediterranean cooking to season meat, poultry, soups, and omelets. The dried form is stronger than the fresh. It may be used in any dish instead of thyme. Chamomile (*Anthemis nobilis*) [D] is native to Europe and Asia. The aromatic flower heads are used dried in herbal teas and other infusions and sometimes in the manufacture of vermouth and other apéritifs, as well as lotions and in hair rinses. Mint (*Mentha*) [E] has many species and varieties. In some parts of the world the strongly flavored leaves are cooked whole with young summer vegetables and used, finely chopped, in jellies and chutneys. It is also used to flavor cool summer drinks, cups, and juleps. It is relatively unknown in French cuisine but is a common seasoning in the Middle East, where it is often added to chutneys and yogurts.

taste than fresh ones and are therefore used in much smaller quantities. The essence of some herbs, particularly parsley, chervil, and mint, is lost when they are dried. The cook can always have some fresh herbs at hand, for they can be grown in a window box or even in a few pots on a sunny kitchen window sill. Some herbs, such as thyme, rosemary [3A], and bay, tolerate prolonged cooking, but others, including chervil [1D], dill [2A], and fennel [1B], are best added at the last minute so that their aromatic qualities are not lost.

Fines herbes and their uses

The French term *fines herbes* is applied to a mixture of very finely chopped herbs. It usually consists of parsley and chives, and sometimes of parsley only, but it should correctly also include chervil and tarragon [3D]. In former times salad burnet, chopped mushrooms, and shallots were part of the *fines herbes* mixture. These herbs are usually added to quickly cooked dishes, particularly omelets, or sprinkled as a garnish over meat and fish dishes and young vegetables. They may also be incorporated in butters and sauces.

Gremolata, an Italian version of *fines herbes*, is made of finely chopped parsley and anchovy, crushed garlic, and grated lemon rind. *Gremolata* is used to season many Milanese dishes.

Potpourri and pomanders

In addition to their other uses, aromatic herb mixtures can be enriched with dried, scented flowers to make up a potpourri. Sweet marjoram [2C] and sprigs of rosemary [3A] can be mixed with flowers, petals, or small buds of clover, roses, and verbena and with the leaves of scented geraniums. Potpourris are sometimes put in cloth bags but are most often seen in decorative china containers, which may be placed in closets or on table tops to release their scent throughout a room.

Pomander balls may be made from oranges, lemons, or limes impregnated with a mixture of herbs and spices. They were once believed to be effective protection against infection.

KEY

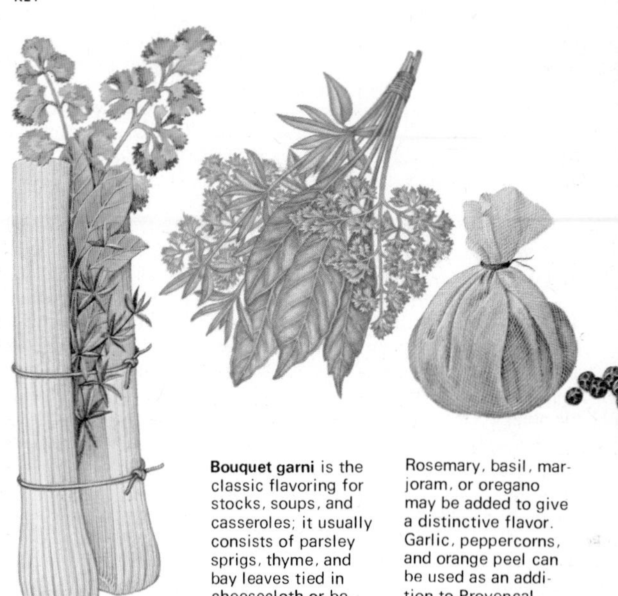

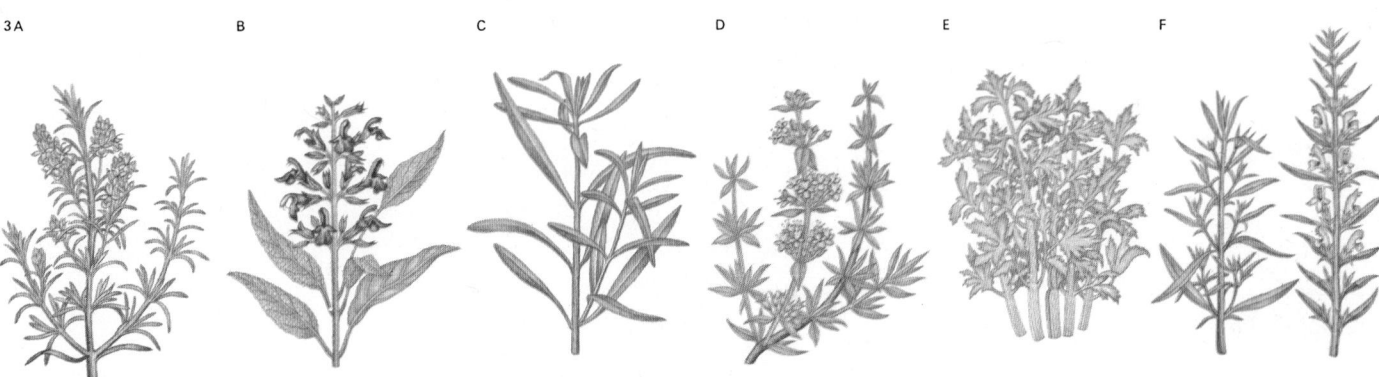

Bouquet garni is the classic flavoring for stocks, soups, and casseroles; it usually consists of parsley sprigs, thyme, and bay leaves tied in cheesecloth or between celery sticks. Rosemary, basil, marjoram, or oregano may be added to give a distinctive flavor. Garlic, peppercorns, and orange peel can be used as an addition to Provençal casseroles.

3A B C D E F

3 Rosemary (*Rosmarinus officinalis*) [A] is a strongly flavored herb that can be reminiscent of camphor. Small sprigs are used to season lamb, pork, veal, rabbit, and grilled fish. It is particularly popular in Italy. Sage (*Salvia officinalis*) [B] comes from the Mediterranean. The aromatic leaves are commonly used in stuffings for poultry and meat and in sausages. In Germany and Belgium sage is used to flavor eels. Tarragon (*Artemisia dracunculus*) [C] is popular in French cooking. The aromatic leaves are used, finely chopped, in sauces, butters, soups, salads, and vinegars. Thyme (*Thymus vulgaris*) [D] has a pungent aroma and when dried retains much of its flavor. It is a favorite of Mediterranean cooks for casseroles, vegetable stews, and soups, with fish and in stuffings for meat and game. It is an essential ingredient of a *bouquet garni*. Celery (*Apium graveolens*) [E] is a favorite salad vegetable, and the leaves are equally useful. The feathery, pale-green foliage can be used, finely chopped, to flavor soups, salads, veal and chicken stews; small, whole leaflets make attractive garnishes when watercress is scarce. The leaves are sometimes dried and used instead of celery salt. Summer savory (*Satureja hortensis*) [F] is a member of the mint family. The pungent leaves should be used young, before the herb flowers.

4A B C D E

4 Sorrel (*Rumex acetosa*) [A] leaves may be cooked whole like spinach or made into a purée with butter to be served cold with fish, fatty meat, and poultry; the young bitter leaves can be used in small quantities to season soups and salads. Myrtle (*Myrtus communis*) [B] is an evergreen aromatic shrub from the mountains around the Mediterranean and is used to season lamb. The scented, purple-black berries, which follow the white flowers, were formerly dried and used like pepper. Borage (*Borago officinalis*) [C] is native to southern Europe and was introduced to northern Europe by the Romans. The hairy leaves have a cucumber scent and flavor and are most often used in iced drinks; young leaves, finely chopped, may be added to salads, yogurts, and cream cheese. In Italy borage is used as a stuffing for ravioli, boiled like spinach or fried in batter. The pale blue flowers are sometimes candied and used to decorate cakes, desserts, and confectionery. Angelica (*Angelica archangelica*) [D] has many uses in cookery. Its stems, leaves and seeds have a characteristic musky flavor. Young stems are candied or crystallized and used to decorate cakes and desserts. The leaves are cooked as vegetables in many northern countries and they can also be used to flavor orange marmalade. Young shoots can be blanched and added to salads. Roots and seeds are used in the manufacture of liqueurs, vermouth, and gin. Salad burn (*Sanguisorba minor*) [E] is another herb with a cucumber flavor. It is used fresh to flavor salads and salad dressings. The outer leaves are bitter and only young, tender, center leaves should be used.

Berries, nuts, and olives

Of all the fruits eaten by man the strawberry *(fragaria)* is one of the most prized. The Indians of Chile were cultivating plump, aromatic strawberries [1] long before Europeans reached South America. In the early eighteenth century these plants were brought to Europe and crossed with an already established North American sweet variety. A new strawberry (the one eaten today) was produced, combining the size of the one with the excellent flavor and color of the other.

The red raspberry *(Rubus idaeus)* [1] is native to most European countries, although the best crops come from temperate areas, where summer days are long. Different varieties of the fruit have been developed for other conditions all over the world. A yellow raspberry is also grown in England as is the hybrid loganberry [1]—a cross between the raspberry and a North American Pacific coast species of blackberry. Other types of hybrid blackberry developed in California are the boysenberry and the phenomenal berry, similar to the loganberry but with slightly larger fruit.

The hardy blackberry [1], with its trailing brambles and clusters of fruit, is a familiar wild plant in many places. The black mulberry *(Morus nigra)* has been cultivated for centuries both for its dark red fruits and for its ornamental attraction. The white mulberry *(M. alba)* originated in China and its leaves are used in silkworm culture.

Fruits for the epicure

Blueberries, bilberries, and whortleberries are all species of *Vaccinium*. Cranberries [1], native to Europe and America, also belong to this genus. Their crimson, acid fruit make an agreeable sauce or jelly to accompany turkey or venison. The scarlet berries of the rowan or mountain ash are inedible when raw, but, cooked and jellied, they lend a tart contrast to game and venison. Red, black, and white currants *(Ribes)* [1] are familiar as garden plants and have been grown in Europe since the fifteenth century. Rich in vitamin C, black currants were once regarded as a cure for sore throats but are now gathered to make fruit syrups, jams, and jellies. Red currant jelly is used in France with game stews and in Britain with roast lamb.

Closely related to the currant is the gooseberry *(Ribes grossularis)* [1], whose greenish fruits have been a common sight in English gardens since 1600. This deciduous plant flourishes in northern climates even up to the Arctic Circle. The red, green, or yellow berries can be sweet or acid, smooth or hairy, some making a reasonable dessert when fully ripe. They are excellent for bottling, jam, and pies and for making the English pudding called gooseberry fool.

Nuts for the confection box

The sweet almond *(Prunus amygdalus)* [5B] is one of the world's most popular nuts and is indigenous to the eastern Mediterranean. Those called Jordan almonds are particularly fine for making sugared almonds. Sweet almonds are an essential ingredient of marzipan and dainty *petits fours*, and bitter almond provides the essence to flavor confectionery. One of the most delicious sweetmeats is the candied *marrons glacés* of southern France, made from the large

CONNECTIONS

See also
356 Seeds and spices
358 Culinary and medicinal herbs
362 Fiber and oil crops
456 How flowering plants reproduce

1

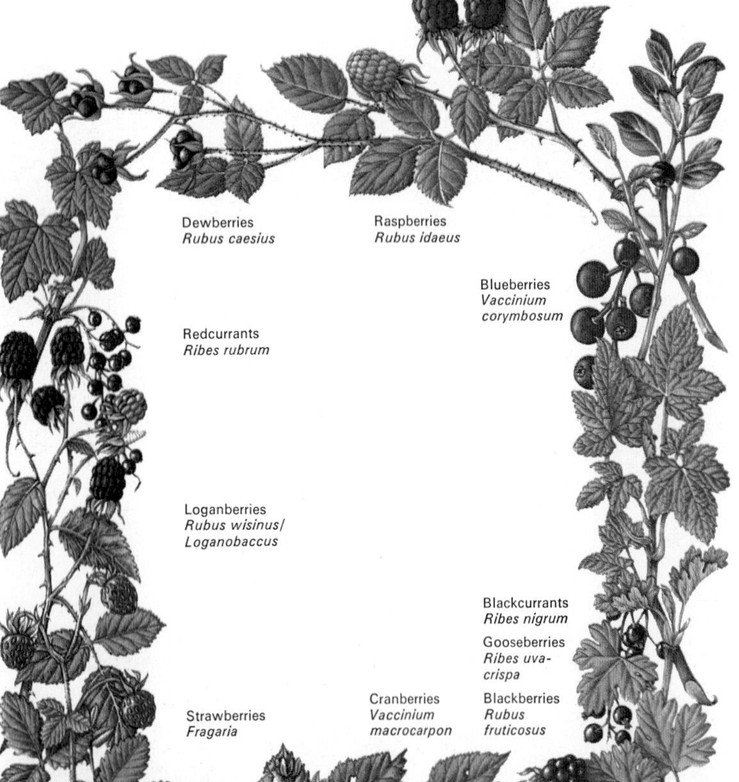
Dewberries
Rubus caesius
Raspberries
Rubus idaeus
Blueberries
Vaccinium corymbosum
Redcurrants
Ribes rubrum
Loganberries
Rubus wisinus/ Loganobaccus
Blackcurrants
Ribes nigrum
Gooseberries
Ribes uva-crispa
Strawberries
Fragaria
Cranberries
Vaccinium macrocarpon
Blackberries
Rubus fruticosus

1 Succulent European fruits such as the raspberry have been popular and widespread since ancient times. The soft red flesh of this berry makes it an ideal fresh desserts. Blueberries and black currants are both rather acid and these fruits are better cooked or made into jellies. Gooseberries make a delicious filling for tarts and pies. The soft purplish-black fruit of blackberries does not keep for long and these should be used as a pie filling soon after picking. The cranberry is most often used to make preserves and sauces or to add flavor to meat. Juicy red strawberries, eaten fresh with cream and sugar, are one of the most popular berries. Sweet loganberries are served stewed with sugar. Red currants, grown in Europe since the fifteenth century, are also eaten fresh as a dessert, or as an excellent jelly. The dew berry is similar to the blackberry but has a trailing stem and the fruit is generally thought to possess a finer flavor.

2

2 The olive is one of the oldest crops in the world. Both immature green and ripe black olives are bitter and inedible before processing. But treated with an alkaline solution and soaked in brine—an early process still in use today—the olive becomes a noble delicacy. The olive tree grows quite slowly, but may live for more than 1,000 years. There are hundreds of named varieties of olive.

3

3 Oil from fresh olives was extracted by a primitive press. Today, mills clean the fruit and crush it coarsely between grinders. The pulp is collected in cloths and pressed between heavy racks. Called virgin oil, the product of this first pressing is of fine quality. But as the pulp is subjected to further pressings the liquid obtained becomes inferior. The oil is washed to remove bitterness and filtered for bottling. Some varieties of olive tree are grown primarily for their oil, a commodity prized by the ancient Greeks who used it to anoint their bodies. Sometimes the oil-bearing fruit is beaten from the trees, although in many Mediterranean groves it is picked by hand. Today the processing of olive oil is an extremely important industry. The fruity green olive oils of Tuscany, Greece, and Cyprus are strong in flavor. More delicate virgin oil from the Provençal olive is used for salads and mayonnaise. Tunisia is another major olive oil producing region. There are other vegetable oils in use for cooking and salads. Walnut oil, even more expensive than olive oil, is kept by cooks for dress salads for special occasions. Peanut oil, largely produced in West Africa, is tasteless and is therefore used as a general-purpose oil for frying and for salads.

European chestnut *(Castanea sativa)* [5C]. Chestnuts also are roasted.

The pecan *(Carya illinoensis)* [4C], one of the finest of oily nuts, has a mild but distinctive flavor much in demand for baking and confectionery. In the United States, where it is extensively cultivated, it is also popular as a dessert nut. The elongated, brown shell of the pecan holds a fruit similar to a walnut to which it is related. The brazil nut [Key B] *(Bertholletia excelsa)*, indigenous to the Amazon valley, is among the choicest dessert nuts on Christmas tables.

Nuts as side-dishes and delicacies

Walnuts are a favorite at any holiday feast. Although the black walnut *(Juglans nigra)* of North America is used in sweet dishes, the pronounced flavor of most walnuts is an ideal contrast to the richness of caramelized sweets, layer-cakes, and sugary pastries. In France, fresh walnuts, accompanied by a glass of new wine, are eaten with hot bread, coarse sea salt, and sweet butter. Roasted hazel nuts [4A] are served with the local wine at Avellino, a small town near Vesuvius, in Italy, hence their specific name *Corylus avellana*. These slow-roasted, pale golden-brown nuts have been famous since Roman times. The shiny, round, hard-shelled Macadamia or Queensland nut is yet another kind served with drinks.

The pistachio *(Pistacia vera)*, a pale green, finely-textured nut, is prized as an ingredient in pâtés and sausages and as a coloring for confections. The waxy, ivory-colored seeds of a considerable number of species of pine are invaluable as a seasoning for savory dishes. The fruits of Roman or stone pine *(Pinus pinea)* [5B] are used by the Italians as a sweetly sour stuffing for sardines.

Peanuts or groundnuts *(Arachis hypogaea)*, native to tropical South America, were cultivated by the ancient Incas and Mayas. Peanuts, which are not true nuts but pulses, like peas, are a major source of edible oil. They are used for their rich dominating flavor in Oriental cooking, and in the West salted peanuts are served as snacks. The taste of cashew nuts *(Anacardium occidentale)* [4B] is enhanced by roasting.

KEY

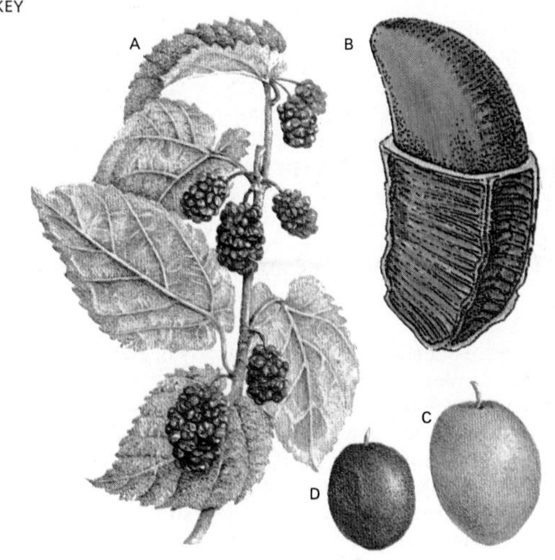

A
B
C
D

Black mulberries (*Morus nigra*) [A] grow on short, squat trees cultivated in Eurasia and North America for their fruits. Brazil nuts *(Bertholletia excelsa)* [B] grow on a large Amazonian tree. Olives *(Olea europaea)* are picked green [C] before they ripen or as black olives [D] after they ripen.

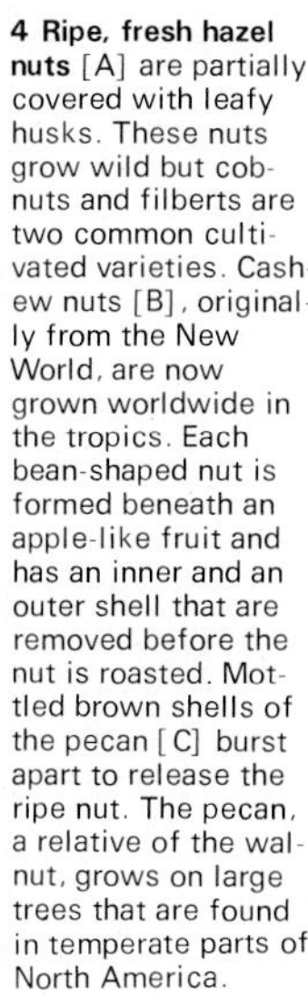

4 Ripe, fresh hazel nuts [A] are partially covered with leafy husks. These nuts grow wild but cobnuts and filberts are two common cultivated varieties. Cashew nuts [B], originally from the New World, are now grown worldwide in the tropics. Each bean-shaped nut is formed beneath an apple-like fruit and has an inner and an outer shell that are removed before the nut is roasted. Mottled brown shells of the pecan [C] burst apart to release the ripe nut. The pecan, a relative of the walnut, grows on large trees that are found in temperate parts of North America.

4 A

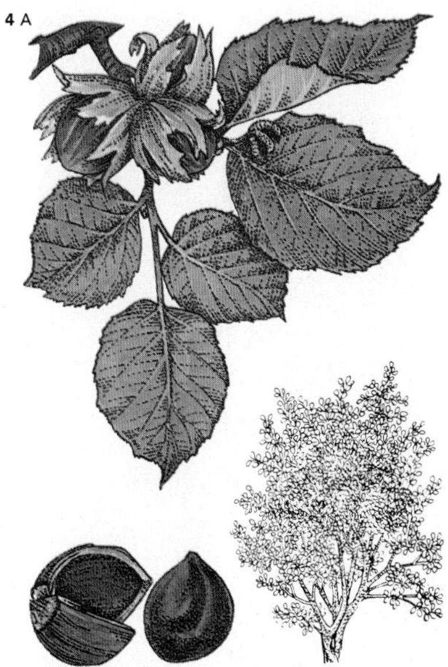

B

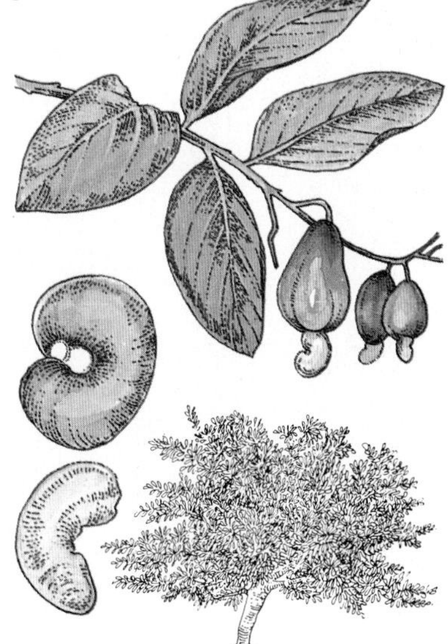

C

5 A

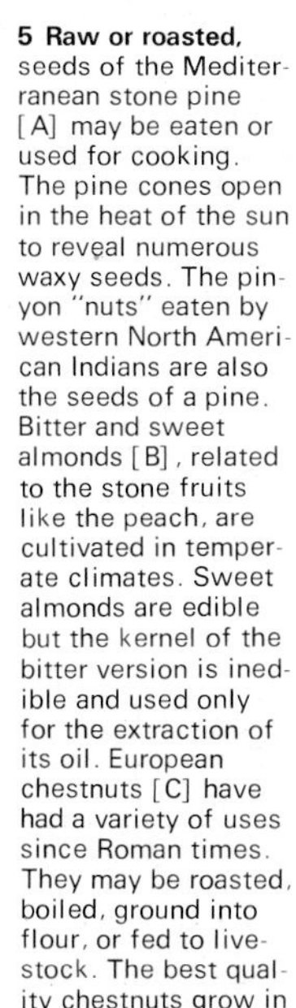

5 Raw or roasted, seeds of the Mediterranean stone pine [A] may be eaten or used for cooking. The pine cones open in the heat of the sun to reveal numerous waxy seeds. The pinyon "nuts" eaten by western North American Indians are also the seeds of a pine. Bitter and sweet almonds [B], related to the stone fruits like the peach, are cultivated in temperate climates. Sweet almonds are edible but the kernel of the bitter version is inedible and used only for the extraction of its oil. European chestnuts [C] have had a variety of uses since Roman times. They may be roasted, boiled, ground into flour, or fed to livestock. The best quality chestnuts grow in southern Europe.

B

C

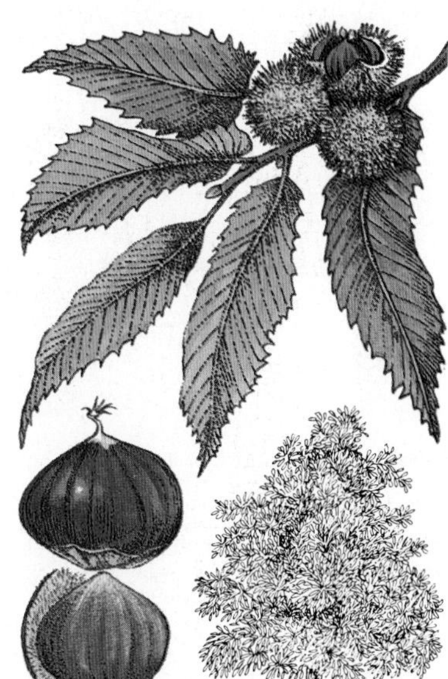

Fiber and oil crops

Men cultivate plants not only for food but also for their oil and fiber content. Vegetable fibers may be obtained from the fruit, leaves, or stems of plants. Fibers consist largely of cellulose, a long organic molecule of the sugar or carbohydrate family that forms the walls of plant cells and makes up as much as 90 percent of the cell. Characteristically fibers are strong and pliable, allowing plants to bend without snapping.

Types of plant fiber

Archeological evidence from caves in Mexico and the American southwest reveals that fibers were being used more than 10,000 years ago. In addition to using flax, hemp, and other fibers to make ropes, nets, or sacks, early peoples made crude fabrics by pounding the fibrous tissues of certain trees and plants into flat paperlike sheets of "bark-cloth," such as the Polynesian *tapa* still made today. By 3000 BC cotton was being spun into yarn and woven into cloth in India, while the manufacture of linen was well developed in Egypt even earlier than in India.

Fibers from different parts of a plant have varying characteristics. Bast fibers come from the outer layer of the stems of plants like flax and hemp. Made up of long overlapping cells, they are embedded in a cementing material that must be removed before the fibers can be peeled apart. Bast fibers are known as "soft fibers" and are very flexible. They can be made into rope or twine or woven into coarse, heavy-duty sacking, and flax can also be woven into a soft, fine fabric known as linen [6]. Hemp [3], jute [4], and flax [5] are the most important commercially, and some nations' economies are dependent upon them.

Soaking, or retting, the long stems in water partially decomposes the material that binds bast fibers together. The stems are then beaten and passed through rollers that separate the softened fibers from the mucilaginous matter. Jute fibers are stripped away by hand.

Leaf fibers, obtained mostly from perennial plants, are part of the vascular structure of leaves. They have a stiffer texture and are much shorter than bast fibers. They are processed in rolling machines that crush the leaves, scrape off nonfibrous matter, and wash it away with jets of water. These hard fibers are generally too stiff to be made into fabrics. Their major use is as cord, twine, brush bristles, and coarse sacking. The most important leaf fibers are sisal, henequen, and abaca.

Seed fibers grow as fine hairs on the seeds of certain plants [1]. Each individual fiber is a single, elongated cell. Cotton [Key], coir, and kapok are the only seed fibers of any major commercial value. Of the three, only cotton is suitable for spinning into fine yarn [2]. Kapok is mainly used as stuffing or insulation, and coir is made into ropes, sacks, and brushes.

Vegetable oils for the human diet

Vegetable oils are essential to the human diet and contain more energy per unit of weight than any other food. Unlike mineral oils, they consist primarily (over 95 percent) of triglycerides—combinations of glycerol and stearic, lauric, oleic, linolenic, and other similar fatty acids.

CONNECTIONS

See also
330 Staple foods: legumes
360 Berries, nuts, and olives
1620 Fibers for fabrics
1622 Making cloth

1 The cotton plant is a shrublike annual native to subtropical regions the world over. After rapid flowering, small green seedpods (bolls) develop. The cottonseeds within the bolls sprout a mass of fine fibers. When mature, the bolls rupture and a soft cloud of cotton erupts. The crop is harvested either by hand or machine and then ginned to separate the seeds from the fibers. Next, it is cleaned, carded, and spun into yarn. Of the four different species of cotton now cultivated, American Upland and Egyptian are the most important. The former accounts for approximately 85% of the world's cotton production.

1

Cotton *Gossypium sp.*

2

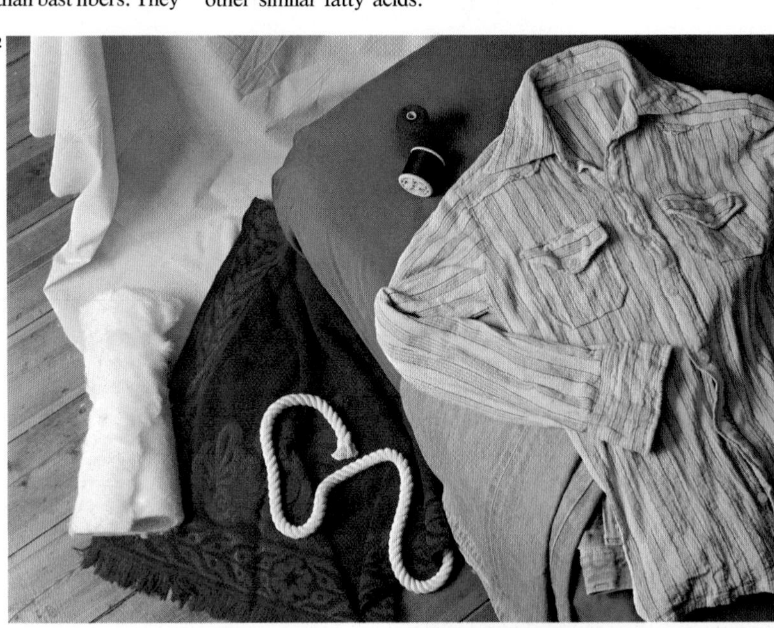

2 Cotton products date back at least to 3000 BC in India and Central America. The highly durable and versatile fiber has been used for countless purposes ever since. The longest, highest quality fibers are made into laces and fine fabrics, while coarser fibers are used to make sheets, carpets, blankets, sailcloth, and numerous industrial products such as thread, film, plastics, and paper.

3 A

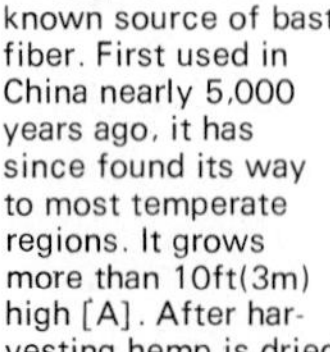

Hemp *Cannabis sp.*

B

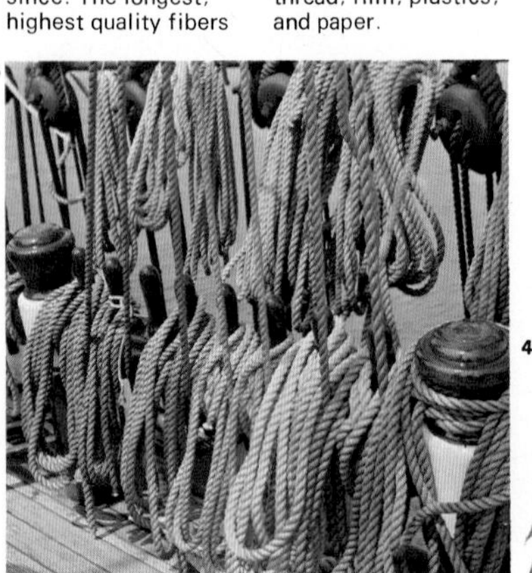

3 Hemp is a well-known source of bast fiber. First used in China nearly 5,000 years ago, it has since found its way to most temperate regions. It grows more than 10ft(3m) high [A]. After harvesting hemp is dried and then ripped apart for the fibers found in its long, woody stem. These yellowish to gray fibers are stronger than flax but far coarser. They are easily twisted into rope or twine or else woven into sacking and other coarse fabrics. Hemp was in demand in the days of sail when it was used for rope [B]. Today, sisal and synthetic fibers are cheaper and more durable. Oil is extracted from hemp seeds. Hemp sap or resin contains the drug tetrahydrocannabinol.

4 Jute is native to India. This tall annual plant yields a fine bast fiber that is cheap, easy to bleach and dye, and can be readily woven into coarse fabrics, sacking, ropes, and twine.

4 Jute *Corchorus sp.*

5 Flax *Linum sp.*

5 Flax thrives in moist temperate climates. One species, *Linum usitatissimum*, is cultivated for its fiber and rich oil seeds. After harvesting, flax stems are retted to soften the fibers which are spun into yarn and then woven into fabric.

6

6 Flax and jute products exploit the different qualities of their fibers. Bed and table linens are fabrics made from flax that combine strength with fineness and pliability. Linen is also highly absorbent and is used for dish towels. Flax also can be made into rag pulp for cigarette papers. Jute is a coarse strong fiber that can be produced cheaply and is therefore made into rope or materials such as hessian and burlap for sacking and furnishing uses.

Extraction of oil from the seeds and fruits of plants is possible only after the oil-bearing cells are first ruptured by heat pressure. Typically, seeds are hulled, then coarsely ground and baked to reduce their moisture content as much as possible. They are then fed into hydraulic or screw presses that crush the seeds to release their oil content. Alternatively, the ground and dried seeds are passed through a solvent bath consisting of hexane, carbon disulfide, or similar volatile hydrocarbons. The oil and solvent are then separated by distillation. This highly efficient process leaves less than one percent of the oil remaining in the seed pulp.

Vegetable oils have both culinary and industrial uses. Early Mediterranean civilizations, for example, not only consumed olive oil but also used it as a grease and lubricant. Other oils were made into soaps, burned in lamps, or used to make paints and varnishes.

Demand for vegetable oils has risen spectacularly. Today soybeans are the single most important source of vegetable oil. The oil (16–18 percent by weight) is extracted from the beans by the solvent process. If it is to be made edible, the oil is further refined to be sold as an odorless, almost colorless cooking oil with free fatty acids removed. Edible soybean oil that is used for margarine (an emulsion of oil, skim milk, flavoring, and preservatives) or shortening is also hydrogenated. Hydrogenation turns unsaturated fats into saturated ones that are solid at room temperatures. Apart from soybeans, the most important of the edible oils [7] are extracted from peanut, corn, cottonseed, rapeseed, sunflower, coconut [9], and olive.

Industrial oils

The main industrial oils [8] are soybean, castor, tung, and linseed, all of which contain more free fatty acids and other contaminants such as resins and sterols than do edible oils. Industrial oils are used in the manufacture of soaps, detergents, plasticizers, cosmetics, paints, varnishes, synthetic alkyd resins, and a variety of other chemicals.

KEY

Cotton is a valuable plant that provides both fiber and oil. The fiber grows on the seeds and is separated from them by ginning. The oil is extracted from the seeds. Cotton cultivation is a major activity of such regions as the southern United States, where ripe bolls were once picked by hand.

7

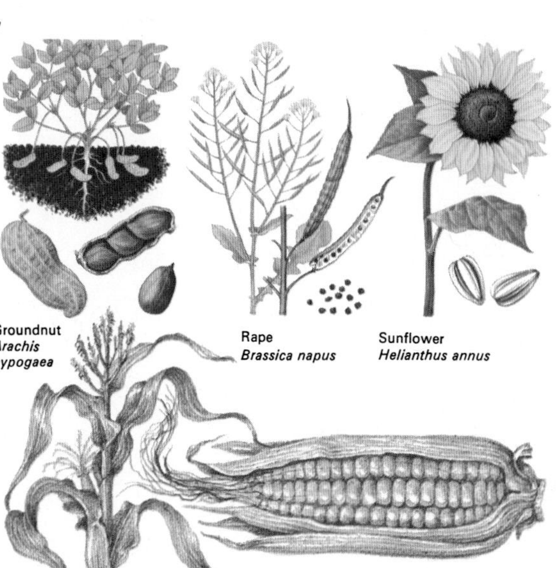
Groundnut *Arachis hypogaea*
Rape *Brassica napus*
Sunflower *Helianthus annus*
Maize (corn) *Zea mays*

7 Seeds and fruits of many plants provide edible oils. Sunflower seeds yield a light, high quality oil used in margarine, shortening, and confectionery. Rapeseed and corn germ both have an oil content ranging from 40% to 50%. Peanuts are the next most important source of vegetable oil after soybeans.

8

Linseed *Linus sp.*
Almond *Prunus amygdalus*
Castor *Ricinus communis*
Pine *Pinus sp.*

8 Industrial uses are found for castor and linseed oil in lubricants, chemicals, plasticizers, paints, varnishes, and printer's inks. Volatile oils such as almond and pine, which bear the essence of a plant's fragrance, are used as scents in soaps and perfumes and as flavorings in food.

9

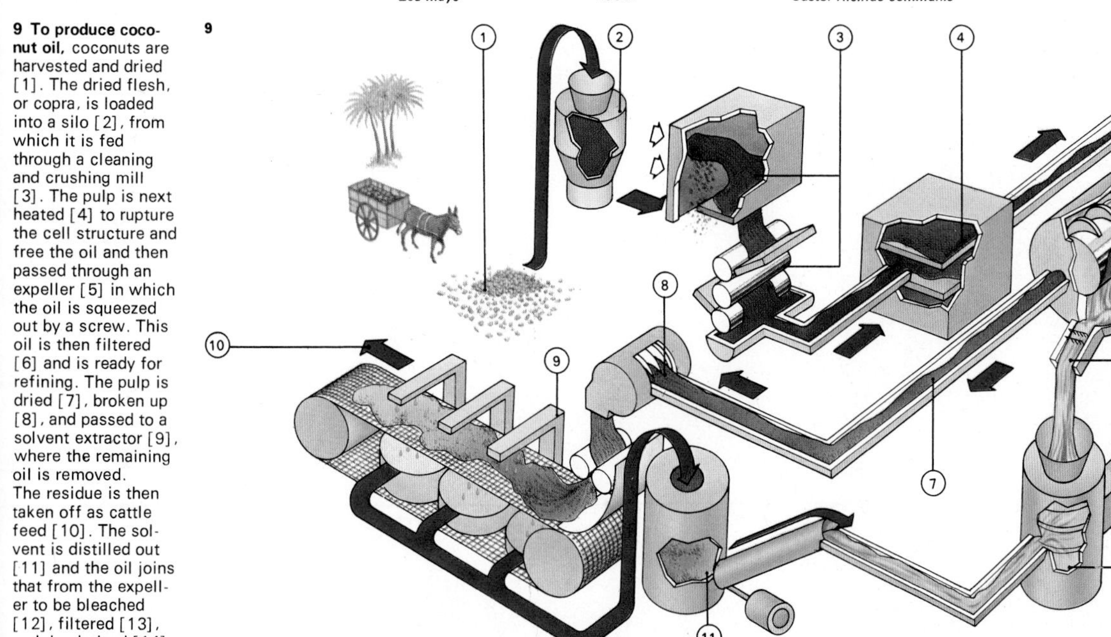
1
2
3
4
5
6
7
8
9
10
11
12
13
14

9 To produce coconut oil, coconuts are harvested and dried [1]. The dried flesh, or copra, is loaded into a silo [2], from which it is fed through a cleaning and crushing mill [3]. The pulp is next heated [4] to rupture the cell structure and free the oil and then passed through an expeller [5] in which the oil is squeezed out by a screw. This oil is then filtered [6] and is ready for refining. The pulp is dried [7], broken up [8], and passed to a solvent extractor [9], where the remaining oil is removed. The residue is then taken off as cattle feed [10]. The solvent is distilled out [11] and the oil joins that from the expeller to be bleached [12], filtered [13], and deodorized [14].

Forestry

Forestry is the art and science of managing stands of growing trees and their associated soils—and, by extension, plant and animal life—so that they yield the greatest possible benefits to mankind. Timber, firewood, and pulpwood for papermaking are the main economic products of forests. Woodlands are also valued for soil conservation, safeguarding of water supplies, wildlife preservation, scenery, and recreation.

Every good forest manager normally aims to bring these objectives into balance by applying the concept of multiple-use forestry, although, in most cases, profitable timber production is the main objective.

In most countries much, or even all, of the forest area is government-owned. Where woodlands are privately owned, it is usual to find some degree of government control, because the long-term objectives are too important to the nation to be left entirely to the discretion of individual owners.

Natural woodland

Natural forests once covered nearly two thirds of the world's land surface, but clearing land for farming has reduced this figure to barely one third. Forests remain mainly on mountainous or remote regions or on other slopes or sites unsuited to agriculture. The world's 10 billion acres (4 billion hectares) of forest yield 2 billion tons of timber annually, equivalent to half a ton of wood for each of the Earth's inhabitants. This yield is only 1 percent of the volume of standing timber. Foresters usually aim at sustained yield, so that forests provide a steady supply of timber year after year.

Natural forests still dominate vast areas of the northlands, particularly those of Canada, northern Europe, Scandinavia, the Soviet Union, and many other mountainous regions. In the north-temperate zone most forest trees are conifers, which yield softwood used in vast quantities for building, packaging, and paper. Farther south, the temperate-zone broad-leaved trees, such as oak, ash, beech, birch, and sycamore, dominate the native woodlands and provide temperate-zone hardwoods valued for specialized uses, such as furniture making.

In many tropical regions of the Americas, Africa, Asia, and northern Australia, tropical broad-leaved trees grow in extensive dense rain forests or, where rainfall is lower, in open savannas. Most of the many and varied hardwoods they produce are mainly used locally, but the best of them, such as teak, mahogany, greenheart, and rosewood, are exported and used worldwide.

Selective cutting

Selective cutting [3] provides the simplest means of producing useful timber with the least disturbance to the environment and at the lowest cost. After a detailed study of the trees growing in an area, including their rate of growth and replacement by self-sown seedlings, a skilled, experienced forester draws up a working plan. Under this, each portion of the forest is tackled in turn, possibly one tenth being dealt with each year for ten years, after which the working cycle is repeated. Workers fell selected mature trees, creating gaps that will be filled gradually by natural seedlings. They thin out

CONNECTIONS

See also

368 Trees: problems of climate and disease
366 The modern tree nursery
592 Northern evergreen forests
594 Northern temperate woodlands
598 African rain forest
600 Forests of Southeast Asia
440 The cone bearers
442 Pines and other conifers
450 Flowering trees, shrubs, and climbers
1624 Making paper

1
2
3

1 Natural forests can attain equilibrium with their surroundings and endure for thousands of years. As individual trees age and are toppled by wind, fungal decay, or lightning, they are replaced by younger trees springing from self-sown seed. In this view of a north European forest the principal trees are Scotch pine [1], Norway spruce [2], and birch [3]. Trees harvested by man are often replaced.

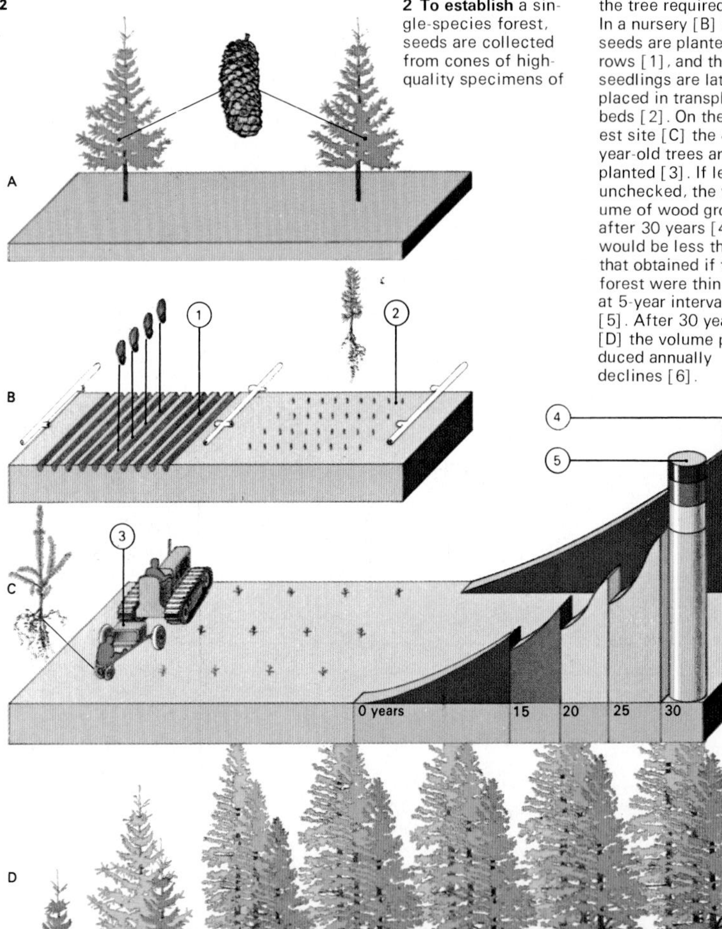

A
B
C
1
2
3
4
5
0 years
15
20
25
30

2 To establish a single-species forest, seeds are collected from cones of high-quality specimens of the tree required [A]. In a nursery [B] the seeds are planted in rows [1], and the seedlings are later placed in transplant beds [2]. On the forest site [C] the 4-year-old trees are planted [3]. If left unchecked, the volume of wood grown after 30 years [4] would be less than that obtained if the forest were thinned at 5-year intervals [5]. After 30 years [D] the volume produced annually declines [6].

1
2
3
4
5
6
7
8

3 Selective cutting is a way of obtaining regular yields with minimum disturbance to the environment. Because trees of different kinds and ages stand side by side, they are also called multi-species or uneven-aged. A typical Oregon forest may have lodgepole pine arack *(Larix occidentalis)* [4], Douglas fir *(Pseudotsuga menziesii)* [5], ponderosa pine *(Pinus ponderosa)* [6], and red pine *(Pinus resinosa)* [8]. Trees are selected every few years for felling [1], and the logs are hauled out by tractor [7]. A tree must be removed while it is still healthy. As the trees compete for sunlight, water, and nutrients, the weaker trees are suppressed by the stronger ones. Seeds from existing trees produce saplings that grow up in the gaps caused by felling. Large logs are sold to sawmills for cutting into lumber and veneer; smaller ones are used for paper pulp.

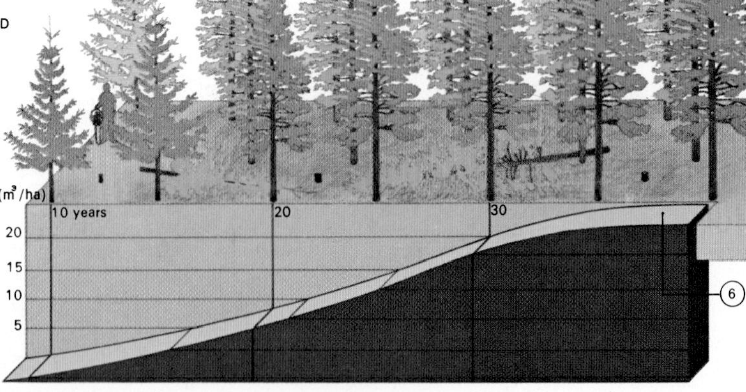

D
(m^3/ha)
10 years
20
30
20
15
10
5
6

groups of smaller, still immature specimens. This method causes minimum disturbance to the forest canopy, soil, wildlife, and scenery. It is favored in national parks and in mountainous regions where soil erosion or even avalanches might follow clearcutting on exposed slopes.

Clearcutting

Even-aged, single-species forests [2] are the obvious choice where people have to reforest bare land to increase a country's timber supplies, replace useless scrub with worthwhile trees, or repair devastation caused by past clearcutting or forest fires. By this method, trees are grown like a farm crop, although over a much longer period of time, to meet the needs of expected future markets at fair profits. A careful choice is made of the most profitable tree for the land available, and this often proves to be a foreign one. For example, Monterey pine *(Pine radiata)*, native only to California, is widely grown in South America, South and East Africa, Australia, and New Zealand, and Australian eucalyptus trees, such as *Eucalyptus globulus*, are planted in India.

Selected seed, which can be kept in cold storage for several years if necessary, is sown in well cultivated and fertile soil in nurseries, usually in spring. The resulting seedlings are transplanted, when one or two years old, to transplant beds to give them more growing space. One or two years later the saplings are planted, either by hand or (on easy ground) by machine, at their final positions in the forest. As they grow taller, the forester protects them against diseases; insect pests; weeds; browsing animals such as sheep, deer, and rabbits; and, above all, against fire.

After 15–25 years the first harvests begin. A proportion, often about one quarter, of the trees is harvested as thinnings to give the others more growing space. This thinning process is repeated every few years until the crop is considered mature. Then, at an age of from 30 to 40 years for spruce and pine, to perhaps 200 years for oak, the whole forest is harvested in the final felling [8]. The land is then replanted with its next tree crop.

KEY

Forest rangers must keep a constant vigil in their towers for any sign of a forest fire. Today there is a great demand for trained professional foresters and forest technicians by private industry as well as by the US government. Many colleges and universities offer 4-year programs in forestry leading to a bachelor of science degree.

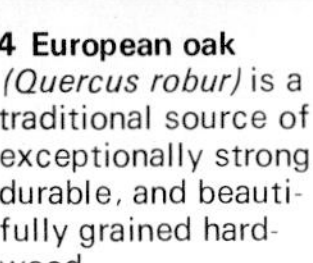

4 European oak *(Quercus robur)* is a traditional source of exceptionally strong, durable, and beautifully grained hardwood.

5

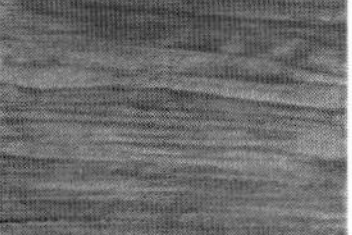

5 Teak *(Tectona grandis)* grows in the jungles of southern India, Burma, and Indonesia. Outstanding strength, resistance to chemicals, workability, and attractive golden-brown color insure its use internationally in making furniture and building boat decks and trim.

6

6 American mahogany *(Swietenia mahogani)*, native to rain forests of the Caribbean region, attracted early Spanish explorers with its firm, red-brown, lustrous, and readily worked timber. It is used to build strong, high-grade furniture and in the boatbuilding industry.

7

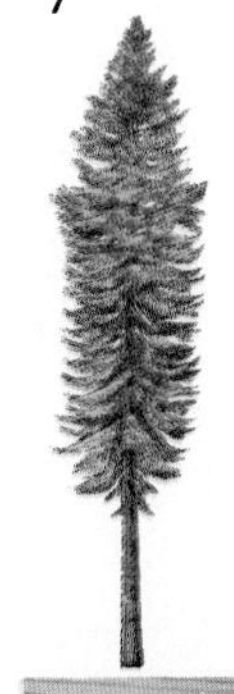

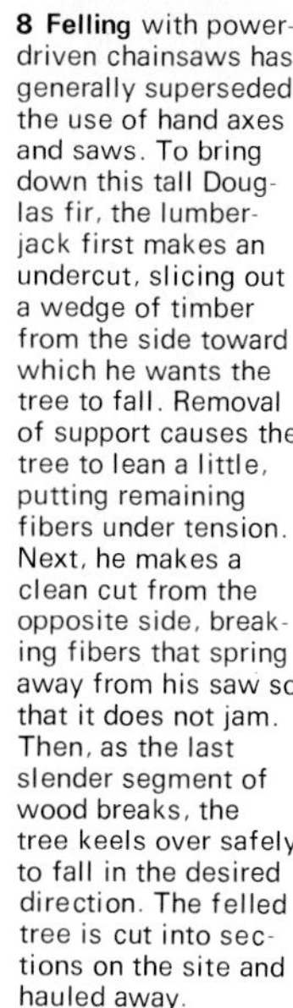

7 Douglas fir *(Pseudotsuga menziesii)*, which forms vast forests in western North America, is now extensively planted in Europe. Its fast-growing timber holds strong, dark, summer-wood bands, fitting it for exacting construction work, cabinetmaking, and heavy-duty plywood.

8

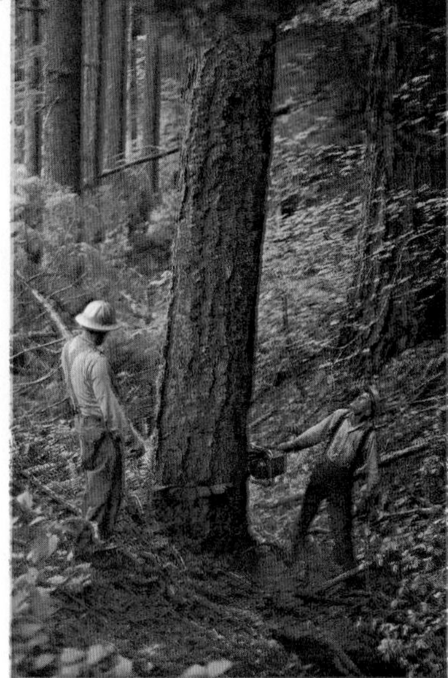

8 Felling with power-driven chainsaws has generally superseded the use of hand axes and saws. To bring down this tall Douglas fir, the lumberjack first makes an undercut, slicing out a wedge of timber from the side toward which he wants the tree to fall. Removal of support causes the tree to lean a little, putting remaining fibers under tension. Next, he makes a clean cut from the opposite side, breaking fibers that spring away from his saw so that it does not jam. Then, as the last slender segment of wood breaks, the tree keels over safely to fall in the desired direction. The felled tree is cut into sections on the site and hauled away.

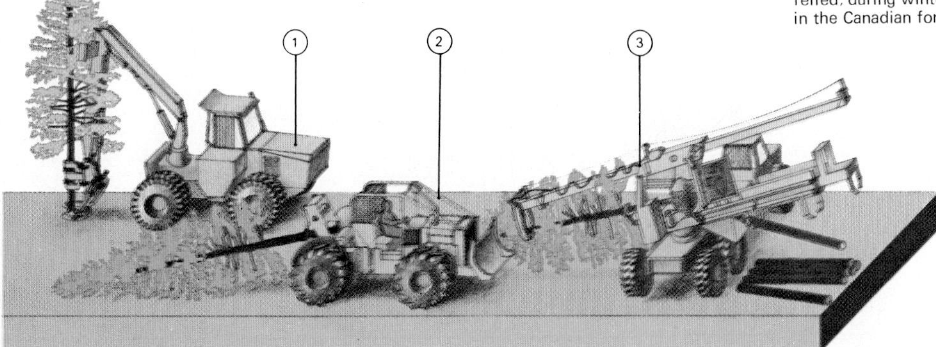

1
2
3

9 In Sweden, Canada, and the USSR, even-aged crops are now sawed or sliced down by a felling machine [1], which cuts the tree near the base, using movable jaws to lay the trunks in conveniently placed bundles. These are then dragged from the felling site by a skidder [2] and delivered to the processor [3]. The telescopic jaws of the processor feed the tree, butt first, into a ring of rotating blades that remove the branches. It also saws the resulting logs into standard lengths.

10

10 Floating logs down rivers is the traditional, cheapest way of transport from upland forests to sawmills sited at river mouth ports. These logs are felled, during winter, in the Canadian forest. They are then drawn on sleds pulled by tractors over ice-covered roads to lie on the ice of a frozen stream. When the spring thaw comes, boatmen guide them downstream, and they float freely. At the sawmill, they are halted by a boom, then stored, still floating, in a pool until each in turn is drawn to the endless chain that lifts it ashore to be processed into lumber.

The modern tree nursery

Botanist-explorers have brought to garden, park, and arboretum thousands of species that once lived in distant and perhaps largely unapproached habitats. In a more prosaic way, nurserymen have contributed almost equally to the great many types of trees available.

An explorer brings home a new species or a new variety of a known species. The nurseryman frequently crosses one species with another to produce a hybrid with a better commercial "performance"—that is to say, one that is easier for an amateur to establish, perhaps with a faster growing period or more attractive blossoms than either of its parents.

Special cultivation

The nurseryman also keeps a careful watch on his seedbeds for any interesting deviant. Many of the most planted trees today have been selected from mutants that normally must be maintained by man. A few "cultivars" (the varieties selected for their desirable qualities) reproduce themselves faithfully from seed, but a great number can be kept in existence only through the arts of propagation that bypass the sexual system: rooting, cuttings, layering, or grafting. Otherwise, the mutant strain is lost. Cultivars produced by interspecific hybridization are usually sterile and only vegetative means of propagation can be used.

The names of many notable nurseries of the past are preserved in the names of plants they have bred or selected: Lucombe of Exeter, Späth of Berlin, Vilmorin of Paris. Veitch of Chelsea. These names are as familiar to the committed gardener as the great names of today—Gulf Stream of Virginia; Wayside Gardens of Mentor, Ohio; Hillier, Treseder of Truro, England; Hesse of Bremen, Germany.

The greater part of the work of a commercial nursery, however, is simply the production of a wide range of plants up to the packaged stage for the customer. The modern trend inevitably is to confine production to species and cultivars that have the greatest public demand. The nursery illustrated below [3] is modeled on one that sets out to do the opposite.

Moving established trees

Trees grown in nursery conditions are the easiest to replant; much of the cultivation that has gone into them has been to this end. It is possible, with care, to move established trees and replant them in a more suitable situation. Large trees are clearly the most difficult and require either a large labor force or a huge machine. Even then, the tree will not survive unless laborious preparations, beginning perhaps two years or more before, are made. Trenches are dug, first around one side of the tree, then the other—with a year in between diggings—and filled with leafmold. The tree then fills the leafmold with fibrous feeding roots to make a compact root system that can be moved without half of it being lost. In nurseries on light sandy soils trees may be moved each year so that deep roots do not develop; the compact ball of fibrous roots that forms makes transplanting easy.

The easiest trees to move, and ones that amateurs can shift around within their own gardens, are typical garden conifers, the cypresses and cedars, which have small

CONNECTIONS

See also
364 Forestry
368 Trees: problems of climate and disease

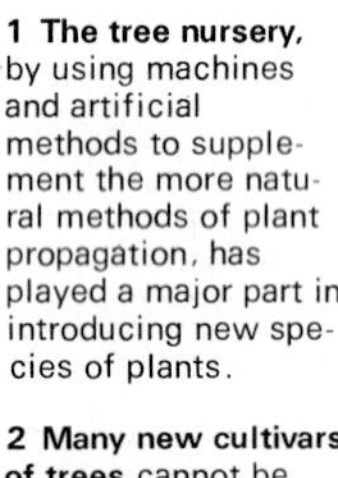

1 The tree nursery, by using machines and artificial methods to supplement the more natural methods of plant propagation, has played a major part in introducing new species of plants.

2 Many new cultivars of trees cannot be grown from seed and it is necessary to propagate them vegetatively (avoiding the normal sexual processes) by means of cuttings or grafts, for example.

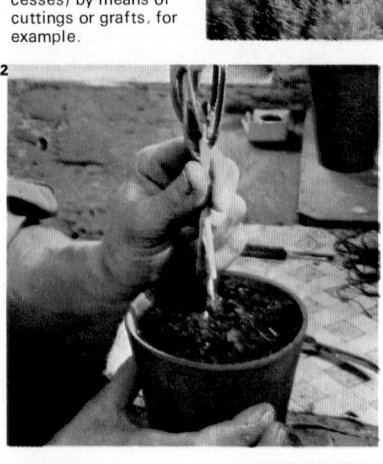

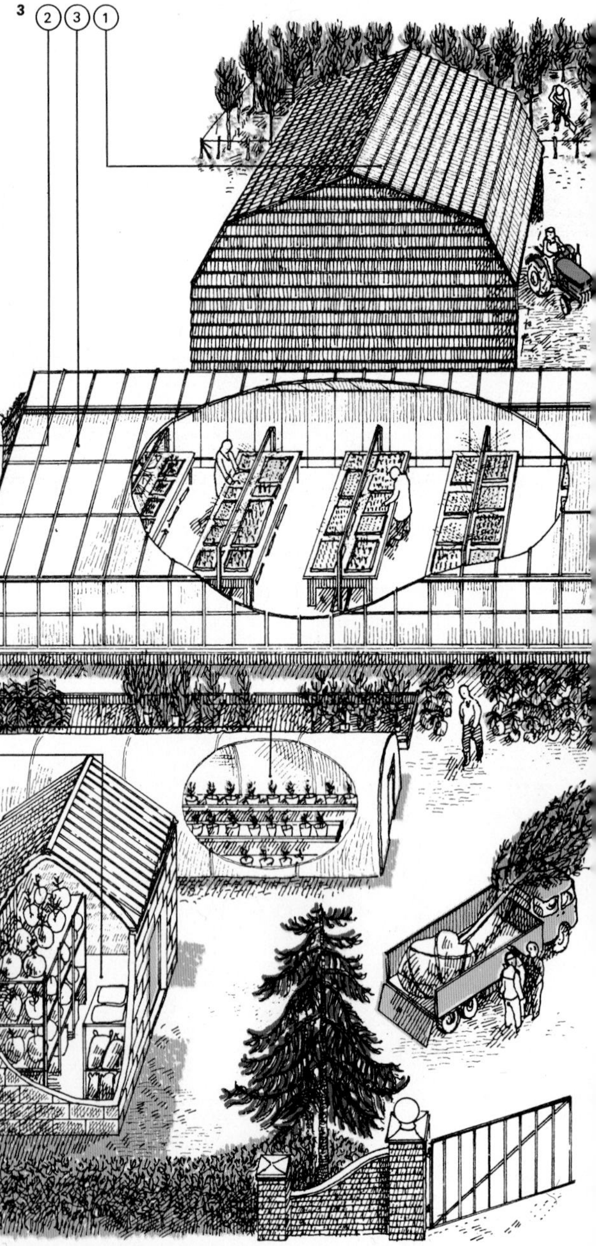

3 In this nursery, an open barn [1] holds tractors and implements. There is a cutting and grafting house [2]; if cuttings do not root, grafting onto quick-rooting stocks is practiced. The mist house [3] has benches fitted with spray bars that maintain a heavy mist in the air around the boxes of cuttings, producing ideal conditions for the cuttings to root. Seeds of popular trees are sown in quantity [4], the flow being regulated by an operator sitting on zones of dense root close to the soil surface. It is easy for two men in a day to prepare a new hole, unearth and transplant a tree of up to 20ft (6m), losing hardly any root. With a strong stake or guy ropes, and regular watering for at least a year, success is very likely.

Planting a tree can be simple—and is, for example, in forestry plantations where tens of thousands of trees are planted. Holes are made, the trees inserted and the soil made firm. But care and attention improve the chances of success with garden trees. "Basin planting," with the tree placed in a little hollow, will encourage moisture flow in dry areas as, in contrast, "mound planting," with the tree raised slightly above ground level, helps where the ground is very wet.

Best planting times

In regions where winter conditions are severe, all planting is best left to early or mid-spring, when the ground is thawed and not too sodden. In more temperate areas, deciduous trees are best planted about the time their leaves fall. Their roots can grow surprisingly well in mild winter weather, giving them a better chance to become established than if they were planted in the spring. And cold spring winds are also less likely to dehydrate them if they have had a winter in the ground [Key].

In the same regions, evergreen can be planted either in the early autumn or spring, but if in the spring, not until the ground has a temperature of not less than 41°F (5°C) and the danger of cold, drying winds is over. Broadleaved evergreens can have some of their leaves cut off to reduce water loss through transpiration.

Trees in pots or containers are, in theory, safe to plant at any time. Obviously the best planting season for them is the same as for any other trees. If they are planted in midsummer, they must be watered well and often. A tree that appears to be flourishing may have been in its container too long so that the soil is filled with a dense tangle of roots. To ensure a good start, the soil should be shaken off and the roots untangled and spread carefully in the hole when planting.

KEY

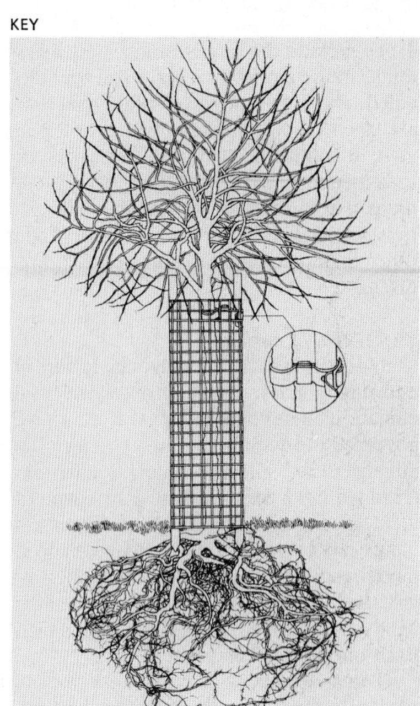

The most important thing for a newly planted tree is security from having its roots disturbed. Semi-standard and larger trees must be tied firmly to a stake for the first two years after planting. A practical form of tie is a plastic belt with a buckle passing through a band that keeps the tree and stake apart (inset). Damage by animals can be prevented by means of a special plastic sleeve or wire guard that covers at least the bottom 2ft(60cm) of the trunk. In areas with hot summers, the bark of young trees may become scorched after they have been planted. Paper wrapping is one method of shielding the trunk from the sun.

the trailer. Seeds in bulk and cuttings awaiting handling are kept in a cool 37°F(3°C) building [5] or a cold frame. Cuttings can be kept in good condition for months. Some have survived after being carried across the world, their stems stuck in a potato. Tunnel houses [6] of polyethylene sheets are economical greenhouses for the protection and nurturing of young plants just struck from cuttings for a "weaning" period. Modern potting is carried out by machine in the potting shed [7]. Rooted plants from the mist house or frames are potted up in the hundreds, once a laborious task for human hands. Container-grown trees are stored in container beds full of damp sand and peat [8]. These trees, and the bigger ones in pots or cans in front of the mist house, are ready for sale at any time. A tractor with a spray bar [9] sprays lines of seedlings with insecticides or selective weed killer. Another tractor [10] undercuts the young trees with a blade to prevent formation of tap roots. Some beds have permanent irrigation pipes and in these [11] seed is hand sown. The covered rows at the back of the bed have mist pipes for starting cuttings in summer. An area is permanently planted with stock trees [12]. Administrative buildings adjoin a locked storage area [13].

Trees: problems of climate and disease

Trees include the largest and oldest living things in the world. Some are so huge, dignified, and apparently everlasting that they are often taken for granted as almost permanent landscape features. Yet, despite their beneficent role in helping to provide oxygen in the air that we breathe, trees are most menaced today by humans. Their other major problems—animal pests, fire, diseases, and climate—are less threatening.

The effects of climate

Climate is one of the most crucial factors in deciding which trees will grow where, and climatic changes over millions of years have governed the evolution of tree species. Relatively recent climatic changes have determined the present natural distribution of most species around the globe. Fossil remains left by trees, in turn, have enabled modern science to establish prehistoric patterns of climate—even to the prevailing winds that carried tree seeds and pollen from one area to another.

The ancestors of all trees were tropical plants. In the tropics the seasonal temperature changes are usually small; what alters most from one time of the year to another is rainfall. Most tropical plants are evergreen and grow either continuously or intermittently whenever there is enough moisture. The montana zones are exceptional regions within the tropics—the equatorial Andes, for example, or Mounts Kenya and Kilimanjaro in Africa—where temperatures decline with altitude. The high slopes and "meadows," are characterized by dwarf forests of low-growing alpine trees and shrubs.

Temperate-zone trees are adapted to changing seasons. They are called "hardy" because they are adapted to withstand the rigors of long spells of freezing temperatures and fluctuating conditions.

Ecological niches

A graphic illustration of how trees find their most favorable climatic environment can be seen along the course of a mountain range that runs from north to south. In the western ranges of the United States and Canada [2], the pattern of each tree's range from south to north tells the story. In the Sierras a species may find its ecological niche at high altitudes. In the Cascades and in the Coast Range similar basic climatic conditions—including the length of time that the snow lies on the ground and the number of days during which the temperature is high enough (above 40°F, or 4.4°C) for the tree to grow and ripen new wood—force this same species right down to sea level.

Once a tree is moved (or its seed is planted) out of its accustomed zone, it is in potential danger. A larch from Siberia, if moved to a milder climate, might be expected to luxuriate in the longer growing season while still being totally hardy. What actually happens in practice is that it is "lured" out of dormancy too early in the spring by higher temperatures than it "expects." As a result, it starts growth, only to be cut back eventually by late spring frosts. If this happens repeatedly the tree may die.

The converse happens when a southern tree is transplanted north. It may be relatively safe in the spring, for bud-break will just be delayed. But if growth continues late

CONNECTIONS

See also
364 Forestry
366 The modern tree nursery

1 A

B

C

1 D

1 E

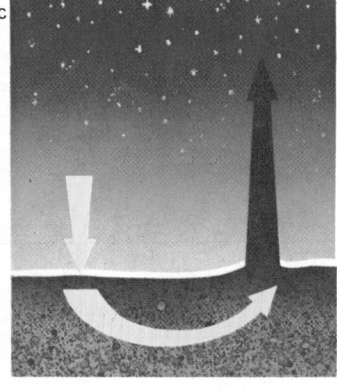

1 Cause and effect of frost: where clouds or a tree canopy insulate the layer of warm air at ground level from the open sky, heat cannot escape, so frost is unlikely [A]. On a night without clouds [B] heat is free to escape and the soil temperature falls below that of the air. The soil takes heat from the air near the ground [C] and as a result produces radiation frost. Cold air, which gathers in a thin layer at ground level, flows downhill, collecting in hollows and valleys, which thus become frost "pockets" [D]. The height to which the hollows fill with frost is marked by the dead lower branches of trees. The house and garden [E] are protected from frost because it is stopped from flowing downhill by the trees.

2 A

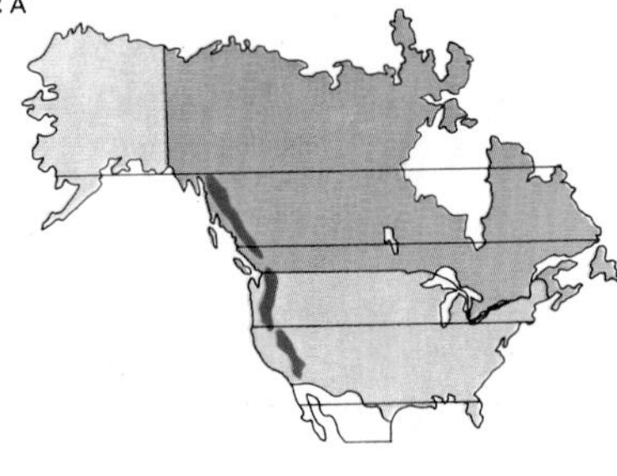

2 B

Alpine fir
Bigleaf maple
Black cottonwood
Douglas fir
Engelmann spruce
Grand fir
Mountain hemlock
Ponderosa pine
Sugar pine
Western juniper
Western red cedar
Western white pine
Sierras
40°N
Cascades
50°N
Coast Range
60°N
4,267
3,962
3,658
3,353
3,048
2,743
2,438
2,134
1,829
1,524
1,219
914
610
305
m
14,000
13,000
12,000
11,000
10,000
9,000
8,000
7,000
6,000
5,000
4,000
3,000
2,000
1,000
ft

2 The mountains of western North America [A] reach from British Columbia's coast range in the north, through the Cascades of Washington and Oregon to the Sierras of California. The foreshortened cross section [B] plots the altitudes at which the same tree species occur. In the south, western white pine grows at 9,000ft (2,740m); in the north it has come down to 2,500ft (760m) to find the same growing conditions. These conditions are, in the main, dependent on the length of the growing season, at temperatures above about 40°F(4.4°C). There are exceptions to the rule. These are brought about by purely local rather than general conditions—chiefly where competition from other species is increased. The species described in the diagram are mainly conifers—the firs and pines of temperate mountain environments.

in the northern summer, the new wood may be still soft and immature and therefore susceptible to frost kill in the early northern autumn.

More surprising is the difficulty trees experience in moving from the west coast to the east of North America—or from the Orient to Europe. Western conifers are as unhappy in New England as oaks from Ohio are in Britain or France. On the other hand, spruce trees native to subarctic conditions in Canada and Norway are widely used for reforestation in Western Europe.

An extreme example of upset is that of a cold climate tree that is moved to the subtropics. What happens here is that its buds may fail to open at all. Built into its schedule is the need for a cold spell (winter) to break its dormancy. If there is perpetual warmth, it will remain dormant and in all probability will die.

Seed origin is of the greatest importance. The forester's object is to extend the growth period of his trees as far as he can without risking frost damage. He has little room for maneuver, but if he can add even a week to the growing season by getting his seed from 100 miles (160km) farther south without injury to the trees, he may add a whole year's growth in 20 years.

Many temperate zone trees can stand being frozen solid while they are dormant. What is most harmful, and can sometimes kill, is winter drought. When the ground is frozen, and no water is available to the roots, high winds and, often, low humidity continue to evaporate water from the branches. As a result, the tree begins to dry out. On evergreens this shows in the browning of the leaves by the end of even a normal winter.

Pests and disease

If the climate—the weather and its vagaries—provides the principal influence on a tree, a more immediate threat may be posed by some microscopic vector of death, such as insects or bacteria to which a tree is home and food. Most of these tiny creatures do no harm; others, such as the elm bark beetle, distribute a fungus that has killed trees the world over.

KEY

Fir trees completely shrouded by snow resemble an army of ghosts high in the mountains of Hokkaido, northernmost of Japan's large islands. Snow, which protects tiny plants from the more severe effects of cold, dry winds, provides vital protection to evergreens in the intense cold and dry sunshine of the mountains. Prevailing winds deform trees in an exposed situation by stunting or preventing growth on the windward side. New shoots can grow only in the shelter of old ones and the tree takes on a characteristic shape, with its branches and foliage trailing to leeward.

3

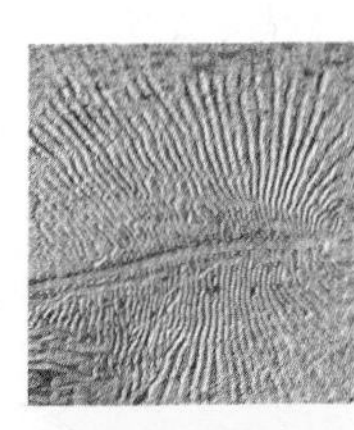

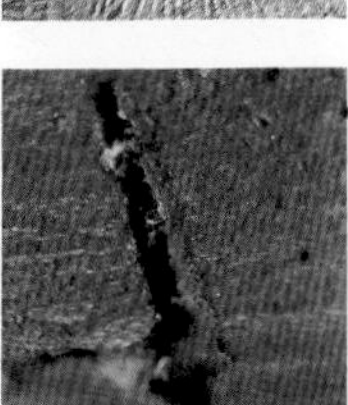

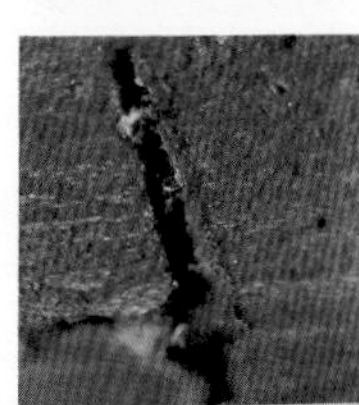

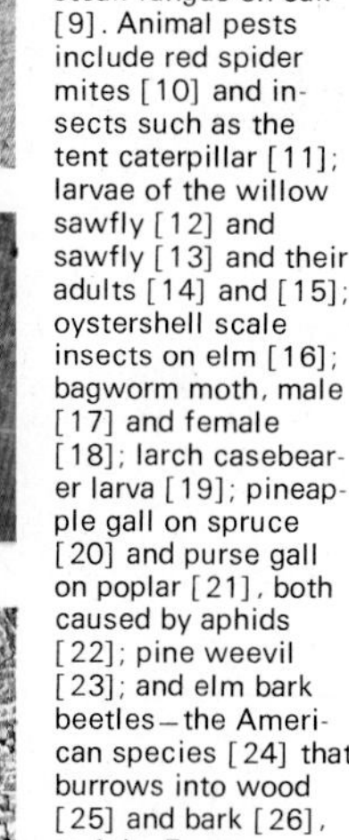

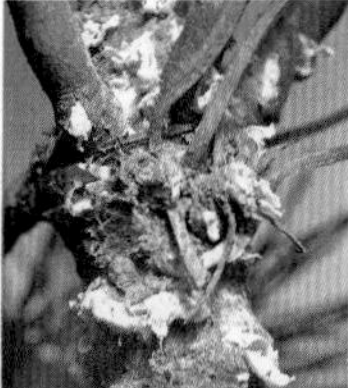

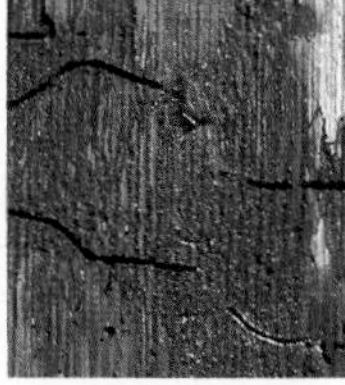

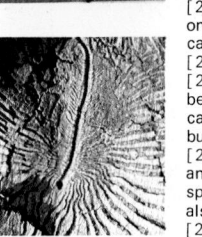

3 Trees can be attacked by many organisms. Fungal and bacterial pests include anthracnose on sycamore [1]; rust fungus on linden [2]; downy mildew [3]; chestnut blight [4]; honey fungus on pine [5]; fireblight of cotoneaster [6]; bacterial canker on poplar [7]; white pine blister rust [8] and beefsteak fungus on oak [9]. Animal pests include red spider mites [10] and insects such as the tent caterpillar [11]; larvae of the willow sawfly [12] and sawfly [13] and their adults [14] and [15]; oystershell scale insects on elm [16]; bagworm moth, male [17] and female [18]; larch casebearer larva [19]; pineapple gall on spruce [20] and purse gall on poplar [21], both caused by aphids [22]; pine weevil [23]; and elm bark beetles—the American species [24] that burrows into wood [25] and bark [26], and the European species [27] that also damages wood [28] and bark [29]

Farm stockbreeding and management

Until mechanical power replaced the ox and the horse, animal husbandry was a part of every farm's working life. Farms entirely without livestock are still in the minority. In the United States, for instance, farm revenue from livestock is normally more than twice that from all crops. About three-fifths of this comes from cattle and sheep and two-fifths from pigs and poultry.

Livestock management

Breeding and management have a combined aim: the most profitable production of meat, milk, wool, or eggs, in environments ranging from entirely natural to wholly man-made. Thus, domesticated species have been spread, partly by selection of types best suited to conditions (for example, range cattle and various sheep breeds) and partly by changing the environment—for example, providing shelter and an improved diet. The more such changes are made, the more breeding aims must be changed to suit the new conditions.

Cattle (synonymous with wealth in some languages) are managed in both ways. They may live entirely by grazing or be completely confined and even have fresh grass brought to them from the field. The beef cow should produce and rear a calf a year, while the dairy cow provides a profit from her milk. The whole routine of the dairy farm revolves around the milking [5], which takes place twice a day. For milk production the cow must be mated to calve annually for each lactation of about 305 days. Her feed is scaled to her yield of milk and the calf is reared away from her.

Sheep, in all but the most extreme conditions (for example, in Icelandic winters), are seldom housed and live by grazing—sometimes on crops especially sown for them. Flocks grazing in mountain areas in summer may be moved to lower ground for the winter feeding and spring lambing. Lambing and shearing remain the shepherd's biggest tasks.

Except in the tropics, the pig—once a forager in woods and wastelands and housed only for fattening—has moved under cover. New-born pigs thrive only in warmth. The main cost of rearing thereafter is food; a pig that is cold burns food to keep warm instead of using it to put on weight. Modern pig rearing is designed to speed up growth by regulating temperature and restricting movement. Many of the same considerations apply to poultry.

Selective breeding

Breeding for improved production is easiest with species that mature early and produce many young in a year [1], but an outstanding male animal, whose attributes are inherited by his descendants, can have a vast effect within a few generations. This process has been greatly accelerated by the wide adoption of artificial insemination [3], especially in cattle. The semen of an outstanding sire can be stored in a freezer and used for mating after he is dead. Or, it can be shipped to distant countries when the transfer of live animals would be too expensive or would be a disease risk.

Ancestors of more than one type have usually contributed to the make-up of existing breeds. The new type has then been fixed by a period of close inbreeding. This

CONNECTIONS

See also
372 Cattle for beef and milk
376 Pigs and sheep
382 Poultry and egg pr duction
416 Principles of heredi
308 The farming corpor tion
306 The small farm
310 Farm machinery an buildings
472 Flatworms, flukes, and tapeworms
474 Earthworms, clamworms, and roundworms

1

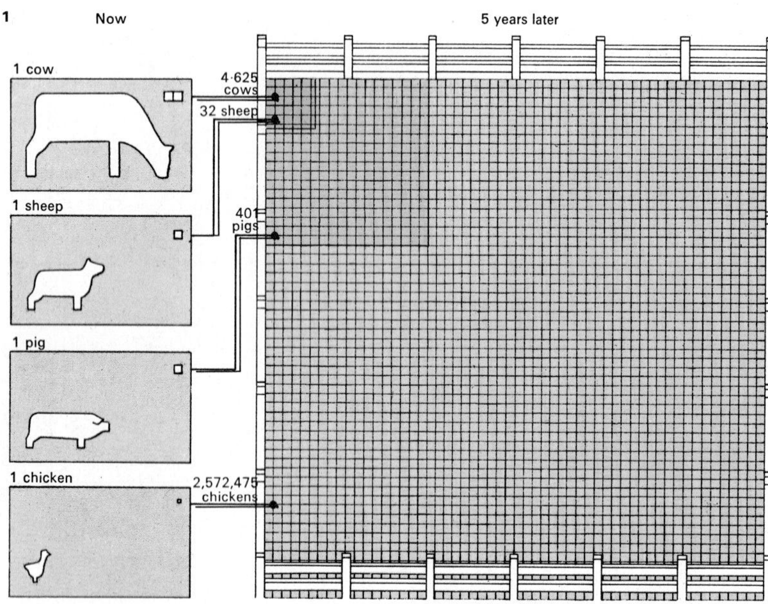
Now
5 years later
1 cow
4·625 cows
32 sheep
1 sheep
401 pigs
1 pig
1 chicken
2,572,475 chickens

1 Rapid change in a livestock population is easiest where generations are short and numbers in each generation large. The development of inbred lines for crossing to provide commercial stock has resulted in major improvement in pig and poultry performance. Upgrading of cattle is facilitated by using superior sires in successive generations and selecting progeny on performance.

2

Border Leicester
Friesland
Dorset Horn
Clun Forest
Colbred

2 New sheep breeds may be produced by introducing desired attributes from foreign types. The basis of the British Colbred sheep was the Friesland, a Dutch milk breed with a high rate of reproduction but was unsuitable for meat. Crossing involved three different British breeds. The Colbred, used for fat lamb production, retained some of the extra prolificacy. Many breeds are similarly created.

3 A

B

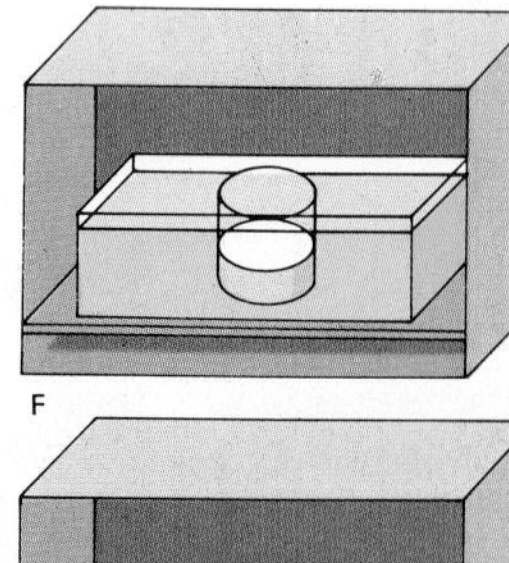

C

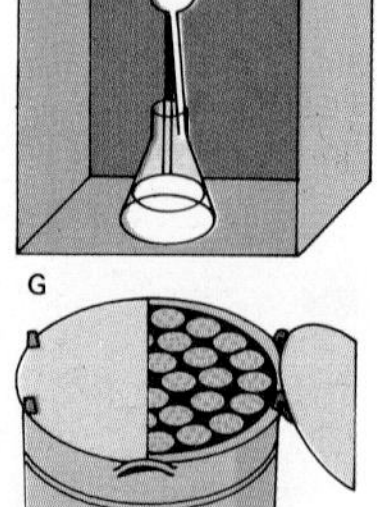

D

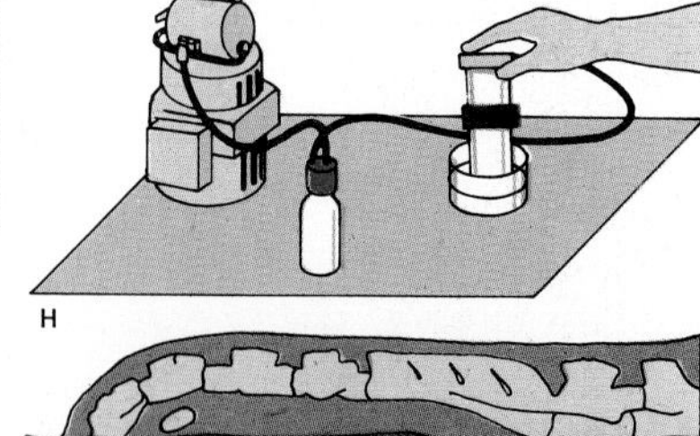

E

F

G

H

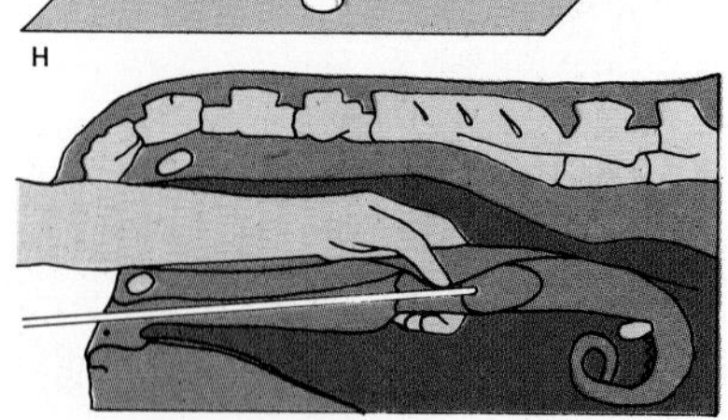

3 Artificial insemination is in world-wide use. Semen, collected from the bull on a dummy or "teaser" cow [A], is kept warm in water [B] and a buffer added. It is diluted [C] and put into plastic "straws" [D], which are corked and prepared for storage [E]. The straws are then cooled for seven hours at 4°C(39°F) [F] and stored in liquid nitrogen freezers [G]. When needed, the semen is thawed and introduced into a cow's uterus through a catheter [H].

cannot be carried too far without a considerable risk of diminished vigor and inherited defects. Cross-breeding to overcome this danger is a regular commercial practice, particularly with sheep and beef cattle, where hardy breeds are often mated to less hardy but more rapidly maturing varieties.

Improvement of performance within breeds has come to depend increasingly on detailed records: yields of milk and eggs and speed of growth and feed economy in meat animals. This entails elaborate testing procedures and statistical analysis of records. The computer has become a necessary tool of large breeding organizations that sell stock or semen to commercial farms.

The greater the emphasis on economic performance, the more the livestock farmer must rely on specialist advice and the results of scientific research. Animal nutrition has become a field of study in itself, as has the design of housing and equipment.

Veterinary care

Above all, increasingly dense populations of animals must be kept healthy. Consequently, the role of the veterinarian is now very important and he must be an expert in preventive medicine [7] as well as in the diagnosis and treatment of clinical disease when it appears. The history of stock farming is punctuated by occasional outbreaks of infectious diseases that are now controlled by closing frontiers, strict quarantine, and by slaughtering the affected animals and their contacts [8].

Vaccination is still considered the most effective method of disease prevention in countries where infection is rare and frontiers easily closed. Elsewhere, vaccination has reduced the risk, although, for success, the strain of the infection must be effectively typed. Vaccination, for instance, has greatly reduced the impact of foot-and-mouth disease and undulant fever. Other diseases, including bovine tuberculosis, hog cholera, and anthrax, which once caused serious stock losses and even human illness, are now wholly or partly wiped out in most advanced countries. But there are always some risks, especially where husbandry is primitive and disease endemic.

KEY

A championship at one of the big shows is the culmination of many breeders' dreams. Prizewinning animals, such as this Holstein cow, are greatly sought after for breeding.

4

4 The driving of sheep and cattle from summer mountain pasture to winter quarters and back again in spring (called "transhumance") is widely practiced. Flocks and herds move up the slopes as the season advances, always on new, fresh grass. This is the usual procedure in the mountain states where most of the U.S. sheep industry exists. For farm flocks, pasture rotation is recommended.

5

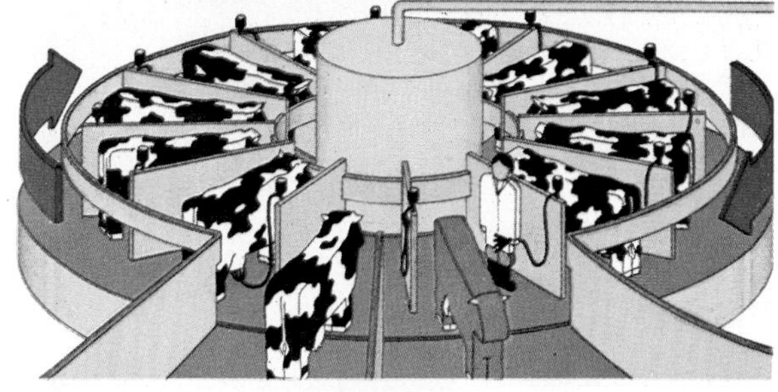

5 Cows move on a revolving platform in one type of labor saving milking setup. The milker need not move to fix and remove the unit on the teats of each cow. The turntable's speed is set at the average milking time of the herd and slow milkers may be sent around again. Yields are automatically measured and the milk is piped to the dairy. The milker can adjust the quantity of feed given to each cow during milking.

6 A

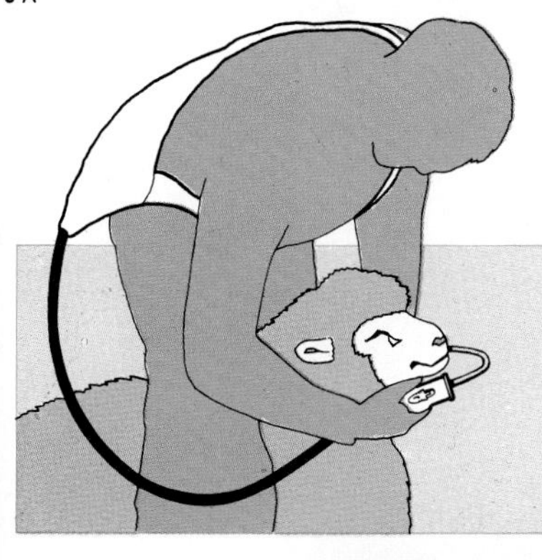

B

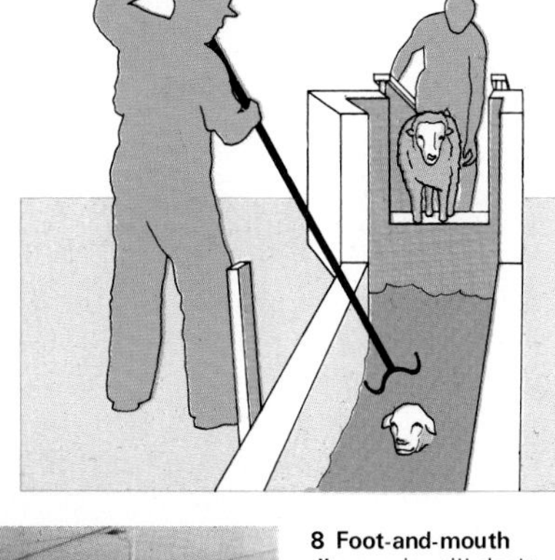

6 Internal and external parasites cause weight loss and discomfort in farm animals and may carry more serious consequences. To control them sheep are given routine doses of a drench [A] against those internal parasites that infest the digestive tract and the lungs. A number of external parasites, which thrive in the shelter of the fleece, have to be dealt with by dipping sheep completely in a disinfectant bath [B]. This must cover the whole of the animal including the head. The dipping vat is now often replaced by a chute, through which the sheep are driven between a series of jets.

7

7 Vaccination is now a matter of routine; here young pigs are being treated by injection. Infections can spread quickly among a herd kept in buildings under intensive systems. For pigs and poultry, oral vaccines, which can be mixed in feed or drinking water, have also been developed. The period of protection is sometimes limited. Vaccinations may need to be highly specific against particular strains of the organism that can cause the disease.

8

JCB

8 Foot-and-mouth disease is still dealt with in North America and Britain by the slaughter of all possible contacts. The carcasses are burned or buried to avoid further infection. Where the disease is more frequent, susceptible livestock are vaccinated. The disease is seldom fatal to adult animals, but its effects on production can be catastrophic. There are several strains of the virus endemic in some parts of the world and vaccines must be prepared.

Cattle for beef and milk

Cattle, first domesticated in Neolithic times, can be selected to serve a wide range of needs and to adapt to many environments. In early settled agriculture the same beasts served as power units for cultivation and haulage, as milk animals, and, finally, as a source of meat. The first use has almost disappeared in developed countries and the aim of modern breeders is to improve the yield and composition of milk and to increase weight gain rapidly and economically.

Ancient lineage and modern stock

Improvement of cattle on a regional basis has a long history, especially in areas where feed was abundant. From the sixteenth century onward the big cattle of the Low Countries had an important influence on breeding in many parts of Europe. But detailed records of pedigrees were not available until toward the end of the eighteenth century. Then a growing demand from the urban population for meat stimulated such pioneer British improvers as Robert Bakewell (1726–96) who developed Longhorns in Leicestershire and Robert Colling (1749–1820), who, with his brother Charles (1750–1836), bred what were the first modern Shorthorns at their farm in Yorkshire. They opened the way for the establishment, over the next 100 years, of breed societies and herdbooks covering all the major breeds. The result was that outstanding animals could be more easily identified and the influence of these beasts extended by a wider use of their descendants, particularly in the male line.

This process has been greatly accelerated by the general adoption, over the last 30 years, of artificial insemination. As a result of this process an outstanding bull may sire several thousand offspring. Using frozen semen, "matings" are possible in any part of the world, even after a bull is dead. His genetic influence on such factors as milk and butterfat yield in his daughters can be precisely measured by comparing their performances with those of cows in the same herds sired by other bulls. Expert inspection of these cattle will also indicate the bull's influence on body conformation. Measuring the genetic contribution of a bull used for siring beef cattle is more difficult, but progeny records of growth rate and feed consumption give useful information.

A good beef animal must not only grow quickly and economically but also must carry the main weight of lean muscle in those parts of the carcass preferred by consumers—the hindquarters and back. Heavy bone is wasteful to the butcher and fat, although some is needed for flavor and tenderness, is now little in demand. The characteristics of the three most prominent beef cattle types are quite different: the ubiquitous Hereford is docile and able to thrive under fairly rough conditions; the Angus is a smaller animal but regarded by many as the producer of the best beef; while the French Charolais has great size.

Dairy and dual-purpose animals

The pure dairy cow presents a strong contrast to cattle bred purely for beef. As much of her food as possible must be converted into milk, not muscle. She needs a large digestive system and a well shaped and capacious udder. Two specialist breeds of this kind are the Ayrshire from Scotland and

CONNECTIONS

See also

370 Farm stockbreeding and management

304 History of agriculture

378 Cuts of meat

374 Dairy produce and cheese

380 Pork, ham, sausages and processed meats

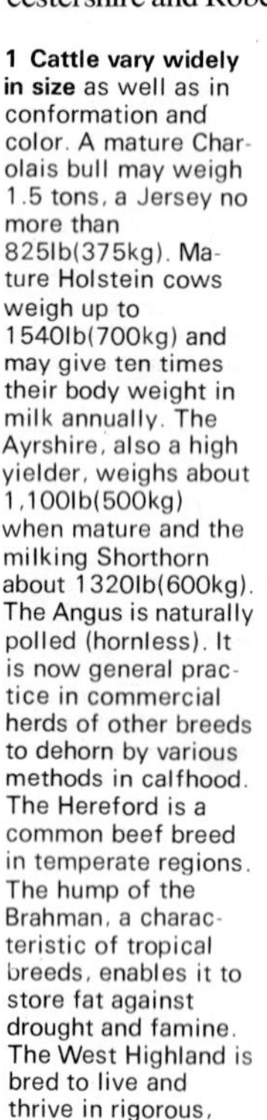

1 Cattle vary widely in size as well as in conformation and color. A mature Charolais bull may weigh 1.5 tons, a Jersey no more than 825lb(375kg). Mature Holstein cows weigh up to 1540lb(700kg) and may give ten times their body weight in milk annually. The Ayrshire, also a high yielder, weighs about 1,100lb(500kg) when mature and the milking Shorthorn about 1320lb(600kg). The Angus is naturally polled (hornless). It is now general practice in commercial herds of other breeds to dehorn by various methods in calfhood. The Hereford is a common beef breed in temperate regions. The hump of the Brahman, a characteristic of tropical breeds, enables it to store fat against drought and famine. The West Highland is bred to live and thrive in rigorous, upland habitat.

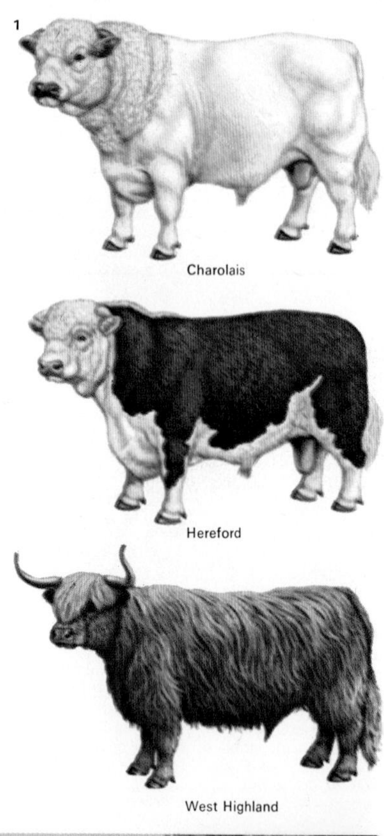
1
Charolais
Hereford

West Highland

Holstein
Ayrshire
Shorthorn

Angus
Jersey
Brahman

2 African cattle such as the longhorned Ankole are the mainstay of many pastoral tribes outside tsetse fly infested areas. Progressive eradication of this pest has widened their range.

3 Mountain meadows provide rich summer pasturage in the Swiss Alps up to the snowline. The cattle are brought up from the valleys where they spend the winter under cover. The main breeds are the Simmenthal and the Brown Swiss illustrated.

the Jersey from the Channel Islands; the latter is the smallest of all widespread modern breeds, giving milk containing the highest percentage of butterfat—from 5% to 6%.

Much of the world's meat and milk supply comes from cattle that can be regarded as dual purpose. Of these the most numerous are the black and white Holstein cattle, which originated in the Netherlands but which now show local variations of type. The Holstein (called Friesian in Europe) is a large animal that produces heavy yields of milk whose composition has been greatly improved since the advent of artificial insemination. It has largely supplanted other once-prominent US dairy breeds, such as the Ayrshire, Guernsey, and Jersey.

In a beef-breeding herd the sole revenue is from the calves. In a pure dairy herd most of the male calves have little value for rearing. To overcome this, in many commercial herds only the very best cows are mated with a dairy bull—to provide replacement heifers—while the remainder are mated to a beef bull to provide cross-bred calves suitable for beef production. In order to make these cross-breeds easily identifiable, breeders use a bull that will pass to the progeny such distinguishing features as the white face of the Hereford.

Specialized breeds

There is still a great demand for breeds of cattle that are adapted to particular environmental niches. Examples include the somewhat slow-growing but extremely hardy Highland cattle of Scotland, which can survive the northern winter in the open, and a wide range of European breeds. In Africa cattle must be capable of surviving long periods of drought and also be resistant to local conditions that European breeds cannot tolerate. In tropical and subtropical areas much use is being made of the humped Brahman cattle of India and Southeast Asia. These have been widely used in breeding programs for the hotter areas of Australia and the Americas, most notably in the development of the Santa Gertrudis of Texas. Some work has been done on improving the American bison, or buffalo, and has resulted in the "beefalo" crossbreed.

KEY

The English engraver Thomas Bewick depicted this freshly milked Holstein in about 1800. This breed was already noted for its yield and has been bred for milk for about 2,000 years. Holstein cattle originated in the Netherlands.

4

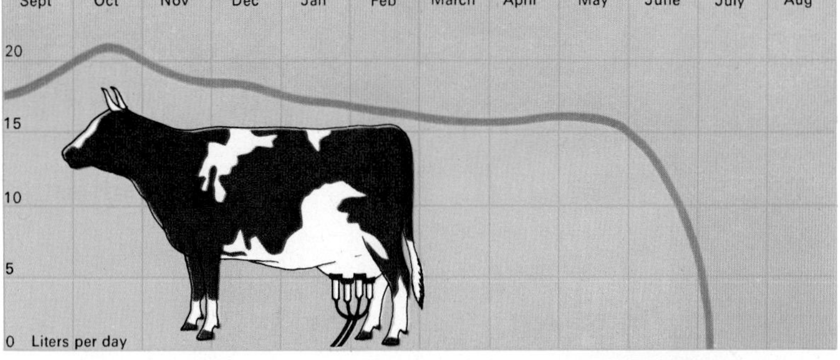

Sept
Oct
Nov
Dec
Jan
Feb
March
April
May
June
July
Aug
20
15
10
5
0 Liters per day

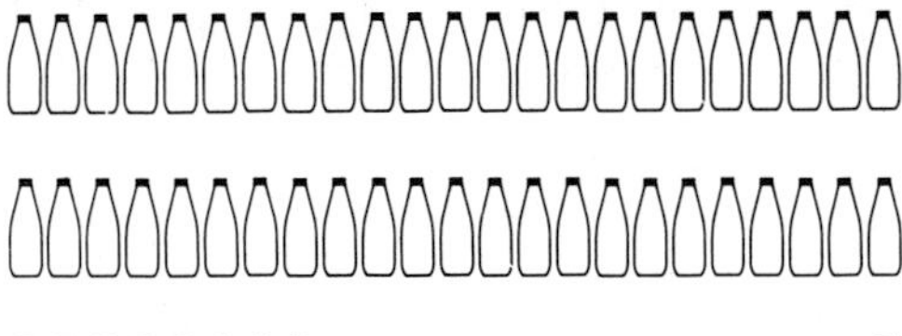

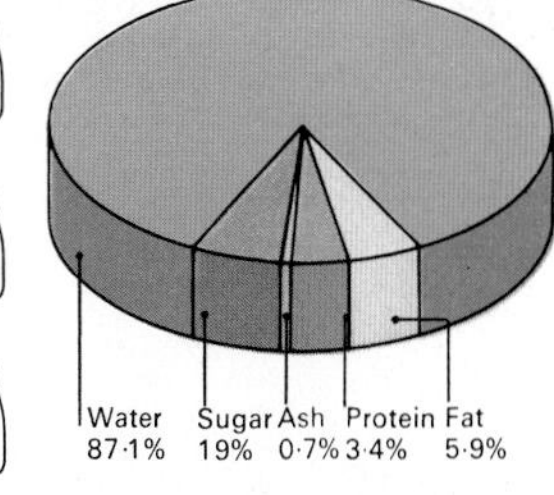

50 liters milk
Water 87·1%
Sugar 19%
Ash 0·7%
Protein 3·4%
Fat 5·9%

4 Autumn calving is necessary in areas where fresh milk is in demand all year. An average dairy cow, giving about 815gals(2,700liters) over 10 months, will have a lactation curve that rises to a peak about six weeks after calving, falls gradually during the winter and briefly rises again when she goes out to grass in the spring. Although milk is usually about 87% water, its fat and sugar content are an important source of energy in the diet and its protein is of high quality and easily digested. Calcium and other minerals are also important nutrients. Selective breeding of dairy cattle aims at increasing the total yield of milk solids.

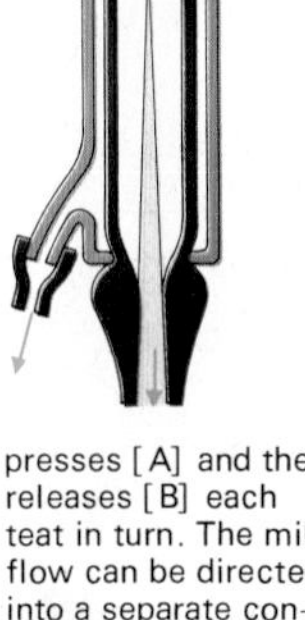

5 A
B

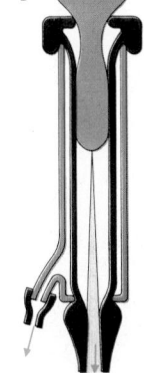

5 In machine milking the cow is conditioned to let down milk as if she were feeding her own calf. A partial vacuum holds the rubber teat cup in place and a varying pressure of air through the valve presses [A] and then releases [B] each teat in turn. The milk flow can be directed into a separate container or, as in large modern installations, piped directly to a cooling tank in the dairy.

6

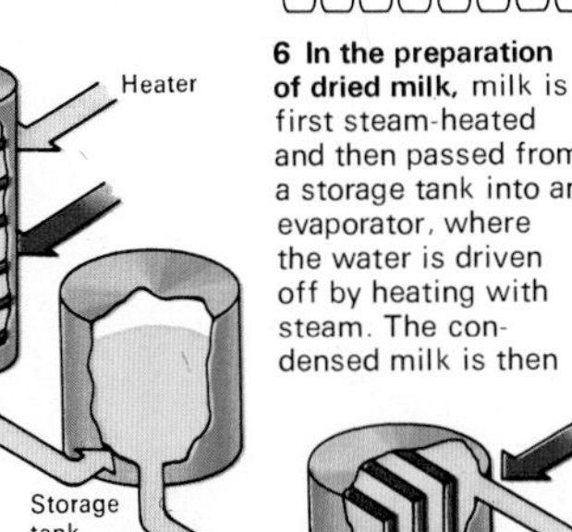

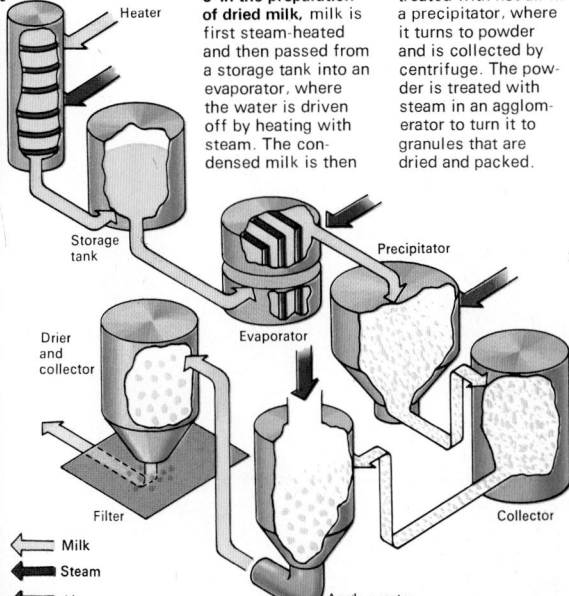

Heater
Storage tank

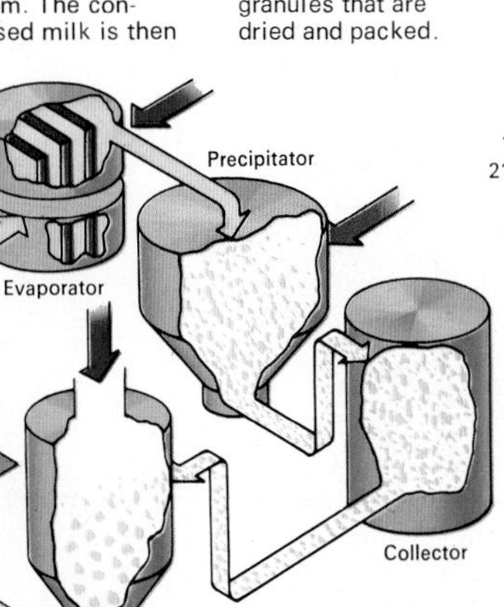

Precipitator
Evaporator
Drier and collector
Filter
Collector
Agglomerator
Milk
Steam
Air

6 In the preparation of dried milk, milk is first steam-heated and then passed from a storage tank into an evaporator, where the water is driven off by heating with steam. The condensed milk is then treated with hot air in a precipitator, where it turns to powder and is collected by centrifuge. The powder is treated with steam in an agglomerator to turn it to granules that are dried and packed.

7

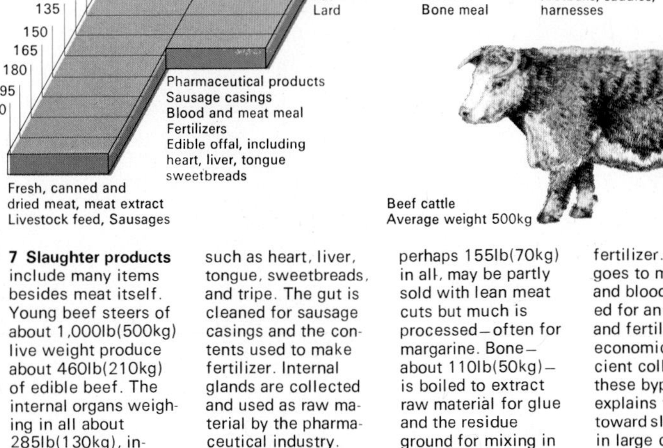

Weight in kg 15
30
45
60
75
90
105
120
135
150
165
180
195
210
Lean
Internal organs
Fat
Bones
Skin and waste
Blood
Blood meal
Fertilizers
Leather for shoes, clothes, upholstery
bookbindings
footballs, saddles, harnesses
Glue
Fertilizer
Bone meal
Fat
Lard
Pharmaceutical products
Sausage casings
Blood and meat meal
Fertilizers
Edible offal, including heart, liver, tongue sweetbreads
Fresh, canned and dried meat, meat extract
Livestock feed, Sausages
Beef cattle
Average weight 500kg

7 Slaughter products include many items besides meat itself. Young beef steers of about 1,000lb(500kg) live weight produce about 460lb(210kg) of edible beef. The internal organs weighing in all about 285lb(130kg), include edible offal such as heart, liver, tongue, sweetbreads, and tripe. The gut is cleaned for sausage casings and the contents used to make fertilizer. Internal glands are collected and used as raw material by the pharmaceutical industry. Fat, accounting for perhaps 155lb(70kg) in all, may be partly sold with lean meat cuts but much is processed—often for margarine. Bone—about 110lb(50kg)—is boiled to extract raw material for glue and the residue ground for mixing in animal feed, or as fertilizer. The hide goes to make leather and blood is collected for animal feed and fertilizer. The economic and efficient collection of these byproducts explains the trend toward slaughtering in large commercial abattoirs.

Dairy products

Man began supplementing his diet with the milk of animals long before he began to make records of his activities. References to milk and dairy products in both the Bible and the Hindu Vedas indicate that these were traditional foods long before the birth of Christ. Today, although milk is a popular nutritious drink, more than two thirds of the world's milk is converted into other products, principally butter, cheese, ice cream, yogurt, and evaporated, dried, or condensed milk. Dairy products are also used as animal feed and can even be converted into plastics. Before the recent intensive development of petrochemical plastics, casein (the main protein in milk) was used in the manufacture of a wide range of products from buttons to billiard balls.

Milk and milk treatment methods

The choice of dairy animals varies from culture to culture. The major dairy producers—the United States, Europe, New Zealand, and Australia—use cow's milk for nearly all of their dairy products. In Asia both cow and buffalo milk are used, and in the Mediterranean region the chief milk animals are sheep and goats. Other sources of milk for human consumption include reindeer, yaks, and camels.

Apart from its by-products, milk itself now comes in a variety of forms. Consumption of raw milk, which goes sour quickly and is easily contaminated, is less and less common in the developed countries. Most milk is pasteurized by heating it to kill all disease-carrying organisms and most of those that cause souring. Milk is also usually homogenized by emulsifying fat particles so they will not rise to form a layer of cream. Milk preservation is a large industry. The most widely used form of preserved milk is dried milk, which is usually made from skim milk with a minimal fat content [1]. The fats are removed from milk by a large centrifuge, called a cream separator, which separates whole milk into fat-free skim milk and cream. Most skim milk is dried, but some is sold for animal feed. Condensed and evaporated milks are made by reducing the milk's water content. Condensed milk is often sweetened.

Cream, butter, and ice cream

Cream, which is the fatty part of whole milk, is sold for table use and it is also used in the preparation of butter, ice cream, and cream cheese.

Butter was probably the first product to be made from milk, and it continues to be one of the most important dairy products. It is manufactured from full cream, which is agitated until the fat globules and solids in the cream clump together. The resulting semisolid—butter—has little protein, but its high fat content [1] makes it a good energy food. Buttermilk is the liquid residue from butter making. Its slightly sour taste makes it a popular and refreshing drink.

Until the advent of refrigeration, ice cream, a favorite dish in the courts of seventeenth-century Europe, graced only the tables of the rich. Today it is a popular food [3] for everyone. Although the trend in recent years has been to replace dairy products with vegetable oils in making frozen desserts, ice cream made in the traditional manner continues to be preferred in most countries.

CONNECTIONS

See also
372 Cattle for beef and milk
422 Bacteria and viruses

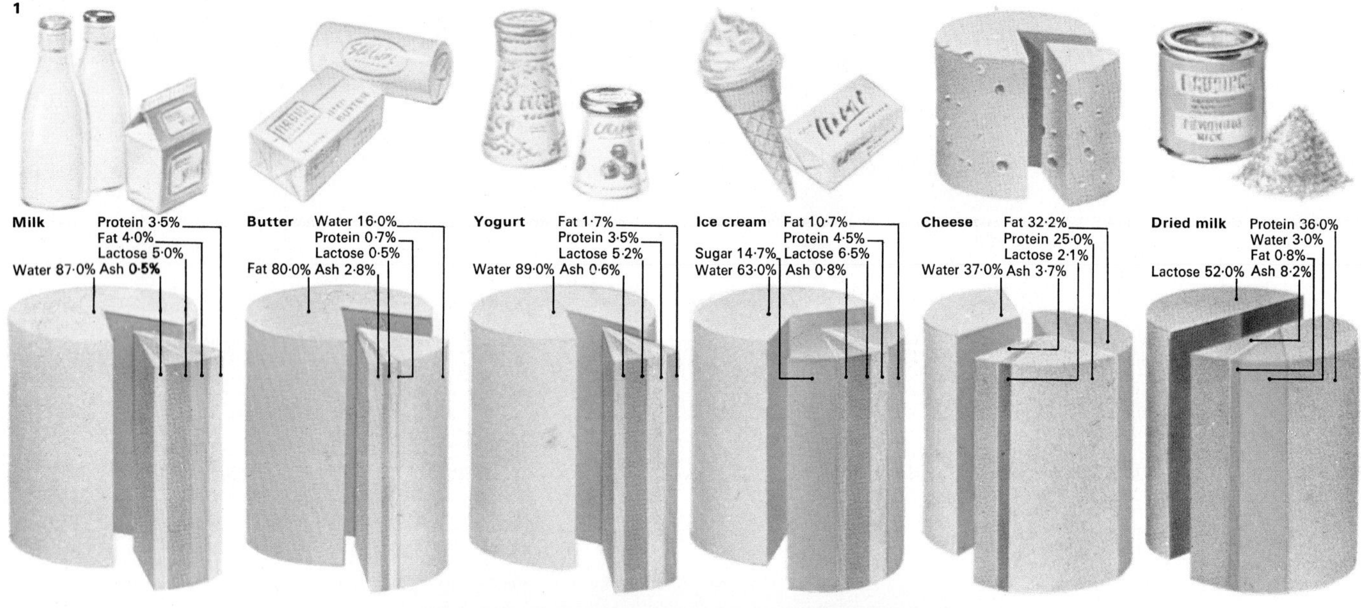
1
Milk
Protein 3·5%
Fat 4·0%
Lactose 5·0%
Water 87·0%
Ash 0·5%
Butter
Water 16·0%
Protein 0·7%
Lactose 0·5%
Fat 80·0%
Ash 2·8%
Yogurt
Fat 1·7%
Protein 3·5%
Lactose 5·2%
Water 89·0%
Ash 0·6%
Ice cream
Fat 10·7%
Protein 4·5%
Sugar 14·7%
Lactose 6·5%
Water 63·0%
Ash 0·8%
Cheese
Fat 32·2%
Protein 25·0%
Lactose 2·1%
Water 37·0%
Ash 3·7%
Dried milk
Protein 36·0%
Water 3·0%
Fat 0·8%
Lactose 52·0%
Ash 8·2%

1 Milk products have the same basic consituents—water, protein, fat, lactose, and minerals (ash)—as does milk itself, but in different proportions.

2 Butter molds were very popular in the nineteenth century and are still used in some fine restaurants. Their function was to turn a foodstuff into an attractive table decoration.

PURE ICES

3 Ice cream, once a luxury food, is an inexpensive treat sold all over Europe and America by street vendors, cafes, dairy stands, and groceries.

4 Dried milk is one major contribution that the world's richer nations, who are often large dairy producers, can make to the Third World. Despite intensive use of milk in America, Europe, Australia, and New Zealand, surpluses often arise. Dried milk is easily stored and transported, and, when reconstituted, can provide a significant proportion of protein and nutritional requirements.

Cheesemaking and yogurt

Cheese is made from ripened milk curds. If made from whole milk it contains most of the food value of milk. Although there are really only three categories of cheese (soft, hard, and blue), variations in the process of making it produce over 2,000 different kinds. The main variables are the types of milk used, the conditions under which the milk-yielding animal was fed, and the method of maturing the cheese [5].

Despite the great number of variations, the basic method of cheese-making is the same everywhere. First, a curdling agent is added to the milk to precipitate the solids. The solidified casein, fat, and other water-insoluble constituents are called the curds, and the remaining liquid is known as whey. The curds are then broken or cut to release most of the whey and left to drain. They are then broken up, salted, and put into molds. Finally, the cheese is ripened. This is one of the most important stages in cheesemaking, because the length of time and the conditions under which a cheese is matured are critical. The action of bacteria at this stage creates the cheese's characteristic taste and appearance.

Cream cheese differs from other cheeses in that it is rarely ripened. Cream cheese can be made at home by allowing milk to sour naturally, adding rennet to coagulate the milk, wrapping the curds in cheesecloth, and hanging them up to drain. The cheese can be eaten after a day. Processed cheese is a factory product made by sterilizing the cheese instead of ripening it. When canned or vacuum packed, it can be stored indefinitely.

Yogurt, originally a Middle Eastern food, is a semisolid fermented milk food, characterized by a smooth texture and slightly sour taste. It is traditionally made from goats' milk by a process of fermentation in which a small amount of yogurt from a previous batch is used to start a new ferment. Most commercial yogurt [1] is usually made from cow's milk and dried milk solids, which are fermented with cultured bacteria. Yogurt's lactic-acid content is believed by many to make it a valuable aid to digestion.

KEY

Unhygienic dairies of the early 19th century bear little resemblance to the clean, sanitary plants established as a result of improved technology and strictly enforced health laws.

5

5 Health laws have altered the quality of cheeses, but the best ones are still made by traditional methods. Here, Roquefort is matured in caves to induce the "blueing" caused by bacteria.

6

6 Factory-produced cheeses are easily stored and marketed. They are made in large molds, then cut up and vacuum packed. Hygienic conditions tend to produce somewhat tasteless cheeses.

7

PROVOLONE
GALBANI
DANISH BLUE CHEESE
DANABLU DANMARK
DOLCELATTE
Galbani

7 Many cheeses are instantly recognizable by their distinctive appearance. Some of the more famous cheeses are illustrated here.

1 Provolone
2 Parmesan
3 Samsoe
4 Edam
5 Gouda
6 Mimolette
7 Blue Cheshire
8 Fontina (Danish)
9 Stilton
10 Cheddar (Canadian)
11 Gloucester
12 Cheddar (English)
13 White Wensleydale
14 Ricotta
15 Bleu de Bresse
16 Dunlop
17 Mozzarella
18 Jaalsberg
19 Danish Blue
20 Caciocavallo
21 Leicester
22 Feta
23 Fontina (Italian)
24 Gruyère
25 Monterey Jack
26 Tome au Raisin
27 Lancashire
28 Caerphilly
29 Edelpilzkäse
30 Limburger
31 St Nectaire
32 New England Sage
33 Red Windsor
34 Brick
35 Port Salut
36 Gorgonzola
37 Vacherin
38 Epoisses
39 Emmenthal
40 Dolcelatte
41 Tilsiter
42 Pont l'Evêque
43 Livarot
44 Quargel
45 Roquefort
46 Banon
47 St Marcellin
48 Camembert
49 Münster
50 Brie
51 Bel Paese
52 Maroilles

Pigs and sheep

Throughout the world pigs and sheep exist as both wild and domesticated animals. Wild pigs are largely found in damp, open woodlands in the Old World from northern Europe to Southeast Asia. Wild sheep live in mountainous regions of Asia, North America, and the Mediterranean, but the many different breeds of domesticated sheep thrive in nearly all habitats.

Pig breeding

The pig is one of nature's most efficient and omnivorous scavengers. The first records of the domestication of the pig—a very efficient provider of meat—date back to about 4000 BC in Southeast Asia from where it spread to China and the Middle East. The wild boar was domesticated independently in Europe in about 3000 BC.

More recently pig breeders have concentrated on producing animals with the ability to convert feed into lean meat rather than unwanted fat and on rearing females capable of giving birth to larger litters. Today's "improved" females are ready to breed when they are 7 to 8 months old and will produce litters of more than 10 piglets within 16 weeks of conception. If properly fed, managed, and housed, a healthy sow will produce more than 20 piglets a year.

Before being slaughtered piglets are fed varying amounts of food. These depend on the different market requirements—fresh pork, cured bacon and hams, and a wide variety of processed foods such as sausages, pies, and canned meat products [2]. For pork and bacon production today the hog growers and packers demand meat-type hogs. Lard breeds are no longer in demand. Most commercial pigs are now crossbreeds or planned hybrids between two or three pure breeds.

Pig rearing and pork production

It is a popular misconception that pigs are dirty animals. Given well-planned living conditions pigs will keep themselves cleaner than most other domestic animals. But if they are crowded together in pens that do not provide easily identified sleeping and eating areas their natural preference for cleanliness is upset. In hot conditions pigs always need water in which to cool themselves because they have few, and inefficient, sweat glands. The pig uses its snout to forage for food and a large herd of pigs kept on free range will quickly turn a wet field of grass into a sea of mud. But good grass and forage root crops can provide adult breeding pigs with a large proportion of their diet, and open air pig-keeping methods are still popular and profitable in areas where the climate is mild and the soil free-draining. Because pigs dislike extremes of heat and cold most farmers now keep fattening pigs in intensive housing conditions. Well-designed pig houses are equipped with mechanical feeders and manure disposers designed to provide maximum comfort and encourage rapid growth rates on scientifically balanced rations [4]. In such conditions well-bred pigs will reach market weight of 180 to 220 pounds at approximately five to six months of age. Pigs are slaughtered at various weights depending on their use as either meat or bacon. Pigs have become big business in the form of large factory-scale units. Some of the largest such

CONNECTIONS

See also
370 Farm stockbreeding and management
308 The farming corporation
310 Farm machinery and buildings
380 Pork, ham, sausages, and processed meats
378 Cuts of meat

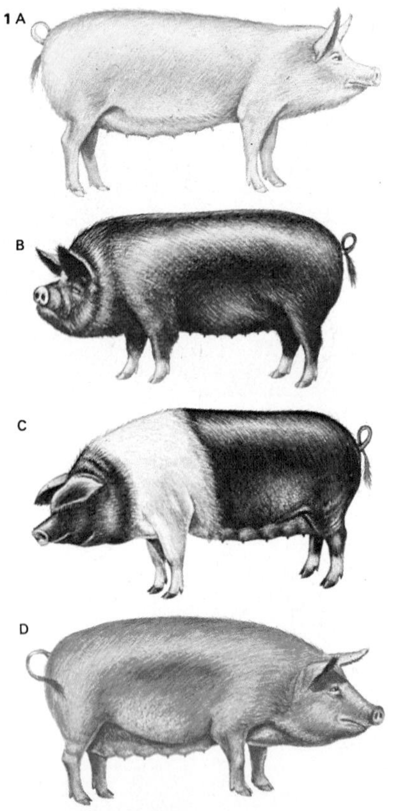

1 A
B
C
D

E
F
G
H

1 Purebred pigs vary widely in the quality of meat that they produce. The Large White [A], known as the Yorkshire in countries where it has been imported, is the predominant pure breed in Britain and popular in the United States. The Berkshire [B] has not been as popular as some breeds in the United States but is used to some degree in both purebred and commercial operations. The Hampshire [C], with its characteristic white belt, has been widely used in crossbreeding programs. The sandy colored Tamworth [D], originally a forest pig, is now a minor breed in North America and Britain. Different types of Landrace pigs [E] have made an impact in the United States. Most famous is the Danish type, bred specifically for lean bacon. Poland China [F] and Chester White [G] pigs are popular US breeds along with the long red Duroc [H].

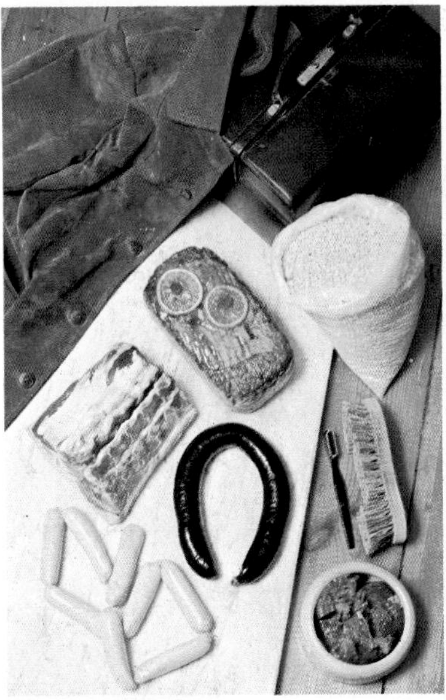

2 Processors of pork products claim that "nothing is wasted but the squeal." Pig meat is used in a wide variety of ways, including fresh pork and cured ham and bacon. The less desirable cuts are incorporated in loaves and sausages and the congealed blood in puddings. Pig bristle is used for a variety of brushes and the hide is used for gelatin or converted to a variety of leather goods.

3 Pigs have played an important part in human culture, from the "unclean" animal of Islamic and Jewish cultures to being the most common meat provider in China and a member of the family in parts of Melanesia. Many Oceanic tribes measure wealth in terms of the number of pigs owned. They are reluctant to eat them. In the United States pig raising is an important food production industry. Here members of a 4-H club learn proper care and handling.

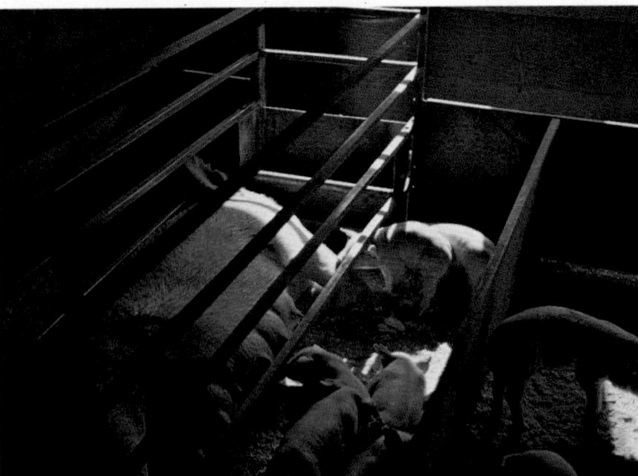

4 A modern pig farm ensures that its animals are fed carefully balanced rations. The trend toward scientific pig feeding has been accelerated by rearing to meet the human demand for low-fat pork and bacon. In the wild pigs are efficient scavengers and their natural diet consists of roots, fallen fruits, and nuts. And although pigs are valuable recyclers of domestic table refuse and other waste foods, today's pigs require controlled diets.

units are to be found in the corn belt area, especially in Iowa, Illinois and Indiana. The main risk of factory-scale pig production is disease, which can travel quickly through large intensive units.

Sheep for wool and meat

Sheep are multipurpose animals [8] that were first domesticated about 8,000 years ago but were not bred for their fleece until a thousand years later. The wealth of medieval England was built on sheep kept for their wool, but today's largest sheep producing nations are Australia and New Zealand. Spanish Merinos were taken to Australia from Europe and fine Australian Merino wool is still considered to be the best in the world. Purebred Merino flocks are still important in Australia, but breeders have introduced other stock to improve meat content at the expense of wool quality.

In New Zealand, wool takes second place to meat production. Crosses between the English Romney and Border Leicester breeds have helped establish a thriving market lamb export trade [7].

Sheep have evolved in different ways in different countries. The Finnish Landrace and Russian Romanov breeds are noted for their ability to produce twins, triplets, and even quints. Breeders in the United States and Europe are beginning the use these breeds to increase production in their sheep flocks. Texel sheep from the Netherlands, which produce compact carcasses, are also being used in crossing programs in Europe to boost meat yield and quality.

The British breeds of sheep show more variation than in most other countries and there are sound geographic reasons for this. Hardy upland breeds, including the Scottish Blackface, Cheviot, Swaledale, and Welsh Mountain, thrive on high rough grazings unsuited to cattle and crop production; at intermediate and lowland levels crossbred sheep are preferred. A popular crossbred ewe is obtained by crossing the small hill ewes with larger longwool breeds such as the Border Leicester. This ewe is in turn often crossed with a lowland ram like the Suffolk or Dorset Down to produce early maturing market lambs.

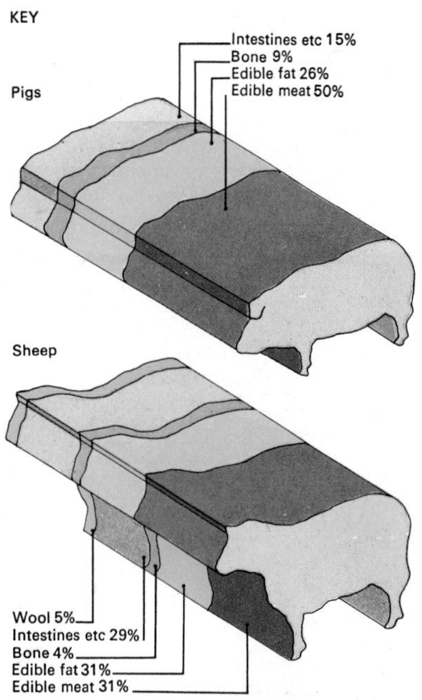
KEY
Pigs
Intestines etc 15%
Bone 9%
Edible fat 26%
Edible meat 50%
Sheep
Wool 5%
Intestines etc 29%
Bone 4%
Edible fat 31%
Edible meat 31%

Domestic breeds of pigs and sheep are constantly being improved by selective breeding to increase the proportion of usable parts of the carcass. Efficiency at converting food into meat is a prime consideration in pig-breeding, but sow productivity and the viability of a litter are also important. There are hundreds of breeds of sheep, mostly bred for a particular characteristic, such as wool, meat, or milk, and so it is difficult to give a breakdown of the weight of an average sheep. Many sheep, however, are bred for a number of different purposes and a multipurpose sheep can show a compromise between high meat and wool production.

5
A
B
C
D
E
F
G
H

5 Many sheep breeds have been based on European breeds such as those illustrated here. Merinos [A], originally bred in Spain, are famed worldwide for the fine quality of their wool. Karakul sheep [B] are the source of Persian lamb. Dutch Texels [C] produce heavy white fleece and are used in crossing programs for their compact carcasses. Blackface sheep [D] are native to Scotland and noted for their hardiness and quality mutton; their fleece is used to make tweed and carpets. Welsh Mountain sheep [E] are lighter and smaller but thrive on their native hills. Borders [G] are also hardy. English Romneys [F], crossed with Leicesters, helped found the New Zealand export trade. The Suffolk [H], which originated from crosses of Norfolk Horn ewes and Southdown rams, is a popular crossing ram for market lamb production.

6

6 High-speed mechanical sheep-shearing methods were pioneered in Australia and New Zealand. On large stations with small staffs they are a necessity. Efficient facilities for holding large numbers of sheep and presenting them for shearing are essential for the skilled worker to achieve maximum output. To meet seasonal needs, contract shearers serve many large farms.

7

7 Fertile soils and an equable climate make New Zealand an excellent country for intensive sheep husbandry on hills and lowlands. Crossbred stock produce market lambs – mainly for export and wool.

8 Sheep provide meat and wool plus milk and a wide variety of manufactured products. Hides are used for coats, hats, and gloves, for book bindings and bags. Parchment, an early type of writing paper, was made of untanned sheep hide.

8

Cuts of meat

Most meat eaten in the Western world is bought cut and prepared from meat markets or supermarkets, although with the increasing availability of domestic freezers many people now buy half or quarter carcasses and prepare the meat themselves. This costs less and saves time in shopping.

Commercial butchering

Meat is, broadly, beef, veal, mutton, lamb, and pork. After an animal has been slaughtered, the edible viscera and organs are removed to be sold separately as variety meats (liver, kidneys, heart, tongue, brains, and so on). Some organs are used in processed meats or as pet food. Some variety meats are highly nutritious but are unappetizing to many people. Liver and kidneys, in particular, supply protein, vitamins, and many of the minerals and trace elements essential to a proper diet.

Brains and sweetbreads—the thymus—are easily digested and are excellent as the basis for restorative meals for invalids. Tripe needs special attention—blanching and scrubbing—but that is normally done by the packer. The classic dish tripes à la mode de Caen is simmered in a very low oven for 24 hours. Beef and lamb tongue is usually boiled.

All meat, with the exception of pork and veal, benefits from aging, or hanging, a matter of literally hanging the carcass for a few days under refrigeration while enzymes break down connective tissue and make the meat tender. The process, which takes about a week for lamb and mutton and about two weeks for beef, also improves flavor.

Meat cutting and hanging

Butchers prepare meat to produce cuts that will command the best prices. Most people equate quality with tenderness (although in fact some less tender cuts carry more flavor). Hindquarters of beef, legs of lamb and pork, and lamb chops are preferred.

Beef should be bright cherry red in color, firm, fine-grained, and marbled with streaks of fat. The outside fat should be a rich cream in color and slightly crumbly.

Veal [2], the meat of calves less than 12 weeks of age, is rarely aged. Its characteristic pale color is caused by lack of muscle pigment, which is more concentrated in older animals. The flesh should be plump, fine-grained, and soft and velvety in texture.

Mutton is considered best when the sheep is at least two years old before it is killed. It is a highly flavored meat much enjoyed in Great Britain but not popular in the United States. It should be red with white fat and firm, fine-grained flesh. As mutton may be tough, it should be marinated before it is cooked to avoid dryness.

Lamb refers to sheep less than 12 months old. It is very tender and, because of its relatively high fat content, easily cooked. Lamb is popular throughout the world, especially around the Mediterranean basin. Very young milk-fed lamb is regarded as a great delicacy. Lamb is popular because of its tenderness, the ease with which it is cooked, and its flavor. Much lamb is exported by Australia and New Zealand.

Lamb is at its best when the animal is between three and five months old [5]. It should be plump and light pink in color, with fine, hard, opaline fat.

CONNECTIONS

See also
380 Pork, ham, sausage, and processed meats
372 Cattle for beef and milk
376 Pigs and sheep

1 Beef is preferred by the Western world to almost all other meat. In the United States the annual per capita beef consumption is approximately 110 lbs vs. 65 lbs for pork and 3 to 5 lbs each for lamb and veal. The classic English dish is roast beef with Yorkshire pudding, a batter cooked around and under the roast. The tradition of eating roast beef on Sunday began in the last century.

1 Brisket: used for pot roasts or corned beef
2 Shoulder and neck: the basis for stews, casseroles and curries
3 Ribs: roasted or cut into steaks for broiling
4 Loin: makes the best steaks and roasts including fillet, porterhouse and T-bone
5 Top round and bottom round: cut from the round end and roasted, steaked, or salted
6 Rump steak: highly flavored; best grilled or roasted whole
7 Cuts from the flanks: used for flank steak; trimmings are used for ground beef
8 Shin of beef: stewed, casseroled or minced
9 Cow heel: boiled to provide aspic, a clear jelly

2 Veal is far more popular in Europe, especially Italy and Germany, than in the United States. It is a tender meat.

1 Breast of veal: can be pot roasted, braised or boiled
2 Shoulder: usually boned, stuffed and roasted
3 Neck: used for pies stews and goulashes
4 Middle neck cuts: best pot roasted or braised
5 Cutlets: from the best end of the neck
6 Loin: best roasted or cut into chops
7 Fillet: provides the tenderest and tastiest portions
8 Leg: can provide an excellent roast although it is far better when thinly sliced into escallopes and fried or grilled
9 Knuckle: makes excellent fricassees and casseroles

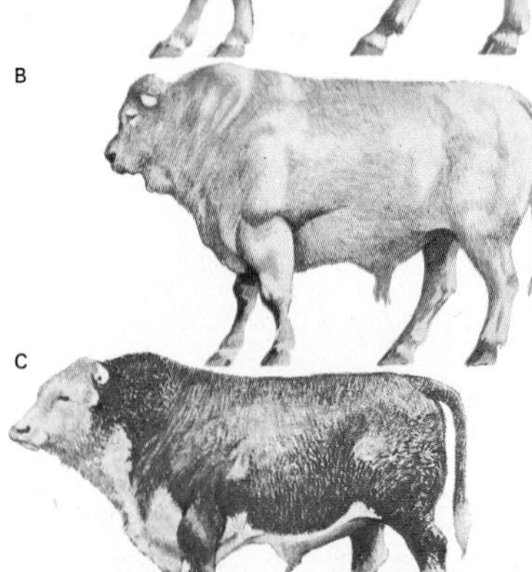
3 A
B
C

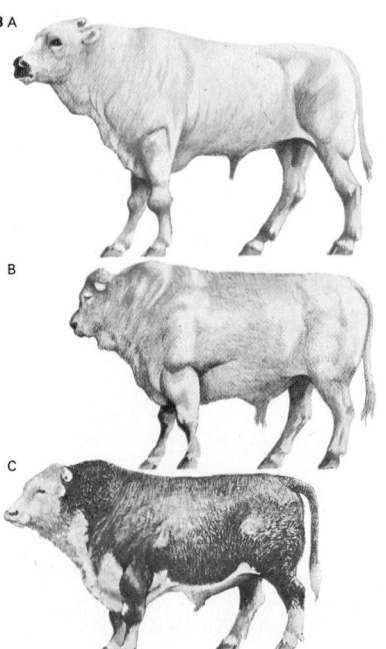

3 The oldest recognized breed of cattle and the heaviest, is the Italian Chianina [A]. Bred in Tuscany since ancient times, the Chianina grows fast and is slaughtered at an earlier age than other cattle. The finest French beef cattle are the white Charolais [B], named after the area in Burgundy where they originated. They are always fed on grass and as a result their meat is extremely lean and yet tender. White-faced Herefords [C] are the result of generations of breeding by cattle farmers in Hereford, England. The breed has been exported all over the world, principally to the United States, Canada, South America, and Australia.

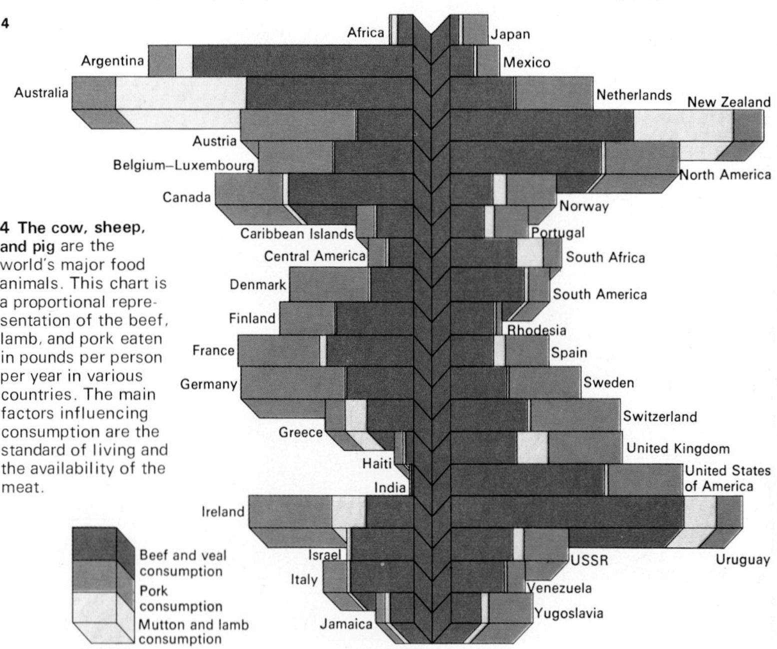
4
Africa
Japan
Argentina
Mexico
Australia
Netherlands
New Zealand
Austria
Belgium–Luxembourg
North America
Canada
Norway
Caribbean Islands
Portugal
Central America
South Africa
Denmark
South America
Finland
Rhodesia
France
Spain
Germany
Sweden
Switzerland
Greece
United Kingdom
Haiti
United States of America
India
Ireland
Israel
USSR
Uruguay
Italy
Venezuela
Jamaica
Yugoslavia
Beef and veal consumption
Pork consumption
Mutton and lamb consumption

4 The cow, sheep, and pig are the world's major food animals. This chart is a proportional representation of the beef, lamb, and pork eaten in pounds per person per year in various countries. The main factors influencing consumption are the standard of living and the availability of the meat.

Pork, a good source of protein and vitamin B, must be carefully chosen, not kept too long, and well cooked to eliminate the danger of trichinosis. The meat should be pale pink, lean, with white, firm fat, and have a thin skin. It should yield to pressure, springing back readily. Pork is safe to eat provided it is kept refrigerated and clean and is thoroughly cooked. If the meat still looks raw after it has been cooked, it should be more adequately cooked or avoided.

Cooking meat

Meat is often wiped with a damp cloth before it is cooked, and surplus fat removed. The most common methods of cooking meat are (1) dry heat cookery, such as oven- or pan-broiling and roasting or baking, and (2) moist heat cookery, as in simmering or stewing and braising. Pan-frying combines the two methods.

The less tender portions of meat can often be improved by marinating before cooking. A marinade—an inexpensive one can be made of onions, water, and vinegar—breaks down the connective tissue and gives the meat greater tenderness and flavor. The best marinades are made from brandy, wine, and herbs.

Roasting is done in an oven (wrapping the meat in aluminum foil helps seal in the flavor and prevents splattering of the oven; the meat is basted with its own juices). Small roasts may get dry, and a glass of wine or meat stock is often added to them halfway through the cooking process.

Pot roasting is a method of cooking a roast in a heavy closed pan on an open element. The meat is first seared by browning in a frying pan and then placed in the saucepan with the fat yielded by the frying. It is then left to cook normally in its own juices.

Stewing and braising are similar—the meat is cut into pieces and cooked in water—but when it is to be braised it is first seared in a frying pan. Meat may be stewed or braised with vegetables, for a casserole.

Only the most tender cuts of meat should be roasted, broiled, or fried. Steaks, whether grilled or fried, should be done quickly to preserve the natural juices.

KEY

A B C D

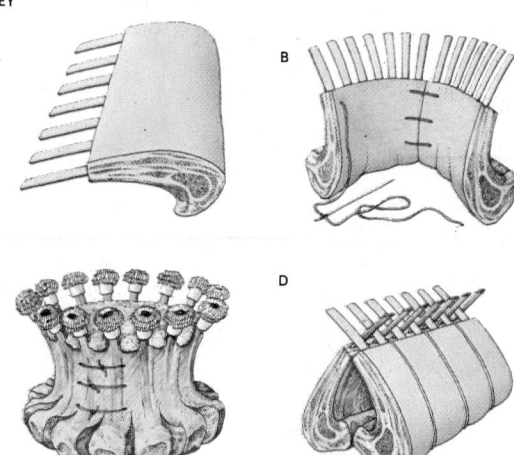

Crown roast [C] and Guard of Honor [D] are elegant ways of preparing a traditional roast. The starting point for both is the full rack or rib section, with the ribs "frenched" [A]. To make the crown roast, the two ends are stitched together [B] and the center stuffed; to make the Guard of Honor, the racks are interlocked and the hollow stuffed.

5

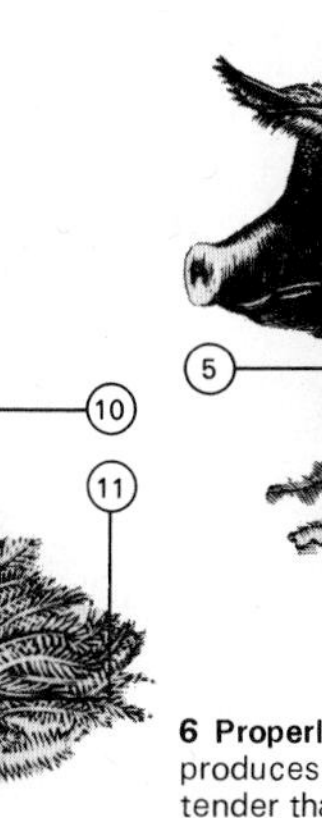

5 Lamb is immensely popular in the Middle East, where it is often cooked on a spit over an open fire. It benefits from the use of herbs; the tradition of serving it with mint sauce is an Arab innovation. Three-month-old lamb is the tastiest.

1 Breast of lamb: though fatty, it is succulent; it is usually roasted after being boned and stuffed
2 Shoulder: often roasted whole but can be boned and stuffed
3 Head: used as a basis for stock, broths and soup
4 Neck: best stewed or casseroled
5 Middle neck cuts excellent for braising but can be grilled
6 Best end of neck: cut into chops or roasted whole
7 Top loin: prime roasting meat which can be spit-roasted whole
8 Loin: usually cut into chops but can also be roasted
9 Leg: roasted whole or cubed for shish kebab
10 Shank: usually sold with the leg: even though mainly bone, the meat portions have a pronounced flavor
11 Lamb's trotters: can be boiled to provide thickening for gravies and sauces or slowly baked for eating

6

6 Properly fed pork produces a meat so tender that nearly all the carcass can be roasted or fried. A great delicacy is roast suckling pig. Young pigs are often roasted whole with herb stuffing.

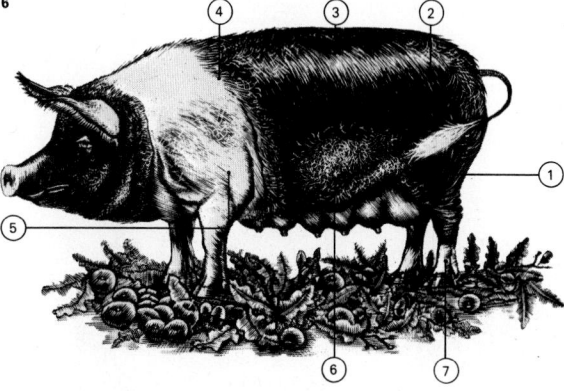

1 Ham: usually roasted and the skin scorched so that crackling forms
2 Loin: can be roasted or cut into chops and fried, baked or broiled
3 Foreloin: best roasted whole or cut into chops
4 Spare ribs: grilled, fried or braised
5 Shoulder: casseroled whole or boiled
6 Bacon or side-cured: smoked and sliced for bacon
7 Hocks and feet: still considered a great delicacy, they are boiled and can be served either hot or cold or used to flavor casseroles and pâtés

7 A

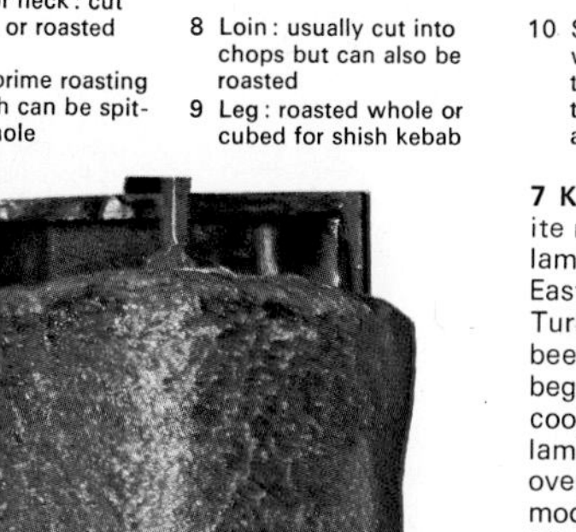

B

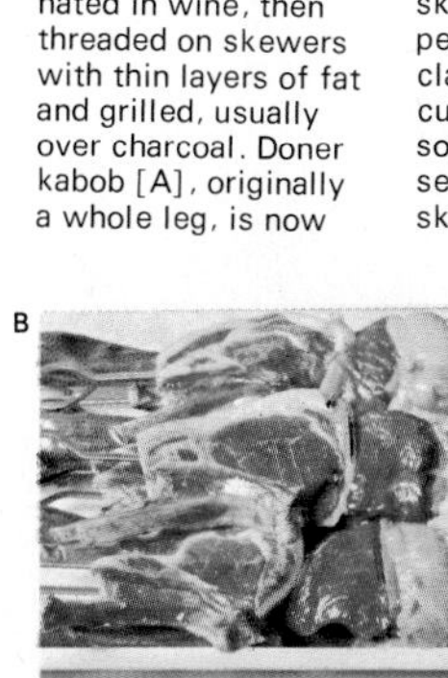

7 Kabobs are a favorite method of serving lamb in the Middle East. The word is Turkish for "cooked beef." The tradition began when soldiers cooked freshly killed lamb on their swords over open fires. In modern shish kabob [B] the meat is marinated in wine, then threaded on skewers with thin layers of fat and grilled, usually over charcoal. Doner kabob [A], originally a whole leg, is now often minced lamb mixed with herbs into the shape of a leg. It is roasted on a vertical spit and then sliced. Kabobs are usually served with rice and raw vegetable salads. Lamb, veal, and pigs' kidneys are also excellent when cooked on skewers with peppers and onions. In classical French cuisine they are soaked in brandy and served flaming on a skewer at the table.

8

8 Goats are bred mainly in countries where the pasture is too poor for sheep; the desert areas of the Middle East, for example, and the mountainous regions of Greece and the Balkans. Old goat needs long cooking; indeed, many recipes suggest slow simmering overnight. Very young kid can be sweet and tender and is often roasted whole, like suckling pig. In the Middle East, kid is a great delicacy and is often stuffed with rice, raisins, and nuts. The goat has been a general purpose animal, providing both meat and milk.

Pork, ham, sausages, and processed meats

Pork, the fresh meat of the domestic pig, is one of the most popular and certainly one of the most versatile of meats. High in protein and a good source of the B vitamins (thiamin, niacin, riboflavin) pork products are highly nutritious. The pig was first domesticated in Southeast Asia in about 4000 BC and its omnivorous habits and undemanding nature make it a relatively easy animal to rear. It produces more edible meat per unit of carcass weight than most other food animals and, in spite of its proscription under Judaic and Islamic law (which consider it unclean), it has long been a staple of Western and Eastern cuisines.

Curing pork

Pork may be eaten fresh or cured. Great care must be taken when cooking fresh pork; it should never be eaten rare (underdone) because the larvae of the parasite *Trichinella spiralis* can infest pork meat in temperate climates and can be killed for certain only by long, slow cooking.

The best cured pork comes from the prime parts of the pig—the hind legs, or hams [1], and the loin. The curing of pork is an ancient process that began in Roman times or even earlier and its purpose was to preserve the meat for the winter. The comparatively recent introduction of winter feed for the animals, and of refrigeration as a means of storage, have lessened the need for curing as a method of preservation. Flavor is now a main reason for curing. The ham is removed from the pork carcass and is cured, wet or dry, usually in salt or in brine, often with sugar or sometimes molasses or maple syrup. The cured meat may then be smoked with various hardwoods. Regional favorites, such as Irish hams, are smoked over peat, which gives them a very distinctive taste. Nutrition plays an important part in the ultimate flavor of the specialty hams—pigs from Parma, Italy are fed on parsnips, Virginia pigs on peanuts and peaches, and Kentucky pigs on wild acorns, beans, and clover. Some of the world's most famous hams, including *Bayonne, Parma,* and *Westphalia,* may be eaten uncooked. Lesser-known German, French, and Polish country hams such as *Lachsschinken* and *Losoiowa* can also be eaten raw. Other fine hams, such as Prague ham, *Pražská šunka,* are cured, smoked and left to mature in preparation for final cooking.

Bacon comes from the belly (side) of the pork carcass and is cured in brine or dry cured. It may be bought smoked or unsmoked ("green"). In the United States cured, smoked bacon is generally sold sliced and packaged but may be merchandised "slab" or "chunk" style. Scandinavian countries, particularly Denmark, have long specialized in the intensive production of high-grade lean bacon, primarily for export. The pigs are especially bred for this purpose and both age and breeding play an important role in the quality of the final product.

"Little bags of mystery"

Pork is also the basic ingredient of many types of sausage [3]. The origins of this food (the word derives from the Latin *salsus,* meaning salted) are obscure, and the earliest references to its consumption appear in

CONNECTIONS

See also
378 Cuts of meat
376 Pigs and sheep
372 Cattle for beef and milk

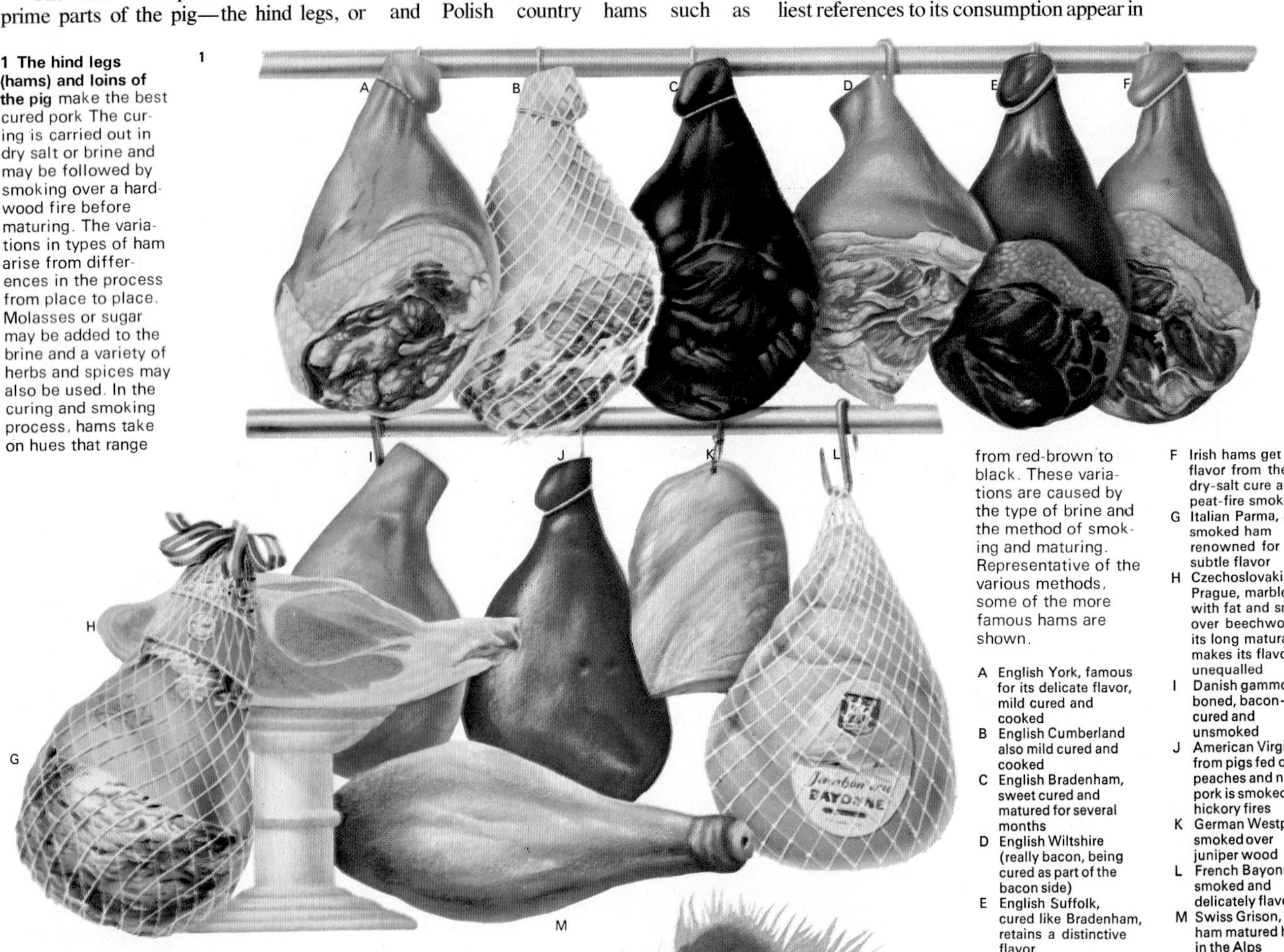

1
A
B
C
D
E
F
G
H
I
J
K
L
M
BAYONNE

1 The hind legs (hams) and loins of the pig make the best cured pork The curing is carried out in dry salt or brine and may be followed by smoking over a hardwood fire before maturing. The variations in types of ham arise from differences in the process from place to place. Molasses or sugar may be added to the brine and a variety of herbs and spices may also be used. In the curing and smoking process, hams take on hues that range from red-brown to black. These variations are caused by the type of brine and the method of smoking and maturing. Representative of the various methods, some of the more famous hams are shown.

A English York, famous for its delicate flavor, mild cured and cooked
B English Cumberland also mild cured and cooked
C English Bradenham, sweet cured and matured for several months
D English Wiltshire (really bacon, being cured as part of the bacon side)
E English Suffolk, cured like Bradenham, retains a distinctive flavor
F Irish hams get their flavor from the dry-salt cure and peat-fire smoking
G Italian Parma, a raw smoked ham renowned for its subtle flavor
H Czechoslovakian Prague, marbled with fat and smoked over beechwood fires: its long maturation makes its flavor unequalled
I Danish gammon, boned, bacon-cured and unsmoked
J American Virginia, from pigs fed on peaches and nuts; the pork is smoked over hickory fires
K German Westphalian, smoked over juniper wood
L French Bayonne, smoked and delicately flavoured
M Swiss Grison, a raw ham matured high in the Alps

2

2 The wild boar of Europe *(Sus scrofa)* and that of Asia *(S. vittatis)* are the direct ancestors of modern domestic swine breeds. Wild boars are extinct in Britain because of over-hunting and the loss of the forests, but they can still be found throughout Europe and Asia. They were introduced into North America and can today be found in the Appalachians. The boar is still hunted for game, usually with dogs. In France the flesh of the *marcassin* (a term for a wild boar up to six months old) is considered a great delicacy. Pigs were first domesticated in Southeast Asia and today there are two main varieties—the long-backed Chinese pig and its heavier cousin, the European variety.

Homer's *Odyssey*. In the Middle Ages the plain, rather humble sausages of classical times were transformed, by the use of mixed meats and exotic flavorings and spices, into the forerunner of today's products. Known rather derisively in Victorian times as "little bags of mystery," sausages consist of a filling of chopped or minced meat or meats, plus seasonings, preservatives, and sometimes cereal and dried milk products, all stuffed either in an edible casing made from the animal's intestine or into cellulose casings, later to be removed. Sausages may be divided into two main categories. The "dry" sausages, or *charcuterie* (from the French *chair cuite,* meaning cooked meat of the pig) are ready to eat. They include the ubiquitous *salami,* traditionally made from pork meat and lard, although Hungarian *salami* should contain donkey meat; Italian *mortadella,* which is often studded with pistachio nuts; and various types of liver and garlic sausages. The second type of sausage, known as "wet," must first be cooked. Wet sausages include the German *Frankfurter* and *Bratwurst,* Italian *zampone* (encased in the skin from a pig's trotter), Spanish *chorizo,* the famous *saucisson de Toulouse* from France, and regional specialties, such as the haggis from Scotland, blood or black puddings from France, Germany, and Britain.

The sausage, which began as one of the world's first convenience foods and a means of using up odd scraps of meat, now occupies an important and integral part of international cuisine.

The pig stripped bare

The fact that there is very little wastage from the carcass of a pig has contributed to its worldwide popularity and exploitation as a food animal. Liver, heart, tongue, and brains are all sold as delicacies. Trotters, snouts, heads, tails, ears, and chitterlings (small intestines), although in declining demand, are still widely bought for human consumption. Pig skin is used for leatherwork, such as handbags and wallets, as well as for making gelatin. Pork fat is rendered to make lard, and bones are ground for animal feed or fertilizer.

KEY

In a medieval print a swineherd knocks down acorns for fodder. Pigs have been reared in Europe from *c.* 3000 BC.

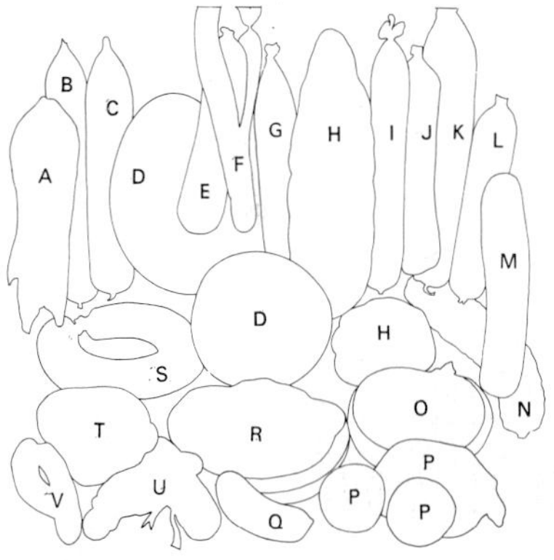

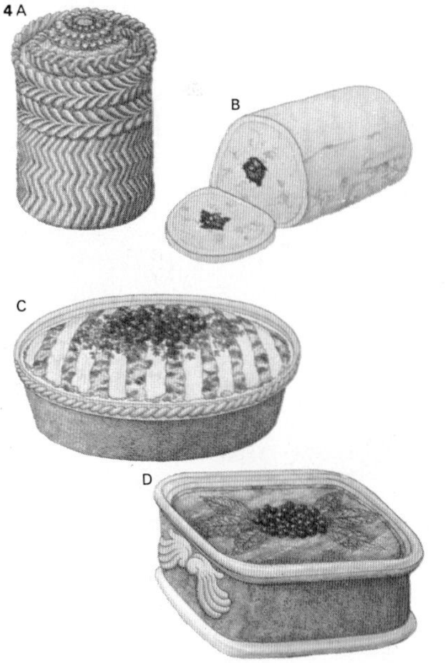

3 Sausages made from chopped meat mixed with other foods and stuffed into a casing, are part of a culinary tradition that is centuries old and stretches back to ancient Greece, being mentioned in Homer's *Odyssey* in the 9th century BC. Pork is particularly suited to sausage-making and all parts of the pig can be used, including the liver (in *Leberwurst*) and the blood (in *boudin* or black pudding). Beef is often mixed with pork or may be used alone. Sausages are also made from other meats and even fish. Finally, sausage is a very convenient vehicle for the new "non-meat" proteins, such as soybean protein, either alone with a filler or mixed with traditional sausage meats. Some sausages are shown.

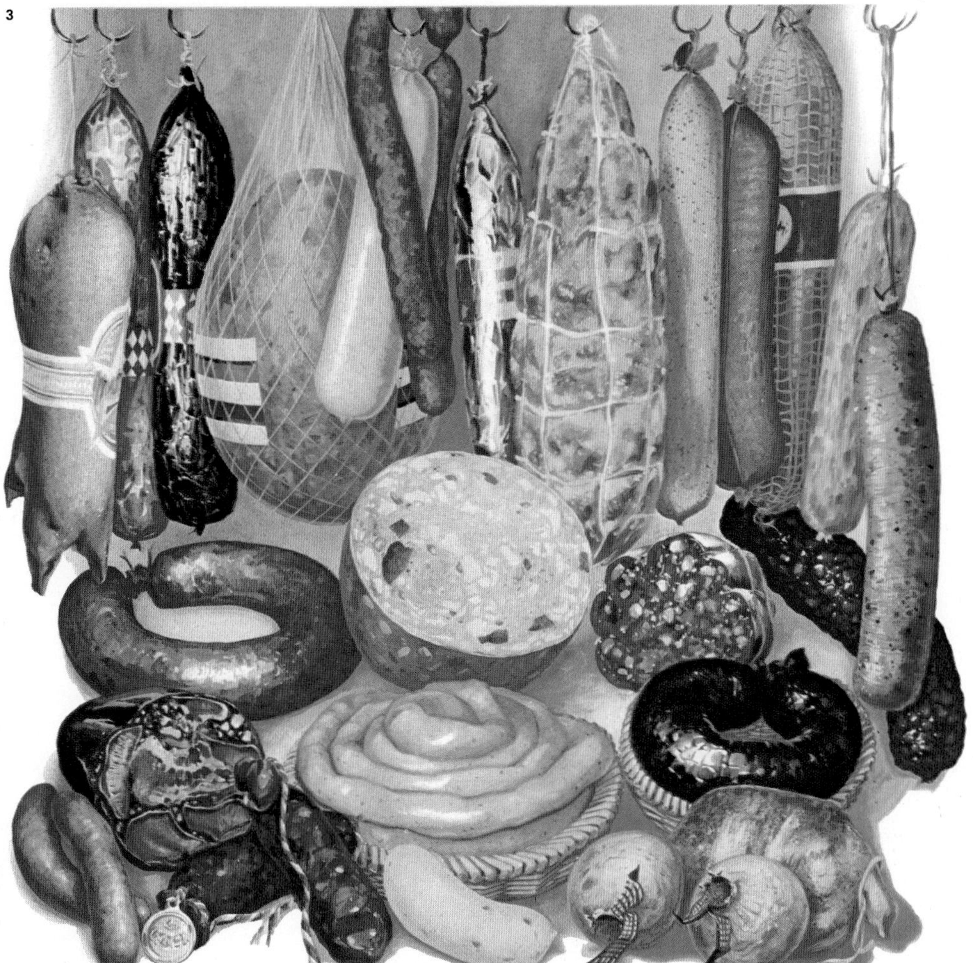

A Italian *zampone*
B Polish *krakowska*
C Polish *debowiecka*
D Italian *mortadella*
E German *Leberwurst*
F Polish *kabanosy*
G Italian *salami*
H French *saucisson sec*
I Hungarian *salami* with donkey meat
J German *cervelat*
K Italian *crespone*
L Italian *cotechino*
M German *Bratwurst*
N German *Mettwurst*
O French *boudin*
P Scottish *haggis*
Q French *boudin blanc*
R English *Cumberland sausage*
S Polish *wiankowa*
T German *Blut Zungerwurst*
U Spanish *chorizos*
V German *Frankfurter*

4 Pâtés are made of minced pork, veal, rabbit, game, or liver flavored with herbs, spices, and wine or brandy. A terrine is a pâté cooked and kept in an earthenware pot such as the hare pâté [A], the *pâté de campagne* [C], and the pheasant pâté [D]. The French *pâté de foie gras* [B] is made from the extra-rich and enlarged livers of force-fed geese and always includes large pieces of truffles. An even more exotic pâté is that made in New Caledonia from fruit bats.

Poultry and egg production

The modern trend throughout livestock farming is toward more intensive methods. In this, specialists in poultry have set the pace; since the 1920s poultry production has changed beyond recognition. Barnyard fowl have given way to egg and broiler factories controlled by a decreasing number of large, integrated organizations. The largest broiler chicken companies control their own feed production, house construction, slaughtering, and freezing plants, and many even have wholesale outlets.

As a result of the revolution in poultry raising, small chicken farmers who once made a comfortable living from 1,000 laying hens have been forced out of business. Poultry as a sideline, too, has been discontinued on many farms, except for direct sale of fresh eggs for which a premium must be charged to cover high production costs. The old-fashioned five- to six- month-old cock chicken reared outside on corn stubbles has been replaced by the broiler, a bird that is mass produced in controlled-environment houses. These birds are ready for market in 8 to 10 weeks. Turkey and duck farming is becoming equally intensive and today only small flocks of geese and some waterfowl and game birds are still produced in traditional open air range conditions.

Breeding poultry for profit

Among livestock, poultry were the first to receive serious attention from geneticists, who had discovered that planned cross-breeding of selected pure and inbred lines of plants could give dramatic increases in production. Tailor-made hybrids for egg and broiler chicken production quickly ousted the old pure breeds [1] such as the Rhode Island Red, White, Black and Brown Leghorns, Light Sussex, and crosses between them.

Hybrid poultry breeding [5] started seriously in the United States in the mid-1930s and today only a few small independent breeders are left. Poultry breeding for egg and broiler production is dominated by large international companies based in the United States and Canada. These organizations sell grandparent stock from their closely controlled breeding programs to licensed multiplier breeders and hatcheries farther down the production pyramid in many different countries. Royalties are charged on day-old chicks produced and these are then sold to commercial producers of eggs, broilers, and turkeys.

The genetic make-up of modern hybrids is changing all the time and most are now described purely by code name. They are advertised and sold on their performance specifications proved in trials [3]. These include eggs per bird, size and weight over a given period, and the ability to convert expensive balanced rations into eggs or poultry meat. Resistance or immunity to disease is also included in the sales specfication.

The technology of intensive rearing

The other reasons for the rapid changes in poultry farming methods lie in twentieth-century technology. The development of the incubator to replace the mother hen sitting her seasonal clutch of eggs was the first major step toward factory farming of poultry [2]. Artificial incubation led to an immediate increase in egg production.

CONNECTIONS

See also
308 The farming corporation
370 Farm stockbreeding and management
384 Poultry and game
528 The anatomy of birds
530 How birds reproduce

1

A Australorp
B Cornish
C Dorking
D Leghorn
E New Hampshire
F Plymouth Rock
G Rhode Island Red
H Light Sussex

1 Commercial hybrid poultry, bred specifically for eggs or meat, are descended from a variety of pure breeding birds. The most productive egg-laying strains have been derived from Leghorns and Rhode Island Reds. Pure White, Brown, or Black Leghorns are lightweight birds. The object in the breeding of table chickens is efficient food conversion and rapid growth, plus the maximum amount of leg and breast meat. Today's broilers are based on heavier, less active breeds like the New Hampshire, Plymouth Rock, and Light Sussex. The Dorking and Cornish are old English meat breeds; the Australorp is a new Australian strain.

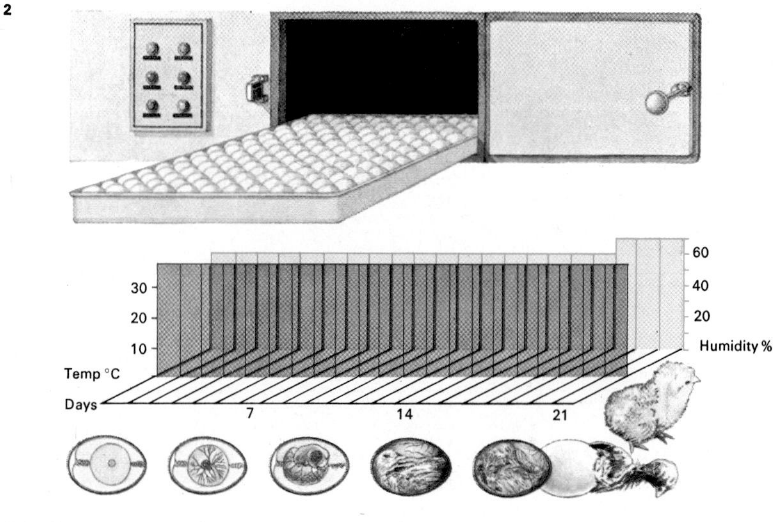

2

Temp °C
10
20
30
Humidity %
20
40
60
Days
7
14
21

2 Mechanical incubation of fertile hens' eggs in heated and ventilated cabinets has transformed poultry production into an industry. Each egg is kept in the incubator for 21 days. A temperature of 99.75°F(37.65°C) is maintained. Humidity is kept at 60%, then raised to 70% for the last three days before hatching.

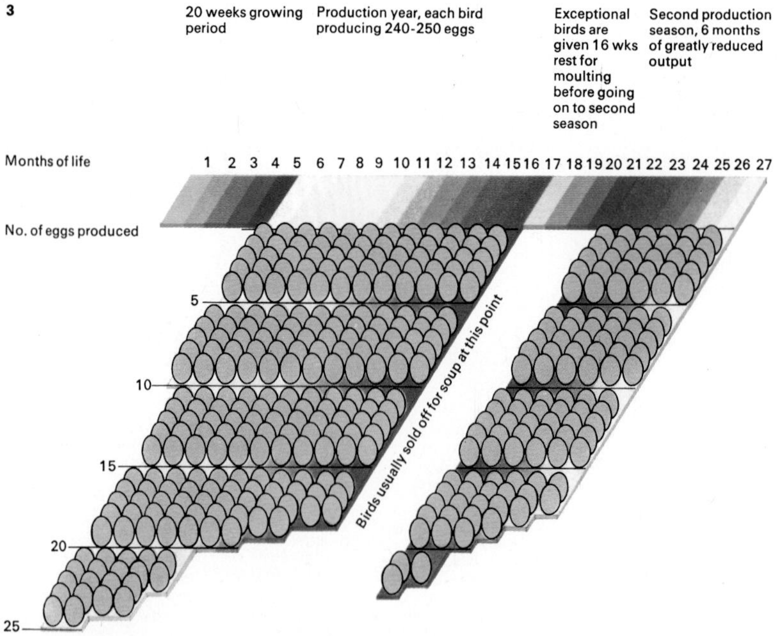

3

20 weeks growing period
Production year, each bird producing 240-250 eggs
Exceptional birds are given 16 wks rest for moulting before going on to second season
Second production season, 6 months of greatly reduced output
Months of life
1 2 3 4 5 6 7 8 9 10 11 12 13 14 15 16 17 18 19 20 21 22 23 24 25 26 27
No. of eggs produced
5
10
15
20
25
Birds usually sold off for soup at this point

3 Modern egg production is a highly intensive and carefully costed business. The efficiency of different laying strains is compared since producers need to know how long it takes different breeds and hybrids to grow to maturity, the number and sizes of eggs laid, and the amount of food needed to maintain the bird and produce the eggs. Most modern hybrid strains grow to maturity in about 20 weeks and are then kept in laying cages for approximately 12 months before they go into molt. During this period they produce 240–250 eggs. Occasionally they are allowed a second season – six months of greatly reduced output – but usually they are slaughtered.

Compared with other farm livestock the life cycle of poultry is short and the number of eggs and potential offspring produced is much higher. A modern hen reaching maturity in five months can lay well over 200 eggs a year. Fertile hen, duck, and turkey eggs can be moved long distances to a central incubator plant and carefully boxed day-old chicks then sent all over the world.

Except for waterfowl, most poultry lend themselves to highly intensive housing and production methods. Egg production was the first aspect to become intensive on a large scale and most laying birds are now housed in cages of different types. The latest laying cages have automatic feeding, watering, and egg collection. Waste droppings are removed mechanically from three or four tier cages, or allowed to build up in pits under single-tier flatdecks or staggered tiers of cages.

It has been proved that poultry, like plants, respond to variations in light length and intensity. Therefore, the light pattern for laying birds in windowless houses is gradually increased from the onset of laying to simulate a perpetual spring when birds in their natural state lay most eggs. Well insulated and fan-ventilated, humidity-controlled houses provide an even temperature and, in addition, artificial heat is used for replacement chick rearing and broiler chicken production. Most broilers are still produced on comfortably littered solid floors, but more controlled cage-rearing methods have appeared. The main drawback to wire-floored cages for table birds has been that they cause breast blisters.

The case for intensive methods

Intensive poultry-rearing methods, which have cut the cost and increased the efficiency of egg and poultry meat production and changed chicken meat from an expensive luxury to a competitively priced source of meat, are condemned as unnatural and cruel by advocates of more natural open range farming methods. Poultry producers claim, however, that their intensive methods must be meeting all the birds' comfort and nutritional requirements or production would suffer.

KEY

The days of the traditional farm where poultry survived on scraps from the kitchen and pickings from the farmyard have largely disappeared with the advent of intensive rearing methods. Today the poultry industry is based on large numbers of birds housed under one roof.

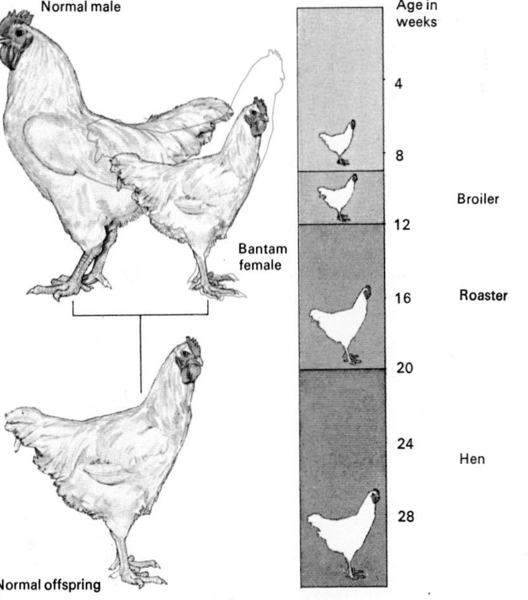
Normal male
Bantam female
Normal offspring
Age in weeks
4
8
12
16
20
24
28
Broiler
Roaster
Hen

4 Various techniques are used for breeding poultry. The female of a dwarf or bantam strain of White Plymouth Rock is economical on feed but when crossed with the male of a normal sized strain it produces normal sized offspring. Desirable traits in table birds include early feathering, which aids immediate sexing, and white plumage, which gives a cleaner carcass when the bird is dressed. A dressed bird can be marketed under different names according to its age when killed. A bird 9-12 weeks old is a broiler or fryer, from 12-20 weeks it is a roaster, and older than that it is a stewing bird.

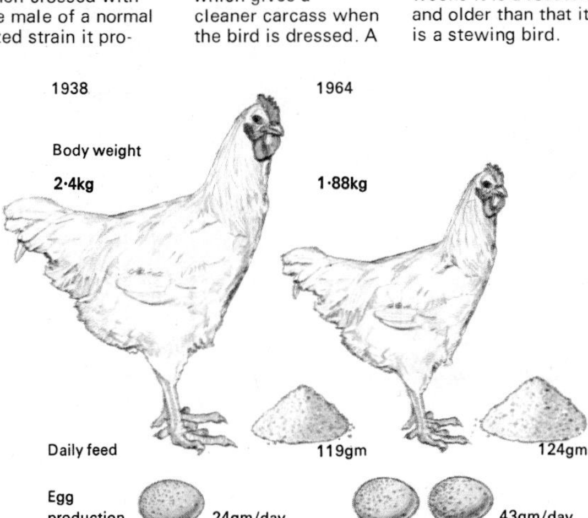
1938
1964
Body weight
2·4kg
1·88kg
Daily feed
119gm
124gm
Egg production
24gm/day
43gm/day

5 Increase in egg production has been dramatic since selective poultry breeding started in earnest in about 1945. The increase has been achieved by selecting smaller, more fertile hybrid layers. Although their eggs are smaller, the hens eat less food per egg produced than birds laying large eggs, and are twice as efficient at converting food into eggs compared with their ancestors. The feeding of scientifically balanced rations has also raised efficiency.

6
A
B
C
D
E
F
G
H
I
J
K
L
M
N
O
P

Geese
A Chinese
B Roman
C Egyptian
D Greylag
E Toulouse
F Embden

Ducks
G Buff Orpington
H Muscovy
I Khaki Campbell
J Aylesbury
K Pekin
L Indian Runner White
M Rouen

Turkeys
N Beltsville
O Broadbreasted Bronze
P Black Norfolk

6 Ducks and geese were domesticated over 3,000 years ago. Turkeys reached Europe in the 1500s.

Poultry and game

Today's most universally eaten meat is probably the domestic chicken, which is raised almost everywhere in the world, in places ranging from back yards to huge factories. The Romans bred chickens for the table and are reputed to have drowned the birds in red wine to impart a finer flavor. In the Middle Ages, chicken was fare fit for kings and lords only; the poor kept the birds for eggs and new chicks and killed a hen only when it became too old to lay eggs. Chicken [2A, 2B] is now one of the least expensive of all meats. Most chickens are bred and raised to be marketed as roasting birds, varying from tiny poussins to family-sized broilers.

Goose, turkey and duck

Goose [2C, 2D] was considered the finest poultry of all for festive occasions until ousted by the turkey in the sixteenth and seventeenth centuries. Roast goose was a favorite dish of Queen Elizabeth I and was traditional on Michaelmas Day, September 29. In Victorian days, goose was the principal Christmas bird, sometimes in the form of a Yorkshire speciality, goose pie, which consisted of a boned goose stuffed with smaller boned birds and encased in a rich pastry crust. In Scandinavia, Germany, and parts of France, goose is still eaten on festive occasions. The Strasbourg goose is especially fattened and the large liver used for *foie gras*; the meat is salted, cooked, and potted and the preserved meat, *confit d'oie*, keeps for several months.

Turkey [2E] was introduced to Europe from America in the sixteenth century. It quickly replaced goose in popularity because of its larger size and its firmer, less fatty meat. In Britain and North America it is now traditional at Christmas and weddings and in the United States also at Thanksgiving.

Duck [2H] is the most expensive type of poultry; it is difficult to breed under confinement conditions and the proportion of meat to bone is small. The French Rouen duckling is prepared and cooked with its own blood, which gives a special flavor and red color to the meat. Nantes duckling is plumper and the meat paler; it is often cooked *à l'orange*. Gourmets maintain that the Chinese methods of preparing and cooking duck, such as Peking and Szechwan duck, are superior to any other recipes. These involve spicing the exterior of the bird with honey and wind-drying it before roasting.

Game animals and birds

Quails and squabs are domesticated varieties of game birds and classified as such in many countries, notably the United States, France, and Italy. In Britain, quails [2F] for the table are imported frozen from Japan although a few farms are now producing them commercially. Squabs [2G] are a type of pigeon, bred to be eaten young while still tender.

Man's first food consisted of birds' eggs, roots, berries, and wild vegetables, a scant diet that he had to supplement by killing game animals. These included elephants, bison, moose [1A], reindeer, and wild pigs. As the nomadic existence in search of food was replaced by communitylife, with tilling of fields and breeding of cattle, game hunt-

CONNECTIONS

See also
382 Poultry and egg production

1
A
B
C
D
E
F
G
H
I
J
K
L
M
N
O
P
Q
R
S

1 Game animals and birds of the world include the moose of North America and northern Europe [A], one of the largest and rarest of game animals; the black bear [B]; the blackbuck [C], a typical antelope from India, prized for its meat and for trophies; the red deer or elk [D]; the wild boar [E]; such ground game as the rabbit [F] and the hare [G], different species of which are prolific throughout the world; the gray squirrel [H]; mallard duck [I], the largest of the wild ducks; the wild Canada goose [J]; the wild turkey [K], indigenous to North and Central America; the mourning dove [L], hunted in North America; partridge [M], woodcock [N], wild guinea fowl [O], and pheasant [P], regarded as the finest game birds; the golden plover [Q], now protected in many countries; the great bustard [R], one of the largest flying birds, found chiefly in Europe; and the lark [S], regarded as a delicacy in France, especially for pâtés.

ing became less important as a source of food, although furs and skins were still needed for clothing. But big game became scarcer and many of the original species are now extinct in many areas.

Red deer, called elk in North America, [1D] are still distributed throughout Europe, Asia, and North America. Deer meat is known as venison.

The wild boar [1E] no longer roams the dense forests of Europe as it did when it was the target of medieval royal hunts. The elaborately decorated boar's head, complete with polished tusks, rarely forms the centerpiece at banquets.

Venison and rare game birds remained the prerogatives of the rich, while the poor satisfied their craving for meat with wild rabbit [1F], hare [1G] and squirrel [1H], most often made into stews and pies.

In Europe and China, pheasant [1P] is the favorite and most expensive game bird; the meat of the hen is more tender than that of the cock, which is the larger bird and distinguished by its brilliant tail feathers. Partridge [1M], woodcock [1N], wild duck [1I], and guinea fowl [1O] are also popular. In most countries, game birds are protected by law during certain months of the year; they may not be killed in the so-called "closed" seasons. These vary from country to country and from state to state, but usually include nesting periods.

Hanging of game birds

All game—birds and mammals—should be hung for a time to tenderize the meat and develop the flavors. The hanging period depends on individual taste (some people prefer their game "high"), on the weather, and on the age of the game. Young game birds, best roasted and grilled, are hung for a shorter time (usually seven days) than older game, which is more suitable for casseroles.

Peacocks and swans are now prized for their ornamental features and not for the gastronomic qualities with which the Middle Ages endowed them. In most countries, small songbirds are protected by law, but in France they are not and the blackbird, lark [1S], and thrush are considered great delicacies.

KEY

This 19th-century engraving shows a busy English market day. The poulterer supplied whatever game was in season as well as chicken, duck, and giblets. The upper classes of the 18th and 19th centuries were prodigious eaters. A typical menu of the late 18th century included "A couple of rabbits smothered with onions, a neck of boiled mutton, and a goose roasted with currant pudding and a plain one".

2 Most popular chicken breeds like the White Leghorn [A] and Rhode Island red [B] are for table use and egg production; few chickens are free-range today, most being confinement-reared for expanding markets. Domestic geese, now in dwindling supply, include the Chinese goose [C], bred from the Siberian swan goose, and the Greylag goose [D]. The turkey [E] has replaced the goose in popularity and availability and is the traditional festive bird in Britain and North America. Quail [F] is a migratory bird coming to Europe from Africa for the summer, but the birds seen in poulterers' shops have been bred on poultry farms. The squab or dovecote pigeon [G] is a domesticated version of the wild species; it is becoming rare and consequently an expensive delicacy. Species of farmyard ducks vary from country to country; in Britain the Aylesbury duck [H] is the favorite breed, which, like the Pekin breed, is derived from the wild mallard.

2

Commercial fishing

The sea is a vast hunting ground for food for man. But fish are caught in commercial quantities in relatively small areas, where the conditions are favorable to the growth of phtyoplankton (minute plants) on which many marine organisms feed. Regions where cold water wells up to the surface from deeper levels are particularly rich in phytoplankton, and, although they make up only about one percent of the area of the sea, half the annual catch of fish is taken in them. Fin fish make up about 90 percent of the catch. Among the remaining ten percent are seafoods of high commercial value, such as mollusks and crustaceans. Of the total catch, about half is processed to make animal feed.

The danger of overfishing

Throughout history it has been assumed that the seas would provide fish in unlimited quantities; the size of the catch appeared to be directly related to improvements in the fishing industry's technology. But in the modern world developed nations have become so efficient at catching fish that they have disturbed the delicate balance between hunter and prey. The rate at which major known fish stocks are being replaced has now fallen behind the rate at which fish are being caught.

Fish catches rose rapidly from the mid-1950s, but statistics show that on a world basis a period of positive decline has now begun. The peak year was 1970, when a world catch of 69.6 million tons was recorded. Since then the annual catch has been cut back to about 65 million tons [7].

Diminishing stocks and fishing control

In recent years, fish stocks have been depleted by various natural events as well as by overfishing. The Peruvian anchoveta fishery—which provided the world's largest annual catch of a single species—was destroyed by the appearance of El Niño, a warm sea current that invaded the area, disturbing the environment for the fish, with the result that the shoals disappeared. The loss was partly offset by the sudden development of a market for Alaskan pollack, regarded as a cheap alternative to cod. Caught in the northeast and northwest Pacific Ocean, Alaskan pollack has replaced anchoveta as the world's largest catch of a single species.

Because supplies of fish have decreased, estimates of future production have been revised. At one time it was thought that 200 million tons of fish could by caught each year without drastically depleting stocks. Now, even assuming development of unexploited resources and effective international control of fishing, the maximum potential yield of marine species of fish, crustaceans, and mollusks is estimated at about 118 million tons.

Fish stocks are a food resource capable of self-replenishment, but they can continue to provide protein for the world's growing population only with careful management. The depletion of whale stocks should provide fishing nations with a grim example of the folly of uncontrolled hunting of fish. Until there is international agreement about the perils of such overfishing, however, too many boats will continue to chase too few fish. Progress toward international agree-

CONNECTIONS

See also
392 Fish of the ocean deeps
394 Shellfish and other seafoods
390 Fish of ponds and rivers
388 Fish farming
626 Animals of the ocean
512 The life of fish
514 Unusual fish
516 Fish of seas and rivers

1
Trawl warps
Aft starboard gallows
Radar
Trawl winch
Navigation lights
Gallow block of fore starboard gallows
Towing block
Cran basket
Windlass

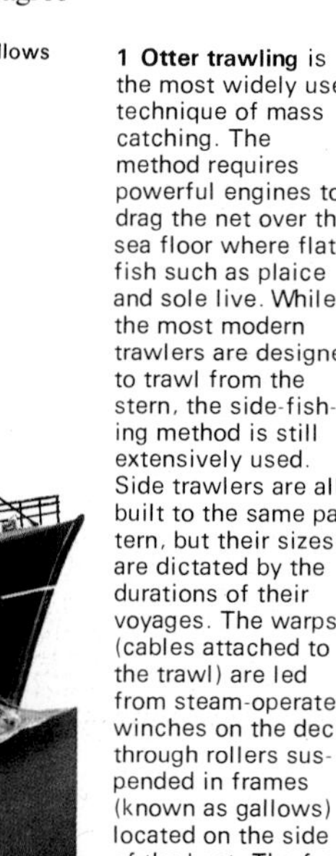
1 Otter trawling is the most widely used technique of mass catching. The method requires powerful engines to drag the net over the sea floor where flatfish such as plaice and sole live. While the most modern trawlers are designed to trawl from the stern, the side-fishing method is still extensively used. Side trawlers are all built to the same pattern, but their sizes are dictated by the durations of their voyages. The warps (cables attached to the trawl) are led from steam-operated winches on the deck through rollers suspended in frames (known as gallows) located on the side of the boat. The freeboard is low to make it easier to haul the catch aboard for cleaning and sorting.

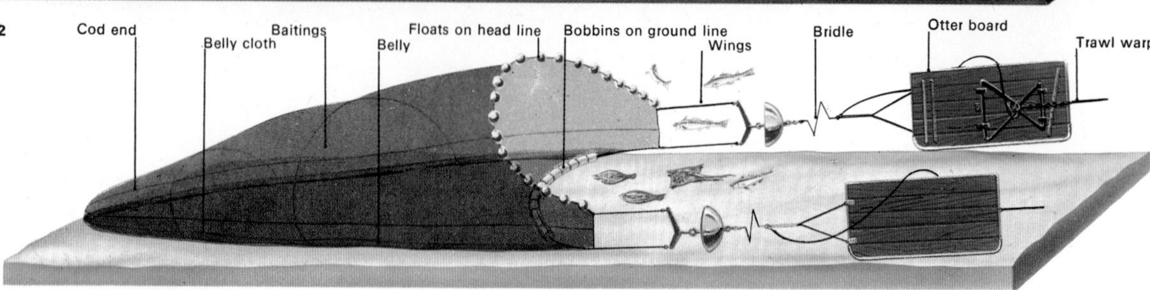

2
Cod end
Baitings
Belly cloth
Floats on head line
Belly
Bobbins on ground line
Wings
Bridle
Otter board
Trawl warp

2 The warps of an otter trawl are connected to otter boards—heavy steel or wooden panels that are linked to each wing of the net by bridles. When the net is under tow, the otter boards are forced apart, keeping the mouth of the net open horizontally. Floats on the head line and bobbins (heavy rollers) on the ground line keep the net open vertically. The underside, or belly, of the net is lined with hide "chafers" to protect it from obstructions on the sea floor. The tapered cod end of the net is secured by a rope that permits quick release of the catch after it is hauled aboard.

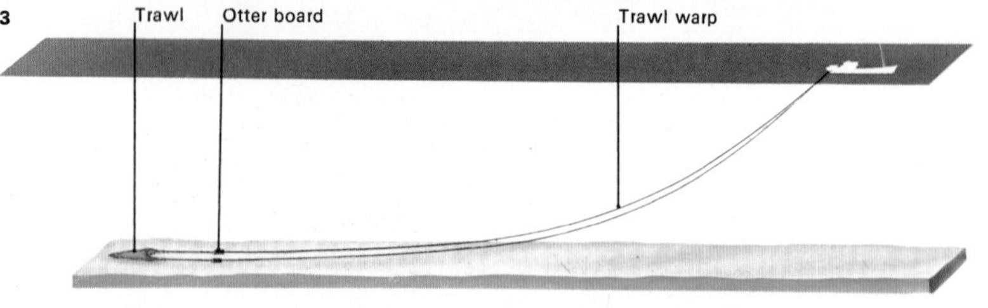

3
Trawl
Otter board
Trawl warp

3 Fishing gear is under great strain when in use. On a deep-sea trawler, a single tow under full power can last as long as three hours, with the trawling gear streaming out as far as 1mi(1,600m) from the ship. With the trawl extended that far, there is a danger of other trawlers in the area cutting across the gear, which can result in a lost net. To minimize this risk, two cones (or, more usually, a cran basket) are hoisted on the forestay to warn other vessels.

ments on the control of fishing has been intermittent, and no effective, concerted scheme for managing the oceans' food stocks has been devised.

Apart from the effort to achieve direct, internationally agreed controls on fishing through catch quotas and net-size regulations, the best hope of conserving fish stocks lies in the establishment of wider territorial limits around national coastlines. Moves to widen these limits restrict the activities of highly developed fishing nations. As the great ocean-roaming fleets (mainly Soviet, Japanese, West European, and American) are forced to accept catch limitations within many of their traditional fishing grounds, the pattern of fishing inevitably will change. Nations will restructure their fishing fleets to concentrate their efforts within new limits, but the pressure they put on stocks within their own waters will still need strict supervision.

Finding new commercial species

Important as conservation measures are, an increase in food production from the sea also depends on the marketing of species that have previously been ignored and on new fish-farming techniques. Already the potential of fish farming is becoming recognized, but it will be many years before such farms will significantly increase the total world supply.

Some nations are beginning to exploit fish species that are not widely eaten now. In the waters of the Antarctic, for instance, krill, a shrimplike creature that is the food of the baleen whale, can be found in massive swarms and is attracting trawlers to this remote region. Although krill is plentiful, the question of how it is to be marketed has yet to be resolved. Experts are investigating the possibilities of using it for animal feed.

Alternative species found in very deep water [9] also present a marketing problem. The unattractive appearance of some of these fish tend to make them hard to sell. The profitability of catching them will probably depend largely on their marketability in other forms—such as fillets—and on a shortage of familiar species, but new commercial species could be quickly overfished.

KEY

Stern trawling, like most modern fishing methods, is so efficient that the survival of some fish stocks is threatened. There are also destructive side effects: trawl nets wreck the sea floor and catch species that, although not eaten, are an integral part of the ocean's food chain.

4

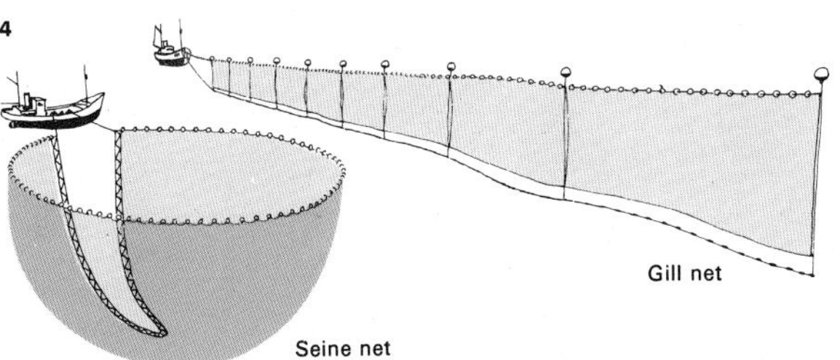

Gill net
Seine net

4 Purse seining and gill netting are two common fishing methods. The purse seine is used to surround shoals of pelagic (open-sea) species. A rope running around the bottom of the net is drawn tight, trapping the fish. The gill net is held in a vertical position by floats and weights and is "shot" across the expected path of the schools of fish, which are caught by the gills as they try to swim through.

5

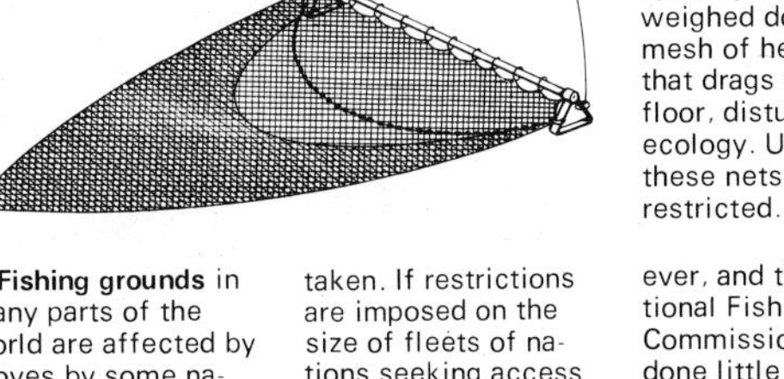

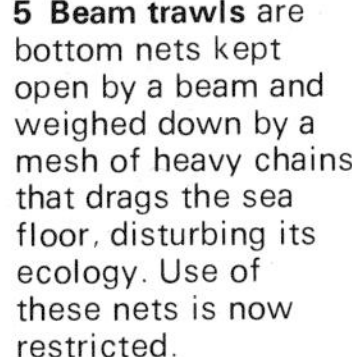

5 Beam trawls are bottom nets kept open by a beam and weighed down by a mesh of heavy chains that drags the sea floor, disturbing its ecology. Use of these nets is now restricted.

6

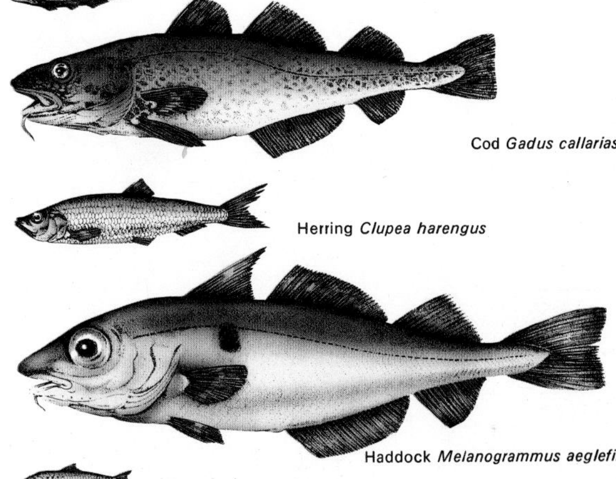

Anchoveta *Cetengraulis mysticetus*
Cod *Gadus callarias*
Herring *Clupea harengus*
Haddock *Melanogrammus aeglefinus*
European pilchard (sardine) *Sardinops sp*

6 Large-scale commercial fishing is concentrated on relatively few species. Mainstays of the world catch over recent years have been anchoveta, herring, haddock, cod, and sardine. Until 1972, anchoveta provided the largest catch. In 1970, the peak year, more than 13 million tons of anchoveta were landed. But in 1973 the catch declined to just less than two million tons, although in 1975 stocks showed signs of recovery. Catches of Alaskan pollack have overtaken other major species.

7

1966 67 68 69 70 71 72 73
Million tons
12
10
8
6
4
2
Anchoveta
Herring
Cod
Haddock
Pilchard

7 World catches of several major species of fish have shown a decline since the 1960s. Catches of anchoveta (used mainly as a feed) showed a particularly spectacular fall between 1971 and 1973. During this period, Peru's lead in fish production was overtaken by nations such as Japan, active in the north Pacific.

8 Fishing grounds in many parts of the world are affected by moves by some nations with coastlines to broaden to 200mi(320km) the zones in which they may control the size of catches that are taken. If restrictions are imposed on the size of fleets of nations seeking access to these zones, major changes could be expected in the patterns of fishing. The dangers of overfishing will remain, however, and the International Fisheries Commission has done little to protect endangered species; international supervision is of limited value unless it is accepted by all fishing nations.

8

Industrial fishing grounds Subsistence fishing

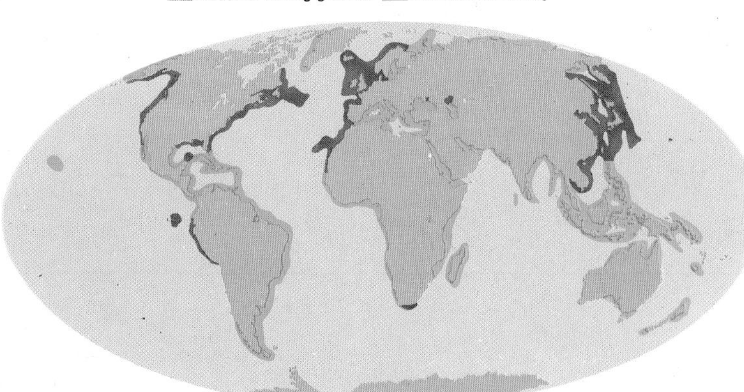

9 A

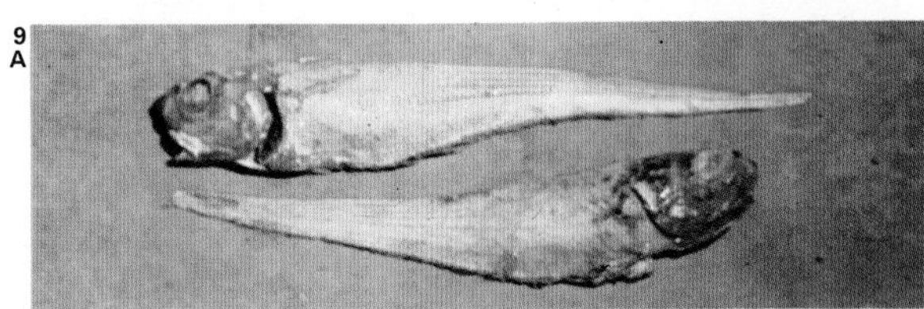

B

9 Some deep-water species have proved to be very palatable although their gruesome appearance may deter some people from buying them. Fished at depths of 2,600 to 3,600 ft, species such as the grenadier or rattail [A] and red director [B] could provide an alternative to fish with depleted stocks.

Fish farming

In one form or another, man has been farming fish for more than 4,000 years, but the development of scientific fish farming (or aquaculture) began only recently. It has come at a time when most of the major commercial fish species are either at or near the limit of their potential yield.

Importance of aquaculture

The total annual production from aquaculture is still no more than five million tons, but is increasing as research and modern technology provide new techniques for the fish farmer. In some developing countries aquaculture is an important part of the economy, providing both food and work.

In terms of output, China leads the world in fish farming. Estimates of production vary, but it is well over two million tons annually—about 40 percent of China's total fish and shellfish supply. Aquaculture is also important in India and Indonesia, which provide, respectively, about 38 and 22 percent of the fish eaten. The Soviet Union, the Philippines, Thailand, Japan, and Taiwan are also fish-farming nations. In the United States and Europe, much of the development in fish farming—apart from shellfish culture—has so far been concentrated on technological research rather than on production.

Mangrove swamps, estuaries, lakes, fresh and salt water lagoons, shallow coastal waters, and artificial ponds are all being utilized for fish farming. According to recent estimates, about 7 million acres (3 million hectares) of water surface are under cultivation. Some experts believe this could be increased to 70 million acres (30 million hectares) in the foreseeable future and that world farmed fish production could reach 40 to 50 million tons by the year 2000.

The choice of animals available to the fish farmer includes mollusks, crustacea, and fin fish. Mollusk culture (mussels [1], oysters [2], clams [7], and so on) is well established, especially in North America, Europe, and Japan, and many countries have some method of oyster farming. The development of intensive hatchery systems during the last 40 years has made available mass rearing techniques for many mollusks.

Farming of crustaceans (which include shrimps and prawns) [3] has developed more slowly and is mainly found as a semiculture that makes use of the water in artificial ponds formed when rice fields are flooded. Mass rearing of shrimps or prawns for general sale has not yet been achieved, but almost certainly will be in the near future.

Many species of fresh-water fish can be farmed, with varying degrees of success. These include carp, tilapia, catfish, trout [4], salmon [5], and eels. The only salt water fish farmed in any numbers are milkfish and sea bream, although experiments are taking place to widen the choice of farmable marine fish to include flatfish (sole, turbot, halibut, and plaice).

Techniques employed in aquaculture

Aquaculture techniques are many and varied, but fall into four categories. First, the young can be reared through the most vulnerable stages of their lives for release into lakes or the sea to supplement natural stocks (for example, trout and sturgeon). A

CONNECTIONS

See also

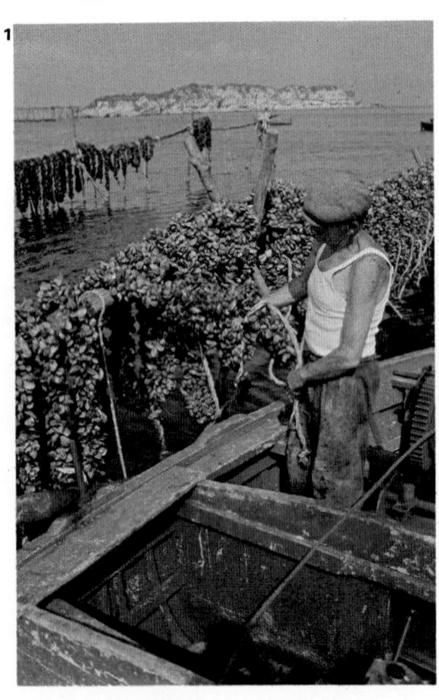

1 The edible mussel (*Mytilus edulis*) is cultivated on ropes hanging from stakes or similar structures driven into the sea bottom (as here in northern France), or on ropes suspended from floating rafts (as in Spain). Both methods first involve the collection by settlement of mussel "seed," or "spat." The "seed" may then be transferred to farming areas free from predators or pollution.

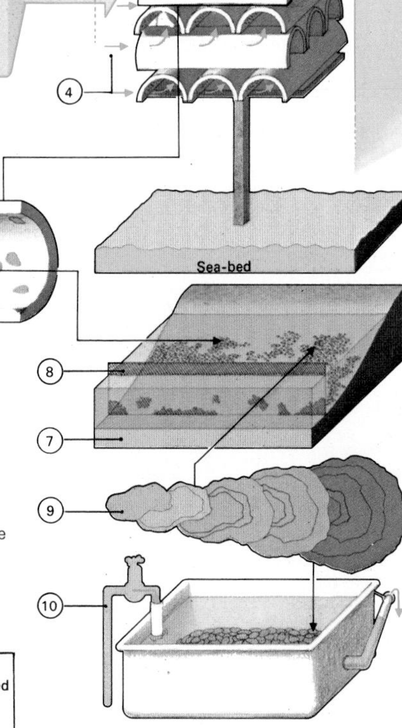

Sea level
Sea-bed

2 Cultivation of the European "flat" oyster *(Ostrea edulis)* is one of the earliest examples of aquaculture, known since Roman times. It involves the collection of larval animals, "spat," and their subsequent growth in protected tidal bays and estuaries. The sexually mature oyster [1] begins to spawn in the spring as the seawater temperature rises. When a spawning, or "spat fall," occurs, the growers set down artificial spat collectors in the water to which the tiny larval oysters [2] can attach themselves. Around the Brittany coast of France spat collectors are usually curved, lime-covered roof tiles [3] stacked just clear of the ocean floor at right angles to facilitate water circulation [4] The young (about 50 to a tile) are left until winter when, as orange-colored "seed oysters" [5], they are pried [6] from the tiles and planted out in growing beds [7], or "parcs," where they feed on microscopic particles brought in by the tides. Parcs may be protected by nets [8] to help prevent attack by predators. After about 18 months the beds are dredged and the oysters sent by barge to fattening grounds, also in the estuary. The oysters are allowed to grow for about five years, each year adding a new layer to their shell [9]. Then they are gathered from the estuary and, before marketing, left for a few days in sterile seawater to cleanse them [10].

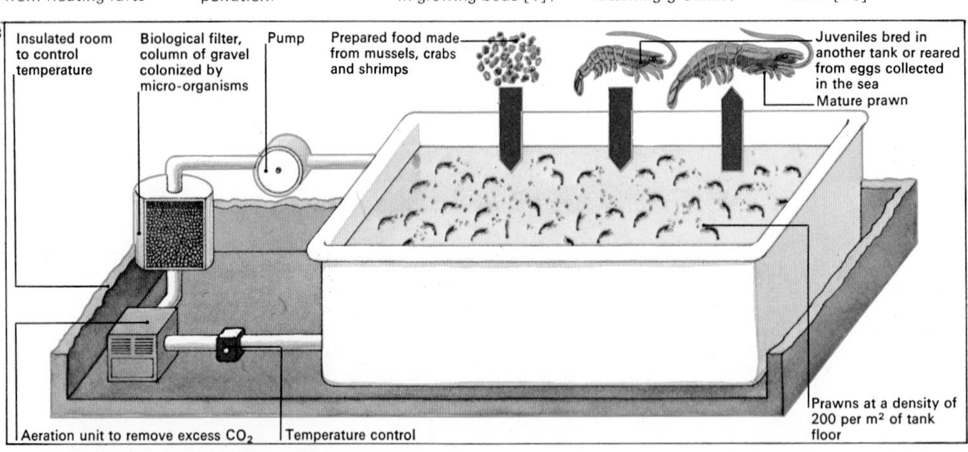

Insulated room to control temperature
Biological filter, column of gravel colonized by micro-organisms
Pump
Prepared food made from mussels, crabs and shrimps
Juveniles bred in another tank or reared from eggs collected in the sea
Mature prawn
Prawns at a density of 200 per m² of tank floor
Aeration unit to remove excess CO_2
Temperature control

3 Several species of prawns and shrimps can be reared under controlled environmental conditions. Some fast-growing tropical prawn species are considered particularly suitable since they provide three or four crops a year. Eggs are obtained either from captive stock or from egg-bearing females caught wild. Mass-rearing techniques are used through the juvenile stages. Then the young prawns are fattened in an enclosed circulation system, shown here, where water at a controlled temperature is recycled by pump through the rearing tank. Dangerous toxic waste products excreted by the prawns must continuously be removed by filters like those used for purifying sewage.

second method is to capture immature wild fish and marine animals. Confined in enclosures, they may be left to forage for themselves or provided with supplementary feed. The species best adapted to this kind of cultivation include milkfish, mullet, shrimp, oysters, and mussels.

Third, eggs from wild parents can be gathered, incubated, and farm-reared to a marketable size. In the most sophisticated form of fish farming, eggs are hatched and the young reared so that a growing brood stock is maintained. The operator therefore achieves full control over the life cycle of the animals and may be able to breed them selectively. Trout, salmon, catfish, carp, and oysters [2] are successfully farmed in this way.

Technological developments

Although most fish farming is still based on techniques of partial culture, it is in the carefully controlled intensive-rearing system that most technological developments are taking place. For example, closed-circuit water recycling enables the farmers to remove waste products—mainly ammonia, urea, and feed or waste solids—and return clean water to the rearing facility [3]. Fish grow more rapidly in warm water. For this reason, some fish farms are located near power stations and farmers can make use of the warm waste water from cooling towers, previously regarded as a pollutant, in the recycling process to accelerate growth rates of fish and shellfish, thus saving on heating costs. In the United States the effluent from a thermal power station has been put to good use in the rearing of mollusks and lobsters, and in Britain flatfish have been grown in heated water flowing from a nuclear power station.

Successes in catfish culture systems [Key] and in farming the Atlantic salmon [5] demonstrate the exciting possibilities for fish farming. Many factors must be considered, however. These include feed costs in relation to product value, disease control in intensive systems, increasing costs where labor-intensive methods are used, and, for some species, consumer resistance to accepting them as food.

KEY

Among the most impressive examples of industrial-scale fish farming is the pond culture of catfish, seen here in Arkansas. It has achieved small industry status in the United States.

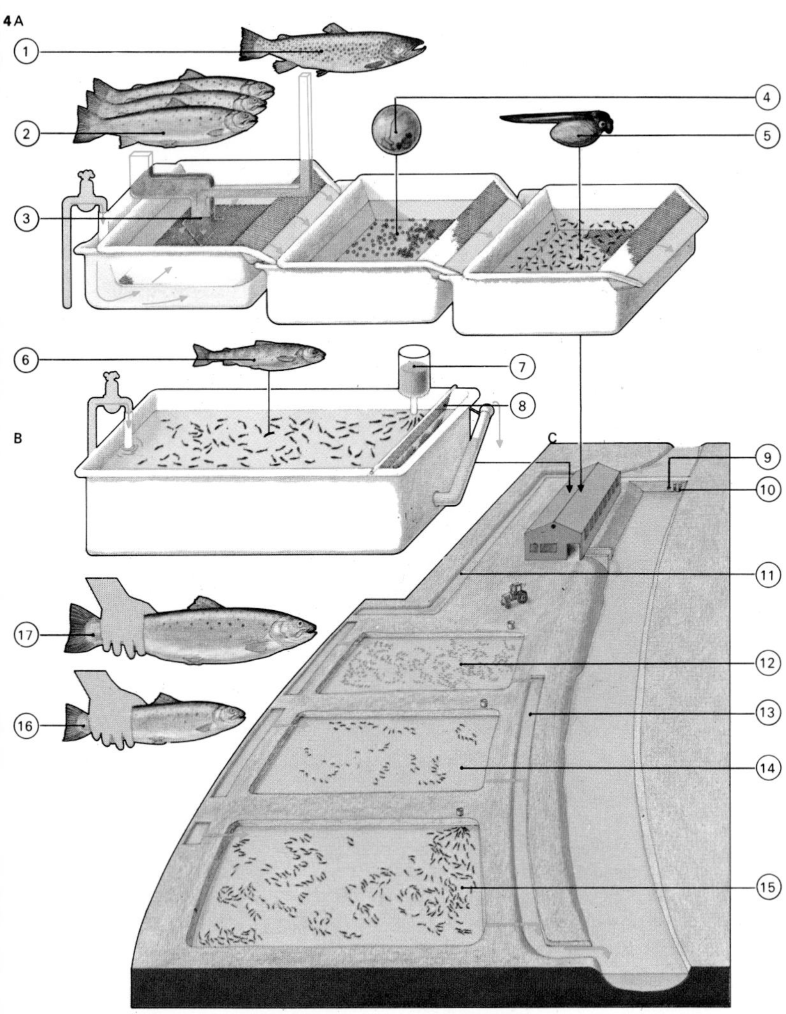

4A
1
2
3
4
5
6
7
8
B
C
9
10
11
12
13
14
15
16
17

4 In trout farming the operator can achieve complete control over his stock throughout its life cycle. The hatchery process [A] involves the removal of milt from male fish [1] and eggs from female fish [2]. The eggs are fertilized [3,4] and placed in an incubator, and when the alevins (larval fish)[5] have absorbed their yolk sacs, they are transferred to the fry tank [B]. There the fry [6] are fed automatically [7] and are prevented from escaping by a perforated screen [8]. When the fish are sufficiently developed they are removed to the fish farm [C]. Water from a river is diverted by a dam [9] incorporating an eel pass and fish ladder [10], and flows to the tanks by a channel [11]. The first pond [12] accommodates fish up to one year old. Water is returned to the river by an outlet channel [13]. Fish are held in the second pond [14] until two years old [16] and in the third [15] until three years old [17]. These are kept for breeding.

5

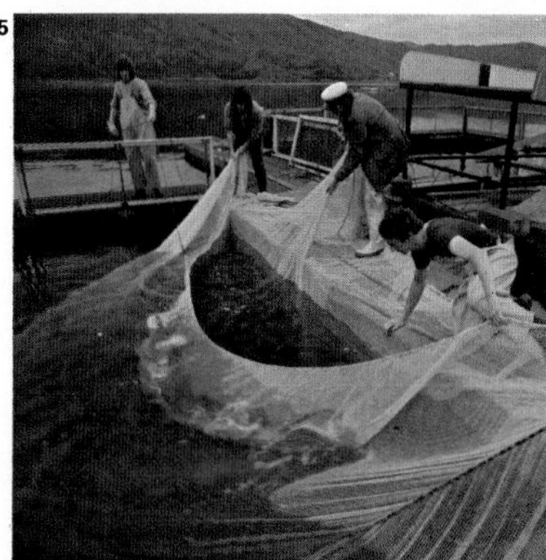

5 The salmon is migratory; it must move from fresh to salt water. Salmon eggs are incubated and the young fish reared throughout their early life stages in fresh water. But when the important "smolt" stage is reached they must be transported to seawater where they are normally kept in floating pens. Here Atlantic salmon (*Salmo salar*) are harvested from cages in a Scottish sea loch.

6

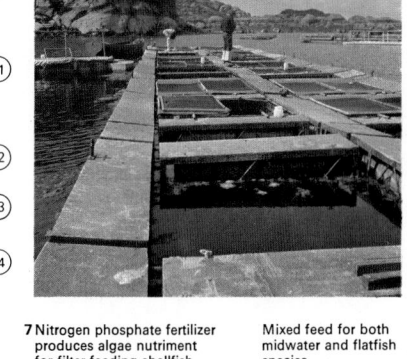

6 Flatfish, particularly turbot and Dover sole, have been shown to be suitable for farming. After being reared in a nursery they are fattened in cages in sheltered tidal waters.

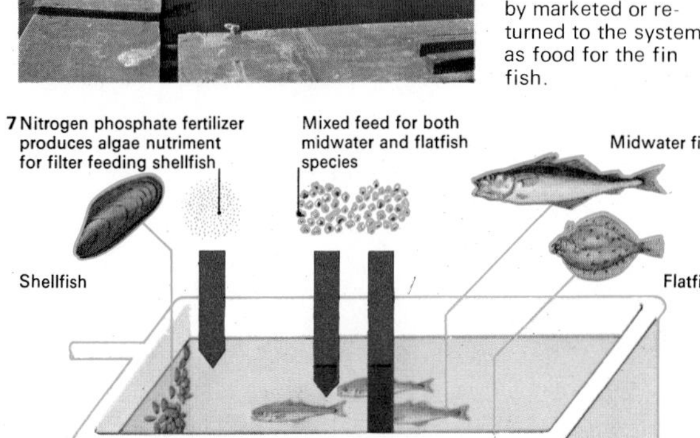

7 Nitrogen phosphate fertilizer produces algae nutriment for filter feeding shellfish
Mixed feed for both midwater and flatfish species
Midwater fish
Shellfish
Flatfish

7 Two or more species of fish or shellfish can be reared together in a "polyculture" system. The shellfish may either by marketed or returned to the system as food for the fin fish.

Fish of ponds and rivers

Rivers and other inland waters throughout the world support a rich and varied fish population, but it is chiefly in the Northern Hemisphere that freshwater fish are favored as a popular source of food. This is probably because of the much larger areas of continental land mass in the Northern Hemisphere, which result in a greater fish distribution in inland waters.

Fish of northern and southern rivers

All members of the salmon family—including trout, whitefish, and char—are native to northern rivers; sturgeon inhabit rivers of North America, although the species of this highly prized fish from which caviar is obtained is found in the rivers of the Soviet Union and the Balkans and in the Black and Caspian seas.

Apart from introduced species, these popular freshwater fish are absent from most waters south of the Equator, but many Southern Hemisphere rivers are inhabited by native species of good food value. The New Zealand river whitebait, for example, which are the young of several *Galaxies* species, are much appreciated delicacies; and the golden perch, also known as callop, is indigenous to Australian rivers.

The perch family of northern waters is represented in the Southern Hemisphere by a related freshwater family, the cichlids, widely distributed throughout Africa and most of South America. The cichlids are, confusingly, known as bream (a different European fish) in southern Africa.

The carp family numbers more than 1,500 species. Many of these are minute (the minnows) and of no culinary interest, but the mirror, or common carp, which may weigh up to 15lb (6kg), is highly valued in Europe. The carp [3] inhabits rivers and ponds of North America, Europe, and Asia.

The migratory eel

Freshwater eels have been valued for their compact, rich, and oily flesh since ancient times; wealthy Romans bred eels for the table in large fish ponds near river banks. Smoked eel is a delicacy particularly prized in northern European countries. Eels are distributed throughout the temperate zones of the world, apart from South America and the west of North America. The European eel, like the salmon, is a migrant. It begins its life in the Sargasso Sea and drifts on the ocean currents toward European rivers, the same way that American forms reach American rivers.

Eels spend most of their young and adult lives in fresh waters. Adult eels return to the Sargasso Sea to spawn, after which they die. The Japanese eel, like the European species, is widely eaten, in contrast to the American species, which is not much valued for food.

While young hatched eels migrate from their parents' spawning grounds in the sea to spend their adult lives in fresh waters, the Japanese ayu, a relative of the smelts, does the opposite. It spawns in rivers of Japan and Korea where the currents are strong and the water temperature low. After mating the adult fish dies. The fry float on the currents down to the sea where the young fish remain until sexually mature. At the age of about 18 months, the ayu return to the rivers for spawning.

CONNECTIONS

See also
616 Lakes and rivers
516 Fish of seas and rivers
392 Fish of the ocean deeps
394 Shellfish and other seafoods
388 Fish farming
386 Commercial fishing

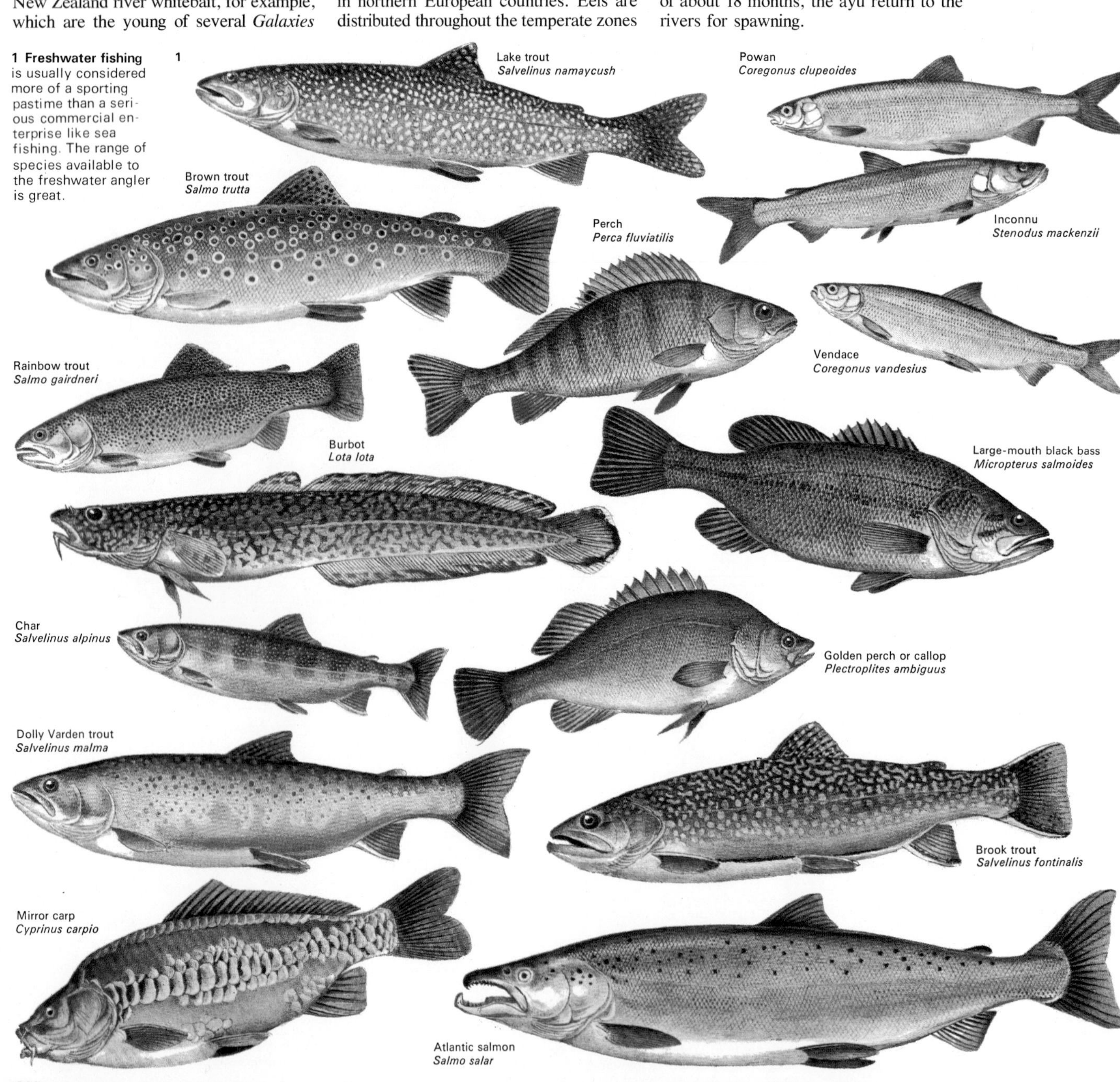

1
Lake trout
Salvelinus namaycush
Powan
Coregonus clupeoides
Brown trout
Salmo trutta
Inconnu
Stenodus mackenzii
Perch
Perca fluviatilis
Vendace
Coregonus vandesius
Rainbow trout
Salmo gairdneri
Burbot
Lota lota
Large-mouth black bass
Micropterus salmoides
Char
Salvelinus alpinus
Golden perch or callop
Plectroplites ambiguus
Dolly Varden trout
Salvelinus malma
Brook trout
Salvelinus fontinalis
Mirror carp
Cyprinus carpio
Atlantic salmon
Salmo salar

1 Freshwater fishing is usually considered more of a sporting pastime than a serious commercial enterprise like sea fishing. The range of species available to the freshwater angler is great.

Fishing for salmon and trout

Freshwater food is not as abundant in the Northern Hemisphere as it once was. Many species have been almost destroyed by overfishing or pollution; once prolific, the sturgeon is now so rare that its price puts it beyond the reach of most people.

The Atlantic salmon [Key], once very common in New England streams, has now become relatively rare. It also once ascended London's Thames River, but it was eliminated from these waters by 1870. It has, however, returned both to New England waters and the Thames in recent years. A hazard for this species has been the discovery, recently, by Danish and Greenland fishermen of the salmon's main feeding grounds in the Atlantic, not far from the coast of Greenland. Massive and indiscriminate netting of immature salmon in these waters led to an outcry from land-based net fishermen and rod-and-line anglers in the 1960s when catches declined. At the same time, a fungal disease attacked the salmon, reducing their numbers still further.

Fishing for trout and salmon and angling for other freshwater fish are becoming increasingly popular. Trout and salmon tend to be scarcer and therefore more expensive to pursue than other fish that are usually found in local rivers, lakes, and canals. Often freshwater fish, which are not always easy to cook or good to eat, are returned to the water after being caught and weighed for competitions. Freshwater salmon average 10lb (4.5kg) and can reach 40lb (18kg).

European brown trout inhabit all kinds of freshwater environments and are now widely distributed in North America. The rainbow trout tends to prefer still waters (lakes and ponds), but can also thrive in certain river conditions. Some brown trout occasionally adopt the habits of migrating salmon and swim down the rivers to estuaries, where they manage to survive in briny conditions and can grow to very great weights. Neither the salmon nor the trout (brown or rainbow) should be confused with the so-called sea trout, or weakfish, a kind of croaker that is also sometimes misnamed salmon. It, too, is good to eat.

KEY

A

B

The Atlantic salmon is born in fast-flowing rivers on both sides of the North Atlantic. At this stage it is known as a fingerling and after two years it becomes a parr. It journeys down river as a smolt, maturing in the estuary before setting out to live in the ocean in an area from the Arctic southward to latitude 40°N. The return migration from the Atlantic begins after four years, when the salmon has reached its maturity [A]. It may cross more than 3,000mi(4,800km) to reach its spawning grounds in the fresh water of the river [B] where it was born. After the laying and the fertilizing of the eggs the salmon generally dies.

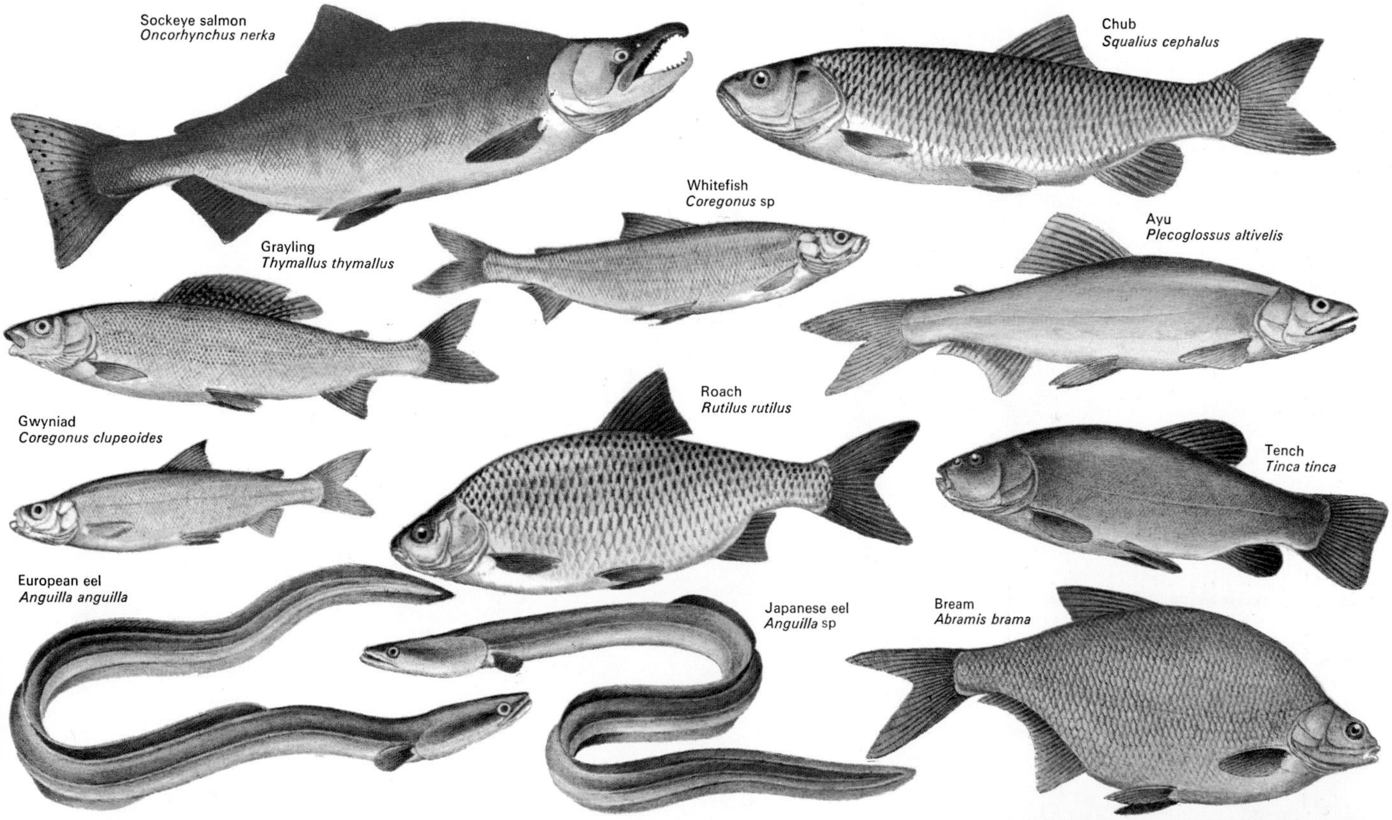

Sockeye salmon *Oncorhynchus nerka*

Chub *Squalius cephalus*

Whitefish *Coregonus* sp

Ayu *Plecoglossus altivelis*

Grayling *Thymallus thymallus*

Roach *Rutilus rutilus*

Gwyniad *Coregonus clupeoides*

Tench *Tinca tinca*

European eel *Anguilla anguilla*

Japanese eel *Anguilla* sp

Bream *Abramis brama*

2

2 The carnivorous northern pike *(Esox lucius)* belongs to the family Esocidae an old-established fresh-water group of North America and Eurasia. It inhabits rivers and lakes among dense colonies of water plants. Young pike live in shallow water, feeding on larvae and the fry of other fish. When the pike matures it moves into deeper water. The elongated, flecked body is camouflaged by the plants from which the pike darts out to devour fish, waterfowl, and even small mammals. One of the most vicious predators of fresh waters, the pike is equipped with a large and voracious mouth bearing backward-curving, sharp teeth from which no prey can escape once it is caught. The northern pike can grow to a length of 4.5ft(1.4m) and attain a weight of 45lb(20kg). It is widely fished for sport and also for food, as the firm, white flesh is greatly valued for its flavor. Pike are raised in fish hatcheries.

3

3 The common carp *(Cyprinus carpio)* originated in the Caucases and has been introduced throughout the Northern Hemisphere. Carp bones excavated from Greek Stone Age sites show the importance of fresh-water fish in prehistoric times. Many varieties have been bred, including the European mirror carp. The ornamental golden carp of Japan symbolizes bravery, inherent in the carp's struggle upstream to spawn.

Fish of the ocean deeps

Rich in protein, and in some cases more easily obtained than meat animals, fish have for centuries formed part of the diet of many peoples. More recently fish have been processed as feed for animals. The fish of the seas, however, are not merely a supply of nourishment for man; on an even larger scale they provide food for each other and are part of natural food cycles in the oceans.

Man has fished the shallow margins of the seas from earliest times, but not until he found methods of preserving catches—using ocean-going ships—did deep-sea fishing get underway. Various nineteenth-century developments included the large-scale building of trawlers, the introduction of railroad transportation from fishing ports to inland cities, and the establishment of canning factories. Today the fleets of trawlers that fish the grounds off Greenland, Newfoundland, and Japan for several months at a time are floating factories complete with deep-freeze equipment.

Scientifically developed fishing methods and the easier means of preserving catches and transporting them today have caused the fishing industry to become an international rather than a national concern. In spite of the prolific breeding habits of marine fish, indiscriminate fishing of some established grounds has led to a falling population in some species.

Cold northern waters

Fewer species of fish inhabit the colder waters of the North Atlantic than the warmer Mediterranean and Pacific areas. But these fish, particularly the Atlantic herring [8] and the members of the cod family [3, 9], are caught in vast quantities. A female herring is less fertile than a female cod but still lays about 50,000 eggs each year. The herring population is held in check by other fish that feed on the numerous eggs. In spite of this, a large proportion of the eggs survive and develop through various stages to the mature herrings that are fished for throughout the year by fleets following their migrations.

The herring is among the most nutritious of all fish. In addition to protein it contains vitamins A and D, as well as minerals such as iron and calcium. It is marketed fresh or frozen, salted, cured, smoked, canned, and pickled, and some people regard fresh or canned herring roe as a delicacy. Cod [3] is another important species for the fishing industry on both sides of the North Atlantic. A related species lives in the North Pacific, but most commercial cod fishing is confined to the deep cold waters of the Atlantic. For some nations, the cost involved in reaching such far-off fishing grounds has made cod an expensive food fish, although it is cheaper than its close—but less abundant—relative, the haddock [20]. Spotted dogfish [18], halibut [13], and pollack, or pollock (also known as saithe), are other species found in cold seas. Skate [2] and whiting [9] are also fish of cold waters, although they do not inhabit the extreme North Atlantic. Farther south—as far as the African coast—John Dory [14], mackerel [15] (related to the tuna), sole [17], and turbot [12] are the most important catches.

Mediterranean waters

The temperate Mediterranean Sea supports numerous species of fish. Several kinds of

CONNECTIONS

See also
386 Commercial fishing
394 Shellfish and other seafoods
388 Fish farming
390 Fish of ponds and rivers
626 Animals of the ocean

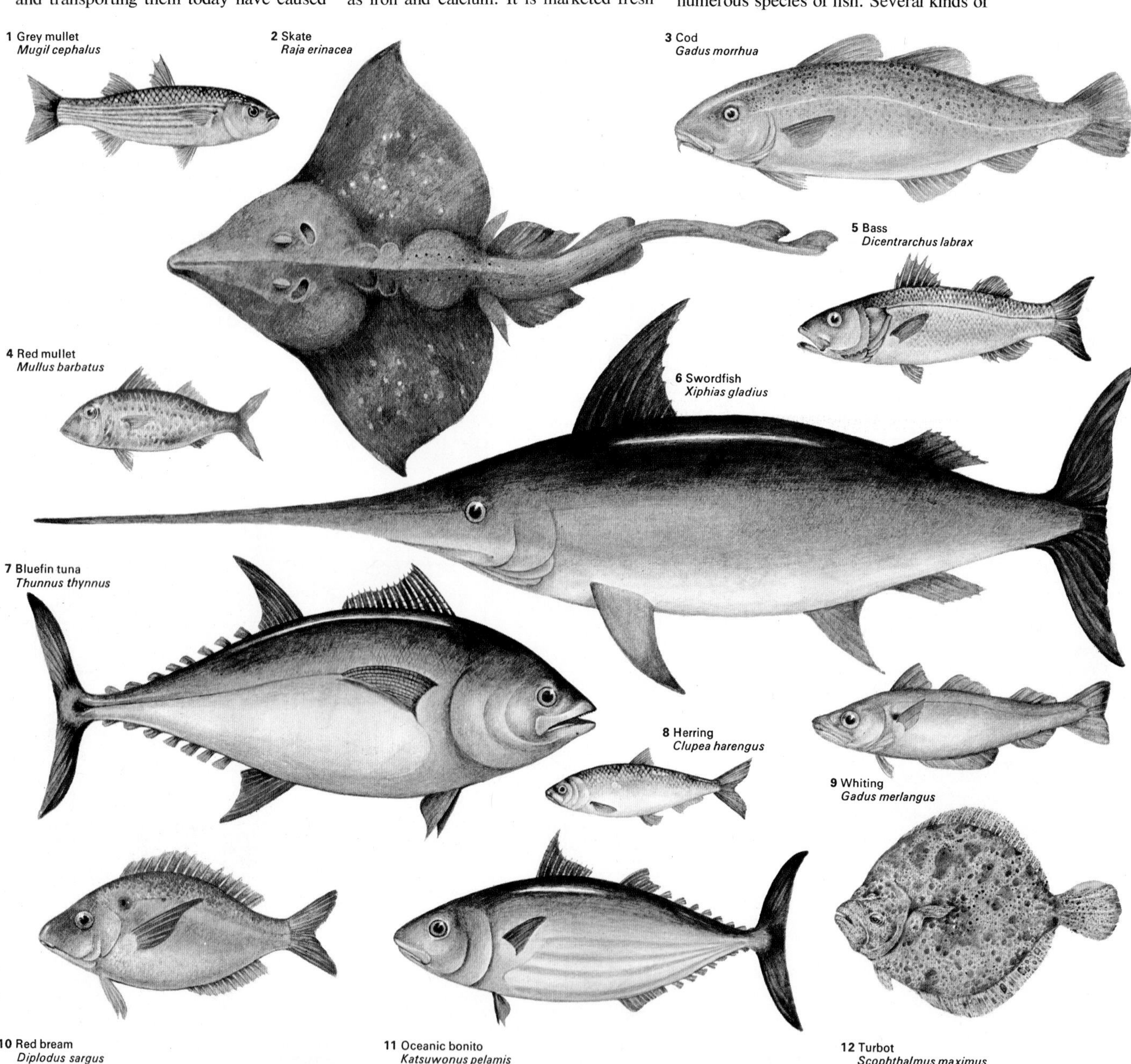

1 Grey mullet *Mugil cephalus*

2 Skate *Raja erinacea*

3 Cod *Gadus morrhua*

4 Red mullet *Mullus barbatus*

5 Bass *Dicentrarchus labrax*

6 Swordfish *Xiphias gladius*

7 Bluefin tuna *Thunnus thynnus*

8 Herring *Clupea harengus*

9 Whiting *Gadus merlangus*

10 Red bream *Diplodus sargus*

11 Oceanic bonito *Katsuwonus pelamis*

12 Turbot *Scophthalmus maximus*

sea bream [10] are caught for their delicate flesh, along with the popular sardines and anchovies. Related species of the latter are also found in waters of the Pacific off North and South America.

The red mullet [4], known in France as *rouget,* is considered by many to be a Mediterranean speciality and was in classical times as expensive as Atlantic salmon is today. The name "red mullet" is often given to another species of Mediterranean fish, the gurnet or gurnard, which while similar in coloring has coarser flesh.

The true red mullet can also be found in parts of the Atlantic off southern England and the southern United States. The goatfish, abundant in the Indian and Pacific oceans, is related to the red mullet.

The ugly anglerfish is regarded as a delicacy in Venice and it is also one of the components of a true Marseilles bouillabaisse. In North America, however, where it is more plentiful, the anglerfish is rarely used for anything but pet foods.

Another plentiful fish of the Mediterranean is the silvery bass [5], a related species of which is found off the shores of the United States. Swordfish [6], tuna [7], and oceanic bonito [11] are frequently caught during the summer months in Mediterranean waters, although their breeding grounds are in warmer seas.

Fish of tropical waters

Both the bluefin [7] and bonita [11] tuna belong to warm oceans, but many related species inhabit the Mediterranean Sea and South Atlantic Ocean (although they are rarely sighted north of the Bay of Biscay). The swordfish has a similar distribution pattern.

The red snapper [16] is a native of the Gulf of Mexico, whereas the Atlantic croaker [19] lives off the coasts of the United States and South America. Members of the croaker family are known throughout the world by different names, depending on their habits and resemblances to other types of fish. In South Africa one kind is the *kabeljou* (from the Dutch name for cod) and in Australia another species of croaker is the mulloway.

KEY

Trawlers range far and wide in the search for fish, using modern technological aids such as echolocation. Consumer demand can lead to international incidents. As catches fall off, trawlers go farther afield, "invading" seas that are claimed as the exclusive territory of other nations. Many coastal countries have extended their national limits in order to conserve remaining fish stocks, and "fish wars," with damage to nets and ships, have been common. The "cod war" between Britain and Iceland in the mid-1970s was typical.

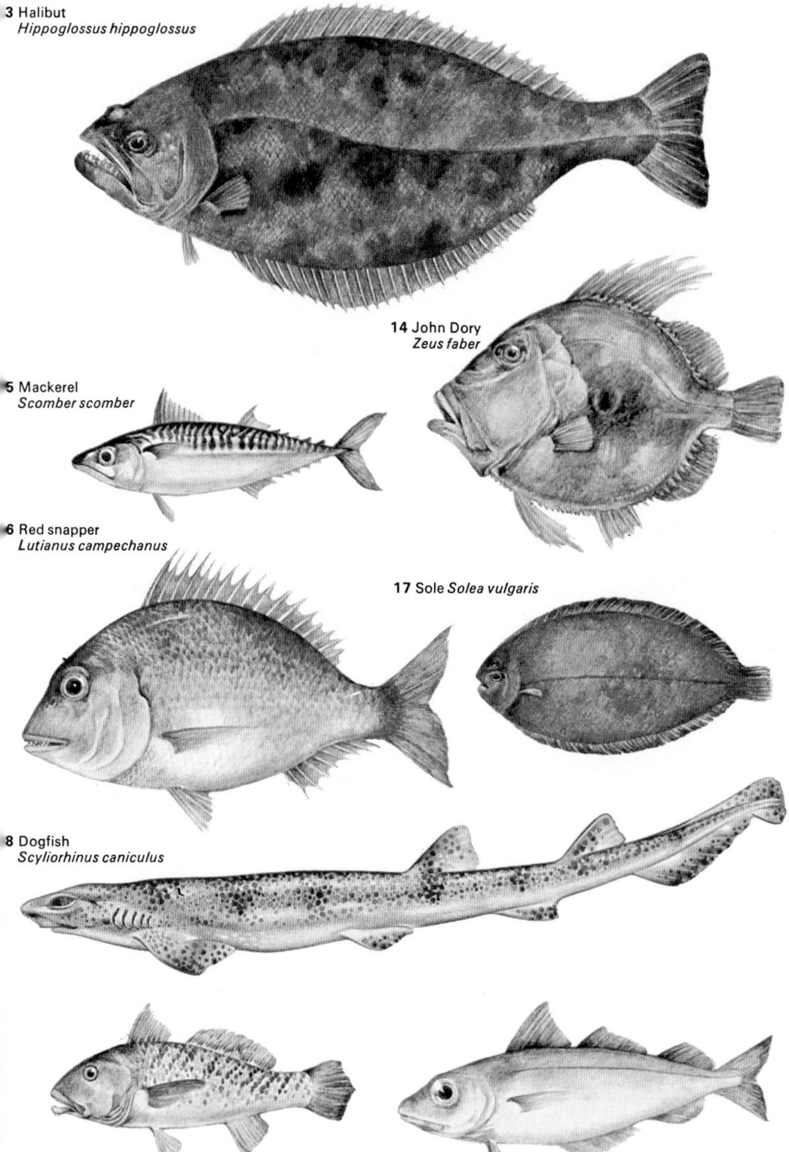

3 Halibut
Hippoglossus hippoglossus
14 John Dory
Zeus faber
5 Mackerel
Scomber scomber
6 Red snapper
Lutianus campechanus
17 Sole *Solea vulgaris*
8 Dogfish
Scyliorhinus caniculus
9 Croaker
Micropogon undulatos
20 Haddock
Gadus aeglefinus

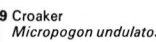

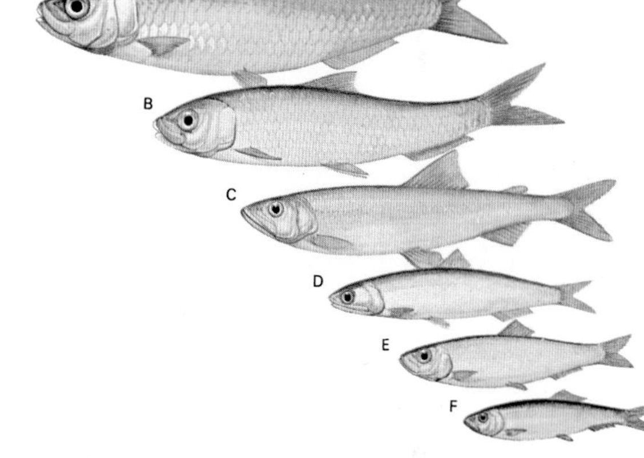

21 A
B
C
D
E
F

21 The adult Atlantic herring at 3 years of age has matured through a series of stages, all of which are used by man as food. Adult herrings [A] are sold fresh or salted, cured whole (as bloaters, bucklings, and kippers), and pickled as fillets (matjes and rollmop herrings). Soft and hard roe is sometimes sold fresh but usually canned. At stage [B] herring are frequently sold as pilchards, a closely related species, and used for canning. At stage [C], herrings are often miscalled sardines, again a closely related species, and like the true sardines canned in oil or tomato, either whole, skinned, or boned. Young herring [D] may be smoked whole but are more usually sold as whitebait. At stage [E] herrings are often called sprats or brislings, although these are a different species, and like them are lightly smoked before canning in oil. The tiny herrings [F] sold as anchovies (a different species) are fried whole and also exported as pastes, concentrated sauces, or as fillets.

22 Tora fugu
Fugu rubripes rubripes

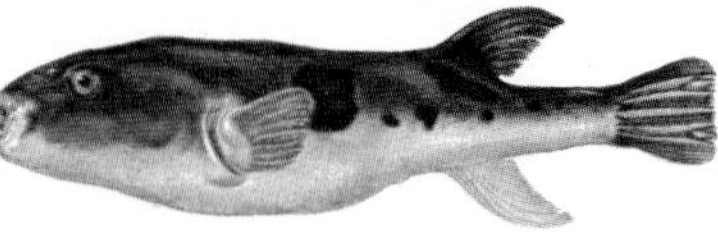

22 The Japanese puffer fish is poisonous like other species of puffers and blowfish. Although poison from a badly prepared puffer fish can be fatal, the flesh is delicate, appetizing, and perfectly safe once the harmful liver and ovaries are removed competently. The puffer fish (in Japan known as *toro fugu*) is regarded as a gourmet's choice, and may be one of the dishes in a western style hors d'oeuvres.

Shellfish and other seafoods

Coastal and inland waters the world over are inhabited not only by fish but also by numerous other animals that have become an increasingly important source of food. Among these sea creatures are the highly prized shellfish, easily obtained when uncovered at low tide or when washed up on to beaches and the banks of estuaries.

Shellfish fall into two separate categories: the crustaceans with jointed shells, which include lobsters, spiny lobsters, crabs [1], and shrimps [5], and the mollusks, such as mussels, oysters, clams, and cockles [2], squids [Key D], and octopuses.

Today a steadily rising demand coupled with limited or falling supply has led to increasing prices for all types of shellfish in North America and Europe, where lobsters, shrimp, and oysters have become luxury foods. The traditional American clambake, which includes lobster as well as clams, is now an expensive feast.

King of the shellfish

Many gastronomes consider that as salmon is the king of fish, so lobster is supreme among the crustaceans. There are three valued species of true lobster—the large *Homarus americanus,* which lives off the eastern coast of the United States (chiefly in the area of Maine), the lobster of European waters, *Homarus vulgaris*, and the Norway lobster (*Nephrops norvegicus)*, also known as Dublin prawn and scampi.

Lobsters are caught alive in "pots." These are actually wooden or metal cages baited with food. The lobster can enter easily, but once inside cannot escape. The pots are weighted down on the sea bed with rocks or stones and attached to a float on the surface to mark their location. The delicious white, firm flesh and the scarcity of lobster combine to make this shellfish one of the most prized of all food delicacies. The female lobster is generally preferred to the male, partly because it has a larger body, with more tender flesh, and partly because of the eggs (known as coral) that are carried in the tail and are considered a delicacy.

The spiny, or rock, lobsters (most of them in the genus *Palinurus*) resemble the true lobsters but lack the prominent claws and their antennae are extremely well developed. Most of the meat is contained in the large, fan-shaped tail. Spiny lobsters are larger and heavier than true lobsters and their flesh is sometimes more tender. European sea catches come from the eastern Atlantic and the Mediterranean, but a related species, the Western Indian spiny lobsters, abounds in the Caribbean Sea. The California spiny lobster is also valued for food, as is the commercially important South African rock lobster *(Jasus lalandei)*.

Oysters and crabs

Oysters have been eaten since the earliest times. They were certainly known to the ancient Greeks, who used the shells to cast votes at elections. The Romans supplemented local supplies by importing oysters from Britain. Until the mid-nineteenth century oysters were commonplace fare in some areas, where they were used as ingredients in peasant cooking until the seemingly inexhaustible oyster beds were badly depleted. Since then, the price of oysters has risen astronomically. Most of the oysters

CONNECTIONS

See also
388 Fish farming
478 Life between two shells
480 Squids and octopuses
476 Land and sea snails
486 Crabs and lobsters
490 Crustaceans and other arthropods
392 Fish of the ocean deeps
390 Fish of ponds and rivers

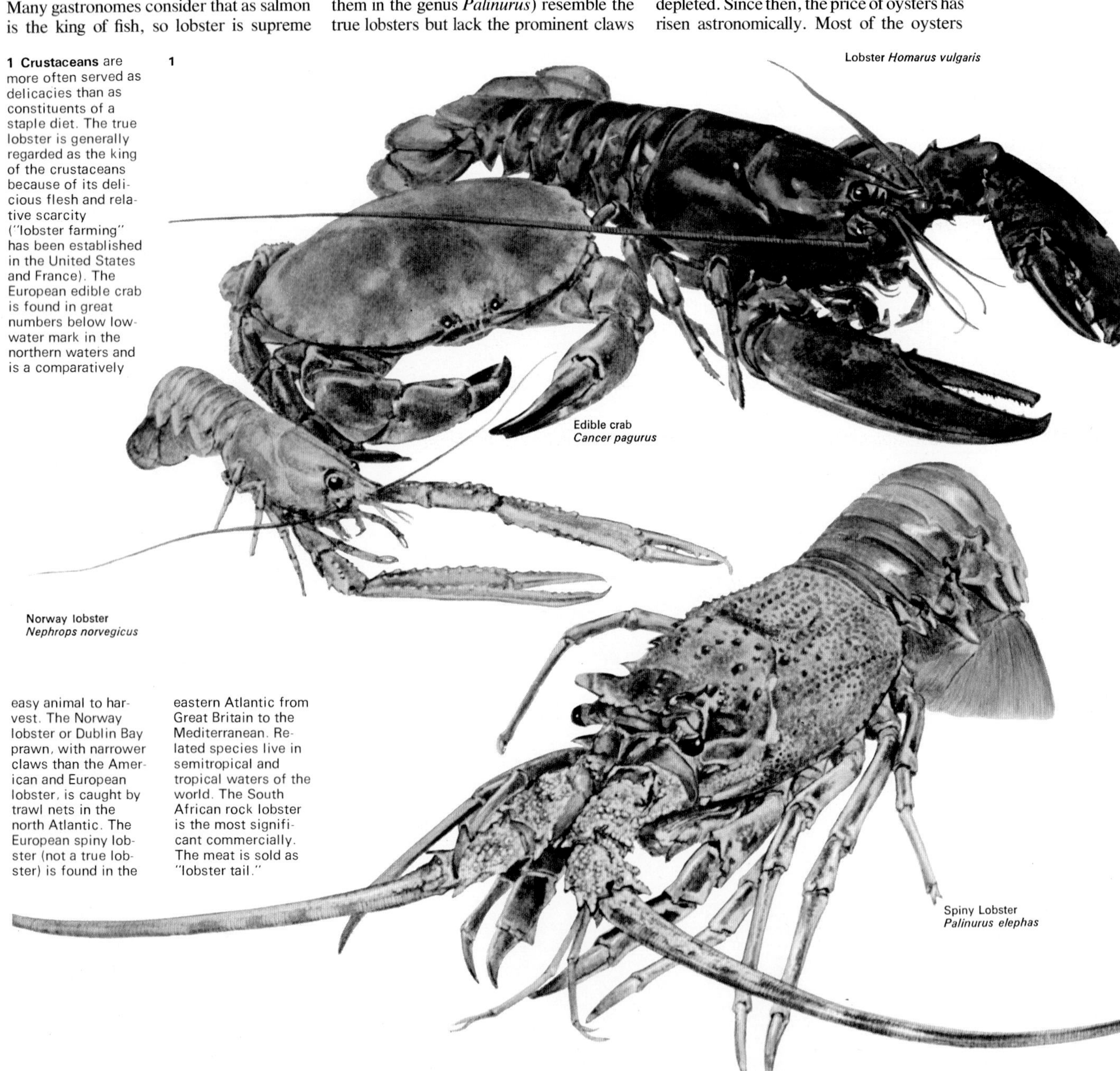

1
Lobster *Homarus vulgaris*
Edible crab
Cancer pagurus
Norway lobster
Nephrops norvegicus
Spiny Lobster
Palinurus elephas

1 Crustaceans are more often served as delicacies than as constituents of a staple diet. The true lobster is generally regarded as the king of the crustaceans because of its delicious flesh and relative scarcity ("lobster farming" has been established in the United States and France). The European edible crab is found in great numbers below low-water mark in the northern waters and is a comparatively easy animal to harvest. The Norway lobster or Dublin Bay prawn, with narrower claws than the American and European lobster, is caught by trawl nets in the north Atlantic. The European spiny lobster (not a true lobster) is found in the eastern Atlantic from Great Britain to the Mediterranean. Related species live in semitropical and tropical waters of the world. The South African rock lobster is the most significant commercially. The meat is sold as "lobster tail."

marketed today come from protected beds and undersea farms established in parts of Europe, the United States, Japan, and Australasia. Oysters are valued more for their flavor than for any particular food content.

The clam is extremely popular in North America, where it may be served and eaten raw. It is also cooked in traditional New England chowders. Crabs, on the other hand, are abundant in all seas, and they are among the most widely eaten of shellfish. The Kamchatka [4], also known as the Japanese crab, is larger than most edible species and, like the giant Tasmanian crab, commands higher prices because of its comparative rarity.

Mussels are even more common than crabs and are much used in Mediterranean cuisines. Other less expensive shellfish include European cockles, whelks, and winkles [2], popular at the seaside.

Squid, octopus, and sea urchin

In North America and northern Europe there is little demand for mollusks of the cephalopod order, which include cuttlefish, squid, and octopus. These are all tentacled creatures, distinguished by their well-developed heads and active life styles. They also possess an ink sac from which they squirt a dark fluid into the water in order to confuse pursuers. Around the Mediterranean, squid, octopus, and cuttlefish are highly valued; cuttlefish is also among the national dishes of China, Japan, and some Pacific islands.

Octopus is popular in Greece and Cyprus, where dried and grilled pieces of the tentacles are served as appetizers (the tentacles of squid are used for the same purpose in Italy). Octopus flesh is extremely dry and tough and must be beaten to break down the fibers before it is cooked.

Sea urchins are spine-covered marine animals (related to sea stars) that cling to rocks in warm waters throughout the world. They have long, sharp, movable spines sticking out from a hard limy shell that protects the soft parts inside. Popularly known as sea eggs, the urchins are a specialty of Marseilles, France. They are cut open, cleaned, and served raw.

KEY

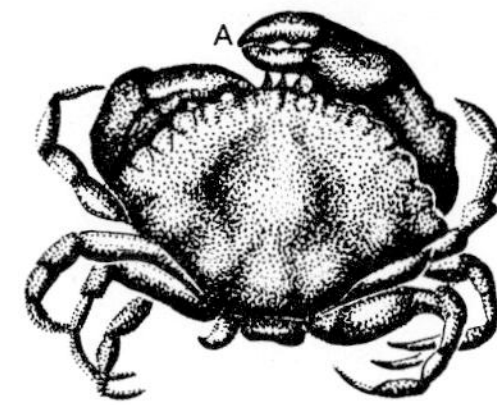
A

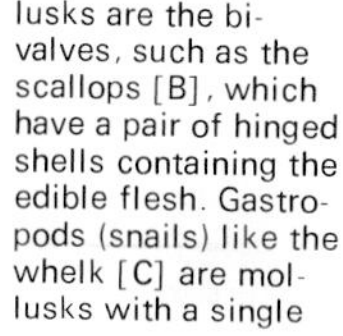
B

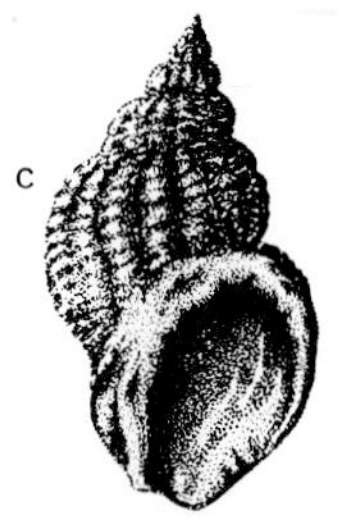
C
D

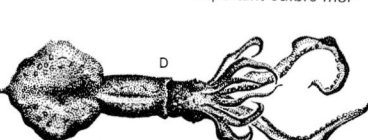

A wide range of seafood is found in most of the world's oceans. Shellfish varieties include crustaceans and the mollusks. A typical crustacean is the edible crab [A]. When the animal is cooked the shell is broken open and the flesh inside is eaten. The most important edible mollusks are the bivalves, such as the scallops [B], which have a pair of hinged shells containing the edible flesh. Gastropods (snails) like the whelk [C] are mollusks with a single shell. Cephalopods, the tentacled mollusks such as the squid [D], usually have no shell and most of the animal can be eaten.

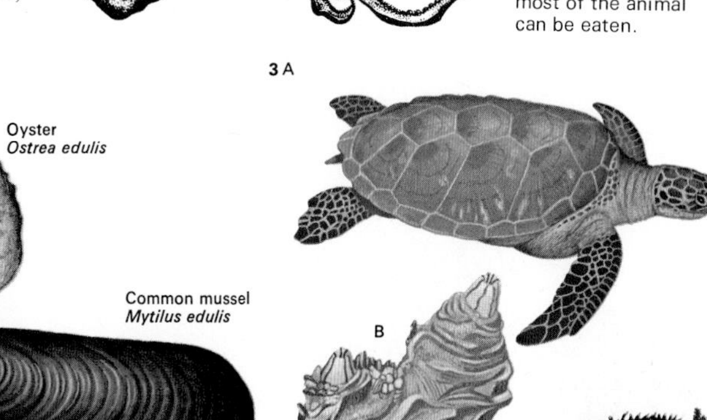
3 A
B
C

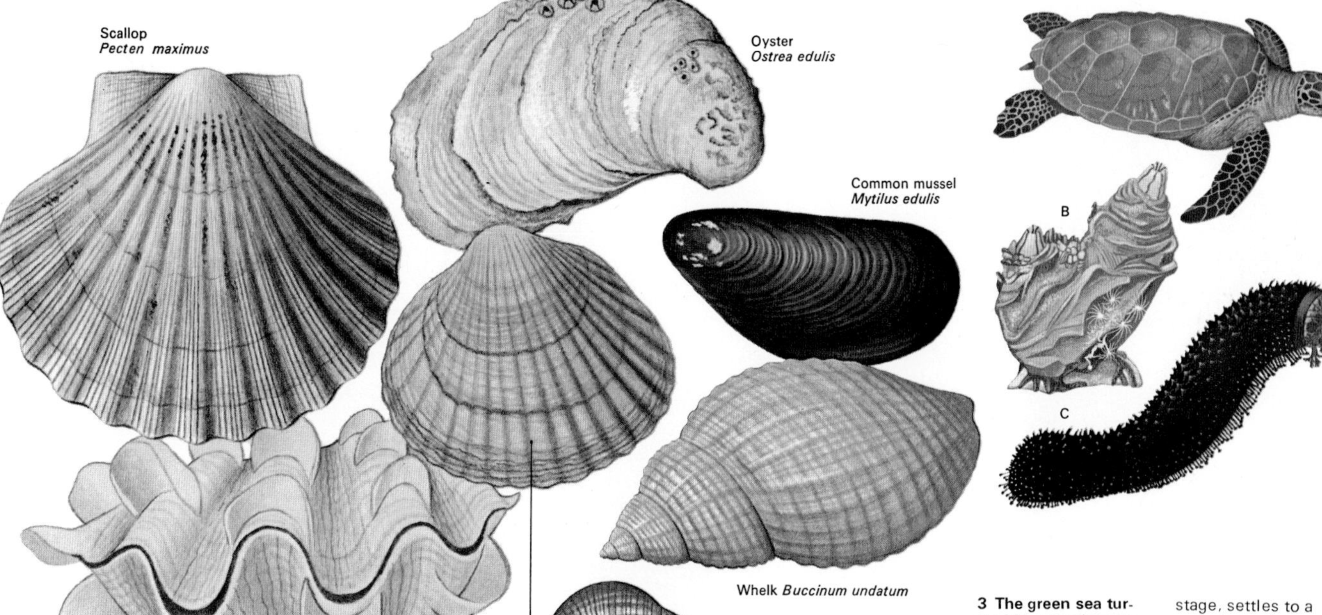
2
Scallop
Pecten maximus
Oyster
Ostrea edulis
Common mussel
Mytilus edulis
Whelk Buccinum undatum
Winkle
Littorina littorea
Frilly clam
Tridacna squamosa
Cockle Cardium edule

2 Bivalves and gastropods are the most important mollusks to be harvested. They are mostly found in shallow coastal waters and are quite easily collected. Scallop shells have been used as decorative embellishments since Roman times and were taken as emblems by the pilgrims to the church of St James of Compostela; in France the scallop is known as the pilgrim shell or *coquilles Saint Jacques*. Oysters, once a cheap seafood, are today one of the most expensive luxury foods, often eaten raw and on ice with lemon and brown bread, usually during winter. The common mussel is an inexpensive shellfish, particularly appreciated in French and Spanish cooking as the basis for soups and stews. Cockles are popularly known as the poor man's oyster in Europe and like them may be eaten raw, although they are more often marketed cooked and shelled. Whelks are also sold cooked and shelled and are traditionally eaten with vinegar and brown buttered bread; they are also used as fish bait. Many species of clam may be eaten raw, or alternatively can be grilled or used in any of the well-known American clam recipes. Winkles, or periwinkles, are smaller relatives of whelks; they may be eaten raw or cooked. A long pin is needed to extract the flesh.

3 The green sea turtle [A], a marine reptile, is rated as one of the world's delicacies. It lives offshore in warm waters of the Atlantic and Pacific, but comes ashore to lay eggs. Turtles are exported from Australia, South America, and Africa, but the finest come from the West Indian islands and are used in the famous turtle soup. Sea fig [B], or *figue de mer*, is a sea squirt, a primitive creature that, after a free-swimming larval stage, settles to a sedentary existence on rocks near the shore. It is gathered and eaten at its adult stage, and, despite its leathery covering, it is considered a delicacy in France. Sea cucumber [C] is an elongated relative of the starfish. About two dozen species of sea cucumbers are harvested in the Indian and Pacific oceans, where a food product, *bêche-de-mer*, is prepared from the body wall of the animal.

4

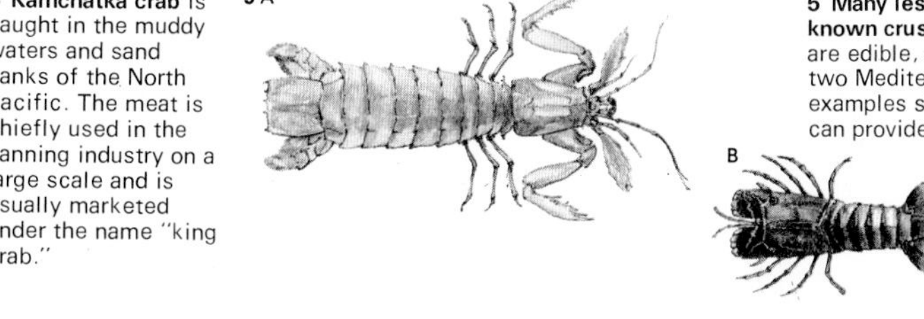
5 A
B

4 Kamchatka crab is caught in the muddy waters and sand banks of the North Pacific. The meat is chiefly used in the canning industry on a large scale and is usually marketed under the name "king crab."

5 Many less well-known crustaceans are edible, and the two Mediterranean examples shown here can provide the base for excellent soups. The mantis shrimp [A] lives in shallow water and has an average length of 8in (20cm). Large specimens of the creature known in France as *petite cigale* [B] may be prepared and served like lobster.

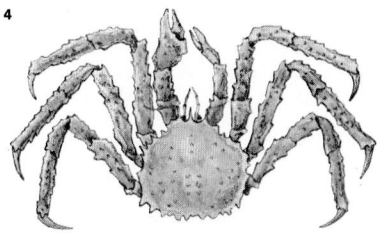

Food preservation

Almost all food, whether plant or animal in origin, is subject to deterioration and eventual decay. If it is not properly preserved, bacteria and molds start to grow, fats begin to oxidize and turn rancid, and enzymes within the food cause tissues to break down.

The rate at which food decays depends on its composition and on where it is stored. Soft berries, shellfish, and milk all begin to spoil within a few hours. On the other hand, chocolate, root crops, and nuts will often keep for weeks without any special precautions for storage. Food that is kept in cool, dry conditions [Key] keeps much longer than food stored in warm, humid surroundings.

Traditional methods of preservation

Methods of preserving food have been known since ancient times. One of the earliest was to dry food in the sun [2] or beside a fire, thereby evaporating much of its water content and reducing the rate at which chemical and biological processes of decomposition (which are water-dependent) make it unfit to eat. A variation of drying is smoking [3]; the chemicals in the smoke greatly increase the storage life of foods. Drying and smoking are widely employed, especially among nomadic peoples.

Salt [1] has been used as a preservative for thousands of years. It extends the storage life of foods by inhibiting the growth of bacteria. Salt and spices are both used to make food more palatable, especially if it has already begun to deteriorate.

Almost all agricultural societies are familiar with fermentation and its preservative effects. The chemical products—alcohol, acetic acid, and sometimes lactic acid—that are formed during fermentation inhibit the growth of decay-causing organisms. A similar process is that of pickling in vinegar, alcohol, brine, or syrup [4]. Foods that are placed in baths of brine or some fermented liquid absorb the liquid and resist decomposition.

Heat sterilizing and canning

One of the major modern methods of food preservation is canning [6]. Although the principle of heat-treating food to destroy decay- and disease-carrying organisms was explained by the French scientist Louis Pasteur (1822–95) in the mid-1800s, the art of canning had been discovered earlier. In 1809, after 14 years of experiment, the Frenchman Nicolas Appert (1749–1841) found that certain foods would keep for months at room temperature if they were first sealed in glass bottles and then heated in boiling water. In the following year the same process was carried out using steel cans. Canning at first required up to five hours' heating.

Today, canning is generally an automatic process during which raw food is washed, sorted, cooked, canned, and packaged by machine. Heat treatment of the can takes little more than half an hour. The canning process also preserves the nutritional value of foods.

Refrigeration and freezing

Other common methods of food preservation are cooling and freezing, based on the principle that biochemical processes are slowed down and eventually halted as the

CONNECTIONS

See also
1820 Everyday machines and mechanisms 3

1 Fresh meat and vegetables were once not available during long sailing voyages. Before the invention of canning, travelers had to eat dried, smoked, or pickled foods. Salted beef was a staple in the seafaring diet. Slabs of beef were packed in dry salt or a saline brine inside large wooden casks. A salt solution of 10–15% was generally effective in preserving the meat throughout a long crossing.

2 The risk of spoilage is greatly diminished in food that is dried, as most microorganisms and processes of decomposition require the presence of moisture. Dried meat, or pemmican, is eaten by nomadic peoples. A traditional method of drying is by exposing fish, meat, or fruit to the sun and wind. In Norway gutted fish are sliced open and then placed flat upon large wooden drying racks angled to face the sun.

3 Preservation by smoking is an age-old technique used to cure meat, fish, and cheese. Smoking serves to dehydrate food and to coat its surface with chemicals that retard decomposition and inhibit the growth of molds and bacteria. In a typical smokeroom, the food is hung by hooks from the ceiling and the floor covered with a smoldering layer of sawdust. The smoking process lasts for at least 24 hours.

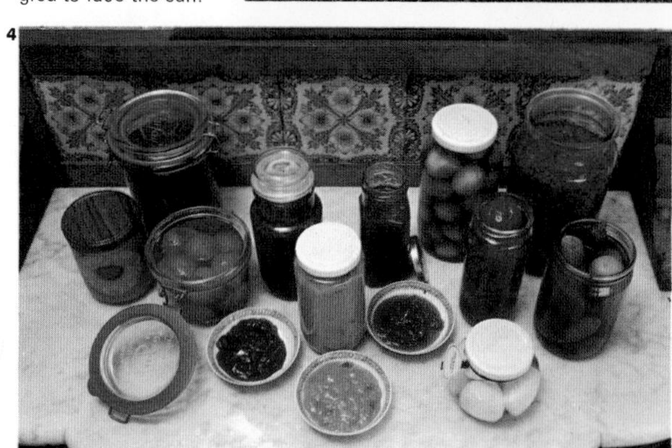

4 In pickling, a salt brine controls the kinds of changes that the food undergoes. Instead of decay taking place, fermentation occurs within the food tissues and produces acids that act as preservatives. Pickled foods may remain edible for many months. Today, however, pickling is more important as a flavoring process because bottled and canned foods can be relied on as having been sterilized by heat treatment.

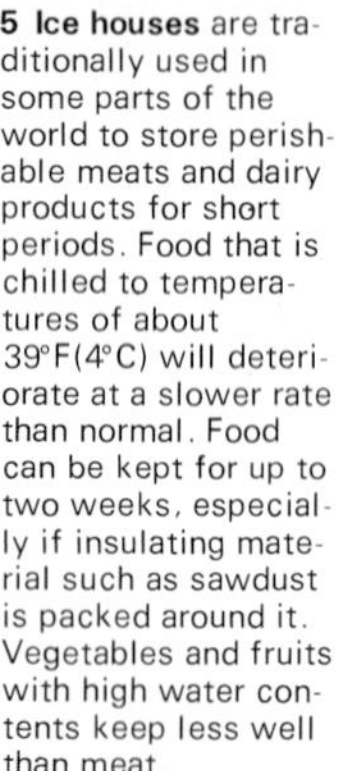

5 Ice houses are traditionally used in some parts of the world to store perishable meats and dairy products for short periods. Food that is chilled to temperatures of about 39°F(4°C) will deteriorate at a slower rate than normal. Food can be kept for up to two weeks, especially if insulating material such as sawdust is packed around it. Vegetables and fruits with high water contents keep less well than meat.

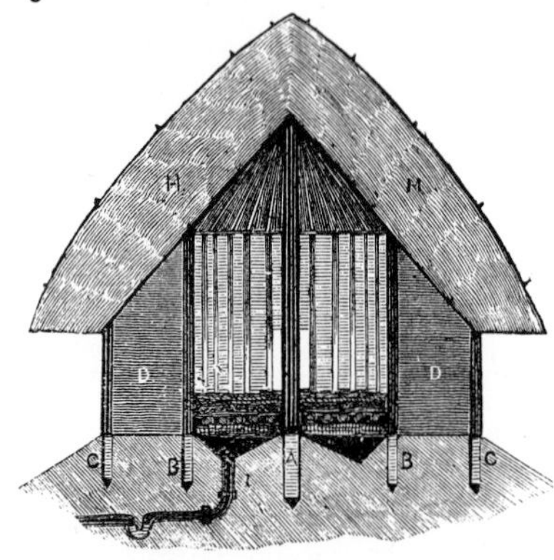

6 Canning is the process in which food is placed in containers (traditionally tin-lined steel, but today often plastic-lined aluminum cans), heated to 240°F(115°C) and then sealed under a vacuum. A brief heating of the can kills any bacteria that cause decay or that might otherwise contaminate the food. Modern canning machinery will sort, wash, cook, and can foods automatically, producing many cans a minute.

temperature drops. Cooling is an ideal way of preserving the freshness of food [5]. As early as 2500 BC in India and Egypt, food containers were wrapped in wet rags. The heat loss caused by evaporation was an efficient cooling technique. Long before this, however, cellars and caves were being used as storage rooms for food, and inhabitants of cold regions have always been familiar with freezing techniques. Even the process of freeze-drying [7], or dehydrating and freezing, was known to some.

Food will keep fresh if it is stored in a cool, dry place. Below 39°F (4°C) most fruits and vegetables will keep for up to a week. Freezing denies water to microorganisms, bringing their growth to a standstill although not necessarily killing them. They are revived when the food is thawed out.

If food is frozen gradually, as in a domestic freezer, large slivers of ice form within it. These crystals rupture the cell tissue so that the food loses its moisture and texture when it is thawed out. The flavor and texture of delicate fruits and vegetables can be ruined by slow freezing.

Ascorbic acid and a range of sulfites and benzoates are commonly used food preservatives. Minute amounts of these chemicals check the growth of bacteria, molds, and yeasts. In addition, foods are treated with a wide variety of antioxidants, bleaching chemicals, neutralizers, and stabilizers in order to preserve their original "garden fresh" appearance.

A fairly recent process of food treatment uses irradiation techniques [7]. Although complete sterilization by this method requires doses of radiation so high that food tissues are destroyed, lower pasteurizing doses are effective in killing many organisms and halting sprouting. Radiation prolongs the storage life of food, although it must still be kept refrigerated or stored in hermetically sealed containers.

In the past 200 years, great strides have been made in the techniques of food preservation. It has become possible for consumers in most parts of the world to obtain meat, vegetables, and fruit in "fresh" condition although they may have been stored for weeks or even months.

KEY

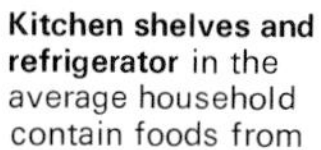

Kitchen shelves and refrigerator in the average household contain foods from almost every corner of the globe. Modern methods of preserving and packaging food have made it possible to eat fruit and vegetables all year round.

7

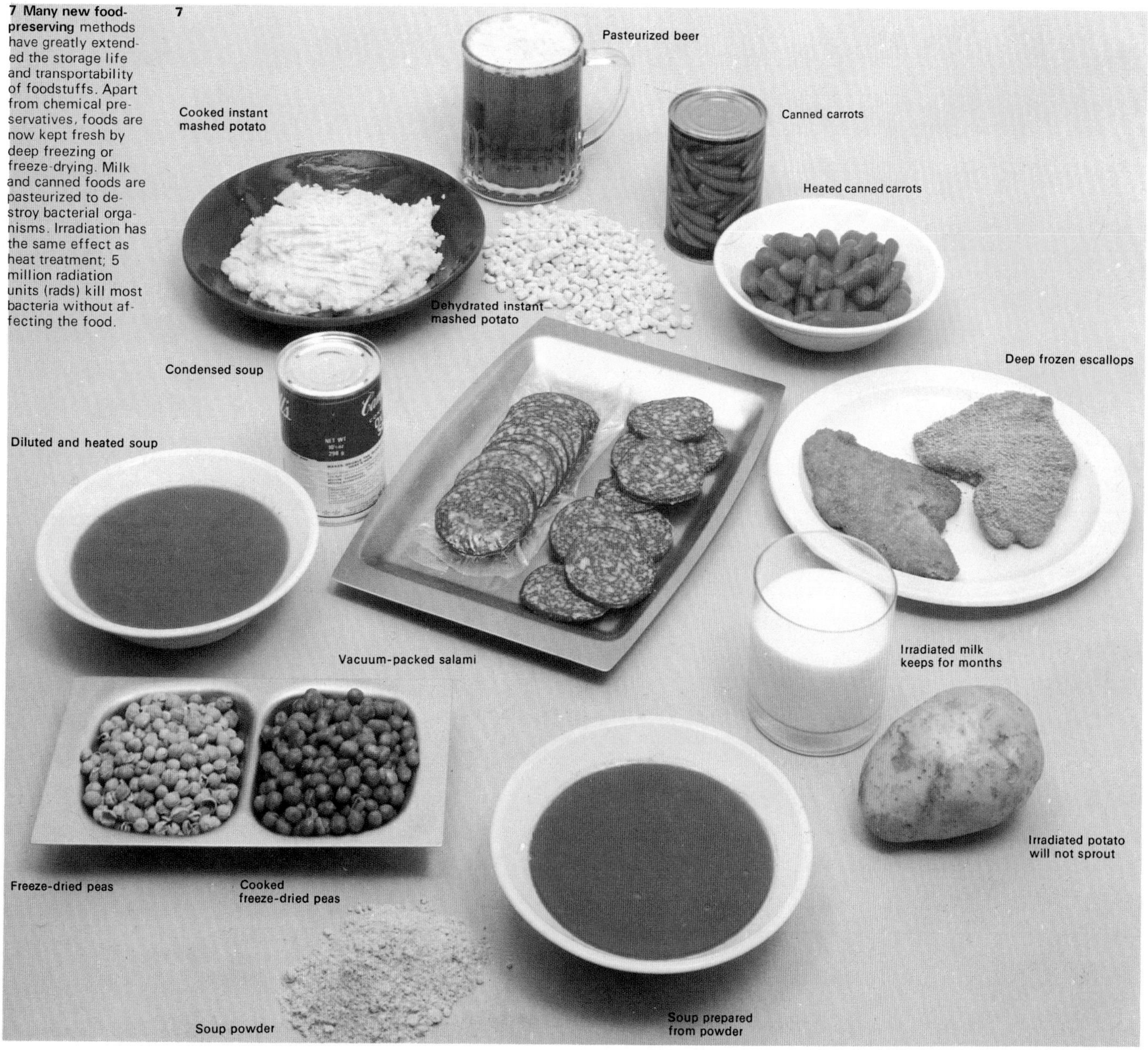

7 Many new food-preserving methods have greatly extended the storage life and transportability of foodstuffs. Apart from chemical preservatives, foods are now kept fresh by deep freezing or freeze-drying. Milk and canned foods are pasteurized to destroy bacterial organisms. Irradiation has the same effect as heat treatment; 5 million radiation units (rads) kill most bacteria without affecting the food.

Pasteurized beer

Cooked instant mashed potato

Canned carrots

Heated canned carrots

Dehydrated instant mashed potato

Condensed soup

Deep frozen escallops

Diluted and heated soup

Vacuum-packed salami

Irradiated milk keeps for months

Irradiated potato will not sprout

Freeze-dried peas

Cooked freeze-dried peas

Soup powder

Soup prepared from powder

The future of food

In his *Essay on the Principle of Population* published in 1798, Thomas Malthus (1766–1834) put forward the idea that the human population was growing faster than the supplies of food needed to keep it alive. He concluded that if population were permitted to increase unchecked a food crisis would eventually result and war and disease would reduce the population to a level compatible with existing foods supplies [9].

To date, the crisis that Malthus predicted has not materialized. In spite of several serious famines in the last 200 years and the persistence of widespread malnutrition, which afflicts 15 percent of the world's population, people of affluent countries are better nourished today than ever before.

Why Malthus was wrong

Malthus was wrong because he could not possibly foresee the dramatic changes that would greatly increase man's ability to produce more food. The first of these changes began with the rapid expansion in agricultural land that occurred when vast areas of fertile land were opened up in North America, Australia, and, to a lesser extent, South America during the nineteenth century. The invention of the steam engine, and later the discovery of the principles of refrigeration, enabled the produce grown on those continents to be shipped to the newly industralized nations in Europe, thus greatly increasing their food supplies and increasing the variety in their diets.

Perhaps more important were the scientific advances that eventually led to man's being able to grow more food from each acre of land. In 1840 Baron Justus von Liebig (1803–73) discovered that man could replace the nutrients extracted by crops from the land. This important discovery led to the development of the fertilizer industry and to the eventual widespread use of inorganic fertilizers by farmers. Another major advance was the discovery by Gregor Mendel (1822–84) of the laws of inheritance. The growth in the knowledge of genetics that followed eventually led to its practical application. New higher-yielding crops were bred [5], as were increasingly productive livestock [4].

These and developments such as the discovery of chemical pesticides enabled man to grow more food on the land. At the same time, he began to look more and more to the sea as a source of food. Sea-going trawlers, together with mechanical refrigerating machines, meant that people living away from the coast could purchase and eat fresh fish [3].

Food for the future

Population projections suggest that a great effort will have to be made over the next 50 years if widespread starvation is to be avoided. The United Nations predicts that by AD 2000 there will be 6.5 billion mouths to feed. How can they all be satisfied?

Obviously, food production is going to have to increase above its current level. Following the conventional approach, this might possibly be done either by bringing more land under cultivation or by further intensifying production on land already being cultivated, or by doing both these things. Unfortunatlely, this approach presents several problems. Most of the best agricultural

CONNECTIONS

Read first
302 World food resources

See also
628 Endangered mammals
636 Constructive man

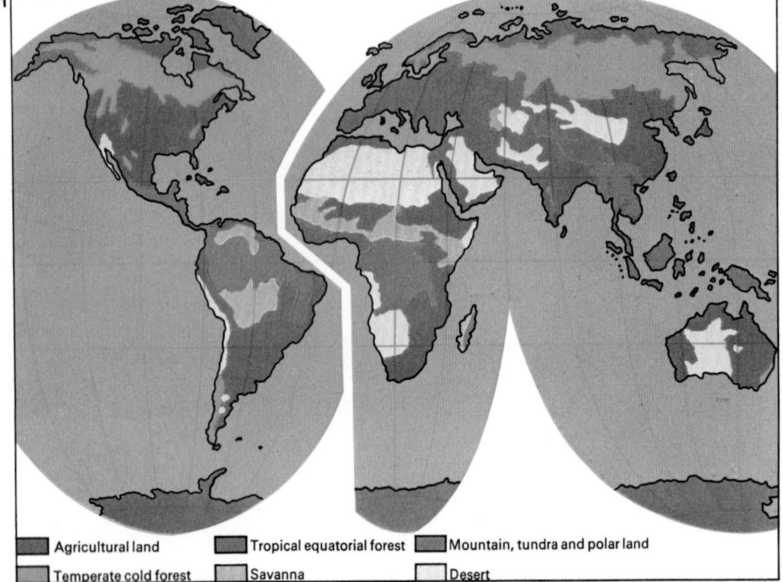

Agricultural land
Tropical equatorial forest
Mountain, tundra and polar land
Temperate cold forest
Savanna
Desert

1 Potential arable land of 4 billion acres (1.5 billion hectares) is as yet unexploited. The most fertile land has long been under cultivation and what remains is marginal land where the cost of bringing it into production is high. This new land will produce high crop yield only with difficulty because of the severe limitations imposed by soil fertility, topography, and adverse climatic conditions.

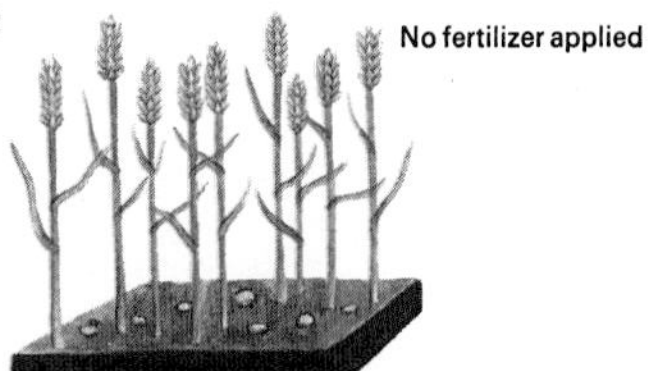

No fertilizer applied

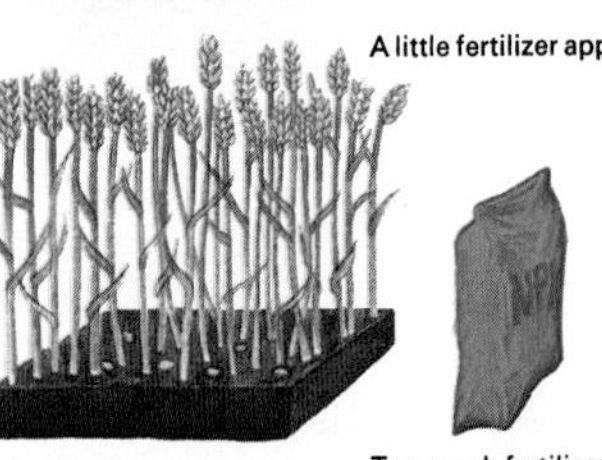

A little fertilizer applied

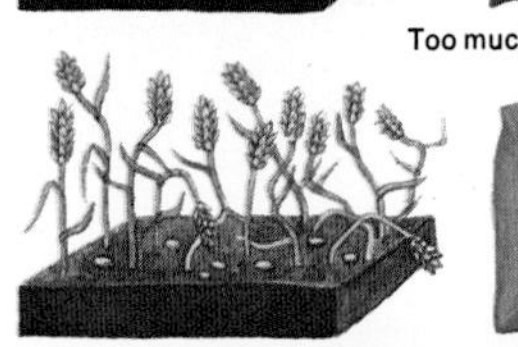

Too much fertilizer applied

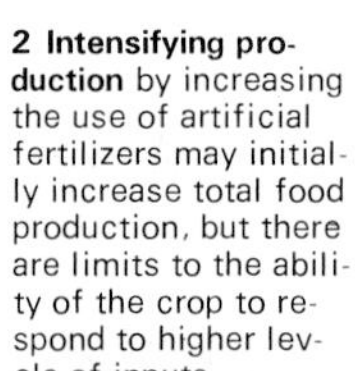

2 Intensifying production by increasing the use of artificial fertilizers may initially increase total food production, but there are limits to the ability of the crop to respond to higher levels of inputs.

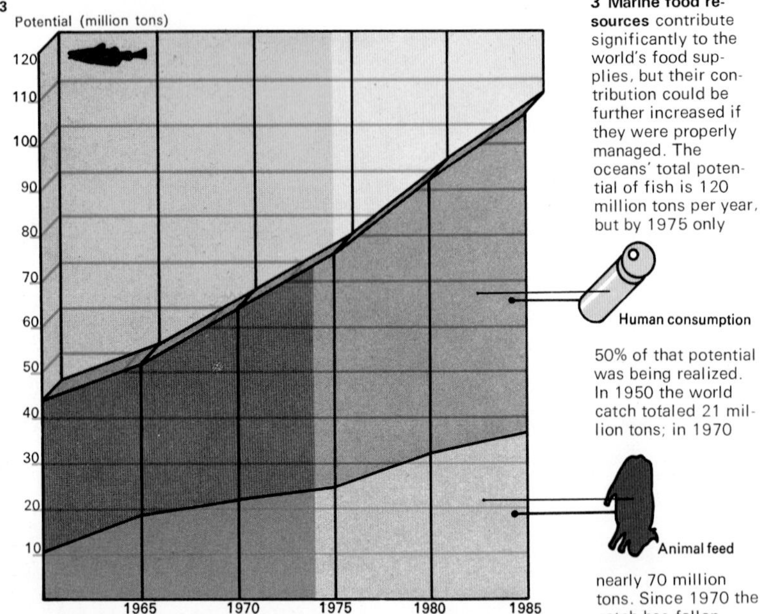

Potential (million tons)
120
110
100
90
80
70
60
50
40
30
20
10
1965
1970
1975
1980
1985
Human consumption
Animal feed

3 Marine food resources contribute significantly to the world's food supplies, but their contribution could be further increased if they were properly managed. The oceans' total potential of fish is 120 million tons per year, but by 1975 only 50% of that potential was being realized. In 1950 the world catch totaled 21 million tons; in 1970 nearly 70 million tons. Since 1970 the catch has fallen, largely as a result of overfishing the commercial table species and also because of the disappearance of the anchovies (used in large quantities for animal feed) off the coast of Peru in 1972. Conflict over fishing rights is increasing and several nations have established an extension of the existing 12-mi(19-km) limit to 200mi(320km). Despite overfishing there still remain regions such as the Indian Ocean that have not yet been exploited for food.

4 The beefalo is an experimental hybrid of an American bison and a domestic beef animal. It can convert grass and other roughage to meat better than conventional beef breeds, and may help to increase world food production.

land in the world is already under cultivation. To bring the remaining 4 billion acres (1.5 billion hectares) of potential agricultural land into production may prove costly [1]. Much of this land is found in tropical areas such as the Amazon and Congo basins, which are covered with thick jungle. If the protective canopy of trees were indiscriminately removed and the land plowed up to grow crops, heavy tropical rains would soon transform the soils into barren laterite (a soil rich in iron and aluminum oxides but devoid of mineral nutrients such as potassium and nitrates).

The use of higher levels of inputs such as fertilizers would be limited by their availability and cost [2]. Because of the law of diminishing returns, higher applications of fertilizer do not result in correspondingly higher yields. Consequently, unless increased fertilizer production were earmarked for land that currently receives very little fertilizer (and most of this land is found in the developing world), its use could result in more expensive food. In addition, the application of more fertilizer could lead to severe pollution of water supplies. Given the population projections and the limitations imposed on increasing food supplies by conventional methods it appears that well-planned approaches must be adopted.

Simultaneous attacks on the problem

It is important to work simultaneously on three fronts: to increase food production; to improve the global distribution of food supplies; and, finally, to limit the growth in demand for food by curbing the expansion in the world's population.

An increase in food production requires both conventional and nonconventional methods. Nonconventional methods include the development of new crops, animals, and foods. If the increased food production is to benefit the world as a whole, then its distribution must be improved from the present situation in which about 33 percent of the world's population eats much more than half the food. Initially this can best be done by ensuring that the increase in food production occurs primarily in the developing nations of the world.

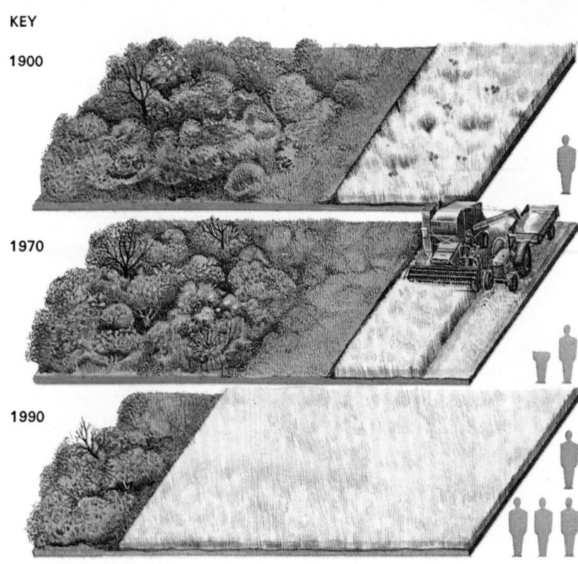
KEY
1900
1970
1990

World food production has increased four-fold since 1900 although the area of potential cropland under cultivation has remained the same. By 1990, 83% of potential cropland will have to be cultivated to support the increased population.

5

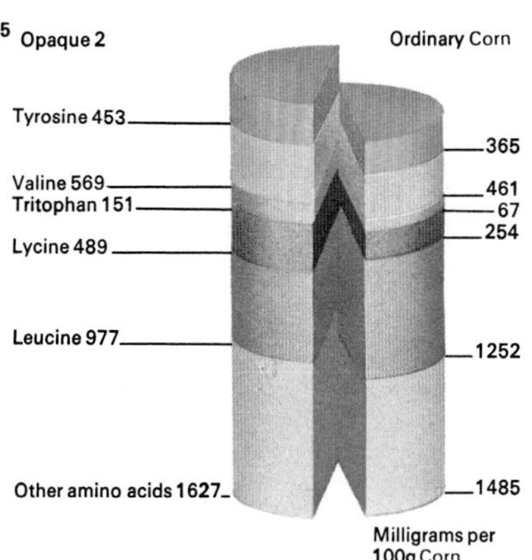
Opaque 2
Ordinary Corn
Tyrosine 453
Valine 569
Tritophan 151
Lycine 489
Leucine 977
Other amino acids 1627
365
461
67
254
1252
1485
Milligrams per 100g Corn

5 High protein grains could improve nutrition, particularly in the poorer nations of the world where grain is a major source of protein. The development of Opaque 2 varieties of corn has already increased the effective protein yield of these varieties 25 percent above that of ordinary corn. This has become possible because of the higher lysine and tryptophan content of Opaque 2 varieties.

6

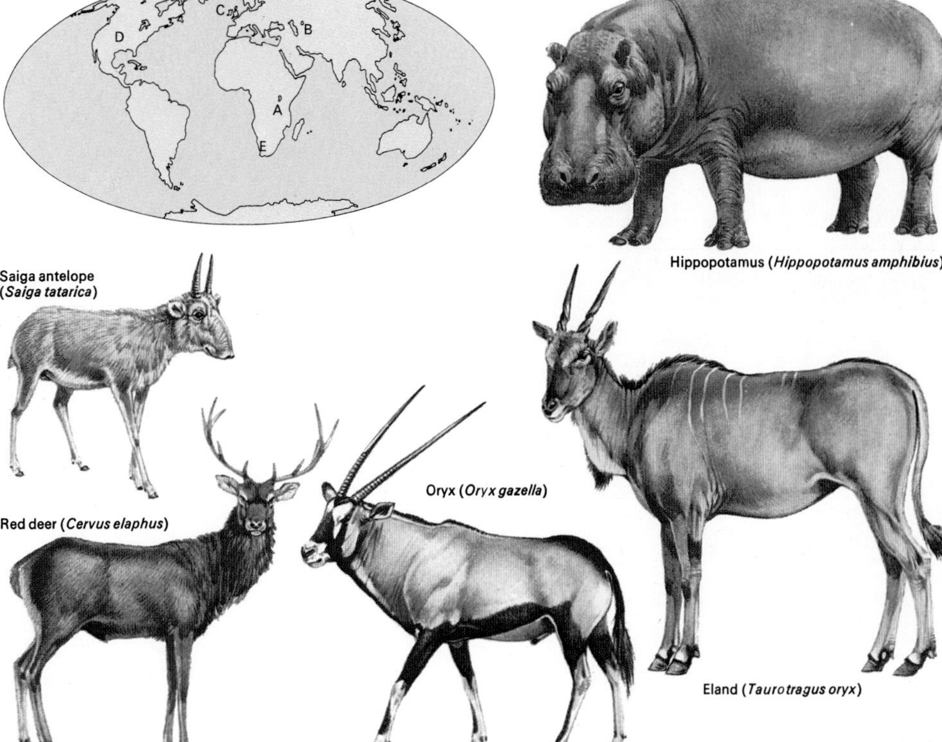
A
B
C
D
E
Hippopotamus (*Hippopotamus amphibius*)
Saiga antelope (*Saiga tatarica*)
Red deer (*Cervus elaphus*)
Oryx (*Oryx gazella*)
Eland (*Taurotragus oryx*)

6 Protection and sensible culling of wildlife stocks enable species to thrive and at the same time provide meat. In Ugandan game parks [A] the hippopotamus has been culled for meat. The saiga antelope is found in the Soviet Union [B] and is harvested for meat, leather, and horns. The red deer is more efficient than any domestic animal at converting the poor moss and grasses of the Scottish Highlands [C] into meat. The eland of East Africa is now bred in Africa and the United States [D] for meat. The oryx is one of the few meat producing species that can live in deserts [E].

7

7 New foods that make use of crops not generally eaten by people in the Western world are being developed. One is textured vegetable protein made from soybean. Protein extracted from leaves may one day also be used for food.

8

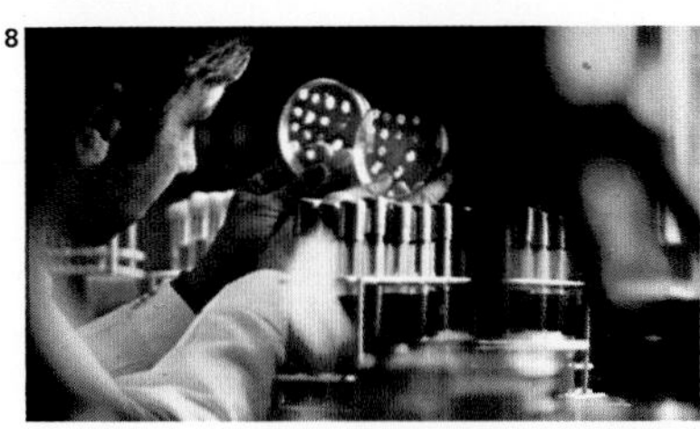

8 New animal foods are being developed by the growing of bacteria, algae, fungi, and yeasts on hydrocarbons. If successful, this could release large quantities of high protein products, such as fish and legumes, for human consumption.

9

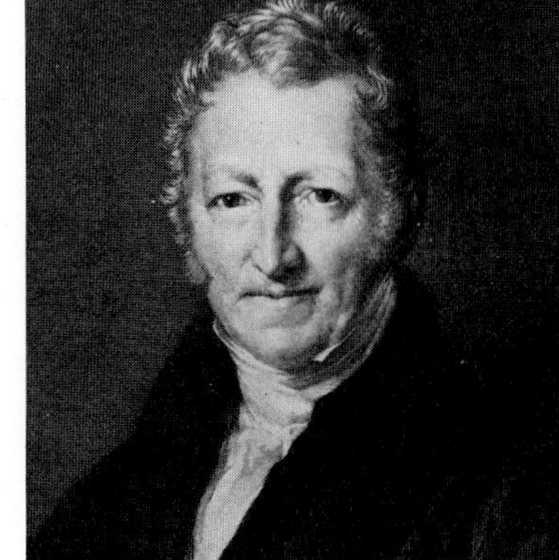

9 Malthus suggested that population tends to expand more rapidly than food supplies and that a food crisis is inevitable. This crisis has been avoided so far, but it may materialize unless ways are found to curb world population growth.

LIFE ON EARTH

LIFE ON EARTH

by Professor Salvador E. Luria

Life is the phenomenon, so far observed only on the crust of the Earth, by which a portion of matter achieves an unusual degree and variety of organization maintained by a flow of chemical energy.

Interpretations of the phenomenon of life vary according to the interests and viewpoints of different observers. To primitive man, projecting into nature around him his inner feeling of wonder, life was a mysterious essence pervading all the universe. To theologians life is the most obvious manifestation of a specific intervention of divine will within matter. More specifically, to Judeo-Christian theologians life is evidence of a spiritual creationism culminating in man himself, the possessor of a perfectible soul.

To most scientists life is a natural phenomenon, fully obeying all physical laws but also exhibiting specific features of organization that reflect the properties of certain substances under certain conditions of quality, quantity, and time. The program of a science of life is to interpret life in terms of a theory that embodies no force or principle *external* to physical matter. Hence the apparent exceptionality of life phenomena among the totality of natural phenomena requires the introduction of some unique *internal* principle.

The life phenomenon would be approached differently by different scientists—a physicist, a chemist, a biologist—each looking at life mainly from the viewpoint of his specialty.

To the physicist the exceptionality of life phenomena would appear mainly as a pattern of organization maintained by a lasting, unusually high level of chemical activity even at the relatively low temperatures that prevail on the Earth's surface. This chemical activity is an indication that in the molecules of living organisms not all atoms are bound by the strongest possible bonds. Conversion of weak to stronger bonds releases energy. Since natural processes tend to release energy spontaneously, weak bonds tend to be replaced by stronger bonds and chemical activity tends to become minimal. Faced with the high levels of chemical transactions that continue to take place in living organisms, the physicist would attribute them to the singular propensity of two atoms, oxygen and nitrogen, to form between themselves and with other atoms a peculiar class of "medium-strength" bonds. These bonds, in molecules such as O-O, are weaker in energy per single bond than the stable bonds in molecules such as water (H-O-H), but are stronger than the bonds in unstable molecules such as chlorine gas (Cl-Cl).

The medium-strength bonds confer to molecules a specific, "just-right" mixture of stability and chemical reactivity. They are stable enough to last a reasonable length of time, so that some catalysts are needed to accelerate chemical changes; and yet their tendency to be converted to stronger bonds with release of energy makes them "restless." The reverse process, the conversion of strong bonds to medium-strength bonds, requires a trapping of external energy. The physicist would note that such trapping is the essence of photosynthesis, the process that today provides almost all of the energy for life on Earth.

The chemist, who is a specialist physicist, would agree with his confrere but would add as a characteristic of life the unique property of the carbon atom to enter into stable chemical combinations with an enormous variety of atomic groups. Organic chemistry—the chemistry of carbon compounds—is the chemistry of life. Among the stable chemicals of living organisms the chemist would single out as most remarkable a unique class of molecules present in every organism, essentially deoxyribonucleic acid, or DNA, whose famous double-helix structure was discovered by James Watson and Francis Crick in 1953. DNA resembles crystals in its degree of intrinsic spatial order and stability, but superimposes upon these qualities an enormous amount of "chemical information" usable for life processes. Whereas a crystal is a monotonous, repetitive assembly of identical patterns of atoms, like a mosaic of identical marbles that can grow only by accommodating additional marbles at its outer edges, the "aperiodic crystals" of DNA, to use the famous phrase of Ervin Shroedinger in his book *What Is Life?* (1944), are like computer tapes. Just as sequences of magnetic signals on a computer tape encode messages of words, numbers, or sounds, so on DNA the sequence of certain chemical groups,

---

Institute Professor of Biology and Director of the Center for Cancer Research, Massachusetts Institute of Technology; Nonresident Fellow of the Salk Institute of Biological Studies; Co-recipient of the Nobel Prize for Medicine; Fellow of the American Academy of Arts and Sciences; Member of the National Academy of Sciences; Fellow of the American Philosophical Society; author of *Life: The Unfinished Experiment; Thirty-Six Lectures in Biology*, etc.

like letters of an alphabet, embodies messages of unlimited variety and unique specifications. These messages, our astute chemist would surmise, are the program of life: the set of directions that masterminds the myriad of chemical reactions in living organisms.

The biologist does not start from physical and chemical facts alone. He notices first the immense variety of living organisms, from human beings and giant trees to microscopic bacteria and submicroscopic viruses. He recognizes the existence of species as natural groups of highly similar organisms. He seeks for unity in variety and finds it in the similarity of certain functions and processes: chemical exchanges; reactivity to the ambience; maintenance of form; cycles of birth, growth, and death. He puts order into variety, classifying organisms in terms of similarities of forms and activities.

Once an ordered classification has emerged, the quest for the origin of variety—that is, for meaningful relationships—leads the biologist (if he is a Charles Darwin) to divine the underlying principle: evolution. Life suddenly becomes not only a dynamic process of chemical exchanges but a historical progression.

Darwinian evolution, the only intrinsic principle of life science, took form in the mid-19th century as the culmination of the scientific revolution, the convergence of the Newtonian view of the physical world with the humanistic historicism of 18th-century philosophers. In its present form the theory of evolution envisages a single historical process embracing the entire world of living organisms, as well as that of dead fossil ones, in a continous sequence of events. Similarities between organisms are interpreted as common ancestry; the more recent, the closer are the similarities. Discontinuities—the missing links—are traced to the disappearance of species and groups of species. The species of organisms that actually exist are a small sample of all those that might have existed, most of them having failed ever to emerge. What to the superficial observers appears as a chaos of existent forms acquires the rationally understandable order of a complex but natural process of probabilistic survival. What is, is what has survived and prospered.

Organic evolution

The modern theory of evolution, as developed since Darwin's time in the light of contemporary biochemistry and genetics, invokes two driving natural forces: hereditary variation and natural selection. Hereditary variation, readily apparent even within highly homogeneous species of plants or animals, is traced to *mutations,* that is, to chance changes in the DNA molecules that constitute the hereditary material, the tape with the program of life. Mutations arise by mistakes in the synthesis of new copies of DNA molecules and by other accidents. Once a mutation arises in an organism of a given species, the mutated DNA can spread among the members of the species through its replication. Through the mixing of heredities, which is the essence of sexual reproduction, the mutant DNA can become associated with a variety of genetic make-ups in individual members of a species. Once such hereditary variety has arisen within a species, different individuals will function differently in a given environment, and the effects of selective pressure become apparent.

Natural selection is simply the outcome of a process of *differential reproduction.* The more successful members of a species are those represented by more descendants in later generations. Differential reproduction results in numerical expansion or reduction of certain species and can even lead to their disappearance.

As expressed in the aphorism *Chance and Necessity* (the title of a famous book by Jacques Monod) the history of life is the interplay between random, accidental changes in hereditary material and the inexorable pressure of selection by differential reproduction.

The performance of life

Each living organism is the manifestation of its hereditary material interacting with the environment that surrounds it. Its performance will decide its destiny in evolution. How does life performance unfold? That is, how are the instructions of the genes carried out and made responsive to the outside world?

At the present stage of evolution all essential life processes take place within *cells.* A cell is a chemical factory that provides near-optimal conditions for the chemical reactions programmed by the genes. Genes—segments of hereditary material—participate in these processes uniquely as *templates.* That is, they serve as chemical molds both for the generation of new copies of the genes themselves—a process called *replication*—and for the fashioning of tools used in chemical catalysis and for the scaffolding of cells and organs. The genes are DNA filaments consisting of sequences of chemical groups called *nucleotides.* The tools are *proteins,* consisting of chains of substances called *amino acids.* Each gene is the tape for one protein chain. Between a gene and its specific protein products there intervenes a transient mediator substance, ribonucleic acid, or RNA. This is but a slightly different version of the gene tape, which, being free to move away from the gene itself, makes it possible to convey the message to the cellular sites where proteins are made. Biologists, borrowing the linguists' jargon, say that the information of the genes—the code of life—is *transcribed* into messages of RNA, which are then *translated* according to a unique decoding process into the molecular structure of protein.

Whereas DNA genes and most RNA messages are used only in the way that linear tapes are used in a computer, a protein, after being fashioned as a linear object under direction of a linear RNA template, acquires its final, functional shape by "balling up" into a specific tridimensional tangle, an object whose shape and surface details are dictated only by the gene-directed sequence of its amino acids. Thus the unidimensional wisdom of each gene tape, translated into a linear protein backbone, gives rise to a tridimensional protein molecule whose outward structure bears no likeness to the shape of the gene. And yet it is the structure of the protein, with its unique surface pattern of chemical groups, that will act in the chemistry of the cell and whose functional effectiveness will be tried by natural selection.

The replication of the genes is itself catalyzed by a set of specific proteins. By their own activity the genes fashion the cellular machinery and renew themselves. Thus does life grow.

The effectiveness of proteins has no direct effect on the properties of the genes themselves. There is no inheritance of characters acquired by an organism through its functional response to specific environmental conditions. Only by its effect on differential reproduction of the organism is the functional effectiveness of proteins tested in evolution.

The functioning of any given gene is not invariable in time. It is regulated by the intrinsic program of the organism, the set of genes as a whole, which has evolved in such a way that it unfolds by its own logic and can also respond to the demands of the external world. Thus in simple organisms such as bacteria, transcription of a given gene is turned on or off in response to environmental signals, so that each needed protein that the organism can make is made in just the needed amount. Encounter with a potentially useful food may evoke the appearance of a protein catalyst that digests it. Likewise, finding an essential substance (such as a vitamin) ready-made in the environment can decrease the synthesis of those proteins that would otherwise manufacture that substance. At least in bacteria, this regulation of the function of the genes by the external milieu is astonishingly precise.

In the development of a complex organism such as man, different genes function at different times in different cells, even though all cells of a given individual have the same genes. So long as the growing embryo or fetus remains in the relatively uniform environment of the mother's womb, differentiation expresses almost exclusively the unfolding of the intrinsic program of the genes. Later, when the newborn meets the changing milieu of the world, differentiation continues as an interplay of nature and nurture. The environment—the ecological reality—fashions the organism and also tests it for its capacity to reproduce and flourish.

Life, matter with a program

The essence of what has been outlined above is that life is the property of that portion of matter that becomes organized by a program—a set of genes. The program varies from organism to organism, yet has a common general structure in all organisms and controls its own reproduction by directing the synthesis of the complicated machinery of a chemical factory, the living cell. In complex organisms the program includes directions for the selective expression of certain genes. Evolution is the story of changes in program tested rigorously in the arena of natural selection. Throughout the living world, despite complexity, the organization of the program—DNA—and the basic machinery for its translation—protein synthesis—have remained similar.

Two major questions may be posed: How did the program come into existence? And how did evolution bring into existence not only simple cells but also large elaborate organisms of great complexity?

Gene evolution

It is now tentatively held that life developed first by chemical reactions occurring in a "prebiotic" environment, that is, an environment not fashioned by the activities of life itself. By virtue of the local high temperatures generated by radioactivity and by solar radiation in the newly formed Earth the prebiotic environment contained a "hot thin soup," with high concentrations of carbon, nitrogen, and oxygen in compounds rich in those medium-strength bonds in which our physicist saw the springboard of the chemical machinery of life. Laboratory experiments have shown that a series of compounds likely to have existed early on the Earth's crust can in fact give rise spontaneously in the test tube to the very building blocks of present-day life molecules—nucleic acids and proteins.

At first the processes that finally led to life must have proceeded haphazardly, producing here-and-there local concentrations of large molecules resembling DNA and proteins. In a pleasing coincidence with the biblical story of the fashioning of man from clay, the early process may actually have been catalyzed by certain clays. This process became enormously accelerated when chance events gave rise to some organic molecules that could replace clays as catalysts in the synthesis of other complex molecules. A key step was presumably the appearance of molecules of certain nucleic acids that, acting as genes, directed the production of catalysts that copied the genes themselves. Thus a "feed-ahead" process started; life as a self-propelled program was on its way. The final, critical step in the transition from hot thin soup to organized life was the "invention" of the cell: the appearance of catalysts that could generate molecules capable of forming a closed enveloping membrane with suitable properties of selective permeability for various classes of chemicals.

Once cellular life had come into being, it must have used up relatively quickly the prebiotic store of organic compounds. As early as the midpoint of the five billion years of the age of our planet the expansion of life probably had become dependent on the radiant energy of sunlight.

Out of many blind alleys, one line of descent was successful and gave rise to the glorious family of animals and plants that today populates the Earth.

Extraterrestrial life

Did life evolve elsewhere than on Earth? There is every reason to believe that the other planets of our Solar System lack the conditions needed for life to arise. Searching for life there is probably a futile and wasteful venture.

Among the planets that presumably surround other suns in our and other galaxies one must assume that there exist many that resemble Earth and on which some life will probably have developed. Only if such extraterrestrial life has evolved to the stage of sending, receiving, and decoding signals will we on Earth have a chance to learn of its existence by our own signal-detecting technology.

Life's complexity

A human being consists of about ten trillion cells of different degrees of variety. Billions of liver cells, for example, are almost identical to each other and function in similar manner as processors of foods. But of the billions of brain cells probably not any two are "wired" identically: each cell takes up a unique function within the network that receives, processes, and responds to signals and functions in thinking and talking.

Most plants and animals have evolved sex, which requires at each generation not one but two ancestors. And yet single-celled organisms such as bacteria and protozoa still live and thrive. What forces made simplicity useful here, complexity valuable there? Complexity was not just selected for the opportunity it provides for large organisms to devour small ones, since plants and trees evolved enormous complexity without generally becoming predators. At some points in evolution size as such must have been at a premium, permitting the development of specialized organs. Since cells must remain small in order to keep the reasonable ratio of surface to volume they need to carry out their chemical processes, increase in size required multicellular organization. This in turn permitted and indeed required the delegation of various functions to different parts of an organism—as in a tree whose leaves get light and gases from the atmosphere while the roots receive water and minerals from the soil. Thus, large organisms came to consist of organ systems, among which an exquisitely precise division of labor and coordination of function became established.

Yet even the most superbly functioning organism is not an ideally perfect instrument. It is only a compromise of adaptations brought about by natural selection acting on the limited materials that evolution makes available to it at any one time. Disease, decay, and death are the obvious expression of the compromise aspect of life.

Life and purpose

Few concepts are harder for the nonscientist to internalize than the absence of purpose beneath the apparently purposeful adaptiveness of the evolutionary process, an adaptiveness that gives organisms their high degree of efficiency within their natural environments. A human eye almost seems made to see. A tree leaf looks as if it had been made to convert light energy to chemical bonds. Both adaptations exist because the series of genetic changes that produced them happened to give the organism some reproductive advantage at some critical times in some critical situations. Life evolved not by problem-solving but by meeting emergencies.

How superbly was this done over and over again! Alone among the mollusks, for example, the octopus shares with vertebrates a camera-type eye—a chamber with a lens at the front and an image-sensitive layer at the back. These were two separate inventions that evolved at different times in two separate lines of descent. The two inventions, however, need not have occurred fully independently of each other. Perhaps some common ancestors of mollusks and vertebrates already possessed a set of genes that provided a background upon which one or more genetic changes could build a useful camera eye. Such changes may by chance have occurred twice—in the octopus line and in the vertebrate line—under circumstances that favored the establishment of this visual device. The conclusion to be drawn is that significant evolutionary adaptations usually stem not from single genetic events but from series of events occurring within a line of descent and cumulatively creating a favorable opportunity.

Once an organ has come into existence, if it continues to perform a useful function for a long time, another process sets in: the perfecting of the organ by accumulation of genetic changes that improve its function. Such persistence of evolution in a given direction was almost certainly responsible for the astonishing speed at which certain organs became perfected. The most outstanding but not unique example is the development of the human brain. Within less than a million years, fewer than 100,000 generations, this organ grew to double its size. It made possible human speech and human language. For the first time since the dawn of time a new force entered the story of life: human consciousness and, with it, conscious purpose. Through domestication of plants and animals, through their mastery over the environment, however still limited in range and wisdom, humans began to alter their own environment on earth and even started exploring other planets.

Through domestication man himself became a powerful agent of biological evolution, an agent using conscious purpose rather than blind instinct. Again nature and nurture interacted: by conscious purpose man created new varieties of roses, and in turn the roses' loveliness and scent inspired human emotions and human will.

Human beings themselves became, at least in part, the biological products of their own will through their conscious and social rather than purely instinctual choice of mates and, more important, through the impact of human activities on the environment. Thus *Homo sapiens* is at least partially a domesticated animal species. We have by no means removed ourselves from the forces of natural selection, but have learned to contain them to some extent by our will and our technology. Our social environment changes our lives far more rapidly than does genetic evolution.

Yet full harmony between human and nonhuman life, and between life and its inanimate surroundings, has not been reached and may never be reachable. Consciousness provides mankind with the awareness of death, the negation of life—the "absurd" of the human condition as defined by existential philosophers. The tension between the enjoyment of life and the awareness of death becomes the source of humanity's efforts to transcend its own destiny through religion and science and art.

In its rash if justifiable pride, thinking mankind believed at first that its own purpose was nature's purpose and that its reason was a reflection of a rational will external to nature. The science of life has taught man humility. Our passage on Earth has no more discernible purpose than that of the octopus in the ocean or of the birds in the sky. Yet, out of the apparent meaninglessness of all life man has fashioned science and art, ideals and goals. His mind has developed to the point where he is now aware that the meaning of his life is what he, with his limited yet powerful wisdom, can give to it by his own activities.

Life and its origins

Life should be easy to define—a horse, for instance, is quite clearly alive, whereas a lump of rock is not. The nature of life is something that has puzzled biologists for centuries, but the basic feature of all living organisms is their ability to produce identical copies of themselves [Key].

The essentials of life

The simplest of all living creatures [4] consists of a single living unit, the cell. More complex creatures are made up of many hundreds, even millions, of cells, but living organisms all share a number of essential characteristics, as well as the all-important one of reproduction. These are responsiveness to the environment (usually including movement [5] of some sort), growth, and the ability to harness the energy sources of the environment to their own use; this they do through the action of molecules called enzymes, found within the cell.

Plants and animals differ essentially only in the way in which the basic activities of life are carried out. Thus, animals move about, whereas plants show complex and organized movement within their cells. Animals have sophisticated nervous systems with which to monitor their surroundings; plants are sensitive to stimuli such as light and gravity. And while plants use the sun's energy to synthesize many chemical components, ultimately all animals depend on plants as an energy source.

For life to be maintained, a balance must exist between the energy-producing capacity of an organism and all its energy-utilizing functions—such as growth and movement and cell maintenance and repair. Within a living plant or animal, every enzyme system designed to construct new molecules in the body is balanced by other systems that break down molecules to release energy. The dynamic equilibrium of these two systems represents the organism's metabolism.

In spite of the immense variety of living organisms, both in form and complexity, they are all fashioned out of the same kinds of molecular building blocks [6]: proteins, carbohydrates, nucleic acids, and fats. Nucleic acids carry the genetic instructions that are passed from parent to offspring; proteins perform structural jobs and also take part as catalysts (enzymes) in the myriad chemical reactions that make an organism alive; carbohydrates and fats both provide sources of energy and building blocks for all types of organisms.

How life began

Establishing the origin of life depends on discovering how these chemicals were created. When the Earth was created by cosmic events—probably some 4.5 billion years ago—it was lifeless. Its noxious atmosphere and blazing hot temperature [1] were incapable of supporting living organisms.

Before even the simplest life forms could begin to establish themselves on the maturing Earth one essential step had to be taken: the evolution of the chemicals of life. This step—or, rather, countless series of random events—began the process by which the hostile atmosphere of hydrogen, methane, ammonia, and water vapor that enveloped the primitive Earth evolved into

CONNECTIONS

See also

1 Some 4 billion years ago conditions on Earth were unsuitable for life. The atmosphere was composed of hydrogen, methane, ammonia, and water vapor. There was very little—if any—oxygen. The sun's ultraviolet rays blazed through this nonprotecting layer onto the rocks and water below; volcanoes and thunderstorms were frequent; the heat was intense. The first step for the emergence of life was the creation of life-related molecules such as amino acids from the atmospheric gases. Energy was supplied by the sun, lightning, volcanoes, and meteorites. The newly formed basic life molecules were polymerized by the sun's heat into proteins, nucleic acids, and carbohydrates.

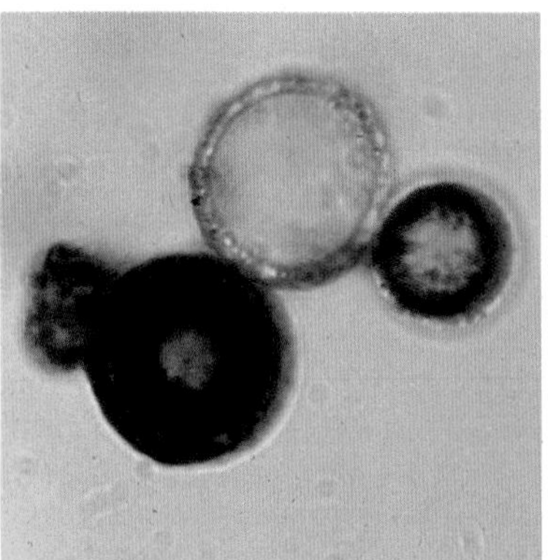

2 The most primitive cells formed on the early Earth may have been simple structures known as protein spheroids. These have none of the detailed architecture of the single-celled organism. Laboratory experiments show that protein molecules suspended in water, heated, and agitated will form tiny spheres roughly the same size as cells, with similar surrounding envelopes.

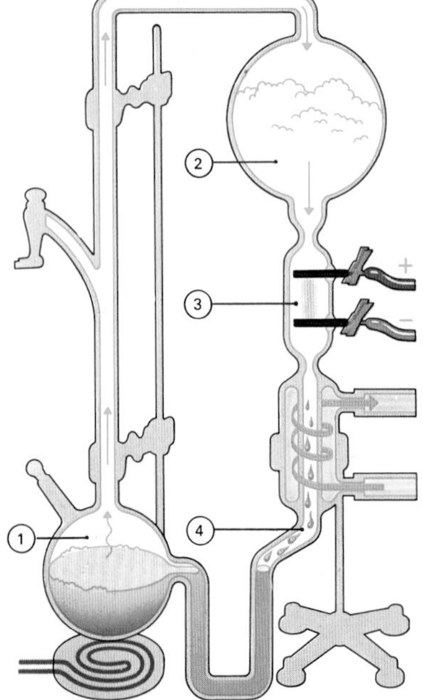

1
2
3
4
+
–

3 Conditions on the primitive Earth were re-created by the US scientists Miller and Urey. They mixed hydrogen, ammonia, and methane gases [1]. Then these gases were further mixed with water vapor [2] and were subjected to electrical discharge [3], any liquid forming [4] being condensed back into the lower flask. This liquid was found to contain four amino acids commonly used in natural protein synthesis, some fatty acids, and other life-related molecules.

a life-supporting cushion of oxygen, carbon dioxide, and nitrogen.

The formation of carbohydrates, proteins, nucleic acids, and fats probably took place as a result of favorable chemical conditions prevailing on the primitive Earth. They almost certainly did not arrive on the Earth conveniently pre-formed, as some Victorian scientists speculated, and there is enough evidence to suggest that the atmosphere of the primitive Earth provided all the necessary ingredients to generate the more complex components of life-supporting molecules.

Scientists have managed to re-create in the laboratory the conditions they think existed on the primitive Earth [3]. The first major experiment along these lines was performed in 1953 by Stanley Miller (1930–) and Harold Urey (1893–) at the University of Chicago. They passed an electric spark through a "primitive atmosphere" for one week. When they analyzed the "soup" they had created they found a number of molecules characteristic of life, including four amino acids commonly present in proteins, a number of fatty acids, and urea—another biologically important molecule. Since then, representatives of all the classes of life-related molecules have been forged under conditions similar to those that must once have been prevalent on the young Earth.

The chemistry of the maturing Earth depended on natural energy resources such as ultraviolet light and heat from the sun, flashes of lightning, heat from volcanoes, radioactivity, and the intense pressure and temperature generated when huge meteorites crashed into the Earth's surface.

The "primordial soup"

Over millions of years there was a gradual build-up of vital fats, sugars, amino acids, and nucleic acid components that formed a "primordial soup." In order for life proper to begin, however, those substances had to be fused together. The central part of the chemical evolution of life was the production of the nucleic acids; it is these molecules that direct the activities of the cell and that have the ability to replicate themselves.

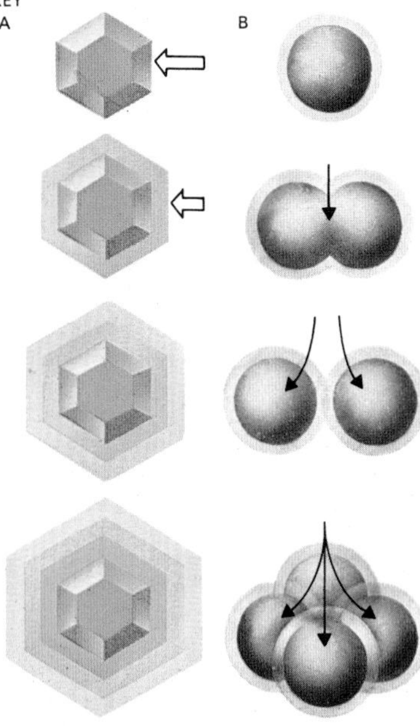
KEY
A
B

Growth and reproduction are two of the keys of life. A nonliving crystal [A] can enlarge its size by aggregating more and more molecules to its surface. But this is not growth in the living sense. Organisms that are alive [B] grow via the essential process of biosynthesis: raw materials are obtained by the growing organism, broken down into simpler units, then reconstructed to fit in with the organism's demands. Nonliving crystals, though they can grow, cannot perform the all-important "life" activity—unlike living cells they cannot split themselves into two identical offspring which can themselves grow and divide.

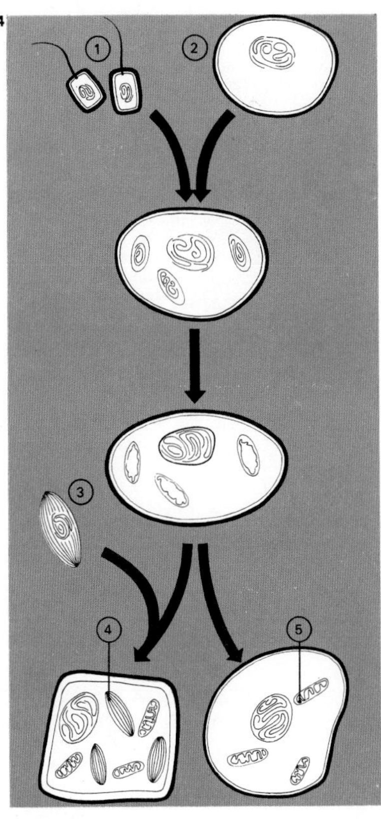
4
1
2
3
4
5

4 The first sophisticated single-celled organisms may have been produced by the aggregation of less complicated structures. The accidental engulfing of nucleic acids and enzymes (proteins) by a protein spheroid may have been the basis of a regular cell. A simple cell like this could probably carry out some basic chemical reactions to pursue simple life processes. A big advance could have been achieved if these basic cells [2] were to engulf other smaller cells, such as primitive bacteria [1] or algae [3]. Some scientists believe that the sausage-shaped structures, mitochondria [5], which perform many of the energy-releasing reactions in the cells, are descendants of ancient bacteria engulfed in this way. Similarly, the green structures in plant cells, chloroplasts [4], may once have existed separately as algae.

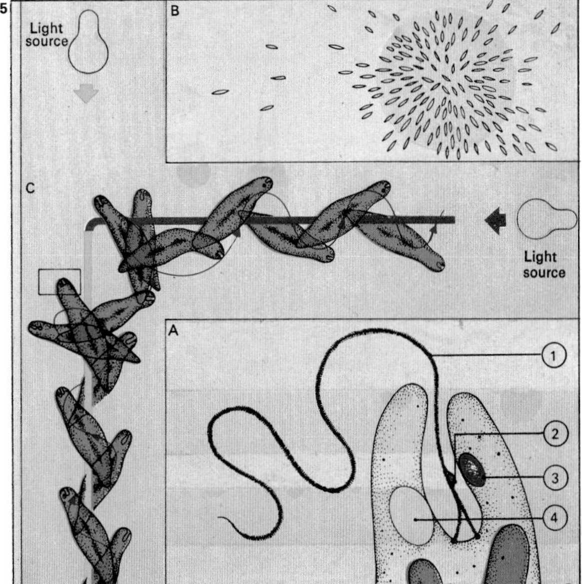
5
Light source
B
C
Light source
A
1
2
3
4

5 The single-celled organism Euglena, like other living creatures, can respond to its environment, move, and feed. [A] *Euglena* is equipped with a whiplike flagellum [1] whose action aids movement. Light is detected by a photoreceptor [2], which is periodically shaded by a stigma [3]. Excess water within the cell is expelled via a contractile vacuole [4]. *Euglena* reacts to light [B] by moving toward it in a spiral fashion [C], keeping its photoreceptor illuminated but periodically shaded by the stigma. The creature can change direction if the light source is moved from one position to another.

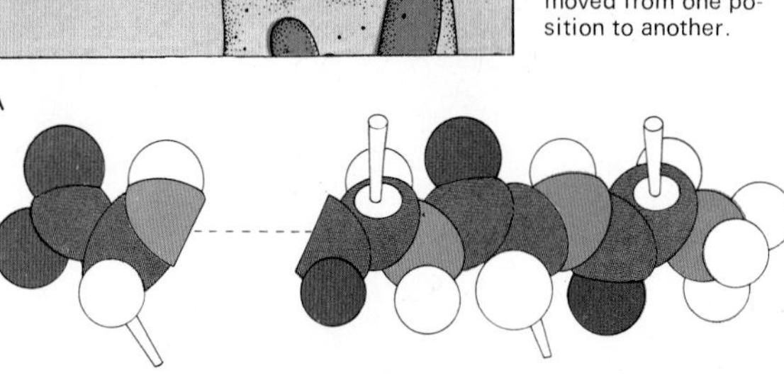
6 A

6 The molecules of life include proteins [A], carbohydrates [B], and fats [C]. Cell proteins act as building materials and as enzymes; carbohydrates and fats supply energy.

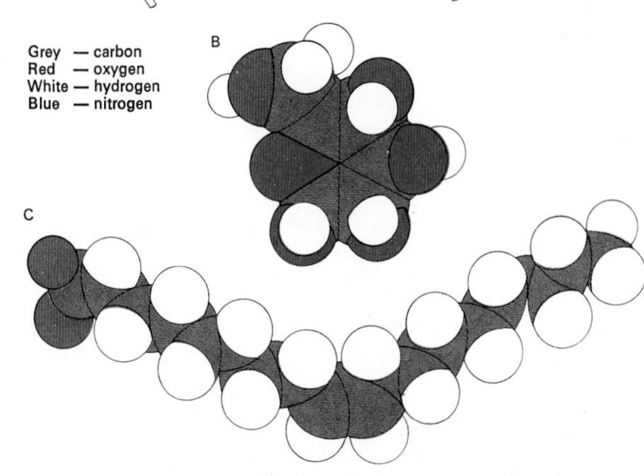
Grey — carbon
Red — oxygen
White — hydrogen
Blue — nitrogen
B
C

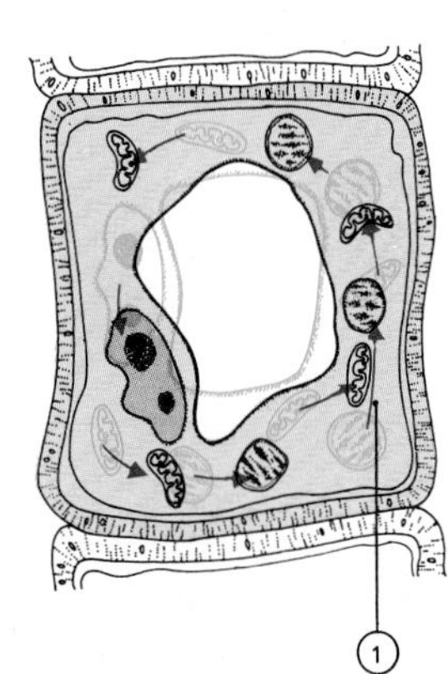
7 A
1

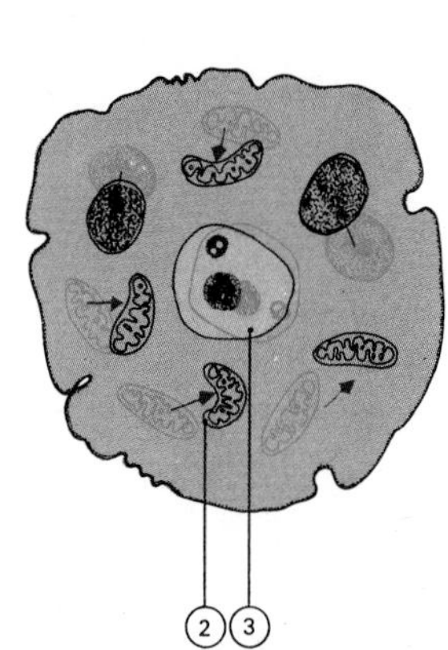
B
2
3

7 Movement of the ground substance, or cytoplasm, within cells is characteristic of life. In plants [A] streaming of the cytoplasm sweeps the organelles within the cell into circular motion [1], a process known as cyclosis. Within an animal cell [B] the organelles, such as the mitochondria [2], may change shape or move independently. Or the cell nucleus [3] may spin continuously. In some human cells the nuclei rotate completely every 3.5 minutes.

Evolution of life

The history of the Earth is one of ceaseless change. This is particularly true of the plants and animals that inhabit its every corner, from mountain heights to ocean depths. The way living things have changed since life began is the story of evolution [Key, 4].

Life's beginnings

We do not know how life began, but it is almost certain that the first living organisms must have appeared in the ocean and fed on the organic molecules surrounding them, breaking them down to obtain their chemical energy without the help of oxygen. Perhaps more than a billion years later the important green chlorophyll pigments developed and enabled some organisms to create food substances from water and carbon dioxide using the energy of sunlight. So the first plants appeared, the "primary producers" or fixers of solar energy on which all other life forms depended.

The evidence that evolution has taken place is copious. The most irrefutable part of this evidence is the fossil record [3]. Fossils do not in themselves prove that evolution has occurred, for each of them could have come into being independently. But fossils recovered from successive geological eras show a distinct progression and also show that animals were adapted to cope with the conditions prevailing on Earth during their lifetime [2].

Other evidence for evolution has come from the study of living animals and plants. Comparative anatomy of the limbs of animals with bony skeletons, for example, leaves little doubt that the hand of man has bony equivalents in the pectoral fin of a fish. Each is adapted for a particular way of life but is built to a fundamental plan that indicates that fish and men share common ancestors. Embryology—the study of development—provides similar examples and so does animal behavior. The hornbills of India and Africa, for instance, although they are different species, plaster up their nests in almost identical ways. At a biochemical level affinities of descent are shown by similarities in such features as the chemical composition of the blood proteins.

The overwhelming evidence of the fossil record that evolution has occurred as a process of gradual development by which animals and plants compensated for changes in their circumstances was not accepted until the late nineteenth century. Indeed, it was not until the eighteenth century that scientists and philosophers even thought of studying objectively the way in which species had arisen. The French philosopher Montesquieu (1689–1755) was one of the first to put forward the idea that "in the beginning there were very few species and they have multiplied since." The adaptation of the then newly discovered flying lemurs on the island of Java suggested this to him.

Evolution by natural selection

Another Frenchman, the naturalist Georges Buffon (1707–88), was the first to suggest that ape and man have a common ancestry. Buffon, like Charles Darwin (1809–82) who followed him, incurred ridicule from his peers. It was Darwin, however—and Alfred Russel Wallace (1823–1913)—who first drew attention to the process of evolu-

CONNECTIONS

See also
406 Life and its origins
410 The world before man
418 Evolution: classical theories
420 Evolution in action
646 Primate to hominid
1570 Toward the chemistry of life
1572 The chemistry of life: biochemistry
1574 Polymers: giant molecules
276 Earth's time scale
1186 Exploration and science 1750–1850
1442 Alchemy and the Age of Reason
834 Myths of spring

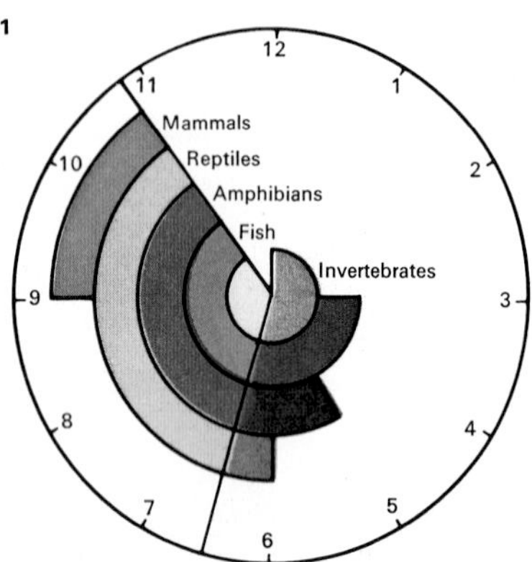

1
12
1
2
3
4
5
6
7
8
9
10
11
Mammals
Reptiles
Amphibians
Fish
Invertebrates

1 The time scale of evolution can be compared to a clock. If midnight is regarded as the beginning of the clear fossil record about 600 million years ago, by the end of the Paleozoic era at 6:30 invertebrates, fish, and amphibians were well established and reptiles had evolved. At the end of the Mesozoic at 10:45 mammals had come to the fore, and in the last 1.25 hours they have been dominant.

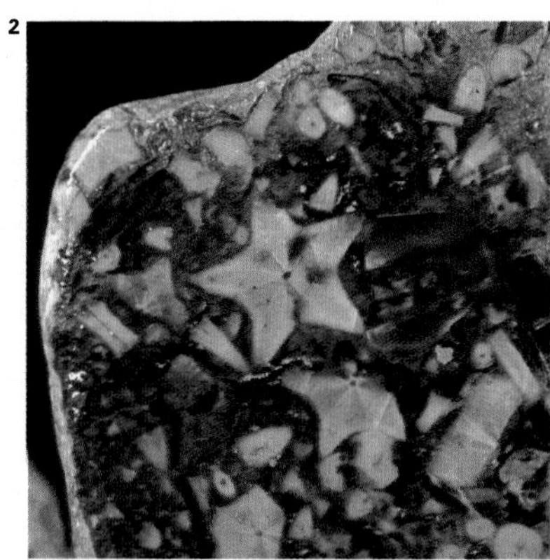

2 The five-rayed disks that make up the stem of an extinct crinoid or sea lily *(Pentacrinus)* are common fossils in sedimentary Jurassic rocks. More than 5,000 fossil crinoids are known, the oldest of which dates from the Ordovician period, over 430 million years ago. Their hard skeletons fossilized easily and most marine limestones contain fragments or even whole fossils.

3 Although the primeval sea teemed with life, notable absentees were the vast array of fish. Instead, during the Cambrian and Ordovician periods, there was a host of creatures without backbones. Most of these invertebrates are now extinct. Many others, including those illustrated here, have descendants still alive today. The crinoids are virtually unchanged, but most of them are extinct.

3 Graptolite, Jellyfish, Giant nautiloid, Clam, Coral, Brachiopod, Crinoid, Sea snail, Trilobite, Sea scorpion, Brittle star

tion by natural selection and in so doing took the scientific world by storm.

Natural selection is the process by which successful organisms survive while unsuccessful ones do not. Mixing of parental stock and changes (mutations) in genetic material ensure that in every species individuals begin life with small but important differences. Competition for scarce resources tends to eliminate the weakest in favor of those that are strongest or most adaptable and who will therefore produce more offspring.

The species and classification

The process of evolution by natural selection is essentially a conservative one. Animals and plants have not changed over the millennia for the sake of changing but only to compensate for changes in their environmental circumstances. In species well adapted to a stable environment, most mutations are thus unfavorable and individuals carrying them soon die out because they cannot survive long enough to reproduce. In fluctuating environments variety in the gene pool is at a necessarily high premium because only those populations that have "left their options open" will survive.

The unit of evolution is the species because it represents the unit of mating. Plants and animals of the same species can mate and produce viable offspring while organisms more distantly related cannot. The naming and grouping of species is designed not only for identification purposes but to reflect evolutionary relationships. Species that are presumed to have a single common ancestor are grouped together in a genus, and the Latin name, or binomial, for each consists of the generic name first, followed by the specific name. Cats are thus classified in the genus *Felis* of which there are several species such as *Felis pardalis,* the ocelot, and *Felis sylvestris,* the European wildcat.

Related genera are grouped together into larger groups or families and several families together make up an order. Related orders are members of the same class and several classes form the largest practical unit of classification, the phylum.

KEY
A Conifers
Ginkgos
Cycads
Seed ferns
Ferns
Flowering plants
Horsetails
Club mosses
Psilophytes 2
Bryophytes
Algal ancestor
B Chordates
Arthropods
Peripatus
Advanced worms
Molluscs
Echinoderms
Brachiopods
Rotifers
Primitive worms
Flatworms
Jellyfish
Protozoan ancestor

Steps in the evolution of plants [A] have been the development of a vascular system [1], roots [2], leaves [3], cone seeds [4], frond seeds [5], and flowers [6]. Invertebrate animals [B] have evolved a gut [7], a body cavity [8], a complex internal structure [9], and segmented bodies [10]. Some have shells [11], others have legs [12].

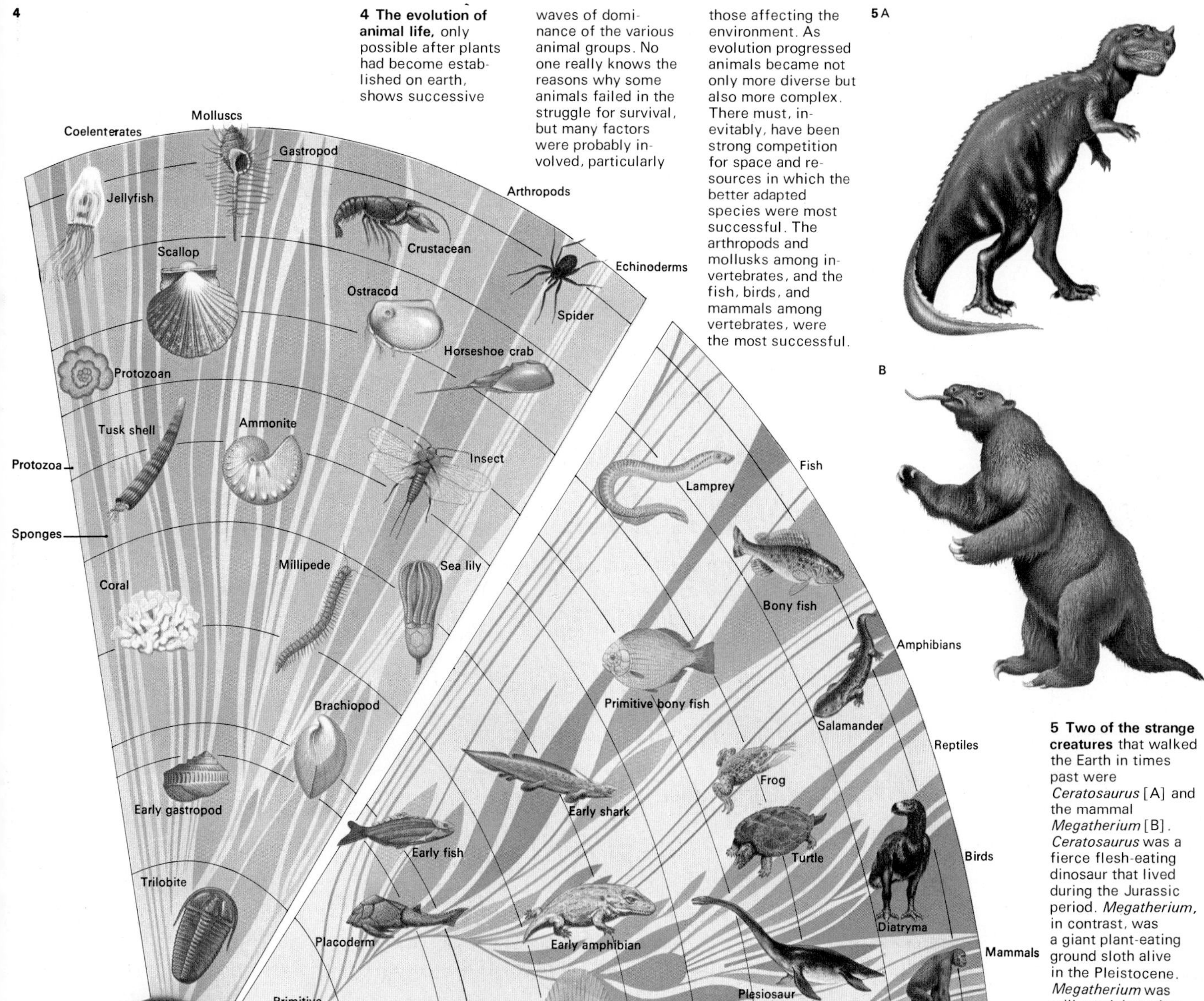

4
Coelenterates
Molluscs
Gastropod
Jellyfish
Arthropods
Scallop
Crustacean
Echinoderms
Ostracod
Spider
Horseshoe crab
Protozoan
Tusk shell
Ammonite
Protozoa
Insect
Sponges
Fish
Lamprey
Millipede
Sea lily
Coral
Bony fish
Amphibians
Brachiopod
Primitive bony fish
Salamander
Reptiles
Frog
Early gastropod
Early shark
Early fish
Turtle
Birds
Trilobite
Diatryma
Placoderm
Early amphibian
Mammals
Plesiosaur
Primitive chordates
Pelycosaur
Primate
Precambrian
Cambrian
Ordovician
Silurian
Devonian
Carboniferous
Permian
Triassic
Jurassic
Cretaceous
Tertiary
Quaternary
5A
B

4 The evolution of animal life, only possible after plants had become established on earth, shows successive waves of dominance of the various animal groups. No one really knows the reasons why some animals failed in the struggle for survival, but many factors were probably involved, particularly those affecting the environment. As evolution progressed animals became not only more diverse but also more complex. There must, inevitably, have been strong competition for space and resources in which the better adapted species were most successful. The arthropods and mollusks among invertebrates, and the fish, birds, and mammals among vertebrates, were the most successful.

5 Two of the strange creatures that walked the Earth in times past were *Ceratosaurus* [A] and the mammal *Megatherium* [B]. *Ceratosaurus* was a fierce flesh-eating dinosaur that lived during the Jurassic period. *Megatherium,* in contrast, was a giant plant-eating ground sloth alive in the Pleistocene. *Megatherium* was still surviving when early man migrated to South America. By then *Ceratosaurus* had been extinct for 130 million years.

The world before man

The story of the Earth's evolution, unfolding over a vast span of millennia, begins with an empty stage. Although the fabric of the Earth's crust is some 4.6 billion years old, the first stirrings of life did not disturb the barren expanses of its surface until about 1 billion years after its formation. A further 3 billion years were to elapse before the appearance of creatures that left recognizable fossils.

The time scale of evolution

From studies of the Earth's crust, scientists have distinguished three broad geological eras following the long awakening of the Precambrian. They are the Paleozoic (Greek for "ancient life"), Mesozoic ("middle life"), and Cenozoic ("recent life"). Each is divided into richly diverse periods and the Cenozoic, spanning about 65 million years, is subdivided into epochs.

Although the origin of life remains a subject for continuing speculation, it was not until the publication of Darwin's theory of evolution in 1859 that the argument became the province of scientists as well as philosophers. Modern paleontologists have confirmed much of his intelligent guesswork. Great advances in particular have been made in the dating of fossil remains. The discovery of the basic genetic material known as deoxyribonucleic acid (DNA) has also increased understanding of two contrasting mechanisms in evolution. One is the way in which species reproduce themselves faithfully and the other is the process by which new species of animals and plants come into being. The second involves mutation—minute changes in DNA instructions.

The first vital seeds of this continuing argument were sown in the Precambrian period, when for some 4 billion years the land lay barren and devoid of life. Although there was no free oxygen in the atmosphere, the primeval oceans of that desert world already contained the basic constituents of life. Primitive organic structures, such as bacteria and algae, were the first to evolve and, with their appearance about 3 billion years ago, the Earth reached a turning-point in its history.

Following on from early soft-bodied forms, the shelled creatures of the Cambrian period provided the earliest yield of fossil remains, the most numerous being the many-legged trilobites. It was not until the Ordovician period that the first fishlike vertebrates (the jawless fish) began to appear [1]. By the time that jawed fish had evolved, toward the end of the Silurian, marine plants were moving to the shore.

The first land dwellers

At last, as the Devonian period opened, there were living things on land as well as in the sea. This was a time of great topographical change. The crust of the Earth rose and fell, throwing up huge mountain ranges, and the oceans advanced and receded several times, exposing mud that was rich in organic materials. As lush vegetation grew up to carpet bare rock, the first insects appeared. By the end of the period the first vertebrates had emerged on land. These were the amphibians—descended from the lobe-finned fishes that had started to crawl from their fresh-water pools.

CONNECTIONS

See also
408 Evolution of life
560 Fossils: the life of the past
276 Earth's time scale
562 Plants of the past
564 Fossils without backbones
566 Fish and amphibians of the past
568 Toward life on land
570 Reptiles of the past
572 The age of reptiles
574 Mammals of the past
576 The age of mammals
646 Primate to hominid

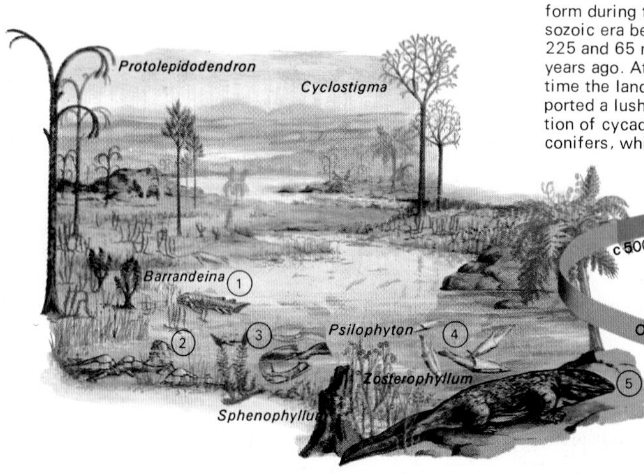

1 The age of fishes began in the mid-Paleozoic era about 400 million years ago. For some 4 billion years, the land had been barren and lifeless and all living things dwelled in the sea. It was not until the first strong-stemmed plants, descended from algae, invaded the land that animal life could come ashore. Scorpions, spiders, and insects prepared the way for the first amphibians.

1 *Dipterus*
2 *Pterichthys*
3 *Drepanaspis*
4 *Pteraspis*
5 *Ichthyostega*

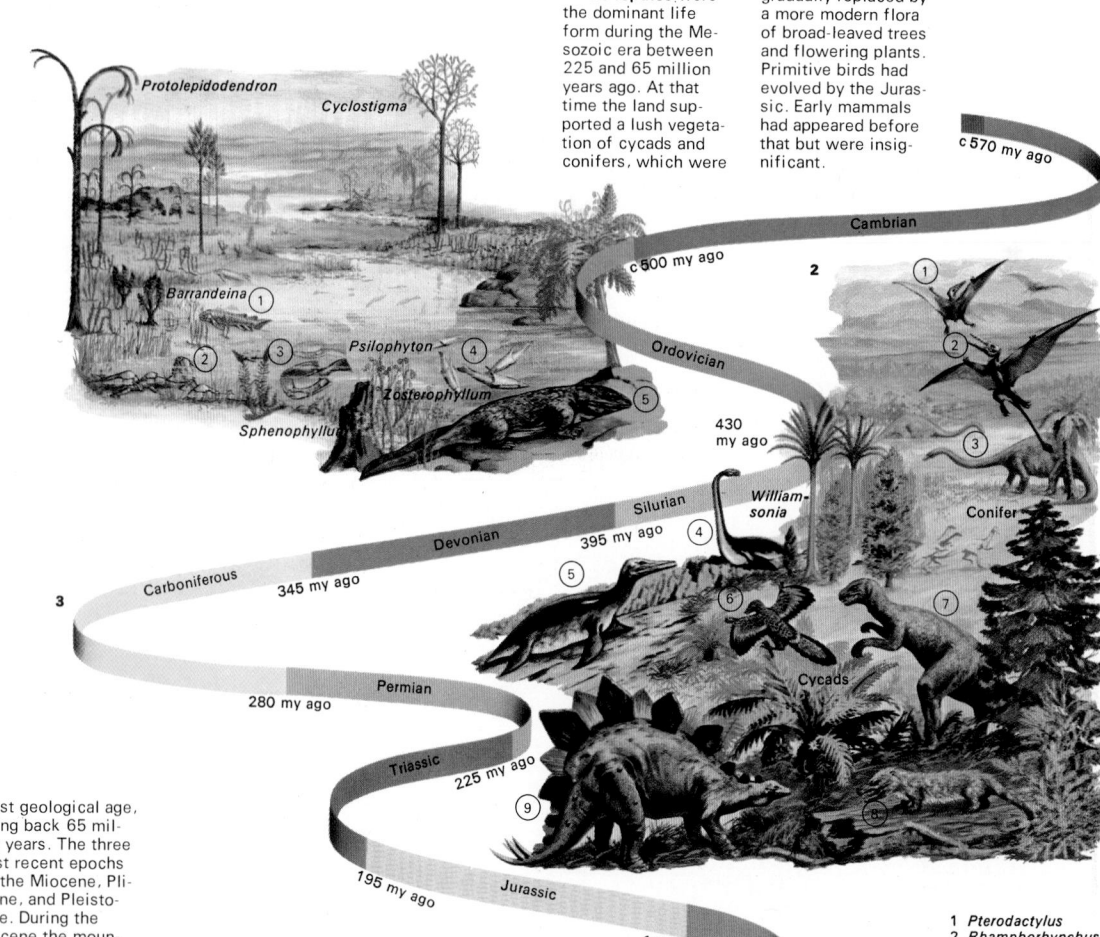

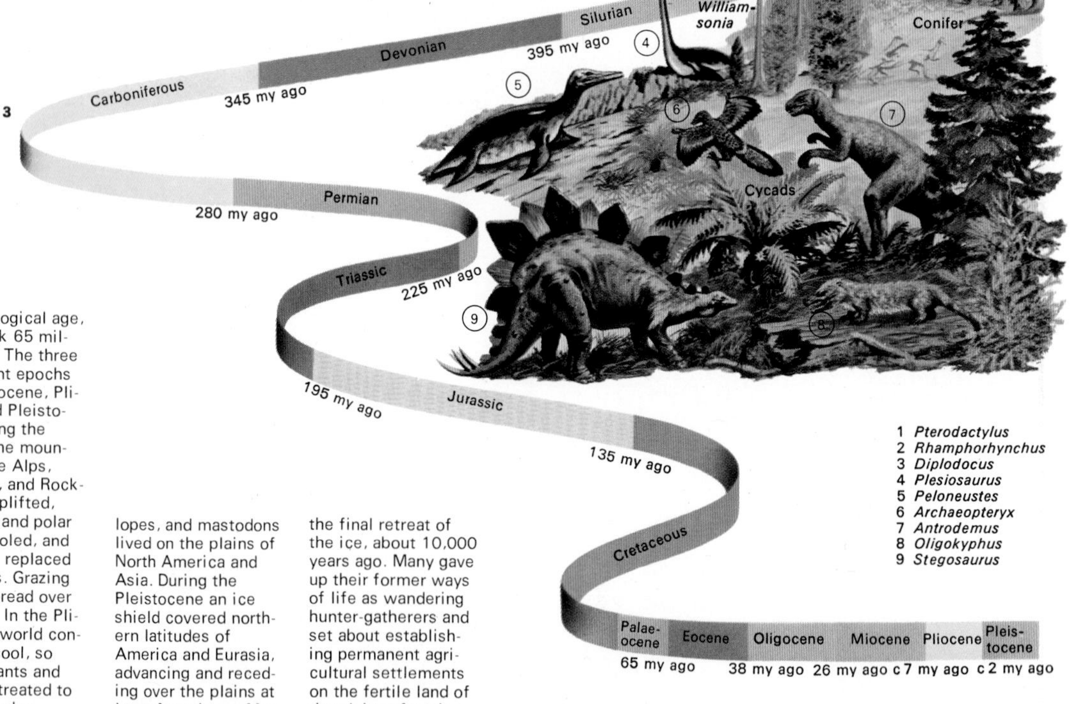

1
Protolepidodendron
Cyclostigma
Barrandeina
Psilophyton
Zosterophyllum
Sphenophyllum

2 The reptiles were the dominant life form during the Mesozoic era between 225 and 65 million years ago. At that time the land supported a lush vegetation of cycads and conifers, which were gradually replaced by a more modern flora of broad-leaved trees and flowering plants. Primitive birds had evolved by the Jurassic. Early mammals had appeared before that but were insignificant.

2
Williamsonia
Conifer
Cycads

1 *Pterodactylus*
2 *Rhamphorhynchus*
3 *Diplodocus*
4 *Plesiosaurus*
5 *Peloneustes*
6 *Archaeopteryx*
7 *Antrodemus*
8 *Oligokyphus*
9 *Stegosaurus*

3
c 570 my ago
Cambrian
c 500 my ago
Ordovician
430 my ago
Silurian
395 my ago
Devonian
345 my ago
Carboniferous
280 my ago
Permian
225 my ago
Triassic
195 my ago
Jurassic
135 my ago
Cretaceous
Palaeocene
Eocene
Oligocene
Miocene
Pliocene
Pleistocene
65 my ago
38 my ago
26 my ago
c 7 my ago
c 2 my ago

3 The major stages of life's evolution can be depicted as a ribbon spanning an interval of 600 million years. During that time a remarkable and ever-changing succession of life forms has populated the Earth. Geological periods are the major divisions of this vast time span. They are shown to scale along the ribbon that winds through reconstructions (illustrations 1, 2, and 5) of three of the most significant ages, the Paleozoic, Mesozoic, and Cenozoic. The latter is the latest geological age, dating back 65 million years. The three most recent epochs are the Miocene, Pliocene, and Pleistocene. During the Miocene the mountains of the Alps, Himalayas, and Rockies were uplifted, temperate and polar regions cooled, and grasslands replaced the forests. Grazing animals spread over the plains. In the Pliocene the world continued to cool, so tropical plants and animals retreated to lower latitudes. Camels, horses, antelopes, and mastodons lived on the plains of North America and Asia. During the Pleistocene an ice shield covered northern latitudes of America and Eurasia, advancing and receding over the plains at least four times. Men began farming after the final retreat of the ice, about 10,000 years ago. Many gave up their former ways of life as wandering hunter-gatherers and set about establishing permanent agricultural settlements on the fertile land of the plains after the last ice age.

In the Carboniferous period the reptiles developed. These new animals did not have to return to water to lay their eggs. The cotylosaurs, or stem reptiles, were a simple group that gave rise to many new forms, the most significant development from them being the mammallike reptiles that proliferated during the Permian. Some of these evolved into the first mammals during the arid conditions of the Triassic.

Curiously, it was the thecodonts—small in size, but one of the most successful reptile groups—that evolved into some of the biggest creatures that ever lived, the dinosaurs [2]. Not all members of the vast dinosaur family were giants, however: the meat-eating *Podokesaurus,* for example, was only the size of a chicken. But among the long-necked vegetarians that lived during the late Jurassic and early Cretaceous periods were the 82-ft (25-m)-long *Diplodocus,* and *Brachiosaurus,* which, weighing more than 50 tons, was the heaviest land animal of any era.

Recent theories suggest that the dinosaurs and other Mesozoic reptiles, including the flying pterosaurs, may have been warm-blooded and more like mammals than reptiles in behavior. Certainly they gave rise to warm-blooded descendants, such as birds, which may have evolved directly from one of the two orders of dinosaurs. The first mammals in this age of reptiles were probably monotremes—egg-layers like the present-day duck-billed platypus.

The end of reptile dominance

Toward the end of the Mesozoic Era, sweeping geological changes altered the face of the Earth. Gradually the single large continent had been breaking up into separate land masses [Key]. But now the slow-moving drama of evolution suffered a change of cast: for no apparent reason, the dinosaurs and many other dominant forms, such as the great swimming and flying reptiles, died out. With their demise came the birth of a new era, the Cenozoic, and the way was cleared for the proliferation of mammals [5] and, ultimately, for the arrival of man's direct ancestor.

KEY

The shifting continents began as a single "supercontinent," Pangaea. The outlines of the present continents correspond to a network of cracks formed 200 million years ago.

Pangaea began to split in two major blocks 180 million years ago. The southern block later subdivided.

1 Trenches.
2 Mid-ocean ridges
3 Transverse faults
→ Direction of drift

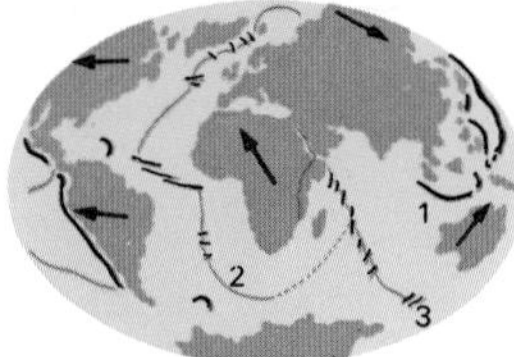

The rift between the eastern and western continents reached northward splitting Greenland from North American about 65 million years ago.

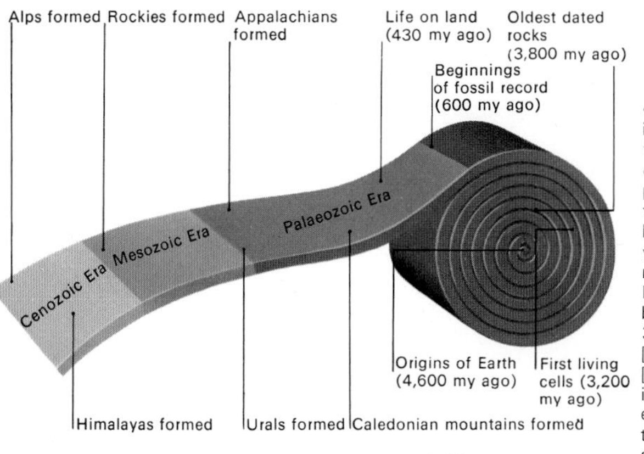
4A
Alps formed
Rockies formed
Appalachians formed
Life on land (430 my ago)
Oldest dated rocks (3,800 my ago)
Beginnings of fossil record (600 my ago)
Cenozoic Era
Mesozoic Era
Palaeozoic Era
Origins of Earth (4,600 my ago)
First living cells (3,200 my ago)
Himalayas formed
Urals formed
Caledonian mountains formed

4 Fossils preserved in rocks provide a fragmentary record of life on Earth in past ages. There are few traces of life before 600 million years ago, but the rocks reveal the first living organisms—bacteria—dated to 3.2 billion years ago [A]. The time chart [B] traces the steps in evolution from the earliest evidence through the appearance of the first fish and land dwellers to the age of mammals.

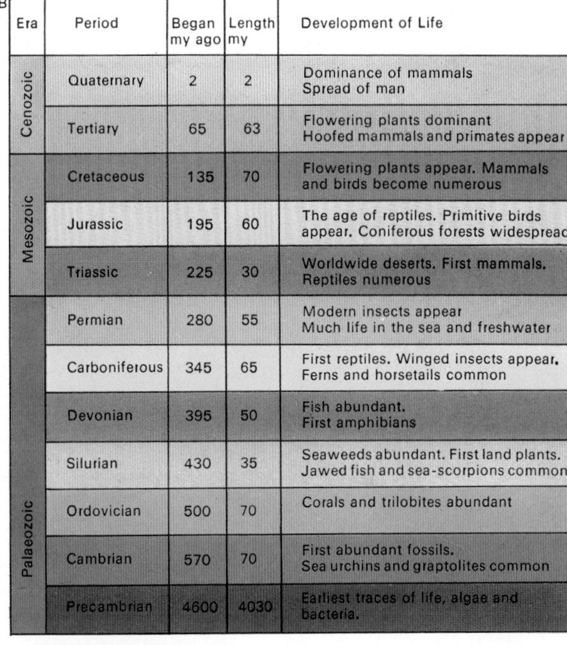
4B

Era	Period	Began my ago	Length my	Development of Life
Cenozoic	Quaternary	2	2	Dominance of mammals Spread of man
	Tertiary	65	63	Flowering plants dominant Hoofed mammals and primates appear
Mesozoic	Cretaceous	135	70	Flowering plants appear. Mammals and birds become numerous
	Jurassic	195	60	The age of reptiles. Primitive birds appear. Coniferous forests widespread
	Triassic	225	30	Worldwide deserts. First mammals. Reptiles numerous
Palaeozoic	Permian	280	55	Modern insects appear Much life in the sea and freshwater
	Carboniferous	345	65	First reptiles. Winged insects appear. Ferns and horsetails common
	Devonian	395	50	Fish abundant. First amphibians
	Silurian	430	35	Seaweeds abundant. First land plants. Jawed fish and sea-scorpions common
	Ordovician	500	70	Corals and trilobites abundant
	Cambrian	570	70	First abundant fossils. Sea urchins and graptolites common
	Precambrian	4600	4030	Earliest traces of life, algae and bacteria.

5 Mammals evolved as warm-blooded offshoots of reptilian stock and became predominant in the Cenozoic. Before this, flowering plants also overtook other forms of vegetation and spread throughout the world. The relatives of many modern mammals can be seen among early Tertiary forms.

1 *Indricotherium*
2 *Uintatherium*
3 *Moeritherium*
4 *Hyracotherium*
5 *Diatryma*
6 *Brontotherium*
7 *Arsinoitherium*
8 *Andrewsarchus*

5

The cell in action

Cells are the basic units of life, the blocks of which all living things are built. Most are minute structures—measuring a few thousandths of a millimeter in diameter—and in a human being, for instance, there are roughly 100 million million of them existing together in organized harmony. But whether a cell lives totally independently, as do bacteria and single-celled organisms (protists), or as part of a more complex multicellular organism, such as a horse or a human, it has the basic potential to utilize raw materials in its environment and to reproduce itself.

A closer look at the cell

Cells can be thought of as simple sacs packed with the molecules (particularly proteins, nucleic acids, fats, and carbohydrates) needed for life. This was the picture that biologists had of cells until they developed sophisticated techniques for examining cell structure and activities more closely. Only then did they realize that the internal architecture of the cell is organized in a complex way to perform its many functions.

There are many varieties of cell shape [2, 5]. Animal cells, for example, may be roughly spherical, as in the liver; spiky as in bone; flat, as in the skin surface, or elongated like nerve cells, which may send long fibers from one part of the animal to another. Despite these differences, which reflect differences in function, there is an underlying pattern in cell construction because all cells have a share in the properties and requirements of total organisms.

At its simplest [Key] the cell can be seen as a sphere with a thin outer membrane (the plasma membrane) containing a smaller, denser sphere (the nucleus) suspended in a jellylike substance (the cytoplasm). Use of the electron microscope, however, has revealed a high level of organization.

Detailed analysis of the cell's plasma membrane [4] has led to the concept of it being a sandwich with layers of protein forming the "bread" and fat molecules providing the "filling." The membrane is not merely a boundary wall but is actively involved in cell operations. For instance, materials are constantly passing in and out of the cell [7, 8, 9] and there seem to be special areas in the membrane that work as selective transport channels, constructed in such a way that passage is permitted only to those substances that are needed.

The plasma membrane is the meeting point between the inside and the outside of the cell and is thus involved in communication. Some neigboring cells establish closer contact by means of minute filaments (desmosomes), which overlap between the cells. The plasma membrane also possesses special receptors on its surface with which other chemical messengers, such as hormones, interact.

Information and energy

Inside nearly all cells the most prominent structure is the nucleus without which the cell dies. It is there that all the genetic information (coded in the genes) is stored in structures called chromosomes as deoxyribonucleic acid (DNA), which has the remarkable ability to replicate itself. Also inside the spherical nucleus is the nucleolus, involved in the synthesis of proteins.

CONNECTIONS

See also
406 Life and its origins
414 The genetic code
416 Principles of hered
1570 Toward the chemis of life
1572 The chemistry of li biochemistry
1574 Polymers: giant molecules
430 The way plants wo
1562 Chemicals in soluti
1478 The scale of the un verse
740 The body's natural d fenses

1

Cell membrane
Smooth endoplasmic reticulum
Nucleus
Nucleolus
Nuclear membrane
Cytoplasm
Rough endoplasmic reticulum
Ribosome
Golgi body
Mitochondrion
Lysosomes

1 Animal cells are all built to the same basic pattern. The nucleus is a membrane-bound sac containing the genetic material of the cell. The genetic information is encoded in deoxyribonucleic acid (DNA). This is combined with various proteins to form chromosomes. The nuclear membrane is perforated by pores that may be important in controlling exchange of substances between the nucleus and cytoplasm. The cytoplasm contains numerous small structures called organelles. Prominent are the mitochondria, small sausage-shaped bodies that are responsible for energy production. Scattered in the cytoplasm are several multilayered membrane systems: the smooth endoplasmic reticulum, the rough endoplasmic reticulum, and the Golgi body. The smooth endoplasmic reticulum is concerned with the manufacture of lipid (fat) molecules while the rough endoplasmic reticulum manufactures proteins destined for export from the cell. The granular nature of the rough endoplasmic reticulum is created by the presence of globular ribosomes on the surface of its membranes and it is on the ribosomes that proteins are assembled. The Golgi body is thought to modify some proteins. Lysosomes contain enzymes concerned with breaking down some larger molecules that enter the cell.

There is a continual flow of messages from the nucleus to the cytoplasm carrying instructions for the manufacture of specific proteins. These messages are translated into proteins on globular structures known as ribosomes. Proteins destined for release from the cell are made on the ribosomes situated on an extensive network of membranes, the rough endoplasmic reticulum, designed to effect rapid removal of newly made proteins to the exterior through the plasma membrane. Proteins for internal use are made on ribosomes floating free in the cytoplasm.

Proteins play an essential part in cell activities. As enzymes they work as catalysts to promote the many reactions that go on in every cell. They can also work as hormones, in which case they may be modified before release. Modification and transport is thought to be effected by another membrane structure, the Golgi apparatus [6].

Scattered throughout the cytoplasm are sausagelike structures, the mitochondria [3], which are packed with enzyme systems designed to metabolize fatty acids and other energy-releasing molecules. Because the mitochondria produce all the cell's energy they are known as its powerhouses. Other enzyme-packed structures dispersed in the cell are lysosymes. The enzymes they contain are responsible for digesting many materials—including noxious ones—entering the cell.

The cells of plants

Plant cells [Key] differ from animal cells in a number of ways and have, for example, a tough cellulose coat surrounding the filmy plasma membrane. An important feature of most plant cells is their green color and this is produced by the substance chlorophyll contained in packets known as chloroplasts. The chloroplasts are responsible for exploiting the Sun's energy to manufacture carbohydrates in photosynthesis. Many plant cells possess one or more spaces, or vacuoles. They contain cell sap and sometimes, as in the alga *Spirogyra*, the nucleus is suspended in the center of one of the vacuoles on strings of cytoplasm.

KEY

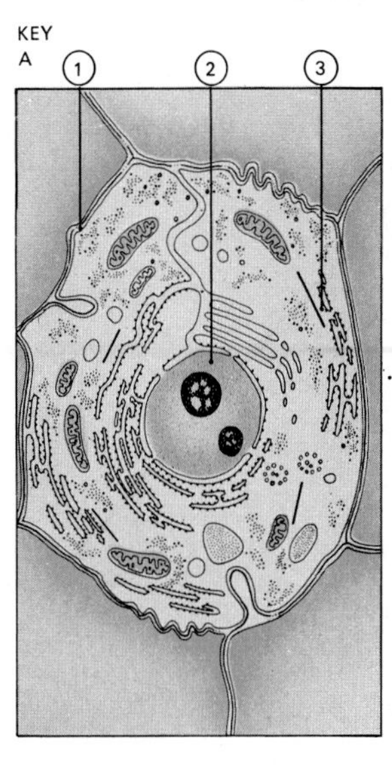
A
1
2
3

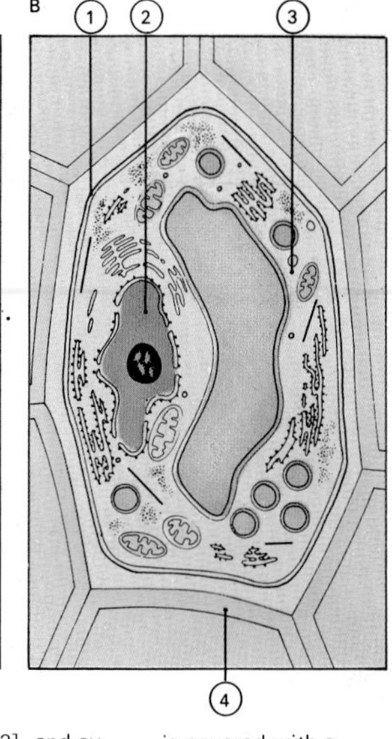
B
1
2
3
4

Both animal [A] and plant [B] cells have a cell membrane [1], nucleus [2], and cytoplasm [3]. But in plants the cell wall is covered with a rigid coating of cellulose [4].

2

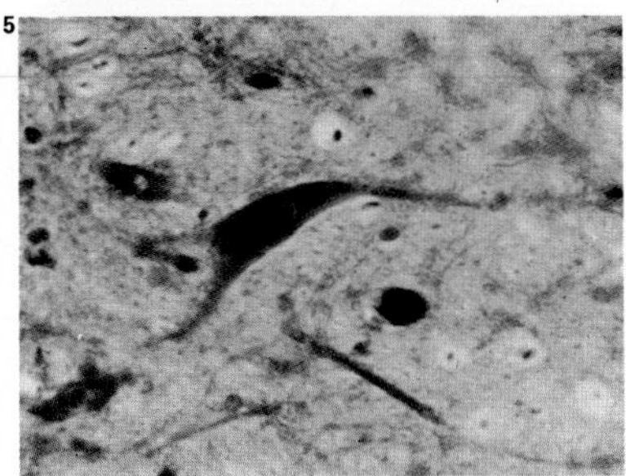

2 The function of muscle cells is to contract and so they are packed with special protein fibrils, made of actin and myosin. These interact to make the cell shorten. The extra energy needed to effect contraction is provided by the activity of an abundance of sausage-shaped mitochondria.

3

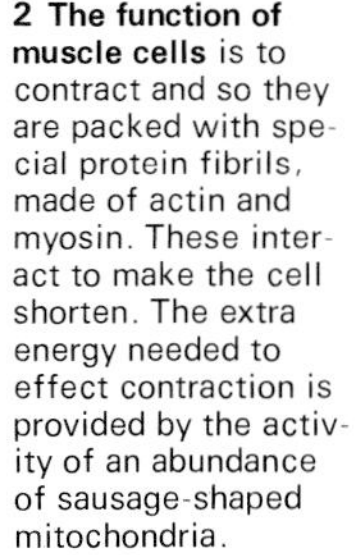

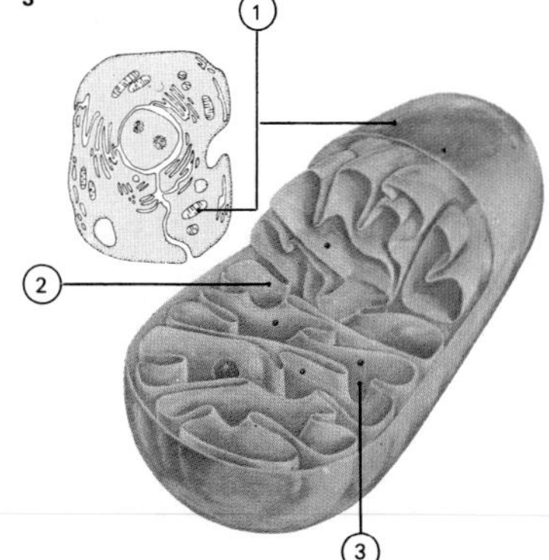
1
2
3

3 Mitochondria [1] are the cell's powerhouses: enzymes within them metabolize nutrients to release energy in a form, ATP (adenosine triphosphate), that can be used for synthesis of cell materials. The mitochondrion has two membranes: a smooth outer one and a much-folded inner one [2]. Scattered spherical granules in the mitochondrion [3] collect essential calcium ions.

4 The cell membrane [A], magnified 2 million times, appears layered. Models of the membrane show fat globules [B], fat layers [C, E], and a protein channel [D].

4

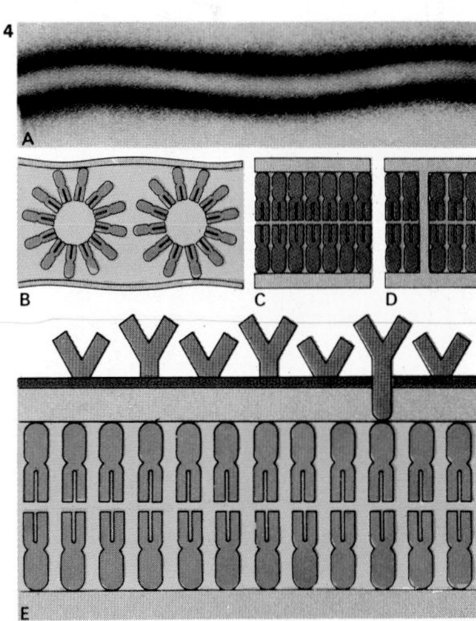
A
B
C
D
E

5

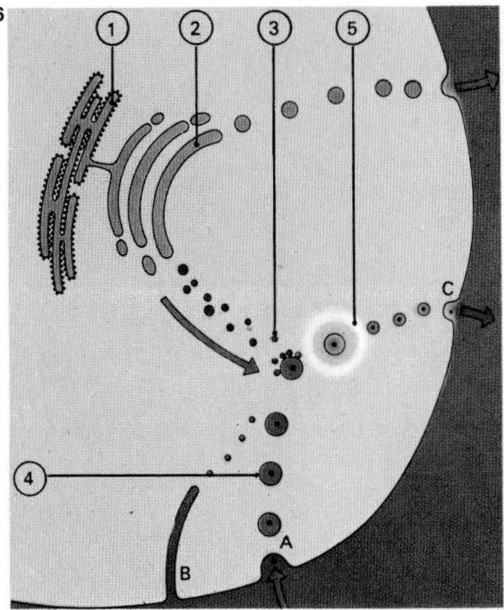

5 Nerve cells send messages from one area of the body to another and are therefore elongated. Messages are received by small fibrils, or dendrites, at the end nearest the cell body (the central dark area) and pass down the long fiber, the axon, to other nerves or perhaps directly to a muscle or gland.

6 Large particles can enter the cell via an infolding of the membrane [A, B]. These vesicles [4] fuse with lysosomes [3] containing digestive enzymes. Digestion products [5] are absorbed and waste products are ejected [C]. Materials made by the endoplasmic reticulum [1] may leave via the Golgi body [2].

6

1
2
3
5
4
C
B
A

7

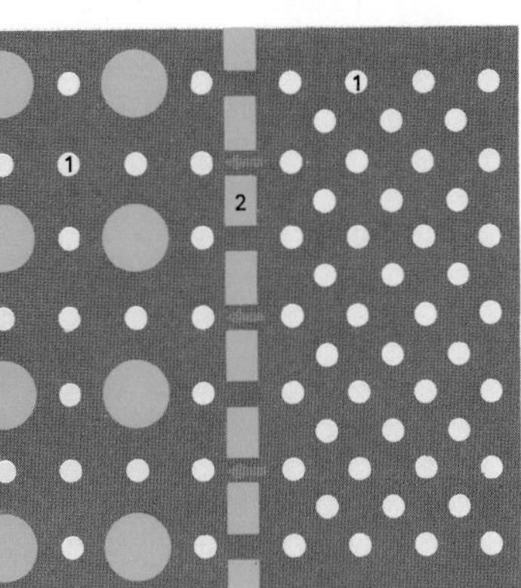
1
1
2

7 Molecules may enter cells in different ways depending on the environment that exists within the cell and outside it. Transfer of molecules [1] may occur by diffusion when their concentration is higher outside the cell membrane [2] than it is inside it. This is a passive process and continues until the concentrations are equal on each side of the membrane. Molecules move into the cells of the alimentary tract by diffusion during digestion.

8

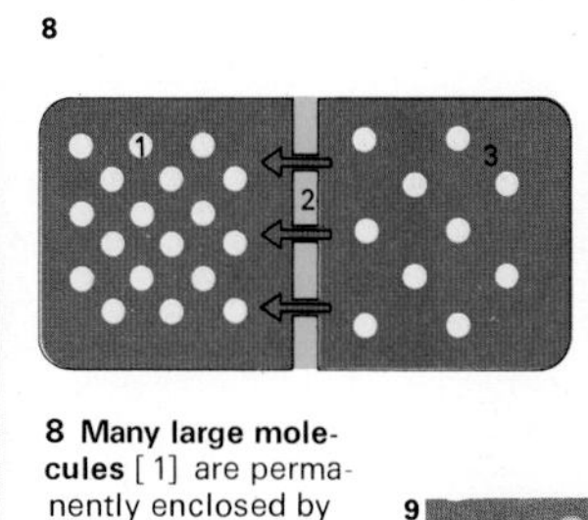
1
2
3

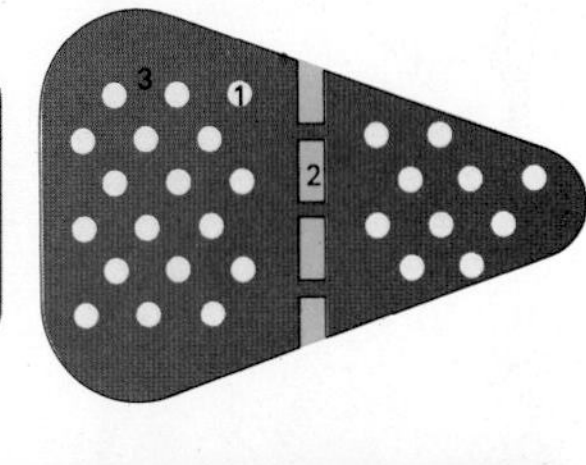
3
1
2

8 Many large molecules [1] are permanently enclosed by the cell membrane [2]. The more concentrated they become the more they attract water [3]. This water movement is osmosis.

9

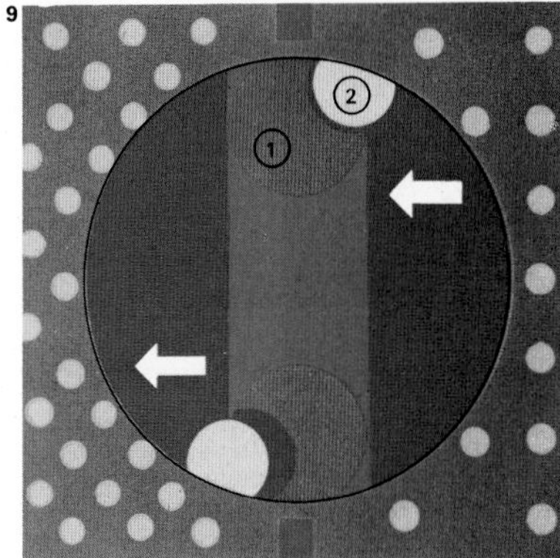
1
2

9 Cells can take in molecules from low to high concentrations by active transport requiring energy. Carrier molecules [1] in the membrane bind to the incoming molecules [2] on one side of the membrane and release them on the other.

The genetic code

Inside every living cell, in its nucleus, is a master plan that governs both the minute-to-minute activities of the cell itself and those of the whole organism. The nucleus also contains the genetic information passed from parent to offspring in the reproductive process. The life plan is encoded in the form of a molecular substance called deoxyribonucleic acid (DNA). The DNA molecule has two characteristics essential to its role at the center of life: the ability to store information and to make exact copies of itself.

The code secret

The DNA molecule is a long strand too fine to be seen even with the most powerful optical microscope. It is arranged in the form of a twisted rope ladder with millions of rungs—the double helix [Key]. The sidepieces are made up of alternating units of phosphate and deoxyribose sugar. Each rung contains a linked pair of chemical compounds called nucleic acid bases. There are only four of these bases—adenine (A), thymine (T), cytosine (C), and guanine (G). Because of their differing but complementary structures, A can link only with T while C can link only with G. The order in which the bases present in the nucleotide units of DNA (a nucleotide unit consists of a nucleic acid base with a sugar and a phosphate attached) are arranged on one side of the ladder, therefore, precisely determines the order of bases on the other side. When a DNA strand is divided it will always re-form in the same pattern [2], although the pattern is different for every individual.

On the DNA blueprint there is a specific code for each type of protein manufactured in the cell. The codes are contained in segments (called genes) of the DNA ladder, each containing from several hundred to a few thousand rungs. It is the precise sequence of base units on these rungs that makes up a protein code and one gene is thought to code for one polypeptide chain (part of a protein). Other genes are concerned with the regulation of the translating machinery for making specific proteins.

This translation mechanism from code to protein is extraordinarily elegant. A protein is built out of a long chain of amino acids. These acids, together with the energy needed to synthesize them into protein, are supplied to the cell by food. Once inside the membrane of the cell (in the cytoplasm) they are collected according to the instructions of the DNA and brought to the cell's manufacturing plant, the ribosome.

To achieve this, certain genes in the DNA order a substance called ribonucleic acid (RNA) to deliver to the ribosome a blueprint for the protein required [4]. Part of the DNA ladder temporarily untwists and separates down the middle. The messenger RNA is a substance chemically similar to DNA. The main differences between them are that the RNA is single stranded, contains the sugar ribose, and has the base uracil (U) instead of thymine. In the synthesis of messenger RNA [5] one strand of the DNA ladder acts as a template and the RNA is made as a complement to it. The messenger RNA then travels to the ribosome where it serves as a mold for the assembly of a protein. Other RNA molecules, called transfer RNA, are each coded to collect a specific amino acid and bring it to the right

CONNECTIONS

See also
412 The cell in action
406 Life and its origins
416 Principles of heredity
408 Evolution of life
1570 Toward the chemistry of life
1572 The chemistry of life biochemistry
1574 Polymers: giant molecules

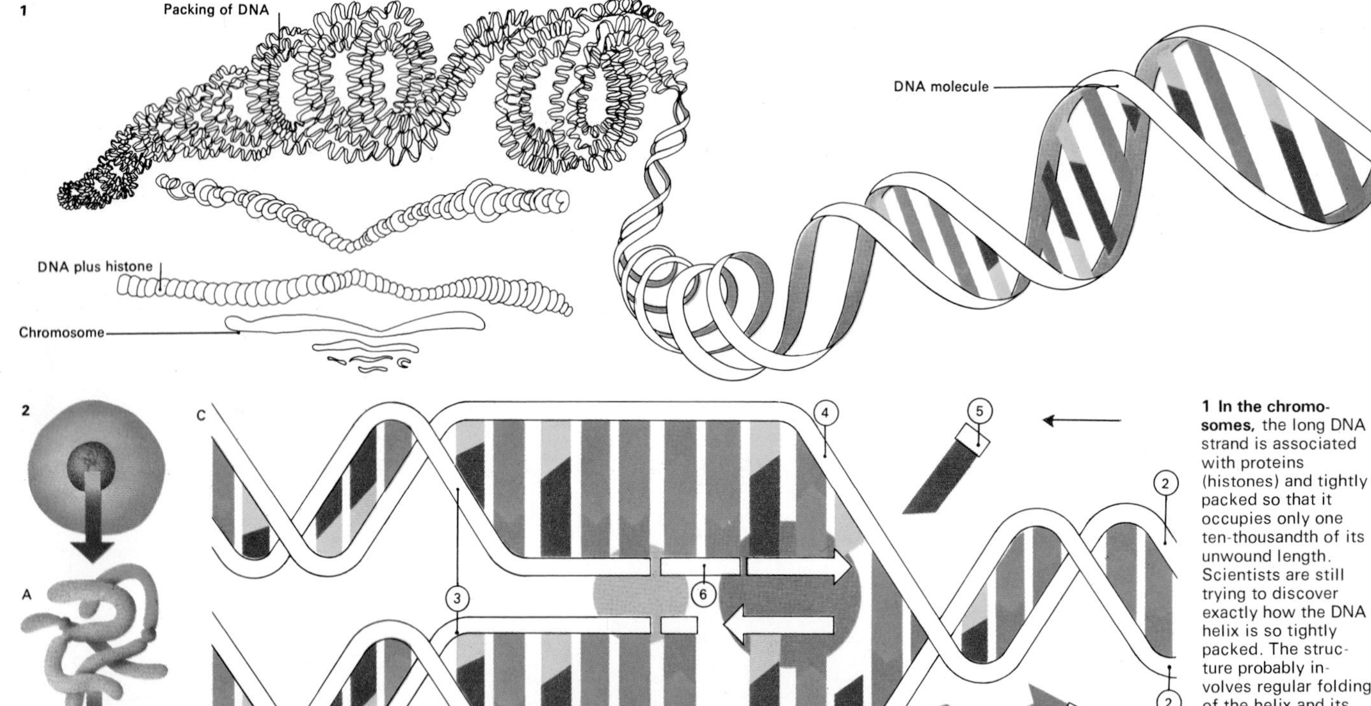

1
Packing of DNA
DNA molecule
DNA plus histone
Chromosome
2
C
A
B
1
2
3
4
5
6
Thymine
Cytosine
Adenine
Guanine
Deoxyribose phosphate chain
DNA polymerase enzyme
DNA ligase enzyme
3A
B

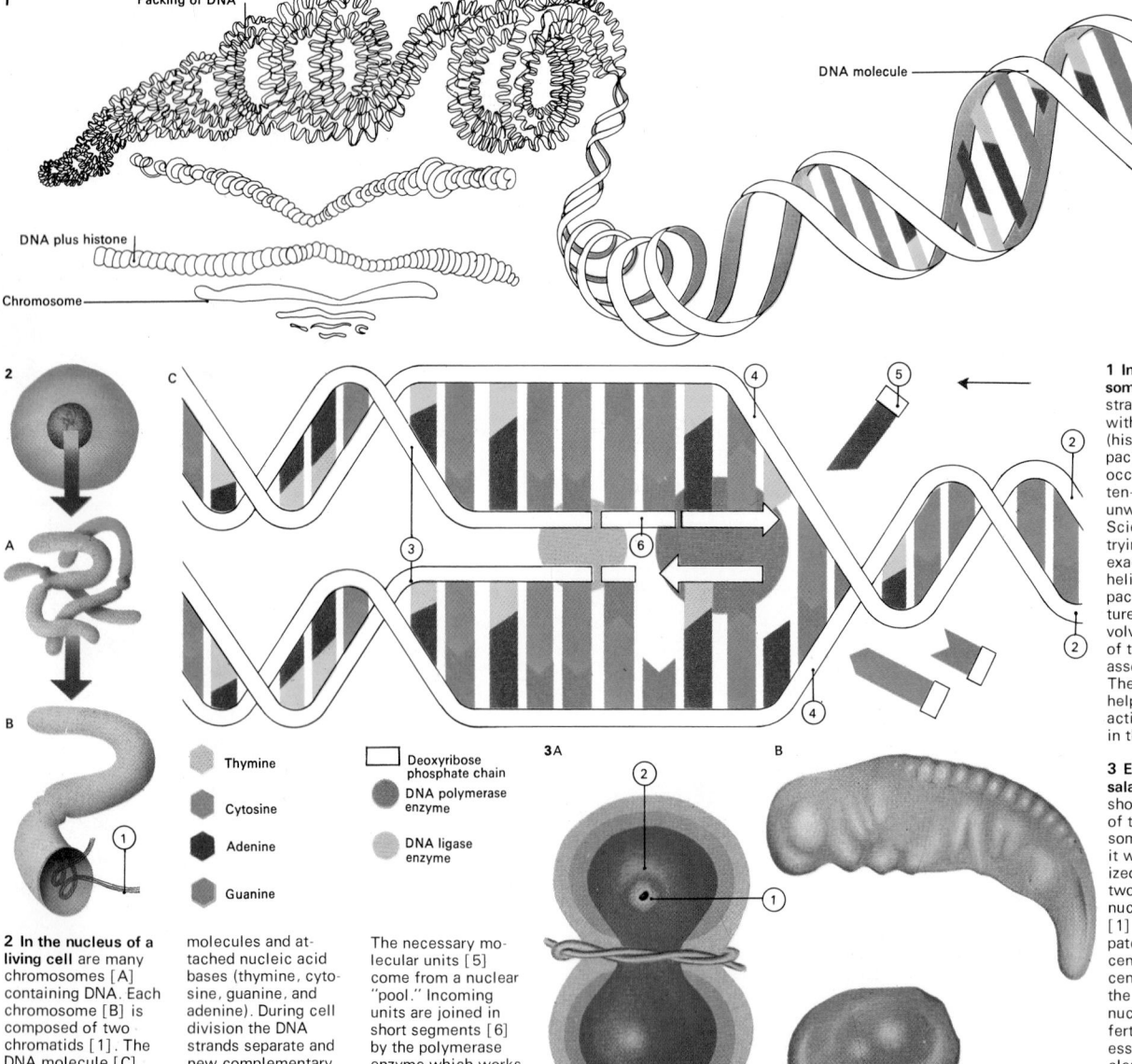

1 In the chromosomes, the long DNA strand is associated with proteins (histones) and tightly packed so that it occupies only one ten-thousandth of its unwound length. Scientists are still trying to discover exactly how the DNA helix is so tightly packed. The structure probably involves regular folding of the helix and its associated proteins. These proteins also help to control the activity of the genes in the DNA.

2 In the nucleus of a living cell are many chromosomes [A] containing DNA. Each chromosome [B] is composed of two chromatids [1]. The DNA molecule [C] also has twin strands [2], each consisting of a backbone of sugar and phosphate molecules and attached nucleic acid bases (thymine, cytosine, guanine, and adenine). During cell division the DNA strands separate and new complementary daughter strands [3] are formed using single parent strands [4] as templates. The necessary molecular units [5] come from a nuclear "pool." Incoming units are joined in short segments [6] by the polymerase enzyme which works in opposite directions on each strand. Segments are sealed by the ligase enzyme.

3 Experiments with salamander eggs show the importance of the nucleus and something of the way it works. The fertilized egg is split in two [A] leaving the nucleus in one half [1] plus a grayish patch, the gray crescent [2]. This crescent, formed under the influence of the nucleus just after fertilization, is as essential as the nucleus to development [B]. The half with neither gray crescent nor nucleus shrivels and dies.

place on the assembly line. The code word for each amino acid is composed of three base units of the DNA. Different triplet sequences (called codons) of any of the four base units—such as GUG or GAA—can produce 64 possible code words. Since there are only 20 amino acids, some amino acids may have more than one code word.

Protein manufacture

Protein synthesis takes place as the ribosome moves along the messenger RNA mold and the correct transfer RNAs, loaded with their specific amino acids, move in to recognize the triplet sequence; the amino acids are then released from their RNA carriers and are linked together in the specified order. The proteins so formed may be actively functional, such as the enzymes; or catalytic proteins, which participate in all biochemical reaction; or structural, such as the collagen found in the skin.

There are also chemical signals that trigger genes to dispatch particular messenger RNAs. Similarly, other chemical signals switch off genes and stop further protein production. The structural genes that carry the code information for specific proteins do not exist in isolation. Each is associated with controlling elements in a genetic unit. Countless genetic units are linked together on the long DNA molecular strand. And the DNA strand itself is wrapped up in association with certain proteins [1]. At cell division this nuclear material forms chromosomes. In humans, there are 23 pairs of chromosomes and, when dividing, these are thick enough to be seen with an ordinary microscope.

DNA duplication

The precise base-pairing in the double helix explains the ability of the DNA to duplicate itself accurately during cell division and pass on a copy of its genes from one cell to the next. When a cell divides [3], the DNA ladder splits down the middle and two new halves are synthesized by an enzyme called DNA polymerase. Each cell contains one old and one new DNA strand, ensuring that the new ladder has the same sequence as the parent.

KEY

The double helix is the thread of life and is the name given to a ladder of deoxyribonucleic acid (DNA) that forms a long molecular coil in chromosomes. The chemical structure in this ladder encodes genetic instructions in cells of every living organism. A model of the DNA strand shows the characteristic winding of the double helix. Its structure was discovered in England in 1953 by James Watson and Francis Crick at Cambridge University and by Maurice Wilkins at the University of London. The significance of their work in advancing knowledge of biology was recognized by the award of a joint Nobel prize in 1962.

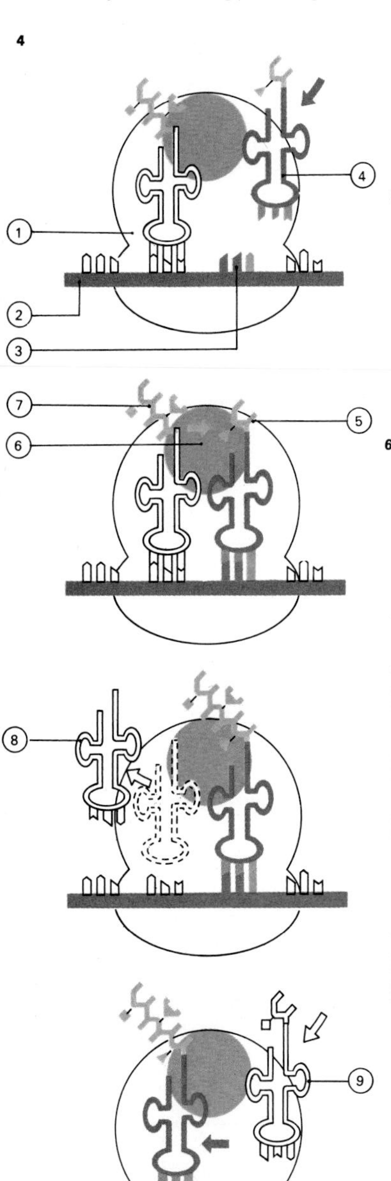
4
1
2
3
4
5
6
7
8
9
Uracil
Cytosine
Adenine
Guanine
Enzyme

4 Proteins are assembled on particles known as ribosomes [1]. The code for the protein structure is contained in messenger RNA [2]. Each amino acid in the protein is encoded by a triplet of bases called a codon [3]. Molecules of transfer RNA [4] bring the required amino acids [5] to the ribosomes, where the enzyme peptidyl transferase [6] links the amino acid to the growing peptide chain [7]. Once its amino acid has been transferred, the transfer RNA moves away [8] and a new one arrives [9]. The strand of messenger RNA moves relative to the ribosome so new codons are presented for translation.

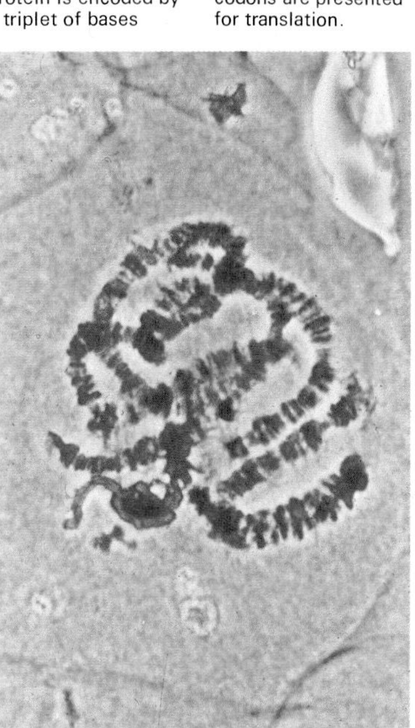
6

6 Certain chromosomes have distinct bands which correspond to single genes. When these become active, synthesizing messenger RNA, the band expands to form chromosome puffs, as seen with a powerful microscope.

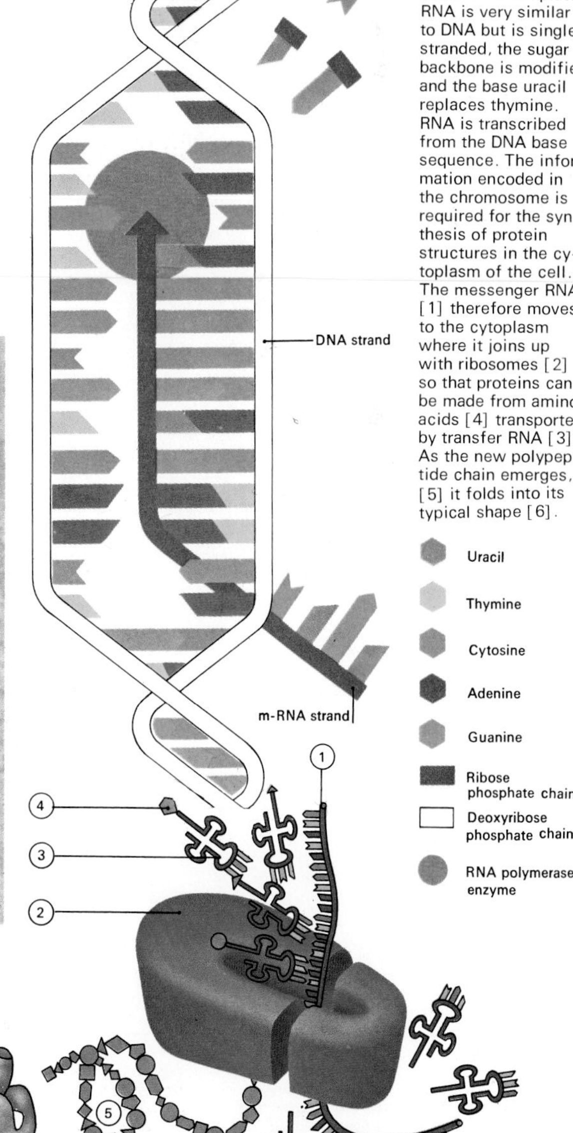
5
DNA strand
m-RNA strand
1
2
3
4
5
6
Uracil
Thymine
Cytosine
Adenine
Guanine
Ribose phosphate chain
Deoxyribose phosphate chain
RNA polymerase enzyme

5 Messenger RNA molecules are made by using one DNA strand as a template. RNA is very similar to DNA but is single-stranded, the sugar backbone is modified and the base uracil replaces thymine. RNA is transcribed from the DNA base sequence. The information encoded in the chromosome is required for the synthesis of protein structures in the cytoplasm of the cell. The messenger RNA [1] therefore moves to the cytoplasm where it joins up with ribosomes [2] so that proteins can be made from amino acids [4] transported by transfer RNA [3]. As the new polypeptide chain emerges, [5] it folds into its typical shape [6].

Principles of heredity

Heredity is the mechanism by which characteristics are passed from parent to offspring. These characteristics include obvious features such as eye color or stature as well as the hidden parameters of body metabolism such as structure and quantity of enzymes. Such characteristics are said to be inherited by the offspring from the parents. The study of the mechanism of heredity is called genetics.

Mendel and genetics

Genetics is a relatively young science but the forces of heredity have been appreciated for a very long time. Ten thousand years ago, when man was on the threshold of organized agriculture, he quickly realized that better crops could be raised by actively crossing the good strong plants that had arisen by accidents of nature. But until the middle of the nineteenth century nobody was concerned with how selective breeding worked nor with the factors involved in the passing on of characteristics through the generations. The great breakthrough was achieved by an Austrian monk, Gregor Mendel (1822–84) [2], but his work was ignored for many years.

In his monastery Mendel investigated the inheritance of characteristics, or traits as they are often called, using pea plants as his experimental material [3]. He examined flower color, texture of the pea seed, and the size of the plant. The first stage of his experiments required two different strains of pea to be crossed, forming what is called a hybrid. By looking at the resulting hybrids he obtained some idea of the interactions of characters. For instance, whenever he crossed tall plants with short ones, no matter which plant donated the pollen, all the hybrids were tall. He said that the factor for "tallness" was dominant over that for "smallness" in these plants; the factor for "smallness" was said to be recessive.

In a series of such experiments Mendel demonstrated dominance and recessiveness of other characters. For instance, red flowers are dominant to white and smooth peas are dominant to wrinkled. The next step was to allow the hybrid plants to self-fertilize, a technique that permitted the recessive traits to reappear: self-fertilized hybrid tall plants yielded some small and some tall offspring. But the important thing was the ratio in which the two types appeared. There were always three times as many with the dominant trait.

The importance of genes

To explain his results Mendel postulated the existence of "factors," or genetic elements (now known as genes), a pair of which was needed for each character. In the case of stem size, for example, there would be two genetic elements for tallness *(TT)* or one for tallness *(T)* and the other for shortness *(t)*. Because tallness is dominant, a *Tt* plant has a tall stem. The only way a plant can have a short stem is to double the dose of the shortness gene *(tt)*.

When the two members of a gene pair are identical, as in *TT*, the organism is said to be homozygous for that character; a mixture, such as *Tt*, is a heterozygote. Once a gene pair is recognized, it identifies the genotype of an organism, whereas the actual appearance of the organism is its

CONNECTIONS

See also
414 The genetic code
418 Evolution: classical theories
420 Evolution in action
1574 Polymers: giant molecules
660 Family of man: how peoples differ
316 Improving crops
322 Plant genetic resources
370 Farm stockbreeding and management
710 The causes of illness: 1
688 Heart and blood circulation
398 The future of food
462 Sex in the animal world

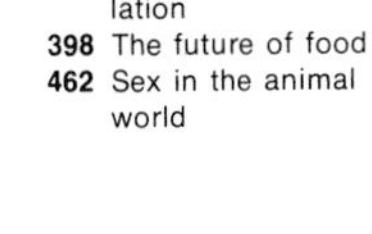

1 The basis of sexual reproduction is the fusion of gametes from the male and female (sperm and egg). In this way genetic material from two individuals intermingles to create a new individual. The result is a tremendous variation between members of the same species. In humans, although there has been an estimated one hundred billion people born, no two have been alike (apart from identical twins). Gametes are produced by reduction division, or meiosis, resulting in cells with only half the normal number of chromosomes. When the two gametes fuse at fertilization the correct number is restored.

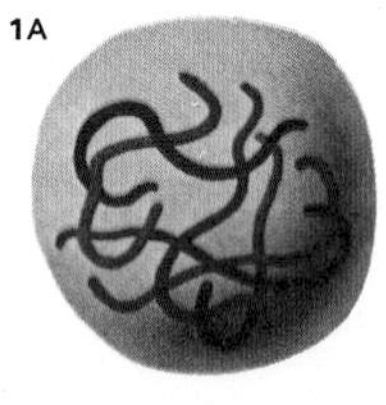

[A] In a cell destined to form sperm the chromosomes appear at cell division as thin strands.

[B] The chromosomes become thicker and arrange in pairs: one each from the mother and father.

[C] Later each member splits itself lengthwise with each part connected at one point only.

[D] "Crossing over" occurs with an exchange of genetic material, important in generating diversity.

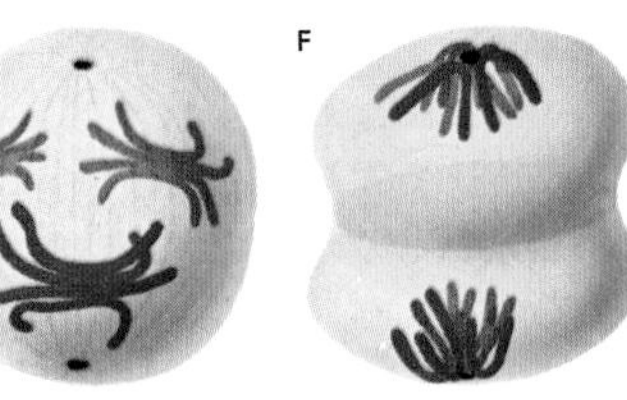

[E] The chromosome pairs align themselves around a spindle structure; they then separate.

[F] The paired chromosomes are parted by contractile fibers and migrate to the spindle poles.

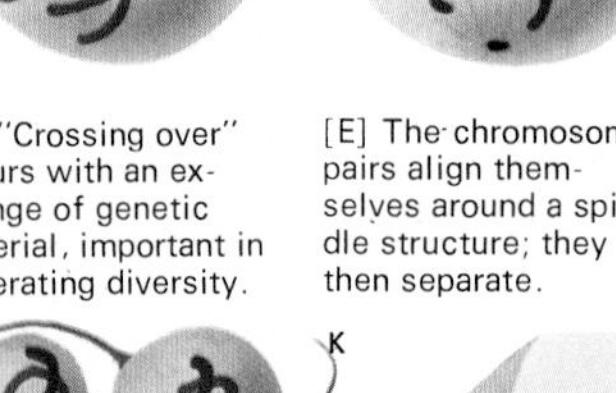

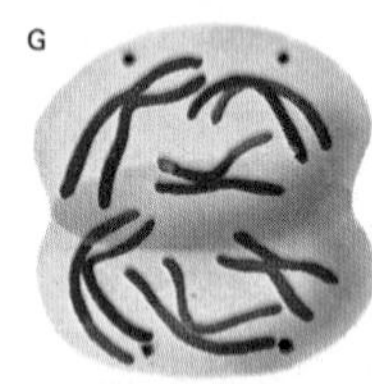

[G] The centrioles (the spindle-forming bodies) separate to form four poles.

[H] Unlike the earlier division there is now no exchange of genetic material.

[I] After the new spindles are formed the chromosomes migrate in 4 groups.

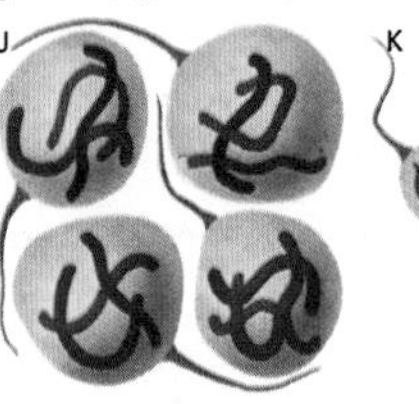

[J] The 4 sperm are produced, each with half the normal number of chromosomes.

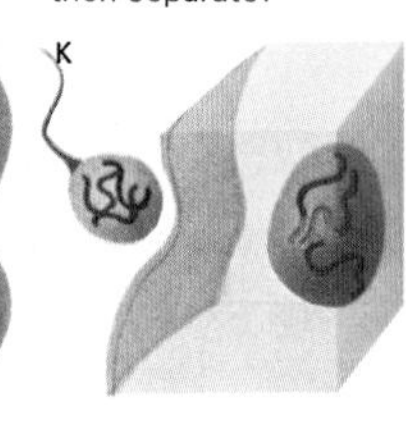

[K] A similar reduction division occurs in the formation of the egg.

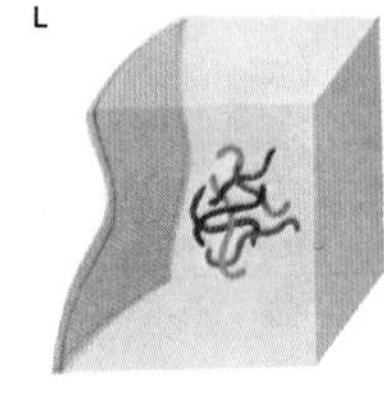

[L] New cells have the full complement of chromosomes and parental genes.

2 Gregor Mendel is the father of genetics. He was profoundly interested in science and performed many experiments on inheritance in pea plants. By analyzing mathematically the outcome of crosses between different strains of peas he was able to establish the basic laws of inheritance. Mendel sent his results to a Swiss botanist who thought them unimportant. The value of the work, published in an obscure journal, was not realized until some time after Mendel's death.

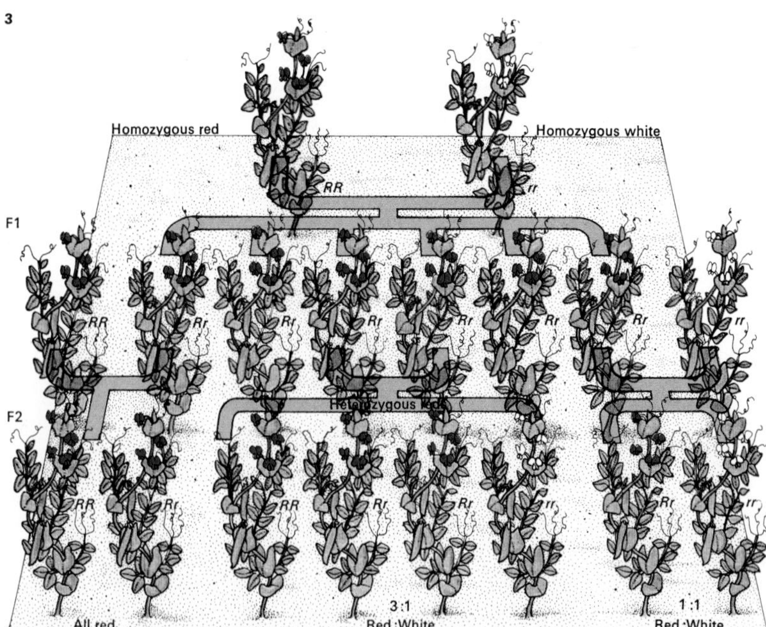

Homozygous red
Homozygous white
RR
rr
F1
RR
Rr
Rr
Rr
Rr
Rr
rr
F2
Heterozygous red
RR
Rr
RR
Rr
Rr
rr
Rr
rr
All red
3:1
Red:White
1:1
Red:White

3 Mendel used garden peas to demonstrate dominant and recessive inheritance. Pure-breeding plants were assumed to carry two similar genes (to be homozygous) for red *(RR)* or white *(rr)* flowers. The first (F_1) generation of progeny were all red, suggesting that the red gene was dominant. All the members of this F_1 generation were thus *Rr* in constitution. This was proved in the second (F_2) generation backcrosses between the two parental types and the offspring. All the progeny of red-red crosses were red. Of the red-white crosses half were red and half white. Crosses between F_1 progeny gave a 3:1 ratio of red to white flowers.

phenotype: if the genotype of a pea plant is heterozygous *Tt* its phenotype will be tall.

Mendel's experiments laid the foundations for understanding inheritance. We now talk of genes, not genetic elements; we know that characters are usually governed by a collection of genes, not just one; and we know that genes are part of the chromosomes located in the nucleus, a discovery made by an American, Walter Sutton (1877–1916), 30 years after Mendel's death. Humans have 46 chromosomes in each cell, made up of 23 pairs; one set of the pair comes from the mother and the other set from the father [Key]. This means that for every character a gene (or genes) from the mother interacts with a gene of the father to produce the phenotype of the offspring.

Sex chromosomes and sex linkage

The double set of chromosomes is achieved when a sperm fertilizes an egg (ovum) [1]. The sperm contains one half of the male set while the ovum contains half of the female set. When they join to create an embryo the full complement is restored. Of the 23 chromosome pairs, one is different in that the two chromosomes in this pair are not identical in size. This is the sex chromosome pair: the sex chromosomes are denoted X, which is big, and Y, which is small. A person whose genotype has two X chromosomes is female, an XY is male.

The difference between X and Y chromosomes gives rise to a number of so-called sex-linked diseases of which hemophilia [5] and color blindness [6] are best known. The gene for hemophilia, a disease in which the blood clotting mechanism is defective, is recessive and is located on the X chromosome. For a female to have this disease, therefore, she must have a double dose of the hemophilia gene, one on each of the X chromosomes. The Y chromosome lacks the portion that contains the hemophilia (or the anti-hemophilia) genes. A male will therefore suffer from hemophilia if the culprit gene appears on the X chromosome because there is nothing on his Y chromosome to counteract it. Inbreeding is dangerous because harmful recessive traits are more likely to be expressed phenotypically.

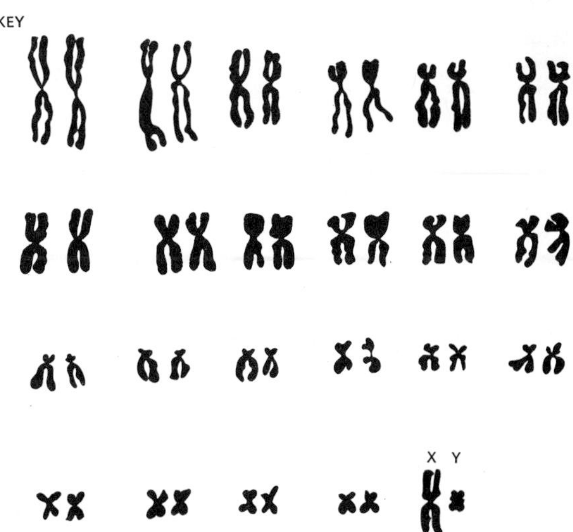
KEY
X Y

The chromosomes are the carriers of genetic information. The human chromosomes are 46 in number and consist of 23 pairs. In each pair one chromosome comes from each parent. One pair is responsible for sex determination. In the male, they are dissimilar and are known as X and Y.

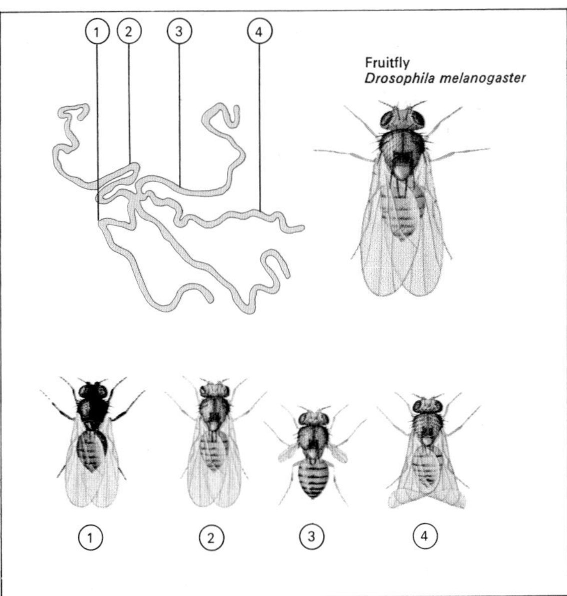
1
2
3
4
Fruitfly
Drosophila melanogaster
1
2
3
4

4 The fruit fly *(Drosophila melanogaster)* is a favorite of geneticists because it takes up little space, reproduces every 10 to 15 days, and its cells contain only four pairs of chromosomes. Geneticists have mapped many genes on these chromosomes: for example, genetic damage at point 1 produces bar-shaped eyes; at 2, sepia bodies; at 3, lack of wings; and at 4, curly wings. *Drosophila* also has giant chromosomes whose basic structure can be seen by looking at cells in the salivary glands. They have bands across them and each band is now thought to correspond to a gene.

5 Queen Victoria's family numbered among its male members several hemophiliacs. It seems that Queen Victoria herself received, from one of her parents, a gene for hemophilia that had changed spontaneously from the norm – that is, it had mutated. Her father was normal and there is no evidence that her mother was a carrier of the gene. Through various marriages this hemophilia gene spread through many European royal families. It affects mainly males because the gene is carried on the X chromosome. Males have an XY complement of sex determining chromosomes so that if the hemophilia gene is present on the X, the individual will have hemophilia. Victoria's family also share other obviously inherited characteristics such as those of facial features.

6

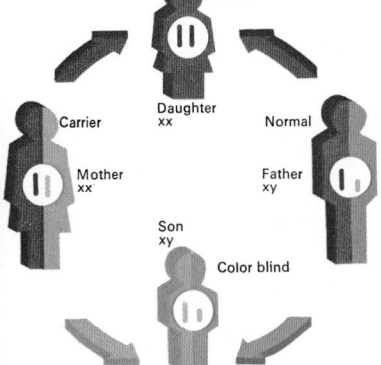

Normal
Daughter
xx
Carrier
Normal
Mother
xx
Father
xy
Son
xy
Color blind

6 Color blindness is also a sex-linked trait. The recessive gene for color blindness (*c*) is carried on that part of the X chromosome for which there is no corresponding portion on Y. A woman may carry one such gene but not show it. Because she has two X chromosomes the second will probably bear the dominant gene for normal color vision (*C*), making her *Cc*. If any son inherits the X chromosome with the *c* gene, he will be color blind.

7 In Mendel's early experiments he dealt with traits that were either one thing or the other – red flowers or white: wrinkled peas or smooth. But because most characters are influenced by more than one gene they tend to appear in a kind of spectrum. Height in humans spreads from short to tall. There is a pool of genes contributing to this factor making for a so-called normal distribution with an average in the middle between two extremes.

Evolution: classical theories

The word evolution means an unfolding, a gradual development, and it is a word that has become closely linked with the origin of animal and plant species as they exist today. Scientists now believe that through millions of years of the changing environments on Earth simple organisms have developed into more complex ones, each better adapted to prevailing conditions than its predecessor. It is generally accepted that the ultimate survival of a new form is determined by a process known as natural selection, or the survival of the fittest—a theory associated with the name of Charles Darwin (1809–82) [Key].

Ideas about the origin of species

Darwin published his theory of evolution in 1859 in a book whose full title is *On the Origin of Species by Means of Natural Selection, or the Preservation of Favoured Races in the Struggle for Life,* but which is popularly called *The Origin of Species.* He suggested that the development of species is a continual process, and implied that man himself must have evolved from an apelike stock. This was considered by many to be an heretical proposal. The first edition of the book, some 1,200 copies, was sold out on the day of publication, an indication of the prevailing interest in the subject.

After much critical examination by scientists, and a great deal of public scorn and derision directed at man's supposed origins from among the apes, the theory of natural selection was assimilated and has remained central to later ideas on evolution.

The modern conception of species as such began with John Ray (1627–1705) in the seventeenth century, and was established fully by Carolus Linnaeus (1707–78) in the following century. It was the Linnaean classification system that really emphasized the relationship between similar species, the variations that so impressed Darwin in his observations.

One theory about the origin of species that held sway for a long time, and encompassed the Christian view on the creation of man, suggested that species were created spontaneously, perhaps sequentially, after a series of disasters. But the obvious relationships between species that emerged from studying Linnaeus's classification of organisms forced people to look for the origin of species in a process of gradual change—an evolution. It was Georges Buffon (1707–88) who first seriously suggested that the environment had an important effect on the evolution of species. This idea was developed by Jean Baptiste Lamarck (1744–1829), and it is his name that is attached to the suggestion that species inherit characteristics that their parents have developed in adapting to the environment.

The basis of Lamarck's theory

Lamarckism proposes that changes in external environments create new needs in the species living there [6]. These new demands lead to new patterns of behavior that may involve modifying the use of existing organs, thereby altering their structure. It is these altered structures that the offspring are thought to inherit. For instance, Lamarckian theory proposes that giraffes have long necks because of their repeated attempts to reach food in high trees.

CONNECTIONS

See also
416 Principles of heredit
420 Evolution in action
406 Life and its origins
408 Evolution of life
560 Fossils: the life of th past
538 Island birds
410 The world before ma
1442 Alchemy and the Ag of Reason
1186 Exploration and science 1750–1850
646 Primate to hominid

1 On December 27, 1831 Darwin set sail on board HMS *Beagle* at the beginning of a five-year expedition. The *Beagle* explored extensively around South America, and as the ship's naturalist, Darwin made an enormous collection of samples of plants, animals, and rocks. It was during the voyage of the *Beagle* that Darwin amassed the data that led to his theory of natural selection.

1

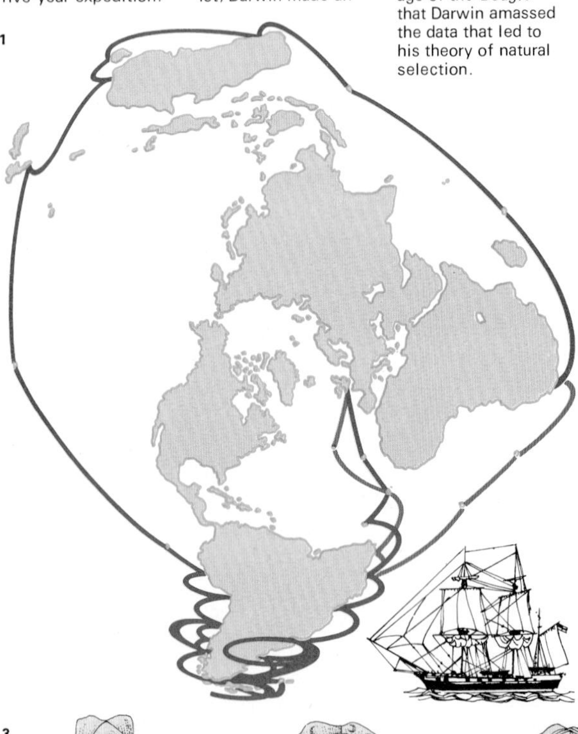

2

The Galápagos Islands
Pinta (*T.e. abingdoni*)
N
Marchena (*T.e. Darwini*)
San Salvador
Darwin's route
Fernandina
Santa Cruz
San Cristobal (*T.e. chathamensis*)
Isabela (*T.e. microphyes*)
Santa Maria (*T.e. elephantopus*)
Española (*T.e. hoodensis*)

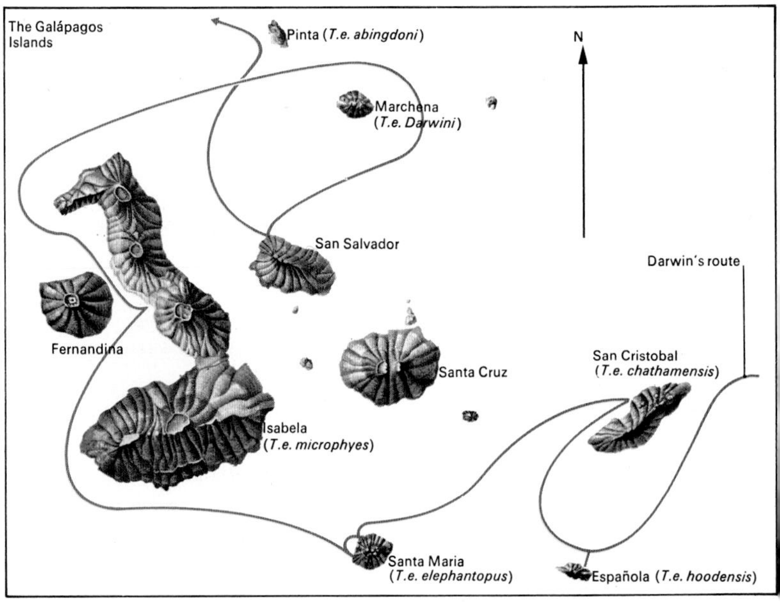

2 While on the Galapagos Islands, Darwin discovered specimens that convinced him that a new explanation was needed of the origin of species. He was especially intrigued and puzzled by the similarities and differences among the giant tortoises, *Testudo elephantopus*, a different subspecies of which inhabited each island. Selected shells of the tortoises are shown in illustration 3.

3 The giant tortoises can all be regarded as varieties (subspecies) of *Testudo elephantopus*, a species believed to have originated from another kind of South American tortoise that somehow drifted to the islands. The shells vary from island to island. Many of the original dozen varieties are now extinct or becoming rare because introduced animals are destroying their food, eggs, and young.

3

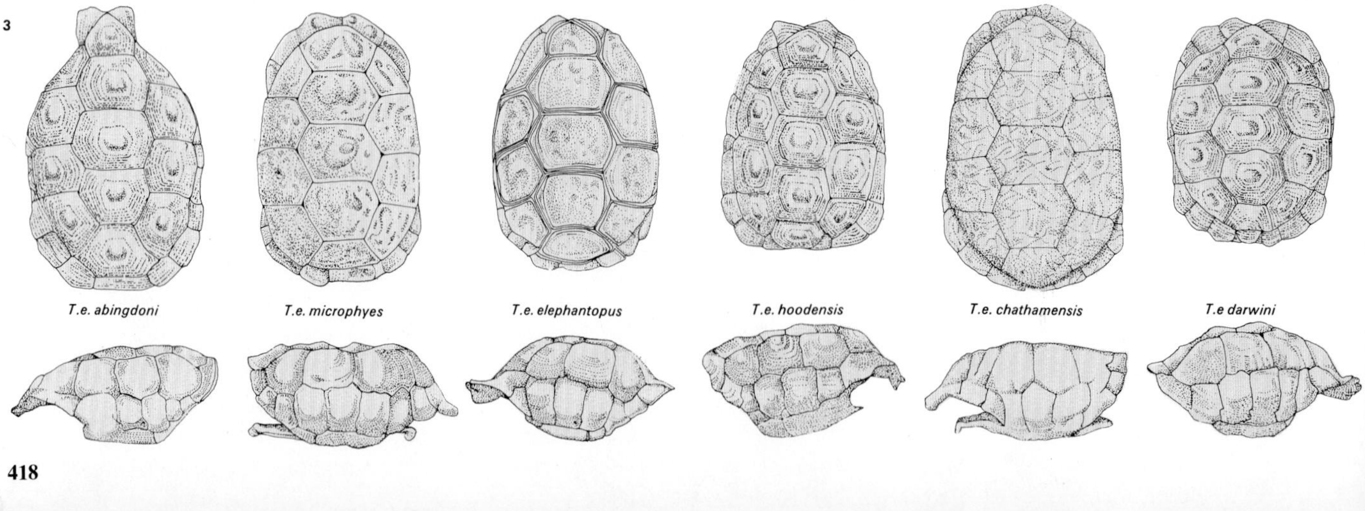

T.e. abingdoni | *T.e. microphyes* | *T.e. elephantopus* | *T.e. hoodensis* | *T.e. chathamensis* | *T.e darwini*

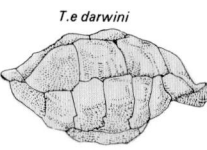

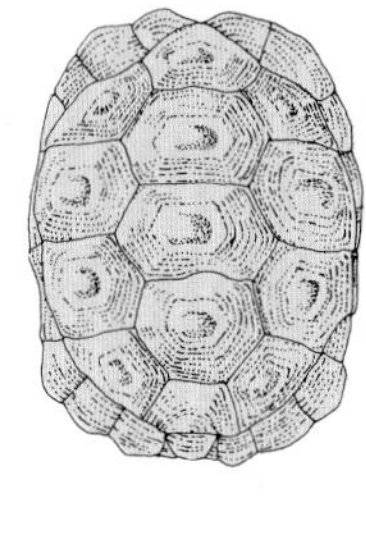

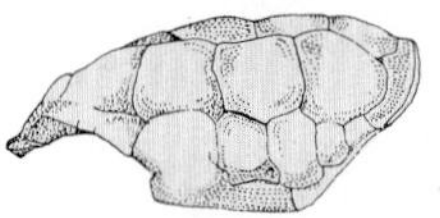

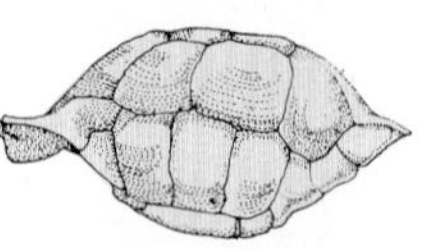

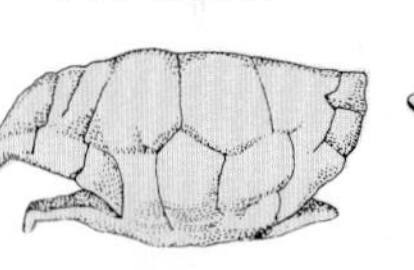

Lemarckism, with its emphasis on the perfectability of species, attracted a lot of support, some of it after Darwin's natural selection theory was published. But in fact the laws of inheritance do not allow Lamarckian inheritance to operate. As we now know from modern genetics, characteristics are passed from parent to offspring by means of the genes in the germ cells (the ones that form gametes), and structural changes in distant parts of the body do not modify the genetic constitution of the germ cells or indeed of any cells.

The fruits of Darwin's voyage

Darwin had sailed on HMS *Beagle* [1] as the expedition's naturalist and returned five years later a confirmed evolutionist, the transformation having taken place on the Galapagos Islands. In all his explorations during the voyage, Darwin was impressed by the subtle variation between species [3], particularly among the finches on the Galapagos Islands [5]. Darwin noticed that in almost all organisms there is a massive production of potential offspring (whether eggs or spores), and that only a few survive. Life, then, was a struggle for existence. The next important step in the development of Darwin's ideas was his recognition of the individual variation within populations.

The combination of these two points produced a third: those variants that survived to adulthood in the struggle for life were, presumably, the ones most fit to do so. Darwin supposed that individual variation could be inherited by offspring from their parents. He therefore saw evolution operating through the natural selection of inheritable variations.

Darwin first developed his theory of natural selection as early as 1838 but felt unable to publish it, perhaps because it went so much against his father's beliefs. Eventually he was virtually forced into publishing when Alfred Russel Wallace (1823–1913) sent him a short paper on his theory on evolution, a theory that matched Darwin's own exactly. The two men presented a joint paper to the Linnaean Society in 1858, and Darwin published *The Origin of Species* a year later.

KEY

The Englishman Charles Robert Darwin developed the theory of natural selection in evolution.

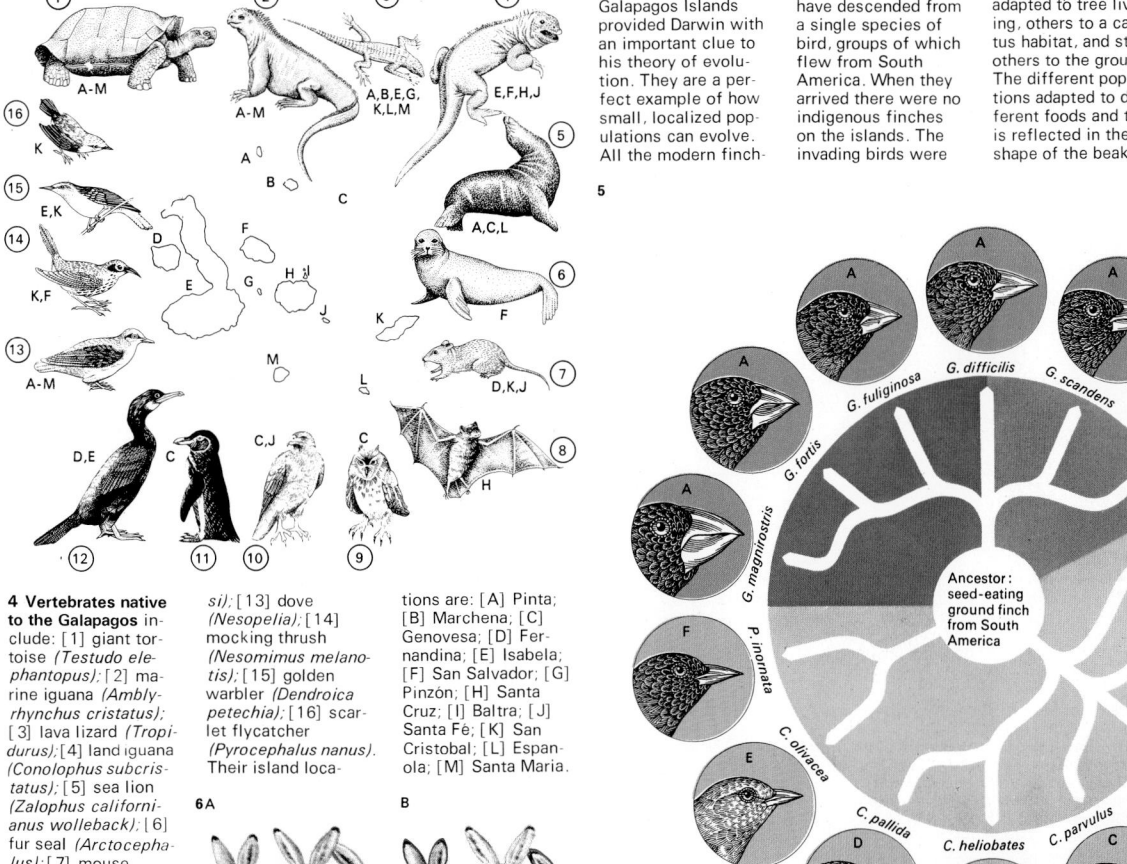

4

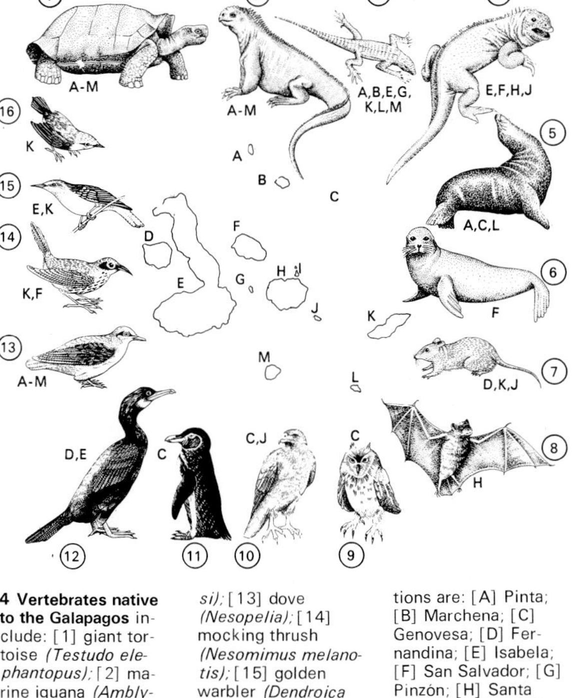

1
A-M
2
A-M
3
A,B,E,G,
K,L,M
4
E,F,H,J
5
A,C,L
6
F
7
D,K,J
8
H
9
C
10
C,J
11
C
12
D,E
13
A-M
14
K,F
15
E,K
16
K

4 Vertebrates native to the Galapagos include: [1] giant tortoise *(Testudo elephantopus)*; [2] marine iguana *(Amblyrhynchus cristatus)*; [3] lava lizard *(Tropidurus)*; [4] land iguana *(Conolophus subcristatus)*; [5] sea lion *(Zalophus californianus wolleback)*; [6] fur seal *(Arctocephalus)*; [7] mouse *(Oryzomys)*; [8] bat *(Lasiurus)*; [9] short-eared owl *(Asio flammeus)*; [10] hawk *(Bute.)*; [11] penguin *(Spheniscus mendiculus)*; [12] flightless cormorant *(Nannopterum harrisi)*; [13] dove *(Nesopelia)*; [14] mocking thrush *(Nesomimus melanotis)*; [15] golden warbler *(Dendroica petechia)*; [16] scarlet flycatcher *(Pyrocephalus nanus)*. Their island locations are: [A] Pinta; [B] Marchena; [C] Genovesa; [D] Fernandina; [E] Isabela; [F] San Salvador; [G] Pinzón; [H] Santa Cruz; [I] Baltra; [J] Santa Fé; [K] San Cristobal; [L] Espanola; [M] Santa Maria.

5 The finches of the Galapagos Islands provided Darwin with an important clue to his theory of evolution. They are a perfect example of how small, localized populations can evolve. All the modern finches are thought to have descended from a single species of bird, groups of which flew from South America. When they arrived there were no indigenous finches on the islands. The invading birds were all seed eaters. Some adapted to tree living, others to a cactus habitat, and still others to the ground. The different populations adapted to different foods and this is reflected in the shape of the beak. The ecological and geographical separation allowed divergent evolution until separate species developed. Today there are 14 species on the islands classified in six separate genera.

5

A *Geospiza* sp
B *Platyspiza* sp
C *Camarhynchus* sp
D *Cactospiza* sp
E *Certhidea* sp
F *Pinaroloxias* sp

G. difficilis, G. scandens, G. conirostris, P. crassirostris, C. psittacula, C. pauper, C. parvulus, C. heliobates, C. pallida, C. olivacea, P. inornata, G. magnirostris, G. fortis, G. fuliginosa

Ancestor: seed-eating ground finch from South America

Food source: Seeds; Buds and fruit; Insects

Habitat: Trees; Ground; Cacti

6A B

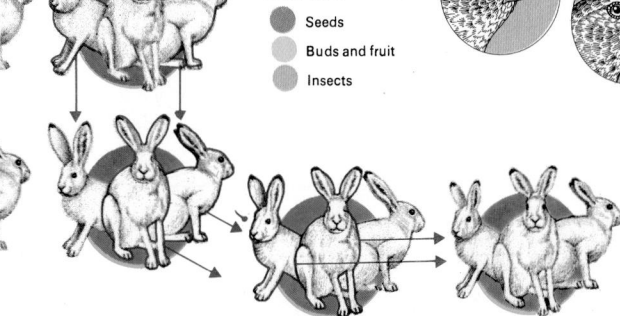

6 The contradictory concepts of evolution proposed by Lamarck and Darwin are illustrated by Arctic hares. According to Lamarck, all of the hares have ears of the same size initially [A]; the influence of the environment causes them to become shorter and this is passed on through the generations. Darwin said that all the hares originally had ears of different lengths [B] but that those with the shortest ones survived better and were able to breed most successfully.

Evolution in action

Since its publication in 1859, Charles Darwin's theory on the origin of species has enjoyed varying popularity, sometimes being almost totally eclipsed by contemporary ideas. But, modified and improved by new data and new concepts, the theory has survived in essence and remains central to current views on evolution.

The key word in Darwin's theory is variation: he continually emphasized the subtlety of the variations within a species. This phenomenon is known as continuous variation. In contrast, there are often striking differences between species and these are termed discontinuous variations. Emphasis on these forms of variation led to the first challenge to Darwinism.

The challenge to Darwin's theories

In 1894 William Bateson (1861–1926) published a book, *Materials for the Study of Variation*, in which he pointed out with some force the difference between continuous and discontinuous variation. It was then an easy step to suggest that evolution may have progressed through jumps provided by discontinuous variation, rather than by the smooth slides of continuous variation.

Bateson's implication was taken up enthusiastically by Hugo de Vries (1848–1935). In observations of cultivated plants he noticed that there occasionally appeared a variant strikingly different from the rest. Such variations, he insisted, were outside the range of continuous variation. De Vries named this phenomenon "mutation," a totally new concept in the origin of variation, and one that could presumably explain the appearance of discontinuous variations. Out of all this emerged the mutation theory of evolution. Evolution, it suggested, was mediated through sudden spontaneous changes rather than depending on natural selection acting on continuous variations. At about that time the work of Gregor Mendel (1822–84) on inheritance was rediscovered, after almost 40 years of obscurity. Genetics as a real science was then born, and it seemed to support the mutation theory as against orthodox Darwinism.

With the reality of chromosomes and the notion of genes now before them, it was easy for geneticists to envisage evolution in terms of major jumps. For instance, X rays and certain drugs could inflict change within a chromosome, and rearrangement of the chromosomes themselves also occurred. Both of these chromosomal changes could induce physical changes in the organisms involved.

The results of chromosomal reordering

One dramatic example of a new species emerging as a result of chromosomal change was a plant, *Spartina townsendii*, more commonly known as cord grass. A count of chromosomes on this grass totaled 126. This grass was clearly a hybrid between two other species of *Spartina*, one with 56 chromosomes and the other with 70. The new species thrived and multiplied phenomenally, a good example of a new species created by discontinuous variation filling an ecological niche and surviving. This type of process, although probably not uncommon in plants, is rare in animals of any complexity because such doubling of chromosomes, outside the norm of stan-

CONNECTIONS

See also

418 Evolution: classical theories
414 The genetic code
416 Principles of heredity
582 Isolation and evolution
614 Life on islands
544 Monotremes and marsupials
434 The lichens
292 Pollution of the air

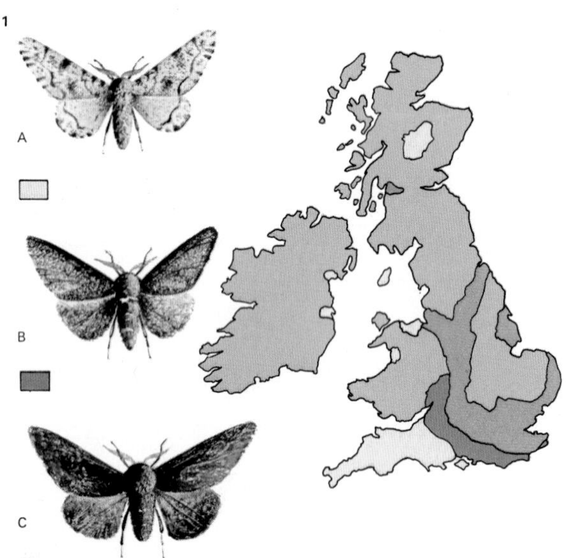

1
A
B
C

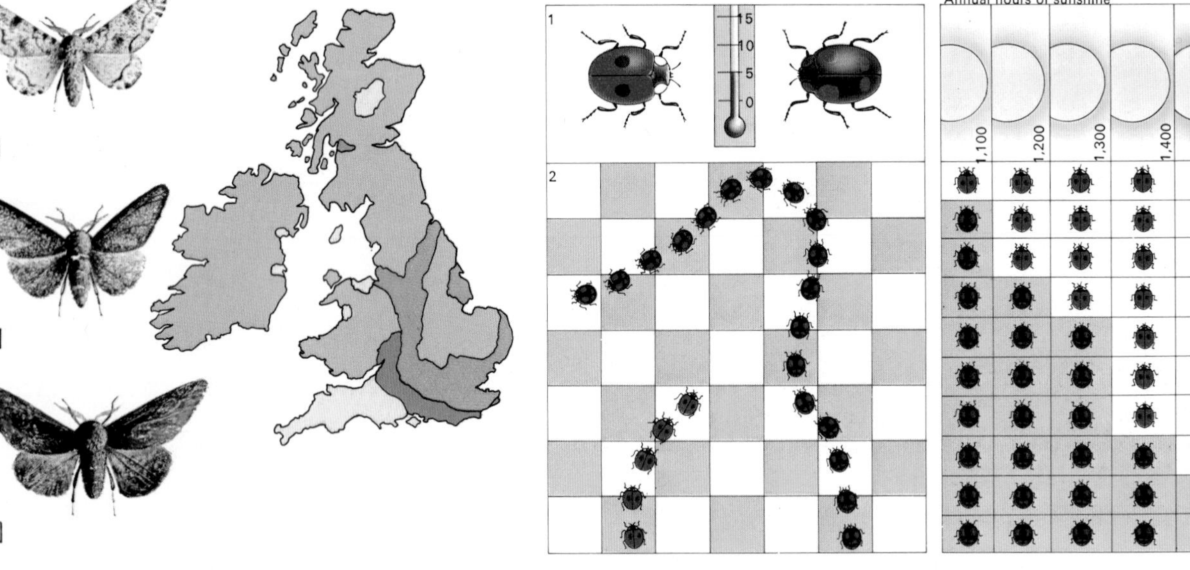

2 A
B
Annual hours of sunshine
1
15
10
5
0
2
1,100
1,200
1,300
1,400
1,500
1,600
Percentage melanics
90
80
70
60
50
40
30
20
10
0

1 The peppered moth *(Biston betularia)* [A] of Europe originally lived on lichen-covered trees where its light color gave some protective camouflage. During the 1800s industrial pollution killed much of the lichen and covered trees with soot. The light colored moths were now more easily seen by predators and two darker forms, *insularia* [B] and *carbonaria* [C], evolved. The darker moths were better camouflaged and soon became abundant in industrialized areas. [A] now thrives in non-industrial areas and the darkened, but not black form [B] is found in semi-industrial zones. This is an example of evolution in action.

2 The typical two-spot ladybird has two black spots on a red background, but melanic forms have the colors reversed. The melanic forms, or morphs, appear more frequently if there is little sunshine and are more active at lower temperatures, as is shown here. A ladybird of each form is chilled for 30 minutes at 41°F (5°C) [1]. The activity of the two forms is recorded as the number of squares each enters in a set time [2]. The melanic form is found to be more active [A]. The frequency of each form in the population is plotted against the hours of sunshine. In areas of low sunshine, the melanic forms are more common [B].

Yellow 1–5 bands
Pink 1–5 bands
Brown 1–5 bands
Yellow
Pink
Brown

3 The shells of the snail *Cepaea nemoralis* can be of three different colors: pink, yellow, or brown. A series of bands may be superimposed on the shells. The proportion of colors and banding varies, depending on the ecology of the habitat and the ability of the predator thrush to recognize them. In short turf [A] the greenness and uniform nature of the background favors the yellow unbanded snail. In beech wood [B] the degree of banding depends on the leaf carpet. In rough herbage [C] yellow banded snails are best camouflaged. Leaf litter [D], in a deciduous wood, favors brown, unbanded shells.

3
A
B
C
D

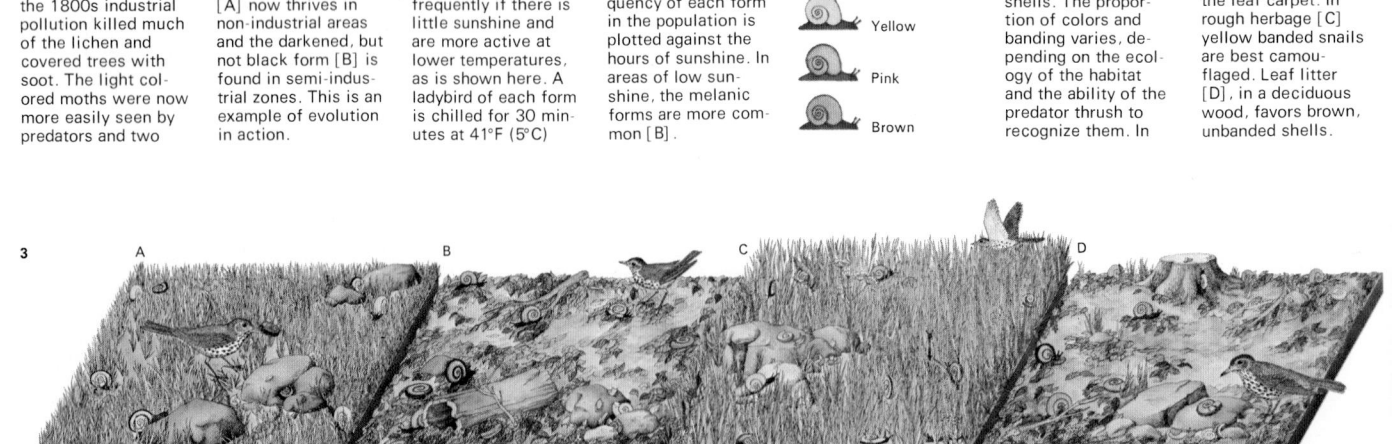

dard sexual reproduction, generally leads to sterile or inviable offspring [5].

Mutational events are undoubtedly important in evolution. The hereditary information in genes is written in a code of nucleotide bases, triplets of which represent single amino acids. If one of these bases is altered, a new amino acid may be coded, slightly altering the structure of the protein for which the gene carries the total information. A changed amino acid in an unimportant part of the protein molecule has no effect on the organism's phenotype, and it is the phenotype upon which the forces of natural selection act.

A mutation in a crucial area of the molecule, however, may make itself felt. And the degree of modification in the phenotype depends on the number of genes that are responsible for that particular character. If the character is determined by a single gene, mutation in that gene may have a dramatic effect, in other words producing a discontinuous variation; but if a battery of genes combine to shape that character, mutation in one of them may have only minimal effect, producing continuous variation. It is clear, then, that a sharp distinction cannot be made between orthodox Darwinism and the mutation theory. The principle of selection remains sound, and the new synthesis of ideas has become known as neo-Darwinism.

The problem of altrusim and the individual

By its nature, selection acts on the individual. It is the survival of individuals that overall makes a group of them (a population) successful; it is on the individual that the forces of the environment act. And yet this emphasis on individual rather than group selection has thrown up the problem of explaining altrusim in animals, a trait that undoubtedly exists. For example, a worker bee will sting an invader to defend the hive, and die in the act. How can suicide be favored by natural selection and survival of the fittest? The answer to this puzzle is that other individuals carrying genes identical with those possessed by the now dead individual have been given a better chance to survive and pass on those genes.

KEY

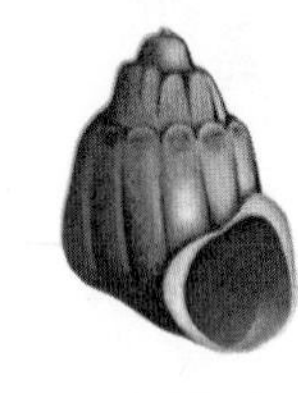

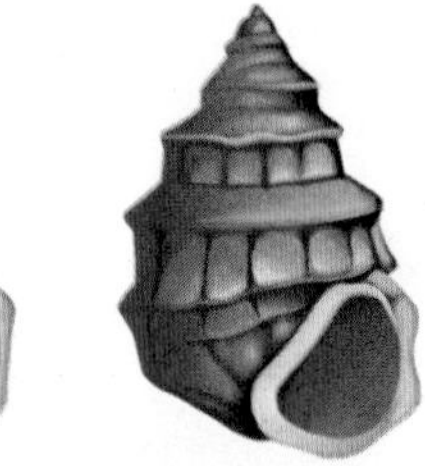

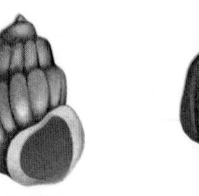

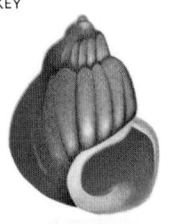

10 million years old
3 million years old

A series of fossil shells from successive layers of rock illustrates how small, almost imperceptible changes in structure can give rise to large changes that are obvious at first glance. Despite this, all the shells are members of the same species, a fact that would not be known without such a full fossil record. They range from three to 10 million years old.

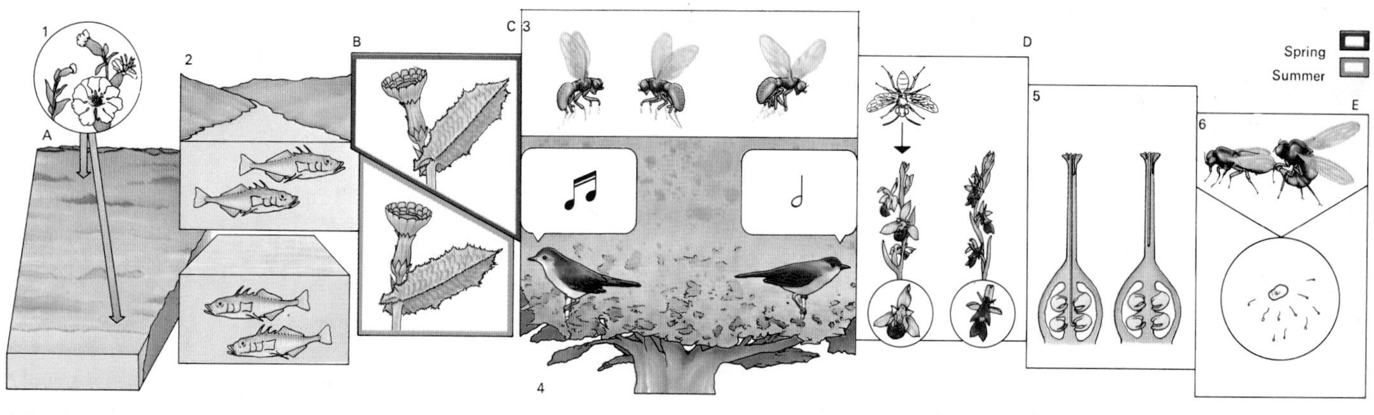

4
Spring
Summer

4 Species are kept distinct in a number of ways. One form of isolation is habitat [A]. Hybrids of sea campion and bladder campion are viable [1], but normally do not occur because one grows on the seashore and the other in meadows. Three-spined sticklebacks have two populations in Belgium—one marine, the other freshwater [2]. Eventually two distinct species may develop. Of two species of *Lactuca* [B] one flowers in spring, the other in summer. The chances of cross-fertilization are thus reduced. Isolation is also caused by behavioral differences [C]. Fruit flies [3] have a complex courtship so that related species are unlikely to mate; if they do [E], the gametes are usually incompatible or the egg is unacceptable to the sperm [6]. In blackcaps and garden warblers [4] the song is highly specific. Mechanical isolation [D] exploits the senses of insects, flowers having different colors and structures. If transferred, pollen often does not grow a tube reaching the ovule [5].

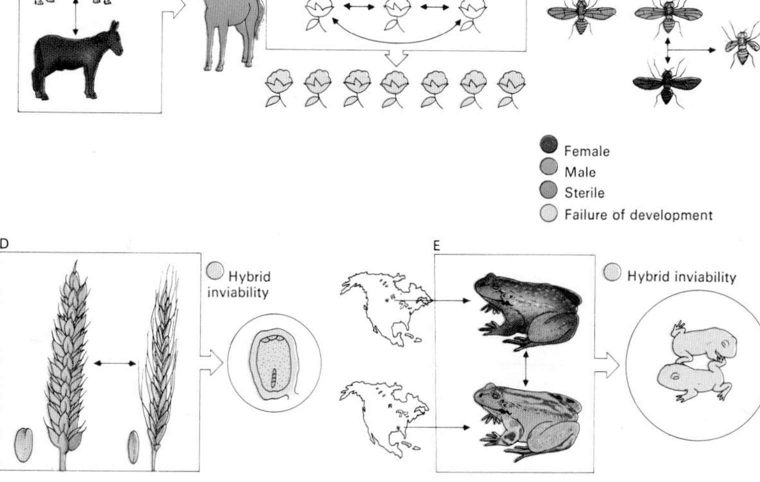

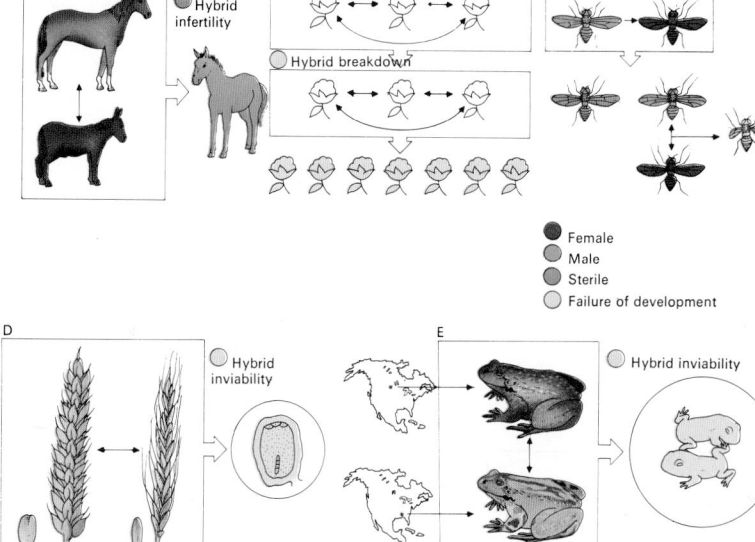

5 A
Hybrid infertility
B
Hybrid breakdown
C
Female
Male
Sterile
Failure of development
D
Hybrid inviability
E
Hybrid inviability

5 Sometimes species (and even subspecies) are kept distinct by incompatability of genetic material after mating. The mule [A] produced by a mare and a male donkey is sterile, as is a hinny, the cross between a stallion and a female donkey. If a fertile (viable) hybrid is formed from different species and is then mated with one of its parents, weak or sterile offspring arise, as in certain cotton plants [B] and fruit flies [C]. Related species of wheat *(Triticum aestivum)* and rye *(Secale cercale)* [D] and different races of the North American leopard frog *(Rana pipiens)* [E] can produce hybrid seeds or eggs respectively, but the embryos fail to develop.

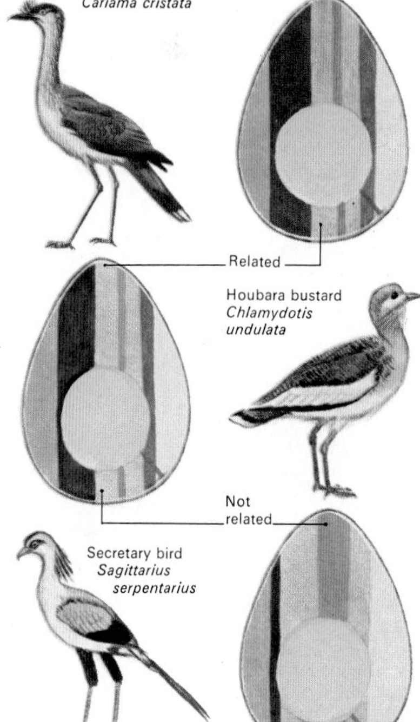

6
Crested seriema
Cariama cristata
Related
Houbara bustard
Chlamydotis undulata
Not related
Secretary bird
Sagittarius serpentarius

6 Many species of birds are similar in appearance because of convergent evolution, but by comparing the proteins of the white of the eggs their true relationships can be established.

Bacteria and viruses

Bacteria and viruses are the smallest forms of life on earth; about 250,000 of them would cover the period at the end of this sentence. They are simple entities, but they are not primitive [1]. They have a capacity for survival in inhospitable places and an ability to adapt to new conditions that puts them among the most successful of living things.

Although associated with disease, death, and decay, the role of bacteria in returning essential nutrients to the soil, and in making complex foods that can be used by other living creatures, means that they are essential to the balance of nature.

Viruses and their effects

Viruses have been described as "living chemicals." They neither feed, breathe, grow, reproduce on their own, nor move, yet once within a living cell [4] they can take control of it and subvert it from its ordinary activities to the production of new viruses. All living cells are susceptible to attack by viruses—even bacteria fall victim to a special type of virus, the bacteriophage ("bacteriaeater") [5]. Virus "particles," seen under the microscope, are the infectious agents, bundles of chemicals traveling from one "victim" cell to the next.

Viruses are made up of a core of hereditary material surrounded by an envelope of protein; they are not true cells. Plant virus particles [2] enter living cells through damaged cell walls, while animal virus particles [3] are taken up by the cell as if they were morsels of food. Bacteriophages inject themselves into their victims. Once inside, the viral hereditary material takes control, diverting its victim's cellular machinery to new virus production.

Viral infection is usually specific. A particular virus will attack only one organism, or only one part of that organism. Virulent viruses destroy the cells they attack with the release of the new viruses—these cause diseases such as yellow fever, poliomyelitis, influenza, the common cold, and smallpox. Latent viruses do not harm their victims, but may coexist with them for long periods before becoming virulent.

Antibiotic drugs are comparatively ineffective against viruses, but living cells produce antibodies that give immunity to viral attack, and vaccination with killed virus can be used against diseases such as poliomyelitis. Interferon, a substance produced naturally by living cells in response to viral attack, prevents viral multiplication, but has proved difficult to use medically.

The ubiquitous bacteria

Unlike viruses, bacteria are cellular, but their cells are much more simple than those of higher organisms and vary greatly in size and shape [6, 7, 8]. Bacteria are found everywhere and can live in conditions that defeat more complex organisms. They have been found 6 miles (9km) below the surface of the ocean, floating in the upper atmosphere, attached to rocks washed by the spray from boiling springs, and in small pockets of liquid water in otherwise frozen soil. When conditions worsen some bacteria produce a resistant resting stage, the endospore, the most resistant living thing known. Even boiling will not kill some.

Some bacteria invade the bodies of other organisms and can therefore be

CONNECTIONS

See also
412 The cell in action
406 Life and its origins
710 The causes of illness: 1
740 The body's natural defenses
312 The living soil
1766 Water supply
374 Dairy produce and cheese
396 Food preservation
320 Organic farming
398 The future of food
1746 Nuclear, chemical, and biological warfare

1 Microorganisms vary greatly in size. On the scale shown, a large filamented bacterium would be too large for the page, while the smallest virus would scarcely be visible. Microorganisms are measured in microns (μ). One μ equals a millionth of a meter. [A], [B], and [C] are various bacteria. *Haemophilus influenzae* [D] is a large virus and [E] is a mycoplasma, the smallest known free-living cell.

2 Tobacco mosaic virus "particles" each take the form of a long, hollow rod [A], measuring 300 millimicrons in length and 18 millimicrons in diameter. Ribonucleic acid (RNA) forms a helical spine [1] around which the protein units [2] are arranged. This virus was the first to be isolated from its host plant and purified. Infected leaves were ground up and the virus was precipitated out. This showed that a living organism could be handled like a chemical.

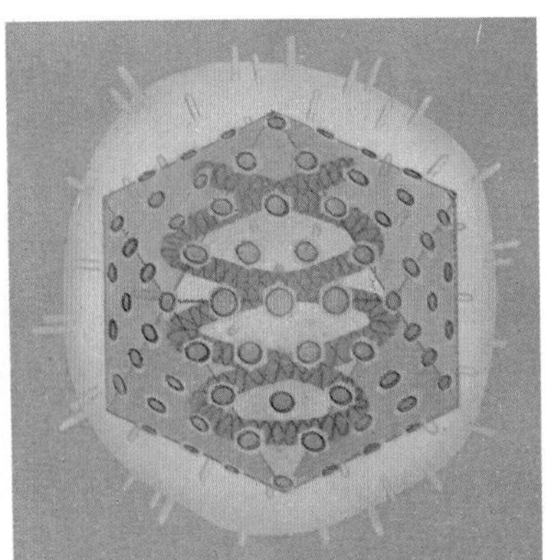

3 Chickenpox and shingles are caused by a typical animal virus, the herpes "particle." Its DNA core is surrounded by 162 protein units in the shape of a solid with 20 plane faces.

5 Bacteriophages, the most complex of viruses, infect bacteria. Each particle consists of a head [1], a protein tail surrounded by a retractable sheath of protein units [2], and tail fibers [3].

4 Viruses can live and multiply only within living cells. The viral hereditary material substitutes for that of the host as a blueprint for the creation of more viruses. In multiplying they may cause disease. Cowpox, for example, is caused by *Vaccinia* virus, one of the largest viruses. It can enter the host cell by special chemical means. A pocket is induced in the host's cell membrane [A], which the virus particle enters and then crosses [B]. Once inside, the viral core with its hereditary instructions, is released into the cell contents [C], and the production of new viruses begins.

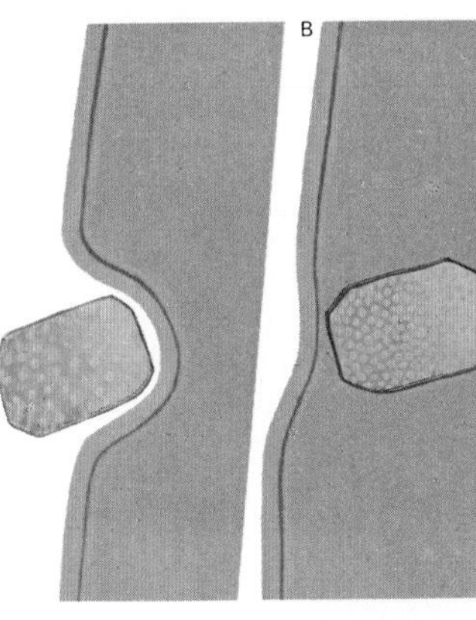

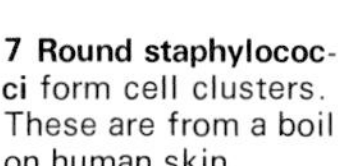

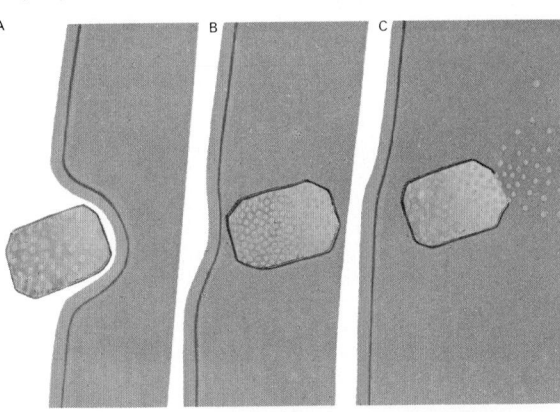

6 Typhoid is caused by the rod-shaped bacterium named *Salmonella typhi.*

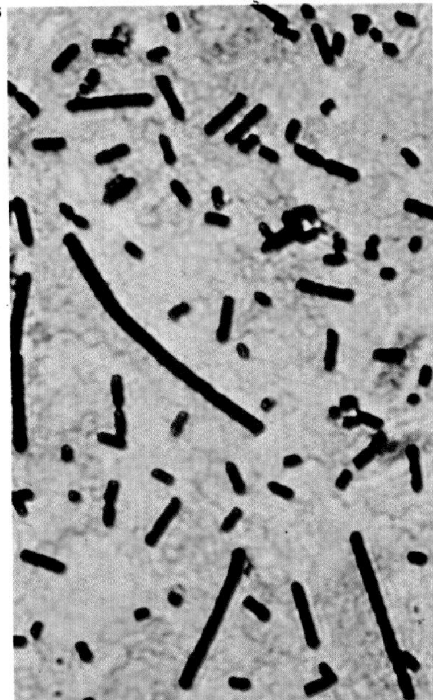

7 Round staphylococci form cell clusters. These are from a boil on human skin.

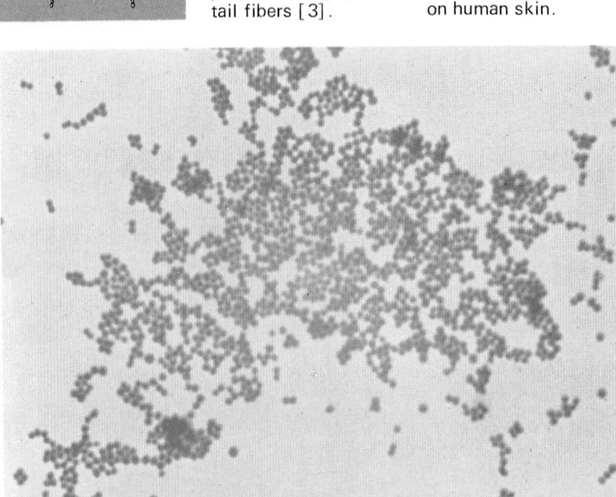

dangerous. Bacteria gain entrance through wounds or with the intake of infested food and water. Once inside they must resist their victim's defense mechanism, chiefly phagocytes (cells that would engulf them) and antibodies that would destroy them. Some bacteria have slimy capsules on their outer surface that phagocytes cannot attack. Others are able to live within the phagocyte after being engulfed; some bacteria produce camouflage substances that give the invaded cell the illusion that no invasion has taken place and therefore no antibodies are produced.

Harmful and helpful

Bacteria can harm in three ways: by clogging vital passages through sheer numbers; by producing poisonous substances—tetanus (toxin) produced by the soil organism *Clostridium tetani* is one of the most poisonous substances known—and by producing an allergic reaction in their victims. Antibiotics have been effective against bacterial infections for some time, but bacteria are appearing that are resistant to these chemicals. Bacteria multiply rapidly, dividing once every ten minutes in good conditions, so the chances of mutants arising, resistant to antibiotics, are high.

Bacteria living within other creatures are not always harmful. The bacteria living in the rumen of cows, sheep, and goats help the animal digest plant cellulose [12].

The mycoplasms, smallest of all cellular creatures and perhaps an intermediate stage between viruses and bacteria, can exist in nature by living on sewage, but may also live in animals, where they cause diseases.

Bacteria break down dead bodies and return the vital substances contained within them to the soil. Without the continual recycling of these vital building blocks, life could not continue. Man makes use of bacteria in sewage systems to render organic waste harmless, in composting [13], and in making cheese, butter, and vinegar.

Between bacteria, viruses, and other creatures a fine balance is constantly maintained in which coexistence is the dominant theme. Invasion leading to disease and death is the exception rather than the rule.

KEY

A bacterium is bounded by a rigid wall [2] outside which may be a simy capsule [1]. A fine membrane [3] surrounds the cell contents. The hereditary material [4] lies free within the cell, together with the machinery that manufactures the cell substance [5]. Some bacteria appear hairy [6] and some bear flagella [9]. Granules of storage material [7, 8] are also found in some bacteria, such as *Chlorobium*.

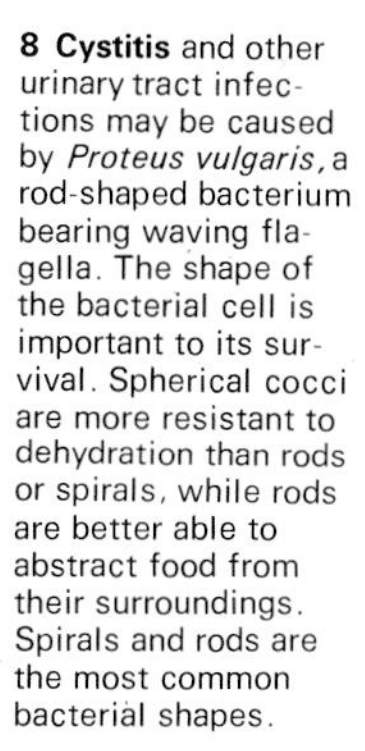

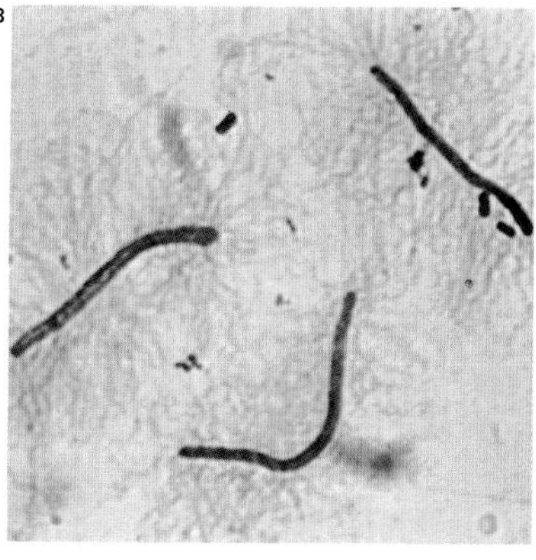

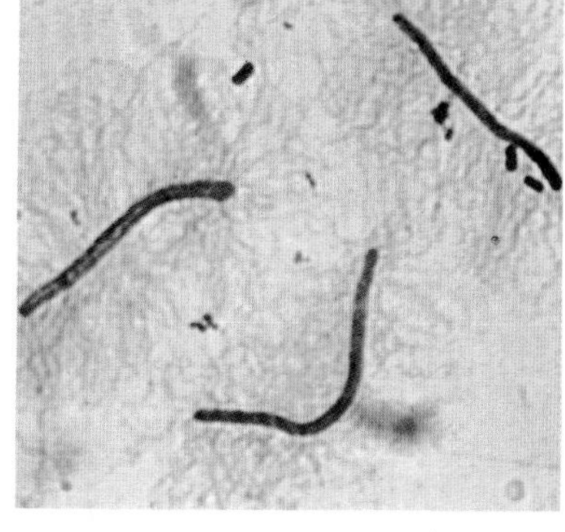

8 Cystitis and other urinary tract infections may be caused by *Proteus vulgaris*, a rod-shaped bacterium bearing waving flagella. The shape of the bacterial cell is important to its survival. Spherical cocci are more resistant to dehydration than rods or spirals, while rods are better able to abstract food from their surroundings. Spirals and rods are the most common bacterial shapes.

9 Bacteria acquire energy in several different ways. All bacteria must either elaborate their own food using light or chemical energy, or find it ready-made. Some do not need oxygen—they are anaerobic. *Actinomyces* [2] causes rotting in compost heaps [9] while *Rhodopseudomonas* [4] lives in the mud at the bottom of lakes. *Leptospira* [6] lives in the human kidney, causing a form of jaundice. Others, such as *Gallionella* [3] need oxygen, while some, such as *Rhizobium* [1], fix nitrogen in the root nodules [8] of leguminous plants. *Bacillus anthracis* [7] causes anthrax in hoofed animals. Some bacteria can live with or without oxygen. *Rhodospirillum* [5], for example, obtains its energy from chemical reactions when oxygen is available and from light when oxygen is sparse.

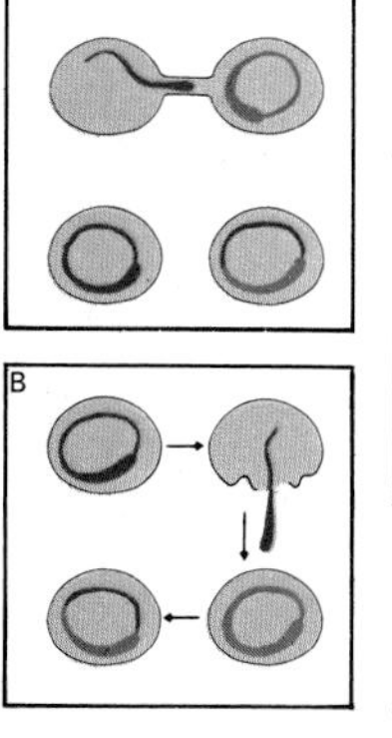

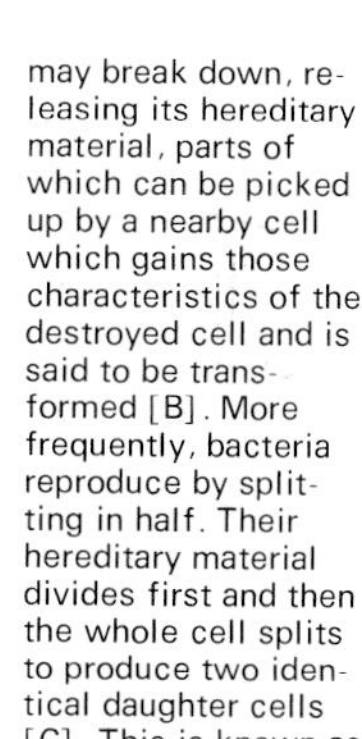

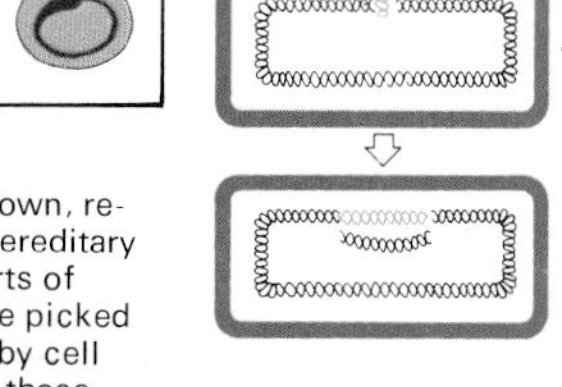

10 Mating behavior in bacteria can be similar to sexual reproduction [A]. The "male" forms a tube through which part of the hereditary material passes to the "female." The resulting cell shows some of the characteristics of the "male." The process is called conjugation. More unusually, a bacterial cell may break down, releasing its hereditary material, parts of which can be picked up by a nearby cell which gains those characteristics of the destroyed cell and is said to be transformed [B]. More frequently, bacteria reproduce by splitting in half. Their hereditary material divides first and then the whole cell splits to produce two identical daughter cells [C]. This is known as fission.

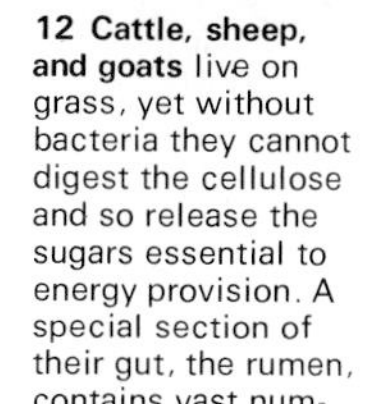

11 Viruses multiplying in a cell can pick up a part of their victim's hereditary material by mistake [A] and carry it to a second victim where it becomes incorporated in the new host's hereditary material. Specific genes can be so transferred [B]. This is transduction.

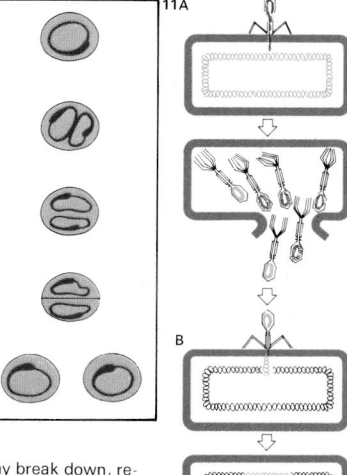

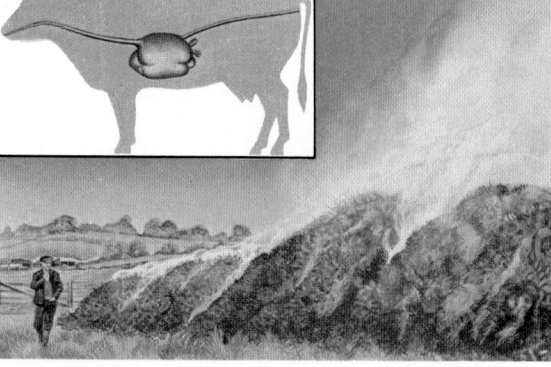

12 Cattle, sheep, and goats live on grass, yet without bacteria they cannot digest the cellulose and so release the sugars essential to energy provision. A special section of their gut, the rumen, contains vast numbers of bacteria and other organisms that break down the complex plant cellulose structure into simpler sugars.

13 Compost heaps usually comprise soil, dead plant matter, and manure. Bacteria break these materials down into simpler substances, many of them nitrogenous, which can be used as fertilizer. As a result of bacterial activity energy is released as heat and a compost heap may become very hot and burst into flames when air enters.

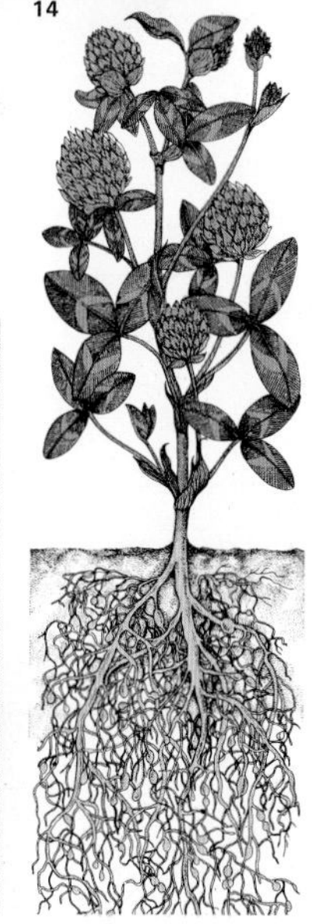

14 All living things need nitrogen but only certain bacteria can assimilate nitrogen directly from air. Nodules on the roots of leguminous plants contain bacteria that help "fix" nitrogen and convert it to a usable form.

The plant kingdom

Traditionally, the plant kingdom is studied in two distinct groups, the lower or non-seed-bearing plants and the higher or seed-bearing plants. The lower plants include algae, mosses, horsetails, and club mosses, while the higher plants consist not only of the profusion of flowering plants but also of ferns and most trees and shrubs.

The history of the plant kingdom is one of increasing complexity from the simple single-celled algae of the Precambrian era, which could only survive in water (some fossil algae are 2.5 billion years old), to the flowering land plants of today, of which the first records date back to the Cretaceous, some 130 million years ago [Key]. The conquest of the land by plants involved a number of specialized and complex adaptations. These included the development of an internal water and food transport system (vascular system) and a mechanism to ensure fertilization without the need for water.

Many plants have two forms, one sexual, the other asexual, or vegetative. This is known as alternation of generations. In the simplest plants the sexual form is the dominant; in land plants there has been a shift of emphasis to the asexual phase, culminating in the flowering plants where the sexual phase is reduced to a few cells.

Early plant types

Today, more than 400,000 species of plants have been described and it is thought that all are descendants of a small fraction of the progeny of earlier species. Most of those early species, less fitted for competition under natural conditions, became extinct. Ancestry of the major groups of plants can be traced to simple single-celled plants similar to *Euglena* [1], which reproduce asexually by mitosis, the process by which a nucleus reproduces itself without any change in the number of chromosomes.

Relatively early in the evolutionary tree, fungi [3] and mosses and liverworts [4] appeared. The latter group, called Bryophyta, has developed multicellular sex organs and shows affinities with the ferns and horsetails. The fungi (Eumycophyta) developed independently of green plants as a highly specialized group containing no chlorophyll (the green matter that uses the sun's energy to manufacture food) and are therefore unable to obtain food by photosynthesis. Fungi are either parasites on other living creatures or saprophytes that obtain energy from dead organic matter. They have evolved to produce a great number of species diverse in form and function and are of importance in the economy of the living world: as important decomposing agents, with the bacteria, they are the scavengers of the plant kingdom. Lichens are a combina tion of two plants—an alga and a fungus.

Ferns, club mosses, and horsetails

Among the next group of plant types are the ferns [5], club mosses, and horsetails [6]. These include about 10,000 species and as a group show much variety of form—in particular the specialization in which cells for conducting water up the stem form a central tube of dead tissue. These tubes may then split into parallel tubes and branches. With the development of the vascular system and a growth tissue (cambium), plants of larger and more complex shape became possible.

CONNECTIONS

See also
412 The cell in action
422 Bacteria and viruses
430 The way plants work
432 Algae and seaweeds
434 The lichens
436 Mosses and liverworts
438 Ferns and horsetails
440 The cone bearers
444 Flowering plants: two seed leaves
452 Flowering plants: one seed leaf
1574 Polymers: giant molecules
742 Origins of curative medicine
1814 Cosmetics and perfumes
1468 Shape and symmetry

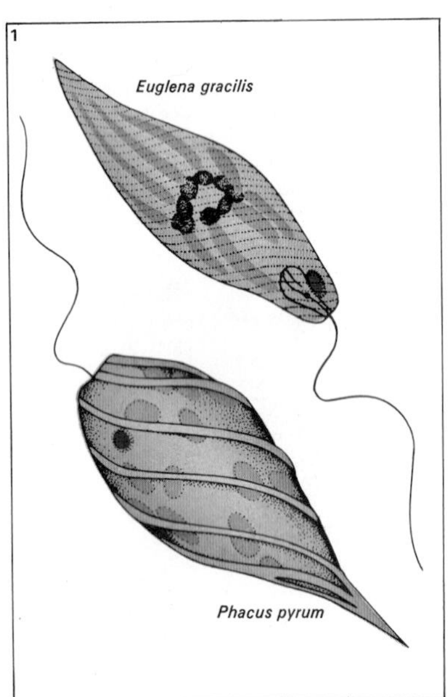

1
Euglena gracilis
Phacus pyrum

1 Euglenoids are among the simplest of all plants. *Euglena* species are microscopic, single-celled algae containing chlorophyll that live by photosynthesis. Borderline organisms that are also regarded as single-celled animals by zoologists, Euglenoids have a worldwide distribution in fresh and salt water, and these are just two of about 10,000 species of single-celled plants.

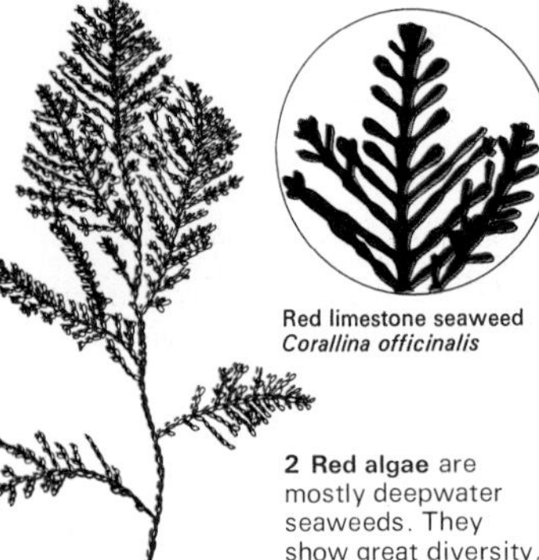

2
Red limestone seaweed
Corallina officinalis

2 Red algae are mostly deepwater seaweeds. They show great diversity, from unicellular to ribbon species.

3
Fly agaric fungus
Amanita muscaria
4
Moss
Atrichum undulatum

3 Fungi contain no chlorophyll and must live as parasites on green plants or as saprophytes on dead or decaying matter.

4 Mosses and liverworts are together classified as bryophytes, a group that has multicellular sex organs and no true conducting, or vascular, system. There are about 25,000 species occurring in all parts of the world, but most individual plants are small and inconspicuous. They are important in the formation of soils in many barren regions.

5
Hart's tongue fern
Phyllitis scolopendrium

5 Ferns, unlike bryophytes, are mostly large plants. Anatomically they differ from bryophytes in having special water-conducting cells. They also have a region of growing cells—cambium—which allows the development of larger plants such as the tree ferns of tropical regions. Ferns have an interesting life cycle. The typical "fern plant" is the asexual stage. It produces spores that grow into the inconspicuous sexual stage.

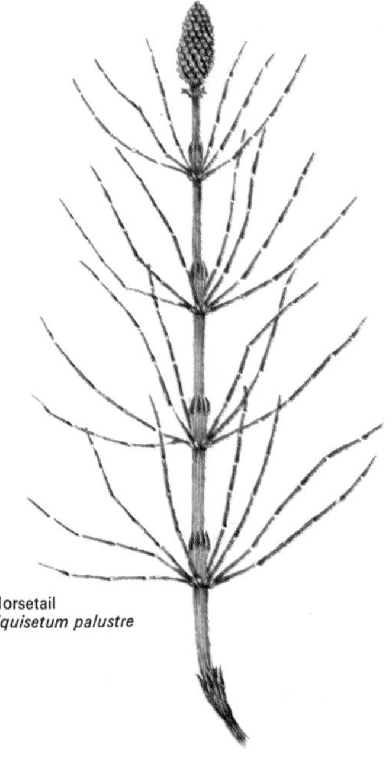

6
Horsetail
Equisetum palustre

6 Horsetails are allied to ferns and have cylindrical leaves and jointed stems. The spores are produced in conelike structures at the tips of fertile stems. They are "living fossil" relatives of giant Devonian trees.

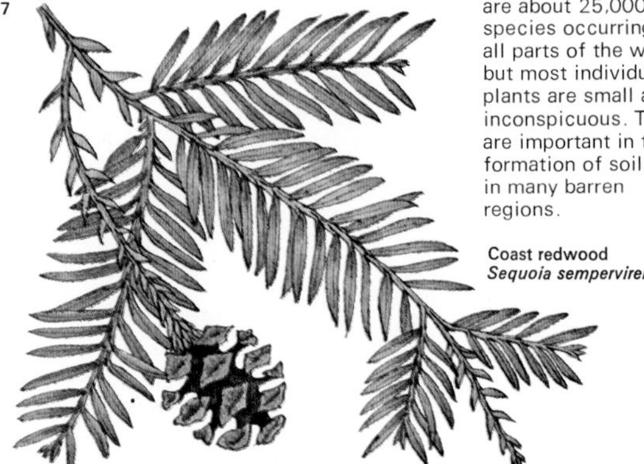

7
Coast redwood
Sequoia sempervirens

7 Gymnosperms are one of the two main groups of seed-bearing plants. They bear "naked seeds," actually unenclosed ovules; male pollen and female ovules are borne separately on leaves, in cones, or in catkinlike structures. The largest class of gymnosperms is that of the cone-bearing conifers. The conifers are wind-pollinated and seed fertilization can be a complex process, taking many years for the development of pollen and maturation of the seed.

The primitive life cycle with two generations, one sexual (gametophyte) and one asexual (sporophyte) became more complex. In ferns the gametophyte generation is suppressed and gives rise to the dominant sporophyte plant body.

The range of seed plants

A major development was the evolution of the angiosperms and gymnosperms—distinguished by the formation of seeds during reproduction [7] and [8]. These form the main vegetation over most of the fresh water and land surfaces of the earth and some specialized plants have even adapted to such inhospitable regions as salt marshes, tundra, and deserts. The number of seed plant species is estimated at more than 250,000 and included in them is a fascinating variety of form and size.

All the plants in this group produce seeds, almost all by sexual reproduction. Pollen grains are produced by male organs and egg cells form in the female ovule. A pollen grain then fuses with an egg cell to produce an embryo in a seed. The cycle from seed to seed-producing plant can vary greatly in length and many annual weeds have very rapid life cycles—shepherd's purse *(Capsella bursa-pastoris)* can complete a life cycle in 21 days. After producing seeds shepherd's purse dies, but perennial plants can live to a great age. Some specimens of the bristlecone pine *(Pinus aristata)* may be nearly 5,000 years old.

Angiosperms may be distinguished from other types by their flowers [10], which normally have conspicuous petals and leaf-like sepals surrounding the reproductive organs. Although gymnosperms do not have flowers, they do have obvious pollen-producing organs and ovules. Bark surrounding the stems of woody seed plants is another characteristic of the group.

Vascular plants have special pores or openings in leaf surfaces called stomata [12]. These normally have two kidney-shaped guard cells capable of shrinking and swelling to close or open the pores and by this means the rate at which water droplets evaporate from the surfaces of the plant can be controlled.

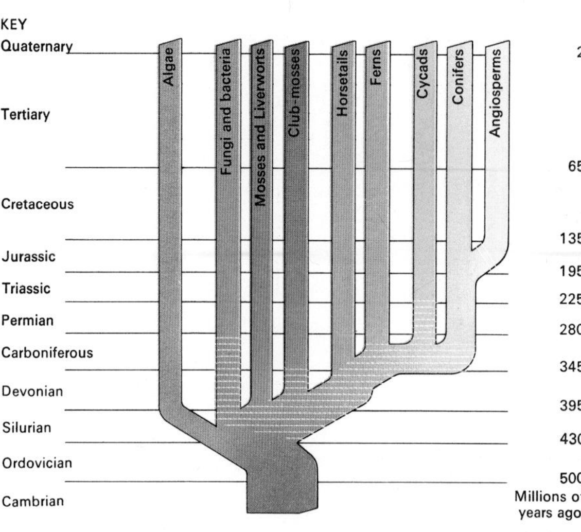

KEY
Quaternary
Tertiary
Cretaceous
Jurassic
Triassic
Permian
Carboniferous
Devonian
Silurian
Ordovician
Cambrian
Algae
Fungi and bacteria
Mosses and Liverworts
Club-mosses
Horsetails
Ferns
Cycads
Conifers
Angiosperms
2
65
135
195
225
280
345
395
430
500
Millions of years ago

Plants have developed through the ages from simple unicellular algae to the complex flowering plants that exist in the world today. Fossil records have been found of most major plant groups. Although these records provide a broad outline of plant evolution, they do not give a complete picture. Because of the relative scarcity of plant fossils the relationships of plant groups are still uncertain.

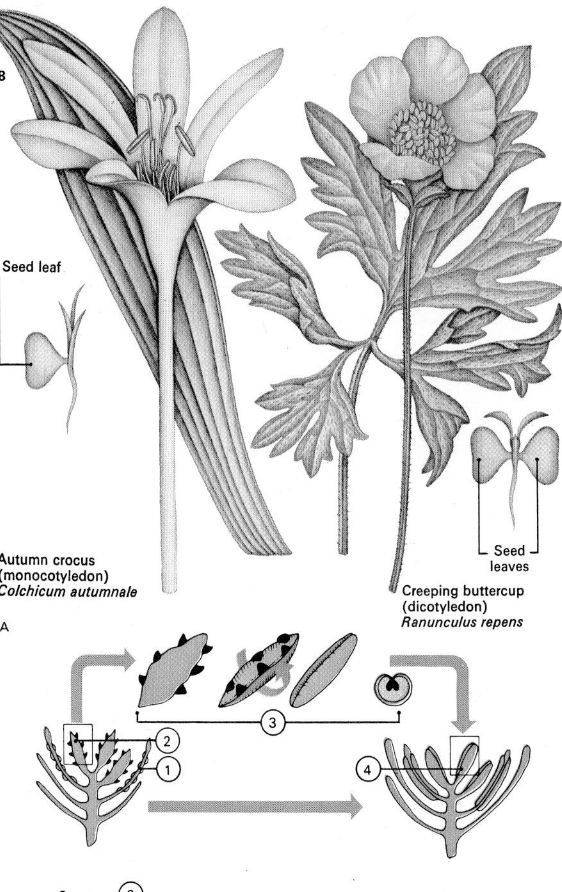

8
Seed leaf
Autumn crocus (monocotyledon) *Colchicum autumnale*
Seed leaves
Creeping buttercup (dicotyledon) *Ranunculus repens*

8 Angiosperms are seed-bearing plants with ovules enclosed in ovaries. They are divided into monocotyledons (one seed leaf) and dicotyledons (two seed leaves).

9 Angiosperm fruits show an evolutionary sequence from one ovary with many ovules, as in the custard apple *(Annona)* [A], to an ovary with one ovule, as in wheat *(Triticum)* [E], or a number of ovaries with many ovules, as in the tomato *(Lycopersicum)* [F]. The cherry *(Prunus)* [B], walnut *(Juglans)* [C], and orange *(Citrus)* [D] represent intermediate stages with one or many ovaries and one ovule.

10 Flowers contain the sex organs of higher plants. Some such as the buttercup *(Ranunculus)* [A] have large petals [1] and honey-guide markings [2]. A flower plan is shown [3]. Daisy family flowers comprise a number of florets. In cornflowers *(Centaurea)* [B] these are central and fertile [4] or sterile and marginal [5]. Poplar *(Populus)* has small, open male [6] or female [7] flowers.

11 Two major theories exist for the way flowering plants evolved. The euanthemum theory [A] suggests that the ancestral flower was fernlike with separate male [1] and female [2] parts, or sporophylls. These then folded over [3] to produce parts of the flower [4]. The pseudanthemum theory [B] supposes that flower evolution began with a complete flower head with both male [5] and female [6] flowers, which gradually [7, 8] became condensed.

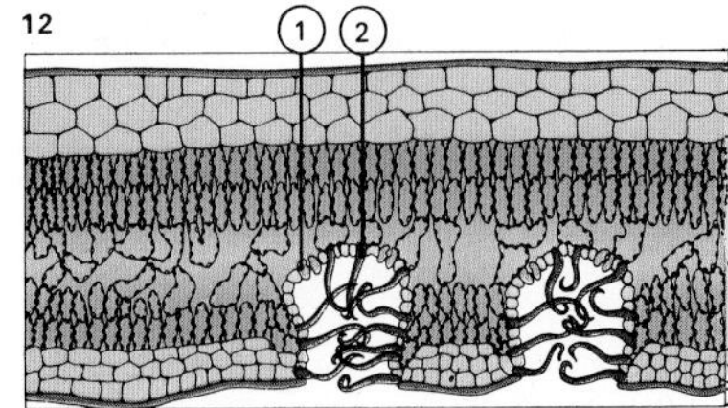

12
1
2

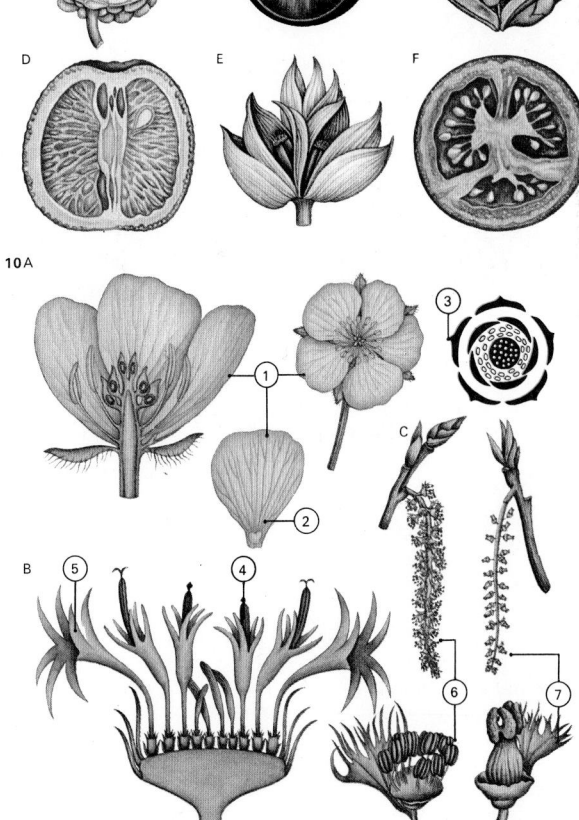

12 A stoma is a pore in the surface layer of cells of leaf or stem, characteristic of seed plants and of the ferns. Each stoma is surrounded by guard cells [1] or hairs [2], which control retention or loss of water as vapor from the plant.

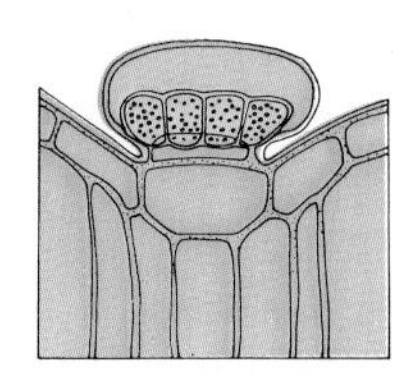

13

13 Outer cells of leaves may form hairlike projections, some of which are specialized secretory cells. The section through the epidermis of a *Thymus* leaf shows a club-shaped gland containing the scented oil of thyme secreted by the plant.

Yeasts and molds

Molds and mildews, rusts and smuts are all fungi, members of a vast group of organisms which, like animals, cannot manufacture their own food and, like plants, have no organs of locomotion to go in search of it. All fungi are therefore either parasites, forced to live in or on other living things, or saprophytes [6] living on dead and decaying organic matter. The fungi, a group comprising 100,000 or more distinct species, include not only the microscopic single-celled yeasts [11] but also the familiar mushrooms, toadstools, and puffballs.

Harmful and helpful fungi

Although fungi are chiefly the enemies of the green plant, certain species will attack animals—some trap and kill nematode worms [8], while others cause disease in insects [9]. Athelete's foot and ringworm in man are also fungal diseases. These are minor irritations, however, compared with the enormous problems that fungal diseases cause agriculturists. Roots and shoots, foliage, leaves, and fruits of plants are all subject to attack [Key].

Fungi do have their uses, however. Yeasts yield alcohol by causing the fermentation of sugars, the central process in the making of wine and beer. Bakers use yeast in their dough—the fungus produces bubbles of carbon dioxide, making the bread rise. Many fungi produce antibiotics, substances that can be used to control bacterial diseases in man and other animals. The members of the genus *Penicillium* [4] are among the most important to man. Species of this genus are not only the source of the antibiotic penicillin (produced by *Penicillium notatum*), but are also used in cheese-making. Many forest trees enjoy mutually beneficial liaisons (mycorrhiza) with fungi—the fungus receives nourishment from the tree which, in turn, receives extra mineral salts from the fungus.

With the exception of the single-celled yeasts, all fungi are constructed of fine filaments called hyphae. These are surrounded by a stout wall made not of cellulose, as in green plants, but of another carbohydrate, fungal chitin, which is similar to the material found in the shells of insects and crustaceans. These filaments ramify through the substance on which the fungus lives, forming a loose network called a mycelium. In some species elaborate and substantial fruiting bodies are produced by the combination of many thousands of fungal filaments.

Fungal classification

Because fungi cannot search out food, their only hope of finding new sites for colonization is to produce reproductive spores and distribute them widely. The methods of sexual reproduction and spore dispersal so developed are very distinctive and form the basis of fungal classification. Those fungi in which sexual reproduction has never been observed are lumped together in a category called "fungi imperfecti." Among them are the grey molds, the ringworm fungus, and the wilt fungi. Most other fungi are grouped together as either phycomycetes, ascomycetes, or basidiomycetes, depending on the way in which they produce their spores.

There are about 1,800 species of phycomycetes; members of the group are simple fungi that do not produce complex

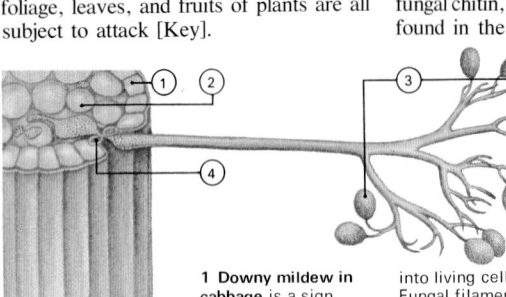

CONNECTIONS

See also
428 Mushrooms and toadstools
424 The plant kingdom
434 The lichens
350 Beer and brewing
328 Bread and pasta
374 Dairy products
398 The future of food
368 Trees: problems of climate and disease
738 Preventive medicine
724 Diseases of the skin
318 Protecting crops
312 The living soil

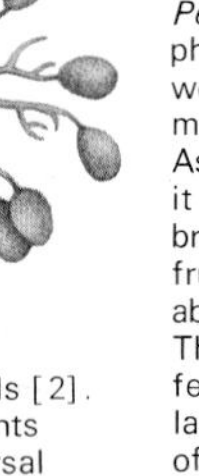

3

1 Downy mildew in cabbage is a sign of attack by *Peronospora parasitica*, a fungus that enters the plant through the epidermis [1] then ramifies, sending forked feeding tubes into living cells [2]. Fungal filaments bearing dispersal spores (conidia) [3] cause the white mildewy appearance. The spore-bearing filaments emerge through the stomata [4] of the plant.

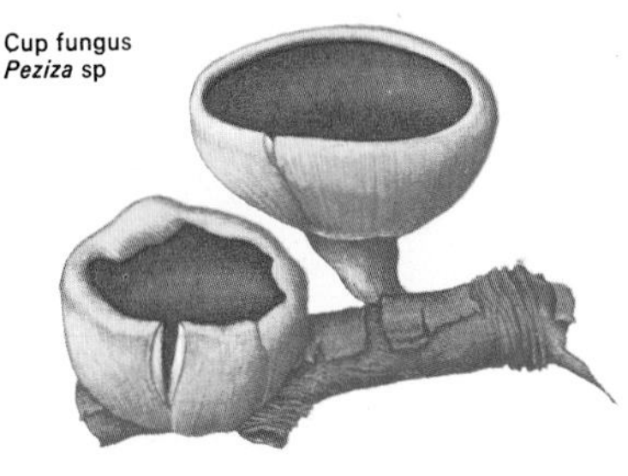

2A
Cup fungus
Peziza sp

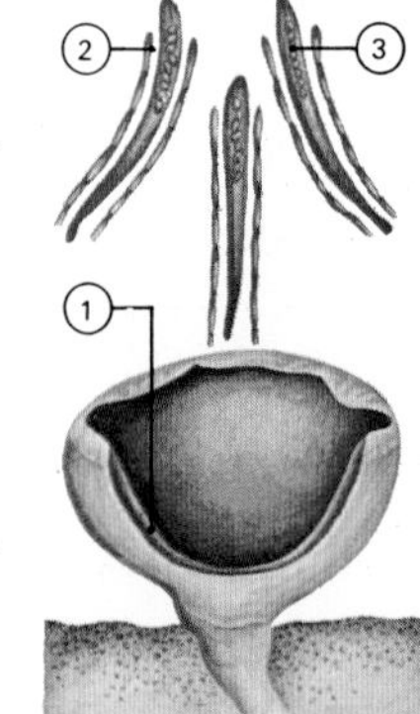

B
1
2
3

2 The cup fungus *Peziza* lives saprophytically on dead wood and organic matter in the soil. As its name suggests it forms a cuplike, brightly colored, fruiting body [A], above the ground. This bears [B] the fertile hymenium layer [1], consisting of sterile hairs [2] and spore-containing asci [3], which point toward the light. The eight ascospores produced in the sacline cell are shot 1in (2.5 cm) into the air.

3 Black rust of wheat is caused by *Puccinia graminis*, a fungus that divides its complex life cycle between two hosts. In early summer, spores [B] on an infected wheat plant [A] are dispersed to infect other wheat. Later, new resting spores [C] are produced. These survive the winter on wheat stubble and germinate [D] in the spring, producing spores to infect the barberry plant [E], on which a form of sexual reproduction [F] produces another wheat infector.

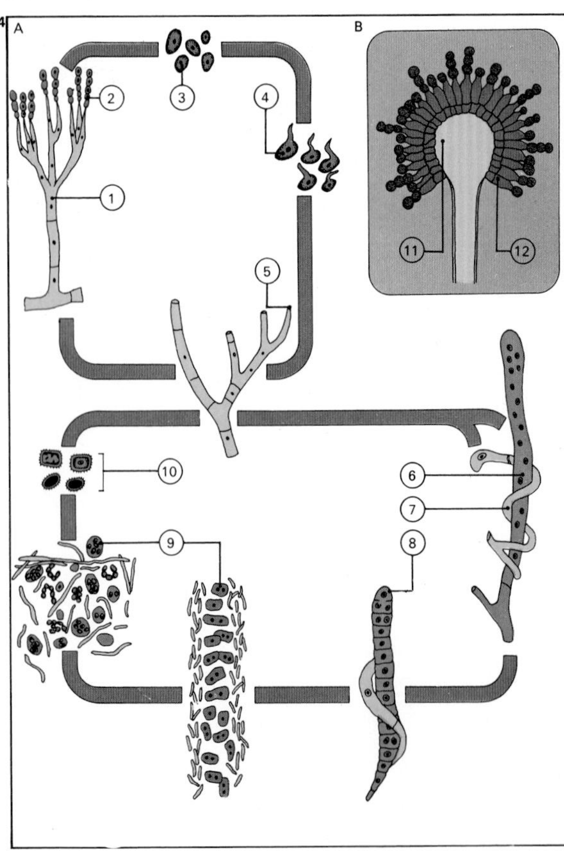

A
B
1
2
3
4
5
6
7
8
9
10
11
12

4 The blue mold *(Penicillium)* [A] reproduces asexually and sexually. Chains of asexually produced conidia [2] are borne on a hypha [1]. Released [3], the spores germinate [4] to produce new hyphae [5]. Sexual reproduction follows the formation of a female hypha [7] which spirals around a male one [6] and fuses with it [8]. The contents of the hyphae mix and asci [9] containing ascospores [10] are produced. *Aspergillus* [B] produces a vesicle [11], from which spore-bearing stalus emerge [12].

5 Slime molds, more like animals than fungi, resemble individual ameba at one stage. Later the cells join to form a large, multinucleate sporing structure.

fruiting bodies. They include many water molds, downy mildews [1], bread molds [6], and the chytrids, many of which parasitize algae and other fungi. These species produce dispersal spores asexually, either within a special structure, the sporangium (spore-producing body), or at the end of an erect hypha (the externally produced spores are called conidia). They also have a form of sexual reproduction: two identical-looking specimens of bread mold may, in fact, come from different mating strains. When these strains meet, chemical substances pass between them, there is a recombination of nuclear material and, in favorable conditions, a resistant spore is produced.

Ascomycetes form the largest class of fungi and some form stable relationships with algae to produce lichens. Most ascomycetes can reproduce asexually by conidia, but their chief characteristic is the sexually produced ascus, a saclike cell in which ascospores (generally eight) are produced. Some ascomycete fruiting bodies are edible—good examples are the morel and the truffle. The group includes the cup fungi [2], the flask fungi, the powdery mildews, and the yeasts.

The toadstools, bracket fungi, puffballs, and stinkhorns are basidiomycetes, a group that also includes the rusts [3], smuts, and the commercially significant fungus *Serpula lacrimans*, the cause of dry rot in wood. This fungus produces rhizomorphs—long, creeping strands of fungus that can even grow over dry brick to spread the infection farther. The basidiomycete species all produce four basidiospores on short stalks at the end of a short, clublike basidium. The wind must catch the discharged spores if they are to be dispersed effectively.

Entering the host

When fungal spores land on a suitable host plant they germinate in the surface moisture, producing a germ tube that gains entry either by piercing the host's outer covering or epidermis, or by growing in through open stomata [1]. Soil fungi can usually gain entrance through the delicate root cells, but some fungi cannot attack living tissue and must enter through wounds or dead matter.

KEY

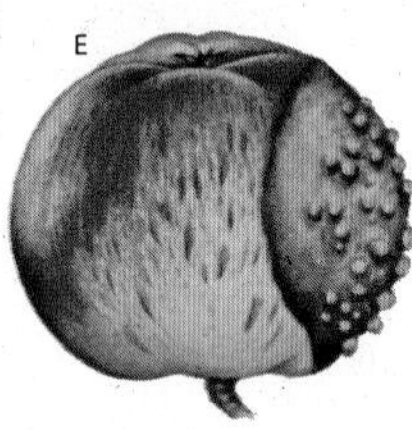

Victims of fungal attack include barley [A], susceptible to loose smut, and rye [B], here bearing ergots of dangerous *Claviceps purpurea*. Potato crops may be ruined by the potato blight *(Phytophthora infestans)* [C], which attacks the leaves. Wart disease of the potato tuber is caused by *Synchytrium endobioticum* [D]. Apples that become infected with *Venturia inaequalis* turn brown and rot [E].

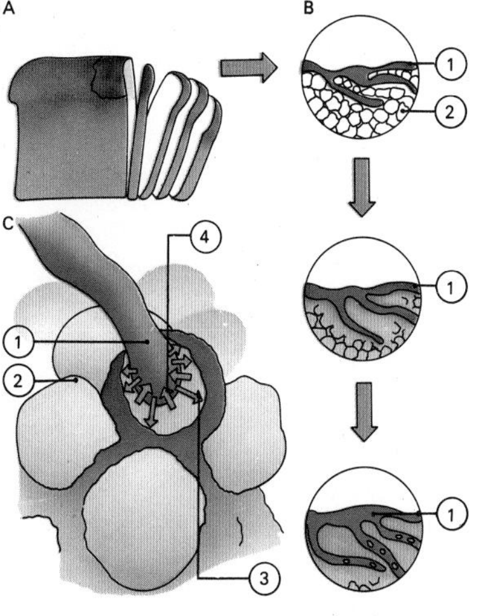

6 The common mold *Mucor* lives on dead organic material and is easily grown on damp bread [A]. Within several days the bread sprouts a forest of black pinlike *Mucor* fruiting bodies. The mycelium [B] of the threadlike hyphae [1] ramifies through the bread particles [2]. [C] Digestive enzymes [3] are secreted to break down the food outside the hyphae and allow it to be absorbed [4].

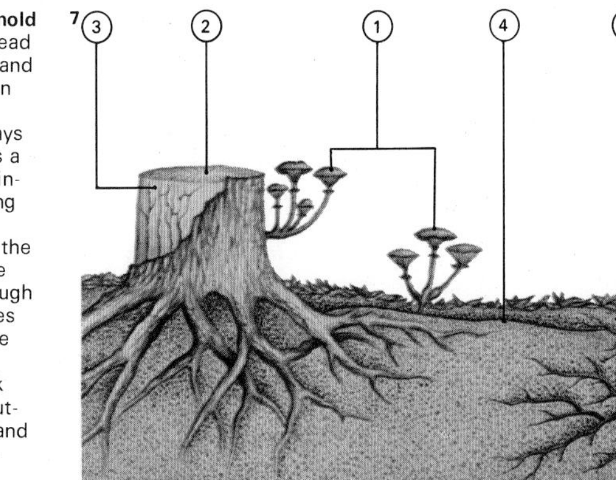

7 The honey fungus *(Armillaria mellea)* is a basidiomycete with conspicuous fruiting bodies [1]. These occur on dead tree stumps [2] where they grow as saprophytes. From the hyphae [3] in the dead stump rhizomorphs—black, rootlike strands [4]—creep out through the soil to attack the roots of live trees [5]. The fungus kills living tissue, forming a suffocating network below the bark of the tree.

8 Some fungi can trap, kill, and digest eelworms. The fungus *Dactylella bembicodes* grows as a mass of threads [1] in rotting wood, which is a favorite haunt of nematode worms. The worm trap [2] consists of a small ring of cells on a short stalk like a lasso. Once in the "noose," the victim [3] is trapped by the suddenly inflating cells [4]. Ramifying fungal hyphae then penetrate [5] the victim, which is eventually absorbed entirely by the fungus.

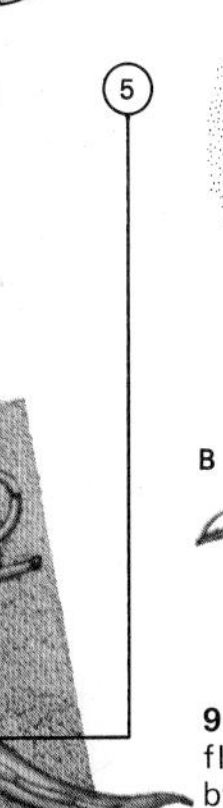

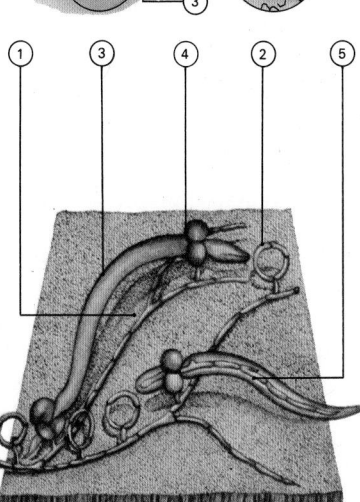

9 A fly dies from fly cholera caused by the phycomycete *Entomophthora muscae*—grim proof that some animals, mostly insects, fall victim to fungal diseases. Spores of the fungus adhere to the fly's body and a germ tube penetrates its skin. The fungus [B] grows inside the fly and eventually plugs its entire body with hyphae. Spore bearing filaments break out all over the dead fly, squirting spores in a great halo around the corpse [A].

10 Tumors and galls are abnormal growths on plants caused by parasites. Fungi, bacteria, and viruses, as well as some small animals cause plant galls. These are seen as rapid and uncontrolled cell growth, but rarely kill the plant. It seems certain that substances produced by the invader set off the gall-making process, but their exact composition remains a mystery.

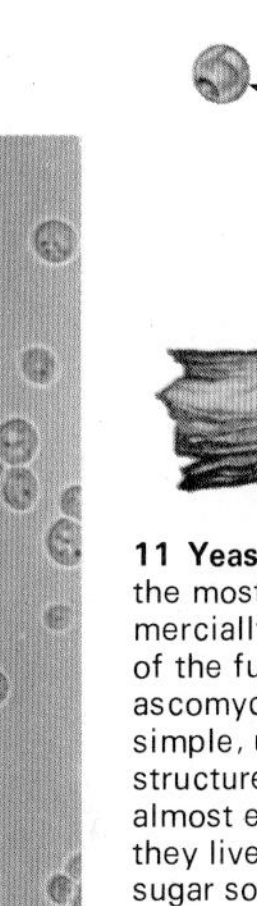

11 Yeasts are among the most commercially important of the fungi. These ascomycetes are simple, unicellular structures. Present almost everywhere, they live in weak sugar solutions (such as are found on fruit surfaces).

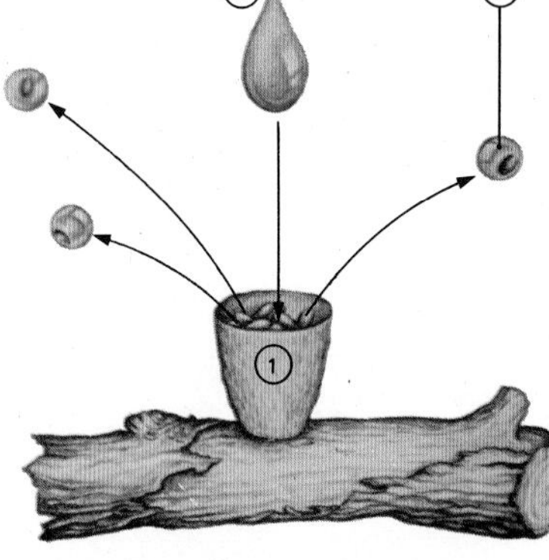

12 Transport by rain is a novel method of spore dispersal. The basidiomycete bird's-nest fungus *(Crucibulum vulgare)* has a fruiting body like an open vase [1]. Rain [2] bouncing off the inside of the cup removes spore tissue [3].

Mushrooms and toadstools

Mushrooms and toadstools, sprouting from the earth with their diminutive, fleshy "umbrellas," are among the most familiar fungi known to man. Botanists classify them in the Basidiomycetes—a name given to them because their spores are formed on special structures called basidia.

Most people use the term "mushroom" when referring to edible members of the class and "toadstool" when describing poisonous fungi. Botanists or, more specifically, mycologists (botanists who study fungi) make no such distinction. The term "mushroom" is used as a collective name to include all the larger Basidiomycetes—the gill-bearing fungi (agarics), fleshy fungi with pores (boletes), bracket fungi (polypores), fairy clubs, puffballs and their allies, stinkhorns, jelly fungi, and others. The term "toadstool," on the other hand, is lapsing into disuse.

The life cycle of an agaric

The life cycle of an agaric [Key] begins with the germination of two basidiospores. Each of these carries half the hereditary (genetic) material of the species. When they germinate, each basidiospore produces an extensive system of branching threads (hyphae), collectively known as a mycelium. This penetrates the material on which the fungus grows. Usually, before any agaric fruiting bodies such as the typical mushroom umbrella can be produced, there must be a fusion of the complementary mycelia. The fruiting bodies are thus produced from a mycelium, which is perennial, with complete hereditary material. A microscopic examination of the resulting fruiting bodies shows that the gills (on the underside of the umbrella) are densely covered with basidia—each with four spines (sterigmata) at their apex, producing a single basidiospore to repeat the cycle of growth.

Methods of spore dispersal

Mushrooms produce enormous numbers of spores during their very short life; an ordinary field mushroom about 4in (10cm) in diameter will produce some 16,000 million spores in a period of about six days.

Except in puffballs and their relatives, basidiospores are discharged explosively from the basidium and although they move only a fraction of an inch, this is sufficient to carry them clear of the fertile surface. They then fall free of the parent and are dispersed by the breeze.

Raindrops help to disperse the spores of puffballs [1], bird's nest fungi, and earth stars (*Geastrum*) [3]. A number of puffballs that grow in deserts are released from the sand when ripe and are blown far away by the wind, scattering their spores.

The spores of some mushrooms, especially those that grow in dung, such as *Coprinus,* are dispersed by animals. Small rodents such as squirrels may carry agaric fruiting bodies for some distance before partially eating them. Slugs and snails also disperse spores over shorter distances. The stinkhorns [2] and their allies are a group of fungi specifically adapted to spore-dispersal by insects. *Aseroe rubra,* for example, attracts insects not only with its powerful smell of carrion, but also by means of the bright red color of its fruiting body.

CONNECTIONS

See also
426 Yeasts and molds
424 The plant kingdom
434 The lichens
710 The causes of illness:1
712 The causes of illness:2
730 Alcoholism and drug abuse
742 Origins of curative medicine

1 Puffballs provide a familiar example of the kind of fungi whose spores are dispersed by the action of raindrops. When ripe, the fruiting body is made up of a thin, perforated, papery wall enclosing a mass of powdery spores. When a raindrop falls on the fungus, the wall is momentarily depressed and functions like a bellows as it puffs out a small cloud of spores.

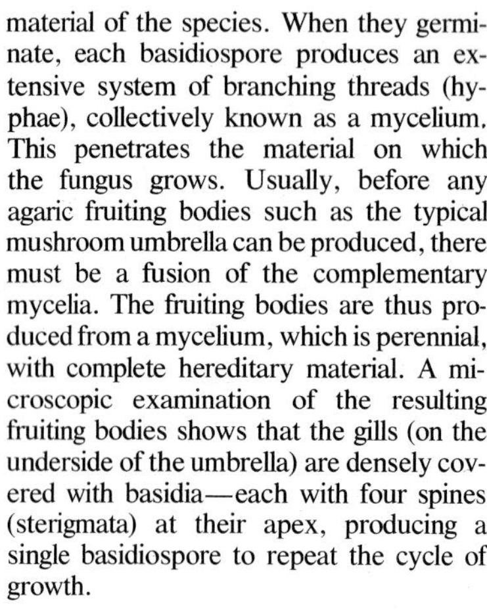

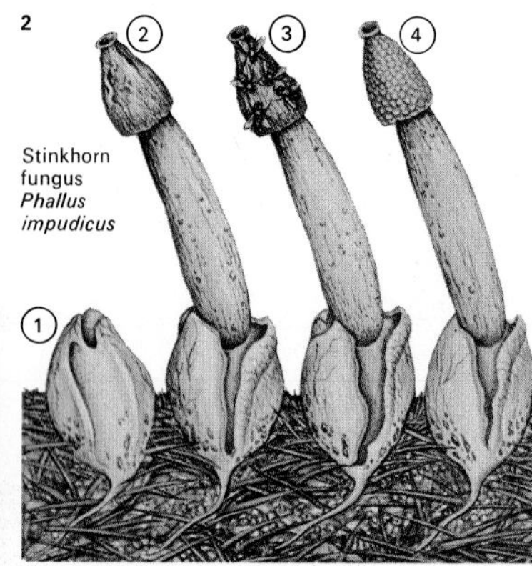

2
Stinkhorn fungus *Phallus impudicus*
1
2
3
4

2 Stinkhorns start from a whitish "egg" [1] that is about 2in (5cm) across. Inside its thin skin is a thick layer of jelly surrounding the immature fruiting body (receptacle). When ripe, the receptacle ruptures the egg and carries the glutinous olive spore mass [2] on its conical reticulated cap [4]. Flies, attracted by the putrid smell, eat the gluten [3] and fly away with spores in their gut.

3 The spores of earth stars are dispersed by raindrops in the same way as those of true puffballs. The fungus, which is at first globular or bulb-shaped, eventually splits into a number of rays. These are grouped around a central thin, papery spore sac that has a distinct opening through which the spore clouds are released. In *Geastrum triplex* the rays curl under the fungus and push it clear of leaf litter, in this way exposing it more effectively to the rain. The rays of other species curl over to enclose and protect the spore sac in dry weather and open again during rainy periods.

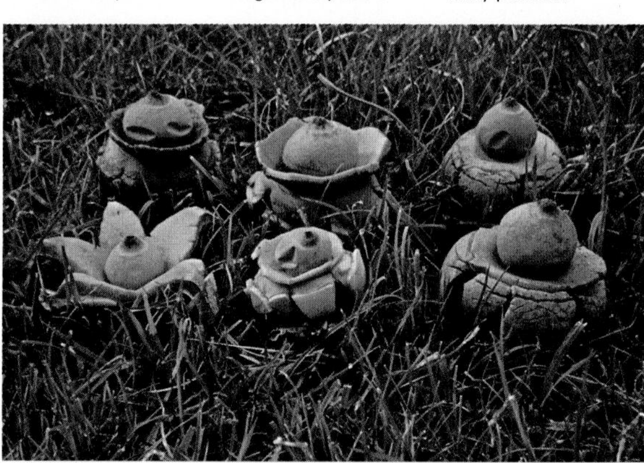

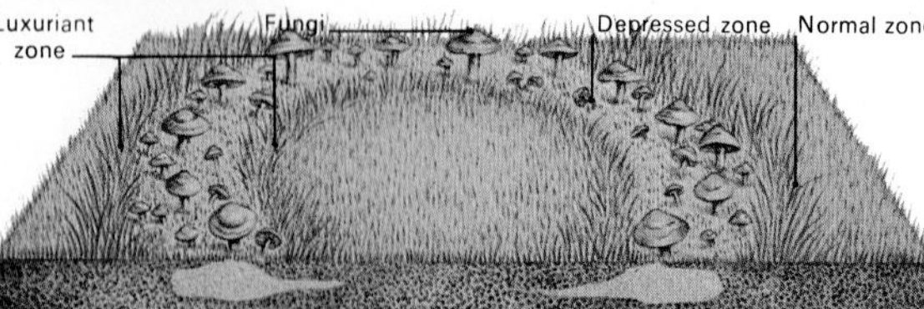

4 A
Luxuriant zone
Fungi
Depressed zone
Normal zone

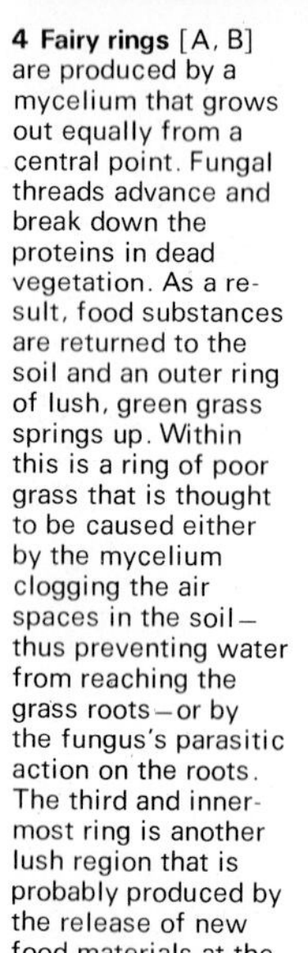

4 Fairy rings [A, B] are produced by a mycelium that grows out equally from a central point. Fungal threads advance and break down the proteins in dead vegetation. As a result, food substances are returned to the soil and an outer ring of lush, green grass springs up. Within this is a ring of poor grass that is thought to be caused either by the mycelium clogging the air spaces in the soil—thus preventing water from reaching the grass roots—or by the fungus's parasitic action on the roots. The third and innermost ring is another lush region that is probably produced by the release of new food materials at the death and decomposition in the soil of the old fungal mycelium.

5 The bracket fungus *(Laetiporus sulphureus)* grows chiefly on old oaks. It is easily recognizable when young by its juicy tiers of orange fruiting bodies, but the colors fade with age.

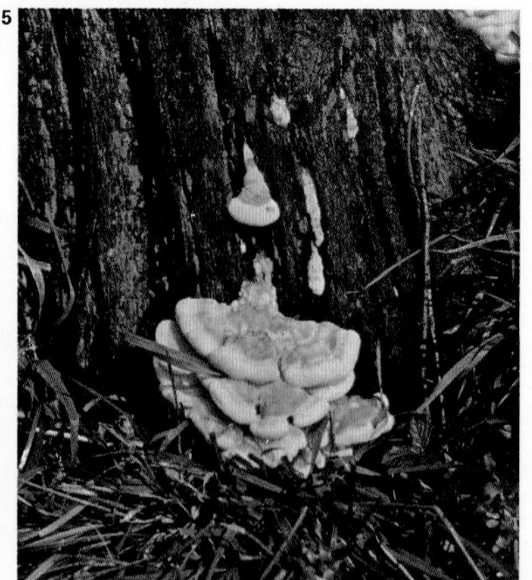

6 The cauliflower fungus *(Sparassis crispa),* which measures up to 10in (25cm) across, grows at the base of conifer trunks and forms intricate masses of small lobes. The popular name comes from the fruiting body, which resembles a large waxy cauliflower head, has a spicy smell, and is edible. Several species grow in woods in North America and Eurasia and all are very similar. These other species are also edible. Some polypores of deciduous woodlands are somewhat similar but have far fewer and thicker lobes.

Mushrooms, even when green, lack chlorophyll and as a result are unable to manufacture their own carbohydrates by means of photosynthesis. Instead they obtain their carbohydrates from the breakdown of complex organic substances in humus and other vegetable debris, or by living parasitically on trees, as many bracket fungi do. But many woodland agarics form a special kind of association with the roots of various trees. These fungi form a sheath of mycelium around a tree's rootlets and from this numerous branching threads penetrate between or into the cells of the roots. Deep penetration of the root is usually prevented by a reaction from the tree that inhibits the fungal growths. Such a relationship is known as a mycorrhiza and infected roots are believed to be better able to absorb nutrients from poor soils, thus benefiting the tree. The fungus, in its turn, obtains various organic substances from its host.

Some mushrooms, the bracket fungi [5] in particular, cause losses in forestry by injuring or killing trees. Among these are the birch polypore *(Piptoporus betulinus)*, a familiar sight wherever birches grow, and the large perennial, brown, woody brackets of *Gandoderma applanatum,* whose stratified fruiting bodies with tube-layers are commonly found on the trunk and branches of beech and other trees.

Poisonous and nonpoisonous mushrooms

Many mushrooms are edible and tasty [6, 7], but some kinds are deadly and there is no infallible way of distinguishing between edible and poisonous species in the kitchen. The only safe way is to learn from an expert. The most dangerous fungus is the death cap [8]. Any mushroom with a white cap, white gills, and a stem bearing a ring and a sheathed base should be avoided. The yellow staining mushroom [8], easily confused with the field mushroom, is mildly poisonous. In general all boletes are safe to eat except for those with red pores and red marks on the stem. Most puffballs are also edible if eaten while still white inside, but the earth balls *(Scleroderma)* should be avoided.

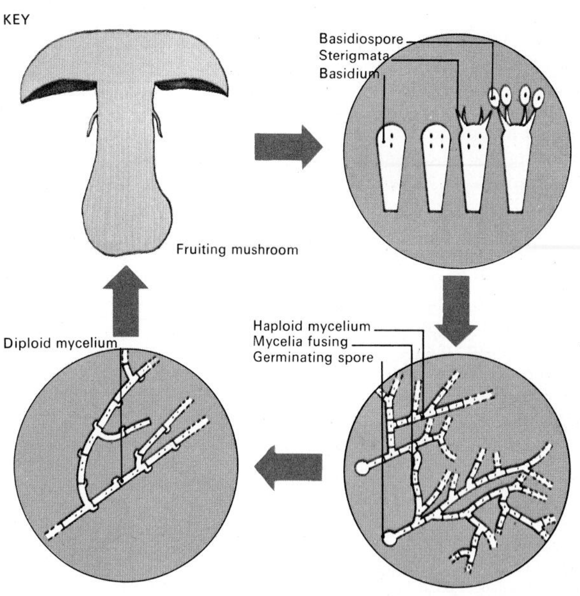
KEY
Basidiospore
Sterigmata
Basidium
Fruiting mushroom
Haploid mycelium
Mycelia fusing
Germinating spore
Diploid mycelium

The life cycle of a field mushroom is typical of higher fungi, but the mycelia may also produce an asexual (mold) stage.

7

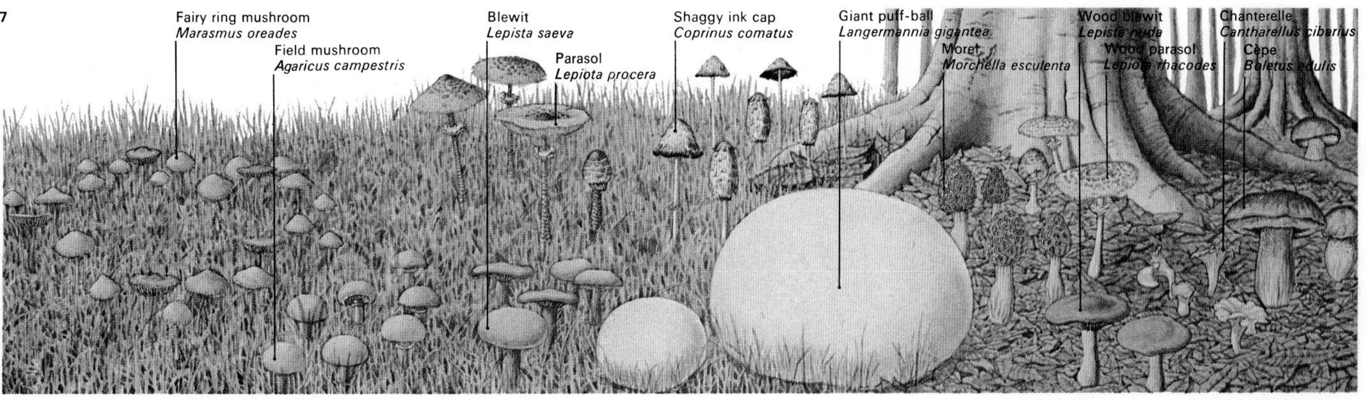
Fairy ring mushroom
Marasmus oreades
Field mushroom
Agaricus campestris
Blewit
Lepista saeva
Parasol
Lepiota procera
Shaggy ink cap
Coprinus comatus
Giant puff-ball
Langermannia gigantea
Moret
Morchella esculenta
Wood blewit
Lepista nuda
Wood parasol
Lepiota rhacodes
Chanterelle
Cantharellus cibarius
Cèpe
Boletus edulis

7 Edible mushrooms are numerous. The fairy ring mushroom *(Marasmius oreades)* is rather leathery, with a bell-shaped cap that varies from reddish tan when wet to buff when dry. It can be dried and used for flavoring soups. The common field mushroom *(Agaricus campestris)* can be recognized most easily by the color of the gills. These are pink at first but eventually turn purplish brown. The blewit *(Lepista saeva)* and wood blewit *(L. nuda)* are closely related but the former grows in pastures while the latter is a woodland species. The parasol *(Lepiota procera)* is different from the wood parasol *(L. rhacodes)* in that it grows in pastures, has brown, snakelike markings on the stalk and flesh that does not turn reddish when it is bruised. Shaggy ink caps, or shaggymanes *(Coprinus comatus),* have distinctive cylindrical white caps resembling closed umbrellas. When ripe, the gills turn black and the entire cap drips away as an inky liquid. Giant puffballs *(Langermannia gigantea)* may reach 12in (30cm) across and weigh more than 2.2lb (1kg). Morels *(Morchella esculenta)* have a characteristic conical honeycomblike cap. Chanterelles *(Cantharellus cibarius)* are top-shaped and fleshy, with thick, irregularly branched gills. They have a smell of apricots. The cèpe *(Boletus èdulis)* has a tan to dark yellow or red-brown cap.

8

Death cap
Amanita phalloides

Fly agaric
Amanita muscaria

Yellow staining mushroom
Agaricus xanthodermus

Devil's boletus
Boletus satanas

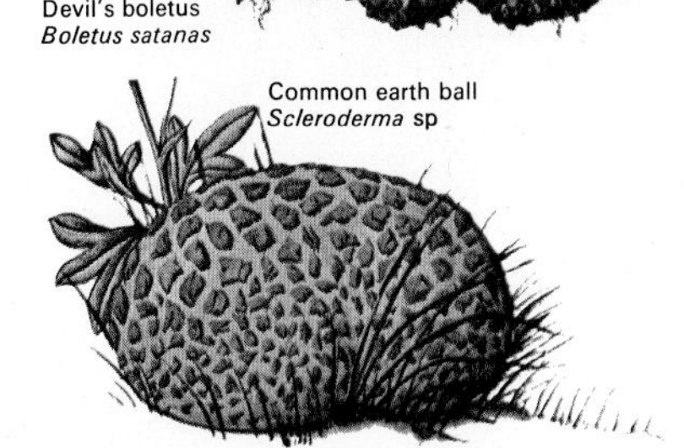
Common earth ball
Scleroderma sp

8 Poisonous mushrooms are not always easily recognizable, even by experts. Fungi of the genus *Amanita* develop a membrane that forms a kind of envelope or veil covering the entire plant. One species, the death cap, is so highly poisonous that it is usually lethal to human beings. It is most commonly found under oak and beech and has a yellowish green, indistinctly streaky cap about 3.5in (9 cm) across. The gills are white, and the stem, which is also white, bears a pendulous ring and has a sheathed base. Fly agarics *(A. muscaria)* grow under birch trees with which they form a mycorrhizal association. Their red caps with pyramidal white scales are unmistakable. The yellow staining mushroom can easily be confused with the field mushroom because it grows in similar places. It turns bright yellow when cut or bruised. The plant is only mildly poisonous and some people are unaffected by it. The devil's boletus *(Boletus satanas),* which has a pale cap, red pores, and a red network on the stem, grows in woodlands of eastern and western United States. The common earth balls *(Scleroderma),* unlike true puffballs, have a thick rind.

The way plants work

Green plants and a few specialized bacteria manufacture all the food that sustains life on earth. Their raw materials are water, carbon dioxide, and sunlight. No matter where plants live, they must have adequate supplies of those essentials and they have evolved special structures to ensure this.

Photosynthesis in green plants

All green plants, which range in size from microscopic single-celled algae to trees over 325ft (99m) in height, have at least two features in common. First, the cells of all plants are surrounded by a firm wall of cellulose [1]; it may be less than 0.001mm thick but it gives the plant structural strength. Second, all green plants contain the pigment chlorophyll, which gives them their green color and which is vital for photosynthesis, the process by which they manufacture their own food. Chlorophyll is responsible for capturing energy from the sun, which is then used to power the chemical processes of food manufacture.

Even plants that look brown or red—some seaweeds for example—contain chlorophyll, although its greenness is masked by the presence of other pigments. A few plants have no chlorophyll and must either live parasitically on other plants (for example dodder which parasitizes nettles) or establish a mutual dependence with them (a symbiosis) as the bird's-nest orchid does with a fungus. Leaves on parasitic plants are often reduced to mere scales.

Although virtually any part of a plant can contain chlorophyll, the leaves [3] are specialized for photosynthesis and are especially rich in the pigment. In the process of photosynthesis the sun's energy is used to split water in the plant into oxygen and hydrogen. The oxygen is released, but the hydrogen is used to convert carbon dioxide from the atmosphere into sugars (carbohydrates) through a series of complex chemical reactions involving enzymes. The sugars can then be converted into all the other chemicals found in the plant.

Food manufactured in the leaves of plants is transported for use in other parts of the plant through tissue called the phloem. This is a series of elongated cells arranged in a system of "veins" running through the plant. The cells are separated from each other at their ends by perforated plates called sieve plates. Fine strands of living material pass through these plates and some researchers believe that these strands are responsible for transporting the food.

The water system

Water moves through a green plant's conducting or vascular system in xylem cells which are associated with the phloem cells in the veins. Together, the xylem and phloem are called vascular bundles. Xylem cells form a series of long tubes strengthened by stout cell walls. To offset evaporation from the plant surface, water is absorbed by the roots and passed up to the leaves [5] by forces that include osmosis (a special type of diffusion) and capillary action (the raising of water in very fine tubes), and which are so strong that water can be raised hundreds of feet to the top of the highest tree.

Most plants, whether aquatic or terrestrial, remain anchored in one place, although

CONNECTIONS

See also

412 The cell in action
456 How flowering plan
reproduce
444 Flowering plants: tw
seed leaves
448 Woody flowering
plants
452 Flowering plants: or
seed leaf
440 The cone bearers
438 Ferns and horsetail
436 Mosses and liverwor
432 Algae and seaweeds
312 The living soil
1572 The Chemistry of lif
biochemistry
1574 Polymers: giant
molecules

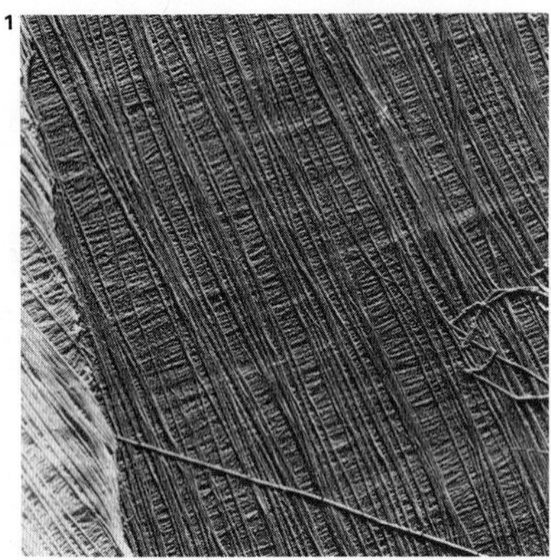

1 The plant cell wall is formed by two layers of cellulose fibers. As shown in this photo made with an electron microscope, these fibers lie parallel to each other in the inner layer but criss-cross in the outer layer. Cells communicate with one another through strands of living tissue that pass through fine holes in the cell wall. The holes may aggregate to form pits in the walls.

2 All the hereditary information needed to create a whole plant is contained in the genetic material of a single cell. Cells of a carrot plant [1], taken from the leaves [2], storage root [3] or branch roots [4] and grown in coconut milk, will all give rise to plantlets [5]. From these plantlets entire carrot plants will grow. Known as totipotency, this phenomenon occurs only rarely in nature.

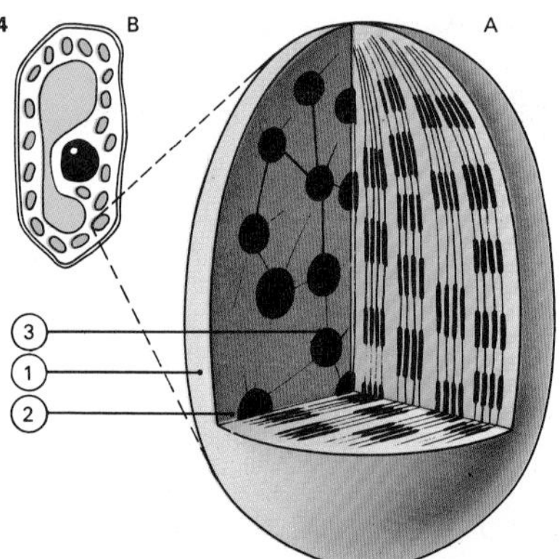

B
A
3
1
2

4 A single chloroplast [A], typical of those found in a palisade cell [B] of a land plant, is contained in a membrane [1]. Its internal structure comprises a series of minute plates called lamellae, each a few molecules thick. Chlorophyll molecules are found chiefly on these membranes in areas called grana [3]. Between the grana is a granular mass called the stroma [2].

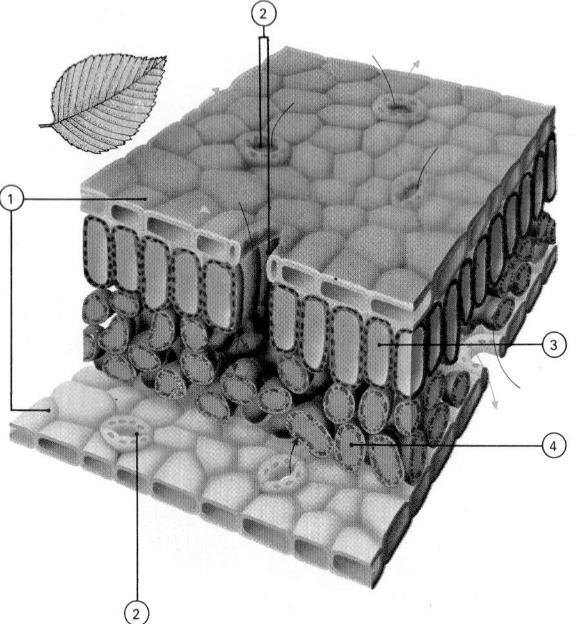

2
1
3
4
2

3 Both surfaces of a leaf are protected by epidermal cells [1], covered with a waterproof cuticle that prevents excessive water loss. These impermeable surfaces are pierced by small holes called the stomata [2], found mostly on the leaf's lower surface. Through them water vapor, oxygen, and carbon dioxide enter and leave the leaf. Below the epidermis on the upper side is the palisade layer [3], which consists of cylindrical cells filled with chloroplasts where photosynthesis chiefly takes place. Below the palisade layer is the spongy mesophyll [4] where the products of photosynthesis are stored before being transported to other parts of the plant.

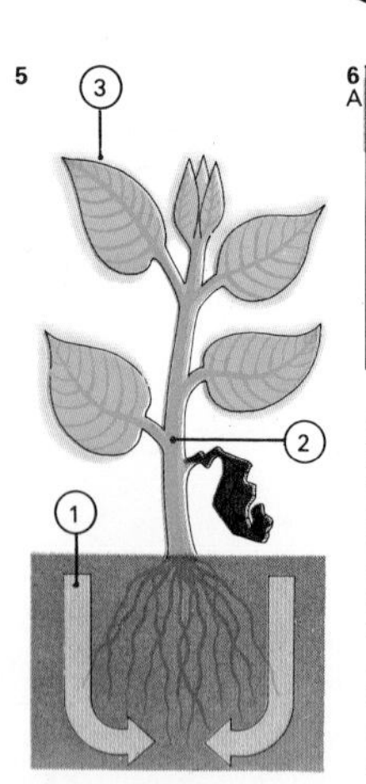

3
2
1

5 Water is absorbed by tiny hairs on the roots of a plant [1]. It is passed upward in the xylem tissue [2] and evaporates through the stomata. This transpiration process helps to cool the leaves and aids absorption of mineral salts.

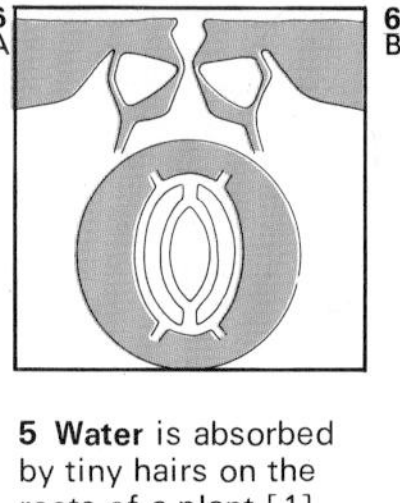

6 A

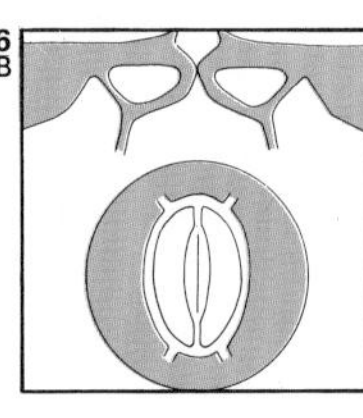

6 B

6 Stomatal apertures are bordered by special doorlike guard cells. The stomata usually open in light [A] to allow photosynthesis and close in darkness [B] to prevent water loss. Modified stoma of desert plants aid water retention.

Some microscopic algae move through the water by thrashing whiplike flagella or hairlike cilia. Water plants are flexible and frondlike to ride with the currents. Land plants orient their green leaves so that the flat surfaces face the sun. The roots of land plants are firmly embedded in the soil. The shape and form of a plant can vary enormously with its environment.

Unlike animals, plants have no sophisticated nervous system. Their growth is controlled by hormonal substances. These are produced in one part of the plant and transported to another, where they exercise their influence. Some hormones, including the auxins, the gibberellins, and the cytokinins, promote growth. Other hormones inhibit growth, and still others influence processes such as the ripening of fruit.

All plant hormones affect plant growth in various ways. Auxin, for example, is chiefly responsible for the elongation of plant cells, but it also plays a part in the initiation of rooting and in controlling abscission—the process by which a plant 'cuts off' dead leaves and ripe fruits before they are shed. Gibberellins play various roles in plant growth but are especially known for their ability to stimulate growth in dwarf plants [7]. Cytokinins are important in the regulation of plant cell division [13].

The importance of sunlight

Sunlight, vital to plants for photosynthesis, also helps to regulate plant growth. Plants grown in the dark are spindly and yellowish [12] because there is no destruction, by light, of auxin and no formation of chlorophyll. Phytochrome, a chemical sensitive to red light, is part of the internal clock that tells a plant how long the day is and thus what time of year it is. Some plants flower regardless of the length of day, but others will flower only when days are long or when days are short [11]. This is important ecologically because the best time for flowering and setting seed differs in various parts of the world. The sensitivity of phytochrome to red light causes that part of a plant's hereditary material regulating growth and development to be "switched on."

KEY

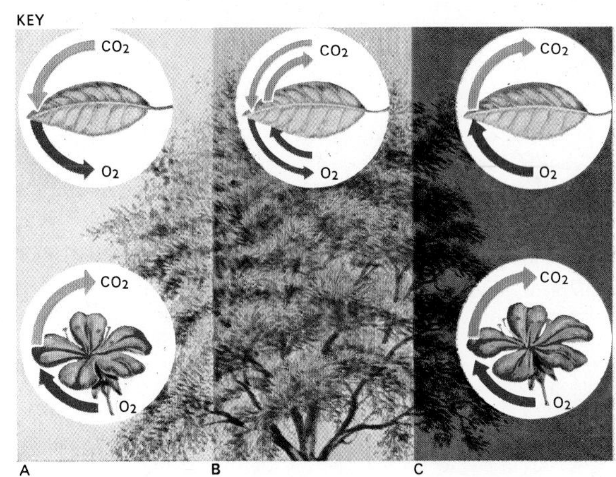

CO2
O2
A
B
C

Trees, like all plants, breathe continuously, using oxygen (O_2) and releasing carbon dioxide (CO_2). During the day photosynthesis takes place in the leaves faster than respiration and only the uptake of carbon dioxide and the release of oxygen can be detected [A]. In twilight photosynthesis slows down and all oxygen given off is used in respiration while all the carbon dioxide given off in respiration is used in photosynthesis. This is called the compensation point [B]. At night the process of photosynthesis is halted and it is easy to detect carbon dioxide release and oxygen intake [C].

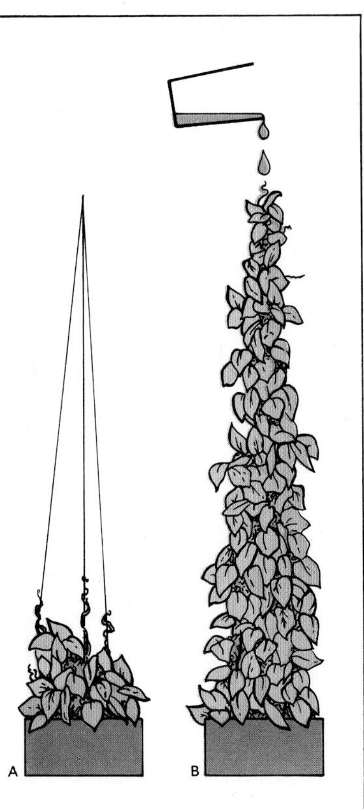

A
B

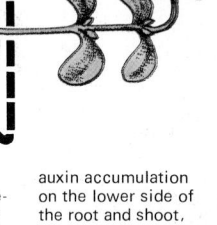

7 A dwarf bean [A], after treatment with a solution containing gibberellic acid, grows as tall as a normal bean [B]. This hormone is one of several able to modify inherited growth patterns.

8

8 Plant stems bend toward the light because the growth hormone auxin, produced in the tip, is diverted to the shaded side of a plant where it stimulates markedly faster growth.

9

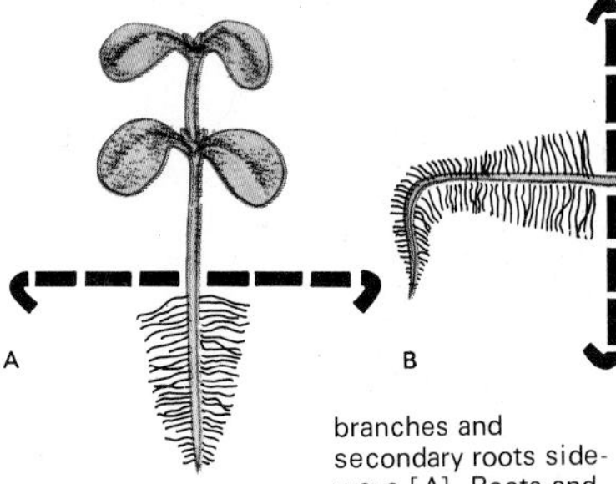

A
B

9 Plant response to gravity is called geotropism. Roots normally grow downward, stems upward, branches and secondary roots sideways [A]. Roots and shoots of a plant on its side [B] will try to regain their former positions. Deposited starch grains promote auxin accumulation on the lower side of the root and shoot, stimulating vertical growth in the shoot but inhibiting it in the root, which then grows downward.

10 A

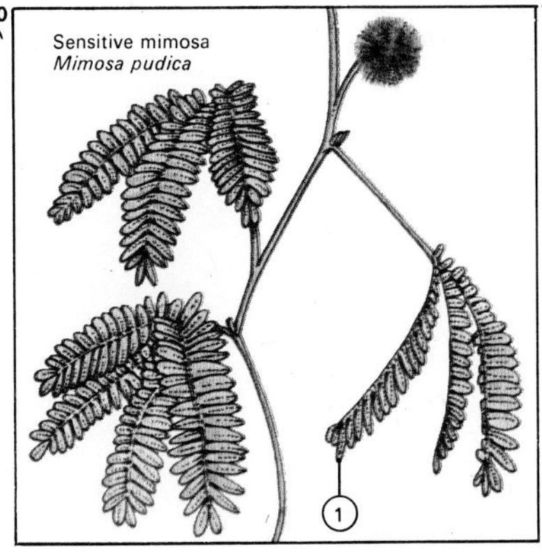

Sensitive mimosa
Mimosa pudica
1

10 B

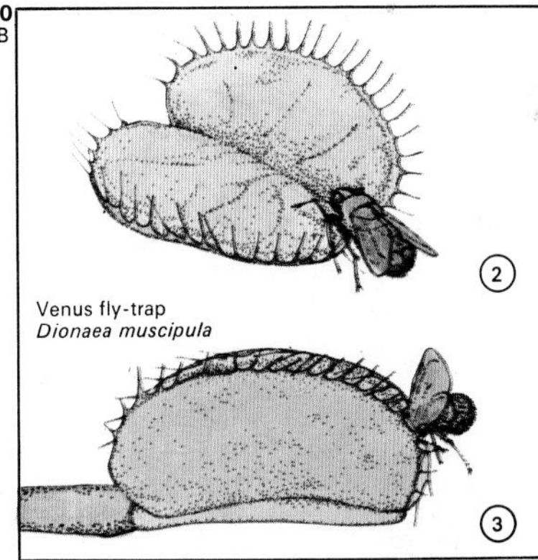

Venus fly-trap
Dionaea muscipula
2
3

10 Movements of plant parts are sometimes caused not by growth but by changes in the structure of the plant's cells. In the sensitive mimosa [A], leaflets [1] are attached by special cells, the pulvini. If a leaf is shaken these cells lose water and the branch may suddenly sag. The Venus fly-trap [B] is a carnivorous plant. When an unwary insect touches hairs on the leaf [2] a trap is sprung [3].

11

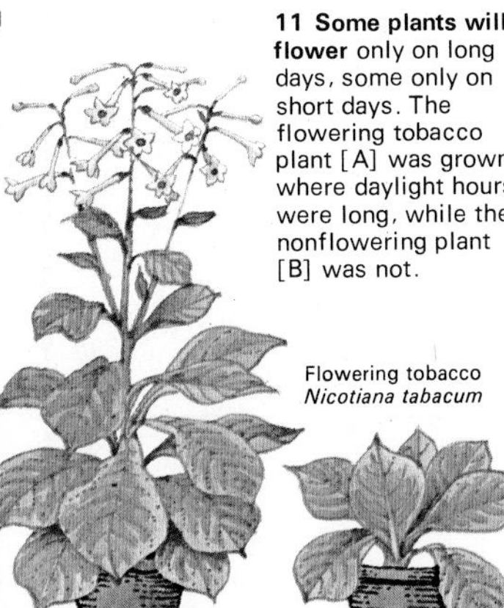

Flowering tobacco
Nicotiana tabacum
A
B

11 Some plants will flower only on long days, some only on short days. The flowering tobacco plant [A] was grown where daylight hours were long, while the nonflowering plant [B] was not.

12

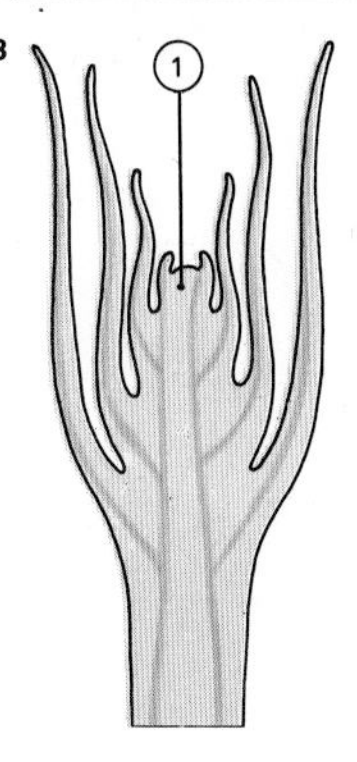

A
B

12 The effect of light on the growth of plants is called photomorphogenesis. One mustard seedling has been grown in the light [A]. Another of the same age and genetically identical has been grown in darkness [B]; it is tall and spindly and its leaves and roots have not developed. Light is essential for the development of all green plants and a seedling will use up all the stored food in its seed leaves in an attempt to grow toward the light.

13

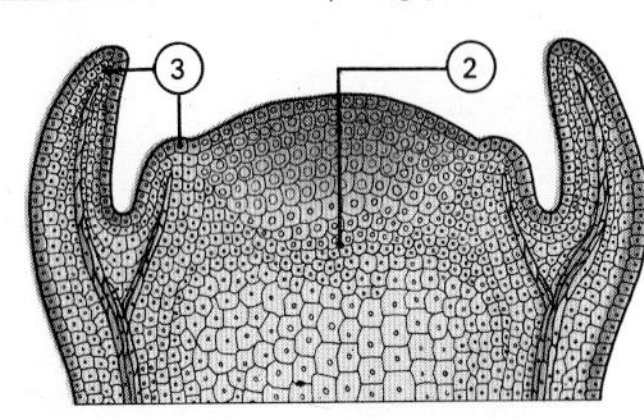

1
3
2

13 New cells are manufactured chiefly at the tips of the roots and shoots of plants by a process called apical growth. The shoot apex of a vascular plant [1] consists of a small group of cells, the meristem, which divides to produce more cells, so the tip constantly grows away from the roots. Dividing cells [2] produce leaf primordia [3] and in the axil of each leaf is a bud that could develop into a new branch. The apical bud may prevent the growth of lateral buds with an inhibiting hormone; this is apical dominance

Algae and seaweeds

The simplest plants are those in which a single cell is capable of independent existence. These, together with their multicellular relatives, are called algae and there are about 20,000 species of them in the world today. Algae are technically distinguished from higher plants by the absence of a sterile cell layer around the sexual cells and, although some algae can be large and complex, they never attain the degree of anatomical differentiation of flowering plants and ferns.

The classification of algae

Algae are a rather loose assemblage of not very closely related organisms that can be classified into 11 major groups based on differences in pigmentation, cell-wall composition, nature of reserve food materials, and type of organelles—parts of cells doing special work—present in cells. These groups are the blue-green algae (Cyanophyta), red algae (Rhodophyta), diatoms (Bacillariophyta), yellow-green algae (Xanthophyta), golden-brown algae (Chrysophyta), dinoflagellates (Pyrrophyta), cryptomonads (Cryptophyta), brown algae (Phaeophyta), euglenoids (Euglenophyta), green algae (Chlorophyta), and stoneworts (Charophyta).

All the groups of algae possess chlorophyll "A," the green pigment primarily responsible for photosynthesis, the process by which the plant converts light energy into chemical energy. Indeed, the green algae have the same pigments in the same proportions as the higher plants and are thought to be the ancestral stock from which these have evolved over millions of years. In other groups the accessory pigments differ in nature or in proportions, giving them their characteristic colors. These may, however, be much modified both in different species and according to environmental conditions.

Blue-green algae [7] are in many respects more like bacteria than like other algae. They lack true organelles, have little or no power of movement and no truly sexual reproductive processes. In all the other groups each cell has a true nucleus (an organelle with its own surrounding membrane), which controls important cell processes such as division, and one or more plastids—organelles that contain the photosynthetic pigments. In most groups (except the red algae) there are at least some species or stages bearing flagella—thin, flexible, hairlike structures that beat rhythmically and serve as the principal means of locomotion. In some groups—the brown algae [4, 5], for example—they are restricted to reproductive cells. Differences in number, position, and kind of flagella occur among different major groups and help to distinguish them. Some nonflagellate algae, particularly certain diatoms, are capable of quite rapid gliding movements.

Natural habitats of algae

Algae occur in almost all possible habitats to which adequate light penetrates. They may color permanent snow and ice fields red or green, may multiply rapidly in small temporary puddles (thus often giving rise to stories of colored rain), and have been found in hot springs at temperatures of up to 185°F (85°C). They abound in brackish and

CONNECTIONS

See also
424 The plant kingdom
622 The seashore: life b tween the tides
434 The lichens
430 The way plants wor
562 Plants of the past
236 Oceanographic exp ration

1 Chlamydomonas [A] has a cup-shaped plastid [1], two equal flagella [2] and a red eyespot [3]. It usually reproduces by division of the cell contents [B] into 4 to 16 motile cells (zoospores) that then disperse. In sexual reproduction the divided products (gametes) fuse together in pairs [C, D] after release, forming a nonmotile resting stage [E] that produces four zoospores [F] when conditions are favorable. The organism lives mostly in fresh water, especially stagnant pools, where it swims about in response to the light. The red eyespot is sensitive to light and determines the direction in which the organism moves.

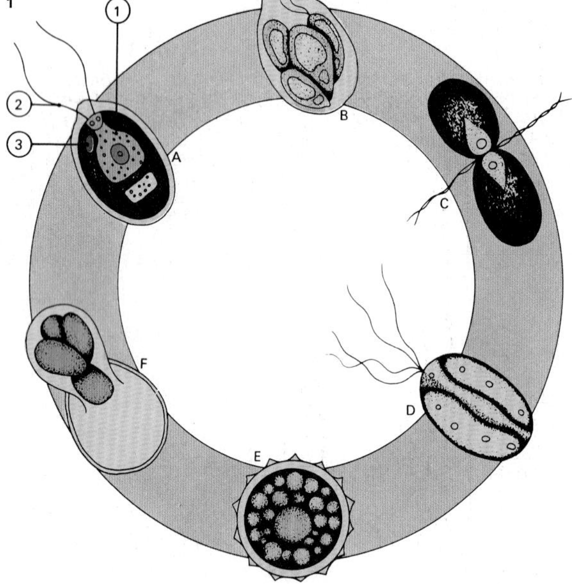

1
A
B
C
D
E
F

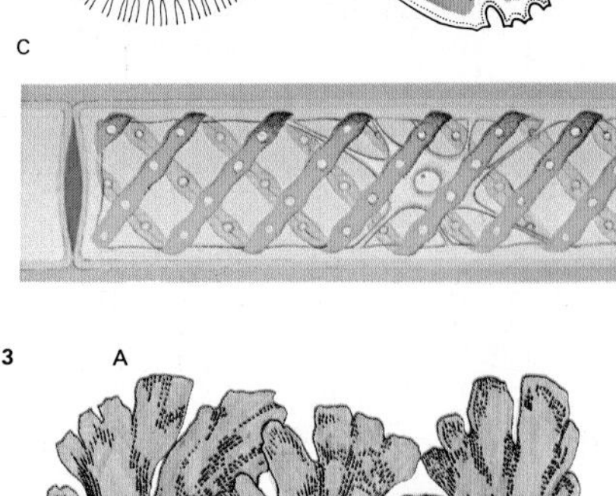

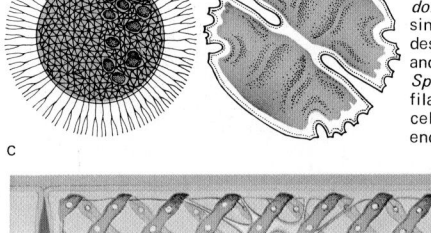

2A
B
C

2 Kinds of algae include *Volvox* [A] with motile *Chlamydomonas*-like cells; single-celled desmids [B], varied and beautiful; and *Spirogyra* [C], whose filaments consist of cells joined end to end.

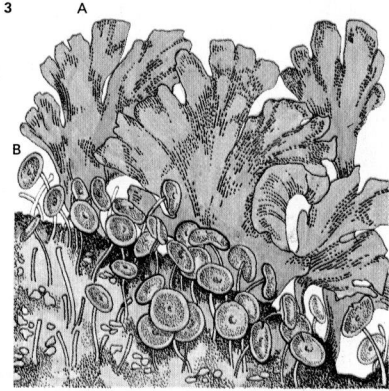

3 The sea lettuce or green laver *(Ulva lactuca)* is a familiar seaweed [A] that is occasionally eaten. *Acetabularia* [B] is one of a group of lime-encrusted green algae from tropical and subtropical seas. It resembles a delicate toadstool and has been widely used and studied by scientists because the single-celled stalk, up to 2in (5cm) high, can be cut into two living parts with and without a nucleus.

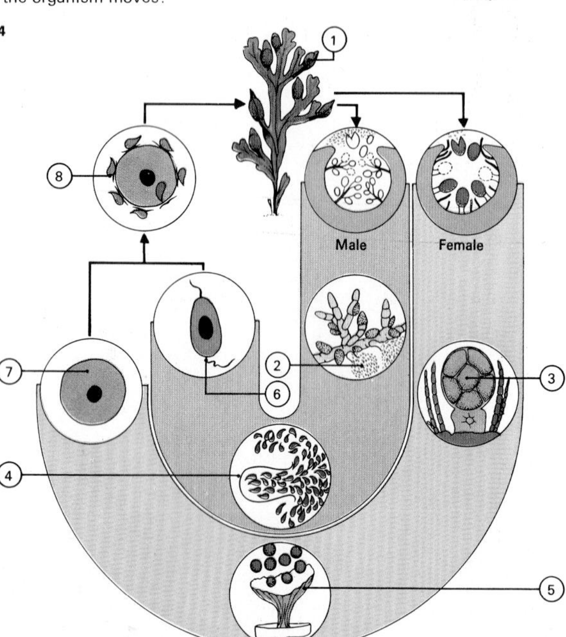

4
Male
Female

4 The life history of Fucus is often used as an example of the brown algae because species of this genus are common. The most usual form of reproduction is a specialized sexual process. On the tips of certain fronds are swollen areas known as receptacles [1]. Male and female reproductive organs are produced on separate plants in cavities in the swollen areas. Male reproductive organs (antheridia) are released in spring as orange slime [2]. Female reproductive organs (oogonia) [3] are similarly released as a green slime. When the seaweed is covered by the tide the antheridia [4] and oogonia [5] burst, releasing the reproductive cells into the water. The male gametes [6], 64 per antheridium, have two unequal flagellae, which they use to propel themselves. They fuse [8] with nonmotile egg cells [7], eight per oogonium, in the water. In a few other groups the gametes are as in *Fucus*, but in most groups all the gametes produced are mobile. In all these groups nonsexual reproduction also occurs: the contents of some cells divide and are released as motile zoospores, which become new plants.

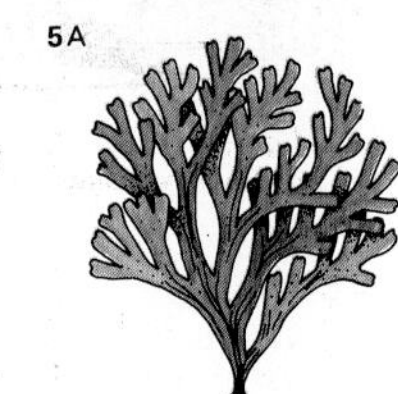

5A

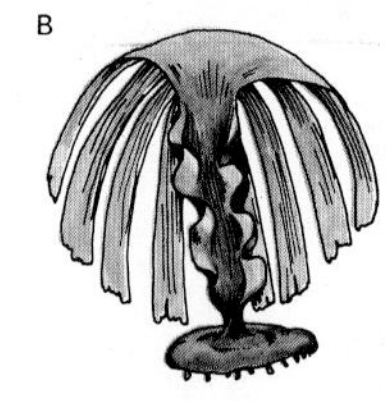

B

5 Brown algae range from small filamentous types to large plants with elaborate structures. *Dictyota* [A] is anchored by rhizoids and has thin flat fronds. New plants are all of this kind. But in many brown algae two different kinds of plants are produced. In furbelows, *(Saccorhiza polyschides)* [B], the zoospores produce microscopic filaments, which in turn produce gametes. Fusion of gametes results in the growth of a plant with fan-like fronds.

marine waters and are found even in saline pools where the salts are crystallizing out. Although the smaller forms are individually inconspicuous they may multiply rapidly enough to color the water. The Red Sea was so named because of the frequency in its waters of a reddish blue-green algae, *Trichodesmium*. Such water blooms may cause fish and other aquatic organisms to suffocate, taint drinking water, and, as is the case with Red Tide organisms (certain dinoflagellate species), poison the water with powerful toxins. Algae also play an important role in purifying sewage effluents by removing dissolved substances and keeping the waters oxygenated.

Some algae remain suspended in the upper layers of the water and together with small drifting animals form the plankton that is a rich food source for higher animals. Others, known as benthic forms, occur on or among bottom deposits or become attached to plants and animals on the bottom. These are limited in development by their need for adequate light for photosynthesis, but in very clear waters may be found at depths of as much as 655ft (200m). The richest vegetation on the seacoast occurs just below the level exposed to air by receding tides, but a wide variety of species live between tides, often forming distinctive zones at different levels characterized by particular species.

Algae also inhabit nonaquatic regions. Large numbers grow in the upper layers of soils (even in deserts), on buildings, trees and other terrestrial plants, and even in animals such as some sponges, flatworms, and shellfish. Algae even grow on corals.

Fossilized deposits

In most of the major groups of algae some or nearly all members have lime or silica deposited either in the cell walls or as a form of external shell. These hard parts are readily preserved as fossils and, indeed, fossil diatom deposits 3,000ft (914m) thick have been found. Such fossilized forms can give an indication of the ages of the groups to which they belong. Among red algae the calcareous corallines were well developed 500 million years ago. Ancient calcareous green algae are also known.

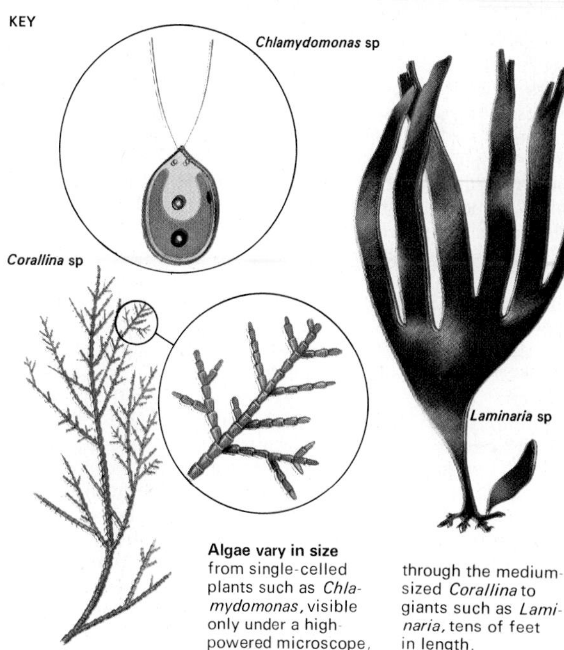
KEY
Chlamydomonas sp
Corallina sp
Laminaria sp

Algae vary in size from single-celled plants such as *Chlamydomonas*, visible only under a high-powered microscope, through the medium-sized *Corallina* to giants such as *Laminaria*, tens of feet in length.

6
D
D
G
F
A
C
B
H
E

6 The red algae are mainly marine. Dulse *(Palmaria palmata)* [A] is a common edible species, as are Irish moss *(Gigartina stellata)* [B] and laver *(Porphyra umbilicus)* [H]. *Dumontia incrassata* [C] is common in shallow intertidal pools. It dies in late summer but new plants appear in spring. *Phymatolithon polymorphum* [E] is a common encrusting coralline species, living between and below tide lines. The beautiful crimson fronds of *Heterosiphonia plumosa* [F] grow best below the tide line, while the stiff, dark red fronds of *Ptilota plumosa* [G], are found growing on the oarweed *(Laminaria hyperborea)* [D].

7 The blue-green algae are a primitive but successful group well represented in terrestrial, marine, and fresh-water habitats, being particularly abundant in muddy places such as salt marshes and paddy fields. They consist of simple cells aggregated into loose or regular colonies such as *Dermocarpa*, or filaments—branched or unbranched. The colonies may be embedded in a gelatinous matrix. Reproduction is vegetative or by nonmotile spores. Some filamentous types such as *Anabaena* are capable of converting atmospheric nitrogen into ammonia.

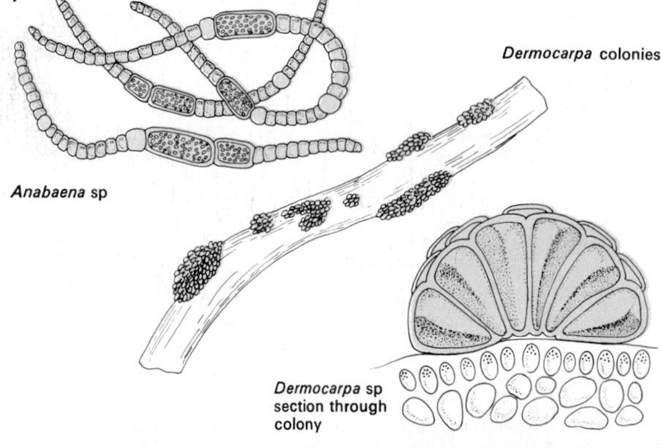
7
Dermocarpa colonies
Anabaena sp
Dermocarpa sp section through colony

8 The uses of seaweeds are many and varied. Traditionally they have been used as manure and for food, for which they are specially cultivated in Japan. They once provided a source of iodine and soda (for glassmaking). Today jellylike substances are extracted—agar from red algae and alginates from brown algae. These are colorless, tasteless, and odorless and are used for growing microbes, food canning, and for making nonfat creams (edible and cosmetic), emulsifiers for paint, beer, ice cream, pills, capsules, for film emulsion and thread. Fossil diatoms provide abrasives and are used in making toothpastes, filters, and insulating materials.

8

The lichens

Lichens occupy some of the most forbidding regions of earth, establishing themselves in environments where few other species of living things are able to survive. They are found farther south and farther north than any other type of plant. In the Himalayas they have been found at altitudes of more than 18,500ft (5,643m).

Distribution and structure

Lichens can adapt themselves to almost any kind of surface. They will grow on sun-baked rock in arid deserts, on the backs of weevils, or in the bleached skulls of dead animals. One species *(Verrucaria serpuloides)* is continuously submerged in freezing Antarctic waters; another *(Lecanora esculenta)* travels on the wind. And although lichens are on the whole highly sensitive to industrial pollution, in Britain *Lecanora conizaeoides* has increased in areas of high industrial pollution.

There are some 15,000 known species of lichens, classified into three main groups on the basis of their characteristic growth forms. The foliose (leafy) lichens [3] flourish in regions where the rainfall is heavy. Crustose (crust-forming) lichens [2], which cling close to a surface, are resistant to drought and prevail in deserts. The fruiticose (stalked) lichens absorb water in the form of vapor and are particularly suited to humid climates. As a result, lichens vary greatly in both size and appearance. Some have filaments that reach lengths of 9ft (2.75m) or more. Other lichens are smaller than a pinhead.

Lichens arise from the association between two distinct plant types, algae and fungi, and provide one of the most successful examples of the symbiotic relationship called "mutualism"—a term used to describe the beneficial partnership that can develop between two dissimilar organisms.

The algal partner of a lichen belongs to either the blue-green algae (Cyanophyta) or to the green algae (Chlorophyta). Most fungal members belong to the fungal group known as Ascomycetes, which derive their name from the ascus or sac in which they form their reproductive cells. With very few exceptions, a lichen is the product of a single species of fungus and a single species of algae. The most common algae (found in more than 50 percent of lichens) is the single-celled green algae *Trebouxia*.

Lichens are extremely slow-growing plants. Most crustose types rarely grow more than .04in (1mm) in a year. Other types grow a little faster but rarely exceed more than 0.4 in (1 cm) a year. It follows, therefore, that the larger lichens are extremely old—some that occur in the Arctic are thought to be more than 4,000 years old. A technique known as lichenometry uses lichens for dating rock surfaces. The ages of glaciers and of the giant stone heads that are found on Easter Island in the South Pacific have been determined by applications of this technique.

The roles of fungi and algae

The great ages attained by lichens indicate that they have evolved a highly organized and well balanced relationship between the algal and fungal partners. The exact nature of that relationship, however, is still not entirely clear. The algal partner is a simple green plant that, like other green plants,

CONNECTIONS

See also
432 Algae and seaweeds
426 Yeasts and molds
424 The plant kingdom
430 The way plants work
292 Pollution of the air
428 Mushrooms and toadstools
1812 Color chemistry

1 By mapping lichens it is possible to pinpoint areas of high and low pollution in a given region and to assess what importance factors such as wind direction, elevation, and ground shape have on the sources of pollution. The diagram shows the monitoring of such a region, based on specific lichens and of the green alga *(Pleurococcus viridis)* found on oak trees compared with a graph indicating the varying levels of the poisonous gas sulfur dioxide (SO_2). Few lichens are found where the SO_2 concentration is high: the result is a "lichen desert." Outside this is a "struggle zone," which merges into the normal lichen flora. A British study, however, has shown that some species, such as *Leconora conizaeoides*, have increased distribution in areas of high SO_2 concentration. Some species of lichen occur in more than one zone. Species present in zone 1 are *Usnea articulata, Lobaria amplissa;* zone 2 – *amplissa, Usnea subfloridans;* zone 3 – *Usnea subfloridans, Parmelia caperata;* zone 4 – *Graphis elegans, Parmelia caperata, Parmelia saxatilis;* zone 5 – *Lecidea scalaris, Parmelia saxatilis;* zone 6 – *Lepraria incana, Pleurococcus viridis;* zone 7 – *Pleurococcus viridis, Lecanora conizaeoides.*

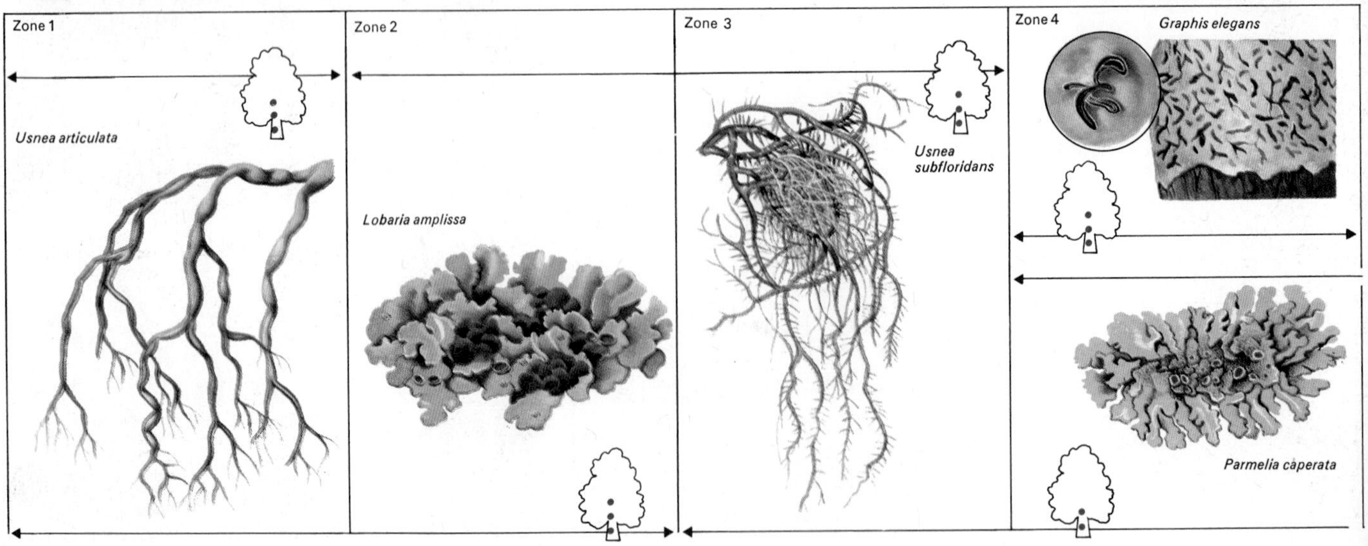

1
Location on oak tree
Branches
Trunk
Base
SO2 mg/m³
0
30
40
45
65
100
140
180
Zone 1
Zone 2
Zone 3
Zone 4
Zone 5
Zone 6
Zone 7
Usnea articulata
Lobaria amplissa
Usnea subfloridans
Graphis elegans
Parmelia caperata

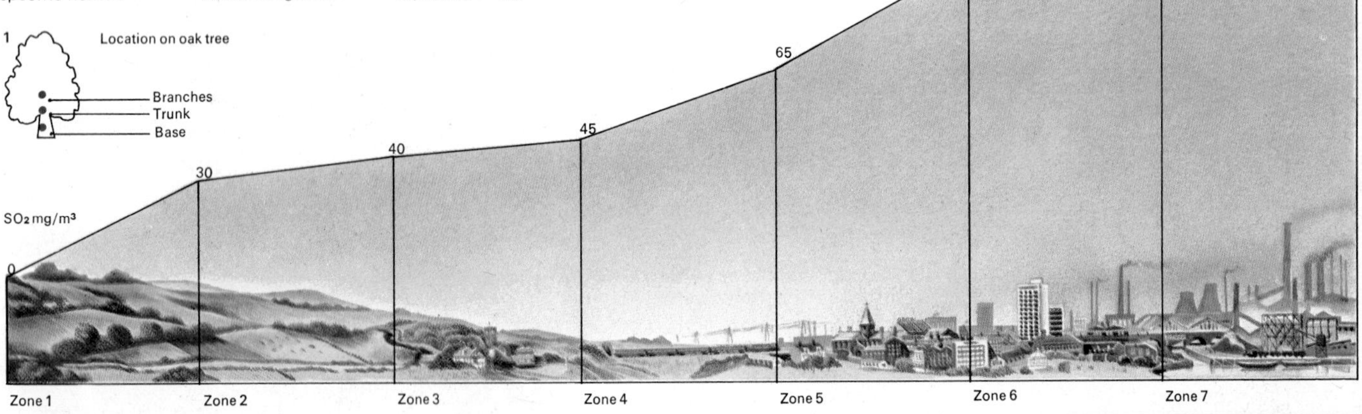

manufactures its food by the process of photosynthesis—the conversion of the carbon dioxide and water vapor contained in the air into carbohydrates by exposure to light. On the other hand, the fungal partner does not have any of the green matter (chlorophyll) that is essential for photosynthesis.

The simple carbohydrate formed in the algal layer is excreted, absorbed by the fungus, and transformed by it into a different carbohydrate. This carbohydrate flow is the basis of the symbiotic relationship that has developed in the lichen. The transfer of nutrients from algae to fungus is swift; fungi have been found to convert sugars derived from algae into fungal products within three minutes of the start of photosynthesis. The algae may also provide the fungus with vitamins and stimulate the growth of the lichen. For its part, the fungus takes in water vapor, which accelerates the rate of photosynthesis in the algae, while the fungus provides shade for the algae underneath—some algae such as *Trebouxia* dislike strong light.

The uses of lichens

Lichens have many uses—as food for animals (reindeer obtain two-thirds of their food supply from lichen 3 [4]), as nesting material for birds and as protection and homes for hundreds of species of small invertebrates such as mites, beetles, snails, and moths. Man also has derived benefit from lichens. For more than two centuries Iceland moss *(Cetraria islandica)* has been prescribed for chest ailments. Usnic acid, present in some lichens, is used to combat infection from superficial wounds and also in the treatment of tuberculosis. Modern medical research has revealed the existence of antibiotic substances effective against diseases such as scarlet fever and pneumonia. Litmus is derived from *Roccella* species of lichen.

Lichens are particularly sensitive indicators of atmospheric pollution [1]. Radioactive derivatives of strontium and cesium are absorbed and retained in high concentrations. This poses a great threat to the reindeer and, ultimately, to Eskimos and other northern peoples who eat them.

KEY

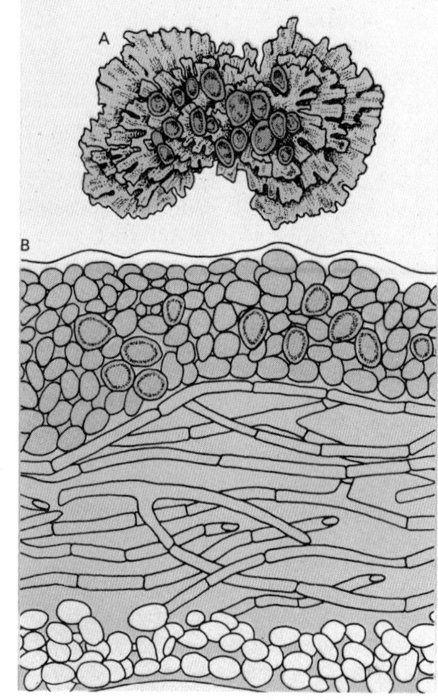
A
B

Lichens arise from the mutually beneficial partnership that can develop between algae and fungi. *Xanthoria parietina* [A] is commonly found along coasts on rocks and on the walls and roofs of many buildings. The bright orange, saucer-shaped fruiting bodies (apothecia) differ little in structure from those of an isolated fungus. A section through a lichen [B] shows a thin upper layer of tightly packed fungal strands. Embedded in this upper layer are isolated green algal cells. The main body of the lichen is made up of enmeshed fungal strands, below which is another thin layer of fungal strands.

2

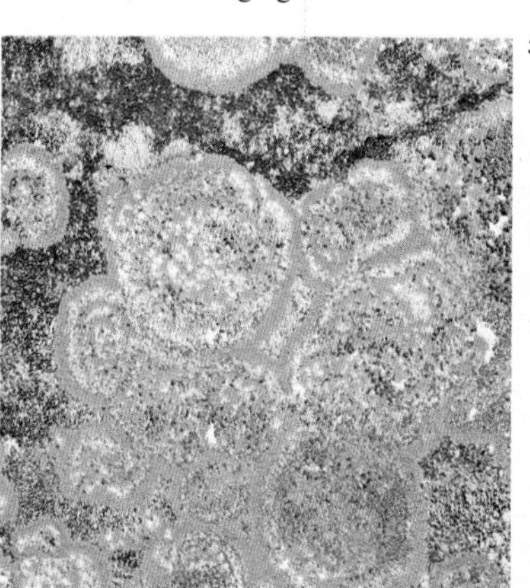

2 Encrusting lichens cling close to the surface to which they attach themselves. The species shown here is *Caloplaca heppiana*. It is frequently found growing on walls and tombstones. (This and similar species of lichen can be used for dating purposes.) Such lichens are often brightly colored – the pigment being derived from the fungal partner.

3

3 A typical leafy lichen is the tree lungwort *(Lobaria pulmonaria)*, one of 70 species which are mostly subtropical. The tree lungwort occurs in the northern temperate zone. Its "leaves" can grow to lengths of 4in (10cm). When wet they are bright green; when dry, yellowish brown. Reproduction is by means of spores produced in cup-shaped structures on the "leaf" surface.

4 Reindeer moss, *Cladonia rangiferina* [B], is the staple diet of reindeer [A] in the long months of the Arctic winter when there is little other green vegetation available for consumption. Other deer and musk oxen also graze large quantities of it. Lichens contain a high proportion of carbohydrates that provide the energy required in such extreme conditions. Lichens, however, are low in other nutrients. When animals feed exclusively on lichens symptoms of protein deficiency appear. In Scandinavia species of *Cladonia* are used to make alcohol and sugar.

4 A

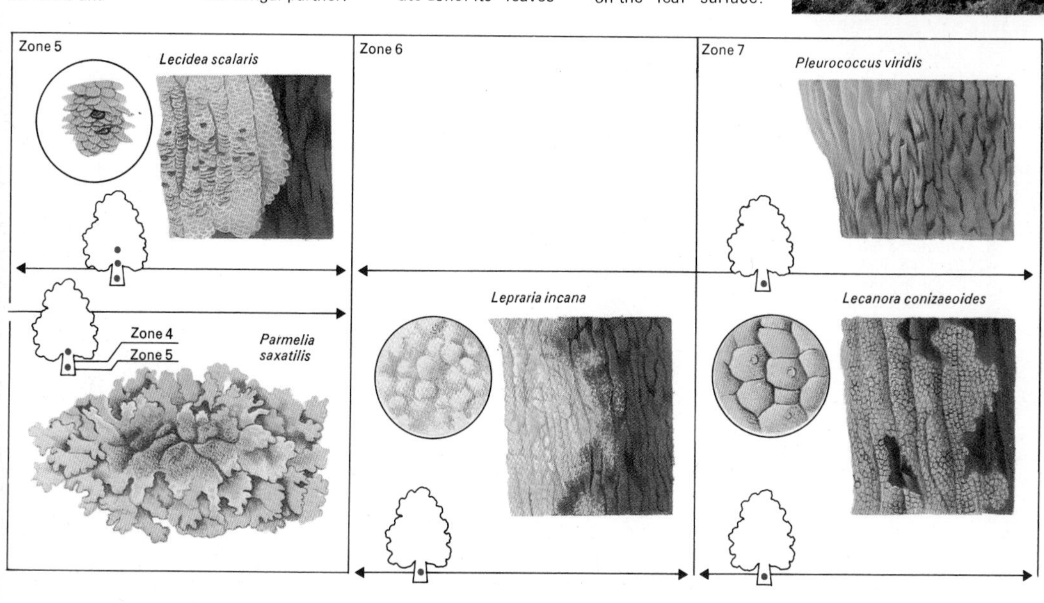
Zone 5
Lecidea scalaris
Zone 6
Zone 7
Pleurococcus viridis
Zone 4
Zone 5
Parmelia saxatilis
Lepraria incana
Lecanora conizaeoides

4 B

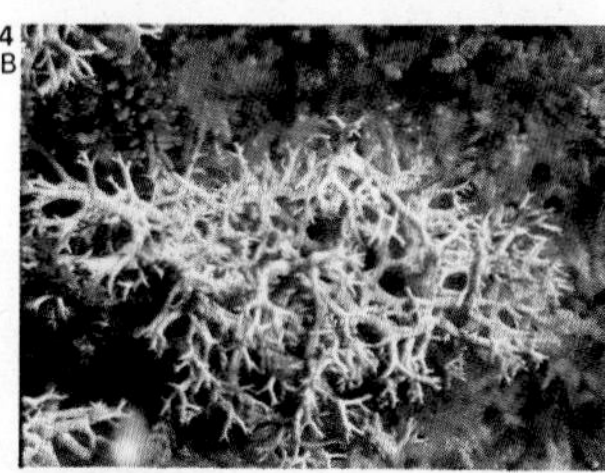

5

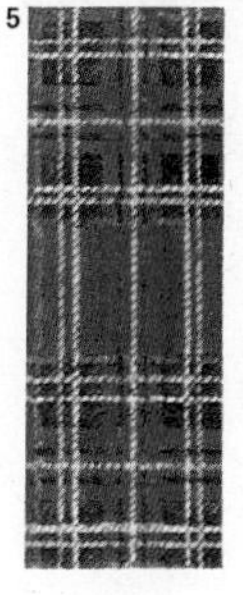

5 Lichen extracts were once used to color the cloth for Scottish kilts. The lichens colored the cloth yellow, brown, red, and purple. Intermediate colors were obtained by overdyeing. Lichen extracts are now used in the manufacture of an antibiotic, perfume, and litmus.

Mosses and liverworts

Mosses, liverworts, and hornworts—collectively known as the bryophytes—are among the simplest and most primitive of land plants. The mosses total some 14,000 species, the liverworts about 8,000, the majority of both groups being tropical. Most species favor moist, shady habitats in soil or dead leaves or on bark or rocks. Some mosses, however, are able to survive many months of drought and desiccation.

The structure of bryophytes

It is generally assumed that the bryophytes evolved from green algae and they still retain many primitive features that reveal this ancestry [Key]. Mosses and their allies are structurally very simple. Some bryophytes bear a superficial resemblance to flowering plants but although they appear to have stems, leaves, and roots these structures are much simpler than in higher plants. Liverworts are so called because they are often roughly liver-shaped and in the Middle Ages were reputed to be good for liver disease.

Leafy liverworts, such as *Lophocolea*, a common liverwort found on damp logs and tree stumps, display "leaves" carried on a central "stem." In the mosses, this adaptation is taken a step further, and the thallus shape is lost completely.

The differences between mosses and leafy liverworts can be seen externally. The leaves of liverworts never have a central midrib and are nearly always in two or three rows. Moss leaves are never divided in shape and are rarely in more than one row. The rhizoids—the fine hairlike structures that root the plant in the soil and absorb nutrients—are made up of a single cell in the liverworts, but have many cells in the mosses. They also differ in the shape of the capsule—the spore-containing structure—and in the way that the spores are dispersed. In liverworts, the capsule is oval or spherical and the spores when mature are dispersed through four longitudinal splits that develop in the capsule wall. In mosses, the capsule is usually cylindrical and often has a lid that is shed when the spores are nature, exposing a circle of "teeth" round the open "mouth" [1] of the capsule.

Unlike higher plants, most bryophytes have no specialized cells to conduct water and food around the plant, nor do they possess woody tissues that could support a large plant body. As a result, all bryophytes are comparatively small plants.

Reproduction in bryophytes

Despite all of these primitive features, bryophytes show significant adaptations to life on land compared with their algal ancestors, which are nearly all confined to water. The most significant adaptation to the land habit is a pattern of alternation of generations in which the plants producing sexual organs are dominant and the plants producing asexual spores are virtually parasitic on the dominant form [1].

Alternation of generations is the rule in virtually all plant species. It implies that there are two distinct stages in the plant life cycle: one that has only one complete set of chromosomes and another, formed as a result of sexual reproduction, that has two sets of chromosomes, one from each parent. In the algae, both generations may

CONNECTIONS

See also
424 The plant kingdom
438 Ferns and horsetails
432 Algae and seaweeds
562 Plants of the past
282 Energy resources: coal

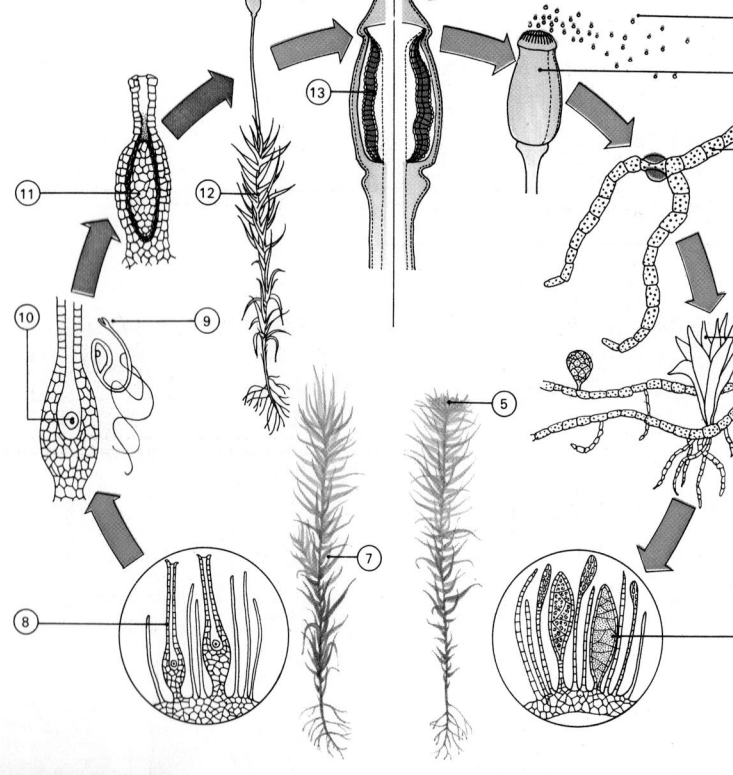

1 The life cycle of a moss, *Polytrichum*, begins with the dispersal of the tiny spherical spores through gaps in the teeth guarding the apex of the capsule [1]. The spores [2] germinate to form a branched filament, the protonema [3]. The upper parts turn green and buds appear on those filaments that grow into a plant [4]. Mature male [5] and female [7] *Polytrichum* plants are similar. Male sex organs [6] are borne in a flowerlike open cup at the shoot apex. Female sex organs [8] are borne in a cluster, also at the shoot apex. Male sperm [9] swim from male to female plant and fertilize the egg [10]. This develops into an embryo [11] that gives rise to the moss sporophyte generation. The sporophyte borne on the female [12] consists of a stalk and capsule holding spores [13] which were produced by meiosis.

2 The thallus of the liverwort *Marchantia* in cross-section [A] shows unspecialized cells [1] bounded by surface layers [2]. Scales and rhizoids [3] are found on the lower surface. The moss "stem" [B] shows a central cylinder of cells [4] that conducts water up the stem. The surrounding cells [5] conduct food. Unspecialized cells [6] lie between these and the outer epidermal layer.

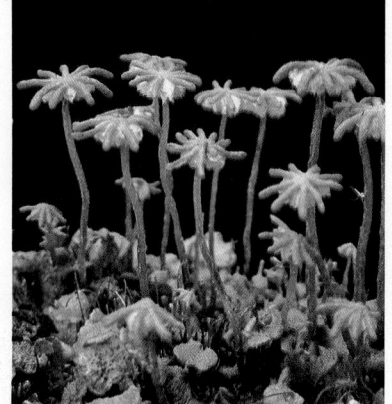

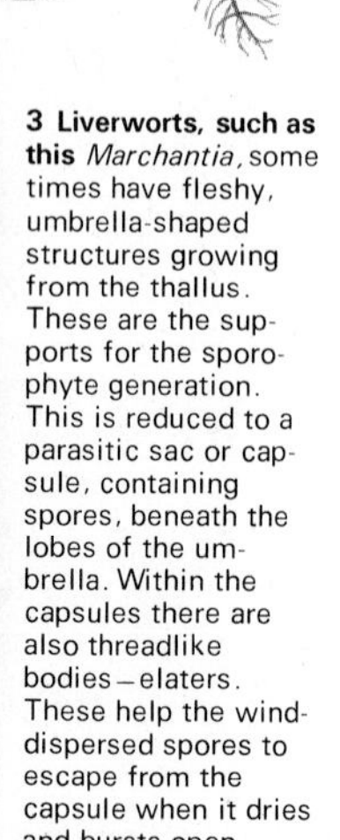

3 Liverworts, such as this *Marchantia*, some times have fleshy, umbrella-shaped structures growing from the thallus. These are the supports for the sporophyte generation. This is reduced to a parasitic sac or capsule, containing spores, beneath the lobes of the umbrella. Within the capsules there are also threadlike bodies—elaters. These help the wind-dispersed spores to escape from the capsule when it dries and bursts open.

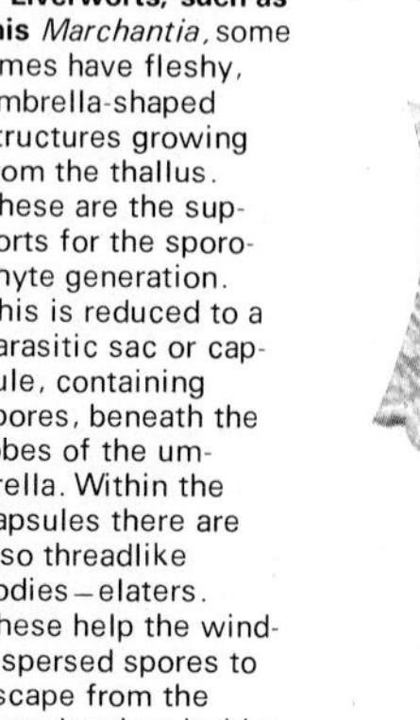

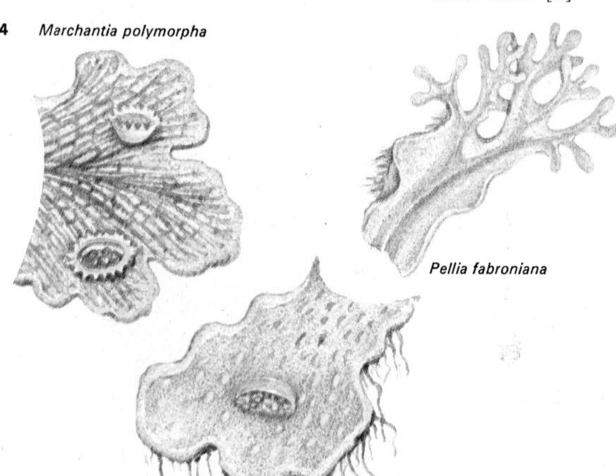
Marchantia polymorpha
Pellia fabroniana
Lunularia cruciata

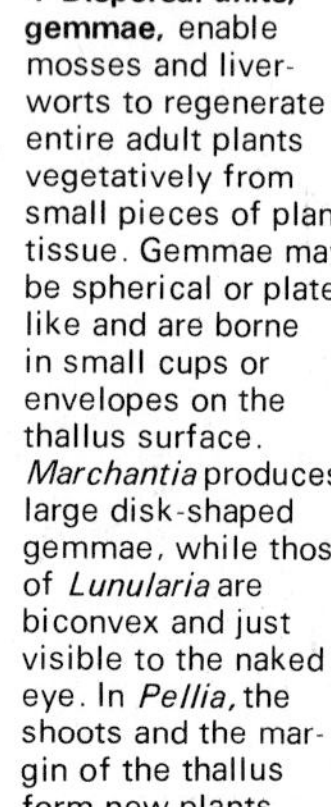

4 Dispersal units, gemmae, enable mosses and liverworts to regenerate entire adult plants vegetatively from small pieces of plant tissue. Gemmae may be spherical or plate-like and are borne in small cups or envelopes on the thallus surface. *Marchantia* produces large disk-shaped gemmae, while those of *Lunularia* are biconvex and just visible to the naked eye. In *Pellia*, the shoots and the margin of the thallus form new plants.

appear identical, but in the bryophytes each is distinct.

The reason for separate generations is that bryophytes need water for sexual reproduction. The male sperm must swim—using two whiplike flagella—to the female egg. Because the male reproductive organs and the female reproductive organs may be borne on separate plants, there must be an unbroken film of water extending from the male organs to those of the female. On land, this occurs only during rainfall or after a heavy dew, so the evolution of sexual reproduction was less dependable as a means of colonizing new environments. The bryophyte response was to find a way of making each mating much more effective; the fertilized egg became not a mature bryophyte plant but a spore-producing organism, or sporophyte, dependent on the mature plant for its food. Each of the thousands of spores produced as a result of one mating could give rise to a new plant.

In both mosses and liverworts, the sporophyte consists of a foot embedded in the tissues of the bryophyte plant. This foot usually develops a long stalk and a capsule that contains and disperses the spores. *Anthoceros,* the hornwort, is distinct from all other bryophytes because its spore-producing structure consists of only foot and capsule.

Bryophytes can also reproduce vegetatively, often from small detached fragments. Many have developed specialized deciduous shoots or groups of cells called gemmae from which the entire adult plant can regenerate [4].

Important bryophytes

Sphagnum [6], the moss of peat bogs, is another untypical bryophyte as well as the only one of any commercial importance. Because it is able to soak up and retain large amounts of water it can be used as a surface mulch for water conservation. Dried and partially decomposed it may be added to heavy clay soils to improve their texture. Peat is dug and burned as a fossil fuel in some parts of northern Europe. Bryophytes also prevent erosion and retain surface water and help to break down rocks to soil.

KEY

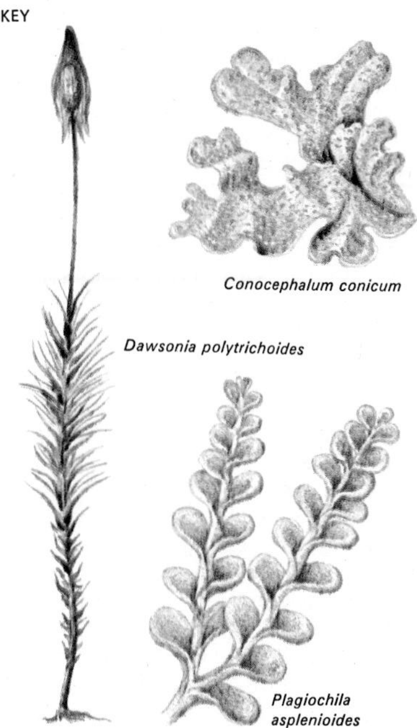
Conocephalum conicum
Dawsonia polytrichoides
Plagiochila asplenioides

Mosses and liverworts are almost certainly descended from algae and show stages in the development of a land habit. The thallose liverwort *Conocephalum conicum,* for example, with dark green, ribbonlike branches, looks rather like a thalloid green algae. *Plagiochila asplenoides* shows a new development—the thallus has become divided to give the appearance of a central "stem" bearing large rounded "leaves." This development is most marked in mosses (*Dawsonia polytrichoides* is an Australian example) where the plant grows in an upright manner and the "leaves" and "stem" are well developed.

5

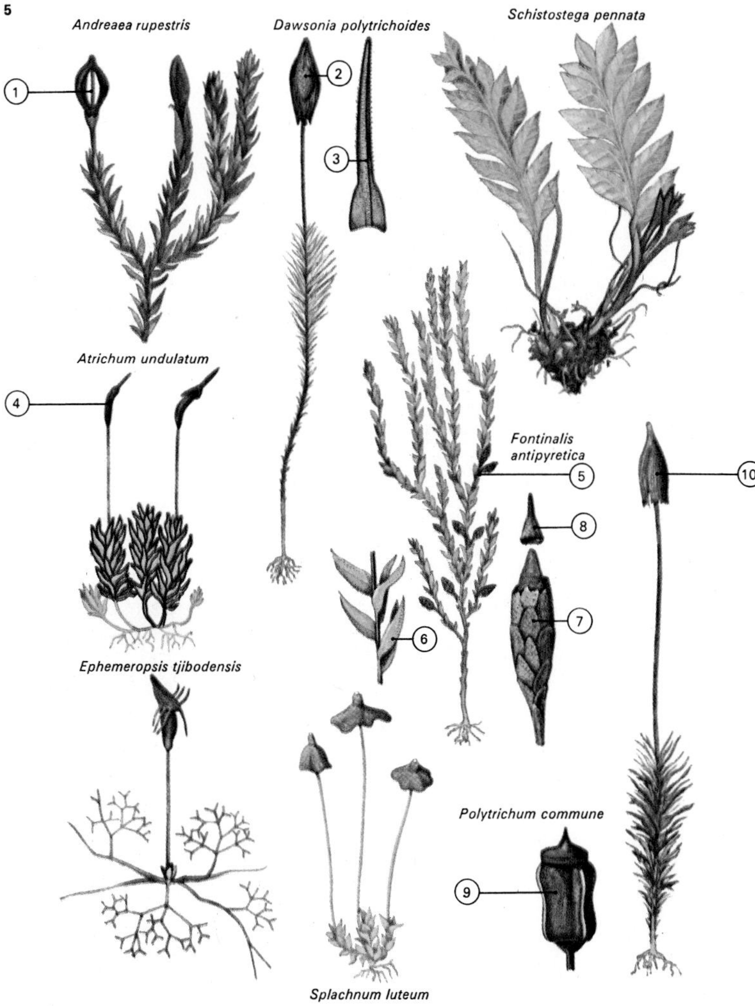
Andreaea rupestris
Dawsonia polytrichoides
Schistostega pennata
1
2
3
Atrichum undulatum
4
Fontinalis antipyretica
5
10
8
7
6
Ephemeropsis tjibodensis
Polytrichum commune
9
Splachnum luteum

5 Mosses vary in growth and color according to species. *Andreaea rupestris* is dark reddish-brown with tiny capsules [1] that open by four longitudinal slits. *Dawsonia polytrichoides* is an Australian species with a distinctive capsule [2] and thin, pointed leaves [3]. *Schistostega pennata,* a European moss, has flattened, translucent leaves. *Atrichum undulatum,* common on open lands and in woods, has a capsule [4] with a long, pointed cap. *Fontinalis antipyretica* is an aquatic moss whose boat-shaped leaves have a sharp keel [6]; the capsules are oblong or cylindrical [5, 7] and there is a pointed cap [8]. *Ephemeropsis tjibodensis* has an extensive protonema, while the mature plant is small. *Splachnum luteum* has a spore-producing body that resembles an umbrella. *Polytrichum commune* is extremely common and has a boxlike capsule [9]. It bears a long, golden brown cap [10] which is released before the spores are dispersed.

6

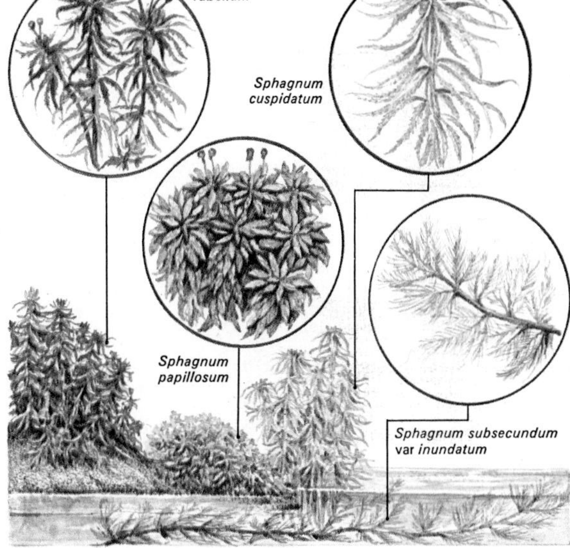
Sphagnum rubellum
Sphagnum cuspidatum
Sphagnum papillosum
Sphagnum subsecundum var inundatum

6 The peat mosses *(Sphagnum)* can absorb and retain enormous amounts of water—over 25 times their own dry weight. They can reproduce asexually extremely efficiently by separating off branches. As a result, open stretches of water that are colonized by *Sphagnum* species are drained by the ever-encroaching moss, while the level is raised by dead and decaying moss tissue accumulating on the surface. At an early stage in the formation of a peat bog, the water surface is covered with a dense mat of *Sphagnum* and other species, forming a treacherous "quaking bog." These bogs are capable eventually of supporting large trees and in time the swamp is replaced by woodland.

7

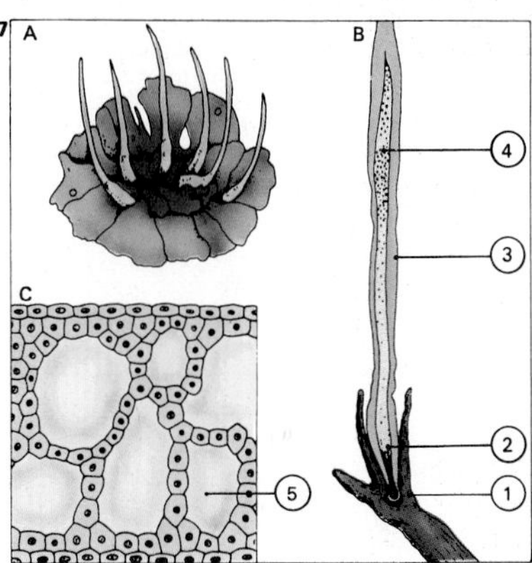
A
B
C
4
3
2
1
5

7 The hornwort *(Anthoceros)* [A], is a rare plant found in moist, shady places. Long sporophytes [B], growing from the upper surface of the plant, are fed from the gametophyte [1] by a foot [2]. Fertile spores [3] develop from the tissues around the sterile central column [4] and are released when the capsule splits. The plant [C] often has cavities [5] containing colonies of blue-green algae.

Ferns and horsetails

Ferns, horsetails, and club mosses, the pteridophytes, are among the most primitive vascular plants, that is, plants that have a system of tubes (a vascular system) to conduct water and food around the plant [2]. This characteristic they share with seed plants and, like the mosses and liverworts, they have a life cycle [1] that shows well-marked alternation of generations.

The pteridophyte life cycle

The leafy plant, or sporophyte, is the dominant stage in the pteridophyte's life cycle and is involved with the production of asexual spores. When they germinate, fern spores give rise to small, insignificant plants (prothalli) that look like liverworts. These are called gametophytes because they produce the sex cells. For male and female sex cells to come together, fuse, and give rise to a new spore-producing plant, water is essential in order that the male cells can "swim" to the female cells. This need for water explains why most ferns and horsetails can exist only in damp environments and also why they are called cryptogams, a name that means "hidden marriage." To early botanists the sexual lives of ferns were a mystery because they did not produce easily visible structures such as pollen, fruits, and seeds in the way that flowering plants do.

Where ferns are found

Ferns and horsetails have become greatly reduced in numbers from their abundance in the Carboniferous period [Key], but this does not mean that they are no longer important in the plant population. One has merely to see a hillside of bracken turn golden-brown in autumn to realize that some species of fern are still very common. In forests and jungles, the enormous complex fronds of tropical ferns, quite unsuited to dry or exposed habitats, are ideally suited to capturing the maximum amount of light available in the forest shade. Ferns also occur in many other habitats—even as far north as the Arctic tundra—and can grow in amazing abundance in suitable places.

There are about 10,000 species of ferns. The greatest number and diversity (about 2,500 species) are found in Southeast Asia, where ferns and horsetails [7] cover much of the jungle floor and also grow in the boles of the trees. In contrast there are only about 150 species of ferns and fern allies to be found in Europe and in North America.

Useful and ornamental species

Few pteridophytes are of economic importance but some are eaten, especially in Japan. Spores of the club moss *Lycopodium*, which form a very light, mobile powder, were once used for demonstration purposes in physics experiments to reveal the vibration patterns on an object, such as a drum skin, that was generating sound. An extract of the male fern *(Dryopteris)* was once commonly employed as a highly effective and relatively safe vermifuge or "worm powder" for human beings. Bracken *(Pteridium aquilinum)* is one of the very few ferns regarded by man as a "weed." With its rapid growth and persistence it overtakes large areas of pasture land and burned-over land. The trunks of certain tree ferns are used for construction in the tropics.

CONNECTIONS

See also
424 The plant kingdom
560 Fossils: the life of the past
562 Plants of the past
436 Mosses and liverworts
282 Energy resources: coal
568 Toward life on land
572 The age of reptiles
596 Woodlands of Australasia

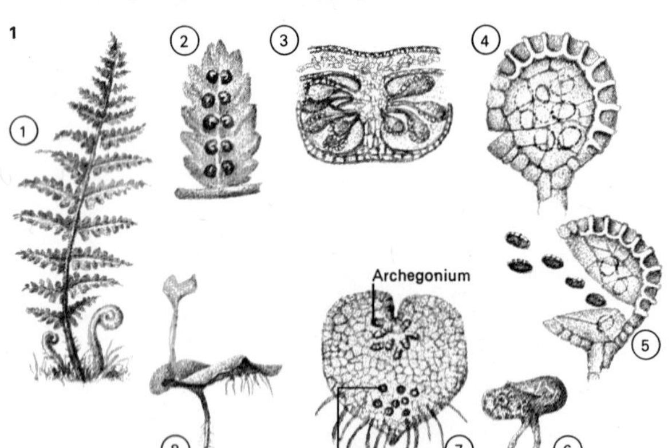

1
Archegonium
Antheridium

1 The dominant plant in the life cycle of *Dryopteris*, the male fern, is the spore producer [1]. From brown patches, the sori [3], on the leaf undersides [2] asexual spores [5] are produced from sporangia [4]. The spores germinate in damp places [6] Each forms a heart-shaped prothallus [7] that measures 0.5-0.75in (1-2cm) long. On the underside of the prothallus, male (antheridia) and female (archegonia) organs containing sex cells (gametes) are formed. The motile male gamete swims to and fuses with the female. Then a new sporophyte forms [8].

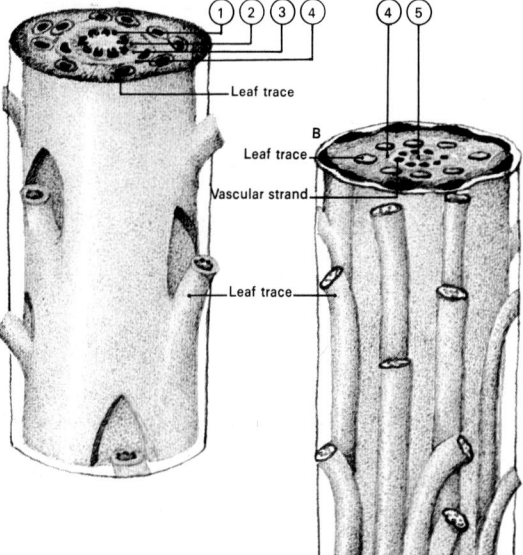

2A
Leaf trace
B
Leaf trace
Vascular strand
Leaf trace

2 Ferns have more primitive systems for conducting water and mineral salts than do flowering plants. The xylem or water-conducting tissue [1] is made up of tracheids, single elongated cells with stiffening. Instead of the xylem and phloem (food-conducting tissue) [2] being arranged in bundles as they are in higher plants there is a more primitive arrangement. The simplest fern stem [A] consists of a solid mass of xylem completely surrounded by phloem, pericycle [3], and endodermis [4]. This is a protostele. Another arrangement, the solenostele [B], may be hollow or contain pith [5].

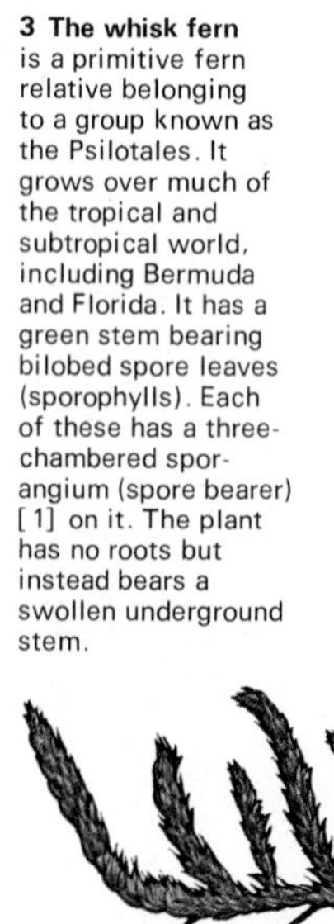

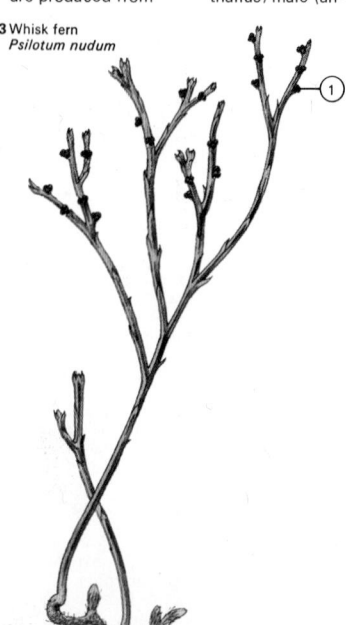

3 Whisk fern
Psilotum nudum

3 The whisk fern is a primitive fern relative belonging to a group known as the Psilotales. It grows over much of the tropical and subtropical world, including Bermuda and Florida. It has a green stem bearing bilobed spore leaves (sporophylls). Each of these has a three-chambered sporangium (spore bearer) [1] on it. The plant has no roots but instead bears a swollen underground stem.

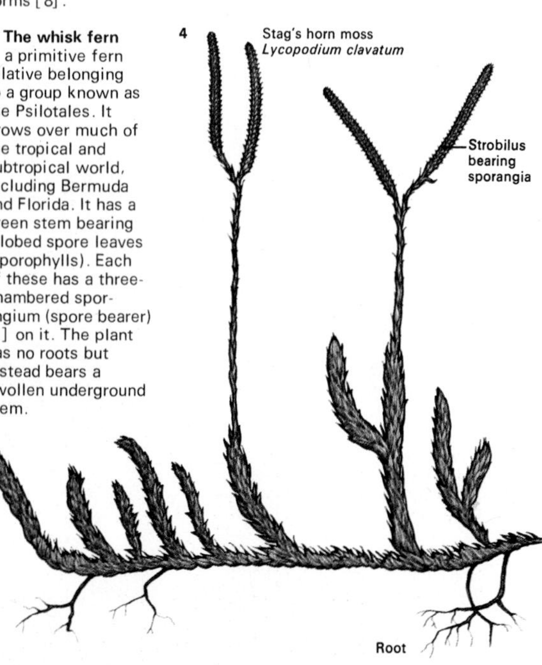

4
Stag's horn moss
Lycopodium clavatum
Strobilus bearing sporangia
Root

4 Club mosses are widespread descendants of a plant group that reached its peak in the Carboniferous. Fossil remains are found in coal. The types that remain today, like stag's horn moss, grow in many niches.

5 Selaginella is a relation of the club mosses but differs in that its leaves have a small outgrowth at the base, known as the ligule. Many species are restricted to tropical rain forests where they flourish in the perpetual humidity.

Many ferns are grown in gardens and greenhouses because once established they tolerate conditions unsuitable for most flowering plants. During the reign of Queen Victoria (1837–1901) there was a craze for fern collecting, and certain types of fern, especially the so-called filmy ferns [11] with very delicate leaves only one cell thick, were collected and grown in Wardian cases (sealed glass boxes). Particularly in Britain and Europe, this led to a serious depletion of some ferns in the wild. Certain other genera such as *Woodsia,* a fern of high mountain regions, were also over-collected.

Many varieties of the various fern species found in the wild are grown in gardens. Some bear such names as *Phyllites scolopendrium* "palmatum" (palmate, or hand-shaped, harts-tongue) and *Asplenium trichomanes* "cristatum" (crested maidenhair spleenwort). Many of the more common fern species can be grown in shady spots in gardens where the soil is poor.

Certain ferns, such as *Salvinia* and *Azolla* species [8], live totally in water. These two genera are native to tropical and subtropical regions but are grown widely. Water ferns can form large mats over ponds and *Azolla* often turns a beautiful crimson.

The horsetails *(Equisetum)* are fern allies that vary from small creeping plants to scramblers reaching up to about 30ft (9m). Many of the species have much silica (sandlike material that is rough and scratchy) in their stems. The rough horsetail, or common scouring rush *(Equisetem hyemale),* was once used for scouring pans and can still be bought in music shops for shaving down and smoothing the reeds of clarinets and saxophones. Horsetails are weeds that are almost impossible to eradicate.

True ferns can often be recognized even when they do not resemble ferns by the characteristic way in which the new shoot tips unroll. In ferns they appear to unwind like a spring, a phenomenon known as "circinate vernation." Thick-stemmed ferns in the early stages of shooting resemble the carved scroll at the head of a violin and have been given the common name "fiddleheads."

KEY

1 2 3 4 5 6

Tertiary

Cretaceous

Jurassic

Triassic

Permian

Carboniferous

Devonian

Silurian

The true relationships between pteridophytes are not known because of a lack of fossil evidence. The number of living species is small compared to their abundance in Carboniferous period, which was truly the age of ferns. It was in this period that enormous beds of plants were fossilized to form coal seams. The modern groups that remain are the Psilotales [1], club mosses [2], the selaginellas [3], quillworts [4], the horsetails [5], and the ferns [6].

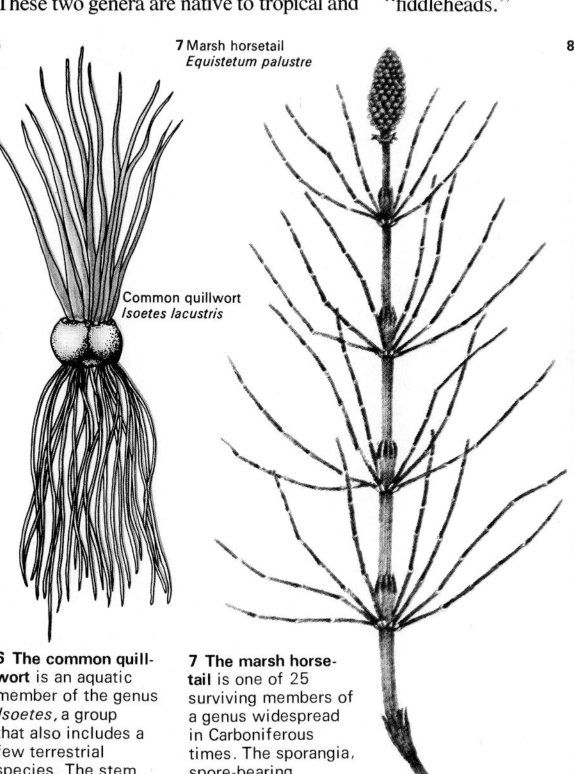
6
7 Marsh horsetail
Equistetum palustre
Common quillwort
Isoetes lacustris

6 The common quillwort is an aquatic member of the genus *Isoetes*, a group that also includes a few terrestrial species. The stem of the plant is compressed into a tuberlike structure.

7 The marsh horsetail is one of 25 surviving members of a genus widespread in Carboniferous times. The sporangia, spore-bearing tissues, are grouped into cones that may tip branched shoots.

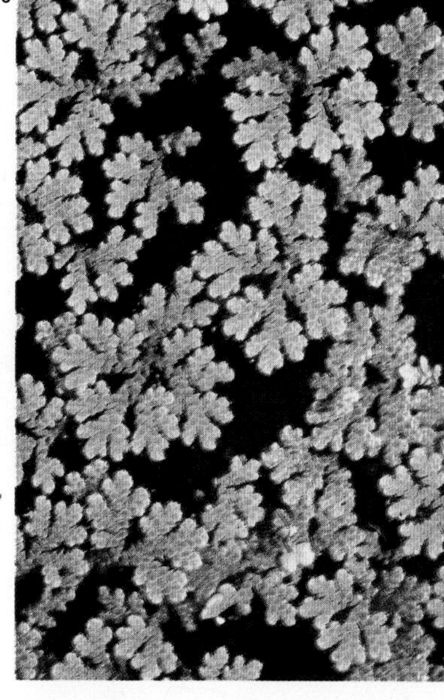
8

8 The water fern *(Salvinia)* occurs in Africa and grows so rapidly that it may completely choke lakes and ponds. During construction of the Kariba dam on the Zambezi, two species were allowed to meet and hybridize. This hybrid showed such vigor that in a short while this "man-made" species, named *Salvinia molesta,* caused serious economic problems.

9 Royal fern
Osmunda regalis
1
2

9 The royal or flowering fern flourishes in wet, peaty areas all over the world. Similar in appearance to a locust tree, it is often collected for gardens; as a result, European representatives are becoming rare. The fronds of the fern show a marked difference between those that are sterile [1] and those that are spore bearing [2]. The fronds may grow to 10ft (3m) long.

10 The tree ferns, such as *Dicksonia,* build up a trunk of leaf bases like palms. Most tree ferns are tropical, but this species *(Dicksonia antarctica)* is found in temperate eastern Australia.

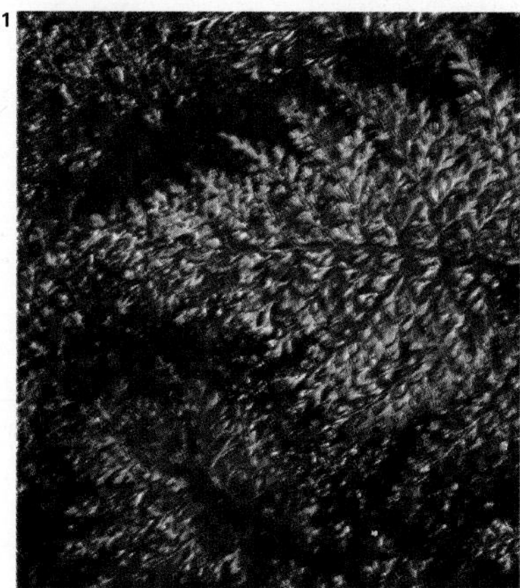
11

11 The delicate, humidity-loving filmy ferns have fronds that are only a single cell thick. In Victorian times they were much collected and grown with great care in so-called Wardian cases or greenhouses.

12

Stag's horn fern
Platycerium bifurcatum

12 The stag's horn fern has flat, spreading basal leaves that are often brown. These may create a "plate" from which forked, fertile fronds project. Its distribution is from tropical Africa to India and Australia.

The cone bearers

A significant proportion of the world's vegetation is classified as gymnosperms—plants with naked seeds. The group—which includes the conifers, whose seeds are normally borne in structures called cones—consists of about 66 genera with 600 species that are woody plants, mostly with bark. They have primitive male and female "flowers," and all have two or more seed leaves or cotyledons.

Development of gymnosperms

Gymnosperms were of great importance in prehistoric times. They were a highly varied group that dominated the flora in the Mesozoic era more than 220 million years ago. Today they are represented only by a relatively small remnant of those earlier species, but they still form a very important section of the world's flora, including such well-known trees as firs, pines, and yews.

The seed plants differ from the ferns, or pteridophytes, in the alternating generations between sexual and asexual, or spore-producing, stages. As the male and the female cells of the sexual generation became specialized in ferns and primitive gymnosperms, the male cells were motile, with whiplike flagellae that enabled the sperms to move through water or a film of moisture. This happens in cycads and ginkgo, but the "swimming" stage has disappeared in the pine and all flowering plants, thus releasing them from the restriction of needing water for the last stage of the fertilization process.

In conifers fertilization is a complex process that takes a long time. In the pine *(Pinus)* it takes three years for the pollen grains to mature. Each grain has two wings to facilitate wind pollination and a mature tree can produce about 2.2lb (1kg) of pollen each year, which may be blown for some hundreds of miles downwind. The pollen grain landing on a female cone can take a year or more to grow in and fuse with the cell inside, and two more years may pass before the cone is mature.

Groups of gymnosperms

There are five main subgroups of gymnosperms. The Cycadales are tropical, palmlike trees known as tree ferns or cycads [12]. The cones of cycads can be very large, and in one species, *Encephalartos caffer,* cones weighing 92lb (42kg) have been reported—the largest cones known on any plant. Another species, the Australian *Macrozamia,* has cones 2ft (60cm) long.

The Ginkgoales group contains only one living genus and one species, namely the maidenhair tree *(Ginkgo biloba)* [10]. It was thought that this species, too, had become extinct as a wild plant, but in recent years Chinese botanists have found some wild maidenhair trees, thus confirming that it does still exist in the wild state. It is a common avenue tree in American cities. The group that includes yews and podocarps is known as the Taxales and all its members have fleshy fruits. They are the only gymnosperms that do not produce cones. The fourth group of gymnosperms, the Gnetales, including the *Welwitschia* [11], are a very small and specialized class.

Most important of the gymnosperms are the Coniferales, the group that contains 48 out of the total of 66 gymnosperm genera.

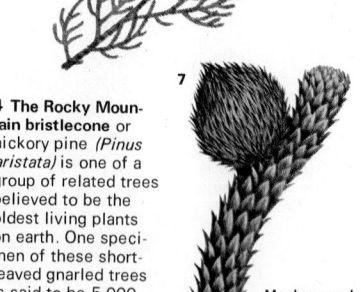

CONNECTIONS

See also
442 Pines and other conifers
424 The plant kingdom
592 Northern evergreen forests
562 Plants of the past
560 Fossils: the life of the past
568 Toward life on land
364 Forestry
1624 Making paper
448 Woody flowering plants
366 The modern tree nursery
368 Trees: problems of climate and disease

1

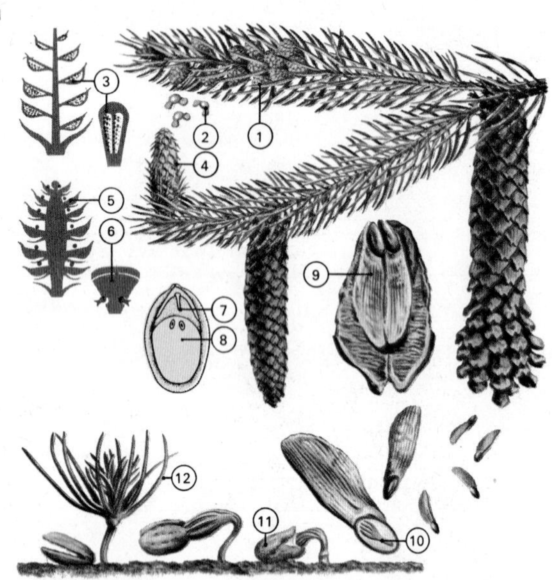

2

2 The wood of coniferous trees is called softwood because it is easily worked. Characteristic of gymnosperms is the absence of vessels in the vascular or water- and mineral-conducting system. In cross section the softwood shows a single type of cell tracheid or fiber [1]; when magnified this looks square in outline. Large tracheids laid down in spring alternate with smaller summer tracheids forming annual rings [2]. The tubes serve mainly as space for the transport of sap through minute openings called pits [3]. At right angles to the rings, rays [4] radiate from the center for movement of sap and water through the trunk.

1 The reproductive cycle of the Norway spruce starts when pollen grains [2] from under scales [3] of the male cone [1] blow onto two unfertilized eggs [5] on scales [6] of the female cones [4]. The pollen grain nucleus passes down the tube [7] and fuses with the female nucleus [8] to form a winged seed [9]. Seeds disperse and the embryo [10] germinates [11, 12].

3 100m 75 50 25 20 15 10 5 0

3 The California redwoods *(Sequoia sempervirens)* are magnificent examples of cone-bearing trees. The tallest tree in the world, growing in Redwood Creek Valley, California, is 367ft (112m) tall and has a girth of about 46ft (14m) at 5ft (1.5m) above the ground.

4

4 The Rocky Mountain bristlecone or hickory pine *(Pinus aristata)* is one of a group of related trees believed to be the oldest living plants on earth. One specimen of these short-leaved gnarled trees is said to be 5,000 years old.

5

Willow-leaf podocarp
Podocarpus saligna

5 Podocarps or yellow-woods are native to tropical mountains. They bear berrylike cones, some of which are edible. This willow-leaf podocarp grows in the Andes.

6

Mediterranean cypress
Cupressus sempervirens

6 True cypress trees are evergreen conifers of North America, Europe, and Asia. The Italian form of the Mediterranean cypress *(Cupressus sempervirens stricta)* is commonly planted in formal gardens.

7

Monkey puzzle
Araucaria sp

7 The Chilean pine, better known as the monkey puzzle, has characteristically stiff, dark green leaves on tiered branches. Resin from the bark is used in medicinal preparations and seeds of the large female cones are edible.

8 Common juniper
Juniperus communis

8 Junipers are chiefly Northern Hemisphere evergreens. The fruits, although commonly called berries, are true cones with overlapping scales that look like berries. The fruits of one species are used to flavor gin.

These are mainly evergreen, temperate trees with needlelike or scalelike leaves [Key] and they often form the dominant vegetation in colder parts of the world, being especially abundant in temperate forests both north and south of the Equator. Economically they are of great importance as timber trees. Conifers are often grouped together as "firs" and most have softwood timber containing resin. This is formed in minute canals that run through the wood giving the characteristic turpentine smell to freshly sawn softwood and is the commercial source of many useful resins.

The recognition of conifers

The "firs" comprise a diverse group of trees, most of which can be identified by the shape of their cones and the number and grouping of their leaves or "needles." In the pines, for example, there are only two, three, or five needles together. In cedars *(Cedrus)* the needles are in bundles or clusters of many individuals, firm and evergreen. The larches *(Larix)* [9], also have needles in clusters but are deciduous.

When the young twigs remain green through the summer the conifer may be a yew *(Taxus)* if the needles are long but short-stalked; Japanese cypress *(Cryptomeria)* if the leaves are small scales grouped in spirals, or a California big-tree *(Sequoiadendron)*. Among trees on which the needles are arranged in two rows on short shoots that are soft to the touch and fall in autumn, the swamp cypress *(Taxodium)* has these short shoots arranged singly, while the dawn redwood *(Metasequoia)* has the short shoots opposite in pairs on the stem. Another distinction is a clear stalking of the needles; where this occurs and the tree top overhangs, it is a hemlock *(Tsuga)*. The Douglas fir *(Pseudotsuga taxifolia)* has sharp-pointed buds and lemon-scented needles. The silver firs *(Abies)* have characteristic round scars where needles are pulled off, while a spruce *(Picea)* needle takes a small piece of stem with it.

The conifer trees are mostly evergreens. One of the exceptions is the larch, which is deciduous. The dawn redwood, like the ginkgo, is a "living fossil."

KEY

A B C D

Conifers can be identified by their shapes, needles, and cones. The Scotch pine *(Pinus sylvestris)* [A] has a flattened crown and triangular cones. The larch *(Larix species)* [B] is one of the few deciduous conifers. It has open cones. The Norway spruce *(Picea abies)* [C] has long, pendulous cones and is the European Christmas tree. The Douglas fir *(Pseudotsuga taxifolia)* [D] has light-brown cones, 2-4in (5-10cm) long, with pointed scales and long, soft, flat needles.

9 A

B

9 The larch genus includes about a dozen species that are native to the cool temperate regions of the Northern Hemisphere. Some of them are among the most commonly planted timber trees. Larches grow tall and straight, and their coarse-grained, hard, heavy, rot-resistant wood is used in making ships' masts, telegraph poles, and mine timbers. But many people also grow larches purely for ornament because of their pleasing shape. In forests [A] the trees grow rapidly, and disease-resistant types can be selected. In the open [B] larch trees grow a fine regular crown. Larches are deciduous and cones on bare twigs appear in early spring. [C] Male flowers are small, silvery, and inconspicuous; female flowers, the familiar red-purple "larch roses," are followed by green cones.

C Larch
Larix sp
Female cone
'Larch rose'
Male cone

10

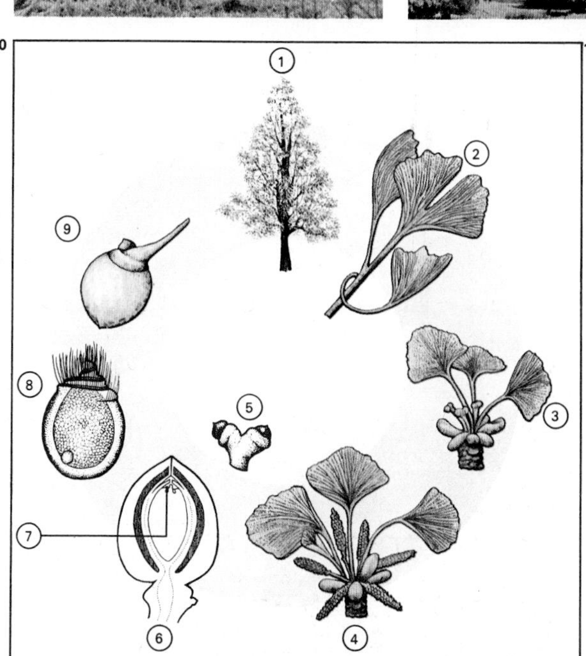

1
2
3
4
5
6
7
8
9

11 *Welwitschia* sp

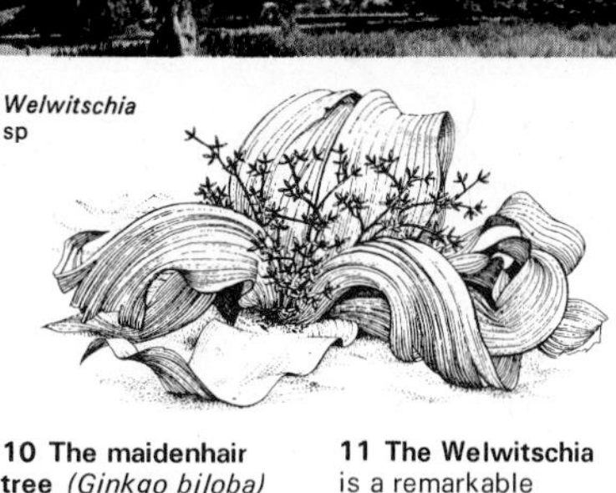

12

Seed fern (Cycad)
Cycas revoluta

10 The maidenhair tree *(Ginkgo biloba)* [1] has typically lobed leaves [2] with parallel veins. The sexes are separate: female trees bear ovules [3], male ones [4] produce pollen. The young ovule [5] matures into a structure [6] equipped to receive pollen. On landing on the ovule, pollen is drawn into the pollen chamber [7]. Two large motile spermatozoids [8] are produced, fertilization takes place, and a naked seed is formed [9].

11 The Welwitschia is a remarkable woody plant, the sole member of its family. It is adapted to desert life by restricted water loss, and it grows only in parts of South-West Africa.

12 Cycads have a long history dating back to Triassic times. They look like palms or ferns and today are found in the tropics. *Cycas revoluta,* from Japan, is widely grown in warm areas, and in greenhouses in cooler regions.

Pines and other conifers

The conifers, as their name suggests, are plants with cones. What makes them most remarkable is their size and longevity. Conifers are by far the largest plants on earth, and at their tallest—the maximum is 367ft (112m)—literally "reach for the sky." For man a century is a remarkable lifespan, but some conifers live for a thousand years.

The conifers are classified into eight families, and of the 50 genera 33 are confined to the Northern Hemisphere. Nearly all are evergreens with tough, dark-green needlelike or scalelike leaves and they form dense and deeply shaded forests.

Man has used conifers for hundreds of years, particularly for timber and for paper-making, and these trees have the added advantage of being able to thrive on poor, thin soil where arable farming is impossible. Conifers add wood to their stems faster than broadleaved trees do and can thrive even where the Sun's rays are weak.

Conifers are also ornamental and have graced gardens and palaces since ancient times. Their upstanding, formal appearance adds elegance to man-made architecture.

CONNECTIONS

See also

440 The cone bearers
592 Northern evergreen forests
608 Mountain life
364 Forestry

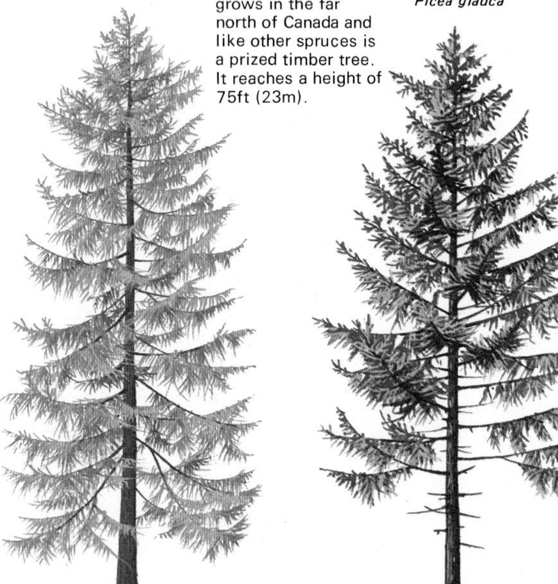

1 Tamarack *Larix laricina*

2 White spruce *Picea glauca*

1 The tamarack or American larch of eastern North America can grow to a height of 60ft (18m). Like other larches this conifer is unusual in being deciduous and not evergreen. All are classified with the pines (family Pinaceae). They have resinous, weather-resistant timber.

2 The white spruce grows in the far north of Canada and like other spruces is a prized timber tree. It reaches a height of 75ft (23m).

3 Lawson cypress *Chamaecyparis lawsoniana*

4

5

5 The Scotch pine *(Pinus sylvestris)* is seen here in the setting from which its name is derived—on the shores of a Scottish loch. This tree, which can grow 2 to 3 ft (0.6 to 0.9m) a year for 20 or 30 years is the best known of the family Pinaceae. All pines *(Pinus)* have two kinds of leaves; there are brown, scale leaves on the long shoots and needle-shaped ones on the short shoots.

6 The Norway spruce *(Picea abies)* is the commonest species of *Picea* and Europe's tallest native tree, reaching a height of 180ft (54m). It is seen here growing in the Italian Tyrol, in the Alps. The tree may live more than 1,000 years and may not reach maturity (as shown by the production of cones) until it is 30 years old. It can tolerate shade and thus forms thick forests.

4 The cypresses are well known as ornamental garden trees and include golden varieties. This species, *Cupressus macrocarpa*, which grows to a height of 150ft (46m) is shown here in a Mediterranean setting. All of the 15 to 20 species are distinguished by scalelike leaves.

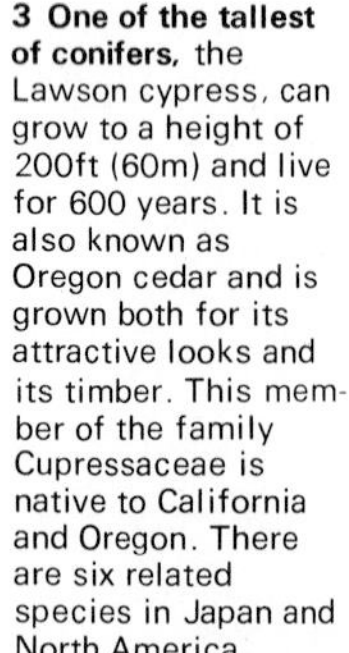

3 One of the tallest of conifers, the Lawson cypress, can grow to a height of 200ft (60m) and live for 600 years. It is also known as Oregon cedar and is grown both for its attractive looks and its timber. This member of the family Cupressaceae is native to California and Oregon. There are six related species in Japan and North America.

6

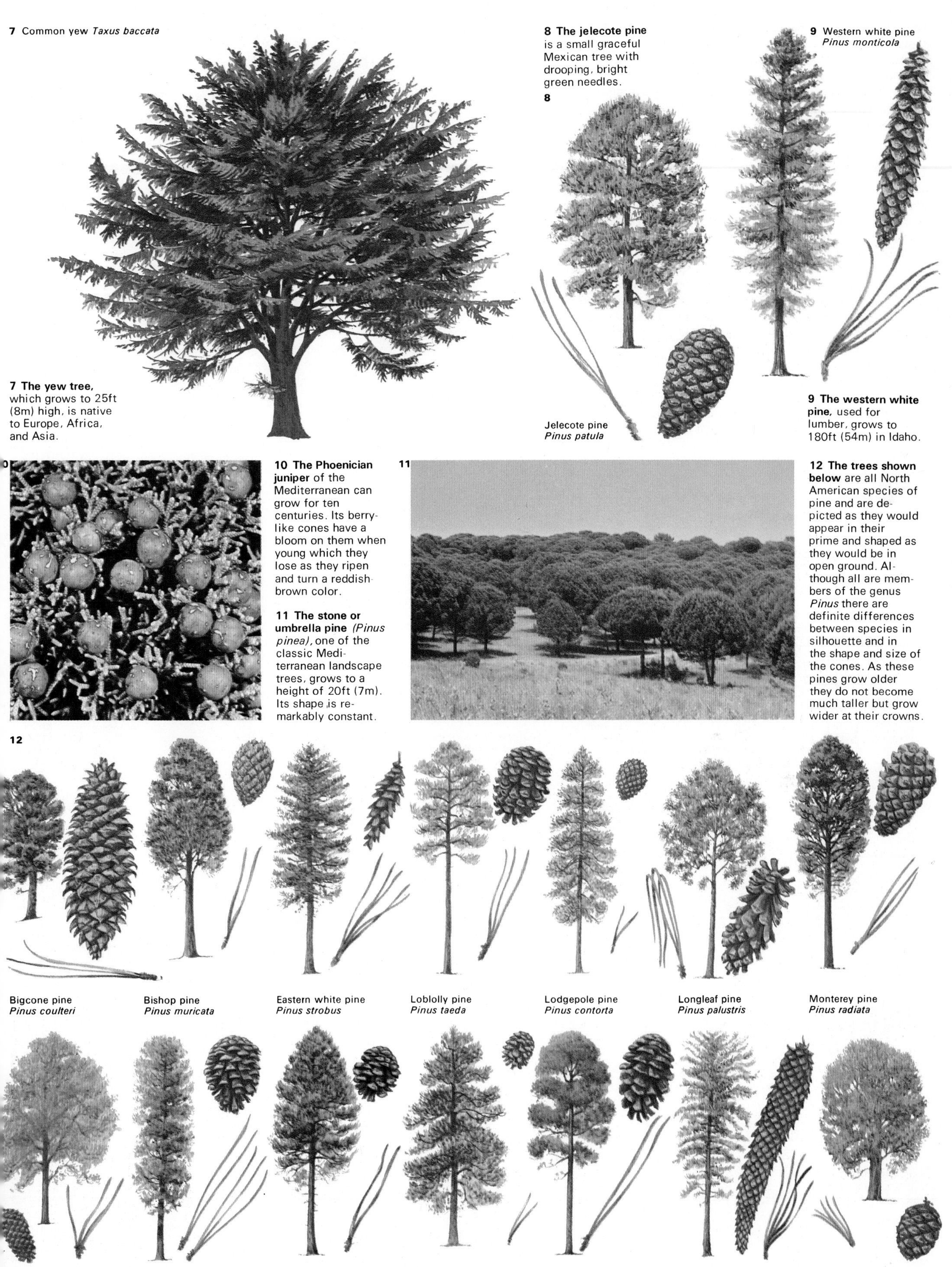

7 Common yew *Taxus baccata*

7 The yew tree, which grows to 25ft (8m) high, is native to Europe, Africa, and Asia.

8 The jelecote pine is a small graceful Mexican tree with drooping, bright green needles.

8

Jelecote pine
Pinus patula

9 Western white pine
Pinus monticola

9 The western white pine, used for lumber, grows to 180ft (54m) in Idaho.

10

10 The Phoenician juniper of the Mediterranean can grow for ten centuries. Its berry-like cones have a bloom on them when young which they lose as they ripen and turn a reddish brown color.

11 The stone or umbrella pine *(Pinus pinea)*, one of the classic Mediterranean landscape trees, grows to a height of 20ft (7m). Its shape is remarkably constant.

11

12 The trees shown below are all North American species of pine and are depicted as they would appear in their prime and shaped as they would be in open ground. Although all are members of the genus *Pinus* there are definite differences between species in silhouette and in the shape and size of the cones. As these pines grow older they do not become much taller but grow wider at their crowns.

12

Bigcone pine
Pinus coulteri

Bishop pine
Pinus muricata

Eastern white pine
Pinus strobus

Loblolly pine
Pinus taeda

Lodgepole pine
Pinus contorta

Longleaf pine
Pinus palustris

Monterey pine
Pinus radiata

Pitch pine
Pinus rigida

Ponderosa pine
Pinus ponderosa

Red pine
Pinus resinosa

Shore pine
Pinus contorta

Slash pine
Pinus elliottii

Sugar pine
Pinus lambertiana

Whitebark pine
Pinus albicaulis

Flowering plants: two seed leaves

Most of the flowering plants belong to a group that botanists call the dicotyledons because within the seeds of these plants the embryo has two separate seed leaves, or cotyledons, attached to it. Such plants have a characteristic internal anatomy [Key]. The many woody shrubs and trees among dicotyledons provide useful timber, but the nonwoody dicotyledons are just as valuable to man because many are food plants.

Worldwide dicotyledon distribution

Nonwoody dicotyledons occur almost everywhere; each continent has a large population, including the Arctic and the Antarctic. These plants fill many different ecological niches and colonize all types of habitats except permanent snow and ice, from natural regions such as marshes, forests, rocky cliffs, and pastures to totally manmade areas such as walls, roofs, roadsides, and demolition sites.

Ornamentals and food providers

Almost all families of dicotyledons provide plants that are used for food or grown as ornamentals. Many buttercups [1] and their relatives (family Ranunculaceae) are grown as ornamental garden flowers. These include anemones, pasqueflowers, delphiniums, and clematis. In the mustard family (Cruciferae) a few species such as stocks, wallflowers, honesty, and alyssum are grown as garden flowers, but much more important are the cabbage and its many relations of the genus *Brassica*. Cabbage, brussels sprouts, cauliflower, broccoli, curly kale and many other cabbagelike vegetables are all different forms of a single plant species. Other crucifers are rape (a turnip crop), which is an important source of vegetable oil, and both black and white mustard. Rutabagas and turnips, which revolutionized stock farming in the eighteenth century, also belong to this family. Another important crop family is the Solanaceae or nightshade family, which includes the potato, tomato, and many drug sources such as deadly nightshade and henbane. The daisy family (Compositae) [7] provides not only many decorative flowers but also artichokes (Jerusalem and globe), lettuce, chicory, and endive, and oil crops such as sunflower. The rose family (Rosaceae) is represented by orchard fruits (apples, pears, plums, peaches), blackberries, raspberries, strawberries, and garden flowers throughout the temperate world. Among the latter are geums, lady's-mantles, *Kerria, Dryas* and, of course, roses. Besides food and ornamental plants, certain families, such as the mint family (Labiatae), with its many aromatic species, have been used from ancient times as flavorings. These include mint [11], thyme, sage, basil, and marjoram. Fruits of certain families are also aromatic and are known as spices. Examples from the carrot family (Umbelliferae) are dill, fennel, coriander and caraway seeds. The roots of a few species are also used as spices. Among these are horseradish, in the mustard family, and the licorice, which is a legume.

Other plant families yield fibers for clothing or rope-making. The mallow family (Malvaceae) is represented by the cotton plant, and flax belongs to its own family (Linaceae). Hemp, or *Cannabis sativa*

CONNECTIONS

See also
446 Flowers of fields and roadsides
424 The plant kingdom
456 How flowering plants reproduce
452 Flowering plants: one seed leaf
448 Woody flowering plants
430 The way plants work
604 Life in the desert
330 Staple foods: legumes
332 Staple foods: tubers
362 Fiber and oil crops
334 Vegetables
336 Green salads

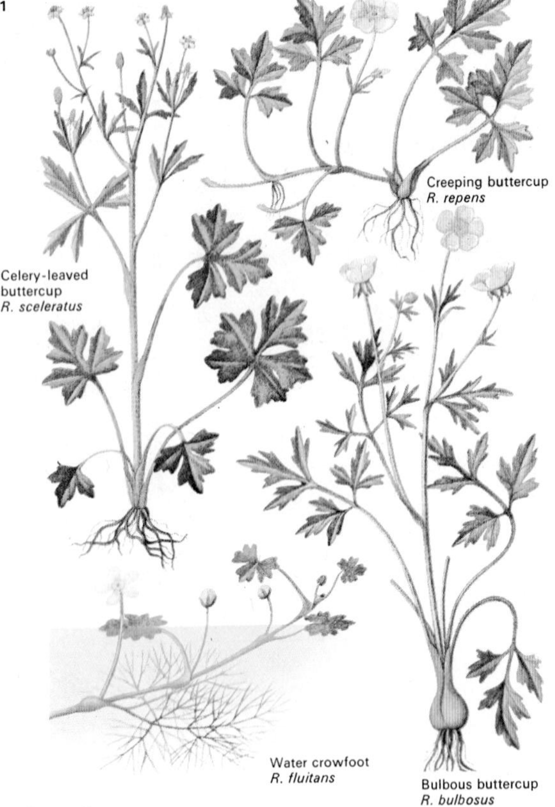

1
Celery-leaved buttercup
R. sceleratus
Creeping buttercup
R. repens
Water crowfoot
R. fluitans
Bulbous buttercup
R. bulbosus

1 Buttercups are common plants of the family Ranunculaceae that vary greatly in shape and size. They occur in many ecological niches from water to fields. The crowfoots are generally aquatic and have white flowers. Their leaves are of two kinds—floating and submerged. Other buttercups of different species grow on dry land, but each occupies a separate habitat and has distinctive anatomical characteristics. *Ranunculus bulbosus*, for example, as its name suggests, has an underground bulb. Both the creeping and bulbous buttercups are prolific weeds of fields, roadsides, and gardens.

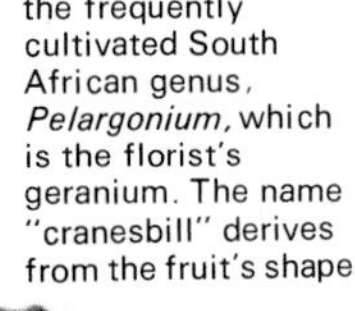

2 The meadow cranesbill is a beautiful plant common on grassy roadsides. There is a rare variety that has white flowers. Closely related is the frequently cultivated South African genus, *Pelargonium*, which is the florist's geranium. The name "cranesbill" derives from the fruit's shape.

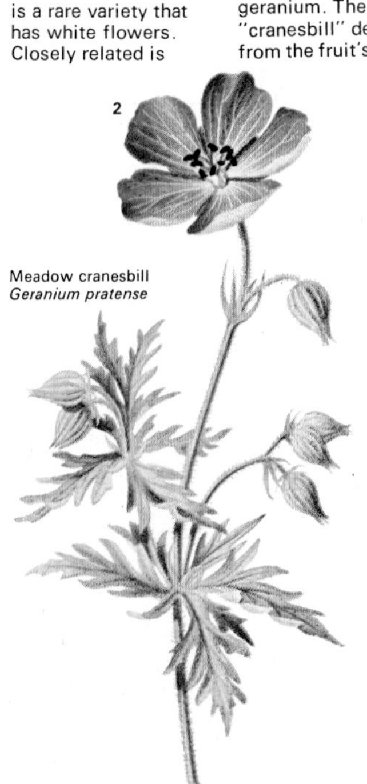
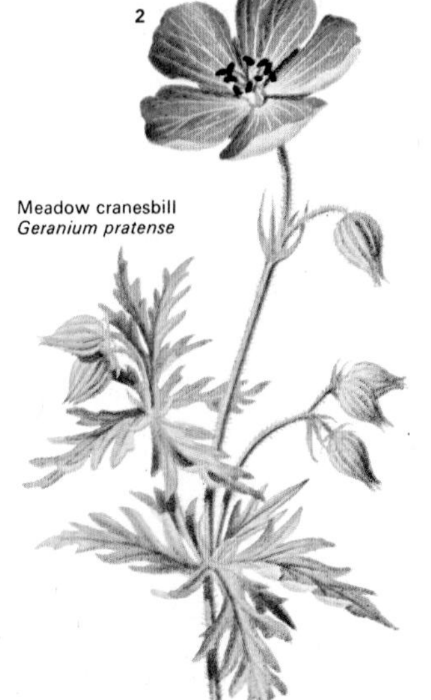

2
Meadow cranesbill
Geranium pratense

3

Deptford pink
Dianthus armeria

3 The Deptford pink is a member of the family Caryophyllaceae and is closely related to garden carnations. It has a wide range and is found on sandy soils throughout Europe; it has also been introduced to North America. Although it is a rare plant there, local populations may be quite extensive.

4 Grass of Parnassus is not a grass but is related to the saxifrages. It occurs in damp grassland in Europe, temperate Asia, and North America. The pretty five-petaled white flower has gleaming golden pinheads called staminodes that entice insects to visit the plant in search of nectar. This is the only means the plant has of attracting insect visitors, which then pollinate it. The flower stalk has a heart-shaped leaf.

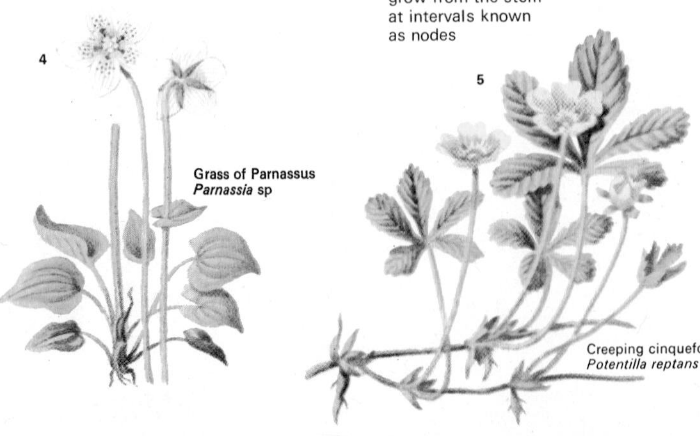

4
Grass of Parnassus
Parnassia sp
5
Creeping cinquefoil
Potentilla reptans

5 The creeping cinquefoil is a member of the widespread rose family and occurs as a common weed in gardens and fields. It has yellow flowers and leaves with five leaflets like the fingers of a hand. The roots grow from the stem at intervals known as nodes

6 The rue-leaved saxifrage is a rare plant of rocks, walls, and dry soils. It is a member of the widespread family Saxifragaceae. The name, which in Latin means "breaker of rocks," illustrates the kind of stony habitat that this plant and its relatives occupy. Saxifrages are frequently grown in the rock garden—examples are *S. aizoon*, which lines a north slope or the shade of a large rock, and *S. hosti*, which forms silvery rosettes.

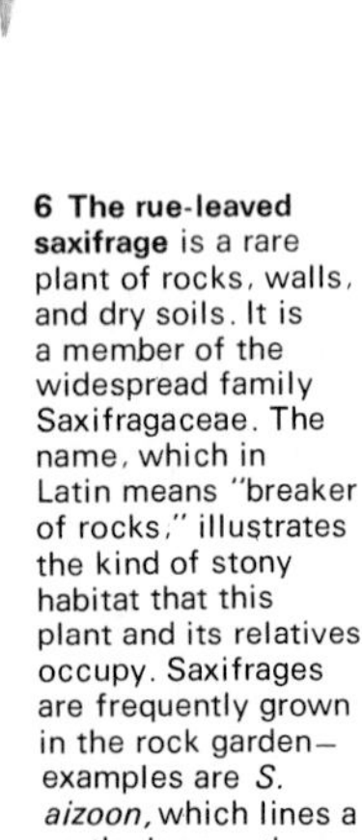
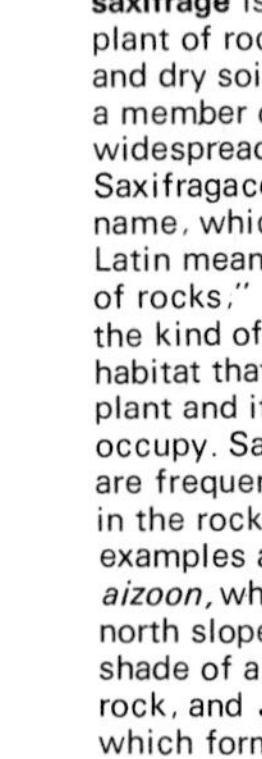

6
Rue-leaved saxifrage
Saxifraga tridactylites

(family Cannabiaceae) provides the drug cannabis (marijuana) and also yields the familiar rope fiber. Some herbaceous dicotyledons grow where the supply of nutrients is very poor, such as in bogs.

Insectivorous plants

Plants have evolved to fill low-nutrient niches and in order to obtain the missing nutrients (especially nitrogen) some resort to trapping and digesting insects. These insectivorous species belong to several families. They include the sundews, butterworts, bladderworts, and the pitcher plants of the genera *Sarracenia* and *Nepenthes,* which are found in the tropics and subtropics. These plants have many different ways of catching their food. Sundews *(Drosera)* trap insects by means of "fly-paper." They have short tentacles coated with sticky adhesive and insects passing close to the plants or landing on them get stuck. The plants then produce digestive enzymes that dissolve the insect and the plants absorb the nutrient fluid. Butterworts *(Pinguicula)* behave similarly, but produce the adhesive over the whole leaf surface.

Bladderworts *(Utricularia)* grow in water and have traps, each one of which is a small vesicle with a door and signal hairs growing near it. When a small water creature touches these hairs, the door opens and both water and creature rush into the trap, where digestive enzymes break down the food. The pitcher plants are basically pitfall traps that attract insects and other small creatures to the top of a container, often by the promise of nectar. The victim eventually slips on the smooth surface and falls into a soup of enzymes where hairs directed downward trap it until it drowns. The best known insectivorous plant is the Venus flytrap *(Dionaea muscipula),* the leaf of which has a hinged trap at its tip with touch-sensitive hairs. These will not respond to a single touch, but require a short burst of touches, such as that given by a moving insect, to trigger a response, bringing the two halves of the trap together with a sudden snap. The trapped prey is then dissolved and digested.

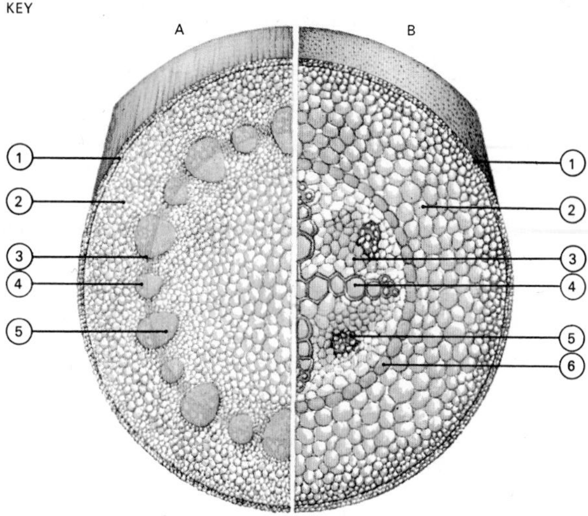
KEY
A
B
1
2
3
4
5
6

The hallmarks of a dicotyledon show in its stem [A] and root [B]. Both are covered by epidermis [1] surrounding a cortex [2], inside which the growing layer or cambium [3] builds vascular bundles containing water-conducting xylem [4] and food-conducting phloem [5]. In the root the pattern is cross-shaped and there is an endodermis [6].

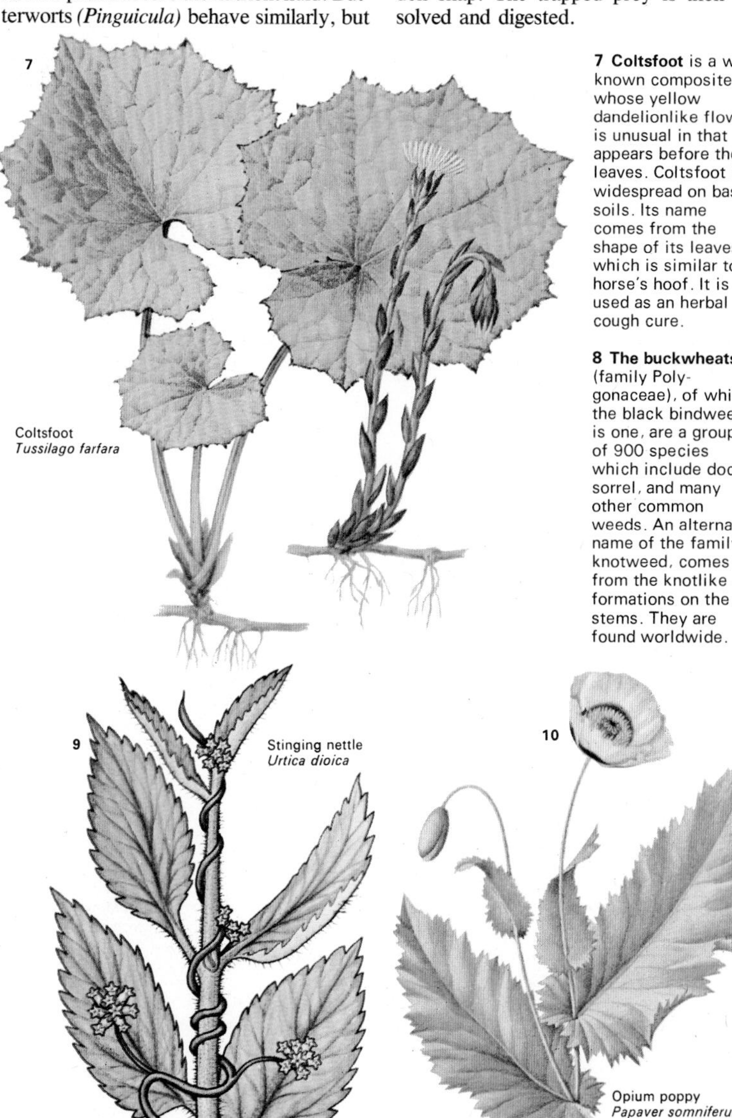
7
Coltsfoot
Tussilago farfara
9
Stinging nettle
Urtica dioica
Dodder
Cuscuta sp

7 Coltsfoot is a well-known composite whose yellow dandelionlike flower is unusual in that it appears before the leaves. Coltsfoot is widespread on basic soils. Its name comes from the shape of its leaves, which is similar to a horse's hoof. It is used as an herbal cough cure.

8 The buckwheats (family Polygonaceae), of which the black bindweed is one, are a group of 900 species which include dock, sorrel, and many other common weeds. An alternate name of the family, knotweed, comes from the knotlike formations on the stems. They are found worldwide.

8

Black bindweed
Polygonum convolvulus

9 The parasitic dodder attacks few plants except the stinging nettle. It feeds by means of haustoria, outgrowths of the stem that enter the host plant.

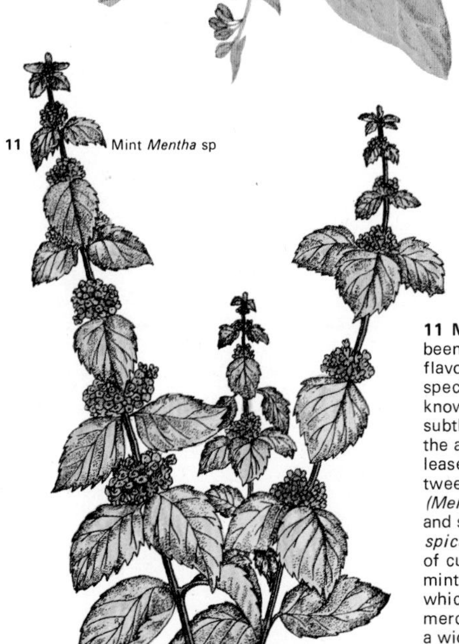
10
Opium poppy
Papaver somniferum
11
Mint *Mentha* sp

10 The opium poppy has been cultivated since the Middle Ages. The drug opium and its derivatives, morphine and heroin, are extracted from the latex of the seed pods. The seeds themselves are used as cattle food and as a source of oil. It is probably of European origin.

11 Mint has long been used as a food flavoring. Many species of mint are known and they show subtle differences in the aromas they release. Crosses between water mint *(Mentha aquatica)* and spearmint *(M. spicata)* are the basis of cultivated peppermint *(M. piperita),* which is commercially grown on a wide scale in the United States and used to flavor chewing gum, toothpaste, and many drugs.

Flowers of fields and roadsides

Of all the world's flowering plants the nonwoody members of the dicotyledon group (plants with two seed leaves) are the most numerous. Of the total of 200,000 dicotyledon species, which are grouped into over 250 families, more than half are nonwoody herbs. Many of these herbs are cultivated in gardens and greenhouses in temperate regions, where they are treated as ornamental plants or as vegetables.

The largest families of dicotyledons include both familiar and useful herbs, such as the buttercups (Ranunculaceae), the brassicas (Cruciferae), the spurges (Euphorbiaceae), the roses (Rosaceae), the legumes (Leguminosae), the carrots (Umbelliferae), the nettles (Labiatae), the potatoes (Solanaceae), and the daisies (Compositae).

Although many of these herbs are employed by man as foods and flavorings, many others are weeds that hamper his agriculture, crowding his plants and robbing them of valuable nutrients. Most weed plants have extremely efficient reproductive mechanisms and many of them spread vegetatively as well as by means of seed.

CONNECTIONS

See also
444 Flowering plants: two seed leaves
424 The plant kingdom
318 Protecting crops
358 Culinary and medicinal herbs
336 Green salads

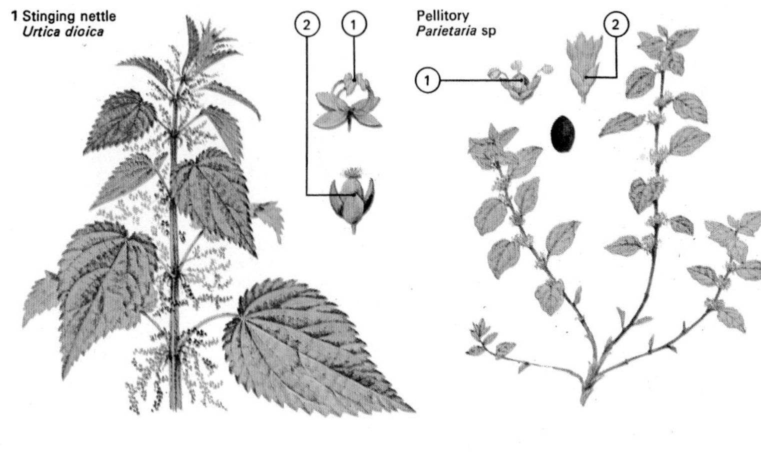

1 Stinging nettle
Urtica dioica
2
1
Pellitory
Parietaria sp
1
2

1 The stinging nettle, a common weed of neglected gardens, and the pellitory are two of the few species of the family Urticaceae that grow in temperate regions. Native to Eurasia and naturalized in North America, each plant bears both male [1] and female [2] flowers. There are 35 species of *Urtica* and all of them have bristlelike stinging hairs, which are long, hollow cells. The tips of these are toughened with silica and they are easily broken off. When the plant is touched the hairs penetrate the skin like surgical needles; the tips are lost and the poison contained in the cells is released. The pellitory is essentially a nettle that does not sting. Both it and the stinging nettle have been used in herbal medicine.

2

Sage
Salvia sp

Thyme
Thymus vulgaris

Marjoram
Origanum vulgare

Lavender
Lavendula sp

Rosemary
Rosmarinus officinalis

2 Many culinary herbs such as those illustrated here, are members of the family Labiatae. Their forms vary, although members of this family can be recognized by their squarish stems and distinctively shaped flowers. Their characteristic smell is caused by aromatic oils in their leaves and stems. The oils are contained in capsules near the surface and they are released on drying or bruising. Some of these oils are used in the manufacture of perfumes. The leaves are used for seasoning.

3

3 The dahlia "tuber" consists of a bunch of swollen roots. These contain food materials that the plant can use to overwinter and they also serve as a means of vegetative reproduction.

4 *Crassula falcata*

4 The succulent *Crassula falcata* is a South African member of the large order Rosales. As in many plants that live in hot, dry climates, its leaves are fleshy and can store water, thus enabling the plant to withstand long periods of drought. Nearly all the plants in the crassula family (Crassulaceae) are found in subtropical Africa, temperate areas of Asia, and in Mediterranean regions. They are often found on rocks and mountainsides.

5 The French or Provence rose and *Escallonia,* although in different families, share common grouping in the order Rosales. The French rose, from the Mediterranean, is one of the many rose species from which cultivated varieties have been derived.

6 Large, watery fruits are a common feature of the cucumber and its relations in the family Cucurbitaceae. The plants are generally large and covered with coarse hairs and many have tendrils that help them climb and scramble. Although most of the fruits are edible, those of *Bryonia* are unusual in being small, red, and poisonous. Dried fruits of the gourds are used in Mexico to make musical instruments called maracas.

7 This stonecrop is a plant of central and eastern Europe that lives on rocky ground. It is related to the rose and often cultivated in rock gardens. There are more than 500 *Sedum* species.

9 The common ragwort may grow as either a biennial or a perennial. It is a member of the family Compositae, grows to 4 ft (1.3m) high, and may be harmful to sheep if eaten by them.

10 Persicaria, or lady's thumb, is a weed that is hard to eradicate. It is widespread on farmland. Other members of the buckwheat family (Polygonaceae) include dock, sorrel, and rhubarb.

13 Curled dock gets its name from the wavy margins of its leaves. This plant (family Polygonaceae) is related to sorrel. Application of dock leaves is a country remedy for nettle stings.

8 The common dandelion (family Compositae) is one of the most widespread of grassland perennial weeds. It is hard to eradicate because it reproduces both vegetatively and by means of air-borne seeds.

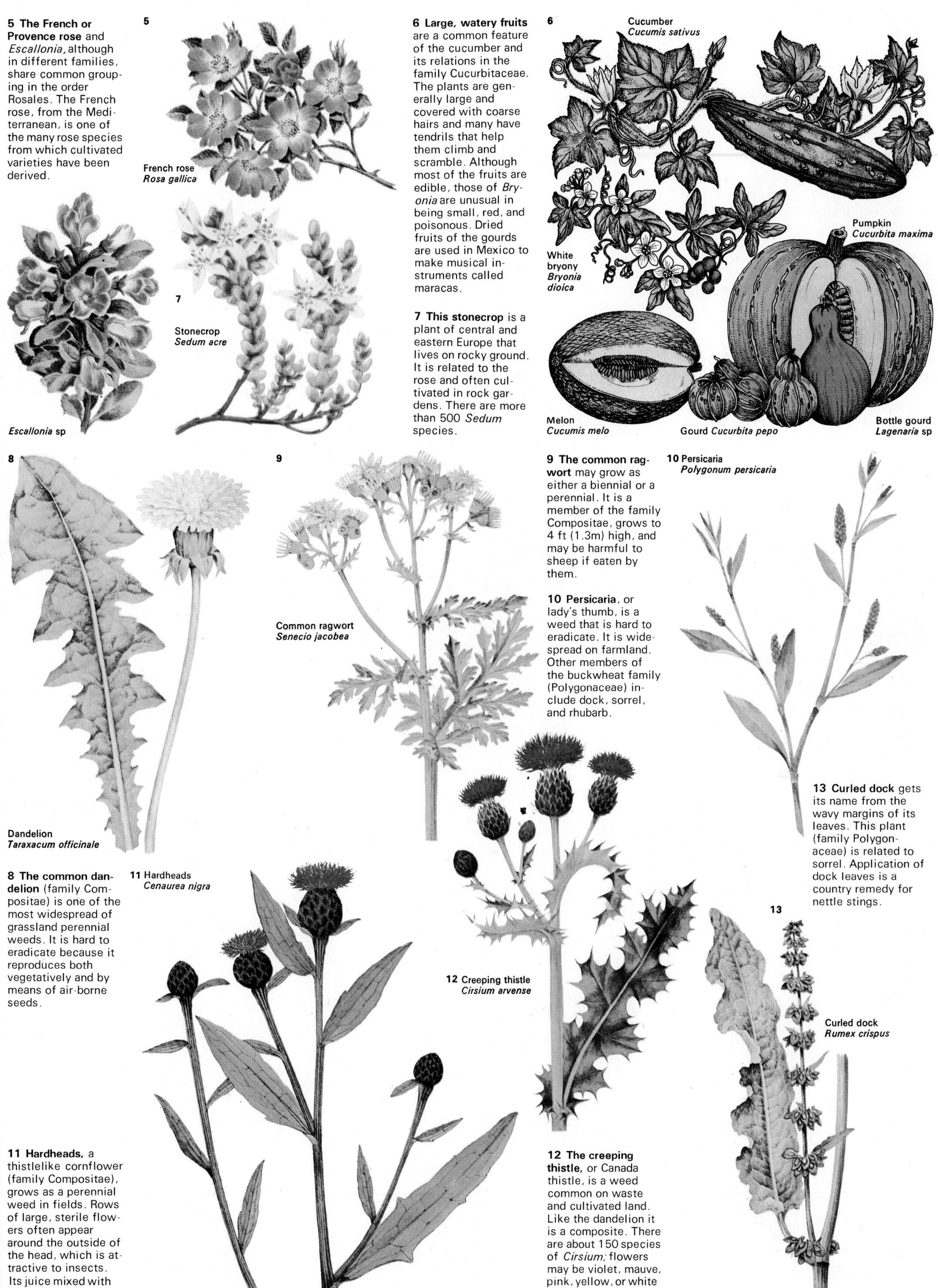

5
French rose
Rosa gallica
Escallonia sp
7
Stonecrop
Sedum acre
6
Cucumber
Cucumis sativus
White bryony
Bryonia dioica
Pumpkin
Cucurbita maxima
Melon
Cucumis melo
Gourd *Cucurbita pepo*
Bottle gourd
Lagenaria sp
8
Dandelion
Taraxacum officinale
9
Common ragwort
Senecio jacobea
10 Persicaria
Polygonum persicaria
11 Hardheads
Cenaurea nigra
12 Creeping thistle
Cirsium arvense
13
Curled dock
Rumex crispus

11 Hardheads, a thistlelike cornflower (family Compositae), grows as a perennial weed in fields. Rows of large, sterile flowers often appear around the outside of the head, which is attractive to insects. Its juice mixed with alum is a dye.

12 The creeping thistle, or Canada thistle, is a weed common on waste and cultivated land. Like the dandelion it is a composite. There are about 150 species of *Cirsium;* flowers may be violet, mauve, pink, yellow, or white in color.

Woody flowering plants

The world's flowering trees, although they appear to be quite different from the rest of the Earth's flora, do not in fact form a distinct botanical category. Most of them are simply flowering plants (angiosperms) that possess woody stems. All living trees, with the exception of the gymnosperms such as conifers and ginkgo, are flowering trees. These are divided botanically on the basis of the number of seed leaves or cotyledons they possess; monocotyledons have one seed leaf and the dicotyledons have two.

Relatively few monocotyledons are flowering trees and those that are, unlike dicotyledonous trees, produce no wood. The most familiar are the several hundred palm species, such as the date *(Phoenix dactylifera)* and the coconut *(Cocos nucifera)*. Most tree species are dicotyledons and the majority grow in the world's tropical forests. Many valuable wood trees make up this group, including teak, ebony, and mahogany. In contrast, the temperate regions support fewer tree species. Oak, ash, beech, and birch are the four most common temperate trees. They grow in mixed woodlands, often accompanied by other species such as the hickory, or (less usually) form single-species forests, as in the case of the black beech [6] of New Zealand.

Size and growth of trees

The key to the size of trees lies in a continuous ring of cells within the trunk known as the cambium [1]. The multiplication of these cells, which lie just below the bark, results in growth. The cells produced by the cambium rapidly become specialized as elements of the transport system within the trunk, by which water, food substances, and essential mineral salts are carried through the trunk, branches, and leaves.

The tree's structural and mechanical strength—provided by its woodiness—is a consequence of the fate of the cells produced by the cambium. As the cells of the water transporting system, known collectively as the xylem, enlarge and age they gradually become invested with layers of lignin, a tough substance related chemically to cellulose. Lignin provides a rigidity that helps trees to stand erect.

Division of the cambial cells does not proceed at a steady rate. In temperate trees growth is much faster in summer than in winter. As a result the woody cells that arise in the summer months appear as lighter-colored rings when the tree trunk is cut across. Because this is a yearly cycle of growth the tree's age is easily determined by counting the number of these annual rings. In tropical trees growth patterns follow the cycle of wet and dry seasons.

The bark that covers the tree is a product of a special tissue, the cork cambium. This protective covering for the all-important cambium varies greatly in thickness and consistency from species to species. The bark of the silver birch, for example, is thin and papery, while that of the cork oak is extremely thick and porous. In some savanna trees the bark is even fire-resistant.

Leaves and photosynthesis

Trees, like all other green plants, produce the food they require by photosynthesis. This is a process in which energy from the

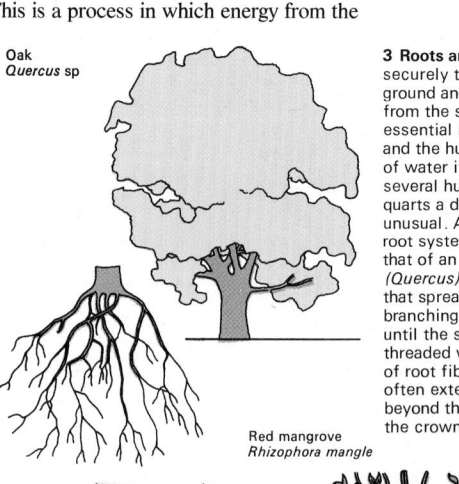

CONNECTIONS

See also
444 Flowering plants: two seed leaves
450 Flowering trees, shrubs, and climbers
594 Northern temperate woodlands
364 Forestry
368 Trees: problems of climate and disease
346 Vines and grapes
354 Coffee, tea, and cocoa
356 Seeds and spices
360 Berries, nuts, and olives
338 Temperate fruits
340 Tropical fruits

1

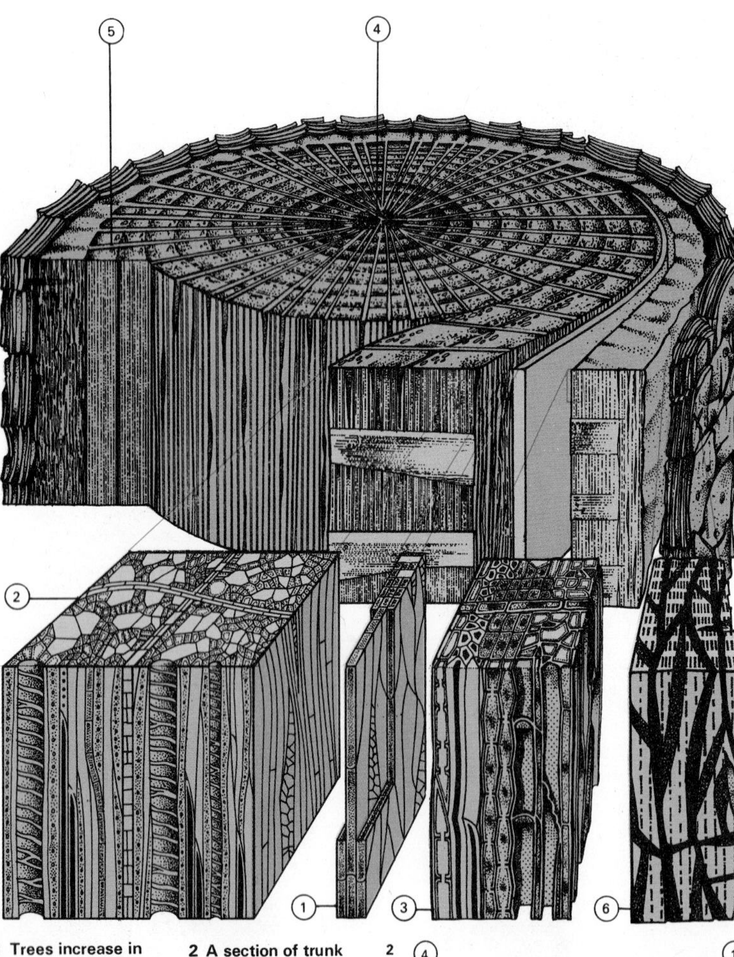

1 Trees increase in girth by rings of new wood produced annually in temperate zones but less often in the tropics. The cambium [1] produces xylem [2] and phloem [3]. They are alive but the heartwood [4] is dead. The medullary rays [5] allow the transport of food across the trunk. Bark [6] is a protective outer coating.

2

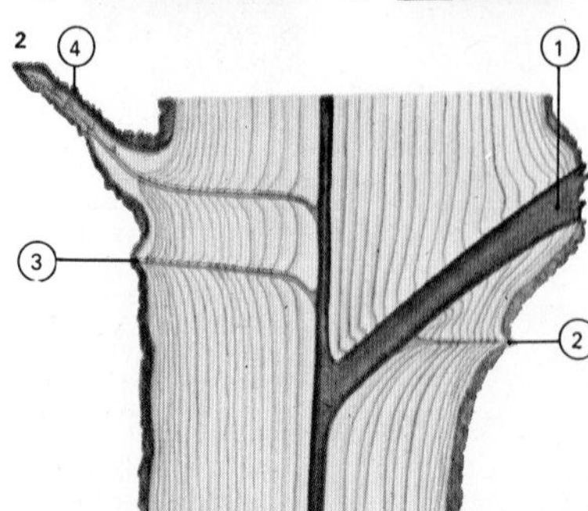

2 A section of trunk is cut here to show how buds are held in reserve in case the main shoot is lost. After a mature branch has been broken off [1] a "suppressed" bud [2] begins to grow. A totally suppressed bud [3] grows just enough to keep pace with the thickening of the trunk. A short shoot [4] may grow into a branch.

3 Oak *Quercus* sp

Red mangrove *Rhizophora mangle*

White mangrove *Avicennia officinalis*

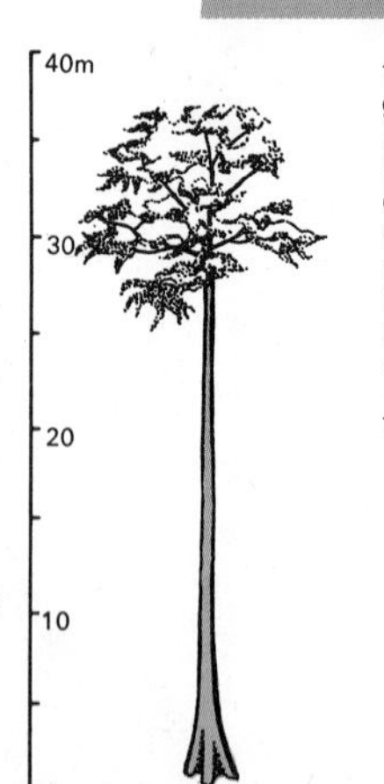

40m
30
20
10
0

Tropical forest tree

3 Roots anchor a tree securely to the ground and take up from the soil the essential minerals and the huge quantity of water it needs—several hundred quarts a day is not unusual. A fibrous root system such as that of an oak *(Quercus)* has roots that spread outward branching repeatedly until the soil is threaded with a mat of root fibers that often extends far beyond the reach of the crown of the tree. The red mangrove *(Rhizophora mangle)* rises above its swampy habitat on stilt roots that enable it to survive changes in the mud level. The white mangrove *(Avicennia officinalis)* sends roots upward in the airless mud to enable them to obtain oxygen. Root systems develop in different ways. The shallow roots of tall rain-forest trees concentrate in the humus-rich topsoil and grow flangelike buttresses that support the trunk. These can grow to 13 ft (4m) up and out. The black alder *(Alnus glutinosa)* is another resident of waterlogged places that has supporting roots. Although root structures vary, their purpose is the same.

Sun is trapped by the green pigment chlorophyll in the leaves and used to build food materials from water and carbon dioxide. The leaves of trees show a profusion of shape and size and may be simple or complex. Near the extremes of the scale are the small, simple leaves of the birch measuring up to 2in (5cm) in length and the giant leaves of the rubber plant, which can be more than 12in (30cm) long.

Each leaf on a tree has a limited life, which depends on climatic factors. In many temperate trees all the leaves are shed every autumn and reappear in spring [4]. These trees are described as deciduous. In contrast, evergreens are those in which the leaves die and are replaced at random every two or three years. Large numbers of tropical trees are evergreen but those that endure a dry season are often deciduous.

In temperate regions the flowers of trees are generally unspectacular, often to such a degree that they appear to the casual observer to be nonexistent. The reason for this lack of floral flamboyance is that these trees are wind pollinated and do not need to attract living pollinators such as insects. Those woody plants that are pollinated by insects—most shrubs, climbers, and tropical trees—produce large, colorful, often scented flowers [7, 8].

The results of successful pollination—the fruits of trees—are as varied as the flowers. The winged fruits of the maple and ash, the huge nuts of tropical trees such as the coconut, the fleshy fruits of apples and plums, and the pealike pods of the acacia are some familiar examples.

The future of flowering trees

The distribution of flowering trees over the Earth has varied greatly since these plants made their first appearance. For example, analysis of pollen remains shows that preglacial European woodlands contained not only the familiar modern trees but also those regarded as alien species, such as magnolias and rhododendrons. Were it not for their removal by man, forests would still cover huge areas of the globe. Only in recent years has man made any attempt to conserve the trees of temperate regions.

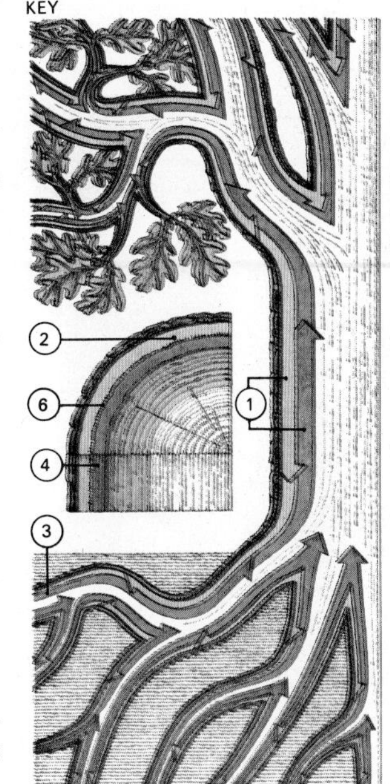
KEY
2
6
4
3
1

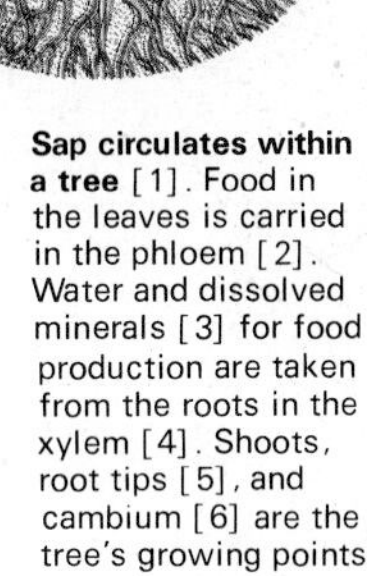
5

Sap circulates within a tree [1]. Food in the leaves is carried in the phloem [2]. Water and dissolved minerals [3] for food production are taken from the roots in the xylem [4]. Shoots, root tips [5], and cambium [6] are the tree's growing points.

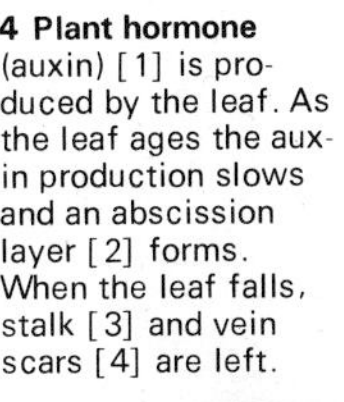
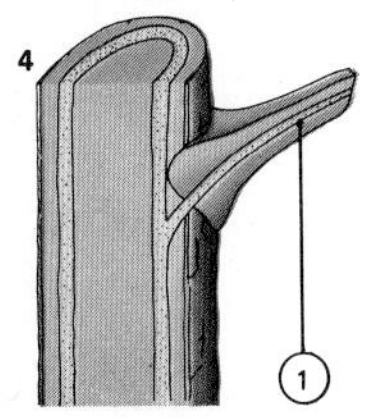
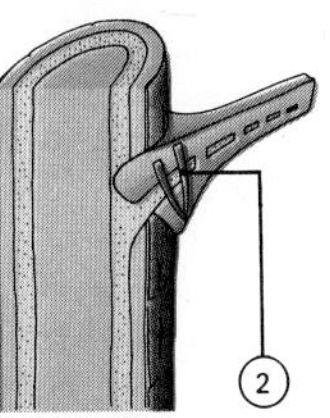
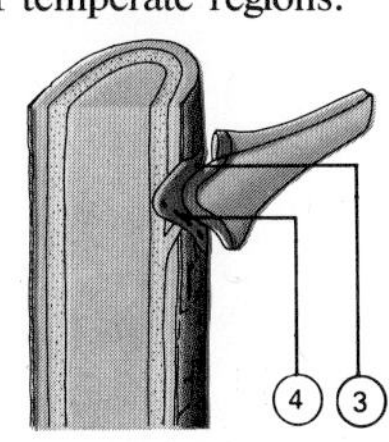
4
1
2
4
3

4 Plant hormone (auxin) [1] is produced by the leaf. As the leaf ages the auxin production slows and an abscission layer [2] forms. When the leaf falls, stalk [3] and vein scars [4] are left.

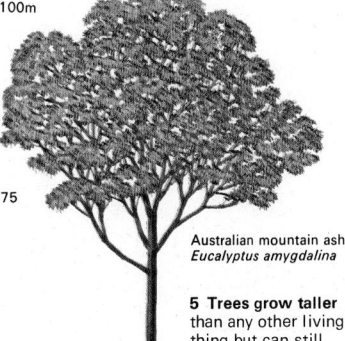

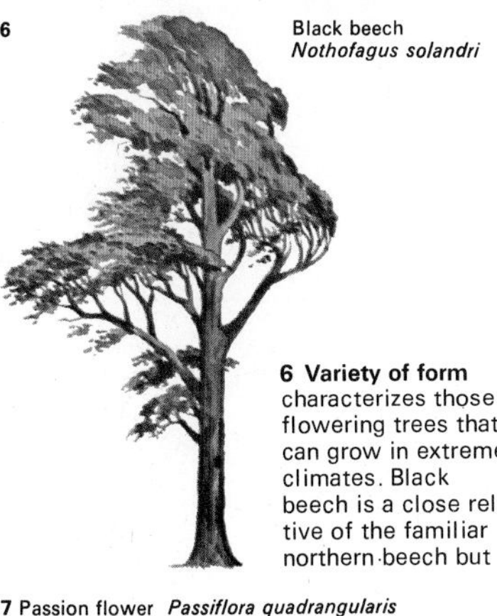
6
Black beech
Nothofagus solandri

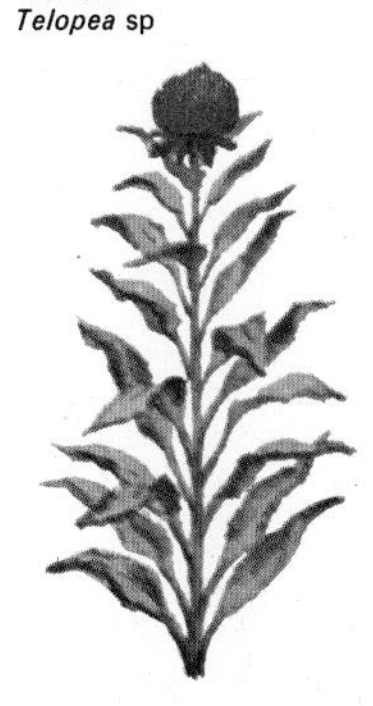
Waratah
Telopea sp

6 Variety of form characterizes those flowering trees that can grow in extreme climates. Black beech is a close relative of the familiar northern beech but grows in New Zealand where high rainfall and fertile soils produce jungle conditions. Growing to 100ft (31m), with evergreen sprays of tiny leaves up to 0.75in (2cm) long, black beech forms vast one-species forests of great beauty. Waratah is the floral emblem of New South Wales, Australia. A small shrubby plant with blooms up to 4in (10cm) long, it grows in near-desert conditions.

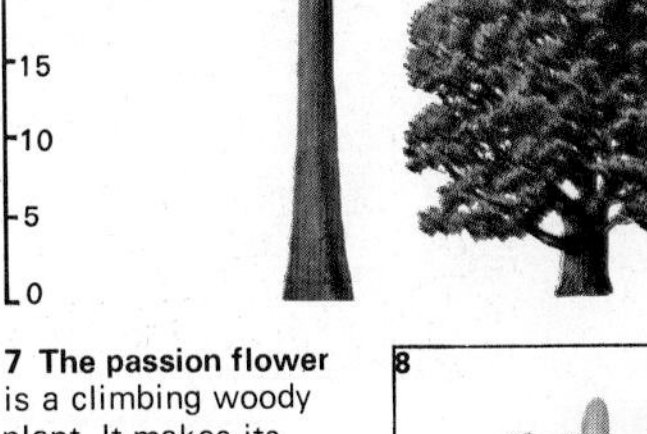
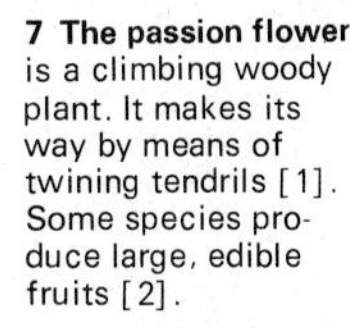
5
100m
75
50
25
20
15
10
5
0
Australian mountain ash
Eucalyptus amygdalina
English oak
Quercus robur
Frailjon
Espeletia sp
Bonsai tree

5 Trees grow taller than any other living thing but can still survive in miniature form. If the roots are restricted either artificially, as in bonsai perfected in Japan, or by natural means as when a seed germinates in very thin soil on a mountain, a fully formed tree only a few inches high will result. The California redwood, the tallest tree, is closely rivaled by a eucalyptus such as the mountain ash of Australia. The eucalyptus can grow as much as 45 ft (14 m) in two years. All parts of this tree are rich in oil. It is also grown for its hard timber. The English oak is one of 450 species of oak that grow as trees, bushes, and shrubs. It enlarges slowly—about 15 ft (4.5m) in 10 years—but produces wood of great strength. *Espeletia* grows on snowy ledges over 1,300 ft (400m) up in the Sierra Nevada.

7 Passion flower *Passiflora quadrangularis*
1
2

7 The passion flower is a climbing woody plant. It makes its way by means of twining tendrils [1]. Some species produce large, edible fruits [2].

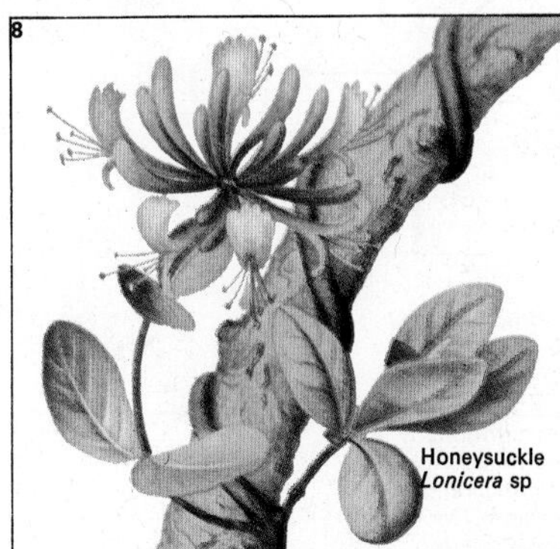

8
Honeysuckle
Lonicera sp

8 The honeysuckle twines its stem around its tree hosts. Saplings can be marked for life by its spiraling stem; such wood was once prized for walking canes. In extreme cases the host is completely strangled as the honeysuckle stops sap flow. The honeysuckle is insect-pollinated and the flowers have male and female parts.

Flowering trees, shrubs, and climbers

Most of the world's flowering trees are noted more for their shape and form than for their flowers. Nearly all of the broadleaved species (as distinct from narrow-leaved conifers) are deciduous and are members of the group of plants known as dicotyledons.

During the evolution of the flowering trees, shrubs, and climbers the great step forward came with insect pollination rather than wind pollination. One advantage of this is that there is no need for trees to grow in large stands in order for pollination, and thus fruit formation, to be successful.

Most trees with significant, attractive flowers belong to one of three plant families, the Magnoliaceae (magnolias), the Rosaceae (roses) and the Leguminosae (peas). Of these the rose relatives are the most important economically because they often bear edible fruits—apples, pears, plums, and cherries—for which they are cultivated. The fruits of many other tree families are eaten by man and include the olives (Oleaceae), figs (Moraceae), walnuts and pecans (Juglandaceae), chestnuts (Fagaceae) and oranges (Rutaceae).

CONNECTIONS

See also
448 Woody flowering plants
424 The plant kingdom
440 The cone bearers
742 Origins of curative medicine
1590 Bark, hide, and ho
1618 Rubber and plastic
342 Sugar and honey

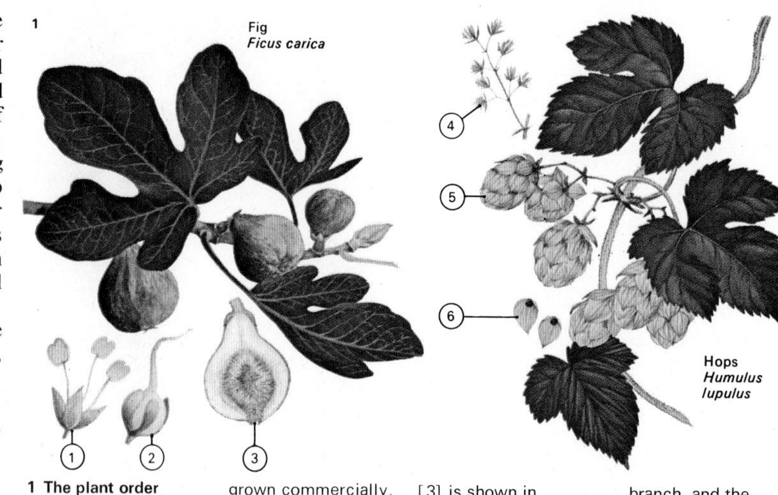
1
Fig
Ficus carica
1
2
3
4
5
6
Hops
Humulus lupulus

1 The plant order Urticales contains a number of diverse families as widely different as the elms, figs, hops, and stinging nettles. Many of these are grown commercially. The fig is grown for its fruit in warmer areas of the world. Male flowers [1] and female flowers [2] are found on the same tree. The fruit [3] is shown in section. Hops are cultivated in many countries and are used to flavor beer. Shown here are the male flower [4], the fruit [5] on a branch, and the seeds [6]. The other member of the Urticales that is commercially important is the elm, which is grown for its versatile timber.

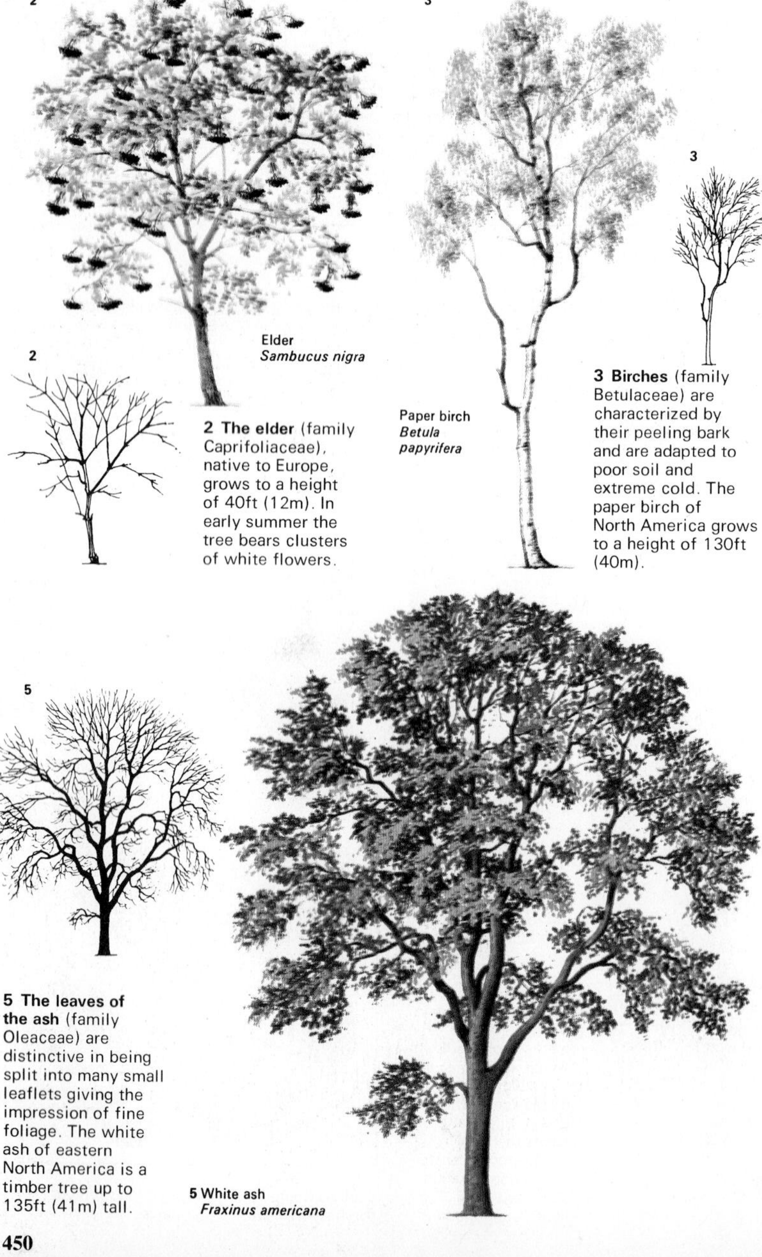
2
Elder
Sambucus nigra
2
3
Paper birch
Betula papyrifera
3
5
5 White ash
Fraxinus americana

2 The elder (family Caprifoliaceae), native to Europe, grows to a height of 40ft (12m). In early summer the tree bears clusters of white flowers.

3 Birches (family Betulaceae) are characterized by their peeling bark and are adapted to poor soil and extreme cold. The paper birch of North America grows to a height of 130ft (40m).

4 The lindens (family Tiliaceae) have some of the largest leaves found on deciduous trees. Of these the largest—12in (30cm) long—are on the American linden (basswood) of North America.

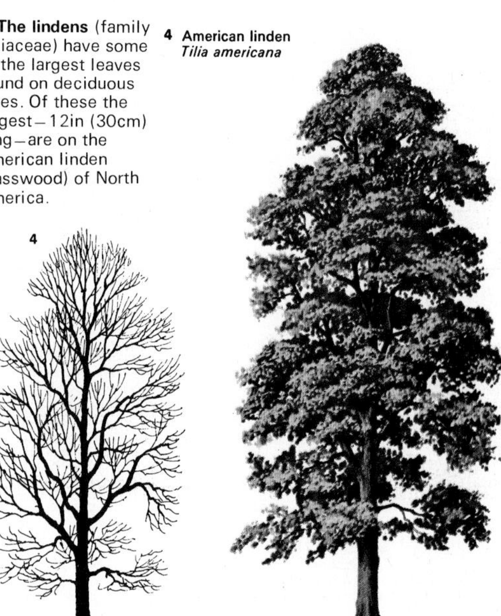
4
4 American linden
Tilia americana

5 The leaves of the ash (family Oleaceae) are distinctive in being split into many small leaflets giving the impression of fine foliage. The white ash of eastern North America is a timber tree up to 135ft (41m) tall.

6 European willow
Salix caprea

6 The willows (family Salicaceae) are fairly small trees, the European willow growing to 35ft (10m). The seeds are light, wind dispersed, and contain little food. They often grow by water where rapid germination is effected.

6

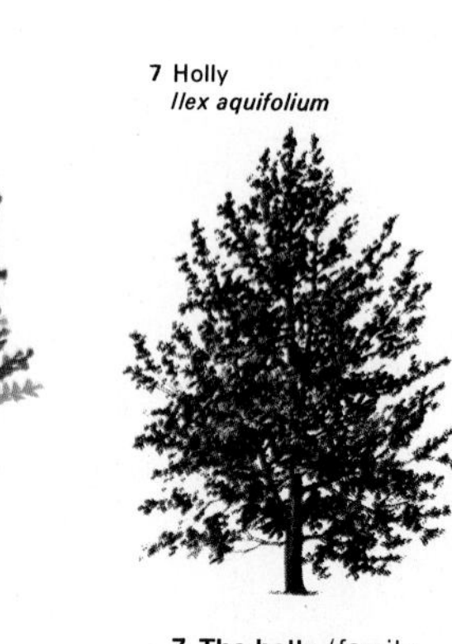
7 Holly
Ilex aquifolium

7 The holly (family Aquifoliaceae), with its thick foliage of evergreen thorned leaves, is planted as a windbreak and for ornamental purposes. Its red, winter berries create a striking contrast to the dark foliage. It grows to 70ft (21m).

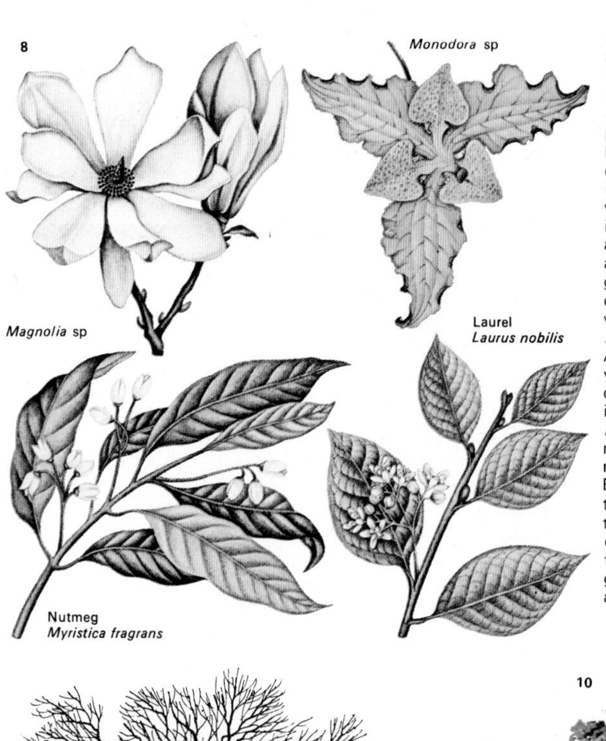
8
Monodora sp
Magnolia sp
Laurel
Laurus nobilis
Nutmeg
Myristica fragrans

8 The plant order Magnoliales includes the magnolia and the nutmeg and consists entirely of woody plants. They have been introduced for ornamental purposes in many parts of the world. The magnolia is indigenous to Asia and North America and is a popular garden plant because of its early pink and white blooms. *Monodora* is a West African jungle tree yielding spices and drugs. It is cultivated in the West Indies. *Myristica* is the nutmeg tree and is native to the East Indies. *Laurus*, the laurel, is native to the Mediterranean countries, where its fruits and leaves are gathered for spices and medicines.

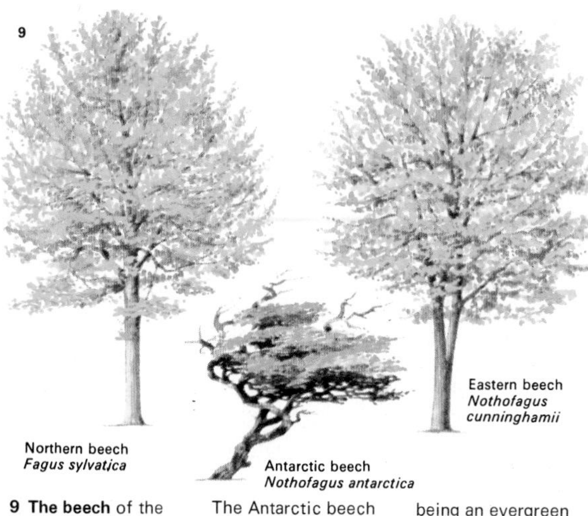
9
Eastern beech
Nothofagus cunninghamii
Northern beech
Fagus sylvatica
Antarctic beech
Nothofagus antarctica

9 The beech of the Northern Hemisphere (family Fagaceae) does well on chalky soil. Male flowers grow in clusters and are separate from the female ones. The Antarctic beech is 100ft (30m) tall and grows in the Andes and in south-eastern Australia and New Zealand. It differs from its northern cousin in being an evergreen species. The eastern beech of Australia is in the same genus as Antarctic, but like the northern beech attains a height of up to 120ft (36m).

10 Black walnut
Juglans nigra

10 The walnut (family Juglandaceae) is a decorative tree prized for its fruits and its fine timber. The nuts are pressed to give an edible oil. It grows to 160ft (49m) and is one of the last trees to gain its leaves in the spring and first to lose them in the autumn. Most of the 15 species of walnut are found in the Northern Hemisphere.

10

11

11 The umbrella tree (family Magnoliaceae) is popular in gardens. There are 80 species of *Magnolia;* the one shown here, from North America, grows to 45ft (13m).

11 Umbrella tree
Magnolia tripetala

12

Hawthorn
Crataegus sp

12 The hawthorn (family Rosaceae) is an ideal tree for hedge planting because of its hardiness and its display of thorns. It grows to 35ft (11m) and its heavily scented blossom is conspicuous in spring and early summer.

12

13

13 The sycamore-maple (family Aceraceae), largest of the maples, can grow to 110ft (34m). It is also the fastest growing, reaching its full height in 60 years. Its leaves, however, are prone to attack by various fungus diseases.

13 Sycamore maple
Acer pseudoplatanus

Flowering plants: one seed leaf

Flowering plants—called angiosperms—are the most dominant form of vegetation on earth. The angiosperms are divided botanically into two groups, the monocotyledons and the dicotyledons. The names of these two groups indicate the number of seed leaves, or cotyledons, contained within the seed; monocotyledons have one seed leaf and dicotyledons have two seed leaves.

Distinguishing features

The monocotyledons and dicotyledons are distinguished by several other features. In the monocotyledons the food and fluid transport system is grouped into closed, scattered, vascular bundles [1]. The leaves have parallel veins and usually no distinct central vein or midrib [4]. The flower parts of monocotyledons are arranged in threes, usually with three or six petals. Those few species that are woody have no bark.

The food and fluid transport system of the dicotyledons is made up of vascular bundles arranged as a single ring within the stem. The leaves have a network of veins and a distinct midrib. Flower parts have a five-, a four- or, more rarely, a two-fold arrangement. There are many woody species, all of which have bark.

Throughout the world there are some 55,000 species of monocotyledons, forming about a quarter of all flowering plants and including the grasses, palms, and orchids. They show a considerable range of form, and leaf size in this group can vary from a fraction of an inch to the 65-ft (20-m) long leaf of the raffia palm *(Raphia ruffia)*. The flowers of many families also show considerable variety and include the lilies (Liliaceae) [8], orchids (Orchidaceae), pineapples and other bromeliads (Bromeliaceae), as well as the palms (Palmaceae), sedges (Cyperaceae), and grasses (Gramineae). There are more examples of monocotyledons on the following pages.

Flowers of vivid beauty

The flowering monocotyledons include many of the most beautiful and ornamental garden plants, as well as decorative aquatic plants [5]. The lilies are widespread garden plants, together with species of narcissus (Amaryllidaceae) and irises (Iridaceae). Other striking examples in this group are the bird of paradise flowers and canna flowers [11].

The orchid family [10] displays a particular wealth of brilliant blooms, but even the most irregular and intricately shaped of orchid flowers still retain the characteristic three-fold monocotyledon arrangement of the flower parts, although this may be hard to detect. Another large group of versatile and curious monocotyledon plants is found in the pineapple family. Most of these grow on other plants, especially trees (as such they are called epiphytes); a few are terrestrial plants. Members of the pineapple family grow throughout the American tropics, in deserts, jungles, or on salt-saturated beaches, and from sea level to mountain slopes. A characteristic of many plants in this family is that the color of the leaves changes when they flower.

Monocotyledons are widely distributed. They range from palms, which flourish in the tropics, to the bog cottons [6], which

CONNECTIONS

See also

454 Grasses, reeds, and rushes
424 The plant kingdom
444 Flowering plants: two seed leaves
584 Northern grasslands
456 How flowering plants reproduce
600 Forests of Southeast Asia
326 Staple foods: grains
342 Sugar and honey
362 Fiber and oil crops
322 Plant genetic resources
398 The future of food

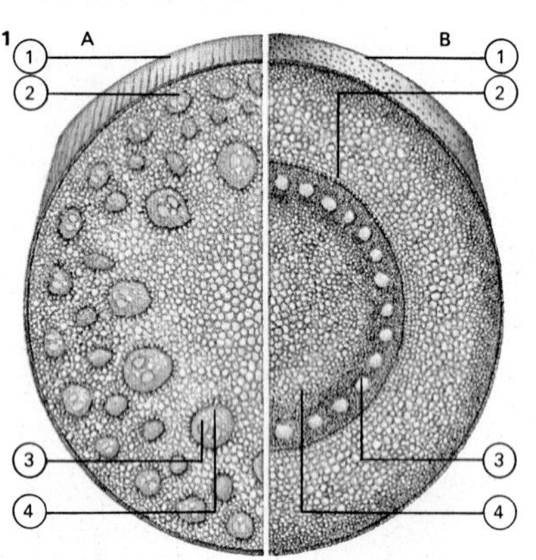

1
A
B
1
2
3
4

A Stem cross-section
1 Epidermis
2 Fibre bundle
3 Phloem
4 Xylem

B Root cross-section
1 Epidermis
2 Endodermis
3 Xylem
4 Pith

1 Monocotyledonous stems have an irregular arrangement of the food- and fluid-carrying tubes, the phloem and xylem. In the stem [A] they are scattered, but in the root [B] are central.

2

Date palm
Phoenix dactylifera

2 The date palm, with its graceful columnlike trunk, can grow to 100 ft (30 m) in height and live for 200 years, often in arid conditions. The tree bears either male or female flowers and its fruit has been a staple food in North Africa and India for centuries.

3

Screw pine
Pandanus sp.

1

3 Screw-pines, with their characteristic stilt roots (1) above ground, are a feature of tropical Asia, the islands of Polynesia, and the Indian Ocean. A few kinds grow in Africa. In some areas they form the dominant vegetation. Their tough, pliable leaves are made into mats and baskets.

4 A

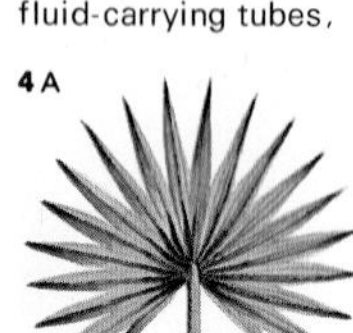

B

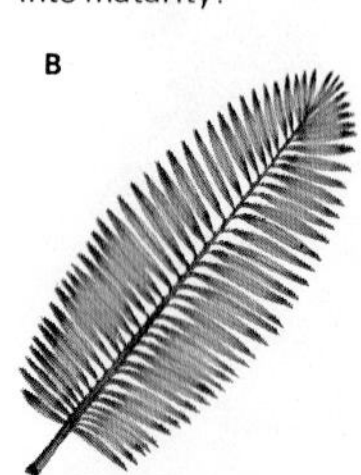

4 Palm leaves are mostly either palmate (handlike) [A] or pinnate (featherlike) [B]. They are large and stiff and, when in bud, are folded in pleats that shake out as the leaves unfold into maturity.

5

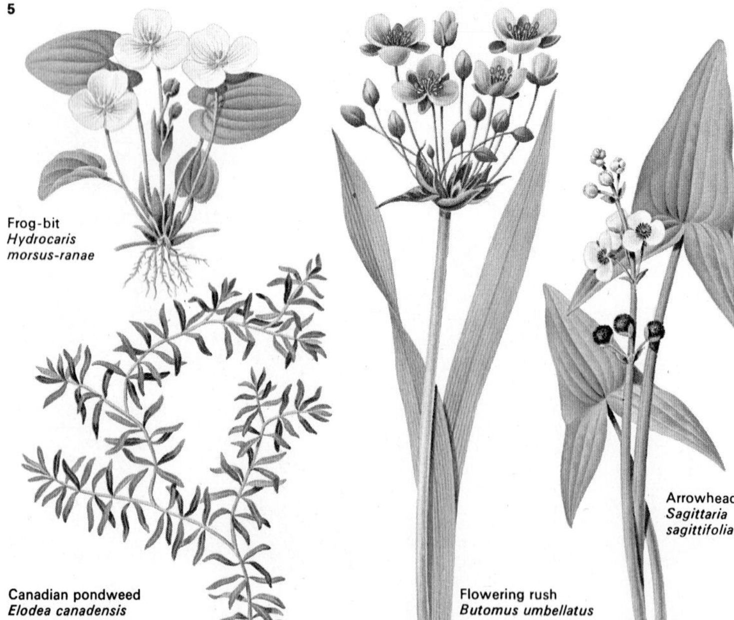

Frog-bit
Hydrocaris morsus-ranae
Canadian pondweed
Elodea canadensis
Flowering rush
Butomus umbellatus
Arrowhead
Sagittaria sagittifolia

5 Aquatic monocotyledons clearly show a parallel leaf venation and those with conspicuous flowers, such as frog-bit, flowering rush, and arrowhead, have the typical three petals. The plants can be rooted or free-floating and may grow their leaves and flowers above the surface. Canadian pondweed, which is free-floating and submerged, has tiny flowers that grow on long stalks to the surface. Other species have small flowers that open under water, some consisting only of an ovary and stamens.

6

Bog Cotton
Eriophorum sp

6 Bog cotton, a sedge found in arctic tundra and cold bogs, is recognized by its white, cotton-plumed, nodding seed heads.

cover vast expanses of the Arctic tundra. Many of these single-seed leaf plants provide food, such as grain crops useful to man.

Valuable food plants

The palms are of immense economic importance to man because they produce food, timber, wax, oil, sugar, wine, and fiber. Species of palms vary greatly in size and form. A few are slender climbers, but most have a characteristic appearance of woody trunks without branches, topped by a crown of large, stiff leaves. They have small individually inconspicuous flowers, usually in large clusters, and the variable fruit may be berries (the date) or drupes (the coconut).

The coconut palm *(Cocos nucifera)* is used in many ways and is considered to be the most valuable of all palms. Another valuable species, the date palm *(Phoenix dactylifera)* [2], has flower clusters that may contain as many as 10,000 blossoms. To ensure good yields of fruit, growers sometimes hang branches of male flowers on the flowering female tree. Dates are especially nutritious and in northern parts of Africa they are a staple food of man and animals. Dates are also cultivated in the US southwest.

The banana plant (Musaceae), providing a staple food of the tropics, is one of the largest of monocotyledonous herbs [11]. It looks like a large-leafed palm and bears fruit only once.

Members of the grass family are perhaps the most important of all the plants worldwide. The family is a large one, containing more than 600 genera and 10,000 species. Grasslands flourish in regions where rainfall totals 10–30 in (25–75cm) annually. Many grass species are vital in the form of crops such as grain or green pasturage, or for such products as fibers and building materials.

Bamboos [9] are grasses and with a few exceptions are tropical. The mountain species are able to withstand the cold of high localities. The woody, hollow stems, which are tough, stringy, and braced by solid cross joints, have great strength. The bamboo grows profusely in Southeast Asia and its stems can even be used for reinforcing concrete in roads and foundations.

KEY

Meadow grass
Poa pratensis

Meadow grass is an important hay and green pasture grass in North America and Europe and as such it is an economically valuable member of the large and widespread grass family (Gramineae). The flower of the grass is a minute spikelet, usually arranged in open branching clusters known as panicles. The flowers are cross-fertilized by the wind, and the single ovule then develops into a seed or grain. Grassland will evolve readily wherever forest or scrub cover is sparse and where there is sufficient moisture and nutrients in the soil. Vast areas of the world are natural grasslands, for example the steppes of Asia and the North American prairies.

7

Bluebell
Endymion non-scriptus

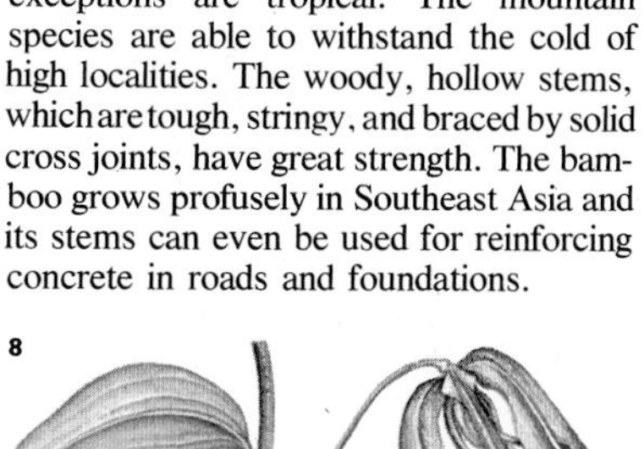

8

Climbing lily *Gloriosa simplex*

8 The climbing lily is a native of Africa. The lily family includes cultivated species and is widespread and varied. Many of the most fragrant and beautiful flowering plants are of this family.

9 The bamboos are tropical members of the grass family Gramineae. They vary greatly in height, with giant species growing to 120 ft (37 m), and are often found in dense, impenetrable clumps.

9

7 The European bluebell is a spring flowering bulb found in woodlands throughout Europe. Most bulbous plants, for example tulips and daffodils, are monocotyledons. The bulbs are food storage organs for the plants and provide for vegetative reproduction.

10 The California lady's slipper orchid is so named from the distinctive slipper shape of the large concave lower petal or lip. There are 50 species of lady's slipper orchid, in a variety of showy colors and shapes, growing in tropical and temperate areas.

11 Flowers of the banana group, Zingiberales, such as the bird of paradise, Indian shot, banana, and ginger grow in humid tropics and are often spectacular. Although it is hard to detect at a glance, these irregular and intricately shaped flowers all have the three-fold monocotyledon arrangement.

10

Californian lady's slipper orchid
Cypripedium californicum

11

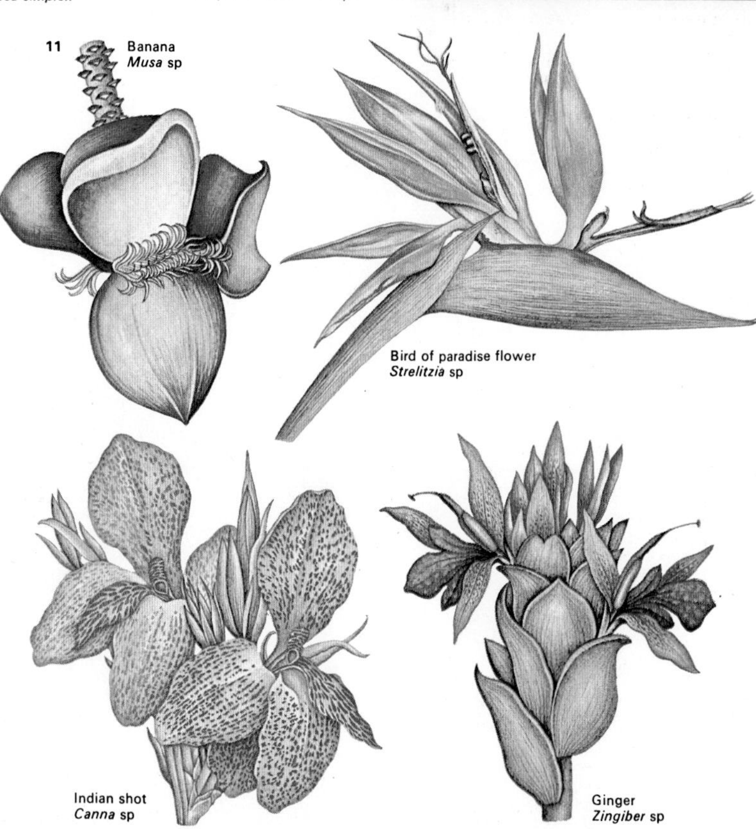

Banana
Musa sp

Bird of paradise flower
Strelitzia sp

Indian shot
Canna sp

Ginger
Zingiber sp

Grasses, reeds, and rushes

The group of plants that includes the grasses, palms, lilies, orchids, reeds, and rushes is known as the monocotyledons and comprises some 55,000 species grouped into 31 families. The monocotyledons, mostly herbs and found worldwide, include some of the earth's most useful and attractive plants. From the grass family [2] (Gramineae) come many of man's staple food crops, including wheat *(Triticum)* and sorghum *(Sorghum)*, and luxury foods such as sugar from the sugar cane *(Saccharum)*.

Bamboo [7], another grass, is a building material widely used in Asia. The papyrus [6] (family Cyperaceae) was used as a writing material by the ancient Egyptians. Other monocotyledons are used to brighten man's homes and gardens. Some of the most fascinating of these are the bromeliads (Bromeliaceae) [1] and the tradescantias [4] (Commelinaceae)—trailing plants that are widely grown. Monocotyledons are found in such diverse habitats as desert, where the century plant [3] *(Agave)* thrives, and marshland, where bulrushes [5] (family Typhaceae) are common.

1 The bromeliads (family Bromeliaceae) come from the New World tropics. Some, such as *Aechmea fasciata*, are epiphytes—that is, they grow on trees, large cacti, rocks, and other supports, but do not obtain nourishment from them. The leaves of many bromeliads form a "vase" that catches and holds water and dissolved minerals. Within the vase entire life cycles of small animals and plants may occur.

1 Bromeliad
Aechmea fasciata

CONNECTIONS

See also
452 Flowering plants: on seed leaf
456 How flowering plant reproduce
584 Northern grasslands
1624 Making paper
1620 Fibers for fabrics
872 Communication through writing: 2

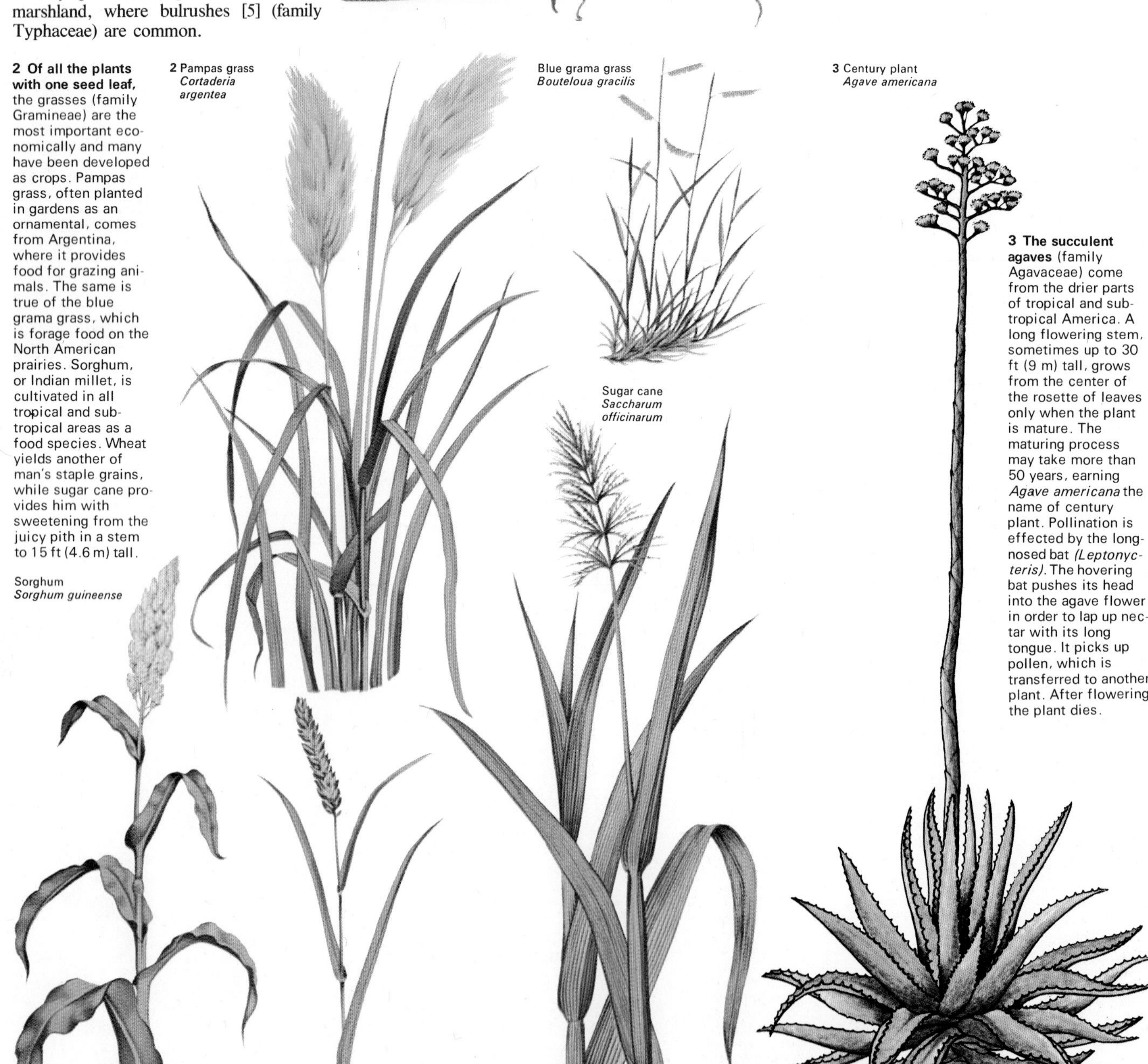
2 Pampas grass
Cortaderia argentea
Blue grama grass
Bouteloua gracilis
3 Century plant
Agave americana
Sugar cane
Saccharum officinarum
Sorghum
Sorghum guineense
Wheat
Triticum aestivum

2 Of all the plants with one seed leaf, the grasses (family Gramineae) are the most important economically and many have been developed as crops. Pampas grass, often planted in gardens as an ornamental, comes from Argentina, where it provides food for grazing animals. The same is true of the blue grama grass, which is forage food on the North American prairies. Sorghum, or Indian millet, is cultivated in all tropical and subtropical areas as a food species. Wheat yields another of man's staple grains, while sugar cane provides him with sweetening from the juicy pith in a stem to 15 ft (4.6 m) tall.

3 The succulent agaves (family Agavaceae) come from the drier parts of tropical and subtropical America. A long flowering stem, sometimes up to 30 ft (9 m) tall, grows from the center of the rosette of leaves only when the plant is mature. The maturing process may take more than 50 years, earning *Agave americana* the name of century plant. Pollination is effected by the long-nosed bat *(Leptonycteris)*. The hovering bat pushes its head into the agave flower in order to lap up nectar with its long tongue. It picks up pollen, which is transferred to another plant. After flowering the plant dies.

4 Boat lily
Rhoeo discolor
Wandering Jew
Zebrina pendula

4 The tradescantia family (Commelinaceae) comprises over 300 species, mainly found in tropics and subtropics throughout the world. Most are creeping plants but some, including the boat lily, have upright habits. Wandering Jew is one of the many tradescantia species cultivated for the beauty of its leaves, which are variegated. The flowers are often small, few, and inconspicuous, but in some species are large with violet-colored petals and six bright yellow, pollen-bearing anthers. Vegetative reproduction is assisted by the formation of roots at the leaf bases. The Wandering Jew makes an ideal basket plant.

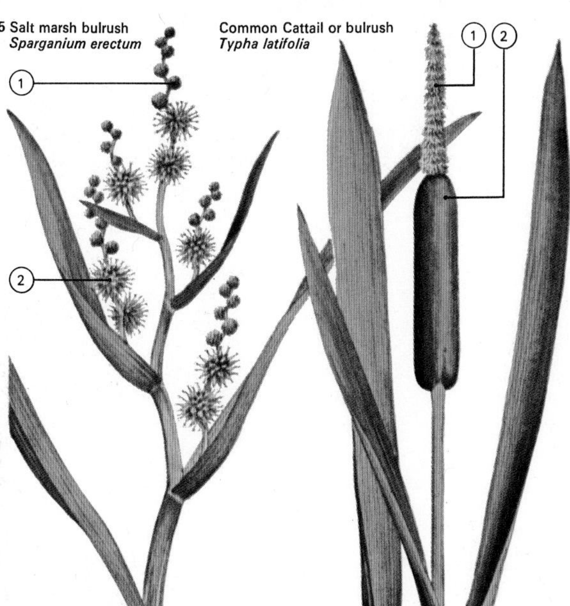
5 Salt marsh bulrush
Sparganium erectum
Common Cattail or bulrush
Typha latifolia
1
2
1
2

5 The bur-reeds and cattails (or bulrushes) of the families Sparganiaceae and Typhaceae are usually found in swamps and at water margins. Both male [1] and female [2] flowers are borne separately on the same plant. In cattails they are on the same head.

6 The sedges and clubrushes (family Cyperaceae) are a widespread group of plants usually found in waterlogged acid soils. Pendulous sedge grows in large clumps in damp, shady woods, while salt marsh bulrush grows in tidal marshes. Papyrus, from which an ancient writing material was made, is a member of the same family.

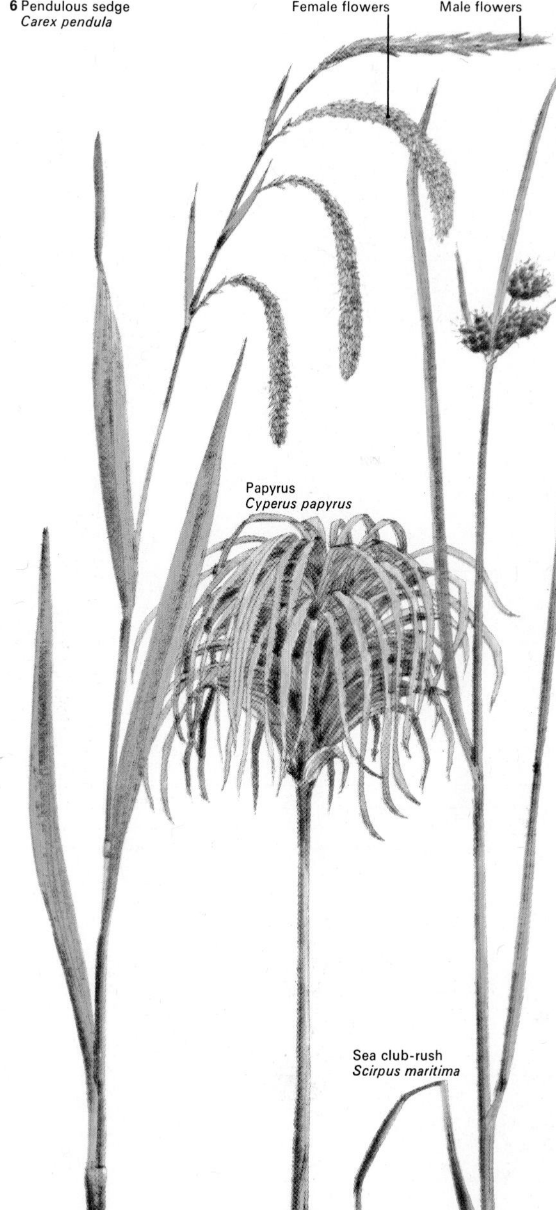
6 Pendulous sedge
Carex pendula
Female flowers
Male flowers
Papyrus
Cyperus papyrus
Sea club-rush
Scirpus maritima

7 The bamboos are woody members of the grass family that vary in height from a few inches to 100 ft. Bamboos often grow in dense, impenetrable clumps in tropical regions, but some, such as *Arundinaria alpina*, grow on mountain sides and can withstand cold conditions. Because of their abundance, strength, and unusual stem structure [1] (woody and hollow with solid, stiffening cross joints), bamboos are used by man for many purposes, including the building of houses and furniture. Large canes are used as pipes in irrigation systems. Young shoots can be eaten and many people regard them as a delicacy.

7 *Arundinaria japonica*

1

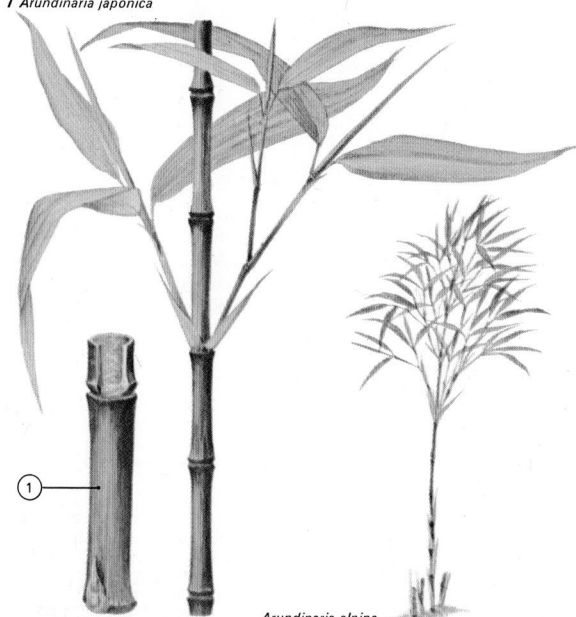

Arundinaria alpina

How flowering plants reproduce

The profusion of rainbow colored, richly scented, and curiously shaped flowers that exists throughout the world is an essential part of the plant kingdom's adaptation for sexual reproduction, although nearly all plants can reproduce asexually and sexually. Asexual reproduction [9] can take place by simple budding, by means of bulbils (bundles of swollen leaves), rhizomes (underground stems) or tubers (swollen parts of roots or stems). Or, in a few so-called apomictic species such as dandelions, seed can be produced without sexual fusion. Sexual reproduction is effected through specialized organs in which a male cell fuses with a female cell. This gives rise to a new plant that combines the characteristics of both parents.

Sexual reproduction

Plants that reproduce sexually may either have the male and female organs in the same flower (bisexual), or in different flowers on the same plant (monoecious) or on different plants (dioecious). As the flower bud is formed and the flower parts develop, so the male and female organs differentiate. The female part consists of the ovary, in which there is the ovule (embryo seed) and from which projects the stigma (the pollen receiver) on a stem, or style, of varying length. The male organ is the stamen, made up of an anther bearing pollen grains, and the stalklike filament. Most pollen grains are carried by wind or animals—frequently insects—to the ovule, which contains the egg nucleus and in which, after fertilization, the young embryo subsequently develops to give rise to a seed and eventually to a new plant [4].

Pollen grains, too small to be seen individually by the human eye, can be detected as "dust" when shaken from the anthers of flowers. But when magnified, pollen is seen to vary greatly in size and shape and electron microscopy has revealed remarkable structuring of ridges and hollows in the outer coat of each pollen grain. In many flowering plants there is a physical affinity between the shape of the pollen grain and the surface cells of the female stigma, contributing to successful fertilization. In the primrose, for example, there are two distinct flower types [Key] but the structure of the pollen grains is such that those from one type fit the stigmas of the other and vice versa, thus ensuring cross pollination.

The evolution of flowers

In the earliest and most simple types of flowers, pollen was transferred from stamens to stigmas by wind. Many trees have wind-pollinated flowers, often forming catkins. The male flowers are simple and open in structure to facilitate pollen dispersal. Pollen is produced in very large quantities so that, from the cloud of pollen released as catkins toss in the breeze, there is a high chance of some grains at least falling on ripe stigmas of a nearby female flower of the species. The full range of diversity of flower adaptation is found in flowers pollinated by animals [1]. The direct transfer of the pollen by a creature provides greater efficiency in fertilization, but to ensure that it will occur the flower must attract the required insect (or other animal) pollinator. To this end many flowers have bright colors, and

CONNECTIONS

See also
444 Flowering plants: two seed leaves
452 Flowering plants: one seed leaf
324 Plant propagation
322 Plant genetic resources
316 Improving crops
318 Protecting crops
338 Temperate fruits
340 Tropical fruits
356 Seeds and spices
360 Berries, nuts, and olives
366 The modern tree nursery
398 The future of food

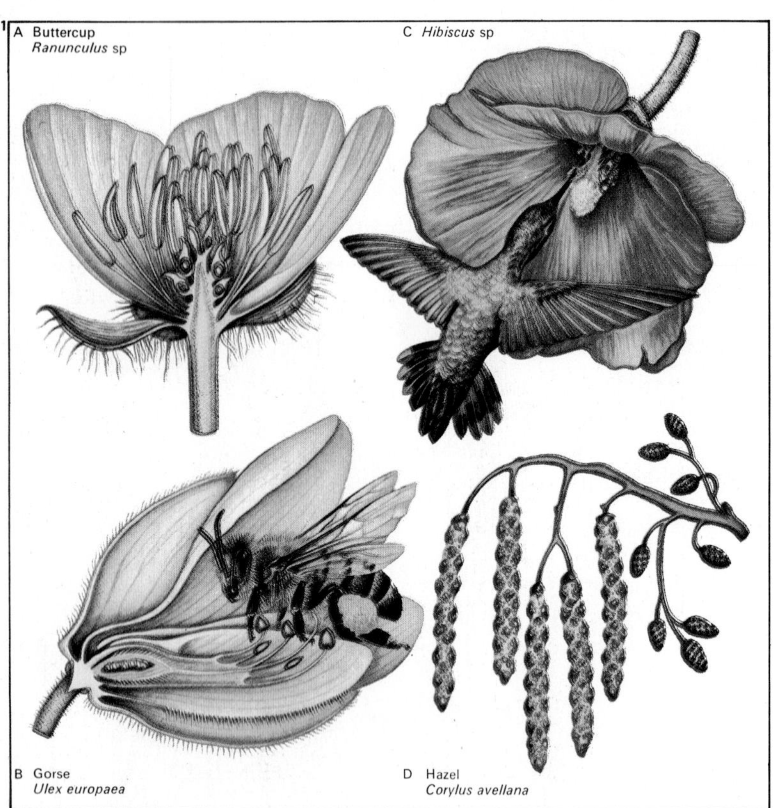

1
A Buttercup
Ranunculus sp
C *Hibiscus* sp
B Gorse
Ulex europaea
D Hazel
Corylus avellana

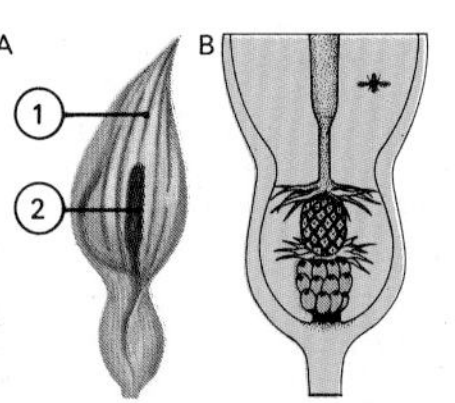

2 A
1
2
B

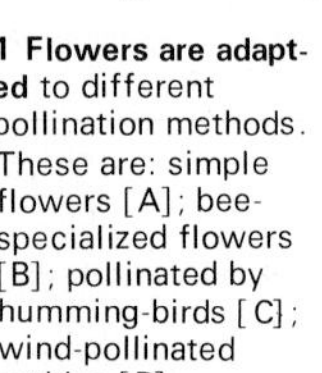

C

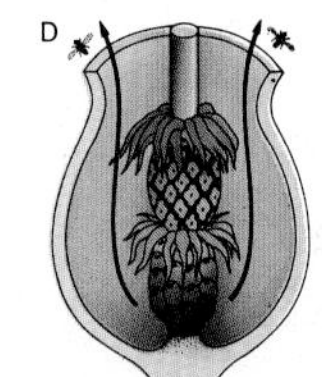

D

1 Flowers are adapted to different pollination methods. These are: simple flowers [A]; bee-specialized flowers [B]; pollinated by humming-birds [C]; wind-pollinated catkins [D].

2 The cuckoopint of Europe *(Arum maculatum)* [A] is remarkably adapted for pollination. As the spathes [1] unfurl [B] the exposed spadix [2] heats up releasing a carrion scent attractive to owl-midges. These insects crawl down, and pollinate the female flowers and become trapped in a ring of hairs [C]. The midges are dusted with pollen and escape as the hairs wither [D].

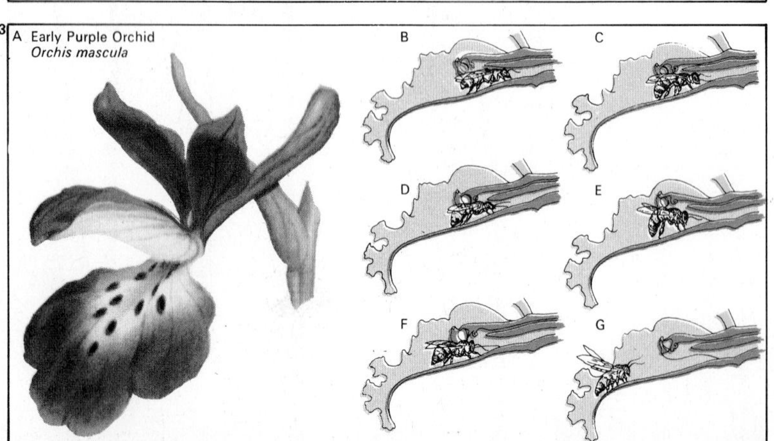

3
A Early Purple Orchid
Orchis mascula
B
C
D
E
F
G

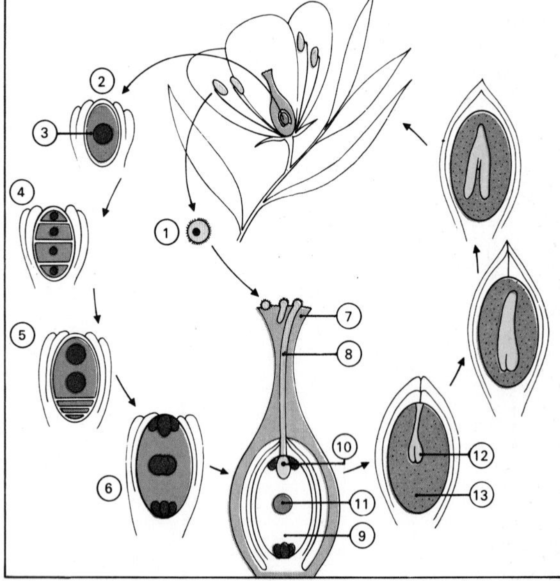

4
1
2
3
4
5
6
7
8
9
10
11
12
13

3 In the pollination of the early purple orchid [A] the bee enters with a bundle of pollen (a pollinium). As it backs out, the pollinium is left on the stigma. The bee's back is smeared with liquid to which the pollinium sticks [B-G].

4 Flower maturation involves pollen production [1] and ovule development [2]. The ovule [3] divides repeatedly [4, 5] to form an embryo sac [6] containing eight nuclei. When pollen lands on the stigma [7] a pollen tube [8] forms and the male nucleus passes down it, dividing in two. In the ovule [9] one fertilizes the egg nucleus [10], the other fuses with one polar nucleus [11]. The embryo [12] develops within nutritious endosperm [13].

studies of the sight capacity in bees and other insects have shown them to be particularly receptive to certain colors. The petals of flowers are modified leaves—in wind-pollinated flowers they are usually small and mostly green. In insect-pollinated flowers the petals are often large and showy and the green pigment found in leaf cells is replaced by pigments that provide a new color range. Yellow and white pigments are primitive colors found in the simpler flowers, while red, purple, and blue pigments are found in more advanced flowers. Orange is an uncommon natural flower color and completely black petals are unknown in the wild.

Flower shape and scent

Many intricate flower shapes have evolved as a result of the plant/insect relationship. In each insect-pollinated flower there are glands producing nectar and scents enticing the insect to visit [2]. In the petal markings of most flowers there is a pattern of honey guidelines that are sometimes black to direct the feeding insect to the parts of the flower necessary for pollination. Simple flowers that are open and saucer-shaped have nectar at the petal bases in the center and can be pollinated by any visiting insects. More specialized flowers are tube-shaped and the tube often fits one particular type or species of insect exactly.

Orchids have a complex pollination mechanism, with flowers often shaped, marked, and scented to resemble an insect and some even have furry-textured petals [3]. Equally specialized are long-tubed flowers whose nectar can only be reached by long-tongued butterflies and moths, birds with long, curved bills [1] or even bats. Where the evolutionary lines between plants and pollinators run parallel, animals are able to feed from and pollinate flowers through mutual adaptation.

After fertilization, flower petals and stamens wither and the ovary develops into the ripening fruit containing the seed. There are many adaptations for seed dispersal including wings, parachutes [5], and explosive mechanisms [7] to ensure that the seeds are carried far enough to colonize new soil.

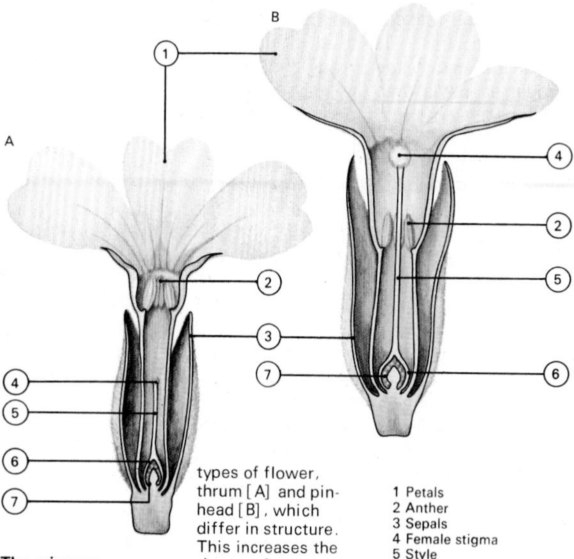

KEY
A
B
1 Petals
2 Anther
3 Sepals
4 Female stigma
5 Style
6 Ovary
7 Ovules

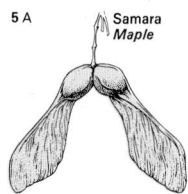

The primrose *(Primula)* has two types of flower, thrum [A] and pin-head [B], which differ in structure. This increases the chance of cross-pollination.

5 A
Samara
Maple
5 B
Cypsela
Tragopogon

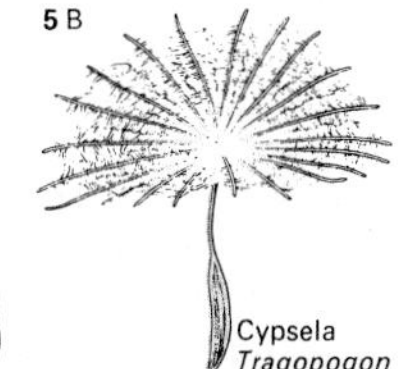

5 Some plant seeds are shaped for wind dispersal. Air currents lift the winged maple samara [A] some distance away. The parachuted cypsela of goat's beard [B] floats on the breeze.

6 Man and animals assist seed dispersal when fruits with hooked spines become caught on fur or clothing. This trouser leg carries burr-marigold, bedstraw, and agrimony.

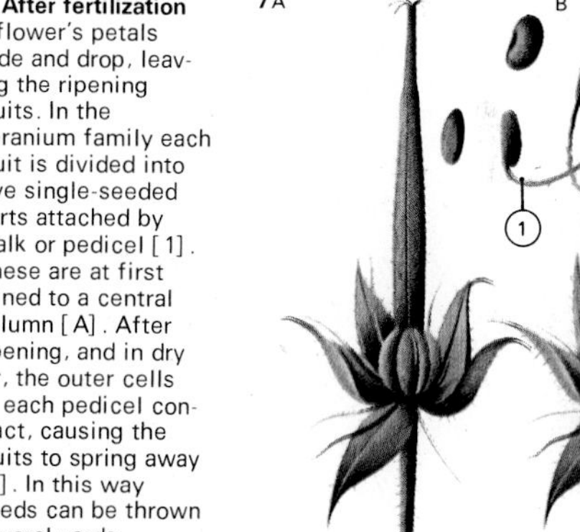

7A
B

7 After fertilization a flower's petals fade and drop, leaving the ripening fruits. In the geranium family each fruit is divided into five single-seeded parts attached by stalk or pedicel [1]. These are at first joined to a central column [A]. After ripening, and in dry air, the outer cells of each pedicel contract, causing the fruits to spring away [B]. In this way seeds can be thrown several yards.

8 Berries, pollen, and nectar form the staple diet of many birds and small mammals, and often there is an intricate interdependence between the plants and animals. In Australia, parrots [1] and parakeets [2] swinging in the gum tree branches [3] to seek out fruit will shake the tasseled flowers, and pollen grains that dust their feathers (or are caught on their tongues) will be carried to new plants. Honey-eaters [4], with long, curved bills, and honey possums [5], with narrow noses and long tongues, use these adaptations for feeding on the rich nectar of the *Banksia* flowers [6–9]. Others such as the dormouse possum [10] carry pollen grains caught in their fur or whiskers.

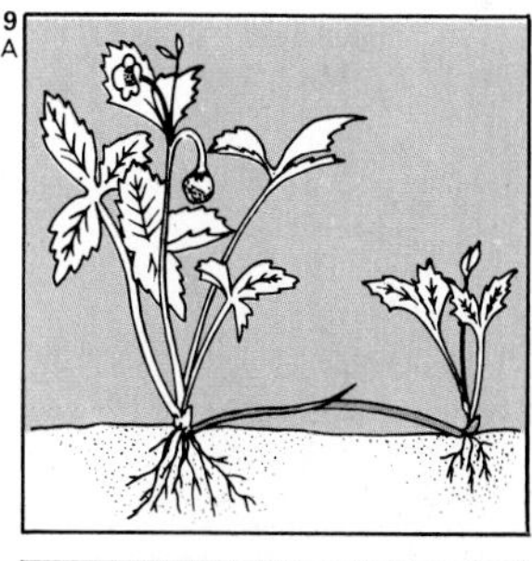

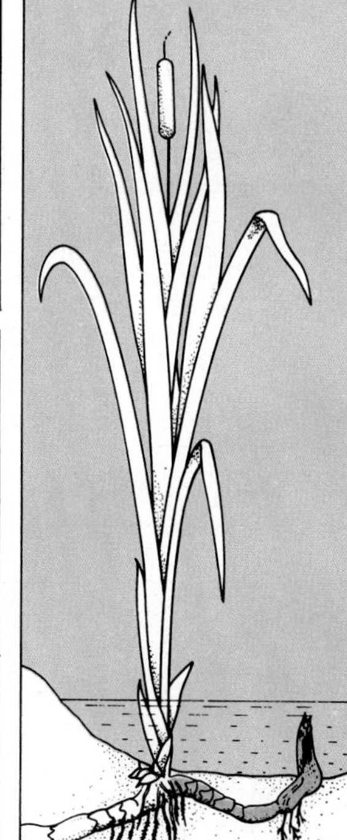

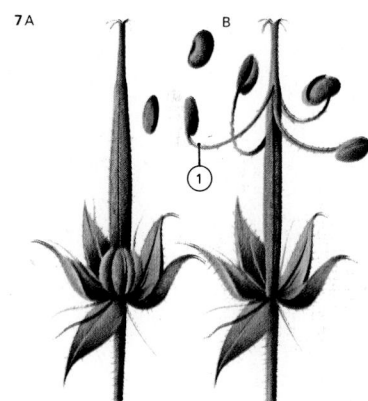

9 New plants may arise by a variety of asexual methods. In the strawberry [A] they spring from creeping stems, in the bulrush [B] from swollen underground stems or rhizomes, and in the wild onion [C] from bulbils in the flower.

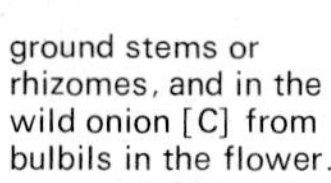

The animal kingdom

All animals are made up of a cell or cells with a nucleus that contains the cell's genetic specifications. The main groups into which the animal kingdom is divided are known as phyla and the most primitive phylum is that of the Protozoa, animals that are made up of just one single nucleated cell. This means that each individual protozoan must be completely self-sufficient, with special structures (organelles) to perform those functions essential to all cells and those that in many-celled animals are shared between different tissues.

From sponges to mollusks

Although there are protozoans that live in colonies, the great step that separates them from all other animal forms is that which led to the development of interdependent groups of cells with a distinct form. The phylum Porifera, which contains the sponges, is the most primitive multicellular phylum and sponge cells retain a high degree of independence. The Coelenterata are more complex and the members of this phylum have differentiated tissues. These animals are composed essentially of a gut and a ring of tentacles. Sessile, or anchored, forms, such as *Hydra* and sea anemones, may also have a foot. The others, such as the jellyfish [3] are free-swimming.

Apart from the small phylum of Ctenophora—the sea walnuts or comb jellies—which are very like the coelenterates, the next three major phyla in the evolutionary tree consist of worms—flatworms (Platyhelminthes) [4], roundworms (Nematoda) [5], and the segmented worms (Annelida) [6].

The phylum Mollusca contains more than 80,000 species, which makes it second in number among the invertebrates only to the arthropods. Mollusks are most conspicuous for their external shells; the marine gastropods and bivalves provide the varied and fascinating sea shells that litter the world's beaches. The most important class of mollusks other than the Gastropoda [7] and the Bivalvia are the Cephalopoda—the squids and octopuses. In some of these the shell has become internal, and in *Octopus* [8] it has disappeared.

External and internal skeletons

There are about one million known species of arthropods, of which the most numerous fall into three classes: Crustacea—the lobsters [9], shrimps, and crabs; Arachnida—spiders [10], ticks, and scorpions; and Insecta [11]. The arthropods have colonized every conceivable ecological niche on land, in the air, and in water. They, like annelids, are characterized by a segmented body, but this has been modified to such an extent that it is often only apparent during the larval phase; but more importantly, they feature an external protective skeleton. Most also have compound eyes and complex nervous systems.

The Echinodermata are marine animals which, although invertebrates, have an internal skeleton. The most familiar of these are the starfishes [12] and sea urchins. There are many minor invertebrate phyla but the majority of the remaining invertebrates belong to the Hemichordata, which is a subphylum of the Chordata and contains the marine acorn worms. About 95 percent of animal species are invertebrates, and nu-

CONNECTIONS

See also
408 Evolution of life
410 The world before m
484 The joint-legged an mals
492 The classification o insects
510 The classification o fish
526 The classification o birds
540 The classification o mammals
646 Primate to hominid
578 Regions of the eart zoogeography
460 Animal anatomy
1478 The scale of the un verse

1

2

Sarcodine
Amoeba proteus
African buffalo
Syncerus caffer

1 Amebas are single-celled animals that belong to the class Sarcodina. The protozoans flourish wherever there is moisture and they range in size from the microscopic blood parasite *Pseudoplasmodium* to the freshwater ciliate *Spirostomum*, which is 0.1in (3mm) long. Because it is difficult classifying single-celled organisms as animals or plants, they are often grouped as the Protista.

2 The African buffalo is one of the large mammals, made up of millions of cells organized into specialized tissues. With a height of 4.9ft (1.5m), the buffalo is many millions of times larger than the largest protozoan. Mammals have colonized most environments in which protozoans can flourish; and some protozoans, such as *Trypanosoma*, parasitize mammals. *Trypanosoma* causes sleeping sickness.

3

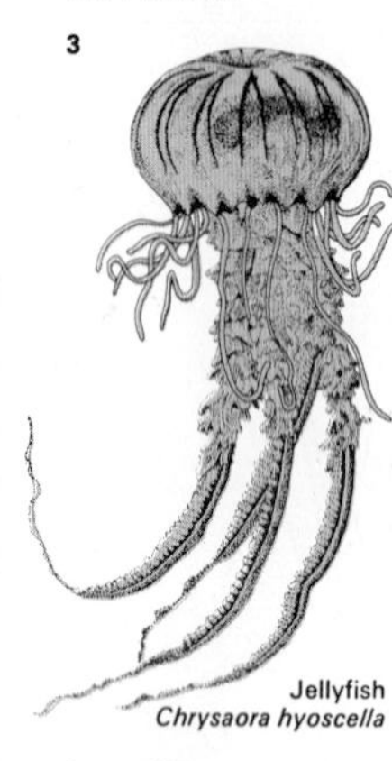

Jellyfish
Chrysaora hyoscella

3 Jellyfish belong to the Coelenterata, the first unambiguously metazoan or multicellular animal phylum, sharing with the Ctenohpora (comb jellies) the feature of radial symmetry.

4 Parasitic tapeworms are members of the phylum Platyhelminthes. All are flattened and bilaterally symmetrical. Parasitic flukes and free-living flatworms are also in the phylum.

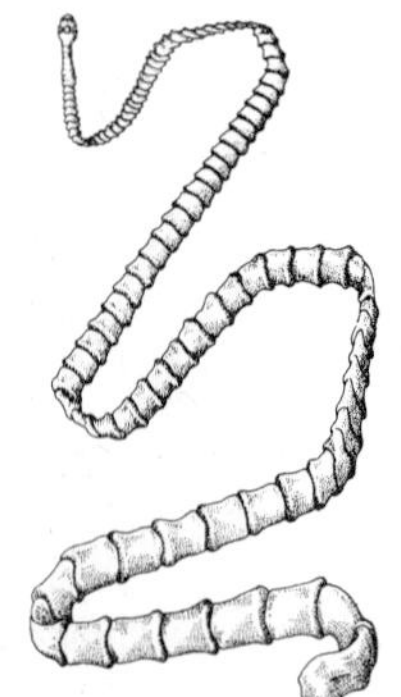

4 Tapeworm
Taenia solium

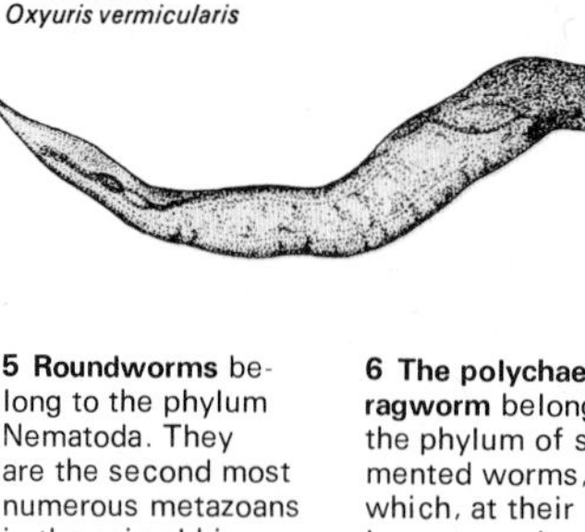

5 Threadworm
Oxyuris vermicularis

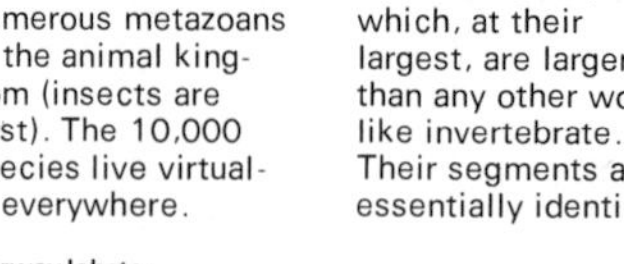

5 Roundworms belong to the phylum Nematoda. They are the second most numerous metazoans in the animal kingdom (insects are first). The 10,000 species live virtually everywhere.

6 Ragworm
Nereis diversicolor

6 The polychaete ragworm belongs to the phylum of segmented worms, which, at their largest, are larger than any other worm-like invertebrate. Their segments are essentially identical.

7

7 The freshwater snail, *Viviparus viviparus*, belongs to the largest class of mollusks, the Gastropoda, with more than 35,000 species. Bivalves and cephalopods are also mollusks.

8

Octopus
Octopus vulgaris

8 The octopus, a mollusk that has lost its shell in the course of evolution, belongs to the cephalopods. This group includes the 65-ft (20-m) giant squids, largest of all the invertebrates.

9 The lobster belongs to the arthropod phylum and is one of the jawed (mandibulate) species. It represents the Crustacea, the only primarily aquatic arthropod class, which is made up of more than 30,000 distinct species.

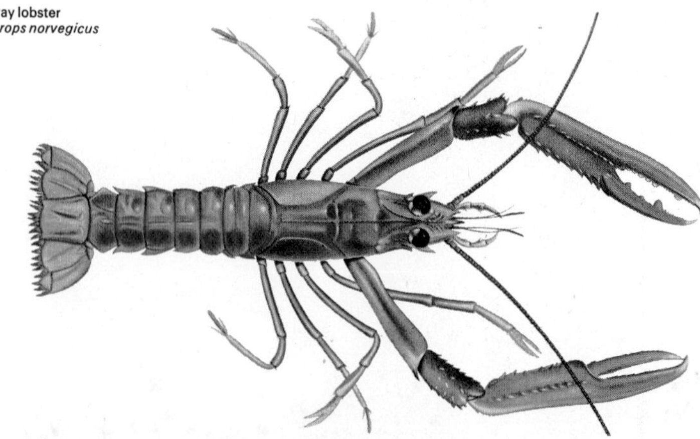

9 Norway lobster
Nephrops norvegicus

merically arthropods are the most important group, because they constitute three-quarters of all animal species. The vertebrates constitute just one subphylum of the chordates and all have backbones. The other small subphyla include the tunicates, or sea squirts, and the lancelets. They have no true backbones but only an internal rod called a notochord at some stage in their development.

Fish, amphibians, reptiles, birds, mammals
The group Pisces, the fish, is by far the largest group of vertebrates and is also the oldest in evolutionary history. The two principal kinds of fish are the cartilaginous, or sharklike fish, and the bony fish [13], which comprise the larger and more advanced group.

The Amphibia, the frogs, toads [14], newts, and salamanders and a few legless wormlike species—the caecilians—are the survivors of the first group of vertebrates to develop legs, enabling them to emerge from the waters in which life began. But they have not quite abandoned the aquatic habit: their eggs are still laid in water or moist environments, and the larvae breathe through gills.

The reptiles [15] made the final break with the water through the development of eggs with shells, for protection and preservation of moisture, and yolks for nourishing the embryo. The living reptiles are the snakes, lizards, turtles, and crocodilians. These are mainly tropical species because their cold-bloodedness makes them too sluggish to survive in colder climates. To a zoologist birds [16] seem little more than "glorified reptiles." They have an essentially reptilian anatomy but a warm-blooded metabolism, hollow bones, and feathers.

The mammals [2], the hairy animals, are the only other warm-blooded class of vertebrates. They are defined by their protracted care of the young which they nurture internally or in a pouch (except for the egg-laying monotremes, such as the platypus) and feed with milk from their mammary glands for a varying period after birth. Behavioral complexity and intelligence reach their peak in the mammals.

KEY
Land
Man
Lepidoptera
Birds
Primates
Hymenoptera
Marsupials
Insects
Mammals
Onychophora
Monotremes
Reptiles
Amphibians
Spiders
Penguins
Whales
Arthropods
Bony fish
Segmented worms
Crustaceans
Cartilaginous fish
Vertebrates
Roundworms
Snails
Molluscs
Protochordates
Spiny-headed worms
Squids and octopuses
Flatworms
Rotifers
Coelomates
Echinoderms
Ctenophores
Jellyfish
Sponges
Plants
Protozoans
Fossil forms
Water
Bacteria
Viruses

0 Tarantula
Aphonopelma sp

10 Spiders, scorpions, mites, and ticks are arachnids and belong to the chelicerate, or jawless, division of the Arthropoda. Among arthropods, Arachnida are second to Insecta in number.

11 The butterfly is one of the most beautiful of the Insecta, which is a huge class of arthropods containing some 1,000,000 species, more than all the other animal species put together.

11 Asian swallowtail
Papilio philoxenus

12

Common seastar
Asterias rubens

12 The starfish has hard projecting spines, forming part of its internal skeleton. This is the most important feature characterizing the phylum to which it belongs, the Echinodermata. The name means "spiny-skinned." The starfish has a central mouth located on the underside of its body. It eats mussels, snails, oysters, and clams, and is found in all seas except polar.

3 Catfish
Silurus glanis

13 Fish were the first vertebrates to develop jaws. They belong to the class Pisces of the subphylum Vertebrata and are an evolutionary landmark in terms of the emergence of man.

14 The toad belongs to the order Anura, whose members are the commonest of the three amphibian orders. The Amphibia were the first of the tetrapod vertebrate classes—the four-footed land animals.

14 European green toad
Bufo viridis

15

Boa constrictor
Constrictor constrictor

15 The boa constrictor belongs to the Serpentes, a specialized group of Reptilia, the first vertebrate class to be completely independent of water. The other reptilian orders have legs.

16 The stonechat, one of the 8,600 species of the vertebrate class Aves, belongs to the most diverse vertebrate group after the fishes. Almost all the special features of bird physiology can be traced to the requirements of flight.

16

Stonechat
Saxicola torquata

Animal anatomy

All animals, from the microscopic protozoan ameba to the huge African elephant, share the same essential requirements. They must be able to obtain a supply of food and oxygen, get rid of unwanted waste products, reproduce themselves, move, and be capable of monitoring and responding to the environment in which they live. In the single-celled ameba these tasks are easily fulfilled; oxygen, for example, is obtained by diffusion through the cell membrane.

Layers of cells

During evolution, animals were able to become more complex only because their body plans were organized in a way that allowed the essential life processes to continue. The first big jump from the protozoan body plan came with the appearance of the coelenterates—sea anemones and their relations. In these multicellular creatures the body is a simple tube bounded by two layers of cells—the outer ectoderm and the inner endoderm [Key].

True organs did not arise until animal anatomy had taken another step forward—the development of a third layer of cells, the mesoderm, between the ectoderm and the endoderm. The simplest animals to have three cell layers are the platyhelminths, or flatworms. From this mesoderm layer there arise muscles, reproductive organs, and excretory cells. The ectoderm forms the outer layers of the body as well as the nervous tissue, along which coded information is conveyed to and from different body parts. The simple flatworm body is the first on the evolutionary tree to have a recognizable head containing clusters of nerve cells or ganglia and also primitive eyes.

The three-layer body plan provided the potential for enormous evolutionary advance and this arrangement is found in all the remaining groups of animals. Despite this, animal bodies can still be thought of as tubes, and in all animals from the sea anemone onward digestion takes place in the innermost tube—the gut—which is lined with endoderm.

The gut also contains bands of muscular tissue derived from mesoderm cells. The purpose of these muscles is to move food from mouth to anus. In the flatworm this process is accompanied by waves of contraction down the whole of the animal's body. Little evolutionary advance was possible until the development of a separate fluid-filled cavity, the coelom [Key].

The simplest animals to have a coelom are the annelids—the earthworms and their allies—and in these creatures the coelom is easily visible in a cross-section. In higher animals the coelom is barely detectable because it is filled with numerous organs.

The segmented body plan

The most striking feature of annelid anatomy is its division into segments [1]. A closer, internal study shows that all of these are essentially identical, apart from those at the head end [6], where there is some concentration of nerve tissue, and at the tail. For annelids, the greatest advantage of the segmented body plan is as an aid to movement. In other invertebrate animals, however, different body segments have become specialized to do different

CONNECTIONS

See also
458 The animal kingdom
468 Sea anemones, hydras, and corals
472 Flatworms, flukes, and tapeworms
474 Earthworms, clamworms, and roundworms
484 The joint-legged animals
508 Threshold of the vertebrates
512 The life of fish
520 The life of reptiles
528 The anatomy of birds
542 The life of mammals
662 An introduction to body and mind
646 Primate to hominid
682 Skull, skeleton, and joints
1468 Shape and symmetry

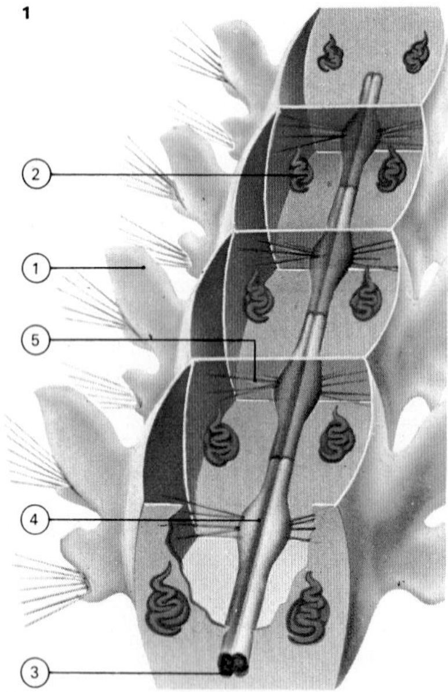

1
2
1
5
4
3

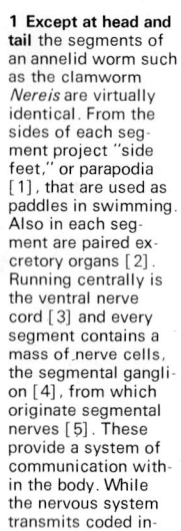

1 Except at head and tail the segments of an annelid worm such as the clamworm *Nereis* are virtually identical. From the sides of each segment project "side feet," or parapodia [1], that are used as paddles in swimming. Also in each segment are paired excretory organs [2]. Running centrally is the ventral nerve cord [3] and every segment contains a mass of nerve cells, the segmental ganglion [4], from which originate segmental nerves [5]. These provide a system of communication within the body. While the nervous system transmits coded information, the blood system conveys oxygen to all the body cells.

2 Although totally different in evolutionary origin, man and the crayfish depend on similar anatomical systems to circulate blood, digest food, and perform other body functions. But the crayfish has a hard external skeleton while man, in common with other vertebrates, has an internal skeleton to which muscles are attached. The segments of the crayfish body show some specialization.

Blood system
Nutrition
Reproduction
Excretion
Respiration
Nervous system
Skeleton
Endocrine system

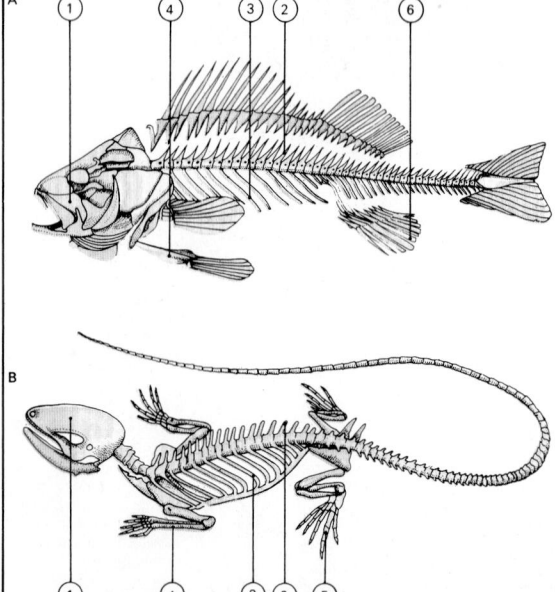

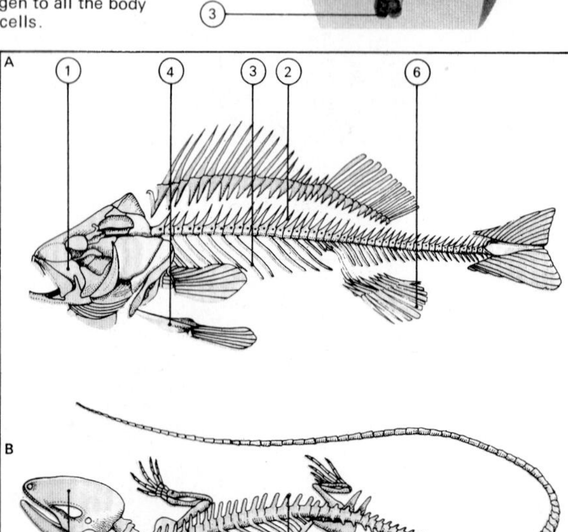

3
A
1
4
3
2
6
B
1
4
3
2
5

3 Fish, reptiles, birds, and mammals are all vertebrates with essentially similar skeletons. The fish [A] and the lizard [B] both possess similar skeletal features such as a skull [1], a backbone [2], ribs [3], and limb support bones [4]. The lizard's foot [5] is an evolutionary development of the fish's fin [6] and has the five-toed pattern typical of vertebrates.

4 The differences between the skeletons of a bird [A] and a mammal [B] reflect the differences in their ways of life. The limb bones of birds [1] are reduced and fused as are those of the backbone [2]. The mammal, having no need for lightness, tends to have larger and heavier bones.

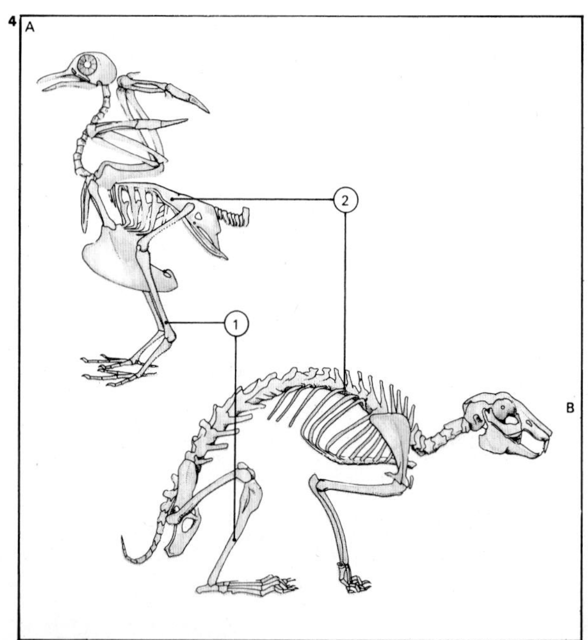

4
A
2
1
B

jobs. This is particularly so in the arthropods [2], a group that includes the insects. In these animals the segments are equipped with jointed appendages but these are modified to form structures such as legs and mouthparts. Internally, sex organs, a heart to push blood through the circulatory system, and other organs are positioned in particular segments. There is a head with a simple brain and, usually, compound eyes.

External and internal skeletons

Small, soft-bodied animals such as worms have little need of any body supports, and have no skeleton, but the arthropods have developed an external skeleton that serves the dual purpose of protection and the provision of rigid material to which muscles are attached. Such an arrangement does impose limitations, however, for it means that the animal cannot grow without molting this skeleton. Not until the skeleton was formed internally did animal anatomy take another big step forward. This occurred in the primitive chordates. These animals possessed a notochord, the forerunner of the backbone.

The chordate body, like that of the annelids, is divided into well-defined segments. These are related to the development of the backbone because each one contains bands of muscles—myotomes—attached to the notochord and whose contractions enable the animal to swim.

It is only a small step from this body plan to that of a fish. Like all animals with backbones [3, 4], the fish has a body divided into head, trunk, and tail, the latter lying behind the anus. It also has a chambered heart and a blood system divided into veins, arteries, and capillaries. In the fish, oxygen is obtained from the surrounding water by gills well supplied with blood vessels.

The next really significant anatomical advance came with the emergence of life on land. For the first time animals breathed through lungs and had internal skeletons strong enough to support four well-defined limbs, each with a five-toed foot, on which the body could be raised off the ground. Other advances on the vertebrate plan [3, 4, 5] are essentially adaptations to different modes of life.

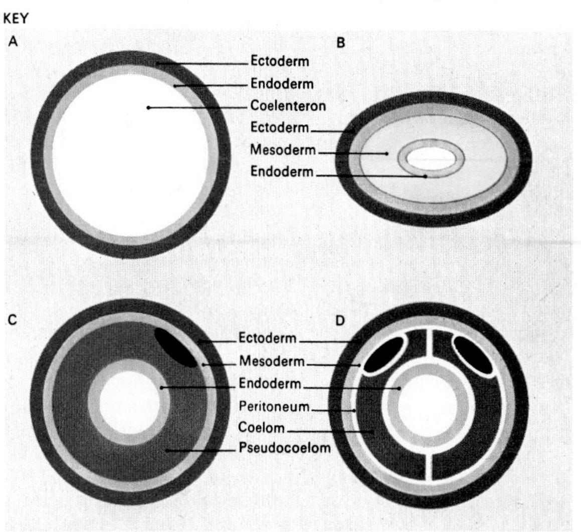

KEY
A
B
Ectoderm
Endoderm
Coelenteron
Ectoderm
Mesoderm
Endoderm
C
D
Ectoderm
Mesoderm
Endoderm
Peritoneum
Coelom
Pseudocoelom

Sections cut across animal bodies show increasing complexity. The two-layered coelenterate body [A] and the three-layered flatworm body [B] are both simple tubes. All higher animals [D] have an additional cavity, the coelom. The pseudocoelom of roundworms [C] differs in its lining.

5

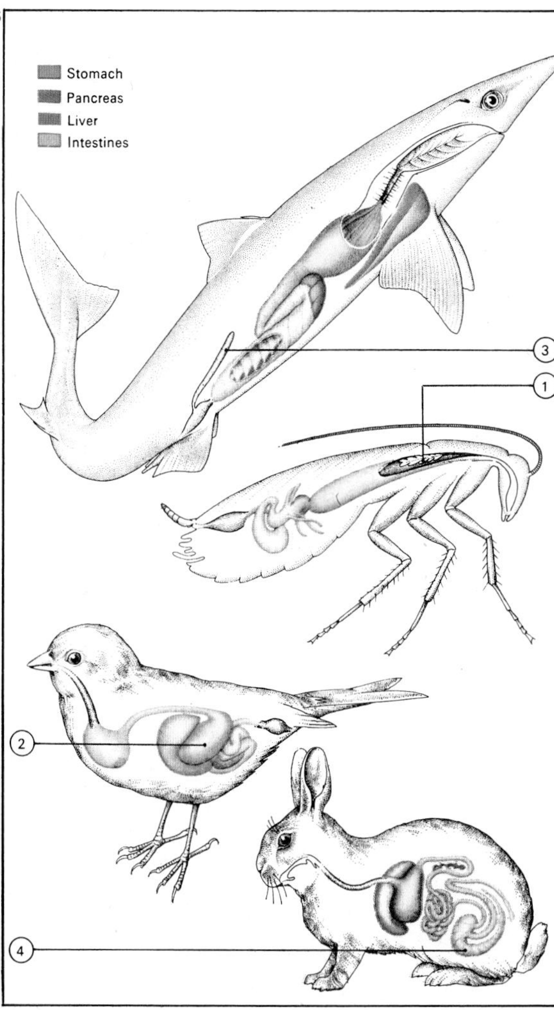

Stomach
Pancreas
Liver
Intestines
3
1
2
4

5 The tubular digestive system consists of an intake opening, the mouth, leading to a storage and processing chamber, the stomach. This is followed by the intestines where the absorption of digested food takes place. Associated with the intestines and involved in digestion are the liver and the pancreas. Differences in animal digestive systems are the result of dietary dissimilarities. The insect has a gizzard [1] with "teeth" for grinding food. A bird's gizzard [2] is a modified stomach with a horny lining. It contains small stones that are used to grind food. The fish has a rectal gland [3] to excrete excess salt. The rabbit has an enlarged caecum [4] that is the site of cellulose digestion.

6

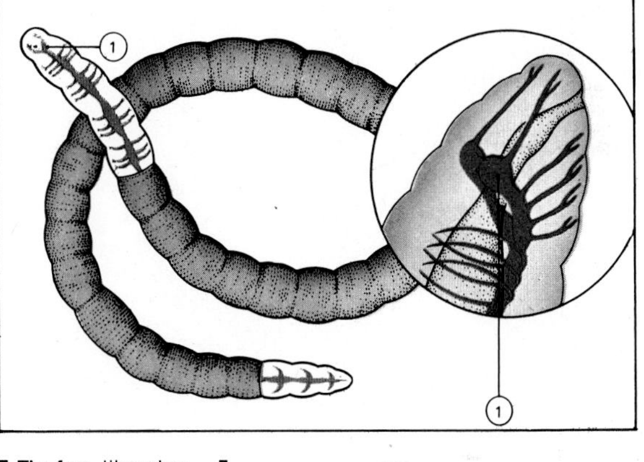

1
1

6 The nerve cord of the earthworm is specialized at the "head" end of the animal to form cerebral ganglia [1] This development makes possible a range of coordinated responses to the environment such as, for example, in finding food, in burrowing, and in mating. The outer covering of the body of the earthworm bears receptors that respond to light, temperature changes, and chemicals, as well as to touch.

7

7 The frog, like other vertebrates, has a well defined head containing a lobed brain. The cerebrum is concerned with learned behavior, the optic lobes with vision, the olfactory lobes with interpreting smells, and the cerebellum with balance and the coordination of movement. No single area of the frog's brain shows any dominance over the others, but compared with a fish the cerebrum is larger.

8

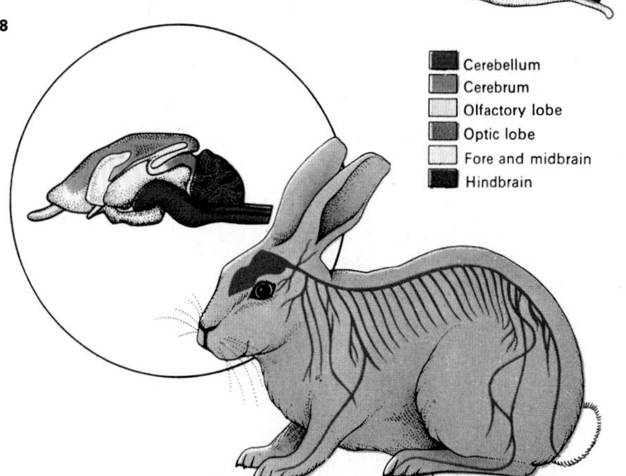

Cerebellum
Cerebrum
Olfactory lobe
Optic lobe
Fore and midbrain
Hindbrain

8 The brain of the rabbit, like that of other mammals, is remarkable for the size of its cerebrum and its cerebellum. These are associated, respectively, with the large range of voluntary movements the animal performs and with the very fine degree of muscular coordination achieved. The size of the optic and olfactory lobes is an indication of the importance of the senses of sight and smell. In man the cerebrum overshadows all other parts.

Sex in the animal world

In the natural world all sexual activity is directed to one end: the fusion of male and female sex cells, or gametes, to form the first cell of a new organism. The means to that end are many. In flowering plants, for example, the male sex cells, or pollen, may reach the female sex cells by being borne on the wind or carried by animals. In the animal kingdom the male and female gametes are, respectively, spermatozoa and eggs [Key], and their fusion may take place either inside or outside the female body. In all living organisms vastly more sex cells are produced than are ever shed or fused, and this seems to be a natural insurance policy for fertility.

The evolution of sex

Why did sex evolve? Many primitive animals reproduce simply by budding and in principle there is no reason why humans should not do the same. But sex, by bringing together the inherited characteristics of two parents in a new combination, makes for greater variety in the offspring. In evolutionary terms this variety is the essence of survival, for variety offers a wide choice on which the forces of natural selection can operate. It provides the material for an infinite number of genetic variants within a species and for vigorous offspring, and it allows for the "storage" of genes that are not immediately useful. These genes, inherited from one parent, are dominated or "disguised" by genes from the other.

Bringing the sexes together

The first requirement for mating is to bring the two animals together at the right moment [1]. In many species this is achieved by the secretion of chemicals known as pheromones by the female. The male traces her by sense of smell, sometimes extremely sensitive, as in moths, which are able to detect one or two molecules of female pheromone borne on the wind [5]. Other animals may rely more on other senses. Male frogs, for example, have special mating croaks with which they attract females. The tones of the male's croak only reaches the right pitch when he is old enough to mate. Until then, females ignore him.

The most spectacular ways of bringing the sexes together are the elaborate visual displays of some animals—from the "dance" of the red-bellied male stickleback in the mating season to the courtship rituals of some birds which may flaunt their plumage like the peacock or even build a decorative lovenest like the bowerbird.

Many of the mating calls and visual displays of animals serve a dual function. Not only do they bring the two sexes of the same species together, but they also ensure that the two sexes in different species are kept apart. The behavioral ritual has to be exactly right or the female will not respond. The same applies to pheromones; the chemicals must be exactly the right ones, sometimes even in exactly the right proportions, or the male will not court the female. This is why so much evolutionary energy has been expended on extravagant or subtle ritual and decoration in the mating season. It plays a vital part in the process of reproductive isolation by which similar species can live in the same territory and yet remain separate.

CONNECTIONS

See also
416 Principles of hered
464 Principles of anima behavior
530 How birds reprodu
700 Reproduction
556 How mammals beha
558 How primates beha
476 Land and sea snail
480 Squids and octopus
830 Types of ritual
1814 Cosmetics and perfumes
370 Farm stockbreedin and management

1
8
10
2
7
6
9
3
5
4

1 Sexual reproduction in one form or another has evolved in most life forms. Some mosses [1] have male and female sex cells on different plants; sperm is carried to the egg on a film of moisture. Many plants, such as foxglove [2], have female eggs and male pollen on one plant. Earthworms [3] are also hermaphrodites (with both sex organs) but nonetheless mate with a reciprocal exchange of sperm. In some single cells [4], mating involves only the exchange of small pieces of genetic material rather than a complete package. Sticklebacks [5] and frogs [7] fertilize their eggs externally. In many other creatures such as dragonflies [6], finches [8], field mice [9], and rabbits [10] fertilization is internal. Fertilization in all reptile, bird, and mammal species takes place internally.

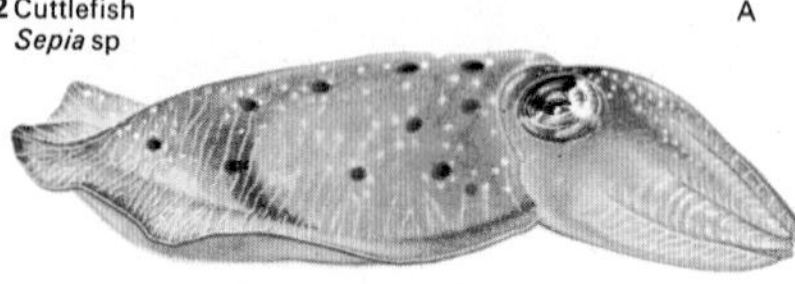

2 Cuttlefish
Sepia sp
A

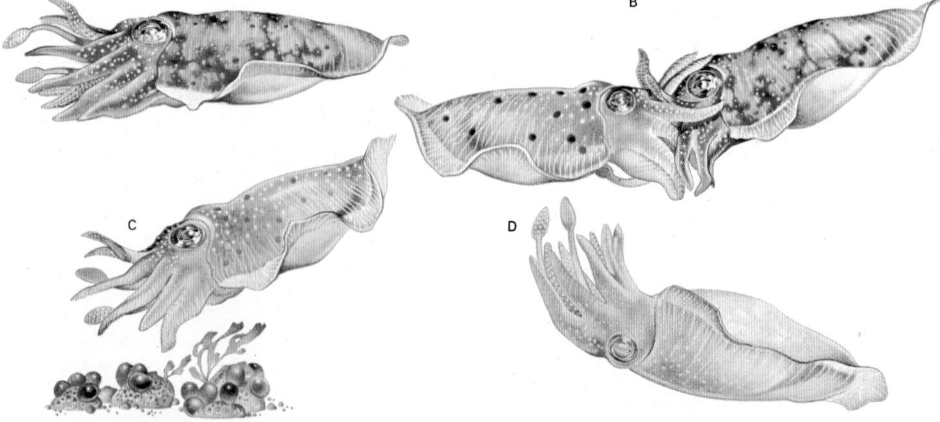

B
C
D

2 The male cuttlefish courts a female [A] by displaying to her, often turning red all over as he does so. The two animals then join [B], either side by side or head-to-head, with their tentacles entwined. The male then transfers a package of sperm—a spermatophore—to the female's mantle cavity using a modified tentacle, the hectocotylus, which may then drop off. The male then dies [D]. So does the female, but not until after she has laid her eggs on the sea bed [C].

There are several mechanisms, once male and female have been brought together, for the final step of fusing the genetic information of the two. Some single-celled organisms have a special structure on the cell surface that effects the transfer of small pieces of DNA (the material containing the genetic blueprint) from one organism to another. In hermaphrodites, such as the earthworm or the snail, the behavior of the two partners is identical, each transferring sperm to the other. In terrestrial species with distinct sexes, fertilization is usually internal, the male inserting a penis or some analogous organ into the female to deposit the sperm. Sometimes, as in most aquatic species, the eggs are laid first and fertilized externally afterwards, while cuttlefish and squids, in which fertilization is internal, make use of specialized tentacles for transferring sperm to egg [2].

Socio-sexual relations

The social aspects of sex range far beyond courtship and mating. The hormones that burnish the plumage of the male mallard and bring a scarlet color to the belly of the stickleback are also the ones that in many species cause aggressive behavior between males. Rutting deer engage in ritual encounters that, although they may not represent fighting in the strict sense, certainly appear hostile from a human point of view.

In insects socio-sexual relationships can be extremely complex. The honeybee queen monopolizes the attentions of the male drones, whose sole function is to fertilize her eggs. The workers, which build, clean, forage, and act as nursemaids for the entire colony, are females prevented from reaching sexual maturity by the food they receive and by chemicals (pheromones) that they lick from the queen.

In higher animals living in colonies or herds it is usual for a single male to dominate other males and gain exclusive access to a large number of females. In deer and seals, for example, a male gathers around him a harem of many females [6]. Among seals the younger bulls may not acquire harems for many years after they have reached sexual maturity.

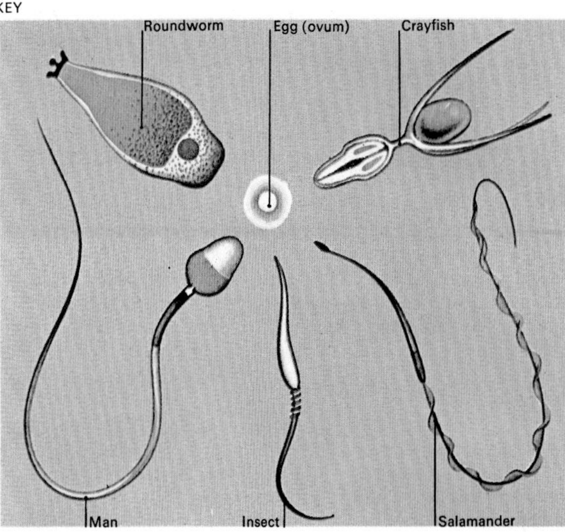

KEY
Roundworm
Egg (ovum)
Crayfish
Man
Insect
Salamander

At the moment of fertilization, the main goal of sexual activity, the sperm from the male partner enters the egg from the female, each carrying genetic material. Sperm vary in shape and size from species to species but can be grouped into two categories: flagellate and non-flagellate types.

3 The courtship and mating ritual of the Uganda kob begins when the male circles the female with a prancing gait, his head held high to display the white patch on the throat [A]. He sniffs her vulva [B], causing her to squat, and can detect by her smell that she is in heat. He then tests her willingness to mate with a sharp kick [C] probably a relic of fighting behavior. If she is ready the male quickly mounts her [D].

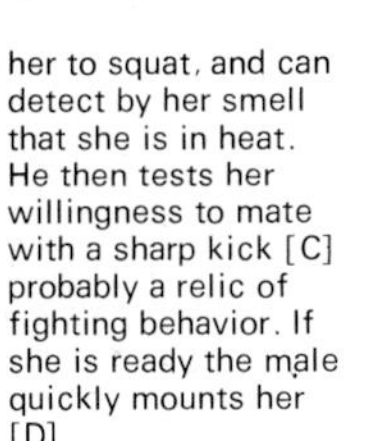

3 Uganda kob
Kobus kob tomasi
A
B
C

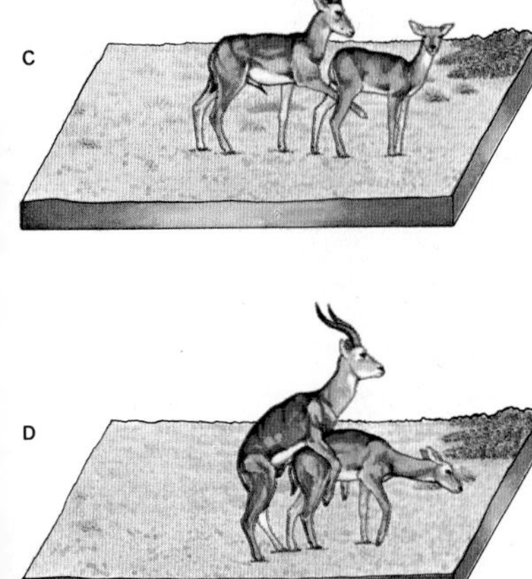

D

4 The pairing of the wandering albatross *(Diomedea exulans)*, which breeds on islands in the Subantarctic, takes place by way of an elaborate ritual involving both auditory and visual signals. This ritual establishes a pair bond. The sequence begins with neck stretching and bill clapping [A] followed by bowing of the heads in a preening posture [B]. The birds then stretch toward one another [C] with more bill clapping, "nibbling" at one another's bills. The male then circles the female with wings open; she turns on the spot, always facing the male [D], until finally both stand with necks stretched and wings open [E] as the preliminary to mating.

4 A
B
C
D
E

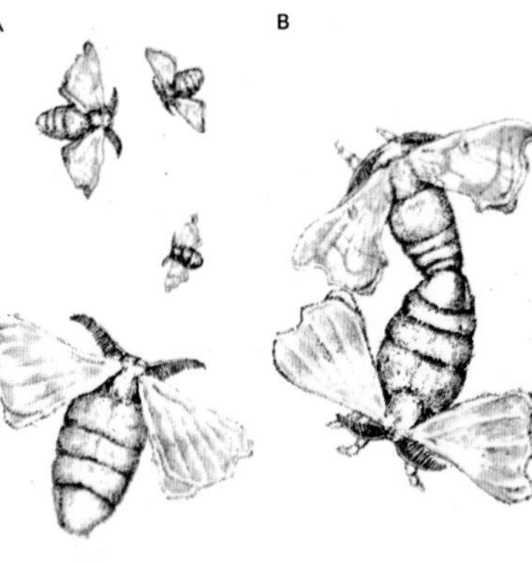

5 A
B

C

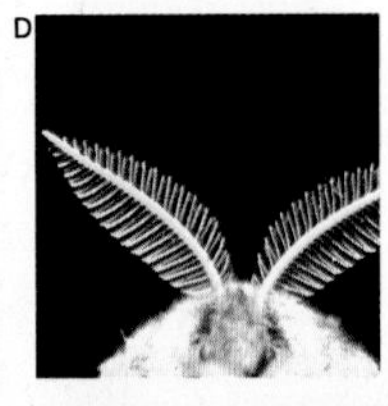

D

5 A male moth detects a female [A] by a "sex scent" or pheromone she secretes from a gland on her leg. He "smells" this scent by means of sensory receptors on his antennae [D] that enable him to detect very small quantities of the pheromone. After copulation [B] and fertilization the female seeks out a suitable larval food plant, such as mulberry, on which to lay her eggs [C].

6

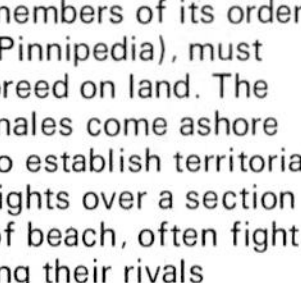

6 The South American sea lion *(Otaria byronia)*, like other members of its order (Pinnipedia), must breed on land. The males come ashore to establish territorial rights over a section of beach, often fighting their rivals fiercely. As the females come ashore the bulls try to gather a harem of 10, which precipitates more inter-male rivalry. Soon after the females have landed they give birth to single pups (conceived the previous year) after which the bulls mate with them. For most seals and sea lions the gestation period is from 250–365 days. It is so variable because delayed implantation is known to occur in some species.

Principles of animal behavior

Animals must be observed in their natural habitats if their behavior is to be understood, because much of their innate behavior has evolved to enable them to survive, feed, and reproduce in those habitats [1]. Instinctive patterns of animal behavior have been molded by the demands of the environment in the course of evolution and reflect the animal's evolutionary history in just the same way that its skeleton does. Insects provide excellent study material for investigating innate animal behavior because, unlike mammals, their actions are not modified by a higher intelligence.

The basis of behavior

An animal's action—a cat pouncing on a mouse, a peacock spreading its tail to the hen, a spider spinning its web—is determined by three factors. One is the external stimulus—the mouse or the peahen. The second is its own sense organs and nervous system, which determine what the animal can see, hear, and feel and also what behavior patterns it can produce in response. The third is the state of its body chemistry, such as its state of hunger or, for example, the level of its sex hormones.

Not only do the sense organs of animals give them widely varying amounts and types of information about the world about them, but studies of animal behavior have made it clear that, for each species, there are certain stimuli that have special significance. These, known as sign stimuli, may be visual, like the red belly of the male stickleback during the breeding season, which induces the female to spawn, or chemical, like the chemical released by the female moth to attract the male. Chemical sign stimuli are known as pheromones. Sign stimuli trigger what are known as innate releasing mechanisms (some sign stimuli are called releasers), which lead to the expression of stereotyped behavior [Key].

Feeding behavior

Both the stimuli and the behavior triggered by them vary enormously in complexity. One of the most primitive patterns is that involved in the feeding behavior of the frog [4]. Frogs perceive as prey any relatively small moving object in their field of vision and the detection of such an object releases a rapid dart of the tongue in its direction. But while the feeding behavior of the frog is barely more than a reflex, the feeding behavior of some insects involves complex social signs. Most famous of these is the dance of the worker honeybee [2], which won its discoverer, Karl von Frisch (1886–), a Nobel Prize in 1973. A worker bee that has found a food source returns to the hive and performs a "dance" that conveys to other workers information on the location and nature of the food. The dance causes the workers to leave the hive in the direction encoded in the forager's movements.

A fact of which beekeepers are only too aware is that honeybees become enraged at the approach of a thunderstorm, the result of their sensitivity to changes in atmospheric electricity. Recent studies suggest that they begin to show the first signs of annoyance as the electrical oscillations approach ten kilohertz when a thunderstorm is on the way, but it has been noticed also that

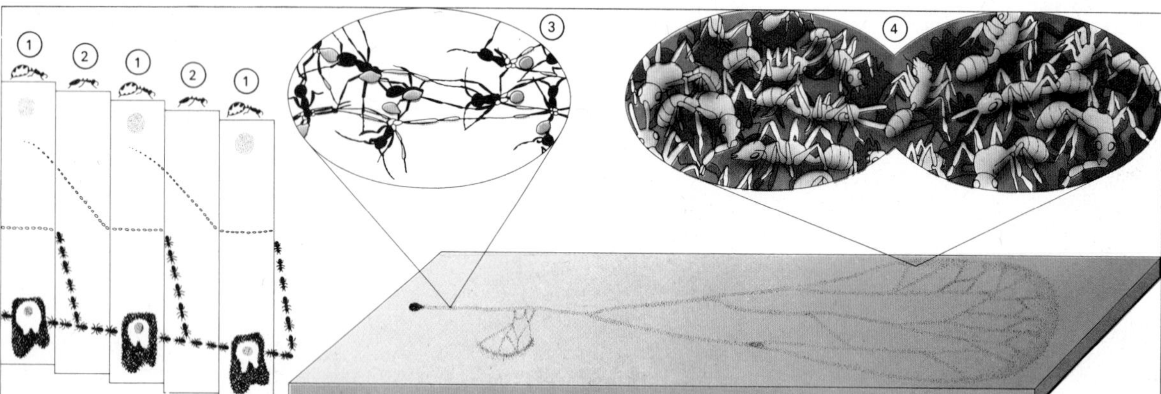

1 Army ants *(Eciton burchelli)* of the tropics are found in colonies made up of soldiers and two kinds of worker ant, with a queen whose function is to lay eggs and produce more ants. Army ants undergo an alternating rhythmic cycle of static [1] and nomadic [2] phases. In the static phase, eggs are laid by the queen and the colony remains in one bivouac for two or three weeks. During the nomadic phase, raiding swarms leave the bivouac but instead of returning, set up fresh bivouacs each night. The advancing front of a swarm on the move is a dense mass of ants [4], while the bivouac is made by ants that are attached to each other to form chains and bridges [5].

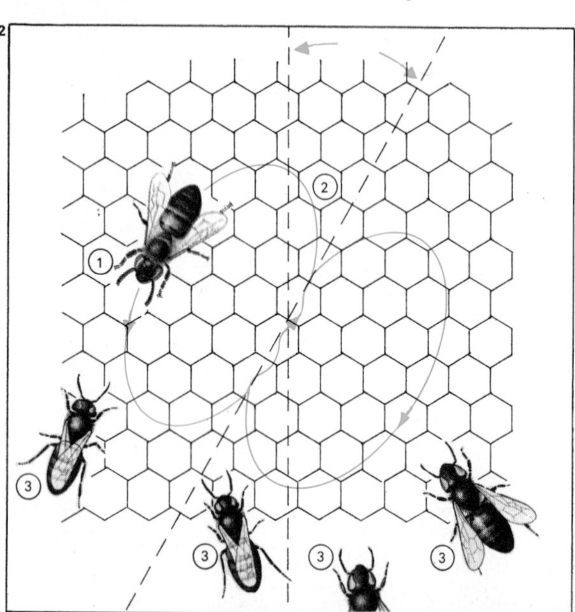

2 The dance of the honeybee stimulates worker bees at the hive to go out and find food sources whose location is encoded in the messenger bee's movements. The messenger [1] moves in a figure eight [2]; the angle at which it dances indicates the position of the food source in relation to the sun, and the duration of abdominal flicks during the straight run is proportional to the distance of the food from the hive. When other workers [3] go out for food they follow the messenger's directions and, furthermore, gather nectar only from flowers that have the same scent as that returned to the hive by the messenger bee.

3 Locusts are types of grasshoppers that respond to overcrowding by migrating in huge swarms. In the solitary *(solitaria)* form [A], the locust is relatively inactive. The *gregaria* form is distinguished by the darker color of the immature insects, or nymphs. A *gregaria* female [B] is shown laying eggs, or ovipositing. The eggs hatch into flightless nymphs, which in crowded conditions gather into an army and set off in search of food. The nymphs mature on the way and take to the air as a swarm, a relentless plague that devastates everything in its path and often ruins vast areas of cropland as it moves across the country.

other influencing factors include increased atmospheric moisture and a fluctuating concentration of negatively charged ions. Without these, it has been observed, electricity alone will not infuriate the insects.

The gregarious feeding behavior of some insects often has terrifying consequences. At a given level of overcrowding, African locusts [3] gather into a vast, rapacious swarm.

In army ants [1] social behavior is as rigid as that of honeybees, with different forms performing different and highly organized functions in the colony. Army ants bivouac in a solid column formed from the linked bodies of their fellows in a cylinder up to 39 in (1m) across, with the queen and larvae in the center. During the day, foraging parties of ants disperse in fan-shaped swarms. For most ants, the signals that control cooperative behavior are chemical.

The voracious behavior of ants and locusts is the evolutionary outcome of the need to feed. In the caddisfly larva [5], this necessity has given rise to an amazing chain of behavioral responses resulting in its clothing itself in a private fortress. In this case, each stage of the building triggers the next stage, until the protective home is finished.

Instinct and learning

In higher animals, behavior is such an intricate mixture of the learned and the instinctive that the two components become almost impossible to separate, but in insects, where instinct is predominant, the contribution of learning can clearly be defined. Digger wasps, for example [6], deposit their eggs in holes in the ground stocked with prey and then set out on a hunting expedition in which they capture further prey to take back to the next hole. The choice of prey is entirely innate and is based partly on visual clues but also on smell (for digger wasps that capture bees cannot distinguish bees from other insects of about the same size on sight alone). The return to the next hole after a hunting trip, however, entails learning. The wasp circles the hole for a few seconds before leaving and remembers its appearance so that it recognizes it after a trip lasting an hour or more.

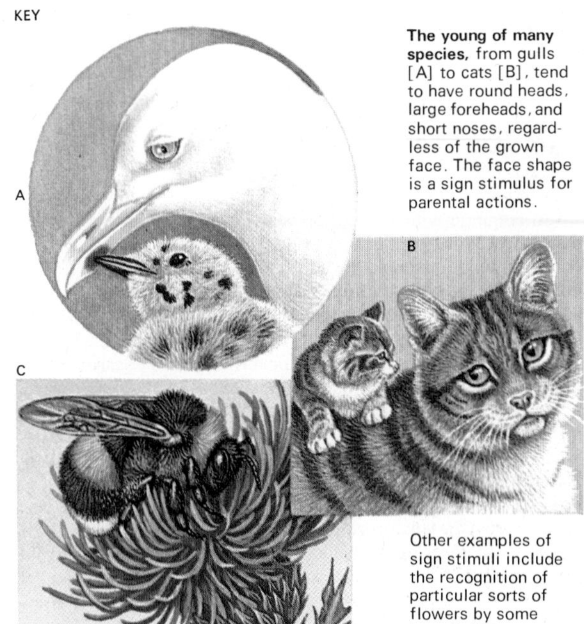

KEY
A
B
C

The young of many species, from gulls [A] to cats [B], tend to have round heads, large foreheads, and short noses, regardless of the grown face. The face shape is a sign stimulus for parental actions.

Other examples of sign stimuli include the recognition of particular sorts of flowers by some insects [C].

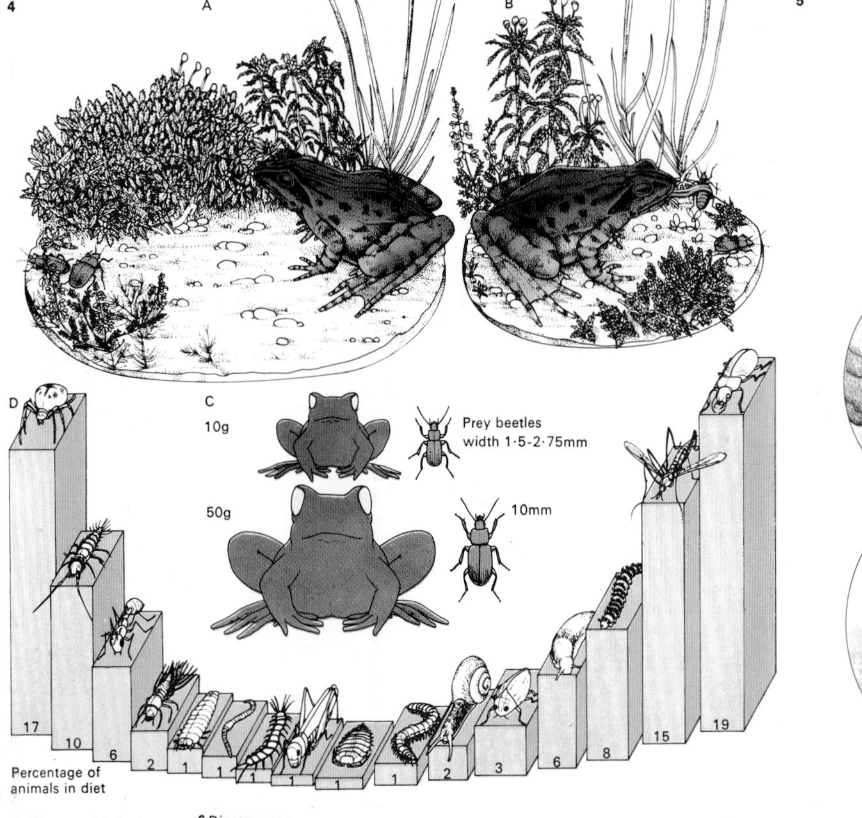

4
A
B
C
D
10g
50g
Prey beetles
width 1·5-2·75mm
10mm
17
10
6
2
1
1
1
1
1
1
2
3
6
8
15
19
Percentage of animals in diet

4 The motionless hunter, the common European frog, like all frogs, feeds by catching prey only when it comes in reach of its tongue [A, B]. The size of prey the frog will eat depends entirely on its own size – whether it can open its mouth wide enough to accommodate the meal [C]. The usual diet of the frog includes insects of all kinds [D], according to their seasonal availability, but beetles make up the greatest proportion.

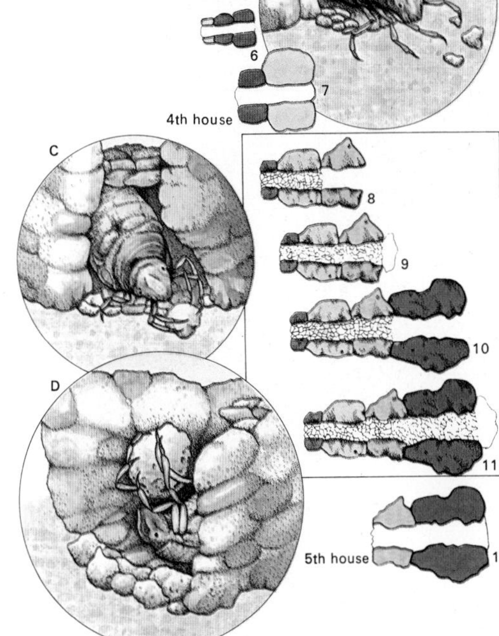

5
A
B
C
D
1st house
2nd house
3rd house
4th house
5th house
1
2
3
4
5
6
7
8
9
10
11
12

5 Caddisfly larvae build a total of five houses [A] through their larval development, one for each of five molts and each bigger than the previous one. Cross sections show the series of houses [A1–7] and how they are enlarged by stones [8–12]. In between, during molts, the larva blocks off the opening. The larva filters out small stones by raking [B], it rejects large stones [C] by touch. The stones are fitted together [D] by silk spinning.

6 Digger wasp
Sphex sp

A B C D

6 The female digger wasp learns the landmarks around a nest hole [A, B]. If the conspicuous pine cones [C] are moved, the wasp searches in vain for the nest [D].

Single-celled animals and sponges

The single-celled organisms that are regarded as being the simplest forms of animal life are protozoans, members of the large group, or phylum, of living creatures known as the Protozoa. They number more than 30,000 species and nearly all of them are invisible to the naked eye, growing no larger than the size of a pinhead.

In common with all other animals, the majority of Protozoa are mobile and take in complex food materials that are broken down inside the body to provide energy. In addition they all need water to survive and although the majority are either marine or freshwater species a significant number live as parasites within higher animals, including man, where they may cause a variety of diseases.

Methods of locomotion

Protozoa are divided into four main classes depending on the ways in which they move. Members of the class Mastigophora bear one or more of the threadlike structures—flagella—whose beating action propels the animal forward. All the Ciliata are equipped with many hairlike projections known as cilia [3]. These lash in a synchronized pattern and in doing so produce movement. The members of the class Sarcodina move by means of pseudopodia, extensions of the protoplasm with which their cells are filled. The Sporozoa all lack specialized structures for locomotion.

Varieties of Protozoa

The Protozoa with flagella include members of the genera *Euglena* and *Chlamydomonas*—all of which contain chlorphyll and thus photosynthesize—plus the dinoflagellates encased in a cellulose capsule, which are found in the plankton. *Trypanosoma* is a parasite that lives in man, where it causes sleeping sickness. The trumpet-shaped *Stentor* is a remarkable ciliate which, when feeding, attaches itself to a water plant.

The sarcodines are also a diverse group. *Amoeba proteus* is a common free-living representative; others, such as species of *Entamoeba* live within the human gut, some of them as parasites. The plankton contains foraminiferans, marine species that secrete calcareous shells around their bodies. Radiolarians and heliozoa form comparable shells of silica.

As exceptions to the rule of diversity, all sporozoans show a high degree of uniformity. They are all parasites and lack the cell parts (organelles) necessary for locomotion and feeding—they have no need to move and they take in predigested food. They also have unique life cycles incorporating both asexual and sexual reproductive stages in which spores, each bearing hundreds of offspring, are produced.

Most protozoa reproduce asexually by splitting in two, a process called binary fission. When fully grown, an equal division of cytoplasm and nucleus takes place and "daughter" organisms are formed [5]. In adverse conditions some flagellate (Mastigophora) and some ameboid (Sarcodina) species secrete a hard and impervious protective cyst with which they surround themselves and in which the cell may duplicate itself. When the environment is again favorable the cyst breaks open and releases the offspring, which reproduce asexually.

CONNECTIONS

See also
458 The animal kingdo
406 Life and its origins
422 Bacteria and virus
624 Life in the oceans
312 The living soil
710 The causes of illness: 1
732 Diseases of the Th World
506 Invertebrate odditi
476 Land and sea snai
1478 The scale of the ur verse
432 Algae and seaweed

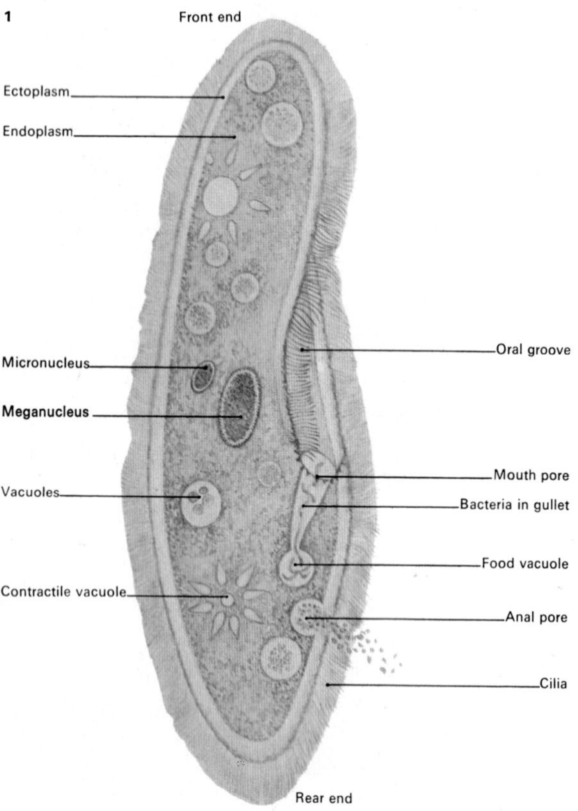

1
Front end
Ectoplasm
Endoplasm
Micronucleus
Meganucleus
Vacuoles
Contractile vacuole
Oral groove
Mouth pore
Bacteria in gullet
Food vacuole
Anal pore
Cilia
Rear end

1 Paramecium is a specialized single-celled animal. The outer layer of the cell, the ectoplasm, is bounded by a tough skin through which many tiny hairs, or cilia, protrude. Regular beating actions of the cilia produce locomotion. The oral groove extends into the inner granular endoplasm, forming a blind-ended gullet. Food particles are pushed into the gullet by ciliary action and enclosed in vacuoles. As food vacuoles circulate through the endoplasm their contents are digested by enzymes. Undigested and unabsorbed materials are expelled via the anal pore. The water content of the cell is controlled by the action of the two contractile vacuoles. Of the two nuclei present, the larger, or meganucleus, controls all day-to-day activities of the cell, while the smaller micronucleus is concerned with cell reproduction.

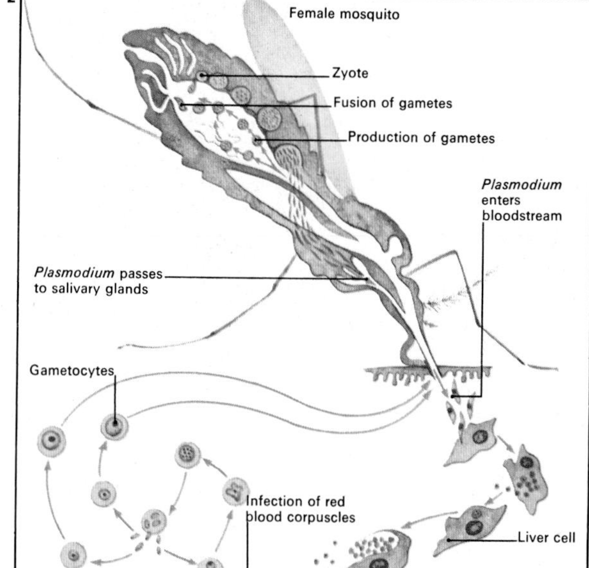

2
Female mosquito
Zyote
Fusion of gametes
Production of gametes
Plasmodium enters bloodstream
Plasmodium passes to salivary glands
Gametocytes
Infection of red blood corpuscles
Liver cell

2 The malaria-producing protozoan *Plasmodium vivax*, when injected into the human blood stream by an infected female *Anopheles* mosquito, rapidly invades the liver cells and multiplies. As cells rupture the plasmodia escape and infect other cells. In blood cells numerous cycles of multiplication, cell rupture, and invasion occur before sex cells (gametocytes) appear. If another mosquito takes up the infected cells, gametocytes divide within its stomach, forming gametes. These fuse to produce zygotes, which release plasmodia to enter salivary glands and repeat the cycle.

3 Protozoa move about in three main ways. Sarcodines move by means of streaming protoplasmic extensions [A]. The forward flow of inner plasmasol, coupled with a continuous reversible change of fluid plasmasol into the outer, jellylike plasmagel, produces movement. Mastigophora are equipped with flagella whose whiplike beating actions [B, C] pull the organism along. Ciliata have numerous tiny beating cilia [D] to propel them.

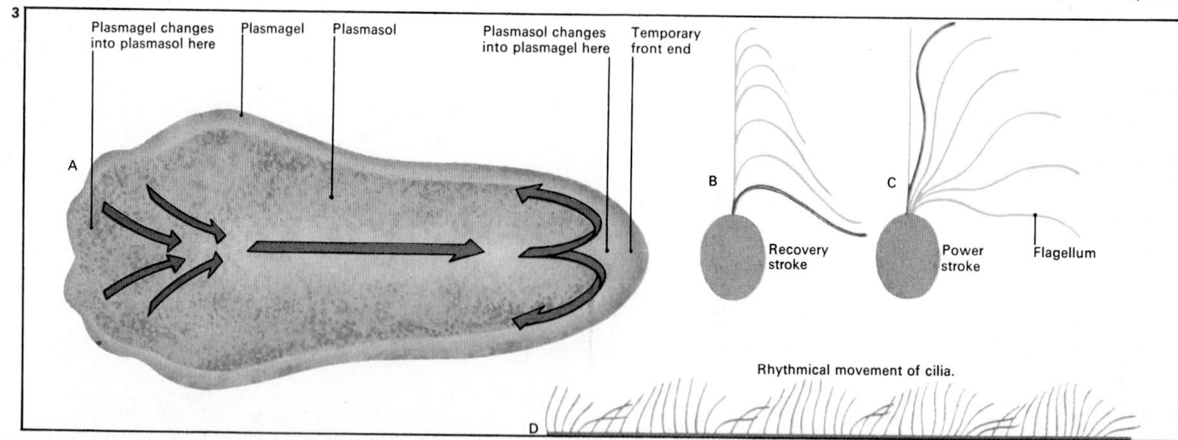

3
Plasmagel changes into plasmasol here
Plasmagel
Plasmasol
Plasmasol changes into plasmagel here
Temporary front end
A
B
C
Recovery stroke
Power stroke
Flagellum
Rhythmical movement of cilia.
D

Sexual reproductive methods also occur in Protozoa. *Paramecium* [1, 4], generally reproduces sexually by conjugation; two individuals of different strains fuse side by side and, after nuclear divisions and interchange of nuclear material, they separate. Further division of each organism takes place, producing eight daughter cells, four from each, with nuclei of mixed parentage.

The structure of sponges

Sponges are simple creatures formed through the aggregation of many cells. They are not considered true metazoans because they do not have tissue layers. They are classified in the phylum Porifera.

All sponges are sedentary aquatic animals and are divided into three main classes. Calcareas, such as *Sycon, Leucosolenia,* and *Grantia,* bear an internal skeleton built up of "needles" of calcium carbonate. The glass-sponges, or Hexactinellida, are equipped with skeletons containing silica. Most representatives of the third class, the Desmospongiae, possess a skeleton composed of the protein spongin, as in the case of the common bath sponge *(Spongia mollissima)* [6], but others bear a skeleton of spongin and silica.

The basic structure of sponges consists of a sac with a large opening at the top and numerous perforations in the side walls. The outer layer of the sac is formed by a mosaic of flattened "covering" cells. The inner layer is composed of "collar" cells with whiplash flagella like those of the flagellate protozoa. Numerous cells, some like amebas and others employed in the secretion of skeletal substance, lie sandwiched between inner and outer strata, forming the middle or mesenchyme layer.

Sponges reproduce asexually by budding. Buds may separate from the parent and grow into new individuals or remain attached to form a branched colony. Sexual reproduction in sponges begins with the formation of sperm and eggs from undifferentiated mesenchyme cells. Although most sponges are hermaphrodites, self-fertilization is rare. Sperm released from one sponge are carried by water to the eggs of another and fertilization follows.

KEY

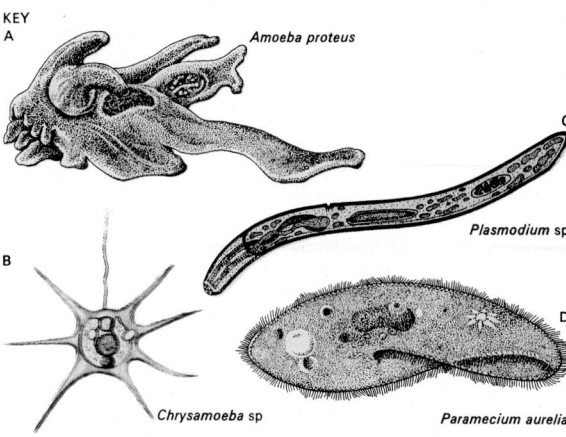

A *Amoeba proteus*

B *Chrysamoeba* sp

C *Plasmodium* sp

D *Paramecium aurelia*

Protozoans can be divided into four classes on the basis of the way in which they move about. Sarcodines, such as *Amoeba proteus* [A], move by means of pseudopodia, extensions of their protoplasm. Pseudopodia are also used to form food cups for the capture of prey. Most sarcodines are free-living protozoans. Locomotion in Mastigophora [B] is produced by whiplike flagella. Sporozoa, which include the malaria-producing *Plasmodium* [C], are all parasitic and lack specialized locomotor structures. The class Ciliata contains a majority of free-living (nonparasitic) species such as *Paramecium* [D] that move by ciliary action.

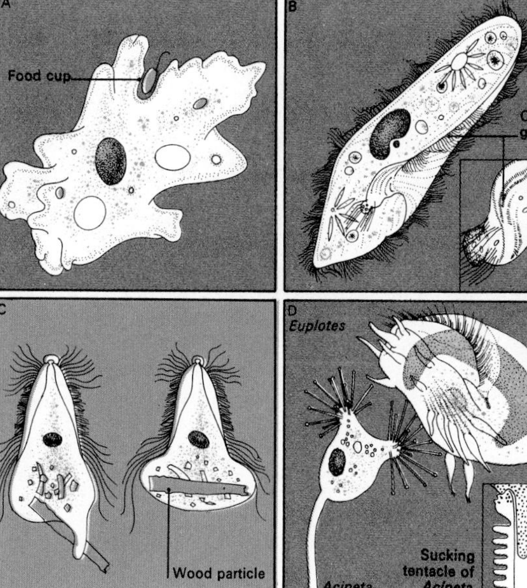
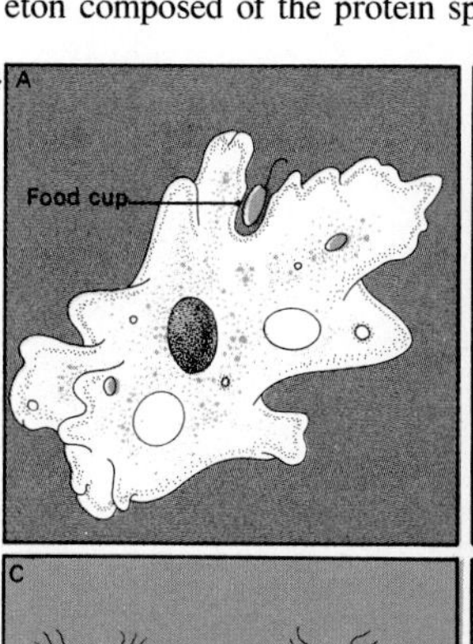

4 A
Food cup

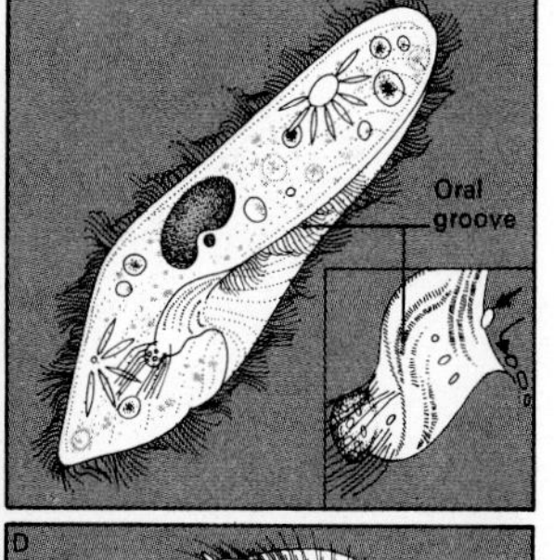

B
Oral groove

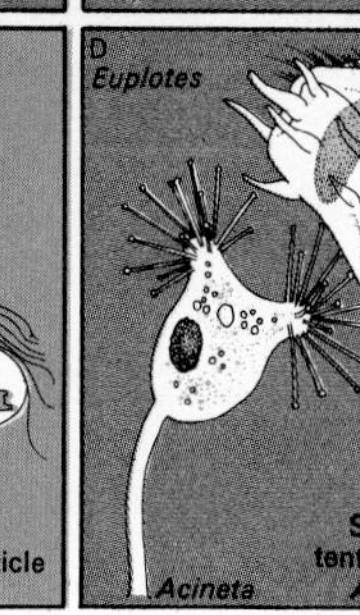

C
Wood particle
D
Euplotes
Sucking tentacle of Acineta
Acineta

4 Like other animals protozoans feed on complex organic food materials to obtain energy. Ameba [A] engulfs materials by forming food cups around them with special pseudopodia. Food is later broken down within vacuoles by the action of digestive enzymes. *Paramecium* [B] feeds primarily on bacteria drawn into the oral groove by the cilia. *Trichonympha* [C] are symbiotic protozoans that live in the guts of termites. They engulf wood particles that the termites cannot digest themselves. *Acineta* [D] feed only on specific species of ciliates, such as *Euplotes*. These are often several times larger than the *Acineta* themselves.

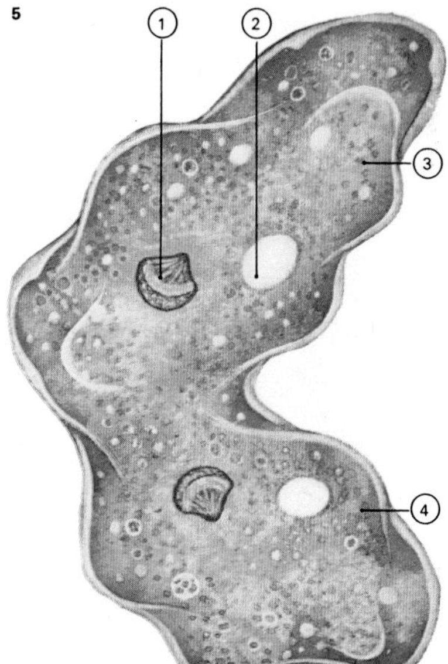

5
1
2
3
4

5 Asexual reproduction in protozoans takes place by binary fission. In amebas this simply involves the splitting of one cell into two equal parts. The process starts with the appearance of chromosomes in the nucleus, which become shorter and thicker. Chromosomes, each made up of two chromatids, line up across the cell while contractile vacuoles [2], having previously replicated, begin to separate. The chromatids are drawn apart [1] and the cytoplasm starts to split into equal halves. With chromosome division complete, the cytoplasm finally divides. The two resulting daughter amebas [3, 4] are identical.

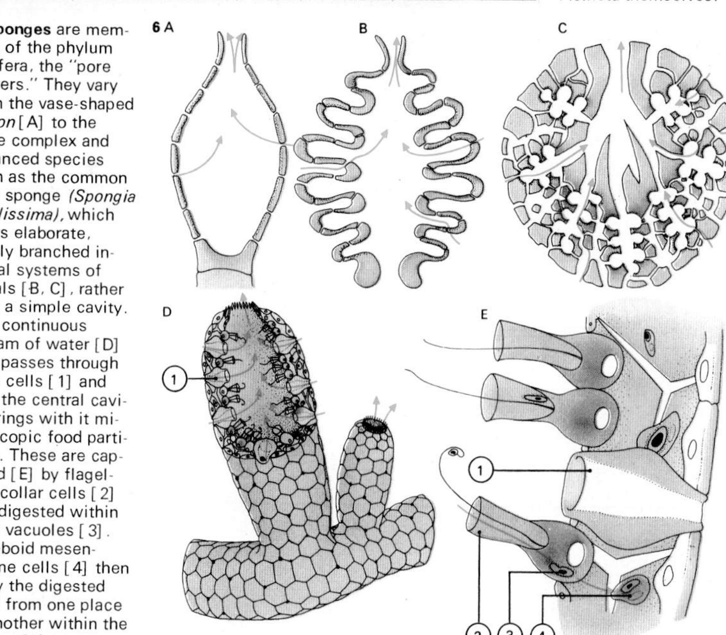

6 A
B
C
D
E
1
2
3
4

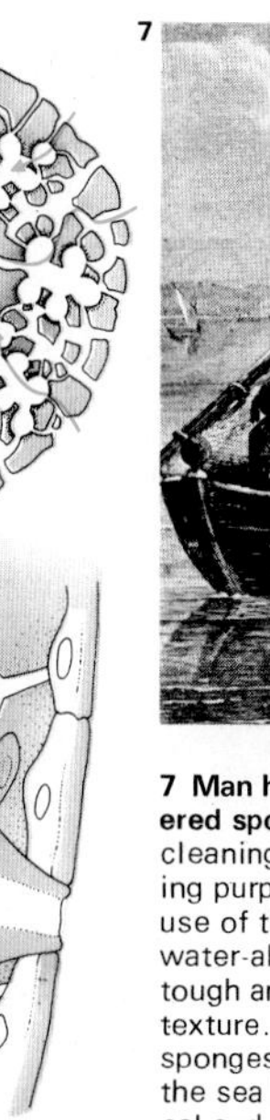

6 Sponges are members of the phylum Porifera, the "pore bearers." They vary from the vase-shaped *Sycon* [A] to the more complex and advanced species such as the common bath sponge *(Spongia mollissima)*, which bears elaborate, highly branched internal systems of canals [B, C], rather than a simple cavity. The continuous stream of water [D] that passes through pore cells [1] and into the central cavity brings with it microscopic food particles. These are captured [E] by flagellate collar cells [2] and digested within food vacuoles [3]. Ameboid mesenchyme cells [4] then carry the digested food from one place to another within the walls of the sac.

7

7 Man has long gathered sponges for cleaning and polishing purposes, making use of their soft, water-absorbent, yet tough and durable texture. Commercial sponges are found on the sea bed in tropical and subtropical waters. In deep waters they are collected by divers, but in shallow coastal areas they can simply be pulled up from the ocean floor by using trident-like poles. Once collected, the sponges are dried to kill the thin layer of protoplasm that surrounds the horny skeleton. Further cellular material, and the shells and skeletons of the organisms trapped within the fibrous remains, are removed by repeated pounding of the sponge. It is then washed, dried, and trimmed before it is used commercially.

Sea anemones, hydras, and corals

Flowerlike sea anemones, rocklike corals, and translucent, tentacled jellyfish are among the most attractive creatures in the ocean. Diverse though they may seem, these animals are all coelenterates [Key], a group numbering more than 9,500 species, all of which are aquatic and most of which inhabit marine shallows.

Corals, jellyfish, and fresh water hydras are all classified as coelenterates because they possess a large, central body cavity, or coelenteron (hence their name). The body is made up of a concentric arrangement of body parts and cells are organized into rudimentary tissues. The cells work in co-operation as elements of the whole, not as independent members of loose cell aggregates as in sponges.

The coelenterates are the first animals on the evolutionary tree to show this level of organization and they all share a similar pattern of tissue arrangement. There is an outer layer of cells, the ectoderm, and an inner layer, the endoderm, separated by mesogloea, a gelatinous material that may be only a thin film, as in *Hydra,* or that may form the bulk of the animal, as in the jellyfish.

Coelenterates such as sea anemones are solitary animals, but others, such as the plantlike *Obelia,* are made up of a colony of several sub-individuals, or polyps. When these polyps are not identical the animal is said to be polymorphic; some marine colonies have separate polyps for feeding, for protection, for reproduction, and even special structures for floating.

Phases of development

The life history of many coelenterates shows two distinct phases—a free-swimming or medusoid stage followed by a sessile, or polyp, stage of attachment and growth—which means that some species have both bottom-living and open-water forms. In different coelenterates, however, there is a different emphasis of these two phases and this explains why these animals show such a variety of form. In *Obelia* [5], for example, the medusoid phase is relatively brief and followed by a longer, predominant period of attachment, a cycle typical of the coelenterate group called the Hydrozoa. When mature, the *Obelia* colony gives rise to reproductive polyps, which each then produce new medusae of their own.

Among the Scyphozoa, or true jellyfish, the situation is reversed and it is the medusa that predominates. In the third coelenterate sub-group, the Anthozoa, which includes the corals [6–8] and sea anemones [4], the attached phase predominates and there is no medusoid phase. In these types, eggs and sperm are shed directly from the gonads and pass out through the mouth. The fertilized eggs then divide to form balls of cells that settle and grow into new individuals.

There are, however, some exceptions to this systematic grouping, especially among the Hydrozoa. *Hydra* [1], for example, has no medusa and its life history resembles that of the sea anemone—except that the sperm and eggs develop on the outside instead of on the inside of the polyp. And a few hydrozoans have a dominant medusa and a polyp stage that is either minute or does not occur at all.

CONNECTIONS

See also
470 The jellyfish
458 The animal kingdom
624 Life in the oceans
460 Animal anatomy
622 The seashore: life between the tides
564 Fossils without backbones
268 Coastlines
248 Sedimentary and metamorphic rocks

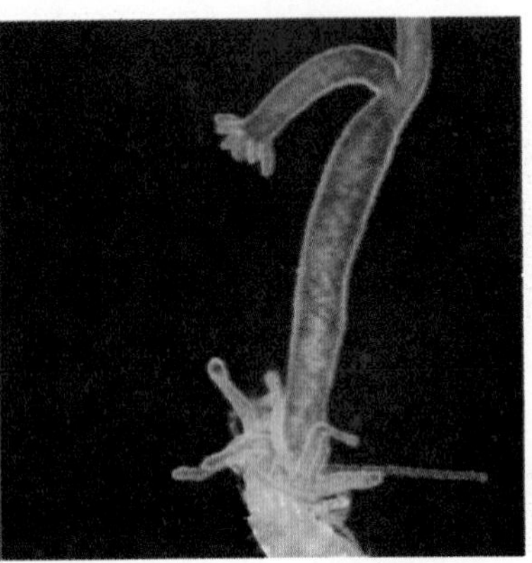

1 Species of Hydra are found throughout fresh water of the world with the exception of frigid zones. When feeding, *Hydra* narrows its body and allows its extended tentacles to trail freely. If a water-flea or some other potential food source brushes against the tentacles, the nematocysts discharge, partially paralyzing the prey. Next, the tentacles contract and draw the victim toward the mouth to be eaten.

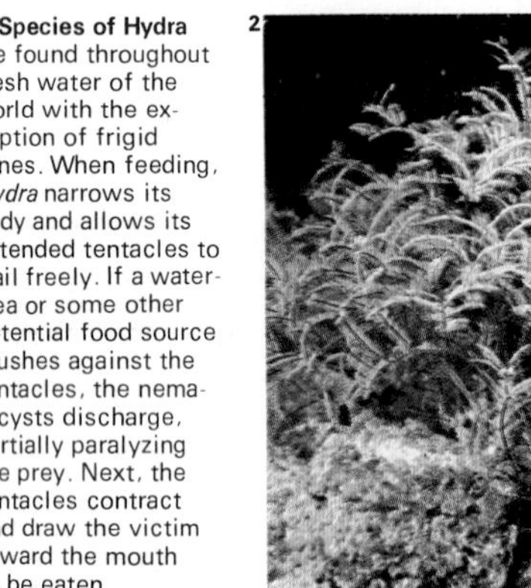

2 The stinging hydroid *(Lytocarpus philippinus)* is one of the colonial coelenterates. The colony arises from a single individual that has produced buds in much the same way as its solitary cousins, with the difference that the new polyps remain attached to their parent. The coelenteron forms a continuous cavity and the end result is a branching collection of hydroid polyps.

3 Budding is one method of asexual reproduction. When conditions are good, a small bulge [1] forms on the parent *Hydra*. This grows into a new individual and eventually detaches itself.

4 The dahlia anemone *(Tealia felina)* belongs to the group of coelenterates known as sea anemones. They can be found stuck firmly to rocks below the high-tide line. When left exposed by the receding tide the anemone reduces itself to a compact, bloblike mass. When covered by water the tentacles expand, ready to trap any small crabs or fish that stray within reach.

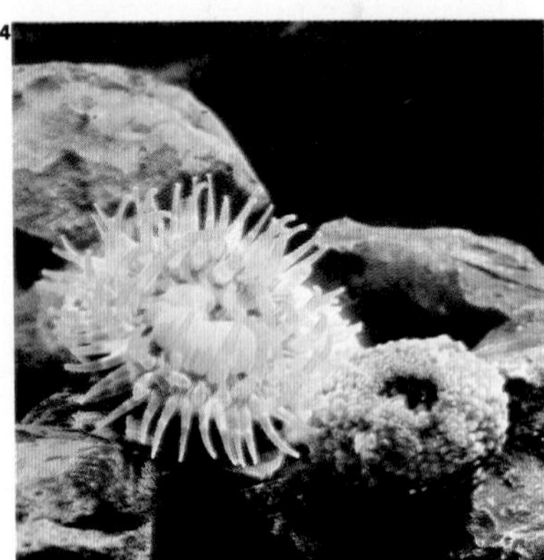

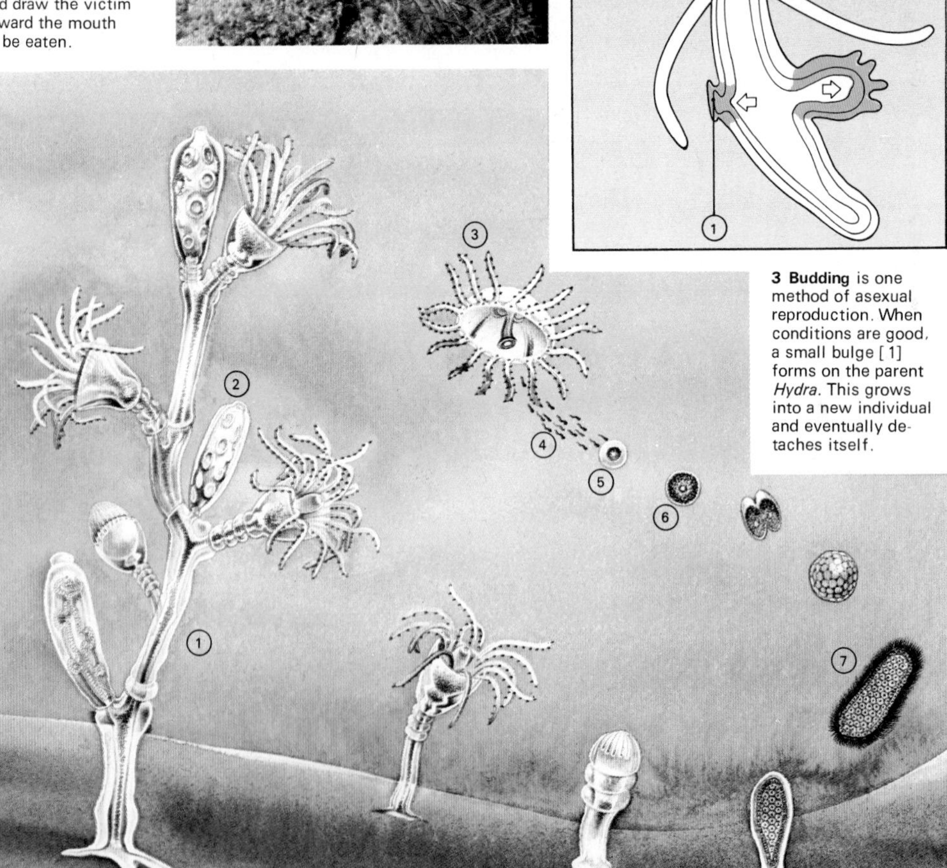

5 A mature colony [1] of *Obelia* bears reproductive polyps [2] concerned solely with production of the free-swimming, or medusoid, form [3] that carries *Obelia's* reproductive organs. Once separated from the parent colony the medusae shed their sperm [4] or eggs [5] into the water. The fertilized egg [6] subdivides to form a ciliated larva [7] that swims until it finds a suitable surface on which to settle. Here it grows and buds asexually, becoming in turn an *Obelia* colony.

Compared with the complexities of their sexual lives, the asexual reproduction of coelenterates is relatively straightforward; a *Hydra* can bud [3] a new individual from its body, a sea anemone divides itself in two. Asexual reproduction may also result in the formation of colonies of individual polyps that are linked by a continuous inner cavity (coelenteron). This ability of the coelenterates to reproduce asexually means that they have considerable powers of regeneration; a mere fragment broken from an animal may be able to grow into a complete new individual.

How coelenterates feed

In most coelenterates feeding is assisted by the tentacles that surround the mouth. Liberally armed with stinging "cells" (nematocysts) [9], these tentacles paralyze the prey and draw it toward the captor. All the tentacles cooperate, bending to attach themselves to the victim and thrusting it into the coelenteron. The mouth then closes and the endoderm cells secrete digestive enzymes into the central gastric cavity. The food is broken down either into soluble products available for immediate absorption or into small particles that can be engulfed by the endodermal cells. The residue of the meal is expelled, by means of contractions of the body, through the reopened mouth.

Powers of movement

All coelenterates can move, although motion may be restricted to mere bending of the tentacles and shape changes. All movements are made possible by the muscle fibers in the cells of both the ectoderm and endoderm. In addition, the base of the sea anemone is richly endowed with muscles that enable it to move over rocks with a gliding action. *Hydra* can perform similar movements, but it may also change position more rapidly by a kind of somersaulting action.

Even the simplest of coelenterate movements requires some degree of coordination. This coordination is the responsibility of a diffuse network of nerve cells that runs through the tissues and forms a primitive nervous system.

KEY

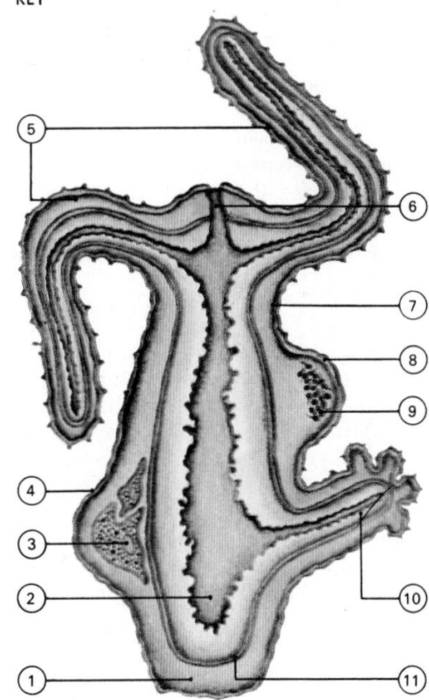

5
6
7
8
9
4
3
2
10
1
11

A hydroid polyp—shown here in schematized longitudinal section—illustrates some of the characteristics of coelenterates. The mouth [6], surrounded by a ring of tentacles[5] bearing stinging cells, opens directly into the digestive cavity, or coelenteron [2]. The body wall is constructed of an outer layer of cells known as the ectoderm [7]. This is separated from the inner layer, or endoderm [11], by a jelly-like layer, the mesogloea [1]. Coelenterates may reproduce by budding [10] or by a sexual process in which sperm [9] generated by a testis [8] fertilize the egg [3] shed by an ovary [4].

6

6 Staghorn coral is a widespread species of coral. At first glance it may not be obvious that corals are living animals, since the individual polyps are enclosed in stony, protective cups. The individual polyps of coral resemble small sea anemones but these warm-water species tend to live colonial rather than solitary existences.

7

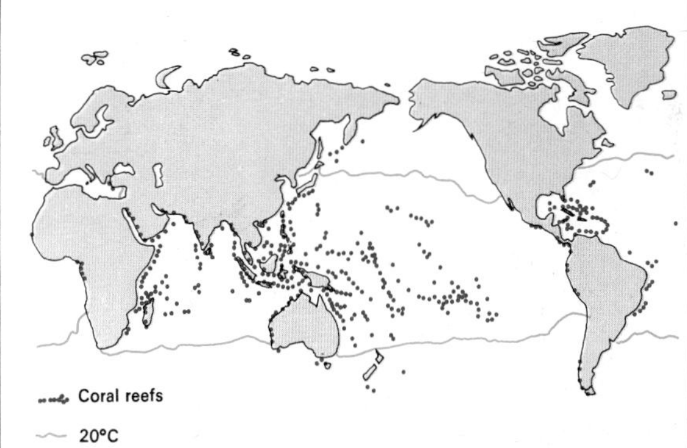

Coral reefs
20°C

7 Reef-building corals—like those of the Great Barrier Reef fringing the Australian coast—grow only in the tropical oceans bounded by the 68°F (20°C) isotherm shown on the map. As the polyps bud and divide, so the colony expands upward and outward. The resulting masses of limestone long outlast the polyps that secreted them. Corals can be exquisitely colored but most are either pale or white.

8

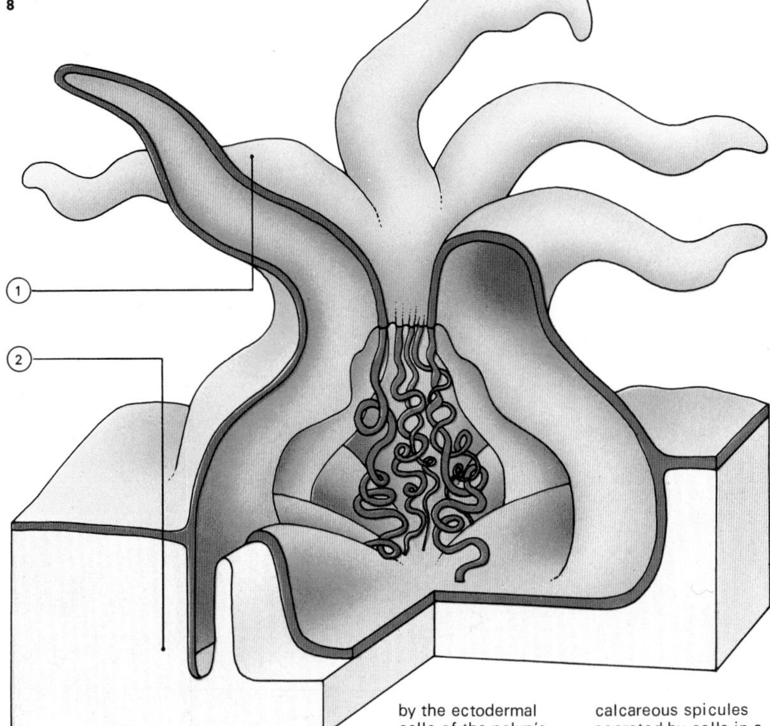

1
2

8 A coral polyp [1] lies embedded in its protective cup [2]. In stony corals—the type shown here—the cup is made of calcium carbonate (limestone) secreted by the ectodermal cells of the polyp's outer surfaces. In other groups, such as sea pens, the skeleton is internal and is formed of horny or calcareous spicules secreted by cells in a central and conjoined mesogloeal layer, thus providing support to the whole branching colony.

9

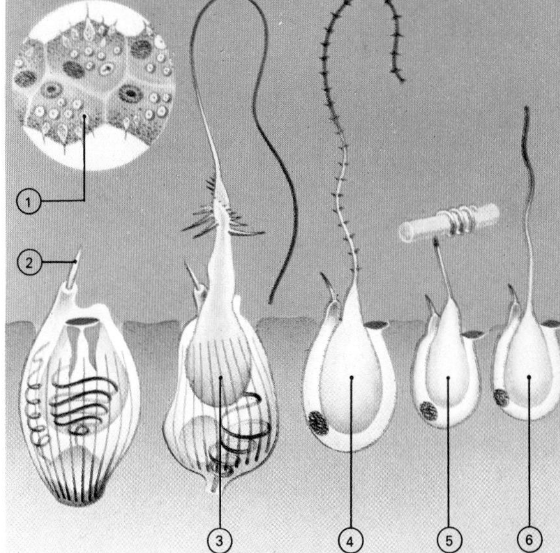

1
2
3
4
5
6

9 Nematocysts, or stinging capsules [1], are the coelenterates' weapons of offense and defense. Located in greatest concentration over the tentacles, they play an essential role in feeding. Some [3] inject a paralyzing poison into the prey; some nematocysts [4, 6] are able to secrete a sticky substance; while others [5] are equipped with coiling threads. Projecting from one side of each nematocyst is a small hair [2], which acts as a trigger. When the hair is touched by a passing animal the nematocyst fires. The mechanism of firing is not fully understood, but is thought to depend on a sudden pressure increase of the fluid within the capsule. Each nematocyst fires only once, after which it is discarded.

The jellyfish

The fearsome Portuguese man-of-war might seem to have little in common with *Hydra,* the sea anemones, and corals, but all of them are coelenterates. Jellyfish belong to the classes Scyphozoa (true jellyfish) and Hydrozoa (among which they form a separate subdivision called the Siphonophora). The Scyphozoa are typically free-swimming, bellshaped individuals while the hydrozoan jellyfish are colonies of animals that behave as an individual. Each member of the colony is modified to perform a particular function such as feeding or swimming. The siphonophore colonies are always free-floating or swimming instead of being attached like other hydrozoans.

The scyphozoan group

A scyphozoan, or true jellyfish [Key] and a simple polyp such as *Hydra* are both built with the same kind of body plan. In all coelenterates, the ectoderm (outer layer of cells) is separated from the endoderm (inner layer) by jellylike mesogloea. There is so much mesogloea in the jellyfish that it makes up most of the animal's bulk.

Jellyfish come in diverse shapes and sizes, but all share the basic "umbrella" form, frequently with a margin fringed with tentacles. The mouth lies at the center of the underside of the umbrella, usually separated from the gastric cavity proper by a short tube, the manubrium. The corners of the mouth are often drawn out into trailing fronds, the mouth lobes. The fronds consist of membranes, folded and narrowing to a point. In *Aurelia* [1], the moon jelly common to all the world's oceans, these mouth lobes bear ciliated (hair-fringed) grooves surrounded by nematocysts (stinging cells) that paralyze the small prey on which *Aurelia* feeds. The cilia sweep the prey up through the mouth and into the gastric cavity where digestion then takes place.

Many jellyfish are bulky and need an efficient system of moving food, oxygen, and waste products around their bodies. This is provided by a branching series of pouches and radical canals that link the central gastric cavity with a narrow circular canal running around the margin of the bell. The ciliated lining of these canals keeps a current of water circulating freely to carry the materials along.

The free-swimming medusoid (bell-shaped) stage plays a highly important part in the life of the Scyphozoa. The medusa is a vehicle for the gonads (sex organs) and is the form in which the animal passes most of its life.

Jellyfish swim by a kind of jet propulsion, alternately opening and shutting the bell and so thrusting themselves through the water. The jelly counteracts the movement of the muscles, restoring the animal to the open shape when the muscles relax.

An active free-swimming existence clearly demands more sophisticated sense organs than those needed by an animal permanently attached to rocks or seaweed. Many jellyfish have light-sensitive areas near the margin of the bell which detect light intensity and thus the surface of the water. A series of statocysts (balancing organs) permits the animal to stay upright in the water. These two systems are important because jellyfish are slightly denser than seawater and, as a result, sink unless they

CONNECTIONS

See also
468 Sea anemones, hydras, and corals
626 Animals of the ocea
458 The animal kingdom
712 The causes of illness: 2

1 The life cycle of the jellyfish Aurelia includes the adult medusoid form [A] with four violet, horseshoe-shaped gonads around its mouth. Testes and ovaries are on separate individuals. Sperm emerges from the mouth and enters the female's gastric cavity. Each fertilized egg grows into a ciliated larva [B], which is released and settles on a rock or similar surface [C]. It grows into a small polyp called a scyphistoma [D] and at the right temperature divides into eight-armed buds called ephyrae [E]. These break free [F] to become adults.

2 The colonial hydrozoan Velella is made up of a colony that lives at the sea surface. It is supported by an oval float bearing a vertical sail, which allows it to be wind-driven. There are three kinds of polyps: a large feeding polyp just below the float [1]; an outer ring of protective polyps with stinging cells [2]; and between these two there is a cluster of reproductive polyps [3].

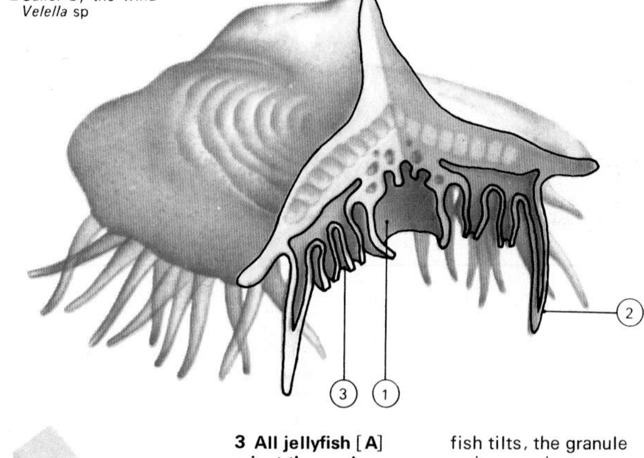
2 Sailor-by-the-wind
Velella sp
2
3
1

1

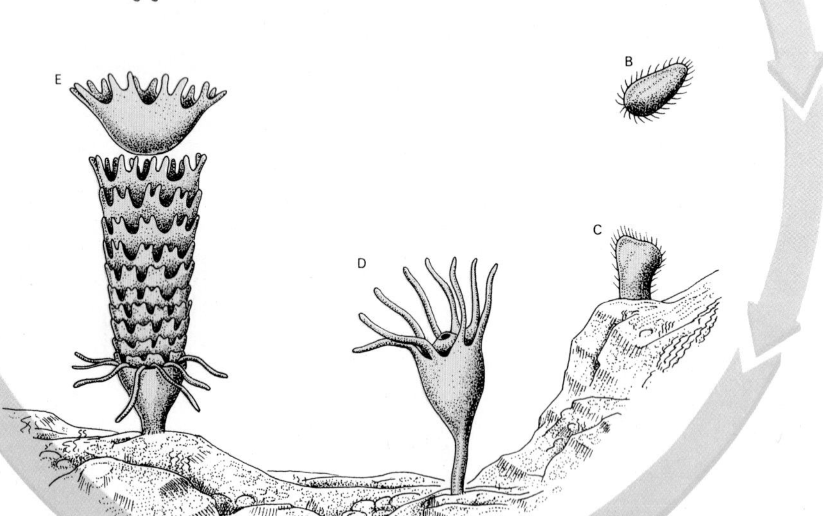
A
B
C
D
E
F

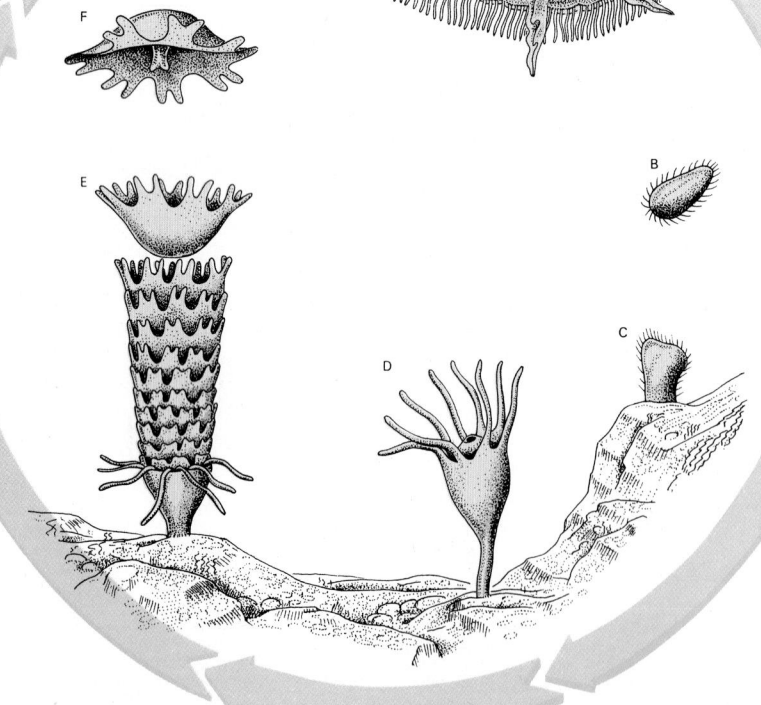

3 All jellyfish [A] orient themselves by means of balancing organs called statocysts [B]. Each is a fluid-filled sac [1] enveloping a solid hanging granule called a statolith [2]. When the jellyfish tilts, the granule swings against an adjacent sensory process [3] that sends nerve impulses to the contractile cells of the umbrella. Extra contraction on one side causes the animal to right itself.

3

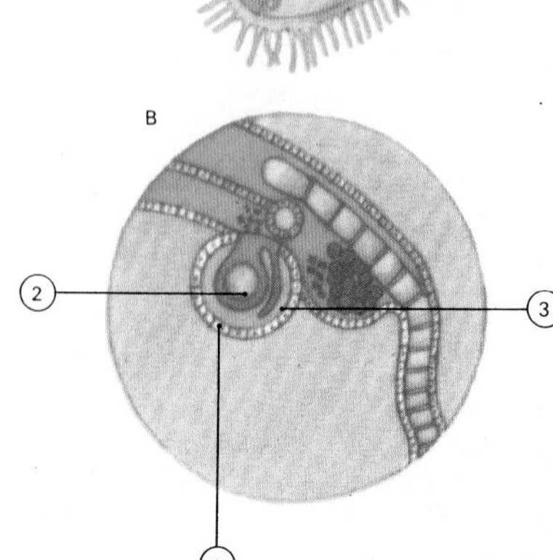
A
B
2
3
1

keep on pulsating. A jellyfish that was unable to distinguish "up" from "down" could easily swim directly toward the sea bottom, and away from its normal habitat.

The hydrozoan group—the siphonophores
The second group of jellyfish, the unattached colonial hydrozoans, show a high degree of polymorphism. *Velella* [2] illustrates several of the polyp types, but it is by no means the most complicated. Its feeding, reproductive, and protective polyps hang from the underside of a gas-filled float, itself thought to be a modified medusoid. Medusoids contribute to the swimming bells that propel siphonophores which do not rely on the wind for movement. *Physophora* has both a float and swimming bells which drag the rest of the polyps behind them. A similar arrangement is found in *Muggiaea* except that this jellyfish has just one large swimming bell at the head of the colony and no float.

Physalia, the Portuguese man-of-war [4], is without doubt the best known of the colonial hydrozoans and its appearance is justifiably frightening to human swimmers. Its sting is extremely painful and the appearance of large fleets of *Physalia* off bathing beaches can be regarded as a local disaster. The man-of-war paralyzes fish—its normal food—with its long, stinging tentacles and then pulls its inert prey in toward the waiting mouths of the feeding polyps.

The comb jellies
The Ctenophora [5], or comb jellies, are a phylum that is separate from the coelenterates but has much in common with them. Both share the inner and outer layers separated by a jellylike mass. The typical ctenophore tends to be rounded with a gastrovascular cavity opening from a mouth that is located at the lower pole. At the opposite end is a small sense organ that keeps the animal in balance and corresponds to the statocyst of the true jellyfish. Ciliated bands around the body drive comb jellies through the water. Some ctenophores have tentacles, and these are armed with adhesive cells (not stinging cells as in coelenterates), used in capturing prey.

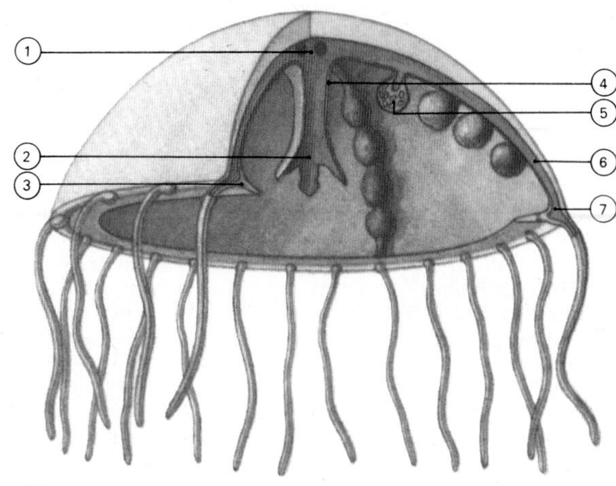
KEY
1
2
3
4
5
6
7

The diagram of a scyphozoan jellyfish shows the gastric cavity [1] opening to the exterior through a mouth [2] at the end of a stalklike organ (manubrium) [4]. The cavity is continuous, via a series of radial canals [6], with a circular canal [7] around the margin of the bell. The margin bears tentacles and sense organs connected by nerve rings [3]. The gonads [5] open into the gastric cavity.

4 *Pelagia noctiluca*

4 Many beautiful species of jellyfish float in the world's oceans. The Portuguese man-of-war *(Physalia)* is not a true jellyfish but a colony of hydrozoans. The tentacles may grow to about 60ft (18m) long. It feeds mainly on fish up to 12in (30cm) in length. Although an inhabitant of tropical waters, it is sometimes found in temperate seas. Species of *Chrysaora, Rhizostoma,* and *Cyanea* are found in the Atlantic Ocean but they are rarely seen close inshore. The largest species of cyanea *(C. arctica)* has been recorded as having a bell measuring 12ft (3.7m) across, with tentacles more than 100ft (30m) long. A jellyfish that lives in warm seas and is responsible for luminescence in the water is *Pelagia noctiluca.* The sea wasps (e.g. *Chironex)* of the tropical Pacific are among the most dangerous animals known, despite their small size—about 12in (30cm). Some possess a poison that can kill a man. *Porpita* is a colonial species like *velella.*

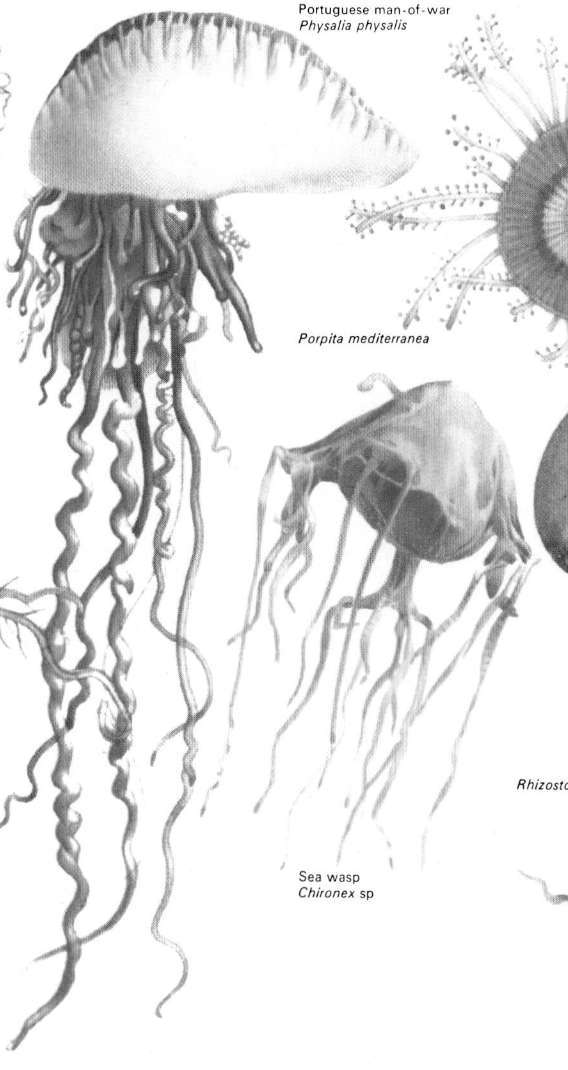

Portuguese man-of-war
Physalia physalis

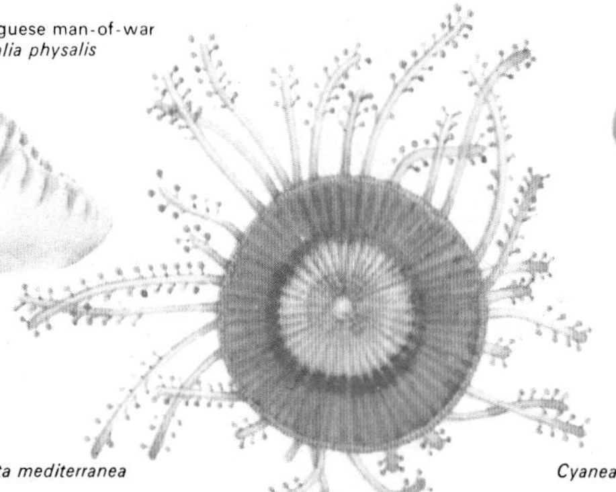

Porpita mediterranea

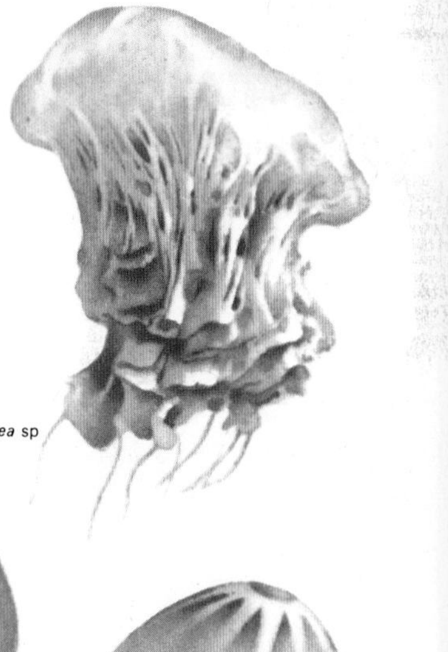

Cyanea sp

5

Sea gooseberry
Pleurobrachia sp

Sea wasp
Chironex sp

Rhizostoma sp

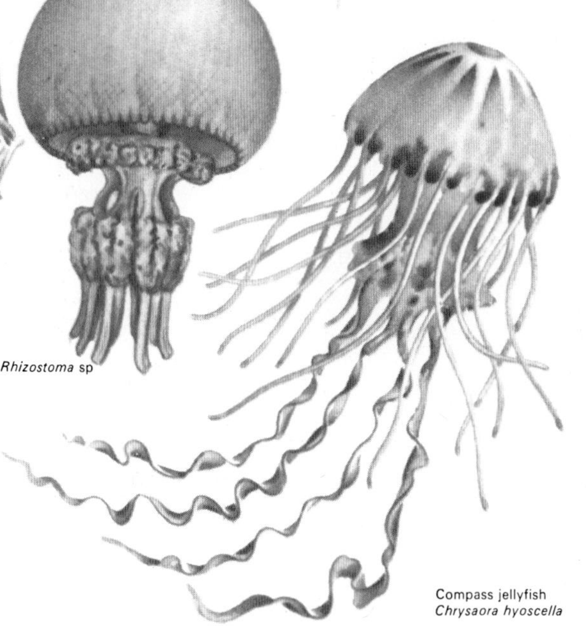

Compass jellyfish
Chrysaora hyoscella

5 The sea gooseberry, *Pleurobrachia,* is a member of the phylum Ctenophora. It swims by co-ordinated beating of the rows of cilia that lie in eight bands stretching almost the whole distance from pole to pole. It has long tentacles that sweep the water for small animals. These are periodically "wiped" off near the mouth located at the lower pole. They are common in coastal waters all over the world and may grow to 1.5in (3.8cm) in diameter.

Flatworms, flukes, and tapeworms

Flukes and tapeworms are two groups of parasitic animals with deadly potential to both man and his domestic animals. These creatures, whose effects, worldwide, have considerable economic significance, are placed zoologically together with the free-living flatworms in the phylum Platyhelminthes. All of them have simple bodies and all are bilaterally symmetrical—that is, the two halves that lie on either side of a line drawn from head to tail are mirror images.

The life of flatworms

The free-living flatworms, or turbellarians, [1] are simple, ribbon-like creatures with no circulatory system and only a single opening into the gut. The inner and outer cell layers, the endo- and ectoderm, characteristic of the coelenterates (the sea anemones and their relatives) are separated, however, by a third mass of cells—the mesoderm. The mesoderm is responsible for the formation of muscles and reproductive organs. Indeed, the appearance of true organ systems is in itself a further advance over the coelenterate body plan.

Most of the free-living flatworms are aquatic. They move by creeping (effected by muscle contraction) or by beating of the hairlike cilia with which their surface layers are usually covered. These flatworms, which are carnivorous, use their pharynx (the tube that links the mouth with the intestine) for feeding. The pharynx is pushed out and pressed onto the food; then with muscular movements it tears off particles which pass into the intestine.

Flatworms are the most primitive group of animals to possess a true excretory system; tubes running down either side of the body and opening to the exterior by excretory pores serve to link a series of "flame cells." These cells, so called because of the bundle of hairlike projections, or cilia, constantly flickering within them, are thought to be responsible for regulating the water content of the worms.

A concentration of nervous tissue at the front of the flatworm [2] forms a primitive "brain" into which run the nerve bundles from two primitive eyes. Most species shun the light and track food largely by the use of organs sensitive to chemicals (chemoreceptors). Flatworms respond rapidly to waterborne chemicals released by a potential source of food. As soon as they sense even a weak solution of these chemicals, they move toward the higher concentration.

The life of flukes

The simplest form of parasitism is attachment to the outside of the host's body and a number of flukes (or trematodes) have adopted this style of life. *Gyrodactylus,* for example, can be found attached by suckers and hooks to the gills of the fish on which it feeds. But more important to man are the internally parasitic flukes such as *Schistosoma* [5], the genus responsible for bilharzia or schistosomiasis, and the liver fluke *Fasciola* [4], which commonly infests the bile ducts of sheep.

Apart from the obvious need to attach themselves to their host and feed, the requirements of internal parasites are fairly simple. Thus the organs of movement, digestion and sense are reduced and the surface cilia are replaced by a tough cuticle.

CONNECTIONS

See also
458 The animal kingdom
460 Animal anatomy
474 Earthworms, clamworms, and roundworms
710 The causes of illness:1
732 Diseases of the Third World
312 The living soil
506 Invertebrate oddities
370 Farm stockbreeding and management
376 Pigs and sheep

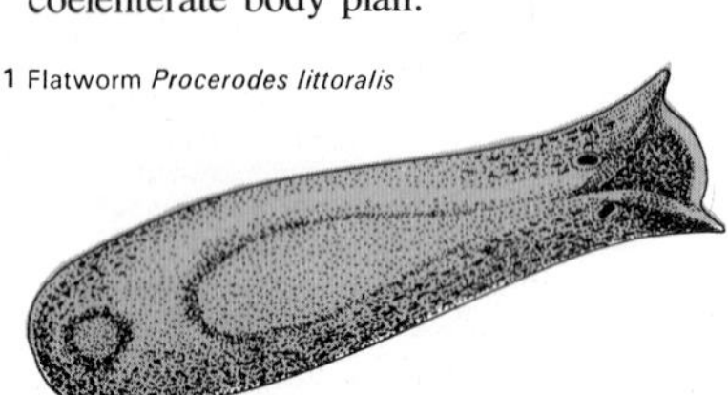
1 Flatworm *Procerodes littoralis*

1 The free-living flatworm named *Procerodes littoralis* grows to a length of 0.75in (2cm) and lives on the rocks of the seashore. It belongs to a group called the Turbellaria, most of which are aquatic and many marine. The ribbon-like body—which ensures that oxygen and waste products have only a short distance to diffuse—is advantageous for an animal with no vascular system.

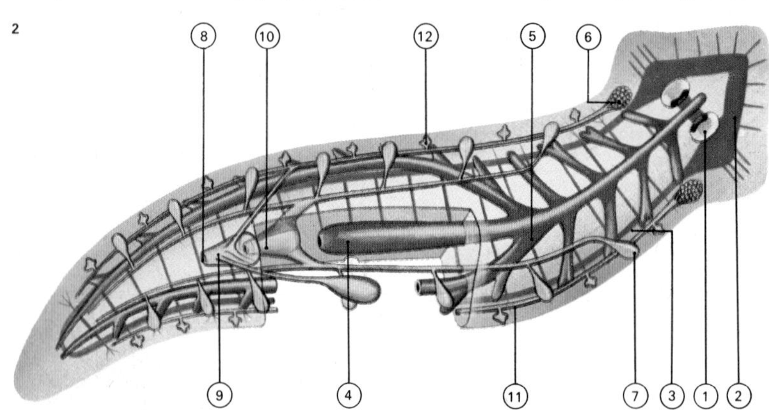

2 Turbellarian flatworms have sensory, reproductive, and digestive systems. In some, the head has simple eyes [1] located over a brain [2] from which runs a pair of nerve cords [3]. A pharynx that can turn inside out [4] opens into a branching gut [5]. All species are hermaphroditic with ovaries [6] and testes [7]. A genital pore [8] leads to the genital chamber [9] in which lies the penis [10]. On passing down the oviducts [11] eggs are fed by yolk glands [12].

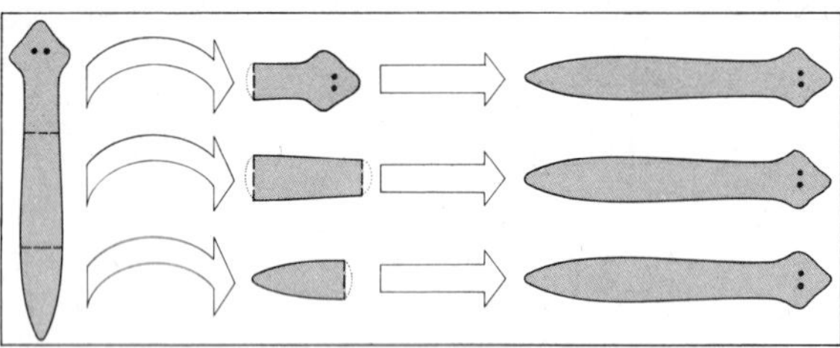

3 The flatworms have remarkable powers of regeneration. Cut into three, each segment will form a whole new worm. Indeed, free-living flatworms often divide asexually. Adaptability of the group is further demonstrated by starving them: when food is in short supply they not only shrink in size, but actually digest their own organs. Later, the missing organs are regenerated.

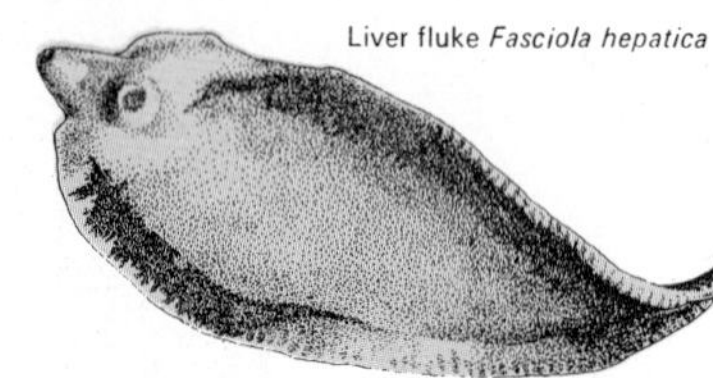
Liver fluke *Fasciola hepatica*

4 The liver fluke *(Fasciola hepatica)* is parasitic in the bile ducts of sheep and cattle. Its powers of reproduction are enormous; it may produce over 40,000 eggs that leave the host with its feces. The eggs hatch to form free-swimming larvae that enter the intermediate host, a freshwater snail. Further changes take place until a tiny, tailed version of the adult fluke bores its way out of the snail, crawls up the stem of a plant, and is eaten by a sheep.

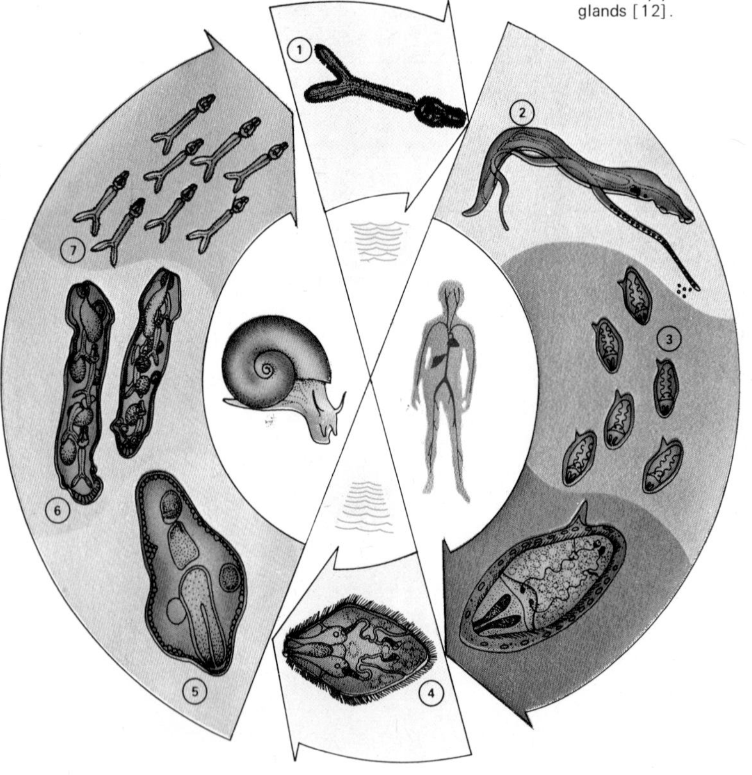

5 Adult human blood flukes of each sex [2] live in the blood vessels of the gut—causing abscesses and internal bleeding (schistosomiasis, common in Africa and Asia). The eggs [3] leave via bladder or intestine and on reaching water hatch to release free-swimming larvae [4] that penetrate the tissues of a snail. Further development [5, 6] gives rise to thousands of cercariae [7, 1] that escape into water and enter man through his skin.

Reproductive organs, on the other hand, must be enlarged because the offspring of the parasite face severe hazards as they search for a new host. All flukes, therefore, have massive and prolific organs of reproduction which ensure that even if 99 percent of the eggs are lost a few will survive to enter the body of another host.

The animal harboring the adult fluke is said to be the "final" host. To facilitate transmission between final hosts there may be one or more intermediate hosts. *Schistosoma* [5] uses just one intermediate, the Chinese liver fluke *(Clonorchis)* uses two—a snail followed by a fish. These intermediates are used as staging posts in which the parasites multiply their numbers.

The life of tapeworms

In tapeworms (or cestodes) [6] simplification of the anatomy is carried still further. A digestive system is absent—for an animal that lies bathed in the predigested contents of its host's gut has no need to do more than absorb the necessary food. Only the head of the tapeworm [8], armed with

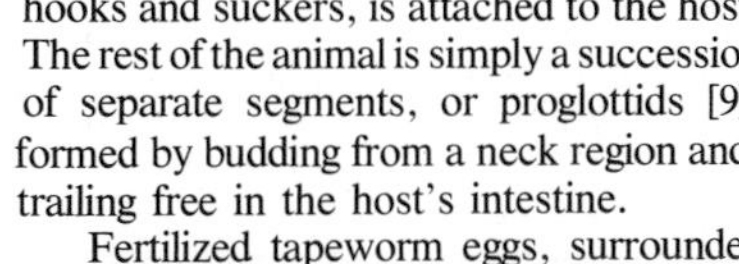

hooks and suckers, is attached to the host. The rest of the animal is simply a succession of separate segments, or proglottids [9], formed by budding from a neck region and trailing free in the host's intestine.

Fertilized tapeworm eggs, surrounded by yolk and a protective shell, are stored in the tapeworm's uterus. At the end of the tape each segment is essentially a sac of eggs; a few segments at a time become detached and pass out with the host's feces. Like the flukes, tapeworms [7] may have one or more intermediate hosts. *Diphyllobothrium,* the fish tapeworm found in the intestines of men, dogs, and cats and which may be up to 90ft (27m) long, has two intermediates; *Taenia solium,* the pork tapeworm, has only one. The eggs of *Taenia* shed from the human gut hatch only if eaten by a pig. The pig's digestive juices dissolve the shell and a small six-hooked embryo emerges to bore its way through the intestine, enter the bloodstream and eventually reach a region of muscle. There it encysts as a bladderworm [10], until eaten by another human, when the life cycle repeats.

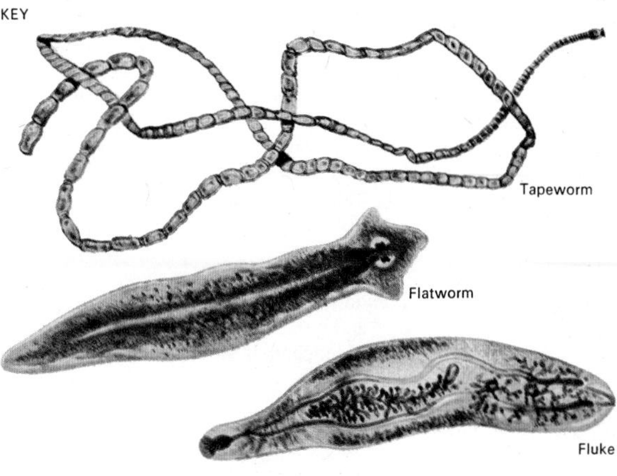

KEY
Tapeworm
Flatworm
Fluke

Three groups of animals—free-living flatworms, parasitic flukes, and tapeworms—comprise the Platyhelminthes. Some of the best known of the Platyhelminthes are parasitic and these offer an excellent illustration of the modifications most characteristic of a parasitic way of life. Thus the flukes have hooks and suckers, a complex reproductive system, and reduced sensory equipment, while the segments of the tapeworm are devoid even of a gut, because food exists in their environment ready-made. These creatures are little more than bags of reproductive organs.

6 The pork tapeworm *(Taenia solium)* is parasitic in man and may reach a length of over 14ft(4m). The intermediate host is the pig, which becomes infected through eating human feces. Reinfection is avoided by cooking pork well.

6

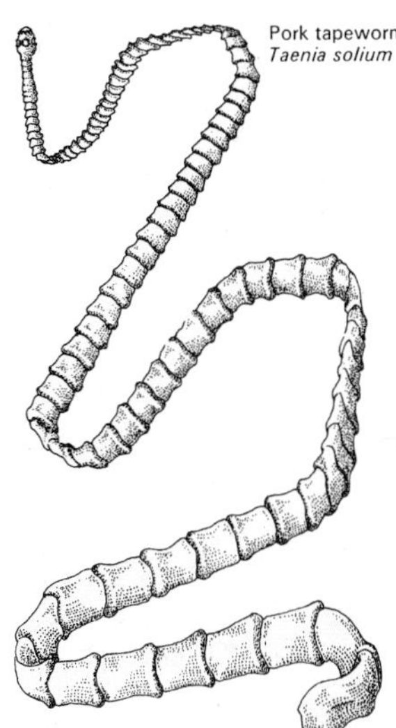

Pork tapeworm
Taenia solium

7

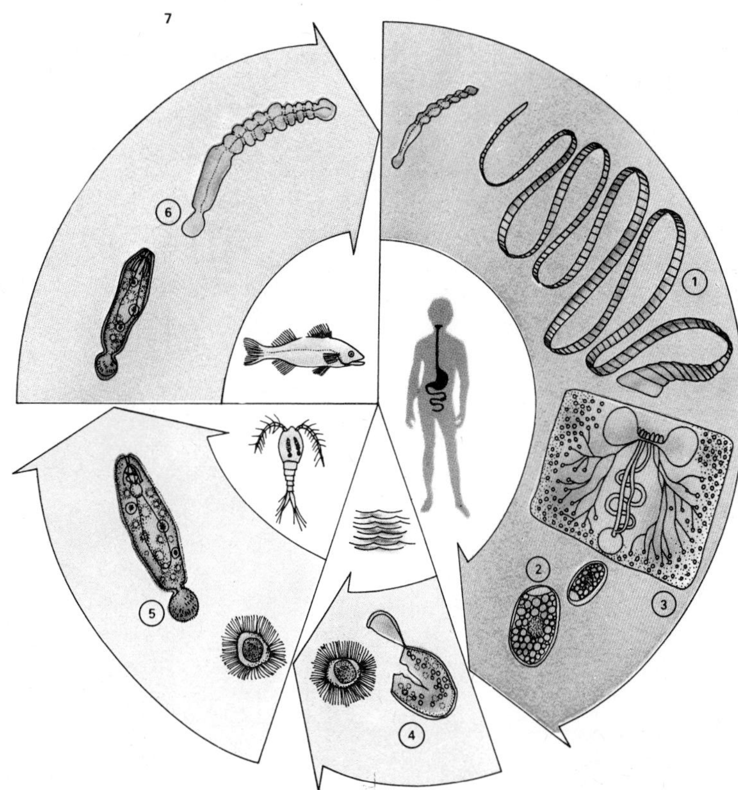

7 The broad tapeworm *(Diphyllobothrium latum)* is a human parasite with two intermediate hosts; the water flea and many freshwater fish. The adult worm [1] lives in man's intestine where it may grow to a length of many yards. The terminal segments—shown enlarged [3]—detach and as many as 13 million eggs [2] may be discharged every day in the feces. In water the eggs hatch into embryos [4] and are eaten by water fleas; here they develop into the first larval form [5]. If the flea is eaten by a fish the larvae penetrate its tissues to form secondary larvae [6]. If an infected fish is then eaten uncooked by a man these secondary larvae are released. Using their small hooks they attach themselves to the wall of the gut and develop into adult worms in about three weeks.

8 The head, or scolex, of a tapeworm is the point of attachment to the host. Hooks and suckers hold the worm firmly to the wall of the gut, making it extremely difficult to remove. And as long as the head remains, new segments can always grow.

8

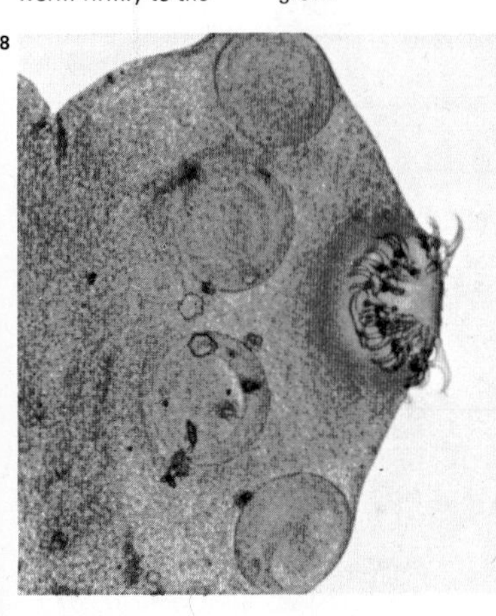

9

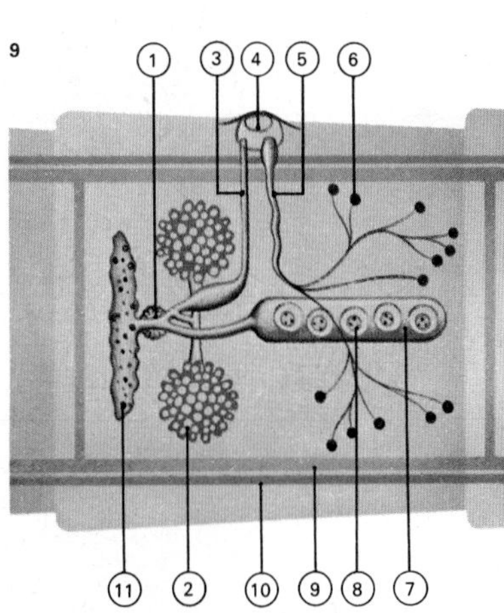

9 Apart from the excretory canals [9] and nerve cords [10], a tapeworm segment is largely reproductive organs. A branching testis [6] leads into a sperm duct [5] which opens along with a vagina [3] into a genital pore [4]. Eggs from ovaries [2] receive products of shell [1] and yolk [11] glands. Uterus [7] stores self-fertilized eggs and embryos [8].

10 "Measly meat" is infested with large numbers of cysts of tapeworm larvae.

10

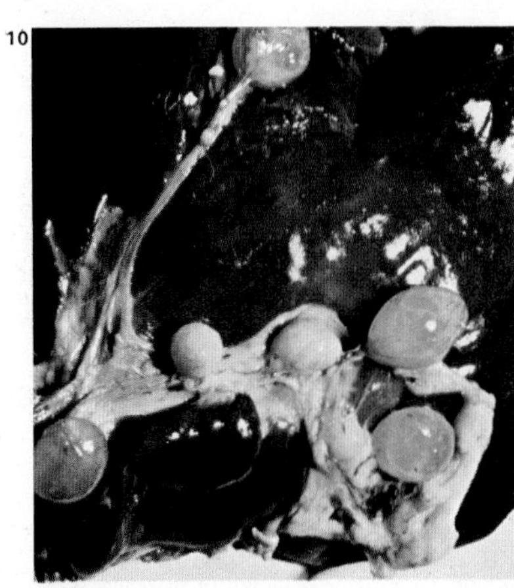

Earthworms, clamworms, and roundworms

Earthworms and clamworms as well as the leeches are all segmented worms and are grouped together in the phylum Annelida. These worms number more than 7,000 species and although they are found all over the world, in fresh water, in seawater, and on land, they are far less widespread than the 10,000 species of roundworms [Key]. Almost every habitat has been occupied by round, or nematode, worms, which are usually classified in the phylum Nematoda, although sometimes they are treated as a subdivision of the phylum Aschelminthes.

The life of roundworms

Nearly all vertebrate animals, and many invertebrates, have parasitic roundworms living within them. The roundworms most important to man are the parasitic species that cause disease. The intestinal inhabitant *Ascaris lumbricoides* sometimes causes pain and diarrhea, usually in children [4], while the filaria worm *Wuchereria bancrofti* is the causative agent of elephantiasis. Hookworms, guinea worms [6], whipworms, and giant kidney worms are all nematodes that cause disease in man. Other nematodes are free-living, but wherever they occur they do so in large numbers.

Adult roundworms are generally spindle-shaped [1]. They have thin, inflexible body walls that restrict their movements to whiplike body contortions. Most possess a simple, tubular alimentary tract and a primitive excretory system consisting of an H-shaped arrangement of canals that opens via a pore at the front of the body. The high pressure of body fluids probably forces excreta into the canals and out of the body. The nervous system is also built on an H-shaped plan and although the system is a simple one, roundworms have sensory structures that respond to touch, chemical, and light stimuli.

In many roundworms, including the human (and animal) parasite *Ascaris lumbricoides*, the two sexes are separate and males are smaller than the females [4]. Males are equipped with only a single testis, females with a pair of ovaries. During copulation the male injects sperm into the female. The sperm crawl like amebae toward the eggs, and fertilization takes place within the female. The female *Ascaris* can lay up to 200,000 eggs a day and these are eliminated in the feces of the host. Characteristically, parasitic nematode worms have very complex life cycles, often involving several hosts and developmental stages.

In hermaphroditic roundworms, where both testis and ovaries are present, sperm are produced first and then stored. As eggs are released stored sperm fertilizes them. In all species fertilization produces a zygote, which becomes enclosed in a protective cyst. Juvenile worms grow inside these cysts but on escaping pass through up to four larval stages before becoming adults.

Bristleworms, earthworms, and leeches

Segmented worms are divided taxonomically into three classes. The polychaetes—the clamworms and bristleworms—are predominantly marine and have bristle-covered "paddles" called parapodia on the body. Bristleworms include the burrowing lugworms *(Arenicola),* tube-forming fan worms [8], such as *Sabella* and *Serpula,*

CONNECTIONS

See also

458 The animal kingdom
460 Animal anatomy
622 The seashore: life between the tides
710 The causes of illness
312 The living soil
370 Farm stock breeding and management
506 Invertebrate oddities

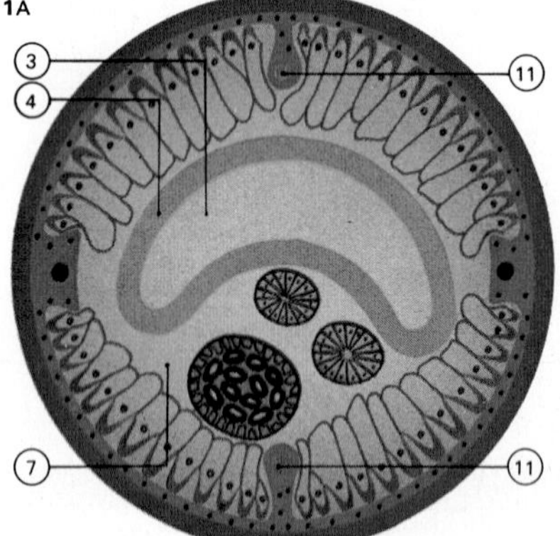

1A
B

1 Roundworms and earthworms show distinct differences. An earthworm [B] has a true coelom [1], a fluid-filled body cavity formed by the splitting of the mesoderm into inner and outer layers. The inner "splanchnic" mesoderm gives rise to a muscular layer [2] around the intestine [3] while the outer "somatic" layer has longitudinal [4] and circular [5] muscle layers. There is also a coelomic lining [6]. A female *Ascaris* [A], a parasitic roundworm of man, has a pseudocoelom [7], a cavity formed by the coalescing of fluid-filled spaces within the mesoderm. The intestine [3] lacks a muscular coat and only longitudinal muscle bands [4] are present. Blood vessels [8, 9] and developed excretory organs [10] are present only in the annelids. Both have cords [11].

3 Mating in earthworms begins with the formation of a slime tube around the front portions of two worms close together. Sperm, released from the vasa deferentia, pass along grooves in the body to the sperm receptacles of the annelid partner. The worms then separate. The clitellum then secretes a cocoon, which becomes part of the slime tube and glides down the body picking up ripe eggs from the oviducts and sperm from sperm receptacles. Once the tube leaves the worm, the cocoon becomes sealed. Inside, fertilization takes place and small worms develop rapidly.

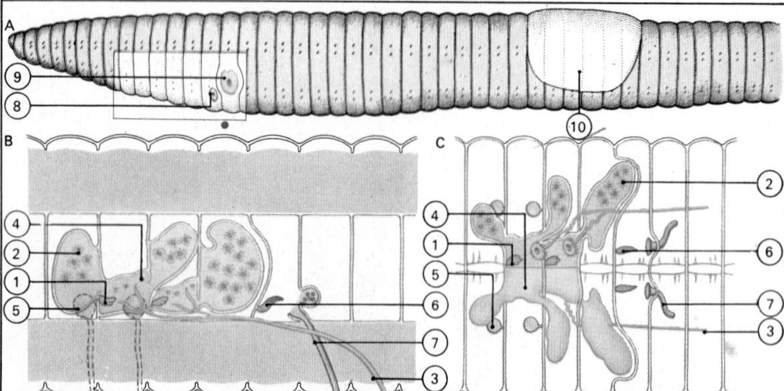

A
B
C

2 Earthworms are hermaphrodites that practice reciprocal cross-fertilization. The earthworm's internal reproductive organs consist of many paired structures (side view B; top C). In the testes [1] male germ cells are produced. These subsequently develop into sperm within the seminal vesicles [2]. The vasa deferentia [3] conduct sperm from testes sacs [4] to the male openings on the lower surface (segment 15). Partners' sperm are stored in receptacles [5] in segments 9 and 10 before fertilization occurs. In the ovaries [6] eggs are produced and these pass to the female pores (in segment 14), via the oviducts [7]. Externally [A] the openings of oviducts [8] and the vasa deferentia [9] are visible as well as the clitellum [10], the region of glandular epidermis that secretes the cocoon. During mating the clitellum rests against the area of genital openings of the partner. After exchange of sperm fertilization occurs in the cocoon.

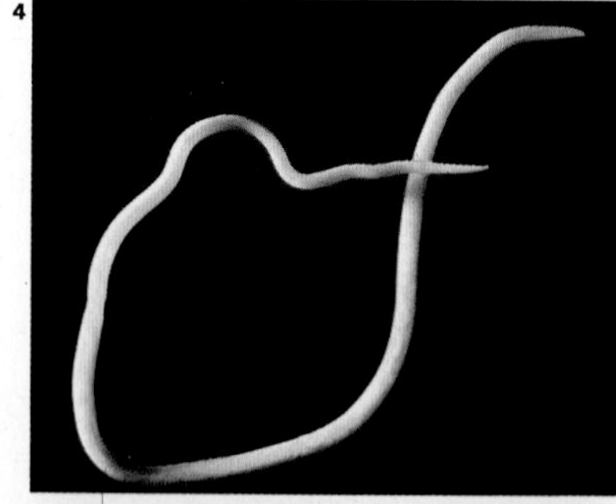

4 The parasite *Ascaris lumbricoides* inhabits human and pig intestines where it is harmless except in large numbers, when it can block the gut. The female roundworm grows to 12in (30cm).

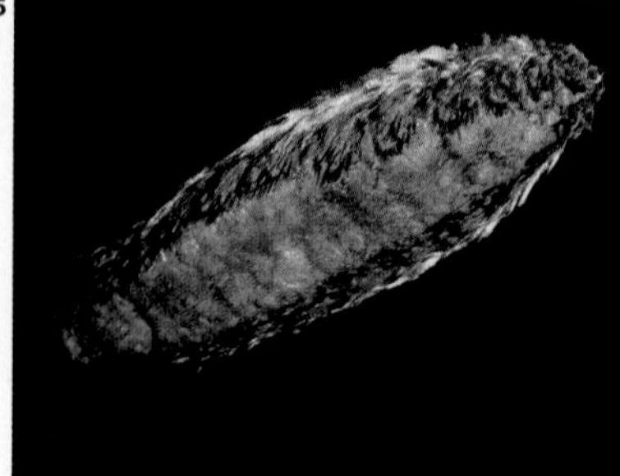

5 The sea mouse, or aphrodite (*Aphrodite aculeata*), is an unusual polychaete annelid worm found on the sea bed just offshore in temperate waters where it feeds on dead animals. These creatures, which measure 3–6 in (7.5–15 cm) in length, are occasionally washed up on beaches after storms. Partly concealed among its its iridescent hairs are dark, hollow spines thought to contain poison. If spines penetrate they cause irritation.

and the more mobile clamworms *(Nereis)* [10] and palolo worms [8]. The class Oligochaeta contains earthworms *(Lumbricus)* and freshwater worms such as *Tubifex*.

Earthworms are nocturnal, burrowing animals and come to the surface only after heavy rain, when the water has cut off their underground air supply. Earthworms feed on decaying plant and animal matter, and soil. Their burrowing aids soil cultivation by allowing air and water to reach the soil.

The third class of segmented worms, the Hirudinea, or leeches, are flattened animals. Some are parasitic but many others are free-living. Parasitic leeches live outside their hosts and suck their blood. Leeches [7] always have bodies divided into 33 primary segments. In parasitic species the gut is merely a reservoir for predigested food.

The bodies of all annelid worms consist of rows of identical segments. The body wall is equipped with circular and longitudinal muscle fibers and the intestine is surrounded by a thick muscular coat [1B]. There is a simple blood circulatory system and a digestive system consisting of a tubular tract modified according to the feeding habits of the species. The excretory and nervous systems are also in segments. The nervous system is composed of a ventral nerve cord along which are spaced concentrations of nervous tissue—the ganglia—within each segment. The ganglia of the front segments, however, have become combined to form a primitive brain.

Reproductive behavior

The reproductive behavior of annelids is varied [3]. In bristleworms sexes are separate and testes or ovaries are present in many of the body segments. Gametes are released as these segments split open, and fertilization occurs externally.

Earthworms and leeches are hermaphroditic and gonads are present only in specific segments. Self-fertilization is rare and copulation involves a pairing of worms during which exchange of sperm takes place. Sperm and eggs are released into a mucous bag that contains a cocoon, which is slipped off the body and inside which the fertilized eggs develop.

KEY

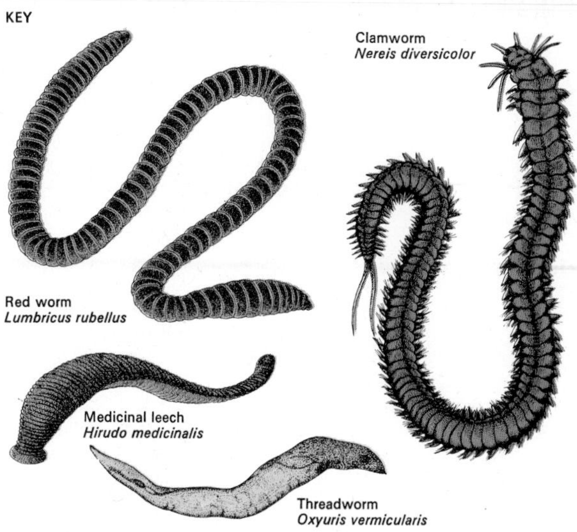
Clamworm
Nereis diversicolor
Red worm
Lumbricus rubellus
Medicinal leech
Hirudo medicinalis
Threadworm
Oxyuris vermicularis

The annelids and roundworms comprise over 21,000 animal species. The marine clamworm, the red earthworm, and the leech are all representatives of the phylum Annelida. The threadworm, or pinworm, is a parasitic roundworm of the phylum Nematoda, which often inhabits the human intestine.

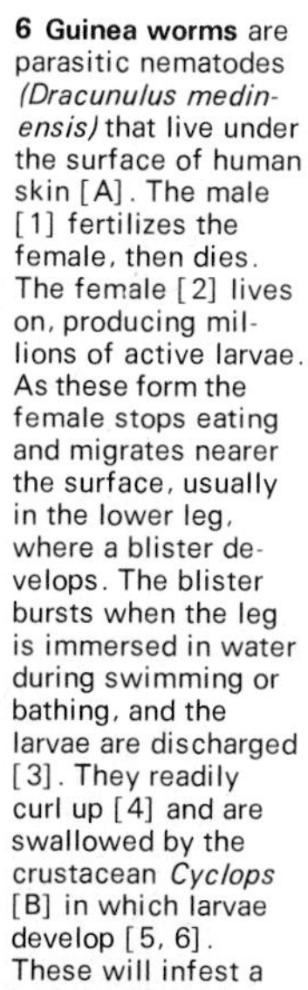

6 Guinea worms are parasitic nematodes *(Dracunculus medinensis)* that live under the surface of human skin [A]. The male [1] fertilizes the female, then dies. The female [2] lives on, producing millions of active larvae. As these form the female stops eating and migrates nearer the surface, usually in the lower leg, where a blister develops. The blister bursts when the leg is immersed in water during swimming or bathing, and the larvae are discharged [3]. They readily curl up [4] and are swallowed by the crustacean *Cyclops* [B] in which larvae develop [5, 6]. These will infest a human who drinks the water.

6

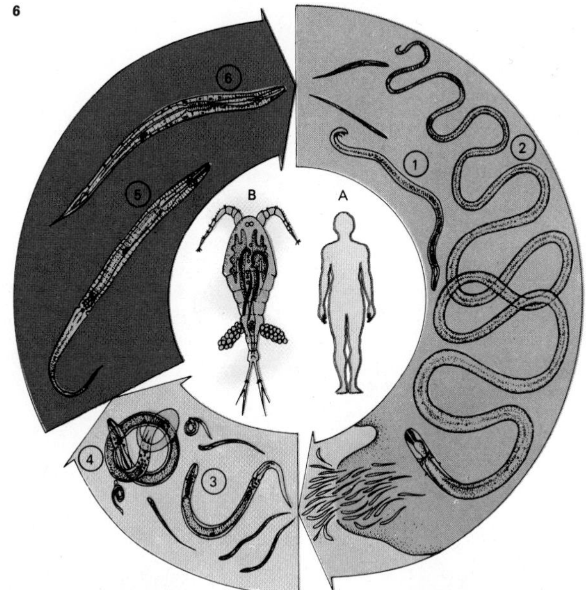
6
5
1
2
B
A
4
3

7

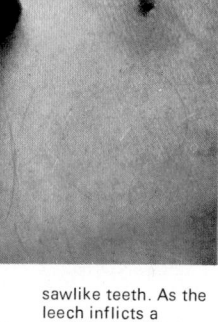

7 Leeches are common in tropical and temperate regions in freshwater habitats and feed on a variety of small animals. Many leeches feed as external parasites and suck the blood of animals. They were once used for medicinal bleeding. Leeches attach themselves with suckers at each end of the body. The anterior sucker surrounds the mouth which, in many leeches, is armed with three sawlike teeth. As the leech inflicts a wound, as on this human arm, it injects a blood anticoagulant—hirudin. At one meal a leech can take ten times its weight in blood, food for up to nine months.

8

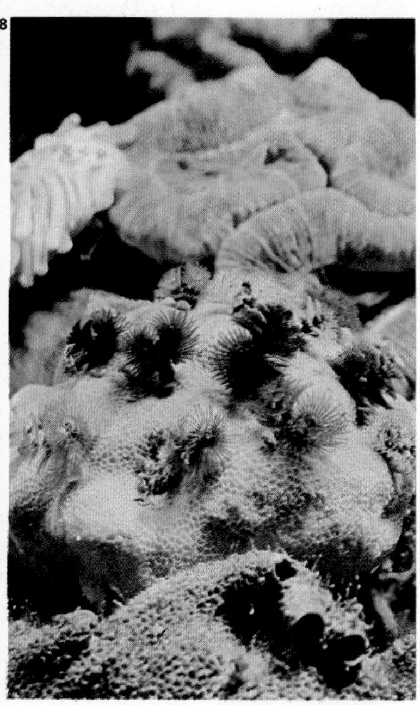

8 Feather worms are polychaetes of the subclass Sedentaria—so named because they live within tubes that they build in the sand. The front portions of their bodies are above the surface and bear many featherlike structures that function as respiratory gills and food collectors. Beating cilia covering the gills direct small organisms toward the mouth. The worms shown are *Spirographis*.

9

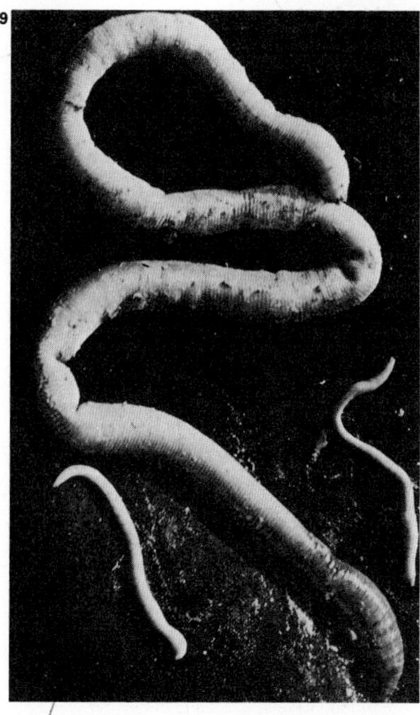

9 Giant earthworms, such as this *Megascoloides australis*, live only in moist tropical regions. They can grow to as much as 12ft (3.7 m) in length. Also shown are two common earthworms, which rarely grow to more than 6in (15cm).

10

10 Clamworms *(Nereis)* are marine polychaetes. They live in burrows in the mud or in fine sand on the seashore, occasionally pushing their heads above the surface to feed. Wavelike motions of their bodies create currents that draw water through the burrows, bringing in fresh supplies of oxygen and carrying away carbon dioxide and nitrogenous wastes. They are predators, feeding on small marine animals, but they also consume planktonic organisms and detritus from the mud.

Land and sea snails

CONNECTIONS

See also
478 Life between two shells
480 Squids and octopuses
482 Shells of the world
458 The animal kingdom
622 The seashore: life between the tides
582 Isolation and evolution
732 Diseases of the Third World
466 Single-celled animals and sponges

Mollusks, of which more than 80,000 species are known, are a group of extraordinary diversity, encompassing creatures as different as the periwinkle, the clam, and the giant squid. Traces of the basic mollusk plan can be detected throughout all members of the group, but this is often greatly modified.

The mollusk body plan

Mollusks [Key] are soft-bodied creatures with a visceral mass containing such organs as those of digestion and reproduction covered by a sheet of tissue called the mantle. A space enclosed by the overlap of the mantle is called the mantle cavity. The tissue layer covering the outer surface of the mantle, the epithelium, secretes the shell, which is usually calcareous and is one of the most obvious characteristics of most members of the group. Beneath the visceral mass lies the foot, a fleshy muscular pad of tissue often important in movement.

The chitons [1], although specialized, show the basic body plan in its simplest form. The digestive system has a mouth (bearing a rasping "tongue," or radula for feeding), stomach, intestine, and anus discharging into the mantle cavity. Chitons have a heart and blood vessels that make for a simple circulatory system, paired excretory organs, gills that project out into the mantle cavity, and a nervous system with ganglia (concentrations of nerve cells) and nerve cords. In the course of the chiton life cycle, as in other mollusks, the fertilized egg develops into a kind of larva called a trochophore that swims by means of the bands of beating cilia that surround its body.

Torsion and its effects

At first glance, at least a few of the gastropods (mollusks with a broad, flat foot and undivided mantle) appear also to have held fairly closely to the basic mollusk plan. The limpet [2], for example, has a simple conical shell and an apparently straightforward anatomy. On close inspection, however, that anatomy is not as simple as it first seems. During development from the larva the whole of the visceral mass becomes twisted upon the foot. This process, known as torsion, has several predictable consequences. The gut, instead of being straight, performs a U-turn, while the nervous system, its cords no longer parallel, is twisted into a figure eight. Most striking is the repositioning of the gills and the opening of the anus into the mantle cavity; both are now at the front instead of the back.

Torsion may have stemmed from the evolutionary advantages of having a clean flow of water into the mantle cavity and over the gills.

The mechanics of torsion are simple but elegant. The trochophore larva develops into a further form, the veliger, characterized by expansion of its areas of cilia. The rudiments of the adult shell and foot also become apparent. Then, with the head and foot remaining stationary, the viscera rotate through a half circle, bringing the mantle cavity both forward and upward.

Shells and their loss

The other factor that makes recognition of the mollusk body plan difficult in many gastropods is the coiling of the shell. This has

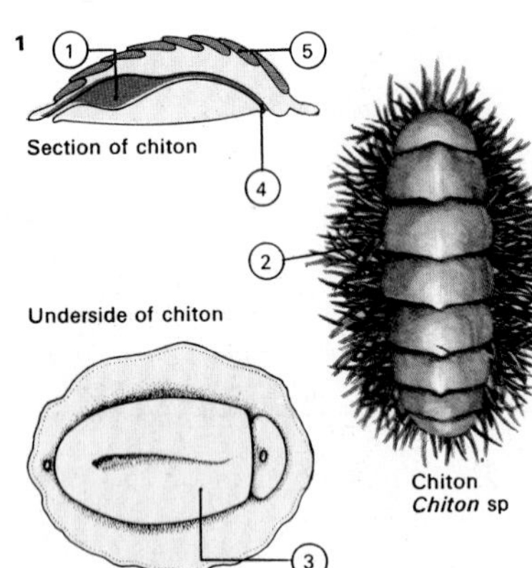

1
5
Section of chiton
4
2
Underside of chiton
3
Chiton
Chiton sp

1 Chitons, or coat-of-mail shells, are among the most primitive of the mollusks. Their bodies are covered with eight overlapping calcareous plates [5] and in some cases a fringe of calcareous spines [2] as in *Chiton*. On the underside is an oval, fleshy foot [3] fronted by a degenerate head with a mouth [4] leading straight into the gut [1]. If dislodged from the rocks, chitons will curl up.

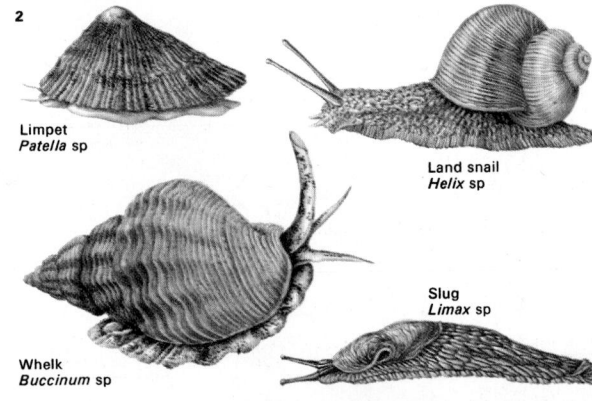

2 The gastropods (or univalves) have exploited many habitats and adapted accordingly. Limpets, with their conical shells, are some of the simplest. More widespread are gastropods with coiled shells. Some, such as the whelk, inhabit the sea; others live in fresh water and on land. There are tree snails and even those that live in sand dunes. A few gastropods, such as slugs, have abandoned their shells.

Limpet *Patella* sp
Land snail *Helix* sp
Whelk *Buccinum* sp
Slug *Limax* sp

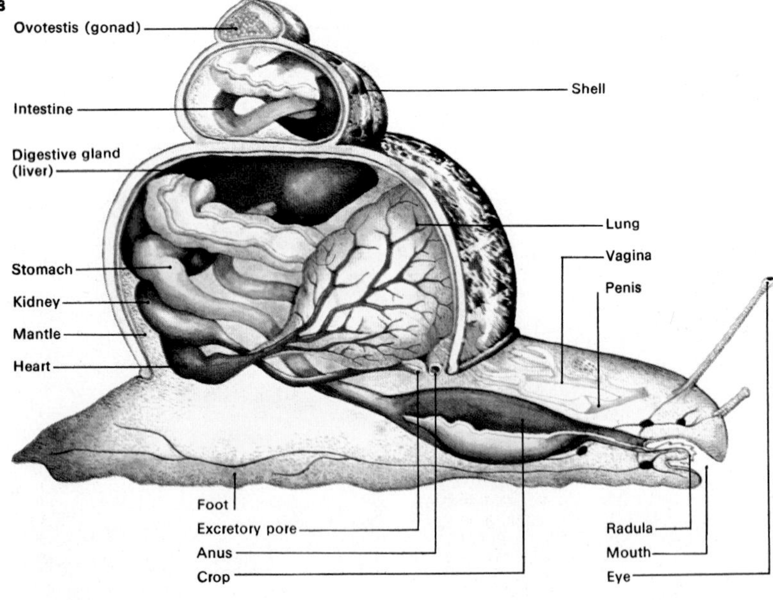

Ovotestis (gonad)
Shell
Intestine
Digestive gland (liver)
Lung
Vagina
Penis
Stomach
Kidney
Mantle
Heart
Foot
Excretory pore
Anus
Crop
Radula
Mouth
Eye

3 The anatomy of a land snail shows a well developed head with sensory tentacles and eyes. The foot is flattened and used for creeping. The layout of the internal organs is asymmetrical because of torsion and the coiling of the visceral hump within the shell. The mouth, inside which lies the radula, opens into an esophagus that leads to the stomach and gut. Because of the changes due to torsion the anus opens toward the front of the animal instead of at the rear as in chitons. Most gastropods respire through a gill located in the mantle cavity, but in the pulmonate group to which land snails belong, this organ has been lost. Instead, the lining of the mantle cavity is liberally supplied with blood vessels, the whole surface acting as a lung. Air moves in and out through a small opening called the pneumostome. The nervous system is made up of paired cerebral ganglia and nerve cords reaching to the foot and the viscera.

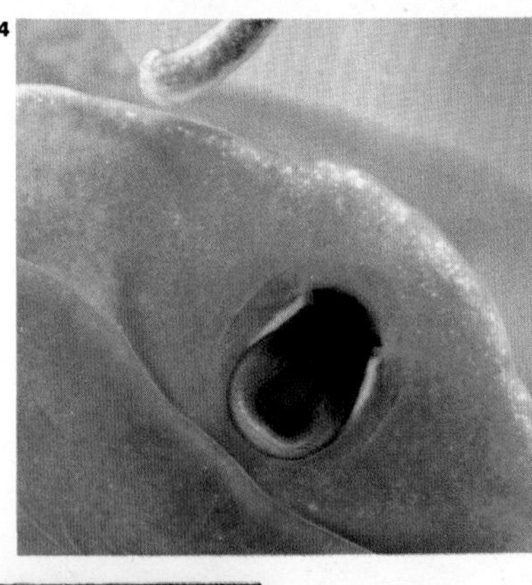

4 The radula of the pond snail Limnaea, like that of all gastropods, is a file-like rasping organ rooted within a sac just inside the mouth. It is especially well developed in species such as limpets, which graze on the algae growing on rocks. As the radula moves backward and forward out of the mouth, the food is scraped and macerated. As the radula and its teeth are worn down, more teeth are formed.

5 A land snail creeping across glass shows that it proceeds by a series of wavelike muscular contractions in the undersurface of the foot. These waves originate at the rear of the animal and pass forward along its length. Copious secretions of mucus thoroughly lubricate the surface of the foot, aiding its progress and giving it improved adhesion to the base. Most other gastropods also follow this characteristic means of locomotion.

been achieved by a loss of symmetry in the visceral mass and the disappearance of one of the members of some of the paired organs. But odd though the coiling may seem it is an arrangement that is far more satisfactory than mere elongation of the shell to an unwieldy length.

The snails [3] in particular have proved remarkably adept at exploring new habitats, both aquatic (marine and freshwater) and terrestrial. Yet the move to land is always a difficult one, and in the case of the gastropods has demanded a change-over of gills to a kind of air-breathing lung.

A shell undoubtedly confers advantages upon its owner in the way of protection and support. But it also restricts mobility. As a result, some groups—such as the land and sea slugs—have either evolved a reduced shell, or lost it altogether.

Sea slugs, or nudibranchs, belong to the opisthobranch division of the gastropods and include some of the more colorful and unusual species such as the Spanish dancer *(Hexabranchus)* [11]. Associated with the reduction or loss of the shell in opisthobranchs are two further changes: the uncoiling of the visceral mass and unwinding, or detorsion. The change restores some measure of the lost body symmetry.

The gills, again as a result of shell loss, are visible in many members of this group. But in one division the "gills" covering the upper surface do much more than respire. Indeed, by origin they are not really gills at all, but outgrowths of the body surface—called cerata—each of which encloses an outgrowth, or diverticulum, of the gut.

Members of this nudibranch group that feed on coelenterate hydrozoan polyps (relations of sea anemones) are somehow able to remove their stinging capsules (nematocysts) undamaged and transfer them to the gut diverticula in the cerata. The sea slug thus ingeniously makes use of its victim's defenses to defend itself. When the animal is attacked it exudes nematocysts through small pores in the cerata. A predator taking in water containing these nematocysts is stung. And if the attacker persists, it may provoke the harassed mollusk into detaching whole cerata full of stinging cells.

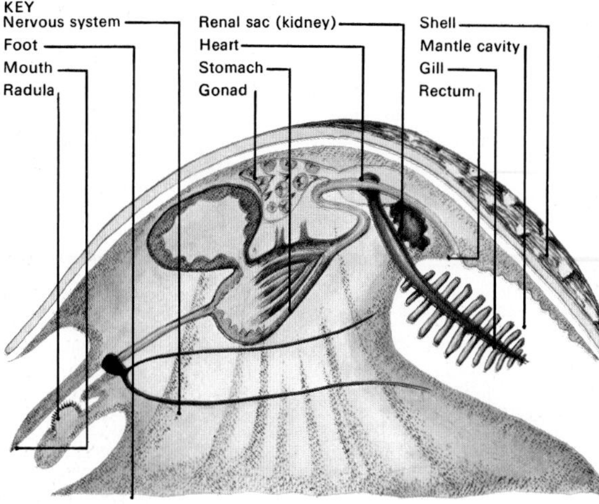
KEY
Nervous system
Foot
Mouth
Radula
Renal sac (kidney)
Heart
Stomach
Gonad
Shell
Mantle cavity
Gill
Rectum

A section through a generalized mollusk shows the body mass, protected by a shell, comprising three components: head, visceral mass, and a large muscular foot. The mouth leads to a stomach and intestine, which discharges through an anus. Respiration is through gills in the mantle cavity. All mollusks are variations on this plan, although it is more obvious among chitons than in the squid and octopus.

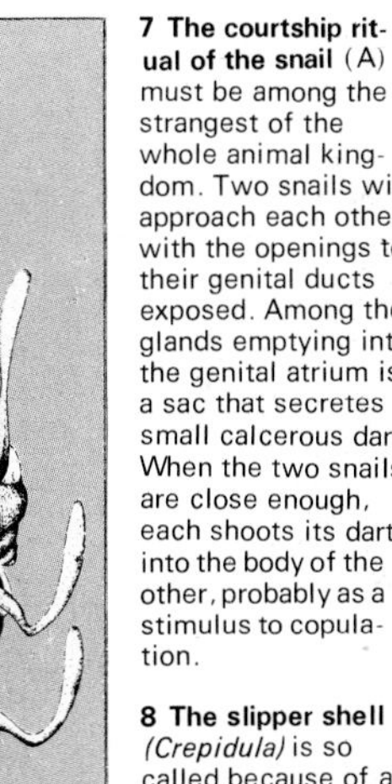
6
5
4
3
2
1

6 The shelled sea butterfly (*Limacina*) belongs to an unusual group that swims by means of flat elongations of the foot. The downward thrust of these "paddles" [1, 2] provides lift. The paddles are then looped upward in a slower recovery stroke [3–5] and the cycle is repeated.

7 The courtship ritual of the snail (A) must be among the strangest of the whole animal kingdom. Two snails will approach each other with the openings to their genital ducts exposed. Among the glands emptying into the genital atrium is a sac that secretes a small calcerous dart. When the two snails are close enough, each shoots its dart into the body of the other, probably as a stimulus to copulation.

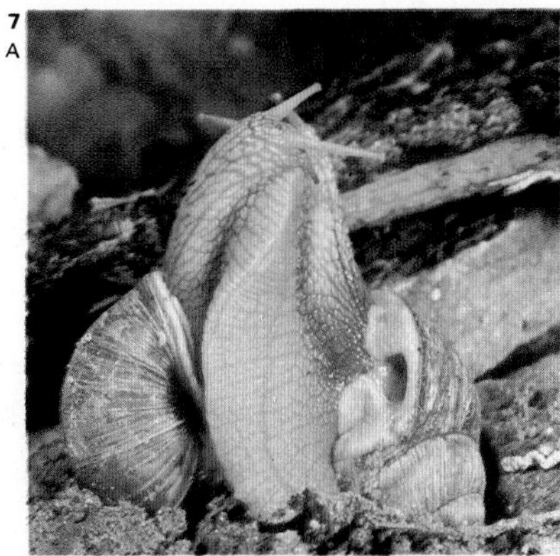
7
A

Most gastropods have separate sexes, but land snails are hermaphroditic [B], an ovotestis producing both sperm and eggs. At copulation the penis of each partner is inserted into the vagina of the other and sperm is transferred in a packet called a spermatophore. Sperm is then stored in a special chamber, the spermatheca, from which it is released as required. The fertilized eggs are laid in the soil.

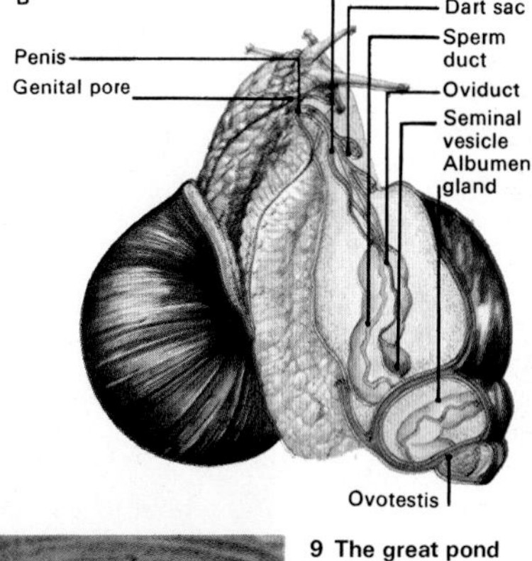
7
B
Penis
Genital pore
Vagina
Dart sac
Sperm duct
Oviduct
Seminal vesicle
Albumen gland
Ovotestis

8 The slipper shell *(Crepidula)* is so called because of a ledge inside the shell that makes it look like an upturned slipper. *Crepidula* is a static creature that tends to live in chains of up to nine or ten individuals. Younger arrivals settle on the backs of their elders. The sex of each animal depends on its position in the chain, females at the bottom, males at the top. They thus change sex with age.

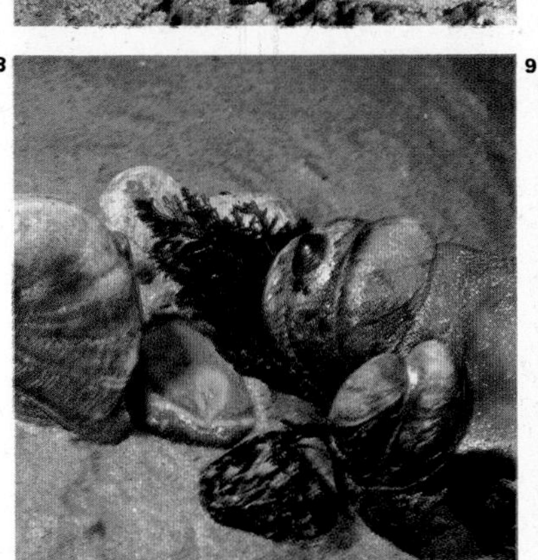
8

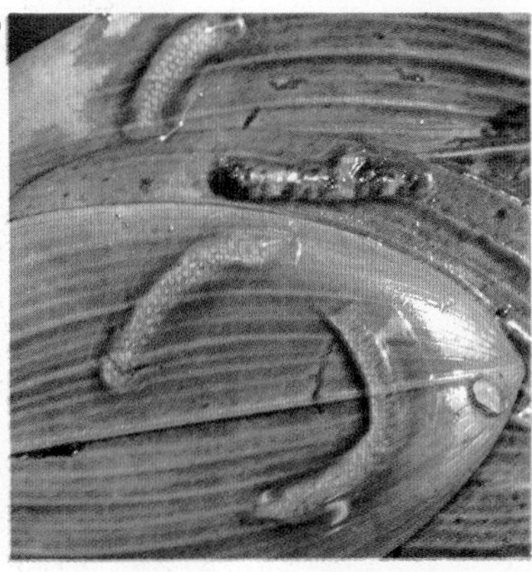
9

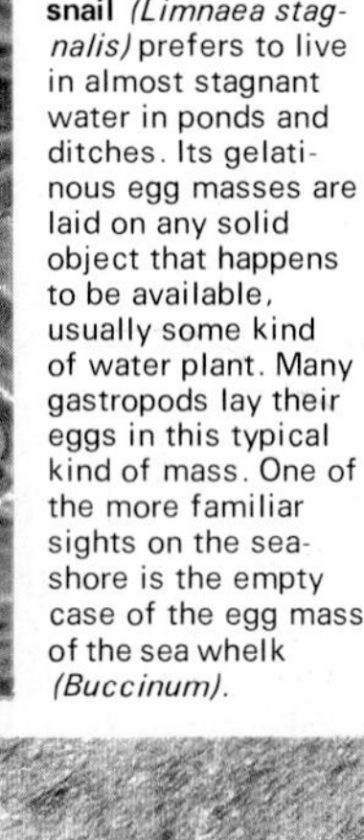

9 The great pond snail *(Limnaea stagnalis)* prefers to live in almost stagnant water in ponds and ditches. Its gelatinous egg masses are laid on any solid object that happens to be available, usually some kind of water plant. Many gastropods lay their eggs in this typical kind of mass. One of the more familiar sights on the seashore is the empty case of the egg mass of the sea whelk *(Buccinum)*.

10

10 Color in gastropods is not confined to the shell. The western Australian species *Amoria grayi* has a slim, translucent, yellowish shell, while its body is covered with rust-colored striations.

11 The spanish dancer *(Hexabranchus)* is an inhabitant of the Great Barrier Reef of Australia. Shell and mantle cavity have been lost and the animal has reassumed bilateral symmetry and become sluglike in appearance.

11

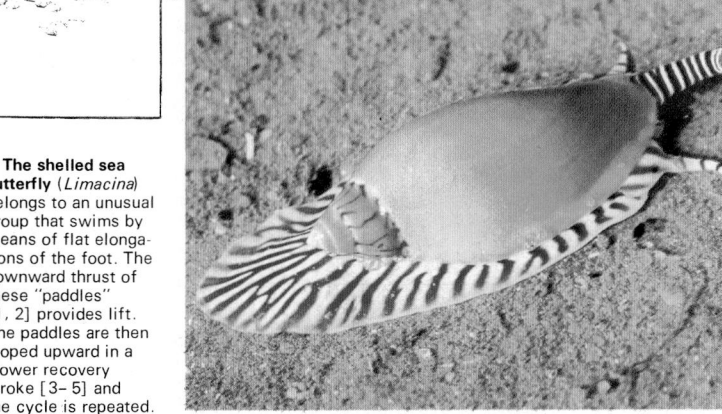

Life between two shells

The soft-bodied animals—the mollusks—are subdivided into three main groups: the snails or gastropods; the squids and octopuses, or cephalopods; and the bivalves. The bivalves include representatives that are interesting in their ways of life (the rock-boring piddocks), their appearance (the razor clam), and gastronomically (the mussel, the oyster).

Bivalves, as their name implies, have hardened, calcium-containing shells like those of snails, but instead of being in one piece the shell is divided into right and left halves. The two shells are joined along their "back," or dorsal margin, by a horny hinge. When the animal is relaxed and feeding there is a gap between the two halves; when it is disturbed a pair of powerful muscles attached to the shells pulls them tightly together.

Structure of bivalves

The bulk of the bivalve body lies toward the hinge of the shell and is covered by a structure called the mantle. This grows outward on either side of the body and forms a lining on the inside of both shell halves. It is the outer layer of the mantle that is responsible for secreting the shell. A muscular foot—flattened from side to side, extensible, and often used in burrowing—projects from the body into the cavity separating the halves of the mantle.

If one shell and half the mantle of a bivalve are removed the most obvious structures exposed are the gills which, besides serving as organs of respiration, are used in feeding. Bivalves are filter feeders [3]. In most, tubular extensions of the mantle form a pair of siphons, one for the entry of a current of water, the other for its exit. This current is maintained by the beating action of hairline cilia with which the gills are liberally covered. Water is drawn in through tiny pores in the gills and eventually ejected by way of the discharge siphon. Particles of food are strained out and trapped in the layer of sticky mucus, a substance similar in consistency to human saliva, that covers the gill surfaces.

From there trapped food passes to the edge of the gills farthest away from the hinge and larger particles such as silt fall off into the mantle cavity. The remainder, still entangled in a string of mucus, moves forward to the palps surrounding the mouth. Further sorting then takes place and selected particles enter the mouth and pass into the stomach and gut where they are digested.

Digestion and reproduction

A paired gland surrounding the stomach is the chief organ of digestion in bivalves. In addition, in many species, a transparent rod called a crystalline style projects from a pouch into the stomach. The style contains carbohydrate-splitting enzymes. Cilia in the pouch make the rod rotate and rub against an area of the stomach known as the gastric shield. As the style is worn away the enzymes it contains are released into the stomach contents. Digestion is completed in the intestine, which follows a twisted course to the anus. This opens into the mantle cavity near the discharge siphon, thus ensuring removal of feces in the outgoing water.

CONNECTIONS

See also
476 Land and sea snails
480 Squids and octopus
482 Shells of the world
622 The seashore: life b tween the tides
388 Fish farming
394 Shellfish and other seafoods
458 The animal kingdor

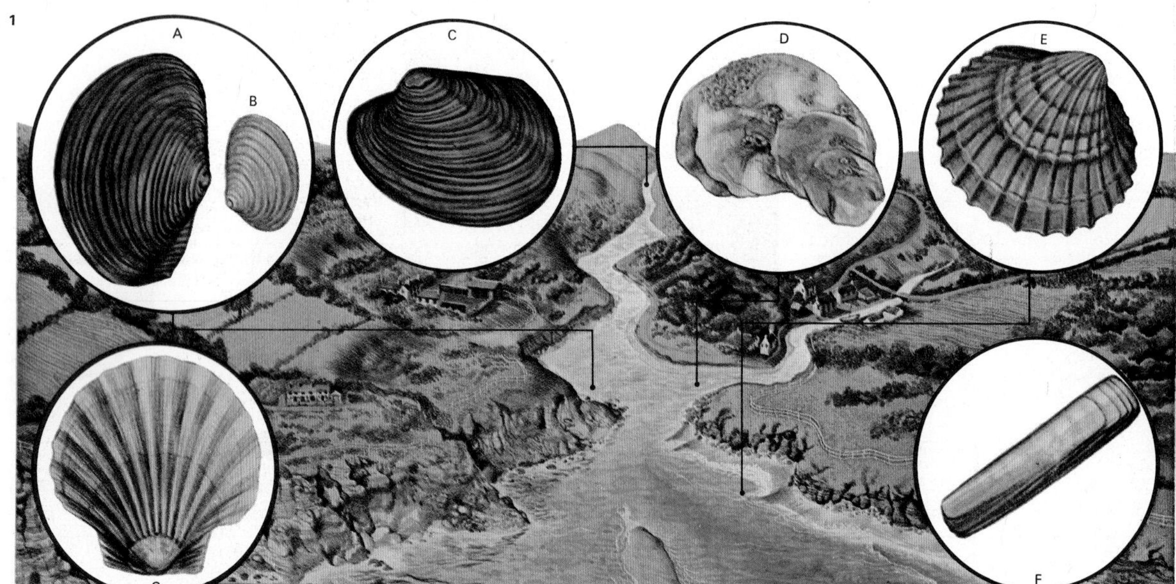

1
A
B
C
D
E
F
G

1 The distribution of bivalves depends on such factors as the force of wave action, tidal movement, and the nature of the substrate. The pearl mussel *(Margaritifera)* [A] is a freshwater species. The swan mussel *(Anodonta)* [B] and the river pea mussel *(Pisidium)* [C] are both freshwater species but can also be found in the lower reaches of tidal rivers. The oyster *(Ostrea)* [D] lives in estuaries and creeks while the common European cockle *(Cardium edule)* [E] can be found on the middle and lower seashore. The jackknife clam *(Ensis siliqua)* [F] burrows in the lower shore. The scallop *(Pecten maximus)* [G] is off shore.

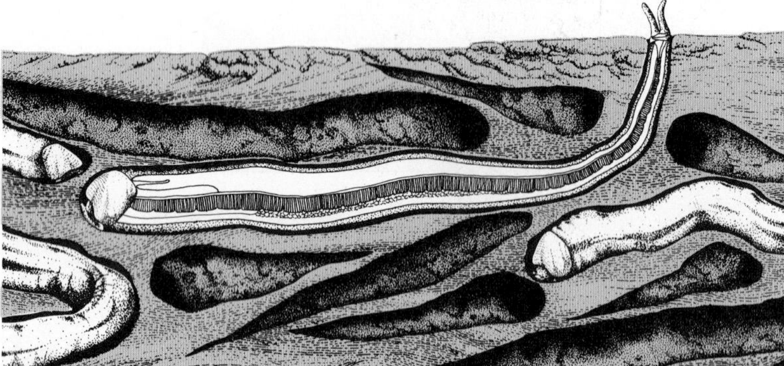

2 A

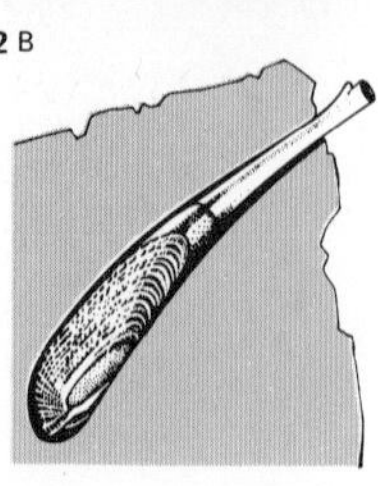

2 B

2 Many bivalves burrow in sand or mud but a few species spend their lives in submerged wood or even rocks. The shipworm *(Teredo)* [A] measures up to 12in (30cm) in length. The shell is much reduced, the halves having been modified to act as a drill by which its wormlike body is able to penetrate wooden pilings and ships' hulls—doing much damage in the process. As the bivalve grows it lengthens its burrow, lining it with a calcareous layer secreted by the mantle. Even more remarkable are some of the piddocks (e.g. *Pholas dactylus*) [B], which bore their way into rock; using the foot as a lever they move their shells backward and forward to scrape the rock and slowly hollow out a burrow.

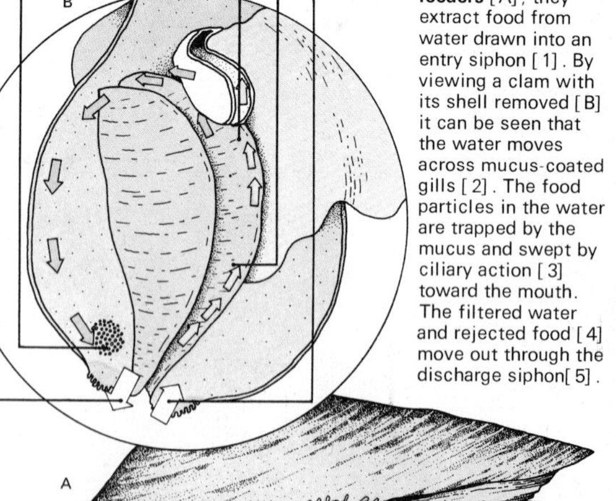

3
4
3
2
1
B
5
A
5
1

3 Bivalves are filter feeders [A]; they extract food from water drawn into an entry siphon [1]. By viewing a clam with its shell removed [B] it can be seen that the water moves across mucus-coated gills [2]. The food particles in the water are trapped by the mucus and swept by ciliary action [3] toward the mouth. The filtered water and rejected food [4] move out through the discharge siphon [5].

Paired excretory organs lie on either side of the heart and a "kidney" in each extracts waste products and discharges them via a bladder into the gill passages and then to the exterior. Bivalves have a three-chambered heart whose single muscular ventricle pumps blood into arteries that run to the foot, mantle, and the body organs. Many of the tissues of the body are permeated not by capillaries, as in higher animals, but by blood spaces or sinuses. Sinuses in the foot permit sand-burrowing—the foot swells and elongates as extra blood is pumped into it. Blood then returns via a series of veins to the heart.

Bivalves have simple reproductive systems with paired gonads and no glands. The sexes are separate and most allow the spermatozoa and ova to escape into the water where, in marine species, they form part of the plankton. Some freshwater bivalves brood their young, while others release a larval stage called a glochidium that passes through a brief parasitic phase in the gill chambers of fish before assuming independent adult existence.

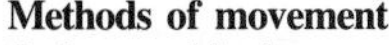

Methods of movement

Sedentary bivalves, such as mussels, spend their lives attached to a firm base by a bundle of threads called the byssus. These threads are secreted by a gland in the foot, and anchor their owner with surprising strength—a necessity if the animal is to avoid being swept away by the force of the waves. A more common mode of life, found in such bivalves as cockles and razor clams, is sand-burrowing [5] by means of a mobile foot. The deeper penetrating forms often have long siphons for reaching surface water for respiration and feeding.

In contrast to the sand-burrowing species the shipworm [2A] burrows into wood by back and forth rotation of its shells. Some piddocks can even burrow into rock. The animal must periodically cease boring and project the edge of its mantle onto the surface of its reduced shells to deposit a fresh layer of calcium carbonate.

In most bivalves the head is reduced or absent and sensory organs are generally insignificant. But the animals do react to waterborne chemicals, vibration, and light.

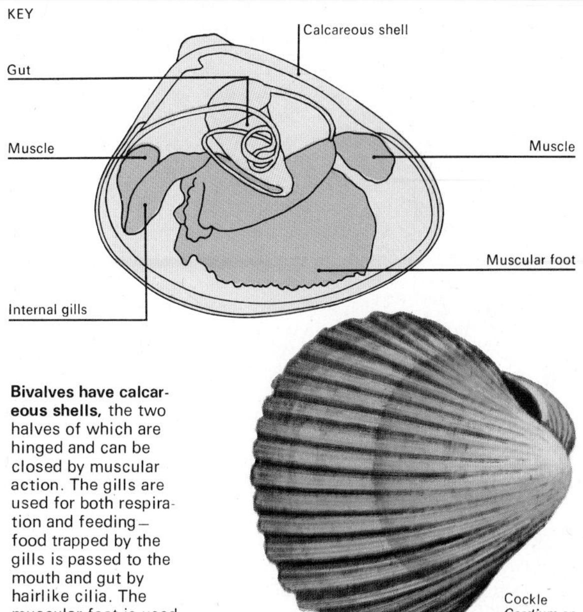
KEY
Calcareous shell
Gut
Muscle
Muscle
Muscular foot
Internal gills
Cockle
Cardium sp

Bivalves have calcareous shells, the two halves of which are hinged and can be closed by muscular action. The gills are used for both respiration and feeding—food trapped by the gills is passed to the mouth and gut by hairlike cilia. The muscular foot is used during burrowing.

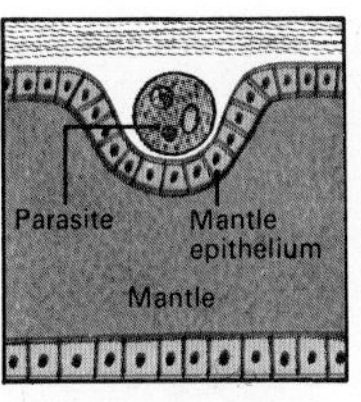
Parasite
Mantle epithelium
Mantle

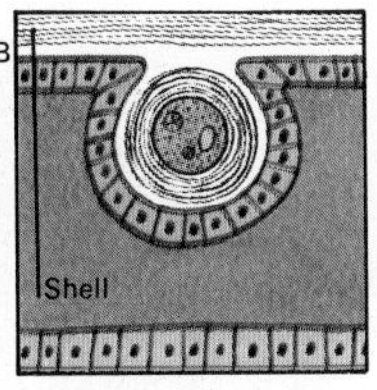
B
Shell

C
Pearl

4 Pearl formation is the result of a foreign body—often a parasite or a grain of sand—lodging between the shell and the epithelium of the oyster's mantle [A]. The mantle first surrounds the embryo pearl with its own covering or epithelium [B]; this proceeds to secrete concentric layers of pearly material—mother-of-pearl—actually thin sheets of calcium carbonate comparable with those lining the whole shell. These layers serve to isolate the foreign body [C]. Pearls can sometimes be found in Atlantic pearl oysters but they are seldom big enough to be of much value.

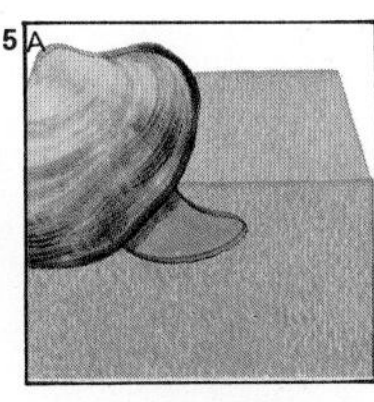
5 A

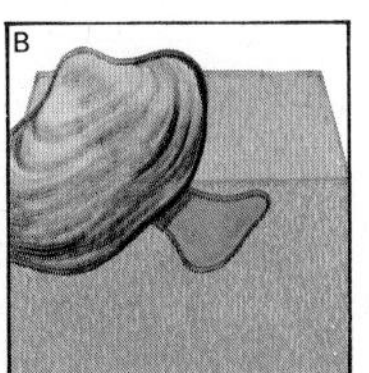
B

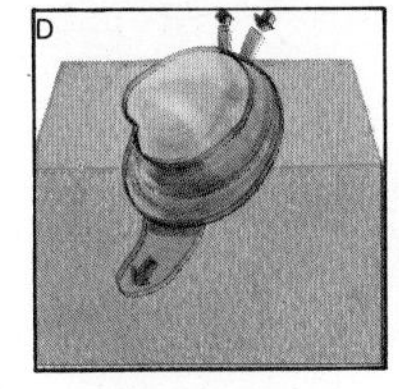
D

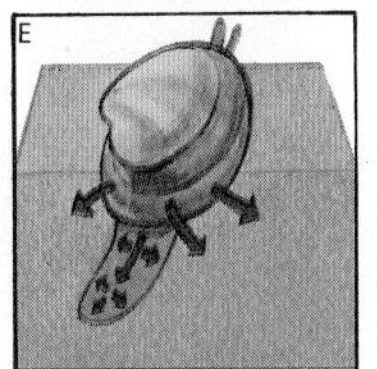
E

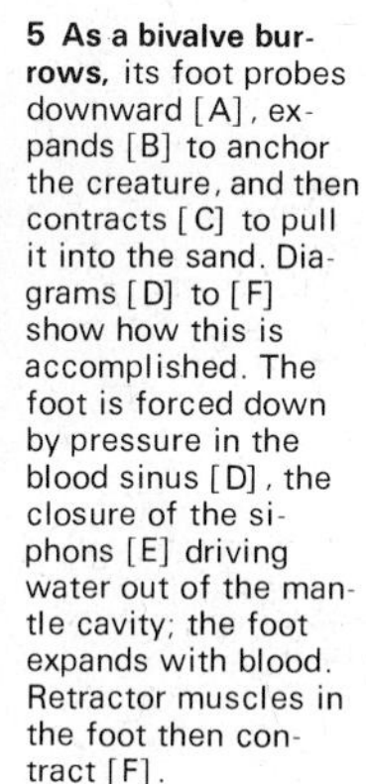

5 As a bivalve burrows, its foot probes downward [A], expands [B] to anchor the creature, and then contracts [C] to pull it into the sand. Diagrams [D] to [F] show how this is accomplished. The foot is forced down by pressure in the blood sinus [D], the closure of the siphons [E] driving water out of the mantle cavity; the foot expands with blood. Retractor muscles in the foot then contract [F].

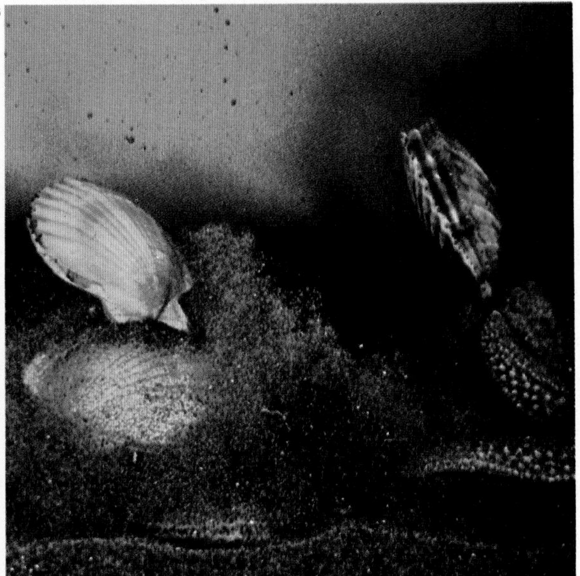

6 Scallops are notable among bivalves in being able to escape predators by "swimming." The great scallop *Pecten maximus* starts life firmly attached to a substrate but later detaches to take up a free life on the sea bottom. It can sense the presence of predators—notably starfish—chemically. The shell at once snaps shut, the closure of its two halves forcibly expels a water jet, and the creature escapes. Water can be expelled on either side of the hinge, making the scallop move in the opposite direction. The queen scallop *(Chlamys opercularis)* can even position a flap of tissue in its mantle cavity to determine the direction of its water jet—and thus the direction of its movement.

7 In oysters, as in most bivalves, the sexes are separate. Eggs and sperm are shed into the water and after fertilization the embryo develops into a free-swimming trochophore larva with rudiments of a shell and a bundle of cilia for propulsion and feeding. As the shell enlarges, the second, or veliger, larval form develops. This has a well-muscled foot, a bivalve shell, and internal organs. The spat, or young oyster, remains free-swimming for some two weeks before settling down and attaching itself to a suitable surface. Some bivalves go through a brief parasitic phase that aids dispersal. The larva of these species—a glochidium—must attach itself to a fish for development to take place. Afterward the young bivalve abandons its host to take up an independent existence in the ocean.

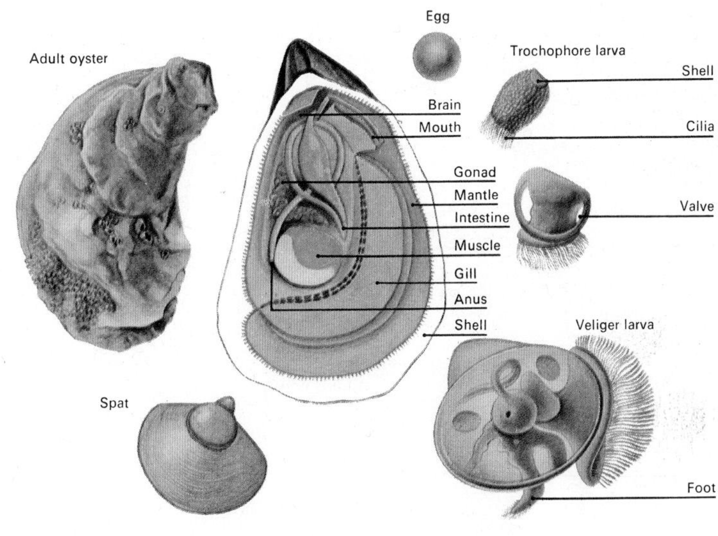
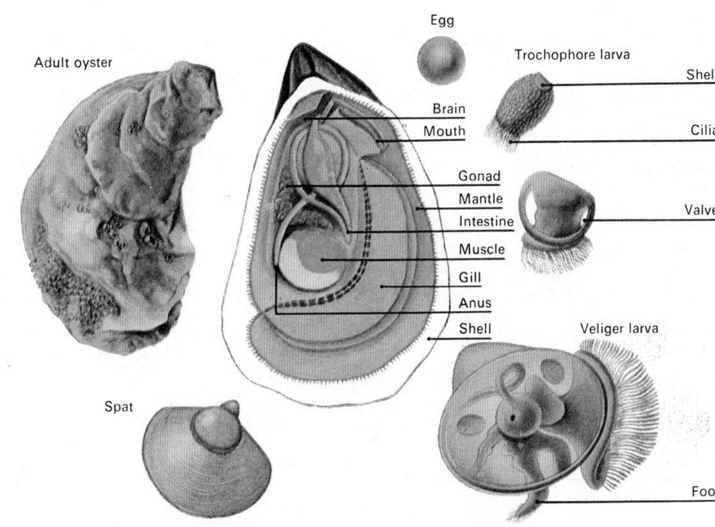
7
Egg
Adult oyster
Trochophore larva
Shell
Brain
Mouth
Cilia
Gonad
Mantle
Intestine
Valve
Muscle
Gill
Anus
Shell
Veliger larva
Spat
Foot

Squids and octopuses

Cephalopods, the animal group that includes squids, octopuses, cuttlefish, and nautiloids, have always held a peculiar fascination for man. Some of these creatures—particularly the squids—grow to an enormous size and may have lent credence to the legend of the "sea serpent." As mollusks the cephalopods are related to such shelled animals as snails, mussels, and clams, but are far more advanced and include the largest and most intelligent of the invertebrates. Cephalopods are "jet-propelled" mollusks that live in the sea and have their foot divided to form a number of tentacles or arms surrounding the head.

Support, movement, and respiration

Because most cephalopods have internal shells or no shell at all, their relationship to other mullusks is not immediately apparent. The shell itself, where it exists, is markedly different from that of other mollusks. In *Nautilus* it is still in evidence; in the octopus it is completely absent; in the squid it survives as a thin, horny plate (the pen), which serves as an internal skeleton. In the cuttlefish the shell forms the cuttlebone, which serves both as a supporting structure and an organ of buoyancy. The bone is divided (like the shell of the nautilus) into a series of chambers, the youngest (most recently formed) of which contain gas.

Cephalopods are far more active than other mollusks and therefore require an efficient respiratory system. This is provided by the mantle, which pumps a constant current of water in and out of the mantle cavity and over the gills [Key]. Deoxygenated blood is forced through each gill by a separate gill heart. Oxygenated blood passes from the gills to a single main, or systemic, heart that distributes it to the vessels and capillaries of the rest of the body. Contractions of the mantle also enable most cephalopods to move with great speed when necessary [4]. Water is drawn into the mantle cavity and then expelled as a jet.

Well-developed sense organs

The feature that most distinguishes cephalopods from their lowlier mollusk relatives is the extraordinary development of their sense organs and nervous system—a feature that reflects their active life style.

The large cephalopod brain, which encircles the esophagus directly between the eyes, is made up of several masses of nervous tissue (ganglia) that in most lower invertebrates are spread throughout the body. The nervous system of a squid incorporates a number of exceptionally large and long nerve cells called "giant fibers," which scientists have used widely in studying the physiology of nerves.

Cephalopods have chemical sense organs and balancing organs but their most striking features are the eyes [8]. Even a cursory glance at a section of a cephalopod eye is sufficient to reveal its resemblance to the eye of a vertebrate. Within the globe can be seen an outer window, or cornea, a lens, a sensitive layer, or retina, and an opaque backing layer, or choroid. Yet there is no direct evolutionary relationship between mollusks and vertebrates. The arrangement of the cells in the retinas of the two groups is quite different, as is the focusing

CONNECTIONS

See also
476 Land and sea sna
478 Life between two shells
482 Shells of the worl
626 Animals of the oc
564 Fossils without backbones
462 Sex in the animal world
1812 Color chemistry
1454 Mathematical curv

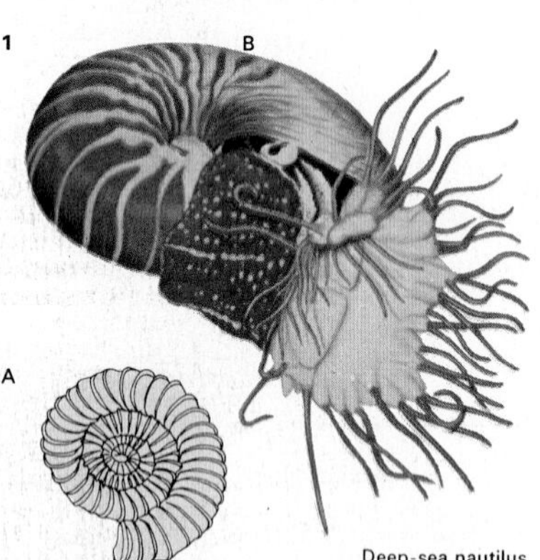
1
B
A
Deep-sea nautilus
Nautilus pompilius

1 Nautilus is the only surviving genus of the original cephalopod stock, the nautiloids. The fossilized shells of extinct relatives, the ammonoids [A], are quite common. About 100 million years ago there were probably some 2,500 species. Today there are three species of *Nautilus*. One of them, the deepsea nautilus, *Nautilus pompilius* [B], is a deepsea species that lives in tropical Pacific waters.

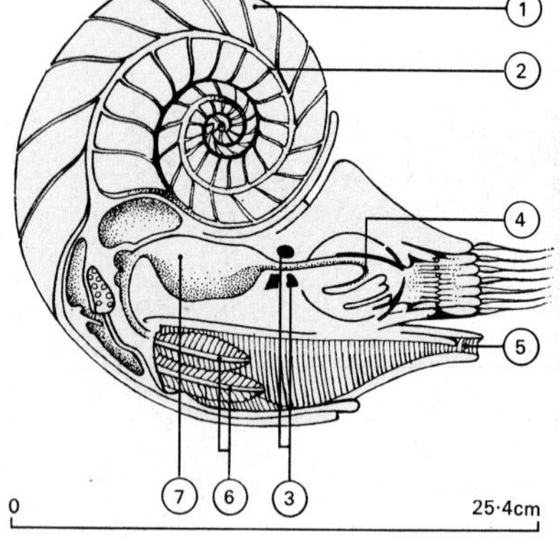
2
1
2
4
5
7
6
3
0
25·4cm

2 A section through Nautilus shows the shell [1] and siphuncle [2] wound in a spiral. Just behind the tentacles lies the mouth [4] leading to the intestine [7]. *Nautilus* has an advanced nervous system with a brain [3], and respires by means of gills [6] that are located in the mantle cavity. It swims by forcing a jet of water out of its mantle cavity and through the siphon [5].

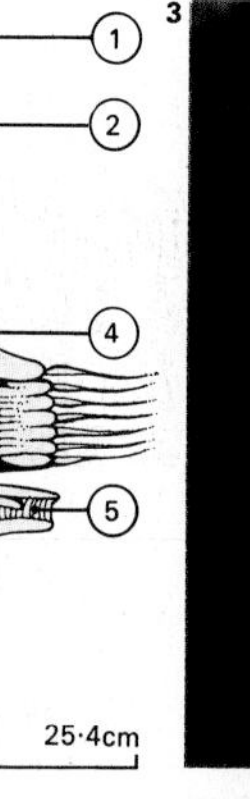

3 The cuttlefish *Sepia officinalis* lives on the sea bottom where it feeds on shrimp. It is able to uncover these by blowing jets of water at the sand of the sea bed. In a similar way the animal can bury itself by blowing the sand from below and allowing the particles to fall back onto its upper surface. The cuttlefish is a master of camouflage; as the environment changes, its surface displays rippling patterns of color change—the product of many thousands of expandable bags of pigment, each one under control of the nervous system.

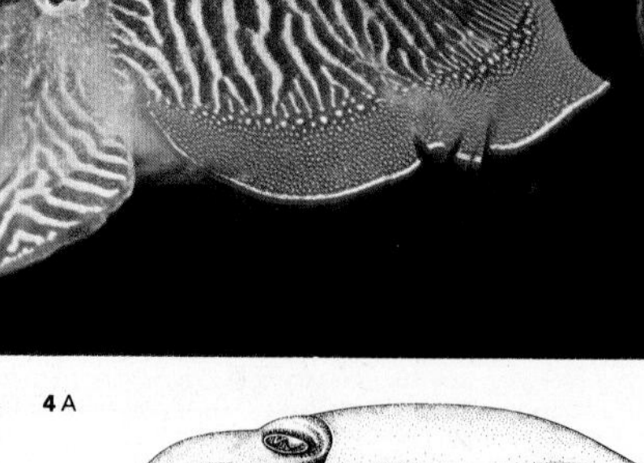
4 A
B
C

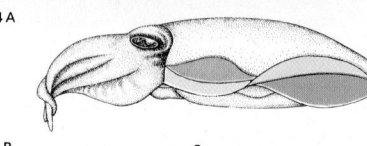

4 The most elegant of movers among the cephalopods is the cuttlefish. When moving slowly [A], as in hunting, for example, it swims by means of a series of undulations in its lateral fins. When it accelerates [B, C], it closes the opening of its mantle cavity, constricts the powerful muscles in the wall of the mantle, and forces a jet of water through its siphon. The siphon may be moved through any angle, so the cuttlefish can use this mechanism to steer itself in any direction it chooses. All cephalopods share this system of jet propulsion, which allows them to make a rapid escape from possible danger whenever necessary.

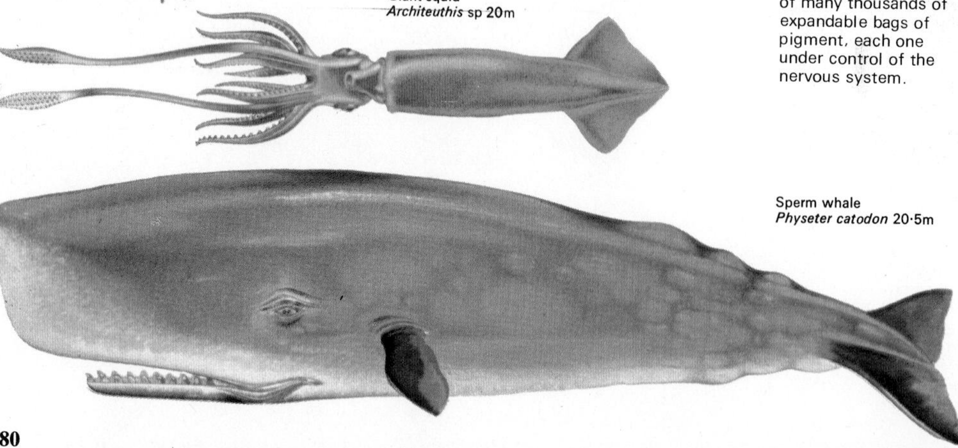
5
Octopus 9m
Giant squid
Architeuthis sp 20m
Sperm whale
Physeter catodon 20·5m

5 Cephalopods vary enormously in size. *Sepiola*, the little cuttle, is seldom longer than 1.5in (4cm), although some octopuses reach a length of 29ft (9m). But even these huge creatures are dwarfed by the giant squid *(Architeuthis)*, which grows to 65ft (20m) long. This begins to compare with the size of that other giant of the oceans, the sperm whale *(Physeter catodon)*. The comparison is significant because the squid forms a major part of the sperm whale's diet. Evidence of conflict between these two species is provided by the scars of huge sucker marks occasionally found on the whale's tough skin.

mechanism. The overall resemblance is a result of evolutionary convergence by which two differing groups have solved the same problem—that of vision—in a similar manner.

Patterns of behavior

Their powerful sense organs and large brains allow cephalopods to achieve complex behavior patterns and account for their pronounced ability to learn. These attributes are clearly valuable assets to predatory animals that feed on such prey as crabs and lobsters, which have the strength and equipment to fight back. All cephalopods are swift and powerful hunters. The tentacles that surround the mouth, armed with suckers on muscular stalks, help to seize the victim and thrust it between the horny jaws. Squids and cuttlefish have two tentacles that are longer than the rest. Normally at least partly retracted, these can be shot out at great speed to capture moving prey. The octopus uses a less graceful but equally effective technique; it jumps on its prey, using its tentacles to enfold the victim.

Many cephalopods, especially the deep-sea forms, are capable of producing light—a phenomenon known as bioluminescence. This may be useful to illuminate the way, or as an attraction or a warning signal, and can be generated either in special tissues or by bacteria that live symbiotically in various parts of the cephalopod body. One cuttlefish *(Hetereteuthis)* can even release a luminous cloud of bacteria when disturbed.

The reproductive behavior of cephalopods is complex; approaches between cuttlefish, for example, may involve sophisticated color changes. During the breeding season a male approached by another cuttlefish deepens its color. If the newcomer fails to change likewise, it is assumed to be female. Both male and female have a single gonad (organ producing sex cells) that discharges into the mantle cavity. The male collects its sperm into a small packet, the spermatophore, and transfers this to the female using a specialized arm called a hectocotylus. Various glands associated with the female gonad produce yolk and shell for the eggs.

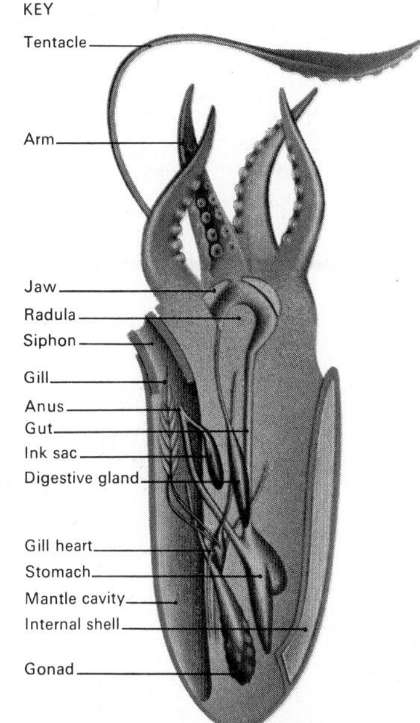
KEY
Tentacle
Arm
Jaw
Radula
Siphon
Gill
Anus
Gut
Ink sac
Digestive gland
Gill heart
Stomach
Mantle cavity
Internal shell
Gonad

The cephalopods, or "head-footed" animals, such as this cuttlefish, are the most advanced of the mollusks. The mouth is surrounded by sucker-bearing tentacles and equipped with horny jaws. A muscular mantle covers the cavity that houses the gills. Through these, a pair of gill hearts pump blood. All cephalopods can move by forcing a jet of water out of the mantle cavity and through a tube, the siphon. A dark fluid is discharged from the ink sac when the animals are excited or frightened. The shell is large and external in nautiloids, smaller and internal in squids and cuttlefish, and completely absent in octopuses.

6 Common octopus
Octopus vulgaris

6 The octopus has eight tentacles surrounding its mouth (unlike the squid, which has ten). The common Atlantic octopus *(Octopus vulgaris)* is a native of warm waters but can be found in the North Atlantic.

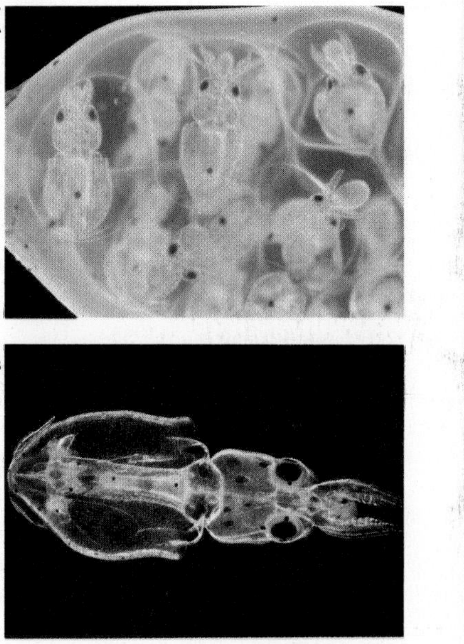

7 The squid *(Alloteuthis sublata)* lays its eggs in gelatinous capsules as do all cephalopods. Shortly before hatching [A] the developing squids are clearly visible through the sac wall. On hatching [B] young squids resemble adults but are transparent.

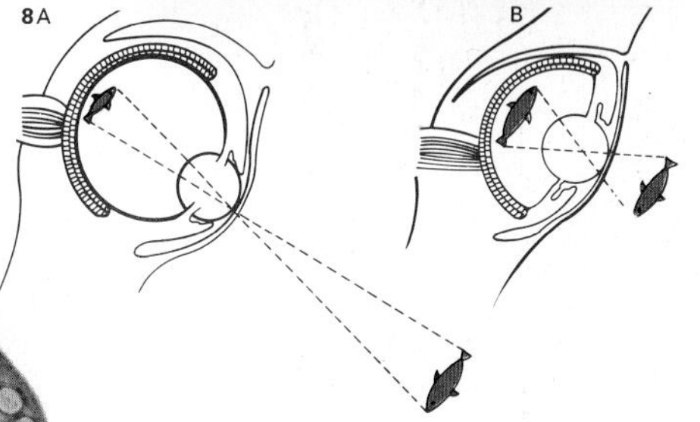

8 The cephalopod eye resembles that of vertebrates but evolved independently. Focusing is achieved by changing the distance between retina and lens [A, B], not by lens shape changes.

9 Tooth shell
Dentalium sp

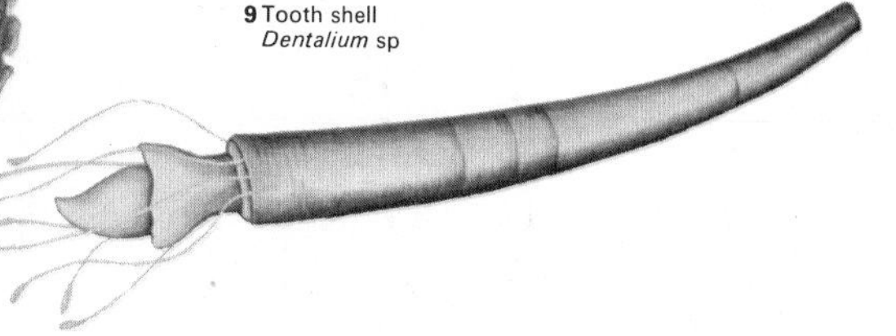

9 The scaphopods, or tooth shells, are a small group of burrowing mollusks, measuring up to 5in (13cm) long, which look like, but are not related to, cephalopods. Their bodies are enclosed in tubular shells, their heads tentacled.

Shells of the world

More than 80,000 species of mollusks have been identified and named. These animals, many of which have shells, are second only to the arthropods in abundance.

Mollusks are grouped zoologically into six or seven classes, depending on whether a group of shell-less deep-sea burrowing forms is placed with the chitons in the class Amphineura or given their own class, Aplacophora. The most primitive mollusks belong to the class Monoplacophora, which consists of only one living genus, *Neopilina*. Another small group, the tusk shells (class Scaphopoda), has 200 species.

The three remaining mollusk classes are the largest and best known. The two-shelled mollusks, or bivalves (class Bivalvia), include many familiar shellfish such as clams, mussels, and scallops. The sea and land snails are grouped together in the class Gastropoda and include some of the most interesting and beautiful of all the mollusks. Members of the class Cephalopoda, many of which have lost their shells, include the squid and the octopus. These advanced mollusks show a rudimentary intelligence.

1 Before it was dredged from the Pacific in 1957, *Neopilina* was known only as a fossil.

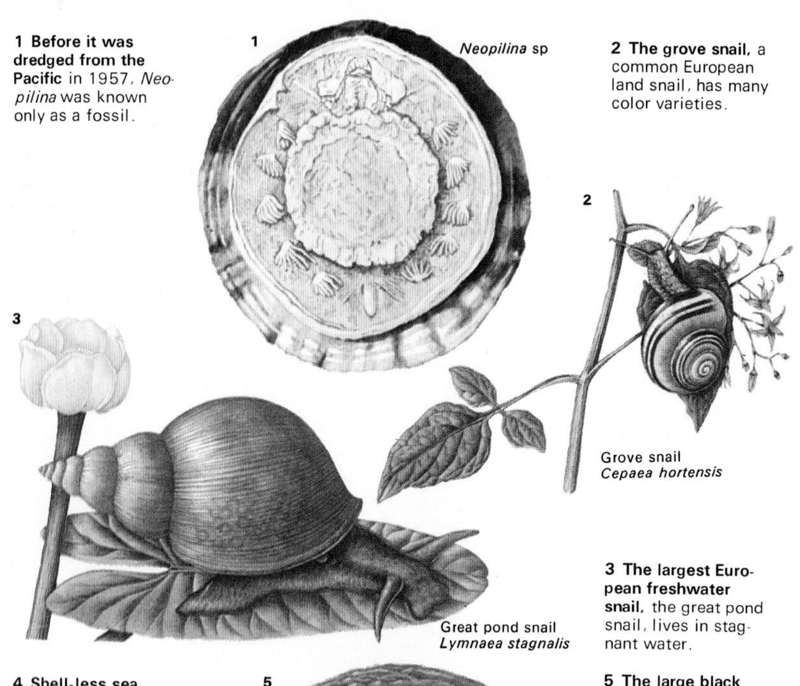

Neopilina sp

Grove snail *Cepaea hortensis*

Great pond snail *Lymnaea stagnalis*

2 The grove snail, a common European land snail, has many color varieties.

CONNECTIONS

See also
476 Land and sea sna
478 Life between two shells
480 Squids and octopu
616 Lakes and rivers
622 The seashore: life tween the tides
1812 Color chemistry

3 The largest European freshwater snail, the great pond snail, lives in stagnant water.

4 Shell-less sea slugs, many of them brightly colored, are found worldwide.

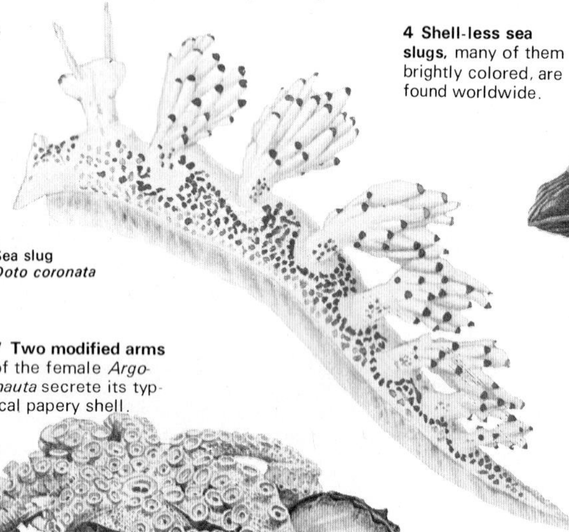

Sea slug *Doto coronata*

5 The large black slug can also be brown or orange.

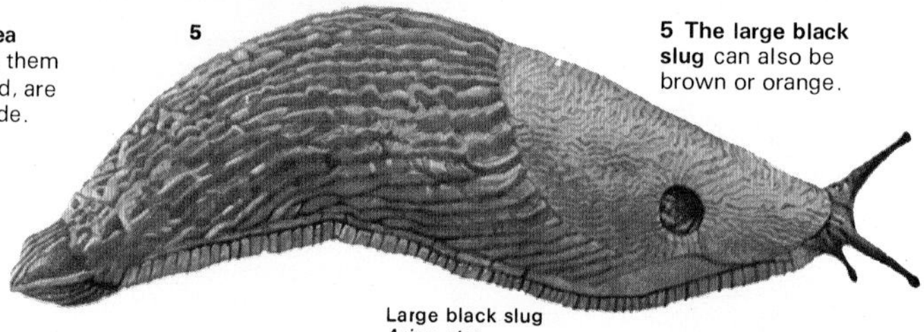

Large black slug *Arion ater*

7 Two modified arms of the female *Argonauta* secrete its typical papery shell.

Paper nautilus *Argonauta* sp

8 This, the largest top shell, is 6in (15cm) long and lives in the Pacific. It is used for buttons.

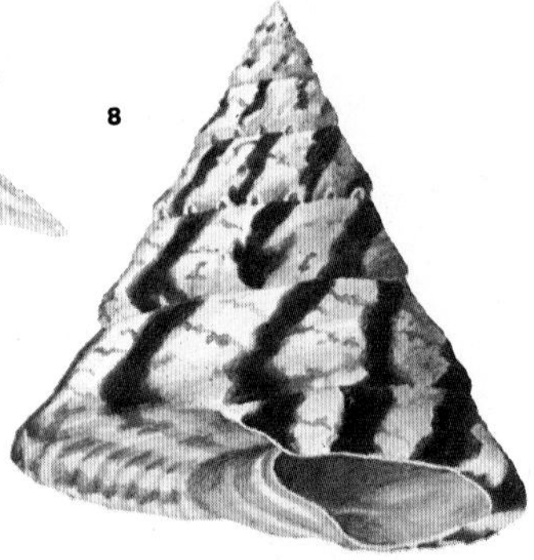

Top shell *Trochus niloticus*

6 This miter shell of the Indo-Pacific is a large species measuring 5in (12.5cm) long.

Miter shell *Mitra papalis*

9 The red abalone of California is a popular food of both man and sea otters.

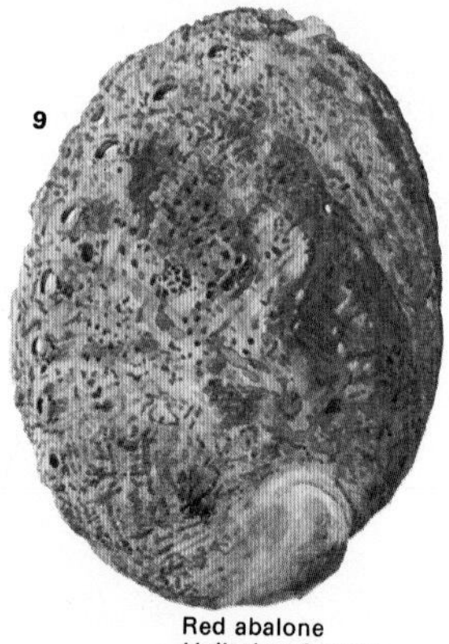

Red abalone *Haliotis rufescens*

12 Giant clams are the largest bivalve mollusks, weighing over 500lb (225kg).

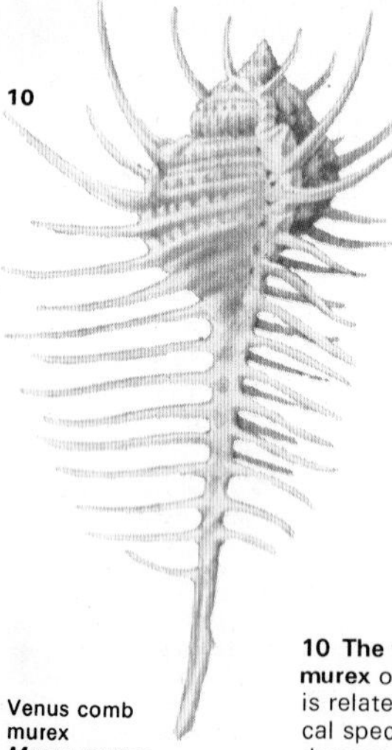

Venus comb murex *Murex pecten*

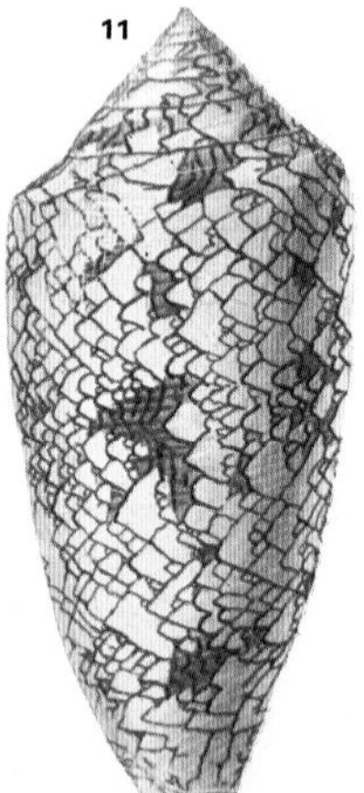

Cone shell *Conus textile*

10 The venus comb murex of the Pacific is related to a tropical species that produces a purple dye.

11 There are many species of the poisonous tropical cone shells. This one is 3.5in (8cm) long.

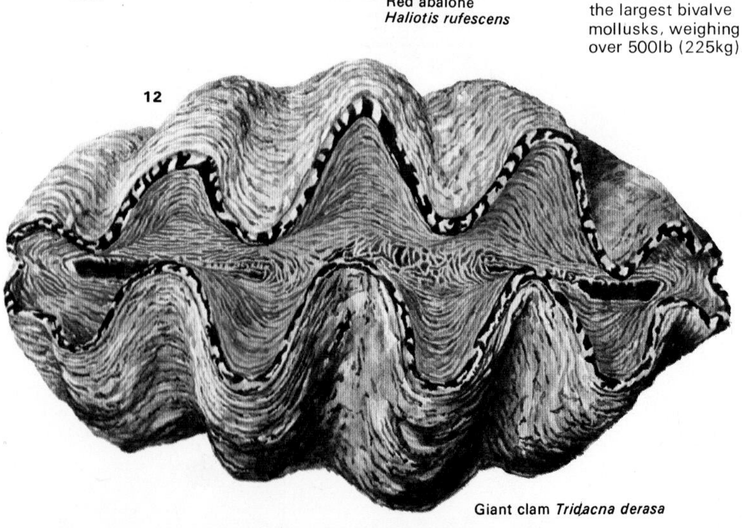

Giant clam *Tridacna derasa*

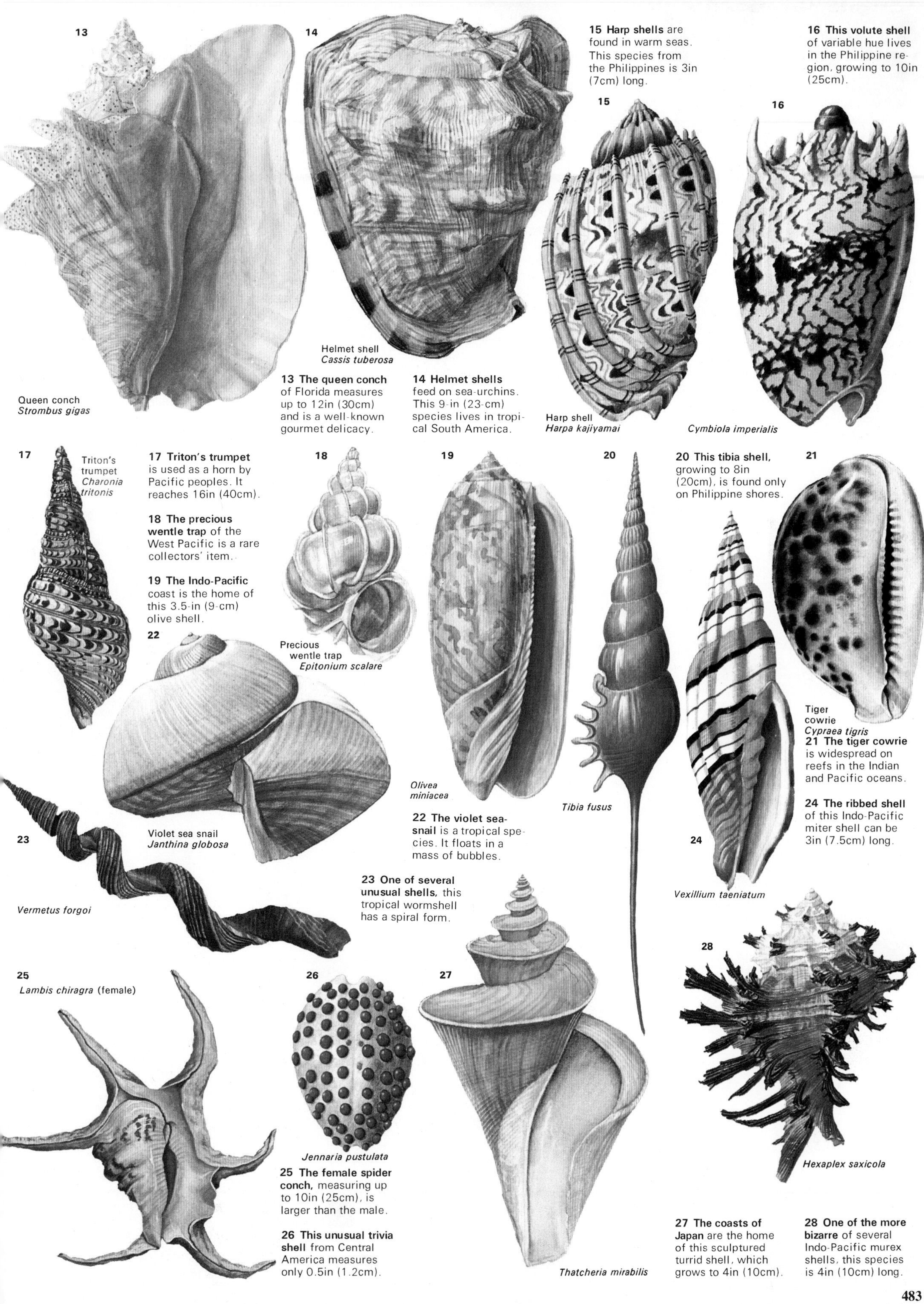
13
14
15
16
17
18
19
20
21
22
23
24
25
26
27
28

Queen conch *Strombus gigas*

Helmet shell *Cassis tuberosa*

13 The queen conch of Florida measures up to 12in (30cm) and is a well-known gourmet delicacy.

14 Helmet shells feed on sea-urchins. This 9-in (23-cm) species lives in tropical South America.

15 Harp shells are found in warm seas. This species from the Philippines is 3in (7cm) long.

Harp shell *Harpa kajiyamai*

16 This volute shell of variable hue lives in the Philippine region, growing to 10in (25cm).

Cymbiola imperialis

Triton's trumpet *Charonia tritonis*

17 Triton's trumpet is used as a horn by Pacific peoples. It reaches 16in (40cm).

18 The precious wentle trap of the West Pacific is a rare collectors' item.

19 The Indo-Pacific coast is the home of this 3.5-in (9-cm) olive shell.

Precious wentle trap *Epitonium scalare*

Olivea miniacea

20 This tibia shell, growing to 8in (20cm), is found only on Philippine shores.

Tibia fusus

Tiger cowrie *Cypraea tigris*

21 The tiger cowrie is widespread on reefs in the Indian and Pacific oceans.

Violet sea snail *Janthina globosa*

22 The violet sea-snail is a tropical species. It floats in a mass of bubbles.

24 The ribbed shell of this Indo-Pacific miter shell can be 3in (7.5cm) long.

Vexillium taeniatum

Vermetus forgoi

23 One of several unusual shells, this tropical wormshell has a spiral form.

Lambis chiragra (female)

Jennaria pustulata

25 The female spider conch, measuring up to 10in (25cm), is larger than the male.

26 This unusual trivia shell from Central America measures only 0.5in (1.2cm).

Thatcheria mirabilis

27 The coasts of Japan are the home of this sculptured turrid shell, which grows to 4in (10cm).

Hexaplex saxicola

28 One of the more bizarre of several Indo-Pacific murex shells, this species is 4in (10cm) long.

The joint-legged animals

The phylum Arthropoda—literally "joint-legged" animals—is by far the largest and most diversified group of creatures in the animal kingdom and must be regarded as one of the most important developments in animal evolution. Arthropods are of obscure origin but it is most likely that they arose from primitive annelid (segmented worm) stock [Key], possibly from animals rather like modern velvet worms [1], more than 600 million years ago.

Diversity and common features

The phylum Arthropoda contains a great many familiar animals such as insects, spiders, scorpions, centipedes, and crustaceans (crabs, shrimp, and lobsters), and also more unusual forms such as horseshoe, or king, crabs, sea spiders, and the parasitic ticks and mites. The numbers of individuals in many species are enormous and the number of arthropod species in the animal kingdom far exceeds that of all other animals put together. About 80 percent of the known species of animals are arthropods. The basic characteristics that all arthropods share are the tough, segmented, external skeleton (exoskeleton) covering the whole of the body (the internal anatomy of which also shows some segmentation) including the jointed limbs and a nerve cord running ventrally along the length of the animal (as in many other invertebrates but not in vertebrates). The heart, if present, is simple and situated dorsally.

There are variations on the basic theme, for arthropods have evolved over a long period of time and through diverse branches and it is not surprising that several kinds of arthropod are recognizable as belonging to that group only by experts. Some parasitic forms, for example, have lost most of their organs and look more like plant growths in the tissues of other animals. Only their typically arthropod larvae betray them. Others are so small—both winged and wingless species—that they have missed attention for centuries and bear little superficial resemblance to the great marine crustaceans or exotic butterflies and moths. But there must also be many thousands of species waiting to be described for the first time.

All of the arthropod organs have been modified in various ways during evolution and even the heart may be absent. But the dominant feature of the group, the tough exoskeleton [4] upon which so many of the other features depend, is always present in at least some stage of the life cycle.

The exoskeleton, which has contributed so greatly to the success of the arthropods, also imposes certain restrictions on them. It is excellent as a protective covering, but one-piece armor would prevent any movement. This problem was overcome by the simple solution of dividing the external skeleton into a number of separate plates. The plates are joined together by a thin, flexible membrane. The legs are also segmented and are composed of several tubelike elements hinged by a membrane.

The rigidity of the exoskeleton

The rigidity of the exoskeleton also complicates growth. The cuticle (outermost skin) can stretch between segments to a certain extent, but for any real overall increase in size the animal has to molt its outer covering

CONNECTIONS

See also

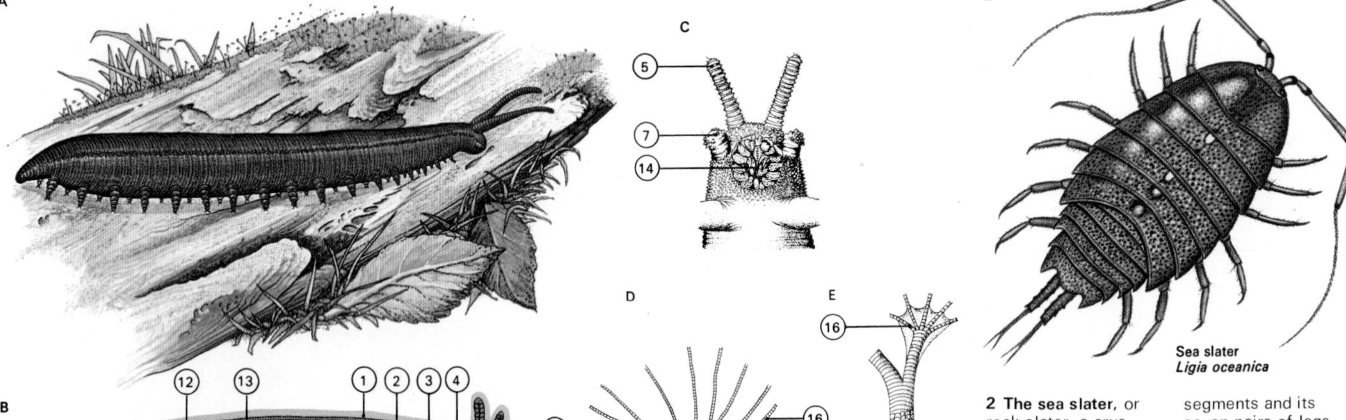

1 A
C
5
7
14
2
D
E
16
15
B
12
13
1
2
3
4
5
6
11
10
9
8
7
Sea slater
Ligia oceanica

1 Velvet worms such as *Peripatopsis* [A] have features [B] typical of both arthropods (the cuticle [1], heart [2], haemocoel [3], and the antennae [5]) and annelid worms (eye [4] and excretory organs [11]). Slime glands [8] discharge through oral papillae [7]. The mouth [6] has jaws [14] and leads to the gut [9]. The underside of the head is shown [C]. Paired nerve cords [10] coordinate movement. Female reproductive organs comprise ovaries [12] and uteri [13]. Spiracles (respiratory openings) [15] and tracheae [16] of *Peripatopsis* [D] and insects [E] are only superficially similar.

2 The sea slater, or rock slater, a crustacean of the order Isopoda, which also includes pill bugs, has a simple, typically arthropod structure. Its armored exoskeleton is jointed between the body segments and its seven pairs of legs, borne on the thorax, are all very similar in proportions (Isopoda means "equal feet"). Appendages beneath the abdomen function as gills for breathing in water.

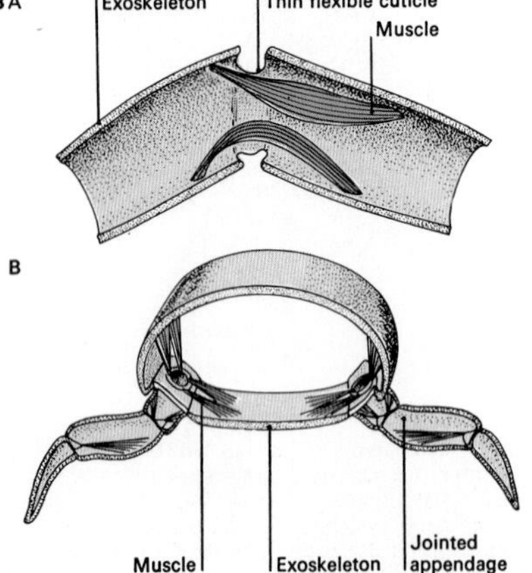

3A
Exoskeleton
Thin flexible cuticle
Muscle
B
Muscle
Exoskeleton
Jointed appendage

3 The support of muscles for movement is a major function of the exoskeleton. The muscles are attached across a joint [A], as in vertebrates, but inside the skeleton. The contraction of one muscle of a pair and the relaxing of the other results in movement at the flexible joint. A cross section through the body at a leg insertion [B] shows the part played by muscle attachment points and by the thin flexible cuticle at joints allowing movement.

4

1
3
2

Epicuticle
Chitinous endocuticle
Epidermis
Basement membrane

4 The exoskeleton in the Crustacea is hardened by the deposition of calcium salts. As a result most crustaceans, such as the crayfish, have very tough shells consisting mostly of a cuticle [1] secreted by the epidermis. Special glands [2] in the connective tissue secrete the waterproof epicuticle. Epidermal bristles [3] detect various stimuli.

and expand before the new skeleton hardens. During that time it is very vulnerable.

The renewal of the exoskeleton places heavy demands upon the animal. The new covering requires a great deal of material for its production and only marine arthropods such as crabs and lobsters with abundant food supplies and available minerals can grow to a large size.

Although excellent as a protective covering the exoskeleton is relatively heavy. With increase in size the exoskeleton becomes proportionately heavier and imposes a size limit on terrestrial arthropods and, more significantly, on flying species.

Success of the group

In spite of the problems inherent in the basic arthropod body plan, the group has been remarkably successful within its limitations. One arthropod or another has managed to colonize every habitat invaded separately by all the other groups. The insects, of course, are among the most proficient of flying animals. Indeed, certain fliers are, for their size, the fastest of all living things.

Many arthropods, of various groups, can both produce and perceive sounds. Some moths, for example, use ultrasound for confusing the hunting techniques of bats and possibly for other purposes too. Other senses in arthropods are also well developed. They can detect not only airborne vibrations but also those of the surface upon which they are resting. The chemical senses of taste and smell are highly developed and play an important role in communication between individuals of many species. The eyes are extremely well developed in many arthropods and vision can extend beyond man's visible spectrum into either the infrared or ultraviolet zones. The eyes of some insects, for example, can detect the plane of polarization of light from the sky and use it in navigation.

Arthropod muscles are relatively efficient and very powerful. The claw of a large lobster, for example, can crush a man's wrist. The flight muscles of higher insects such as flies possess the remarkable ability of contracting so rapidly that the wings beat at up to 1,000 times a second.

KEY

Annelida (Earthworms, etc)
Onychophora (Velvet worms)
Pycnogonida (1)
Merostomata (2)
Arachnida (3)
Crustacea (4)
Chilopoda (5)
Diplopoda (6)
Pauropoda (7)
Symphyla (8)
Pterygota (9A)
"Apterygota" (9B)

Arthropods
1 Sea spiders
2 Horseshoe crabs
3 Spiders, scorpions, etc
4 Crabs, lobsters, etc
5 Centipedes
6 Millipedes
7, 8 (no English name)
9A Winged insects
9B Wingless insects

The phylum Arthropoda can be divided into nine classes with living representatives and five classes composed of extinct species. The arthropods are the most successful of all invertebrate groups on land, in the water, and the air.

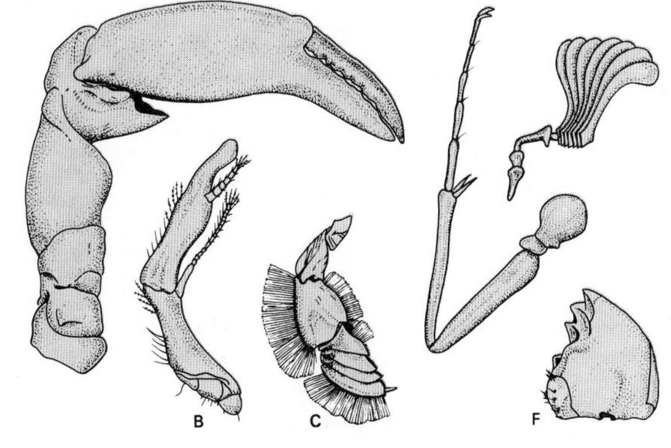

5A
B
C
D
E
F

5 The jointed limbs of arthropods were originally for locomotion, like the legs on the rock slater's thorax. They have since become modified for different functions, even in the same animal. Examples of these adaptations are a claw [A] and sperm guide [B] of a crustacean; a swimming leg of a water beetle [C]; a walking leg of a ground beetle [D]; an antenna of a cockchafer [E], and a chewing mandible of a cockroach [F].

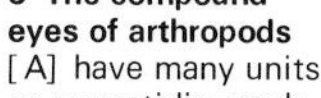

6 The compound eyes of arthropods [A] have many units, or ommatidia, each covered with a transparent corneal lens [1]. Underneath is the photoreceptor unit [2] that connects with the optic nerve [3]. The ommatidia work together or separately, in the dark [B] or the light [C]. In the dark, pigment in the screening cells [4 and 6] is withdrawn so that the photopigment cells [5] and receptor cells [7] act together to receive the light focused by the crystalline cone and corneal lens secreted by the corneagen cells. But in the light the pigment from the screening cells isolates the ommatidia, which send separate messages to the brain via nerve fibers [8].

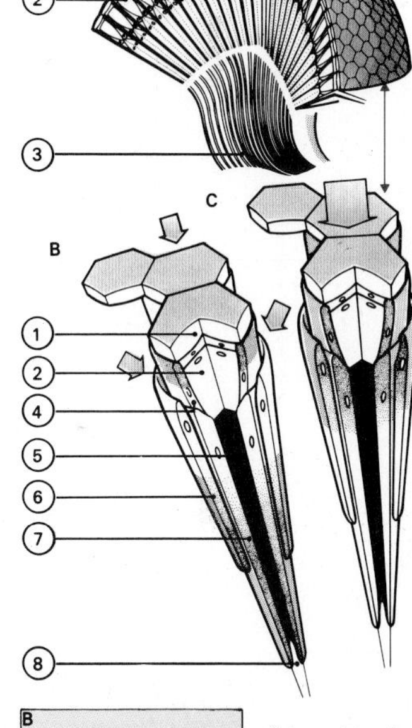

6A
1
2
3
B
C
1
2
4
5
6
7
8

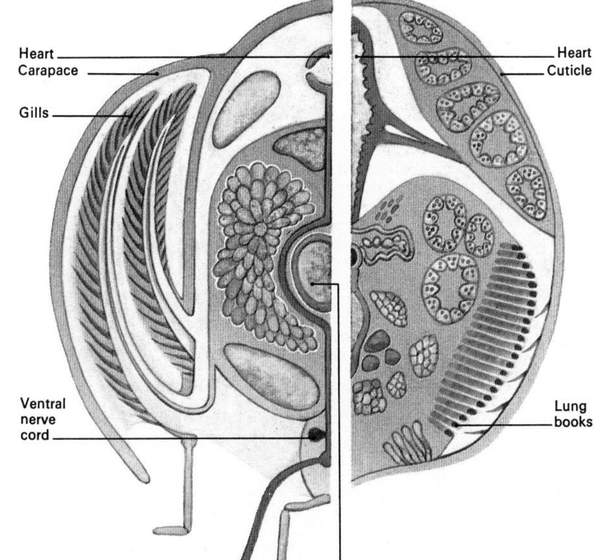

7A
B
Heart
Carapace
Gills
Ventral nerve cord
Heart
Cuticle
Lung books
Intestine

7 The breathing apparatus of arthropods is shown in the cross sections through a water-dwelling lobster [A] and land-dwelling spider [B]. In lobsters and other crustaceans, a carapace (a plate of the skeleton) covers a gill chamber through which water circulates. Blood passing through the gills returns to the heart for pumping to the blood spaces in the body. Most spiders have pairs of book lungs made up of "leaves," each containing circulating blood and enclosed in a "vestibule" full of air. This opens to the outside by means of spiracles. As in crustaceans, the blood returns to the heart after oxygenation to be recirculated.

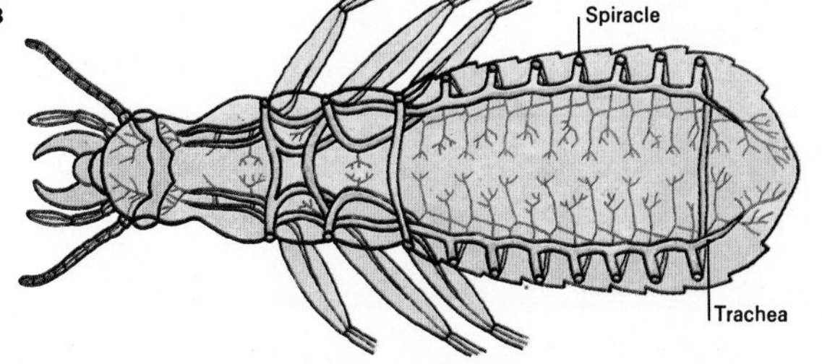

8
Spiracle
Trachea

8 Insects, being terrestrial animals, run the risk of drying out and therefore have a severely limited area open to the outside air. Respiration is by a system of tracheae, or tubes, opening to the outside by pairs of spiracles along the abdomen.

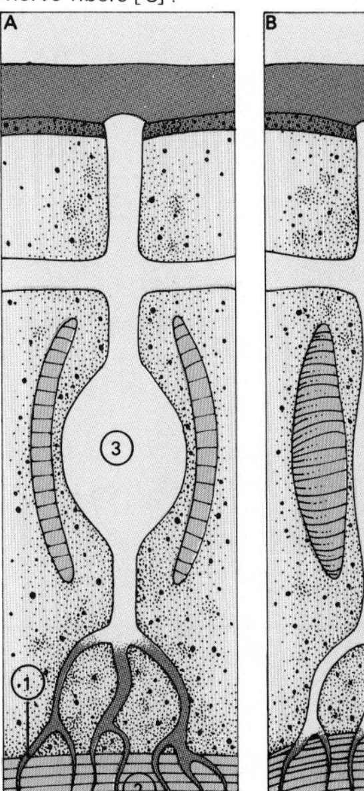

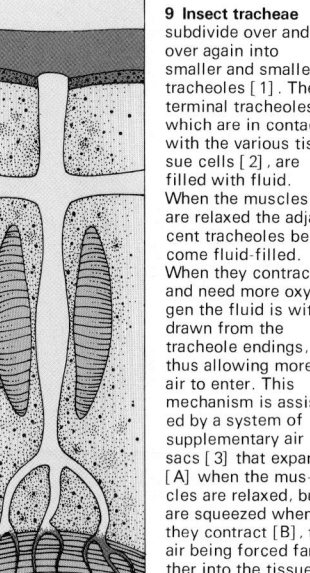

9A
3
1
2
B

9 Insect tracheae subdivide over and over again into smaller and smaller tracheoles [1]. The terminal tracheoles, which are in contact with the various tissue cells [2], are filled with fluid. When the muscles are relaxed the adjacent tracheoles become fluid-filled. When they contract and need more oxygen the fluid is withdrawn from the tracheole endings, thus allowing more air to enter. This mechanism is assisted by a system of supplementary air sacs [3] that expand [A] when the muscles are relaxed, but are squeezed when they contract [B], the air being forced farther into the tissues to supply oxygen.

Crabs and lobsters

The crabs, lobsters, crayfish, prawns, and shrimp, together with such creatures as woodlice, water fleas, and barnacles, are all members of the zoological class Crustacea. This class is a subdivision of the larger group or phylum Arthropoda (the joint-legged animals) to which the insects also belong.

Diversity of forms

The Crustacea number more than 30,000 species and are one of the most diverse of all animal groups. They vary in form from the familiar lobster to the barnacles, which look more like mollusks than crustaceans, and in size from the giant Japanese spider crab *(Macrocheira kaempferi)*, measuring 10–13ft (3–4m) from claw tip to claw tip, to the copepods of the ocean plankton that may be only a fraction of an inch in diameter.

Crustacean life-styles are as diverse as their body forms although most live in water or in damp surroundings. The crabs and lobsters are largely scavengers, while the greatly modified barnacle *Sacculina*, which looks more like an undifferentiated sac of tissue than a crustacean, lives as a parasite within crabs. The mantis shrimps are active predators, the gribble *(Limnoria)* is a wood-borer, and the cleaner shrimp *(Stenopus)* feeds on external parasites of fish. In return for its "cleaning services" the shrimp obtains immunity from potential predators. Many crustaceans, including the sedentary barnacles, are filter feeders, extracting food particles from the water in which they live by forcing a constant flow of it through their bodies.

Characteristics of crustaceans

The typical water-dwelling crustacean has a body covered with a hard shell, or exoskeleton. This external skeleton is composed of protein and chitin and hardened with lime salts. Also typical is the segmented body form, as seen in the Norway lobster [Key], although the middle body section (the thorax) is often concealed by a large plate of skeleton (the carapace).

Generally, each segment of the crustacean head and body carries a pair of legs or other appendages [6]. These appendages have become modified to perform different functions. On the head, for example, the typical appendages are the first and second antennae, which are used as sensory receptors, and the mandibles and first and second maxillae, which are used for taking in and crushing food. The thorax bears three pairs of maxillipeds (which are also employed in pushing food toward the mouth), the chelae, or pincers for food capture, plus four pairs of walking legs. Under the abdomen are five pairs of swimmerets used, as their name suggests, in locomotion, but some of them may be modified for reproductive purposes. The crustacean abdomen ends with a pair of appendages known as uropods. These, with the tip of the abdominal skeleton (the telson), form a tail fan that is used for steering during swimming or, when flicked vigorously down and under, shoots the animal backward in quick retreat.

Most crustaceans breathe dissolved oxygen from the surrounding water either through gills or through most of the body surface; exceptions to the rule are the woodlice and the extreme parasitic forms. The

CONNECTIONS

See also
484 The joint-legged animals
490 Crustaceans and other arthropods
564 Fossils without backbones
552 Whales, porpoises, and dolphins
622 The seashore: life between the tides
624 Life in the oceans
388 Fish farming
394 Shellfish and other seafoods

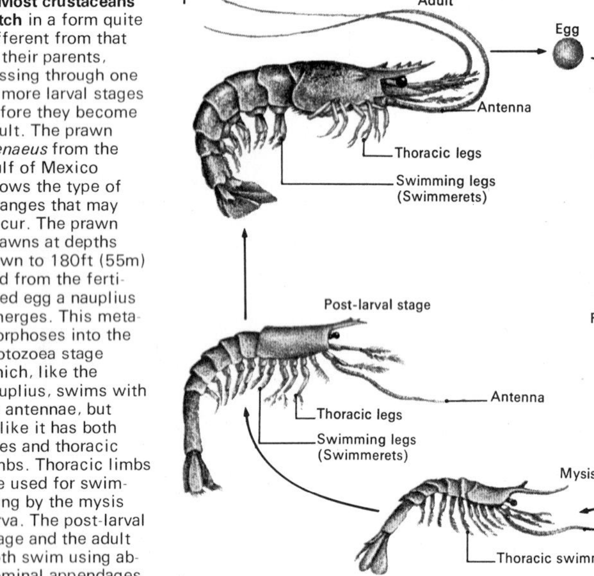

1
Adult
Egg
Antenna
Antenna
Thoracic legs
Nauplius
Swimming legs (Swimmerets)
Antenna
Protozoea
Post-larval stage
Antenna
Thoracic legs
Swimming legs (Swimmerets)
Mysis
Antenna
Thoracic swimming legs

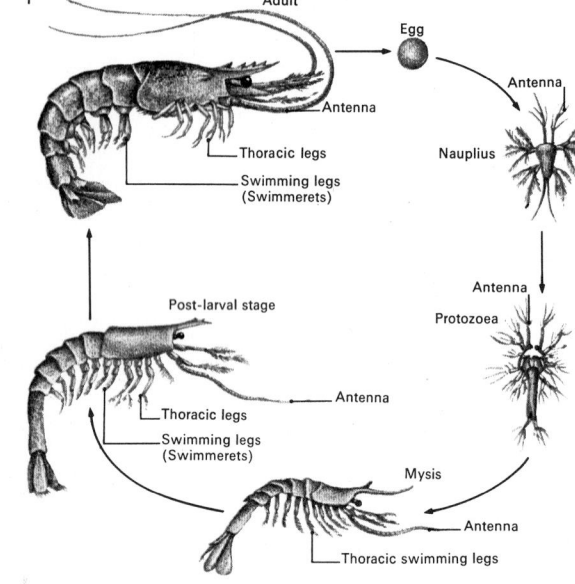

1 Most crustaceans hatch in a form quite different from that of their parents, passing through one or more larval stages before they become adult. The prawn *Penaeus* from the Gulf of Mexico shows the type of changes that may occur. The prawn spawns at depths down to 180ft (55m) and from the fertilized egg a nauplius emerges. This metamorphoses into the protozoea stage which, like the nauplius, swims with its antennae, but unlike it has both eyes and thoracic limbs. Thoracic limbs are used for swimming by the mysis larva. The post-larval stage and the adult both swim using abdominal appendages.

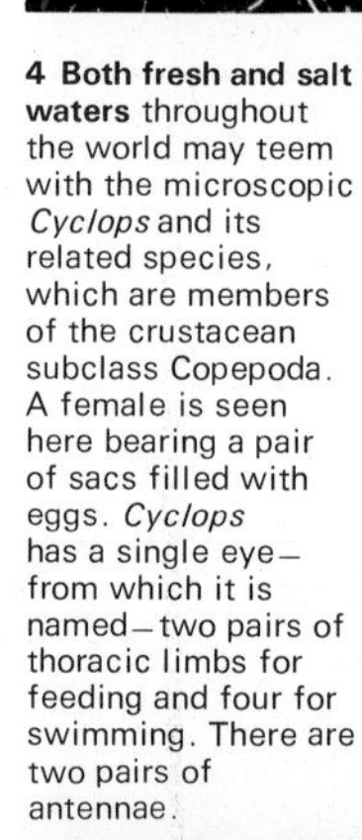

2 The eggs of the squat lobster are attached to the female on special abdominal appendages. The abdominal swimmerets secrete a substance to which the eggs stick. They are held beneath the abdomen, partly covered by the tail, in a large mass. Females carrying eggs in this way are said to be "in berry." After the eggs have hatched the larvae may also cling to the female's swimmerets for a time.

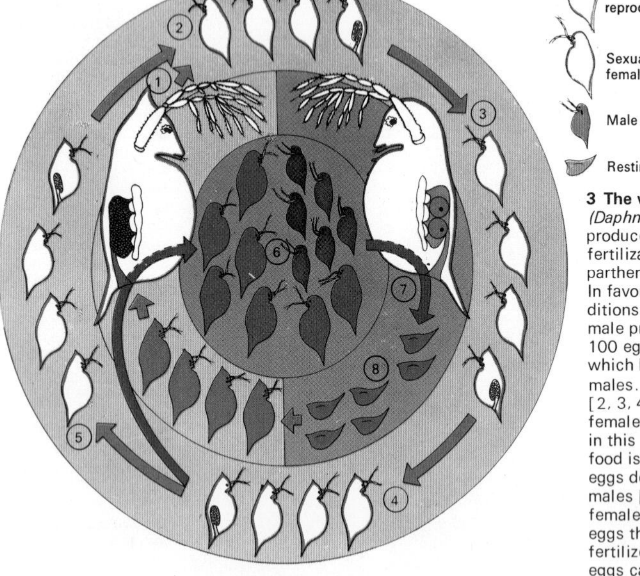

3
Good conditions
Bad conditions
1
2
3
4
5
6
7
8
Parthenogenetically reproducing female
Sexually reproducing female
Male
Resting egg

3 The water flea *(Daphnia)* can reproduce without fertilization, that is, parthenogenetically. In favorable conditions [1] the female produces up to 100 eggs, all of which hatch into females. Generations [2, 3, 4, 5] of females can be born in this way. When food is scarce some eggs develop into males [6] and the females produce eggs that must be fertilized [7]. These eggs can survive harsh conditions [8].

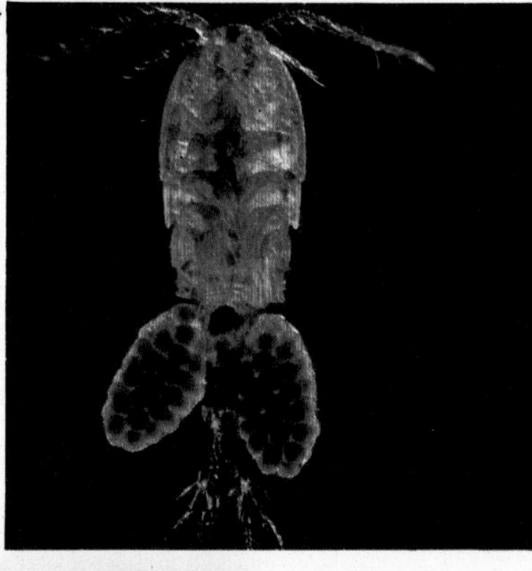

4 Both fresh and salt waters throughout the world may teem with the microscopic *Cyclops* and its related species, which are members of the crustacean subclass Copepoda. A female is seen here bearing a pair of sacs filled with eggs. *Cyclops* has a single eye—from which it is named—two pairs of thoracic limbs for feeding and four for swimming. There are two pairs of antennae.

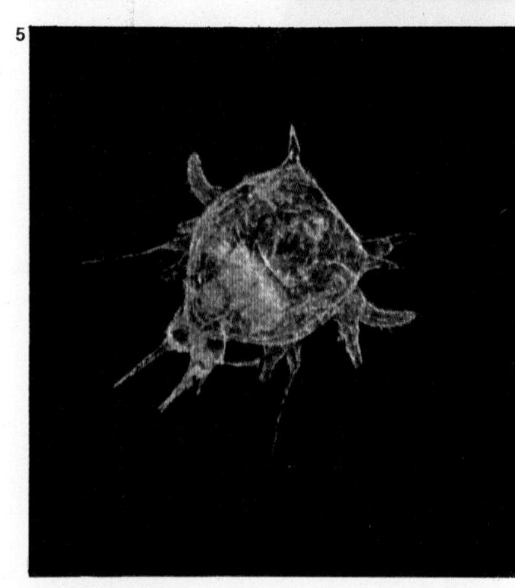

5 The nauplius larva is found in so many Crustacea that it can justifiably be called the basic larval form. The nauplius usually has a simple triangular or shieldlike unsegmented body with a single eye and three pairs of appendages. The first pair are simple and sensory; the second pair, the antennae, are very well developed with two branches covered with special hairs, or setae, and are used for swimming. A pair of mandibles is employed in feeding.

gills of crabs and lobsters are thin-walled, leaflike outgrowths that originate at or near the bases of the appendages of the thorax. They are enclosed in a chamber covered by a downgrowth of the carapace on each side and a current of water flows over them maintained by the beating of a paddlelike organ at the base of the second maxilla. In the woodlice and other similar crustaceans, however, the gills are modifications of the appendages of the abdomen and in many of the smaller crustaceans the body surface itself acts as a gas-exchanger. But whatever their structure, the gills of all crustaceans must remain wet and this explains why most crustaceans are confined to watery habitats.

The sense organs of crustaceans, particularly the eyes and antennae, are well adapted to the needs of these animals. The paired eyes of crabs and lobsters are borne on stalks and like those of insects they are compound. But in copepods they are simple, single, and central—one copepod is in fact named *Cyclops* [4] after the legendary Greek giant with the same characteristic. The two pairs of antennae are used to detect vibrations, maintain balance [7], and also serve as sensors of "taste" and "smell."

Like other creatures that are encased in hard external skeletons, Crustacea can only increase in size if they undergo successive molts [8]. Many crustaceans have the ability to regenerate lost parts [9] such as claws and eyes, and often do this following the rejection of an injured part by self-amputation.

Most Crustacea develop from eggs laid by the female [2]. In some species, including water fleas [3], young can be produced by parthenogenesis. Larval development is generally in several stages [1], but most species have a nauplius larva [5].

Food for others

Throughout the world crustaceans play a major role in aquatic food webs, both freshwater and marine, as the food of larger animals. Freshwater ponds teem with microscopic *Daphnia* and *Cyclops;* seashores shelter millions of sand hoppers beneath seaweed and other flotsam; and in the sea one group, known as krill, provides food for fish, squid, jellyfish, and some whales.

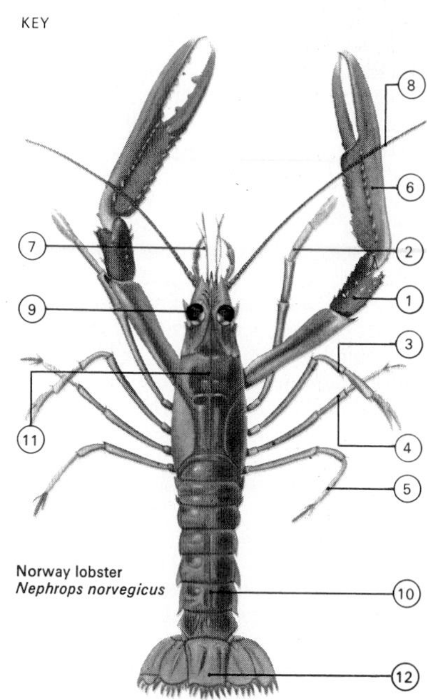
KEY
Norway lobster
Nephrops norvegicus
1
2
3
4
5
6
7
8
9
10
11
12

The Norway lobster, a small, burrowing form up to 8in(20cm) long found off northeast Atlantic coasts, is a typical crustacean. With the crabs, crayfish, prawns, and shrimps it is classified in a sub-group, or order, called the Decapoda (literally, 10 legs). These legs are borne in pairs [1-5] the first of which is enlarged to form nipping claws, or chelae [6]. Of the two pairs of antennae [7, 8] the second may be far longer than the body. With the eyes [9] they are the principal sense organs. The body segments are obvious only on the abdomen [10] for the thorax is covered by a hard carapace [11]. The tail bears a fanlike telson [12].

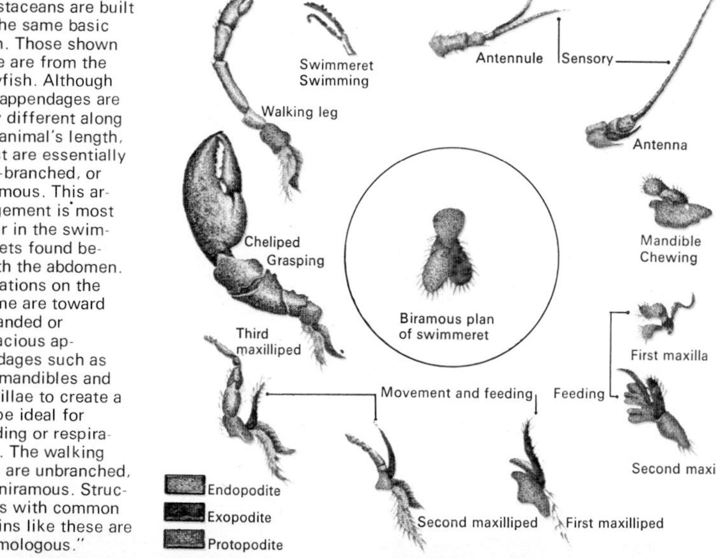
6
Swimmeret
Swimming
Walking leg
Antennule
Sensory
Antenna
Cheliped
Grasping
Mandible
Chewing
Biramous plan
of swimmeret
Third
maxilliped
First maxilla
Movement and feeding
Feeding
Second maxilla
Endopodite
Exopodite
Protopodite
Second maxilliped
First maxilliped

6 The segmented appendages of all crustaceans are built to the same basic plan. Those shown here are from the crayfish. Although the appendages are very different along the animal's length, most are essentially two-branched, or biramous. This arrangement is most clear in the swimmerets found beneath the abdomen. Variations on the theme are toward expanded or foliacious appendages such as the mandibles and maxillae to create a shape ideal for feeding or respiration. The walking legs are unbranched, or uniramous. Structures with common origins like these are "homologous."

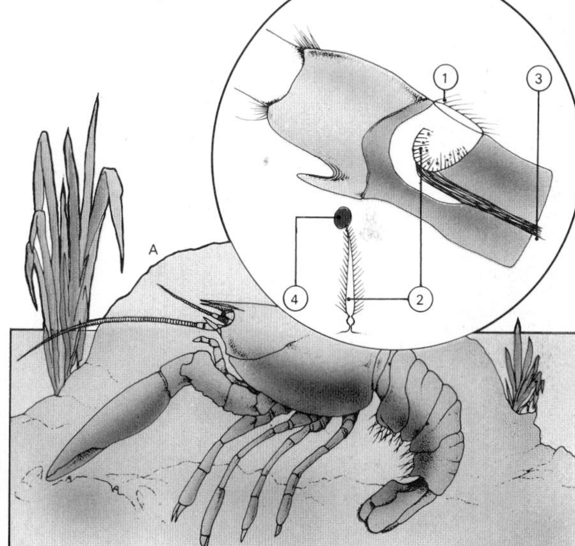
7
B
1
3
A
4
2

7 The balancing organs of Crustacea, as in this crayfish [A], are situated at the bases of the first antennae. Each organ of balance, or statocyst [B], lies in a cavity protected by a fringe of bristles, or setae [1], and consists of a series of setae [2] onto which sand grains [4] are stuck with a special secretion. As the animal moves, the grains also move and set up stresses on the setae that stimulate sensory cells. These send messages to the brain through the statocyst nerve [3]. New sand grains have to be incorporated each time the crayfish sheds its exoskeleton.

8
A

B

8 Molting, or ecdysis, in Crustacea, as in other arthropods, is essential if the animal is to grow. When the crab is ready to shed its shell [A] the membrane between carapace and abdomen is ruptured, and the animal begins the slow process of withdrawal [B], which may take several hours, starting with the head and ending with the abdomen. Immediately after the molt the animal absorbs water and expands before the skeleton hardens.

9 The crabs and many related crustaceans are able to regenerate portions of their limbs. This ability is connected with the phenomenon of autotomy whereby a claw or walking leg may be cast off [A] if trapped. The damaged appendage is snapped off along a built-in line of weakness and then slowly regenerates [B]. It usually takes many moltings for a lost part to be replaced completely.

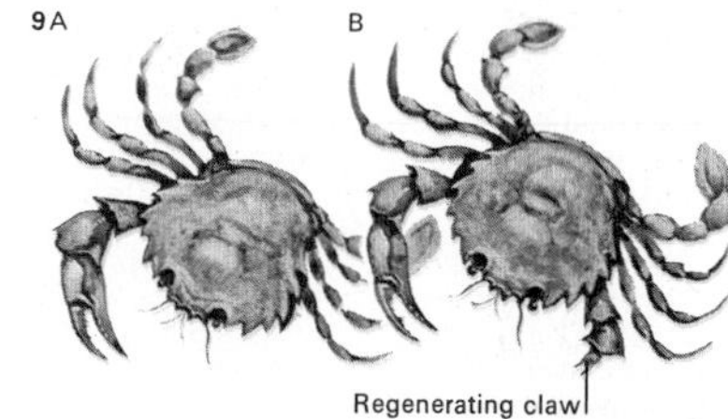
9A
B
Regenerating claw

Spiders and scorpions

A widespread and successful animal group, spiders, scorpions, and their relatives are collectively termed arachnids (class Arachnida) by naturalists. They have a long evolutionary history [Key]. The earliest known fossil arachnids are from the Palaeozoic era. Fossil scorpions occur in Silurian rocks (430 million years old) and fossil spiders are known from the Devonian of Scotland (395 million years old). Their ancestors were aquatic, but most modern and fossil spiders are terrestrial and many are found in extremely arid regions. Their aquatic ancestry is evident in their possession of modified gills (book lungs), although the more advanced members of the group possess air tubes (tracheae) that appear externally as spiracles on the abdomen [1].

Spider versus insect

It is likely that the earliest spiders fed upon insects, before the latter evolved wings, and caught them on the ground in the same way as present day wolf spiders. The development of insect flight opened another niche for the spiders who countered with the evolution of webs and snares to capture flying prey. Insects became masters of the air, but spiders joined the "aerial plankton" (creatures that live hanging in air or blown on its currents), suspended on silk threads.

The best known of the arachnids are the spiders. Many species are found in or near human dwellings and their webs are well known [6]. Spiders are generally disliked because a number of species (such as the black widow) have bites that can be dangerous to humans. But the bite of the large "tarantulas" is not as serious as is generally believed and most can be readily handled.

Spiders as skillful hunters

The main significance of the spiders in the natural order lies in the role they play as predators upon the insects. There are more than 20 times more insect species than spiders, of which there are about 40,000 species. From sea level to at least 22,000ft (6,700m) spiders pursue insects with a variety of traps and maneuvers adapted to fit the habits of their prey [9]. Nocturnal spiders take up the hunt when diurnal ones rest, so that insects are not safe at any time of the day or night. Spiders have devised a great variety of ways of capturing their prey. Some spiders jump upon their prey, others lasso them, and many varieties net and snare their victims.

The number of spiders in the world is enormous, a fact first emphasized by the British expert on spiders, W. S. Bristowe (1901–) in 1939. He found that an English field contained around two million spiders per acre.

The production of silk [7] has been one of the spiders' keys to success. With it, they are able to fashion a number of accessories that aid them in their struggle for existence. Not only are their traps made of silk, but also their shelters and breeding structures, as well as the parachutes that allow the wind to carry them from one place to another. The thinnest spider silk has greater tensile (stretching) strength than the equivalent thickness of steel wire.

Spiders are equipped with poison glands that they use to quiet and kill their prey before their silken webs, or they them-

CONNECTIONS

See also
484 The joint-legged animals
490 Crustaceans and other arthropods
458 The animal kingdom
608 Mountain life
712 The causes of illness: 2
464 Principles of animal behavior
604 Life in the desert
312 The living soil

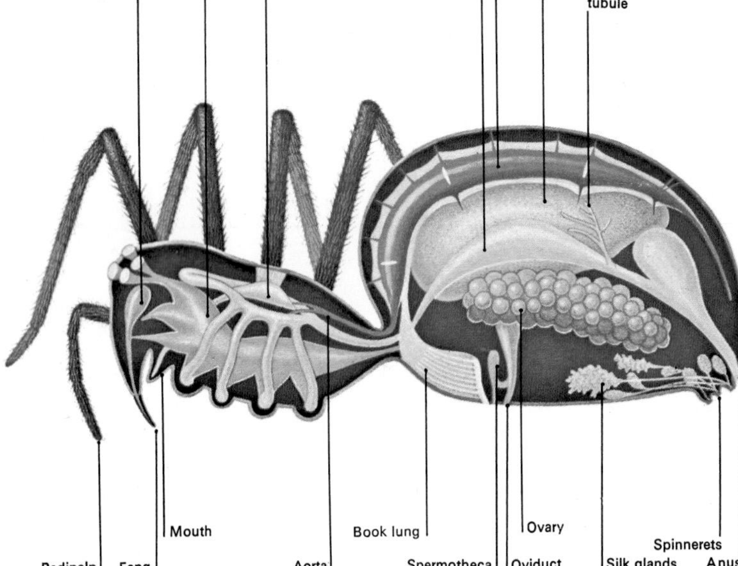
1
Poison gland
Brain
Sucking stomach
Intestine
Heart
Liver
Malpighian tubule
Pedipalp
Fang
Mouth
Aorta
Book lung
Spermotheca
Ovary
Oviduct
Silk glands
Spinnerets
Anus

1 Spiders and other arachnids differ from other arthropods in having bodies divided into two sections. Head and thorax are united in a cephalothorax, or prosoma, joined to the abdomen by a narrow stalk, or pedicel. There are four pairs of walking legs and the eyes are simple, not compound. There are no antennae. Straight hairs on the appendages carry out sensory functions. The mouth parts are chelicerae or fangs, and behind them are limblike pedipalps with sensory and feeding functions. In male spiders they are modified for the transfer of sperm. Excretory organs (Malpighian tubules) open into the hind gut.

2 Garden spider *Araneus diadematus*

2 The garden spider is a well-known species often found hanging in its complex and beautifully structured web, spun where there are insects to be caught.

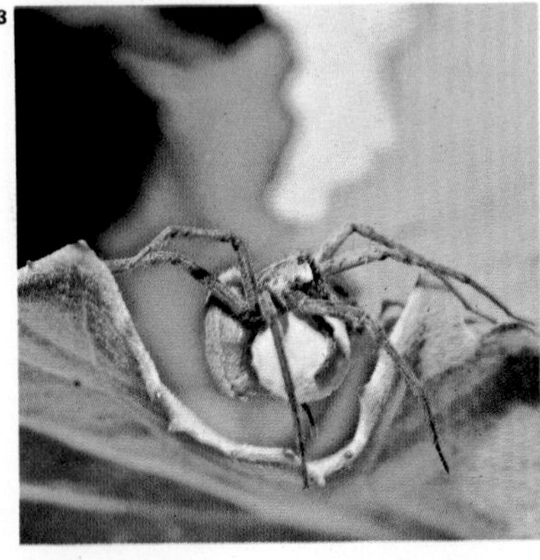

3 A female spider discharges her fertilized eggs into a saucer of silk which is then enclosed in a silken sac or cocoon. This may be hidden in the soil, in a tree trunk, or attached to the roof of a cave or to plants. In some cases the cocoon will be guarded by the female. Some species of spiders camouflage their cocoons, while others, such as this hunting spider *(Pisaura mirabilis)* protect them by carrying them around with them until the eggs hatch.

4 Newly hatched spiders are vulnerable because they cannot defend themselves nor can they feed or spin silk until after they go through their first molt. These young garden spiders hatch from eggs in cocoons that are hidden and often guarded by the female. Young spiders sometimes remain together as a ball and if disturbed will quickly disperse in an explosion of bodies and color.

5 Scorpions produce their young alive, not from eggs. Newly born scorpions are carried around on their mother's back, as some spiders carry their young. Scorpion embryos develop in special brood chambers in the mother's body, so when they are born they have only to climb onto her back. They are able to hang on securely by means of small suckers on their feet and are carried about for days or even weeks—depending on their species and the prevailing conditions—living on the remains of their embryonic yolk supply. As with spiders, scorpions are unable to leave the female until after the first molt. They become adult after six or seven molts, a process takes about a year in most of the species.

selves, are badly damaged by the struggles of their victims. Species with the more virulent toxins can deal with prey, or enemies, that are much bigger than themselves.

Small but prolific mites

Less well known than spiders, but an equally successful arachnid group, is the order Acarina, which includes the ticks and mites. These small creatures are easily overlooked, except in the case of the many ectoparasitic species (those living on the surface of their host). Mites and ticks are found on large numbers of vertebrates and invertebrates. All the ticks are blood-suckers and many of them carry diseases in both wild and domesticated animals and man. They are responsible for considerable loss of life. The mites too are of economic importance, many of them as parasites of both plants and animals. Some are beneficial, being involved in the breakdown of plant material in the soil.

The scorpions [5] are a group of arachnids limited to the earth's warmer regions. They have an ancient fossil history and are a homogeneous group; all 600 or more species are easily recognized as scorpions.

The sting of the scorpion is used mostly in defense and only rarely for killing prey, the virulence of its poison varying among species. In only a few does the venom prove a threat to human life, for example, species in the family Buthidae. In most it is almost harmless. Scorpions capture their prey with their pincers, technically called the pedipalps.

The harvestmen, or daddy longlegs (order Opiliones), are known to most people. These animals are spiderlike but they may be distinguished by the lack of the narrow pedicel between cephalothorax (a union of the head and thorax) and abdomen, and their extremely long legs. They are found throughout the world in low-growing vegetation and in leaf litter, where they feed largely on small insects.

The wide distribution of arachnids and the fact that spiders are carnivorous makes their role in the world's food chains a vital one.

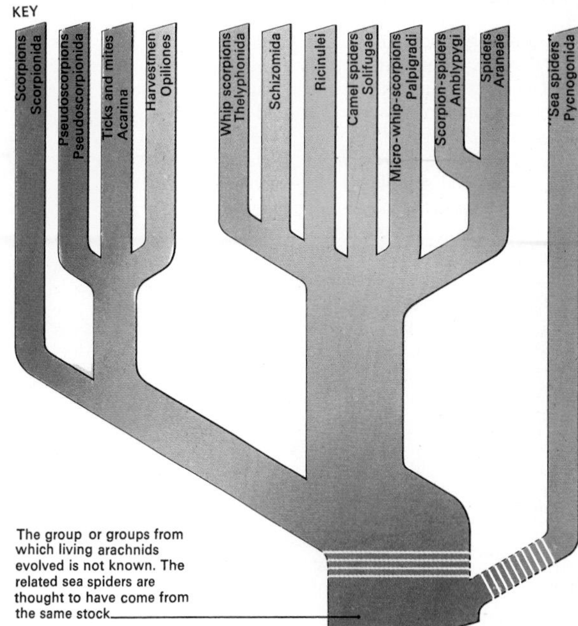
KEY
Scorpions
Scorpionida
Pseudoscorpions
Pseudoscorpionida
Ticks and mites
Acarina
Harvestmen
Opiliones
Whip scorpions
Thelyphonida
Schizomida
Ricinulei
Camel spiders
Solifugae
Micro-whip-scorpions
Palpigradi
Scorpion-spiders
Amblypygi
Spiders
Araneae
"Sea spiders"
Pycnogonida
The group or groups from which living arachnids evolved is not known. The related sea spiders are thought to have come from the same stock

6 The orb webs of spiders are spun from silk with great accuracy to specific designs of various types. A bridge is first constructed between two supports and then the orb is fashioned beneath. Radiating spokes support a spiral whose gummy thread is extruded from the silk glands. The gum layer is broken into beads by the spinner's stretching the thread and letting go with a snap.

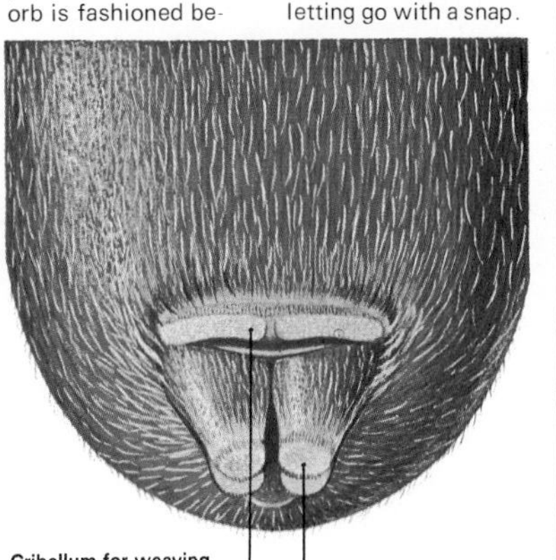
Cribellum for weaving bands of silk
Spinnerets

7 Spiders' silk is produced in special silk glands and distributed by the spinnerets. A variety of glands produce different kinds of silk for specific parts of the web, for binding prey and for the egg cocoon. Parts of the glands produce the gum for snare lines. The spinnerets have many minute spinning tubes at their tips. Each thread consists of many filaments fused together for strength.

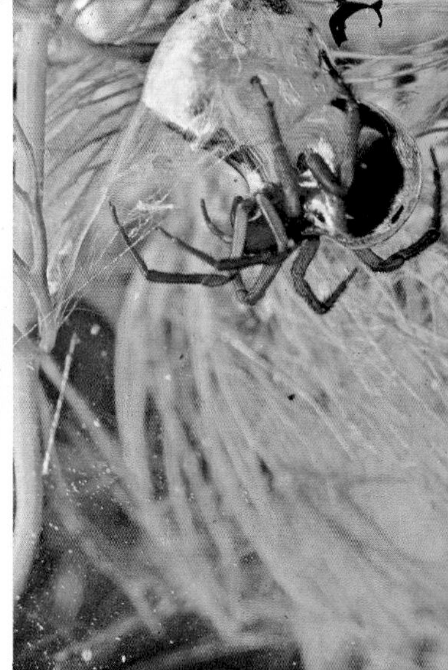

8 The water spider *(Argyroneta aquatica)* is found in temperate Europe and Asia and is the only spider that spends most of its life beneath the surface of the water. The hairs covering its body trap a film of air which is taken underwater to a bell of silk that is attached to water plants. The spider breathes the air in the bell, emerging only at night to hunt. Eggs are laid in the bell.

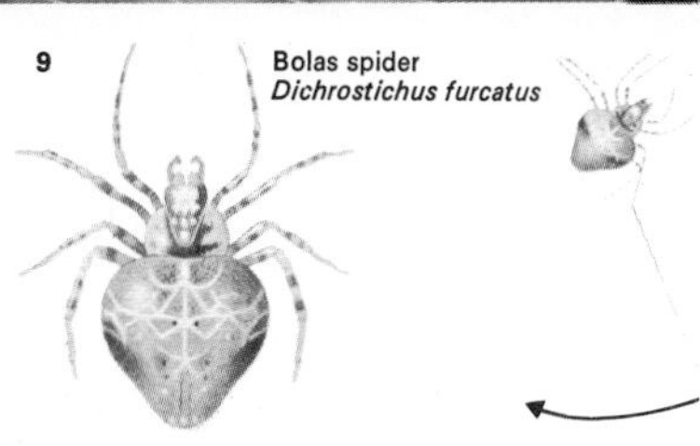
Bolas spider
Dichrostichus furcatus

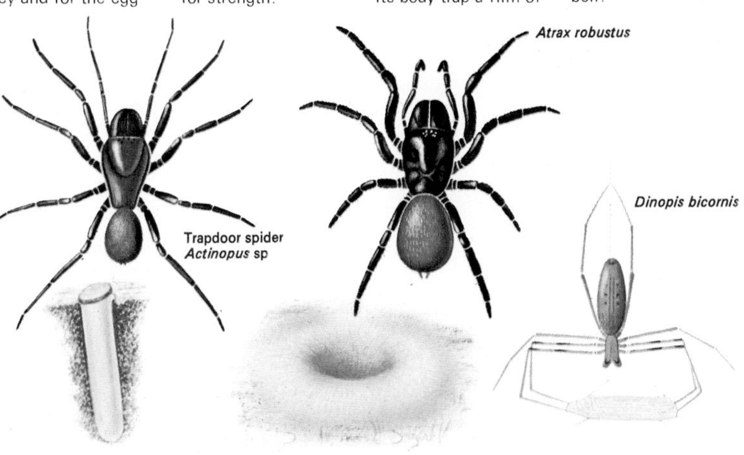
Atrax robustus
Trapdoor spider
Actinopus sp
Dinopis bicornis

9 Spiders show great ingenuity in the ways in which they trap prey. Tropical bolas spiders suspend a sticky gum droplet on the end of a silk thread and swing it to and fro like a pendulum. Passing insects are attracted to it and become ensnared. Trapdoor spiders may make complex burrows from which they dig side chambers to which they can retreat in safety from flooding. The Australian funnelweb spider *(Atrax robustus)* has a silken burrow with a funnel-shaped entrance. Its prey slips down the funnel to be ensnared below and killed by the spider's venomous bite. The ogre-faced spider *(Dinopsis bicornis)* hangs from a strong thread holding a sticky net stretched between its legs. When a suitable victim passes near, the spider casts the net over it. As the victim struggles it becomes more enmeshed and immobilized in the net.

Crustaceans and other arthropods

The joint-legged creatures are together classified in the phylum Arthropoda, the group that includes the insects. Those that are not insects, some of which are illustrated here, total more than 90,000 species. These are divided almost equally between the class of the spiders and scorpions, the Arachnida, with more than 50,000 species, and the class Crustacea, which includes the lobsters, shrimp, and crabs, with more than 30,000 species. Among the remainder the millipedes and centipedes constitute two groups that together contain more than 11,000 species. The other classes all number less than 450 species each.

All these joint-legged animals have bodies organized in a similar way but show an amazing variety of shapes and sizes. Apart from the spiders, scorpions, and their relatives, most are water-dwellers, and planktonic forms are an important link in the food chains of larger marine animals such as fish. Many are more directly important to man either as a source of food (crabs, shrimp, lobsters) or as his enemies (poisonous spiders and parasitic ticks).

2 Sea spiders are members of a small class of the arthropods known as the Pycnogonida; their name comes from their spiderlike appearance. Unlike spiders, however, they are marine and have from four to six pairs of walking legs. The body is so narrow that some of the digestive tract extends into the long legs. One species spans 2ft (60cm).

CONNECTIONS

See also
484 The joint-legged animals
486 Crabs and lobsters
488 Spiders and scorpions
622 The seashore: life between the tides
458 The animal kingdom
394 Shellfish and other seafoods

2 Sea spider *Nymphon rubrum*

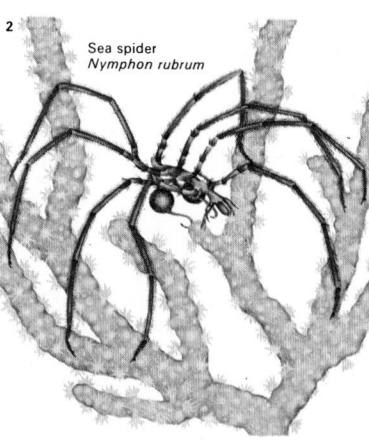

1 King crab *Limulus polyphemus*

1 The king, or horseshoe, crab is not a crab at all – it is a primitive arthropod closely related to fossil forms and allied to spiders and scorpions. This marine species measures up to 2ft (60cm) long.

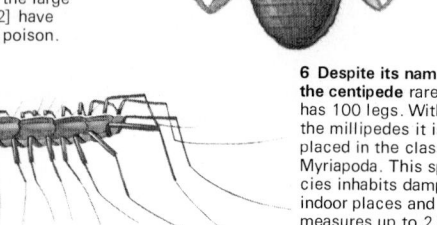

3 Harvestman *Phalangium africanum*

3 The North African harvestman has many relatives throughout the world, including North America where it is known as daddy longlegs. This minute scavenger measures up to 0.5in (12mm).

4 Pseudoscorpion *Chelifer cancroides*

4 All the false or pseudoscorpions are small. This species lives in houses and is about 0.3in (8mm) long. The small chelicerae [1] contain silk glands; the large pedipalps [2] have pincers and poison.

5 The mouthparts of the harvest mite, an arachnid parasitic on vertebrate tissue during the early part of its life, are borne on a "false head". The total body length of this species is only 0.04in (1mm).

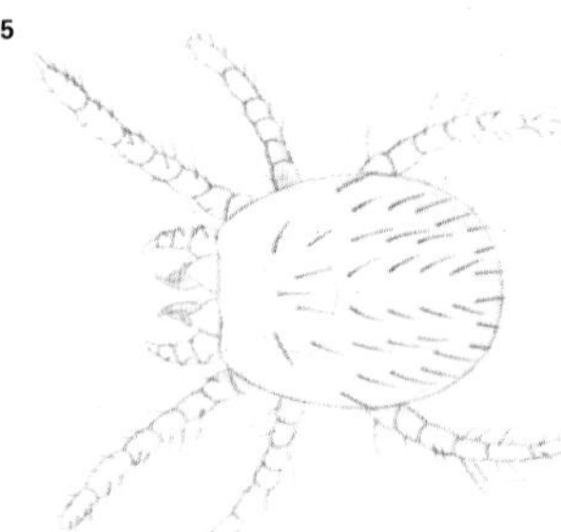

5 Harvest mite *Trombicula autumnalis*

7 Pill millipedes have the peculiar ability to roll up when disturbed. They differ from centipedes in having two rather than one pair of legs on each body segment. This one is 0.75in (2cm) long.

6 House centipede *Scutigera coleoptrata*

6 Despite its name, the centipede rarely has 100 legs. With the millipedes it is placed in the class Myriapoda. This species inhabits damp indoor places and measures up to 2 in (5cm) in length.

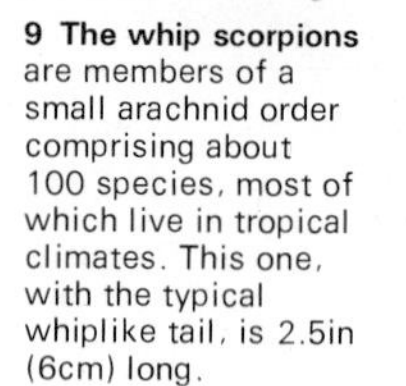

7 Pill millipede *Glomeris marginata*

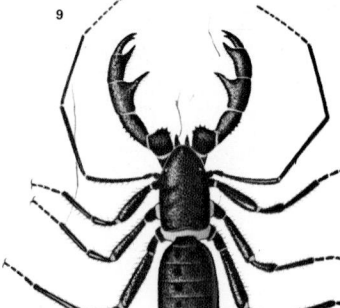

9 The whip scorpions are members of a small arachnid order comprising about 100 species, most of which live in tropical climates. This one, with the typical whiplike tail, is 2.5in (6cm) long.

10 Little-known arachnids, the 37 species in the order Ricinulei are found in leaf mold and caves in tropical Africa and America. None grow to more than 0.4in (1cm) long. This one is African.

8 Bird Spider *Sericopelma communis*

9 Whip scorpion *Mastigoproctus giganteus*

8 A hummingbird is the victim of this fiercely predatory bird spider from Panama which measures about 2.5in (6cm) long. Often wrongly called a tarantula it is relatively harmless – its venom is about as potent as that of a bee.

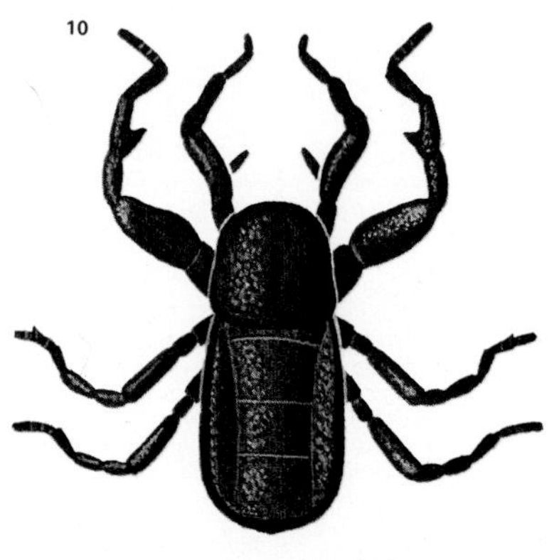

10 Ricinuleid *Ricinoides afzeli*

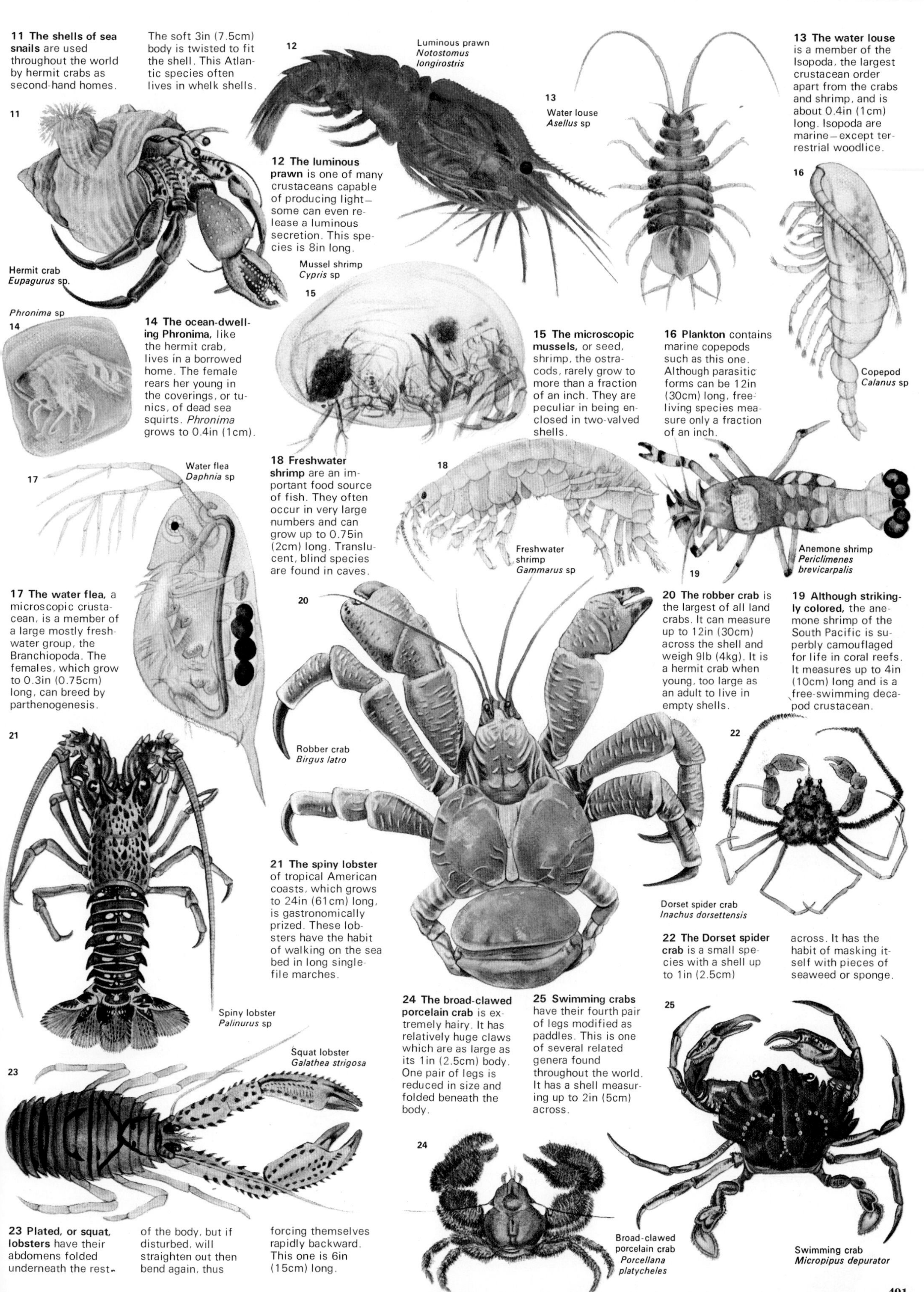

Hermit crab
Eupagurus sp.
Luminous prawn
Notostomus longirostris
Water louse
Asellus sp
Mussel shrimp
Cypris sp
Phronima sp
Copepod
Calanus sp
Water flea
Daphnia sp
Freshwater shrimp
Gammarus sp
Anemone shrimp
Periclimenes brevicarpalis
Robber crab
Birgus latro
Dorset spider crab
Inachus dorsettensis
Spiny lobster
Palinurus sp
Squat lobster
Galathea strigosa
Broad-clawed porcelain crab
Porcellana platycheles
Swimming crab
Micropipus depurator

11 The shells of sea snails are used throughout the world by hermit crabs as second-hand homes. The soft 3in (7.5cm) body is twisted to fit the shell. This Atlantic species often lives in whelk shells.

12 The luminous prawn is one of many crustaceans capable of producing light—some can even release a luminous secretion. This species is 8in long.

13 The water louse is a member of the Isopoda, the largest crustacean order apart from the crabs and shrimp, and is about 0.4in (1cm) long. Isopoda are marine—except terrestrial woodlice.

14 The ocean-dwelling Phronima, like the hermit crab, lives in a borrowed home. The female rears her young in the coverings, or tunics, of dead sea squirts. *Phronima* grows to 0.4in (1cm).

15 The microscopic mussels, or seed, shrimp, the ostracods, rarely grow to more than a fraction of an inch. They are peculiar in being enclosed in two-valved shells.

16 Plankton contains marine copepods such as this one. Although parasitic forms can be 12in (30cm) long, free-living species measure only a fraction of an inch.

17 The water flea, a microscopic crustacean, is a member of a large mostly freshwater group, the Branchiopoda. The females, which grow to 0.3in (0.75cm) long, can breed by parthenogenesis.

18 Freshwater shrimp are an important food source of fish. They often occur in very large numbers and can grow up to 0.75in (2cm) long. Translucent, blind species are found in caves.

19 Although strikingly colored, the anemone shrimp of the South Pacific is superbly camouflaged for life in coral reefs. It measures up to 4in (10cm) long and is a free-swimming decapod crustacean.

20 The robber crab is the largest of all land crabs. It can measure up to 12in (30cm) across the shell and weigh 9lb (4kg). It is a hermit crab when young, too large as an adult to live in empty shells.

21 The spiny lobster of tropical American coasts, which grows to 24in (61cm) long, is gastronomically prized. These lobsters have the habit of walking on the sea bed in long single-file marches.

22 The Dorset spider crab is a small species with a shell up to 1in (2.5cm) across. It has the habit of masking itself with pieces of seaweed or sponge.

23 Plated, or squat, lobsters have their abdomens folded underneath the rest of the body, but if disturbed, will straighten out then bend again, thus forcing themselves rapidly backward. This one is 6in (15cm) long.

24 The broad-clawed porcelain crab is extremely hairy. It has relatively huge claws which are as large as its 1in (2.5cm) body. One pair of legs is reduced in size and folded beneath the body.

25 Swimming crabs have their fourth pair of legs modified as paddles. This is one of several related genera found throughout the world. It has a shell measuring up to 2in (5cm) across.

The classification of insects

Insects are the most numerous of all living creatures, representing about 80 percent of all animal species. There are more than 1,000,000 known species and probably as many again are still to be discovered.

There are enough insect fossils and primitive living forms to serve as a guide to the evolution of the 29 orders into which all insects are classified. Most of the evidence dates from the advent of the Carboniferous period some 345 million years ago, when a number of winged insects inhabited the coal-forming swamps of the period.

Primitive insects

Insects are thought to have evolved from a centipedelike ancestor from which they differed principally in having only three pairs of legs. Each pair is attached to one segment of the thorax—the middle part of the body. The most primitive of modern insects are possibly the wingless species belonging to four orders that were once grouped together as the "Apterygota." Of these, the order Thysanura [4] seems to resemble the hypothetical ancestral form most closely.

The Collembola [1] and Protura [2] may have evolved from a creature similar to a dipluran [3], but the two groups have become modified in different ways. The Collembola have a peculiar forked structure on the abdomen that acts like a spring and enables them to jump considerable distances. In the Protura the antennae are absent and the front legs have taken over some of their functions. The Thysanura are structurally the most advanced of the "Apterygota," but differ in not having their mouthparts enclosed in a cavity.

The next major development was the evolution of the wings and the power of flight. Two orders—Ephemeroptera [5] and the Odonata [6]—are combined under the Palaeoptera, or "ancient wings." Their wings cannot be folded or laid over the back at rest. Those insects that can fold wings at rest [orders 7–29] are grouped together in the Neoptera, or "new wings."

The seven orthopteroid orders (7–13) are considered to be the least advanced of the Neoptera. Most of these have simple mouthparts and are predominantly herbivorous. The order Plecoptera [14] is an evolutionary offshoot with many archaic features. The hemipteroid orders show a steady progression from the primitive, nonspecialized mouthparts of the Psocoptera to those of the Hemiptera [19], which have developed piercing and sucking mouthparts to feed on sap or blood.

A significant development in the nature of the insect life cycle gave the remaining orders [20–29], a great advantage over their more primitive relatives.

Greater flexibility

The young insects that hatch from the eggs of the more primitive orders resemble the adult insect. These are the "apterygote" and exopterygote orders [1–19]. The young, known as nymphs, undergo a series of molts from which they emerge as fully developed adults. In the remaining orders, the endopterygotes [20–29], a larva that does not resemble the adult hatches from the egg. This larva (a caterpillar, maggot, or grub) usually eats food that is entirely different from that eaten by the adult. Eventually the larva

CONNECTIONS

See also

484 The joint-legged animals
494 The world of insects
496 Locusts, sucking bugs and dragonflies
498 Advanced insects
500 Colorful bugs and beetles
502 A variety of advanced insects
458 The animal kingdom
564 Fossils without backbones

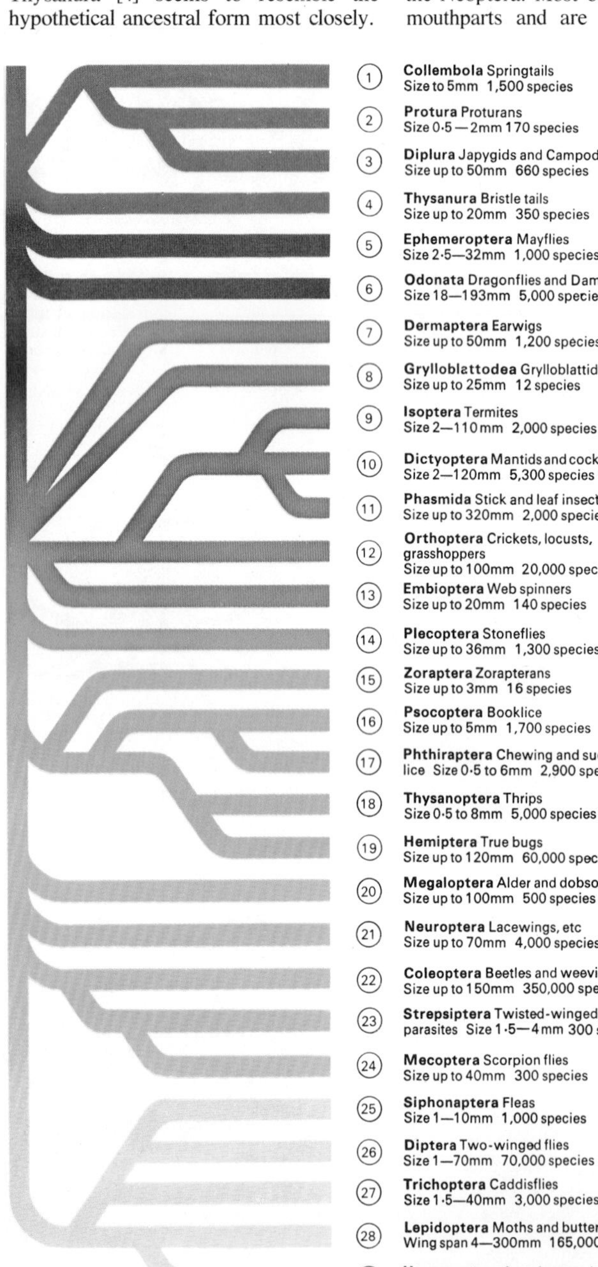

1 **Collembola** Springtails Size to 5mm 1,500 species
2 **Protura** Proturans Size 0·5—2mm 170 species
3 **Diplura** Japygids and Campodeids Size up to 50mm 660 species
4 **Thysanura** Bristle tails Size up to 20mm 350 species
5 **Ephemeroptera** Mayflies Size 2·5—32mm 1,000 species
6 **Odonata** Dragonflies and Damselflies Size 18—193mm 5,000 species
7 **Dermaptera** Earwigs Size up to 50mm 1,200 species
8 **Grylloblattodea** Grylloblattids Size up to 25mm 12 species
9 **Isoptera** Termites Size 2—110mm 2,000 species
10 **Dictyoptera** Mantids and cockroaches Size 2—120mm 5,300 species
11 **Phasmida** Stick and leaf insects Size up to 320mm 2,000 species
12 **Orthoptera** Crickets, locusts, grasshoppers Size up to 100mm 20,000 species
13 **Embioptera** Web spinners Size up to 20mm 140 species
14 **Plecoptera** Stoneflies Size up to 36mm 1,300 species
15 **Zoraptera** Zorapterans Size up to 3mm 16 species
16 **Psocoptera** Booklice Size up to 5mm 1,700 species
17 **Phthiraptera** Chewing and sucking lice Size 0·5 to 6mm 2,900 species
18 **Thysanoptera** Thrips Size 0·5 to 8mm 5,000 species
19 **Hemiptera** True bugs Size up to 120mm 60,000 species
20 **Megaloptera** Alder and dobson flies Size up to 100mm 500 species
21 **Neuroptera** Lacewings, etc Size up to 70mm 4,000 species
22 **Coleoptera** Beetles and weevils Size up to 150mm 350,000 species
23 **Strepsiptera** Twisted-winged insect parasites Size 1·5—4mm 300 species
24 **Mecoptera** Scorpion flies Size up to 40mm 300 species
25 **Siphonaptera** Fleas Size 1—10mm 1,000 species
26 **Diptera** Two-winged flies Size 1—70mm 70,000 species
27 **Trichoptera** Caddisflies Size 1·5—40mm 3,000 species
28 **Lepidoptera** Moths and butterflies Wing span 4—300mm 165,000 species
29 **Hymenoptera** Ants, bees and wasps Size 0·2—120mm Over 110,000 species

'APTERYGOTA' — The orders of wingless insects. The Thysanura are considered to be the most primitive of the living insect orders. The Collembola, Protura and Diplura have no eyes and are now thought not to be true insects. Most species live in damp places.

PALAEOPTERA — The two most primitive orders of winged insects belonging to widely different lineages. They have non-folding wings.

ORTHOPTEROID ORDERS — These orders are grouped together because they are thought to be evolved from a common ancestor. They are considered to be the most primitive of the orders with 'modern' wings although the Isoptera has species with a well-organized social system. The orders Isoptera, Dictyoptera and Orthoptera contain some of the most destructive insect pests.

PTERYGOTA

An order not closely related to the adjacent groups.

HEMIPTEROID ORDERS — This group of orders is thought to have a common ancestor. Many members of the Hemiptera are important plant pests. The species of Phthiraptera—the chewing and sucking lice — are mostly parasites feeding externally. The booklice (Psocoptera) can cause minor damage to books and stored food.

NEOPTERA

NEUROPTEROID ORDERS — The most advanced of the insects are included in this group which contains some of the most numerous and widespread species. Some species of Hymenoptera — bees, wasps, ants — are highly organized social insects. The ovipositor is often long, especially in some parasitic species and some sawfly species use it as an efficient drill. About a third of all insect species belong to the order Coleoptera — the beetles and weevils. They are found in almost every available habitat. Many species are economically important pests of crops and stored products, some are predators of pests and others, such as the dung beetles, have an important ecological role.

1 North American springtail *Isotoma andrei* 1·2mm

2 European proturan *Acerentomon* sp 1·8mm

3 Campodeid *Campodea folsomi* 4mm

4 Common silverfish *Lepisma saccharina* 8mm

5 North American mayfly *Hexagenia limbata* 5mm

6 Emperor dragonfly *Anax imperator* 75mm

7 Common earwig *Forficula auricularia* 15mm

changes into a pupa, or chrysalis, which may lie dormant for many months while a metamorphosis, or rearrangement of the body tissues, transforms the larva into a mature adult insect.

The differences in habit of the larva and adult have allowed endopterygote insects to exploit extremely diverse habitats. The endopterygote orders contain 84 percent of insect species and most of those of economic importance.

Adaptive radiation

The Hymenoptera [29] are a large group whose fundamental structure varies little and differs greatly from other endopterygotes. This group shows the culmination of insect social behavior as exhibited by the social ants, bees, and wasps. The Coleoptera [22], the largest order in the animal kingdom, have distinctly modified hard forewings that cover the rear flying wings. The solidity of the external skeleton and the adaptability of its basic design have been important factors in allowing the adult to invade many hostile environments.

The remaining endopterygotes form a group centered around the once abundant Mecoptera. The Lepidoptera [28] are recognized by their scale-covered wings and most have the mouthparts specialized into sucking tubes to exploit nectar as a food source. The evolution of this order, and of some of the Diptera [26], coincides closely with that of the flowering plants.

The Trichoptera [27] are an offshoot of the Lepidoptera with hairy wings and chewing mouthparts. The larvae are aquatic.

The Diptera fly with their forewings only, the hind pair being modified into halteres, which act as gyroscopic balancers during flight. The larvae of this order show greater adaptive specialization than any other group of insects. The blood-sucking habit of many of the adult Diptera is associated with their importance as transmitters of diseases.

Closely related to the Diptera are the Siphonaptera [25], which have become wingless and laterally compressed. As with the Phthiraptera [17], all are externally parasitic on warm-blooded animals.

KEY

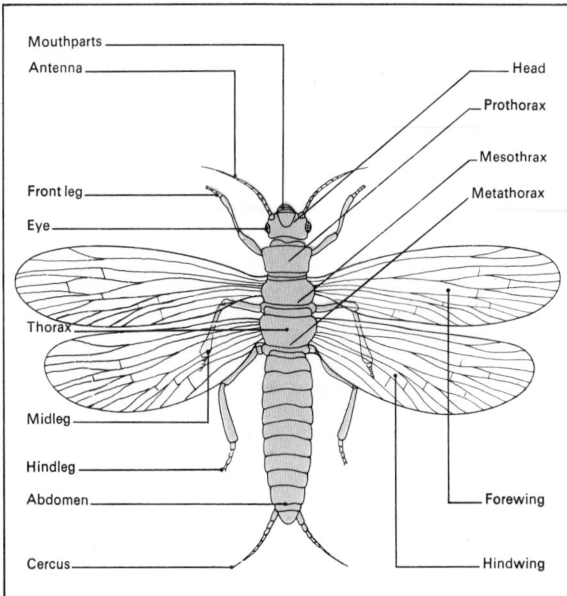
Mouthparts
Antenna
Head
Prothorax
Mesothrax
Metathorax
Front leg
Eye
Thorax
Midleg
Hindleg
Abdomen
Forewing
Cercus
Hindwing

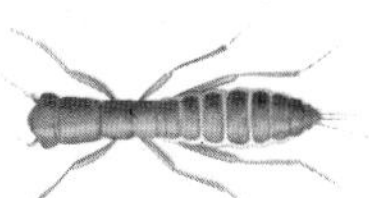

North American grylloblattid *Grylloblatta* sp 20mm

African termite *Amitermes hastatus* 30mm

Praying mantis *Sphodromantis lineata* 90mm

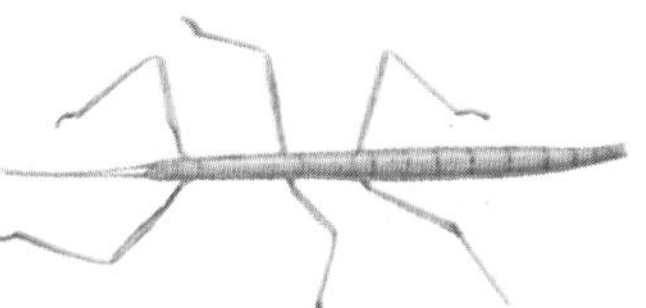

A Stick insect *Carausius morosus* 85mm

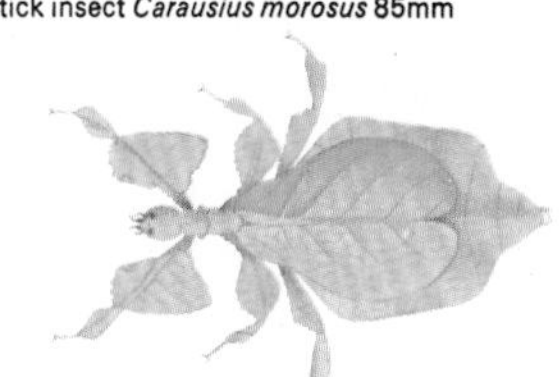

B Leaf insect *Phyllium crurifolium* 90mm

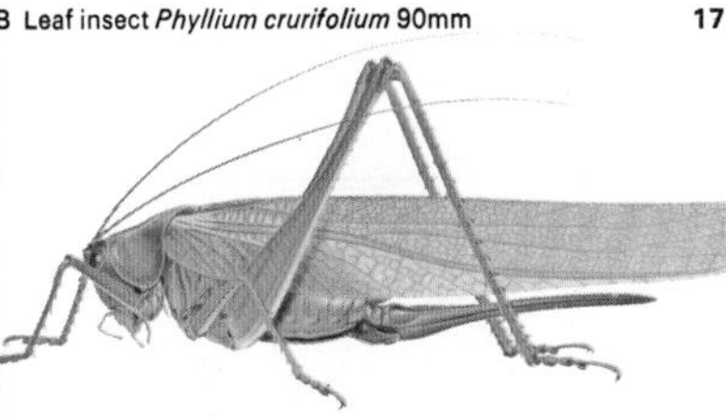

Great green bush cricket *Tettigonia viridissima* 50mm

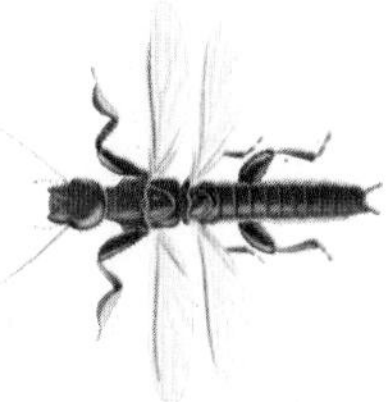

13 Indian web spinner *Parembia major* 2mm

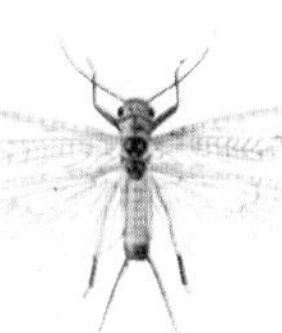

14 European stonefly *Perla bipunctata* 20mm

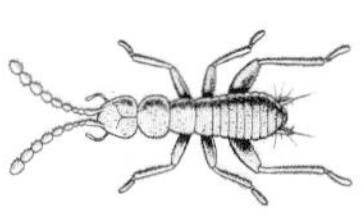

15 African zorapteran *Zorotypus guineensis* 2·5mm

16 Winged psocid *Lachesilla pedicularia* 1·2mm

17 Body louse *Pediculus humanus* 4mm

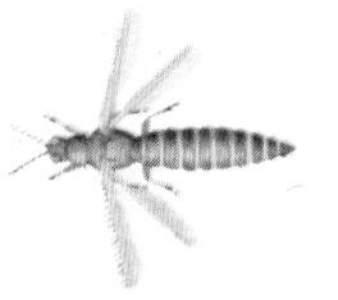

18 Onion thrips *Thrips tabaci* 1·4mm

19 Shield bug
Eurydema ornatum 20mm

20 European alderfly
Sialis lutaria 20mm

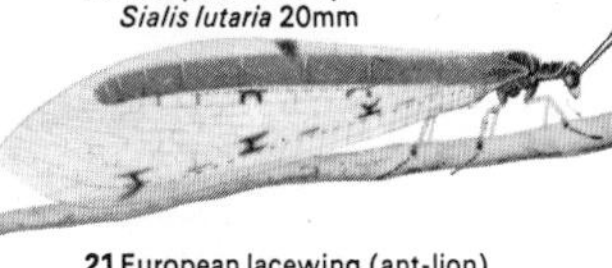

21 European lacewing (ant-lion)
Euroleon europaeus 20mm

22 Dung beetle
Onthophagus sp 15mm

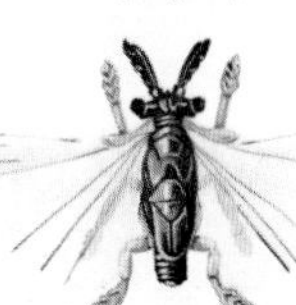

23 North American stylops (male)
Stylops shannoni 4mm

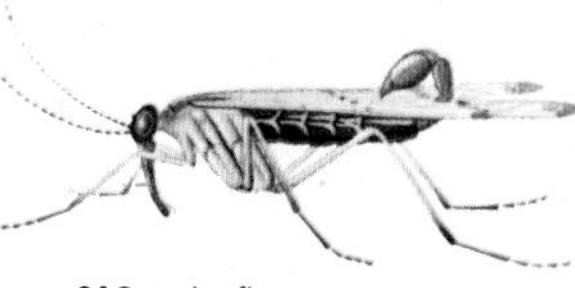

24 Scorpion fly
Panorpa sp 25mm

25 Rat flea
Xenopsylla cheopis 3mm

26 Hover fly
Volucella pellucens 15mm

27 Caddisfly
Phryganea grandis 25mm

28 A European swallowtail butterfly
Papilio machaon span 70mm

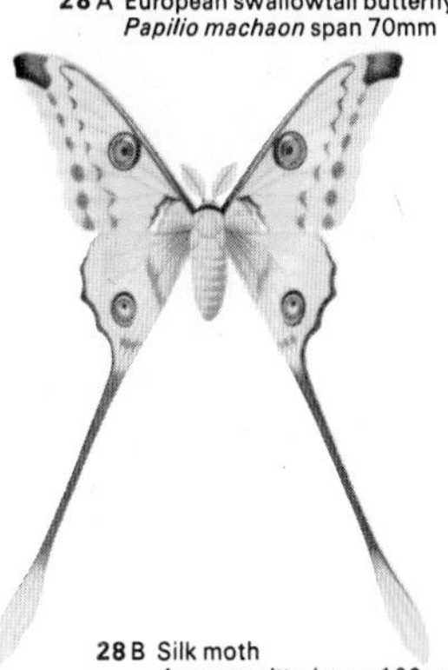

28 B Silk moth
Argema mittrei span 100mm

29 Vespid wasp
Eumenes sp 15mm

The world of insects

The animals that inhabit the Earth total about one and a quarter million species. Of these, some 80 percent are insects, animals classified in the phylum Arthropoda, the group of joint-legged creatures. Numbers alone indicate the success of the class Insecta but they have also colonized the world more widely than any other group.

The ubiquitous insects

There are only a few marine insects; some are surface dwellers, others live between tide marks and one midge even lives on the sea bed. But wherever else other animals go, so do the insects—either as free-living forms adapted to an enormous variety of habitats or as parasites living in or on other animals. The insects are a dominant life form from the arctic to the equator. Some exist beneath the snow and ice, others in deserts, still others in salt lakes and hot springs. In southern California there is even a species of small fly that spends part of its life in pools of crude petroleum.

One of the chief factors in insect success is their ability to fly [2]; apart from the more primitive forms, most species have achieved the freedom of the air, enabling them to colonize new areas and habitats, to escape from predators, to find mates, and to prospect for food much more easily than their nonairborne invertebrate relatives.

Although the insects have scored a great evolutionary success through their powers of flight, their weight/wing ratio is such that theoretically, flight should not be possible. Actually, however, their wing muscles build up energy and then release it rapidly, the speed of the wing-beat compensating for a theoretical lack of lift.

Insect size and shape

Size has also been important in the evolutionary success of insects. When they first appeared about 400 million years ago, the scale of the environment was similar to that of today and the insects adapted to it, fitting into the many ecological niches on land that were waiting to be occupied. Insects are comparatively small—although there is a fossil dragonfly with a 2.5ft (76cm) wing span.

Another important factor in the success of the insects is their possession of a horny outer covering, the exoskeleton. Although it has to be shed during growth, and thus imposes regular periods of vulnerability, this exoskeleton is extremely light and tough. Chitin is the basis of the insect skeleton; it is flexible. It is made waterproof by a waxy surface layer or by the hardener "sclerotin." The prevention of water loss is essential for land insects. And the material of which the skeleton is composed is so malleable that insects take on a variety of shapes, particularly in the various appendages. Wings, wing covers, legs, ovipositors, mouthparts, bristles, scales, antennae, and other appendages all illustrate the ways in which the chitinous exoskeleton may be molded.

The insect body is divided into three main parts: the head, thorax, and abdomen [1]. The head bears the principal sense organs and mouthparts and encloses the brain, salivary glands, and foregut. The thorax bears the wings, basically two pairs—on the second and third of the three

CONNECTIONS

See also
492 The classification of insects
496 Locusts, sucking bugs, and dragonflie
498 Advanced insects
500 Colorful bugs and beetles
502 A variety of advancec insects
464 Principles of animal behavior
484 The joint-legged animals
318 Protecting crops

1 The internal anatomy of all insects, including this honey bee, is all contained and protected within the confines of the tough, flexible exoskeleton. The typical insect body contains organs of digestion, respiration, circulation, excretion, and reproduction. There are muscles through which movement is effected and a nervous system that coordinates and controls insect actions on the basis of information received by the sense organs, most important of which are the large compound eyes and the feelers, or antennae. The body is in three parts; head, wing-bearing thorax, and abdomen.

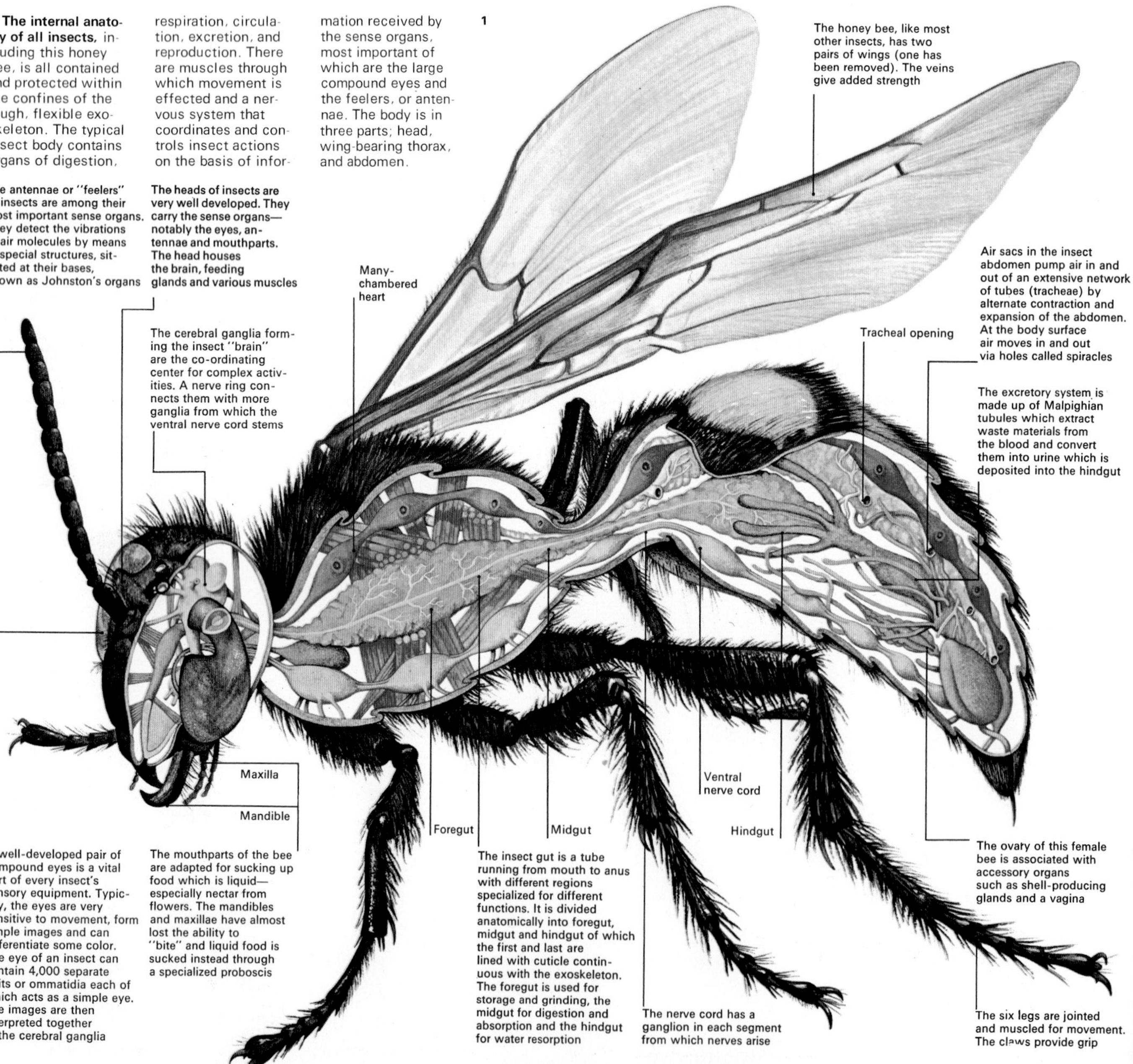

1

The honey bee, like most other insects, has two pairs of wings (one has been removed). The veins give added strength

The antennae or "feelers" of insects are among their most important sense organs. They detect the vibrations of air molecules by means of special structures, situated at their bases, known as Johnston's organs

The heads of insects are very well developed. They carry the sense organs—notably the eyes, antennae and mouthparts. The head houses the brain, feeding glands and various muscles

Many-chambered heart

Air sacs in the insect abdomen pump air in and out of an extensive network of tubes (tracheae) by alternate contraction and expansion of the abdomen. At the body surface air moves in and out via holes called spiracles

Tracheal opening

The cerebral ganglia forming the insect "brain" are the co-ordinating center for complex activities. A nerve ring connects them with more ganglia from which the ventral nerve cord stems

The excretory system is made up of Malpighian tubules which extract waste materials from the blood and convert them into urine which is deposited into the hindgut

Maxilla

Mandible

Ventral nerve cord

Foregut

Midgut

Hindgut

A well-developed pair of compound eyes is a vital part of every insect's sensory equipment. Typically, the eyes are very sensitive to movement, form simple images and can differentiate some color. The eye of an insect can contain 4,000 separate units or ommatidia each of which acts as a simple eye. The images are then interpreted together in the cerebral ganglia

The mouthparts of the bee are adapted for sucking up food which is liquid—especially nectar from flowers. The mandibles and maxillae have almost lost the ability to "bite" and liquid food is sucked instead through a specialized proboscis

The insect gut is a tube running from mouth to anus with different regions specialized for different functions. It is divided anatomically into foregut, midgut and hindgut of which the first and last are lined with cuticle continuous with the exoskeleton. The foregut is used for storage and grinding, the midgut for digestion and absorption and the hindgut for water resorption

The nerve cord has a ganglion in each segment from which nerves arise

The ovary of this female bee is associated with accessory organs such as shell-producing glands and a vagina

The six legs are jointed and muscled for movement. The claws provide grip thoracic segments—plus the three pairs of legs. The abdomen consists typically of 11 segments and carries the copulatory organs [3] and, when present, stings that are modified ovipositors.

The jointed legs of insects give them great mobility. This is increased still further by the wings, whose structure and movement, like those of the limbs, depend very much on the nature of the insect skeleton. This excellent mobility has been a contributory factor in the interference of insects in the life of man. The locust, for example, combines great fecundity with the power of flight, which means that enormous flocks of countless millions can move quickly to a new area to continue their ravages on crop plants when one such food source is depleted.

Patterns of behavior

The members of the class Insecta show a great variety of behavioral adaptations, particularly in their reproduction. Courtship, mating, and care of the young may be remarkably sophisticated, particularly in the social insects—the ants, bees, and wasps of the order Hymenoptera, and the termites, which are members of the order Isoptera. The social organization of one insect species, the honey bee *(Apis mellifera)* is especially efficient, involving both different castes—workers, drones, and queens—and a division of labor between workers of different ages. This second system is not rigid but can be modified according to the changing needs of the hive as a whole.

Despite the high level of organized behavior in the beehive, and the success of the insects as a group, insect behavior is largely instinctive. This involves a genetic "programming" of the animal as a result of which it responds to particular stimuli in a specified way appropriate to the demands of the environment. Intelligence, as applied to human activities, does not enter into this. Thus, although moths of certain species have evolved mechanisms for avoiding bats by unpredictably erratic flight, or by producing bursts of ultrasonics to jam the bats' "sonar," they cannot avoid the attraction of bright lights, which is often fatal.

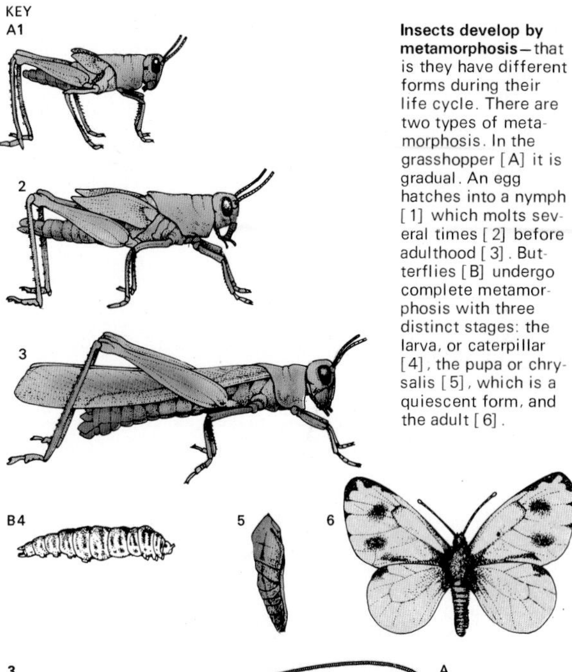

KEY
A1
2
3
B4
5
6

Insects develop by metamorphosis—that is they have different forms during their life cycle. There are two types of metamorphosis. In the grasshopper [A] it is gradual. An egg hatches into a nymph [1] which molts several times [2] before adulthood [3]. Butterflies [B] undergo complete metamorphosis with three distinct stages: the larva, or caterpillar [4], the pupa or chrysalis [5], which is a quiescent form, and the adult [6].

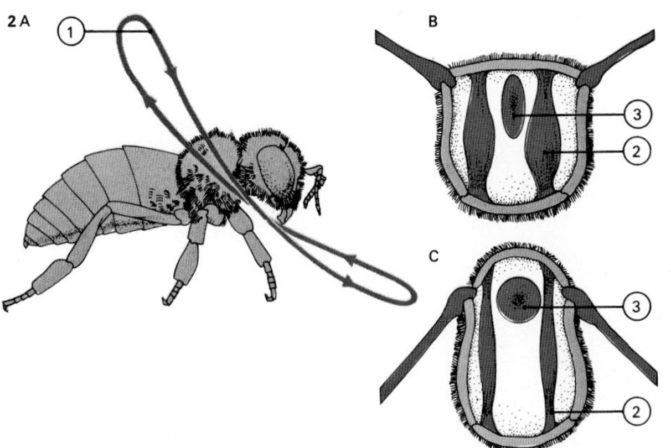

2 A
B
C

2 Most insect wings provide only enough support for powered flight and not for gliding. In the honey bee [A] the two pairs of wings are connected in flight. The pattern of the wing stroke is a figure eight that gives more lift and thrust on the down stroke [1]. This is made more efficient by wing twisting so that there is little air resistance on the upstroke. The wings move as levers and are powered indirectly by muscles that change the shape of the thorax [B, C]. The vertical muscles [2] contract to control the up beat while longitudinal muscles [3] contract to power the down beat.

3 Male and female insects, like these cockroaches, may be similar in external appearance. In the male [A], however, sex organs comprise a pair of testes [1] producing sperm. This then passes to the mushroom gland [3] for storage. A conglobate gland [2] "packages" sperm during copulation. Two sets of ovaries [4] in the female [B] produce eggs to be fertilized. Egg cases are made by shell glands [5].

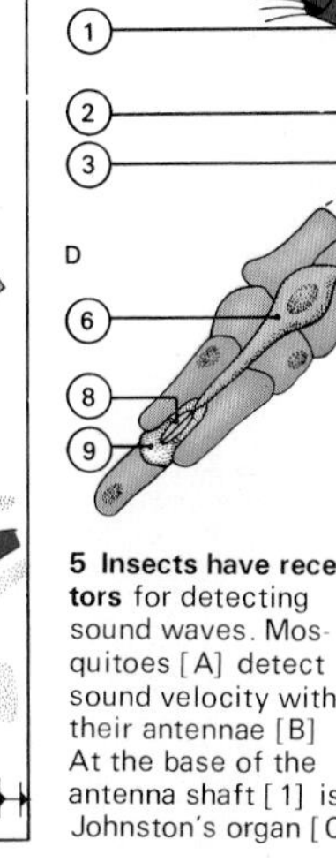

4
A
B
C
D

4 Signaling sounds are produced by many insects. In the order Orthoptera, which includes the grasshoppers, locusts, and crickets, sound production is well developed in males. Sounds are made by stridulation, in which vibration is set up by the scraping of one hard surface against another. In crickets [A] the forewings, or tegmina, are specially modified for this purpose [B], for each bears a scraper [1] and a file [2]. When the wings are rubbed together [3] vibrations are set up which produce sounds. Individual variations are created by the "mirrors" [4]. The vibrations of each tooth [C] produces sound of a particular frequency as in the graph [D].

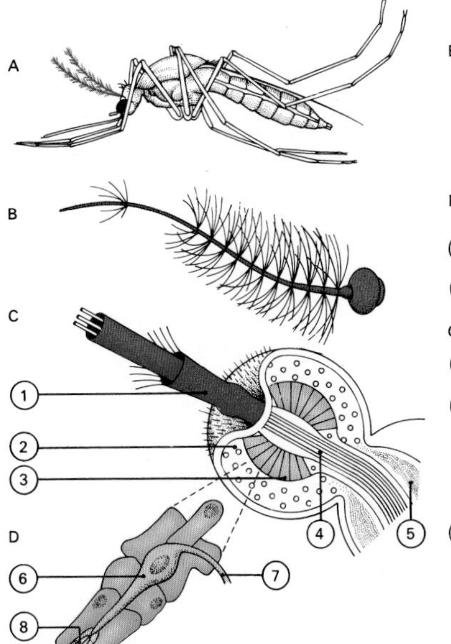

5
A
B
C
D

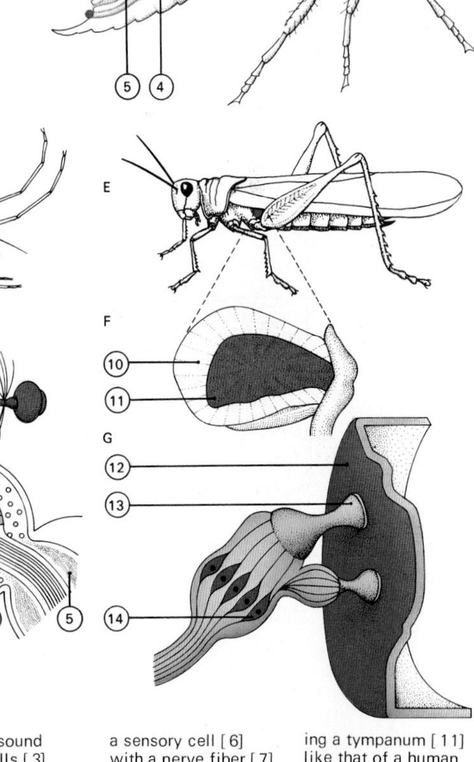

E
F
G

5 Insects have receptors for detecting sound waves. Mosquitoes [A] detect sound velocity with their antennae [B] At the base of the antenna shaft [1] is Johnston's organ [C] containing sound receptor cells [3] and their nuclei [2]. These send impulses via nerve fibers [5] to the brain, where they are interpreted as sounds. Blood vessels and nerves pass through the organ [4]. Each receptor unit [D] contains a sensory cell [6] with a nerve fiber [7] and a sensory hair [8] with a protective cap [9]. The sound receptors on the abdomens of grasshoppers [E] respond to changes in the air pressure. They consist [F] of a rigid frame [10] supporting a tympanum [11] like that of a human ear. In detail [G] the tympanic membrane [12] carries a supporting process [13] for sensory units formed as in [D]. The nuclei of the sensory cells [14] give off nerve fibers to the brain.

Locusts, sucking bugs, and dragonflies

There are more than 1,000,000 known living insect species and almost all of them have wings. Truly wingless insects are primitive forms grouped together in the subclass Apterygota, while winged insects belong to the subclass Pterygota. Winged insects are further classified into two major groups on the basis of their developmental changes or metamorphosis. The more primitive of these are known as the Exopterygota, or "insects with outside wings," because the wings can be seen developing on the exterior of the animal. The other group, called the Endopterygota, or "insects with inside wings," includes the more advanced insects such as butterflies, whose wings do not appear on the outside of the pupa stage of the life cycle.

From egg to adult

In the Exopterygota a type of larva called a nymph (basically a minature adult) emerges from the egg [5]. The proportions are different from those of the adult, as they are in most young animals; there is little indication of wings and the nymph is sexually immature. But otherwise it is clearly the young form of the adult that it will become.

The nymph grows by gradual progressive stages, or instars, the exoskeleton being molted between instars so that the insect can rapidly swell and harden the new exoskeleton that has been prepared beneath the old one. The more primitive species tend to have the largest number of instars. Mayflies (order Ephemeroptera), for example, molt 30 times or more, while locusts molt only four or five times. At each molt there is an increase in the relative wing size and gonad development as well as in general proportions. In the Endopterygota the wings develop on the inside of the larva and on the outside of the pupa. Winged insects may also be classified into two groups according to whether the wings are folded along the abdomen or not (Paleoptera and Neoptera).

The mode of life of the nymph is basically the same as that of the adult; it lives more or less in the same place and eats the same type of food. There are, however, some notable exceptions. Dragonflies [6] and damselflies (order Odonata) are an exception in that the nymphs are aquatic while the adults are free-flying forms.

A further and remarkable exception to the general rule in exopterygotes that all individuals of a species are similar is seen in the termites, or "white ants" (order Isoptera). These insects are fairly closely related to the cockroaches (order Dictyoptera) but have shown an evolution of social organization convergent with that of ants, bees, and wasps (order Hymenoptera). Not only are there different castes in one nest, but some of the castes—workers and soldiers—are sterile forms of either sex in an arrested nymphal stage of development.

The problem of insect pests

Advanced insects of the endopterygote group cause a great deal of human misery and death through the diseases they carry, but only a few exopterygotes, such as the human louse [7], do this. Yet Exopterygota such as locusts can do an almost unbelievable amount of damage to standing crops. One species alone—the desert locust *Schis-*

CONNECTIONS

See also
492 The classification of insects
494 The world of insects
500 Colorful bugs and beetles
498 Advanced insects
502 A variety of advanced insects
484 The joint-legged animals
732 Diseases of the Third World
318 Protecting crops
368 Trees: problems of climate and disease

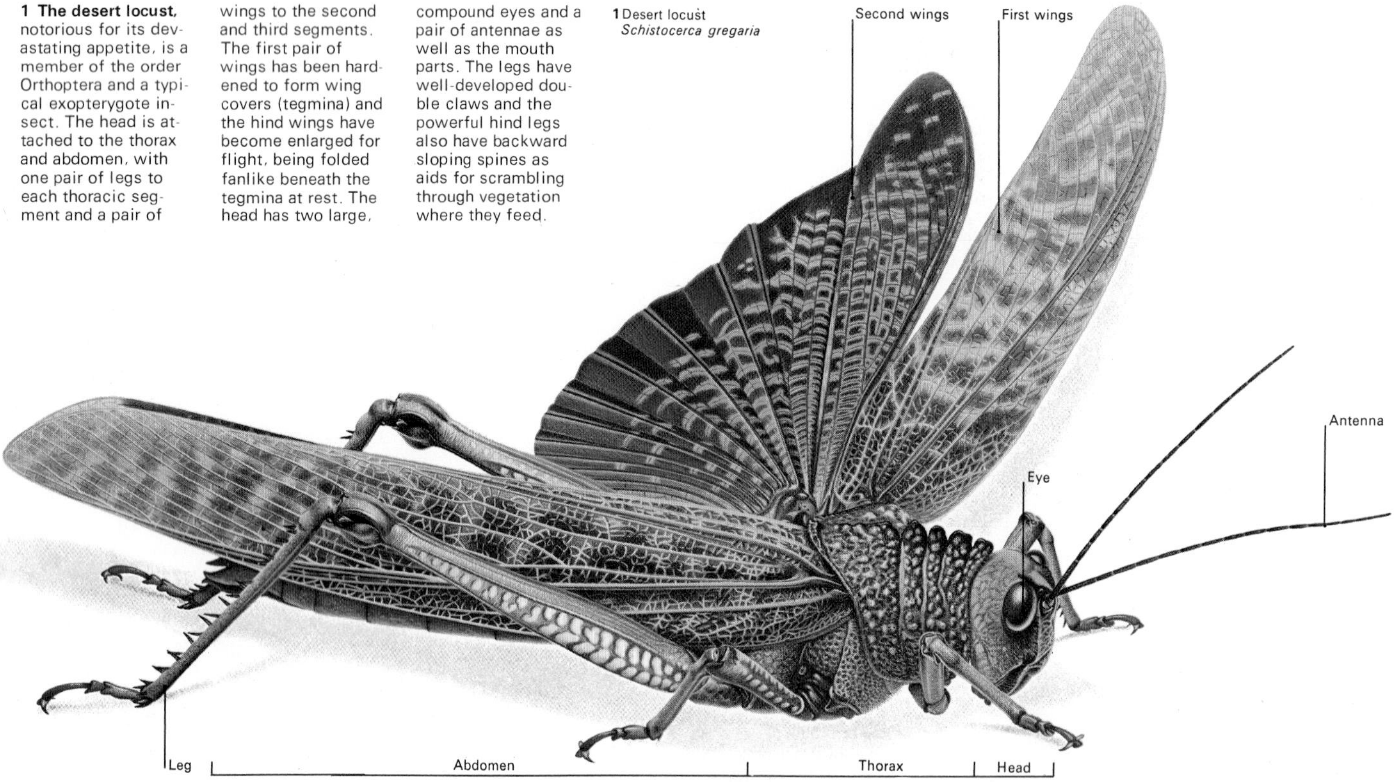

1 The desert locust, notorious for its devastating appetite, is a member of the order Orthoptera and a typical exopterygote insect. The head is attached to the thorax and abdomen, with one pair of legs to each thoracic segment and a pair of wings to the second and third segments. The first pair of wings has been hardened to form wing covers (tegmina) and the hind wings have become enlarged for flight, being folded fanlike beneath the tegmina at rest. The head has two large, compound eyes and a pair of antennae as well as the mouth parts. The legs have well-developed double claws and the powerful hind legs also have backward sloping spines as aids for scrambling through vegetation where they feed.

1 Desert locust *Schistocerca gregaria*

Second wings
First wings
Antenna
Eye
Leg
Abdomen
Thorax
Head

2

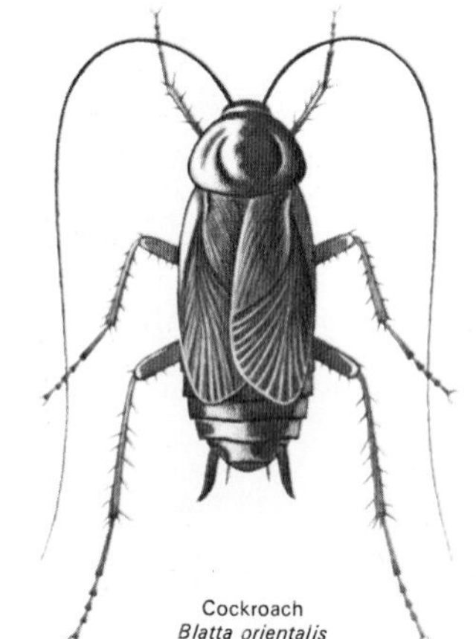

Cockroach
Blatta orientalis

2 Cockroaches (order Dictyoptera) are unspecialized insects that live by scavenging. This species, often called a water bug, is 1in (2.5cm) long and has been introduced worldwide. Cockroaches are nocturnal. Their egg cases hold 16 eggs.

Egg case

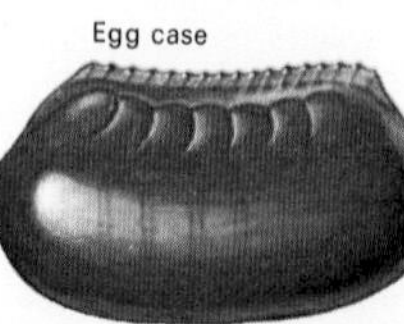

3

Earwig
Forficula auricularia

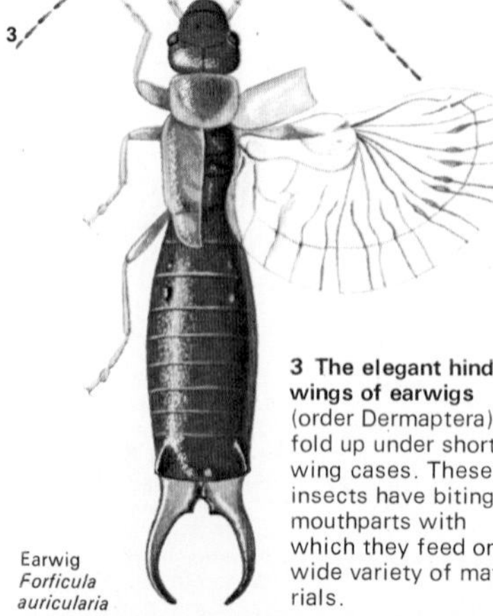

3 The elegant hind wings of earwigs (order Dermaptera) fold up under short wing cases. These insects have biting mouthparts with which they feed on a wide variety of materials.

4

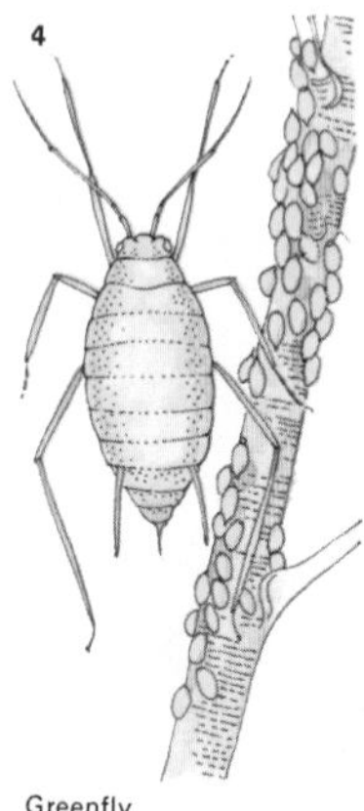

Greenfly
Aphis sp

4 Aphids or plant lice of the order Hemiptera and family Aphididae are small insects about 0.25in (3mm) long. They are often serious crop pests as they occur in enormous numbers. Throughout the world the 2,000 or more species probably do more damage than any other insect pests. Most aphids have remarkable reproductive powers as the females may produce young parthenogenetically, that is without fertilization by a male; one reason for their number.

tocerca gregaria, which was responsible for the eighth plague of Egypt—may directly affect more than ten percent of the human population of the world. It breeds rapidly after unusually heavy rains, and can then suddenly spread out into more than 20 percent of the world's terrestrial habitat, eating all green plants in its path.

The attack on plants

Locust swarms consist of countless millions of insects, blackening the sky across a front of many miles. In a bad year they cause hundreds of millions of dollars worth of damage and contribute to the death by starvation of thousands of people. The red locust *(Nomadacris septemfasciata)* and the migratory locust *(Locusta migratoria)* have been effectively controlled by extensive international effort and expense but the desert locust remains a serious problem.

One of the features that has led to the success of the exopterygote insects is their chewing mouthparts. A number of groups have modified their mouthparts over evolutionary time to produce an apparatus adapted for sucking the juices of plants and animals. The bugs (order Hemiptera) of the suborders Homoptera, which include aphids [4] and the cicadas, and the Heteroptera (including the shield bugs), are among the scourges of the horticulturalist; their habit of sucking the juices of plants provides a route for the entry of disease-causing organisms. These bugs and also thrips of the order Thysanoptera [8] may thus damage crops indirectly and directly.

The same principle, with respect to animal hosts, applies to lice [7]. And when present in large numbers even relatively lowly insects such as earwigs [3] and mole crickets [9] can cause considerable harm to the plants on which they feed. No one who grows plants can avoid supporting one or more species of exopterygote insects unless he expends an enormous amount of time, money, and energy on their control.

In their way some of the Exopterygota may be said to be as successful as their more advanced and more numerous relatives, the Endopterygota. But there are few exopterygotes of use to man.

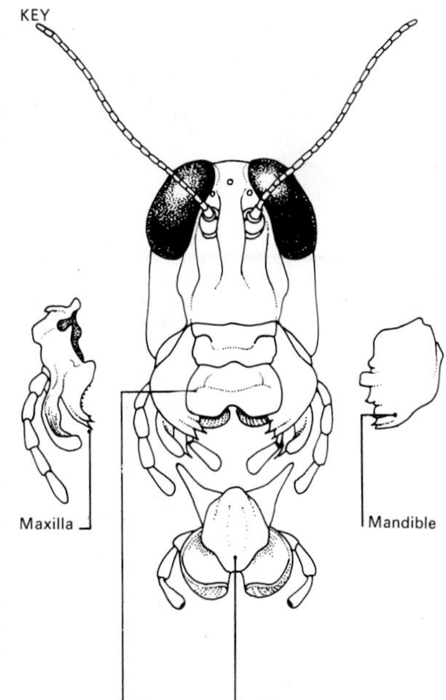

KEY
Maxilla
Mandible
Labrum
Labium

The chewing mouth parts of exopterygote insects are one of the keys to the animals' success. The head-on view of a locust shows the basic pattern. There are three pairs of units: the mandibles, the maxillae, and the labium, or second maxillae, with an extension of the head skeleton, the labrum, providing frontal protection. The mandibles are very strong and are used for chewing the resistant plant cellulose that forms the staple diet. The first and second maxillae both have sensory and manipulatory parts by means of which the food is tested and subsequently guided between the mandibles and into the gullet.

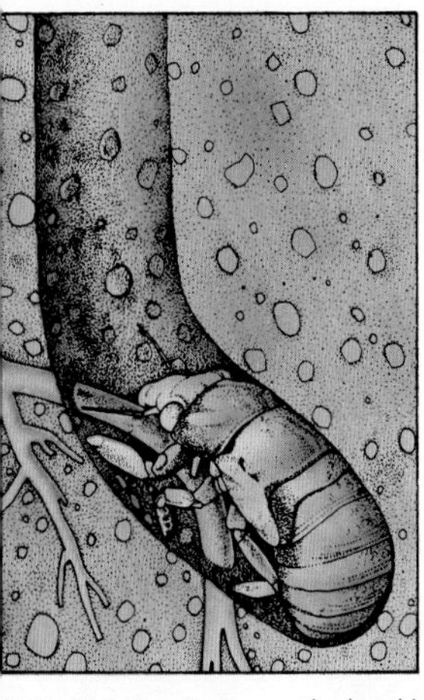

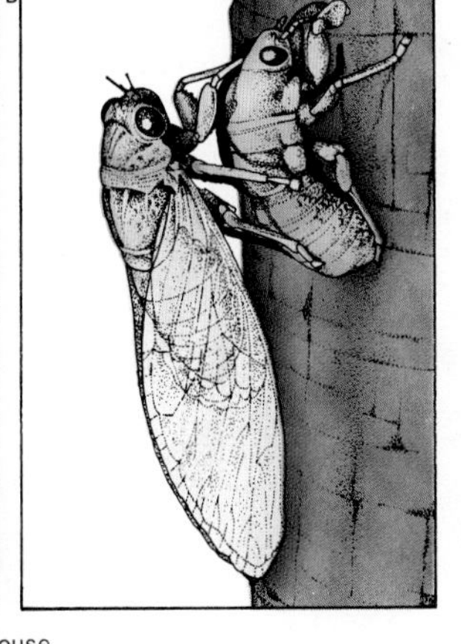

B

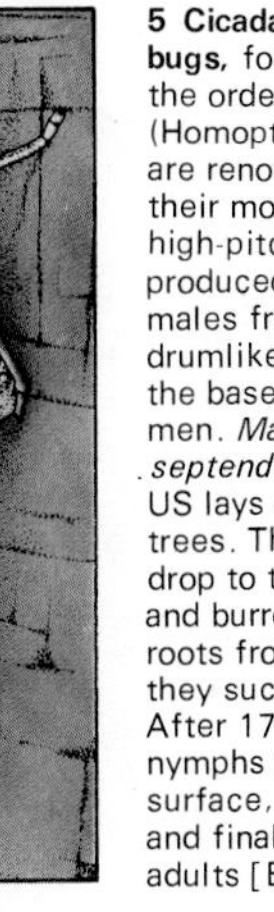

5 Cicadas are true bugs, forming part of the order Hemiptera (Homoptera). They are renowned for their monotonous, high-pitched sound, produced only by males from a pair of drumlike organs at the base of the abdomen. *Magicicada septendecim* of the US lays eggs in trees. The nymphs drop to the ground and burrow to the roots from which they suck sap [A]. After 17 years the nymphs return to the surface, climb a tree and finally molt into adults [B].

6 A Dragonfly *Anax imperator*

B Nymph

6 An incomplete metamorphosis, such as occurs in dragonflies (order Odonata), may be an adaptation to take advantage of different habitats. The adult form [A] of *Anax imperator* is a fast-flying predator on other insects while the nymph [B] is aquatic, preying on a variety of life in freshwater ponds.

7 Sucking lice (order Phthiraptera) are small, wingless external parasites of mammals. The human louse exists as two races: the body louse, which lives in the body clothing, and the head louse, which lives in the hair of the head on which it lays its eggs or "nits." Lice are dangerous because they transmit typhus, trench fever, and relapsing fever.

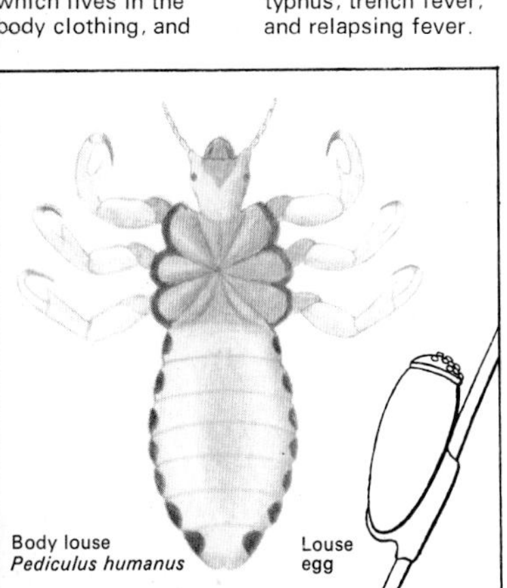

Body louse
Pediculus humanus
Louse egg

8

1

2

Onion thrip *Thrips tabaci*

8 Thrips are tiny pests of the order Thysanoptera. They are significant for the damage they do to crops and for carrying disease. They have simple, fringed wings (or none at all) and unusual mouthparts with which they suck plant juices. The onion thrips in both adult [1] and nymphal [2] stages infest a number of hosts to which they may transmit the tomato spotted wilt virus.

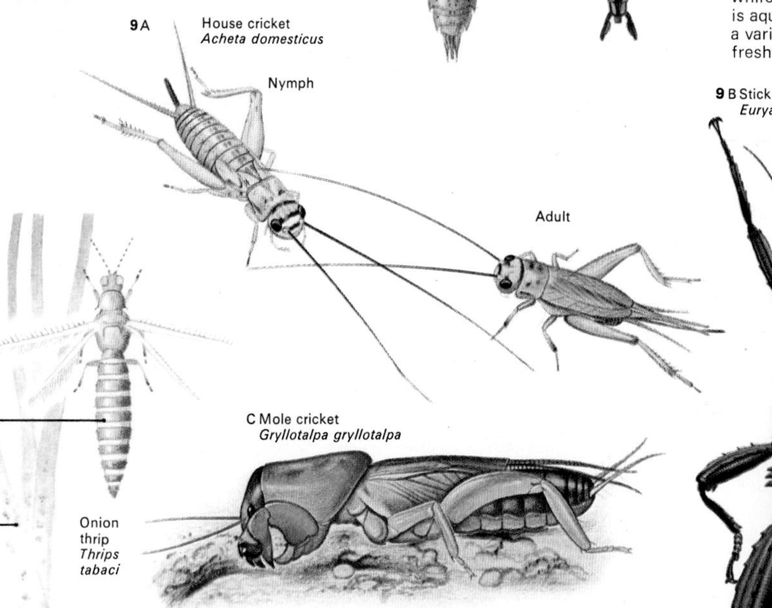

9A
House cricket
Acheta domesticus
Nymph
Adult
C Mole cricket
Gryllotalpa gryllotalpa

9 B Stick insect *Euryacantha horrida*

9 A great variety of form exists among exopterygote insects. The cosmopolitan house cricket [A] is particularly common in warm places where food is prepared and cooked and it often inhabits bakeries. The stick insects [B] of New Guinea are highly modified for the purposes of camouflage, mimicking the plants on which they live. These adaptations may seem bizarre, but the mole crickets are even more unusual. This species of North Africa and Eurasia has greatly enlarged front legs for digging the burrows in which it lives.

Advanced insects

Of all insects, those that have a four-stage life cycle—egg, larva, pupa, adult—are the ones that are both most advanced and most successful. They total more than two-thirds of the 1,000,000 different insect species and include such familiar groups as the moths and butterflies (more than 160,000 species), beetles (more than 350,000 species), bees, wasps, and ants (about 110,000 species), and true flies (about 75,000 species). Because of their numbers and worldwide distribution they are of great biological importance. To man they are both a help and a hindrance.

The butterfly life cycle

The butterfly has a life cycle [1] typical of advanced insects. After mating the female lays her eggs on a selected food source, which may be completely different from that of the adult. The eggs hatch in a matter of a few days (or even a few hours) into larvae (caterpillars). It is during this larval stage that many insects do great damage to crops and caterpillars such as those of the cabbage white butterflies may strip leaves down to bare "ribs" in a matter of only a few days.

The complete metamorphosis of the larva to the adult stage is via a "resting" phase, the pupa chrysalis. Within the pupa larval tissues are transformed into those of the adult imago. The most dramatic changes include the development of wings and the muscles to power them and also, in many insects, a complete change in the feeding apparatus—in the butterfly from chewing larval mouthparts to sucking adult ones.

The life of the adult insect is frequently short and serves only as a dispersal and reproductive phase. Many adult insects do not even feed but rely solely on the energy derived from fat stores laid down in the voracious larvae. Some adult insects will, if they emerge late in the year, hibernate over winter and delay egg laying until spring.

Keys to success

The advantages conferred on those insects that undergo complete metamorphosis (the endopterygotes) are manifold. Differences between the food eaten by the adults and larvae allow the larvae to exploit food resources that are not available to the adults. The larvae, because they are not involved in reproduction, can be highly camouflaged or live inside their food source—in plant stems or dung, for example—and are thus well protected against predators, such as birds. The immobile pupa, although it is helpless and needs protection from enemies, is necessary for the great change to the adult. The pupa stage also endows the advanced insects with an effective, enforced dormancy period during adverse seasonal weather conditions.

The evolution of advanced insects has favored those species in which the end of the pupal phase coincides with the onset of conditions conducive to adult survival, and thus the survival of future generations. The flying adult stage increases the chances of successful mating and allows dispersal of the fertilized eggs over a wide area.

The endopterygote insects play a major role in the maintenance of land ecosystems. They form the principal food of many birds and most bats; they act as the chief plant

CONNECTIONS

See also

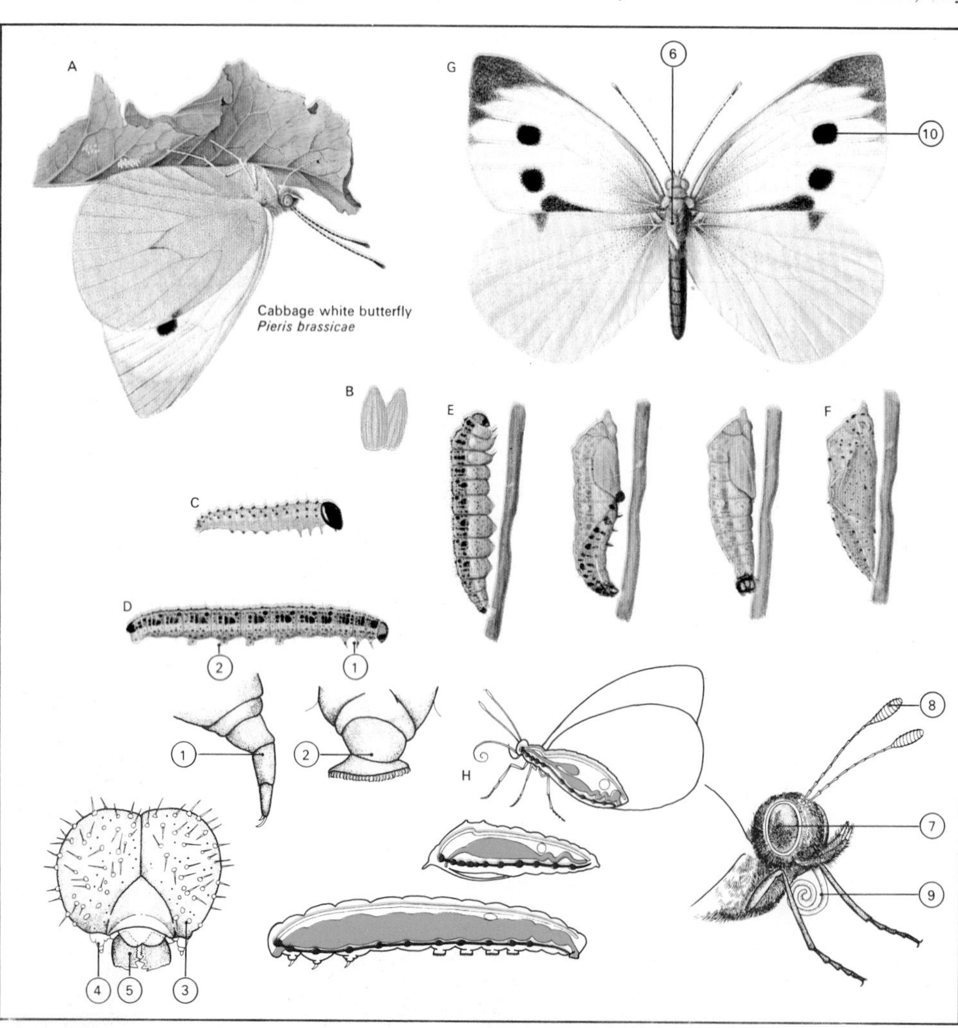

1
A
G
6
10
Cabbage white butterfly
Pieris brassicae
B
E
F
C
D
2
1
1
2
8
H
7
9
4
5
3

1 The cabbage white butterfly has a complete metamorphosis. The female [A] lays her eggs [B] on the underside of leaves in batches of 100 or more. The eggs hatch into the first stage larva, or caterpillar [C]. The larva molts successively and after four molts is fully grown [D]. It has three pairs of "true" legs [1], which represent the butterfly's legs, and four pairs of prolegs [2]; claspers at the end of the abdomen; and mandibles [5] for chewing. The head bears rudimentary eyes [3] and antennae [4]. After the fifth molt [E] the caterpillar's skin hardens to form the case of the pupa, or chrysalis [F]. Inside this case the tissues of the catepillar reorganize to form the butterfly [G], which shows the typical insect head, thorax, and abdomen. The thorax [6] bears two pairs of wings and three pairs of legs. The head has large compound eyes [7], clubbed antennae [8], and a coiled proboscis [9]. The internal systems [H], including those of the nerves [red], blood [yellow], and digestion [blue], become more complex at each stage. Soon after emergence from the chrysalis, the adult butterflies mate. The male is recognizable by its lack of forewing spots [10].

2 Houseflies [A] eat any liquefiable organic matter. The mouthparts [B] consist of a proboscis folded beneath the head when not in use. This extends and its expanded apex spreads over the food [1]. Digestive juices are pumped onto the food to liquefy and partially digest it. Left behind on the food are digestive juices as well as bacteria. Flies may thus carry diseases.

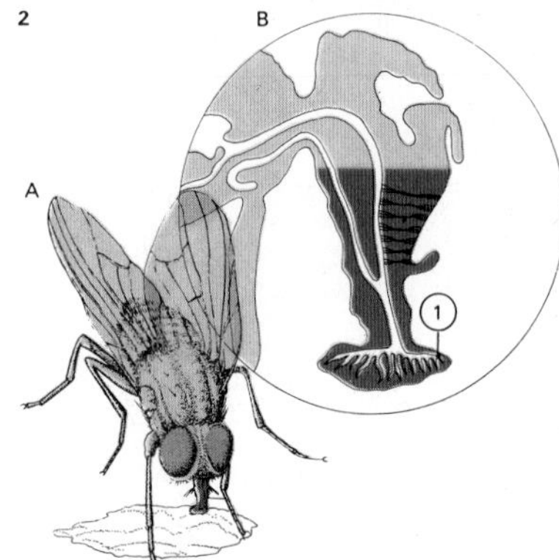

2
B
A
1

3 Like houseflies, craneflies are true flies of the order Diptera. The hindwings are reduced to special balacing organs, the halteres [1]. In flight these vibrate with the wings. Any deviation from the stable flight path is detected by the halteres and corrections made by the fly. The operation is similar to that of an autopilot on an aircraft. The inset shows a fly deviating from its flight path and the halteres correcting for this, thus enabling the fly to return to a stable course.

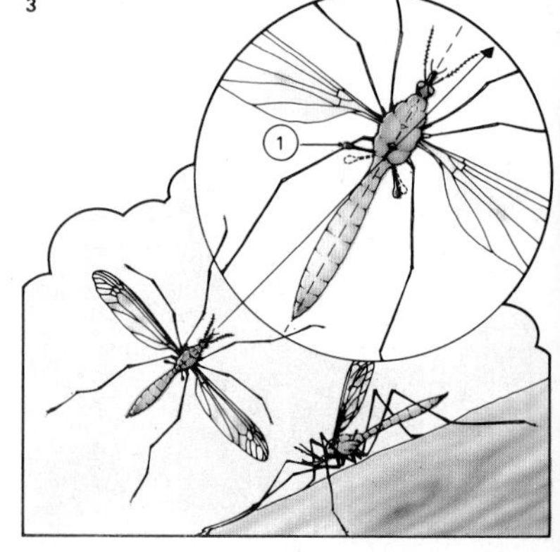

3
1

pollinators and contribute enormously to the disposal of dead organisms and waste matter. Many feed on the green plants essential to all animal life, and also form fundamental links in freshwater food chains. They include, however, especially in tropical regions, carriers of disease [2].

Helpful and harmful insects

The benefits insects confer on man are many. Pollination by insects is essential for many crops, including most fruits. Bees [8] are the most important pollinators and also make honey, one of the oldest crops taken by man. Other products derived directly from insects include beeswax, used in polishes, and silk from the cocoons of the silkworm moth.

The advanced insects are used by man in the field of biological pest control. This may be done by introducing an insect as a predator or parasite. In California, for example, the cottony-cushion scale *(Icerya purchasi)* was successfully controlled by the introduction of the Australian ladybird beetle *(Rodolia cardinalis)*. Such insects exercise this type of control constantly and help to prevent many potential pests from becoming actual ones.

Scavenging insects, such as dung beetles [4], are also vital. When cattle were first introduced to Australia the accumulated dung rendered grazing lands useless until dung beetles that could utilize it were introduced. On the debit side insects can cause great economic damage. Insect pests may damage crops and stored products and also carry diseases fatal to man and livestock. Malaria is carried by mosquitoes, while the tsetse fly *(Glossina)* carries nagana and sleeping sickness, diseases afflicting cattle and man, respectively.

Crop damage can be severe. The boll weevil *(Anthonomus grandis)* causes annual losses of $200 million to the US cotton crop, while in the absence of chemical or biological control the codling moth *(Carpocapsa pomonella)* can cause losses in apple yields of up to 50 percent. The Colorado beetle *(Leptinotarsa decemlineata)* has spread rapidly wherever potato plants have been grown.

KEY

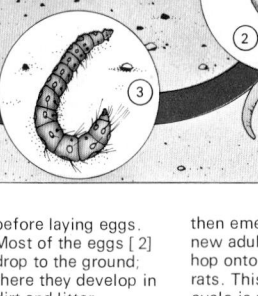

Bubonic plague is transmitted to man by the bite of the rat flea *(Xenopsylla cheopis)*, order Siphonaptera. The adult rat flea [1] feeds on rat blood before laying eggs. Most of the eggs [2] drop to the ground; there they develop in dirt and litter. Hatched larvae [3] feed on this before pupating [4] and then emerging as new adults, which hop onto passing rats. This type of life cycle is very adaptable because it includes a resting, resistant pupal phase.

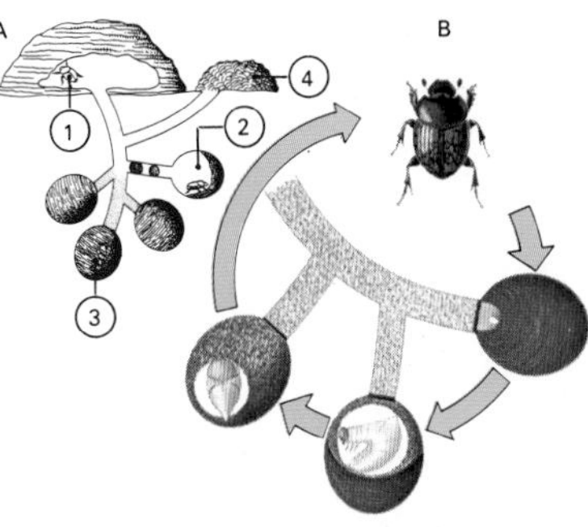
A
B

4 Typical of many insects that benefit from the feces of mammals are the dung beetles (order Coleoptera). The adult beetles of the genus *Onthophagus* construct brood chambers for their young [A] under cow dung. The male excavates the dung from below [1] and passes it to the female, who fills the brood chambers with it [2], lays an egg in each, and seals them [3]. Spoil is taken to the surface [4]. The eggs hatch into larvae, which feed on the dung until fully grown when they pupate [B]. On emerging, the adults dig to the surface.

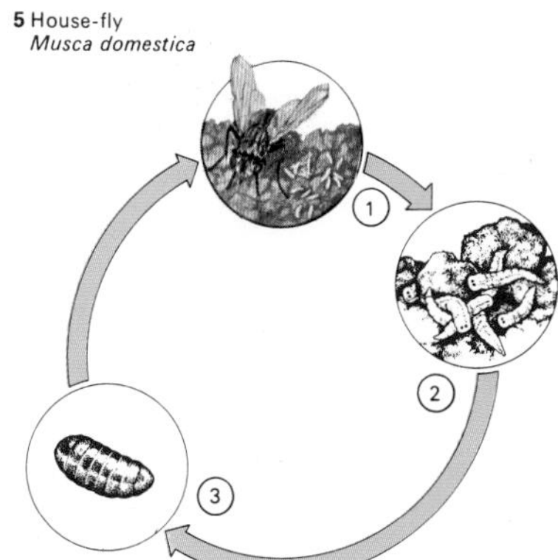
5 House-fly
Musca domestica

5 The housefly life cycle takes 8–40 days. Eggs are laid [1] in batches of 100 or more and, depending on the temperature, hatch in 1 to 5 days. The larva [2] pupates [3] after a minimum of 5 days.

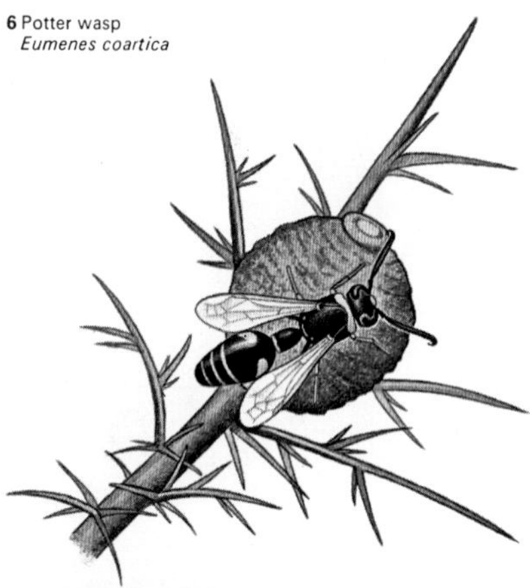
6 Potter wasp
Eumenes coartica

6 The potter wasps build clay pots attached to plants. They paralyze caterpillars with their stings and place them inside. The female lays an egg in each pot and the emerging larvae feed on the comatose but living caterpillars.

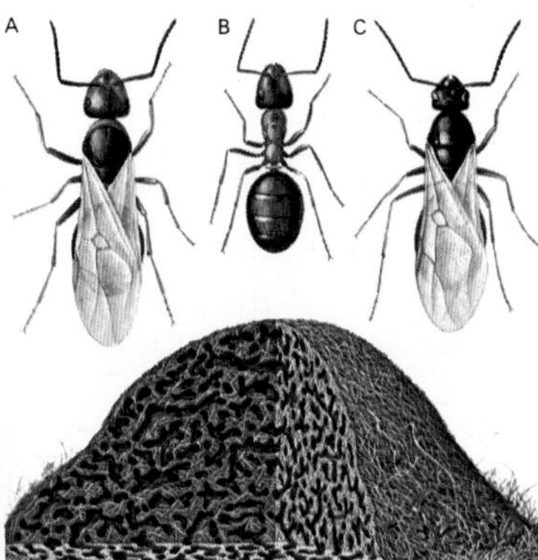
A
B
C

7 Colonies of the European wood ant *(Formica rufa)* may contain half a million ants, of three castes—queens [A], female workers [B], and males [C]. The queens and males are winged for their mating flights. Nests of pine needles create mounds 3ft (91cm) or more high. The queen discards her wings and lays eggs in brood chambers. The eggs are tended by workers, who also feed the larvae when they hatch. The ant pupae, often called "ants' eggs," are also attended by workers.

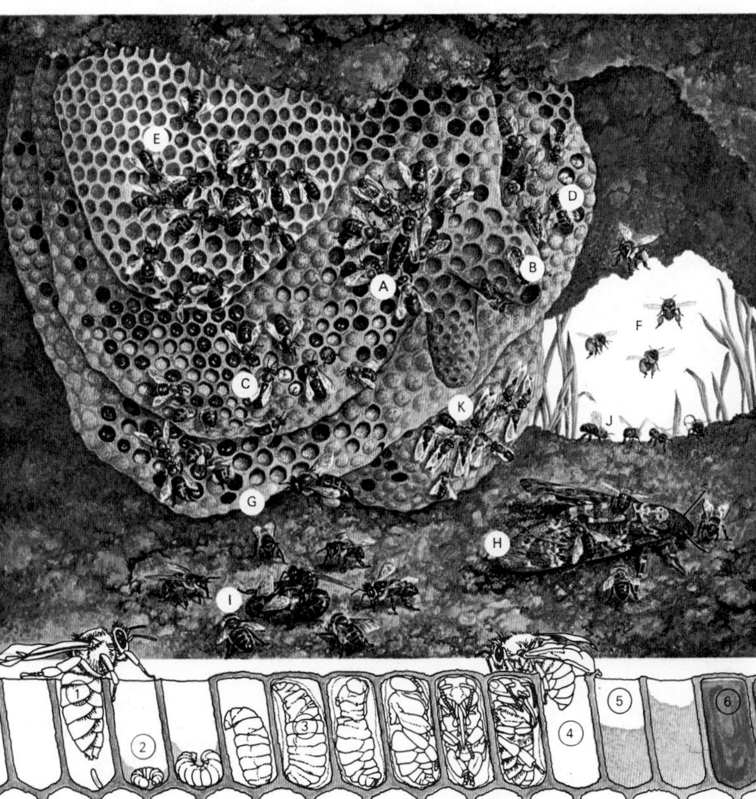
8

8 A strong colony of the honeybee *(Apis mellifera)* may have 80,000 sterile female workers, a fertilized queen [A], and a few hundred males, or drones. The colony is organized to maintain a constant internal environment. The queen [1] lays up to 1,500 eggs a day; fertile eggs in queen cells [B] and worker cells, unfertilized eggs in drone cells. The larvae [2] are fed by the workers and when the larvae pupate [3] workers cap the cells. Emerging bees [4] do domestic tasks for ten days, including helping workers [C] and drones [D] to emerge. Then they begin comb-building [E]. They take food from foraging workers [F] and store it [G] in pollen [5] or honey [6] cells. They also remove debris or intruders [H], including other queens [I]. The hive is cooled by wing fanning [J] or kept warm by huddling [K]. After three weeks all the workers become foragers.

Colorful bugs and beetles

The orders of bugs (Hemiptera) and beetles (Coleoptera) are often regarded with distaste and distrust and lumped together in popular language as "beetles." They are, however, distinct groups that are not even closely related. Between them they represent nearly half the known number of insects, the beetles numbering more than 350,000 species, the bugs more than 50,000 species. Some of the most spectacular bugs and beetles are illustrated.

Bugs and beetles are found in almost every habitat on earth and exhibit a wide variety of shape and size. They include some of the largest, heaviest, and most colorful insect species. A common characteristic of all bugs is their piercing and sucking mouthparts with which they extract their liquid diet from plants or animals. The beetles, in contrast, usually have chewing mouthparts employed equally efficiently on plants and animals. Most bugs and beetles have one pair of wings used for flight. The other pair is modified and hardened as a protective covering in all beetles and partially or completely in bugs.

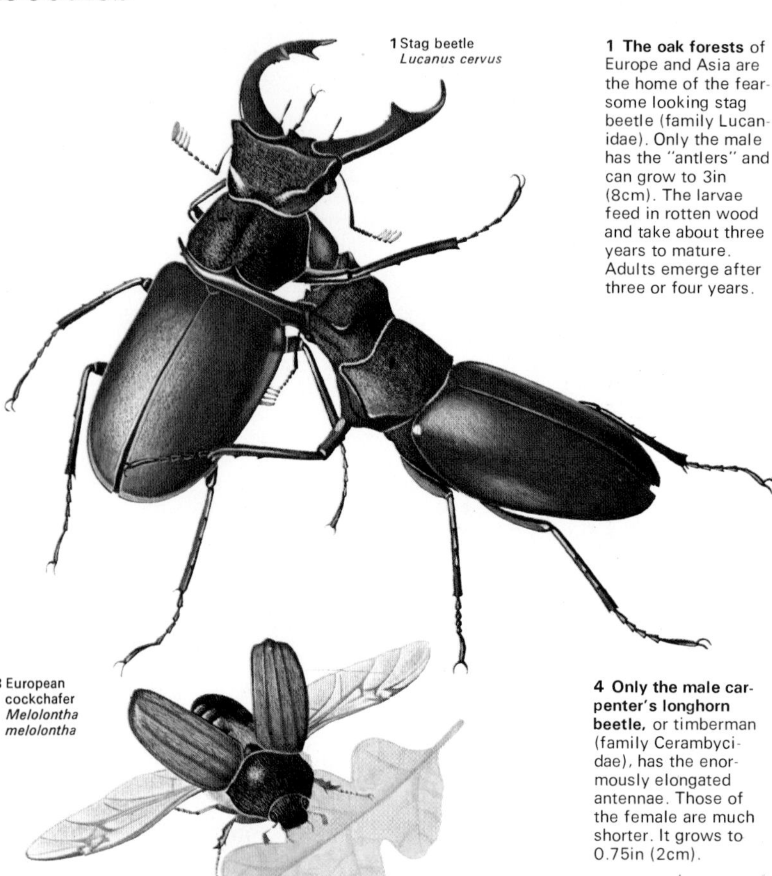

1 Stag beetle *Lucanus cervus*

1 The oak forests of Europe and Asia are the home of the fearsome looking stag beetle (family Lucanidae). Only the male has the "antlers" and can grow to 3in (8cm). The larvae feed in rotten wood and take about three years to mature. Adults emerge after three or four years.

CONNECTIONS

See also

496 Locusts, sucking bugs, and dragonflies
498 Advanced insects
492 The classification of insects
494 The world of insects
502 A variety of advanced insects
484 The joint-legged animals
464 Principles of animal behavior

2 Great silver water beetle *Hydrophilus piceus*

3 European cockchafer *Melolontha melolontha*

3 The common cockchafer, or maybug (family Melolonthidae), is a familiar beetle in Europe. It appears in vast numbers every three or four years. The adults, to 1.5in (4cm), eat leaves.

4 Only the male carpenter's longhorn beetle, or timberman (family Cerambycidae), has the enormously elongated antennae. Those of the female are much shorter. It grows to 0.75in (2cm).

4 Carpenter's longhorn beetle *Acanthocinus aedilis*

6 The bold yellow stripes of the European wasp beetle are thought to warn off potential predators. It grows to 0.6in (1.51cm) and is classified in the same family as the timberman.

6 Wasp beetle *Clytus arietus*

2 The great silver water beetle (family Hydrophilidae) was popular in Victorian aquariums but is now rare through overcollection. It is one of the largest water beetles reaching 2in (5cm).

5 The ground beetle is one of several species of the genus *Carabus* (family Carabidae) found in North America, Europe, and Asia. It measures about 1in(2.5cm) long and is an active predator.

5 Ground beetle *Carabus problematicus*

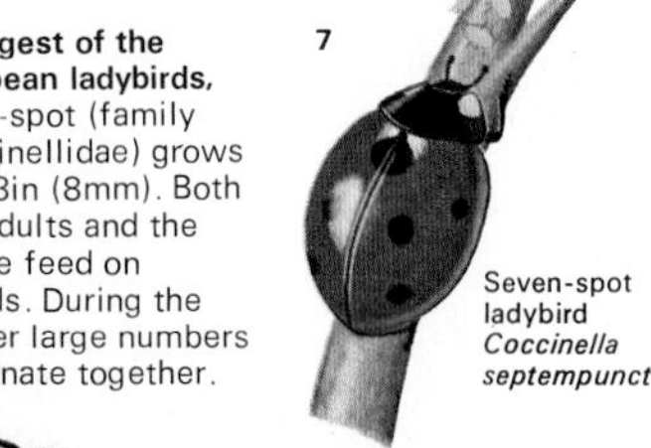

7 Largest of the European ladybirds, the 7-spot (family Coccinellidae) grows to 0.3in (8mm). Both the adults and the larvae feed on aphids. During the winter large numbers hibernate together.

7 Seven-spot ladybird *Coccinella septempunctata*

8 Hercules beetle *Dynastes hercules*

8 The beetle with the longest known tip to tail measurement is the Hercules beetle of tropical Central America (family Scarabaeidae). Including the "horn" it grows to about 6in (15cm) long. As with the stag beetle only the male possesses the elongated horns, the function of which is unknown. Most members of the group to which this species belongs are tropical American.

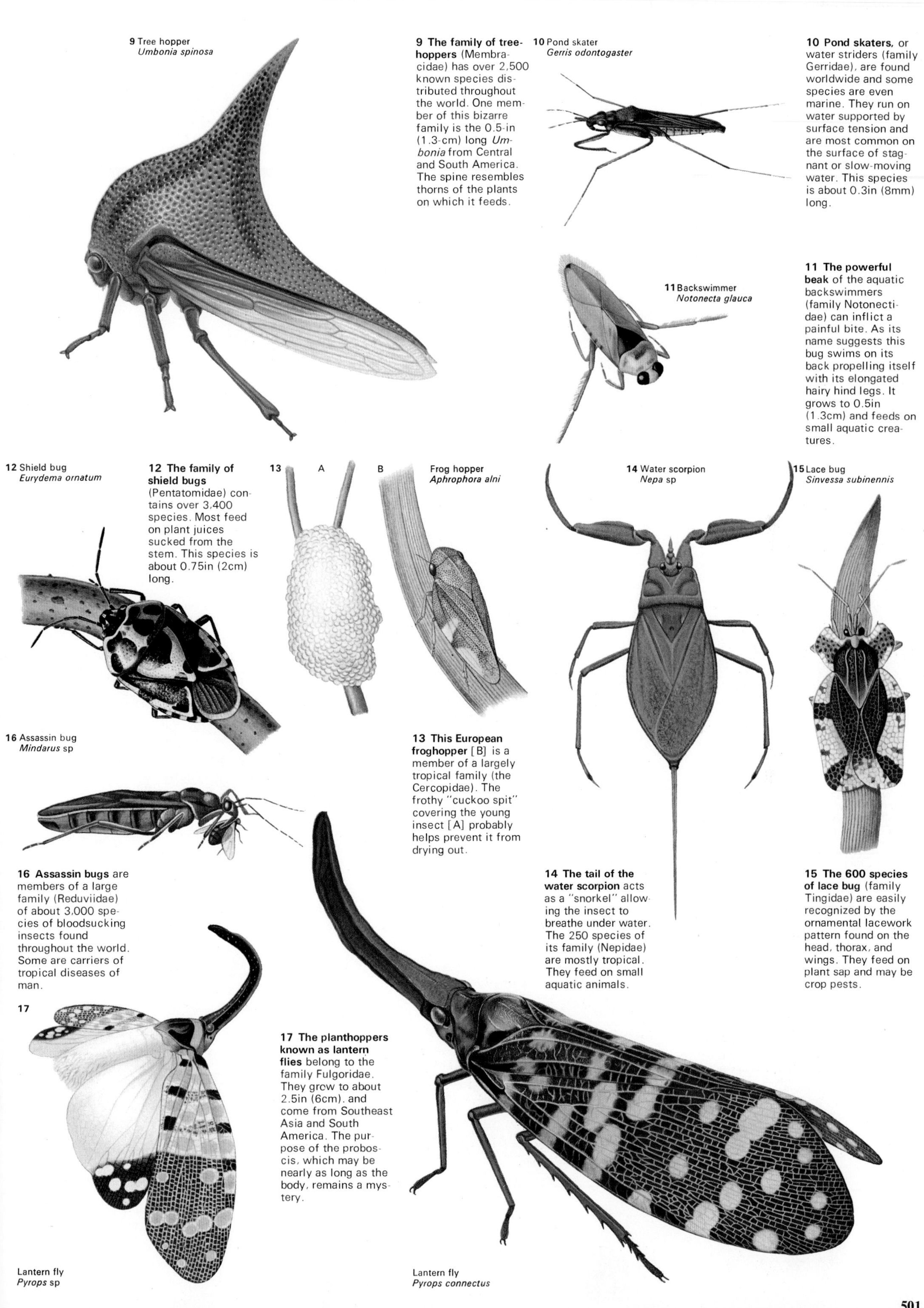

9 Tree hopper
Umbonia spinosa
10 Pond skater
Gerris odontogaster
11 Backswimmer
Notonecta glauca
12 Shield bug
Eurydema ornatum
13
A
B
Frog hopper
Aphrophora alni
14 Water scorpion
Nepa sp
15 Lace bug
Sinvessa subinennis
16 Assassin bug
Mindarus sp
17
Lantern fly
Pyrops sp
Lantern fly
Pyrops connectus

9 The family of tree-hoppers (Membracidae) has over 2,500 known species distributed throughout the world. One member of this bizarre family is the 0.5-in (1.3-cm) long *Umbonia* from Central and South America. The spine resembles thorns of the plants on which it feeds.

10 Pond skaters, or water striders (family Gerridae), are found worldwide and some species are even marine. They run on water supported by surface tension and are most common on the surface of stagnant or slow-moving water. This species is about 0.3in (8mm) long.

11 The powerful beak of the aquatic backswimmers (family Notonectidae) can inflict a painful bite. As its name suggests this bug swims on its back propelling itself with its elongated hairy hind legs. It grows to 0.5in (1.3cm) and feeds on small aquatic creatures.

12 The family of shield bugs (Pentatomidae) contains over 3,400 species. Most feed on plant juices sucked from the stem. This species is about 0.75in (2cm) long.

13 This European froghopper [B] is a member of a largely tropical family (the Cercopidae). The frothy "cuckoo spit" covering the young insect [A] probably helps prevent it from drying out.

16 Assassin bugs are members of a large family (Reduviidae) of about 3,000 species of bloodsucking insects found throughout the world. Some are carriers of tropical diseases of man.

14 The tail of the water scorpion acts as a "snorkel" allowing the insect to breathe under water. The 250 species of its family (Nepidae) are mostly tropical. They feed on small aquatic animals.

15 The 600 species of lace bug (family Tingidae) are easily recognized by the ornamental lacework pattern found on the head, thorax, and wings. They feed on plant sap and may be crop pests.

17 The planthoppers known as lantern flies belong to the family Fulgoridae. They grow to about 2.5in (6cm), and come from Southeast Asia and South America. The purpose of the proboscis, which may be nearly as long as the body, remains a mystery.

A variety of advanced insects

Butterflies and moths, wasps, bees, and ants are among the best-known insects and a small selection of the many interesting species are illustrated here. These insects are members of two of the most advanced insect orders. The butterflies and moths are classified in the order Lepidoptera, the bees, ants, and wasps in the order Hymenoptera. The families of moths and butterflies include some of the most beautiful insects, while the bees, wasps, and ants are remarkable for the high degree of social organization shown by some members, particularly the honeybees. The most economically important species of moths are those from which silk is obtained.

The known species of butterflies and moths total 165,000; bees, wasps, ants, and their allies number 110,000. Both groups are distributed worldwide and many species of Lepidoptera conflict with man's interests, being ranked among the most noxious of agricultural and forest pests. Their caterpillars can be particularly voracious. One species of moth, the vampire moth, is known to suck the blood of large mammals.

1

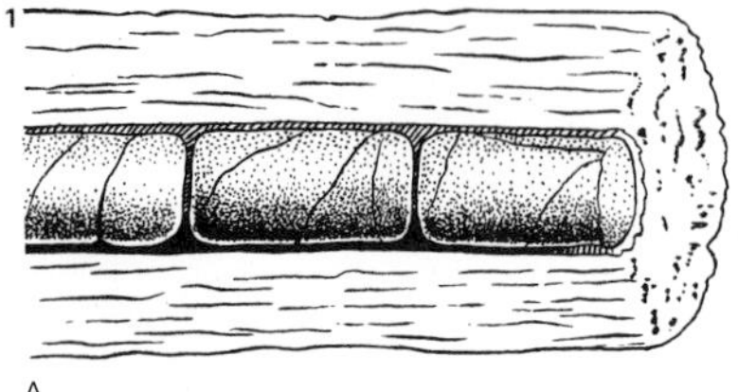

A

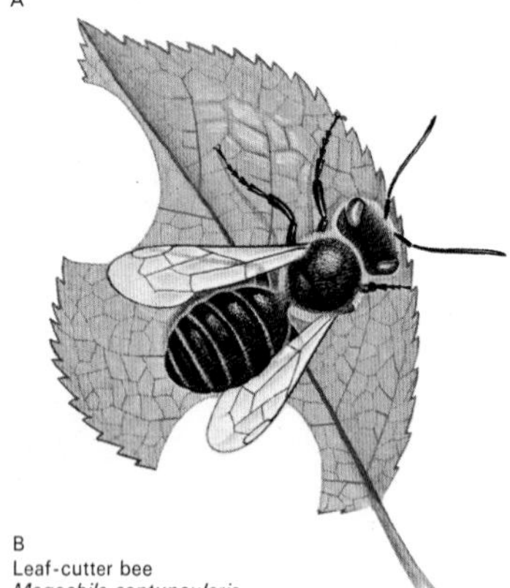

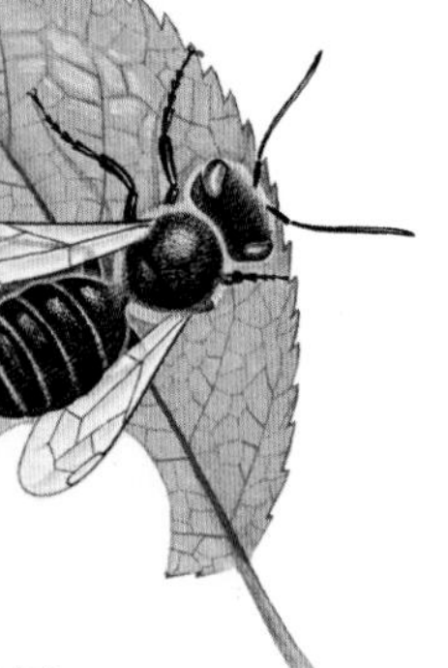

B
Leaf-cutter bee
Megachile centuncularis

1 The heavily built solitary Megachile bees (family Megachildae) are known as leaf-cutters. This name comes from their habit of cutting large disks out of leaves with their jaws [B]. The leaf sections are used to line the egg cells [A] built in dead twigs Each cell is filled with pollen, one egg is laid on top and the cell sealed. Pollen is collected on the hairy underside of the abdomen. This bee grows to about 0.5in (1.2cm) in length at maturity.

2 The solitary hairy-legged mining bee belongs to the family Melittidae. Of all bees this group has the largest "pollen baskets" on the hind legs. The bee excavates a nest shaft with cells at the end, each containing pollen and one egg.

CONNECTIONS

See also
498 Advanced insects
492 The classification of insects
494 The world of insects
500 Colorful bugs and beetles
484 The joint-legged animals
632 Endangered species

2

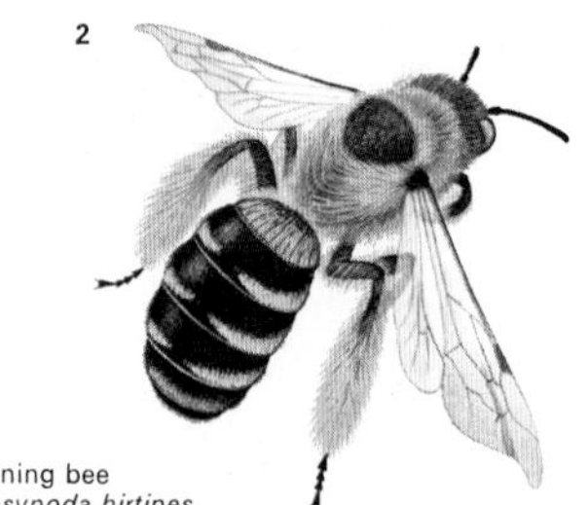

Mining bee
Dasypoda hirtipes

3

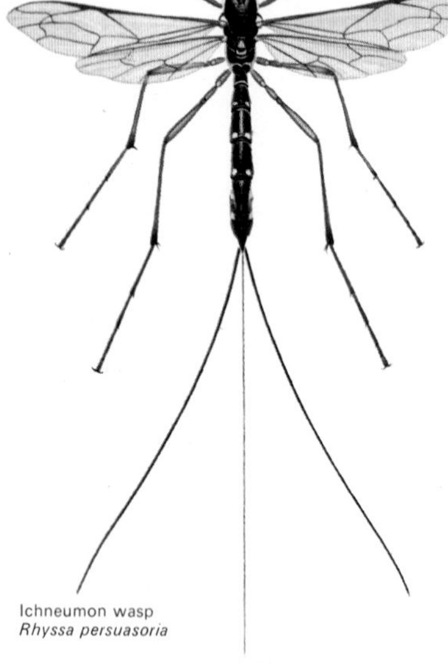

Ichneumon wasp
Rhyssa persuasoria

3 The ichneumon wasp (family Ichneumonidae) has a long ovipositor here shown separated from its coverings. It is used to lay eggs under the skins of insects. This species is 1.2in (3cm) long.

4 The mud-dauber wasps (family Sphecidae) are found worldwide but abound in the tropics. The nest cells of these solitary wasps are stocked with insects and a single egg is laid in each.

4

Mud-dauber wasp
Sceliphron sp

5

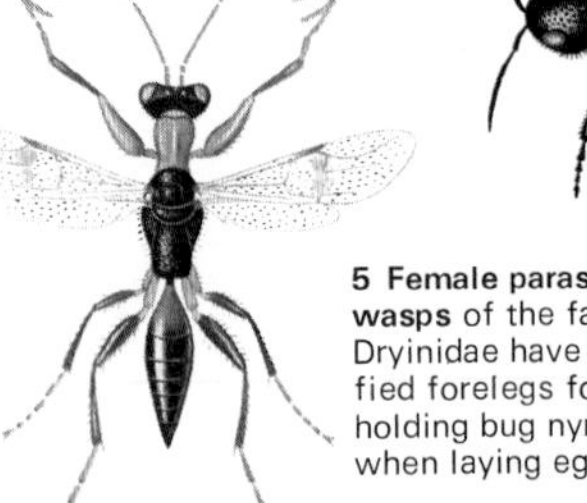

Dryinid wasp
Megadryinus magnificus

6

Velvet ant
Mutilla europaea

5 Female parasitic wasps of the family Dryinidae have modified forelegs for holding bug nymphs when laying eggs.

6 The velvet ant (family Mutillidae) is a wasp (the female is wingless). It lays eggs in nests of solitary wasps and bees.

7 Ants of the subfamily Dorylinae are commonly known as army, driver, or legionary ants. Nomadic tropical species, they roam forested areas in long columns feeding on small animals.

7

Army ant
Cheliomyrmex andicolus

8

Bulldog ant
Myrmecia forficata

8 The Australian bulldog ants (subfamily Ponerinae) are large, aggressive, and have pincerlike mandibles. They grow to 1in (2.5cm) and make subterranean nests for a few dozen ants.

10 All true social wasps belong to the family Vespidae. Many species, such as this one, are solitary; even the true social species may form only small colonies.

9 Many species of the family of gall wasps (Cynipidae) cause cancerlike growths—galls—on plants. These provide food and shelter for the developing larvae. This species produces oak galls.

10 Vespid wasp
Eumenes sp

9

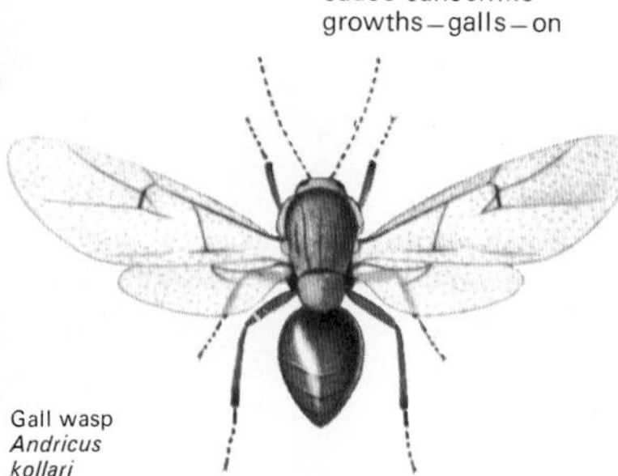

Gall wasp
Andricus kollari

11

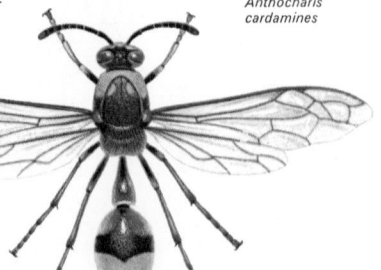

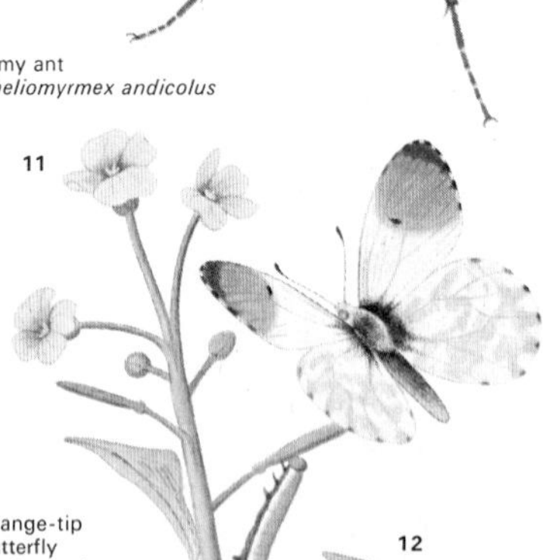

Orange-tip butterfly
Anthocharis cardamines

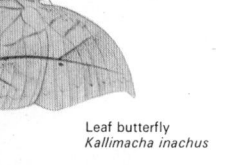

11 The orange tip butterfly (family Pieridae) lays its eggs on plants of the cabbage family, especially the lady's smock *(Cardamine pratensis)*. The chrysalis is attached with a silken girdle.

12 Mimicry is strikingly shown by the leaf butterfly of Asia, which even has "veins" in its wings.

12

Leaf butterfly
Kallimacha inachus

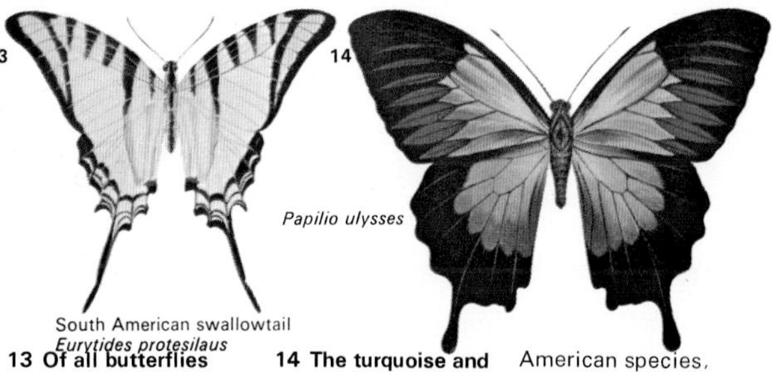

Papilio ulysses

South American swallowtail *Eurytides protesilaus*

13 Of all butterflies the swallowtails (family Papilionidae) are among the most beautiful. This South American species, like other members of the family, has the typical hind wing "tail" extensions.

14 The turquoise and brown swallowtail of New Guinea has a wing span of about 4in (10cm).

European swallowtail *Papilio machaon*

16 Brilliant colors, "tail streamers," and a slow flight are characteristic of one of the best-known groups of butterflies—the swallowtails of the family Papilionidae. The caterpillars feed on various plants of the carrot family (Umbelliferae). The chrysalis is attached to the food plant and stays dormant until the following spring. Swallowtails are distributed worldwide but like other European and North American species, these butterflies are becoming rare because their food plants are being destroyed with herbicides and by bog drainage.

Papilio zalmoxis

15 Africa is the home of several species of swallowtail. This large green species is one of those lacking the typical "tails." It is found in West Africa.

Papilio polyxenes

17 This is one of the 15 species of swallowtail found in North and Central America and also in Cuba. Its measurement from wingtip to wingtip is about 3in.

Graphium weiskei

18 New Guinea is the home of this swallowtail, one of the smaller but typical species. Its wing span is 2.5in (6cm).

Iphiclides podalirius

19 The scarce, or sail, swallowtail lives in the warmer parts of Europe but is becoming increasingly rare. The caterpillars feed on the leaves of blackthorn.

Viceroy *Limenitis archippus*

Monarch butterfly *Danaus plexippus*

20 A form of protection that has evolved by some animals, particularly butterflies, is mimicry. A harmless species evolves the external appearance of a harmful form that predators have learned to avoid. The American monarch butterfly, for example, is poisonous to birds due to the presence of cardenolide, a heart poison, and is rapidly regurgitated if devoured. The monarch is mimicked by the viceroy. The bright coloration on the wings is repeated on the undersides of the wings of both butterflies so that they are conspicuous. The butterflies are members of two different families.

European swallowtailed moth *Ourapteryx sambucaria*

22 The swallowtail moth is a common species found from north-central and southern Europe to Siberia. Its caterpillars eat ivy, sloe, and hawthorn. It belongs to the family Geometridae.

Hawk moth *Herse convolvuli*

21 Hawk moths (family Sphingidae) such as the convolvulus hawk are found worldwide. Many have a long "tongue" used to extract nectar from tubular flowers and often feed on the wing.

Skipper butterfly *Ochlodes venata*

23 There are about 3,000 species of the skipper butterflies (family Hesperiidae) found throughout the world. The large skipper of Europe has a wing span of 1.2in (3cm). The name is derived from erratic flight.

Lackey moth *Malacosoma neustria*

24 The caterpillars of the lackey moth (family Lasiocampidae) a European relative of the North American tent caterpillar, live on bushes and trees, which they strip. Eggs are laid in a collar around a twig.

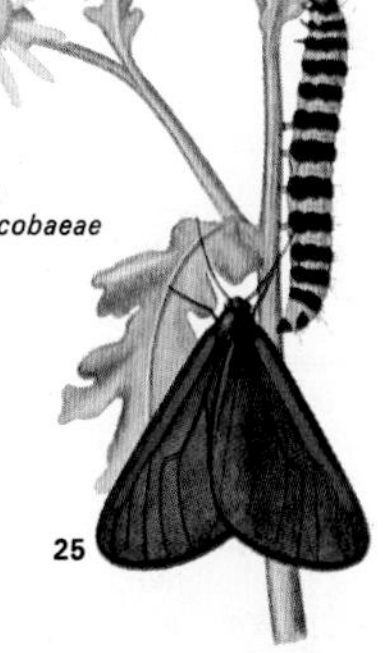

Cinnabar moth *Callimorpha jacobaeae*

25 The cinnabar moth (family Arctiidae), seen here alongside its caterpillar, is found in Europe. Its bright color warns of its unpleasant taste. The caterpillars feed mainly on ragwort.

Starfish and sea urchins

Echinoderms, the group of "spiny-skinned" animals [1] that includes the starfish and sea urchins, are found throughout the world's oceans, on the sea bottom, in rock cavities and shallow coastal waters, and buried deep in sand. There are more than 5,500 species grouped into 5 classes.

Echinoderm classes

Sea urchins (class Echinoidea) are often more familiar as beautifully symmetrical ornaments than as living animals bristling with sharp, often poisonous spines [Key]. The largest species is *Sperosoma giganteum* of Japan with a 12in (30cm) diameter, but most are only about 3in (7.5cm) across. The flattened sand dollars belong to the same group. Starfish and cushion-stars (class Asteroidea), are among the most colorful creatures in the sea. The 20-rayed star *(Pyconopodia)* of Puget Sound is 3.3ft (1m) across, but some cushion stars, with their short arms, are only 0.5in (1.2cm) in diameter. Less familiar are the peculiar limp sea cucumbers (class Holothuroidea) that crawl along the sand; the brittle stars and basket stars (class Ophiuroidea), often found massed together in isolated patches on the sea bottom; and the primitive sea lilies (class Crinoidea), found in deep water.

All these echinoderms, although it is not obvious in the sea cucumbers, have pentamerous symmetry—that is, the body can be divided into five parts around a central axis. They may have evolved from a mobile bilateral ancestor that became sedentary, took on a more adaptive radial symmetry, and then resumed a free-moving existence.

The starfish and sea urchin seem unlikely relatives, but if the five arms of the starfish were drawn above the center of the animal and sewn together, the result would be similar to the body form of the urchin. Another common feature is the external skeleton of bony plates just under the skin. In sea urchins, the plates are fused to form a rigid box, but in sea cucumbers they are reduced to microscopic spines.

How echinoderms move and feed

Most echinoderms move, even if slowly. Starfish, and to a greater extent sea urchins, have inflexible, rigid skins and for movement must rely mainly on peculiar small appendages called tube feet, which are blind-ended sacs arising from an internal system of water-filled tubes in the body cavity, or coelom. The feet are extended and retracted hydraulically to produce movement. The sea urchin is clothed in bands of tube feet armed with suckers [3] that can be extended beyond the long spines when a vertical rock is to be climbed.

Starfish use the rows of feet on the undersides of their arms to cling to rocks in heavy seas [2]. Brittle stars and basket stars move by wriggling their long arms. Sea lilies are mainly sedentary. Their flexible arms are attached to a stalk that is anchored to rocks or sand. (Their relatives, the feather stars, are stalkless and free swimming.)

Sea lilies feed on organic particles that fall through the water around them. The particles are caught in grooves on the arms and are moved by hairlike cilia. The sea urchin shuffles over rocks, rasping off tiny plants and animals, using an elaborate chewing apparatus. Waste is ejected

CONNECTIONS

See also
458 The animal kingdom
508 Threshold of the vertebrates
506 Invertebrate oddities
564 Fossils without backbones
622 The seashore: life between the tides
408 Evolution of life
1468 Shape and symmetry

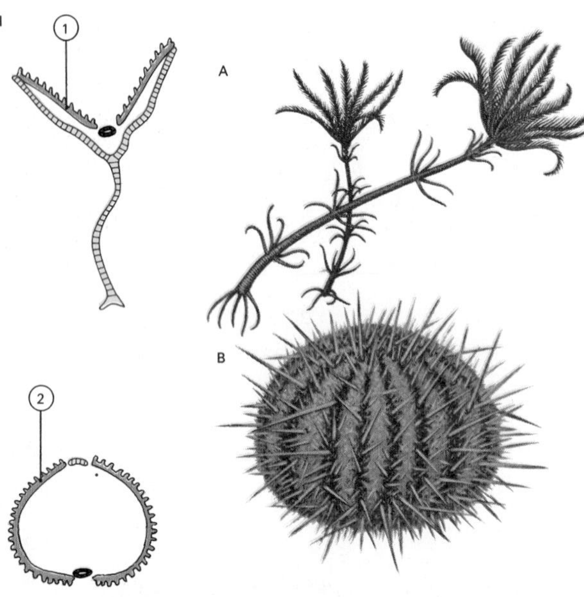

1
A
B

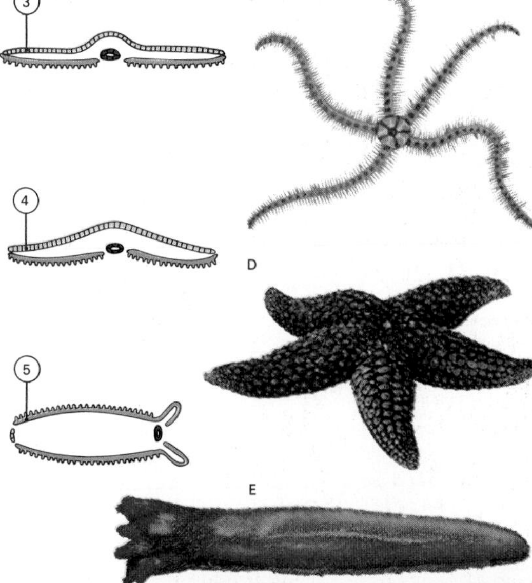

C
D

1 Although diverse in body shape, these creatures are all "spiny-skinned" animals, or echinoderms. The five groups—sea lilies [A], sea urchins [B], brittle stars [C], starfish [D], and sea cucumbers [E]—all have the same basic body plan [1–5], with a body pattern that has structures present in fives. They all possess locomotory tube feet [blue], which are part of an internal system of canals filled with fluid, an external skeleton of calcareous plates embedded under the skin [yellow], and a mouth [red] to rake in food and sometimes to give out waste. They are all marine and mostly live on sand or on rocks.

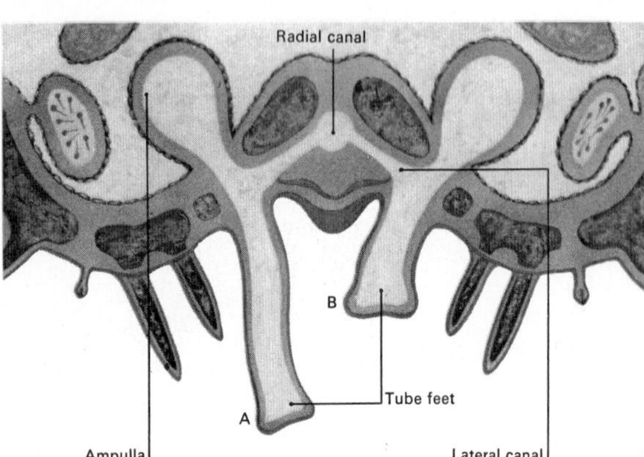

2
Radial canal
B
A
Tube feet
Ampulla
Lateral canal

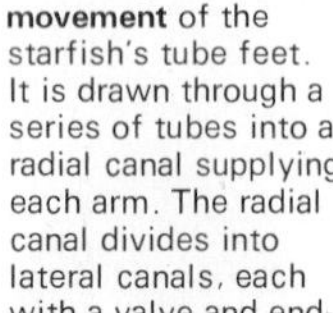

2 Water powers the movement of the starfish's tube feet. It is drawn through a series of tubes into a radial canal supplying each arm. The radial canal divides into lateral canals, each with a valve and ending in a bulblike ampulla and a foot. During movement the ampulla contracts, the lateral canal valve closes, and water is forced into the foot, which elongates [A], swings forward, and adheres to the substrate. Longitudinal muscles then contract, shortening the foot [B] and forcing fluid back into the ampulla. Each foot is controlled by an intricate system of nerve fibers and works independently, but during forward movement all the feet in the leading arm or arms move in the same direction.

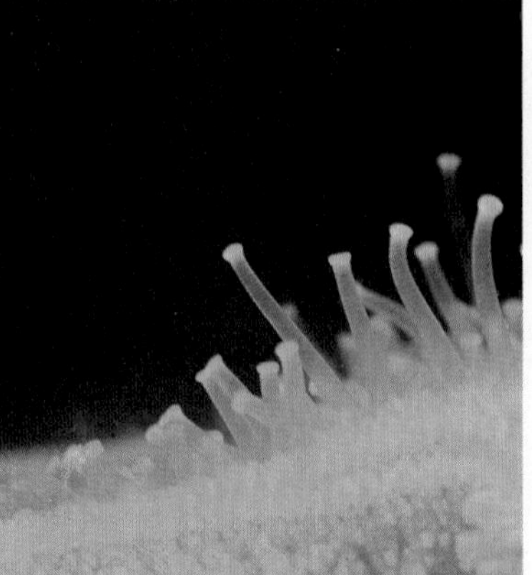
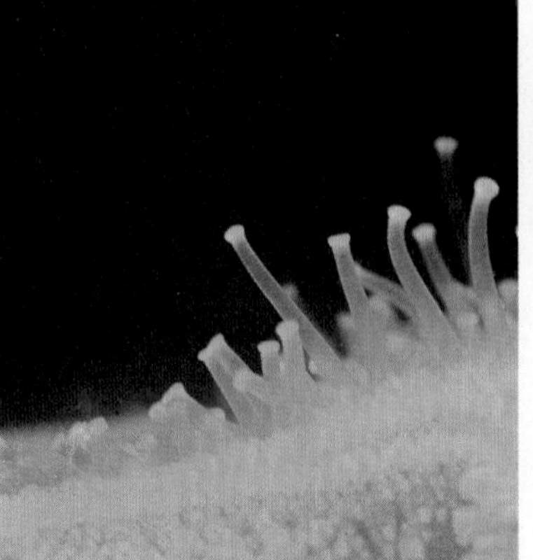

3 The tube feet of a sea urchin are seen, in close-up, to be capped by suction pads. When the feet contact a solid surface, the center of the sucker is withdrawn, producing a vacuum and adhesion. Contraction of muscles and removal of water from the feet lift them from the surface once more. In this way the sea urchin can move rapidly over rocks and even climb vertical surfaces.

4 To open up a bivalve, the starfish makes use of the adhesive force of its tube feet, which it firmly attaches to the two shell valves. By applying a strong, steady pressure the starfish opens the two shells far enough to push part of its stomach into the body of its prey and start to digest it outside its body. Stomach juices reduce the soft parts of the shellfish to a semi-liquid mass that can then be drawn into the stomach. The empty shells are discarded.

through a hole in the top of the shell. With nerve endings highly sensitive to touch [5], most of the starfish seek out shellfish. They open bivalve mollusks [4] using adhesive tubular feet. Others swallow crustaceans, mollusks, and small fish, and the crown-of-thorns starfish *(Acanthaster planci)* lives on coral polyps in the Pacific Ocean. Sea cucumbers extract nutrients from sand.

Means of protection

With no rapid means of escape, most echinoderms have some means of protection against enemies. Most familiar are the sharp spines of sea urchins, such as those of the hat-pin sea urchin *(Diadema setosum)*, which rests on the sand in the shallow water of the Great Barrier Reef and can inflict painful wounds. The spines can also be rotated like a drill and used to burrow into rocks and sand for shelter. Sea cucumbers of the genera *Holothuria* and *Actinopyga* shoot out sticky white threads through the anus to ensnare enemies. They can also eject their viscera through their mouths and later regenerate a new set.

The power of tissue regeneration of echinoderms is remarkable. The common Pacific sea star *(Linckia)* can lose all its arms, but if a small piece of one remains attached to the central disk, it will regenerate five new arms. The brittle star *(Ophiothrix fragilis)* can break into pieces if it is handled roughly, each piece regenerating into a new individual. Regeneration is also a means of reproduction. A single male brittle star *(Ophiactis savignyi)* colonized a reef in the West Indies and by self-dividing formed the whole reef population.

Sexual reproduction involves separate males and females. Females shed eggs into the seawater, where they are fertilized by sperm from the male. In the spring spawning each female sea star may release up to two million eggs. Some cold-water echinoderms brood their eggs. In a California sea cucumber *(Thyone rubra)*, development takes place in the coelom and the young leave through the anus. Others brood eggs on the body surface. In most echinoderms fertilized eggs develop into mobile larvae [7].

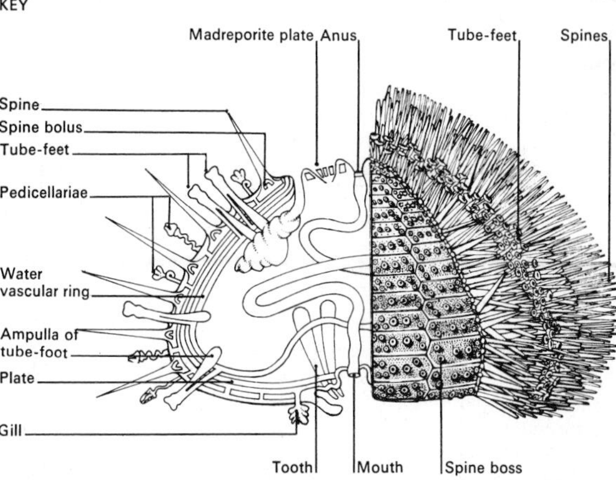
KEY
Madreporite plate
Anus
Tube-feet
Spines
Spine
Spine bolus
Tube-feet
Pedicellariae
Water vascular ring
Ampulla of tube-foot
Plate
Gill
Tooth
Mouth
Spine boss

Sea urchins are the only echinoderms in which the calcareous plates under the skin are fused to form a rigid box, or test. Sharp, sometimes poisonous, spines are used for protection, for burrowing into rocks, and, in conjunction with five columns of tube feet, for locomotion. Between the spines, pincerlike pedicellariae prevent anything settling on the test. The mouth is equipped with five movable teeth that rasp encrusting organisms from the rocks. Surrounding the mouth, five pairs of gills are the chief centers of respiration, exchanging oxygen for carbon dioxide.

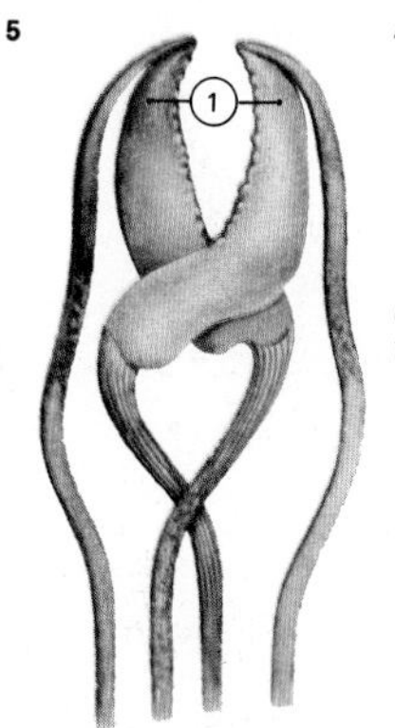
5
1
A
Cross-jawed pedicellaria
B
Straight-jaw pedicellaria
C
Tridactyl pedicellaria
D
Stalked pedicellaria

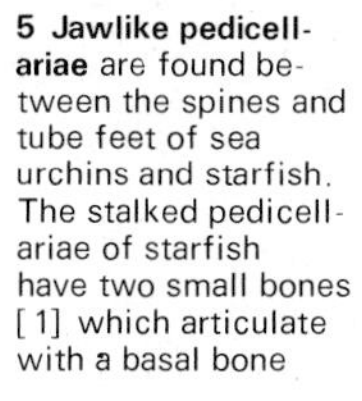

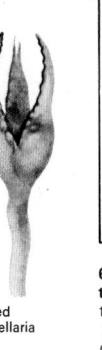

5 Jawlike pedicellariae are found between the spines and tube feet of sea urchins and starfish. The stalked pedicellariae of starfish have two small bones [1] which articulate with a basal bone in a scissors [A] or forceps [B] arrangement. Sessile [C] and stalked [D] pedicellariae of sea urchins have three jaws using a pincer-like movement. The jaws are operated by muscles; if touched on the outside they open; touched on the inside, they snap shut. Some are poisonous and are used for defense; most capture small prey and prevent organisms "lodging" on the body surface.

6 A B C

6 If accidentally turned on its back, the common seastar *(Asterias rubens)* is capable of righting itself. The tip of one arm is twisted [A] so that the rows of tube-feet can grip a hard or rocky surface. With this initial foothold, the rest of the arm gradually turns and moves backward [B] so that the body folds in half. The three gripping arms now pull the body over, so that, in a slow somersault, the starfish has regained its normal position [C].

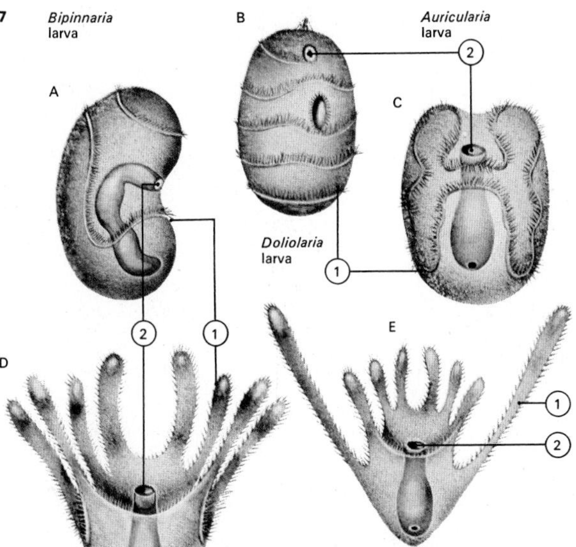
7
Bipinnaria larva
A
B
Auricularia larva
C
Doliolaria larva
D
Echinopluteus larva
E
Ophiopluteus larva
1
2

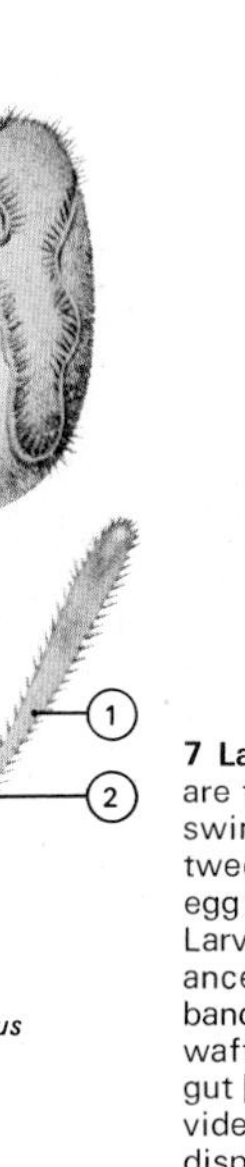

7 Larval echinoderms are the free-swimming stage between the fertilized egg and the adult. Larvae vary in appearance, but most have bands of cilia [1] to waft food into the gut [2] and to provide a means of larval dispersal. Two-week-old starfish larvae [A] have two ciliated bands; three-day-old sea cucumber larvae [C] have a single band, which later breaks into rings [B]. Sea urchin larvae [D], and basket star larvae [E] have extended larval arms.

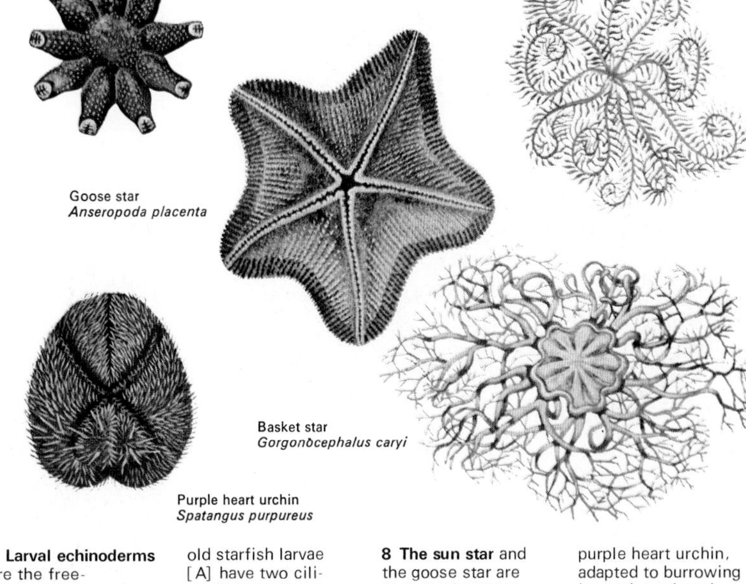
8
Purple sun star
Solaster endeca
Feather star
Antedon bifida
Goose star
Anseropoda placenta
Basket star
Gorgonocephalus caryi
Purple heart urchin
Spatangus purpureus

8 The sun star and the goose star are both sea-bottom dwellers and they illustrate the diversity of shapes within the class Asteroidea. The feather star, a crinoid, lives on the continental shelf and temporarily attaches itself to rocks. The purple heart urchin, adapted to burrowing in sand, mud, and gravel, is found offshore from Norway to the Mediterranean. The basket star is a deepwater inhabitant of the North Atlantic.

Invertebrate oddities

The animals without backbones, the invertebrates, are a huge group of organisms comprising about 95 percent of all animal species and found in every available habitat on earth. The main groups of invertebrates have been described on the previous pages, but there are, in addition, many small, bizarre groups, some of which are illustrated here. Most of these are aquatic; those that are not have often assumed parasitic habits inside other animals.

Although they may appear insignificant, many of these "odd" invertebrates play an important part in the food chains of other animals—the marine species, for example, may be eaten by shrimp, the shrimp by fish, and the fish by man. And to the zoologist the description and investigation of these animals, many of them too small to be seen with the naked eye, provide an endless source of fascination and discovery.

The invertebrates were the first animals to appear on earth and it may be that these rare groups will provide more clues about the early steps in the evolution of the higher animals, including man himself.

CONNECTIONS

See also
458 The animal kingdom
466 Single-celled animals and sponges
472 Flatworms, flukes, and tapeworms
474 Earthworms, clamworms, and roundworms
484 The joint-legged animals
504 Starfish and sea urchins
508 Threshold of the vertebrates
564 Fossils without backbones

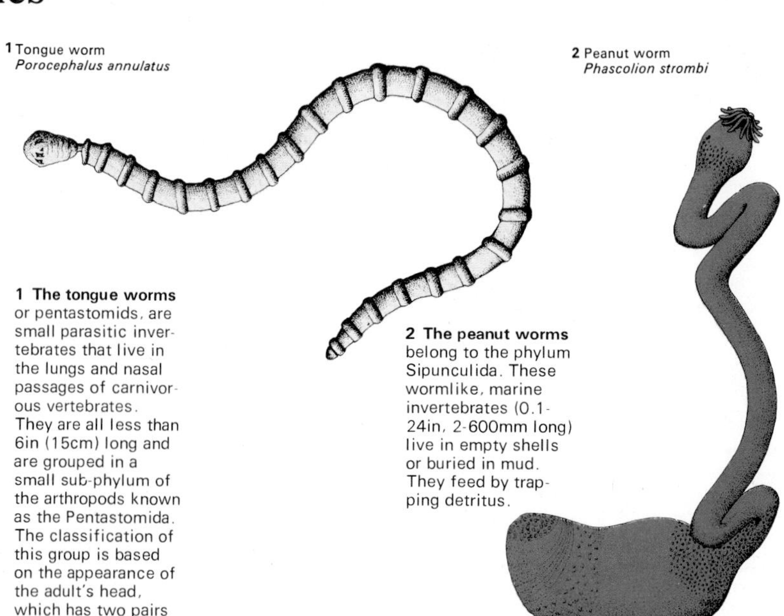
1 Tongue worm *Porocephalus annulatus*

2 Peanut worm *Phascolion strombi*

1 The tongue worms or pentastomids, are small parasitic invertebrates that live in the lungs and nasal passages of carnivorous vertebrates. They are all less than 6in (15cm) long and are grouped in a small sub-phylum of the arthropods known as the Pentastomida. The classification of this group is based on the appearance of the adult's head, which has two pairs of small, clawed projections.

2 The peanut worms belong to the phylum Sipunculida. These wormlike, marine invertebrates (0.1-24in, 2-600mm long) live in empty shells or buried in mud. They feed by trapping detritus.

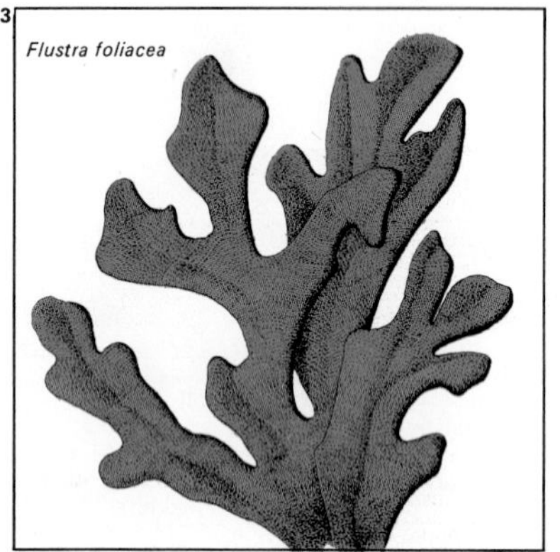
3 *Flustra foliacea*

3 The colonial, sedentary Flustra appears at first sight more like a plant than an animal. In fact it is made up of numerous small creatures called zooids that secrete protective skeletal shells around themselves. *Flustra* is a member of the phylum Ectoprocta (Bryozoa). Starting life as a single zooid it forms a colony by budding. The zooids remain connected internally.

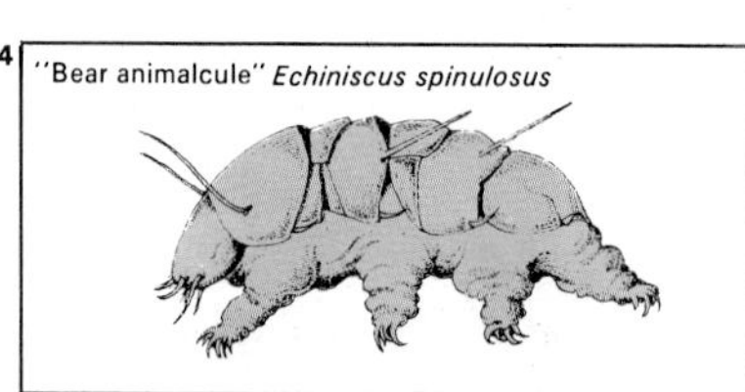
4 "Bear animalcule" *Echiniscus spinulosus*

4 The "bear animalcules," or tardigrades, are very small invertebrate relations of the arthropods. Most are less than 0.02 in long and inhabit the film of water covering mosses.

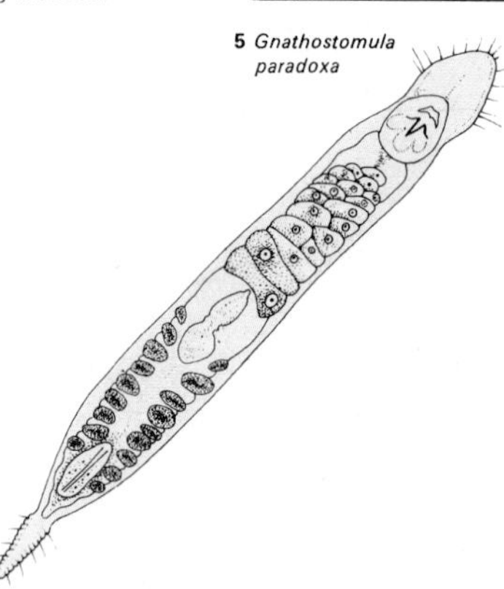
5 *Gnathostomula paradoxa*

5 Marine muddy sand is the home of minute, transparent wormlike animals of the group Gnathostomulida, which are related to the freeliving flatworms. They are all less than a millimeter long and have heads bearing long, hairlike cilia. The body is covered with short cilia. Both male and female sex organs are found in each individual, but reproduction is by cross fertilization. About 50 species are known.

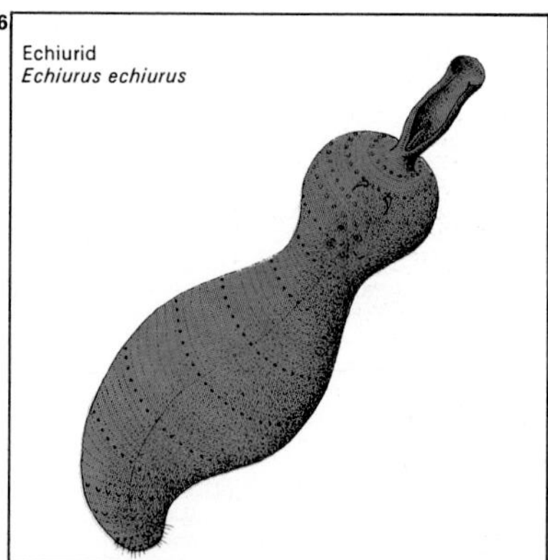
6 Echiurid *Echiurus echiurus*

6 The echiurids are a small phylum of wormlike invertebrates that live buried in sand or mud on the sea bottom or inhabit rock crevices. They feed on detritus that is spread over the substratum. They trap it using a large tubelike mouth or proboscis. These worms, ranging from 0.1 to 24in (2 to 600mm) long have some similarities in anatomy to earthworms (Annelida) and may be related.

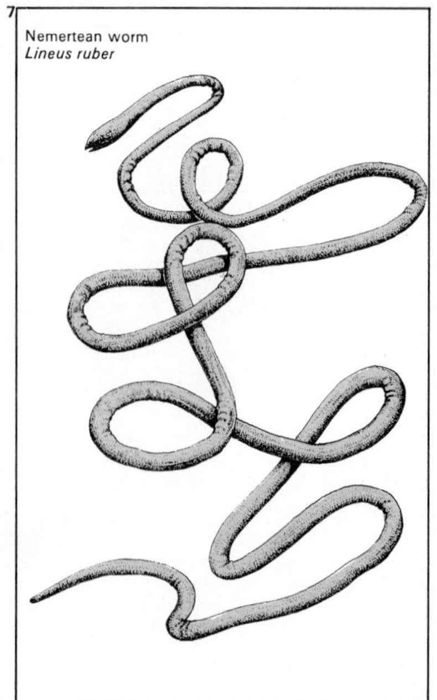
7 Nemertean worm *Lineus ruber*

7 Most nemertean, or ribbon, worms live in the seas of the Northern Hemisphere. These unsegmented creatures, which may be up to 90ft (27m) long, live in shallow waters where they feed on both live prey and detritus. Under certain conditions the body of the worm may spontaneously break up into fragments that can stay alive and even regenerate into new individuals. A few nemertean worms live as parasites in other invertebrates.

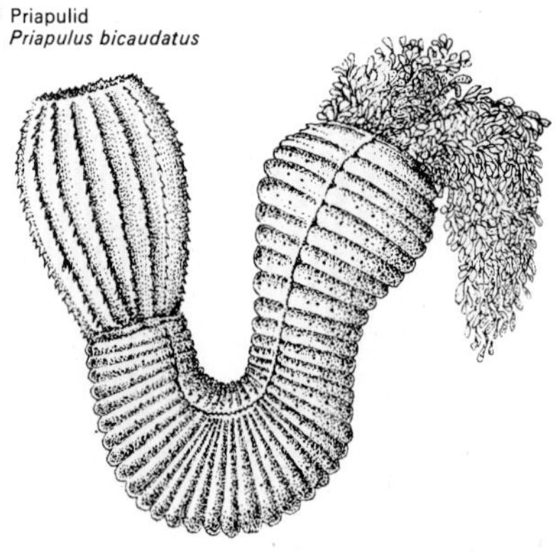
8 Priapulid *Priapulus bicaudatus*

8 The priapulids are a group of cylindrical worms that inhabit the muddy bottoms of coastal waters in the colder parts of the oceans to depths of about 26,000 ft (8,000m) in both hemispheres. Apart from *Priapulus* only one other genus, *Halicryptus*, is known. The relationship of these animals to other invertebrates remains a mystery, but their anatomy is somewhat similar to that of the nematodes (roundworms). The species illustrated measures 2in (5cm) in length.

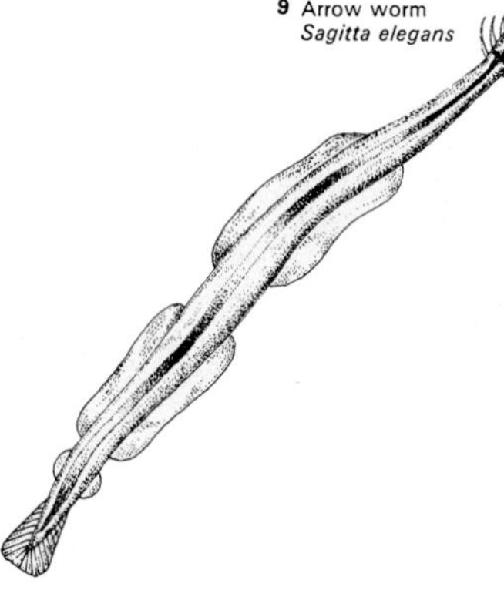
9 Arrow worm *Sagitta elegans*

9 The arrow worm is a member of a small phylum known as the Chaetognatha and is common in the sea's plankton in all the oceans of the world. Although they usually move only in ocean currents, these animals are capable of swimming. They vary in length from 1-4in (2.5-10cm) and each worm contains both ovaries and testes. Reproduction is by self-fertilization and the first stages in the development of the embryo take place inside the tubular body of the adult arrow worm.

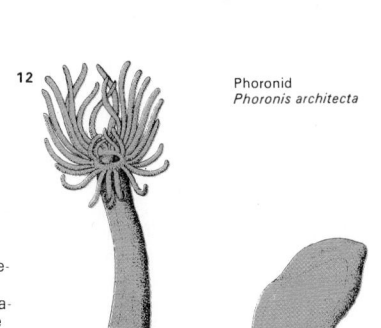

10 *Pedicellina cernua*

11 Rotifer *Trichotria tetractis*

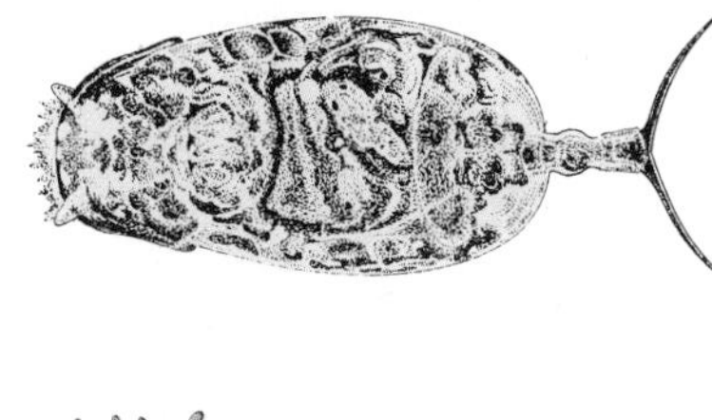

11 The rotifers, or "wheel" animalcules, are microscopic creatures found chiefly in fresh-water lakes and ponds. They belong to the phylum Rotifera. The head end has a ciliated crown that spins small organisms into the mouth.

13 *Moniliformis moniliformis*

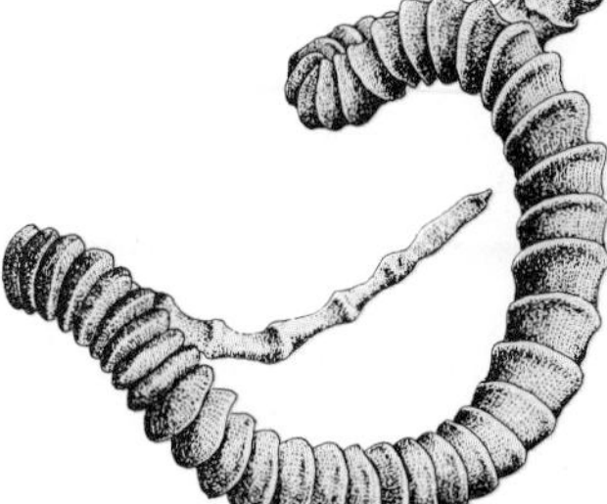

12 Phoronid *Phoronis architecta*

10 Pedicellina is a small sessile invertebrate that lives in the sea. It is only 0.1in (2.5mm) in height and lives attached by a short stalk to rocks, shells, and pieces of wood, or to other animals such as crabs and sponges. It is a member of a small phylum, the Endoprocta, and forms colonies that look like those of the coelenterate *Obelia*. A ring of up to 24 tentacles surrounding the "body," or calyx, is used for trapping food particles. The calyx contains the digestive and reproductive organs.

12 The phoronids are a group of sea dwelling, detritus-feeding worms of which only about 15 species are known. Most are less than 8 in (200 cm) long and live in tough tubes of chitin attached to rocks or buried completely in the sand.

13 Moniliformis is a parasitic invertebrate worm belonging to the phylum Acanthocephala (spiny-headed worms), a small group of animals consisting of about 600 species. All are parasites and all have simple bodies but complex life cycles involving several hosts, one of which is usually an insect. The primary hosts are vertebrates and may be freshwater or marine fish, birds, snakes, or rodents. Some of these parasites grow to 20 in (50 cm) but most average 2-5 in.

14

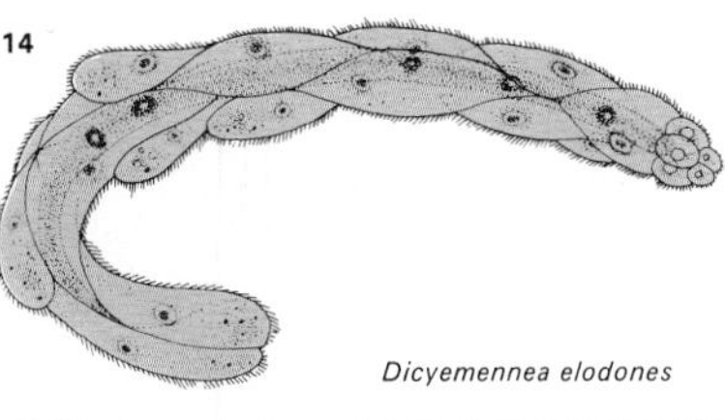

Dicyemennea elodones

14 Dicyemennea is a tiny parasitic invertebrate found mainly in cephalopod mollusks. Its body consists of one internal reproductive cell and 24 other cells. It belongs to the phylum Mesozoa.

16 Pogonophoran *Lamellisabella johanssoni*

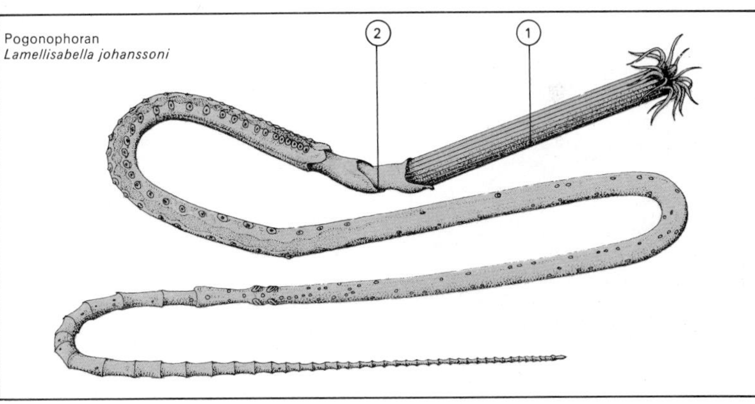

2
1

15 The lamp shells, marine invertebrates that superficially resemble mollusks, are grouped in the phylum Brachiopoda. They live attached to rocks or, like *Lingula*, buried in mud or sand. Modern brachiopods are mostly less than 2 in (5cm) across and number about 260 species but the group reached its height in the Devonian, some 370 million years ago. More than 30,000 fossil species have been found.

15 Lamp shell *Lingula anatina*

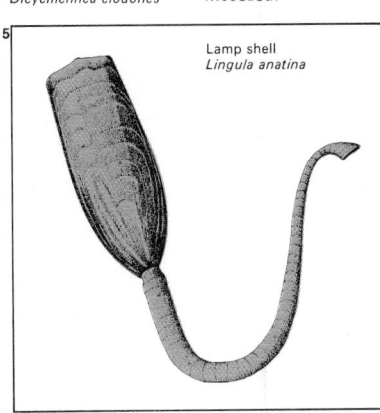

16 The pogonophorans inhabit chitinous tubes on the deep ocean bed. Their bodies are divided into three regions: The protosome [1], bearing tentacles, a short mesosome [2], and a long "trunk," or metasome. The first specimen was discovered in 1900, but the group was not accorded its own phylum until 1955. The 80 known species are from 2-14 in (5-35 cm) long.

17 Kinorhynch *Echinoderes dujardini*

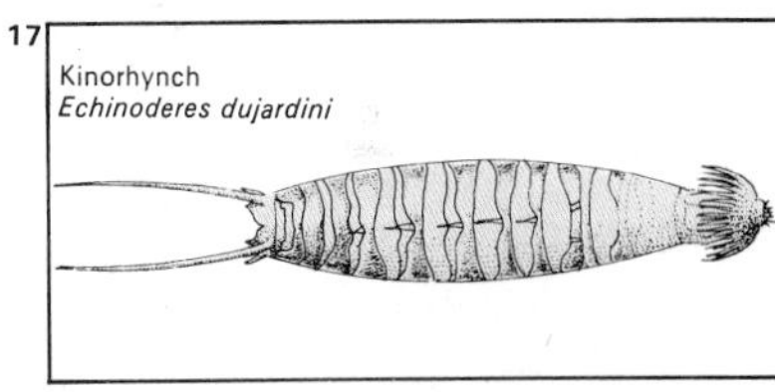

20 Radiolarian *Hexacontium* sp

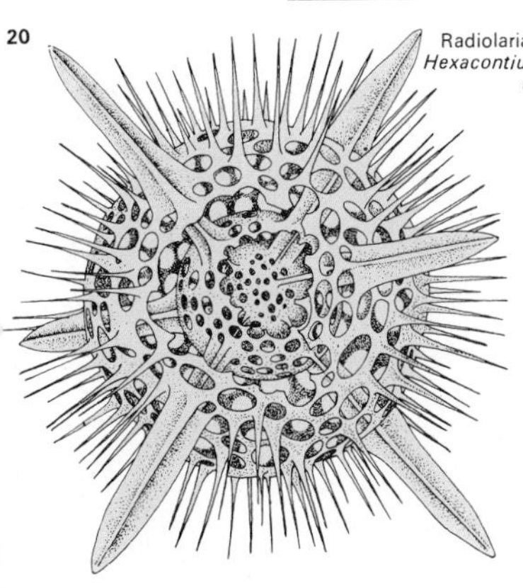

18

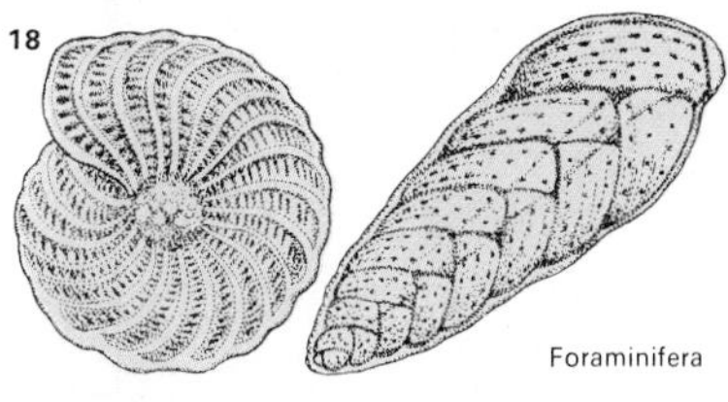

Foraminifera

18 The shells of Foraminifera, when enlarged, look like snail shells. In fact they are made by minute single-celled creatures that spend their lives among, and feed upon, diatoms.

17 The kinorhynchs are microscopic marine animals of the phylum Kinorhyncha. The cylindrical kinorhynch body is divided superficially into 13 joints, or zonites. The head is retractable and bears long spines. Biologists think that these creatures are close relations of the rotifers for, like them, they possess adhesive glands. Most kinorynchs are less then 0.04 in (1mm) long.

19 Venus's flower basket is a deep-sea sponge (phylum Porifera) that grows to 10 in (25cm) in length. The skeleton is of silica. A species of shrimp often lives trapped within the sponge's body.

19

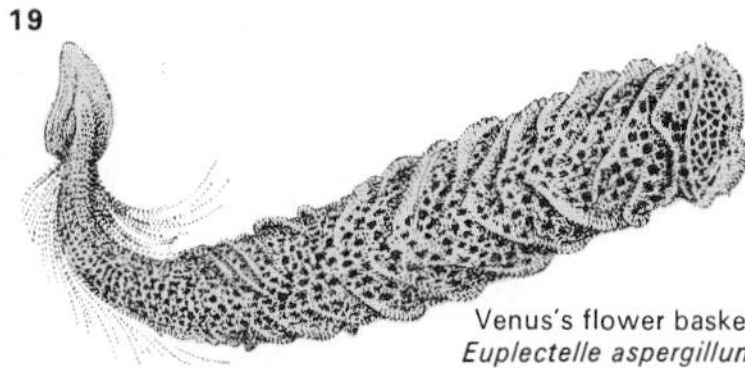

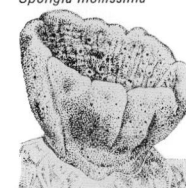

Venus's flower basket *Euplectelle aspergillum*

22 Calcareous sponge *Leucosolenia botryoides*

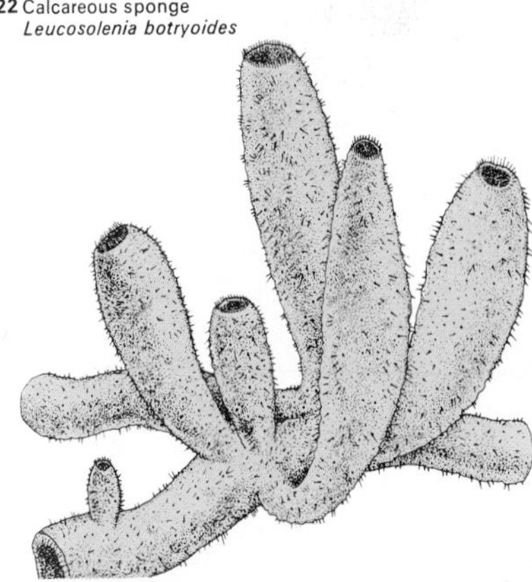

20 The radiolarian *Hexacontium* has an ornate skeleton composed of three concentric spheres that are pierced by hundreds of radiating spicules. The skeleton is very hard and made of silica. Radiolarians divide asexually simply by multiple splitting. These marine ameboid protozoans have existed for millions of years. Their fossil skeletons have been found in rocks of about 65 million years ago. Radiolarians capture food with pseudopods, flowing extensions of cytoplasm.

21 Bath sponge *Spongia mollissima*

21 The bath sponge is an inhabitant of warm seas such as the Caribbean and the Mediterranean. After harvesting, the sponge is dried, beaten, and washed to remove hard debris so that the only part remaining is the spongin "skeleton."

22 Shallow coastal water of the Atlantic is the home of this calcareous sponge. Its name is derived from its supporting skeleton, which is composed of calcium carbonate spicules. Each vase-shaped part is about 2 in (5cm) in height.

Threshold of the vertebrates

All animals with backbones, including man, are chordates. The essential feature that all chordates share, and after which they are named, is the notochord, a stiffening rod running the length of the body [Key]. Animals with backbones are known as vertebrates and are descended from a line of creatures that appear small and insignificant. These animals, the early chordates, possibly arose in the early Cambrian some 570 million years ago. Their exact ancestry is still a mystery, but they are probably related to echinoderms—the starfish and their relations.

Chordate characteristics

The chordate notochord is the forerunner of the backbone and is the basis for the attachment of segmentally arranged muscles, the myotomes. Above it lies a tubular nerve cord, the anterior, or "head," end of which is enlarged and folded to form a brain. In addition all true chordates show some evidence of paired gill openings and have a tail behind the anus. These features are often only apparent in the embryo.

The modern remnants of the early chordates, or protochordates, from which all the animals with backbones arose, are a few highly specialized "left overs" of a group that millennia ago was probably numerous and highly successful. These comparative rareties are classified in three subphyla known as the Hemichordata (the acorn worms), the Urochordata (the tunicates, or sea squirts) and the Cephalochordata (the lancelets, or amphioxi). The most primitive true vertebrates are hagfish and lampreys.

Acorn worms and sea squirts

The acorn worms, marine mud burrowers, are creatures whose physical make-up has some features of the echinoderms and some of the true chordates. Some acorn worms have the tubular nerve cord and most have gill slits, but the slits are used for feeding rather than breathing; and although acorn worms possess an internal structure that looks like a notochord, this is formed in the embryo in quite a different fashion from a true notochord. The adult worm may resemble a simple chordate but the larval stages of its development [6] are almost identical to those of starfish and sea urchins; this is evidence for citing the echinoderms as vertebrate ancestors.

Sea squirts [4, 13], peculiar saclike animals most of which spend their sedentary lives attached to the sea bottom, have few typically chordate features except for gill slits. It is the free-swimming sea squirt "tadpole larva" that reveals the sea squirt's place in the chordate line, for some zoologists argue that vertebrates may have arisen by a process (known as neoteny) in which the tadpole larva [Key] did not mature into an adult [7] but became sexually mature in its larval form.

The sea squirts are so called because many of them push out a jet of water when they are disturbed. Water is constantly drawn into and pushed out of the sea squirt body, and food and oxygen are removed in the process. The other popular name of "tunicate" comes from their inert cellulose sac, or tunic.

Of all the protochordates the lancelets are the most fascinating, because these

CONNECTIONS

See also
458 The animal kingdom
504 Starfish and sea urchins
512 The life of fish
460 Animal anatomy
564 Fossils without backbones
566 Fish and amphibians of the past
408 Evolution of life
410 The world before man

1

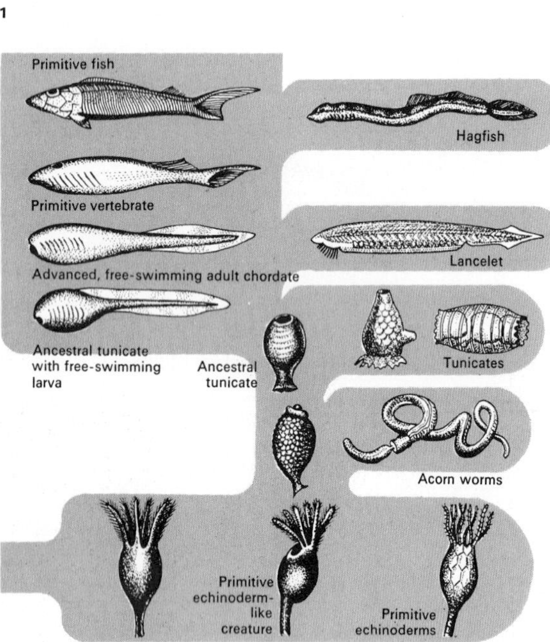

Primitive fish
Hagfish
Primitive vertebrate
Lancelet
Advanced, free-swimming adult chordate
Ancestral tunicate with free-swimming larva
Ancestral tunicate
Tunicates
Acorn worms
Primitive echinoderm-like creature
Primitive echinoderms

1 The exact course of early vertebrate evolution is impossible to trace but protochordates provide what clues there are. Similarities between larval acorn worms and echinoderms suggests that they descended from echinodermlike creatures. The tunicates may have been the first creatures to have gill slits, but a more significant step seems to have been the development of sex organs in tunicate "tadpole" larvae and of a notochord. Free-swimming adult chordates then appeared and the lancelet is most probably a side branch from the mainstream of evolution, which resulted in the fish, the first of the true vertebrates.

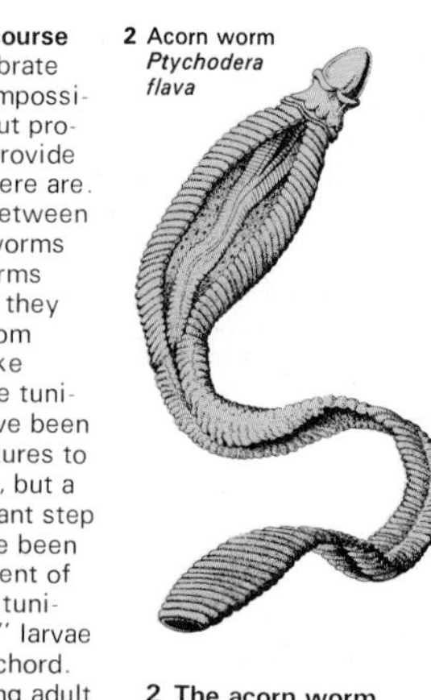

2 Acorn worm
Ptychodera flava

2 The acorn worm lives in mud and sand on the bottom of inshore marine waters, trapping detritus and plankton in its acorn-shaped proboscis. It is classified as a hemichordate, or enteropneust.

3

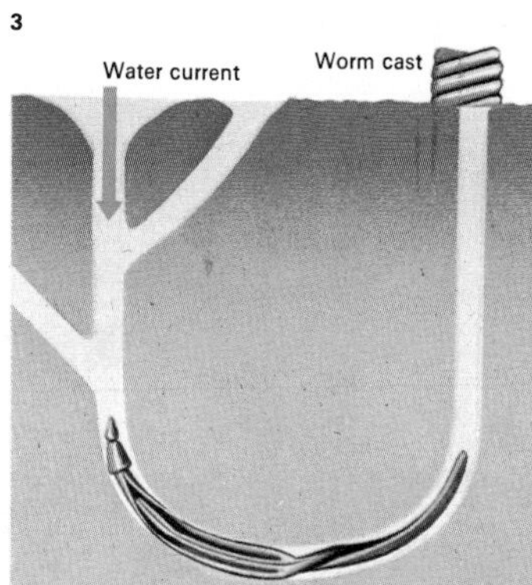

Water current
Worm cast

3 Worm casts on the beach can be made by burrowing acorn worms such as *Balanoglossus*. The worms live in tubes in the sand, the walls of which the worm secretes. As a result of its feeding habits the worm's alimentary tract becomes filled with sand and it is this that is discharged at low tide to form the familiar curled worm cast. Acorn worms vary from 0.75in (2cm) to 7.5ft (2.5m) long.

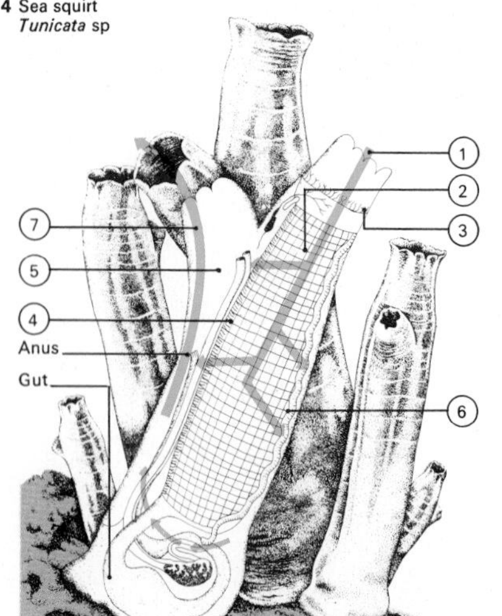

4 Sea squirt
Tunicata sp
1
2
3
7
5
4
Anus
Gut
6

4 The sedentary sea squirt feeds by a filter mechanism. Water containing food and oxygen is drawn in a steady stream through one siphon [1]. It then enters the pharynx [2] whose aperture is protected by a ring of tentacles [3]. The internal water current is created by hairlike cilia lining the gill slits [4] and passes through them into the atrium [5] and out via the atrial siphon [7]. Mucus, secreted by the endostyle [6], traps food particles. This mucus is then rolled into a rope and passed into the gut for digestion. The anus discharges waste into the atrial siphon.

5

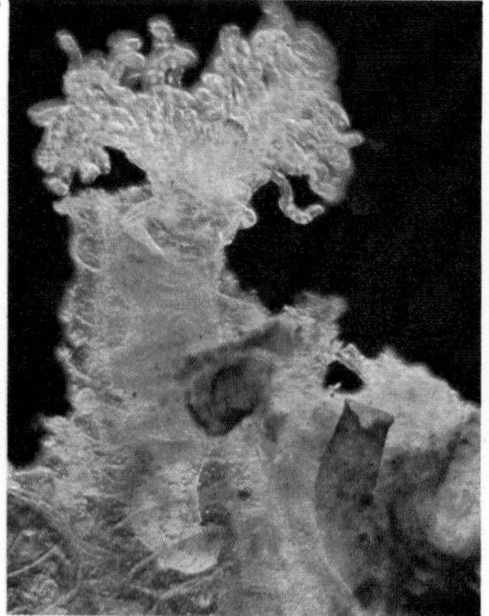

5 A branched tube is the home of each individual of *Rhabdopleura*, a colonial relative of the acorn worm. New individuals are produced by asexual budding from the creeping base of the animal, the stolon. *Rhabdopleura* is 0.20in (5mm) long.

6

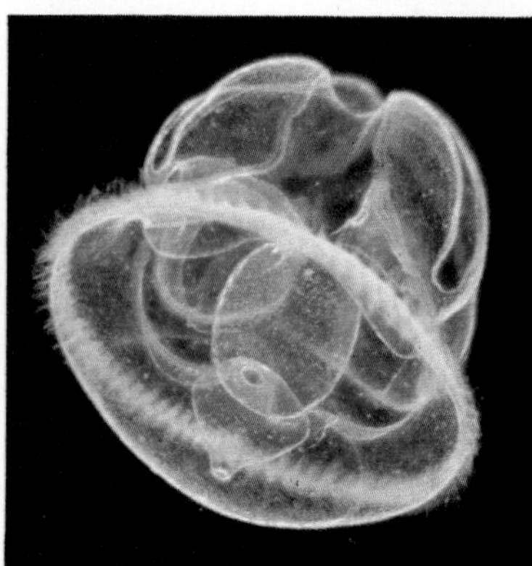

6 The larva of the acorn worm is known as a tornaria. This larva is one of the mainstays of the evidence that the early chordates, the vertebrate ancestors, evolved from echinoderms, for the tornaria is so like the larva of some starfish that for many years it was mistaken for one of them. The significant difference is that the tornaria has the gill clefts typical of chordates. The tornaria is part of the zooplankton and is seen here magnified more than 30 times in size.

small creatures, most of which are sand burrowers on the beaches of the warmer seas, have simple bodies bearing all the hallmarks of the chordates. Running nearly the whole distance from head to tail is a notochord below the typically hollow chordate nerve cord. Just behind the lancelet mouth on each side of the body lie more than 100 pairs of gill slits. These are used both for filtering food and for extracting oxygen from seawater. Like other protochordates the adult lancelet is the result of metamorphosis from a larva.

Hagfish and lampreys

The earliest true vertebrates to appear in the Ordovician period were fishlike creatures that were possibly ancestral to the hagfish [12] and lampreys [10]—the most primitive vertebrates known today. Neither the hagfish nor the lampreys have jaws, but both have a skeleton made of cartilage and have large notochords as well as gill slits. All lampreys and hagfish have tubular nerve cords lying above the "spine." The head of the lamprey bears organs of taste, smell, and hearing and well developed eyes, while the hagfish head has a cluster of sensory tentacles around the mouth but poorly developed eyes.

Hagfish and lampreys are far from the most attractive of fish, in looks and in habits. The hagfish are ocean scavengers, feeding on any dead or dying fish, crustaceans, or mollusks they can find. On locating a dead fish the hagfish actually enters it through the gills or anus and devours the body contents, leaving only skin and bones.

The world's species of lamprey can be divided into two groups according to their feeding habits. One group is parasitic and individuals attach themselves to their hosts with huge suckerlike mouths, break through the flesh with rasping teeth [11], and suck out the blood. When the lamprey has eaten its fill it releases its oral grip and in doing so may inflict a fatal wound. Free-living lampreys live only a few months. They feed normally as larvae but after metamorphosis the gut degenerates. The adult cannot feed and lives only long enough (4 to 11 months) to spawn.

KEY

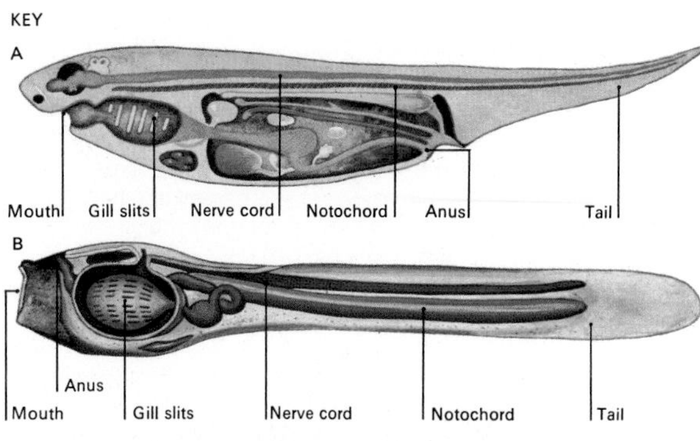
A
Mouth
Gill slits
Nerve cord
Notochord
Anus
Tail
B
Anus
Mouth
Gill slits
Nerve cord
Notochord
Tail

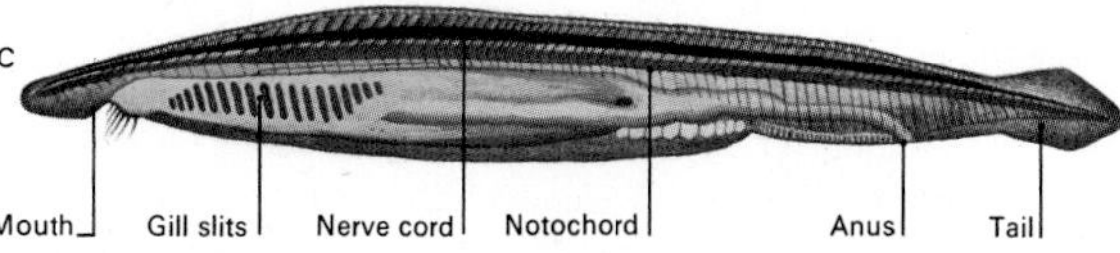
C
Mouth
Gill slits
Nerve cord
Notochord
Anus
Tail

All chordates conform, at some stage in their life cycle, to a generalized body plan [A]. This has a stiffening rod, the notochord, above which is situated a tubular nerve cord. Gill slits behind the mouth are used in respiration and there is a post-anal tail. In the sea squirt chordate features are obvious [B] in the "tadpole" larva's tail. The lancelet, or amphioxus [C], has all the chordate characteristics.

7 The adult sea squirt [C] is formed through metamorphosis of the "tadpole" larva, which attaches itself [A] to a firm substrate then undergoes gradual maturation [B] using the yolk [1] for food.

8 The lancelet, a resident of sandy shores in temperate and tropical seas, is placed in the subphylum Cephalochordata. It has a fishlike body but a notochord rather than a true backbone.

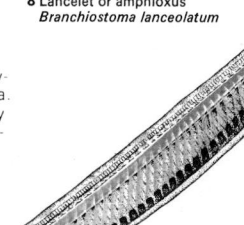

8 Lancelet or amphioxus *Branchiostoma lanceolatum*

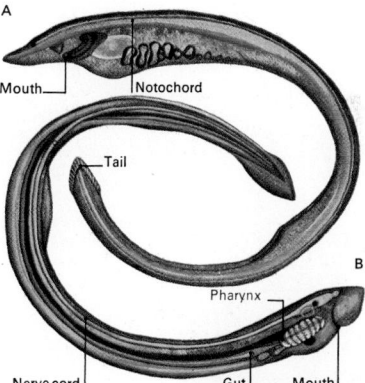

9 The ammocoete larva, the immature lamprey [B], is especially interesting because it resembles embryos of higher vertebrates. Unlike the larva of amphioxus [A] it has a heart, eyes, and ears as in vertebrate embryos, as well as such typical chordate features as the notochord. Until metamorphosis was observed this was thought to be a species quite distinct from the lamprey.

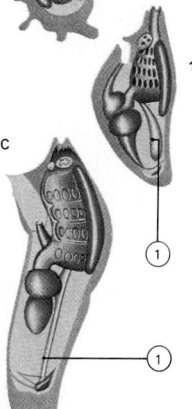

10

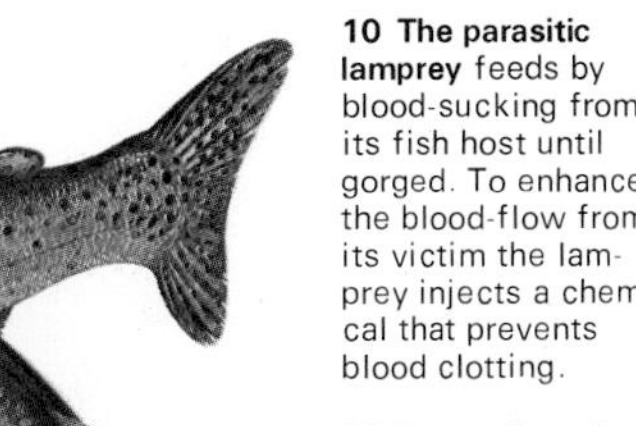

Trout *Salmo* sp

Lamprey *Petromyzon* sp

10 The parasitic lamprey feeds by blood-sucking from its fish host until gorged. To enhance the blood-flow from its victim the lamprey injects a chemical that prevents blood clotting.

11

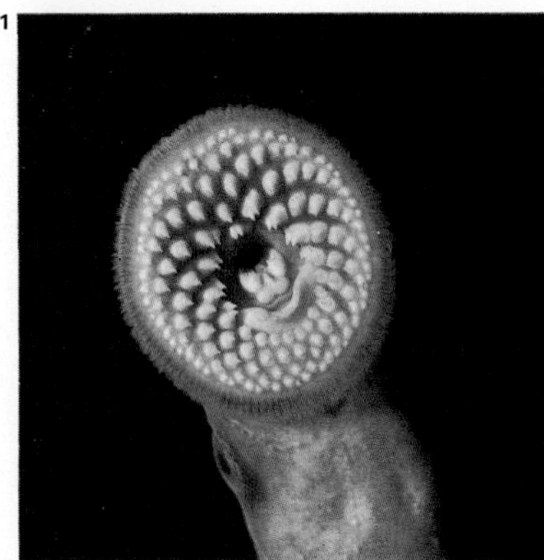

11 Rows of rasping teeth arm the inside of the lamprey's mouth. These are used to penetrate a fish's blood circulation while the perimeter of the mouth acts as a suction device.

12 Slime hag *Bdellostoma* sp

12 Hagfish scavenge the flesh of dead and dying fish using sucking mouths and rasping tongues. At the same time they produce vast quantities of mucus from pairs of slime glands and this is thought to protect the hag and to make its prey die more quickly. All the 21 known species of hagfish are marine and have retained the basic body organization of the first vertebrates, the jawless fish of 450 million years ago. They are among the most primitive vertebrates.

13

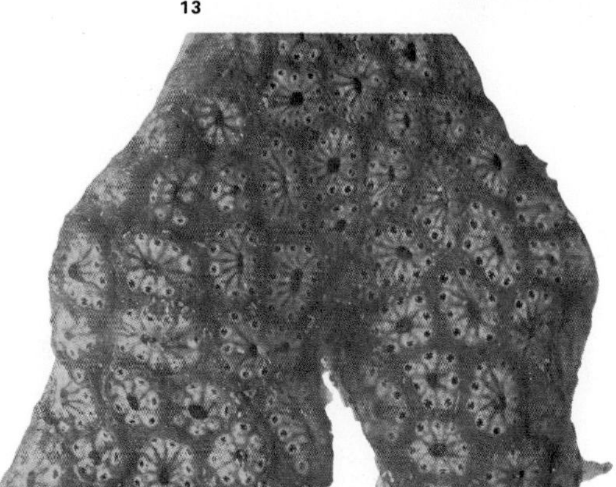

13 The star sea squirt *(Botryllus schlosseri)* is seen here encrusting the brown seaweed *Fucus:* This tunicate is a colonial species and classified in the subphylum Urochordata and the class Ascidiacea. The colony of tunicates may share the same body covering—the test or tunic that gives them their name. Several *Botryllus* individuals share one water exit, or exhalent siphon. Each exit is surrounded by 3 to 12 "petals," the inhalent siphons.

The classification of fish

Apart from the primitive jawless fish or Agnatha—hagfish and lampreys—all fish belong to one of two great classes: the cartilaginous fish, or Chondrichthyes, and the bony fish, or Osteichthyes.

Cartilaginous fish

On the evolutionary scale [Key] the cartilaginous fish are the more primitive of the two classes. They include the sharks, skates, and rays, and their skeletons are composed not of bone but of gristly cartilage. Some dwell on the sea bottom while others, notoriously ferocious predators, swim in mid and open waters.

There are about 620 species of cartilaginous fish, divided zoologically into three groups: the typical sharks (Elasmobranchii), the skates and rays (Batoidea), and a rather odd-looking group of uncertain ancestry, the chimaeras (Holocephali). A characteristic of most cartilaginous fish is the heterocercal tail whose top half is longer than the bottom [1].

Most sharks are fast-moving hunters and are by nature fish-eaters, but they will, in exceptional circumstances such as severe hunger, attack mammals, including humans. Skates and rays are found patrolling the ocean floor feeding on shellfish.

The largest of the cartilaginous fish are ironically the least ferocious and represent no threat to most of their undersea neighbors. The whale shark, which reaches a length of 60ft (18m), the basking shark 46ft (14m), and the awesome manta ray, which has a "wing span" of 20ft (6m), feed only on plankton and other minute marine animals. For all their immense size the whale and basking sharks feed on small creatures and have comblike structures on their gills through which they strain their food.

Most cartilaginous fish, such as the blue shark and smooth dogfish, give birth to live young, but some lay large, yolky eggs which, before being laid, are individually encased in a tough, leathery cover. After the eggs have hatched, the empty cases can often be found on the seashore and are popularly known as "mermaids' purses" Fertilization is internal and the male has modified pelvic fins, a portion of which, the claspers, conduct sperm into the female during mating.

All cartilaginous fish, with the exception of sawfish and some species of ray, live in the sea. By contrast the 20,000 species of bony fish are found in both sea and fresh water throughout the world.

Classification of bony fish

Bony fish belong to two subclasses, the Crossopterygii and the Actinopterygii. Very few of the former have survived to modern times, for they are at the base of the evolutionary branch that led to land animals. The best known of them is the coelacanth *(Latimeria)* [2], which was believed to be extinct until one was fished up from off the African coast in 1938. Its lobed fins have fleshy bases that actually look like the beginning of a limb. The other surviving crossopterygians are the lungfish [3], which can breathe air into a primitive version of lungs. They belong to the order Dipnoi and are found in tropical conditions.

The Actinopterygii are the typical modern ray-finned fish. The most primitive,

CONNECTIONS

See also
512 The life of fish
514 Unusual fish
516 Fish of seas and rivers
458 The animal kingdom
508 Threshold of the vertebrates
460 Animal anatomy
566 Fish and amphibians of the past
632 Endangered species
624 Life in the oceans
626 Animals of the ocean

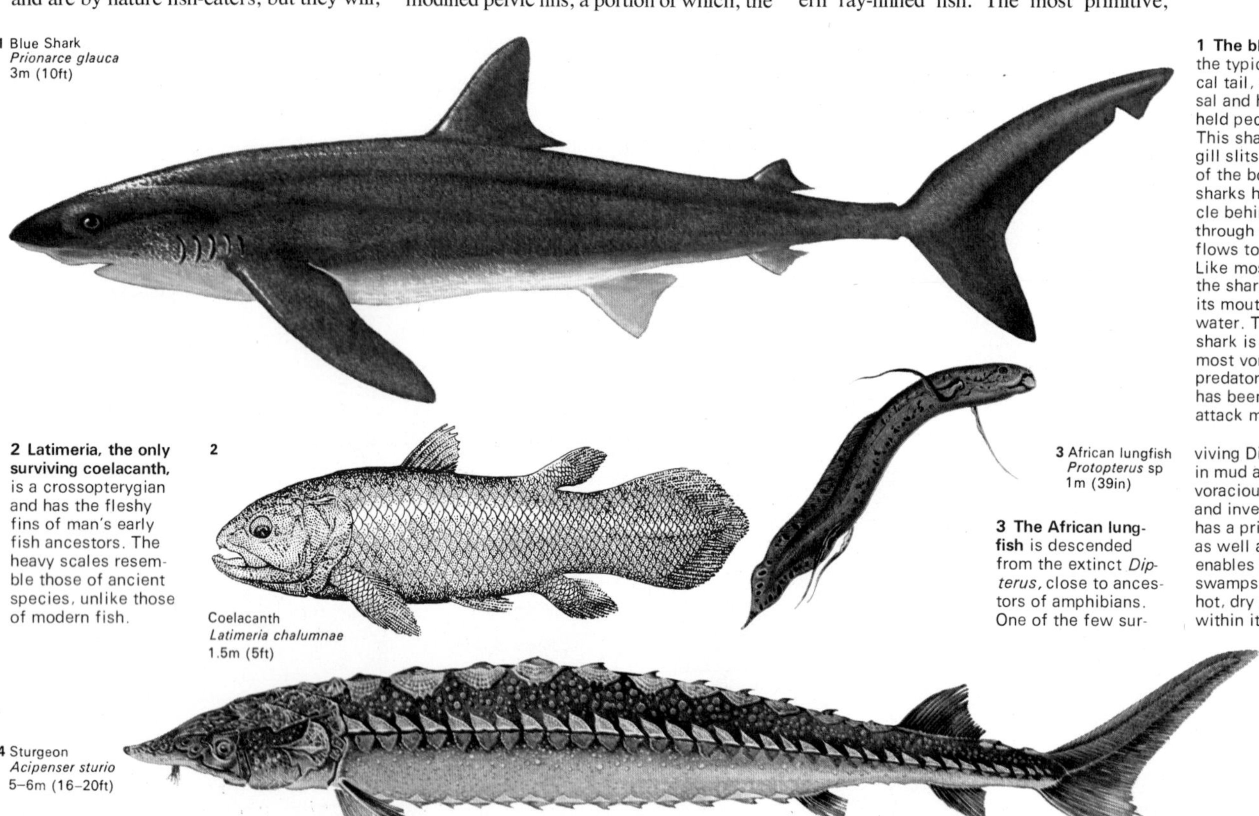
1 Blue Shark
Prionarce glauca
3m (10ft)
2
Coelacanth
Latimeria chalumnae
1.5m (5ft)
3 African lungfish
Protopterus sp
1m (39in)
4 Sturgeon
Acipenser sturio
5–6m (16–20ft)

1 The blue shark has the typical heterocercal tail, pointed dorsal and horizontally held pectoral fins. This shark has five gill slits in each side of the body. Many sharks have a spiracle behind each eye, through which water flows to the gills. Like most other fish, the shark also uses its mouth to take in water. The blue shark is among the most voracious of all predatory fish, and has been known to attack mammals.

2 Latimeria, the only surviving coelacanth, is a crossopterygian and has the fleshy fins of man's early fish ancestors. The heavy scales resemble those of ancient species, unlike those of modern fish.

3 The African lungfish is descended from the extinct *Dipterus,* close to ancestors of amphibians. One of the few surviving Dipnoi, it lives in mud and feeds voraciously on fish and invertebrates. It has a primitive lung as well as gills. This enables it to live in swamps and survive hot, dry summers within its cocoon.

4 The Atlantic sturgeon belongs to the Chondrostei, the most primitive group of actinopterygians, or ray-finned fish. Its heterocercal tail and cartilaginous skeleton are reminiscent of the shark's. Some species also have a spiracle. Its scales are shiny and large (known as ganoid) like those of the early bony fish. The sturgeon is not a fierce fish; it swims at the bottom of the sea, snuffling out invertebrate food with its long, sensitive snout, or rostrum. The adult fish swims up the river to lay its much-prized eggs. Caviar is processed from the ovary before the fish can spawn.

5 The alligator gar belongs to the Holostei, a group of actinopterygians that lived in the Triassic 225 million years ago. Its thick scales probably differ little from those of its ancestors. Like them, it has a short, symmetrical tail that is a forerunner of the homocercal tail of teleosts. The gar feeds on small fish, which it catches with its well-developed lower jaw. The alligator gar travels along the surface of the water using its tail like a propeller.

5 Alligator gar
Lepisosteus spatula
3m (10ft)

which are also the most sharklike of the bony fish, belong to the infraclass Chondrostei. They share some characteristics with the cartilaginous fish, such as the heterocercal shape of the tail, and they are bottom-dwelling scavengers. But their eggs, unlike those of the cartilaginous fish, are small and fertilized externally. This group includes the highly prized sturgeon [4], a fish whose eggs are the source of caviar.

The infraclass Holostei, including the bowfin and garfish [5], now contains only the freshwater remnants of a once large seawater group. Its members are fast swimmers, usually with truncated heterocercal tails.

The largest group of ray-finned fish are the members of the infraclass Teleostei. They are the culmination of the evolutionary line and seem to be perfectly adapted to life in water. Their tails are completely symmetrical and with the buoyancy imparted by their swim bladders they do not need rigid paired fins. Many species have developed a streamlined form for maximum speed and minimum friction while swimming, but the locomotion of each type of teleost is adapted to its mode of life. Thus the flatfish "creep" along the sea bottom while the pike is built for speed.

Diverse modern bony fish

Teleosts have probably evolved along three main lines to give rise to eight super orders of living fish. The first line includes the eels (Elopomorpha) [9] and the prolific herring (Clupeomorpha). The second line consists of peculiar tropical freshwater fish (Osteoglossomorpha). The salmon and trout (Protacanthopterygii) [6] belong to the most primitive group of the third line while most freshwater fish, including carp and roach, belong to a more advanced group, the Ostariophysi [7]. The cod and angler fish (Paracanthopterygii) and exotic creatures such as flying fish (Atherinomorpha) are also advanced groups, but the final superorder, the Acanthopterygii, whose members are typically fish with spiny fins, is much the largest and most diverse. It includes the stickleback [8] and the seahorses, the perch, mackerel, flatfish, and puffer fish.

KEY
Cyclostomata
Holocephali
Elasmobranchii
Batoidea
Crossopterygii
Chondrostei
Holostei
Teleostei
Agnatha
Chondrichthyes
Osteichthyes
Actinopterygii

Living fish are classified into two major groups, or classes, and one minor one. The smallest group is the Agnatha, the primitive jawless fish, which includes, the modern lampreys and hagfish. From these evolved the cartilaginous fish, the Chondrichthyes, which are further divided into three subclasses. About 400 million years ago the second large group, the bony fish, or Osteichthyes, branched from the cartilaginous fish. Most modern fish are classified in the subclass Actinopterygii, the main subdivision of the Osteichthyes. The Actinopterygii is made up of three infraclasses, the largest of them being the infraclass Teleostei.

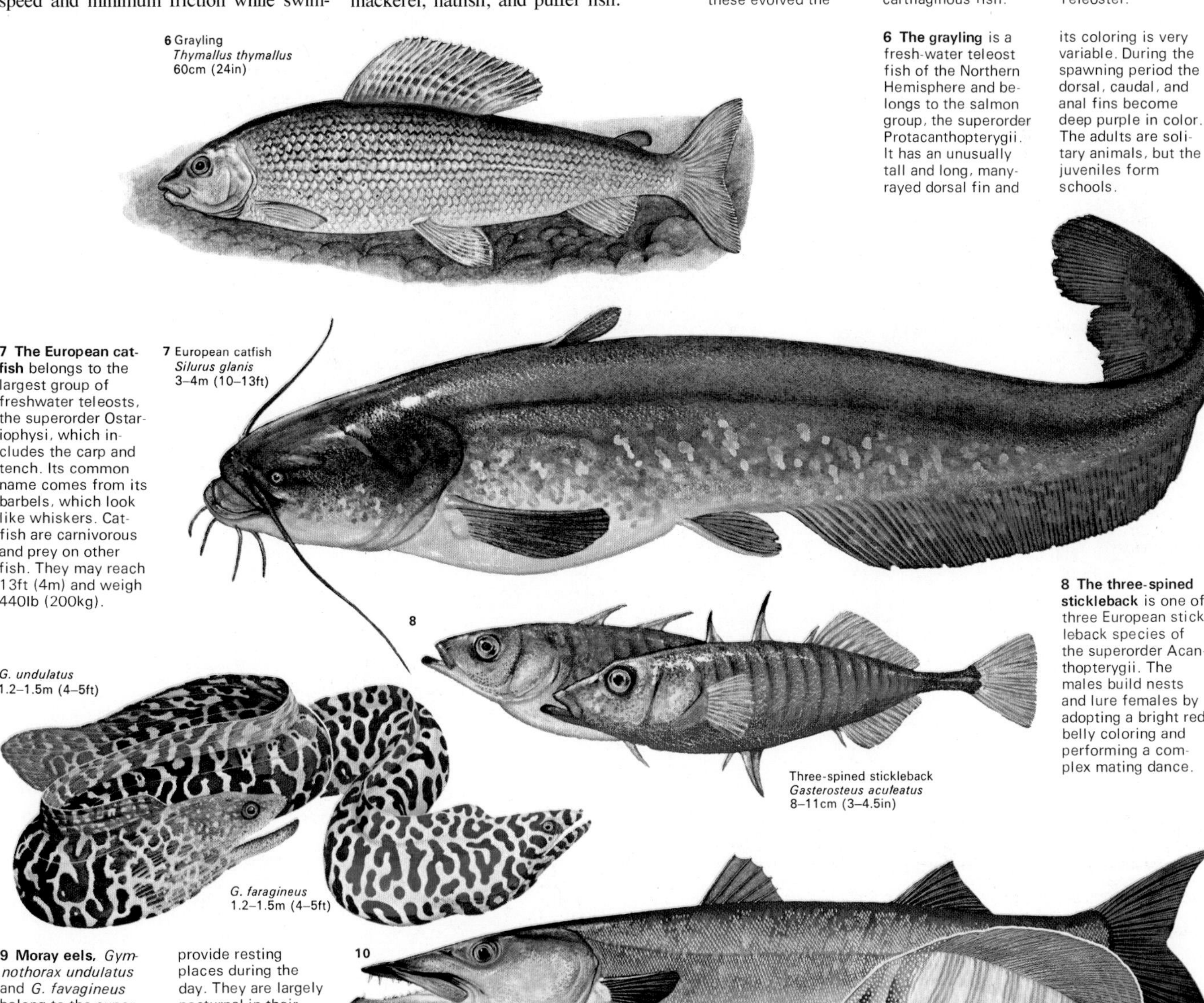

6 Grayling *Thymallus thymallus* 60cm (24in)

6 The grayling is a fresh-water teleost fish of the Northern Hemisphere and belongs to the salmon group, the superorder Protacanthopterygii. It has an unusually tall and long, many-rayed dorsal fin and its coloring is very variable. During the spawning period the dorsal, caudal, and anal fins become deep purple in color. The adults are solitary animals, but the juveniles form schools.

7 European catfish *Silurus glanis* 3–4m (10–13ft)

7 The European catfish belongs to the largest group of freshwater teleosts, the superorder Ostariophysi, which includes the carp and tench. Its common name comes from its barbels, which look like whiskers. Catfish are carnivorous and prey on other fish. They may reach 13ft (4m) and weigh 440lb (200kg).

8 Three-spined stickleback *Gasterosteus aculeatus* 8–11cm (3–4.5in)

8 The three-spined stickleback is one of three European stickleback species of the superorder Acanthopterygii. The males build nests and lure females by adopting a bright red belly coloring and performing a complex mating dance.

9 *G. undulatus* 1.2–1.5m (4–5ft)

G. faragineus 1.2–1.5m (4–5ft)

9 Moray eels, *Gymnothorax undulatus* and *G. favagineus* belong to the superorder Elopomorpha, which includes the congers, the largest of the eels. Moray eels are found in all tropical seas and favor rocks and areas of broken ground that provide resting places during the day. They are largely nocturnal in their habits and seldom move during the day except to poke their heads out of their hiding places and snap at passing prey. They can inflict severe bites.

10 Northern barracuda *Sphyraena borealis* 45cm (18in)

Sail-finned surgeon fish *Zebrasoma veliferum* 30cm (12in)

10 The northern barracuda and a sail-finned surgeon fish appear to have little in common, but both are members of the highly advanced order Perciformes, the largest order of spiny-finned fish.

The life of fish

Fish can be thought of as the most successful of the vertebrates, the animals with backbones. They are not only more numerous than all other vertebrates, but there are also more species of fish—probably not less than 23,000 of them. Fish vary widely in shape and habits. Some live in seawater and some in fresh; some lurk in the depths while others swim just below the surface; some feed peacefully on seaweed or plankton and some on marine invertebrates and many are aggressive predators that feed on other fish or even on amphibians or land animals.

The bodies of fish

All fish breathe by pumping water past their gossamer-thin gills [4], whose numerous folds offer a large surface area for the intake of oxygen in exchange for waste carbon dioxide. Water is pumped by movements of the mouth and pharynx and, in bony fish, by the opercula (gill covers).

The typical fish shape has evolved over millions of years to allow for maximum speed and agility in the water. The most predatory of the bony fish are the best swimmers; they can cruise at speeds of between three and six times their body length per second and can turn within one body length. The evolutionary breakthrough for the bony fish came with the development of air bladders to keep them afloat. The cartilaginous fish such as sharks, whose skeletons are composed of "gristle," or cartilage, instead of bone, do not have air bladders and sink if they stop swimming. Their "shoulder," or pectoral, fins give them lift, but many cartilaginous fish have become bottom-dwellers. The bony fish, however, released from the constant need for lift, can use their pectorals as brakes or paddles for swimming backwards; this adds to their flexibility in movement and allows them to feed in a much greater diversity of niches.

Fish vary greatly in speed and staying power and their different abilities are reflected in their muscle proteins. As a result, red meat comes from fast swimmers such as tuna, or powerful fish with endurance such as migrating salmon, and white meat from slow-moving flatfish such as sole.

Modern fish also have the advantage of having shed the protective heavy armor of their ancestors. Cartilaginous fish, being predators, have no need of such armor and have developed, instead, a tough, abrasive skin. In bony fish the armor has been refined into the familiar light, delicate coat of overlapping scales that protects the fish without hampering its movements.

The senses of fish

For coordination of movement when hunting, fleeing, or schooling (for mutual protection), a highly developed set of receptors has evolved that keeps fish informed of their environment. Sharks, for example, have an acute sense of smell for locating prey. Most fish have keen eyesight and react readily to the yellows and greens of their watery world. Many have good hearing, which is used socially to pick up mating or schooling noises, or sometimes as part of a kind of echolocation system in which the fish's own sounds help in the detection of objects in the water. The hearing mechanism forms part of the labyrinth, an organ essential to all fish,

CONNECTIONS

See also
510 The classification of fish
514 Unusual fish
516 Fish of seas and rivers
624 Life in the oceans
626 Animals of the ocean
508 Threshold of the vertebrates
566 Fish and amphibians of the past
1496 Pressure and flow
692 Breathing and the lungs
616 Lakes and rivers

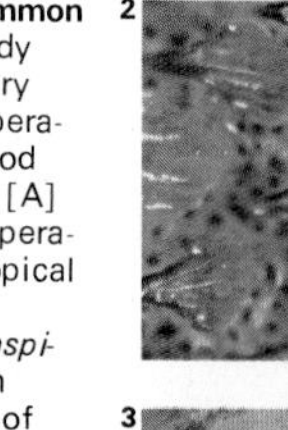

1 Fish share common features, but body temperatures vary with water temperature. Thus the cod *(Gadus morhua)* [A] has a lower temperature than the tropical triggerfish *(Balistoides conspicillum)* [B]. Fish swim by means of muscular bodies and tails such as those of the American eel *(Anguilla rostrata)* [C], and by fins as can be observed in the trunkfish *(Lactophrys triqueter)* [D]. The mudskipper *(Periophthalmus chrysospilos)* [E] has specialized pectoral fins for moving across the mud. Gills, that appear as five paired openings in the ray *(Raja clavata)* and the dogfish *(Scyliorhinus caniculus)* [F], are used for breathing. Typical bony fish (Teleosts), such as the cichlid *(Labeotropheus fulleborni)* [G], have skin covered with bony scales. Most fish lay eggs; the herring *(Clupea harengus)* [H] probably lays 50,000 at a time.

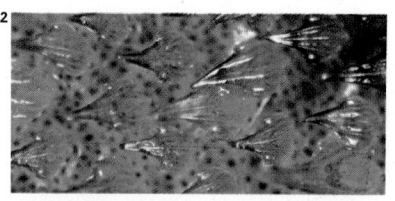

2 Fish with gristly skeletons, such as sharks, have tough, flexible skins. The scattered, thornlike scales (denticles) that grow on their skin are similar in structure to the teeth lining their jaws.

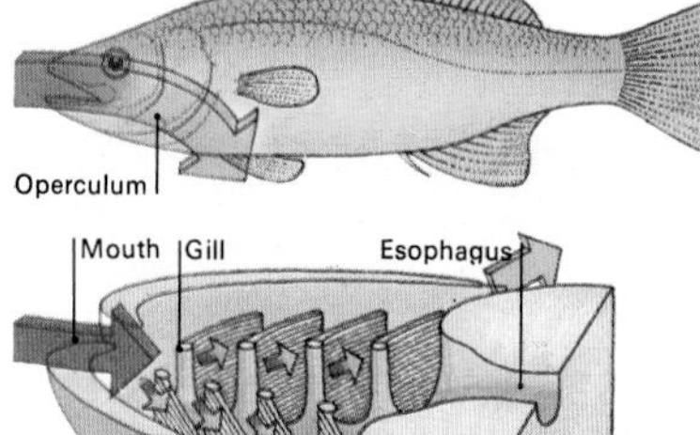

3 Bony fish have thin, overlapping cycloid or ctenoid scales that protect them from predators but do not hamper movement. Ctenoid scales have spines on the rear edge for extra protection.

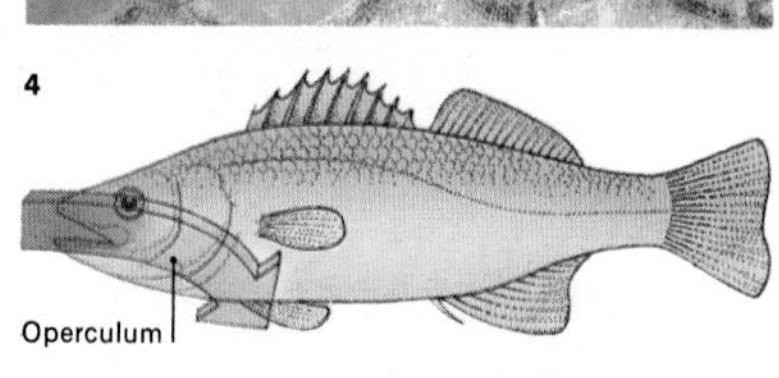
Operculum

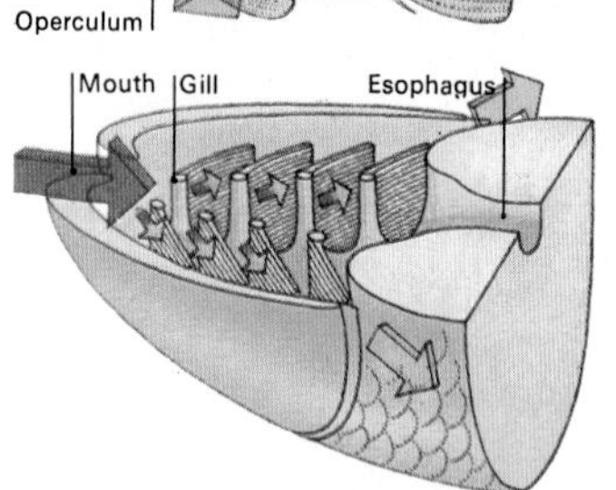
Mouth
Gill
Esophagus

4 Gills are the breathing organs of most fish. When a fish breathes it opens its mouth, draws in water, then shuts its mouth again. This forces a continuous stream of water [arrowed] through the gill slits, over the gills, and out into the surrounding water. Oxygen from the water is absorbed into blood vessels in the gills while carbon dioxide is carried out by the water expelled through the gills.

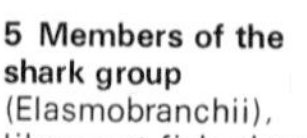

5 Members of the shark group (Elasmobranchii), like most fish, thrust through the water by means of a wave of muscular contraction that spreads down the body. Up to 40 percent of this thrust may be supplied by the tail, which also helps to keep the fish swimming in a straight line.

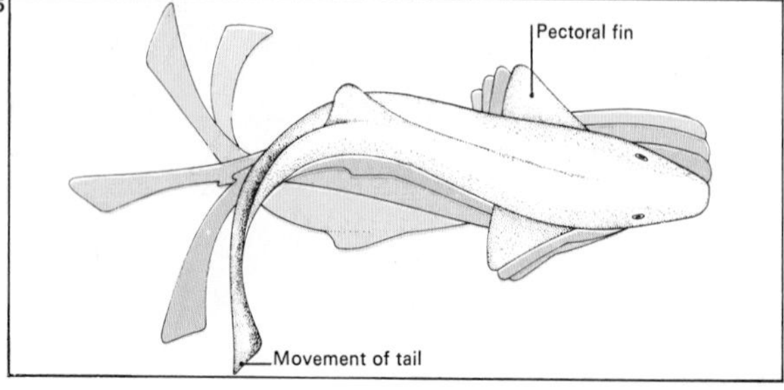
Pectoral fin
Movement of tail

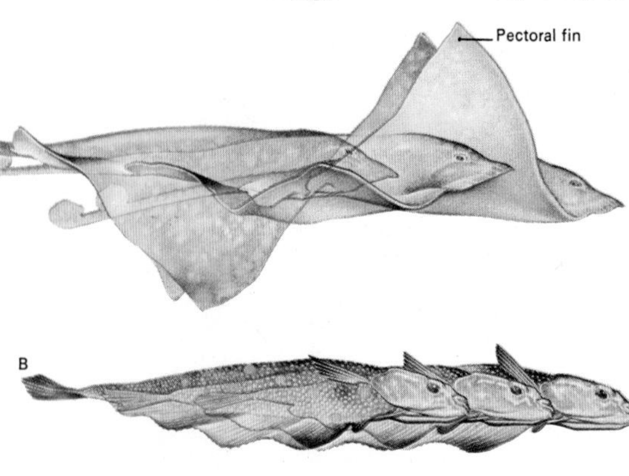
Pectoral fin
A
B

6 Bottom-dwelling fish are much poorer swimmers than their more streamlined cousins. Most are sedentary bottom-feeders relying on camouflage for protection. If threatened, rays [A] swim by flapping their pectoral fins and flatfish [B] by undulating their dorsal and anal fins.

hat signals position in space and angular acceleration and is crucial to the fish's balance vhen swimming. Fish also possess a unique rgan that puzzled land-dwelling man for a ong time. This is the so-called lateral line 10], that works on a similar principle to the ertebrate ear, but instead of detecting ound waves in air it picks up pressure vaves due to movement in water. This rgan gives the fish a kind of "distant touch ense" for objects that are moving at a disance.

All this information is pooled in the cenral nervous system where special centers re built onto the basic brain regions [11] hat deal with automatic functions such as espiration and heartbeat. The ears, abyrinth, and lateral line are linked to the indbrain by the cranial nerves. The large lfactory bulb, the organ of "smell," or hemical reception, is joined to the cererum in the forebrain. Chemoreception is hought to be very important to fish for uccessful navigation, feeding, and mating. The most advanced part of a fish's brain, where behavior that has been learned is controlled, is the optic lobe, which is connected to the eyes. The cerebellum has the task of coordinating sensory information for the fine control of movement.

How fish reproduce

Fish use various methods of reproduction [12]. Some reproduce by fertilizing eggs within the body; in some fish the female first lays the eggs and these are then fertilized by the male outside the body; and a few fish are hermaphrodites. But whatever their method of reproduction, fish are enormously prolific. A cod may produce eight million eggs at a time, and most fish produce tens of thousands. The young are usually microscopic and exist at first in the form of animal plankton. Most of them perish before reaching adulthood, but nevertheless many survive. Scientists have estimated, for example, that there are about a trillion herrings in the Atlantic. The teeming seas not only signify the tremendous success of the fish as an animal, but also provide a rich and in many areas, an often vital source of protein for man.

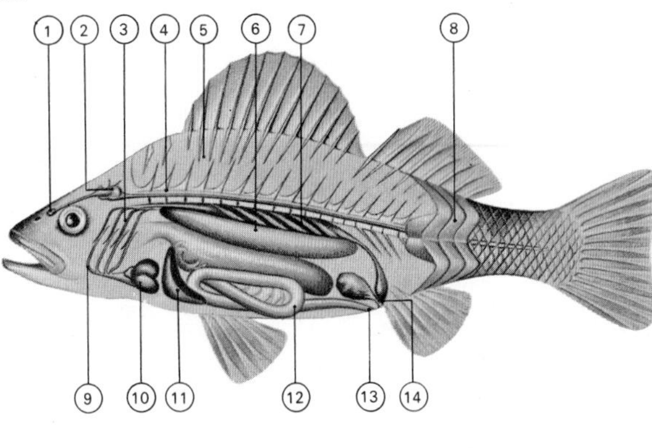
KEY

Fish, the first of the vertebrates, have a backbone [4] that keeps the body rigid against the powerful contractions of the muscles (myotomes) [8] during movement. Fins are based on supporting rods [5] that may be made of cartilage or formed from modified scales. A bony fish has an air bladder [6] above the gut [12]. The ventral aorta [9] takes blood to the branchial arteries [3] which are protected by the opercula. The brain [2] is quite well developed and the olfactory bulb [1] is particularly prominent in sharks. The kidneys [7] lie paired under the vertebral column. The liver [11] is located behind the heart [10]. The gut empties at the anus [13] just in front of the urogenital opening [14].

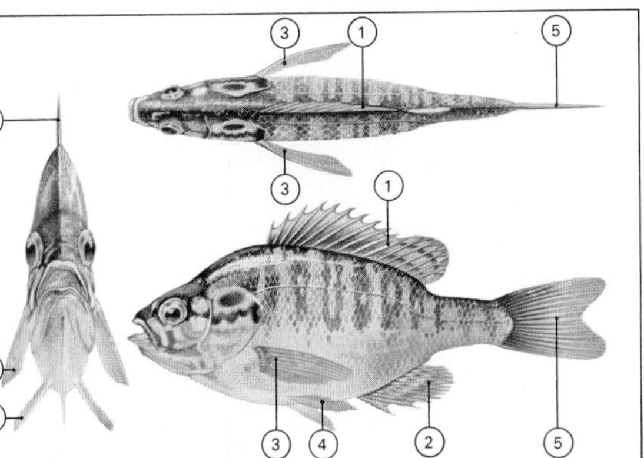

7 The fins of bony fish serve as fine controls for movement. The dorsal [1] and anal [2] fins prevent rolling. The pectoral fins [3] often serve as brakes, and the pelvic fins [4] control a tendency to pitch upward as the fish slows down. The paired fins also control rising and diving. They are used to produce rolling movements. The caudal [5], or tail, fin serves as an efficient propeller.

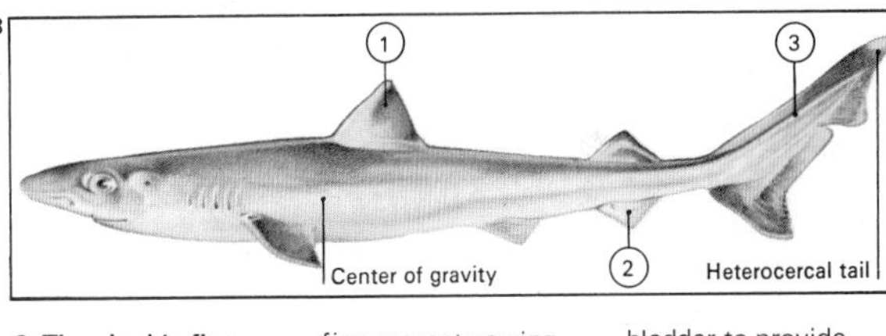
Center of gravity
Heterocercal tail

8 The shark's fins serve to stabilize its body as it swims. The dorsal [1], anal [2], and caudal [3] fins prevent yawing (deviating off course). Most important for the sharklike fish, which have no air-bladder to provide buoyancy, are the tail and the pectoral fins, which give lift and keep the nose level.

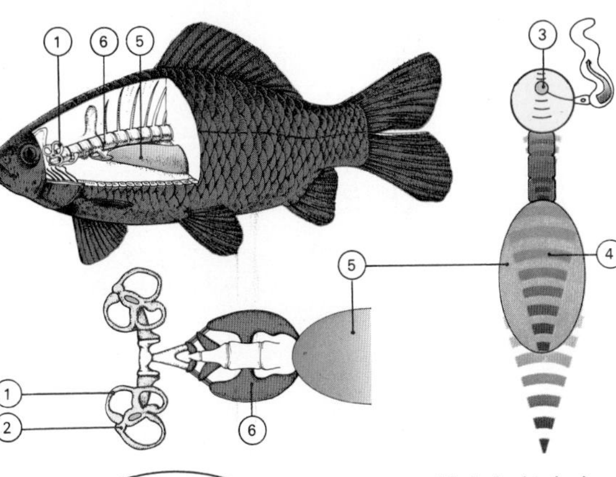
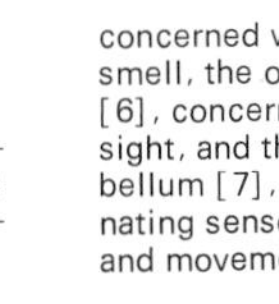

9 The ear of a fish serves for hearing and for positional sense. The fluid in three semicircular canals [1] shifts in response to changes in movement and transmits this to three ampullae [2]. There sensory cells that transmit the message to the central nervous system are stimulated. For hearing, otoliths [3] are moved by sound waves [4] from the air bladder [5], transmitted in some by an ossicle chain [6].

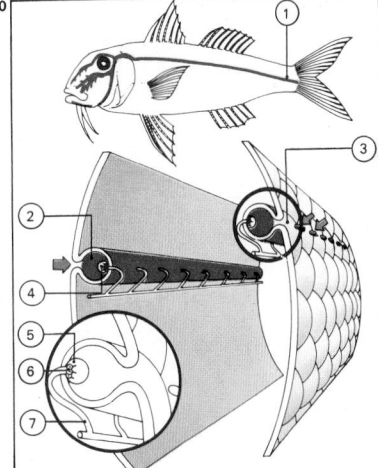

10 The lateral line organs [1] transmit information about the movement of water to the fish brain. The lateral line itself (shown on a red mullet) runs from head to tail on either side of the fish. It consists of a fluid-filled canal [2] with pores [arrowed] opening to the water through scales [3]. Behind each pore is a sensory organ, the neuromast [4]. This is made up of a gelatinous mass, the cupula [5], with a cluster of sensory hair cells [6] whose fibers combine in a nerve [7] running to the brain.

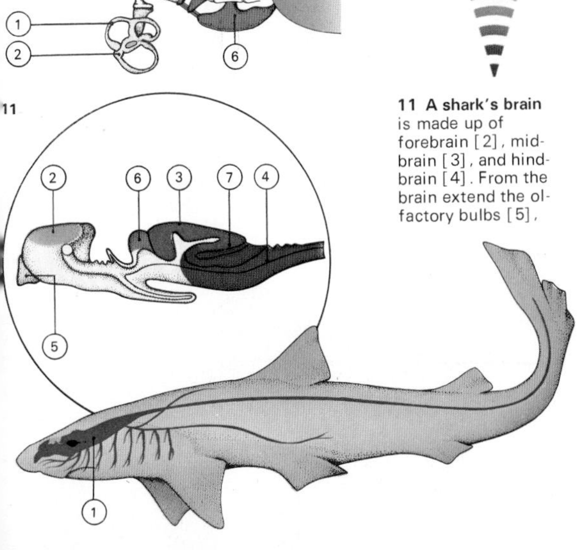

11 A shark's brain is made up of forebrain [2], midbrain [3], and hindbrain [4]. From the brain extend the olfactory bulbs [5], concerned with smell, the optic lobes [6], concerned with sight, and the cerebellum [7], coordinating sensory input and movement.

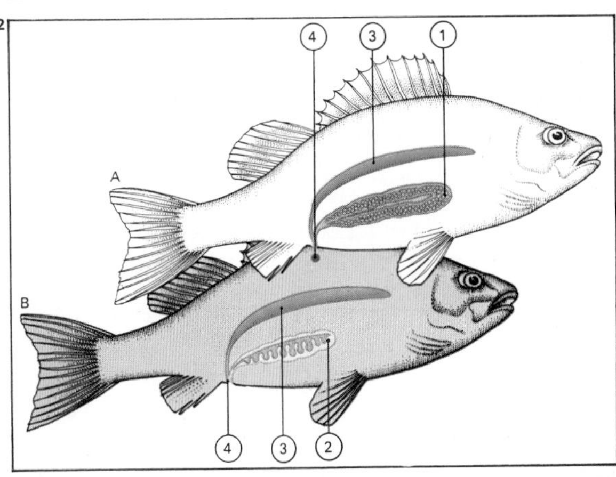
A
B

12 The reproductive organs of the perch are typical of bony fish. The ovary [1] of the female [A] and the testis [2] of the male [B] are entirely separate from the kidney [3] but expel their products through the same opening, the cloaca [4]. The eggs are fertilized outside the female's body.

Unusual fish

Fish have evolved, over a period of 400 million years, an amazing variety of special adaptations to the different environments in which they live. Some of the deep-sea fish—those that lurk at least 9,850ft (3,000m) down in the abyssal depths—display the most bizarre shapes. In contrast the tropical fish of the coral reefs [1] have some of the most brilliant coloring to be found anywhere in the animal kingdom. Each peculiarity, ugly or beautiful to human eyes, has its own significance to the fish.

Defense and attack

Deep-sea fish have two special problems: the high density of water more than 600ft (180m) down, which they overcome by having a lightweight skeleton; and the gloom, which, for many, is adequately coped with by the possession of luminous organs. Some fish provide their own luminosity through photophores, which are modified mucus glands. But others use light from luminous bacteria that colonize certain organs located where the fish can reveal them, for example, by a fold of skin. Luminous organs are exploited by abyssal fish to attract not only members of the same species and opposite sex but also other species on which they feed.

Many deep-sea fish have weak jaws with large teeth, in contrast to some of the coral reef fish that have powerful armored jaws. One group of these, the parrot fish, bites off chunks of coral, which are ground up and expelled, after passing through the gut, as a cloud of chalk dust. The vivid iridescent colors of these fish are made up from the interplay of a few pigments—black, red, orange, or yellow. This remarkable range of colors is involved in sexual display, but poisonous species may also use coloration as a warning to predators.

A notoriously voracious predator is the small piranha [9], which has formidable teeth and an aggressive temperament so that it actually poses a threat to species as large as man. The puffer fish [3] protects itself, as its name suggests, by puffing itself up in order to appear twice its real size and perhaps to deter attempts by other species to swallow it.

The puffer manages a temporary change in its shape by a special adaptation of its gullet, but many fish, such as the seahorse [6], have evolved more profound and permanent adaptive changes in form. A fairly typical feature of bottom-dwelling deep-sea fish is the possession of a long thin tail, which, by increasing the length of the lateral line, helps the fish detect prey more easily. At the other end of the scale is the flying fish [2]. The spectacular adaptation of its pectoral fins allows it to glide for several yards through the air when propelled from the water by its tail.

Adaptations of the sexes

Sometimes through evolution of form, the two sexes of one fish species become very different. The most grotesque example of such sexual dimorphism is that of the deep-sea anglerfish *Photocorynus* in which the male never grows larger than about 4in (10cm) and leads a parasitic life permanently attached to the female [5]. The virtue of this arrangement is that the female in a sparse population does not have to scour the dark

CONNECTIONS

See also
512 The life of fish
510 The classification of fish
516 Fish of seas and rivers
626 Animals of the ocean
632 Endangered species
616 Lakes and rivers
618 Wetlands: marshes and swamps
620 Salt marshes and coastal swamps

1 The fish of tropical coral reefs are often brightly colored. Many, such as the moorish idol *(Zanclus canescens)* [A] and the longnose butterfly fish *(Chelmon rostratus)* [D], are striped for camouflage. The forceps fish *(Forcipiger longirostris)* [E] has false, rear "eyes" to confuse predators such as the triggerfish *(Balistipus)* [B]. Safety from predators is, for the clown anemone fish *(Amphiprion percula)* [F], provided by the shelter of a sea anemone's arms and, for the cleaner wrasse *(Labroides)* [G], by its eating of the parasites that infect the predators. The parrot fish *(Scarus)* [C] feeds on coral, which it bites off in large pieces with its bony jaws.

2 A Flying fish *Cypselurus opisthopus*

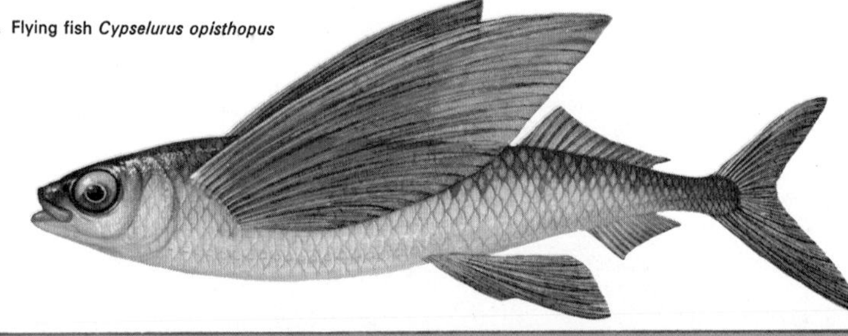

B

2 The flying fish [A] has developed wing-like pectoral fins that enable it to glide through the air. To emerge from the sea [B] it holds its fins close to its body, takes off from the crest of a wave then spreads its fins to climb and glide.

3 Blue trunk fish *Ostracion* sp

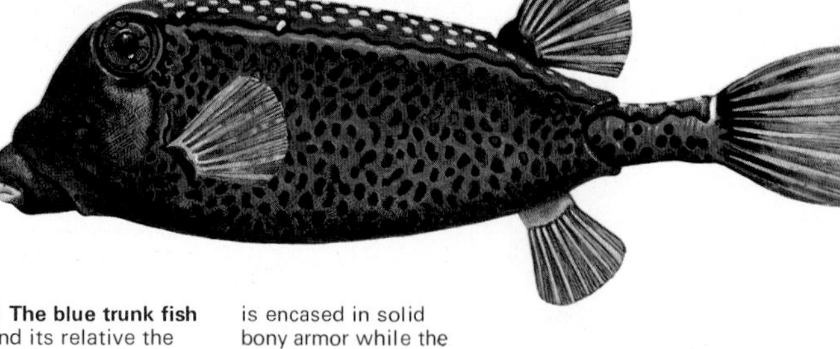

Puffer fish *Spheroides spengleri*

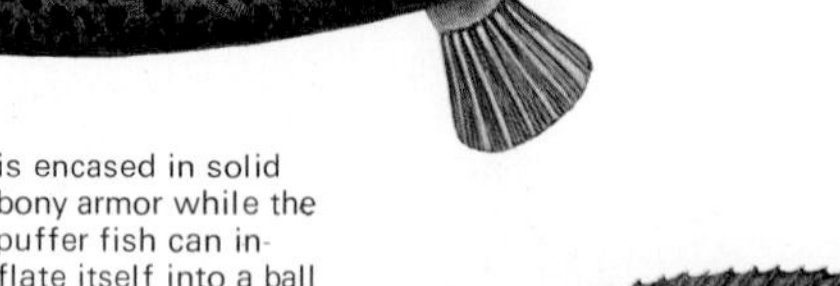

3 The blue trunk fish and its relative the glove, or puffer, fish have unique defense mechanisms. The body of the trunk fish is encased in solid bony armor while the puffer fish can inflate itself into a ball shape when danger threatens.

4 African cichlid fish *Haplochromis burtoni*

4 The female of the African cichlid fish carries her fertilized eggs in her mouth. After about 12 days the eggs hatch and the young fish form a school around her head. If danger threatens, the female "calls" her offspring back into her mouth. After about five days the young depart.

ocean depths to search out a mate every time she has eggs ready for fertilization.

Some fish have reproductive habits as bizarre as the differences between the appearance of the sexes. In the case of the seahorse, for example, the male has developed a pouch and it is he who nurtures the developing young, instead of leaving them unguarded as is usually the case. Many cichlid fish [4] retain the conventional division of reproductive labor between the sexes but some females appear to spit their young into the world, as a result of their practice of hatching the eggs in their mouths. As soon as the eggs are laid the female takes them into her mouth. In some species, the male has egglike specks located around the anal opening so that the female, while attempting to pick up the extra "eggs," takes in his sperm and fertilizes the real eggs.

For fish such as eels [7], salmon, and steelhead trout spawning can be the end of a very long journey. Salmon return to their native streams to breed after spending a year or more at sea. Pacific species are known to arrive back after traveling between 1,000 and 2,000 miles (1,600 and 3,200km) and the evidence suggests that they are able to recognize their general course by means of a sun-compass sense of direction; and the details of the last parts of their journey by using their sense of smell.

Electric fish

Electric organs [8] have developed independently in no less than four families of bony fish and also in some of the cartilaginous torpedoes and rays. These organs are all thought to be derived from muscle and are usually arranged in a series of plates forming an organic battery. Some fish are capable of generating large voltages. One of them, the electric eel *(Electrophorus)*, which lives in the Amazon, can generate up to 550 volts. These large voltages are probably used for protection or paralyzing prey; most fish that possess electric organs live in muddy or turbid water where visibility is restricted. These fish generate weak electric fields which are thought to enable them to navigate and find prey but not to kill it.

KEY

Fish live in almost all aquatic habitats. Some have become adapted to living in extremely inhospitable regions. The grouper inhabits the warm waters of tropical coral reefs while from the freezing Antarctic seas come ice fish. In torrential streams the modified fins of *Sewellia lineolata* serve as suckers. Fish even inhabit caves; the blind cave barb is an African example of a cave fish from Zaire.

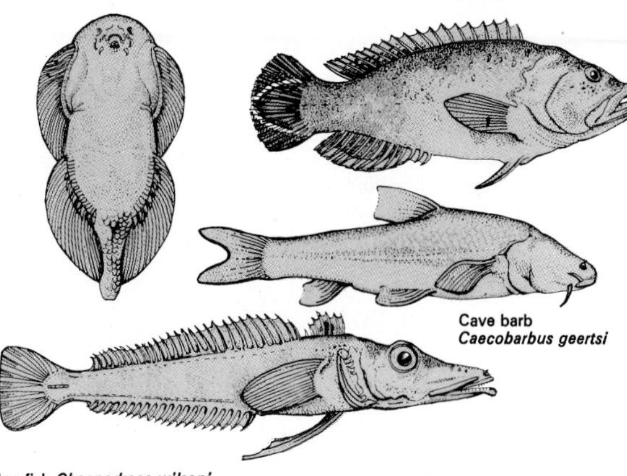

Sewellia lineolata (underside)
Grouper *Cephalopholis urodelus*
Cave barb *Caecobarbus geertsi*
Ice fish *Chaenodraco wilsoni*

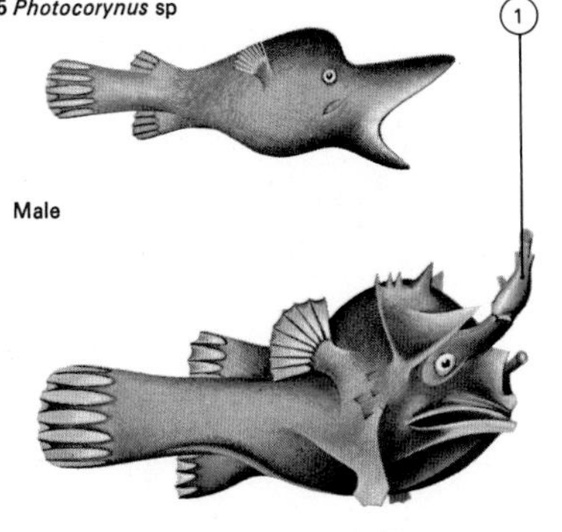

5 *Photocorynus* sp
1
Male
Female

5 The deep-sea anglerfish *Photocorynus* presents an extreme example of sexual dimorphism. The male, which is a fraction of the size of the adult female, has no independent existence but lives parasitically attached to her. He latches on by his mouth [1] to a special protuberance just above her snout and takes his nourishment from her. In return he supplies her with sperm to fertilize the eggs.

6 The seahorse is related to the pipefishes and lives in tropical and temperate seas. It is the only fish with a prehensile tail, which it uses to cling to seaweed. Another distinctive feature is that the male looks after the eggs, carrying them in a pouch in his belly until they hatch. The seahorse swims weakly with an upright stance and is mostly carried along by ocean currents.

6 Seahorse *Hippocampus* sp

7

European eel *Anguilla anguilla*

7 The life history of the European freshwater eel starts in the Sargasso Sea where the adults spawn and then die. The tiny larvae, known as leptocephali, are swept slowly northward on the Gulf Stream. It then takes them three years to reach the coasts of Europe where they exchange their somewhat fishlike shape for that of tiny transparent "glass eels," or elvers. During the next stage they migrate inland up the rivers as yellow eels. This phase lasts for about a year and then gradually over the next six years the adult eels change from yellow to silver. Not until they are about 10 years old do they start the journey back to the Sargasso Sea to spawn. What induces and guides the migration of eels is still something of a mystery. But it is now thought that very few European eels return to the Sargasso Sea. Most of the adults spawning there seem to have made their way down from the coasts of North America, and European eels probably come from these. Many biologists, however, believe that the American eel is a distinct species.

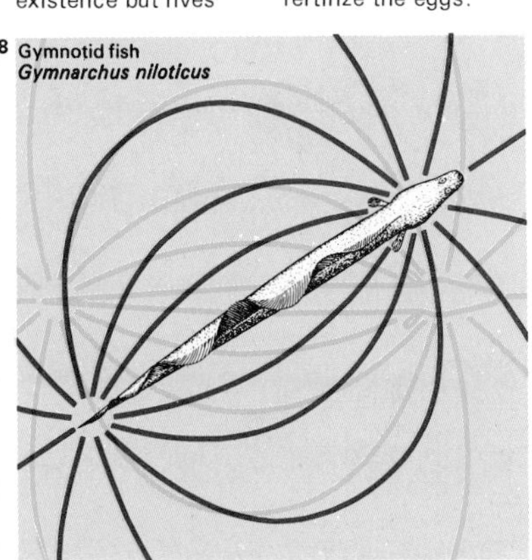

8 Gymnotid fish *Gymnarchus niloticus*

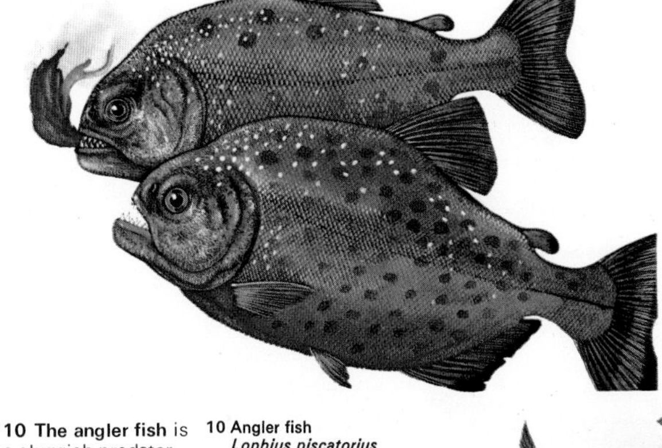

9 Red piranha *Rooseveltiella nattereri*

9 The red piranha of South America is notorious for its ferocity which, allowing for popular exaggeration, is still formidable. It has powerful jaws full of very sharp teeth, and makes up for its small size – 14in (35cm) long at the most – by often swimming in large schools. These represent a threat to larger fish and sometimes to swimming land animals and man. They feed in bouts rather than continuously and locate their prey by means of their sense of smell which leads them, particularly, to any flesh that has already been torn and is bleeding.

8 This gymnotid fish is one of the so-called electric fish. It belongs to the weakly electrogenic species that emit regular pulses of current from electric organs modified from muscle or nerve. Their stiff-spined posture enables such fish to detect objects in their environments as disturbances in the electrical field. Special centers in the nervous system control the electric impulses but how the information is interpreted by such electric fish is not yet known.

10 The angler fish is a sluggish predator that lies half concealed in mud waving an appendage developed from the dorsal fin. Smaller fish, attracted by the lure, approach the angler and are sucked into its huge, tooth-rimmed mouth.

10 Angler fish *Lophius piscatorius*

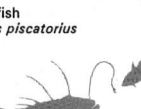

Fish of seas and rivers

Fish are found in an extraordinarily wide range of shapes and sizes. This reflects the many ways in which they have become adapted to the various conditions and habitats that the world's seas and fresh waters have to offer. Many fish that live in weedy habitats, for example, have peculiar outgrowths from their bodies [13] while others are decorated with intricate color patterns. Both these kinds of adaptations are forms of camouflage, as is the ability of some fish to change color to merge with their surroundings. Features of fish that live in muddy waters are the sensory barbels around the mouth [12], which are used in locating food.

Predatory fish [1] are generally sleek and streamlined with large mouths and sharp teeth. Flatfish [8], in contrast, feed on the sea bottom and are slow moving. Fish of many kinds are vital to man as a source of food, particularly the cods [9], herring [6], and flatfish. Fish are also the source of fishmeal, which is used as fertilizer and as pig and poultry feed. The fish, in turn, often feed upon other fish.

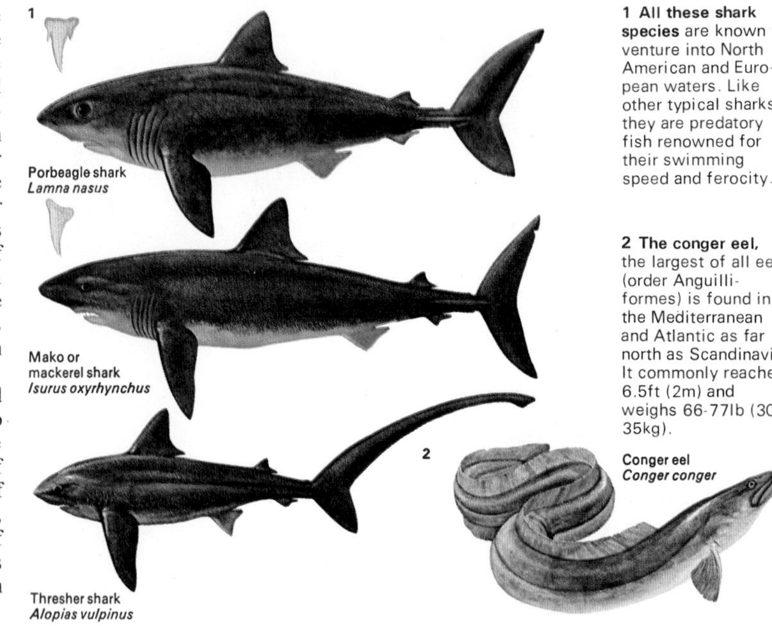
1
Porbeagle shark
Lamna nasus
Mako or
mackerel shark
Isurus oxyrhynchus
Thresher shark
Alopias vulpinus
2
Conger eel
Conger conger

1 All these shark species are known to venture into North American and European waters. Like other typical sharks, they are predatory fish renowned for their swimming speed and ferocity.

2 The conger eel, the largest of all eels (order Anguilliformes) is found in the Mediterranean and Atlantic as far north as Scandinavia. It commonly reaches 6.5ft (2m) and weighs 66-77lb (30-35kg).

CONNECTIONS

See also
512 The life of fish
510 The classification of fish
514 Unusual fish
626 Animals of the ocean
386 Commercial fishing
388 Fish farming
390 Fish of ponds and rivers
392 Fish of the ocean deeps
616 Lakes and rivers

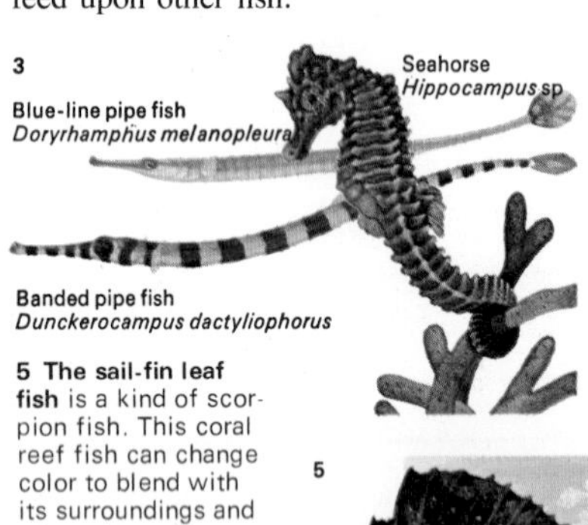
3
Seahorse
Hippocampus sp
Blue-line pipe fish
Doryrhamphus melanopleura
Banded pipe fish
Dunckerocampus dactyliophorus

3 One of the ocean's oddities, the seahorse, is related to the pipefish and to the stickleback. These fish have bodies covered, in varying degree, with bony plates and have tubular snouts.

5 The sail-fin leaf fish is a kind of scorpion fish. This coral reef fish can change color to blend with its surroundings and when alarmed may "act dead" by drifting upside down.

5
Sail-fin leaf fish
Taenianotus triacanthus

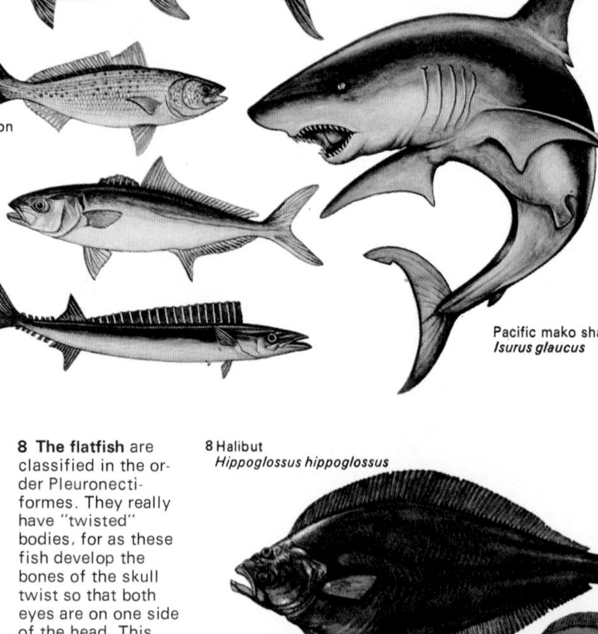
4
Catfish
Tandanus tandanus
Golden perch
Plectroplites ambiguus
Murray cod
Maccullochella macquariensis
Tiger flathead
Neoplatycephalus richardsoni
Southern bluefin tuna
Thunnus thynnus maccoyii
Australian salmon
Arripis trutta
Kingfish
Seriola grandis
Pacific mako shark
Isurus glaucus
Barracouta
Thyrsites atun

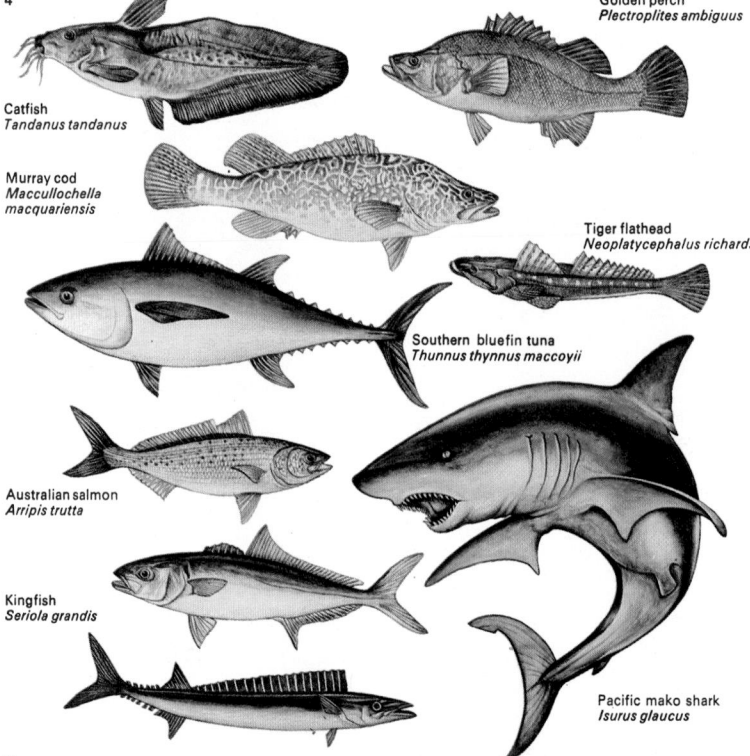

4 Australian waters are inhabited by about 2,000 species of fish. Sharks and barracoutas patrol the seas and inland waters abound in freshwater types, including the catfish and the murray cod.

6 One of man's most important food fish is the herring. It is classified in the order Clupeiformes and is found on both sides of the North Atlantic. Its average length is 12in (30cm), but the size range is great.

6 Herring
Clupea harengus

7 Weedy regions of rivers and backwaters in southern Asia are the home of the knife fish. The fish are named after their vertically compressed shape. Their color varies widely, even within one species, which makes them hard to identify.

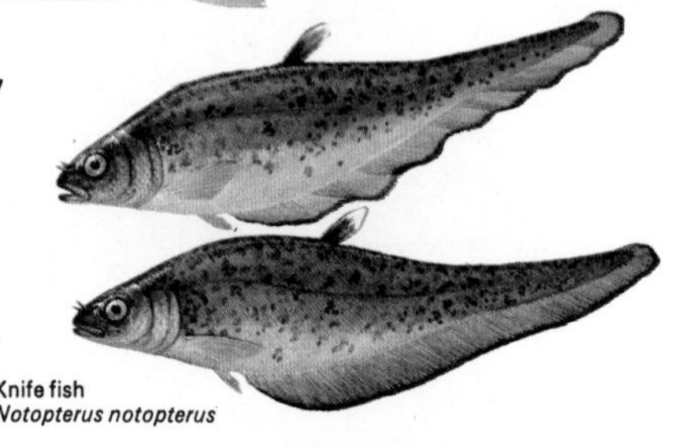
7
Knife fish
Notopterus notopterus

8 The flatfish are classified in the order Pleuronectiformes. They really have "twisted" bodies, for as these fish develop the bones of the skull twist so that both eyes are on one side of the head. This side becomes the back of the mature flatfish and takes on a heavy pigmentation while the other, the "blind" side, remains nearly white [1]. Some species can change color as they move from rocky to sandy ocean bottom and vice versa.

8 Halibut
Hippoglossus hippoglossus

Flounder
Platichthys flesus

1

Dab
Limanda limanda

Turbot
Scophthalmus maximus

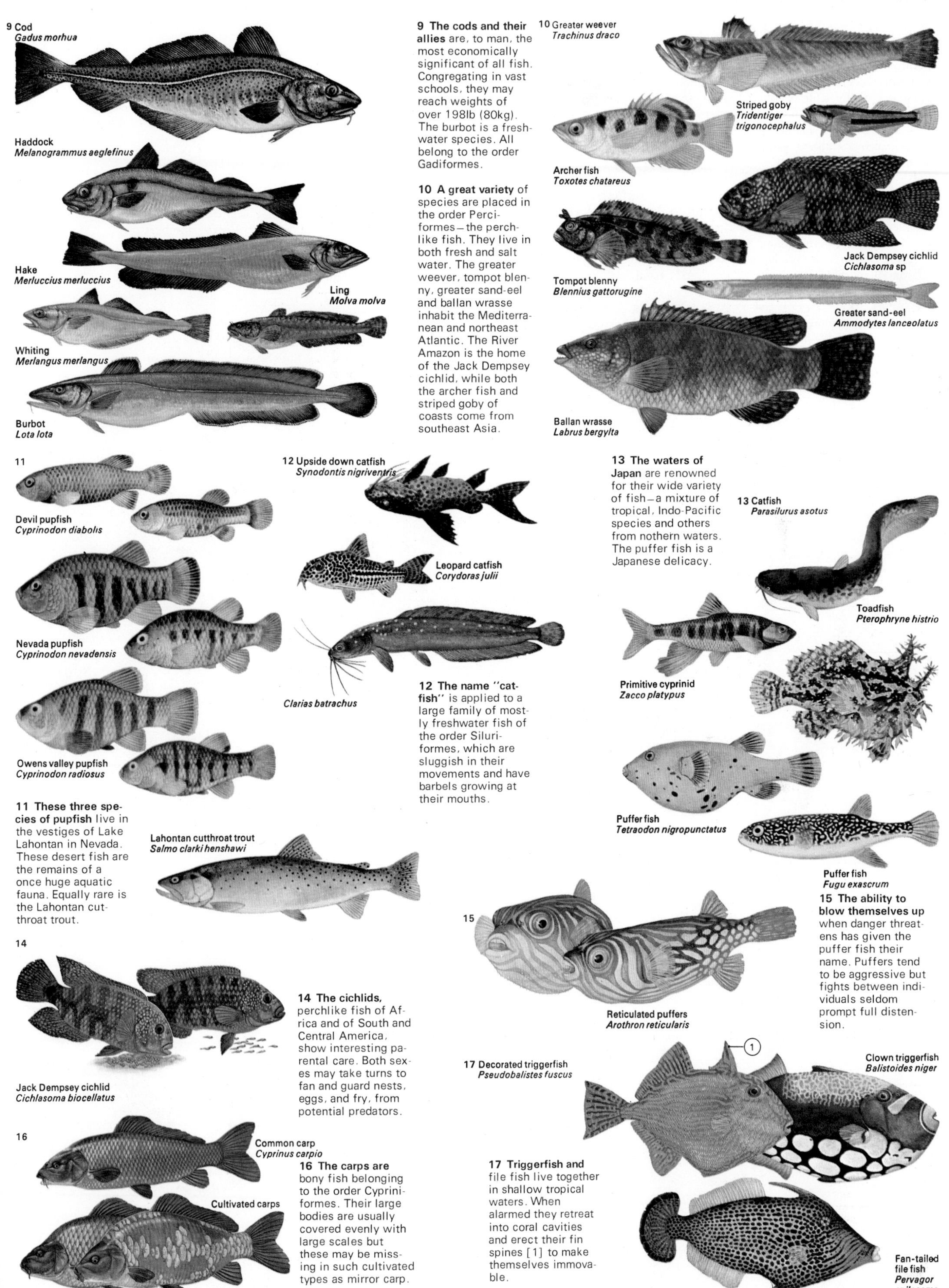
9 Cod
Gadus morhua
Haddock
Melanogrammus aeglefinus
Hake
Merluccius merluccius
Ling
Molva molva
Whiting
Merlangus merlangus
Burbot
Lota lota
10 Greater weever
Trachinus draco
Striped goby
Tridentiger trigonocephalus
Archer fish
Toxotes chatareus
Jack Dempsey cichlid
Cichlasoma sp
Tompot blenny
Blennius gattorugine
Greater sand-eel
Ammodytes lanceolatus
Ballan wrasse
Labrus bergylta
11
Devil pupfish
Cyprinodon diabolis
Nevada pupfish
Cyprinodon nevadensis
Owens valley pupfish
Cyprinodon radiosus
12 Upside down catfish
Synodontis nigriventris
Leopard catfish
Corydoras julii
Clarias batrachus
13 Catfish
Parasilurus asotus
Toadfish
Pterophryne histrio
Primitive cyprinid
Zacco platypus
Puffer fish
Tetraodon nigropunctatus
Puffer fish
Fugu exascrum
Lahontan cutthroat trout
Salmo clarki henshawi
14
Jack Dempsey cichlid
Cichlasoma biocellatus
15
Reticulated puffers
Arothron reticularis
17 Decorated triggerfish
Pseudobalistes fuscus
1
Clown triggerfish
Balistoides niger
Fan-tailed file fish
Pervagor spilosoma
16
Common carp
Cyprinus carpio
Cultivated carps

9 The cods and their allies are, to man, the most economically significant of all fish. Congregating in vast schools, they may reach weights of over 198lb (80kg). The burbot is a freshwater species. All belong to the order Gadiformes.

10 A great variety of species are placed in the order Perciformes – the perchlike fish. They live in both fresh and salt water. The greater weever, tompot blenny, greater sand-eel and ballan wrasse inhabit the Mediterranean and northeast Atlantic. The River Amazon is the home of the Jack Dempsey cichlid, while both the archer fish and striped goby of coasts come from southeast Asia.

11 These three species of pupfish live in the vestiges of Lake Lahontan in Nevada. These desert fish are the remains of a once huge aquatic fauna. Equally rare is the Lahontan cutthroat trout.

12 The name "catfish" is applied to a large family of mostly freshwater fish of the order Siluriformes, which are sluggish in their movements and have barbels growing at their mouths.

13 The waters of Japan are renowned for their wide variety of fish – a mixture of tropical, Indo-Pacific species and others from nothern waters. The puffer fish is a Japanese delicacy.

14 The cichlids, perchlike fish of Africa and of South and Central America, show interesting parental care. Both sexes may take turns to fan and guard nests, eggs, and fry, from potential predators.

15 The ability to blow themselves up when danger threatens has given the puffer fish their name. Puffers tend to be aggressive but fights between individuals seldom prompt full distension.

16 The carps are bony fish belonging to the order Cypriniformes. Their large bodies are usually covered evenly with large scales but these may be missing in such cultivated types as mirror carp.

17 Triggerfish and file fish live together in shallow tropical waters. When alarmed they retreat into coral cavities and erect their fin spines [1] to make themselves immovable.

The life of amphibians

Amphibians evolved from fishlike ancestors 350 million years ago in the upper Devonian period. At that time fern-fringed swamps provided ideal humid conditions for the first conquest of the land by animals with no means of conserving their body water.

Fossil evidence indicates that the first amphibians resembled giant salamanders with elongated heads and well developed tails. These animals, often more than 40in (1m) long, moved slowly and clumsily, carrying their heavy bodies from one pool to another. By the Carboniferous period, many different amphibian forms had evolved. These creatures led slow but untroubled lives with little competition from other animals and an abundance of food.

Adaptation difficulties

The change from life in water to life on land posed many problems and it took the amphibians many millions of years to become adapted. In fact, amphibians never completely adapted to this harsher environment and still need water for breeding. To move efficiently on land, the amphibians developed strong muscles and interlocking backbones to lift their bodies off the ground [8]. The limbs of many of the earlier amphibians were awkward structures with large bones and widely expanded hands and feet, though they showed the typical five-fingered (pentadactyl) limb pattern of higher vertebrates. In order to breathe, the amphibians used a new method of respiration that involved paired air sacs or lungs.

Of the many amphibian groups that once existed, there are only three modern orders: the Anura (frogs and toads), the Urodela (newts and salamanders), and the smallest group, the Apoda, or caecilians, (legless, blind, and burrowing forms).

There is a great diversity of frogs and toads with over 2,000 species adapted for life in habitats which, apart from wet lands, include tropical forests, grassland, and even deserts. A common feature of frogs and toads is that they undergo a complete change in form (known as metamorphosis) during their life history [1].

Male frogs and toads usually call to attract females for breeding and also in response to danger. Both sexes have vocal organs but only those of the male are fully developed. The typical croaking noise is produced by vibrations of the vocal cords. Air is passed backward and forward between the lungs and the vocal pouches, formed below the mouth.

Nearly all temperate species of frogs and toads migrate to water in the spring. They find their way with the help of special sensory cells—osmoreceptors—in their mouths. Certain ponds seem to be especially attractive, and enormous numbers congregate there in the mating season. The males usually precede the females and then attract them by calling.

The amphibian skin

The larval forms of frogs, toads, newts, and salamanders all have external gills for respiration in water but these are lost in most adult forms. Mature frogs can breathe in three ways [Key]. They use their lungs when highly active, the floor of the mouth (buccal cavity) when feeding, and their moist skin when resting or hibernating. The

CONNECTIONS

See also
458 The animal kingdom
566 Fish and amphibians of the past
568 Toward life on land
460 Animal anatomy
524 Unusual reptiles and amphibians
464 Principles of animal behavior
632 Endangered species
604 Life in the desert

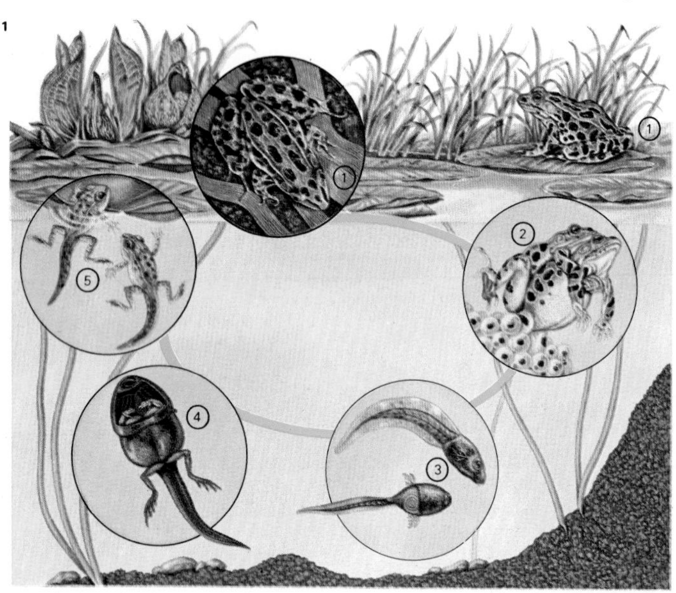

1 The life cycle of the North American leopard frog *(Rana pipiens)* begins when the adult frog [1] leaves the long grass of a wetland meadow and returns to a pond or stream to breed [2]. A few days after the eggs hatch, the tadpoles have external gills [3]. After 8 weeks hind limbs are well developed [4]. Young frogs at 3 months have all limbs developed but still have a tail [5], which is later lost.

2 The phenomenon of neoteny is seen in parts of the range of the Mexican tiger salamander. Spermatophores [1] are picked up by the female [2] and the fertilized eggs are laid on water weed [3]. The aquatic larva has external gills [4]. Sometimes, the fully-grown sexually immature larva [5] can reproduce. At high iodine concentrations, sexually mature larvae will metamorphose.

3 The fire salamander *(Salamandra salamandra)* is the largest European salamander, attaining a length of 11 in (28 cm). It lives in hilly, wooded areas and has striking warning colors.

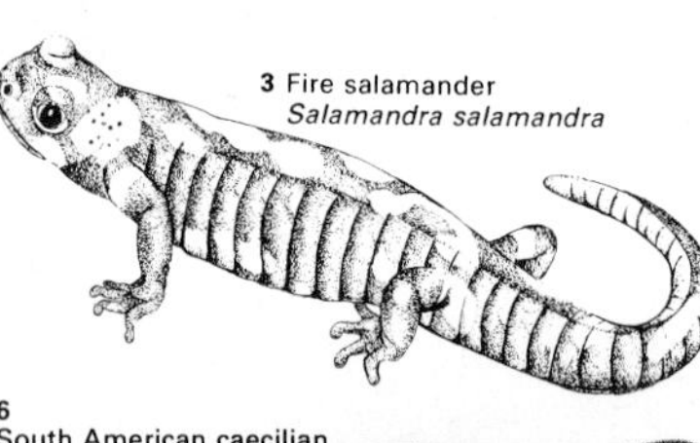
3 Fire salamander
Salamandra salamandra

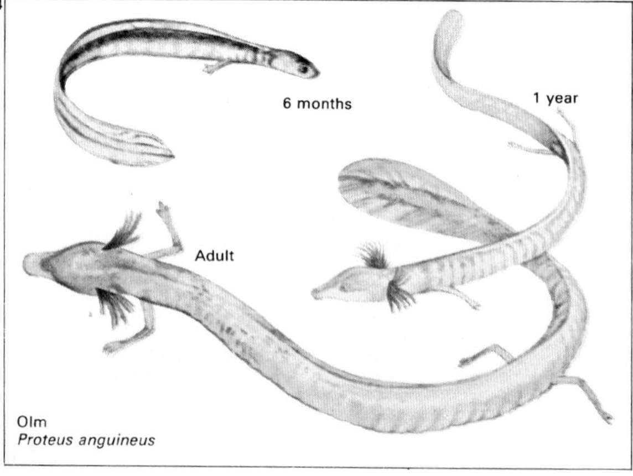
6 months
1 year
Adult
Olm
Proteus anguineus

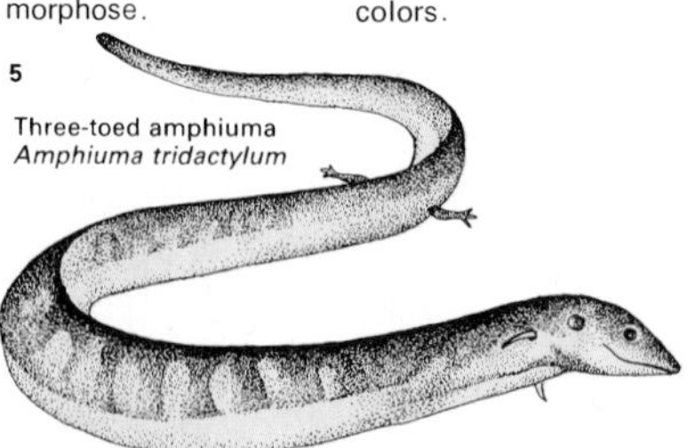
5
Three-toed amphiuma
Amphiuma tridactylum

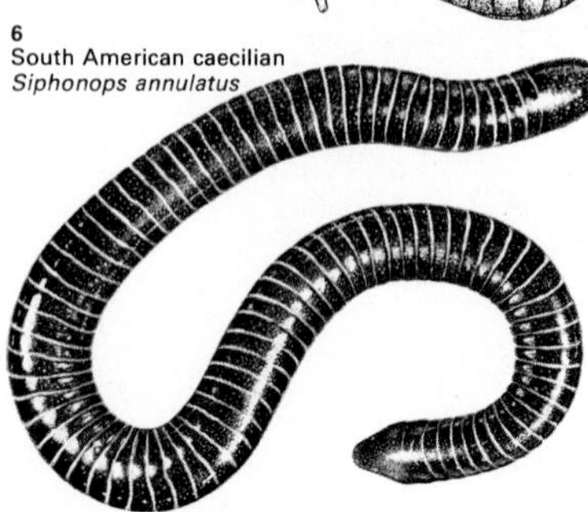
6
South American caecilian
Siphonops annulatus

4 The olm *(Proteus anguineus)* is a neotenous amphibian that lives in caves. The young have eyes and are pigmented like salamanders but these features disappear in the adult form.

5 The three-toed amphiuma *(Amphiuma tridactylum)* grows to a length of 40in (1m) and is found in southeastern United States. It is nocturnal and spends most of its time in water.

6 The wormlike *Siphonops annulatus* is a typical member of the caecilian group. It is blind, lives underground, and probably feeds on earthworms. Caecilians live only in subtropical and tropical regions of the world. This species comes from South America. It guards its eggs and grows to 20in (50cm).

skin is kept moist by secretions from mucous glands in the outer layer, the epidermis. The skin may also contain poison glands, which are well developed in tropical frogs such as *Dendrobates* and *Phyllobates*. The virulent poison secreted is used on arrows by South American Indians to paralyze prey such as birds and monkeys. Many of the poisonous amphibians are brightly colored, thus warning predators to leave them alone. The use of color for camouflage is highly developed in the amphibians. Three layers of pigment cells in the skin can produce color changes by expansion and contraction.

Tailed and legless amphibians

Newts and salamanders show less deviation from the generalized amphibians than do the more specialized frogs and toads. The body shape is usually lizardlike with a distinct head. Adult and larval forms are very similar and do not generally show the complete metamorphosis typical of frogs and toads. There are 8 families with approximately 225 species. Like frogs and toads, they generally breed in the water. Most of them lay eggs and internal fertilization is common. The male releases a packet of sperm, taken up by the female.

Newts become brightly colored during the breeding season and there is often an intense courtship display. Some salamanders exhibit neoteny, in which the breeding adult retains features of the young larvae, such as well-developed external gills and unpigmented skin. There are several families whose members are perennially larval in form—the mudpuppies, for example.

The tropical caecilians are the smallest and least well known group of amphibians. Many are burrowing [6] and all are limbless, showing such interesting primitive features as the retention of scales in the skin. They have vestigial eyes whose function is largely replaced by special sensory "tentacles" with which they feel their way through the earth. One of the better known species is the Ceylonese caecilian *(Ichthyophis glutinosus)*, first studied at the end of the nineteenth century.

KEY

The common European frog. *(Rana temporaria)*, uses its lungs [6], skin [9], and mouth [3] for breathing. By means of the hyoid bone [5], which lowers the cavity floor, air is drawn through the nostrils [2]. The frog's eyes [1] are set high on the head for improved vision. The flip-out tongue [4] is used to catch food. The heart [8] has two atria and one ventricle. The eardrum [7] is visible on the surface.

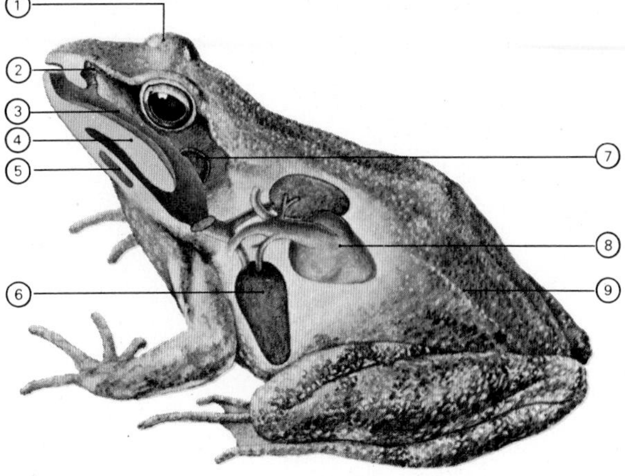

1
2
3
4
5
6
7
8
9

7

Surinam toad *Pipa pipa*

Dendrobates sp

Marsupial tree frog *Gastrotheca ovifera*

South American tree frog *Cerathyla* sp

7 Specialized breeding methods are used by many different species of frogs and toads. In tropical areas, eggs may be laid in a nest of leaves or attached to a twig over a stream or pond, so that when the tadpoles hatch they fall into the water to continue developing. These methods have the merit of giving protection from predators in the vulnerable egg stage. Another protective step is for the parents to carry the eggs. The male of the European midwife toad *(Alytes obstetricans)* winds the eggs around his hind feet and carries them until they hatch. The ultimate in parental care is shown in tropical species whose young hatch directly from the female's back. Frogs that show this degree of protective care produce fewer young but the chances of survival are much greater than in species that lay a large number of unprotected eggs. The male Surinam toad *(Pipa pipa)* courts the female by uttering metallic calls, then holds her in his arms. The sticky eggs are fertilized as they are laid singly and moved onto the female's back, sinking in so that the skin covers them. The young do not go through a true tadpole stage but hatch out from the female's back 3–4 months later. The South American tree frog *(Cerathyla)* carries her eggs in a basket-shaped hollow on her back until they are ready to hatch in a cup of rainwater formed in a leaf. The tadpoles of the South American frog *Dendrobates* are carried on their father's back but their development is completed in the water. In the "zip-bag" birth of the marsupial tree frog *(Gastrotheca ovifera)*, about 20 fully-formed young frogs hatch out from a pouch on the female's back.

8

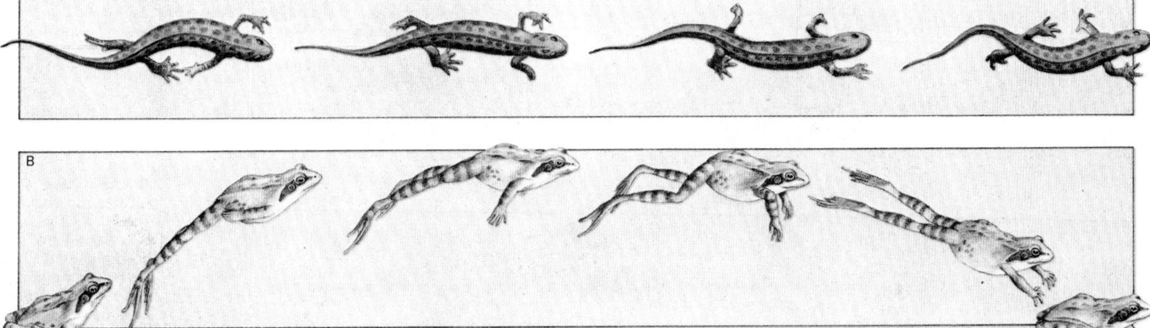

A
B

8 Amphibians move on land by various methods. [A] A newt walks by raising its body onto legs that act like levers. The backbone acts like a girder by carrying the weight of the body. When frightened, a newt can wriggle along on its belly. [B] A frog's long hind legs give very good leverage for jumping. Both legs are thrust out simultaneously to produce a highly effective leap.

The life of Reptiles

Reptiles have inhabited the earth longer than man and all other mammals, and longer than the birds. Indeed, early reptilians were the ancestors of both the other classes, and their descendants continue to share with birds such characteristics as the laying of shelled eggs and the possession of a single knob on the back of the skull fitting it to the backbone and a single bone in the middle ear.

Reptiles appeared about 300 million years ago, descendants of the early amphibians. In the course of time, some grew to huge proportions, like the dinosaurs, but for the past 70 million years they have mostly been small animals, except for the modern Crocodilia, which represent both relations and contemporaries of the long extinct dinosaurs.

Reptilian orders

Four main orders of reptiles, totaling some 6,000 species, exist today. Tortoises and turtles, of the order Chelonia, are perhaps the most primitive group, with skulls like the earliest reptiles, the cotylosaurs. The crocodiles and alligators are members of the Crocodilia, while snakes and lizards, most recently evolved and most numerous of the reptiles, belong to the order Squamata. The tuatara, sole surviving member of the order Rhynchocephalia, lives in New Zealand and existed as a species 200 million years ago, before the dinosaurs came into existence.

Turtles [4, 7] have shells, typically with a horny layer covering a bony box derived from the backbone and ribs plus bony plates that originate in the skin. It is an effective armor, but heavy. Land tortoises are slow-moving, with legs adapted for weight-bearing; they sometimes have elephantine feet. The most common chelonians are the amphibious freshwater forms with flatter shells than those of land tortoises. Their toes are webbed and they eat mainly animal food, while land tortoises are largely vegetarian. Sea turtles are completely aquatic and their limbs have become flippers. The chelonian has no teeth but deals with its food with horn-rimmed jaws, the front legs assisting in the tearing process.

Crocodiles and alligators are found in lakes and rivers throughout the tropics. They use their muscular, flattened tails for driving themselves through the water and their webbed feet for steering. The sharp, conical teeth with which they are armed are good for seizing their prey but less efficient at cutting up a carcass. To overcome this drawback the crocodile can spin over in the water with its victim in its grasp, until part is torn off. It retains its sharp bite into old age, for it continually grows new teeth to replace the old ones. The alligator differs from the crocodile in its dentition. The large fourth tooth of a crocodile's lower jaw sticks up inside the upper jaw whereas in the alligator it disappears into a pit inside the upper jaw [8].

Snakes and lizards

The Squamata, the lizards and snakes, share many similarities despite the obvious differences between them. Lizards usually have five-toed limbs; snakes are legless. Lizards usually have eyelids, visible external ear openings, and small scales under the

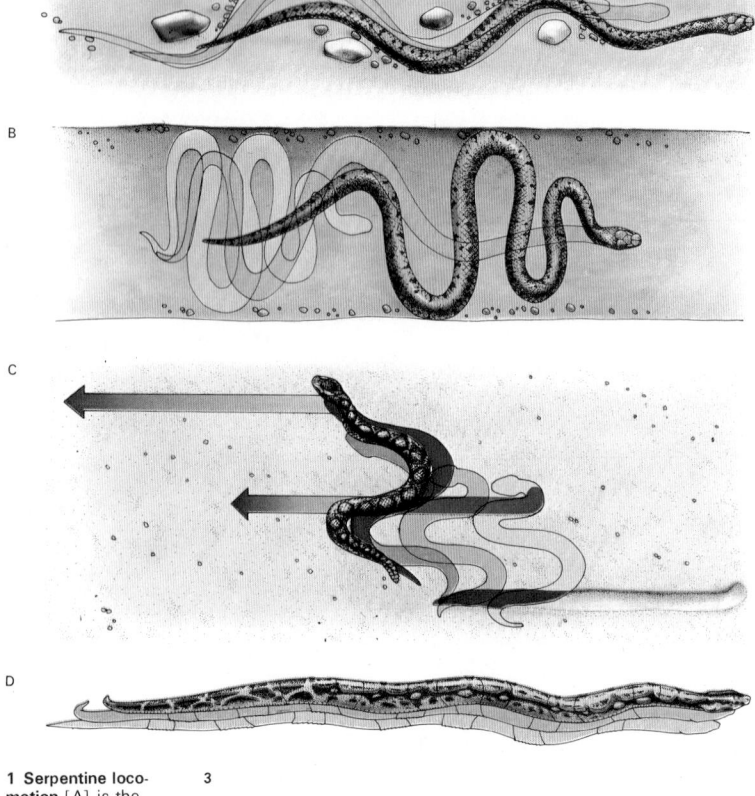

CONNECTIONS

See also
458 The animal kingdo
522 Snakes, lizards, an turtles
524 Unusual reptiles ar amphibians
570 Reptiles of the pas
572 The age of reptiles
604 Life in the desert
632 Endangered specie

1 A

B

C

D

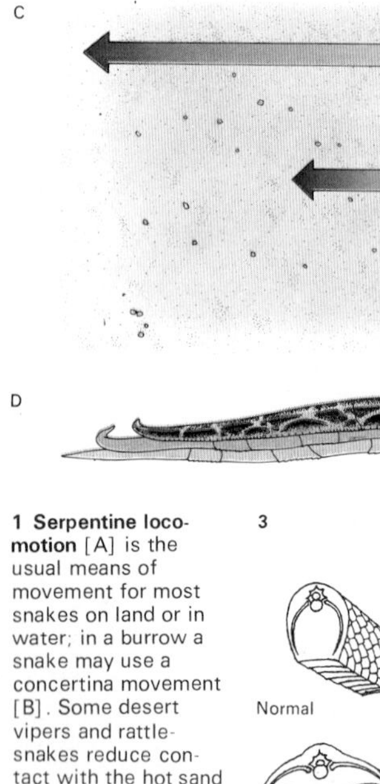

1 Serpentine locomotion [A] is the usual means of movement for most snakes on land or in water; in a burrow a snake may use a concertina movement [B]. Some desert vipers and rattlesnakes reduce contact with the hot sand by "sidewinding" [C]. A boa constrictor moves in a straight line by contraction of its belly muscles [D].

2

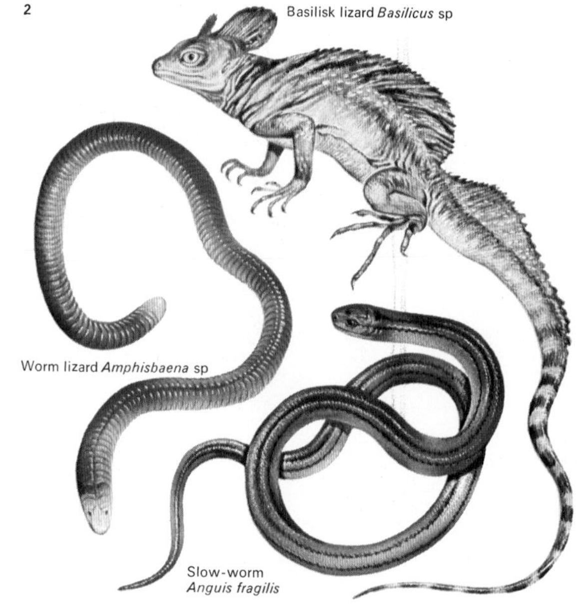

Basilisk lizard *Basilicus* sp
Worm lizard *Amphisbaena* sp
Slow-worm
Anguis fragilis

2 Lizard locomotion shows several variations on the typical four-footed method. Basilisk lizards can run at 7mph (11kph) on their hind legs alone. At these speeds the long tail acts as a counterbalance. Worm lizards are legless burrowers that tunnel by ramming the ground with blunt, strong-skulled heads. In existing tunnels they move like earthworms, pulling their rings of scales forward in groups. The slow-worm belongs to a family of lizards that includes some with normal legs and feet, but like many burrowing or semiburrowing species of lizards this one is limbless.

3

4

Normal
In flight
Flying snake *Chrysopelea pelias*
Freshwater spiny soft-shelled turtle
Trionyx spiniferus
Sea-dwelling loggerhead turtle
Caretta sp

3 The flying snake glides between trees by flattening its undersurface.

4 Some reptiles are well adapted to a life in water, both fresh and salt. Several families of turtles are found in lakes and rivers, while all of the true sea turtles belong to one of two families. The leatherbacked sea turtle is the only member of the family Dermochelidae; all the remaining sea turtles are placed in the family Cheloniidae. The sea turtles possess flippers, but the freshwater species usually have only modified webbed feet.

belly as well as on the back. Snakes have no true eyelids, no external sign of ears, and possess a single row of large scales along their bellies.

Most lizards are carnivorous, feeding on insects and other small prey, but some larger species such as monitors prey upon vertebrates. They tend, like other reptiles, to spend much of the time immobile, waiting for the prey to approach before they grab it, or make a short rush for it. Iguanas and some skinks are among the few vegetarian lizards. Camouflage and immobility are main defenses used by lizards, but monitors use both claws and teeth to protect themselves and even small lizards may bite if cornered. Others protect themselves by shedding part of their tail at a special breaking point, leaving it behind to confuse the predator. A replacement is then grown.

In movement, most lizards have a straddling gait. Many climb, and the gecko, which has ridges and microscopic spines under its toes, can walk on a smooth ceiling. The flying dragon of southeast Asia is a lizard that glides using flaps of skin.

Big eaters

Most snakes move by bending their bodies from side to side using muscles along the backbone. The sides of their bodies grip the ground. Some species, however, have adapted to other means of locomotion [1, 3]

All snakes are carnivores, swallowing their prey whole. Jaws loosely joined to the skull and to one another permit an enormous gape [10], and allow prey much wider than the snake's head to be engulfed by "walking" the jaws alternately around it. In this way a 16ft (4.8m) rock python has been known to swallow whole a 130lb (59kg) impala, and a 26ft (8m) anaconda a 100lb (45kg) peccary.

Large snakes such as these suffocate their victims by constriction. Others have poisonous bites. The most dangerous of these are the front-fanged snakes, the cobras, whose venom mainly attacks the nervous system, and vipers and rattlesnakes, whose poison affects the blood and tissues [10]. Venomous snakes usually flee before a threat, but some use a deterrent display or warning colors as a defense.

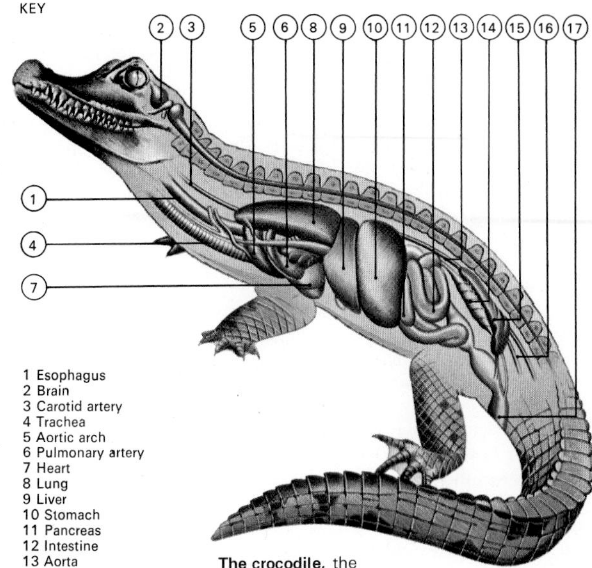
KEY
1
2
3
4
5
6
7
8
9
10
11
12
13
14
15
16
17

1 Esophagus
2 Brain
3 Carotid artery
4 Trachea
5 Aortic arch
6 Pulmonary artery
7 Heart
8 Lung
9 Liver
10 Stomach
11 Pancreas
12 Intestine
13 Aorta
14 Testes
15 Kidney
16 Posterior vena cava
17 Cloaca

The crocodile, the largest reptile, has remained unchanged since the time its relative, the dinosaur, vanished.

5

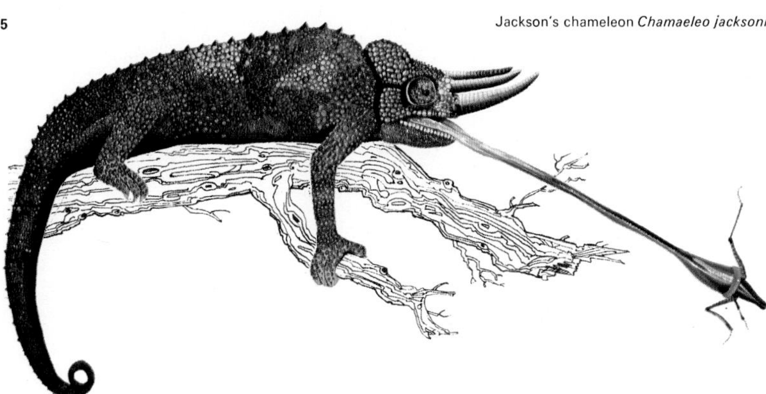
Jackson's chameleon *Chamaeleo jacksoni*

5 Flicked out in 0.04 sec, a chameleon's tongue tip is sticky and partly prehensile, giving the insect victim no chance. In locating food, the eyes swivel independently until prey is sighted, then focus together. Another remarkable characteristic of this reptile is its ability to change color. Color changes are activated largely by changes in light, a signal from the eye passing via the nervous system to pigment cells in the skin. Most chameleons are well adapted for climbing, with toes fused and grouped to form grasping hands and feet. The toes have sharp claws that aid in climbing.

6

A

B

C

6 The egg-eating snake [A] gulps eggs, cracks and rejects the shells. The boa constrictor [B] coils round its prey, suffocating it. The tentacled fishing snake [C] seizes fish in back-fanged jaws.

7

7 The alligator snapper, *Macrochelys,* has a lure for fish on the back of its tongue—a pink projection that is wriggled like a real worm. Fish are attracted to this bait and swim close to the snapping jaws.

8

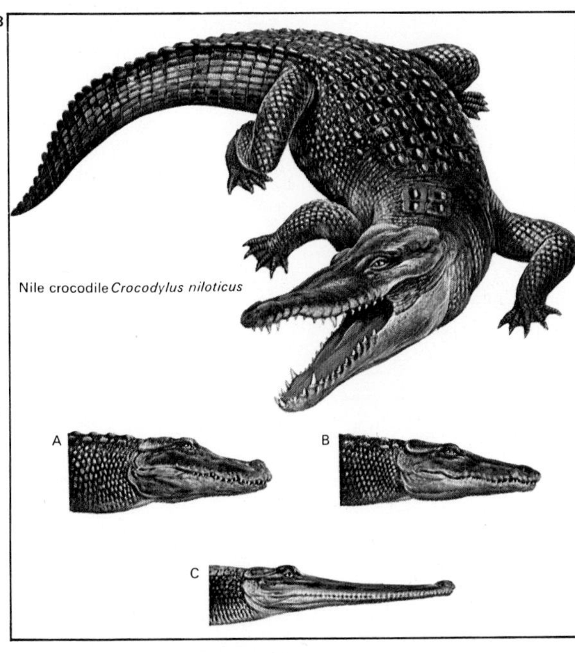
Nile crocodile *Crocodylus niloticus*
A
B
C

8 Large alligators [A] and crocodiles [B] are powerful enough to kill and feed on animals up to the size of a cow. The specialized gavial [C] has long, thin jaws which it swings from side to side snapping at fish in the vicinity.

9

A
B

9 The fangs of the Indian cobra [A] are at the front ot its jaws, and well-placed for delivering the venom. Back-fanged snakes such as the boiga [B] generally have smaller fangs.

10

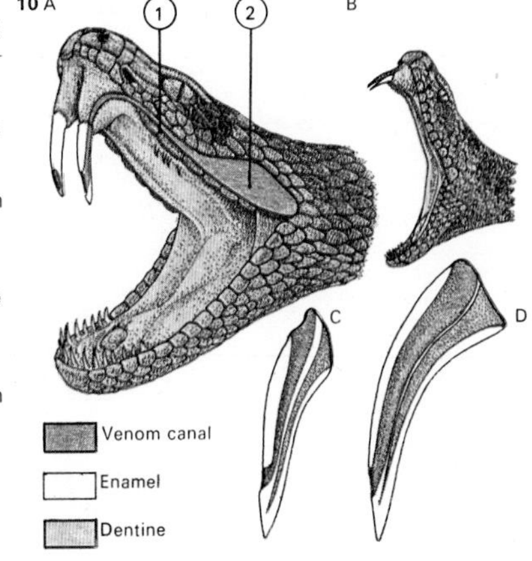
A
1
2
B
C
D
Venom canal
Enamel
Dentine

10 Snake venom is produced in modified salivary glands, delivered in certain snakes by grooved teeth. In rattlesnakes [A] and other vipers, venom is squeezed down a duct [1] from the venom gland [2] into hollow fang. The fangs are erected and the huge gape [B] becomes apparent as the snake strikes. Three kinds of cobra spray venom at their adversaries' eyes. Their fangs have forward-directed orifices [C], unlike the "hypodermic" fang [D].

Snakes, lizards, and turtles

There are over 6,000 species of reptiles living in the world today. They comprise about 25 species of crocodiles, 250 species of turtles and tortoises, 2,800 of snakes, and 3,000 of lizards. Most reptiles live in the tropics [Key], but a few hardy species, such as the common lizard, the adder, and the greater snake, are found above the Arctic Circle, and one lizard species lives in Tierra del Fuego.

Temperature regulation

Most reptiles cannot tolerate cold. Reptiles are cold-blooded animals. They have no built-in control over their body temperature and take on the temperature of their surroundings, to within a few degrees. Reptiles are most active when they are warm and they are best suited to tropical climates. Cold makes them sluggish and eventually kills them. But reptiles can control their temperature to some extent [11] by basking in the sun when cold and so raise their temperature even above that of the surrounding air, but they are not able to maintain constant temperatures like mammals. Even with body temperatures as high as those of mammals they may produce energy only one-tenth as fast. Behavior that takes advantage of heat when available and avoids cooling is important.

In the tropics, reptiles may avoid large fluctuations in body temperature, but far from the Equator or at high altitudes it is not so easy. In temperate zones, low winter temperatures make active life impossible for reptiles, and they survive only by hibernating.

Reproduction and growth

All reptiles reproduce by laying eggs. Crocodiles and pythons may lay up to 100 in a clutch, and sea turtles lay even more, but most lizards and snakes have smaller clutches. The eggshells are hard in tortoises and crocodiles, but in other species are usually leathery. The eggs are fertilized within the female before laying. All male reptiles, with the exception of the tuatara, have an intromittent organ—single in turtles, tortoises, and crocodiles, double in lizards and snakes—which is turned outward from the genital opening, the cloaca, for mating. Most reptiles have no family life and the eggs are abandoned after being laid, although they are often buried first. Warmth from the sun or decaying vegetation incubates them.

Some reptiles retain their eggs inside the oviducts until hatching, or even afterward, so that the young are born alive—a condition known as ovoviviparity. This process is particularly common in species that live in hostile surroundings, such as deserts or cold regions, and it has the advantage that the mother protects the developing embryos.

Newly-hatched reptiles are miniatures of their parents, ready to fend for themselves. Poisonous snakes can bite immediately after hatching. The rate at which reptiles grow depends on food and warmth. An alligator in suitable surroundings might grow an average of 1in (2.5cm) a month for the first years of its life and pythons might grow three times as fast as that. Reptiles grow quickly until sexual maturity, which is reached in less than a year by some small lizards but not until ten years or more by

CONNECTIONS

See also
520 The life of reptiles
524 Unusual reptiles and amphibians
570 Reptiles of the past
572 The age of reptiles
632 Endangered species
604 Life in the desert
712 The causes of illness:2

1

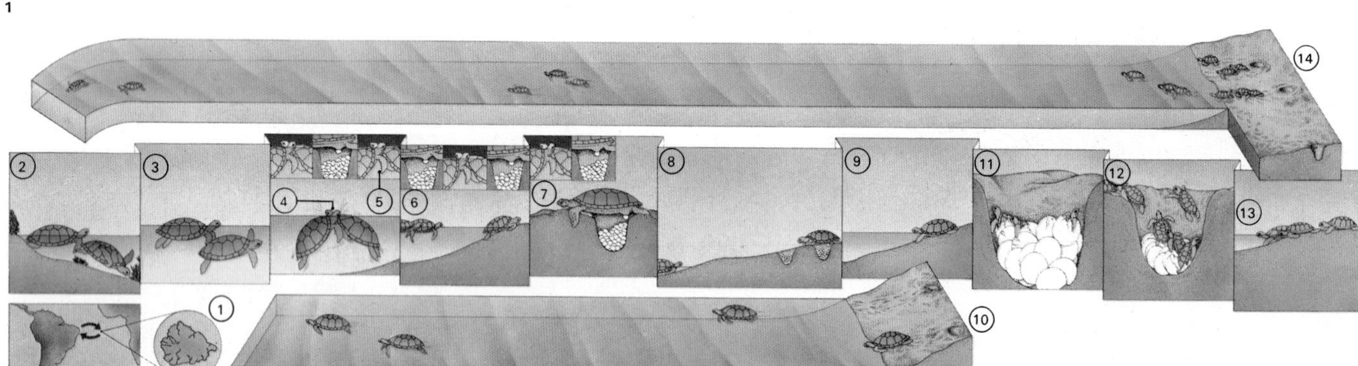

1
2
3
4
5
6
7
8
9
10
11
12
13
14

1 The green turtle *(Chelonia mydas)* ranges through tropical seas but the number of major breeding sites is small. In the Atlantic, Ascension Island [1] is used by turtles that feed on eelgrass and algae in warm shallow coastal waters off South America [2]. By unknown means the turtles navigate [3] 1,375 miles (2,200km) to Ascension in December. Courtship and mating [4] take place just off shore. Females may mate several times [5] but sperm can be stored for long periods and several clutches [insets] can be fertilized from one mating. The female leaves the water [6] at night. She lays hundreds of eggs in a season in sandy pits [7]. When the eggs are covered and camouflaged [8] she returns to the sea [9] and after the breeding season [10] returns to Brazil. After incubating for up to 10 weeks, eggs hatch [11] almost simultaneously. The baby turtles emerge together [12] at night and scramble toward the sea [13] and head for open water [14].

2 Anolis lizard
Anolis roquet extremus

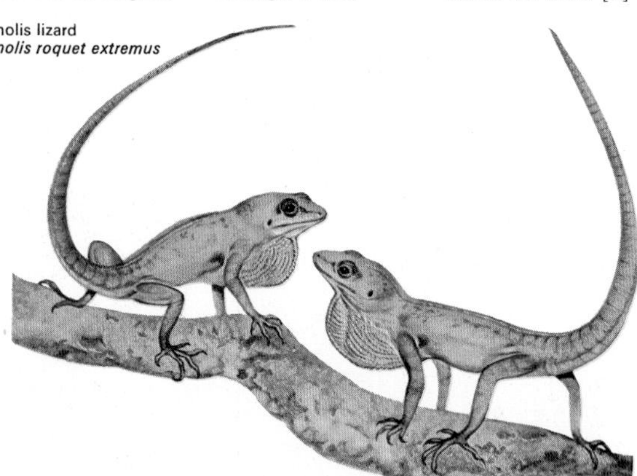

4

5 A

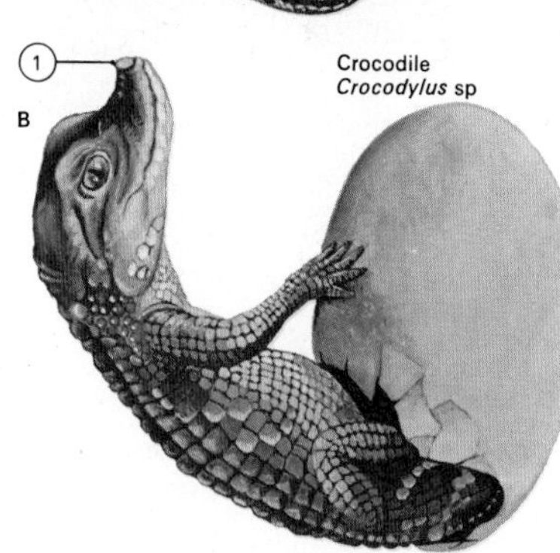

Blue racer
Coluber constrictor
1
B
Crocodile
Crocodylus sp

2 Anolis lizards display to each other by raising their bodies and tails and flashing the brightly colored dewlap. This is an aggressive display between males. Other lizards display with flashing colors and by bowing to each other.

3

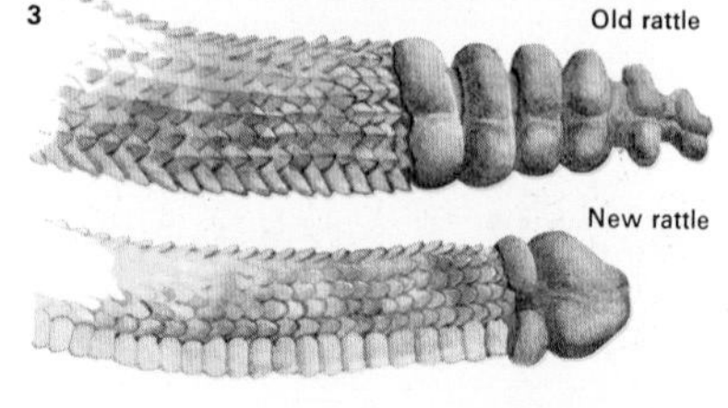

Old rattle
New rattle

3 A rattlesnake's rattle begins at birth with a hard button on the tail. Each time the skin is shed, a new tip forms, but the segments from the old skin remain. In this way a rattle is built up of a series of hard, hollow pieces connected together.

4 The "combat dance" is a display of ritual fighting by pairs of rival male snakes over territory. Venomous snakes, such as these rattlers, do not attempt to bite but merely try to push each other to the ground to establish superiority.

5 Reptile embryos have special devices with which to cut themselves out of the egg. Hatching crocodiles [B] and turtles have a special horny thickening of the skin on the snout [1] called the egg-caruncle. The hatching blue racer snake [A], like other snakes and lizards, employs an egg-tooth, which develops in the midline of the upper jaw. The tooth is large, very sharp and projects forward. After hatching it is no longer of any use and is then discarded.

some tortoises and crocodiles. Unlike mammals, reptiles may continue to grow when adult, although more slowly.

The sense organs

The sense organs of reptiles vary. Crocodilians have reasonable eyesight, with the slit pupils characteristic of nocturnal animals, but cannot distinguish colors. Their hearing is good and their sense of smell is probably adequate. Turtles and tortoises have good vision and respond to colors; they also react to scents, but their hearing is limited. Like many reptiles, they hear low notes best.

Lizards that are active during the day probably have the best reptile vision, seeing sharply and in color, as would be expected from their use of color in display. Hearing is less acute, the animals responding, if at all, to the lower end of the sound scale. The exceptions seem to be the geckos, which have good hearing, and these and crocodiles are the only reptiles to produce much sound themselves. The sense of smell varies.

There is an unusual sense organ, called Jacobson's organ [9], found in all reptiles but especially well-developed in snakes and in several families of lizards. It is made up of two small cavities in the roof of the mouth and is used in conjunction with the tongue. The organ is lined with scent-sensitive cells and the twin cavities may explain why snakes and some lizards have a forked tongue. Jacobson's organ helps a snake's sense of smell and many snakes can follow a trail by using it. Snakes also have unusual eyes. These are covered with a special transparent scale, which replaces the two lids, and a sideways-moving nictitating membrane (third eyelid), which is normal reptile equipment. Snakes are colorblind and they also lack the external eardrum that is present in other reptiles. Although they have internal ears, snakes are deaf to airborne sounds but sensitive to ground vibrations.

Some snakes possess heat detectors—sense organs that are unknown in other vertebrates. These take the form of large pits [10] on the face of rattlesnakes and other pit vipers and a series of smaller pits lined with sensitive cells around the lips of some pythons and boas.

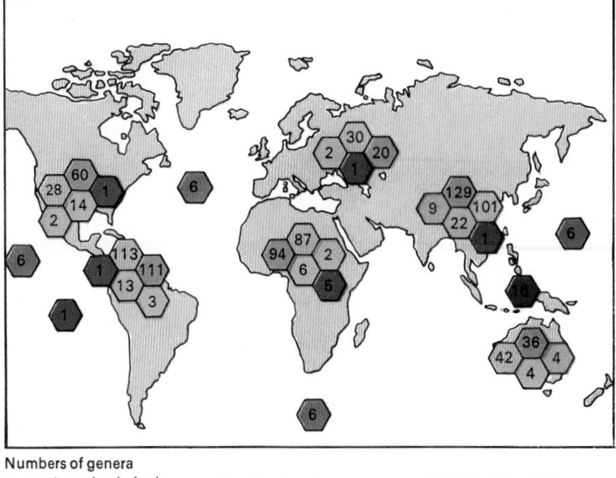
KEY
Numbers of genera
Aquatic chelonia
Terrestrial chelonia
Lizards
Snakes
Crocodilians
Marine turtles
Marine lizards
Marine snakes

Tropical regions are the home of many reptile species. Numbers on the map refer to the genera present in each area. Although they come ashore to breed in particular areas, sea turtles are widely distributed throughout the warmer oceans. The only genus of marine lizard lives on the Galapagos Islands. Australasia has relatively few genera.

6 Indian python *Python molurus*

6 Parental care is shown by few reptiles. Some snakes, such as cobras and pythons, coil around their eggs, and female crocodiles and alligators guard their nests. Because these animals are cold-blooded, they cannot keep the eggs warm, so the main effect of their presence is to deter potential predators. But there is some evidence to show that a brooding Indian python may produce heat by muscular contraction. Some lizards "brood" eggs too. The skink *(Eumeces obsoletus)* actually cleans and turns the eggs, helps the young to hatch, and then grooms them for more than a week.

7 The longest reptile that was reliably recorded was a reticulated python of 32ft (10m). The anaconda is reputed to grow larger still but while it must be the heaviest species of snake, the most acceptable record of its length is only 30ft (9m). The longest poisonous snake is the king cobra, at 18ft (5.5m). Several kinds of crocodiles may occasionally reach 20ft (6m). The giants among lizards are the Komodo dragons of Indonesia with lengths of up to 10ft (3m). Largest of the chelonians is the leatherback turtle, more than 6.5ft (2m) long and weighing more than half a ton. Galapagos and Seychelles giant tortoises are the largest on land. The smallest lizards are New World geckos *(Sphaerodactylus)* which, excluding the long tail, average only 0.75in (1.8cm) in length.

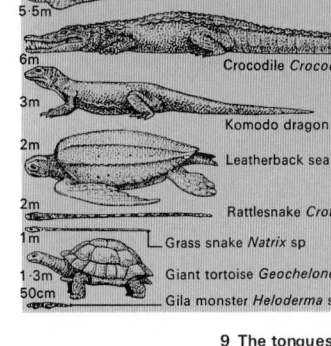

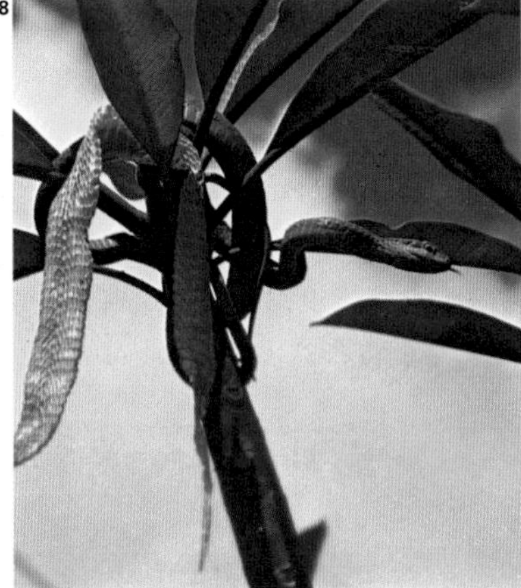

8 A snake sheds its skin regularly. The old skin undergoes chemical changes as a new layer of cells comes into readiness below. The old skin splits, usually around the lips, the snake wriggles out, and the old skin is often left as an inside-out colorless case. Colors show up brilliantly on the newly molted snake, as in this African boomslang *(Dispholidus)*.

9
1
2
3

9 The tongues [1] of lizards and snakes convey particles to Jacobson's organ [2] where smells are detected. Originally part of the nose [3], the organ became separated and well developed.

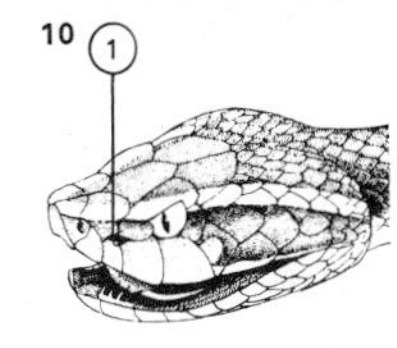
10
1

10 A sensory pit [1], sensitive to infrared radiation, is located on either side of the face of pit vipers like rattlesnakes. Even in darkness they can detect and strike at warmblooded prey such as mice.

11 A
B
C
D

11 Reptiles may control body temperature by variations in behavior. In the morning, when it needs to absorb heat, a horned lizard lies with flattened body on a sloping surface in order to absorb as much as possible [A]. Later, when less heat is needed, it turns its head to the sun and presents a smaller surface to the rays [B]. Finally, during the hottest part of the day, the lizard may seek shelter from the sun [C] or burrow into cooler soil [D].

Unusual reptiles and amphibians

The amphibians and reptiles are two groups of cold-blooded vertebrates, most of which lay eggs. The amphibians, numbering more than 2,000 species, include frogs, toads, newts, salamanders, and caecilians, and the 6,000 reptile species include the snakes, lizards, crocodiles, and turtles. They range in size from 0.75in (2cm) tree frogs that live in bromeliad "vases," to the 25ft (8m) constricting snakes.

Amphibians, because they must keep their skins moist in order to breathe, are found in wet and humid situations. Most species of amphibians live in the tropics where they can take advantage of the hot, wet climate. Reptiles are also more numerous in tropical than in temperate regions, but do not rely on the presence of water in order to survive. They are common desert animals and in this environment avoid becoming overheated by hiding during the day.

No amphibians and relatively few reptiles live in the sea. Most marine reptiles—the sea snakes are an exception—come ashore to breed.

CONNECTIONS

See also

520 The life of reptiles
522 Snakes, lizards, and turtles
518 The life of amphibiar
568 Toward life on land
570 Reptiles of the past
572 The age of reptiles
632 Endangered species

1 European green tree frog *Hyla arborea*

2 Box tortoise *Terrapene carolina*

Soft-shelled turtle *Amyda ferox*

Tropical hawk-billed turtle *Eretmochelys imbricata*

1 The European green tree frog—like all tree frogs (of which there are more than 200 species)—has disks at the ends of its toes that enable it to grip slender branches of the trees in which it lives. It is found throughout central Europe, southern Italy, and eastward to Asia. When frightened, or when the sky becomes overcast, it changes color from bright green to grey for camouflage.

2 Tortoises and turtles have a massive bony shell [1] made of plates of keratin that are fused to the backbone [2] and ribs [3]. Most can pull back their heads under the shell when danger threatens. The North American box turtle spends most of its time on land, whereas the soft-shelled turtle and the tropical hawk-billed turtle are both entirely aquatic. All turtles, however, lay eggs on land.

3 Bell's ceratophrys *Ceratophrys ornata*

3 The horned frog, Bell's ceratophrys, lives in Argentina. The horns are outgrowths of the upper eyelids. The horned frog uses its large pointed teeth to attack other frogs, which it eats.

4 Boulenger's arrow-poison frog lives at high altitudes in the South American Andes. It is easily caught and local people use a venom secreted from its skin to poison the tips of their arrows.

4 Boulenger's arrow poison frog *Atelopus boulengeri*

5 Green turtle *Chelonia mydas*

5 The green turtle lives in tropical seas but has to go ashore on sandy beaches to lay its eggs. This turtle has a flat shell and limbs well adapted for swimming. It is valued as a source of food.

6 Two-toned arrow poison frog *Phyllobates bicolor*

6 The two-toned arrow-poison frog is native to Peru. The male incubates the tadpoles on his back, as do many arrow-poison frogs. The rim of the frog's upper jaw is armed with small teeth.

7 The timber rattlesnake is common in the northeastern United States and southern Canada. Highly venomous, it grows 6.5ft(2m) long and is found in groups of a hundred or more in winter.

7 Timber rattlesnake *Crotalus horridus*

8 Boa constrictor *Constrictor constrictor*

8 The boa constrictor is a large snake that grows up to 12ft(3.6m) long. It lives in underground holes or in trees in many areas of tropical America. It preys on birds and small mammals such as rats and agoutis, which it kills by entwining them in its coils and crushing them until they suffocate.

9

Wagler's pit viper
Trimeresurus wagleri
Mangrove snake
Boiga dendrophila
Banded sea snake
Laticauda colubrina
Dog-headed water snake
Cerberus rhynchops

9 Snakes found in mangrove swamps of Southeast Asia include tree-living species and species that have adopted an aquatic way of life. The two arboreal snakes have become adapted to different feeding methods. The bird-eating *Boiga* moves rapidly in order to catch its prey, while Wagler's pit viper is more likely to lie in wait for prey, which it detects with its heat-sensitive pits. The aquatic snakes hunt fish and mollusks for food.

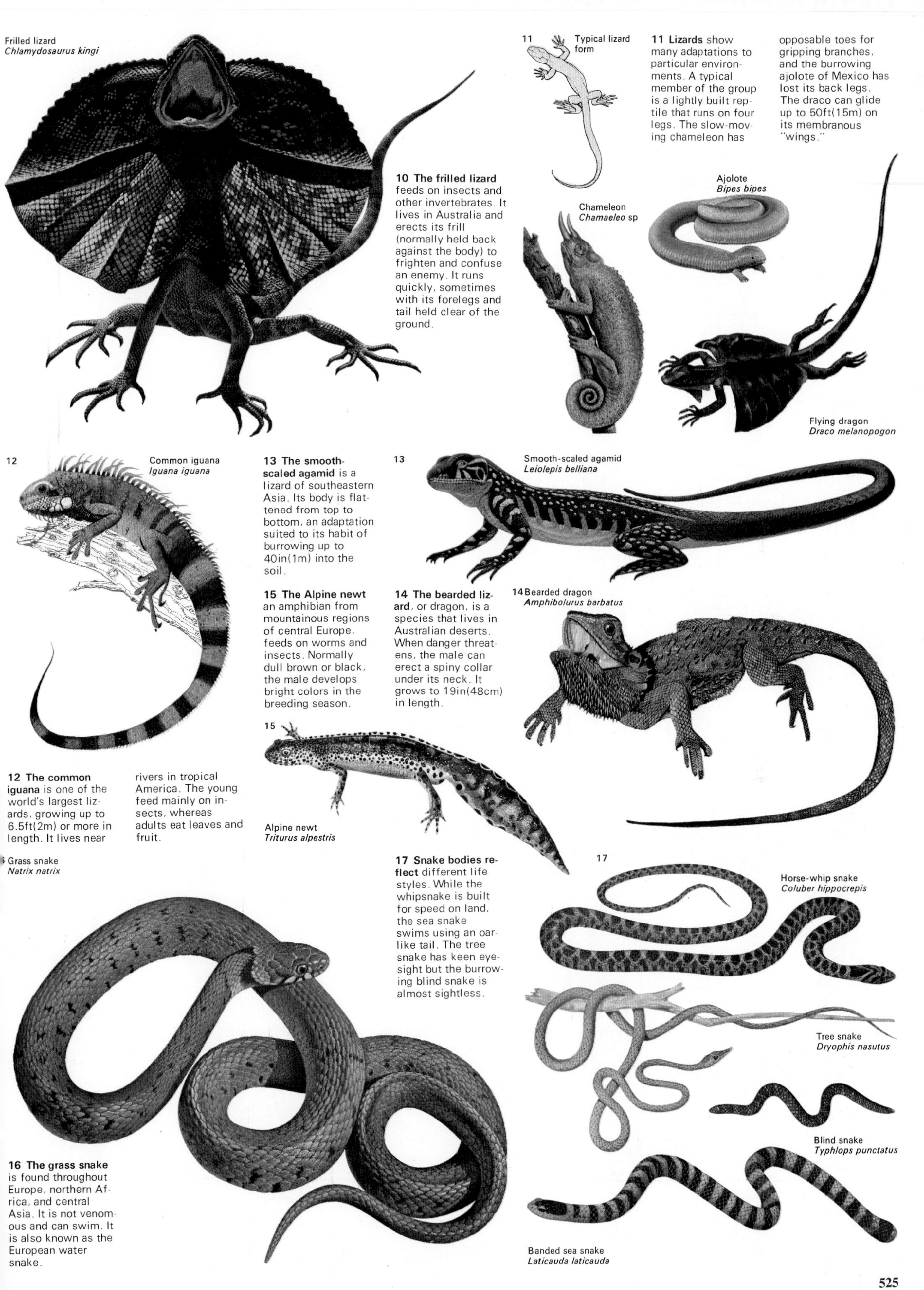
Frilled lizard
Chlamydosaurus kingi
11
Typical lizard form
Chameleon
Chamaeleo sp
Ajolote
Bipes bipes
Flying dragon
Draco melanopogon
12
Common iguana
Iguana iguana
13
Smooth-scaled agamid
Leiolepis belliana
14 Bearded dragon
Amphibolurus barbatus
15
Alpine newt
Triturus alpestris
16 Grass snake
Natrix natrix
17
Horse-whip snake
Coluber hippocrepis
Tree snake
Dryophis nasutus
Blind snake
Typhlops punctatus
Banded sea snake
Laticauda laticauda

10 The frilled lizard feeds on insects and other invertebrates. It lives in Australia and erects its frill (normally held back against the body) to frighten and confuse an enemy. It runs quickly, sometimes with its forelegs and tail held clear of the ground.

11 Lizards show many adaptations to particular environments. A typical member of the group is a lightly built reptile that runs on four legs. The slow-moving chameleon has opposable toes for gripping branches, and the burrowing ajolote of Mexico has lost its back legs. The draco can glide up to 50ft(15m) on its membranous "wings."

12 The common iguana is one of the world's largest lizards, growing up to 6.5ft(2m) or more in length. It lives near rivers in tropical America. The young feed mainly on insects, whereas adults eat leaves and fruit.

13 The smooth-scaled agamid is a lizard of southeastern Asia. Its body is flattened from top to bottom, an adaptation suited to its habit of burrowing up to 40in(1m) into the soil.

14 The bearded lizard, or dragon, is a species that lives in Australian deserts. When danger threatens, the male can erect a spiny collar under its neck. It grows to 19in(48cm) in length.

15 The Alpine newt an amphibian from mountainous regions of central Europe, feeds on worms and insects. Normally dull brown or black, the male develops bright colors in the breeding season.

16 The grass snake is found throughout Europe, northern Africa, and central Asia. It is not venomous and can swim. It is also known as the European water snake.

17 Snake bodies reflect different life styles. While the whipsnake is built for speed on land, the sea snake swims using an oar-like tail. The tree snake has keen eyesight but the burrowing blind snake is almost sightless.

The classification of birds

The study of wildlife is possible only if each specimen can be labeled adequately and unambiguously. The system of labeling birds currently in use was propounded by the Swedish naturalist Carl von Linné (1707–78), whose name is more familiar in its Latinized form of Carolus Linnaeus. He proposed that every living creature should have a "binomial" consisting of a generic and a specific name. The carrion crow, for example, belongs to the genus *Corvus* and is specifically *Corvus corone*. Each of the 8,600 bird species has its own name.

The basis of grouping

Several genera of closely related birds are grouped together in families and when more than one family is considered to have descended from a single ancestral form then these families are grouped in the same order. In the case of the Corvidae, the family to which the crow belongs, the appropriate order is the Passeriformes [28]—the largest bird order, containing 57 families, including finches, family Fringillidae, the starlings, family Sturnidae, the thrushes, family Muscicapidae, and the swallows, family Hirundinidae. All the 28 orders of birds are classified in the class Aves and the subphylum Vertebrata (the backboned animals).

Although birds are placed in their respective groups largely on the basis of anatomical and behavioral comparisons, in recent years the analysis of the egg—and especially of the proteins in the egg white—has been used. This procedure has caused controversy among taxonomists because affinities of various bird groups have been suggested that do not agree with traditional ideas. The taxonomic problems created by several aberrant groups have been solved, however, by egg-white analysis. The hoatzin—long given a family of its own—is now, as a result of this technique, considered to be a strange cuckoo and placed in the family Cuculidae which, with the turacos, form the order Cuculiformes [20].

Examination of the anatomy of the flamingos (family Phoenicopteridae), showed similarities to the storks (family Ciconiidae, order Ciconiiformes) but studies of their behavior and feather lice suggested relationships with the ducks and geese (family Anatidae, order Anseriformes). On the evidence of egg-white proteins, however, flamingos are now thought to be more closely related to herons (family Ardeidae) of the Ciconiiformes.

Convergent evolution

The several species of large ground-dwelling birds—the ostrich, rhea, emu, and cassowary—all resemble each other quite closely but are thought to have arisen independently and as such are examples of a phenomenon called convergent evolution. They are thus classified in separate orders—the ostrich in the Struthioniformes [1], the rhea in the Rheiformes [2], and both the cassowary and the emu in the order Casuariiformes [3].

The strange New Zealand kiwi also has its own order, the Apterygiformes [4]. Similarly the divers are alone in the order Gaviiformes [5], the grebes in the Podicipediformes [6], and the penguins in

CONNECTIONS

See also
528 The anatomy of bi
530 How birds reprodu
532 Birds and migratio
534 Bird life and variet
536 How birds behave
630 Endangered birds
538 Island birds
458 The animal kingdo
570 Reptiles of the pas

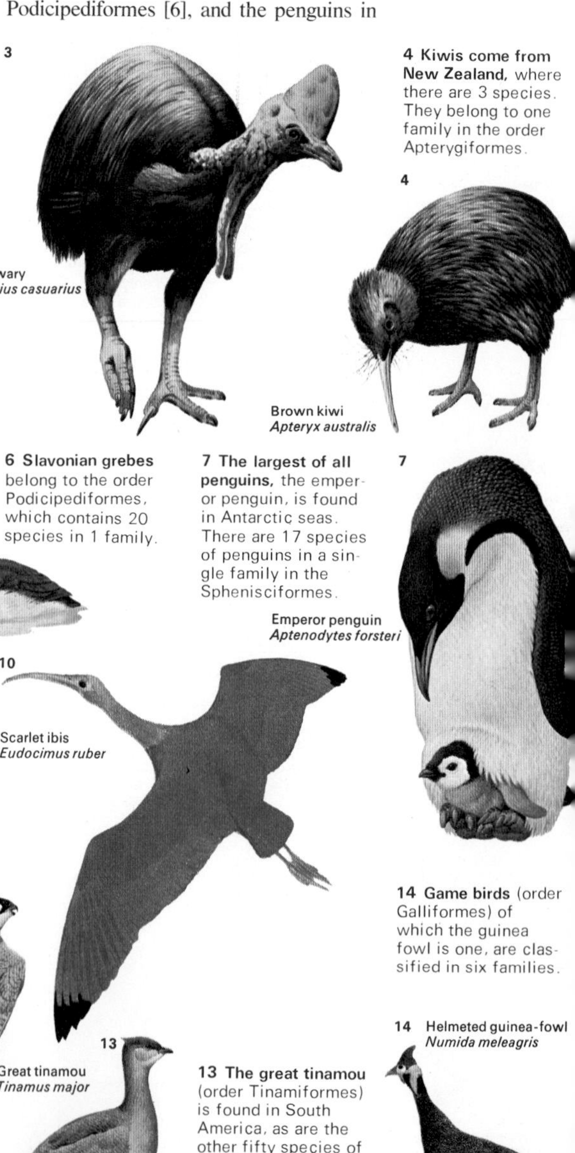

1 Ostrich *Struthio camelus*

1 Africa is the home of the ostrich, the largest living bird. The single species is the only member of the order Struthioniformes.

2 Greater rhea *Rhea americana*

2 The South American rhea is ostrich-like. Its order, the Rheiformes, has two species.

3 Cassowary *Casuarius casuarius*

3 The cassowary and emu of Australasia belong to separate families in the Casuariiformes.

4 Brown kiwi *Apteryx australis*

4 Kiwis come from New Zealand, where there are 3 species. They belong to one family in the order Apterygiformes.

5 Arctic loon *Gavia arctica*

5 The Arctic loon is one of 4 species of the order Gaviiformes found in the Arctic regions.

6 Slavonian grebe *Podiceps auritus*

6 Slavonian grebes belong to the order Podicipediformes, which contains 20 species in 1 family.

7 Emperor penguin *Aptenodytes forsteri*

7 The largest of all penguins, the emperor penguin, is found in Antarctic seas. There are 17 species of penguins in a single family in the Sphenisciformes.

8 Great shearwater *Puffinus gravis*

8 The great shearwater is a sea bird of the order Procellariiformes, which contains four families.

9 Darter *Anhinga anhinga*

9 The darter, tropic bird, gannet, cormorant, pelican, and frigate bird families are placed in the order Pelecaniformes.

10 Scarlet ibis *Eudocimus ruber*

10 The scarlet ibis is a colorful member of one of the six families in the order Ciconiiformes.

11 Black swan *Cygnus atratus*

11 From Australia comes the black swan, one of the 147 species of the duck family in the order Anseriformes.

12 Hobby *Falco subbuteo*

12 Diurnal birds of prey in the order Falconiformes include the falcon, vulture, osprey, and hawk families. The hobby is a typical falcon.

13 Great tinamou *Tinamus major*

13 The great tinamou (order Tinamiformes) is found in South America, as are the other fifty species of the order.

14 Helmeted guinea-fowl *Numida meleagris*

14 Game birds (order Galliformes) of which the guinea fowl is one, are classified in six families.

the Sphenisciformes [7]. The families of tube-nosed sea birds, the petrels, albatrosses, and shearwaters are in the order Procellariiformes [8]. The six families in the order Pelecaniformes [9] are water-dwellers.

The six families of large, long-legged wading birds—herons, the shoebill, the hammerhead, storks, ibises, and flamingos—are placed together in the order Ciconiiformes [10]. The ducks, geese, swans and screamers are Anseriformes [11].

Family relationships

Diurnal birds of prey, including the vultures, are placed in five families and combined in the order Falconiformes [12]. The single family of terrestrial game birds of South America, the tinamous, have an order, the Tinamiformes [13], to themselves. Pheasants, grouse, guinea fowl, and turkeys are all ground-dwelling game birds classified with the remarkable megapode family of Australasia and the South American curassow family in the order Galliformes [14].

Many of the Gruiformes [15] are aquatic. Those that are terrestrial, such as the bustards and hemipodes, fly only rarely. Wading behavior is a feature of several Charadriiformes [16], an order that includes the plovers, avocets, gulls and auks.

The sandgrouse are a one-family order, the Pteroclidiformes [17], as are the pigeons and doves of the Columbiformes [18], and the parrots of the Psittaciformes [19]. The Strigiformes [21], owls and barn owls, is composed of just two families.

Nocturnal life styles and large mouths are the features shared by most birds in the five families of the order Caprimulgiformes [22], a group that includes the frogmouths and nightjars; and small feet and legs characterize and give the name to the order Apodiformes [23], the group to which the swifts and hummingbirds belong. Some rather peculiar birds, the mousebirds, or Coliiformes [24], and the trogons, or Trogoniformes [25], make up two single-family orders. The spectacular kingfishers, hornbills, and cuckoo-rollers represent three of the nine families in the order Coraciiformes [26], while the Piciformes [27] are the woodpeckerlike birds.

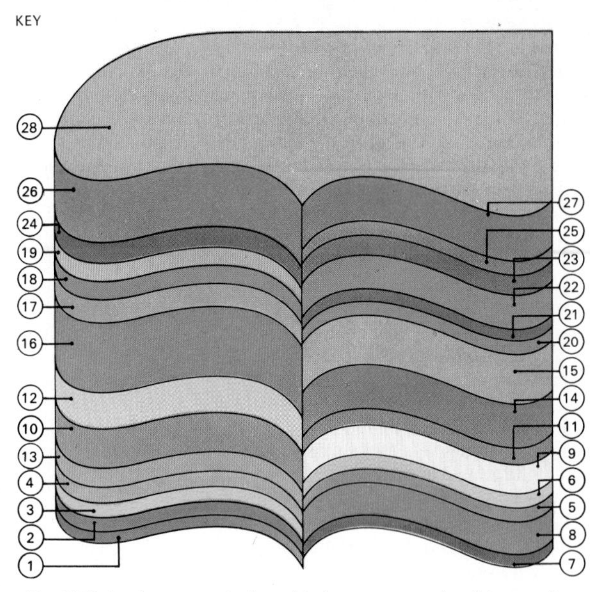
KEY
28
26
24
19
18
17
16
12
10
13
4
3
2
1
27
25
23
22
21
20
15
14
11
9
6
5
8
7

The 28 bird orders are arranged in evolutionary sequence, starting with the most primitive at the bottom. The numbers on the diagram refer to the illustrations below.

15

15 A rare bird from North America is the whooping crane. It is classified in the order Gruiformes, the members of whose twelve families are mostly waders.

Whooping crane
Grus americana

16

Ruff
Philomachus pugnax

16 The ruff (order Charadriiformes) is a member of one of the sixteen families forming this group.

17 Pallas' sandgrouse
Syrrhaptes paradoxus

17 Dry grasslands and deserts are the home of the sandgrouse (order Pteroclidiformes).

18

18 The Australian crested pigeon belongs to the single family in the order Columbiformes.

Crested pigeon
Ocyphaps lophotes

19 One of the widespread parrot family in the order Psittaciformes is the blue and yellow macaw.

19

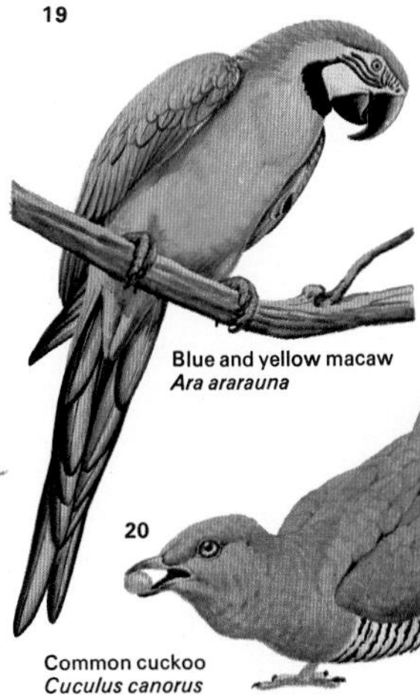

Blue and yellow macaw
Ara ararauna

20 The cuckoo belongs to the larger of two families that make up the order Cuculiformes.

20

Common cuckoo
Cuculus canorus

21 Snowy owls of the Arctic belong to one of two owl families, both mostly nocturnal, that together make up the order Strigiformes.

21

Snowy owl
Nyctea scandiaca

22

Pennant-winged nightjar
Macrodipteryx vexillarius

22 Large-mouthed insect-eating birds such as the nightjar make up the order Caprimulgiformes.

23

Andean hillstar
Oreotrochilus estella

23 Hummingbirds and swifts are classified in three families in the order Apodiformes.

24

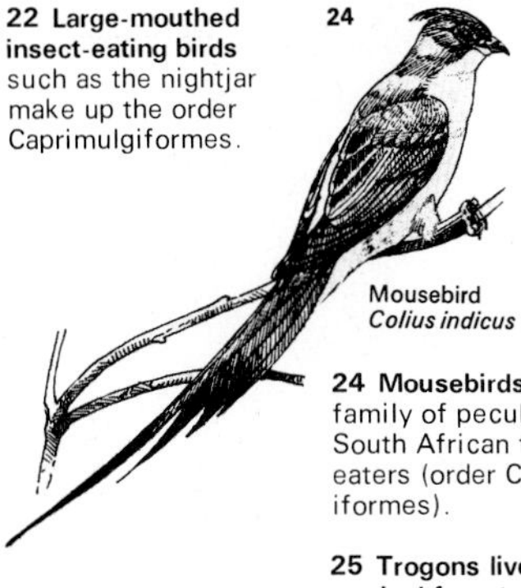

Mousebird
Colius indicus

24 Mousebirds are a family of peculiar South African fruit-eaters (order Coliiformes).

25

Indian trogon
Harpactes fasciatus

25 Trogons live in all tropical forests. The single family makes up the order Trogoniformes.

26

26 Kingfishers, hornbills, and bee-eaters are three of the nine families in the order Coraciiformes.

Kookaburra
Dacelo gigas

27

Rufous-tailed jacamar
Galbula ruficauda

27 Woodpeckers and their allies make up a worldwide group that includes jacamars and toucans. The six families are all classified in the order Piciformes.

28

Green jay
Cyanocorax yncas

28 The largest order of birds is the Passeriformes, with more than half the living species. It includes crows, tits, antbirds, and finches.

The anatomy of birds

Birds are the only group of vertebrate animals (apart from bats) that are capable of true flight, as distinct from mere gliding. Although they are masters of the air they are also at home on land or in the water, and some—certain ducks for example—are efficient in all three. The development of feathers has been crucial to this success. Feathers undoubtedly came before flight. They were evolved, like fur, for insulating a warm-blooded body and were only later used as airfoils. Birds were probably feathered for millions of years before they flew. But many other developments were also necessary.

Physical adaptations for flight

The adaptations of a bird for flight involve all of the principal structural and behavioral features of the animal. The structural changes center on the development of strength with lightness. Therefore the bones are hollowed or honeycombed or molded into thin, curved plates to make them light yet strong enough for the jobs they have to perform. The light beak takes the place of heavy teeth and the feather covering is very light—even though it may weigh more than the skeleton. A series of air sacs in the body cavity, connected with the lungs, assist in respiration.

The rearrangement of bones to deal with the mechanical stresses in an animal that walks on its hind legs and flies with its front ones is seen principally in the pectoral (shoulder) and pelvic (hip) regions. The pectoral girdle is firmly attached to the breastbone so that the body is efficiently suspended from the wings in flight [7]. This is brought about by an extra development of the coracoid bones, which are absent in mammals. Similarly, the pelvic girdle is so strengthened and arranged that the hind legs can efficiently carry the bird's weight on the ground and especially they can act as shock absorbers on landing. Because bones are so delicate, they have been strengthened by fusion. As in mammals, the three bones of the pelvic girdle on each side are fused together and to the backbone. There has also been a fusion of vertebrae in the spine, from the last thoracic (chest) one through all the lumbars and sacrals to the first few caudal (tail) vertebrae. These fused vertebrae form the synsacrum, which supports the pelvic girdle and lets the legs and wings function efficiently without the need of bulky trunk muscles.

Limbs and feathers

The limb skeleton of birds is also much modified from the basic vertebrate arrangement. The bones of the lower leg and the tarsal (ankle) bones of the foot have become elongated and fused to provide an extra joint in the limb [11]. The thigh bone of birds is usually concealed in the body wall and feathers. An unusual feature of the hindlimb is the mechanism for ensuring a good perching grip. The toe flexor muscles originate above the knee. Their tendons pass in front of the knee, behind the ankle, and beneath the toes. When a bird's leg is flexed (bent), as when perched, this arrangement ensures that the toes grasp tightly even during sleep.

In the forelimb the "hand" is much reduced, the few remaining bones being

CONNECTIONS

See also
530 How birds reproduc
526 The classification of birds
532 Birds and migration
534 Bird life and variety
536 How birds behave
538 Island birds
460 Animal anatomy
570 Reptiles of the past

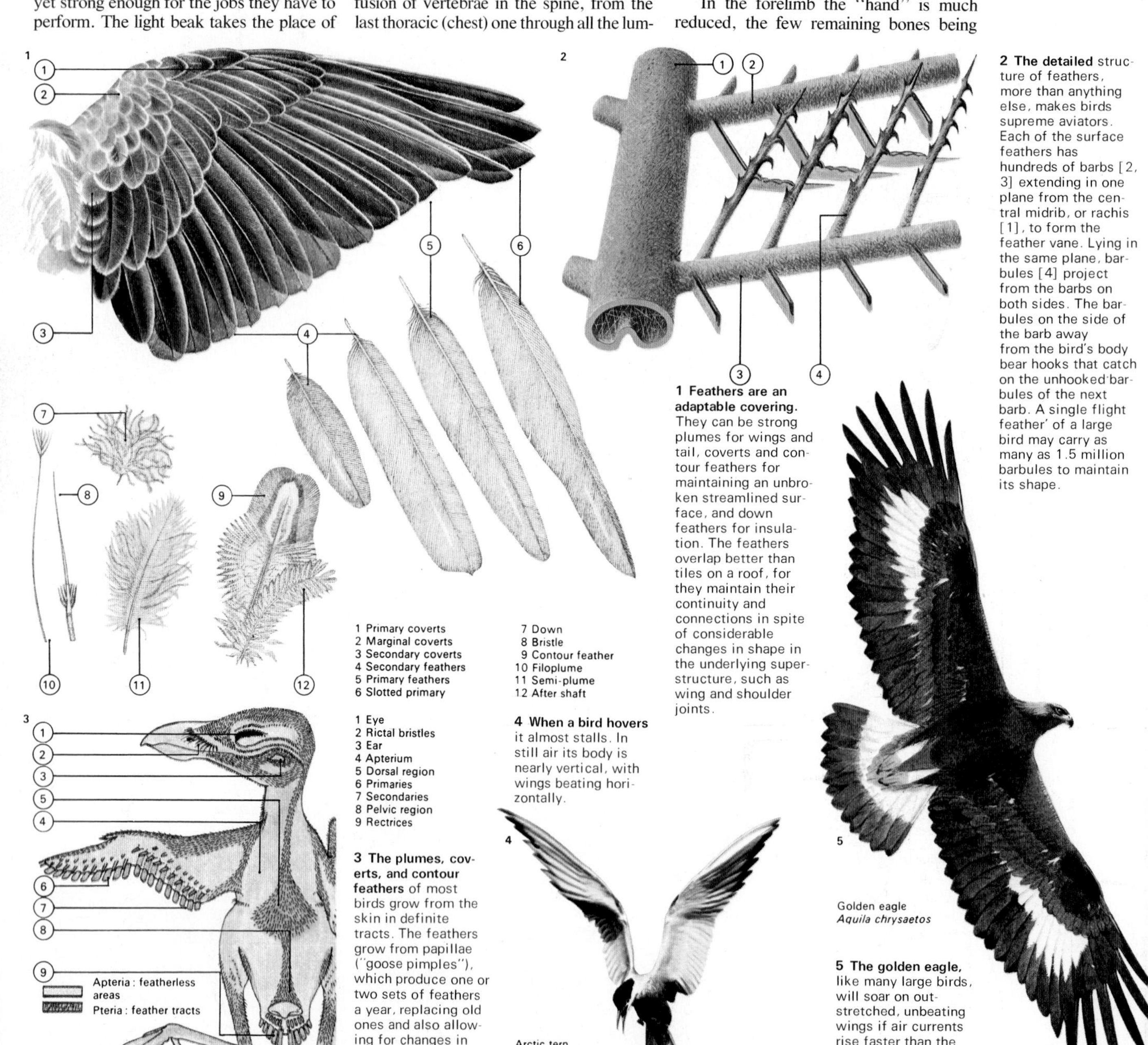

1
2
3
4
5
6
7
8
9
10
11
12
1 Primary coverts
2 Marginal coverts
3 Secondary coverts
4 Secondary feathers
5 Primary feathers
6 Slotted primary
7 Down
8 Bristle
9 Contour feather
10 Filoplume
11 Semi-plume
12 After shaft
1 Eye
2 Rictal bristles
3 Ear
4 Apterium
5 Dorsal region
6 Primaries
7 Secondaries
8 Pelvic region
9 Rectrices
Apteria: featherless areas
Pteria: feather tracts
Arctic tern
Sterna paradisaea
Golden eagle
Aquila chrysaetos

1 Feathers are an adaptable covering. They can be strong plumes for wings and tail, coverts and contour feathers for maintaining an unbroken streamlined surface, and down feathers for insulation. The feathers overlap better than tiles on a roof, for they maintain their continuity and connections in spite of considerable changes in shape in the underlying superstructure, such as wing and shoulder joints.

2 The detailed structure of feathers, more than anything else, makes birds supreme aviators. Each of the surface feathers has hundreds of barbs [2, 3] extending in one plane from the central midrib, or rachis [1], to form the feather vane. Lying in the same plane, barbules [4] project from the barbs on both sides. The barbules on the side of the barb away from the bird's body bear hooks that catch on the unhooked barbules of the next barb. A single flight feather' of a large bird may carry as many as 1.5 million barbules to maintain its shape.

3 The plumes, coverts, and contour feathers of most birds grow from the skin in definite tracts. The feathers grow from papillae ("goose pimples"), which produce one or two sets of feathers a year, replacing old ones and also allowing for changes in color.

4 When a bird hovers it almost stalls. In still air its body is nearly vertical, with wings beating horizontally.

5 The golden eagle, like many large birds, will soar on outstretched, unbeating wings if air currents rise faster than the bird loses height.

largely fused to form an attachment for the primary flight feathers. The first remaining digit forms a support for the alula, which acts as a slot to prevent stalling at low flight speeds. The secondary flight feathers are attached to the ulna in the forearm. Together with the remarkable structure of feathers [1, 2], this results in a wing of extreme efficiency and adaptability that functions as a propeller as well as an airfoil.

Feathers in flight

The flight feathers of the wing (remiges) and those of the tail (rectrices) provide lift, thrust, and guidance in flight, but their aerodynamic properties are not fully understood. In normal flapping flight [8] the wing is beaten strongly downward and forward and then more quickly upward and backward. On the down strike the wing has such a high angle of attack that it would stall if the primary feathers did not act as individual adaptable airfoils to prevent this. Each feather twists up and back along its length so that the total resultant thrust is strongly forward, the separation of the feather tips assisting this. Also, at a certain angle of attack, the alula lifts forward from the front of the wing creating a "slot" to cut down turbulence over the airfoil and reduce the risk of the wing stalling. Birds capable of flying slowly have particularly well-developed wing slots (large spaces between the primary feathers); for example, those of the golden eagle *(Aquila chrysaëtos)* [5] may take up as much as 40 percent of the total wing area when in use.

At the other extreme from eagles and vultures, seabirds such as the albatrosses have long thin wings. These birds rarely flap their wings but soar in the wind, principally by gliding and accelerating downwind and then turning and climbing sharply upwind until they almost stall. Their flight is so highly specialized that on still days albatrosses are "grounded."

The specialized wings of hummingbirds, in which flight feathers are primaries only, may beat up to 50 times a second or more while the bird is hovering, the stroke being horizontal and powered in both forward and backward directions.

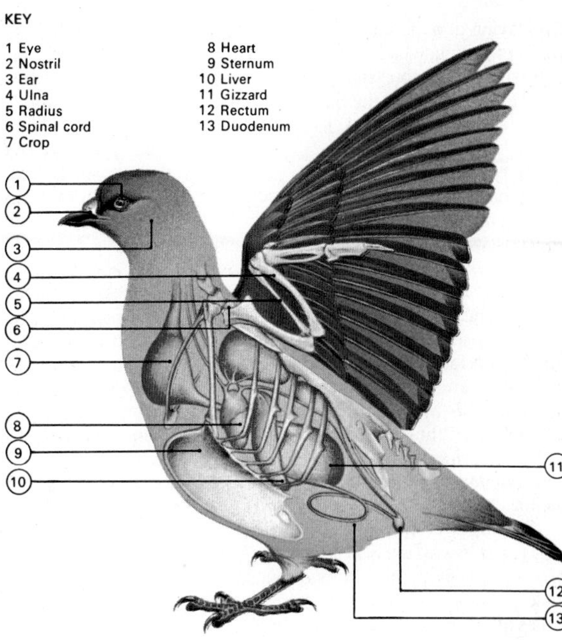
KEY
1 Eye
2 Nostril
3 Ear
4 Ulna
5 Radius
6 Spinal cord
7 Crop
8 Heart
9 Sternum
10 Liver
11 Gizzard
12 Rectum
13 Duodenum

6

Whinchat
Saxicola rubetra

6 On landing, a bird reduces its speed. This is usually achieved by swinging the body into an upright position with its tail spread and its wings beating against the direction of flight.

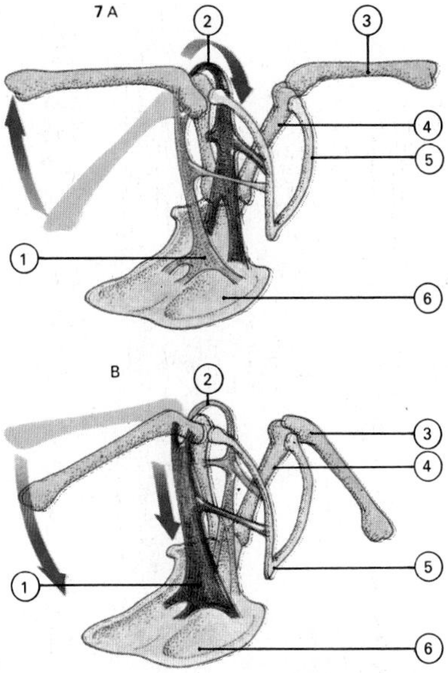

7A

B

7 The flight muscles (pectoralis overlying supracoracoideus) [1] are attached to a large-keeled sternum [6] and a pair of struts, the coracoids [4], between the sternum and the shoulder joint. This includes part of the wishbone (fused clavicles) [5] and the scapulae (shoulder blades). The joint forms a pulley through which the tendon of the supracoracoideus [2] passes to be inserted on top of the humerus [3]. Therefore the wing is pulled up when the supracoracoideus contracts [A] and down when the pectoralis contracts [B].

8 The wing movements of the mallard *(Anas platyrhynchos)* show something of the intricacies of flapping flight. The upper arm acts as an airfoil as in gliding flight. The main thrust is developed by the wing tip, which moves much faster than the rest of the wing.

Mallard
Anas platyrhynchos

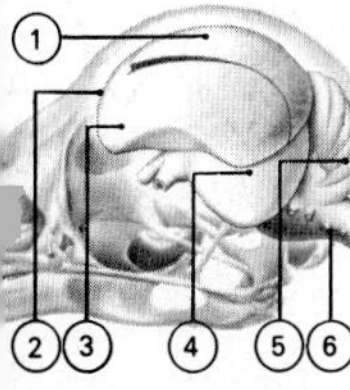

1 Cerebral cortex
2 Olfactory bulb—small birds have poor sense of smell
3 Corpus striatum
4 Large optic lobes
5 Cerebellum—muscular co-ordination centre
6 Medulla oblongata—origin of most of cranial nerves

9 Birds have "instinct" brains for the coordination of complex inborn behavior patterns and a well-developed corpus striatum that controls these activities. Mammals possess "intelligence" brains with a highly developed cerebral cortex. The bird's cortex is well enough developed for advanced types of learning to occur, and this, with instinctive behavior, the power of flight, and good eyesight, permits a wide range of complex activities.

10

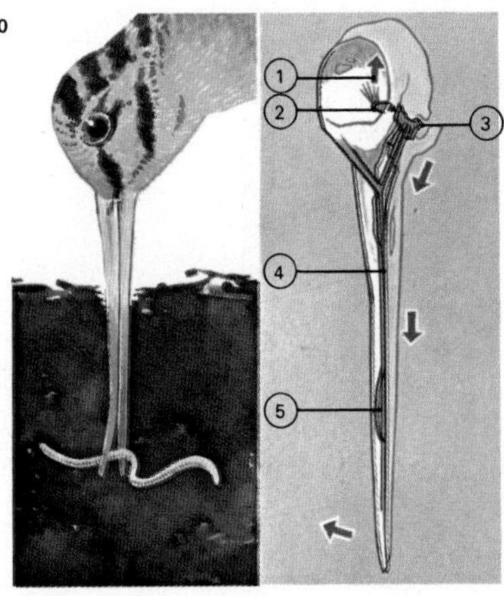

10 Most manipulations are performed by the bill. The woodcock shows how complex such procedures can be when it plunges its bill deep into mud to take a worm. When it has reached its prey, the bill tip is opened by the quadrate bones [2] rocking forward in their seating [3] when muscles [1] contract. This pushes forward on the jugal bones [4]; these in turn push the tip of the upper beak open beyond a thin, hinge-like area [5].

11

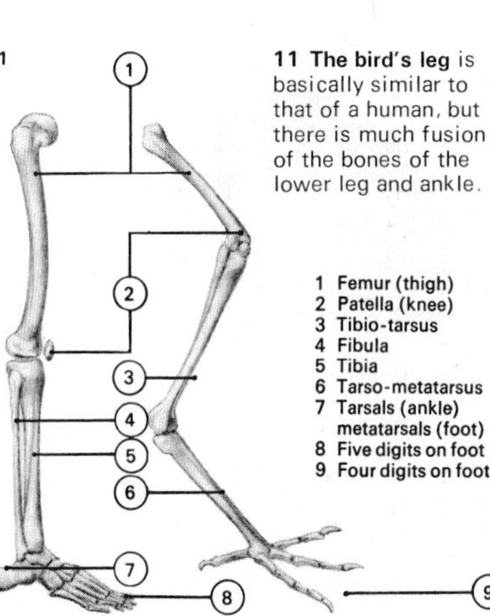

11 The bird's leg is basically similar to that of a human, but there is much fusion of the bones of the lower leg and ankle.

1 Femur (thigh)
2 Patella (knee)
3 Tibio-tarsus
4 Fibula
5 Tibia
6 Tarso-metatarsus
7 Tarsals (ankle) metatarsals (foot)
8 Five digits on foot
9 Four digits on foot

How birds reproduce

The laying of a clutch of bird's eggs is the result of mating, which in turn is the result of courtship. The courtship displays [1] of birds are as varied as the birds that employ them and are essential to procreation.

Courtship displays

To human eyes some bird display may not seem apparent, as in the robin. But this is a species with a highly developed song. Songbirds have evolved their characteristic songs for the establishment and maintenance of the pair-bond, as well as for territorial advertisement and warning off intruders. In species of similar appearance living in the same area, such as the willow warbler *(Phylloscopus trochilus)* and the chiffchaff *(P. collybita)*, the differences in song seem to be the principal means of both specific and individual recognition, to the birds as well as to humans.

The most complex bird courtship displays are those of the bowerbirds and other members of the family Ptilonorhynchidae, widespread in Australasia. Not only are the males of many species very brightly colored but many also have outstanding powers of mimicry and build elaborate display grounds (bowers) in which they conduct their courtship. Some species build mounds, huts, or avenues; the ground and their buildings may be decorated with fruits, flowers, shells, or bones; some species even paint their bowers with a mixture of saliva and dried grass, charcoal, or fruit pulp.

Nests and eggs

The nests of birds [4, 5, 7], where the eggs are laid, vary from mere scrapes in the ground as made by birds such as plovers and stilts, to large intricately-woven and even communal structures like those of the weaver birds (Ploceidae). Some birds, such as the auks (Alcidae), make no nest at all, and lay their eggs on the bare rock. An extreme case is the emperor penguin *(Aptenodytes forsteri)*, which incubates its egg on its feet, covered with a flap of its feathered belly, through 64 days and nights of darkness and cold in the Antarctic winter.

The bird's egg [6] is an adaptation for embryonic development on dry land. It is a closed system: within the shell when it is laid there is provision for the nourishment of the growing embryo, room for it to develop, mechanical protection, and a means of dealing with waste material. Birds' eggs are uricotelic; that is, the excretory product (waste) of the embryo is largely uric acid. This is a highly insoluble substance and therefore does not dissolve in the embryo's body fluids. It remains inert in the egg and is left behind when the fully-developed embryo hatches.

The formation of an egg in the oviduct [Key] follows a carefully controlled sequence of events. After fertilization by sperm received from the male, the egg proper—ovum plus nutrient yolk—passes down the oviduct. It is then covered by the protective jellylike albumen, or "white," of the egg, then by the two shell membranes and the shell. The last is deposited in layers and is followed, finally, by a thin cuticle. The pigments that give the egg its specific and even individual appearance are deposited mainly in the outer layers of the shell and in the cuticle. They consist of two basic colors:

CONNECTIONS

See also
528 The anatomy of bir
536 How birds behave
534 Bird life and variet
462 Sex in the animal world
532 Birds and migratio
382 Poultry and egg production
830 Types of ritual

1
Ruffed grouse
Bonasa umbellus
Yellow-thighed manakin
Pipra mentalis
Blackcock
Lyrurus tetrix
Ruff
Philomachus pugnax
Greater bird of paradise
Paradisaea apoda
Hawfinch
Coccothraustes coccothraustes
Kingfisher
Alcedo atthis
Adélie penguin
Pygoscelis adeliae
Great frigatebird
Fregata minor
Shag
Phalacrocorax aristotelis
Gannet
Morus bassanus
Black-headed gull
Larus ridibundus
Robin
Erithacus rubecula
Jackdaw
Corvus monedula
Pochard
Aythya ferina
Pintail
Anas acuta

1 Courtship leads birds into a wide variety of displays. The most obvious is male adornment as with the plumage of the bird of paradise and the grouse. Bizarre movements often accompany plumage development, as in manakins and penguins. Simple feeding gestures can also be significant, as in robins and kingfishers. Hawfinches tend to be courtly in their approach. If stress builds up, the "cut-off" gesture shown here by black-headed gulls who are head flagging, often reduces tension.

2 Adélie penguin
Pygoscelis adeliae

2 Between Adélie penguins, courtship includes the presentation of nest stones by the male. This reinforces the attraction of the birds to a particular spot to which they return yearly. The birds occupy "rookeries" in the Antarctic spring (Sept/Oct), traveling more than 200 miles (320km) over sea, ice, and snow to reach them. They usually hatch their two eggs after 35 days.

3

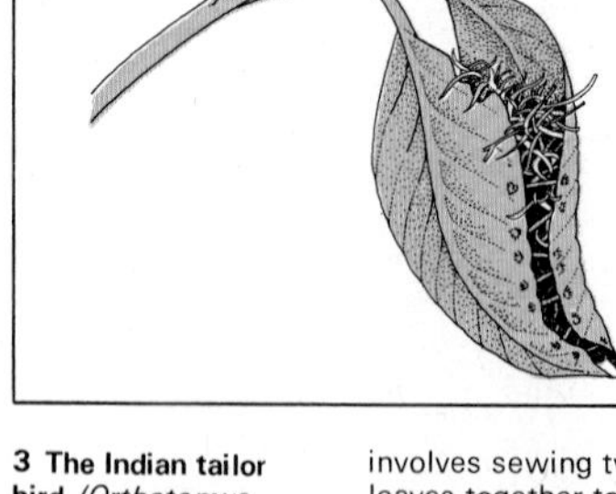

3 The Indian tailor bird *(Orthotomus sutorius)* is one of the species that has fitted in with human development, occupying gardens and verandas where there are suitable plants for nest-making. This involves sewing two leaves together to make a basket, inside which a nest is built. The bird makes holes in the leaf margins with its bill and "sews" the edges together with cotton or grass.

4 Cave swiftlets *(Collocalia fuciphaga)* make their nests in the walls and roofs of caves. The nests are often in total darkness and the birds use a form of echolocation for navigation. The principal nest material is saliva, sometimes mixed with feathers or other materials, depending on the species. Pure saliva nests are highly prized in the Orient for making bird's nest soup.

4

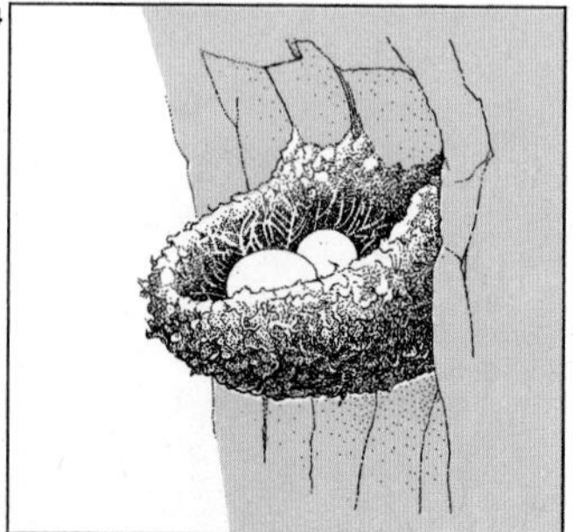

5 The rufous ovenbird *(Furnarius rufus)*, of Brazil and Argentina, lays its three to five eggs in a conspicuous domed nest of mud and straw. This gives it a local name of *el hornero* (the baker).

5

red-brown and blue-green. Varying combinations and intensities of these two pigments give a wide range of egg patterns.

Some of the most strikingly colored eggs are those of birds that nest on the ground in the open, such as the plovers, gulls, terns, and nightjars. The eggs of tinamous are unusual in that they have the appearance of polished porcelain and a range of colors including chocolate, grey, purple, and near-black.

Shapes and sizes

The shapes of birds' eggs vary considerably, from the well-known ovoid to the almost spherical eggs of some birds of prey and the pear-shaped ones of plovers and guillemots. There is also a great range of size in birds' eggs from the largest, that of the ostrich, to the smallest hummingbird's egg. The egg of an ostrich *(Struthio camelus)* averages 6–8in (15–20cm) long and weighs about 3.5lb (1.5kg). That of the bee hummingbird *(Mellisuga helenae)* is only 0.45in (11.4mm) long and weighs about 0.18oz (0.5gm); less than one 3,000th of the weight of an ostrich egg. The largest egg was laid by an extinct bird, the elephant bird *(Aepyornis maximus)*, from Madagascar. Its fossilized eggs are 13in (32.5cm) long and must have weighed about 27lb (12.3kg). The relative size of a bird to its egg varies too, the larger birds tending to have relatively smaller eggs. Small birds produce eggs one-eighth of their weight or more, while in the larger species the proportion may be less than one-fiftieth.

The bird's egg is such an efficient structure for protecting the growing embryo inside that it is necessarily difficult to break out of. The hatching bird therefore has to employ a special combination of "equipment" and behavior in order to get out of its shelly prison. By means of an egg-tooth at the tip of the upper bill and a series of vigorous upward nods of the head, the chick makes a series of ruptures ("pips") around the blunt end of the egg, turning counterclockwise on its axis as seen from that end, until enough of the shell has been cracked to enable the chick to break the rest with one blow.

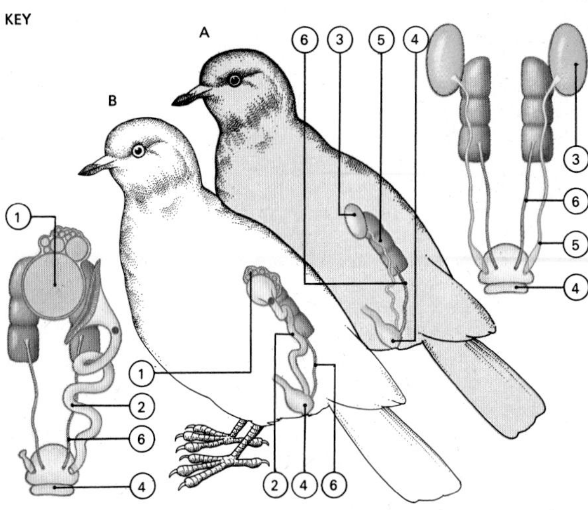

KEY
A
B

In adult pigeons, the male [A] and female [B] urinogenital systems have basic similarities. In the female, the reproductive system is made up of the left ovary [1] and the oviduct [2] only, the right side being reduced to leave room for the relatively large egg. Eggs and sperm from ovaries and testes [3] pass to the cloaca [4] via the oviduct and vasa deferentia [5]. Kidney ducts [6] also open into the cloaca.

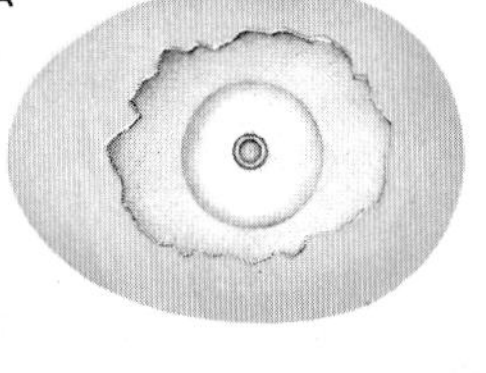

6A

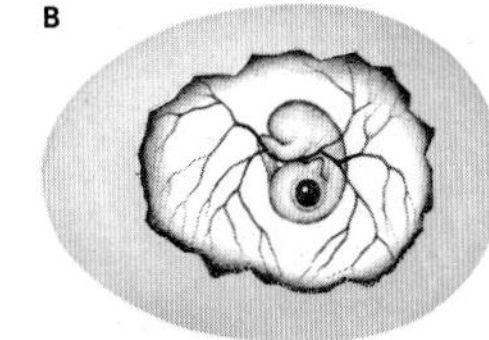

B

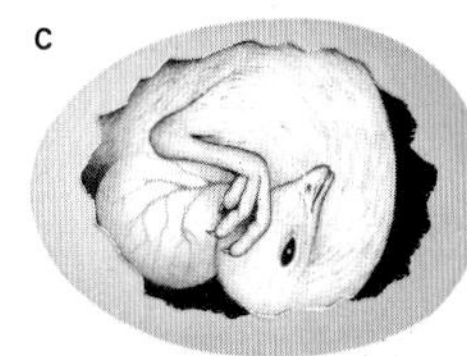

C

D
E

6 The chicken's egg is surrounded by a strong calcareous shell that has two lining membranes. These enclose the albumen that surrounds the yolk, on top of which is the ovum [A]. A fertilized egg develops quickly if incubated, the heart pumping blood after only three days. After nine days, capillaries extend over the yolk, transporting nutrients to the developing chick [B]. This is ready to hatch after 21 days [C]. Downy chicks [D] such as chickens or ducklings can follow the parents as soon as they are dry after hatching, and are called nidifugous. Nidicolous young are almost helpless [E].

7

A
B
C
D

7 The lapwing nests in open fields [A] while the little tern [B] and the ringed plover [C] nest on the seashore. Eggs and chicks [D] and often the adult birds of these and other ground-nesters match their surroundings almost to perfection and are said to be cryptically colored. This camouflaging of the young is most effective when they crouch motionless at a predator's approach.

8

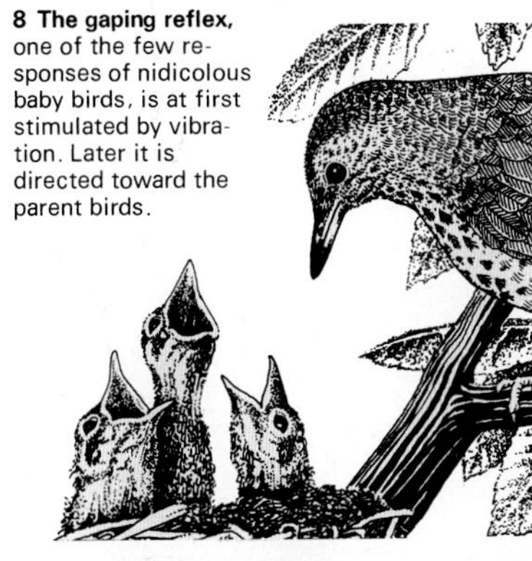

8 The gaping reflex, one of the few responses of nidicolous baby birds, is at first stimulated by vibration. Later it is directed toward the parent birds.

11

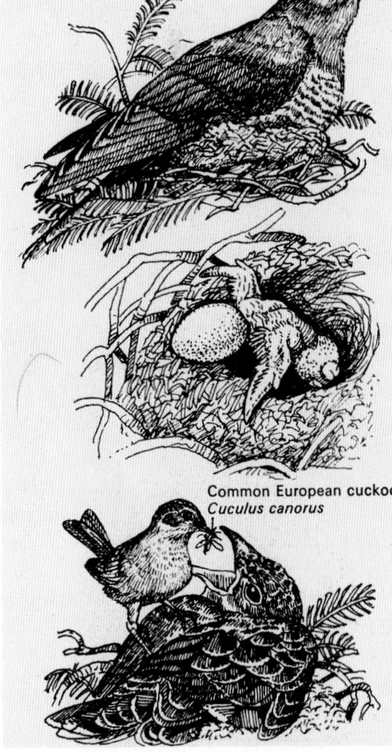

Common European cuckoo
Cuculus canorus

11 "A cuckoo in the nest" is serious if the species is the common European cuckoo. This bird lays its egg in the nests of a small host species. The nestling ejects its nestfellows, thus receiving all its foster parents' attention.

9 Red-billed dwarf hornbill
Tockus camurus

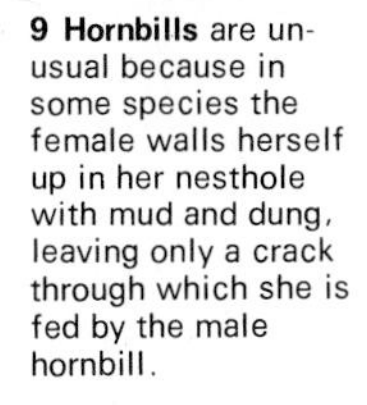

9 Hornbills are unusual because in some species the female walls herself up in her nesthole with mud and dung, leaving only a crack through which she is fed by the male hornbill.

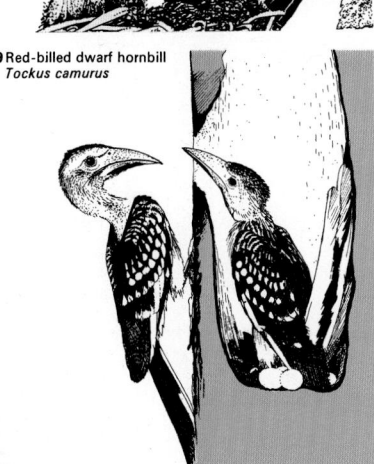

10

Female
Koklass pheasant
Pucrasia macrolopha
Male

10 Pheasants such as the koklass illustrate the differences between the sexes that exist in many birds. The males generally sport bright attractive colors while the female is cryptically colored for protection while incubating.

Birds and migration

Birds owe much of their success as a group to their unusual powers of migration. The phenomenon of migration, for the scientist bewilderingly complex and for the animal extremely exhausting, is deep-rooted in many species and has undoubtedly exerted great influence on their evolution. The change in residence of migrants parallels changes in appearance, diet, or even the behavior of some of the more sedentary bird species.

The longest journeys

True migration involves a regular, seasonal movement between one area, in which the animal breeds, and another, in which the climatic and other conditions are more suitable when the breeding season is over. Thus some bird species, particularly wildfowl and plovers, breed in the tundra and migrate to temperate regions for the winter. Others, particularly insect-eaters of the Northern Hemisphere, such as the swallows and warblers, breed in temperate lands and move south to winter in the tropics. In the Southern Hemisphere, the migratory movements are largely in the other direction, though the greater land area in the Northern Hemisphere means that there are more species moving south than north.

Bird migration varies hugely in its scope [Key]. The greatest travelers, particularly the sea birds, may fly almost from pole to pole and many land birds also make long trans-equatorial migrations. At the other extreme, some species may move only from an island breeding area to the coast or from mountain breeding areas to winter quarters in the valleys. Sea bird colonies provide a vivid example of local movement, with vast numbers of breeding birds moving from their coastal nest sites to a much wider dispersal area over the open sea.

The misfits: "partial migrants"

Not all bird species show the consistent, cohesive movements that characterize the true migrants. These "partial migrants" are species in which not all individuals behave uniformly; some may go on a post-breeding migration, others may not. This inconsistent behavior may provide a clue to some of the selection pressures involved in the evolution of migration. These species may be at the edge of their "comfortable" winter range, and some individuals will be poorly adapted to local conditions. These birds will tend to move out for the winter.

Migration does not, strictly speaking, include movements such as irruptions [3], or extension of range, even though birds often travel greater distances in the process. Extensions of range are largely the result of a preferred food source becoming available over a wider area. An impressive extension of range has been seen in the collared dove [6] and the fulmar petrel *(Fulmarus glacialis)* of the eastern Atlantic. In this century the collared dove spread westward from Asia to the Atlantic by 1955, and 20 years later had reached Iceland.

The origins and mechanics of migration

The evolutionary origin of migration is extremely complex and is as yet incompletely understood. The phenomenon is undoubtedly related to the necessity of finding appropriate food and weather for the raising of

CONNECTIONS

See also
536 How birds behave
528 The anatomy of birds
534 Bird life and variety
538 Island birds
630 Endangered birds
514 Unusual fish

1 A

Present breeding range
Present wintering range
Former range

Whooping crane
Grus americana

1 The perilous migration of the whooping crane, *Grus americana,* is carefully observed by wildlife conservation officials in Canada and the United States. From the safety of their remote breeding grounds in southern Mackenzie District, Canada, these large birds, which reach a height of 5ft (1.5m), begin their annual winter migration to the Aransas National Wildlife Refuge on the Gulf Coast of Texas. [A] Even there this endangered species is vulnerable to weather conditions; the entire whooping crane population of about 50 birds could be wiped out if the area were to be hit by a severe hurricane. At one time the breeding areas of the whooping crane were the coastal marshes of Louisiana and the interior of the North American continent. The golden plover, *Pluvialis dominica,* has its summer breeding grounds in arctic Canada. The adult birds start their annual migration before the fledglings are able to fly; these are left to make the journey on their own. The plovers first stop on the coasts of Labrador and Nova Scotia, where they feed. They then begin their nonstop flight to the northern coast of South America, where they take a brief rest before reaching their final destination – the pampas of Argentina – in September. In January they fly back to the northern tundra, this time passing over the Gulf of Mexico and the American Great Plains. [B] The golden plover thus makes a round trip of 15,000mi (24,000km).

B

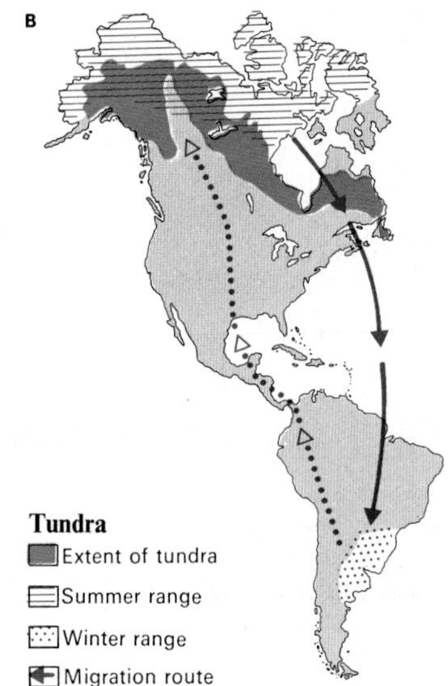

Tundra
Extent of tundra
Summer range
Winter range
Migration route

Golden plover
Pluvialis dominica

a brood. The migratory instinct has probably been developing over a period of 40 to 50 million years and, though greatly influenced by the Pleistocene glaciations, did not originate with them. Migratory movements are governed by inherited factors but initiated and guided by environmental influences. Individuals of a migratory species will thus show "migratory restlessness" at the onset of the migration period, even though there is little climatic indication that the season is changing. The weather may then delay or accelerate departure and to some extent modify the route taken. Despite these occasional deviations, when the birds get lost or blown off course, the direction of migration remains remarkably constant.

The physiological mechanisms behind these great powers of navigation and orientation are still a mystery. If the means by which migrating birds compute their bearings is still not clear, it is well established that they use landmarks when convenient and sky signs, almost certainly both the sun and the stars. Recent studies prove that Adélie penguins navigate by the sun. Nevertheless, many birds apparently follow a magnetic bearing rather than a bearing to a particular point on the earth's surface.

The habits of certain species show that they have an innate knowledge of the migratory route. The young of these species depart in autumn before or after their parents. Individual adult birds displaced laterally by humans while on migration will resume their flight on release on exactly the same magnetic bearing, finishing up with the same lateral displacement from their destination. On the other hand, some birds can navigate back home after an unusual displacement. One famous example of the innate migratory urge is that of a Manx shearwater *(Puffinus puffinus)* that was taken by plane to Boston, Massachusetts, from its burrow on Skokholm Island, south Wales. It was back on its nest 12.5 days after release in America—ten hours before the mail arrived giving details of its release. How the bird managed to find its way over this distance, with no landmarks to guide it, and in such a remarkably short time, still remains a mystery.

KEY

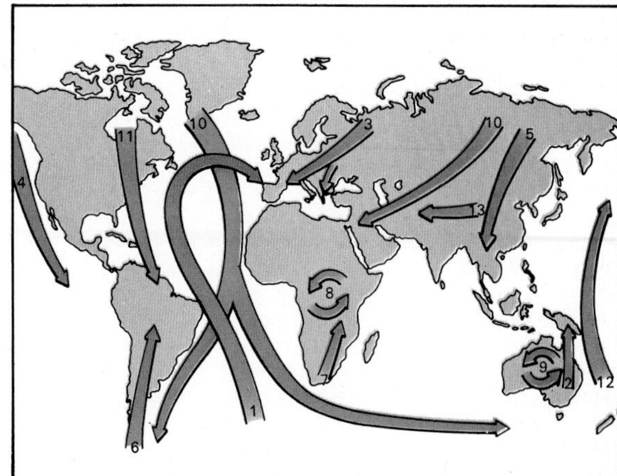

When migrating, many birds travel along fairly well defined flightpaths or flyways. These often follow winds or sea currents [1, 2], land contours, or coastlines [3, 4]. Birds from high latitudes move toward the Equator [5, 6, 7] during the winter. Some travel many thousands of miles [10, 11 12]. In Eurasia east-west movements occur [13]. On large land masses such as Australia and Africa fruit-eaters and insectivores follow seasonal food sources [8, 9].

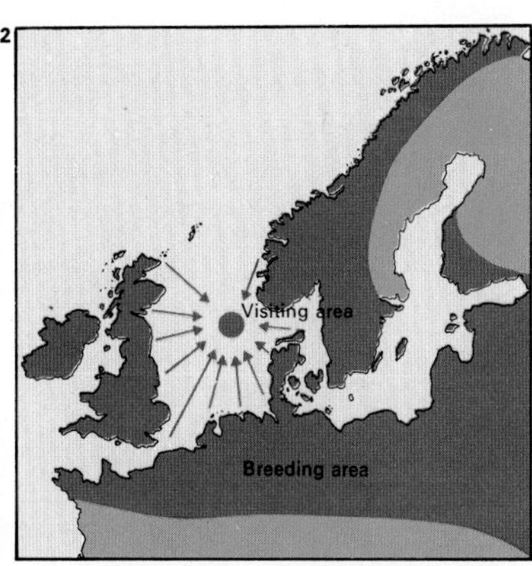
Visiting area
Breeding area

2 Shelduck *(Tadorna tadorna)* undertake mass post-breeding migrations from the northwest European coasts to Heligoland to sit out flightless molting periods. They return in smaller parties.

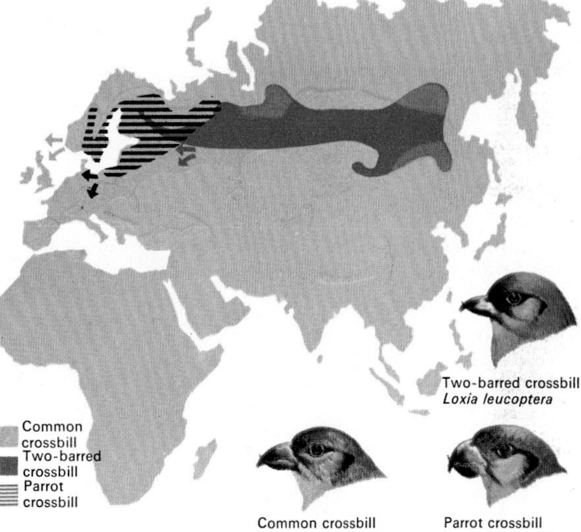
Common crossbill
Two-barred crossbill
Parrot crossbill
Two-barred crossbill *Loxia leucoptera*
Common crossbill *Loxia curvirostra*

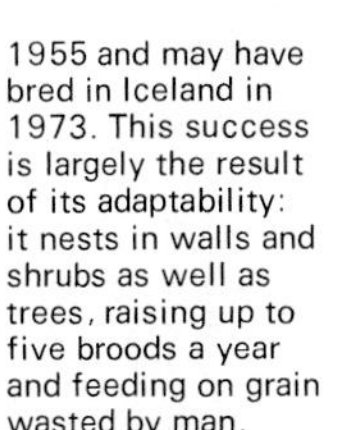
Parrot crossbill *Loxia pytyopsittacus*

3 Irruptions are special "migratory" movements that occur irregularly in a few species as a response to unusual food conditions. The crossbills of Eurasia, for example, may leave their normal breeding areas in large numbers, moving south and west to exploit exceptional crops of their main food, conifer seeds. The parrot crossbill, the heaviest-billed, specializes in tough pine cones, while the common crossbill has an intermediate bill and prefers spruce. The two-barred species, which has the lightest bill, is restricted to larch cones. These species do not usually set up new long-term populations.

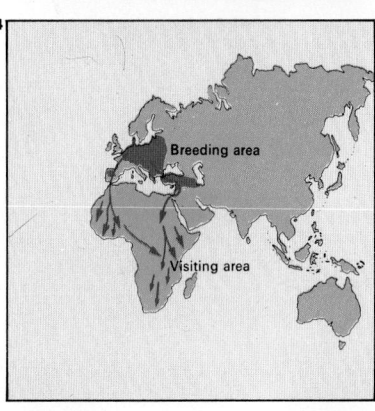

4 The European populations of the white stork *(Ciconia ciconia)* winter largely in steppes and deserts of southern Africa. Flying via land they avoid long sea crossings with poor soaring conditions.

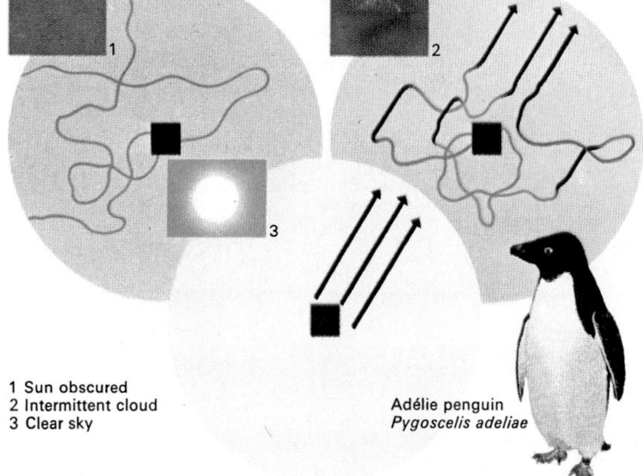
1
2
3
1 Sun obscured
2 Intermittent cloud
3 Clear sky
Adélie penguin *Pygoscelis adeliae*

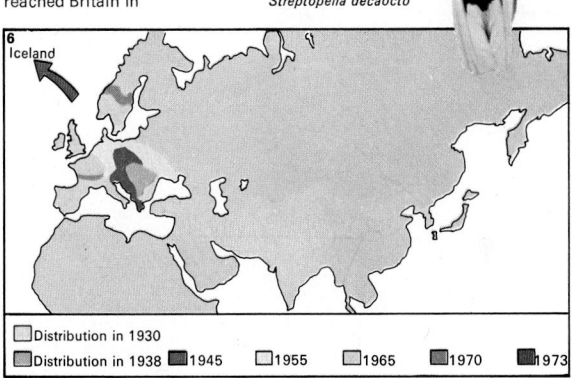

5 The penguins navigate by sky signs just as flying birds do. Faced with a return journey to the breeding grounds of up to 200 miles across snow and ice, Adélie penguins *(Pygoscelis adeliae)* use the sun to aid their accurate homing navigation. This was conclusively proven when birds were taken hundreds of miles from home and released on featureless terrain. With the sun obscured, the navigation of the displaced birds was erratic, but with a clear view of the sun they were able to orient themselves accurately. Intermittent cloud gave intermediate results. How the birds compensate for the daily movement of the sun is unknown.

6 Extensions of range are not examples of true migration. The collared dove spread slowly from Asia early this century and had reached Hungary by 1928. Then its rate of progress increased and its range was extended by 1,200 miles in 20 years. It reached Britain in 1955 and may have bred in Iceland in 1973. This success is largely the result of its adaptability: it nests in walls and shrubs as well as trees, raising up to five broods a year and feeding on grain wasted by man.

Collared dove *Streptopelia decaocto*

Iceland

Distribution in 1930
Distribution in 1938 1945 1955 1965 1970 1973

Bird life and variety

Within the limits imposed by their special adaptations for flight, birds show a remarkable range of form and habit. The largest living bird is the ostrich *(Struthio camelus)*, which stands up to 8ft (2.4m) tall and weighs up to 300lb (136kg), while the smallest is the bee hummingbird *(Mellisuga helenae)*, less than 2.5in (6.3cm) long and under 0.1oz (2.5gm) in weight. In fact, the world population of bee hummingbirds—about 100,000—would weigh approximately the same as a pair of large ostriches.

Limitations of flight

The size of birds imposes a limit on their ability to fly, for weight increases proportionally more than lifting area as size increases. A heavier bird therefore needs proportionally more power for its weight. The trumpeter swan *(Olor buccinator)* is probably the heaviest living flying species, with a weight of up to 38lb (17.2kg). Its 10ft (3m) wingspan is exceeded only by that of the wandering albatross *(Diomedea exulans)*, which may be 11.5ft (3.5m) or more. It would be interesting to know the flying abilities of the apparently larger, but extinct, giant condor *Teratornis*, which lived in the Pleistocene period, some two million years ago.

The flying abilities of birds, coupled with their capacity for maintaining a high body temperature, have made possible a range of ecological and behavioral variation seen in few other groups. The 8,600 species (approximately) of birds are distributed throughout almost every part of the world from the poles to the tropics.

Breeding and feeding

Birds breed almost anywhere except in the sea. Nests may be on or in the ground, in holes in trees, cliffs, or buildings, in low bushes or the tallest trees, even floating on still water. Some species nest in enormous colonies, others make no nest at all, laying their eggs on the ground or on cliff ledges. The "mound builder" birds (Megapodidae) use the heat from the fermentation of rotting vegetation, or hot sand, to incubate their eggs. And the emperor penguin *(Aptenodytes forsteri)* breeds in the depths of the Antarctic winter. The male bird incubates the egg. He stands on ice at temperatures below −76°F (−60°C) for 64 days holding a single egg on his feet before the chick hatches.

A remarkable variety may also be seen in feeding habits. Birds have adapted to all the principal food sources. Different avian predators specialize in feeding on a great range of prey organisms, from the smallest invertebrates to birds and mammals several times their own weight. Some birds store food and use the stores in winter; others feed on parasites that live on mammal skins, the skin tissue itself, and on blood. The Egyptian vulture *(Neophron percnopterus)* casts stones at ostrich eggs to break them open, and one Galapagos finch *(Camarhynchus pallidus)* forces insects out of tree holes and crevices by means of a cactus spine or twig held in its bill.

Some birds are parasites upon other avian species. The European cuckoo *(Cuculus canorus)* is a well-known example. This species, like the brown-headed cowbird *(Molothrus ater)* of North America

CONNECTIONS

See also
526 The classification of birds
530 How birds reproduce
532 Birds and migration
536 How birds behave
538 Island birds
630 Endangered birds
606 Desert birds and mammals
582 Isolation and evolution
420 Evolution in action
634 Destructive man

1
1
2
3
4
5
6
7
8
9
10
11
12
13

1 Reproductive isolation through different plumage and displays in closely related species can be clearly seen in the ducks of the genus *Anas* and the American wood warblers of the genus *Dendroica*. In North America there are 13 *Anas* species of dabbling ducks—or "puddle" ducks—and 20 *Dendroica* warblers. Several species often live together and must be reproductively isolated in order to avoid producing unhealthy hybrids. This is achieved by a combination of color, form, movement, and vocalization that is distinctive for the male of each species, together with an instinctive preference on the part of the female for the male who gives the "correct" display. Thus, half a dozen species of ducks may be found on the same stretch of water, even in the breeding season, without any significant confusion occurring. The same applies to the warblers. In both the *Anas* ducks and the *Dendroica* warblers the distinctiveness of the males is enhanced by a striking breeding plumage. The females are very similar in appearance, apparently even to the birds themselves. *Anas* and *Dendroica* males in the post-breeding season are extremely difficult to identify, even for an expert.

Wood warblers
Dendroica spp

1 Blackpoll warbler *D. striata*
2 Magnolia warbler *D. magnolia*
3 Townsend's warbler *D. townsendi*
4 Blackburnian warbler *D. fusca*
5 Chestnut-sided warbler *D. pensylvanica*
6 Black-throated blue warbler *D. caerulescens*
7 Prairie warbler *D. discolor*

Dabbling ducks
Anas spp

8 Gadwall *A. strepera*
9 Pintail *A. acuta*
10 Cinnamon teal *A. cyanoptera*
11 Mallard *A. platyrhynchos*
12 Blue-winged teal *A. discors*
13 Common teal *A. crecca*

and some other species, lays its egg in the nest of a "host" bird, leaving the host to rear the young. Other birds, such as the skuas (family Stercorariidae) are kleptoparasites, forcing neighboring sea birds to disgorge their food.

The plumage of birds shows a wide range of form, pattern, and color. Some species are brighter than the most exotic flowers or jewels, others are as somber as desert sand or the blackest night. Some of the brightest species are the pheasants (family Phasianidae) and the birds of paradise (family Paradisaeidae).

An additional and unusual example of behavioral variety in birds is that of the satin bowerbird *(Ptilonorhynchus violaceus)*. Like the other bowerbirds, all found in Australia and New Guinea, the male of this species builds a bower of twigs on the ground in which to display himself to the female. The bower has a floor of twigs and is open at each end. The sides lean together to form a roof. The floor of the bower is decorated with bright objects such as feathers and flowers. It is orientated north-south so that the bird is not dazzled by the sun when displaying. Additionally, this species "paints" its bower with fruit pulp held in a spongy wad of fiber retained in the bill. The male bird may display for several months, posturing with the display objects held in the bill until, with the seasonal appearance of insect food for the young, mating takes place in the bower.

Learning by experience

Bird behavior, although advanced, does not necessarily indicate "intelligence." But the variety of bird behavior increases through "insight learning." This may occur when tits (family Paridae) and crows (family Corvidae) learn to haul in a length of string in order to obtain food attached to the end. That this kind of behavior may involve insight is suggested by the results of experimental work with crows, parrots (family Psittacidae), and finches (family Fringillidae), showing that they can learn to "see into" a situation and modify their behavior accordingly. Such abilities may increase enormously the variety of bird activity.

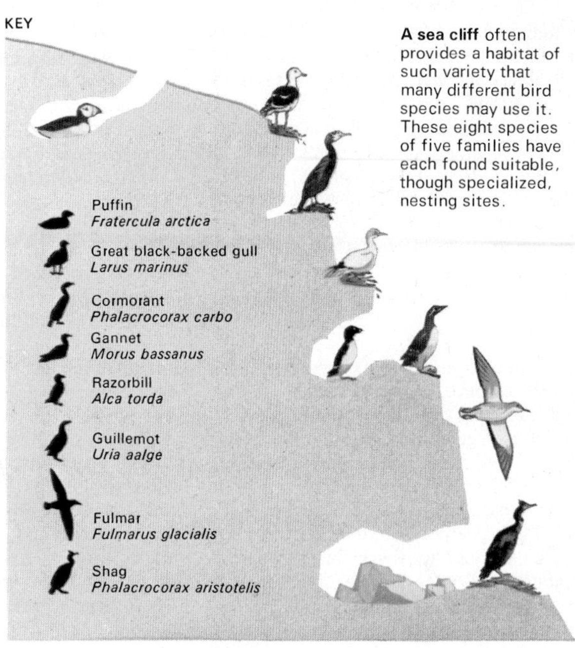
KEY
Puffin
Fratercula arctica
Great black-backed gull
Larus marinus
Cormorant
Phalacrocorax carbo
Gannet
Morus bassanus
Razorbill
Alca torda
Guillemot
Uria aalge
Fulmar
Fulmarus glacialis
Shag
Phalacrocorax aristotelis

A sea cliff often provides a habitat of such variety that many different bird species may use it. These eight species of five families have each found suitable, though specialized, nesting sites.

2
Jackass penguin
Spheniscus demersus

2 Penguins are the most aquatic of all birds, the 18 living species showing a mastery of their element that enables them to prey on fast-swimming fish with great success. The jackass is typical in its streamlined form, flipperlike wings, and steering-paddle feet placed far back. The feathers have been modified to form a close-fitting, scale-like wet suit, and the specific markings are largely on the head.

3 Puffin
Fratercula arctica

3 The common puffin is a marine bird that finds its prey—primarily fish—entirely under water. Its aquatic adaptations are less extreme than those of the penguins. It is not so streamlined, the feet are not so far back (thus it does not have to stand bolt upright), and the wings are still used for flight. But it can catch smaller or slower-moving fish for itself or for its unfledged chick.

4 Great hornbill *Buceros bicornis*

4 The 45 species of hornbills are found in tropical Africa and Asia. The enormously developed bill seen in the great hornbill is used for display and nesting purposes rather than for feeding.

5 Toco toucan
Ramphastos toco
8

5 Toucans are the New World counterparts of the hornbills, some 35 species being found in the forests of tropical America. But they have even bigger and brighter bills than the hornbills.

6 Sword-billed humming-bird
Ensifera ensifera

6 The hummingbirds of the Americas, numbering more than 300 species, live largely on nectar. Some use tubular tongues to suck nectar from flowers and may add to their diet insects trapped in or near blooms. Others have brushlike tongues.

7 Double-collared sunbird
Nectarinia mediocris
New Holland honeyeater
Phylidonyris novaehollandiae

7 The sunbirds, numbering 104 species, fill the nectar-feeding niche in Africa, Asia, and to some extent in Australia. The double-collared sunbird of the Kenya mountains conserves heat by lowering its body temperature at night.

8 The 167 species of honeyeaters are the main insect- and nectar-feeding birds in Australasia. Long isolation without much competition has resulted in a wide adaptive range of form, of which the New Holland honeyeater is typical.

How birds behave

Studies of bird behavior were long hampered by the idea that birds had little learning ability and were mainly creatures of instinct. This misconception was based largely on birds' lack of brain structures similar to those of the cerebral cortices of mammals. Recent tests indicate, however, that birds have learning capacities in some areas that are exceeded only by the highest mammals [8, 9, 10], as well as unmatched navigational skills. Bird behavior is a mixture of the learned and the instinctive.

Instinctive behavior

Instinct can be seen at its most blind in the habits of birds in the incubation of their eggs. Herring gulls, for example, will sit on any large egg at the expense of their own. Much instinctive behavior [3] takes the form of intricate sequences known as fixed action patterns. These are inherited and tend to be stereotyped; they can be seen in such activities as fly-catching by insect-eating birds, or in nest-building. They are also a conspicuous feature of courtship. It is possible to cross closely related species to produce hybrids whose courtship and nesting behavior has elements of the patterns of each parent, as in lovebirds [5]. This rigidity of behavior is thought to be essential in the process of keeping species distinct by preventing mating among them.

Signs and rituals are also involved in territorial behavior [2]. Most birds have well-defined territories within which they are noisier and livelier, and they generally seem to behave as if they are more at home in these territories than outside of them. Such birds defend their territories from intruders of the same species—or strictly speaking from any animal or inanimate object resembling the species. In the European robin the red breast is the sign stimulus for defensive behavior [1]. Such behavior, however, rarely involves a fight; instead, the defending bird engages in a stereotyped threat display—a sign that the intruder should retreat. The intensity of display depends on the distance from the territorial center. Cautious "sparring" occurs at the edge of a bird's territory but fighting may be involved at the center.

Displacement and imprinting

A bird sometimes finds itself in a situation that elicits two conflicting behavior patterns. At the boundaries between their territories, for example, males may be torn between fight and flight. And in the mating season many birds have to overcome their natural aversion to physical contact. Once the level of sex hormones reaches its peak the sex drive swamps the aversion, but there is a stage at which the two tendencies more or less balance. In such situations the bird resorts to actions known as displacement activities. These activities take the place of the normal expression of the animal's innate drives. The male bird may preen its feathers or peck at something [7] instead of approaching a female.

In most of these behavior patterns there is an innate recognition of a specific inducing stimulus. But much bird behavior is modified by experience and some is entirely learned. An example of pre-programmed behavior with a single learned component is the phenomenon known as imprinting [4]. Newly hatched ducks, geese, and chicks

CONNECTIONS

See also
464 Principles of animal behavior
530 How birds reproduc
532 Birds and migration
528 The anatomy of bir
534 Bird life and variety
526 The classification of birds
556 How mammals beha
558 How primates beha
830 Types of ritual
538 Island birds

1 The threat posture of a European robin defending its territory is designed to display the red breast [A] and varies according to the position of intruders [1]. A defending robin adopts posture [B] when the intruding bird is above it, but posture [C] if the intruder is below it. If the threat display fails as a deterrent the defending robin may actually launch an attack [D] against the intruder.

2 Rigid demarcation of territory can be observed even when birds gather in large social groups. An example is the uniform spacing between nests in a colony of gannets *(Morus)*.

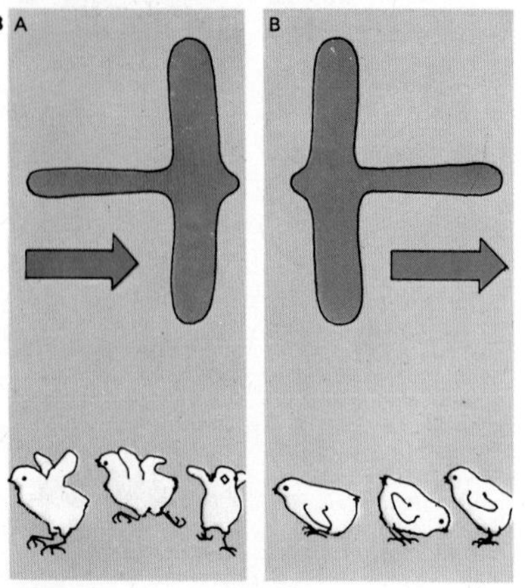

3 Instinctive fright reaction to predators flying overhead is shown by chicks. The same cardboard model of a bird that induces fear of short-necked, long-tailed predators [A] is ignored if the direction of movement is reversed so that it looks like a long-necked, short-tailed and therefore harmless species [B].

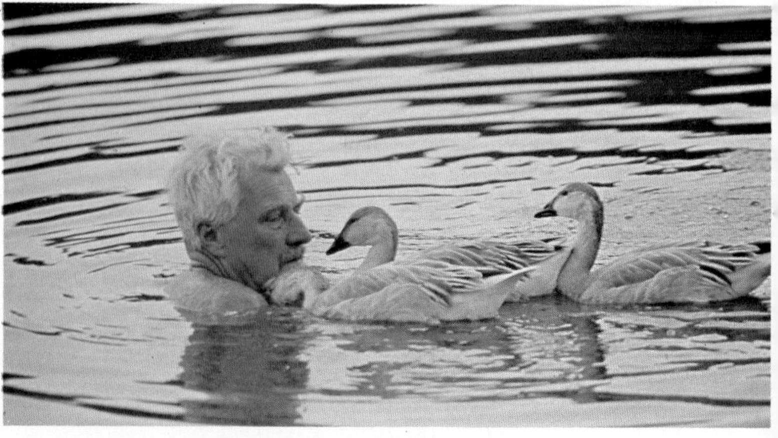

4 Goslings became "imprinted" to Austrian ethologist Konrad Lorenz, who studied the behavior of tame geese.

will imprint on and follow the first moving thing they see. This is usually their mother, but experiments have shown that baby birds will imprint upon a range of objects.

In imprinting the behavior is pre-programmed but there is no innate recognition of the parents. This knowledge is quickly learned and the young bird tends to adopt as its parent the first large moving object it sees. Not only will the young bird follow this object as a parent, later it will direct sexual advances toward it, as demonstrated by the experiments of Konrad Lorenz.

This kind of following is simple, automatic, and innate, but more complex behavior, such as the production of the bird's characteristic song, sometimes involves a subtle combination of innate and learned influences [6]. Some young song birds, if reared in isolation, produce a song that has roughly the right length and number of notes for its species but the wrong tune. If a group of chaffinches, for example, is reared together without adults, it develops its own version of the species song, quite distinct from that of the wild male.

Navigational expertise

One of the most striking examples of learning in birds is still shrouded in mystery, namely the ability of many birds to home accurately (as opposed to the innate directional migration of young birds, which has no learned component). Recently experiments have begun to reveal the complex combination of signals a homing pigeon uses to orient itself. One of these is certainly the sun. But because pigeons can orient themselves even under overcast skies, it seemed that there must be some other kind of "map."

Some researchers hit on the idea of fitting pigeons with small bar magnets. The idea was that pigeons might have a sense that enables them to pick up information about the Earth's magnetic field. If that sense were upset they might be unable to find their way home. It was found that pigeons bearing magnets could navigate in sunny conditions but became disoriented under heavily overcast skies. There are still many unanswered questions about the pigeon's navigational system, however.

KEY

Herring gulls will sit patiently on abnormally large models of their own eggs, ignoring their real eggs. The normal stimulus for incubating behavior is the real egg and the outsize egg acts as a supernormal stimulus. The rigidity of instinctive behavior compels the birds to be "tricked" in this way, but in nature such behavior aids bird survival.

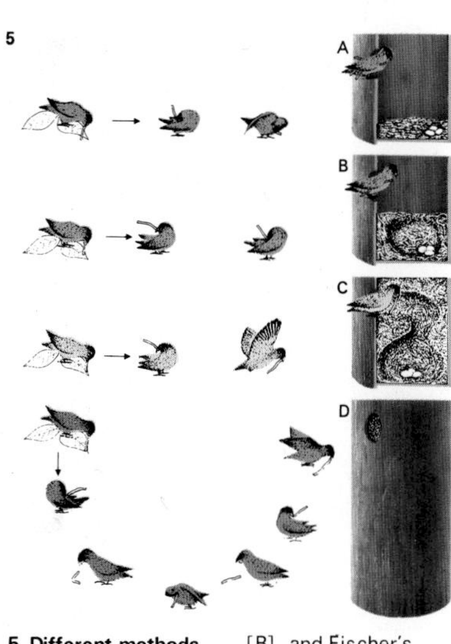
5
A
B
C
D

5 Different methods of carrying material and nest-building are shown by Madagascar [A], peach-faced [B], and Fischer's lovebirds [C]. Hybrids [D] show conflicting patterns and can not breed.

6 A
B

6 The development of bird song is the result of a combination of innate and environmental influences. A bird will usually produce some kind of song however it is reared, but if a songbird is deafened at birth or if it is reared in total isolation and cannot hear adult male songs [A], it will produce a totally abnormal sound pattern in its own song [B]. A songbird learns to sing during the first four months of life and after that the song pattern cannot be changed.

7A
B
7 C
D

7 Displacement behavior occurs when conflicting instincts are aroused. Rival male blackbirds [A], torn between fight and flight, may settle for pecking at leaves, whereas herring gulls [B] may react to a threat by pulling at grass. A threatened oystercatcher [C] may resolve the same conflict by taking refuge in "sleep." Sex-shy avocets [D] channel their drives into preening (for the male) or bill-dipping (for the female), overcoming innate drives before progressing to mating.

8 Blue tit
Parus caeruleus
9 Jay
Garrulus glandarius
10 Raven
Corvus corax

8 Blue tits learned to peck through milk bottle tops to drink the cream. They not only learned where to find bottles but also to distinguish the colors of tops and select bottles richest in cream.

9 Ability to adapt to a novel situation is demonstrated by jays and other birds that can be taught to obtain food attached to a string by pulling up the string and anchoring it with a foot.

10 Ravens and other birds have been found capable of counting up to seven. Presented with a series of marks, they can associate these with the same number of marks on a box containing a reward.

Island birds

When islands first emerge from the sea, only nesting sea birds and turtles can find a use for such barren hulks of rock and coral. Land-based birds arriving at this stage must either depart or perish; only after vegetation is well established can these species have any chance of surviving. Purely insect-eating species must wait even longer before the island can provide a life-supporting food supply. Those few birds that do settle tend to become more specialized and diversified than their mainland counterparts in order to exploit the relatively few feeding niches.

Over a quarter of all island species have become extinct through over-specialization, and the fortunes of the remainder turn on the delicate ecological balance of their habitats, the smaller the island the finer the thread on which survival depends. On the smallest islands extinction may follow natural fluctuations in population, and the arrival of man, with his introduction of rival bird species and predators, does nothing to improve their survival. Hunting is also a major factor in the decline or extinction of many island birds.

CONNECTIONS

See also
630 Endangered birds
526 The classification of birds
582 Isolation and evolution
418 Evolution: classical theories
614 Life on islands
534 Bird life and variety
536 How birds behave

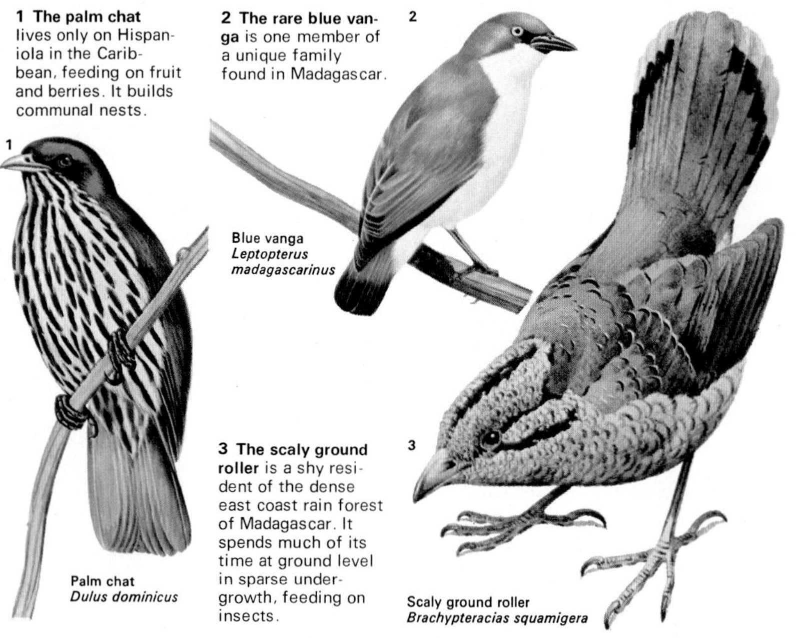

1 The palm chat lives only on Hispaniola in the Caribbean, feeding on fruit and berries. It builds communal nests.

1 Palm chat
Dulus dominicus

2 The rare blue vanga is one member of a unique family found in Madagascar.

2 Blue vanga
Leptopterus madagascarinus

3 The scaly ground roller is a shy resident of the dense east coast rain forest of Madagascar. It spends much of its time at ground level in sparse undergrowth, feeding on insects.

3 Scaly ground roller
Brachypteracias squamigera

4 The Bornean bristle-head is so rare that little is known about it. It lives in lowland forests, feeding on insects.

4 Bornean bristle-head
Pityriasis gymnocephala

5 The world population of the Narcondam hornbill is confined to one island in the Bay of Bengal. Its numbers, 400, are controlled by lack of nest sites.

5 Narcondam hornbill
Rhyticeros narcondami

6 Cuckoo roller
Leptosomus discolor

6 The cuckoo roller, the sole surviving member of its family, lives high in the forests of Madagascar and surrounding islands feeding mainly on insects.

7 The Papuan hawk owl is a rare nocturnal resident of New Guinea. Nothing is known of its breeding behavior. It feeds on insects and rodents.

7 Papuan hawk owl
Uroglaux dimorpha

8 Victoria crowned pigeon
Goura victoria

8 The large Victoria crowned pigeon, now protected, was hunted for the magnificent plumes on its head. Unlike other New Guinea pigeons, it flew into the open when disturbed and was easy to shoot.

9 Black-mantled goshawk
Accipiter melanochlamys

9 The black-mantled goshawk is one of eight species found in New Guinea. It ambushes smaller birds at water holes, flying in to seize its prey on the wing.

10 Emerald dove
Chalcophaps indica
11 Luzon bleeding heart
Gallicolumba luzonica
12
Pheasant pigeon
Otidiphaps nobilis
PHILIPPINES
NEW GUINEA
Key to distribution
Luzon bleeding heart
Pheasant pigeon
Nicobar pigeon
Emerald dove
13 Nicobar pigeon
Caloenas nicobarica
14
15
16 Tui
Prosthemadera novaeseelandiae
17
18
Fernbird
Bowdleria punctata
Kokako
Callaeas cinerea
Princess Stephania bird of paradise
Astrapia stephaniae
Magnificent riflebird
Ptiloris magnificus
19
20
Rifleman
Acanthisitta chloris
21
New Zealand pigeon
Hemiphaga novaeseelandiae
Kea
Nestor notabilis
22
Takahe
Notornis mantelli
23
Brown kiwi
Apteryx australis
24
Iiwi
Vestiaria coccinea

10 The buff and green colors of the emerald dove match the background of the evergreen and deciduous forests in South Asia, where it is widespread in shady wooded ravines.

11 The Luzon bleeding heart pigeon is one of five related species confined to the Philippines.

12 A shy, crow-sized bird, the pheasant pigeon is capable of only short bursts of flight. It inhabits dense hill forests of New Guinea and adjacent islands.

13 The Nicobar pigeon is a ruff-necked species that inhabits densely forested islands from Malaysia to the Solomon Islands. It lives mainly on hard seeds, but also on fruits and insects.

14 A quiet, subdued bird, the Princess Stephania bird of paradise is much sought after by New Guinea tribesmen for its tail plumes.

15 The magnificent riflebird is an agile climber in its search for insects. It is sombre-looking until seen in the rays of the New Guinea sun.

18 The fernbird has been forced to retreat as New Zealand marshlands have been reclaimed.

16 The tui of New Zealand mimics other birds.

17 The kokako of New Zealand has a fine song.

21 The forest dwelling New Zealand pigeon was saved from extinction by protective measures.

19 A New Zealand mountain parrot, the kea feeds mainly on carrion. It was the victim of an extermination campaign when falsely branded as a sheep-killer.

20 The rifleman is the commonest of the three living species of a unique New Zealand bird family.

22 The takahe, a giant rail, was thought extinct until rediscovered in 1948 in New Zealand.

24 The iiwi is a long-billed, nectar-feeding honeycreeper fairly common on Hawaii.

23 The brown kiwi is the commonest of the three New Zealand kiwi species. It seems less vulnerable to predators than the others. It lives in forest areas where it feeds on worms and insects.

The classification of mammals

The mammals, the animal group of which man is a member, are the most highly organized and among the most successful of all the creatures on earth. From humble origins as contemporaries of the dinosaurs they have evolved to become the dominant animal form on our planet, despite the fact that compared with other groups their numbers are relatively few.

Common characteristics

All mammals share several common characteristics. They are all warmblooded, are usually hairy, have relatively large brains, and suckle their young. Monotremes, although mammals, lay eggs, but all other mammals give birth to live young. Female mammals, except monotremes, have a placenta by which the young are nourished before birth. The placenta is only poorly developed in marsupials and part of its function is replaced by a pouch.

Zoologists classify mammals on the basis of their anatomy and behavior and as a result they recognize 19 groups or orders of mammals. Each order contains mammals alike in essential features—most primates, for example, have brains with large and dominant cerebral hemispheres. The animals in each order are further classified into families and each family consists of creatures that share closer relationships to each other than to those of other families. Thus all the great apes in the family Pongidae resemble each other more closely than they do the Old World monkeys of the family Cercopithecidae. The number of families in each mammal order varies widely. An indication of the relative size of each order is given on these pages by the illustrations of representatives of each order.

The classification of mammals also reflects their age in evolutionary terms, the monotremes being the most primitive and ancient. The most advanced mammal order, by this reckoning, is that of the seals (Pinnipedia) because its members appeared most recently; the primates are well down the list. A different set of criteria produces a completely new picture. A classification based on brain development places the primates at the head of the list, closely followed by the whales and dolphins.

During the early part of the Tertiary period, starting about 65 million years ago, the mammals found a vast range of habitats available to them due to the extinction of the dinosaurs, and evolved along many and varied lines. Several of these early mammal groups themselves became extinct after a few million years and changing conditions left even highly successful orders with only a few surviving representatives. Thus the elephant, hyrax, and aardvark represent orders (Proboscidea, Hyracoidea, and Tubulidentata, respectively) that have only one modern family remaining.

The orders of mammals

The two most primitive mammal orders, the Monotremata [1] and the Marsupialia [2] are very different from the remainder. The monotremes lay eggs, whereas marsupials such as the kangaroos possess pouches in which the immature young are suckled.

The Insectivora [3] are the least specialized of all the placental mammals. The insectivores resemble most closely the

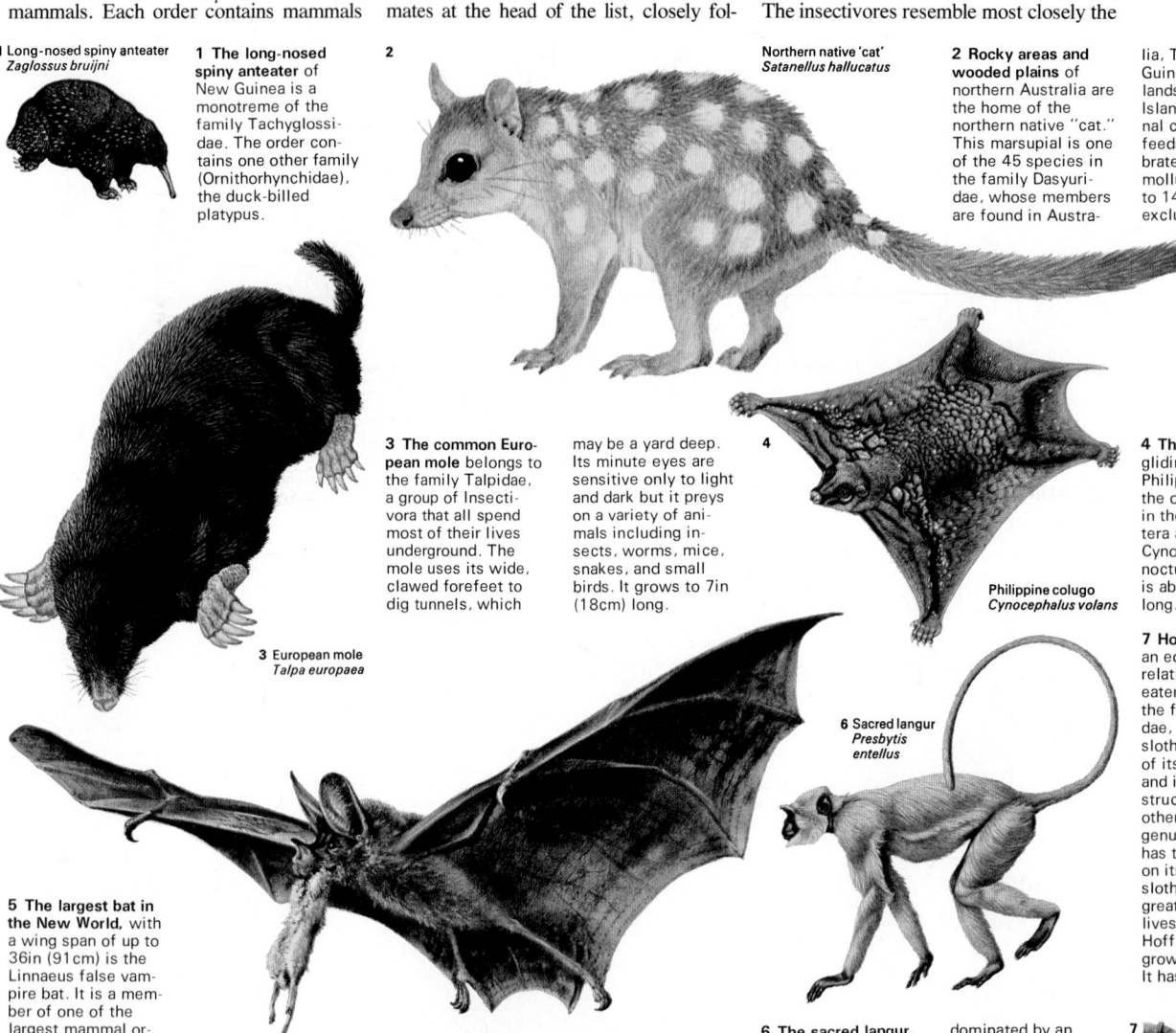

CONNECTIONS

See also
458 The animal kingdom
542 The life of mammals
544 Monotremes and marsupials
546 Rodents, insect-eaters, and bats
548 Hoofed mammals
550 Flesh-eating mammals
552 Whales, porpoises, and dolphins
554 Primates: relatives of man
646 Primate to hominid
574 Mammals of the past

1 Long-nosed spiny anteater
Zaglossus bruijni

1 The long-nosed spiny anteater of New Guinea is a monotreme of the family Tachyglossidae. The order contains one other family (Ornithorhynchidae), the duck-billed platypus.

2

Northern native 'cat'
Satanellus hallucatus

2 Rocky areas and wooded plains of northern Australia are the home of the northern native "cat." This marsupial is one of the 45 species in the family Dasyuridae, whose members are found in Australia, Tasmania, New Guinea, the Aru Islands, and Normanby Island. It is a nocturnal creature that feeds on small vertebrates, insects, and mollusks. It grows up to 14in (35cm) long, excluding the tail.

3 European mole
Talpa europaea

3 The common European mole belongs to the family Talpidae, a group of Insectivora that all spend most of their lives underground. The mole uses its wide, clawed forefeet to dig tunnels, which may be a yard deep. Its minute eyes are sensitive only to light and dark but it preys on a variety of animals including insects, worms, mice, snakes, and small birds. It grows to 7in (18cm) long.

4

Philippine colugo
Cynocephalus volans

4 The colugo, the gliding lemur of the Philippines, is one of the only two species in the order Dermoptera and the family Cynocephalidae. This nocturnal vegetarian is about 16in (40cm) long.

5 Linnaeus false vampire bat
Vampyrum spectrum

5 The largest bat in the New World, with a wing span of up to 36in (91cm) is the Linnaeus false vampire bat. It is a member of one of the largest mammal orders, the Chiroptera, and is further classified in the family Phyllostomidae. The bat's name betrays its feeding habits for it does not suck blood like a true vampire but feeds on rodents, birds, insects, and fruit.

6 Sacred langur
Presbytis entellus

6 The sacred langur, found in forests of Southeast Asia, is an Old World monkey, a primate, and belongs to the family Cercopithecidae. Like other primates, the sacred langur is a social creature and lives in a group comprising up to 40 individuals dominated by an adult male. These monkeys are known as leaf monkeys, and they have a vegetable diet that includes fruits and flowers as well as foliage. They are arboreal animals, and grow to about 40in (1m) long, with tail.

7 Hoffman's sloth is an edentate and a relative of the anteaters. It is placed in the family Bradypodidae, along with other sloths, on the basis of its sluggish habits and its skeletal structure. And like other members of the genus *Choloepus* it has two clawed toes on its forefeet. All sloths spend the greater part of their lives upside down. Hoffman's sloth grows to 2ft (65cm). It has no tail.

7 Hoffman's sloth
Choloepus hoffmanni

ancestors from which all these mammals are derived. They have the least specialized teeth and relatively small bodies and brains.

The bats, grouped together in the order Chiroptera [5], are closely related to the insectivores but their bodies are modified for flying. They are the only true flying mammals. The "flying" lemur (Dermoptera [4]) only glides from tree to tree.

Primates [6], the mammal order to which man belongs, are all very similar in appearance and show various degrees of adaptation to life in trees. Only man among the primates is exclusively ground dwelling and he is the most "intelligent" of all mammals. The two orders Edentata [7]—the anteaters, sloths, and armadillos—and Pholidota [8]—the pangolins—contain species that are toothless or peg-toothed and highly specialized for living on a diet of ants and termites. Only the tree sloths among the edentates feed on leaves.

The Lagomorpha [9], the rabbits, hares, and pikas, and the Rodentia [10]—although they both have similar gnawing teeth—are not closely related to each other. And while there are only two families of lagomorphs, the rodent families number about 33 and are the most numerous and widespread of all mammals. Mammals that are adapted for eating flesh on land are all grouped together in the order Carnivora [12].

The aquatic mammals

Three mammal orders have returned to the water, the environment that their amphibian ancestors left many millions of years before. The Cetacea [11], the whales and dolphins, are wholly adapted to this lifestyle and never return to land, but the seals, order Pinnipedia [13], must breed on shore.

The other aquatic group, the sea cows, or Sirenia [16], are a small group closely related to the elephants, or Proboscidea [14], and the hyraxes, the Hyracoidea [15]. The sole survivor of an archaic group is the aardvark, order Tubulidentata [17].

The two remaining mammal orders both consist of hoofed beasts or ungulates. The Perissodactyla [18] have an odd number of hoofed toes whereas the Artiodactyla [19] have an even number.

KEY

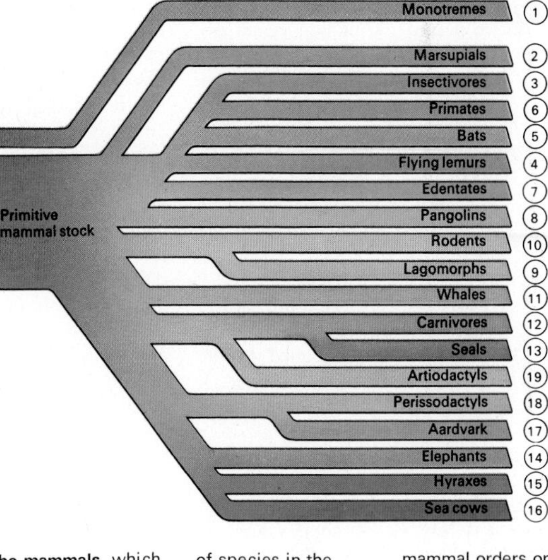
Primitive mammal stock
Monotremes 1
Marsupials 2
Insectivores 3
Primates 6
Bats 5
Flying lemurs 4
Edentates 7
Pangolins 8
Rodents 10
Lagomorphs 9
Whales 11
Carnivores 12
Seals 13
Artiodactyls 19
Perissodactyls 18
Aardvark 17
Elephants 14
Hyraxes 15
Sea cows 16

The mammals, which all developed from a shrewlike ancestor, underwent a period of rapid development of species in the Eocene period. Although many groups have become extinct, all the 19 modern mammal orders originate from that period. Chart numbers refer to the illustration numbers below.

8

Giant pangolin *Manis gigantea*

8 The giant pangolin of Africa belongs to one of the smallest mammal orders, the Pholidota, which consists of just one family, the Manidae, and one genus, *Manis*. It grows to 5.5ft (168cm), with tail.

9 Cotton-tail *Sylvilagus* sp

9 The cotton-tail is a New World lagomorph of the family Leporidae, all of which have typically short, furry tails and long ears. Cotton-tail species range in length from 11 to 20in. (27.5 to 50cm).

10 Bandicoot rat *Bandicota indica*

10 The largest order of mammals, to which this bandicoot rat belongs, is the Rodentia. Its family, the Muridae, includes all the other Old World rats and mice. The bandicoot rat is found in India and the Far East and is up to 24in (62cm) long.

11 Common porpoise *Phocaena phocoena*

11 The common porpoise is grouped with the whales and dolphins in the order Cetacea. Both porpoises and dolphins are in the family Delphinidae. Porpoises grow from 4 to 7ft (1.2 to 1.5m) long.

12 Ocelot *Felis pardalis*

12 The ocelot of the Americas is a member of the flesh-eating mammal order (Carnivora). It measures from 31–58in (80 to 147cm) long and is grouped with all other cats in the family Felidae.

13 Grey seal *Halichoerus grypus*

13 Turbulent waters around North Atlantic rocks are the preferred habitat of the grey seal of the order Pinnipedia and the family Phocidae. Males grow to 9ft (3m) and females to 7.5ft (2.25m) long.

14 Indian elephant *Elephas maximus*

14 Only one family of elephants, the Elephantidae, exists today—once there were six. The Indian elephant is one of the two surviving genera of the order Proboscidea. It grows to 20ft (6.4m) long.

15

Rock hyrax *Procavia capensis*

15 The rock hyrax is one of nine living species in the order Hyracoidea and the family Procaviidae. This African animal grows to about 15in (38cm) long and lives in colonies of over a hundred.

16

Dugong *Dugong dugon*

16 Sea cows of the order Sirenia inhabit coastal waters. They grow from 8 to 13ft (2.5–4m) in length. Each family, Dugongidae (dugongs) and Trichechidae (manatees), has but one genus.

17 Aardvark *Orycteropus afer*

17 The termite eating aardvark is the sole survivor of the mammal order Tubulidentata and the family Orycteropodidae. Its name comes from the Afrikaans word meaning "earth pig" and this refers both to its habit of digging deep burrows and to its appearance. It may measure up to 5ft (1.5m) in length and weigh up to 154lb (70kg). Apart from the head region it is covered in bristlelike hair. Aardvarks are found where ant and termite food abounds, south of the Sahara.

18 The woolly tapir belongs to the Tapiridae, which with the horses and rhinoceroses constitute the Perissodactyla, the order of hoofed, odd-toed animals. This tapir is an Andean species and grazes on grass and other low-growing vegetation. Like other tapirs it is a docile creature and a good runner, swimmer, and diver. The woolly tapir may grow to 7.5ft (2.5m) long.

18

Woolly tapir *Tapirus roulini*

Hippopotamus *Hippopotamus amphibius*

19

19 Hoofed mammals with an even number of toes are grouped together in the order Artiodactyla. The hippopotamus has a family of its own, the Hippopotamidae. It is a water-loving mammal that was once common in deep water habitats all over Africa but is now, due to man's ravages, severely restricted in range. The heavyweight hippopotamus tips the scales at between 3 and 4.5 tons. The largest animals grow to about 15ft (4.6m).

The life of mammals

The first mammals emerged at some time in the Triassic period 200 million years ago, and they were probably similar to living shrews and opossums. The story of mammal evolution is one of growing independence from the immediate pressures and constraints of the environment. Mammals became able to regulate their body temperature automatically and to maintain it at a constant level in heat or cold, usually above that of their surroundings. The infant mammal is protected with warmth and a guaranteed food supply during the earliest and most vulnerable part of its life. And the mammalian brain has developed to the point where the animal is capable of exercising some control over its environment.

How temperature is controlled

Temperature control in mammals is effected largely by means of skin glands and by blood vessels located just below the skin. A part of the brain, the hypothalamus, incorporates a mechanism for detecting changes in blood temperature. If the temperature is too high, activity in the hypothalamus causes the blood vessels of the skin to dilate so that blood heat can be more readily lost. To encourage this, the sweat glands secrete liquid onto the skin so that it is cooled by evaporation. When the temperature is too low, the skin blood vessels are constricted, the sweat glands dry up, and another reflex comes into play to erect the fur (or in the case of man the meager remnants of it). In a respectably furry animal, the fluffed up hairs make an effective insulating layer. When the skin temperature is uncomfortably low, reflex shivering is induced so that heat is generated by the work of the muscles. Many mammals, especially marine species, have layers of insulating fat beneath their skins.

Within the warm cocoon of its mother's body, the unborn mammal is insulated from the environment for up to the first year or so of its life, and most are provided with nourishment by a specially developed organ, the placenta. Nutritional care of the young continues after birth, with suckling.

Mammals have many features in common, but one of the most outstanding characteristics of the group is extreme diversity [1], particularly in body form. A vast array of animal types has radiated from the small insectivore ancestors, and these vary enormously in habit and life style.

Diversity of mammals

There are herbivores with hoofs, carnivores (flesh eaters) with claws, omnivores of all kinds, animals that burrow, nest, or build dams; animals with and without teeth, tails, or toes. By strange adaptations of body form, the mammal has gained the mastery of land, sea, and air. Kangaroos, by the enormous development of the hindlimbs, bound over the huge areas of the Australian outback. The fleetest sprinters come from the ungulates, deer and antelopes, and from the carnivores—especially the big cats. Squirrels and primates move along tree branches with ease and grace; the sloth is so completely adapted to an arboreal existence that it is virtually unable to walk on the ground.

Otters, coypus, beavers, and many other carnivores and rodents are proficient swim-

CONNECTIONS

See also
540 The classification of mammals
460 Animal anatomy
700 Reproduction
686 Skin and hair
574 Mammals of the past
576 The age of mammals
554 Primates: relatives of man
606 Desert birds and mammals
662 An introduction to body and mind
544 Monotremes and marsupials
552 Whales, porpoises, and dolphins

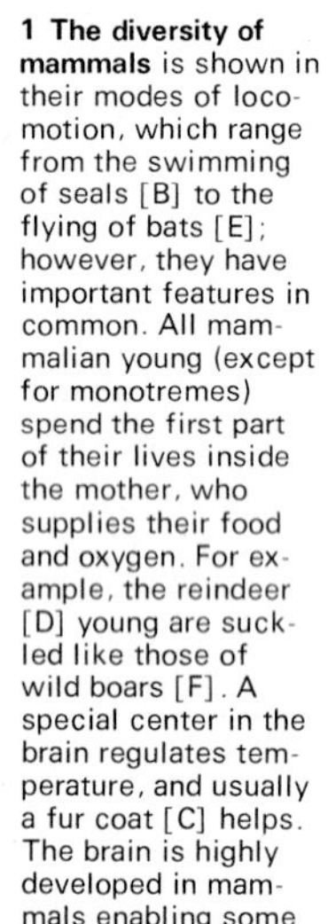

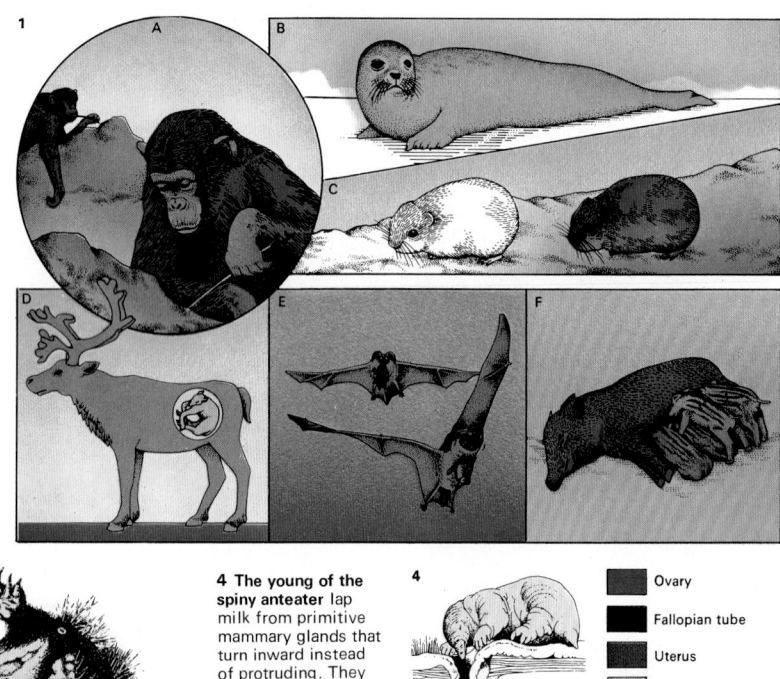

1 The diversity of mammals is shown in their modes of locomotion, which range from the swimming of seals [B] to the flying of bats [E]; however, they have important features in common. All mammalian young (except for monotremes) spend the first part of their lives inside the mother, who supplies their food and oxygen. For example, the reindeer [D] young are suckled like those of wild boars [F]. A special center in the brain regulates temperature, and usually a fur coat [C] helps. The brain is highly developed in mammals enabling some [A] to use tools.

3 The spiny anteater, or echidna *(Tachyglossus aculeatus)* has a primitive cloaca and mammary glands. It lacks separate urogenital and gut openings and has no true nipples.

4 The young of the spiny anteater lap milk from primitive mammary glands that turn inward instead of protruding. They lick the milk off the mother's fur.

5 The marsupial mouse *(Dasyuroides byrnei)* has no pouch. As a result, the helpless young are obliged to cling to their mother's fur.

6 The long-nosed bandicoot *(Perameles nasuta)* has a pouch that faces backward. This reversal stems from the animal's vigorous burrowing habits, which would otherwise fill the pouch with earth and harm the young.

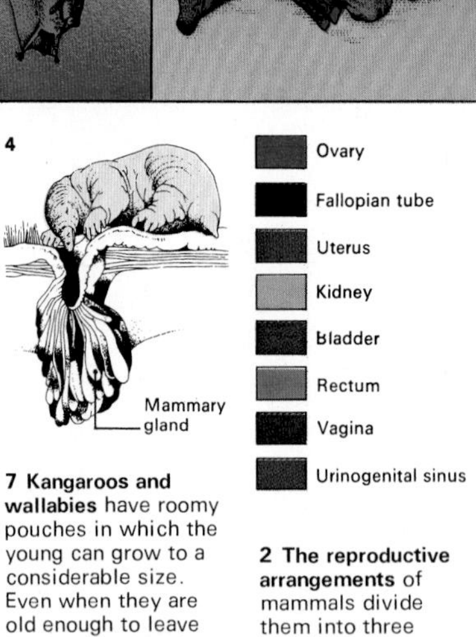

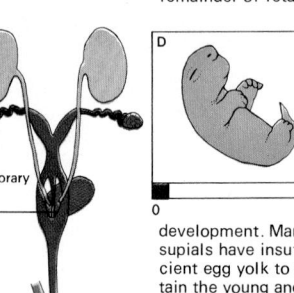

Mammary gland
Ovary
Fallopian tube
Uterus
Kidney
Bladder
Rectum
Vagina
Urinogenital sinus

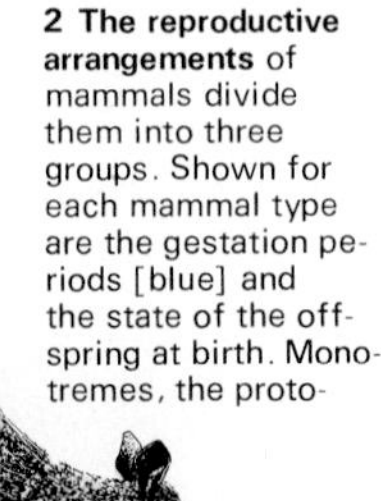

7 Kangaroos and wallabies have roomy pouches in which the young can grow to a considerable size. Even when they are old enough to leave it, young kangaroos return to the pouch in order to feed.

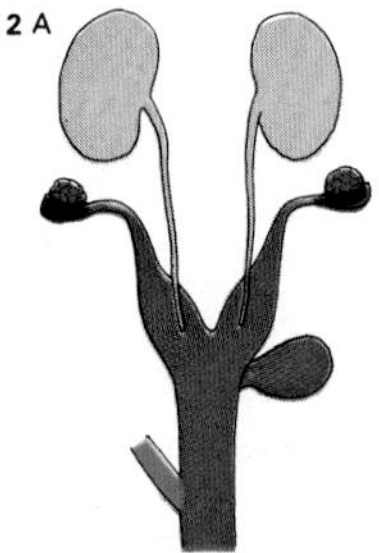

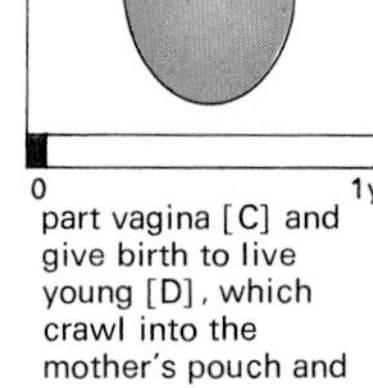

0
1yr

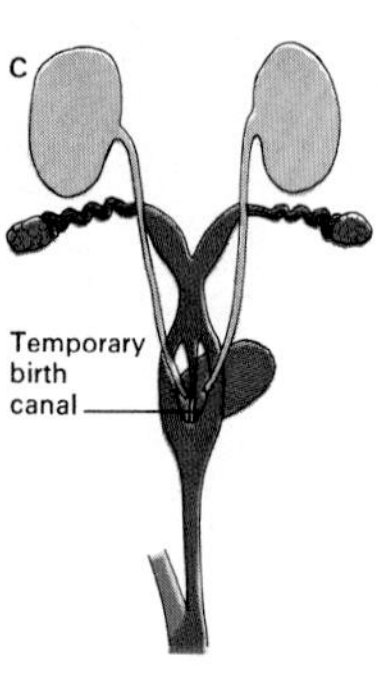

Temporary birth canal

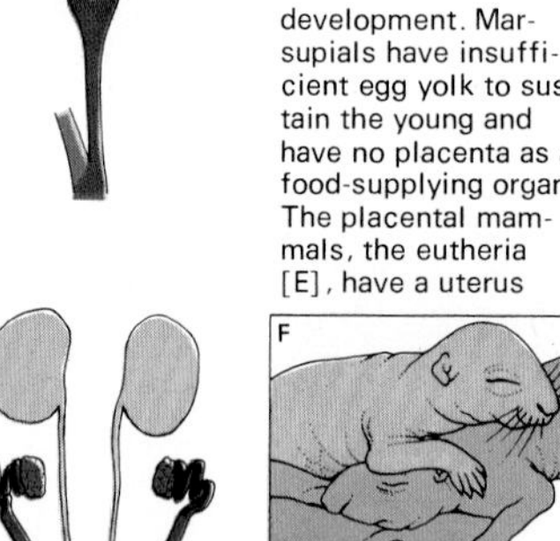

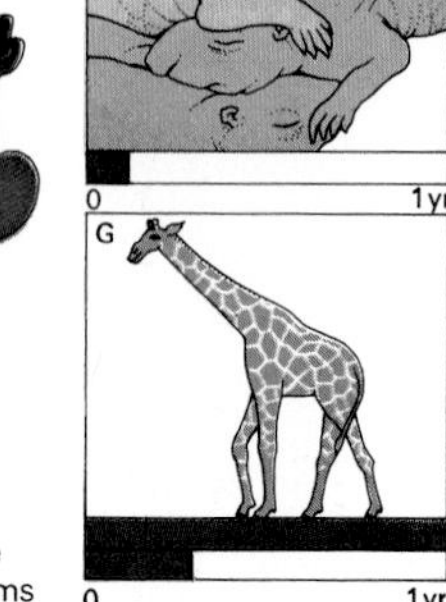

2 The reproductive arrangements of mammals divide them into three groups. Shown for each mammal type are the gestation periods [blue] and the state of the offspring at birth. Monotremes, the prototheria, have female reproductive systems [A] resembling those of reptiles and produce eggs [B]. Thus the young develops outside the mother's body. Marsupials, the metatheria, have a two-part vagina [C] and give birth to live young [D], which crawl into the mother's pouch and live there for the remainder of fetal development. Marsupials have insufficient egg yolk to sustain the young and have no placenta as a food-supplying organ. The placental mammals, the eutheria [E], have a uterus that can carry the young to an advanced stage of development ranging from the immature rat [F] to the fully formed giraffe [G].

mers and lead a semiaquatic life; but some mammals have really "taken the plunge," exchanging fingers for flippers and down the ages losing their legs. Seals, sea lions, sea cows, and most completely of all, the whales and dolphins [11] have abandoned the land to return to the ocean from which vertebrates painfully emerged so many millions of years ago.

The bats are the only flying mammals. Others, such as the so-called flying squirrel, may prolong what is really no more than a leap by passively holding out sheets of loose skin and gliding. But only the bat has wings that flap—as well as its personal version of a sonar system, using a continuous emission of ultrasonic bleeps to locate obstacles and potential food sources that it cannot see.

Diversity from genetic development

The remarkable diversity of form among mammals has developed during a relatively short period in evolutionary terms. Reptiles and amphibians, over a much longer time, have diversified much less dramatically. The embryos of vertebrates resemble each other during the early stages of development and there is not much difference between the appearance of a fish and a human embryo to begin with. But as development progresses mammalian embryos begin to show characteristic mammalian features and reach a stage at which they all look very similar to one another and quite different from the "lower" orders of vertebrates.

This is presumably because the genes that regulate early development have changed little in the course of events leading to the emergence of mammals. Those that control later development, however, have clearly evolved very fast. It is now believed that the diversity of the mammals is the result of an explosive acceleration in the rate of change of the genes regulating critical developmental events—genes whose activities are still not understood, but which are responsible not only for features such as the elephant's trunk, the neck of the giraffe, and the camel's hump, but also for the development of the cerebral hemispheres of the brain—an organ that in turn is able to initiate complex behavior patterns.

KEY

Male

Female

5 4 2 7 6 1 3 7

Eutherian, or placental, mammals have reproductive systems typified by that of the rabbit. The erectile penis [1] is inserted into the female vagina [2], and sperm is emitted from the testes [3]. This enters the uterus [4] to fertilize ripe ova descended from the ovaries [5]. Urinogenital tracts [2, 6], separate from the rectum [7], replace the cloaca.

8

8 The spiny anteater has two problems in reproducing itself. The first problem arises from the presence of spines on its back instead of hair. This makes copulation in the normal belly-to-back position painful. The second is the absence in the male of an erectile penis, which means that the genital openings must be brought as close together as possible for fertilization. So the spiny anteater mates belly-to-belly or tail-to-tail.

9 Two foxes that control their body temperatures differently. The Arctic fox [A] is protected from cold by a thick fur coat that turns white in winter. Its ears are small and almost submerged in hair to prevent heat loss. The fennec fox [B] lives in the Sahara and has enormous ears whose copious blood supply and large surface area makes them a very efficient device for losing heat. The temperature range over which the fennec fox must survive starts somewhat above where that of the Arctic fox leaves off.

9 A Arctic fox
Alopex lagopus

– +
50 40 30 20 10 0 10 20 30 40 50 60
degrees centigrade

B Fennec fox
Fennecus zerda

– +
50 40 30 20 10 0 10 20 30 40 50 60
degrees centigrade

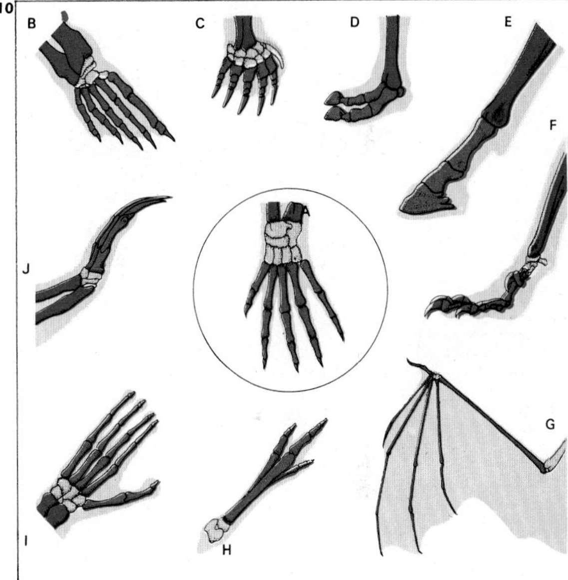

10
B
C
D
E
F
J
G
I
H

10 The feet of mammals have evolved in many different ways from the basic mammalian foot [A] possessed by the earliest shrewlike mammals. Seals [B] have developed evenly graduated toes for a webbed paddle. Moles [C] have truncated toes for leverage when digging. The camel's two toes [D] are padded for walking on sand. Horses have a hoof [E] instead of claws, and elongated feet for speed, as has the cheetah [F]. Bats [G] have enormously elongated digits to support wings. Kangaroos' toes [H] are for hopping. Lemurs [I] and sloths [J] have forelimbs for grasping trees.

11 Bottle-nosed dolphin
Tursiops truncatus

Dorsal nostril (blowhole)

Streamlined body

Dorsal fin for stability

Tail flukes for propulsion

Toothed jaws

Sunken eye aids streamlining

No external ear

Flippers are modified forelimbs

Young are born tail-first

No hindlimbs

11 The dolphin has come full circle in evolutionary history and has returned to the sea. Typically mammalian features are not very easily recognizable because of the dolphin's streamlined and fish-like body. After birth of the young, which feed from teats close to the genital opening, each female dolphin separates itself from the school with one other female. Dolphins have well-developed social lives and are considered to be highly intelligent.

Monotremes and marsupials

Monotremes and marsupials are the two most primitive groups of living mammals. The monotremes bear the marks of their reptilian ancestry in their bony structure as well as in the feature that gave them their name, for monotreme means literally "single hole" and refers to the fact that excretory and reproductive functions are both served by one passage, the cloaca. In higher mammals there are separate excretory and genital tracts.

Monotremes: the egg-laying mammals

The three surviving genera of monotremes, the duck-billed platypus *(Ornithorhynchus)* [1] and the Australian and New Guinea echidnas *(Tachyglossus* and *Zaglossus)*, all lay eggs that have a typically reptilian soft leathery shell, and the latter take the hatched young into a temporary pouch. The young feed on milk secreted from modified sweat glands, which, however, are not combined into a single milk duct ending in a nipple. Although the monotremes have fur to help maintain body temperature, the temperature-regulating mechanism is not well developed and, as a result, they tend to be cooler and have a more variable body temperature than higher mammals.

Both kinds of monotremes have developed marked specializations peculiar to their different ways of life. The platypus has webbed feet as well as its ducklike bill to equip it for a mud-grubbing aquatic existence [1]. The spiny echidna has long claws and a pointed nose for digging ants out of their nests. Neither has teeth but the platypus bill has a horny ridge that is used to demolish hard-skinned crustaceans.

Marsupial characteristics

Although the pouch is the distinguishing characteristic that comes to most people's minds when they think of marsupials, strictly speaking the important zoological point is not the presence of the pouch but the absence of the placenta, an internal organ designed to nourish the fetus within the mother. (Many American opossums, for example, generally lack a pouch.) The egg yolk plus uterine secretions nourish the embryonic marsupial for the first few days and in some cases a primitive placenta forms. The young animal then crawls, still in an unformed fetal state, into its mother's pouch and latches on to a nipple for sustenance during its development.

Both the marsupial mother and the fetus are highly specialized for this arrangement. The fetus, for example, develops its forelimbs far in advance of its hindlimbs for the long climb between the vagina and pouch. The mother's teats are muscular organs that inject milk into the young.

Only in the New World and Australasia have marsupials survived. In South America they are represented principally by the opossums and the rat opossum of the Andes; one kind of opossum has also settled most of North America. Marsupials are classified into two main groups, the polyprotodonts and the diprotodonts. Polyprotodonts, which literally means "many front teeth," have more than three incisors in each jaw. Diprotodonts, "two front teeth," are more specialized, and have only two projecting teeth in the lower jaw for grazing.

CONNECTIONS

See also

542 The life of mammals
540 The classification of mammals
590 Australian desert grasslands
596 Woodlands of Australasia
578 Regions of the Earth: zoogeography
582 Isolation and evolution
628 Endangered mammals
574 Mammals of the past

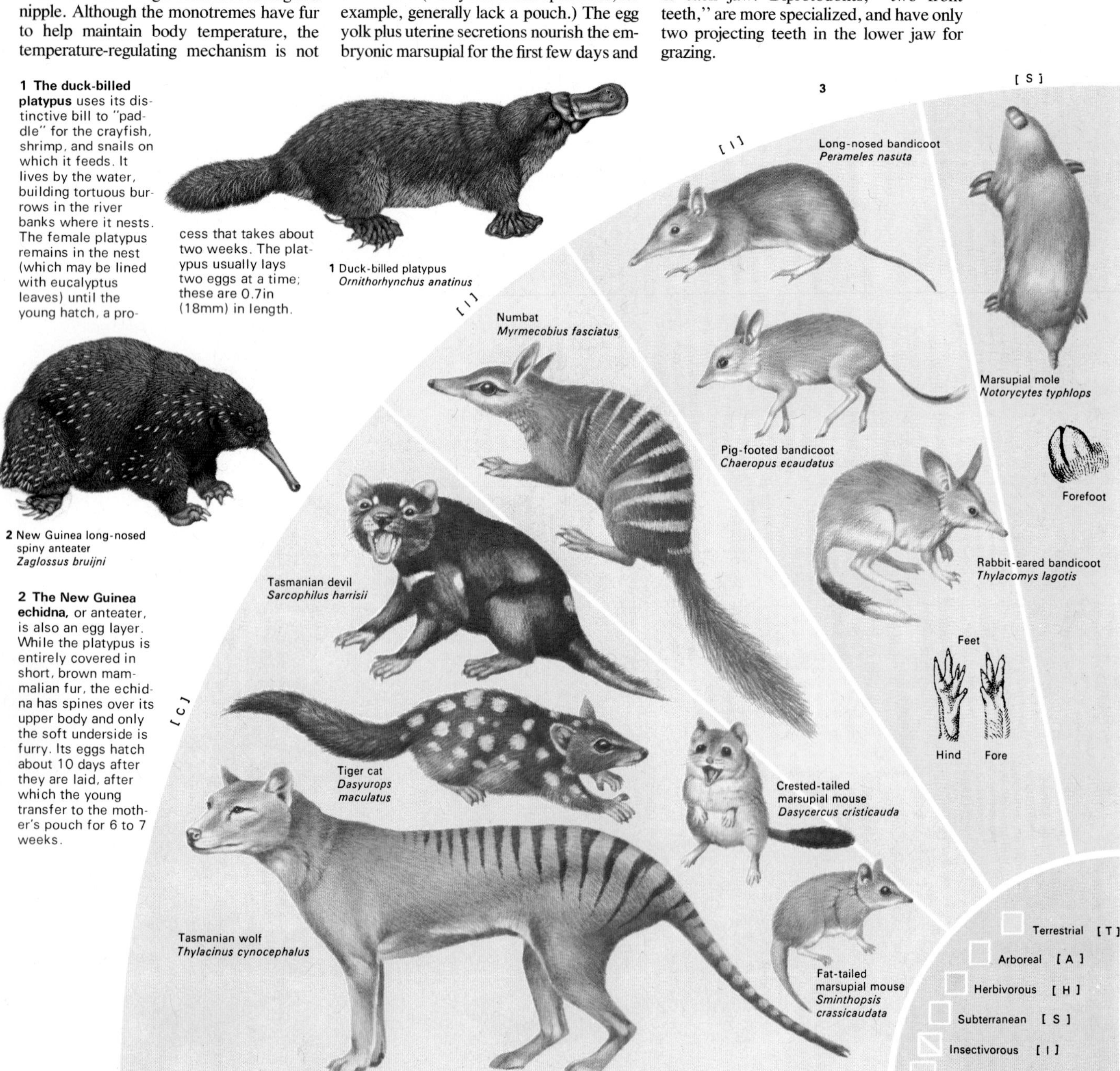

1 Duck-billed platypus
Ornithorhynchus anatinus
2 New Guinea long-nosed spiny anteater
Zaglossus bruijni
3
[I]
Long-nosed bandicoot
Perameles nasuta
[S]
Marsupial mole
Notorycytes typhlops
Forefoot
[I]
Numbat
Myrmecobius fasciatus
Pig-footed bandicoot
Chaeropus ecaudatus
Rabbit-eared bandicoot
Thylacomys lagotis
Tasmanian devil
Sarcophilus harrisii
[C]
Feet
Hind
Fore
Tiger cat
Dasyurops maculatus
Crested-tailed marsupial mouse
Dasycercus cristicauda
Tasmanian wolf
Thylacinus cynocephalus
Fat-tailed marsupial mouse
Sminthopsis crassicaudata
Terrestrial [T]
Arboreal [A]
Herbivorous [H]
Subterranean [S]
Insectivorous [I]
Carnivorous [C]

1 The duck-billed platypus uses its distinctive bill to "paddle" for the crayfish, shrimp, and snails on which it feeds. It lives by the water, building tortuous burrows in the river banks where it nests. The female platypus remains in the nest (which may be lined with eucalyptus leaves) until the young hatch, a process that takes about two weeks. The platypus usually lays two eggs at a time; these are 0.7in (18mm) in length.

2 The New Guinea echidna, or anteater, is also an egg layer. While the platypus is entirely covered in short, brown mammalian fur, the echidna has spines over its upper body and only the soft underside is furry. Its eggs hatch about 10 days after they are laid, after which the young transfer to the mother's pouch for 6 to 7 weeks.

The American marsupials, with the exception of the rat opossum, are all polyprotodonts. They have failed to develop a typical diprotodont feature—the fusion of the two digits for purposes of hair-combing.

Australian marsupials

Australian marsupials [3], which have had 130 million years to evolve without competition from placental mammals, are much more varied than their American relatives. They fall into four rough groupings, defined by their feeding habits—omnivorous, insectivorous, carnivorous, and herbivorous.

The American opossums (family Didelphidae), which generally have rudimentary pouches, are insectivorous or omnivorous [4, 5]. The bandicoots, also omnivorous or insectivorous, occupy a family of their own and have developed backward-facing pouches. This is a special trait of marsupials that dig or burrow and serves to protect the young from flying earth thrown up by the mother's excavations.

Carnivorous marsupials, numerous in Australia, include parallels to the placental cats and wolves, though all are quite small. The insectivores include the marsupial mole, numerous pouched "mice" (which occupy the niche taken up by the shrews of the placental group) and the South American rat oppossum.

The most specialized of the marsupials are the Australian diprotodonts. All have developed rodentlike teeth for gnawing vegetation or, in kangaroos and wallabies, for shearing grass. This group contains three genera of "flying" mammals, including the flying squirrel *(Petaurus)*. Apart from the squirrellike phalangers, there is the wombat of similar size and habits to such large placental rodents as marmots and woodchucks and the Australian koala.

The kangaroos and wallabies invite no easy comparison with placental equivalents. They alone have developed the peculiarly powerful hind legs and muscular tails that have given the group its name—the macropodidae, meaning big feet. But they are unique in other respects, combining gnawing types of teeth with grazing habits and often a very large body size.

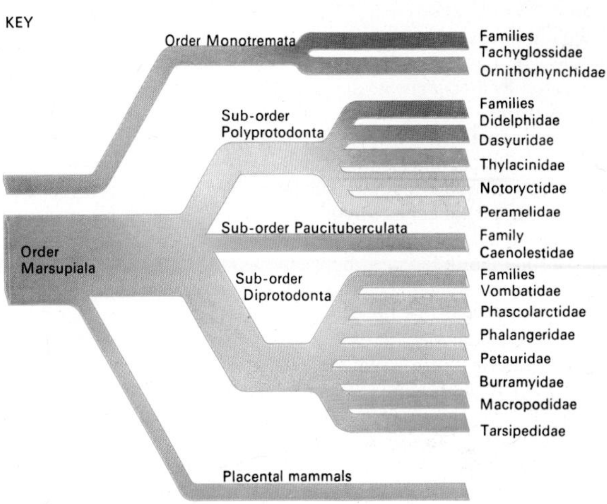

KEY
Order Monotremata
Families
Tachyglossidae
Ornithorhynchidae
Sub-order
Polyprotodonta
Families
Didelphidae
Dasyuridae
Thylacinidae
Notoryctidae
Peramelidae
Order
Marsupiala
Sub-order Paucituberculata
Family
Caenolestidae
Sub-order
Diprotodonta
Families
Vombatidae
Phascolarctidae
Phalangeridae
Petauridae
Burramyidae
Macropodidae
Tarsipedidae
Placental mammals

Only two branches of monotremes, the egglaying mammals, exist today: the spiny echidnas of Australia and New Guinea and the Australian duck-billed platypus. They belong to the subclass Prototheria and although specialized are the most primitive mammals. Spiny echidnas develop a temporary pouch. Monotremes and marsupials—Metatheria—lack the true placenta of placental mammals—Eutheria. Marsupials live only in Australasia and the New World; about 250 species exist.

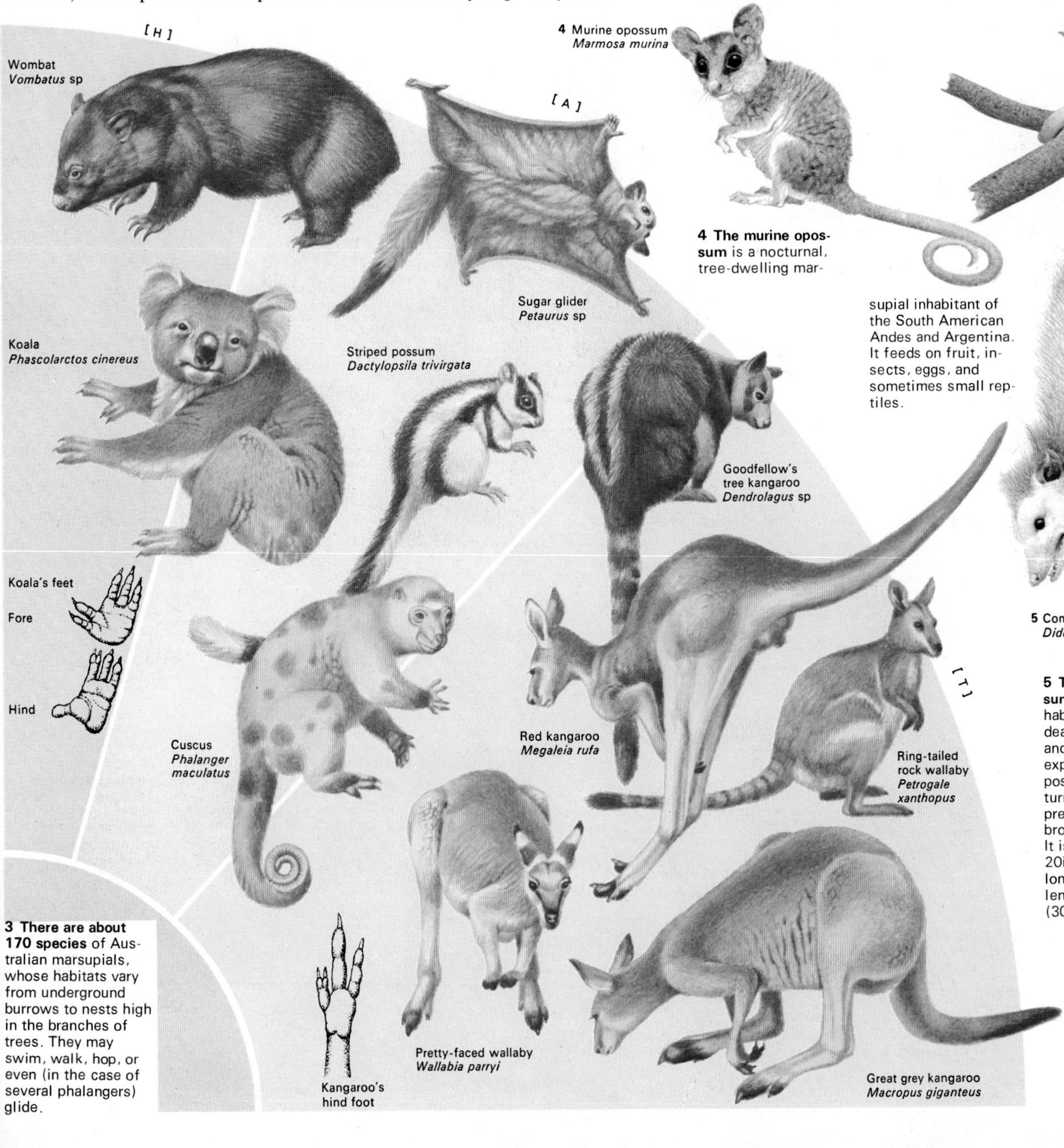

[H] Wombat *Vombatus* sp

[A] Sugar glider *Petaurus* sp

Koala *Phascolarctos cinereus*

Striped possum *Dactylopsila trivirgata*

Goodfellow's tree kangaroo *Dendrolagus* sp

Koala's feet: Fore, Hind

Cuscus *Phalanger maculatus*

Red kangaroo *Megaleia rufa*

[T] Ring-tailed rock wallaby *Petrogale xanthopus*

Pretty-faced wallaby *Wallabia parryi*

Kangaroo's hind foot

Great grey kangaroo *Macropus giganteus*

3 There are about 170 species of Australian marsupials, whose habitats vary from underground burrows to nests high in the branches of trees. They may swim, walk, hop, or even (in the case of several phalangers) glide.

4 Murine opossum *Marmosa murina*

4 The murine opossum is a nocturnal, tree-dwelling marsupial inhabitant of the South American Andes and Argentina. It feeds on fruit, insects, eggs, and sometimes small reptiles.

5 Common opossum *Didelphis marsupialis*

5 The common opossum is familiar for its habit of feigning death when surprised and gave rise to the expression "playing possum." It is a nocturnal animal with a prehensile tail and broad feeding habits. It is between 13 and 20in (33–50cm) long, with a tail length of 12in (30cm).

Rodents, insect-eaters, and bats

Two out of every five species of mammals in the world are rodents (order Rodentia), the chisel-teethed gnawing animals. The insectivores fall into two groups, first those classified in the order Insectivora, and second other insect-eating animals, namely the bats (order Chiroptera), the anteaters (order Edentata), the pangolins (order Pholidota), and the aardvark (order Tubulidentata).

Despite the differences between them, which are mainly connected with feeding, the Rodentia and the Insectivora share a number of common features and these are, in turn, similar to those of early mammals. For example, they are mostly small, built to a simple plan, and are five-toed.

Rodents range in size from the capybara [1] of South America, which is as large as a small pig, to the African pygmy mouse *(Musminutoides)*, which averages about 3in (7.6cm) in length, only slightly smaller than the European harvest mouse *(Micromys)*.

Rodents and rabbits

Rodents are found in almost every habitat the earth has to offer, apart from the sea. Most live on the ground, but niches from treetops (squirrels) to underground burrows (mole rats) have been exploited; beavers and some others have even become adapted, though not totally, to life in water, having webbed feet and heavy waterproof fur. Rodents move in various ways. On the ground, progression is usually by running, as with the Patagonian cavy, or "hare," or by leaping, as with the jerboas. Above the ground, rodents may climb or glide, as seen in the tree squirrels and flying squirrels [2].

Rabbits and hares, and their relatives the pikas, belong to the order Lagomorpha, a word that means "hare-shaped." Although they resemble rodents, lagomorphs have different kinds of gnawing teeth [Key B 5]. Compared with rodents, there are few species in the rabbit group, but it is nevertheless highly successful, with vast numbers of individuals. Hares differ from rabbits in having longer hind legs and ears that are longer than their heads [10]. Rabbits and hares can walk, but they usually hop over the ground and can move at great speed when danger threatens. Pikas are the smallest of the group. They are easily distinguished by their small ears, almost complete lack of a tail, and the possession of all four legs of equal length.

The insect-eaters

The group of mammals belonging to the order Insectivora has a long evolutionary history. Fossil insectivores are known from rocks of the late Mesozoic age. These creatures shared their world with the dinosaurs, but they and their descendants survived when the great reptiles died out. Today, members of the order Insectivora are found in all parts of the world except for the polar regions and Australasia (where the insect eaters are monotremes and marsupials) and live in a wide range of habitats from mountains to lowland rivers, and from tundra to tropical forest. They include a number of widely differing forms, but all feed on insects or other small invertebrates. Most widespread are the ever-hungry shrews, the smallest of all mammals. Somewhat larger, though no less voracious, are the moles. Moles are all burrowing animals that loosen

CONNECTIONS

See also
540 The classification o[f] mammals
542 The life of mamma[ls]
588 South American grasslands
602 New World tropics
606 Desert birds and mammals
556 How mammals beha[ve]
1802 Radar and sonar
574 Mammals of the pa[st]
578 Regions of the Ear[th:] zoogeography

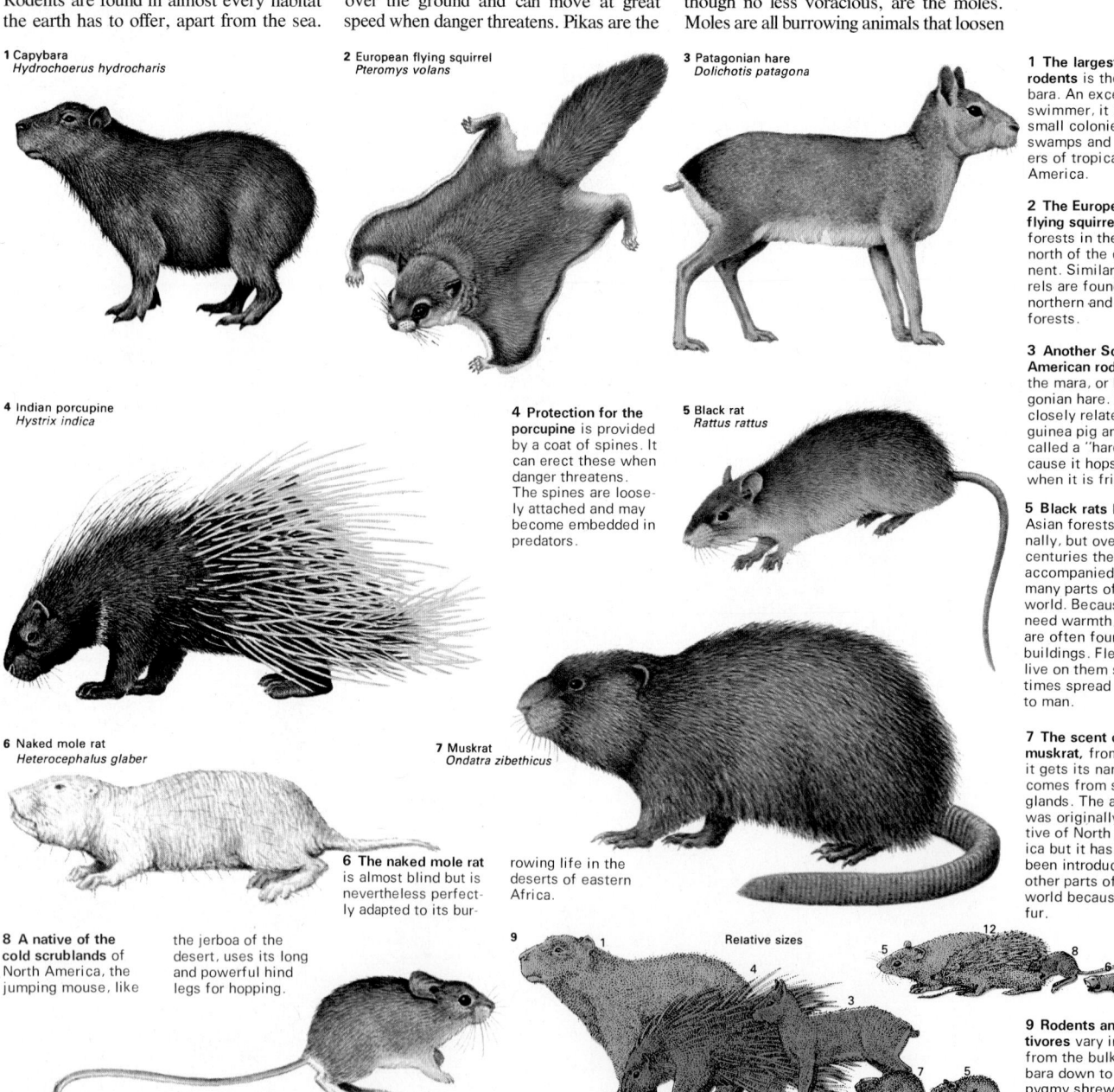

1 Capybara
Hydrochoerus hydrocharis

2 European flying squirrel
Pteromys volans

3 Patagonian hare
Dolichotis patagona

1 The largest of all rodents is the capybara. An excellent swimmer, it lives in small colonies in swamps and near rivers of tropical South America.

2 The European flying squirrel lives in forests in the far north of the continent. Similar squirrels are found in both northern and tropical forests.

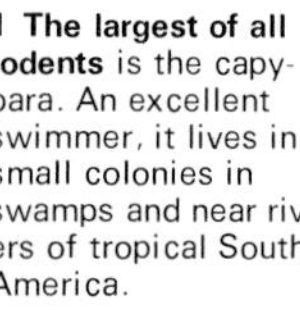

3 Another South American rodent is the mara, or Patagonian hare. It is closely related to the guinea pig and is called a "hare" because it hops away when it is frightened.

4 Indian porcupine
Hystrix indica

4 Protection for the porcupine is provided by a coat of spines. It can erect these when danger threatens. The spines are loosely attached and may become embedded in predators.

5 Black rat
Rattus rattus

5 Black rats lived in Asian forests originally, but over the centuries they have accompanied man to many parts of the world. Because they need warmth, they are often found in buildings. Fleas that live on them sometimes spread disease to man.

6 Naked mole rat
Heterocephalus glaber

7 Muskrat
Ondatra zibethicus

6 The naked mole rat is almost blind but is nevertheless perfectly adapted to its burrowing life in the deserts of eastern Africa.

7 The scent of the muskrat, from which it gets its name, comes from special glands. The animal was originally a native of North America but it has since been introduced into other parts of the world because of its fur.

8 A native of the cold scrublands of North America, the jumping mouse, like the jerboa of the desert, uses its long and powerful hind legs for hopping.

8 Jumping mouse
Zapus hudsonius

9 Relative sizes

9 Rodents and insectivores vary in size from the bulky capybara down to the tiny pygmy shrew, one of the world's smallest mammals.

the soil with their short, powerful forelimbs and shoulder their way through to consolidate a tunnel around their bodies. Still larger are the hedgehogs [12], which are native only to the Old World. They are protected by a coat of spines that has the advantage, rare in animal armor, of being fairly lightweight. The porcupine [4], among the rodents, has the same kind of protection, but there is no close relationship between it and the hedgehog.

The bats

Most bats [15, 16], the only flying mammals, eat insects. Their wings are attached to their forelimbs, which are long and slender and have elongated finger bones that support the fragile membrane. The rear of each wing is attached to the bat's hind legs and is sometimes extended to include the tail. Bats make up almost a quarter of all placental species. They owe their success probably to the fact that they occupy a niche left vacant by the diurnal birds, since bats are nocturnal insect-eaters. They feed mainly on night-flying creatures such as beetles and moths, which they detect with a highly sophisticated sonar system [17]. There are far fewer bats in temperate regions than in the tropics, where their diet comprises a much wider range, including blood, fish, and fruit.

Many other groups of animals eat insects. They include the pangolins [13] of the tropical Old World, which are armored with overlapping horny plates, giving them the appearance of animated pine cones. Some species can climb trees. In the tropical New World there are no pangolins but their place is taken by the anteaters. These belong to a curious South American order called the Edentata ("animals with no teeth"). This is a misleading name because some members of the group—the tree sloths and armadillos—are equipped with many teeth, although these are degenerate structures that lack enamel and are restricted to the back of the mouth. The anteater's extremely weak jaws [Key D] are long and tubular, and its mouth forms a tiny slit at the end. Its long, sticky tongue flicks out like a whiplash to scoop up the termites on which it feeds.

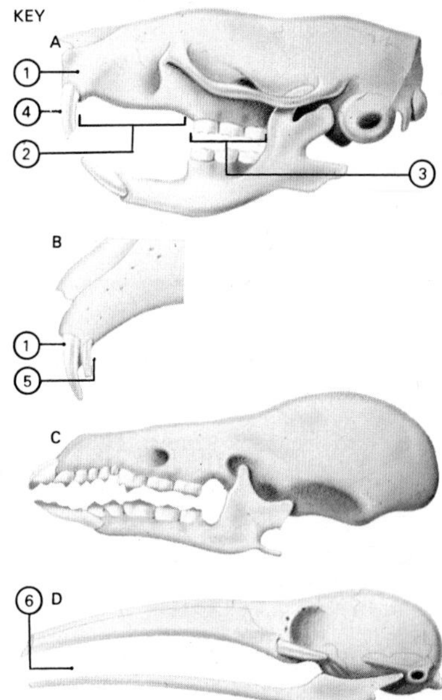
KEY
A
B
C
D
1
2
3
4
5
6

The teeth of animals betray their feeding habits. Rodents such as rats [A] and lagomorphs such as rabbits [B] have gnawing incisors [1] that are open-rooted and continue growing for life. Then comes a toothless gap, the diastema [2], followed by grinding teeth [3]. Rodents have a single pair of incisors in both upper and lower jaws, and only the front surface is enameled [4]. Lagomorphs have a second, smaller pair of incisors [5] that lie behind the main upper teeth, which are fully enameled. The teeth of insectivores such as shrews [C] have sharp shearing edges. Pangolins and anteaters [D] feed on ants and have long, toothless jaws [6].

10 Jack rabbit
Lepus californicus

10 The jack rabbit of North America, so called, is actually a hare, and its huge ears are a clue to its correct classification. It squats in a scrape in the ground, whereas the true rabbit lives in a burrow. Young jack rabbits are born fully furred.

11 Grant's desert mole *(Eremitalpa granti)*, from South Africa, is a golden mole. These resemble true moles but are in a different family.

11

Grant's desert mole

12 Long-eared hedgehog
Hemiechinus sp.

12 A coat of spines protects the long-eared hedgehog, which lives in dry regions ranging from the Near East to Mongolia. The hedgehog hunts by night and rests in a burrow during the day.

16
1
2
3
4
5

13

African tree pangolin
Manis tricuspis

13 The African tree pangolin is an unusual animal. Its short, powerful forelegs are armed with sharp claws that help it to climb and tear open the nests of tree ants on which it feeds. Its tail also helps its progress through the trees by curling around branches or by pressing its overlapping scales against the trunks.

14 North American pygmy shrew
Microsorex hoyi

14 One of the smallest of all mammals is the North American pygmy shrew. It measures only about 3.5in (9cm) overall and weighs less than 0.1oz (3gm). Like all shrews, it is highly active but has only a short life span.

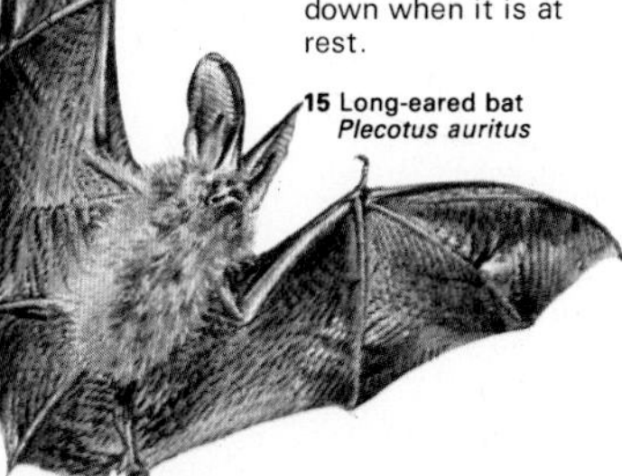

15 Long-eared bat
Plecotus auritus

15 This long-eared bat is found in the temperate regions of Europe, Asia, and North Africa. It holds its long ears erect in flight and folds them down when it is at rest.

16 Bats are flying insectivores. The big-eared bat *(Macrotus mexicanus)* [1] is typical. The fisherman bat *(Noctilio leporinus)* [2] takes fish from surface water. The vampire bat *(Desmodus rotundus)* [3] slices the skin of a tapir and laps blood. Long-tongued bats *(Glossophaga soricina)* [4] feed on nectar and pollen, whereas the wrinkle-faced bat *(Centurio senex)* [5] prefers pulpy fruit.

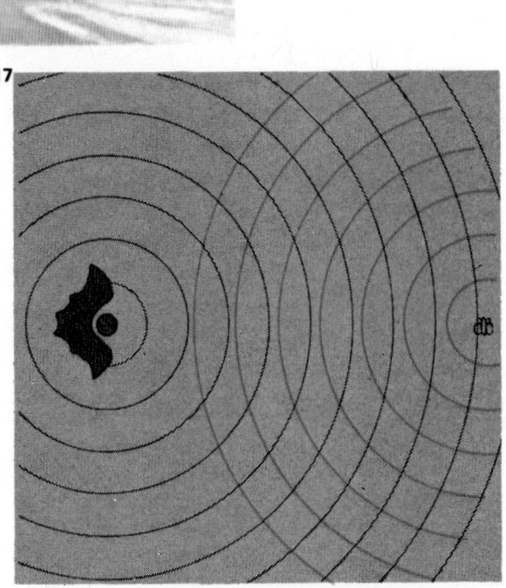
17

17 Almost all bats use echolocation with which to navigate and find their food. As they fly, they emit a series of high-pitched squeaks, each lasting about 1/500 of a second at a rate of about 50 a second. These signals bounce off any object in their paths and the resulting echo is detected by the bats' sensitive ears. Acting on this information, the bats can then take the necessary action.

Hoofed mammals

There are more than 200 different species of hoofed animals, or ungulates, of which the horse and cow are the most familiar. All hoofed animals are mammals and all are herbivores, most feeding on tough vegetation which they masticate with specialized and complex teeth. Hoofs are large, flat toenails that developed in the course of evolution as a result of the tendency of some animals to stand and walk on their toes rather than using the full length of the foot in the way that man and his close relatives do. This has the advantage of increasing the length of the leg by the length of the foot, and sometimes by that of the toes, resulting in a longer stride and faster movement.

Odd-toed and even-toed animals

Most hoofed mammals belong to two great orders: the even-toed, or Artiodactyla, which have two or four toes on each foot; and the odd-toed, or Perissodactyla, which have a variable, but almost always an odd number of toes. There are approximately 190 species of even-toed mammals and roughly 15 species of odd-toed mammals. There is, in addition, another group of hoofed mammals, the subungulates, which includes animals as diverse as the elephant, the rock hyrax, and the sea cow, which has forelimbs developed as flippers and no hind limbs.

The herbivores

The ungulates arose from early mammalian stock at the start of the Cenozoic era some 60 million years ago, but by the Eocene, some 20 million years later, many had become large, heavy-bodied herbivores a number of which were destined to be replaced, in the Miocene, by fleet-footed grazers. Even in the early days of the ungulates three distinct groups began to emerge. Thus, although the cow group (even-toed) and the horse group (odd-toed) may seem linked, they have a long history of separate evolution.

Of the two main groups, the even-toed species have proved to be the better survivors, for almost all of the medium to large plant eaters in the world belong to this group. The more primitive even-toed species include the Old World pigs and the New World peccaries, which have four well developed toes on each limb. They are omnivorous and their dentition is less specialized than in many other forms. Hippopotamuses, which retreat to water during the daytime, come ashore to feed at night. Camels, which are primitive cud-chewers highly adapted for desert life, have only two toes on each foot, as do their South American relatives the llamas. These animals all have some upper front teeth.

The upper front teeth of the other even-toed ungulates, which are all cud-chewers, or ruminants, are missing and are replaced by a horny pad. They can take in food tremendously fast, however, often using the tongue to tear at vegetation. The food is passed to a holding compartment in the stomach and regurgitated later to be masticated thoroughly before being swallowed a second time, after which digestion proper starts. One advantage of chewing the cud is that food that may have been gathered in dangerous areas and rapidly eaten can be digested later in a place of comparative

CONNECTIONS

See also

540 The classification of mammals
542 The life of mammals
586 Grasslands of Africa
628 Endangered mammals
1590 Bark, hide, and horn
556 How mammals behav
636 Constructive man
372 Cattle for beef and milk
376 Pigs and sheep
582 Isolation and evolution
578 Regions of the Earth zoogeography

1

African elephant
Loxodonta africana

1 The African elephant is the largest land mammal; a big male may stand at nearly 12ft (4m) and weigh over 7 tons. The tusks are upper incisor teeth that continue to grow throughout its life.

2 The aardvark, which measures up to 5ft (1.5m) long, is a subungulate found in much of Africa. It is rarely seen for it is nocturnal and extremely shy. Its presence may be detected by the large burrows it digs, using the hooflike claws on its forefeet. It feeds chiefly on termites and ants, which it catches with its long tongue, coated with sticky saliva. It also eats vegetation.

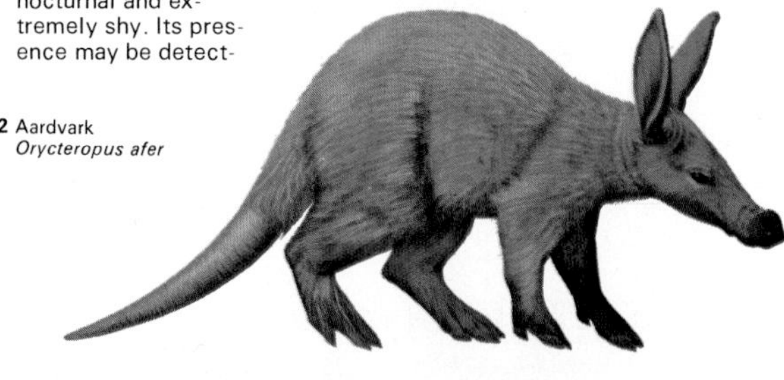

2 Aardvark
Orycteropus afer

5

Florida manatee
Trichechus manatus

3

Rock hyrax
Procavia capensis

3 Several species of rock hyrax live in parts of Africa and the Near East. They are small, superficially rodentlike animals, living in rock crevices or in borrowed burrows in forested areas.

4 A

B

C

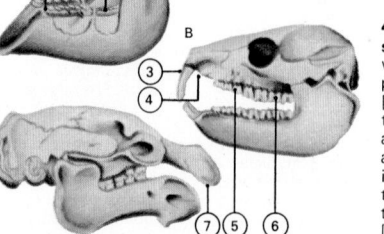

4 The dentition of subungulates varies widely. In the elephant's lower jaw [A] the larger molar tooth [1] is replaced as it wears out by another tooth growing forward [2]. In the rock hyrax [B] the upper incisors [3] grow continuously. The lower incisors point forward like small tusks. There is a big gap [4] between these and the grinding premolars [5] and molars [6] In the manatee [C] the incisors are replaced by horny pads [7] behind fleshy lips.

5 The manatees are subungulates of the tropical coasts of the Atlantic, although one species travels as far north as Georgia. The fleshy lobes on the upper lip are sufficiently mobile to seize food and pass it along to the manatee's mouth.

safety. Deer, giraffes, antelopes, cattle, sheep, and goats are all ruminants.

Odd-toed animals were at one time more numerous than at present; today only horses, rhinoceroses, and tapirs survive. The rarity of the first two is largely the result of persecution by man, and the true wild horses and asses and the three species of Asiatic rhinoceroses are among the rarest mammals in the world, although the zebra is relatively common in parts of Africa. No odd-toed animal chews the cud and none has any true horns, those of the rhinoceros being made of compressed hair. The rhinos have three toes on each foot, the tapirs have four on the front feet and three on the hind feet, while horses (including donkeys and zebras) have lost all but the large central toes of each foot. The way weight is carried by the legs is therefore completely different from that of the even-toed animals.

Elephants, hyraxes, and sea cows

The subungulates are the smallest group of hoofed animals. Two species of elephant survive to the present day in Africa and southern Asia, the sole remnants of an order of giant animals that once inhabited most of the world. Their size alone distinguishes them from all other land mammals, but the possession of a trunk and the peculiarities of the teeth, which include two tusks in the upper jaw and only four other teeth, also sets them apart.

A group of animals found in Africa and the Near East and thought to be closely related to the elephants is that of hyraxes, small, dumpy yet agile creatures that live socially in forested or rocky areas. All have hooflike nails on the four front toes and a large claw on the innermost of the three hind toes.

Fossil remains have shown that the early relatives of the sea cow were similar to those of the elephant. Now, however, the sea cows are entirely aquatic, living in tropical rivers and offshore areas where they feed on water vegetation. They are large, placid, sluggish animals that swim by means of a tail fluke. The forelimb is transformed into a paddle and in some species this carries small flattened fingernails.

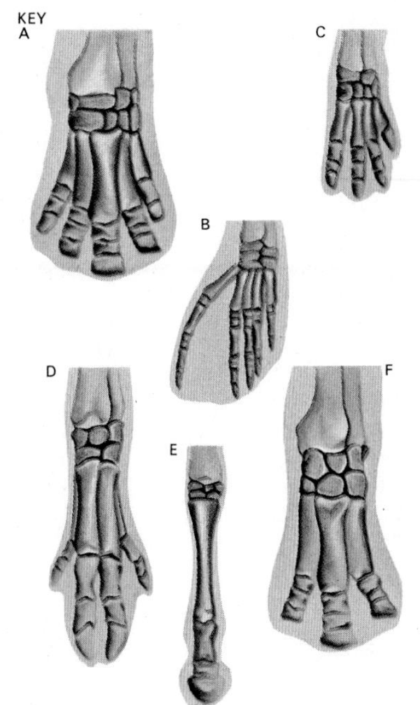
KEY
A
B
C
D
E
F
Forearm
Wrist (carpals)
Metacarpals
Phalanges

The front limbs of a selection of hoofed animals show that the same sequence of joints occurs however many the toes. The elephant's foot [A] has 5 toes slightly spread and backed by tissue pad. The manatee's flipper [B] and the rock hyrax's trotter [C] both have a handlike skeleton. The pig [D] has 4 toes but walks on only 2. The horse's "hand" [E] contains only one toe, with the last of the finger bones carrying the hoof, while the rhinoceros [F] has three toes to each foot.

6
Common eland
Taurotragus oryx
Water buffalo
Bubalus bubalis
Hippopotamus
Hippopotamus amphibius
Reindeer
Rangifer tarandus
Vicuña
Vicugna vicugna
Giraffe
Giraffa camelopardalis
Red river hog
Potamochoerus porcus
Indian chevrotain
Tragulus meminna
Burchell's zebra
Equus burchelli
Mouflon
Ovis ammon
Malayan tapir
Tapirus indicus

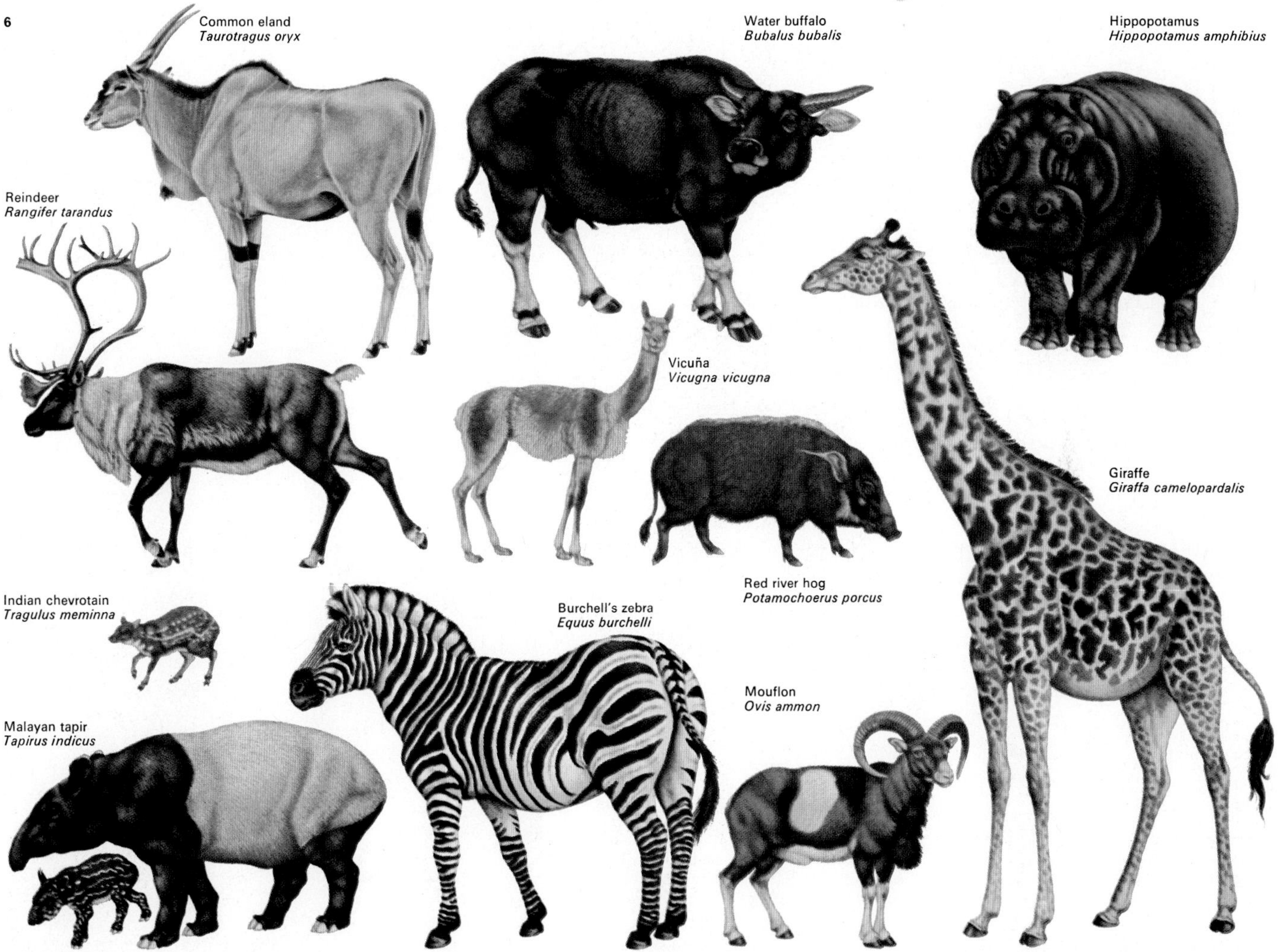

6 Hoofed mammals include many species economically important to man. The eland is the largest of the antelopes. Recently attempts have been made to domesticate it for its excellent milk, meat, and hide. The water buffalo is found as a wild animal in some parts of India but has been domesticated in much of the tropical world. The hippopotamus, an African animal, is found in rivers, lakes, and swamps, in social groups. The reindeer migrates vast distances between summer and winter feeding grounds. Both male and female carry antlers. The vicuna is a South American relative of the camel and lives in small herds in arid or mountainous areas. Its numbers have been greatly reduced by hunters seeking its fine silky fleece. The red river hog, so-called because of its reddish bristles, is found in Africa. It lives in family groups and forages at night. Chevrotains live in SE Asia and Africa. They are small, shy, nocturnal animals that inhabit dense bush. The males develop long tusks. Burchell's zebra is the commonest of the striped horses of Africa. Why it is striped is a puzzle, for it lives in family groups in open country where the stripes seem to make it more obvious. The Malayan tapir is a shy, nocturnal inhabitant of dense forests in SE Asia. The mouflon is a mountain dweller found only in the remoter parts of Sardinia and Corsica. It is related to the ancestor of the domestic sheep, whose fleece has been developed from the wool layer beneath the mouflon's top coat of coarse fur. The long neck of the giraffe enables it to reach trees up to a height of 18ft (6m). It tears off vegetation from the tree tops for food.

Flesh-eating mammals

Many kinds of animals are flesh-eaters. Land mammals of this type are classified zoologically into the order Carnivora (which includes cats, hyenas, dogs, weasels, bears, raccoons, and civets), a group in which most of the members are adapted to preying on other creatures.

One group of mammals (the seals, sea lions, and walrus) became adapted—although not completely—to existence in water. These are treated by most authorities as the order Pinnipedia, but are sometimes grouped as a suborder within the Carnivora because both groups are descended from a common mammalian ancestor that lived in the Eocene over 50 million years ago.

Some members of these two groups have diverged from a strictly carnivorous way of life. Thus the hyena [5], although a ferocious hunter, also feeds on carrion, bears [6] eat a variety of food including fruit and leaves, the aardwolf [10] feeds almost exclusively on termites, and the walrus [12] feeds on marine shellfish.

The Carnivora are native to almost all parts of the world except Australia, New Zealand, and many Pacific islands, while the seal group has members distributed on the shores of temperate and polar seas.

The carnivorous life style

Successful carnivores are well equipped for preying on other animals and all are built on a relatively primitive plan, with a long, fairly flexible body and tail. The terrestrial species have well-developed and often long legs. Among the dogs are several long-distance runners, and among cats is the cheetah, the world's fastest sprinter. Even the short-legged carnivores can move rapidly over short distances. The proportions of the head differ in the various groups of flesh-eaters, but certain features are common to all of them. Most have well-developed canine teeth with which they hold their prey, comparatively small incisors (cutting teeth), and two pairs of shearing molars, or carnassial teeth, adapted to flesh-eating needs. The carnassials have special cutting edges that act like scissor blades.

Carnivores have fairly good eyesight; in many the eyes are sufficiently far down the face to give some degree of stereoscopic vision and this helps them to judge distances when pouncing on prey. Their sense of smell is usually well developed and their sense of hearing is acute. Most carnivores are intelligent animals—this is because they must be versatile opportunists if they are not to be outwitted by their prey.

Social, marine, and subterranean carnivores

Most carnivores are solitary creatures, although the young often depend on their mothers—or occasionally both parents—for a long time after birth. Two exceptions are the dogs, which usually live and hunt in packs, and lions, which form prides of males, females, and juveniles. Lions may also hunt singly or in pairs. Another "great cat," the tiger, is a lone hunter living in jungle, unlike the lion—which lives in open grassland. Most of the big cats gorge their kill in one meal and follow this with a drink and a long period of rest.

In the temperate parts of the world, members of the weasel family have occupied many niches. Some are found in

CONNECTIONS

See also
540 The classification of mammals
542 The life of mammals
586 Grasslands of Africa
628 Endangered mammals
556 How mammals behave
552 Whales, porpoises, and dolphins
608 Mountain life
578 Regions of the Earth: zoogeography
1590 Bark, hide, and horn

1

1 The black-backed jackal feeds in typical carnivore fashion, using the large, slicing carnassial teeth at the back of its mouth to cut the meat into chunks small enough to swallow. Most carnivores have toes connected with a web of skin that endows flexibility yet gives enough strength for digging. Carnivores sometimes dig for their prey; at other times they excavate or enlarge a hole for a den. The jackal lives in family groups but many canids travel in large packs. As a result the task of hunting becomes less onerous for each individual and the prey is shared by the pack.

2

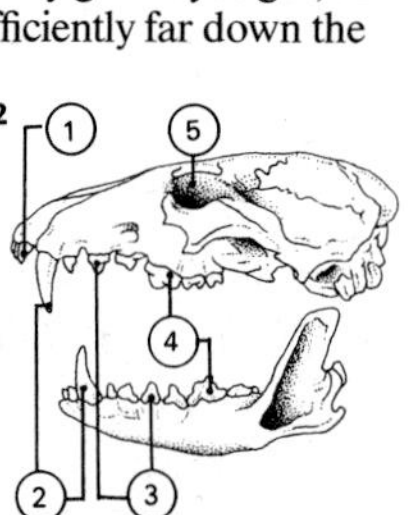

1
5
4
2
3

2 A carnivore's skull bears small, nipping incisor teeth in the front of the mouth [1], large tearing canine teeth [2], and a series of premolar and molar teeth for slicing and crushing food [3]. The fourth upper premolar tooth and the first lower molar have cutting edges that slice against each other. These are known as the carnassial teeth [4] and are characteristic of carnivores. The orbit [5], or bony cavity that contains the eyeball, is large, open, and directed forward.

3 Leopard
Panthera pardus

3 The leopard and the "black panther," a color phase of the leopard, are found in tropical rain forests of Africa and Asia and feed on any animal that they can overpower. The leopard is one member of the cat family *(Felidae)* of which the Siberian tiger is the largest and the South African black-footed cat the smallest. Most cats, including the leopard, are solitary, secretive animals that live in forests or dense scrub where they are camouflaged by beautiful spotted or striped coats. Many cats can climb and some, including jaguars and tigers, can swim well when it is necessary.

4 Banded mongoose
Mungos mungo

4 The banded mongoose is a social animal. It lives in groups of about 15 individuals that travel daily in compact formation to cover a circular territory. They eat insects, mice, and reptiles.

6

6 The brown bear *(Ursus arctos)* is found in North America, Europe, and Asia. Many forms have developed, differing widely in color and size. An island race, the Kodiak bears from coastal Alaska may weigh up to 1,600lb (725kg) and are the largest land carnivores. Bears will eat almost anything, including fish, carrion, plant food, and even honey when they can get it. They doze through the winter months but do not hibernate fully.

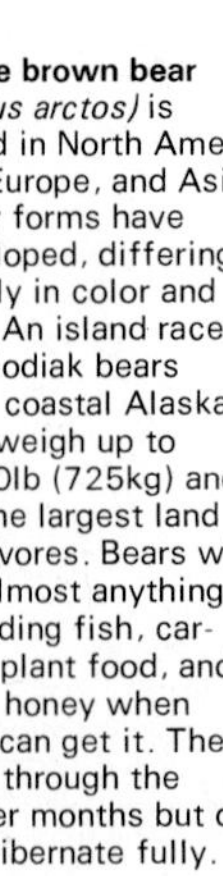

5 Hyena
Crocuta crocuta

5 The spotted hyena lives in the savannas of Africa. It feeds as a scavenger, taking the remains of a lion's kill, but it is also an efficient hunter and competes with lions. Its powerful jaws can crush bones that even a lion could not crack.

water (the otters), some in trees (martens), and others (weasels) are small enough to follow their prey into underground burrows. The badgers dig vast underground tunnel systems from which they emerge at night to forage. No carnivore, however, has become completely adapted to a subterranean way of life. In the tropical Old World, mongooses [4], genets [11], and their relatives hunt mostly small, ground-living prey, although there are some that eat insects or fruit. In the New World and parts of the Old, mongooses have their counterparts in the raccoon group [8], which embraces a wide range of animals including fruit-eaters. The marine carnivores—the seals [13], sea lions [14], and walruses [12] feed mainly on fish and mollusks.

Because of their way of life, the seals have evolved a highly streamlined form. They have, unlike the whales, retained their body fur but like them have a thick layer of insulating blubber beneath the skin. The seals are skillful swimmers; their limbs are modified into flippers, the forelimbs being used for propulsion in the eared seals and walrus and the hindlimbs in the true seals. On land, seals are clumsy creatures, although the eared seals can turn their hindlimbs forward, which enables them to walk and even run. The true seals cannot do this and drag themselves by their flippers.

Seals come ashore to breed and at this time they are highly gregarious, although the males are also intensely competitive. Breeding colonies of seals can contain up to a million animals in an area of only 19 sq mi.

Scent glands and skin

Most carnivores except the seals possess a pair of anal scent glands that produce an odoriferous fluid for defining territories, attracting a mate, or in some cases as a means of defense, the most notorious example of the latter being the skunk [7]. Most of these scents are offensive to human beings, but some have a sweet component and are used as bases for perfumes. Many flesh-eating animals, especially the cats, weasels, and seals, have pelts of great softness and beauty and have been hunted almost to extinction for their skins.

KEY

Flesh-eating mammals (carnivores) were among the earliest of placental mammals to appear. Primitive carnivores (creodonts) lived alongside the last of the dinosaurs. Early in the Tertiary era catlike and doglike forms evolved from and replaced the creodonts. All modern members of the order Carnivora are descended from these two groups. The bear and raccoon are the least specialized for flesheating.

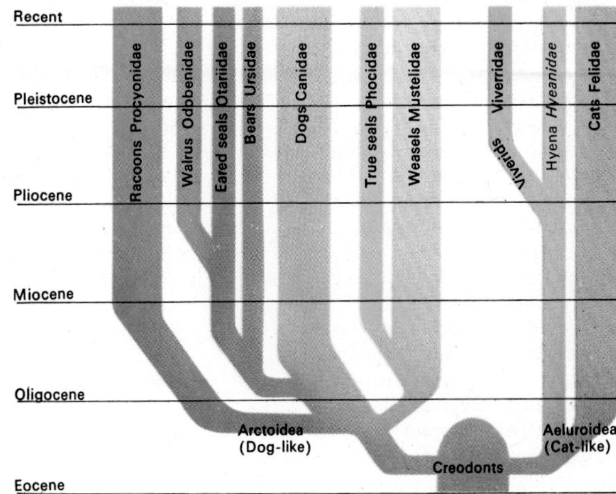

Recent
Pleistocene
Pliocene
Miocene
Oligocene
Eocene
Racoons Procyonidae
Walrus Odobenidae
Eared seals Otariidae
Bears Ursidae
Dogs Canidae
True seals Phocidae
Weasels Mustelidae
Viverrids Viverridae
Hyena Hyaenidae
Cats Felidae
Arctoidea (Dog-like)
Aeluroidea (Cat-like)
Creodonts

7 Skunk *Mephitis mephitis*

7 The skunk's fur is boldly striped in black and white and serves as an unmistakable warning to would-be predators, for it is well able to look after itself. If molested, the skunk ejects a foul-smelling liquid from its anal scent glands.

8 Raccoon *Procyon lotor*

8 A most adaptable carnivore is the raccoon, which is found in many parts of North America. It eats almost any kind of food, climbs and swims well, and often lives close to man.

9 Kinkajou *Potos flavus*

9 The kinkajou is an oddity among carnivores because it has a prehensile tail. It uses this as it climbs among the tree tops of tropical America in search of the soft fruit that is its main food.

10 Aardwolf *Proteles cristatus*

10 The aardwolf, of the savannas of southern and eastern Africa, is related to the hyenas but lacks their strong jaws and teeth and feeds almost exclusively on termites and insect larvae, varying its diet with mice and eggs of ground-nesting birds. It may gain protection by mimicking the striped coat of the hyena.

11 Genet *Genetta genetta*

11 There are six genet species. One, *Genetta genetta,* lives in Europe; the rest inhabit forest and dense brush in Africa. These nocturnal animals spend the day in rock crevices, hollow trees, or any similar shelter. They feed on the ground, eating rodents, birds, and any other animals that they can catch. The civet cat *(Civettictis civetta),* a close relative, is one of the sources of commercial musk.

12 A unique relative of the sea lion, the walrus is assigned a family of its own. It feeds on mollusks which it rakes up from the sea bottom with its tusks. A large male (a bull) may be more than 7ft (3m) long and weigh a ton. The tusks may reach 40in (1m) in length.

12 Walrus *Odobenus rosmarus*

13 Bearded seal *Erignathus barbatus*

13 The bearded seal *(Erignathus barbatus)* is a maritime carnivore that lives in small groups in Arctic waters. Like all seals it has a streamlined body that is heavily insulated with fat.

14 S. American sea lion *Otaria byronia*

14 South American sea lions breed in large, widely distributed colonies. One bull guards a harem of up to nine females and may be very aggressive.

Whales, porpoises, and dolphins

The whales comprise a group that includes, along with the large marine animals of that name, all the smaller species such as porpoises and dolphins. All are members of the mammal order Cetacea. The whales are not only the largest but also among the most intelligent animals that have ever lived. Today modern whaling methods threaten the continued existence of many species.

The origins of whales

The whales, with the carnivores, are thought to be descended from a common mammalian ancestor that lived in the Cretaceous period more than 65 million years ago. While most of the carnivores developed on land, the ancestors of the whales took to the water and became completely adapted to an aquatic way of life. As they evolved, tail flukes developed for locomotion, the hindlimbs disappeared, and the forelimbs became modified to form balancing and steering paddles.

There are two main groups of whales: the baleen whales, of which the relatively few species vary from 20 to 100ft (6–30m) in length and the largest weigh more than 100 tons, and the toothed whales, which are far more numerous and mostly much smaller [Key]. The baleen whales have no teeth but carry instead triangular plates of horny material in the roofs of their mouths. These "whalebones" [10] are used to strain krill (small shrimplike organisms) and other floating and weak-swimming forms from the seawater. Most toothed whales have large numbers of simple, cone-shaped teeth in their mouths and feed on fish and squids.

Whales are the only mammals that live the whole of their lives in water. Unlike seals they do not even return to the land to breed. Although they are aquatic creatures they must surface at regular intervals to take in oxygen and release waste carbon dioxide. The nostrils, situated at the top of the head, are tightly closed during submergence.

Whale life and development

All whales can hold their breath for a long time—some of them for up to two hours. But if water enters a whale's lung it drowns as any other air-breathing creature would. The distinctive spout that displays the presence of a whale, thrown up just before it surfaces, is a mixture of water and condensed vapor from the animal's breath.

Whales have been known to dive to depths of 4,800ft (1,500m) and they are able to do this by means of various physiological adaptations. Before diving the air in the whale's lungs is changed completely: to do this the whale breathes several times in quick succession. During the dive the heartbeat slows and blood is shunted from the muscles to the brain. The centers in the brain that control breathing, unlike those in man, are relatively insensitive to the increase in carbon dioxide in the blood and as a result the whale is not "forced" to take another breath when the carbon dioxide concentration rises.

Whales are able to grow large because their bodies are supported by water. The blue whale *(Sibbaldus musculus)* [11] is the largest animal ever to have lived; sizes of up to 113ft (34m) have been recorded for the female blue whale. Almost all traces of hair and fur have been lost, but these insulating

CONNECTIONS

See also
540 The classification of mammals
542 The life of mammals
628 Endangered mammals
550 Flesh-eating mammals
624 Life in the oceans
634 Destructive man
1802 Radar and sonar
780 Language development
486 Crabs and lobsters
298 Pollution of the sea
864 Communication through speech: 1

1 La Plata dolphin *Stenodelphis blainvillii*

1 The La Plata dolphin is representative of the freshwater dolphins and is found in the estuary of the Rio de la Plata of South America. The Ganges dolphin *(Platanista gangetica)* and Amazon dolphin *(Inia geoffrensis)* occur in the respective rivers, and yet another *(Lipotes vexillifera)* is found in Lake Tungting Hu on the Yangtze River. The long, beaked snout is characteristic and contains large numbers of teeth–up to 222 in the La Plata dolphin. Except for the Amazon dolphin, the river dolphins are virtually blind and orientation and food location are achieved by means of sound and touch.

2 Bottle-nosed whale *Hyperoodon ampullatus*

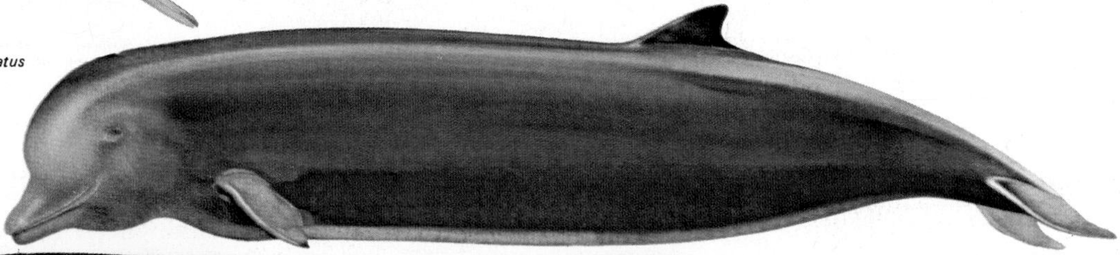

2 The bottle-nosed whales belong to the groups called beaked whales. They have only one or two pairs of teeth and feed on squid and fish. They range in length from 14 to 40 ft (4.5 to 13m).

3 Narwhale *Monodon monoceros*

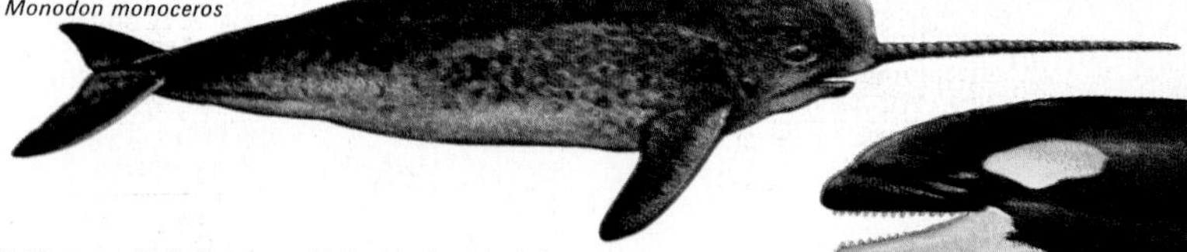

3 The narwhale is found in Arctic seas. It reaches a length of 11 to 16ft (3.6 to 5m). The distinctive tusk can grow to 9ft (2.8m) in length. It is generally found only in the male and develops from the left tooth of a pair in the upper jaw. The function of the tusk is not known. Narwhales eat fish and squid.

4 Killer whale *Orcinus orca*

4 The large triangular dorsal fin and the black and white body are the two obvious features of the killer whale *(Orcinus orca)*. It is found mostly in polar seas and is generally considered to be the most ferocious of the whales. Any creatures in the sea are considered food by the 30-ft (9-m) killers.

5 Beluga *Delphinapterus leucas*

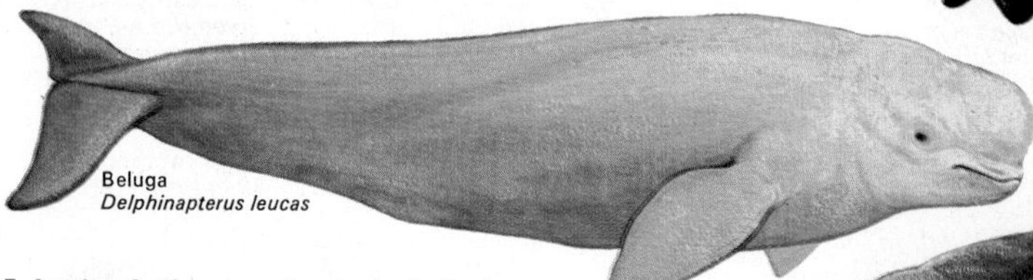

5 Another Arctic species of whale is the beluga. It usually travels in a school that may number hundreds. Its food consists of many species of fish and squid. It grows to 17ft (4.25m).

6 Bottle-nosed dolphin *Tursiops truncatus*

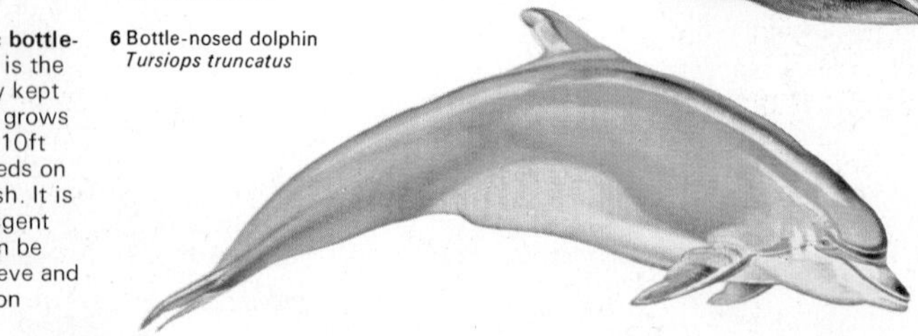

6 The Atlantic bottle-nosed dolphin is the one commonly kept in captivity. It grows to a length of 10ft (3.6m) and feeds on a variety of fish. It is a highly intelligent animal and can be taught to retrieve and carry objects on command.

7 Pilot whale *Globicephala* sp

7 The pilot whale or blackfish is often seen in schools containing several hundreds. It grows to 26ft (8.5m) in length and can weigh over 2,200lb (1,000kg). It feeds mostly on squid. If frightened near a sloping shore a whale school may become stranded and die. The three species of pilot whale are found in most oceans except the polar seas. They migrate between warm and cold waters depending on the season. Breeding takes place in warm water. They have a life span of about 50 years. The Newfoundland whaling industry was based on hunting the large schools of pilot whales.

devices are replaced by thick layers of fat or blubber beneath the skin. The efficiency of the blubber as an insulator is so great that the heat produced in the decomposition of a dead whale can cook and char the flesh.

Whales lack of a sense of smell and cannot see very well. As a result they have to rely greatly on their senses of hearing and touch. Whales also make a wide range of sounds and some of these have been shown to involve communication between individuals. This may be so elaborate that it comprises a primitive language. Sound is used for both echolocation of prey and orientation—the strandings of some species on sandy beaches may be due to an absence of echo reflection.

Whales and dolphins are found in all the oceans of the world and some dolphins live in freshwater rivers [1] and lakes. Many whales, especially those from the colder seas, migrate to warmer waters to breed. One of the best known is the California grey whale *(Eschrichtius glaucus)* [8], which makes its annual migrations to the lagoons and estuaries of Baja (Lower) California.

Young whales can be up to a third of the size of the female. They are born tail first to ensure that they do not drown during birth. The female pushes the young to the surface to take its first breath and suckles it from teats lying in slits on either side of the genital opening. To allow the young whale to suckle and breathe simultaneously the female floats on her side and ejects the milk forcibly.

The endangered species

The species of whales most threatened by man are those of the open oceans whose carcases are used to produce oil. These include, in particular, the sperm whale *(Physeter catodon),* the blue whale *(Sibbaldus musculus)* [11], the humpback *(Megaptera novaeangliae),* and the finback whale *(Balaenoptera physalus).* Properly managed, however, the world's whale stocks could still provide man with a large, steady source of food as well as allowing him to study these fascinating and unique creatures. Instead, he seems determined to exterminate them.

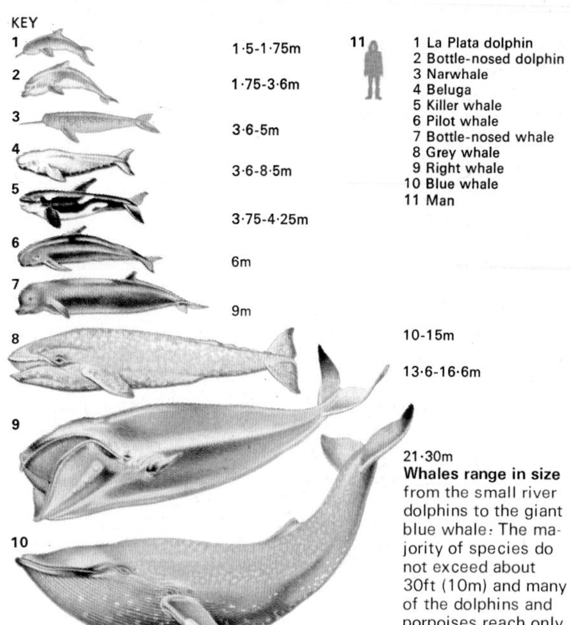
KEY
1 1·5-1·75m
2 1·75-3·6m
3 3·6-5m
4 3·6-8·5m
5 3·75-4·25m
6 6m
7 9m
8 10-15m
9 13·6-16·6m
10 21·30m
11
1 La Plata dolphin
2 Bottle-nosed dolphin
3 Narwhale
4 Beluga
5 Killer whale
6 Pilot whale
7 Bottle-nosed whale
8 Grey whale
9 Right whale
10 Blue whale
11 Man

Whales range in size from the small river dolphins to the giant blue whale. The majority of species do not exceed about 30ft (10m) and many of the dolphins and porpoises reach only 9ft (3m).

8 California grey whale *Eschrichtius glaucus*

8 The grey whales are confined to the North Pacific. There are two populations, one living on the eastern side and one on the western side. From the northern seas they migrate south in winter to breed in the shallow, warmer seas of Baja California and South Korea. They feed on plankton strained from water by means of baleen plates in their mouths. Baleen was the whalebone of commerce.

9 Right whale *Eubalaena* sp

9 The right whales are found in all the world's oceans including subtropical waters. There are three genera—the Greenland right whale *(Balaena)*, the black right whale *(Eubalaena)*, and the pygmy right whale *(Caperea)*. They are all rare because of overhunting. Their name derives from the fact that they were the "right" whales to hunt. They grow to 55ft (18m) in length.

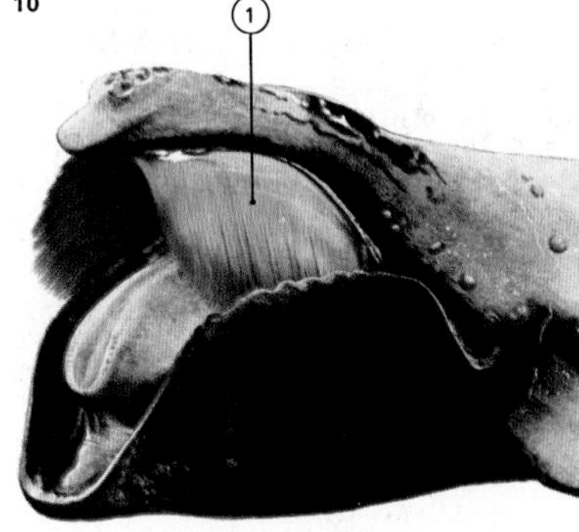
10
1

10 The head of a baleen whale is enormous and is about a third or a quarter of the animal's total length. Fringing each side of the mouth is a series of baleen plates [1] that act as food strainers. When feeding, the whale swims through swarms of small crustaceans and other plankton animals and when enough have been trapped it dives, closes its mouth, and swallows.

11 Blue whale
Sibbaldus musculus

11 The largest animal in the history of the earth is the blue whale. It grows to a length of 90ft (30m) and can weigh 125 tons. It usually travels at speeds of 10 to 12 knots. Its other name of sulphurbottom whale is derived from the film of yellowish microscopic algae that sometimes forms on its undersurface. It inhabits polar seas and only rarely enters tropical oceans, but it does move to warmer waters to breed. It, like the right and grey whales, feeds on krill, which it strains from the water with plates of baleen. Its stomach can hold about two tons of food. It is rarely encountered in schools and seems to be a rather solitary animal. It is now protected, though possibly too late to save it from extinction, following overhunting by whalers. Two related and endangered species are the finback whales *(Balaenoptera)* and the hump back whales *(Megaptera novaeangliae)*, both also protected.

Primates: relatives of man

Man, as a mammal, is a member of a group of mainly tropical creatures called primates. Like other mammals the earliest primates [Key] were contemporaries of the last of the dinosaurs. Today, the nonhuman primates, which include the monkeys and apes, abound in warmer parts of the world. They are in many respects a conservative group and retain (as does man) a number of primitive skeletal features, such as the collarbone long since discarded by many other mammals. They have also kept, as few others have, the primitive number of five toes on each foot.

In evolutionary terms, primates have undergone few physical changes. Such specializations as they do show are almost all toward perfecting them to a tree-dwelling life and even man still retains many of these features. The earliest primates to take refuge in trees differed little from their insect-eating ancestors on the ground.

Variety of lower primates

The tree shrews (Tupaiidae) of Southeast Asia [1] are thought to represent an early stage of primate development. They can be regarded as "living fossils." Indeed, some authorities exclude them from the primates proper and group them with the insectivores or place them in their own separate order. They are active, squirrellike animals with long tails, pointed faces, large eyes and small ears. As they climb in search of food—mainly insects—they grasp the branches with their clawed fingers and toes. This grasping ability [8] is amplified in all other primates. It enables them to make more use of small branches than nongrasping clawed species can and, when at rest, to handle food and other objects.

The prosimians of Africa and Asia are an array of species including the lemurs (Lemuridae) from Madagascar [7]. Many have hands and feet with opposable thumbs and great toes; that is, the first digit can be rotated and crossed over the palm of the hand or ball of the foot [8]. These creatures can hold firmly whatever they grasp and their handling power is enhanced by the development, on most toes, of flat nails rather than claws. The bush babies, pottos, lorises (Lorisidae), although retaining the doglike naked nose of the lower primates, have large eyes and a short snout which makes them look more human than their Lemur relatives, at least facially.

The tarsier (Tarsiidae) [2], similar in many respects to the other prosimians, has an even more human-looking face. Its huge eyes look directly forward and the face has shrunk beneath them, enabling the animal to achieve a high degree of stereoscopic vision. This is a necessity (as is its foot structure) if the tarsier is to leap about in its forest home. It must judge distances, like other primates, with accuracy. This is possible with eyes that look forward rather than to the side. With the shortening of the face there is a tendency for the sense of smell to become less acute. The face is similar to that of the higher primates. The tarsier's brain is larger and more complex than that of its near relatives.

Man's closest relatives

Animals belonging to the highest group of primates are called anthropoids (An-

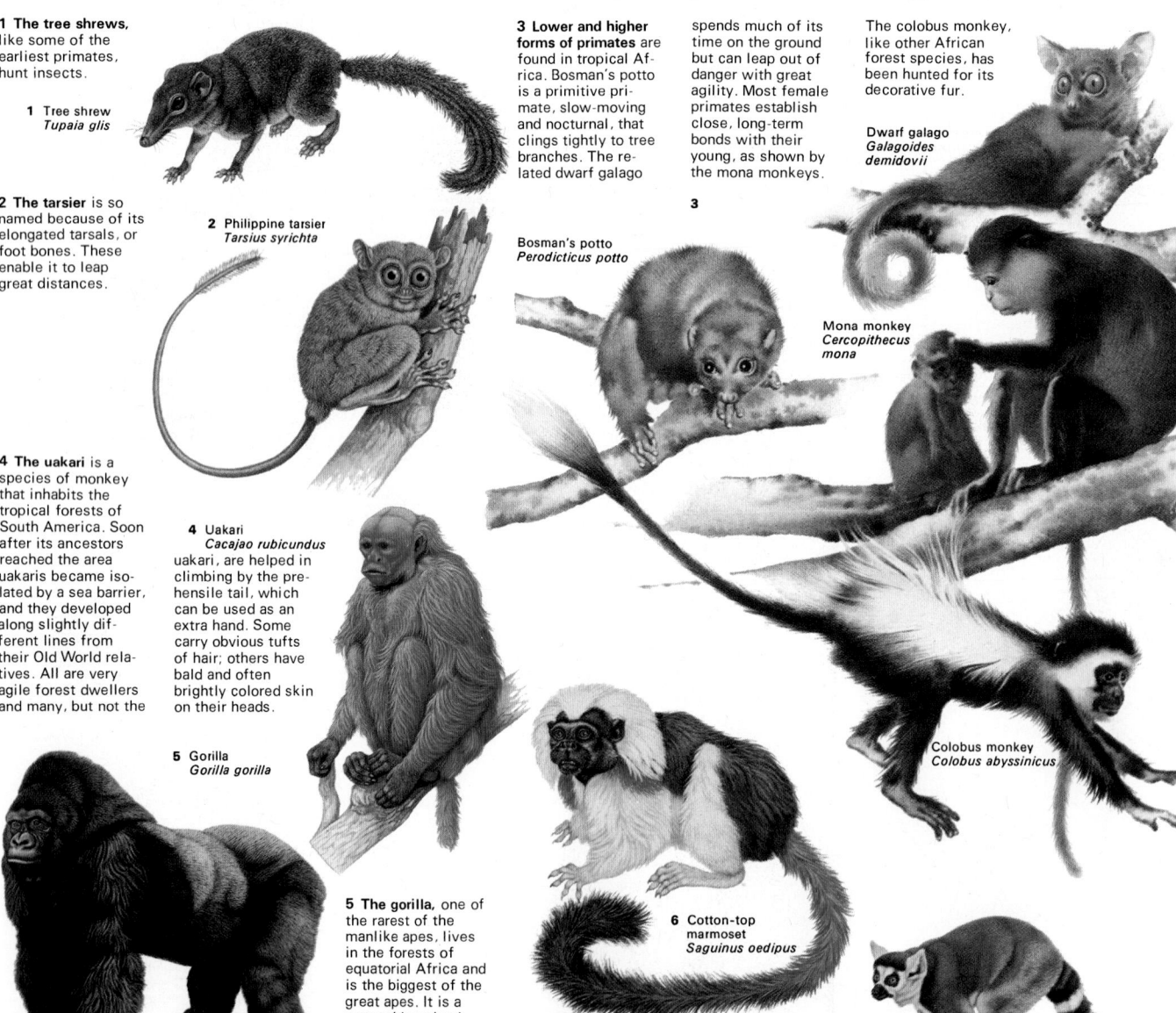

CONNECTIONS

See also
542 The life of mammals
646 Primate to hominid
558 How primates behave
658 Family of man: today's peoples
660 Family of man: how peoples differ
540 The classification of mammals
628 Endangered mammals
598 African rain forest
602 New World tropics
600 Forests of Southeast Asia
662 An introduction to body and mind
674 Sight and perception
574 Mammals of the past

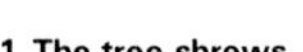

1 The tree shrews, like some of the earliest primates, hunt insects.

1 Tree shrew *Tupaia glis*

2 The tarsier is so named because of its elongated tarsals, or foot bones. These enable it to leap great distances.

2 Philippine tarsier *Tarsius syrichta*

3 Lower and higher forms of primates are found in tropical Africa. Bosman's potto is a primitive primate, slow-moving and nocturnal, that clings tightly to tree branches. The related dwarf galago spends much of its time on the ground but can leap out of danger with great agility. Most female primates establish close, long-term bonds with their young, as shown by the mona monkeys. The colobus monkey, like other African forest species, has been hunted for its decorative fur.

3

Dwarf galago *Galagoides demidovii*

Bosman's potto *Perodicticus potto*

Mona monkey *Cercopithecus mona*

Colobus monkey *Colobus abyssinicus*

4 The uakari is a species of monkey that inhabits the tropical forests of South America. Soon after its ancestors reached the area uakaris became isolated by a sea barrier, and they developed along slightly different lines from their Old World relatives. All are very agile forest dwellers and many, but not the uakari, are helped in climbing by the prehensile tail, which can be used as an extra hand. Some carry obvious tufts of hair; others have bald and often brightly colored skin on their heads.

4 Uakari *Cacajao rubicundus*

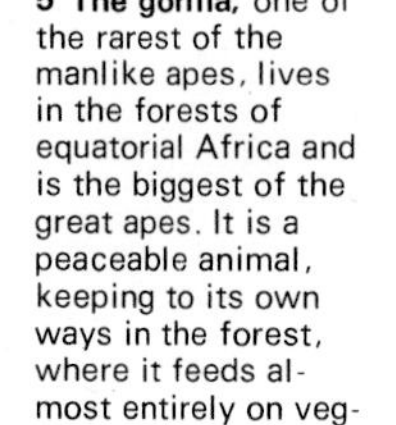

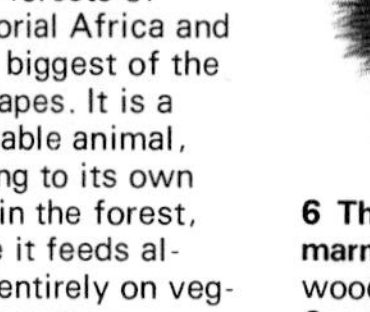

5 Gorilla *Gorilla gorilla*

5 The gorilla, one of the rarest of the manlike apes, lives in the forests of equatorial Africa and is the biggest of the great apes. It is a peaceable animal, keeping to its own ways in the forest, where it feeds almost entirely on vegetable matter.

6 Cotton-top marmoset *Saguinus oedipus*

6 The cotton-top marmoset is found in wooded areas of South America.

7 Ring-tailed lemur *Lemur catta*

7 The ring-tailed lemur is a prosimian found only on Madagascar.

thropoidea). They include monkeys and apes, as well as man, and many lead complex social lives in which individuals live as families and the young are cared for over a long period. Communication among these primates is also highly developed.

Two groups of monkeys are known. One is found in the tropical New World (South and Central America) [4], while the other inhabits the Old World tropics (Asia and Africa). Some species are found in cooler areas, such as the foothills of the Himalayas or in Japan. The main difference between the two is their nose shape. Old World monkeys have their nostrils closer set, which gives them a pronounced nose. The nostrils of New World monkeys are set wide apart giving them a flattish nose.

Grasping, or prehensile, tails are found only in species of New World monkeys, but all monkeys, with the exception of the New World night monkeys, or douroucoulis, are diurnal; they sleep at night and are awake during the day. Both types of monkeys are social animals, living in groups with a well-developed hierarchy. Some Old World forms, such as the baboons, have largely deserted the trees to take up life on the ground. But they are still good climbers and when threatened can scamper to safety among branches or rocks.

The lesser and great apes

The apes are distinguished from monkeys by their greater size, their bigger and more complex brains, and their complete lack of a visible tail. The siamangs and the gibbons of Southeast Asia, referred to as the lesser apes, are spindly-limbed forest acrobats [9] that can travel at high speed through the tree tops, leaping and swinging by their arms. The great apes, which include the orang-utans, gorillas [5], and chimpanzees, are all larger and heavier creatures. They spend much of their time on the ground, although they retreat to the branches to sleep.

Man's evolutionary relationship with the great apes is particularly close. Apart from man's much larger brain, the main bodily differences are associated with the ape's specialization to a forest life and man's to open-country living.

KEY: Pleistocene, Pliocene, Miocene, Oligocene, Eocene, Paleocene, Cretaceous — Human stem, Ape stem, Old World monkey stem, New World monkey stem, Tarsiers, Lemurs, Lorises, Insectivore stem; Earliest apes; Anthropoids; Prosimians

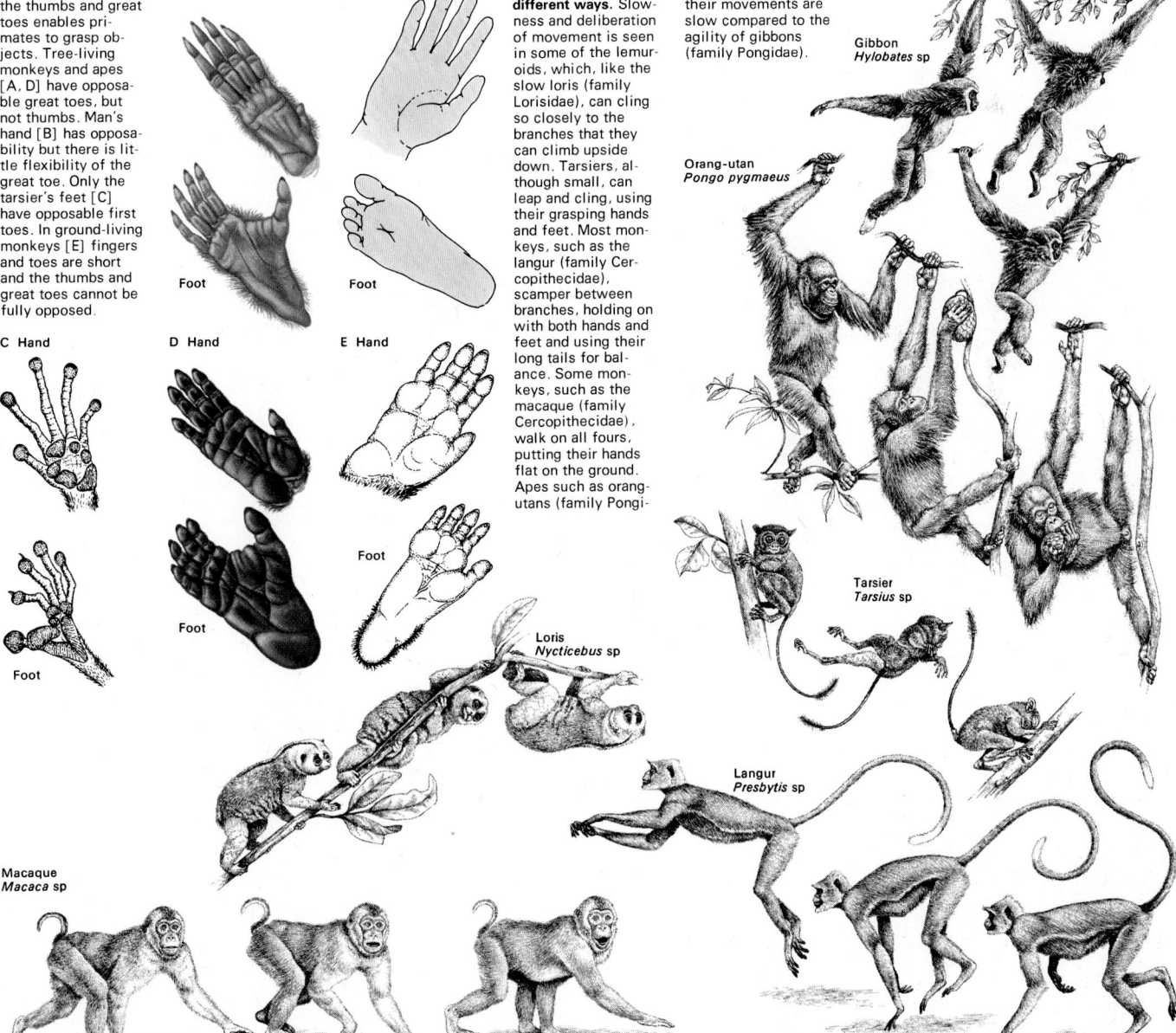

A family tree of primates shows that the earliest members of the group were closely related to the insectivores, as are today's tree shrews (illustration 1). In the Paleocene and Eocene epochs, lemurs flourished in many parts of the world. Today they are found only in Madagascar and the Comoro Islands. Both the New World and the Old World monkeys probably evolved from tarsierlike ancestors during the Oligocene epoch. The first true apes appear later in the Miocene and they gave rise to man's immediate ancestors.

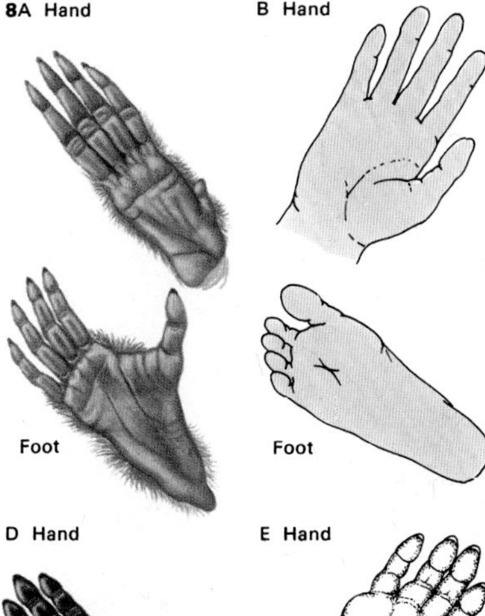

8A Hand
Foot
B Hand
Foot
C Hand
Foot
D Hand
Foot
E Hand
Foot

8 The opposability of the thumbs and great toes enables primates to grasp objects. Tree-living monkeys and apes [A, D] have opposable great toes, but not thumbs. Man's hand [B] has opposability but there is little flexibility of the great toe. Only the tarsier's feet [C] have opposable first toes. In ground-living monkeys [E] fingers and toes are short and the thumbs and great toes cannot be fully opposed.

9
Gibbon
Hylobates sp
Orang-utan
Pongo pygmaeus
Tarsier
Tarsius sp
Loris
Nycticebus sp
Langur
Presbytis sp
Macaque
Macaca sp

9 Primates move in different ways. Slowness and deliberation of movement is seen in some of the lemuroids, which, like the slow loris (family Lorisidae), can cling so closely to the branches that they can climb upside down. Tarsiers, although small, can leap and cling, using their grasping hands and feet. Most monkeys, such as the langur (family Cercopithecidae), scamper between branches, holding on with both hands and feet and using their long tails for balance. Some monkeys, such as the macaque (family Cercopithecidae), walk on all fours, putting their hands flat on the ground. Apes such as orang-utans (family Pongidae) do climb, but their movements are slow compared to the agility of gibbons (family Pongidae).

How mammals behave

Mating and feeding, the primary needs for survival, provide the drives for much animal behavior. Whatever the drives that stimulate the animal, its encounters—whether sexual or aggressive—always tend to be surrounded by rituals. These rituals are probably most varied among the mammals.

Rituals associated with copulation and those associated with aggression may be hard to distinguish within one species although both commonly involve genital sniffing. In some rodents the female is larger and fiercer than the male and sex play may take the form of a battle from which the male may not escape without injury.

Group survival patterns

Much of the social behavior of mammals is directed toward the survival of the species as a whole. Wolves hunt in packs to enhance their chances of cornering prey and the prey in their turn have developed ways of thwarting bands of predators. In the musk ox [1] this involves the formation of "phalanxes," an effective tactic.

Cooperation of this sort involves communication between the members of the species, and in mammals this is both widespread and diverse, reaching its most sophisticated level in whales and dolphins and in man and other primates. One of the most familiar nonverbal phenomena is the warning system of rabbits, which thump with their hind feet and flash their white tails as they retreat from danger [3]. Mammalian signals are not just visible or audible; touch and smell [4] are also important.

The importance of smell

The importance of smell as a stimulus is easy to underestimate from the human point of view, but is crucial to the behavior of many mammals. Many male mammals are equipped with scent glands that attract females and from the female's smell the male can tell if she is in heat—that is, in the fertile phase of her sexual cycle. Responses to the scents produced, which are known as pheromones, can be quite subtle and unexpected. Pregnant female mice, for example, will abort their young if they are put in a cage with a male of another strain. This does not occur if they are put into an empty cage, so the phenomenon has been attributed to a pheromone. Effects of a similar kind may underlie the natural regulation of population density that has been noticed in many colonial species of mammals.

The sense of smell may be vital in establishing the bond between a mother and her young [2]. A kind of olfactory "imprinting" seems to occur among some ungulates, hoofed mammals, that give birth to one or two young and then have to keep track of their offspring in a moving flock or herd. The imprinting takes place immediately at birth and enables the mother to recognize her own offspring.

Exclusive bonds between a mother animal and her own young are not always the rule among mammals. Prairie dogs, which are actually large rodents, live in populous colonies that for part of the year are divided into smaller territories containing groups of one or two adult males with females and young. The young are suckled indiscriminately by any female and

CONNECTIONS

See also
464 Principles of animal behavior
558 How primates behave
700 Reproduction
876 Origins of human society
830 Types of ritual
536 How birds behave

1

1 A herd of musk oxen forms a powerful phalanx in a bare landscape to make a defensive ring of bulls around the more vulnerable cows and calves, which are protected in the safety of the center. Living in the harsh Arctic tundra of northern Greenland and Canada the musk ox *(Ovibos moschatus)* has natural, predatory enemies in the wolf packs of that inhospitable region. Instead of scattering as the pack attacks, the oxen muster together with their great horns pointing outward. This tactic shows how the basic drive to flee from danger by running away has been superseded by the development of a social instinct requiring communication, coordination, discipline, and courage. In their defensive formation the oxen can defy the wolf pack, but if discipline broke down the pack would quickly attack and pull them down.

2

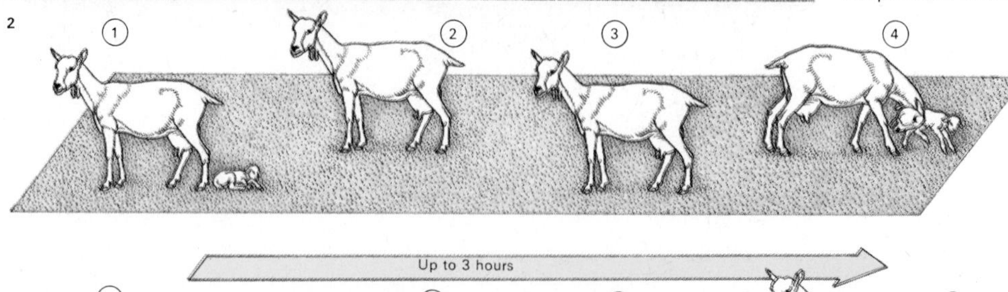
1
2
3
4
Up to 3 hours

5
6
7
8
5 minutes

2 Imprinting is responsible for the bond that is formed between a female animal and her offspring within hours, possibly even minutes, after the birth. The female goat soon learns to distinguish her own young from others in the herd. The immediate postnatal nuzzling and licking is probably necessary to imprinting. If immediately after the birth [1] the kid is removed [2, 3] for 3 hours, the mother will reject it, butting or even biting it [4] to drive it off. If immediately after the birth [5] the mother is allowed a mere 5 minutes of licking and nuzzling her offspring [6] before a similar 3-hour separation [7], she will usually accept and suckle the kid when it is returned to her [8]. The rapidly formed bonding between the female and her offspring is probably essential to the survival of those animals living in herds that are constantly on the move, like the reindeer *(Rangifer tarandus)*.

groomed in a friendly way by any male. The same kind of system is found in small communes of African hunting dogs. Here, however, conflict can arise between the females who compete to suckle the young.

The most common source of conflict between mammals is competition for females during the breeding season. This is the underlying reason for the ritual clash of antlers among deer and is one of the defining features of dominance hierarchies in animal groups: the more dominant males have access to larger numbers of females.

The weak and the strong

Much ritualized animal behavior is concerned with preventing competition from ending in harm to either competitor within a species. Dogs and wolves, for example, have recognized signals of threat and submission. A dominant wolf stands stiffly, hair raised, growling through bared teeth. The subordinate animal deters attack by crouching with ears flattened in submission.

Dominance and subordination signals also occur in rats, both between members of one colony and between the members of a colony and intruders. It is believed that members of the same colony recognize one another by smell and that intruders are immediately liable to attack. The attacker adopts an arch-backed posture and moves around the intruder, flank-on, chattering his teeth. The intruder may adopt a submissive posture—by lying down—and thus prevent actual attack. If he fails, the next move will be leaping and biting.

A curious social phenomenon observed in rat colonies is that of the fatal effect of social stress [5]. An intruder, or a rat low in the dominance hierarchy of a colony, may be subjected to so much threat that he literally gives up and dies.

Mammalian behavior is not always directly controlled by the primary drives of mating and feeding but has come to reflect the complex demands of social life. Limited freedom from the immediate demands of hunger and sex can be seen in an everyday context in the willingness of dogs to run errands. Social play is also common among many wild animals.

KEY

Two male rats in competition for a female threaten [1], attack [2], and bite [3]. A female not in heat [4] rejects a male but submits [5] when in heat.

1
2
3
4
5

3 A

1

2

3

B

5
4
6
7
8
21 March—11 April
24 May—13 June
C
Blue—Adult
Green—Young

3 A colony of wild rabbits [A] occupies a warren made up of a system of burrows that perform various functions. In spring [1] rabbits graze the pasture around their warren, stripping it of grass and leaving nettles, ragwort, and ground ivy to flourish. The rabbit population is swollen by young twice a year [C] for each female. In the summer and the autumn [2] rabbits destroy pastures and crops. In winter [3] they may eat such crops as winter wheat. The cross-section cut through a typical rabbit warren [B] shows a bolt-hole [4] offering a quick refuge, [5] a breeding burrow lined with leaves and grass and [6] young venturing above ground where they encounter predators such as the fox and hawk [7, 8] that deplete the rabbit population.

4 Black-tailed deer [A] have scent glands on their ankles. They use the glands, called tarsal organs [1], for recognition. Members of a herd [B] sniff one another's tarsal organs [2]. Fawns recognize their mothers by similar ankle sniffing [3]. When a stranger [4] enters the herd's territory its smell betrays it at once.

5 A strange rat [A] entering a colony may be subjected to social stress [B] severe enough to prove fatal. It may not have suffered any physical injury.

4 A

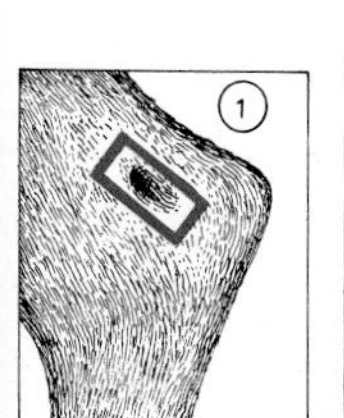
1

B

2
3
4

5 A

B

How primates behave

Primate behavior is a source of fascination for humans as the evolutionary predecessor of their own. But the behavior of many primates is radically different from that of man. Most species are social, but a few, particularly the nocturnal prosimians, are solitary [1]. In addition to the endlessly fascinating question of the mental abilities of subhuman primates [Key] the social organization of these mammals is also significant.

Interpreting social signals

Most of the more advanced primate species live in troops with a clearly defined role structure, the dominant males (usually the older and larger) being allowed first choice of both food and females. By comparison with other groups, primates make elaborate use of facial expression, in addition to posture, in order to signal dominance or submission [3]. Aggressive facial expressions often involve bared teeth and other signs that would be recognized as threatening by a human. But the interpretation of specific signals is not always obvious in human terms; for instance, curling of the lip is believed to signal pleasure in gorillas whereas in humans it portrays anger. Roaring and breast-beating, however, are more easily deciphered as hostile although they may also express exuberance and fear. The correct submissive response is to shake the head slowly from side to side, avoiding the gorilla's eyes.

Within a troop, and subject to the constraints of the dominance hierarchy, primates are in general sexually promiscuous. A female chimpanzee has been seen to accept as many as seven males in succession. Sexual activity is not limited to the estrous period (fertile period) of the female. In rhesus monkeys, copulation seems to be stimulated by a pheromone (a chemical that is smelled) produced by the female only during estrous; but chimpanzees seem to copulate at more or less any stage of the estrous cycle. This dissociation of sexual behavior from its immediate reproductive function is generally seen as a reflection of the advanced thinking abilities and need for social cohesion of primates. Their play, through which they gain much experience, is more elaborate than that of other advanced mammals. The reasoning capacity of the more intelligent primates is certainly well developed but it is only recently that detailed observations of animals living in the wild have supplemented those in the laboratory in confirming this.

Weaponry and skills

Tests conducted in the wild have proved decisively that chimpanzees habitually use sticks and stones as tools [5] or weapons. The immediate reaction of a troop of savanna chimpanzees confronted with a stuffed leopard was to retreat in fear to a nearby group of trees. The adults made much noise and then cautiously advanced and began throwing sticks in the direction of the leopard. When it did not move the boldest chimpanzees came closer and began striking it with sticks. After the stuffed head became detached from the body the chimpanzees realized that the leopard was harmless and went over warily to sniff it. Finally they ignored it altogether and wandered off. Baboons [4] show similar behavior in the

CONNECTIONS

1 Lemurs, primitive primates from Madagascar, are mostly solitary animals. The weasel lemur *(Lepilemur mustelinus)* never forms groups larger than a mother-child pair. By day [A] this lemur sleeps in a hole in a tree or in a nest of leaves and twigs. At dusk it wakes to feed on bark and leaves [B]. It is active at night within its home range [C] – a radius of some 160ft (50m) from its nestsite. It returns at dawn [D].

1
A
B
C
D

2 The orang-utan *(Pongo pygmaeus)*, one of the intelligent great apes, lives in the tropical rain forests of Sumatra and Borneo. Orang-utans live in small groups of up to six individuals. Mother and infant [A] comprise the basic family unit and all feed mainly on fruit [B]. Adult males [C] are larger and heavier, usually live apart, and have pronounced cheek pads that have evolved for display purposes.

3
A

B

3 Facial expressions are important in the social interactions of rhesus monkeys. The

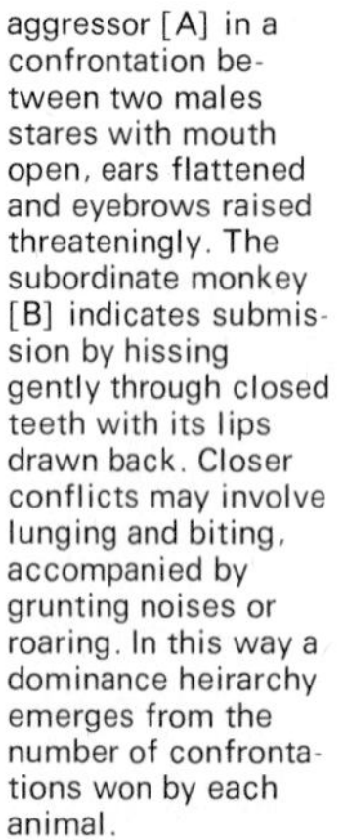

aggressor [A] in a confrontation between two males stares with mouth open, ears flattened and eyebrows raised threateningly. The subordinate monkey [B] indicates submission by hissing gently through closed teeth with its lips drawn back. Closer conflicts may involve lunging and biting, accompanied by grunting noises or roaring. In this way a dominance heirarchy emerges from the number of confrontations won by each animal.

4 Baboons live in troops with well defined dominance hierarchies and engage in cooperative hunting. The troops may be relatively small and, to avoid inbreeding, there seems to be a system whereby young males periodically transfer from one troop to another when they have reached their full adult size at about six to eight years of age. The females do not transfer and their troops have traditional home ranges into which others rarely intrude.

wild and have been seen trying to frighten a team of researchers by dropping stones on them from a safe distance.

Despite the artificiality of the conditions, some of the most revealing observations and rigorous tests on primates have been made in the laboratory. Studies made of mother chimpanzees, for example, have demonstrated how they encourage the independent climbing skills and movements of their infants. And a famous series of experiments has shown that the social development of rhesus monkeys depends heavily on the mother-infant bond initially and later on interactions with other infant monkeys.

Laboratory tests of rhesus monkeys have shown they can grasp abstract concepts such as "oddness." If given training in a special test apparatus the monkey can learn to select an object because it has a different shape or color from others [6].

Language experiments

A rich source of controversy concerning primate behavior is whether apes are capable of language, the crucial human achievement. US researchers have bypassed the problem of apes' inability to produce human sounds by teaching them sign language as used by the deaf and dumb. Apes taught this language by people fluent in it who were responsible for their day-to-day care as infants learned words fast and could use them in an appropriate context. What they have not yet been able to do, however, is string them into sentences with a clear syntax. However, some experiments in which apes were taught to use shapes that stood for words showed that these animals could construct sentences on their own.

Ethologists point out that this kind of experiment is only meaningful in the context of the apes' ecology and natural communication system. Researchers have counted as many as 36 distinguishable sounds made by certain monkey species and found that different sounds are used in complex combinations. Enough is now known to make it clear that the sound signals of these animals are used exclusively for conveying social information.

KEY

The problem-solving abilities of chimpanzees enable them to work out novel solutions to practical dilemmas by the use of tools. Confronted with a bunch of bananas hanging too high for it to reach, a chimpanzee is capable of reasoning that, by putting a box beneath the bananas and using this as a step, it will raise itself to a level at which the fruit can be reached. While many animals make use of various materials for building purposes, the cognitive process involved in solving complex problems by the regular use of tools has evolved in only man and the higher primates.

5

5 The high intelligence of chimpanzees is demonstrated in their practice of "fishing" for termites. This involves a sequence of behavior that is quite complex in logical thought. The first step is for the chimpanzee to find a suitable twig. This is thrust into a hole in a termite mound where the termites will attack the intruding object. The chimpanzee then withdraws the twig, to which a number of termites remain clinging, picks off the insects with its mobile lips, and eats them. This sequence of behavior, with its regular use of an accessory tool (the twig), has been observed in wild chimpanzees in many parts of Africa. It is a remarkable example of the way in which the curiosity and puzzle-solving ability that have been seen in laboratory tests on chimpanzees is actually applied to life in the wild.

6A

B

6 A monkey's intelligence enables it to grasp the concept of "oddness" in a laboratory test using covered food wells, one of which contains a reward. In [A] the objects covering the wells are the same color but two are cubes and one is a pyramid. The monkey quickly learns to choose the pyramid. In [B], given two blue objects and a red one all of different shapes, it then selects the pyramid proving that it has learned to recognize shape.

Fossils: the life of the past

Fossils, traces of dead organisms found in the rocks of the earth's crust, reveal what life was like at the time the rocks were formed [1]. It is through the study of fossils (the name comes from the Latin meaning "something dug up") that the evolution of life on Earth has been traced and affinities revealed between groups of animals and plants, both living and extinct.

Fossilized organisms may be found in many different states of preservation, but only rarely totally intact. Usually only the hard parts are preserved or only the shape impressed on some other material. In trace fossils [2] only the footprints or some other signs of an animal's passing are left.

Other more unusual types of fossils include gastroliths and coprolites. Gastroliths are smooth, rounded pebbles often found within the rib-cages of dinosaurs and swimming reptiles. These were swallowed by the animal possibly for the same reason that a modern fowl swallows gravel, to help grind up food in the stomach. Coprolites are fossilized dung and are most commonly associated with Tertiary mammals or Carboniferous fish. Such fossils as these give valuable clues to the diets and life habits of extinct animals.

Myths and mystery

Fossils have not always been recognized for what they are. Although ancient Greeks such as Herodotus (*c.* 485–425BC) noted their similarity to living animals and plants, later civilizations did not have the philosophies to account for them. Whole mythologies were built around fossils; mammoth skulls found on the Greek islands may have given rise to the Cyclops legends because the fused nostril cavity suggests a single eye socket. The American Indians regarded dinosaur skeletons as the remains of great serpents that lived beneath the surface of the earth and died when they came too close to the light. Christian chronology, based as it was on biblical events and dating the Creation at about 4000 BC, made no attempt to account for the time involved in turning sediments into rock and raising mountains, so the true nature of fossils was obscured for many hundreds of years. For centuries they were regarded as sports of nature or as tricks of the devil conjured up to test the faith of the people. Those who were convinced that they represented the remains of once living organisms could account for them as the remains of creatures destroyed in the Great Flood. Not until the beginning of the nineteenth century did paleontology (the scientific study of fossils) become a recognized science.

Fossil investigation

The detailed study of fossils, rather like a crime investigation, involves the piecing together of many diverse fragments of evidence; a vast number of techniques are used [6]. The fossil may be a huge dinosaur skeleton, which must be attended to by a large number of people on the spot where it is found, or it may be a microscopic structure found in the depths of a piece of rock and revealed in laboratory studies.

Initially, in the case of the dinosaur, the bones have to be removed from the matrix [6], encased in some protective substance, and transported to a museum or laboratory,

CONNECTIONS

See also
406 Life and its origins
562 Plants of the past
408 Evolution of life
410 The world before man
564 Fossils without backbones
270 The record in the rocks
566 Fish and amphibians of the past
568 Toward life on land
570 Reptiles of the past
572 The age of reptiles
574 Mammals of the past
576 The age of mammals

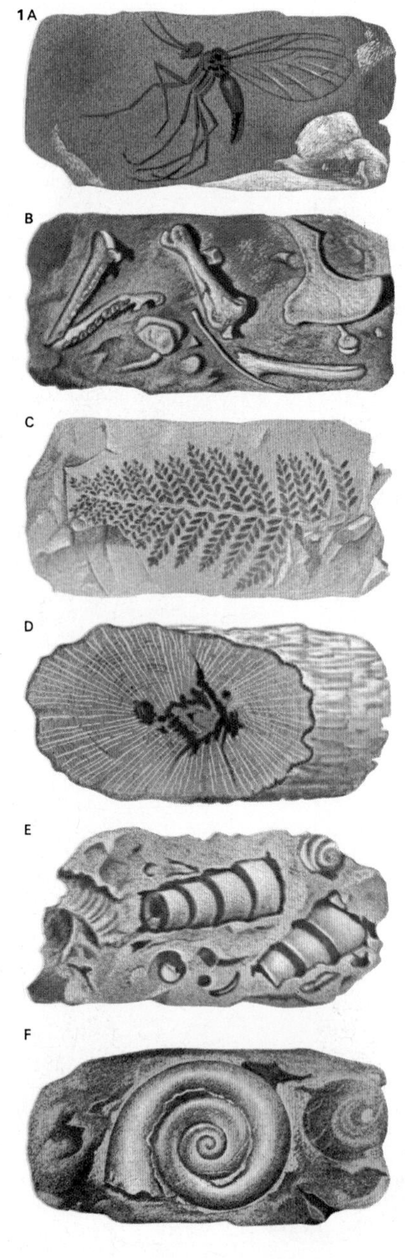

1A
B
C
D
E
F

1 Fossils are the remains or traces of animals and plants of past times, found preserved in rock. The preservation can take place in a number of different ways. In some cases the organism is preserved in its entirety [A] when it becomes embedded in an antiseptic medium. Examples of these are insects entombed in amber and mammoths buried whole in frozen mud. The hard parts may be preserved unchanged [B] when an antiseptic medium encases them after the soft anatomy has decomposed. Mammal bones are preserved in tar pits like this. More often only very little of the original material is left [C], as in the fossils of fern leaves preserved in Carboniferous shale as a thin film of the carbon constituents. Sometimes the original tissues are replaced, molecule by molecule, by another substance to give an exact replica of the original. Fossil wood replaced by silica is an example of this [D]. The organism may rot away completely after its burial [E] leaving a hole called a mold in the shape of the original. Molds of Tertiary water snails are often found. After a mold has formed it may fill with minerals deposited by percolating ground water, giving a solid with the external shape of the original, called a cast. Calcite casts of ammonites are common [F].

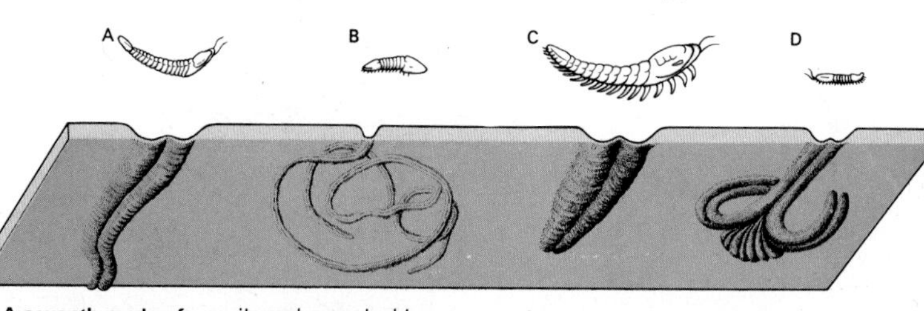

2
A
B
C
D

2 A seventh mode of fossilization is one in which no part or shape of an organism is preserved—only the footprints, burrows, and feeding trails. These are known as trace fossils and are valuable as indicators of the life styles of extinct creatures. Sometimes an animal is known only from its fossil traces. For some animals these consist of tunnels or tunnel systems which are given group names according to their shapes and complexity. Trilobite traces called *Repichnia* [A] are long and fairly straight; the *Pascichnia* types [B] are meandering and cover a wide area. The *Cubichnia* burrow types [C] are usually short and straight and those of *Fodinichinia* [D] radiate from one spot.

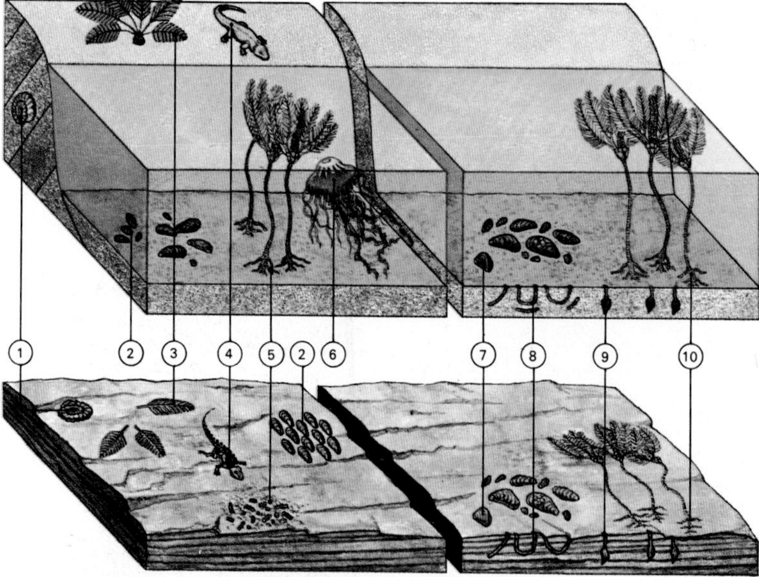

3A
B
1
2
3
4
5
2
6
7
8
9
10

3 Fossils lie in two kinds of assemblies: one that does not reflect the life style of the organisms (called a death assemblage, or thanatocoenosis), or one that does (a life assemblage, or biocoenosis). Features of a thanatocoenosis [A] include derived fossils [1], fossils of an earlier age removed from a rock eroded at the time of deposition of the assemblage, shells disarticulated and aligned with the current [2], plant and animal remains from another environment brought in after death [3, 4], and fragile creatures, such as crinoids, broken and scattered [5]. Some soft-bodied creatures, such as jellyfish [6], are never fossilized. A biocoenosis [B] has shellfish in their living positions [7], burrows and burrowing organisms undisturbed [8, 9], and crinoids still in one piece [10]. A thanatocoenosis is the result of currents and erosion disturbing the remains while in a biocoenosis there has been little or no disturbance of the fossil remains.

careful note and measurements first having been taken of the position in which the bones are found. The nature of the surrounding rock is also noted because this gives valuable information about the environment in which the creature lived. In the laboratory the bones are cleaned and treated to make them less fragile. Usually the individual bones are cast in plaster or a plastic material so that a facsimile of the skeleton can be assembled and put on display while the actual specimens are preserved for research purposes.

The dinosaur remains are then compared to the hard parts of modern animals and reconstruction is made, usually by means of a painting or a model, showing the appearance of the animal when alive. The color of extinct animals is never preserved and is a matter of informed guesswork. When microfossils are studied, a promising looking rock is taken into the laboratory, sliced up, and treated with solvents. These either corrode rock and fossil at different rates, causing the fossil to stand out in relief or corrode only the rock, leaving the fossil.

The fossil hunters

Anyone with sufficient interest can find and collect fossils, but to identify them and study them in depth requires a thorough knowledge of animal and plant anatomy. To locate fossils with accuracy an understanding of earth movements and processes that give rise to the preservation of organisms is also necessary. This will enable the fossil hunter to interpret the clues that they give about past conditions. Once they are removed from their matrix, all fossils must be treated with respect and preserved.

Although fossils may be collected as a hobby, they are used by the paleontologist as the identifying "fingerprints" of a particular rock bed. An otherwise featureless bed of limestone containing fossils of a particular short-ranged species found at one locality can be identified at another locality by the presence of that fossil species. Or knowledge of the rates of animal and plant evolution can be used to give an age to the sedimentary rocks in which identifiable fossils are found. This branch of geology is known as stratigraphical paleontology.

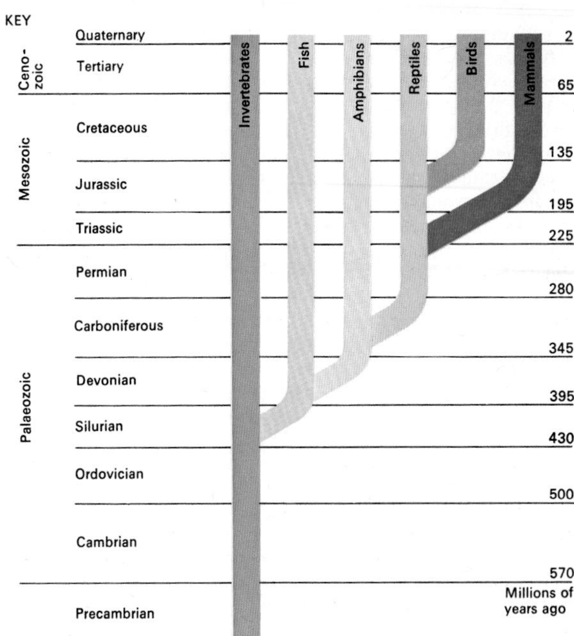

KEY
Quaternary
Tertiary
Cretaceous
Jurassic
Triassic
Permian
Carboniferous
Devonian
Silurian
Ordovician
Cambrian
Precambrian
Ceno-zoic
Mesozoic
Palaeozoic
Invertebrates
Fish
Amphibians
Reptiles
Birds
Mammals
2
65
135
195
225
280
345
395
430
500
570
Millions of years ago

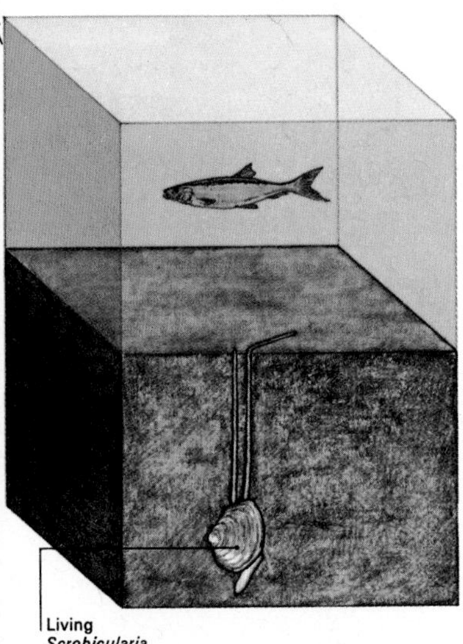

Living
Scrobicularia
Fossil
Scrobicularia

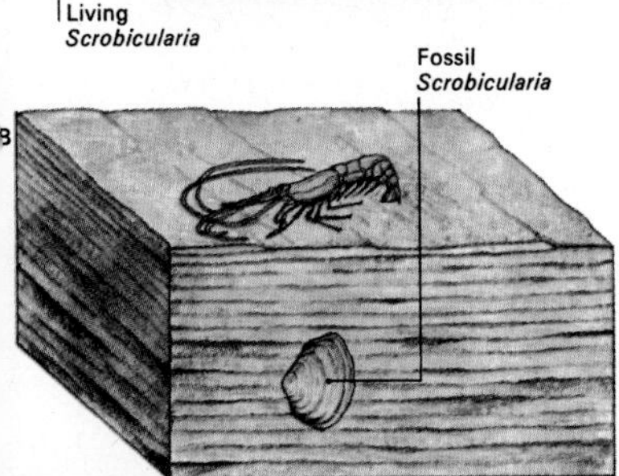

4 A facies fossil is indicative of a particular environment of deposition. The shellfish *Scrobicularia* lived only in oxygen-free mud [A]. It shows that such muds formed the rock in which it is found fossilized [B]. The prawn and fish were mobile, not dependent on the mud, and thus are not facies fossils.

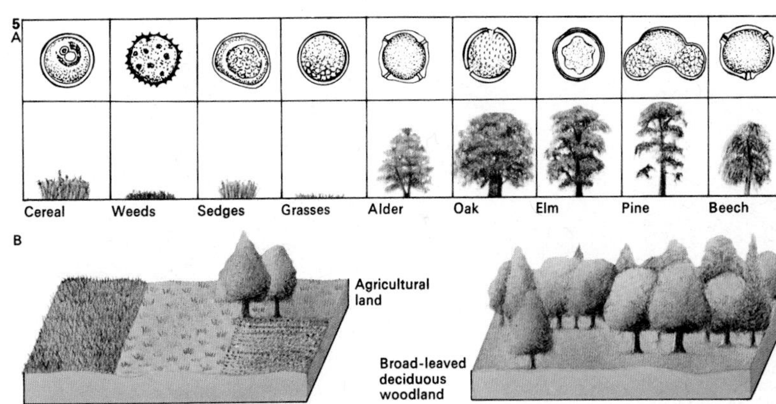

Cereal
Weeds
Sedges
Grasses
Alder
Oak
Elm
Pine
Beech
Agricultural land
Broad-leaved deciduous woodland

Coniferous woodland
Tundra

5 The study of microscopic fossils, micropaleontology, includes the study of pollen grains [A] found at different depths in recent soils. They indicate changing vegetation—and thus changing climates—over the past few million years [B]. This study is known as palynology.

6 A fossil in a rock such as this belemnoid [A] is often unprepossessing and sometimes it takes a paleontologist to recognize it. It is actually the internal stiffening rod of a squidlike animal. The fossil hunter must work with the find wherever the specimen is discovered. The removal of the fossil from the rock [B] can take place on the spot but usually the fossil and matrix are carefully transported back to the laboratory where the right equipment, preserving fluids, and technicians are on hand. Sometimes, if the fossil and the rock are of two very different materials—such as a calcite shell embedded in shale—removal is easy. More often the task involves months of laborious work, scraping away the embedding material from around the valuable specimen for use by paleontologists in attempts to reconstruct the past. The end product, after all this, is a prepared and mounted specimen [C], a solid reminder of life that may have flourished millions of years before man.

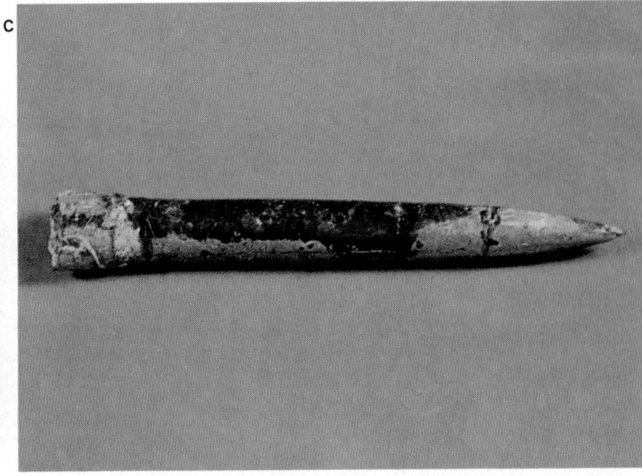

Plants of the past

The earliest traces of life on Earth are those of plants; simple, one-celled organisms spawned in the primeval ocean, the result of a rich "broth" of materials absorbed from the earth and atmosphere. These first traces occur in Precambrian rocks, 2 to 3 billion years old, in North America and South Africa.

Fossil evidence of plant life is hard to come by, for plants do not fossilize easily; they tend to lack durable hard parts and are usually destroyed by weather or chemical processes before they can be preserved in the rocks. Such plants that have become fossilized, however, are exhaustively studied by paleobotanists and from them much has been deduced about the history of plant life on Earth.

Importance of plants

Of the two biological kingdoms, plants and animals, the plant kingdom is by far the most important and arose first. The earliest traces of animals do not appear until the early Cambrian, some 570 million years ago, in Australia. Plants take in energy directly from sunlight and use it in the synthesis of food. Without these foods the food chains that involve the animal kingdom would have no starting points: with no plants there would be nothing to feed the herbivores, with no herbivores there would be nothing to feed the carnivores. But at first the importance of plants was even greater. The early atmosphere of the earth was probably so rich in carbon dioxide that animals could not have survived. Plants made animal life possible, since the process of food production involves the removal of carbon dioxide from the atmosphere and the production of free oxygen. For these reasons it is assumed that once evolution began to transform the first living protoplasm into more complex forms of life, the plants evolved first.

The first recognizable plants were one-celled algae [1], in which all vital processes take place in a single cell. As time passed more specialized algae developed. They consisted of more than one cell and various processes such as reproduction were carried out by different parts of the plant. These plants resembled present-day seaweeds. By this time animals, too, had developed; herbivores fed on these seaweeds and carnivores evolved to feed on the herbivores in turn.

Life out of the water

All this early activity took place in the sea—the land and its atmosphere were too alien and hostile for much to happen there. Some algae became adapted to fresh water and it is from these algae that land plants are thought to have evolved. In time physiological changes occurred that enabled the plants to spend more time exposed to the atmosphere. The most important of these changes was the evolution of a vascular system that could carry water up from the base where it was available and synthesized foodstuffs down from above [2]. With the formation of light-trapping organs held toward the sun [7], and a system of reproduction that would work in the air, the true land plant had evolved. The atmosphere probably resembled that of today, with a higher proportion of carbon dioxide.

CONNECTIONS

See also
560 Fossils: the life of t[he] past
408 Evolution of life
270 The record in the rocks
272 Clues to the past
274 Geology in the fiel[d]
276 Earth's time scale
282 Energy resources: coal
424 The plant kingdom
438 Ferns and horsetai[ls]
440 The cone bearers

1 A

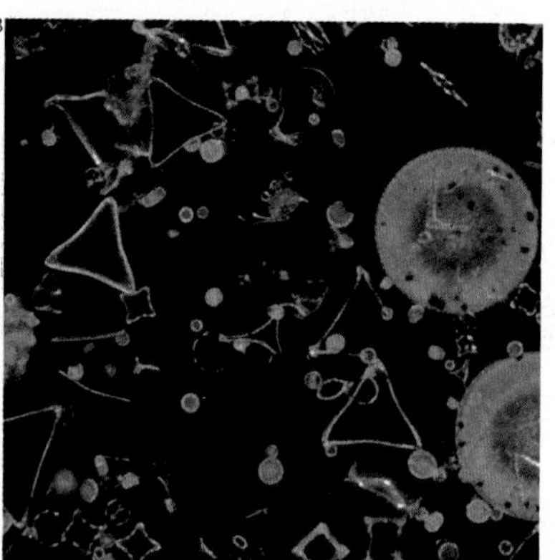
B

1 The earliest plants, the primitive algae, are known from the rock structures (stromatolites) they produced [A]. These were created by the fossilization of concentric layers of mud and algae. Other fossil algal remains commonly found are the "shells" of diatoms [B]. These small, brown algae have been abundant since the Cretaceous period. The diatomaceous earths are composed entirely of their shells.

2 A

B *Nematophyton*

2 To live on land plants needed "plumbing" equipment—a means of transporting water up from the roots and foodstuffs down from the leaves. This is done by means of the vascular system, a network of tubes throughout the plant. In modern plants this is well organized, but extinct plants such as *Nematophyton* had a trunk [A] consisting entirely of tubes of two widths [B] for transport.

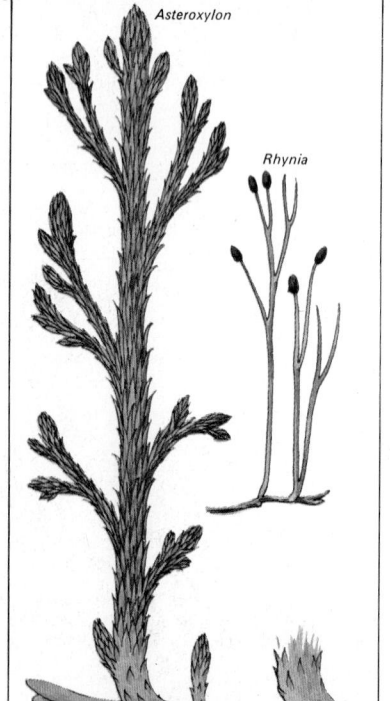

3 *Asteroxylon* *Rhynia*

3 The earliest land plants known from detailed fossils are psilopsids preserved by a freak volcanic eruption during the Devonian in Scotland. *Asteroxylon* grew to a height of 40in (1m) and *Rhynia* grew to a height of 20in (50cm).

4

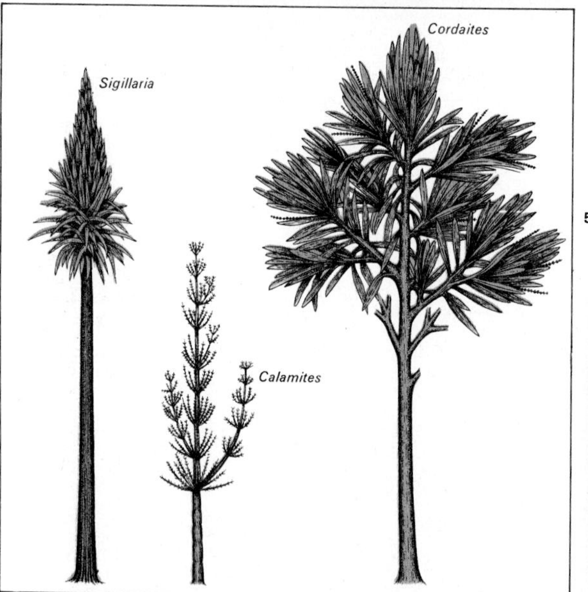
Sigillaria
Cordaites
Calamites

4 The vegetation of the great coal forests consisted of lycopods (clubmoss relatives), horsetails, and primitive gymnosperms. *Sigillaria* was typical of the lycopods, growing to a height of 100ft (30m) in very marshy ground. *Calamites* was a 30ft (9m) horsetail that grew as "reed beds" in the waters of the swamps. Drier areas supported gymnosperms such as *Cordaites*, a primitive member of the conifers. The undergrowth consisted mainly of ferns.

5

5 The great size of the coal forest trees is evident in this picture of a fossil *Sigillaria* stump. Although most trees of the Carboniferous forests lost all their recognizable structures on being decomposed and compressed into coal, sometimes the shapes of roots ("stigmaria") and fallen trunks are preserved in the sands and muds on which they grew when the ground was clear of other plant remains. These remains are most often found in "seat earths" underneath coal seams.

During the Devonian and Carboniferous, over 300 million years ago, plants developed a great variety of complex forms. These were still primitive by today's standards, being close relatives of the horsetails, club mosses, and ferns [Key], but nevertheless they formed vast forests [4, 5] and adopted all the growing habits of modern plants—trees, bushes, creepers, undergrowth, and the like. They grew in such numbers that the thick layers of their rotting remains became solidified into the present-day coal beds [6]. One feature that characterized this flora was its lack of a self-contained reproductive body—the seed.

The evolution of the seed

The seed evolved during the Carboniferous but the seed-bearing plants did not come into their own until the Permian; in the Triassic (225 million years ago) the dominant plants were gymnosperms [8] such as the conifers.

During the Cretaceous, which began about 135 million years ago, the angiosperms [9], or flowering plants, came to the fore and a flora was established that was closely related to today's. For the past 130 million years no major plant group has arisen, but there has been an enormous proliferation of grasses and herbs with a correlated influence on the animals associated with them.

Because the division of the geological column is based on the stages of evolution of animal life, the story of plant evolution does not fit easily into the time scale. In essence, the earth's flora consisted entirely of algae up to Silurian times—halfway through the Paleozoic era, the age of invertebrates. Then land plants—consisting of mosses and liverworts (bryophytes) and ferns, horsetails, and club mosses (pteridophytes)—evolved and dominated the flora until the Permian, the end of the Paleozoic. Gymnosperms were the dominant plant forms from the Triassic until the beginning of the Cretaceous, halfway through the Mesozoic, the age of reptiles. At this time the angiosperms became widespread and continued their dominance until the present day.

KEY

The fronds of this fossilized fern have been preserved as a thin film of residual carbon pressed between beds of shale, the most common method of plant fossilization.

6

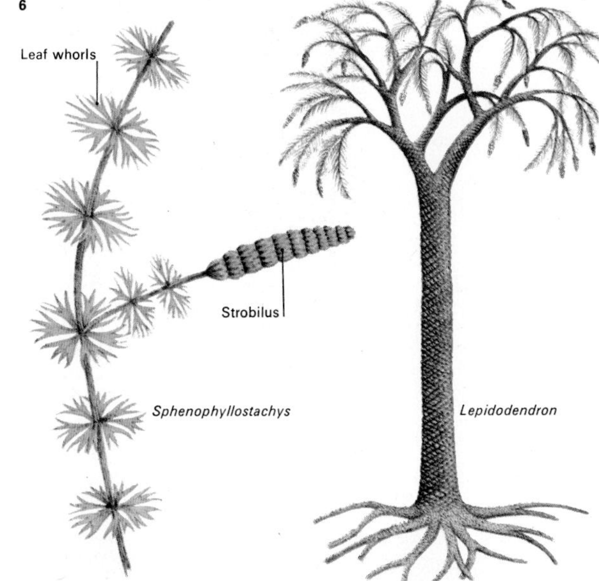

Leaf whorls
Strobilus
Sphenophyllostachys
Lepidodendron

6 A creeping form that made up part of the undergrowth of the coal forest was the horsetail *Sphenophyllostachys*. Whorls of six leaves 0.75in (2cm) long sprouted at intervals from the stem and spores were formed in a strobilus, or cone, on a side branch. *Lepidodendron* was one of the largest of the Carboniferous lycopods, growing to a height of 100ft (30m). The trunk had a characteristic diagonal pattern of leaf scars and it branched dichotomously (repeatedly into two equal parts) to give a crown of branches with strap-shaped leaves. Under the ground the stem branched dichotomously to produce a woody rootstock.

7

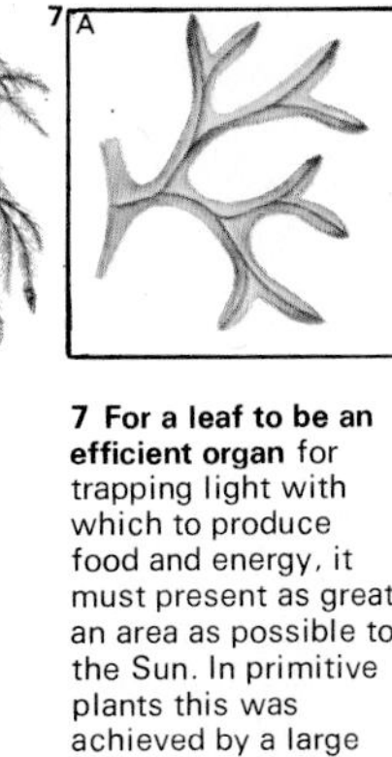

A

B

C

7 For a leaf to be an efficient organ for trapping light with which to produce food and energy, it must present as great an area as possible to the Sun. In primitive plants this was achieved by a large number of branches. It is thought that outgrowths of these branches coalesced, forming single plates of wider surface from which true leaves evolved [A, B, C]. The primitive position [D] of reproductive bodies [1] is at the ends of dichotomously branched stalks. More advanced forms show a reduction in the branching [E], which is carried still further in some fossil ferns [F].

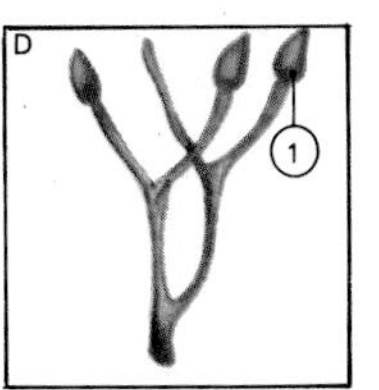

D
1

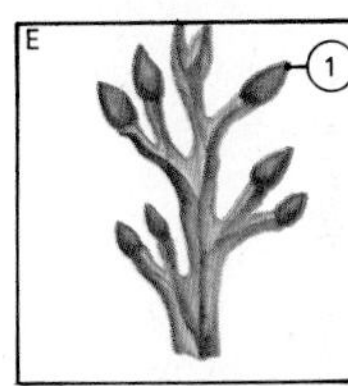

E
1

F
1

8

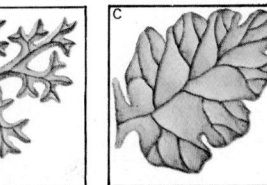

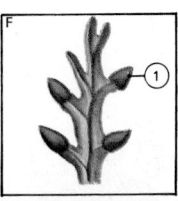

4
1
3
2

8 From the Triassic to the end of the Jurassic, the gymnosperms were the dominant plants. These resembled the modern gymnosperms—the conifers and the cycads—and were characterized by the possession of true seeds. These seeds were open to the air rather than borne in enclosed fruits. The early Mesozoic gymnosperms were mostly conifers and cycadeoids (or Bennettitales). The latter were closely related to the cycads and consisted of a bulbous trunk that may have carried "flowers," surmounted by palmlike fronds. Examples include *Williamsonia* [1] and *Bennettites* [2]. Contemporary conifers include species of *Voltzia* [3] and *Araucarites* [4].

9

A
B

9 Angiosperms, higher plants with enclosed seeds, took over from gymnosperms when the dinosaurs roamed the Earth at the beginning of the Cretaceous. Since then the flora, both herbs and trees, has remained very similar to that of the present day. The leaf shown is that of a plane *(Platanus)* [A] preserved in sediments of the Mesozoic, and is about 100 million years old. The structure of this leaf is almost identical to that of a modern specimen [B].

Fossils without backbones

The most abundant and significant fossils in the rocks of the Earth's surface are those of invertebrates. These range in size from microscopic creatures to cephalopods with coiled shells 6ft (1.8m) in diameter, and in age from the early Cambrian, 570 million years ago, to historic times.

Joint-legged creatures and shells

Some of the earliest fossils are those of the arthropods, which are found from the Cambrian onward. These are the joint-legged animals that have shells of chitin—today's insects, spiders, crabs, and lobsters. In Cambrian times they were represented by the trilobites [1] and other strange creatures. The trilobites were generally unspecialized marine animals with bodies divided into a large number of similar segments. They flourished during the lower Paleozoic, but started to wane during Devonian times and by the end of the Permian were extinct. The closely related eurypterids [3] had a shorter range—Ordovician to Devonian—but while they lived they were the terror of inshore waters, one, *Pterygotus*, being 10ft (3m) long and carrying great lobsterlike claws. Ostracods are another important group of fossil arthropods. They were encased in a pair of tiny, almost microscopic, shells hinged along the back. These shells had characteristic decorations and are valuable as index fossils. The distribution of each species through time is well known, and when a recognizable species is found in a rock the age of the rock can be determined.

Arthropods were among the first animals to colonize land, the millipede *Archedesmus* being found in Devonian rocks. Insects evolved soon afterward and the Carboniferous forests sheltered such creatures as *Meganeura* [4]—a dragonfly the size of a parrot. The arachnids and simpler insects were well established by the upper Paleozoic, while the flies and social insects did not develop until the upper Mesozoic. Mollusks are another major group of organisms with a long ancestry. The tentacled mollusks—the cephalopods—have been found as far back as the Cambrian. These first cephalopods, called nautiloids, had straight, conical shells but later many of them developed curved as well as tightly coiled shells. From nautiloids of the Upper Paleozoic evolved the ammonoids, which reached their peak in the Jurassic. Unlike the straight-walled chambers of nautiloid shells, ammonoids have completely folded partitions between chambers [10]. Ammonoids make excellent index fossils because of their great variety in shell shapes and ornamentation [11, 12] and the short time range of each species. Ammonoids died out during the general change of fauna at the end of the Mesozoic and since then the cephalopods have been represented only by the squid, cuttlefish, octopus, and nautilus.

The snails and the bivalves, the other chief members of the mollusk group, have also been present since the Cambrian, but not until the Tertiary did the bivalves became the important "sea shells" that they are today. During the Paleozoic and Mesozoic their ecological niche was occupied by a primitive group, the brachiopods, which superficially resembled

CONNECTIONS

See also
560 Fossils: the life of the past
410 The world before man
476 Land and sea snails
478 Life between two shells
480 Squids and octopuses
484 The joint-legged animals
486 Crabs and lobsters
496 Locusts, sucking bugs, and dragonflies
508 Threshold of the vertebrates
270 The record in the rocks

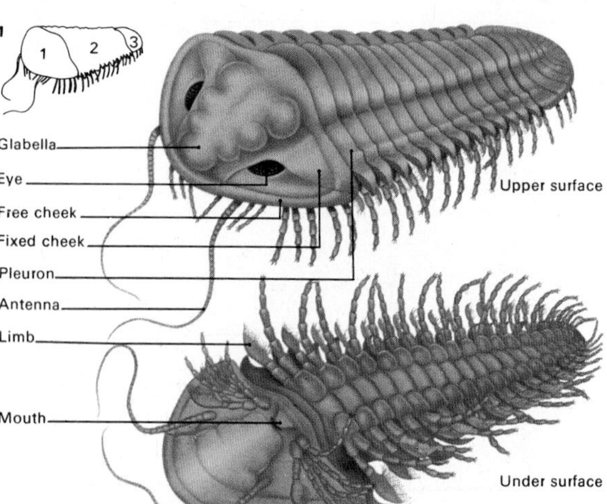

1
2
3
Glabella
Eye
Free cheek
Fixed cheek
Pleuron
Antenna
Limb
Mouth
Upper surface
Under surface

1 A trilobite resembled a modern woodlouse, being covered by a chitinous skeleton. This was divided into the cephalon [1], or headshield, which carried sensory organs, and the glabella, a bump that housed the stomach; [2] the thorax, a region of articulated segments below each of which was a pair of legs; and [3] the pygidium, or tail shield. Each limb consisted of a jointed appendage for walking and swimming along with gills and a paddle that swept food particles toward the mouth.

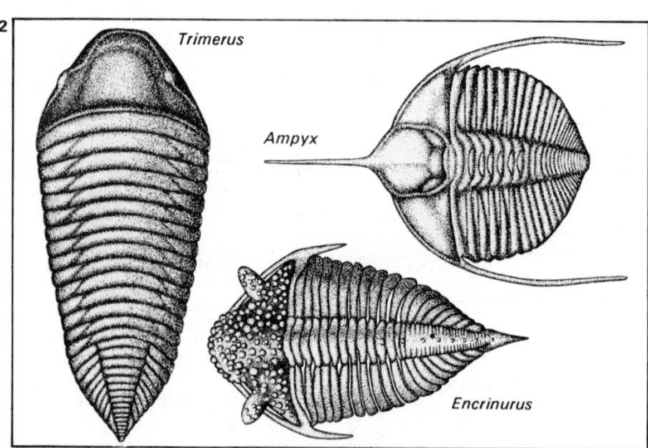

Trimerus
Ampyx
Encrinurus

2 Trilobites adapted to their environment in a variety of ways. *Trimerus* was a burrower, *Ampyx* was a lightweight swimmer, and *Encrinurus* was a slow-moving bottom dweller.

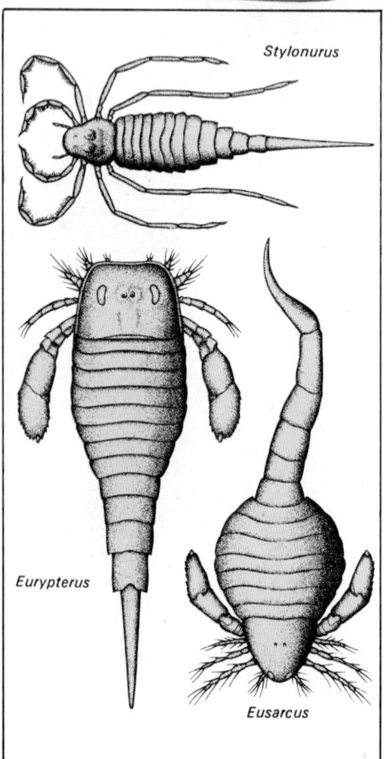

Stylonurus
Eurypterus
Eusarcus

3 The eurypterids, distantly related to the trilobites and placed in the same group as horseshoe crabs, included the great sea scorpions of the Silurian and the Devonian. Although some carried claws and grew to a length of 10ft (3m), those shown here were smaller. *Stylonurus* was a long-legged form found in Silurian and Devonian rocks. *Eurypterus* of the Devonian was the first of the group to be discovered. *Eusarcus* was scorpionlike. These lived only in Silurian seas but later forms moved into brackish and fresh water.

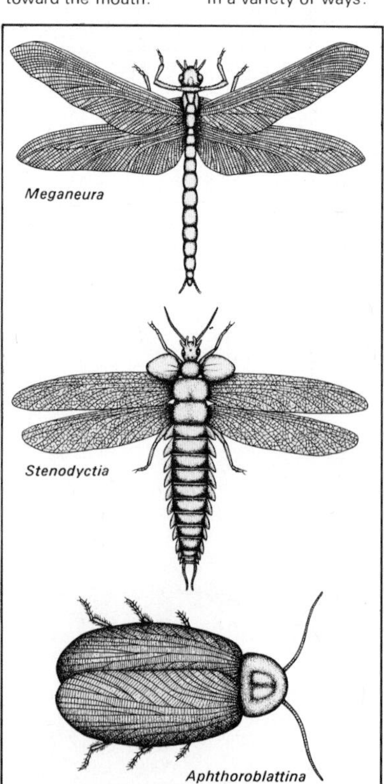

Meganeura
Stenodyctia
Aphthoroblattina

4 Insects appeared in the Devonian and flourished in the Carboniferous. These included an archaic dragonfly called *Meganeura*, with a wingspan of about 31in (79cm); *Stenodyctia*, which was a generalized type; and *Aphthoroblattina*, a cockroach.

5 This trilobite is *Ogygiocarella* and was preserved in Ordovician rocks 500 million years old.

6 The fossil of the extinct lobster *Eryon* was found in 140 million-year-old Jurassic limestone.

them—being sessile (sedentary) and having their soft anatomy enclosed in two shells—but were not related to them. They have been declining in importance since the end of the Mesozoic and have been largely replaced by the bivalves.

Development of corals

The corals are an important group of fossil organisms and can be divided into three groups, two of which are extinct. The first group, called the rugose corals because of the wrinkled appearance of the outer skeleton, were mostly solitary organisms, looking like the related sea anemones but encased in cup-shaped shells. Some later rugose corals were colonial, consisting of more than one individual. They appeared in the middle Ordovician, reached their peak in the lower Carboniferous, and died out in the Permian. The second group, the tabulate corals, were all compound, consisting of large numbers of small individuals. They appeared in the middle Ordovician, flourished in the Silurian and Devonian, and became extinct in the Permian. The third group, the scleractinian corals, are the reef-building corals of today. They did not appear until the middle Triassic and have been mostly colonial in habit.

Some vertebrate relatives

The phylum known as the chordates, to which man belongs, includes several groups of small, apparently simple wormlike animals. An early offshoot of this phylum may have given rise to the graptolites—communal drifting organisms that were abundant in the oceans of Ordovician and Silurian times [7]. Their evolution took place rapidly from the complex types of the lower Ordovician to the straight, simple forms of the Silurian, making them good index fossils for identifying the featureless black shales of the lower Paleozoic.

The echinoderms—the starfish, sea urchins, and sea lilies—are probably close to the ancestors of the vertebrates and, because they are mostly covered with armor, they tend to fossilize easily. Certain Carboniferous limestones are made up largely of crinoid (sea lily) plates.

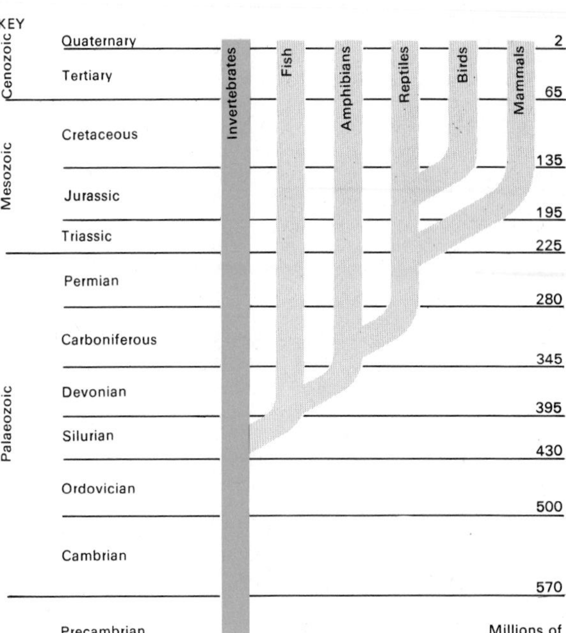
KEY
Cenozoic
Mesozoic
Palaeozoic
Quaternary
Tertiary
Cretaceous
Jurassic
Triassic
Permian
Carboniferous
Devonian
Silurian
Ordovician
Cambrian
Precambrian
Invertebrates
Fish
Amphibians
Reptiles
Birds
Mammals
2
65
135
195
225
280
345
395
430
500
570
Millions of years ago

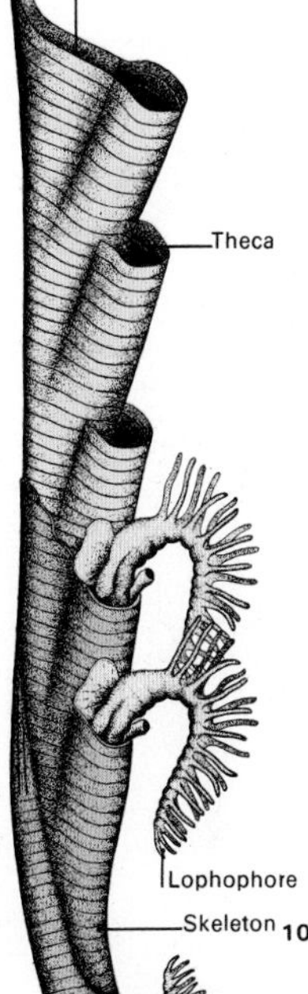
Common canal
Theca
Lophophore

7 The graptolites were free-floating colonial organisms that abounded in the seas of Ordovician and Silurian times. They did not grow much above 4in (10cm) long and started off with a single individual (zooid) produced by sexual means. Subsequent zooids grew from the side of the original and budded off from one another producing the characteristic shape of the particular species. Each zooid rested in a cup called a theca and was connected to all the others by a common canal. The chitin skeleton had an outer layer secreted by an outer skin. Each zooid carried a feathery feeding organ (lophophore).

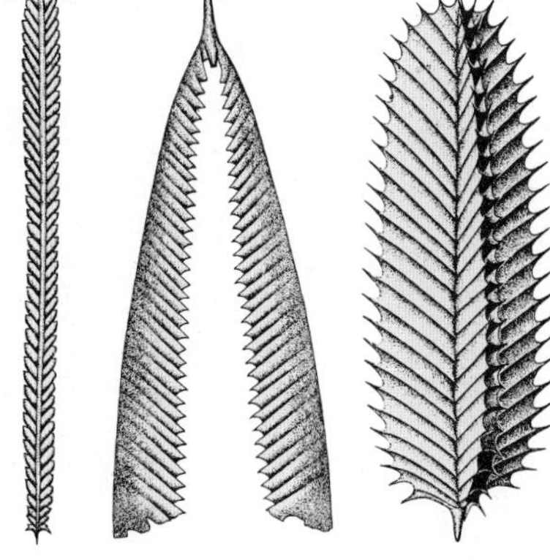
A
B
C

8 Graptolite genera can be recognized by the shape and arrangement of their thecae (cases) and of their branches (stipes). *Diplograptus* [A] had two stipes joined together growing upward back to back. *Didymograptus* [B] had two stipes separately growing downward, and *Phyllograptus* [C] had four stipes joined together along their length growing upward with long and spiny thecae.

9 The rapid evolution of the graptolites and the fact that they are found all over the world makes them ideal index fossils. The presence of large numbers of *Didymograptus* in this shale identifies it as being of Lower Ordovician age. Slightly older or younger shale have different graptolites.

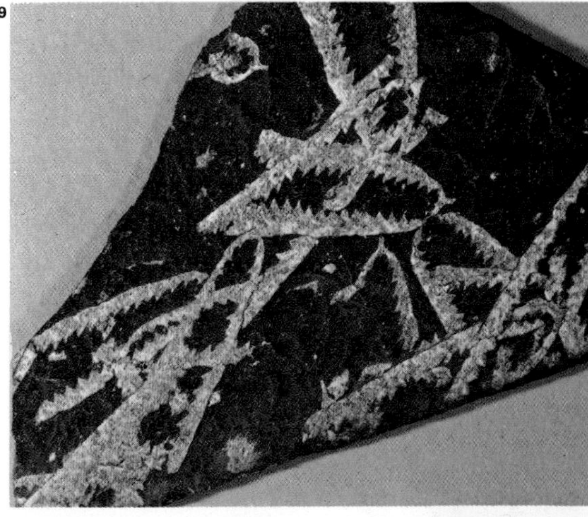

Skeleton
Zooid

10 Ammonoids had a soft anatomy similar to that of the modern nautilus, which lives in the open end of its shell. As the animal grew it secreted more shell and moved forward into the new part, walling off the old section with a septum. The walled-off chambers were used for buoyancy, being supplied with air from a tubelike passage, or siphuncle, connecting them all. The septa met the shell wall in suture lines that had identifiable patterns for each species and became more complex as the group advanced. [A] shows a primitive *Ceratites* suture, [B] *Hildoceras*, and [C] advanced *Baculites*. The arrow shows the position of the siphuncle and the direction of the head.

11 Many ammonoids can be identified by the ornamentation on the shell. *Promicroceras* [A] had ribs, *Douvilleiceras* [B] had tubercles, *Harpoceras* [C] had a keel, *Hildoceras* [D] had a longitudinal series of ridges, and *Kosmocaras* [E] had its aperture guarded by a pair of small paddle-shaped flaps.

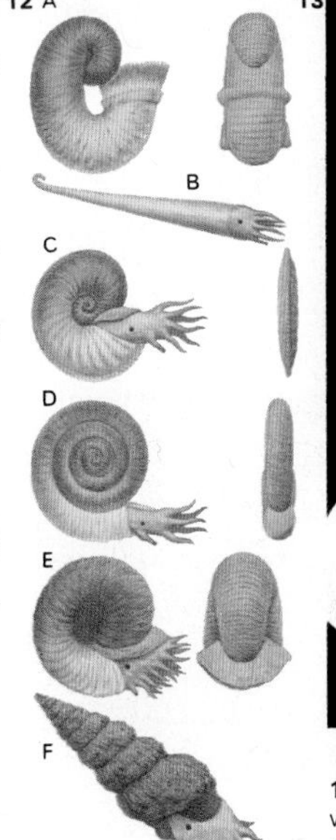
A
B
C
D
E
F

12 The shape of an ammonoid's shell determined its mode of life. *Scaphites* [A] was a passive drifter; *Baculites* [B], *Amaltheus* [C], and *Dactylioceras* [D] were streamlined active predators; inactive *Cadoceras* [E] only moved up and down by varying its buoyancy; and snaillike *Turrilites* [F] was confined to living on the bottom of the sea.

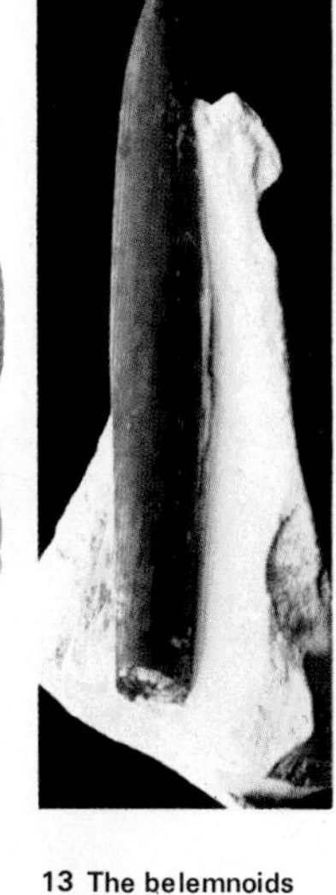

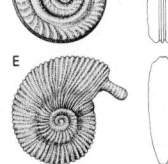

13 The belemnoids were related to the ammonoids, but were squidlike with pen-shaped shells.

Fish and amphibians of the past

Vertebrates, the animals with backbones, are believed to have evolved from invertebrate chordates, such as the tunicates and lancelets. These, in turn, are thought to have shared a common ancestry with primitive attached echinoderms similar to sea lilies. Early chordates that developed rings of bone around the notochord—called vertebrae—gave rise to the first vertebrates.

Toward the age of fish

The first recognizable skeletal features of early vertebrates would have been the jointed support for the main muscular system—the backbone—and a box to contain the brain, namely the skull. This is more or less the layout of the earliest and most primitive fish, the agnathans [1]. These Silurian forms had no jaws, the mouth being merely a sucking organ. They breathed through gills which were paired and supported on bony outgrowths. As time progressed the first pair of gill supports moved forward and became hinged to the skull to form the jaws, and bony structures evolved to support proper fins. The true fish had developed.

The jawed fish are divided into three groups: the Placodermi, armor-plated fish of the Devonian; the Chondrichthyes, cartilage-skeletoned sharks and rays that have existed since the Devonian; and the Osteichthyes, bony fish that also appeared in the Devonian and represent the major type of fish found in the seas today.

The Devonian period is known as the age of fish because during this time all three groups of fish came to the fore and dominated the seas. Even in those early times the bony fish were divided into the ray-finned and lobe-finned types. The ray-finned fish are what we think of as typical—swimming by means of paired fins supported by a "ray" of bony outgrowths and balancing by means of a "swim bladder" of air within the body. The lobe-finned fish have their fins supported by muscular lobes and in some instances the swim bladder is connected to the gullet to form a lung. After Devonian times the lobe fins decreased in importance and today are represented only by one marine species, the coelecanth. Before that they were to play a very significant role in the history of life.

The Devonian lobe-finned fish lived in freshwater lakes of the Northern Hemisphere. These lakes would occasionally dry out, killing everything that lived in them [5]. Some of the lobe-fins, however, with their ability to breathe out of the water, and their lobed fins providing a clumsy but serviceable means of locomotion on land [6], could exist, at least for short periods, out of the water. Often this was enough to enable them to find their way to the next pond. As time passed the bones in the lobe were formed into a more efficient support and the first land-going limbs were developed.

Life comes ashore

The early limb, built of two main sections and five digits at the end, became the basic pattern of all land vertebrates to follow. The earliest amphibian, *Ichthyostega* [8] from the upper Devonian of Greenland where forests of sizeable land plants were beginning to grow, had the early tetrapod limb but

CONNECTIONS

See also
560 Fossils: The life of the past
568 Toward life on land
410 The world before man
512 The life of fish
510 The classification of fish
408 Evolution of life
518 The life of amphibians

1

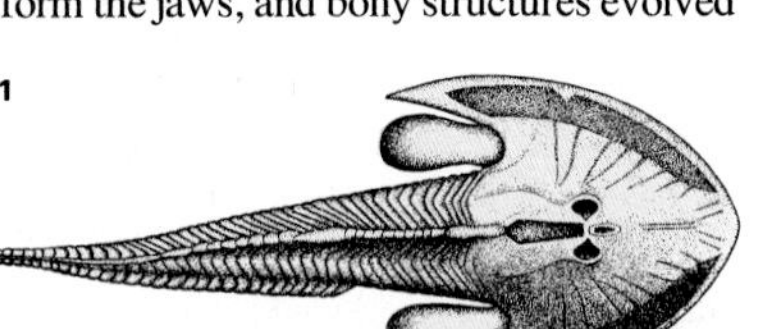

1 One of the jawless fish of the Silurian was *Cephalaspis*. It had a triangular head shield bearing the mouth and paired fins beneath, and a pair of vibration-sensitive organs on the upper surface.

2

2 Dinichthys was an armored placoderm. With a length of 30ft (9m), it was a fearsome fish of the Devonian seas.

3

3 Drepanaspls was a Devonian agnathan. It was a flattened bottom dweller with a complicated pattern of armor.

4

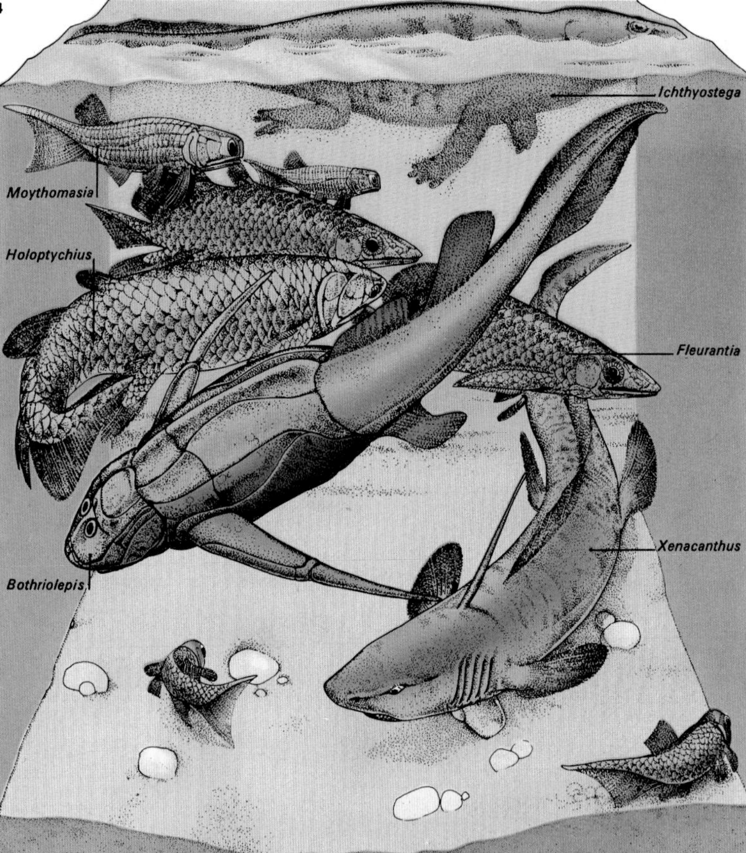

Ichthyostega
Moythomasia
Holoptychius
Fleurantia
Xenacanthus
Bothriolepis

4 The typical habitats of Devonian fish were inland seas, many of which existed among the freshly formed mountain chains of the northern continent of that time. Shown here is a selection of the fish types found in such an area. *Bothriolepis* was a placoderm reaching a length of 9in (24cm). Its head and body were armored as were the first pair of fins. *Xenacanthus* was an early member of the Chondrichthyes and had many sharklike features. It swam by means of paired, leaf-shaped fins and had a long, pointed tail. It was 2.5ft (75cm) long. *Moythomasia* was one of the ray-finned Osteichthyes while *Holoptychus* was one of the lobe-finned type. *Fleurantia* was a lobe-finned lungfish similar to the ancestral stock that gave rise to the first amphibians such as *Ichthyostega*, shown here on the surface of the water.

5

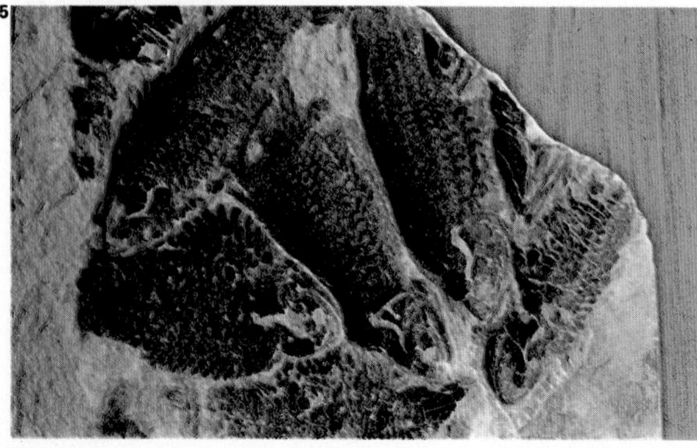

5 As the Devonian desert pools dried out the inhabitants crowded together in the last drop of moisture and died, like these *Holoptychius* from Scotland. Land vertebrates evolved from creatures that survived such conditions.

6

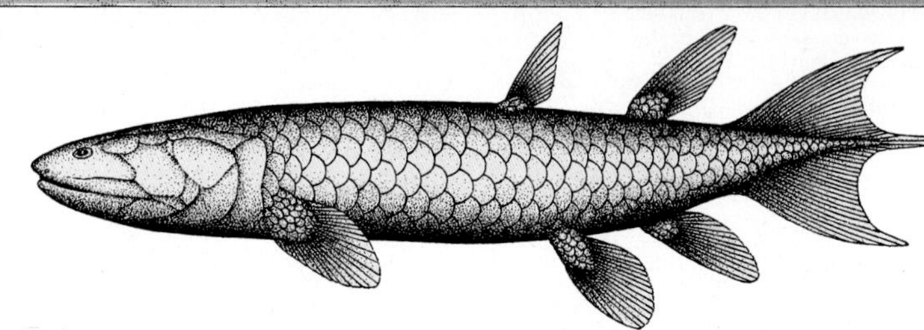

6 To be able to live out of the water a fish would need a lung system for breathing and at least one pair of muscular leglike fins to allow it to travel. These features are found in the Devonian 2ft (60cm) long lobe-fin *Eusthenopteron*.

also retained fishlike characteristics in the bones of the skull and in the tail.

By the time of the Carboniferous, amphibians were plentiful and they mostly belonged to one extinct group called the labyrinthodonts—so called because of the convoluted nature of their tooth enamel. These had a much more powerful vertebral column than *Ichthyostega,* reflecting the fact that they spent much more time out of the water. They probably had the same general life style as modern amphibians, spending most of their adult life on land and returning to the water to lay eggs. The fishlike tadpoles would have lived in the water only until they were mature.

Adaptations of amphibians

The Carboniferous amphibians adapted swiftly to the different ecological niches offered by the dry-land environments and they were all carnivores, the smaller ones eating the insects that abounded in the coal forests and the larger ones living like crocodiles and eating either fish or members of their own kind in the swamps.

Other Upper Paleozoic amphibians, unrelated to the labyrinthodonts, adopted very different and specialized modes of life. Some spent all their time in the water, adopting a snakelike body. One such creature was *Dolichosoma* [10]. Others became flattened and their skulls grew into broad, flat horns, the purpose of which is obscure. These, like *Diplocaulus* [11], probably lived in the mud on the bottoms of pools.

The labyrinthodonts and other specialized amphibians became extinct by Triassic times, leaving only the direct ancestors of modern frogs and salamanders. But some time before this, the amphibians gave rise to an intermediate group that was to abandon the water altogether and become reptiles. These, the seymouriamorphs, showed advanced features, especially in the reptilian nature of the limbs, although the skull and vertebrae remained distinctly amphibian. Typical of this group is the Permian *Seymouria* [13], which, however, could not be the direct ancestor of the reptiles since primitive reptiles are known from the Carboniferous.

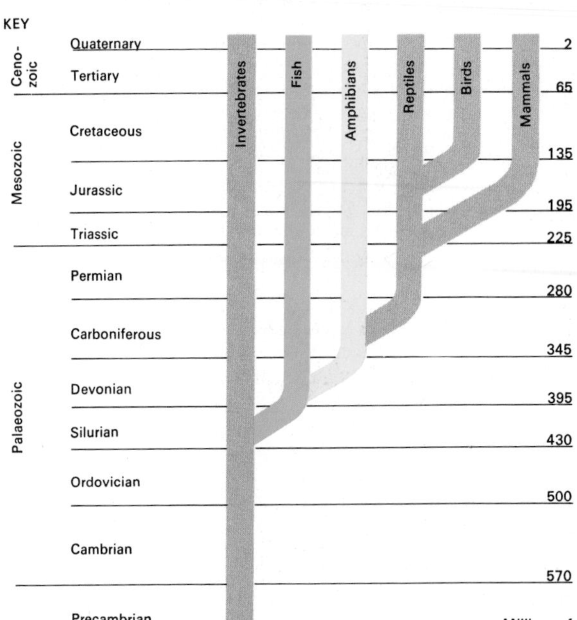
KEY
Cenozoic
Mesozoic
Palaeozoic
Quaternary
Tertiary
Cretaceous
Jurassic
Triassic
Permian
Carboniferous
Devonian
Silurian
Ordovician
Cambrian
Precambrian
Invertebrates
Fish
Amphibians
Reptiles
Birds
Mammals
2
65
135
195
225
280
345
395
430
500
570
Millions of years ago

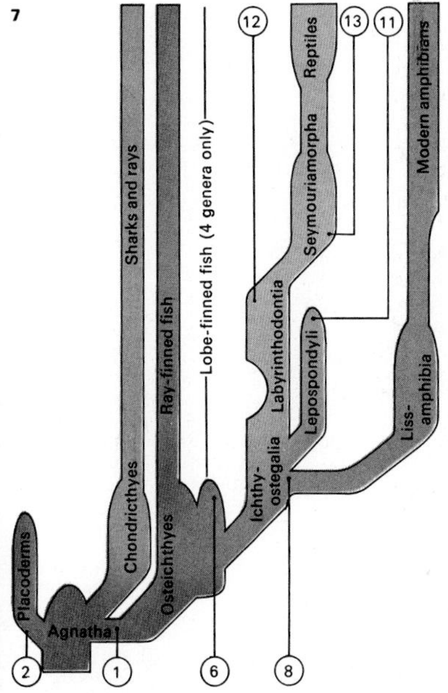
7
Placoderms
Agnatha
Chondricthyes
Sharks and rays
Osteichthyes
Ray-finned fish
Lobe-finned fish (4 genera only)
Ichthyostegalia
Labyrinthodontia
Seymouriamorpha
Reptiles
Lepospondyli
Lissamphibia
Modern amphibians
12
13
11
2
1
6
8

7 Amphibians and advanced fish evolved from primitive Devonian forms. The numbers refer to the illustrations.

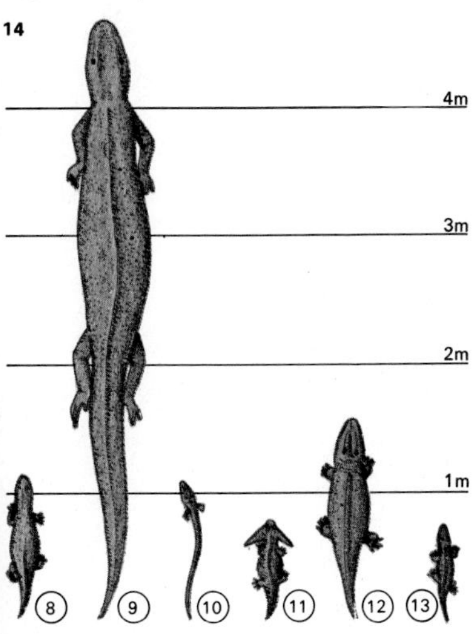
14
4m
3m
2m
1m
8
9
10
11
12
13

14 The sizes of the Upper Paleozoic amphibians varied as much as their shapes, as the illustrations show.

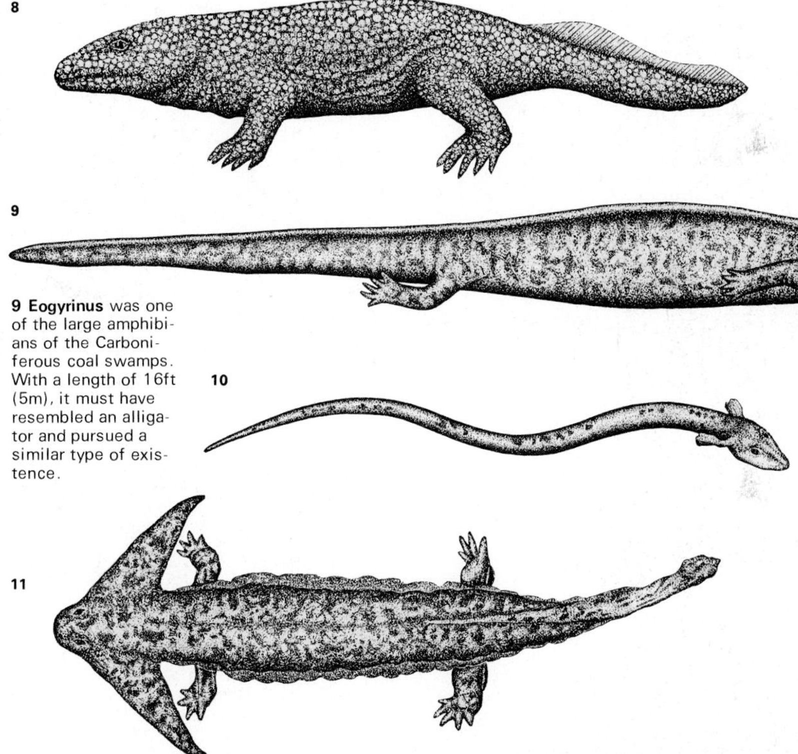
8
9
10
11
12
13

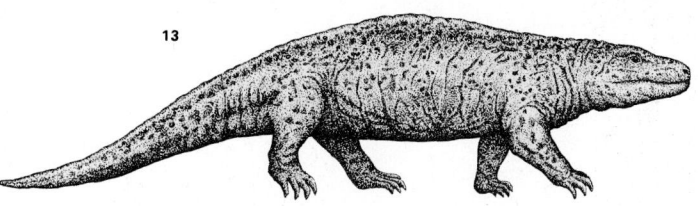

8 Icthyostega is the earliest and most primitive amphibian known. Found in Devonian deposits of Greenland, it had a typical amphibian body about 40in (1m) long but retained a fish skull and tail.

9 Eogyrinus was one of the large amphibians of the Carboniferous coal swamps. With a length of 16ft (5m), it must have resembled an alligator and pursued a similar type of existence.

10 Dolichosoma shows the adaptability of the Carboniferous amphibians. It was 40in (1m) long and had no limbs, giving it an appearance that suggests an eellike mode of life.

11 Diplocaulus was a Permian amphibian that reached a length of 2ft (60cm). Its peculiarity was its boomerang-shaped skull, which suggests that it lived in mud at the bottom of ponds or lakes.

12 Eryops was a massive Permian amphibian typical of the bulky forms that developed just before the age of amphibians passed into that of the reptiles. It was 5ft (1.5m) long and was well adapted for life on land.

13 Seymouria was a Permian amphibian so advanced that there is still much discussion as to whether it was an amphibian or a primitive reptile. It was 2ft (60cm) long and the bones of its limbs were distinctly reptilian.

Toward life on land

The Paleozoic era spans the 345 million years between the beginning of the Cambrian period and the end of the Permian [Key]. During the Lower Paleozoic era (the Cambrian, Ordovician, and Silurian periods), life was confined to the sea. It came ashore during the Upper Paleozoic era (in the Devonian, Carboniferous, and Permian periods) and developed into the innumerable forms known today.

Tell-tale fossils

Evidence of life on Earth has been found in rocks 3 billion years old, but it is only since the beginning of the Cambrian period some 570 million years ago that the record has been clear. Before then all living organisms were soft-bodied and they fossilized only under exceptional conditions [1]. After the beginning of the Cambrian, several groups of animals developed hard parts that were easily fossilized, and since then enough remains have been preserved to provide a detailed picture of ancient environments.

During the Cambrian period [2], a time of low lands and mild climates, the most prominent creatures were arthropods (jointlegged animals) of various types, the most important of which were the trilobites (segmented marine creatures). Because of their great age, Cambrian rocks provide only fragmentary fossil evidence, but enough exists for environments to be reconstructed in detail.

The Ordovician deposits [3], 500 million years old, indicate that there was a great submergence of the lands with the spread of shallow seas. Fossil evidence from the seas shows that the arthropods continued to develop and there had arrived on the scene a number of cephalopods (mollusks), some of them very large with shells and tentacles. The most prominent shellfish during those times were the brachiopods, which only superficially resemble the more familiar bivalves. In modern times bivalves have taken over and brachiopods are now rare.

The trends of life on the sea bottom during Ordovician times continued into the Silurian period, 430 million years ago. In this period came the development of massive coral reefs, the rise of the first vertebrates, and the first tentative land forays of primitive plants. Much dry land appeared as mountain ranges rose from the sea. Extensive deposits from the Ordovician and Silurian periods have been found in parts of Europe, North and South America, and Australasia, and it is because such detailed remains have been found in particular localities that the ecology of entire periods can be reconstructed.

Life reaches the land

Life began to reach the land in earnest during the Devonian period [4], 395 million years ago. The land plants that flourished at that time released great quantities of oxygen into an atmosphere previously too rich in carbon dioxide to support animal life out of the water. Once a certain level of oxygen had been established, the way was open for the colonization of the land by arthropods, such as mites and millipedes. These were followed by vertebrates, starting with lobe-finned fish and progressing to amphibians. Most of this activity took place at the edge of shallow inland waters, away from

CONNECTIONS

See also

566 Fish and amphibians of the past
560 Fossils: the life of th[e] past
408 Evolution of life
410 The world before ma[n]
518 The life of amphibian[s]
282 Energy resources: coal
510 The classification of fish
508 Threshold of the ver[-]tebrates

1

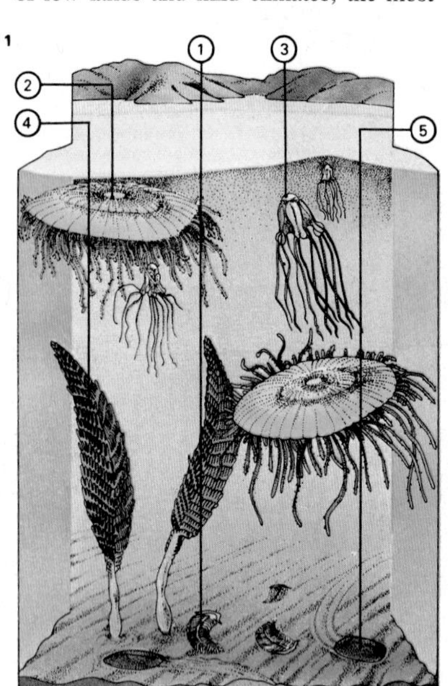

1
3
2
4
5

1 Really ancient fossils dating from before the Cambrian period, some 570 million years ago, are extremely rare. This is because organisms before that time were simple and lacked hard parts that fossilized easily, and also because rocks older than this are usually badly deformed, destroying all traces of organic remains. But occasionally individual organisms such as lime-secreting algae are found in these ancient rocks, some of which are 2.5 billion years old. The best Precambrian fossil assemblage so far discovered dates from just before the beginning of the Cambrian and was found at Ediacara in south Australia. The rocks indicate that there was a shallow sea environment with a sandy bottom inhabited by soft-bodied creatures such as wormlike *Spriggina* [1]; *Eoporpita* [2], and *Kimberella* [3], jellyfish; *Arborea* [4], a sea pen; and *Dickinsonia* [5], an invertebrate of uncertain affinities.

2

4 5 7 6 1 9 3 2
8
10

2 Fossils of the Cambrian period are more widespread because many groups of organisms developed preservable hard parts. The most prominent of these were the arthropods, including the segmented trilobites. Cambrian fossils have been found in all parts of the world but a particularly good fauna of about seventy genera is known from the middle Cambrian Burgess shales of British Columbia. This rock sequence indicates a deep-water environment that was suddenly poisoned by a seepage of gas. Among arthropods found there are 8in (20cm) trilobites such as *Olenoides* [1] and *Ogygopsis* [2], and 0.75in (2cm) *Agnostus* [3]. Other arthropods include malacostracans [4], *Naraoia* [5], *Burgessia* [6], *Sidneya* [7], *Marella* [8], *Waptia* [9] and *Emeraldella* [10]. As well as these there were sponges, worms, jellyfish, and seaweeds. This fauna is typical of the middle Cambrian, although the mode of preservation is not.

3

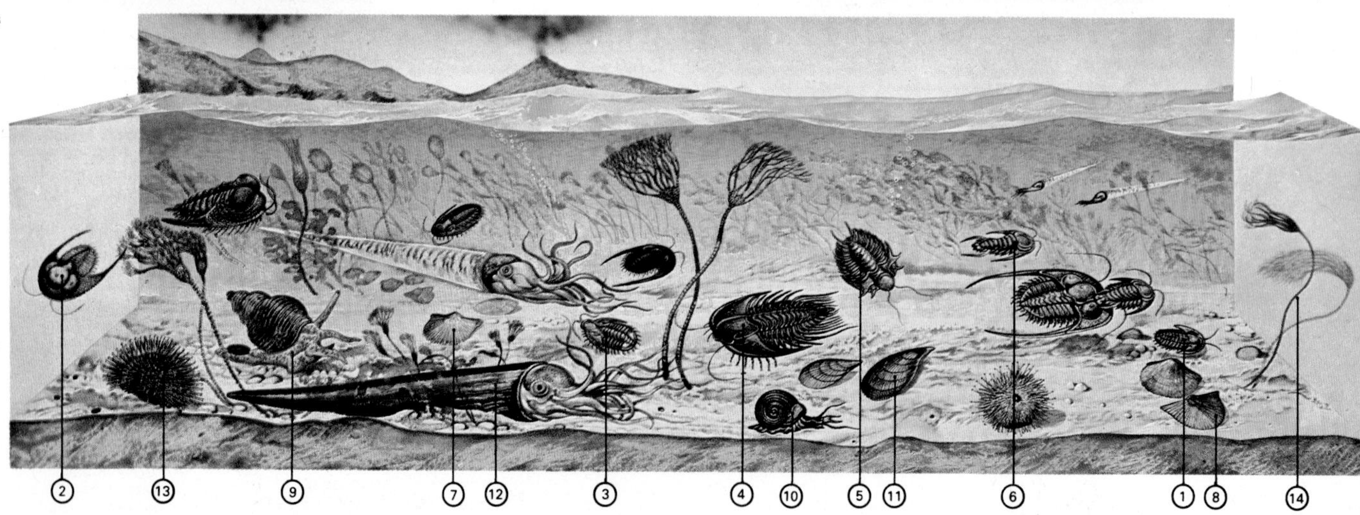

2 13 9 7 12 3 4 10 5 11 6 1 8 14

3 In Ordovician times living things had diversified even more and their fossils are abundant. A deep-sea trough covered the area of the British Isles separating land masses of rising mountains in the north from low relief in the south. This restoration has been based on an upper Ordovician fauna from Scotland. The seas toward the edge of the trough contained trilobites that grew up to 12in (30cm) long such as *Proteus* [1], *Tetraspis* [2], *Phillipsinella* [3] *Paracybeloides* [4], *Sphaerocoryphe* [5] and *Remopleurides* [6]; brachiopods such as Sampo [7] and *Raphinesquina* [8]; snails such as *Cyclonema* [9] and *Sinuites* [10]; bivalves such as *Byssonchia* [11]; shelled cephalopods such as *Orthoceras* [12]; and echinoderms such as *Aulechinus* [13] and the sea-lilies [14]. This trough persisted into Silurian times.

the destructive chaos of the ocean beaches. Most fish by that time had jaws, which meant that, unlike their ancestors, they were able to bite and eat their neighbors. Many fish evolved bony armor as a means of self-protection. It was at that time, too, that ancestors of sharks first appeared.

The conquest of the land by vertebrates was basically a matter of survival. The lobe-finned fish lived in pools that periodically dried out. When this happened they were forced to move to the next water. As time passed the fish became better adapted and were able to spend much longer periods out of water. From these came the amphibians, which lived in water for only part of their life cycle. The process of mountain building that had begun in the Silurian period reached its climax in the Devonian.

From forests to deserts

By the time the Carboniferous period [5] was under way, 345 million years ago, land plants had firmly established themselves and vast forests of ferns and giant club mosses had spread over well-watered, fertile lowlands. These were the swamps that were eventually buried and compressed to form our present coalfields. Amphibians of many shapes and sizes slithered in the green gloom of the undergrowth, while above them, between the patterned trunks, droned enormous insects, some of them with 24in (60cm) wing spans [5]. On higher ground, above the steaming valleys and deltas, a more open vegetation of ferns and primitive conifers flourished. Simple reptiles evolved from amphibian stock during the Carboniferous period, but did not become dominant until a later period.

The transition from the Carboniferous into the Permian period [6, 7], 280 million years ago, was accompanied by a change, for reasons that are not clear, from forest to arid conditions, together with an ice age in the Southern Hemisphere. During that time the reptiles successfully spread over the land. They had an advantage over their amphibian ancestors in that they could live out of water and had better constructed skeletons. Toward the end of the period some developed mammallike features.

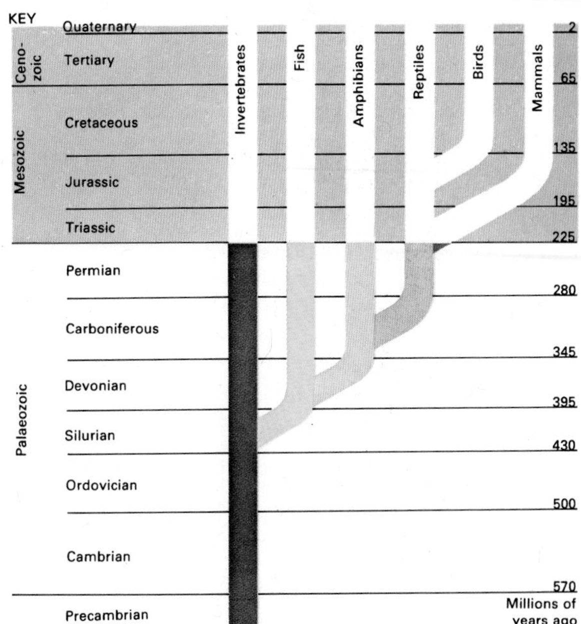

KEY
Quaternary
Tertiary
Ceno-zoic
Cretaceous
Jurassic
Triassic
Mesozoic
Permian
Carboniferous
Devonian
Silurian
Ordovician
Cambrian
Precambrian
Palaeozoic
Invertebrates
Fish
Amphibians
Reptiles
Birds
Mammals
2
65
135
195
225
280
345
395
430
500
570
Millions of years ago

4

3
1
2
6
4
5

4 Northern Scotland had inland seas in Devonian times. On the shores of these grew psilophytes, the earliest land plants to possess a water-conducting system. They included *Psilophyton* [1], *Rhynia* [2] and *Asteroxylon* [3], 8in (20cm) tall. The earliest known animals also lived there. These were mites, *Protocarus* [4] and the millipede *Archedesmus* [5]. When the waters dried up, lungfish such as *Dipterus* [6] survived buried in the mud. The remains of these organisms were preserved when a nearby volcano erupted and buried them in silica-rich deposits. Thus there are many fossils.

5

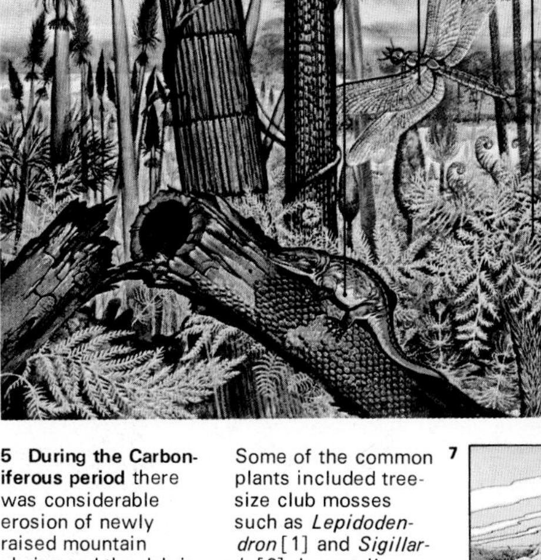

7
5
1
4
3
6
2

5 During the Carboniferous period there was considerable erosion of newly raised mountain chains and the debris that was washed off them formed vast deltas in the Northern Hemisphere. These deltas supported the great coal forests consisting of primitive plants grown to tree size. Some of the common plants included tree-size club mosses such as *Lepidodendron* [1] and *Sigillaria* [2], horsetails, calamites [3] and tree ferns, *Medullosa* [4]. The animal life included giant insects such as *Meganeura* [5] and *Stenodictya* [6] and amphibians such as *Diplovertebron* [7].

6 During the Permian period the humid forests and swamps gave way to mountains and deserts in the Northern Hemisphere. The reptiles had evolved by that time and these were far better adapted than the amphibians to withstand the rigors of desert life. They became diversified to fit the new conditions. One group, the pelycosaurs, developed strange backfins supported on elongations of the vertebrae. These fins may have been temperature-regulating structures, absorbing heat when turned toward the sun and radiating heat when turned away. *Dimetrodon* with a huge fin [A] was a flesh-eating pelycosaur that attained a length of about 10ft (3m). *Edaphosaurus* [B] with a shorter fin was another 10ft long pelycosaur, but one with gentle herbivorous habits.

6

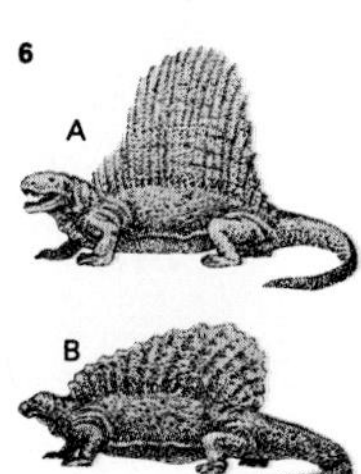

A
B

7

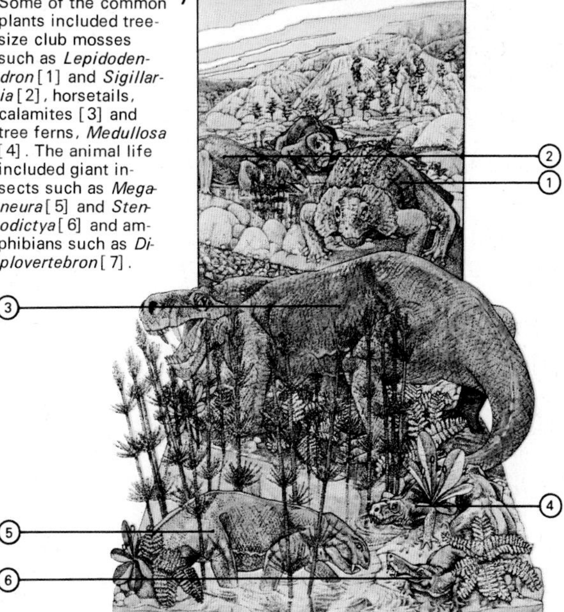

2
1
3
4
5
6

7 The Permian deserts of the southern continents were at times subjected to ice ages. In between these glacial periods they supported a sparse vegetation of horsetails, conifers, ferns, and seed-ferns. Among these lived a variety of reptiles that ranged from the extremely primitive to others that displayed advanced mammallike characteristics, showing them to be the ancestors of the mammals to come. Fauna found in the Permian beds of South Africa includes primitive reptiles, such as *Pareiasaurus* [1], and mammallike types of reptiles, such as *Endothyodon* [2], *Lycaenops* [3], *Hofmeyria* [4], *Dicynodon* [5], and *Chorosaurus* [6].

Reptiles of the past

Once primitive amphibians had finally emerged from the water in the Devonian period (345–395 million years ago), animal life on land had begun. By the Carboniferous (280–345 million years ago) the first reptiles had appeared, turning their backs completely on their watery ancestry.

To do this, the aquatic amphibian larval stage—the tadpole—had to be dispensed with and the yolk-filled hard-shelled egg, protected from drying out by membranes and able to develop on land, was evolved.

Study of the fossil record

The skeletons of the earliest reptiles and amphibians were so alike that it is difficult to distinguish between them. The only accurate identification lies in the way the eggs were produced, which is almost impossible to tell from the fossil record.

The oldest fossil reptile known is *Hylonomus*, a lizardlike creature about 39 in (1m) long, found preserved among the stumps of coal-forest trees of the Upper Carboniferous. It was one of the cotylosaurs, or "stem reptiles," a very basic group, from which all others developed. The cotylosaurs appeared in the Carboniferous, flourished in the Permian and vanished in the Triassic period.

The skeletons of these creatures differed from those of the amphibians in having a firmer backbone and well-articulated wrists and ankles, features that were to give rise to the more specialized limbs of their successors—as well as a taller, narrower skull, hinting at a greater brain development. Reptiles also possess scales, which were probably lacking in their amphibian forebears. These scales are not analogous to those of the ancestral fish but were a new development.

The cotylosaurs expanded rapidly into their newly conquered environment and gave rise to a large number of new and experimental forms. Many of these were short-lived, but one of the most successful groups was the thecodonts [2].

Thecodonts and dinosaurs

Some of the thecodonts—the name means "socket-toothed" and refers to their dental arrangement—stood on their hind limbs and adopted a semi-upright mode of movement balanced by a long tail. This freed the forelimbs for other purposes such as grasping, although the animal could have resumed a four-footed stance when resting. The thecodonts were small creatures but they were to evolve into some of the biggest animals that ever lived—the dinosaurs.

The word *dinosaur*, meaning "terrible lizard," was coined by the pioneer paleontologist Richard Owen, in 1842, to describe a number of reptilian finds that were coming to light in England at that time. "Dinosaur" is no longer a precise term scientifically, but is a convenient category that includes the orders Saurischia and Ornithischia.

The Saurischia—meaning "lizard hips"—are so named because the bones of the hip resemble those of a lizard [3]. The group is subdivided according to the arrangement of the bones of the feet—theropods had feet superficially like mammals and sauropod feet resembled those of lizards. The theropods were the two-legged, meat-eating dinosaurs and they appeared in

CONNECTIONS

See also
410 The world before man
560 Fossils: the life of the past
572 The age of reptiles
520 The life of reptiles
522 Snakes, lizards, and turtles
408 Evolution of life

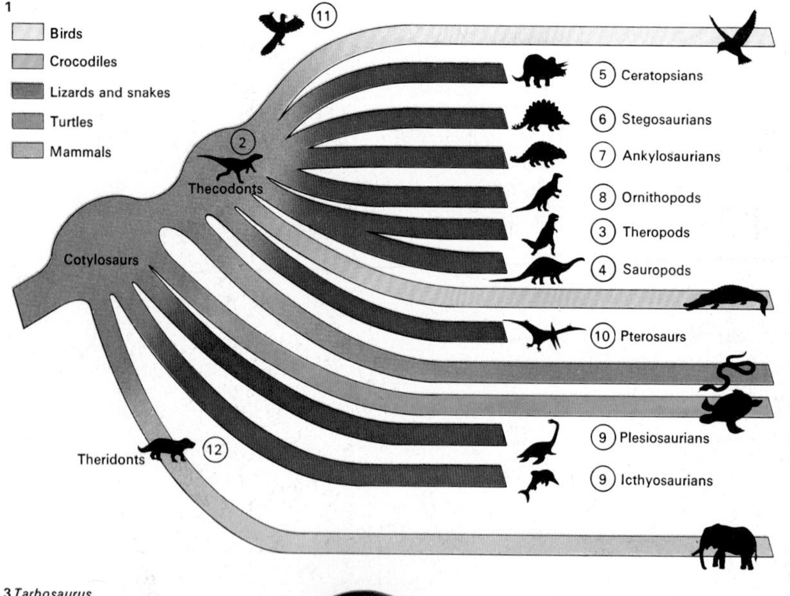
1
Birds
Crocodiles
Lizards and snakes
Turtles
Mammals
11
2
Thecodonts
Cotylosaurs
5 Ceratopsians
6 Stegosaurians
7 Ankylosaurians
8 Ornithopods
3 Theropods
4 Sauropods
10 Pterosaurs
9 Plesiosaurians
9 Icthyosaurians
Theridonts
12

1 The diversification of reptiles from the most primitive amphibianlike cotylosaurs took place in the Upper Paleozoic and gave rise to the thecodonts and other groups, living and extinct.

2 *Scleromochlus*

2 The thecodonts, or "socket-toothed reptiles," were fairly small lizardlike animals that gave rise to some of the strangest beasts that ever lived. Some adopted a two-legged stance, leaving the forelimbs free. This is evident in many of their descendants and although most of the dinosaurs reverted to a four-footed stance, their forelimbs remained short. The thecodont *Scleromochlus* had a length of 39in (1m).

3 *Tarbosaurus*
4
Atlantosaurus

3 The theropods were great carnivorous, lizard-hipped dinosaurs. The terrifying *Tarbosaurus* was 40 ft (12m) long.

4 The sauropods, herbivorous dinosaurs of the end of the Jurassic, were the largest beasts ever to live on land. *Atlantosaurus (Apatosaurus* or *Brontosaurus)* was 66ft (20m) long.

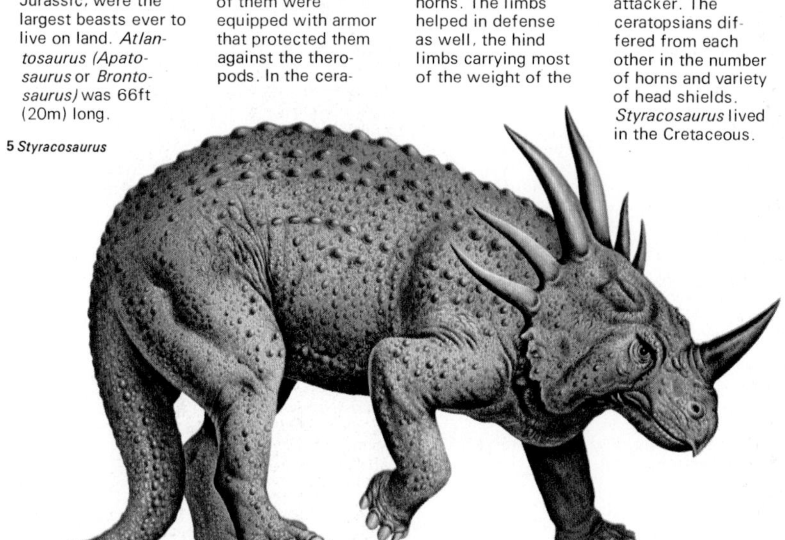
5 *Styracosaurus*

5 The bird-hipped dinosaurs were herbivorous and most of them were equipped with armor that protected them against the theropods. In the ceratopsians the armor took the form of head shield and horns. The limbs helped in defense as well, the hind limbs carrying most of the weight of the body and the forelimbs turning it quickly to face an attacker. The ceratopsians differed from each other in the number of horns and variety of head shields. *Styracosaurus* lived in the Cretaceous.

a great variety of sizes: *Podokesaurus* was chicken-sized, whereas at the other end of the scale *Tyrannosaurus* and *Tarbosaurus* were 40 ft (12 m) long. The sauropods were the huge, long-necked vegetarian dinosaurs that flourished in the upper Jurassic and lower Cretaceous [4]. *Diplodocus* was 82 ft (25m) long; *Brachiosaurus* weighed 50 tons.

The herbivores and early birds

The Ornithischia—meaning "bird hips" —had hip bones arranged like those of a bird and were herbivores. They are classified into four groups. Ceratopsia [5], rhinoceroslike with an arrangement of armor on the head, lived in the upper Cretaceous. *Triceratops* was typical of this group, with three forward-pointing horns and a bony neck frill. Stegosauria were late Jurassic and early Cretaceous forms that had armor mounted vertically down the back. *Kentrurosaurus* was similar to *Stegosaurus* [6] but had an armor of spines rather than plates. The Ankylosauria, squat creatures from the upper Cretaceous, had a tight mosaic of armor plates upon their backs and *Ankylosaurus* [7] had a bony club on the end of its tail. The last of the four Ornithischia groups, the Ornithopoda [8], differed from the other three in having a bipedal stance and a lack of armor. Several of these—among them the duck-billed *Anatosaurus*—possessed features that suggest that they were semiaquatic.

Some experts believe that the dinosaurs and other fossil reptiles, including the flying pterosaurs [10], were warm-blooded and more like mammals than reptiles in their behavior. If so, the restorations should show the animals in a more active stance.

The first birds [11] may have evolved from semi-upright thecodonts and—if the warm blood theory is correct—it seems likely that feathers were first developed from scales for insulation and that the power of flight came later.

Some offshoots of the cotylosaurs returned to the sea [9]. But the most significant offshoot was that which first produced mammallike reptiles with mammallike teeth and limbs, and finally in the Triassic the first primitive mammals.

KEY

Era	Period	Millions of years ago
Cenozoic	Quaternary	2
	Tertiary	65
Mesozoic	Cretaceous	135
	Jurassic	195
	Triassic	225
Palaeozoic	Permian	280
	Carboniferous	345
	Devonian	395
	Silurian	430
	Ordovician	500
	Cambrian	570
	Precambrian	

Invertebrates, Fish, Amphibians, Reptiles, Birds, Mammals

6 The armor of the stegosaurians, as in *Stegosaurus*, consisted of a double row of bony plates mounted vertically along the spine. These beasts lived in the Upper Jurassic.

6 *Stegosaurus*

7 The ankylosaurians were also a heavily armored group but they were squat animals and their armor was arranged as a compact mosaic over their backs. Some form of weapon was usually present on the tail. The 20ft (6m) *Scolosaurus* lived in the Upper Cretaceous.

7 *Scolosaurus*

8 *Iguanodon*

8 The ornithopods were bipedal, herbivorous, bird-hipped dinosaurs that usually lacked armor. *Iguanodon* of the Lower Cretaceous was 33 ft (10m) long.

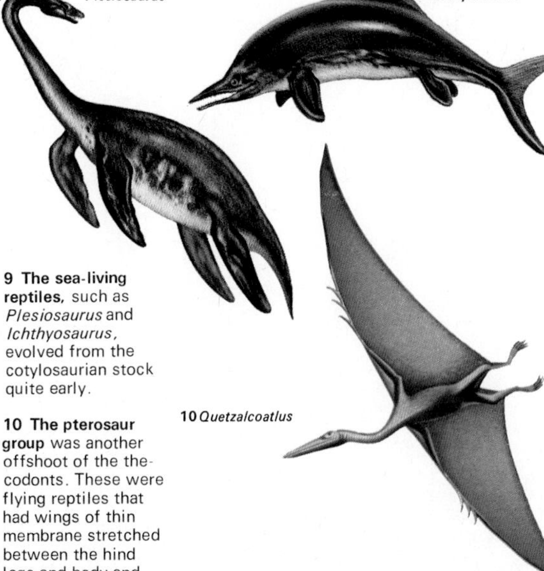

9 *Plesiosaurus* *Ichthyosaurus*

10 *Quetzalcoatlus*

9 The sea-living reptiles, such as *Plesiosaurus* and *Ichthyosaurus*, evolved from the cotylosaurian stock quite early.

10 The pterosaur group was another offshoot of the thecodonts. These were flying reptiles that had wings of thin membrane stretched between the hind legs and body and extended fourth digit in the forelimb. This enormous form recently found from the Upper Cretaceous was named in 1975. Its wing span was 50 ft (15m).

11 Archaeopteryx was the earliest known recognizable bird and dates from the Upper Jurassic. The presence of wings and feathers defines it as a bird, but the skeleton is quite reptilian. The wings, instead of being the specialized flying limbs of modern birds, were really elongated thecodont forelimbs, complete with claws. The tail was a lizard's tail and the skull had teeth. The small breastbone shows it was a poor flyer. It is believed to be descended from bipedal, running and climbing thecodonts.

11 *Archaeopteryx*

12 A

12 The line of the theriodonts, mammallike reptiles, formed an early and important offshoot from the primitive cotylosaurs. They resembled the mammals in their teeth, limbs, and stance. Many types have been found, ranging from reptiles with some mammal traits, such as *Titanophoneus* [A], to virtual mammals, like *Oligokyphus* [B].

B

The age of reptiles

The age of reptiles began about 225 million years ago and ended, for no known reason, about 65 million years ago. The Mesozoic era, as it is called, was made up of the Triassic, Jurassic, and Cretaceous periods. During that time reptiles dominated land, sea, and sky, and evolved into what were some of the largest land animals that ever lived—the mighty dinosaurs.

Reptiles return to the sea

The oldest period of the Mesozoic, the Triassic [1], saw a perpetuation of the desert environment established during the preceding Permian period. Mountain ranges that had arisen during the Permian in the Northern Hemisphere were worn down to arid hills and plains with scattered salt lakes. Plant life differed little from that of the previous era, consisting mostly of ferns and horsetails in the moist areas and conifers such as *Voltzia* and *Araucarites*, which resembled modern monkey-puzzle trees, on the drier hill slopes. While the desert environment had changed little, this was not true of its inhabitants. The complex interaction of living things that prevailed in the oceans during the Paleozoic was swept away and replaced by a new order of existence. The cephalopods of the time—early relatives of modern squids and octopuses—had developed into ammonoids, an advanced group with bodies encased in chambered shells that was to dominate the seas of the Mesozoic.

In the seas and estuaries aquatic reptiles were becoming prominent. Some groups that had evolved from amphibians to lead a totally dry-land existence found it advantageous to return to the sea. As a result, they adopted aquatic features, such as webbed feet and streamlined bodies, that enabled them to exploit their ancestral environment as expertly as their fish forebears.

On land, the reptiles were extremely versatile. *Kuehneosaurus* even took to the air on primitive gliding wings. The mammals had evolved, but they were tiny and left few remains. Among the land-dwelling reptiles was a lizardlike creature, a thecodont, no bigger than a turkey, that began to walk on its hind legs, leaving its forelimbs free for grasping or balancing. This small creature was the ancestor of the great dinosaurs that were to dominate the Earth.

During the Jurassic period [2, 3], about 190 million years ago, the single large continent that had been in existence during most of the Upper Paleozoic was splitting up due to continuing continental drift. The main crack ran from north to south, eventually widening to become the Atlantic Ocean, with Europe first separating from North America, followed by Africa from South America. Humid climates returned to the continents and lush vegetation grew over most of the world.

The coming of the dinosaurs

The jungles of the Jurassic consisted mostly of ferns and tree ferns, with stands of conifers. The Bennettitales—gymnosperms that resembled cycads—with their thick, stumpy trunks and crowns of fernlike leaves, provided the closest things to flowers—rosettes of seed-bearing cones. Reed beds of horsetails grew by the shallow waters. These were the jungles in which the

CONNECTIONS

See also
570 Reptiles of the past
410 The world before man
560 Fossils: the life of the past
520 The life of reptiles
522 Snakes, lizards, and turtles
408 Evolution of life

1
8
7
1
6
2
3
9
4
11
10
5

1 Central Europe in Triassic times was covered by a shallow, limy sea surrounded by low-lying desert plains. The animal life in this sea was completely different from earlier kinds. The sudden diversification of the reptiles that was taking place on land was evident in the sea as well and several groups adopted features that equipped them for a sea-going existence. *Placodus* [1] retained a familiar reptilian shape but had webbed feet and a flattened tail to help it to swim and rounded, knoblike teeth for crushing shellfish. It attained a length of 6.5ft (2m). *Nothosaurus* [2] belonged to the group ancestral to the sea-living plesiosaurs of the Jurassic and Cretaceous and showed an elongation of the neck and a shortening of the tail, both plesiosaur features. It ate fish and had a length of 10ft (3m). Most fishlike was the 6.5ft (2m) *Mixosaurus* [3], an early ichthyosaur. It had limbs modified into paddles and the start of a fishlike tail and dorsal fin. These creatures fed on fish such as *Thoracopterus* [4], a flying fish, and *Semionotus* [5]. The invertebrate fauna was typical of the Mesozoic, with the ammonoids, cephalopods with coiled shells, very much in evidence. They differed from one another by the ornamentation on the shells, *Cladiscites* [6] having longitudinal ribs and *Trachyceras* [7] transverse ribs. Shellfish were a mixture of brachiopods like *Coenothyris* [8] and *Tetractinella* [9], and bivalves such as *Miophoria* [10]. Sea lilies like *Encrinites* [11] flourished. The bodies of these creatures were buried in the limy mud of the sea bottom, which was later solidified into limestone, then raised to form the Alps. These organisms were found fossilized in northern Italy and represent an important scientific find.

2
11
7
5
9
8
3
2
4
10
1
6
12

2 In the region of Bavaria during the Jurassic period there was a series of islands and quiet, shallow lagoons. Fine-grained limestone was slowly precipitated in them, preserving the remains of animals and plants that lived in the area. The most significant fossil from these deposits is *Archaeopteryx* [1]. This is regarded as the first bird because it had wings and feathers, but some experts claim it was a reptile because of its lizard-like skull, tail, and fingers. Also flying above the lagoons were pterosaurs, the gliding reptiles such as *Pterodactylus* [2] and the long-tailed *Rhamphorhynchus* [3]. They ranged in size between that of a sparrow and of an eagle. *Archaeopteryx* was crow-sized. The sea abounded in swimming reptiles that were even better adapted to life in the sea than those of the Triassic. These included *Ichthyosaurus* [4], which was fish-shaped, *Plesiosaurus* [5], with its long neck, and *Steneosaurus* [6], a sea crocodile. Up to 23ft (7m) long, they ate fish such as the early banjo fish [7], *Macrosemius* [8] and *Mesodon* [9]. Also in the lagoons lived squidlike belemnoids [10] and lobsters, prawns, and king crabs. In the undergrowth of the islands and along the mud banks of the shoreline ran the smallest dinosaur, *Compsognathus*, [11] which was the size of a chicken, and *Homoeosaurus* [12], a lizardlike creature related to the modern tuatara.

great dinosaurs of the Jurassic period lived. There was ample vegetation to support the herbivorous sauropods and bird-hipped dinosaurs, which were preyed upon by the carnivorous theropods. Also present were the gliding pterosaurs, crocodiles, and the early mammals.

Most of the remains of those ancient land creatures that can be seen in museums today were preserved because they fell into water and were buried by sediments when they died. Such a rare and fortunate combination of circumstances occurred in Bavaria where, in Upper Jurassic times, fine-grained limestone was gently precipitated into shallow lagoons. The animal and plant life preserved by this process has provided a full picture of the specialization of reptiles into an abundance of swimming and flying types, from fishlike icthyosaurs to the appearance of the first true bird.

Last of the dinosaurs

The Cretaceous period [4, 5], which began about 135 million years ago, was a time of spreading, shallow seas. There the swimming reptiles reached the peak of their dominance, as did the ammonoids. On land, ferns and cycads gave way to the more familiar willow, maple, and oak. These lands supported the last and greatest of the dinosaurs. Flying reptiles also grew to enormous sizes at the end of the period and one pterosaur had a wing span of 50ft.

At the end of the Cretaceous period a number of sweeping changes took place in the Earth's animal life. The dinosaurs died out, as did the specialized swimming and flying reptiles, together with the ammonoids and belemnoids. Nobody knows why this happened although many theories have been advanced to account for it. The most plausible explanation is that the environments, after tens of millions of years of stability, began to change, draining the swamps, altering the climate and modifying vegetation. The dinosaurs were unable to adapt to the radically new life demanded of them. Whatever the reason, the reptilian life of the Mesozoic became extinct more than 65 million years ago, leaving the mammals to emerge into dominance.

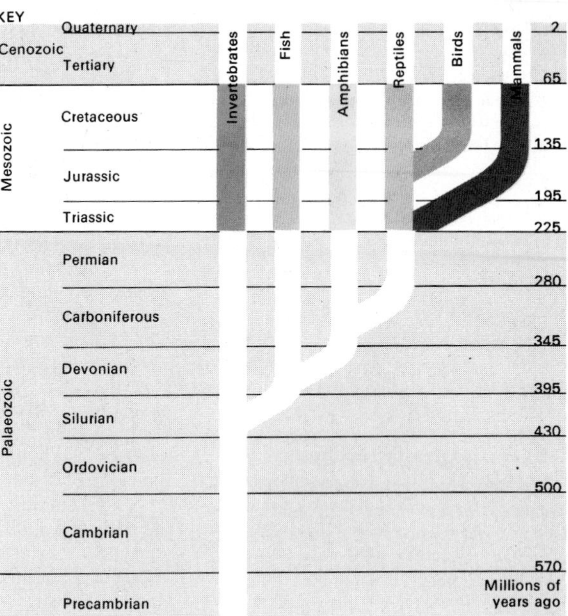
KEY
Cenozoic
Quaternary
Tertiary
Mesozoic
Cretaceous
Jurassic
Triassic
Palaeozoic
Permian
Carboniferous
Devonian
Silurian
Ordovician
Cambrian
Precambrian
Invertebrates
Fish
Amphibians
Reptiles
Birds
Mammals
2
65
135
195
225
280
345
395
430
500
570
Millions of years ago

3 In the Upper Jurassic of North America there is a sequence of rocks called the Morrison formation that is famous for the bones of giant dinosaurs found in it. During the Upper Jurassic the Rocky Mountains were just beginning to rise and material washed off them was spread by sluggish, winding streams to form a low fertile plain to the east. The sandspits and mudbanks of these rivers, destined to form the rocks of the Morrison formation, gave rise to a lush vegetation of horsetails [1], ferns, cycadlike plants, and conifers. Among these browsed the herbivorous dinosaurs, which were preyed on by the theropods. The most common plants were conifers [2], tree ferns [3], *Williamsonia* [4] and other Bennettitales [5], and the ginkgo tree [6], which was widespread at that time. The herbivorous dinosaurs that fed on them included the huge sauropods *Atlantosaurus (Apatosaurus* or *Brontosaurus)* [7] and *Camarasaurus* [8], the armored *Stegosaurus* [9] and the ornithopod *Camptosaurus* [10]. These were preyed on by the theropod *Antrodemus* (or *Allosaurus*) [11] and crocodiles [12] that were very like modern types. Primitive mammals [13] were present, but were still small and insignificant.

4 The Cretaceous landscape of North America differed from the Jurassic in that modern trees began to replace the forests of ferns and Bennettitales. The animal life, however, did not undergo any major change and the dinosaurs were still the dominant life form. Although many of these became truly enormous, some of them were of quite modest size. On land were the horned dinosaurs, the ceratopsians, ranging in size from *Triceratops* [1], 23ft (7m), to *Brachyceratops* [2], 6.5ft (2m). The theropods that fed on them were huge like *Tyrannosaurus* [3] at 39ft (12m), but there were also small theropods. *Ornithomimus* [4] was 13ft (4m) long and built like an ostrich. It probably fed on small lizards and eggs. They lived at the end of the Cretaceous just before the dinosaurs died out.

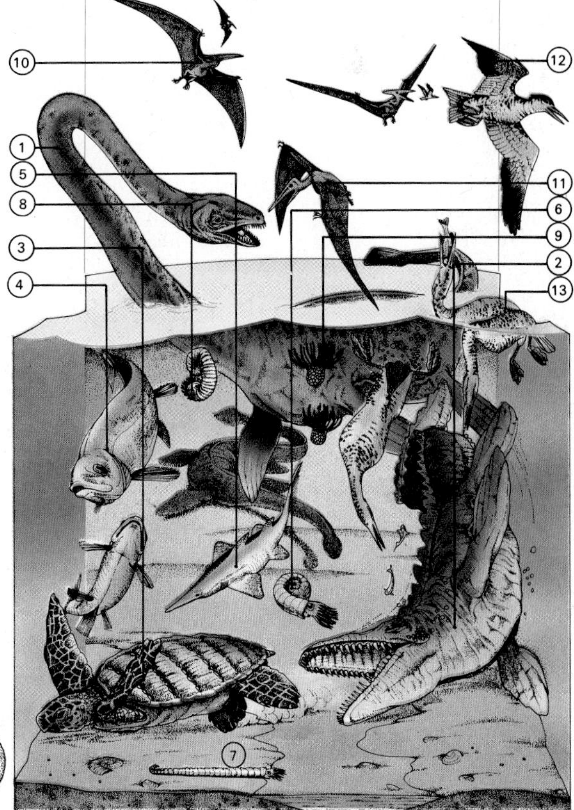

5 The seas of the Cretaceous period were rich in microscopic limy algae, the shells of which accumulated on the sea floor to form great deposits of chalk. The greatest sea creatures of the time were the reptiles: the 50ft (15m) plesiosaur *Elasmosaurus* [1], 66% of which was neck, the great mosasaur *Tylosaurus* [2], and the turtle with a 10ft (3m) shell *(Archelon)* [3]. Fish included the 10ft (3m) long herring *Portheus* [4] and the living "ghost shark" *Scapanorhynchus* [5]. Ammonoids such as *Acanthoceras* [6], *Baculites* [7], and *Scaphites* [8] still existed. The sea-lily *Uintacrinus* [9] was free-swimming. Above soared the pterosaurs *Pteranodon* [10] and *Nyctosaurus* [11]. Specialized sea birds like *Ichthyornis* [12] and flightless *Hesperornis* [13] existed.

Mammals of the past

In the early days of reptile evolution during the Permian and Triassic periods, the line was established that was to lead to the mammals and eventually to humans. The line was established by certain reptiles with features that later came to characterize the mammals.

Mammalian characteristics

These mammalian characteristics include warm-bloodedness and hair (unfortunately impossible to determine from fossil evidence), which are both temperature-regulating systems. A reptile can operate only with short bursts of activity followed by long periods of rest. A mammal, on the other hand, can live a continuously active existence. To support this it needs more food and a more efficient digestive system; thus different cutting, tearing, and chewing teeth evolved. The secondary palate appeared, enabling an animal to eat and breathe at the same time. Each half of the lower jaw became a single solid bone and an advanced hinge permitted a more precise chewing action. With this simplification of the jaw, the bones "left over" from the old reptile lower jaw were incorporated into the ear and made hearing more efficient. But the most significant difference between mammals and reptiles is in reproduction. A mammal bears its young alive in a more or less fit state to face the world. In contrast, reptile development usually takes place in an unprotected egg.

Ancient mammalian groups

Despite the advantages conferred by mammalian anatomy and physiology, the new line did not catch on for some 160 million years. During the Mesozoic the mammals existed in several orders, all of which consisted of small creatures resembling shrews. These differed from one another in their teeth, but very little is known about them for their remains are scattered and fragmentary. They suffered a fate similar to that of the early reptiles—extinction—and only one line really came to anything. These were the pantotheres that gave rise to the marsupial and placental mammals. One of the ancient groups is represented today by the monotremes—the echidna and duck-billed platypus. These are true mammals, although they lay eggs.

The extinction of most orders of reptiles at the end of the Mesozoic left the environments empty and the small mammals expanded and diversified to fill the void. They produced hoofed animals to browse the forest and graze the plains, carnivores to feed on the herbivores, rodents to live in the undergrowth, primates to climb trees, bats to fly, and whales to swim in the seas, while the original mode of life was continued by the insectivores. All this evolutionary advance took place within a few million years of the extinction of the great reptiles.

Tracing the evolutionary lines

This spectacular evolution of the mammals began in the Tertiary period a mere 65 million years ago, so the remains of the extinct mammals tend to be better preserved than those of the great reptiles that preceded them, and evolutionary lines of the horses are well known, from the tiny *Hyracotherium* (formerly *Eohippus*) to the

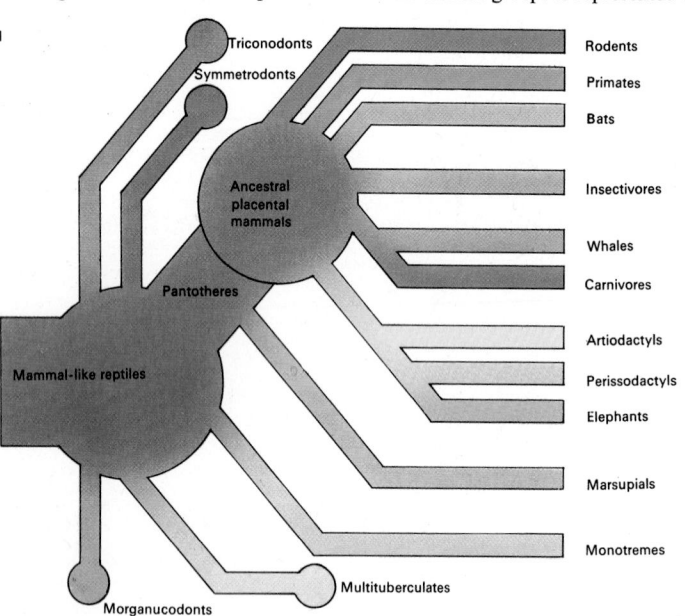

CONNECTIONS

See also
576 The age of mammals
408 Evolution of life
410 The world before ma
560 Fossils: the life of th past
646 Primate to hominid
540 The classification of mammals
542 The life of mammals
546 Rodents, insect-eaters, and bats
554 Primates; relatives o man
578 Regions of the earth zoogeography

1

Triconodonts
Symmetrodonts
Ancestral placental mammals
Pantotheres
Mammal-like reptiles
Morganucodonts
Multituberculates
Rodents
Primates
Bats
Insectivores
Whales
Carnivores
Artiodactyls
Perissodactyls
Elephants
Marsupials
Monotremes
Living mammal groups

1 Mammals evolved in the Triassic from reptiles with mammallike characteristics. They formed several groups, each possibly descended from different lines. Of these groups all but two have died out; one of those – the monotremes – has only two living examples, the platypus and the echidna. The other group, the pantotheres, has diversified into a wide range of marsupial and placental mammals. Little is known about the other early groups because fossils are rare; they remain small, enigmatic creatures differing from each other in the shape and the arrangement of their teeth.

2 *Megazostrodon*

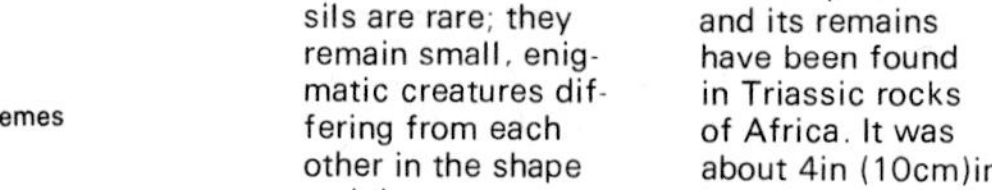

2 Megazostrodon was one of the earliest pantotheres and its remains have been found in Triassic rocks of Africa. It was about 4in (10cm) in length and was built rather like a reptile. It can be regarded as being very close to the ancestor of modern mammals. Its appearance was typical of that of all primitive mammals during the time of reptile dominance.

3 The marsupials, a group of mammals that carry their young in pouches, developed early and some grew to a large size. *Diprotodon* was a Pleistocene wombat as large as a grizzly bear.

4 The rhinoceros group is a division of the perissodactyls (odd-toed ungulates) that has existed for a long time. The earliest known is *Hyrachyus* [A], a dog-sized creature from the Eocene. This developed into *Baluchitherium* [B], the largest land mammal ever, 16ft (5m) high. Later members, such as the woolly rhinoceros [C], were the size of today's rhinoceros.

3 *Diprotodon*

4

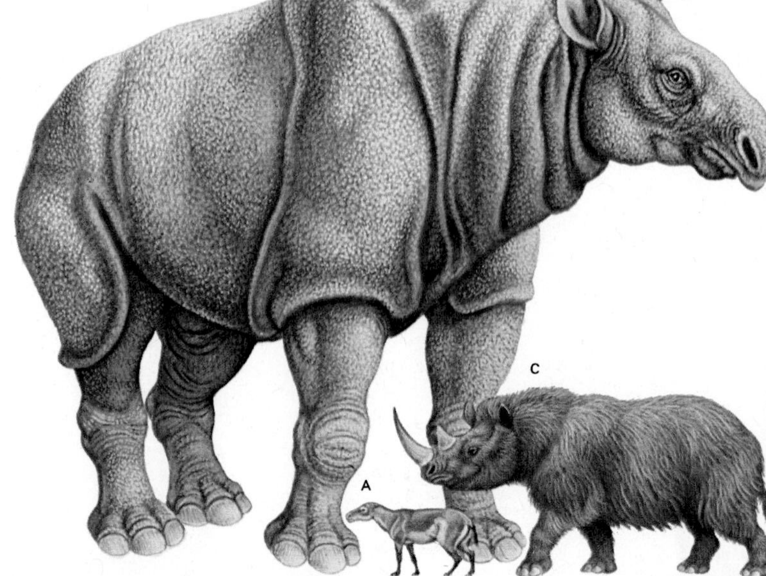

B
C
A

present-day *Equus*. The evolution of the titanotheres—elephant-sized rhinoceros-like herbivores—can be traced from the dog-sized *Eotitanops* of the Eocene to the massive *Brontotherium* that lived just before the extinction of the line some 40 million years later. But most evolutionary lines cannot be followed directly and only the remains of creatures that were offshoots from the main branch have been found. Many of the offshoots, such as rhinoceroses and elephants, specialized in widely differing modes of life.

Certain mammals, however, showed what is known as convergent evolution, in which unrelated creatures adopt similar life-styles and evolve to look like one another. *Coryphodon* of the Eocene behaved and looked like the hippopotamus but was not related to it. *Stenomylus* was a camel that looked more like a gazelle.

Carnivores as we know them developed in Oligocene times, quite late in the history of mammals. They were preceded by the archaic carnivores—the creodonts—which were quite generalized meat-eating creatures. These probably gave rise to the whales as well as to the advanced carnivores such as the great wolves and cave bears of the Quaternary. Most of the cats throughout the Tertiary and Quaternary (such as *Hoplophoneus* of the Oligocene and *Smilodon* of the Pleistocene) had long saberlike teeth as their weapons. With these they made powerful slashing attacks, wounding their victims so deeply that they bled to death. This was an efficient way of killing the large, thick-skinned animals that abounded at that time. Modern cats, on the other hand, have smaller teeth and can run down fast grazing animals and kill them by breaking their necks.

An extinct side branch from the ungulate stock gave rise to the uintatheres—rhinoceroslike animals with six horns and powerful tusks. Chalicotheres were horse-like creatures with claws instead of hoofs.

The primates developed rapidly during the Tertiary from tree shrews and tarsierlike creatures in the Eocene, through lemurs to monkeys and apes in the late Tertiary. One of these lines developed into man.

KEY
Ceno-zoic
Mesozoic
Palaeozoic
Quaternary 2
Tertiary 65
Cretaceous 135
Jurassic 195
Triassic 225
Permian 280
Carboniferous 345
Devonian 395
Silurian 430
Ordovician 500
Cambrian 570
Precambrian
Invertebrates
Fish
Amphibians
Reptiles
Birds
Mammals
Millions of years ago

5 Extinct elephants differed from each other in the shape of the head. After the tapirlike Eocene ancestral *Moeritherium* [A], the body size soon reached that of today's elephants. *Trilophodon* [B], from the Miocene, had four tusks. The Miocene *Deinotherium* [C] had a pair of downward curving tusks in the lower jaw, and *Platybelodon* [D], also from the Miocene, had its lower tusks expanded and flattened into a kind of shovel for scooping waterweed. *Mammuthus* [E], the Pleistocene woolly mammoth, was adapted to cold.

5
A
B
C
D
E

6 The armadillo family was represented in the Pleistocene by glyptodonts such as 10ft (3m) long *Daedicurus*, which was heavily armored and carried a bony club on the end of its heavy tail.

7 Brontotherium resembled a rhinoceros but was not closely related, being a member of the extinct titanotheres. It stood *c.* 10ft (3m) high and lived in the Oligocene.

8 Sivatherium was a giraffe, although it looked more like a moose than today's giraffes. It was heavily built and carried two pairs of horns on its head, a small pair above the eyes and a large pair farther back.

6 Glyptodont
Doedicurus

7 *Brontotherium platyceras*

8 *Sivatherium*

9 *Oxyaena*

9 Carnivorous mammals evolved to feed on the newly developed herbivorous mammals. The early carnivores, called creodonts, were quite unlike any we know today. They included animals such as *Oxyaena*. It was not until late in the Eocene or the Oligocene that the more modern carnivores, replaced them. These carnivores were, even then, divided into the groups that are now familiar—cats, dogs, raccoons, civets, and weasels. *Ursus spelaeus*, the cave bear, was one of the larger Pleistocene carnivores but modified its feeding habits and lived on roots and nuts. A very different descendant of the creodonts is the whale. It adopted its fishlike form rapidly, as in the Eocene *Zeuglodon*, but has since evolved socially and mentally.

Cave bear
Ursus spelaeus

Zeuglodon

10 Primates began to evolve from Cretaceous insectivores that resembled tree shrews. *Notharctus* was an Eocene lemur on the road to man.

10 *Notharctus*

The age of mammals

Earth's most recent geological history, the last 65 million years or so, is known as the Cenozoic era and is made up of the Tertiary and Quaternary periods. During that time landforms and climates changed slowly to what they are now.

Mammals make their bow

The first 27 million years of the Tertiary are made up of the Paleocene and Eocene [1] epochs. It was during this time that mammals first began to play a dominant role in the life of the planet. The complete extinction of the great reptiles of the Mesozoic left the forests and plains deserted; as a result, the then humble mammal evolved within a few million years into a vast number of different forms that could make full use of the empty environments. The first mammals appeared in the Triassic. These were tiny animals known principally from their teeth—their fragile bones are rarely preserved. After these came the marsupials (pouched animals) and the placentals (animals that are nourished inside the mother's body). The placentals became dominant in the early Tertiary. So rapid was their evolution that all modern groups of mammals were represented by the Eocene, including marine kinds such as whales and flying kinds such as bats. Birds also began to resemble their modern counterparts, although some became highly specialized and developed into creatures such as the ferocious, flightless, 6ft (1.8m) high *Diatryma*, which must have behaved like the smaller carnivorous dinosaurs. Bivalves and gastropods such as we have today appeared in the seas together with modern types of fish.

The Oligocene, which embraced the next 10 million years of the Tertiary, provided a continuation of the Eocene environment during which basic stocks of animal life became specialized. Horses, which appeared early in the Eocene in the form of *Hyracotherium (Eohippus),* remained as forest-dwelling browsers but became a little larger. Rhinoceroslike creatures appeared such as *Arsinoitherium,* which had two small horns above the eyes and an enormous pair pointing forward above the nose, and the titanotheres, which were the size of elephants and carried great Y-shaped horns on their noses. These creatures only superficially resembled the true rhinoceroses that roamed the plains at this time.

Runners of the plains

During the next 13 million years—the Miocene [2]—the climate became more temperate. Grasslands flourished as the forests dwindled, and more animals became adapted to life in the open. Horses became longer legged and their toes, which originally had numbered four in front and three behind, became fewer. In this way the animals became adapted to running on the plains, while their teeth became more suitable for eating grass than leaves. An Eocene camel, *Protylopus,* had been about the same size as the first horse. But in the Miocene, along with other running creatures, camels grew leggier and better adapted to the plains. This was a time of upheaval in the earth. The Alps and Himalayas were being pushed up, the Andes were still rising and there was volcanic activity in North America.

CONNECTIONS

See also
574 Mammals of the past
560 Fossils: the life of the past
410 The world before man
408 Evolution of life
540 The classification of mammals
542 The life of mammals
556 How mammals behave
646 Primate to hominid

1

1 In Eocene times much of the Northern Hemisphere was a subtropical lowland supporting swamps of modern plants such as swamp cypress [2], nipa palm [5], sabal palm [10] and magnolia [3]. Mammals had become common by this time. In detail they might have looked odd to us, but in general their shapes and life styles would not have differed much from today's animals. The hippopotamuslike *Coryphodon* [6] lived on river banks and fed on the roots torn up by its powerful tusks. In the forests lived the tiny early horse *Hyracotherium* [8] that had a height of about 12in (30cm) at the shoulder. It was adapted for life in the undergrowth and its teeth were suitable for cropping leaves rather than grass. The birds, too, had spread and evolved into types that would be recognized today. *Halcyornis* [1] was a kingfisher that lived above the waters of the swamps and streams. *Lithornis* [11] was a vulture that was very similar to the vultures flying today. The gannetlike *Odontopteryx* [9] was a coastal bird that fed on sea fish. Its beak was serrated with rows of barbs that resembled sharp teeth. Nobody knows for certain what color these birds were. The colors shown here are purely guesswork and based on the plumage of related modern birds. After the great reptiles of the Mesozoic had disappeared, only the more humble forms, such as lizards and snakes, lived on. In this particular area the remains of crocodiles [4] and the river turtle *Podocnemis* [7] have been found. Both these animals were virtually identical with types that are found in present-day rivers and swamps.

After the Miocene came the Pliocene, lasting about 10 million years. The huge, unwieldy mammals of earlier ages had died out and the animals that replaced them looked very much like the kinds we know today. The most important innovation toward the end of the Pliocene was the appearance of an early hominid, *Australopithecus,* who walked upright on the plains of Africa and used simple tools.

The coming of the ice ages

The lowering of temperatures at the end of the Pliocene heralded the coming of the Pleistocene [3] ice ages about two million years ago. This was also the beginning of the Quaternary period—the age of man. The glaciers came and went four times in response to a changing climate and the animal life of the Northern Hemisphere had to adapt to it. The animals living in what are now temperate latitudes were Arctic forms with thick fur and were able to subsist on conifers, birches, and lichens. The woolly mammoth, the mastodon, and the woolly rhinoceros lived in this manner and fell prey to early man with his hunting skills. South of the ice sheets, *Smilodon,* a saber-toothed "tiger," wrought havoc among the heavy, slow-moving ground sloths and the mastodons. Glacial conditions did not affect the whole of the world, nor were they continuous even in the glaciated areas. Warm periods occurred between the advances of the ice sheets, and during such times even elephants lived in latitudes as far north as the British Isles.

The Holocene, or Recent, which dates from the end of the Pleistocene, is such a short epoch (about 10,000 years) that it cannot really be regarded as a distinct geological division. The modern pattern of climatic zones with different weather conditions is probably exceptional, and more stable worldwide climatic conditions seem to have existed throughout geological time—for example, during the times when the deserts of the Permian and the forests of the Eocene covered the land. The last ice sheet has barely receded and there is a distinct possibility that today's environment is merely another Pleistocene interglacial stage.

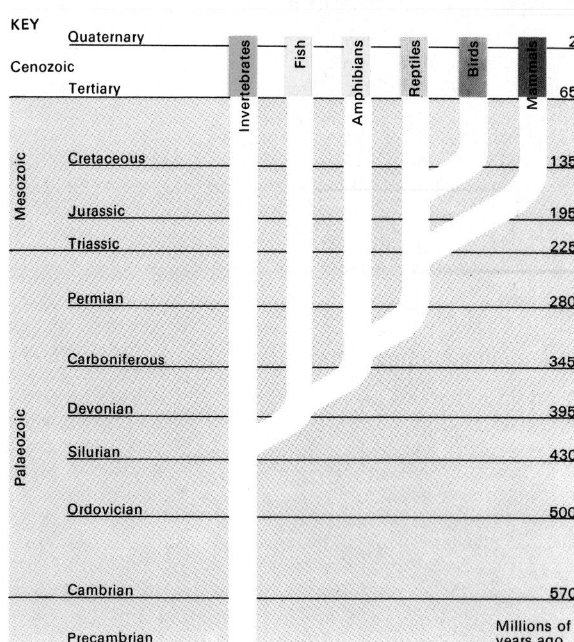
KEY
Cenozoic
Quaternary
Tertiary
Mesozoic
Cretaceous
Jurassic
Triassic
Palaeozoic
Permian
Carboniferous
Devonian
Silurian
Ordovician
Cambrian
Precambrian
Invertebrates
Fish
Amphibians
Reptiles
Birds
Mammals
2
65
135
195
225
280
345
395
430
500
570
Millions of years ago

2 During the Miocene the forests that were typical of the lower Tertiary thinned out and were replaced by open grasslands. Running animals roamed these plains in herds. The plains of the lower Miocene of North America looked very much like the savannas of today. The Rocky Mountains were still being pushed up and this process was accompanied by great volcanic activity. Primitive horses had evolved into *Parahippus* [1], which showed a reduction of toes to three on each foot (from the original four on the forefeet), and an adaptation of teeth to grazing. *Dinohyus* [2] was a pig as large as an ox. A corkscrew-shaped burrow [3], given the name *Daemonelix,* may have been occupied by some kind of rodent not yet identified. *Diceratherium* [4] was a small, two-horned early rhinoceros. *Stenomylus* [5] was a long-necked camel that lived in herds as do today's antelopes. *Moropus* [6] was related to the horse but had claws instead of hooves.

3 A good selection of Pleistocene animals, south of the ice sheets, representative of an almost modern fauna was found in the tar pits of California at Rancho La Brea. These pits trapped unwary creatures and their struggles attracted scavengers and predators that were themselves trapped. Familiar looking animals, such as rabbits, weasels, wolves, horses, bison, and storks died here, as did many creatures that are now extinct such as mammoths.

1 Rabbit *Lepus* sp
2 Weasel *Mustela* sp
3 Giant ground sloth *Paramylodon* sp
4 Lion *Panthera atrox*
5 Mammoth *Mammuthus imperator*
6 Mastodon *Mammut americanus*
7 Stork *Ciconia maltha*
8 Camel *Camelops* sp
9 Dire wolf *Canis dirus*
10 Horse *Equus* sp
11 Bison *Bison antiquus*
12 Sabre-toothed "tiger" *Smilodon* sp
13 Giant condor *Teratornis* sp

Regions of the Earth: zoogeography

Zoogeography is the study of the geographical distribution of animals that attempts to explain why, for example, kangaroos are found only in Australia and ostriches only in Africa. It is broad in its concepts and demands knowledge not only of present-day geography but also of the patterns and timings of changes in the location of land masses during the earth's development.

The drifting continents

The present-day distribution of animal species can be explained largely by the theory of continental drift. According to this theory the continents were once a huge land mass called Pangaea, which—over millions of years—split into parts that drifted to their present positions, taking with them their resident animals.

The theory of continental drift has firm backing in the fossil record. The fossil skull of *Lystrosaurus,* a reptile from the Triassic of over 200 million years ago, has been found in Antarctica. Similar fossils have been found in South Africa and the rock structures in which they were embedded are so closely linked that continental drift is the only plausible explanation.

For convenience of study the earth is divided into six main zoogeographical regions [Key]. The ecological conditions of the regions vary, and even within the same region there may be huge variation. The Palaearctic region, which stretches from the Arctic north of Siberia to the tropical Far East, provides an extreme example of this.

Most animals have precise ecological requirements and for this reason they occupy specific ecological niches. Those with wide tolerances, such as rats, locusts, or starlings, are regarded as pests, while those with narrow tolerances may be rare species. Because many kinds of vegetation are common to all regions, a certain number of common ecological niches are found in all of them. The species of animals filling similar niches vary from region to region, leading to characteristic differences between the fauna of one region and another.

The continents became separate so long ago that in each one evolution has taken place "in parallel." Similar adaptations to similar ecological niches has produced so-called ecological equivalents [3].

Some species are without equivalents because of unsuitable physical and climatic conditions; for example, there are no truly arboreal leaf-eating mammals—the equivalents of the Ethiopian and Neotropical monkeys—in the Palaearctic and Nearctic.

The Australian example

Adaptation and the process of natural selection are the keys to an understanding of zoogeography. Their operation can best be described by the example of the continent of Australia. It broke off from a southern continental land mass, called Gondwanaland, at the end of the Mesozoic era just when the pouch-bearing mammals, the marsupials, were beginning to evolve from a primitive mammalian stock. The island continent drifted eastward and was eventually isolated from the later evolution of the placental mammals that took place farther north, although land bridges may have existed for many millennia between Australia and both

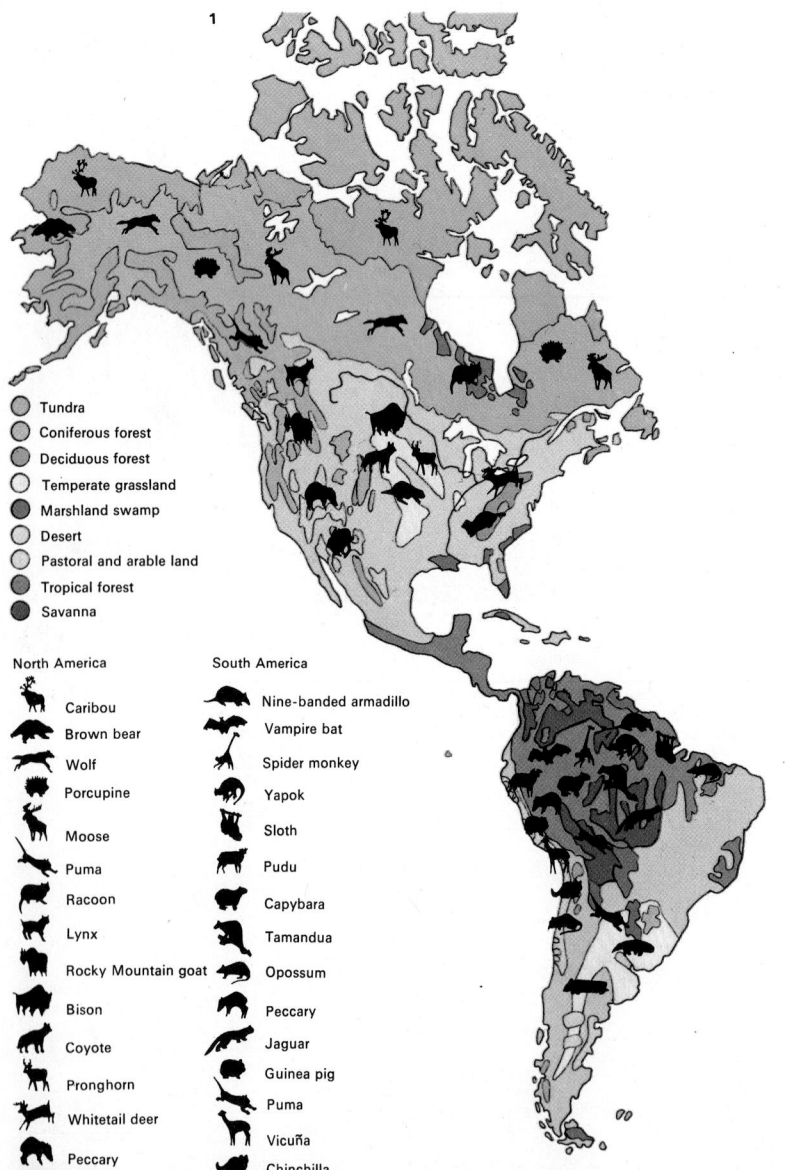

CONNECTIONS

See also
580 The basis of ecology
582 Isolation and evolution
654 Spread of man: 1
458 The animal kingdom
544 Monotremes and marsupials
540 The classification of mammals
418 Evolution: classical theories
420 Evolution in action

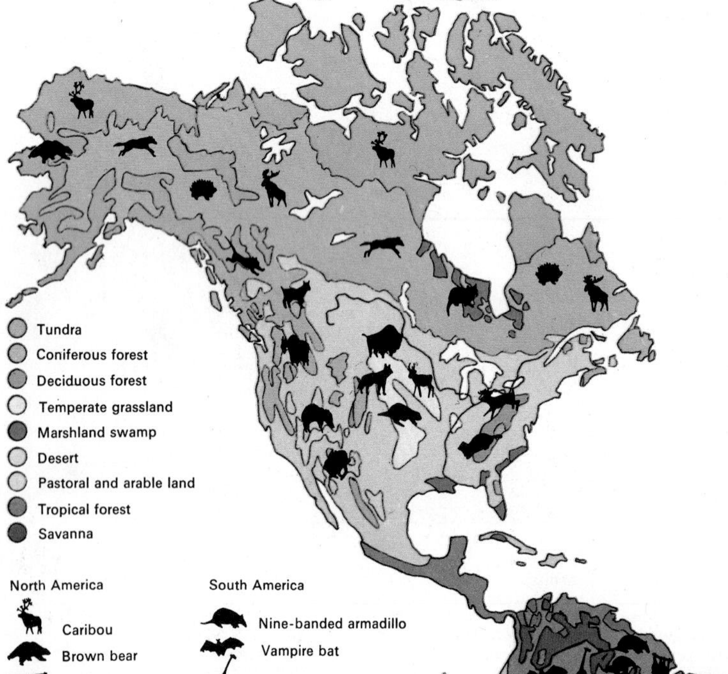

1
Tundra
Coniferous forest
Deciduous forest
Temperate grassland
Marshland swamp
Desert
Pastoral and arable land
Tropical forest
Savanna
North America
Caribou
Brown bear
Wolf
Porcupine
Moose
Puma
Racoon
Lynx
Rocky Mountain goat
Bison
Coyote
Pronghorn
Whitetail deer
Peccary
Prairie dog
Skunk
Cottontail rabbit
South America
Nine-banded armadillo
Vampire bat
Spider monkey
Yapok
Sloth
Pudu
Capybara
Tamandua
Opossum
Peccary
Jaguar
Guinea pig
Puma
Vicuña
Chinchilla
Caenolestes
Giant anteater
Fairy armadillo

1 The Nearctic and Neotropical regions comprise the New World, but are quite distinct from one another. The fauna of North America resembles that of Eurasia—possibly a result of the existence (more than a million years ago) of a land bridge where the Bering Sea is today. Even the most "American" animals betray this ancient tie. The moose *(Alces alces)*, an inhabitant of the coniferous forest belt, is the same species as the European elk. Brown bears *(Ursus arctos)*, of which the grizzly is a particularly large race, are distributed throughout the Northern Hemisphere, and wolves *(Canis lupus)* still roam the forests of North America, Asia, and Europe. South of the Mississippi, the fauna is basically Neotropical because the area was recolonized from South America during the last Ice Age. South America was isolated for much of the Tertiary period. So, in the absence of competition with successive new colonizations, its fauna evolved into countless species found nowhere else. Among the most curious and well known of these unique species are the armadillos, different species of which are to be found both in open grassland and thick cover. All seven species of sloth come from the dense Neotropical forests of South America.

2 Alfred Wallace (1823–1913) gave his name to the Wallace Line, his version of the sea barrier (between the islands of Indonesia) that prevented Australasian and Indo-chinese species from intermingling.

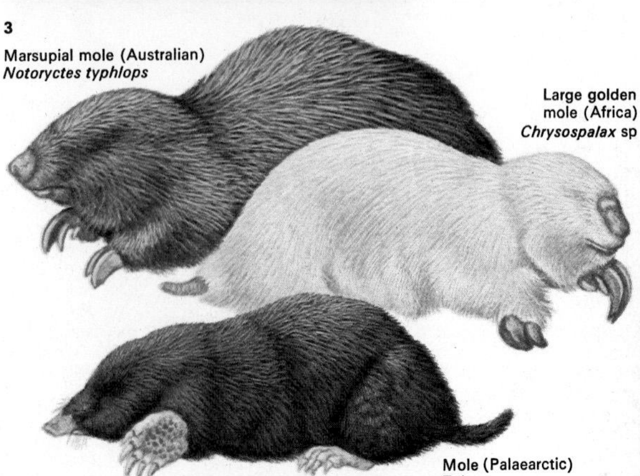

3
Marsupial mole (Australian)
Notoryctes typhlops
Large golden mole (Africa)
Chrysospalax sp
Mole (Palaearctic)
Talpa sp

3 Ecological equivalents of the mole have evolved in Australia and Africa. All have a similar shape of body and foot, but are not closely related. The Australian mole is a marsupial.

South America and Antarctica, which the placentals failed to use.

Faced with a welter of unoccupied niches and no mammalian competitors, the Australian marsupials slowly began to evolve into a mass of forms each suited to a particular niche, a process called adaptive radiation.

The Australian fauna can be described as relict—left behind by the march of evolution because of severe physical barriers that prevented the spread of animals. Today, many islands support relict faunas and the best known of these is Madagascar. Its fauna, rich in primitive mammals, birds, and reptiles, suggests what the fauna of Africa was like many millions of years ago.

Barriers to invasion

Faunal characteristics of regions are maintained by the presence of barriers preventing new invasions. If the barriers remained inviolable from their origins, faunal differences would today be greater than they actually are. But continental shifting of the Earth's crust creates new barriers and destroys old ones. Each destruction allows a new invasion and mixing of species. Since the Pleistocene, which began about two million years ago, the fauna of Britain has received many elements of European fauna because of the temporary existence of land bridges linking it with northwest Europe. Ireland was cut off sooner and more completely, so the Irish fauna is much less varied. The Bering Sea is now a formidable barrier to animal dispersal but in earlier times it was a highway between the Nearctic and Palaearctic regions.

Animals with good powers of dispersal may not be deterred by even the most formidable barriers. Flying animals and ocean-dwelling species are frequently dispersed over several regions. Whether or not they can survive in another region depends on the existence of suitable food and climate. Sometimes animals are introduced accidentally into new regions, either by man or by chance. The occurrence of species in inexplicable places demonstrates that zoogeographical regions are, to a degree, arbitrarily drawn and not strict divisions.

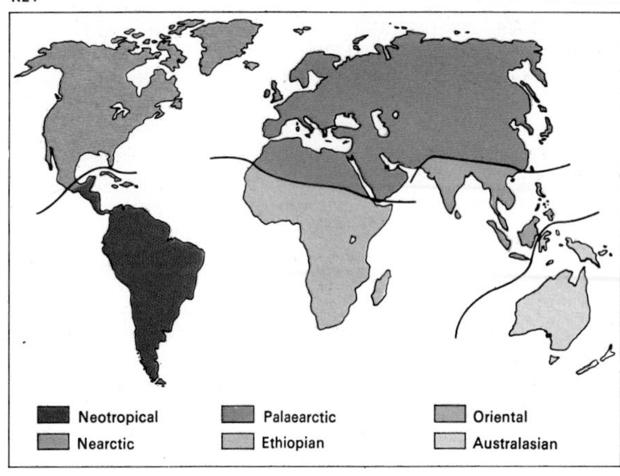
KEY
Neotropical
Nearctic
Palaearctic
Ethiopian
Oriental
Australasian

The six main zoogeographical regions of the world are all, apart from the Oriental region, continental land masses. For some purposes the Palaearctic and Nearctic are grouped together as the Holarctic. The divisions between regions are arbitrary and animals with good powers of dispersal may be found in more than one region. Each region has a characteristic fauna typified by certain species—the result of evolution at different places and times and of the different injections of species that the drifting land masses received.

4

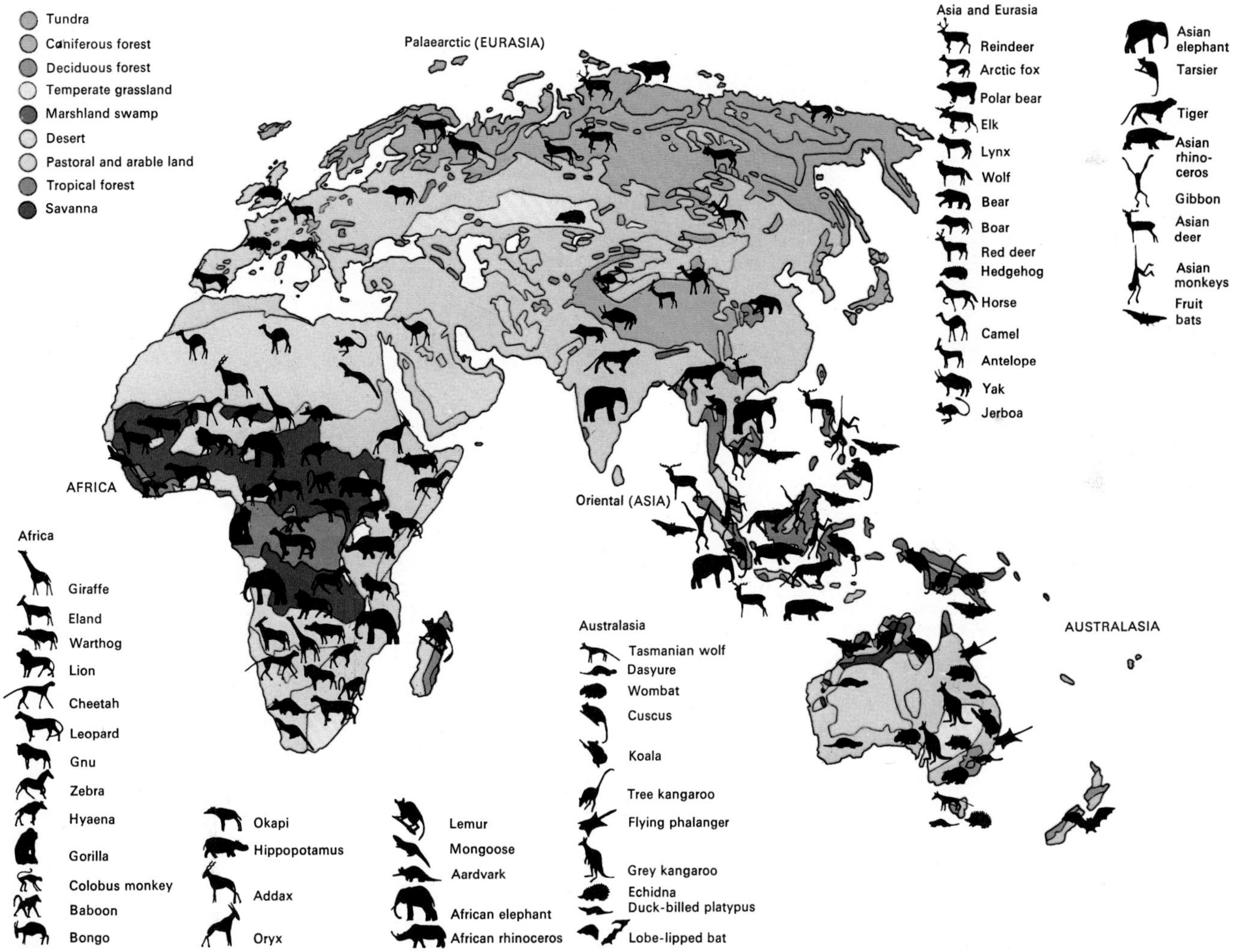

Tundra
Coniferous forest
Deciduous forest
Temperate grassland
Marshland swamp
Desert
Pastoral and arable land
Tropical forest
Savanna

Palaearctic (EURASIA)

AFRICA

Oriental (ASIA)

AUSTRALASIA

Asia and Eurasia
Reindeer
Arctic fox
Polar bear
Elk
Lynx
Wolf
Bear
Boar
Red deer
Hedgehog
Horse
Camel
Antelope
Yak
Jerboa

Asian elephant
Tarsier
Tiger
Asian rhinoceros
Gibbon
Asian deer
Asian monkeys
Fruit bats

Africa
Giraffe
Eland
Warthog
Lion
Cheetah
Leopard
Gnu
Zebra
Hyaena
Gorilla
Colobus monkey
Baboon
Bongo
Okapi
Hippopotamus
Addax
Oryx
Lemur
Mongoose
Aardvark
African elephant
African rhinoceros

Australasia
Tasmanian wolf
Dasyure
Wombat
Cuscus
Koala
Tree kangaroo
Flying phalanger
Grey kangaroo
Echidna
Duck-billed platypus
Lobe-lipped bat

4 The Palaearctic region stretches from western North Africa and the Persian Gulf to the north of Siberia. Its eastern limit is the Bering Sea. A large area—Arctic tundra and permafrost—is inhabited by polar bears, Arctic foxes, and reindeer. To the south lie coniferous forests and temperate deciduous woodlands. Both are rich in species; the Ice Ages and the consequent climatic effects caused all but the most tolerant species to move south. The Ethiopian region encompasses Africa from the Sahara southward and includes southern Arabia. Straddling the equator, the region is mostly tropical and typified by dry, highly seasonal grassland. Much of west and central Africa is covered by tropical rain forest and is inhabited by essentially arboreal species such as gorillas, monkeys, and lorises. The grasslands support huge herds of grazing and browsing herbivores and their predators—the "big game" of Africa. Many of these species roamed far into the Palaearctic before the formation of the Mediterranean Sea barrier (evidenced by the discovery of fossil hippopotamuses under the streets of London). The Australian region, separated from Gondwanaland during the Cretaceous, was populated mainly by opossumlike marsupials that radiated into adaptive niches similar to the ones filled by placental mammals on other continents. Its many primitive species, such as the duck-billed platypus, lungfish, and flap-footed lizard, have never been in competition with the more successful forms that evolved later, and so have survived. Much of the region is desert and arid scrub and supports an impoverished fauna.

The basis of ecology

No organism alive on Earth is an isolated individual. Every plant and animal is a member of a dynamic community known as an ecosystem [8]. An ecosystem is a complex that consists not only of living creatures but also of nonliving matter and of radiant energy from the Sun. The limits of any ecosystem—such as a forest or a stretch of seashore—are always arbitrary because they are drawn by man; this whole planet is one huge ecosystem. The concept remains relevant, however, to the study of ecology, a branch of biological science. The aim of ecology is to analyze ecosystems in detail and to account not only for the effects of each organism on the ecosystem as a whole but also for the influence of the whole system on the individual plants and animals of which it is composed.

Producers, consumers, and decomposers

Energy is the basic essential of all ecosystems—without a ready supply of usable energy life cannot continue. Green plants make their own foods by the process of photosynthesis; using the plentiful atmospheric components carbon dioxide and water, and energy from sunlight, they are able to synthesize sugars. These sugars retain, in their chemical bonding, some of the sun's energy, and this can be released and used to build the more complex chemical compounds needed by the plant for building its structural and reproductive elements, such as its conducting channels, flowers, and seeds.

Unlike plants, animals cannot make their own foods. Instead they "steal" energy from plants and from other animals by eating them; they can live only at the expense of other living organisms. Within any ecosystem green plants are thus known as producers or fixers of energy, while animals are consumers. The organisms that feed on the dead bodies of plants and animals, causing their decay, are decomposers. In any particular ecosystem, producers, consumers, and decomposers live together, rely on each other, and adapt to each other. The more well defined their boundaries of influence become, the more the ecosystem is said to become closed.

Complex ecosystems may include many thousands of species, all interrelating with each other to some degree. Their interactions include feeding and the provision of food, but plants and animals can also provide various kinds of shelter or protection, nesting material and homes for each other.

Links in the food chains

The fundamental food-providing relationships between the organisms in an ecosystem are often expressed in terms of diagrams known as food chains [7]. Most commonly these consist of a sequence of species that are related to each other as prey and predators, and most chains are tied to each other by cross linkages to form food webs that quickly become too complex to be mapped.

The energy flow within each food chain is remarkably constant and nearly always conforms to the "ten percent rule." According to this rule ten percent of energy is transferred at every link in the chain. Thus a herbivore obtains ten percent of the calories in the plants it eats and so on. This 90 per-

CONNECTIONS

See also
578 Regions of the earth: zoogeography
582 Isolation and evolution
220 Climates
620 Salt marshes and coastal swamps
612 Life on the tundra
602 New World tropics
586 Grasslands of Africa
604 Life in the desert
606 Desert birds and mammals
594 Northern temperate woodlands
624 Life in the oceans
610 Polar regions
254 Earth's water supply

1

2

2 The tropical rain forest is the richest of all the biomes. Although large animals are few, small ones proliferate in an environment offering a huge supply of available energy in the ecosystem.

3

1 The montane biome is found in polar, temperate and tropical regions. At the greatest altitudes organisms are few and their interrelations finely balanced to overcome energy shortages.

4

4 In the harsh conditions of the desert, plants and animals are restricted in numbers to those able to cope with the extremes of temperature and with the regular conditions of drought.

3 All the world's grasslands are classified by ecologists as the grassland biome. Although each one contains different selections of species, they all share certain common characteristics, such as a large variety of herbivorous animals. The savanna illustrated here also supports many predatory animals and carrion-feeding scavengers. The trees and bushes provide food and shelter for animals on the savanna.

5

5 The temperature forest biome supports many fewer plant and animal species than its tropical counterpart. This is, however, one of the most complex natural biomes. Its trees are deciduous.

6

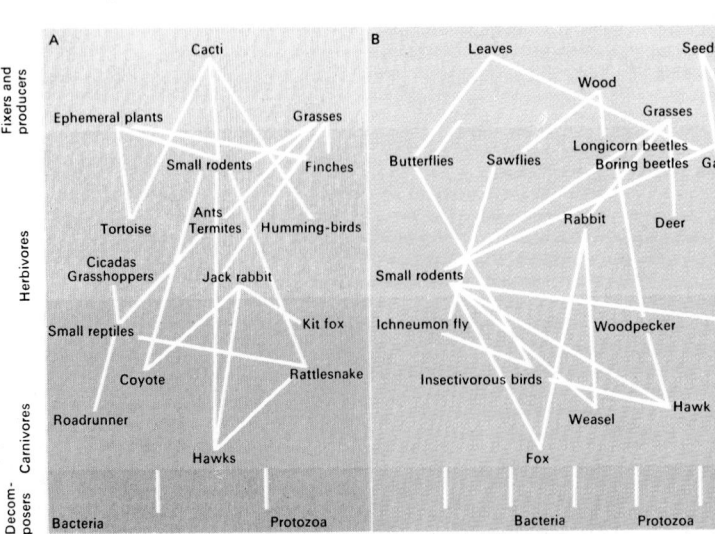

6 The life forms of the ocean are far greater in numbers than those that exist on land. They range from the largest of living creatures, the blue whale, to microscopic plankton on which it feeds.

7 All plant and animal communities are organized along essentially similar economic lines. Ecologists represent these in terms of diagrams known as food webs. In them, plants are the primary producers because they alone are able to fix solar energy and use it to synthesize complex food materials from the simple ingredients of carbon dioxide and water. The Sun's energy is locked in chemical bonds within the plant and is used by herbivores. These animals are, in turn, preyed on by carnivores. In most ecosystems the food webs are complex and some degree of simplification is essential to make them easy to understand. The desert food web [A] is essentially simple. In this North American example the cacti are the dominant fixers and producers, the coyotes and hawks the chief species of carnivores. In temperate woodland [B] the complex food web reflects the fact that the biome has remained stable for millions of years. Insects are a significant food source for many woodland birds. The plant pastures of the huge ocean biome [C] are the algae, the majority of which are minute diatoms. Every sea creature depends ultimately on the algae for its essential food supply. Mountain life [D] tends to form a simple food web. In the Himala-

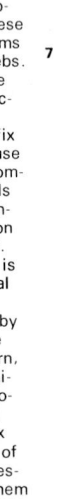

7

Fixers and producers
Herbivores
Carnivores
Decom-posers

A
Cacti
Ephemeral plants
Grasses
Small rodents
Finches
Ants
Termites
Tortoise
Humming-birds
Cicadas
Grasshoppers
Jack rabbit
Small reptiles
Kit fox
Coyote
Rattlesnake
Roadrunner
Hawks
Bacteria
Protozoa

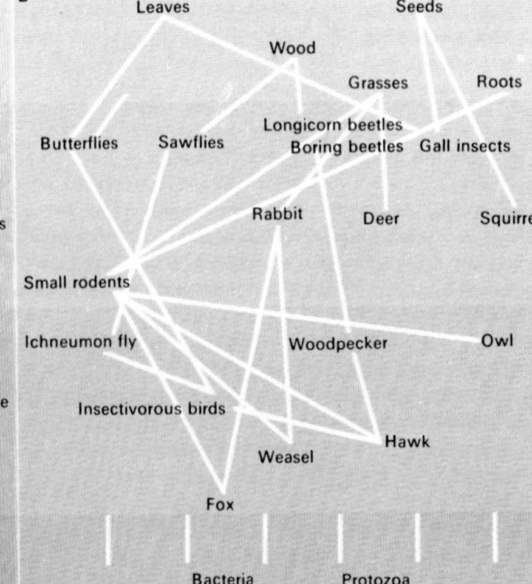

B
Leaves
Seeds
Wood
Grasses
Roots
Butterflies
Sawflies
Longicorn beetles
Boring beetles
Gall insects
Rabbit
Deer
Squirrel
Small rodents
Ichneumon fly
Woodpecker
Owl
Insectivorous birds
Hawk
Weasel
Fox
Bacteria
Protozoa

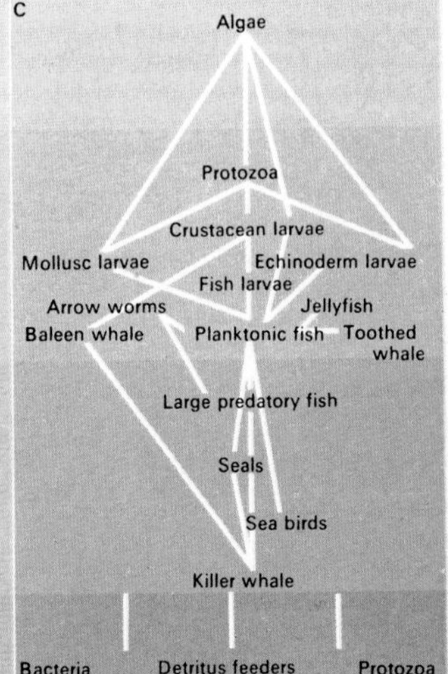

C
Algae
Protozoa
Crustacean larvae
Mollusc larvae
Echinoderm larvae
Fish larvae
Arrow worms
Jellyfish
Baleen whale
Planktonic fish
Toothed whale
Large predatory fish
Seals
Sea birds
Killer whale
Bacteria
Detritus feeders
Protozoa
Mixed feeders

cent reduction in available energy determines the length of the food chain: the animals at the end of a chain, such as foxes, yield too few calories to make preying on them worthwhile.

Ecosystems do not arise suddenly but mature over many years [9], gradually becoming more complex. Generally speaking, the older the ecosystem the more species it is likely to contain. At its height, and in its final and most long-lived form, the ecosystem is known as a climax community.

The formation of an ecosystem

New environments (such as a newly-formed pond, a field recently devastated by fire, or a glacier bed from which the ice has retreated) develop by succession. At first they attract only the hardy species of plants that can survive without shelter and a few animals capable of living among them. These pioneers are usually capable of rapid reproduction and the plants among them include lichens and mosses and many weed species. These early settlers in the chain of succession modify the environment by adding humus and nutrients to the soil, provide shelter from the sun and wind, and make it more hospitable to other creatures. As more organisms move in, more habitats (known as ecological niches) become available. In a maturing ecosystem the early colonizers may die as new, more stable species exert their competitive superiority.

The surface of the globe can be divided ecologically into ten broad regions determined by their natural vegetation [Key]. These regions, along with such areas as the sea [6] and the polar ice caps, are often referred to as biomes. Some of the world's most complex ecosystems are found in the tropical rain forest [2], where productivity is high and conditions have been stable for many millions of years. Some of the most simple ecosystems occur in polar regions, where there is less energy available and where few organisms have had time to adapt to the new environment exposed after the retreat of the ice sheets.

Just as ecosystems are built up so they may be destroyed, either naturally or, more probably, through the interference of man.

KEY

Evergreen trees and shrubs
Coniferous forest
Deciduous forest
Temperate rain forest
Monsoon forest
Tropical rain forest
Thorn forest
Grassland and savanna
Arid scrub and desert
Alpine tundra and ice

Ecologists divide the Earth into regions known as biomes, each characterized by a pattern of natural vegetation or, as in the sea and in lakes and rivers, by the nature of its water. The land biomes vary from the tropical forest, teeming with plant and animal life, to the cold, treeless tundra carpeted with lichens, grasses, and low-growing shrubs.

8 A
B
C

8 The basic unit of ecology is the individual plant or animal [A]. Many individuals, like this Arctic hare, are genetically distinct from others of their kind. Others, like the grass plants on which the hare feeds, reproduce vegetatively and form part of a "clone" of individuals, all of which are identical. The population [B] to which any individual belongs is isolated, either wholly or partly, from other populations of the same species. The Arctic hare of northern Greenland may thus differ genetically from that of Siberia. The ecosystem [C] is an assembly of animals and plants interacting with each other and the environment. Ecosystems can be simple or complex. A simple system could consist of unicellular algae sects, and insect-eaters. A complex ecosystem such as that of the tropical rain forest may consist of thousands of plants and animals interacting with each other in a variety of ways.

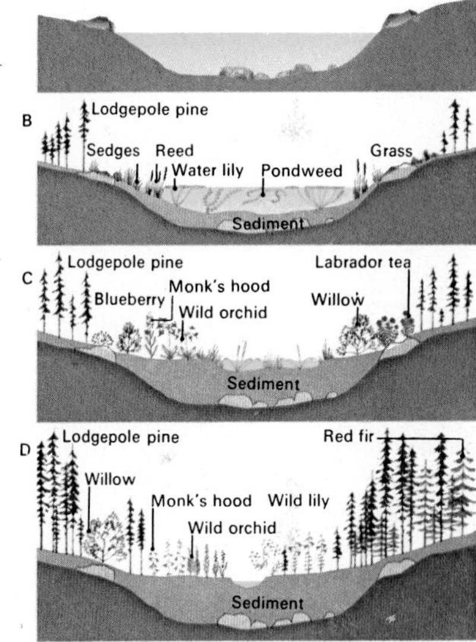
9
A
B
Lodgepole pine
Sedges
Reed
Water lily
Pondweed
Grass
Sediment
C
Lodgepole pine
Labrador tea
Monk's hood
Blueberry
Wild orchid
Willow
Sediment
D
Lodgepole pine
Red fir
Willow
Monk's hood
Wild lily
Wild orchid
Sediment

9 Ecosystems do not arise overnight but evolve gradually. A shallow glacial tarn [A] is transformed to a forest [D] in a timespan of a few thousand years. The first living organisms to colonize it are algae whose spores are carried there by the wind. Larvae of flying insects feed on the algae and their debris accumulates on the bottom. Bacteria and protists recycle the nutrient salts and small animals and plants enter the system. Surrounding sediments now fill the tarn [B], marsh plants spread inward and land plants [C] replace them as the ground consolidates. The final, stable ecosystem is known as the climax community.

yas, whose web is depicted here, the herbivores are the predominant form of animal life and are preyed on by only a few carnivores. The tropical rain forest [E] is the home of many highly specialized plants and animals, all of which take their place in the complex food web. Epiphytes, for example, are plants adapted to live on other plants. On the forest floor fallen leaves and dead wood are very rapidly decomposed. The rich variety of savanna life [F] reflects a mature ecosystem. As in the woodland biomes, stable conditions persisting for many millennia have allowed many species to become established in the savanna and to develop a similarly complex food web.

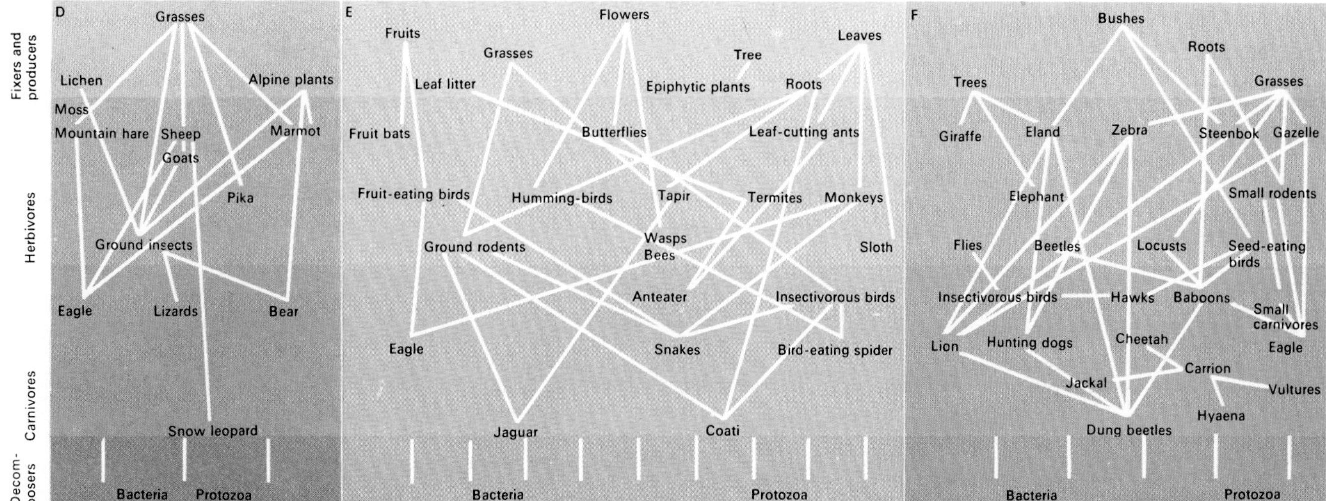
Fixers and producers
Herbivores
Carnivores
Decomposers
D
Grasses
Lichen
Alpine plants
Moss
Mountain hare
Sheep
Goats
Marmot
Pika
Ground insects
Eagle
Lizards
Bear
Snow leopard
Bacteria
Protozoa
E
Flowers
Fruits
Leaves
Grasses
Tree
Leaf litter
Epiphytic plants
Roots
Fruit bats
Butterflies
Leaf-cutting ants
Fruit-eating birds
Humming-birds
Tapir
Termites
Monkeys
Ground rodents
Wasps
Bees
Sloth
Anteater
Insectivorous birds
Eagle
Snakes
Bird-eating spider
Jaguar
Coati
Bacteria
Protozoa
F
Bushes
Roots
Trees
Grasses
Giraffe
Eland
Zebra
Steenbok
Gazelle
Elephant
Small rodents
Flies
Beetles
Locusts
Seed-eating birds
Insectivorous birds
Hawks
Baboons
Small carnivores
Lion
Hunting dogs
Cheetah
Eagle
Carrion
Jackal
Vultures
Hyaena
Dung beetles
Bacteria
Protozoa

Isolation and evolution

According to the theory of evolution, all living plants and animals have derived from simple ancestral stocks. Scientists have classified more than one million animals and half a million plants into separate species. This classification is first made on the basis of physical appearance and, in organisms that appear to be similar, the difference in species is confirmed by the fact that they do not interbreed freely in the wild. So, although it is possible in captivity to breed a cross between a lion and a tiger, the lion and the tiger are nevertheless still classified as separate species since they do not interbreed naturally.

The development of species

How then do different species develop from a homogeneous population? If one imagines such a population inhabiting a fairly large area and having a large gene pool, then the forces of natural selection will, in time, produce groups of individuals that are adapted to live in specific habitats. If new habitats become available, groups of animals or plants will colonize them and adapt to explot them fully. The new population will have undergone adaptive radiation [2].

The new groups may become distinct enough to be regarded as separate subspecies, or races. Occasionally, they may diverge farther from the parental stock in such a way as to eliminate or decrease the ability to exchange genetic material with either the parent stock or with other populations derived from the parent stock. They then can be described as different species.

Geographical isolation

The most obvious barrier to reproduction—and often the first step in the process of specialization—is that of geographical isolation. This depends primarily on the habits and dispersal power of the species concerned. Birds have a large dispersal power but other creatures are limited in their range. Land snails on the Pacific Islands, for example [Key], inhabit wooded valleys that are separated from each other by rocky ridges. In the valleys the frequency of different species of snail varies. It seems that the original populations wandered into one or more of the valleys and that the ridges between the valleys kept them separate. Large physical barriers [1], such as oceans and mountains, not only separate populations of the same species but also keep families and orders apart, as is shown by the development of the marsupials of both Australia and South America.

Reproductive isolation also occurs when two or more related species inhabit the same geographical area. The barriers to gene exchange can take two forms, acting either by deterring fertilization because of differences in behavior or by lowering the survival potential or fertility of any hybrids.

Isolation by habitat [3] is most common in plants but also evident in some animals. Individual plant species are often adapted to a specific soil condition and their hybrids are unable to survive in either habitat.

Reproductive isolation

In animals one of the most important isolating mechanisms is mating preference, which is widespread in animals inhabiting the same geographical areas. One of the

CONNECTIONS

See also
408 Evolution of life
418 Evolution: classical theories
420 Evolution in action
614 Life on islands
580 The basis of ecology
578 Regions of the earth: zoogeography
608 Mountain life
600 Forests of Southeast Asia
538 Island birds
476 Land and sea snails

1

Sumatra, Java and Borneo were once linked to continental Asia and New Guinea was joined to Australia. Between these two regions active volcanoes threw up new islands and these have been invaded by flora and fauna from both mainlands.

Oriental fauna

Endemic species derived from Oriental (brown animal in green circle) and Australasian (brown animal in red) fauna.

Australasian fauna

Green—Oriental fauna
Red—Australasian fauna

1 Natural barriers such as deep ocean channels separate the animals of the world into distinctive groups. These barriers have served as isolating mechanisms, keeping apart not only species but also whole families of animals. One striking example is the juxtaposition of the flora and fauna of Southeast Asia and Australasia. The biologist Alfred Russel Wallace (1823–1913) drew a dividing line where the fauna and flora of Southeast Asia were distinct from those of Australasia. This was later modified by the naturalist Thomas Henry Huxley (1825–95). Even later, the German biologist Max Weber drew a new line marking the point of balance between the two faunas. Later he modified this to mark the sea channel that forms a barrier to the spread of land mammals. Between Weber's and Wallace's line is an area of faunal mixing where animals and plants have managed to cross the channels.

Wild buffalo
Bubalus bubalis
2 Gaur
Bos gaurus
Banteng
Bos banteng
Yak Bos grunniens
Anoa
Anoa depressicornis
m ft
1
3
2
1
0 0

2 Adaptive radiation can be seen in the cattle of Southeast Asia, which, although related, occupy different environments. The gaur is found in the hilly forests, while the wild buffalo, ancestor of the domestic variety, roams the upland swampy areas. The banteng lives in Java, where it is sometimes domesticated. Yaks, also domesticated, are adapted to withstand the cold of Tibet and central Asia. The anoa lives in wet, hilly regions of the Celebes.

most striking differences between closely related species is the ability of individuals to recognize breeding partners of the same species. Elaborate courtship displays and differences in color ensure that only individuals of the same species mate. Other cues to breeding partners may include smell, the distinctive calls of most species of birds, and even the croaking of frogs and the singing of crickets. Without these specific stimuli many animals will not mate.

It was long believed that in animals the differences in the genitalia of different species led to reproductive isolation where, for example, the male genitalia could not physically fit into the female genitalia. Recent observations have shown that this kind of mechanical isolation is not really significant among animals, where behavioral isolation mechanisms play the primary role. In plants, however, mechanical isolation can be essential to keeping species apart. Differences in flower structure prevent pollination and fertilization between species. Plants exploit the activities of animals to spread their genes; differences in flower structure, color, and scent attract various kinds of pollinators to different species. This reduces the chances of cross-pollination between two unrelated species. In California, for example, there are related species of a flower *(Penstemon)* that have different sized flowerheads. The different species are pollinated respectively by large bees, smaller bees, and solitary bees and wasps. Another species has a long tubular flower and is adapted to pollination by hummingbirds.

If fertilization does occur between different species it is quite likely that one of the three mechanisms may be at work. Often the first generation hybrid is weak because of abnormal genetic matching; it rarely survives to reach reproductive maturity. Or, the hybrids, although healthy, are often sterile, as is seen in the mule—the offspring of a horse and a donkey. When the hybrids are healthy and reproductively active, the third possible mechanism comes into play by leading to a gradual breakdown of genetic viability in succeeding generations. As a result, the hybrid line dies out.

KEY
1 *A. fulgens* (Niu)
2 *A. cestus* (Wailupe)
3 *A. fuscobasis* (Palolo)
4 *A. stewartii* (Manoa)
5 *A. turgida* (Alea)
OAHU

Many species of agate snail *(Achatinella)* live on the Hawaiian island of Oahu, most of them in a small area of adjacent valleys. Individuals remain close to their point of hatching. The rocky ridges that seperate the valleys are an effective barrier to migration for these relatively immobile animals. Over thousands of years the snails have been geographically isolated and, as a result, the species have remained quite distinct.

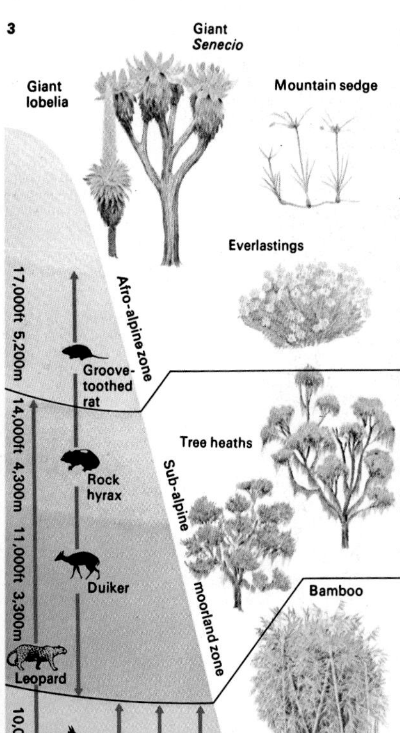
3
Giant *Senecio*
Giant lobelia
Mountain sedge
Everlastings
Afro-alpine zone
17,000ft 5,200m
Groove-toothed rat
14,000ft 4,300m
Rock hyrax
Tree heaths
Sub-alpine moorland zone
11,000ft 3,300m
Duiker
Leopard
Bamboo
10,000ft 3,000m
Bushbuck
Mole-rat
Monkey
Bamboo montane forest zone
Forest hog
8,500ft 2,700m
Bush baby
Elephant
Bongo
Buffalo
Tree hyrax
6,800ft 2,100m
Rhinoceros
Tropical forest trees
Savanna

3 Zones that vary with altitude can lead to the formation of different habitats that are best exploited by different species of plants and animals. This can be clearly observed on Mount Kenya, which rises 17,057ft (5,199m) in equatorial Africa. High up on this mountain there is a specialized flora and mammals include the groove-toothed rat, the hyrax, and the duiker. Lower down the mountain, in the sub-alpine zone, tree heaths dominate the vegetation. Mammals are similar to those found higher up, but leopards and hunting dogs appear as predators in this zone. The bamboo montane forest supports a wide variety of animals, including omnivores, such as monkeys and pigs, and browsing animals, such as antelopes and elephants. Below the forest is the grassy savanna.

4 Vegetation zones in mountainous regions may not always be uniform because the high land forces winds laden with moisture to rise. As they do so, the water they carry is dropped and they blow down the other side of the range as waterless, desiccating airflows.

A zonal plan of Mount Kenya shows that, where the rainfall is less heavy, areas of scrub and dry land replace the montane forest that covers the north of the massif. This affects many animals that depend on particular vegetation for food and shelter.

4
A Dry scrub
B Afro-alpine
C Sub-alpine
D Moorland
E Bamboo
F Montane forest
G Savanna

Vertical scale in metres
4,900
4,300
3,600
3,000

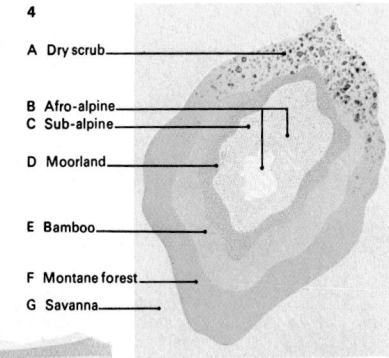

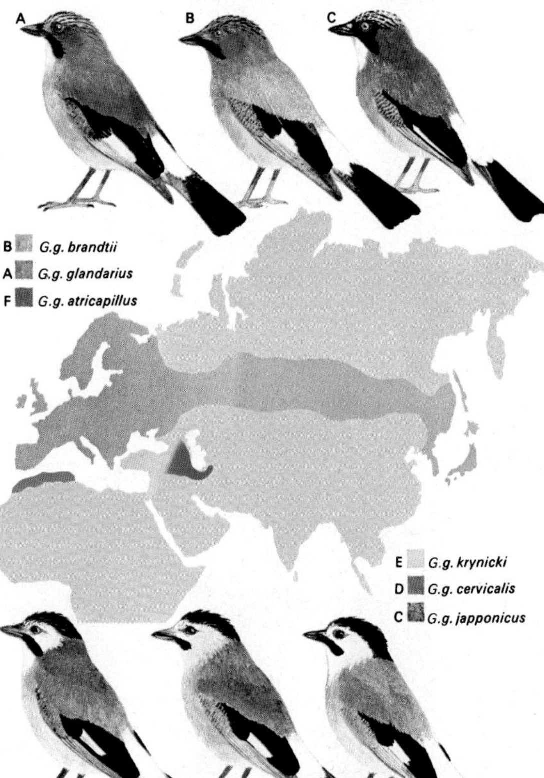
5
A
B
C
B G.g. brandtii
A G.g. glandarius
F G.g. atricapillus
E G.g. krynicki
D G.g. cervicalis
C G.g. japponicus
D
E
F

5 More than 20 recognized races of jay are found in Eurasia, ranging from western Europe to the islands of Japan. The jay is primarily a bird of deciduous woodlands that feeds mainly on acorns wherever it can find them. But it is a versatile feeder and can live on a variety of seeds, fruits, buds, insects, and even eggs and small birds. In some areas it has taken to coniferous forests, where it feeds on seeds of certain pines. Many species of birds are widely distributed and show marked local variation in the color of their plumage in different parts of their range. Where bird populations overlap, there is a gradual transition of features from one race to another, as the different populations freely interbreed. These populations are regarded only as subspecies, or races. The birds at the extremes of their ranges are unlikely to interbreed and they may in time become separate species.

Northern grasslands

Grasses were among the last families of flowering plants to evolve. They have more than made up for lost time, however, and are now the dominant plants over much of the world. In general they are found where rainfall is too low to support tree growth, yet above the level at which semi-desert conditions prevail; grazing animals and fire help to promote their growth. Northern Hemisphere grasslands include the prairies of North America, the steppes of Europe and central Asia, and grassy areas extending along the valleys of some of the great rivers of eastern Asia.

Grasses and grass eaters

Winds sweep unimpeded across the steppes and the prairies and the grasses make use of them for pollinating their flowers. Unlike those of many other plants, grass flowers [1] are not large, gaudy, sweet-scented, or provided with nectar. Instead they possess the bare minimum of stamens with abundant lightweight, non-sticky pollen grains and stigmas to be pollinated by them. During their development the reproductive parts are surrounded by protective scales, which later enfold the seed. The stamens and stigmas are ripe for only a comparatively short time, but the amount of pollen produced is so large that when the plant is shaken by the wind pollination is almost inevitable.

One reason why the grasses are successful lies in their compact with the grazing animals. The growing point in grasses lies close to the ground and when the foliage is cropped at a higher level it does little harm because the cut leaves simply continue to grow upward with little or no interruption in the growth pattern. As a result the grazing animals can feed without damaging their food supply.

Large grazing animals are abundant in grasslands within the temperate areas. But their numbers are relatively few where they were once present in the millions. Experts estimate that in 1700, before the coming of the white man to the prairies, more than 60 million bison [2] wandered over the plains, in addition to large numbers of pronghorn. In Asia, herds of wild horses, asses, and saiga antelopes [3] abounded. In both continents these large animals had been almost eliminated by the end of the last century; in 1899 fewer than 550 plains bison survived. Careful conservation has gone some way to restoring populations, particularly with regard to the saiga and the pronghorn over part of their respective ranges. All these large mammals are herd animals that migrate when the food supply becomes scarce, so the grass is never overgrazed or badly trampled. They were once accompanied by predators, principally wolves, but as the great wild herds were destroyed the predators were also doomed.

A variety of animals

Small mammals were also once abundant on the plains but, unlike the large creatures, they were sedentary [4]. Some, such as the North American prairie dogs and the Eurasian susliks, lived in great colonies that at one time often included several million individuals in a single "township." These animals feed mainly on the grasses, eating the roots as well as the leaves, but often also renewing the plant growth because of their

CONNECTIONS

See also

454 Grasses, reeds, and rushes
586 Grasslands of Africa
588 South American grasslands
590 Australian desert grasslands
578 Regions of the earth: zoogeography
580 The basis of ecology
540 The classification of mammals
526 The classification of birds
520 The life of reptiles
492 The classification of insects

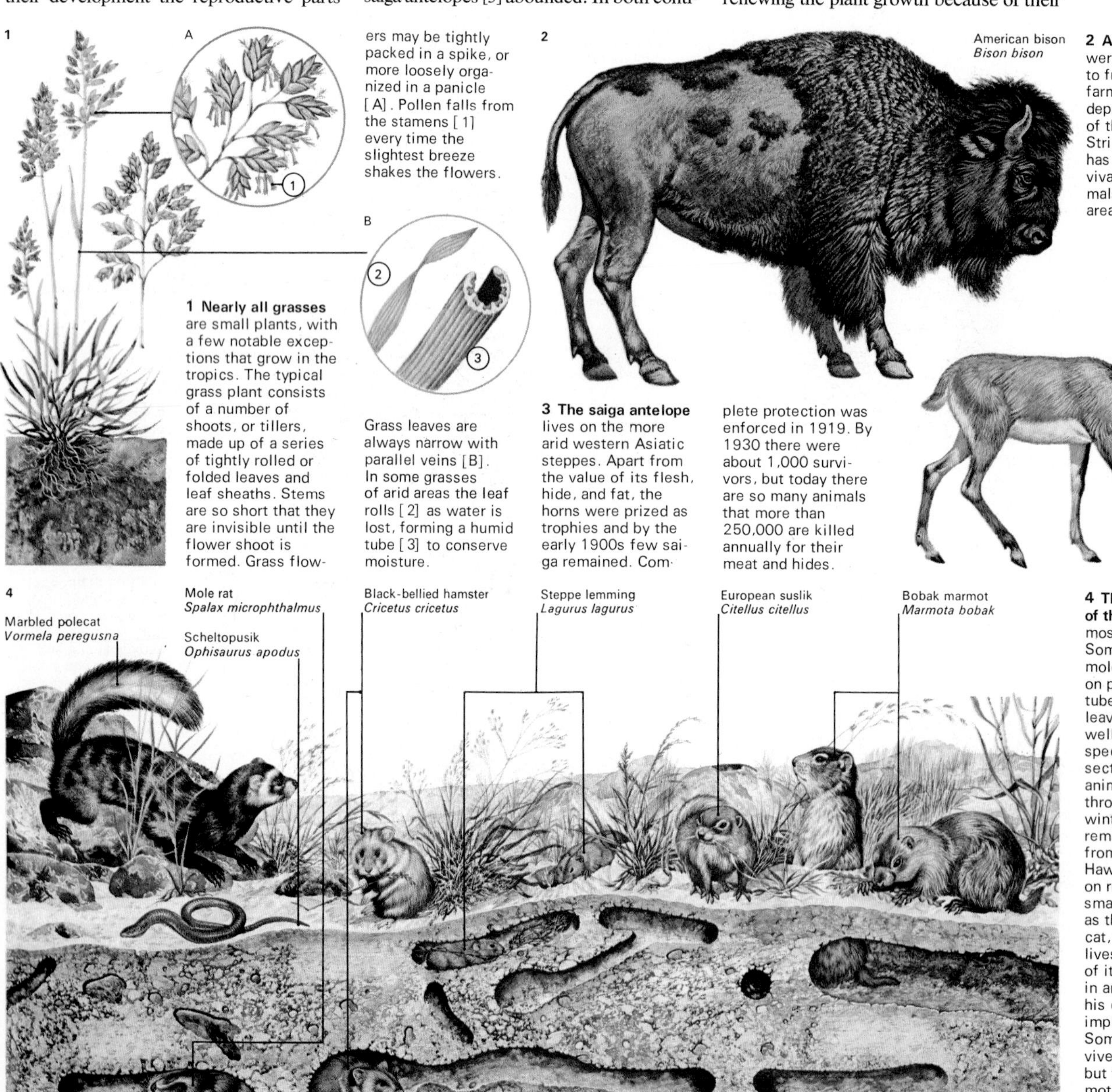

1
A
B
2
3
American bison
Bison bison
Saiga
Saiga tatarica
4
Marbled polecat
Vormela peregusna
Mole rat
Spalax microphthalmus
Scheltopusik
Ophisaurus apodus
Black-bellied hamster
Cricetus cricetus
Steppe lemming
Lagurus lagurus
European suslik
Citellus citellus
Bobak marmot
Marmota bobak

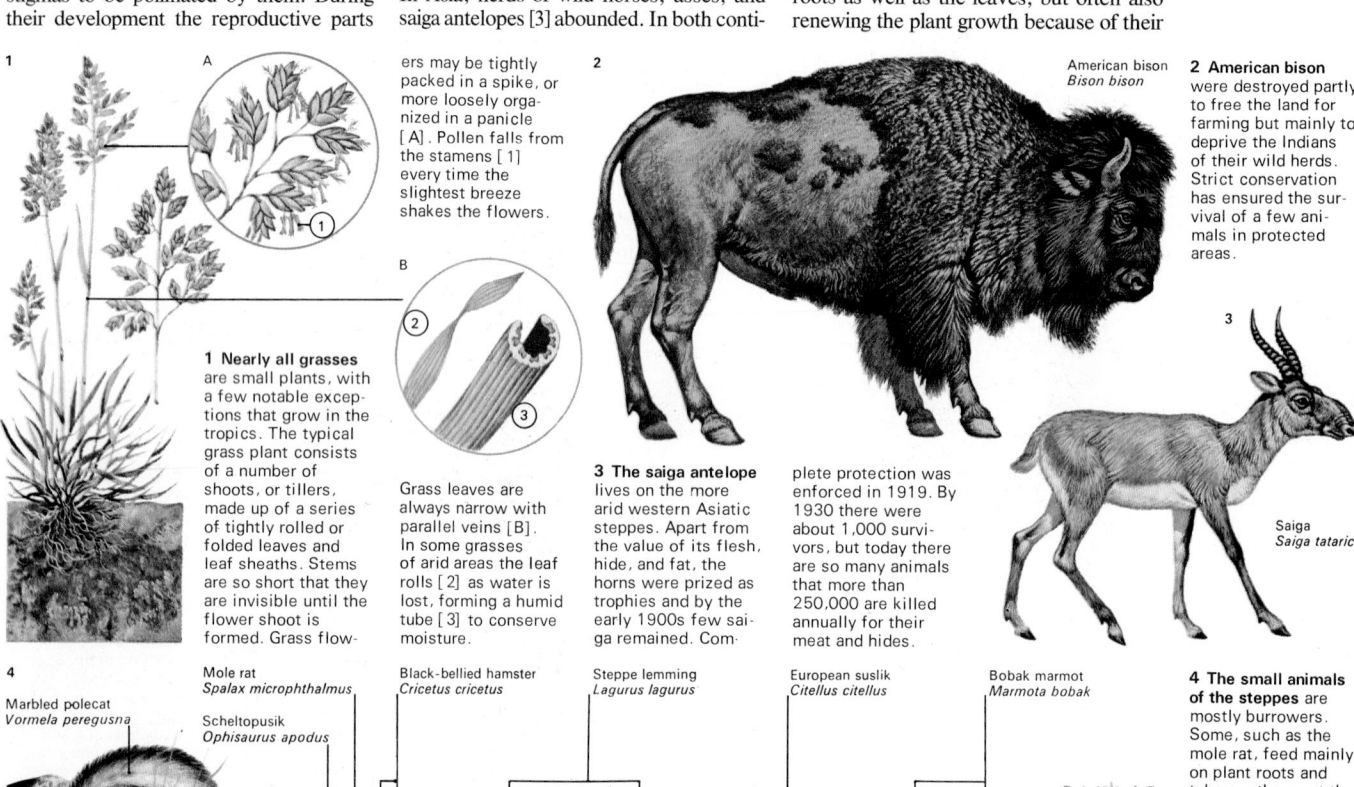

1 Nearly all grasses are small plants, with a few notable exceptions that grow in the tropics. The typical grass plant consists of a number of shoots, or tillers, made up of a series of tightly rolled or folded leaves and leaf sheaths. Stems are so short that they are invisible until the flower shoot is formed. Grass flowers may be tightly packed in a spike, or more loosely organized in a panicle [A]. Pollen falls from the stamens [1] every time the slightest breeze shakes the flowers. Grass leaves are always narrow with parallel veins [B]. In some grasses of arid areas the leaf rolls [2] as water is lost, forming a humid tube [3] to conserve moisture.

2 American bison were destroyed partly to free the land for farming but mainly to deprive the Indians of their wild herds. Strict conservation has ensured the survival of a few animals in protected areas.

3 The saiga antelope lives on the more arid western Asiatic steppes. Apart from the value of its flesh, hide, and fat, the horns were prized as trophies and by the early 1900s few saiga remained. Complete protection was enforced in 1919. By 1930 there were about 1,000 survivors, but today there are so many animals that more than 250,000 are killed annually for their meat and hides.

4 The small animals of the steppes are mostly burrowers. Some, such as the mole rat, feed mainly on plant roots and tubers; others eat the leaves and seeds as well, while many species also eat insects. A number of animals hibernate through the harsh winters and some remain underground from August to April. Hawks and owls prey on rodents, and so do small mammals, such as the marbled polecat, which often lives in the burrows of its victims. Man, in an effort to protect his crops, is the most implacable foe. Some animals survive his persecution, but the bobak marmot is not one of these and has now disappeared from areas where it was once numerous.

habit of gathering and storing seeds. The burrows of these animals are not very deep, but in digging them they turn the soil over, sometimes bringing up material of a different mineral type from below.

Birds of the grasslands include plant- and seed-eaters that parallel the mammals in their activities. Some, such as the bustards, are large and reluctant to fly, a propensity that has increased their rate of destruction. There are also many smaller species of birds that feed both on seeds and insects. They in turn may fall prey to several species of falcons [8], hawks, and eagles.

Other predators include large numbers of reptiles [9, 10], which may feed on eggs or young birds, as well as small mammals whose underground homes they can enter. The insects of the grasslands [11] are an important part of the fauna and repeat in miniature the pattern of primary herbivores and hunters and scavengers, which are not well represented among the bigger creatures. Insects and other invertebrates may lack universal appeal, but they are important in the economy of the grasslands because they stimulate soil fertility and help to hold erosion in check.

The most important of the grassland animals is man, who underwent essential stages in his evolution in tropical grasslands and who has subsequently spread to other environments. He is, however, still mainly dependent on grasslands for his food; all cereals are cultivated grasses and most of man's domestic animals are grazing species that still need grass for their survival.

The threat to the grasslands

It is ironical that although man has greatly increased the area of the world's grasslands, mainly by the destruction of forests, which he has replaced with short-lived farm crops, he has in many areas of the world destroyed the grasslands by overgrazing and returning too little to the soil. Sometimes, in his attempts to improve productivity with heavy-yield farm crops, he has plowed up the land and harmed the delicate balance between plants and animals. This has often led to erosion and as a result the desert has encroached in many areas.

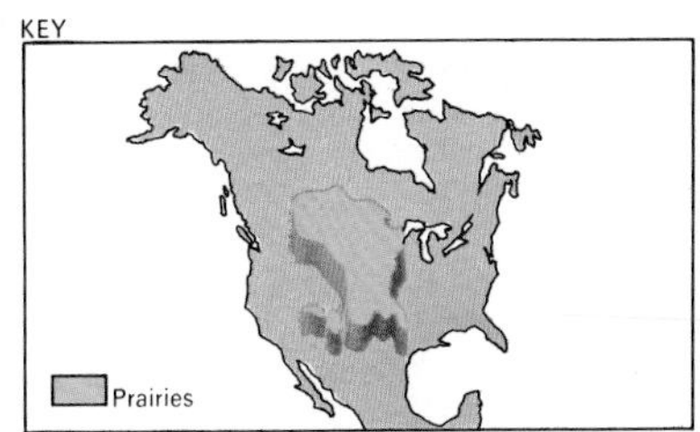
KEY
Prairies

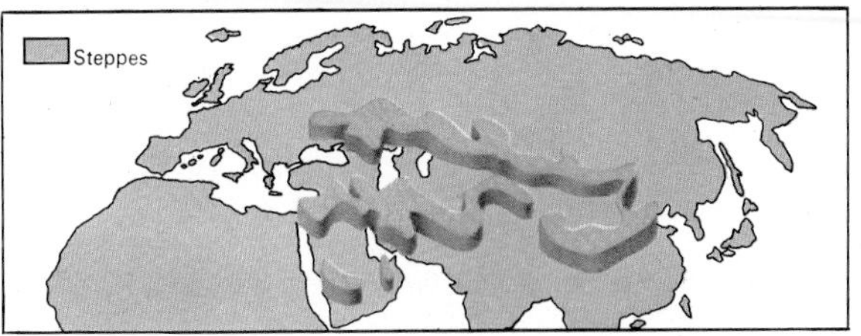
Steppes

The prairies of North America occupy much of the central part of the continent. They are almost entirely surrounded by forests and only in the southwest do grasslands yield to desert regions in the shadow of the Rockies. In the Old World the natural grasslands, or steppes, start in eastern Europe and stretch across the Eurasian land mass in a great belt that is bounded on the south by semidesert and scrub, and on the north by forests. North of Mongolia the steppe becomes discontinuous as it is broken by trees. But the steppe reasserts itself on the plains of Inner Mongolia and in the northeast of the Soviet Union.

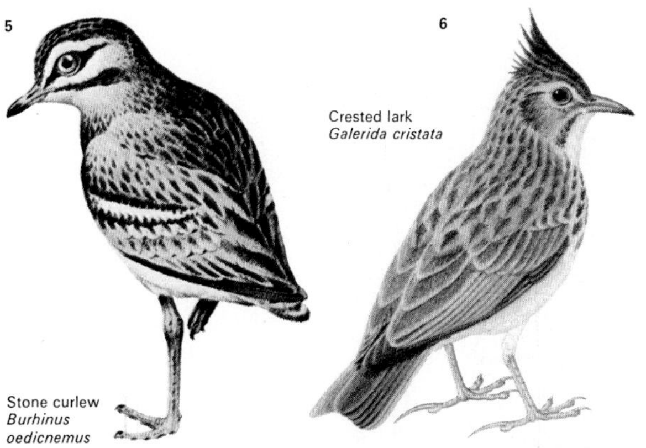
5
6
Crested lark
Galerida cristata
Stone curlew
Burhinus oedicnemus

5 The stone curlew was once common on grasslands from Britain to eastern Europe. As a result of its ground-nesting habit and reluctance to fly it has disappeared from many of its former haunts.

6 The crested lark, fearless of man, is common in dry Old World grasslands.

7
Burrowing owl
Speotyto cunicularia

7 The burrowing owl, from the grasslands of North America, lives in unused burrows.

8
Prairie falcon
Falco mexicanus

8 The prairie falcon is a bird of the arid southern and western parts of the prairies. It scans the ground from heights up to 100ft (30m) for the small animals and birds that make up its diet.

9 Rattlesnake *Crotalus* spp

9 Rattlesnakes are common over much of the grassland and desert regions of North America. The amount of venom they produce far exceeds that needed to kill the rodents that form their usual prey. Snakes use it to protect themselves against large predators, but they are not normally aggressive and try to avoid a confrontation by warning of their presence. Their unmistakable and menacing rattle is produced by "bells" of hard skin on the end of the tail.

10
Bull snake
Pituophis sp

10 The bull snake, which grows up to 4ft (1.2m) long, is one of the many snakes found in the prairie region, where it preys on the abundant rodents. It is nonpoisonous but suffocates its prey with its strong, constricting coils.

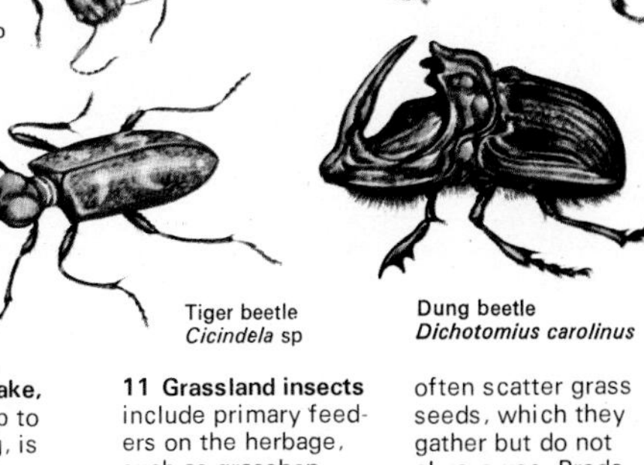
11
Lubber grasshopper
Brachystola sp
Harvester ant
Pogonomyrmex sp
Tiger beetle
Cicindela sp
Dung beetle
Dichotomius carolinus

11 Grassland insects include primary feeders on the herbage, such as grasshoppers, and more general feeders such as ants. Ants are smaller, but the huge colonies in which they live may alter the soil where they burrow. They also often scatter grass seeds, which they gather but do not always use. Predators, such as ground beetles, abound. The scavenging dung beetle fills a niche by breaking down the dung of other animals and returning it to the soil.

Grasslands of Africa

Savanna grassland covers much of Africa from the Sahara to the Cape. Only in the west does it give way to the dense tropical forest of the Zäire River basin and the West African coast and to the Namib Desert. The grassland is not a uniform area, but ranges from dry steppe and subdesert in the north and southwest (on the fringes of the Sahara and Kalahari Deserts) through thorn scrub to open savanna woodland in the equatorial region. The landscape is bisected by watercourses and granite hills, and much of the southern area is modified by farming.

Distinct types of savanna

The transitions between the various types of savanna are distinct and each type has its own characteristic fauna and flora. The open woodlands are characterized by fire-resistant trees such as *Brachystegia* and *Isoberlinia,* which are replaced in drier areas by acacias (thorn scrub) and baobabs. The vegetation of the open areas is a mixture of grasses and herbs with acacias.

Ecologically, the savanna is a highly complex system of interdependent components. The food of the large herds of grazing animals—the grasses and herbs—is resistant to drought, fire, and grazing and quickly recovers from their effects. Many savanna grasses reproduce by underground runners and can spread rapidly. The trees and bushes are protected from excessive browsing by long thorns covering the trunks and branches.

A bewildering number of savanna animals exploit their environment in a variety of different ways. Among the browsers there is a vertical zoning of feeding habits [Key]. Giraffes and elephants feed on the trees—giraffes on the topmost shoots and elephants on the upper shoots and the bark. Black rhinoceros, eland, kudu, and gerenuk browse on lower shrubs and trees, with the lowest branches, often only inches above the ground, providing food for steenbok and dik-dik. The grazing animals utilize the grasses in different ways. Zebras feed on the coarse tops, the leafy center is eaten by wildebeeste and topi, and gazelles crop the shoots at ground level. Underground roots are eaten by warthogs grubbing.

Feeding on the herds of grazing animals are a number of large predators. One of the best known is the lion [5], which lives in family groups and catches its prey in a short rush from cover. Two other cats are also found on the savanna: the leopard, which often kills from cover at waterholes, and the cheetah, which is capable of outrunning gazelles over a short distance. Small packs of hunting dogs [6] roam the savanna, working as teams and pursuing their prey until it is exhausted and falls victim to their snapping jaws. The hyenas are both predators and scavengers. No young animal is safe from them and no bone is too large for their powerful jaws to crack.

Rodents and hares

In addition to the large and spectacular animals, many small animals, not often seen, live in the savanna. Like the larger animals they occupy a particular niche. The numerous rodents and hares feed on seeds and herbs and in turn provide food for foxes, snakes, small cats, and birds of prey. Many kinds of mongooses, civets, and weasels

CONNECTIONS

See also
584 Northern grasslands
588 South American grasslands
590 Australian desert grasslands
578 Regions of the earth: zoogeography
580 The basis of ecology
540 The classification of mammals
492 The classification of insects
526 The classification of birds

1

1 Baobab tree *Adansonia digitata*
2 Umbrella thorn *Acacia* sp
3 Candelabra tree *Euphorbia* sp
4 Whistling thorn *Acacia* sp
5 Weaver bird nests Family Ploceidae
6 Red oat grass *Themeda triandra*
7 Giraffe *Giraffa camelopardalis*
8 Topi *Damaliscalus korrigum*
9 Impala *Aepyceros melampus*
10 Waterbuck *Kobus defassa*
11 Cape buffalo *Syncerus caffer*
12 Oxpecker *Buphagus* sp
13 Marabou stork *Leptoptilus crumeniferous*
14 Crested guinea fowl *Guttera edouardi*
15 Tawny eagle *Aquila rapax*
16 Common agama *Agama agama*
17 Banded mongoose *Mungos mungo*
18 Puff adder *Bitis arietans*

1 The African savanna, with its flat-topped acacias, supports large herds of herbivorous mammals. Their predators, being mainly nocturnal, are less often seen. But birds, from the busy weaver to the scavenging marabou stork and vegetarian guinea fowl, are as conspicuous as the game.

2

2 The masked weaver builds a nest of woven grass. Its foundation is a ring of knotted strands to which the walls and then the roof are added. An entrance hole is left underneath the nest.

prey on the small savanna animals. Two animals of special interest are the meerkat and the ratel. The meerkat, or yellow mongoose, is a sociable burrowing animal living in large warrens and feeding on insects, spiders, and millipedes. Also living in burrows, the ratel, or honey badger, is best known for its association with the honey guide—a small brown bird. When this bird finds a bees' nest it attracts the ratel with a particular call and leads it to the nest. The ratel digs out the nest with its powerful claws and both animals share in the feast.

Variety of bird life

Great numbers of birds inhabit the savanna, many more than live in the tropical rain forest. Ostriches often accompany the grazing herds; so do storks and egrets, which feed on disturbed insects. The majestic kori bustard and the snake-eating secretary bird can also be seen striding through the grass. The nests of weaver birds [2], like huge fruit, adorn many acacias, and overhead the circling vultures and soaring eagles scan the ground for carrion and small animals.

In summer vast numbers of birds migrate from Europe and Asia to the savanna regions to escape the severe northern winter. This enormous variety of birds feeds on seeds, berries, and insects and is in turn preyed upon by hawks, owls, and falcons.

Because of the seasonal rains, migration is a major feature of life on the savanna. During the dry season the wildebeeste and other animals move to areas where rain has fallen and the grass is growing. During the migrations many thousands of animals, particularly wildebeeste, die through drowning and starvation. Scavengers and predators, notably vultures and hyenas, take full advantage of this superabundance of easily obtained food. Such is the richness of their environment, however, that the numbers of wildebeeste soon recover.

The delicate balance of the savanna ecosystem is easily upset, especially by man. Fortunately, enlightened governments—aware of the unique nature of the wildlife heritage—have set aside large areas of the savanna as inviolable sanctuaries.

KEY

Vertical feeding patterns of savanna herbivores reduces competition between species. The giraffe [4] takes leaves 18ft (6m) up, leaving the lowest ones for the tiny dik-dik [11].

1 Springbok
2 Eland
3 Kudu
4 Giraffe
5 Warthog
6 Black rhinoceros
7 Elephant
8 Vervet monkey
9 Gerenuk
10 Steenbok
11 Kirk's dik-dik

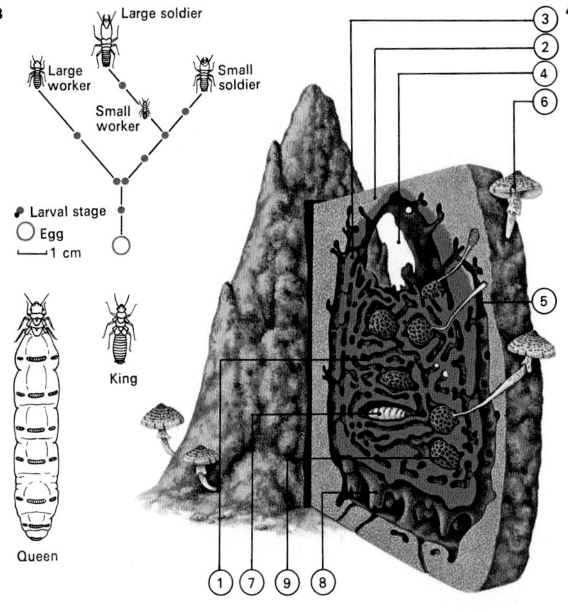

3
Large soldier
Large worker
Small soldier
Small worker
Larval stage
Egg
1 cm
King
Queen

1 Nest
2 Outer wall of termitarium
3 Wall of nest
4 Air space within nest
5 Chimneys to regulate the temperature of the nest
6 Fungus growing from mound
7 Queen's chamber
8 Base pillars supporting nest
9 Fungus gardens

3 A termite mound, with its blank exterior, gives no hint of the complex system of chambers and tunnels within. Thick, hard walls deter most predators and chimneys can be opened or closed to regulate the temperature. The mound is developed from a hole occupied by a mated male and female. The female (queen) only produces eggs, which become either workers or soldiers. Termites feed on wood and leaves brought in by foraging workers, and on fungus grown on feces in special fungus gardens inside the mound.

4

4 A typical savanna scene might have a herd of Grant's gazelle *(gazella granti)* feeding on grass. The open plains are dotted with wide-topped acacias and clumps of small bushes.

5 Prides of lions, often with several adult males, are commonly seen lazing in the shade of a tree. Lionesses, which lack manes, do most of the killing, often working as a team to stalk prey. Lions themselves have no natural enemies except man.

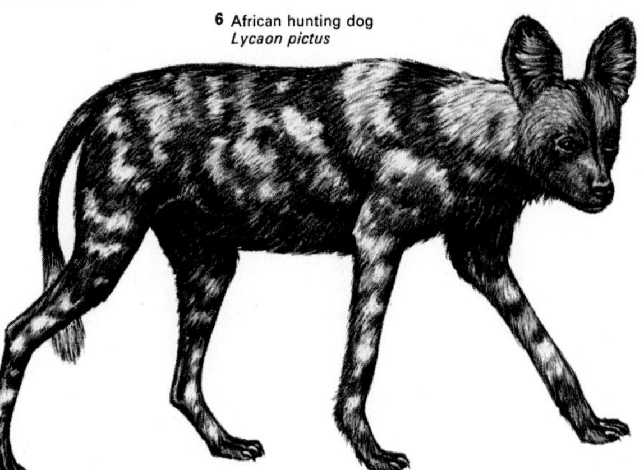

6 African hunting dog
Lycaon pictus

6 African hunting dogs are gregarious animals that live in packs of from 6 to 20 individuals. They hunt in an organized manner, taking turns to chase their prey animal until it is exhausted.

5 Lion
Panthera leo

South American grasslands

From the Brazilian highlands and dense forests of the Amazon southward to the barren lands of Patagonia, and from the eastern slopes of the Andes to the Atlantic Ocean, stretches a vast ocean of grassland. This is a region where droughts are frequent and where torrential downpours penetrate only the top layers of soil. As a result, trees are unable to compete with shallow-rooted grass plants that take the available water.

Grassland and climate

The type of grassland, and therefore the kind of animals it supports, depends largely on rainfall and temperature. Hot, dusty summers, cold, windy winters, and alternate periods of drought and heavy rainfall have produced the huge expanse of temperate grassland called the Argentine pampas [1]. On this plain, formed by layers of soil weathered from the Andes and carried eastward by rivers toward the sea, the controlling influence of soil moisture on vegetation is clearly apparent. On the wetter eastern side the grass grows in tall, coarse tufts and eventually merges into forest. The fertility of this part of the pampas has been used by man for wide-scale ranching and agriculture and, as a result, the landscape has been considerably modified. On the drier western and southern margins bare soil patches are found between clumps of prairie grass, and drought-resistant bushes and small scrub trees replace the grassland. Further west the scrub gives way to desert.

Animals large and small

Most of the large mammals that inhabited these grasslands when South America was an isolated continent disappeared about three million years ago when the isthmus of Panama was formed and carnivores traveled southward from North America. The carnivores were unable to cope with conditions successfuly, and eventually died out. As a result the only animals found in the South American grasslands today are those that have managed to adapt to the climate and food supplies of the area. The only mammal of any size on the pampas is the pampas deer *(Blastocerus campestris)* [2] and the largest animal inhabitant is a bird, the rhea *(Rhea americana)* [10]. This flightless bird is well suited to an open habitat. Its long legs give it an elevated view of its surroundings and enable it to run at more than 30mph (50kph). In spite of the absence of large mammals, at ground level the grasslands teem with life. There may be as many as 100 surface insects per square foot, particularly grasshoppers and butterflies. They, and numerous lizards, snakes, and spiders provide food for the predatory birds and mammals.

It is the small mammals, however, that have made best use of the ground cover and are most characteristic of the grasslands. Many of them solve the problems of climatic extremes and a lack of suitable hiding places by living underground for at least part of their lives and, as a result, burrowing rodents such as the viscacha *(Lagostomus maximus)* [4] and the noisy tucu-tucu *(Ctenomys talarum)* are among the most successful grassland inhabitants. For much of the day they remain hidden in their underground tunnels, coming out to feed only in the safety of darkness. The wild guinea

CONNECTIONS

See also
584 Northern grasslands
586 Grasslands of Africa
590 Australian desert grasslands
578 Regions of the earth: zoogeography
580 The basis of ecology
540 The classification of mammals
526 The classification of birds

1

1 The flat Argentine pampas covers more than 350,000 sq miles (500,000 sq km). In the east moist Atlantic winds promote the growth of rich, tall grass; but near the Andes a hot, dry climate produces an arid steppe land with bare soil patches between tufts of prairie grass and drought-resistant bushes. Many pampas animals in these harsh regions live underground for at least part of their lives.

2

Pampas deer
Blastoceros campestris

2 The pampas deer is one of the few herbivorous mammals of any size to be found on the South American grasslands. Its numbers have now been seriously reduced as a result of overhunting and the destruction of its habitat by cultivation.

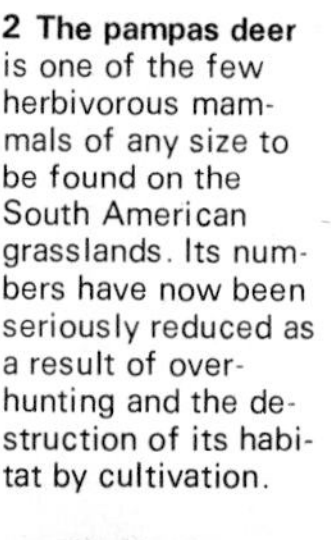

3 Giant armadillo
Priodontes giganteus

Six-banded armadillo
Euphractus sexcinctus

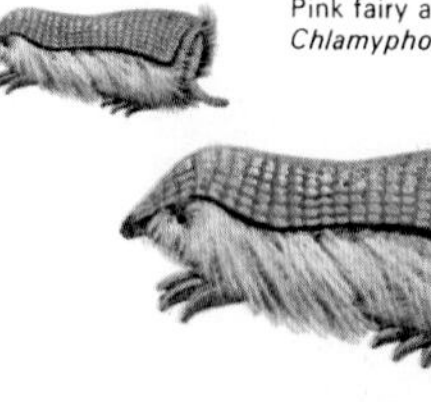

Pink fairy armadillo
Chlamyphorus truncatus

3 The 21 species of armadillo are among the most abundant and widespread of South American mammals. Uniquely protected by plates of bone joined with skin, a few of them, such as the three-banded armadillo, can roll themselves into round balls when threatened. But most escape predators by rapid burrowing. Armadillos vary in size from the giant armadillo, 5ft (1.5m) in length and weighing up to 110 lb (50kg), to the fairy armadillo which is only 5in (13cm) long and spends most of its life underground. Armadillos are regarded as pests in some areas but they do help man by ridding his crops of harmful insects and other small animals.

Five-toed armadillo
Cabassous centralis

Hairy armadillo
Chaetophractus villosus

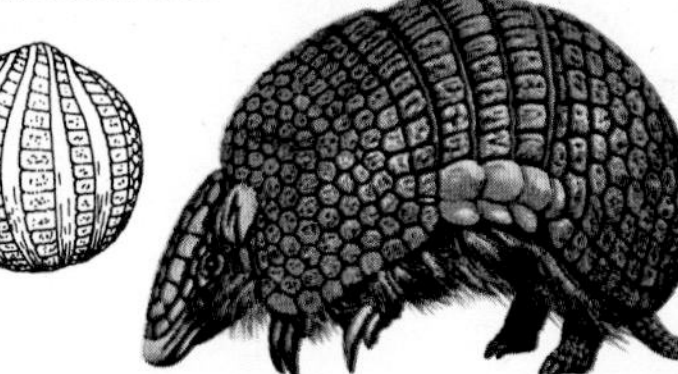

Three-banded armadillo
Tolypeutes matacus

pig *(Cavia aperea)* [4], which lives above ground, seeks protection by forming large colonies of up to several hundred and only emerges from tufts of grass to feed.

Rodents form a large part of the diet of grassland predators such as the pampas fox *(Dusicyon gymnocercus)* and Azara's opossum *(Didelphis azarae)*. But extremes of climate and erratic rainfall make food supplies unreliable, so many predators will eat almost anything they can find. Numerous other predators, such as armadillos [3], skunks, and anteaters, forage in the grass for the abundant insect life. Birds such as the smooth-billed anis *(Grotophaga ani)* and the aptly named cattle tyrant *(Machetornis rixosus)* [7] find their food by following grazing animals. They then catch the thousands of insects disturbed from the ground vegetation.

Many of the birds of the pampas are migrant visitors. In autumn the golden plover *(Pluvialis dominica)* leaves the harsh conditions in the tundra and flies nearly 7,500 miles (12,000km) to winter in the grasslands before returning to its nesting grounds in spring. Many northern shore birds, such as redshanks and sandpipers, also migrate there in winter to take advantage of the fish and insects of marshy areas.

The Chaco and its wildlife

Large expanses of water are also typical of an area to the north of the pampas called the Chaco—a transitional zone between the grassland and the tropical forests of the Amazon that lacks a specialized fauna but attracts animals from neighboring zones. Sluggish rivers spread out over a large plain to form swamps. These become shallow lakes during the heavy summer rains and form a paradise for water birds such as limpkins, ducks, and noisy screamers [9]. The swamps, often inhabited by the giant anteater *(Myrmecophaga tridactyla)* [6], are interspersed with patches of grassland and deciduous forest. The forest is the home of the giant armadillo *(Priodontes giganteus)* [3] and the elusive maned wolf *(Chrysocyon brachyurus)*, [5] which, although well adapted to plains life, seeks the shelter of trees.

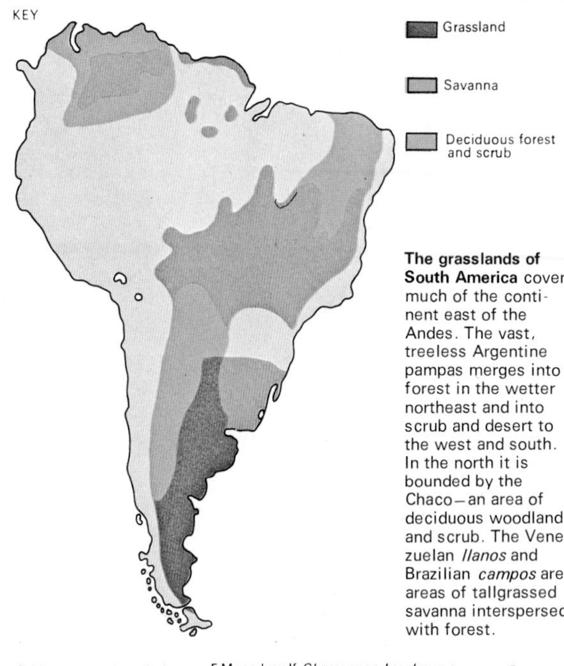
KEY
Grassland
Savanna
Deciduous forest and scrub

The grasslands of South America cover much of the continent east of the Andes. The vast, treeless Argentine pampas merges into forest in the wetter northeast and into scrub and desert to the west and south. In the north it is bounded by the Chaco—an area of deciduous woodland and scrub. The Venezuelan *llanos* and Brazilian *campos* are areas of tallgrassed savanna interspersed with forest.

4

Mara
Dolichotis patagona
Viscacha
Lagostomus maximus
Burrowing owl
Speotyto cunicularia
Cavy
Cavia aperea

4 The viscacha digs a system of tunnels that it shares with the burrowing owl and the mara, or Patagonian hare. By stripping the surrounding area of vegetation the viscacha can detect approaching predators. The pampas cavy nests at the base of grass tufts.

5 Maned wolf *Chrysocyon brachyurus*

5 The shy, nocturnal maned wolf, like other plains predators, will eat almost anything from small animals to fruit.

6 Giant anteater
Myrmecophaga tridactyla

6 The giant anteater rips open termite mounds and scoops up the termites with its sticky tongue. Its shaggy coat protects it from bites.

7

Cattle tyrant
Machetornis rixosus

7 The cattle tyrant is a flycatcher that perches on the backs of hoofed mammals waiting for insects disturbed by the grazing animals. It has an erectile crest of feathers.

8 Crested caracara
Polyborus plancus

8 The crested caracara, a ground-dwelling falcon that is both hunter and scavenger, searches the grassy plains for food both living and dead with a characteristic head-bobbing walk.

9

Southern screamer
Chauna torquata

9 The southern screamer haunts marshy areas of the pampas with harsh cries. Its slightly webbed feet enable it to walk on floating vegetation.

10 Common rhea
Rhea americana

10 The flightless rhea, or South American ostrich, a bird that lives in open country, roams the pampas in flocks of up to 30, feeding on vegetation and insects. It stands up to 4.6ft (1.5m) tall and can detect approaching danger even in high grass. When threatened it can run faster than a horse.

Australian desert grasslands

Two-thirds of Australia's 3 million square miles (8 million sq km) is semi-arid land supporting only tough grasses [5] and scattered acacia and gum trees. Less than 10in (25cm) of rain falls during the year, daytime temperatures average 90°F (32°C), and a dry wind blows. Inhospitable to man, these dry grasslands are the home of many of the symbolic animals of Australia [1, 3] such as the kangaroo, emu, koala, and kookaburra, as well as flocks of parrots, cockatoos, and budgerigars—all animals that cope with the dry conditions.

Making the most of water

The "outback" of the interior has largely been created by drying winds from the southeast and west. These are forced to release their moisture prematurely by the Great Dividing Range in the east and cold currents off the west coast. The "desert" lies at the limit of penetration of rain from the north and south and consequently may one year receive rain in winter, another in summer, and another not at all. The animals and plants are opportunists—they make the most of the water when it comes. The dull porcupine grass *(Triodia)* [4] bursts into a yellow sea of blossom on the red desert sand. The mulla mulla *(Trichinium manglesii)* springs up and produces fluffy pink flowers. Aromatic gum, or eucalyptus, trees such as the river gum *(Eucalyptus camaldulensis)*, which line the banks of dry rivers and watercourses, bear unique flowers whose stamens provide vivid colors.

Many plants are adapted to prevent excessive loss of precious water. Acacia leaves are reduced to flattened leaf stalks and those of the desert oak *(Casuarina decaisneana)* to needles that hang in fringes. Porcupine and cane grasses have thick, waxy cuticles and saltbush leaves *(Atriplex)* are coated in salts.

Australia's unique marsupials

The grasses and trees provide food, shelter, and nesting materials for the animal inhabitants. These animals entered Australia when it was still part of the land mass known as Gondwanaland (which included present-day Africa, South America, Southeast Asia, and Antarctica before continental drift) and were able to evolve unhindered by competition from placental animals when it became an island at the end of the Mesozoic era. The result is a unique set of animals with a trend toward nonaggressive behavior, a herbivorous diet, and a tolerance for arid conditions.

The name "koala" means "the animal that does not drink." These timid marsupials, or pouched mammals, live on an extremely restricted diet of eucalyptus leaves, which provide all the moisture they need. The fat-tailed marsupial "mouse" *(Sminthopsis crassicaudata)* stores fat "for a rainy day" in its tail. Kangaroos, which feed on triodia grass and saltbush, can survive long periods of drought. The wombat *(Vombatus)*, like several of its neighbors, digs a long underground burrow, often more than 10ft (3m) long, where it can escape the excessive heat and dryness of the day and the cold of the night. Many smaller marsupials, such as the insectivorous bandicoots and jerboa marsupial "mice" come out only at night. The primitive egg-laying echidna,

CONNECTIONS

See also

544 Monotremes and marsupials
578 Regions of the Earth: zoogeography
580 The basis of ecology
584 Northern grasslands
586 Grasslands of Africa
588 South American grasslands
606 Desert birds and mammals
526 The classification of birds
540 The classification of mammals

1

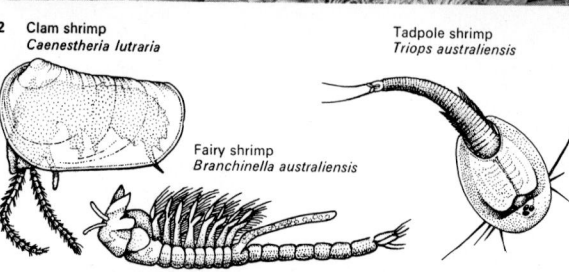

1 Koalas and kangaroos, which symbolize Australia, are only two of a wide variety of unique animals (see illustration 3) that have evolved since Australia became an island about 80 million years ago. In the vast, flat, desertlike interior covered with hardy grasses and fire-resistant eucalyptus and acacia trees the marsupials – "pouched" animals – and even stranger monotremes, like the echidna, were able to adapt unhindered by competition from placental mammals. The number and diversity of birds are equally impressive. The emu is the world's second largest bird and the parrot family has its stronghold here. The lizards, many of them nocturnal, have made the most successful adjustment to desert life. Amphibians, notably frogs, make use of temporary desert pools, and there are numerous species of insects.

2 Clam shrimp *Caenestheria lutraria*

Fairy shrimp *Branchinella australiensis*

Tadpole shrimp *Triops australiensis*

2 Tiny crustaceans like these shrimplike animals take advantage of temporary freshwater desert pools, which form during rain storms. When the pools evaporate the crustaceans die, leaving behind covered eggs that survive drought to hatch when conditions are favorable.

or spiny anteater, one of Australia's two monotreme species, is heavily armed with spines and when threatened can either roll into a ball or rapidly dig itself into the desert soil. It scoops up desert insects with its long, whiplike tongue.

Birds, reptiles and insects

Birds of the desert grasslands are usually seen more often than mammals. Colorful flocks of galahs, the most common cockatoos, nectar-feeding lorikeets, and green and yellow budgerigars congregate around water holes, often dug by ranchers for their cattle. These birds are constantly on the move in search of water and breed only after the rains. The uncertain water supply means that the kookaburra, a giant kingfisher, no longer finds most of its food in pools but searches for insects and snakes on the ground and in the trees. The emu, Australia's largest bird, changes from a diet of seeds to new-grown grass when the rains arrive. The mallee fowl *(Leipoa ocellata)* lays eggs in mounds of vegetation and sand. The vegetation ferments with the aid of dampening rain and the sun's heat and incubates the eggs. By altering the amount of nest material the male mallee fowl is able to regulate the incubation temperature.

Reptiles include dragon-lizards such as the frilled lizard, which erects a frill when threatened, small and large monitors, and skinks, which scuttle between clumps of porcupine grass in search of insects. Some snakes, such as the carpet python, are harmless to man, but most, like the death adder and king brown snake, are deadly. Male frogs call females to ponds only in wet conditions so that the tadpoles will develop quickly before the next dry season. In the period following the rains the grassland is full of insects—flying termites, bees, mantids, grasshoppers, and beautiful butterflies.

The dingo is one of Australia's few placental mammals but it is not indigenous. Now considered by many to be the same species as the domestic dog *(Canis familiaris)*, it probably returned to the wild after being introduced by the aborigines when they arrived in Australia about 30,000 years ago.

KEY

Stony desert
Mountain desert
Sand desert
Shield desert
Claypan desert

Two-thirds of Australia is flat desert formed by dry winds blowing across the interior. More than 2,000 species of plants and hundreds of animals have adapted to its aridity.

3 A selection of the birds and animals of Australia (shown in illustration 1), many of them unique to that continent and its off shore islands, is keyed here as follows:

1 Koala *Phascolarctos cinereus*
2 Sulphur-crested cockatoo *Cacatua galerita*
3 Galah *Kakatoe roseicapilla*
4 Cockatiel *Nymphicus hollandicus*
5 Budgerigar *Melopsittacus undulatus*
6 Kookaburra *Dacelo gigas*
7 Crimson-winged parrot *Aprosmictus erythropterus*
8 Lace monitor *Varanus varius*
9 King brown snake *Pseudechis australis*
10 Tawny frogmouth *Podargus strigoides*
11 Sugar glider *Petaurus breviceps*
12 Black kite *Milvus migrans*
13 Dingo *Canis dingo*
14 Wallaroo *Macropus robustus*
15 Great red kangaroo *Macropus rufus*
16 Great grey kangaroo *Macropus giganteus*
17 Emu *Dromiceius novaehollandiae*
18 Northern native cat *Satanellus hallucatus*
19 Brolga crane *Grus rubicunda*
20 Bearded dragon *Amphibolurus barbatus*
21 Red-tailed cockatoo *Calyptorhynchus magnificus*
22 Wedge-tailed eagle *Aquila audax*
23 Termite mound
24 Sand monitor *Varanus* sp
25 Echidna *Tachyglossus aculeatus*
26 Rainbow bee-eater *Merops ornatus*
27 Hairy-nosed wombat *Lasiorhinus latifrons*
28 Rufous rat kangaroo *Aepyprymnus rufescens*
29 Turquoise grass parrot *Neophema pulchella*
30 Long-nosed bandicoot *Perameles nasuta*
31 Rainbow lorikeet *Trichoglossus haematodus*
32 Frilled lizard *Chlamydosaurus kingi*
33 Giant stick insect *Didymuria violescens*
34 Little quail *Turnix velox*
35 Agile wallaby *Wallabia agilis*
36 Cicada *Platylomia* sp
37 Common marsupial mouse *Smihthopsis murina*
38 Carpet python *Morelia argus*
39 Checkered swallowtail *Graphium* sp
40 Jerboa marsupial mouse *Antechinomys spenceri*
41 Death adder *Acanthophophis antarcticus*
42 Holly cross toad *Motaden bennetti*
43 Common Australian crow butterfly *Euploea core*

4 The characteristic grass of the Australian interior is the prickly porcupine grass *(Trioda)*, which grows in huge pincushions in the red sand between saltbush and blue-bush scrub. With an extensive deep root system and leaves with hard cuticles assisting moisture-retention, the grass is adapted to withstand long droughts and to exploit brief rains.

5 Savanna woodland forms a continuous strip along the north coast and continues south inland from the Great Dividing Range with isolated areas in the southwest. The vegetation depends on over 20in (50cm) of rain a year. The trees (mainly eucalypts) grow fairly close together and the undergrowth is a mixture of grass and shrubs.

Northern evergreen forests

The northern coniferous forests stretch like a broad ribbon across the Northern Hemisphere, from the Pacific coast of Canada eastward to the Kamchatka Peninsula [Key]. In North America and Europe these vast tracts of land are known as the boreal forest and in Asia as the taiga—a Russian word meaning a dark and mysterious woodland. The southern boundary is marked by the blending of the pine trees and the deciduous tree varieties, although much land has now been cleared for agricultural purposes. In the northern extreme the trees are hemmed in by the vast open wastes of the frozen tundra. This wide climatic zone contains very few tree species, but scattered throughout the forest are glacier-scoured lakes and slow-flowing rivers that provide a varied habitat for many animals.

Food from the pine trees

The beaver *(Castor fiber)* [2], widespread throughout North America and recovering its numbers in Europe and Asia after being hunted almost to extinction, creates its own particular niche in the habitat. Both the male and female of the species, which pair for life, engage in felling trees with their sharp front incisors and damming a stream to form a pond with a high water level. In the middle of the pond they build a lodge where they live and raise a family of up to 12 individuals. A supply of young twigs is stored under water as a food supply for use during the long, harsh winter.

The main supply of food for most of the resident animals is furnished by the coniferous trees, which provide an ample but unvaried diet of seeds, buds, bark, and young needles. The yield of these coniferous products directly controls the numbers of animals that the forest supports. Many have become specialist feeders, particularly the birds and smaller mammals. The pine grosbeak *(Pinicola enucleator)* feeds on the young buds, seeds, and needles, while the crossbills *(Loxia)* specialize in taking the buds, seeds, and needles of pine and spruce. The European nutcracker *(Nucifraga caryocatactes)* and the Siberian jay *(Perisoreus infaustus)* open the cones with their strong bills. The capercaillie *(Tetrao urogallus)* and hazel grouse collect seeds that have dropped to the ground. The seed-eating mammals include the northern red-backed vole *(Clethrionomys rutilus)* and the wood lemming *(Myopus schisticolor)* of Eurasia.

Many animals store up food for the winter. The Eurasian red squirrel *(Sciurus vulgaris)* collects and hides cedar seeds and nuts in the hollows of trees and, for a special delicacy in the long, cold, dark months, impales mushrooms on ends of branches.

From winter into summer

The brown bear *(Ursus arctos)* and the Eurasian badger *(Meles meles)* relax in a deep sleep and let the cold winter months pass, using up a reserve of fat that they accumulate in the autumn when food is more plentiful. The spring and summer bring relief to the beleaguered forest and, as the snows melt, young tender shoots provide sustenance for the herbivores. Multitudes of insects, a plague to man but a boon to insectivorous birds and mammals, swarm through the forest. The moose

CONNECTIONS

See also
- **440** The cone bearers
- **608** Mountain life
- **594** Northern temperate woodlands
- **612** Life on the tundra
- **578** Regions of the Earth: zoogeography
- **580** The basis of ecology
- **540** The classification of mammals
- **526** The classification of birds

1

1 Siberian jay *Perisoreus infaustus*
2 Pine marten *Martes martes*
3 Great grey owl *Strix nebulosa*
4 Lynx *Felis lynx*
5 Pine grosbeak *Pinicola enucleator*
6 Capercaillie *Tetrao urogallus*
7 Eurasian flying squirrel *Pteromys volans*
8 Northern bat *Eptesicus nilssoni*
9 Black woodpecker *Dryocopus martius*
10 Wood-boring beetle
11 Willow tit *Parus montanus*
12 Siberian ruby throat *Luscinia calliope*
13 Elk *Alces alces*
14 Wolverine *Gulo gulo*
15 Boar *Sus scrofa*
16 Willow grouse *Lagopus lagopus*
17 Brown bear *Ursus arctos*
18 Reindeer *Rangifer tarandus*
19 Wolves *Canis lupus*
20 Eurasian ground squirrel *Eutamias sibiricus*
21 Pupa of longhorn beetle
22 Pygmy shrew *Microsorex hoyi*
23 Siberian weasel *Mustela sibirica*
24 Ichneumon wasp *Rhyssa* sp
25 Siberian tit *Parus cinctus*
26 Crossbill *Loxia* sp
27 Pine weevil *Hylobius* sp
28 Nutcracker *Nucifraga caryocatactes*
29 Snowy owl *Nyctea scandiaca*
30 Blue hare *Lepus timidus*
31 Raven *Corvus corax*
32 Greenshank *Tringa nebularia*
33 Pika *Ochotona hyperborea*
34 Brambling *Fringilla montifringilla*
35 Stoat *Mustela erminea*
36 Arctic fox *Alopex lagopus*
37 Masked shrew *Sorex cinereus*
38 Root voles *Microtus oeconomos*

1 The northern edge of the pine forest abuts on to the stark tundra terrain. In this Eurasian boreal forest the winters are long and severe, but the snow is loosely packed and the soil remains unfrozen for most of the year. This allows animals to burrow for the winter in comfort, and ensures that insects are available for the insectivores. The evergreen conifers guarantee a continuous food supply of seeds, twigs, and buds throughout the year and most of the animals spend their time in only a restricted area of the forest, rather than migrating. Carpeting the forest floor is a layer of pine needles, which provides a habitat for carpenter ants, carabid beetles, and spiders. Other spiders construct their webs under loose bark on tree trunks or decaying timber. Rotten wood is a home for insects such as ants.

(*Alces alces*) [4] (known as the elk in Europe and Asia), which is the largest member of the deer family, can then stop stripping the bark of trees or grubbing for mosses and lichens in the snow and resume browsing on small shrubs and trees or aquatic plants.

The moose may be the tallest animal in the forest, but the heaviest in North America was a woodland race of bison (*Bison bison*); and in Eurasia it was the European woodland wisent (*Bison bonasus*). Once widespread throughout both continents, these animals have been hunted to near extinction and now survive only in protected herds of a few hundred individuals. Another animal rescued from extinction is the sable of Eurasia (*Martes zibellina*), which for many years has been hunted for its valuable fur. Active conservation management has succeeded in restoring the sable population to the numbers living more than 200 years ago.

Common predators

The sable is carnivorous and drives its cousins the ermine (*Mustela erminea*) and the Siberian weasel (*Mustela sibirica*) from their home range. But these two animals are numerous in other regions along with other members of the mustelid family, such as the weasel (*Mustela nivalis*). A predator that is widespread throughout all of the northern forests of the world is the lynx (*Lynx*), a member of the cat family. It specializes in hunting hares and its numbers fluctuate according to the food supply.

The brown bear is perhaps the largest predator of the forest, but the most ferocious is the wolverine (*Gulo gulo*), which is amazingly strong for its size and takes prey as large as reindeer. The wolf (*Canis lupus*) lives on the edge of the forest. It makes hunting forays into the forest in packs to bring down reindeer and moose.

Smaller mammals, birds, and fish fall prey to marauders of the sky, such as the golden eagle (*Aquila chrysaëtos*), the goshawk (*Accipiter gentilis*), the snowy owl (*Nyctea scandiaca*), and in North America the bald eagle (*Heliaeetus leucocephalus*), the esteemed national symbol of the United States.

KEY

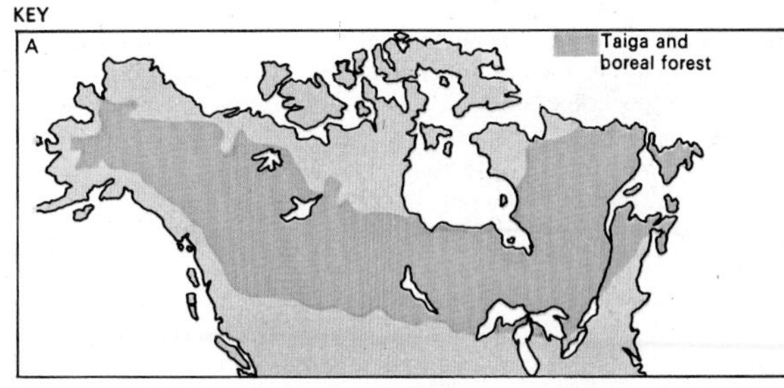
A
Taiga and boreal forest

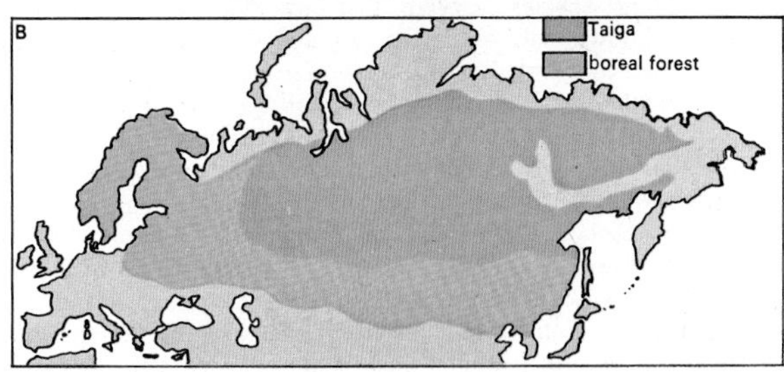
B
Taiga
boreal forest

Evergreen forests stretch across the northern portions of North America [A], Europe, and Asia [B]. To the south are mixed deciduous forests, to the north, sparse tundra.

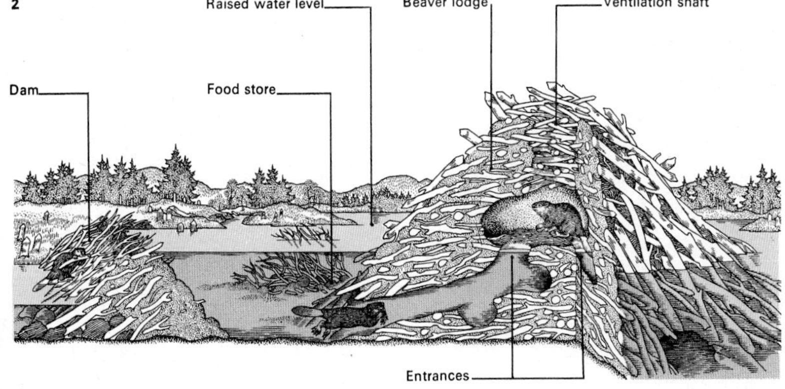
2
Raised water level
Beaver lodge
Ventilation shaft
Dam
Food store
Entrances

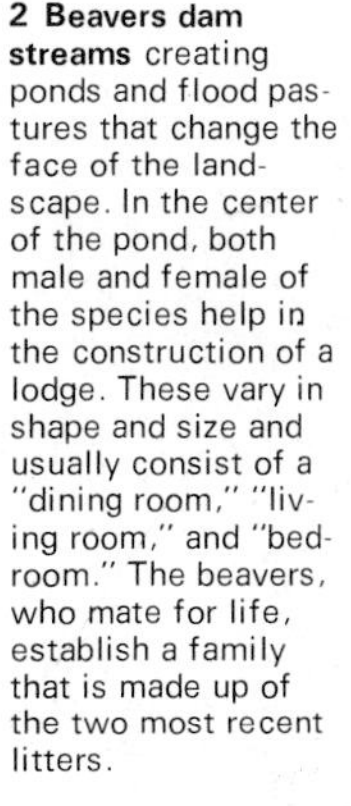

2 Beavers dam streams creating ponds and flood pastures that change the face of the landscape. In the center of the pond, both male and female of the species help in the construction of a lodge. These vary in shape and size and usually consist of a "dining room," "living room," and "bedroom." The beavers, who mate for life, establish a family that is made up of the two most recent litters.

3 The beaver fells young trees with its powerful incisors and takes them to the dam or lodge in the middle of the pond.

3 Beaver
Castor fiber

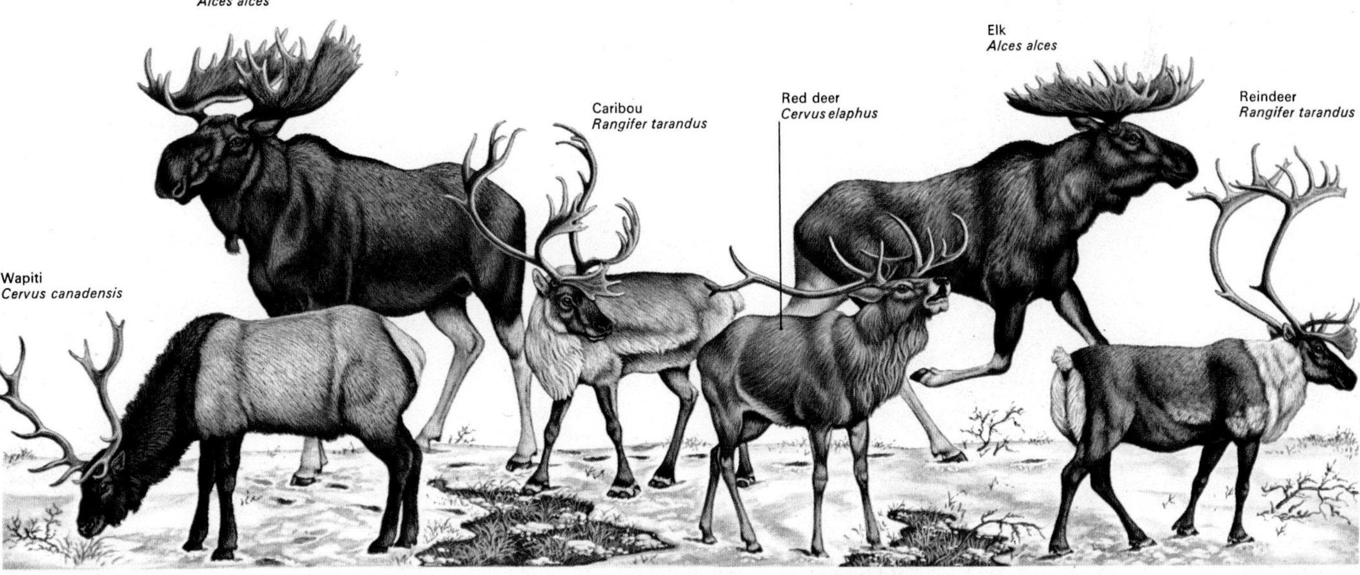
4
Moose
Alces alces
Elk
Alces alces
Caribou
Rangifer tarandus
Red deer
Cervus elaphus
Reindeer
Rangifer tarandus
Wapiti
Cervus canadensis

4 The tallest animal living in the forests of North America is the moose. It is identical with the elk that roams the European and Asian woodlands. The wapiti, which is confusingly known as the elk in North America, is second only to the moose in size. It is the American counterpart of the red deer, which is widespread in Eurasia, feeding on mountain pastures in summer and going down to the forest valleys in winter. Caribou are found in large herds throughout the tundra region of North America. They feed on low-growing vegetation, especially lichens or reindeer moss (*Cladonia*). Caribou are called reindeer in Europe and Asia. There they lead a semidomesticated life under the care of nomadic herdsmen.

5
American mink
Mustela vison

5 The American mink is found in many parts of North America. It has webbed feet and thick fur and it is equally at home in water and on land. Mink are mainly active at night and feed on a wide variety of small animals. They are farmed for their valuable pelts, but many have escaped and returned to the wild. The mink is a member of the family Mustelidae, which includes weasels, ermines, polecats, badgers, wolverines, skunks, and martens.

Northern temperate woodlands

Broadleafed forests consisting of a mixture of deciduous tree species are characteristic of much of the temperate zone of the Northern Hemisphere [Key]. In the past, forests of this sort were greater in extent, but they have been reduced in area by climatic changes and by man's activities in creating more agricultural land.

Remnants of the former grandeur of the temperate woodlands can still be seen in China and North America. In forests there several plant species survive that are otherwise known only as fossils or cultivated species in Europe and western Asia. They include the dawn redwood *(Metasequoia glyptostroboides)*, a deciduous conifer and the maindenhair tree *(Ginkgo biloba)*, both from China, and the tulip tree *(Liriodendron tulipifera)* from North America.

Man's activities in the forests have been almost entirely destructive. Over most of western Europe, for example, little of the original woodland remains. Many of the trees that do exist there have been planted or managed by man, who has subdued forests to his needs, often destroying them completely to make farmland. Whenever once forested land is abandoned it is quickly covered by scrub. If this were left, a succession of trees would gradually become dominant until, after two or three centuries, a forest would arise once more.

The woodland community

The trees in temperate forests are generally smaller than those of tropical forests, but all of the major plant groups are represented among the many species found in the northern woodlands. The trees themselves are dominant, but there are other woody species, such as the honeysuckle and ivy, supported by the trees. Where there is enough light, there may be an undergrowth of hazel and hawthorn or other smaller trees. Below this is a ground layer of herbaceous plants that must complete their life cycle in the spring months because of the lack of light once the trees and undergrowth are in full leaf. When light and warmth increase in the early part of the year, these plants flower in rapid succession.

Most trees also flower in springtime, bearing catkins whose pollen is spread by the wind and would otherwise be impeded by leaves. The relatively few exceptions, particularly some of the more southerly woodland species, such as limes and chestnuts, are insect-pollinated and flower later. Many kinds of lower plants, particularly the ferns and mosses, like the shade and dampness of the woodlands and are often abundant in forests. Fungi come into their own as the trees die, for their function is largely that of recycling agents; they break down the woody tissues and return them to the soil.

Animals of the woodlands

Animals in temperate woodlands are mostly small. The largest European animals, the aurochs *(Bos primigenius)*, wild oxen, became extinct in the seventeenth century and only a small number of European wisent *(Bison bonasus)* survive in the eastern forests of the continent. In North America the wood bison, a race of the American bison *(Bison bison)*, has been greatly re-

CONNECTIONS

See also
448 Woody flowering plants
450 Flowering trees, shrubs, and climbers
580 The basis of ecology
596 Woodlands of Australasia
578 Regions of the Earth: zoogeography
338 Temperate fruits
492 The classification of insects
526 The classification of birds

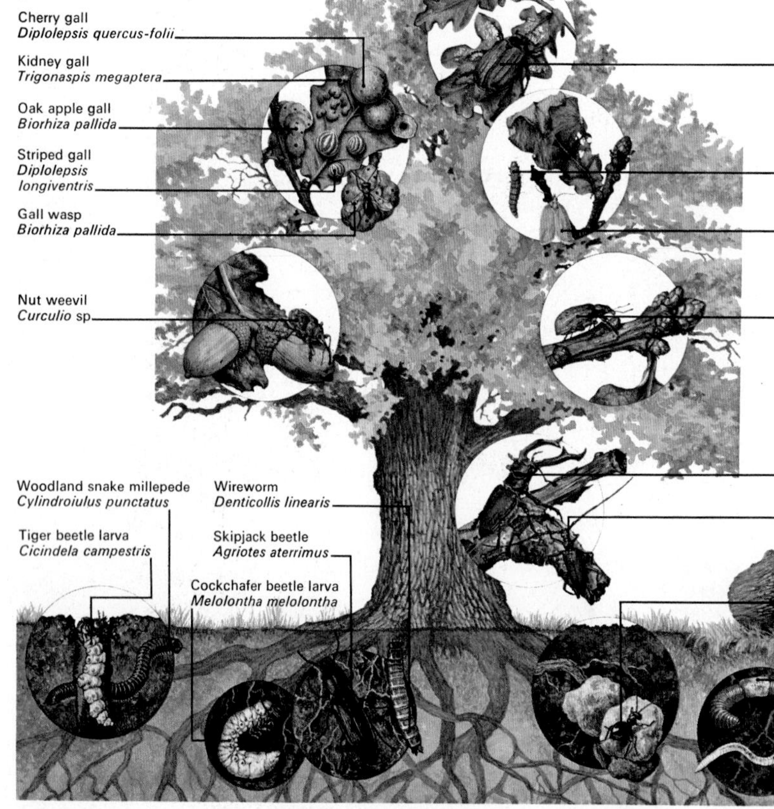

1
Cherry gall
Diplolepsis quercus-folii
Kidney gall
Trigonaspis megaptera
Oak apple gall
Biorhiza pallida
Striped gall
Diplolepsis longiventris
Gall wasp
Biorhiza pallida
Nut weevil
Curculio sp
Cockchafer beetle
Melolontha melolontha
Moth larva
Acrobasis consociella
Green tortrix moth
Tortrix viridana
Weevil
Phyllobius pyri
Greater stag beetle
Lucanus cervus
Longhorn beetle
Cerambyx cerdo
Woodland snake millepede
Cylindroiulus punctatus
Wireworm
Denticollis linearis
Tiger beetle larva
Cicindela campestris
Skipjack beetle
Agriotes aterrimus
Cockchafer beetle larva
Melolontha melolontha
Root gall
Biorhiza pallida
Marsh worm
Lumbricus rubellus
Pot worm
Mesenchytraeus setosus

1 An oak tree supports a wealth of small animal life (typical European species are shown). In the spring swarms of caterpillars, bugs, and beetles feed on the new leaves but do little lasting harm because the oak offsets the loss by putting out a late growth. For some beetles the oak offers safety to their young. Larvae of the weevil *Phyllobius* live in twigs, those of the stag beetle in dead wood, and the nut weevil in acorns. Other species of larvae find safety in galls, the abnormal growths on a tree, that form where the minute grubs feed. Beneath the tree a variety of worms break down fallen leaves and litter. Millipedes, worms, and larvae feed on soft, rotting plants and roots. The voracious larva of the tiger beetle digs a deep hole in which to hide and catch unwary insects, while the colorful adult beetle hunts small forest invertebrates.

2 The forest floor supports a different microcommunity from that of growing trees (typical species of eastern North America are shown). Small creatures are constantly active in breaking down the dead tissues of the forest litter and returning the components to the soil for use by plants. Tiny insects bore into the tissues, preceding the many fungi, bacteria, and other invaders that continue the process until the breakdown is completed. These organisms can be extremely specialized. In most cases they require a particular species of plant or tree, which will be tackled only when it is in a particular state of dryness or humidity. Many tiny creatures are the prey of hunters such as beetles and the slimy salamanders; the bigger kinds may be taken by birds and forest mammals. Foxes and badgers, for instance, will often eat worms and grubs when hungry.

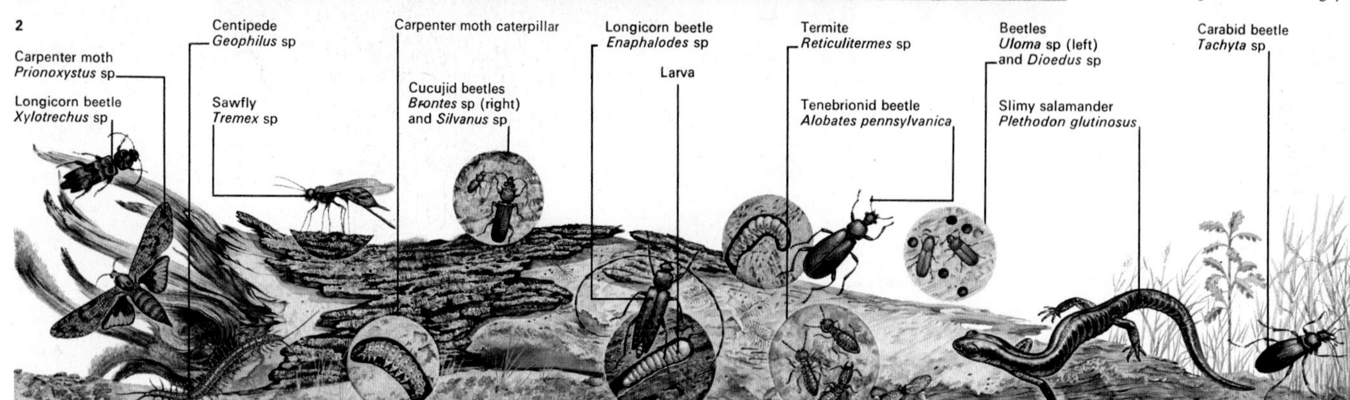

2
Carpenter moth
Prionoxystus sp
Longicorn beetle
Xylotrechus sp
Centipede
Geophilus sp
Sawfly
Tremex sp
Carpenter moth caterpillar
Cucujid beetles
Brontes sp (right)
and Silvanus sp
Longicorn beetle
Enaphalodes sp
Larva
Termite
Reticulitermes sp
Tenebrionid beetle
Alobates pennsylvanica
Beetles
Uloma sp (left)
and Dioedus sp
Slimy salamander
Plethodon glutinosus
Carabid beetle
Tachyta sp

duced in numbers, and deer are now the largest creatures of most of the temperate woodlands. The biggest of these, the moose *(Alces alces)*, is found in the more northern forest areas in Europe although it is more common in North America.

The paucity of large animals in the northern forests does not mean that the forests lack animal life, but rather that its richness depends on specialization, which is better achieved by small creatures. The common European oak *(Quercus robur)* is said to support more than 300 animal species [1]. Some of these, such as squirrels, depend partly on other plants. But many small animals are tied both to one kind of tree as well as to a particular part of it—a leaf, twig, or root—for their specialized existence. At all levels, from the canopy to the ground, there is a web of interdependent species [3].

The yearly food cycle

With the springtime growth of the plants there is a resurgence among the animals. Many small creatures emerge from hibernation to feed on the new leaves and to become themselves the food of numerous predators, including invertebrates, small birds, and insectivorous mammals.

Later in the year the first flush of animal and plant life disappears, but at no time are the woods empty of animal life. Even in winter grubs continue to bore their tunnels through the trunks of the trees. When a tree dies it still supports a host of small organisms, such as fungi, ants, and beetles, whose task is to assist in the speedy breakdown of the wood so that the soil is not impoverished by the loss of a tree. There are always small creatures, especially worms, at work in leaf litter on the forest floor, converting the autumn leaf fall into humus in the soil.

The trees influence life far beyond their own boundaries. Their need for water draws it from as far as their roots will reach. It is taken through the woody tissues and finally much of it is lost to the atmosphere via the leaves. A single large tree will, during spring and summer, pass hundreds of gallons of water to the atmosphere in a day.

KEY

Forest is the natural ground cover wherever there is sufficient moisture in the temperate regions. In North America, only remnants are left of the great temperate deciduous forests that once covered much of the eastern half of the continent.

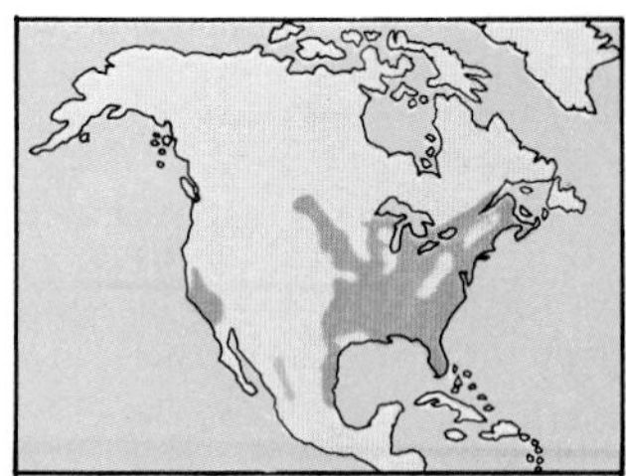

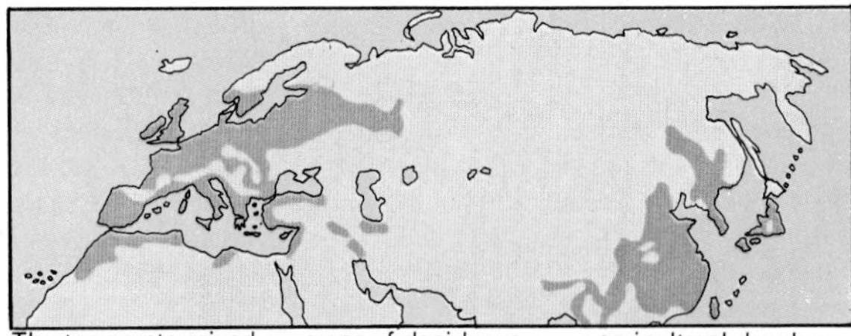

The temperate mixed woodlands of Europe extend from the British Isles across central Europe into the USSR. Beyond the Mountains of Tibet there are further areas of deciduous forest in eastern China. Oak, ash, beech, and chestnut are typical trees of Europe's forests. Vast areas have been cleared for urban and agricultural development, and in some places the natural growth is being replaced with faster-growing conifers.

3

1 Woodcock *Scolopax* sp
2 Fox *Vulpes* sp
3 Wood sorrel *Oxalis* sp
4 Horn of plenty *Craterellus* sp
5 Dormouse *Muscardinus* sp
6 Woodmouse *Apodemus* sp
7 Sparrowhawk *Accipiter* sp
8 Wood anemone *Anemone* sp
9 Bluebell *Endymion* sp
10 Violet *Viola* sp
11 Slow-worm *Anguis* sp
12 Oak *Quercus* sp
13 Honeysuckle *Lonicera* sp
14 Wood ant *Formica* sp
15 Wood warbler *Phylloscopus* sp
16 Birch *Betula* sp
17 Butterfly *Pararge* sp
18 Parasite wasp *Ichneumon* sp
19 Hornet *Vespa* sp
20 Bush cricket *Tettigonia* sp
21 Glow-worm *Lampyris* sp
22 Earwig *Forficula* sp
23 Red underwing moth *Catocala* sp
24 Hover fly *Myiatropa* sp
25 Nightingale *Luscinia* sp
26 Ash *Fraxinus* sp
27 Tree creeper *Certhia* sp
28 Woodpecker *Dendrocopos* sp
29 Tawny owl *Strix* sp
30 Grey squirrel *Sciurus* sp
31 Nut weevil *Curculio* sp
32 Galls
33 Purple emperor *Apatura* sp
34 Green woodpecker *Picus* sp
35 Elm *Ulmus* sp
36 Humble bee *Bombus* sp
37 Great tit *Parus* sp
38 Roe deer *Capreolus* sp
39 Badger *Meles* sp
40 Hart's tongue fern *Phyllitis* sp
41 Fly agaric *Amanita* sp
42 Wasp beetle *Clytus* sp
43 Primrose *Primula* sp
44 Ground beetle *Carabus* sp

3 The trees of an English oak wood provide nourishment and shelter for many species of wildlife. Some species are primarily dependent on the trees for their food, while others are predators, finding their food among the herbivores. In its natural state, a broadleaved woodland usually contains mixed plant species. If the soil is acid, birches are often present; where it is alkaline, ash trees and ferns can often be found. Elm usually grows in hedgerows or at the edge of a wood. Among the smaller plants the woody honeysuckle is supported by other trees. The spring-flowering herbs include primroses, violets, wood anemones, wood sorrel, and bluebells. Two common large fungi present are horn of plenty and fly agaric. Of the woodland mammals only the dormouse and woodmouse are confined to the forest. Foxes, badgers, deer, and squirrels use it as a source of food and shelter. The grey squirrel, an introduced species from North America, has largely replaced the native red squirrel in Britain, but it is not present in the rest of Europe. Woodland birds include the ground-dwelling woodcock, rarely seen because of its camouflaged coloring and shy ways. The great tit is a resident, while the wood warbler and nightingale are migrants, taking advantage of the summer wealth of insects. The tree creeper searches the bark for small insects but the woodpeckers feed on grubs extracted with their long bills. Birds of prey are the day-hunting sparrowhawk and the nocturnal tawny owl, which feed on small mammals and other birds. Many of the insects have short adult lives and can be seen for only a few weeks in the breeding season.

Woodlands of Australasia

Despite its large area, only a small proportion of the Australian land mass is covered with true forest. Temperate forest covers the southern portion of the Great Divide, the mountain ridge separating the eastern coastal plain from the interior, extending to the southeastern corner. In contrast, the forest of the northern coastal areas is tropical. Of the large islands that form the remainder of the Australasian region, New Guinea is clothed with tropical rain forest and New Zealand and Tasmania largely with temperate trees [Key].

The effects of isolation

The animals and plants of the region have close equivalents in other parts of the world but relatively few representatives. This is because of the long period of isolation from other major continents. The less advanced forms of life, including, insects, reptiles, and amphibians, are unique to the Australasian forests. Among them are many primitive, or "relict," species—the hallmarks of millennia of isolation and of island living—including primitive "tailed" New Zealand frogs *(Leiopelma)* which live near mountain tops, and two families of egg-laying mammal, the platypus *(Ornithorhynchus anatinus)* of temperate Australian streams and the spiny echidnas, or anteaters, of eastern Australia and New Guinea.

Temperate and tropical trees

The trees of the temperate forests comprise many genera unique to the world's southern continents. They include many species of aromatic gum *(Eucalyptus)* and southern beeches *(Nothofagus)*. In the damper areas, giant tree ferns *(Dicksonia)* abound [1, 2].

Australasia's tropical forests, very similar to those of the Oriental region, include large-leaved tropical trees such as stilt-rooted mangroves *(Sonneratia)* and trees with edible fruits—coconut palms *(Cocos)*, bananas *(Musa)*, and breadfruit *(Artocarpus)*. In the humid forest of New Guinea there are some peculiar "living fossils" found only in the southern Pacific region. They include the winter's barks of the family Winteraceae, the spiky monkey-puzzles *(Araucaria)*, and members of the primitive podocarp family, Podocarpaceae, of which the "plum yew" *(Podocarpus)* bears succulent "cones."

Like the trees among which they live, many of the mammals of the Australasian forests are unique and almost all (apart from some bats and rodents) are marsupials. The canopy, inhabited by primates in other forests, is here the home of tree kangaroos *(Dendrolagus)* and the many species of arboreal phalangers, among them the recently rediscovered Leadbeater's possum [5] and the koala "bear" [4]. The single koala species is confined to the eucalyptus forests of eastern Australia. There, koalas are fully protected from the depredations of man, who once slaughtered them for their fur.

The predators within the forest are the varied species of native "cat," but no longer are the forests of the southeast roamed by the pouched "wolf" or its attendant "devil." The forest and scrub of Tasmania are now the only homes of the Tasmanian devil *(Sarcophilus harrisii)*, which feeds on a wide variety of animal food, including carrion. When the pouched wolf, or

CONNECTIONS

See also
544 Monotremes and marsupials
578 Regions of the Earth: zoogeography
594 Northern temperate woodlands
580 The basis of ecology
1260 Colonizing Oceania and Australasia
526 The classification of birds

1
Wagga Wagga
Melbourne
Devonport
Hobart
Red river gum *Eucalyptus camaldulensis*
Snow gum *Eucalyptus niphophila*
2400m
Blue gum *Eucalyptus saligna*
Tree fern *Dicksonia antarctica*
Waratah *Telopea* sp
Bass Strait
Snow gum *Eucalyptus pauciflora*
Black beech *Nothofagus* sp
1600m
Mountain ash *Eucalyptus regnans*
Mulga scrub
Red river gum
Sclerophyll forest
Snow gum (*niphophila*)
Snow gum (*pauciflora*)
Mixed forest
Mangrove
Mountain ash
Snow gum (*pauciflora*)
Black beech
Beech forest

1 The effects of local climatic differences can be seen in the trees found along a line through a southern portion of the Great Divide and Tasmania. The westward-facing mountain slopes are much drier than those facing east and on them grow the dry, "hard-leaved," or sclerophyll, forests of eucalyptus. Only in the moist areas can species of tree ferns survive. The prevailing winds often warp the growth of beech and snow gum.

2
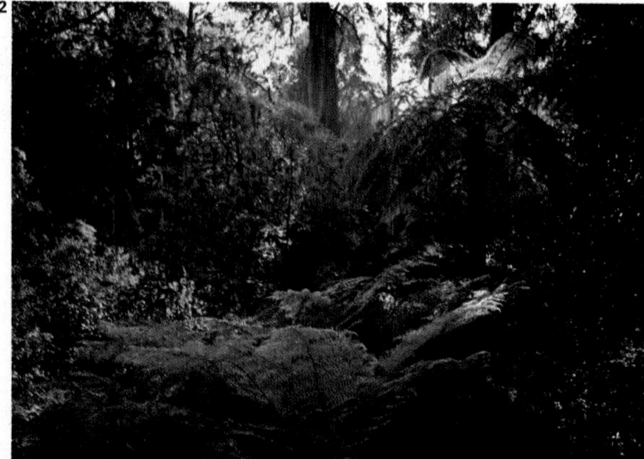

2 Tree ferns and eucalyptus abound at the edge of a typical "wet" forest area of New South Wales. In the depths of this type of forest the lyrebird builds its domed nest of sticks and moss on a tree stump or ledge.

3 Corroboree frog
Pseudophryne corroboree

3 The corroboree frog is at home in cold, damp moss at high altitudes in the Australian alps. Any accumulation of water in the moss is sufficient for it to lay its eggs in and for tadpole development.

4
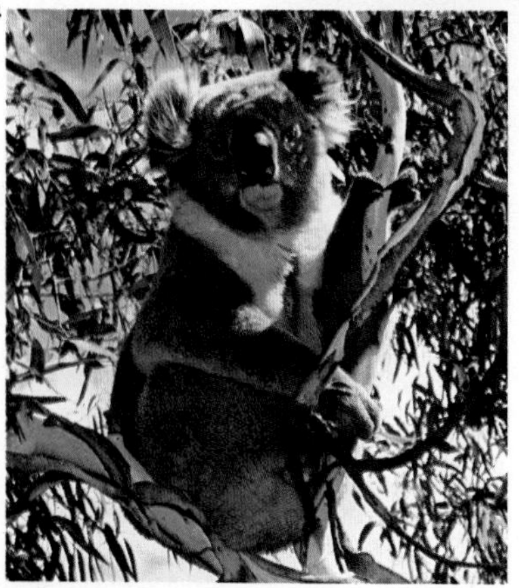

4 The koala (Phascolarctos cinereus) was once slaughtered for its fur, but the animal is now protected. Confined to the southeastern states of Australia, koalas feed on about 12 species of eucalyptus, or gum tree. They rarely come to the ground and spend most of their lives in the tree tops eating leaves and young bark. They are mostly solitary, but an adult male usually has a small harem which he guards jealously. The maximum body length is about 33in.

5 Leadbeater's possum
Gymnobelideus leadbeateri

5 Leadbeater's possum was at one time thought to be extinct as no specimens had been seen since 1909. In 1961, however, the species was rediscovered in a dense mountain ash forest in the highlands near Marysville, Victoria. It is completely arboreal and its paws are adapted to its life style, being very wide at the tips with strong, short claws. This phalanger displays great agility in pursuit of its insect prey, which it catches by night.

thylacine *(Thylacinus cynocephalus)*, was more common, accompanying Tasmanian devils fed on the remains of the wolves' kill. The last specimen of thylacine to be seen was shot in 1930.

Fliers of the forests

New Zealand forests contain only two native species of land mammals, both of them bats, the wattled bat *(Chalinolobus tuberculatus)* and the New Zealand short-tailed bat *(Mystacina tuberculata)*. Unusually, the chief herbivores are birds. The most spectacular of these, the moas, were hunted to extinction by the original migrants, the predecessors of the Maoris, for food and feathers. Other peculiar birds of New Zealand still living are the three species of flightless kiwis *(Apteryx)* and a rare ground parrot, the kakapo *(Strigops hapbroptilus)*.

Some of the most strikingly colored and vocal inhabitants of the Australasian forests are the many varieties of birds, a great number of which are found nowhere else in the world. The most magnificent of these are inhabitants of the tropical forests of New Guinea and include the birds of paradise (family Paradisaeidae), the bowerbirds (family Ptilonorhynchidae) [6], and several unique species of pigeons, among them the slate blue and crested crowned pigeons *(Goura)*, the largest of which is almost the size of a turkey—about 39in (1m).

Parrots abound among the branches of both tropical and temperate trees. One of the most familiar is the sulfur-crested cockatoo *(Cacatua galerita)*, a popular cage bird the world over. Harsh and strident parrot calls resound through the forest canopy, while in the densely vegetated undergrowth of the temperate southeast the male lyrebird [8] indulges in his ventriloquist song, throwing his voice in a remarkable assortment of calls borrowed from others.

From crown to floor, the forests are occupied by nectar-eating honeyeaters, insect-eating thornbills, fantails and Australian robins. Although some birds, such as the rock warbler of the Hawkesbury Sandstone area of Sydney, have a restricted range, others, such as the golden whistler [7], are widespread.

KEY

Tropical rain forest

Temperate rain forest

The forests of Australasia are of two distinct types: temperate and tropical, each supporting a unique selection of plants and animals. The temperate forest of southeast Australia is the one on which man has had the most effect, but even here high rainfall and fertile soil may produce jungle.

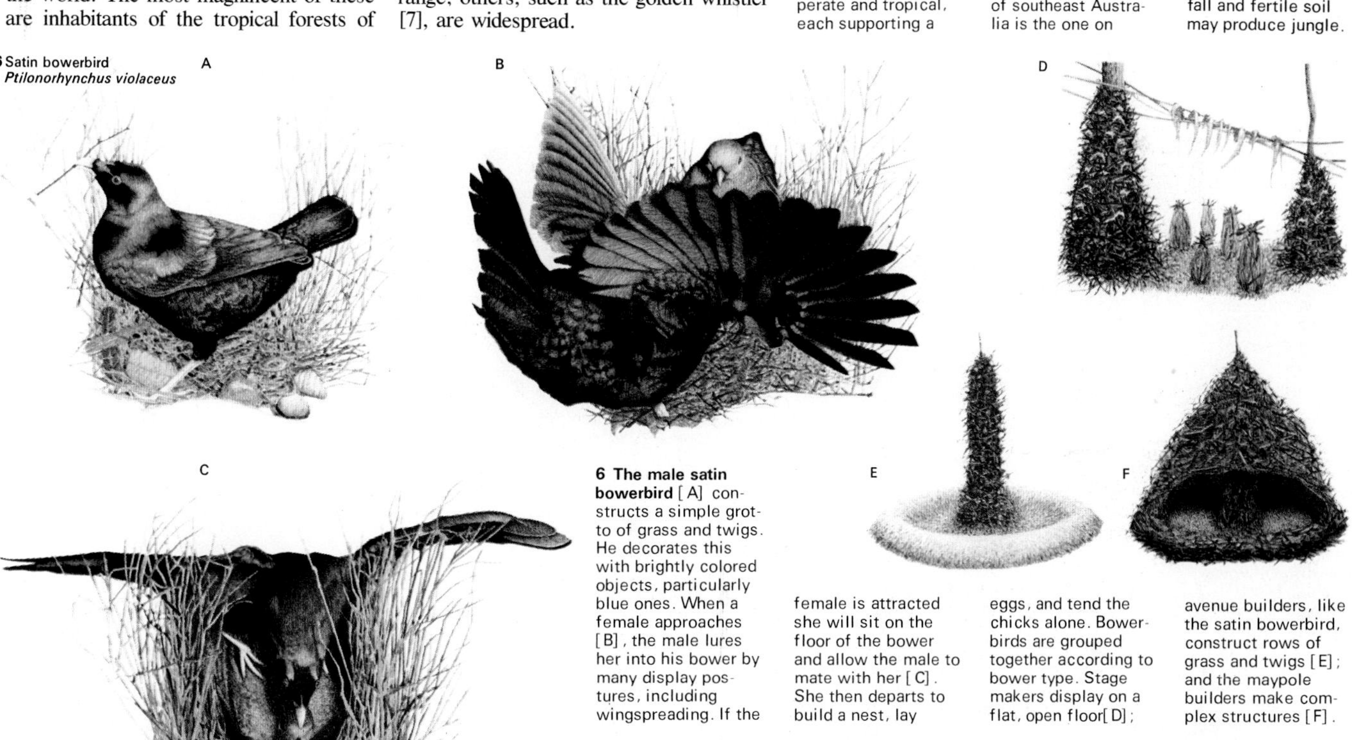

6 Satin bowerbird
Ptilonorhynchus violaceus
A
B
C
D
E
F

6 The male satin bowerbird [A] constructs a simple grotto of grass and twigs. He decorates this with brightly colored objects, particularly blue ones. When a female approaches [B], the male lures her into his bower by many display postures, including wingspreading. If the female is attracted she will sit on the floor of the bower and allow the male to mate with her [C]. She then departs to build a nest, lay eggs, and tend the chicks alone. Bowerbirds are grouped together according to bower type. Stage makers display on a flat, open floor [D]; avenue builders, like the satin bowerbird, construct rows of grass and twigs [E]; and the maypole builders make complex structures [F].

7
Tasmania
Louisiade Archipelago
Tanimbar Islands
Golden whistler
Pachycephala pectoralis

7 The golden whistler is a bird found in many different forms on the islands around the Australian coast. Bill shape, as shown here, varies considerably among island races, and reflects the way in which each has become adapted to feed in different kinds of forest.

8 Superb lyrebird
Menura superba

8 The secretive and shy lyrebird is rarely seen by man because it hides in densely vegetated gullies in the most inaccessible parts of the temperate forest. The female lyrebird is remarkably fastidious, for she carries all the droppings from the nest and puts them in a stream.

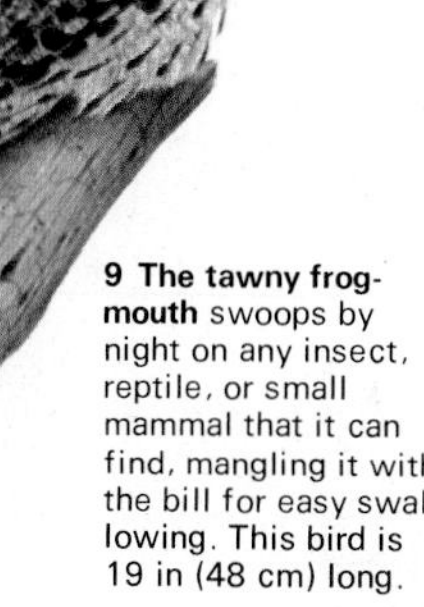

9 Tawny frogmouth
Podargus strigoides

9 The tawny frogmouth swoops by night on any insect, reptile, or small mammal that it can find, mangling it with the bill for easy swallowing. This bird is 19 in (48 cm) long.

African rain forest

A tropical forest is a deceptive place. No other habitat is so complex or supports such a teeming variety of animals. Yet a visit there may reveal little more than hosts of butterflies and an occasional bird. Since many of the animals are nocturnal, they stay hidden by day in their leafy sanctuary. Some remain in burrows in the ground litter and others seldom, or never, venture down from their arboreal homes. They are betrayed only by forest sounds; a distant crashing of monkeys through the foliage, for example, or the resounding shrieks of hornbills as they feed in the canopy.

The forest vegetation

Rain forests such as those of Africa [Key] are found in tropical regions where rain falls in heavy storms throughout the year. In such places temperatures average 81°F (27°C), varying little between night and day, and the air is moist and humid.

The vegetation of the rain forest [3], forever pushing upward toward the Sun, forms a series of distinct layers. On top, scattered tall trees, or emergents, many with flanged buttresses formed from root and trunk for support, reach above the thick-spread canopy layer. In the middle, smaller trees with long, oval crowns compete for narrow shafts of sunlight penetrating the foliage. Below the smaller trees, palms and shrubs exist in a twilight microclimate and merge into a relatively sparse ground layer of shrubs and tree seedlings. Matting the tree trunks are creepers and woody vines (lianas). Wherever the sunlight reaches the ground, herbs, shrubs, creepers, and tree seedlings are woven into a dense undergrowth.

Everywhere in the forest is an ever-growing, evergreen tangle of plant life. Species that grow on other plants, the epiphytic ferns, lichens, and orchids, lodge in sunny branches in the canopy or shady nooks farther down. Some rely on litter accumulating around their roots for food and moisture while others absorb water through hanging roots. Strangler figs bring death to their host trees; germinating in the tree bark they send down roots that eventually surround the trunk and cause it to rot away.

The African rain forests contain more than 7,000 species of evergreen and deciduous flowering plants and the virtual non-seasonal climate means that at any time of the year there is a supply of leaves, flowers, and fruits for the animals.

Life in the trees

The way in which the forest is formed into well-defined layers means that animals can live and feed in different habitats at different heights from the ground. Herbivores, such as the colobus monkeys, stay fairly rigidly within a particular layer, while predators, such as genets, are forced to make journeys from the ground to the canopy in search of bird, small mammal, and insect prey.

The whole forest is a finely balanced ecosystem where the animals not only feed in different layers but also at different times. Monkeys and birds tend to be diurnal and most forest mammals nocturnal. At night the tiny bush babies such as the dwarf galago *(Galagoides demidovii)* emerge from their nests to search for flying insects [7] and fruit.

CONNECTIONS

See also
600 Forests of Southeast Asia
602 New World tropics
596 Woodlands of Australasia
580 The basis of ecology
578 Regions of the Earth: zoogeography
448 Woody flowering plants
526 The classification of birds
554 Primates: relatives of man

1

Okapi 1·6m *Okapia johnstoni*

Water chevrotain 30cm *Hyemoschus aquaticus*

Chequered elephant shrew 30cm *Rhynchocyon* sp

Forest genet 40-50cm *Genetta tigrina*

Banded duiker 50cm *Cephalophus zebra*

Four striped squirrel 20cm *Funisciurus* sp

Bongo 1·3m *Taurotragus eurycerus*

1 Stripes and spots work equally well as disruptive camouflage for many shy forest mammals. Blending in with patches of sunlight and dark vegetation, nocturnal animals such as the banded duiker and genet remain motionless and hidden by day and emerge to feed at night. The okapi, a relative of the giraffe, is a daytime feeder. The horizontal stripes imitate the sun's rays as they penetrate the forest canopy. The hoofed mammals are smaller than their relatives in open habitats. A compact body and small or backward-pointing horns facilitate movement through tangled bushes. Bongo and duiker pass under low bushes with odd, crouching runs. Dimensions given for the chevrotain, okapi, duiker, and bongo are heights at the shoulder; for the genet, shrew, and squirrel, they are head and body length.

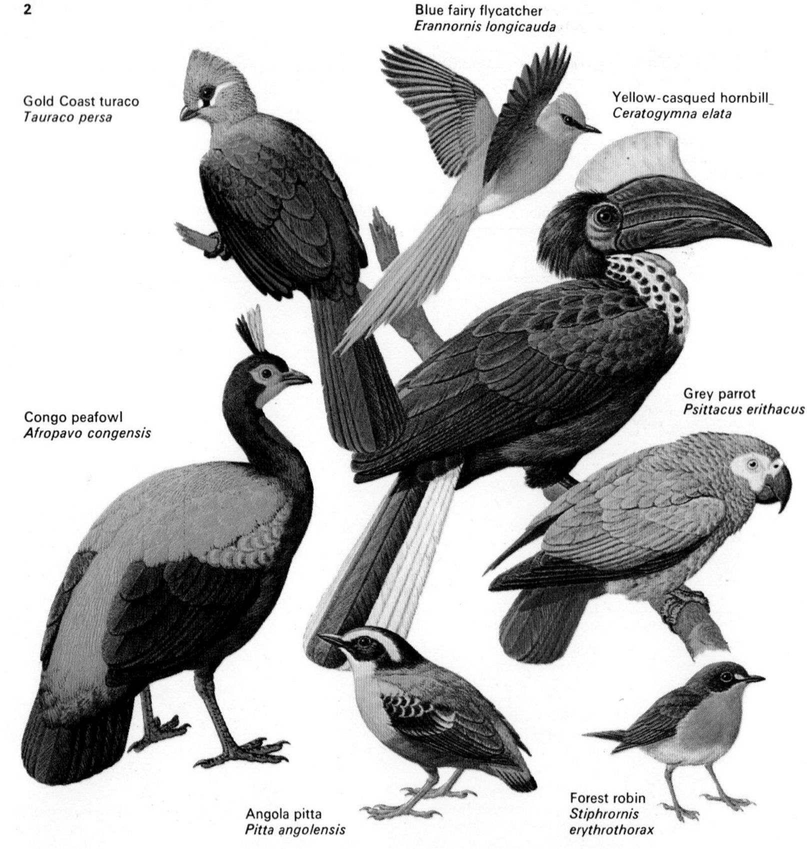

2
Blue fairy flycatcher
Erannornis longicauda
Gold Coast turaco
Tauraco persa
Yellow-casqued hornbill
Ceratogymna elata
Grey parrot
Psittacus erithacus
Congo peafowl
Afropavo congensis
Angola pitta
Pitta angolensis
Forest robin
Stiphrornis erythrothorax

2 Rarely seen but continuously heard, forest birds tend to leap among the trees rather than fly around the forest. High in the canopy the Gold Coast turaco and heavily-built yellow-casqued hornbill crash noisily from branch to branch in search of their staple diet of fruit, while the grey parrot is often seen in small flocks flying over the tops of the trees. Many of the smaller birds feed on insects and other small invertebrates. The blue fairy flycatcher finds them in the trees, while the forest robin and Angolan pitta, aptly called the "jewel-thrush" because of its brilliant coloration, grub among the humus of the forest floor. The pitta is a particularly hard bird to detect as it has the ability to throw its voice like a ventriloquist. The Congo peafowl, a ground-dwelling bird related to the Asiatic peacock, was not discovered by Europeans until 1937.

3

Dwarf galago
Red colobus

100ft
30m

Diana monkey
Python
Great blue turaco

50ft
15m

Chimpanzee
Grey-cheeked mangabey

25ft
7·5m

Gaboon viper
African civet
Tullberg's rat
Okapi

3 A variety of tree heights provides different levels at which forest animals may live. The tallest trees emerge through the canopy and may reach 200ft (60m) from the ground. Below, a canopy of interlocking tree crowns 50 to 100ft (15-30m) high forms the roof of the forest. In the middle layer, 25 to 50ft (7.5- 15m), trees with long, narrow crowns are less intermeshed. The trees up to 50ft (15m) high form a lower layer that merges with shrubs and herbs.

In the canopy the nocturnal and omnivorous Beecroft's tree hyrax *(Dendrohyrax dorsalis)* screams loudly as it scurries up and down the tree trunks. The red-backed flying squirrel *(Anomalurus erythronotus)* [5] glides between trees on extended wings of skin, and the African linsang *(Poiana richardsoni)* emerges from its nest in thick, tangled vines to hunt for insects and small vertebrates.

On the ground, night-browsing mammals, such as the bushbuck *(Tragelaphus scriptus),* start to forage, while in the forest litter the African civet *(Civettictis civetta)* hunts for small rats, mice, and shrews.

At dawn the monkeys begin to feed. Distinguished by their long black-and-white coats, the colobus *(Colobus polykomos)* sit in groups of up to 20 animals, eating leaves and grooming each other. All the permanently arboreal monkeys are lightweight animals able to reach the leaves and fruit at the very end of slender branches.

In the forest canopy the crashing of branches may be caused by monkeys—black-cheeked, white nosed guenons *(Cercopithecus ascanius)* or diana monkeys *(C. diana)*—leaping between trees, or it may be noisy hornbills, turacos [2], and wood-hoopoes, jumping from branch to branch.

In the middle layer of trees, grey-cheeked mangabeys *(Cercocebus albigena)* feed on fruit. The ranges of the monkeys may overlap but each species uses a different kind of leaf or fruit as its main diet. The monkeys share the trees with arboreal snakes, chameleons, and frogs as well as invertebrates living in the soil around the epiphytic plants that grow on the trees.

The ground-dwellers

Not all forest primates are arboreal. The vegetarian gorillas *(Gorilla gorilla),* although they can and do climb trees, prefer to pick leaves from ground vegetation. These animals, together with the forest elephants, buffalo, and the okapi *(Okapia johnstoni),* are among the few large terrestrial mammals of the rain forest. More numerous are the squirrels, mice, rats, and tiny elephant shrews [1] that live in the ground vegetation.

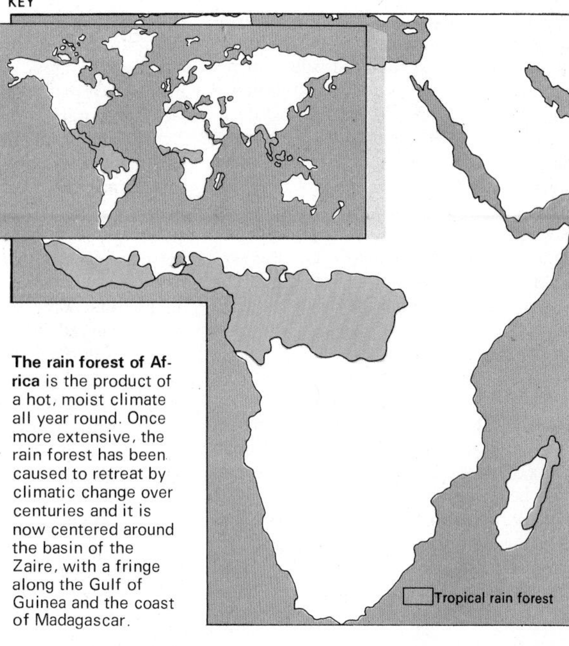
KEY
Tropical rain forest

The rain forest of Africa is the product of a hot, moist climate all year round. Once more extensive, the rain forest has been caused to retreat by climatic change over centuries and it is now centered around the basin of the Zaire, with a fringe along the Gulf of Guinea and the coast of Madagascar.

4 **Along the banks of muddy rivers** below the canopy the rain forest is an interwoven complex of different plant species. The crowns of small trees overlap, and smooth, unbranched tree trunks are festooned with woody lianas and creepers. The undergrowth is a network of ferns, herbs, and tree seedlings, while the forest floor is littered with rotting leaves, fruits, and tree trunks, which provide nutrients for the growing plants. Very dense ground vegetation is usually characteristic of secondary forest. In virgin forest the scarcity of light at ground level confines undergrowth to scattered clumps of shade-tolerant shrubs.

5
Diana monkey
Cercopithecus diana
Red-backed flying squirrel
Anomalurus erythronotus
Red colobus
Colobus badius
Moustached monkey
Cercopithecus cephus

5 **The monkeys and squirrels** are some of the most agile of the treetop inhabitants, moving cautiously among the branches or taking spectacular leaps from tree to tree. The red-backed, or scaly-tailed, flying squirrel runs up tree trunks, steadied by pointed scales on the underside of its tail, and then glides between trees on wings of skin between elbows and feet. The diana and mustached monkeys use opposable thumbs to grip the branches and seem to crash their way haphazardly among the tree tops, unlike the red colobus, which uses its hind legs to make precision jumps between branches.

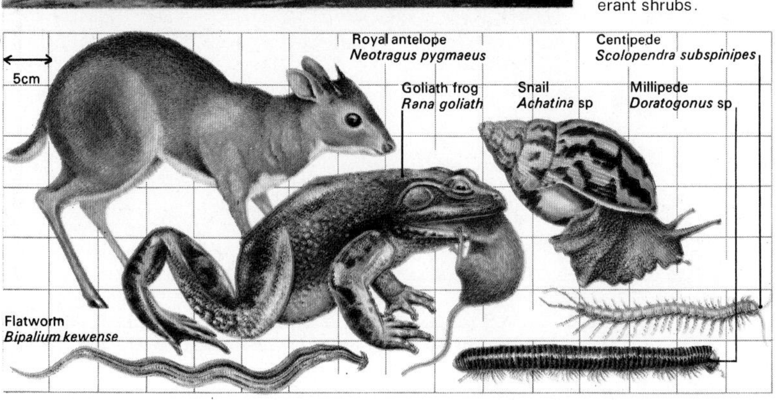
6
5cm
Royal antelope
Neotragus pygmaeus
Centipede
Scolopendra subspinipes
Goliath frog
Rana goliath
Snail
Achatina sp
Millipede
Doratogonus sp
Flatworm
Bipalium kewense

6 **Extremes of size** are common in tropical rain forests. A warm, moist climate has allowed some invertebrates and cold-blooded vertebrates to become giants, while life in dense undergrowth has led to the evolution of dwarf herbivorous mammals. The royal antelope stands only 12in (30cm) at the shoulder and is the smallest antelope in the world. In contrast, the goliath frog, of deep forest pools, can grow up to 32in (81cm) from nose to extended hind limb. It feeds on many small animals, including mice, rats, and lizards. On the forest floor, feeding on dead plant material, live the giant millipedes that grow to 12in (30cm) in length. Also on the forest floor are the active predatory centipedes and the giant snails and enormous flatworms.

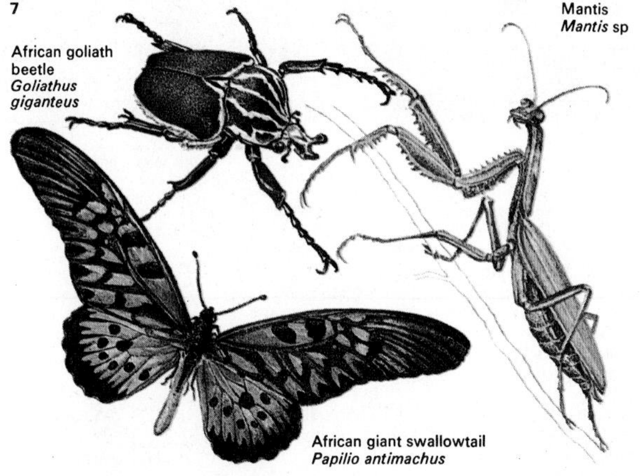
7
African goliath beetle
Goliathus giganteus
Mantis
Mantis sp
African giant swallowtail
Papilio antimachus

7 **Tropical forest insects** are the biggest in the world. The goliath beetle may grow up to 4in (10cm) long and the unique wings of the poisonous swallowtail span 10in (25cm). Some predatory kinds of mantis are large enough to feed on lizards.

Forests of southeast Asia

Rain forests are the natural vegetation of major parts of southeast Asia and the Indian subcontinent [Key] but as a result of man's activities, they have virtually disappeared in large areas, especially in India, Bangladesh, and Indochina. Where they still exist in climates of high constant temperatures and high rainfall, they exhibit the greatest diversity of plants found anywhere in the world. With animals ultimately dependent on plants for food, the forests have also provided for the development of one of the richest animal communities in the world.

Forest communities

Trees growing in the southeast Asian rain forests are taller than their related species in African and South American rain forests, with the "emergents" often reaching a height of more than 225ft (70m). These giant trees begin branching only at about 145ft (44m) above the ground, but produce wide, spreading crowns, with thick, leathery leaves adapted in shape to allow rapid drainage of rain from their surface. Their most striking feature is a thick buttressed trunk. Because the thin but nutritious soil supports only a shallow rooting system, the buttresses—often 35ft (11m) high—are needed to provide stability against buffeting winds and rain.

The animal community of the emergent zone is made up almost exclusively of birds, insects, and bats. Because the climate lacks marked seasonal changes, trees can flower and fruit throughout the year, thus providing animals with a continuous supply of food. Hornbills *(Buceros* and *Aceros)* feed on the fruits of the "emergents" using their strong, curved bills to push through the foliage; butterflies, bees, and wasps feed on the nectar of flowers, and fruit-eating bats, (Megachiroptera), strip trees of their produce. Swifts *(Hemiprocne* and *Chaetura)* fly high above trees, feeding on insects, while eagles *(Ictinaetus* and *Spilornis)* and other birds of prey hover above, waiting to pounce on small vertebrates.

The forest canopy

Below the emergent zone is the forest canopy where the crowns of buttressed trees, fig trees, and trees producing such exotic fruits as durians, mangosteens, and rambutans merge to form a continuous layer of leafy vegetation about 145ft (44m) above the ground.

The canopy is a home and major food source for many animals. There, gibbons *(Hylobates)* and the Malayan and Sumatran siamangs *(Symphalangus syndactylus)* swing from branch to branch in search of fruit, leaves, and flowers. Orang-utans, found only in Borneo and Sumatra, forage for fleshy fruits. The giant squirrel *(Ratufa)* leaps between trees in search of nuts, fruits, and even birds' eggs. Minivets *(Pericrocotus)* flit between branches, feeding on insects, while fruit-eating barbets *(Megalaima)* may be found nesting in holes in trees. Insects abound and provide food for insectivorous bats.

The middle zone of the rain forests is composed of trees adapted to shade and high humidity, 98 to 110ft (30–33m) high, bearing deep, narrow crowns and trunks and branches covered in flowers. A tangle of ferns that live on trees, climbing lianas

CONNECTIONS

See also
598 African rain forest
602 New World tropics
620 Salt marshes and coastal swamps
596 Woodlands of Australasia
580 The basis of ecology
582 Isolation and evolution
526 The classification of birds
578 Regions of the Earth: zoogeography

1 Southeast Asian forests contain perhaps the richest populations of animals and plants in the world. A single acre of forest may contain 60 different species of trees, and an island may support more than 150,000 species of animals. A few are shown in this picture, with a key on the opposite page. Within forests most animals forage for food beside watercourses or lakes where vegetation is less dense and where light penetrates. Many animals in the forest are adapted for specialized feeding, for colonizing a particular niche, or for moving about within the layers of the forest.

2 Ants form a bridge

Two leaves are drawn together

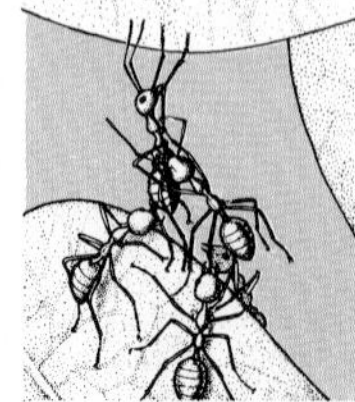

Leaf edges are held together before gluing

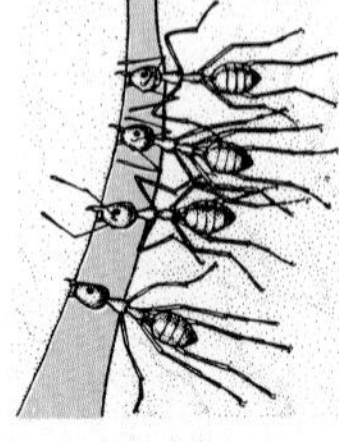

2 Weaving ants *(Oecophylla smaragdina)* are commonly found in all rain forests of southeast Asia. They build nests in trees and bushes by binding living leaves together with silken threads. Although the ants are unable to produce silk, their larvae bear silk glands. Construction of a new nest commences when a team of worker ants forms a bridge between two leaves. While one set of workers draws the leaves together a second set commandeers the silk-secreting larvae (not shown) to spin a web of silk across the gap, thus gluing and sealing the leaves together.

and vines, and parasitic "strangler" figs, wrapped and twisted around the branches and trunks of canopy trees, also add to the foliage.

Many of the animals of the middle layer are highly adapted for movement between trees. Several species of lizards *(Draco)*, frogs *(Rhacophorus)*, squirrels *(Aeromys)*, and flying lemurs *(Cynocephalus)* bear extensible flaps of skin that allow them to glide large distances from tree to tree.

The binturong *(Arctictis binturong)* has claws and a prehensile tail for climbing, while the long tails of langurs *(Presbytis)* and proboscis monkeys *(Nasalis larvatus)* are used only for balancing as they leap between the branches. The more terrestrial macaques *(Macaca)* possess much smaller tails. The calm, humid climate of the middle layer has also allowed flying insects to evolve enormous wings [3], which they use in their search for specific flowers and fruits.

The shrub layer

In primary rain forests the shrub layer is rather sparse and consists mainly of woody plants and young growing trees, which reach a height of about 18ft (5.5m). Where light penetrates to the inner forest, or in secondary forests, this layer becomes much denser and bears numerous broad-leaved herbaceous plants. On the margins of rivers and lakes palm trees and mangroves thrive. Such areas are the home of the nocturnal tarsier *(Tarsius)* which leaps from branch to branch as it searches for lizards, spiders, and insects. The leopard *(Panthera pardus)* sits on an overhanging bough awaiting its prey. Arboreal pit vipers *(Trimeresurus)*, pythons *(Python)*, and tree snakes *(Boiga)*, which feed on small mammals, reptiles, and birds, wrap themselves around the thick branches. Broadbills *(Calyptomena)*, shamas *(Copsychus)*, and flycatchers *(Terpsiphone)* fly swiftly through the foliage. But by far the most numerous animals of southeast Asian rain forests are the insects—highly camouflaged stick insects and leaf insects, grasshoppers, crickets and cicadas, beetles, butterflies and moths, and ants, bees, and wasps—of which more than 100,000 species have been described.

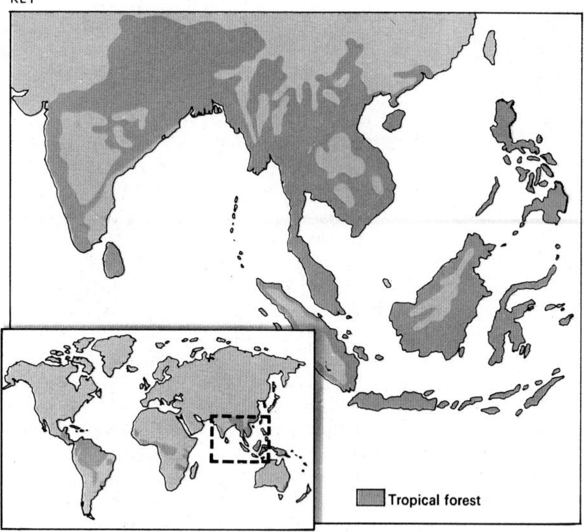

KEY
Tropical forest

Rain forests would grow in all the areas shown in blue on the map were it not for man. They are now found only in western India, Sri Lanka, Burma, Thailand, Laos, Malaysia, the Philippines, Borneo, Sumatra, and the Celebes.

1, 14 Gibbons *Hylobates* spp
2, 11 Colugo *Cynocephalus* sp
3 Flying lizard *Draco volans*
4 Stick insect *Carausius* sp
5 Lesser-green broadbill *Calyptomena viridis*
6 Tarsier *Tarsius* sp
7 Green pit viper *Trimeresurus* sp
8, 13 Hornbills *Buceros* spp
9 Leaf insect *Pulchriphyllium* sp
10 Orchid mantis *Hymenopus coronatus*
12, 16 Flying foxes *Pteropus* spp
15 Brahminy kite *Haliastur indus*
17 Prevost's squirrel *Sciurus prevosti*
18 Tree shrew *Tupaia* sp
19 Yellow-crowned bulbul *Pycnonotus* sp
20 Langurs *Presbytis* sp
21 Orang-utan *Pongo pygmaeus*
22 Sumatran rhinoceros *Didermoceros sumatrensis*
23 Malayan tapir *Tapirus indicus*
24 Banded linsang *Prionodon linsang*
25 Indian darter *Anhinga melanogaster*
26 Tiger *Panthera tigris*
27 Muntjac *Muntiacus* sp
28 Sun bear *Helarctos malayanus*
29 Jungle fowl *Gallus* sp
30 Adjutant stork *Leptoptilus dubius*
31 Black-naped blue monarch *Hypothymis azurea*
32 Fishing cat *Felis viverrina*
33 Moon rat *Echinosorex* sp
34 Crab-eating macaques *Macaca irus*
35 *Graphium* butterfly
36 Crocodile *Crocodylus* sp
37 Small-clawed otter *Aonyx* sp
38 Indian three-toed kingfisher *Ceyx erithacus*
39 Binturong *Arctitis binturong*
40 Mangrove snake *Boiga dendrophila*
41, 45, 56 Soldier crabs *Dotilla mictyroides*
42 *Appias* sp
43 Butterfly *Prothoe* sp
44, 51, 54 Fiddler crab *Uca* sp
46, 50 Mudskippers *Periophthalamus* spp
47, 48 Swallowtails *Papilio* spp
49 *Atrophaneura* sp
52 White-breasted water hen *Amaurornis phoenicurus*
53 Blue-winged pitta *Pitta brachyura*
55 *Python reticulatus*

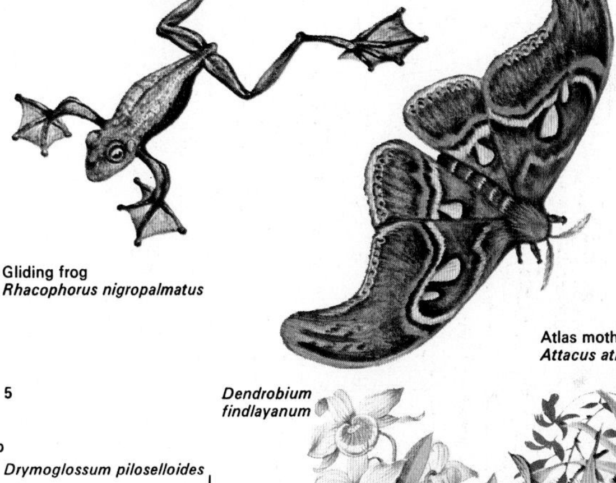

3
Gliding frog
Rhacophorus nigropalmatus
Atlas moth
Attacus atlas

3 The atlas moth and the gliding frog are relatively common inhabitants of rain forests in southeast Asia. With a wing span of up to 12 in (30cm) the atlas is the largest Asian moth and has the greatest wing span of any lepidopteran. The gliding frog of Malaysia is equipped with webbed feet that act as flat planing surfaces and allow it to glide more than 40 to 50ft (12–15m) between trees.

5
Dendrobium findlayanum
Drymoglossum piloselloides
Phalaenopsis heideperle
Vanda tricolor
Averrhoa bilimbi
Coelogyne massangeana

4 Rafflesia arnoldi [A] is a rare parasitic plant, bearing neither stem nor leaves, that grows on the branch of one species of vine in Malaysia. Measuring up to 40in (1m) in diameter, it is the world's biggest flower. [B] Germinating *Rafflesia* seeds produce strands of cells [1] that penetrate the water and food conducting channels of the host plant [2] to absorb water and nutrients. The bloom lives for less than a week.

5 Mosses, lichens, ferns, and orchids grow on branches of canopy trees, where they receive sunlight and are nourished by humus in the bark. Accumulations of these epiphytes, or air plants, collect water and provide a suitable home for a varied host of invertebrate animals.

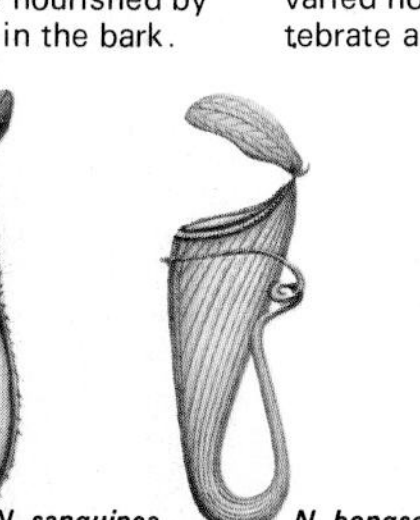

N. sanguinea
N. bongso

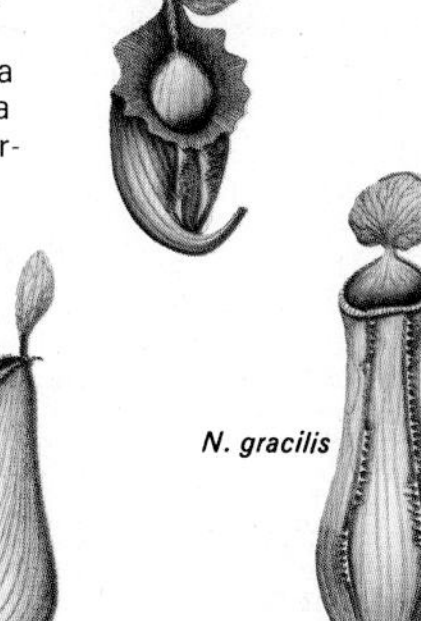

6
N. rajah
N. ampullaria
N. gracilis

6 The pitchers of the Nepenthes genus of plants are expanded leaves modified for catching insects. Ants, flies, and beetles are lured to the pitchers by the scent of nectar and become trapped. Insects are probably taken in to obtain nitrogen, which is scarce in the heavily leached soil. There are about 60 different *Nepenthes* species found only in the Malayan archipelago.

New World tropics

Enveloping the basin of the great Amazon River in a shroud of dense vegetation is the greatest continuous mass of rain forest in the world. The abundance of water and the warm, humid climate support dense stands of trees that are festooned with creeping and climbing lianas. The forest floor receives little light and is the home of dark-colored animals that prefer a cool, damp environment. High above is the forest canopy, a continuous collection of tree tops broken only by tall, scattered emergent trees. It is here that most of the light is filtered out and where an abundance of animal life resides.

The exuberant vegetation provides a wide range of habitats for a remarkable variety of animals, although they are not usually densely distributed and the visitor may, in fact, see few of them. The lack of seasonal variation in temperature guarantees a supply of food throughout the year.

Fish, insects, and birds

The number of different species of fish in the rivers and insects in this tropical rain forest is so vast that they have never been fully classified. Small predators, especially the birds, grow fat at their expense, living in colonies along the banks of the rivers. The insects are remarkable not only for their numbers but also for their size and way of life. The Hercules beetle *(Dynastes hercules)* measures up to 6in (15cm) in length and is rivaled in size only by the bird-eating spiders *(Theraphosa),* which grow up to 10in (25cm) across, feeding on small animals of all kinds. Butterflies are remarkable for their beautiful coloring but some of the most fascinating insects are the ants. Leafcutter ants *(Atta)* dissect leaves and carry them off to build compost heaps where they "farm" the fungi on which they feed.

The birds of the forest represent the most diverse adaptations to the numerous habitats and exploit the various food sources without undue competition. They include macaws, pigeons, tanagers, and the delicate hummingbirds, all of which feed almost entirely on plants and their products. The insectivores are specialized in their feeding habits: swifts take insects in flight, woodpeckers feed on bark insects, cuckoos eat venomous wasps, and a whole family, the antbirds (Formicariidae), feeds entirely on the abundant supply of ants, even deriving their name from this prey. High in the canopy, hawks and owls patrol the forest, preying on reptiles, birds and small mammals.

Mammals and other land animals

In comparison to the birds, mammals are poorly represented. Land mammals tend to be small, like the shy brocket deer *(Mazama),* which is only 3ft (91cm) long. The habitat usually occupied by deer is exploited by such rodents as the agouti *(Dasyprocta)* and the paca *(Cuniculus paca).* But the region also boast the largest rodent in the world, the peaceful capybara *(Hydrochoerus hydrochaeris),* which lives in large family groups on the banks of the rivers. Two of the strangest creatures in this land of contrasts are the anteater and the tapir. The great anteaters, or ant "bears" *(Myrmecophaga tridactyla),* are solitary animals that roam the swampy areas of the forest, while another anteater, the taman-

CONNECTIONS

See also

598 African rain forest
600 Forests of Southeast Asia
596 Woodlands of Australasia
294 Misuse of the land
580 The basis of ecology
578 Regions of the Earth: zoogeography
526 The classification of birds
488 Spiders and scorpions
448 Woody flowering plants
340 Tropical fruits

1

1 Epiphytic orchid *Oncidium* sp
2 Tree *Vochysia* sp
3 White-headed capuchins *Cebus apella*
4 Scarlet macaw *Ara macao*
5 Three-toed sloth *Bradypus tridactylus*
6 Howler monkeys *Alouatta* sp
7 Common opossum *Didelphis marsupialis*
8 Epiphytic orchid *Cattleya* sp
9 Bromeliad
10 Tiger butterfly *Heliconius ethillus*
11 Tree *Cecropia* sp
12 Brocket deer *Mazama* sp
13 Tamandua *Tamandua tetradactyla*
14 Termite nest
15 Scarlet ibis *Eudocimus ruber*
16 Brown coati *Nasua narica*
17 Epiphytes
18 Great anteater *Myrmecophaga tridactyla*
19 Roseate spoonbill *Ajaia ajaja*
20 Keel-billed toucan *Ramphastos sulfuratus*
21 Liana flowers *Cephaelis* spp
22 Ruby and topaz humming bird *Chrysolampis mosquitus*
23 Capybara *Hydrochoerus hydrochaeris*
24 South American river turtle *Podocnemis expansa*
25 Arrow-poison frog *Dendrobates* sp
26 Paca *Cuniculus paca*
27 Bird-eating spider *Theraphosa leblondi*
28 Tapir *Tapirus terrestris*
29 Jaguar *Panthera onca*
30 Giant water lily *Victoria amazonica*
31 Red and blue leaf-hopper
32 Leafcutter ants *Atta* spp

1 The dominant features of the forest are the trees and the water; as a result, most of the animals living there are either arboreal or aquatic, and sometimes both. Every niche in this enormous habitat is fully occupied with a bewildering collection of animals and plants. The huge trees are supported by special outgrowths of root and trunk and are festooned with long lianas. Epiphytes, such as the startlingly beautiful orchids and bromeliads, abound on tree trunks and branches. The numerous rivers provide homes for millions of fish. There are a number of aquatic or semiaquatic creatures that use the river as their base. These include reptiles such as terrapins, caimans and anacondas. Wading birds, such as the roseate spoonbill and scarlet ibis, are also found on or by the river. Many animals live at the water's edge, browsing on aquatic plants. They include the tapir and the world's largest rodent—the capybara. The shy paca roams the forest floor amid millions of insects and many species of frogs and reptiles. But most animals live high up the forest canopy. There, troops of monkeys show off their acrobatic skills and the sloth lives up to its name with its funereal progress through the branches. Most of the birds also live in the canopy. They range in size from the big-billed toucan to the tiny hummingbird that flits from flower to flower like an iridescent jewel. The solitary jaguar is fond of water and often chases tapirs and capybaras right into the river. It also feeds on fish and caimans, which it catches in shallow parts of the river.

dua *(Tamandua tetradactyla),* has become arboreal. The tapir *(Tapirus),* a relation of the horse and rhinoceros, belongs to a family of animals that was formerly widespread but is now confined to Central and South America and similar habitats of southeastern Asia. It is nocturnal and feeds on vegetable matter. Other ancient residents include marsupials, made up mainly of opossums, of which the common opossum *(Didelphis marsupialis)* is found as far north as New England. The only aquatic marsupial, the yapok *(Chironectes minimus),* hunts by night for frogs, fish and crustaceans.

In the higher levels of the tree canopy the inhabitants vary from extremely agile, acrobatic monkeys to slow-moving sloths—both the three-toed *(Bradypus)* and the two-toed *(Choloepus)* kinds. The monkeys differ from their counterparts in the Old World, having evolved quite separately. They are divided into two groups, the marmosets and the cebid monkeys. Marmosets are the smallest primates in the world; the pygmy marmoset *(Cebuella)* grows only 3 to 4 in (7–10cm) in length. The cebids are more diverse in their appearance. They include the agile spider monkey *(Ateles);* the howler monkey *(Alouatta),* which has the most powerful vocal call of all the primates, and whose roars can be heard for miles; and the only truly nocturnal monkey, the large-eyed douroucouli *(Aotus).* Bats also abound in the forest. Some, such as the fruit bats, are herbivorous, others are insectivorous, and still others entirely carnivorous. One of the most notorious is the vampire bat *(Desmodus rotundus),* which pierces the skin of warmblooded animals with its sharp teeth and drinks the blood.

Numerous predators

The vast array of animal life supports many predators, including larger reptiles such as the giant anaconda *(Eunestes murinus),* the smaller boa constrictor *(Constrictor constrictor),* and caimans. The largest mammalian predator is the jaguar *(Panthera onca),* one of the resident cat family that includes the puma *(Felis concolor),* ocelot *(Felis pardolis),* margay *(Felis weidii),* and the jaguarundi *(Felis yagouaroundi).*

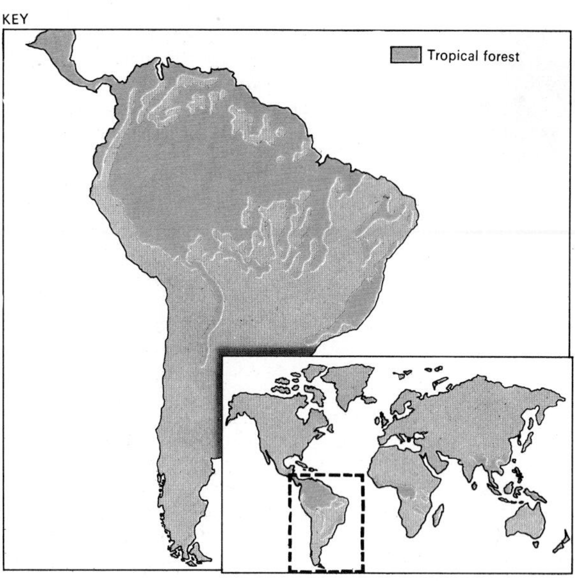

KEY
Tropical forest

The great South American rain forest covers the low-lying Amazon basin and extends eastward to the Guianas and westward to the foothills of the Andes mountains.

2

2

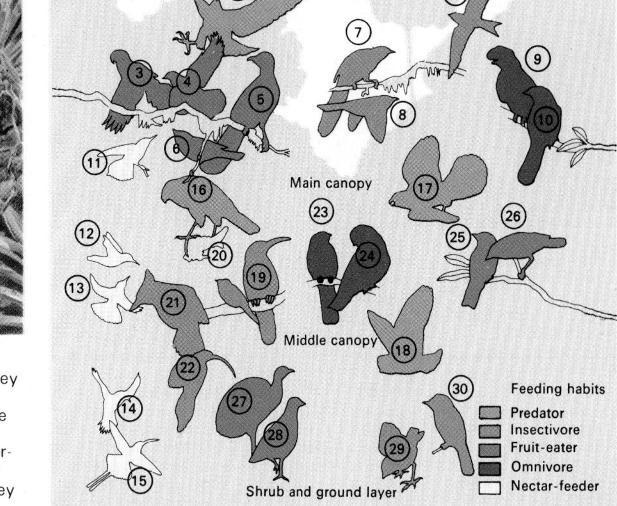

1
2
7
9
3
4
5
8
10
11
6
16
Main canopy
17
23
26
12
25
20
24
19
13
21
Middle canopy
18
22
30
Feeding habits
27
14
28
Predator
Insectivore
29
Fruit-eater
Omnivore
15
Shrub and ground layer
Nectar-feeder

2 The birds of South American forests are more numerous and vividly colored than any others. The complex ecosystem provides an abundance of habitats and a very wide variety of food to sustain them. The unvarying climate ensures a year-round food supply and, as a result, birds do not have to migrate to escape harsh conditions. These factors also mean that birds need move only within a restricted area. Most of them have short, wide wings for maneuvering between the trees. The swifts rarely enter the forest but hunt for insects over the canopy. Their wings are long and narrow for fast flying. The most abundant foods are insects and the fruits of plants, and many forest birds feed on these. Hummingbirds feed on both insects and nectar. Many daytime birds of prey feed only on other birds but some, like eagles, also eat mammals. Owls normally hunt at night and feed on any prey they may catch.

1 Crested eagle *Morphnus guianensis*
2 White-collared swift *Streptoprocne zonaris*
3 Hyacinth macaw *Anodorhynchus hyacinthinus*
4 Short-billed pigeon *Columba nigrirostris*
5 Blue-throated piping guan *Pipile pipile*
6 Silver-throated tanager *Tangara icterocephala*
7 Squirrel cuckoo *Piaya cayana*
8 Rufous-browed pepper-shrike *Cyclarhis gujanensis*
9 Ornate umbrella-bird *Cephalopterus ornatus*
10 Cayanne jay *Cyanocorax affinis*
11 Black-eared fairy *Heliothryx aurita*
12 Fork-tailed woodnymph *Thalurania furcata*
13 Bronze-tailed plumeleteer *Chalybura urochrysia*
14 Band-tailed barb-throat *Threnetes ruckeri*
15 Long-tailed hermit *Phaethornis superciliosus*
16 Semi-collared hawk *Accipter collaris*
17 Collared forest falcon *Micrastur semitorquatus*
18 Spectacled owl *Pulsatrix perspicillata*
19 Great jacamar *Jacamerops aurea*
20 Rufous-capped spinetail *Synallaxis ruficapilla*
21 Chestnut woodpecker *Celeus elegans*
22 Red-billed scythebill *Campyloramphus trochilirostris*
23 Black-throated trogon *Trogon rufus*
24 Cock-of-the-rock *Rupicola rupicola*
25 Red-capped cardinal *Paroaria gularis*
26 Brazilian tanager *Ramphocelus bresilius*
27 Grey-winged trumpeter *Psophia crepitans*
28 Marbled wood-quail *Odontophorus gujanensis*
29 Black-bellied gnat-eater *Conopophaga melanogaster*
30 Grey-throated leaf-scraper *Sclerurus albigularis*

Life in the desert

A desert is defined as an area with less than 10in (25.4cm) rainfall a year. No two deserts are the same. They are of two types, known as cold or hot deserts [Key] depending on whether they are cold or warm in winter.

The distribution of deserts

Cold deserts are found in North America (the Great Basin), northern Asia (Gobi), and South America (Andean plateau-puna). The hot deserts are found in southern North America and Mexico (Mojave, Colorado, Arizona-Sonora, Baja California, and Chihuahua), in South America (Chile and Peru coast), northern and southern Africa (Sahara, Kalahari-Namib), the Middle East (Sinai, Arabian), and Australia. The plant and animal life supported by the desert is as varied as the people who share the same environment. But there is one factor common to them all: to a greater or lesser degree they have had to adapt to the harshness of desert life caused by the lack of water and shelter and the extreme changes in temperature. Temperatures as high as 134°F (56.7°C) have been recorded in Death Valley, California, and as low as −40°F (−40°C) in the Gobi. All living organisms in the desert—plants, insects, reptiles, birds and mammals—depend upon water in some measure, but they have evolved a capacity for surviving on the barest minimum during times of drought.

Desert plants and insects

Desert plants (or "xerophytes") have adapted in a variety of ways [3]. Some plants can become dehydrated without permanent injury. Older leaves may dry up and die but young leaves, though drying and turning brown, will continue to grow when watered again.

Plants may also evade drought. The life cycle of a plant such as the Californian poppy is completed within so short a space of time that during the most arid months of the year it is below the surface in seed form, where it can lie dormant for several years without rain [4]. An interesting phenomenon of some desert plants is that only part of the seed germinates at the first watering; other parts must be subjected to several falls of rain before growth of the seedling is possible. This helps to ensure their survival.

Drought resistance is the most usual method of survival. Some plants shed leaves, so that they need less water to stay alive. Others grow extraordinarily deep roots to tap the reservoirs of water deep underground. Mesquite and acacia trees, for example, grow roots to a depth of 50ft (15m), while those of shrubs such as *Atriplex halimus* grow 60 to 70ft (18–21m). Another way is for plants to develop root systems over a wide but shallow area to take maximum advantage of a brief fall of rain. Such root systems can run for more than 1,000 yards (915m). Some plants die back to ground level, surviving the drought as tubers and bulbs, while others store excess moisture within their stems to be used as required. Many succulent plants *(Aloe, Crassula)* have leaves that are adapted for water storage. The long, silky hairs covering such cacti as *Cephalocereus* also help to prevent water loss. Desert plants provide shelter [1] for many animals, including varieties of birds, reptiles, and moths.

CONNECTIONS

See also
606 Desert birds and mammals
590 Australian desert grasslands
588 South American grasslands
266 Winds and deserts
430 The way plants work
314 Water and irrigation
520 The life of reptiles
632 Endangered species
580 The basis of ecology

1 The Joshua tree *(Yucca brevifolia)* is one of the few plants able to survive in the Mojave Desert. It plays host to a large number of animals. Dependent insects include weevils *(Yuccaborus)* [3] and termites *(Paraneotermes)* [6] while the yucca moth *(Tegeticula alba)* [5] is the tree's major pollinator. Small mammals, among them the pack rat *(Neotoma magister)* [7], build their homes at the tree base. Birds, including the small cactus wren *(Campylorhynchus brunneicapillus)* [1], Scott's oriole *(Icterus parisorum)* [2], and the gila woodpecker *(Centurus urdoygialis)* [4], attracted by insects, nest among the leaves. Reptiles, such as the desert night snake *(Hypsiglena torquata deserticola)* [8] and the night lizard *(Xantusia vigilis)* [9] soon arrive to consume some of the abundant food.

2 The desert, often thought of as a barren, inhospitable place, can support a wealth of plant life The hot deserts of Mexico and North America are the home of most of the world's 1,500 species of cacti. These plants, which range in height from less than 1in (2.5cm) to over 50ft (15m), are the ones most often associated with the desert landscape. The prickly pear *(Opuntia)* and the tall upright giant saguaro *(Cereus giganteus)* seen here are two of the most common and spectacular.

3 The cactus form is generally cylindrical to reduce evaporation. Few cacti (family Cactaceae) [1,2,3,4,7,10] have leaves, but many have sharp thorns or spines to discourage animals from eating them. The cactus shape may be seen in other desert plants [11, 12], but most have succulent [5, 8,9] or reduced [6] leaves. These plants belong to several families including the Crassulaceae [6] Stapeliaceae [12], Euphorbiaceae [11], Liliaceae [5,9], and the Aizoaceae [8].

Key to species
1 *Eriocactus* sp
2 *Astrophytum* sp
3 *Mammillaria* sp
4 *Lobivia* sp
5 *Gasteria* sp
6 *Crassula* sp
7 *Stetsonia* sp
8 *Lithops* sp
9 *Haworthia* sp
10 *Cereus* sp
11 *Euphorbia* sp
12 *Stapelia* sp

4 When rain falls in the desert after a dry period the land may be rapidly transformed into a colorful and exotic meadow. The seeds have lain dormant, awaiting water to complete their germination before bursting into life.

Insects exist in great numbers in the desert and they play an important part in the survival of the other desert-dwellers, some of which are exclusively insect-eating. The adaptation of these small desert inhabitants to the aridity and heat varies enormously [5, 8]. Some, such as the harvester ant, are physically unsuited to the terrain and so make their nests deep underground where they are only slightly affected by temperature. The harvester ant makes brief foraging expeditions above ground to collect seeds, most of which are stored against times of drought.

Many insects are nocturnal, sheltering during the day under rocks or just below the ground's surface. Diurnal insects (those that are active only by day) have either long legs to lift their bodies above the hot sands, or the ability to fly, or climb onto plants. Most insects avoid dehydration by secreting on their cuticles a thin layer of wax that is relatively impermeable to water vapor. This layer is also impermeable to oxygen and carbon dioxide so a mechanism has evolved whereby the gases can cross the shell while water loss is kept to a minimum. Breathing is controlled via special apertures, the spiracles, which are opened only to facilitate respiration when a sufficient level of carbon dioxide has accumulated in the body.

Reptiles—the best survivors

Reptiles form another group of desert creatures, and it is probably the group that feels most at one with its habitat [12, 13]. They are cold-blooded animals—unlike birds and mammals—which makes it impossible for them to maintain internal heat, so they must rely on the sun to warm the surrounding air and ground in order to raise their body temperature. In extreme heat, however, their bodies become so hot that it is often necessary for them to take shelter. They also have to find less exposed places at night to protect themselves from the cold. Snakes are more numerous in the desert than any other reptiles but because they are often nocturnal hiding by day, they are less obvious than the lizards that scurry about in the sunlight.

KEY

Deserts are found in all the continents of the world and make up about 14 percent of its total land mass. The Sahara, which is the largest desert, has an area of roughly 3.5 million square miles (900 million hectares). Although deserts are easily recognizable, they are often difficult to define, but any area receiving less than 10in (25.4cm) of rain a year can be thought of as one. The boundaries of deserts are also hard to define as few deserts consist of totally barren sand. Instead there is a fringe zone where desert vegetation merges imperceptibly with that of the surrounding area. Sand is not a regular desert feature. Deserts can consist of stones, rocks, or even salt.

5

Tenebrionid beetle
Stenocara sp

6 Scorpion
Buthus occitanus

7 Camel spider
Galeodes sp

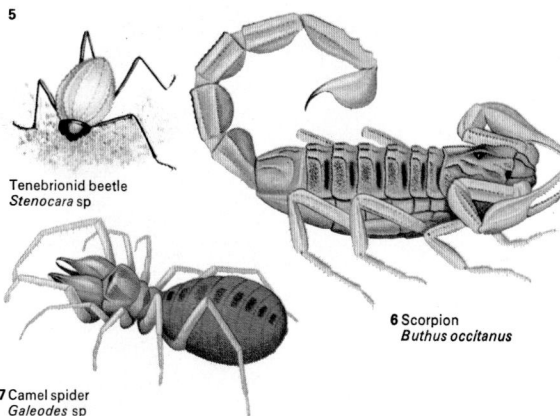

5 Tenebrionid beetles are well represented among desert beetles. They live in sand dunes into whose safety they plunge at the first hint of danger.

6 Scorpions can withstand great heat. They live on spiders and insects but will also attack other scorpions.

7 Camel spider is a name for solifugid, meaning "fleeing from the sun," there are over 800 species mostly nocturnal.

8

Honey ant
Myrmecocystus melliger

8 Some honey ants are living food stores accepting honey from the rest of the colony. Their abdomens distend to form food-filled globes from which others feed in drought periods.

9 Locusts are destructive desert grasshoppers. An average swarm is made up of one billion individuals which, collectively, need to eat 3,000 tons of food each day to survive. Although there is a naturally high mortality rate, they present a serious problem to farmers as they are unpredictable and difficult to control. The young congregate in dense masses and march across country.

9

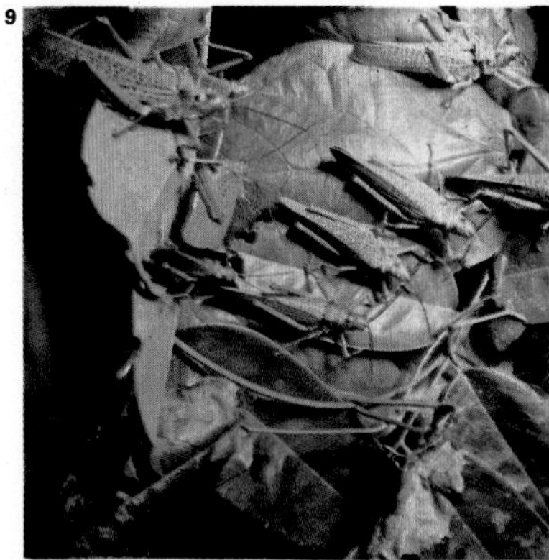

10 Pupfish are relics of an aquatic fauna that once populated the southwestern North American desert zones when there were extensive lakes rather than arid sands. Male and female Owens Valley pupfish, together with several other species of fish, may still be found in water pools, which are in fact vestiges of former large lakes.

10

Male

Female

Owens Valley pupfish
Cyprinodon radiosus

11 Spadefoot toad
Scaphiopus couchi

11 The spadefoot toad, so-called because of the digging appendages on the hind feet, is one of several species of desert toads. It lives in a burrow for most of the year, emerging at night to feed on insects. If it rains, the toad goes to the nearest pool, where males and females mate and the eggs are laid. The tadpoles then develop rapidly and by the time the waters have dried up have become mature adults, ready for burrowing.

12

Banded gecko
Coleonyx variegatus

12 The banded gecko is one of a great many species of gecko inhabiting desert regions. It is nocturnal, hiding under rocks during the day and foraging for insects at night.

13

Desert tortoise
Gopherus sp

14 Skink
Scincus scincus

13 Desert tortoises are perfectly adapted to their environment. The heavy shell, a protection from extreme heat (and cold) and from predators, houses two storage sacs for excess moisture.

14 The Old World skink is sometimes known as "sand fish." It seems to swim through the sand, pushing itself along with its flattened toes, which are fringed with scales. It spends much of its time feeding just beneath the surface.

Desert birds and mammals

There are fewer birds and mammals, especially large ones, in deserts than in other regions, but a surprising number do manage to survive in this harsh and forbidding environment. They can only do so by adaptations of their behavior, life processes, and external coverings.

The adaptable camel

Because of its usefulness to man, the camel *(Camelus dromedarius)* [Key] is one of the commonest and best known of the larger desert mammals. Unlike many other large, wild desert mammals, such as the addax *(Addax nasomaculatus)* [2], which is now threatened with extinction, domesticated camels are increasing in numbers.

The camel has a remarkable ability to withstand heat, and its body temperature can fluctuate by as much as 12°F (about 7°C) without causing it distress. During the day the camel's body may heat up slowly to 105°F (40°C), and during the night may drop to 93°F (33.9°C). The camel's hump, which is a fat store, contributes indirectly to the control of its body temperature. The lack of insulating fat beneath the skin allows heat to escape easily, and the animal's thick, woolly fur reduces the entry of heat.

The camel is also unusually adapted to reduce its water loss from breathing, sweating, and excretion. If man lost water amounting to 12 percent of his body weight, he would die of "explosive heat" because, as water is lost, blood decreases in volume and becomes thicker, slowing down the circulation. Internal heat can no longer be dissipated from the skin and death quickly follows. The camel, however, can lose up to 25 percent of its body weight in water and still maintains its blood volume by removing water from the body tissues. The camel's sweating reflex is not activated until its body temperature reaches about 105°F (40°C), which means that its water loss is correspondingly reduced. It also urinates sparingly—about 1.75 pints a day in summer.

Antelopes and cats

The increasingly rare addax is a member of the large cattle family (Bovidae), which includes the antelopes and sheep. It is even more resilient than the camel in that it does not need to drink water at all because it takes in the moisture it needs by eating plants. Simply by sniffing the air, the addax can locate from great distances an area where rain has fallen. As a result, it can live in arid regions that no other mammal could tolerate, not even the well adapted scimitar-horned oryx *(Oryx tao)*—another animal related to the addax—which is at home in the Libyan and Sahara deserts.

A well-known desert antelope is the graceful and fleet-footed gazelle *(Gazella)*. That only a relatively few animals remain is an indictment of the "sportsmen" who shoot them from motorized vehicles—proving that even swift species such as these can be wiped out by such methods.

Relatively few large carnivores live in deserts. The cat family is well represented, but the only big cat is the cheetah *(Acinonyx jubatus)* of Africa and Asia, the fastest land animal in the world. It is exceptional in its habits because, unlike the other members of its family, it does not stalk and pounce on an unsuspecting prey, but runs it down. The

CONNECTIONS

See also
- **604** Life in the desert
- **590** Australian desert grasslands
- **588** South American grasslands
- **628** Endangered mammals
- **526** The classification of birds
- **540** The classification of mammals
- **266** Winds and deserts

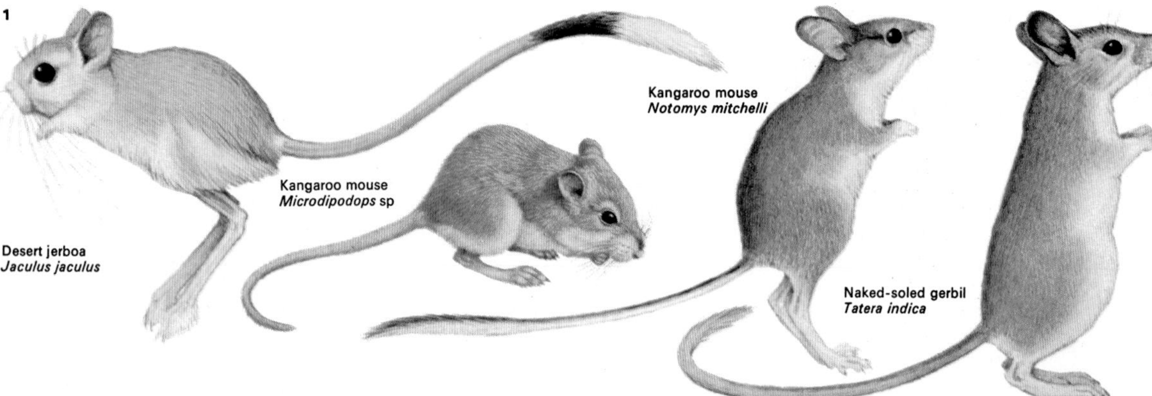

1
Desert jerboa
Jaculus jaculus
Kangaroo mouse
Microdipodops sp
Kangaroo mouse
Notomys mitchelli
Naked-soled gerbil
Tatera indica

1 Desert rodents exist in large numbers, having successfully adapted to their environment by living in burrows. They include the desert jerboa, kangaroo mouse, and naked-soled gerbil. They can make long, swift leaps with their powerful hind legs to escape from predators. Using their tails as rudders, they can alter course in mid-air. They are also protected by their sensitive hearing.

2
Addax
Addax nasomaculatus

2 One of the larger desert mammals is the Saharan addax. This antelope often falls to the hunter, who prizes its meat and fine skin. As a result, it is now a much-endangered species. Like many other desert dwellers, it does not need liquid water to survive, but obtains the necessary fluids from its food. It has a well-developed sense of hearing but lacks the speed to flee successfully from danger.

3 Pallas' cat lives in burrows or among the rocks of the Asian deserts. It is an agile hunter, whose body length does not usually exceed 20in (50cm). It feeds on a variety of small birds and rodents.

3 Pallas' cat
Felis manul

4 A hardy desert animal from Australia is the red kangaroo. Although widely distributed across the continent, its numbers have been reduced by hunting and the fencing of sheep ranges. Its urinary system, like that of the ground squirrel and kangaroo rat, has evolved to cope with desert conditions and its urine is highly concentrated. This desert mammal drinks only in periods of extreme heat and drought. Kangaroos such as this species are famed for their jumping ability. Studies have shown this to be a more energy-conserving way of moving than the normal four-legged gait.

4 Red kangaroo
Macropus rufus

5
Kit fox
Vulpes velox
Fennec fox
Fennecus zerda

5 The kit fox and the fennec are similar but unrelated desert mammals. The kit fox is from the New World, the fennec from the Old, and both have adapted in the same way to desert life. This is a case of convergent evolution—the development of similar characteristics by animals or plants of unrelated species. Both are nocturnal and live in burrows. They feed on insects, lizards, rodents, and birds, which they detect with their large and sensitive ears.

small desert cats [3] tend to be nocturnal, lying in wait for their prey.

Very few members of the dog family inhabit deserts, but those that do are all similar in color and appearance [5]. They are generally small with large ears and usually hunt by night.

Rodents are the commonest of the small desert mammals. Most are nocturnal and pass the day in burrows. There, where the air is more humid than it is outside, they remain cool. Many do not drink, obtaining all their water from plants. Some are known to obtain water by the oxidation of the carbohydrates in their food, which is mainly dry seeds. They also have highly efficient kidneys that extract most of the water from their urine. Jumping as a means of movement has been developed in many of these desert rodents [1]. Although they all look similar, they are not closely related and inhabit different continents. Jerboas *(Jaculus)* and gerbils *(Tatera)* are from Africa and Asia. Species of kangaroo mouse are from North America *(Microdipodops)* and Australia *(Notomys)*.

Birds of the desert

Many birds live in the desert, from the tiny elf owl *(Micrathene whitneyi)* [6] to the flightless ostrich *(Struthio camelus)*, the largest bird in the world. Desert birds may feed on seeds or water-rich plants such as cacti, but many, such as the roadrunner *(Geococcyx californianus)* and the elf owl, both of the North American Southwest, are predators, getting all the water they need from other animals. Birds that are mixed feeders, such as Pallas' sandgrouse *(Syrrhaptes paradoxus)* from Central Asia, are often migrants or nomads and can move quickly if conditions become unfavorable.

Ostriches are well adapted to desert life. They obtain their water from the plants they eat and they merge well into the pale tones of the desert landscape when squatting on the ground. If threatened while on the nest, which is just a shallow scoop in the earth, the hen bird presses her long neck flat along the sand, making herself difficult to distinguish. This attitude has perhaps given rise to the mistaken belief that ostriches bury their heads in the sand as a form of defense.

KEY

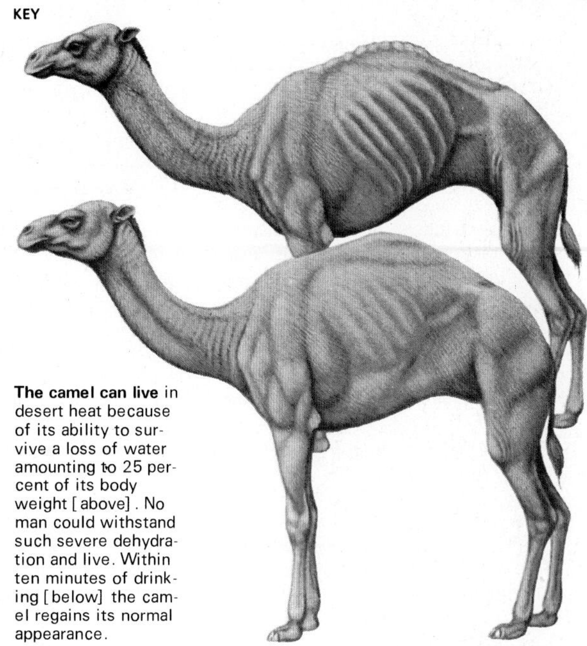

The camel can live in desert heat because of its ability to survive a loss of water amounting to 25 percent of its body weight [above]. No man could withstand such severe dehydration and live. Within ten minutes of drinking [below] the camel regains its normal appearance.

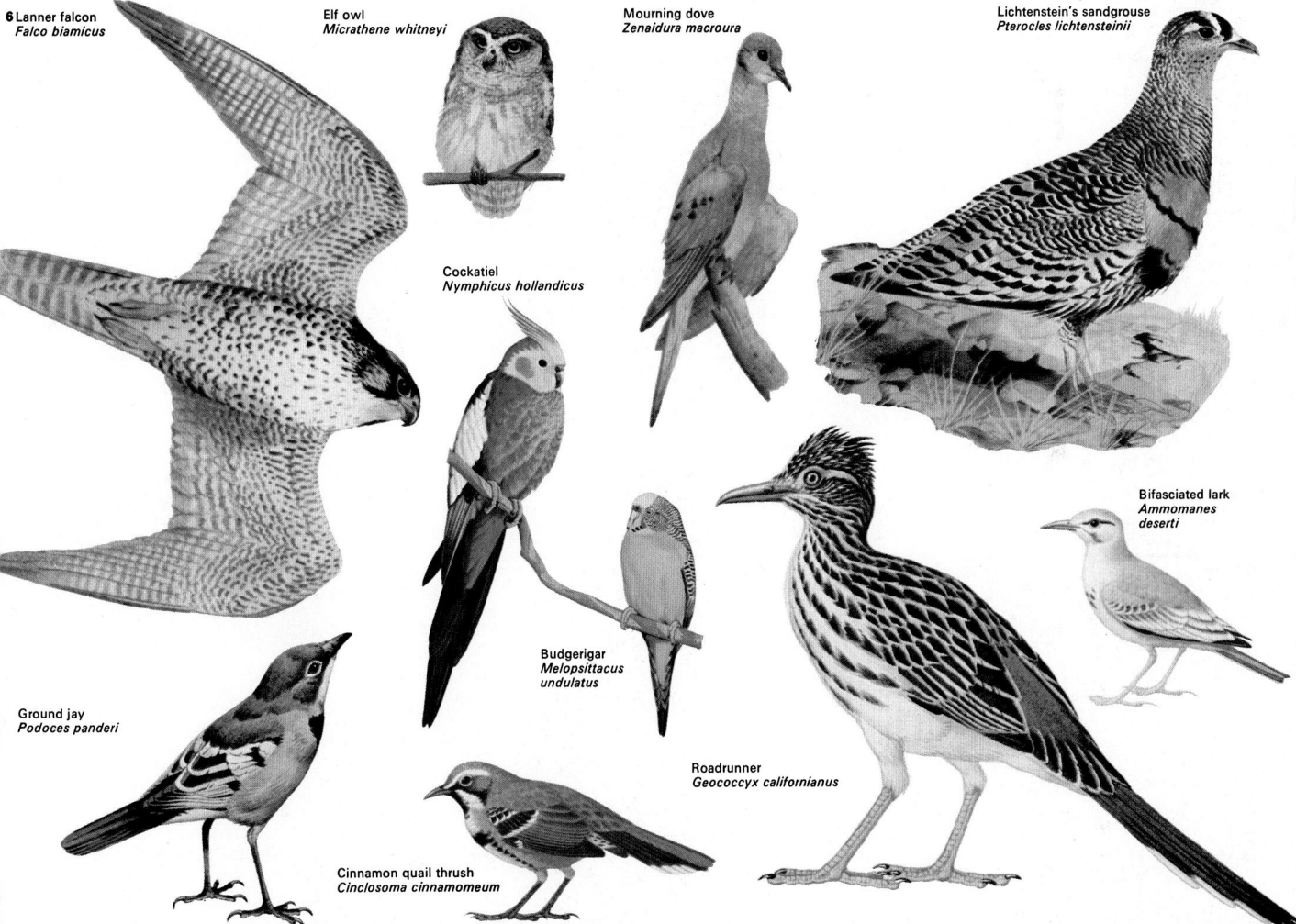

6 Lanner falcon *Falco biamicus*

Elf owl *Micrathene whitneyi*

Mourning dove *Zenaidura macroura*

Lichtenstein's sandgrouse *Pterocles lichtensteinii*

Cockatiel *Nymphicus hollandicus*

Bifasciated lark *Ammomanes deserti*

Budgerigar *Melopsittacus undulatus*

Ground jay *Podoces panderi*

Roadrunner *Geococcyx californianus*

Cinnamon quail thrush *Cinclosoma cinnamomeum*

6 Typical desert birds include the lanner falcon, which feeds mainly on other birds. It has been a popular bird with falconers for thousands of years in Africa and Asia. The New World elf owl is one of the smallest of the owls, about 6in (15cm) long. It often nests in cacti, using the abandoned nests of the gila woodpecker, and feeds on insects and occasionally on small birds. The North American mourning dove can withstand a variety of climatic conditions and so is at home in the desert. It breeds throughout most of the year. Lichtenstein's sandgrouse is unusual in that the parents carry water in their crops and then regurgitate it into the mouths of their chicks. The budgerigar is the native name for a little Australian parakeet well known as a cage bird in many parts of the world. In the wild it lives in large flocks in the semi-deserts of Australia, as does the widespread cockatiel. The roadrunner is noted among desert birds for its expertise in killing snakes. It does this by a series of quick stabs with its long, pointed beak. It rarely flies, but is a very fast, agile runner. The bifasciated lark of Africa and Asia has an unusually strong bill for digging grubs and ant lions from the sand to supplement its diet of seeds. The ground jay, so called because it has become almost totally ground-based, uses its wings only to increase its running speed. Its grey plumage effectively camouflages it in the desert. It nests in burrows or beneath bushes. The Australian cinnamon quail thrush can survive the most severe drought. It seldom drinks and gets its needed water from eating insects.

Mountain life

Mountains make up about five percent of the Earth's land mass. The world's great mountain ranges are not confined to any one latitude but are found in all continents. Specifically, they are the mountain ridge from Alaska to the southern tip of South America, which includes the Rockies and the Andes; the great range separating east and west Antarctica; the Appalachians of eastern North America; the various ranges of the Eurasian land mass, including the Alps, Pyrenees, and Caucasus mountains; and the Himalaya range [2, 3] between the Palearctic and Oriental regions. In Africa there are the Atlas in the north and several isolated mountainous regions in Ethiopia, Kenya, and Rwanda. Australia has one major range—the Great Divide of the eastern coast.

Mountain zones

The plants and animals of mountains comprise different species according to their locality but all share adaptations essential to survival in this habitat and some of these adaptations are very similar to those of plants and animals found in polar regions. The range of life on a mountainside is very wide, for in terms of climate a difference in altitude of 200ft (70m) is equivalent to 1° of latitude—roughly 70 miles (110km). This is due to sharp decreases in temperature and increases in precipitation up the mountainside.

Mountain plants reflect changes of climate by showing a definite vertical zonation. This is modified by the distance from the Equator. Mount Kilimanjaro, 19,340 ft (5,595m) in Africa, shows all the possible mountain zones—tropical forest, deciduous forest, and coniferous forest which merges into the alpine zone at the tree line. Topping the alpine zone are snow and ice. Mountains in temperate regions, such as the Sierra Nevada, [1], have no tropical zone, while those at even higher latitudes, as in the northern Rockies, have no temperate zone. Herbivorous animals, ranging from insects to mountain goats, show a similar zonation because their distribution is limited by food sources, but mountain carnivores tend to be more mobile.

As in all other habitats, the plants and animals of mountains are affected by such factors as soil, cover, and competition. But because of the harsh environment of the higher zones the number of species able to survive is limited.

Plant adaptations

Plants are the basis of the mountain food chains. Plants of the alpine zone [5] are either short, compact and virtually stemless or have supple shoots and stems. These adaptations enable them to survive cold, strong winds. Many mountain plants have extensive root systems to provide anchorage against the wind and to increase their chances of obtaining water on dry slopes. The common alpine cushion plants stand only an inch or two high yet their roots may penetrate more than 3ft (0.9m) down into the soil. Water conservation is enhanced by such adaptations as waxy coverings on the leaves; the alpine edelweiss *(Leontopodium alpinum)* has leaves covered with hairs that trap heat and reduce water loss. To combat freezing, plants such as the mountain crow-

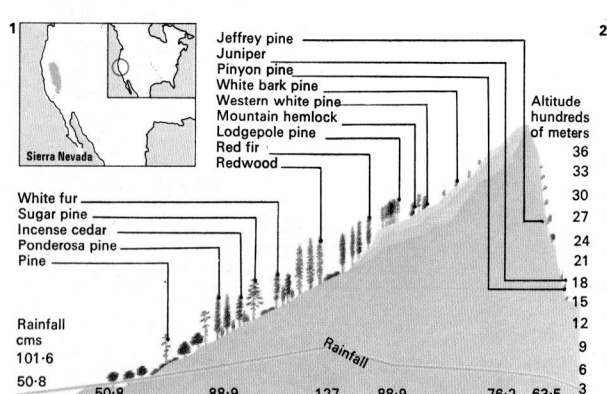

CONNECTIONS

See also
582 Isolation and evolution
610 Polar regions
612 Life on the tundra
592 Northern evergreen forests
440 The cone bearers
580 The basis of ecology

Sierra Nevada
Jeffrey pine
Juniper
Pinyon pine
White bark pine
Western white pine
Mountain hemlock
Lodgepole pine
Red fir
Redwood
White fur
Sugar pine
Incense cedar
Ponderosa pine
Pine
Rainfall cms
101·6
50·8
Altitude hundreds of meters
36 33 30 27 24 21 18 15 12 9 6 3
Rainfall
50·8 cms 88·9 127 88·9 76·2 63·5

1 The Sierra Nevada of California is a classical example of the botanical zonation typical of most mountains. Shown here in cross-section, it illustrates the influence of rainfall, altitude, slope, and aspect in determining the distribution of mountain vegetation. Although the climate is temperate, deciduous trees are replaced by semi-desert scrub because of low rainfall. The western slope has a higher rainfall and thus a richer and more varied selection of plants than the dry easterly slopes of the mountain.

Altitude Hundreds of meters
64 61 58 55 52 49 46 43 40 37 34 30 27 24
Chiru antelope *Pantholops hodgsoni*
Yak *Bos grunniens*
Tibetan wild ass *Equus hemionus kiang*
Bharal *Pseudois nayaur*
Nayan *Ovis ammon hodgsoni*
Tibetan gazelle *Procapra piticaudata*
Shapu *Ovis orientalis*

2 Several species of large, hoofed mammals (ungulates) live in herds with side-ranging territories on the steep slopes and high grazing areas of the Himalayas and the Hindu Kush. Herds of chiru antelope roam over large areas of scant vegetation. Yaks, protected by dense, matted coats, also survive in high bleak areas where they often feed only on mosses and lichens. The Tibetan wild ass has the greatest vertical range of the animals shown here. It can withstand long periods without food and water. The Tibetan gazelle and the bharal, nayan, and shapu sheep are all less well equipped to endure the cold and so live in lower regions as a means of survival, feeding on the grassland plains.

3 The Himalayan alpine zone extends near to the summit of Mt Everest 29,030ft (8,848m) high. Animals are limited in numbers and range by availability of food at about 16,500ft (5,000m). Alpine choughs *(Pyrrhocorax graculus)* [1] eat insects and worms. The golden eagle *(Aquila chrysaëtos)* [2] flies far in search of carrion or small animals. The Tibetan pika *(Ochotona ladacensis)* [3], feeds on small green plants, storing some for winter. Stalking, rather than waiting in ambush, the snow leopard *(Uncia uncia)* [4] preys on both the Himalayan ibex *(Capra ibex sakeen)* [5] and bharal sheep *(Pseudois nayaur)* [6], which roam the slopes in search of small plants.

foot *(Ranunculus glacialis)* have a rich cell fluid that acts as an antifreeze. The alpine soldanella *(Soldanella alpina)* can even melt snow by releasing heat from the breakdown of carbohydrate within its cells.

In the alpine zone the summer growing season lasts only a few weeks. As a result most alpine plants are perennials. The cushion pink *(Silene acaulis)* may take ten years to flower, but when it does bloom several hundred flowers may appear. This low but concentrated reproductive rate probably occurs because it takes a long time for the plant to build up sufficient food reserves to enable it to flower. Many mountain plants are self-pollinating, a mechanism that ensures fertilization in a situation where there are few flying insect pollinators. For the same reason wind-pollinated species outnumber insect-pollinated ones.

Animal life on mountains

Many mountain animals tend to stay on high slopes and peaks throughout the year but can avoid extreme conditions in a number of ways. Larger herbivorous animals of the alpine zone, such as sheep, goats, and antelopes—and their attendant carnivores—migrate to lower, snow-free slopes in winter. Marmots *(Marmota)*, and to a lesser extent ground squirrels *(Citellus)*, hibernate. The marmots gorge in the summer and lie dormant in burrows during the winter, slowly using up their stored energy supplies. The European snow vole *(Microtus nivalis)* remains active in winter in its underground home, using hoarded food. Pikas *(Ochotona)* often remain above ground in winter, living on dried plant material they have hidden beneath rocks [8].

Birds [7] are well adapted to altitude. Their dense covering of feathers provides excellent insulation. Many insects can tolerate cold conditions above the tree line because their body fluids have a low freezing point. The glacier flea *(Isotoma saltans)* can withstand being frozen solid for short periods, while springtails (Collembola) have survived being trapped in ice for several years. Most insects of high altitudes, however, remain dormant over the winter in hollows beneath snow-covered rocks [6].

KEY

Mountains close to each other, such as the Tatra and more southerly Bucegi mountains of central Europe, have similar vegetation, but the altitudes at which individual zones occur may vary. This variation is a reflection of differences in climatic conditions of the regions.

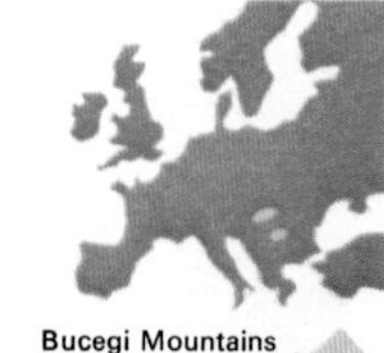

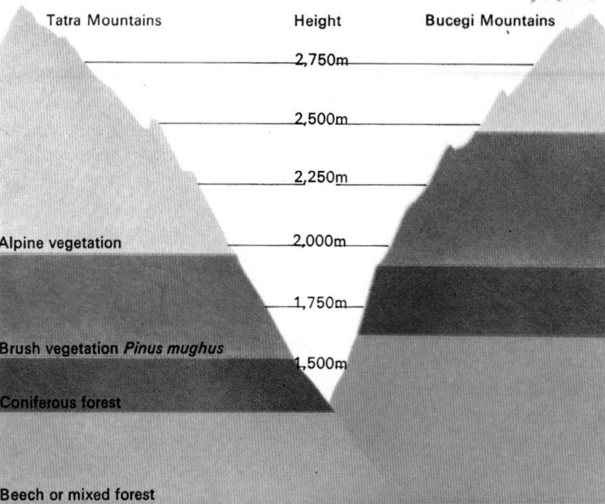
Tatra Mountains
Height
Bucegi Mountains
2,750m
2,500m
2,250m
2,000m
1,750m
1,500m
Alpine vegetation
Brush vegetation *Pinus mughus*
Coniferous forest
Beech or mixed forest

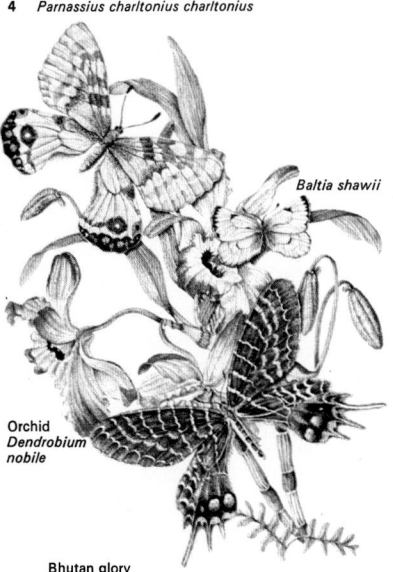

4 *Parnassius charltonius charltonius*

Baltia shawii

Orchid *Dendrobium nobile*

Bhutan glory *Armandia lidderdalei*

4 Butterflies are found at nearly all mountain levels. *Parnassius charltonius charltonius* lives at heights of 17,000ft (6,000m) in the Himalayas. Most mountain butterflies are darker than related lowland species, which allows them to absorb the maximum of heat and protects them from the sun's ultraviolet rays. Among common species of the mountain regions of Turkestan, Tibet, Mongolia, and the Himalayas are *Baltia shawii and Armandia lidderdalei.* Like most mountain insects, they fly close to the ground to avoid high winds. They feed on nectar which they obtain from orchids and other flowering alpine plants.

5

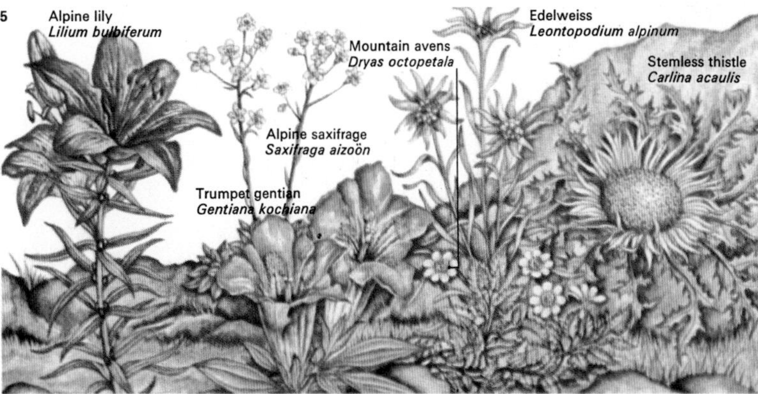
Alpine lily
Lilium bulbiferum
Mountain avens
Dryas octopetala
Edelweiss
Leontopodium alpinum
Stemless thistle
Carlina acaulis
Alpine saxifrage
Saxifraga aizoön
Trumpet gentian
Gentiana kochiana

5 Mountain plants are most often short, supple, and compact, with leaves and petals that show a variety of adaptations to cold and windy conditions. The alpine lily is a perennial plant and is among the tallest of all alpine species. But it has an extremely supple stem and thus can bend in the wind. The well known edelweiss of the Alps shows another adaptation to mountain life. The plant is covered with a thick layer of white hairs that act as a heat trap. The trumpet gentian has large, thin and flat leaves to absorb a maximum amount of radiant energy. The mountain avens and alpine saxifrage are both small, low-lying perennial plants, particularly common in northern Europe. The stemless thistle is found in rocky places of mountain regions throughout western Europe.

6

1
2
3
4
5
6
7
8

6 The insects and other arthropods of the high Himalayas are usually confined to three locations. Hollows under rocks shelter attid spiders [1], pseudoscorpions [2], carabid beetles [3], and millipedes (Diplopoda) [4]. Springtails (Collembola) [5] and mites (Acarina) [6] live on rock surfaces. Beside meltwater streams stoneflies (Plecoptera) [7] and mayflies (Ephemeroptera) [8] are found. Many live on seeds and pollen deposited on the mountain by wind.

7 Snow finch
Montifringilla nivalis

7 The snow finch, *(Montifringilla nivalis)*, is commonly found in mountainous parts of Eurasia. It lives at heights up to 15,000ft (4,500m) and feeds on insects and the seeds of various alpine plants.

8 The Asian pika *(Ochotona lacadensis)* occupies a habitat 18,000ft (5,400m) up in the Himalayas. Its small, round body and short ears are adaptations to reduce heat loss.

8 Asian pika
Ochotona lacadensis

Polar regions

The northern and southern polar regions of the earth [Key] share the same hostile characteristic of intense cold. In almost every other way they are different. The Arctic is almost entirely frozen ocean surrounded, for the most part, by land. The Antarctic on the other hand, is a land mass pressed down beneath a great raft of ice, a lost continent that at one time, before the continents drifted apart, was much warmer.

The polar climate

The common feature of both regions—their coldness—stems from their being located at the ends of the earth's axis. When one pole is tilted for its summer toward the sun, the other is tilted away into an endless night. They are cold because they receive their sunlight more obliquely than any other part of the world, for received heat is related to the angle at which the Sun's rays strike the surface. Finally, the cold is intensified because the ice acts as a mirror that reflects solar energy back into space.

The contrast between the polar regions is most marked in the forms of life that each supports. The Arctic includes among its inhabitants one of the largest and most powerful of predators, the polar bear *(Thalarctos maritimus)* [1]. The Antarctic boasts as its only true terrestrial animals a handful (63 species) of insects, the largest of which is a wingless mosquito.

Ruthless trackers and ocean giants

The polar bear has adapted perfectly to life in the frozen ocean. It is able to spend most of its life in water, insulated from the cold by thick, greasy fur. A solitary animal, the polar bear patrols the ice in search of its prey, particularly the ringed seal *(Pusa hispida)* [1]. When the seal's head appears through a breathing hole in the ice the bear stuns it with a single blow from its powerful front leg. During the harshest of the winter months pregnant female bears hole up in ice caves beneath the surface [2]. The young are born in March or April, usually two at a time. The family leaves its den within the next two months—once the sun has become warm enough—and for the next two years the cubs learn to hunt.

The polar bear is hunted by the Eskimo. The Arctic fox *(Alopex lagopus)* [1] will also trail the bear, for in lean times it will live off the bear's droppings.

The subpolar waters around the edges of the permanent Arctic ice are covered only by broken pack ice during the summer and these nutrient-rich waters support hosts of seals, including the ribbon seal *(Histriophoca fasciata)*, the hooded seal *(Cystophora cristata)* [6], and the walrus *(Odobenus rosmarus)* [1], hunted by the Eskimo for its meat and for its valuable ivory tusks.

The marine mammals of both north and south include the remnants of once huge populations of whales, reduced to a fraction of their former numbers by over-hunting. Among them are the blue whale *(Sibbaldus musculus)*—at around 115 tons, the largest living mammal—which feeds by straining the abundant plankton and small crustaceans through a horny sieve that hangs at the sides of its mouth.

One of the most fascinating creatures of the Arctic waters is the narwhale *(Monodon*

CONNECTIONS

See also

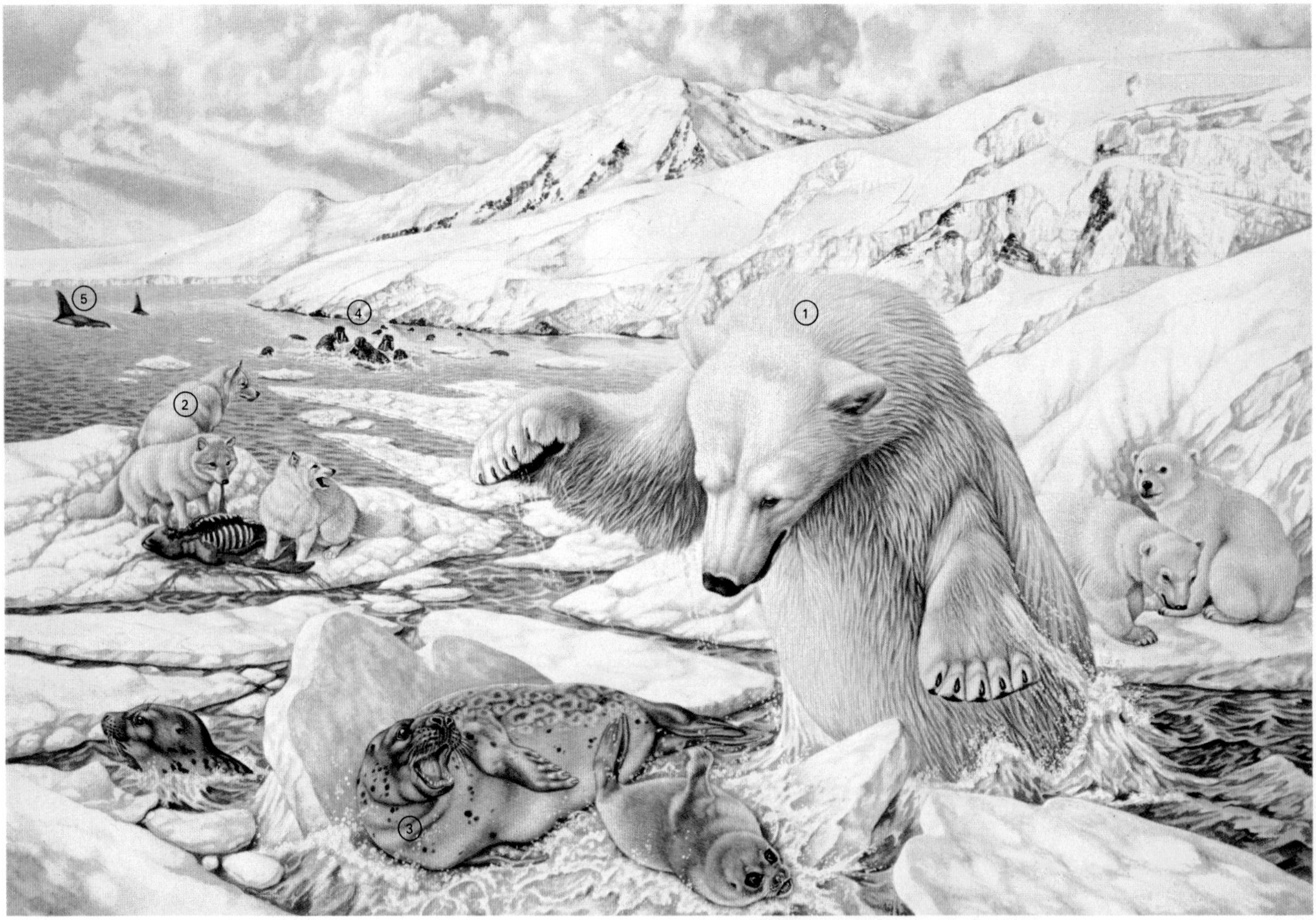

1 Two carnivorous predators, the polar bear *(Thalarctos maritimus)* [1] and the Arctic fox *(Alopex lagopus)* [2], head the food chain of the ice cap surrounding the North Pole. The polar bear feeds chiefly on the seals of the species *Pusa hispida* [3] and young walruses *(Odobenus rosmarus)* [4], although it may itself fall prey to the killer whale *(Orcinus orca)* [5]. The Arctic fox feeds mainly on carrion left behind by the polar bear. Seals feed on abundant fish and squid, while the walrus grubs on the ocean bottom for mollusks and crustaceans. In the early spring young polar bears are born in caves that have been shaped out beneath the snow. The polar bear is protected from the cold by a thick fur coat that traps a layer of insulating air. In contrast the seal is insulated by a layer of subcutaneous fat or blubber.

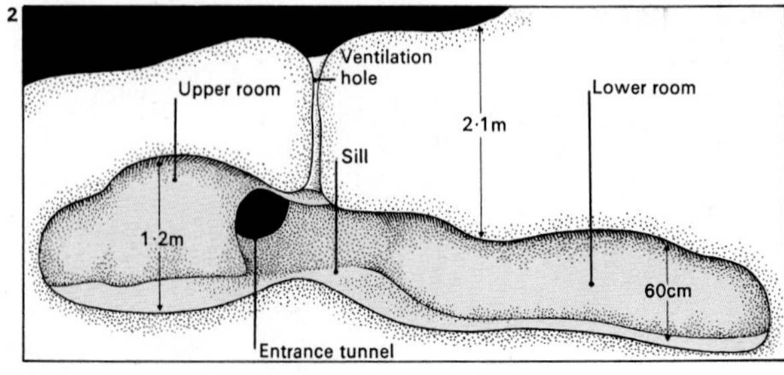

Ventilation hole
Upper room
Lower room
2·1m
Sill
1·2m
60cm
Entrance tunnel

2 As the winter approaches all pregnant female polar bears, most other females, and some adult males seek out a rock or ice den and spend the cold months in sleep. Here, too, the young are born—usually two cubs who remain with their mother for two years.

monoceros), the unicorn of the sea, which has a long single tusk. The narwhale feeds mainly on squid and is an amiable animal, often using its tusk as a sword for "fencing" matches with its fellows.

Considerable areas of North America and Eurasia fall within the Arctic Circle. These are the bleak, treeless tundra lands that support only grasses, mosses, and lichens. During the summer they are visited by wandering herds of caribou, and swarms of insects breed in the meltwater pools. The insects and the fresh, transient vegetation attract millions of migrant birds to feed, away from the crowded temperate regions. Of the 100 or more birds that breed in the tundra all but five or six are migrants.

The Antarctic seals

Summer and winter, most of the great mass of the Antarctic is lifeless, containing as it does 90 percent of the world's ice. Only on its fringes is life to be found in the form of huge colonies of penguins and seals.

The four species of seal for whom Antarctic waters are home are the southernmost mammals in the world: the Weddell seal *(Leptonychotes weddelli)* [9], the crabeater seal *(Lobodon carcinophagus),* the Ross seal *(Ommatophoca rossi)* [8], and the leopard seal *(Hydrurga leptonyx)* [10].

Each has its own particular life style. The Weddell seal always remains inshore while the others range far out to sea. The crabeater seal earns its name from its feeding habits; it gulps in large quantities of water and squirts this out through fanlike teeth that form a fine mesh at the gum margins, to sieve out the small crustaceans. The leopard seal is a fierce predator, cruising the edges of the ice pack in pursuit of its favorite dish, the Adélie penguin *(Pygoscelis adeliae).* The leopard seal preys also on the pups of other seal species, on squid, and on fish.

The Adélie is the most common of the Antarctic penguins, of which there are five species; largest is the emperor *(Aptenodytes forsteri)* [5], about 40in (1m) high. Other birds are well represented, including the skua *(Catharacta skua),* which preys on penguin eggs and chicks.

KEY

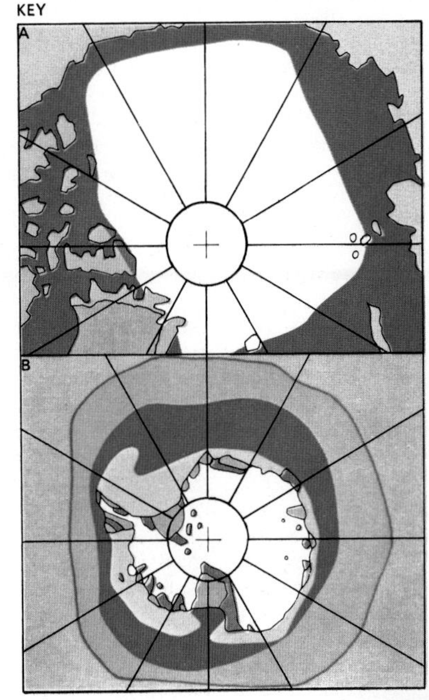

A
B

At the ends of the earth are, to the north, the frozen ocean and marginal tundra of the Arctic [A]; to the south, the lost continent of Antarctica beneath its blanket of ice [B]. In neither region does the temperature ever rise much above 50°F (10°C). At one time, however, the Antarctic enjoyed a subtropical climate, but continental drift took it to its present position. This separation and the savagery of its climate have excluded purely terrestrial mammals, in contrast with the Arctic, which supports a surprisingly diverse fauna despite the harshness of an icy, almost sunless environment. Even man survives there.

3 The gyrfalcon lives throughout the Arctic regions taking birds after a chase on the wing instead of striking from above like the peregrine falcon.

3 Gyrfalcon *Falco rusticolus*

4 Glaucous gull *Larus hyperboreus*

4 A greedy predator—like some other gulls—the glaucous gull nests on Arctic and North Atlantic cliffs and islands. It takes a wide variety of prey, ranging from small mammals to the eggs of birds.

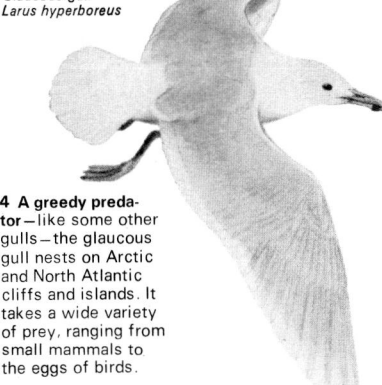

5 Largest of the penguins, the emperor breeds on the ice packs and small islands around the coastline of the Antarctic continent. The female lays a single egg that is then passed into the care of the male, who carries it on his feet for the two-month incubation period. The female spends this time at sea but returns for hatching and brooding. The emaciated male now returns to the sea to feed greedily.

5

Emperor penguin ***Aptenodytes forsteri***

6 Hooded seal *Cystophora cristata*

6 The grotesque nose of the hooded seal inflates during the breeding season to intimidate his rivals and to attract females.

7 Banded seal *Histriophoca fasciata*

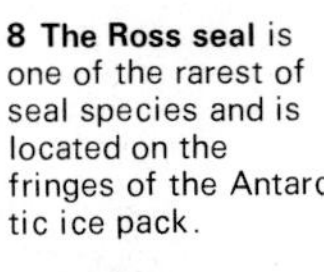

7 The banded seal, found exclusively in the Arctic waters of the Pacific south and west of the Bering Strait, is one of the smallest of seal species.

10 The hunter of the southern oceans is the leopard seal. This solitary animal hunts along the edge of the pack ice in search of its favorite prey—the Adélie penguin. This continual persecution produces one of the unusual sights of Antarctica—the reluctance of individual Adélies to enter the water (when they are most vulnerable to attack). The leopard seal varies its diet with squid, fish, and the pups of other seals.

8 The Ross seal is one of the rarest of seal species and is located on the fringes of the Antarctic ice pack.

8 Ross seal *Ommatophoca rossi*

9 Weddell seal *Leptonychotes weddelli*

9 The southernmost mammal, the Weddell seal, chews breathing holes in the ice when the sea is frozen over.

10 Leopard seal *Hydrurga leptonyx*

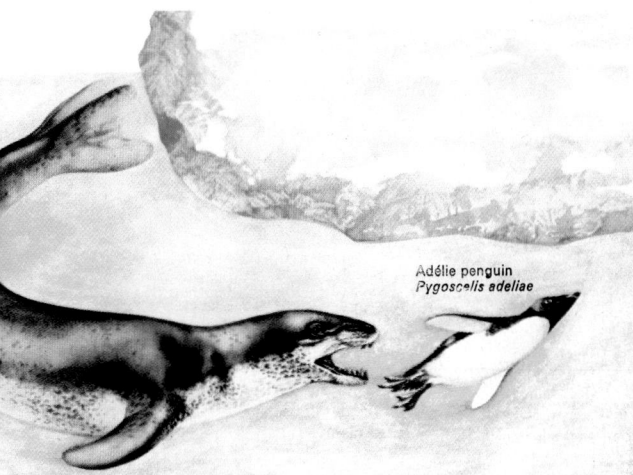

Adélie penguin *Pygoscelis adeliae*

Life on the tundra

The great ice sheets that covered much of North America and Eurasia in geologically recent times have retreated to the far north and the high mountains. Around their fringes, however, there remains a vast cold region known as "the barren grounds" in North America and the tundra (from the Finnish for a treeless plain) in the Old World. Despite their different names, the two areas are similar and have about 75 percent of plant and animal species in common. The area occupied by the tundra lies between 60° and 70°N latitude. It begins roughly where the average temperature of the warmest month reaches 50°F (10°C). Temperature is one of the limiting factors for tree growth.

Harsh climatic conditions

Within the tundra, darkness and cold are the principal controls on life. At the Arctic Circle the sun does not rise above the horizon at the winter solstice, and north of the circle the darkness is more prolonged. Over much of the tundra there is no sunlight for several months of the year. This is compensated for, to some extent, by the continuous daylight of summer, and the plants and animals cram much of their activity into this short period of light.

The cold is equally important and part of the geological inheritance. The subsoil is totally frozen, a condition known as "permafrost" [Key]. It is at least 2,000ft (610m) deep in Greenland and may be deeper in other places. Only the surface soil thaws in the summer. This is known as the active zone and may be as deep as 10ft (3m), or as shallow as 3in (7.6cm), but in either case it supports all life in the area, both plant and animal. Yet the soil in it is likely to be waterlogged because water cannot drain through the frozen zone. The frequent freezing and thawing causes the soil to rise in small "blisters," and stones collect in the hollows between them. The resulting formations are known as polygons and stone rings. Such precipitation as there is almost all falls as snow, equivalent to at most 20in (51cm) of rainfall a year.

There are some high mountains in the tundra, but mostly the land is low-lying, dotted with little lakes and pools, and crisscrossed by small meandering rivers. In the "low arctic" of the southern tundra, plant cover may be complete; farther north in the "high arctic" strong winds may sweep away the scanty soil and rooted plants become restricted to crevices and sheltered places. Lichens may be the only plants visible.

Tundra food chains

The larger plants of the tundra are mostly woody, forming knee-high forests of birch and willow, with mature trees often only a few inches high [1]. Many members of the heather family are present. Most are berry-bearers and form an important part of the diet of many tundra animals—even the polar bear will gorge itself on cranberries in the autumn. The woody plants are augmented and often overgrown by herbaceous plants, which in summer provide a brief blaze of color.

The animal life of the tundra is surprisingly rich for an environment that seems so inhospitable. Large animals include the musk ox [3] and in the summer the caribou.

CONNECTIONS

See also
608 Mountain life
592 Northern evergreen forests
434 The lichens
610 Polar regions
548 Hoofed mammals
532 Birds and migration
580 The basis of ecology

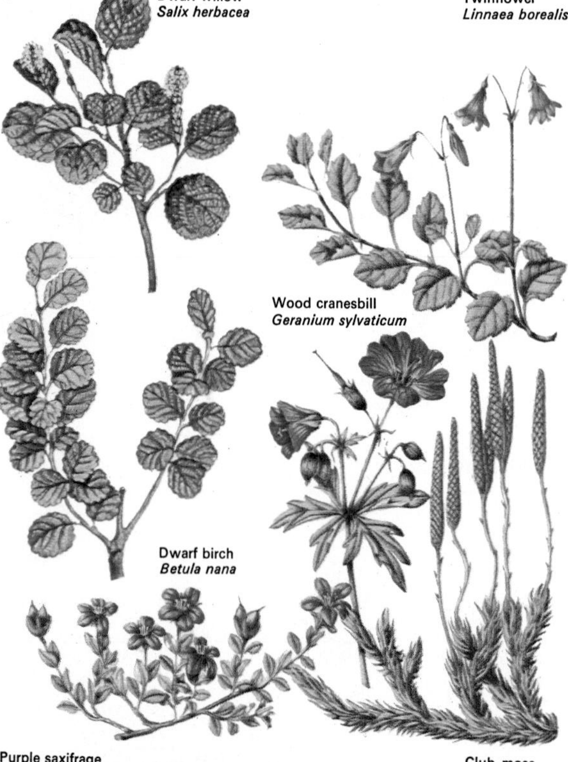

1
Dwarf willow
Salix herbacea
Twinflower
Linnaea borealis
Wood cranesbill
Geranium sylvaticum
Dwarf birch
Betula nana
Purple saxifrage
Saxifraga oppositifolia
Club-moss
Lycopodium sp

1 The vegetation of the tundra is almost all prostrate. A dwarf birch that grows up to 40in (1m) high is exceptional. Usually this plant is much smaller, as are dwarf willows, even when they are mature "trees." Beneath birch and willow is a rich growth of mosses and lichens that form the equivalent of a shrub layer in a temperate forest. Here *Lycopodium*, a club moss, is found. This small plant may spread over the ground for many acres, but is a poor reminder of the great scale trees of the past to which it is closely related. The wood cranesbill is one of the brilliant summer flowers of the tundra. Purple saxifrage is also found on many southern mountains, forming part of a flora referred to as "arctic alpine." *Linnaea* commemorates the great Swedish botanist Linnaeus, who made a journey to the tundra of Finland.

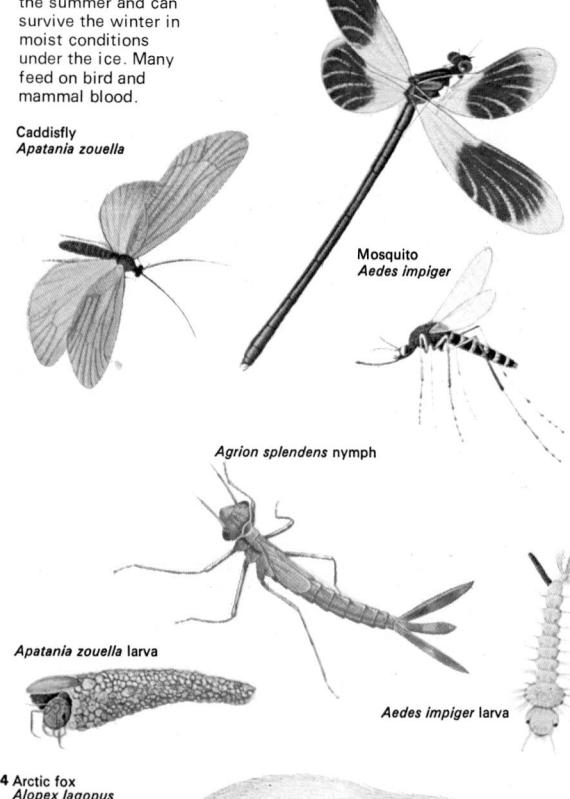

2 Most tundra insects spend their larval lives in the ephemeral pools of the summer and can survive the winter in moist conditions under the ice. Many feed on bird and mammal blood.

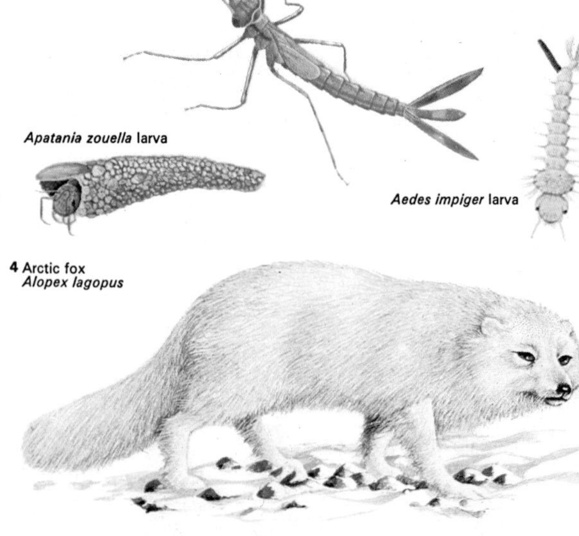

2 Dragonfly
Agrion splendens
Caddisfly
Apatania zouella
Mosquito
Aedes impiger
Agrion splendens nymph
Apatania zouella larva
Aedes impiger larva
4 Arctic fox
Alopex lagopus

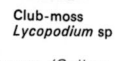

3 Musk oxen *(Ovibos moschatus)* are the largest animals found in northern Canada and Greenland. They have disappeared from the Old World, which they inhabited in the Ice Age. Their extremely thick coats protect them from cold, but they become exhausted if they have to cross thick snow in search of food. If threatened, the herd bunches together, presenting lowered heads and heavy horns to the attacker, providing a good defense.

4 The arctic fox is a circumpolar tundra resident. It exists in two forms: the blue form, which is smoky grey all the time, and the brown form, which changes to white in the winter. The population fluctuates with the availability of food, following the rise and fall of lemming numbers. Man is the fox's chief enemy; he kills it for its thick coat.

Smaller predators include wolves, arctic foxes [4], and wolverines, which feed mainly on the arctic ground squirrel, voles, and lemmings. These mammals are adapted to the cold with thick, warm fur and, under the skin, a heavy layer of fat. The danger of frostbite to their extremities is reduced by their compact shape and their short faces, ears, and tails.

Migratory birds

Few birds are resident in the tundra, but every year, drawn by the migratory urge, millions of ducks, geese, and shorebirds [5], among others, travel to the far north to nest and feed. This is the time of plenty for the arctic fox, which haunts the bird colonies, taking what it can of weak or injured chicks. It hides those that it cannot eat, and some of these caches remain, frozen, as supplies for the winter. The basis for much of the bird life on land is the huge number of insects, including mosquitoes and other biting flies [2].

The sea is as rich as the land is poor, and the summer flush of plankton supports a huge web of life, including seals, whales, and sea birds [6], most of which migrate to the far north to feed on the abundance of the waters. For a short time the temperature rises and activity and life abound. By August, however, the hours of daylight have become noticeably shorter, the temperature drops, and the first sleet heralds the winter. Insects die, leaving their eggs and larvae to winter beneath the ice covering the pools or in the shelter of snow-covered vegetation. The birds, their reproductive mission complete, fly southward in great flocks to spend the winter months in temperate and subtropical areas. Reindeer and caribou, followed by the wolves, migrate south, leaving only the musk oxen and the hardy arctic fox.

Yet even in summer the tundra, for all its apparent abundance, is an area where species are few but populations are large, and where the delicate balance of predators and prey is easily upset. Wildlife populations, often made up of prey such as small mammals, may fluctuate greatly between superabundance and paucity. The lemmings [8] are the best known of the animals that undergo this population swing.

KEY

A

Summer

Winter

1 metre

Waterlogged

Permafrost

Frozen ground

The ground surface of the tundra thaws in summer but stays waterlogged as the permafrost impedes drainage [A]. In winter it freezes, but small mammals [B] survive in burrows.

B

5 Small shorebirds, such as dunlin, turnstone, and knot, migrate north each spring to nest in the tundra. Like them, long-tailed duck and brent geese return south to feed on mudflats once families are reared. The snowy owl (immature shown) moves slightly south in the hardest weather.

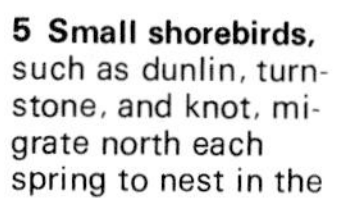

5 Dunlin *Calidris alpina*

Turnstone *Arenaria interpres*

Knot *Calidris canutus*

Long-tailed duck *Clangula hyemalis*

Brent goose *Branta bernicla*

Snowy owl *Nyctea scandiaca*

6 Arctic loon *Gavia arctica*

Arctic skua or parasitic jaeger *Stercorarius parasiticus*

6 Both skuas and loons breed on the tundra but they migrate to the oceans in winter. The arctic loon, or black-throated diver, feeds on fish. The skua eats rodents or fish it steals from gulls.

7

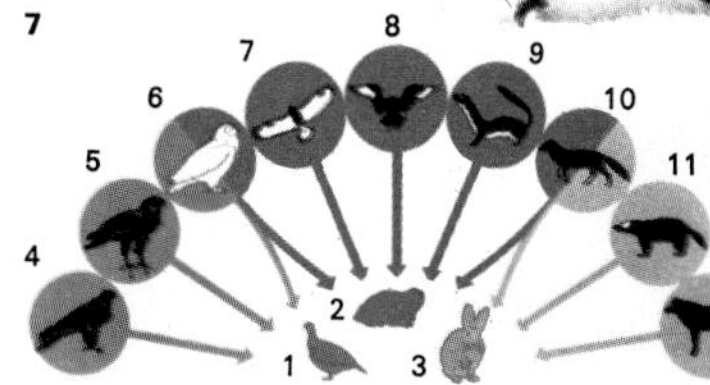

1
2
3
4
5
6
7
8
9
10
11
12

7 The herbivorous ptarmigan [1], lemming [2], and arctic hare [3] are the principal prey of a range of predators, such as the gyr and peregrine falcons [4, 5], short-eared owl [6], rough-legged hawk [7], pomarine jaeger [8], ermine [9], arctic fox [10], wolverine [11], and wolf [12]. Because the predators tend to be nomadic, wandering from poor areas to richer ones, there is little danger of their food becoming scarce.

8 Norway lemmings have a 4-year cycle of abundance [A]. A small population can, under favorable conditions, build up to great numbers. These attract predators, but lemmings continue to multiply and deplete their food supply. Popularly supposed to commit mass suicide, many lemmings die through attempting to migrate. They may drown while crossing rivers or when they reach the sea. Yearly lemming activity [B] is above and below the snow.

8 A

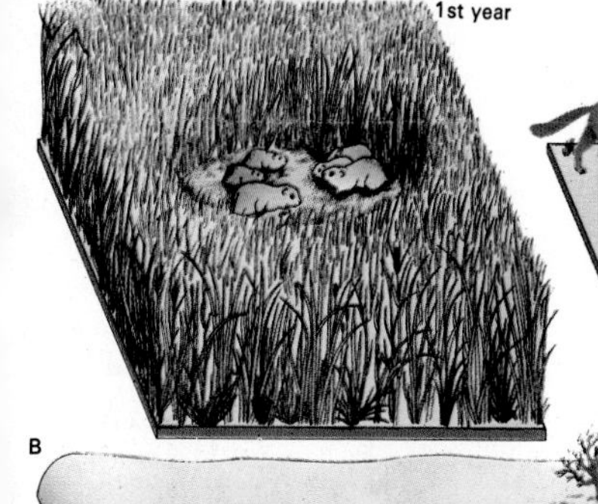

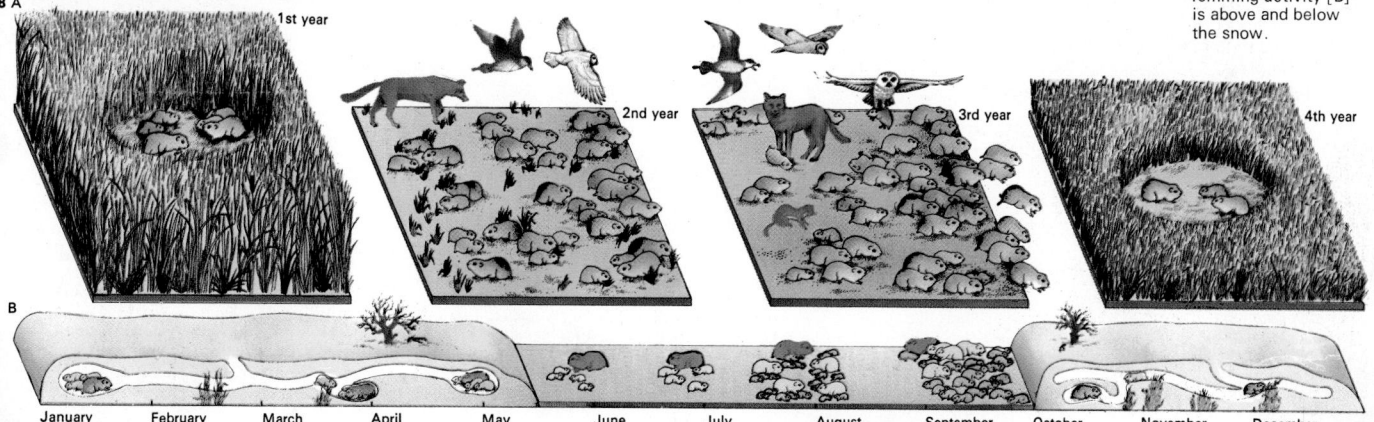

1st year

2nd year

3rd year

4th year

B

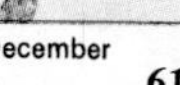

January February March April May June July August September October November December

Life on islands

Oceanic islands produced by the eruption of undersea volcanoes are, for some time afterward, unsuitable for any kind of life. Eventually, however, the lava cools and the area begins to become habitable. Chance is an important factor in colonization, but some organisms will manage to reach the land [Key] and in time even the most remote islands will become populated.

Certain kinds of vegetation and animals are adapted to travel to islands by air or sea [1]. Some plants produce numerous spores or very light airborne seeds, such as those of the daisy family (Compositae) that stand a better chance of making a sea crossing than do the large, heavy fruits of forest trees. Some plants have seeds that may be carried by birds, either hooked to their plumage or in mud on their feet. In a few cases seeds are carried in a bird's digestive system but the speed at which birds digest their food limits the chances of the seeds' surviving long journeys. Some plants, notably the "coco de mer," the unusual Seychelles double coconut, have well-protected floating seeds adapted to be spread by the sea. But it is doubtful whether most seeds can survive immersion for more than a few weeks.

Among the animals, many tiny creatures are carried in the upper air currents. Aphids and minute spiders form a large part of this "aerial plankton." Most die before they are dropped but a few survive to fall on dry land and colonize new areas. At lower altitudes large insects and birds whirled along by a storm may reach land thousands of miles from their starting points.

The successful colonies

Water travel is more difficult for land-dwelling animals. Gigantic rafts of vegetation [3], which are sometimes swept down to the sea by tropical rivers in flood, can become floating islands able to carry a number of small, tree-living animals to distant landfall. The most successful colonists, however, are the reptiles, and the fauna of most tropical islands includes lizards and tortoises. Inside the timbers of a vegetation raft the grubs of beetles and other insects continue to gnaw their way, unaware of their changed circumstances. They may hatch out far from the place where the eggs were laid. The beetle fauna of many islands consists largely of wood-boring forms.

Once ashore on an oceanic island a degree of luck is needed to ensure survival. An animal arriving on a barren island will soon die from lack of food or water. But should the basic needs of life be available the new arrivals may find themselves in an open environment in which the ecological niches have remained unfilled. The adaptability inherent in every living organism enables the newcomers to occupy some part of the available living space. In many instances [8] the descendants of a single species have diverged widely to form several new and different species adapted to the conditions on an island.

Certain trends can be seen among animals and plants on islands. One is increase in size for, in general, the lack of competition allows larger organisms to take what food is available. If predators are rare the need to be small or swift for protection will disappear. Giant forms, particularly of reptiles, can be found on tropical islands.

CONNECTIONS

See also
582 Isolation and evolution
538 Island birds
418 Evolution: classical theories
630 Endangered birds
1260 Colonizing Oceania and Australasia

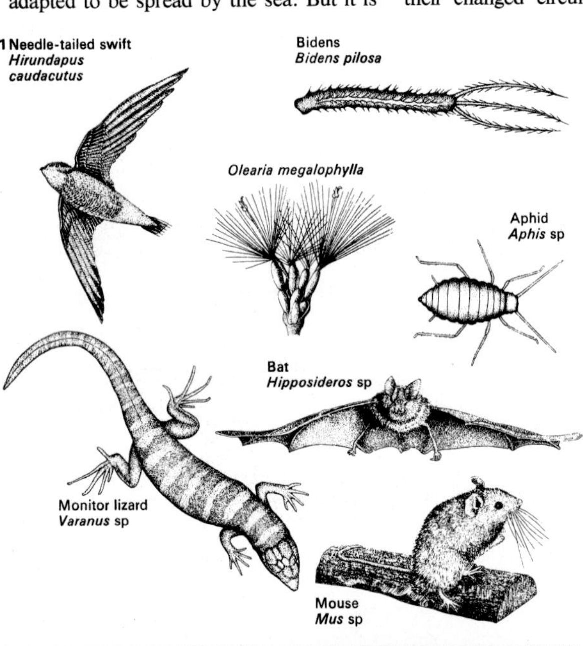

1 Needle-tailed swift
Hirundapus caudacutus
Bidens
Bidens pilosa
Olearia megalophylla
Aphid
Aphis sp
Bat
Hipposideros sp
Monitor lizard
Varanus sp
Mouse
Mus sp

1 Many kinds of organisms are likely to colonize islands. They include a number of medium-sized birds such as the swift, since smaller ones are unlikely to survive the journey and big ones are not so easily blown off their course. The birds may carry fruits like those of *Bidens* hooked in their plumage. Tiny insects, such as aphids, might be carried by air currents, along with plumed fruits of plants such as *Olearia*. Lizards can survive long-distance sea travel on vegetation rafts, as can rats, mice, and other small animals. Bats, too, will make short sea journeys and even survive long ones, thus colonizing new lands.

2 Hoop pine *Araucaria cunninghamii*
Phyllocladus hypophylla
Drimys winteri

2 Some islands far from land are of continental origin. Their rocks, plants, and animals proclaim this, for the same species may also be found on major land masses. The plants illustrated grow in New Guinea. Their seeds cannot survive in sea-water nor are they adapted for transport by animals or the wind.

3 Tropical rivers in flood will sometimes sweep downstream huge masses of timber and creepers tangled together into rafts of vegetation. As these floating islands reach the sea they are still the home of many animals. But each day farther from land these creatures become fewer. First to go are the bigger mammals, such as the monkeys, which may have been clinging to the branches and cannot survive the reduced size of their habitat and the cooler sea temperature. The reptiles and some insects, which have lower metabolic rates and are relatively inactive, can last longer and perhaps make a successful landfall in a place where there may be a food source sufficient to enable them to survive.

Micromus drepanoides
Micromus halaekalae
Micromus vagus
Micromus lobipennis

4 The lacewings that have reached the Hawaiian islands have undergone great changes to adapt them to life where flight can mean destruction by being blown out to sea. In some species, such as *Micromus drepanoides* and *M. vagus*, wings have become large and heavy with angular corners, thus making flight almost impossible. In other forms the hindwings are almost totally absent *(M. lobipennis)*. Some species with reduced hindwings have forewings that are studded with thickened areas that increase their weight and hamper flight as in *M. halaekalae*.

Birds and insects are often markedly larger than their ancestors, and plants may evolve from herbaceous types into treelike forms.

Islands are windy places and organisms that have been blown there may be blown off again. Successful colonizers often lose their power of flight and many species of flightless birds [5] are known in remote places. Flightlessness and large size are often combined and giant flightless birds, such as the extinct elephant birds of Madagascar, and outsize flightless insects, such as the lacewings of Hawaii [4], inhabit remote islands.

The chance to survive

Although large animals cannot reach distant islands, they are sometimes cut off from the main population by changes in sea level. When this happens the opposite kinds of changes occur to those found in birds on remote islands. Large mammals make heavy demands on their environment and because islands tend to be restricted in size the smaller creatures, whose needs are simpler, stand the best chance of survival. Examples of this can be seen on many continental islands. The race of sika deer *(Cervus nippon)* found in Japan, for example, is smaller than the mainland forms. An extreme case is that of elephants and hippopotamuses isolated on Mediterranean islands some two million years ago, during the Pleistocene, by rising sea levels. Fossil evidence shows that these creatures developed into miniature forms as small as Shetland ponies.

The arrival of man

Plants and animals of remote islands often survived in a very delicate ecological balance until the arrival of man. To humans, the large, slow creatures meant little more than a convenient food supply and in many cases [6] they were virtually wiped out soon after their discovery. The lack of natural enemies often led the animals to be so trusting that their destruction was the more certain. The introduction of domestic animals, especially pigs and goats, has in many cases also caused the destruction of the unique flora of some islands, as well as bringing the native animals to the point of extinction.

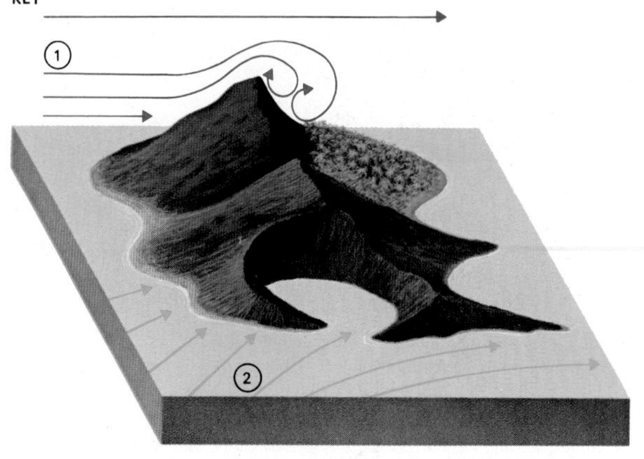
KEY
1
2

An island rising from the ocean bed, far from any land, can be colonized by plants and animals in only a limited number of ways. Those that do reach it arrive largely by accident. If the island stands in the path of regular strong winds, such as the trade winds [1], spores and lightweight seeds and tiny animals may be blown there. If it lies within a hurricane belt, storms may bring larger insects and birds that have been blown off course, while sea currents [2] may deposit vegetation carrying seeds and also small creatures.

5
Flightless cormorant
Nannopterum harrisi
6 Dodo
Raphus cucullatus
7
Tuatara
Sphenodon punctatus

5 The flightless Galapagos cormorant, like other island birds, dives for food near the shore and after hunting spreads its nonfunctional wings out to dry, just as its flying relatives do.

6 The dodo, now extinct, lived securely on Mauritius. When predators arrived it succumbed.

7 The tuatara is a rare "living fossil," surviving in the security of a few small islands off the coast of New Zealand. At one time relatives of this animal were abundant over much of the world.

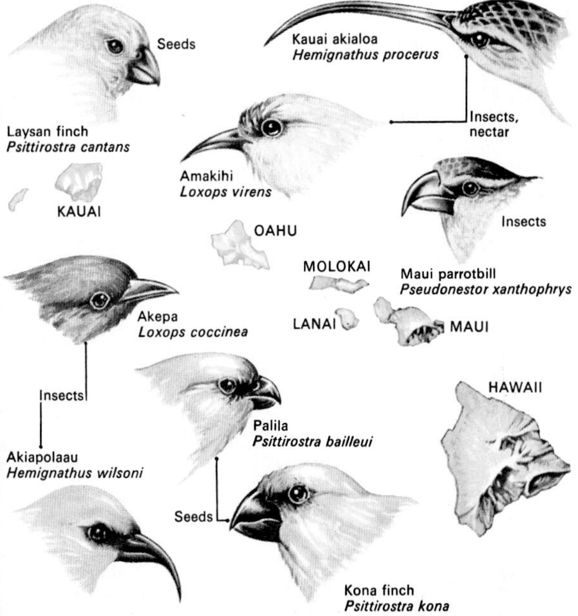
8
Seeds
Laysan finch
Psittirostra cantans
Kauai akialoa
Hemignathus procerus
Insects, nectar
Amakihi
Loxops virens
KAUAI
OAHU
Insects
MOLOKAI
Maui parrotbill
Pseudonestor xanthophrys
Akepa
Loxops coccinea
LANAI
MAUI
HAWAII
Insects
Palila
Psittirostra bailleui
Akiapolaau
Hemignathus wilsoni
Seeds
Kona finch
Psittirostra kona

8 The honey-creepers of the Hawaiian islands probably have as a common ancestor a species of New World tanager or warbler that long ago colonized the islands. Their beak shapes show that some feed on nectar, others on insects or seeds. Among them they fill a variety of ecological niches on the islands.

9 The plumed fruits of dandelionlike plants (family Compositae) are carried long distances by the wind. On remote islands they often develop into treelike plants adapted to extremes of climate or other conditions. Species of *Dubautia* and *Argyroxiphium* of Hawaii and *Scalesia* of the Galapagos are all woody and treelike in form.

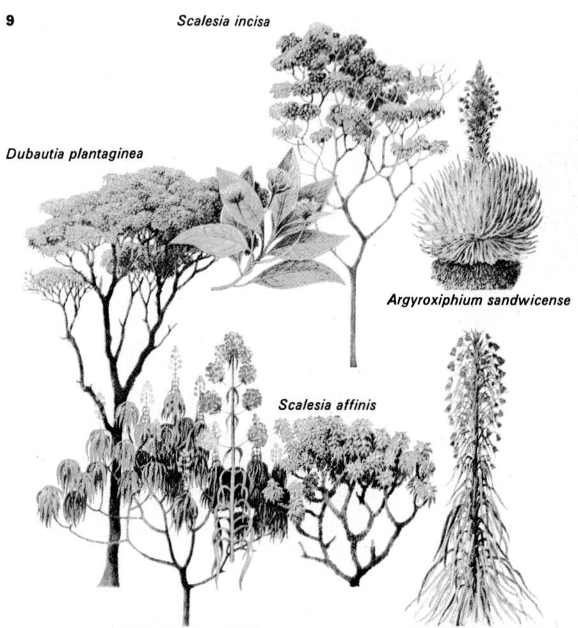
9
Scalesia incisa
Dubautia plantaginea
Argyroxiphium sandwicense
Scalesia affinis
Scalesia pedunculata
Argyroxiphium virescens

Lakes and rivers

The overwhelming mass of the world's water is oceanic, its freshwater lakes and rivers covering a minute area by comparison, but fresh waters provide a wide variety of habitats and these are occupied by a diverse selection of specialized plants and animals. For the purposes of plant and animal study rivers are divided into a series of "reaches," depending on the distance from the ocean, each characterized by a dominant fish species. The classification below is based on European rivers but can be adapted to suit rivers anywhere.

The reaches of a river

The typical river begins high in the mountains as a small stream, with occasional sharp falls, trickling over rocks. This is referred to as the upper cascade reach, an area of cold, clear, and pure water with few inhabitants, although some insects, and the bullhead *(Cottus gobio)* may be present. Downstream, where the water is still clear and cold and the slope still steep, an amalgamation of small torrents forms the trout reach. There is a sharp increase in the number of fish species, many of them using the pebbles that accumulate in sheltered spots for breeding. Salmon will penetrate upstream to the lower part of the trout reach, but they thrive better in deeper, pebbly areas. These are to be found in the grayling, or minnow, reach.

In the grayling reach the well oxygenated water still flows rapidly, but it is deeper and more suited to salmon. The turbulence of the water prevents many plants from rooting at the edge of the stream but the high oxygen content encourages a wealth of small animals, such as crustaceans, worms, insects, and their larvae. The grayling reach is followed by the barbel reach. The slope of the river is easing, the flow less headlong, but it is still cool, clear, and well aerated.

The last reach before the estuary is the bream reach, which winds slowly across a flat landscape. The water is warm and murky with suspended silt. The oxygen level is lower but it may be augmented in the summer by the many plants growing in what is often biologically the richest part of the river supporting a wide variety of fish.

The last stage of the river's life is the estuary, where salt water from the ocean penetrates and changes its character. Estuarine waters are a unique environment and are not strictly part of the river, which shares them with the sea. Some riverine species—the pike and perch among them—may occur in several reaches, but most are restricted to the section that is their native habitat.

Life in lakes and ponds

A lake may be part of a river, or its birthplace, and ponds may dot the valleys and plains through which the river passes. The difference between a lake and a pond is based on the depth of the water. Area alone does not turn a pond into a lake, although a large pond is sometimes given the nominal status of lake. In a pond rooted plants may grow from any part of its silty bed because its water is uniformly warm and poorly oxygenated in summer. On the edge of the lake conditions may be pondlike but beyond, where the lake's bed may fall to great depths, no rooted plants can grow.

CONNECTIONS

See also
516 Fish of seas and rivers
518 The life of amphibians
258 Rivers and lakes
510 The classification of fish
476 Land and sea snails
454 Grasses, reeds, and rushes
296 Pollution of rivers and lakes
618 Wetlands: marshes and swamps
580 The basis of ecology
496 Locusts, sucking bugs, and dragonflies

1

1 No part of the living space provided by a pond is neglected. Plants root in the muddy bottom or float on the surface. Some animals, such as *Tubifex* worms or midge larvae, bury themselves in the silt, but most are more active, gliding over the mud like the flatworms, undulating through the water like the leech, or jogging upward like the water fleas. The larvae of pond insects are the food of newts and fish, which are in turn fed on by birds.

1 Dragonfly *Aeschna grandis*
2 Water starwort *Callitriche* sp
3 Great diving beetle *Dytiscus marginalis*
4 Great pond snail *Lymnaea stagnalis*
5 Pea mussel *Pisidium amnicum*
6 *Tubifex* worm
7 Moorhen *Gallinula chloropus*
8 Pond skater *Gerris* sp
9 Newt tadpole *Triturus vulgaris*
10 Hornwort *Ceratophyllum demersum*
11, 12 Water spider and nest *Argyroneta aquatica*
13 Great ramshorn snail *Planorbis corneus*
14 Toad tadpole *Bufo bufo*
15 Larva of great diving beetle *Dytiscus marginalis*
16 Blood worm *Chironomus* sp
17 Mayfly *Cloëon dipterum*
18 Arrowhead *Sagittaria sagittifolia*
19 Dragonfly nymph *Libellula quadrimaculata*
20 Water boatman *Notonecta glauca*
21 Wandering snail *Lymnaea pereger*
22 Three-spined stickleback *Gasterosteus aculeatus*
23 *Hydra oligactis*
24 Great crested newt *Triturus cristatus*
25 Damselfly nymph *Agrion virgo*
26 *Aplecta hypnorum*
27 *Cyclops* sp
28 Common frog *Rana temporaria*
29 Horse leech *Haemopsis sanguisuga*
30 Ivy-leafed duckweed *Lemna trisulca*
31 Minnow *Phoxinus phoxinus*
32 Frogbit *Hydrocharis morsus-ranae*
33 Mallard *Anas platyrhynchos*
34 Kingfisher *Alcedo atthis*
35 Damselfly *Coenagrion puella*
36 Water crowfoot *Ranunculus aquatilis*
37 Water scorpion *Nepa cinerea*
38 Toad spawn *Bufo bufo*
39 Saucer bug *Ilyocoris cimicoides*
40 Water flea *Daphnia* sp
41 *Bithynia tentaculata*
42 Freshwater sponge *Spongilla lacustris*
43 Water mites *Hydrarachna globosa*
44 Caddisfly larva *Limnophilus flavicornis*
45 Painter's mussel *Unio pictorum*
46 Water louse *Asellus aquaticus*
47 *Planaria gonocephala*

The water is cold and dark even in midsummer and separated from the upper water—warm and containing life forms—by a thermocline, or region of abrupt temperature change. There is some mixing of the two water zones during winter storms but in summer the two water bodies exist separately in the same basin.

Plant life in lakes and rivers includes some planktonic floating organisms—richer in lakes and ponds than in rivers, where they would be swept away by the current. In the still waters of the pond larger plants, such as frogbit and bladderwort, are rootless, but most are attached to some kind of firm substrate. Occasionally they grow up through several feet of water—the water lily is one such plant. A common feature of stream plants is the possession of dissected underwater leaves that reduce the drag of the flowing water, plus broad surface leaves that catch the sunlight. In their protected environment most water plants have tissues that are unable to support themselves in air yet have great power to resist the relentless tug of the water.

Ponds, lakes, and rivers support a rich animal life wherever the worst effects of man's presence have not polluted the water. Lakes are often large enough to support a fish population of such numbers that a fishing industry can also be maintained.

Amphibians, birds, and mammals

Apart from the species that visit fresh water to drink, lakes and ponds are also inhabited by creatures of two worlds, the amphibians who spawn in the waters and whose tadpoles lead an aquatic life until they metamorphose. Even afterward they must remain in or close to a moist environment to prevent drying out. Many birds, some of them adapted for swimming by having webbed feet and dense feathers naturally waterproofed with oil, form part of the freshwater populations, as do many mammals. Some of these, such as the muskrat and the coypu, are herbivorous; others, such as the mink and the otter, are carnivores. Among the invertebrates, every major phylum except the echinoderms (starfish and sea urchins) has freshwater representatives.

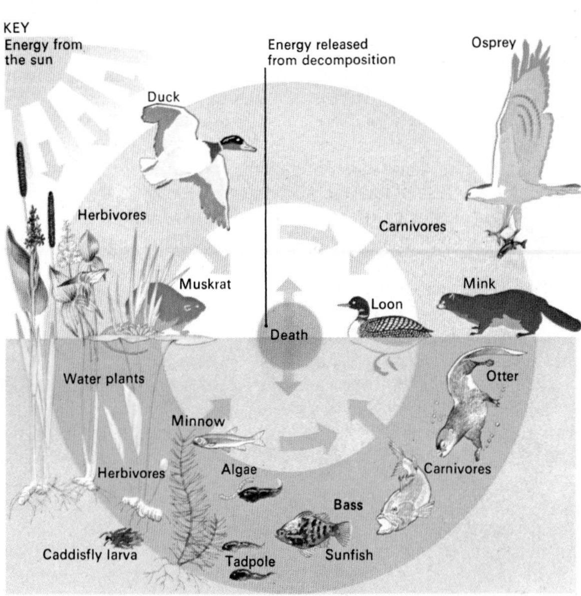

KEY
Energy from the sun
Energy released from decomposition
Osprey
Duck
Herbivores
Carnivores
Muskrat
Mink
Loon
Death
Water plants
Otter
Minnow
Herbivores
Algae
Carnivores
Bass
Caddisfly larva
Tadpole
Sunfish

A river, pond, or lake is a largely self-contained microcosm taking energy from the sun and minerals from the land.

2 Mayfly *Rhithrogena semicolorata*
Caddisfly *Plectrocnemia conspersa*
Caddisfly larva net *Plectrocnemia conspersa*
Black fly larva *Simulium* sp
Mayfly nymph *Baetis rhodani*
Mayfly nymph *Rhithrogena semicolorata*
Caddisfly larva net *Hydropsyche fulvipes*

2 In the upper cascade reach the rush of a mountain torrent is usually unbearable for most animals. The few inhabitants spend only their immature phases here. Some caddis larvae attach themselves to boulders by silk webs to avoid being swept away, while black fly larvae hang on with hooks at the rear end. Some mayfly larvae are streamlined swimmers; those with flattened forms cling to large stones and let the water flow past.

3

3 Some animals can survive even in the hot springs that bubble up from the earth in areas of volcanic activity. To the heat is added a high mineral content, but the conditions do not seem to bother a New Zealand water snail *(Lymnaea tomentosa)*[2] and a damsel fly nymph of the genus *Ischnura* [3], which occur in water up to 95°F (35°C). A beetle *(Laccobius)*[4], some rotifers [1], and the carp *(Cyprinus carpio)*[5] can stand even higher temperatures, and a nematode *(Tylocephalus)* [6] has been recorded in water up to 176°F (80°C). This is the limit of life: above it, protein coagulates and organisms die.

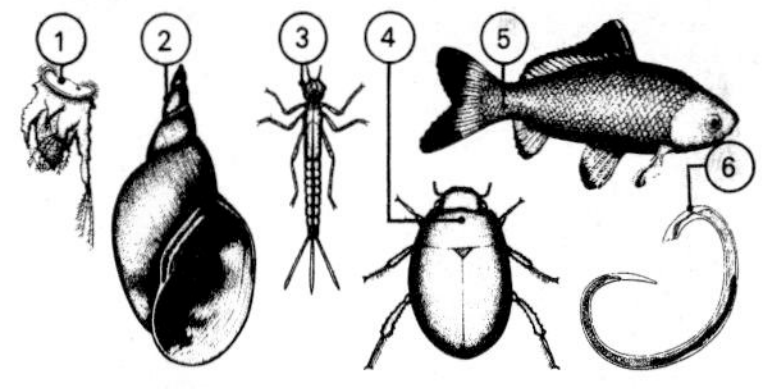

1
2
3
4
5
6

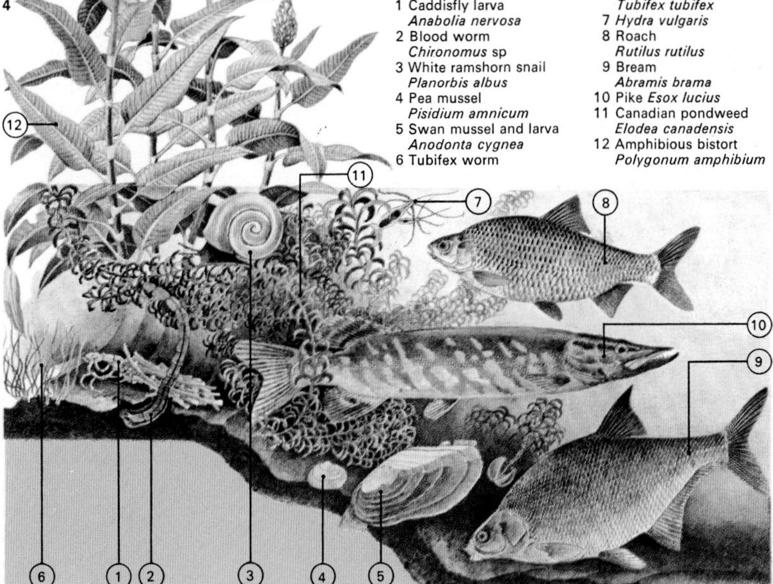

4
12
11
7
8
10
9
6
1
2
3
4
5

1 Caddisfly larva *Anabolia nervosa*
2 Blood worm *Chironomus* sp
3 White ramshorn snail *Planorbis albus*
4 Pea mussel *Pisidium amnicum*
5 Swan mussel and larva *Anodonta cygnea*
6 Tubifex worm *Tubifex tubifex*
7 *Hydra vulgaris*
8 Roach *Rutilus rutilus*
9 Bream *Abramis brama*
10 Pike *Esox lucius*
11 Canadian pondweed *Elodea canadensis*
12 Amphibious bistort *Polygonum amphibium*

4 In lower reaches, dense growth such as Canadian pondweed—introduced into Europe where it choked many watercourses like a form of natural pollution—tangles with *Potamogeton* and amphibious bistort. In the silt bed *Tubifex* worms and some midge larvae are buried. Their red hemoglobin enables them to use what little oxygen the water contains at this level. A few freshwater dwellers are filter feeders, like the swan mussel and the small related pea mussel. Many more are plant feeders like the ramshorn snail that glides over plants. Caddis larvae, of different species from those of fast streams, protect their bodies with cases made of sand grains or vegetable debris, some neatly, some in a haphazard manner. Deep-bodied, slow-moving fish, such as roach and bream, are found here, making a rich living off the wide range of plants and animals in the habitat. In turn, they are preyed on by the fierce, lurking pike.

5 Pond dwellers endure greater changes of living conditions than those of any habitat other than the seashore. The contrast for them is most marked in winter, when silt accumulates and the surface freezes over. At this time frogs, turtles, some fish, and other animals become dormant or hibernate in the muddy bottom, but those that remain active rarely suffer from oxygen deficiency. As the ice forms, air bubbles are trapped underneath it and from this sufficient gas diffuses into the water to sustain the life of the pond throughout the cold winter months.

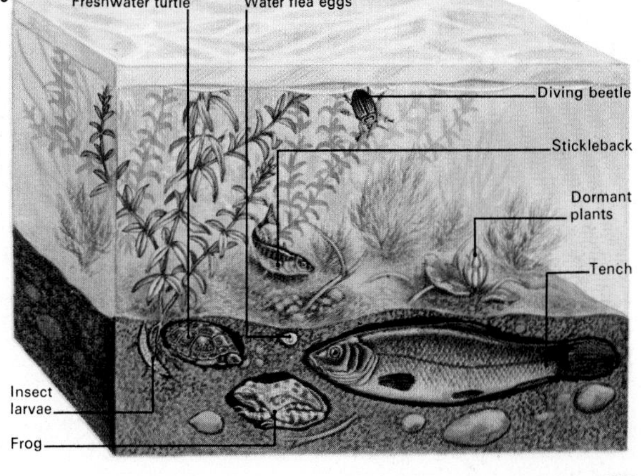

5
Freshwater turtle
Water flea eggs
Diving beetle
Stickleback
Dormant plants
Tench
Insect larvae
Frog

Wetlands: marshes and swamps

Wetlands are the most difficult of all the major environments to define and describe concisely. They may be regions of meandering rivers in the Arctic or of ephemeral lakes in the tropics. They may be acid upland bogs, with a flora and fauna quite different from that of alkaline lowland peat marshes, only a few miles away, or they may be areas of slow-flowing water such as the "River of Grass" constituting the Florida Everglades. The one factor all these habitats share is water—usually poorly oxygenated—in which there is an astonishing richness of life. The term "wetlands" has been coined to cover all of these varied habitats; as normally used it excludes lakes and rivers and saltwater estuaries.

Luxuriant plant life

Few woody plants can stand continuously waterlogged conditions; thus the luxuriant plant growth often found in wetlands is usually made up of herbaceous plants. Some wetland plants are adapted to slight waterlogging, others to life afloat in stagnant water and many to intermediate conditions.

The extreme acidity of many wetland areas means that nutrients, trapped in the peat at the bottom of the water, are not available to the plants. Some have overcome this by developing a carnivorous way of life. Using modified leaves, pitcher plants, Venus fly-traps, sundews, and butterworts, for example, trap insects or other small animals, which they consume by the use of enzymes. The minerals from the tissues of these animals compensate for the deficiency of minerals in the wetland environment.

Animal life of wetlands

The animal life of wetlands is usually very rich. These regions are often regarded by man as areas of little use so that animals find in them a secure haven. Some large mammals are specialized for a wetland life, with adaptations of the feet, in particular. These often spread to take the creature's weight on sinking ground. Even reindeer, which spend much time in swampy tundra areas, have toes that spread to carry their body weight.

Other mammals and birds may have swamp-adapted feet [Key], but it is in some of the lower animals that the most complete adaptations to a wetland life take place. Crocodiles and many other reptiles are well adapted to life in tropical swamps where, because they are air-breathers, the poorly aerated water does not bother them. Many tropical amphibians have adaptations involving carrying the young with them, a reflection of the ephemeral quality of many of the ponds and waterways that are their homelands.

Fish of swampy areas are usually deep-bodied animals, better able to weave among thick-growing vegetation than the streamlined fish of fast-flowing or open waters. Most can survive reduced oxygen levels and in the tropics, where the warm water can hold very little oxygen, many have the ability to breathe air. This they do in a variety of ways—in some the gill chambers have become richly supplied with blood capillaries and act as lungs; in others, such as some of the loaches, part of the gut takes over the task of absorbing oxygen,

CONNECTIONS

See also
616 Lakes and rivers
620 Salt marshes and coastal swamps
294 Misuse of the land
510 The classification of fish
526 The classification of birds
540 The classification of mammals
454 Grasses, reeds, and rushes
580 The basis of ecology

1 Matetite reed *Phragmites* sp
2 Hammerhead stork *Scopus umbretta*
3 Hippopotamus *Hippopotamus amphibius*
4 Saddle-billed stork *Ephippiorhynchus senegalensis*
5 Sitatunga *Tragelaphus spekei*
6 Black crake *Limnocorax flavirostra*
7 Water cabbage *Pistia stratiotes*
8 Swamp worm *Alma emini*
9 Bichir *Polypterus* sp
10 Catfish *Malapterurus* sp
11 Papyrus *Cyperus papyrus*
12 Malachite kingfisher *Corythornis cristata*
13 Herald snake *Crotaphopeltis hotamboeia*
14 African spoonbill *Platalea alba*
15 Lily trotter *Actophilornis africana*
16 Water-lily *Nymphaea* sp
17 Shoebill *Balaeniceps rex*
18 Squacco heron *Ardeola ralloides*
19 Marsh mongoose *Atilax paludinosus*
20 Snail *Biomphalaria sudanica*
21 Lungfish *Protopterus aethiopicus*

1

1 A swamp in the Upper Nile valley is dominated by papyrus, the paper reed, which grows to a height of 12ft (3.5m) or more. Other plants that mask the open water include water lilies and water hyacinths. The largest swamp animal is the hippopotamus, which inhabits shallow rivers and lakes over much of Africa. Hippos usually live in groups, leaving the water at night to feed. The sitatunga is far more secretive than the hippo and is rarely seen. If in danger it will submerge with only its nostrils showing, for long periods if need be. The many birds are almost all long-legged relatives of the herons. They feed on small animals, particularly insects, which swarm throughout the swamp.

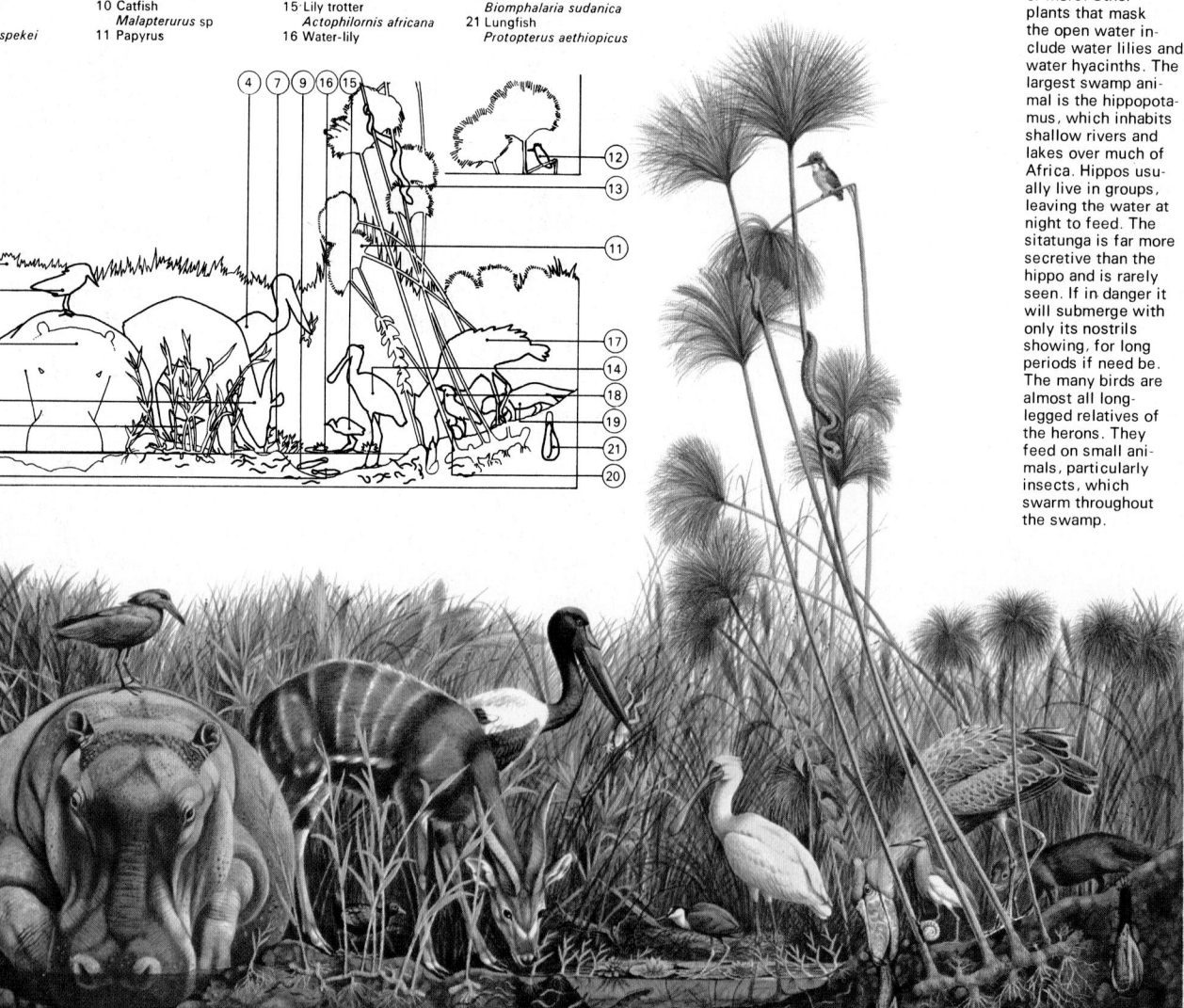

and in the mailed catfish even the stomach has become specialized to serve as a lung.

The true lungfish [2] are all found in the tropics of the southern continents, living in streams or pools that are subject to deoxygenation or even complete drying out. It is from relatives of early lungfish, the lobe-fins, that the first land-dwelling animals, the early amphibians, are thought to have evolved, for they, too, are thought to have been able to survive the desiccation of their swampland habitats.

Among the invertebrates, most freshwater snails breathe by means of lungs rather than gills. These lungs permit the animals to survive should their ponds dry up. Most of these mollusks can stand adverse conditions—even the freezing of their swampy homes in wintertime—by growing a mucus shield over the mouth of the shell and entering a state of dormancy until more favorable conditions return.

All of the insects that inhabit swamps are also air-breathers, as are the larvae of midges and mosquitoes. These have snorkellike tubes at the hind ends of their bodies, which they can push up to the surface of the water. A number of other larvae, such as those of dragonflies and water beetles, have gills, but in both these cases the adults breathe air because they leave the water for at least part of their lives, often in order to find a mate and thus complete the life cycle of their species.

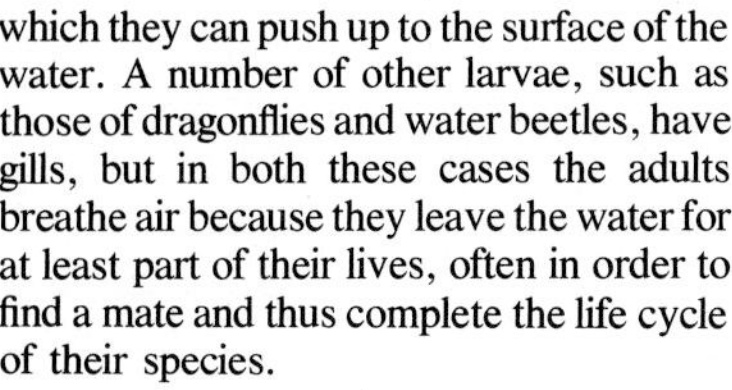

Man and the wetlands

Because wetlands cannot be farmed easily man has tended to ignore them until relatively recently. But today, with the need for more land, many swamp and marsh areas have been drained. This has often reduced the numbers of disease-carrying organisms, such as mosquitoes, adding further impetus to the drainage programs. Nevertheless, wetlands have an importance beyond their own boundaries because they often act as a reservoir of water for distant areas and are frequently the seasonal home of many species of migratory birds. Naturalists and conservationists have realized this for many years and some of the earliest conservation attempts were on behalf of wetlands.

KEY

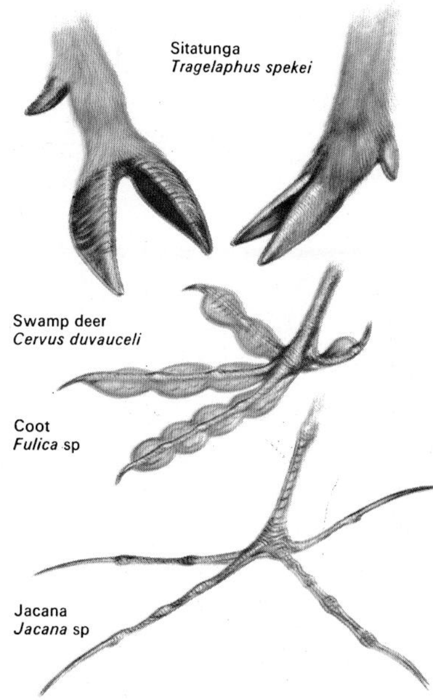
Sitatunga
Tragelaphus spekei
Swamp deer
Cervus duvauceli
Coot
Fulica sp
Jacana
Jacana sp

Animals of wetlands run the risk of becoming bogged down in the soft, quaking ground that lies at the water's edge, so they frequently develop large, weight-spreading feet. Among birds the long toes of herons are examples of this adaptation. Foot adaptation takes an extreme form in the jacana, which can walk on floating vegetation. Some waterside birds have partly webbed feet. In the coots and sun grebes the adaptation takes the form of lobes along the toes, which, as well as spreading their weight, helps them to swim. Both the swamp deer of India and the sitatunga, an African antelope, have long, loosely jointed toes.

2

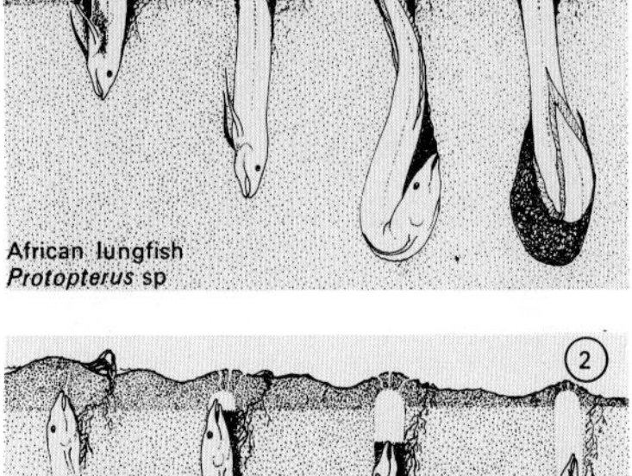
African lungfish
Protopterus sp
2
1

2 The lungfish is related to extinct creatures that were the first vertebrates to live on dry land. Today it is found in tropical regions of the three southern continents. The South American and Australian species can survive complete deoxygenation of the water by breathing air. The African species *(Protopterus)* can live through total dehydration of its environment by burrowing into the mud while it is still damp and eveloping itself in a mucus cocoon. This dries to form a protective case [1]. Air from the disturbed mud filters through a porous "lid" [2] at the top of the case.

3 The boat-billed heron is a bird of Central and South America that lives mainly in the freshwater parts of mangrove swamps. It is secretive and nocturnal, like the night herons of the northern continents. Little is known of its habits, but it has been observed standing or walking slowly in shallow water, using its broad bill to scoop up shrimp and other invertebrate prey.

3 Boat-billed heron
Cochlearius cochlearius

4 The matamata, a South American turtle, has a bossed carapace that resembles a lump of dead, waterlogged wood. The flaps of tissue that dangle from its head and neck look like inviting scraps of food to the small denizens of the unruffled tropical waters where the matamata lives. The inquisitive amphibians or fish do not discover their mistake until it is too late. In spite of its grotesquely flattened head, the matamata has huge, if feeble, jaws and a greatly distensible throat. It sucks in a huge volume of water, bearing any nearby small animals in with the water.

4 Matamata
Chelys fimbriata

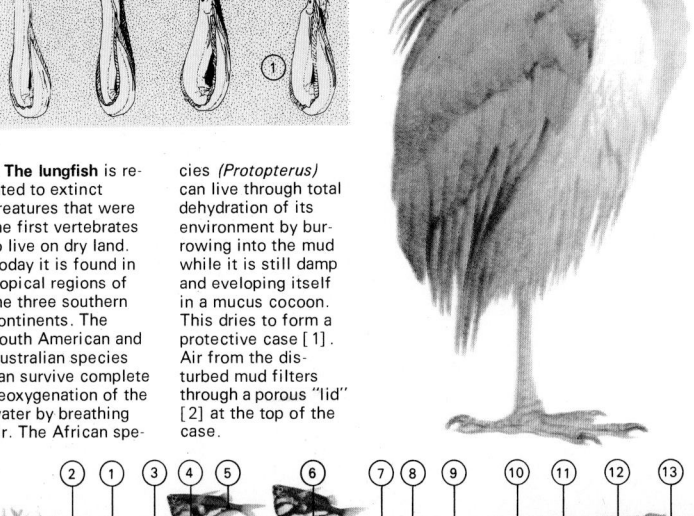

5 Much of the vast Amazon basin is drained by meandering, swampy streams. Electric fish such as the electric eel *(Electrophorus electricus)* can stun their prey with charges of up to 600 volts. Here, too, lives the arapaima, the world's largest freshwater fish, weighing up to 200lb (90kg). Some of the nearby faster flowing waters abound with shoals of piranha *(Serrasalmus natteri)*, which are among the most voracious of all vertebrates. Hunting in "packs," they can reduce a large animal to a skeleton within minutes.

1 *Symphysodon discus*
2 *Hyphessobrycon innesi*
3 *Boulengerella lateristriga*
4 *Anostomus anostomus*
5 *Carnegiella strigata*
6 *Leporinus fasciatus*
7 *Prochilodus insignis*
8 *Metynnis schreitmuelleri*
9 *Serrasalmus natteri*
10 *Gymnotus carapo*
11 *Gymnorhamphichthyes hypostomus*
12 *Electrophorus electricus*
13 *Oxydoras niger*
14 *Pseudoplatystoma fasciatum*
15 *Ancistrus cirrhosus*
16 *Auchenipterus nigripinnis*
17 *Corydoras myersi*
18 *Arapaima gigas*
19 Young *Arapaima gigas*
20 *Osteoglossum bicirrhosum*

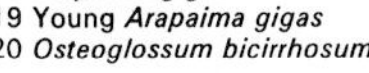

5

2
1
3
4
5
6
7
8
9
10
11
12
13
14
15
16
17
18
19
20

Salt marshes and coastal swamps

The boundaries between sea and land are not always exact and throughout the world complex transition zones exist. In the temperate regions of the world they are represented by salt marshes; while in the tropical regions mangrove swamps [2] flourish on many coasts. Both areas are highly productive and present a habitat that has a unique and populous fauna. The plant species that compose the marshes and swamps are especially adapted to withstand the presence of salt water and periodic immersion by tides [Key].

Salt marsh succulents

Many plants of the salt marsh are succulent, their stems and leaves swollen with water stored in special tissues. Salt marsh plants suffer from a lack of water in much the same way as desert plants because it is difficult for them to extract water from the sea. The reason for this "physiological drought" is that the concentration of mineral salts in sea water is similar to that inside the plant cells and, as a result, little water is able to move into those cells.

Another problem faced by salt marsh plants is lack of oxygen. To overcome this, many plants develop aerial roots that grow like periscopes above the surface of the mud. The tolerance of salt concentrations, and of the length of time of inundation by the tide, varies from species to species and thus there is a division into zones [1].

In the mangrove swamps of Southeast Asia growing near the sea are *Sonneratia* species [2] with a wild array of aerial roots sprouting from branches and trunks. The stands behind them are of *Rhizophora*, which have roots that lie just above or below the ground. Growing behind these are *Bruguiera* with their roots buried in the mud, leaving only small spikes jutting above the surface. The mangrove roots trap sediment that accumulates to form muddy banks; these present a new habitat to be colonized by more trees. In this way the stilted forest takes over the shoreline.

One of the characteristic animals of the mangrove forest is the mud skipper [5], a tiny fish that can live out of water and walk across the mud. Millions of small fiddler crabs *(Uca)*, each with one outsize claw, scuttle along the mud seeking refuge beneath it when the tide rises or danger threatens. The vast number of mollusks, crustaceans, and fish that live on the quantities of organic debris provide prey for monitor lizards *(Varanus salvator)*, saltwater crocodiles *(Crocodylus porosus)*, and various extremely venomous sea snakes, such as the banded sea snake *(Laticauda colubrina)*.

Mangrove birds and mammals

The mangrove snake *(Boiga dendrophila)* lives on birds that flock to the mangrove swamps to take fish and shellfish. These include the graceful fish eagles *(Haliaeetus leucogaster)* and the tall adjutant storks *(Leptoptilos javanicus)*. Mammals include the long-tailed macaque *(Macaca irus)*, which is also known as the crab-eating monkey. As their name suggests, the members of the clan spend their time on the mud flats watching for any crabs that disappear down their burrows. When the crab reappears it is skillfully grabbed, torn apart, and

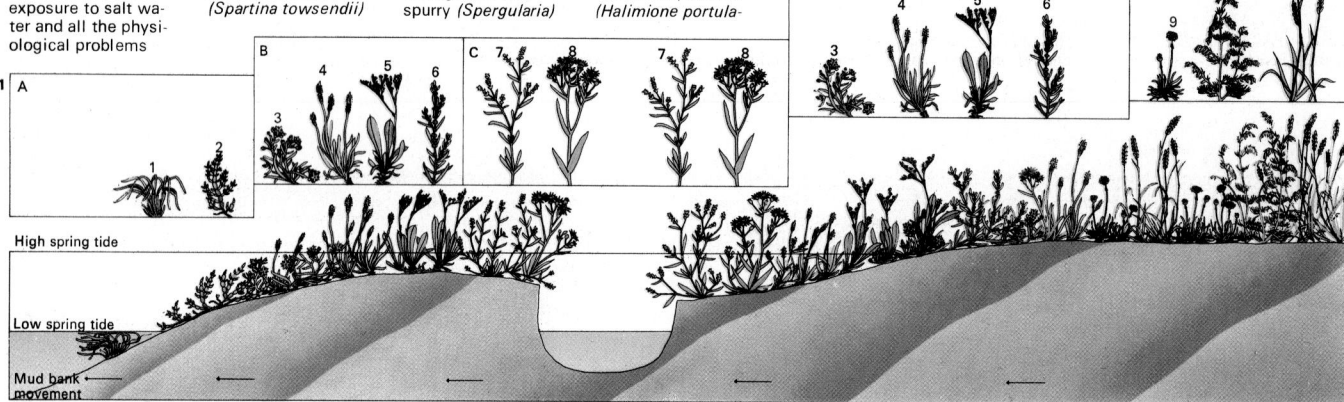

CONNECTIONS

See also
618 Wetlands: marshes and swamps
622 The seashore: life between the tides
600 Forests of Southeast Asia
580 The basis of ecology
412 The cell in action
430 The way plants work
448 Woody flowering plants

1 On a typical temperate salt marsh a distinct division of plants can be seen, which reflects the plants' abilities to withstand periodic immersions by the tide and thus their exposure to salt water and all the physiological problems this involves. The primary colonizers [A] of the bare mud are the eel grass *(Zostera)* [1] and saltwort *(Salicornia)* [2]. At the beginning of the 20th century the sea cord grass *(Spartina towsendii)* became a major colonizer of the bare mud zones of many European salt marshes. The general marsh community [B, C, D] contains a number of different plants, among them sea spurry *(Spergularia)* [3], sea plantain *(Plantago maritima)* [4], sea lavender *(Limonium)* [5], and sea blight *(Sueda maritima)* [6]. On the hummocks and edges of creeks [C] are found sea purslane *(Halimione portulacoides)* [7] and sea aster *(Aster tripolium)* [8]. These grow only in the better-drained areas. At the edge of the marsh, in the areas with the least likelihood of inundation, are found [E] thrift *(Armeria maritima)* [9], sea wormwood *(Artemesia maritima)* [10], and sea couch grass *(Agropyron)* [11].

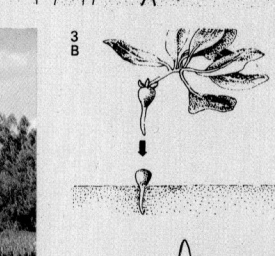

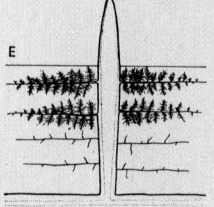

1

A
B
C
D
E
High spring tide
Low spring tide
Mud bank movement

2

2 Moving forever seaward, the mangrove forests [C] claim new territory for the coastline. A section through a mangrove swamp [B] shows the distribution and zonation [A] of the various species of mangrove. The pioneer mangrove *(Sonneratia)* [D] has large numbers of aerial roots (pneumatophores) by means of which it is able to breathe. Lateral roots form from these [E].

1 *Sonneratia* zone
S. griffithii, S. alba

2 *Rhizophora* zone
R. mucronata, R. apiculata

3 *Bruguiera* zone
B. parviflora,
B. gymnorniza
B. cylindrica, B. sexangula

4 Palms *Nypa* spp

2 A

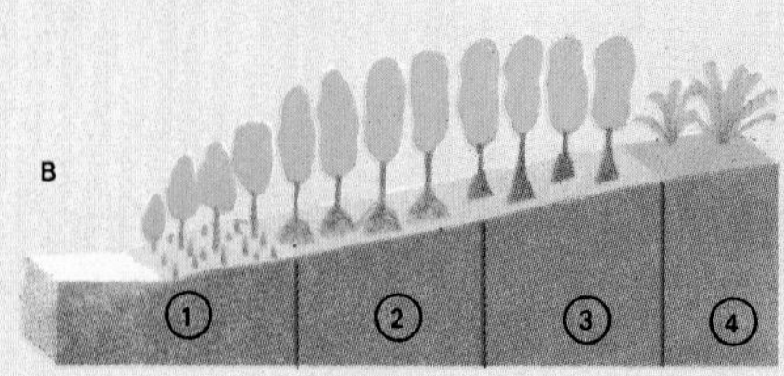

B

C

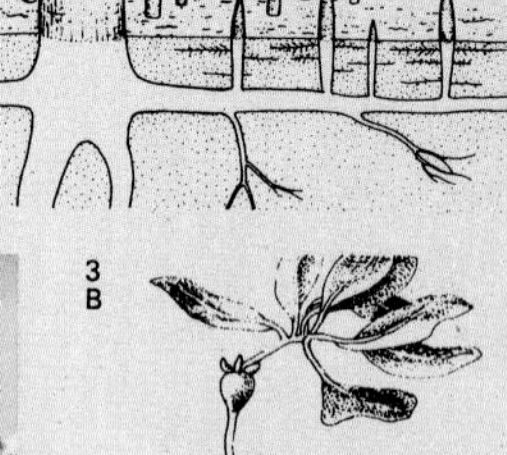

D

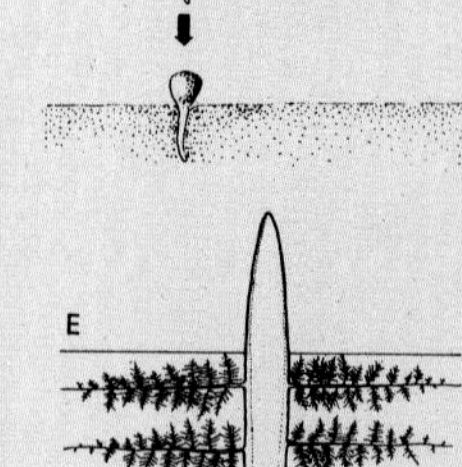

E

3 A

3 B

3 The seeds of the *Rhizophora* mangrove germinate before they leave the parent plant [A]. When they fall from the tree their roots stick in the mud [B] and the seedlings become established before the tide can wash them away.

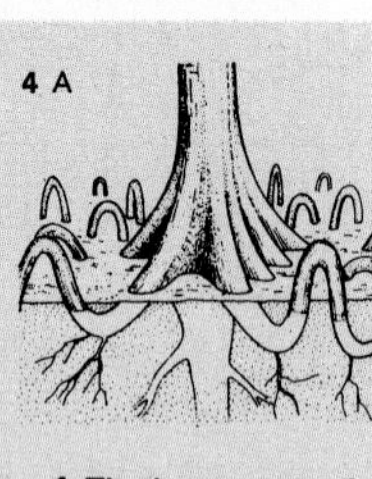

4 A

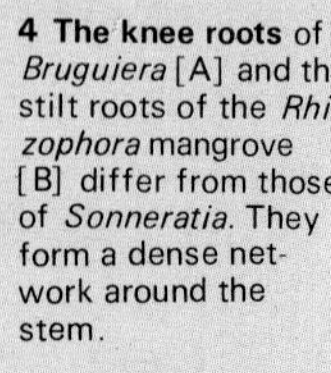

4 The knee roots of *Bruguiera* [A] and the stilt roots of the *Rhizophora* mangrove [B] differ from those of *Sonneratia*. They form a dense network around the stem.

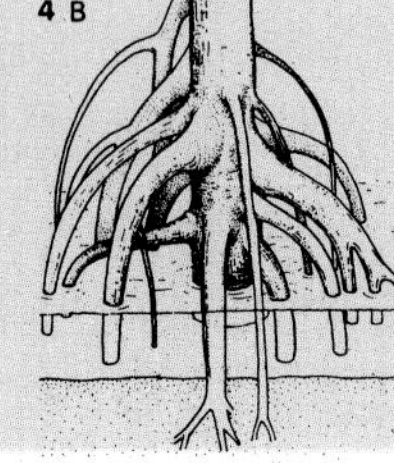

4 B

devoured. Found exclusively in the mangroves of Borneo are the rare proboscis monkeys *(Nasalis larvatus)* [7], grotesque-looking creatures with large nasal appendages that hang over mouths and chins of the males. Despite their appearance they are peaceful animals. They live in troops of 15 or 20 and feed on leaves of the *Sonneratia caseolaris* mangrove.

Marshland communities

The salt marshes of the world, although not as dramatic as the mangrove swamps, are no less productive. Many of the estuaries and coastal marshes serve as nurseries for a wide variety of animals. Many fish and invertebrates lay their eggs in these sheltered regions and the newly hatched young are less vulnerable in the protective, shallow waters. The division of plant species into zones is also affected by the tidal range and reflects individual tolerances to salt concentrations and periods of covering by the tide. The lower reaches, which may be submerged at all times, may be colonized by eel grass *(Zostera),* which provides food for the brent geese *(Branta bernicla),* or by meadows of turtle grass *(Thalassia),* the food of the green turtle *(Chelonia mydas).* Adjoining this zone are expanses of saltwort *(Spartina),* which are tolerant to high salt concentrations. These provide detritus vegetation that feeds mollusks, crustaceans, and birds.

Farther toward firm ground is a general salt marsh community that is accustomed to the salt concentrations but not to prolonged immersion in seawater. The richest feeding grounds for visiting birds are those that are exposed for long periods each day. The open marsh provides food for wigeon and brent geese, and the maze of channels and pools criss-crossing the area yields food for opportunist feeders such as gulls and shelduck [10]. The best adapted of all birds are the shorebirds, such as the redshank [11].

The area of the Camargue in southern France is a patchwork of fresh and saltwater marshes adjoining the Mediterranean. A multitude of birds and flocks of greater flamingos present a dramatic spectacle among the less exotic species.

KEY

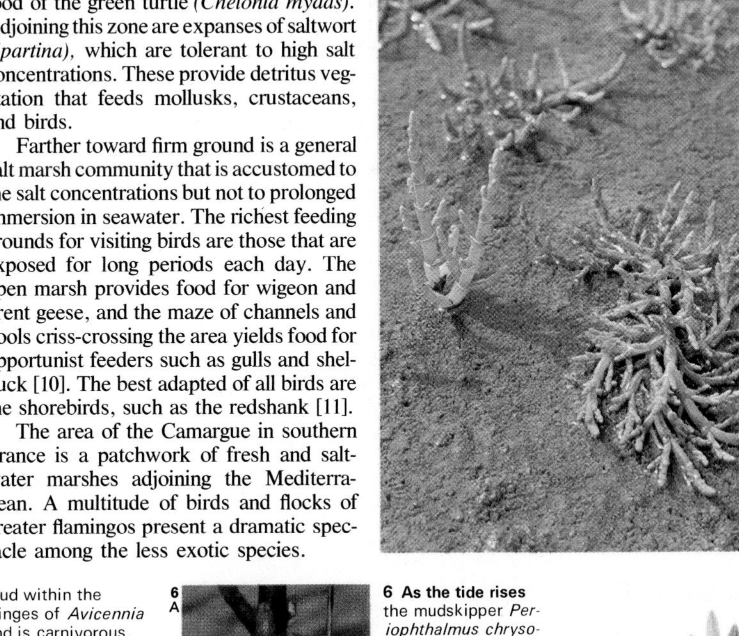

Plants of the genus Salicornia are among the first colonizers of sandy and muddy shores. There are about 35 species worldwide, commonly called saltwort, glasswort, or samphire, all so similar in appearance that they are almost impossible to tell apart. Small plants have an upright growth but larger plants tend to sprawl. They have minute leaves and a succulent form, which are adaptations to conserve water. Although they live in wet conditions, the soil contains a lot of salt and this prevents water from being freely available to the plants. These and other plants adapted to living in a salty environment are known as halophytes.

5 The mudskippers of mangrove swamps are fish that live as much out of the water as in it. Each species [B] feeds on a different diet and occupies a separate niche in the mangrove mud. *Boleophthalmus boddaerti* is found at the seaward edge of the swamp and feeds on algae. Mudskippers exert strong territorial rights at breeding time *Periophthalmus chrysopilus* builds a circular burrow in the mud to which it attracts a female with a series of leaps. In contrast *Periophthalmodon schlosseri* makes its home on the firmer mud within the fringes of *Avicennia* and is carnivorous. Courtship of the mudskippers involves a typical mouth-to-mouth display [A].

5

A *B. boddaerti*

B

Boleophthalmus boddaerti *Periophthalmus chrysopilus* *Periophthalmodon schlosseri*

6 A

6 As the tide rises the mudskipper *Periophthalmus chrysopilus* climbs the mangrove trees [A] and clings to them with a sucker [B].

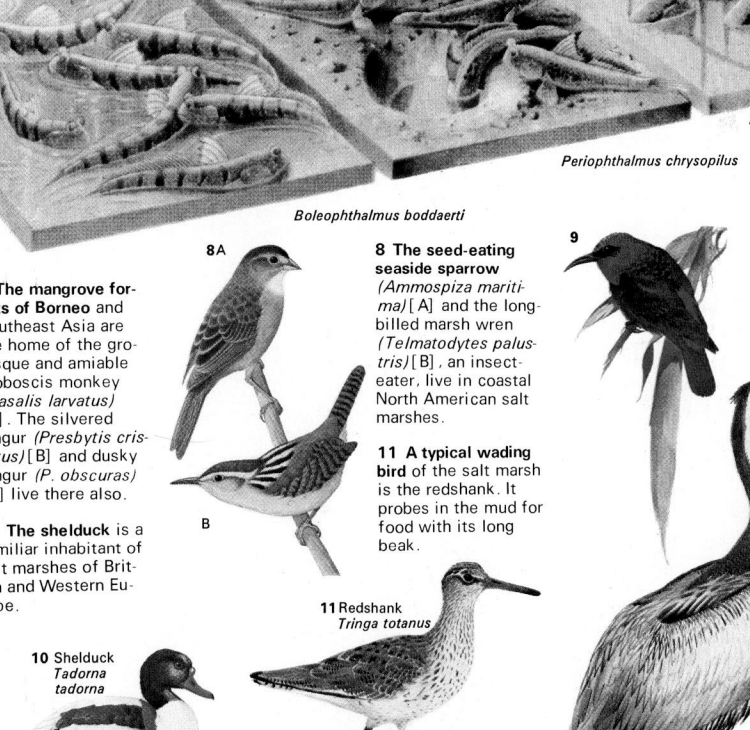

B

7 A

C
B

7 The mangrove forests of Borneo and Southeast Asia are the home of the grotesque and amiable proboscis monkey *(Nasalis larvatus)* [A]. The silvered langur *(Presbytis cristatus)* [B] and dusky langur *(P. obscuras)* [C] live there also.

10 The shelduck is a familiar inhabitant of salt marshes of Britain and Western Europe.

8A

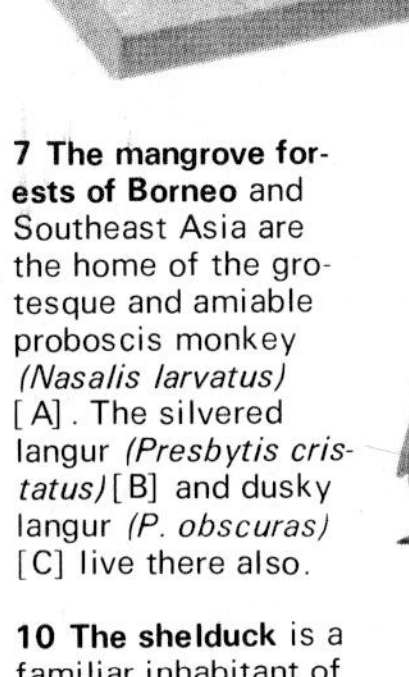

B

8 The seed-eating seaside sparrow *(Ammospiza maritima)* [A] and the long-billed marsh wren *(Telmatodytes palustris)* [B], an insect-eater, live in coastal North American salt marshes.

11 A typical wading bird of the salt marsh is the redshank. It probes in the mud for food with its long beak.

10 Shelduck *Tadorna tadorna*

11 Redshank *Tringa totanus*

9

9 The red-headed honey eater *(Myzomela erythrocephala)* is one of 20 related species of mangrove swamps in Australasia.

12 Brown pelican *Pelecanus occidentalis*

12 The brown pelican has a large bill with a distensible pouch that it uses to catch the fish on which it feeds. It lives on the coasts of tropical America.

The seashore: life between the tides

The shore lies between the land and the sea, allied to both yet belonging to neither. It is a zone defined by the daily rise and fall of the tides, washed by salt water, but also exposed to the effects of drying air.

Types of beaches

The type of beach is dependent on its hinterland—hard rocks give a cliffed and rocky shore while softer rocks give a sandy or muddy beach—and on the effectiveness of the waves in eroding the rocks.

On shingle or pebble beaches it is impossible for plants to grow because the action of the waves causes the stones to rub together and grind off any life form that attempts to gain a foothold. The only animals on a pebble beach exist at the edge of the high tide mark.

Other factors that have an important influence on beach fauna and flora are its aspect and degree of slope. Shallow, sloping beaches offer a far greater area for the development of animals and plants than do steeper beaches. The effect of the tide on seashore life is also altered by the degree of slope, because the steeper the slope the fiercer are the waves. On a steeply sloping beach the waves have a greater scouring action, preventing all but the most tenacious animals and plants from securing a foothold.

Once seaweeds do obtain a hold on shallow, rocky shores they exert great modifying influence on wave action. Beneath their sheltering fronds large numbers of less well adapted plants and animals are able to find a secure home.

Life on beach zones

The beach can be divided into a series of zones [7] according to how far it is influenced by the water. At the edge of the land is the splash zone, normally wetted only by sea spray but still affected by the maritime influence. Below this is the upper shore, extending from the level of high spring tides down to the average high tide level. The middle shore runs from there to average low tide level and the lower shore from that point to extreme low spring level. A walk from the upper shore to the low tide line shows that the plants and animals change with their level on the beach. This zonation is one of the most characteristic features of the seashore.

The beach as a whole is the most variable of all environments. When the tide is out the drying effects of the wind and sun threaten the plants and animals of the upper shore. If they are not to dry out they have to be well protected. In summer the beach and the rock pools may warm up considerably, but they are cooled quickly when the water comes splashing back. At low tide the salinity of rock pools may increase with evaporation or decrease if there is heavy rainfall. The acidity of rock pools is low during the daytime when the plants are photosynthesizing but may increase sevenfold at night when they are producing carbon dioxide. Most plants and animals are adapted to live in a narrow range of temperatures, salinity, and acidity, but the organisms of the shore can stand continuous large variations in their environment.

The plants of the shore are almost all seaweeds [7]. These are entirely different

CONNECTIONS

See also
432 Algae and seaweeds
476 Land and sea snails
478 Life between two shells
482 Shells of the world
468 Sea anemones, hydras, and corals
474 Earthworms, clamworms, and roundworms
486 Crabs and lobsters
504 Starfish and sea urchins
528 The anatomy of birds
268 Coastlines
620 Salt marshes and coastal swamps
580 The basis of ecology

1 A

B

C

1 Barnacles, sea snails, and seaweeds are typical of seashore life. Barnacles [A] feed by opening their shelly plates when submerged, catching minute, suspended food particles. Many sea snails, such as the dog whelk [B], eat flesh. A dog whelk rasps through the shells of barnacles and mussels with its strong, filelike tongue (radula) to reach the unprotected animal inside. Seaweeds do not have roots but attach themselves to rocks with holdfasts [C].

2 Sand hoppers or beach fleas live near the top of the beach where the last energy of the waves has thrown the detritus of the sea. Huge numbers of these small animals are found living in decaying seaweed, sand, and even fine gravel, which may be fairly dry. They are valuable scavengers of dead material and in turn create an abundant food supply for shorebirds such as turnstones on the upper shore.

2

Sand hopper *Orchestia gammarella*

3 Sand burrowers

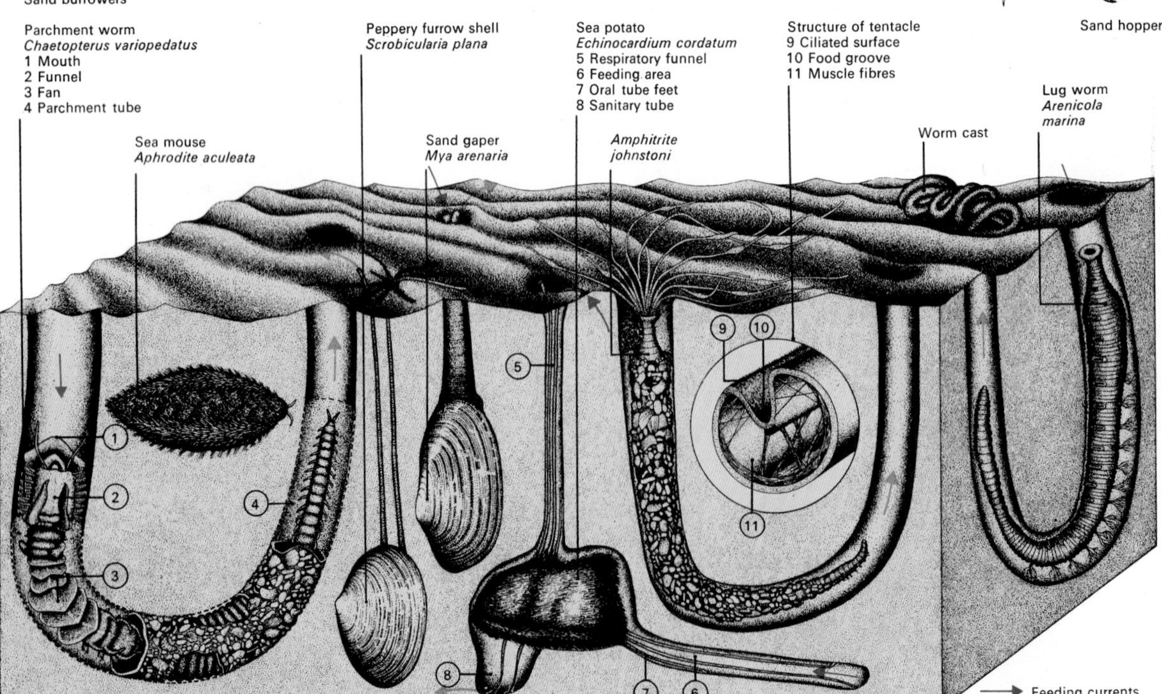

Parchment worm
Chaetopterus variopedatus
1 Mouth
2 Funnel
3 Fan
4 Parchment tube
Sea mouse
Aphrodite aculeata
Peppery furrow shell
Scrobicularia plana
Sand gaper
Mya arenaria
Sea potato
Echinocardium cordatum
5 Respiratory funnel
6 Feeding area
7 Oral tube feet
8 Sanitary tube
Amphitrite johnstoni
Structure of tentacle
9 Ciliated surface
10 Food groove
11 Muscle fibres
Worm cast
Lug worm
Arenicola marina
Feeding currents

3 The surface of a sandy beach at low tide gives few clues to the amount of life hidden beneath it. The principal inhabitants are worms and bivalves of many kinds, but other animals, such as burrowing sea urchins and crabs may also be present. Most bivalves depend on the planktonic richness of the sea for their food. When the sand is covered at high tide they push siphons up to the surface and pump a flow of water that circulates through their gill system. By this means oxygen is removed and food particles are trapped. Worms may use specialized tentacles or, like the lugworm, eat sand to swallow the tiny inhabitants of the water film around each grain.

from land plants in that they have no roots, stems, leaves, flowers, or fruit. Supported and bathed in seawater, they absorb all the nutrients they need directly from the sea. All photosynthesize, but in many the green of the chlorophyll is masked by other pigments that assist photosynthesis at low light levels or screen the chlorophyll from intense light. Defended against desiccation by sticky mucilage, they are often unattractively slimy objects when found at low tide or when cast up on the beach. Under water they are transformed, for their structure allows the graceful, swaying fronds to be carried toward the light.

Animals of the shore

Among the animals of the shore, most of the major groups, or phyla, are represented. Often brightly colored and of bizarre shape, to many people they are one of the great attractions of the seaside. On the middle and upper shore in particular, many of the animals are protected against the battering force of the waves by heavy shells, although others creep into burrows or cracks in rocks in times of storm or at low tide. Most are more or less sedentary but they produce planktonic larvae that float off in the water and may colonize other beaches.

The feeding patterns of beach animals are complex. A few animals eat the seaweeds, but the larger algae are generally inedible, although their smaller relatives of the open sea are the basis of all life in the oceans. Some animals are carnivores [1], some are scavengers [2], and many are filter feeders, finding food in what they can strain from the floating life of seawater. A variant is found in the sand eaters [3], which ingest vast amounts of sand in order to devour the tiny animals whose homes are the jackets of water that surround each sand grain.

Apart from recreation, man has comparatively little use for the seashore. In some places minor industries are based on collecting mollusks or crustaceans or even the algae. Unfortunately most seaweeds cannot be digested by man or most other large animals unless processed to provide useful minerals (particularly iodine) and mucilage.

KEY

The shore crab (*Carcinus* sp) is most active at high tide. It hides under stones or in seaweed at low water.

The fiddler crab (*Uca* sp) remains in its burrow during high water but is active on the beach when the tide is out.

4

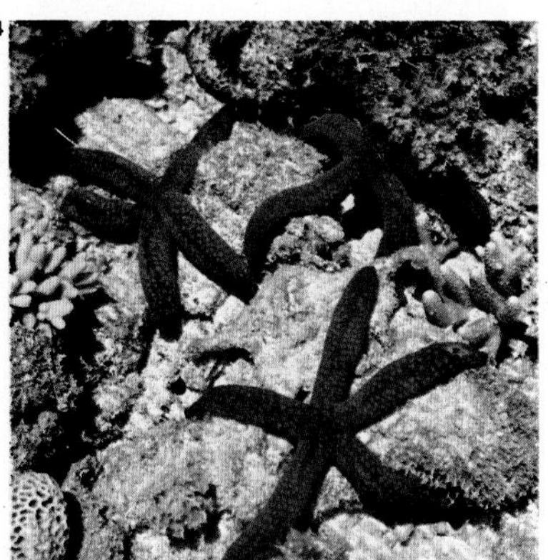

4 Starfish live mostly on the lower shore although they may be cast higher up the beach by the tide. *Linckia laevigata* comes from Pacific coral reefs, which are a special type of shore.

5

5 Sea slugs are snails without shells but unlike land slugs they are frequently beautiful. This one is crawling over a red seaweed. They owe their protection, in part, to their unpalatable taste.

7 Most living things are closely zoned to a narrow part of the shore and no single species of plant or animal is found in all zones. Among algae, green species live on the higher levels of the shore although channeled wrack, a brown weed, is often found on rocks at the landward edge of the beach. Brown weeds generally belong to the middle of the shore although the oarweeds extend below the bottom of the tide line. The fragile-looking redweeds grow on the lower shore. Animals are also zoned. Sometimes there is an association between a particular species and a seaweed, such as that between the flat periwinkle and bladder wrack. Those that can endure the greatest desiccation and varied conditions live at the top of the shore, while those animals that require greater stability are found closer to the sea.

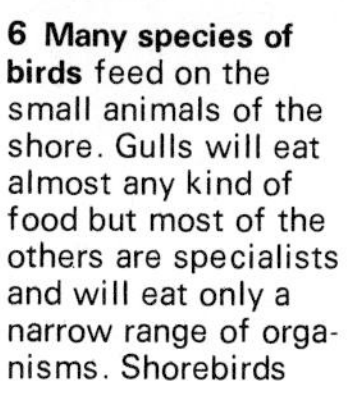

6 Many species of birds feed on the small animals of the shore. Gulls will eat almost any kind of food but most of the others are specialists and will eat only a narrow range of organisms. Shorebirds such as the redshank probe the mud with long, thin bills. The oyster-catcher can open cockle shells at a blow. The bills of eider ducks crush the shells of crabs and sea urchins with little difficulty.

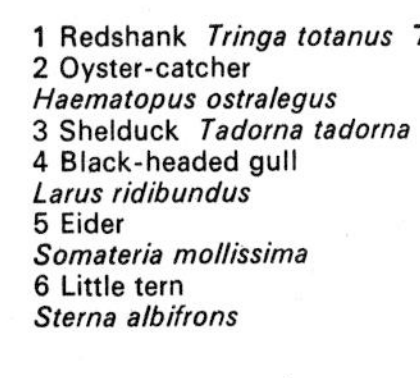

1 Redshank *Tringa totanus*
2 Oyster-catcher *Haematopus ostralegus*
3 Shelduck *Tadorna tadorna*
4 Black-headed gull *Larus ridibundus*
5 Eider *Somateria mollissima*
6 Little tern *Sterna albifrons*

6

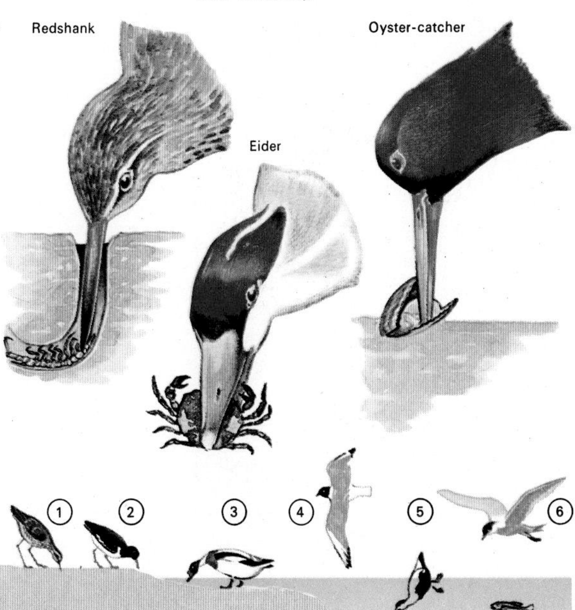
Redshank
Eider
Oyster-catcher
1
2
3
4
5
6

7

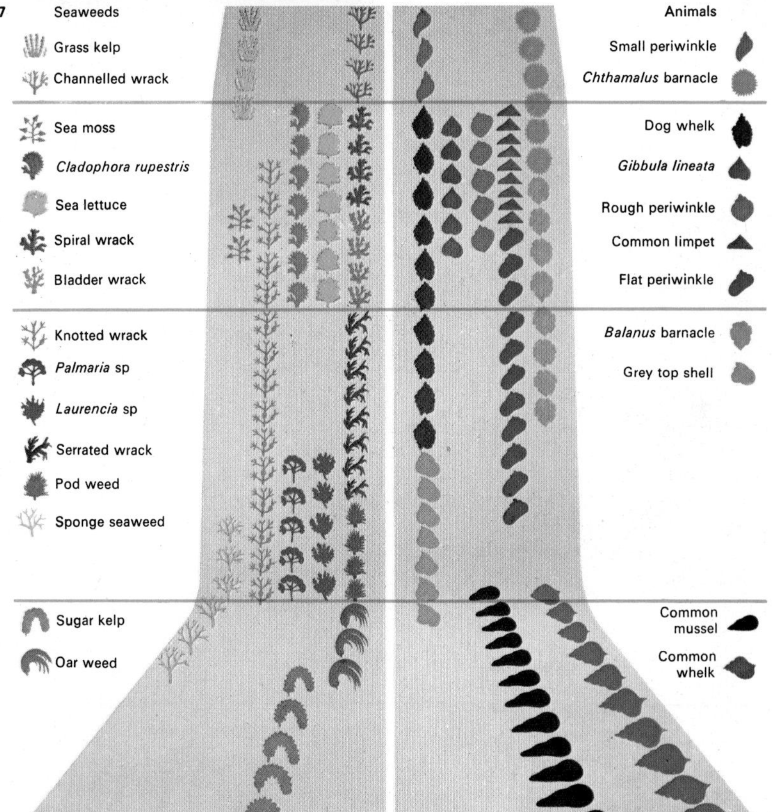
Seaweeds
Grass kelp
Channelled wrack
Sea moss
Cladophora rupestris
Sea lettuce
Spiral wrack
Bladder wrack
Knotted wrack
Palmaria sp
Laurencia sp
Serrated wrack
Pod weed
Sponge seaweed
Sugar kelp
Oar weed
Animals
Small periwinkle
Chthamalus barnacle
Dog whelk
Gibbula lineata
Rough periwinkle
Common limpet
Flat periwinkle
Balanus barnacle
Grey top shell
Common mussel
Common whelk

Life in the oceans

More than two-thirds of the Earth's area is taken up by the oceans. These great bodies of water not only cover a huge area but also have immense depth—on average more than 12,000ft (3,650m). Thus the oceans offer a vast, three-dimensional living space to countless plants and animals.

The richness of marine life at any one place is largely determined by the current systems of the ocean. Where two currents, or a current and a land mass, interact so as to draw deep water to the surface, they carry fresh nutrients into the upper, lighted zone and animal and plant life thrive.

The pyramid of life

The oceans are, for the greater part, cold, dark, and comparatively still. This would appear to give life little chance, yet it is thought that all life started in the sea, and it continues to flourish there. All the modern phyla of animals can be found in the sea and some have never left it. Among the arthropods, an important group virtually unrepresented in the oceans is the insects. Instead the crustaceans (the shrimp and their relations) are extremely abundant in number and species. The smallest of these crustaceans are dependent for food on small marine plants that are the basis of a vast pyramid of life [5] that includes the squid, fish, birds, and mammals with which the seas abound. So wide is the base of the pyramid that the natural destiny of more than 90 percent of all sea creatures is to be swallowed by other animals.

Although nearly all oceanic organisms are found in the upper, light regions, even the greatest depths support some life, dependent on a slow rain of organisms from above. Creatures living on the sea bottom are referred to as benthic, while those leading a free, active life are known as pelagic. The latter may be subdivided into those strong enough to swim against the currents when they wish—the nekton—and those too small or feeble to do anything but drift with the current—the plankton. Small plants are, in turn, known as phytoplankton [1], while planktonic animals are the zooplankton [Key]. Members of the zooplankton may be the young of large creatures. During this phase of their lives they disperse as widely as possible, or they may be a permanent planktonic component, as are the arrow worms and minute crustacean copepods. In either case they are the basis of all larger life forms in the sea.

Pastures of the deep

If an attempt is made to assess the productivity of the sea in terms of the dry weight of the plants produced in a year, a given area of the sea appears to be as rich as an equal area of land and the richest estuaries are equivalent to land-growing forests. The big difference is that whereas on land plants have developed into multicellular forms large and strong enough to support themselves, in the sea this has never been necessary, for the water supports the individual cells. Many of the millions of plant cells that go to make up a forest are for support or are employed as conduction channels and are not involved in photosynthesis, and thus in food production. In the open sea, where plants are all single-celled, every cell is capable of photosynthesis and is potentially productive.

CONNECTIONS

See also
626 Animals of the ocean
466 Single-celled animals and sponges
468 Sea anemones, hydras, and corals
470 The jellyfish
516 Fish of seas and rivers
552 Whales, porpoises, and dolphins
222 The sea and seawater
224 Ocean currents
236 Oceanographic exploration
298 Pollution of the sea
622 The seashore: life between the tides
386 Commercial fishing
392 Fish of the ocean deeps
432 Algae and seaweeds

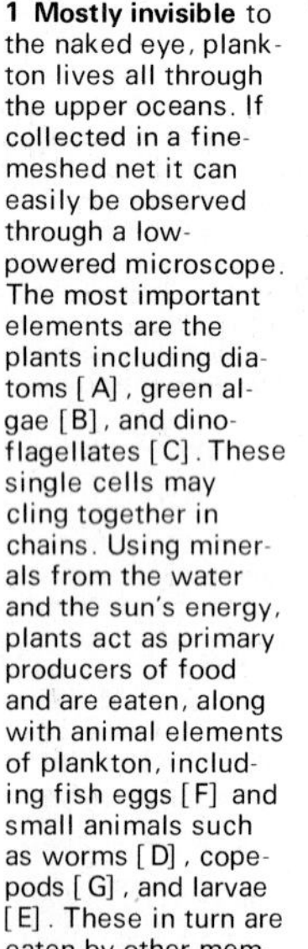

1 Mostly invisible to the naked eye, plankton lives all through the upper oceans. If collected in a fine-meshed net it can easily be observed through a low-powered microscope. The most important elements are the plants including diatoms [A], green algae [B], and dinoflagellates [C]. These single cells may cling together in chains. Using minerals from the water and the sun's energy, plants act as primary producers of food and are eaten, along with animal elements of plankton, including fish eggs [F] and small animals such as worms [D], copepods [G], and larvae [E]. These in turn are eaten by other members of the pyramid.

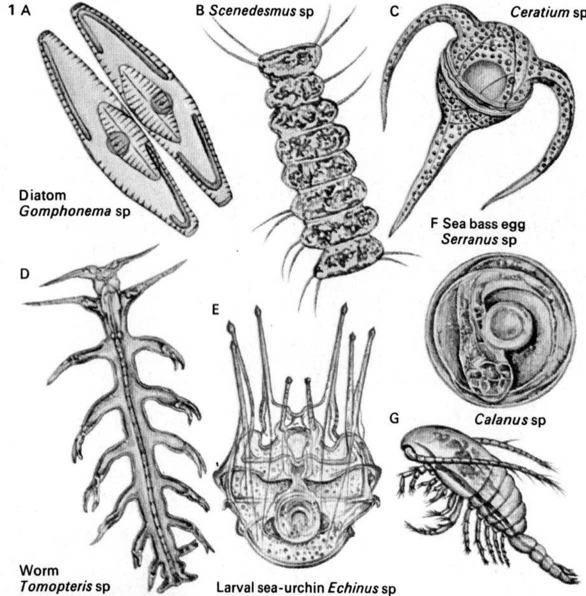

1 A
Diatom
Gomphonema sp
B *Scenedesmus* sp
C
Ceratium sp
D
Worm
Tomopteris sp
E
Larval sea-urchin *Echinus* sp
F Sea bass egg
Serranus sp
G
Calanus sp

2 The wandering albatross, the largest of all sea birds, is an inhabitant of the southern oceans and only comes ashore on remote islands to breed. Its wings are ideally shaped for effortless gliding.

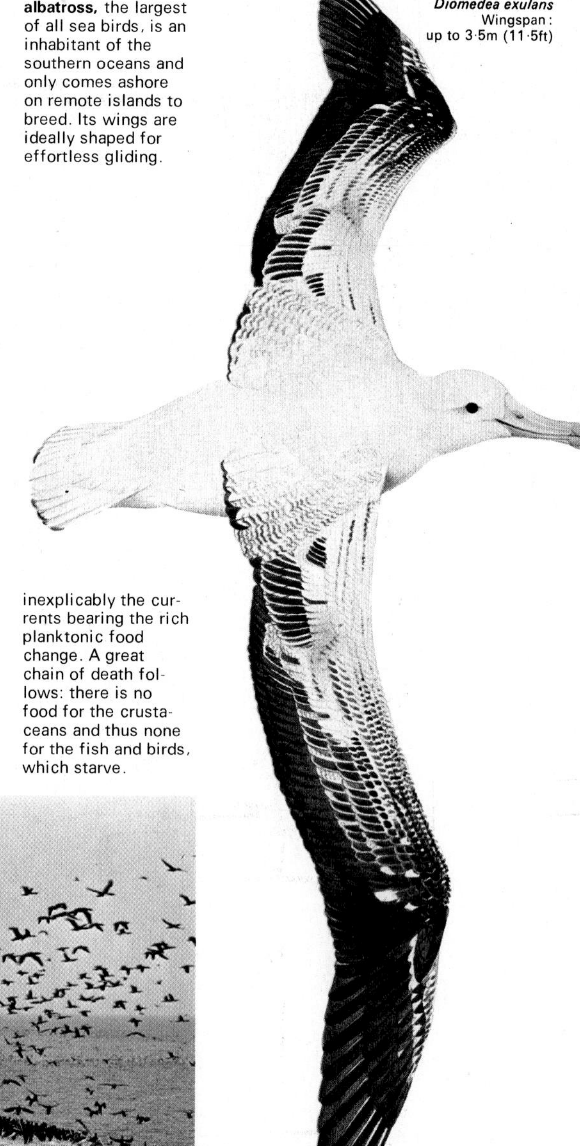

2
Great wandering albatross
Diomedea exulans
Wingspan:
up to 3·5m (11·5ft)

3

3 Strange animals, such as this bizarre fish, live far down in the cold, dark depths of the sea—all of them carnivores or scavengers dependent for food on the sunlit waters above. Many bear luminous organs. In fish, crustaceans, and squid the luminous organ can be a complex structure with a lens and a reflecting layer that increases the penetration of light through the water. The light may be used to help locate prey or discomfort predators, or as a pre-mating signal.

4 Huge numbers of cormorants, pelicans, and other birds of the west coast of South America feed on the anchovies that thrive in the cold waters of the Humboldt Current. The droppings of these birds return minerals to the sea but certain islands are used for nesting and here the accumulated droppings, or guano, makes a thick deposit that is removed by man and used as fertilizer. Occasionally and inexplicably the currents bearing the rich planktonic food change. A great chain of death follows: there is no food for the crustaceans and thus none for the fish and birds, which starve.

4

The distribution of the phytoplankton is not uniform over the oceans. As on land, there are barren areas or deserts where plant life is sparse and, in contrast, places where it is so abundant that the water is opaque green or brown. Because plant life requires both sunlight and nutrient salts, phytoplankton is produced only in the first few hundred feet below the surface, to a depth at which sufficient sunlight penetrates.

The need to strain food from water has given rise to an enormous diversity of filtering mechanisms in almost all groups of marine invertebrates, from the minute animals that drift in the plankton to those that live buried in or lie upon the bottom of the ocean. By maintaining a constant current of water through their bodies these animals are able to extract the nutrients they need.

Creatures of the reefs

A very special ocean habitat is that of the coral reef. The reef itself is a complex of coral colonies whose architects are minute coral polyps, coelenterate animals related to the jellyfish and sea anemones. The polyps are able to extract calcium carbonate from seawater and use it to create solid support. They grow only in warm seas where the winter temperature never falls below 68°F (20°C), often in close association with algae. The two have a complex interdependence because the algae release substances useful to the coral polyps and in return are supplied with nutrients. The polyps, by making important mineral nutrients available to the algae, help promote their healthy growth.

The high rate of nutrient turnover in the reef results in a complex and highly organized community of living creatures. It has been estimated, for example, that there are more than 3,000 species of animals living in the Great Barrier Reef. These include an abundance of jellyfish and sea anemones and of brightly colored fish, shrimp, crabs, starfish, sea slugs, and sea cucumbers. In many animals the color is used as a camouflage. Against its many-hued background, the boldly striped clownfish, for example, merges with its surroundings.

KEY

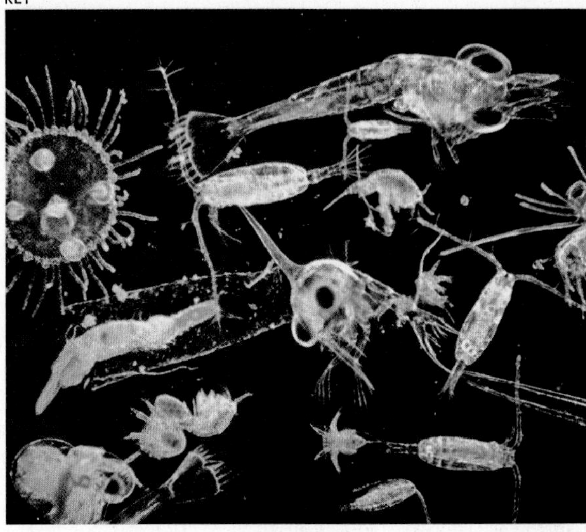

Plankton contains some adult animals, but most of this mass of floating marine organisms consists of larval forms. Kept afloat in the water by means of weight-spreading spines or tiny beating cilia, they are swept far away from their parents. Some species become sedentary when adult.

5 Macaroni penguin
Eudyptes chrysolophus
Height: up to 71cm (28in)

Upper jaw of crabeater seal

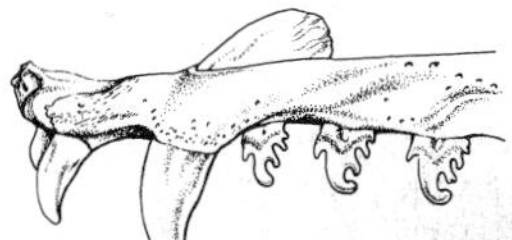

Crabeater seal
Lobodon carcinophagus
Length: up to 2·6m (8ft)

Common diving petrel
Pelecanoides urinatrix
Length: up to 25cm (10in)

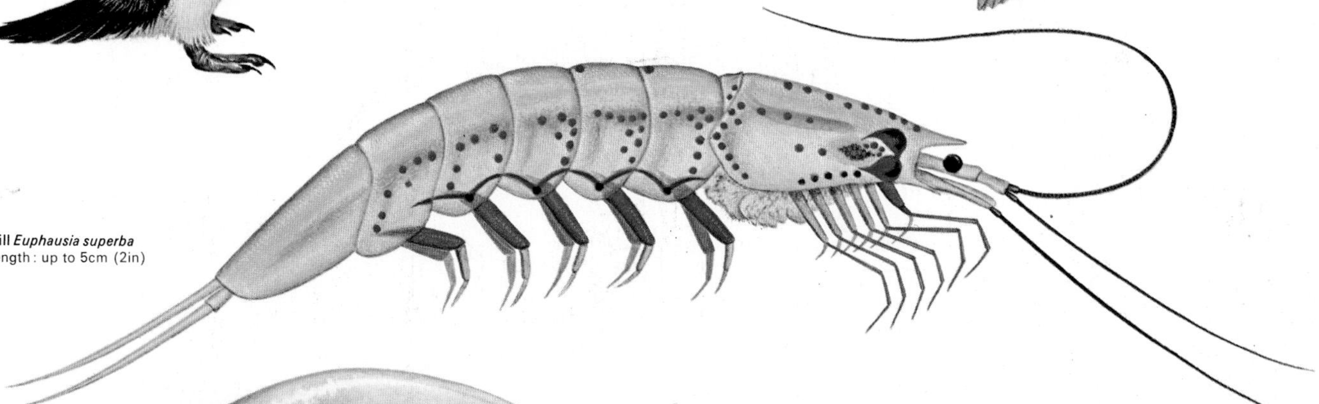

Krill *Euphausia superba*
Length: up to 5cm (2in)

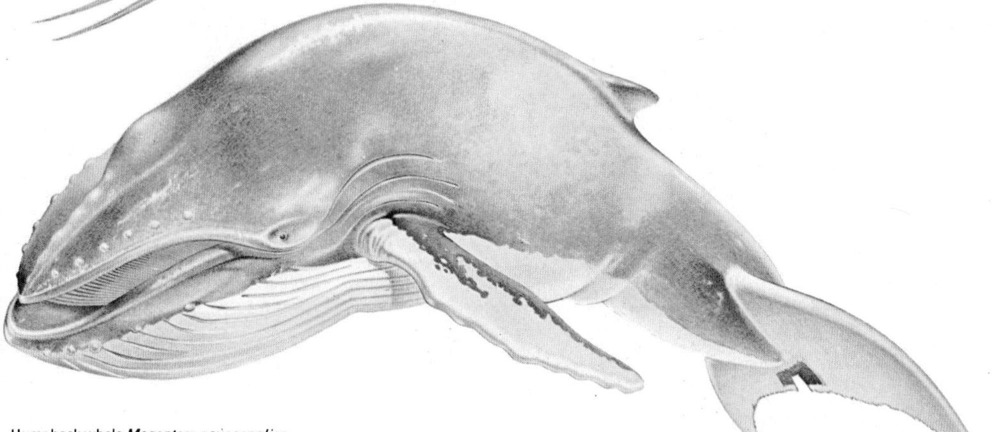

Humpback whale *Megaptera novaeangliae*
Length: up to 15·2m (50ft)

5 The shrimplike krill, some of the most important animals of the plankton, are about 2in (5cm) long when fully grown. They belong to a group of crustaceans (found in all oceans) characterized by luminescent organs along their sides, on their undersides, and heads. *Euphausia superba* is the most important species of the Antarctic seas for it supports much of the warm-blooded life of the southern oceans. Many birds, including the Adélie and macaroni penguins and shearwaters, eat it almost exclusively, as do the crabeater seal, the blue whale, and the humpback and other baleen whales. In its first year a blue whale eats up to 450 tons of krill. Commercial harvesting of krill may further reduce the chances of survival of the whales.

Animals of the ocean

The oceans of the world are a continuous mass of some five billion tons of water. But far from being uniform from surface to floor the ocean is divided into several regions [Key], each with its own typical forms of life. The most varied and spectacular of these are animals; their distribution is determined by the interaction of such factors as light, temperature, pressure, salinity, currents, waves, and tides.

The sunlit zone

The smallest animals of the ocean are concentrated in the upper, or euphotic, zone [1] into which the most light penetrates; they are known as zooplankton. Most are copepods, krill, and other small crustaceans, but the zooplankton also includes the eggs and larvae of many sea creatures, worms, comb jellies, snails, and jellyfish.

The smallest zooplankton are the chief herbivores of the ocean, grazing on the microscopic plants, or phytokplankton, that form the basis of the ocean food chains. Larger zooplankton, including small fish and also invertebrates such as large jellyfish, live either as carnivores or as detritus or "carrion" feeders living on dead matter.

All parts of the oceans are inhabited by fish, but those of the superficial euphotic zone are largely zooplankton feeders and many are small, immature fish that are themselves the prey of larger fish. The herrings *(Clupea)* and their allies, however, consume phytoplankton as a significant portion of their diet. It is because they can use the ocean's plant resources that the herrings provide the bulk of man's ocean harvest.

While fish can swim in search of food, many large jellyfish are passive surface drifters. The Portuguese man-of-war *(Physalia physalis)* has a float with a "sail" that puts it at the mercy of the sea winds.

The number of small fish in the euphotic zone tends to increase at night. These fish migrate upward from the lower, pelagic zone and this movement seems to be a protective mechanism because predators are generally less active during the hours of darkness.

At night the upper layer of the ocean is illuminated by the light produced biologically by the constituents of the plankton. It has been suggested that rather than putting the plankton at a disadvantage it protects them, for the light makes plankton feeders such as small fish easily visible to the larger ocean carnivores; the very presence of fish seems to excite the plankton into light production.

Sea-dwelling mammals, such as whales, seals, and dolphins can dive deep into the ocean, but regularly inhabit the uppermost layer of the open ocean because they must surface to breathe. The baleen whales are further limited by the distribution of their food supply, namely small invertebrates and fish.

Predation and protection

The middle, or mesopelagic, zone of the ocean holds myriads of fish, accompanied by larger invertebrates, such as squid, octopuses, and prawns. This is the habitat of the sea's active predators, but it is one with no shelter. To survive the threat of large carnivores the creatures of the mesopelagic must either be armed with powerful defen-

CONNECTIONS

See also
624 Life in the oceans
466 Single-celled animals and sponges
468 Sea anemones, hydras, and corals
432 Algae and seaweeds
480 Squid and octopuses
486 Crabs and lobsters
490 Crustaceans and other arthropods
504 Starfish and sea urchins
516 Fish of seas and rivers
522 Snakes, lizards, and turtles
222 The sea and seawate
224 Ocean currents
228 The sea bed
236 Oceanographic exploration

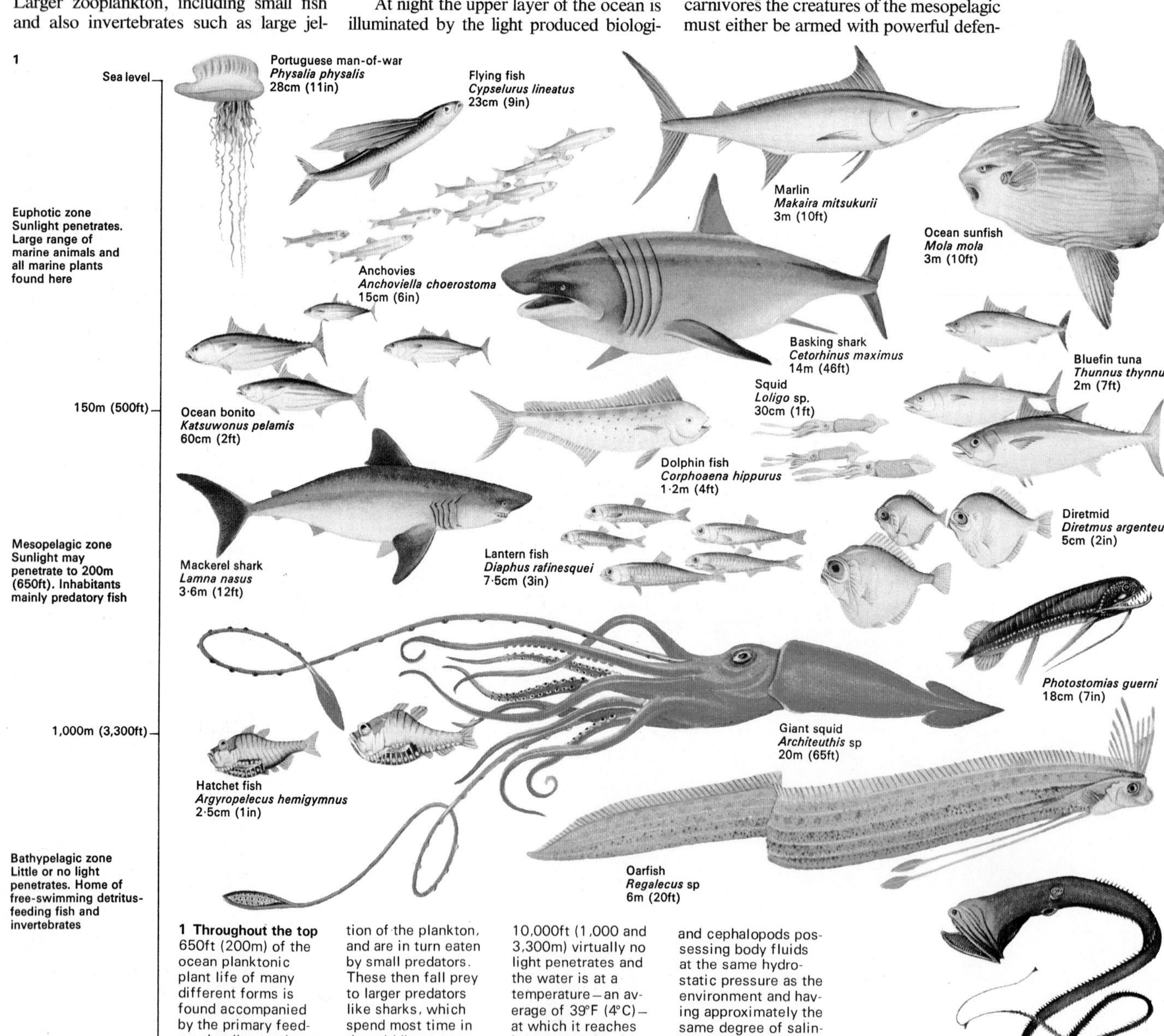

1
Sea level
Euphotic zone Sunlight penetrates. Large range of marine animals and all marine plants found here
150m (500ft)
Mesopelagic zone Sunlight may penetrate to 200m (650ft). Inhabitants mainly predatory fish
1,000m (3,300ft)
Bathypelagic zone Little or no light penetrates. Home of free-swimming detritus-feeding fish and invertebrates
3,000m (10,000ft)
Abyssal pelagic zone
Portuguese man-of-war *Physalia physalis* 28cm (11in)
Flying fish *Cypselurus lineatus* 23cm (9in)
Marlin *Makaira mitsukurii* 3m (10ft)
Ocean sunfish *Mola mola* 3m (10ft)
Anchovies *Anchoviella choerostoma* 15cm (6in)
Basking shark *Cetorhinus maximus* 14m (46ft)
Bluefin tuna *Thunnus thynnus* 2m (7ft)
Squid *Loligo* sp. 30cm (1ft)
Ocean bonito *Katsuwonus pelamis* 60cm (2ft)
Dolphin fish *Corphoaena hippurus* 1·2m (4ft)
Diretmid *Diretmus argenteus* 5cm (2in)
Lantern fish *Diaphus rafinesquei* 7·5cm (3in)
Mackerel shark *Lamna nasus* 3·6m (12ft)
Photostomias guerni 18cm (7in)
Giant squid *Architeuthis* sp 20m (65ft)
Hatchet fish *Argyropelecus hemigymnus* 2·5cm (1in)
Oarfish *Regalecus* sp 6m (20ft)
Gulper eel *Saccopharynx harrisoni* 1·4m (4·5ft)

1 Throughout the top 650ft (200m) of the ocean planktonic plant life of many different forms is found accompanied by the primary feeders that live on them. These tend to travel about in schools, in the wake of the greatest concentration of the plankton, and are in turn eaten by small predators. These then fall prey to larger predators like sharks, which spend most time in the middle or mesopelagic zone of the open ocean. In the range of depth between 3,300 and 10,000ft (1,000 and 3,300m) virtually no light penetrates and the water is at a temperature – an average of 39°F (4°C) – at which it reaches its greatest density. The life below 3,300ft is made up of free-swimming fish, crustaceans, and cephalopods possessing body fluids at the same hydrostatic pressure as the environment and having approximately the same degree of salinity. At night some mid-water dwellers migrate to the surface to feed on other animals.

sive apparatus, such as the stinging cells of the jellyfish, or be adept swimmers equipped with sensory apparatus efficient enough to detect the approach of potential enemies. For this reason the most streamlined of all fish, both prey and predators, are found in the mesopelagic zone and include such species as the oceanic bonito *(Katsuwonus pelamis)* and the mackerel shark *(Lamna nasus)*. Other protective mechanisms of pelagic fish include schooling behavior [2] and bioluminescence [3].

Deep-water dwellers

Animals of deep, or bathypelagic, waters are largely dependent for food on the rain of debris from the mesopelagic and euphotic zones above them. In this habitat more than 2,000 species of fish and about the same number of large invertebrates have so far been discovered. Many of them have been located with the help of baited cameras; others have been found in the stomachs of whales and swordfish.

The problems of life at great depth—inky darkness, cold, and crushing pressures—have resulted in the evolution of many curious but beautiful species [6]. The majority of deep-sea fish are 12in (30cm) or less in length and most swim with their mouths permanently agape. Although often dark-colored, more than 60 percent of all deep-sea animals possess light-producing organs. Their bioluminescence is used for recognizing neighbors and mates and confusing predators.

On the sea bottom the fauna vary according to the distance from the surface, but most bottom dwellers are detritus feeders. Most of these benthic species are found in the comparatively shallow waters of the continental shelves. There, mussels and other bivalves, fan worms, sea cucumbers, crabs, and sea urchins and other echinoderms live with flatfish.

The life of the abyssal ocean is much less well documented, but explorations to depths of more than 6,500ft (2,000m) off the coast of California have revealed fauna that include species known to be adapted to the near-freezing temperatures of Arctic waters.

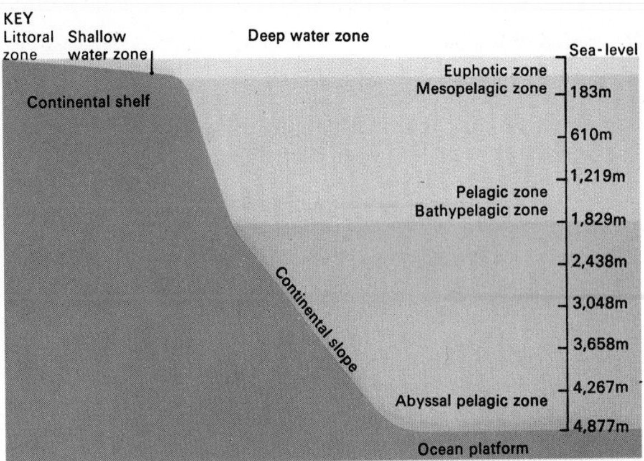

KEY
Littoral zone
Shallow water zone
Deep water zone
Sea-level
Euphotic zone
Mesopelagic zone
183m
Continental shelf
610m
1,219m
Pelagic zone
Bathypelagic zone
1,829m
2,438m
Continental slope
3,048m
3,658m
4,267m
Abyssal pelagic zone
4,877m
Ocean platform

The ocean layers from the translucent surface waters through the twilight zone to the depths of eternal gloom provide a range of habitats to which the varied species of the ocean are adapted. The "conventional" fish shape of the tuna and the shark, which live in the euphotic and mesopelagic zones, is in marked contrast to the highly specialized forms of the abyssal zone. The herbivores of the ocean are concentrated in the euphotic zone, carnivorous predators in the mesopelagic zone and detritus feeders on the sea bottom. Materials are constantly carried back to the surface by the upwelling and mixing of seawater.

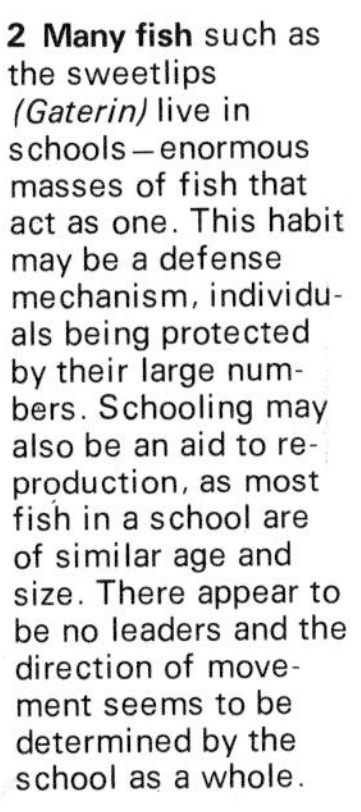

2 Many fish such as the sweetlips *(Gaterin)* live in schools—enormous masses of fish that act as one. This habit may be a defense mechanism, individuals being protected by their large numbers. Schooling may also be an aid to reproduction, as most fish in a school are of similar age and size. There appear to be no leaders and the direction of movement seems to be determined by the school as a whole.

3 The hatchet fish *(Sternoptyx diaphana)* is typical of the luminous fish of the bathypelagic zone. It possesses "cold light" luminous organs in its body that supply the only light to waters of this depth. Its large mouth is typical of predatory deep-sea fish. In the sunless depths there are very few prey species and a large mouth is essential if a fish is to obtain enough food to survive.

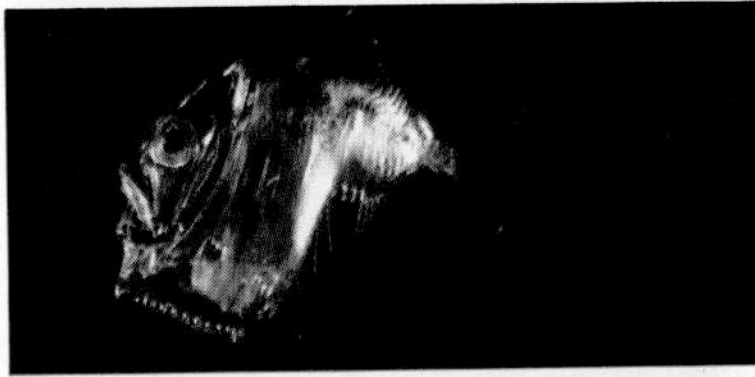

4 The catshark, or skamoog *(Holohalaelurus regani)*, is a member of a family of small sharks (Scyliorhinidae) that is found worldwide. This species inhabits coastal waters of South Africa. Like many of this family it feeds mainly on or near the sea bottom. Its sharp, needlelike teeth point inward. This arrangement ensures that even if slippery prey struggles, it is securely held.

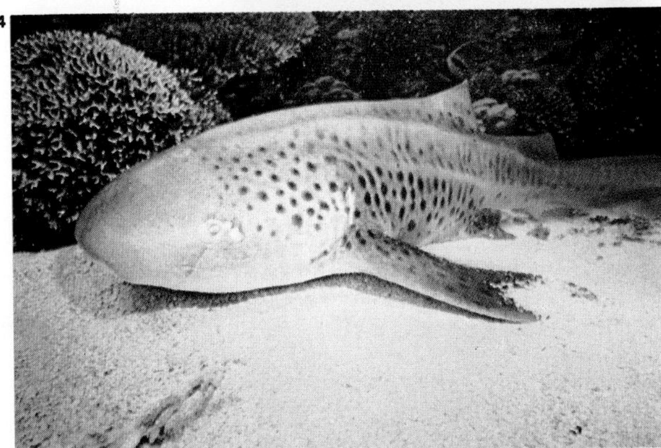

5 The stonefish *(Synanceja verrucosa)* is typical of shallow water bottom-feeders in that it is superbly camouflaged to match the colors and textures of its background. As a further means of discouraging its enemies it is equipped with sharp dorsal spines. When these come in contact with an enemy a poison is injected that is near-deadly to man. The stonefish lurks on the bottom in wait for its prey, on which it "pounces," using its pectoral fins.

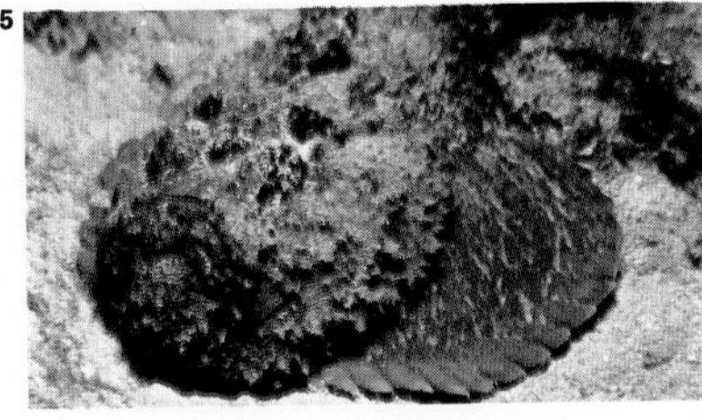

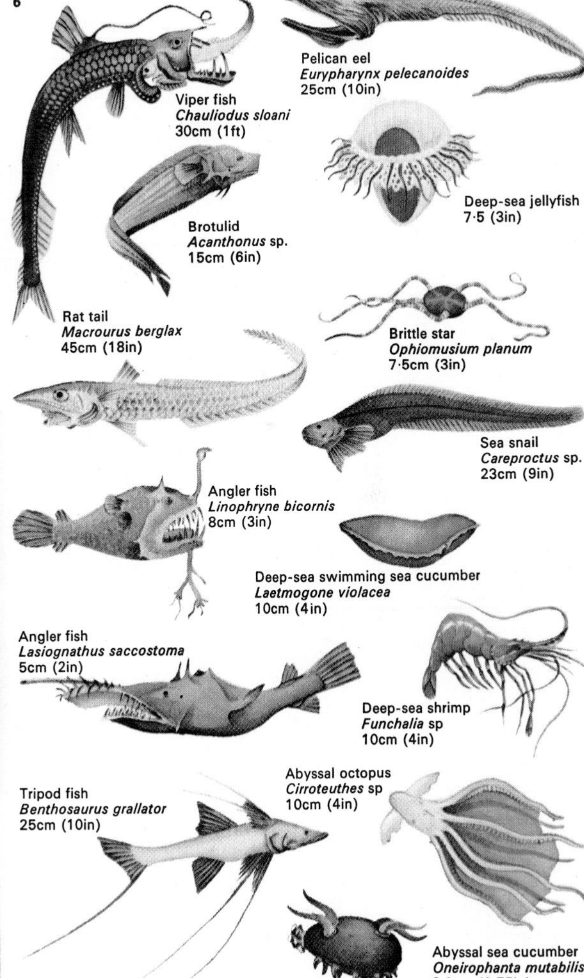

6
Pelican eel
Eurypharynx pelecanoides
25cm (10in)
Viper fish
Chauliodus sloani
30cm (1ft)
Deep-sea jellyfish
7·5 (3in)
Brotulid
Acanthonus sp.
15cm (6in)
Rat tail
Macrourus berglax
45cm (18in)
Brittle star
Ophiomusium planum
7·5cm (3in)
Sea snail
Careproctus sp.
23cm (9in)
Angler fish
Linophryne bicornis
8cm (3in)
Deep-sea swimming sea cucumber
Laetmogone violacea
10cm (4in)
Angler fish
Lasiognathus saccostoma
5cm (2in)
Deep-sea shrimp
Funchalia sp
10cm (4in)
Abyssal octopus
Cirroteuthes sp
10cm (4in)
Tripod fish
Benthosaurus grallator
25cm (10in)
Abyssal sea cucumber
Oneirophanta mutabilis
0·2cm (0·75in)

6 Below 10,000ft (3,000 m) life in the world's oceans includes a range of animals, many of them weirdly shaped, adapted to living in near-freezing water at extremely high pressures. The only glimmers of light in this pitch-dark region come from the bioluminescent organs that many of them possess. About 75% of the free-swimming species of fish in this region, representing 90% of the individuals, have light organs. These fish are small, few larger than 12in (30cm) in length. Many deep-sea, bottom-dwelling fish, such as the rat tails, grow a little longer, although much of this elongation is accounted for by the tail. Few of these bottom forms have light organs, but feed in darkness.

Endangered mammals

Extinction is a natural process. Fossils reveal that there have been countless thousands of animal species on Earth that no longer exist. Man had nothing to do with their disappearance. But in the last few hundred years the pace of extinction has quickened; since 1600 at least 36 species of mammals have become extinct and another 120 are now in danger. A few of these have simply reached the end of their natural timespan. Evolution has passed them by and they are gradually declining under the relentless competition of animals better adapted to live and breed. But at least four out of every five endangered animals are rare because of man's deliberate or unthinking actions.

Man's responsibility

Man has always been a hunter. Indeed, some zoologists believe that ancient man played a part in the extinction of many Ice Age (Pleistocene) mammals, presenting these beasts with an enemy they were not equipped to cope with. Most frequently, however, primitive hunting of wild animals for food and skins rarely caused any extinctions. When an Eskimo hunted the polar bear [Key] with dog sled and spear, his prey had a good chance of fighting back or escaping. Today, the snowmobile and the repeating rifle make killing very much easier and external demand has pushed up the value of skins. If the polar nations—the United States, Canada, Denmark, Norway, and the Soviet Union—had not signed a convention in 1973 prohibiting all hunting except for scientific purposes or by traditional methods, the polar bear might have become extinct.

The threats to mammals

Three factors have totally altered the effects of man the hunter on wildlife: modern technology, the world market, and man's explosive increase in numbers. The odds have shifted dramatically against the hunted, and the prospect of selling a skin for a high price has increased the hunter's motivation even further.

Man's greed has sent many species to the edge of extinction, a process that started when seamen from sailing ships clubbed to death thousands of puppy seals on the Arctic ice, boiling them down in huge vats to extract the blubber. The same process has continued into the 1970s as Soviet and Japanese whaling fleets have used explosive harpoons and giant factory ships to decimate the whales of the Antarctic Ocean.

Most dramatic of all has been the plight of the blue whale [5], the largest animal to have lived on the Earth. One hundred feet (30m) long and weighing up to 150 tons, three times heavier than the most massive dinosaur, the blue whale was once so plentiful that 200,000 of them lived in the Antarctic. By 1963 there were fewer than 1,000. Since then, under complete protection in all oceans, the blue whale seems to have slowly increased in numbers.

Most endangered mammals, however, are not threatened by any deliberate act of man. Some, especially those that live in water, suffer from the effects of pollution [6]. The Pyrenean desman [7], for instance, is an aquatic mole, an insectivorous animal not unlike a water shrew, that swims in the

CONNECTIONS

See also
630 Endangered birds
632 Endangered specie
634 Destructive man
636 Constructive man
638 Zoos and botanic g dens
294 Misuse of the land
298 Pollution of the se
540 The classification o mammals

1

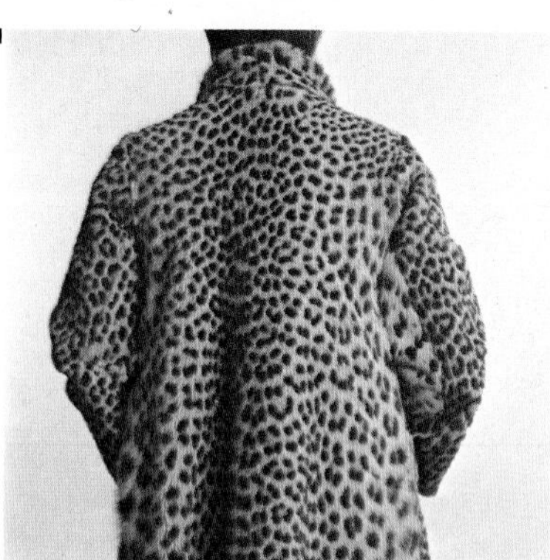

1 The fashion for fur coats threatens the survival of spotted cats of all kinds. The cats most in danger include the leopard, from which this coat was made, the jaguar, ocelot, and snow leopard.

2 The tiger was once common throughout Asia. An inhabitant of wooded areas and jungle, it has suffered much from the reduction of its habitat, but its greatest threat comes directly from man because of the increased availability of firearms. Reserves have been established in India for the protection of the tiger.

2

Tiger *Panthera tigris*

3 The remaining 50 protected specimens of the Javan rhino are still threatened by poachers in Indonesia. The powder made from its horn is erroneously believed to be a sexual stimulant.

5 Blue whale *Sibbaldus musculus*

3

Javan rhinoceros *Rhinoceros sondaicus*

4

Kouprey *Bos sauveli*

4 The kouprey, a wild ox of the Cambodian forests, has probably already been hunted to extinction by soldiers. It could have been important in improving the strains of domestic cattle.

5 The blue whale is the largest animal the Earth has ever known. It has been almost exterminated for its meat and oil but is now thought to be recovering, although fewer than 1,000 remain.

6

6 Wrecked supertankers, such as the *Torrey Canyon,* shown here in the last hours before it sank in March 1967, threaten birds and mammals. Oil discharged by such wrecks impairs the insulating effect of fur, and as a result sea otters, for example, may die of exposure. Other threats at sea include dumped pesticides, which can contaminate supplies of food throughout the ocean.

7 The monk seal is extinct in the Caribbean, nearly gone in the Mediterranean, but survives in Hawaii. The sea otter thrives again off California, but the Pyrenean desman is on the decline.

Pyrenean desman *Galemys pyrenaicus*

7

Monk seal *Monachus* sp

Sea otter *Enhydra lutris*

clear mountain rivers of southern France, Spain, and Portugal. The development of those streams for irrigation or hydroelectric power, and their pollution by pesticides or other chemicals, is depriving the desman of the pure, highly oxygenated water that is its only possible habitat.

Introduction and destruction

Another hazard is the introduction of alien forms of wildlife. The monotremes, or egg-laying mammals, of Australia have suffered from many such introductions, starting with the dingo or hunting dog, which the aborigines took with them 10,000 years ago.

Undoubtedly the greatest danger of all is the destruction of natural habitats [8]. As man plows up the grasslands, fells the rain forests, dams the rivers, drains the marshes, and builds roads, towns, and cities everywhere, the specialized habitats of animals with restricted distributions are squeezed until they disappear. Many mammals vanish with their habitats. The great prairies of the United States, over which the Plains Indians once hunted bison, are today turned over to grain and cattle. Bison survive only in a few reserves and smaller mammals such as the prairie dog and the black-footed ferret that preys on it have almost vanished [9].

The ethical argument for saving endangered mammals is a powerful one. Do we want our children to know a rhinoceros only from picture books? But the practical reasons are even more compelling; man needs wild mammals as genetic resources for the future. Cattle, for example, are unsuited to many parts of Africa and Australia and natural populations of wild antelope, deer, and kangaroo are already being ranched instead. In Asia, the rare wild ox called the kouprey [4] could play a role by hybridization with the domesticated zebu cattle of India.

Conservation is indivisible. To save a rare mammal such as the indri [9] the Madagascan rain forest that is its home must also be preserved. And in conserving the rain forest, we safeguard the wild plant *Coffea bertrandii,* which may one day allow breeders to develop caffeine-free coffee.

KEY

Polar bear
Thalarctos maritimus

Wildlife's main eneny is man: the polluter, the destroyer of wilderness, the introducer of alien species, and the hunter. Today at least 120 mammal species are in danger of extermination. The polar bear *(Thalarctos maritimus)* is now on the increase under international protection.

8

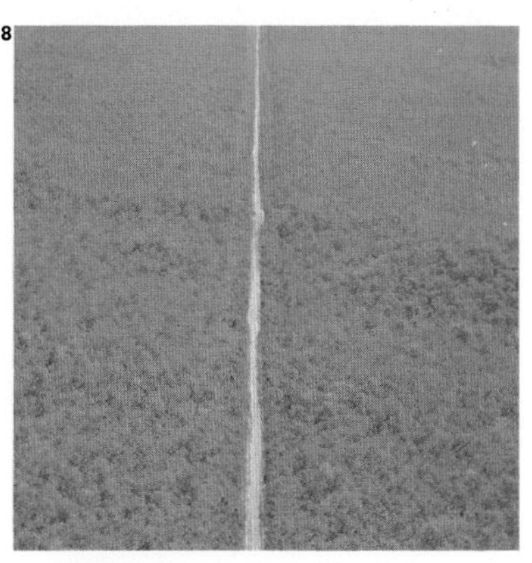

8 The biggest threat to wildlife is the damage to habitats caused by developments like the Trans-Amazonian Highway. The destruction of the wilderness destroys the homes of the animals with it.

9

Pygmy hog *Sus salvanius*

Indri
Indri indri

Spanish lynx
Felis lynx pardina

Spectacled bear
Tremarctos ornatus

Black-footed ferret
Mustela nigripes

9 The pygmy hog lives in the *terai,* a belt of grass and woodland along the Himalayan foothills that is being carved up by local cultivation, tea estates, and forestry. The indri is a handsome tree-living lemur from the Madagascar rain forests, which are increasingly being cleared. The spectacled bear lives in forests on the high slopes of the Andes; although human settlement has reduced its numbers, it is still widespread in Ecuador and Bolivia. The Spanish lynx needs wilderness to hunt its prey and is now confined to a few inaccessible sierras and the Doñana National Park in the Guadalquivir delta. The black-footed ferret lives in the prairies of western North America. The ferret is disappearing along with its main prey—prairie dogs—which have been deliberately poisoned because their burrows are hazardous to livestock.

10

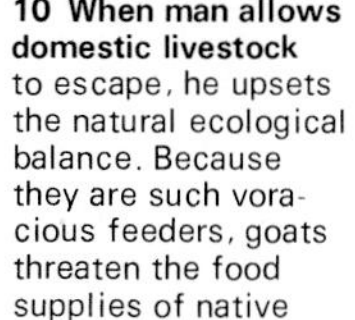

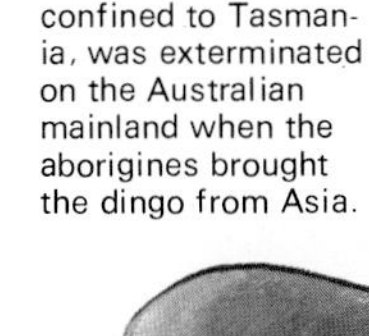

10 When man allows domestic livestock to escape, he upsets the natural ecological balance. Because they are such voracious feeders, goats threaten the food supplies of native mammals.

11 The onager has been pushed by domestic livestock onto the most barren pastures in northern Iran. The insect-eating Cuban solenodon is threatened by competition from the introduced mongoose, while the thylacine, very rare and confined to Tasmania, was exterminated on the Australian mainland when the aborigines brought the dingo from Asia.

11 Onager
Equus hemionus onager
Cuban solenodon
Solenodon cubanus
Thylacine
Thylacinus cynocephalus

Endangered birds

There are about 350 species and subspecies of birds in danger of extinction, but they are not spread evenly among the continents. Most endangered are birds with a naturally restricted range—those that live in remote or small habitats or on oceanic islands.

The regional scene

Of the total, there are 30 endangered species in the Palearctic (Eurasian) region; 8 in Europe and North Africa, and 22 in Asia north of the Himalayas. On the whole, Palearctic birds are widely distributed over their huge land mass, but local birds of prey, such as the Spanish imperial eagle [4], are still threatened.

The Ethiopian region (Africa) with 16, the Oriental region (southeast Asia) with 38, and the Nearctic region (North America) with 39, again have relatively few endangered birds. But species such as the ivory-billed woodpecker [2], which requires undisturbed forest swamps, and the whooping crane [1], which breeds on remote subarctic lakes, have suffered from habitat loss and overhunting respectively.

The Neotropical region (South and Central America), and even more so the Australasian region, have a more primitive bird fauna than the great continents of the Northern Hemisphere. Their unique forms of bird life are probably on the way out—on an evolutionary time scale. And man has greatly hastened the process by destroying habitats and by introducing predatory mammals such as dogs, cats, pigs, goats, weasels, rats, and foxes. These attack ground-nesting or flightless birds or damage the vegetation on which the birds feed. As a direct result, 69 Neotropical and 41 Australasian birds were on the endangered list in 1975.

Island birds at risk

The greatest number of threatened species, 117 in all, come from the oceanic islands, where isolated environments house only a relatively few species that originally emigrated from the continents. Once on the islands, many of these birds evolved distinct races and even totally new species, and the restricted size of their new homelands meant that they never built up large populations. Man has threatened these birds by destroying vegetation, by introducing competitors or enemies, and by hunting. The Pacific Ocean islands have an alarming total of 84 endangered species. The Hawaii group is a striking example, with no fewer than 29 species from several families threatened.

Overall, 32 percent of all endangered bird species are believed to be rare primarily because of natural causes. Hunting threatens another 24 percent, introduced predators 11 percent, and introduced competitors 3 percent. For the remaining varieties, destruction of habitat is the greatest threat, endangering 30 percent.

Organizations to the rescue

The statistics of threatened birds, together with those of animals and plants, are compiled by the International Union for Conservation of Nature and Natural Resources (IUCN), an international scientific organization with headquarters in Switzerland. The IUCN has compiled detailed *Red Data*

CONNECTIONS

See also
628 Endangered mammals
632 Endangered species
634 Destructive man
636 Constructive man
638 Zoos and botanic gardens
538 Island birds
294 Misuse of the land
296 Pollution of rivers and lakes
298 Pollution of the sea
526 The classification of birds

1 Whooping crane
Grus americana
2
Ivory-billed woodpecker
Campephilus principalis

1 The whooping crane, whose family goes back to the beginning of the age of mammals, was already declining when the white man first colonized North America. No nests were found between 1922 and 1955, and then the only remaining colony was discovered in Wood Buffalo National Park, Canada. In 1975 there were about 50 whoopers. The birds migrate 2,300 miles (3,700km) to winter in Texas and risk being shot *en route* by sportsmen who mistake them for sandhill cranes. Whooping cranes lay two eggs a year but rear only one chick. Some eggs have been taken for captive breeding to supplement the wild flock.

2 The ivory-billed woodpecker is one of the rarest birds in the world. An inhabitant of southeastern United States, it may already be extinct. It resides in primeval swamp forests and is extremely shy and may desert its nest even if it is only watched. Indian chiefs once adorned their belts with its bill and plumes; now logging has removed the big trees in which it breeds.

3
Puña grebe
Podiceps taczanowskii

3 The flightless puña grebe is confined to the shallow water of Lake Junin, 13,400ft (4,084m) up in the Peruvian Andes. The lake is becoming increasingly polluted with mine effluent, sewage, and runoff from eroded farmland. It is possible that this potential tourist attraction may be made a national park.

4

Imperial eagle
Aquila heliaca

4 The Spanish imperial eagle once ranged over Morocco, Algeria, Spain, and Portugal. By 1975 it bred in only a few remote Spanish sierras and in Europe's last great wilderness, the Coto Doñana national park near Seville. This is probably Europe's most threatened bird, with fewer than 100 individuals surviving. Although it has been well protected in its Doñana breeding grounds, it may soon die out completely unless farmers outside the protective limits of the park can be persuaded to stop shooting it.

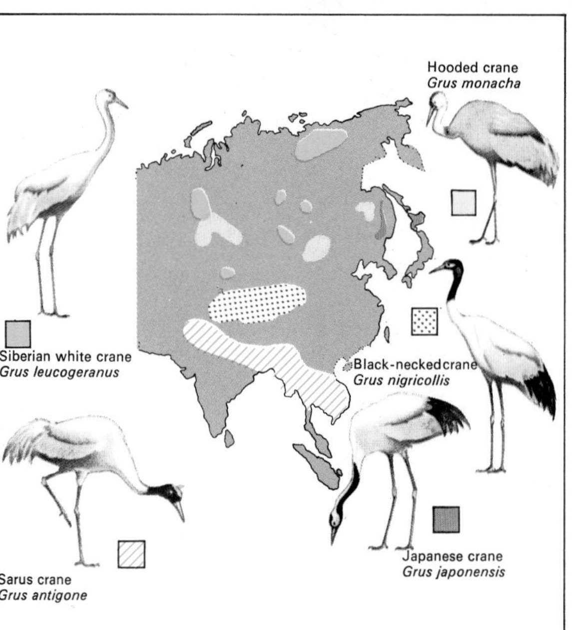

5
Hooded crane
Grus monacha
Siberian white crane
Grus leucogeranus
Black-necked crane
Grus nigricollis
Sarus crane
Grus antigone
Japanese crane
Grus japonensis

5 The Asian cranes are survivors from the warm, wet swamps of the Pleistocene. Never common, their numbers have been greatly reduced by hunting and the loss of the wide marshlands in which they nest and winter. The magnificent Japanese crane plays a major part in the nation's folklore and legend and was rigidly protected by the medieval nobility. It breeds rapidly in captivity and 33 percent of its population is now in zoos. Carefully protected today, it is slowly on the increase. The hooded crane, which winters in Japan, is also increasing its numbers. Less is known of the black-necked crane, which nests on remote lakes deep in the highlands of central Asia.

Books for all endangered mammals and birds and for some reptiles, amphibians, fish, and plants.

An IUCN fact sheet describes the present and former distribution of every threatened species, its estimated numbers, the presumed reasons for its decline, the numbers held in captivity and their breeding potential, and the protective measures already taken and those proposed. The sheets are color-coded: green pages are for those species that are off the immediate danger list and red for those that are on the verge of extinction.

Experts from IUCN decide, on a strictly scientific basis, what must be done to save each species and draw up action plans in consultation with authorities in each country. But implementing these schemes is another matter and here the World Wildlife Fund (WWF) plays a key role. WWF has an international organization based near Geneva, but it also has national groups in many countries. It is a propagandist and fund-raising body, charged with persuading national governments to take action to save the world's living heritage and with raising the money that alone makes IUCN's plans possible. IUCN and WWF work closely together, but they have distinct roles. WWF cannot lay claim to IUCN's scientific expertise, which goes far beyond the sphere of endangered species to include every aspect of the rational use of natural resources, whereas IUCN does not involve itself in WWF's political and financial activities.

Together, IUCN and WWF have pulled a number of birds back from the brink and focused attention on many others. Without them, the Coto Doñana in southwestern Spain would not have provided a sanctuary for the imperial eagle [4], and the unique Galapagos hawk [10] might have disappeared entirely. But although money and advice are necessities, in the last resort conservation depends on the determination of the local people. Unless, for example, pollution ceases in Lake Junín in Peru, the puña grebe [3] will become extinct, and the monkey-eating eagles [6] of the Philippines will disappear unless hunters stop answering the demand for specimens.

KEY

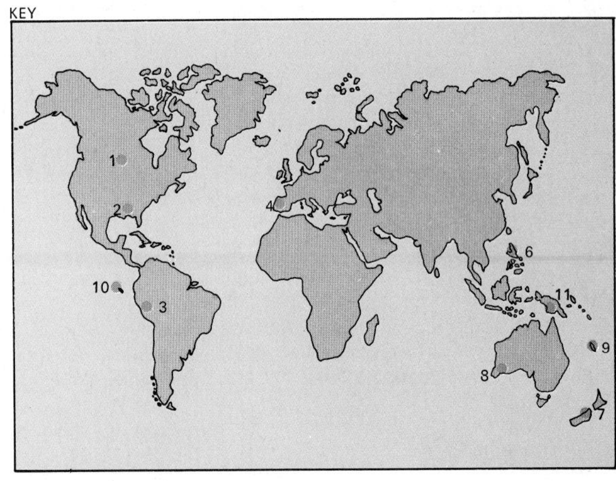
1
2
3
6
8
9
10
11

Birds in danger are found in all the zoogeographical regions of the world. The species illustrated on these pages are keyed numerically in this map. Nearly a third of the world's total of endangered birds resides on oceanic islands. The chief reason for this is that they have tended to become highly specialized in habitats that are severely restricted in area. Man has posed a three-fold threat to bird species through destruction of their habitats, by the introduction of predators and competitors, and by hunting and egg collecting.

6 Monkey-eating eagle *Pithecophaga jefferyi*

6 The impressive monkey-eating eagle of the Philippines has been reduced to fewer than 100 individuals. The causes are destruction of their forest habitat and a demand for specimens.

7 Kakapo *Strigops habroptilus*

8 Noisy scrub bird *Atrichornis clamosus*

7 The New Zealand ground owl parrot, or kakapo, began to decline with the arrival of the Maoris. Predators introduced from Europe and deforestation have reduced its numbers to fewer than 100.

8 The noisy scrub bird of Western Australia lives in dense coastal scrub. Until rediscovered in 1961 at Two People Bay, near Albany, it had not been recorded since 1889 and was thought to be extinct.

10 Galapagos hawk *Buteo galapagoensis*

10 The unique Galapagos hawk lives only on the Galapagos Islands. Habitat destruction by goats and shooting by chicken farmers have reduced the population to about 200 birds. Protective measures, for example the removal of the introduced goats, are beginning to prove successful.

11 King of Saxony bird of paradise *Pteridophora alberti*

11 The King of Saxony bird of paradise is one of the world's rarest birds and now on the verge of extinction. Its range extends from the Snow Mountains to the Central Highlands of New Guinea. The export trade in plumes was banned in 1924, but illicit trading continues. Its survival is also threatened by the destruction of its forest habitat.

9 Kagu *Rhynochetos jubatus*

9 The mysterious kagu, a virtually flightless raillike bird, is confined to the remote forests of New Caledonia. It is threatened by introduced predators such as cats, pigs, rats, and dogs.

Endangered species

A great deal is known about some 300 mammals and birds thought to be in danger of extinction, but very little about the many other threatened species. One estimate suggests that 20,000 plant species may be threatened, but detailed information exists for only a few hundred of them. There is a little more data about amphibians and about endangered reptiles, such as snakes, turtles, lizards, and crocodilians, as well as freshwater fish, at least in North America and Europe. But there is an almost total lack of knowledge about endangered butterflies [7–10] and other invertebrates, nor is it known how many marine inhabitants are threatened by pollution.

Value of wildlife

In all, 50,000 or even 100,000 species of animals and plants may be endangered, largely as a result of man's activities. The Washington Convention (1973) banning trade in rare species and their products has not solved the problem. Some of the world's disappearing wildlife has no obvious value to man, but because all organisms are ultimately interdependent, the loss of one or two of them can critically affect others in such a way that species of economic importance may become involved.

Many endangered species, however, have actual or potential economic value in themselves. The marine turtles [1], for example, are the basis of an industry in meat, eggs, shell, and oil, and if they were carefully harvested or even farmed they could provide income for many more years. Komodo dragons [2] may seem useless curiosities, but tourists visiting Indonesia pay to see these huge carnivorous lizards.

Some fish species may seem useless at present, but the need to produce food from the most unlikely sources may give them value in the future. The endangered Moapa dace [5], for example, which is found only in a few warm springs in Nevada, might one day be used to breed fish that could be grown commercially in the heated effluent from electrical power stations. Sport fishermen pay to fight unusual fish like the Gila trout [6].

Insects are often involved in biological control of pests as natural predators or parasites to reduce the numbers of a plant or animal harmful to man. The relentless spread of impenetrable thickets of a South American cactus across the sheep lands of Australia was stopped only with the help of a moth from the Argentine. Its caterpillars feed naturally on the cactus, and when the moth was introduced to Australia 60 years after the cactus, it soon gnawed the pest to the ground.

Endangered plants

Endangered plants have perhaps even more potential uses than threatened animals, although some flowers are worth saving for their beauty alone. The fragrant Calabrian primrose [11], for example, might prove profitable for seed and garden firms. But other plants have provided man with a remarkable variety of useful products. Drugs such as aspirin and the heart medicine digitalis; drinks such as tea and coffee; all of the vegetables and fruits; pepper, nutmeg, and other seasonings; jute and other fibers;

CONNECTIONS

See also
628 Endangered mammals
630 Endangered birds
634 Destructive man
636 Constructive man
638 Zoos and botanic gardens
294 Misuse of the land
296 Pollution of rivers and lakes
424 The plant kingdom
510 The classification of fish
518 The life of amphibians
520 The life of reptiles

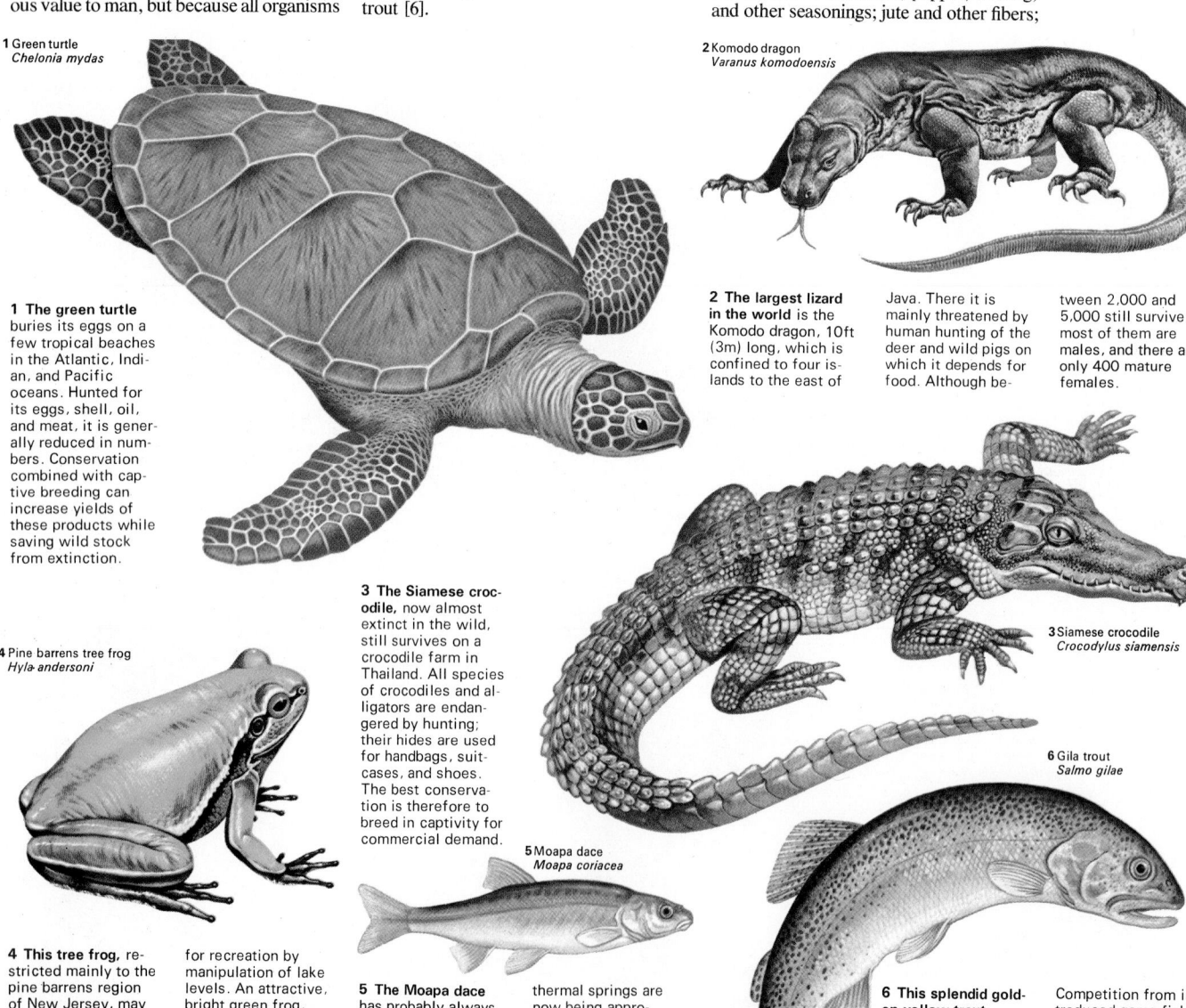

1 Green turtle
Chelonia mydas
2 Komodo dragon
Varanus komodoensis
3 Siamese crocodile
Crocodylus siamensis
4 Pine barrens tree frog
Hyla andersoni
5 Moapa dace
Moapa coriacea
6 Gila trout
Salmo gilae

1 The green turtle buries its eggs on a few tropical beaches in the Atlantic, Indian, and Pacific oceans. Hunted for its eggs, shell, oil, and meat, it is generally reduced in numbers. Conservation combined with captive breeding can increase yields of these products while saving wild stock from extinction.

2 The largest lizard in the world is the Komodo dragon, 10ft (3m) long, which is confined to four islands to the east of Java. There it is mainly threatened by human hunting of the deer and wild pigs on which it depends for food. Although between 2,000 and 5,000 still survive, most of them are males, and there are only 400 mature females.

3 The Siamese crocodile, now almost extinct in the wild, still survives on a crocodile farm in Thailand. All species of crocodiles and alligators are endangered by hunting; their hides are used for handbags, suitcases, and shoes. The best conservation is therefore to breed in captivity for commercial demand.

4 This tree frog, restricted mainly to the pine barrens region of New Jersey, may also survive in a few small colonies in Georgia and North Carolina. Its swampland habitat is being steadily drained for industrial and housing development and for recreation by manipulation of lake levels. An attractive, bright green frog, which is also collected for the pet trade, it hardly ever breeds in captivity. At least 70 other amphibian species are endangered by changes in the environment.

5 The Moapa dace has probably always been confined to a few warm springs at the headwaters of the Moapa River in Nevada, with its numbers never much higher than the present 500-1,000. The thermal springs are now being appropriated for commercial purposes, and alien introductions, such as bullfrogs and the mosquito fish *(Gambusia)*, are altering the delicate ecological balance.

6 This splendid golden-yellow trout, unique to the Gila River in New Mexico, has been depleted by felling of watershed forests, causing erosion, and dam building, leading to fluctuating water levels. Competition from introduced game fish has reduced it still further, and the Gila trout is now confined to Diamond Creek and other streams. A conservation program has shown good results.

timbers, dyes, and hundreds of other substances were all developed from what were originally wild plants. The use of defoliants has endangered, if not exterminated, one of them. The source of the yellow pigment gamboge yellow, the tree *Garcinia hanbury*, has been severely threatened in its native habitat in Vietnam and Cambodia.

What to do?

For a few of these endangered animals and plants special reserves can be set up, but all must rely on man for the preservation of their habitats. The chain of reserves established by the Indian government to save the tiger from extinction is of equal value to hundreds of less dramatic but equally endangered species. There is no way of conserving the tiger in the wild without conserving the complex ecosystem of which it forms a part. Similarly, protection for the giant otter means protection for a whole area of the Amazonian rain forest.

There are some endangered species, of which the marine turtles and the crocodiles are good examples, where the risk comes from over-exploitation by man. Here there are several ways in which conservation can be designed to ensure that a renewable resource remains to enrich future generations. One method is to limit the number of animals that may be killed or eggs that may be taken. Countries from Borneo to the West Indies are trying to do this for the green turtle [1] with the aim of taking no more than a suitable crop. Another technique is to collect turtle eggs and hatch them in captivity, releasing the young when they are a year old and past their most vulnerable stage.

A third method is to breed the animals entirely in captivity, as happens on crocodile farms in several countries [3], so that the best quality hides can be collected from known sources and a complete ban placed on killing animals in the wild. A fourth possibility is semidomestication. One day, herds of adult turtles may be pastured on seaweed and cropped for eggs and meat.

These methods of conservation all reflect a growing respect for wildlife and a desire to perpetuate species that are in danger of dying out completely.

KEY

The use of insecticide sprays, the fashion for reptile-skin handbags and wallets, and the incorporation of pressed flowers into goods such as bookmarks, all threaten a huge number of species. As many as 20,000 plant species may be in danger of extinction and, unlike the threatened mammals and birds, the number of endangered plants, insects, fish, reptiles, and amphibians is largely unknown.

7 Insecticides, collectors, and the destruction of habitats are three main threats to butterflies, but little is known about the decline of many once common species such as the splendid Apollo, found over much of Europe and Asia.

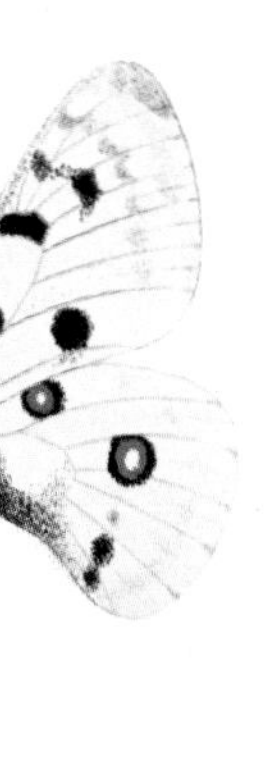

7 Apollo butterfly *Parnassius apollo*

8 Large copper butterfly *Lycaena dispar*

8 The last individual large copper butterfly in Great Britain was recorded in 1848. Extinction there resulted from over-collecting and local disappearance of the caterpillars' food plant, the great water dock, with the draining of the fens in eastern England. The Dutch race, which has become rare for similar reasons, was introduced to Wood Walton Fen, England, from the Netherlands in 1927.

9 Victoria birdwing *Ornithoptera victoriae*

9 Collectors and forest clearance for agriculture threaten the Victoria birdwing in New Guinea. A single birdwing once fetched $1,875 at an auction in Paris.

10 Brown glasswing *Dircenna varina*

10 The Trinidad subspecies of the southern brown glasswing of Ecuador is confined to the southern part of the island. It lives in scrub, much of which has been destroyed by agricultural fires.

11 Calabrian primrose *Primula palinuri*

11 The Calabrian primrose, a sweet-smelling species, is limited to two areas near Cape Palinuri, in southern Italy. Greatly reduced by grazing and picking, it needs total protection in the wild.

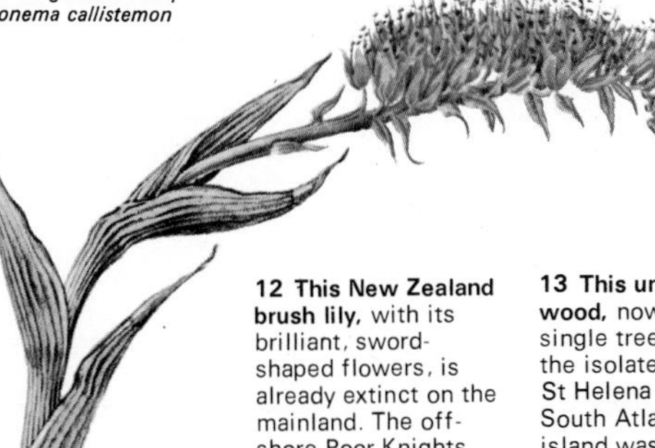

2 Poor Knights brush lily *Xeronema callistemon*

12 This New Zealand brush lily, with its brilliant, sword-shaped flowers, is already extinct on the mainland. The offshore Poor Knights and Hen and Chickens islands were made reserves and protect the species from the wild pigs.

13 St Helena redwood *Trochetia erythroxylon*

13 This unique redwood, now down to a single tree, stands on the isolated island of St Helena in the South Atlantic. The island was once thickly forested but has been eaten bare by goats introduced since discovery by Europeans in 1502.

14 Cooktown orchid *Dendrobium bigibbum*

14 The Cooktown orchid, emblem of Queensland, Australia, although protected, is avidly collected from the north Australian rain forests for sale and cultivation. Its flower hangs from small pockets of humus in which it lives.

Destructive man

Of all the creatures alive on Earth man is the most destructive. As Mark Twain expressed it, "Man is the only animal that can blush or needs to." For millions of years man has been destroying his environment by activities usually attributed to his intelligence. What is meant, of course, is that man's superior intellectual ability, his power to reason, has enabled him to seek and find ways of exploiting his environment that have never been discovered by other animals. This intelligence has largely protected him from the adverse effects of this exploitation.

The overcrowded planet

It is now becoming increasingly clear, however, that the Earth's resources are not limitless. The rate of change and the number of new methods of extracting and exploiting natural resources continue to increase. The greater "wealth" produced by these new methods enables an ever-growing human population to survive on the planet, although paradoxically it does not raise the overall standard of life for these millions—there are more people today than ever before living at unacceptably low standards. And as the human population grows it becomes necessary to devise even more ingenious methods of supporting the increased numbers.

There are many signs that the Earth's natural systems are approaching the limits of their ability to cope with growing human numbers, and advanced technology is rapidly using up natural resources. The ability of the environment to recover from these massive attacks is also in doubt.

Vanishing forests

Initially, destructive man was no more than a minor nuisance to nature. His tree-felling was of no great consequence because the forests soon returned to their former area and density after man had moved on. This system of agriculture [7] is still practiced in some areas: unfortunately, due to expanding human populations and diminishing available land, the slash-and-burn cultivators return to the same patch of forest within two or three years, rather than after a generation or more. As a result, the soil has no time to recover between successive onslaughts.

Apart from the demands of agriculturists, the world's great forests are under increasingly acute pressure from the timber industry. The tropical rain forests, thought to be the most ancient wild habitats on earth, are fast vanishing. It has been estimated that every minute some 14 acres (5.6 hectares) disappear. The results are manifold. Animal species are exterminated and huge numbers of valuable and potentially valuable plants wiped out. The significance of this is that all man's cultivated vegetables were once wild plants and that many drugs he depends on are plant derivatives.

The rain forests often grow on poor, infertile soil and when the forest cover is removed all that is left is barren desert. Forest destruction has led to erosion, flooding, and adverse climatic changes. But still the clearance goes on, partly because trees represent a source of income but also for more primitive reasons. Man still regards wild forest as something to be tamed.

CONNECTIONS

See also
628 Endangered mammals
630 Endangered birds
632 Endangered species
636 Constructive man
638 Zoos and botanic gardens
292 Pollution of the air
294 Misuse of the land
296 Pollution of rivers and lakes
298 Pollution of the sea
302 World food resources
552 Whales, porpoises, and dolphins
304 History of agriculture
318 Protecting crops
878 Stages of social evolution

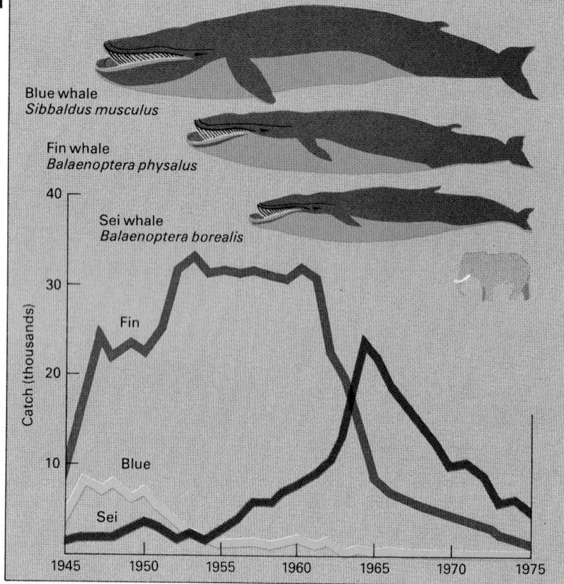
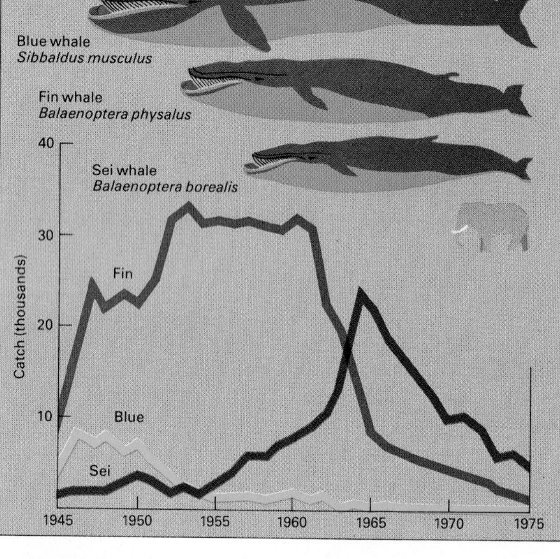

1
Blue whale
Sibbaldus musculus
Fin whale
Balaenoptera physalus
Sei whale
Balaenoptera borealis
Catch (thousands)
40
30
20
10
Fin
Blue
Sei
1945
1950
1955
1960
1965
1970
1975

1 The whaling industry is among the most efficient, ruthless, and myopic of all man's industries based on the exploitation of the animal kingdom. So effective has whale-catching become, with its huge factory ships, sonar, radar, and spotting aircraft, and its explosive harpoons, that the great whales are easy prey. The whales, properly harvested, could provide an enormous and continuing source of fat and protein. Instead the industry, until recently, greedily overkilled the whales, reducing species after species to near extinction. The graph shows the decline in numbers killed of three species.

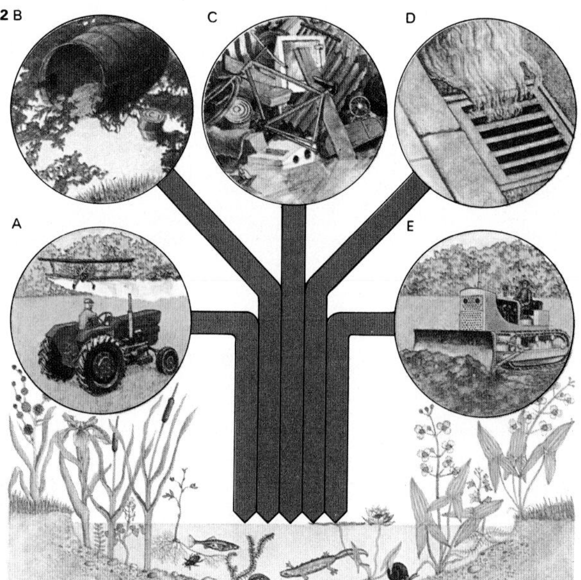

2 B
C
D
A
E

2 Modern man has little use for ponds as watering places for animals, but instead of preserving these thriving ecosystems he has destroyed many of them through pollution and land reclamation. Pond life is threatened by the excessive use of fertilizers, pesticides, and herbicides [A]; by the rusty residue from dumped cans and other metal [B]; and by rubbish dumping on a larger scale [C]. Other pollutants reach ponds as run-off from road drains [D] and contain oil, rubber deposits, petroleum, and tar. Bulldozers [E] of developers obliterate ponds to make room for homes.

3 A
B
C
D
E

3 Grasslands can support a wide range of wild animals—grazers, browsers, predators, and burrowers—all making use of different parts of the system [B, C, D]. Many are migrants, which allows the grass to regenerate. Some grasses are well adapted to withstand fire, and one species sends its seedlings spiraling below ground away from the heat [A]. The coming of man and too many domestic cattle has spelled disaster [E]. The large protected herds compact the soil, overgraze the grass, and turn grassland to desert.

4 The destruction of grassland by cattle is particularly severe in the Masai lands of East Africa. And the Masai do not cull their cattle for food but rather regard them as wealth.

Other habitat types are being destroyed around the world for much the same reasons. Other forms of destruction, however, are more insidious because their effects are less immediately obvious. Man has introduced alien animal and plant species into new environments, often with motives no more "evil" than to bring familiar creatures with him to a new land to remind him of home. The consequences have been disastrous when the native fauna and flora have been unable to compete successfully with these introductions.

Man the overhunter and polluter

Man has overhunted with ferocious prodigality, both for food and for sport. He has tried to graze his cattle on semi-arid lands where they do not do well but simply oust the better adapted native wild animals. He has introduced rabbits, donkeys, and goats to oceanic islands as a future source of food with an unfailingly tragic effect on the simple and fragile ecosystems. In the sea he has overfished [1] to such an extent that yields have declined drastically.

Man's greatest threat to his environment lies in his technology. Rivers and inland waters, and even some seas, have been stripped of their wildlife by the tide of noxious industrial waste and untreated sewage that is pumped into them. While the Rhine and Danube rivers are grossly polluted, and the Baltic and Mediterranean seas are fast becoming sterile, it is still barely recognized that it costs more to counteract the effects of pollution than to install nonpolluting processes initially.

The construction of dams for irrigation or hydroelectric power can have serious ecological drawbacks. The Aswan High Dam in Egypt has blocked the nutritious flow of silt to Lower Egypt and has affected the inshore fisheries in the eastern Mediterranean by reducing the flow of Nile water to the sea. The silt itself, building up behind the dam, is already a major problem.

The chemical revolution on the farm has increased yields but may ultimately prove self-defeating. An insect pest may become resistant to one pesticide, while some pesticides kill the predators of the pests.

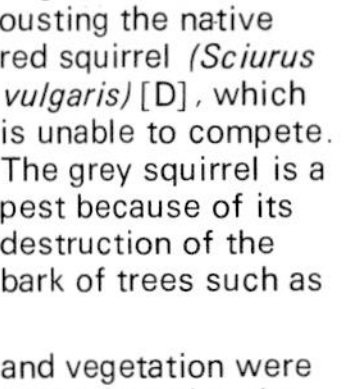

KEY
A
B
C
D
E
Grey squirrel
Sciurus carolinensis

Man's introduction of alien or exotic species has resulted in the destruction of the environment because the effects of the introductions were unforeseen and often disastrous. The grey squirrel, for example, was introduced to Britain from its native North America in the early 19th century. It has now spread [A] to a large part of the UK, ousting the native red squirrel *(Sciurus vulgaris)* [D], which is unable to compete. The grey squirrel is a pest because of its destruction of the bark of trees such as beech, maple, larch, and oak [B]. It also feeds on cereals [C], as well as buds, shoots, birds' eggs, and young birds [E]. The red squirrel was not nearly so destructive.

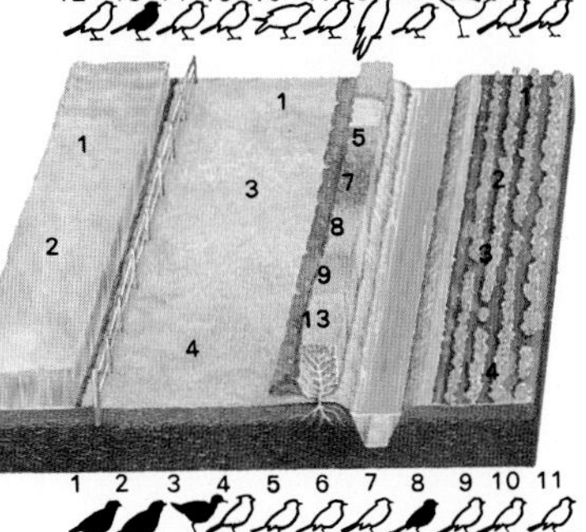

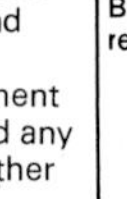

Key to birds
1 Partridge
2 Pheasant
3 Lapwing
4 Skylark
5 Dunnock
6 Wren
7 Blackbird
8 Corn bunting
9 Yellowhammer
10 Chaffinch
11 Robin
12 Blue tit
13 Whitethroat
14 Great tit
15 Songthrush
16 Carrion crow
17 Long-tailed tit
18 Kestrel
19 Greenfinch
20 Moorhen
21 Reed bunting
22 Sedge warbler

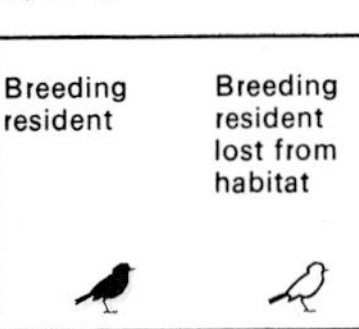

Key to symbols
Breeding resident
Breeding resident lost from habitat

5 As man's numbers have increased, along with his growing technological expertise, so the demand for land has risen. All man's activities seem to need more and more land. And not only is the land itself vanishing but the acres that remain are being farmed more intensively. This diagram shows the effect on bird life of the modern trend toward one-crop agriculture and its ruthless removal of such traditional country features as hedges, streams, ponds, and trees. These features are thought by some farmers to interfere with efficient agricultural practice in an age when farming is increasingly mechanized. Fortunately farmers are coming to realize that the retention of pockets of natural habitat, even on the most modern farms, can repay them amply. Apart from aesthetics, the insect-eating birds they support, for example, can be more efficient than any chemical insecticide. Here, 22 European species have been reduced to four by the removal of the stream and hedges, and the altered environment has not attracted any new species, either breeding or nonbreeding.

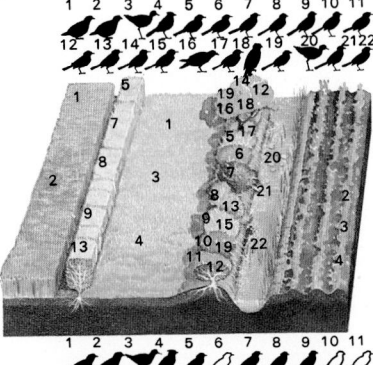

6 Early European settlers were lured to the prairies of the American West by the vast, fertile land. The native wildlife and vegetation were well adapted to the region's extremes of climate. Man, however plowed the land, planted crops, and introduced domestic cattle. No longer held together by protective grasses, the soil simply blew away in many areas during a prolonged drought in the 1930s, leaving a dust bowl. At the time, the farmers were driven away but some land has now been reclaimed.

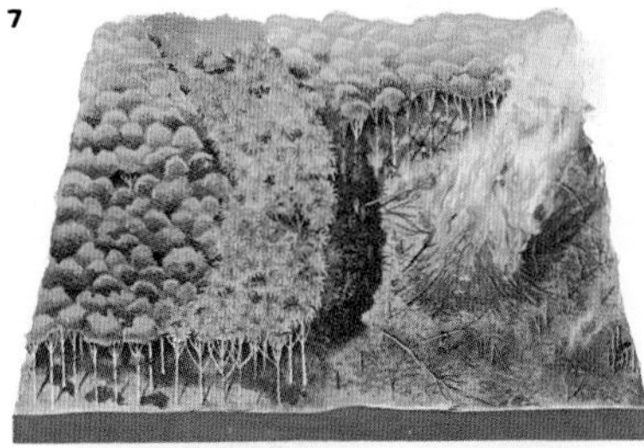

7 The great forests of West Africa have long been felled by man to provide space for growing crops. The technique shown here is called slash and burn. Because the forests grow on infertile soils the cleared areas will support a crop for only a year or two. The people then move on to a new area and repeat the process. Unfortunately, the diminishing forests and increasing human populations cause the cultivators to return before the soil can recover.

Constructive man

It is only in the past century that active attempts have been made to preserve and nurture nature's treasures. The world's first national park, Yellowstone in Wyoming and adjacent parts of Montana and Idaho, was founded in 1872.

Connections with hunting

Conservation on a limited scale, practiced often by lone saints, dreamers, and enthusiasts, has a much longer history, however. Faeroe Islanders and Icelandic fishermen have been gathering sea birds and eggs for centuries on a controlled basis that gives them a good harvest while allowing the birds to maintain their population at a stable level, year after year. Henry VIII of England introduced laws governing the seasons during which certain animals could be hunted, and the Inca kings of South America reserved exclusive rights to wear robes made from the wool for which the vicuña [6] alone was hunted. Protective regulations existed in the Plymouth Colony, and almost all of the American colonies had closed seasons by 1775.

Nature conservation, and especially animal conservation, has long been closely connected with hunting. Indeed, the need for conservation arose as the result of man's hunting activities. The first marked impact of man on his environment, as measured by the extinction of animal species, took place some 10,000 to 15,000 years ago. Fossil records show how man in Paleolithic times began to gain ascendancy over his fellow inhabitants of the earth. Whole species disappeared in Europe and—spectacularly—in the Americas, as man spread down from the Bering Straits, exterminating giant sloths, bears, lions, wolves, bison, mastodons, and mammoths along with the dependent scavengers, such as giant vultures and birds of prey.

Early conservationists were invariably hunters. Their goal was to husband their quarry and to make sure there would always be an abundance of game. The early nature reserves were often royal hunting preserves. Today the conservation movement is much more broadly based, but hunters still play an important part. Two outstanding examples are the activities of Ducks Unlimited of the United States and the Wildfowlers' Association of Great Britain and Ireland.

Modern conservation began to gather momentum around the turn of the century, and by the third quarter of the century many environmental groups, such as the Sierra Club, the National Wildlife Federation, the Wilderness Society, and Friends of the Earth, were exerting significant influence on US public opinion and legislation. In addition, there were hosts of large and small societies, national and local, devoted to studying birds or lichens or reptiles, or to acquiring land for preservation—all of them involved in conservation. Internationally, there are four main bodies concerned with nature conservation. They are the Fauna Preservation Society (founded in 1903), the International Council for Bird Preservation (founded in 1922), the International Union for Conservation of Nature and Natural Resources (IUCN—founded in 1948), and the World Wildlife Fund (founded in 1961). IUCN is in some sense the senior of these four bodies. The World Wildlife

CONNECTIONS

See also
638 Zoos and botanic gardens
634 Destructive man
628 Endangered mammals
630 Endangered birds
632 Endangered species
288 Energy for the future
388 Fish farming
398 The future of food
586 Grasslands of Africa

1 

1 Wildlife conservation is achieved locally by setting up reserves and national parks. To live a natural life most animals need a fairly large area in which conditions are as close as possible to their wild habitat and in which human disturbance or settlement is minimal. This does not necessarily mean the exclusion of all humans; many reserves in North America, and this one in East Africa, are visited by tourists. Also, it is often necessary to have a staff of game wardens to guard against poachers and encroachment by loggers, farmers, and other kinds of developers.

2 

3 

3 Yellowstone National Park in the United States was the first such park in the world and is still one of the biggest and best. It is visited by millions of people each year who have the chance to see creatures such as this bull moose *(Alces alces)*. At certain times of year, citylike traffic jams develop on the park's road system. The future prospect is that access to the world's nature reserves will have to be controlled ever more strictly if damage to the natural habitat is to be avoided. In the developing countries, increasing pressure is being placed on wildlife reserves as city people seek escape and spiritual refreshment from the strain of urban life.

2 Nature reserves need not be large. To protect rare orchids like these, or a single plant threatened with extinction, such as the Indonesian *Rafflesia,* areas smaller than an acre can be set aside.

4 The eggs of the green turtle are a great delicacy in Asia. In Malaysia, conservationists run a hatchery to protect enough eggs to ensure that turtles will keep returning to the beaches.

4 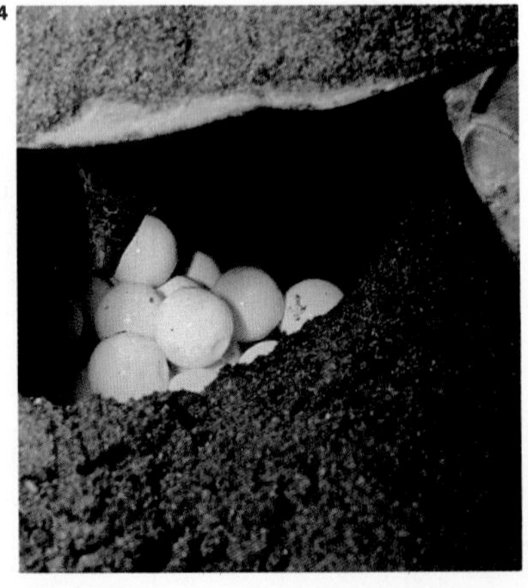

Fund has branches in nearly 30 countries and is a voluntary fund-raising organization whose main aim is to produce money to finance the conservation programs worked out by IUCN. Both of these organizations have their headquarters in Morges, Switzerland.

Safeguarding the habitat

Following the impetus given by the establishment of Yellowstone National Park in the United States [3], the method of saving animals and plants by safeguarding the habitat itself spread widely. There are now some 1,200 areas in the United Nations List of National Parks and Equivalent Reserves. These parks, in one hundred countries, are paralleled by countless smaller areas with similar objectives around the world. They include game reserves [1], nature reserves, forest reserves, sites of special scientific interest, areas of outstanding natural beauty, and marine reserves. The world's largest national park is the North-East Greenland National Park, of 275 million acres, while at the other end of the scale are many nature reserves of less than an acre, often for the protection of a single plant [2]. In Indonesia, for instance, reserves have been created to protect *Rafflesia,* the largest flower in the world, but this method of conservation still makes any species vulnerable to chance destruction.

The vital task of conservation

People everywhere are coming to realize the importance and urgency of saving wild animals, wild plants, and wild places for future generations [4, 5, 7, 8]. Nearly 1,000 different kinds of animals are threatened with extinction, and perhaps 20,000 plants (ten percent of all the world's flowering plants).

The 1972 Conference on the Human Environment in Stockholm, held under United Nations auspices, and the subsequent establishment of the United Nations Environment Program, are indications that the nature conservation movement is approaching maturity and that conservation is being accepted as one of the most important tasks of our time.

KEY

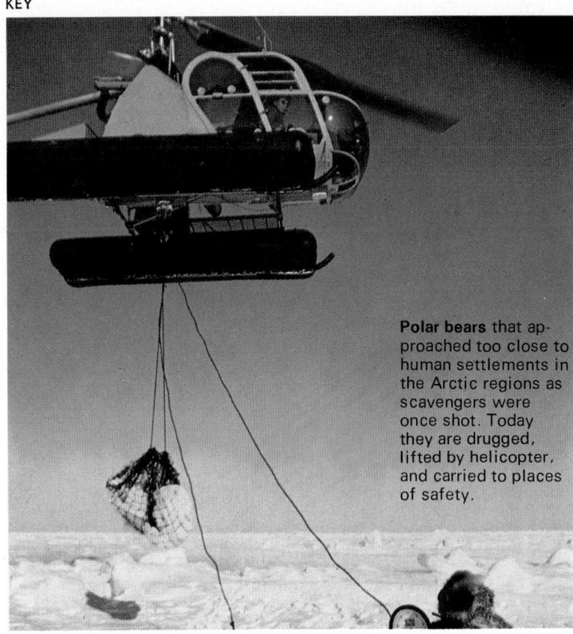

Polar bears that approached too close to human settlements in the Arctic regions as scavengers were once shot. Today they are drugged, lifted by helicopter, and carried to places of safety.

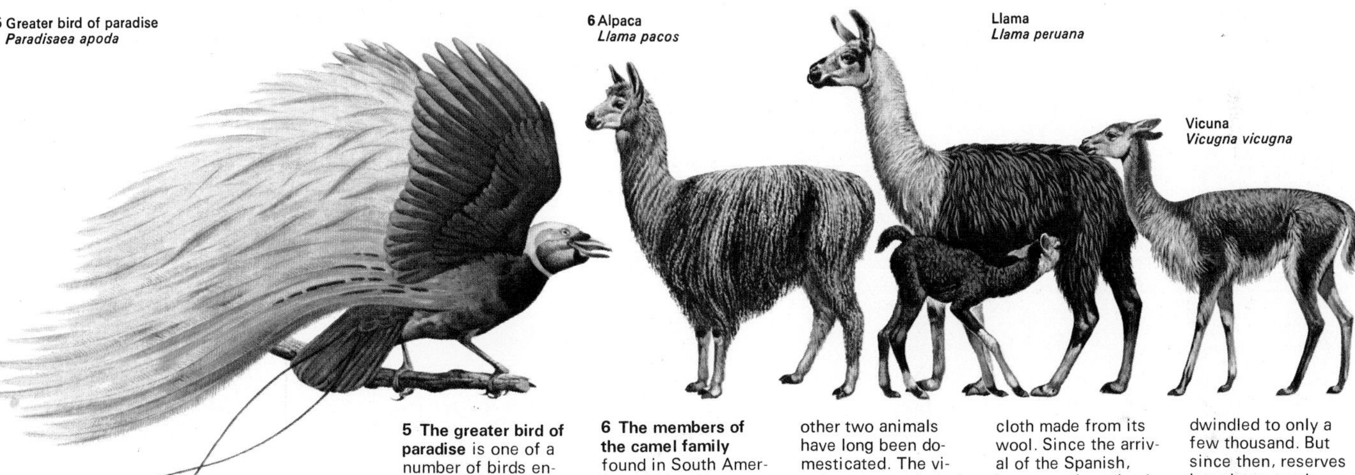
5 Greater bird of paradise *Paradisaea apoda*
6 Alpaca *Llama pacos*
Llama *Llama peruana*
Vicuna *Vicugna vicugna*

5 The greater bird of paradise is one of a number of birds endangered by the demand for their brightly colored feathers. Strong conservation laws are needed to control this trade.

6 The members of the camel family found in South America are the alpaca, llama, and vicuña together with a fourth species, the guanaco. Only the vicuña and the guanaco are wild; the other two animals have long been domesticated. The vicuña once numbered millions in its home in the high Andes and was carefully conserved by the Inca kings who alone were allowed to wear cloth made from its wool. Since the arrival of the Spanish, however, the animal has been heavily exploited for its valuable wool, which is considered the finest in the world. By 1970 vicuña numbers had dwindled to only a few thousand. But since then, reserves have been established to protect the species in Peru and Bolivia, and conservation measures have produced a slow increase in numbers.

7

7 The orang-utan is endangered by the demands both of zoos and of individuals who consider it a status-symbol pet. Conservation authorities in Borneo and Sumatra (the only places where it is found) now confiscate any animals illegally owned and send them to centers like this one in Sumatra, where they are retrained for life in the wild before being released.

8 Osprey *Pandion haliaetus*

8 Ospreys are now protected by such means as a 24-hour watch maintained on their nesting tree during the breeding season. They are one of the examples of protected birds of prey. Such birds used to be persecuted as a result of a widespread, but erroneous, view that they are pests that kill domestic animals or compete with human hunters for the same prey. In fact, a healthy population of birds of prey is necessary to keep other species in balance.

Zoos and botanic gardens

Whether the animals ever actually went into the Ark two by two is a matter for conjecture. But without doubt mankind has been making collections of living animals for a very long time. The ancient Egyptians, the Chinese, and the Romans all had their court menageries; so too did the kings of England—at the Tower of London—for some 600 years until the nineteenth century. The first zoo existed in Austria in the fifteenth century; others followed, until in 1752 the Emperor Franz I founded the Garden at Schönbrunn outside Vienna, the oldest zoo still in existence. The Madrid Zoo opened in 1775, the Paris Zoo in 1793, and the London Zoo in 1826.

Zoo development

The disadvantage of older zoos is that they were designed more for the convenience of spectators than that of animals [Key]. As a result these once-proud establishments now have to struggle to find the increasingly large sums of money necessary to bring their enclosures up to the more enlightened standards of today [1, 2, 3].

Many German zoos were destroyed during World War II and so had to be completely rebuilt. Fortunately, this process coincided with new developments in zoo design and these zoos are now among the best in the world. A more open kind of zoo is the parklike establishment, typified by the Hamburg Zoo, which was laid out by Karl Hagenbeck in 1907; the Rome Zoo, designed by the same architect; the Zoological Society of London's Whipsnade Park; and the San Diego Wild Animal Park, the world's largest zoo, with more than 1,000 kinds of animals. There is another new kind of zoo, a commercially-motivated development of the park type, whose advantages can best be appreciated by first examining what purposes zoos should serve and if they are justifiable.

While the early zoos existed purely to display exciting or exotic animals for the amusement of their royal owners, today responsible zoologists and zoomen (the two are not necessarily synonymous) generally agree that it is only justifiable to keep animals in captivity for education, conservation, or scientific research. In other words, a zoo should have a serious purpose, with the exhibition of animals purely as "entertainment" or for status very much a subsidiary factor in zoo planning.

Education and research

It is not difficult for a zoo to run a good educational program. Much depends on adequate labeling of the exhibits, but the zoo can also publish and distribute informative guidebooks and organize school lecture tours. Education can often succeed by simply displaying the animals attractively; it is not educational for the public to see decaying food inside dirty cages.

The contribution made by zoos to conservation [5] is more uneven. It is said that zoos can help by breeding rare animals [7] and in due course reintroducing them to the wild; however, there are not many successful examples. The European bison—once reduced to a few captive specimens but now thriving in more or less natural conditions on the Polish–Soviet border—is one. Another is the successful breeding of ne-ne

CONNECTIONS

See also
636 Constructive man
634 Destructive man
628 Endangered mammals
630 Endangered birds
632 Endangered species
1186 Exploration and science 1750–1850
556 How mammals behave
558 How primates behave

1 The modern aviary at the Bronx Zoo manages to combine good architecture with satisfactory surroundings for the animals that live inside. This is proved by the number of birds that regularly breed within its confines. But it is not only impressive to look at from the outside; it is a walk-through aviary that allows visitors to enter the birds' own environment, however briefly. This is an enjoyable—and educational—experience, even for the families who keep birds as pets, and enables thousands of yearly visitors to learn a great deal about the birds' habits.

2 Progressive zoos can create enclosures that provide a more natural life for their animal inhabitants and at the same time give the public a reasonably accurate idea of how the animal would behave in the wild. By constructing a well-planned enclosure [B], a zoo could approximate the surroundings in which a female black African rhinoceros and her young offspring would go through a typical 24-hour activity pattern. In their savanna grasslands, [A], these animals are normally solitary, apart from a close mother-infant relationship [11]. An intrusive adult male will be driven off [9]. A typical day might begin with a drink [1] about 2am. Then the mother and young will follow well-worn paths to areas where they feed on scrubby plants and woody herbs [2, 4], before moving toward shade [5]. From 9am until late afternoon, they rest and sleep [3, 6,], often cooling themselves by wallowing in dust-filled depressions [7]. Their activity increases toward nightfall [8, 10]. Unfortunately for zoo visitors, rhinos are naturally least active during the daytime hours.

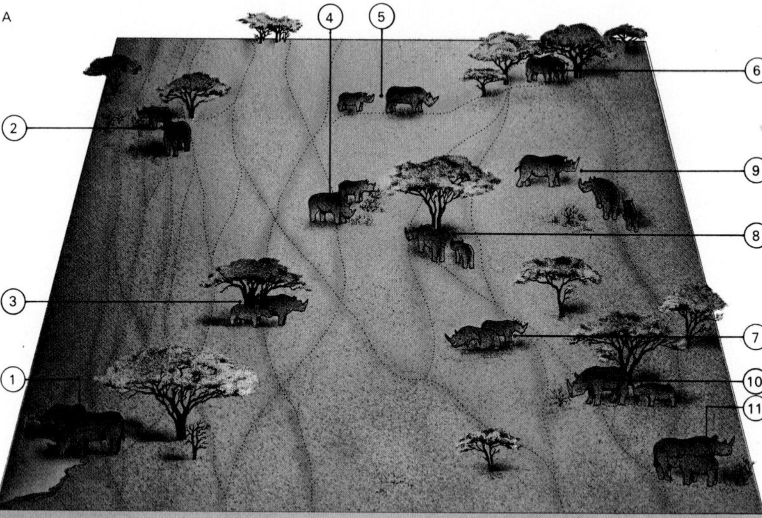

2A
1
2
3
4
5
6
7
8
9
10
11

3 Rhinos need hard ground to walk on (soft, muddy pasture is unnatural to them) and they need dusty wallows to lie in. They also need trees or man-made structures to rest beneath or rub against. Visitors to zoos sometimes get the impression that an animal's enclosure is in some way unsuitable merely because it does not correspond with the kind of surroundings they would like to live in themselves. Good zoos explain each animal's needs.

2B

or Hawaiian geese at the Wildfowl Trust in Gloucestershire, England, and their reintroduction to Hawaii [4].

Many good zoos, like good botanic gardens [8], have substantial programs of scientific research. Often this research tells us more about the behavior of captive animals than about their wild relatives. Nevertheless, this is important if it means that zoo animals will live longer, happier lives than they would otherwise. Some zoos, especially New York's Bronx Zoo, maintain an active program of field research, often with great emphasis given to conservation.

Conventional city zoos are constantly improving their facilities, partly to make them more attractive to visitors [9] but even more with the animals' health and happiness in mind. Some years ago, London Zoo spent £250,000 on a rhino and elephant pavilion that proved unsuitable for the animals inside because insufficient thought was given to their needs. The same mistake would not be made today. A new enclosure for big cats at the same zoo, completed in 1976, is a marvelous example of how to display the optimum number of animals in a confined space so that the needs of both public and animals are served in the best way possible.

Safari parks

One modern zoo development, that looks at first sight to be an excellent one, has some retrograde aspects. It is the mushrooming growth of the drive-through "safari parks." Unfortunately, too many safari parks are owned and run by organizations that are commercially motivated, and education, conservation and even animal husbandry are sometimes secondary to the profit motive. Many keepers are inexperienced and poorly paid and frequently no one is interested or knowledgeable enough to train them. The animals' welfare may be subordinated to the public's enjoyment and the animals become sick.

The good zoo, therefore, will increasingly be supported out of public funds, or be a nonprofit society. It will concentrate on education and will specialize in small groups of animals.

KEY

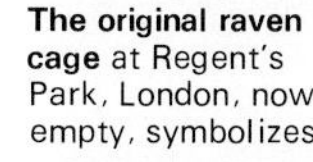

The original raven cage at Regent's Park, London, now empty, symbolizes the historical zoo concept—that of a menagerie where it was more important to create an interesting enclosure than to consider the creature inside.

4 Ne-ne *Branta sandvicensis*

4 The ne-ne, or Hawaiian goose, illustrates how zoos can play a part in conserving wild creatures. This bird was declining in its native Hawaii and was in danger of becoming extinct when some were sent to Britain. There, with great expertise, they were bred in captivity until some could be sent back to their native habitat. Hundreds have been reintroduced in this way.

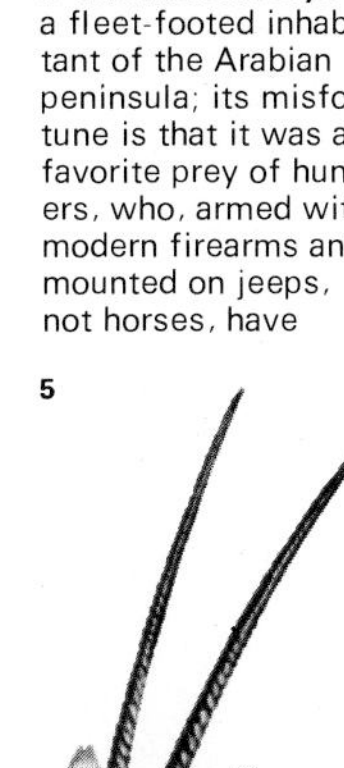

5 The Arabian oryx is a fleet-footed inhabitant of the Arabian peninsula; its misfortune is that it was a favorite prey of hunters, who, armed with modern firearms and mounted on jeeps, not horses, have probably exterminated the animal in the wild. Luckily, a few were saved in time and now there exist flourishing captive herds at two zoos in the United States; the first was in Phoenix, Arizona.

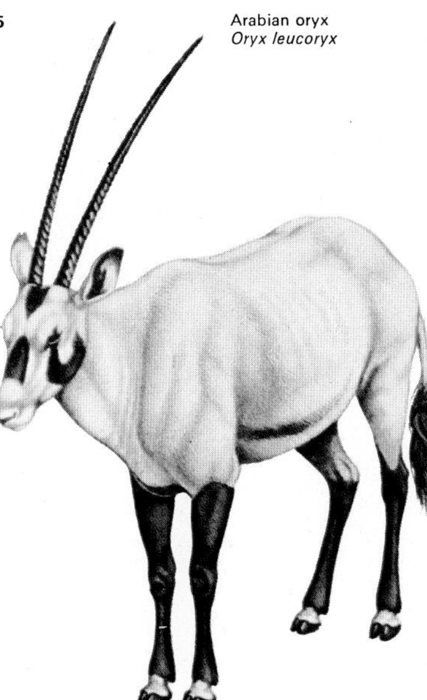

5 Arabian oryx *Oryx leucoryx*

6 **6 A lone gorilla** or other animal was once a common sight in zoos that felt they had to have a "representative" collection with many different animals. Not only were they without the knowledge needed to cope with thousands of species but they also tended to collect solitary individual beasts. Now it is considered better to have breeding pairs and family groups of fewer species.

7 **7 Breeding** is usually regarded as the yardstick for judging a zoo—on the reasonable assumption that an animal is unlikely to breed if it is not happy. But some animals defy their keepers' best efforts. Cheetahs, for example, never used to breed in zoos. In several zoos the problem has now been solved. Part of the solution requires the separation of the males and females until the time is ripe for them to mate.

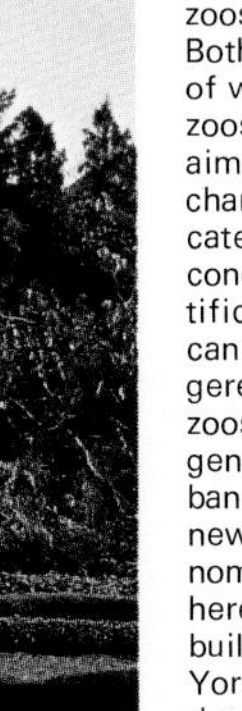

8 **8 Botanic gardens** are for plants what zoos are for animals. Both are collections of wild species. Like zoos, botanic gardens aim to breed their charges and to educate visitors. They conduct much scientific research and can cultivate endangered species. Like zoos, they can act as gene banks (or seed banks) to produce new varieties of economic plants. Shown here is the main building of the New York Botanical Garden. The gardens cover 230 acres.

9 **9 Young polar bears** are potent crowdpullers. However richly-endowed zoos may be, nearly all depend largely on income from the public. Many zoos have found that attendance increases dramatically when they have a notable animal birth. It is a happy coincidence that baby polar bears are so popular, for their species is endangered. If a zoo can breed them successfully, it can fulfill serious aims and benefit financially as well.

MAN

MAN

by Professor Loren Eiseley

In desert places, when heat currents disturb the air, one can occasionally see "dust devils," little whirlwinds which may start rotating at some particular spot. They pick up impetus, tower into several feet of spinning sand, leaves, and dust, and go hesitantly marching across the landscape. Sometimes they quickly die out, but, rarely, they assume gigantic proportions and go roaring with a dreadful purposefulness into the settled lands. Man, who like everything in the material universe is composed of spinning electrons, has about him some of the same deceptive qualities.

The biped whose ancestry can be tracked across whole geological eras into a creature no larger than a diminutive rat, and whose intellectual powers only began to be strikingly prophetic during the last Ice Age, scarcely deserves the generic title he has given to himself, *Homo sapiens,* Man the wise. It is true he has learned to solve problems, but he creates them in an almost geometric proportion. Unlike the other animals of the planet, he occupies no particular foreordained environment. From the time he acquired speech, he became subject to the whims and vagaries of thought. His true environment is worldwide; with the tool of speech he has cut his way into a new invisible niche, the domain of thought; but thoughts, as we know, are not always rational. They give rise to fanatic, destructive ideologies, the cyclonic element always lurking in man. Particularly in his advanced stages, man occupies not a stable ecological zone but history, and history is, to put it briefly, the ephemeral land of the dust devils. Even as history it does not stay fixed. It is constantly reinterpreted in the light of the present, which itself is destined to become history.

Benjamin Franklin Professor of Anthropology and the History of Science, University of Pennsylvania; Curator of Early Man, University of Pennsylvania Museum; Fellow of the American Academy of Arts and Sciences; Fellow of the American Philosophical Society; Fellow of the National Institute of Arts and Letters; Fellow of the American Anthropological Association; Council Member of the National Parks Advisory Board; Recipient of Bradford Washburn Gold Medal (Boston Museum of Science), Joseph Wood Krutch Medal (US Humane Society), Lecomte du Noüy Award, John Burroughs Medal, National Phi Beta Kappa Science Award; author of *The Immense Journey; Darwin's Century; The Firmament of Time; The Unexpected Universe; The Invisible Pyramid; The Man Who Saw Through Time,* etc.

Man has been called the time-binder, because with the tool of words he binds the generations together. He is the only animal on Earth who knows and is able to communicate intellectually that there have been generations before him and will be after him. Furthermore, he can similarly transmit into the far future, by means of writing, knowledge of the thought and inventions of the past. In this respect he is the most burdened animal alive, and this fact has occasioned vast neurological adjustments in his infancy. Just how, or in what specific branch of the human evolutionary family collectively known as the *Hominidae* these adjustments first began to be made, is unknown, but without them man could not be the creature he is. His surviving relatives, the great apes—the gorillas, for example—are born with an average cranial capacity of some 280 cubic centimeters. After birth the gorilla brain grows at an average pace until, at the age of about 14 years, this giant beast will possess a brain ranging around 470 cubic centimeters.

At birth the human cranial capacity is only slightly larger than the gorilla's, averaging around 330 cc. The reason lies in the fact that the human infant, like the gorilla, has to enter the world through a birth canal of limited dimensions. Nature has prepared for this event in the case of man in a curious way. Unlike that of the gorilla, the brain of the human child grows with a prodigious spurt in the second year of life, its capacity shooting upward to almost 1,200 cc and going on to reach 1,375 cc by its fourteenth year. This is a very remarkable alteration in brain growth. It means that the human brain, the time-binder, the speech-user, is born in an extremely larval and immature condition that is rapidly rectified by an almost explosive rate of growth after birth.

This is why, in comparison with other animals, the human offspring seems so dependent upon parental care. Its body is engaged in enlarging *after birth* the brain that will have to master speech and the social world about it—to take on, in short, the transmitted social habits and learning of the human world into which it is born and of which it will be expected to be a part. Nature has somehow provided in the course of evolution that this exponential growth of the child's brain after birth will evade the trap of the narrow birth canal and still create a fully functioning human being. The start of the process lies lost in the mists of prehistory, perhaps more than three million years ago. Man likes to boast of his conscious achievements, but his brain and his most important invisible tool, speech, are the gifts of that mysterious nature that has never ceased to intrigue his capacity for discovery.

Homo sapiens is the last of his kind left upon Earth. In his case no living fossils, no ancestral types survive to tell us about his earlier behavior. What we learn must be from fossil remnants of bone, or from the behavior of living primitive societies of our kind that in a few places around the world, notably Australia, have drifted on in a kind of autumnal twilight. At best such people are racially distinct from ourselves but in no way represent the very first men. They speak languages as adequate for their purposes as our own; they can acquire and use our cultural appurtenances. Their "deficiencies," as western man would regard their uncivilized state, seem to be the product of long isolation or environmental vicissitudes such as those experienced by the Eskimos. One would not expect the latter to be practicing agriculture in the Arctic, but in their own way they are a mechanically gifted people. Many such isolates have achieved a balance with nature that would be the envy of a modern environmentalist struggling with pollution.

Nonliterate societies, which at one time embraced all of humanity—writing being then unknown—are historically shallow. The people are still time-binders in that the institutional structures and corpus of beliefs that make up the society can be passed verbally from one generation to another, but it is a propensity of the human mind to clothe what it learns orally in myth and legend after the passage of a few generations. Without the assistance of the written word, the place from which the people originally came may be lost or once-living men may be transformed into deities so that plain everyday events become entwined with the supernatural. Similarly, food plants, and the whole of the domestic world, including fire, may be ascribed to the beneficence of individual gods. This attitude may promote extreme conservatism on any matters involving cultural change.

Writing has come late in man's history and equates to a considerable degree with the rise of organized states and at least an incipient urban world. To review the entire history of this invention, which literally gave man a social brain, would demand a book. Only a brief digression is possible. If one draws on the map a triangle with the island of Crete as its apex and the eastern Mediterranean shores (including the valley of the Euphrates and the Nile) as its base, one may assert that within the area of this triangle originated most of the great hieroglyphic systems of the world and, what is more important, the alphabetic system that is used, with variations, throughout most of the present civilized world. Curiously enough, Europe played no part in these original developments.

There is a marked though not total distinction between hieroglyphic systems and the development of the phonetic alphabet mostly in use today. Hieroglyphics preceded the origin and spread of the alphabet and are so involved and complicated that they gave rise to special craftsmen, the scribes. Mastering writing by the hieroglyphic system demands the mnemonic utilization of hundreds of involved characters standing for *ideas,* not just a vowel or a consonant, as in the case of the alphabet. Beginning as simple ideograms, or pictures of objects, hieroglyphics were elaborated with the centuries and became very ornate and complex. Some of these systems are still being discovered and not all can be read, although enormous effort has gone into their decipherment. Abstract and complicated thought could be represented, but the inscriptions, for all the artistic skill expended upon them, were a far more cumbersome method of communication than the alphabet, which some unknown genius drew out of the long experimentation upon hieroglyphs.

Hieroglyphic writing arose in the Near East after 3400 BC. It was impressed upon wet clay with a writing instrument called a stylus. The fortunate chance that the writing was imprinted upon such imperishable material as baked clay tablets has enabled researchers in the last century to unravel many aspects of Mesopotamian history. Egyptian hieroglyphs are probably at least as ancient in their origin as the tablets of Sumer, but along the Nile the most perishable papyrus reed paper upon which the Egyptians wrote has left us less common everyday documentation than is true of the Mesopotamian region. The art style between the two regions is different, and the two systems apparently arose in considerable if not complete isolation from each other, as is evinced by the different materials utilized.

Hieroglyphic systems seem to have emerged and culminated where trade and taxation had taken on growing importance—in other words, where both the state and the trader found a need for precise records of objects and the keeping of accounts. The eastern Mediterranean lying within the triangle we have already mentioned had early witnessed the growth of coastal travel, and farther inland many of the rising cities lay across caravan routes; thus there was an early atmosphere conducive to the invention of writing. Moreover, as hieroglyphics grew complicated, monumental, and more abstract, it became apparent that within the systems there were partial and limited attempts to utilize characters that had direct phonetic implications. Finally, somewhere in the neighborhood of 1800 BC a Semitic coastal people, probably Phoenician, developed a genuine phonetic alphabet. The superiority of the alphabet lies in its simplicity. A limited number of characters (in our own case, 26) is utilized to reproduce all the sounds in a given language. Thus words could be written directly, and elaborate abstractions could be uttered as one read. The way lay open for total literacy. The Phoenicians carried their alphabet to Greece and other trading centers of the Mediterranean world. Different peoples have modified the letters to fit the tongue they spoke, although the invention came but once. All alphabets including our own run back to this single source.

Man had infinitely simplified communication through space and time. Great libraries would arise, dictionaries be simplified and expanded. The social brain that retained the memory of the past would grow beyond the power of any barbarian to destroy it. Printing at last would multiply its products. The priestly monopoly of writing would disappear. Thousands of years went into the development of writing and its culmination in the rise and spread of the phonetic alphabet. Only this now seemingly simple improvement makes it possible to write the word *man* in an encyclopedia and dwell succinctly upon some of his characteristics. He *is* a time-binder; speech and writing have made him so. Speech was a biological gift to man. Writing—his own invention—he devised out of his neurologically expanded brain.

We have previously indicated that man has one great gift or failing, depending upon how he has used it—that, whereas animals are generally confined or adapted to a specific environment, the human species roving in the invisible domain of thought can alter the way it lives. We have already seen that man was once totally illiterate and with much superstition and illusion could pass on his traditions only by word of mouth. Similarly, down to a few thousand years ago, although he had expanded through all the great continents man was solely a hunter and collector of wild plants and vegetables. He had domesticated nothing; he had to seek his living in the open. Because he had invented tools to help him in this process we might call him a successful hunter and fisher, but there we would have to stop.

The meaning of this long pause upon a flat prehistoric plateau is very clear: man did not yet possess the crafts nor the necessary human energy that would enable him to support a large population in any one place. His numbers were growing—his slow driftage over every continent but uninhabitable Antarctica reveals this fact—but his spread was like that of a thin fire over meadow grass. If he tarried too long in a game-filled region, his numbers grew and the game, in turn, decreased. It took many square miles and constant travel to support a small band of 50 to 100 persons of both sexes. So long as this condition obtained, what we call civilization was impossible of achievement. All man's movement was outward, centrifugal. Civilization, by contrast, is centripetal, inward-drawing, city-building. It demands specialization of labor which the hunter cannot afford. Food must exist in sufficient excess to support craftsmen, not simply hunters. In some parts of the world men have lived as hunters and gatherers down into modern times; always they have lived as simple bands of a few score or hundreds. Never have they raised cities.

To break out of this mode of living one basic aspect of man's life had to be altered: the world of the hunter had to give way to the domestication of animals and plants, more particularly the cereal grains such as wheat, which are dry and storable. Once this crucial transformation had been effected, energy would be available for other developments. The ability to utilize surplus meant a rise in human numbers and the division of labor in a variety of directions. Social classes, the rulers and the ruled, were bound to appear along with the bureaucratic state. Man's powers were growing, but with them would vanish the simple democracy of the hunting societies. The god-king, as in Egypt, would appear, and armed professional soldiery would make its appearance.

Slowly the archeologist is pushing back the time of the first small urban concentrations to perhaps 6000 BC in the Near East. Historically speaking, man has been an urban dweller, considering his age, for only a short time. His shift in habits seems to coincide, in some degree, with the final disappearance of the northern ice sheet and the growing desiccation of North Africa and the Middle East. Before the rise of cities and great irrigation works along the Tigris-Euphrates and the Nile, there is evidence of simple people harvesting wild or perhaps already semidomesticated grain with sickles inset with flint blades. As the game herds streamed away with the dying glaciers people were making more use of, and paying more attention to, the plant life about them. Similarly, the acquisition of excess grain made it possible to support the first domesticated cattle.

Nor must fire be neglected. It had been used and carried by the hunters for many thousand years. It had enabled an originally tropical animal to spread far northward. It softened and made more palatable the diet of raw flesh. The warm hearth at the cave mouth strengthened the ties between the early human groupings. Now with the agricultural revolution it aided in the digestion of hard grains. Slowly it improved the cuisine. It did more. In the development of pottery, the kiln was invented and the ground laid for the metallurgy that would follow. Fire was man's first great energy source beyond his own body. Hidden within it, undiscovered, lay the steam power of the industrial revolution.

With the first city-states came the urge for empire: flames rose, walls were battered in, people were enslaved or massacred, old cities were obliterated by the new. The clash of hunters had been brief at best, the people few, food scarce, nothing much in the way of wealth to be coveted, but now the military arts had become professional. The agricultural empires were arising, dominated by men capable of wringing wealth from trade and the massive extension of irrigation. Sails were to be seen in coastal waters and on great rivers such as the Nile. Man had discovered another source of energy—the wind.

Two sides of man's nature were becoming more manifest. On the one side, rapacity, greed, and indifference to human suffering; on the other, a certain tolerance induced by great territorial extensions that brought diverse peoples and customs into contact. The god of the city-state had, perforce, to extend his powers or vanish. During what has been called the time of the axial religions, beginning some 2,000 years ago in Asia, man's thinking grew more concerned with universal values, with ethics, with man's relation to man. In Buddhism, to use just one example, we find a disdain of worldly power, and later Christ speaks across the barrier of peoples when he says, "Other sheep I have which are not of this fold." Long before the dawn of modern science there were those who, in millions, followed simple wayfaring saviors, and there were others, as today, in whom savagery predominated.

The sun-seed empires, which are all postglacial in origin whether in farther Asia, with rice the dominant grain, or in the New World, where maize was domesticated, are all notable for monumental building and beautiful ceramics. Science as we understand it did not exist in that world. Essentially it was a craftsman's world, yet it gave birth early to mathematics and to star-watching. Much of this builder's knowledge was traditional and seemingly passed on orally. Civilizations, even our own, are old and yet paradoxically young as we survey the swinging pendulum of the great ice clock. Man has built his cities and states only in the ten-thousand-year interval since the last ice withdrew. Always before he had simply drifted with the seasons. Now at last he was an organic inventor, an experimenter with plants and animals. Food had given him inventive leisure.

There is one spot of bright sunlight particularly discernible across the millennia—classical Greece. From the 6th to the 3rd centuries BC men speculated about the universe with an openness never quite dared before, even after Rome had swept Greece under its sway. In the long stumbling decline of the great empire whose legacy lay largely in its efficient road system and its aqueducts, little more of a scientific or philosophical nature was achieved. Only by devious and roundabout ways through Arab sources did Greek philosophy rearise with the birth of the modern world. Its outlook, its mood, lie at the root of modern experimental science, although like classical civilization in general the urge toward controlled experiment was not present—or certainly not sufficiently to create a tradition. Man was still, on occasion, the victim of famine and disease. The average age at death was low, the masses lived miserably. Man was and remains an inexperienced city dweller. One foot remained in the forest. People in concert were learning to create gigantic structures, but could they be maintained as viable through the centuries, or even millennia, without falling victim at last to some unseen or unguessed disaster?

When the Black Death, the bubonic plague, devastated Europe in the middle of the 14th century, an estimated third of the population was swept away. The tightly controlled medieval order that had grown up since the fall of the Roman Empire began to crumble. The upper classes proved as susceptible to infection as the peasantry. The fields of the manor house lay abandoned. A dearth of labor brought survivors to seek refuge in the towns. For all the misery and loosening of social ties, a new age was about to be born—an age of great voyages and mercantile exchange closely followed by the scientific twilight that was to usher in the modern world.

In the 15th and 16th centuries Portugal took the lead in devising a new ocean-going ship, the caravel, so rigged that it steered better and, with more than one mast, was able satisfactorily to sail upwind. The influence of the Moors and the fragments of Greek geographical learning that had entered Spain and Portugal with them stimulated the oncoming discoveries of the Renaissance. The medieval world had been tightly circumscribed both religiously and geographically. Ideas of progressive change such as were later to spread in the modern world were nonexistent. The afterlife occupied human attention; man's coming here was, practically, but the prelude to his passing hence. There was scant social mobility in the sharply stratified social classes. Traffic was coastal, and there was little desire to reach beyond the borders of the known world.

The Renaissance ushered in the modern world. To explore its origins would be an intricate task, but printing, a revival of interest in the lost world of antiquity, the introduction of the mariner's compass, and, as we have seen, the social and psychological effects of the Black Death all played their role. The little caravel pressed on to round the Cape of Good Hope and find its way into the mysterious and spice-laden East. Magellan's ship *Victoria* circumnavigated the globe (1519–1522), although her commander perished in the Philippines. Columbus, of course, had previously made his somewhat blundering discovery of America under the mistaken assumption that he had reached the Far East. The world was being opened up geographically as it was shortly to be scientifically. In fact, the changes are intertwined, but of the Renaissance it has been succinctly said that it was "the discovery by man of himself and of the world."

Throughout this period of rapid change in Europe, China, one of the oldest and most cultivated of the sun-seed empires, remained secure and incurious in what it regarded as the middle of a world surrounded by barbarians. The Chinese had never evinced geographical curiosity, convinced as they were that nothing could be learned from inferior peoples. In Central and South America other civilizations had arisen successively in tremendous isolation with their own domestic plants and hieroglyphics. In other parts of the world men either slept under the massive weight of previous great cultures gone downhill, as in Egypt, or led what was largely the life of our Ice Age forebears.

From the 15th century onward, however, Europe is to be characterized by just one word, *inquiry*. All was at stake: man, his works, his world, the stars beyond him. The curiosity of the Greeks, so long buried, was being unearthed again, but this time not in speculation alone but by experiment. In the words of one great spokesman of science, Sir Francis Bacon, "we are not to imagine or suppose but to *discover* what nature is or may be made to do." Experiment properly conducted may enable us in some degree to draw novelty out of nature as the sun-seed empires had unconsciously done long ago when they domesticated and improved upon the plant and animal worlds about them. Now, however, the dawning science of the 16th and 17th centuries was establishing societies and journals to transmit deliberately the results of experiment. Men were beginning to leave their tracks upon nature, the wildest, the most unknown continent of all. As a result, time would expand into vast eras unrecognizable to the theologian; and finally—later on in the 20th century—man, by reason of this same science, would see his numbers mount dangerously and fearful weaponry range overhead. He would gaze far back down his evolutionary pathway and perceive his first ancestry in a tiny insectivore.

As no civilization in history had quite grasped previously, it was now possible through the efforts of the archeologist to realize that civilizations might die like individual organisms struck by some insidious disease or, on the other hand, to achieve great works and then sink into passive somnolence for long millennia unless something stirred them from without. To us of this age science has been the catalyzer bringing impressive gifts, but it has been at the same time subject to man's own blindness and ferocity. After the devastation wreaked scientifically in the wars of this century it is evident that the first happy pride in scientific progress is marked by an equal fear that the equivalent of the Black Death may still linger among us, nurtured by the nature of man and the science he has evoked out of that nature.

So short is the history of urban civilization that we are forced to say we do not know the lengths to which it may be carried. We have stirred the whole many-faceted world into a knowledge of itself and the potentialities of science, yet the first demand has been for weapons and more weapons. The growth of the great urban centers demands an ever-growing bureaucracy to manage them. At what point, one is forced to ask, do these creations become fiscally and humanly unmanageable? At what point does confusion destroy order in the affairs of state? In the 3rd century the Old Mayan Empire arose in the jungles of Central America under a priesthood of mathematical diviners. It prospered and grew in wealth and power for six long centuries, longer than the United States has yet existed. By the 9th century the ceremonial centers lay in ruins. There is no evidence of outside conquest; the Spaniards had not yet come. It is as though the Old Empire had died as quietly as a flower closing, as though its peasantry, growing weary of astronomical divination, had slipped away in the night. There lie the pyramids and carefully dated stelae, but the corpus of belief, the gods, the priests, the remarkably able craftsmen are all gone. The hieroglyphs cannot be read, though the number system can.

No one civilization can represent man any more than one man can be said to represent the whole of humankind. But when experimental science was conceived—"the invention of inventions"—it tied man to man everywhere. There could no longer be a hidden enclave where the seeds of some solitary creation could grow without influence from others. Now all is at stake everywhere, and the human world is knotted together in one great electronic nerve net. Is it for the best? No man can answer. The poet Xenophanes at the end of the 6th century BC wrote: "The gods did not reveal to men all things in the beginning, but in course of time, by searching, they find out better."

The words of Xenophanes were blotted from existence for many centuries, but they survive. Perhaps they carry to us some hidden meaning. Man is a creature of hope. It is part of his better nature. Today we can add no more to Xenophanes' words, though they were written 2,400 years ago. Man and his world are at stake. They have always been since history was entered and the first marks scrawled on clay. We are the last human species left on Earth. When we go, there will be no others. It is well to read the words of Xenophanes again. It just may be he saw a little further than we do. The Greeks had a way of being first.

Primate to hominid

We know that 75 million years ago there were primates in what is now Montana. The primate order is the first or highest order of mammals and includes prosimians (lower primates), monkeys, apes, and man-apes, as well as humans, and thus knowing its earliest appearance is important in tracing human evolution. All primates tend to have relatively large brains, forelimbs with nails and some sort of opposable thumb for grasping [2, 3, 4], and eyes that are set forward in the head, often protected by a bony ridge. In addition, certain evolutionary trends characterize the primate order. These include the tendency to enlargement and complexity in the brain, which involves greater emphasis on visual perception and reduction of reliance on the sense of smell [1, E–H]; the emerging shape of the lower jaw [1, I–L]; and the changing structure of the lower limbs as the species adapts to walking upright on two legs [1, M–P; and 5].

The first primates

Prosimians were the only primates on Earth through the Eocene period, about 55 million years ago. Some Eocene primates were adapted to life in trees, and the grasping action needed for climbing is reflected in their limb structure: thumb and big toe are turned in to face the other digits, claws are replaced by nails, and sensitive touch pads are developed on the ends of the digits [2].

Toward the end of the Eocene period the fossil record shows a great reduction in the number and variety of prosimians. The survivors lingered on in a few isolated places such as Madagascar, Sri Lanka, and Southeast Asia and became nocturnal to avoid daytime predators and competitors.

Old and New World monkeys

In the Oligocene period (38 million to 26 million years ago) primitive monkeys and very primitive apes seem to have developed. New World monkeys, sometimes called platyrrhines (because their noses are flat and broad with nostrils set wide apart), do not seem to have played any part in the evolution of humans. That development probably took place on the European-African-Asian land mass, and Old World monkeys (catarrhines, with nostrils closer together) played a part in it, if only by providing the foundation for the ape forms that may have been ancestors of humans.

Examples of the suborder of primates called Anthropoidea have been found in an extremely rich Oligocene deposit at Fayum in Egypt, which may contain ancestors of African monkeys, *Oreopithecus* (see below), gibbons, great apes, and even humans. Fossil finds from many areas suggest that once monkeys, who now live mainly in the tropics, were more widespread.

Evolution of the ape

The superfamily Hominoidea includes apes, ape-men, and humans. The apes are divided into lesser and great families: the Hylobatidea (which includes gibbons) and the Pongidea (including orangutans, gorillas, and chimpanzees). Of these the great apes are considered closest to humans. Their brains are not only better developed than those of monkeys and prosimians, but they also show the same basic pattern of convolutions as human brains; many fea-

CONNECTIONS

See also
648 The first hominids
650 The first men
652 From ancient to modern man
554 Primates: relatives of man
576 The age of mammals
574 Mammals of the past
540 The classification of mammals
458 The animal kingdom
406 Life and its origins
408 Evolution of life
410 The world before man
418 Evolution: classical theories
420 Evolution in action

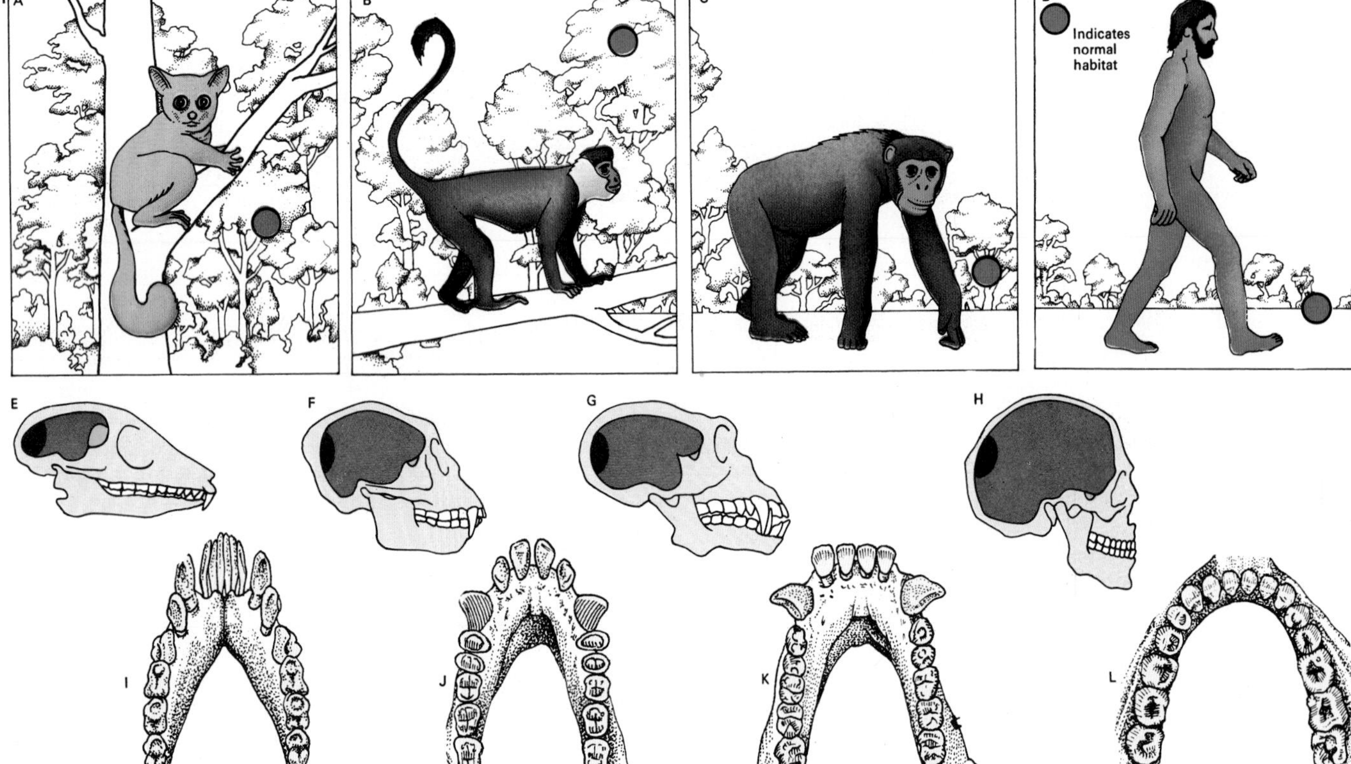

1
A
B
C
D
Indicates normal habitat
E
F
G
H
I
J
K
L

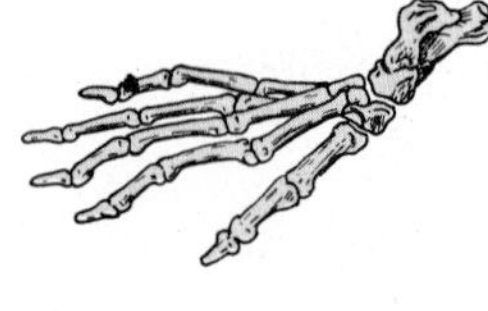
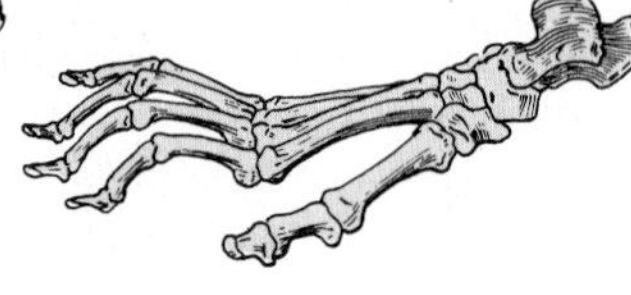
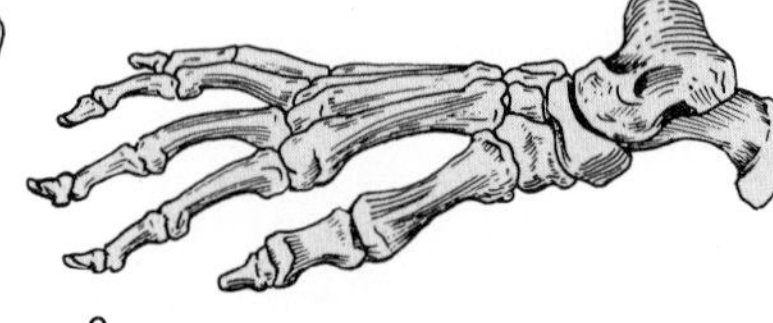
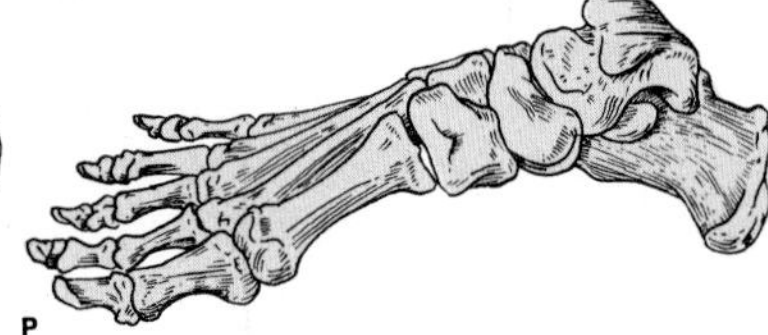

M
N
O
P

1 The primates have evolved through many stages, from the bush baby *(Galago)* [A], guenon *(Cercopithecus)* [B], and Chimpanzee *(Pan)* [C] to man *(Homo)* [D]. This gradual evolution has involved changes to many parts of the body. The skulls [E, F, G, H] of the animals, for instance, show the gradual shortening of the snout and reduction in the size of the teeth, (especially the canines) and jaws. Brain size increases, and the change in the relative importance of the olfactory centers [blue] and the visual centers [black] is noticeable. The shortening of the snout and changes in the arrangement of the teeth [I, J, K, L] have affected the shape of the chin. The dental arcade has altered from a rectangular to a parabolic shape. Locomotion has progressed from vertical clinging and leaping and walking on all fours in the trees (arboreal quadrupedalism) to swinging (brachiation) that required an upright posture. Eventually, the striding walk of man (bipedalism) on the ground developed. The latter was probably successful because once man was upright his visual field was much greater and his hands were freed to carry food and to use tools. The feet [M, N, O, P] also changed. In man the ability to grasp with the feet has been lost. The big toe is in line with the others and is large because it takes most of the force of each stride. Man's foot is unique in being sprung on two arches, one running lengthwise along the foot, the other across the foot.

tures of skull and skeleton are humanlike (particularly those traits related to the erect posture many apes can assume); it may be hard to determine whether a single fossil tooth belongs to an ape or a human.

The earliest known ape fossils come from Fayum. They include *Aegyptopithecus*, the likeliest candidate for ancestor of modern great apes. *Aegyptopithecus* may have been a small animal with a tail. It certainly had a long snout and well-developed teeth.

Few fossil prosimians, monkeys, or apes have left living descendants. Most became extinct. Two of the extinct ape lines are *Oreopithecus* and *Gigantopithecus*. *Oreopithecus* has been dated as early as 14 million years ago; however the best preserved skeletons of this gibbonlike form were found in the brown coal of the Pliocene age (*c.* 7 million years ago). It had long arms and was about the size of a chimpanzee. Although once thought to be a "missing link," recent opinion is that *Oreopithecus* is not on the line between apes and men. The same can be said for *Gigantopithecus*, which some people like to believe survives as the "abominable snowman" of the Himalayas. The oldest remains of *Gigantopithecus* date 6–9 million years ago. It may have been 9ft (3m) tall and weighed 660lb (300kg) [6].

It is among the remarkable fossil apes of the earlier Miocene era (*c.*26–45 million years ago) that we encounter something that looks like a strong contender for a form ancestral to both modern apes and modern humans. The subfamily Dryopithecinae, the great apes of this period, look primitive and nonspecialized in comparison with modern types, and for that reason some genus of the dryopithecines may be the ancestral stock from which the superfamily of Hominoidea later developed. The remains of *Ramapithecus*, a small apelike creature that may be the earliest true human, have been dated from the Miocene and Pliocene eras; but we still have not been able to figure out precisely when the family of Hominidae (ape-men and humans) separated out of the superfamily Hominoidae to form an independent line of evolution [Key].

KEY

10,000 Years ago
30,000
50,000
70,000
100,000
500,000
1 my
Modern man
Cro-Magnon man
Rhodesia man
Solo man
Neanderthal man
Homo sapiens
Homo erectus
Australopithecus
Ramapithecus
Dryopithecines
Gibbon
Orang-utan
Chimpanzee
Gorilla
PLEISTOCENE
PLIOCENE
MIOCENE
OLIGOCENE
EOCENE

An important evolutionary step on the way to man was taken 30 million years ago with the evolution of the apes (present-day forms include orangutan, chimpanzee, and gorilla). The earliest undisputed member of the group is *Aegyptopithecus*, first discovered in 1964. This is probably one of the early apes called dryopithecines and is ancestral to the hominid line. The first dryopithecine was found in France in 1856, but specimens have also been found in Africa and Asia. Some of the African dryopithecines are believed to be ancestors of the chimpanzee and gorilla, while the Asian finds are regarded as early forms of orangutan and gibbon.

2 Primates evolved from a stock that resembles present-day tree shrews. The hand shown is intermediate between a simple five-digit hand and that of a typical primate. It shows the beginning of a specialized thumb although this does not function very differently from the other four fingers. Sensitive finger bulbs are beginning to develop underneath the animal's long claws.

2

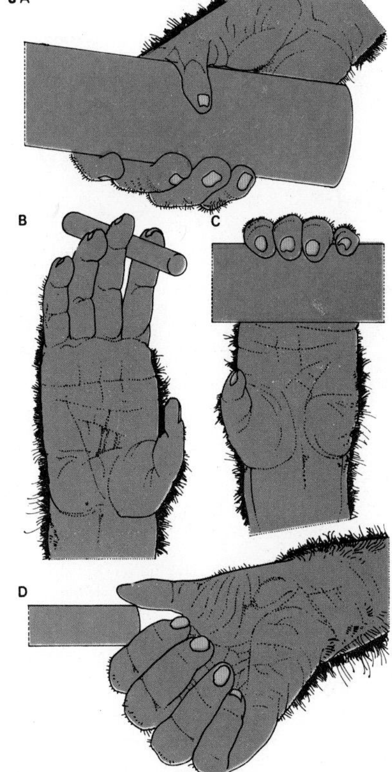

3 A B C D

3 The ape's hand has nails instead of claws and fingertips that are delicate instruments of touch. Although the hand resembles a human's, it cannot perform delicate operations. The power grip [A] is similar to that of man. The ape's equivalent of more precise gripping is shown [B, D]. Compare with the human grips [4A, B, C]. Tree-swinging apes use a hook grip [C] that humans cannot manage.

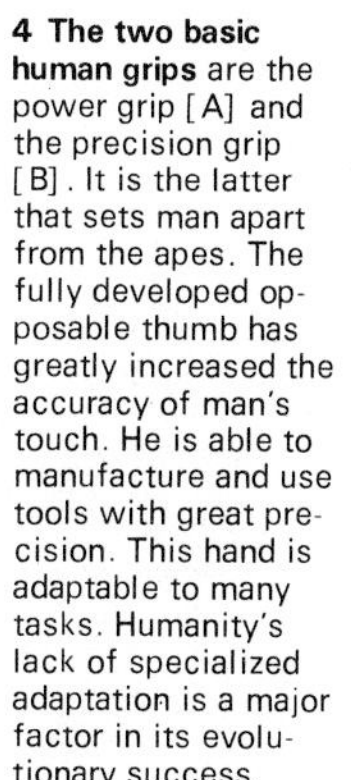

4 The two basic human grips are the power grip [A] and the precision grip [B]. It is the latter that sets man apart from the apes. The fully developed opposable thumb has greatly increased the accuracy of man's touch. He is able to manufacture and use tools with great precision. This hand is adaptable to many tasks. Humanity's lack of specialized adaptation is a major factor in its evolutionary success.

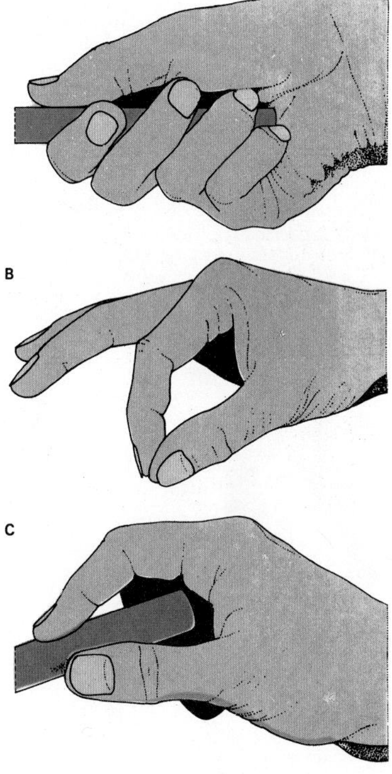

4 A B C

5

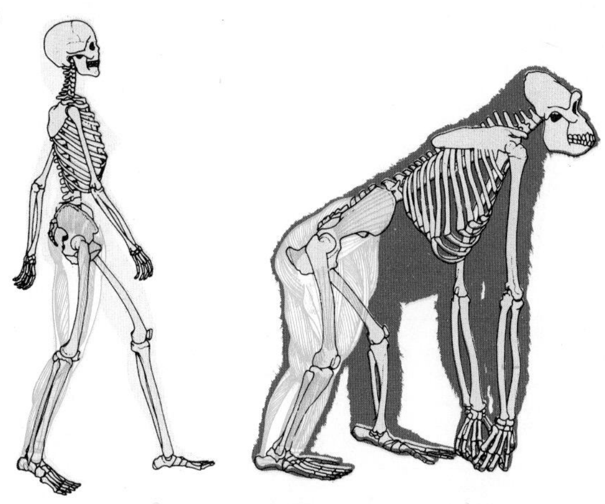

5 The long pelvis of the gorilla is necessary to accommodate the special muscles needed for quadrupedal walking. The big toe is able to grasp branches, and the fingers are curved inward for knuckle walking. In man the pelvis is short and adapted to a striding gait. The skull, unlike that of the gorilla, is balanced on top of the spinal column.

6 Reconstructions of *Gigantopithecus, Oreopithecus*, and a dryopithecine.

6

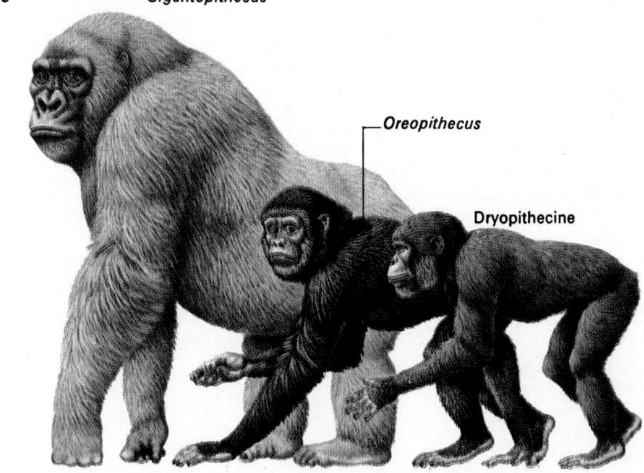

Gigantopithecus
Oreopithecus
Dryopithecine

The first hominids

There is still much doubt about when the first hominid (member of the family Hominidae, which includes ape-men and humans) emerged from ape stock. One possibility is *Ramapithecus*, which lived 12 to 14 million years ago. The fossil evidence is not conclusive (no limb bones have been found, for instance), but these specimens certainly show a mixture of apelike and humanlike traits. Some authorities feel that the human traits dominate, and would place *Ramapithecus* as the first hominid.

Australopithecus

The Australopithecinae, on the other hand, are accepted by all authorities as hominids. These creatures, whether one calls them man-apes or ape-men, are certainly closer to modern man than to the apes. They have certain obviously apelike features: cranial capacities about equal to that of modern great apes and massive projecting jaws. But there are human characteristics in the australopithecines too—in their teeth and their lower bone structure—and close analysis has convinced anthropologists that they are on the line of hominid evolution rather than the line that leads to today's apes.

The first specimen, found in 1924 by Raymond Dart, was named *Australopithecus africanus* (southern-ape of Africa). Other finds were given other names, but the *Australopithecus* name is the one that stuck. It now seems that the various fossil finds—some of which date from as far back as 5 million years ago—can be classed roughly into two groups: the slender, also called "gracile" or "delicate" form *(africanus)* and the robust form, sometimes called *Paranthropus robustus (robustus)*. Various theories have been devised to explain the differences between the two. One says that *africanus* and *robustus* are actually two separate species of the same genus—at least as different from one another as modern humans are from the Neanderthals. Another suggests that the split merely shows racial or even sexual differentiation within the same species—*africanus* being female and *robustus* male. A third idea is that *robustus* represents an evolutionary dead end: the true australopithecine that left no descendants; whereas *africanus* is supposed to have been what led eventually to humans. Finally, some authorities see all *robustus* and some *africanus* australopithecines as a separate species, and only a few selected examples of *africanus* as the forerunners of the subfamily Homininae—humans. Scientists have to come up with explanations that best fit the finds they have made, and in the case of *Australopithecus*, the finds have been so numerous that there is enough evidence to support a number of different explanations of the physical differences in the fossils.

Dating the fossils has also been a matter of some controversy. What seem to be the oldest finds have come from East Africa and Ethiopia. Those from Kenya may be as old as 5 million years, and some specimens from the Omo River have been put at 3 and 4 million years old. The South African sites are later—from the Pleistocene age. Taung and the lowest levels of Sterkfontein are the oldest here, from the late lower Pleistocene. Makapansgat, Swartkrans, and Kromdraai are successively younger—with the last possibly as old as one million years. The

CONNECTIONS

See also
646 Primate to hominid
650 The first men
652 From ancient to modern man
276 Earth's time scale
560 Fossils: the life of the past
562 Plants of the past

1 Australopithecus robustus [A] and *Australopithecus africanus* [B] are hominids, just as is *Homo sapiens* [C]. They are all members of the family Hominidae, which includes ape-men and men. Superfamily Homininae includes humans only.

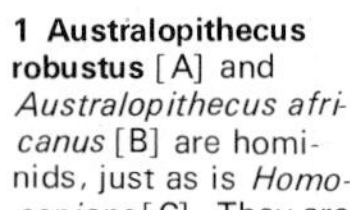

1
A

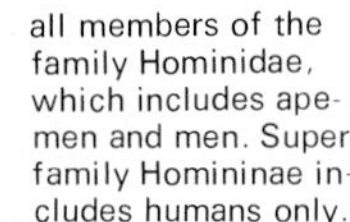

B

C

2 A

B

2 Piltdown man, discovered at Piltdown in Sussex, England, proved to be a fraud. In 1912–13 finds were made by Charles Dawson, Arthur Woodward of the British Museum, and Pierre Teilhard de Chardin. Their explanations of what they found were accepted uncritically because they bore out the popular theory that the enlargement of the braincase occurred before modification of the jaw [A]. Piltdown was said to represent an intermediary stage. It is now believed that the modification of the jaw preceded the enlargement of the braincase [B]. Tests of Piltdown man between 1949 and 1953 revealed a man's skull from about AD 1330 and an orangutan's jaw from AD 1450.

3 The Pleistocene era lasted from about 2,000,000 to 10,000 years ago. During the earlier part of this period the australopithecines roamed Africa. They were gone by the Middle Pleistocene.

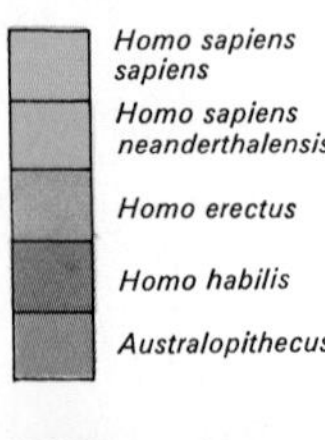

Homo sapiens sapiens
Homo sapiens neanderthalensis
Homo erectus
Homo habilis
Australopithecus

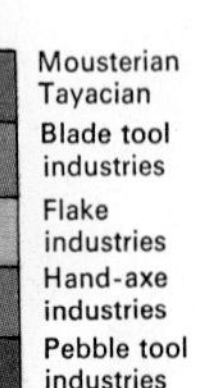

Mousterian Tayacian
Blade tool industries
Flake industries
Hand-axe industries
Pebble tool industries

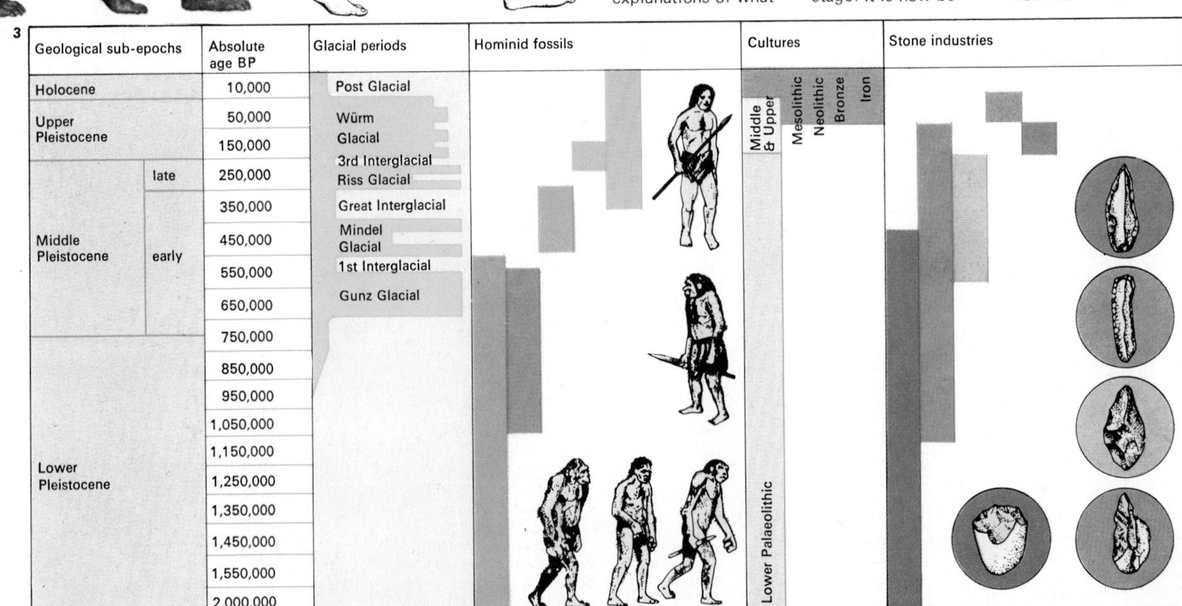

3
Geological sub-epochs
Absolute age BP
Glacial periods
Hominid fossils
Cultures
Stone industries
Holocene
Upper Pleistocene
Middle Pleistocene
late
early
Lower Pleistocene
10,000
50,000
150,000
250,000
350,000
450,000
550,000
650,000
750,000
850,000
950,000
1,050,000
1,150,000
1,250,000
1,350,000
1,450,000
1,550,000
2,000,000
Post Glacial
Würm Glacial
3rd Interglacial
Riss Glacial
Great Interglacial
Mindel Glacial
1st Interglacial
Gunz Glacial
Middle & Upper
Mesolithic
Neolithic
Bronze
Iron
Lower Palaeolithic

finds at Olduvai Gorge in East Africa cover roughly the same time period.

Tool-users

Perhaps the most significant piece of evidence we have about the australopithecines is that they used tools. Stone tools have been found in areas where australopithecines lived and from the times when they lived (although so far none is earlier than 2 million years ago). There is no evidence that any more advanced hominids were in the same areas at the same time. The tools were crudely fashioned of stone, but they represent evidence of a level of cultural development that no apes ever attained. Toolmaking is a peculiarly human accomplishment.

From the tools found we can speculate that the australopithecines were a hunting-and-gathering folk with a technology far in advance of anything else on earth at that time. The life-style pieced together from their remains suggests that they had reached several important landmarks in the development toward *Homo sapiens*. The three most important of these are probably: the switch from forest and tree life to life in the open country and savanna, the beginning of cooperative hunting techniques, and the addition of meat to their diet (other primates are mostly herbivores). All of these opened up new physical, intellectual, and cultural resources that had hitherto been largely unexplored among primates.

Fossils that have features in common with those of Australopithecinae have been found in southern Asia, and some authorities feel that *Meganthropus* from Java is really a representative of *robustus*. The *africanus* form, however, seems never to have left Africa. Early examples of *Homo erectus* may well have existed side-by-side with *Australopithecus robustus* in many parts of the world, but there is no evidence that puts *africanus* and early humans in the same place at the same time. Does this mean that *Australopithecus africanus* is the direct ancestor of the subfamily of Homininae? It could be—but at present we do not have nearly enough evidence to say for sure.

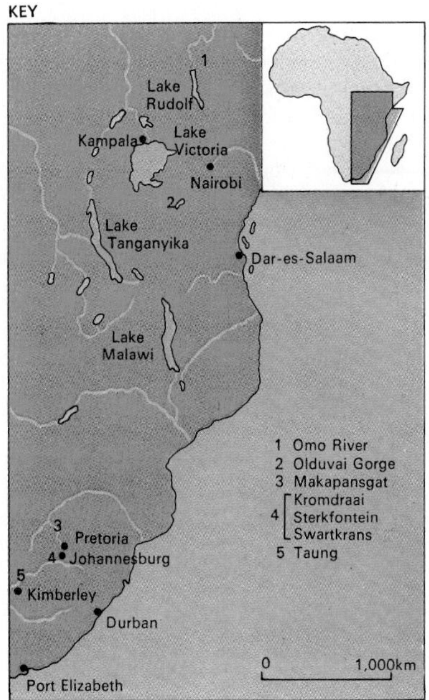

KEY
Lake Rudolf
Kampala
Lake Victoria
Nairobi
Lake Tanganyika
Dar-es-Salaam
Lake Malawi
Pretoria
Johannesburg
Kimberley
Durban
Port Elizabeth
1 Omo River
2 Olduvai Gorge
3 Makapansgat
4 Kromdraai
Sterkfontein
Swartkrans
5 Taung
0 1,000km

The first confirmed australopithecine remains were found in 1924 in the Cape Province. Since then four other sites in South Africa have been unearthed. *Africanus* remains were found at Taung (Cape), Sterkfontein, and Makapansgat (both in the Transvaal), while *robustus* is known from Swartkrans, and Kromdraai (Transvaal). In recent years other important australopithecine discoveries have been made in Tanzania, Kenya, and Ethiopia. The first site to be developed was Olduvai Gorge, which has since yielded a wealth of material. Recent work in the Lake Rudolf area, Kenya, and the Omo River region, Ethiopia, has added to our knowledge.

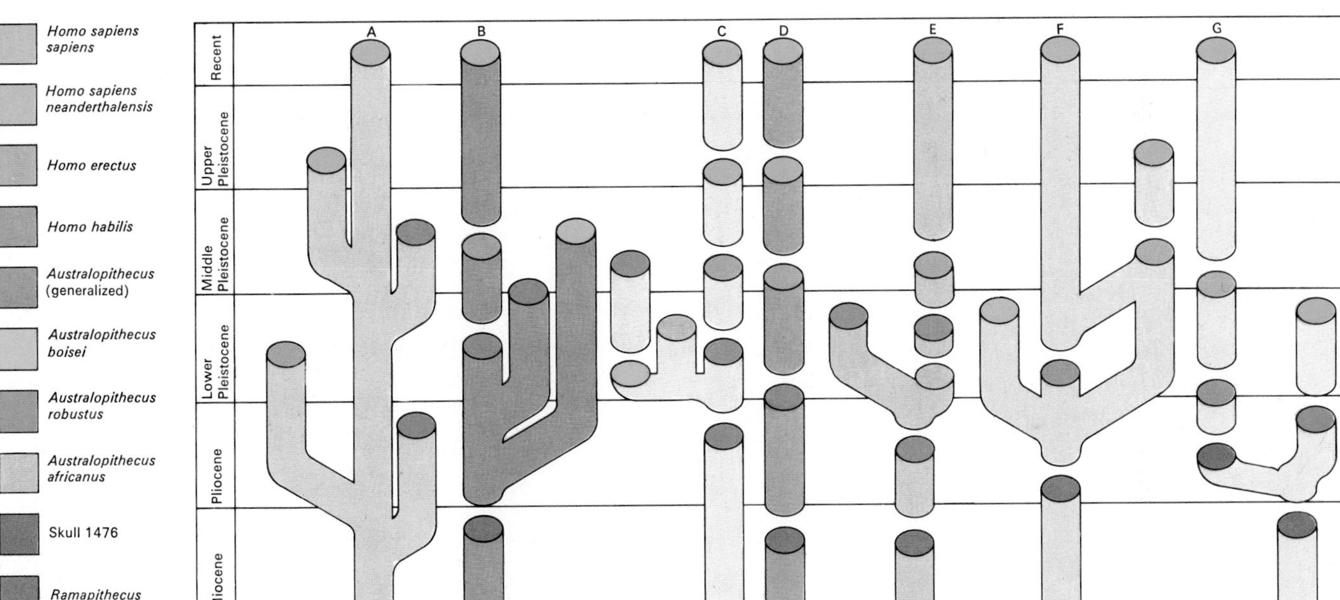

4
Homo sapiens sapiens
Homo sapiens neanderthalensis
Homo erectus
Homo habilis
Australopithecus (generalized)
Australopithecus boisei
Australopithecus robustus
Australopithecus africanus
Skull 1476
Ramapithecus
Recent
Upper Pleistocene
Middle Pleistocene
Lower Pleistocene
Pliocene
Miocene
A
B
C
D
E
F
G

4 Human evolution has been variously interpreted. [A] Le Gros Clark suggests that no known hominid is a direct descendant of any other; [B] John Napier, that *Australopithecus* is two separate offshoots; [C] Philip Tobias, that *Australopithecus* gives rise to the main hominid line; [D] Loring Brace, that each hominid is directly descended from the one before; [E] Desmond Clark, that there are two separate lines of *Australopithecus*; [F] Louis Leakey, that the branches interweave, and that *Homo erectus* is not the forerunner of modern humans; [G] Richard Leakey, that the main stem separated early from *Australopithecus*.

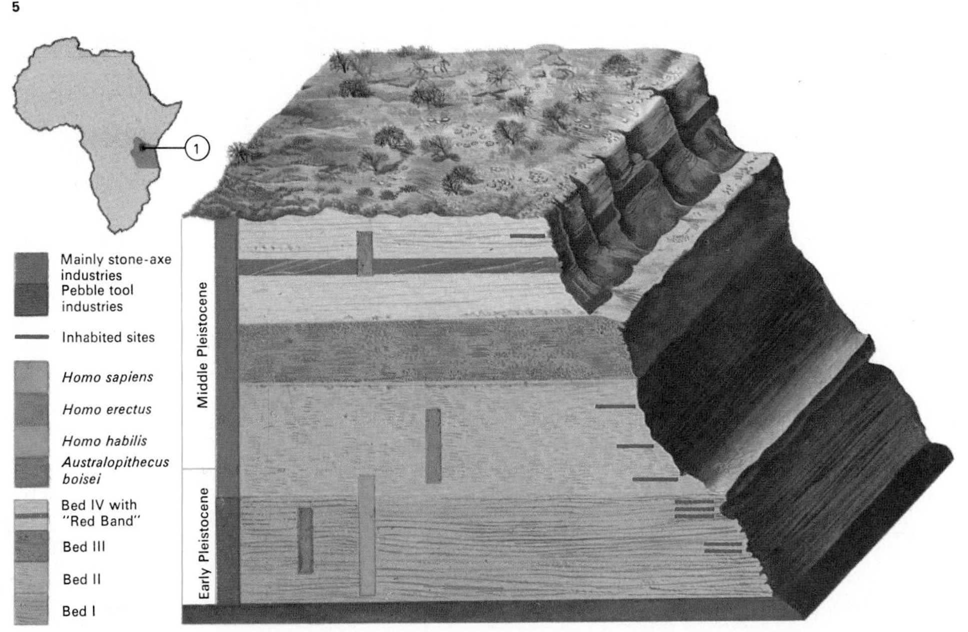

5
1
Mainly stone-axe industries
Pebble tool industries
Inhabited sites
Homo sapiens
Homo erectus
Homo habilis
Australopithecus boisei
Bed IV with "Red Band"
Bed III
Bed II
Bed I
Middle Pleistocene
Early Pleistocene

5 Olduvai Gorge on the Serengeti Plain of Tanzania [1] is 25mi (40km) long and 320ft (100m) deep and is the most famous site in the world for the discovery of the remains of prehistoric humans. The gorge is cut through lake and volcanic sediments. The lake deposits provide an ideal medium for the preservation of fossils, and the volcanic rocks yield excellent material for accurate dating of remains. Louis B. Leakey (1903–72), a British anthropologist and his wife Mary Leakey made many of the sensational finds here, including *Homo habilis*, who is either another australopithecine or the earliest form of human known; testing has been inconclusive.

The first men

The immediate predecessors of *Homo*, or australopithecines—tool-using, ground-dwelling creatures who walked upright and were found mostly in Africa. But reconstructing the evolutionary line between them and above all fixing the point at which *Homo* emerges involves as manny difficulties as tracing the ancestry of the australopithecines themselves.

Homo habilis

In 1964, Dr Louis Leakey (1903–72) announced a new find, which he called *Homo habilis* (handy man) [1], thereby placing this new hominid in the same genus as present-day man. The specimen, which has an estimated brain size of 600cc, came from Bed I of Olduvai Gorge, Tanzania, and was dated at between 1.8 and 1.2 million years old.

Others of a younger age have been found, some of which show characteristics in between those of *Homo habilis* and *Homo erectus*, a specimen of which was discovered at the top of Bed II and is therefore a little older than a half million years. Many authorities believe that *Homo habilis* does not warrant a separate generic or specific division from the slender australopithecines and hence call them *Australopithecus africanus*; others regard them as a separate species, which they call *Australopithecus habilis*. All are agreed, however, that the finds possess some characteristics that are more manlike than most australopithecine remains.

African finds from Olduvai Gorge seem to confirm that *Homo erectus* (erect man) did have an australopithecine ancestor, but some suggest that the two are not directly linked. This view has been strengthened by recent discoveries, particularly that of a hominid from Rudolf, Kenya, with a brain size of just under 800cc and an age of 3 million years. This could mean a very early split in the australopithecines and not a gradual transition between *africanus* and *habilis/erectus*.

Homo erectus

Even in Asia, where most of the *Homo erectus* material has been unearthed, clues about its origins are almost nonexistent [5]. The oldest specimens have been found on Java, where a tantalizing find that could be an australopithecine was also made. But lack of material makes it difficult to link the two. Other *Homo erectus* finds are known from China, Africa, and Europe—enough so that a general picture of the form can be mapped out. The finds date from the Middle Pleistocene (1 million to 500,000 years ago). They have cranial capacities of around 1,000cc; flat, sloping foreheads; large beetling brows; flattened, narrow skulls, the backs of which are sharply angular; and no real chins. The limbs that have been found are closer to those of modern humans than the skulls are. True to his name, *Homo erectus* walked upright in much the same way as modern man.

No tools were found at the earliest sites in Java, but some were associated with the remains of Peking man and from later Java finds. Peking man is the popular name for *Homo erectus* specimens found in the caves of Chou-k'ou-tien, near Peking in China, between 1927 and 1937. Although these specimens were lost in 1941 and only casts

CONNECTIONS

See also
648 The first hominids
652 From ancient to modern man
646 Primate to hominid
1582 Early technology
1586 The stone age
654 Spread of man: 1
656 Spread of man: 2

1
A
B
C

1 Homo habilis [A] is the earliest of the prehistoric men to be placed in the same genus as modern man, that is *Homo*. *Homo erectus* [B] shows a considerably larger brain size than the australopithecines, averaging about 1,000cc. In general the size of *erectus* is not unlike that of modern man [C], and he certainly walked with a striding gait. There are significant changes in his skull, although it may still be termed robust, particularly with regard to the face and jaw. It has been suggested that the initial increase in brain size might be linked to increasing size of the body.

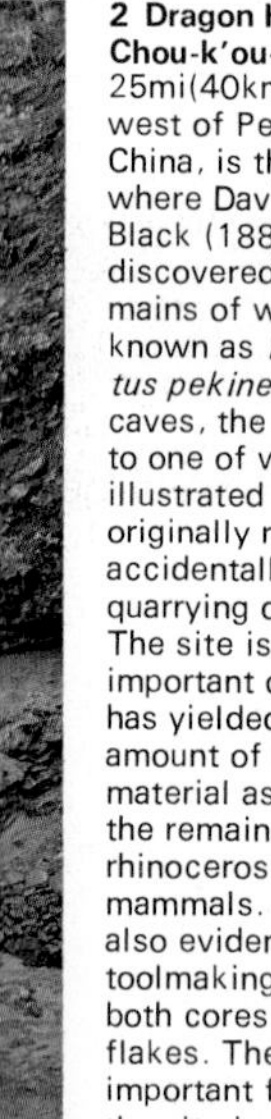

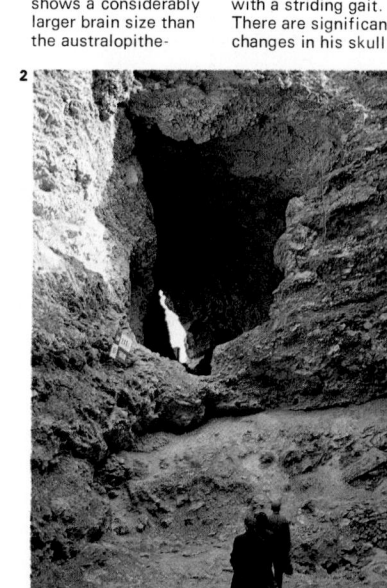

2 Dragon Hill, Chou-k'ou-tien 25mi(40km) southwest of Peking, China, is the site where Davidson Black (1884–1934) discovered the remains of what is now known as *Homo erectus pekinensis*. The caves, the entrance to one of which is illustrated here, were originally revealed accidentally during quarrying operations. The site is a most important one and has yielded a large amount of human material as well as the remains of deer, rhinoceros, and other mammals. There is also evidence of toolmaking, using both cores and flakes. The most important find within the site is evidence of man's use of fire.

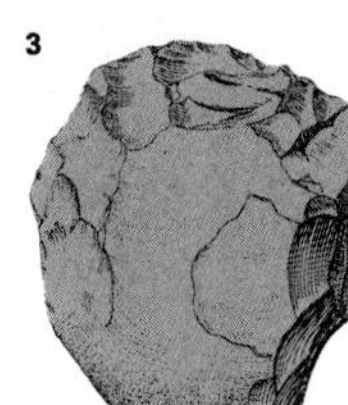

3 Peking man's tools were made of quartz, greenstone, and quartzite. Quartz was the most common material used by the Chou-k'ou-tien culture as shown by analysis of 100,000 tools found at the main site. The tools, which belong to an Oldowan type of culture, were made by simple means. One boulder was hit with another to chip off a few flakes and so form a rough cutting edge. Sometimes it was this remaining core that would be most useful; at other times the finer flakes, which could be retouched, were used. Bones and antlers were also shaped into tools. The hand ax traditions of Europe, Africa, and western Asia are not found in East Asia.

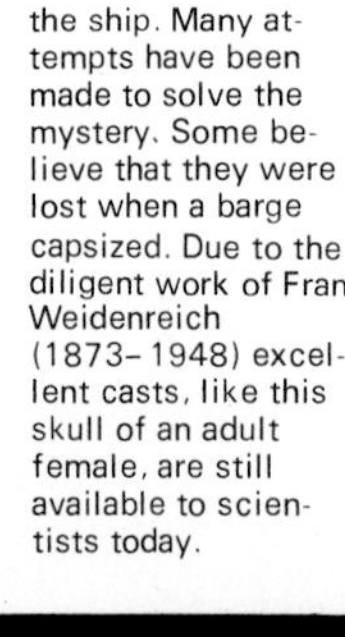
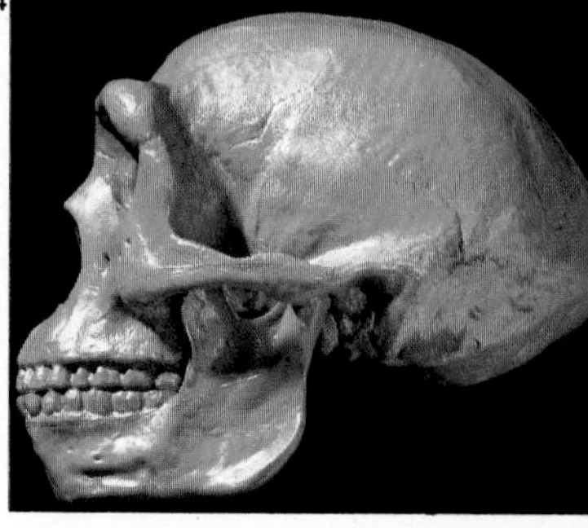

4 The original finds of *Homo erectus* at Chou-k'ou-tien, near Peking, were unfortunately mislaid during World War II. In order to keep them safe their owners, the Geological Survey of China, decided to ship them from China to the United States. They disappeared somewhere between Peking and the ship. Many attempts have been made to solve the mystery. Some believe that they were lost when a barge capsized. Due to the diligent work of Franz Weidenreich (1873–1948) excellent casts, like this skull of an adult female, are still available to scientists today.

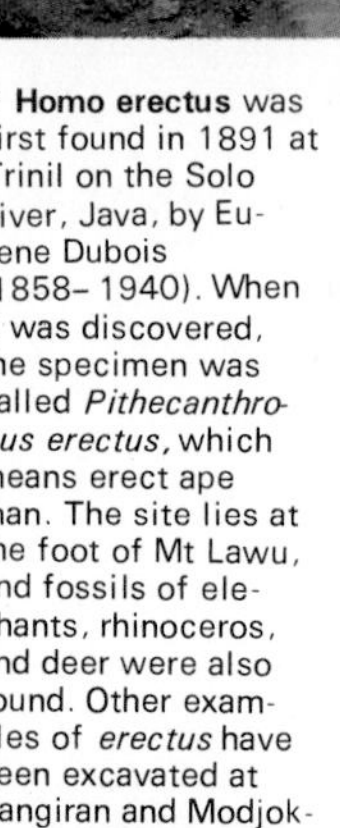

5 Homo erectus was first found in 1891 at Trinil on the Solo River, Java, by Eugene Dubois (1858–1940). When it was discovered, the specimen was called *Pithecanthropus erectus*, which means erect ape man. The site lies at the foot of Mt Lawu, and fossils of elephants, rhinoceros, and deer were also found. Other examples of *erectus* have been excavated at Sangiran and Modjokerto, with younger specimens at Ngandong and Wadjak.

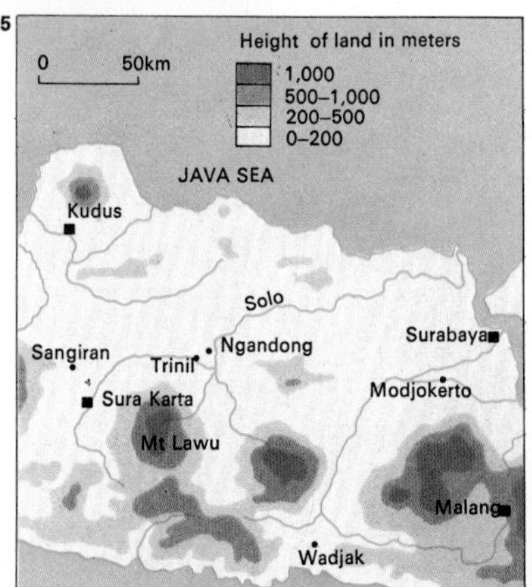

5
Height of land in meters
1,000
500–1,000
200–500
0–200
0
50km
JAVA SEA
Kudus
Solo
Sangiran
Trinil
Ngandong
Surabaya
Modjokerto
Sura Karta
Mt Lawu
Malang
Wadjak

remain, new finds have been made since digging resumed in 1958. *Homo erectus* seems to have been a successful hunter at Chou-k'ou-tien. More important, he had learned to use fire for cooking and presumably for warmth as well.

Homo erectus may or may not have populated Europe and North Africa. Fragments suggest their presence in Germany (the "Heidelberg jaw"), Algeria (Ternifine), and Morocco (Casablanca); as does, to some scholars, a skull found in Greece (Petralona). Olduvai Gorge in East Africa and Swartkrans in South Africa have produced evidence of *Homo erectus*. The fossils from most areas are meager and usually consist of fragments, so that the picture of *Homo erectus* is more than usually hazy. In addition, there are difficulties in dating the material precisely—particularly that discovered before modern dating techniques were evolved. It is possible however, that Java man may be as much as 1,900,000 years old. Some of the remains from Chou-k'ou-tien are from 500,000 to 200,000 years ago. The Heidelberg jaw and some of the bones found at Olduvai Gorge could be older (*c*. 700,000–500,000 years), but the fragments from Casablanca may be only 100,000 years old.

Between Homo erectus and Homo sapiens

In 1965 some milk teeth and a bone from the back of a skull were found at Vertesszöllös, near Budapest, Hungary. They have been dated as coming from 350,000 years ago, and experts say that they seem to show a mixture of features similar to those of *Homo erectus* and *Homo sapiens*. They may represent an intermediate type, and if so, the date of this ancestral form would be a very early one. Other finds at Nice have only recently been fully investigated. Two skulls found in late middle Pleistocene deposits on the banks of the Omo River in southern Ethiopia show widely different characteristics—one (Omo II) being obviously more like *erectus* than the other (Omo I). Yet they seem to have come from the same geological time period. Future finds may clarify the suggested relationship between *Homo erectus* and *Homo sapiens*.

KEY

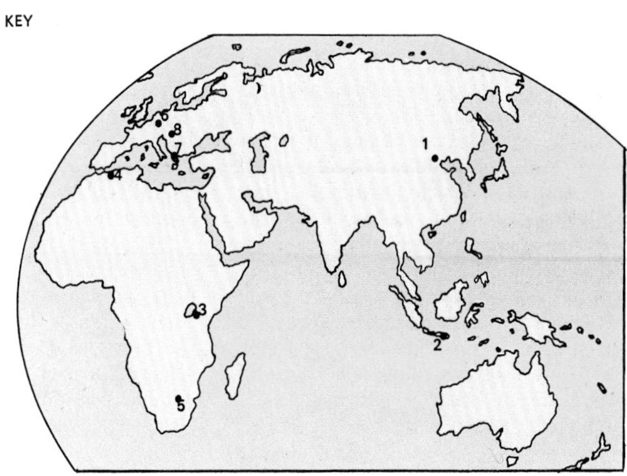

Homo erectus is known from Africa, Asia, and Europe. Much of present knowledge is from the first specimens, those found in China [1] and Java [2]. Originally regarded as completely separate types, they are now considered to be subspecies of *Homo erectus*, sometimes called respectively *pekinensis* and *erectus*. In Africa finds have been made in Olduvai Gorge, Tanzania [3], Ternifine, Algeria [4], and at Swartkrans in South Africa [5]. In Europe the most famous find is that of a jawbone from Heidelberg [6]. Others come from Petralona, Greece [7], and Vertesszöllös, Hungary [8].

6 Paleolithic camps 300,000 years old have been found at Terra Amata (beloved land) in Nice, France. The finds were made in 1966 during building excavations, and a rescue operation involving 300 workers over a six-month period was mounted. The site covered 264 square yards (221sq m), and 35,000 objects were recovered. Although no human remains have been found it would seem that the occupants of the site must have been *Homo erectus* from a footprint that has been found. An examination of the pollen content of the fossilized human feces has revealed that the hunters came to the camp in late spring or early summer. Evidence suggests that part of the site was occupied during 11 consecutive years. The huts, which were oval shaped, ranged in size from 26–48ft (7.8–14.7m) in length and from 13–20ft (3.9–6m) in width. The walls were made of branches pushed down into the sand and propped up by stones. There also appear to have been central supporting posts [1]. Each hut has a hearth [2] protected on the windward side by a screen of stones. Although seafood [3] formed part of the diet, there seems to have been a preference for the young of big game: boar *(Sus scrofa)* [4]; Merk's rhinocerous *(Dicerorhinus merki)* [5]; deer *(Cervus elphus)* [6]; wild ox *(Bos primigenius)* [7]; ibex *(Capra ibex)* [8]; and the extinct elephant *(Elephasmeridionalis)* [9]. The tools were made on the spot and include scrapers [10], cleavers, projectile points, and biface tools [11]. Wooden staves may have been hardened in the fire [12]. The camps were closer to the coast than at present.

From ancient to modern man

There is a considerable time gap between specimens of *Homo erectus,* the earliest members of the genus *Homo,* and unmistakable forms of *Homo sapiens.* The characteristics of *Homo sapiens* that distinguish this form from that of *erectus* include a mean cranial capacity of about 1,350cc, a forehead that is not sloped but vertical, a skull base that is rounded rather than angled, smaller teeth and jaws, and a projecting chin. It used to be thought that "Neanderthal man" was a separate species, but today *Homo sapiens neanderthalensis* is considered only a subspecies of *Homo sapiens*—even though Neanderthals have sloping foreheads, angled skull bases, and other characteristics not usually associated with the general *Homo sapiens* description.

The earliest examples

In tracing the early evolution of *Homo sapiens* a major difficulty has been that the older finds are limited mainly to Europe [Key]. As more and more finds are made however, significant trends in the evolution of *Homo sapiens* are beginning to emerge.

The two specimens usually regarded as having claims to being the earliest sapients were found at Swanscombe, England, and at Steinheim, near Stuttgart, Germany. Both of these came from the Mindel-Riss interglacial period, about 250,000 to 200,000 years ago. The brain volume of the Steinheim specimen is calculated at 1,150cc, and that of the Swanscombe specimen at about 1,300cc, but these estimates are based only on fragments of the skull. Although the brow ridges are more like those of *Homo erectus,* the rounded shape of the back of the skull is more modern than that of Neanderthal man, who appears later. Another find at Fontéchevade, France, of even more modern appearance, is from the Riss-Würm interglacial of 90,000 to 80,000 years ago.

Homo sapiens neanderthalensis

From the early upper Pleistocene there may have been a number of different populations of sapients. The best known are the Neanderthals, who lived during the part of the last and most intense period of glaciation, the Würm, from about 70,000 to 35,000 years ago. The first specimens of Neanderthal humanity were found in 1856 [2]. A few finds indicate that the Neanderthal type was established even earlier than this. Remains from Saccopastore, near Rome, have been dated to the Riss-Würm interglacial. Other finds of the early Würm glaciation have come from Morocco, Libya, and Israel.

Although with his sturdy build and massive brow ridges Neanderthal man was certainly different from modern humans [1], his brain size was, on the average, slightly larger. He was a good hunter [3], with a developed and diversified stone technology (called the Mousterian culture after Le Moustier, where the tools were first found). Bone and wood were also used for tools and weapons. The Neanderthal way of life could be adapted swiftly to harsh climatic changes. Neanderthals tried to alter the sites where they lived with stones, paving, excavations, and the like. This is the first period that provides evidence of deliberate burial practices. In 1908 the fossil of a young Neanderthal buried in a sleeping position

CONNECTIONS

See also
650 The first men
648 The first hominids
646 Primate to hominid
1588 Fire and bronze
1590 Bark, hide, and hor
1592 The iron age
950 The art of prehistory
654 Spread of man: 1
656 Spread of man: 2
880 Simplest human societies
876 Origins of human society
878 Stages of social evo lution
256 Caves and underground water

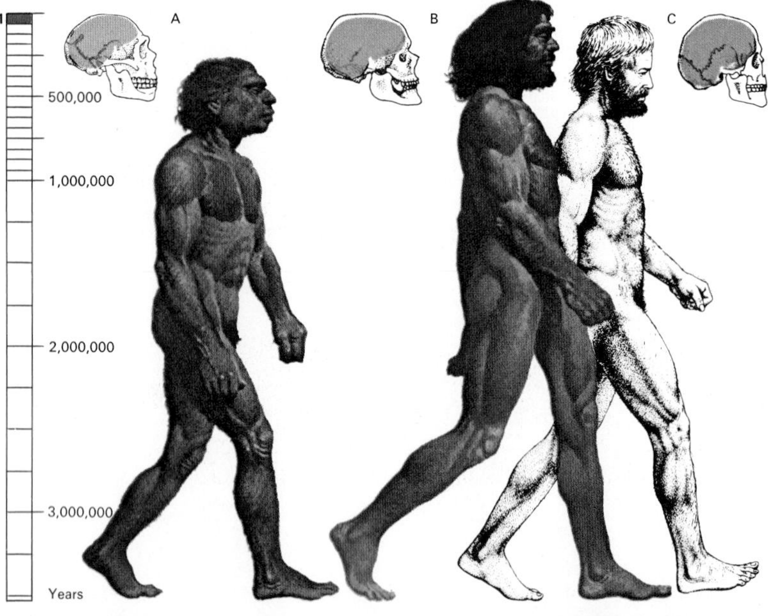

1
A
B
C
500,000
1,000,000
2,000,000
3,000,000
Years

1 Neanderthal man [A], with his large brain but squat build and heavy brows, gave way about 30,000 years ago to Cro-Magnon man [B], whose physical makeup was closer to modern man's [C].

2
>150 meters
125–150
100–125
75–100
<75
Present-day quarries
Neanderthal reserve
Railway
0 1km
Hochdahl
Düsseldorf 10km
Wuppertal 15km
Düssel

2 The site of the first Neanderthal find was the valley of the River Düssel, called Neanderthal, between Düsseldorf and Wuppertal, where farm workers discovered a skullcap in 1856.

3

3 The hunting skills of Neanderthal man must have been well developed. Among his opponents were the woolly rhinoceros and the cave bear, which was 39in (1m) taller than Neanderthal adults. These animals provided not only food but also materials for clothing and for use in the cave. Hunting techniques required a great deal of cooperation within the group. Among different methods used were the stampeding of animals toward narrow gorges or cliff edges and the digging of pits or other forms of ambush. Fire-hardened spears and stone clubs were employed to kill the prey and stone tools to skin it.

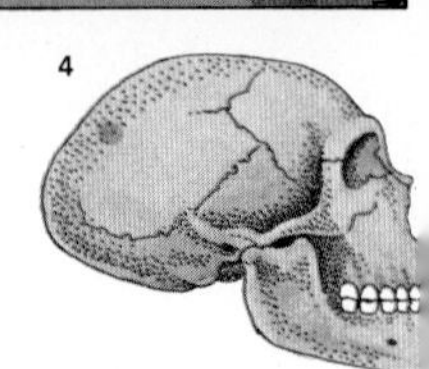

4

4 Was Peking man a cannibal? Some experts feel the hole drilled in the base of this skull is evidence that the brain was extracted through it and eaten, as some cannibal groups have been known to do in more recent times.

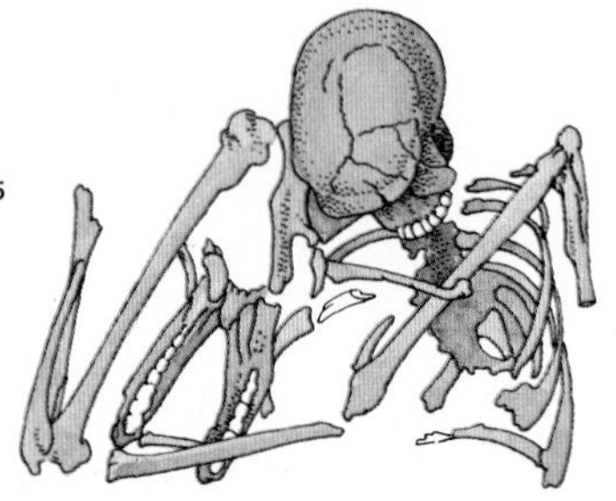

5

5 Ceremonial burial of the dead is suggested by the discovery of a Neanderthal skeleton clasping the jawbone of a boar. The Neanderthals were the first to practice such rites. Ritual burials have been found at Monte Circeo, Italy, and at several sites in France.

was found at Le Moustier. At Drachenlock, in the Swiss Alps, patterns of skulls and bones of cave bears were found, and similar arrangements appear in Austria and Germany. What Neanderthal religious beliefs were, or indeed if these practices are religious ones, we probably will never know.

Other mysteries involving the Neanderthals include exactly what factors may have been at work in shaping their short, powerfully built frames, their large braincases, their particular facial features and heavy limbs. Climate has been suggested as the determining factor, but this fails to account for the variety of climatic changes that actually took place during the Würm glaciation or the ways in which the Neanderthals coped with these changes. Climate has also been blamed for the sudden and total disappearance of evidence for *Homo sapiens neanderthalensis* about 35,000 years ago. In Europe, habitation sites show a period of no occupation at all before the next people (Cro-Magnons) moved in. Possibly some groups survived a drastic climate change or an epidemic only to lose out to the more efficient Cro-Magnons in hunting or in warfare, or to be absorbed into their groups.

Interpretation of remains, called "Neanderthaloid," that show blends of Neanderthal and other traits is equally difficult. There is no hard-and-fast evidence to support any of the contentions that have been made: that there was some intermixture or that there was not, that Neanderthals spread worldwide or that they did not. "Neanderthaloid" specimens have been found at Mount Carmel, Israel; Krapina and Kulna, Yugoslavia; and in China, Java, Zambia, South Africa, Kenya, and Ethiopia.

The last of the ancient hunters

The Cro-Magnon peoples were hunters, as the Neanderthals had been. The earliest representatives of *Homo sapiens,* wherever they are found, are hunting-and-gathering peoples. The first great cultural revolution occurred later—about 7000 to 8000 BC—when hunting gave way to crop cultivation and animal husbandry, and the first step toward modern society was taken.

KEY

1 Swanscombe
2 Channel Islands
3 La Chaise
4 Le Moustier
5 Lacave
6 La Ferrassie
7 La Chapelle-aux-Saints
8 Montmaurin
9 Malarnaud
10 Spy
11 Neanderthal
12 Steinheim
13 Gánovce
14 Sipka
15 Krapina
16 Gibraltar
17 Monte Circeo
18 Kiik Koba
19 Mount Carmel

0 1,000km

Finds of specimens that can be placed in the *Homo sapiens* group are widespread, particularly in Europe. The earliest in geological age, almost 200,000 years old, are those of Swanscombe in England and Steinheim in Germany. Famous sites of Neanderthal and related species are the Neanderthal Valley, Germany, Spy in Belgium, La Chapelle-aux-Saints, Ferrassie, and Le Moustier, all located in France, Monte Circeo in Italy, and Gibraltar. Finds of Neanderthaloids are also widespread in Asia and Africa. Upper Paleolithic men are represented by a number of races such as Cro-Magnons and Predmostians. Man as an agriculturist first appeared in the Middle East about 7500 BC.

6 Caves used for shelter by early man are rarely found unchanged by later natural events. But it is still possible, with experience, to read the story they contain. In this hypothetical cave it is assumed that the river was close to its present level [1] 25,000 years ago when cave painting became widespread. A river terrace [2] shows that the cave was once submerged, leaving an insoluble limestone residue on the floor [3]. As the river cut into its valley, it gradually fell [4], depositing a silt bed [5] Continued deepening of the valley left the cave floor dry. Rock falls blocked the entrance after man left.

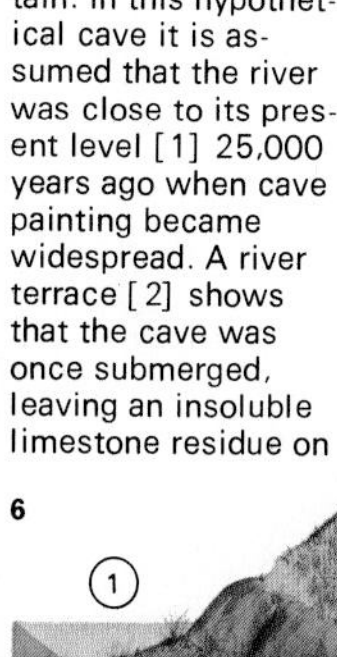

6

At the cave mouth, rock debris conceals layers of ash built up by the fires of the early men who used the shelter of the entrance both to keep a lookout and to cook their food. The ashes have accumulated in three main layers, each denoting a long period of use.

Just inside the mouth of the cave a bird of prey, possibly a buzzard, built its nest. The evidence lies directly below it on the slope of the rock debris where small rodent bones are scattered.

Cave art is found well within the cave and appears to have been part of the hunters' semi-religious efforts to secure both success and safety in hunting the animals depicted.

Stalactites hanging from the roof of the cave have developed over thousands of years as a result of water containing calcium carbonate seeping through the limestone above.

Animal remains are littered through the cave but are heaped at this point because animals have fallen through a hole left by a rock fall.

Rock falls can provide a new entrance to a cave after the mouth has been blocked. Here rock debris and earth from above have totally filled the shaft.

A burrow in the cave floor has been left by a small animal. It was deflected sideways by harder rock, until it could continue downwards, throwing up bones from older deposits. It died at the end of its burrow. This kind of mixing of bones of different ages makes dating difficult.

Evidence of a fairly widespread cave bear cult has been found in carefully prepared arrangements of bear skulls (here in a stone compartment), leg bones and other fragments. Men could hardly have picked a more dangerous opponent, and they could find meat much easier.

Early men buried their dead in various ways. Some buried skulls only, arrayed with possessions or ornaments; others buried men but not women. This skeleton shows evidence of careful arrangement in a sleeping position similar to that of the Grimaldi remains in the Grotte des Enfants, Monaco.

Even the interior of a structurally stable cave changes over a long period of time. Upright stalagmites, produced by the slow seepage of calcium carbonate-rich water through the limestone above, have built up on a large pile of rock that has fallen from the roof.

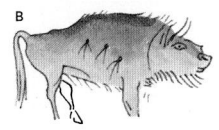

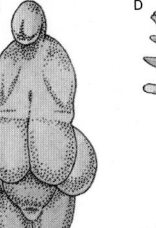

7A

B

C

D

7 The origins of art go back to at least 30,000 BC. Carvings on antlers [A] are among the oldest forms, dating from the Aurignacian period (30,000–22,000 BC). Cave paintings like that of the wounded aurochs [B] were produced by the Gravettian people (22,000–18,000 BC). These paintings may have been magical (helping to trap game) or educational, but they certainly show man's knowledge of animals. The Gravettians decorated ivory and produced Venus figurines and body ornaments [D]. Solutrean people (18,000–15,000 BC) produced fine friezes and the Magdalenians (15,000–8,000 BC) were painters and modelers.

8

8 Mesolithic man lived about 10,000 years ago. His main hunting weapon was the bow and arrow. Other tools that have been discovered reflect changes in the food-gathering pattern, which included fishing, fowling, and sealing. Canoes were used and, in the subarctic regions, skis and sledges were made. Farming was yet to come, but the domestic dog was bred from the wolf by the people of Mesolithic times. They also formed large social groups.

The evidence so far collected by archeologists and paleontologists suggests that the cradle of humankind was in East Africa, about five million years ago, when the Australopithecines first appeared. From the beginnings there, humans spread out to populate and dominate the world. The speed and extent of this dispersal have been largely controlled by humanity's ability to exploit the advantages and overcome the disadvantages presented by climate. For millions of years the wanderings of the family Hominidae as nomadic hunter-gatherers were severely limited by environmental factors. Without the skills needed to fashion tools, build dwellings, or make warm clothing, humankind was completely at the mercy of the elements.

Before Homo sapiens

Long before the evolution of *Homo sapiens* some 50,000 years ago, the restraints of ignorance had been broken. Remains of *Homo erectus* (who emerged more than a million years ago) found in Europe and Asia suggest that humans made the journey from Africa in spite of the difference in climate. Probably more flexible communication (which would have expanded the range and effectiveness of cooperation) together with improvements in tools enabled *Homo erectus* to become a more efficient hunter, and thus to follow new game, feed more mouths, and rear larger families.

The discovery of fire by *Homo erectus* was a crucial event in humanity's fight for survival. The fact that the Neanderthals were able to endure the vicissitudes of an ice age is testament to the importance of fire as well as to the steadily growing abilities of early humanity.

The Neanderthals used fire for warmth and made clothes from animal skins. They devised ingenious ways of trapping animals and coordinated groups for hunting the way military operations are coordinated. Because of skills of this sort, Neanderthals were able to live in locations where earlier hominids would not have been able to survive. Humans had begun to create their own environment, but Neanderthal man could not create the game and the vegetation his hunting and gathering people depended on for food.

Homo sapiens in the ice age

Homo sapiens had made his way all over the world by the Upper Pleistocene. In some areas we must presume that *Homo sapiens sapiens* and *Homo sapiens neanderthalensis* competed for the same resources, although there is no direct evidence of this in the fossil record. We do know, however, quite a lot about certain of the Upper Paleolithic hunting cultures of *Homo sapiens*. The Eastern Gravettian culture, for instance, flourished during a warm period of the last glaciation [1]. Warmer conditions permitted the movement of game along the steppe lands of eastern Europe, between the northern ice sheets and the glaciated mountains of the south. The mammoth was the staple beast of this period (in the same way that the bison was for the Plains Indians in the nineteenth century). It provided meat, clothing from skins, tools from tusks and bones, and even shelter from skeletal structures and hides.

CONNECTIONS

See also
656 Spread of man: 2
650 The first men
652 From ancient to modern man
264 Ice caps and ice ages
266 Winds and deserts

1

1 The Eastern Gravettian culture, which flourished during the upper Paleolithic (35,000–10,000 BC), is remarkable for its sophisticated solution to the problem of shelter. These peoples, living on the edges of the glaciers of Czechoslovakia and southern Russia, an area without natural caves or rock shelters, constructed huts from movable poles covered with animal skins sewn together. The bottom edges of these skins were weighted down with the bones of mammoths, reindeer, and the occasional rhinoceros that was killed. When they were forced to move on in the search for game the huts could be dismantled and transported. The hut floors were scooped out of the soil as a protection against drafts, and there may have been more than one fire per hut as well as the communal hearths outside. There is evidence that surface coal and mammoth tusks provided fuel for these fires. The clothes of these peoples were made from skin, much as those of the Lapps and Eskimos are today. Statuettes were made from clay and ocher. The dead, often painted with ocher, were buried not far from the camp in a shallow ditch protected by mammoth bones and tusks. Included in the graves were everyday goods such as food, arms, and ornaments. Hunting techniques developed considerably during this period, with foliage-covered pits being used to trap big game against which weapons (primarily blades, spears, and clubs made from bone, antlers, and flints) would have been ineffective. Needles, spoons, borers, and end-scrapers were the basic tools at that time.

The last major advance of the ice produced important cultural changes. The Magdalenian people of this period lived much as the pre-white-man Eskimos did; they adapted to the extreme cold and the changes in game and vegetation instead of being driven out or killed off by the climatic shift.

Mesolithic hunters and gatherers

As the ice receded for the last time, human beings followed the herds back north. Some stayed behind, of course, to face different problems in adapting to the changes of the new Holocene era.

The Mesolithic peoples of western Europe lived in a heavily forested region. They inhabited shorelands and other open locations to escape the forest cover [2]. Stone tools were used to cut down trees and to work the wood. Bows and arrows were used extensively for hunting (earlier, spears had been the principal hunting tool). Mesolithic groups caught birds and fish as well as deer. The dog was domesticated, which suggests that there was enough food to allow people to take time out from the search for sustenance and devote it to other pursuits. The rich vegetation provided fruits, berries, and roots.

Pollen counts from sediments of the period show a decrease in tree pollen and an increase in herbaceous pollen at a number of sites—evidence that Mesolithic humanity made clearings to set up temporary camps. The waterways were free of ice, and boats made from skins or canoes dug out from logs were used in the exploration and exploitation of the waterways.

But it was in the rich and fertile river valleys and hilly flanks of the Middle East that humankind took the next step in controlling the environment. A new type of culture originated during the Neolithic period of human prehistory, one based on agriculture and domesticated animals. This was the first great cultural revolution, and from this economic foundation came a population explosion and the first cities, intercultural trade, colonization, and ideas of empire and conquest. It was the threshold of history.

KEY

Even today human beings migrate from place to place. Here a herding group in Afghanistan moves to summer pasture.

2 The forests that grew up as the glaciers retreated to where they are today presented almost as many difficulties as the ice. The new environment forced humans to occupy sites on the sides of rivers and lakes until their technology had developed sufficiently to enable them to clear the trees. Lepenski Vir, a site southeast of Belgrade in Yugoslavia, is typical of the Mesolithic settlements in the Danube basin. Discovered in 1960, the site appears to have been built in about 5000–4600 BC. To achieve level foundations the houses had to be constructed on terraces cut into the sloping bank of the river. They were aligned in rows with their entrances facing the river and varied in size from 6.6 square yards (5.5 sq m) to 35.9 square yards (30 sq m). The floors were of hard limestone plaster covered by a thin red or white burnished surface. The hearths within the houses were elongated pits lined with limestone blocks and were often surrounded by a pattern of thin sandstone blocks. These fireplaces may have been constructed primarily to smoke and dry the fish that were abundant in that part of the river. Lepenski Vir is the name of the large whirlpool that existed at that point in the Danube; it churned up the small organisms on which fish feed. The inhabitants also hunted the red deer, aurochs, roe deer, and wild pigs that were plentiful on the wooded hills. Their hunting and fishing methods are not known, but blocks of stone may have been used to club fish that had been landed alive after being caught in nets and fish traps.

Spread of man: 2

Human beings are now scattered over the face of the earth, but it cannot always have been thus. As far as we know, humanity was, in the earliest stages of its development, confined to eastern and southern Africa. From there groups migrated to Europe, Asia, and beyond. *Homo erectus* and *Homo sapiens neanderthalensis* were established in Europe and Asia as well as Africa during the Pleistocene era, but it seems to have been *Homo sapiens sapiens,* modern man, who pushed on to populate the Americas and Australasia [Key].

Following the herds

It is a mistake to think of these early human beings setting off for new lands like the Pilgrims embarking for America. Most probably, human groups merely followed the herds of game animals as they foraged for food. The herds, in turn, went where the pastures were lushest.

The herds took humanity farther than one might expect. Archeological investigation has revealed, for instance, that human beings have lived in the vast wastes of Siberia for at least 20,000 years, or since the last glacial era. Although barren and cold, this area does support a type of plant growth suitable for grazing mammals. It is likely, therefore, that people followed the herds even to these inhospitable regions. To do so, human beings had to have been able to make warm clothing and shelter—had to be able to create the material culture needed to counteract the harsh effects of the environment.

Land bridges open new worlds

Climate fluctuated widely during the last glacial phase, affecting not only the distribution of game animals and the plants on which they (and humans) fed, but also the level of the oceans. During periods of intense glaciation, when vast quantities of water were frozen, the sea level must have been much lower than it is today. Scientists assume that many land bridges were exposed in this manner. Coastal areas would not have been covered with ice at the periods of maximum glaciation but would have been rather like the Arctic tundra—suitable grazing regions with many lakes.

But the hypothesis of following the herds cannot fully account for the population of Australia, for there are no game herds on that continent. Humans (and dogs) did come there, however, probably over a series of land bridges the traces of which are still to be seen in the chain of islands linking Asia to Indonesia, New Guinea, and Australia itself. The first people to reach Australia got there between 20,000 and 30,000 years ago. This group was in its turn pushed south by a new (biologically distinct) group that comprised the ancestors of the aboriginal people in Australia today. The first group populated the island of Tasmania until systematic efforts by British colonists wiped them off the face of the earth in 1876.

The inhabitants of Melanesia also seem to have had forerunners on the Asian mainland, as the peoples of Micronesia and Polynesia also may have had (although the Kon-Tiki expedition and other evidence suggests a New World origin for some of the peoples of the South Pacific). Here again, some other explanation is needed to ac-

CONNECTIONS

See also

654 Spread of man: 1
952 Beginnings of agriculture
956 The Sumerians 4000–2006 BC
658 Family of man: today's peoples
660 Family of man: how peoples differ
304 History of agriculture

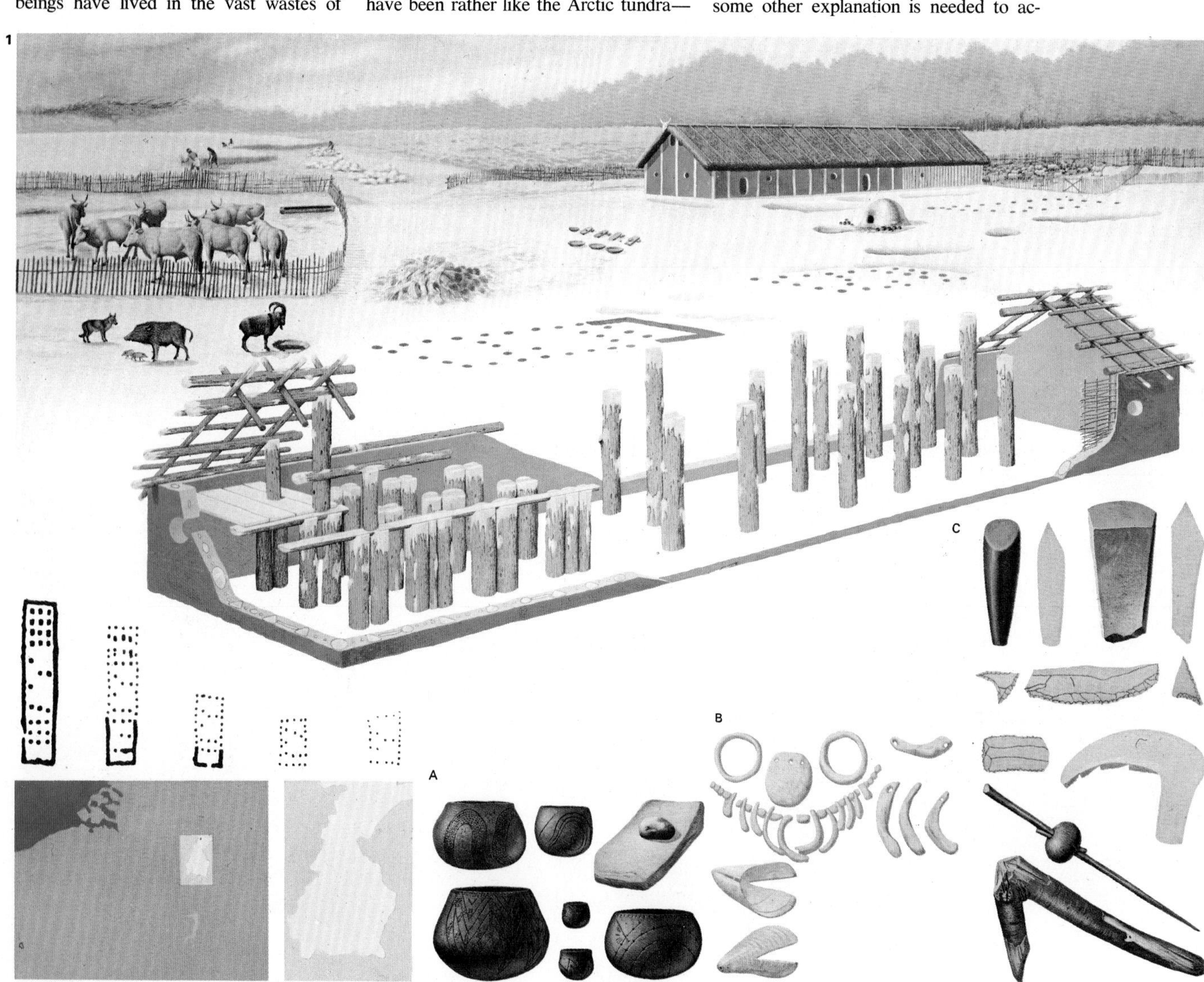

1
A
B
C

1 Sittard, in the Netherlands, is a site dating from the end of the fifth millenium BC when the first mixed farming communities settled in the Meuse valley in Dutch Limburg. These people were part of the Danubian culture complex that spread from Moravia, Bohemia, and central Germany throughout most of Central Europe. They practiced a primitive agriculture, without plow or fertilizer, which was dependent on the soft, fertile loess found across the region. Ten Danubian villages have been discovered in the area, each usually includes about 20 large houses. Plan and construction of these varied, but timber posts and daub walls were basic. Danubian-made artifacts include distinctively incised pottery ware [A], simple bone ornaments and jewelry [B], grinding stones, stone axes, flint arrowheads, and flint sickle blades [C]. They kept cattle, sheep, goats, and pigs, and grew a variety of crops, including barley.

count for these population movements: the urge to explore, forced exile, or another hypothesis that is not based on the idea that the environment determined everything early humans did.

The movement into America

Environment does seem to have been the determining factor in the population of the Americas. Beringia, the land bridge linking eastern Siberia with Alaska, seems to have provided the highway. Both plants and animals spread from Asia to America, and we can assume that hunters followed the caribou, musk oxen, and mammoths, as they wandered east. A precise date cannot be given for humanity's diffusion into North America, but it does seem certain that *Homo sapiens sapiens* was the only member of the family of humankind to have set foot on the soil of the Americas.

The population of the Americas may have occurred in a number of waves. Movement from Beringia to the mainland would have been impossible at certain times because of intervening glaciers, but at other times (between 20,000 and 28,000 years ago and between 32,000 and 36,000 years ago for example) an ice-free corridor seems to have existed between the glaciers of the Rockies and the main ice sheet to the east, providing a passageway for human migration southward.

This "wave theory" of population accounts for the diversity of American Indian peoples now found on the continent. The idea is that newer arrivals pushed the earlier migrants south, remaining distinct population groups while so doing, and thus developed distinct gene pools that would have produced the minor physical differences that characterize the Indians of different regions in the Americas.

All the same, the "wave theory" is just a theory. Most of what we know about the spread of humankind is theory—assumption based on the very little material evidence we have found and the very crude ideas we have developed to account for why humans behave in the ways that they do. The factual basis for this theorizing can be summed up in a chart [2].

KEY

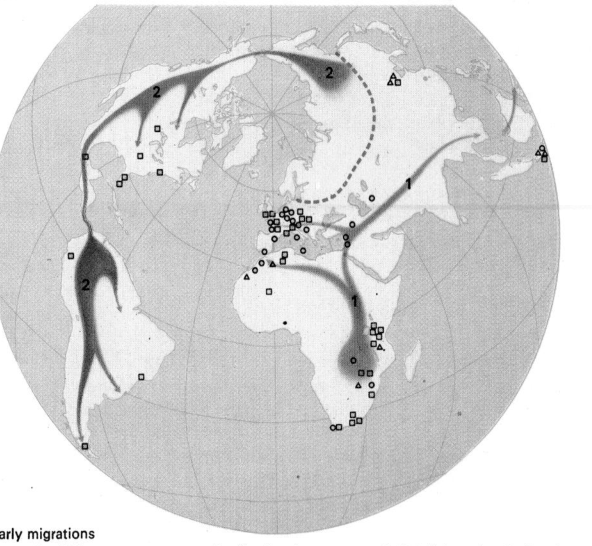

Early migrations
△ Fossils of *Homo erectus*
○ Fossils of Neanderthal man
□ Fossils of early *Homo sapiens*
- - - Expansion of early *Homo sapiens*
1 Possible paths of migrations c. 100,000 years ago
2 Migrations to the Americas c. 35,000-15,000 years ago

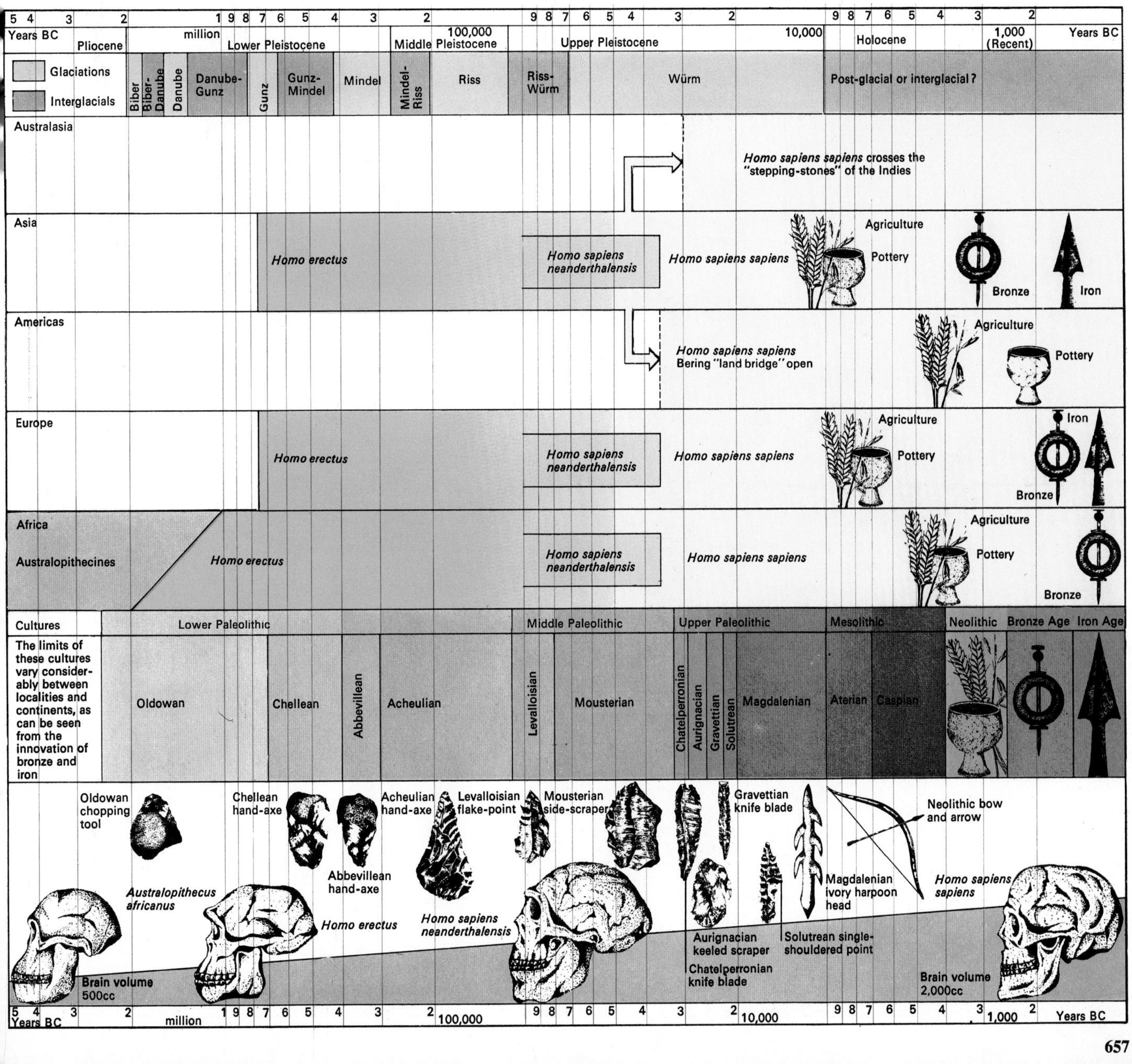

Years BC — million — 100,000 — 10,000 — 1,000 (Recent)
Pliocene | Lower Pleistocene | Middle Pleistocene | Upper Pleistocene | Holocene

Glaciations / Interglacials: Biber, Biber-Danube, Danube, Danube-Gunz, Gunz, Gunz-Mindel, Mindel, Mindel-Riss, Riss, Riss-Würm, Würm, Post-glacial or interglacial?

Australasia: *Homo sapiens sapiens* crosses the "stepping-stones" of the Indies

Asia: *Homo erectus*; *Homo sapiens neanderthalensis*; *Homo sapiens sapiens*; Agriculture; Pottery; Bronze; Iron

Americas: *Homo sapiens sapiens* Bering "land bridge" open; Agriculture; Pottery

Europe: *Homo erectus*; *Homo sapiens neanderthalensis*; *Homo sapiens sapiens*; Agriculture; Pottery; Bronze; Iron

Africa: Australopithecines; *Homo erectus*; *Homo sapiens neanderthalensis*; *Homo sapiens sapiens*; Agriculture; Pottery; Bronze

Cultures: Lower Paleolithic; Middle Paleolithic; Upper Paleolithic; Mesolithic; Neolithic; Bronze Age; Iron Age

The limits of these cultures vary considerably between localities and continents, as can be seen from the innovation of bronze and iron

Oldowan; Chellean; Abbevillean; Acheulian; Levalloisian; Mousterian; Chatelperronian; Aurignacian; Gravettian; Solutrean; Magdalenian; Aterian; Caspian

Oldowan chopping tool; Chellean hand-axe; Abbevillean hand-axe; Acheulian hand-axe; Levalloisian flake-point; Mousterian side-scraper; Gravettian knife blade; Aurignacian keeled scraper; Chatelperronian knife blade; Solutrean single-shouldered point; Magdalenian ivory harpoon head; Neolithic bow and arrow

Australopithecus africanus; *Homo erectus*; *Homo sapiens neanderthalensis*; *Homo sapiens sapiens*

Brain volume 500cc; Brain volume 2,000cc

Family of man: today's peoples

The population groups that most people call "races" are passing episodes in the ongoing evolution of humankind. All the people on earth today are members of the same species, *Homo sapiens*, and what are usually thought of as "racial traits" are probably only the results of adaptation to climate and geography tens of thousands of years ago. Modern transportation and the ability to shield people from the harshest effects of climate have vastly accelerated the breaking down of racial isolation.

What is a race of people?

The word "race" has different meanings but few of them are biologically valid. Hitler's "Aryan race," for example, was originally a linguistic group that included those who spoke Sanskrit as well as those who spoke German. There is no biological "Aryan race." The commonest meaning of race is "cultural or ethnic group." Although there is a fuzzy biological idea behind distinguishing people on the basis of appearance, there is virtually none at all behind distinguishing people on the basis of how they behave. The way people act is almost always a result of training and has nothing to do with biological heredity.

The way people look is not a very scientific way of telling their race, either. Ordinarily it is said that there are three "major races": Caucasoid, Mongoloid, and Negroid [Key], but there is no single "racial trait" that is a surefire indicator of any individual's belonging to one or another of these groups—not even skin color. Some Caucasoids have skin as dark as some Negroids, some Mongoloids do not have the epicanthic fold on the upper eyelid that is common in that group, some Negroids have pointed noses, and so forth. In fact, race is a useful idea only if it is applied to groups of people and not to specific individuals. Within a group we can say that significantly greater numbers of people have this or that feature than have that feature within another group.

There are very few "pure" races left. Thousands of years of migration and interbreeding have done their work. In the United States the "purest" racial groups are Pueblo Indians, Armenians, and people with last names that show Welsh backgrounds (Jones, Owens, etc.). Many Hungarians and Poles have the epicanthic Mongoloid fold; Detroit blacks have nearly 30% European genes; and the successive invasions of Europe by "barbarians," Romans, Mongols, Arabs, and others long ago made the idea of European racial "purity" a biological joke.

Race and genetics

Population groups can be distinguished from one another biologically, as we have said—but some of the old "racial traits" do not stand up to scientific testing. Perhaps the most notorious of these is skin color. There are too many nonbiological factors that may account for the color of a person's skin to make that standard of much use in distinguishing between populations. Other traits, like hair type, physical measurements, the form of the eyes, nose, etc., do have more validity as such standards. But here, too, external factors may modify basic biological tendencies. Scientists need some-

CONNECTIONS
See also
660 Family of man: how peoples differ
894 Prejudice and group intolerance
414 The genetic code
416 Principles of heredity
420 Evolution in action

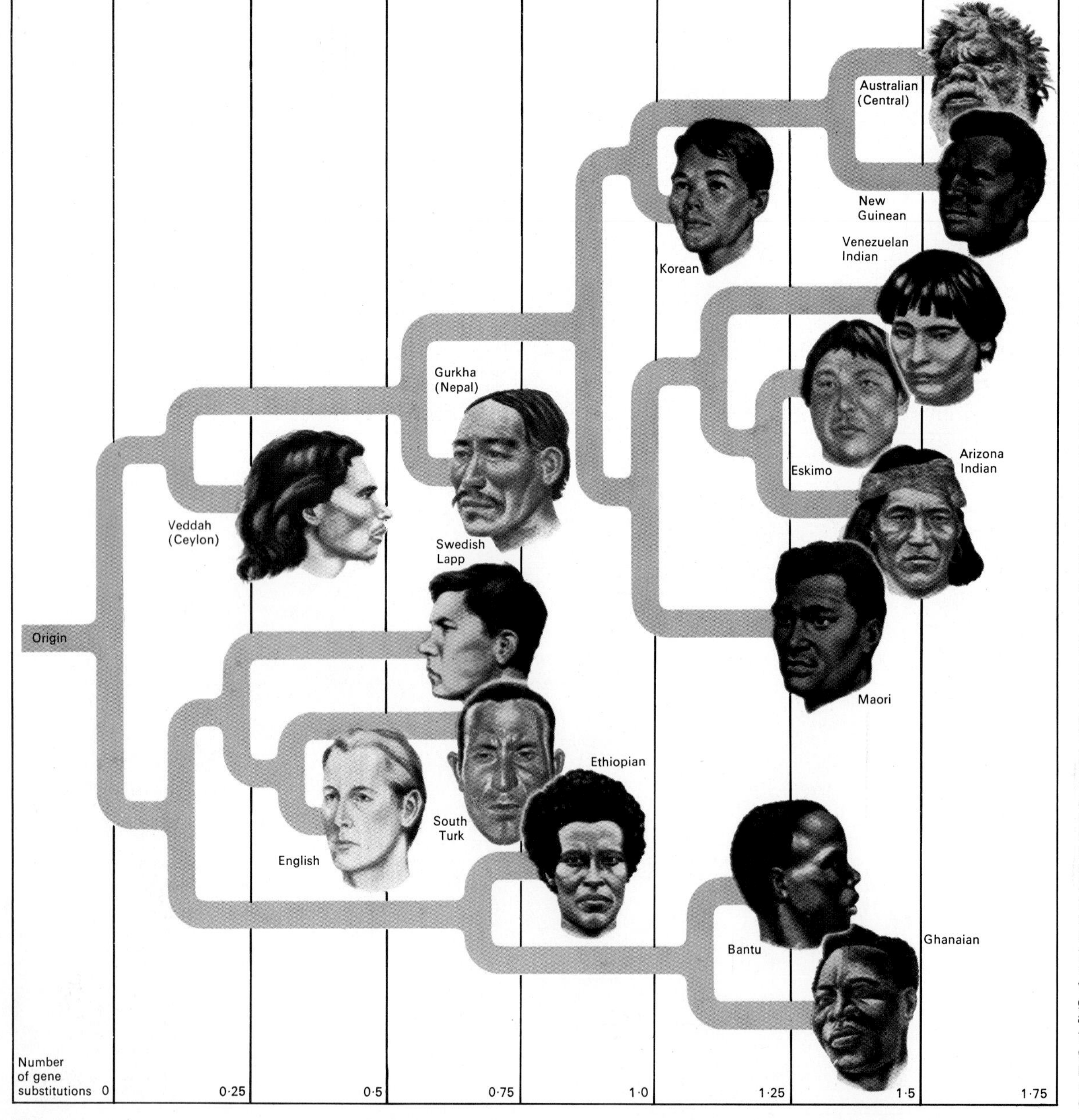

1
Australian (Central)
New Guinean
Venezuelan Indian
Korean
Gurkha (Nepal)
Eskimo
Arizona Indian
Veddah (Ceylon)
Swedish Lapp
Origin
Maori
Ethiopian
South Turk
English
Bantu
Ghanaian
Number of gene substitutions 0
0·25
0·5
0·75
1·0
1·25
1·5
1·75

1 The relationship between various populations can now be assessed accurately by computer analysis of a wide range of inherited traits. These characteristics may be under the control of several genes, as are skull shape and fingerprints, or controlled by a single pair of genes, as are the genetic factors of the blood (such as the various blood groups and enzyme and protein variation). Previously it was only possible to compare the variation of one or two inherited characteristics between a few populations. This computer reconstruction took 15 populations, three from each major area: English, Lapps, and Turks from Europe; Veddahs, Gurkhas, and Koreans from Asia; Eskimos and Venezuelan and Arizona Indians from the Americas; Bantu, Ethiopians, and Ghanaians from Africa; and Australian Aborigines, Maoris, and New Guineans from Oceania. These populations were examined for five blood group systems and the results used to calculate the relationship between them. This is expressed as the number of gene substitutions (variations in the genetic material controlling those particular factors). The final results fitted in well with the geographical distribution and expected relationship of the groups. The computer readings made clear the relatedness of population groups.

thing more precise upon which to base their conclusions.

One answer to this need can be found in genetics. Anyone's physical appearance is, after all, partly the result of genetic determination. What we see is called a phenotype, and the genetic constitution that lies behind it is called a genotype. Genetic biologists seek to know the genotypes associated with racial differences, because the genes are the actual location of whatever differences we think we can see in phenotypes. The most precise studies can be made on those traits that we know are transmitted by a single gene, and most modern research into population groups has concentrated on that area [1].

Race and geography

Genetically distinct population groups will be those whose populations tend to interbreed rather than find mates outside the group. For this reason geography plays an important role in determining race. Even today the effects of geographic isolation can be seen, and geographic classifications are among the most useful that can be made for anyone studying human populations.

There is general agreement that there are six to nine geographically and genetically defined races that take in about 99% of *Homo sapiens*. These include the European (Caucasoid), Asian (Mongoloid), and African (Negroid) groups most people think of as the "major races." But in addition, there are separate classifications for the American (Indian) group and the (East) Indian group. The Australians (Aborigines) constitute another race apart, and the peoples of the South Pacific are sometimes lumped together into yet another race, but more often are divided into Polynesians, Micronesians, and Melanesians.

Within these broad divisions distinctions can be made between local races—groups that constitute separate breeding populations. Tribal groups are often good examples of this, and sometimes modern "ethnic" groups are actually local races in this sense. The definitions are more arbitrary for local races, and researchers have different systems of classification [2].

KEY

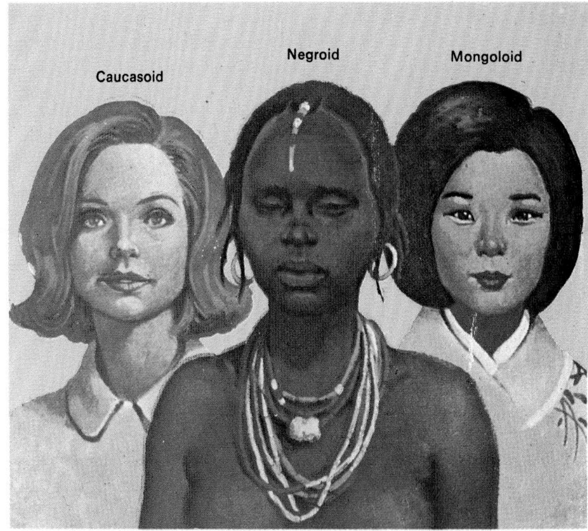
Caucasoid
Negroid
Mongoloid

The human species is often broken down into three major racial groupings: the Caucasoid, Negroid, and Mongoloid. There is, however, no single characteristic that is an indicator of any individual's belonging to one or another of these groups. The concept of race is useful only if applied to groups.

2

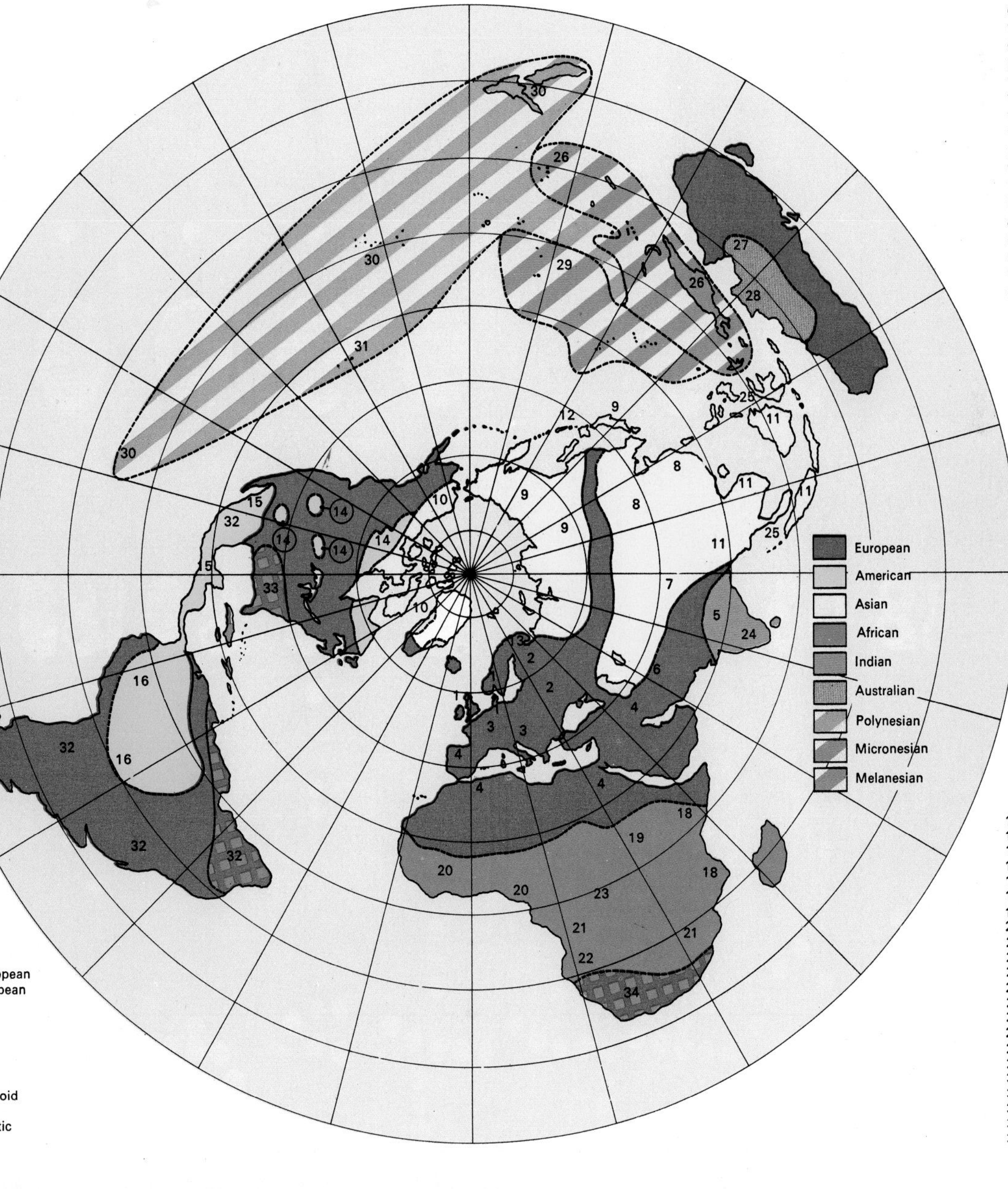

2 Nine distinct races of man are commonly distinguished within the Caucasoid, Mongoloid, and Negroid peoples. This classification is based on the geographical distribution of population prior to modern migrations. For convenience, many of these races have been further divided and the subgroups given separate racial status. Shown is a typical classification of the races of man.

European
American
Asian
African
Indian
Australian
Polynesian
Micronesian
Melanesian

1 Northwest European
2 Northeast European
3 Alpine
4 Mediterranean
5 Hindu
6 Turkic
7 Tibetan
8 North Chinese
9 Classic Mongoloid
10 Eskimo
11 Southeast Asiatic
12 Ainu
13 Lapp
14 North American Indian
15 Central American Indian
16 South American Indian
17 Fuegian
18 East African
19 Sudanese
20 Forest Negro
21 Bantu
22 Bushman and Hottentot
23 African Pygmy
24 Dravidian
25 Negrito
26 Melanesian-Papuan
27 Murrayian
28 Carpenterian
29 Micronesian
30 Polynesian
31 Neo-Hawaiian
32 Ladino
33 North American Colored
34 South African Colored

Family of man: how peoples differ

Humans have studied the differences among population groups of their own species, *Homo sapiens,* for centuries. Serious investigations of racial groups can tell us much about the evolution of humankind, genetics, and other important areas of knowledge. All too often, however, racial studies have been undertaken to make some political point. Thus these trivial differences can produce such terrible results as racism and genocide.

Skin and bones

Among the outward signs of differences between population groups are skin pigmentation and skeletal measurement. Skin pigmentation [Key], although it is probably the most popular way of telling people apart, is one of the least reliable. Skin color results from the presence of melanin, a dark brown pigment found in the epidermis. All races have the same number of melanin-forming cells in their skins, but Africans have more granules of melanin itself in the skin. So do people who have been tanned by the sun, for melanin is produced by sunlight. Not all dark-skinned people are African, even in their ancestry. Australian Aborigines, some peoples of the South Pacific, and certain local races of India also have dark skins. The one thing these groups do have in common is that they live in hot, sunny climates. Melanin seems to act as a protection against the ultraviolet rays in sunlight, and it may well be that dark skin color represents a biological adaptation to life in the tropics.

Body measurement has proved a more reliable means of arriving at useful racial differences than skin color. The length and breadth of human skulls can be measured between specified points and the results used to calculate a cephalic index for the skull in question (breadth/length × 100). Skulls can be classified into three general groups on the basis of their cephalic indices: long-headed (dolichocephalic, less than 75); median-headed (mesocephalic, 75–80); and round-headed (brachycephalic, 80 and up). Although all of these types can be found among members of any one population, certain groups tend toward one or another characteristic cephalic index. Central Europeans, for instance, tend to be round-headed, whereas Australian Aborigines generally are long-headed.

Other skeletal measurements have proven useful. It is obvious that "pygmy" groups are shorter than most other humans, but it is also the case that the ratio between various parts of the anatomy can differ widely among population groups and thus provides a basis for differentiation. Body measurements, however, are greatly affected by nutrition; the better-fed people are, the bigger they tend to be. Thus nowadays the results of skeletal measurement are usually used in conjunction with other methods of determining racial affiliation.

Straight black hair is characteristic of Asian peoples and wooly hair is characteristic of African peoples, but other generalizations about hair and racial type are unreliable. There are racial differences in eye forms, nose forms, and body types as well [1]. Each of these traits is dependent upon a complex gene interaction for its appearance. Those traits that result from a single gene can be more certainly located, and that

CONNECTIONS

See also

658 Family of man: today's peoples

688 Heart and blood circulation

686 Skin and hair

894 Prejudice and group intolerance

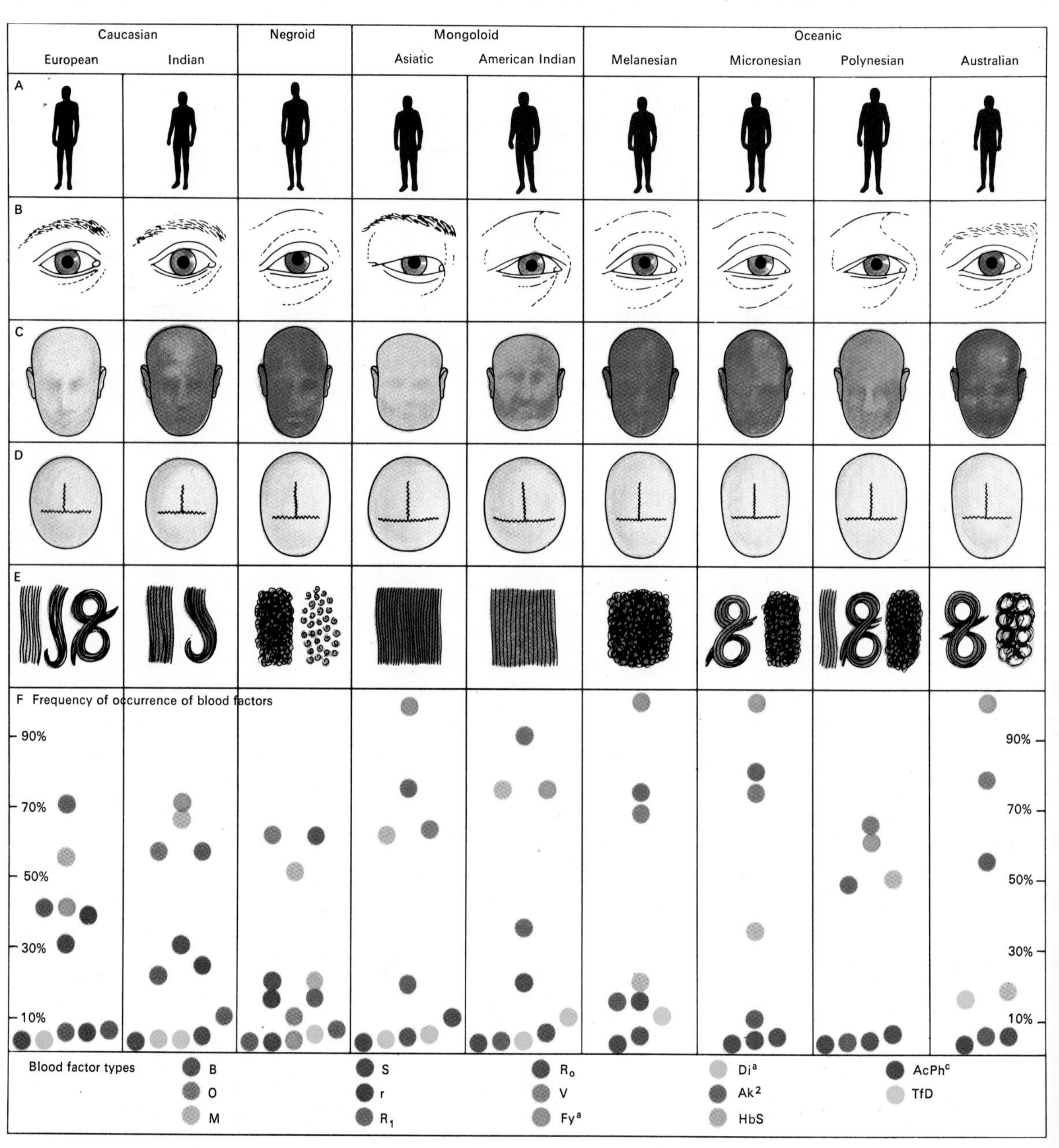

1
Caucasian
European
Indian
Negroid
Mongoloid
Asiatic
American Indian
Oceanic
Melanesian
Micronesian
Polynesian
Australian
A
B
C
D
E
F Frequency of occurrence of blood factors
90%
70%
50%
30%
10%
Blood factor types
B
O
M
S
r
R_1
R_o
V
Fy^a
Di^a
Ak^2
HbS
$AcPh^c$
TfD

1 Until recently anthropological race analysis concentrated on physical features, and races were classified as Caucasoid, Mongoloid, and Negroid. But such external differences are often vague, because of the wide variety of phenotypes that occur in each "race." More recently races have been classified geographically, and this classification is supported by genotypic evidence from blood groups. Shown here are some common physical features that tend to have a higher incidence of occurrence within the population groups depicted. Stature and body type [A] seem to have developed in response to climate. Facially, two obvious traits are that Asians and Amerindians tend to have epicanthic eye folds [B] and that lip eversion tends to occur among Africans. In all races there is a wide range of skin color [C]. A "typical" example of each is shown here. There are three basic skull shapes (seen from above, the wavy line representing the joints between skull bones) [D], while head hair [E] has many different colors and degrees of curliness. Genetic differences between races can best be traced in the frequencies with which blood groups occur within populations. Such groups include the ABO, MNS, Rh, Diego, and Duffy systems, as well as several others [F].

is why scientists today tend to study those traits rather than more obvious physical manifestations.

Blood will tell

Human blood groups are produced by a single set of genes, and millions of people all over the world have had their blood typed. This combination of circumstances has made blood grouping the most widely accepted means of racial population differentiation. Type B blood, for instance, scarcely exists among American Indians or Australian Aborigines, whereas the gene frequency is as high as 40% among African and Asian peoples, and hovers around 12% in Europe. The O antigen has its highest frequency among American Indians, and the A antigen occurs most often in Europe [2]. Other blood groupings have proven equally useful to researchers. Even abnormal blood factors are sometimes helpful. Sickle-celling and thalassemia are blood conditions produced genetically that have been traced to specific local populations in Africa and the tropics (both are associated with immunity to malaria, but a double dose of either gene involved can be fatal).

Genes and intelligence

If genes produce differences in the way people look, isn't it possible that they might produce other differences—in intelligence, for instance? First of all, intelligence is always a culturally defined trait, so an "intelligence test" will measure cultural adaptation better than anything else. Malnutrition and hypertension have measured effects on human intelligence that are not genetic in origin—and both conditions are endemic in poor populations. Intelligence is related to prenatal and immediate postnatal care, family structures, expectations, residence patterns, class background, family income, and how the person taking the test sees himself and the environment. In addition, no research has been able to link other overall behavior patterns to genetic influence [3], so it is correct to say that so far there has been no indication that the race and intelligence of a person are genetically linked.

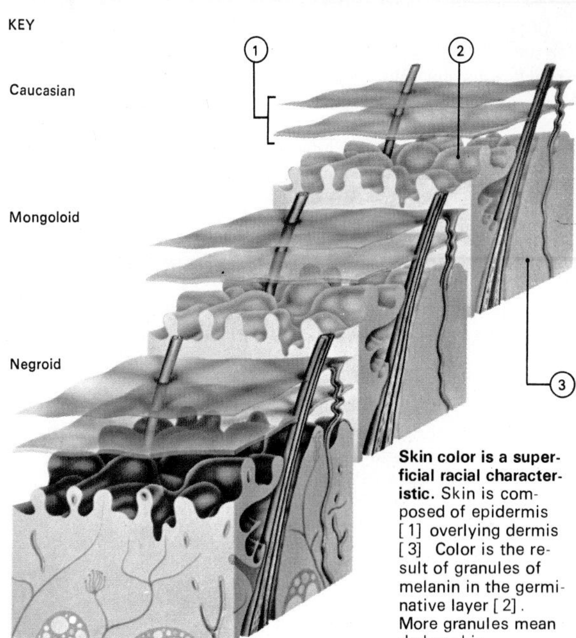
KEY
Caucasian
Mongoloid
Negroid
1
2
3

Skin color is a superficial racial characteristic. Skin is composed of epidermis [1] overlying dermis [3] Color is the result of granules of melanin in the germinative layer [2]. More granules mean darker skin.

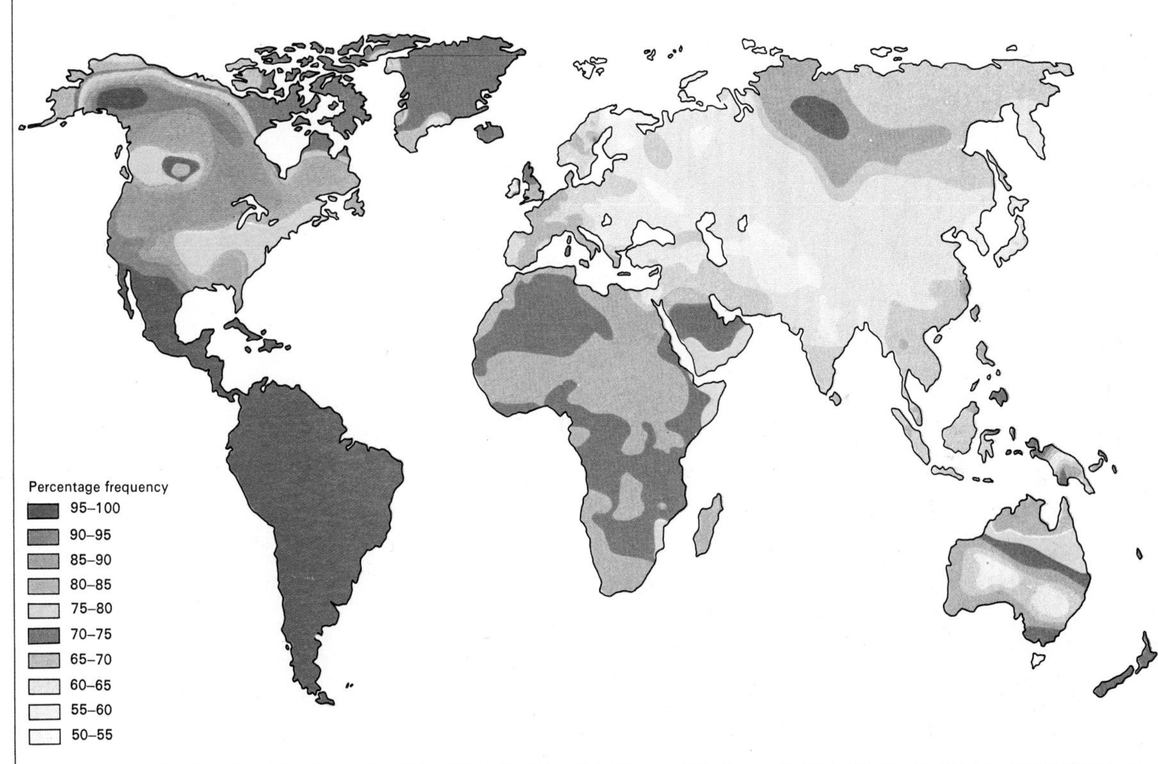
2
Percentage frequency
95–100
90–95
85–90
80–85
75–80
70–75
65–70
60–65
55–60
50–55

2 There is more information available for the ABO system than for all the rest of the blood grouping systems added together. This is largely because of its early discovery but also because it is of major importance in blood transfusion, where it is the main criterion for compatibility of blood types. Shown is the distribution of the O antigen throughout the world. Central and South American Indians have few or no A or B antigens and are therefore very high in O. This probably occurred because the relatively few members of the original colonizing population lacked these antigens. The A antigen is found more often among North American Indians. In Europe the O antigen reaches its highest frequency among people on the Atlantic margins. This may be a remnant population that has been forced westward by population pressures from the east.

3
Bantu
European
Chinese
American Indian
Australian Aborigine
Eskimo
Bushman

3 Behavior is more important in determining what most people see as "racial differences" than is biological race. Costume defines the differences between these people better than physique, although each group has made physical adaptations to its environment, like the steatopygian buttocks of the African Bushmen. More crucial has been cultural adaptation to environment. Humanity's greatest evolutionary strength is its adaptive facility.

An introduction to body and mind

The human body is a dazzlingly complex machine, an apparatus of intricate, interlocking systems [1] in which millions of vital processes take place. But despite this complexity its mechanisms function with amazing efficiency and precision, and its basic structure is in fact relatively uncomplicated.

The interaction of body and mind

While our knowledge of how the body and the mind work mechanically is reasonably advanced, the way in which they interact to produce "the person" remains an unsolved puzzle. That the two are not separate and are related is obvious from what we now know of the psychosomatic diseases. These are physical disorders, such as hypertension and ulcers, that are, in part, caused by psychological factors. We are also aware that attitudes of mind affect the body's susceptibility to attack by diseases. But we are far from unraveling the extent and complexity of the relationship of body and mind. In fact, almost all current research points toward the impossibility of drawing a clear line between the two.

Hardly any better understood is the way in which the brain controls the body and how changes in body function are achieved to maintain optimum working efficiency. Two main systems are involved. The first of these consists of nerve pathways carrying controlling impulses from the brain to the organs themselves. This type of control includes the regulation of breathing and heart rate. Centers in the brain constantly monitor the body's performance and alter breathing and heart rates accordingly.

The second great system, the endocrine system, is chemical and makes use of the bloodstream. The pituitary gland at the base of the brain is its coordinator and also provides the link between it and the brain. In response either to impulses from the brain or to changes in body chemistry, it secretes hormones into the bloodstream. The hormones flow around the body and cause changes in its organs. Many of these changes, such as the control of urine secretion, regulation of metabolism, secretion of hormones to combat stress, are important in maintaining life.

The Hippocratic view of the brain

The problem of how body and mind interact exercised the mind of Hippocrates (*c.*460–*c.*377 BC), the most admired physician of the ancient world. His insight into brain function was remarkable. He wrote: "I hold that the brain is the most powerful organ of the human body . . . Eyes, ears, tongue, hands, and feet act in accordance with the discernment of the brain . . . I assert that the brain is the interpreter of consciousness." This amazing insight into the nature of consciousness was ignored until the eighteenth and nineteenth centuries.

In the Middle Ages the precise observations of the ancients had been lost and speculation took their place. Costa de Luca (864–923), misinterpreting the work of Galen (*c.*130–*c.*200) who was, after Hippocrates, the most distinguished physician of antiquity, described the function of the brain as based on a valve action of the movements of "Pneuma" between the ventricles of the brain.

The idea that messages from the brain were conveyed by fluid flowing from the

CONNECTIONS

See also
412 The cell in action
460 Animal anatomy
664 The nervous system
666 How the brain works
690 Glands and their hormones
542 The life of mammals

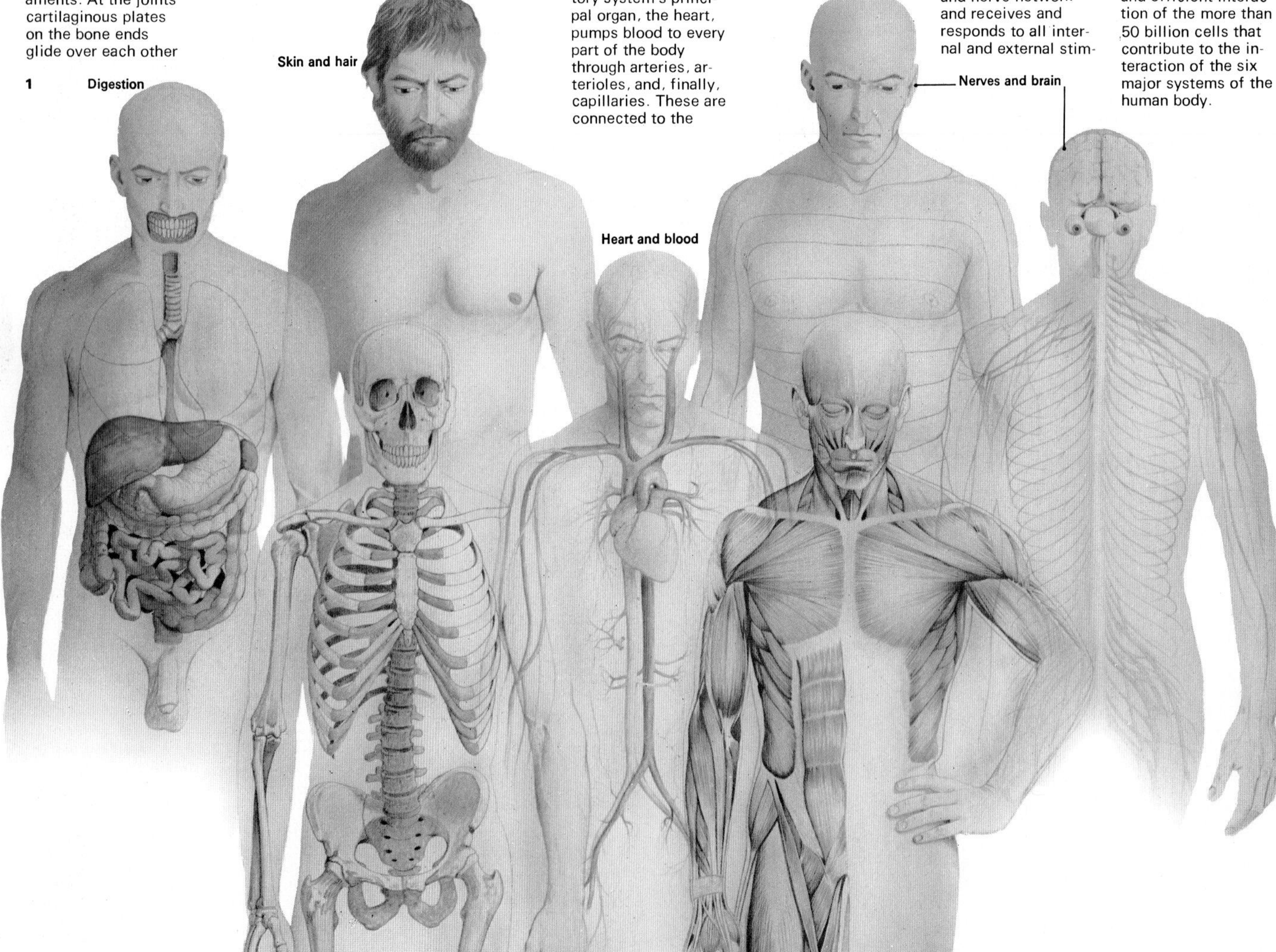

1
Digestion
Skin and hair
Heart and blood
Nerves and brain
Skeleton
Muscles

1 The body has six major systems. The skeletal system is made up of more than 200 bones joined by fibrous ligaments. At the joints cartilaginous plates on the bone ends glide over each other to allow movement. The muscles are the body's motors, making possible its concerted internal and external responses to the environment. The digestive system is concerned with the intake of food, its digestion and then the absorption of its energy-giving and body-building substances. The circulatory system's principal organ, the heart, pumps blood to every part of the body through arteries, arterioles, and, finally, capillaries. These are connected to the venules and veins that return blood to the heart. The skin protects the underlying tissues, regulates body temperature, and helps excrete wastes. The nervous system includes the brain, spinal cord, and nerve network and receives and responds to all internal and external stimuli needing either conscious or unconscious response. The body's healthy and proper functioning depends on the close and efficient interaction of the more than 50 billion cells that contribute to the interaction of the six major systems of the human body.

ventricles down the nerves to the muscles continued until the latter part of the eighteenth century when Luigi Galvani (1737–98), working in Italy, discovered that electricity applied to a frog's leg made the muscles twitch.

Recent theories about the brain

With the coming of the twentieth century scientific knowledge of how the body functions increased. The detailed physiology of respiration and nutrition and the finer details of anatomy and tissue structure came to be understood. Charles Scott Sherrington (1857–1952) in his Oxford laboratories investigated the nervous system and defined in great detail the way in which messages flowed to and from the brain. John Hughlings Jackson (1835–1911), clinician and philosopher, through observations of patients with epilepsy and brain disorders, constructed models of the organization of brain function and the formation of consciousness.

Since the 1940s the understanding of brain function has been changing rapidly. The invention of the vacuum tube and, more recently, the transistor have allowed detailed examination of cellular activity within the brains of both animals and man. The science of biochemistry has led to understanding of the processes that take place deep within the cell and has succeeded in defining the very nature and make-up of the cell itself. Present theories about the functioning of the nervous system and the elaboration of it by consciousness rely heavily on ideas from computer technology.

The brain is now seen as an organ constructed to process the vast amount of information fed to it by the senses. It then constructs a model of the outside world. This model is continually updated by incoming information. There is little doubt that what the brain "sees" depends not only on what is fed to it by the senses, but also on how it wishes to process this information and to interpret its own private world. It would seem that while most people have a common perception of the world, each individual, in addition, has a personal "reality" that remains largely unshared.

KEY

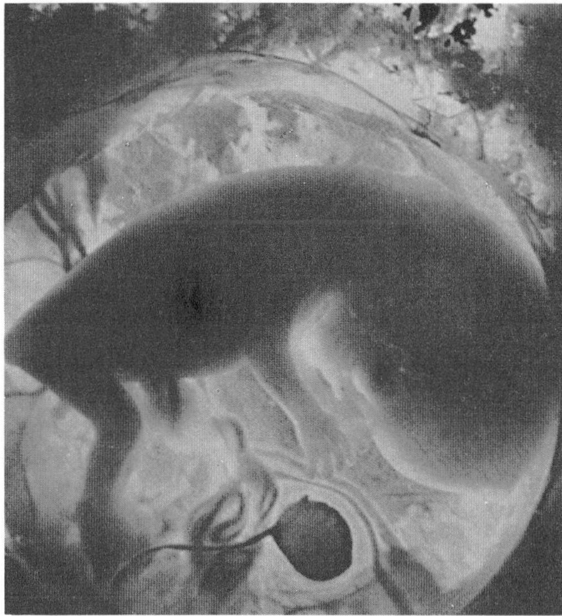

2

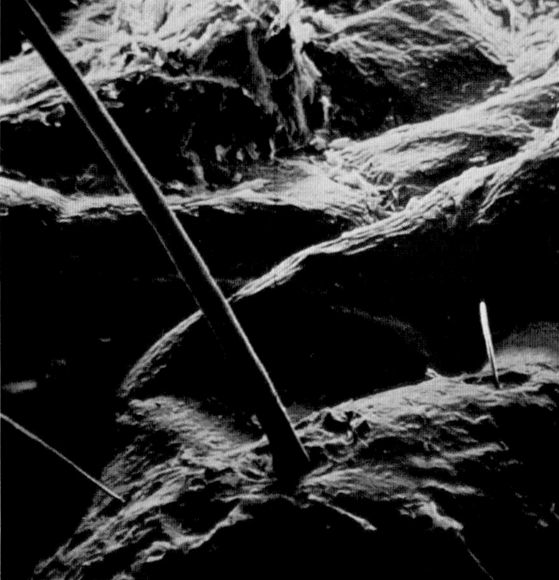

2 Human skin is the body's first line of defense and acts also as an organ of excretion and water regulation. It protects the body from many potentially dangerous chemical, physical, and biological substances. It is waterproof, enabling the body to exist in dry air or be immersed in fresh or salt water. Within the skin, shown here magnified 60 times, lie touch- and pain-sensitive cells and hair follicles.

3

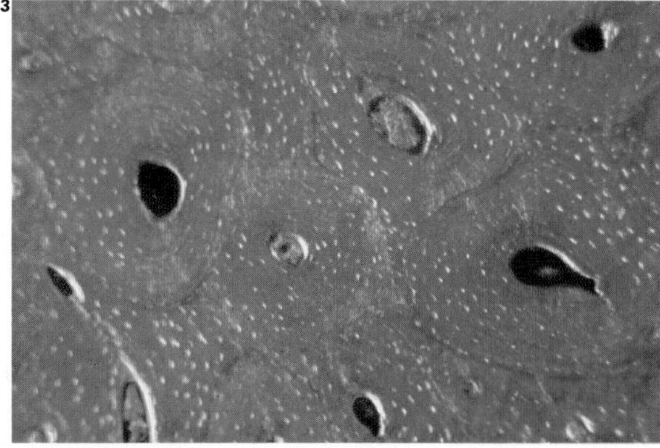

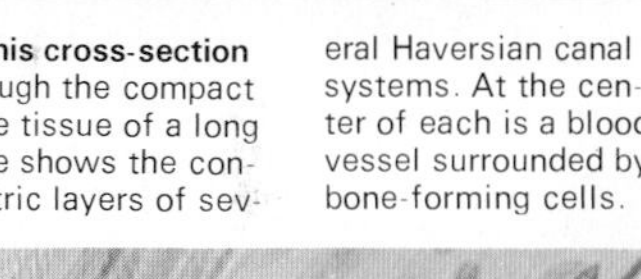

3 This cross-section through the compact bone tissue of a long bone shows the concentric layers of several Haversian canal systems. At the center of each is a blood vessel surrounded by bone-forming cells.

4

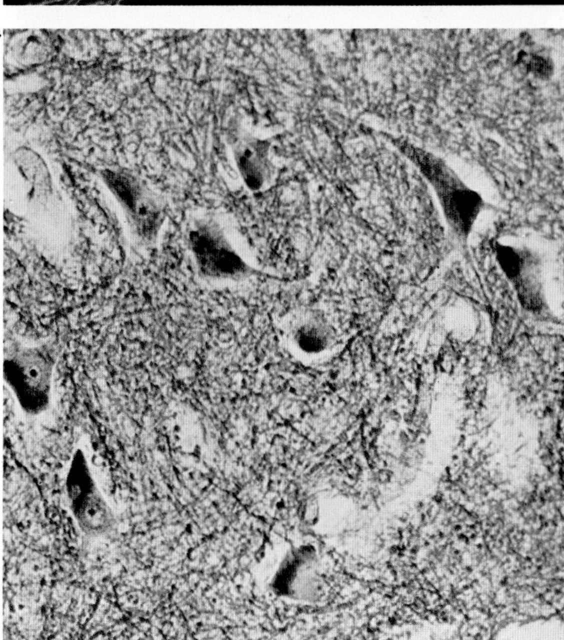

4 The motor cells controlling muscle movement lie deep within the spinal cord. These cells provide the final pathway for impulses arising in the voluntary motor area of the brain. It is these that are destroyed in polio.

5

5 The villi, the fingerlike projections and folds of the small intestines, are seen here in cross-section. They present a large area for the absorption of nutrients from the food reaching the intestine from the stomach.

6

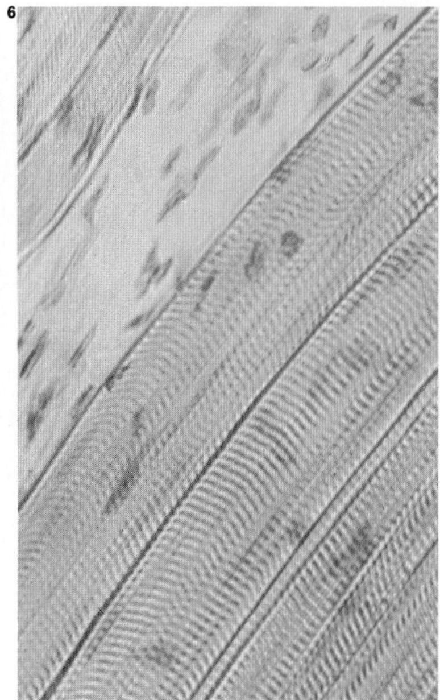

6 Voluntary muscle consists of bundles of fibers. These are divided into bands, which appear as dark lines under a microscope. They contain actin and myosin, two important contractile proteins.

The nervous system

The nervous system is the circuit that brings our bodies to life. It allows us to perceive the world outside and monitor the world within. Through its efficiency we can respond and react to changes in the environment by moving our muscles and coordinating the actions of our various organs.

The structure of the nervous system

The nervous system can be thought of as a number of separate but integrated sections that monitor the environment and instigate and coordinate the body's multiple activities [Key]. The central nervous system (CNS) consists of the brain and spinal cord [1]. Connected to it and running throughout the body is the peripheral nervous system. This has two main parts—the somatic, or voluntary, nervous system and the autonomic, or involuntary, system, which deals with the unconscious control of the body's organs [2]. The somatic deals largely with awareness of sensation and the voluntary control of muscle activity. Information is fed into it through the sensory nerves from the eyes and ears, taste buds, balance organs, and the millions of contact, temperature, pressure, and pain receptors in the skin, which together make up the sense of touch. There are also receptors for sensing the degree of tension in muscles and tendons and for monitoring blood pressure and the levels of oxygen, glucose, and carbon dioxide in the blood. Motor nerves, originating in the CNS, carry information to the muscles and in this way initiate movement.

The cells or neurons that make up the nervous system consist of a cell body, which contains the nucleus, and a long extension called the axon [4]. On the cell body and at the end of the axon are short branches called dendrites. Contact between nerve cells, from the axon of one to the cell body of the next, is established via these dendrites but takes place across a small gap called a synapse. The nerves of the peripheral system consist mainly of axons that run the whole length of the nerve (in the leg this distance may be as much as a yard), while those of the CNS consist mainly of cell bodies with short tracts or bundles of axons. Where cell bodies occur outside the CNS, as with sensory and autonomic nerves, they are collected in groups called ganglia.

How nerves send their messages

Although nerves can be thought of as wires or telegraph cables carrying messages in the form of bursts of electricity, a nerve impulse is more complicated than a surge of electrons traveling along a copper wire. The transmission of an impulse through a living cell involves the movement of electrically charged particles—ions—across, not along, a membrane; in this case the wall of the axon.

At rest (that is, when not conducting impulses) a nerve cell is polarized; the outside of its membrane bears a different electrical charge from the inside. This is because of the different concentrations of sodium and potassium ions on either side of the membrane. Inside is a high concentration of potassium and a low concentration of sodium while the reverse is true outside. When a nerve is stimulated, the arrangement of the molecules in the membrane is altered, allowing potassium ions to leak out and sodium to

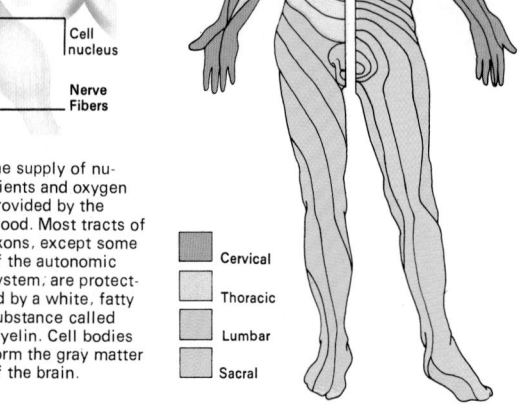

CONNECTIONS

See also
666 How the brain works
722 Diseases of the nervous system
1566 Electrochemistry

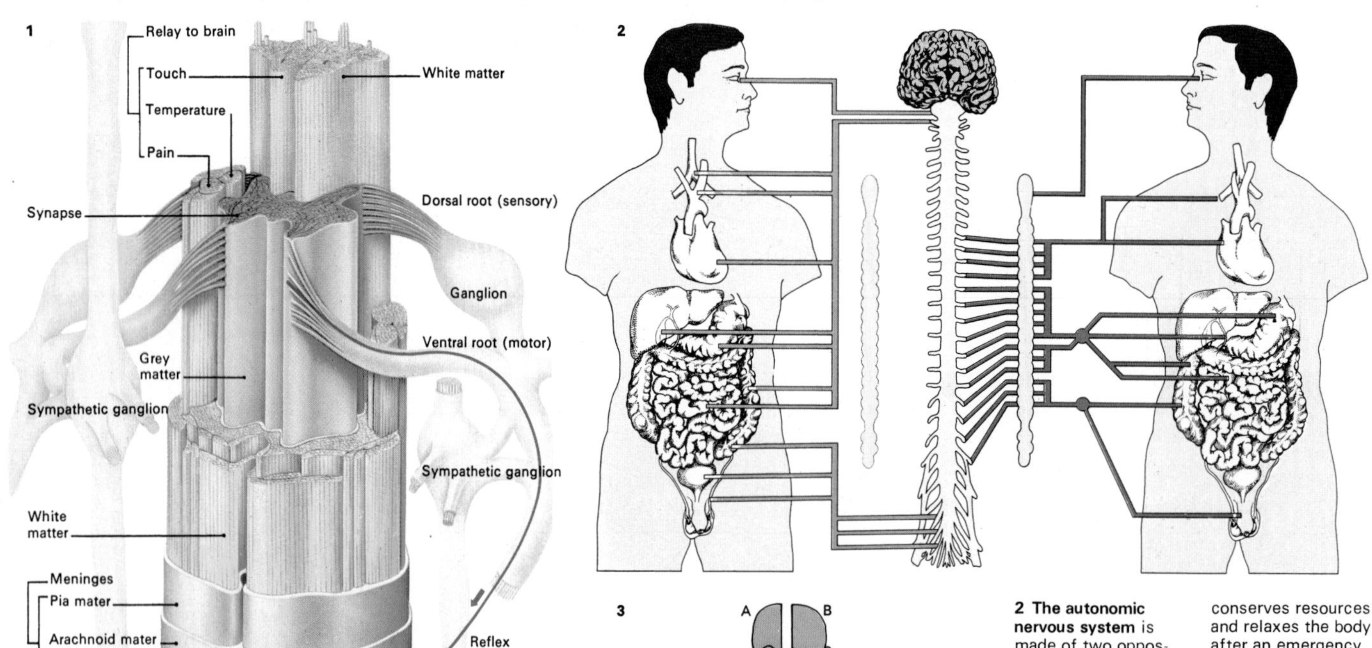
1
Relay to brain
Touch
Temperature
Pain
White matter
Synapse
Dorsal root (sensory)
Ganglion
Ventral root (motor)
Grey matter
Sympathetic ganglion
Sympathetic ganglion
White matter
Meninges
Pia mater
Arachnoid mater
Dura mater
Reflex pathway
Ganglion
Cell nucleus
Nerve Fibers
Synapse
2
3
A
B
Cervical
Thoracic
Lumbar
Sacral

1 The spinal cord is made up of numerous bundles of nerve fibers carrying messages to and from the brain. The pathways cross so that sensations from one side of the body register in the cortex of the brain on the other side. The nervous system needs careful protection. The brain and spinal cord are wrapped in tough membranes called meninges and bathed in a cerebrospinal fluid. This adds an effective watery cushion against jarring, as well as augmenting the supply of nutrients and oxygen provided by the blood. Most tracts of axons, except some of the autonomic system, are protected by a white, fatty substance called myelin. Cell bodies form the gray matter of the brain.

2 The autonomic nervous system is made of two opposing parts; the sympathetic and the parasympathetic. The sympathetic system prepares the body for fight or flight. It can limit the blood supply to the digestive organs, increasing the amount of blood available for muscles and limbs. The parasympathetic system conserves resources and relaxes the body after an emergency or for sleep. Sympathetic nerves [red lines] lead from the spinal cord to nearby nerve chains, the sympathetic chains of ganglia. The parasympathetic nerves [blue lines] lead directly to the organs. This system also controls rate of the heartbeat.

3 Spinal nerves carrying messages to and from the spinal cord serve specific areas of skin known as dermatomes. The 31 pairs, one for each of the bones of the spine (the vertebrae), are subdivided into five groups. As the area served by the last pair of spinal nerves is ill-defined, only the four major groups are shown for the front [A] and back [B] of the adult. The human embryo

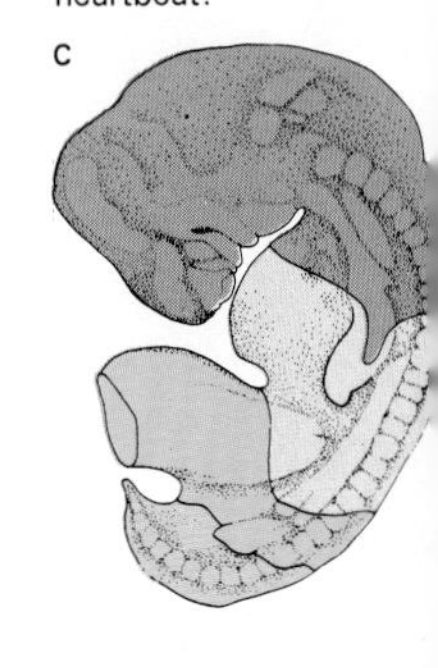
C

[C] shows the same divisions.

leak in. At this moment, the nerve membrane is depolarized and the electrical change causes an alteration in the molecular structure of the next section of membrane, which in turn becomes depolarized. In this way an impulse travels rapidly along the nerve fiber.

Nerve cells are remarkable because they can "communicate" with each other. A stimulated neuron sends messages in the form of the tiny rapid pulses of electricity along its axon, the synapses linking it to other neurons. The electrical impulses cannot themselves jump across synapses, but the signal is passed by causing the release of a chemical transmitter substance that makes the surface of the next neuron develop an impulse [5].

The role of the nervous system

Everything we do requires the mediation of the nervous system, from the flick of a finger to highly coordinated, sophisticated activities. Some simple responses use only particular parts of the nervous system. If someone touches something hot, he pulls his hand away quickly. This simple but essential response is called a spinal reflex [6], since impulses from the sensory nerve endings in the skin need reach only the spinal cord to be acted upon. Impulses generated within motor cells in the spinal cord pass back down the motor neurons of the arm and activate the muscles that move the hand. This reflex is automatic [7] (it can happen during sleep) and is unlearned.

The behavior of very simple animals is made up entirely of reflex movements, but higher animals and humans have greater freedom of action and can respond in a variety of ways to most situations. Reflexes continue to be important in emergencies and for such vital activities as breathing and bowel movements. But most human behavior falls into another category—it is voluntary, learned, and non-reflex. This kind of behavior is made possible because the nervous system can learn from experience and direct its own activities. Since no two people have the same experiences, and no two brains are alike, every nervous system behaves uniquely.

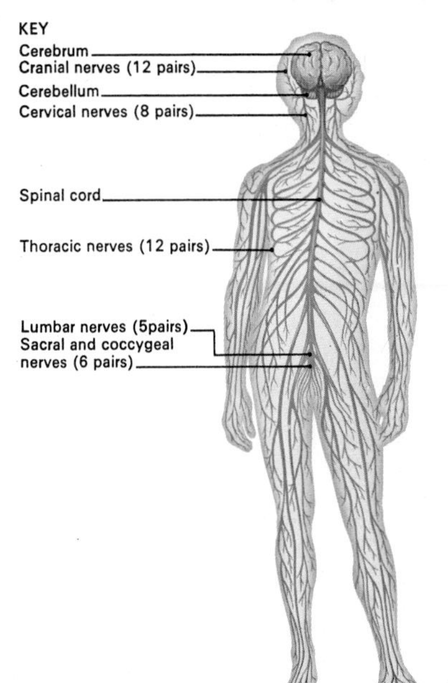
KEY
Cerebrum
Cranial nerves (12 pairs)
Cerebellum
Cervical nerves (8 pairs)
Spinal cord
Thoracic nerves (12 pairs)
Lumbar nerves (5pairs)
Sacral and coccygeal nerves (6 pairs)

The nervous system is divided into two parts: central and peripheral. The central nervous system (CNS) includes the brain and spinal cord. It receives information, makes decisions, and transmits instructions. The peripheral nervous system consists chiefly of nerve fibers leading to and from the CNS. It cannot make "decisions" and acts only as a message transmitter. Here are 12 pairs of such nerves radiating from the brain and 31 pairs from the spinal cord. The peripheral nervous system includes the somatic system, which deals with voluntary actions, and the autonomic nervous system, which controls such organs as the heart and intestines.

4

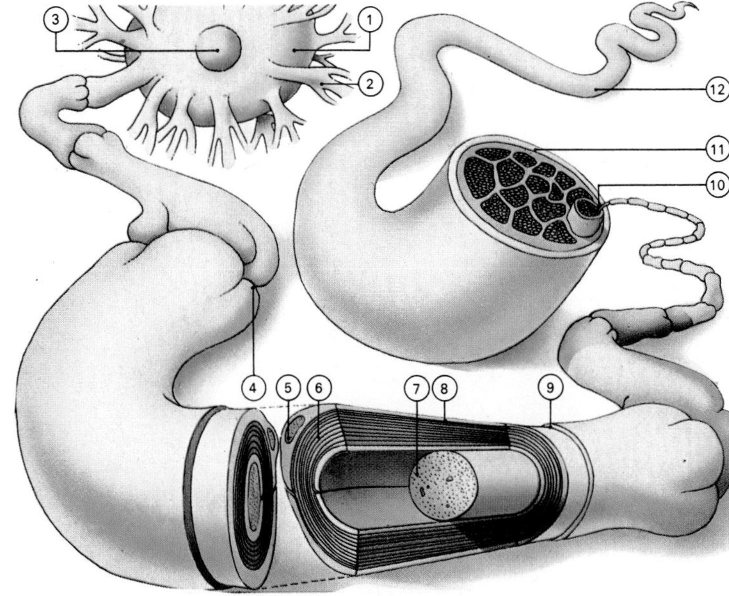

5 Nerve impulses are transmitted by bioelectricity. At the junction between nerve and muscle fibers (the motor end plate) a chemical transmitter is released from the nerve in response to the electrical change produced when the nerve is stimulated. As a result, the muscle fiber contracts. [A] shows a longitudinal section through a motor end plate. [1] shows a nerve axon, with an impulse traveling toward its tip. [2] shows a section though a terminal button of a nerve cell, the part containing acetylcholine, a chemical transmitter. [3] is the synaptic gutter—a muscle fiber membrane greatly folded to form a "gutter" that accommodates the terminal button. [4] is the muscle fiber itself in a relaxed state. [B] is a detailed diagram of the terminal button region, showing the nerve cell about to release the chemical transmitter. [C] demonstrates the release of the chemical transmitter [5] as the nerve impulse reaches the tip of the terminal button. The transmitter causes changes in the permeability of the muscle fiber membrane. [D] shows the contraction of muscle fiber [6]. The permeability change results in an altered electrical state across the membrane, stimulating contraction of the muscle.

5

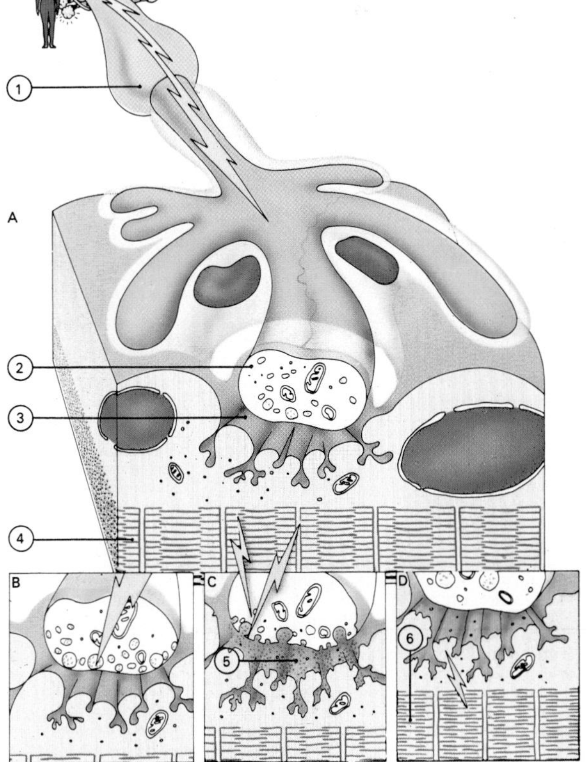
A
B
C
D

4 The structure of a single nerve and myelinated cell fiber is shown. [1] Cell body. [2] Dendrites conducting messages to the cell body. [3] Cell nucleus. [4] Node of Ranvier, a constriction of the myelin sheath. [5] Schwann cell nucleus—the cell secreting the myelin sheath [6] that insulates the axon [7]. [8] Nerve fiber. [9] Endoneurium—interfiber tissue. [10] Perineurium, sheathing fiber bundles. [11] Epineurium sheathing the nerve [12].

6

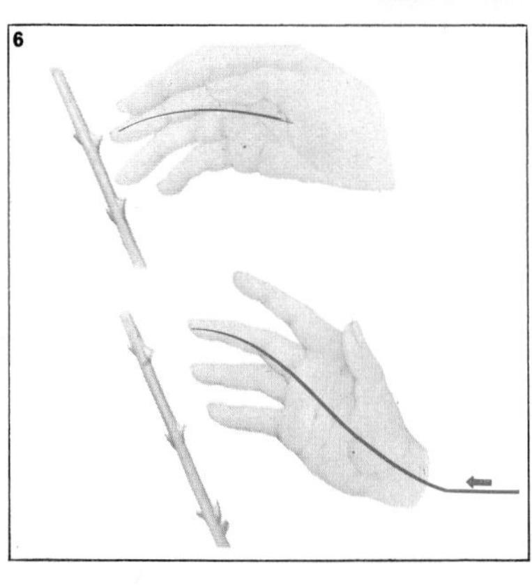

7

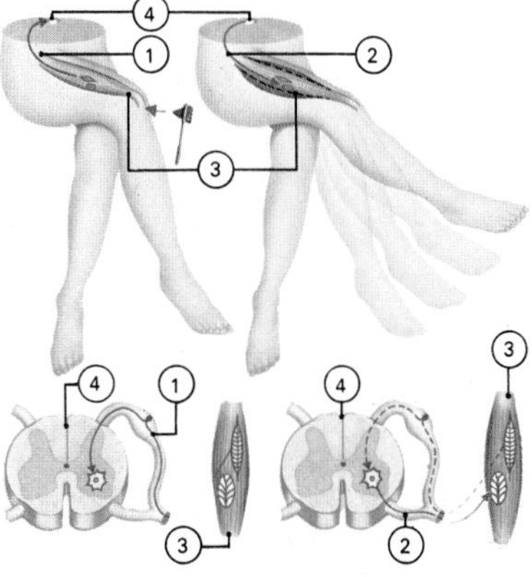

6 Nerve impulses from a pricked finger travel to the brain via the spinal cord, but because the sensory and motor nerves connect at synapses in the spinal cord, reflex withdrawal occurs before the message reaches the level of consciousness.

7 The knee jerk is a simple reflex action, involving only a sensory receptor neuron [1] and a motor neuron [2]. Impulses to and from the muscles [3] traverse only one segment of the spinal cord [4]. This reflex is independent of the brain.

How the brain works

Within the bony protective casing of the skull the brain has a shape and surface somewhat like that of a huge walnut kernel. The major part of the brain has two symmetrical and linked halves with fissures, folds, and wrinkles, and is covered with thin layers of membrane.

Anatomy of the brain

The brain, weighing an average of 3 lb (1,380gm) in a man and 2lb 12oz (1,250gm) in a woman, is made up of about 30 billion cells called neurons. Intelligence is thought to be related in some way to the complexity of the microstructure, the connections between its units, and its biochemistry. At birth the structure of the brain is almost complete, but it continues to grow until the age of 20, both by increasing the size of individual cells and by augmenting the amount of tissue connecting the neurons, which finally makes up some 40 percent of the volume.

The brain is not a homogeneous mass, but has several distinct parts that have developed during evolution [1]. The oldest areas, responsible for such life-supporting functions as breathing, circulation of the blood, and sleeping, are found at the base of the brain joined to the spinal cord, while the more recently developed parts are wrapped around the older areas. They have many folds and thus a large surface area in relation to their volume.

The two hemispheres that make up the cerebrum, the major part of the brain, are mirror images of each other, each chiefly concerned with movements and sensations of one side of the body. The left hemisphere controls the right side and vice versa. Complex behavior such as speech is controlled by one of the two hemispheres—in most people the left hemisphere—which also controls the dominant hand. Thus, if a right-handed person suffers a stroke affecting the left side of the brain, he usually loses the use of the right hand and arm—and also the power of speech.

Structure and function

The hemispheres make up 70 percent of the brain and nervous system, including the nerves of the body. They consist of the cortex [5], an outer layer of gray matter surrounding a thicker layer of white matter made up of nerve fibers, and are connected by a bundle of fibers, the corpus callosum.

Beneath the cortex there are the four lobes of each hemisphere. The occipital lobe at the back of the brain receives and analyzes visual information. The temporal lobes on the side of each hemisphere deal with sound. Certain vivid auditory and visual sensations have also been located here. The frontal lobes are mainly concerned with the regulation of voluntary movements and also have something to do with the use of language. The prefrontal areas of this lobe are thought to be involved with intellect and personality, but their specific functions are still unknown. The parietal lobes are mainly associated with our sense of touch and balance. The senses of taste and smell, poorly developed in humans, are represented by small areas buried in the frontal and temporal lobes.

At the base of the brain is the brain stem, in the medulla, which controls essential ac-

CONNECTIONS

See also

664 The nervous system
668 Mind and brain
670 Memory and recall
672 Potential of the mind
716 Diseases of the circulation
722 Diseases of the nervous system
1672 How computers work
1782 Information retrieval

1 The 30 billion cells of the brain are interconnected with nerve fibers. As in the rest of the nervous system, information is transmitted between the cells in coded form as minute electrical impulses. The nerve fibers appear white because each is insulated by a sheath made of myelin, while the nerve bodies or soma, which are not myelinated, appear gray in contrast. Bundles of nerve fibers run up the spinal cord from the rest of the body to the brain, bringing signals about vital internal functions and external perceptions. After analysis, instructions are sent down the spinal cord to regulate the body's reactions to signals. The brain consists of three distinct units of increasing complexity. The hindbrain consists of the brain stem [A], the cerebellum [B], and medulla and pons [C]. The midbrain is made up of the mammillary bodies [D], the pituitary [E], the thalamus [F], and the hypothalamus [G]. At the top (and covering the other two) is the forebrain, which is made up of twin, structurally similar but functionally distinct units—cerebral hemispheres. Each of these is divided into four lobes: the frontal [H], temporal [I], parietal [J], and occipital [K]. The two hemispheres are connected by a massive bundle of nerve tracts called the corpus callosum [L].

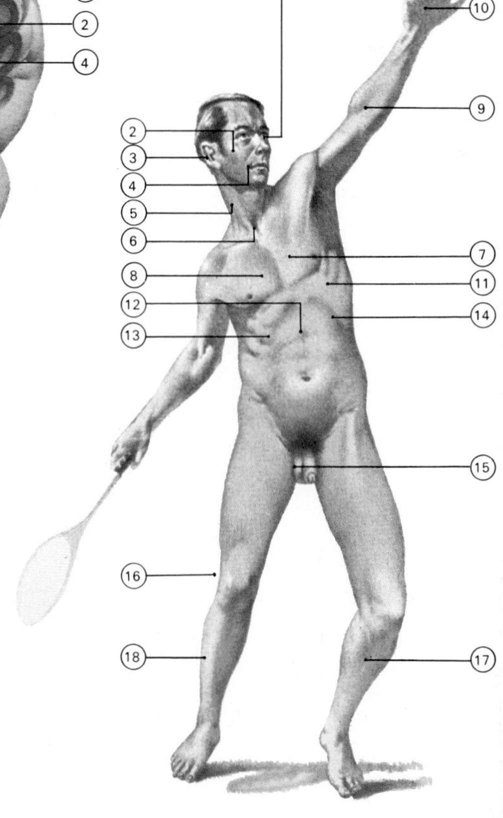

2 How the brain controls the body is still largely a mystery despite modern surgical and laboratory techniques. Partly because its functions are interlinked in a most complex way and partly because of the difficulties of experimenting with humans, the brain remains very much unknown. It is possible to identify some connections between certain parts of the brain and some bodily functions. The principal parts of the brain have been moved apart to show their appearance and relationships, but in real life they are packed tightly in the skull. Optic tracts carry stimuli from the retina of the eye [1] to the occipital lobes. The cortex controls and senses facial movements [2] and also controls hearing [3]. Broca's area of the cerebral cortex controls speech [4]. The cortex controls and senses neck movements [5]. The pituitary controls the thyroid gland [6], which in turn regulates the body's metabolism. The brain stem controls heart rate [7] and respiratory rate [8]. The cortex controls arm movements [9]. The parietal lobe controls judgment of weight, shape, size, and feel [10]. The cortex controls the trunk [11]. The brain stem controls stomach motion and acid secretion [12]. The pituitary affects the adrenal glands [13]. Hormones from the pituitary control the kidney's urine secretion [14]. The pituitary controls the testes [15] and ovaries. The cerebellum controls movement [16]. The pituitary controls the growth of long bones [17]. The cortex controls legs and feet [18].

tivities such as breathing, coughing, and heartbeat. Behind and slightly above this is the cerebellum, which is important for coordinating bodily movement and for maintaining posture and balance. It does not initiate movements but is responsible for their smooth and balanced execution, for maintaining the tension of muscle, and for integrating movements in a complex action such as walking. The two sides of the cerebellum are united by the pons.

Emotional control

Through the brain stem runs the reticular formation, a network of fibers carrying the sensory pathways from the spinal cord to the brain. This diffuse area monitors incoming information from the body's sense perceptors and regulates the level of response. It is also thought to have profound influences on emotional behavior [3].

In the middle of the brain, grouped around the fluid-filled cavities called the ventricles, are regions controlling many of our basic drives. The hypothalamus controls hunger, thirst, temperature, aggression, and sex drive and, by regulating the pituitary gland, is responsible for controlling the secretion of many hormones.

Looped around the hypothalamus is a collection of structures forming the limbic system—the septum, fornix, amygdala, and hippocampus. These are thought to be involved in emotional responses such as fear and aggression and to interact closely to produce mood changes. Also in the middle of the brain lies the thalamus, a tightly packed cluster of nerve cells that relays impulses from the sense organs to the cortex.

The brain normally consumes 20 percent of all the oxygen extracted from the blood. Without oxygen, brain cells are damaged irreparably and die; the brain has no capacity for cell regeneration.

The brain has been likened to a computer, but it is an infinitely more complex structure and much of its functioning still remains a mystery. Although we know to some extent what each part of the brain does, it would be wrong to think that these parts act independently. The brain works as a highly efficient interactive unit.

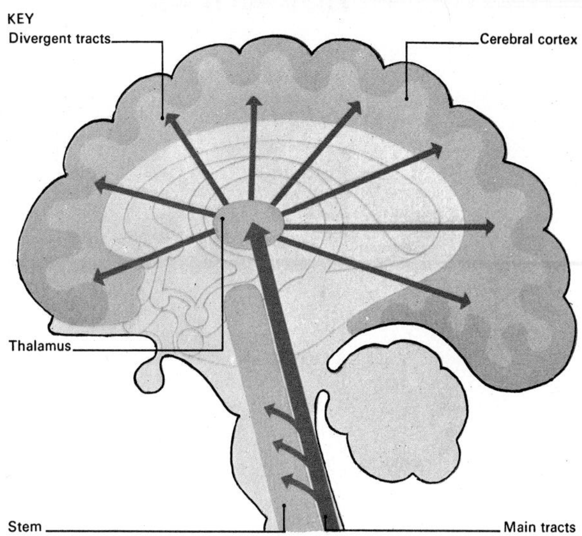
KEY
Divergent tracts
Cerebral cortex
Thalamus
Stem
Main tracts

When the brain is awakened from sleep, sensory information carried by the main tracts stimulates the reticular formation deep in the stem. This area, which regulates the brain's activity, then sends showers of impulses to the thalamus. From here divergent tracts arouse the cerebral cortex.

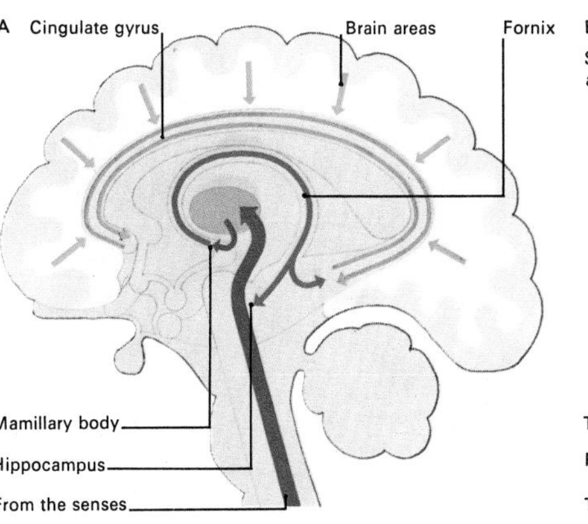
A Cingulate gyrus
Brain areas
Fornix
Mamillary body
Hippocampus
From the senses

B Motor area
Suppressor area
Thalamus
Pathways
Tracts
Cerebellum
Spinal cord

C Limbic system
Input
Pituitary gland
Hypothalamus
Heart and lung rates
Stem
To other organs

3 Identifying areas of the brain that are responsible for such functions as memory, thought, consciousness, judgment, and personality is extremely difficult. Over the past few years, however, various functions have been associated, at least tentatively, with specific areas of the brain [A]. Memory, for example, seems to be linked with the limbic system. One explanation is that impulses from the senses and brain areas enter the limbic system in the middle of the brain and are then passed through the mamillary body, around the fornix to the hippocampus and cingulate gyrus. It is these limbic structures that record impressions and recall them. [B] Movement starts as complex signal patterns in the motor area. These are modified by the suppressor area and then transmitted via nerve tracts to the muscles. Return information reaches the cerebellum through the spinal cord and then, via the pathways and thalamus, helps to coordinate body movement. [C] As far as the emotions are concerned, it has been established that the hypothalamus controls appetite, sex drive, thirst, aggression, and emotion generally. It is thought that impulses from the frontal lobes are integrated in the limbic system and fed to the hypothalamus, which regulates the pituitary gland. Limbic impulses are also responsible for affecting heart and lung rates, and other organs.

4 This grotesque figure, a homunculus, might also be called "sensory man." It shows the parts of the body as they appear to the brain. The physical size of each part is related to the size of the area of the brain controlling that part's activity. The brain clearly assigns importance to particular areas like the hands and fingers, which are very sensitive in order to assess an object's weight, size, texture, and rigidity. This figure shows how the brain "sees," "feels," and "moves" our bodies. The body image on the brain is inverted, so that the feet are controlled by the top of the cortex and facial features at the bottom. Sensations from the left side of the body are "felt" on the right side and vice versa.

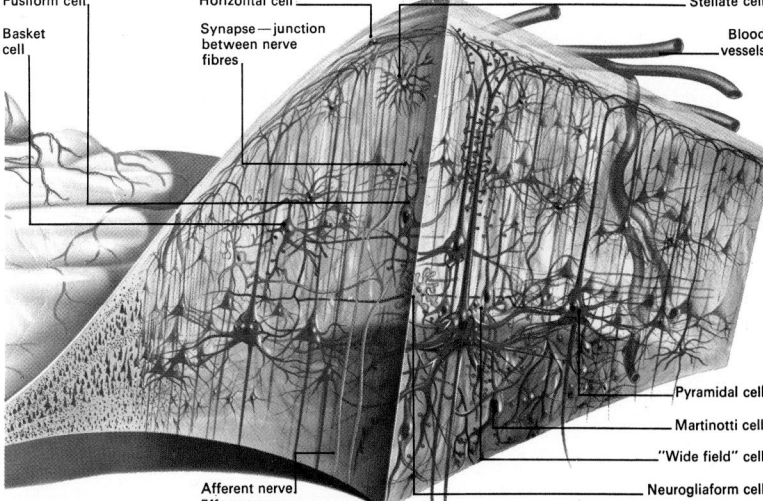

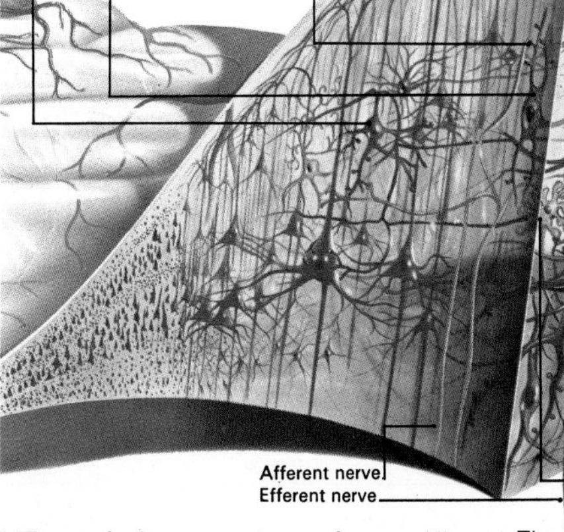
5 Fusiform cell
Basket cell
Horizontal cell
Synapse—junction between nerve fibres
Stellate cell
Blood vessels
Pyramidal cell
Martinotti cell
"Wide field" cell
Neurogliaform cell
Afferent nerve
Efferent nerve

5 The cerebral cortex, as if peeled from the surface of the brain, exposes the various different types of nerve cells with their distinctive organization and fibers running horizontally and vertically. The blood vessels on top of the cortex are also shown. The cerebral cortex varies in thickness from 1.5mm (0.6in) to 3mm (0.12in); it is thickest in the motor region of the frontal lobe.

Mind and brain

Although psychologists, educators, philosophers, and others cannot agree exactly what the mind is, they all acknowledge that the more they find out about it the more amazing it becomes. It has been said, for example, that if mankind wished to use all its current resources to build a computer that could do everything done by the normal human mind, such a computer might have to be the size of our planet—and even then nobody would know how to program it.

Mind and matter

It was once thought that man was made up of mind and matter, matter being something that could be seen and felt, occupying space and having weight, and mind beging a substance present in a person but taking up no space and not able to be weighed, seen, or touched. During the last two centuries the argument went to extremes, some saying that the mind did not exist at all and that everything could be explained in terms of the body, and others saying that everything physical was an illusion and that the only reality was mind. These arguments have subsided, and the most common view suggests that both mind and body exist, each being dependent upon a harmonious interaction with the other. For convenience, the brain is often described as the purely physical matter inside the skull, and the mind is described as "what the brain does."

Until fairly recent times it was thought that the larger the brain the more able the mind. This view was discarded when the brains of deceased people were weighed and no significant correlation was found between the intelligence and mental abilities of the people when alive and the size and weight of their brains. The next theory was that the number of individual brain cells determined the ability of the mind. Again it was found that variations above and below the average of 30 billion cells seemed not to be closely related to a person's mental capacity.

It is possible that the number of permutations and combinations of connections between threadlike filaments called dendritic spines that branch off from each brain cell determines a person's mental ability [2, 3]. The average number of connections for a normal human brain is now known to be so enormous [Key] that previous estimates of individual potential have had to be revised drastically. According to one estimate, between 100,000 and 1,000,000 different chemical reactions take place every minute in the average brain.

Sleep and dreams

A US psychologist, Robert Ornstein, has suggested that the two halves of the brain, the left and right hemispheres, deal with different mental functions. The left side deals with the more academic processes, while the right side deals with the more artistic and imaginative activities [1]. Growing interest in the activities of the right side has led to a number of investigations of the more imaginative, rhythmic, and colorful aspects of the mind.

Much of the work on consciousness has involved studies of sleep. Investigation of sleep deprivation has shown that people seem to be able to function well with very

CONNECTIONS

See also
670 Memory and recall
672 Potential of the mind
666 How the brain works
778 Thinking and understanding
780 Language development
784 Emotional development
812 Aspects of human nature

1 The brain is composed of two halves, the left and right hemispheres, and it has been thought for some time that the left hemisphere controls the right side of the body and vice versa. By recording the origin of brain waves associated with specific types of thought it has been indicated more recently that each hemisphere is also responsible for a different range of mental activities. The left hemisphere is mainly responsible for language, logic, numbers, analysis, critical thinking, and academic activities. The right side of the brain is mainly concerned with imagination, spatial relationships, form, and more artistic and intuitive activities. Humans seem to depend on both sides of the brain. Western societies have tended to emphasize left-hemisphere activity with an education system based mainly on reading, writing, and arithmetic. As a consequence the more artistic side of human endeavor has suffered some neglect to the detriment of the potential capacity and functioning of the brain as a whole. There is some evidence that if both sides of the brain are encouraged to cooperate, creativity, productivity, and the level of general intelligence can be raised. An interesting research sideline is that when both sides of the brain are working in harmony, the body works better, too. A child with jerky handwriting concentrating too hard on academic activity can achieve a remarkable improvement by concentrating on color, while people suffering from such stress-related ailments as ulcers and backache can gain relief apparently through cooperation between the left and right hemispheres of the brain.

little sleep but suffer if they are not allowed to dream [4]. Experiments revealed that those who had little sleep and were allowed to dream were slightly more irritable than usual but otherwise normal. Those who had little sleep but who were not allowed to dream became very disturbed within a few days. A number of them began hallucinating during the day. In other words, the mind needs to dream; if it cannot do so at night, then it must compensate for this lack in waking hours.

The studies concluded that although the normal requirements for sleep vary greatly, most people need to exercise their creative and imaginative faculties through the process of dreaming. Some people, however, require very little sleep and seldom dream.

Further work on dreams and imagination has shown that dreams may be the playground of the mind—stories, plays, and fantastic shows and panoramas that amuse, educate, and sometimes advise and give warning. Dreams have provided inspiration for many works of imagination, notably for the poem *Kubla Khan* by Samuel Taylor Coleridge (1772–1834). Some stories of Edgar Allan Poe (1809–49) were based on his nightmares, and the artist Salvador Dali (1904–) also makes use of the landscape of his dreams. The German chemist Friedrich Kekulé von Stradonitz (1829–96) envisaged the cyclical structure of the benzene ring in a dream and made a significant contribution to chemical knowledge.

Potential of the mind

Recent research indicates that people may be using only a small fraction of their mental potential. But with new understanding of the way in which the mind works and with the beginning of detailed investigation into recall processes, retention, real learning abilities, creative processes, and general mind/body functioning, boundless prospects are opening up. It appears from all the evidence available that the human brain may be the most versatile and finely constructed object known. Only now are some of the basic elements in the brain's infinitely fascinating design beginning to be recognized and studied.

KEY

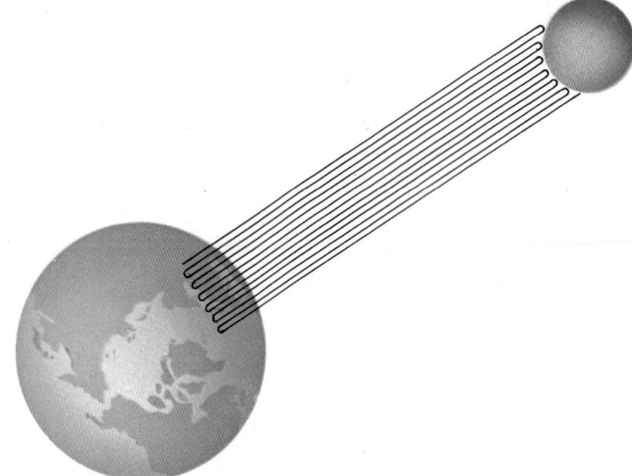

The capacity of the human brain can be expressed in the number of permutations and combinations of connections of which it is capable. A recent estimate put the possible figure at one, followed by 6.5 million miles of zeros. This is a number so large that it would stretch from the Earth to the Moon and back more than 13 times. Such an estimate may even be conservative as it is certain that the full potential of the mind has not yet been realized.

2 Information is transmitted in the brain by electrical pulses at the synapse [A], or tip of the dendritic spines in the conducting cells of the nervous system. Some regions of the cortex have large numbers of these spines [B]. An enlarged diagram of the synapse [C] depicts the transmission of information from one dendrite to another. The more of these connections there are in the brain, the greater the mental ability.

2 A

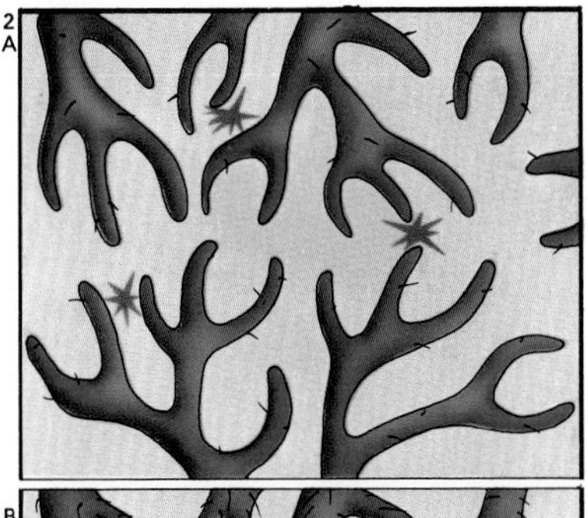

B

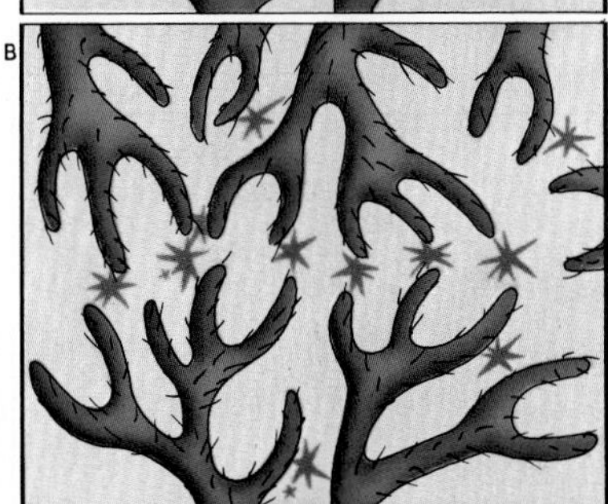

C

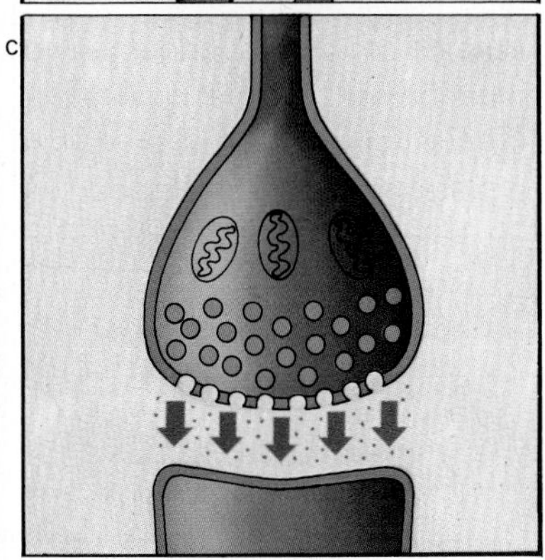

3 A brain cell is like a tiny, multitentacled octopus. From the center, or nucleus, of the cell, the tentacles, or dendrites, stretch out in all directions and on each dendrite there are thousands of minute protuberances called dendritic spines. These connect with each other to form linkage networks between the 30 billion cells of an average brain. Mental activity may increase the number of such connections and facilitate learning.

3

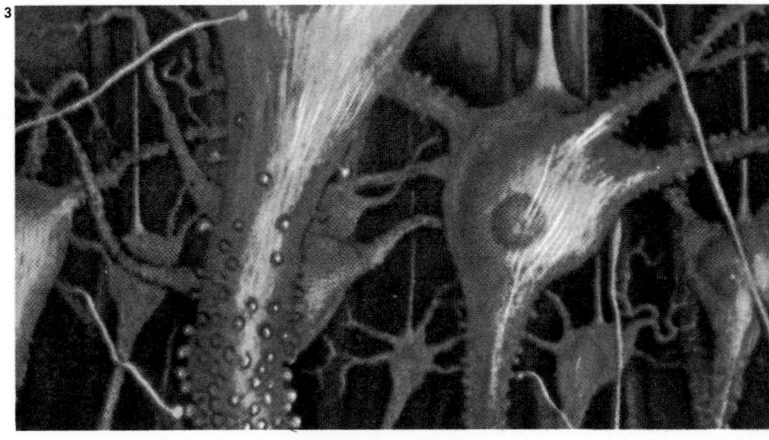

4

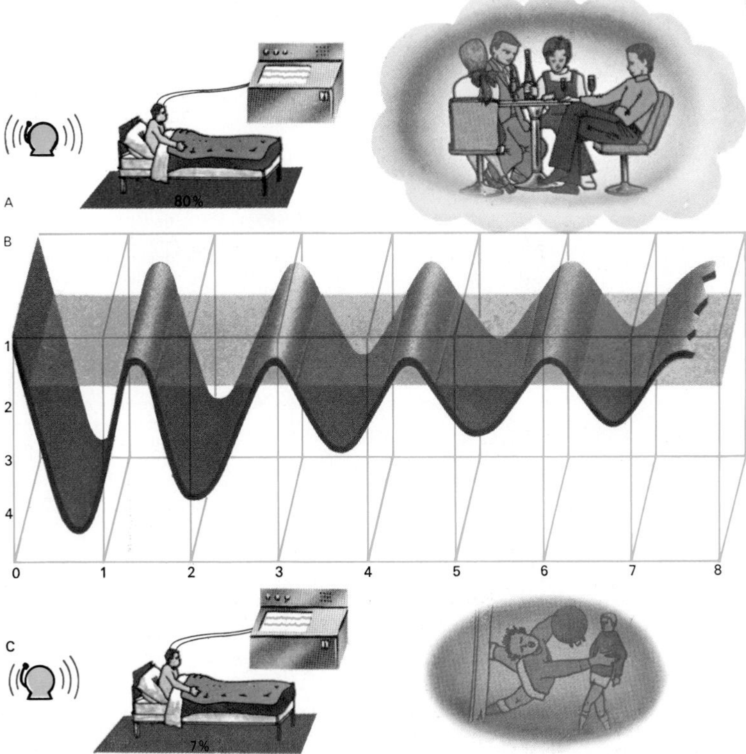
A
80%
B
1
2
3
4
0
1
2
3
4
5
6
7
8
C
7%

4 Depth of sleep can be measured by the fluctuations shown by brainwaves throughout the night [B]. When the waves rise from the deeper levels, rapid eye movements (REM) underneath the eyelids of the sleeper can be seen (pink areas on the graph). Sleep studies have shown that on 80% of the occasions when subjects were awakened during an REM period [A], they gave lengthy narratives of their dreams. Only 7% of subjects awakened during other levels of sleep [C] could recall any dreaming and these were only fragmentary memories compared with the reports from the REM awakenings. It seems clear, therefore, that dreaming is associated with REM sleep. On the graph, the vertical numbers indicate stages in the depth of sleep and numbers on the horizontal axis indicate the hours of sleep.

Memory and recall

The human memory, generally thought to be rather inefficient, is in fact more sophisticated than any computer memory. Memory can be divided into two main parts: retention—the ability to store information; and recall—the ability to retrieve it again. Studies of the human memory reveal that it is excellent at storing information but less reliable at recall—at least without special practice.

Experiment, theory, and experience

Researchers approaching the problem from a number of different angles have all concluded that there is much more stored in our minds than is generally supposed. A Canadian neurosurgeon, Wilder Penfield (1891–), showed that by stimulating the brain electrically he could produce total recall of specific events in people's lives. Dreams, in which characters and events "forgotten" for many years suddenly reappear in perfect clarity, similarly indicate that the information had been stored all the time. Another example is the surprise recall of events until then forgotten that is often triggered by a particular smell, or color, or by returning to a place.

There are probably different mechanisms for "short term" and "long term" memory; short term resulting from active brain processes and long term from chemical changes. But the physical basis of memory is not yet known. One theory is that the astonishing storage capacity of the brain is a product of the almost limitless combinations of the interconnections between brain cells. These connections are stimulated by patterns of activity; repeated reference to information therefore helps recall. It may be that this improvement in performance is the result of strengthening of the chemical bonds involved in memory.

Remembering and forgetting

Most people find their memory is faulty when it comes to recall. The problem is probably not an inherent one, however, but seems to arise from a misunderstanding of how the mind works. Recall can itself be divided into two major areas: recall during learning and recall after learning. During a learning period the mind, like the body when it is exercised, needs periods of activity and rest. If the right period of activity is followed by an appropriate rest period, recall performance improves considerably.

Recall after learning rises for a brief time as the information "sinks in," and then it drops dramatically [2]. This loss of detail can be minimized if certain review techniques are combined with periods of activity and rest. When reading, recall can be improved, for instance, by breaking up learning periods into sessions of between 20 and 40 minutes, during which notes are made. A 10-minute gap is followed by a 10-minute recall period allowing everything remembered to be noted down and compared with the original notes. Memory is reinforced by a 2- to 4-minute review of the same material the next day and then a 2-minute review in the following week.

Faster reading also improves concentration and retention of information, as well as allowing more time for revision of important passages [4]. Aids to faster reading include practice in rhythmic reading with the help of

CONNECTIONS

See also
668 Mind and brain
672 Potential of the mind
778 Thinking and understanding
666 How the brain works
804 An active old age

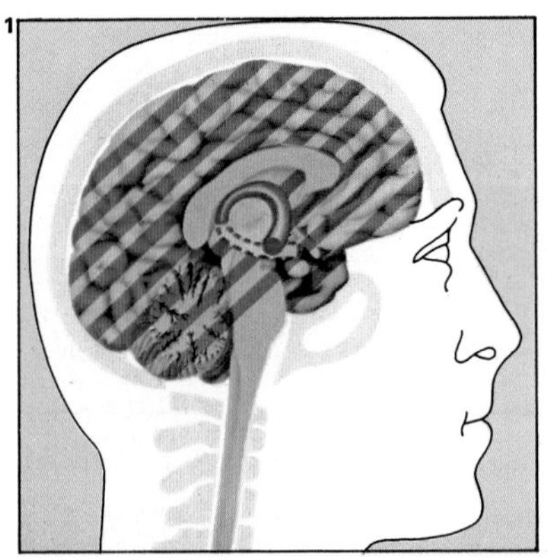

1 Memory processes may take place throughout almost the whole brain (striped area), but certain areas within and bordering on the limbic system—notably the hippocampus and the mamillary bodies—appear to be indispensable to memory. These areas, together with the fornix, form the loop indicated in red at the top of the brain stem. The dotted area recedes into the left hemisphere.

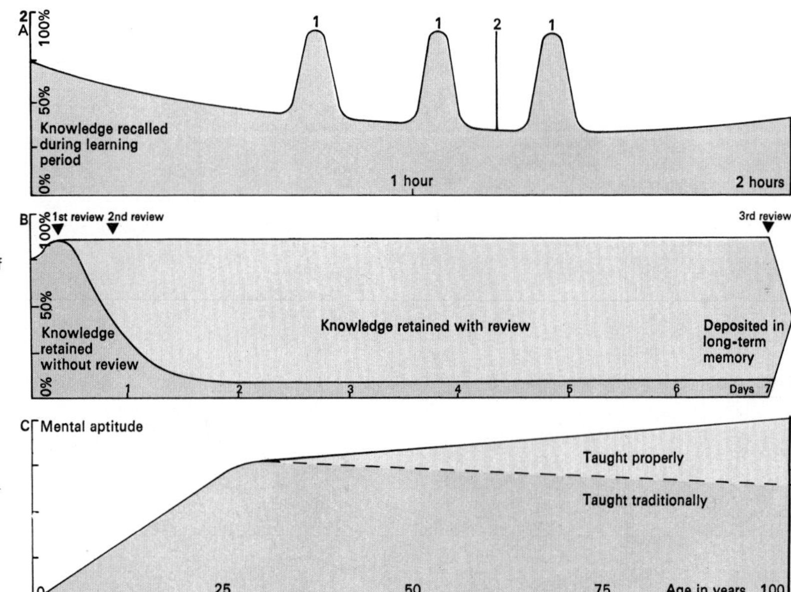
A
100%
50%
0%
Knowledge recalled during learning period
1
1
2
1
1 hour
2 hours
B
1st review
2nd review
3rd review
Knowledge retained without review
Knowledge retained with review
Deposited in long-term memory
1
2
3
4
5
6
Days 7
C
Mental aptitude
Taught properly
Taught traditionally
0
25
50
75
Age in years
100

2 Recall of information being learned varies considerably as time passes [A]. Usually, we recall more from the beginning and end of a learning period and more items that are in some way linked to each other [1] or that stand out from the background material [2]. A period of 20 to 40 minutes seems to maximize understanding and recall. A properly organized review program can prevent rapid decline in recall of detail [B]. Without it, 80% of the material is usually lost within 24 hours. Although mental ability generally declines with age [C], improvement can continue with a review and recall approach.

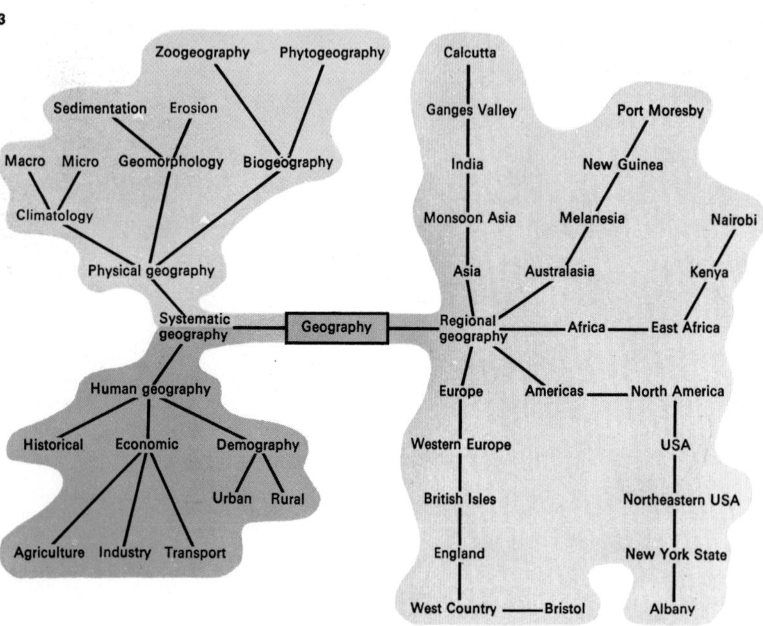
Zoogeography
Phytogeography
Sedimentation
Erosion
Macro
Micro
Geomorphology
Biogeography
Climatology
Physical geography
Systematic geography
Geography
Human geography
Historical
Economic
Demography
Urban
Rural
Agriculture
Industry
Transport
Calcutta
Ganges Valley
India
Monsoon Asia
Asia
Port Moresby
New Guinea
Melanesia
Australasia
Nairobi
Kenya
Regional geography
Africa
East Africa
Europe
Americas
North America
Western Europe
USA
British Isles
Northeastern USA
England
New York State
West Country
Bristol
Albany

3 A form of notetaking, called mind patterns, is based on the way the mind itself organizes information. Key words and key images are linked to form easily recalled networks of facts. Several pages of standard notes on the subject of geography, for instance, can be expressed in a single pattern.

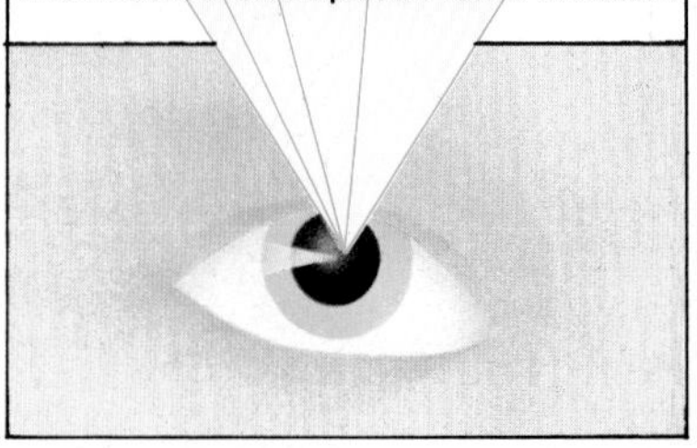
Loem ipsum dolor sit amet, cor
eiusmod tempor incidunt ut lab
Ut enim ad minim veniam, quis
laboris nisi ut aliquip ex ea com
irure dolor in reprehenderit in vo
illum dolore eu fugiat nulla paria
dignissum qui blandit praesent
molestias excepteur sint occae

4 A slow reader who follows only a word at a time is subject to mental wandering because information is entering the mind too slowly. A reader who takes in several words understands and recalls more because information enters the mind in "wholes" in the way it is stored. Advanced reading involves taking in areas of print as the mind selects key words.

a metronome, time tests to encourage higher speeds, and (contrary to popular belief) the use of a finger to follow words and eventually blocks or even pages of words.

When making notes, it helps to use a key word or phrase to sum up sets of diverse information, since this is how the brain stores it [3]. Special memory techniques called mnemonics often use similar methods to accentuate the normal recall processes of associating or linking ideas [5]. Recent studies have shown that a person who can associate ideas in this way will, apart from improving his memory, also improve his creative ability, which depends to a large degree on linking information.

Much of what we "forget" we have in fact never fully taken in, because we have not been concentrating. Many people have considerable difficulty remembering names of people they meet, for example. As a result, they experience mild fear when meeting new people and almost "rehearse" an introduction situation in which they will forget the names. The embarrassment of the imagined situation may also cause them to avoid eye contact with those they are meeting and to give their faces only the most fleeting glance. All this behavior is the opposite of what is needed for recall, for we tend to forget things associated with fear.

Paying attention

In order to remember difficult things such as people's names it is necessary to pay attention, repeat the names, and develop or discover any associations that they may have. This means that during introductions, complete attention should be paid to the face of the other person and any links between outstanding characteristics of the face and name should be made. Sensible repetition of the person's name is also helpful. Repetition tends to build up a more solid "imprint" of a name and will result in a recall of considerably greater duration. These techniques can be generally applied to anything an individual wishes to commit to memory. We are not born with fixed patterns of memory, recall, and retention. It is possible to educate the memory just as practice develops physical or intellectual skills.

KEY

The complexity of the human memory has been underestimated just as the scale of the universe was once underestimated. The more each is explored, the vaster it becomes. Like the astronomer, the psychologist is increasingly using terms such as "limitless" to describe the human memory.

5

5 Mnemonic (memory) systems of various kinds assist recall by organizing information into units that are as easy to store as possible. A simple mnemonic technique is the use of rhyme to learn numbers, dates, or difficult names. Another method is to associate unfamiliar names or facts with familiar ones by making key words into readily remembered images. One form of this technique that has a long history is the placing of objects in regular order within a well-known scene. To recall the objects, the mnemonist moves through the scene "seeing" the objects as he comes to them. Often where abstract things have to be remembered, a visual interpretation will be used. A simple example of the technique is a scene that might be used to remember characters of the nursery rhyme "The House that Jack Built." The characters are placed in order for the mnemonist to come across as he weaves his set path through the mental scene he has constructed. The final verse of the nursery tale (which is already arranged in a mnemonic rhyming system) is: "This is the farmer sowing his corn that kept the cock that crowed in the morn that waked the priest all shaven and shorn that married the man all tattered and torn that kissed the maiden all forlorn that milked the cow with the crumpled horn that tossed the dog that worried the cat that killed the rat that ate the malt that lay in the house that Jack built."

1 Farmer
2 Corn
3 Cock
4 Priest
5 Man
6 Maiden
7 Cow
8 Dog
9 Cat
10 Rat
11 Malt
12 House
13 Jack

Potential of the mind

The most intriguing fields of research into the potential of the mind [Key] are concerned with perception, vision, illusions, hallucinations, and controversial paranormal phenomena such as telepathy and extrasensory perception.

The sense organs are stimulated by various types of physical energy: the eyes by electromagnetic wavelengths; the ears by mechanical vibrations; the nose and tongue by chemicals; and the skin by combinations of pressure and temperature. Perception is the translation of such sensory stimuli, signaled by nerve impulses, into an organized picture of the world.

The problems of perception

Interest in the problems of perception is shared between philosophers, physiologists, and psychologists. Philosophers ask questions about whether things exist independently of our experience of them and how we can test the truth or validity of our observations. Physiologists are concerned with the mechanisms of the nervous system, while psychologists are more interested in the processes relating to learning and knowledge of perception. Illusions and errors are important to them. When we judge something to be of a certain size, for instance, is it actually that size? And if there is a discrepancy between the actual and the perceived, how does that discrepancy arise? Illusions occur if the physiological mechanisms are upset or if there is a misapplication of stored knowledge.

Some psychologists, notably the so-called "atomists," believe that we perceive in units of simple sensations—such as dots, lines, colors and so on—and from these simple sensations we construct a face or a tree or a house. Opposed to this view are the "constructuralists," who think of even basic sensations, such as colored patches, as being derived from neurological processes of which the human being has no consciousness.

Recent theories of perception do not regard experience as primary. Sensations of color, or of the shape of objects, are derived from physical stimuli coded by the nervous system and "read"—as a message is read from the symbolic dots and dashes of the Morse code. Physiologists have found out a great deal about the form of the neural code —trains of electrical impulses—by which the world of objects is signalled to the brain. In 1958 two US physiologists, David Hubel and Torsten Wiesel, reported that neural cells in the brain's striate cortex of a particular orientation respond to lines of a different orientation. The detailed mechanisms of feature recognition are thus beginning to be understood in physiological terms. But how these neural signals are "read" by the nervous system to give perception remains largely mysterious.

Gestalt theories of perception

The Gestalt psychologists of the 1920s and 1930s, such as Kurt Koffka (1886–1941) and Wolfgang Köhler (1887–1967), held that we see organized wholes or configurations (*Gestalten*). These are made up of simple sensations, but the whole is more important than the sum of its parts. Patterns are more important than the elements of those patterns. We "see" dots but perceive a dotted

CONNECTIONS

See also
668 Mind and brain
670 Memory and recall
674 Sight and perceptio
666 How the brain work
778 Thinking and understanding
1724 Man in space

1

1 Computer-processed pictures are part of a research project to discover the least amount of visual information a picture may contain and still be recognizable. Shown is a portrait of Lincoln.

2 A B

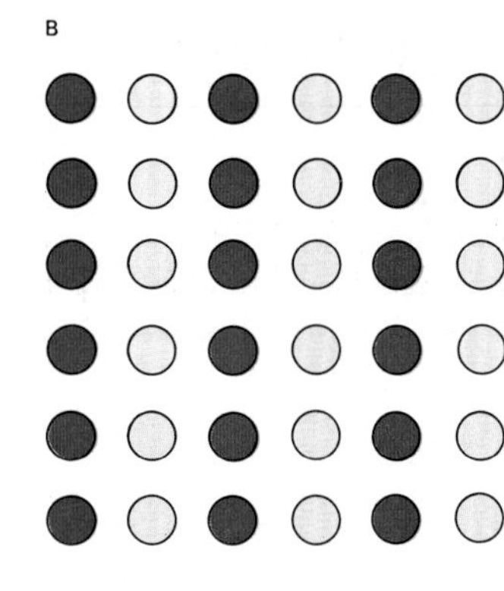

2 Proximity [A] and similarity [B] are two examples of the principles put forward by *Gestalt* psychologists to explain the organization of our perceptions. [A] The horizontal distance between the dots is greater than the vertical distance. Consequently, the dots are perceived as vertical columns. [B] The dots are equally spaced, but because of similarity of color they are still "seen" as vertical columns.

3 A B

3 Optical illusions arise from tricks of perception that occur either in the retina of the eye itself or at the higher cognitive levels of the brain. [A] The bright white triangle that seems to overlap the dark circles and V-shaped lines is an illusion. [B] The central lines in both arrows are the same length, though the bottom one appears to be distinctly the shorter.

4 A B

R
R

4 The mind adjusts size to apparent distance. The moon looks smaller on a near horizon [A] than on a far one [B] as the observer makes a bigger mental enlargement of the retinal image [R].

5 A

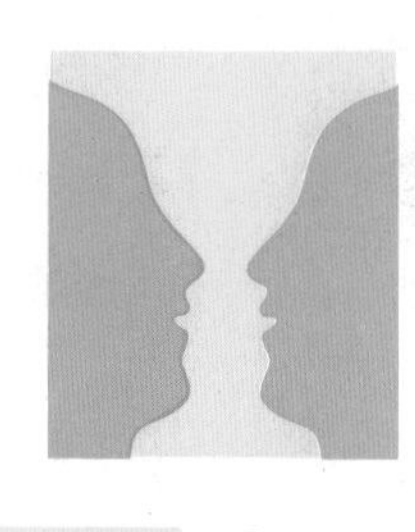

B C

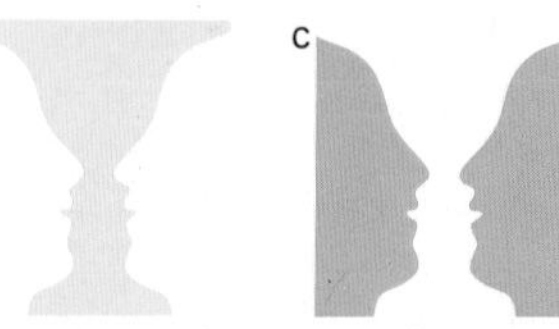

5 A reversal effect can occur when information about foreground and background is ambiguous. The picture [A] may first appear to be a vase [B] but may then begin to look like two faces [C].

6

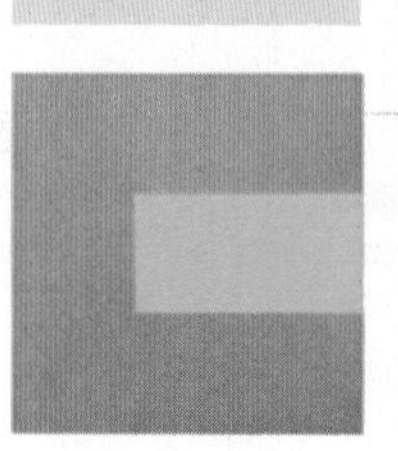

6 Color is a product of the mind's response to varying wavelengths of light reaching the eye, rather than a property of objects themselves. Perception can be changed in the process of adapting to sudden changes of color or to color contrasts. The central color in each pair of pictures is of the same shade and intensity on the left as it is on the right, but the surrounding color fools perception and produces the illusion of slight differences in the central hues.

line. They also postulated a variety of principles of organization that govern our perceptions. The most general of these, called *Prägnanz* (exactness), states that the particular perceived whole will be as good as circumstances allow. "Good," in this context, does not have one all-embracing definition but is rather a series of qualities such as unity, simplicity, symmetry, regularity, proximity, and similarity [2]. These principles govern what we see from the mosaic of stimuli at the eye.

Several optical effects tend to support this *Gestalt* theory. Context, for example, is important in determing what we perceive [5] and there is a remarkable stability or constancy in our perceptions that overcomes changes in direct stimulation. A lump of coal or an orange, for instance, appears to have a constant color even under varied lighting conditions.

The *Gestalt* psychologists believed that perceptions are organized into the (usually simple) shapes of objects by electrical "brain fields" that tend toward simple shapes, in the way that bubbles are spherical because this is their most physically stable form. This idea of "brain fields" as little pictures or models in the brain has been abandoned. The *Gestalt* laws of organization may just as easily be the result of computerlike rules, by which sensory signals are accepted, rejected, and modified to serve as data for perception. For example, similar dots close together are likely to be the edge of an object and are accepted as belonging together because they probably are part of a single object. We see these groupings in arrays of dots, because such rule-following generally leads to appropriate perception of objects from the patterns of stimulation of the receptors.

It is believed that a complex mixture of innate knowledge and data-processing rules underlies perception, although there is disagreement about the relative importance of these two elements. Research on human infants indicates that they are born with an innate perceptual framework, since they can discriminate between complex stimuli even during the very first few days of their lives.

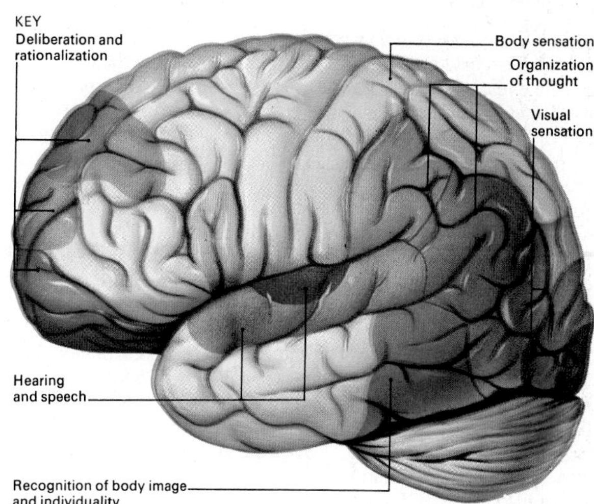
KEY
Deliberation and rationalization
Body sensation
Organization of thought
Visual sensation
Hearing and speech
Recognition of body image and individuality

Five senses were thought to be the sum of man's equipment for experiencing the world: sight, hearing and balance, taste, smell, and touch. It is now thought that we have more than five, including senses of time, direction, and motion. Other senses, such as the ability to respond to magnetic and electrical waves, may lie undeveloped. Shown are skills tentatively associated with various brain areas.

7

8

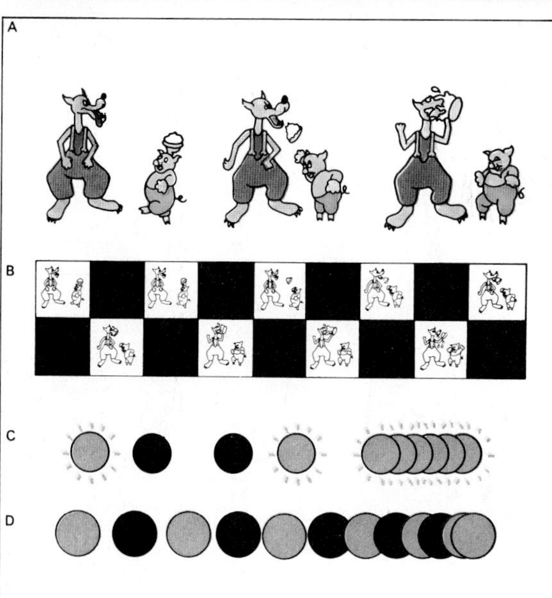
A
B
C
D

8 Cinematic technique relies on basic visual processes to create the illusion of movement. Pictures of objects in different spatial relationships [A] can be seen as moving because of persistence of vision. In the laboratory this is simulated [C] by switching two light on and off in close succession. They appear as a single moving light because the image persists on the retina for several seconds. The shutter of a movie projector [B], by cutting out light between frames, causes visual fusion of images with no flicker. This can also be shown in the laboratory by switching a light on and off [D]. At about 70 flashes per second it ceases to appear to be flashing and seems instead to be a steady light.

7 After-images can produce strong visual effects in the mind. Stare intently at the center of the flag for 40 seconds. Then look at a blank white area where the flag will be seen in its true colors.

9

Soundproofing
Microphone
Experimental control room
Air supply
Subject in water tank

9 Changes in perception seem to occur when stimulation to the brain is reduced to a minimum. In a watery, stimulation free environment designed for research in sensory deprivation, subjects reported strong hallucinations. Some also experienced changes in their mental image of their own bodies; arms felt disconnected from the body and the body actually seemed to change shape, becoming larger, smaller, or distorted. Some subjects also experienced auditory imagery, hearing music, buzz saws, and the chirping of birds. It has been suggested that these changes in perception show that minds need some form of meaningful contact with the environment.

Sight and perception

Sight is one of our principal means of interpreting the world about us. Its instruments are the eyes, which form in the embryo as two "buds" from the brain. It is the brain that decodes the images seen by the eyes.

The anatomy of the eye

Some parts of the eye are directly involved with receiving light, whereas others protect delicate structures [Key]. The protective elements include the eyelids, which are fringed with eyelashes—coarse dust-collecting hairs. The eyebrows, above the lids, may help prevent sweat from running into the eyes. Lining each lid is the conjunctiva, a transparent membrane that loops back to cover the front of the eye. Its low-friction surfaces help the lids to open and close easily and, more important, protect the front of the eye. Under the eyelids are the lacrimal, or tear-producing, glands. Tears, which wash away foreign particles and kill bacteria, are continually secreted onto the conjunctiva through 12 ducts and are normally removed through two canals in the nasal corner of each eye.

The outer coating of the eyeball is the sclera, the tough, fibrous white of the eye. The sclera provides attachment for the six extrinsic muscles [6] that move the eyeball, maintains eyeball shape, and guards delicate inner layers. At the front it is transparent, to allow the entry of light. This part is called the cornea. Lining the inside of the eyeball is the choroid, containing a network of blood vessels; these supply the eye with essential food substances. Toward the front of the eye the choroid becomes the ciliary body, the source of a watery fluid, the aqueous humor. The muscles of the ciliary body also suspend and alter the shape of the lens, a tough biconvex structure made of an elastic capsule filled with fibrous tissue that adjusts the focusing, or "accommodates" [1]. By muscular contraction the lens is made thicker for near vision to give maximum focusing power and is thinnest when a distant object is being viewed.

The lens lies behind the iris, a colored, muscular continuation of the choroid, which, according to inherited characteristics, gives the eye its color [9]. The pupil, a circular opening in the iris, controls the entry of light, for it can change in diameter, by reflex action, from 0.04 to 0.32 (1 to 8mm) [3]. The iris is smallest in bright light, largest in dim light. It closes down for near vision, increasing the depth of field.

Light-sensitive cells

After penetrating the lens light passes through the vitreous humor, the clear jelly filling the eyeball behind the lens. It then falls on the retina, which contains light-sensitive photoreceptor cells, the rods and cones [4]. The 125 million rods are responsible for recognizing light and dark, whereas the 7 million cones are responsible for color vision. The rods are most numerous toward the edges of the retina, and the cones are concentrated at the center, where they are clustered in the fovea, the small area in which vision is most acute.

The rods and cones contain visual pigments whose structure is altered by light. As a result nerve impulses are generated that pass to the brain for interpretation as vision. The pigment in the rods is called

CONNECTIONS

See also
1516 Light and color
672 Potential of the m
666 How the brain wo
696 A healthy diet
416 Principles of hered
1518 Mirrors and lenses
1528 Energy from lasers

1

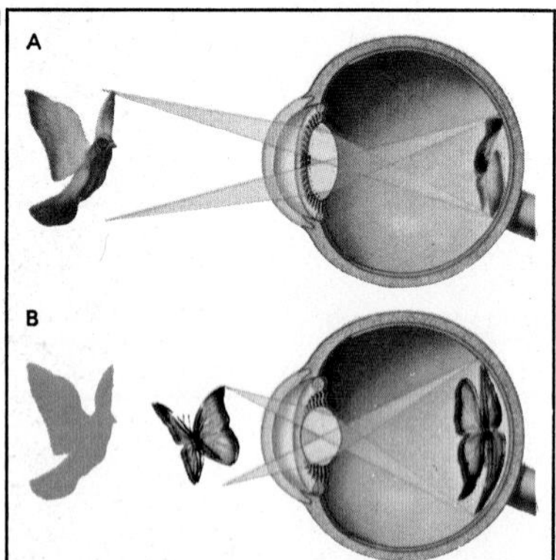

A
B

1 Focusing of light rays from distant objects [A] is mainly done by the cornea with little help from the lens. Ciliary muscles encircling the lens relax and stretch ligaments, which pull the lens flat. Rays from a near object [B] are bent by a thick lens produced when the ligaments slacken as the ciliary muscles contract. This process, called accommodation, is essential for sharp focusing.

2 Light rays from a point on an object are received by the temporal zone of one eye [1] and the nasal zone of the other [2]. The impulses from each, some of which "cross over" at the optic chiasma in the brain [3], then arrive at the opposite side of the brain and can be interpreted by the visual cortex. It is in this way that we perceive objects in terms of their height, width, depth, and color.

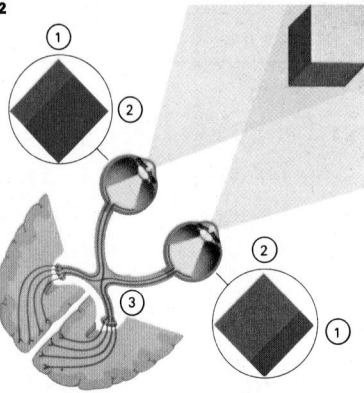

2

3

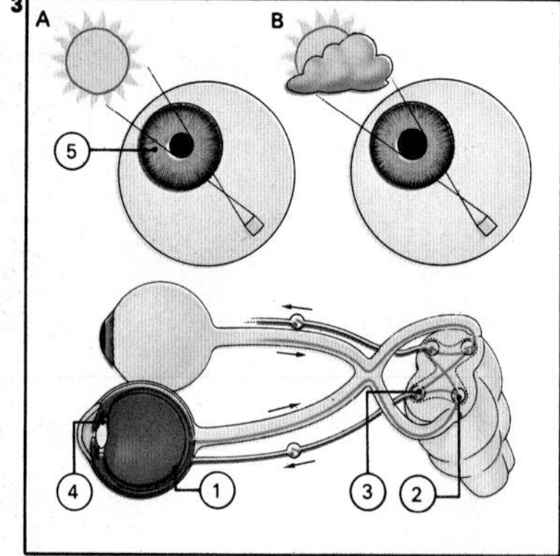

A
B

3 Pupil size changes according to the amount of light. In bright conditions [A] light striking the cells of the retina [1] stimulates impulses to the brain stem [2] and brain centers [3], which cause the pupillary muscles [4] to contract. Radial muscles [5] also stretch and the pupil closes by reflex action to protect the delicate retina. In dull light [B] the muscles contract less, letting more light through.

4

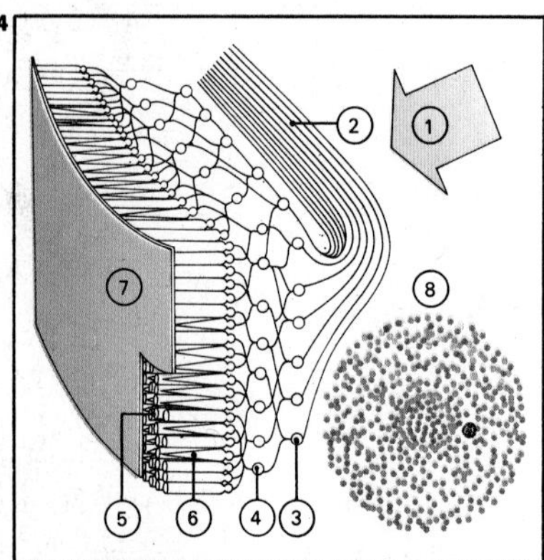

4 Light rays [1] falling on the eye pass through optic nerve fibers [2], ganglia [3], and bipolar nerve cells [4] before reaching the rods [5] and cones [6], the eye's photoreceptor cells found in front of the pigment cell layer [7]. Cones [orange], concerned with color vision, are concentrated in the middle, forming the fovea [8]. Rods [green], effective in black and white, are mostly on the periphery.

5

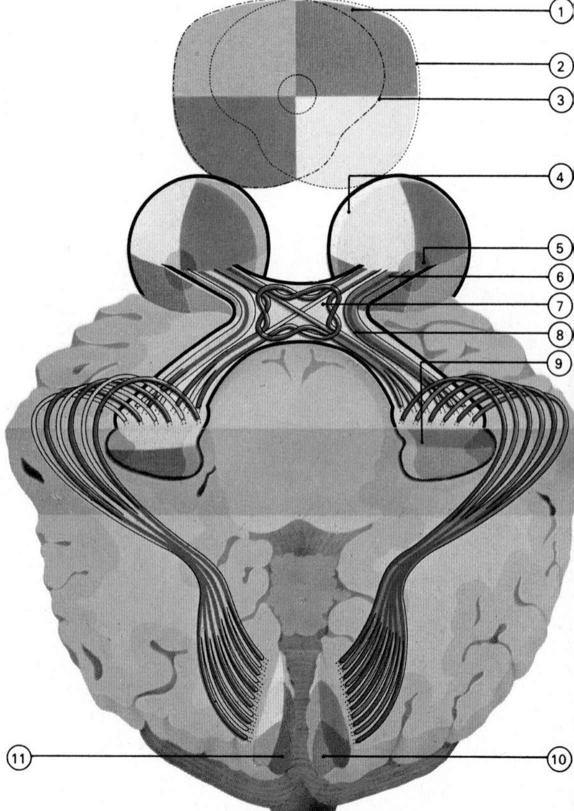

5 The visual field [1] is here divided into four colors. That of each eye [dotted lines] is dissimilar but overlaps [2,3]. The image from the side is indistinct [4] as it falls on the periphery of the retina. The clearest image is formed at the fovea [5]. Information from the retina is taken by the optic nerve fibers [6] to the optic chiasma [7], where "crossing over" takes place. After the fibers leave the optic chiasma they form the optic tract [8], which divides to form the six layers of the lateral geniculate body [9]. The visual cortex in the right hemisphere [10] receives information from the right side of each eye; the visual cortex in the left hemisphere [11] from the left side.

6

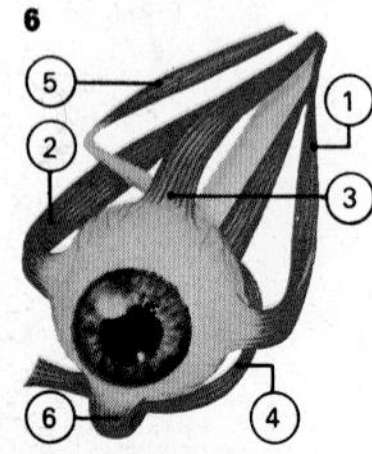

6 The eyeball is rotated by six extrinsic muscles. The lateral rectus [1] moves it away from the midline of the body and is thus in opposition to the medial rectus [2], which moves it toward the midline. The superior rectus [3] and inferior oblique [4] move it upward, while the superior oblique [5] and the inferior rectus [6] move it downward. The movements of the eye, important in perception, ensure that a "fresh" image is constantly presented to the retina.

visual purple, or rhodopsin, and light splits it into retinene and opsin. The cones are of three kinds—"red," "green," and "blue"—and respond to light of those colors. The broad range of tints that we perceive results from "mixing" of the three primary colors [5]. The cones provide precise vision in daytime, but are of little use at night or in dim light.

Both the rods and the cones are connected with ganglion cells and these give rise to one million nerve fibers, which leave the eye at the optic nerve. At this junction, the blind spot, the eye detects nothing. The nerves from each eye lead, after "relay" stations, to the occipital lobe of the cerebral cortex at the back of the brain. Optic nerve fibers are so arranged that impulses from the left side of the visual field of each eye travel to the right side of the brain and vice versa. Crossing over takes place at the optic chiasma situated behind the eyes. Information from each eye is combined by the brain to create stereoscopic vision.

Eye movements are vital for perception. The eyes follow moving objects smoothly, but move in saccadic jerks to select regions of interest and to prevent adaptation of the receptors by continuous stimulation.

The process of perception

Vision results from the stimulation of nerve cells in the retina, signaling patterns of light intensity and color, which are "decoded" by the brain to give perception of separate objects. The most remarkable feature of perception is its ability to convert continuous patterns of energy at the receptors into individual objects and events, in space and time, all from the same kinds of pulses of electricity running along nerve fibers.

Edges—contours—are very important to perception. Orientations of contours stimulate "feature detectors" in the striate cortex. Orientations, angles, and movement are represented separately, by feature detectors "tuned" to these characteristics. Combinations of these signaled characteristics are then put together to form our perceptions of objects. This also requires a great deal of experience stored in the memory.

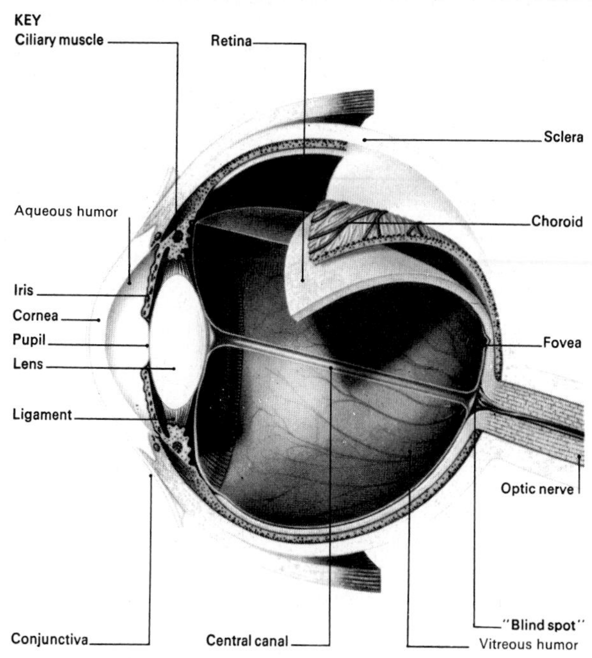
KEY
Ciliary muscle
Retina
Sclera
Aqueous humor
Choroid
Iris
Cornea
Pupil
Lens
Fovea
Ligament
Optic nerve
"Blind spot"
Conjunctiva
Central canal
Vitreous humor

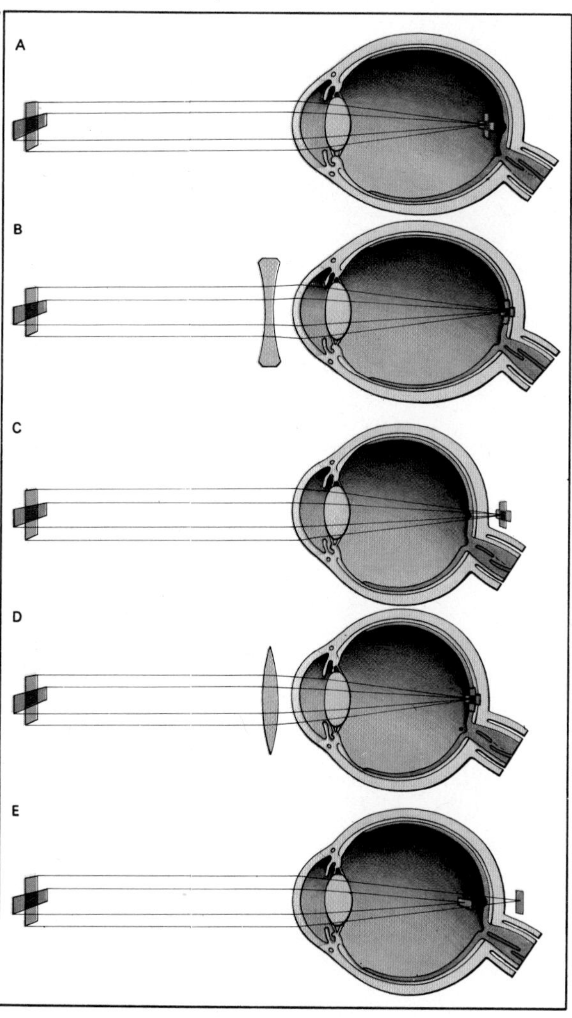
7
A
B
C
D
E

7 Normal vision depends on the refraction, or light-bending, power of the eye and eyeball. Where no defect exists, light rays entering the eye focus clearly on the retina. Myopia [A], or nearsightedness, occurs when the refractive power of the eye is too strong or when the eyeball is elongated. The image then forms in front of the retina. A concave lens is needed [B]. Farsightedness [C] is caused by weak refractive power or a flattened eyeball. The image "forms" behind the retina. A convex lens [D] is needed. In astigmatism [E], which occurs in several forms, refraction is unequal for different orientations because of unequal curvature of the eye in different planes, resulting in distorted vision.

8
A
B
C
D

8 Color blindness of which there are two basic types, means that the individual is unable to tell all colors apart. Normal vision [A] requires red, blue, and green to reproduce all the hues of the spectrum Most color blind people can see only two basic colors and tend to confuse others. This is called dichromatic vision. The most common version of this is the confusion of reds and greens [B], but a few people confuse blue and yellow [C]. Total color blindness [D] is the rarest defect. In this the world becomes nothing but shades of black and white. Approximately 4% of men are color blind compared with 0.5% of women.

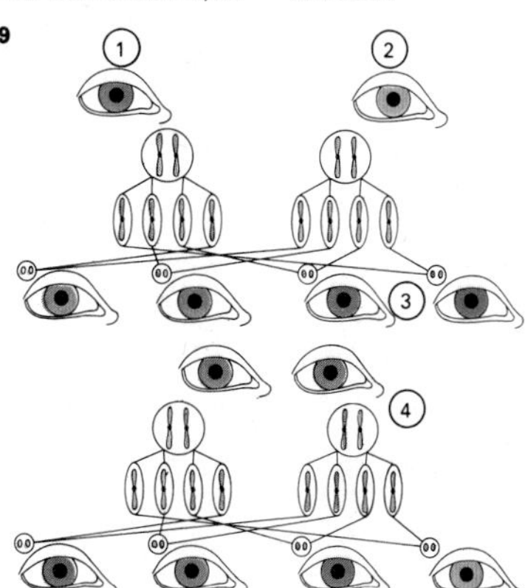
9
1
2
3
4

9 Iris pigments are inherited. In humans the brown gene is dominant over the blue. A man [1] carrying two genes for brown and a woman [2] carrying two genes for blue will bear brown-eyed children [3]. Brown-eyed parents [4] carrying the recessive genes for blue eyes average one blue-eyed child to three brown-eyed. Blue-eyed parents produce blue-eyed children.

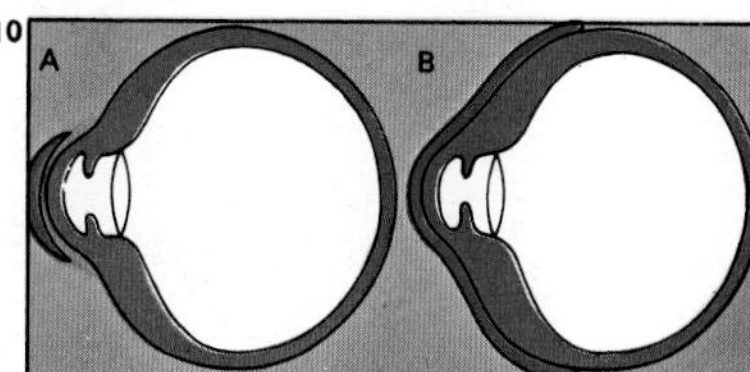
10
A
B

10 Contact lenses are made of plastic or a glass-plastic laminate, and float on the surface of the eye. Two types are the small corneal [A] and the scleral [B] covering the front of the eyeball.

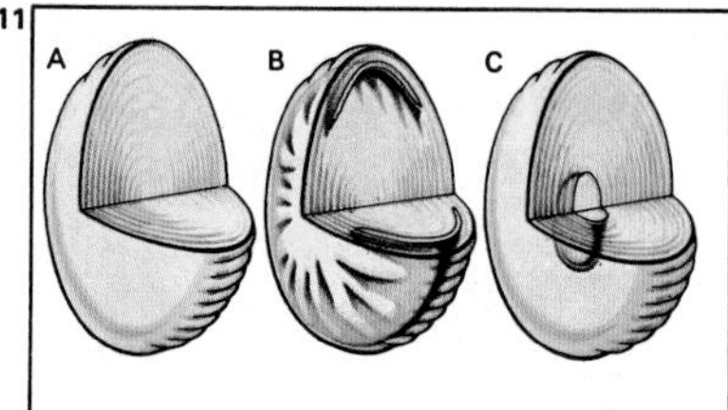
11
A
B
C

11 Cataracts, cloudy changes in the lens, may hinder vision badly, depending on their size and shape. The normal lens [A] is compared with two different cataracts, cortical [B] and dense nuclear [C].

Hearing and balance

The ear functions as a receiver of sound and as a monitor of data concerning posture and balance. The visible ear flap, or pinna, consisting of skin and cartilage, and the auditory canal that it guards are known as the outer ear [Key]. The canal is protected by hairs and modified sweat glands that secrete wax, or cerumen. These trap potentially harmful particles and bacteria.

For protection, the delicate mechanisms of the ear are set deep inside the bone of the skull. At the end of the auditory canal lies the eardrum, or tympanic membrane. On the other side is the cavity of the middle ear, which communicates with the back of the throat through a canal known as the Eustachian tube. This opens into the nose and throat and provides a complementary flow of air from the inside to match the pressure of air from outside the eardrum. This is most dramatically demonstrated if a sudden change in external air pressure—experienced, for instance, in an airplane—causes "popping" of the ears and momentary deafness. Swallowing opens the tube and restores the balance.

Across the cavity of the middle ear, linking the eardrums with the inner ear, are small bones, the malleus (hammer), the incus (anvil), and the stapes (stirrup), collectively known as the auditory ossicles [1]. These, the smallest bones in the body, transmit the vibrations of the eardrum to a membrane, the oval window, which closes off the inner ear. Inside the inner ear is a fluid-filled coiled tube, resembling a snail's shell, called the cochlea [2]. Here the vibrations are converted to nerve impulses that the brain perceives as sound.

How sound reaches the brain

Sound results from wavelike vibrations of air; it has the qualities of amplitude (the height of the waves) and of frequency (the number of vibrations that occur every second). If a sound is loud, then it has a large amplitude, and the higher the pitch of a note the greater the frequency. Most people can detect sounds between 20 and 20,000 hertz (cycles per second) [9].

The pinna not only protects the ear but also serves to direct sound into the auditory canal. Sound waves pass along the canal and vibrate the eardrum. The ossicles respond to the movements of the eardrum and, acting as a series of levers, magnify the intensity of the vibration more than 20 times, although leaving its frequency unchanged. The stirrup passes vibrations to the fluid in the cochlea through the oval window.

The cochlea is divided into two cavities by the basilar membrane, running the length of which is a complex structure called the organ of Corti [3, 8]. Sound waves traveling through the fluid along the membrane cause the sensitive cells of the organ of Corti to vibrate. High notes cause the basilar membrane to vibrate only at its lower end, but low notes set the whole membrane into activity. A complex of more than 30,000 nerve fibers carry the information to the brain.

The intensity of sound, determined by the amplitude of the wave, is measured in decibels (dB). A barely audible whisper is about 20dB, ordinary conversation 60dB, and a jet aircraft at takeoff 140dB. Prolonged exposure to noise above 90dB can

CONNECTIONS

See also
1498 What is sound?
1500 Musical sounds
666 How the brain work
672 Potential of the min
804 An active old age
1698 Cars and society
1752 Airports and air traff

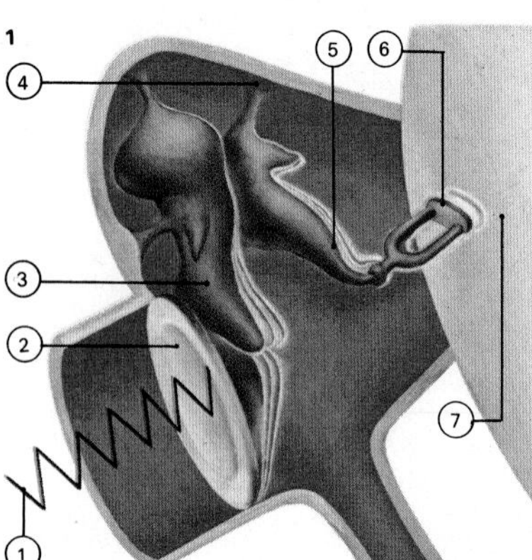

1 Sound waves [1] first strike the eardrum [2] and are transferred to the inner ear [7] by vibrations of the hammer [3], anvil [5], and stirrup [6], which are held in place by ligaments [4].

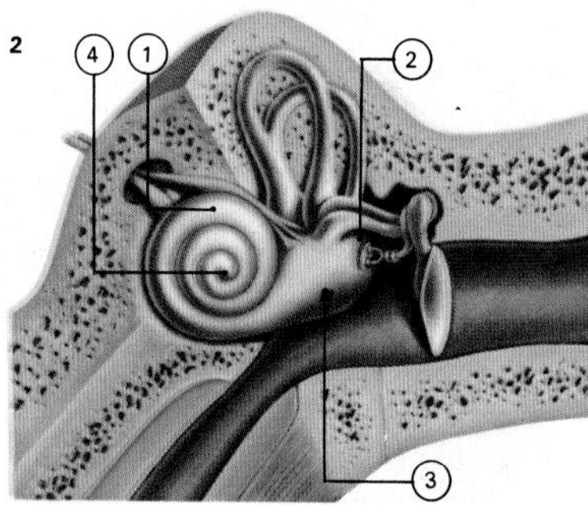

2 Waves pass through the cochlea [1] from the oval [2] to the round window [3]. High frequencies activate the base [4].

3 Compartments filled with fluid [1] in the cochlea carry traveling waves [2]. As these pass along the basilar membrane [3] they activate the sensory cells [4] in the organ of Corti [5].

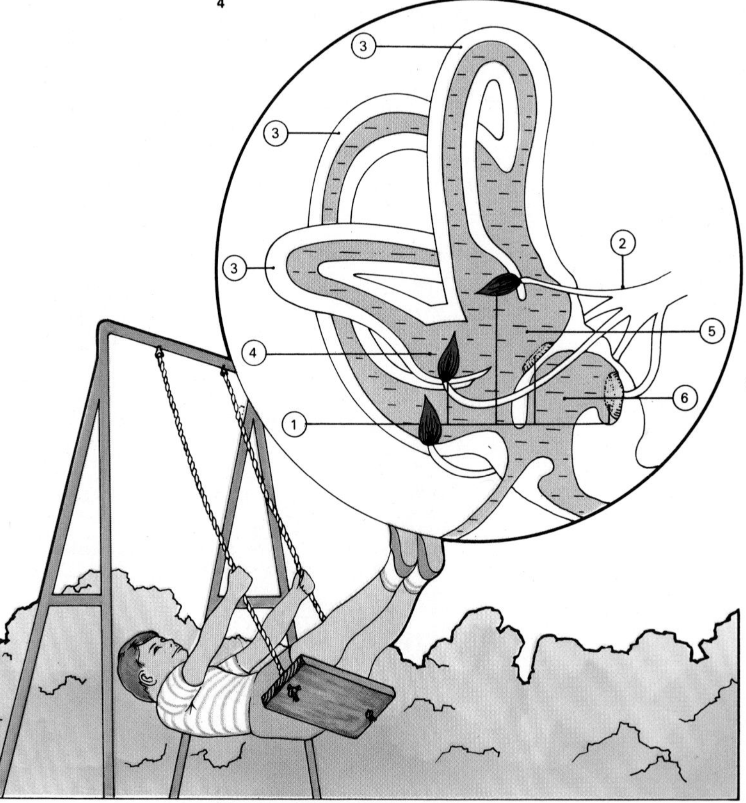

4 The inner ear contains five chambers filled with fluid—the three semicircular canals, the sacculus, and the utriculus. All these contain receptor cells [1], which monitor head movement and relay this information along nerves [2] to the brain. The semicircular canals [3] are set at right angles to each other and can therefore monitor angular movement of the head in any direction. At the base of each canal is a chamber, the ampulla [4], which contains sensory receptors. The utriculus [5] and the sacculus [6] are interconnected and also contain sensitive receptors. These register the position of the head with respect to gravity and allow us to know our orientation.

5 The position of the semicircular canals, the utriculus, and the sacculus are shown here [in red] in relation to the other parts of the ear. Balance also relies on vision, stimuli from the position sensors of limbs, and on cells in the soles of the feet. In some cases, even when the inner ear is defective and not sending adequate signals to the brain, the other senses are able to maintain equilibrium.

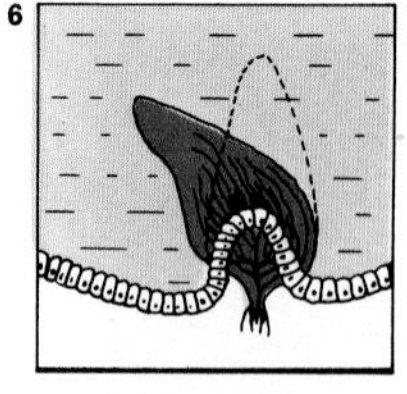

6 Body movement is detected by the ampulla when fluid in the semicircular canals bends the hairs of its receptors. The canals are positioned in three planes, so that any movement will affect the fluid in at least one of them.

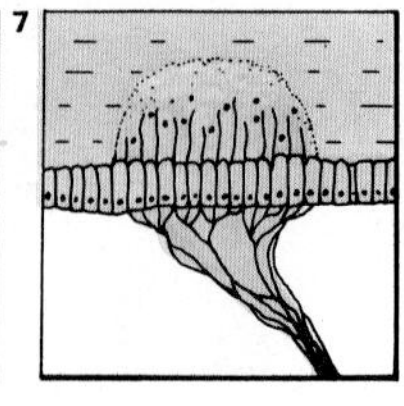

7 The utriculus and sacculus contain hair cells that include small "stones" of calcium carbonate, otoliths. When the head is upright, otoliths press on particular nerve receptors. When the head tilts, they press on other receptors.

lead to temporary deafness. Intensive noise—above 100dB—can cause permanent damage.

Deafness and other hearing defects

Of the two main types of deafness, the conductive form occurs if there is interference with the passage of sound *en route* to the inner ear. This may be caused by a blockage of the auditory canal (often by wax), perforation of the eardrum, fluid, inflammation, or abscess in the middle ear, or by defective growth of the bones in the middle ear. Probably more common is perceptive or sensorinueural deafness, which is caused by damage to or incomplete development of the inner ear. Apart from congenital malfunction, this is brought about by disease, head injuries, virus infections, prolonged exposure to loud noise, or aging [10].

The sense of balance

The inner ear also contains three fluid-filled canals, the semicircular canals and two other chambers, the utriculus and sacculus [4, 5]. These structures function separately from the hearing mechanism and are concerned with balance and posture.

The three semicircular canals are set at right angles to each other and are thus able to detect movements of the head in any plane. At the ends of the semicircular canals are chambers that contain tufts of hair supplied with nerve fibers. Any movement of the head sets the fluid swirling through one, two, or all of the canals. This moves the hairs, whose nerves inform the brain about the body's position [6].

The utriculus and sacculus are the means by which we are able to detect changes in the posture of the body relative to gravity. Like the semicircular canals, these two chambers contain tufts of hair connected to nerves. The hairs are surrounded by a jellylike substance containing minute crystals of calcium carbonate, called otoliths [7]. As the crystals move under the influence of gravity, they stimulate the hairs, which trigger nerve impulses to the brain. The information from these balance organs is integrated with nerve impulses from the eyes to monitor body posture.

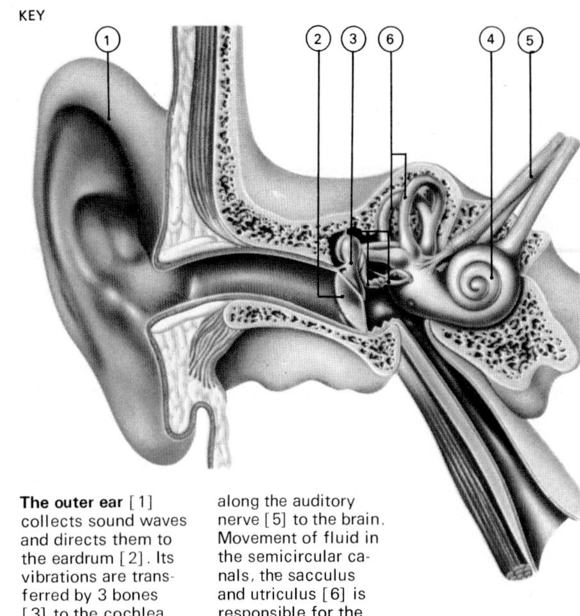
KEY
1
2
3
6
4
5

The outer ear [1] collects sound waves and directs them to the eardrum [2]. Its vibrations are transferred by 3 bones [3] to the cochlea [4]. Impulses run along the auditory nerve [5] to the brain. Movement of fluid in the semicircular canals, the sacculus and utriculus [6] is responsible for the sense of balance.

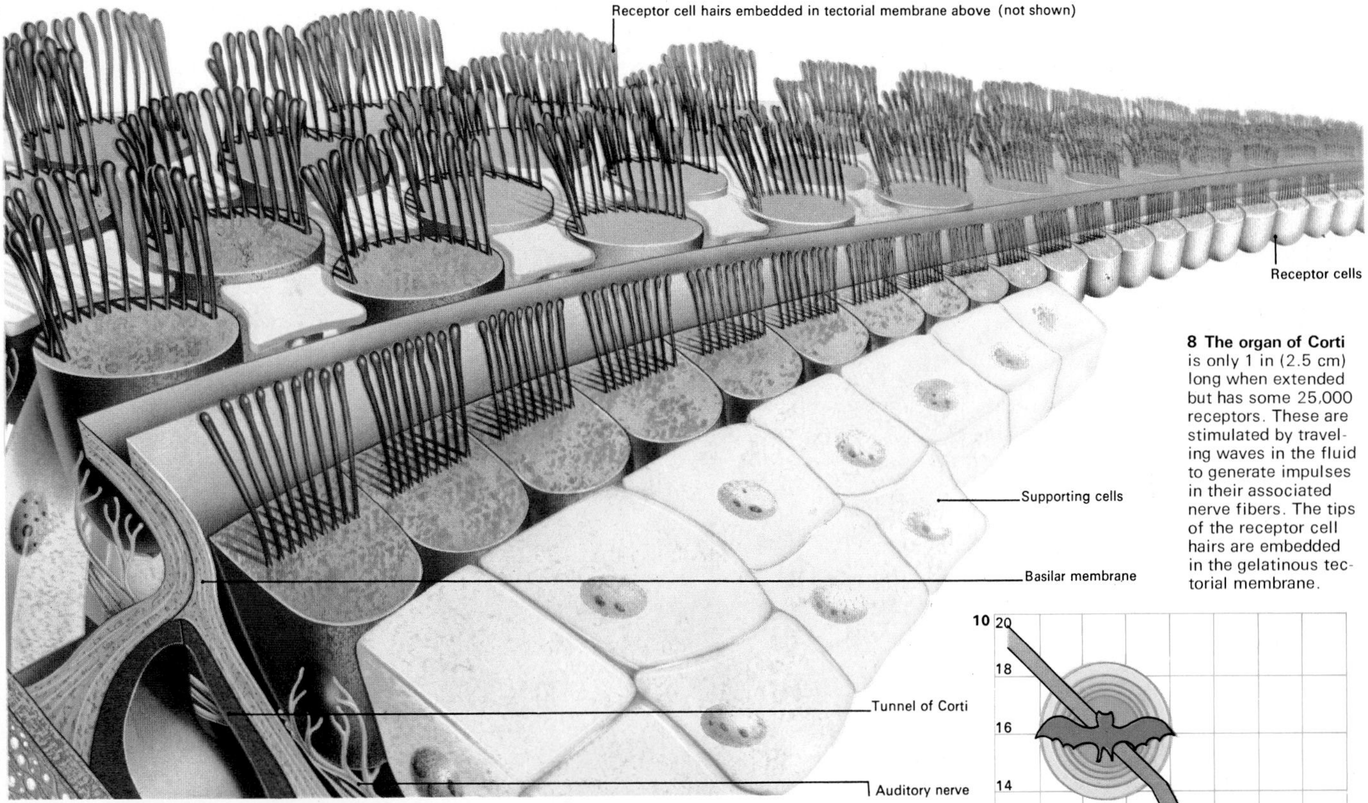

Receptor cell hairs embedded in tectorial membrane above (not shown)

Receptor cells

Supporting cells

Basilar membrane

Tunnel of Corti

Auditory nerve

8 The organ of Corti is only 1 in (2.5 cm) long when extended but has some 25,000 receptors. These are stimulated by traveling waves in the fluid to generate impulses in their associated nerve fibers. The tips of the receptor cell hairs are embedded in the gelatinous tectorial membrane.

9

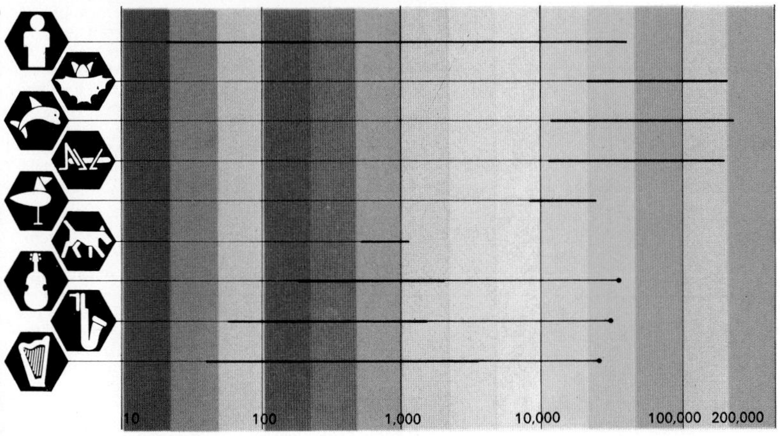

10 100 1,000 10,000 100,000 200,000

9 The human ear can respond to frequencies between 20 and 20 thousand hertz (cycles per second). Many animals can generate frequencies far beyond this range. Musical instruments have both the range of notes that can be played and the overtones (fine lines) that make up their characteristic sounds.

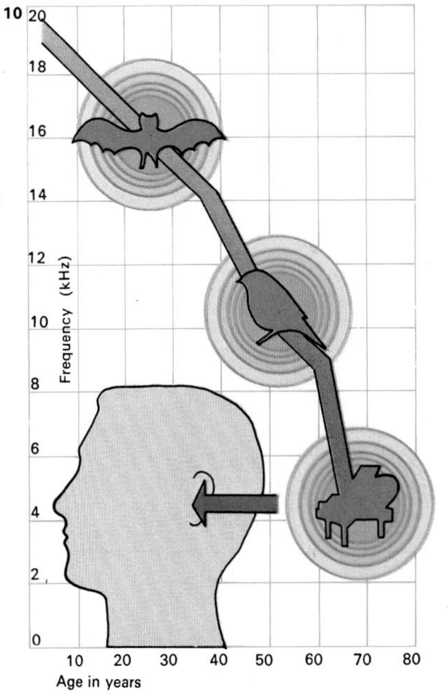

10 Human hearing deteriorates from the late teens on. High frequency response is lost with increasing age.

10

Frequency (kHz): 0 2 4 6 8 10 12 14 16 18 20

Age in years: 10 20 30 40 50 60 70 80

Touch, pain, and temperature

Amid the wealth of information that is constantly fed to the brain is a stream of messages about the sensations of touch, pressure, and temperature. These stimuli, which often demand minor adjustments in our everyday lives, originate in the skin, the body's main contact with the outside world. It is in the skin, therefore (and in the mucous membranes, such as that lining the mouth, that is a modification of surface skin), that some of the human body's most sophisticated and highly complex sensory equipment is located.

Types of receptors

Physical sensations are detected by sensory receptors—specialized nerve extremities that respond best (but not exclusively) to a particular type of stimulus. In the skin these include mechanoreceptors that are involved in detecting touch [2] and pressure [3], and thermoreceptors for sensations of heat and cold [5]. Itch, tickle, and vibration have no specific nerve endings of their own; itching is caused by mild stimulation of the pain receptor, tickle is the result of light agitation of touch receptors, and vibration is felt through pressure receptors.

Sensitivity to a particular stimulus is not necessarily uniform all over the body. Receptive fields may overlap, thus boosting the level of sensation, and in many cases the density of nerve endings varies. There are more touch receptors on the tongue and fingertips, for example, than in body areas such as the back (which explains why it is so difficult to judge how many fingers someone is using to touch your back). Most receptors can adapt to unimportant stimuli and it is for this reason that we do not continuously feel the presence of our clothes.

Significant stimuli are converted into nerve impulses to travel, by way of the spinal cord, to a center in the brain known as the thalamus. The thalamus provides vague awareness (as opposed to fine discrimination) of sensory stimulation, determines its quality, pleasant or otherwise, and may also be responsible for interpreting pain. But the essential function of the thalamus is that of integrating sensory material—grouping together impulses of the same nature from different parts of the body—for transmission to the sensory cortex, the region of the brain that analyzes sensations [1]. Underlying the thalamus is a smaller structure called the hypothalamus, which, among other activities, regulates body temperature.

Pain: variety and interpretation

Pain is the most dramatic and in some ways the most puzzling of the senses that play a part in keeping us alive. Pain is felt in different ways: "bright," or pricking, pain such as that associated with a cut finger is intense, short-lived, and easily localized to the part of the body affected. "Burning" pain is slow to develop, longer-lasting, and less easily localized. "Aching," or visceral, pain is persistent, often nauseating, and may be referred away from the pain source [7]. The anomaly of referred pain is caused by the entry of impulses from the affected area into the spinal cord and their stimulation of nerve fibers from the skin.

Both the sensory end organs and the neural pathways that conduct pain sensa-

CONNECTIONS

See also
686 Skin and hair
820 Meditation and consciousness
672 Potential of the min

1

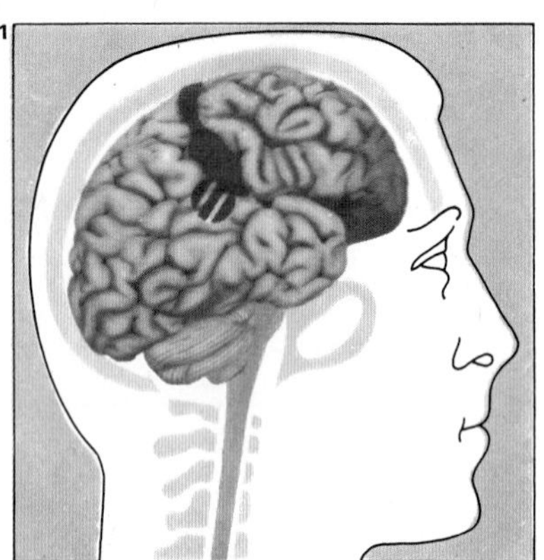

1 The region of the brain that analyzes sensations, such as touch and pressure and heat and cold, is the sensory cortex. The primary area is colored solid red; the secondary area is shown striped.

2A B C

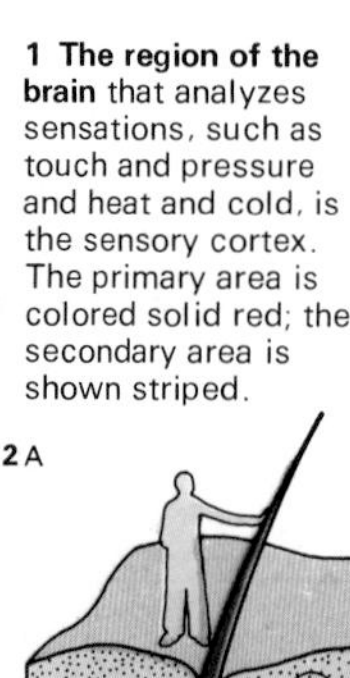

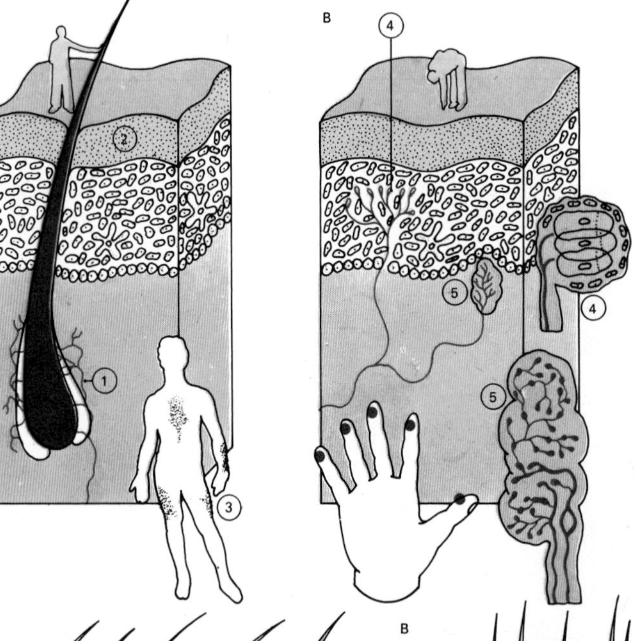

2 The sensation of touch usually results from mechanical distortion of various types of sensory receptors in the skin. Touching a hair [A] affects free nerve endings that form a web [1] around hair follicles beneath the epidermis [2]. These hair end organs are distributed over the body [3]. Mostly found in hairless skin [B], Merkel's disks [4] and Meissner's corpuscles [5] are terminal bulb receptors plentiful in such areas as the fingertips that are especially sensitive to touch. Merkel's disks detect continuous touch while Meissner's corpuscles signal the point and texture of contact. Some free nerve endings can detect both touch and pressure. In the eye [C] receptors of this type [6] serving the epithelium of the cornea [7] above the lens [8] respond to the lightest contact.

3

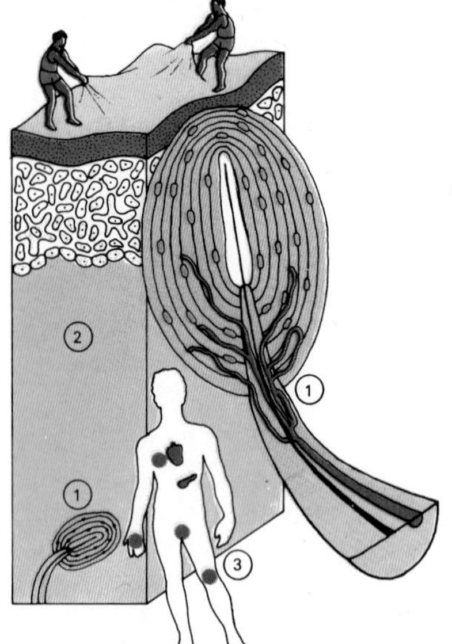

3 Some of the largest sensory receptors in the body are pressure receptors known as Pacinian corpuscles [1], mainly found in the dermis [2] of the skin; they also respond to vibration and stretch. Pacinian corpuscles are distributed [3] both on the body surface and in some internal organs and are particularly abundant in hairless zones such as the palms of the hands and soles of the feet.

4A B

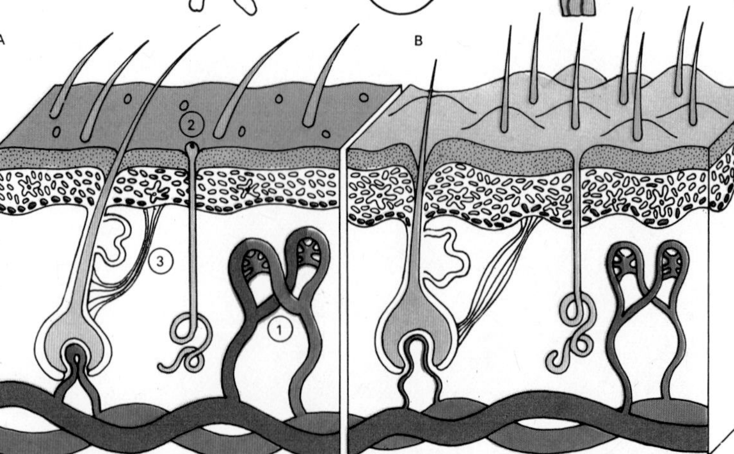

4 Body temperature is adjusted by the hypothalamus of the brain, which signals changes in the skin in response to sensations of heat and cold. A rising temperature [A] causes blushing of the skin as blood vessels [1] dilate to allow heat to be radiated from the surface. Evaporation of sweat [2] and relaxation of hair erector muscles [3] cool the skin. When cold [B], blood vessels constrict, skin looks blue and hair stands on end, causing "goose-flesh."

tions to the central nervous system—the spinal cord and the brain—are so varied that there is dispute about the existence of specialized "pain nerves." Pain may be the result of excessive stimulation of any nerve fiber. Sometimes damage to the neural pathways gives rise to spontaneous pain, referred to the area supplied by the pathway and coupled with sensory loss. Mostly burning in character, spontaneous pain arising from an old injury to peripheral nerves is known as causalgia and is nearly always referred. Similarly, spontaneous central pain occurs when more central structures, such as the spinal cord or the thalamus, have been damaged. The bizarre sensations that are a common legacy of amputation are known as phantom-limb pains. Causalgia, central pain, and phantom-limb pain are known collectively to the medical profession as neurogenic pains.

Both human beings and animals learn quickly to evaluate the experience of pain as a result of events in infancy. There is evidence that undue protection from damage reduces the ability to feel pain or to evaluate painful stimuli. Sensory deprivation of this kind is potentially dangerous in that pain is an important protective sensation—securing withdrawal of the tissues from harmful agents—as well as a useful indicator of disease. Some people suffer from a congenital nervous abnormality that drastically reduces or totally excludes the ability to sense pain—a rare condition known as hypoasthesia. They face a far higher risk of injury.

The psychology of pain

Pain, like all other experience, is entirely subjective and often considerably affected by psychological factors [6]. Soldiers, for example, can suffer fearful wounds in battle without noticing them until later. All the techniques so far available for measuring so-called pain thresholds are open to criticism and all that is known for certain is that men are more sensitive to pain than women, that office workers are more sensitive than manual workers, and anxious people more than calm types. In old age sensitivity to pain tends to be reduced.

KEY

5

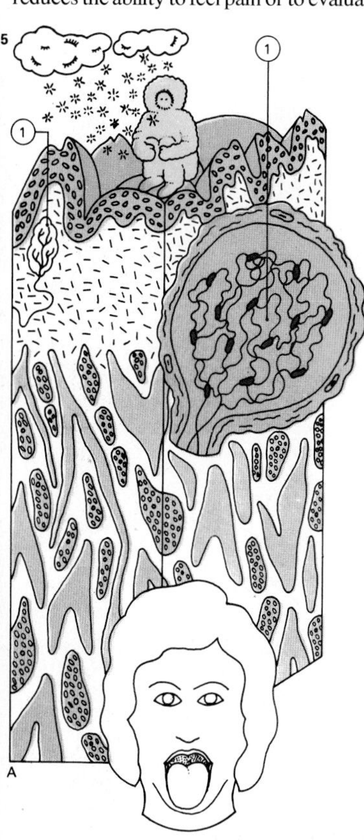

1
1
A

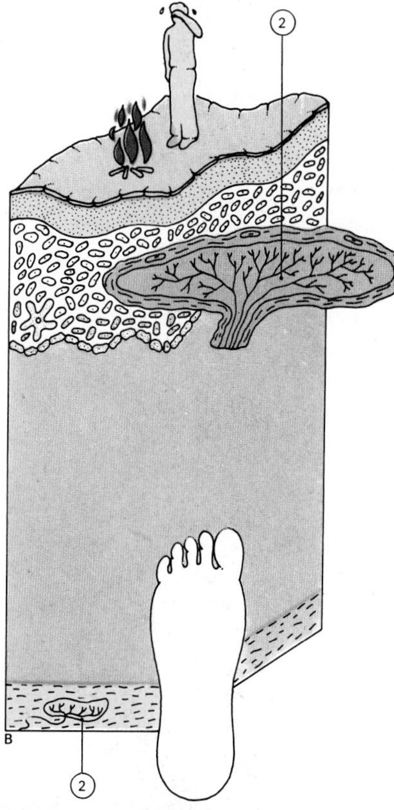

2
2
B

5 Two kinds of skin receptors specialized to detect thermal changes are Kraus end bulbs [1], which respond to cold, and Ruffini corpuscles [2], which react to heat. Kraus end bulbs are most prevalent in the mucosa of the tongue, the conjunctiva of the eye, and the external genitalia. Ruffini corpuscles, found deep in the dermis of the skin, or even in the subcutaneous layer, are flatter in shape and particularly abundant in the soles of the feet.

6

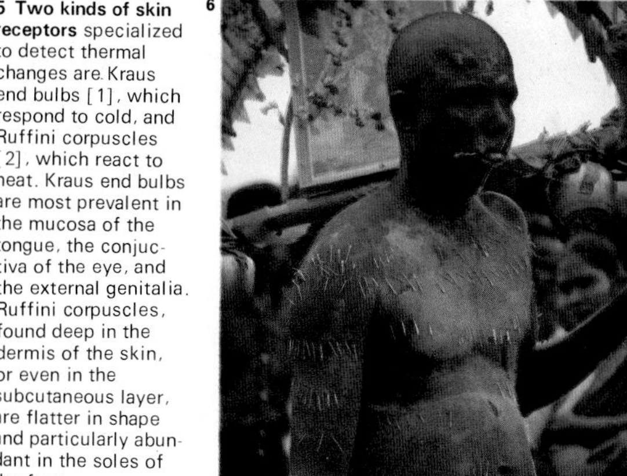

6 Pain is both physical and psychological. Physiologically, it originates from sensory receptors all over the body, but psychological and cultural attitudes seem to override the most powerful pain stimuli to the extent that subjugation of physical sensation is almost a commonplace occurrence at religious ceremonies in the East. This Hindu, taking part in a festival of penitence of Kuala Lumpur, shows no evidence of pain from needles in his skin.

7

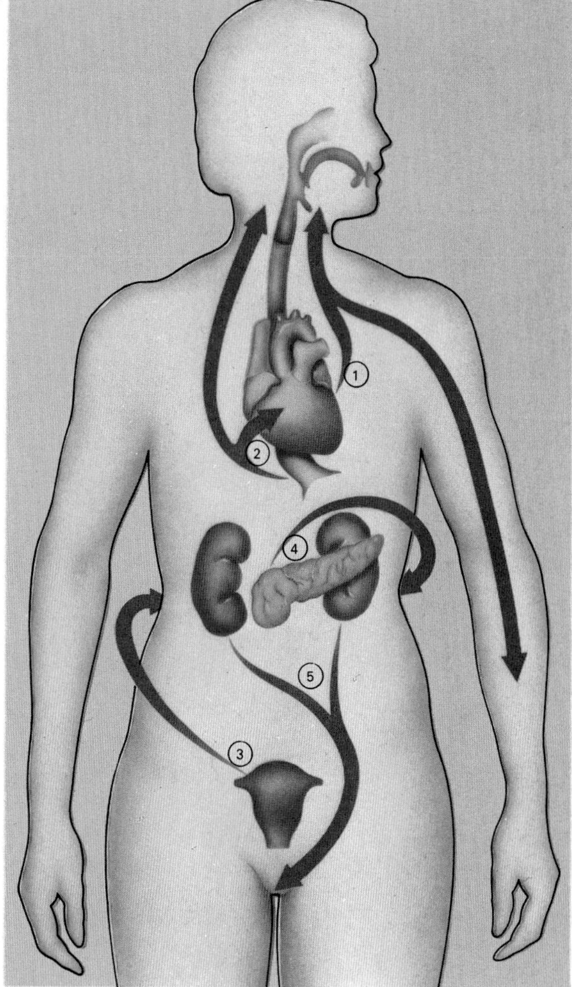

1
2
4
5
3

7 Referred pain is the term used for the sort of visceral pain that makes itself felt somewhere other than the site of the trouble. For example, the condition known as ischemia [1] (a shortage of blood to the heart) causes pain in the base of the neck as well as in the shoulders and arms; acid irritation of the esophagus [2] is felt in the throat and in addition over the heart and in the arms; womb trouble [3] and one or two disorders of the pancreas [4] give rise to backache; and stones in the kidney may set up pain in the groin [5]. As a sign of some internal disturbance referred pain is an important factor in diagnosis, to be considered together with the patient's other symptoms in the accurate location of a disorder.

Smell and taste

The senses of smell and taste together form part of a system that samples the world around us and reports to the brain. They are both chemical senses, separate but closely linked. In humans neither can normally operate at a great distance, and taste, the weaker sense, depends to some extent on the sense of smell to augment it.

The sense of smell (olfaction), centered on two small patches of olfactory epithelium [1] in the nose, detects any airborne odors that reach it. The sense of taste, centered in the tongue, detects chemicals only in the mouth, but the two senses are so interdependent that a foul smell can leave a nasty taste in the mouth and enjoyment of food is a complex response to sensations from the tongue, palate, and nose. The person suffering from a cold, for example, is unable to "taste" food because he has a "stuffed nose."

The sense of taste

The sense of taste enables us to appreciate food and drink and warns us if food has gone stale or is bad. The principal organs of taste are microscopic nerve endings, called taste buds, situated on the tongue and also, to a lesser extent, on other surfaces of the mouth. They are housed in small projections called papillae [2]. Only liquids can be tasted. A solid in a dry mouth creates no sensation of taste, for taste buds are stimulated only when chemicals in food are dissolved by saliva and washed out over the taste buds.

When the receptor cells are stimulated they cause signals to be transmitted along two of the 12 pairs of cranial nerves—the glossopharyngeal and lingual nerves—to the taste centers in the brain [4].

The taste buds register only four basic sensations—sweet, salt, sour, and bitter—although some experts believe that metallic and alkaline tastes can be detected too. Most taste, however, can be considered as combinations of the four basic sensations. Different parts of the tongue detect different tastes [6], and the center of the tongue has no sense of taste.

Touch receptors in the mouth convey information about temperature and texture and the various signals are combined in the brain to give the full flavor sensation. The tongue is also sensitive to irritants such as pepper or the ingredients of curry powder.

How smell works

Smell is less important to humans than the other senses and it is the one about which least is known. It is not nearly as sensitive in humans as it is in many animals and insects. Male moths, for example, can smell female moths several miles away. During evolution our sense of smell has decreased in importance as we have come to rely more on sight and hearing.

The olfactory epithelia are housed in the roof of the nasal cavity [Key]—the narrow, lofty chamber of the nose. The floor of the cavity is the roof of the mouth and its ceiling is the brain case. The whole cavity is lined with mucous membrane, a soft, warm adaptation of the skin that is well supplied with blood vessels.

Glands in the mucous membrane secrete a film of mucus, the viscous fluid that keeps internal surfaces of the cavity moist.

CONNECTIONS

See also
666 How the brain works
678 Touch, pain, and temperature

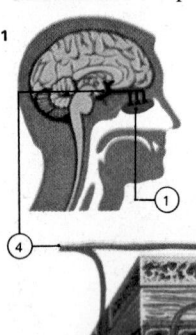

1

1 Olfactory membrane; located at the roof of the nasal cavity
2 Specialized nerve cells sensitive to low concentrations of odiferous substances
3 Mucus-covered outer surface of membrane with cilia
4 Olfactory nerve; transmits impulses to brain

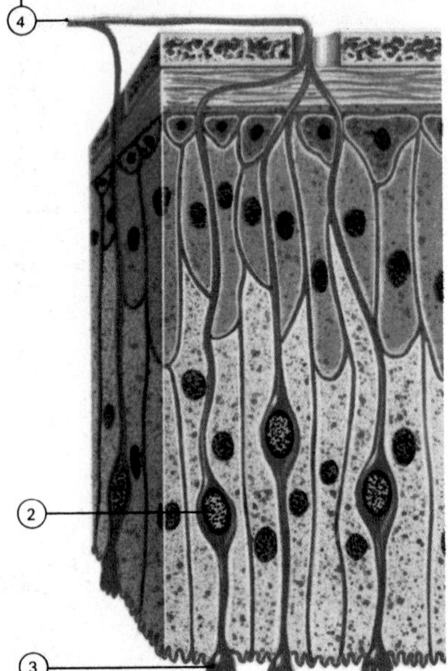

1 Ability to detect smells comes from small organs called olfactory receptors, occupying in the adult about 2 sq in (12sq cm) in the top of the nasal passages. (In comparison, a young rabbit's olfactory surface has the same area as the whole of its skin.) These receptors consist of thousands of hair-bearing cells that are embedded in a layer of mucus-secreting cells. Odiferous substances such as hot foods give off molecules that float through the air. When this air is inhaled and passes over the back part of the nasal passages the molecules dissolve in the mucus. It is believed that a chemical reaction then stimulates the hair to transmit nerve impulses to the olfactory bulbs, which are the two centers dealing with the sense of smell. These pass signals to the brain. A substance must reach the nose as a gas for one to be aware of its odor. Our sense of smell is closely linked with that of taste.

2

2 The tongue, has about 10,000 nerve endings known as taste buds embedded in its surface. These are found in association with minute projections, or papillae, of which there are three sorts. Each taste bud consists of a cluster of taste receptor cells exposed to the surface via a small pore. As food enters the mouth it is moistened by fluid produced both by serous glands in the tongue and by salivary glands in the cheeks (parotid), under the tongue (sublingual), and in the lower jaw (submandibular). Substances in solution then enter the taste buds and stimulate taste receptor cells. Nerve impulses travel via neighboring nerve fibers to the brain. Taste buds can detect up to one part of a chemical in two million. The taste buds in the front and middle of the tongue send messages along the lingual nerve and those at the back of the tongue use the glossopharyngeal nerve. The brain sorts these signals and identifies them as different tastes.

1 Epiglottis, a flap that covers the entrance to the windpipe when food is being swallowed
2 Filiform papilla
3 Fungiform papilla
4 Vallate papilla
5 Entrance to a taste bud
6 Taste receptors
7 Nerve taking taste sensations to the brain
8 Serous gland cell
9 Serous secretion; helps to moisten food

Cilia—microscopic hairs growing from the epithelium—move the mucus continually back toward the throat; sniffing and swallowing help it down toward the stomach.

Air drawn through the nostrils is first filtered by a network of guard hairs, then warmed and partly cleansed by its passage over the sticky surfaces of the nasal cavity. Flowing back toward the lungs, the air passes over the two patches of sensory epithelium in the roof of the nasal cavity. These are made up of many thousands of cells bearing hairs that are connected to the deeply embedded sensory cells.

The detection of smells

How the sensory cells detect odors is not known, but it is believed that molecules of chemical vapor carried in the airstream are deposited on the mucus and in some way sensitize the hairs. These communicate with the cell body beneath them and this in turn initiates an impulse in the associated nerve fibers. The fibers pass from the olfactory membrane to the olfactory bulbs, which are linked directly to the brain [3].

The receptors of the sense of touch in the nose also contribute to the sense of smell. The sharp odor of ammonia, for example, is partly identified by stimulation of the pain receptors in the nose, and the smell of menthol is partly a sensation of coldness.

Although the sense of smell is no longer important in terms of our basic survival, large perfume and deodorant industries thrive on it. The smell receptors in humans can detect an amount of artificial musk equivalent to one drop being diffused throughout a room the size of a concert hall.

The sense of smell adapts rapidly to new odors. If two smells are encountered simultaneously first one is recognized and then the other. But when the receptors become saturated with an odor it quickly fades and this explains how one can tolerate an unpleasant odor after the initial aversion to it. The sense of smell is backed by an excellent memory, and well-trained sense receptors can recognize more than 10,000 different odors. Sensitivity to smells differs between the sexes.

KEY

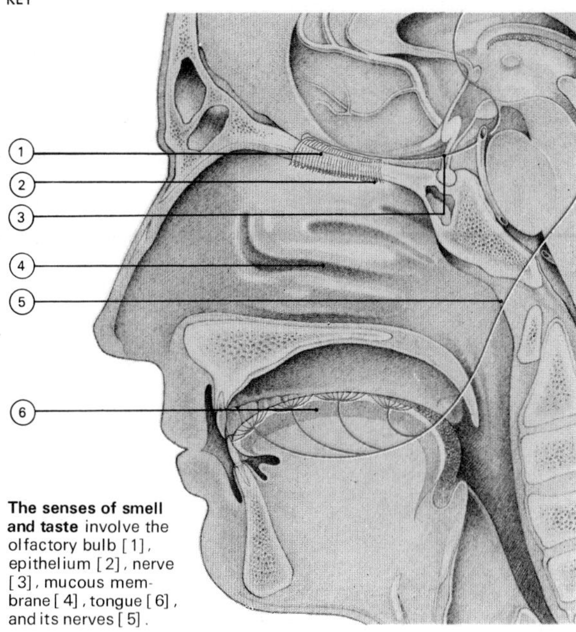
1
2
3
4
5
6

The senses of smell and taste involve the olfactory bulb [1], epithelium [2], nerve [3], mucous membrane [4], tongue [6], and its nerves [5].

3

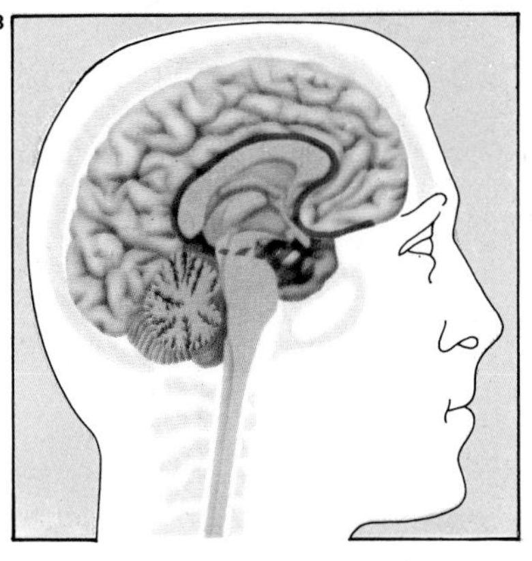

3 The smell pathway in the brain can be traced from the olfactory bulb to the rhinencephalon (the area shown striped here), located deep within the brain.

4 Taste centers in the brain are part of the somato-sensory cortex [A] and the arcuate nucleus of the thalamus [B]. The former controls sensations from the mouth but the latter is thought to be more important.

4

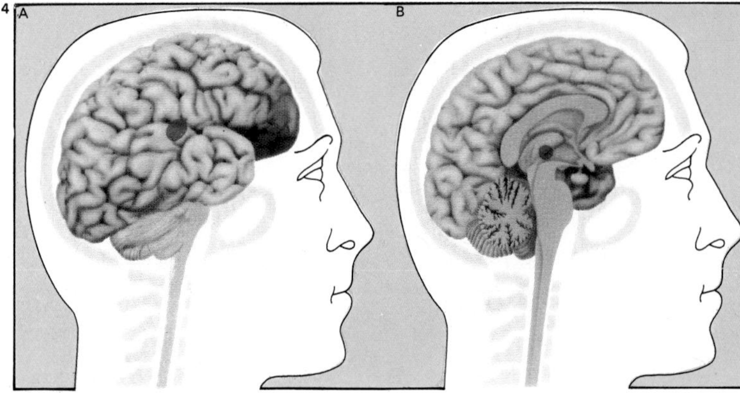
A
B

5

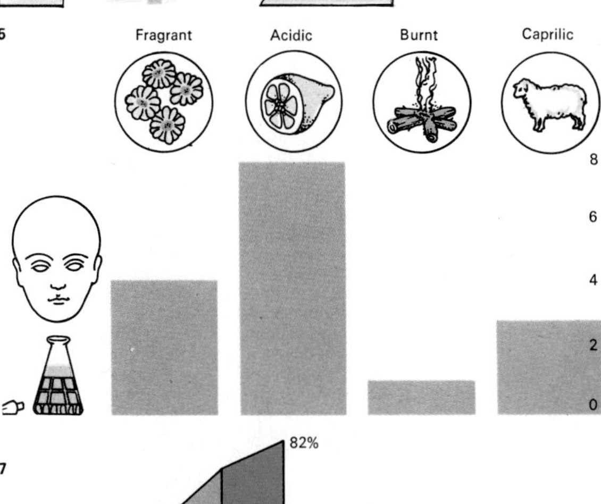
Fragrant
Acidic
Burnt
Caprilic
8
6
4
2
0

5 One classification of odors based on subjective judgments has suggested four basic qualities: fragrant, acidic, burnt, and caprilic (pungent or animal-like). The intensity of each quality has been graded from numbers 0 to 8. In this way the vinegar illustrated here may be designated as 4813 showing that it is "half" fragrant [4], very acidic [8], slightly burnt [1] and moderately caprilic [3].

6

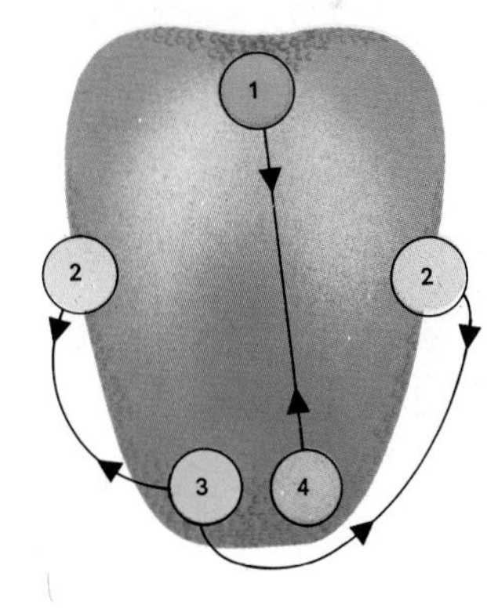
1
2
2
3
4

6 Different areas of the tongue are sensitive to different specific tastes. Bitterness is detected at the back of the tongue [1]; sourness is detected at the sides [2]; saltiness is tasted all over the tongue, but particularly at the front [3]; and sweetness is detected at the tip [4]. Not all taste qualities can fuse with one another but bitter and sweet blend to produce a fused sensation, as do sour and salty.

7

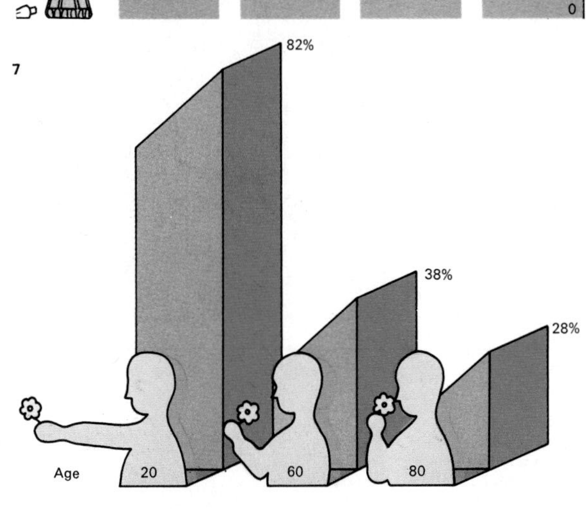
82%
38%
28%
Age
20
60
80

7 Olfactory receptors atrophy as one ages, beginning immediately after birth, so that the sense of smell deteriorates. Shown here are the percentages remaining at the ages of 20, 60, and 80.

8 Human taste buds decline in number with age, especially after 60 and it is largely for this reason that our sense of taste becomes less acute. Here are the number of taste buds in the trench wall of one papilla at the ages of 20, 60, and 80.

8

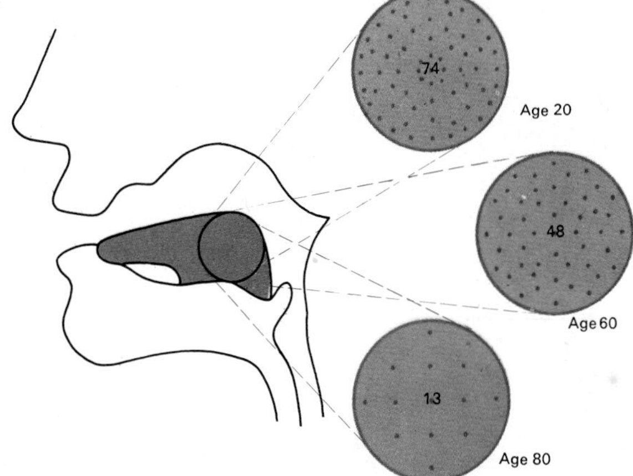
74
Age 20
48
Age 60
13
Age 80

Skull, skeleton, and joints

The bones of the skeleton form a strong scaffolding of protection and support for the human body. Because bone has a high content of calcuim, phosphorus, and other minerals, it appears hard, dry, and rigid. But one third of its composition is a fibrous protein called collagen, and this gives bone a meshwork of pliable threads.

Bone structure and design

If a long bone is soaked in acid, so that the minerals are dissolved, the remaining protein framework is so pliable that it can be tied in a knot. If a bone is heated, destroying the protein, the remaining mineral structure is hard and brittle. The combination of these qualities gives living bone its unique nature. It has strength and rigidity, with resilience and the ability to withstand bending and crushing forces.

Integrated with the bony skeleton are connective tissues. Strong and supple ligaments link bone to bone; springy cartilage cushions the joints where bones meet; and fibrous, inelastic tendons (sinews) are cables attaching muscles to the levers that they move. These connective tissues are as important as bone.

There are four main types of bones. The flat bones such as the shoulder blades, skull vault, and hips, are both strong and light and safely house and support delicate internal organs, as well as provide anchorage for muscles. The irregular bones that form the flexible vertebral column, or spine [2], are separate from each other but are joined together by fibrous ligaments and muscles. The short bones found in the wrist (carpals) and foot (tarsals) are strong, light, and resilient and the long bones in the limbs are strong, hollow, and light—essential for support, leverage, and movement [4].

Bone formation and the skeleton

Bone develops usually from a foundation of cartilage [5], which usually forms a temporary skeleton for the fetus while it grows and expands. Cartilage has an enveloping sheath (the perichondrium) and contains bone-building cells called osteoblasts. When these cells are activated, they absorb soluble calcium salts from the blood and convert them into insoluble salts that are deposited in the cartilage, causing it to harden. This bone-hardening process is called ossification.

Bone tissue develops from centers of ossification [8]. A long bone has three such bone-producing centers. The shaft, or diaphysis, contains one center that becomes active at about the sixth week of fetal development; and each of the cap-like epiphyses, separated from the shaft by a plate of cartilage, also contains one that becomes active, usually after birth. The shaft gradually lengthens until all the cartilage becomes ossified, usually between the ages of 18 and 25 years, after which the bone length can no longer increase.

Adult bone is more likely to fracture than that of a young child in whom the proportion of elastic organic matter is still high, and overstressing causes only a partial fracture. In the elderly a gradual loss of elasticity makes bone more brittle and less resistant to fracture.

The arms, legs, and skull are supported by the spine [Key]. The vertebrae support

CONNECTIONS

See also
684 Muscles and action
720 Diseases of the skeleton and muscles
696 A healthy diet
756 Dentistry
1724 Man in space

1

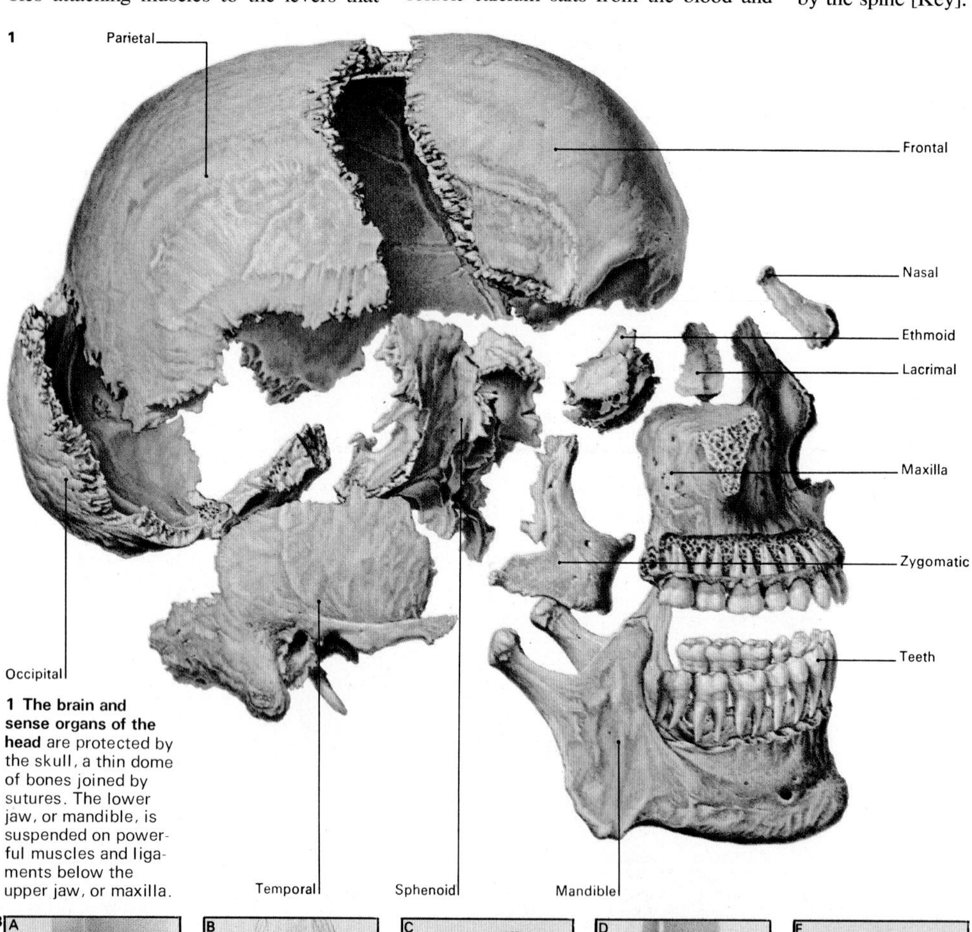

Parietal
Frontal
Nasal
Ethmoid
Lacrimal
Maxilla
Zygomatic
Teeth
Occipital
Temporal
Sphenoid
Mandible

1 The brain and sense organs of the head are protected by the skull, a thin dome of bones joined by sutures. The lower jaw, or mandible, is suspended on powerful muscles and ligaments below the upper jaw, or maxilla.

2

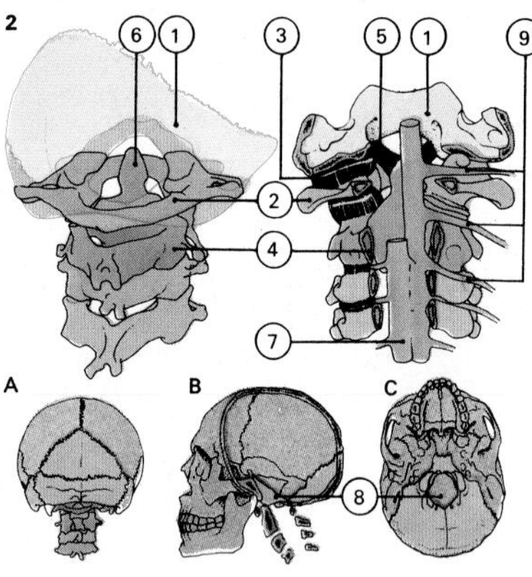

6
1
3
5
1
9
2
4
7
A
B
C
8

2 The vertebral column supports the head and rib cage and protects the spinal cord. The bowl-shaped occipital bone [1] at the base of the skull is attached to the first vertebra, or "atlas," [2] by membranes and by a fibrous capsule [3] that is sandwiched between projections on each bone. The second vertebra, or "axis" [4], is similarly attached to the atlas by a combination of such joints and by ligaments [5]. Turning the head involves movement of the skull and atlas around the central process [6] of the axis. Nodding involves movement of the occipital bone on the atlas. The spinal cord [7] passes through the opening [8] in the occipital bone. Spinal nerves [9] leave through spaces between the vertebrae. The back view [A], side view [B], and bottom view [C] of the skull are shown. The spine is made up of 32–34 vertebrae: 7 in the neck, 12 in the thorax, 5 forming the lumbar region, 5 fused in the sacrum and 3–5 fused in the tail, or coccyx.

3

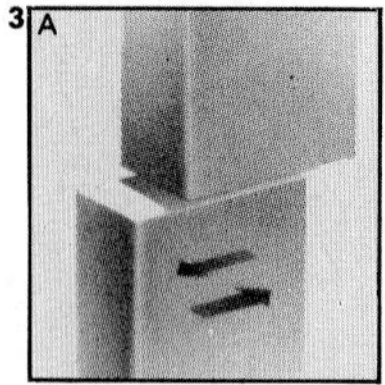

A

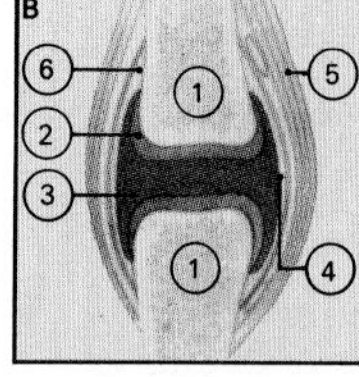

B
6
1
5
2
3
1
4

C

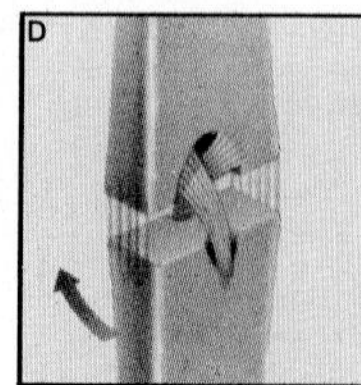

D

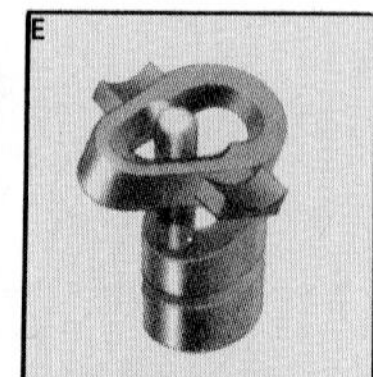

E

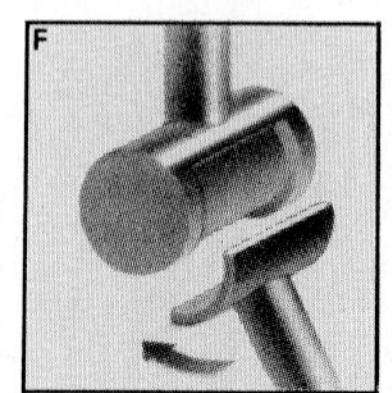

F

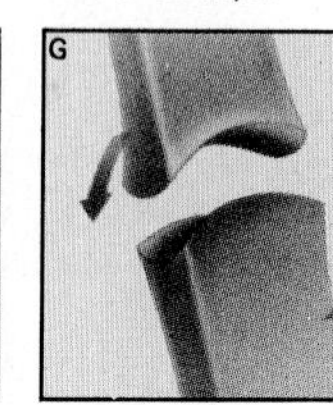

G

3 Simplest of the freely movable joints are gliding joints [A], such as those between the carpal bones at the wrist. Movement is restricted by ligaments. Synovial joints [B] contain fluid to lubricate bearing surfaces. Ball-and-socket joints [C] are found in the hip and shoulder. The socket grips the ball firmly, assisted by ligaments. The hip joints support the trunk's full weight. Internal ligaments [D] help stabilize the knee joint. They cross within the joint, enclosed in synovial membrane where the femur and tibia articulate. Pivot joints [E] are found where the atlas and axis vertebrae articulate and between the radius and ulna. The former allows the head to turn, the latter the forearm to twist. Hinge joints [F] allow movement in only one plane, as at the knee, between humerus and ulna at the elbow, and between the bones of each finger and toe. The saddle joint [G] at the base of the thumb is shaped so that combinations of movements are possible.

1 Bone
2 Cartilage
3 Synovial fluid
4 Synovial membrane
5 Tendon
6 Ligament

the mobile shoulder framework at the pectoral girdle. This includes a pair of collarbones (clavicles) at the front, and a pair of shoulder blades (scapulae) at the back. The clavicles articulate with the breastbone (sternum) at one end, and the scapulae at the other. Attached to the vertebrae are 10 pairs of "true ribs" and two pairs of "floating" ribs.

At the base of the spine is the pelvic girdle, made up of a number of fused bones, which form the framework of the pelvis. The weight of the body is transmitted to the legs through the cup-shaped acetabulum (hip socket) on each side.

Joints and their actions

Joints are formed wherever one bone meets another; some have no movement at all and others have varying degrees of mobility. In this, cartilage plays a vital role; for less freely moving joints, a pad of fibro-cartilage unites bone directly with bone. Displacement of one of these protective pads between the vertebrae can result in the well-known "slipped disk." Where joints are virtually immovable, such as those between the bones of the skull, the bones are tightly dovetailed [1].

In freely movable joints two bones with friction-free hyaline cartilage at the ends are surrounded by a capsule and ligaments [3]. This capsule is lined with a membrane that secrets a fluid in the joint cavity, acting as a lubricating buffer against friction. In large joints such as the knee, external sacs called bursae give additional protective cushioning [7]. (The complaint "housemaid's knee" is the result of the swelling and inflammation of the bursa in front of the knee cap.)

Most bones have hollow cavities that are filled with a spongy bone marrow. Some of this (not in the long bones) forms new red and white blood cells. Only a little more than 0.5lb (225grams) of bone marrow provides the five billion red cells a day that are needed to replace old cells that have become worn out after their 120-day lifetime in the body. Some white cells (a type of leukocyte called a lymphocyte) are also formed in the lymph nodes.

KEY

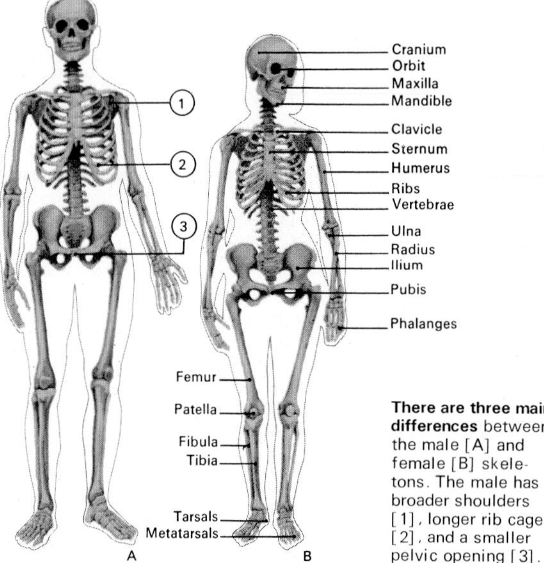
Cranium
Orbit
Maxilla
Mandible
Clavicle
Sternum
Humerus
Ribs
Vertebrae
Ulna
Radius
Ilium
Pubis
Phalanges
Femur
Patella
Fibula
Tibia
Tarsals
Metatarsals
A
B

There are three main differences between the male [A] and female [B] skeletons. The male has broader shoulders [1], longer rib cage [2], and a smaller pelvic opening [3].

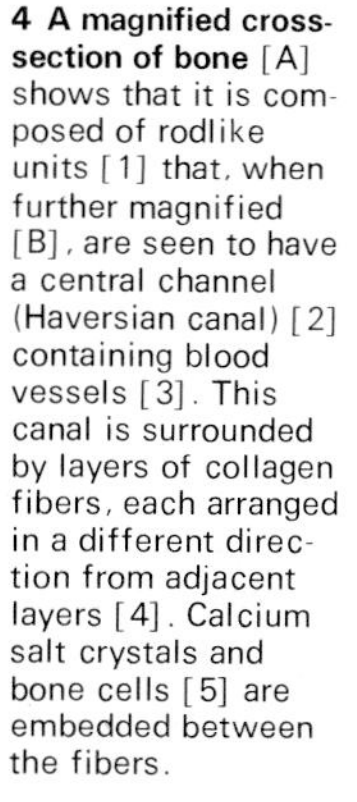

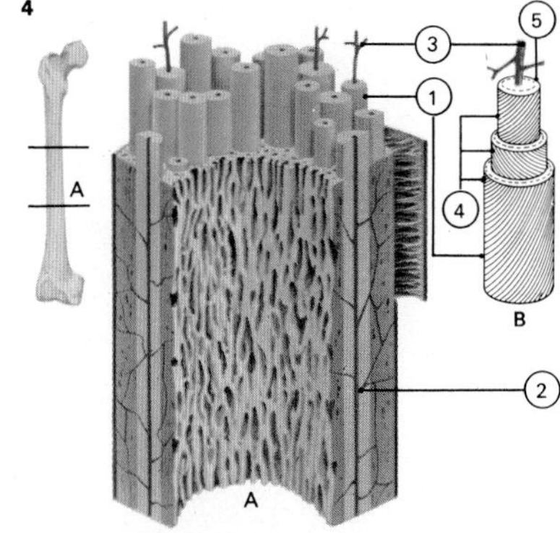

4 A magnified cross-section of bone [A] shows that it is composed of rodlike units [1] that, when further magnified [B], are seen to have a central channel (Haversian canal) [2] containing blood vessels [3]. This canal is surrounded by layers of collagen fibers, each arranged in a different direction from adjacent layers [4]. Calcium salt crystals and bone cells [5] are embedded between the fibers.

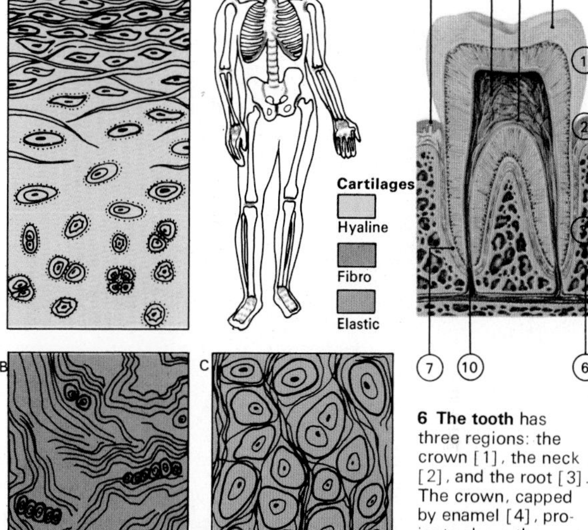
Cartilages
Hyaline
Fibro
Elastic

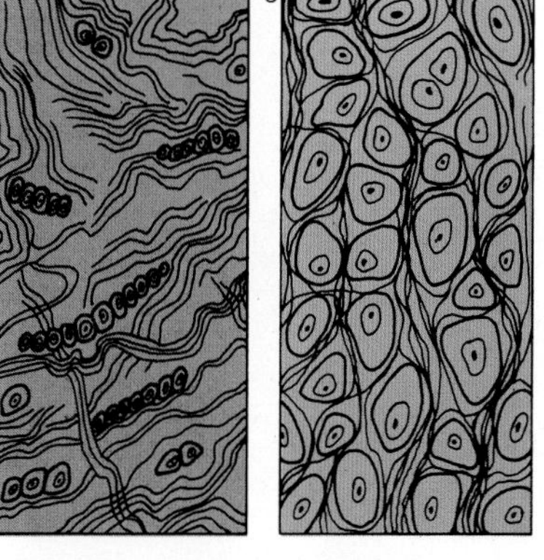

5 The three types of cartilage are composed of cells (chondrocytes) that are embedded, either singly or in groups, within cavities (lacunae) in different matrices. The enlarged cross-sections show [A] hyaline cartilage; [B] fibrocartilage, which contains many collagen fibers; and [C] elastic cartilage with its cells surrounded by dense elastic fibers. [D] shows the locations of the different types in the body.

6 The tooth has three regions: the crown [1], the neck [2], and the root [3]. The crown, capped by enamel [4], projects above the gum [5], the root being fixed in the jaw [6] by a layer of cementum [7]. The connective tissue pulp [8] contains capillaries, nerves, and lymphatics [9]. These enter the tooth at the base through the root canals [10].

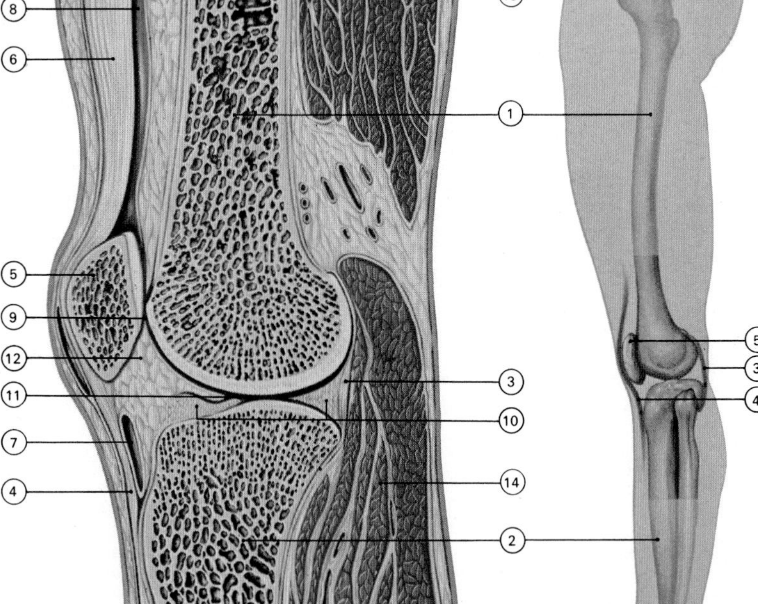

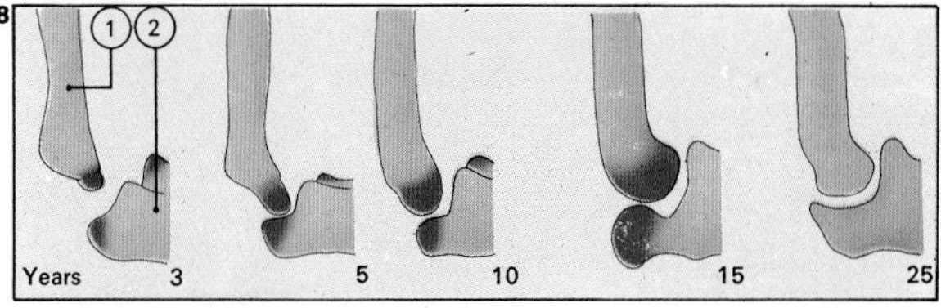
Years 3 5 10 15 25

7 At the knee the femur [1] and tibia [2] are joined by a ligament [3]. Further ligaments [4], attached to the patella [5], form the tendon for the quadriceps muscle [6]. The synovial membrane forms bursae [7,8]. Cartilage [9] covers the articular surfaces and there are two crescents of cartilage [10] between femur and tibia. Synovial membrane and fluid [11] lubricate and fatty pads [12] pack the joint. Biceps [13] and gastrocnemius [14] muscles are shown.

8 Bones lengthen by growth at the epiphyses [red], which are originally cartilage but develop into bone. Shown is the growth of the arm at the elbow, with the humerus [1] and radius and ulna [2], giving growth stages at different ages.

Muscles and action

Muscle, the raw material of movement, is a contractile tissue that makes up from 35 to 45 per cent of the body's weight and powers all its actions—from the merest flicker of an eyelid to the sustained effort needed to run a marathon race. Even during sleep some muscles remain active in order to power vital support systems.

There are three types of muscle, all different in structure and function [1]. Skeletal muscle—the meat on our bones—is strongest and most abundant [3]. Smooth muscle, found in the arteries, intestines, and other internal organs, performs slow, sustained contractions. Cardiac muscle is specific to the heart, generating the powerful contractions that pump blood.

Voluntary muscles

Only skeletal muscle is under natural conscious control—governed directly by the central nervous system—and is therefore described as voluntary muscle. It is networked with blood vessels and nerve endings and consists of fibers up to a maximum of about 12in (30cm) long [Key]. These fibers have the ability to contract along their whole length in response to nerve stimuli, sometimes shortening by as much as a third [4]. Under the microscope the fibers appear striped, which accounts for the name "striped" or "striated" muscle. Each voluntary muscle is bound within its own tough, elastic sheath and is further protected by layers of connective tissue.

Skeletal muscles, mostly attached to bone either directly or through tendons, include flexors to bend joints and extensors to straighten them. Abductor muscles are needed to pull the arm, for example, away from its natural position at the side of the body, and adductors return it to the side. Limbs are twisted by rotators. Each fiber in a muscle has a separate nerve branch; these branches meet at what is called the motor end plate. A nerve impulse from the brain or spinal cord releases a chemical transmitter substance that makes muscle fiber contract.

No single muscle, however, is of much use in isolation. Because contracted fibers require an opposing force to expand, skeletal muscle is mostly arranged in antagonistic blocks with flexors working against extensors and abductors against adductors.

When muscles contract, using energy, heat builds up and carbon dioxide, water, and lactic acid are formed. After strenuous exertion muscles are affected by an accumulation of lactic acid because there is not enough oxygen available for metabolism. This results in an aching sensation and in "heaviness" of the limbs.

Involuntary muscles

Involuntary muscle, the basis of internal support systems, has an equally vital role to play. Both types of involuntary muscle—smooth and cardiac—are in continuous use, maintaining such functions as respiration, digestion, and circulation.

Smooth muscle fibers are arranged in two different patterns, depending on the delicacy of their task. There are multi-unit smooth muscles, for example, in the arteries and in the iris of the eye. There the tiny fibers are separated, contracting only when stimulated by a nerve impulse.

CONNECTIONS

See also
682 Skull, skeleton, an
joints
720 Diseases of the ske
ton and muscles
1572 The chemistry of li
biochemistry
688 Heart and blood circ
lation

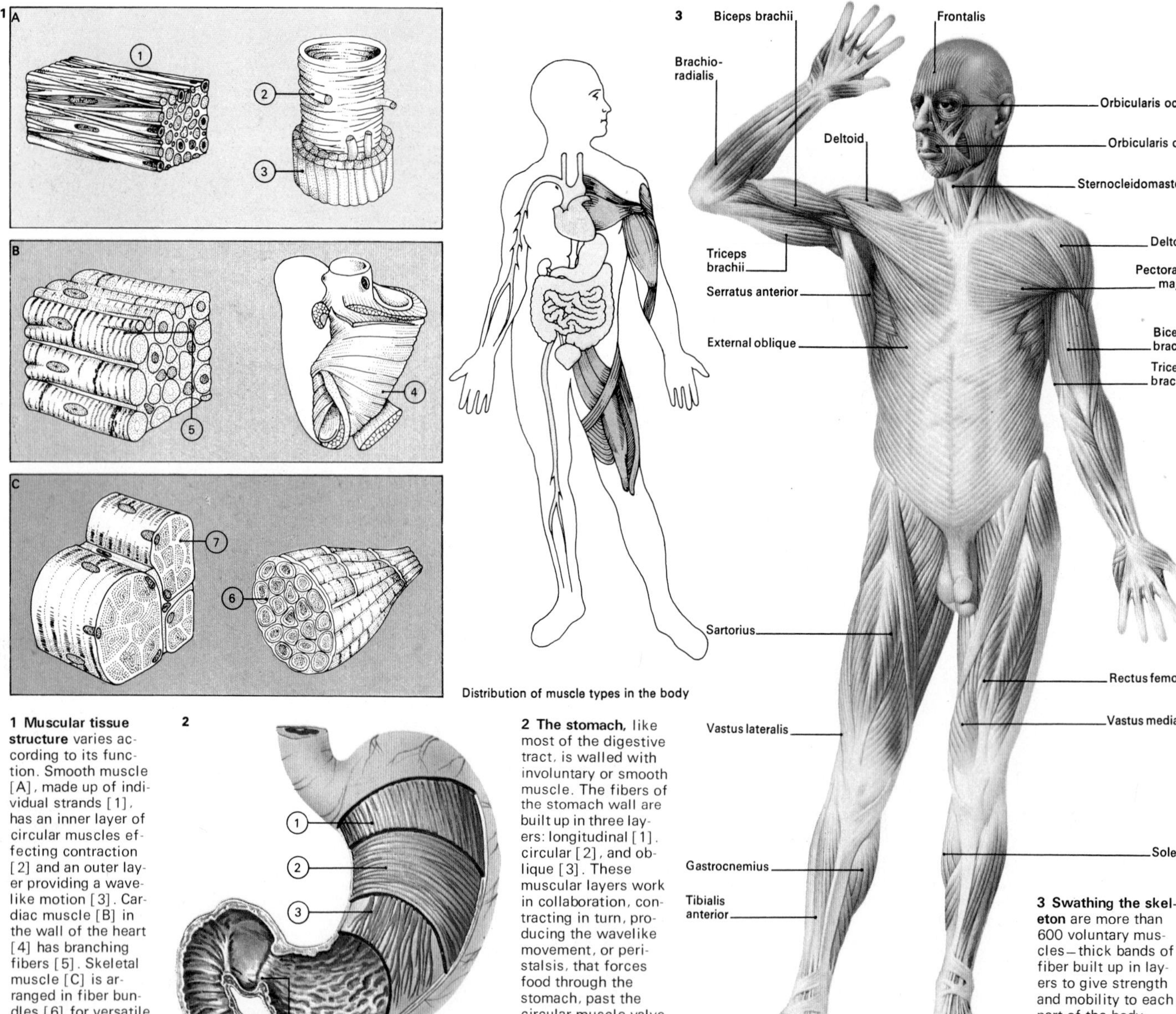

1 A
1
2
3
B
4
5
C
6
7
Distribution of muscle types in the body
2
1
2
3
4
3
Biceps brachii
Frontalis
Brachio-radialis
Orbicularis oculi
Deltoid
Orbicularis oris
Sternocleidomastoid
Deltoid
Triceps brachii
Pectoralis major
Serratus anterior
Biceps brachii
External oblique
Triceps brachii
Sartorius
Rectus femoris
Vastus lateralis
Vastus medialis
Gastrocnemius
Soleus
Tibialis anterior

1 Muscular tissue structure varies according to its function. Smooth muscle [A], made up of individual strands [1], has an inner layer of circular muscles effecting contraction [2] and an outer layer providing a wavelike motion [3]. Cardiac muscle [B] in the wall of the heart [4] has branching fibers [5]. Skeletal muscle [C] is arranged in fiber bundles [6] for versatile function. Each fiber has myofibrils distributed within it [7].

2 The stomach, like most of the digestive tract, is walled with involuntary or smooth muscle. The fibers of the stomach wall are built up in three layers: longitudinal [1], circular [2], and oblique [3]. These muscular layers work in collaboration, contracting in turn, producing the wavelike movement, or peristalsis, that forces food through the stomach, past the circular muscle valve sphincter [4] at the base, and into the adjoining duodenum (small intestine).

3 Swathing the skeleton are more than 600 voluntary muscles—thick bands of fiber built up in layers to give strength and mobility to each part of the body. Skeletal muscles are the largest and most powerful of the three muscle types.

In the kind of smooth muscle found in the viscera—the intestines, bile ducts, ureters and other internal organs—smooth muscle fibers are packed together so densely that they are almost indistinguishable from each other. This is the kind of muscle that powers the wavelike movement known as peristalsis. The antagonistic mechanism vital to muscle function is achieved by the arrangement of two sets of muscle fibers—longitudinal and circular—that compose the muscular wall, and by two sets of autonomic nerves, the sympathetic and parasympathetic.

Early on in the digestive process there is an ingenious mixture of muscle types working in collaboration. This is the esophagus, or gullet, the canal running from the mouth to the stomach. Voluntary muscle rings the upper third of this tube, but sensation of movement ceases as the food reaches the middle section, which consists of mixed voluntary and involuntary muscle. The remaining third is involuntary muscle.

Voluntary and involuntary features are also combined in the bladder. The smooth layers must first relax, allowing the bladder to stretch as it fills with urine, and then contract to expel the contents. The sphincter, a ring of striated muscle that is under conscious control, is the governing mechanism. Kept contracted while the bladder is filling, the sphincter seals off the outlet until, under voluntary direction, it is relaxed, and urine is passed.

Cardiac muscle

Cardiac muscle—the fabric of the heart—is striated like voluntary fibers but it is not normally under conscious control. Highly adaptable, cardiac muscle is stretched as blood enters the heart chambers. The degree of expansion is signalled by pacemaker tissue that sends impulses by conducting tissue to ordinary cardiac muscle cells, ensuring adequate and coordinated constriction to empty the heart completely. Once again the antagonistic principle comes into play and changes in the rate and strength of contraction are governed by stimulation of the sympathetic and parasympathetic nerves.

KEY

Myofibril

Fiber

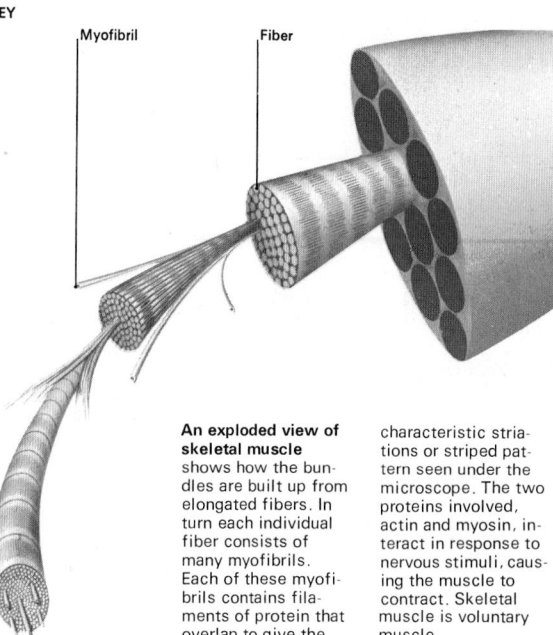

An exploded view of skeletal muscle shows how the bundles are built up from elongated fibers. In turn each individual fiber consists of many myofibrils. Each of these myofibrils contains filaments of protein that overlap to give the characteristic striations or striped pattern seen under the microscope. The two proteins involved, actin and myosin, interact in response to nervous stimuli, causing the muscle to contract. Skeletal muscle is voluntary muscle.

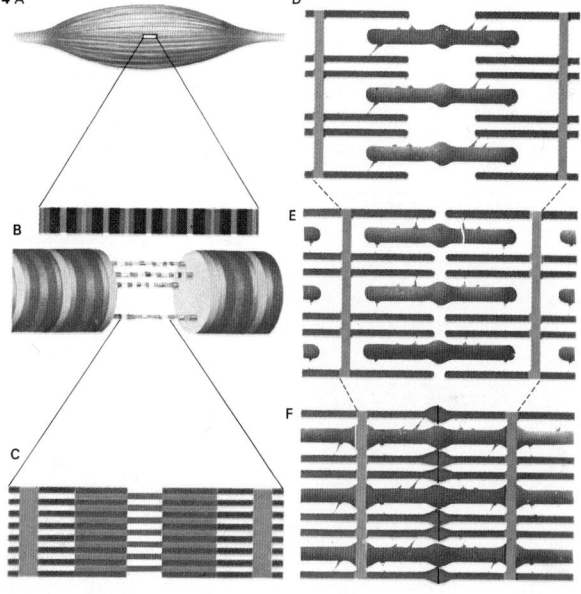

4 A B C D E F

4 Contraction of voluntary muscle [A] is achieved through many elongated cells of fibers [B], made up of fibrils bound together by a membrane. Each fibril [C] contains two different proteins—actin and myosin—laid down in filaments that are arranged in parallel, creating dark bands. Actin filaments show a spiral configuration and the strands of myosin are studded with tiny, knoblike projections [D]. These projections on the myosin filaments [pink] attach themselves to active sites along the actin [brown] in the ratchetlike movement that causes shortening of the muscle fibers [E, F]. Nerve impulses trigger the two proteins.

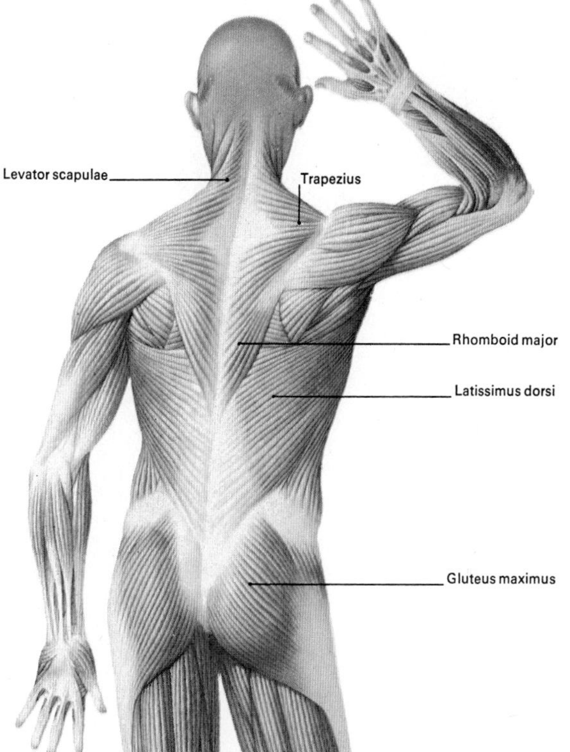
Levator scapulae
Trapezius
Rhomboid major
Latissimus dorsi
Gluteus maximus
Biceps femoris
Iliotibial tract
Gastrocnemius lateral head
Gastrocnemius medial head
Soleus
Tendo calcaneus (Achilles)

5 Chewing and biting, though routine movements, nevertheless require intricate collaboration of skeletal muscles. On each side of the head are five powerful muscles that are chiefly involved in the business of mastication. The buccinator [1] forms the side walls of the mouth. By compressing the cheek, it modifies the position of the food in the mouth. The medial pterygoid [2], which lies horizontally across the side of the face, contracts to lift the jaw. It also produces sideways grinding movements by pulling the lower jaw to one side. The external pterygoid [3], almost at right angles to the medial pterygoid, contracts to protrude the lower jaw and open the mouth. The masseter [4] lifts or closes the jaw by contraction. The temporalis [5], at the side of the head, does the same.

5

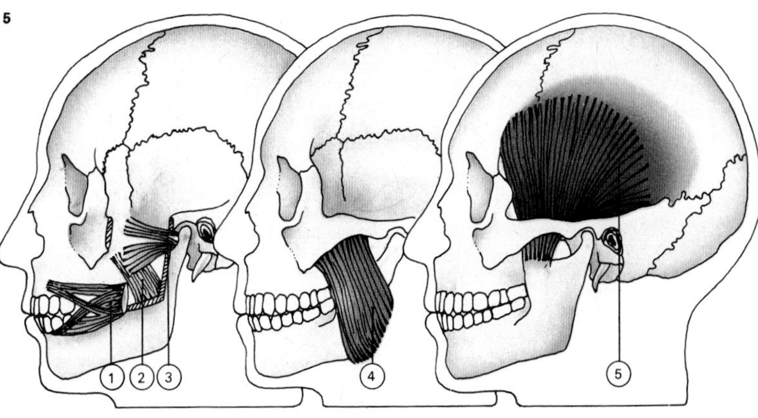
1
2
3
4
5

Skin and hair

Skin is the largest organ of the human body. In an adult it covers a surface area averaging about 2,750sq in (1.75sq m), makes up about 7 percent of the total body weight, and receives roughly one third of the fresh blood pumped from the heart. Versatile in its range of functions, human skin is a waterproof fabric that serves as a first line of defense against injury or invasions by hostile organisms and also has important roles to play as a sensory organ, as an agent of secretion and excretion, and as a modifier of body temperature.

The skin's layered structure

Microscopic examination of the epidermis, or outer skin, reveals five layers through which cells must migrate to replace the dead cells shed from the surface of the skin [1]. In the deepest level of the epidermis, the stratum basale, cells constantly divide to provide the steady supply of fresh cells forming the next layer, the stratum germinativum. As the cells move farther away from the source of blood and nutrients in the underlying dermis they gradually degenerate—by filling with granules of protein waste—and die. Next they form the stratum granulosum, and then the shiny, almost transparent stratum lucidum.

Flattened and laden with keratin—the durable protein of hair and nails and animal horn—these cells finally emerge to form the visible skin—the thick, impervious stratum corneum, or "horny layer." Dead skin flakes away from the surface all the time. It is estimated that the epidermis is totally replaced once every three weeks and that an average lifetime sees the shedding of about 40lb (18kg) of dead skin cells.

The underlying dermis, built around a network of protein fibers, gives the skin its elasticity and strength. Loss of elasticity of the dermis is a feature of aging, characterized by folding or wrinkling of the skin. About 0.1in (3mm) thick, the dermis is interlaced with blood and lymphatic vessels and contains numerous nerve endings, glands, and hair follicles.

Deeper still is the subdermal layer between skin and muscle. Composed of loose connective tissue, this region is heavy with fluid and fat cells that provide insulation, cushion muscles and nerves, and serve as an energy store. It is this subdermal layer of fat (which is thicker in women) that gives shape to the body as a whole.

Hair, nails, and pigmentation

Hair and the nails [2] on the fingers and toes are derivatives of skin; both are made up of modified epidermal cells filled with hard keratin. But whereas hair and nails are nerveless and dead and can be cut without pain, the skin as a whole is acutely responsive to external sensations such as touch, pressure, heat, and pain.

Hair develops as a downgrowth of epidermal cells into the dermis to form a hair follicle set at an angle in the skin [3]. A tube of keratin is pushed up from the follicle to form the hair shaft. Each hair is supplied with its own minute erector muscle and is capable of independent movement—standing on end in response to cold or alarm. What we call "gooseflesh" is equivalent to a bird fluffing out its feathers or a cat's fur standing on end. At maturity the

CONNECTIONS

See also
724 Diseases of the sk
678 Touch, pain, and temperature
660 Family of man: ho peoples differ
542 The life of mamm
1574 Polymers: giant molecules
920 Crime detection
818 Body image and biofeedback
918 Crime prevention
816 Freedom and individuality

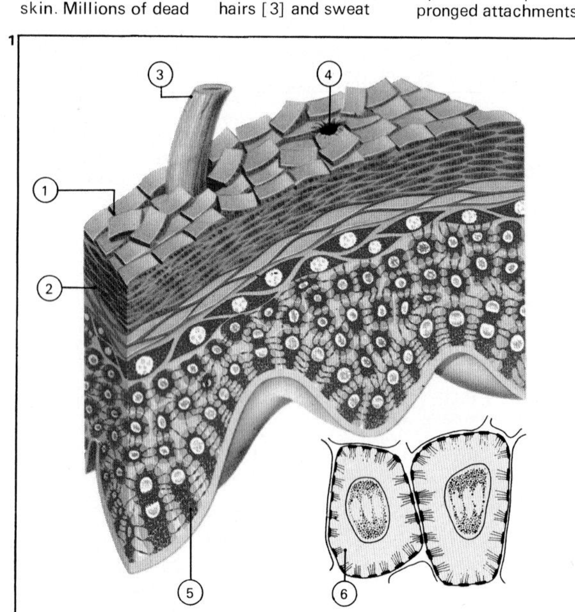
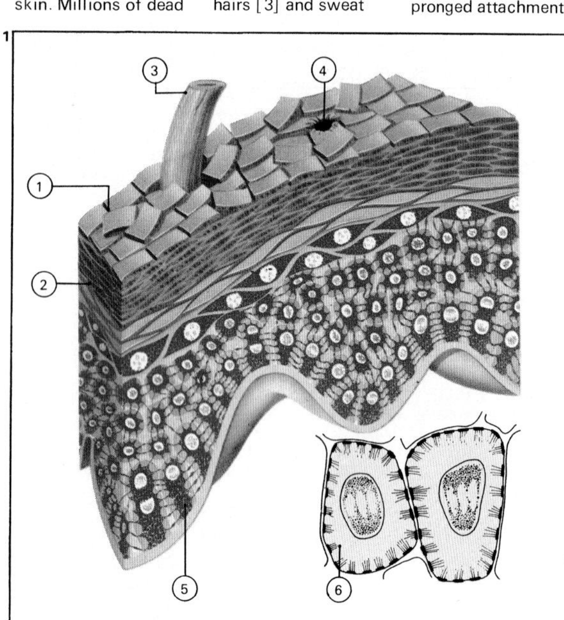

1
2
3
4
5
6

1 The epidermis or outer skin, is covered with flattened (squamous) or tile-like dead cells [1] filled with the protein keratin. It is keratin that toughens and waterproofs the skin. Millions of dead cells are shed (desquamated) from the surface all the time, to be replaced by new cells making their way up from below [2]. Resistant to bacteria, the skin is penetrated only by hairs [3] and sweat pores [4]. The epidermis and the deeper skin, or dermis [5], fit tightly together in a series of corrugations. Epidermal cells [6] cling to each other by means of special pronged attachments.

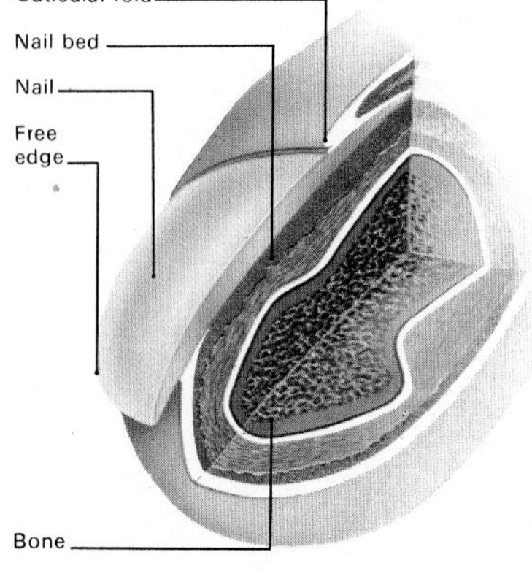

Cuticular fold
Nail bed
Nail
Free edge
Bone

2 Nails, like hair, are derivatives of skin. A useful protective covering for the ends of fingers and toes, nail is made of hard keratin. It rests on the nail bed, formed from the two deepest layers of the epidermis. The cuticle is above the root of the nail and the sensitive quick is located beneath the free edge. The pale half-moon called the lunula lies under the root and represents the active, growing region of the nail.

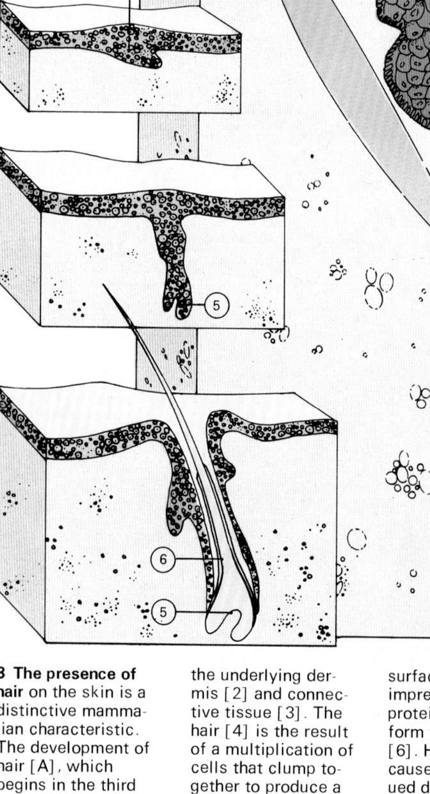

A
B
1
2
3
4
5
6
7
8

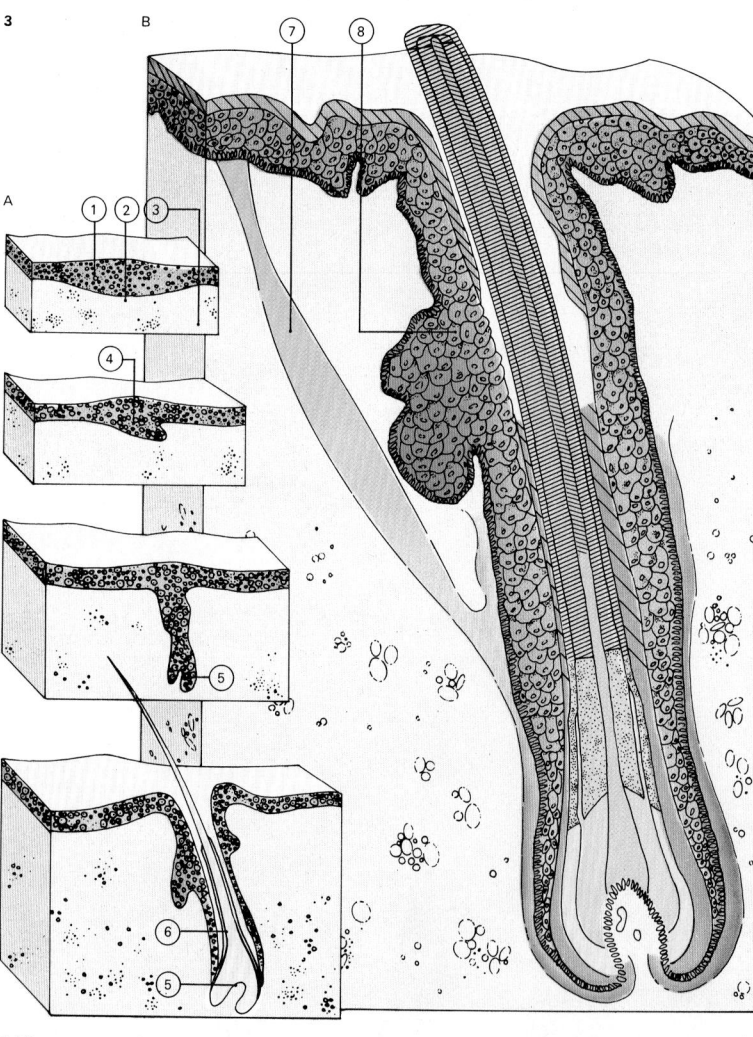

3 The presence of hair on the skin is a distinctive mammalian characteristic. The development of hair [A], which begins in the third month of fetal life, is prefaced by the downgrowth of thickened cells of the epidermis [1] into the underlying dermis [2] and connective tissue [3]. The hair [4] is the result of a multiplication of cells that clump together to produce a papilla [5] at the base of the follicle. Constantly dividing, these cells push upward toward the surface, becoming impregnated with the protein keratin, to form the hair shaft [6]. Hair grows because of the continued division of these "matrix" cells. A cross-sectional view [B] of the hair shaft shows how each hair is equipped with its own erector muscle [7], endowing independent movement. An associated sebaceous gland [8] secretes oily sebum to lubricate the hair and the surrounding skin. The scalp alone is covered with up to 2 million hairs growing about 0.3mm a day.

only parts of the skin free of hair are the undersides of the fingers and toes, the palms of the hands, soles of the feet, and parts of the external genitalia.

Closely correlated, hair and skin color are genetically determined and depend on the amount of pigment—mainly melanin [4]—present in the individual (in the case of red hair there is an additional pigment). Production of melanin in the hair follicles diminishes with age and minute bubbles of air in the shaft makes the hair look gray or white.

A failure in pigment synthesis accounts for the albino state. In albinos melanin cannot be synthesized because an enzyme is missing because of gene mutation. Albinos, therefore, have white skin and hair. Also, with no pigment in the iris, the eyes are extra sensitive to light and they appear pink.

Glands of the skin

Closely associated with all types of body hair are the sebaceous glands, which discharge an oily secretion known as sebum into the hair follicles. Besides lubricating the hair and surrounding skin, sebum also inhibits excess evaporation from the 3 million sweat glands lying coiled in the dermis.

More widespread of the two types of sweat gland are eccrine glands [7] producing the salty sweat that has an important cooling function in hot weather and that also carries away small amounts of waste products such as urea and lactic acid. Apocrine sweat glands, larger and secreting much thicker fluid than the eccrine glands, are concentrated in the armpits and the anal and genital regions. Secretions from the various glands in the dermis help to keep the skin supple, and by absorbing a certain amount of radiation, to prevent sunburn.

Skin does not end at the lips and anus but continues into the body orifices in the modified form of the mucous membrane that lines the nose and mouth, the alimentary canal, and urogenital organs. Lacking the heavily keratinized outer layer of skin proper, this membrane is rich in glands secreting mucus that moistens and protects delicate surfaces and is well endowed with nerve receptors.

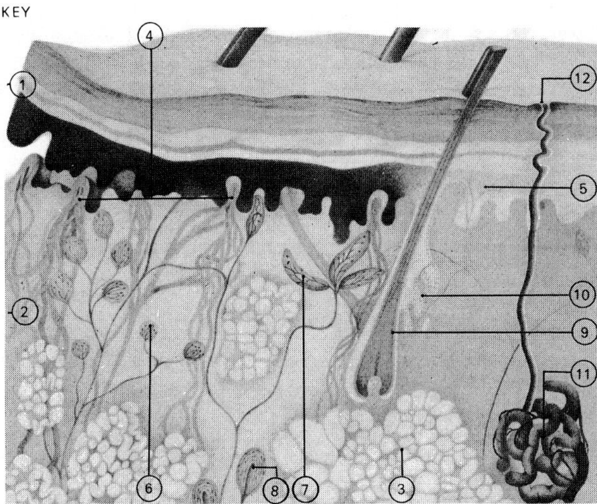
KEY
1
2
3
4
5
6
7
8
9
10
11
12

The skin consists of the epidermis [1], a tough, waterproof outer fabric, and its underlying dermis [2]. A deeper layer of fat cells [3] insulates the body and shapes its contours. Networked in the skin are blood vessels [4] and four types of sensory receptors [5,6,7,8]. Hair pushes up from a follicle [9] and a sebaceous gland [10] secretes lubricant sebum. Sweat glands [11] empty via the pores [12].

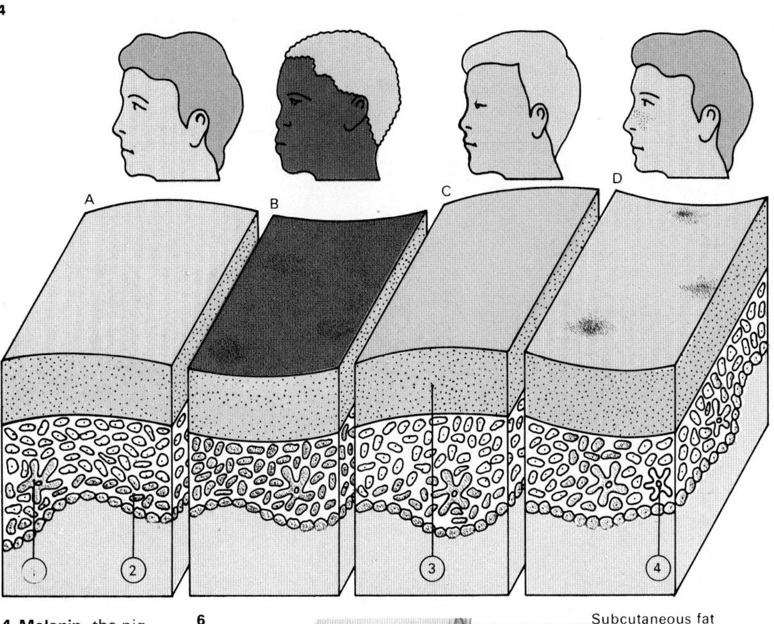
4
A
B
C
D
1
2
3
4

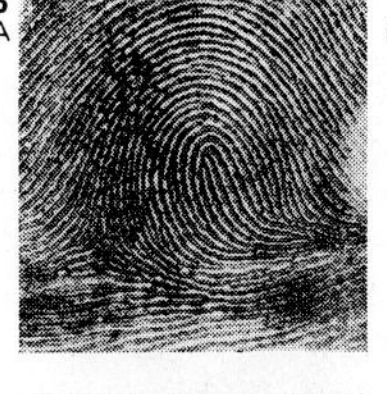
5
A

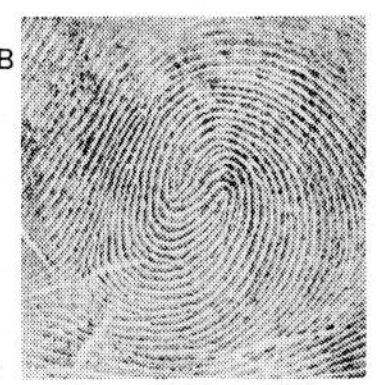
B

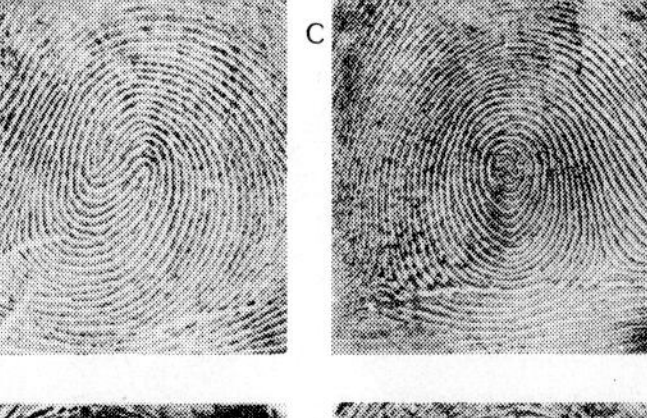
C

D

E

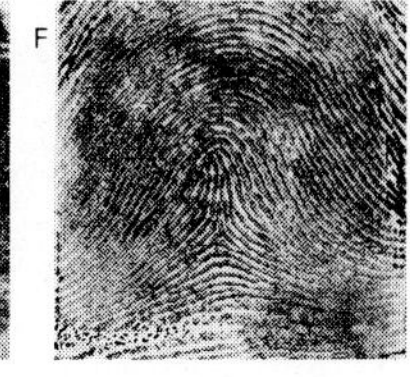
F

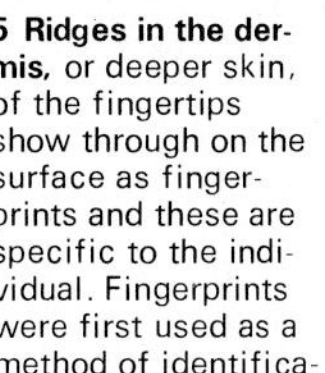

5 Ridges in the dermis, or deeper skin, of the fingertips show through on the surface as fingerprints and these are specific to the individual. Fingerprints were first used as a method of identification to solve a crime almost a century ago. Distinctive patterns include the loop [A], which is most common, the double loop [B], the whorl [C], the central pocket loop [D], the arch [E] and tented arch [F]. Fingerprints remain the same throughout life unless the dermis tissue is destroyed.

4 Melanin, the pigment mostly responsible for skin and hair color, is common to all racial types. It is produced in the epidermis by cells known as melanocytes [1] and injected into the surrounding epidermal cells [2]. When the skin is exposed to sunlight melanin production speeds up to give the Caucasian [A] a protective tan. The skin of the Negroid type [B] radiates heat more efficiently than the lighter skin of his Caucasian and Mongoloid [C] neighbors. Carotene, a yellow pigment found in the horny layer [3], is more abundant in certain Asian races. Freckled skin [D] is caused by pockets of pigment surrounded by inactive melanocytes [4].

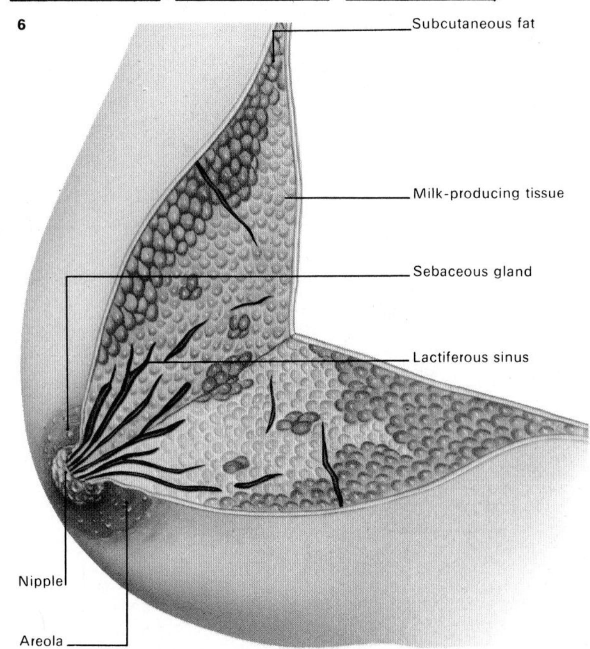
6
Subcutaneous fat
Milk-producing tissue
Sebaceous gland
Lactiferous sinus
Nipple
Areola

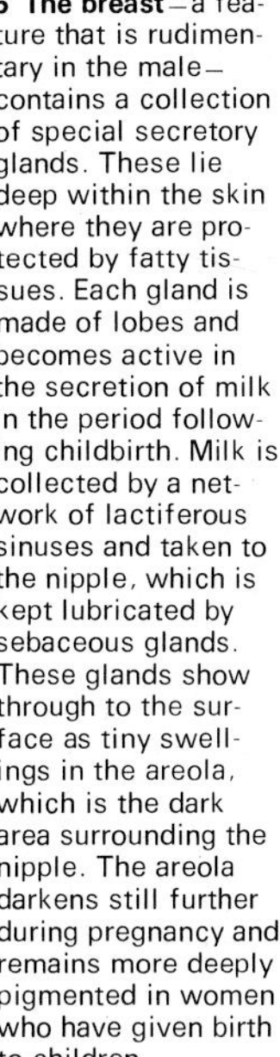

6 The breast—a feature that is rudimentary in the male—contains a collection of special secretory glands. These lie deep within the skin where they are protected by fatty tissues. Each gland is made of lobes and becomes active in the secretion of milk in the period following childbirth. Milk is collected by a network of lactiferous sinuses and taken to the nipple, which is kept lubricated by sebaceous glands. These glands show through to the surface as tiny swellings in the areola, which is the dark area surrounding the nipple. The areola darkens still further during pregnancy and remains more deeply pigmented in women who have given birth to children.

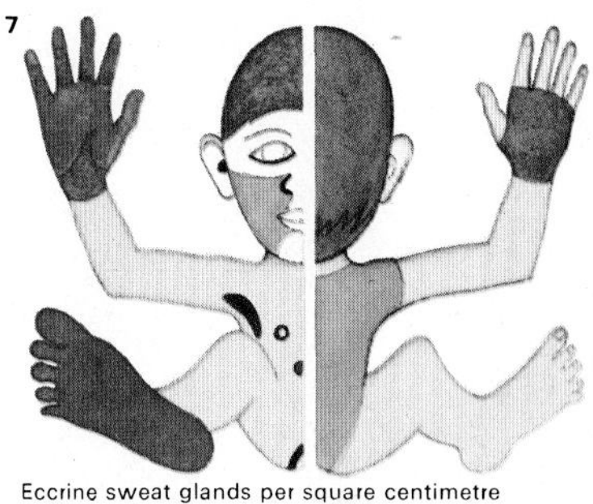
7
Eccrine sweat glands per square centimetre
Less than 100
More than 200
More than 100
More than 300
Specialized glands of the skin

7 Glands of the skin include the abundant sebaceous glands and—less common—ceruminous glands that produce ear wax to protect and lubricate the skin of the auditory canal. Most widespread of the sweat glands is the coiled eccrine type, producing salty sweat. Larger, and yielding a much thicker secretion, the apocrine sweat glands develop in association with the coarse hair of the armpits and the anal and genital regions. They begin to function at puberty.

Heart and blood circulation

It was the English physician William Harvey (1578–1657) who, in 1628, first deduced that the movement of blood is "constantly in a circle." At the time this was a remarkable observation, since Harvey could not have known of the presence of the base network of capillaries that make up the 60,000mi (96,500km) of human micro-circulation [Key], nor of the oxygen that is exchanged between capillaries and tissues.

The function of blood

Every living organism, however primitive, needs a circulatory system to fuel its parts and to remove waste. In the human body this vital exchange is transacted by the versatile fluid known as blood—about 9 pints (5 liters) of it in the adult. It is blood, circulating deep in the tissues, that carries oxygen and nutrients to keep the cells alive and removes carbon dioxide and other waste materials for elimination.

The heart provides the motive power for the circulatory system. Made up of specialized muscle, it consists of two upper chambers, or atria, and two lower chambers, known as ventricles [5]. Blood-flow between chambers and into the aorta and the pulmonary artery is controlled by the four heart valves [7]. The rhythmic action of the heart is regulated by the pacemaker, a modified muscular tissue responsible for the impulses that trigger first the atria and then the ventricles to contract.

How the heart works

The heart is, in effect, a single pump powering a double circuit. In the space of one heartbeat freshly oxygenated blood arriving from the lungs enters the left side of the heart for dispersal to organs and tissues, and deoxygenated blood is pumped via the right side of the heart direct to the lungs [3].

About the size of its owner's fist, the heart begins work in the fourth week of fetal development and continues throughout life. In the adult the heart rate averages 70 to 80 beats a minute, although this resting rate can increase dramatically up to two and a half times in response to stress or exertion. The force of the heartbeat is such that if the body's largest artery—the aorta, arching away from the heart—is severed, a 6-ft (2-m) jet of blood is released.

Freshly oxygenated blood is conducted away from the heart by arteries—thick-walled, muscular vessels, most of which run deep in the tissues to minimize the possibility of damage [6]. Where arteries are present near the surface—as at the wrist—there is a pulse echoing the heartbeat. Arteries branch into arterioles, which in turn break up into a complex network of capillaries [1]. These are the minute structures that thread their way to every part of the body to carry out the vital function of the blood, trading oxygen and other materials for carbon dioxide and waste.

On the venous return side the deoxygenated blood, now carried at low pressure by the capillaries, passes through the larger venules and into the veins. Ultimately two major vessels, the inferior and superior venae cavae, join above the heart and drain spent blood into the right atrium to be pumped to the lungs.

Drawn fresh from the body, blood is a dense, sticky fluid that congeals quickly

CONNECTIONS

See also
716 Diseases of the circulation
692 Breathing and the lungs
684 Muscles and action
698 Keeping fit
416 Principles of heredity

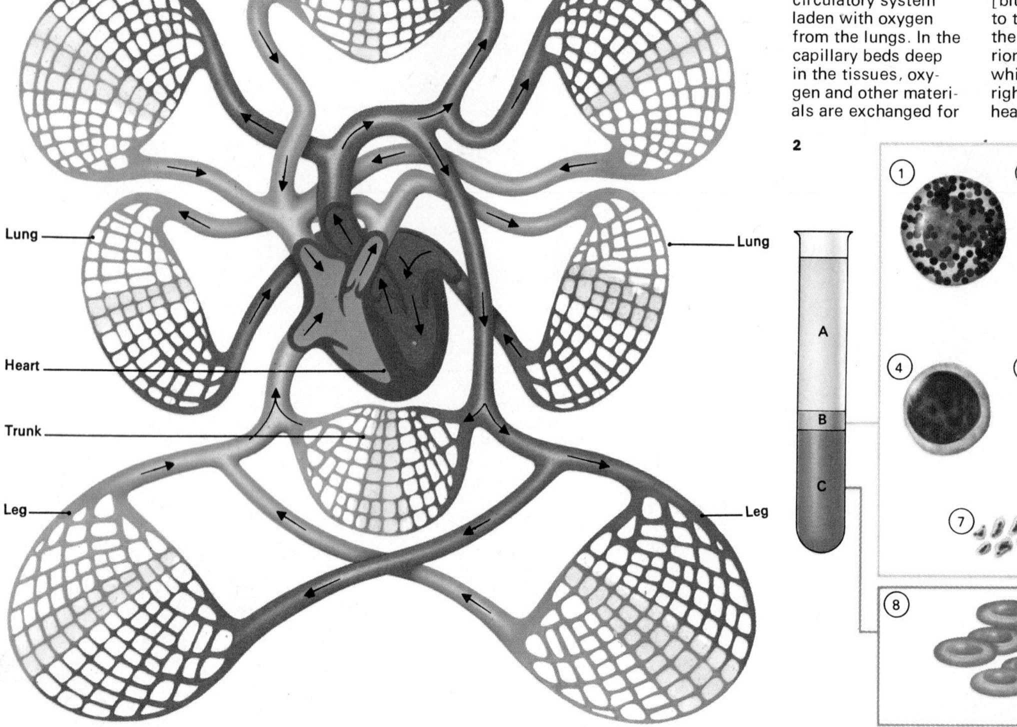
1
Head
Arm
Arm
Lung
Lung
Heart
Trunk
Leg
Leg

1 Fresh blood [red] starts on its long journey through the circulatory system laden with oxygen from the lungs. In the capillary beds deep in the tissues, oxygen and other materials are exchanged for carbon dioxide and waste. Stale or deoxygenated blood [blue] is carried back to two major veins, the inferior and superior venae cavae, which drain into the right atrium of the heart. This blood then enters the pulmonary circulation, to be reoxygenated in the lungs, before being passed back along the pulmonary vein to the left side of the heart to start the journey around the body again.

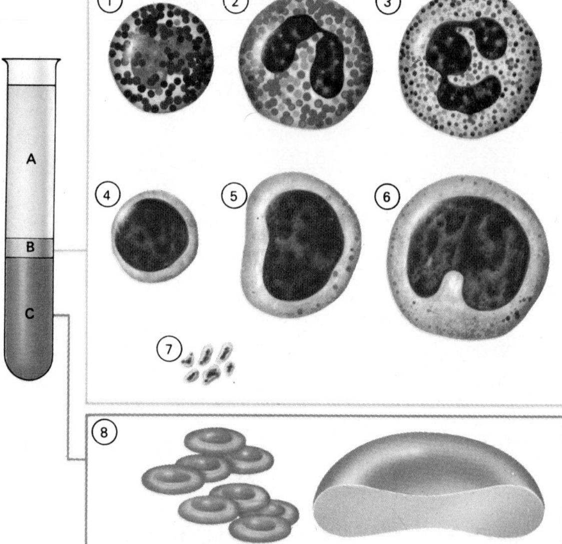
2
A
B
C
1
2
3
4
5
6
7
8

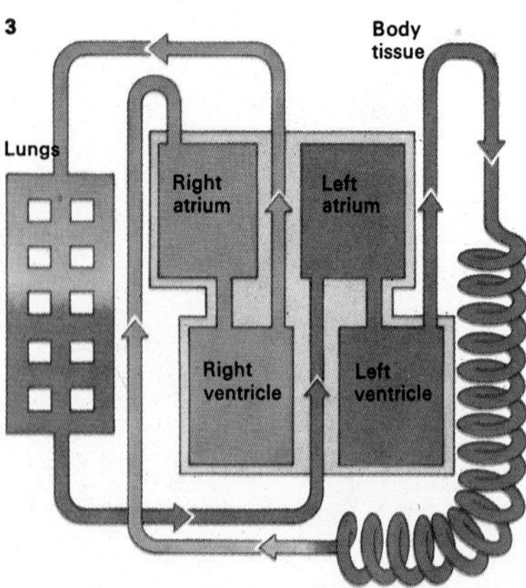
3
Body tissue
Lungs
Right atrium
Left atrium
Right ventricle
Left ventricle

3 The heart is a dual-purpose pump. In the space of a single beat, blood is pumped from the left to the systemic circulation and from the right to the pulmonary circulation for recycling.

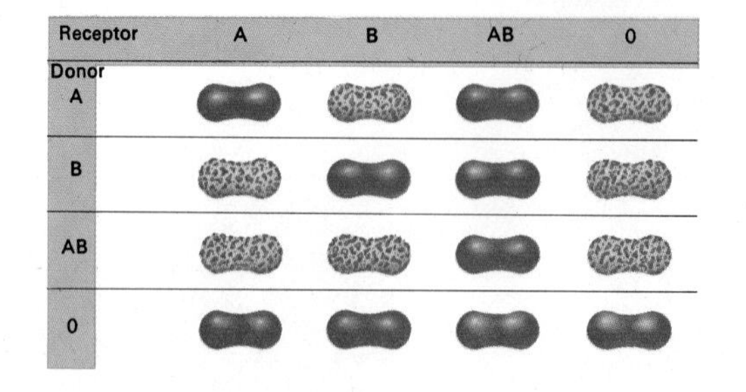
Receptor
A
B
AB
0
Donor
A
B
AB
0

4 The foremost system of blood-group classification in use is the ABO system. The letters A and B relate to types of proteins present in the membrane of red cells. Blood group, therefore, is determined by the presence of A or B proteins or both; people lacking both A and B proteins belong to group O. Accurate cross-matching is vital in transfusions, where incompatible combinations can cause destruction of red cells (represented here by mottled cells), with serious consequences to the recipient patient.

2 Spun in a high-speed centrifuge, blood separates out into plasma [A], layers of white cells, and platelets [B], and red cells [C]. Fluid plasma, almost 90% water, contains salts and proteins. Three main types of white cells, shown in magnification, are granulocytes [1–3], small and large lymphocytes [4, 5], which are involved in the body's defenses, and monocytes [6]. Platelets [7] are vital clotting agents. Red cells [8] are the most numerous.

when exposed to the air. Separated out in the laboratory, it settles into the yellowish fluid known as plasma, which constitutes 55 percent of the volume, and a reddish-brown sediment of fine particles [2].

Plasma, corpuscles, and lymph

Blood plasma is a solution of salts and proteins, similar to the fluid matter of living cells. Serum, the colorless fluid that oozes from a scrape on the skin, is plasma minus fibrin, one of the proteins that helps blood to clot.

The dark sediment consists of vast quantities of red blood corpuscles (erythrocytes), somewhat less of the defensive white blood corpuscles (leucocytes), and platelets (thrombocytes), which play a vital part in blood clotting. Formed in the bone marrow and measuring less than one ten-thousandth of a millimeter in diameter, red blood corpuscles are among the smallest cells in the body. It is the red cells, composed of one-third hemoglobin, that act as vehicles for oxygen. Carried in the bloodstream as oxyhemoglobin, oxygen quickly detaches on reaching target tissues to diffuse through the fine capillary walls.

White blood corpuscles are two to three times the diameter of red cells but almost a thousand times less numerous. Colorless and transparent, they are part of the body's defenses, gliding in and out of blood vessels to accumulate at sites of injury or infection. Also present at the site of a wound are platelets, smallest of the blood particles, which are concerned in the clotting process.

Closely integrated with the circulation of the blood is the lymphatic system. Lymph is the watery medium in which life-giving substances pass through the capillary walls to nourish the surrounding tissues. Basically plasma but with a low proportion of proteins, lymph bathes the cells, where it is known as tissue fluid, before draining away into the separate network of vessels that make up the lymphatic system. Also laden with waste materials, lymph is carried away to be returned to the bloodstream by way of the two jugular veins at the neck's base. Other functions of the lymphatic system include its role in combating illness.

KEY

Carotid artery
Jugular vein
Subclavian artery
Aortic arch
Superior vena cava
Pulmonary circulation
Heart
Basilic vein
Inferior vena cava
Renal circulation
Descending aorta
Brachial artery
Iliac vein
Iliac artery
Femoral artery
Femoral vein

The circulatory system, a 60,000mi (96,500km) network of vessels, takes life-giving blood into every part of the body to replenish tissues and remove waste. From the heart, driving force of the circulatory system, freshly oxygenated blood enters the 1-in (2.5-cm) wide aorta. The aorta branches into major arteries serving the organs and limbs. Arteries divide into arterioles and finally into minute capillaries that, weaving throughout the tissues, serve the body's cells. Spent blood returns by way of venules and veins, to be pumped by the heart back to the lungs, where it is reoxygenated.

5

5 The heart contains four chambers – two atria and two ventricles – and four sets of valves. Blood from the body passes into the right atrium [1], via the venae cavae [2, 3]. Flow of blood into the right ventricle [4] is controlled by the tricuspid valve [5]. Pulmonary arteries [6] conduct blood from the right ventricle to the lungs, while the pulmonary veins [7, 8] carry oxygenated blood back from the lungs to the left atrium [9]. In a parallel manner, the mitral valve [10] controls the flow of blood between the left atrium and the left ventricle [11]. The aorta [12] conducts blood from the left ventricle to all parts of the body.

6 Major vessels of the blood circulatory system are arteries [red] and veins [blue]. Fresh blood flows under high pressure, most of which is lost by the time blood reaches the veins. Veins, therefore, are fitted with cup-shaped valves [1] to prevent backflow. Movement of blood in veins [2] is promoted by the massaging effect of surrounding skeletal muscle [3] or by the adjacent arteries [4].

6

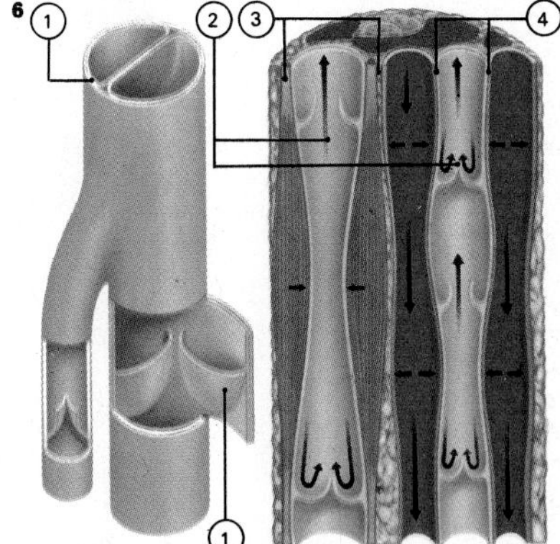

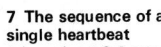

7 The sequence of a single heartbeat takes about 0.9 seconds and begins [A] as the atria [1, 2] fill with blood. Contraction [B] of the atria forces blood past the retaining tricuspid [3] and mitral [4] valves into the ventricles [5, 6]. The thick muscular walls of the ventricles contract [C], snapping shut the atrioventricular valves but causing the semilunar valves [7, 8] to open. With both ventricles fully contracted [D] two streams of blood are forced along the separate routes; fresh blood into the aorta [9], spent blood into the pulmonary artery [10] leading to the lungs.

7 A

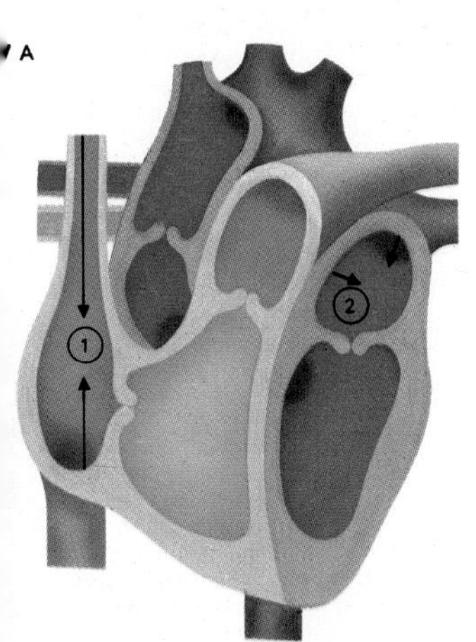

B

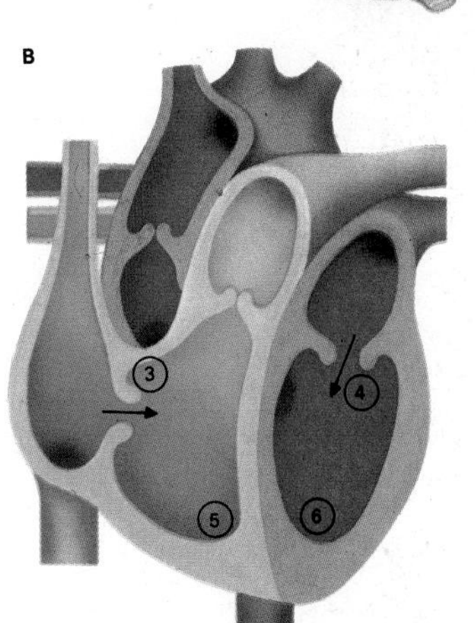

C

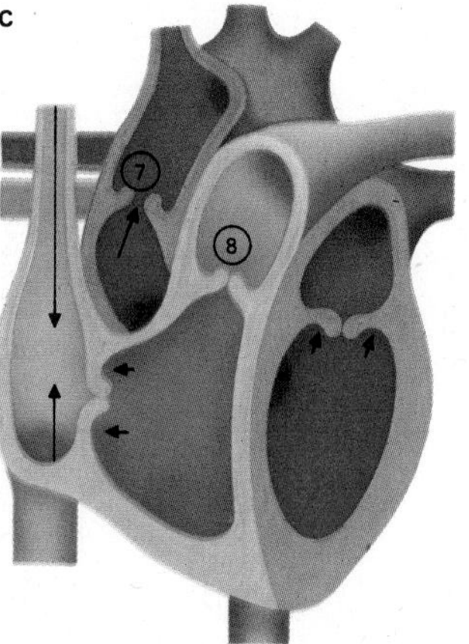

D

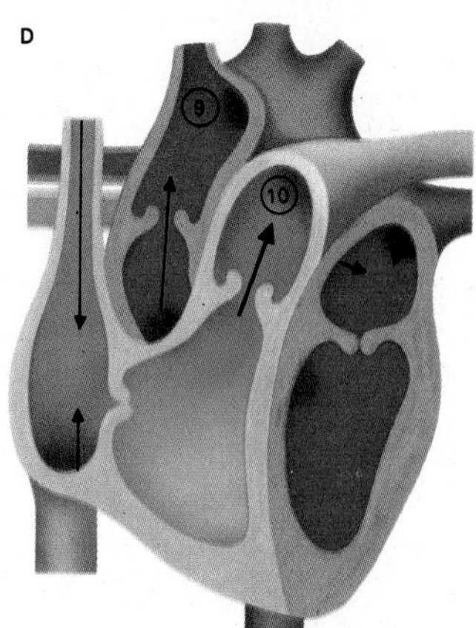

Glands and their hormones

The hormone-producing endocrine glands, working in collaboration with the nervous system, provide a means of controlling various body functions. But whereas the nervous system presides over fast-moving events, the endocrine system governs more widespread processes measured in hours, months, or years. Some hormones are, it is true, involved in rapid events—the "fright, flight, or fight" response, for example, is caused by a sudden increase of adrenaline in the blood—but in general the endocrines govern such processes as metabolism, growth, and development.

Unlike glands of external secretion, which liberate their products to the surface or to the body cavities by way of ducts, the endocrine glands are ductless. These glands of internal secretion take in raw materials from the blood to produce hormones that are released directly into the bloodstream.

The body's master gland

The master gland of the endocrine system is the pituitary [1], measuring only 0.4in (1cm) in diameter and located beneath the brain. The pituitary, sometimes described as the "gland of destiny" because of its importance in development, exercises some control over most hormone systems.

The more important of the pituitary's two main lobes is the anterior, which produces a group of hormones governing the thyroid, adrenal, and sex glands. It is also the source of somatotropin, which controls the growth of tissues and influences fat and sugar metabolism, and of prolactin, which stimulates and sustains milk production in the nursing mother. The posterior pituitary releases two hormones: vasopressin, which acts on the kidneys to control the body's water content, and oxytocin, which is mainly active during labor to help contraction of the uterus.

The two-lobed thyroid [3], operating under direction from the hypothalamus of the brain and the anterior pituitary, embraces the larynx and upper windpipe. Its function is to absorb iodine and other materials from the bloodstream to produce a hormone called thyroxine. It is thyroxine that regulates rates of metabolism all over the body and maintains levels of heat production. The thyroid also produces calcitonin which plays a part in calcium regulation.

The parathyroids are four tiny glands. They cling, limpetlike to the rear surface of the thyroid, but have little in common with the larger gland [3]. Parathyroid hormone (PTH) is vital to the metabolism of calcium and phosphate in the body.

Protecting the body

More versatile are the adrenal glands, located one on each side of the spinal column just above the kidneys. Shaped like a tricorn hat, each gland consists of an outer layer, or cortex, and a central medulla—two distinct areas that differ in their endocrine functions [5]. The cortex produces steroid hormones known as corticoids, including glucocorticoids, important in the metabolism of carbohydrates and proteins; aldosterone, another of the hormones involved in maintaining water-balance through its effect on the kidneys; and small quantities of sex hormones, which supplement the larger amounts produced by the gonads.

CONNECTIONS

See also
726 Diseases of the glands
662 An introduction to body and mind
790 Adolescence
700 Reproduction
702 Pregnancy
706 Birth control
542 The life of mammals

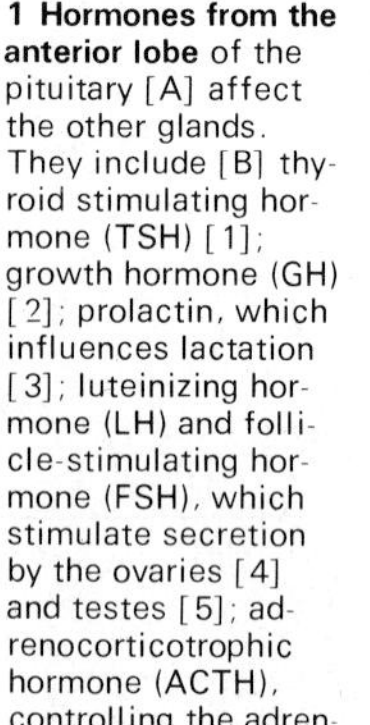
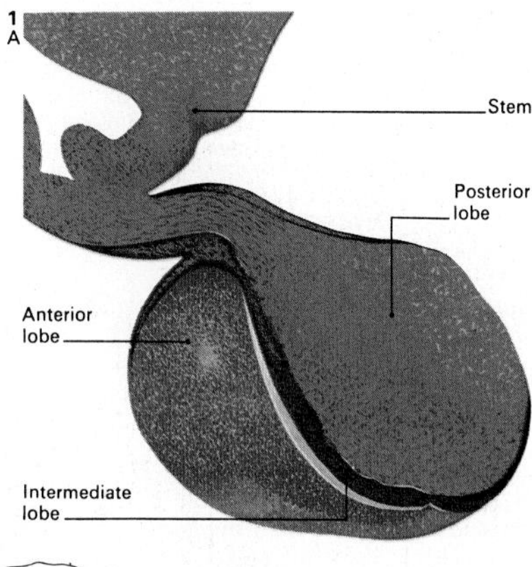

1
A
Stem
Posterior lobe
Anterior lobe
Intermediate lobe

1 Hormones from the anterior lobe of the pituitary [A] affect the other glands. They include [B] thyroid stimulating hormone (TSH) [1]; growth hormone (GH) [2]; prolactin, which influences lactation [3]; luteinizing hormone (LH) and follicle-stimulating hormone (FSH), which stimulate secretion by the ovaries [4] and testes [5]; adrenocorticotrophic hormone (ACTH), controlling the adrenal cortex [6].

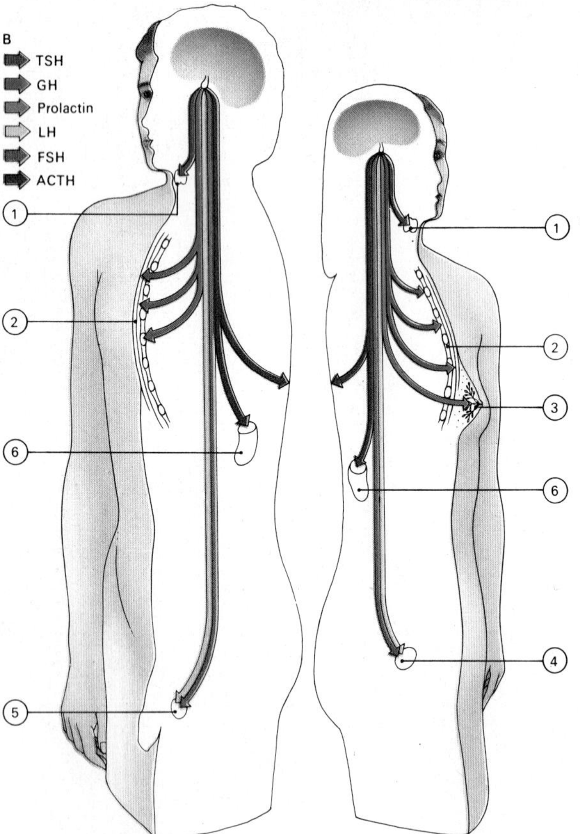

B
TSH
GH
Prolactin
LH
FSH
ACTH
1
2
6
5
1
2
3
6
4

2 Principal hormone of the thyroid [1] is thyroxine, released under control of the pituitary gland [2]. Rich in iodine, thyroxine stimulates energy production in the body cells [3]. An overactive thyroid increases metabolic rate, producing rapid heartbeat, high blood-pressure, and weight loss. Thyroid deficiency lowers resistance to cold. Thyroxine also affects absorption of sugars by the intestine [4] and the blood-cholesterol level [5]. In addition, it has psychological effects—perhaps because of its influence on the adrenal medulla [6]. It is also vital to growth—partly because of its action with the growth hormone [7].

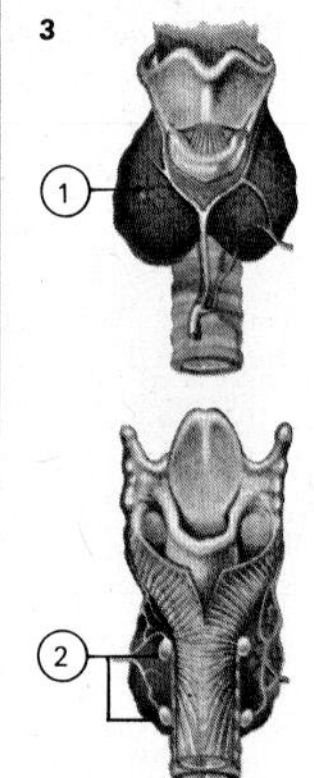

2
1
2
3
4
5
6
7

3 The thyroid [1], curving around the larynx and trachea, has twin lobes joined by an isthmus. Unrelated to their host are the four parathyroid glands [2] lodged on the rear of the thyroid.

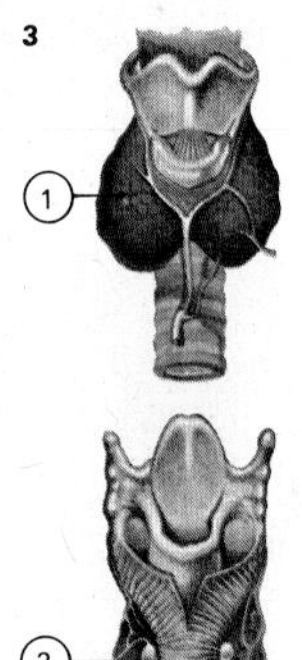

3
1
2

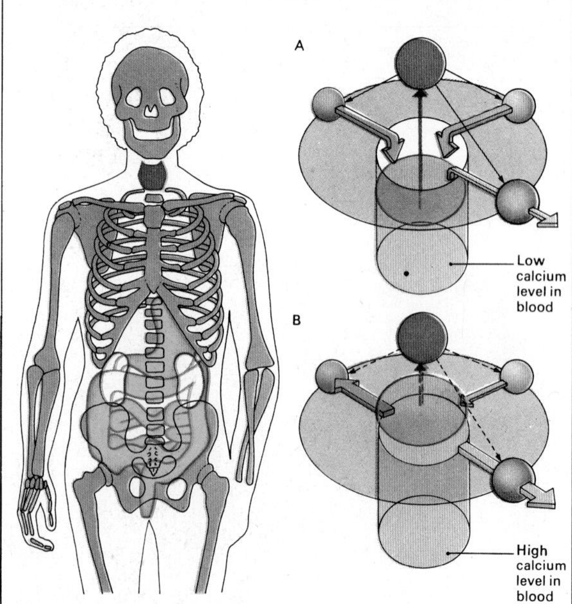

4
A
Low calcium level in blood
B
High calcium level in blood

4 The hormone produced by the parathyroid glands [orange], abbreviated to PTH, has the important function of regulating the level of calcium in the blood. Calcium itself controls secretion of PTH by means of a feedback mechanism. A low blood-calcium level [A] triggers secretion of PTH. This in turn mobilizes calcium from the bones [blue] and aids its absorption from the intestines [green] and reabsorption from the kidneys [pink] to boost the amount that is circulating in the blood. With a high blood-calcium level [B] the sequence is reversed. Production of the parathyroid hormone is inhibited and more calcium is laid down in the bones.

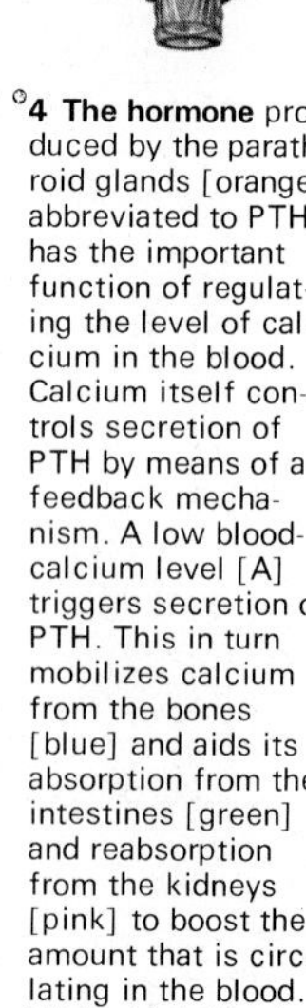

Unlike the adrenal cortex, the medulla is not essential to life. It yields two hormones whose effects resemble those produced by stimulation of the sympathetic nervous system. Adrenaline reinforces the role of the sympathetic nervous system in preparing the body for action in an emergency or stress situation [6]. The other product of the adrenal medulla, noradrenaline, is closely allied to adrenaline chemically.

The pancreas, sometimes called the "salivary gland of the abdomen," secretes pancreatic juice (made up of various enzymes) to aid the digestive process, and this is released to the duodenum by way of the pancreatic duct. But the pancreas also has an important endocrine function, secreting two hormones—glucagon and insulin—which are concerned with the maintenance of blood-glucose level. Sites of production are the tiny islets of Langerhans—small masses of special endocrine cells interspersed throughout the ordinary glandular tissue [7]. Glucagon encourages the breakdown of glycogen, a carbohydrate storage material manufactured in the liver, and this process raises the blood-glucose level. Insulin has the effect of lowering the blood-glucose level by facilitating the uptake of glucose in the muscles. It is failure to produce sufficient insulin that is the cause of diabetes mellitus, or sugar diabetes.

Maleness and femaleness

Stimulated by secretions of the anterior pituitary, the gonads—ovaries in the female, testes in the male—secrete sex hormones. Together with the sex chromosomes, these are responsible for maleness and femaleness—for the bodily characteristics distinguishing the sexes. The testes produce the hormone testosterone. The ovaries produce two hormones, estrogen and progesterone.

Although the endocrine glands may appear to be independent of each other, they do, in fact, achieve a close measure of collaboration, with hormones from one often influencing output from another [8]. With other constituents of the blood the secretions of these ductless glands form a supportive fluid medium for millions of body cells.

KEY

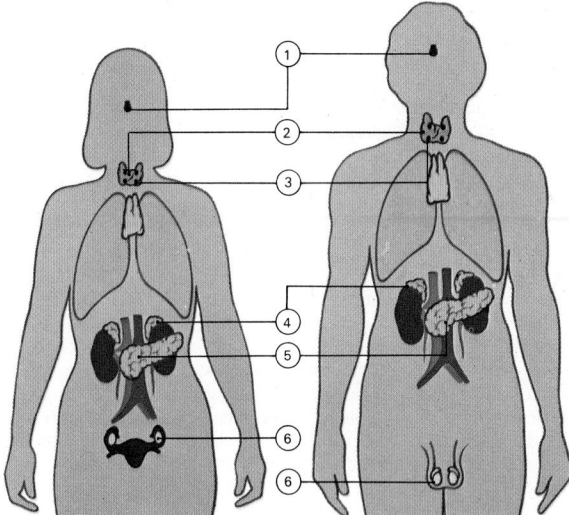

The endocrine glands secrete hormones directly into the blood, which carries them to specific "target" organs. The glands are: [1] pituitary; [2] thyroid; [3] parathyroid; [4] adrenal; [5] pancreas; and [6] ovaries and testes.

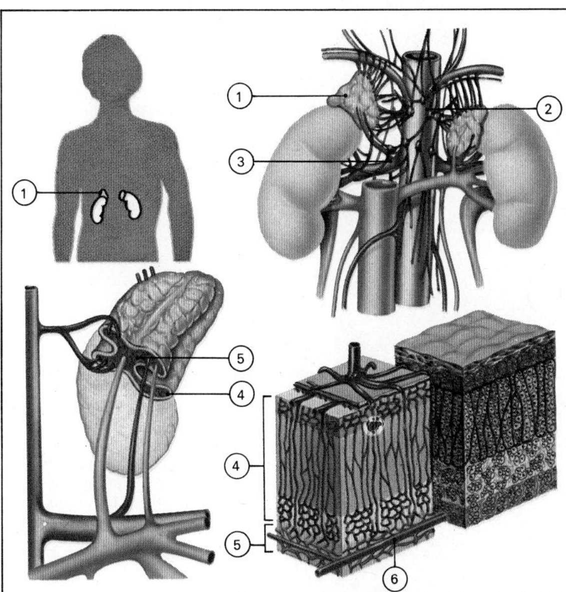

5 Situated just above the kidneys, the two adrenal glands [1] are well supplied with blood entering directly from the aorta [2] and from tributaries of the renal arteries [3]. Each gland consists of two separate functional parts: an outer layer or cortex [4] and an inner medulla [5]. Only the cortex—secreting steroid hormones to control body chemistry—is essential to life. Taking up raw materials from the arteries, the different cell types of the cortex release their products into the veins [6]. The adrenal medulla secretes two hormones which prepare the body for action in emergency.

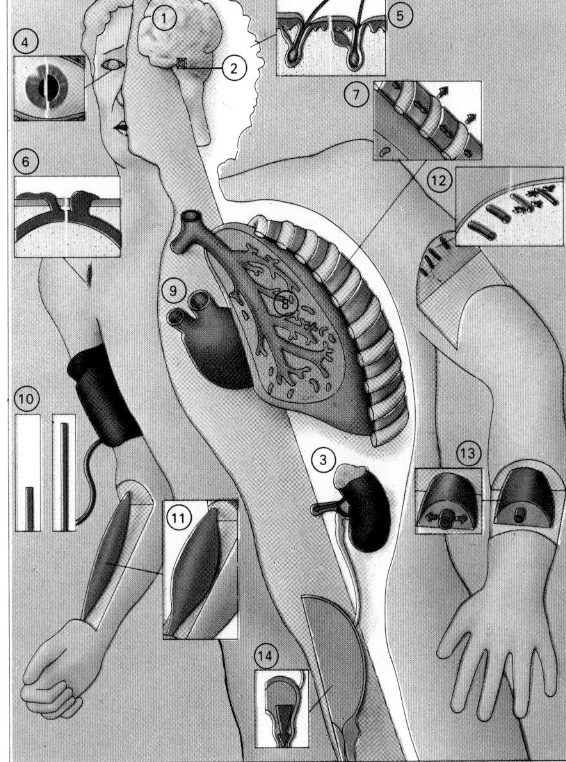

6 A vivid example of a hormone at work is the way in which adrenaline acts in response to fear, a powerful emotion that produces dramatic effects on the body as a whole. It is the sudden release of adrenaline from the adrenal medulla that meets the situation by mobilizing energy output and spurring the body to action. Specifically, fear triggers the following events: [1] an effect in the pituitary's frontal lobe; [2] the hypothalamus of the brain orders the adrenal medulla into production; [3] there is a rapid release of adrenaline; [4] the pupils dilate; [5] hair stands on end; [6] blood readily coagulates; [7] the chest expands; [8] bronchioles dilate; [9] the heart dilates; [10] blood-pressure rises; [11] muscles contract; [12] skin capillaries constrict causing pallor; [13], muscle blood vessels dilate; [14] the bladder evacuates.

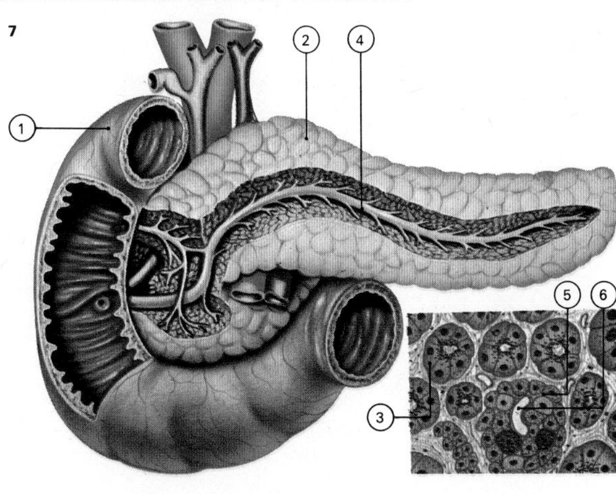

7 The pancreas, lying next to the duodenum [1], is a versatile gland producing both digestive enzymes and hormones. Pancreatic tissue consists of thousands of lobules [2], each containing glandular alveoli [3], where enzymes are produced and released to the duodenum by way of the main pancreatic duct [4]. Glucagon and insulin, the two pancreatic hormones, are produced in the islets of Langerhans [5] grouped around capillaries [6].

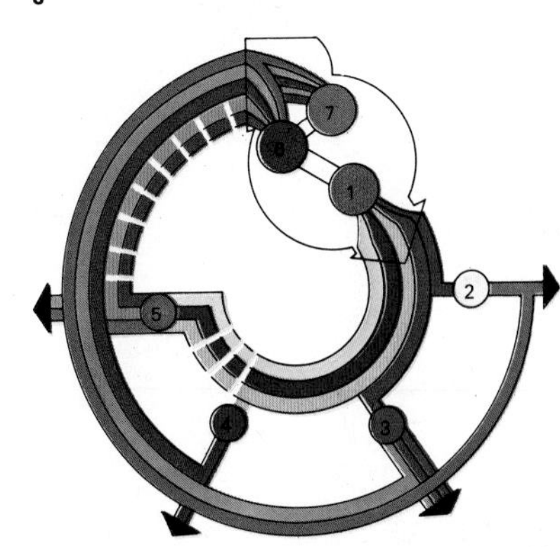

8 A schematic plan of the endocrine system shows the reciprocal action—or feedback mechanism—governing the release of hormones. Most influential is the anterior pituitary [1], secreting "trophic" hormones to trigger production in the thyroid [2], adrenal cortex [3], testes in the male [4], and ovaries in the female [5]. These then affect the hypothalamus [6] and the posterior pituitary [7], which in turn influence the activity of the anterior pituitary.

Breathing and the lungs

Respiration is not simply a matter of breathing in and out; it is something altogether more complex—the process by which energy is released from food. Respiration, of course, involves the chest, lungs, bloodstream, breathing (ventilation), and the intake of oxygen and removal of carbon dioxide (gaseous exchange). But it also involves every other part of the body, because it is at the cellular level that the release of energy occurs.

The structure of the lungs

A continuous supply of oxygen is essential; deprived of oxygen, we rapidly lose consciousness and die. As the body surface is too small to absorb all the oxygen necessary to fuel millions of cells, humans and other complex animals have developed a special internal surface for breathing. This is the lining of the lungs, a vast expanse of up to 750sq ft (70sq m) in the adult—over 40 times the surface of the body as a whole.

The additional value of this internal surface is that it remains permanently moist and is protected to a great extent from damage and from the intrusion of bacteria, fungi, and other threatening organisms. Thin as tissue paper and interlaced with a network of fine-walled capillaries, the internal lining of the lungs absorbs oxygen for rapid transfer to the hemoglobin of the blood. At the same time carbon dioxide, a waste product of cell metabolism, is released from the blood.

The lungs are spongy and delicate rose-pink at birth, darkening to slate-gray or even black in later years. Covered with moist pleural membrane, they fill the deep thoracic (chest) cavity, corresponding to it in shape. The right lung consists of three lobes, the left lung—slightly smaller and indented to make room for the heart—has only two.

The lungs receive air, already warmed and filtered in the mouth or nose, by way of a series of pipes: the pharynx (throat), larynx ("voice box") [3], trachea (windpipe) and, where the trachea forks, the right and left bronchi, which enter the lungs. Inside the lungs the two primary bronchi branch first into smaller bronchi, then into bronchioles—"twigs" of the respiratory tree. In turn the bronchioles subdivide into alveolar ducts leading into the air sacs, or alveoli.

How the lungs work

It is here in these hollow air sacs, lying bunched like microscopic grapes deep inside the lungs, that the actual gas exchange takes place. Capillaries of the pulmonary artery enmesh the alveoli, bringing stale blood close to the fine surface membrane. The alveoli themselves secrete a thin film of liquid, with low surface tension, as a medium for diffusion. The reoxygenated blood then returns via the pulmonary vein to the heart so that it can be pumped once more throughout the body, refueling distant cells with oxygen [4].

When we breathe in, the thorax is enlarged by a tightening of the muscles of the diaphragm (causing it to contract from a dome to a saucer shape) and of the rib cage, which swings upward and outward. As the chest expands, the lungs must also expand, and the air inside them becomes rarefied, forming a low-pressure area [2]. Air rushes

CONNECTIONS

See also
714 Diseases of breathing
688 Heart and blood circulation
698 Keeping fit
238 Man under the sea
512 The life of fish

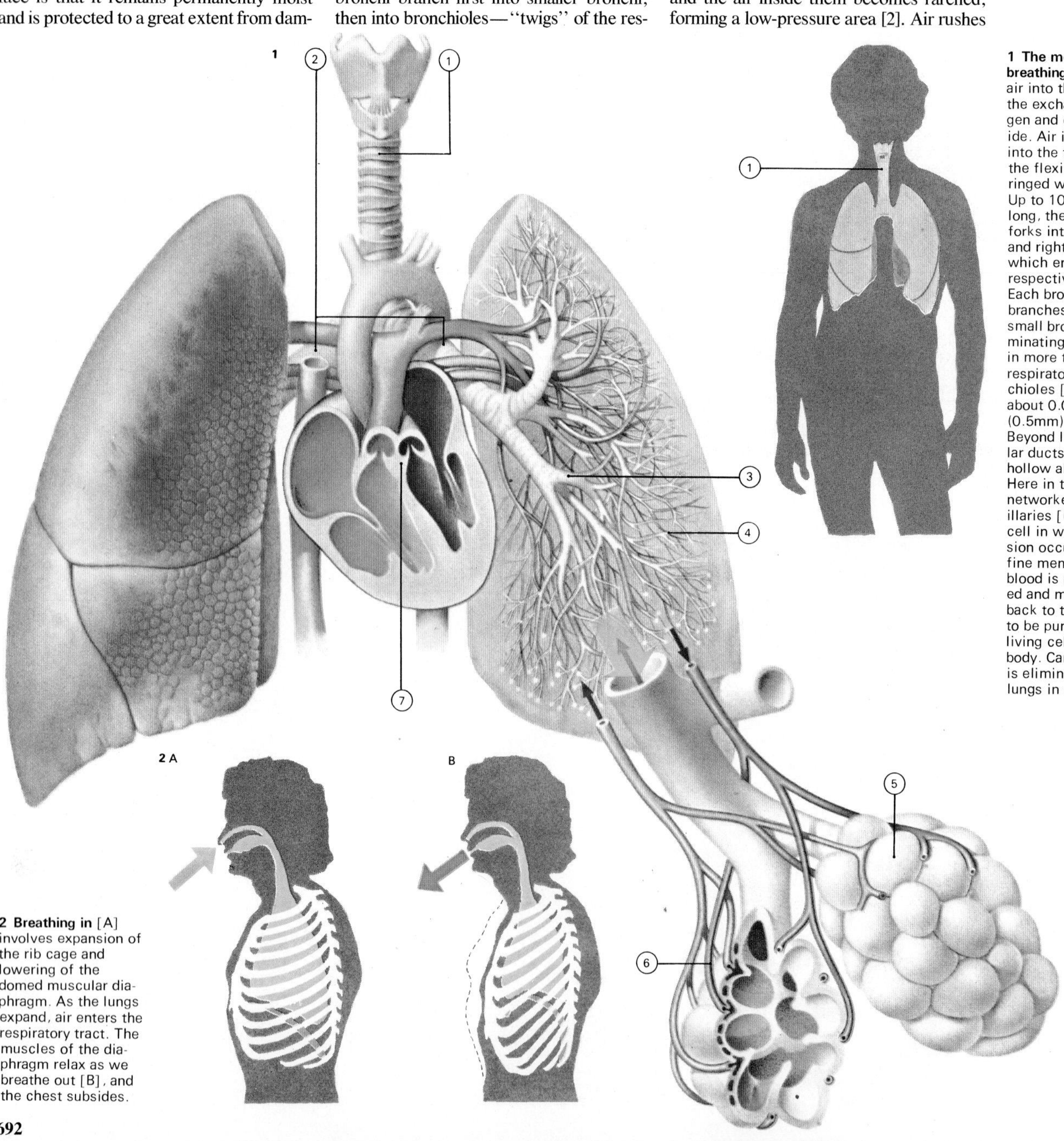
1
2
1
1
3
4
7
5
6
2 A
B

1 The mechanism of breathing introduces air into the lungs for the exchange of oxygen and carbon dioxide. Air is funneled into the trachea [1], the flexible windpipe ringed with cartilage. Up to 10in (25cm) long, the trachea forks into the left and right bronchi [2], which enter their respective lungs. Each bronchus branches into several small bronchi [3], terminating ultimately in more than 250,000 respiratory bronchioles [4], each about 0.02in (0.5mm) in diameter. Beyond lie the alveolar ducts leading into hollow alveoli [5]. Here in the alveoli, networked with capillaries [6] only one cell in width, diffusion occurs across a fine membrane. Stale blood is reoxygenated and makes its way back to the heart [7] to be pumped to each living cell in the body. Carbon dioxide is eliminated from the lungs in expired air.

2 Breathing in [A] involves expansion of the rib cage and lowering of the domed muscular diaphragm. As the lungs expand, air enters the respiratory tract. The muscles of the diaphragm relax as we breathe out [B], and the chest subsides.

down the trachea to restore pressure. Tension in the diaphragm and rib cage muscles slackens and the lungs revert to their resting shape, pulling the thorax back to shape with them and, as they recoil, the air inside them is compressed and some of it is forced out through the trachea.

Quiet breathing—at intervals of from four to six seconds—involves intake of about 0.75pint (0.5liter) of air [1]. Perhaps a third of this lingers in the bronchi and bronchioles, while the remaining two-thirds finds its way to the alveoli. Similarly, we breathe out roughly 0.75 pint at a single expiration. But, with a residual volume of 1.75–2.5 pints, the lungs are never completely drained of air.

Once air reaches the alveoli, oxygen is diffused into the bloodstream and carbon dioxide passes out from the blood to be expelled from the body. In addition to its main purpose—trading fuel for waste products—this exchange maintains the correct level of acidity in the blood. It is acidity level that determines the rate of breathing. If breathing is too slow, there is a build-up of carbon dioxide, causing slight acidification in the blood. This change in acidity is monitored by special cells in the medulla of the brain and elsewhere, and these in turn signal deeper and faster breathing. In this way the acidity level is restored to normal.

Cleaning the air

To cope with the impurities in the air we breathe, the respiratory tract incorporates its own cleansing mechanisms. Supplementing filtration in the upper airways, the cilia—tiny hairs lining the bronchi and bronchioles—are at work all the time wafting mucus, laden with cell debris and foreign particles, upward to the throat (this phlegm is swallowed and disposed of by way of the stomach). Larger particles, including germs, give an excess of mucus, and this has to be coughed up. Both the coughing and sneezing reflexes help blow detritus from the air passages. At the end of the network, the delicate alveoli are kept clean by phagocytes—scavenger white blood cells that engulf dust particles and bacteria.

KEY

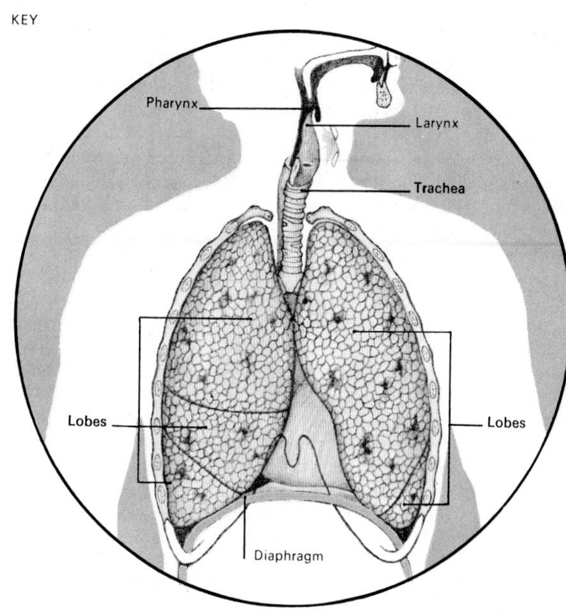
Pharynx
Larynx
Trachea
Lobes
Lobes
Diaphragm

The respiratory system's main components are shown.

3

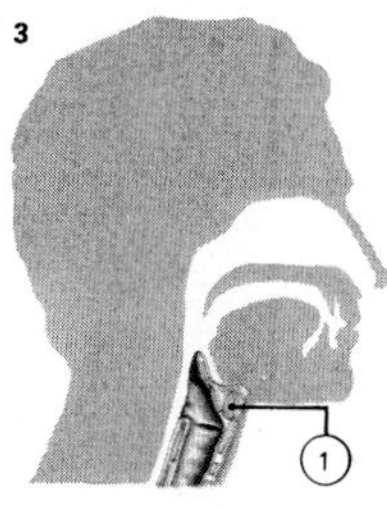
1

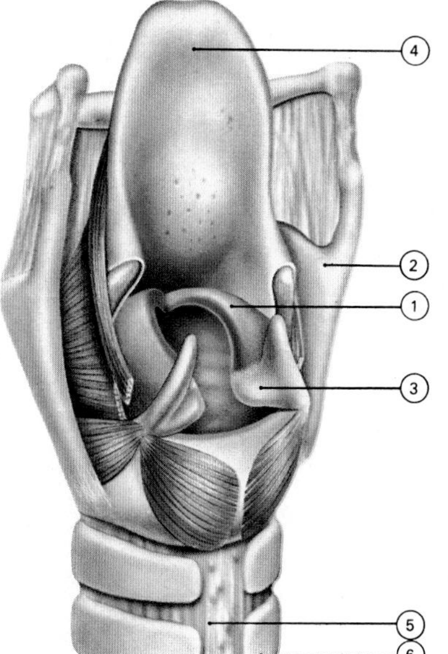
4
2
1
3
5
6

3 Air forced through the larynx or voice box causes the vocal cords [1] to vibrate, producing sound. The vocal cords are fibrous strands that stretch between the thyroid cartilage [2] and the two moving cartilages [3]. The epiglottis [4] drops over the layrnx during swallowing to keep out food. The trachea [5] is supported by rings of cartilage [6].

4

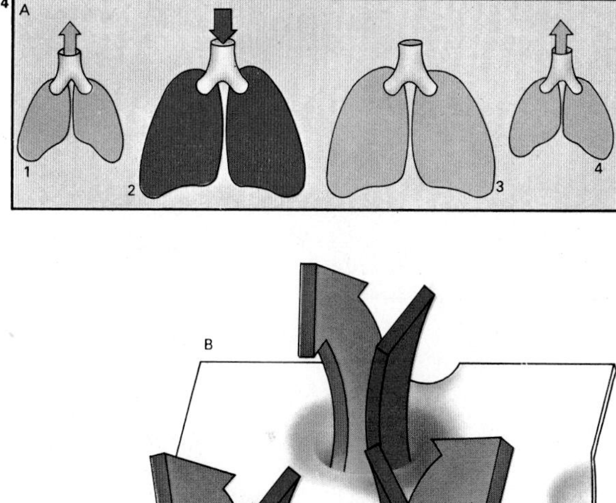
A
1
2
3
4

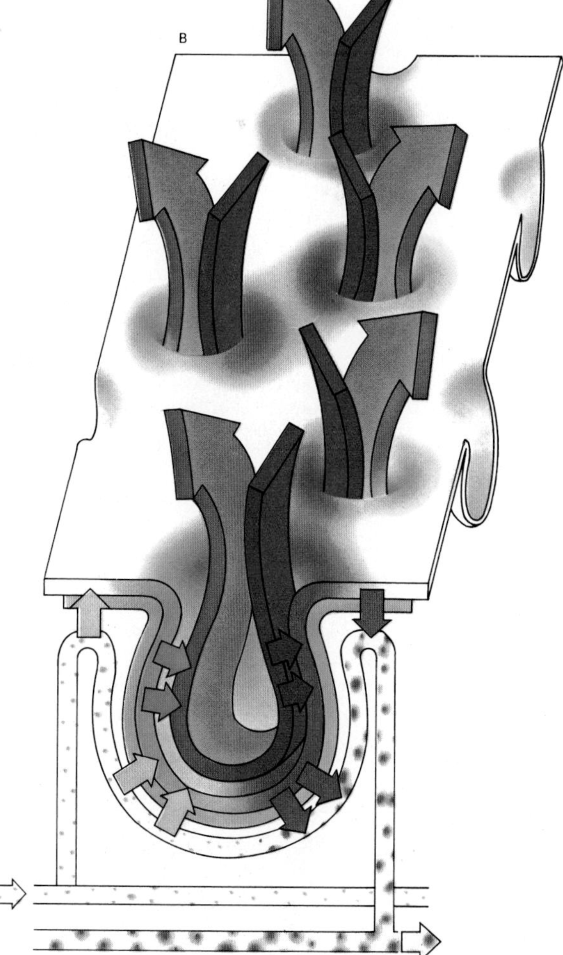
B

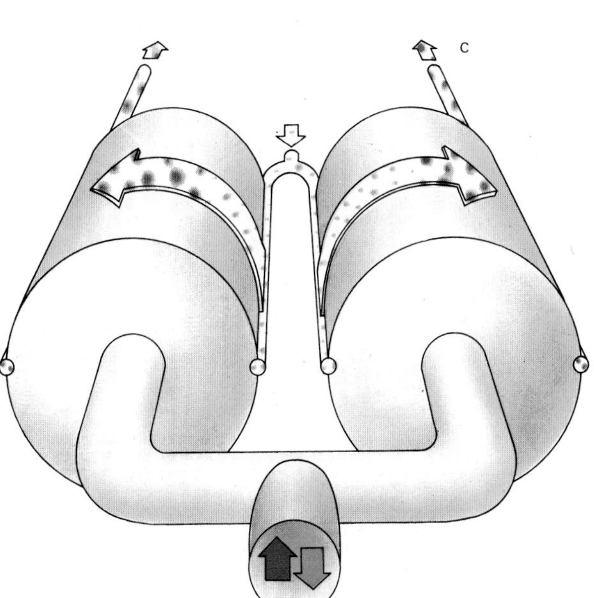
C

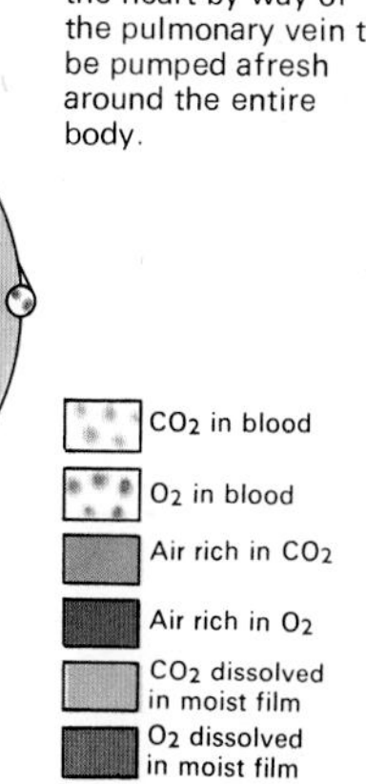
CO_2 in blood
O_2 in blood
Air rich in CO_2
Air rich in O_2
CO_2 dissolved in moist film
O_2 dissolved in moist film

4 The lungs represent the hub of the respiratory cycle. Ventilation [A], a vital part of this cycle, involves [1] exhaling stale air; [2] breathing in fresh air rich in oxygen; [3] the exchange of oxygen and carbon dioxide; [4] the elimination of carbon dioxide. A diagrammatic view of the alveolar surface [B] shows the rapid transaction of oxygen for carbon dioxide. Fresh blood is returned to the main circulation to fuel the body cells. Carbon dioxide is expelled, along with water vapor collected in the moist respiratory passages when we breathe out. For respiration to take place chemicals and oxygen must react together; carbon dioxide and water, the end products of this reaction, must be removed [C]. The pulmonary artery conducts stale blood, dark with reduced hemoglobin, out of the heart. Reoxygenated in the lungs, and now bright red in color, it returns to the heart by way of the pulmonary vein to be pumped afresh around the entire body.

The digestive system

Every one of the millions of living cells within the body needs energy to function—energy that is provided by the food we eat. Placed side by side ten million cells would measure only about 0.04in (1m), yet each cell is a complex biochemical factory that must be supplied with its food energy in a precise form. The vast variety of solids and liquids that are taken into the body therefore require a great deal of processing—both physical and chemical—before they can be assimilated by the cells and used in the vital processes of growth and metabolism.

The process of digestion

Digestion is the process whereby foods are gradually broken down into their basic components: proteins into amino acids (to provide the building blocks for new proteins); carbohydrates (starches) into simple glucose; and fats into fatty acids and glycerol to provide the body with energy. This involves groups of enzymes (the body's chemical catalysts), hormones (chemical messengers), as well as nervous impulses and controlled muscular action.

The intricacies of digestion are perhaps best understood by tracing the fate of a ham and lettuce sandwich during the 24 hours or so that it stays in the digestive tract [3]. This is a good example because it contains the three essential types of food: the ham is largely protein, the bread is rich in carbohydrate, the butter is fat and the lettuce provides a largely indigestible residue of cellulose.

As the sandwich is eaten it is chewed up and mixed with alkaline saliva, which is secreted by three pairs of salivary glands situated around the jaws. The saliva pours into the mouth via small ducts under the tip of the tongue and in the cheeks [1].

At this stage digestion has already begun because saliva contains a digestive enzyme, known as amylase, which acts on starches (in this case the bread) and begins converting them to maltose, a soluble form of sugar.

Each mouthful is formed into a ball-like mass (bolus), which is pushed by the tongue to the back of the mouth and propelled down the gullet (esophagus) into the stomach. It is conveyed not merely by gravity but by peristalsis—strong, rhythmic, wavelike contractions of the esophagus wall.

When it enters the stomach, the food is thoroughly mixed with gastric juice by the churning action of the stomach's strong muscular walls. Between two and four pints (one and two liters) of juice are secreted daily by glands in the stomach lining [2]. This juice consists of strong hydrochloric acid. protective mucus and pepsin, the first digestive enzyme to act on protein in the food (the ham in the sandwich) After an hour or so the sandwich has been reduced to a pulp (chyme) and is ready to go into the duodenum, the first short curved section of the small intestine.

In the small intestine

The small intestine is so called because of its diameter rather than its length, which totals about 23ft(7m). The bulk of digestion and absorption into the surrounding blood supply takes place within its length.

Chyme passing from the stomach into the small intestine encounters another

CONNECTIONS

See also

1572 The chemistry of life: biochemistry
718 Diseases of the digestive system
728 Diseases of the urogenital system
696 A healthy diet
460 Animal anatomy
756 Dentistry

1

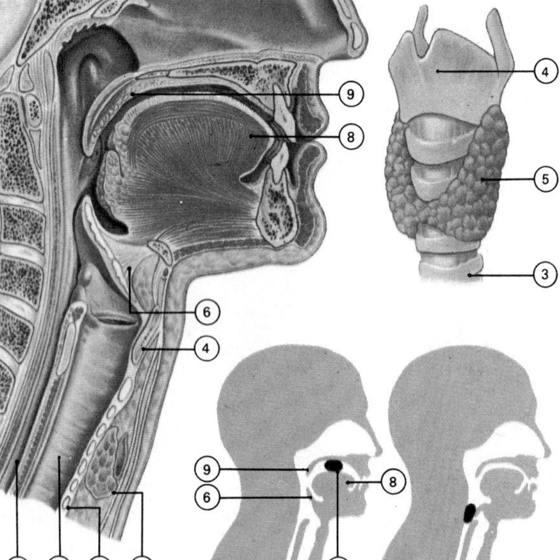

9
8
6
4
5
3
1
2
7
A
B

1 The mouth is a gateway not only to the digestive system but also to the respiratory system. The esophagus [1] lies behind the trachea [2], which is supported by cartilage rings [3]. The larynx is at the top of the trachea and its front is formed by the thyroid cartilage [4], so called because of its proximity to the thyroid gland [5]. The flaplike epiglottis [6] is attached to this cartilage. Food, mixed with saliva, is formed into a bolus [7] and pushed by the tongue [8] into the pharynx. During swallowing [A,B] the soft palate [9] blocks entry to the nose and the epiglottis closes so food does not enter.

2 The digestion and absorption of food takes place within the digestive tract, a coiled tube some 33ft(10m) long that links mouth to anus. Food is passed down the esophagus [1] to the stomach [2], where it is partially digested. Chyme is released into the duodenum [3]—the first part of 23ft(7m) of the small intestine. The duodenum receives bile produced in the liver [5] and stored in the gall bladder [4] and enzymes secreted by the pancreas [6]. Most absorption occurs in the jejunum and ileum, the remaining parts of the small intestine [7]. Any residue passes into the caecum [8], the pouch at the start of the large intestine. At one end of the caecum is the 4in(10cm) long vermiform appendix [9], which serves no useful purpose in man. Feces form as water is reabsorbed in the colon [10]. They collect in the rectum [11] before being expelled through the anus [12]. Many of the wastes that result from cell metabolism are filtered from the blood by the kidneys [13] into urine. This passes down the ureters [14] to the bladder [15], and is voided via the urethra [16].

2

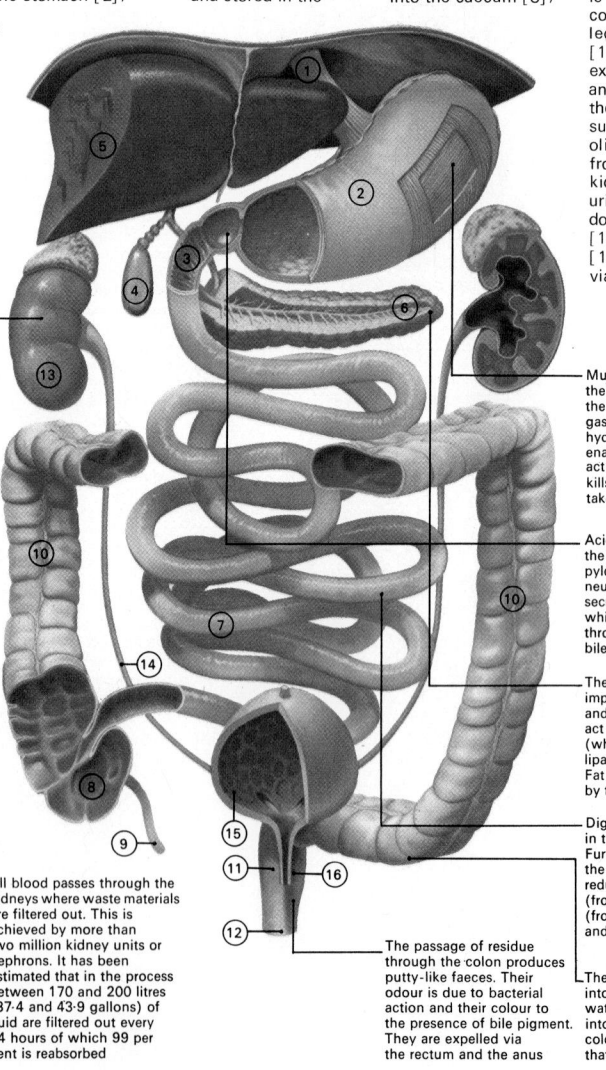

Muscular contraction of the stomach wall churns the food, mixing it with gastric juice which includes hydrochloric acid. This enables the enzymes to act and at the same time kills many of the microbes taken in with the food

Acid chyme squirts into the duodenum through the pyloric sphincter and is neutralized by alkaline secretions of the pancreas which enter the intestine through the same duct as bile from the gall bladder

The pancreas secretes important enzymes: trypsin and chymotrypsin (which act on protein); amylase (which acts on starch); and lipase (which acts on fats). Fat digestion is also aided by the action of bile

Digestion is completed in the small intestine. Further enzymes mix with the food, which is ultimately reduced to amino acids (from proteins), sugars (from starches) and glycerol and fatty acids (from fats)

The residue that passes into the colon contains much water that is reabsorbed into the bloodstream. The colon also contains bacteria that break down cellulose

The passage of residue through the colon produces putty-like faeces. Their odour is due to bacterial action and their colour to the presence of bile pigment. They are expelled via the rectum and the anus

All blood passes through the kidneys where waste materials are filtered out. This is achieved by more than two million kidney units or nephrons. It has been estimated that in the process between 170 and 200 litres (37·4 and 43·9 gallons) of fluid are filtered out every 24 hours of which 99 per cent is reabsorbed

3

24 hours
0
Mouth
Oesophagus
Stomach
Small intestine
Large intestine
Caecum
4
8·5
9·5

3 A typical time scale for the passage of food through the digestive tract relates each part of the system to the time on the clock. Correct timing of the digestive process is essential for two reasons: (1) food must stay in the stomach and small intestine long enough to allow complete breakdown of protein, fat, and carbohydrate, and (2) the residue must pass through the large intestine slowly enough to allow water to be reabsorbed into the body.

dramatic change of environment, this time from acid to alkaline, as it mixes with digestive juices pouring into the duodenum from the pancreas and gall bladder.

The pancreas is a gland about 7in (18cm) long. It plays a vital role in digestion by secreting digestive enzymes that act on carbohydrate, protein, and fat.

The digestive process is further aided by the emulsifying effect of bile, a thick, green, bitter liquid formed by the liver and stored in the gall bladder.

The lining of the small intestine also secretes a whole range of digestive enzymes. Protein, carbohydrate, and fat all finally become amino acids, glucose, and glycerol and fatty acids.

Absorption of these digested substances into the bloodstream is the next essential step in the provision of nutrients to the cells. The lining of the small intestine is heavily folded—to increase its surface area—with thousands of minute fingerlike projections known as villi [4, 6]. These waft to and fro in the intestinal contents, which are thus brought into intimate contact with the rich supply of blood capillaries and lymphatic vessels that lies within each villus.

Amino acids and glucose diffuse across the membrane of the villus into the blood capillaries, and the fatty acids and glycerol enter the lymphatic cells to be transported to the liver, which acts as the body's chief storehouse and also as a breakdown plant and as its chemical factory.

Eliminating waste

By now the sandwich has been digested, absorbed, and processed by the liver. But most of the lettuce remains as indigestible cellulose at the end of the ileum. It passes, together with great quantities of gastric secretions and other debris, through the ileocaecal valve into the caecum, the pouch at the start of the colon, the main part of the large intestine. The principal function of the large intestine is the retrieval of water and important chemicals by reabsorption into the bloodstream. The colon disposes of the waste material—all that remains of the ham sandwich eaten many hours before—through the anus in the form of feces.

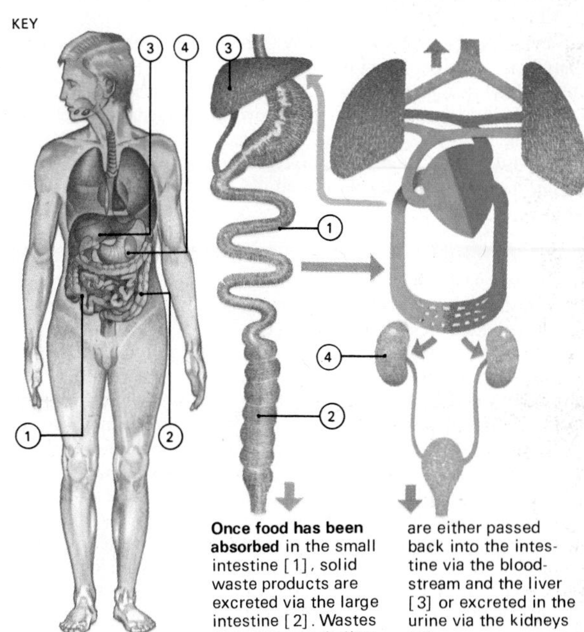
KEY

Once food has been absorbed in the small intestine [1], solid waste products are excreted via the large intestine [2]. Wastes from cell metabolism are either passed back into the intestine via the bloodstream and the liver [3] or excreted in the urine via the kidneys [4].

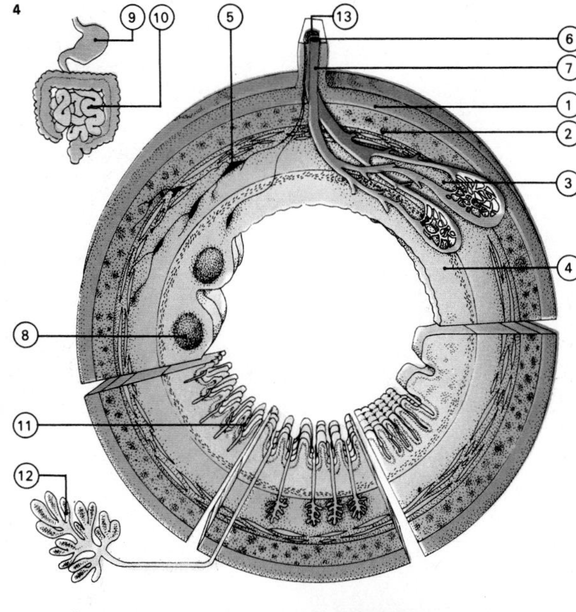

4 The digestive tract has the same basic structure throughout its length. The wall has four layers: the serosa, an outer connective tissue coat [1]; a muscular coat [2]; a submucous coat [3]; and an inner mucous coat [4]. The gut wall is liberally supplied by nerves [5], arteries [6], and veins [7] and with lymph nodes [8]. In the stomach [9] and small intestine [10] the mucosa is greatly folded. In addition, the small intestine's mucosa has many fine projections (villi) [11]. The wall of the duodenum is also perforated by the duct of the pancreas [12]. The tract is suspended from the abdominal wall by the mesentery [13].

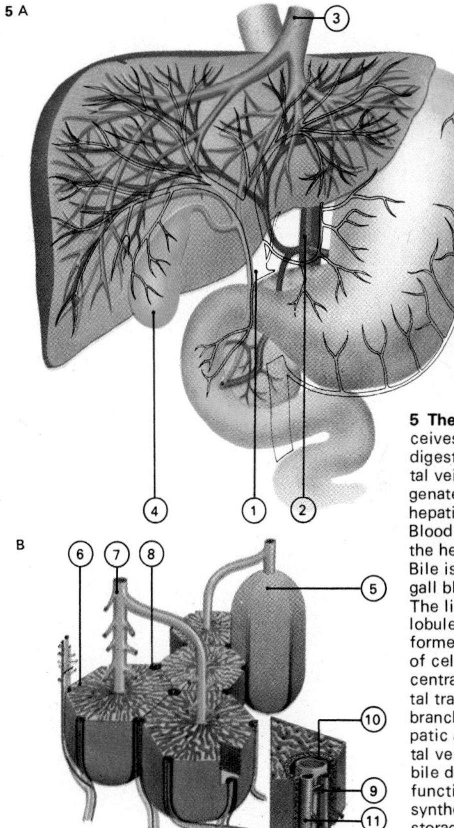

5 The liver [A] receives products of digestion via the portal vein [1] and oxygenated blood via the hepatic artery [2]. Blood is drained by the hepatic vein [3]. Bile is stored in the gall bladder [4]. [B] The liver consists of lobules [5], each formed by columns of cells [6] around a central vein [7]. Portal tracts [8] carry branches of the hepatic artery [9], portal vein [10], and bile duct [11]. Liver functions include synthesis of fats and storage of minerals and vitamins.

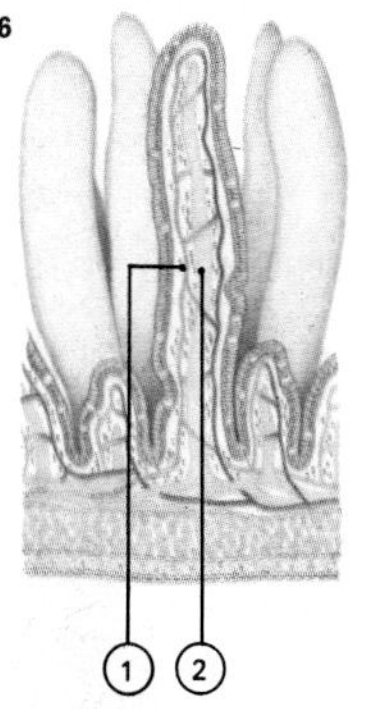

6 The small intestine's internal surface area is greatly increased by the presence of microvilli, microscopic structures covering the surface of each villus. Amino acids and sugars pass into the capillary network [1]; fatty acids and glycerol enter the lymphatic system via a central lacteal [2].

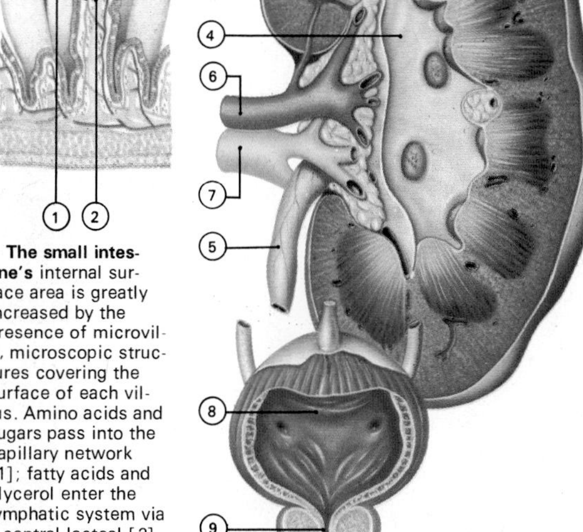

7 In each kidney's fibrous capsule [1] there are three distinct zones: an outer cortex [2]; a medulla region [3] with pyramidal-shaped areas; and an inner pelvis region [4] that leads to the ureter [5]. The renal artery [6] branches repeatedly within the kidney to form a network of capillaries in close association with a complex system of tubules that filter wastes from the blood and convey them to the ureter. The capillaries ultimately unite to form the renal vein [7]. Urine is propelled down the ureter by wavelike contractions into the muscular urinary bladder [8], and this when full contracts, expelling urine from the body down the urethra [9].

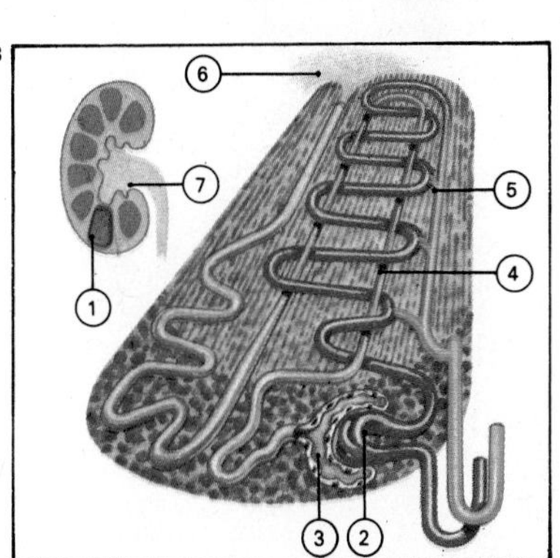

8 In the renal medulla [1] many materials are filtered from the blood via knots of capillaries called glomeruli [2] into Bowman's capsules [3], which are part of the kidney's tubule system. As liquid flows down the tubule or nephron [4], its water content is adjusted and valuable substances are reabsorbed via capillaries [5], leaving only urine [6]. The tubules converge in the renal pelvis [7].

A healthy diet

All living things need food to grow and to maintain life. A person must eat to obtain the energy to fuel muscular activity and basic bodily processes—tissue growth, breathing, heartbeat, and so on. The aim of food nutrition is a balanced diet [Key] supplying just as much energy as needed and no more.

Energy sources

Foods vary widely in their energy value [1]. The most commonly used unit for measuring these differences is the kilogram calorie or kilocalorie (Cal)—the amount of heat needed to raise the temperature of a kilogram of water 1°C. In most diets, the principal energy foods (though not necessarily the highest in caloric value) are carbohydrates, the simplest of which are sugars like glucose. A molecule of sucrose (cane or beet sugar) consists of two simple sugar units chemically linked together. Starch molecules are chains of up to a few hundred such units. Most of the staple foods that provide the bulk of people's diets are plant organs containing starchy food reserves; for example, cereal seeds like wheat, rice, oats, and corn, or tubers like potatoes and yams.

Energy is not available from all carbohydrates. Cellulose is a carbohydrate occurring in all green plants, making up cell walls, the tough fibers of leaves and stems, and the outer coats of cereal grains (bran); these materials are almost unchanged in the human digestive tract. Although without food value, this roughage is useful in helping the passage of food through the digestive system.

Fats are energy-rich foods and certain constituents of fats are probably essential in a balanced diet. They are important foods in wealthy countries, but people living in poverty may eat very little fat and sometimes suffer from a lack of fat-soluble vitamins, especially vitamins A and D. The amount of fat desirable in a healthy diet has still to be established. Many believe that there would be nutritional advantages in a reduction in the high intake of fats common among prosperous communities and in replacement of some animal fats with those of vegetable origin.

Protein molecules are large assemblages of simple units called amino acids. Different proteins contain varying proportions of the 20 or so common amino acids. During digestion, food proteins are broken down into their constituent units, which are absorbed into the blood and then reconstructed into the various proteins needed by the body, including enzymes, contractile muscle protein, and blood-plasma proteins.

Essentials of health

Some amino acids are interconvertible, but about ten are synthesized in the body only very slowly. Sufficient of these "essential amino acids" must therefore be present in any balanced diet. Animal proteins like those in meat, fish, and eggs are rich in essential amino acids. Cereals and vegetables contain comparatively little protein; most plant proteins, moreover, are relatively low in essential lysine and methionine. Many poor people rely largely on plant foods, with meat and fish as rare luxuries, and their protein intake is thus both restricted and of poor quality [7].

CONNECTIONS

See also
1572 The chemistry of life: biochemistry
694 The digestive system
710 The causes of illness: 1
736 Community medicine
732 Diseases of the Third World
734 World health
302 World food resources
398 The future of food
702 Pregnancy
776 Human development
674 Sight and perception
720 Diseases of the skeleton and muscles
326 Staple foods: grains
330 Staple foods: legumes
332 Staple foods: tubers
334 Vegetables
338 Temperate fruits
340 Tropical fruits

1 Weight for weight pure fat supplies 2.25 times more energy than carbohydrate [A]. Any protein surplus to the body's need for tissue growth and repair can also supply energy. Simply to keep their metabolism going, children use far more energy per kilogram of their body weight than older people do [B]; they also need much more protein in proportion to their size.

2A
B
C
D

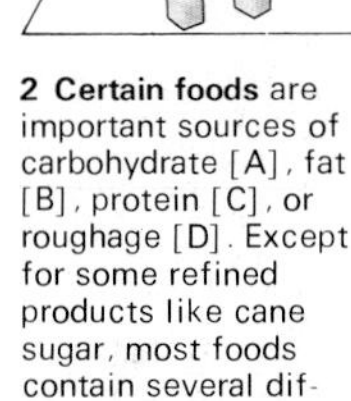

2 Certain foods are important sources of carbohydrate [A], fat [B], protein [C], or roughage [D]. Except for some refined products like cane sugar, most foods contain several different nutrients. Milk provides carbohydrate, fat, protein, calcium, and some vitamins. Even potatoes contain protein and vitamin C as well as energy-rich carbohydrate.

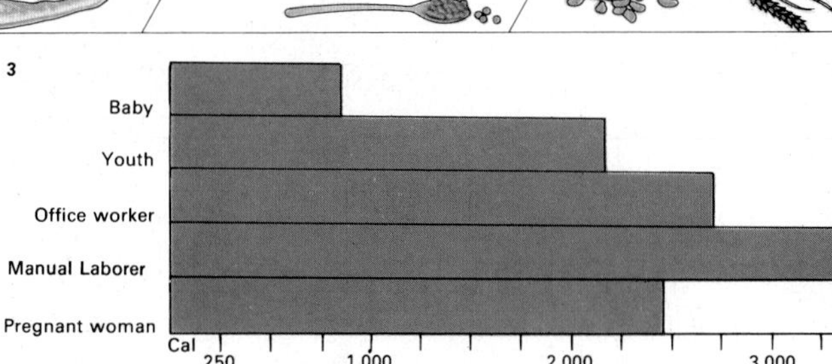

3
Baby
Youth
Office worker
Manual Laborer
Pregnant woman
Cal
250
1,000
2,000
3,000
4,000

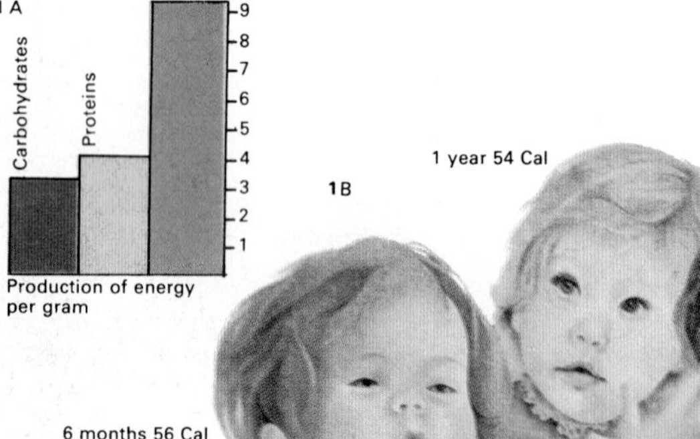

1A
Carbohydrates
Proteins
Fats
Cal
9
8
7
6
5
4
3
2
1
Production of energy per gram
1B
At birth 49 Cal
6 months 56 Cal
1 year 54 Cal
2 years 51 Cal
4 years 47 Cal
8 years 39 Cal
12 years 36 Cal
18 years 26 Cal
70 years 23 Cal

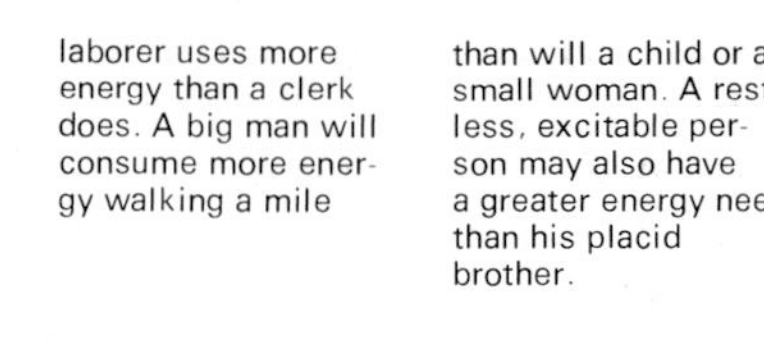

3 People's daily energy needs vary widely. At work, a laborer uses more energy than a clerk does. A big man will consume more energy walking a mile than will a child or a small woman. A restless, excitable person may also have a greater energy need than his placid brother.

Protein-deficiency symptoms [6] usually appear in such communities, especially among young children, who need plenty of protein during the process of growing and building up new cells and tissues. Protein-deficiency diseases include rickets and scurvy.

Dietary influences

A diet of carbohydrates, fats, and proteins alone will not keep people healthy. A wide range of organic compounds, collectively called vitamins [4], and a number of inorganic substances—minerals [5]—are essential in a balanced diet, although many of them are needed in minute amounts only. Mineral and vitamin deficiencies occur even among otherwise well-fed people, especially if they choose a restricted range of foods rather than a varied diet. Iron-deficiency anemia, for instance, is widespread in the developed countries. Many governments therefore require by law the fortification of certain staple foods. Calcium and iron are added to bread flour and vitamins A and D, normally present in butter, are added to the margarine that may replace it.

People's customs and taboos can influence their diet in ways unconnected with the needs of their bodies. Many people like the sweet taste of sugar, for instance, and eat large amounts, even while being aware of the probable consequences—obesity and dental decay. Most western peoples refuse to eat caterpillars and a devout Hindu will not touch beef, although caterpillars and beef are both nourishing high-protein foods. Only in extreme conditions, such as famine, are such behavior patterns likely to break down. Physical idiosyncracies can also affect diet by making certain foods unacceptable: wheat and wheat products are poisonous to people with coeliac disease, while in parts of Asia and Africa, there are many adults who, though quite healthy, cannot digest milk.

When a meal is eaten, the proportion of nutrients actually absorbed by the body depends partly on the efficiency of digestion. This is reduced by anxiety, grief, weariness, or ill humor and enhanced by comfort and tranquility. Digestion also improves when the meal is eaten with enjoyment.

KEY

A balanced diet for a fairly active man would supply about 3,000 calories daily with adequate protein, minerals, and vitamins. The caloric value of foods common in Western diets makes this comparatively easy to achieve.

495 Cal
55 Cal
440 Cal
150 Cal
360 Cal
396 Cal
12 Cal
255 Cal
207 Cal
24 Cal
220 Cal
218 Cal
25 Cal
80 Cal
42 Cal
136 Cal
195 Cal

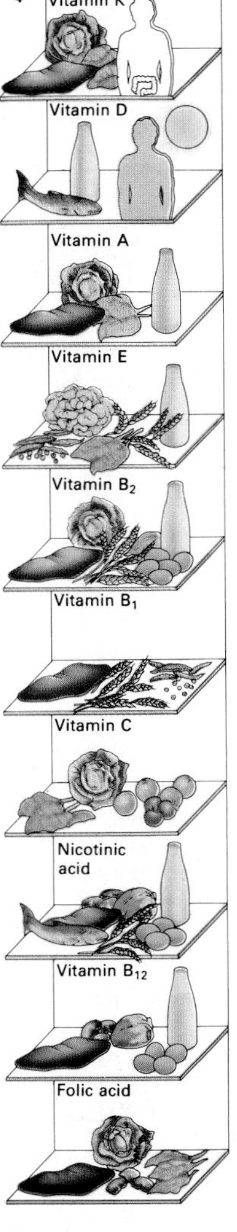
Vitamin K
Vitamin D
Vitamin A
Vitamin E
Vitamin B_2
Vitamin B_1
Vitamin C
Nicotinic acid
Vitamin B_{12}
Folic acid

4 Vitamins essential to health are found in great quantity in liver, milk, green vegetables, legumes, and corn. Fatty foods provide the chief source of vitamins K, D, A, and E, which are soluble in fats and oils. Vitamin K is produced by microorganisms in the gut, while any ordinary diet contains adequate vitamin E. Symptoms of deficiency of these two vitamins cannot therefore be positively identified. Some vitamin D is produced in the skin on exposure to sunlight, but this is insufficient except in sunny climates. Children receiving too little vitamin D cannot absorb calcium properly and their bones become soft and deformed, with swollen joints. This condition (rickets) is also produced by lack of calcium. Vitamin A deficiency leads to eye damage with eventual ulceration and blindness (keratomalacia). Though they are essential nutrients, vitamins A and D are poisonous in large doses. The vitamin B group of water-soluble compounds, including niacin and folic acid, is involved in cell enzyme systems. As vitamin B is generally found in meat and the bran of cereals, deficiencies of it are more likely in poor communities where staple cereals are milled and little meat is eaten. Lack of niacin produces skin eruptions and mental disorder (pellagra). Vitamin C, found in fresh vegetables or fruit, is easily lost in cooking and storage. Lack of it caused sailors to suffer from scurvy, with swollen gums and internal bleeding.

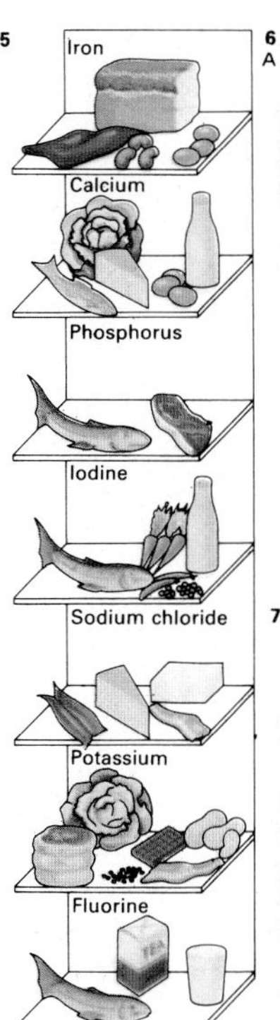
Iron
Calcium
Phosphorus
Iodine
Sodium chloride
Potassium
Fluorine

5 Vital minerals are found in several foods. Those supplying iron help oxygen exchange. Calcium and phosphorus are components of bone, together with magnesium. Iodine is needed for the control of metabolic rate. Although sodium chloride (salt) is found in most diets, extra quantities may be needed in hot countries where people lose salt in sweat. Potassium is important in nerve and muscle function and fluorine, found chiefly in drinking water, is believed to provide protection for children's teeth.

6 A

B
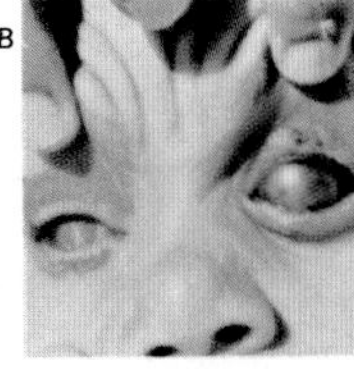
C
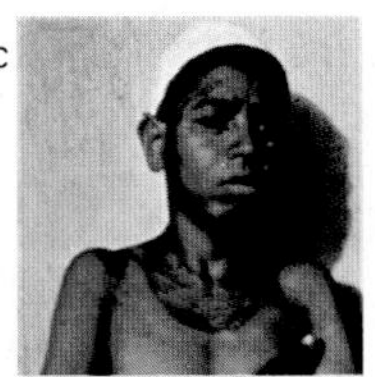
D
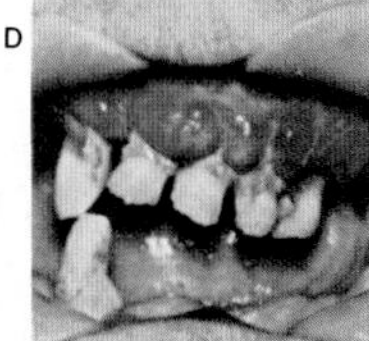
E
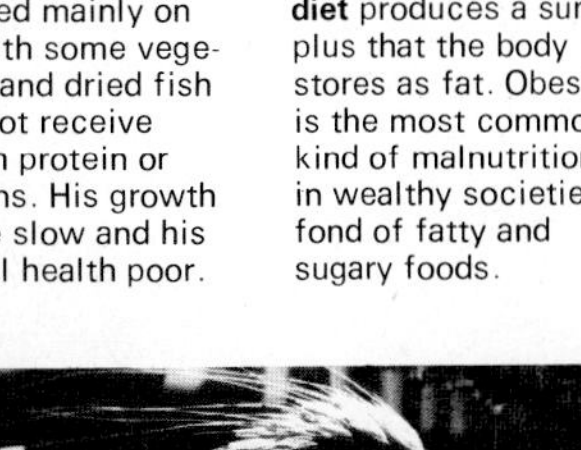
F
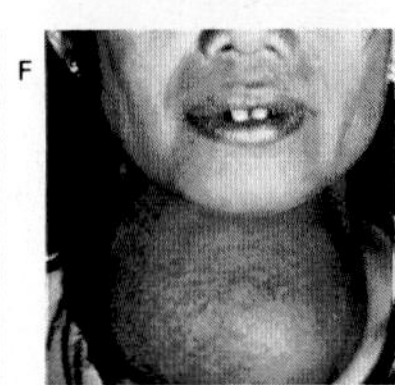

6 Deficiency diseases caused by lack of vitamins include rickets [A], keratomalacia [B], pellagra [C], and scurvy [D]. Kwashiorkor [E] appears in small children who lack protein, often on abrupt weaning. The child's stomach is swollen and its muscles wasted. Growth may be stunted and the brain damaged: iodine deficiency causes thyroid problems [F].

7
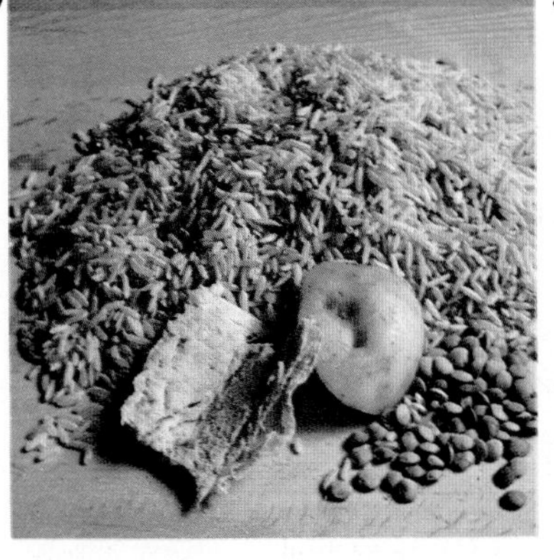

7 A village child in India fed mainly on rice with some vegetables and dried fish does not receive enough protein or vitamins. His growth will be slow and his general health poor.

8

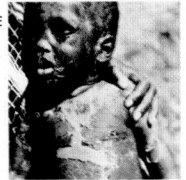

8 An over-rich daily diet produces a surplus that the body stores as fat. Obesity is the most common kind of malnutrition in wealthy societies fond of fatty and sugary foods.

9
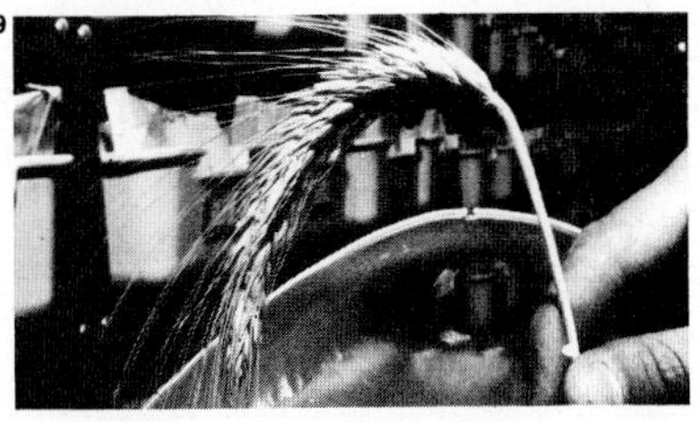

9 New sources of protein for the world's expanding population are being investigated. Farming of fish and big game like antelope is increasing. Geneticists have developed more efficient livestock breeds and new cereals like triticale, which is a heavy-yield wheat-rye hybrid. Yeasts and bacteria from petrochemicals can be made into animal feed but the products are not necessarily suitable for human consumption.

Keeping fit

The purpose of "keeping fit" is to avoid ill health, resist the mental and physical fatigue that makes us vulnerable to infections, and feel more pleasure in being alive. Research the world over affirms the value of a balanced diet, fresh air, sunshine, adequate rest, and some form of regular exercise for everyone, male or female, young or old, fat or thin. There is no doubt that if such a regime were universally followed the numbers of people seeking medical assistance would plunge dramatically, hospitals would be less crowded, and many fatal illnesses could be avoided.

Unfortunately, although the advantages of physical fitness are generally acknowledged, modern man tends to endorse them from his armchair. Sedentary occupations, spectator sports, labor-saving devices, mechanical transportation all tend to encourage more preaching than practice.

The heart of the matter

One of the reasons for the longevity and good health of the physically fit is that they do not put the heart under excessive strain [Key] and so the possibility of heart and blood-vessel diseases is reduced. They also avoid the consequences of weakened muscles, which are the cause of so much back and abdominal trouble.

Some 640 assorted muscles account for about 45 percent of our body weight, and for top efficiency and health these must have strength, endurance (or the ability to store energy), and elasticity, and be kept continually supplied with fuel by the blood. Sensible exercise, carefully suited to each individual (preferably on the advice of a doctor), approached slowly at first and only gradually building up to a sustained level of steady benefit, is the best insurance that all these physical requirements of the muscles will be properly met.

Working out the best method

Most people have learned basic exercises in school—stretching, running in place, lifting weights, and so on—and these are still fundamentally useful, but several new techniques for keeping fit have recently proved especially effective and popular.

Isometrics, developed by the US Marine Corps, is a form of exercise without movement in which one muscle group is exerted against another tensed muscle group for about five to eight seconds [2]. The exercise strengthens or "tones" a particular muscle or set of muscles. This form of exercise is suitable for both men and women, is generally safe to carry out, and can be fit in easily during the most crowded work schedule and can be performed comfortably almost anywhere—even sitting at an office desk.

Exercises involving vigorous movement and extended physical effort—such as running, jumping, fast walking, chopping wood, and most competitive sports—are called isotonics. They can be combined with isometrics to develop both strength and endurance. This combined method is used widely by athletes in intensive training programs.

The Royal Canadian Air Force has also developed a famous fitness program: 5BX, an 11-minute-a-day plan for men, and XBX, a 12-minute-a-day plan for women [4].

CONNECTIONS

See also
696 A healthy diet
692 Breathing and the lungs
716 Diseases of the circulation

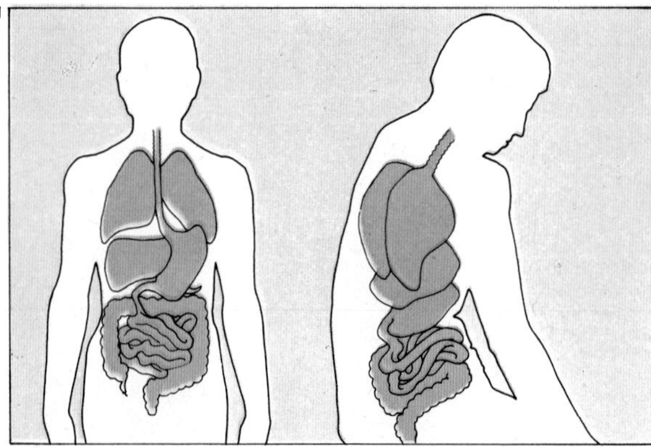

1 Despite his upright posture for the past 14 million years, man still shows the strain of his "new" position by slumping forward, curving his back, rounding his shoulders, and shrinking his chest into his abdomen. The results are neck and back pains and hampered breathing, in turn causing oxygen starvation and impeded blood circulation. Poor posture can lead to sagging, or prolapse, of stomach muscles, and long hours of sitting, to constipation and hemorrhoids. Conversely, over-rigid posture can strain the spine and cause disorders such as lumbago, fibrositis, and muscle strain.

A
B
C

2 Isometric exercises need only take a few moments and can be done almost anywhere, either sitting, standing, or lying down. Props may be just as casual: a towel, desk, doorway, or table can all be useful aids for creating the dynamic tension that strengthens muscles. A doorjamb assists the contraction that helps a woman [A] raise her bustline and also the contractions that firm up leg and stomach muscles [B]. Palms pressed down with force on a desk or table [C] strengthens the upper arms and, for a woman, raise the bustline. Regular isometric exercise can quickly tone up a particular muscle or set of muscles.

The cobra
The cat
The half locust
The half plough
The pose of the camel
The half shoulderstand

3 The aim of yoga exercises is precision and slow harmonized motion, rather than vigor and force. Each one is performed once only and all are combined with deep inhalation and exhalation. The cobra firms breasts, increases spinal flexibility, and tones abdominal muscles. The cat tones throat and chinline and stretches the back and stomach muscles. The half locust firms thighs and buttocks, while the half plough flattens stomach muscles. The pose of the camel makes the spine flexible, strengthens the neck, and firms the jawline. The half shoulderstand invigorates. Yoga exercises should always be learned with the help of a trained teacher.

These require no special equipment and are well suited to urban living.

The 5BX plan is composed of six charts of five exercises each, variously modified for differing ages and gradually increasing in difficulty and effort demanded. XBX is composed of four charts of ten exercises similarly arranged for gradual progress so that there is no undue strain, stiffness, or soreness. Properly followed, these programs maintain weight balance, improve appearance, and keep the body trim and strong.

Yoga and the sauna

The exercises, or "postures," that are one part of the ancient Hindu philosophical system of yoga have been growing in popularity in the West. Originally designed to relax the mind and body for extended meditation, they emphasize harmonious coordination of movement, stretching, and correct breathing. Even a few of the exercises, practiced for 10 or 15 minutes a day, will improve the whole physical system and induce a state of relaxation and well-being [3]. They should, however, be learned under the supervision of a teacher with a full understanding of their overall aim, and they should never be attempted too quickly, without preparation of unused muscles through a gradual loosening process.

Other methods of keeping fit can be combined with the foregoing—massage [5], for instance, can provide a tonic for slack muscles and sluggish circulation, as can the Scandinavian sauna [6], which, if properly used, is often valuable for cleansing the skin, calming the nerves, promoting good circulation, invigorating muscles and joints, and relaxing the entire system.

Ordinary everyday activities pursued vigorously, and any recreation that exercises muscles and stimulates circulation, such as dancing, swimming, riding, bicycling, golf, or tennis, are excellent means of keeping fit. The main objective should be the balancing of all ingredients—rest, calorie intake in proportion to energy output, maintaining good posture and breathing, regular exercise, and an optimistic state of mind.

KEY

Heartbeats per minute

160 150 140 130 120 110 100 90 80 70 60 50

(1) (2)

Lying · Standing · Climbing stairs · Sitting

When a person is physically unfit, his heart is given an extra work load as shown in the number of heartbeats per minute required for various everyday activities. The comparison between someone in poor condition who takes little or no exercise [1] and a person who follows a program of regular exercise [2] shows the value of keeping fit.

4 The exercises for both men and women developed by the Royal Canadian Air Force are carefully graded to increase fitness gradually and without fatigue in 11 to 12 minutes a day. A few are shown.

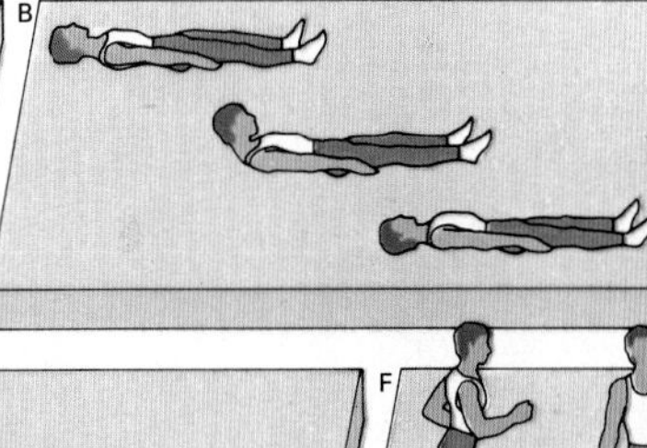

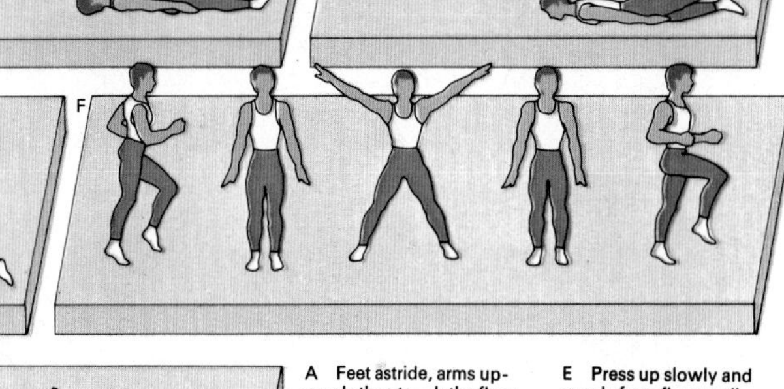

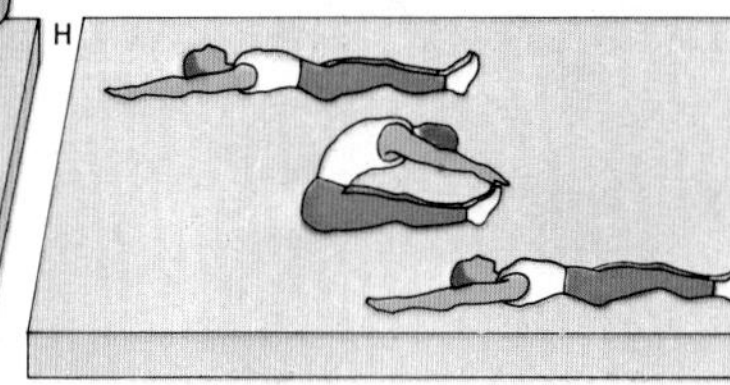

A Feet astride, arms upward; then touch the floor and straighten.
B Lie flat on floor, feet apart, then raise head 15cm (6 ins). off the ground.
C Lie on front, palms under thighs, then raise head and each leg alternately.
D Lie on front, palms under thighs, then raise head and both legs together.
E Press up slowly and evenly from floor until arms are fully extended.
F Running on the spot, interspersed with astride jumps.
G Feet astride, arms upward, then make full circle with hands touching the ground outside each foot.
H Lie on back, arms outstretched, raise trunk.

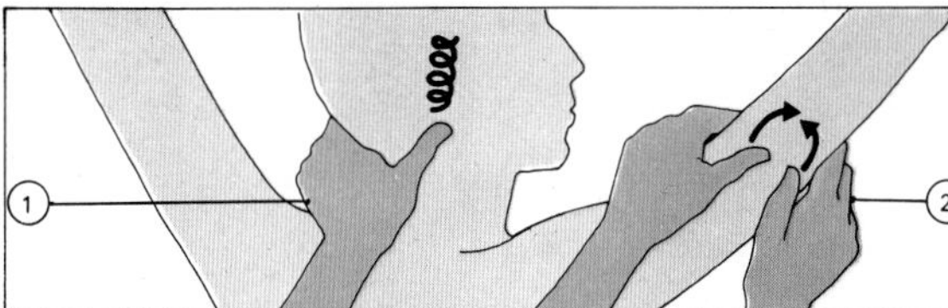

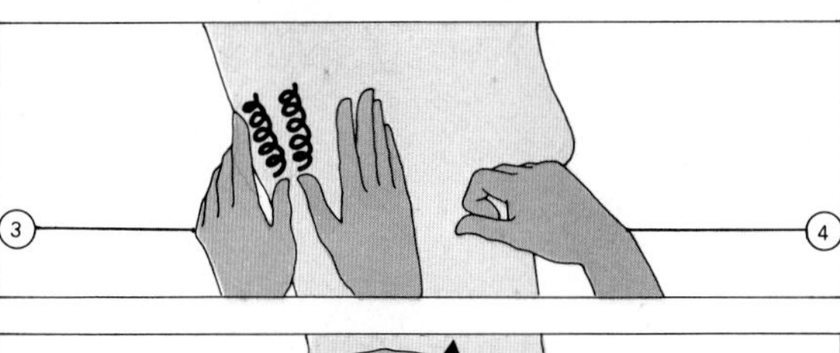

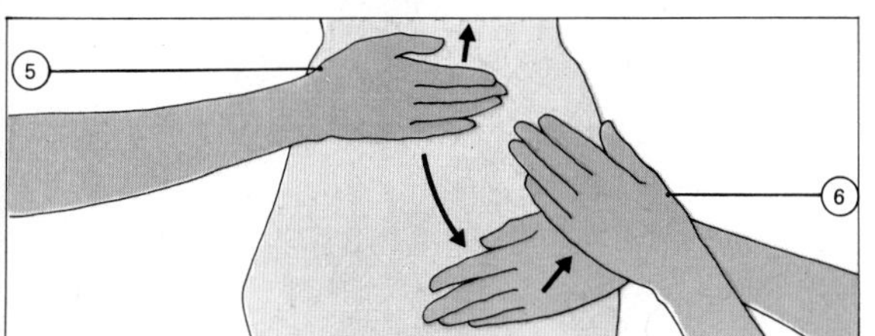

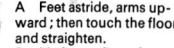

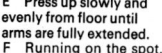

5 Massage, the manipulation of body tissues, is an ancient fitness method that can be physically and psychologically therapeutic. Among the methods used are friction (circular movements) [1, 3]; petrissage (kneeding) [2]; tapotement (tapping) [4, 6]; and effleurage (stroking) [5].

6 In a sauna bath stones are heated on top of a stove to produce a dry heat of 175°–230°F (80°–110°C). Cold water thrown on stones results in steam making the bath feel hotter, although in fact it is not. There is a 50°F (10°C) difference between the floor and the ceiling. The Finns use bundles of twigs to tone up the skin. A cold plunge follows.

Reproduction

Sex in humans has two attributes that are sometime separate and sometimes linked. One is strictly physiological—the creation of a new human being. The other is emotional—the expression of the affection, love, or passion of two people. Few cultures have sought to create children without, at least, affection; many cultures have sought to express love without creating children as a necessary consequence.

The male and female reproductive systems
Reproduction is possible only if a female germ cell (the egg, or ovum) is fertilized by a male germ cell (the spermatazoon). The reproductive system of the human female is designed for the monthly production of these eggs by the ovaries and for the accommodation and nurturing in the uterus of the growing fetus for the nine months until birth. The male system is designed to produce spermatozoa and transfer them to the female reporoductive tract [Key], where they can come into contact with an ovum.

The female external genitals are known collectively as the vulva. At their front limit is the mons veneris or mons pubis, a fatty mound over the pubic bone. Running down from the mons veneris are two folds of skin, the labia majora, which surround two smaller folds, the labia minora. In a cleft between the labia majora is the clitoris, a small organ that is an important source of sexual arousal and corresponds to the penis..

The vaginal opening which lies within the labia is partially or entirely sealed off in virgins by the hymen, a thin membrane that is usually torn at first intercourse, though it can be ruptured earlier by strenuous exercise or injury.

The vagina [2] is a muscular tube some 4in(10cm) long into which the penis is inserted during intercourse. It is here that the sperm-containing semen is deposited at ejaculation. The sperm then pass through a narrow neck, the cervix, into the pear-shaped, 3in(8cm) long uterus, before entering the two fallopian tubes, which are about 4in (10cm) long and connect the uterus with the two walnut-sized ovaries. About every 28 days the ovaries shed a mature egg, which enters a fallopian tube and passes down into the uterus. The ovaries also produce the female sex hormones progesterone and estrogen [5].

Most of the male reproductive system [1] lies outside the body. The visible parts are the penis and the testes, which are suspended in the baglike scrotum. Normally the penis is limp or flaccid but it becomes erect in sexual excitement. Erection [3] occurs when the spongy tissue inside the penis, called the corpora cavernosa, becomes engorged with blood. Continuous production of sperm takes place within the numerous tiny coiled tubes of the two testes. These sperm are then stored in a long tube, the epididymis, which winds over the surface of each testis and ends in the vas deferens, which carries sperm to the ejaculatory duct. The seminal fluid that contains the sperm is produced by the seminal vesicles, the prostate gland, and Cowper's gland, which lie within the body.

Sperm, egg and fertilization
In a single emission of semen, about 250 million sperm may be released. Only a few

CONNECTIONS

See also
706 Birth control
462 Sex in the animal world
702 Pregnancy
414 The genetic code
416 Principles of heredity
728 Diseases of the uro-genital system
704 Giving birth
690 Glands and their hormones
792 Adolescence: sex and independence
790 Adolescence
794 Adulthood: marriage
542 The life of mammals
556 How mammals behave
816 Freedom and individuality

1

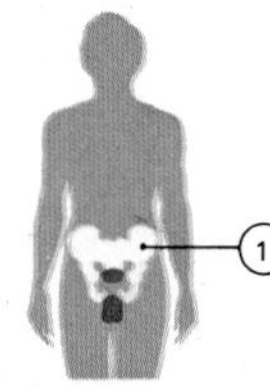

1

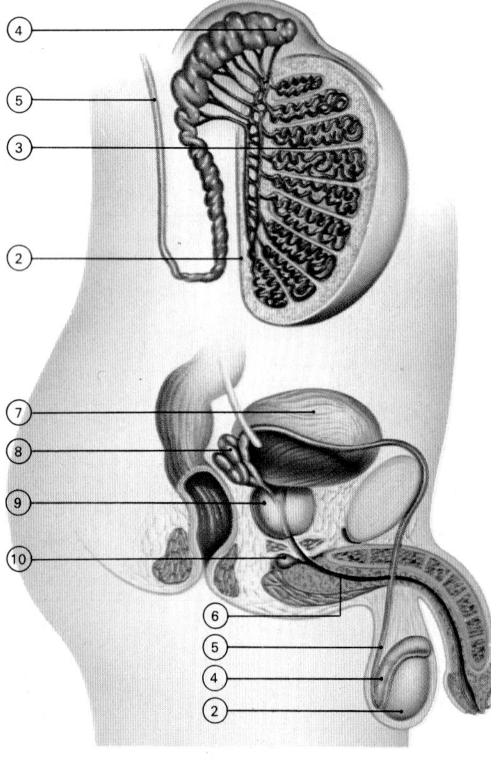

4
5
3
2
7
8
9
10
6
5
4
2

1 The male reproductive system is situated both inside and outside the pelvic region [1]. Outside the body are the testes [2], which every day produce millions of sperm in the convoluted seminiferous tubules [3]. The sperm, formed from the cells lining the outer wall, mature gradually and are pushed towards the center by newly formed cells. They are stored in the epididymis [4]. During coitus, these pass along the vas deferens [5] to the urethra [6], which also carries urine from the bladder [7]. The seminal vesicles [8], prostate [9], and Cowper's glands [10] all secrete fluids into the urethra, producing the semen.

2

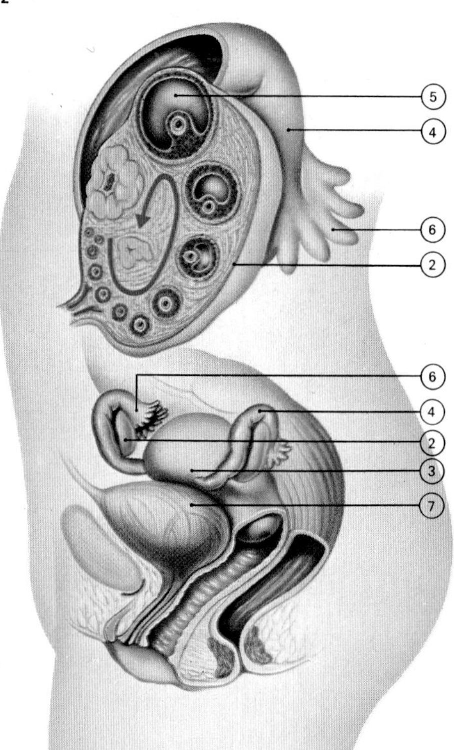

5
4
6
2
6
4
2
3
7
1

2. The female reproductive organs lie within the pelvic cavity [1]. The ovaries [2] usually release just one mature egg each month, which is then transferred to the uterus [3] via one of the fallopian tubes [4]. In the ovaries of the newly born girl are embedded several hundred thousand of the follicles that can potentially develop into eggs [5]. Only a few hundred of them will do so and, when mature, will erupt from the ovary's surface and be caught by the fimbria [6] at the end of the tubes, near the site where fertilization usually occurs. The woman's urinary system [7], unlike the male's, is separate from the genitals.

3

3 Just before orgasm, the penis, exudes drops of seminal fluid that may contain viable sperm, which is why withdrawal is often ineffective as a contraceptive method. At orgasm, muscular contractions occur at the base of the penis and bring about ejaculation.

Erectile tissue
Vas deferens
Prostate
Seminal vesicle
Epididymis
Testis

4 The female genitalia change greatly during arousal and intercourse. The normal state [A] is shown as are changes in the labia, clitoris (arrow), and vaginal opening [B] associated with coitus. Orgasm may cause contractions of the uterus.

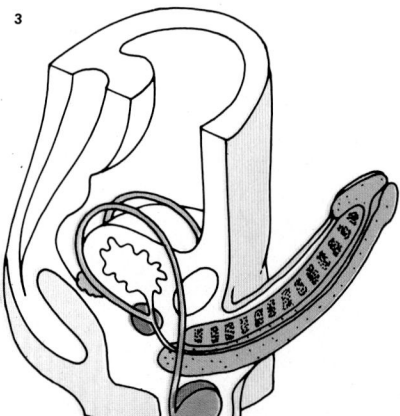

Labia majora
Labia minora
Vagina
Uterus
Clitoris

4A

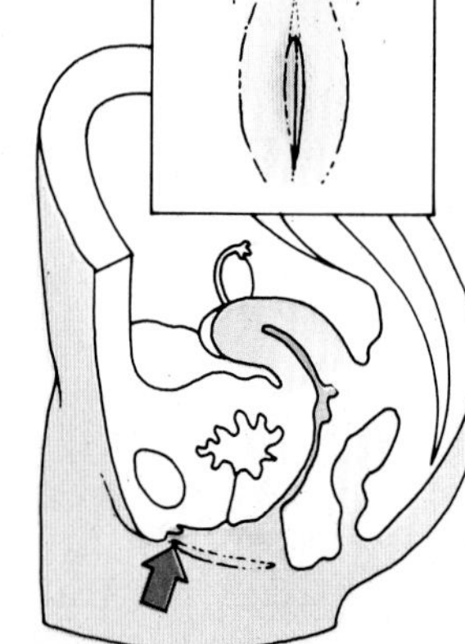

B

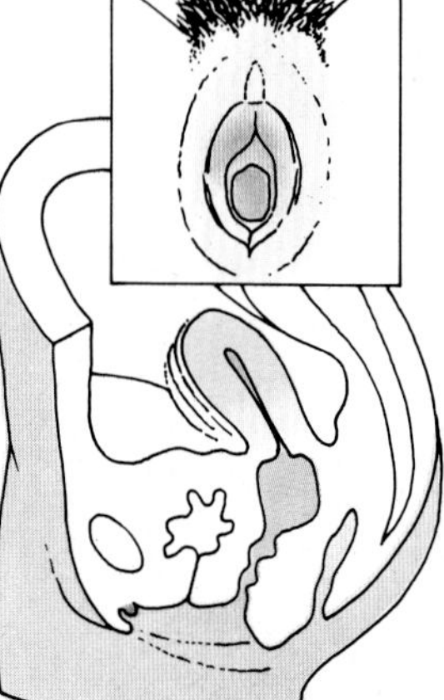

hundred of these minute tadpolelike cells, with flattened heads and long tails, will actually reach the egg high up in the fallopian tube, and only a single sperm will be able to enter the egg [6]. After penetrating the membrane of the ovum the sperm loses its tail and middle section as it enters the egg's protoplasm. The head swells in size and now becomes the male pronucleus. The nucleus of the ovum undergoes similar changes, and then both pronuclei fuse, completing fertilization. The zygote now begins to divide into a number of cells, at the same time moving down the fallopian tube to the uterus. This journey takes about a week to complete, by which time the fertilized ovum has developed into a ball of 32 or 64 cells. The ball fills with fluid and the cells lie on the surface. It is at this stage of development that the young embryo, called the blastocyst, attaches itself to the lining of the uterus. When an egg is not fertilized, it is this uterine lining that is shed during menstruation.

The monthly shedding of the egg by the female occurs between the ages of puberty, at about 12 years, and menopause, in the late 40s—a total lifetime production of perhaps only 500 eggs.

Physiological changes during coitus

Only in recent years have the physiological changes that occur during coitus been scientifically studied. The initial excitement phase is caused by sexual fantasies, stimulation of the senses, and close body contact. In sexual arousal the penis becomes erect and the vagina moist and distended [4]. During the following plateau phase, tension and excitement mount; if stimulation continues and is not deliberately controlled, orgasm results. Tension then subsides and the resolution phase occurs.

Infertility, the inability to conceive, is variously caused. In about 40 per cent of cases it is the result of inefficient sperm production (too few or too sluggish) by the male. In women it is caused by hormonal deficiencies or physical obstruction. Often, childless couples are subfertile and surgical or hormonal treatment (fertility drugs for the female) can change the situation.

KEY

The male and female genitalia, here in coitus, are shown with the ovary [1], uterus [2], cervix [3], penis [4], testis [5], vas deferens [6], seminal vesicles [7], and prostate gland [8].

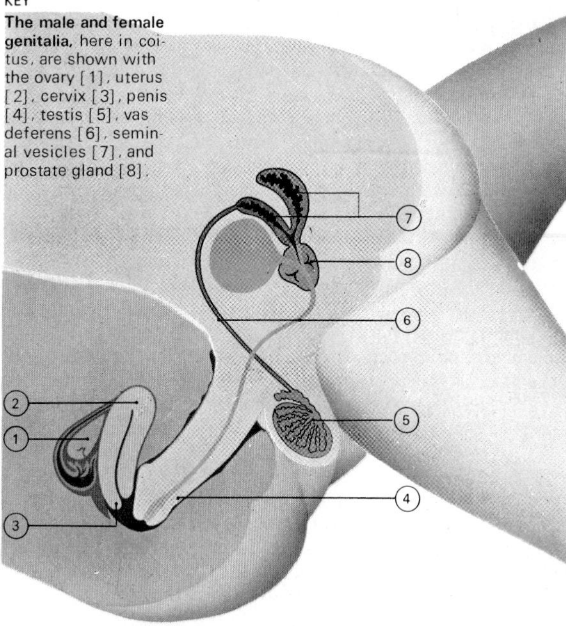

5 The menstrual cycle lasts on average 28 days and occurs regularly from puberty to the menopause. A ripened follicle in an ovary bursts open, releasing a single, minute egg. Empty, the follicle now turns into a corpus luteum (yellow body) which secretes the hormone progesterone, under the influence of LH (luteinizing hormone) produced by the pituitary gland. The hormones work together in the bloodstream to build up the endometrium, or uterine lining. If the egg is fertilized a rich bed is ready for it. If not, during the next 14 days, the corpus luteum withers, ceasing hormone production. The uterine lining then breaks down, causing the menstrual flow of blood to pass through the vagina. A new cycle of some 28 days has now begun. FSH (follicle stimulating hormone) promotes new follicle development.

5
Fallopian tube
Cilia
Follicles
Blastocyst
Muscular layer
Uterus
Fallopian tube
Cilia
Mature follicle
Developing follicle
Endometrium
Fimbria
Cervix
Ovary
Fimbria
Ovary
Vagina

6 Fertilization usually occurs high in the fallopian tube. Many spermatozoa reach the ovum, but only one will fuse with the egg to form the zygote [1]. Cell division begins, the ovum continuing to subdivide [2-4] into two, then four and so on, until a whole ball of cells is formed known as the morula [5]. A fluid-filled cavity develops within the structure, now termed a blastocyst [6]. One week after fertilization, it reaches the uterus and enters the lining [7]. An amniotic cavity [8] develops, and the ball of cells splits to become the two-layered disk [9] which will form the actual embryo. Some six days later, the bottom layer of this germ disk grows to form the yolk sac [10]. Outer cells form the placenta [11]. The cavity grows until joined to the outer layer by the body stalk only [12], which will be the umbilical cord.

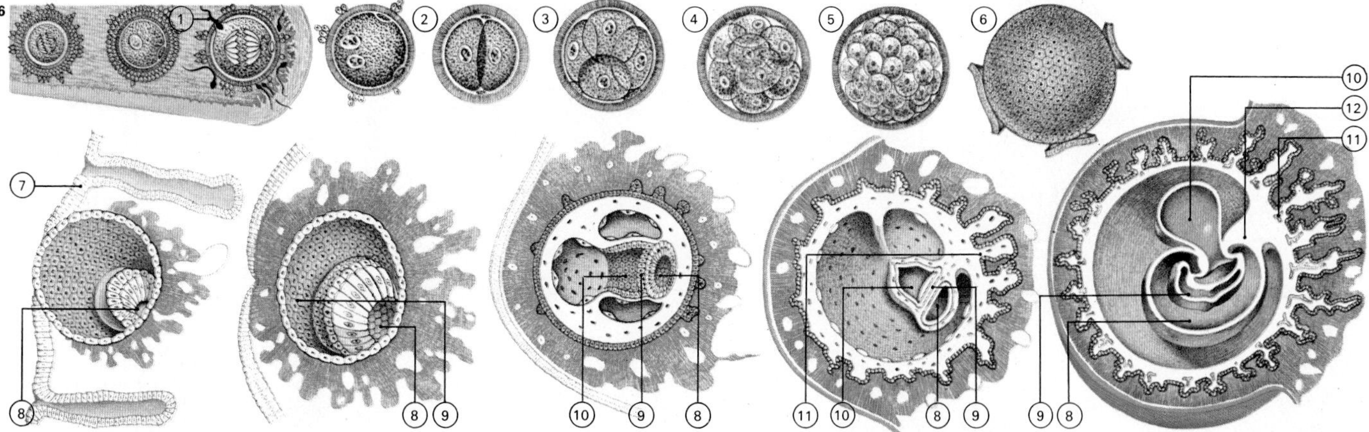

Pregnancy

Pregnancy is the nine-month period during which a single cell is transformed into a human being. A missed menstrual period is usually considered the first sign of pregnancy, but there could be other reasons for a break in the cycle—emotional factors, ill health, or the approach of the menopause. Some other early signs of pregnancy include breast tenderness, morning sickness, nausea, vomiting, fatigue, and sleepiness. Reliable diagnostic tests of pregnancy are carried out on a sample of urine. A pregnant woman's urine contains a special hormone, chorionic gonadotropin (CG). When CG-containing urine is injected in certain laboratory animals, it produces specific effects that would not otherwise occur, thus confirming a pregnancy diagnosis.

Early stages

After confirmation of the pregnancy, it is then relatively straightforward to calculate the approximate date of birth. It is usually done by counting back three months from the first day of the last period and then adding seven days.

Even at this early stage the expectant mother is generally advised to go to her doctor or clinic for examination. A careful medical history will be taken, height and weight measured, blood and urine analyses done, and a physical examination given. A vaginal examination is also usually done to detect any abnormalities. Advice on diet, exercise, and other aspects of prenatal care is given, and regular medical appointments arranged.

Blood tests will be taken at regular intervals. The mother's blood group must be noted in case, at any later stage, a transfusion becomes necessary. They will also identify whether the mother is anemic and, further, whether she is Rh positive or Rh negative. Most people have an Rh (Rhesus) factor in their blood and are therefore termed Rh positive. But some do not. They are the Rh negative group. Special care is needed in the case of an Rh negative woman having a child by an Rh positive man. If the baby's grouping turns out to be Rh positive, then any of the baby's blood that chances to enter the mother's circulation through the placenta will cause production of antibodies. In themselves the antibodies do no harm, but during a subsequent pregnancy these antibodies may get into an Rh positive baby's circulation, causing anemia and jaundice. Potential danger can be avoided by giving an affected child transfusions at birth (or, in extreme cases, while still in the uterus) or by giving the mother a special injection to prevent these antibodies.

Physical changes

During the 40 weeks of pregnancy there is an increase in the breast size because of hormone activity and increased blood supply in preparation for feeding [4]. Some women will also notice an increase in pigmentation of the skin, and a darkening of the area around the nipples will usually begin in about the 14th week, though it may be earlier in dark-skinned women. Morning sickness is another fairly common symptom of pregnancy. Nausea of this kind may be the result of hormonal changes, deficiency of vitamin B, a sudden drop in blood pressure on getting up in the morning, or pressure of

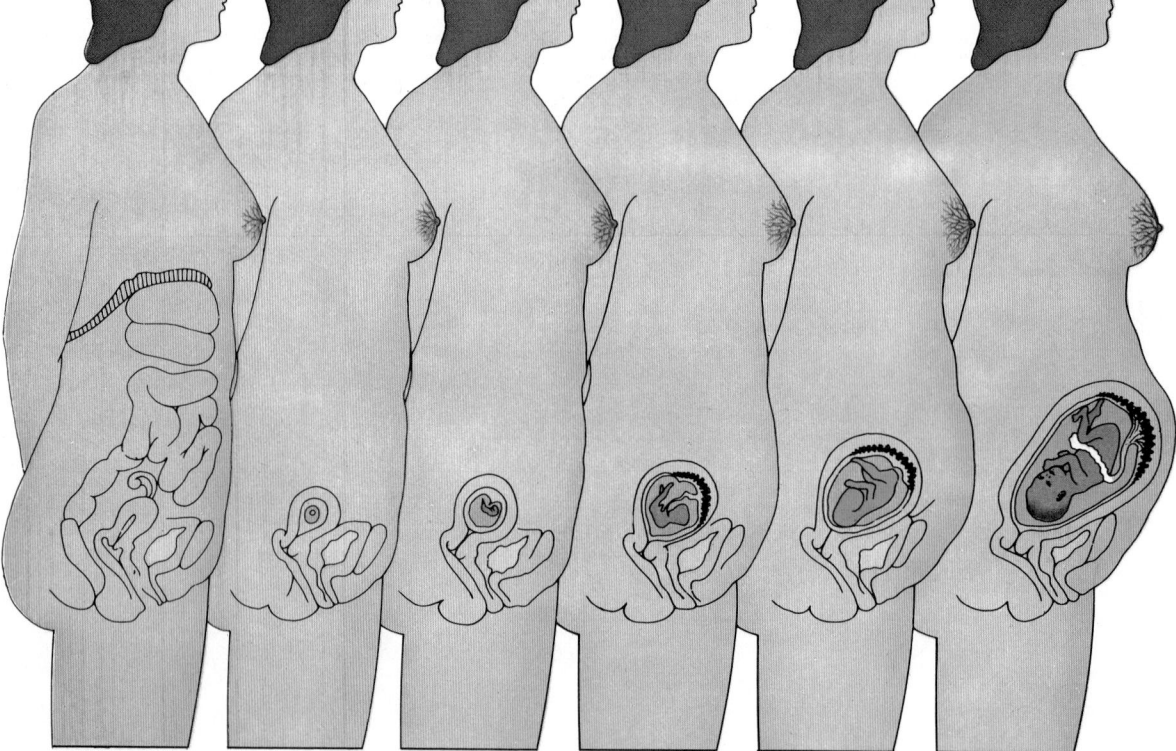

CONNECTIONS

See also
704 Giving birth
700 Reproduction
690 Glands and their hormones
776 Human development
736 Community medicine
808 Questions of life and death
728 Diseases of the urogenital system

1

Missed period
4 weeks
6 weeks
10 weeks
14 weeks
18 weeks

1 After fertilization, the menstrual cycle is normally suppressed because the embryo prevents the uterine lining being shed; at 6 weeks, a tiny newformed embryo is recognizable within the amniotic sac protecting it. The head is forming, as are the brain, chest, and spine, and minute depressions now appear where ears and eyes will develop. By 8–10 weeks, main internal organs are formed, limbs are distinguishable, and the fetus is 1.5in(4cm) long. Facial contours and external genitals soon appear and a fine down (lanugo) will soon cover the fetus. Growth is now rapid; by 22 weeks, strong movement can be felt within the uterus. At 28 weeks, the baby is covered with vernix, a protective greasy matter. Fully formed by 36–38 weeks, the baby's head will engage, descending into the pelvis in readiness for birth, after about 40 weeks.

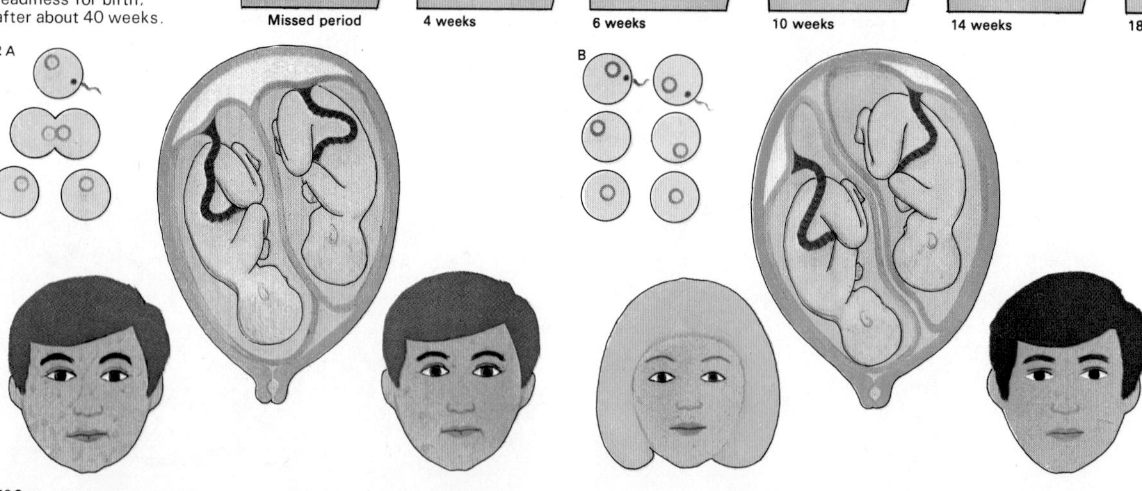

2 A
B

2 Twin births occur approximately once in every 90 deliveries. Identical twins [A] are always the same sex and develop from one egg that splits into two after fertilization, each fetus sharing the same placenta but with its own amniotic sac. Fraternal twins [B] need not be of the same sex; they are only as alike as any two children from one family. They develop as a result of fertilization of two separate eggs by different spermatozoa.

the enlarged uterus. It rarely lasts for more than three months.

Weight will increase, but the general aim should be to gain no more than 18–20lb (8–9kg) throughout pregnancy. Backache is a common complaint in the later stages, but can be prevented by correct posture and well-fitting shoes. The increased urge to urinate is caused by the enlarged uterus pressing on the bladder, and a tendency to constipation may be the result of pressure on the bowels; this can be avoided if plenty of fresh fruit and vegetables are eaten.

Toxemia of pregnancy is an extremely serious condition with symptoms of speedy weight gain, swelling of the hands, feet, and face and an increase in blood pressure. Treatment involves rest, reduction in salt intake, and perhaps the taking of drugs to remove excess fluid and ease the swelling.

A healthy pregnancy

A wholesome diet is vital because the fetus derives all its nourishment from the mother; but there is certainly no need for the mother to "eat for two." She does need a great deal of iron, as the fetus will take a large amount from her system to form its own red blood cells. Providing excess fatigue is avoided, a normal amount of exercise is perfectly safe. Smoking affects the blood supply to the uterus reducing oxygen supply to the fetus. Thus women who smoke more than ten cigarettes a day may retard the normal growth of their fetuses. Drugs should never be taken except under medical supervision.

Rubella (German measles) is known to be potentially dangerous to the fetus if contracted by the mother in her first 12 weeks of pregnancy: it may affect the baby's heart, sight, and hearing. If rubella is contracted after 12 weeks, there is no real risk as the heart, ears, and eyes are already developed.

Earliest fetal movements (quickening) will generally be felt at about 18–20 weeks, reaching their most vigorous at 30 weeks. As early as the seventh week, fetal heartbeats can be distinguished by ultrasonics. Usually at about the 30th week the baby turns so that its head is then down. Normally, after 40 weeks the birth of the child is imminent.

KEY

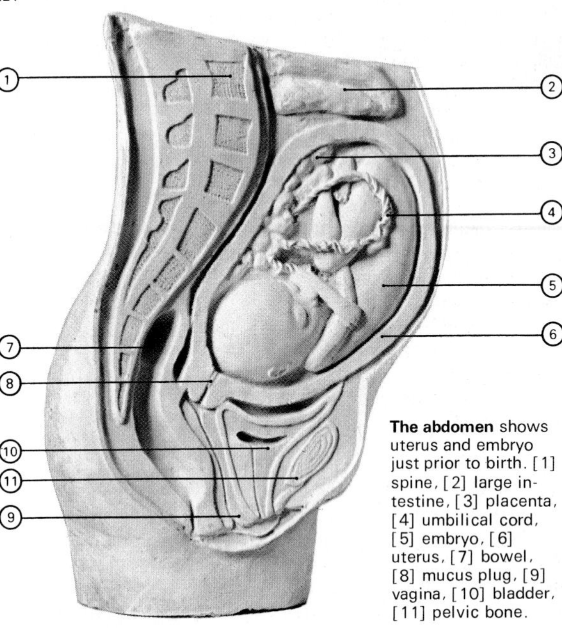
1
2
3
4
5
6
7
8
10
11
9

The abdomen shows uterus and embryo just prior to birth. [1] spine, [2] large intestine, [3] placenta, [4] umbilical cord, [5] embryo, [6] uterus, [7] bowel, [8] mucus plug, [9] vagina, [10] bladder, [11] pelvic bone.

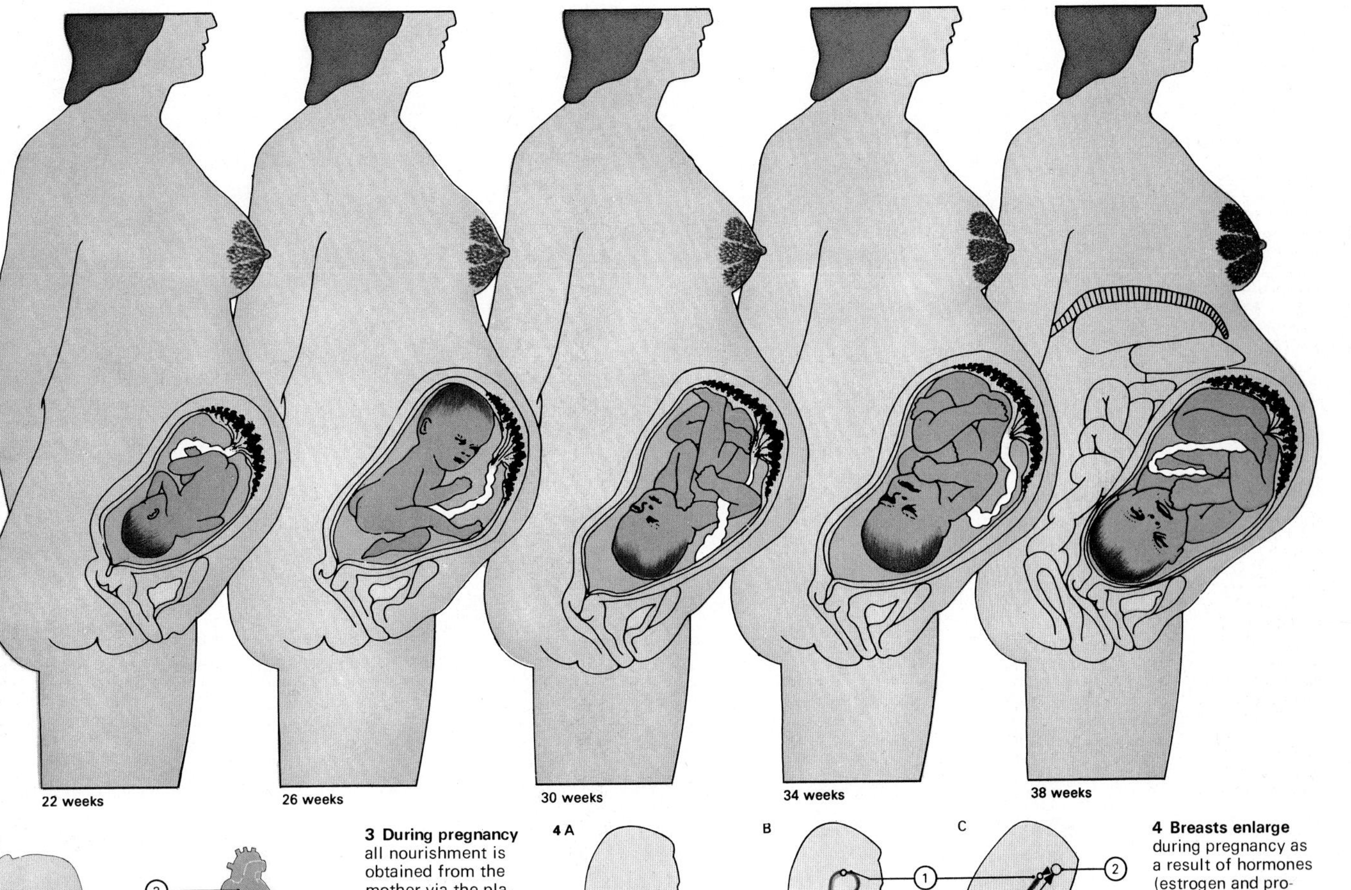

22 weeks | 26 weeks | 30 weeks | 34 weeks | 38 weeks

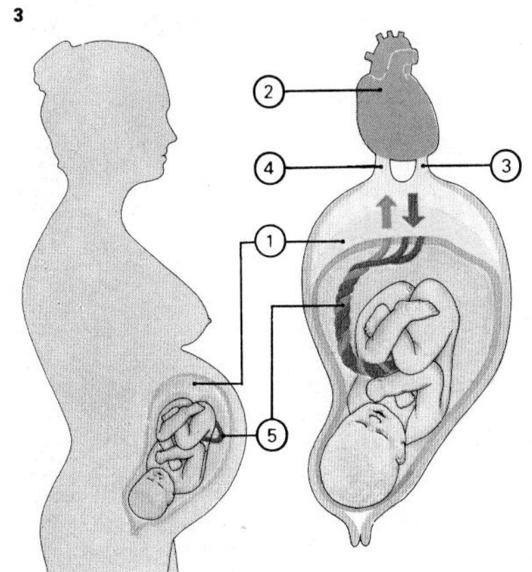
3
2
4
3
1
5

3 During pregnancy all nourishment is obtained from the mother via the placenta [1]. Nutrients are carried in blood pumped by the heart [2] into the placenta via the uterine arteries [3]. Food and oxygen [red] pass continuously from the maternal blood [pale yellow] to the fetal blood [green]. Waste products [blue] pass in the reverse direction entering the mother's bloodstream via the uterine veins [4]. The umbilical cord [5] carries blood.

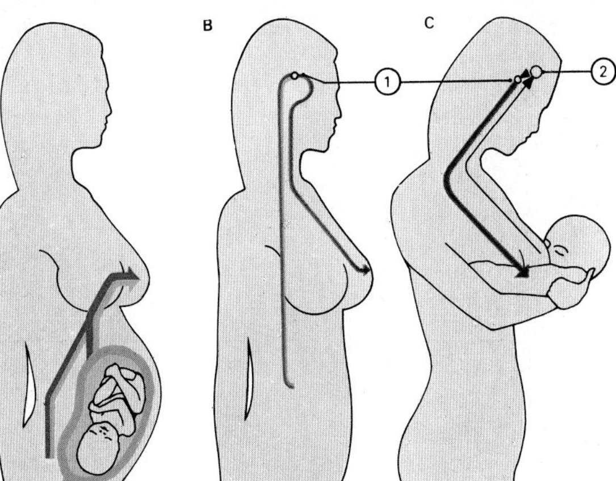
4 A
B
C
1
2

4 Breasts enlarge during pregnancy as a result of hormones (estrogen and progesterone) from the placenta and ovaries [A]. After birth [B] loss of the placenta causes withdrawal of both hormones. Prolactin is then released by the pituitary [1] to stimulate milk production. Oxytocin, which promotes secretion of milk, is also released as the result of suckling [C]. Emotional factors, acting via the hypothalamus [2], are also important.

Giving birth

Birth, or parturition, marks the beginning of a new life in the outside world. It is achieved, at the end of the mother's pregnancy, through a sequence known as labor.

There are various signs that indicate that labor is imminent or already under way. Regular contractions of the uterus, gradually increasing in frequency and strength, are the most common signal. These contractions are definitely rhythmic and cause discomfort, so a mother will usually have no difficulty in distinguishing between the contractions heralding labor and other uterine action commonly experienced during pregnancy, which causes no discomfort, occurs spasmodically, and is thought to be important to growth in the uterus.

Three stages of labor

The birth process is a sequence of three stages. During the first stage [1, 2] the uterus begins to contract vigorously. First the cervix (the neck of the uterus) contracts, and then the vagina dilates. This stage can continue for two to 20 hours, but toward the end of it there is a short transitional period during which the amniotic sac that surrounds the fetus is ruptured. The fluid protecting the fetus then drains away, if it has not already done so—the so-called "breaking of the waters." A feeling of nausea, even slight vomiting, may occur.

The second stage of labor may last from just a few minutes to two hours. Contractions are commonly experienced every one or two minutes and last for about 60 seconds. During these the mother has to push as the baby's head descends through the cervix into the markedly enlarged vaginal passage [3]. This is the actual stage of delivery. In a straightforward birth the head emerges first [4] and is moved so that the baby faces a direction in which the shoulders can emerge more easily [5]. Generally, the rest of the body then slips out quite readily. The baby is held upside down for a short time by the obstetrician or midwife so that any mucus or liquid can drain from the mouth and upper respiratory tract. The baby then takes a first breath of air, no longer reliant on the mother for oxygen, and gives a first cry [Key]. Meanwhile, the umbilical cord will have been clamped in two places near to the baby's body before being cut quite painlessly [8]. Once the mouth and nasal passages are cleared, the baby should breathe normally and skin should change from a bluish tone to pink-red.

The third and final stage, which begins about 15 minutes after the baby has been born, involves the painless expulsion of the placenta (afterbirth) and the remains of the umbilical cord [6]. The placenta is carefully examined to make sure that it is complete. If parts are left inside the mother's body a hemorrhage may result. An intramuscular injection is given to help the uterus contract and to prevent excess bleeding.

The period of six to eight weeks after birth is known as the puerperium, and during this time the mother's organs will return to normal. After delivery, a mother commonly feels elated; but a day or two later she may experience some depression, probably because of a temporary hormonal imbalance. This soon disappears. During the puerperium the uterus shrinks until it is only a little larger than before conception. Milk is

CONNECTIONS

See also
702 Pregnancy
700 Reproduction
752 Development of surgery
688 Heart and blood circulation
830 Types of ritual

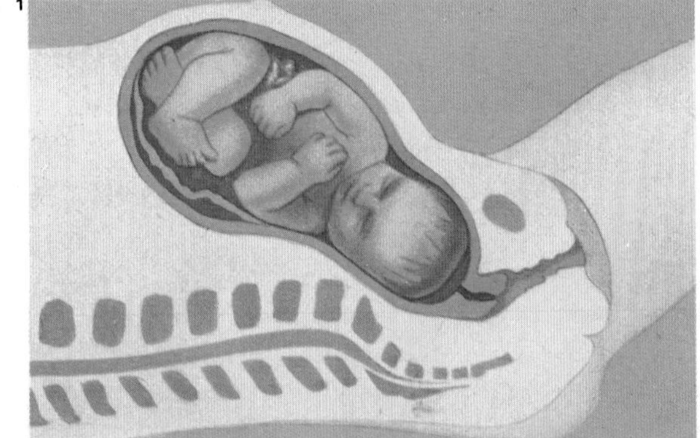

1 At full term the baby's head is engaged in the bowl of the pelvis ready for the journey through the birth canal. In this first stage of labor there may be 5 to 30 minutes between contractions.

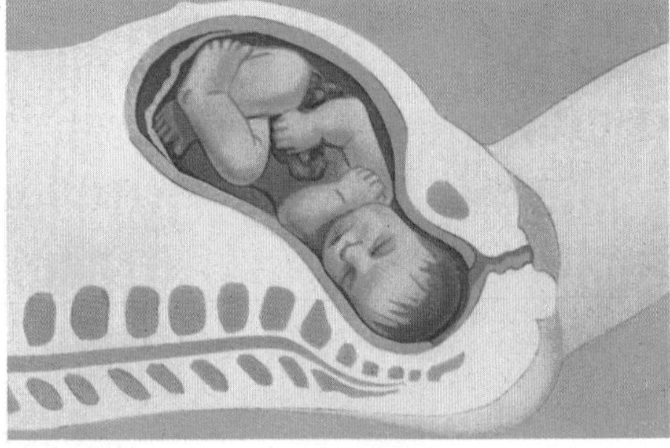

2 Uterine contractions continue to force the baby along, and the head will normally turn sideways, enabling it to pass through the pelvis. Meanwhile, contractions are more frequent.

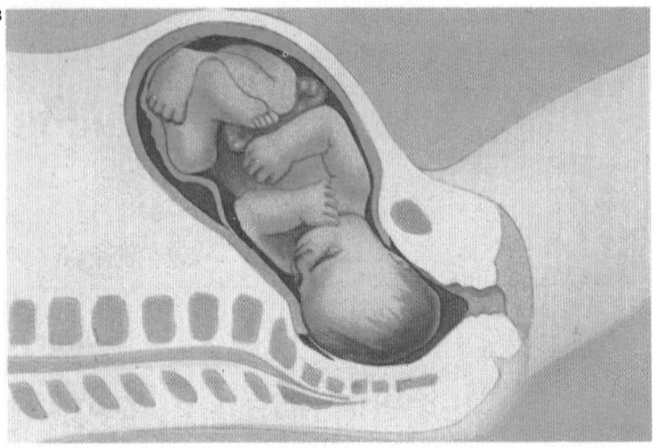

3 The cervix and vagina have now dilated so that they can receive the baby's head as it passes through the pelvis. The mother, "bearing down" with each contraction, helps the baby along.

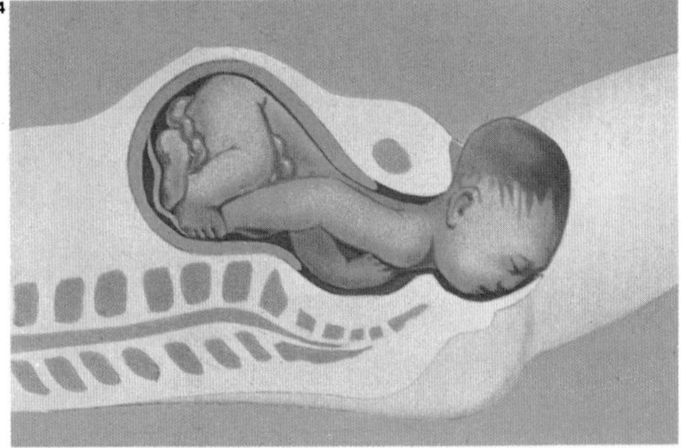

4 The baby's head is now "crowned" and can be seen by the obstetrician or midwife. Once the head has emerged the shoulders are turned to facilitate birth. Contractions continue.

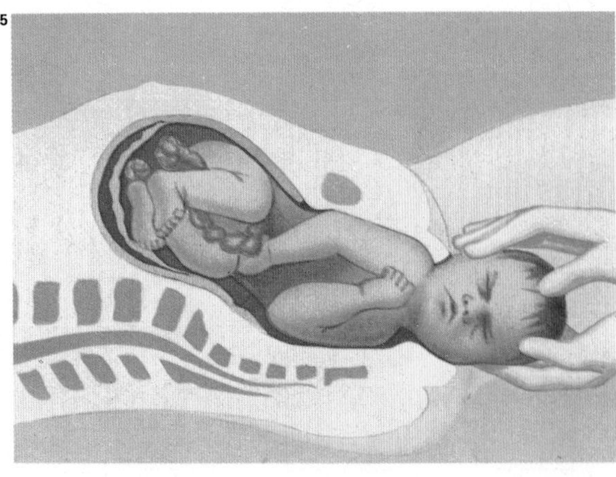

5 The obstetrician or midwife will normally assist with the birth of head and shoulders, after which the body slips out fairly easily. Forceps are sometimes used to help during the delivery.

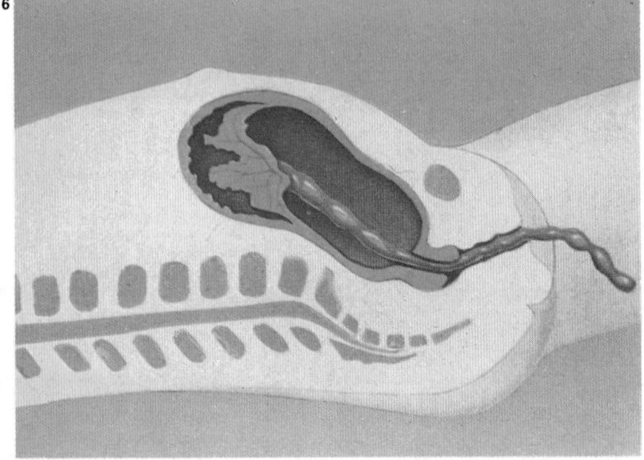

6 In the third stage of labor both the placenta and remains of the umbilical cord are expelled. An injection is normally given to the mother to stem blood loss and to contract the uterus, which returns to normal size after six weeks.

ecreted from the mother's breasts about wo days after birth and continued stimula-ion of the breasts through feeding helps the terus return to its normal proportions.

'ain and labor

Most women experience some degree of ain during childbirth but in a happy and ealthy mother this is overshadowed by eelings of excitement and joy at the birth of er baby. During labor, however, most vomen need some form of pain relief. One ecently developed technique is that of pidural anesthesia [10]. A local anesthetic reezes the nerves to the uterus while the nother remains conscious. Thus she is able o witness the birth and help in the process.

Inhalation anesthesia is also sometimes provided for relief of pain both late in the first stage of labor and throughout the second stage, as required. Analgesic drugs are commonly given by intramuscular injection. These usually reduce discomfort effectively, but care is always taken not to give the drug too late in labor, as it might affect the baby's breathing after birth.

Hypnosis and natural childbirth dispense with drugs and anesthesia, for it is claimed that if the mother is totally relaxed and free of tension she will feel little pain. Hypnosis achieves this through "suggestion;" natural childbirth by encouraging the mother during pregnancy not to be afraid of the birth process and to use special breathing techniques to relieve pain and relax muscles.

Problems at birth

Difficult births are rare, but if the baby is born feet or buttocks first (a breech position) [9], if the mother's pelvis is very small, or if the baby has to be delivered quickly to prevent suffocation, certain medical procedures are carried out. Labor is often induced artificially if there are special reasons for doing so in the interest of the mother or her baby. Forceps—the large surgical tongs—may be used to help the baby out or an incision made in the vagina to ease the pressure on the baby's head. If a normal birth is impossible, a Caesarean operation [11] is performed.

KEY

The baby's body emerges after the head and shoulders,

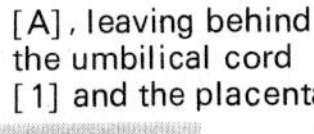

[A], leaving behind the umbilical cord [1] and the placenta

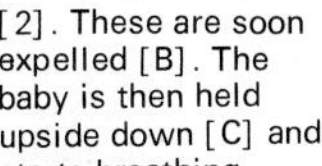

[2]. These are soon expelled [B]. The baby is then held upside down [C] and starts breathing.

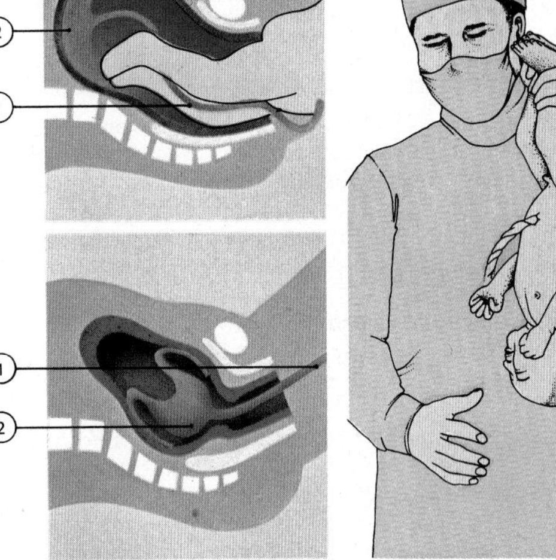
A
2
1
B
1
2
C

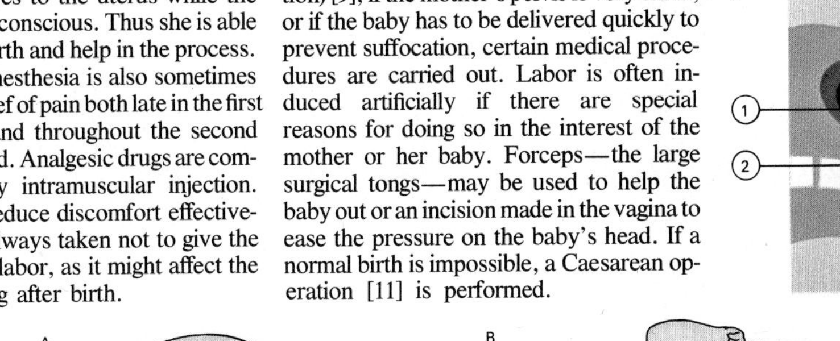
7
A
B

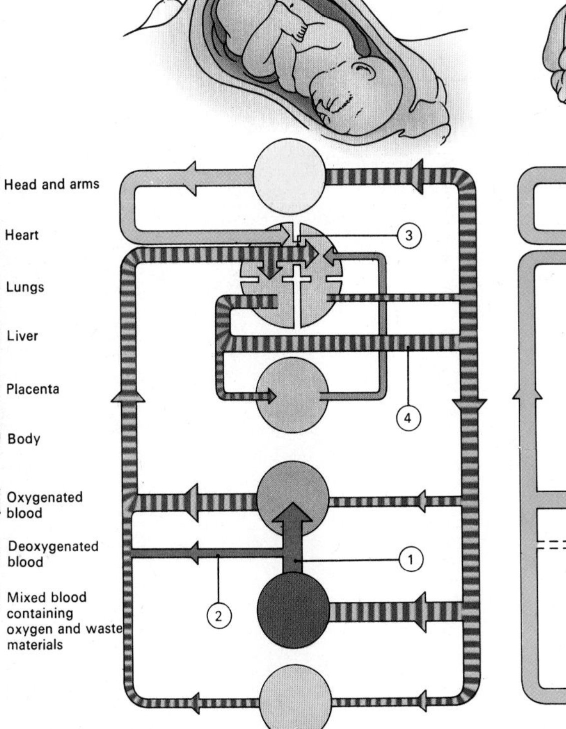
Head and arms
Heart
Lungs
Liver
Placenta
Body
Oxygenated blood
Deoxygenated blood
Mixed blood containing oxygen and waste materials
3
4
1
2

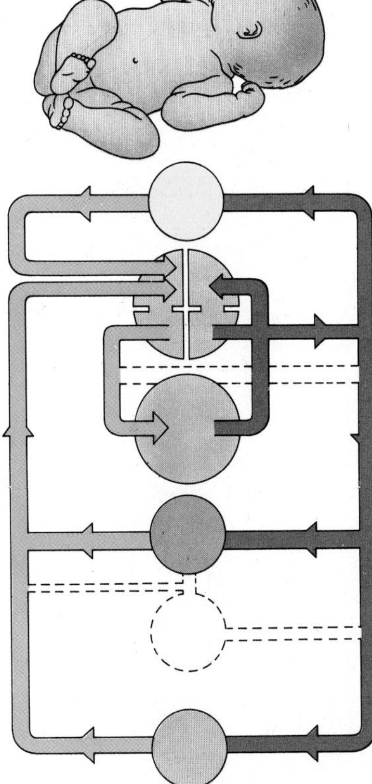

7 Supply of oxygen to the fetus takes place via the placenta, with blood circulation functioning as in [A]. Highly oxygenated blood reaches the fetus via the umbilical vein [1], most passing through the liver, head and extremities. A small amount of blood bypasses the liver through the ductus venosus [2] which closes after birth. In the heart most blood passes through the foramen ovale [3], a movable flap also closing at birth. Blood reaching the right ventricle is also diverted [4] away from the nonfunctioning lung. Once the umbilical cord is cut the baby's own lungs take on the task of oxygenation of blood with changes as shown in [B]. A rise in carbon dioxide concentration stimulates the brain's respiratory center; the newborn baby cries as he takes his first breath.

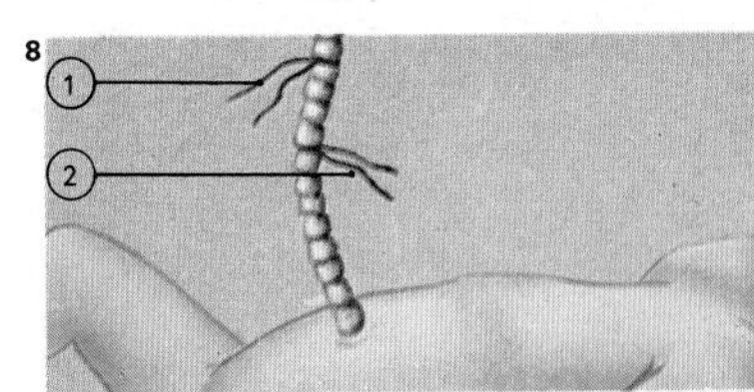
8
1
2

8 The umbilical cord must be cut following delivery, all the mucus having first been removed from the baby's mouth and nose. With the baby lying down, two clamps or knots [1,2] will be placed 6 in and 9 in(15 cm and 23 cm) from the baby so that the cord can be cut between these two points. The baby, now separated from the placenta, is totally on his own.

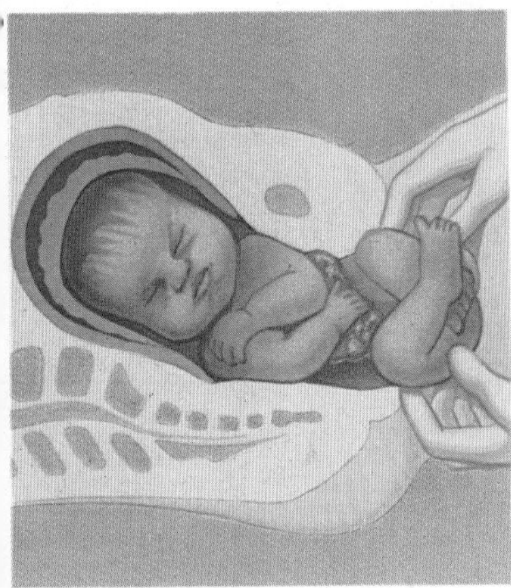

9 A breech baby is one born with feet or buttocks first. Between the 30th and 34th week of pregnancy the baby usually turns so there will be a head presentation. But roughly 1 in every 30 babies fails to do so and remains with the head still lying in the upper part of the uterus. Breech births are not usually difficult, but occasionally the obstetrician will turn the baby in order to avoid any damage to the baby's arms or to the umbilical cord.

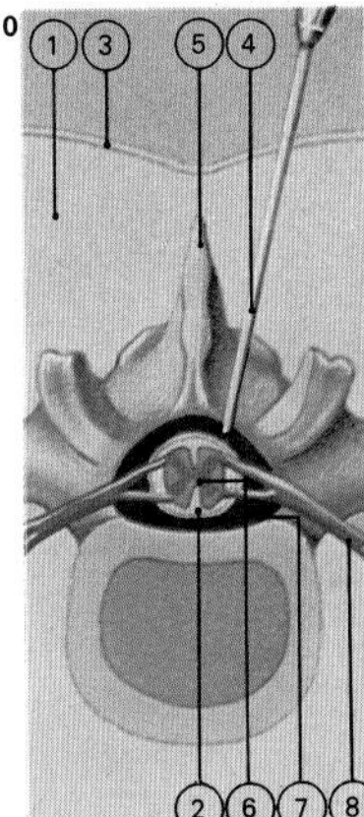
10
1
3
5
4
2
6
7
8

10 Epidural anesthesia provides a painfree labor. A drug is injected through back skin [3] and muscles [1], between vertebrae [5], to epidural space [4] surrounding spinal cord [6], freezing nerves [8] to the uterus.

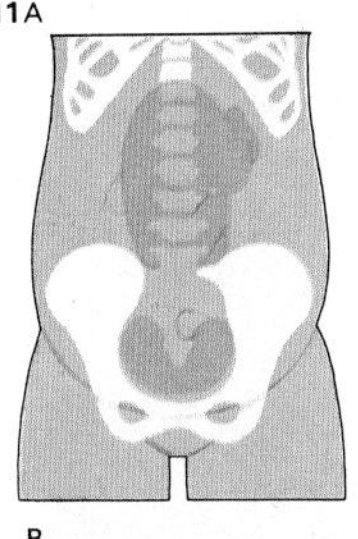
11A

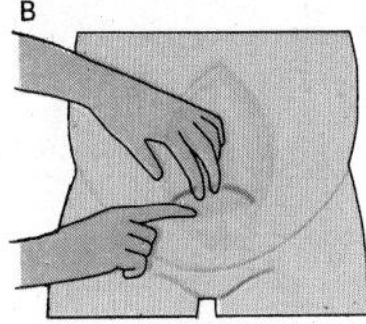
B

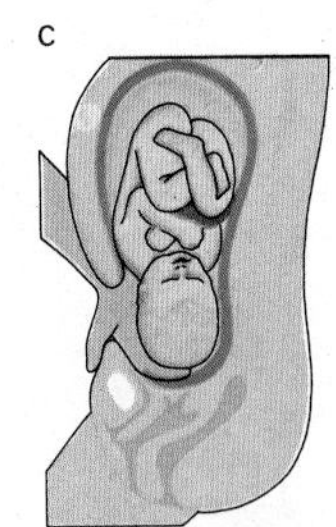
C

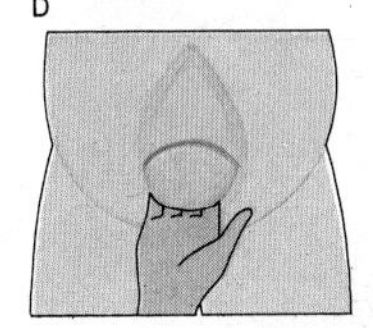
D

11 In the Caesarean section the baby is usually in a normal position [A]. A transverse cut is made in the abdomen [B]. The surgeon places his hand in the uterus [C], easing out the baby [D].

Birth control

All human societies have faced the problem of balancing the need for more hands with the difficulty of feeding more mouths. And most have tried to regulate fertility for personal or economic reasons. Before scientific knowledge of birth control, a wide range of methods was used either to prevent conception or to limit intercourse by ritual taboos.

Development of birth control

In simple societies early methods were often based on sheer superstition. To ward off unwanted pregnancies women wore "magic" amulets made from the tooth of a child, for example, or the testicle of a weasel [3].

Other early methods of controlling conception reflected some knowledge of human biology, or at least close observation of cause and effect. Medical recipes for counteracting sperm date back to about 2000 BC. Vaginal douches of varying efficacy were used, as were simple versions of condoms to sheath the penis or diaphragms to block off the uterus. The "safe period" of women was recognized by a number of primitive peoples and for hundred of years men practiced the oldest method of all, coitus interruptus (removal of the penis before ejaculation).

Opposition to "artificial" methods of birth control led to heated controversy during the nineteenth century when urban overcrowding and soaring birth rates brought the issue of birth control to the attention of social reformers [Key]. The courageous work of such women as Aletta Jacobs (1883–1966), Margaret Sanger (1883–1966), and Marie Stopes (1880–1958) brought gradual acceptance of family planning by women.

The advent of the "Pill"

It was not until the middle of the twentieth century that the emphasis switched from attempts to stop fertilization to methods of intervening in the production of fertile eggs and sperm. In 1955, an American team of biologists led by Gregory Pincus (1903–67) discovered that the hormones estrogen and progesterone, when taken orally, were highly effective in preventing ovulation [2]. By 1966 ten million women throughout the world were estimated to be taking the Pill; the number today may be 40 million.

The success rate of the Pill is such that women have been able to enjoy intercourse without the fear of unwanted pregnancy and without having to employ barrier methods. Although the Pill is generally safe, it does appear to be associated with an increased incidence of phlebitis, stroke, and embolism to the lungs. It is used with caution or not at all in women having high blood pressure, fibrocystic breast disease, or abnormalities of the heart, kidney, or liver, and in women over the age of 40. Since the estrogen compounds found in the Pill can have effects on the breasts and pelvic organs, women using the Pill require periodic medical examinations. Although evidence about the Pill's long-term effects is still limited, fears about loss of fertility seem unfounded. One study has shown that 60 percent of women formerly on the Pill became pregnant in their first cycle, while only 40 percent of other women conceived as quickly. Some women

CONNECTIONS

See also
700 Reproduction
808 Questions of life and death
734 World health
634 Destructive man
690 Glands and their hormones
556 How mammals behave

1 The main methods of birth control are vasectomy [A], the Pill [B], the intra uterine device [C], the diaphragm [D], the condom [E] and rhythm [F]. Coitus interruptus (withdrawal of penis before ejaculation) is practiced but is not reliable and often causes undue strain, both physical and emotional. Spermicidal creams, foaming tablets, and aerosol sprays are not very effective on their own. The douche—an attempt to wash out sperm from the vagina—is not effective. The belief that a woman could not conceive while breast-feeding is not true. Prostaglandins, hormonelike substances now under study, could theoretically be used to induce menstruation in a pregnant woman, but such a method of "birth control" could be seen as a form of abortion. Female sterilization (cutting and tying the Fallopian tubes) is effective but irreversible.

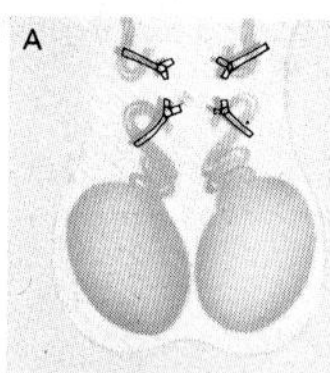

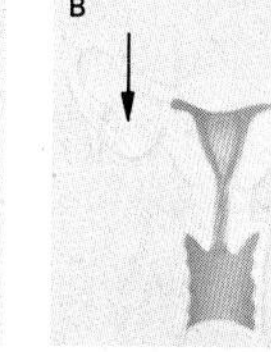

	A	B	C	D	E	F
How it works	Ducts taking sperm from testicles to penis are cut and tied in a minor operation. There is no effect on intercourse.	Taken every day for most or all of the monthly cycle, the Pill inhibits ovulation and may hinder penetration of the sperm into the cervix.	No one yet knows exactly how the IUD works. But it is thought to inhibit implantation of the fertilized egg in the uterine wall.	All types of diaphragms, inserted into the vagina and placed over the cervix, provide a barrier to sperm keeping them from the uterus.	The condom or 'rubber,' rolled on to the penis just before intercourse, provides a barrier to sperm, preventing them from reaching the vagina.	Basically, a couple refrain from intercourse when the woman is most likely to conceive (at least 10 days each month and probably longer).
Possible effects	If both partners want it, there are no psychological problems. Physically, the operation is not risky but there is no guarantee it can be reversed.	Weight gain, nausea, headache, and depression are some possible side effects that a change of pill often helps to alleviate.	Heavy periods do sometimes occur and removal of the IUD may be required. There may be risk of inflammatory pelvic disease.	Generally they are thought to be harmless—except in rare cases of an allergy to rubber or plastic, or sensitivity to a chemical used.	Condoms are harmless—unless the user or his partner is sensitive to rubber. Some couples also find condoms lessen sensation.	Some couples find that restricting intercourse in this way imposes severe strain and tension on their marital relationship.
How to use	A doctor or family planning clinic will advise on surgeons, who carry out this operation. It does not usually involve a stay in the hospital.	The right variety must be prescribed by a doctor or family planning clinic. Periodic check-ups are advisable on grounds of general health.	The IUD must be fitted by a gynecologist. Checkups will be advised. Many IUDs have threads enabling their position to be checked.	Diaphragms must be fitted either by a doctor of the family planning clinic. To be effective they must be used with a spermicidal cream.	Perhaps the most widely sold contraceptive available over the counter, it should only be put on when errection occurs.	Careful records of menstrual cycle and temperature are needed; unreliable if periods are irregular or when sickness alters temperature.
Success rates	Tests are carried out after a few months to check whether seminal fluid is sperm-free. The chance of conception thereafter is usually zero.	The risk of becoming pregnant is almost nil providing the Pill is taken exactly as directed by the physician. Failure rate is less than 1 per cent.	IUDs have been known to come out unnoticed and in some cases pregnancies have occurred. Failure rate is about 3 per cent.	Diaphragms, about as effective as the condom, are dependent on the care with which they are used. Failure rate is about 3 per cent.	Condoms needs care in use; are safest with a spermicide. Some condoms have been known to leak. Failure is about 3 per cent.	Timing cannot be guaranteed. The calendar method is risky, but temperature is more reliable. Failure rate is about 15 per cent.

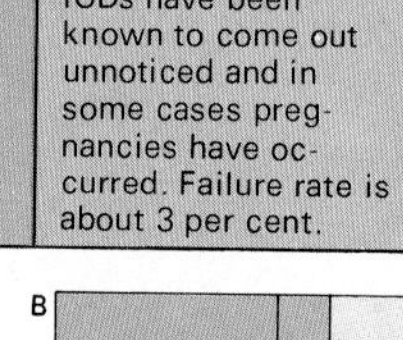

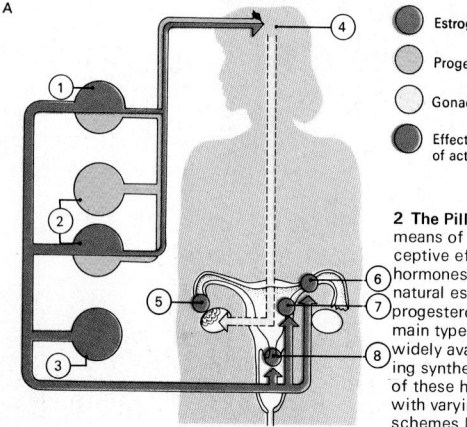

Estrogen
Progesterone
Gonadotrophins
Effective sites of action

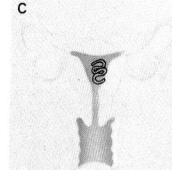

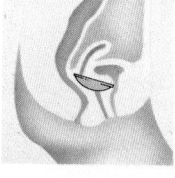

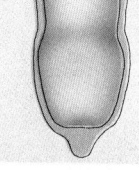

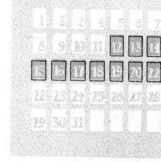

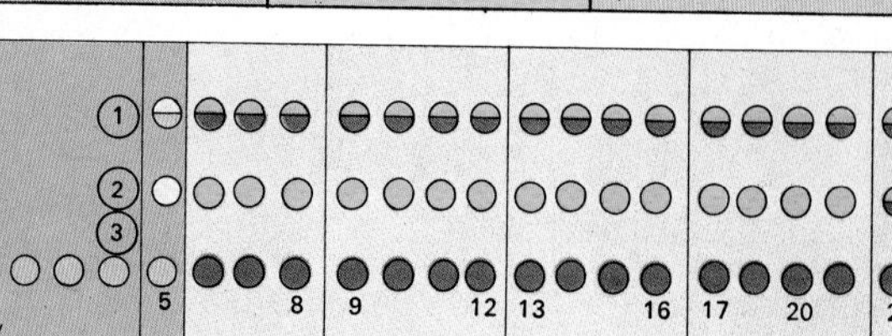

B
1
2
3
1 5 8 9 12 13 16 17 20 21 24 25 28
Day

2 The Pill works by means of the contraceptive effect [A] of hormones similar to natural estrogen and progesterone. Three main types are widely available using synthetic forms of these hormones with varying dosage schemes [B]. The combined pill [1] has both estrogen and progesterone and one pill is taken each day for about three weeks in each monthly cycle. The hormones act together on the anterior pituitary gland [4] to inhibit normal production of gonadatrophic hormones and thus suppress ovulation [5]. Even if an egg is released, the Pill acts further to prevent pregnancy by affecting the oviducts [6] and womb lining [7] and by altering cervical mucus [8]. During the fourth week withdrawal of hormones produces a lighter menstrual period, beginning within three or four days. A month's supply of sequential pills [2] consists of estrogen, which is taken alone for 15 days and then a progesterone-estrogen combination for the following five days. The mini-pill [3] relies on direct progesterone effect only. There is a normal ovarian cycle and menstruation takes place as usual (the first 5 pills are placebos), although the cycle may be more variable than normal.

on the Pill also report increased sexual desire, although reactions are mixed. There are about a dozen "Pills" with varying amounts of estrogen and progesterone.

Among various other methods of birth control, sterilization—particularly vasectomy—is increasingly popular. Other reasonably effective methods include intrauterine devices (IUDs), the diaphragm with spermicidal cream, and the condom. Spermicidal creams and foams used alone are less effective, as is the rhythm method (F). Choice of a method is influenced by medical advice, safety, effectiveness, availability, religious attitudes, cost, and personal aesthetics.

Outlook for developing countries

Researchers are investigating the possibility of a pill that could be taken only once every two weeks and of long-lasting hormone injections or implants that could prevent ovulation (the release of an egg from the ovary). A post-coital, or "morning after," pill is in the experimental stage. Scientists are also trying to develop a pill to be taken by men that would prevent the production of sperm.

Family planning has been most effective in the developed countries where a strong force for the widespread use of contraception has been the Women's Liberation Movement, which stresses the woman's health, welfare, and status. In the Third World, where the threat of starvation is so much greater, the struggle to persuade people to limit family size has unfortunately been less successful [4]. One problem is that the message of population control comes from former colonial powers and is sometimes seen as an attempt to retain dominance. In addition, children are seen variously as symbols of virility (especially in South America), a justification of a woman's life, an insurance policy against old age, and a work force.

The problem of birth control exists not only on the biological front but also as a serious social dilemma in a world of limited space and resources. Education alone seems to offer a long-term solution [5]. The Indian government strongly encourages birth control and offers incentives for sterilization [6].

KEY

Large families like this were common in the West at the end of the last century but are rare now. Family planning began in the Netherlands with the establishment in 1882 of a clinic founded by Aletta Jacobs. Use of a diaphragm—the "Dutch cap"—was explained at the clinic, but this kind of instruction in birth control made slow headway elsewhere. Margaret Sanger set up the first clinic in America in 1916 but it was soon closed and Mrs Sanger was arrested. Similar hostility, including charges of "obscenity," was faced by Marie Stopes, who opened the first British clinic in 1921.

3

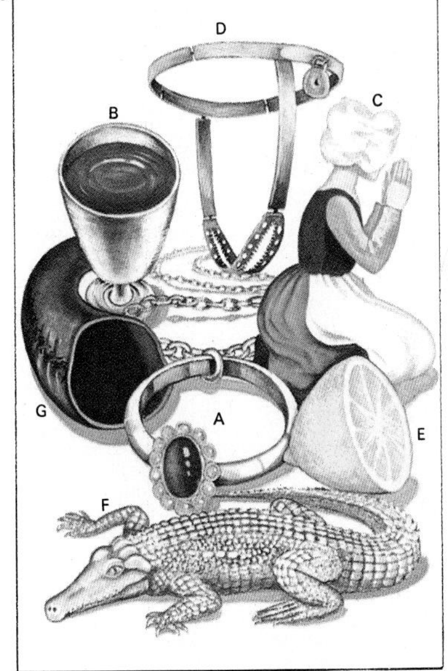

D
B
C
G
A
E
F

3 Early methods of contraception included the wearing of lucky charms [A], the drinking of supposedly "magic" potions [B], and even a resort to fervent prayer [C]. The chastity belt [D] sought to prevent intercourse. Casanova used a lemon [E] as a spermicide, while the Egyptians used the feces of a crocodile [G]. Early condoms [F] were made of sheep or pig intestines.

4

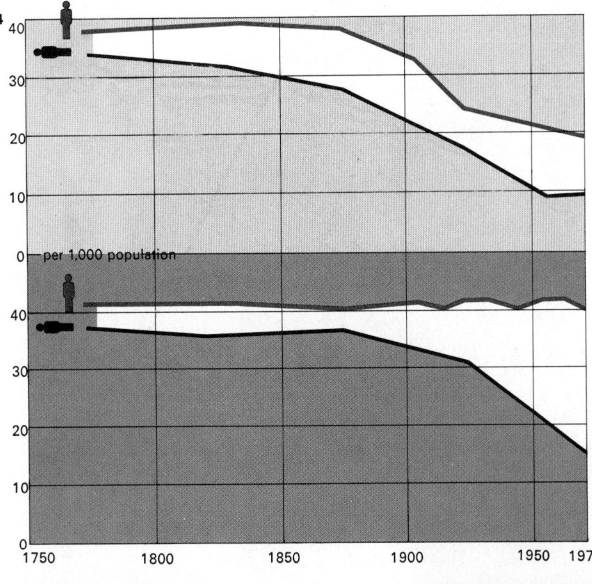

40
30
20
10
0 per 1,000 population
40
30
20
10
0
1750
1800
1850
1900
1950
1970

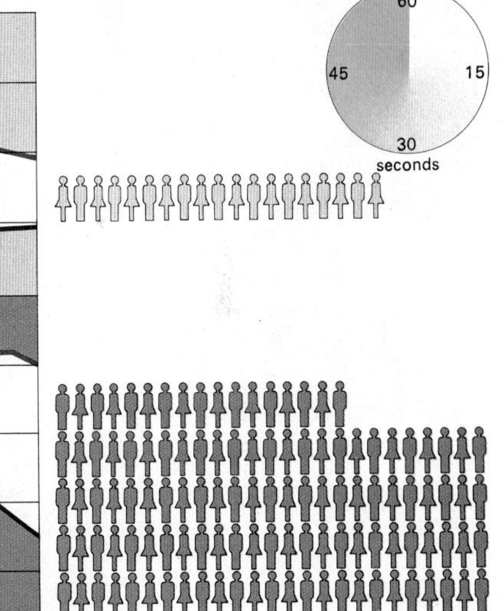

60
15
30
45
seconds
Birth-rate
Death-rate
Developed countries
Developing countries

4 World population reached 1 billion by 1850. But by 1970, largely because of a sharp decline in mortality rates, it had overshot the 3.5 billion mark. Statistics show that in developing countries—in Africa, Asia, Latin America, and parts of Oceania—the birth-rate is far higher than in more industrialized countries of Europe. North America, Japan, Russia, temperate South America, New Zealand, and Australia. This high birth-rate, combined with a fall in deaths because of better nutrition and medical facilities, has meant that the annual rate of increase in population is now far greater in those countries whose ability to provide food or adequate social services is strained. The aim of population control is to reduce this strain on resources and to promote better health and happiness. The graphs show birth and death rates per 1,000 population in developed and developing countries since 1750. The silhouettes beside them represent the current growth in population every 60 seconds.

5

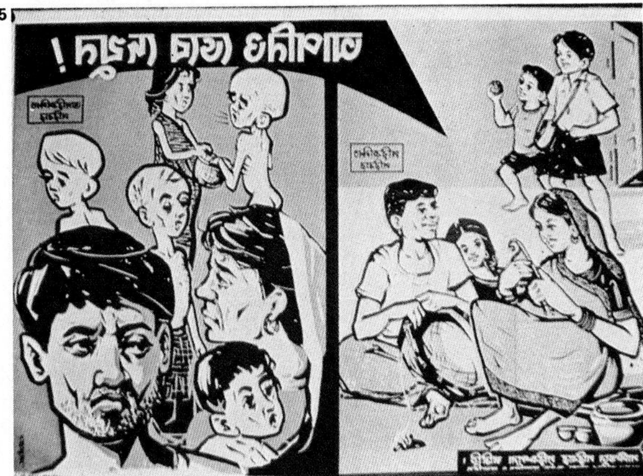

5 Family planning posters are used in India to publicize the advantages of smaller and healthier family units. But some Indians said: "Look at the unlucky man with only three children."

6

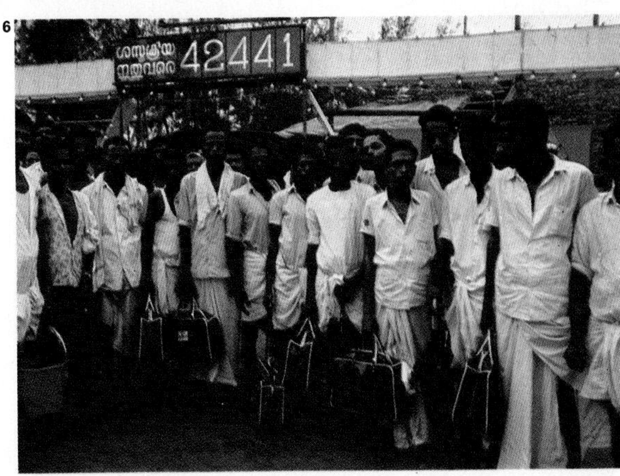

42441

6 After sterilization, a group of men from Kerala in southern India were given an array of gifts—rice, an airline bag, a plastic bucket, an umbrella, a lottery ticket, and cash—incentives in an intensive local campaign for birth control.

An introduction to illness and health

The people who inhabited the earth 20,000 years ago lived the life of hunters, running after their prey and attacking it with stone axes. At the mercy of the weather, they took shelter in caves at night and protected themselves as best they could. For this life humans were as well if not better adapted than any other mammals, with bodies designed to endure long periods without food, to stand up to the heavy exertion of hunting, and to respond quickly to emergencies.

The dangers of comfort

The physical characteristics of modern humans are little different from those of their forebears but are deployed in very different circumstances. Food is plentiful, exercise is rarely taken, and tensions in an urban society are continually high. An early man's appreciation of sweet-tasting berries assured him of an adequate supply of water-soluble vitamins. The same craving for sweet things means that modern man's body is loaded with sugars and other carbohydrates, often in excess of his needs or his body's capacity to absorb them. His sedentary, stressful urban life makes him overweight and tense. In order to feel better he may smoke cigarettes, drink alcohol, or take tranquilizers; palliatives that must, in the long term or in excess, do him harm. The ingenuity of technology means that the human body, which was designed to withstand the privation of a primitive existence, now has to function in a world that has been transformed by intelligence. The body is ill-equipped to deal with the results of that transformation.

The major health problems of developed societies stem from this discrepancy between social and physical evolution. In industrially advanced countries most of the diseases with easily identifiable causes, such as tuberculosis, smallpox, or cholera, have been virtually eliminated and the diseases that increasingly matter are those caused by what may simply be described as an unhealthy existence. High blood cholesterol levels resulting from an unbalanced diet, high blood pressure resulting from stress, obesity, and smoking all add considerably to the chances of heart disease.

Health to difficult to define. It might be described as the subjective assessment of a person's ability to cope with his life; it is only when he feels ill that it is time to visit a doctor. This definition, however, ignores the fact that some diseases do not produce any noticeable symptoms at their onset, and so the tendency in industrial societies is to screen people for diseases before they actually feel ill.

Disease prevention and detection

It is obvious that health checks help to reduce the incidence of epidemic diseases, but such monitoring also helps to reduce mortality from more general causes. The first signs of the conditions that lead to many forms of heart disease or cancer—both scourges of developed societies—can be detected and steps taken to remedy the situation. Studies in the United States have shown that the mortality rate among those who have checkups is lower than normal and that it declines proportionately with the number of checkups that the patient undergoes. A campaign conducted in

CONNECTIONS

See also

768 Psychosomatic diseases and retardation
748 Nonmedical healing
752 Development of surgery
1006 Greek science
826 Astrology
742 Origins of curative medicine
744 Natural remedies
746 Man-made cures

1 Hippocrates, the "father of medicine," was born on the island of Kos *c.* 460 BC. He worked empirically, basing his judgments on observation rather than on preconceived ideas. The Hippocratic Collection, including the Hippocratic Oath that binds doctors to keep their patients' confidences, are medical works by many different authors and are not necessarily of Hippocratic origin.

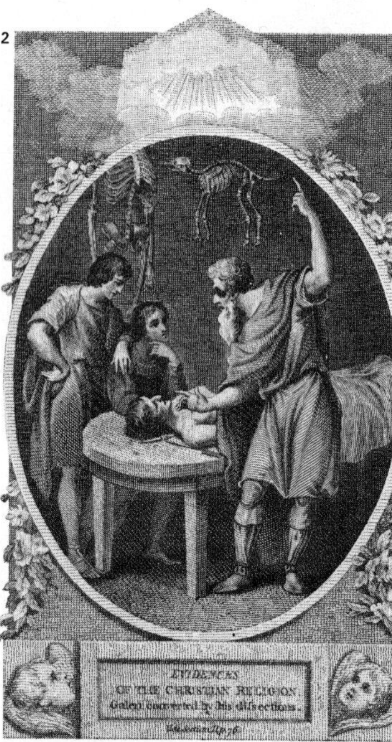

EVIDENCES
OF THE CHRISTIAN RELIGION
Galen converted by his dissection.

2 Galen, who was born in Pergamum in AD 130, was both an anatomist and a physiologist. He proposed the theory that temperament was controlled by the balance of four humors in the body (blood, phlegm, and yellow and black bile).

3 Medicine and astrology were closely linked until the eighteenth century. An astrological chart would be drawn up for the patient and used in diagnosis and prescription. Each sign of the Zodiac was associated with a part of the body, so birth signs indicated the illnesses the subject was prey to. Astrological relationships were also suggested between the Zodiac and the glandular and nervous systems. Aries rules the head and so Arians were said to be susceptible to headaches. Taurus rules the neck and throat, thus making Taureans vulnerable to colds. The arm, shoulder, and lung region is ruled by Gemini, while Leo rules heart, spine, and back. Cancer rules the stomach, making Cancerians prone to indigestion and ulcers. Virgo rules the intestines and the nervous system, with the kidneys under the influence of Libra. Scorpio rules the sex organs and Scorpians were thus highly sex oriented. Knees, bones, and teeth are ruled by Capricorn, so those under this sign were likely to be troubled by dental and orthopedic problems. Sagittarius rules liver, hips, and thighs and Sagittarian women thus tended to have heavy thighs and hips. Pisceans were subject to trouble with their feet, and Aquarians suffered from varicose veins and hardening of the arteries because Aquarius rules circulation.

AVREOLVS PHILIPPVS THEOPHRASTVS PARACELSVS,E
Der hochgelert vnd tiefsinnig natur-kundiger Philippus Theophrastus von Hohenhaim, beider Artzeneien Doctor.
Geboren im Jahr 1493
OMNE DONVM PERFECTVM A DEO: IMPERFECTVM VERO A DIABOLO

4 Paracelsus (*c.* 1493–1541), a Swiss physician and alchemist, broke with the traditions of Galen and revolutionized medical methods. Expelled from his post at Basel University in 1528, he continued with pharmaceutical experiments and encouraged research. He started treatment of venereal disease by mercury and believed that the physician should be alchemist, astrologer, and theologian in order to tend the body, soul, and spirit.

the United States to increase public awareness of health hazards now seems to be contributing to the declining rate of fatal heart disease.

In contrast to those who believe in checkups, some maintain that disease starts when the patient complains of symptoms and that over-anxiousness about health may actually lead to illness. A recent study, in which more than 25,000 English people were examined for diabetes, established that there were more undetected diabetics in the sample than there were known ones and that many of these people were symptom-free.

Another fact in favor of the argument that people are as healthy as they feel is that illness and mental strain are closely linked. Coronary thrombosis is clearly related to a stressful life style. The relationship between stress and illness has been so well defined that it is now possible to calibrate the chances of illness. Each event in a person's life is given a certain score: highest on the list are deaths within a family, followed by deaths of close relatives, changes in the home situation, court appearances, vacations, conferences, and so on. A vulnerability score is obtained from adding up all these points. Recent studies of sailors have shown that the assessment of their vulnerability to illness accorded well with the incidence of illness during voyages.

Fashions in illness

Medicine, as all human institutions, is subject to changing fashion, both in the type and symptoms of disease and in treatment. Before World War I it was fashionable for people suffering from mild psychological illness to display hysterical behavior and no lady's handbag was complete without a bottle of smelling salts to cure an episode of faintness. Today's disease is depression; the symptoms are a slowing down and withdrawal from the situation and the remedy is the antidepressant tablet or tranquilizer. In the 1940s most children had their tonsils removed but tonsillectomy is now seldom performed unless medically necessary. Medical fashion varies not only with the times but from country to country and with socioeconomic group.

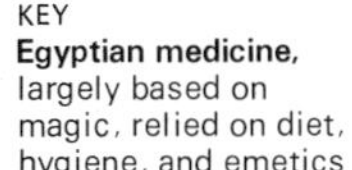

KEY

Egyptian medicine, largely based on magic, relied on diet, hygiene, and emetics (as prescribed by temple priests) for its remedies. Here the god Khemu fashions a man on a potter's wheel while ibis-headed Thoth fixes his life span.

5

5 Leeches, collected from rivers by women who stood in the water and waited for the leeches to attach themselves, were used for blood-letting until recently. Leech salivary glands contain an anticoagulant, hirudin, which has been used to prevent blood clotting, but has been superseded by new drugs.

6

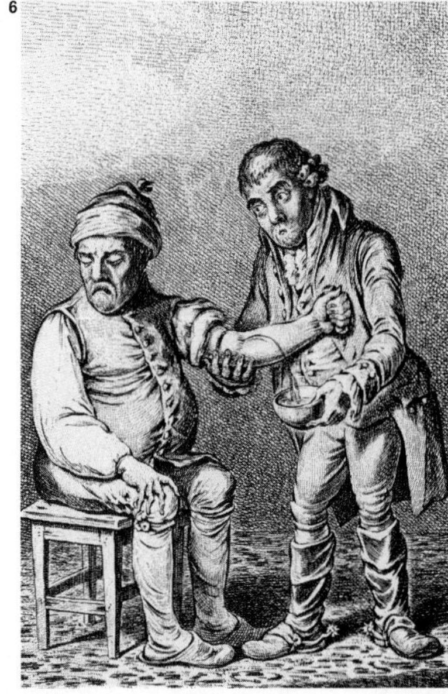

6 Plethora, or excess of blood, was believed by Eristratus (an early teacher in the Alexandrine School of Medicine) to cause many diseases. He actually diminished blood by dietary methods, but his colleagues used blood-letting (phlebotomy) widely and so began a practice lasting for many centuries.

7

7 Mineral springs are found in almost every country, and many cultures have exploited their curative properties. The Romans used hot springs, as did the Crusaders, but spas were most popular in the 1700s and 1800s. Places such as Baden-Baden and Bath became fashionable meeting places for the rich.

8

8 Franz Mesmer (1734–1815), Austrian physician and mystic, was the first man to use hypnosis and had remarkable successes with hysterical patients. He was convinced that cures were the result of "animal magnetism." His theories prompted charlatans to produce devices, such as this tub, claiming to cure all illnesses.

The causes of illness:1

Few people today believe that "evil spirits" are the cause of epilepsy, that those who breathe marshland mists will develop malaria, or that smelly drains lead inevitably to an outbreak of typhoid fever. These ideas, quite firmly held no more than a century ago, have been almost completely dispelled by advances in modern medical science.

The scientific study of the causes of disease (known as etiology), has been so successful that today doctors recognize thousands of disorders, and the discovery of new ones is still a fairly common event. Conveniently, however, nearly all the known causes can be grouped in a few general categories. For example, all the viruses, reckettsias, bacteria, fungi, protozoans and worms that cause disease are included in the category of infectious causes, and all the consequences of injury are grouped in a category called traumatic conditions [3].

Congenital disorders

Congenital causes of disease are traditionally considered first for they act within the womb and cause abnormalities that may be apparent at birth. Harelip, cleft palate, and club foot are examples of common congenital abnormalities. Mongolism [1], deformities of the heart, some of which are responsible for "blue babies," and abnormalities of the nervous system associated with spastic paraplegia, are others. As a class they are caused either by some fault in the chromosomal structure of the fertilized egg or by damage inflicted on the developing embryo in the womb—it is not always easy to decide which.

A developing embryo in the womb can be damaged by diseases contracted by the mother. German measles contracted during the early months of pregnancy, for example, can cause abnormalities of heart and ears (and sometimes of mentality and sight). Other congenital diseases are caused by drugs taken during pregnancy, such as the deformed babies that were born to mothers who had taken thalidomide. The smoking of more than ten cigarettes a day by a pregnant woman may retard the fetus' growth.

The disorders that are transmitted from the parents to the child from generation to generation are known as hereditary disorders. Perhaps the most well-known is hemophilia, a disorder in which the clotting mechanism of the blood is deranged so that trivial injury is followed by prolonged bleeding. Another hereditary condition is phenylketonuria—in which there is an absence of enzymes that metabolize certain toxic phenyls. Untreated, it leads to severe mental retardation, but if detected soon after birth it can be dealt with quite successfully by a diet that is low in the animo acids that give rise to phenyls.

Dietary deficiency

Starvation and malnutrition are obvious causes of disease. Even so, a seemingly ample diet may cause disease if it lacks certain vitamins, the nutrients essential for well-being. Vitamins occur only in certain foods; a diet that consistently lacks a sufficient quantity of a particular vitamin is certain, in time, to give rise to the corresponding vitamin deficiency disease [2]. The

CONNECTIONS

See also

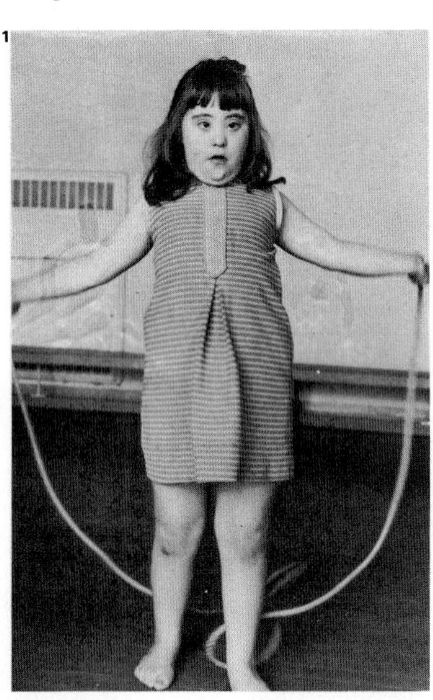

1 Mongolism, a form of mental deficiency associated with certain physical characteristics, is caused by a chromosome imbalance present at birth. Normal cells have 46 chromosomes, whereas mongoloids either have 47 or there may be a rearrangement of chromosomal material between chromosomes. This interferes with the normal control of brain and body growth, producing the flattened face and folded upper eyelid that give the patient an Oriental look. Other features are short arms and legs. The condition, now preferably known as Down's Syndrome, is more likely in babies born to older women.

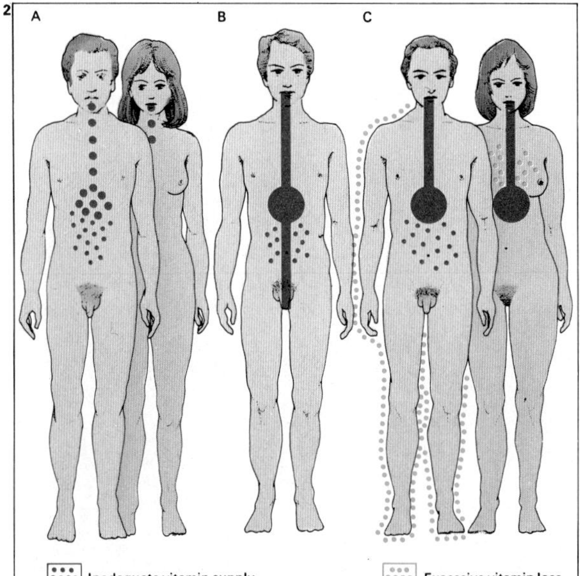

A
B
C
Inadequate vitamin supply
Excessive vitamin loss

2 Vitamins are essential to a healthy diet and lack of them causes a variety of deficiency diseases, such as rickets (vitamin D deficiency), scurvy (vitamin C), and pellagra (niacin). Shortage of vitamins can be caused by a primary food shortage or by diminished food intake [A] resulting from poverty or taboos against eating certain foods. Even when a diet is rich in vitamins, parasitic infections or impaired transport in blood or lymph vessels can reduce absorption [B]. Great physical activity, growth, or excessive loss through sweating or breast feeding [C] creates the need for an increased vitamin intake.

MURPH

3 Accidents are listed under the general heading of traumatic conditions. They range from simple cuts, burns, and scalds to the drastic effects of a highway accident. Doctors put in the same category injuries caused by lightning, electrocution, sunburn, frostbite, and the air pressure problems experienced by flyers or divers. Exposure to radiation from X-ray machines, radioisotopes, or atomic explosions destroys various body cells. Some cells are more easily injured than others. Bone marrow, where red blood cells are produced, is most sensitive, followed by the lining of the stomach and intestines, the skin and sex glands, and lastly cells of the brain and muscles.

scurvy that afflicted sailors on long sea voyages and the beriberi from which thousands of prisoners in Asia died during World War II were caused in this way. The childhood disease of rickets is also caused by vitamin deficiency. In the industrial countries, vitamin deficiency diseases are rare today but occasionally occur in people who, through preference or ignorance, choose to live on very restricted diets. Strict vegetarians, for example, may suffer from lack of vitamins A, D, and E, which are in animal fats.

Several other consituents of the diet are essential for health; important among these is iron. This metal is needed in small amounts to make the hemoglobin in the blood's red cells. A deficiency of iron causes anemia. Another element needed in small amounts is iodine, a shortage of which leads to the swelling of the thyroid gland known as goiter.

Infections and their causes

An enormous number of living things gain entry to the body's tissues, grow there and by so doing cause disease [4]. These infectious agents range in size from viruses so small that they can be seen only with the aid of an electron microscope, to bacteria and protozoa, which can be seen with an ordinary light microscope, and the various small creatures just visible to the naked eye, to the tapeworms that grow to several feet.

The way in which infectious agents cause disease is extremely varied. Viruses are intracellular parasites and the polio virus, for example, causes paralysis by growing in and destroying a particular type of nerve cell in the spinal cord. Bacteria, on the other hand, are largely extracellular and cause their ill effects either by secreting the powerful poisons known as bacterial toxins or by invading tissue. The malaria parasite destroys the blood's red cells and the amebas of amebic dysentery irritate and poison the bowel. The effects of infection or infestation with larger parasites are less well defined but there is little doubt that the debility associated with this type of infection is largely caused by interference with nutrients in food and by loss of blood from the intestinal wall.

KEY

Anatomy classes based on thorough human dissection, like this one at the Barber Surgeons Hall, London, 1581, were the foundation of an understanding of how the healthy body worked, and consequently how diseases were caused. Previously, such scientific knowledge was hampered by a strong taboo against human dissection and an over-reliance on such classical writers as Galen (*c.* AD 130–200). The Belgian Andreas Vesalius (1514–64) broke this tradition.

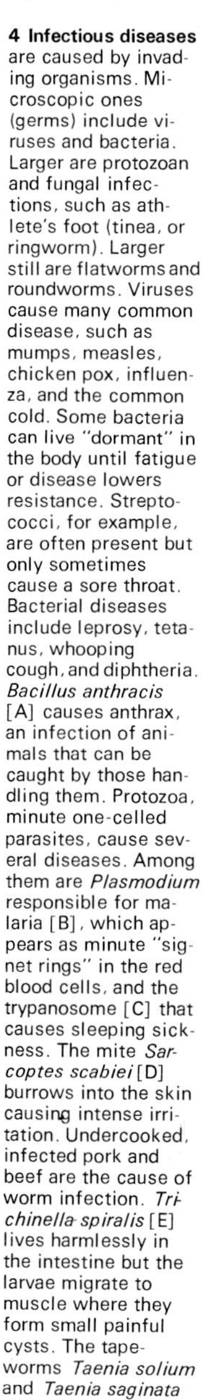

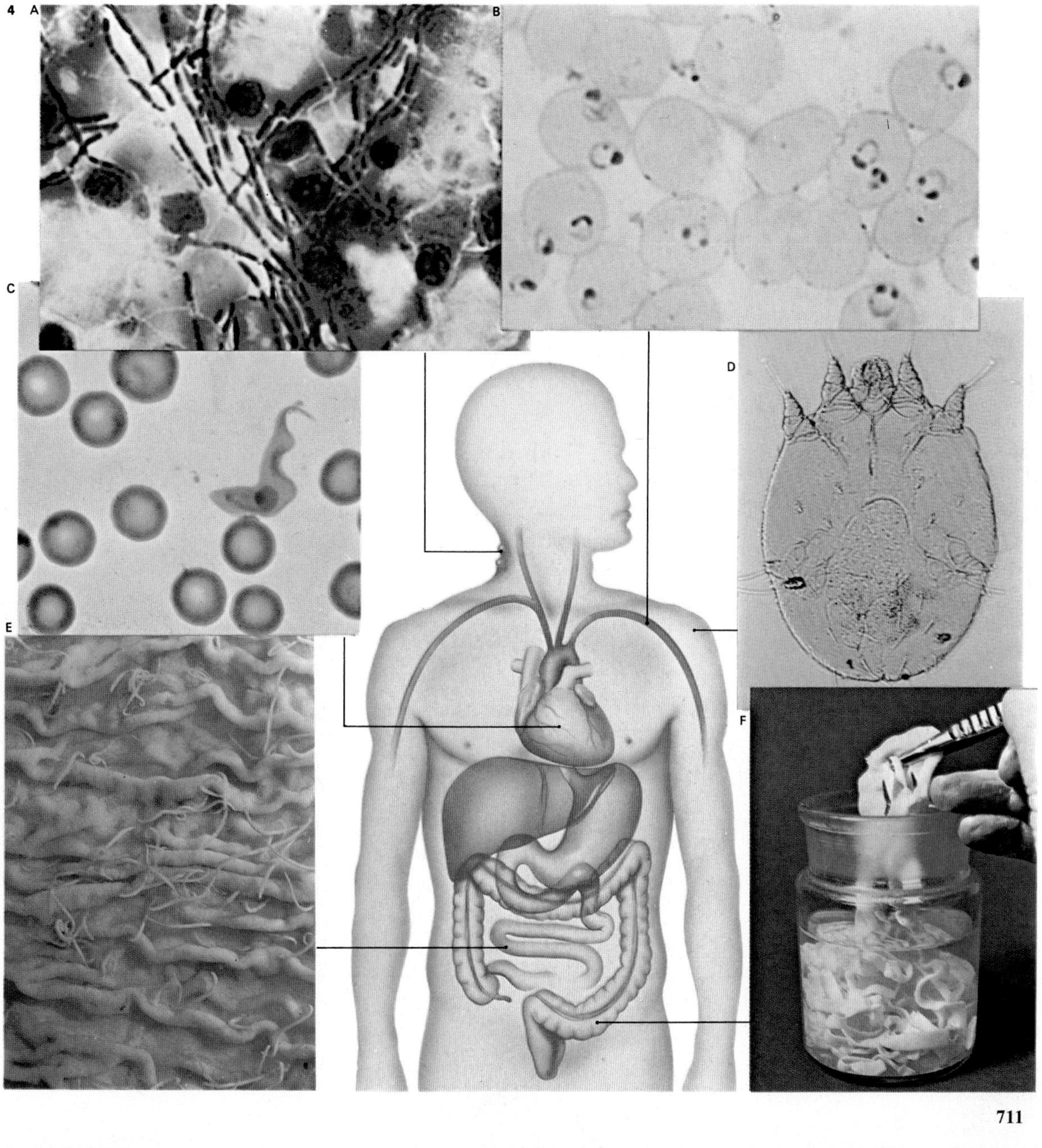

4 Infectious diseases are caused by invading organisms. Microscopic ones (germs) include viruses and bacteria. Larger are protozoan and fungal infections, such as athlete's foot (tinea, or ringworm). Larger still are flatworms and roundworms. Viruses cause many common disease, such as mumps, measles, chicken pox, influenza, and the common cold. Some bacteria can live "dormant" in the body until fatigue or disease lowers resistance. Streptococci, for example, are often present but only sometimes cause a sore throat. Bacterial diseases include leprosy, tetanus, whooping cough, and diphtheria. *Bacillus anthracis* [A] causes anthrax, an infection of animals that can be caught by those handling them. Protozoa, minute one-celled parasites, cause several diseases. Among them are *Plasmodium* responsible for malaria [B], which appears as minute "signet rings" in the red blood cells, and the trypanosome [C] that causes sleeping sickness. The mite *Sarcoptes scabiei* [D] burrows into the skin causing intense irritation. Undercooked, infected pork and beef are the cause of worm infection. *Trichinella spiralis* [E] lives harmlessly in the intestine but the larvae migrate to muscle where they form small painful cysts. The tapeworms *Taenia solium* and *Taenia saginata* [F] are man's largest parasites.

4 A

B

C

D

E

F

The causes of illness: 2

Many of the agents that infect human bodies produce poisonous substances, but there are many poisons that originate outside the body and that are equally damaging [1]. Many of the chemicals used in industry are poisonous, most drugs are poisonous if taken in excess, many plants synthesize poisons in their leaves and fruits, and numerous animals, including some snakes and spiders, use venoms either for attack or defense.

Despite their diverse origins, poisons have a marked similarity of action, for nearly all of them interfere with one or more of the chemical reactions that take place in living tissues. As a consequence of this interference, the poisoned tissue ceases to function properly and, in severe poisoning, may die.

Some poisons lead rapidly to death rather than to illness. Potassium cyanide is probably the best-known rapid poison and it works almost instantaneously by interfering with the intracellular oxidations responsible for the production of the energy used in all living tissues. Any cell that potassium cyanide encounters therefore stops functioning immediately.

The less immediately lethal poisons are those likely to cause lasting illness. These slower poisons can affect many different chemical reactions and so produce different symptoms. Lead poisoning is cumulative, slowly disrupting the formation of red cells, while carbon monoxide rapidly unites so strongly with hemoglobin that it prevents the blood from taking up any oxygen and swiftly results in suffocation of the body's cells.

Tumors and cancers

Neoplastic (new growth) diseases are those that are associated with the growth of tumors. Generally speaking it is the extra growth that brings on the symptoms and so, as the underlying causes for the tumor are often not known [4], they are classified according to size and site of origin.

Tumors vary from harmless warts to the most fatal of cancers. A large proportion are slow growing with little tendency to spread to other parts of the body. This kind of tumor causes disease merely by its presence and its position is more important than its size [5]. A large tumor under the skin of the back many be harmless while a small one, in contrast, can cause disabling disease if it presses on an important or delicate structure such as a nerve and so deranges that structure's function. An acoustic nerve tumor, for example, is harmless in itself but causes deafness.

In contrast to the slow-growing, nonspreading tumors are those that grow rapidly and are capable of spreading to almost any part of the body. These are the cancers. A tumor of this kind causes disease not merely by its destructive effects on the tissue in which it originates and grows, but also by similar effects on any tissue to which it spreads. It is because cancers grow and spread so rapidly that they produce such serious symptoms and are so dangerous.

Degenerative and immunological diseases

Human tissues, like machines, suffer from wear and tear but, unlike machines, they are able in many cases to repair themselves.

CONNECTIONS

See also
710 The causes of illness: 1
758 First aid
428 Mushrooms and toadstools
470 The jellyfish
750 Radiology and radiotherapy
714 Diseases of breathing
724 Diseases of the skin
802 Aging and longevity
804 An active old age
716 Diseases of the circulation
720 Diseases of the skeleton and muscles
740 The body's natural defenses

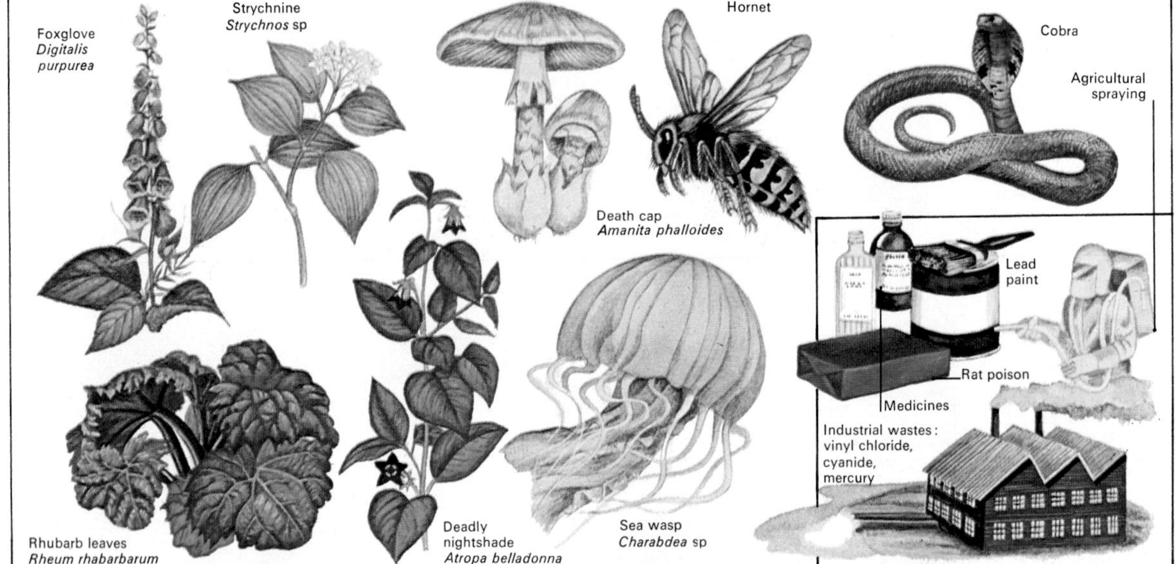

1
Foxglove
Digitalis purpurea
Strychnine
Strychnos sp
Hornet
Cobra
Agricultural spraying
Death cap
Amanita phalloides
Lead paint
Rat poison
Medicines
Industrial wastes: vinyl chloride, cyanide, mercury
Rhubarb leaves
Rheum rhabarbarum
Deadly nightshade
Atropa belladonna
Sea wasp
Charabdea sp

1 Poisons may be inhaled, injected, absorbed through the skin, or swallowed. A few common ones are shown here. Some, such as hornet venom, are mild; others can kill in a few seconds. Most deaths, however, are caused by weaker poisons found in household goods. Children are particularly endangered since they are more sensitive to poisons than adults. The most difficult to avoid are those that occur undetected—for example, the bacterial toxins in contaminated stews and pâtés. In special circumstances quite harmless substances are poisonous: cheese can be lethal to anyone taking certain antidepressants.

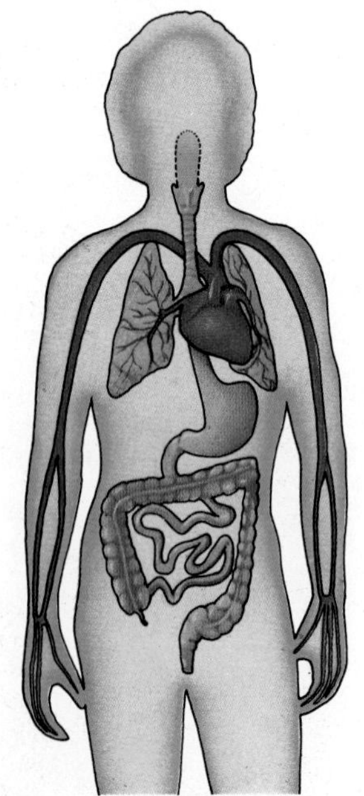

2 A

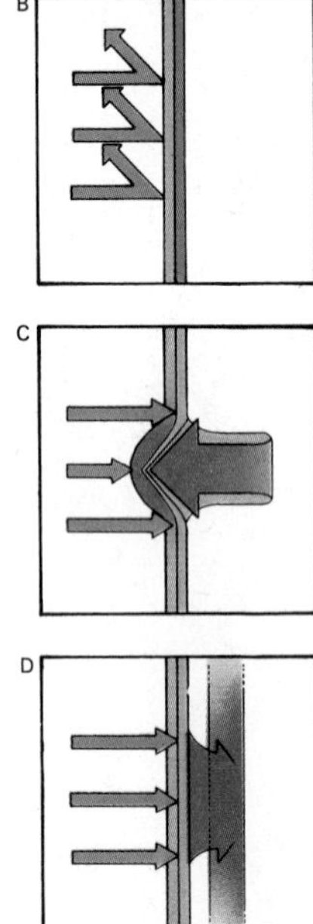

B
C
D

2 Allergies [A] can be caused by almost any substance. Pollen and dust affect the respiratory system [blue]. Some foods upset the digestive system [green]. Drugs, either eaten or injected into the bloodstream [red], cause general reactions. Many substances, on contact with the skin, cause local reactions [pink]. Potential allergens [arrows] have no effect on nonsensitive people [B]. Cells of "sensitized" people are coated with antibodies specific to the allergen [green layer]. Contact with the allergen causes these cells to release histamine, causing inflammation [C]. Antihistamines suppress allergic reactions by blocking histamine action [orange layer] [D].

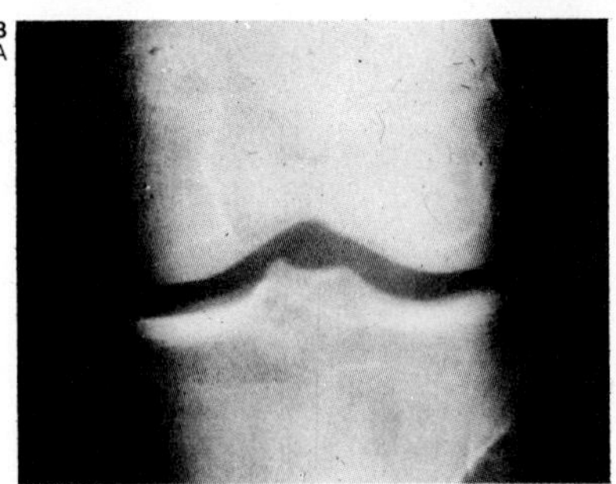

3
A

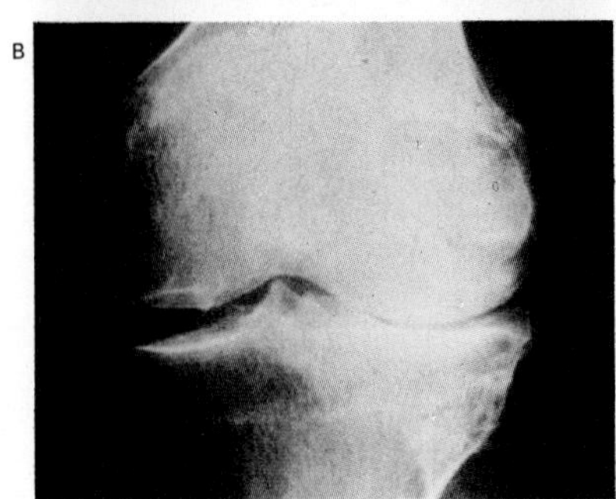

B

3 Osteoarthritis, a painful degenerative condition of the joints, is a common affliction of the elderly. Comparison of X-ray pictures of a normal knee joint [A] and an arthritic one [B] shows the characteristic loss of joint space. The large joints at the knee, hip, and shoulder are most commonly affected, but small joints like those of the hand are often involved. The treatment consists mainly of less activity, heat therapy, and pain killers. In severe cases cures include injections of cortisone drugs, replacing the joint with a plastic one, or even ankylosis, which involves removing any remaining cartilage and immobilizing the joint until the two bones fuse.

With increasing age, however, the reparative ability declines, and as damage outstrips repair, the symptoms of degenerative disease appear. Most common of all degenerative conditions are graying of the hair, baldness, and the loss of elasticity of the lens of the eye, which most middle-aged people suffer from. Far more serious, however, is the painful osteoarthritis that so commonly develops as the surfaces of the joints of elderly people begin to wear [3], and several degenerative conditions of the nervous system, such as Parkinson's disease.

Hardening of the arteries, or arteriosclerosis, when the arteries lose their smoothness and elasticity, leading to angina pectoris, coronary thrombosis, and stroke, is the most important of the degenerative diseases in industrialized countries. It is responsible for more deaths than any other condition.

The immune defenses of the body provide protection against infections and probably against the onset of many cancers. Sometimes, however, the defenses become directed against quite innocuous "enemies" or even against the body's own tissues. Abnormal responses such as these are responsible for hay fever, urticaria (hives), and asthma [2], and also for the far more serious conditions of rheumatoid arthritis and hemolytic anemia. The immune reactions that cause these diseases are similar to those responsible for the rejection of kidney grafts and heart transplants. And occasionally mothers respond to the red blood cells of their unborn infants by producing antibodies that cross the placenta, damage the infant's blood, and result in the child becoming what is commonly known as an Rh baby.

Iatrogenic and idiopathic diseases

Iatrogenic diseases are those that are a consequence of medical care and range in severity from the acceptable side effects of a drug necessarily given in the treatment of a serious illness to the disasters that sometimes follow accidents in operating rooms. Idiopathic diseases are those for which no cause has yet been found, such as the skin disease psoriasis. For this reason they pose considerable difficulties in treatment.

KEY

Cancer is a major killer, particularly in countries with a high life expectancy Research has centered on viruses, for more than 100 viruses have been identified as carcinogens, or external cancer-causing agents, in animals. Positive proof, however, of their ability to cause cancer in man has yet to be fully demonstrated, although some researchers have associated herpes virus with cancer of the cervix.

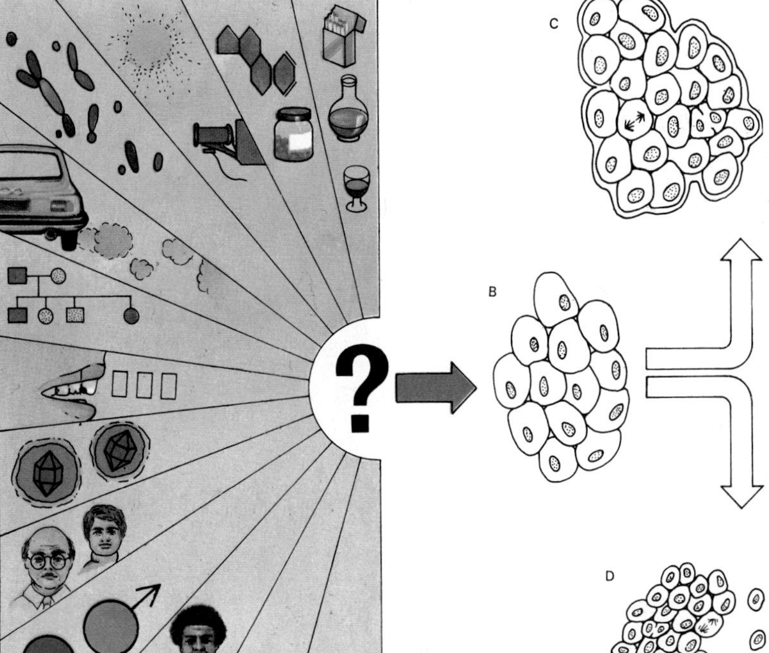

4
A
B
C
D
?

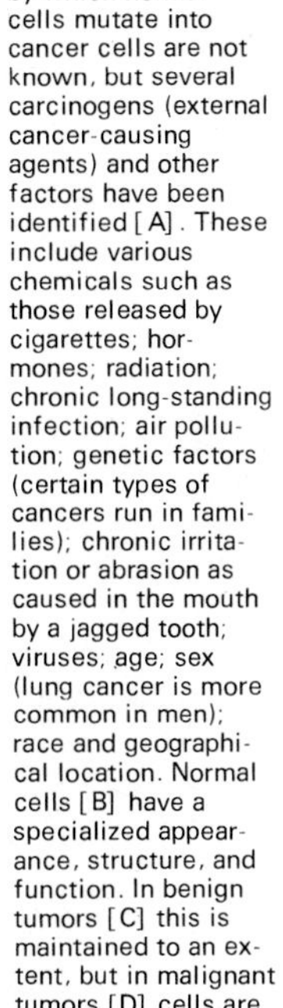

4 The mechanisms by which normal cells mutate into cancer cells are not known, but several carcinogens (external cancer-causing agents) and other factors have been identified [A]. These include various chemicals such as those released by cigarettes; hormones; radiation; chronic long-standing infection; air pollution; genetic factors (certain types of cancers run in families); chronic irritation or abrasion as caused in the mouth by a jagged tooth; viruses; age; sex (lung cancer is more common in men); race and geographical location. Normal cells [B] have a specialized appearance, structure, and function. In benign tumors [C] this is maintained to an extent, but in malignant tumors [D] cells are often grossly aberrant. They also lose their natural ability to stick together and so break away and spread the cancer.

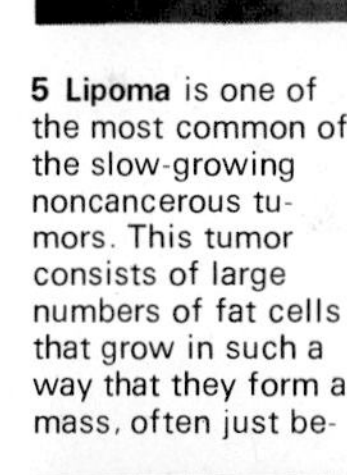

5 Lipoma is one of the most common of the slow-growing noncancerous tumors. This tumor consists of large numbers of fat cells that grow in such a way that they form a mass, often just beneath the skin. Such tumors can be unsightly but they are seldom dangerous. Surgical removal is usually feasible, especially when it is small and this will probably prevent further growth.

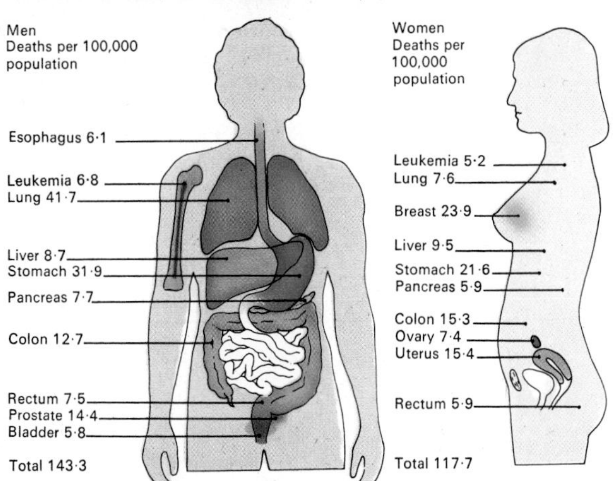

6 Men
Deaths per 100,000 population
Esophagus 6·1
Leukemia 6·8
Lung 41·7
Liver 8·7
Stomach 31·9
Pancreas 7·7
Colon 12·7
Rectum 7·5
Prostate 14·4
Bladder 5·8
Total 143·3
Women
Deaths per 100,000 population
Leukemia 5·2
Lung 7·6
Breast 23·9
Liver 9·5
Stomach 21·6
Pancreas 5·9
Colon 15·3
Ovary 7·4
Uterus 15·4
Rectum 5·9
Total 117·7

6 Cancer causes death by physical obstruction of an essential pipeline, by pressure on normal tissues (such as within the skull), and by crowding of normal tissue. This results in tissue death and consequent loss of the function performed by that tissue. Mortality for the ten most frequent sites of cancer, by sex, in 24 countries in 1970, is illustrated. More men die of cancer yearly than women and lung cancer is the most likely type.

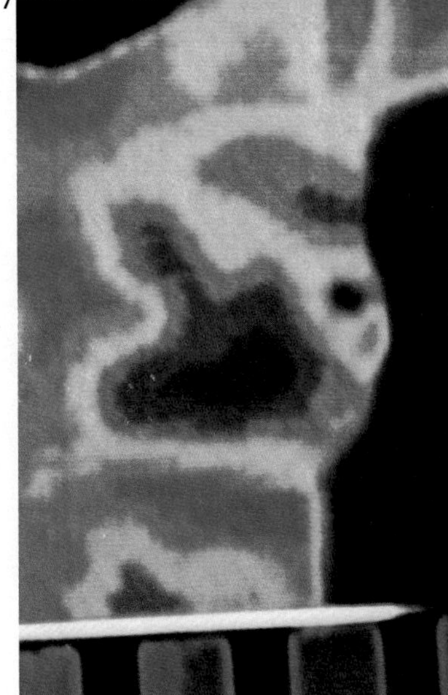

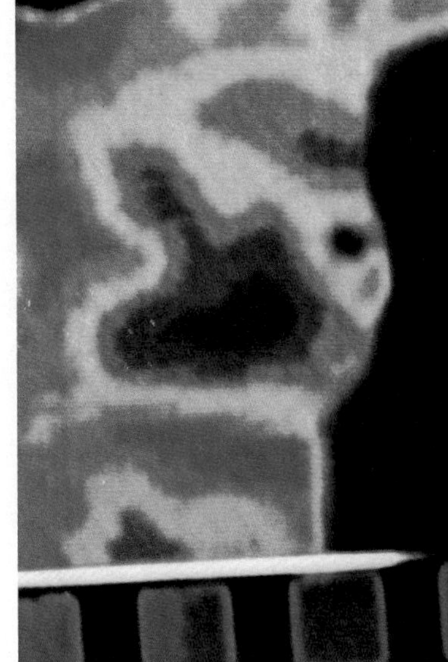

7

7 Early detection highly increases the likelihood of arresting breast cancer. Tests can discover a disease even before outward symptoms appear. Thermography is a technique that measures the surface temperature of the skin. It has been extremely useful in detecting breast tumors. This infrared scanning device displays its information in color on a thermogram. The breast tumor is revealed as a warmer area than the surrounding tissues.

Diseases of breathing

The agents that affect the respiratory passages and the lungs [Key] are basically similar to those that cause disease in other systems. Ports of entry into the body for food, water, or air—the mouth and nose—are also potential sites of weakness in the body's defenses. The lining of the respiratory passages is especially vulnerable to various infections.

The symptoms of infection

The tonsils and adenoids are prominent parts of the lymph system in the throat that help repel infection. Invasion by viruses or bacteria may result in sufficient inflammation to cause tonsilitis [1], in which the throat and neck become sore and swallowing is painful. Many similar viruses of the rhinovirus group can affect the throat, nose, and eyes to cause "the common cold." Infections of respiratory passages are named after the part most affected—larynx (laryngitis), throat (pharyngitis), windpipe (tracheitis), and lung tubes (bronchitis).

When lung tissue itself becomes infected pneumonia develops [3]. Various bacteria can invade the lung air sacs, causing inflammation, increasing blood flow to damaged tissue, and preventing oxygen from entering the blood in sufficient amounts. Toxins, poisonous substances produced by the microbes, further affect the patient. Before the development of antibiotics recovery from pneumonia depended on the ability of the patient's own defenses to fight the illness and mortality was high. Today, appropriate antibiotics mean quicker recovery, providing that pneumonia is not secondary to another serious debilitating disease.

Other bacterial infections of the lung tissues may not initially be as dramatic. Tuberculosis [6], once known as "consumption," may develop slowly before becoming obvious. Many children appear to come into contact with the disease and rapidly develop immunity. With careful treatment a cure can be expected with the drugs now available. Tuberculosis is more likely to occur in people in poor health—the elderly, those with chronic chest disease such as bronchitis and emphysema, and in people with poor general nutrition, such as chronic alcoholics.

The first symptom of a lung disorder is usually interference with breathing. This may take the form of pain, breathlessness, or an inflammation of the nasal membranes. The breathlessness may appear suddenly or slowly, during rest or only on exertion.

Irritants of the air passages

Two lung diseases, bronchitis and emphysema [2], impede the passage of air to and from the lungs. In bronchitis the blockage is often due to the accumulation of excessive mucus; in emphysema to the compression and collapse of air tubes caused by unnaturally distended lung air sacs, or alveoli, in which air has become trapped. Chronic bronchitis is caused by continual irritation of the bronchial mucosa often due to smoke and dust.

It is not surprising that, as the years pass, diseases of the lungs develop, for the respiratory system suffers considerable abuse. This may be from large quantities of fine dust particles that are present in all air,

CONNECTIONS

See also
692 Breathing and the lungs
712 The causes of illness: 2
698 Keeping fit
292 Pollution of the air

1 Air breathed in through the mouth and nose [A] carries with it viruses and bacteria. The tonsils [1] at the back of the mouth and the adenoids [2] in a child are part of the body's defenses against potentially infective microbes. These organisms may lead to inflammation of the tonsils with painful swelling [B], an increased temperature and difficulty in swallowing. The infection may require antibiotic treatment.

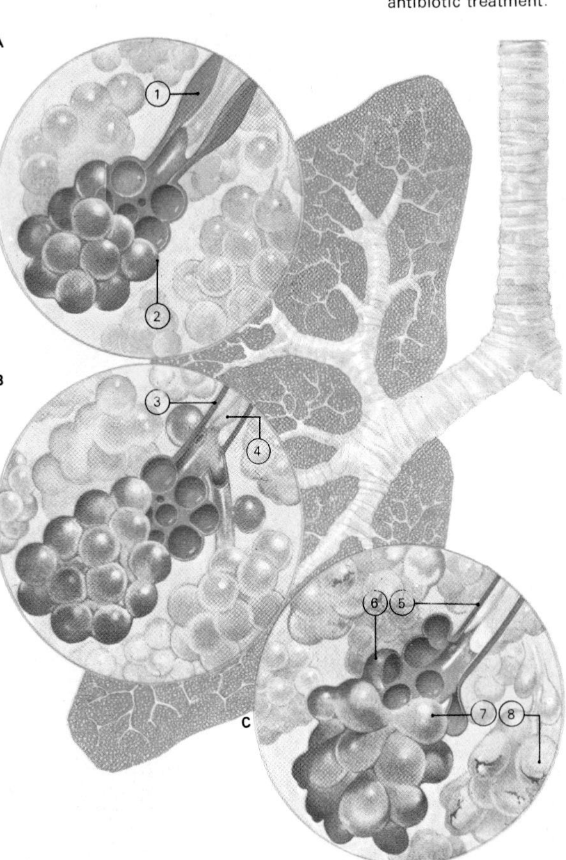

2 A
B
C
1
2
3
4
5
6
7
8

2 Viruses in the air pass down the trachea (windpipe) into the lung tubes (bronchi), where they may cause infection, such as tracheitis and bronchitis with symptoms of cough and fever. Asthma [A], an allergic, generally intermittent, disease, also affects breathing. The small air tubes become narrow [1] and the alveoli overfill [2]. Chronic inflammation of the tubes—called chronic bronchitis [B]—occurs mainly in older people who work in industrial areas and who smoke causing cough and wheezing. The inflamed lining of the bronchial tubes [3] produces excess mucus [4], which is coughed up as phlegm. Inflammation and narrowing of the bronchi [5] lead to difficulty in moving air into and out of the alveoli [6]. The distended alveoli [7] are damaged and some may collapse [8]. The condition, called emphysema [C], prevents normal absorption of oxygen by the blood.

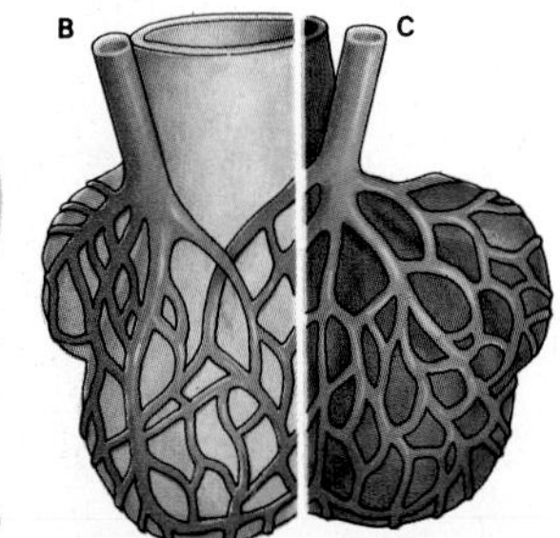

B
C

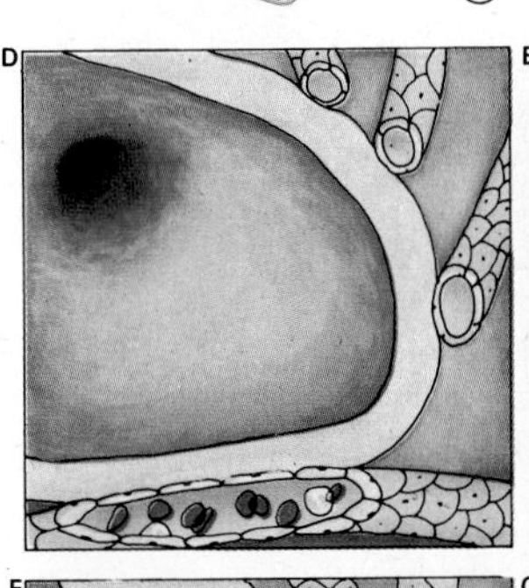

D

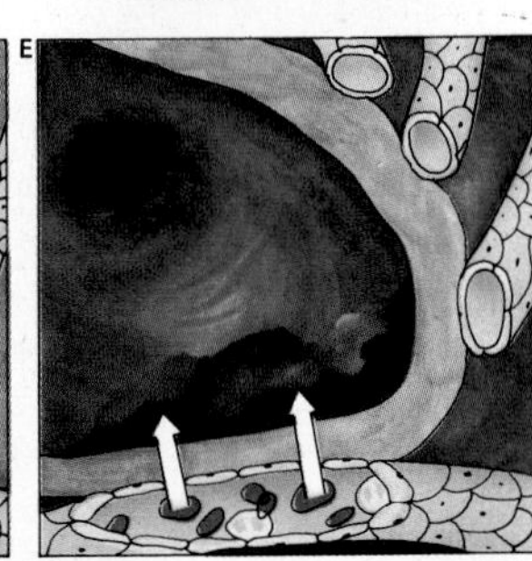

E

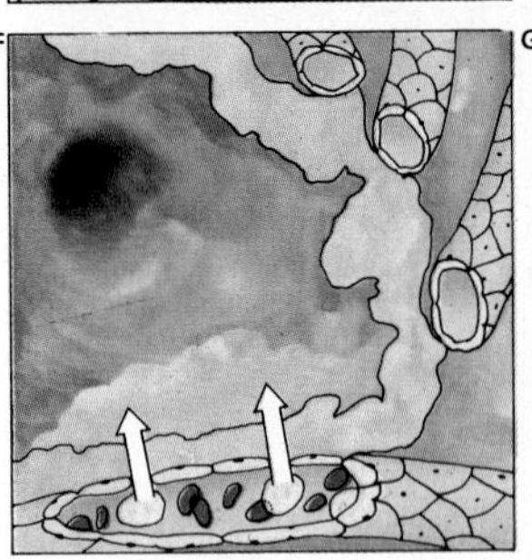

F

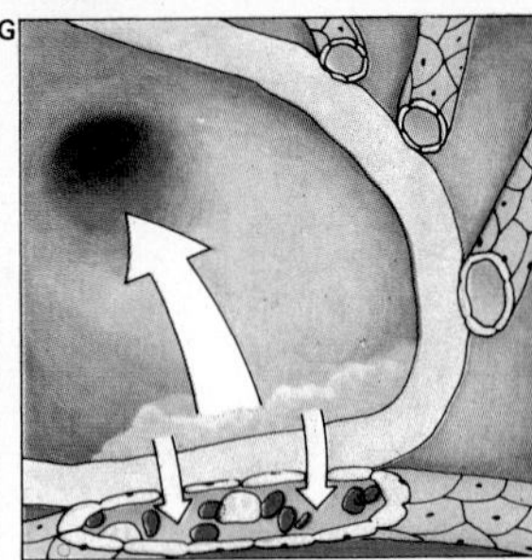

G

3 Infection may affect not only the upper respiratory system and the lung tubes [A], but also the lung tissue and alveoli [1], resulting in pneumonia. This is normally an acute infection caused by bacteria or viruses. The lung alveoli [B] become engorged with blood, inflamed and thickened [C]. Sections through the alveoli seen under the microscope show the stages of the disease. Compared with the normal lung [D], tissue in a pneumonic lung [E] becomes inflamed and the alveoli are invaded by plasma and red and white corpuscles. These form a viscous mass that coagulates, causing acute congestion and airlessness. As the disease progresses [F], some tissue may die and the excess of white corpuscles gives the lungs a gray appearance. During the patient's recovery [G] the dead bacteria, fluid, and inflammatory cells are either coughed up or gradually reabsorbed into the blood stream. Treating the patient with antibiotics speeds recovery, and physiotherapy—which encourages coughing up of infected phlegm—minimizes permanent lung damage.

but are often worse in industrial areas [4]. The lining of the nose, which is equipped with mucus-secreting cells and long hairs, efficiently traps and filters most dust. Not everyone breathes through the nose, but the mouth and upper air passages are also quite efficient traps.

Lung disease can often be traced to a particular irritant; certain industrial processes produce silica particles, which are a particular menace because they reach the alveoli in sufficient amounts to set up, over a period of time, chronic inflammation and scarring. This greatly reduces lung function and increases the risk of lung cancer. Other hazards are forms of asbestos which, when breathed in, increase the risk of cancer of the large air tubes (bronchi). Restriction of the use of such substances, and removal and prevention of coal dust and silica-containing dusts, are important medical preventive measures.

The greatest general threat to the health of lung tissues is smoking [7]. Smoking increases the irritability of industrial dusts, is a major factor in lung cancer, greatly increases the risk of debilitating chronic bronchitis and emphysema, and also has far-reaching effects outside the lungs—it increases the risk of heart disease.

The incidence of different lung diseases varies from country to country and sometimes the reasons for this variation are obscure. Chronic bronchitis and emphysema, for example, have internationally been called the "English diseases," for they have a particularly high incidence in the United Kingdom. More males are affected than females and these diseases are more common in cities.

Allergies: asthma and hay fever

Other inhalants may produce allergic responses. In the summer months grass pollens, for example, produce hay fever, whose symptoms are running noses and eyes, asthma [5], and general ill health in some people. Allergic responses can occur under conditions of prolonged exposure to a highly concentrated foreign material. Thus farmers may suffer asthmatic-type reactions when filling or emptying silos.

KEY

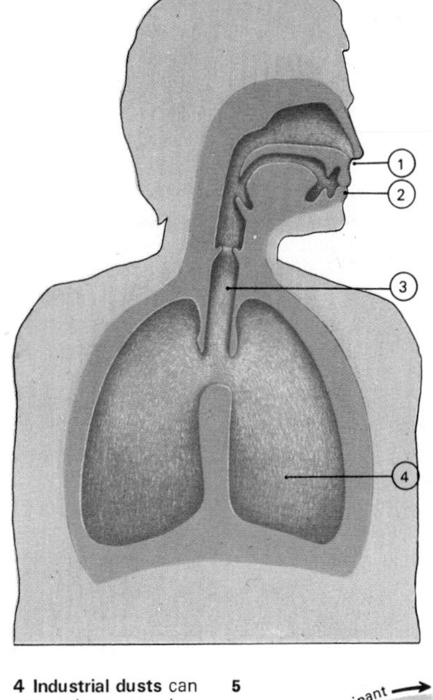

1
2
3
4

An oxygen supply is required for all the body's processes and is taken into the body through the lungs, from which the waste gas carbon dioxide is breathed out. The nose [1] and mouth [2] can both be used for breathing in and out. The nose filters the air, which passes to the windpipe [3], the larger and then the smaller bronchi, before reaching the many million air sacs (alveoli) of the lungs [4]. Many of the disease-causing agents enter the body through the same pathway. Various traps help to deal with these injurious agents, and second-line defenses are available to tackle any that get as far as causing disease.

4

A

B

C

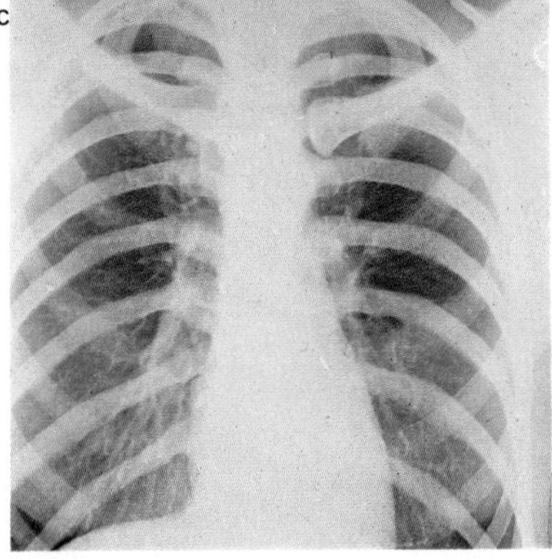

D

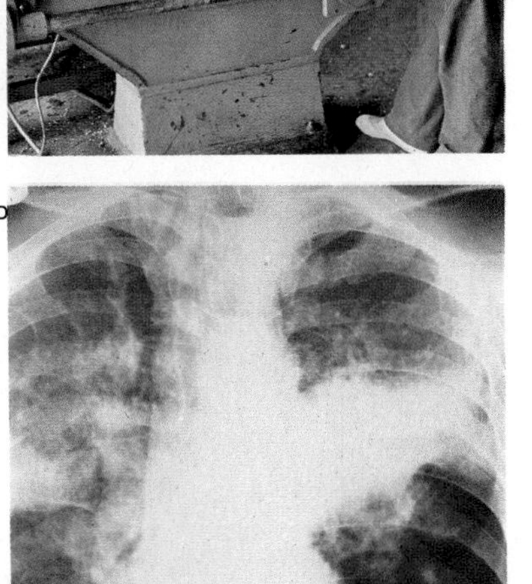

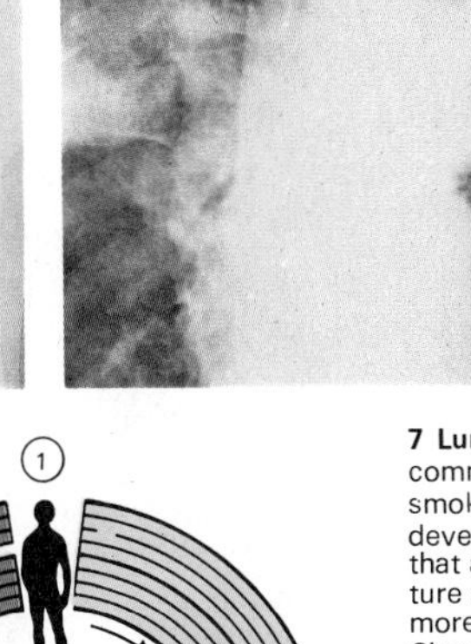

4 Industrial dusts can cause damage to the lungs. Industries whose workers may be particularly threatened are coal mining [A] and those in which fine silica particles occur in the air—granite and sandstone industries, the pottery industry, and metal-grinding processes [B]. In early stages there are no signs or symptoms but gradually breathlessness, a cough, and phlegm develop. The dust causes inflammation and scarring of the lungs and X-ray appearance changes from the normal [C] to one with patchy mottling and scarring in the lungs [D]. Smoking speeds lung damage. Industrial dust removal is an important preventive.

5

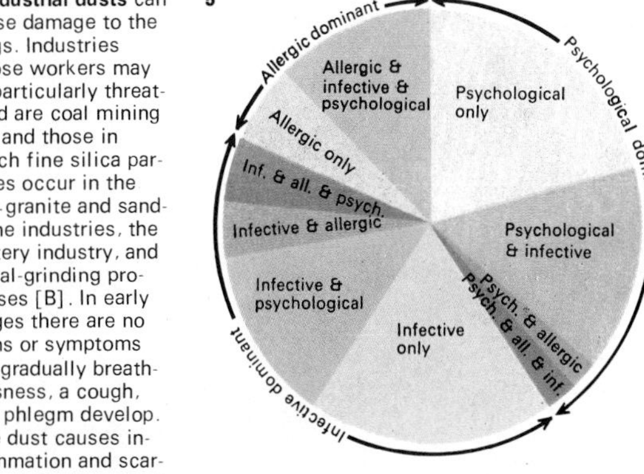

Allergic dominant
Psychological dominant
Infective dominant
Allergic & infective & psychological
Psychological only
Allergic only
Inf. & all. & psych.
Infective & allergic
Psychological & infective
Infective & psychological
Infective only
Psych. & allergic
Psych. & all. & inf.

5 An attack of asthma can be precipitated by a number of factors. These may be psychological, infective, or allergic, or occur in combination. While one factor, such as psychological stress, may be most important, an attack becomes more likely if an infection or an allergy is also present. The size of the segments indicates the relative importance of each cause or combination.

6

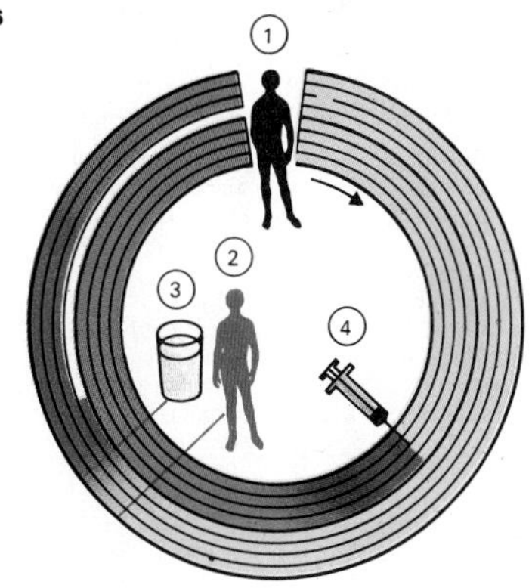

1
2
3
4

6 Tuberculosis normally affects the lung tissues but may spread throughout the body. A healthy person [1] can become infected by inhaling bacteria spread by a tubercular patient [2] or by drinking cow's milk [3] containing bovine tubercle bacilli. A long, often chronic infection follows [red], with a 25 percent mortality risk. Those who recover become immune [green]. Immunization [4] by modified bacilli [orange] also provides protection.

7

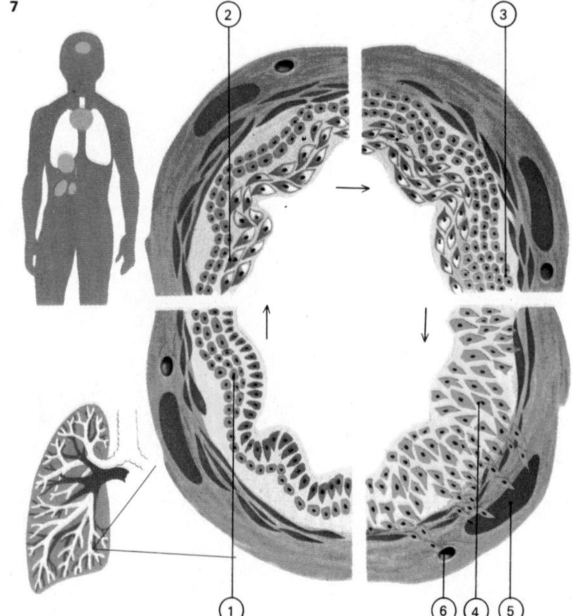

2
3
1
6
4
5

7 Lung cancer most commonly affects smokers. Cancers develop from cells that alter their structure and multiply more rapidly. Changes may occur in cells of the inner or outer lining of the bronchial tubes [1]. Altered malignant cells increase in numbers [2] and extend locally [3] or invade adjacent tissue [4]. In addition, the cancerous cells may spread outside the lung either through blood vessels [5] or the lymphatic system [6].

Diseases of the circulation

Because of the close interdependence of the heart, the blood vessels (arteries, veins and capillaries), and the blood, abnormality or disease of any part [Key] often leads to malfunction of the whole system. Congenital malformation that disrupts the flow of blood through the heart and its major blood vessels, or through both, may lead to a newborn baby appearing blue because the blood is carrying too little oxygen. An operation may be needed soon after diagnosis or perhaps later in childhood to correct the abnormality.

Types of heart disease

The heart and its valves are susceptible to damage by disease. Commonly known is rheumatic fever, which frequently leads to rheumatic heart disease. The damage it causes to the valves in childhood can lead to severe malfunctioning of the heart in later life; a valve-replacement operation often can provide a remedy. The incidence of the disease has been reduced by prompt treatment by drugs.

Occasionally the heart's pacemaker causes irregular beating, or a defect in the conduction of the electrical impulse that causes the beat may lead to a chamber beating out of sequence. These so-called dysrhythmias may be helped by drugs (such as digitalis) but in some cases an artificial pacemaker will be needed [2] and is inserted surgically.

Any decrease in the supply of blood through the coronary arteries to the heart itself can lead to attacks of pain, called angina pectoris, a kind of cramp of the heart muscle that is usually worse after exercise or effort. Severe restriction in the blood supply can cause failure of the heart muscle. This is accompanied by sudden excruciating pain in the chest and is commonly called a heart attack. The usual cause is a thrombosis, or clot, in a coronary artery [1]. Definite causes of coronary thrombosis are still largely speculative. A person who is overweight, takes little exercise, smokes, has high blood pressure (hypertension), a high level of cholesterol in the blood, and a family history of heart disease incurs a high risk of attack.

Defects in arteries and veins

Hardening of the arteries (arteriosclerosis) is a degeneration of the wall of the artery and is a normal part of growing old. It affects all the arteries of the body and can be accelerated and exaggerated by high blood pressure. Atherosclerosis (deposition of fats and cholesterol within an artery) is much more serious. It causes narrow, roughened vessels and may lead to thrombosis. If it occurs in the arteries of the legs, exercise may become painful; a graft may be needed to replace the damaged artery. Atherosclerosis of the aorta may reduce the elasticity of the vessel, producing a bulging of the wall called an aneurysm. This may rupture spontaneously and cause severe hemorrhage that will need emergency medical treatment.

In many cases, the cause of high blood pressure is unknown, but hardening of the small arteries of the kidney is certainly contributory. As high blood pressure makes this condition worse, treatment is needed to break the vicious circle. Several drugs can help. Some act directly to remove adrena-

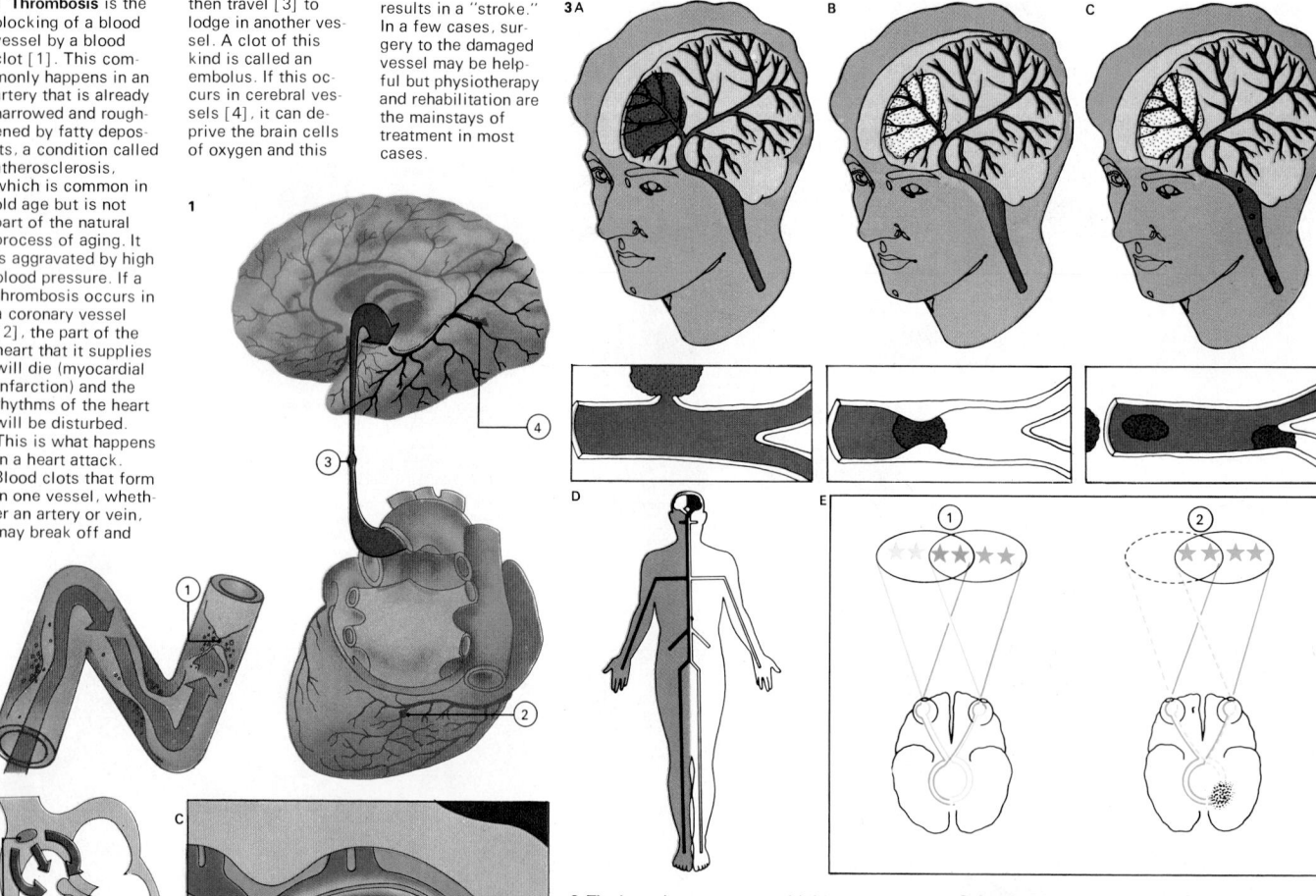

CONNECTIONS

See also

688 Heart and blood circulation
752 Development of surgery
738 Preventive medicine
722 Diseases of the nervous system
698 Keeping fit
416 Principles of heredity

1 Thrombosis is the blocking of a blood vessel by a blood clot [1]. This commonly happens in an artery that is already narrowed and roughened by fatty deposits, a condition called atherosclerosis, which is common in old age but is not part of the natural process of aging. It is aggravated by high blood pressure. If a thrombosis occurs in a coronary vessel [2], the part of the heart that it supplies will die (myocardial infarction) and the rhythms of the heart will be disturbed. This is what happens in a heart attack. Blood clots that form in one vessel, whether an artery or vein, may break off and then travel [3] to lodge in another vessel. A clot of this kind is called an embolus. If this occurs in cerebral vessels [4], it can deprive the brain cells of oxygen and this results in a "stroke." In a few cases, surgery to the damaged vessel may be helpful but physiotherapy and rehabilitation are the mainstays of treatment in most cases.

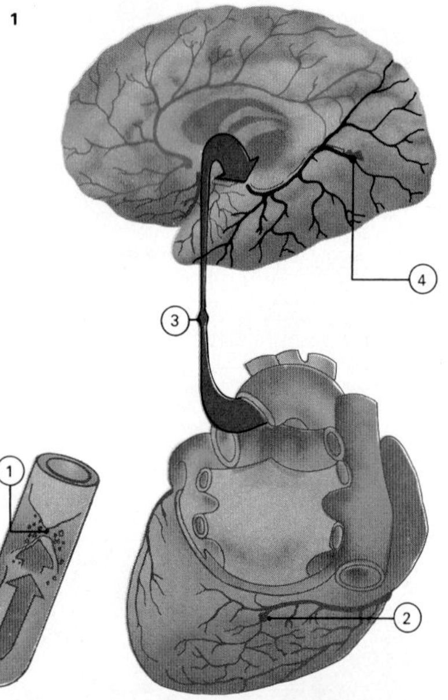

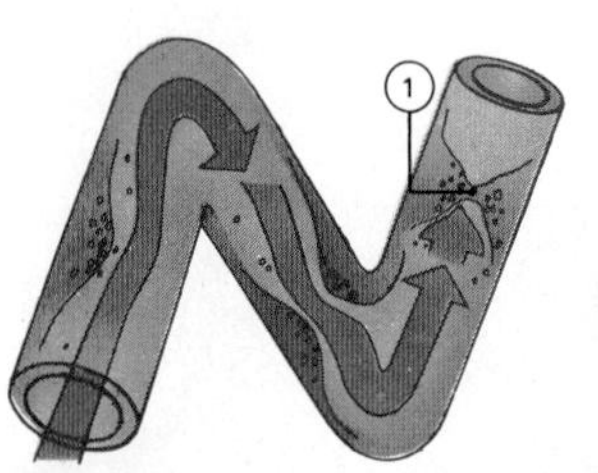

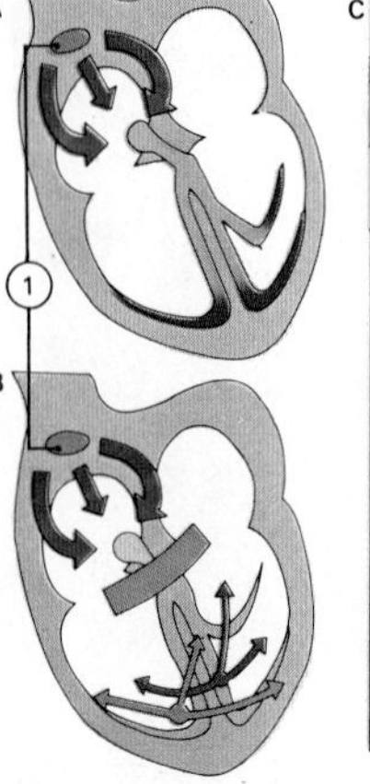

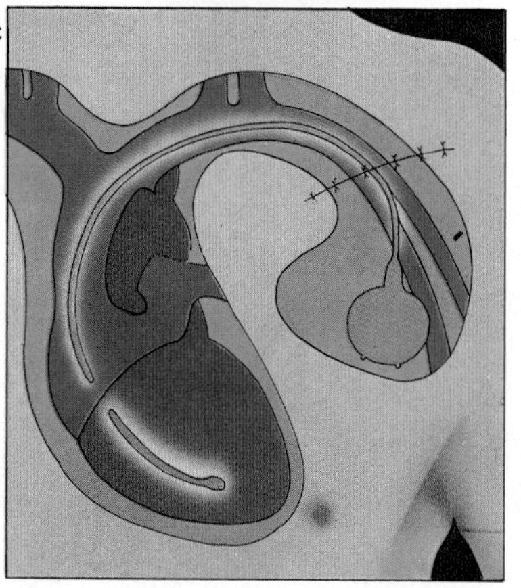

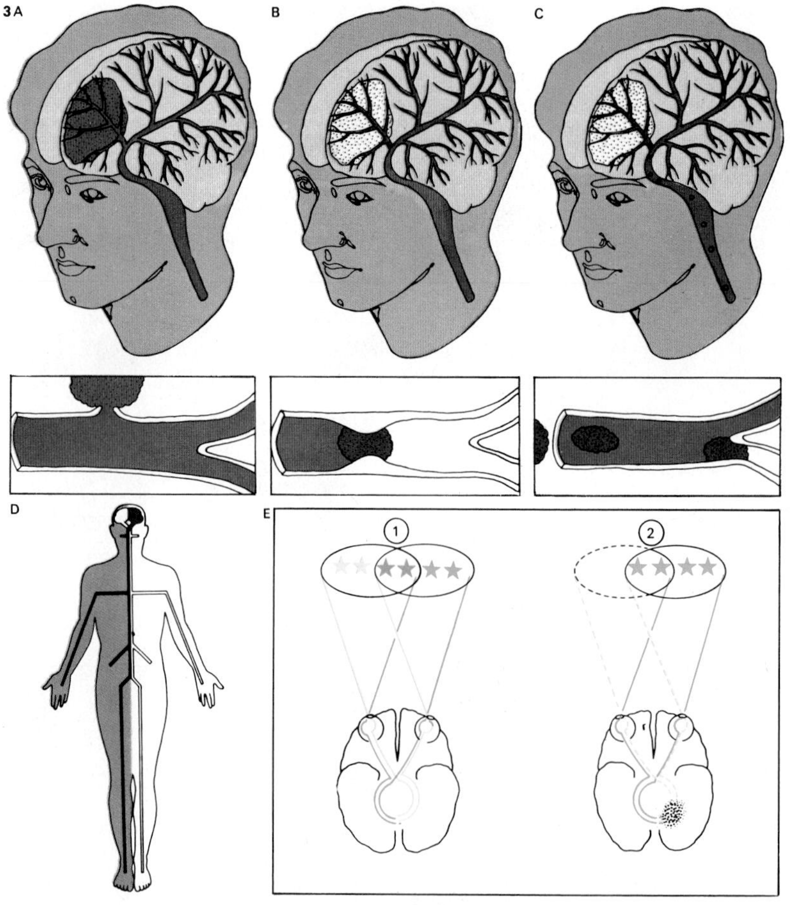

2 The heart has a natural pacemaker [A], the sinoatrial node [1] that controls heartbeat and rhythm. It transmits regular impulses through special conducting tissues, stimulating heart muscle contraction. Defective conducting tissue may result in atria and ventricles contracting in a dissociated way, which may lead to complete heart block [B]. To avoid this possibility, a battery-operated artificial heart pacemaker can be used to stimulate ventricular contraction at a normal rate of 70 to 80 beats per minute. The pacemaker can be placed under the skin of the chest with the electrode leads passing through a great vein to the ventricle [C]. Batteries for the pacemaker are charged periodically.

3 A "stroke" is a disruption of the blood supply to the brain and is caused either by a hemorrhage of a cerebral blood vessel [A], a thrombus [B], or an embolus [C]. The damage (stippled area) may be permanent, but the outcome of a stroke depends on the extent and area of the brain affected by it. The symptoms can range from a temporary loss of speech or other brain function and paralysis of the limbs to sudden death. A stroke on one side of the brain affects the limbs of the opposite side of the body because of the crossing over of nerve tracts in the brain stem [D]. There is a similar effect on the visual cortex [E]. Normal vision [1] is impaired on the left [2] by a stroke on the right.

line (which causes the arteries to contract). Others tranquilize a patient and so reduce the amount of adrenaline he produces. Digitalis helps the heart to pump more vigorously, while drugs called diuretics reduce the fluid in the circulation.

Varicose veins [4] are a common condition, made worse by long periods of standing. Clots can also develop, especially in the legs, when the veins are inflamed (phlebitis), and the legs may be swollen and painful. Venous thrombosis is likely to occur in people who have prolonged periods in bed after an operation or a stroke. The danger of a clot in the legs is that it may break off to become an embolus that travels through the heart and lodges in the lungs. Thrombosis is usually treated with anticoagulant drugs.

Blood defects

Blood is subject to a number of diseases. In anemia there is usually either a reduction in the number of red cells or in the cell's hemoglobin content [5]. The reduction in the oxygen-carrying capacity of the blood causes tiredness and breathlessness. More rarely, disorders of the bone marrow, which makes the blood cells, lead to anemia. Sometimes the red cells are destroyed more quickly than their usual four-month lifespan and are not replaced fast enough.

Leukemia [8] is the name given to a group of diseases characterized by proliferation of abnormal white cells. The patient is likely to suffer from anemia, infection, and bleeding. Drugs, including steroids, that interfere with the reproduction of white cells are used in the treatment of leukemia.

Blood plasma contains various factors needed for the normal clotting mechanism. Deficiency of one, the anti-hemophilic factor, leads to hemophilia [6]. Deficiency in another causes the much rarer Christmas disease, which has similar effects. Treatment with anti-hemophilic factor is needed as soon as possible after the start of spontaneous bleeding to prevent further damage [7]. Unfortunately, the factor lasts in the body less than 24 hours. One hope is that sufficient amounts will be made available so that hemophiliacs can treat themselves.

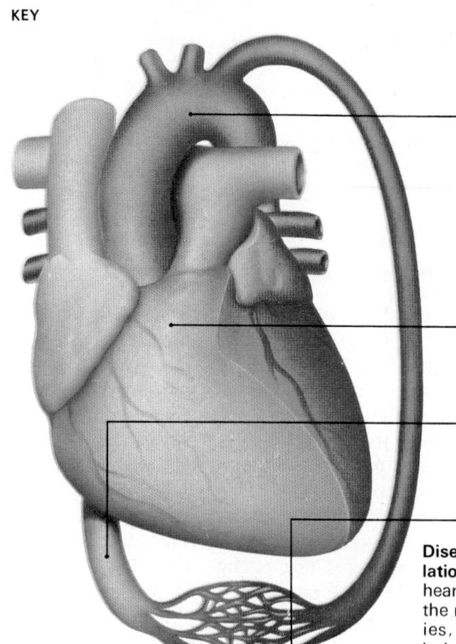
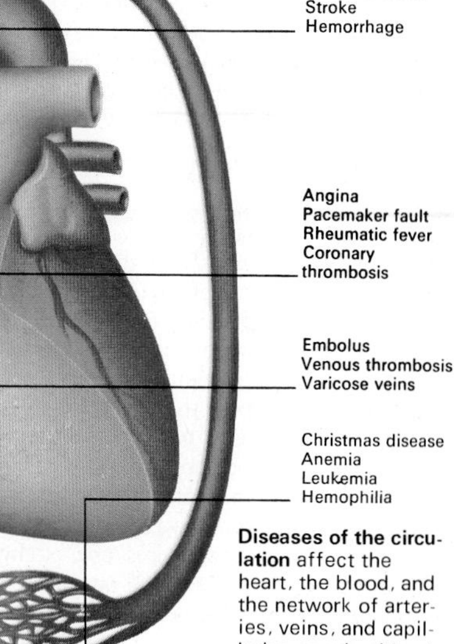
KEY
Arteriosclerosis
Atherosclerosis
Stroke
Hemorrhage
Angina
Pacemaker fault
Rheumatic fever
Coronary thrombosis
Embolus
Venous thrombosis
Varicose veins
Christmas disease
Anemia
Leukemia
Hemophilia

Diseases of the circulation affect the heart, the blood, and the network of arteries, veins, and capillaries carrying blood around the body.

4 Veins normally have a system of valves that enables the blood to travel toward the heart but not back [A]. People whose occupations involve long periods of standing may develop varicose veins. This condition occurs when the valves do not function properly, the veins becoming stretched and distorted [B]. Varicose veins of the lower end of the bowel are called hemorrhoids. If the affected veins fail to respond to simple treatment they may sometimes require surgical removal. When varicose veins become infected and inflamed it is a form of phlebitis [C].

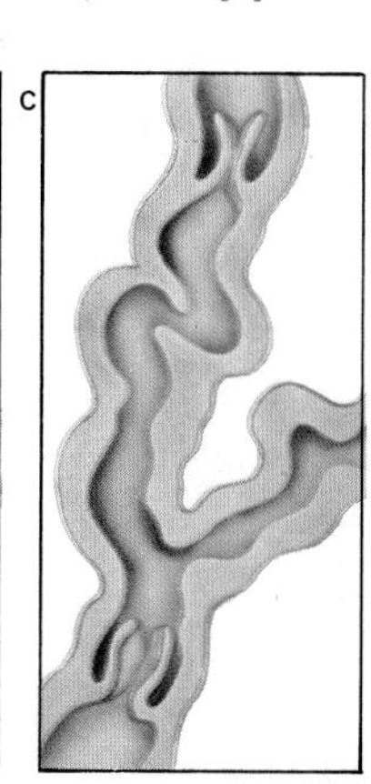
4
A
B
C

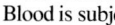

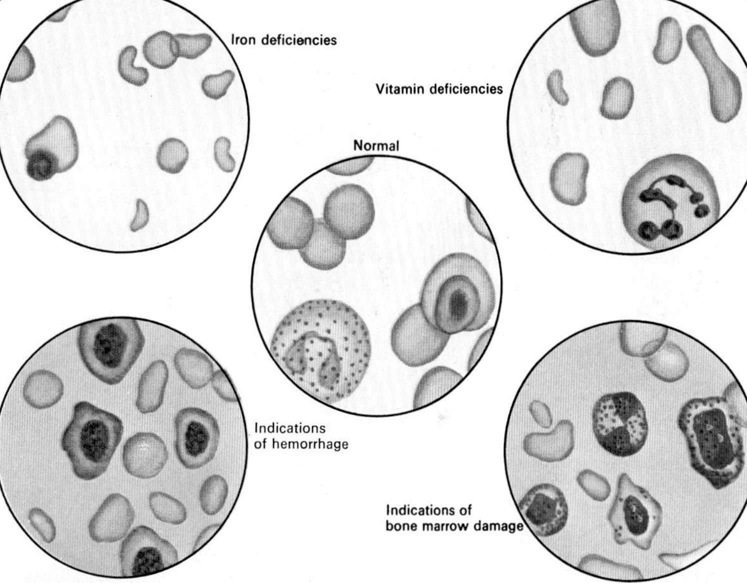
5
Iron deficiencies
Vitamin deficiencies
Normal
Indications of hemorrhage
Indications of bone marrow damage

5 Anemia produces recognizable changes in the red cells of a blood film. Compared with normal blood, iron deficiency shows up in small, pale cells with reduced hemoglobin content. Iron deficiency may be caused by hidden bleeding rather than dietary insufficiency and needs investigating. Lack of either of the vitamins B_{12} or folic acid produces large, pale, abnormally shaped red cells and white cells with multiple nuclei. Diets that lack liver and dairy products like eggs, milk, and cheese (containing vitamin B_{12}) or fresh fruit and vegetables (folic acid), can cause these anemias, but even with an adequate diet the vitamins that are needed may not be properly absorbed. Pernicious anemia, for example, prevents the proper absorption of vitamin B_{12}. After severe hemorrhage or damage, bone marrow may release red cells that are immature or abnormal in some way.

6 The gene causing hemophilia [green] is carried on one of the female (or X) sex chromosomes controlling blood clotting. It does not show in a female carrier [1] because her other X [red] is normal, but when transmitted to the son [2] of a normal male, his Y chromosome [blue] cannot balance it.

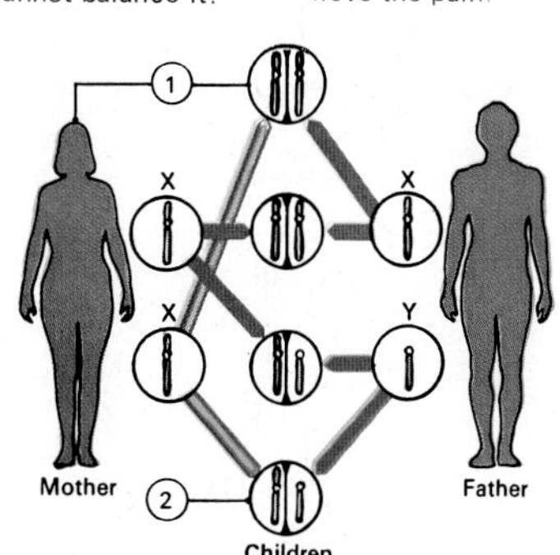
6
1
X
X
X
Y
Mother
2
Father
Children

7 In hemophiliacs, spontaneous bleeding occurs into the joints, which become hot, swollen, and painful. The patient must receive anti-hemophilic factor quickly to stop the bleeding because it can lead to a crippling arthritis. The use of ice packs and analgesics helps relieve the pain.

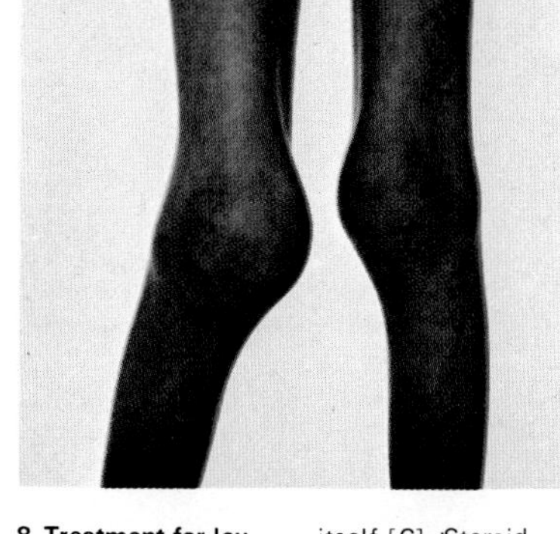
7

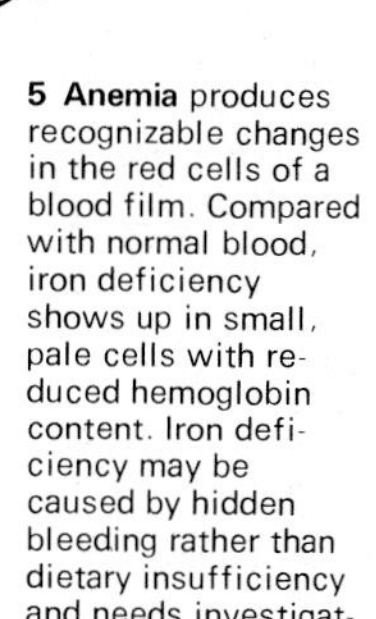
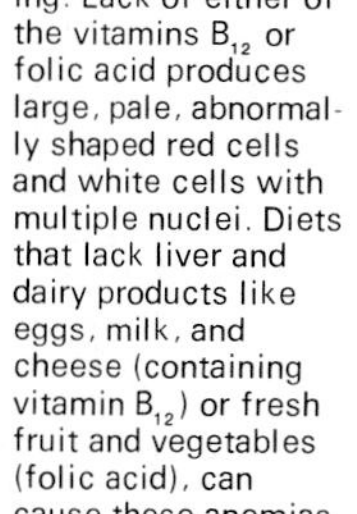
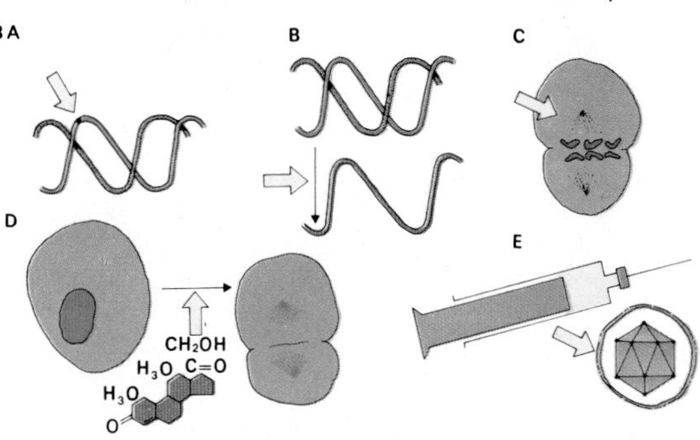
8 A
B
C
D
E
CH₂OH
H₃O C=O
H₃O
O

8 Treatment for leukemia is aimed at preventing the abnormal white cells from reproducing themselves. Drug treatment interferes with the doubling of the genetic material (DNA) prior to division [A, B] or with the division process itself [C]. Steroid drugs also interfere with division [D]. The theory that leukemia is caused by a virus is still only a tentative one, but if proved, could mean new and revolutionary treatment of leukemia by the use of vaccines [E].

Diseases of the digestive system

Disorders and diseases can occur in any part of the gastrointestinal tract. "Indigestion" is something that nearly everyone suffers from occasionally, but if it becomes frequent and persistent then the chances are that disease has affected the digestive system in the region of the esophagus, stomach, or duodenum or perhaps the pancreas, liver, or gall bladder.

The formation of ulcers

The esophagus passes from the throat to join the stomach through an opening in the diaphragm to which it is loosely attached. From middle age this attachment weakens and part of the stomach can become pinched in the opening; this hiatus hernia is quite common. After a meal the acid contents of the stomach can reflux back into the esophagus, causing pain and eventual ulceration. The pain, because of its position, is often called heartburn and is one of the symptoms behind the medical adage "if a patient complains of his heart, examine his stomach; if he complains of his stomach, examine his heart." The reflux may cause regurgitation of fluid into the mouth, probably after bending or straining. Occasionally surgery may be needed, but the usual treatment consists of a weight-reducing diet plus advice on sleeping in a raised position.

The term "peptic ulcer" usually refers to an ulcer found at the lower end of the esophagus, in the stomach or in the duodenum [1]. The cause of ulcers is thought to be increased secretion by the stomach of acid and the enzyme pepsin or a breakdown in the protective mucous secretions of the stomach lining. This acid-pepsin mixture overcomes the protective layer of mucus in the stomach and "eats away" the digestive tract lining. Alcohol, smoking, stress, and O group blood type are all associated with ulcers.

The pain that an ulcer causes is usually felt centrally in the upper part of the abdomen [5]. Its occurrence is related to meal times but often awakens a sufferer between 2 and 3 am. Taking food or antacids usually relieves the pain, as does vomiting. The medical treatment of all ulcers involves relief of stress with rest in bed, a bland diet, the stopping of smoking and the administration of medications, including antacids.

There are many disorders in which the major defect is malabsorption from the intestine of one or more of the minerals, vitamins, or other essential foods. Malabsorption tends to be associated with weight loss, anemia, diarrhea, and vitamin deficiencies.

Malabsorption disorders

Two of the most important malabsorption defects are celiac disease and Crohn's Disease. Celiac disease is caused by an inability to cope with an allergy to gluten, a protein found in wheat and other cereals, while Crohn's Disease is an inflammation of the end part of the small intestine (the terminal ileum) and is also known as regional ileitis. Crohn's Disease can sometimes affect other parts of the small bowel and, rarely, the colon. Typical symptoms include abdominal pain, diarrhea, loss of weight, fever, and anemia.

Ulcerative colitis is an important disease affecting the large bowel. Its cause is a mystery but it involves inflammation that leads

CONNECTIONS

See also
694 The digestive system
710 The cause of illness:
768 Psychosomatic diseases and retardation
750 Radiology and radiotherapy
416 Principles of heredity

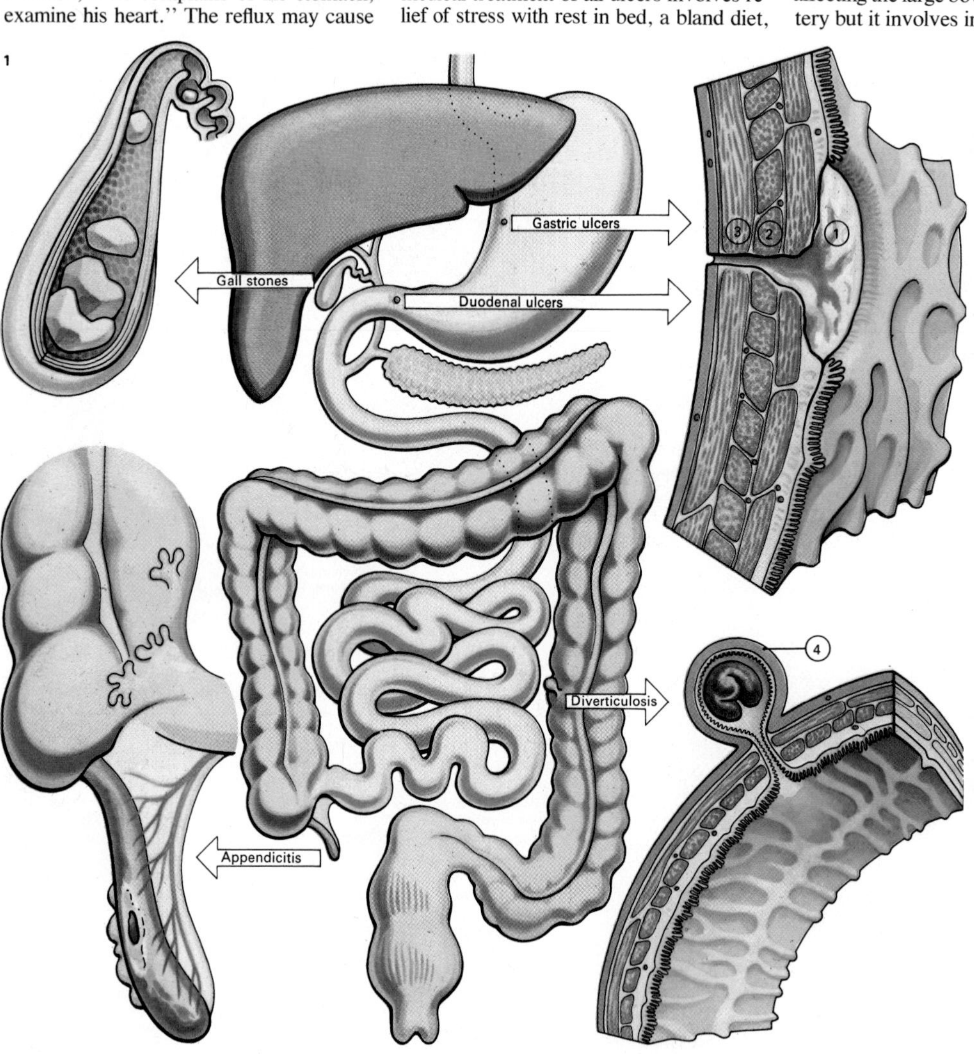

1
Gastric ulcers
Gall stones
Duodenal ulcers
3
2
1
4
Diverticulosis
Appendicitis

1 Five common disorders of the digestive tract are illustrated. Ulcers of the stomach (gastric) or duodenum may penetrate the submucous coat [1], muscle layer [2], and finally perforate the wall [3]. Gallstones occur in 5–10% of the population. They are a classic disorder of the "fs"—the fair, fat, forty, female. They are often associated with gall bladder infections. If stones move out of the gall bladder they cause obstruction to the bile duct and biliary colic. Treatment is surgical removal of the gall bladder. Appendicitis can also demand surgery. It is an inflammation and infection of the appendix. Diverticulosis, or the formation of narrow-necked, saclike diverticulae, [4] commonly occurs in the colon. The disorder is thought to be caused by weakening of the bowel wall and increased internal pressure because of lack of vegetable fiber. As a result, the diverticulae can become obstructed, infected and inflamed.

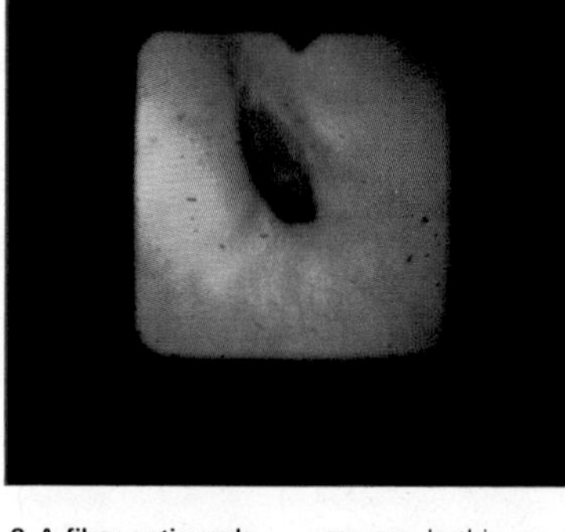

2
A

2 A fiber-optic endoscope, a lighted flexible tube, is used by physicians to look directly into the gastrointestinal tract. In the stomach the instrument can be rotated and pictures can be taken with a camera. In this way it is possible to compare a normal [A] with an ulcerated [B] lining. If an ulcer is present the instrument can remove a piece of tissue for examination in the laboratory.

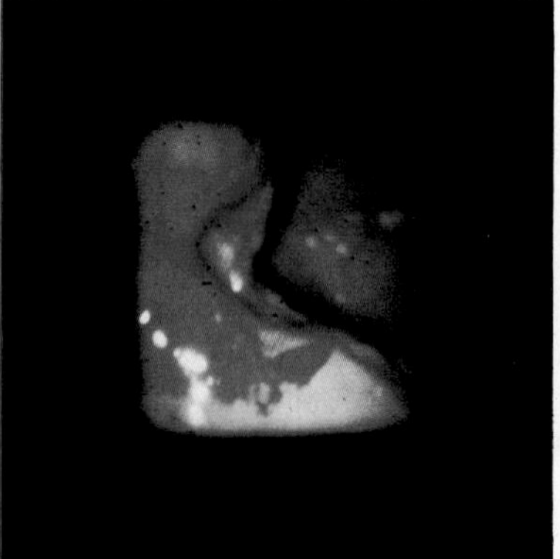

B

3

3 Gallstones are most commonly composed, like these, of a mixture of calcium, cholesterol, and the bile pigment bilirubin. Stones can be made entirely of cholesterol, a fatty substance present in the blood or, more rarely, of bilirubin.

to ulceration. The rectum alone, or sometimes the whole colon, may be affected. Painful attacks of blood-stained diarrhea are typical and in severe cases high fever, anemia, exhaustion, and collapse can occur.

Cancer of the intestine, especially of the stomach and colon, is second only in importance to cancer of the lung. Symptoms include non-specific pain, a change of bowel habits, loss of weight, and intestinal bleeding. In cancer of the stomach loss of appetite, nausea, and vomiting are usual and in cancer of the bowel blockage by feces—intestinal obstruction—may take place.

Jaundice diseases

When the liver and gall bladder malfunction they produce jaundice. Jaundice is a yellow discoloration, most noticeable in the skin, which arises when the amount of bilirubin in the blood is above normal [4]. Liver disease, the breakdown of red blood cells, or the presence of gallstones [1, 3] obstructing the bile duct will cause this. The liver diseases hepatitis and cirrhosis are well known for causing jaundice. Cirrhosis, which may be associated with excess alcohol intake, involves the replacement of normal liver cells with fibrous tissue.

Hepatitis is of two types and each is caused by a different virus. Infectious hepatitis has a relatively short incubation period (15–35 days) and is spread by fecal contamination or the consumption of raw shellfish. Serum hepatitis has a longer incubation period of 40–180 days and is passed mainly by contaminated needles or in blood transfusion. Both diseases cause inflammation of the liver cells and this prevents them from functioning normally and causes an excess of bilirubin, which in turn causes the typical jaundiced coloration of the skin [4].

Apart from the hepatitis viruses, other microorganisms can affect the digestive tract. An example of these are the *Salmonella,* or "food-poisoning," bacteria, which are also responsible for typhoid [6]. Bacteria also cause inflammation of the appendix and thus appendicitis [1]. Other invaders of the digestive tract are amebas and parasites such as roundworms and tapeworms.

KEY

Stomach
Over 35 years
Both sexes: ulcers
Males: cancer

Duodenum
Males 15–25 years: ulcers
All ages
Both sexes: parasites

Small intestine
All ages
Both sexes: viral and bacterial infections
Under 35
Both sexes: appendicitis

Large intestine
Over 50
Both sexes: diverticulosis, colonic hernia, cancer
All ages: amebic diarrhea

Age can be a common factor in some disorders of the digestive system. The diagram shows a few well known examples.

4

Red blood cells
Hemoglobin
Bilirubin
Albumen
Glucuronic acid

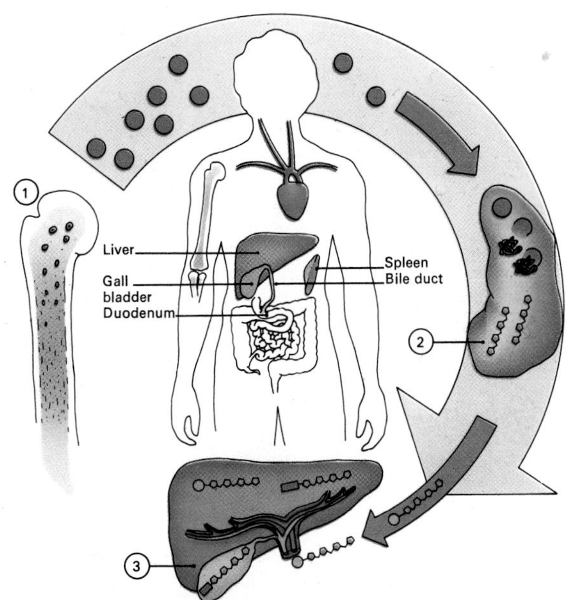

1
Liver
Gall bladder
Duodenum
Spleen
Bile duct
2
3

4 Excessive breakdown of red blood cells causes jaundice. Made in the bone marrow [1], the cells normally have a life of about 120 days before they are removed by the spleen [2]. The red pigment hemoglobin is metabolized to bilirubin and carried to the liver [3] attached to the blood protein albumin. In the liver albumin is removed and replaced with glucuronic acid. This passes to the gall bladder and from there to the gut. Excess of bilirubin produces jaundice.

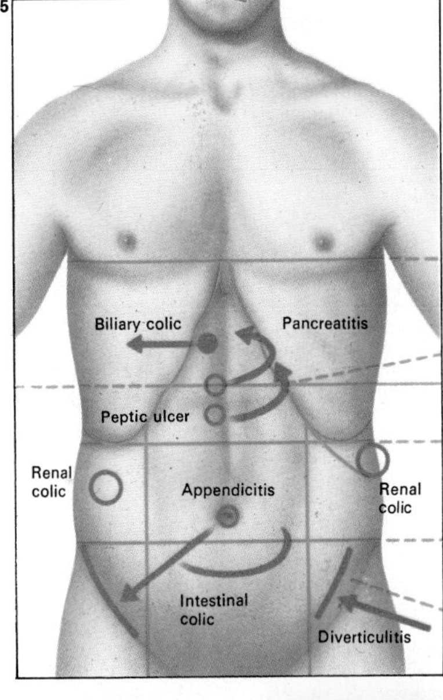

5
Biliary colic
Pancreatitis
Peptic ulcer
Renal colic
Appendicitis
Renal colic
Intestinal colic
Diverticulitis

5 The acute abdomen is the name given to a group of disorders associated with abdominal pains. Colics are pains that wax and wane in intensity. Intestinal colic can occur in food poisoning or intestinal obstruction. Biliary colic is an intense, constant pain starting in the middle and moving to the liver. The pain from a perforated peptic ulcer or inflammation of the pancreas is persistent and "moves" through to the back. Appendicitis usually starts with a pain in the region of the umbilicus, which moves to the area of the right groin. The pain of diverticulitis occurs in the left lower abdomen.

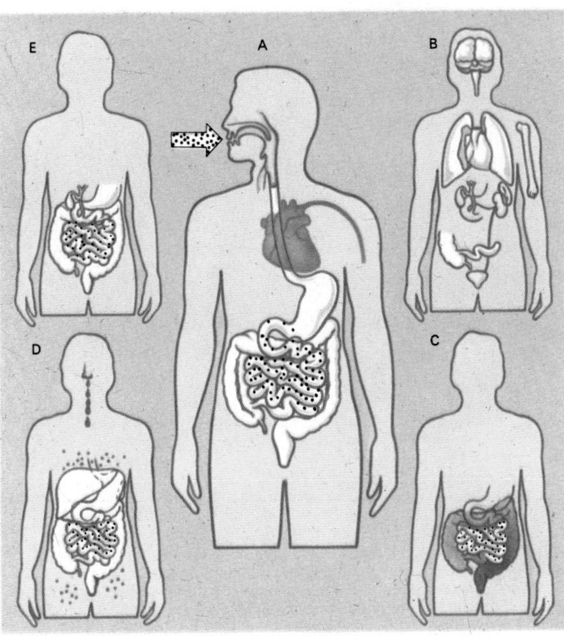

6
E
A
B
D
C

6 The bacterium *Salmonella* causes intestinal infections that may vary from mild gastroenteritis to severe typhoid. Bacteria enter the body [A] from infected food or water and incubate for up to 14 days. In typhoid [B], disease affects many body parts. After incubation [C] diarrhea ensues. Other features of typhoid [D] are nosebleeds and rose spots. Bacteria remaining after an attack [E] make a person a carrier.

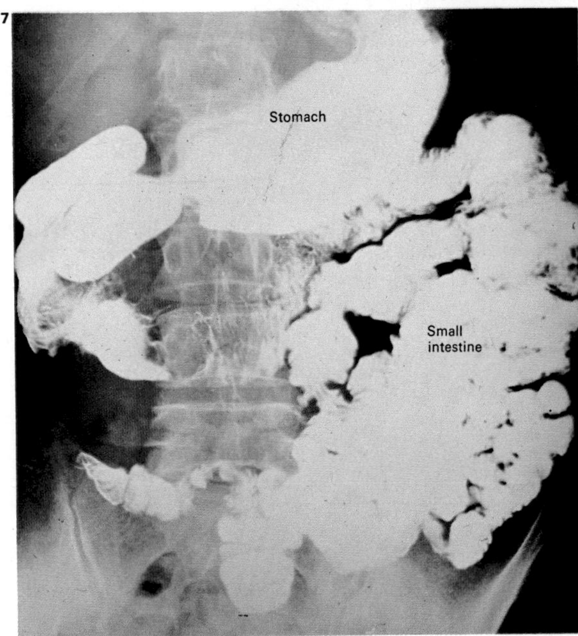

7
Stomach
Small intestine

7 A barium swallow is a common diagnostic procedure. The patient swallows a barium-containing mixture opaque to X rays. Conditions that may be revealed include ulcers, various cancers, and hiatus hernia of the stomach into the esophagus.

Diseases of the skeleton and muscles

The skeleton is the framework on which the body is hung and supported, and the muscles provide movement. Considering the extent of movement in life, and the weight that is supported, it is not surprising that disorders of the musculoskeletal system occur. Not all disorders are the result of wear and tear, however; inherited disorders may also occur, and there are others that may arise during life.

Wear and tear in muscles

The wear and tear disorders are among the most common. Everyone suffers muscular aches and pains at intervals and severe and unaccustomed exercise usually leads to discomfort and stiffness in the muscles the next day. In due course such exercise of muscle will lead to the development of more powerful muscles. In the untrained, sudden movements will more commonly lead to muscle strains, tears of parts of the muscle mass, or tears in the tendons that attach muscle to bone. Such tears are often accompanied by bruising in the muscle; healing can take two or three weeks.

Lumbago, or pain in the lower back, may follow muscle strain resulting from unaccustomed activity. When back pain is accompanied by pain going down the back of one leg the condition is known as sciatica. The pain is caused by pressure on one of the nerve roots that leave the spinal cord and supply the leg via the sciatic nerve. Treatment involves rest in bed on a firm mattress supported by a board. The strain may be on one of the ligaments that run up the spinal column and support the vertebrae.

Excessive pressure on the spinal column can cause the pad, or disk, that cushions each vertebra to be compressed and press upon the nerve root [3]. Treatment requires rest while the tear heals and the disk returns to normal. If rest does not achieve this, surgical removal of the protruding portion of the disk may be necessary.

Other sites at which injury can occur are in the joints between the bones. Bone ends are covered with cartilage and held together by strong fibrous capsules. The capsule of a joint may be torn, and the cartilage may be damaged. In the knee, specialized half-moons of cartilage act as cushions between the femur (thighbone) and the tibia (shinbone). These two cartilages in each knee are attached to the edge of the wearing surface of the knee joint. Sudden twisting of the knee may dislodge a cartilage, tearing its attachment to the bone. Cartilage injuries are common in such sports as football and soccer [6] in which the weight-bearing joints are frequently twisted.

Arthritis and its treatment

Over the years the degree of wear and tear may become excessive and the consequence may be the premature development of osteoarthritis [1] in the joints. This type of arthritis develops in many elderly people in the ankle, knee, and hip. The result is that the joint narrows, movement is restricted, and pain and deformity occur. Osteoarthritis in the hip can be disabling, but it is now possible to replace the hip joint with metal and plastic substitutes and thus restore full mobility.

The other common arthritis, known as rheumatoid arthritis, is not a result of over-

CONNECTIONS

See also
682 Skull, skeleton, and joints
684 Muscles and action
712 The causes of illness: 2
758 First aid
804 An active old age
750 Radiology and radiotherapy

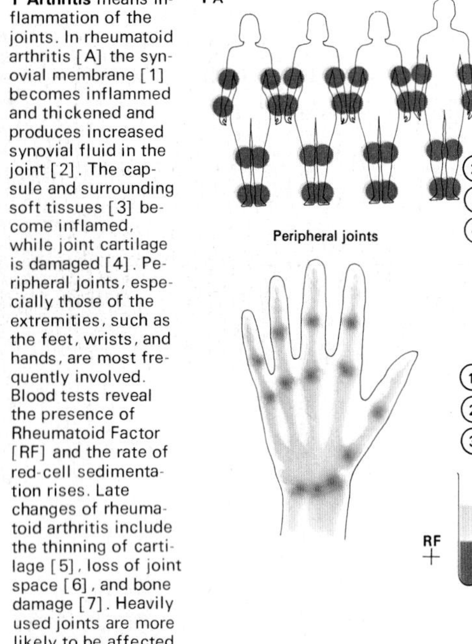

1 A
B
Peripheral joints
Early stages
Stressed joints
RF +
Late stages
RF –

1 Arthritis means inflammation of the joints. In rheumatoid arthritis [A] the synovial membrane [1] becomes inflammed and thickened and produces increased synovial fluid in the joint [2]. The capsule and surrounding soft tissues [3] become inflamed, while joint cartilage is damaged [4]. Peripheral joints, especially those of the extremities, such as the feet, wrists, and hands, are most frequently involved. Blood tests reveal the presence of Rheumatoid Factor [RF] and the rate of red-cell sedimentation rises. Late changes of rheumatoid arthritis include the thinning of cartilage [5], loss of joint space [6], and bone damage [7]. Heavily used joints are more likely to be affected in osteoarthritis [B], and blood tests are normal.

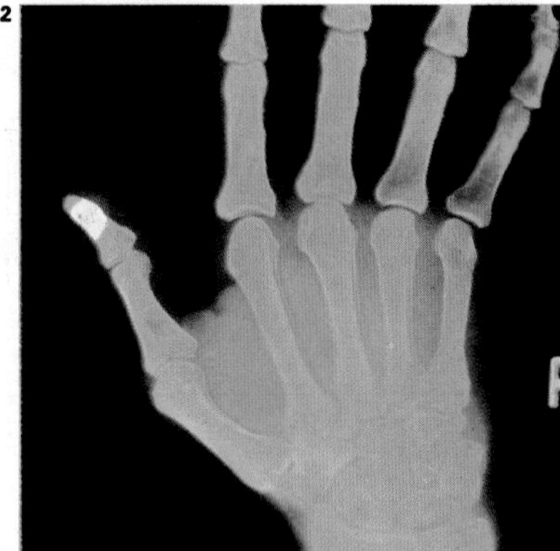

2 The hands are common sites of rheumatoid arthritis. An X ray shows the typical deformity of the joints and the deviation of the fingers toward the little finger side. The cause of rheumatoid arthritis is unknown. Treatment may involve the administration of anti-inflammatory drugs.

3 The spinal column [A] is a series of bones [B] surrounding the spinal cord [1] and separated by disks, or cushionlike pads [2]. These may be pressed from their normal place if the surrounding ligaments tear as a result of strain or degenerative changes. The disk between the fourth and fifth lumbar vertebrae [3] here protrudes toward the back of the vertebrae. Pain, muscle spasm, and restricted movement are common results. The fifth lumbar vertebra [C] (from above) shows the nerve roots [4] leaving the spinal cord. The position of the normal disk [5] is shown pale yellow, while the herniated disk [6] is seen pressing on the nerve root.

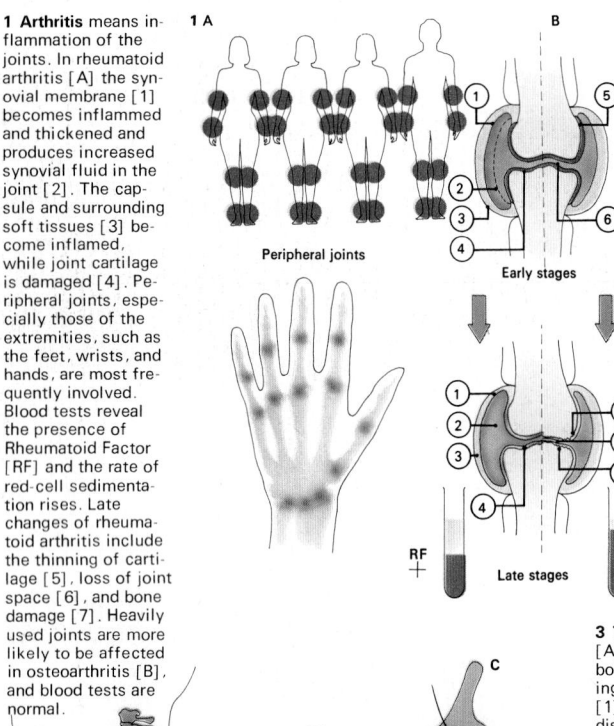

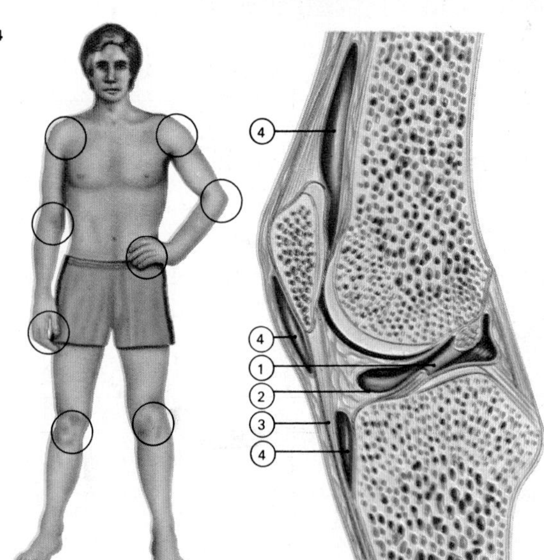

4 Joints are lubricated by synovial fluid [1] produced by a synovial membrane [2]. Around many joints pass tendons [3]. These are protected from rubbing and excess friction by strategically sited sacs, or bursae [4], which are similarly lined and lubricated. Local damage, overuse, or pressure can lead to inflammation and excess production of fluid, (bursitis). Water on the knee, or housemaid's knee, is typical. Trigger finger, and frozen shoulder are often caused by synovitis, while tennis elbow results from damage at the attachment of a tendon. To avoid further strain the joint should not be overused but exercised gently; immobilizing it can lead to stiffness and may be harmful.

use. Women are more likely to be affected than men. The small joints of the hands and feet become damaged and deformed, and elbows, shoulders, and ankles may be affected. The disorder is sometimes part of a more generalized body disturbance, and evidence of widespread inflammation can be detected in blood tests. In both types of arthritis, symptomatic treatment for the pain with analgesics is beneficial, but suppression of the inflammation may be required in rheumatoid disease. This is often achieved by the administration of anti-inflammatory drugs.

Some musculoskeletal disorders are congenital, that is, present from birth. Congenital dislocation of the hip, for example, is sometimes found in infants [7]. The hip joint does not form fully for many years after birth, and initially the socket in which the ball of the femur is held is very shallow. It is easy to dislocate the head of the femur from the socket. In some children this occurs spontaneously and, if not corrected, will cause maldevelopment of the hip. Treatment is simply to splint the leg so that the joint cannot dislocate. Although ungainly, such treatment at an early stage is effective. The longer diagnosis is delayed the more difficult is the cure, and babies are examined shortly after birth for evidence of this fairly uncommon condition.

Treatment by immobilization

Immobilization of an injured part of the musculoskeletal system can be required for many different problems, such as fractures of bones [Key]. Plaster casts may be adequate if the parts of the bones are well aligned. Otherwise internal fixation can be undertaken, in which the bones are held together with pins or plates screwed into the fragments. It is important at every stage after the operation, including the period during which the limb is splinted, that the patient is made to exercise as much as possible, because during the enforced rest wasting of the unused muscles occurs. This can considerably slow full recovery, for building up muscles can be a time-consuming process that requires effort and dedication from the patient.

KEY

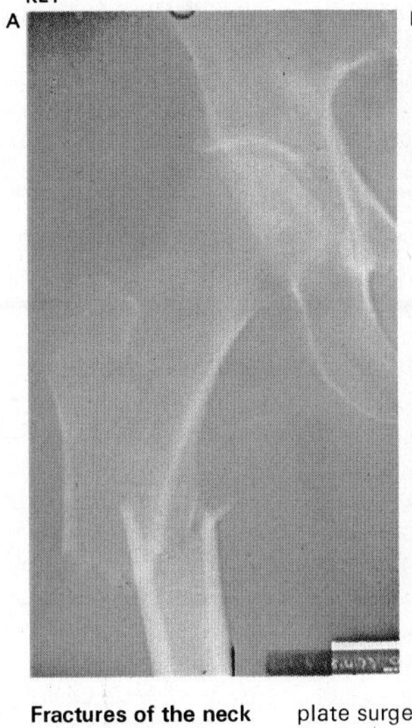
A

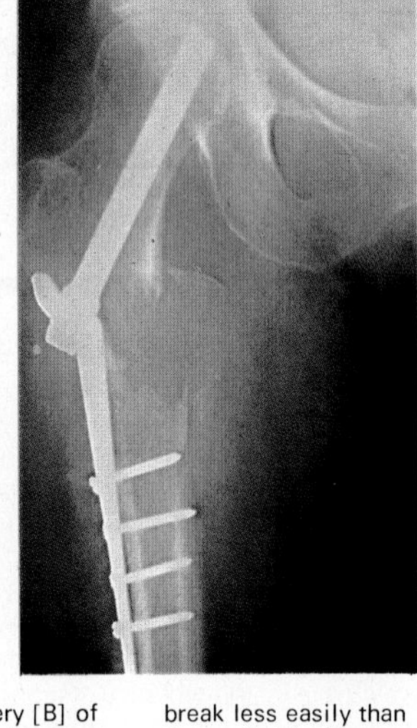
B

Fractures of the neck of the femur [A] are common in old people, who have brittle bones. The X ray shows how pin and plate surgery [B] of the broken fragments can help speed healing and recovery. The bones of the young are more flexible and break less easily than those of old people and when they do break they often cause less damage to surrounding tissue.

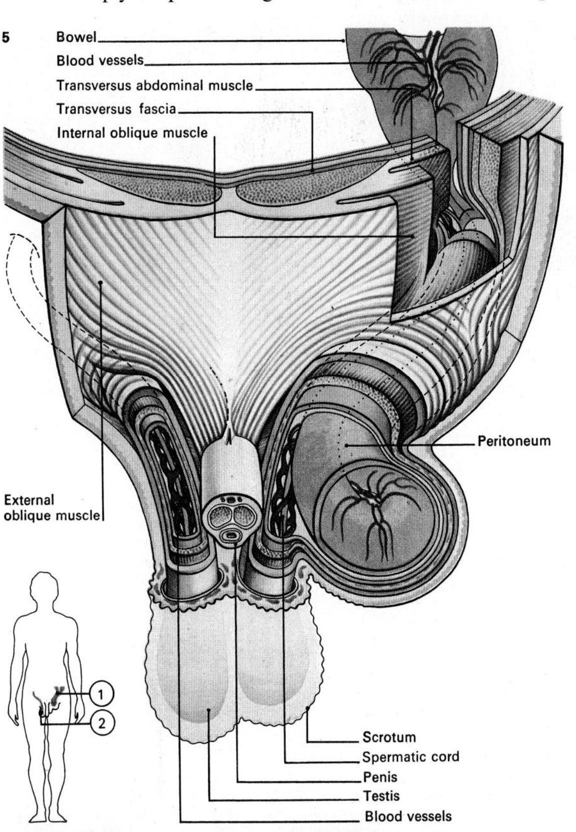
5
Bowel
Blood vessels
Transversus abdominal muscle
Transversus fascia
Internal oblique muscle
Peritoneum
External oblique muscle
1
2
Scrotum
Spermatic cord
Penis
Testis
Blood vessels

5 A hernia, often called a rupture, is the passage of any organ into an abnormal site. Common are those where the bowel [1] slides into the groin [2]. A weakness develops in the abdominal muscles. A loop of bowel insinuates itself along the path of the spermatic cord in the male and appears as a bulge in the groin. Such an inguinal hernia may be controlled by a truss or can be treated surgically.

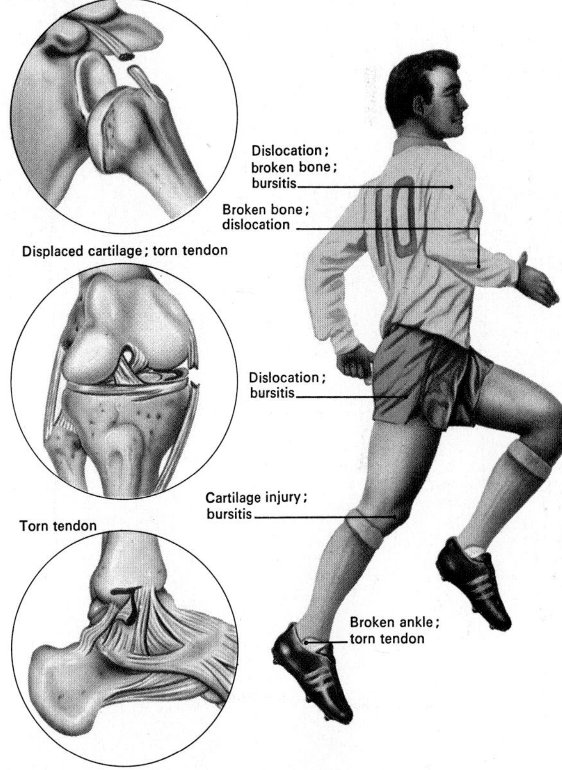
6 Dislocated joint; torn tendon
Displaced cartilage; torn tendon
Torn tendon
Dislocation; broken bone; bursitis
Broken bone; dislocation
Dislocation; bursitis
Cartilage injury; bursitis
Broken ankle; torn tendon

6 In sports such as football, undue stress may be put on bone, tendon, and muscle, and physical fitness is essential to minimize the possible risks. Shown here are some common athletic injuries. Sudden movements and collisions result in dislocated joints or broken bones in the shoulder, the arm, and the leg. Cartilages in the joints may be displaced, while muscles and tendons are strained or torn.

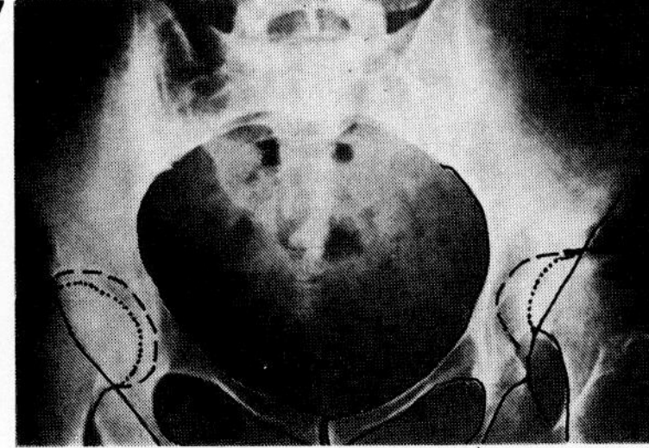
7

7 Congenital dislocation of the hip is a condition found at, or shortly after, birth. It is caused by an increased ability of the head of the femur to slip out of the developing socket. In this X ray, the joint on the left is normal, the one on the right displaced. Characteristic clicking of the hip is checked for in the weeks after birth.

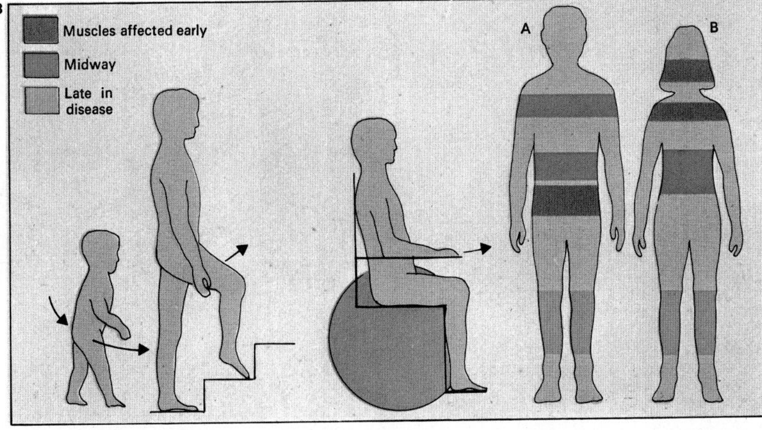
8
Muscles affected early
Midway
Late in disease
A
B

8 Muscular dystrophies are inherited degenerative diseases that cannot be cured. The Duchenne type [A] affects the pelvis, shoulders, trunk, and later the limbs. The disease is first noticed as the child learns to walk with a characteristic waddling gait. He falls frequently and has difficulty in climbing stairs and rising from a sitting or lying position. The facio-scapulo-humeral type [B] affects the face, shoulders, and trunk, and finally the legs.

Diseases of the nervous system

The nervous system is made up of the central nervous system, comprising the brain and spinal cord, and the peripheral nervous system, which carries messages to and from all parts of the body. These two parts of the nervous system vary greatly in their reaction to damage and disease, for while the cells of the peripheral nervous system are resistant to wear and tear, and have some ability to regenerate if partially destroyed, the cells of the central nervous system are susceptible to damage, and once lost are irreplaceable.

Physical damage to the brain

The brain is often compared to a computer, but unlike a computer it does not totally break down from minor damage. The skull provides fairly good protection, but a knockout blow may cause temporary amnesia (loss of memory) or concussion, which can be thought of as temporary brain damage. Even so, recovery is the rule.

Fracture of the skull [1] can cause physical damage to the brain. This, in turn, can result in cessation of activity in body muscles whose actions are controlled directly by the brain.

The most common cause of damage is from within. In some people the arteries of the brain are fragile and can bulge out like weak tires, a condition called aneurysm. The great danger is that the artery may burst, causing bleeding into the brain. This is known as a cerebral hemorrhage; the patient may become paralyzed or may die. A stroke, which involves a sudden loss of cerebral function, may be caused by the hemorrhage of a cerebral vessel or by a blood clot, or thrombus, within a vessel.

Tumors in the brain cause physical damage by the pressure they exert on normal brain tissue and by the replacement of functioning brain tissue with the tumor. In some cases, such tumors can be located and removed by surgery [2].

Effects of toxic chemicals

The brain is also sensitive to chemical damage. Chronic lead poisoning, for example, affecting the central and peripheral nervous system and producing paralysis, has been a problem where lead piping is used for domestic water supplies or when children ingest lead paint particles that have chipped from a wall. In some disorders of metabolism normal body chemicals build up to a level that damages the brain. Phenylalanine, a constituent of body proteins, is one such substance. In the inherited disease called phenylketonuria this substance is created to excess and causes mental retardation, unless the diet is altered.

The chemicals harmful to the nervous system (neurotoxins) can be produced by bacteria that invade the body and reach the brain via the bloodstream or via nerve trunks. The neuritis of diphtheria is caused solely by the toxin the diphtheria bacilli produce. Some bacteria release toxins that affect only nervous tissue. The bacillus *Clostridium tetani,* which causes tetanus [3], produces toxin in the infected wound that passes in the bloodstream to the spinal cord, where it makes the cells controlling the muscles overreact, causing spasm in response to the slightest stimulus. The closely related organism *Clostridium*

CONNECTIONS

See also
664 The nervous system
716 Diseases of the circulation
750 Radiology and radiotherapy
422 Bacteria and viruses
1668 Electronic devices

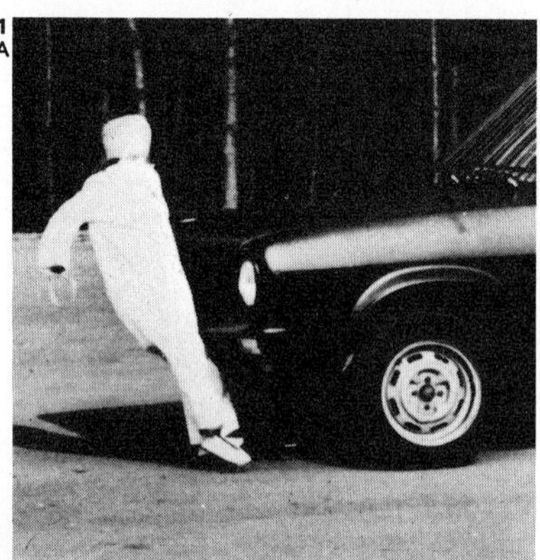

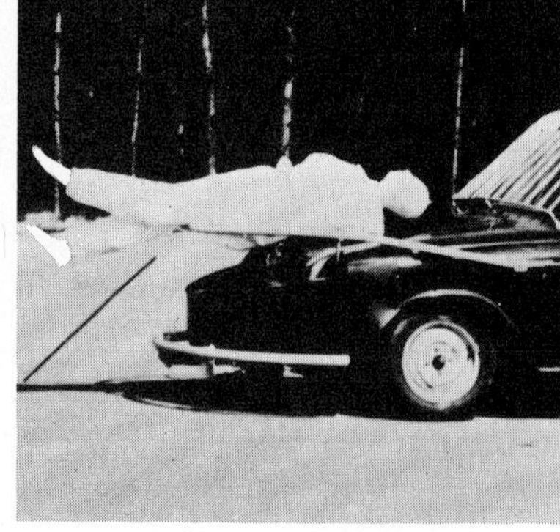

1 Road accidents are a significant cause of brain damage and much research is being conducted to lessen their severity. In a series of experiments a conventional car was shown to knock down a child dummy [A] but "scoop up" an adult dummy [B] at an impact velocity of 10.6mph (17kph). The prototype car [C] with a low, rounded hood picks up the child dummy and reduces head impact.

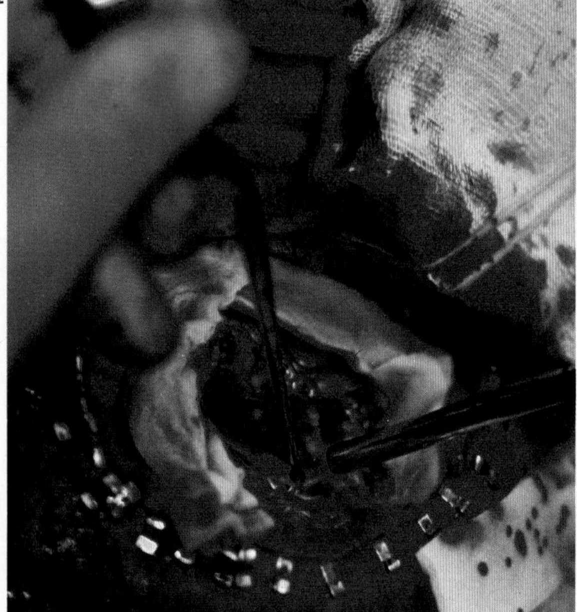

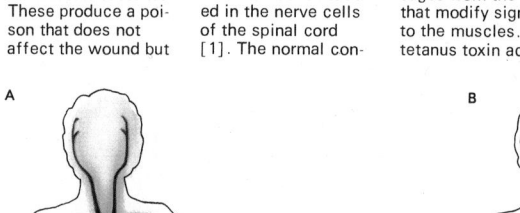

2 Brain surgery is often performed after injury associated with a skull fracture. Such fractures are most commonly caused by car accidents. Brain surgery is usually directed toward stopping bleeding or the removal of blood clots (hematomas). Other types of brain injuries that necessitate surgery include brain tumors and the rupture of weak spots, or aneurysms, in the walls of blood vessels. Diagnosis of brain damage and disease has been revolutionized by the EMI scanner (computerized axial tomography). With this machine the brain can be viewed in serial sections.

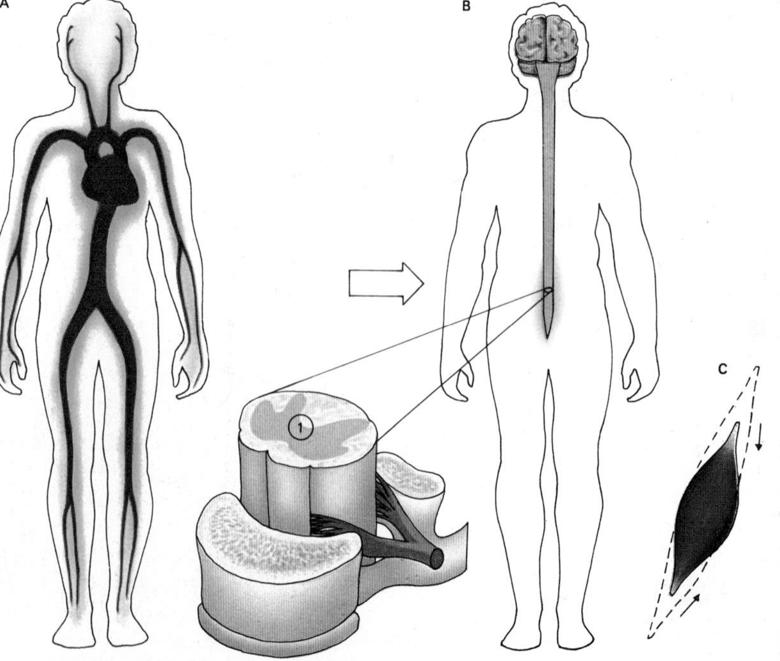

3 A
B
C
1

3 Tetanus, popularly called lockjaw, is caused by wounds infected with *Clostridium tetani* bacteria. These produce a poison that does not affect the wound but is carried [A] by the bloodstream to the central nervous system [B], where it becomes concentrated in the nerve cells of the spinal cord [1]. The normal control of muscle action that takes place in the spinal cord is completed by messages from the brain that modify signals to the muscles. The tetanus toxin acts by blocking the biochemical reactions essential to the completion of the nerve pathway. The muscles cannot relax, and thus go into spasm [C].

botulinum produces a neurotoxin that causes fits, double vision, paralysis, and occasionally death, following the consumption of improperly prepared canned foods.

Some other microorganisms seem to infect the central nervous system preferentially. The rabies virus, for example, specifically attacks the nervous system [7], as does the virus causing poliomyelitis [5].

Some microorganisms that normally cause infections elsewhere find their way into the brain tissue (causing encephalitis) or its surrounding membranes or meninges (causing meningitis). Untreated syphilis can eventually cause an encephalitis, as can measles in about one case in 3,000. The bacteria that cause pneumonia and tuberculosis can both cause meningitis. Advances in immunization [4] have in some cases controlled the spread of infection.

In degenerative diseases of the nervous system a variable pattern of loss of function occurs depending on the particular disease. In multiple sclerosis, for example, seemingly unrelated portions of the nervous system may be sequentially affected over a period of time, often with remissions and exacerbations of the disease process.

Symptoms of disease

Because some parts of the brain perform distinct jobs, the symptoms of disease are often dictated by the area affected. Aphasia, for example, a disturbance in the ability to speak, write, and comprehend words is caused by damage in the area that controls speech. Parkinson's disease, in which the body trembles when at rest but becomes rigid at other times, is the result of destruction of nerve cells at the base of the brain that are involved in the control of movement. The drug L-DOPA now helps 40 percent of all patients with Parkinson's disease. Yet one of the most remarkable things about the brain is that damage to some areas produces no detectable defect, as if other cells take over the damaged ones' activities.

Physiologists specializing in the study of the nervous system have made great advances in discovering the causes of disease, but epilepsy [8]—is one that remains largely a mystery.

KEY

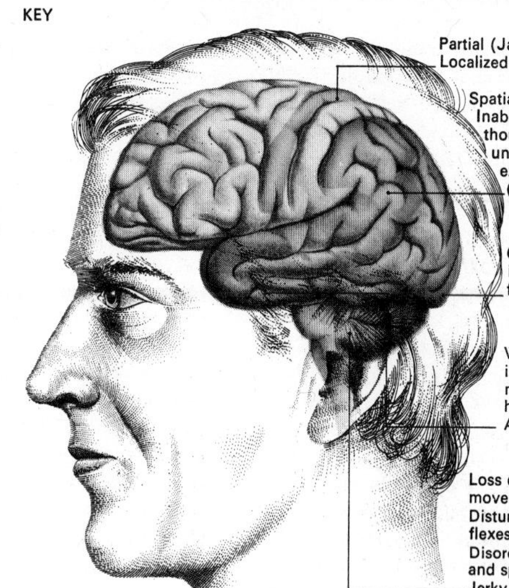
Partial (Jacksonian) epilepsy
Localized muscle paralysis
Spatial disorientation
Inability to express thoughts as words or to understand thought as expressed in words (aphasia)
Crude visual hallucinations such as flashing lights
Visual hallucinations involving patterns of moving color and/or hallucinatory pictures
Auditory hallucinations
Loss of co-ordination in movement
Disturbance of tendon reflexes, posture and gait
Disorders of articulation and speech
Jerky eye movements

The symptoms that result from brain damage may reflect the particular function of the injured area of the brain. Examples of such symptoms are indicated here. The specific effects of certain brain injuries have been of great use in producing physiological "maps" of the brain.

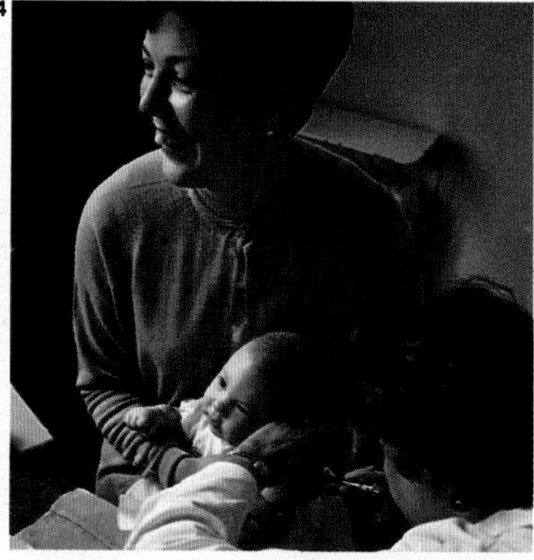

4 An immunization campaign against polio started in the United States and Europe in the 1950's has almost obliterated the disease there. Today babies receive polio vaccine in their first months of life.

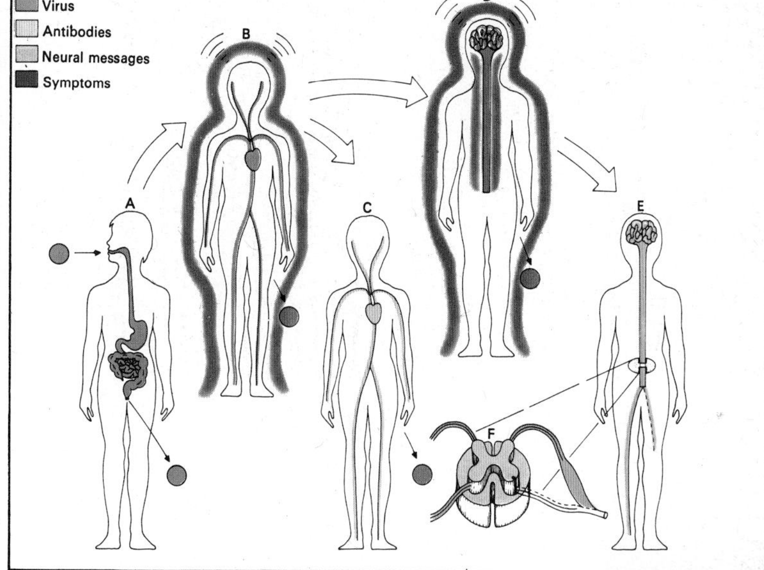
Virus
Antibodies
Neural messages
Symptoms
A
B
C
D
E
F

5 The polio virus enters the body by the nose or mouth [A], incubates in the intestine, and enters the bloodstream [B], causing headaches, fever, and vomiting. The body now "fights back" by releasing antibodies [C], which may effect a complete recovery and also confer immunity against another attack. Or the virus may continue to multiply, reach the brain and spinal cord, and destroy nerve tissue [D]. The result is that the nerves can no longer send out messages to the muscles [E] to effect contraction, and the muscles become paralyzed. The enlarged section of the spinal cord [F] shows the damaged area [black].

6 At a rehabilitation center in Rwanda victims of polio—a disease also known as infantile paralysis because of its preferential attack on the young—receive treatment to restore paralyzed muscles.

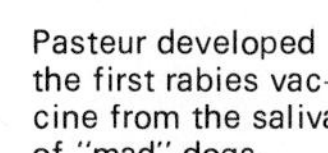

7 Rabies is a fatal disease caused by a virus that selectively attacks the brain. It is caught from the bites of infected animals, particularly dogs and bats. Louis Pasteur developed the first rabies vaccine from the saliva of "mad" dogs.

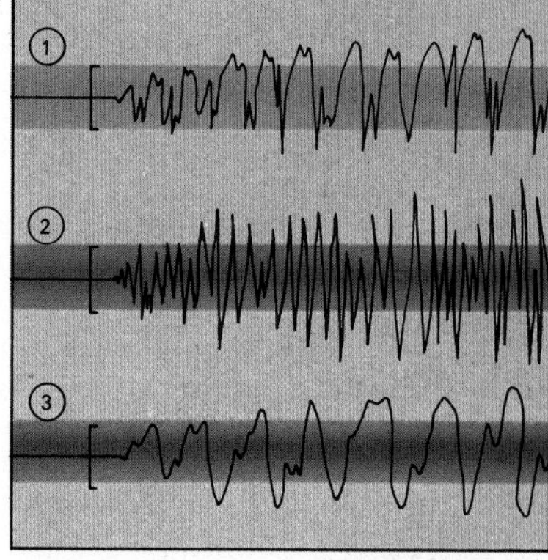
1
2
3

8 Epilepsy is a sudden disturbance in the brain's normal function. During an epileptic seizure the brain shows characteristic electro-physiologic rhythm disturbances that can be recorded on an electroencephalograph. During a "grand mal" [1] the patient generally loses consciousness. Most seizures last a few minutes. In a "petit mal" [2] the unconsciousness may be only momentary. Psychomotor epilepsy [3] is characterized by hallucinations.

Diseases of the skin

The skin has a triple susceptibility to disease [Key]: first, because of its location; second, because of its dependence on the rest of the body; and third, because the skin itself is prone to faulty functioning.

Attack from fungi

Infestations of the outer skin layer (the epidermis) are usually caused by microscopic fungi that use dead cells and skin secretions as food. These fungi are found most often in humid protected regions, the armpits, groin, hair, hands, and feet in particular. Different types of fungi [5] grow in different regions, and although the generic term ringworm [6] may be applied to them, they have nothing to do with worms. The mouth and vagina also may be colonized by the fungus *Candida albicans,* or thrush [7]. These fungal infestations are not usually harmful, although they cause intense irritation. They must be treated, however, as severe complications can result. The skin is also colonized by billions of bacteria. In general these do no harm; often their presence makes it difficult for some dangerous bacteria to take hold. These beneficial bacteria use organic substances on the skin as food; and the major disadvantage of their presence is that the chemical transformation of sweat they cause gives rise to unpleasant odors. Other less wholesome bacteria can be present on the skin and, if these manage to penetrate it through a cut or crack, they can infect a wound or may form an abscess. Similar bacteria may contribute to the development of acne.

Itching and burns

In the industrially developed nations insect infestations of the skin are now rare, but less than 50 years ago infestations by mites, lice, and fleas were common. Indeed, itching caused by insects was so widespread that infestation by the scabies mite, which burrows into the skin and causes irritation, was called "the itch."

Itching is a nonspecific response to any irritation of the skin. It can be psychological in origin, or be caused by a sudden fall in temperature or by excessive sweating. Where redness and swelling are present, they are likely to represent a local toxic reaction to plant or animal stings, for example, or an allergy [4] to a chemical. Eczema and dermatitis are both skin diseases often caused by allergic body responses. They may also be caused by the irritant effect of chemicals that cause direct damage. Many chemicals, ranging from epoxy resins to cleansing powders, can be responsible.

Burns usually result from exposure of the skin to high energy (heat or radiation), although they may be caused by acids. They are divided into degrees, depending on their severity and the depth of the burn. First-degree burns, involving redness of the skin, occur in sunburn [11] and mild overexposure to other sorts of radiation such as Xrays or gamma rays. Second-degree burns are more severe and are associated with blister formation, but still heal without a scar, while third-degree burns involve the full thickness of the skin with loss of sensation and with formation of scars on healing.

Scar formation is the skin's method of repairing severe damage to its surface. Scars are formed after third-degree burns

CONNECTIONS

See also
686 Skin and hair
712 The causes of illness 2
758 First aid
790 Adolescence
422 Bacteria and viruses
426 Yeasts and molds

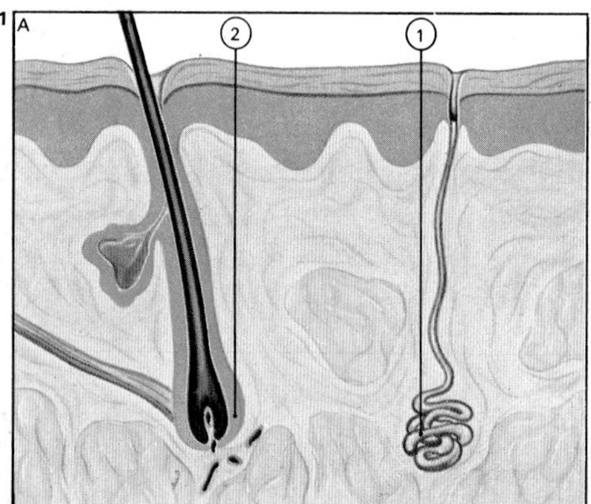

A
2
1

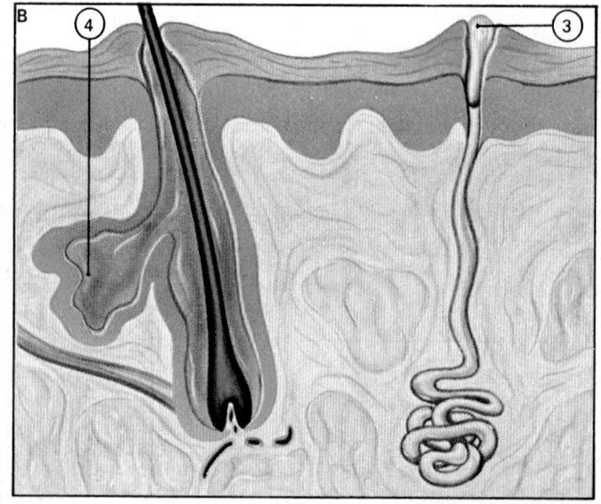

B
4
3

1 The sweat glands [1] and hair follicles [2] of normal skin [A] are subject to disorders and infections [B]. In hot, humid climates, the openings [3] of the sweat glands may become blocked, resulting in rupture of the gland and the inflammation known as "prickly heat." Bacterial infection of the oil-secreting gland that is attached to each hair follicle is one of the causes of acne, in which pustules develop.

4 Hives or urticaria is a reaction shown on the skin in response to the absorption into the bloodstream of a substance to which the body is allergic. The substance is said to act as an antigen. In hives, the itching is caused by the release of histamine, while body enzymes produce the red rash. Strawberries, eggs, nuts, and shellfish are common allergy-producing agents.

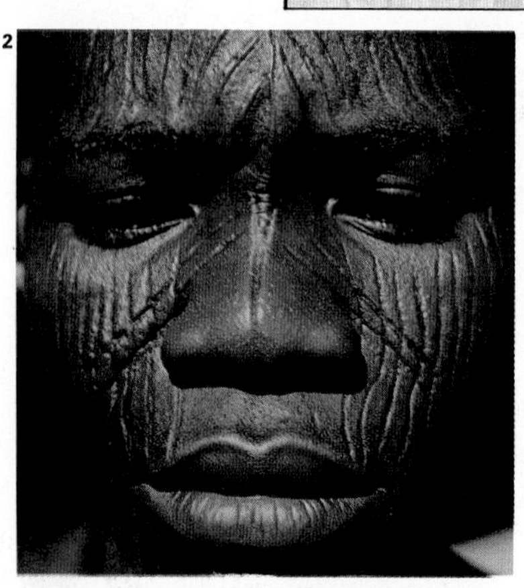

2 Scars form over wounds and burns. Fibroblasts in the wound produce fibrous tissue that joins the broken dermis, and this becomes covered with cuticle. At first the scar is delicate and the presence of many capillaries gives it a red appearance. As the wound heals, the fibrous tissue thickens and the capillaries are lost, so an old scar is hard and white. The faster the edges are joined the less the scar shows.

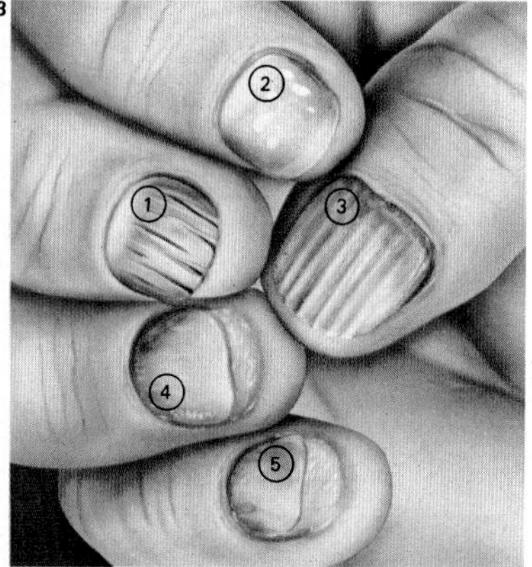

2
1
3
4
5

3 The nails, which develop from the skin beneath them called the matrix, may reflect deficiencies in the diet, for lack of calcium can make them brittle [1], or flecked [2]. A congenital abnormality of the nail-producing tissue can result in ridged nails [3]. Bitten nails often "ingrow" [4] into the surrounding skin, taking with them infective bacteria. The same bacteria gain entry if the cuticle is destroyed [5].

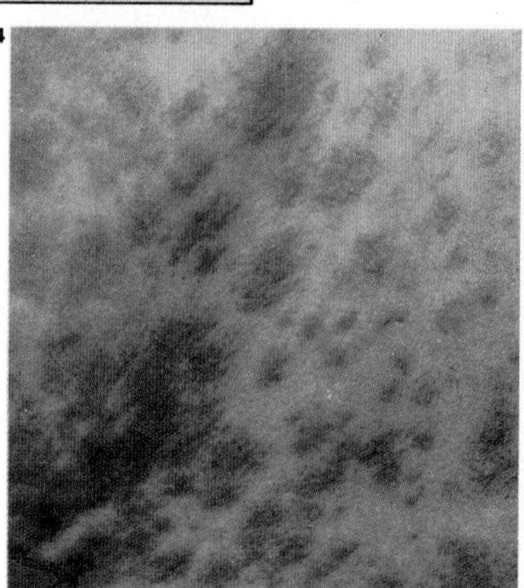

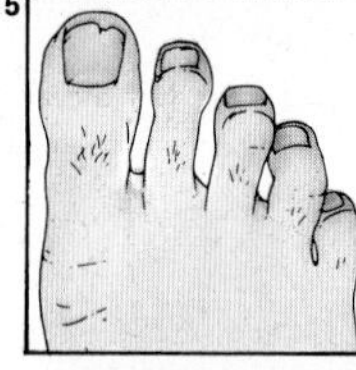

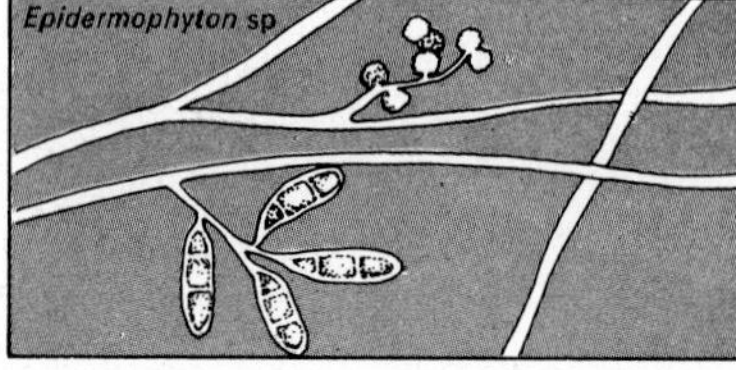

Epidermophyton sp

5 Athlete's foot (misnamed *Tinea pedis,* or ringworm of the foot) is the most common fungal infection of the skin. The affected skin becomes sodden and white, peeling off to reveal a red raw area.

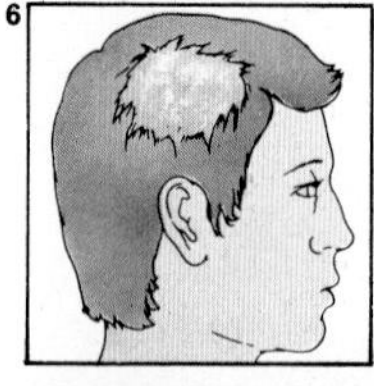

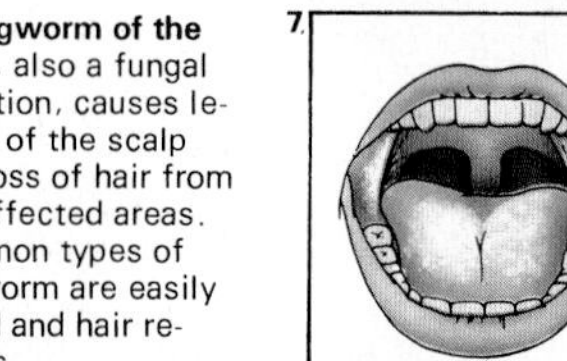

Microsporum andoni

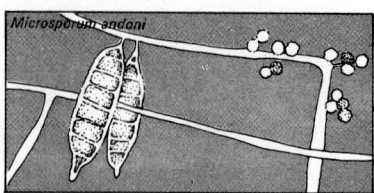

6 Ringworm of the scalp, also a fungal infection, causes lesions of the scalp and loss of hair from the affected areas. Common types of ringworm are easily cured and hair regrows.

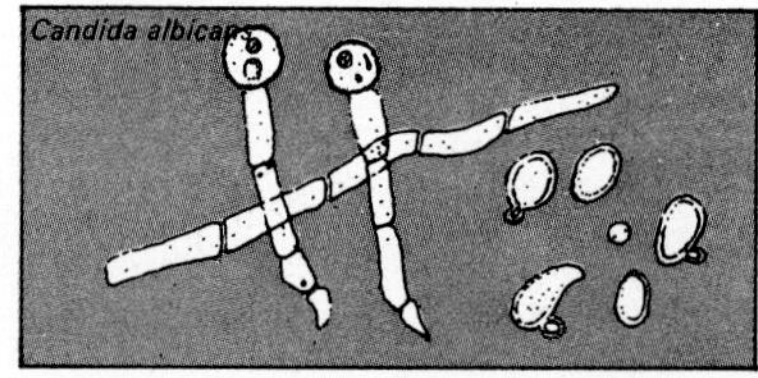

Candida albicans

7 Thrush is the name given to the white patches of infection on the throat, tongue, lips, and palate in young children. The same fungus causes an uncomfortable vaginal infestation in women.

and as a result of wounds or rupture of the skin, as when an abscess bursts. People in some cultures deliberately wound the skin to form scars [2].

Infective agents

Skin problems can be caused by internal infective agents. The viral diseases of childhood, as well as smallpox [9], are examples of diseases in which the infective agent reaches the skin through the bloodstream. The skin problems—rash [8], itching, and the formation of pustules ("pox")—are only one part of the infection and its effects on other organs are the more severe, if less obvious, risks to health; arthritis or osteomyelitis (an infection of bone) can follow.

Direct viral attack of the skin is thought to be the cause of warts, which appear to be contagious. There also seems to be a strong psychological component in their presence; many people never get them, despite constant exposure.

Poor diet and upset metabolism are probably causes of malfunction in the skin's sebaceous glands, which can become blocked through overproduction of oily sebum, producing a local build-up of sebum that can lead to dandruff or acne. Many of the less well-known skin rashes are caused from within the body and affect its metabolism.

Several skin diseases are associated with a breakdown in normal function of the tissues of the skin itself. The most common of these are baldness, or alopecia, in which the hair follicles fail to replace hair as it falls, and the whitening of the hair because of loss of pigment. These both have a strong hereditary component, although they can be caused by other factors.

Albinism [12] is the other genetic disorder of the skin in which pigment-forming cells do not function and hence the albino is pink-skinned, pink-eyed, and white-haired. Birthmarks, in contrast, are localized abnormalities of skin development that involve overpigmentation of the skin (moles) or both overpigmentation and disorders in the blood supply, which are known as port-wine stains.

KEY

The skin is subject to damage from outside: from parasites, chemicals, burning, or wounds. It is also subject to attack by germs and is sensitive to upsets in normal physiology caused by hormonal imbalance [1] or disease [2]. Finally, diseases can result from the faulty function of the skin.

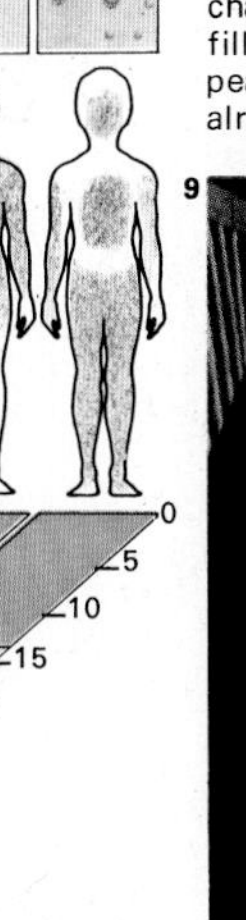

Incubation period
Predromal period
Eruptive period
Recovery period
Infection period
1 Measles *Rubeola* sp
2 German measles *Rubella* sp
3 Shingles *Herpes zoster*
4 Chicken pox *Varicella* sp
5 Smallpox *Variola major*
0
5
10
15
20
25
30
35
40
45 days

8 The common viral diseases are mostly characterized by unsightly and painful rashes. Although these are not the primary result of the infection, their apearance helps to differentiate the diseases.

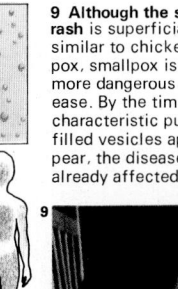

9 Although the skin rash is superficially similar to chickenpox, smallpox is a far more dangerous disease. By the time the characteristic pus-filled vesicles appear, the disease has already affected the other susceptible organs. The vesicles gradually dry out over the ensuing two weeks when complete recovery occurs. Smallpox is now endemic in only two countries. Bangladesh and Ethiopia.

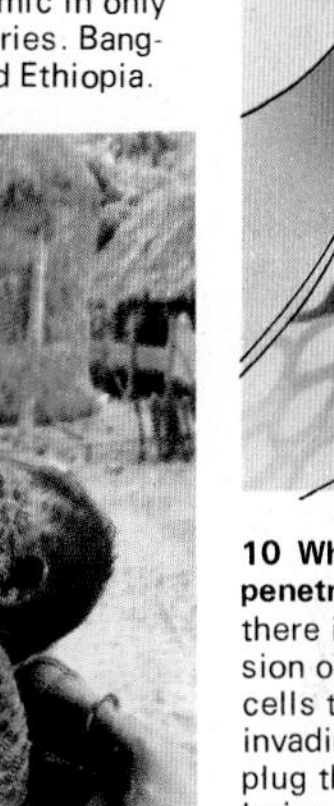

10 When bacteria penetrate the skin there is a local invasion of white blood cells that engulf the invading bacteria and plug the local capillaries [1] to isolate the infection. The mixture of white cells, dead bacteria, and tissue fluids [2] builds up inside the fibrous capsule [3] that develops around the infected area. If the abscess is not lanced, more pus is produced until the skin ruptures.

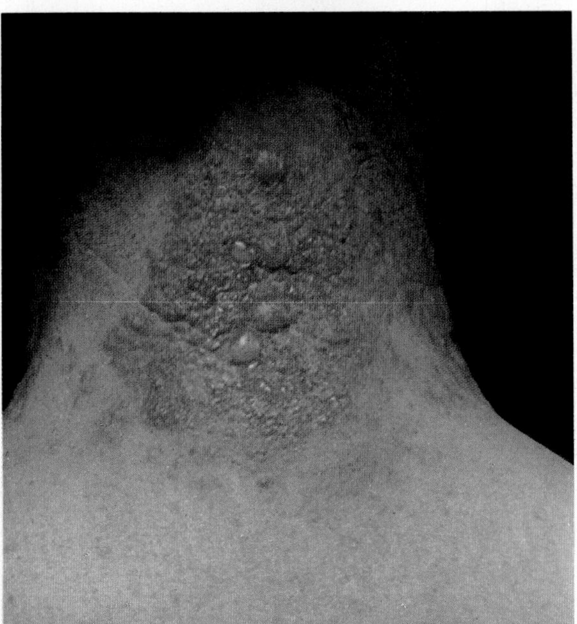

11 The most common form of burning is sunburn, caused by overexposure to the ultraviolet rays of sunlight. Cautious exposure to the sun causes the development of brown pigment, which is the body's natural defense against sunlight. An additional benefit is the formation of Vitamin D. Sunlight has been implicated, however, as one cause of cancer of the skin and excessive exposure to the sun is considered harmful.

12 Albinism can occur in any population. It can be total, that is, a congenital condition, or patchy. The lack of pigment causes sensitivity to strong sunlight. Pink coloration is caused by reflection of light from blood vessels.

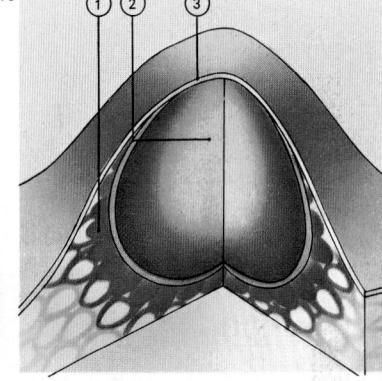

Diseases of the glands

CONNECTIONS

See also
690 Glands and their hormones
696 A healthy diet
750 Radiology and radiotherapy
790 Adolescence

The glands may be divided into two types according to where their secretions go. Those that release their secretions into a duct are called the exocrine glands [8], while those without ducts release their secretions, known as hormones, directly into the blood and are called endocrine glands. The exocrine glands normally release their products to the body surface—for example, sebum to lubricate hair and skin or tears to moisten the eyes—or into the alimentary tract, providing the digestive juices. It is alterations in the activities of the endocrine glands that are normally termed glandular disorders, although infectious mononucleosis is a disorder of the lymph glands.

Diabetes: causes and symptoms

The most common endocrine disorder is sugar diabetes (diabetes mellitus), in which lack of insulin occurs [5]. The major part of the pancreas is exocrine, producing digestive juices, but about one percent of the bulk represents a million clumps of cells called the islets of Langerhans. Lack of insulin secretion from these islets leads to a failure to control the use of the body fuels and building blocks (sugars, fats, and amino acids). In diabetes these are overproduced at the expense of the body tissues and are underused. Sugars, such as glucose, accumulate in the blood and are poured away as waste in the urine.

This great loss of water and urine led the Greek Aretaeus, in the first century AD to call the disease diabetes, after the Greek word for "siphon." Thirst and weight loss occur and high sugar levels encourage infections. The situation can be corrected by insulin injections. When diabetes appears later in life some insulin is produced by the pancreas, but insufficient to keep the metabolism entirely normal. Such patients are often overweight, but with weight loss and controlled intake of carbohydrate foods extra insulin is often not necessary to treat their diabetes.

While longstanding diabetes may lead to circulatory disorders, careful control helps to minimize such problems. Diabetes of varying severity may affect two to three percent of the population in the United States and Europe, but the opposite situation of overproduction of insulin is very rare. It is caused by an insulin-producing tumor of the pancreas, an insulinoma. Blood sugar falls excessively, resulting in hunger, sweating, and altered mental ability.

The thyroid and pituitary glands

The next most common group of glandular disorders consists of those affecting the thyroid gland. Overproduction of thyroid hormone leads to increased demands for food and energy by the body tissues, increased heat production, weight loss, nervousness, and irritability [2]. It may be treated with drugs or thyroid surgery. A lack of thyroid hormone, from failure of the gland, leads to slowness, apathy, weight increase, and susceptibility to cold. It is more common in older people and in those with thyroids that have been overactive in the past. Treatment is by daily thyroid hormone tablets. An enlarged thyroid, or goiter, is caused either by overactivity or underactivity of the gland. Diets deficient in iodine are one reason for goiter.

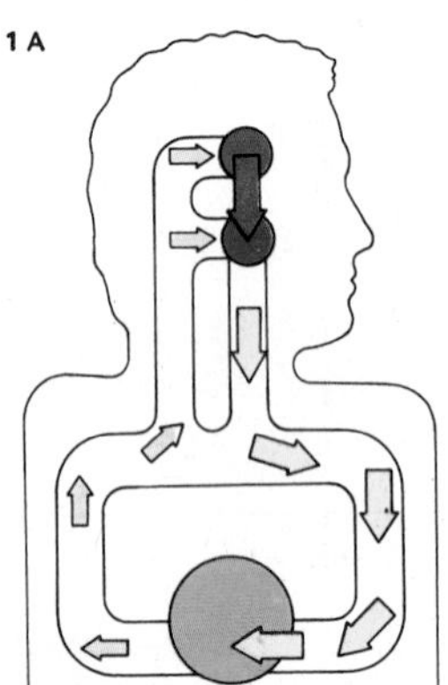
1 A

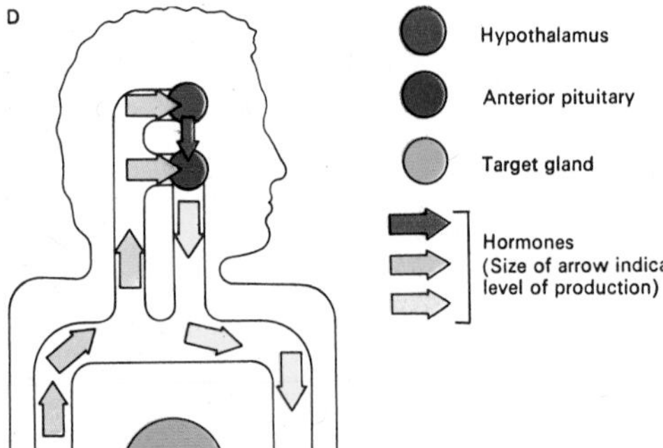
D
Hypothalamus
Anterior pituitary
Target gland
Hormones
(Size of arrow indicates level of production)

1 If one of the target glands on which an anterior pituitary hormone acts is underactive, the feedback of the hormone on the hypothalamus and the anterior pituitary is reduced. Both the hypothalamus (part of the brain) and the anterior pituitary (at the base of the brain) allow increased production of the pituitary hormone, which attempts to stimulate the underactive glands [A]. Alternatively, the pituitary may be underactive despite signals from the hypothalamus and the target gland is also underactive [B]. The opposite may occur, with glandular overactivity. The target gland is overactive despite feedback inhibition of the pituitary [C]. When this is overproducing despite lack of signal from the hypothalamus, the target gland is stimulated to do likewise [D].

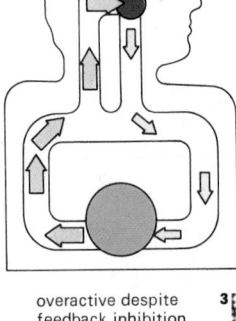

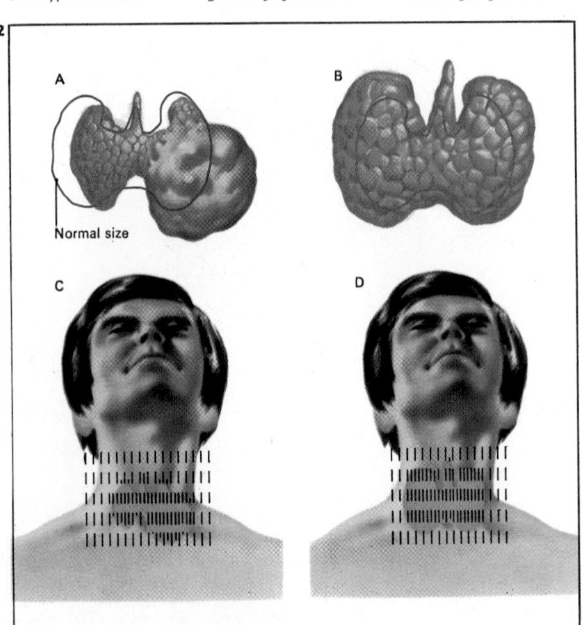
A
B
Normal size
C
D

2 The thyroid gland in the neck may overproduce the thyroid hormone because of a tumor [A] or a generalized enlargement of the organ [B]. One method of assessing this activity is to measure the uptake of iodine into the gland—iodine is necessary to produce thyroid hormone. Radioactive iodine is used in a small dose and the amount in the gland is indicated by the dashes in the thyroid "scans" [C, D].

3 Body size may be affected by glandular disorders in childhood. Anterior pituitary overactivity may cause gigantism, as with this 9.25ft (2.82m) Dutchman. Underactivity is one cause of dwarfism, as with his 36in (0.9m) companion.

Normally the thyroid gland is directed by a hormone from the anterior pituitary gland at the base of the brain [1]. If the thyroid gland fails to produce sufficient thyroid hormone this is registered by the hypothalamus (part of the brain) and the pituitary, which produces thyroid-stimulating hormone in greater amounts in an attempt to restore the normal balance.

Increased pituitary hormone production may, however, be a disorder in its own right, rather than a response to failure of a target gland. If a tumor is present, for instance, hormone production may be excessive. Often only one of the several hormones that the pituitary produces is increased. The effects of such pituitary gland abnormality vary according to which hormone is in excess and the other body tissues and glands that respond.

One such hormone of the pituitary is that which affects the adrenal cortex, part of the adrenal gland that lies just above the kidney. This hormone is adrenocorticotrophic hormone ACTH. Excess ACTH leads to excess steroid hormone production by the adrenal glands. Disturbances of many systems results, with retention of excess salt and water in the body and poor handling of sugar in the body. This disorder, called Cushing's syndrome, may result if the adrenal glands are overactive in their own right.

Other pituitary hormones

Disturbance of one hormone can have marked effects on normal feedback mechanisms as is seen with growth hormone, from the anterior pituitary. Its lack during childhood leads to dwarfism, while overproduction may lead to gigantism [3]. Too much growth hormone in later life leads to acromegaly. This disease is usually first noticed because the sufferer's hats, gloves, and shoes need replacing with larger sizes. The nose, lips, tongue, hands, and feet broaden and enlarge.

The posterior part of the pituitary normally produces antidiuretic hormone, which maintains the correct amount of water in the body. If it is deficient, excess water is lost in the urine; this is diabetes insipidus.

KEY

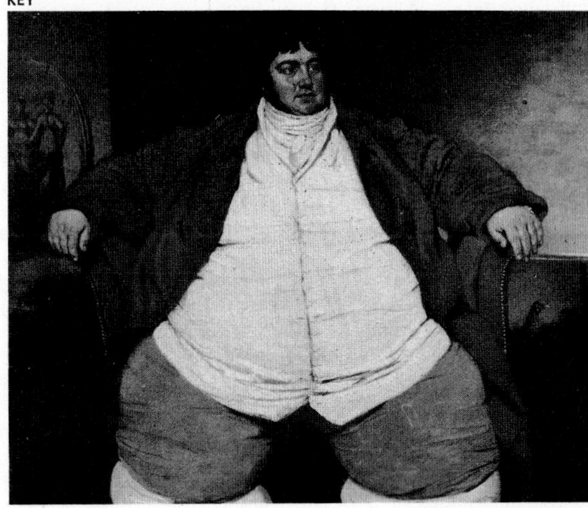

Daniel Lambert [1770–1809] weighed 737lb (335kg). He had a girth of 92in (234cm). The problem of obesity is often justified by sufferers as being the result of a glandular disorder. This is rarely true: overeating is the usual reason. Disorders of the body glands give rise to groups of symptoms characteristic for each condition.

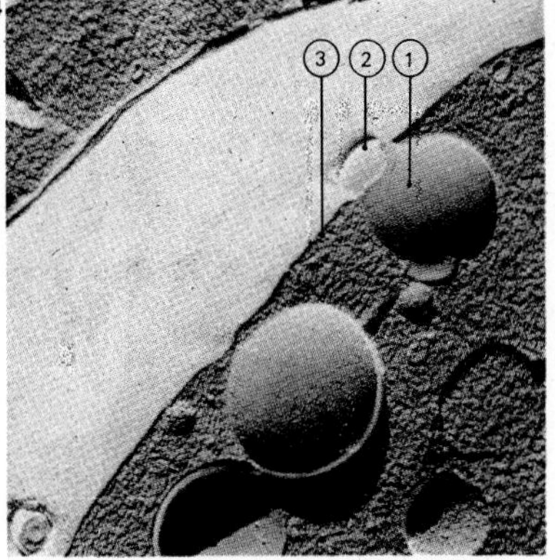
3
2
1

4 Hormones are stored in the cells of a gland in small sacs, or vacuoles [1], until required. Shown is a specially prepared slice through a pancreatic islet cell that makes insulin. When blood glucose levels are high, after a meal the cell discharges the insulin [2] from within these vacuoles through the cell wall [3]. In diabetes insufficient insulin is produced so blood sugar levels rise.

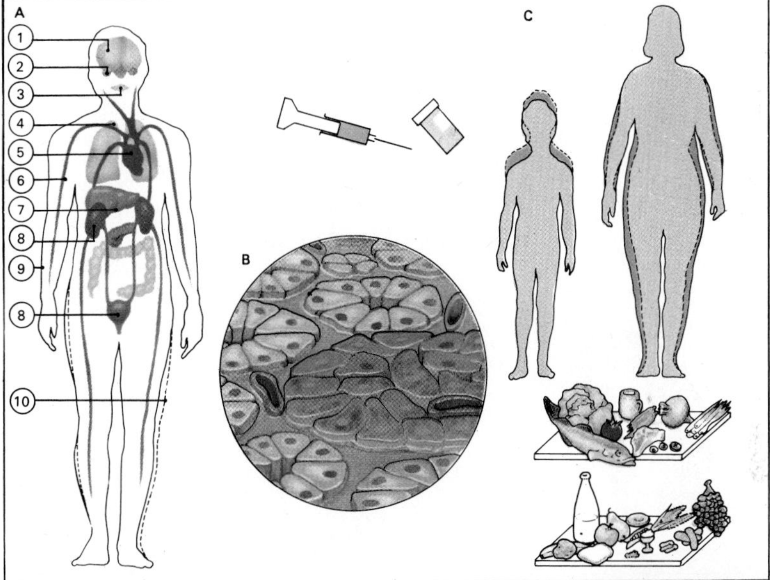
A
1
2
3
4
5
6
7
8
9
8
10
B
C

5 Diabetes mellitus [A] may result in drowsiness and coma [1], impaired vision [2], dry mouth [3], overbreathing [4], cardiac failure [5], high blood sugar levels [6], fatty liver [7], kidney and bladder infections [8], itchy skin and delayed wound healing [9], and loss of weight [10]. It is caused by a lack of the hormone insulin produced in the beta cells of the pancreatic islets of Langerhans (green) [B]. Treatment [C] for juveniles includes a varied, low-carbohydrate diet, usually in conjunction with regular insulin injections. Adults also need a low-carbohydrate diet, but drugs may help to control the disease.

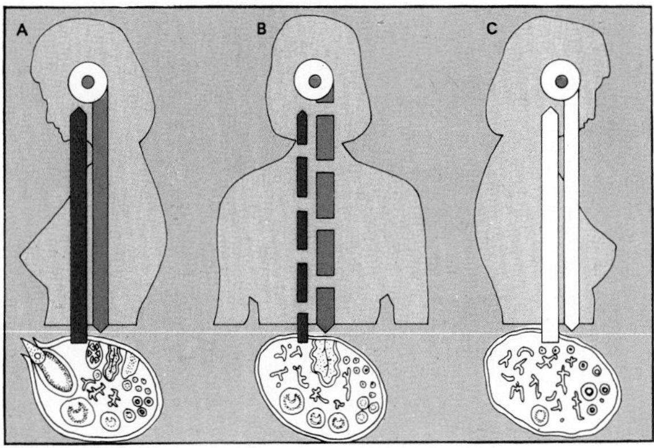
A
B
C

6 Before menopause [A] there is a balanced feedback mechanism between the ovaries, which produce the hormone estrogen [red], and the anterior pituitary gland, which produces ovary-stimulating hormones [blue]. At menopause [B], which usually occurs at 45 to 50, the ovaries cease producing an ovum and thus normal estrogen amounts each month. As a result the pituitary produces an excess of hormones, and the high levels and imbalance are thought to be responsible for the common symptoms of sudden heat sensations, headaches and weight gain. Estrogens can be given as treatment. After menopause [C] hormone production ceases and the symptoms soon disappear.

7 Overactivity of the four parathyroid glands in the neck leads to raised levels of calcium in the blood [A]. Calcium is also lost in the urine where kidney stones and kidney damage result. The bones are weakened as calcium and phosphate are removed from the bone structure [B] in the body's attempt to maintain the high blood levels of calcium. Low levels [C] result if glands are damaged.

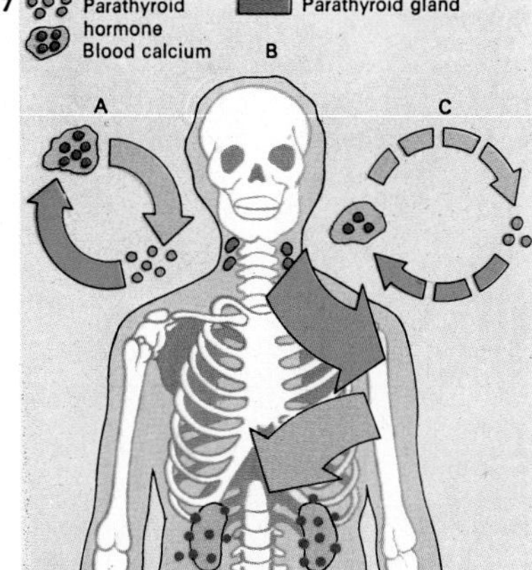
Parathyroid hormone
Blood calcium
Parathyroid gland
A
B
C

8 Apart from the endocrine, or ductless, glands, there are other glands that do not secrete their products directly into the bloodstream but via ducts to the appropriate site. These exocrine glands are affected by their own disorders. A sufferer from mumps has a viral inflammation of the parotid gland. This is one of the salivary glands that produce saliva to moisten the food and begin food digestion. Mumps may affect other glands, such as the ovaries and testes.

Diseases of the urogenital system

While the urinary and genital systems serve very different functions, they are often considered together, for they share anatomical parts [Key]. The openings of these systems, the exits for urine, the penis in men and the vagina in women, are potential points where infections from outside may enter [1]. Symptoms may include difficult urination as in cystitis (inflammation of the bladder), blood in the urine [2], back pain, and disturbances such as fever and sweating.

How infections start

Urinary infections are much more common in females, perhaps because the shorter urethra (the tube from the bladder to the outside) provides an easier path for invading bacteria than in the male. Of the 300ml (0.6 pint) or so of urine in the full bladder all but 1–2ml are normally passed. If bladder emptying is only partial, as may occur in the male with an enlarged prostate [4], any bacteria that reach the bladder are more likely to cause an infection as they are not adequately washed away. Congenital anatomical abnormalities present in the urinary tract, or the development of stones in the kidney, favor bacterial infections.

Stones are formed from an accumulation of mineral substances filtered by the kidneys during the formation of urine. Stones may cause intense pain (ureteral colic) if they block or move down the ureter. If the kidney tubules, which are part of the kidney's two million or so filtering units (nephrons), are defective—either congenitally or as a consequence of pyelonephritis (severe kidney infection)—crystals of calcium salts may be deposited. Stones may form also in patients with gout.

The urogenital system can pick up infections during sexual intercourse. These venereal disorders are of various types [5, 6, 7]. They can produce both local symptoms at the time of infection and also permanent problems such as sterility. Effects of syphilis may become apparent only after a period of years, when circulatory and nervous system diseases occur. The advent of antibiotics allowed these diseases to be cured when promptly treated by specialists. Less serious but much more widespread are vaginal infections causing irritation and discharge. These may be caused by fungi, especially *Candida albicans* (thrush), or microscopic amebalike organisms of the genus *Trichomonas*.

Sterility may be caused by venereal diseases and by other disorders of the urogenital system. These disorders include the retention of one or both testicles inside the male body (the testicles normally descend to the exterior before birth) and malformation, damage, or disease of the testes or ovaries that impair their ability to produce viable sperm or eggs.

Kidney diseases

Kidneys may fail to function adequately either suddenly or slowly, and for many reasons. Less than 25 percent of kidney tissue is necessary for normal removal of waste matter from the blood and life is possible with even less than this. If kidneys fail completely, it is now possible to use a machine [3] to do their job. This kidney dialysis machine, connected into the blood system, can remove waste material from

CONNECTIONS

See also
694 The digestive system
700 Reproduction
750 Radiology and radiotherapy

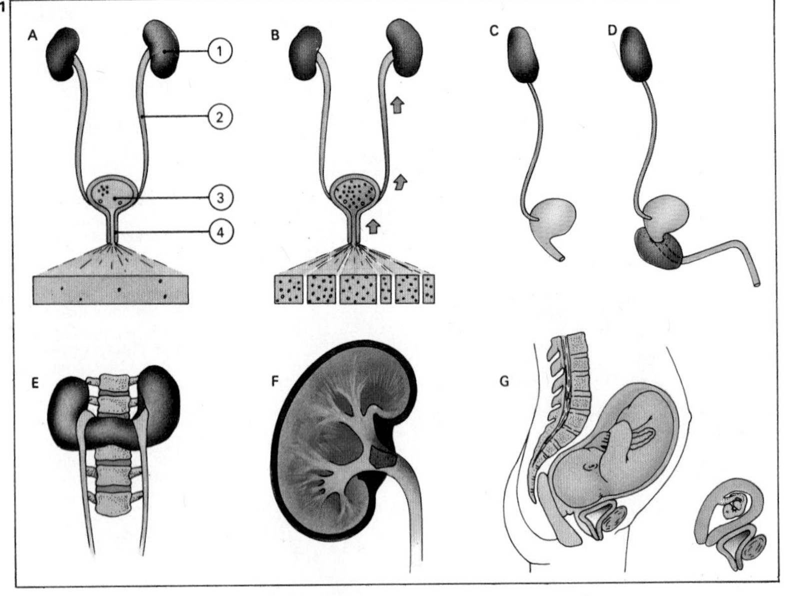
A
B
C
D
E
F
G
1
2
3
4

1 The urinary tract [A] consists of the kidneys [1], ureters [2], bladder [3], and urethra [4]. Infection of the tract [B] first affects the urethra and bladder, giving symptoms of cystitis with painful and frequent urination. If the infection spreads to the kidneys it may cause fever and back pain. A number of factors may lead to infection. The short urethra in the female [C] provides easy access for bacteria, while enlargement of the prostate in the male [D] may prevent the bladder emptying completely. Inherited abnormalities of the kidney, such as "horseshoe" kidney [E], and disorders such as kidney stones [F], predispose to urinary infection. More frequent urination during pregnancy [G], is partly caused by distortion of and pressure on the bladder and encourages infection.

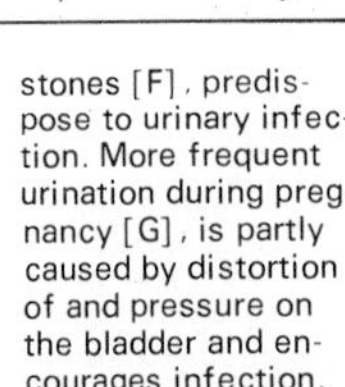

2 Indications of diseases or infections of the urinary tract can often be found by routine examination of urine. Abnormal contents such as blood, pus, and proteins can give some information on the type of disease and the part of the urinary system that is affected. Kidney diseases such as glomerulonephritis [A] are indicated by protein in the urine. In serious stages [B] the protein and red or white blood cells or cellular debris may coagulate into tiny cylindrical urinary casts. Damage to the kidney or bladder or both [C] is indicated by blood in the urine, and infection of the system can occur [D].

3 A kidney dialysis machine is used if nearly all kidney units, or nephrons, fail, bringing the danger of death from an accumulation of waste products in the patient's blood. The patient can be connected in a hospital, or later at home, to a filtering system that removes the impurities from the blood. One or more sessions a week are usually required to pass the blood with its impurities through a solution that has the correct concentration of salts.

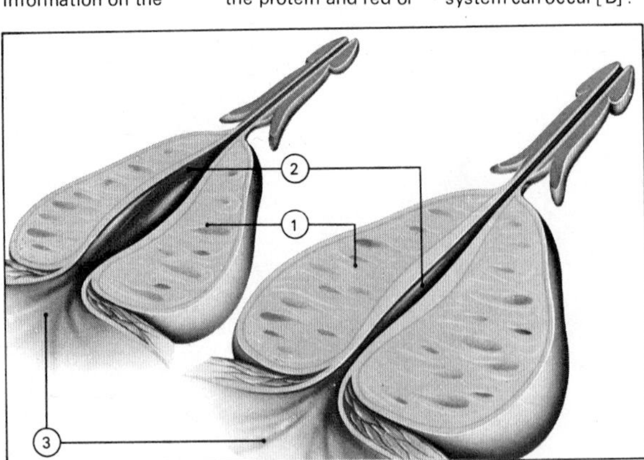
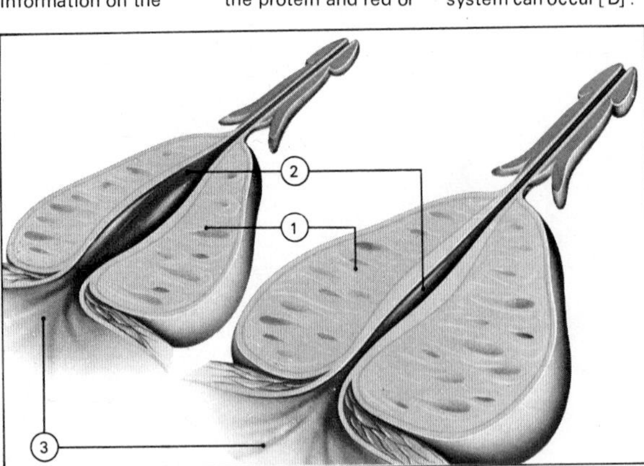
1
2
3

4 The prostate gland [1] is a partly glandular, firm structure that circles the male urethra [2] at the base of the bladder [3]. It produces some of the seminal fluid in which sperm are ejaculated. With increasing years, the gland enlarges, normally a harmless process; however, it may constrict the urethra and prevent adequate urination. Urine becomes increasingly difficult to pass. Infection can occur, the kidneys may be damaged, and complete and painful stoppage of the flow may result. Treatment is usually required when this happens and also if urination is too frequent. This involves surgical removal of at least part of the gland.

the circulation. Alternatively, a diseased kidney can be replaced by a transplanted kidney. It is important that the transplanted kidney be carefully matched and drug treatment is necessary to help prevent the body's rejection of the transplant.

Sudden kidney failure may occur if the blood pressure and flow through the kidneys drop too low—as after hemorrhage or severe burns. It is also a feature of acute glomerular disease, where extensive swelling and inflammation is found in the glomeruli parts of the filtering units.

Many disorders can result from chronic renal (kidney) disease in which the ability of the kidney to remove the waste materials from the blood gradually deteriorates. The breakdown products of proteins are dealt with particularly badly by the failing kidney, and limitation of protein foods may be an essential part of the medical treatment.

Types of tumors

Like other parts of the body the urogenital system is affected by tumor formation. Bladder tumors may be benign or malignant. They may be single or multiple polyps (wartlike growths) that can cause blood to appear in the urine. Often polyps can be removed through a cystoscope—a tube inserted through the urethra by which the inside of the bladder can be inspected and treated.

The genitalia and reproductive organs may also show tumor growth. Tumors of the testes are uncommon, but the female reproductive organs are common sites for both benign tumors, often called fibroids, and malignant ones, known as cancers. It has been found that cancer of the body of the uterus (womb) is more likely in women who have had no children. Similarly breast cancer is a little more common in those women who have no children, or in whom the first child was born when the mother was older than 30. In contrast, cancer of the cervix, or neck of the womb, seems to occur in women with several children, and there is some evidence that its incidence is influenced by factors in the male. Circumcision of the penis appears to reduce the risk to the female.

KEY

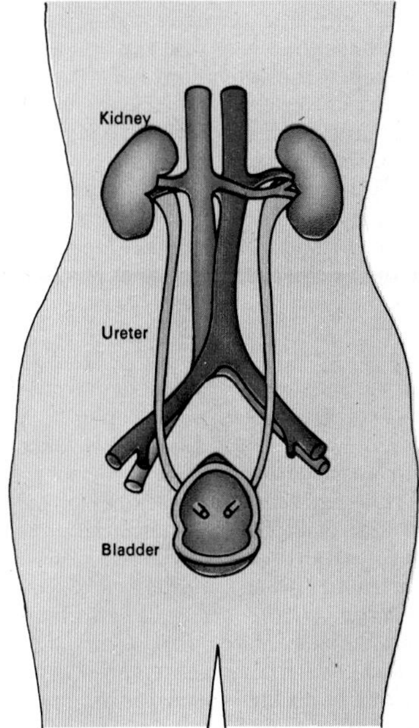
Kidney
Ureter
Bladder

The urinary system consists of two kidneys and ureters draining into a bladder and urethra. Its function is mainly the production and excretion of urine, thus maintaining the water and chemical balance of the body. Disorders of, or damage to, the kidneys may prevent normal urine production, while an enlarged prostate gland in the male may prevent the free passage of urine down the urethra. Stones, often of calcium salts, may form in the kidneys, while tumors may grow in the urinary tract. As in other tissues, infection can occur. The system is somewhat more vulnerable than others since the exit for urine may be an entry for bacteria.

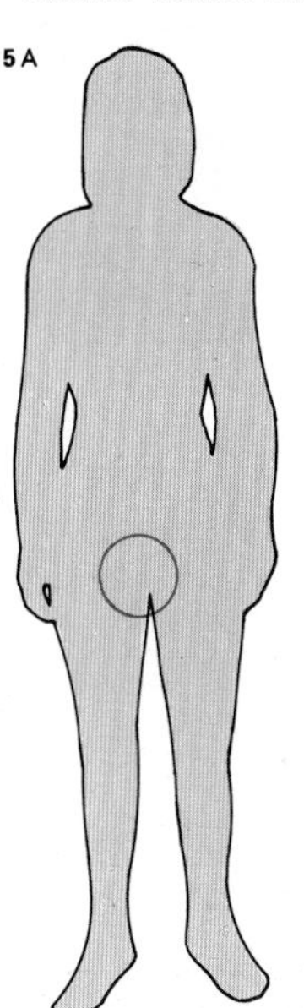
5 A

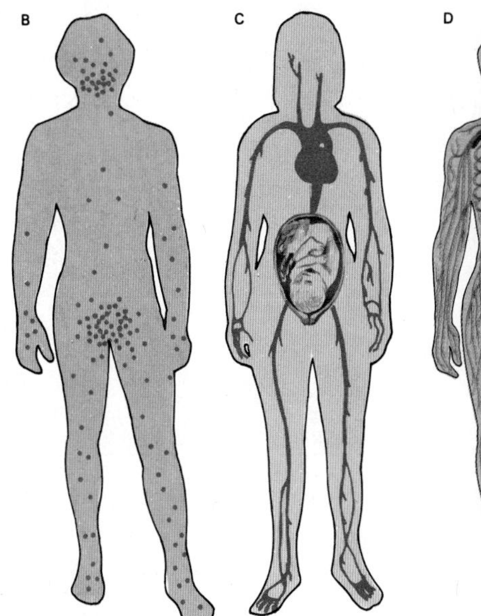
B
C

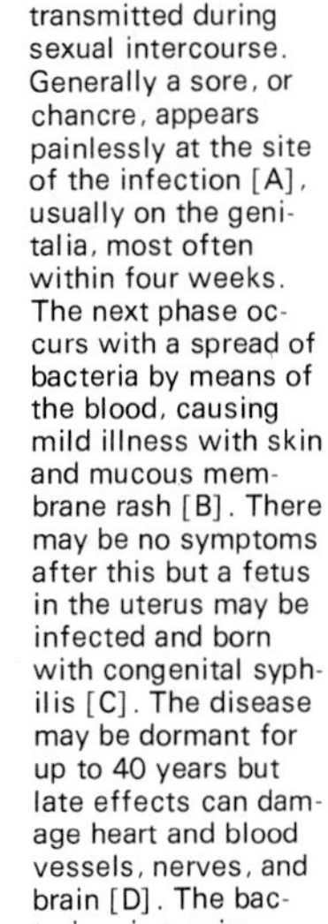
D

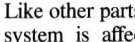

5 Syphilis is an infectious disease transmitted during sexual intercourse. Generally a sore, or chancre, appears painlessly at the site of the infection [A], usually on the genitalia, most often within four weeks. The next phase occurs with a spread of bacteria by means of the blood, causing mild illness with skin and mucous membrane rash [B]. There may be no symptoms after this but a fetus in the uterus may be infected and born with congenital syphilis [C]. The disease may be dormant for up to 40 years but late effects can damage heart and blood vessels, nerves, and brain [D]. The bacterium is a spirochete [E].

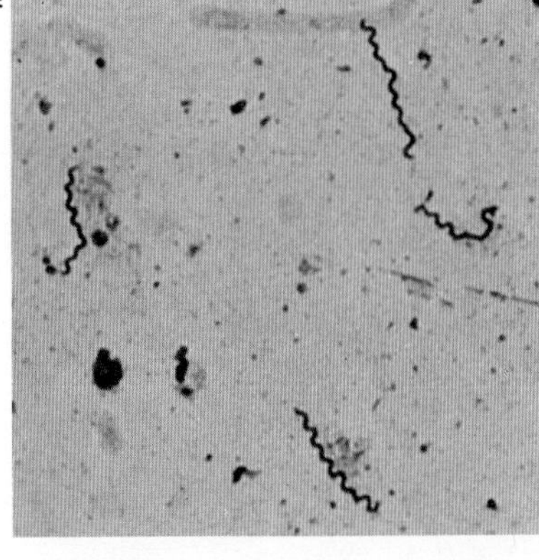
E

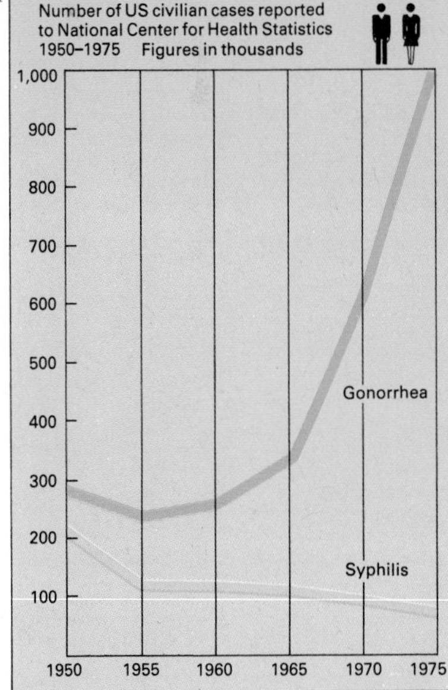
7
Number of US civilian cases reported to National Center for Health Statistics 1950–1975 Figures in thousands
1,000
900
800
700
600
500
400
300
200
100
Gonorrhea
Syphilis
1950
1955
1960
1965
1970
1975

7 Cases of venereal disease have shown rapid increases in many countries. This cannot be accounted for simply by more open discussion of the condition and greater willingness to come forward and be treated. The rise may be related to increased promiscuity. Incidents of gonorrhea have increased to a greater extent than those of syphilis. Apart from the common cold, gonorrhea probably represents the most common infectious disease in humans.

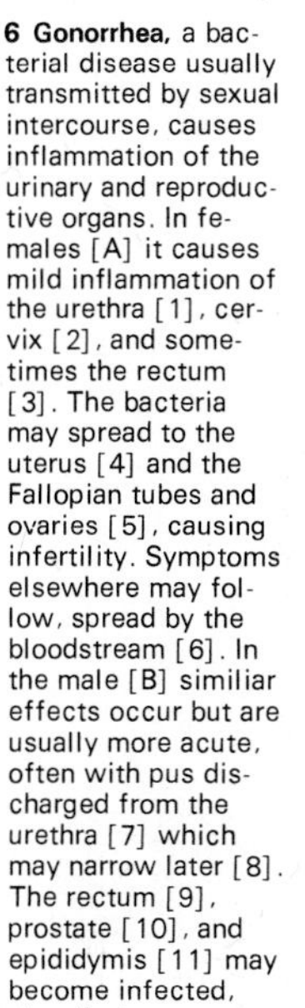

6 Gonorrhea, a bacterial disease usually transmitted by sexual intercourse, causes inflammation of the urinary and reproductive organs. In females [A] it causes mild inflammation of the urethra [1], cervix [2], and sometimes the rectum [3]. The bacteria may spread to the uterus [4] and the Fallopian tubes and ovaries [5], causing infertility. Symptoms elsewhere may follow, spread by the bloodstream [6]. In the male [B] similiar effects occur but are usually more acute, often with pus discharged from the urethra [7] which may narrow later [8]. The rectum [9], prostate [10], and epididymis [11] may become infected, also. Early treatment is essential.

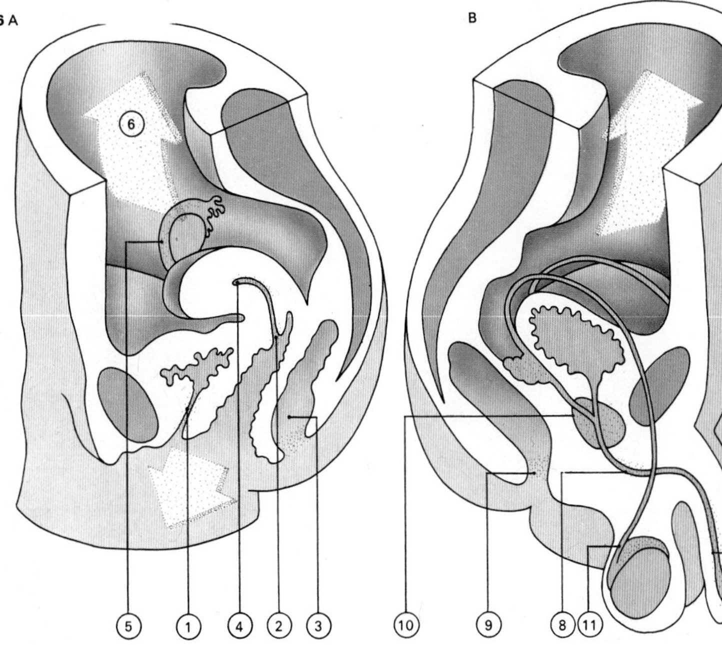
6 A
B
6
5
1
4
2
3
10
9
8
11
7

Alcoholism and drug abuse

In every known society some people take substances that cause alterations of consciousness. There are two main groups of such substances, alcoholic drinks such as beers, wines, and spirits, and drugs such as cannabis, mescaline, cocaine, heroin, and LSD. Some of these are relatively mild and harmless, except when taken in repeatedly large doses; others, even in small doses, set up a dependence that can totally dominate the individual, change behavior, and affect social relationships.

Susceptibility to alcohol

Alcoholics are drinkers who depend on alcohol to such an extent that eventually they show noticeable mental or physical disturbance. Most alcoholics are persistent heavy drinkers [1], but various patterns of alcohol abuse have been identified. Some drink steadily over many years and suffer physical damage in late middle age as a consequence. Others can function quite well without alcohol for long periods but when exposed to alcohol cannot control the amount they drink. Most alcoholics are middle aged and male, although there are signs that more young people and more women are abusing alcohol.

Alcoholism usually develops slowly. The alcoholic often begins by relying on alcohol to ease anxiety or depression, which it does briefly. Tolerance to alcohol develops rapidly, however, and increasing amounts are drunk to obtain relief. Gradually, the alcoholic develops physiological dependence on alcohol so that when deprived of it he exhibits withdrawal symptoms [3]. These include nausea and vomiting, tremors, memory lapses, epileptic fits, and delirium tremens [4]. Pathological drinking is invariably accompanied by difficulties at work caused by absenteeism or drunkenness, family and marital disharmony, financial difficulties, and mental and physical ill health.

Physical complications of alcohol abuse include gastritis, peptic ulceration, cirrhosis of the liver, inflammation of the pancreas, and damage to the heart muscles. Brain damage with severe memory impairment is not uncommon. Psychiatric complications include severe depression with marked guilt feelings, which may become so severe that they end in suicide.

Treatment of alcoholism is aimed at developing an awareness on the part of the alcoholic that he has a problem with drink. Some experts believe there is a form of metabolic fault in alcoholics and complete abstention seems to be necessary in most cases. Psychotherapy, aversion treatment, and drugs are among the methods used to help achieve this.

The dangers of drug dependence

Drug dependence means the repeated non-medicinal use of a drug causing harm to the user or to others. All drugs can be dangerous and should be treated with extreme caution, irrespective of social attitudes that tend to glamorize the use of certain drugs. Drugs have been produced from a bewildering variety of plants, but a large group, including morphine and heroin, are derived from the poppy and are called opiates [Key]. New addictive drugs have been developed in laboratories.

CONNECTIONS

See also
760 Introduction to mental health
770 Physical cures for mental illness
746 Man-made cures
792 Adolescence: sex and independence
916 Changing patterns of crime
428 Mushrooms and toadstools

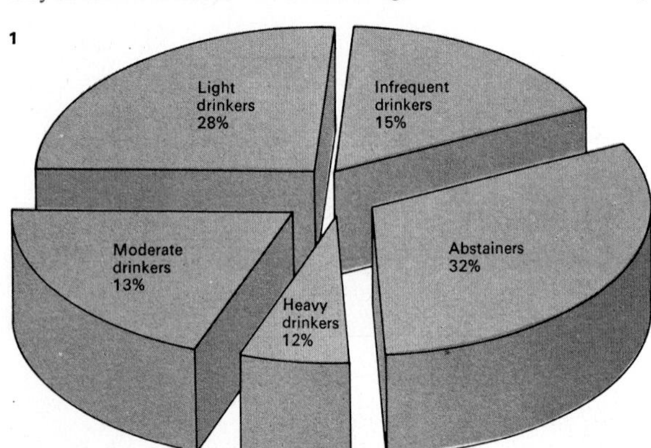

1
Light drinkers 28%
Infrequent drinkers 15%
Moderate drinkers 13%
Heavy drinkers 12%
Abstainers 32%

1 Drinking categories in a US survey assumed that abstainers drank less than once yearly, infrequent drinkers less than once monthly, light drinkers at least once monthly but not more than one drink (a bottle of beer or single measure of spirits) per session; moderate drinkers at least once monthly, three to four drinks per session; and heavy drinkers almost daily, with up to five drinks.

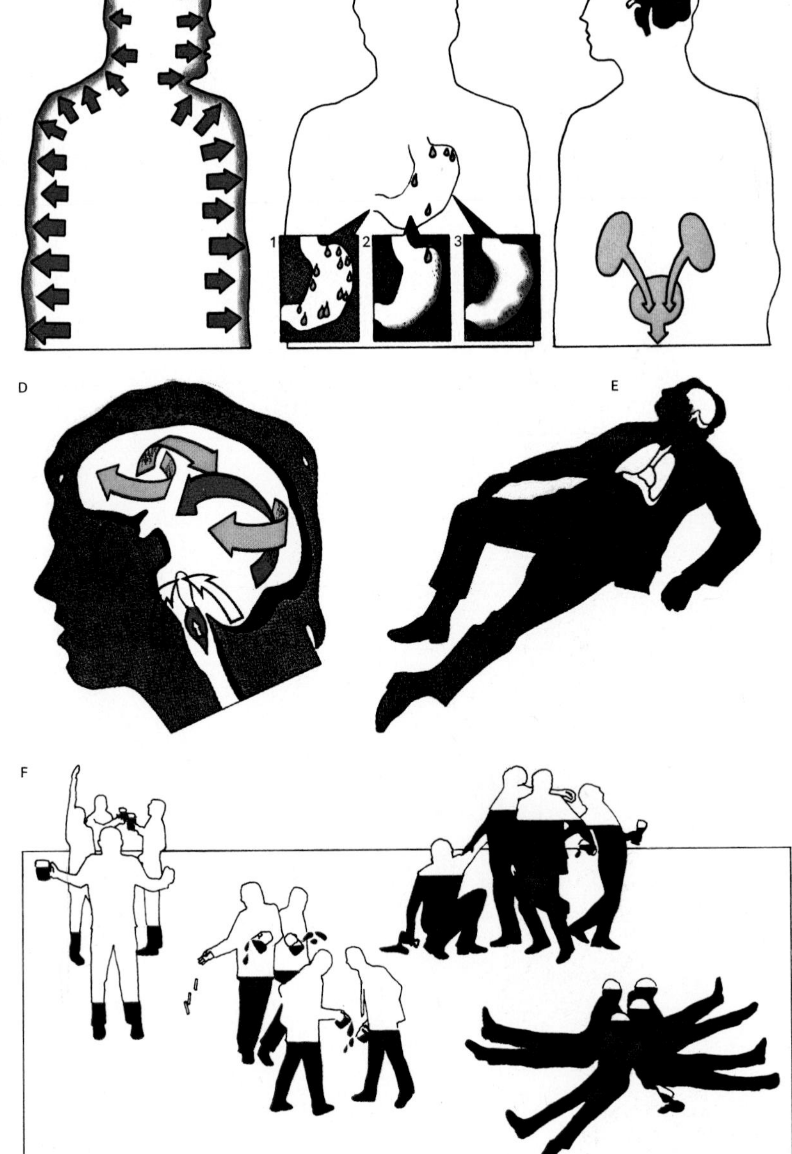

2
A
B
C
1
2
3
D
E
F

2 Short-term effects of alcohol on the body include dilation of skin blood vessels [A] and a drop in temperature. Gastric secretion [B] is increased at a low concentration (20mg alcohol/100ml blood) [1] but is inhibited at higher concentrations [2] and the stomach lining is irritated [3] Inhibition of the pituitary gland in the brain causes increased production of urine [C]. Vital centers in the brain are depressed [D]. Judgment, self-criticism, perception, and motor skills are impaired and sleepiness, coma, and even death may occur [E]. Drinkers may become irritable, disorderly and, finally, comatose [F].

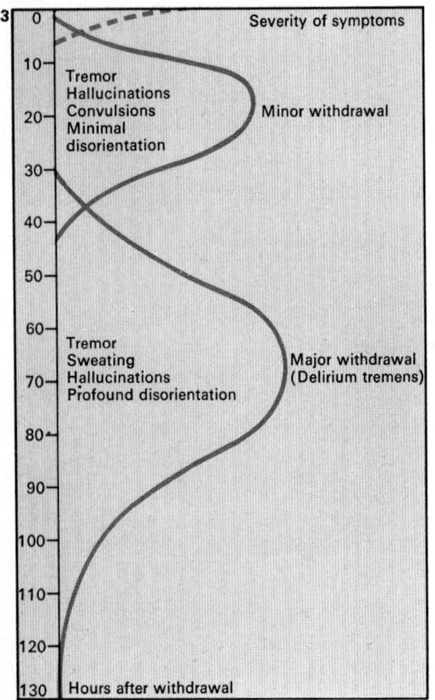

3
Severity of symptoms
0
10
20
30
40
50
60
70
80
90
100
110
120
130
Tremor
Hallucinations
Convulsions
Minimal disorientation
Minor withdrawal
Tremor
Sweating
Hallucinations
Profound disorientation
Major withdrawal (Delirium tremens)
Hours after withdrawal

3 Withdrawal symptoms can follow cessation of drinking after a heavy or chronic intake of alcohol. They can be relatively slight, occurring within 8 to 48 hours of withdrawal, or quite severe, extending over 3 to 8 days.

Addicts who cannot finance their habit (the rapidly developing tolerance to opiates means that ever-increasing doses are required) often turn to crime to finance their addiction. Deprived of his "fix" (jargon for injectable dose), the addict experiences severe restlessness, vomiting, diarrhea, and insomnia, eight to twelve hours after his last dose. Such symptoms last from three to seven days and can end in death. Complications of drug addiction include overdose, liver damage, general infection, and pneumonia.

Dependence on the so-called soft drugs (the barbiturates and the minor tranquilizers) is a serious problem, given the popularity of these drugs in the treatment of insomnia [5] and anxiety. Such drugs differ in their ability to produce tolerance and physiological dependence, but their use, depending on the personality and social pressures involved, can in time lead to the abuse of other drugs, such as the opiates and LSD.

Illusion, hallucinations, altered time sense, distorted judgment, confusion, and disorientation are experienced in LSD "trips." There have also been reports of recurrences of the drug's effects weeks or even months after the end of a trip. No withdrawal symptoms occur after taking LSD. Amphetamines [6] produce a rapid onset of euphoria and in large doses can cause a severe paranoid psychosis. Discontinuance after long-term abuse frequently causes depression, fatigue, and apathy.

The cannabis controversy

Whether *Cannabis sativa,* a euphoriant and relaxant derived from Indian hemp, is a dangerous drug of addiction or a harmless pleasure remains controversial. The dried leaves of the hemp are termed marihuana, the resin obtained from the flowering tops, hashish. In moderate doses, cannabis can produce a sense of excitement, heightened awareness, and well-being followed by a phase of tranquillity and then fatigue.

Drug dependence can be treated by maintaining the addict on a controlled dose of his drug, by replacing the drug by a similar, but less potent, synthetic, or by controlling withdrawal under supervision.

KEY

Opium smoking was fostered in China during the 19th century by European traders intent on profit, particularly the British, who crushed a Chinese attempt to stop traffic in the drug. By the mid-century so-called opium dens were sordid features of Chinese cities. Although Europeans were less addicted, opium, laudanum, and morphine were legal and common drugs in Europe as well as America.

4

A

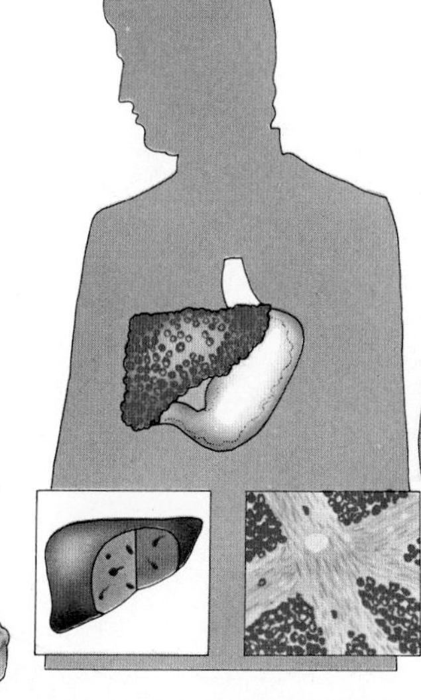

B

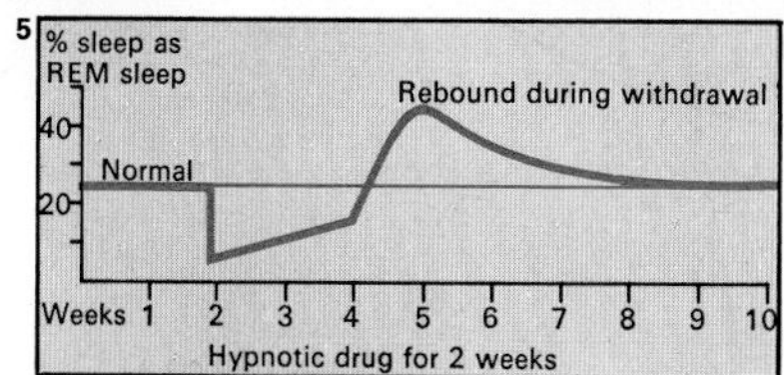

C
D

4 People who drink heavily often eat poorly [A] and, in the long run, malnutrition can result. Inflammation of the stomach and disease of the liver (cirrhosis) produce further loss of appetite. In cirrhosis [B], the liver is damaged either by the direct toxic effect of alcohol or by its effect on nutrition. Normal liver tissue is replaced by fibrous scar tissue. Deficiency of vitamin B1 damages the long nerves to the limbs, resulting in peripheral neuritis [C]. A sufferer loses touch sensitivity. Delirium tremens [D], characterized by extreme agitation and visual hallucinations, is a serious withdrawal effect.

5

% sleep as REM sleep
40
20
Normal
Rebound during withdrawal
Weeks 1 2 3 4 5 6 7 8 9 10
Hypnotic drug for 2 weeks

5 Sleeping pills reduce the amount of REM (rapid eye movement) sleep when dreaming occurs. But REM sleep is higher than normal after withdrawal of the drug, with effects similar to delirium.

6

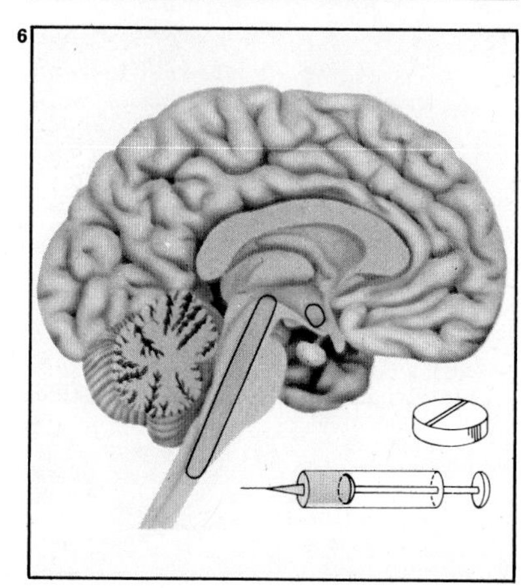

6 The amphetamine group of stimulant drugs acts on the brain in the region of the reticular formation and hypothalamus (yellow). They can be taken as tablets or injected intravenously to decrease fatigue, increase alertness, and lift mood. Tolerance develops rapidly, making progressively larger doses necessary. The euphoria, which follows injection particularly, is short-lived and gives way to depression. Severe paranoid states can occur.

7

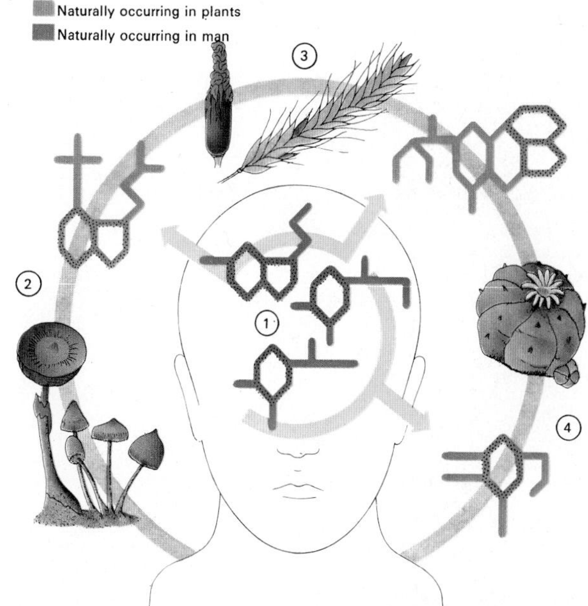

Naturally occurring in plants
Naturally occurring in man
3
2
1
4

7 The hallucinogenic drugs may produce their effects because they are similar structurally to substances [1] thought to be neurochemical transmitters. Three of the most common naturally occurring hallucinogenic substances are psilocybin, LSD, and mescaline. Psilocybin [2] is extracted from the psilocybe family of mushrooms. LSD [3], a highly potent hallucinogen used extensively for therapy by some psychiatrists, was first isolated from a fungus, *Clariceps purpurea,* which causes ergot of rye. Mescaline [4], which has played an important role in the religious rituals of certain Mexican Indian tribes, is obtained from the peyote cactus.

Diseases of the Third World

Health or lack of disease depends, among other things, on quantity and quality of diet; effective control of housing, food standards, and water and sewage systems; and the availability of doctors, drugs, and hospitals should a disease occur. This is a measure of the problem facing most of the developing countries, which make up approximately 70 percent of the world's 4 billion people. All these factors are expensive and presuppose a solid industrial base—something that many Third World countries lack. Hence their health problems are immense: the life expectancy of a newborn baby in such a country is still about 35 years—about the same as it was in Western societies in the fourteenth century.

Insect-borne diseases

The diseases that still affect so many people fall into two main groups—infectious disorders and nutritional ones. The most important infections that occur in tropical countries are those spread by insects, which carry disease from person to person or from animals to people.

First among these insect-borne diseases is malaria, still one of the world's greatest killers. It is caused by a tiny parasite that is carried from man to man by the *Anopheles* mosquito [Key]. When a mosquito sucks blood from an infected person the parasites are sucked into the insect's stomach along with the blood. They breed and ten days later their offspring can be found in the mosquito's salivary glands. From then on the insect will inject a dose of parasites into anyone it bites.

The main symptoms of malaria are high fever, headache, and violent shivering. While some species of the malaria parasite are relatively benign others often cause chronic ill health or death. Treatment is with drugs such as chloroquine, but prevention is a better solution. There are three types of prevention: killing the mosquitoes [1]; stopping them from biting people; and the administration of protective drugs.

Other mosquito-borne infections include various types of filariasis [3], common in the Pacific, the Far East, and Africa, and yellow fever, a serious virus disease that occurs in west Africa and South America. For many years yellow fever has prevented the development and cultivation of much of the South American hinterland. Prevention is the same as for malaria but immunization is an added precaution.

Several other insects are disease carriers. Leishmaniasis [4], dengue fever, and phlebotomus fever are all spread by sandflies and cause much suffering and economic disruption, especially in the Middle East. Rat fleas still continue to spread bubonic plague in some Third World countries, [5] while the tsetse fly is responsible for trypanosomiasis or sleeping sickness [6]. Lice are the carriers of ordinary typhus, while tick typhus is spread by dog ticks and scrub typhus (tsutsuga muchi) is carried by rat mites; rat fleas carry murine typhus. Rickettsial diseases are spread by insects.

Diseases of insanitation

Almost as important as the insect-borne diseases are those of poor sanitation. These depend for their spread on the contamination of drinking water or food by human

CONNECTIONS

See also
734 World health
696 A healthy diet
472 Flatworms, flukes, and tapeworms
466 Single-celled animals and sponges
422 Bacteria and viruses
706 Birth control

1

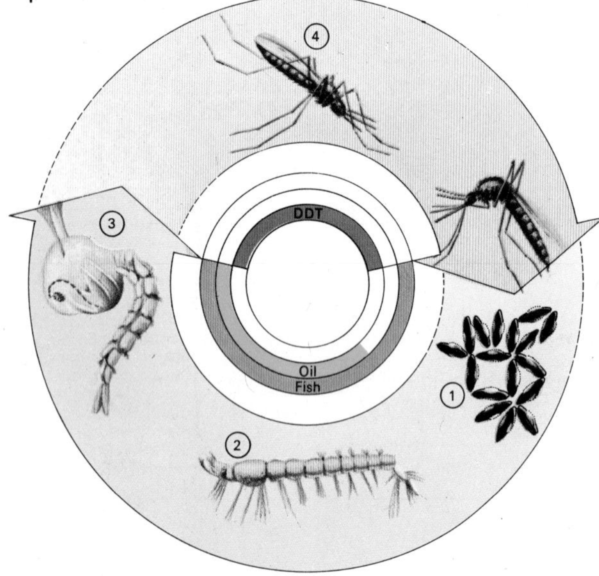

4
3
DDT
Oil
Fish
1
2

1 The malaria parasite is carried by the *Anopheles* mosquito, which thrives in areas with stagnant water. The female lays her eggs in water [1]; from them larvae [2] develop. These go through a pupal stage [3] before developing into adult mosquitoes [4]. Insecticides such as DDT can be used to kill the adults, while spraying oil on stagnant water destroys the larvae and pupae. Guppies in infested waters will attack all three waterborne stages.

2

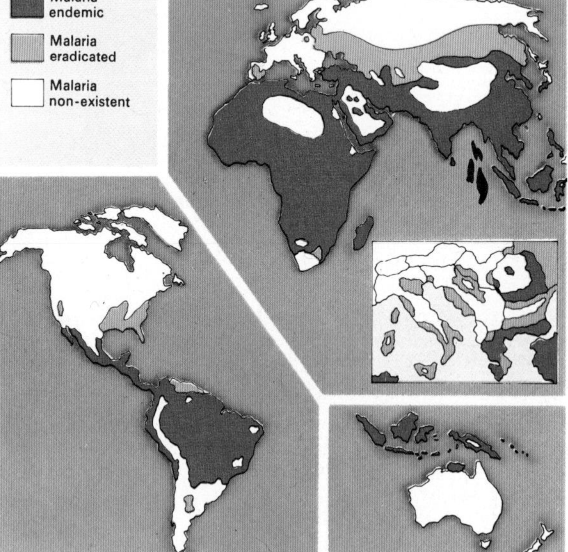

Malaria endemic
Malaria eradicated
Malaria non-existent

2 These maps indicate the areas of the world from which malaria has been eradicated and those in which it is still a danger to life.

3

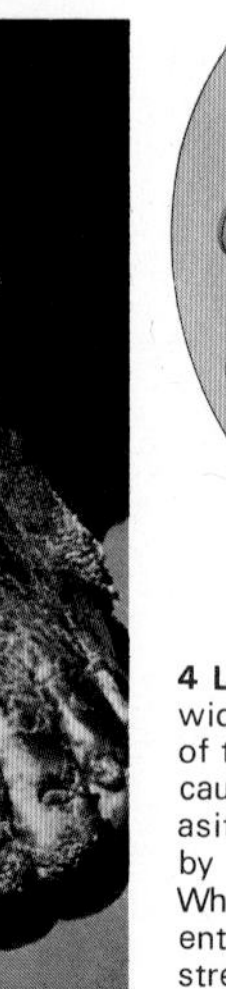

3 Elephantiasis is one of the most dreadful types of filariasis, which is usually caused by the minute filarial worm *Wuchereria bancrofti.* These worms are injected into the human bloodstream by the bite of an infected mosquito.

4

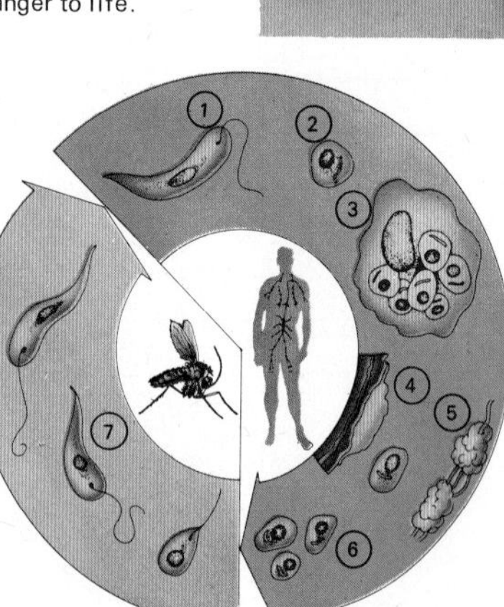

1
2
3
4
5
6
7

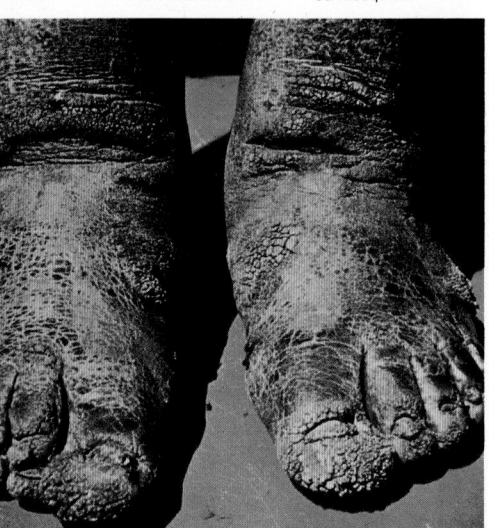

4 Leishmaniasis is a widespread disease of tropical countries, caused by a tiny parasite that is spread by infested sandflies. When the parasite enters the bloodstream [1] it changes form [2] and is ingested by a white blood cell [3]. The parasite multiplies in the cell and its "descendants" may attack the skin [4] or lymph nodes [5]. If the victim is bitten by another sandfly, parasites [6] will enter the insect and mature into forms that can infect other humans [7].

5

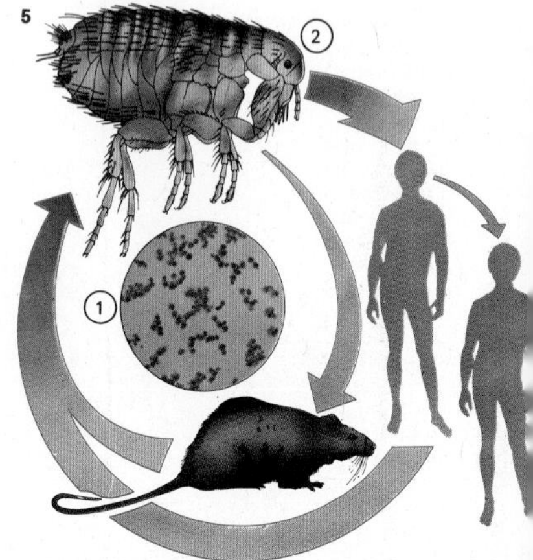

2
1

5 Bubonic plague ("Black Death") may still occur, especially in the Indian subcontinent. It is caused by a germ *Pasteurella pestis* [1], which can live in man, rats, fleas [2], and some other animals. If an animal has the infection, the fleas that feed on it will ingest the germ. A man bitten by these fleas will probably develop the disease—and may spread the infecting organism to others via his breath.

feces. The linked problems of disposing of excreta and of providing pure drinking water are both difficult and costly to solve.

Infections that are spread by this "fecal-oral route" include many kinds of nonspecific diarrhea as well as typhoid, paratyphoid, cholera, various types of food poisoning, bacillary and amebic dysentery, and probably polio as well. Of this group the disease that caused most concern in the 1970s was cholera [7], which spread alarmingly from its base in the Far East to much of the world in recent years, including south of the Sahara desert for the first time.

Other sanitation-related infections to which the Third World populations succumb include hookworm and other worm infestations, which produce anemia and chronic invalidism; and the tropical disease bilharzia, or schistosomiasis [9]. The economic effects of bilharzia, a crippling disease that drastically reduces the ability to work, are severe.

Less important numerically are leprosy and yaws (both spread by prolonged personal contact only, and both now treatable) and rabies, which is caught from animals, especially dogs, and is almost untreatable. The last of the important infectious diseases is smallpox, although this seems to be well under control and is confined to Bangladesh and Ethiopia.

Nutritional disorders

The well-known vitamin deficiency diseases such as pellagra, beriberi, and scurvy are not now of enormous importance in the Third World, partly because it is relatively easy to provide the essential vitamins.

Far more serious are outright starvation and the related disease of kwashiorkor, or protein starvation. Half the world still goes hungry and in areas such as North Africa, where crops have been hit repeatedly by drought, or Bangladesh, where floods have destroyed food supplies, millions of people find it desperately hard to obtain any kind of food. As the world's population grows inexorably, and as the amount of protein available per mouth gets less and less, it seems that the problem of starvation is likely to worsen.

KEY

30m (100ft)

Mosquitoes find their victims in two stages. Carbon dioxide, which humans exhale, first sets them flying. If they then sense a current of warm, wet air such as every person gives off, they home in on it. Some persons are bitten more often than others because they are warmer and wetter. Repellents interfere with accuracy of the mosquitoes' sensors.

6

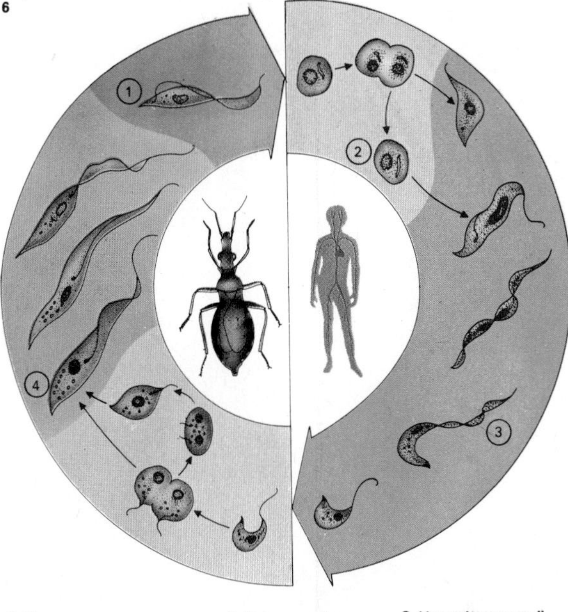

6 Trypanosome infections cause African sleeping sickness and South America's Chagas' disease. The parasite of sleeping sickness [1] enters the blood following a bite of a tsetse fly, or, in Chagas' disease, when fecal matter from a cone-nosed bug enters a skin abrasion or the eye. In sleeping sickness it reproduces [2] and is ingested by other bugs [3], where more parasites develop [4].

7 Cholera is one of the many diseases that spread because of poor hygiene. Human feces containing cholera germs contaminate food or water [A]. The victim ingests them and they incubate in his small intestine [B]. They then produce severe, often fatal diarrhea [C]. The patient may survive if his gross dehydration can be corrected with intravenous fluid [D]. If such therapy is undertaken promptly (and if no kidney damage has occurred), he can fully recover [E].

7A B C D E

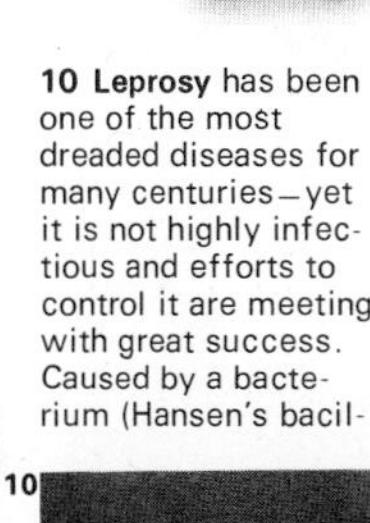

8 Unsanitary conditions associated with food, water supply, or sewage disposal are a sure way to spread disease. This Afghanistan meat market, perched over an open sewer, could spread infection.

8

9

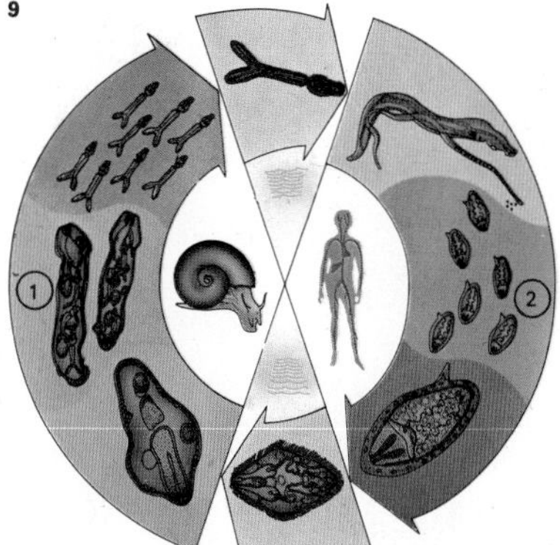

9 Bilharzia (schistosomiasis), named after Theodor Bilharz, who identified it in 1851, today affects about 200 million people in tropical countries. It is caused by a minute parasite that spends part of its life cycle in freshwater snails [1] and part in water, where it can penetrate the skin of anyone washing or bathing [2]. The invading parasite lays up to 40,000 eggs as an adult. These interfere with blood flow and destroy tissues of liver, lungs, and kidneys.

10 Leprosy has been one of the most dreaded diseases for many centuries—yet it is not highly infectious and efforts to control it are meeting with great success. Caused by a bacterium (Hansen's bacillus), it is thought to be passed on only by prolonged close contact. It mainly attacks the skin and the nerves and may produce either trivial alterations in the tissues or gross deformities.

10

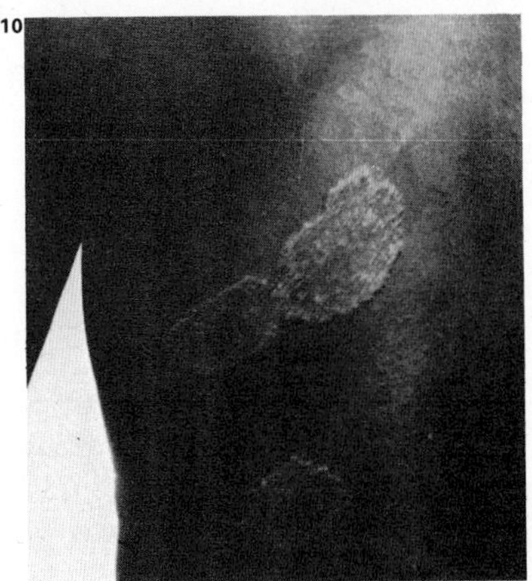

World health

The World Health Organization (WHO) defines "health" as "a state of complete physical, mental, and social well-being, and not merely the absence of a disease."

The object of WHO is to try to achieve such a state of well-being for as many as possible of the world's peoples. It may seem that such a target is far off, when so many millions of people suffer from disease and malnutrition. But in fact today's pattern of health and disease is in many ways far better than that of past centuries. In Western countries at least, men and women are living longer and healthier lives than ever before—even though "warning signs" in the shape of diseases of "civilization" (such as lung cancer and coronary thrombosis) are appearing with much greater frequency.

Health problems in the Third World

Even in the poorer parts of the world there have been great improvements in health care during this century. Immunization against infectious diseases has helped to control such once-dreadful scourges as smallpox [7], and energetic measures against the mosquitoes, flies, and ticks that carry disease are slowly helping to defeat killer infections such as malaria, yellow fever, and typhus.

The health problems of the poorer two-thirds of the world are still far from being solved, however, a fact easily demonstrated by the mortality figures of various nations [4]. In the less well-off countries there are high mortality rates among the young (in Nigeria over 180 babies out of every 1,000 die in their first year) and survival into later life remains the exception rather than the rule [1].

Several factors account for this situation. One is that the tropical climate of many developing countries encourages the development and expansion of the organisms that cause infectious diseases. Another is that providing and maintaining good health care for a rapidly expanding population poses difficult economic problems. In much of the world infant mortality is high simply because there are no proper facilities for looking after mothers and babies. Those babies who survive infancy may die in childhood because of malnutrition. And those who achieve adulthood may die young because of lack of adequate medical care during illness or maternity. People who are weakened by malnutrition, and who have no doctor within reach, are easy targets for any kind of disease and especially the virulent tropical infections. These diseases need not be confined to the tropics. Today's air travel means that such infections can be carried to all parts of the globe in a short time. Monitoring the spread of such diseases is one of the major challenges to world health.

Organizations to the rescue

It was to deal with all these difficult and complex problems that the United Nations set up the World Health Organization in 1948 [Key]. By the mid-1970s WHO was active in more than 130 different countries and cost $1,000,000,000 a year to run.

The functions of WHO are to act as a clearing house for medical information; to carry out research (especially in the field of epidemiology); to administer international

CONNECTIONS

See also
732 Diseases of the Third World
736 Community medicine
1386 Underdevelopment and the world economy
706 Birth control
1382 The United Nations and its agencies

1 Developed and developing countries vary greatly in the availability of health care and this is reflected in the average age of their populations. Comparison of the percentage of the populations of the United States and Papua New Guinea over age 75 [A], or of their general age distribution curves [B], shows marked differences. In developing countries generally, with high birth rates and low life expectancy, the average age is often below 20 and the number of persons living into their 40s and 50s is relatively small. In developed countries most people survive early childhood.

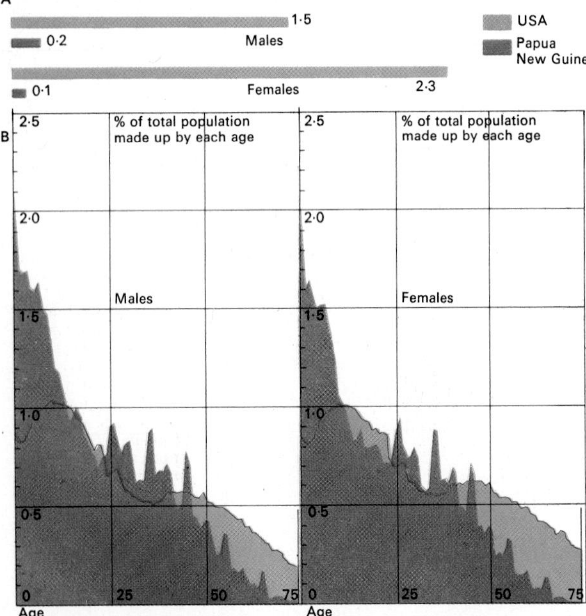
1 % of population over 75
A
1·5
0·2
Males
0·1
Females
2·3
USA
Papua New Guinea
B
% of total population made up by each age
Males
Females
2·5
2·0
1·5
1·0
0·5
0
25
50
75
Age

2

England and Wales
Total hospitals 2,531
Specialist mental hospitals 152

Denmark
Total hospitals 170
Specialist mental hospitals 17

USA
Total hospitals 7,123
Specialist mental hospitals 519

Japan
Total hospitals 7,974
Specialist mental hospitals 769

France
Total hospitals 3,805
Specialist mental hospitals 274

Peru
Total hospitals 285
Specialist mental hospitals 9

1974 Totals

2 While physical disease gradually declines, many types of mental illness are increasing, especially in industrialized countries. Despite the importance of mental health the total number of specialist mental hospitals giving constant, skilled attention remains low.

4 A

Infant mortality (per thousand): Nigeria 187·0, India 139·0, Chile 91·6, USA 19·8, Japan 15·3, Sweden 13·0

Developing countries · Developed countries

B

Life expectancy (years): 57, 41, 37, 74, 71, 71

3

People per doctor · People per bed

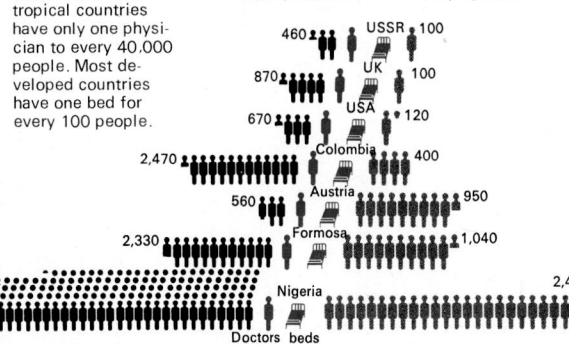

	People per doctor	People per bed
USSR	460	100
UK	870	100
USA	670	120
Colombia	2,470	400
Austria	560	950
Formosa	2,330	1,040
Nigeria	44,620	2,410

Doctors beds

3 A nation's health facilities can be measured by the number of people per doctor and the number of people per hospital bed available. A comparison of several countries provides interesting results. The Soviet Union has more doctors per capita than any other country in the world; in contrast, some tropical countries have only one physician to every 40,000 people. Most developed countries have one bed for every 100 people.

4 National wealth is the key to good health, as found in developed countries. It can secure balanced diets, good living conditions, and expert medical attention. High infant mortality and reduced life expectancy are indicators of poor health and are common in developing countries where such benefits are not readily available. In Sweden, Japan, and the United States, fewer than 20 babies in every thousand die during the first year. In Nigeria the figure is nearly 200 [A]. Similarly, life expectancy [B] in the same three developed countries is over 70 years, but in Nigeria a newborn baby can only expect (on average) to live to 37. Much of Africa and parts of Asia have similar low life-expectancy levels.

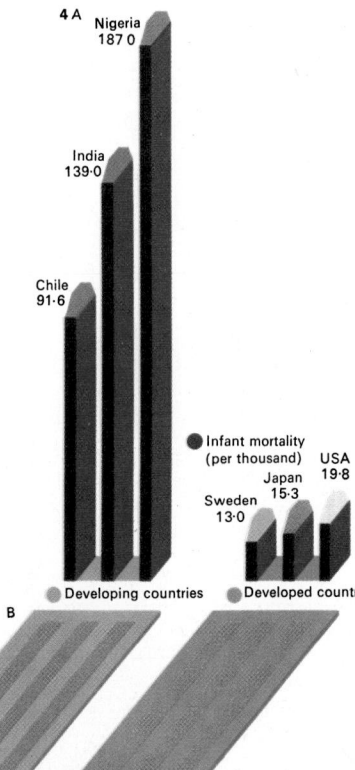

sanitary regulations, especially in connection with travel and quarantine; to finance international research programs, including studies of cancer and tuberculosis; and to help individual countries train medical staff and to fight disease [9].

In this last field WHO does much to provide vaccines, antibiotics, and other medicines. It also helps disseminate health education information, which is of great importance where disease and overpopulation are often the result of ignorance.

The question of overpopulation now looms large in current thinking on world health. It is generally recognized that there are too many people in the world for its nutritional resources and health care facilities to cope with. More and more people are going to starve to death (or die from lack of medical treatment) unless populations can be limited. Much current world health work is devoted to fertility control research and to teaching people about the urgent need for family planning.

Part of the solution to present problems will lie in increased food production, and in this field WHO works closely with one of the UN's other semi-autonomous bodies, the Food and Agriculture Organization (FAO), which has done much to improve world health by research into new crops and new fertilizers and by educating people in better techniques of farming. Unfortunately, it seems almost certain that whatever scientific breakthroughs are achieved in this field, there may never be enough food to feed even the world's present population.

Hope for the future

If there is to be any hope of a future for the Third World, renewed efforts must be made to eradicate the dangerous communicable diseases of the developing world and to prevent the spread of the "diseases of civilization" of the West. People must be educated in the ways of good health and more health personnel must be provided. More food must be grown. If all this can be achieved, then there will be hope that the advances of this century may be shared by a far wider proportion of the world's population than at present.

The World Health Organization (WHO), whose symbol is shown here, is a semi-autonomous unit within the United Nations organization. It is based in Geneva, and is active in more than 130 countries, mostly in the Third World.

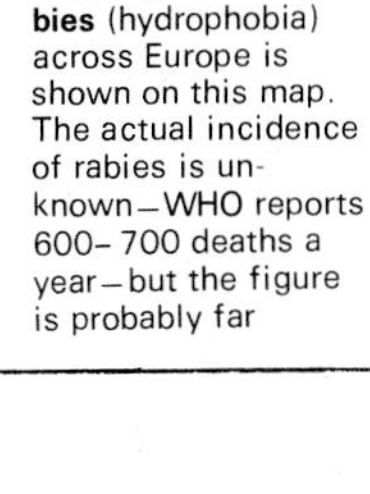
1972
1970
1973
1964
1963
1963
1965–6
1970
1970
1962
1973
1961

5 Cholera spread in the early 1960s from its "base" in the Far East with alarming rapidity. Some cholera germs had changed their nature and this new variant was called the "El Tor" type. Although cholera has not been seen in most Western countries since mid-Victorian times, by the mid-1970s, as the map shows, it was breaking out in southern Europe, aided by increased air travel.

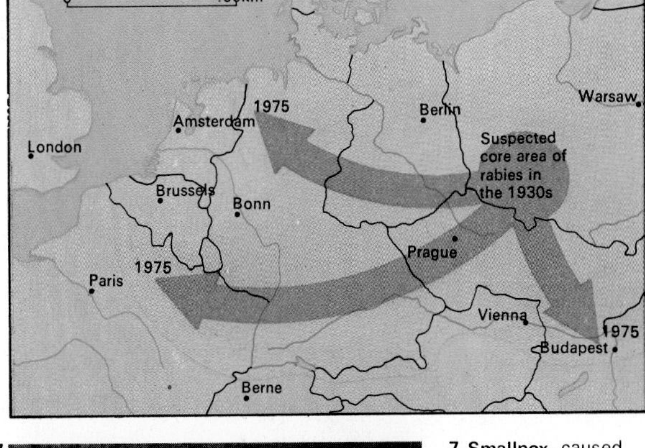
0
400km
London
Amsterdam
1975
Berlin
Warsaw
Suspected core area of rabies in the 1930s
Brussels
Bonn
Paris
1975
Prague
Vienna
1975
Budapest
Berne

6 The spread of rabies (hydrophobia) across Europe is shown on this map. The actual incidence of rabies is unknown—WHO reports 600–700 deaths a year—but the figure is probably far higher. The virus of this terrible disease is spread by dog bites (although even a lick from an infected animal may prove fatal). Foxes and other wild animals can also be carriers of the disease.

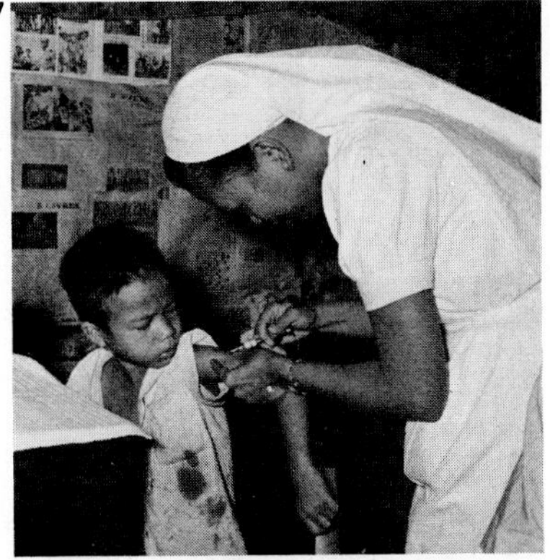

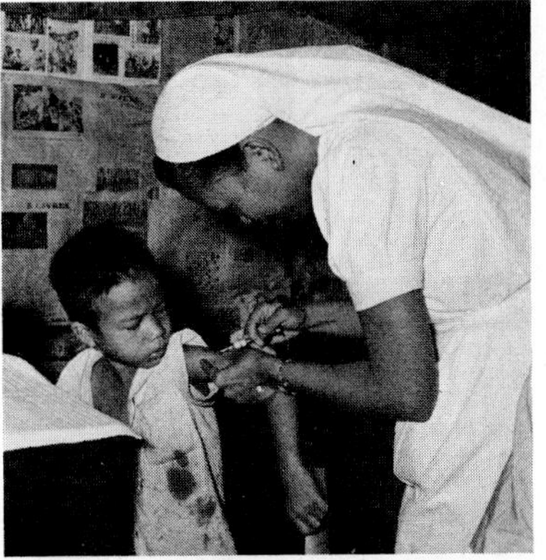

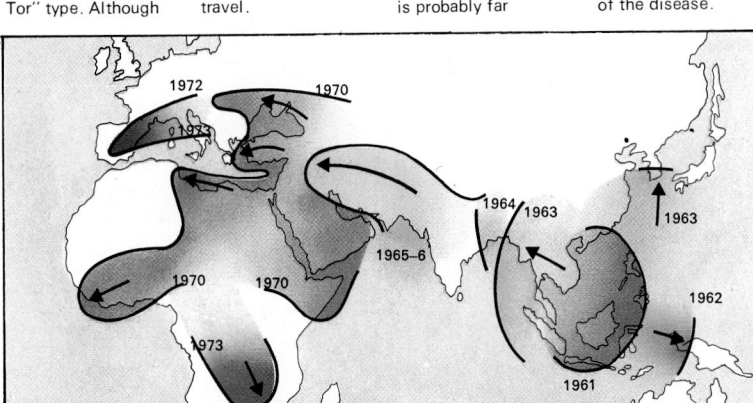

7 Smallpox, caused by a virus that is spread by contact with an infected human, was once a world scourge that killed or disfigured thousands of people (even in the most economically advanced countries) every year. Now it has been driven back so nearly to total extinction that many Western countries have abandoned routine vaccination of infants against it. Travelers may still need immunization.

8 The thin, wasted muscles and protruding bones of these beggars in Calcutta, India, are almost a badge of the developing countries and a sign of the tremendous problems facing them. These problems are exacerbated by the natural disasters (typhoons, flooding, and droughts) that seem to plague them.

9 Regular, small scale clinics, like this one at Keneba, Gambia, for fighting malaria, contribute significantly to the control of disease. Particularly in areas of poor transportation and few ancillary services, this type of center, tailor-made for local conditions, is more effective than prestigious hospitals of the Western type.

Community health

Anyone who has suffered from an attack of food poisoning after a meal in a restaurant, caught influenza from someone on a bus or fleas from a hotel bed, or developed athlete's foot after visiting a public swimming pool knows only too well how the health of the individual depends on the efforts of the whole community.

People cannot function properly when they are ill; in the same way, a society cannot function properly unless its members are healthy. As a measure of self-protection, therefore, every community takes steps to promote the health of its members. This is increasingly important as the size of the community increases, both because the results of ignorance, negligence, or incompetence can potentially affect many more people and because disease can spread more rapidly.

The scope of community health

Social medicine has two major functions: preventing disease and, if that fails, curing it. The second includes the building of hospitals and clinics, the training of nurses and doctors, and the financial support of sick people and their families. This aspect of social medicine is relatively expensive, both because of the cost of the facilities needed and because of the loss of productive work. The preventive aspect of social medicine is less dramatic and goes largely unnoticed, yet it affects all of us all of the time.

On one level these measures range from the proper disposal of the dead to the myriad regulations, typical of almost all countries today, that control building standards; density of population in towns and cities; the numbers of people that can be carried on ferries or seated in theaters; conditions for workers in factories; and permissible levels of airplane noise, emissions from car exhausts, and industrial toxic wastes. The tragedy during the 1950s and 1960s in Minamata, Japan, where unsupervised dumping of paper-mill effluent into the sea caused the death or disablement through methyl mercury poisoning of those who ate fish or shellfish caught in the area, highlights the need for stringent community action to ensure public health. The same vigilance is needed in testing new drugs or similar products thoroughly before they are approved for general use.

A clean water supply

The giant Roman aqueducts that are still scattered across Europe [6] and the ingenious system of underground cisterns or *qanaats* that honeycombed ancient Persia, attest to the vital importance that every community has attached to water. And the linked needs of providing houses with a regular supply of pure drinking water and taking away sewage in such a way that the two do not mix are still major preoccupations of health authorities. The contamination of water with even tiny amounts of feces can cause an epidemic of dysentery, cholera, typhoid, or hepatitis.

The risk is greatest in developing countries, where these diseases are endemic (being highest when an earthquake, typhoon, flood, or other disaster disrupts the normal facilities), but they can occur even in a country as proud of its cleanliness as Switzerland. An outbreak of typhoid in Zermatt

CONNECTIONS

See also
1766 Water supply
1768 Sewage treatment
738 Preventive medicine
696 A healthy diet
292 Pollution of the air
296 Pollution of rivers and lakes
314 Water and irrigation
984 The Persian Empire of the Achaemenids
734 World health

1 The risk of infection from contaminated food is high, and so all stages of its production, storage, processing, and preparation are carefully regulated and monitored. Imported food is subject to the same standards and is rigorously checked both to ensure adequate hygiene and to prevent any new animal and crop pests or diseases not already endemic in the country from being introduced.

2 Tuberculosis of the bone and brain has been largely eradicated in developed countries over the last 40 years by stringent control of milking herds. Cows are tested every year for the presence of tuberculosis bacilli by injecting them with tuberculin. A positive reaction (swelling under the skin as shown here) indicates they carry the disease and can pass it in their milk to humans.

3 Efforts by restaurant and hotel managements to maintain standards of cleanliness, proper waste disposal, adequate toilet facilities, and staff health are checked regularly by official inspectors.

4 Animals must be slaughtered in accredited abattoirs both to ensure painless death and to enable the meat to be inspected for such infections as tapeworms and tuberculosis.

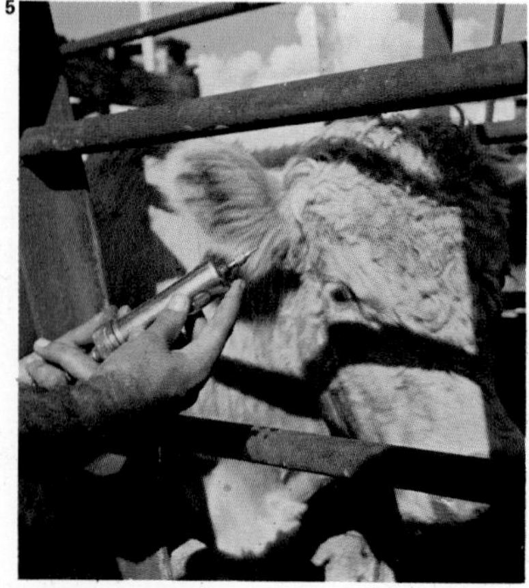

5 Vaccination of cattle against contagious abortion, or brucellosis, not only prevents the loss of calves but also protects humans who drink the milk from the unpleasant undulant or Malta fever.

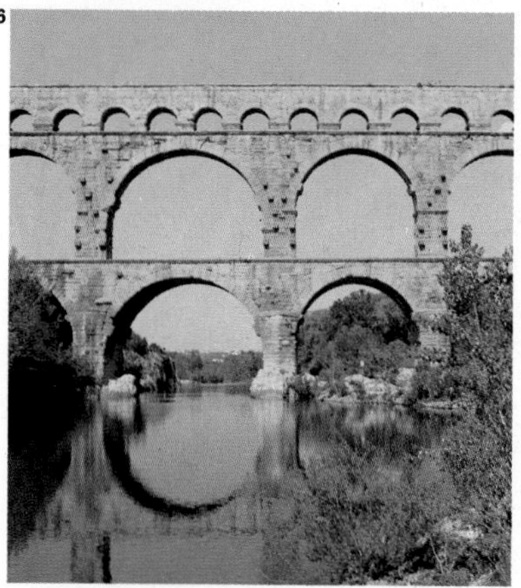

6 The Pont du Gard, near Nîmes, France, is one of the best known of the Roman aqueducts still standing. The longest built was the 57mi(92km) Acqua Marcia from the upper Aniene valley to Rome, only 7mi(11km) were above ground.

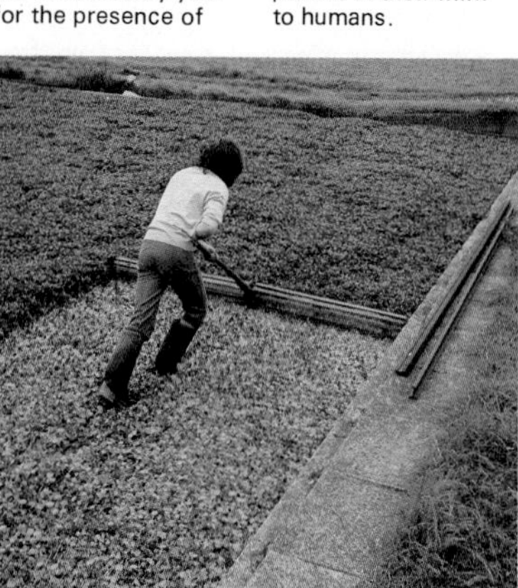

7 Even fresh vegetables can be a potential source of disease. Watercress, for example, can carry on its leaves the eggs of the sheep liver fluke *(Fasciola hepatica)*, a parasitic flatworm that causes liver "rot." Part of its life cycle is spent in the freshwater snail, so every effort is made to prevent infected snails entering the beds. All the water in well-managed watercress farms is drawn from wells or springs that carry no risk of infection, and sheep are kept away.

in 1963, which affected 313 people and killed three before it was finally eradicated, was traced to faulty sewage disposal.

Water must be properly collected—from springs, rivers, or deep bore holes—stored, purified (usually with chlorine, although ozone is sometimes used), and then distributed. In some parts of the world fluoride is added in minute quantities (1 or 2 parts per million) because experiments have shown that its presence decreases the incidence of tooth decay. Constant tests are carried out at all stages to make sure that no contamination from sewage or other impurities takes place.

The technology exists to clean sewage so thoroughly (and in the process remove the river, lake, and sea pollution that is such a feature of industrial countries) that the water can be re-used; but the costs involved in these processes are high and, all too often, the priority is regrettably low.

A further advantage of an adequate water supply is that it makes a water-carried sewage system possible. Such a system, if linked by proper sewers [10] to sewage treatment plants, greatly reduces the danger of diseases spreading, particularly those such as food poisoning, poliomyelitis, and dysentery that are transmitted from feces to food by flies.

Maintaining food standards

All stages of the production of food, from growing and processing to preparation and eating, must be carefully regulated. Techniques for the improvement of food include the addition of vitamins to such common foods as margarine and bread, the pasteurization of milk [8] to prevent the spread of tuberculosis and brucellosis, the inspection of meat to exclude tapeworm infestation [4], and the addition of iodine to salt to combat goiter.

But no matter how high the quality of food it can still become a danger to health if it is not properly handled. Thus there are laws to ensure hygienic conditions in food factories, food stores, and restaurants [3]. The aim is to prevent, as far as possible, food becoming contaminated with any toxin or infectious agent.

KEY

Public wash-houses were common in many European cities up to the 1930s. Erected by the authorities, they were heralded as a great advance in hygiene and even of substantial moral benefit to the "poorer" classes. Those built in villages simply provided cold running water and scrub boards, but later public wash-houses were equipped with large boilers for hot water and even steam-driven spin dryers. Rising wage levels and the advent of cheap electric washing machines largely removed the need for them and they have been replaced by private commercial coin-operated laundries equipped with washing machines and dryers.

8

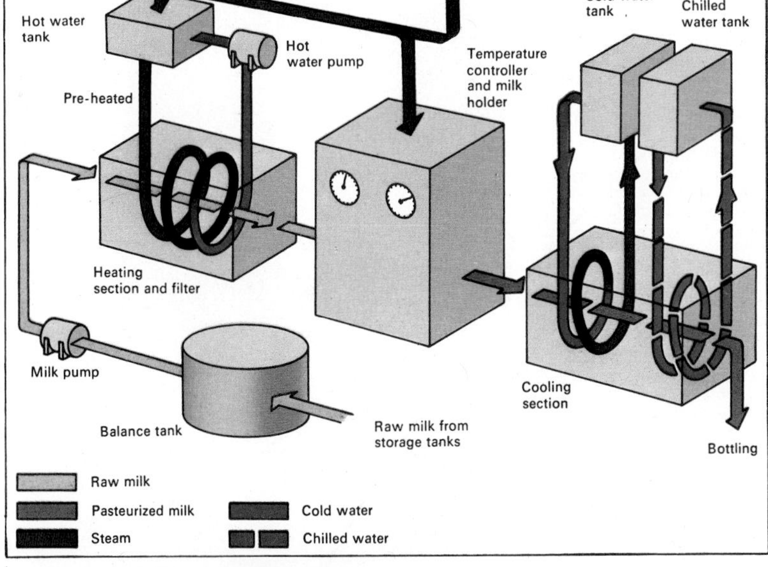
Steam injection
Steam supply
Hot water tank
Hot water pump
Cold water tank
Chilled water tank
Temperature controller and milk holder
Pre-heated
Heating section and filter
Milk pump
Balance tank
Raw milk from storage tanks
Cooling section
Bottling
Raw milk
Pasteurized milk
Steam
Cold water
Chilled water

8 Pasteurization of milk destroys the bacteria that cause tuberculosis and undulant fever. In the process, named after Louis Pasteur (1822–95), the milk is heated to 144°–160°F (62°–71°C), which is lethal to most bacteria but not high enough to alter the quality of the milk. As fewer cows carry infectious diseases, pasteurization's main use is in improving the keeping qualities of milk.

9

9 Unwanted solid refuse can be disposed of by dumping and by incineration. Refuse poses wide environmental problems through its increasing volume and the use of materials that break down slowly.

10

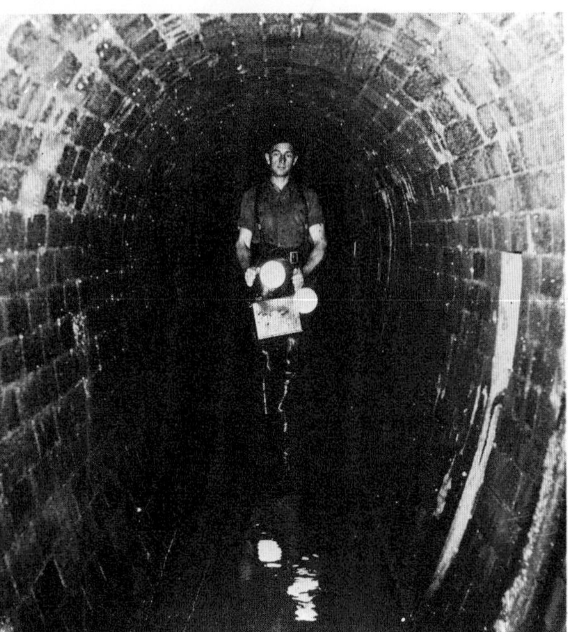

10 Providing adequate facilities for disposing of storm water and sewage from homes and industry is a major health responsibility of local government. Drains and sewers remove such waste for treatment before it is discharged into the sea.

11

11 Many diseases are spread by infected animals or their parasites. Rabies is mainly transmitted through infected saliva and biting by foxes, coyotes, wolves, dogs, skunks, raccoons, and cats. Bats, too, are an important potential source of rabies. Transmission from infected vampire bats to domestic animals and airborne spread to animals and man from bat droppings occurs.

Preventive medicine

Preventive medicine is the sum of all those measures—general physical checkups, vaccinations, dental visits, and eye examinations—that forestall illness either by entirely preventing its occurrence or by catching it so early that it can be easily and quickly treated. Waiting for teeth to ache before visiting the dentist could mean extensive filling or extraction.

Care before birth

Understandably, preventive medicine is most in evidence and most widely accepted during pregnancy. Indeed, the process often begins even before conception. At this stage it is often possible to predict the chances of parents with a genetic defect producing a diseased child, and to help them make a decision for or against parenthood. A woman carrying the trait for hemophilia, for example, might decide against bearing a child on being told that any daughters, while not vulnerable, would have a 50 percent chance of being carriers and that any sons would have a 50 percent chance of suffering from the disease.

During pregnancy, an expectant mother makes regular visits to a physician so that the progress of the fetus and her own health can be monitored. She is checked to ensure that she is not gaining too much weight, that her blood pressure is not too high, that she is not suffering from diabetes, and that she has not contracted syphilis [4] or any of the diseases specific to pregnancy. Particular vigilance is exercised against the metabolic disorder called toxemia of pregnancy.

These prenatal visits also guarantee early action in the event of complications such as narrowness of the birth canal or malposition of the placenta. Monitoring the fetus assures its viability and health and that, at the end of pregnancy, it is in the correct position in the womb for easy delivery.

In recent years a sophisticated new process has been developed to monitor the fetus—amniocentesis [1]. This technique, usually employed when it is suspected that the fetus may have some hereditary defect, involves passing a small hollow needle through the mother's abdominal wall into the bag of fluid, the amniotic sac, in which the fetus lies. A little of the fluid is withdrawn and the cells that it contains are grown in tissue culture. These cells are then examined for abnormalities of their chromosomes and chemistry. Not all the abnormalities identified by this method have an ominous significance; however, the discovery of the characteristics of Down's syndrome and Tay-Sach's disease (which causes blindness and severe mental retardation) will force the physician to consider ending the pregnancy prematurely.

Vaccines versus disease

In the early years of life preventive medicine is largely concerned with ensuring proper nutrition and with vaccination against the common infectious diseases of childhood.

The use of vaccines began in 1796, when Edward Jenner (1749–1823) demonstrated the capacity of *Vaccinia* virus to provide protection against smallpox. Today in the temperate countries of the world the objective is to vaccinate all infants during the first year of life against

CONNECTIONS

See also
736 Community medicin
710 The causes of illness: 1
702 Pregnancy
768 Psychosomatic diseases and retardati
808 Questions of life ar death
1186 Exploration and science 1750–1850

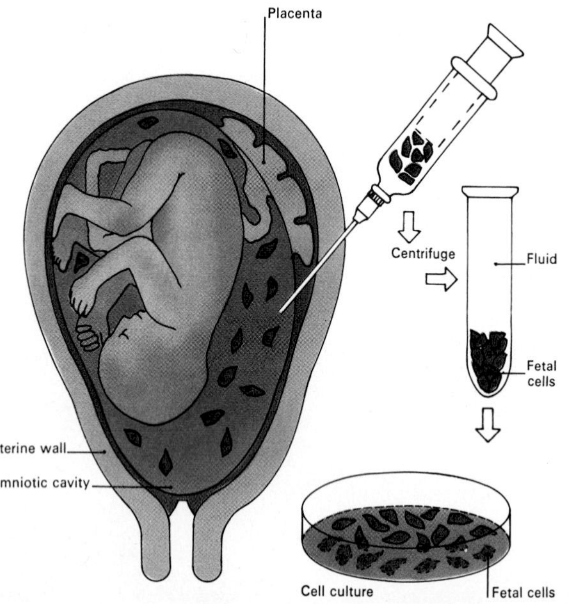

1
Placenta
Centrifuge
Fluid
Fetal cells
Uterine wall
Amniotic cavity
Cell culture
Fetal cells

1 Amniocentesis—the extraction by needle puncture of cells from the fluid around the fetus—greatly increases the chance of identifying the presence of hereditary diseases. At present the fetus' sex and some 40 of the more than 1,600 genetic diseases can be detected after the cells have been grown in culture. The best time for the "tap" is about the 16th week of pregnancy. Problems with using this technique include bleeding, infection, premature labor, and the risk of damage to the fetus. The possibility of its being used for eugenics or genetic engineering and prenatal sex determination raises ethical questions.

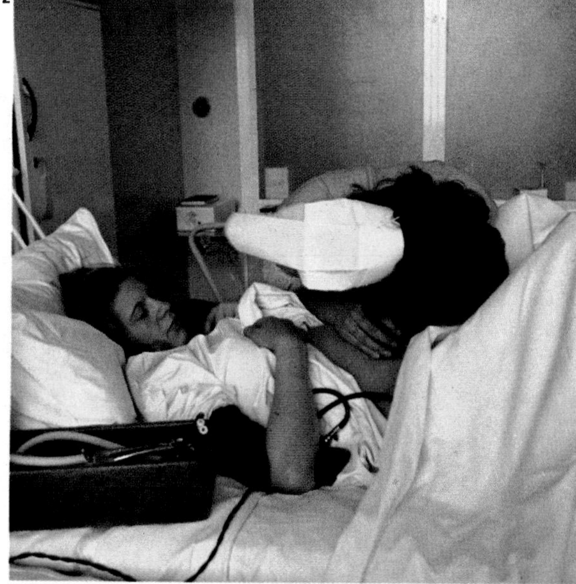

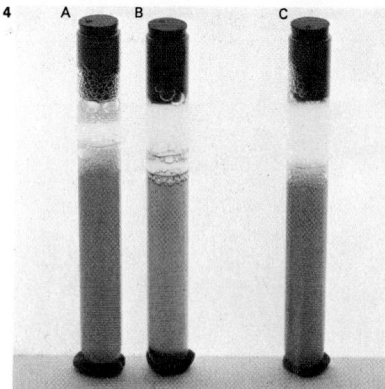

2 The fetal heartbeat becomes clearly audible through the obstetrician's special stethoscope after 28 weeks. More advanced electronic devices can detect the heartbeat as early as seven weeks.

3 Vaccines are produced by artificially cultivating the illness-causing viruses or bacteria. They are collected from infected animals or humans and grown in conditions suited to fast development as here. The microorganisms produced are washed, centrifuged in a sterile salt solution, and killed. The viruses are finally weakened to make them less virulent. A dose injected into the body induces the body to form antibodies which combat the disease.

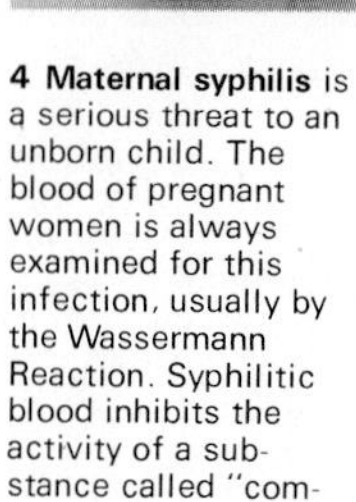

4
A
B
C

4 Maternal syphilis is a serious threat to an unborn child. The blood of pregnant women is always examined for this infection, usually by the Wassermann Reaction. Syphilitic blood inhibits the activity of a substance called "complement," which dissolves especially prepared red blood cells of sheep. These test tubes show positive control [A], a negative control [C], and a positive test [B]. Fever-causing diseases such as malaria can produce a false positive.

diphtheria, tetanus, whooping cough, poliomyelitis, and measles. So effective have these programs been that, with the exception of whooping cough, all these diseases are increasingly rare. Tuberculosis has presented more enduring problems, but mass miniature radiography [6, 9] for early diagnosis and the use of powerful antibiotics have reduced the threat of this disease.

In some circumstances extra vaccinations are provided on a more selective basis. German measles (rubella) vaccine is used for adolescent girls who have not had the disease, to prevent the risk of an attack during pregnancy. There are also influenza vaccines, rabies vaccine for the staffs of zoos and quarantine centers, and anthrax vaccine for veterinarians and wool handlers. The length of time for which these vaccines give protection varies. For cholera it is six months, for yellow fever a lifetime.

Preventive medicine for adults

In later years the emphasis in preventive medicine changes from absolute prevention of infectious illness to early diagnosis by periodic checkup for the illnesses that threaten middle-aged persons.

A physical examination combined with measurement of blood pressure, an X ray of the chest, an electrocardiogram, and an examination of the urine for the sugar of diabetes would constitute a typical check for the more common diseases of middle age [8]. In more elaborate examinations the blood is tested in a multichannel analyzer machine for abnormalities.

For women, there are extra hazards associated with their reproductive systems, and special clinics are becoming more common in developed countries. The functions of such clinics include early diagnosis of cancer of the breast and of the cervix. Careful palpation of each breast often reveals lumps suggestive of cancer, but more complex methods using soft X rays (including xeromammography) and heat sensors (thermography) are sometimes used [5]. Examination of the cervix is usually accomplished by the cervical smear method in which the cells from the cervix are smeared on a glass slide and examined [7].

KEY

Central nervous system
Poliomyelitis
Rabies
Salivary glands
Mumps
Throat
Diphtheria
Whooping cough
Spinal cord
Tetanus
Lungs
Influenza
Liver
Hepatitis
Yellow fever
Lungs
Intestines
Skin
Anthrax
Intestines
Typhoid
Small Intestine
Cholera
Skin
Measles
German measles
Smallpox
Lymph glands
Bubonic plague

The prevention of infectious diseases through vaccination is an important part of preventive medicine. The administration of most vaccines causes the production of substances known as antibodies in the blood of the vaccinated person. These, either alone or in concert with other components of the blood plasma or with the white blood cells, attack invading microbes and prevent infection. The effects of antibodies are quite specific and those induced by a vaccine intended to prevent one infectious disease give no protection against other diseases. Shown are the various diseases (and the sites of their attack) that can be combated by vaccines.

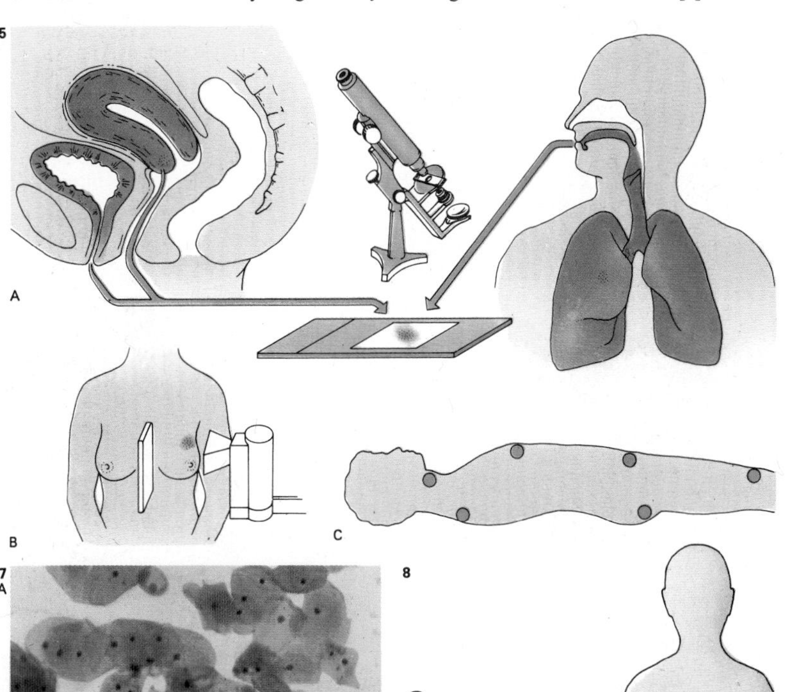

5
A
B
C

5 Early detection of cancer is the best way of minimizing tissue damage and death. Screening tests include microscopic examination of cells [A] and mammography [B], an X-ray technique used to detect breast lumps and to determine whether they are malignant. This crucial early detection is aided by individual alertness to certain danger signals [C] including hoarseness, difficulty in swallowing, breast lumps, change in bladder habits, unusual bleeding or discharge, a persistent sore, and an obvious change in a mole.

6 Mass miniature radiography is a cheap way of examining the lungs by X ray and has been instrumental in the campaign to eradicate tuberculosis. X rays passing through the patient's chest fall on a fluorescent screen to form a picture similar to that on an X-ray plate. This picture is photographed and the small photographic negative can then be examined by the radiologist.

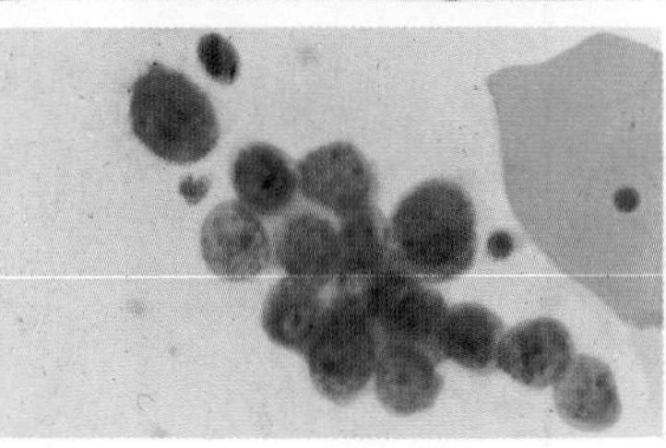

7
A

B

7 Microscopic examination of cells can help detect several different cancers. A smear taken from the cervix during what should be a yearly examination would reveal whether the cells are normal [A] or have undergone cancerous changes [B]. Cells from the urinary tract shed with urine may indicate kidney, ureter, or bladder cancer. Lung cancer may be verified by examination of sputum, while oral cancer can often be detected by examining cells scraped from the mouth.

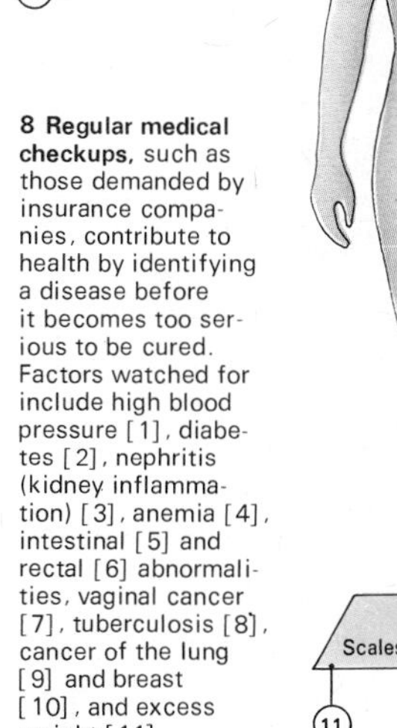

8
X-rays
8
9
10
Blood pressure test
1
2
Blood test
3
4
Barium swallow
Rectal exam
5
6
Cervical smear
Urine test
7
2
3
Scales
11

8 Regular medical checkups, such as those demanded by insurance companies, contribute to health by identifying a disease before it becomes too serious to be cured. Factors watched for include high blood pressure [1], diabetes [2], nephritis (kidney inflammation) [3], anemia [4], intestinal [5] and rectal [6] abnormalities, vaginal cancer [7], tuberculosis [8], cancer of the lung [9] and breast [10], and excess weight [11].

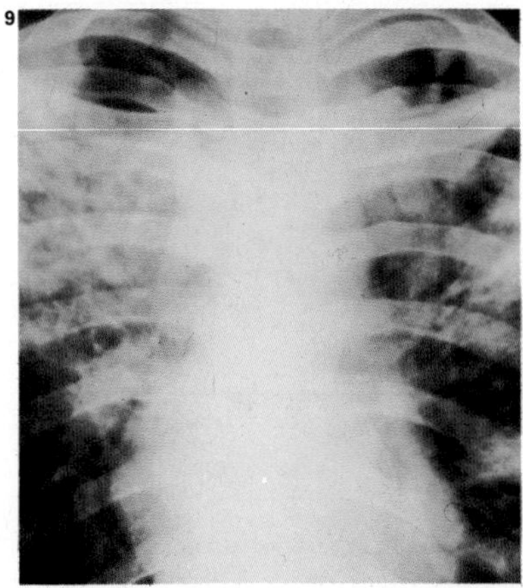

9 Tuberculosis infection causes a thickening of the lung tissue that impedes the passage of X rays through the lung. A shadow, such as that seen at the top of the lungs, is therefore produced on the X-ray plate. The heart shows as a bulge.

The body's natural defenses

A characteristic of all living matter is a certain resilience to disease and damage. The human body possesses a formidable array of such natural defenses [Key]. If we are threatened our bodies have many resources at their disposal. These include an early-warning system of muscular reflexes to keep us away from harmful stimuli; frontier defenses such as skin; the blood-clotting mechanism plus an emergency regime for dealing with excessive blood loss; a chemical immunity system to overwhelm or neutralize potentially harmful germs; and mechanisms for the natural repair of damaged bone and soft tissue.

Invading microorganisms

There are several distinct groups of potentially harmful germs or microorganisms. They are, in order of size, viruses, bacteria, and protozoa, and they can invade the body by way of contaminated food or water, during contact with other people or animals, through a wound, or they may be inhaled directly in the air we breathe. Many, however, are harmless.

The three frontiers through which these organisms invade are the skin (and the mucous membrane lining the mouth, vagina, and other orifices, which is a derivative of skin) and the respiratory and digestive tracts. The skin has a slightly acid surface and is too cold and hostile an environment for most germs. An additional safeguard is sweat, which contains an enzyme able to break up bacteria. Delicate membranes such as those of the vagina are protected by acid secretions and by the presence of harmless bacteria that subdue disease-producing forms.

At the entrance to the respiratory tract hairs in the nostrils filter out some unwanted particles; others are trapped in the mucus lining the nasal passages and are disposed of by way of the stomach. Farther on, foreign matter is wafted away by microscopic hairs known as cilia that line the trachea and bronchi of the lungs. And patrolling the internal surfaces of the lungs are special scavenger cells that engulf intruding organisms and signal a warning to the immune system. In the digestive tract—possibly the most hostile frontier of all—germs are destroyed by stomach acidity or by digestive enzymes produced in the intestine.

If these various threshold defenses fail, bacteria, viruses, and the rest are free to set to work in the body, damaging tissue or releasing toxins (poisonous substances) to cause illness. Yet these germs usually cause disease only if they are allowed to muster in force—a situation often forestalled by the flushing action of various body fluids.

The immune system and tissue repair

When intruders do manage to take hold, they achieve the status of antigens. Now it is the turn of the immune system, the body's own chemical warfare division, to produce the antibodies necessary to fight off infection. A defensive mechanism dispersed throughout the tissues, the immune system consists principally of front-line troops known as lymphocytes. These are particular kinds of white blood cells produced in the bone marrow, thymus, and spleen and found in the lymph nodes that are located throughout the lymphatic system [5].

CONNECTIONS

See also

712 The causes of illness: 2

412 The cell in action

688 Heart and blood circulation

742 Origins of curative medicine

744 Natural remedies

746 Man-made cures

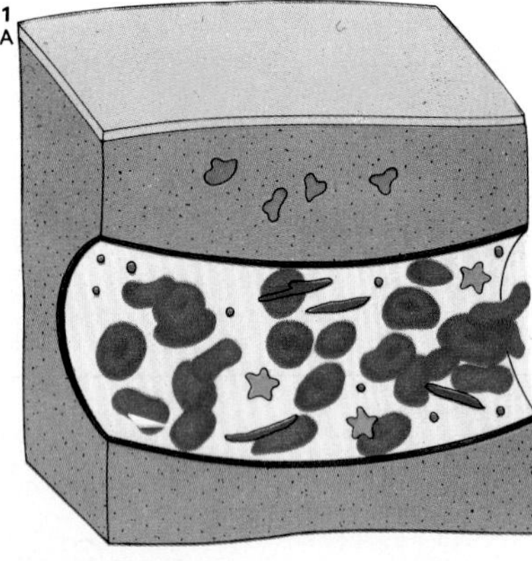

1
A

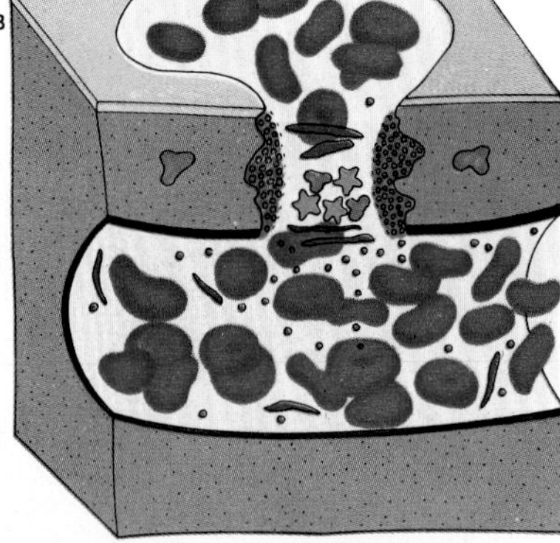

B

D

1 The blood clotting mechanism is the result of a complex chain reaction involving various substances in the blood. Through the interaction of blood platelets, plasma, and tissue-clotting factors the soluble protein fibrinogen breaks up into fibrin threads and forms a mesh across the wound. Prior to injury [A] the fibrinogen circulates in the plasma. At the moment of injury [B] the platelets plug the wound while the clotting reaction takes place. Fibrin threads are laid down [C] across the site. Platelets and blood cells become trapped in the fibrin web [D]. This semi-solid mass shrinks, extruding serum (a yellowish fluid) and the clot is formed.

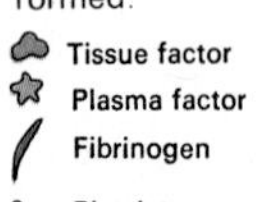

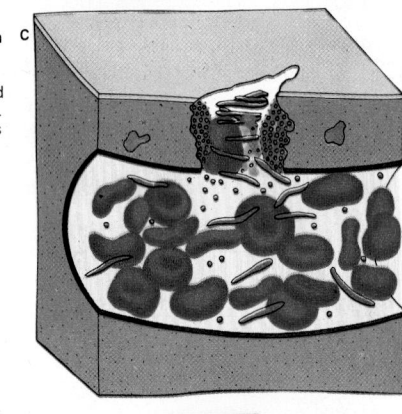

Tissue factor
Plasma factor
Fibrinogen
Platelet
Red blood cell
Fibrin

2 White cells are important in defense against bacterial infection such as that following entry of a splinter. The most numerous type, polymorphonuclear leucocytes [1], surround infecting microbes [2] and prevent them from spreading to adjacent tissue. Many polymorphs may be killed in the process and these form the pus. More replace them and the infection is eliminated.

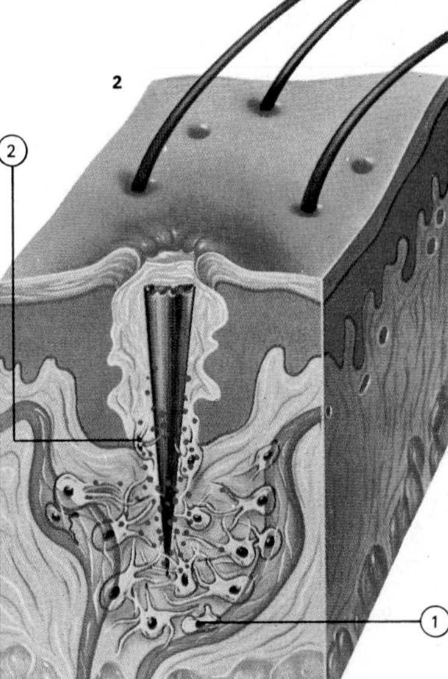

2
2
1

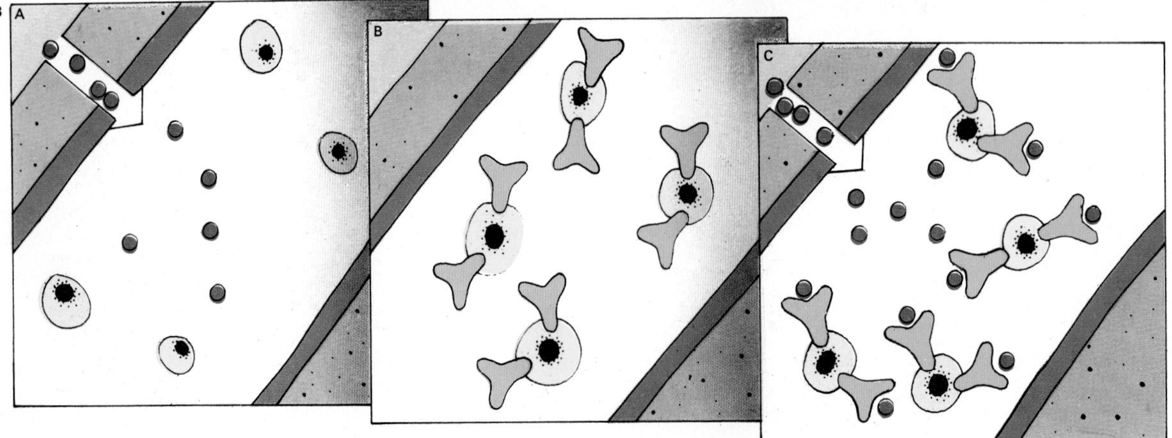

3
A
B
C

Antigen

Antibody

Antibody/antigen complex

3 When an antigen enters the blood [A], it causes a proliferation of small lymphocytes (yellow symbols) with specific membrane-bound antibodies [B]. These remain in the bloodstream for some time. If the same antigen [C] attacks again, the antibodies neutralize it.

The outstanding feature of lymphocytes and other disease-fighting cells is their ability to "recognize" specific antigens and to produce precisely the right antibodies to combat them. Antibodies work in different ways and each offers protection against only one disease. Some cause the antigens to clump together, making it impossible for them to spread; some coat the invaders with a substance that makes them more readily ingestible by phagocytic cells such as macrophages; and others neutralize the harmful toxins that are released by antigens [3]. In some abnormal cases, the body's defenses turn against its own tissues, producing an autoimmune disease.

A sequel to victory over infection is the repair of tissue [6]. Wounds are healed by the arrival of fibroblasts—cells that lay down fibers forming a scaffolding into which new cells grow from surrounding tissue.

Blood clotting and conservation

An important protective mechanism in the case of an open wound is the coagulation of blood [1]. The clotting process depends on various physical and chemical changes but is ultimately related to the conversion of the soluble fibrinogen of the blood plasma into the jellylike protein known as fibrin. Threads of fibrin form the blood clot and it is this that arrests the bleeding [4].

The body also employs techniques to make good the effects of blood loss. If the hemorrhage is severe there is a fall in blood pressure. The severed vessel narrows and there is a tendency for the inner lining to stick to itself. Other blood vessels near the surface of the body become constricted, thus conserving an adequate supply of blood for direction to vital organs such as the heart and brain. Contraction of the spleen may add a pint or more of blood to the general circulation to compensate for the amount lost. Also, since it is not immediately vital to replace red cells, the blood vessels borrow fluid from the tissues to restore volume to the circulation and bring blood pressure back to normal. In this way, with a natural "transfusion" of tissue fluid, a human being can survive the loss of up to a quarter of his blood.

KEY

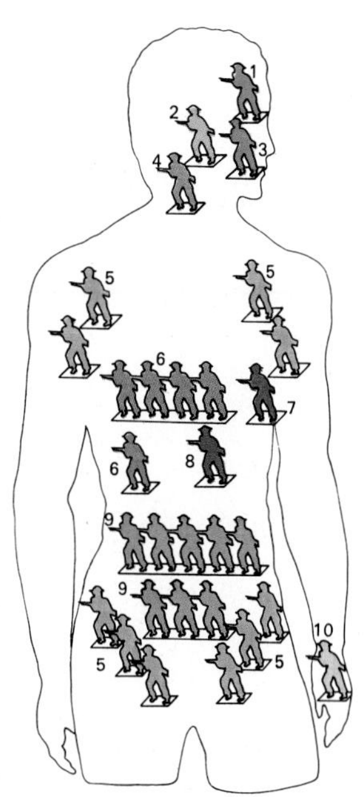

1
2
3
4
5
5
6
7
6
8
9
9
10
5
5

The body fields an array of defenses apart from the skin [10]. Lachrymal glands [1] secrete tears to wash away foreign particles. Lymphoid tissues, important in the destruction of germs, include the adenoids and tonsils [2]. Saliva [3] is an effective barrier fluid. Foreign matter is trapped by mucus in the nose and throat [4]. Lymph nodes [5] release protective white blood cells. The liver [6] destroys germs and produces substances vital in blood clotting and tissue repair. A source of defensive white corpuscles is the spleen [7]. Acid in the stomach [8] kills many germs; those reaching the intestine [9] succumb to enzymes.

4 A wound is first sealed by a blood clot [A]. As healing progresses macrophages move in [B] to remove wound debris such as dried blood, bacteria, and damaged cells. When the fresh layer of skin grows across the site [C], the remains of the blood clot are sloughed off in the form of a scab.

Macrophage
Debris
Blood clot
Epidermis
Dermis

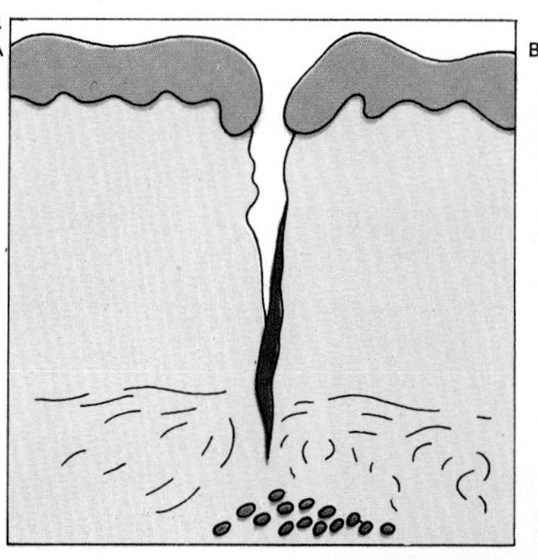

4
A

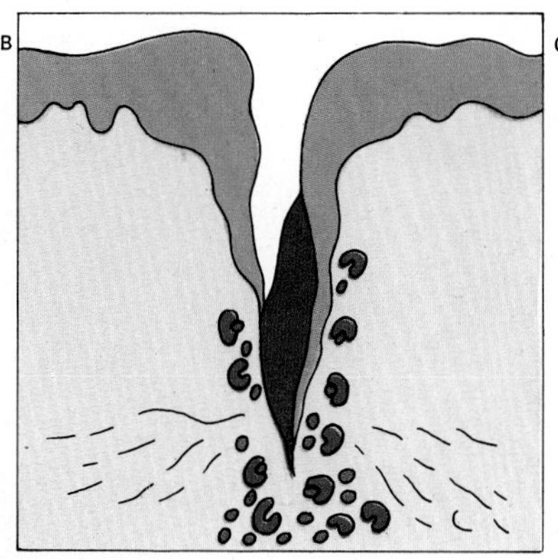

B

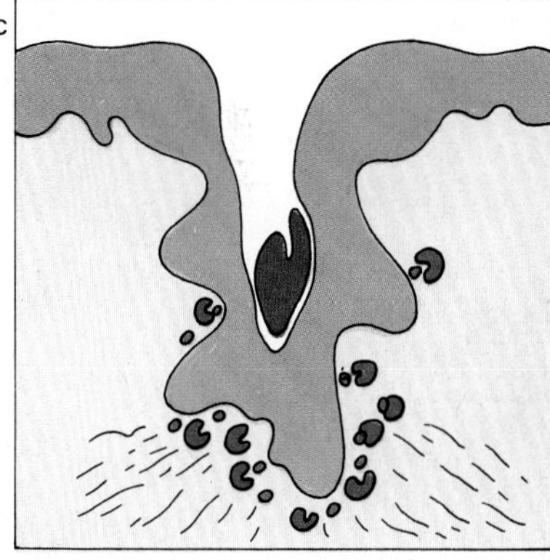

C

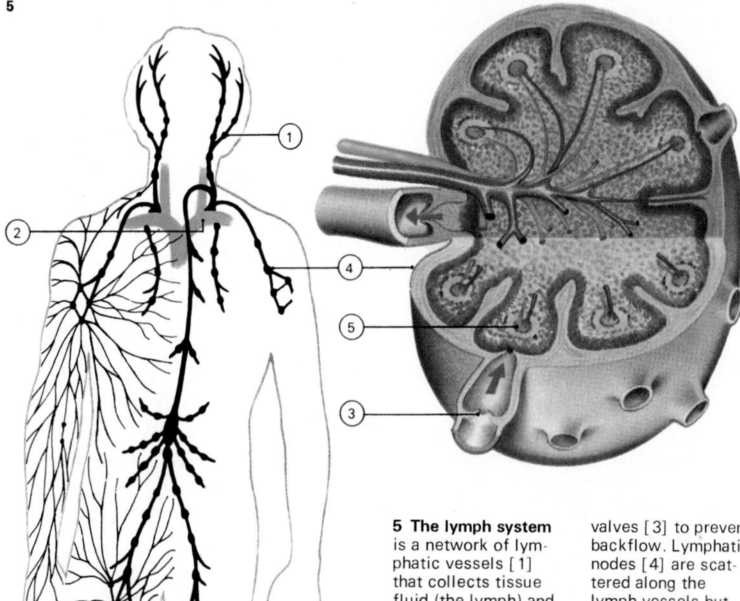

5
1
2
4
5
3

5 The lymph system is a network of lymphatic vessels [1] that collects tissue fluid (the lymph) and conducts it back to the bloodstream at the large subclavian veins [2]. In the process it transports nutrients from blood to cells and cell wastes back into capillaries. Lymph drains through the system, but the lymphatics possess valves [3] to prevent backflow. Lymphatic nodes [4] are scattered along the lymph vessels but particularly in the neck, armpits, and groin. In the tissue around the nodes microorganisms are destroyed by macrophage cells, while antibody-synthesizing white blood cells, the lymphocytes, are produced in the lymph nodules [5].

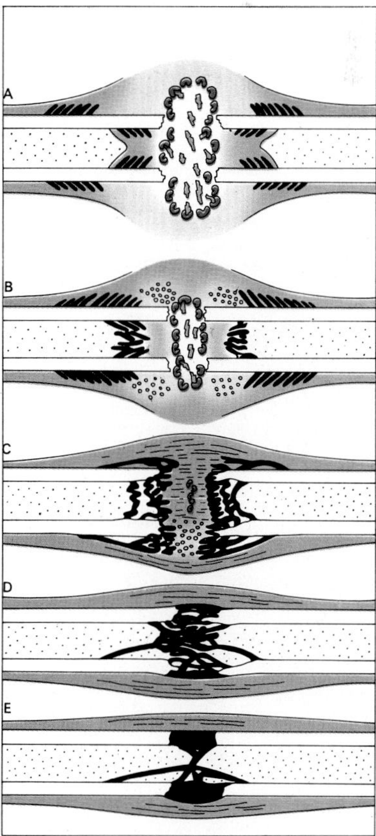

6
A
B
C
D
E

Macrophage
Debris — old bone
Bone
Bone marrow
New bone
Blastema
Connective tissue
Cartilage

6 Fracture is the term used for any break in a bone, whether or not the bone penetrates the skin. After an injury of this kind inflammation sets in and a blood clot forms, sealing the ends of damaged vessels [A]. Macrophages invade the site and remove the wound debris; then after one or two days, long, thin fibroblasts lay down a mesh or grid on which new tissue can grow [B]. A blastema or area of new growth develops and new bone is forged that links the broken ends [C]. Later remodeling strengthens the bone, restoring its true shape [D, E]. At least four to six weeks are required for a fracture to heal completely.

Origins of curative medicine

The practice of medicine in one guise or another predates written history, and much of our knowledge of its early forms is therefore a matter of conjecture. It seems likely that medicine did not emerge as a specialized craft until settled communities developed. Then men learned about different plants—which were good to eat; which were poisonous; and, presumably, which appeared to alleviate symptoms of the various diseases that were probably as prevalent then as now. Certainly, from the first written records, it appears that fevers and coughs were common.

Religion, magic, and medicine

Curative medicine was apparently often allied with religion, as it was in Egypt [3]. The administration of medicinal materials was accompanied by complex rituals and incantations, and it is quite possible that the psychological therapy of the rituals was as effective as the medications, which were often chosen on magical grounds.

One of the basic tenets of magic is the principle of correspondence, known also as the doctrine of signatures. This magical principle asserts that—by analogy—there are connective links between different things. Plants were seen to have similarities with different aspects of the human condition; so, for example, the flat, mossy liverworts were used until the eighteenth century in the treatment of liver ailments simply because their shape resembled that of the liver.

A related belief concerned the transference of powers of one sort or another between objects [Key]. When a cannibal ate the heart of a strong warrior whom he had slain in battle, he believed that some of the dead man's strength would pass into him. By the same token, mummified flesh was at one time a popular remedy, presumably because anything that had survived death so well would help the eater to do the same.

The converse of this is the passage of bad qualities from the sick person to some other person or object. As much early medicine was based on magical beliefs, it is not surprising that many ailments were interpreted as possession or attack by a malevolent being. Such beliefs may well have prompted surgery, some of the earliest evidence of which is found in trephined skulls from prehistoric sites. Trephining—making a hole in the skull—was an operation performed presumably as a way of letting an evil spirit out of the sufferer's head. Excess pressure in the brain may lead to behavior that could be interpreted as demonic possession, so this operation may, ironically, have been of value to those who survived.

In the first millennium AD, victims of "elf-shot" (lightning) in some parts of Europe were buried up to their necks in the ground, so that the malignancy would be transferred to the earth. In more recent times, rheumatism sufferers slept in contact with healthy slaves in order to transfer the rheumatic pains to them. A continuing and medically baseless cure for rheumatism is the wearing of copper bracelets.

Later theories of anatomy and medicine

As civilization developed, many of the early magical practices continued in a distorted

CONNECTIONS

See also
744 Natural remedies
746 Man-made cures
708 An introduction to illness and health
752 Development of surgery
748 Nonmedical healing
740 The body's natural defenses
428 Mushrooms and toadstools
354 Coffee, tea, and cocoa

1 A
B
C

1 Pliny the Elder (AD 23–79) [A] wrote *Historia naturalis*, for centuries a source of information about herbal remedies. Later, John Gerard (1542–1612) [B] and Nicholas Culpeper (1616–54) [C] both produced best-selling herbals. Plants were the first medicines used and still form the basis of much of today's curative medicine. Catalogs of plants effective against disease are always popular.

2
A
B
C
D
E
F
G
H
I
J

2 Herbalists still sell assorted plant materials and claim curative properties for them. Here are sandalwood [A], camomile [B], Chinese herb teas [C], blue mallow [D], kola nuts [E], rose petals [F], rose hip [G], comfrey [H], marigold [I], and cinnamon [J].

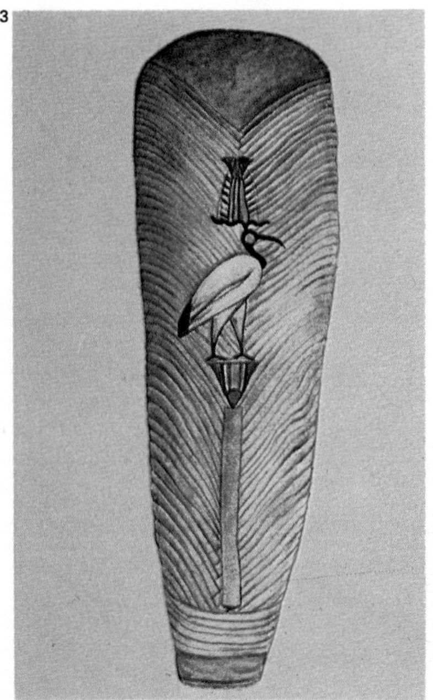

3

3 Hundreds of mummified ibises were found at what may be the tomb of Imhotep (*fl. c.* 2900 BC), who was probably Pharaoh Zoser's physician. The ibis-headed Thoth was chief of the Egyptians' healing gods.

4

4 Animals' teeth, antlers, or horns, bats' blood, and toad poison are among the traditional ingredients of the witches' brew. The handprint is widely used in Eastern countries to keep away evil spirits—as the copper bangle is intended to ward off rheumatism. Not all folk remedies are unpleasant: opium and gin are used now more for pleasure than pain.

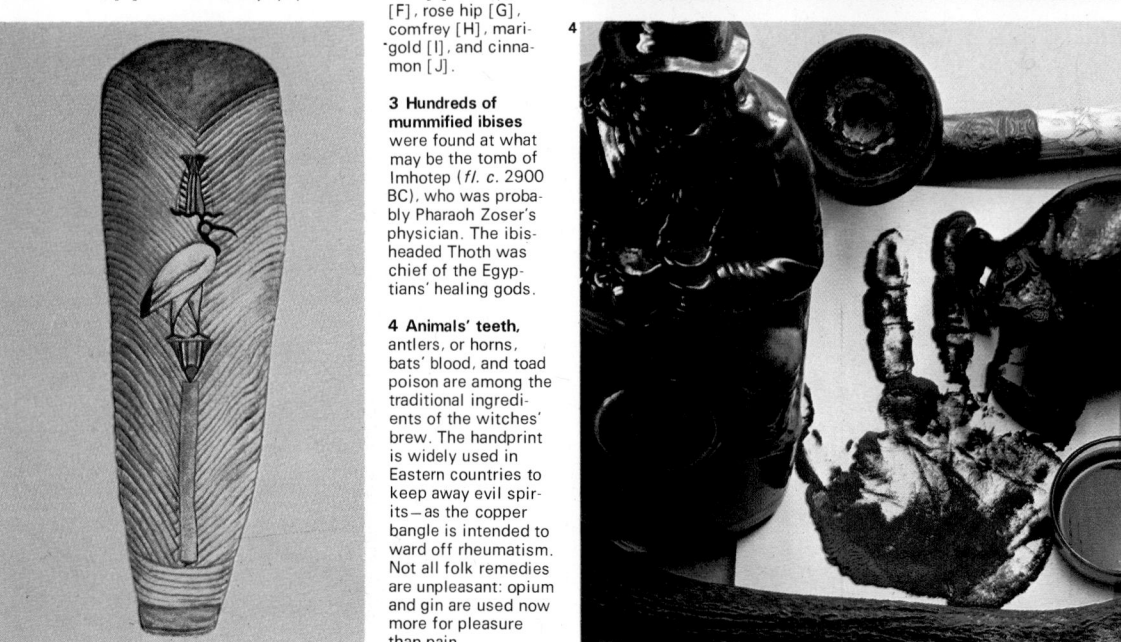

form. The Greek division of bodily principles into four "humors"—blood, phlegm, yellow bile, and black bile—reflected their philosophic view of the universe as being composed of the four elements—earth, air, fire, and water. Long after the alchemists had discovered that matter consisted of more than these four, the humors were still the basis of medical practice. To restore health, it was believed necessary to find treatments that would restore the balance between them. Chinese medicine was based on a similar maintenance of balance, but the principles were called yin and yang (negative, feminine, and dark versus positive, masculine, and light). Drugs were prescribed to restore harmony between these two principles.

Ancient cures still used

Although the early systems of medicine were not based on scientific premises, not all the cures proposed were useless. Presumably doctors then were observant enough to note when a plant substance was genuinely effective. In some early civilizations there were strict laws to keep the doctor on his toes. About 5,000 years ago, in Babylon, a doctor who killed his patient was liable to have his hands cut off. Similar penalties for bad medicine existed in ancient Egypt, with the consequence that in medical papyri the doctor is frequently advised, after a description of symptoms, to effect a diagnosis, not to treat the patient at all, but let nature take its course.

From the Indian, Egyptian, Greek, and Chinese civilizations, written accounts of the diseases and cures of the times have come down to us. In many cases, materials originally used medicinally have now become widely used for nonmedicinal purposes because of their pleasant taste [9]. Examples are rhubarb, tea, coffee, and tobacco. Some of the very early medications are still used in medicine, because the scientific basis for their activities is now understood. What is surprising is the continuing use of many others in which no curative properties have yet been discovered [5] for example, rhinoceros horn as an aphrodisiac, or ginseng as a cure-all.

KEY

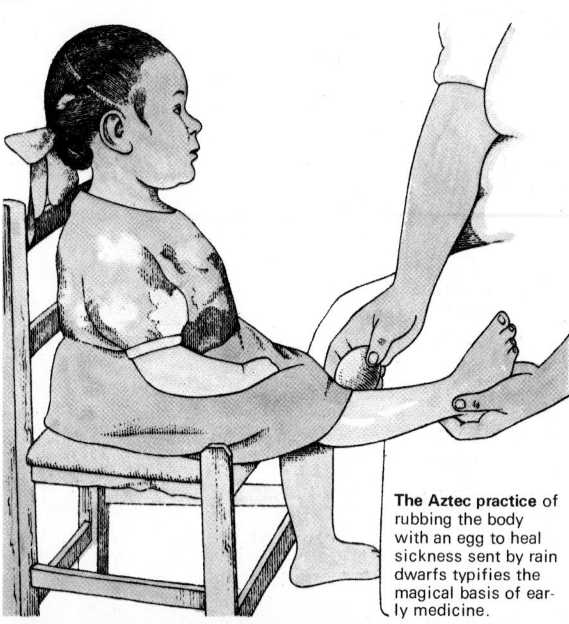

The Aztec practice of rubbing the body with an egg to heal sickness sent by rain dwarfs typifies the magical basis of early medicine.

5

5 Quack doctors peddling useless patent medicines are a perennial feature of human history. A familiar stereotype is the glib opportunist who toured the Wild West in a covered wagon. Mobility was essential so that he could move on before the fraudulence of his cures was exposed.

6

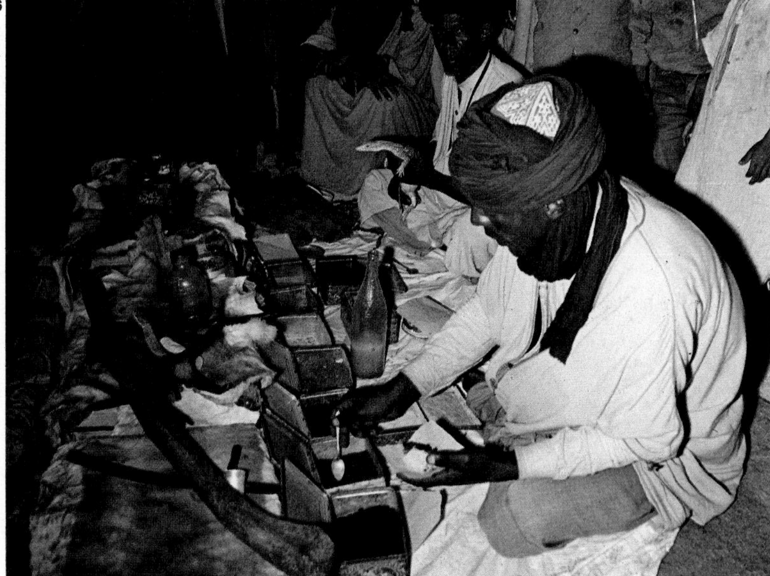

6 While herbalists' shops survive in Western countries, in the less developed parts of the world the local medicine man does a thriving trade, compounding remedies from plant extracts in the marketplace, with little competition from orthodox doctors. The photo shows one at work in Goulimine, Morocco.

7 A

B

C

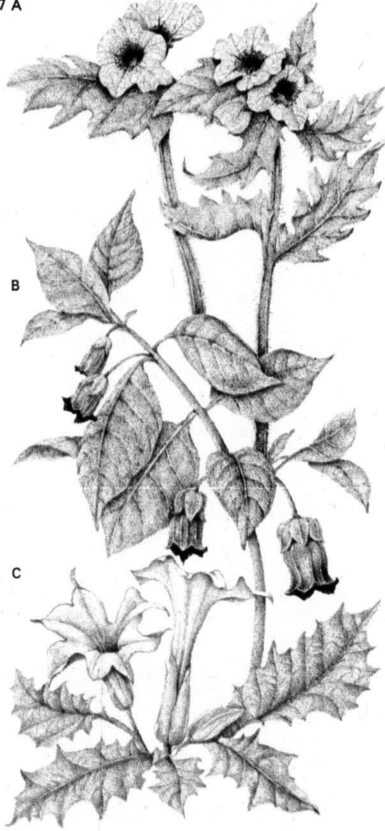

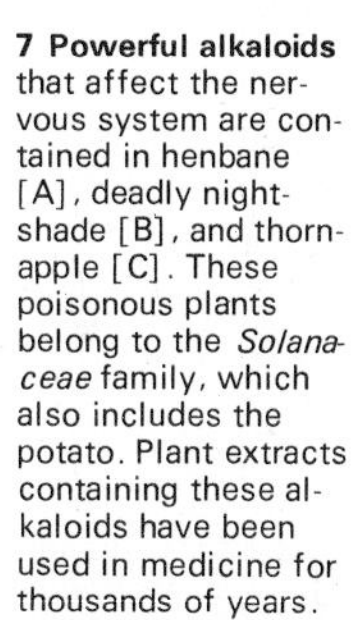

7 Powerful alkaloids that affect the nervous system are contained in henbane [A], deadly nightshade [B], and thornapple [C]. These poisonous plants belong to the *Solanaceae* family, which also includes the potato. Plant extracts containing these alkaloids have been used in medicine for thousands of years.

8 Andean Indians have chewed the leaf of the coca shrub to combat fatigue for hundreds of years. In 1860, when folk medicine was being rapidly overtaken by science, the leaves were found to contain the valuable local anesthetic cocaine. Extract of coca leaves was originally a minor ingredient of some cola drinks.

8

Coca *Erythroxylon coca*

9 Tea drinking is a traditional Japanese ritual. One reason for the popularity of tea in many countries is that it contains the alkaloid caffeine (also present in coffee), which is a mild stimulant. Many herbs are used as medicinal infusions.

9

Natural remedies

As civilization developed, the stock of folklore about the curative properties of various substances or rituals was gradually classified. This was the first step toward scientific medicine. Once alleged remedies were listed and classified those that stood the test of time could be noted. It was not until the nineteenth and twentieth centuries that major advances were made in understanding why some plant extracts, for example, had curative properties. Chemistry had advanced to the stage at which the molecular structures of individual substances could be identified, so that they could be synthesized in the laboratory and tested therapeutically.

Early natural remedies

Among the earliest pharmacopoeias (catalogs of medicines) was that compiled by Dioscorides (*fl. c* AD 60), a surgeon in Nero's army. During his travels he made notes about the remedies used in different countries. These notes provided the basis for a tradition that, although largely lost after the fall of the Roman Empire, passed back to Europe from the Arabs in the fifteenth century. At this time pharmacists were known as *aromatarii* because the materials they sold were aromatic substances extracted from plants. Remedies with an animal or mineral base were also used. Paracelsus (*c.* 1493–1541) was as renowned for his cures effected with mercury as for those that used opium.

At this time there was a continuous interplay of different factors that advanced the science of pharmacy on several fronts simultaneously. Although there were several thousand known "remedies" for various ailments, one school of medical theorists still argued that there was, albeit undiscovered, a substance that would cure all ills. This idea of the "cure-all" is in the alchemical tradition of a philosopher's stone that will turn other materials into gold, and the alkahest, or universal solvent, that will dissolve all other substances. In their search for such universal substances the alchemists and their followers stumbled on some useful processes. Raymond Lully (*c.* 1235–1315) is credited with discovering how to prepare pure alcohol. And he, or one of his followers, probably discovered how to react this with acid to produce ether.

The availability of pure alcohol was a great advantage in the preparation of tinctures and essences because many of the active principles in medicinal plants dissolved more readily in this solvent than in water. And as other parts of the world became known, many new plants were added to the pharmacopoeias and mixed with other substances in alcoholic solutions.

Isolating active ingredients

The major problem was to sort out which of the substances were effective and which could be left out. In the eighteenth century, when the physician William Withering (1741–99) was introduced to an old country woman whose secret herbal mixture seemed to be surprisingly effective in cases of heart failure, he had to sort through 20 different ingredients to discover that it was the foxglove leaves that were effective. (The fact that they contained digitalis was not discovered until later.)

CONNECTIONS

See also
742 Origins of curative medicine
746 Man-made cures
708 An introduction to illness and health
730 Alcoholism and drug abuse

1 Carbon
Oxygen
Hydroxyl
Hydrogen
Naturally occurring in plants

1 Aspirin, the most widely consumed drug in the world, is a chemical substance called acetylsalicylic acid. Plants such as willow *(Salix fragilis)* [1], meadow sweet *(Filipendula ulmeria)* [2], and shallon *(Gaultheria shallon)* [3] contain the related substance salicin. The presence of this pain-reliever was the basis of many old remedies. As salicin is too bitter to be taken internally (the same is true of salicylic acid, the first chemical derivative of salicin), it was not until it was made into its acetyl derivative in 1899 that aspirin [4] emerged for common use.

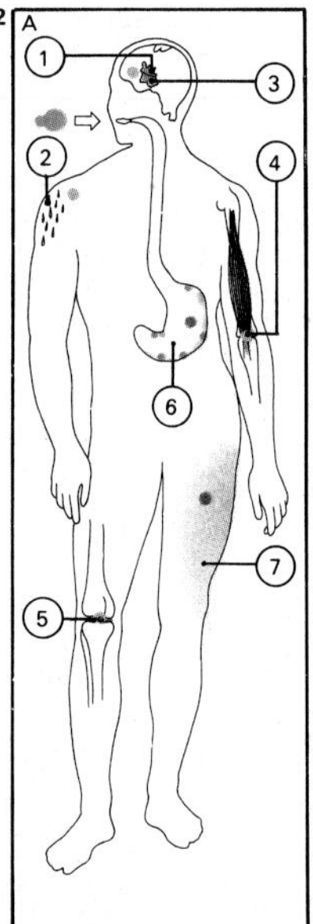
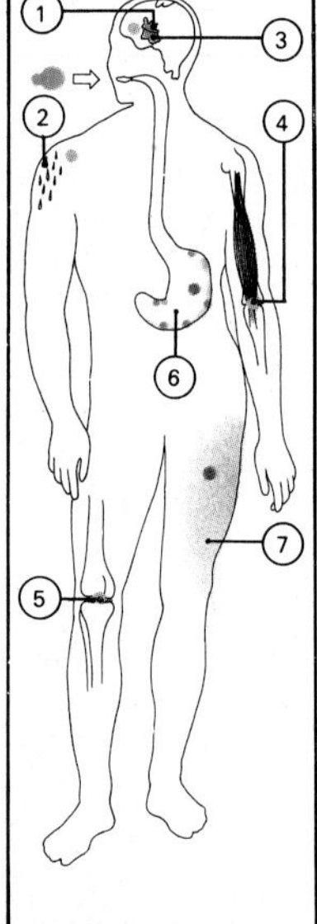

A
B
C

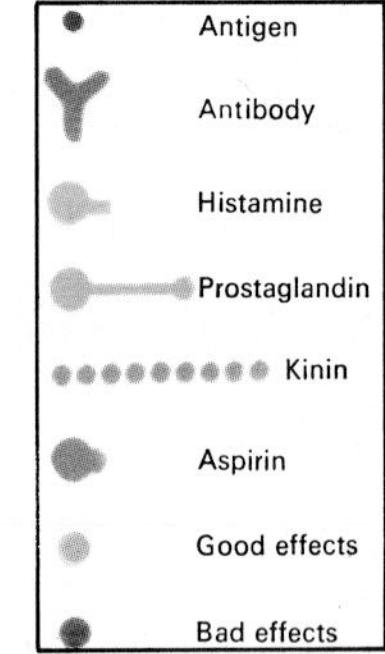

Antigen
Antibody
Histamine
Prostaglandin
Kinin
Aspirin
Good effects
Bad effects

2 Aspirin reduces fever [A] by regulating the brain's temperature control center [1] and by increasing sweating [2]. It reduces pain by cutting reverberatory impulses at the thalamus [3] and inflammation at joints [4, 5]; but it can cause bleeding [6] and skin rashes [7] in some people. Inflammation, produced by an "inflammatory cascade" of prostaglandins, histamine, and kinins [B] in response to an attack of antigens or foreign bodies, is relieved by aspirin's limitation [C] of prostaglandin and kinin production.

3 From the roots of *Rauwolfia serpentina*, reserpine, a valuable tranquilizer, is obtained. Analysis of its chemical structure has led to the development of more effective synthetic tranquilizers with no damaging side-effects.

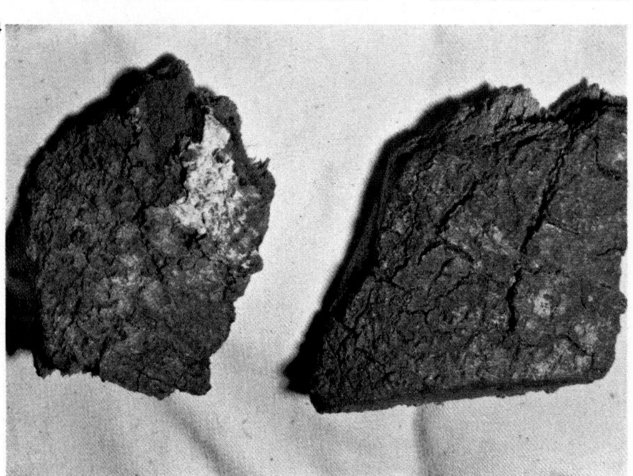

4 Quinine is a bitter substance derived from cinchona bark. Brought from Brazil by the Spaniards, it is a remedy for malaria and has only recently been superseded by synthetic compounds.

By the time the New and Old World had been thoroughly explored the number of natural plant substances with known pharmacological action was enormous. There was opium from poppies [8], emetine (a remedy for amebic dysentery) from the ipecac plant, quinine from cinchona bark [4], castor oil from castor seeds, and salicin from willow [1]. A number of other plant substances with major effects on living organisms was also known, including belladonna, strychnine, and curare [7]. All were used as poisons but are now valuable in medicine. But the physiological effects of these substances are so powerful that they must be used in controlled doses. It was only as the active ingredients were isolated that they could be used quantitatively.

Sophisticated techniques

During the nineteenth century chemistry developed rapidly as an exact science and many plant substances were isolated as pure, crystalline compounds. They were all classed as "organic chemicals," and it was not until 1828 that scientists realized it was possible to make such chemicals in a laboratory. In that year Friedrich Wöhler (1880–82) synthesized urea from ammonia cyanate and changed the entire emphasis of organic chemistry. Until then it had been believed that such substances could be produced only by living processes. Nevertheless, the chemical structures of many pharmacologically useful plant substances are so complex that it is more economical even now to extract them from plants than to make them in the laboratory.

Just how complex some of these substances are was not known until well into the twentieth century, when techniques of molecular analysis were devised. But it is not necessary to understand the structure of a chemical completely in order to modify it. This frequently produces a related substance that shares some properties of the original substance but not others. By trial and error chemists gradually began to improve upon natural remedies, producing analogs of natural compounds that were safer, more effective, or had less unpleasant side effects.

KEY

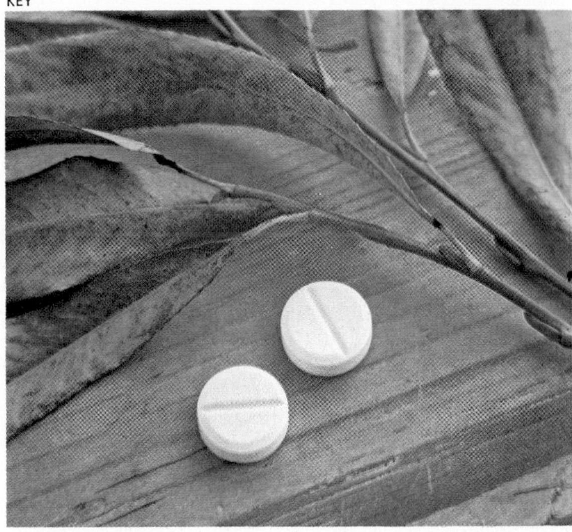

Nearly 2,000 years ago a brew made from white willow leaves was recommended for gout. To kill pain today we take aspirin. Now solely a product of the chemical laboratory, aspirin can also be made from willow brew.

5

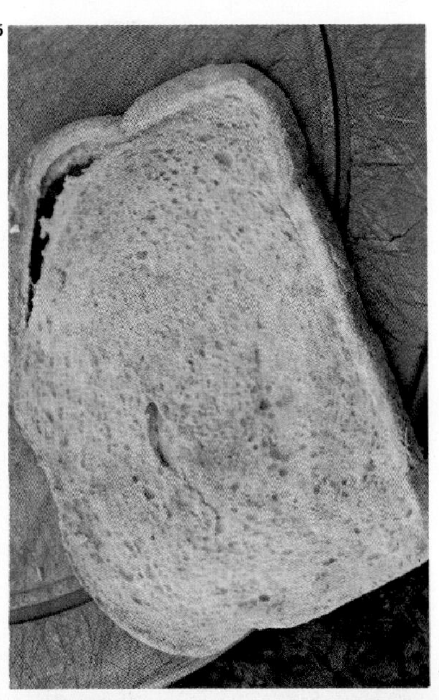

5 Mold on bread is usually viewed with disgust, but it is from variants of one of the common bread molds that penicillin is derived. This is doubtless why "mold poultices" are an old effective remedy.

6 Penicillin is now only one of many antibiotics that kill or inhibit the growth of other microorganisms. This makes them useful in treating bacterial infections. The normal bacterial cell processes [A] are attacked by different antibiotics [B], which may alter cell membrane structure [1] or inhibit cell wall synthesis [2], protein synthesis [3], energy production [4], or DNA replication [5].

6

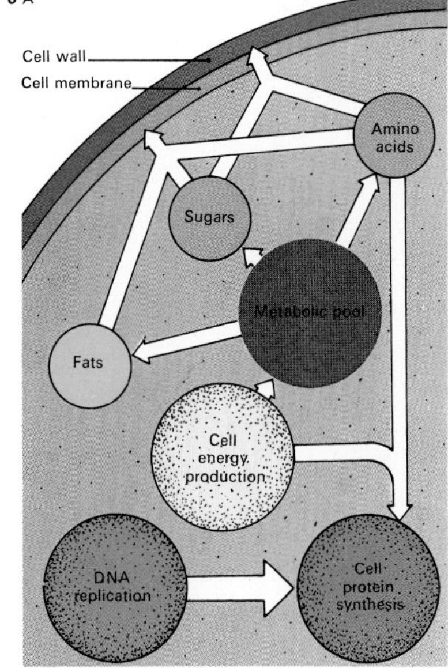

A
B
Cell wall
Cell membrane
Amino acids
Sugars
Metabolic pool
Fats
Cell energy production
DNA replication
Cell protein synthesis
1
2
3
4
5

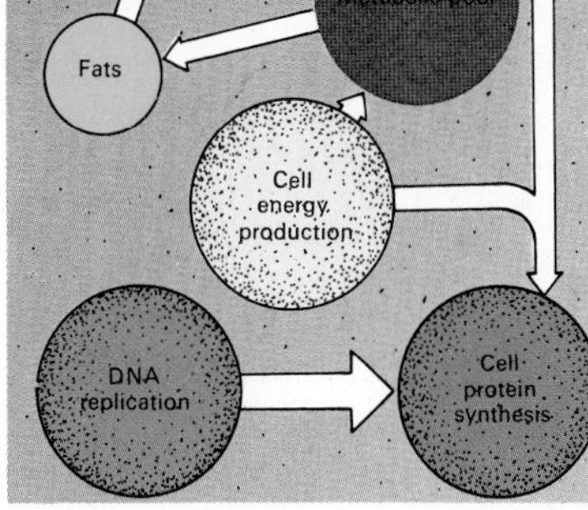

7

7 South American Indians carry pots of raw curare into which they dip their arrows to render them poisonous. This toxic substance is used in controlled doses in surgery for muscular relaxation.

8

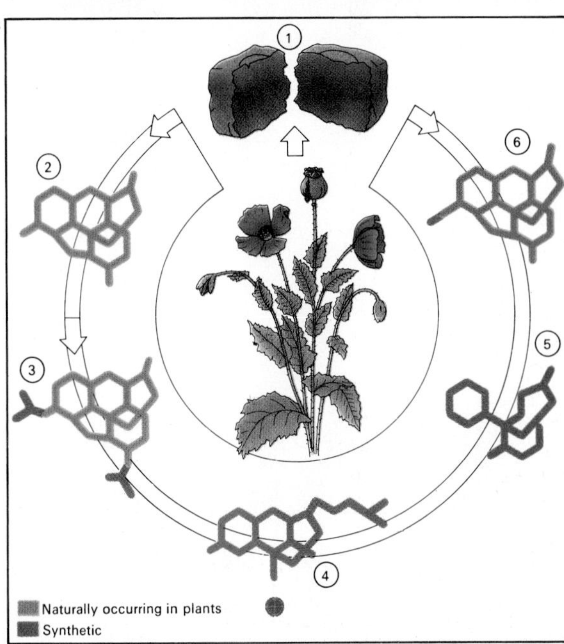

1
2
3
4
5
6
Naturally occurring in plants
Synthetic

8 Most derivatives of opium [1], such as morphine [2], heroin [3], and meperdine hydrochloride [5], although extremely effective pain-killing (analgesic) drugs, are at the same time highly addictive. It is possible in the laboratory to pinpoint those parts of the molecule that are responsible for the analgesic and those for the addictive effect. On this basis drugs such as codeine [6] and pentazocine [4] can be designed.

Man-made cures

At the beginning of the twentieth century most effective remedies were still derived from plants. Now they are produced in factories following directions worked out in chemical laboratories.

The origins of the drug industry

In the late nineteenth century the nature of chemical structures came to be understood and research chemists, notably in Germany, synthesized hundreds of new organic molecular compounds based on carbon atoms. As a result, the idea of a chemically based pharmaceutical industry emerged. Attempts to make synthetic versions of natural compounds on the basis of incomplete knowledge often led to curious results. The first synthetic dye, mauveine, was produced accidentally in 1856.

The result of this discovery was the start of the synthetic dyes industry. Within a few decades hundreds of synthetic dyes had been manufactured. It was from this wealth of new material that chemotherapy, the modern concept of treating disease with chemicals, came into being. The German scientist Paul Ehrlich (1854–1915) [2A] discovered that certain dyes stained only specific tissues when he treated microscopic specimens with them. From this he conceived the idea that some dyes might selectively and safely destroy the microorganisms that caused diseases.

Ehrlich tested 500 different dyes on mice that had been infected with trypanosomes—blood parasites that cause sleeping sickness and other diseases. None of them worked. He then tested other compounds with structures similar to the dyes but which also contained atoms of arsenic. His compound "606," or Salvarsan, although ineffective against trypanosomes, turned out to be effective against the bacteria that cause syphilis; it was manufactured in 1910.

The sulfa drugs and penicillin

Another German scientist, Gerhard Domagk (1895–1964), was responsible for the second great therapeutic discovery to come from the dyes industry. In the early 1930s he discovered that the red dye Prontosil was an effective bacteriostat—a substance that could prevent the proliferation of bacteria in the bloodstream. Until that time the most dangerous part of many surgical operations had been the period after the operation when the patient might die from septicemia—infection from bacteria introduced during the operation.

French scientists soon discovered that only one part of the Prontosil molecule—sulfanilamide—was effective. By the end of the 1930s the sulfa drugs [1] had lowered postoperative mortality dramatically and, in 1938, a bonus appeared in the form of a modified sulfanilamide molecule—sulfapyridine—which was effective against tuberculosis.

At about the same time, the bacteriostatic properties of the penicillin mold, discovered by Alexander Fleming (1881–1955) [2B] in 1928, were being further investigated by Howard Florey (1898–1968) and Ernst Chain (born 1906) [2C]. The development of penicillin manufacture during World War II heralded the age of antibiotics. Many microorganisms were found to contain complex chemicals that would combat other mi-

CONNECTIONS

See also
770 Physical cures for mental illness
1812 Color chemistry
742 Origins of curative medicine
744 Natural remedies
730 Alcoholism and drug abuse

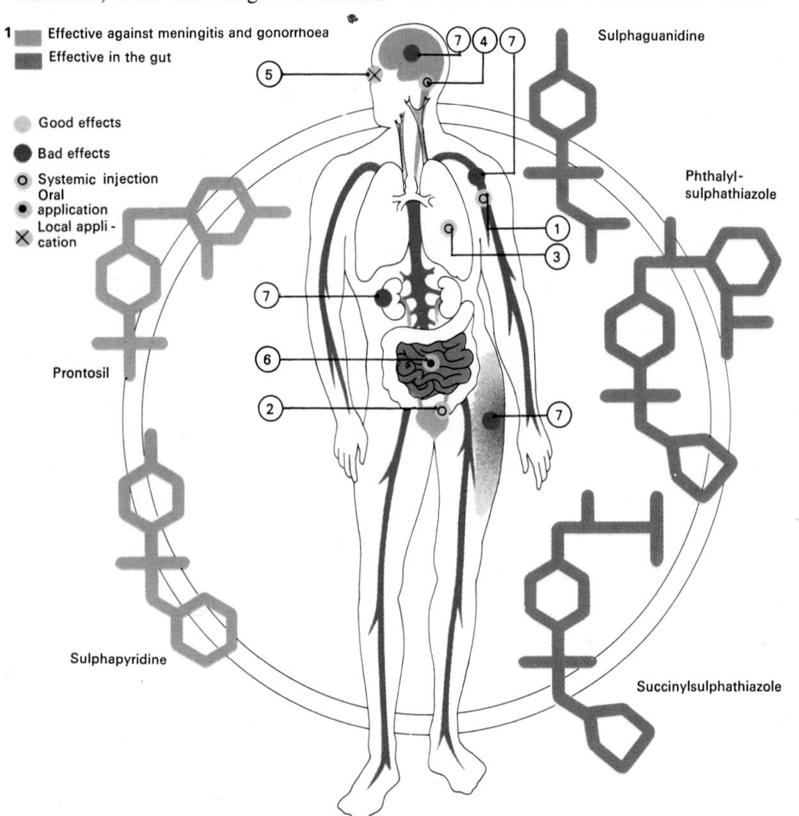

Effective against meningitis and gonorrhoea
Effective in the gut
Good effects
Bad effects
Systemic injection
Oral application
Local application
Prontosil
Sulphapyridine
Sulphaguanidine
Phthalyl-sulphathiazole
Succinylsulphathiazole

1 **The sulfa drugs** act by preventing the multiplication of bacteria and so give the body's natural defenses the chance to overcome them. The drugs combat blood [1] and urinary tract [2] infections, pneumonia [3], meningitis [4], eye infections [5], and alimentary tract [6] infections such as bacillary dysentery. Overdoses [7] can produce skin rashes, raised temperature, impaired kidney function, and anemia.

2 **Paul Ehrlich** [A] is regarded as the founder of modern chemotherapy. He believed that individual chemicals could act against the agents of infection, and his discovery of Salvarsan proved his case. A second era of expansion for the drug industry was based on the accidental discovery by Alexander Fleming [B] that molds could produce antibacterial substances. Ernst Chain [C] who helped in the development of penicillin, took chemotherapy a stage further by suggesting that semi-synthetic drugs would prove useful.

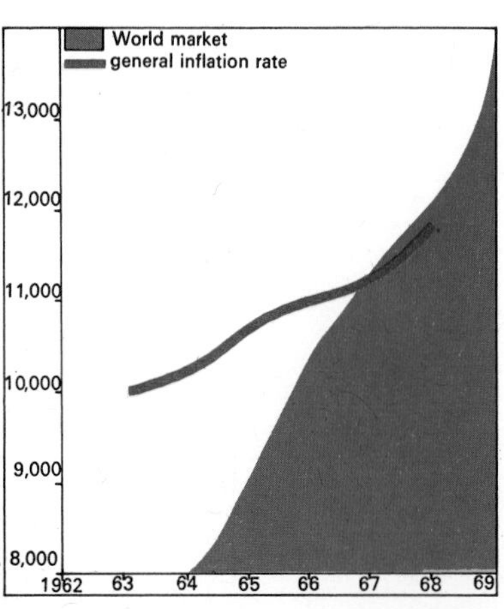

World market
general inflation rate
$ millions
13,000
12,000
11,000
10,000
9,000
8,000
1962
63
64
65
66
67
68
69

3 **The growth** of the pharmaceutical industry during the twentieth century has been astonishing. Many vaccines are available to protect against bacterial and viral diseases. Some, such as Pasteur's smallpox vaccine, contain live microorganisms. Others, like the polio vaccine developed by Jonas Salk, contain killed microorganisms.

croorganisms. Streptomycin was discovered in 1943 and since then dozens of new antibiotics have been discovered and manufactured on a commercial scale [Key].

In most cases it is cheaper to cultivate the microorganisms by fermentation and then extract the active materials, than to synthesize these materials in a laboratory. A compromise between the two approaches was the development of semi-synthetic penicillins in the 1960s. In 1959 the key fragment of the penicillin molecule, 6-aminopenicillanic acid, was isolated. When this is reacted with various organic molecules it is possible to manufacture penicillins that do not occur in nature. These tend to attack microorganisms that have developed resistance to natural penicillins, and they are therefore of greater use therapeutically.

Natural and synthetic products

The concept of modifying natural molecules has spread dramatically through the pharmaceuticals industry. The contraceptive pill, developed in the early 1960s, emerged as the result of the chemical modification of natural sex hormones, which had been isolated in the 1930s. The chemical structures found in human sexual and adrenal cortical hormones are also found in slightly different forms in many living organisms. By chemical modification of a starting material obtained from wild yams, for example, it has been possible to manufacture oral contraceptives.

Many other natural products, such as vitamins and adrenaline, have been synthesized in laboratories and some of them are made commercially by synthetic methods. Adrenaline belongs to an important class of chemical compounds called phenethylamines; this also includes ephedrine, an old Chinese plant remedy now used in asthma treatment and in synthetic amphetamine. Many completely synthetic drugs such as barbiturates have been discovered by accident. The results of unpredicted side effects, such as the impairment of limb development caused by thalidomide, mean that rigorous safety checks must be made. To that end many governments have set up procedures to test new drugs [5].

KEY

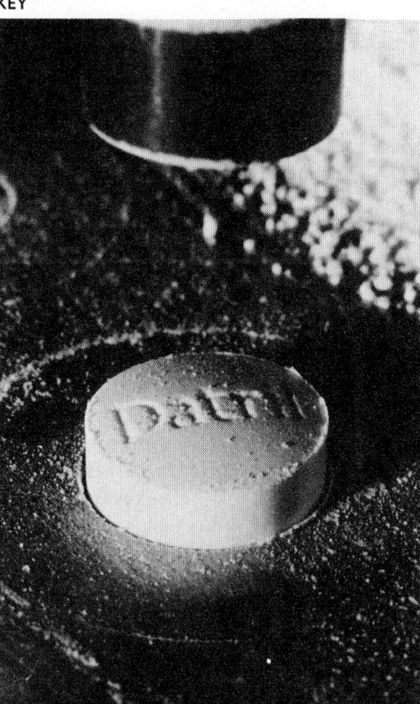
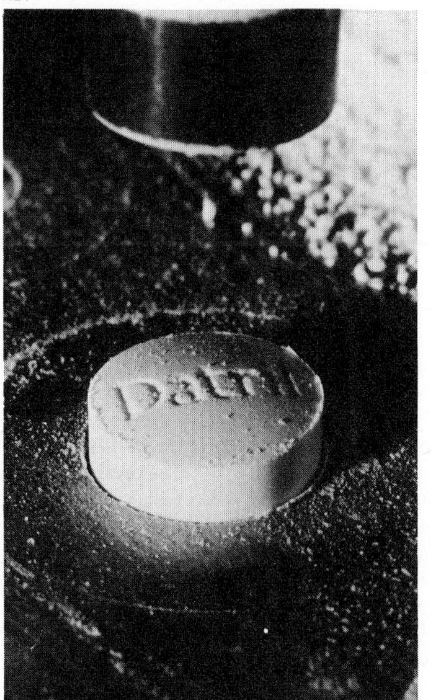

The high-speed tableting machine has supplanted the apothecary's crude apparatus. This is a natural consequence of the need for large amounts of drugs and strict quality control.

4

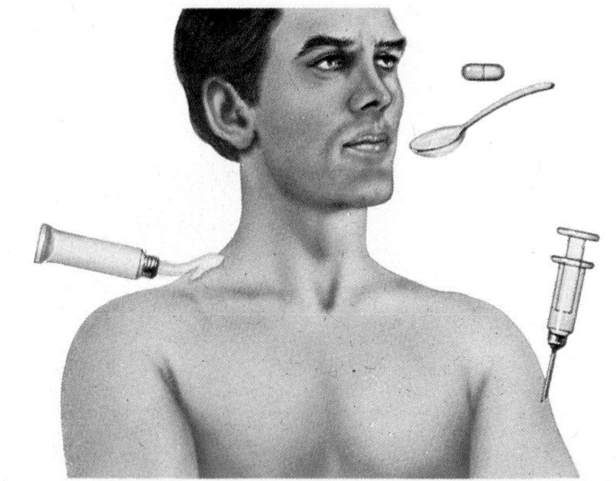

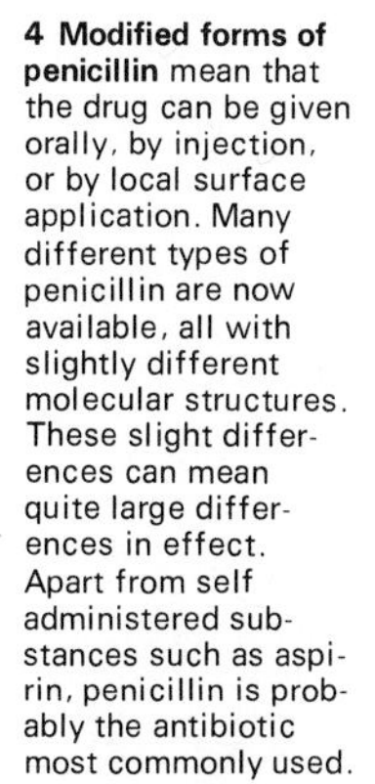

4 Modified forms of penicillin mean that the drug can be given orally, by injection, or by local surface application. Many different types of penicillin are now available, all with slightly different molecular structures. These slight differences can mean quite large differences in effect. Apart from self administered substances such as aspirin, penicillin is probably the antibiotic most commonly used.

5

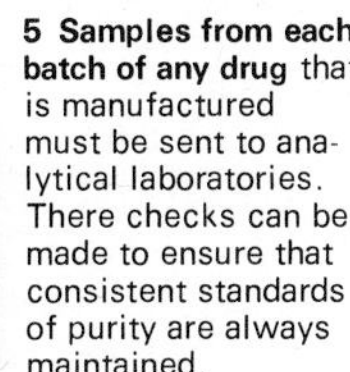

5 Samples from each batch of any drug that is manufactured must be sent to analytical laboratories. There checks can be made to ensure that consistent standards of purity are always maintained.

6

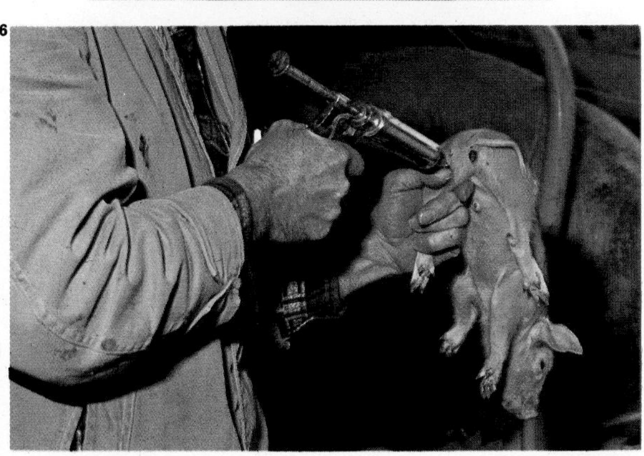

6 Antibiotics have been increasingly used in recent years to keep animals healthy and to combat disease in humans. A disturbing side effect has been that bacteria are becoming immune.

7

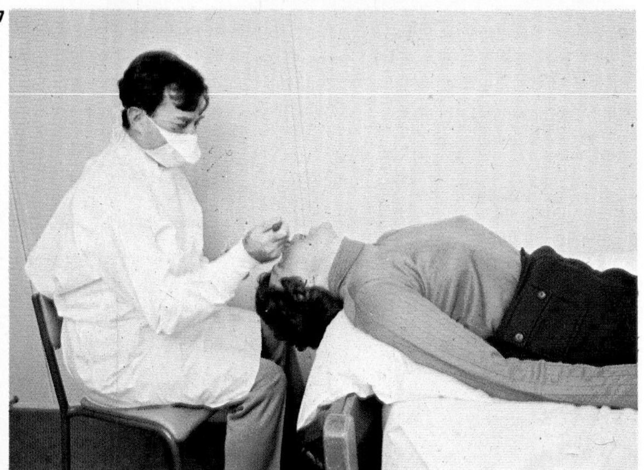

7 Viruses are resistant to most synthetic drugs. To find a cure for viral diseases such as the common cold, scientists experiment, after artificially infecting a volunteer, with complex naturally occurring defense substances.

8

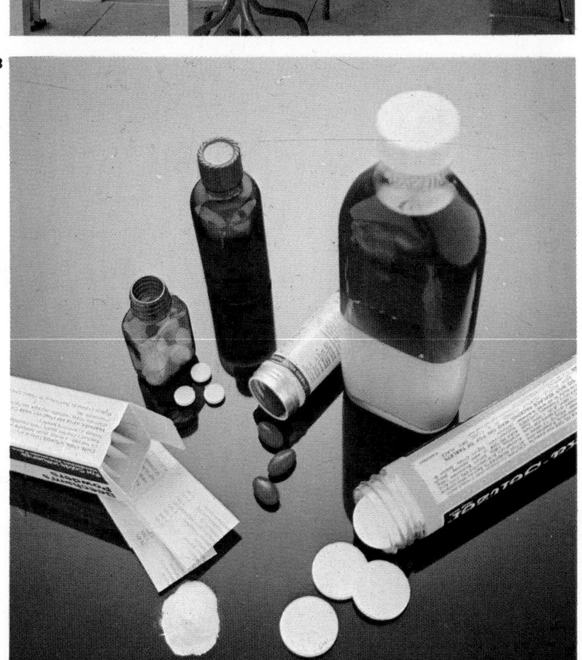

8 Drugs can be formulated for oral consumption as pills, powders, solutions, or suspensions. Different colors and shapes are used to differentiate the thousands of products now marketed.

Nonmedical healing

Nonmedical healing describes any form of healing accomplished without medical or chemical aid, supposedly through the manipulation of the mental or the spiritual being. Verification of illness and cures is difficult in this area, which is thus open to fraudulent practice. But there has been growing interest in the subject, with increasing awareness by the medical profession of the psychosomatic aspects of illness.

Healers and their methods

The many forms of nonmedical healing range through shamanism (the belief in powerful spirits who can be influenced by witch doctors and medicine men) [Key], "laying-on-of-hands," various types of prayer and prayer groups, to meditation and guidance. Also included are placebos (chemically inactive pills or prescriptions that work psychologically, making the patient feel he is taking something therapeutically useful), the so-called psychic surgery of faith healers [3], cleansing of "auras" (fields of energy said to surround all living things), and biofeedback.

Among contemporary faith healers, Kathryn Kuhlman in the United States [1] and Harry Edwards in Great Britain [2] have ministered to thousands of sick people by means of fervent prayers and their conviction of their power to heal through a divine or spiritual agency.

Olga Worrall, who with her husband Ambrose conducted a healing "ministry" in Maryland for more than 40 years, became famous for remarkable results. As "a channel for God's healing power through prayer," she worked with scientists to investigate the power of prayer and reportedly achieved significant results on the growth of plants, apparently influencing germination of seeds and faster growth (compared with that of a control batch) from a distance of as much as several hundred yards.

Many healers combine laying-on-of-hands with their form of mental concentration. Some churches, such as the Pentecostal, incorporate such spiritual healing in their services. Spiritual healing is also an integral part of the New Thought Movement, which includes the churches of Religious Science, and of Christian Science, whose healing principle is "scientific prayer." The World Healing Crusade, headquartered in England, claims cures in more than 100 countries.

The transfer of energy

In the United States, John Scudder claimed significant positive results through combining a breathing technique with "magnetic passes" of his hands over the patient's body, together with a psychological approach to alter the patient's preconceptions of sickness. Norbu Chen, originally Charles Alexander of Kentucky, has applied techniques learned in Tibet in which he "raises his vibrational level" with chanting and meditation until he feels ready to channel the energy of his consciousness to the patient.

Carl O. Simonton in America and Gilbert Anderson of The National Federation of Spiritual Healers in England have claimed promising results in the treatment of terminal cancer through a combination of

CONNECTIONS

See also
708 An introduction to illness and health
818 Body image and biofeedback
742 Origins of curative medicine
820 Meditation and consciousness
850 Religion and the plight of modern man

1 Kathryn Kuhlman's belief in the healing power of faith in God drew thousands to "Miracle Services" at the Andrew Carnegie Auditorium in New York. Working by on-the-spot therapy and prayer, she reportedly helped many people with ailments that had not responded to treatment by conventional medical procedures.

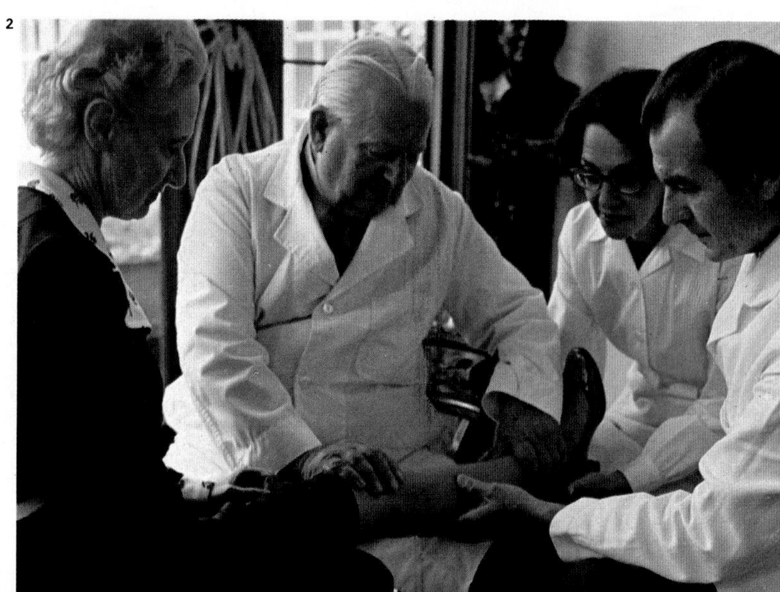

2 Harry Edwards, the best known British faith healer, uses a combination of laying-on-of-hands, sympathy, and understanding. His public demonstrations of healing have filled the Albert Hall, London. His powers have been attributed to the "advice" of Lister and Pasteur as well as to faith.

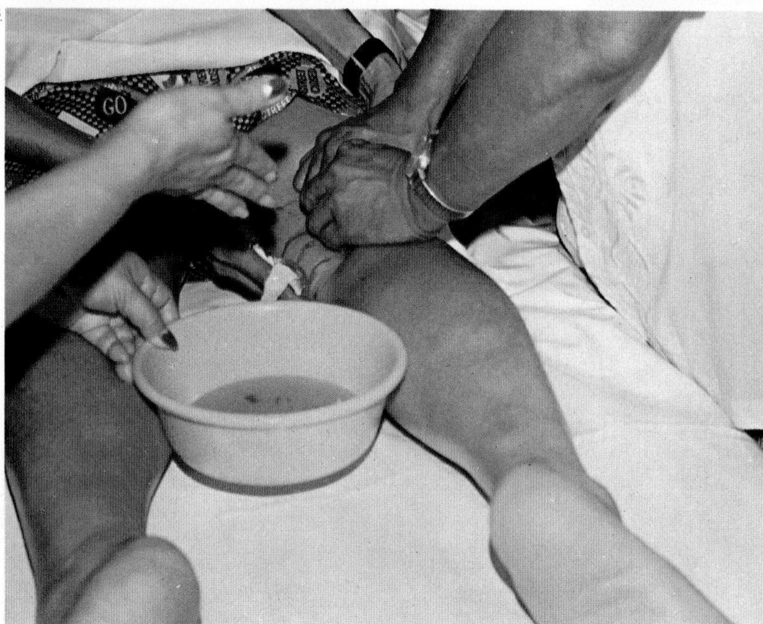

3 "Psychic surgeons" in the Philippines appear to operate on patients without instruments, "cutting" into the body with a finger and opening it up with their bare hands to remove organs or tissues they say cause illnesses. These "operations" have been shown to be fraudulent, with sleight-of-hand and animal blood simulating surgery.

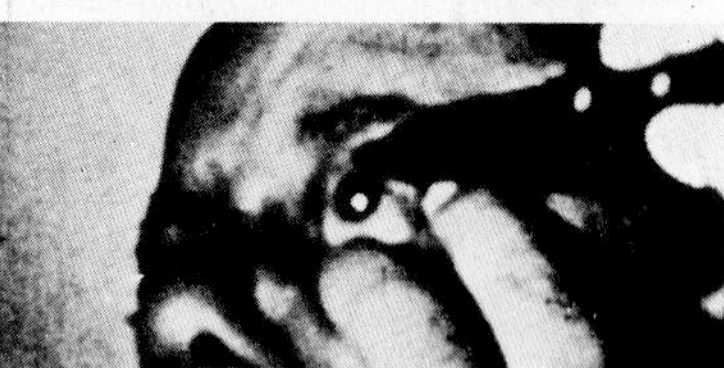

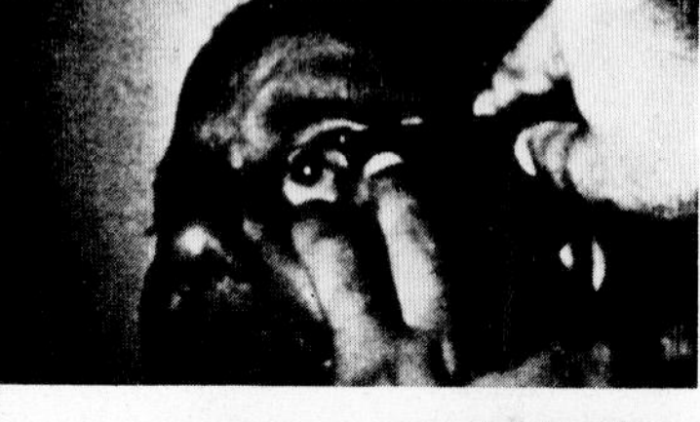

4 Jose Pedro de Freitas, known as "Arigo" (good guy) became famous for successful surgery (such as this removal of an eye cataract) carried out painlessly with any handy knife and without anesthetic. Researchers in 1963 claimed that his skill matched that of doctors.

meditation and laying-on-of-hands and with the patient visualizing the healing of the affected parts.

The long-term effectiveness of all such "miracle cures" has been brought into question by qualified researchers. Psychosomatic medicine, however, does recognize faith as a significant factor in effecting certain kinds of cures.

Biofeedback and acupuncture

Biofeedback, the voluntary control of normally involuntary states, uses the patient's own mind for effecting changes in his physical state by showing him the results of his own state of mind on an instrument. In some way not yet definable he can cause changes in the reading by altering his state of mind, or vice versa. It is possible, for instance, for people with hypertension to lower their blood pressure. Through deep relaxation the patient can relieve tension, headaches, and other symptoms of stress, as well as muscular complaints.

Although the technique of acupuncture dates back at least 5,000 years in Chinese history [5, 6], it first arrived in the West during the 1960s and was brought to prominence only after an investigative visit to China by a group of Western physicians in 1972. Now being applied more widely, it involves the concept of 14 main meridians (12 of them bilateral lines or channels that are said to connect organs deep in the body to surface points), each having a point of stimulation as well as a point of sedation. The organs are "paired," so that if the heart, for instance, is stimulated, the lungs will be sedated.

There are at least 1,000 acupuncture points on the body and possibly many more. When fine steel needles are inserted at an acupuncture point [7] and gently manipulated, they are said to redirect energy flow along the meridians to correct an imbalance. The Chinese called the use of this energy flow "Qi" and it was based on the Taoist yin-yang principle of opposing but complementary aspects of energy which must be kept in balance for health to be assured. The value of acupuncture is still debated in the United States.

KEY

Shamanism is practiced among Polynesian, African, South American, Asian, and American Indian tribes. It has its roots in animism, the belief that spiritual forces pervade the world. The shaman is considered a healer able to control the spirits. Here, a shaman in Africa uses the appropriate words and actions to invoke the favor of the spirits to protect a member of the tribe.

5

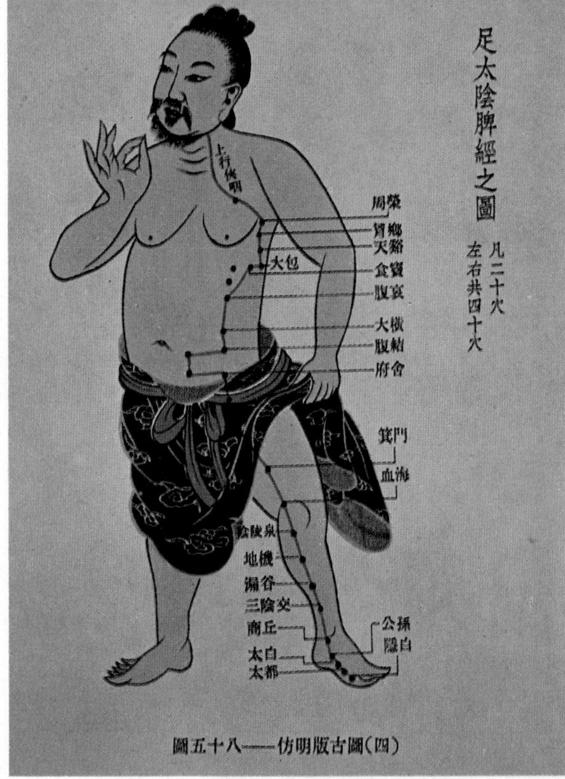
足太陰脾經之圖
凡二十穴
左右共四十穴
太白
隱白
圖五十八——仿明版古圖(四)

5 Acupuncture as a method of curing illness originated in China more than 5,000 years ago. Metal needles are inserted into the skin at specific points, which were mapped on a bronze figure dating from AD 900 and have been illustrated on many charts since then. The points are located on the 14 "meridian channels," of which one is shown here in this nineteenth-century version.

6

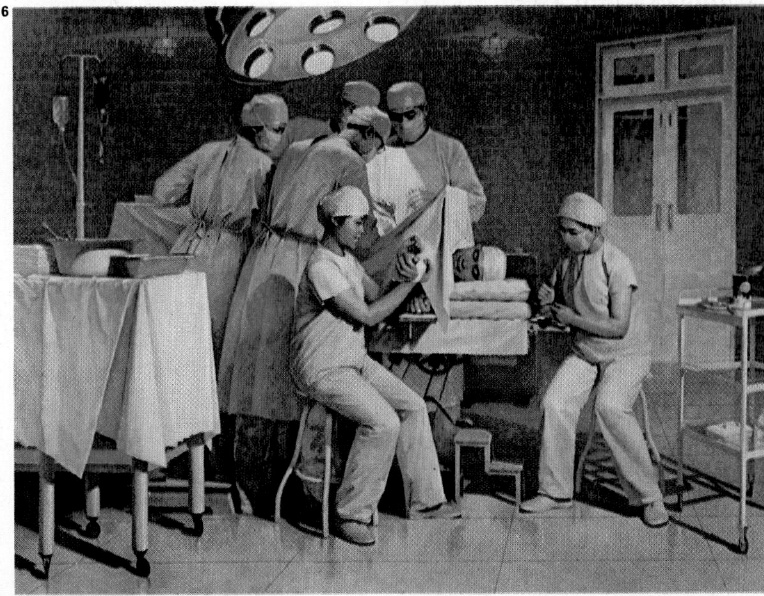

6 In China many kinds of surgery are performed under acupuncture anesthesia. Patients are awake throughout and feel nothing but numbness; they can often walk away from the operating table. The development of acupuncture as an anesthetic began in 1959 when Mao Tse-tung gave acupunturists the status of physicians. Before this time acupuncture was a therapeutic procedure.

7

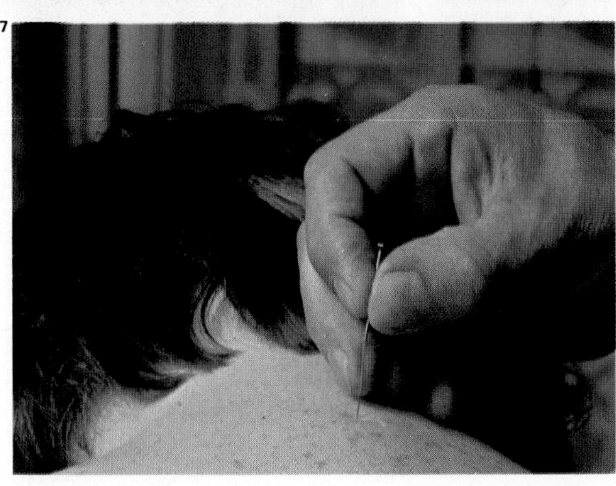

7 Acupuncture procedure involves the rapid insertion of fine steel needles up to 10in(55cm) long at acupunture points, followed by gentle twirling between the thumb and forefinger. This is said to redirect the energy flow along meridians, restoring balance, and correcting the disorder. In a treatment for toothache, for instance, the needle may be inserted in the patient's hand, at an acupuncture point between the thumb and forefinger.

8

8 The use of hypnosis in studying hysteria was pioneered by Jean Martin Charcot (1825–93) at the Salpêtrière Hospital Paris, where Sigmund Freud was one of his students. Hypnosis has been used in many medical fields. In dentistry it has been used to reduce anxiety and has been employed in conditioning processes aimed at reducing or eliminating specific fears. It continues to be used in psychoanalysis.

Radiology and radiotherapy

The effects of radiation may be used for investigating diseases, in diagnostic radiology, and for treating them, in radiotherapy. Much of the early work on the phenomenon of radioactivity was undertaken by Marie Curie (1867–1934) [Key], who, with her husband Pierre (1859–1906) and jointly with Antoine Becquerel (1852–1908), was awarded the Nobel Prize for physics in 1903. In 1911 she was also awarded the Nobel Prize for chemistry for the discovery of radium and polonium. Her death from leukemia was probably caused by overexposure to radiation.

Overexposure illnesses and the long-term effects of atomic bombs point very clearly to the powerful and dangerous effects of radiation waves. By careful and controlled use, however, many of the properties of beta, gamma, and X rays are exploited in medicine for both diagnosis and treatment.

X-ray photography

Most kinds of energy waves are able to pass through some materials and not others. Light waves, for instance, pass through air and also through some liquids (such as water) and even solids (such as glass), but not through walls and doors. X rays, on the other hand, can pass with varying ability through body tissues, but can be blocked and absorbed by other substances such as lead. In the same way that light waves can produce a picture on a photographic plate, so also can X rays activate such a film [1].

In a simple X-ray machine an X-ray source is beamed at the part to be examined and focused onto a photographic film, where the image resembles a film negative. An X-ray picture of a hand, for example, shows bones (which stop X rays quite effectively) as white, the other tissues as grays and the area around the hand (which receives full X-ray exposure) as black. In order to show up other organs within the body more clearly, radio-opaque substances (ones that do not allow X rays through) are used. Barium sulfate is one such substance and is used in barium swallows and enemas to show up the upper and lower intestines respectively [3]. Other substances injected or given by mouth, often containing iodine, are particularly concentrated in certain body organs. This enables better pictures to be obtained of kidneys and bladder.

Scanning techniques

Pictures obtained by conventional X-ray machines are not as clear as ordinary photographs. Organs within the body are seen superimposed upon each other and the picture is a composite one. To see an organ or part within the body with less overlaying detail the technique of axial tomography is used [2]. Here the X-ray source and the detection system or photographic plate are rotated in an arc round the body with the specific organ as the center of the arc. This organ then appears relatively still and in focus, whereas other parts are less clear.

In a major advance this principle has been used in a very sophisticated manner to scan the brain, and using a computer, to integrate the information. The EMI scanner [5] produces a picture of a "slice" through the brain, and can produce a series of such pictures to give a view of the whole brain.

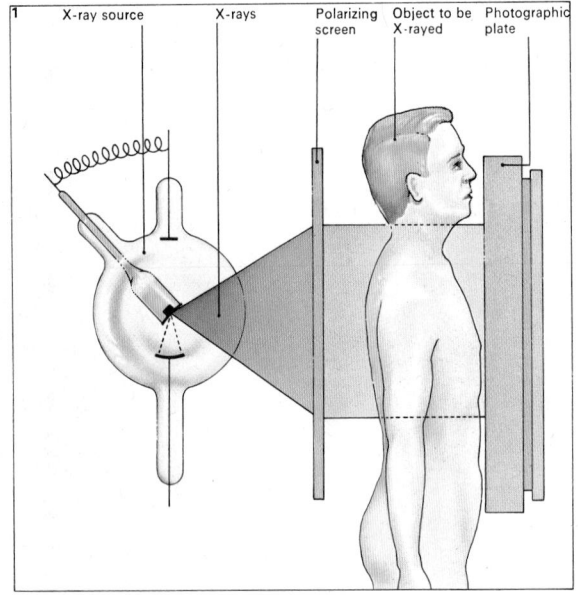

CONNECTIONS

See also
712 The causes of illness: 2
714 Diseases of breathing
718 Diseases of the digestive system
720 Diseases of the skeleton and muscles
722 Diseases of the nervous system
726 Diseases of the glands
728 Diseases of the urogenital system

1

X-ray source
X-rays
Polarizing screen
Object to be X-rayed
Photographic plate

1 The use of X rays in medicine to photograph the body internally has enormously advanced the diagnosis of disease. Since X-ray waves emerge from an X-ray source traveling in several different planes, they are first passed through a polarizing screen. This organizes them into a single plane and so concentrates them. The body's various organs and tissues (skin, bone, brain, lungs, liver, arteries, and so on) absorb varying amounts of the X rays passing through them. Thus the X rays striking the photographic plate are of varying degrees of intensity. The result is an image that resembles a film negative.

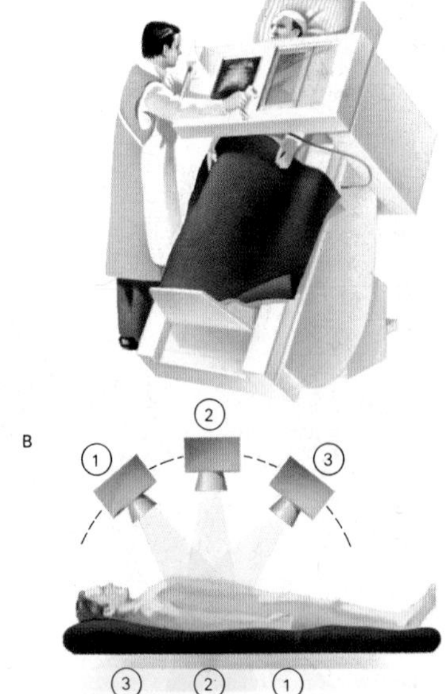

2 A
B
1
2
3
3
2
1

2 Radiology uses X rays to visualize internal parts of the body. Various machines are used to produce X rays of controlled energy levels and to focus the rays and control exposure. A chest X ray [A] can be viewed on a television screen, stored on videotape, or made into X-ray films. To facilitate diagnosis, substances that do not transmit X rays can be swallowed or injected to provide a means of contrast. An X-ray film is a negative and the contrast appears white. By rotating the X-ray source [B] and taking pictures from several angles [1, 2, 3] it is possible to focus on organs in a particular plane of the body.

3

A

B

1

2

3 Barium sulfate is used in radiology to provide contrast in X-ray photography. Internal tissues such as the digestive system and kidneys allow the passage of X rays to varying extents. But when filled with a substance that blocks the X rays, they can be made opaque and show up as white. The barium a harmless paste that passes through and out of the intestines unchanged, can be swallowed [1] or injected into the rectum [2]. When swallowed, it outlines in turn the esophagus, the stomach, and the small intestine [A]. Ulcers, tumors, and alterations of function can be seen. Similarly, the colon, or large bowel, can be photographed [B].

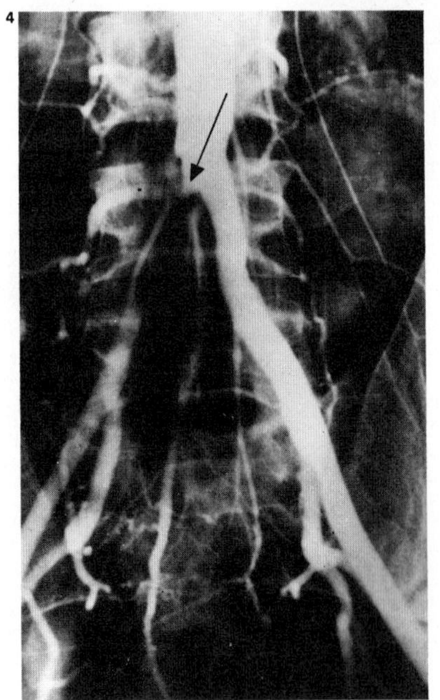

4

4 Arteriography is a specialized technique of radiology developed to show up the inside of arteries so that thickening can be detected. This tissue damage in arteries is the degenerative disease known as arteriosclerosis. It contributes to coronaries and strokes and to poor circulation in the legs. The arteries are shown up by the injection of a radio-opaque dye that reveals irregularities of the vessel wall. The picture here, obtained after injection of a dye into the aorta, shows the large arteries of the pelvis and upper legs and a local narrowing of the artery (arrowed) that is interfering with the blood flow.

By the use of a computer, a very much more detailed and precise picture is obtained. This technique is now likely to replace many of the techniques in which dyes or air are injected as contrasts into the fluids bathing the brain, for these latter procedures are longer, more complicated and potentially dangerous. A computer scanning system is more expensive than conventional machines, but the X-ray dose for the whole procedure is smaller, comparable to that of a skull X ray. The EMI Whole-Body Scanner produces a scan of a body section that is processed in 20 seconds.

X rays are not the only type of radiation that can be used to obtain information about the body. Gamma waves emitted from certain radioactive isotopes (forms of certain elements) are also able to pass through body tissues. Small doses of such isotopes can be injected and a measure of the radioactivity taken up by a particular organ may give evidence about it. The thyroid gland, for example, is responsible for using nearly all the iodine taken into the body. If a radioactive iodine isotope is injected into the bloodstream, the activity of the thyroid can be gauged by measuring its rate of uptake of iodine. This can be done by measuring the gamma waves emitted from the region of the thyroid. In addition, scanning the thyroid will give a picture of the activity of each part of the gland. Parts that are over- or under-active may thus be detected.

Treatment of cancer by radiotherapy

Using high doses of isotopes can cause tissue damage. In treating thyroid cancer doses several thousand times higher than for diagnosis are used to take advantage of this damaging effect to kill the cancer cells. This is the principle of radiotherapy, where high doses of radiation are beamed at tumors to kill them [6]. All living cells are generally sensitive to the effect of radiation, particularly when dividing, and cancer cells are particularly susceptible. Care must be taken to judge the dosage required and to apply it to the correct area. Radiation of a particular energy may be required [7], for some cancers respond better than others to rays of high energy.

KEY

Marie Curie's work on radium led to X-ray and isotope techniques for both the diagnosis and treatment of disease.

5 A

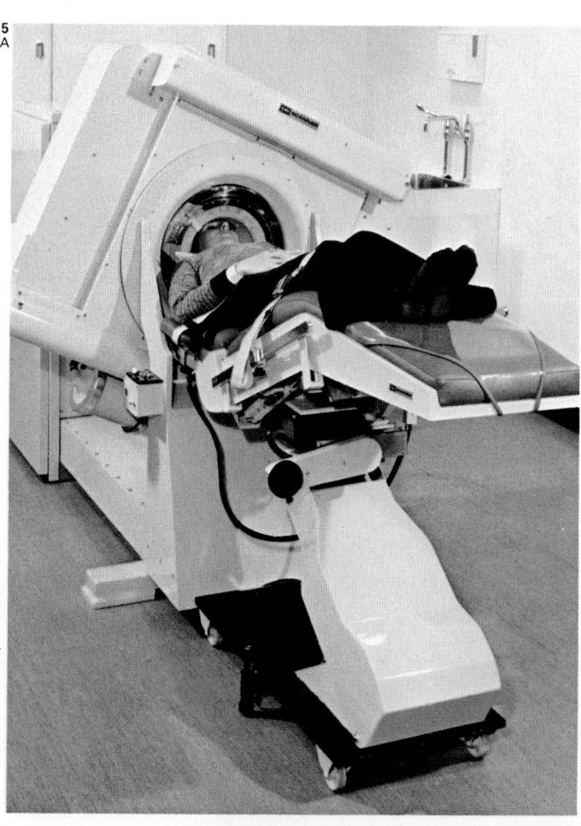

6 Radiotherapy uses radiation to treat disease. Ionizing radiations (beta, gamma, or X rays) cause changes in cells (particularly when they are dividing) and so kill them. This can be used against malignant cells, which are more sensitive to the energy released by irradiation than healthy cells. Treatment of cancer can be by a beam of low-energy rays focused on the skin [A] or of a higher energy [B] focused below the body surface [1], sometimes from more than one direction [2]. A local surface applicator can be used, as in the eye [C] or combined with beam treatment, as in the neck of the womb [D]. Minute radioactive pellets can be placed deep in the body to treat the pituitary [E], or an isotope administered by mouth may be taken up selectively, as is iodine by thyroid cancer, even if the cancer has spread [F].

6

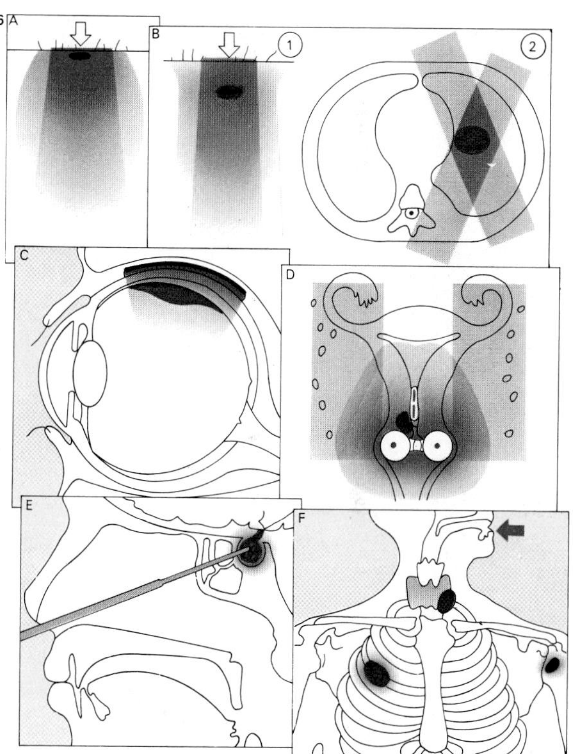
A
B
1
2
C
D
E
F

5 The EMI scanner allows X-raying of the brain through an accurately aligned X-ray source with multiple detectors that move past the patient. Information is fed into a computer and enables a complex picture to be built up. The X-ray unit [A] for examining the brain obtains information easily with low X-ray dose. The Whole-Body Scanner produces pictures of a slice through the body [B]. Shown is the abdomen with the liver (right).

B

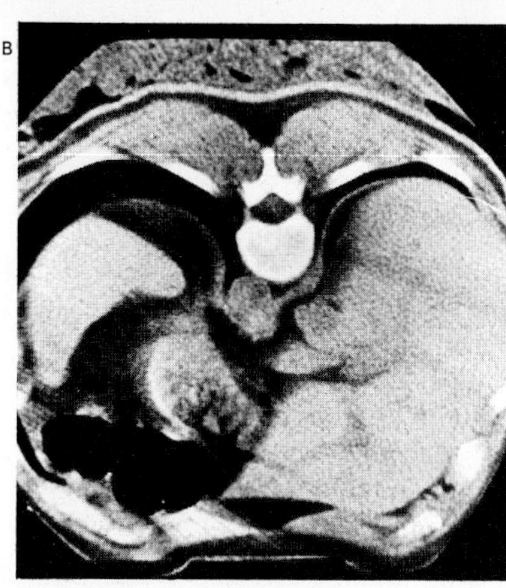

7

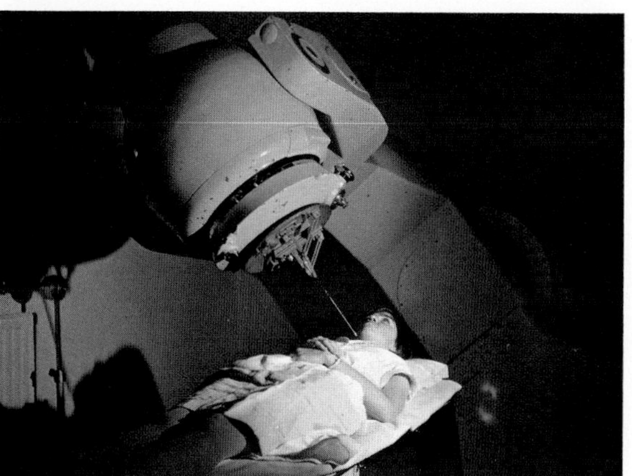

7 To treat a tumor, radiation is delivered by sophisticated machinery with the operators protected by lead screening from the powerful X-ray or gamma-ray source. The patient is also screened so that only a specified area of the body is irradiated for the correct time. Treatment in stages minimizes side effects. The type and energy of the rays are vital for success, and new, very high energy rays can now treat previously unresponsive cancers.

Development of surgery

Surgery is the manual treatment of injuries, deformities, and other disorders. Early peoples probably practiced simple forms, such as setting a fractured limb, binding a wound, lancing an abscess, or pulling a tooth, and there is evidence that they may have attempted delicate operations with some success.

Advances in anatomical knowledge

Even 10,000 years ago "medicine men" were capable of performing the difficult operation known as trephining—the removal of a piece of skull to cure headaches or madness—and the Romans removed endangered babies from their mother's wombs by what came to be known as Caesarean section. But generally surgery was limited to simple external operations. The sophistication of modern surgery is really the result of discoveries made in the last 300 years.

A surgeon's first need is an accurate understanding of the working of the human body. Until late in the Middle Ages surgery remained a primitive trade (closely allied to that of the barber) because neither doctors nor surgeons had any real knowledge of anatomy. The only way to find out is by dissection of the dead, a process looked upon with horror by church and state alike. Only in the fifteenth century was this taboo even partially overcome, but from that time onward doctors were able at last to begin their investigation of the structures that lie within the body. Ambroise Paré (1517–90), the "father" of modern surgery, was one of the earliest to use this new knowledge [1]. Important subsequent landmarks were the demonstration by William Harvey (1578–1657) of the circulation of the blood and the anatomical discoveries of William Hunter (1718–83) and his brother John (1728–93).

Eliminating pain and infection

Even the most exact knowledge of anatomy does nothing to solve the two major problems confronting the surgeon and, more important, the patient—namely pain and infection. It was the nineteenth century that brought about the great revolution that transformed surgery from an agonizingly brutal and dangerous business into the relatively safe and painless one that it is today. The first advance came in 1844 when Horace Wells (1815–48), an American dentist. used laughing gas (nitrous oxide) when extracting a tooth. Within a few years ether [2] and chloroform were also being used to eliminate pain during major surgery. William Morton (1819–1868) pioneered the use of ether (general anesthesia).

The second factor in the surgical revolution was the advent of antiseptic surgery. Until mid-Victorian times it was commonplace for patients to develop lethal post-operative infection. The reason for post-operative infection remained hidden until Louis Pasteur (1822–95) showed that it was caused by germs. The first surgeon to grasp fully the implications of Pasteur's discovery was Joseph Lister (1827–1912), who realized that antiseptic chemicals such as carbolic acid could kill germs and prevent infection of operation wounds. His technique of placing surgical instruments in antiseptic solution, of spraying carbolic acid in the air during operations, and of applying antiseptic dressing to the stitched incision

CONNECTIONS

See also
- 754 Having an operation
- 716 Diseases of the circulation
- 770 Physical cures for mental illness
- 422 Bacteria and viruses
- 1032 Early Oriental and Western science
- 1282 The foundations of 20th-century science
- 1160 Science and technology 1500–1700
- 704 Giving birth
- 706 Birth control
- 756 Dentistry
- 808 Questions of life and death

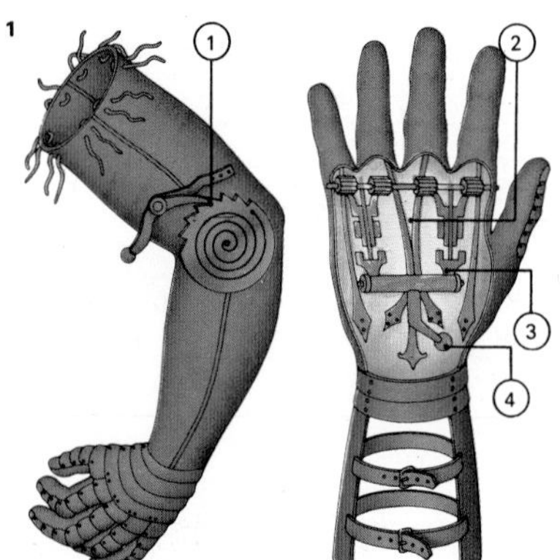

1
1
2
3
4

1 French surgeon Ambroise Paré (1527–90) designed this artificial arm. A ratchet and pawl [1] locked the elbow in any position; springs and catches [2,3,4] opened and then closed the fingers.

2A
B

2 The first "purpose-built" operating tables [A] appeared in the 19th century. They were cumbersome but basically the same as modern ones. The ether inhaler [B] replaced rum as a pain-killer.

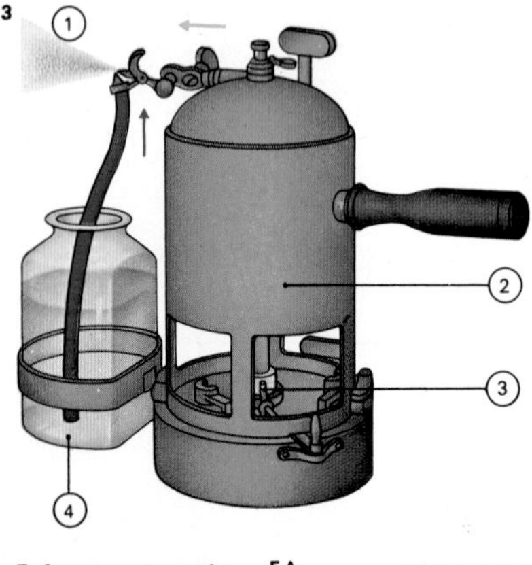

3
1
2
3
4

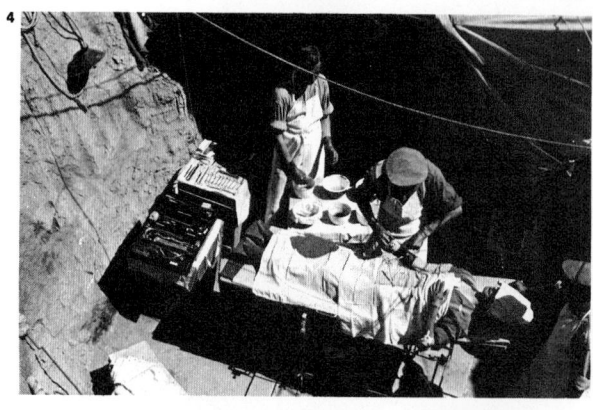

3 The discovery by Pasteur that germs cause infection led to Joseph Lister's introduction of antisepsis—the treatment of wounds with carbolic acid (phenol). Lister (1827–1912) first introduced a hand-operated spray, then a steam model. The steam [1] from the boiler [2]—heated by methylated spirit on a wick [3]—sucked carbolic acid vapor from a jar [4] thus filling the air with an antiseptic mist.

4 Wars accelerate all technologies, not least that of medicine, and the carnage of World War I caused great strides in surgery, particularly in bringing damaged tissues together and keeping patients alive with a saline solution in spite of heavy fluid losses. Here, in a makeshift field operating theater, an army surgeon removes a bullet from the arm of a wounded soldier.

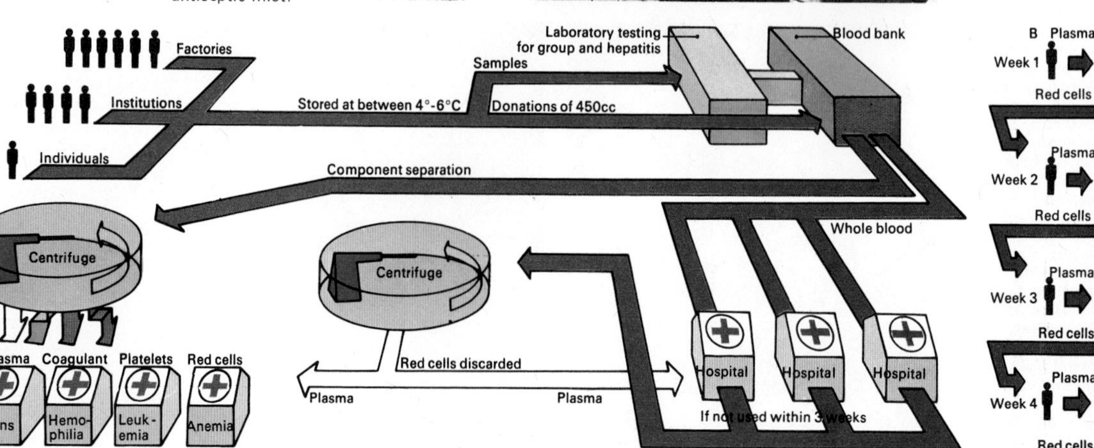

5A
Factories
Institutions
Individuals
Laboratory testing for group and hepatitis
Samples
Blood bank
Stored at between 4°-6°C
Donations of 450cc
Component separation
Whole blood
Centrifuge
Centrifuge
Plasma
Coagulant
Platelets
Red cells
Burns
Hemophilia
Leukemia
Anemia
Red cells discarded
Plasma
Plasma
Hospital
Hospital
Hospital
If not used within 3 weeks
B Plasma
Week 1
Red cells
Plasma
Week 2
Red cells
Plasma
Week 3
Red cells
Plasma
Week 4
Red cells

5 A constant supply of fresh blood from donors [A] to a blood bank is critical, for it deteriorates after three weeks. Blood reaches hospitals whole at 39°–43°F(4°–6°C) or split into its constituent parts by centrifuge. Once separated and dehydrated, plasma can be frozen and kept indefinitely as powder. To increase plasma supplies [B] a donor can give blood 40 times a year instead of the normal three, receiving back his red cells from the previous visit.

dramatically reduced the death rate after surgery [3].

Revolutionary and beneficial as it was, antiseptic surgery began to give way, at the start of the twentieth century, to the modern practice of aseptic surgery, in which the aim is not to kill germs in the operating theater but to exclude them as far as possible from the patient. Surgeons developed an aseptic (germ-free) technique in which the operation site is made bacteria-free by swabbing the skin with a bactericide before an incision is made. Sterile towels, gowns, and masks were introduced and the surgeon and his assistants learned to scrub their hands carefully for a full five minutes before every operation.

The 1920s saw the widespread introduction of blood transfusion [5], which made it possible to replace blood lost during an operation and, at the same time, there arrived refinements in anesthesia to make possible the opening of the chest for lung operations.

Shortly after World War II chest surgeons found ways of inserting a finger into the heart in order to clear a partially obstructed valve. Next it became possible to lower an anesthetized patient's temperature (hypothermia) so much that his heart could actually be stopped for a short time, thus permitting even more delicate operations within it.

Modern innovations in surgery

The advent of the heart-lung machine (which completely takes over the functions of pumping the blood and of breathing) meant that surgeons could take far more time over their complex procedures (with correspondingly better results) and eventually progress to the transplantation of hearts [8]. By the 1960s and 1970s it became possible to transplant other organs (kidneys, liver, lungs, and pancreas), although the incidence of failure is still very high. Indeed, surgery and its technology have advanced to such an extent that it is possible to conceive of a situation in which anyone who has a damaged, defective, or worn out organ will be able to get a working replacement, real or artificial, as well as purely cosmetic devices [6].

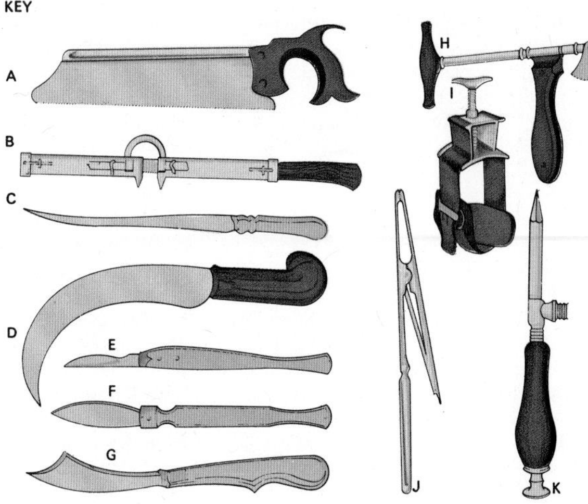
KEY
A
B
C
D
E
F
G
H
I
J
K

Surgical instruments of the 18th and 19th centuries looked crude but were effective. Basic amputation saws [A,B] knives [C,D], and scalpels [E,F,G] have hardly changed. Thal's mechanical saw [H], in which the handle was rotated to move the blade, was sometimes used. Today clamps have replaced tourniquets [I], while forceps [J] now resemble scissors. The trocar [K] was a tube used for drawing off fluids.

6 "Spare parts surgery" has undergone dramatic changes in recent times, making it possible to transplant living organs and fit artificial substitutes within the body. New metals, acrylics, and other plastics have helped overcome the problems of rejection, the refusal of the body to accept the installation of foreign materials. Possible spare parts include [1] surgical wig; [2] "Vitallium" skull plate; [3] plastic nose implant; [4] cosmetic acrylic eye; [5] in-the-ear hearing aid; [6] silicon plastic ear; [7] cosmetic plastic ear; [8] metal jaw-bone; [9] dentures; [10] chin implant; [11] Spitz-Holter valve to control fluid on the brain; [12] electronic larynx; [13] shoulder joint replacement; [14] heart valve replacement; [15] heart pacemaker; [16] filter preventing blood clotting in circulation to the lungs; [17] Dacron heart patch; [18] Dacron artery replacement; [19] elbow replacement; [20] Dacron vein and artery graft; [21] metal bone plate; [22] plastic replacement after removal of a part of small intestine; [23] hip joint replacement; [24] wrist bone replacement; [25] finger joint replacement; [26] thighbone replacement; [27] cosmetic plastic testicles; [28] knee joint replacement; [29] plastic artery graft; [30] artificial leg with knee and ankle movement; [31] shin; [32] arm.

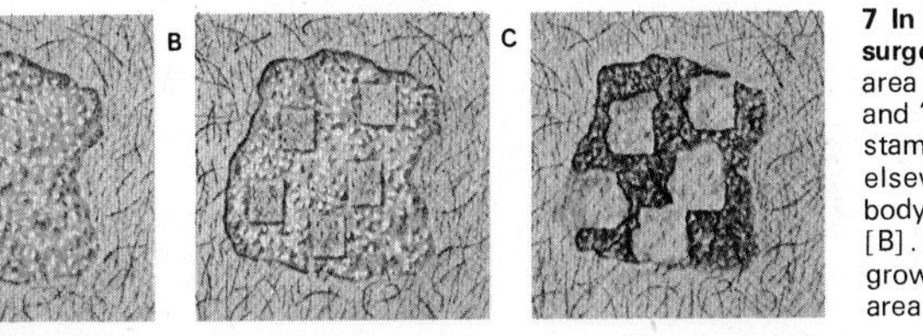
7
A
B
C

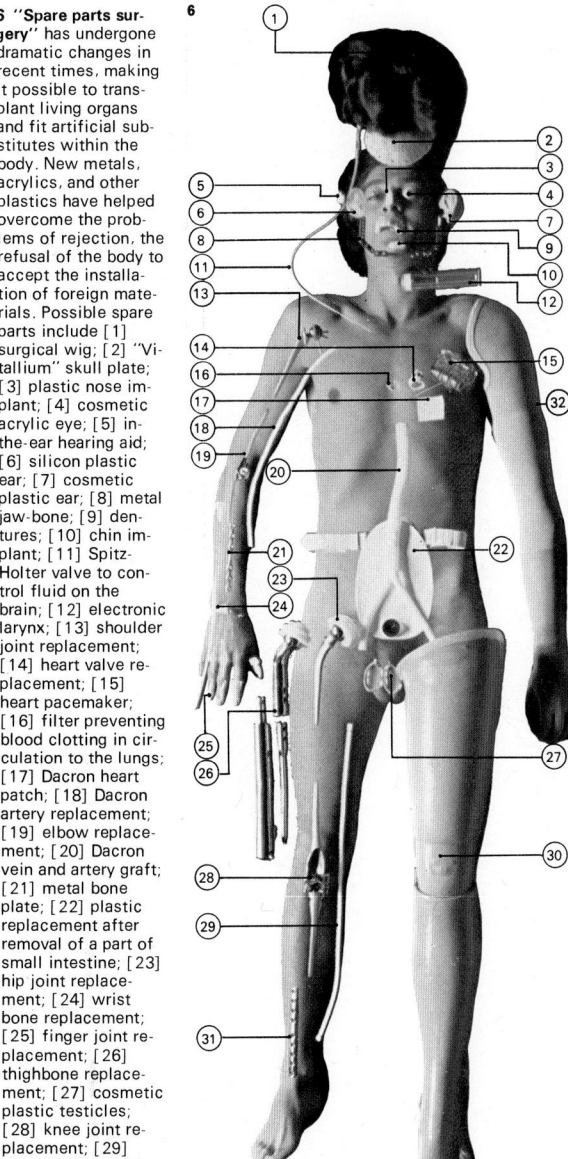

7 In basic plastic surgery, the burned area [A] is cleaned and "postage stamps" of skin from elsewhere on the body are grafted on [B]. Healthy skin grows out until the area is covered [C].

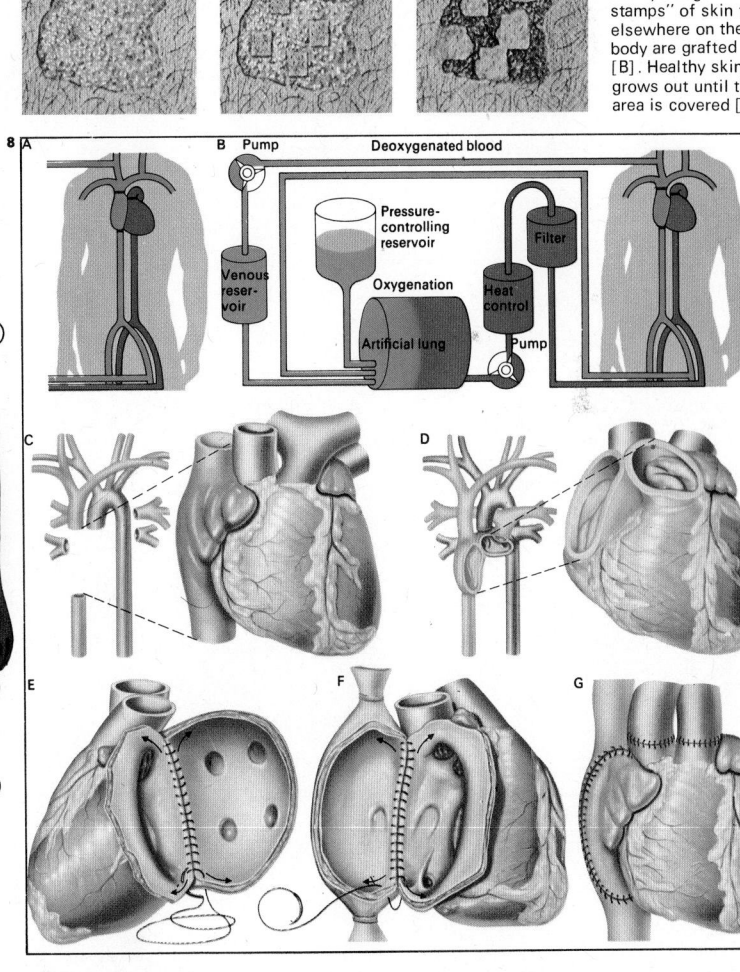

8 A heart transplant involves the removal of a badly diseased heart, replacing it with one from a "donor"—someone who has just died, usually as the result of a road accident. At first, heart-lung machines are connected to both the donor [A] and the recipient [B], to keep their hearts alive. The donor heart is then removed [C] and the recipient's heart is cut out [D], leaving only the top-most part. The donor's heart is now stitched to this "stump," first on one side [E] and then on the other [F]. Salt solution is then pumped through the heart to clear it of air and the final stitching to the great vessels is completed [G]. The recipient's new heart is now stimulated into beating by means of an electric shock. The operation is somewhat rare.

Having an operation

Although advances in modern techniques have made such well-publicized operations as organ transplants and brain surgery relatively safe, these are still only a minute fraction of the total number of operations performed each year.

Common surgical operations

To a certain extent operations are a matter of fashion. In the United States circumcision was, until recently, the most common operation. Virtually the entire male population underwent circumcision shortly after birth. In other countries, however it is becoming quite rare because it is considered really necessary in relatively few cases.

In the United States and many other countries appendectomy (the removal of the appendix) is probably the operation most frequently performed by general surgeons. Other common ones include herniorrhaphy (the repairing of a hernia, or rupture); partial gastrectomy (the removal of part of the stomach, usually for ulcers); cholecystectomy (gall bladder removal); vagotomy (cutting of the nerves to the viscera, again for ulcers); mastectomy (removal of the breast); and hemorrhoidectomy (removal of a hemorrhoid).

The general surgeon may spend a great deal of his time removing benign and malignant tumors from various parts of the body and, in many hospitals, be expected to strip out varicose veins. The latter is also in the province of the vascular surgeon, who carries out operations on blood vessels, such as the removal of aneurysms (swellings) in arteries.

Orthopedic surgeons are responsible for operations on bones, joints, tendons, ligaments, nerves, and muscles. The common procedures they undertake include menisectomy (removal of a damaged cartilage from the knee joint) and operation for the relief of "slipped disks" in the vertebral column.

Urological surgeons deal with the urinary tract and the male reproductive organs. One of their main operations is prostatectomy, or removal of the prostate gland. Gynecological surgeons deal with the female reproductive organs and carry out the extremely common operations of hysterectomy (removal of the womb) and "D and C" (dilation and curettage, or widening of the neck of the womb and scraping of the lining).

Other surgeons specialize in operations on the ear, nose, and throat; the most common operation they perform is probably still tonsillectomy, or excision of the tonsils. Considerably less frequent are the delicate operations carried out by eye surgeons, brain surgeons, and plastic surgeons.

The procedure for surgery

Most people have some sort of operation (though often only a minor one) in the course of their lives, but few understand very much about what is going to happen to them [1]. On admission to a hospital the patient is carefully examined by a resident physician to ensure that he is fit for an operation. The physician may order blood tests or X rays and, if the operation is to be a major one, may ask the blood bank to put aside some blood that has been carefully "cross-matched" with the patient's blood.

CONNECTIONS

See also
752 Development of surgery
806 Death, grieving, and loss

1
2
3
4
5
6
7
8
9
10
11
12

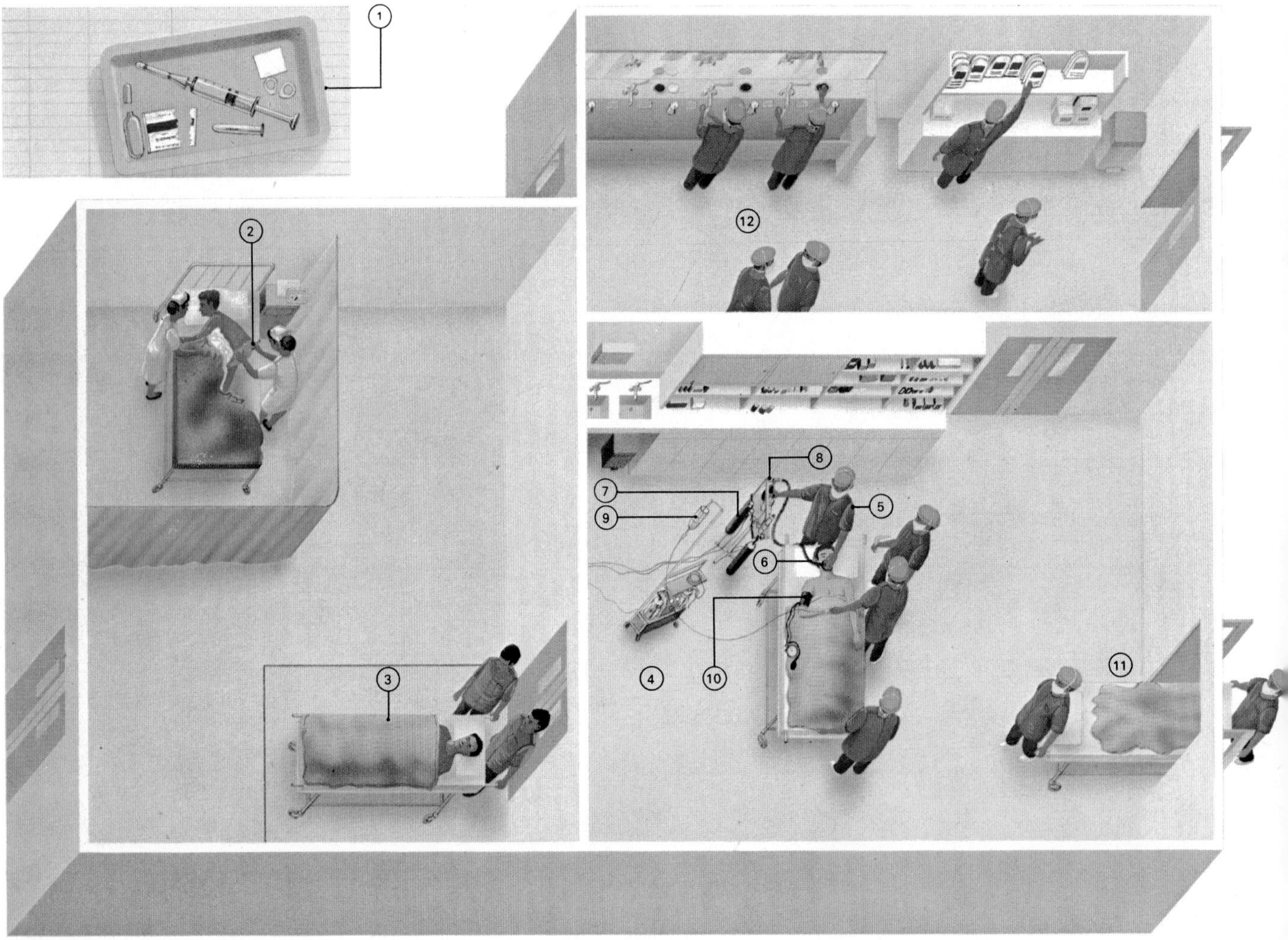

1 Before an operation a pre-medication injection [1] is drawn up into a syringe and administered [2] by a nurse. The "pre-med" takes effect after half an hour or so and then a hospital porter transfers the patient to a stretcher [3] and wheels him into the anesthetic room [4]. The anesthetist [5] "induces" the patient with an anesthetic drug [6]. Administering it into an arm vein makes the effect swift, although sometimes the patient is put to sleep by inhaling gases from the anesthetic machine. This is a movable cart carrying cylinders [7] of oxygen—which has to be administered throughout the operation to keep the patient alive—and of anesthetic gases such as cyclopropane. Oxygen and whatever gas has been chosen by the anesthetist are mixed together and they flow through a black rubber bag [8]. When the patient can no longer breathe for himself, this bag is squeezed manually by the anesthetist or his assistant. After an initial intravenous injection the anesthetist will continue anesthesia with gas as the injection wears off. In the anesthetic room an intravenous "drip" [9] may be set up if it is felt that the patient may need fluid or blood replacement.

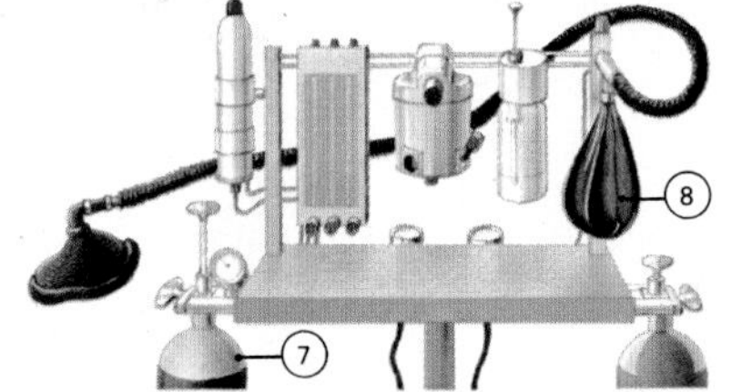

8
7

At some time during the 24 hours before the operation the patient is asked to bathe thoroughly and the skin around the operation site is then shaved. For about six hours before, no food or drink is allowed since, at the start of the anesthetic, such food might be vomited and inhaled into the lungs. An hour or so before the operation a nurse gives the patient a "pre-med" injection, which makes him feel calm and relaxed and dries up chest secretions that might interfere with breathing under the anesthetic.

Eventually the patient is taken to the operating suite. Here the anesthetist gives him an injection into a vein; this produces complete unconsciousness in about ten seconds. The patient is now wheeled into the operating room and placed on the table. The anesthetist places a mask over his face and keeps him unconscious with a mixture of anesthetic gases and oxygen, often supplemented by injections.

The surgeon, his assistants, and the operating room nurse take up their positions. They clean the operation site carefully and place sterile towels around it. The surgeon then makes his incision and probes down to the organ or tissue he is looking for, while his assistants use small forceps to close off any bleeding points. The nurse may be backed by a team of more junior nurses and by technicians.

Most operations are over in about an hour. At the conclusion, the surgeon carefully stitches up the wound and applies a dressing. The patient is then taken to the recovery room where the anesthetist (or a nurse) looks after him until he awakens. From there he may go to the intensive care ward, but more usually he will be returned to his room, where he will be observed carefully for a few hours.

The recovery period

The patient will spend a few days in the hospital after surgery if the operation has been a minor one. Stitches are usually removed about a week after the operation. After discharge from the hospital the patient usually sees the surgeon at least once more before being left in the care of his own physician.

KEY

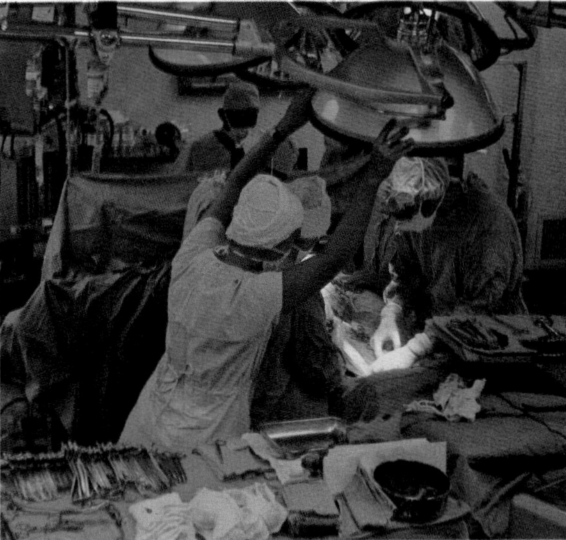

The major types of surgery include treatment of wounds, removal of diseased organs, reconstruction of injured tissue, correction or change of body function, and organ transplants.

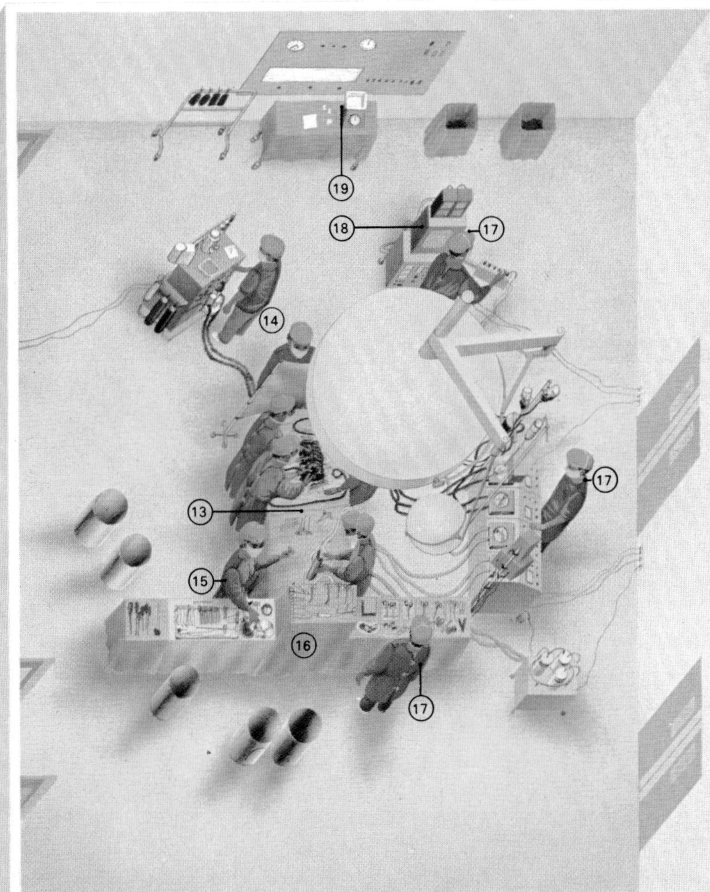

19
18
17
14
17
13
15
16
17

23
24
22

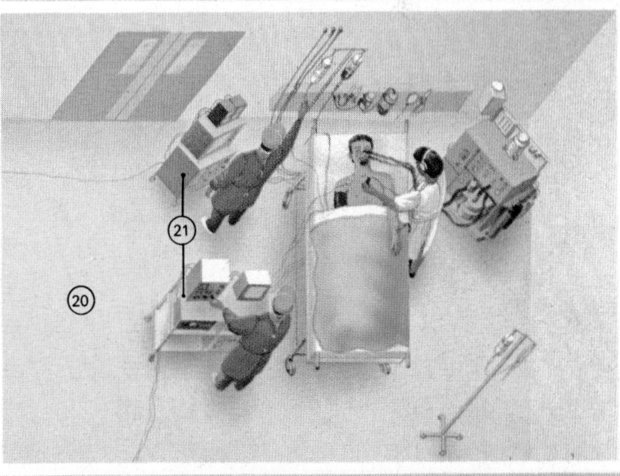

21
20

A blood-pressure cuff [10] and monitoring devices may be applied to his arm before he is finally wheeled [11] into the operating room. Meanwhile, the surgeon, assistant surgeons, nurses, and other staff have been scrubbing up [12]

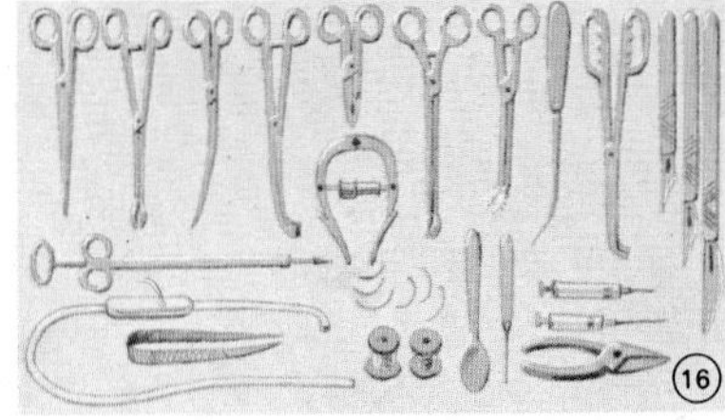

16

and dressing. With the patient on the table [13] they commence the operation while the anesthetist [14] monitors the patient's condition. The operating room nurse [15] passes instruments [16] to the surgeon while other technicians and nurses [17] adjust lights, check blood pressure and brain rhythms [18] and put swabs on a scale [19] to check blood loss. After the operation the patient may need to stay in an intensive care room [20] where machines

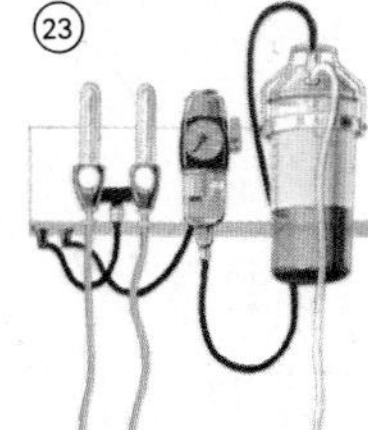

23

[21] monitor his vital functions. He should soon be able to move to a recovery room or a small observation ward [22], which is equipped with oxygen, suction equipment, and dripfeed [23]. Here the nurse [24] will keep an eye on him.

Dentistry

The 5,000-year-old history of dentistry reflects not only man's desire to preserve his teeth but also his attempts to avoid and relieve the agonies of toothache. Despite advances made over the centuries, most people still have dental problems—mainly tooth decay and gum disease.

Dental decay

The teeth become covered by a gelatinous bacteria and food-laden layer [2C] called dental plaque. Decay or caries begins with the breakdown of carbohydrate foodstuffs caught in the plaque by bacteria normally present in the mouth. The bacteria produce acids that dissolve away the protective layer of enamel overlaying the dentine of the teeth [1]. Once the enamel is penetrated, destruction of tooth tissue is rapid.

It is known that decay can be eradicated almost completely by the use of simple and effective preventive measures. These include fluoridation of water supplies, application of fluoride directly on the teeth, control of dental plaque by proper use of the toothbrush and dental floss, and diet.

The action of fluoride on teeth, in strengthening the enamel and increasing resistance to decay, was first recognized less than 40 years ago, although it has benefited people for centuries in places where water supply naturally contains fluoride. Since the 1930s, addition of fluoride to water supplies in selected areas at a level of one to two parts per million has significantly reduced the occurrence of dental decay.

The effectiveness and ease of administration of this form of fluoridation make it attractive, although other measures can be used. They include "painting" the teeth with strong fluoride solutions, adding fluoride to toothpastes and mouthwashes, and "fissure sealing" (a technique whereby susceptible parts of the tooth are sealed by the application of a plastic coating).

Preventive efforts must obviously be directed at children, for teeth, unlike other tissues in the body, cannot repair themselves once they have been damaged. When decay sets in, older established methods of dental treatment in the form of fillings, crowns, extractions, bridges, and dentures must be used. The repair work done by a dentist aims to remove all decay and to stop further destruction by reconstructing the tooth using a filling material—metal, plastic, or composites [4].

Where dental decay is so far advanced that little of the tooth remains, crowns may be required. This involves removing part of the tooth above the gum and building up a crown in porcelain, acrylic, or gold, or in some combination of these materials [5]. Porcelain or porcelain-fused-to-metal crowns may also be used to improve the appearance of front teeth.

More serious damage

While decay can continue for a while quite painlessly, it will eventually cause toothache, which becomes acute once the decay penetrates the nervous and vascular tissue (called the pulp) in the center of the tooth. By this stage an ordinary filling may not be enough to save the tooth, for unless the bacterial contamination of the pulp can be eradicated, an abscess will develop around the root of the tooth, which may have to be

CONNECTIONS

See also

682 Skull, skeleton, and joints
694 The digestive system

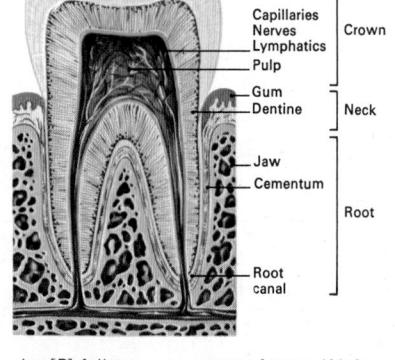

1 The three main parts of a tooth are the crown, the neck, and the root. The crown, capped by enamel, projects out of the gum. The root is held in the bone of the jaw by a ligament embedded in cementum. The delicate pulp contains nerves and blood vessels that connect with the bloodstream and main nerve paths via the root canal. The root and crown underlying the enamel are formed from porous dentine.

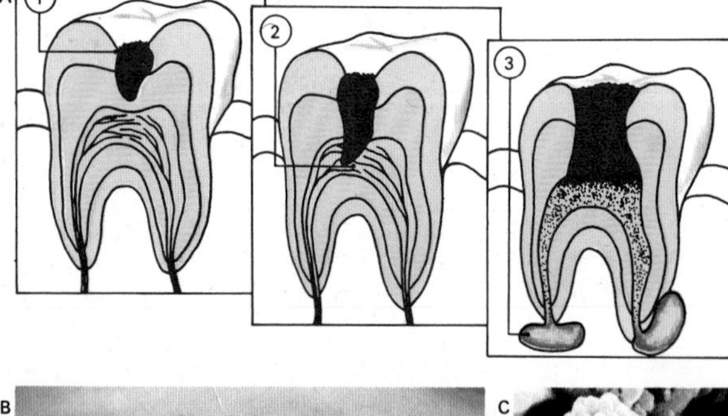

2 Tooth decay (caries) occurs because sugar and other carbohydrates caught in dental plaque (a white film that sticks to the teeth) [C], are turned into strong acid by the fermenting action of bacteria in the mouth. Under the layer of plaque the acid destroys the tooth, first dissolving away the enamel and then eating into the softer dentine, leaving dark, disfiguring stains [B]. Decay [A] starts by attacking the crown [1]. If untreated, it progresses down until it affects the pulp [2]. Once in the pulp, the bacteria begin spreading down the root canal, and an abscess develops around the root, causing pain and swelling [3].

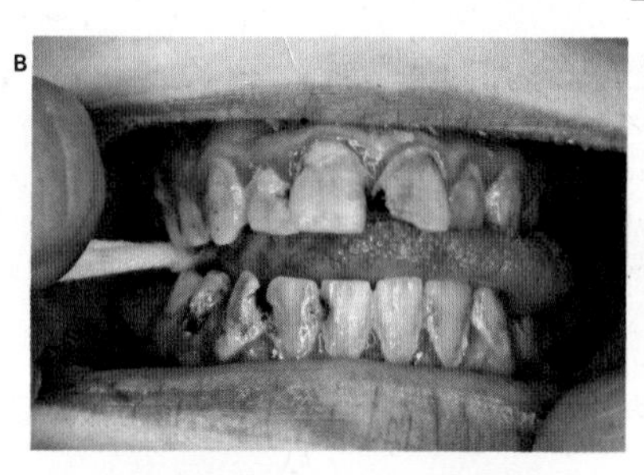

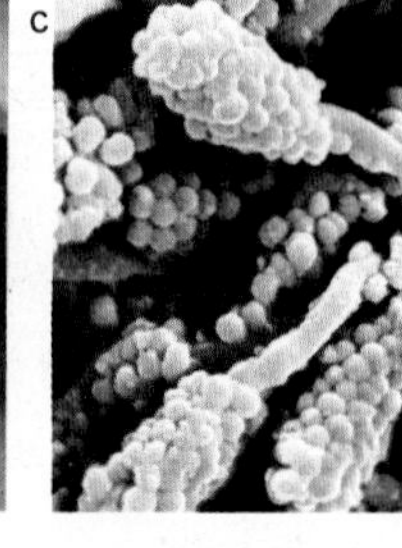

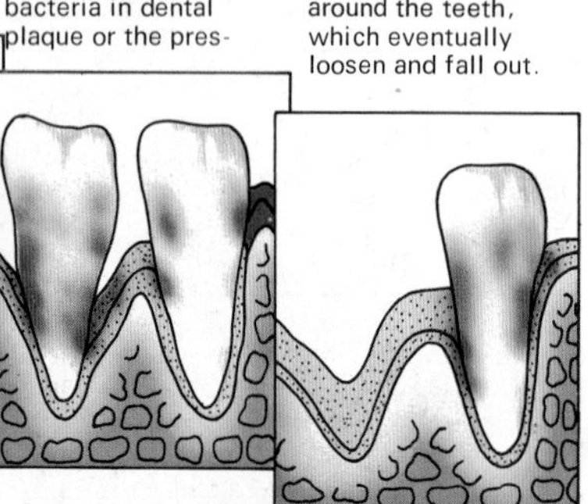

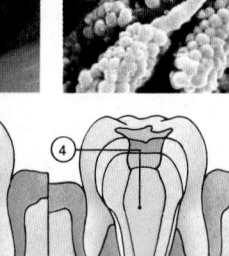

3 Gum disorders are dealt with by periodontists. Gum recession [B] follows infection and inflammation caused by the bacteria in dental plaque or the presence of tartar. If left untreated, this leads to loss of bone [A] around the teeth, which eventually loosen and fall out.

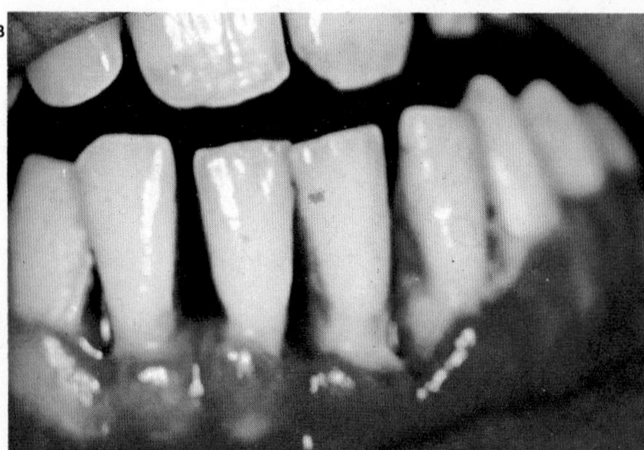

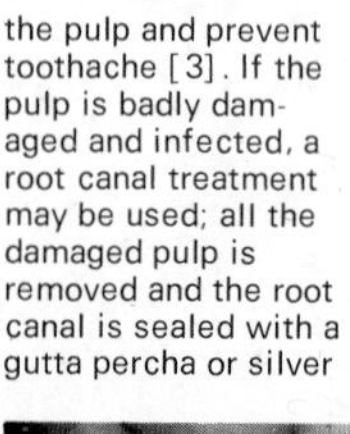

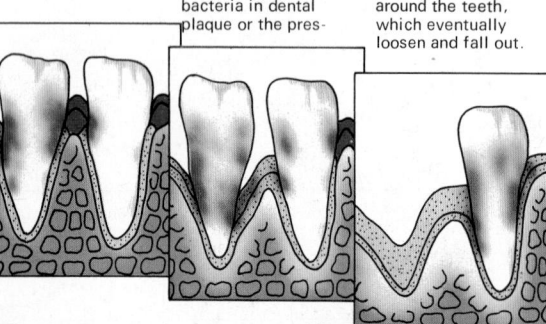

4 To repair decayed teeth, a dentist may use several different types of filling [A]. In the most common procedure, the affected part is cut away [1] and the cavity sealed, usually with a metal filling such as silver amalgam in a back tooth or a white plastic filling in a front tooth [2]. When decay has spread very close to or into the pulp a special sedative lining is placed under the filling to protect the pulp and prevent toothache [3]. If the pulp is badly damaged and infected, a root canal treatment may be used; all the damaged pulp is removed and the root canal is sealed with a gutta percha or silver point [4]. The effectiveness of good dentistry is shown by a case before [B] and after [C] treatment. Decay and a broken down incisor were repaired using silicate fillings and a crown on the incisor.

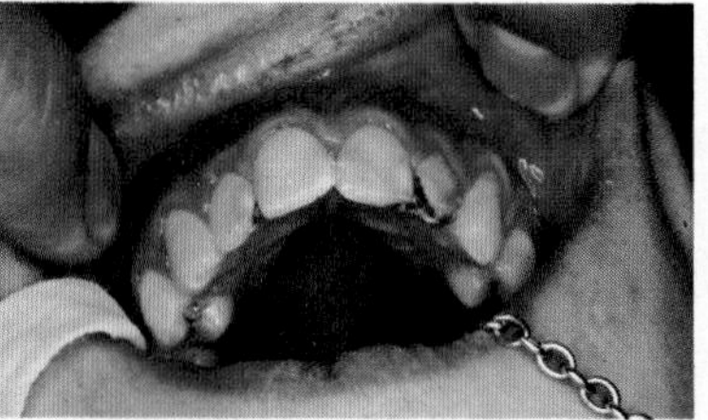

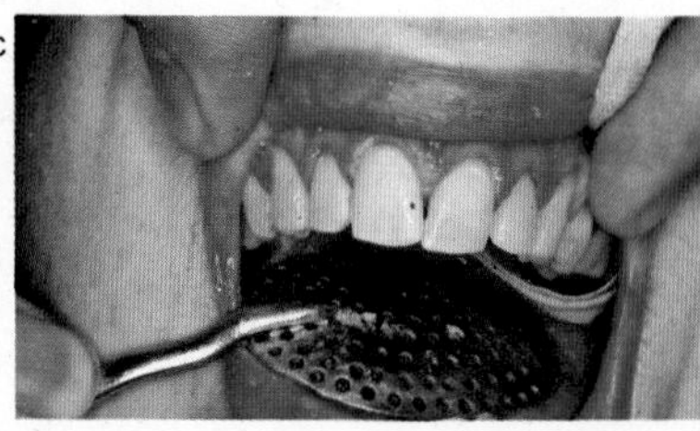

removed. Teeth with inflamed pulps or abscesses can sometimes be saved by a technique known as root canal therapy (endodontia), in which the entire contents of the root canal are removed and replaced by filling material.

As a last resort, a tooth can be extracted under an anesthetic, either local or general. (Where there is an abscess a general anesthetic is sometimes used.) The tooth is firmly gripped by a pair of specially designed forceps and moved in such a way that the surrounding bone yields gently and the tooth can be pulled out. When wisdom teeth remain unerupted, or a tooth is badly broken and decayed, extractions involve cutting back the gums and removing some of the jawbone surrounding the tooth. Such surgical extractions are usually carried out under general anesthetic.

When a tooth has been lost it is important that it be replaced, not only for appearance and to make chewing easier, but also because once a gap exists in the mouth other teeth may have impaired function because teeth tend to migrate into a gap, which causes bite and gum problems. Such gaps can be filled with dentures [6] or bridges [7].

As with dental decay, periodontal or gum disease can usually be prevented by conscientious oral hygiene; however, even when gum disease is established, with loosening of the teeth and gum recession, effective treatment is available. The gums are cut back, the damaged tissue removed [3], and the patient told how to prevent recurrence through oral hygiene.

Specialized forms of dentistry

One of the specialized branches of dentistry is orthodontics, which involves the realignment of tooth positions. Braces may be used to align many teeth in a mouth or may align only a few teeth [8]. Such treatment is most effective in childhood. Orthodontic services are sometimes utilized in the fields of oral and maxillofacial surgery, being used, for example, to treat cleft palates [9]. Repairing fractures to the jaws and facial bones, correcting facial deformities, and treating tumors within the mouth also require special dental skills.

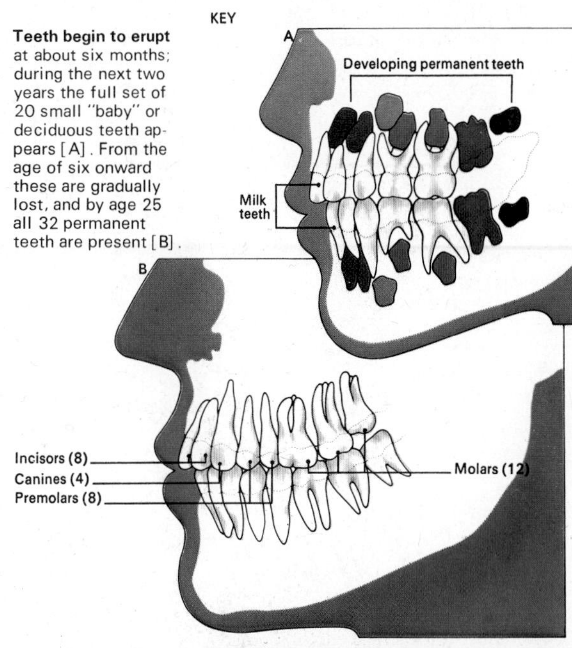
KEY
A
Developing permanent teeth
Milk teeth
B
Incisors (8)
Canines (4)
Premolars (8)
Molars (12)

Teeth begin to erupt at about six months; during the next two years the full set of 20 small "baby" or deciduous teeth appears [A]. From the age of six onward these are gradually lost, and by age 25 all 32 permanent teeth are present [B].

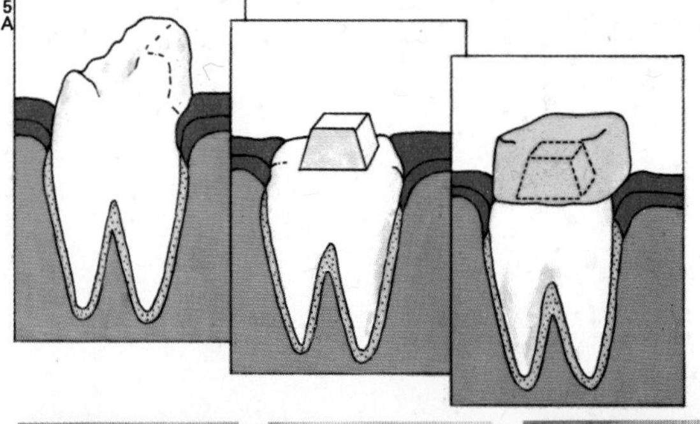
5A

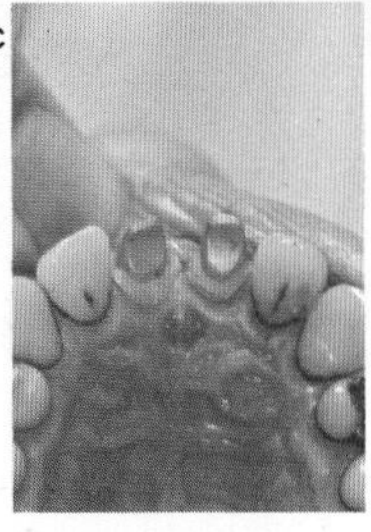
B

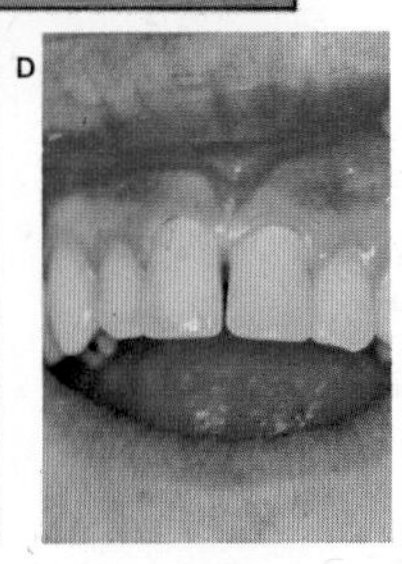
C
D

5 Crowns—gold, porcelain, acrylic, or combinations—are used to repair badly damaged teeth. Where decay has made an ordinary filling impossible [A], the tooth is cut down to a peg, and the dentist takes an impression so that an accurately fitting crown can be made. This is then cemented on to the remaining tooth stump. Even where a tooth has broken off at gum level [B], it can still be restored by first fitting a gold post into the root of the tooth [C] and then using this as a support for the crown [D]. Crowns are also used for cosmetic purposes to replace unsightly discolored or misshapen front teeth.

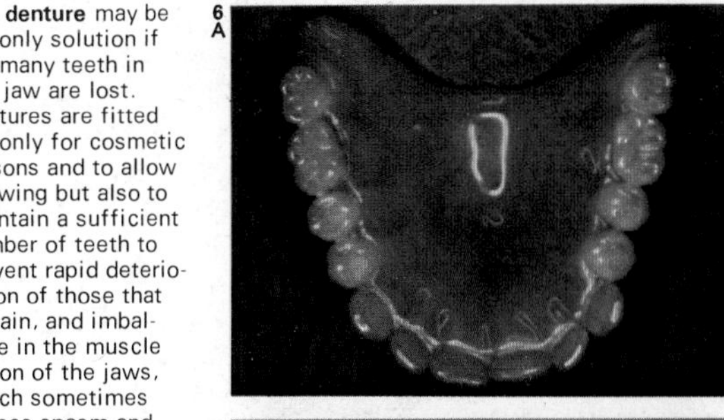
6A

B

6 A denture may be the only solution if too many teeth in one jaw are lost. Dentures are fitted not only for cosmetic reasons and to allow chewing but also to maintain a sufficient number of teeth to prevent rapid deterioration of those that remain, and imbalance in the muscle action of the jaws, which sometimes causes spasm and pain. The making of an accurately fitting denture is a skilled job. An impression is taken of the mouth and a model made to serve as a mold for casting the denture. The extent of a denture varies, as do the materials used to make it. Plastic [A] and metals such as gold or chrome cobalt [B] are common.

7 A missing tooth can be replaced by a bridge construction [A]. The teeth on either side of the gap are cut down to a peg shape so that gold crowns can be fitted over them. A unit of three crowns, one of which replaces the missing tooth, is then cemented into position. If necessary, a bridge can also be made using two teeth on the same side of the gap [B]. One of the teeth used to hold the bridge was badly decayed [C] and needed root canal therapy and the fitting of a gold post [D] before the bridging crowns could be made and fitted [E].

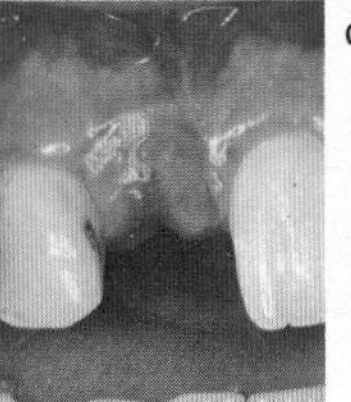
B

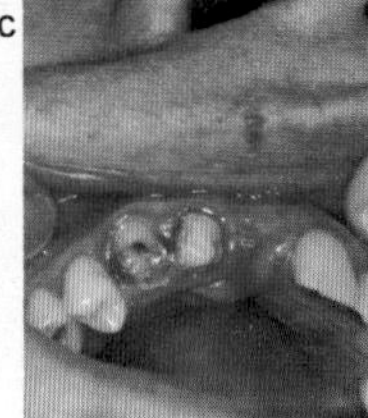
C

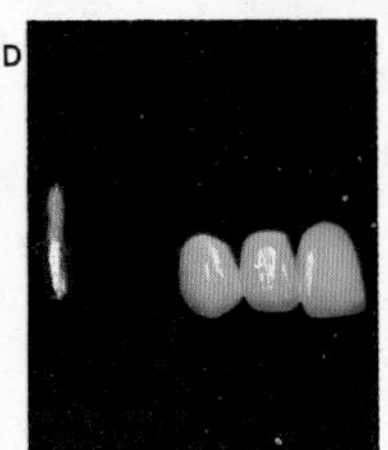
D

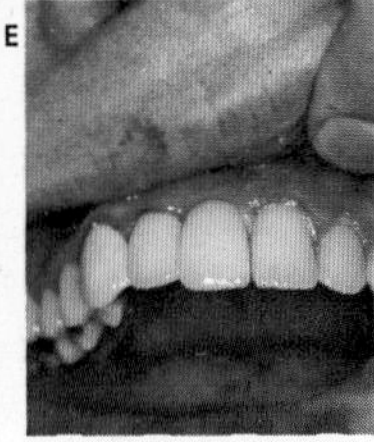
E

8 Orthodontic braces are used to realign misplaced teeth such as protruding upper incisors. A plate clips into the mouth, and stainless steel springs are used to move the teeth gently into line.

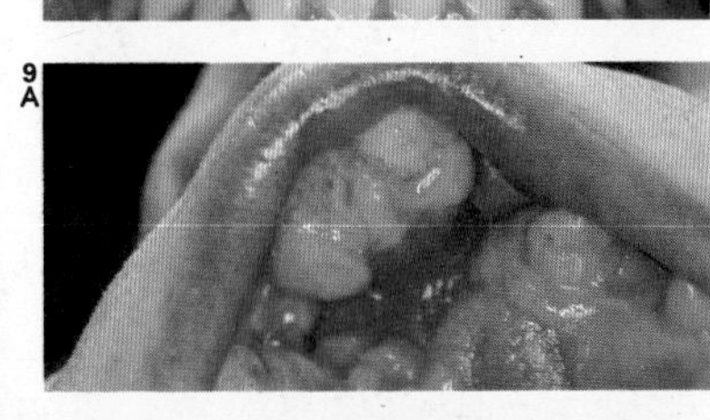
9A

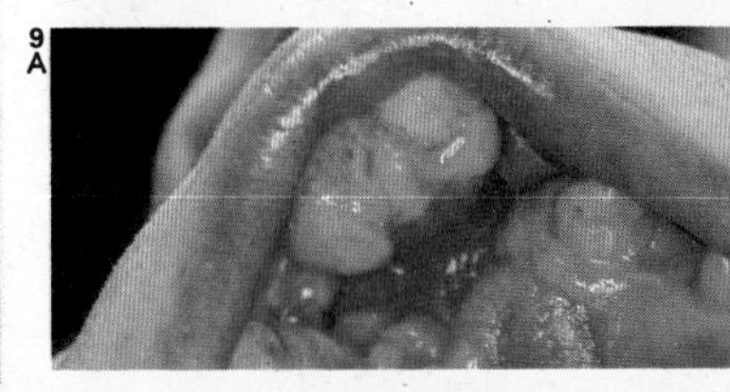

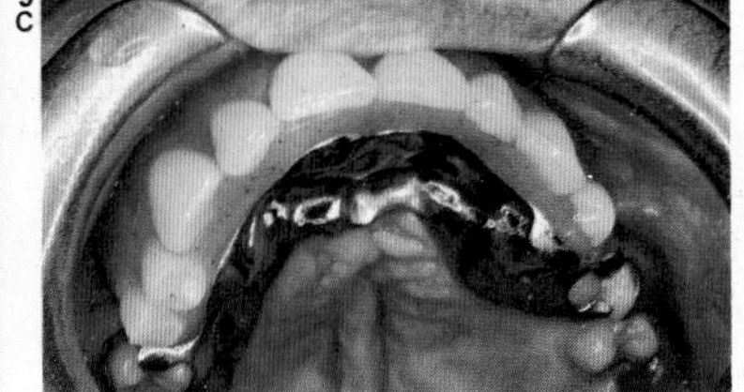
9C

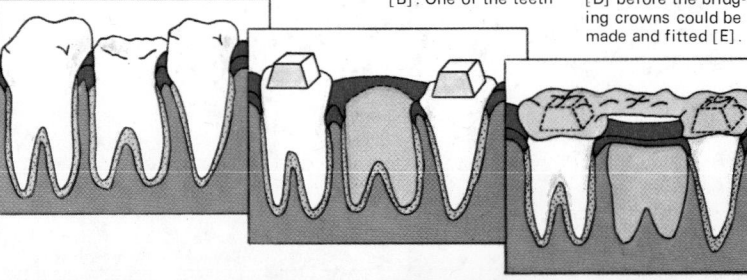

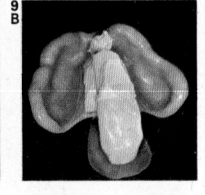

9 A partial cleft palate [A] can be treated by crowning the teeth and clipping a special gold denture [C] to them, which seals the gap. A full cleft palate needs a larger denture [B] with a rubber extension to seal the cleft.

First aid

First aid is emergency attention given after an accident or sudden illness by someone with or without medical, nursing, or other qualifications or experience. Lives are often saved by completely untrained people who simply keep their heads in an emergency, but to give first aid efficiently and safely some form of training is desirable.

In many parts of the world training can be obtained through courses organized by voluntary organizations such as the Red Cross. These courses are well worth taking, especially because some of the techniques once thought of as good first-aid practices are now known to be useless or even dangerous and others are constantly being updated.

The principles of first aid

There are a number of important general principles of first aid that everyone should know because they might save another's life. The first and most important of these is succinctly expressed in the famous Latin phrase *Primum non nocere*—"First of all, do no harm." Inexperienced people may unknowingly act unwisely when faced with someone who is injured or suddenly taken ill. They may attempt to pour drinks into the mouth of the casualty, even an unconscious one, which is a good way to choke him. Or they may try to sit him up or walk him around, when most people who are injured or ill need to be kept lying down. Before giving aid to the casualty knowledge is essential—it might be better not to disturb him at all. And without training heart massage, for example, can be fatal.

Next it is essential to keep calm and to give reassurance. Many people panic at the sight of an injured person and this has a bad effect upon the patient. Keep cool; have someone telephone for an ambulance, stay at the patient's side (unless there is no one else to go for help), and, most important, reassure him that help is on the way.

Ensure breathing; stop bleeding

As far as positive action is concerned, it is vital to keep the air passage open. Many unconscious people die because the passage leading from the nose and mouth to the lungs is blocked by blood or vomit, by loose or false teeth, or by the tongue falling back into the throat. Deaths from blockage can almost always be prevented if someone is there to take action.

When dealing with an unconscious patient prompt action is essential. Tight clothing around the neck should be loosened and any material blocking the air passage should be removed, including dentures. The victim should be turned into the recovery position [1]. In this the face is turned slightly down (to let any fluid flow out) and the head is bent back to ensure that the tongue does not fall back and choke him, which is a real risk if the patient is lying on his back. If his breathing continues to be noisy this is an indication that there is still some obstruction that must be removed.

Any heavy bleeding or hemorrhage must be stopped. If a large artery is spurting or if a major vein is pouring blood any person, but particularly a child, can bleed to death in a few minutes. A tourniquet (a tight bandage above the injury) should not be applied. Equally, one should not attempt to

CONNECTIONS

See also

710 The causes of illness: 1

712 The causes of illness: 2

720 Diseases of the skeleton and muscles

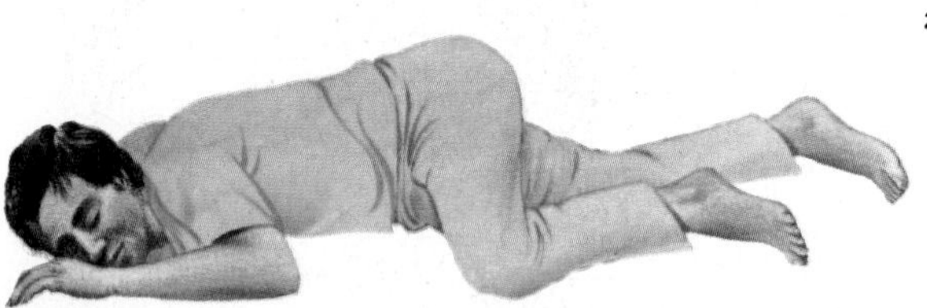

1 Unconscious patients should be placed in this recovery position to avoid danger from choking. The hidden arm is behind the patient to prevent him from rolling over onto his back.

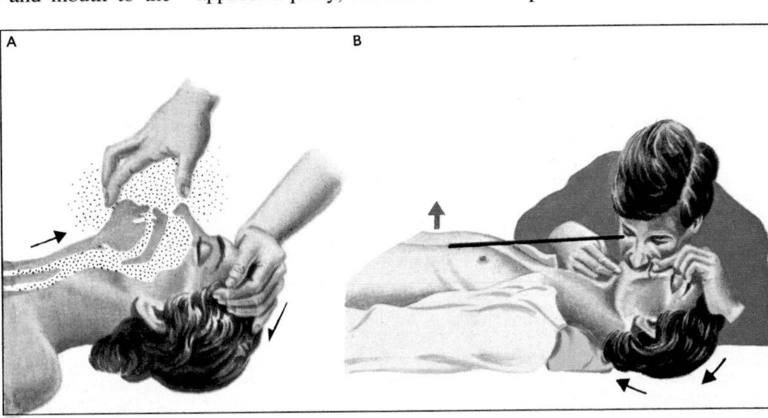

2 The most common method of giving artificial respiration is the mouth-to-mouth system. The mouth and throat are cleared of obstructions [A] and the patient's head is tilted back. The one giving aid holds the nose shut and blows into the mouth [B] until the patient's chest rises, waits for the air to be expelled, then blows again. The rate is 12 breaths per minute for adults, 20 for children.

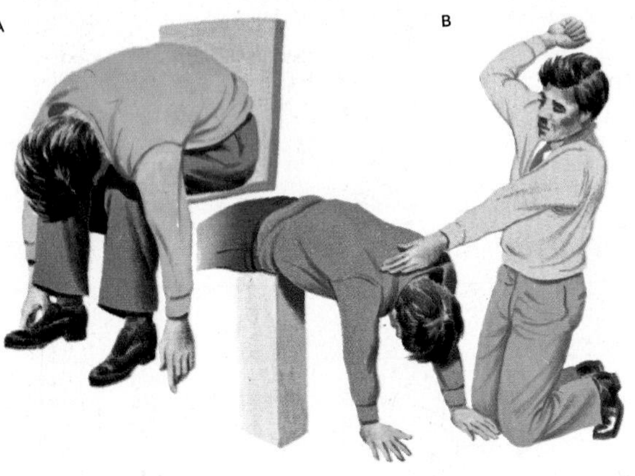

3 Fainting is caused by a failure of the blood supply to the brain. The victim should lie down or sit on a chair [A], head down, then straighten up after a few minutes. Loosen tight clothing around neck, chest, and waist. Lean a choking adult [B] over a table and slap him hard between the shoulder blades. Do not use fingers to remove an object. A child may be held upside down and slapped on the back.

4 The control of a hemorrhage is an important part of first aid. Most nosebleeds can, for example, be controlled by getting the patient to sit up and squeeze the soft part of his nose between finger and thumb for 15 to 20 minutes without interruption [A]. Bleeding from the palm can be effectively controlled by firm and continuous pressure on the place that is bleeding by squeezing a clean pad or handkerchief tightly in the fist [B].

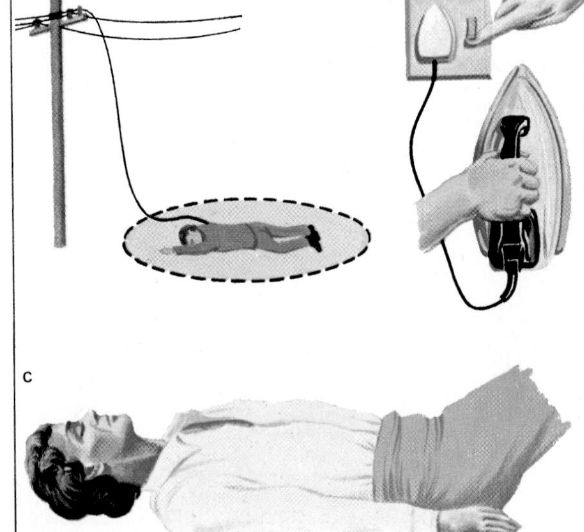

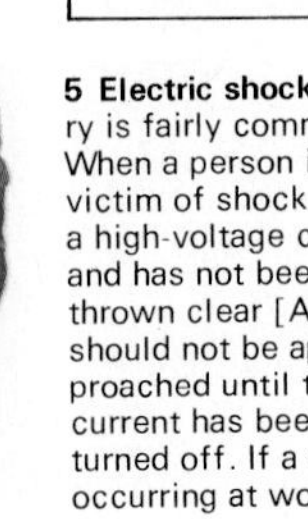

5 Electric shock injury is fairly common. When a person is the victim of shock from a high-voltage cable and has not been thrown clear [A], he should not be approached until the current has been turned off. If a shock occurring at work or home [B] renders a person unconscious, electrical contact must be broken before assistance is given, either by switching off the appliance or pushing the victim away with a dry piece of wood. The next thing is to see if the casualty is breathing, and if not, to give him mouth-to-mouth resuscitation. A badly shocked but conscious person should be laid on his back with legs raised [C] but if unconscious he should be put in the recovery position.

control bleeding by pressing on "pressure points" at some other site. Although nearly everyone seems to have heard of pressure points they are very seldom used in modern first-aid practice. The way to stop bleeding is to press firmly—and keep pressing for at least ten minutes—at the place where the blood is coming out [4]. Ideally, it is best to place a sterile pad on the bleeding site, but in an emergency a clean handkerchief will do. When a person's life is at stake, use the fingers if nothing else is available.

Shock and its treatment

People who have been injured or who may have lost a lot of blood, or those who have had heart attacks, may be in shock. The signs are faintness, giddiness, paleness, clamminess of the skin, shallow, rapid breathing, and a fast but weak pulse.

Shock can prove fatal and it is essential to act to prevent it from developing. Shock is treated or prevented by keeping the patient lying down, preferably with his legs higher than his head (if possible, the lower part of his body should be raised on a rolled-up jacket or similar available object). The patient is then made as comfortable as possible (loosening any tight clothing) and given reassurance, for fright increases shock. Nothing should be given by mouth as fluid swallowed may be vomited and, in an injured or unconscious person, may then flow back into the windpipe. Nor should the patient be heated with hot water bottles and heavy blankets, as overheating dilates blood vessels of the skin, drawing blood away from the internal organs that need this blood in an emergency. These traditional first-aid practices are potentially dangerous to the patient.

No attempt should be made to move a badly injured person unless there is skilled help at hand. Trying to carry someone with broken bones is dangerous unless one is trained and experienced. It is a rule of particular importance where spinal injuries are concerned and these may be present, even if not obvious, in many cases of accident. It is far better to leave the injured person motionless and to wait for an ambulance or other professional help.

KEY

6 A

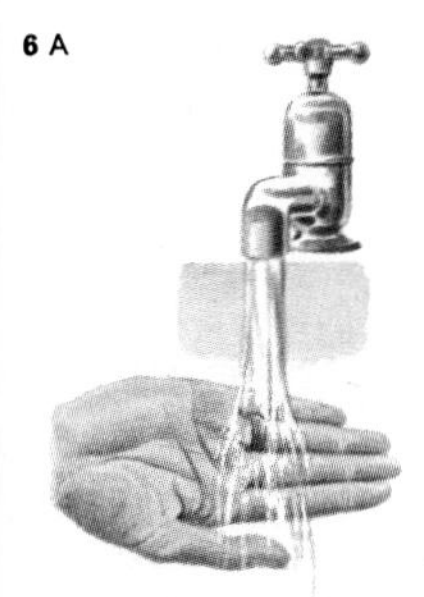

B

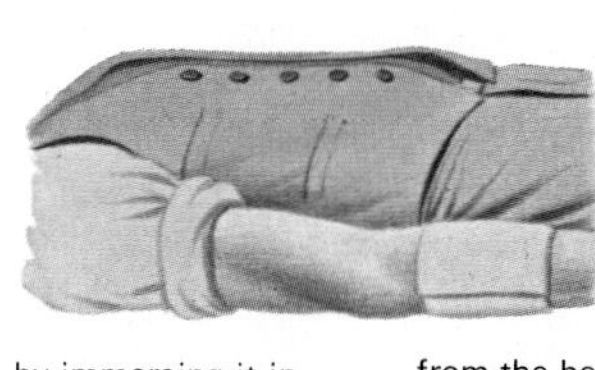

C

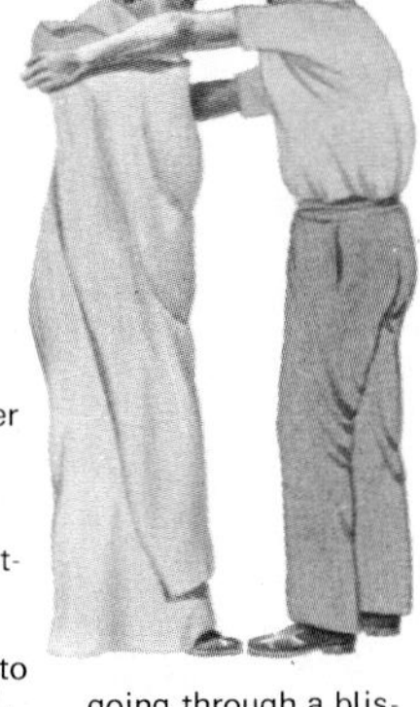

6 Burns caused by dry heat and scalds caused by moist heat are treated similarly. The object is to cool the skin down as fast as possible. Skin damage often occurs after help has arrived because tissues are still very hot. In the case, therefore, of a burn or scald, smoldering or saturated clothes should be ripped or cut off at once; seconds are vital. The affected part should be cooled by immersing it in cold water [A] for at least ten minutes and the casualty asked to lie down [B], if shocked, with his legs raised. No creams or ointments should be used. All that is necessary is to cover the damaged area with a clean dressing such as a sheet. If the rescuer finds the victim with his clothes still on fire, he should at once try to smother the flames with a rug or blanket [C] but if this is impractical, pull him to the ground (which helps to keep flames away from the head) and cover the flames with coats, rugs, etc. He should never be rolled over and over. The extent of burns [D] is measured in the percentage chart [1]. If in doubt burns should always be referred to a doctor or hospital. If large areas are damaged (more than 15 percent in adults and 10 percent in children) it is necessary to treat the patient for fluid loss. A superficial burn [2] rapidly returns to normal, while a slightly deeper one [3] heals after first going through a blistering stage. A deep burn [4] that goes through the epidermis and dermis is still capable of healing if a skin graft is stitched into place. The area from which the graft was taken (hips, buttocks, etc) [5] will soon return to normal.

6 D

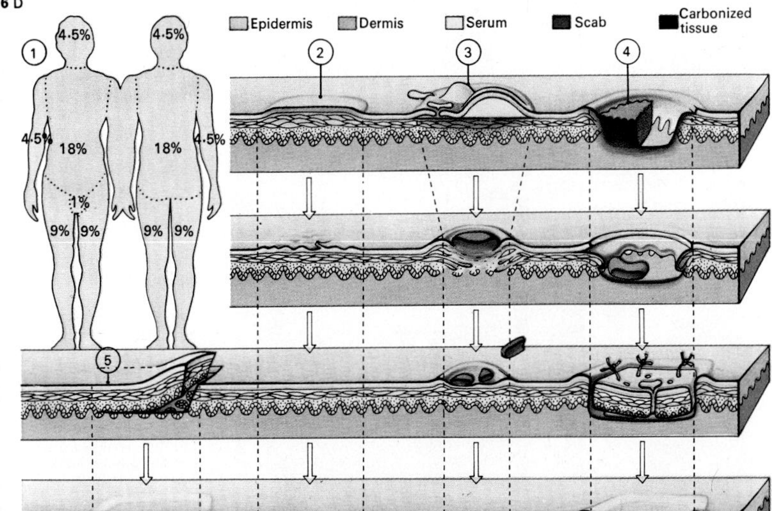
Epidermis
Dermis
Serum
Scab
Carbonized tissue
1
2
3
4
5
4.5%
4.5%
4.5%
18%
18%
4.5%
1%
9%
9%
9%
9%

7 A

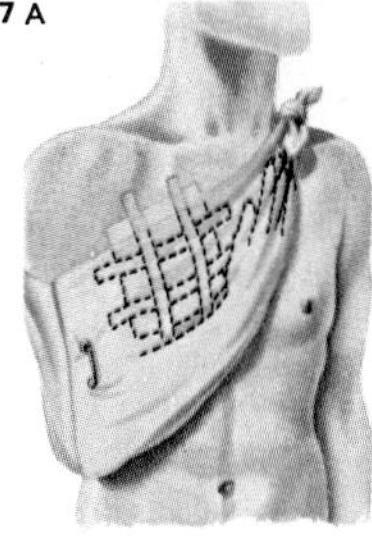

B

C

D

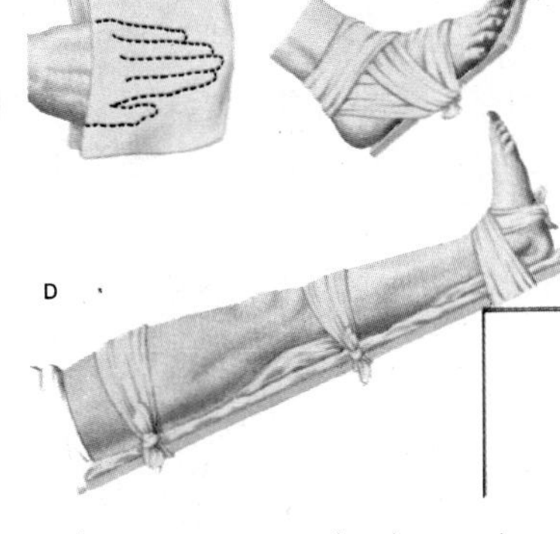

7 A patient with a fractured (broken) bone should not be moved before expert help arrives. Any bleeding should be stopped and wounds dressed to prevent germs reaching the bone ends. The break should be immobilized. This can be done by strapping or bandaging to a splint. For this a piece of wood or metal can be used or, more generally, the patient's own body. For an injured arm, shoulder, or rib [A], a temporary sling is used. A dressing, to protect a fractured finger [B], for instance, can be applied under the sling and held in place by strapping. Suspected fractures of the foot [C] and leg [D] can be splinted as shown. It is important that the bandages should be firm but not too tight and that they should not be put over the suspected fracture.

8 A

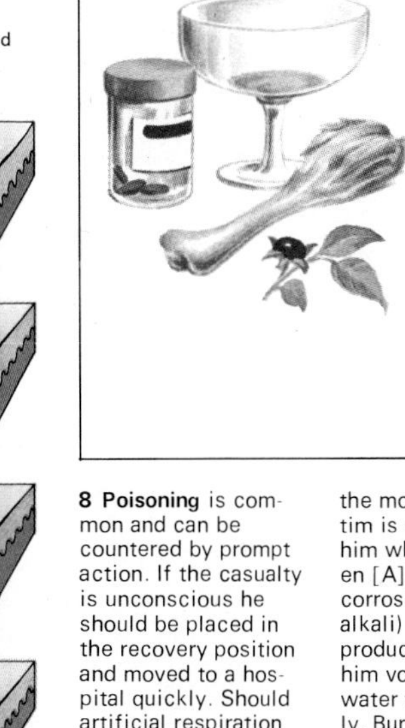

B

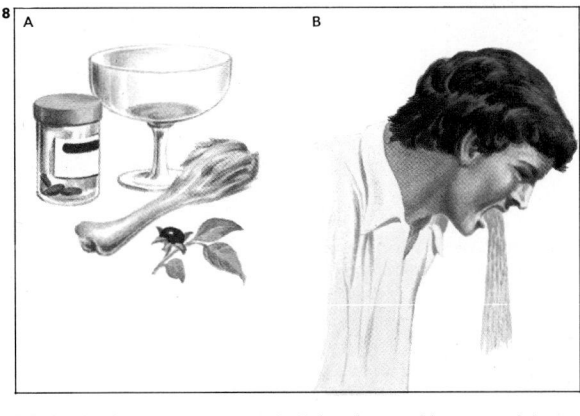

8 Poisoning is common and can be countered by prompt action. If the casualty is unconscious he should be placed in the recovery position and moved to a hospital quickly. Should artificial respiration be necessary beware of any poison around the mouth. If the victim is conscious ask him what he has taken [A]. If it is a corrosive (acid or alkali) or a petroleum product, do not make him vomit; give him water to drink slowly. Burned lips are a clue; they should be splashed liberally with water and the mouth washed. In cases that do not involve either corrosives or petroleum products, the correct action is to induce vomiting [B] by forcing two fingers down the throat after giving water to drink.

Introduction to mental health

Psychiatry, derived from two Greek words meaning "mind" and "medical treatment," is that branch of medicine devoted to the diagnosis, treatment, and prevention of mental illness. There is no clear dividing line between physical medicine and psychiatry. Psychiatry cannot ignore the relationship between bodily condition and mental state, and medicine is increasingly attentive to the way a person's emotional state can precipitate and aggravate physical ill health.

The causes of mental illness

There is never a simple or single cause for mental illness [2]. In practice, a distinction is made between predominantly intrinsic, or endogenous, causes, such as inherited factors, and predominantly extrinsic, or exogenous, causes, such as physical injury and disease, and mental stress such as bereavement, unexpected financial reverses, or the loss of a job. The interaction between a person's basic personality and any physical or emotional stress affects the extent of any subsequent mental reaction. One person may be able to cope with massive stress quite adequately, whereas another may be overwhelmed by a minor setback.

Disorders of the mind

The symptoms and signs of mental illness are grouped under a number of headings: disorders of perception; of thought and speech; of memory; of emotion; of the experience of the self; of consciousness; and motor disorders.

Hallucinations are sensory perceptions without any external, objective stimulus and are a common perceptual disturbance in psychotic illnesses and brain disorders. Symptoms of thought disorder include flights of ideas, in which the thought processes are speeded up; perseveration, whereby the patient "perseveres" with a particular response long after a change in his immediate environment has demanded a different response; and thought blocking, in which there is a sudden arrest of the train of thought and the start of an entirely new one.

In certain disorders (obsessional states for example), the patient recognizes that he is compelled to think about certain things despite his every effort to rid his mind of them. Such compulsion is understood by the patient to originate within him and not as a consequence of some alien activity. In thought alienation, however, the patient experiences his thoughts as being under the control of some external agency. He may believe that others are participating in his thinking or that thoughts are being inserted into or extracted from his head, or that others think his thoughts in unison with him and are aware of his contemplations.

A delusion is a false belief of morbid origin, which is an absolute conviction unamenable to reason or contradiction although usually absurd or impossible. Disorders in the form of thinking are characterized by a fragmentation of the links between successive thoughts and the phenomenon of over-inclusiveness, in which the patient is unable to maintain the boundaries of a concept.

Disorders of memory include disturbances in the registration of material to be remembered (such as by lack of concentration) and in the retention and recall of mate-

CONNECTIONS

See also
730 Alcoholism and drug abuse
762 How mental illness has been treated
764 Psychoses
766 Personality defects and neuroses
768 Psychosomatic diseases and retardation
770 Physical cures for mental illness
772 Behavior therapy
774 Psychotherapy

1 Compared with a "normal" person's view of a scene [A], the neurotically anxious person may feel threatened by his immediate surroundings [B]. Nevertheless, he will maintain contact with reality and be aware that his surroundings are in fact unaltered. The psychotic, however, may experience the same situation in a seriously distorted way [C], believing his impaired perception of external reality to be valid.

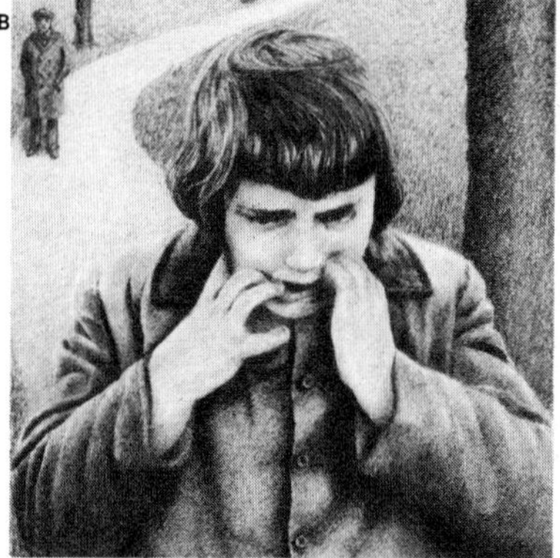

2 Mental health is influenced by widely different factors. Genetic makeup is important; identical twins [A] have a much higher chance of experiencing similar mental states than do normal siblings. Genetic factors are less significant in neuroses, in which emotional trauma, particularly in childhood [B], is more important. Sexual difficulties are traditionally linked with psychiatric disorders, particularly in adolescence [C]. Social isolation [D], to which immigrants and the elderly are vulnerable, causes depression. Some jobs have attendant psychiatric risks [E]: alcoholism in assembly line workers and seamen; depression in house wives and semi-skilled workers; psychosomatic complaints in doctors and businessmen. Some physical disorders, like hyperthyroidism [F], are associated with psychiatric symptoms and it is difficult to separate them from a purely mental condition.

rial. Where there is a pathological memory loss, the gap may be filled with elaborate fabrications, as in alcoholic psychosis.

Emotional disorders consist of variations in the intensity or duration of the emotional response, which may also be inappropriate to the particular situation. The term "affective disorder" refers to a sustained disorder of mood, such as depression or mania, rather than to a transient emotional reaction.

Depersonalization, a disturbance in the experience of the self, occurs when the individual feels himself changed in comparison with his former state. He feels like an automaton and watches his own actions "from outside." In derealization the person perceives the outer world as strange and altered in some significant way. Both these disturbances are experienced on occasion by perfectly healthy people.

Disorders of consciousness are mainly the result of physical causes and include alterations in attention and concentration, a slowing in thinking, and a lack of direction in thought and action. The patient may be disoriented, may manifest disconnected behavior, or may be delirious.

Motor disorders include lack of initiative, retardation in speech and action, and stupor. Major forms of motor disorder in mental illness are psychomotor activity, seen in manic states; catatonic excitement, characterized by stereotypy (monotonous repetition in speech, mannerisms, and movement); and passivity feelings (patients believe their impulses or feelings are controlled by an outside agency).

Major categories of mental illness

There are three major categories of mental illness. The psychoses [1] consist of schizophrenia, manic-depression, paranoid illnesses, the organic psychoses, and psychoses associated with physical disorders. The neuroses consist of anxiety and phobic states, obsessive-compulsive disorders, and hysterical and depressive neuroses. The personality disorders include alcoholism and drug dependence, childhood disorders, and personality anomalies that are not the result of an illness.

KEY

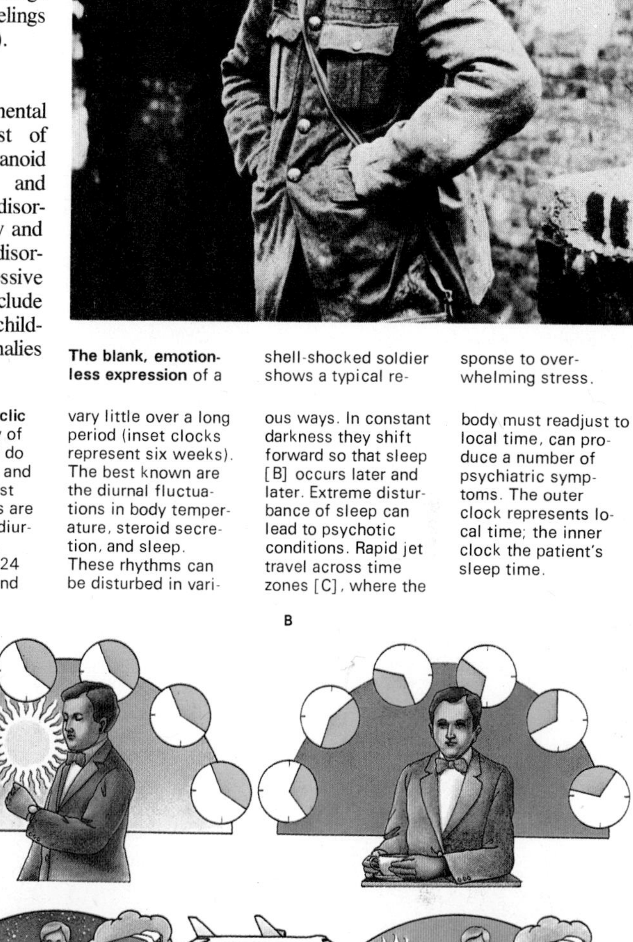

The blank, emotionless expression of a shell-shocked soldier shows a typical response to overwhelming stress.

3

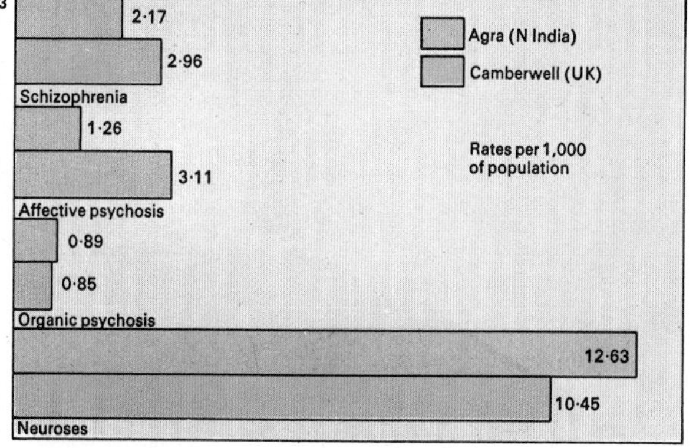

2·17
2·96
Schizophrenia
1·26
3·11
Affective psychosis
0·89
0·85
Organic psychosis
12·63
10·45
Neuroses
Agra (N India)
Camberwell (UK)
Rates per 1,000 of population

3 Variations in the prevalence rates of psychiatric illnesses between different countries may reflect genuine difference, but they may be the result of differing diagnostic practices among psychiatrists or of a marked variation in the availability of psychiatric care. For this reason it is difficult to assess whether one country is more likely to encourage a particular category of mental illness than another. There do, however, appear to be variations in types of neurotic illnesses. For instance, the commonest neurosis in Agra, India, is hysteria, whereas in Camberwell, England, it is depression.

4 Man shows cyclic variation in many of his functions, as do almost all plants and animals. The most prominent cycles are the circadian or diurnal rhythms [A], which are about 24 hours in length and vary little over a long period (inset clocks represent six weeks). The best known are the diurnal fluctuations in body temperature, steroid secretion, and sleep. These rhythms can be disturbed in various ways. In constant darkness they shift forward so that sleep [B] occurs later and later. Extreme disturbance of sleep can lead to psychotic conditions. Rapid jet travel across time zones [C], where the body must readjust to local time, can produce a number of psychiatric symptoms. The outer clock represents local time; the inner clock the patient's sleep time.

4A B C

5 A B

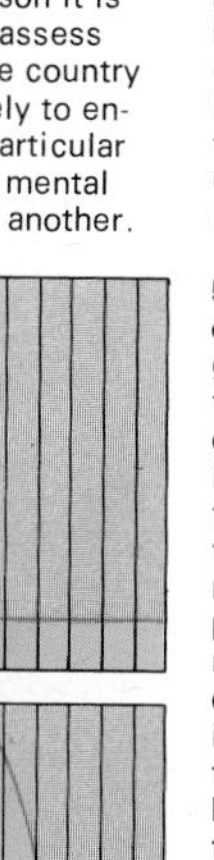

80
70
60
50
40
30
20
10

C

80
70
60
50
40
30
20
10

5 Responses to a set of questions may give indications of the presence and degree of psychiatric illness. The questionnaire is designed to elicit different responses from people with different mental illnesses or disorders of behavior. Questions relate to various areas of behavior or diagnostic categories, such as hysteria, phobia, or thought disorder. Answers are grouped into such categories and the score on each category registered on the graph. The result is a characteristic profile for different mental states. Those shown here are for a neurotic patient [A], a boy suffering from a behavior disorder [B], and a psychiatric patient [C].

How mental health has been treated

In ancient times an individual with a disturbed mind was assumed to be influenced by spirits, demons, gods, or other supernatural forces. As a result, healing practices were generally unsystematic and relied heavily on the power of suggestion.

Madness through history

The theory of the four humors, proposed by the Greek philosopher Hippocrates (*c*.460–377 BC) and the physician Galen (*c*. AD 130–*c*.200), introduced a degree of order and influenced medical thought for over 2,000 years. This theory postulated the existence of four key elements in the body (blood, phlegm, yellow bile, and black bile). Different diseases and different personality temperaments were believed to be associated with the predominance of one or other humor. An excess of black bile or dry phlegm, for example, was considered the cause of melancholia; this condition was treated with physical methods, such as vapors, baths, diet, and emetics.

Arab medicine continued the traditions inherited from Greek medicine, and between the eighth and thirteenth centuries a number of asylums for the insane were opened at Damascus, Cairo, and Baghdad. In Europe, with the spread of Christianity, care of the mentally afflicted was one of the duties of monasteries, other religious houses, and hospitals run by the clergy. The first hospital to be built exclusively for the insane is believed to have been opened at Valencia in Spain, in 1409.

Paradoxically, this greater care and compassion for the mad among the religious institutions coincided with a tendency among ordinary people to reject them, along with paupers, cripples, and other social outcasts. Added to this was medieval Europe's obsession with sorcery, heresy [3], witchcraft, and demonic possession. Many violent or dramatic outbursts of insanity were attributed to these "evil forces" and dealt with by torture, imprisonment, and often death. Yet the most popular treatise of the time, *De proprietatibus rerum,* written by an English Franciscan friar, distinguished between physical and psychological causes of mental illness and prescribed rest, sedation, and music therapy for the violently disturbed.

The seventeenth and eighteenth centuries witnessed a remarkable growth in the scientific basis of medicine and surgery. Theories about mental disturbances, however, lagged behind and the fashion to explain madness in terms of moral flaws, lack of impulse control, and the degeneration of personality flourished. Attempts were made, nonetheless, to explain how the mind worked in physiological and chemical terms, even if these did take unusual forms.

Theory and therapy

Franz Mesmer (1734–1815) blamed mental illness on the accumulation of a magnetic fluid in the body that could be removed by special magnetic powers possessed by certain therapists, such as himself. But "mesmerism" eventually was discredited.

Around this time, Franz Joseph Gall (1758–1828) claimed to have discovered 27 organs within the brain, each responsible for a particular mental function. The better these organs worked, the larger they were

CONNECTIONS

See also
760 Introduction to mental health
922 Changing patterns of punishment
764 Psychoses
766 Personality defects and neuroses
768 Psychosomatic diseases and retardation
770 Physical cures for mental illness
772 Behavior therapy
774 Psychotherapy

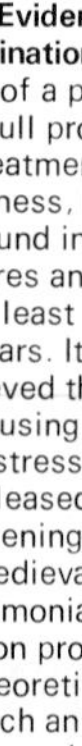

1 Evidence of trephination, the removal of a part of the skull probably as a treatment for mental illness, has been found in many cultures and dates back at least 10,000 years. It was believed that the spirit causing the mental distress might be released through the opening in the skull. Medieval theories of demoniacal possession provided another theoretical basis for such an approach to be readopted.

2 Pilgrimages to the shrines of special saints were made by the mentally ill during the late 12th century. One of the most famous shrines was that of St. John at Ghent. A complex ceremony of offerings, processions, penances, and prayers lasted nine days. This led to the founding, in 1191, of the first reception center for vagrants, paupers, and the insane, which was paid for by the citizens of the town.

3 Insanity has often been linked with magical practices, sorcery, and religious heresy. Girolamo Savonarola (1452–98), the Florentine religious and political reformer who was burned to death for heresy, was almost certainly mentally unstable. There were few medical authorities, however, who distinguished between insanity and heresy. The court physician of the Duke of Cleves, Johan Weyer (1515–88), was prominent among those who insisted that the witches were elderly women who were psychotic rather than evil or possessed, but neither the church nor legal experts agreed. It was not until the latter half of the 17th century that the general persecution of witches ceased.

4 Benjamin Rush (1745–1813) is generally regarded as the father of American psychiatry. A controversial figure, he was a vigorous advocate of blood letting and the use of mechanical devices in the treatment of mental illness. He is better remembered for his progressive views on the need to combine psychological and physiological approaches in the study and treatment of individual patients.

5 Philippe Pinel (1745–1826), on May 24, 1798, with the consent of the Legislative Assembly, removed the chains from 49 insane patients at the Bicetre Hospital in Paris, ushering in a new type of treatment.

6 William Tuke (1732–1822), an English wholesaler of tea and coffee and a philanthropist, founded with his son Henry (1755–1814) the York Retreat (opened 1796). This became an influential institution for the humane care of the insane.

and the more they affected the overall shape of the skull. Phrenology, the art of judging character and mental stability, by the shape and features of the skull, became widely popular until it, too, fell into disrepute around the mid-nineteenth century.

Meanwhile, the era of confining the insane had dawned and large mental hospitals and private madhouses multiplied. Conditions in these institutions were often appalling and treatments relied on physical methods [Key, 7].

A number of progressive pioneers removed the chains, and methods of treatment based on kindness, understanding, limited freedom, and work began to supplant those elaborate mechanical restraints previously in vogue. At the same time, two contrasting trends, both present in amorphous forms for several centuries before, began to crystallize. The first, initiated mainly by German diagnosticians, led to the gradual introduction of an orderly system of classifying mental disease. The second involved the discovery, and subsequently the study, of the unconscious.

Toward modern psychiatry

The French psychologist Pierre Janet (1859–1947) described a hierarchy of mental functions at the bottom of which he placed automatic functioning, such as in catatonic stupors, and at the top, rational, experienced, and conscious activity. Janet's theories, together with the elaborate demonstrations of hypnosis by Jean Charcot (1825–1893) at the Salpêtrière in Paris and the remnants of the theories of mesmerism, magnetism, and phrenology provided the background to the theories of the unconscious of Sigmund Freud (1856–1939).

The twentieth century has witnessed the development and popularization of psychoanalytical theory, particularly in the United States. At the same time, the discovery of the therapeutic efficacy of electrical treatment in severe depressive illnesses, the development of powerful anti-psychotic drugs, such as chlorpromazine, and the slow unraveling of genetic aspects of some forms of mental illness illustrate the progress made in comprehending the biological contribution in psychiatry.

KEY

Bedlam, the popular name for the Bethlehem Royal Hospital, became infamous for its poor treatment of the insane. Public torture was common and a penny tour through the crowded cells was a fashionable pastime in 18th-century London.

7

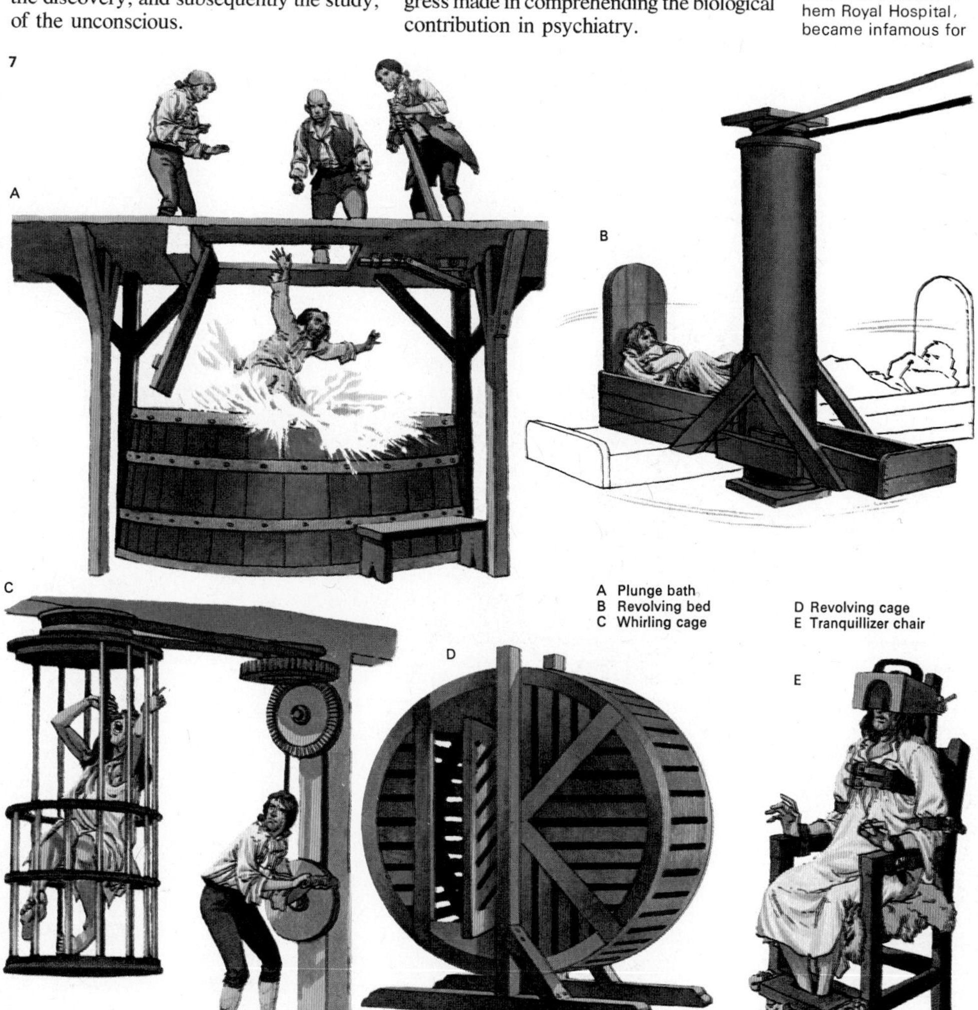
A
B
C
D
E

A Plunge bath
B Revolving bed
C Whirling cage
D Revolving cage
E Tranquillizer chair

7 Elaborate mechanical contrivances superseded, in the 19th century, the physical methods used in earlier periods – the purges, emetics, and bleedings. With the simple intention of subduing violent and manic patients, the most extraordinary contraptions were devised. Leather straps, canvas jackets, muffs, and handcuffs replaced the chains. Patients were fastened in wooden chairs in such a way that only minimum movement could occur. The induction of sudden and intense fear was believed to have a beneficial effect in mental illness with the result that physicians employed whirling chairs, spinning beds, and padded hollow wheels into which patients were strapped and which rotated at speeds of up to 100 revolutions per minute. Such rotation produced vomiting, incontinence, loss of consciousness, and, in a number of cases, death. Another cruel device was the plunge bath. The unsuspecting patient was invited to cross a treacherous floor which gave way, plunging him into a bath of ice-cold water. Benjamin Rush, in America, tried to call attention to the need for therapy and the employment of suitable companions to listen sympathetically to patients.

8 A

8 General paralysis of the insane is a dreaded complication of syphilis appearing some 10 to 25 years after the primary infection. The condition is characterized by severe personality changes, social uncontrollability, impulsiveness, grandiosity, and serious mental deterioration. During the latter half of the last century, before the organic cause had been discovered, physicians looked for psychological causes. The Japanese microbiologist Hideyo Noguchi (1876–1928) [A] put to rest imaginative speculations when, in 1911, he discovered at post-mortem the syphilitic spirochete in the shrunken atrophied brains [B] of patients dying from general paralysis of the insane. His discovery led to a resurgence of hope that similar distinct and treatable causes might be found for other mysterious psychiatric disorders.

8 B

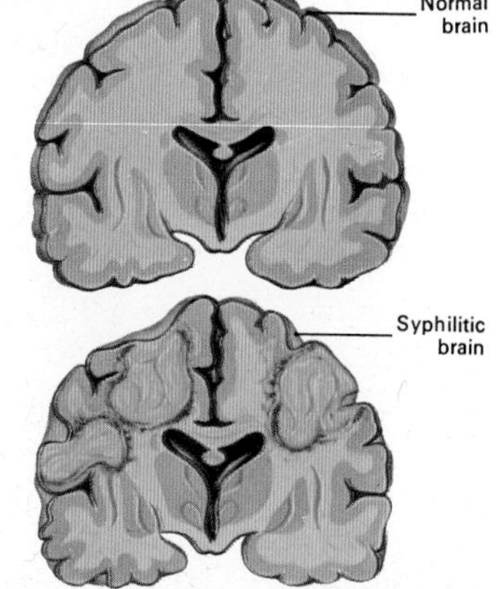
Normal brain
Syphilitic brain

Psychoses

A psychosis is a behavioral disorder typified by a fundamental break with reality and a tortured internal experience [Key]. The major psychosis is schizophrenia. The term psychosis refers to the severe mental disturbances in which there is a detachment from the external world and a disintegration of the internal one.

Schizophrenia

Schizophrenia usually, although not invariably, first occurs at puberty. The most common symptoms include incoherent thinking, lack of emotional response, delusions, and hallucinations [1]. Thought processes are jumbled and the resultant speech is often incomprehensible and illogical. The schizophrenic may receive moving news without any sign of emotional response. He may smile or appear indifferent when told of some personal tragedy or when confronted by a somber scene. Delusions are often bizarre and occur with a strength of conviction that renders them beyond reasonable argument. A schizophrenic in a bar, on being offered a drink by the bartender, might conclude that this was a signal to the other customers that he was a murderer.

The cause of the condition is obscure. The role of genetics, in the light of recent studies of twins, is undoubtedly important, but it is clear that, although necessary, genetic factors may not be sufficient for the illness to appear. Certain emotional stresses, such as family disharmony, physical precipitants such as infection or childbirth, and a number of drugs including amphetamines and LSD, may trigger the illness in predisposed people.

Schizophrenia may be subclassified as paranoid (the patient has delusions of persecution and is mistrustful of everyone); simple (he is apathetic, withdrawn, and uncommunicative); hebephrenic (the patient exhibits silliness and bizarre behavior); and catatonic (he may sit for hours in one position with muscles rigid, unable to feed or look after himself, seemingly unaware of anything around him). Schizophrenia commonly shows as a mixture of these types. Treatment includes drugs (phenothiazines), social rehabilitation, and psychotherapy. The illness usually has serious consequences, and although some patients do recover, permanent damage is the more common outcome.

Paranoia and manic-depression

Paranoia is a term used by some psychiatrists to refer to the mental disorder that occurs when someone has a permanent and unshakable system of delusions and, at the same time, complete clarity and order in thought, action, and will in all other areas. The condition is rare—many cases that begin as paranoia end up showing the characteristic widespread intellectual and emotional deterioration of schizophrenia. Paranoid illnesses occur in some solitary and shy individuals who project their own doubts and insecurities onto others; in a number of deaf people, who may misinterpret comments they do not hear clearly as insulting; and in the morbidly jealous.

The other serious psychosis is called manic-depression. As implied, there are two forms: mania, characterized by excitement, euphoria, grandiose schemes, rapid

CONNECTIONS

See also

760 Introduction to ment
health
770 Physical cures for mental illness
746 Man-made cures
792 Adolescence: sex an
independence
916 Changing patterns c
crime
428 Mushrooms and toadstools

1A
B
C
D

1 Schizophrenia is characterized by disjointed and episodic thought [A] and inappropriate emotional responses [B]. There is a tendency to delusion with the reading of innocent gestures as malicious signals [C]. Hallucinations and illusions occur as when a peaceful country scene seems oppressive or terrifying [D].

flights of ideas, and overactivity; and depression [2]. Patients may suffer from one type or from both.

Psychotic illnesses often occur in association with organic diseases. Many different poisons and various kinds of brain damage may affect the mental state. Psychotic symptoms commonly occur in delirium associated with fever, drug intoxications, and other causes of brain disturbance. Patients in severe delirious states have illusions and hallucinations of the senses, especially vision. Dislocations of their sense of time and space also help to differentiate the organic psychoses from the so-called functional psychoses, schizophrenia and manic-depression.

Brain diseases and psychosis

The most serious brain disorder often appearing with psychotic features is dementia. This is a diffuse cerebral disease in which there is serious intellectual deterioration and emotional impairment. The brain shows general atrophy, there is a loss of brain cells, and there are specific changes in the cerebral cortex. The psychosis may take various forms—manic, depressive, or paranoid. The manic variety is characterized by pointless activity, silly boasting, and a marked overtalkativeness. In the depressive variety, the emotions are rather blunt, there is obvious irritability, and hysterical symptoms may be intermingled with hypochondriacal ones. The paranoid variety is most dramatic—there are often elaborate delusions of gases being pumped into rooms, food being poisoned, spies trying to kill the sufferer, and so on.

Dementia occurring before the age of 60 is commonly termed presenile. Pick's disease, in which there is a circumscribed atrophy of the frontal lobes, and Alzheimer's disease, in which there is widespread atrophy of the brain, may be accompanied by psychotic features. Psychosis can also occur in cerebrovascular disease, with brain tumors, and as a consequence of head injuries. Epilepsy, particularly affecting the temporal lobe, may be accompanied by hallucinations, mood disturbances, and paranoid delusions.

KEY

"The Scream"—Edvard Munch, 1893

2

2 Depression, in psychiatric terms, refers to a condition in which depression is not the only symptom, but is accompanied by insomnia, loss of weight and appetite, diminished libido, feelings of worthlessness and guilt, and suicidal thoughts. Some depressive states may have an obvious precipitating factor such as a bereavement or a broken engagement ("reactive" depression). In others, and particularly in patients predisposed genetically to develop manic-depressive psychosis, the mood disturbance often occurs with little or no obvious provocation ("endogenous" depression). In extreme depression the patient may be severely retarded or markedly agitated. He tends to be preoccupied with feelings of guilt and may explain these by concluding that he has committed some terrible crime or sin for which he is being punished. Depressed patients commonly feel a burden to others, particularly to those close to them, and may attempt suicide to relieve not only their own feelings but also those of their concerned relatives and friends from whom they invariably feel alienated. A delusion sometimes seen in severely depressed people is the so-called "nihilistic" delusion. Influenced by the profound emotional malaise that is central to depression, the patient's mood may become completely negative. He may declare that he has no name, no age, no parents, relatives, wife, or children. He may insist he has no head, no chest, no body—he may deny and resist everything. Treatment in the severe forms of depression is by electric shock and antidepressants. Psychotherapy is helpful, particularly in reactive depression.

Personality defects and neuroses

The neurotic person has obvious abnormal psychological symptoms, but does not show that sharp break with reality that characterizes the psychotic person. Particular neuroses can and do appear for a short time in otherwise healthy people, but they are usually exaggerated versions of normal experiences. All of us have felt depressed, anxious, fearful at some time—what distinguishes the neurotic is quantitative difference from the norm.

Types of neuroses

Classification of neuroses into various categories is fairly arbitrary but is based on the major symptom present. The main neurotic states identified are anxiety neurosis, hysteria, depressive neuroses, and obsessive–compulsive disorders.

The overriding complaint in anxiety neurosis is an excessive fear, often amounting to panic and associated with physical symptoms such as a dry mouth, palpitations, and sweating. It may be complicated by a phobia [3,7], obsession [4], or depression [6].

In the popular mind, hysteria is linked with uncontrollable tantrums and screaming fits. For the psychiatrist the term refers to those symptoms, both physical and mental, such as paralysis, tremor, and amnesia, that are caused by a psychological disturbance and that aim, unconsciously, at escape from a seemingly insurmountable difficulty or the fulfilment of some need.

Hysteria takes two main forms, known as conversion, or mainly physical disturbances [5], and dissociation. The most common of the dissociative states is the fugue, when a patient quite suddenly and without any warning signs wanders off. Such a journey has no plan or destination, is usually accompanied by loss of memory, and often allows the patient to avoid some unpleasant situation.

Allied to fugues are the so-called trances and twilight states when a patient withdraws and insulates himself from the world. More rare but of the same type is the dual, or multiple, personality, when the patient manifests a number of traits that are opposed to each other and poorly integrated. By a process of dissociation a shy, prudish girl may become flirtatious and seductive. In extreme cases patients keep different names and styles for their different personae and when playing one role deny all knowledge of any other.

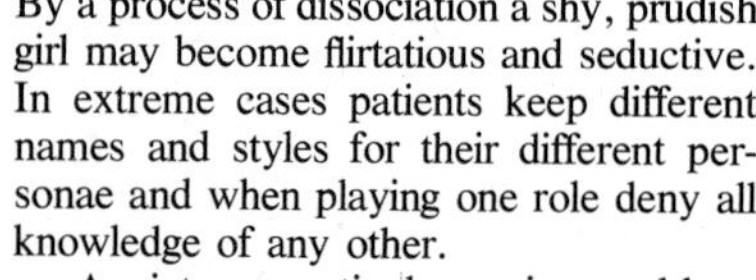

Anxiety, neurotic depression, and hysterical neurosis are the reactions to stress of more-or-less neurotic personalities. The best-balanced individual may react with depression to a severe setback or with anxiety to a major stress. Most of the anxious, depressed, or hysterical patients are more the victims of their own personalities than of outside events.

Personality disorders

Personality disorders are a group of anomalies or deviations that although not the result of a psychosis or other illness, are odd enough to upset or puzzle others and sometimes even the sufferers themselves. Such disorders resemble mental illness and may require psychiatric help and understanding, but the patient is less ill than abnormally developed.

CONNECTIONS

See also
914 Nature and causes c criminality
764 Psychoses
768 Psychosomatic diseases and retardatio
760 Introduction to menta health
762 How mental illness has been treated
770 Physical cures for mental illness
772 Behavior therapy
774 Psychotherapy

1 A sociopath displays recurrent antisocial, delinquent, and criminal behavior in many areas of his life. Data on the prevalence of the disorder are unreliable but it is seen frequently by psychiatrists, usually because of an associated alcohol problem or depression. The family backgrounds of most sociopaths are grossly disturbed. There is commonly a history of parental alcoholism, criminality, separation, divorce, or early death. The first signs usually occur in late childhood or early adolescence and are commonly a restlessness, an unresponsiveness to discipline, and a tendency to be cruel to smaller children or animals. A disturbed school history, with truancy and academic failure, is frequently found, and later the job record is marred by poor performance, unreliability, and an inability to accept even minor criticism. Sociopaths have great difficulty in maintaining close emotional relationships and their marriages are characterized by infidelity, separation, and divorce. Most sociopaths end up with criminal records. Most of them indulge in minor petty delinquency, but a small minority commit brutal and callous acts of physical violence.

1

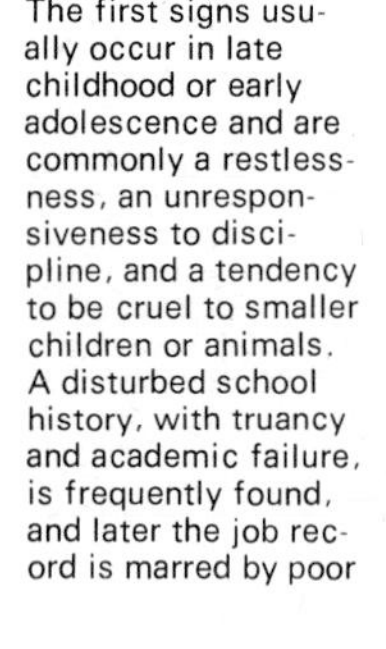

2

2 Inadequate individuals show a low physical and mental strength, a lack of resilience and flexibility, and an inability to cope with stresses. They are often nervous and dependent in early childhood, and their parents are either intensely protective or harsh and rejecting. They are excessively shy, socially and sexually inhibited, egocentric, and introverted. They often lead lonely, somewhat joyless and anxious lives in adulthood.

Some personality disorders are the result of faulty brain development caused by genetic make-up, injury, infection, poisoning, or malnutrition in childhood. Some sex chromosome anomalies also seem to be associated with antisocial behavior, in particular the so-called XXY male who is unusually tall, aggressive, and sometimes of subnormal intelligence. Environmental factors, including early childhood deprivation, parental quarreling, and severe stress, are also known to play their part.

A number of specific categories of personality disorder, including the antisocial [1] and the immature [2], have been described. The paranoid is sensitive and vulnerable, reacting to everyday experiences with an excessive sense of inferiority and humiliation, and likely to be touchy in preserving what he conceives to be his rights. People who have so-called affective personalities have long-standing anomalies of mood—either a predominantly pessimistic attitude to life or the opposite. In contrast, the hysterical or histrionic personality has shallow and changeable emotions and, although unreliable, craves love and attention. The schizoid is notably aloof, shy, and reserved, tending to be markedly introspective and eccentric. Finally, the anankastic or obsessive personality is characterized by a strong sense of insecurity, an excessive caution combined with a stubborn inflexibility, and a rigid perfectionism.

Sexual problems

Various forms of sexual problems are referred to psychiatrists. Some, such as fetishism (the exclusive derivation of sexual pleasure from inanimate objects) are private anomalies of sexual behavior. There are others, however, such as pedophilia (the desire of an adult to engage in sexual activity with children) and exhibitionism (the desire to expose one's genitals to others) that involve public conduct. Transvestitism (dressing in the clothing of the opposite sex) and transsexualism (the wish to be and to function as a member of the opposite sex) are rare but important. These problems are regarded as developmental anomalies rather than as true illnesses.

KEY

The Munchausen syndrome, named after Baron von Munchausen (1720–97), is a severe personality disorder wherein a person malingers or consciously feigns an illness to obtain a desired end. Some people repeatedly malinger, going from one hospital to another, often under a variety of assumed names, but almost always telling the same story, faking the same symptoms, and submitting to innumerable investigations and operations. Chronic malingerers resemble the Baron, who entertained his friends with extraordinary (and patently untrue) tales of his supposed travels so that he eventually gained the reputation of being an incorrigible liar.

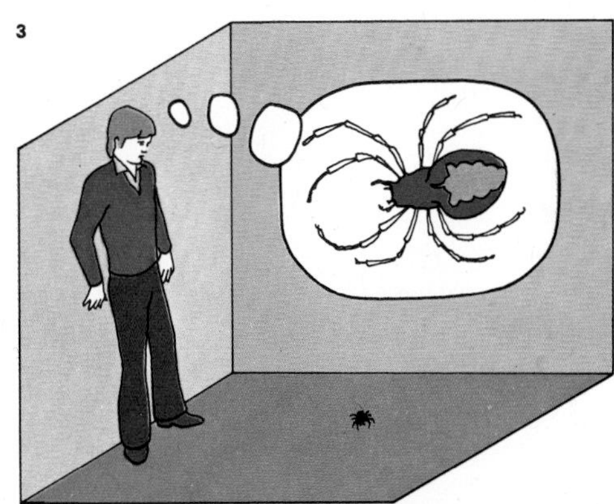

3 Anxiety neurosis may be complicated by a phobia or dread of a specific object or situation. A common phobia is that of "bugs," particularly spiders. Mildly phobic individuals experience anxiety only when required to handle spiders but the severely phobic can become terrified just by thinking about them and will avoid any situation in which there is the slightest chance of further exposure to spiders.

4 In obsessive-compulsive neurosis the patient is occupied with thoughts that do not really interest him and impulses that seem alien. He feels impelled to perform actions that give him no pleasure and that he is powerless to stop. The compulsive rituals may be eccentric (eg, touching objects a given number of times) or involve repetitive activities (eg, cleaning aimed at neutralizing morbid thoughts of dirt).

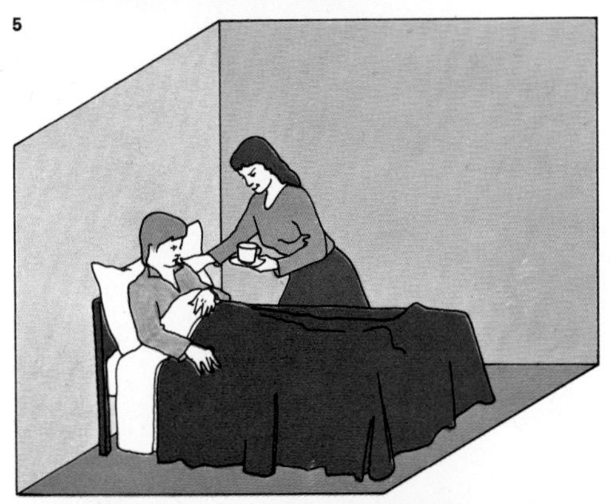

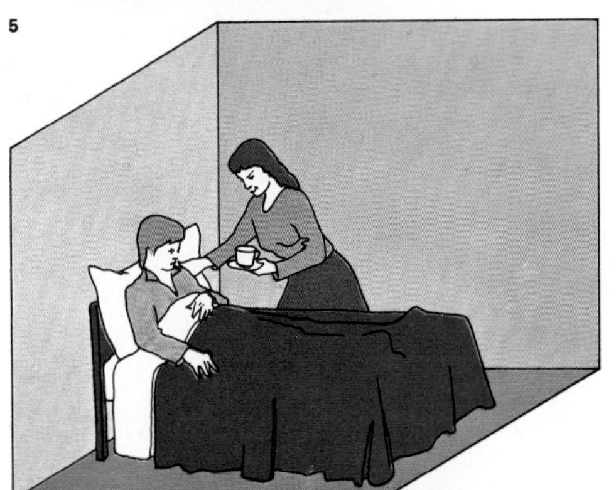

5 A common feature of hysterical or histrionic neurosis is conversion, a physical disturbance psychologically caused. Common symptoms are paralysis, tremor, fits, blindness, deafness, and sensory disturbances. Conversion is a primitive mechanism for dealing with difficult situations. Hysterics differ from malingerers in that, although they may produce illness, they are unaware of what they are doing.

6 Depression is a reaction to the stress or frustration produced by some incident like a loss, grief, or disappointment. Depressive neuroses, as a rule, are an exaggerated form of what happens when the average man is temporarily cast down. The severe weight, appetite, and sleep loss, delusional ideas, and severe guilt feelings seen in manic-depressive psychoses are nearly always lacking.

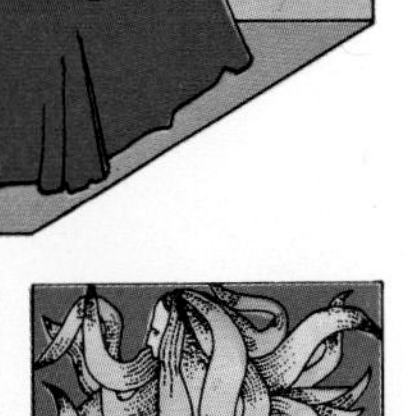
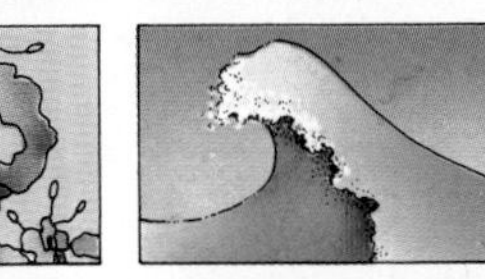

13

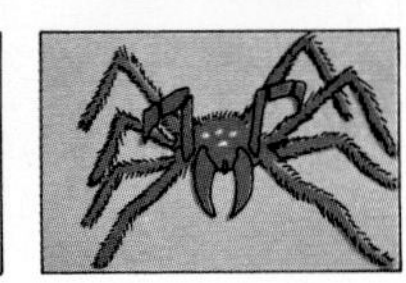
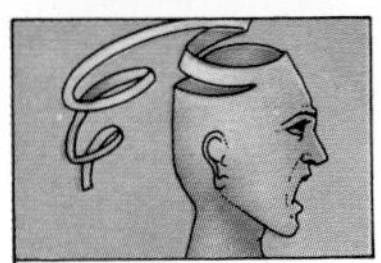
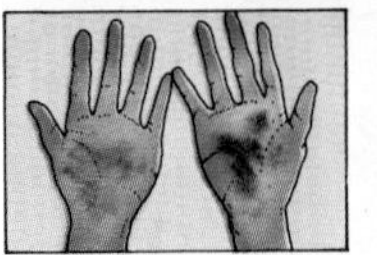

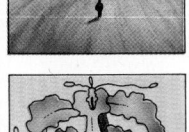

7 Agoraphobia, a fear of open spaces, is commoner in women and includes panic experienced when out alone. Other phobic stimuli are heights, fire, lightning, death, and hair. Fears of flowers, water, and numbers are rarer, but fears of social situations are common, while children are often afraid of the dark. Snakes, closed places (claustrophobia), cats, spiders, insanity, dirt, and mice are other well-known causes of phobia.

Psychosomatic diseases and retardation

Certain physical disorders such as hypertension and bronchial asthma [3] have classically been designated psychosomatic since the early 1930s. In the intervening years, many other conditions have been similarly labeled including anorexia nervosa, gross obesity, psychogenic vomiting, and some abdominal pain.

Psychological factors in illness

There is little agreement on which illnesses are and are not psychosomatic. Their only common characteristic is the assumption that psychological factors play a major role in their complex and obscure causes. Some critics believe the term to be misleading in that the description of some illnesses as "psychosomatic" implies that the remainder are not. In practice there are probably few illnesses in which psychological factors do not play a role. Psychosomatic diseases are believed to be the result of a chronic and exaggerated state of the normal physiological expression of emotion. If persistent, structural damage can result.

There has been much speculation about the possible link between certain personality types and susceptibility to psychosomatic disorders. It has been claimed, for instance, that some sufferers from peptic ulcers may be people who unconsciously want to remain dependent. Such a wish is productive of low self-esteem, however, and runs counter to the adult ego's pride and desire for independence. Accordingly, it is repressed and compensated for by aggression and ambition. The resulting inner conflict produces chronic anxiety, which in turn leads to overproduction of gastric juices and so to ulcers. Similar theories have been advanced for other diseases.

In anorexia nervosa [1] an unwillingness on the part of the patient to develop womanly characteristics, both physical and psychological, with their attendant social and sexual expectations, is thought to dominate the refusal to eat and the attempt to maintain abnormally low weight.

Mental retardation

Mental retardation refers to intelligence defects existing from birth or before full development of the brain irrespective of the cause of the defect. If the IQ of a large sample of people is assessed [7], the same kind of normal distribution curve results as when physical characteristics, such as height or weight, are studied in population samples. IQs between 90 and 110 are considered average. Mental retardation is divided into a number of grades: borderline (IQ 68–85), mild (IQ 52–67), moderate (IQ 36–51), severe (IQ 20–35), and profound (IQ under 20).

Such a grading acts as a rough guide to the capabilities of people falling within each range in terms of possible social adjustment and functioning, ability to learn, and the acquisition of skills. For example, an adult with profound mental retardation requires nursing care and may achieve only a very limited level of self-care. The moderately retarded adult may be able to work in an unskilled or semiskilled capacity under sheltered conditions, whereas the mildly retarded adult can usually achieve a level of social and vocational skill adequate for a minimal level of self-support.

CONNECTIONS

See also
710 The causes of illness
738 Preventive medicine
760 Introduction to mental health
762 How mental illness has been treated
764 Psychoses
766 Personality defects and neuroses
770 Physical cures for mental illness
772 Behavior therapy
774 Psychotherapy
748 Nonmedical healing

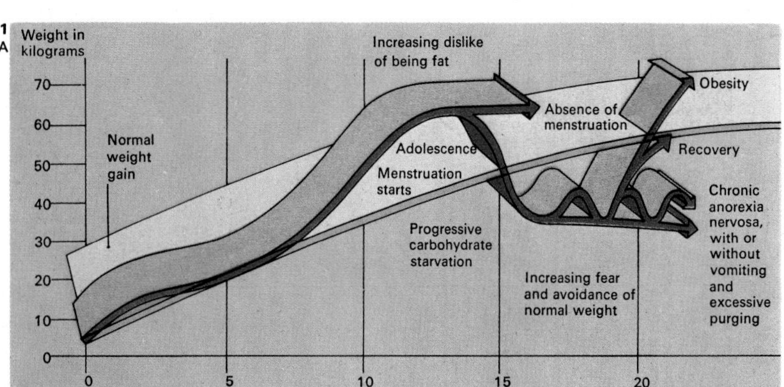

1
A
Weight in kilograms
70
60
50
40
30
20
10
0
Normal weight gain
Increasing dislike of being fat
Obesity
Absence of menstruation
Adolescence
Recovery
Menstruation starts
Chronic anorexia nervosa, with or without vomiting and excessive purging
Progressive carbohydrate starvation
Increasing fear and avoidance of normal weight
0
5
10
15
20
Age in years

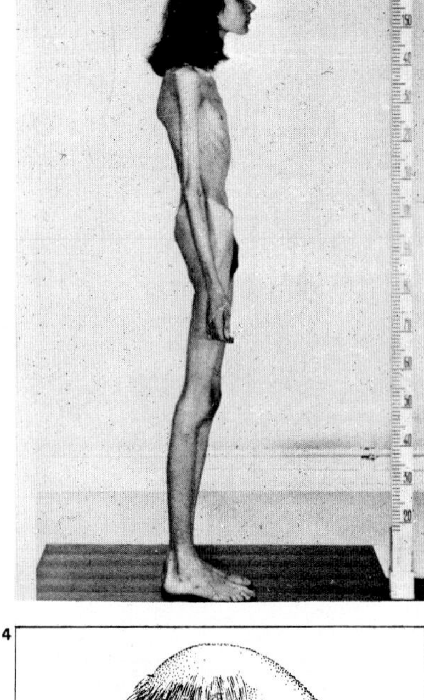

B

1 Anorexia nervosa, a rare condition occurring mainly in young women, sets in around late adolescence [A]. It begins with a distaste for, or a phobia about, fatness that soon develops into an inability to eat, often exacerbated by self-induced vomiting. The result [B] is low body weight, absence of monthly "periods," constipation, and downy hair growth over the normally hairless parts of the body.

2 The "vapors" were a fashionable psychosomatic complaint of distinguished ladies of the 18th century, characterized by dramatic fainting and a variety of nervous fits, sometimes attributed to overtight corsetting. Famous physicians of the day treated attacks of the vapors with such "modern" treatments as electric shocks or a course of baths. Young women were frequent victims.

2

3 Psychosomatic diseases are believed to be the result of excessive and prolonged exposure of a vulnerable organ to the normal physiological changes that are caused by emotion. If persistent, such an emotional reaction can produce structural damage in the organ affected. Major physical diseases in which psychological factors are thought to play a significant causal role, in addition to modifying the way in which such illnesses develop, include bronchial asthma [1], thyrotoxicosis (resulting from overactivity of the thyroid gland) [2], hypertension [3], coronary artery disease [4], peptic ulceration [5], ulcerative colitis [6], and rheumatoid arthritis [7]. There has also been speculation concerning possible links between certain personality types (for example those who want to remain dependent because of low self-esteem) and susceptibility to psychosomatic diseases.

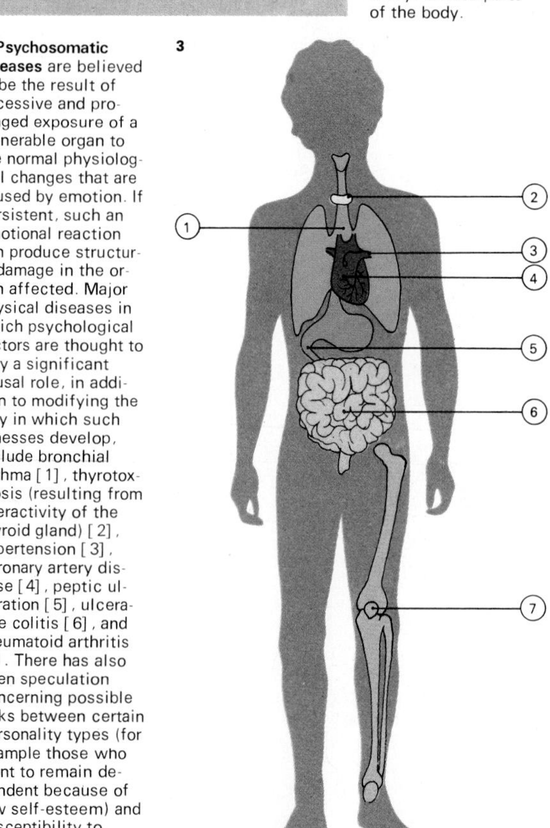

3
1
2
3
4
5
6
7

4

4 Charles Darwin (1809–82), following his journey on HMS *Beagle*, developed a chronic and incapacitating illness, characterized by lassitude; palpitations, headaches, sleeplessness, and tremulousness. There has been much speculation concerning the underlying cause of these symptoms. Analysts have seen them as psychosomatic – a psychological reaction to difficulties in Darwin's relationship with his father, who is usually portrayed as stern and cold.

Causes of mental retardation

Many factors at different stages can cause mental retardation. Some mental defects are the result of genetic diseases. Such conditions include craniostenosis, in which there is premature closing of the cranial sutures (where the bones of the skull are joined) and skull deformity, and a number of serious metabolic disorders, such as phenylketonuria (PKU). Conditions such as mongolism, or Down's syndrome are associated with aberrations of the number or shape of the chromosomes.

Uterine factors in mental retardation include severe dietary deficiency in the pregnant mother giving rise to fetal damage. Virus infections, such as rubella (German measles), contracted by the mother early in pregnancy, can give rise to physical abnormalities and mental deficiency. Irradiation by X rays or from an atomic explosion may damage the fetus, as may certain drugs (such as thalidomide) taken by the mother during pregnancy. Abnormal labor, with prolonged asphyxia and brain trauma during delivery, and premature birth may also result in intellectual deficiencies in the newborn child.

During infancy and early childhood serious infections, such as bacterial meningitis, and encephalitis, and the rare central nervous system involvement in viral conditions such as mumps, measles, and whooping cough, can result in serious mental retardation.

The management of mental retardation can be divided into primary, secondary, and tertiary prevention. Primary prevention includes genetic counseling and those medical measures, particularly in the field of obstetrics, aimed at reducing prenatal, natal, and postnatal complications. Secondary prevention is achieved by the early identification and treatment of hereditary metabolic disorders. Tertiary prevention involves management of the mentally retarded so that the maximum potential of even the most seriously handicapped can be realized. For the mildly subnormal, special schooling may be required [Key]. For the more severely retarded, institutional or residential care may be necessary.

KEY

Treatment of mental retardation involves helping the individual reach his full potential. Special schools teach the mildly retarded the skills they are able to achieve to become useful members of a social group. At a camp for the mentally retarded (shown here) dedicated counselors train retarded children in basic social skills. Many mentally retarded individuals have learned useful occupational skills.

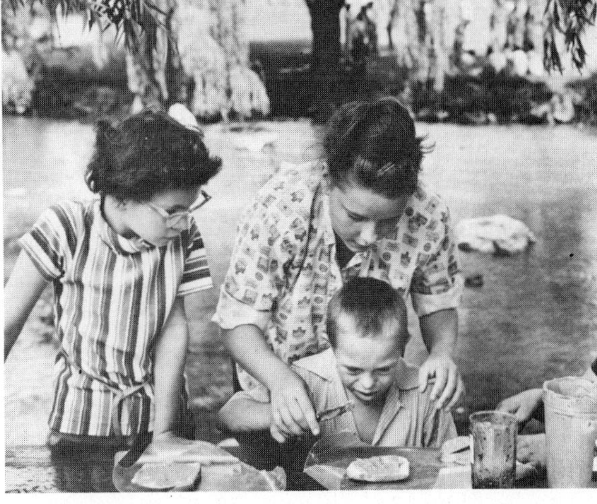

5

5 Alfred Binet (1857–1911), an experimental psychologist at the Sorbonne, Paris, devised a standardized intelligence test to discover mentally defective primary school children. The test was developed from intelligence scales for the investigation of normal and subnormal children. These were extended to become an intelligence test for the 3–15 age range from which modern tests developed.

7

Distribution of IQ in sample population

Number of individuals: 0, 20, 40, 60, 80, 100, 120, 140, 160, 180, 200, 220, 240

Intelligence quotient: 40, 50, 60, 70, 80, 90, 100, 110, 120, 130, 140

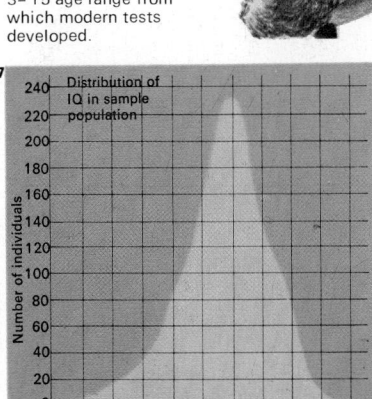

7 The distribution of adult intelligence quotients (IQs) is from a sample of 2,052 people in the United States.

8 This example of dyslexic writing illustrates the bizarre character of the spelling disorders in dyslexia, which may be connected with retardation, although not always. Syllables may be omitted or put in the wrong order and sometimes it is not clear where words end.

8

There are many strange and fasenating fisf, but it seems difecolt to beleaver that some fish are Kapabul of generating ther whone ELEStricaty With Which they can guve a shoc.

the best one of this fish live in Whorm seas. these fish have an orgen behind each ie Which is a mase of sels, roth like a a honeKome.

6 Extremely withdrawn or moderately mentally handicapped children can be helped by using simple behavioral modification techniques. Normally, the child's solitary play is encouraged or "reinforced" by the teacher's attention [A]. But in this instance he is only rewarded by the teacher's full attention when he joins the group [B]. As a check on the treatment the original reinforcement is reinstated [C] which at once encourages the child to revert to his former behavior. The new treatment is started again and the desired behavior—that is, the child playing in the group—is encouraged until it is firmly instilled [D]. In time the teacher can leave the group to its own devices [E] and the child will remain with it. Such behavioral methods are being extended.

6 A B

C D

E

Physical cures for mental illness

Physical treatments in contemporary psychiatry include the use of tranquilizers, sedatives, stimulants, and hallucinogenic-drugs, the application of electroconvulsive treatment (ECT), and certain psychosurgical procedures.

The use of drugs

A tranquilizer is a drug that induces sedation without loss of consciousness even when given in relatively large doses. The most potent tranquilizers are the phenothiazines, of which chlorpromazine (Thorazine) is the prototype. Synthesized in a French laboratory in 1950, this drug soon became widely used to reduce severe agitation or excitement of whatever cause. The phenothiazines appear to have selective effects on the delusions and hallucinatory phenomena seen in schizophrenia and manic depression. As a result they have become the drugs used in the treatment of these conditions. A long-acting phenothiazine, fluphenazine (Prolixin), has been developed that can be given by injection every 2–4 weeks; it maintains schizophrenics in a relatively stable state. The phenothiazines are also used to control excitable behavior in manic states and in confusional states caused by physical disease or drugs. They are not effective in the treatment of depression. Side effects include drowsiness, muscle stiffness, blurred vision, dry mouth, sensitivity of the skin to sunlight, and, occasionally, jaundice.

The most popular group of minor tranquilizers is the benzodiazepines, of which diazepam (Valium) and chlordiazepoxide (Librium) are the best known. These drugs are used in the treatment of phobic anxiety, obsessive-compulsive disorders, and minor anxiety and tension, as well as in the management of the withdrawal symptoms in barbiturate and alcohol dependence. The benzodiazepines may result in dependence.

There are two main groups of antidepressants—the tricyclics, of which imipramine and amitriptyline are the most widely used, and the monoamine oxidase (MAO) inhibitors, of which phenelzine (Nardil) and tranylcypromine (Parnate) are the best known. The tricyclics compare favorably with ECT in the treatment of severe depression characterized by suicidal feelings, guilt, self-reproach, ideas of worthlessness, insomnia, weight loss, and impairment of libido. The MAO inhibitors are less effective in such states but are thought to be useful in mixed anxiety-depressive states and in depressions believed to be reactions to some obvious environmental stress. They are more difficult to use, however, because of undesirable interactions with such commonly used medications as the tricyclic antidepressants, decongestants, and tyramine-containing foods such as cheese, wine, and bean pods. Lithium salts have been found to be useful in the control of mania, although why they work is not clear.

The powerful hypnotic drugs, the barbiturates, once widely used in the treatment of anxiety, have been superseded by the safer benzodiazepines. Because of their tendency to introduce dependence, the barbiturates are now used only as anticonvulsants in epilepsy. Similarly, the amphetamines, stimulant drugs once used to alleviate depression, have been replaced by the antidepressants, but are used to treat hyperac-

CONNECTIONS

See also
746 Man-made cures
752 Development of surgery
666 How the brain works
772 Behavior therapy
774 Psychotherapy
760 Introduction to mental health
762 How mental illness has been treated
764 Psychoses
766 Personality defects and neuroses
768 Psychosomatic diseases and retardation

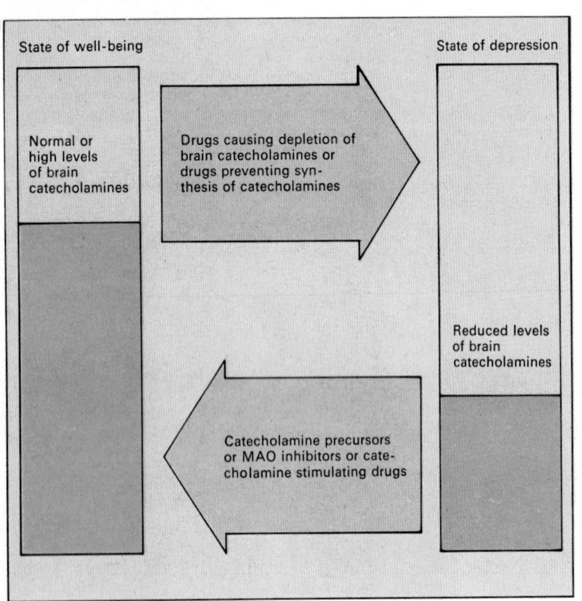

1
State of well-being
State of depression
Normal or high levels of brain catecholamines
Drugs causing depletion of brain catecholamines or drugs preventing synthesis of catecholamines
Reduced levels of brain catecholamines
Catecholamine precursors or MAO inhibitors or catecholamine stimulating drugs

1 The catecholamine theory of depression states that mood change is related to drug-induced changes in the level of chemicals called catecholamines in the brain. The theory is that a feeling of well-being is maintained by a continuous stimulation of certain receptors in the brain by catecholamines, such as adrenaline, noradrenaline, and dopamine. Drugs such as reserpine, a potent substance used in the treatment of high blood pressure, deplete brain catecholamine stores and can cause lethargy, apathy, and severe depression. In contrast, other compounds have been found that produce an increase in brain catecholamines and thus an improvement in mood.

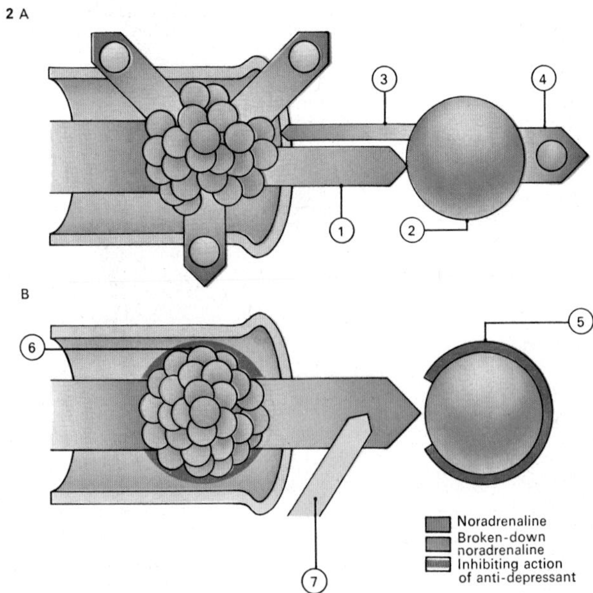

2 A
B
1
2
3
4
5
6
7
Noradrenaline
Broken-down noradrenaline
Inhibiting action of anti-depressant

2 A catecholamine neurotransmitter, noradrenaline, is stored in a nerve ending. On stimulation of the nerve [A] noradrenaline is released [1] and effects the receptor site [2]. Some noradrenaline is reabsorbed by the nerve ending [3] to be used again while the remainder is broken down [4]. Antidepressants [B] may prevent breakdown and reabsorption of noradrenaline, increasing the free noradrenaline at the receptor site. They may also inhibit the breakdown by monoamine oxidase of stored noradrenaline [6]. Other antidepressants increase the receptor site's sensitivity to noradrenaline [7].

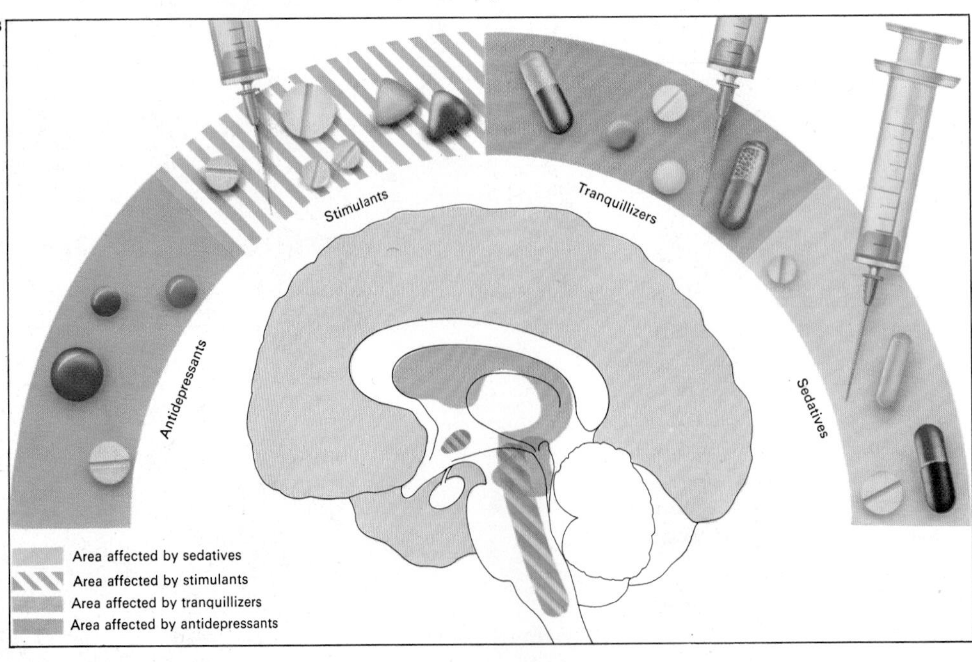

3
Stimulants
Tranquillizers
Antidepressants
Sedatives
Area affected by sedatives
Area affected by stimulants
Area affected by tranquillizers
Area affected by antidepressants

3 Those areas of the brain believed to be affected by antidepressants, stimulants, tranquilizers, and sedatives are shown here. Antidepressant drugs are thought to effect catecholamines stored in the midbrain. Stimulant (drugs) act on the reticular activating system (RAS) and the hypothalamus. Tranquilizer (drugs) also act on the RAS and may suppress RAS response in the cortex. They are also thought to affect the limbic system. Sedative (drugs) such as barbiturates, which are used to induce sleep and as anticonvulsants, have a twofold action on the brain. They act on the RAS and on the cerebral cortex itself, thereby suppressing brain activity.

tive children in whom they have a paradoxical calming effect. The hallucinogenic drugs, LSD and mescaline, were used on an experimental basis in psychiatry until their potential for producing permanent psychoses was appreciated.

Electroconvulsive therapy

Electroconvulsive treatment (ECT) was introduced into psychiatry in the late 1930s. It is still widely used in some hospitals and in severe suicidal depressions may be the treatment of choice. The usual course of ECT consists of 6–8 treatments. The patient is given an anesthetic and a muscle relaxant (which paralyzes the main muscles and thereby reduces the severity of the convulsion). When unconscious, the patient has two electrodes applied to his head. An electric current, usually 80 volts with a duration of 0.1–0.3 seconds, is passed between the electrodes, producing an epileptic discharge and a convulsion, "modified" by the muscle relaxant and manifested by small twitchings of the facial, hand, and feet muscles. There is frequently an associated partial memory loss that is transient, but may take some weeks to clear completely. Studies have revealed that the crucial therapeutic element is the seizure discharge.

Psychosurgery

Psychosurgical operations involve the destruction or removal of normal or apparently normal brain tissue for the purpose of altering certain behavior. Such procedures are among the most controversial in modern psychiatry. The first such operations were popularized by Egas Moniz [6] during the early 1940s, and the so-called "standard" leucotomy (the cutting of certain selected brain fibers) was performed on thousands of chronically incapacitated patients.

The development of potent antipsychotic and antidepressant drugs during the 1950s resulted in a loss of interest in surgical procedures but the development of better operative techniques together with a renewal of interest in brain physiology has given new impetus to this field. Controlled trials of psychosurgical operations are lacking, however.

KEY

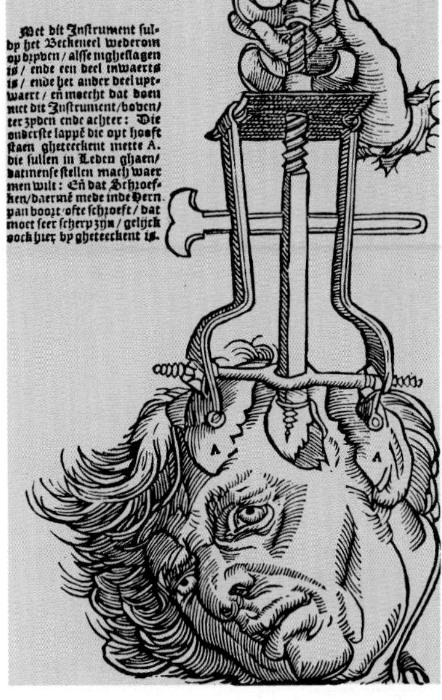
Met dit Instrument sul-
dy het Beckeneel wederom
op drijven / alsse ingheslagen
is / ende een deel inwaerts
is / ende het ander deel upt-
waert / en mocht dat doen
met dit Instrument / boven /
ter zyden ende achter: Die
onderste lappē die opt hooft
staen gheteeckent mette A.
die sullen in Leden ghaen /
datmense stellen mach waer
men wilt: En dat Schroef-
ken / daer mē mede inde Hern-
pan boort ofte schroeft / dat
moet seer scherp zijn / gelijck
ooch hier by gheteeckent is.

The primitive trephination procedures of medieval times were the forerunners of contemporary brain surgery, as a treatment for intractable psychiatric disorders. Historical discoveries have shown that decompression trephining for epilepsy and other brain disorders was common even among Neolithic Gauls and Bohemians, and often repeated as much as five times upon the same person, the excised portions of the skull (rondelles) being used as amulets. In more recent times such procedures have been common among Polynesians, the Aymara of Bolivia, and the Quichua of Peru. Sharpened flints were the instruments used.

4 A major study of the relative effectiveness of ECT, a tricyclic antidepressant (imipramine), an MAO inhibitor (phenelzine), and an inert placebo was conducted with 250 depressed patients. They were divided into four treatment groups. Evaluation after one month showed that 71% of the patients treated with ECT had few or no symptoms, compared with 52% for imipramine, 30% for phenelzine, and 39% for a placebo. This last figure may be taken to indicate the spontaneous short-term remission to be expected in these depressions; some patients get better automatically.

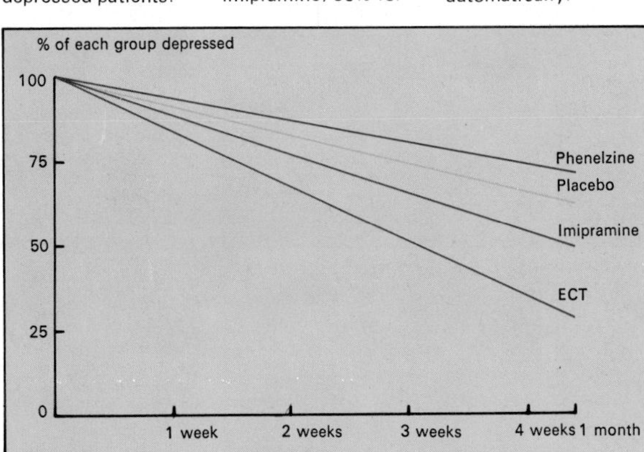
% of each group depressed
100
75
50
25
0
1 week
2 weeks
3 weeks
4 weeks 1 month
Phenelzine
Placebo
Imipramine
ECT

5

5 Ugo Cerletti (1877–1963), an Italian psychiatrist, believed that epilepsy and schizophrenia rarely occurred in the same patient. He suggested that an epileptic convulsion might "protect" the individual against schizophrenia. He induced epileptic seizures in schizophrenic patients, some of whom improved. It is now known that epilepsy and schizophrenia are not antagonistic.

6 Egas Moniz (1874–1955), a Portuguese neuropsychiatrist, impressed by reports that the surgical removal of the frontal lobes in animals eliminated pathological behavioral responses to frustration, suggested that such a procedure might be effective in relieving anxiety in man. His enthusiastic advocacy of such therapeutic procedures led to their widespread adoption.

6

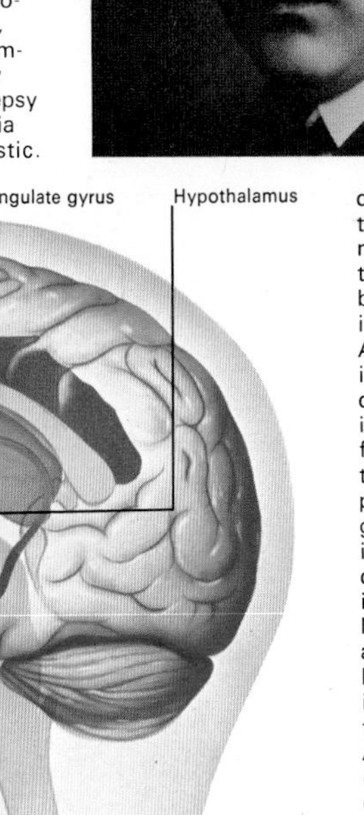

7 The technique of leucotomy, as performed in the early 1940s, consisted of making a burr hole in the side of the head above and in front of the ear. A cutting instrument–a leucotome or thin, sharp knife–was swept in an arc longitudinally, thereby cutting the connections between the frontal lobes and the rest of the brain [A]. The same procedure was then repeated on the opposite side of the head. With development of more precise surgical techniques and with modifications in the theoretical basis of psychosurgery, prefrontal leucotomy became less popular. Today, a probe is introduced through a burr hole [B] and is guided to the target area under X ray control. The area is then destroyed either by the introduction of radioactive seeds through the probe or by the application of intense heat or cold. A favorite target [C] in chronic intractable depression is the inner aspect of the frontal lobe. Destruction of the anterior part of the cingulate gyrus is undertaken in obsessional disorders, of the amygdala in aggressive and hyperactive states, and of centers of the hypothalamus in anxiety states and certain sexual disorders. A combination of centers may also be destroyed. Although Egas Moniz, the pioneer of psychosurgery, was awarded the Nobel Prize in 1949, there is still much dispute about the effectiveness of leucotomy.

7 A

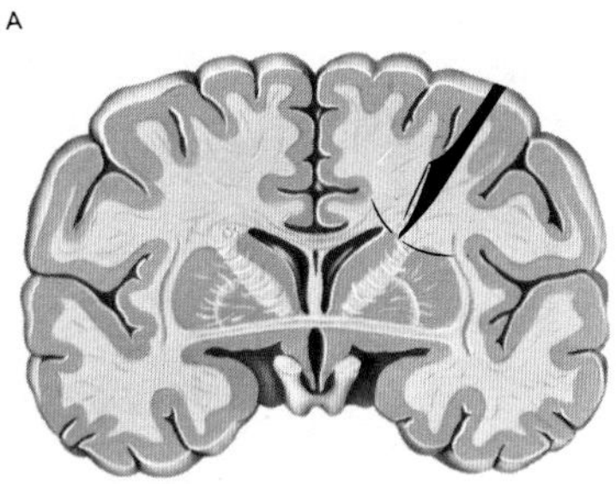

B

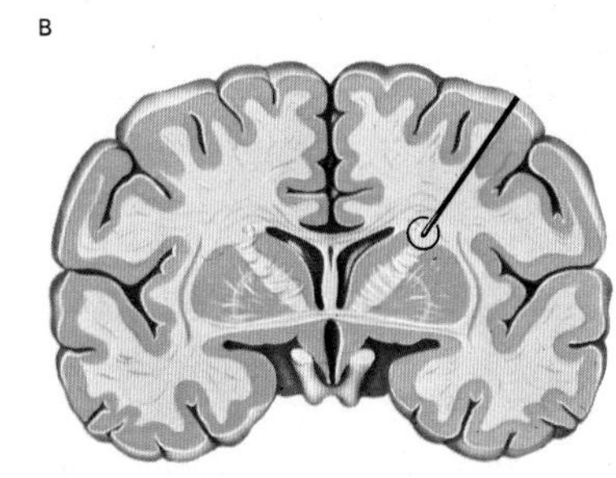

C

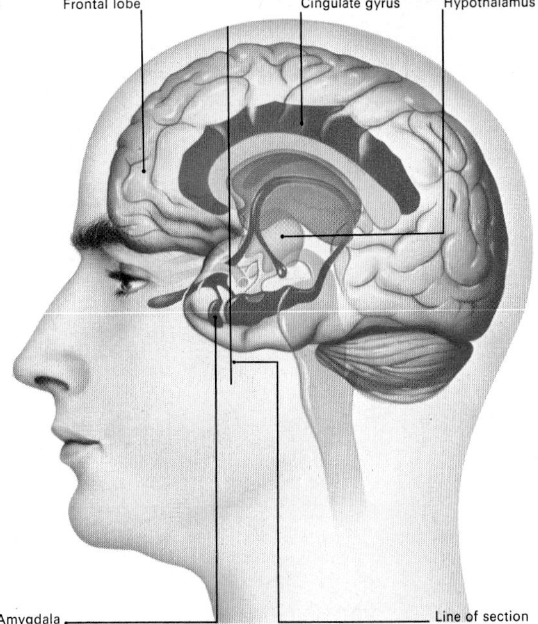
Frontal lobe
Cingulate gyrus
Hypothalamus
Amygdala
Line of section

Behavior therapy

Many psychogists and psychiatrists, concerned with the causes of neuroses or mental illnesses, believe that they result from emotional problems that, once identified, can also point the way to the cure.

Behaviorist psychologists have a quite different approach. They argue that the cause of, say, a phobia about snakes is irrelevant and that the important thing is to get rid of the phobia by working on it directly. The individual learns his behavior. It is therefore possible, the behaviorists argue, for him to unlearn or modify his behavior.

Therapy by conditioning

Behavior theory states that a neurotic reaction is acquired through a simple process of conditioning—the term used by the Russian physiologist Ivan Pavlov (1849–1936) in his experiments with dogs [1]. What is being conditioned is an emotional feeling of fear or anxiety. Such reactions easily give rise to more complex neuroses. A person with a fear of dirt may end up severely crippled by his compulsive need to wash off dirt and with it his fear of contamination.

The behaviorist's answer to such faulty conditioning is to submit it to a process of deconditioning or counter-conditioning. One such method of deconditioning is extinction. In simple extinction the unconditioned stimulus is not repeated when the conditioned stimulus is presented. When applied to Pavlov's original experiments, for example, the bell is rung on a large number of occasions but no food is presented. Gradually the salivary secretion in response to the bell, built up in the earlier experiment, diminishes until it finally disappears completely. Simple extinction is probably responsible for the spontaneous disappearance of some neurotic illnesses.

One reason why all neuroses do not so respond may be that, unlike the Pavlovian dog, human beings can avoid things that frighten them, and this avoidance, by relieving anxiety, serves as a further conditioning stimulus. For example, someone with a fear of spiders will run away from any situation in which he may be exposed to these creatures. His relief reinforces the conditioning process involved so that his phobia for spiders is strengthened. In such a case, behavior therapy is required to force the individual to face up to the noxious stimulus.

Other behaviorist techniques

In systematic desensitization [2], an attempt is made to condition an alternative response to the fear-producing stimulus so that the occurrence of one inhibits the occurrence of the other. Anxiety involves the tensing of muscles. By systematically persuading the patient to relax his muscles while asking him to imagine the feared object (for example, a snake) in its least feared state, the therapist relieves the associated anxiety. Relaxation rather than anxiety is conditioned as a response to the imagined snake. Gradually the therapist works up a "hierarchy" of ever more threatening situations so that eventually the subject is able to tolerate the presence of snakes.

Flooding [3] has been used with some success in the treatment of certain crippling neurotic states, particularly the severe obsessive-compulsive disorders. This involves making the patient experience his

CONNECTIONS

See also
- 770 Physical cures for mental illness
- 774 Psychotherapy
- 778 Thinking and understanding
- 786 Moral development
- 812 Aspects of human nature
- 760 Introduction to mental health
- 762 How mental illness has been treated
- 764 Psychoses
- 766 Personality defects and neuroses
- 768 Psychosomatic diseases and retardation

1 Ivan Pavlov, the Russian physiologist and Nobel prize-winner, proposed the theory of the conditioned reflex as the basic model of mental activity. One of his experiments involved a bell being rung simultaneously with the presentation of food before a dog. Eventually the sound of the bell alone, in the absence of food, caused the dog to salivate. The dog had become conditioned by the experiment to the sound of the bell.

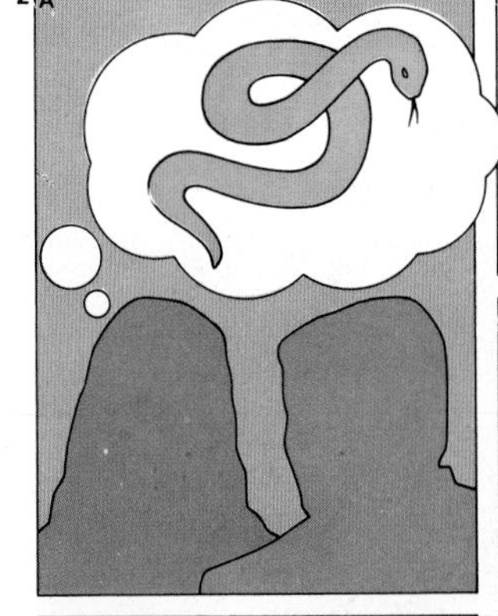

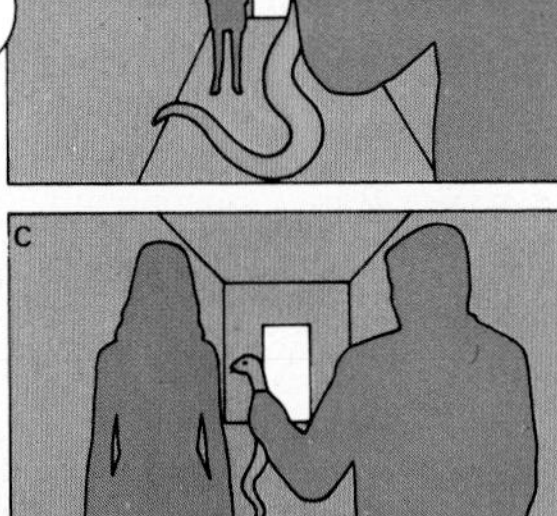

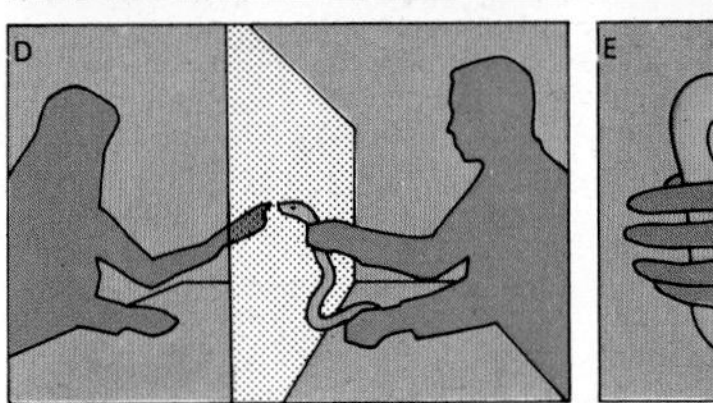

2 Systematic desensitization is a behavior technique used clinically in treating phobias such as the fear of snakes. A reassuring therapist encourages the patient to think about snakes [A] until she can do so without anxiety. She is then confronted with a distant live snake [B], which is gradually brought closer to her [C]. In the final stages of the treatment the patient progresses from touching the snake through a wire screen [D] to handling it by herself [E] without fear. Thus her fear response has been deconditioned and reconditioned into a fearless response brought about by positive reinforcements.

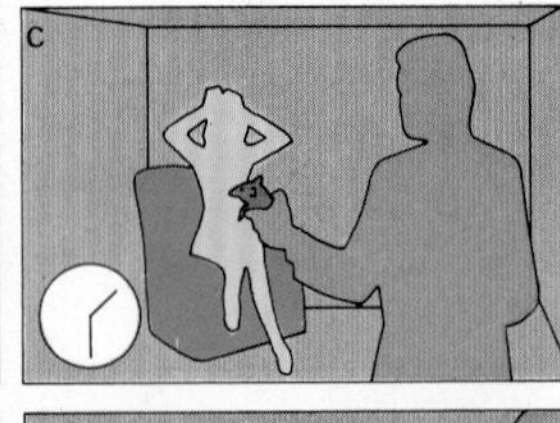

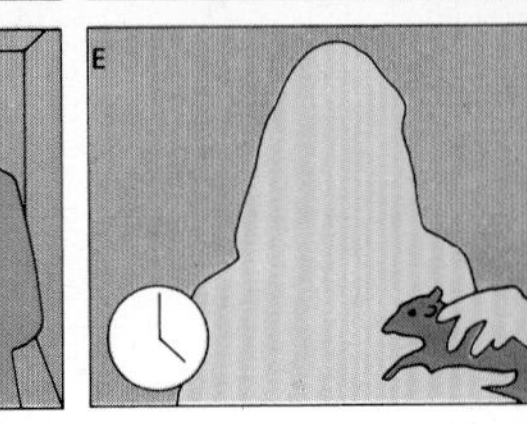

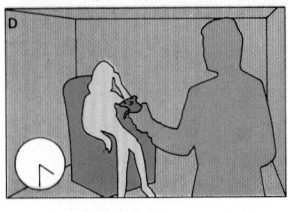

3 The aim of flooding or implosive therapy is to help a patient break the phobic cycle by having her make a deliberate effort to feel and experience her fear without avoiding it. The patient sits in a room while the therapist enters with the feared object, in this case a rat [A]. The rat is taken out of the cage [B] and the patient screams with fear. She becomes progressively more frightened [C], but gradually calms down due to the extinction of her severe anxiety reaction [D]. Finally she is able to hold the rat [E]. The crucial variable is the duration of exposure of the patient to the feared object, for too early a termination of exposure to the rat increases rather than decreases the patient's great fear of the animal.

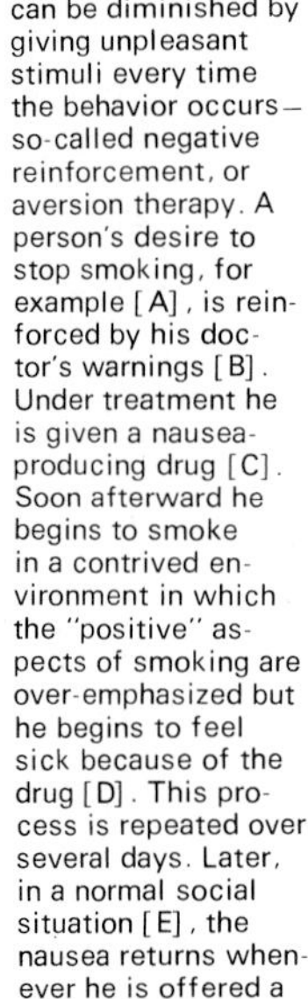

4 Unwanted behavior can be diminished by giving unpleasant stimuli every time the behavior occurs—so-called negative reinforcement, or aversion therapy. A person's desire to stop smoking, for example [A], is reinforced by his doctor's warnings [B]. Under treatment he is given a nausea-producing drug [C]. Soon afterward he begins to smoke in a contrived environment in which the "positive" aspects of smoking are over-emphasized but he begins to feel sick because of the drug [D]. This process is repeated over several days. Later, in a normal social situation [E], the nausea returns whenever he is offered a cigarette. He soon stops smoking [F].

fear fully until it reaches a peak and then diminishes. Aversion therapy [4] has been used in the treatment of sexual deviations (such as exhibitionism and pedophilia) and alcoholism and drug dependence. The noxious stimulus may be a painful shock, or a nausea-producing or paralyzing drug. Following such a course of aversion treatment, the patient is negatively conditioned.

Operant conditioning

Operant conditioning, developed by B. F. Skinner [5] and employed in a number of treatment situations including so-called "token economies" [6], works by means of a mixture of rewards and punishments. If a particular action is consistently followed by a reward ("positive" conditioning), then that particular action is likely to be repeated; if, however, it is followed by a punishment ("negative" conditioning), then the action is likely to cease. It is crucially important for the reward or the punishment to follow quickly upon the behavior in question. Too long a gap results in a failure by the individual to connect the two and hence the conditioning quality of the reward or punishment is low.

Behaviorists make considerable claims for their treatments. But while behavior therapy has a significant role to play in the treatment of neuroses (such as simple phobias) in which there is a single fear-provoking stimulus to be deconditioned, its success rate in more complex states, particularly in the long term, has been questioned. In the treatment of personality disorders behavioral techniques have not to date been very successful, while for the psychoses they have little to offer. In addition, anxieties are often aroused concerning the ethics of certain forms of behavior therapy, particularly aversion therapy. It is felt that behavioral techniques are too much like "brainwashing" or the shaping of a person's character into something that it is not and that this is open to abuse. Behaviorists insist, however, that it is up to the individual to decide whether or not to receive treatment for his problem and that the ethical problems are similar to those of other psychiatric treatments.

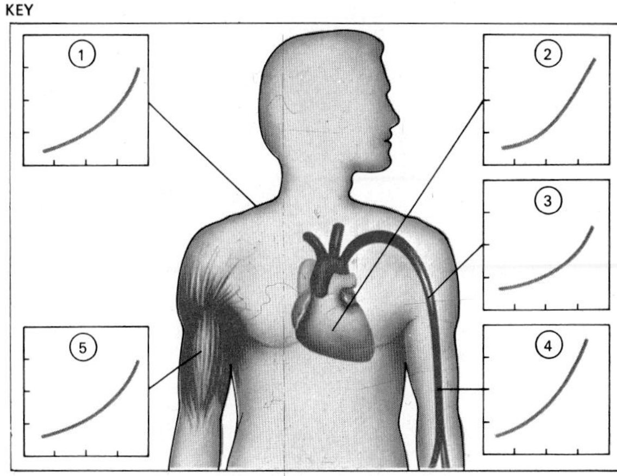
KEY
1
2
3
4
5

Many treatments of neuroses seek to reduce emotional arousal. One way of assessing objectively the degree of emotion experienced is to measure certain physiological changes during treatment. Under stress, the electrical resistance of the skin to the flow of an electric current decreases and the skin conductivity increases [1]. The heart rate accelerates [2] and there is a constriction of the cutaneous blood vessels, causing a rise in blood pressure [3]. Blood flow through the limbs increases [4]. High levels of muscle tone during stress are measured by electrodes [5].

5 The operant conditioning technique was first described by the American B. F. Skinner (1904–) in the 1930s. Whereas Pavlov took a hungry animal and paired a previously neutral stimulus (a bell) with the giving of food to an animal, Skinner waited for an animal to behave in a certain way, and then stepped in with a reward such as food, encouraging the animal to repeat the behavior.

5

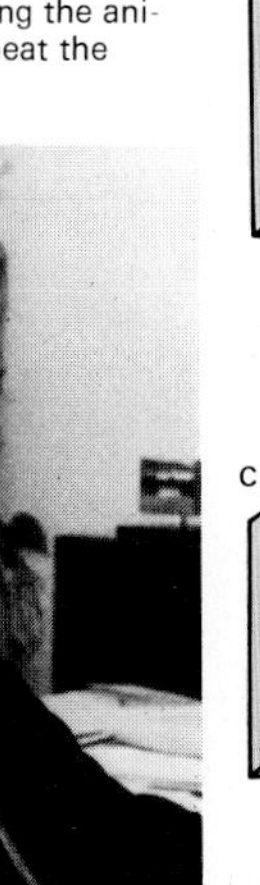

6

A
B

C

D

E

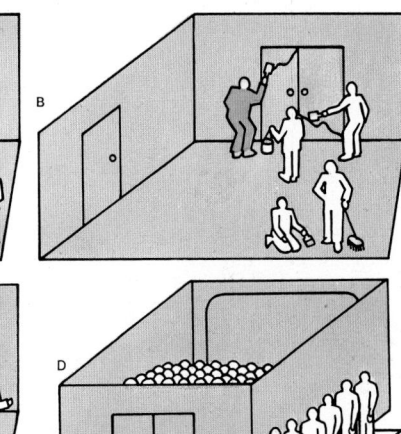

6 Token economies, a technique based on principles of behaviorist psychology, are being used increasingly in the treatment of the mentally ill and handicapped. Many such patients are socially withdrawn and do not participate in group activities [A]. But whenever they do [B] therapists and nurses can reinforce such positive behavior by rewarding them with tokens [C]. These are equivalent to money within the hospital and are exchangeable for goods and privileges such as entertainment [D]. The patient's social behavior can be gradually reshaped in this way and lead to a normal life [E] outside the hospital.

7 The patient's immediate social environment can affect his mental state and behavior, as psychiatrists are now aware. As a consequence, hospital wards have changed from being large and impersonal, with locked doors and few personal possessions [A]. They have been redesigned so that they are smaller, open, and much more social, with outside visitors being actively encouraged [B].

7

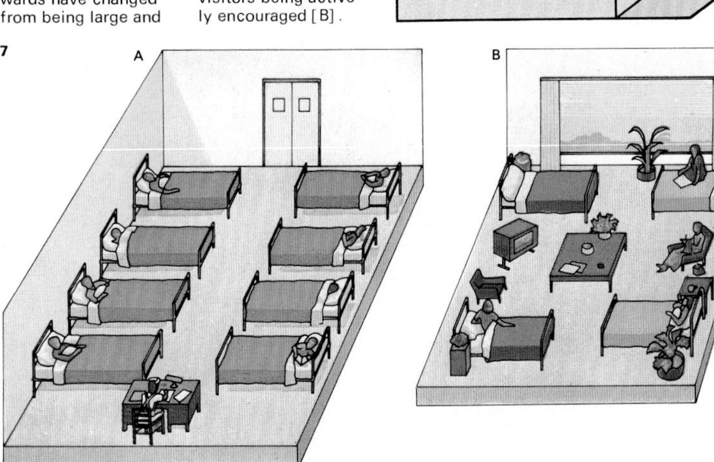
A
B

8

8 William James (1842–1910,) a prominent American psychologist and philosopher and brother of the writer Henry James (1843–1916), laid the foundations of behaviorist psychology. His theory that "emotion" is merely the perception of the bodily changes that accompany stress, while controversial, has greatly influenced clinical psychology. This attention to the outward symptoms of anxiety rather than the inward feelings provided an important theoretical framework for the research of the behaviorists.

Psychotherapy

Psychotherapy is the general term for those forms of treatment in which conversation between the therapist and patient is the primary technique. The object of psychotherapy is not just the removal of symptoms, as with physical treatment of a physical disorder, but an exploration of the patient's personality. Indeed, in many cases the removal of symptoms cease to be as important as the gaining of understanding and insight. To speak of "cure," therefore, as if psychotherapy were a surgical operation, is inappropriate. Most patients go to therapists because their lives are generally unhappy, rather than because they are grossly disturbed.

Psychotherapy may be on an individual or group basis, may be interpretative, supportive, or suggestive, and may be superficial or deep. By interpretative is meant the explanation by the therapist of something obscure or hidden to the patient. For instance, a psychotherapist interprets a dream by attributing to it some meaning over and above that given to it by the patient. Different psychotherapeutic traditions or schools, Freudian or Jungian for example, may give radically different interpretations of the same dream [1]. By supportive or suggestive psychotherapy is meant that the therapist adopts a reassuring or advisory approach. Deep psychotherapy refers to treatment that concentrates on the patient's early life or on repressed areas of his personality; superficial psychotherapy centers on more recent experiences.

Patient and therapist

Not every patient is suitable for psychotherapy. Factors that favor a good response include youth, intelligence, an ability to self-explore, a capacity to tolerate uncertainty, anxiety, and frustration, and verbal skills. Psychotherapeutic techniques are most effectively applied in the treatment of the neuroses and personality disorders, sexual deviations, and childhood disturbances. In addition to the relatively orthodox, analytically based group and individual psychotherapies, there is marital and family therapy, encounter group therapy, counseling, and such less orthodox approaches as Gestalt therapy, primal therapy, psychodrama, and the Japanese Morita therapy.

Until recently, more attention was paid to the particular school of psychotherapy or the therapeutic approach of the therapist than to more personal characteristics. It has become clear, however, that certain factors in the therapist's personality, such as ability to empathize, nonpossessive warmth, sincerity, and open-mindedness are important.

The most intensive form of psychotherapy is individual psychoanalysis. Psychoanalytic theory postulates that the individual defends himself against pain and anxiety by the use of certain mental mechanisms such as repression, denial, and projection. These mechanisms are believed to be characteristically exploited in such neurotic states as hysteria and such psychotic conditions as paranoia. It is these mechanisms that are analyzed and broken down in the psychoanalytic interaction.

Approaches to group psychotherapy

The development of group therapy has meant a greater availability of certain

CONNECTIONS

See also
770 Physical cures for mental illness
772 Behavior therapy
812 Aspects of human nature
760 Introduction to mental health
762 How mental illness has been treated
764 Psychoses
766 Personality defects and neuroses
768 Psychosomatic diseases and retardation

1 A

B

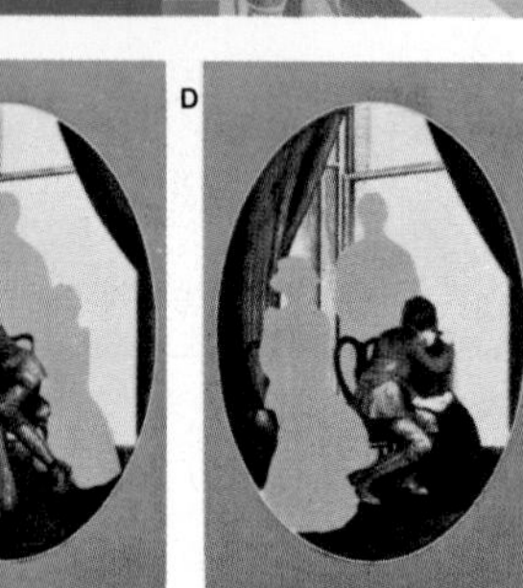

C

D

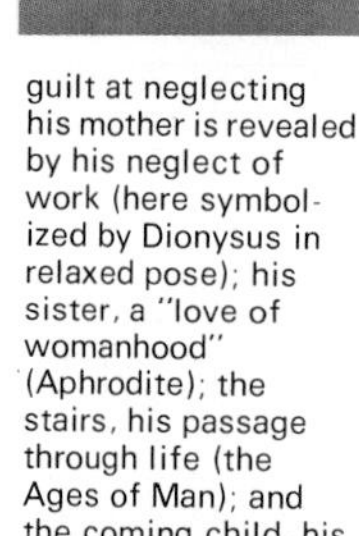

1 Interpretations of dreams vary widely. A young man dreams [A] that he is climbing some stairs with his mother and sister. At the top he is told that his sister is pregnant. For Freud the dream reflected conflict between primitive instincts. This often has roots in a family situation [B]. The stairs represent sexual intercourse, the boy's incestuous wish for his mother [C]. The expected child is an indication of brother/sister sexuality [D]. Jung interpreted the same dream in terms of symbols, or "universal archetypes" [E]. For Jung, the boy's guilt at neglecting his mother is revealed by his neglect of work (here symbolized by Dionysus in relaxed pose); his sister, a "love of womanhood" (Aphrodite); the stairs, his passage through life (the Ages of Man); and the coming child, his rebirth (by spring).

E

2

2 Group psychotherapy is any form of therapy involving more than two patients. Most groups consist of 6 to 10 selected patients. In group analytic psychotherapy, the therapist limits himself to interpreting the dynamics of the group. Verbal confrontation is encouraged but physical contact is minimal.

3

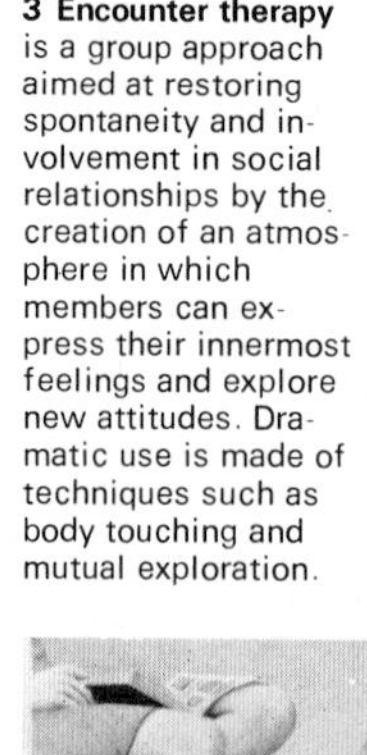

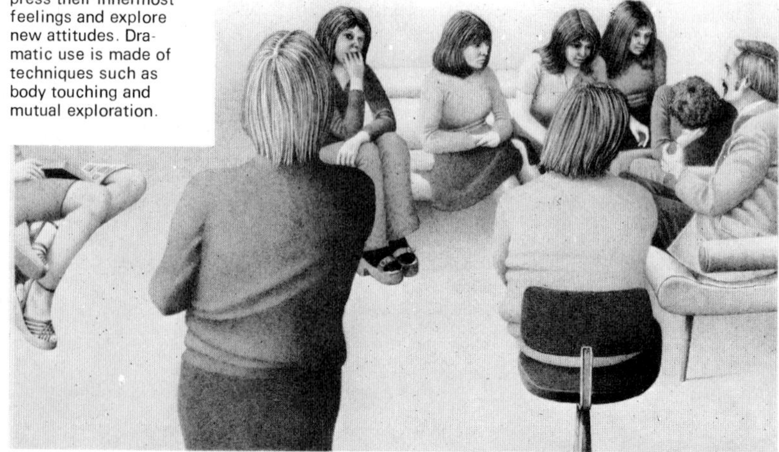

3 Encounter therapy is a group approach aimed at restoring spontaneity and involvement in social relationships by the creation of an atmosphere in which members can express their innermost feelings and explore new attitudes. Dramatic use is made of techniques such as body touching and mutual exploration.

psychotherapeutic approaches. The more orthodox groups [2], which may meet daily or weekly, are run under the leadership of a therapist trained in one of the established analytical schools. Less formal and orthodox groups have evolved over the years under the general label of "encounter" therapy [3]. These groups tend to be less theoretical: they are relatively unstructured, geared to action rather than analysis, and are mainly beneficial to those who do not have severe personality disturbances or mental illnesses.

An offshoot of encounter therapy is marathon therapy, in which the participants and therapists meet continuously for 24–72 hours. Enthusiasts claim that it is effective for couples with marital problems.

Recent developments

Encounter groups often use principles developed by Jacob Moreno, the founder of psychodrama [4]. Janov's primal therapy [5] and Gestalt psychotherapy, with its emphasis on the patient's need to achieve behavioral change through understanding and experience, both involve intense, often exhausting participation and the acting-out of the individual's emotional turmoil.

Such treatments contrast sharply with a Japanese form of psychotherapy, Morita therapy, in which the patient, under the guidance of a specially trained mentor, undergoes a rigid and ritualized form of re-education that requires his participation in a number of prescribed social activities. The patient is discouraged from baring his soul or analyzing his feelings, activities that feed the egocentricity believed to underlie all neuroses.

One therapeutic approach that has developed outside the main medical, analytical, and behavioral traditions is counseling. While concepts taken from medicine, behaviorist psychology, and psychoanalysis are utilized, the major influence is derived from the American psychologist Carl Rogers and his client-centered therapy. Such an approach emphasizes the growth of an equal relationship between therapist and client and the rejection of any imposed system of attitudes or values.

KEY

Sigmund Freud (1856-1939)
Carl Jung (1875-1961)
Alfred Adler (1870-1937)
Melanie Klein (1882-1960)
Jacob Moreno (1889-1974)
Carl Rogers (1902-)

The foundations of psychoanalytic theory and practice were laid by Sigmund Freud. Carl Jung, disenchanted with Freud's teachings, turned for inspiration to philosophy, religion, and metaphysics. Alfred Adler emphasized the importance of man's inferiority feelings. Melanie Klein concentrated on the role of primitive infantile wishes. Jacob Moreno developed psychodrama and Carl Rogers advocated the adoption of noninterpretative psychotherapy.

4

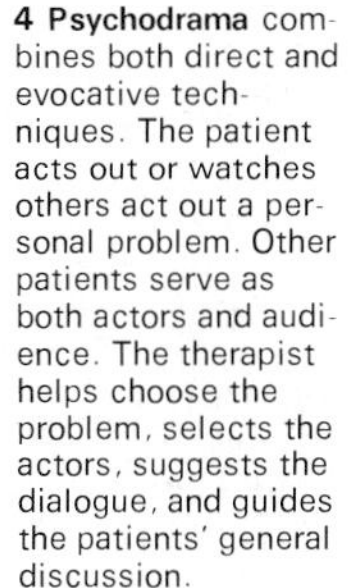

4 Psychodrama combines both direct and evocative techniques. The patient acts out or watches others act out a personal problem. Other patients serve as both actors and audience. The therapist helps choose the problem, selects the actors, suggests the dialogue, and guides the patients' general discussion.

5

5 Arthur Janov's primal therapy portrays neurosis as a defense against pain and seeks to induce cathartic emotional responses. Direct experience of pain is believed to be curative and so the patient is encouraged to undergo a series of "primals"—angry, fearful, sad, or violent outbursts and upheavals.

6

6 Family therapy is a method of psychotherapeutic intervention requiring direct and continual emotional involvement between the family and therapist. For tactical or practical reasons some family members may be excluded from a few sessions, but the focus and benefit is aimed at the whole family.

7

7 Marital therapy is designed to prevent marital disharmony and breakdown. In the typical joint interview, husband and wife are treated together by two trained therapists, one of either sex. Their relationship is explored in depth and skills derived from psychoanalysis are employed in this kind of therapy.

Human development

Physically a baby is an adult in miniature and physical growth is basically a process of enlargement of bones, muscles, fat, and of the baby's internal organs. The human eye may grow as much as 30 percent in the first five years, but it retains its original structure. Such changes are quantitative. Psychological or personality growth, on the other hand, involves marked qualitative changes. How these occur and what factors are most influential in the establishment of the character of the adult are subjects that have produced different interpretations.

Heredity versus environment

Perhaps the area of most controversy is the extent to which the individual is the product of his nature (heredity) or his nurture (environment). Heredity comprises two main elements: those aspects of behavior that are inherent in, or peculiar to, the species *Homo sapiens,* and those aspects determined by being born of two particular individuals. It is the difference between being a man rather than a lion; and being you rather than someone else.

There are some researchers who detect the presence of common human factors in people all over the world—similarities that range from the universality of religion to common patterns of social organization. These imply a common human personality that overrides culture, race, and geography. Noam Chomsky (1928–), the American psycholinguist, for instance, asserts that there is in each of us a model or blueprint of language that accounts for our remarkable ability to master complex linguistic rules early on in life. Nikolaas Tinbergen (1907–), Konrad Lorenz (1903–) and other ethologists (students of animal behavior) have shown the importance of animal heritage in crucial areas of human behavior—for instance in patterns of aggression.

As far as personal heredity is concerned—leaving aside the obvious examples of size, shape, and eye color—there is much (often heated) debate about the extent to which genetic inheritance controls emotional and social development and sets upper limits on intellectual potential.

Opposed to these theories are the so-called behaviorists, headed by B. F. Skinner (1904–), who emphasize the things that each individual is given by being involved in the process of living. This point of view stresses the particular situations and circumstances to which each person is exposed. The behaviorists believe that human beings are, if not good, at least innately "neutral" and that the "evil" in people is a product of their environment [2].

Is the child active or passive?

Within and around the nature/nurture controversy are several related areas of contention. Does the child actively manipulate his environment, trying to shape it to his skills and abilities? Or is he the creature of that environment? Essentially, both the behaviorists and the Freudians follow the latter approach, while thinkers such as Jean Piaget (1896–) favor the former. But although the behaviorists and Freudians agree that environmental influences are paramount, they differ radically in their interpretations of the springs of human per-

CONNECTIONS

See also
812 Aspects of human nature
810 The idea of the person
816 Freedom and individuality
798 Adulthood: from 30 to 40
778 Thinking and understanding
780 Language development
782 Social development
784 Emotional development
786 Moral development
788 The growing child
702 Pregnancy
814 Classifying personality types

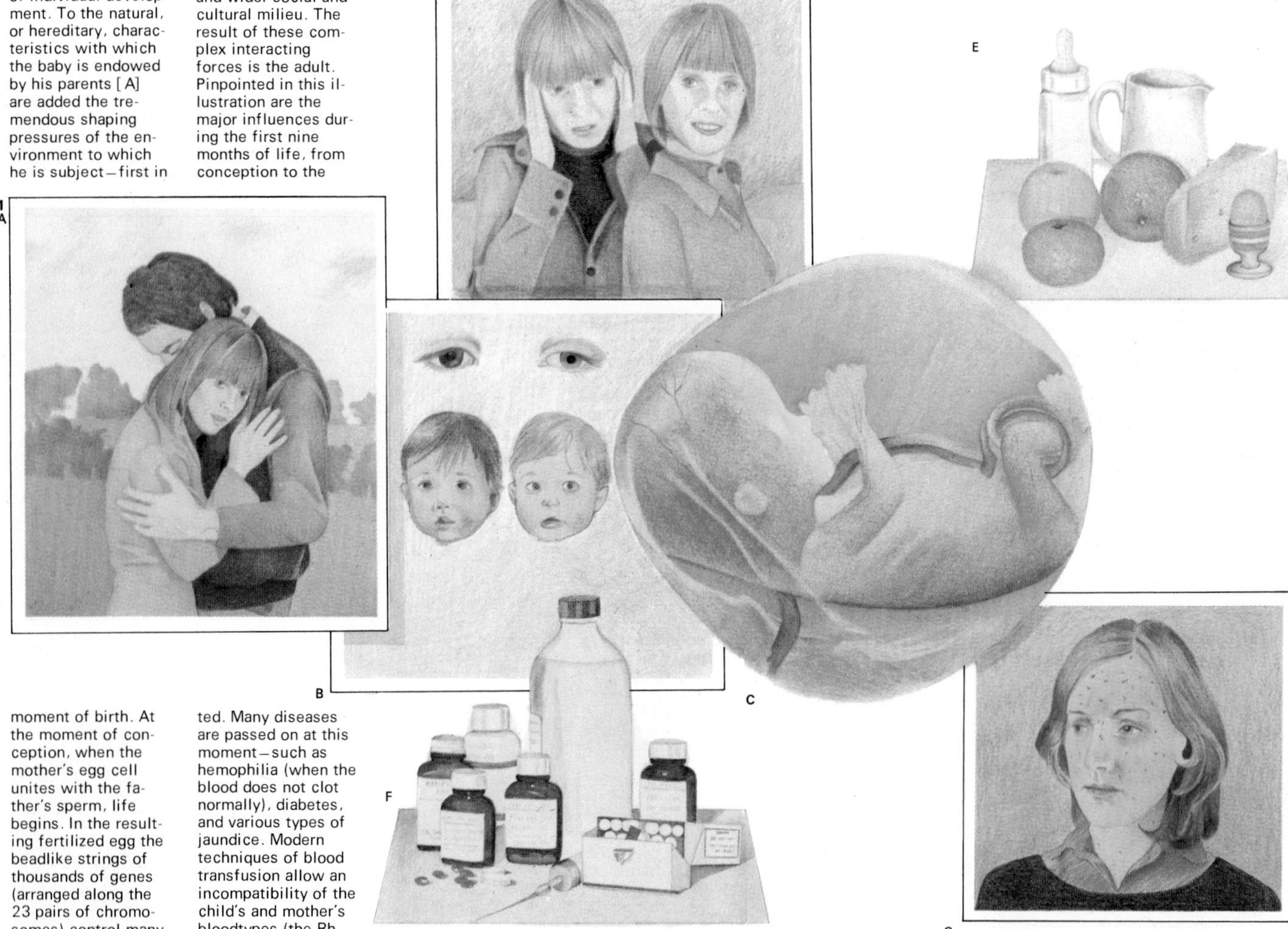

1
A
B
C
D
E
F
G

1 Many factors contribute to the course of individual development. To the natural, or hereditary, characteristics with which the baby is endowed by his parents [A] are added the tremendous shaping pressures of the environment to which he is subject—first in the womb and later in the family circle and wider social and cultural milieu. The result of these complex interacting forces is the adult. Pinpointed in this illustration are the major influences during the first nine months of life, from conception to the moment of birth. At the moment of conception, when the mother's egg cell unites with the father's sperm, life begins. In the resulting fertilized egg the beadlike strings of thousands of genes (arranged along the 23 pairs of chromosomes) control many areas of individual development. The most noticeable and pervasive are physical characteristics [B]. Such factors as sex, shape, stature, hair and eye color, fingerprints, and blood type are all genetically transmitted. Many diseases are passed on at this moment—such as hemophilia (when the blood does not clot normally), diabetes, and various types of jaundice. Modern techniques of blood transfusion allow an incompatibility of the child's and mother's bloodtypes (the Rh factor) to be remedied. Traits such as temperament, intelligence, and disposition are known to be genetically influenced, but how and to what extent is still not entirely clear. The embryo is in the womb for roughly 40 weeks [C]. During that critical time, particularly the first vulnerable nine weeks, it is exposed to many factors that can affect normal growth. The mother's emotional state during pregnancy is important [D]. It is thought that severe or continuing stress can influence the infant's activity level, birth weight, and emotional reactions. Food supply [E], together with the efficient exchange of oxygen and waste products, is crucial. Diets deficient in calcium, phosphorus, iron, and various vitamins are associated with poor development. Many drugs [F] taken by the mother during pregnancy may have an adverse effect on the fetus. Excessive smoking produces smaller babies. Babies born to drug-addicted mothers are also drug-dependent. German measles [G], if contracted during the first three to five months, can lead to a newborn baby with abnormalities in sight, hearing, and brain and heart functions. Untreated syphilis may also seriously affect the fetus.

sonality. If, for instance, a child is afraid of dogs although he has never been attacked by one, the Freudian might argue that the dog's fierceness symbolizes the anger of the child's father. He will say that the child has transferred his fear of his father to the dog. In other words, he will look behind immediate behavior for a deeper or "unconscious" cause. The behaviorists, in contrast, will seek to relate the fear to an actual incident that led the child to conclude that all dogs are dangerous. Persuading the child to face the cause of his fear, they say, will remove it.

Is development continuous

Whether development is continuous—a process of gradual evolution—or whether it proceeds by marked, step-by-step stages, is also a matter of debate. The sequence of psychosexual development put forward by Sigmund Freud (1856–1939) implies that a child's pleasure drive is successively directed to different parts of the body, beginning with the oral and moving through the anal to the genital stage at puberty.

Another argument concerns the direction of development. Does it tend toward a final, ideal goal or is it open-ended and indeterminate? Behaviorists favor the open-ended view. Others, such as Lawrence Kohlberg (1927–   ), believe that there is a desirable endpoint that, when reached, defines and identifies maturity.

Scientific verification for any of these views is difficult. In the nature/nurture controversy the nearest approach to laboratory standards are studies using identical twins raised either with different backgrounds after adoption or together in their natural family.

The various views described are extremes but they illustrate the type and complexity of the problems. Shape, size, and features, for example, depend not only on genetic inheritance but on such purely environmental factors as nutrition and disease both in the womb and later. Heredity, culture, socioeconomic class, and personal experience all play vital parts in the process by which the newborn infant is transformed into a particular kind of adult.

KEY

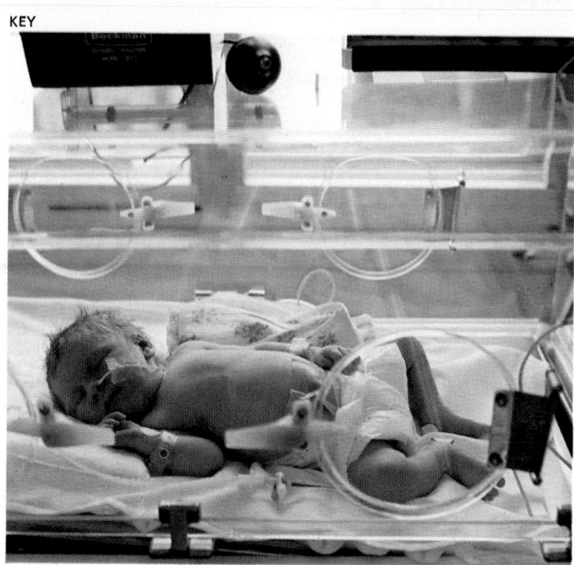

The development of the newborn baby into an adult is subject to many interlinking influences that stretch back to conception and forward to the quality of his environment.

2

A

B

C

D

2 The social environment and culture [A] in which a baby is born and reared exerts a potent and decisive effect on the development of his personality. The atmosphere and values of every culture differ and they are what condition individual assumptions and aspirations. Not least of the ways in which a culture affects individual development is through the methods of child rearing it practices [B]. Size of family [C] and birth order are significant to development. First-born children tend to trust adults more and to conform more to parental models than those born later. Studies show that children with older siblings are usually less aggressive and creative as adults. They adjust better to inequities in communal living. The solitary child is thought to have a richer fantasy life. The physical and psychological characteristics with which the baby is born [D] are instrumental in modifying and molding the environment he grows up in to a considerable extent. Size, sex, temperament, and attractiveness are qualities that affect the people he comes into contact with and so alter the ways that they interact with him. Hereditary differences in the senses, muscle mass, and sensitivity of the central nervous system are among possible factors that determine why some babies are more responsive, alert, and adaptive than others who are reared in the same environment.

Thinking and understanding

Until the early 1950s it was generally believed that a child, at least for the first few months of life, was capable of only dimly appreciating physical sensations. Because a baby's sensory awareness and intellectual ability were supposed to be primitive, he was pictured as existing in a world that amounted to buzzing confusion.

The many talents of the infant

It now appears that within the first few weeks of life a baby can focus his eyes, see one image with both eyes and appreciate detail [1]. He can distinguish between different tastes and smells and between sounds of different frequency and loudness.

As a measure of the speed of this learning process, the baby, at 16 weeks, is able to predict even the trajectory of a ball that he has seen moving but which, during flight, disappears temporarily behind a screen. From birth he also actively selects what he looks at or listens to, attending to those things that differ in brightness, contrast, pattern, or movement from objects he has seen before [Key].

Adults have an organized picture of the world that takes many things for granted. To arrive at this state involves a long, hard journey for the child. Perhaps the most influential researcher into this process was the Swiss psychologist Jean Piaget (1896–). From years of observation and inventive experiment with his own and other children, he formulated the theory that cognitive, or intellectual, growth takes place in a series of four stages or phases: the sensorimotor (up to two years) [2A]; the preoperational (two to seven years) [2B]; the concrete operational (seven to 12 years) [2C]; and the formal operational (12 onward) [2D].

During the sensorimotor stage the infant is constructing a picture of the physical realities of the world by touching, tasting, manipulating, and destroying. By these means the building blocks for later thinking are built up. From then on each stage marks a growing ability to think in abstract terms that moves away from the physical reality of actual objects and involves reaching toward an adult grasp of the world. During the preoperational period the child has difficulty in understanding that an apparent change in an object is not an actual or real change. If two glasses of equal size are filled with liquid and then one is emptied into a taller but narrower glass, the child will maintain that the taller glass has more liquid in it. Later on the child will not be deceived.

Stimulating development

At the center of Piaget's theory is the notion that what propels the child forward from stage to stage is "disequilibrium"—the situation that arises when a child's current picture of his world is shattered by the facts that his observations reveal. A young child will treat a magnet like any other toy, examining its size, weight, and taste until he suddenly discovers that, unlike other objects, it attracts metal. This, according to Piaget, will put the child's world into disequilibrium and compel him to revise his picture of it.

A prominent feature of childhood is the markedly self-centered thinking typical of younger children. They assume that others

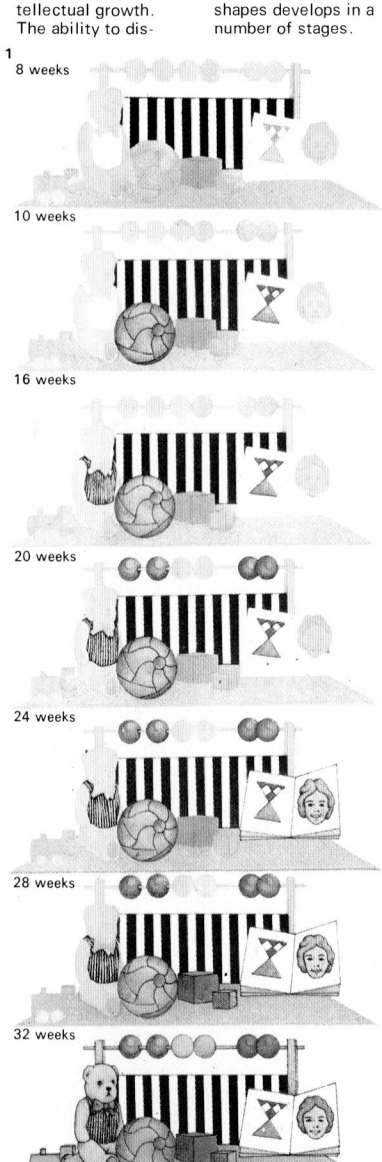

CONNECTIONS

See also
780 Language development
782 Social development
784 Emotional development
786 Moral development
788 The growing child
776 Human development
670 Memory and recall
668 Mind and brain
768 Psychosomatic diseases and retardation
772 Behavior therapy
464 Principles of animal behavior
672 Potential of the mind

1 The acquisition of visual skills is an important part of intellectual growth. The ability to discriminate between lines, patterns, colors, sizes, and shapes develops in a number of stages.

8 weeks
10 weeks
16 weeks
20 weeks
24 weeks
28 weeks
32 weeks

2A

B

I can make the sun move, he follows me around. Sometimes a cloud eats him.
Sometimes God sets him on fire
Sun
Cloud
Tree

C

Look, the sun follows me around.
Large
Medium
Small
How can the sun follow both of us around?

D

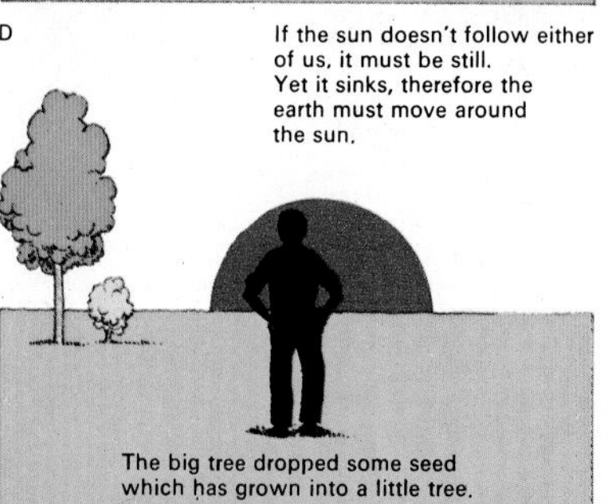

If the sun doesn't follow either of us, it must be still. Yet it sinks, therefore the earth must move around the sun.
The big tree dropped some seed which has grown into a little tree.

2 Jean Piaget, the Swiss psychologist, has shown that intellectual development, although a continuing process of discovery, can be divided into four main stages. In each stage different methods of understanding the world are used, each with its own logic and consistency, even if it does not conform to adult patterns. Piaget states that two processes, which he calls assimilation and accommodation, are essential for this growth. The child either assimilates new information into his existing view of the world, thus filling in more details or, if this is not possible because it does not fit into his past experience, he accommodates the new information by revising his way of thinking. The increasing use by the child of accommodation indicates intellectual growth. For the first 2 years [A] the child is said to be in the sensorimotor stage of development. He understands the world through direct contact with objects and comes to realize that they have a distinct and separate existence. Gradually he learns that they continue to exist even when out of sight. He shows his intelligence through his actions. From 2 to 7 years [B] the child is in the preoperational stage. Thought is more abstract and the image of an object is linked with thoughts about it. The child can also visualize something without seeing it, but thinks everyone shares his view of the world. Unconscious contradictions are common. From 7 to 12 years [C] the child is in the concrete operational stage. He is able to distinguish between present and historic time. He can order and arrange objects according to weight, size, and volume and describe a series of actions (like walking to school), carrying the entire sequence in his mind. From 12 years onward [D] the child is in the formal operational stage. Adolescents are able to use abstract rules to solve problems and they become more preoccupied with thought (and why they are thinking thoughts). They will perceive and explain things in increasingly objective, naturalistic terms. Presented with problems, they will consider possible alternative solutions and choose the one that is most suitable.

3

3 Classical conditioning arises from "association." A child shows unlearned automatic fear of such things as loud noises. If a child sees a rabbit, about which he has no preformed ideas, at the same time as he hears a loud noise, he will begin to associate the rabbit with fear. Soon, the sight of the rabbit alone is enough to make him afraid. The Russian physiologist Ivan Pavlov was the first to observe and record such behavior in his conditioning experiments with dogs.

see, experience, and think about the world in precisely the same way and from the same physical standpoint as they do. Children are only gradually made to realize that theirs is not necessarily the correct or only view. Another change in thinking that takes place during childhood is a decrease in attempts to provide magical explanations.

Learning involves a number of complex mechanisms. The Russian physiologist Ivan Pavlov (1849–1936), basing his theories on the results of his experiments with dogs, showed that we learn to connect impressions or bits of information by the process of association. He rang a bell at the same time as he fed the dogs and their mouths started to water. Soon the ringing of the bell by itself stimulated salivation. This is called classical conditioning [3] and many emotional reactions are learned according to this principle.

Operant conditioning

The American behaviorist B. F. Skinner (1904–) believes that we learn to do things, or not to do things, by observing reactions of those around us. We tend to repeat actions that are rewarded and avoid those that are punished. Our behavior is said to be positively or negatively reinforced. This is called operant conditioning [4] and is a decisive factor in molding many areas of human behavior.

Operant conditioning has been found to exist even in newborn babies. In experiments, babies learned to perform quite complex tasks such as turning their heads twice to the right, three times to the left, and then once to the right. The reward offered was the stimulus of a white light coming on for a few seconds. But once the babies had mastered the rules they lost interest in the experiment [6]. This reveals a crucial point about learning and reward; it is essential to find the right motivation before the child will respond positively and so extend his field of knowledge. The pre-school and elementary education system of Maria Montessori (1870–1952) is based on this self-directing drive to learn and on the belief that the child has creative potential and a right to be treated as an individual.

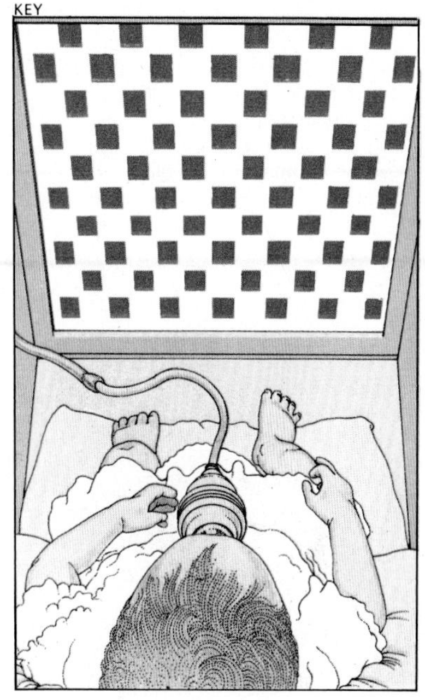
KEY

Technical advances in equipment and procedures have made it possible to carry out sophisticated studies even with week-old babies. These involve the use of electronics, videotape recording, one-way viewing screens, and infrared scans. The apparatus shown tests the baby's ability to respond to a quite complicated learning test. By sucking on the nipple he brings the picture on the screen into sharp focus. Results show that the baby soon learns to master the problem but requires the picture to be changed frequently to retain his interest. The findings show that young children have greater capabilities than had been thought.

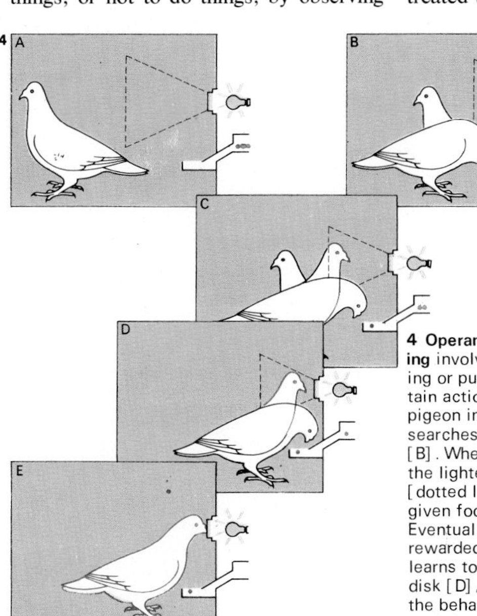
4
A
B
C
D
E

4 Operant conditioning involves rewarding or punishing certain actions. The pigeon in the box [A] searches for food [B]. When it enters the lighted zone [dotted lines] it is given food [C, D]. Eventually it is only rewarded when it learns to peck the disk [D], this being the behavior the experimenter wanted.

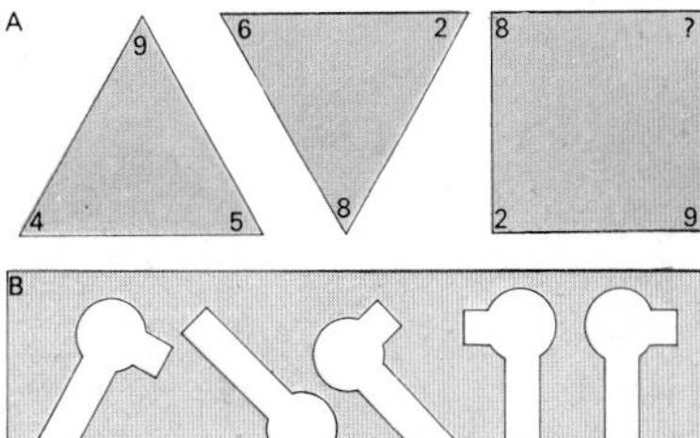
5A
9
4
5
6
2
8
8
?
2
9
B

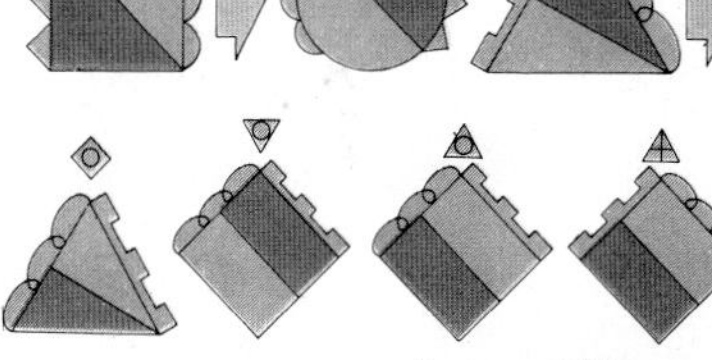
C
?

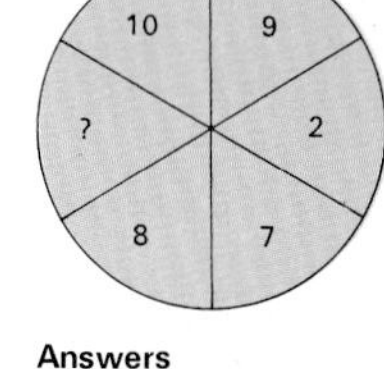
D
10
9
?
2
8
7

5 IQ tests were first devised in 1905 by the Frenchman Alfred Binet (1857–1911) to select slow learners for special courses. Since then they have been used to measure almost everything of importance in intellectual development. Creative ability, productive thinking and problem solving were all assumed to be measurable in a single test. Such tests have become the subject of controversy on the ground that they fail to measure intellectual growth, they do not show ability to learn, and are often loaded in favor of a middle-class cultural approach. Attempts have been made to devise, "culture-free" tests that would avoid this bias. The four examples of culture-free tests measure ability to see links between numbers and shapes. [A] and [D] are numerical tests, [B] and [C] visio-spatial tests.

Questions

A and D: What is the missing number? B: Which is the odd one? C: Which shape on the bottom row gives the correct answer?

Answers

A: The missing number is 3. B: The odd one is the fourth from the left. C: The pairing shape is the third from the left. D: Number 15 is missing.

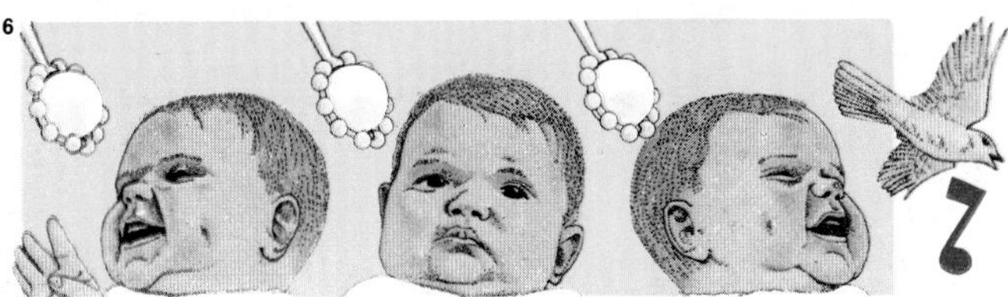
6

6 Habituation—or boredom—is one of the more important factors in discouraging learning and exploration. It is perhaps best illustrated by the common experience of a child soon getting bored with some new toy, such as a rattle. Children react positively to new challenges as long as the rewards for success are changed when they show signs of becoming habituated to them.

7 Chaining is the process of putting together related but separate movements into a coherent, coordinated act. Many of the things that adults do without thinking—such as the seemingly simple opening of a door—in fact involve a complex series or chain of actions. The child has to learn these painstakingly by trial and error. Everything we do is similarly pieced together through the process of chaining.

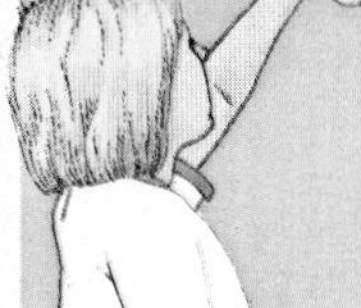
7

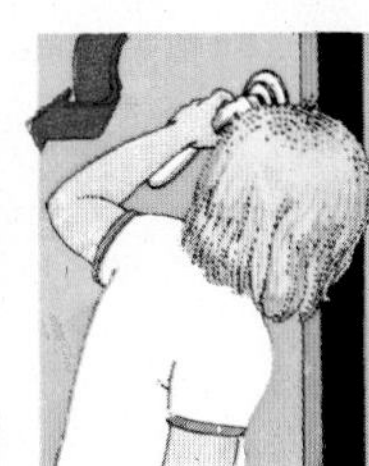

8
A1
B2
A
B
A2
B1
Intelligence
Time

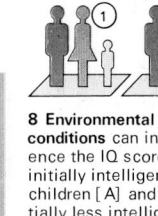

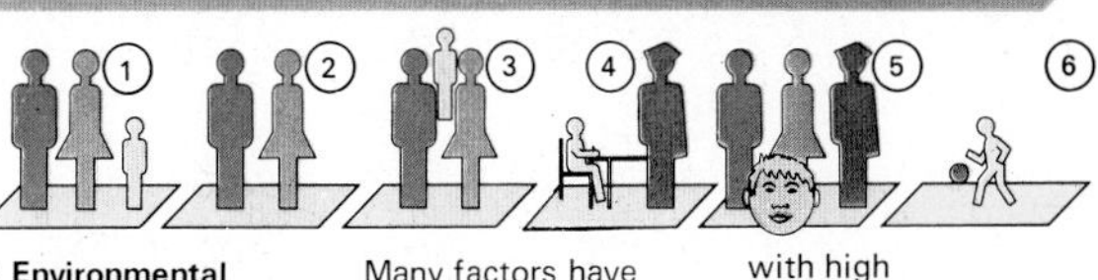
1
2
3
4
5
6

8 Environmental conditions can influence the IQ scores of initially intelligent children [A] and initially less intelligent [B]. This difference may be accentuated [A1, B1] or even reversed [A2, B2]. Many factors have been found to encourage high IQ scores. These include small family size [1], intelligent parents [2] who encourage the child [3], small, well equipped schools with high teacher/pupil ratios [4], where child, teachers, and parents are on good terms [5], and an active life [6]. A child will develop slowly if his environment is deficient.

Language development

The acquisition of language by the child is a remarkable achievement that has fascinated both parents and those who study child development. A central and fiercely debated issue of language development concerns the degree to which language structure and organization are innate or built into the human mind. At one extreme researchers such as Noam Chomsky (1928–   ) maintain that every human being is born with both a natural capacity for language and an already programmed model or pattern in his brain. In contrast the "social learning" theorists, inspired by the work of B. F. Skinner (1904–   ), insist that cultural elements are crucial to language development.

The beginning of language

There is a close interplay between intellectual and language development. From the start the human infant is active and curious and by the first month of life he listens closely to the speech he hears. (The ability to hear is essential to speech development.) Although he can usually distinguish between different speech sounds much earlier, the child is typically a year old before he is able reliably to produce patterns of sounds that are identifiable as distinct words. Apparently the muscular control required for such a feat is gradually acquired, first through crying and then through cooing and babbling.

By the time he is about a year old the infant communicates his feelings and wants by varying the intonation, stress, and frequency of his utterances. Soon afterward, as he truly begins to become a speaking human being, he explores the way in which speech is organized and discovers the systems of rules (grammar) for forming sentences.

This breakthrough is dependent on the parallel development of the child's ability to perceive the world efficiently and to reason about it. He must be able, for example, to retain an abstract image of an object that he has seen, heard, or touched before he can name it or respond to a name. Only in the second year can he hunt for a named object that is absent.

By about two years of age an infant can form rudimentary sentences [2]. He can usually comprehend, as well as express, a variety of fundamental concepts about animate and inanimate objects and about actions and events. He uses such words as "here" and "there," for example, to indicate location and "all-gone" or "all-done" to indicate disappearance or cessation.

At this period, because the child responds positively to a request such as "Please bring me that coat," parents are often misled into thinking that he understands more than he does. The fact is that conversation, particularly with children, is rich in nonverbal cues such as glances or gestures, and it is only in combination with these cues that the child can make sense of the words he hears.

The growth of language

From about the beginning of the third year the child rapidly becomes skilled at comprehending and producing sentences that do not depend on immediate context in order to be understood by others. By about the age of four or five almost all children have mastered the fundamentals of language, al-

CONNECTIONS

See also
864 Communication through speech: 1
866 Communication through speech: 2
778 Thinking and understanding
782 Social development
784 Emotional development
786 Moral development
776 Human development
788 The growing child

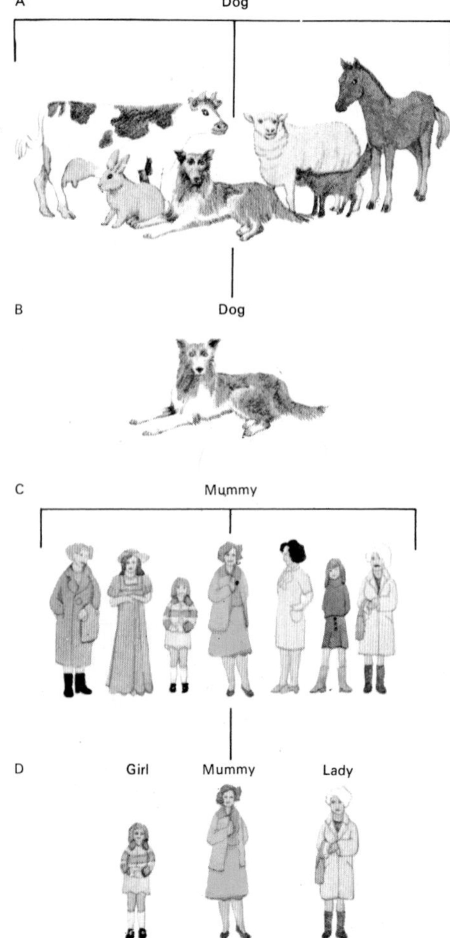

1
A
Dog
B
Dog
C
Mummy
D
Girl
Mummy
Lady

1 Language development in children does not always occur at the same age but most children do show similar steps in language production and comprehension. Typically, a child's first words work as a complete utterance. The word "dog" [A] initially refers to all animals with which the child is familiar. Similarly, "mummy" [C] is used for all females with whom the child comes in contact. The words mean "I see a dog, or some other animal" or "I want mummy or some other female." As the child develops, words gain more specific meanings. "Dog" [B] now refers to only one animal, a dog, and "mummy" refers to the child's mother alone, and he uses other specific words to refer to other females[D].

2

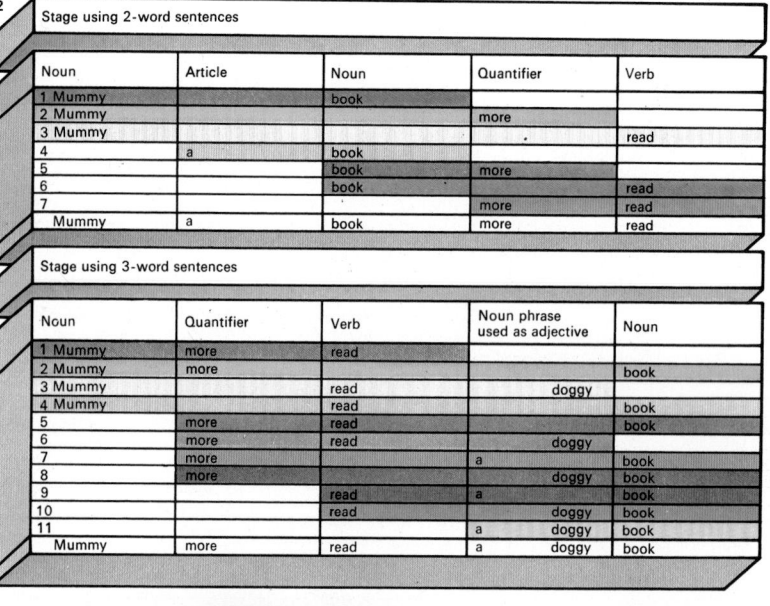

Stage using 2-word sentences

Noun	Article	Noun	Quantifier	Verb
1 Mummy		book		
2 Mummy			more	
3 Mummy				read
4	a	book		
5		book	more	
6		book		read
7			more	read
Mummy	a	book	more	read

Stage using 3-word sentences

Noun	Quantifier	Verb	Noun phrase used as adjective	Noun
1 Mummy	more	read		
2 Mummy	more			book
3 Mummy		read	doggy	
4 Mummy		read		book
5	more	read		book
6	more	read	doggy	
7	more		a	book
8	more		doggy	book
9		read	a	book
10		read	doggy	book
11			a doggy	book
Mummy	more	read	a doggy	book

2 Children soon start to make up rudimentary sentences using first two words, then three. At the two-word stage they choose between easy, unrelated words they hear and know are linked with what they want. They can then construct a number of sentences that express their needs. Once they are using three-word sentences they are already using more complex noun and verb phrases in their speech.

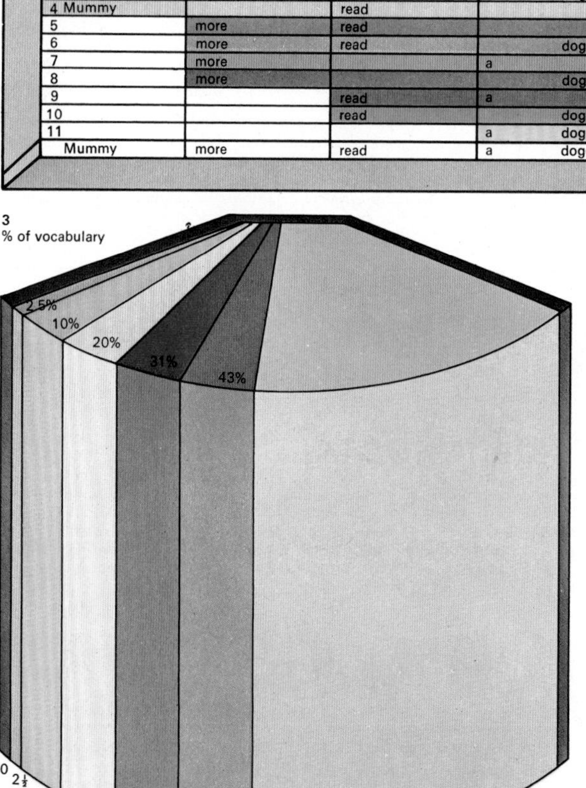

3
% of vocabulary
2.5%
10%
20%
31%
43%
0
2½
5
7½
10
12½
Age

3 The child's vocabulary can be seen as a percentage of his adult vocabulary. The child may use between 1,200 and 2,000 words when he starts school, and be using between 3,000 and 5,000 words at school-leaving age.

though they may have difficulties with certain sounds.

One of the most interesting aspects of language development is undoubtedly that studies carried out in different cultures have shown the universality of the patterns and timings of word use already described. In addition, regardless of the specific language involved, children use similar, non-adult yet nonetheless formal rules in an attempt to impose order on their language almost as soon as they start to talk. They simplify language into telegraphic speech. In doing so they produce characteristically over-regularized "errors" as in the plurals of nouns *(mouses)* and the past tenses of verbs *(holded)*.

What parents can do

Language is not only an intellectual achievement but also largely a social product. Parents therefore play an important role in encouraging their children's interest in and practice of language by talking to them as often as possible, answering questions, describing events, and by reading. In the early stages, when the infant cannot separate individual items from the whole, it is better to make connections between object and word as clear as possible. "Body" is less clear as a word than "hand" or "finger" since it includes so many different parts.

Exactly what type of language is used between parents and children, whether normal adult or stylized "baby talk," does not seem to be very important and is more a question of current fashion than of objective scientific fact. It seems likely that for the first year simplicity and repetition are useful.

One aspect of language development that often disturbs parents is difficulties in speech production. As many as one to two percent of school children, for example, suffer from stuttering, mostly between the ages of six and ten. On the average three times as many boys stutter as girls. There are various reasons why children stutter. But whatever the cause it can set up anxieties, especially at school where fellow pupils are quick to pick on and exploit a weakness.

KEY

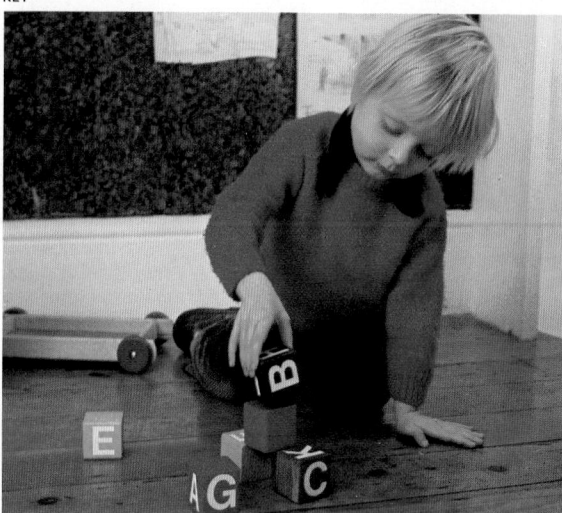

A child's first words usually consist of only one or two syllables, often repeated. Commonly, they are only a part of a word, for example, "og" for *dog*. The parents' active cooperation and interest are essential for language development.

4

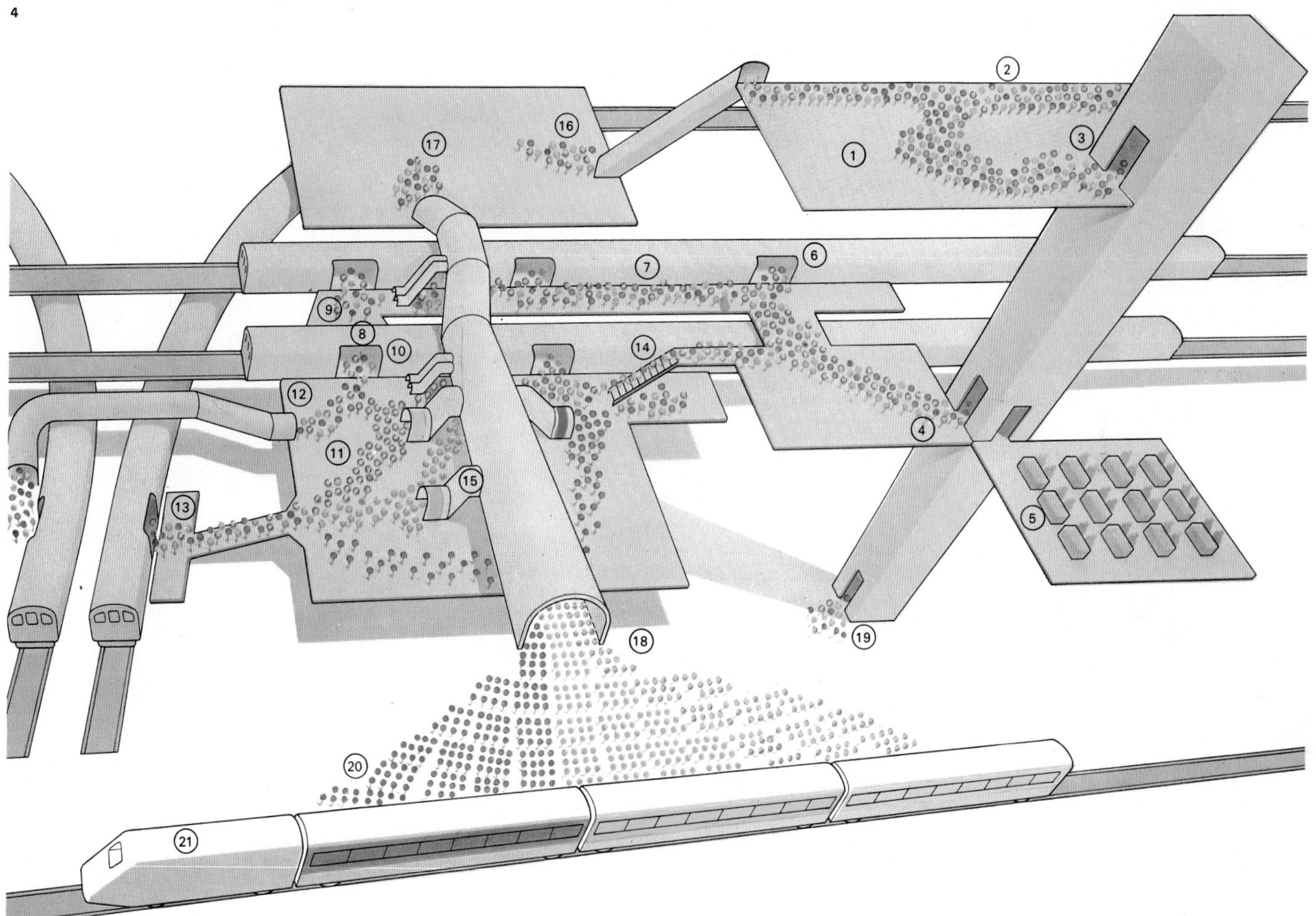

4 The child's rapid grasp of language is extraordinary in view of the complexities involved in making up a sentence. In this diagram the lexicon store [1] is the mind's memory bank for words. Language units assembled here [2] enter an elevator [3] and travel to the deep structure which contains the main rules for language usage. These are the syntax (grammar), the transformational rules, and probably the semantics, or meaning. From a departure area [4] monitored by an overall control center [5] words enter a train [6] to travel around the language system. Between the departure point [7] and arrival point [8] words are given both meaning and syntax. Some words [9] may go on a further journey to acquire more information. Others, which have acquired a grammatical make-up [10], arrive in the transformational area [11]. Here they are sorted into connecting trains according to emphasis, active or passive [12] voice, negative [13] or affirmative moods, and so on. Stray words [14] might cause an ungrammatical sentence if they managed [15] to enter the surface structure. Common words go straight from the lexicon store [16] to the surface structure [17], which governs the final presentation of words. Words emerge [18] ready to take their place in the sentence. Those that have fallen through the deep structure [19] emerge as ungrammatical language. The organized features of a sentence line up in the correct order [20]. A sentence [21] is then ready for the outside world.

Social development

Being human is not just a matter of having an upright posture, prehensile hands, a well-developed brain, and organs that allow speech. These physiological and biological characteristics provide the "what" that makes up the human animal. But turning the "what" into a "who" requires our learning how to be human, and this is achieved through continued contact with our fellow men.

The wild boy of Aveyron

In 1799 a wild boy of about 11 years of age was captured in the forests of Aveyron in southern France by local villagers. He had been abandoned at a very early age, but had miraculously survived alone, living the life of a wild animal. His captors, however, found a human being only in the physiological sense. He could not speak, but grunted like an animal. He walked on all fours and seemed devoid of all the usual signs of human emotional responses such as pleasure or affection. A physician, Jean Itard, took the child into his care, determined to teach him some human characteristics. His success was limited. After several years the wild boy had learned only a few words and could just manage to eat properly and keep clean. Little more could be done, for he had missed the vital social and cultural process that psychologists describe as socialization.

Stages in social development

Social development begins at birth and ends with death, but there is a crucial period in the child's early life during which the "social self" is formed. There seem to be four basic mechanisms that encourage all children in all cultures to become social beings: the desire to obtain regard, acceptance, and recognition from others; the desire to identify with or be like those who are admired and loved; the fear of rejection and punishment; and the tendency to imitate. These four mechanisms influence different aspects of behavior and dominate at different times.

The process begins at birth. The newborn infant has no specific values, attitudes, or beliefs; just a propensity to develop into a social being. All theories of personality, regardless of their specific differences, stress the notion that we learn to be what we are because we interact with others, especially those who are accepting, supportive, and encouraging, while guiding us according to those rules generally considered to be socially desirable.

In most cultures it is the parents who are the main socializing agents, with mothers being particularly influential [1]. We are all affected by prevailing cultural standards, but the environment of the family to which we belong is a more specific and sharply focused influence because it filters and concentrates that culture.

The family's socio-economic class is also crucial because it conditions what is seen as desirable, probable, and possible, and so how we come to regard the world—our aspirations, hopes, and fears. The immediate depth of the family's influence is altered by other influences such as religious and political leaders and the mass media. The importance of these elements varies from time to time, but throughout, the original lessons learned at home are crucial.

CONNECTIONS

See also
- **784** Emotional development
- **786** Moral development
- **790** Adolescence
- **792** Adolescence: sex and independence
- **556** How mammals behave
- **558** How primates behave
- **994** Classical Greece
- **788** The growing child
- **892** The individual in society
- **812** Aspects of human nature
- **776** Human development
- **778** Thinking and understanding
- **780** Language development

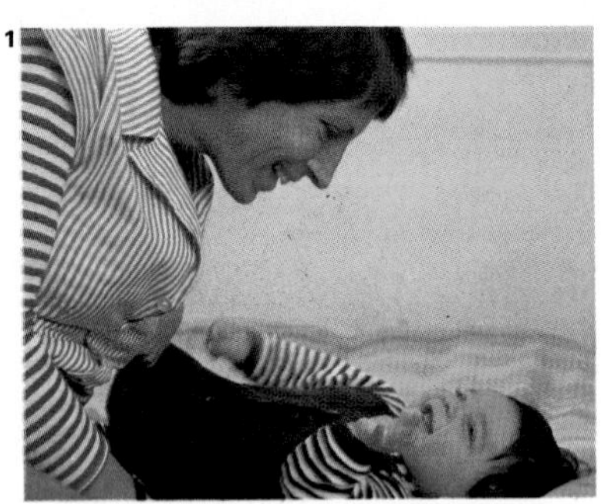

1 The child's early play during his first year primarily involves contact with his mother. He engages little in social play. In the second year, even when in close physical proximity with each other, children are usually quite content to play alone.

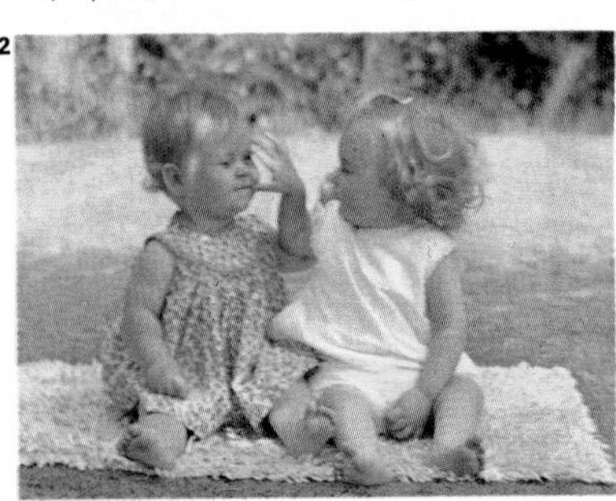

2 As children begin to meet more frequently, toward the end of their second year, play often ends in verbal or physical battles, with each child demanding the toys and other objects or privileges for himself. This phase lasts for six months or more.

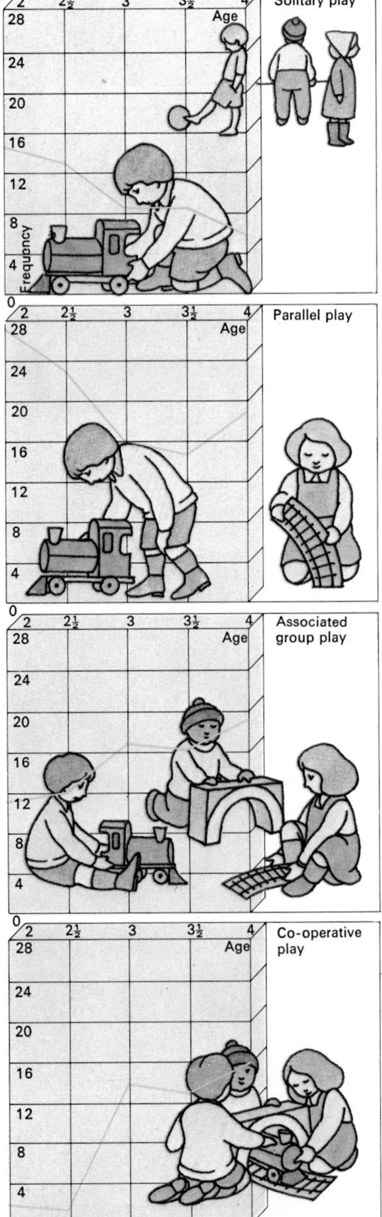

Solitary play
Parallel play
Associated group play
Co-operative play
Age
2
2½
3
3½
4
Frequency
0
4
8
12
16
20
24
28

3 Different types of play serve a variety of purposes for the young child. Both solitary and parallel play, involving little or no social activity and an apparent lack of effort to adapt to playmates, are prominent early in development and then decline between ages 2 and 3. At approximately 3 years, with increasing competence in intellectual, social, and physical skills, children begin to seek out playmates actively. Their play takes on a more reciprocal and communal quality. In associated group and cooperative play children increasingly come to take into account the feelings, skills, and responses of their playmates and others.

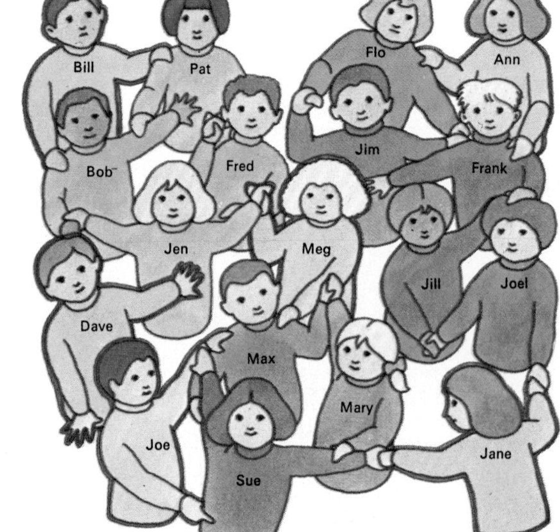

4 January
Bill
Pat
Flo
Ann
Bob
Fred
Jim
Frank
Jen
Meg
Jill
Joel
Dave
Max
Mary
Joe
Sue
Jane

October
Bill
Pat
Fred
Jim
Ann
Flo
Jen
Jill
Dave
Joel
Frank
Bob
Joe
Max
Mary
Jane
Sue
Meg

4 A child's popularity [shown by connections between children] or unpopularity [shown by red outlines], in a school class for instance, changes over time although friendships seem more durable than enmities. Research shows that the popular child appears to be more outgoing, more rewarding of others, and more likely to seek help and approval than clinging affection.

Between the ages of two and five the child goes through a crash course of learning to make his impulses more social. He absorbs rules about property, the rights and welfare of others, and the postponement of gratification of desires. The quality of that period and the way it is handled is critical. Affecting the family situation is the specific interaction between the parents' and the child's different temperaments and those of any brothers or sisters.

After the child is five or six, when he begins to go to school, peer groups take on an increasingly important role in many areas of the child's development. Playing with peers provides the child with the opportunity to observe and practice skills.

The importance of play is shown by its changing patterns [3]. Up to the age of 18 months or so solitary play is normal, and when children are together they tend to fight [2]. Then a change takes place and there is increasing contact with others in group games that involve and encourage friendly contact, reward-giving, the showing of affection, and toy-sharing. That peers imitate behavior has been shown in many experiments in classroom and laboratory [6]. If aggression is met by resistance it tends to diminish or at least shift focus. Studies have shown that when children of four or five see someone giving away toys during a game they are more likely to do the same than those who have not seen a similar model.

Learning sex roles

Biological differences set the stage for sex-role development, and experiments have shown that from a few hours old boys and girls have markedly different patterns of gestures and grimaces during sleep. At the age of two-and-a-half the child is almost fully aware of his or her sexual identity. After this identity has been established it is difficult to reverse. To a varying degree parents convey their own concepts of what is appropriate sex-role behavior—how one should relate to others if they are male or female and what kinds of work are undertaken by each [5]. Peer contact generally supports the cultural attitudes originally conveyed by the child's parents.

KEY

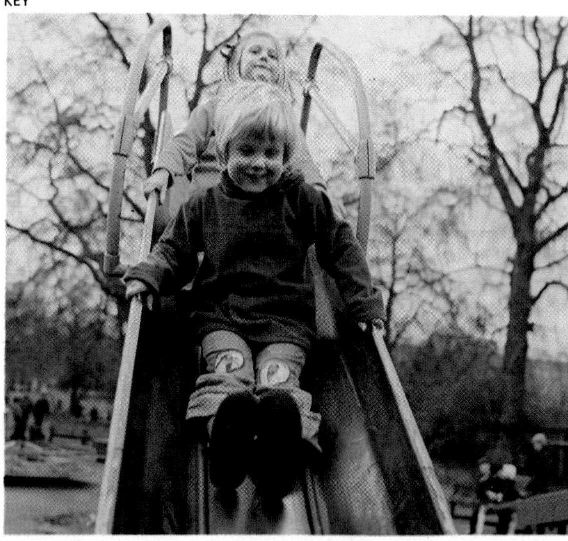

Adults may scoff at children's games of make-believe, but it has been shown that through such games children explore themselves and others, testing different behaviors and attitudes. In games, too, children learn the rules of society.

5 A

B

C

5 Boys and girls follow the unconscious behavior patterns [A, B] presented by their parents almost from birth. In most Western societies males are encouraged to be achievement-oriented, self-reliant and less fearful generally. Girls are taught to be conforming, submissive, and responsible. Increasingly, as stereotyped adult roles dissolve, children are exposed to more ambiguous influences [C].

6 A

46·2%
13·8%

B

31·2%
15·8%

C

54·1%
4%
26%

D

46·9%
10·1%
4%

6 Studies of pre-school children indicate that the more united the group initially, the more aggressive its members will be toward the outsider. Strong friends [A] and weak friends [B] were allowed to play with toys that were then taken away and replaced with less attractive ones. In the resulting frustration the strong friends kicked the experimenter [C]. The weak friends called him names [D]. The proportions of time spent in inter-friend cooperation [brown], interfriend conflict [blue], and aggression to the experimenter [pink] are shown below each picture.

7 A

A
B
C
D
Type of parent
Effect on child's development

7 Parental behavior can be affectionate/permissive [A]; affectionate/controlling [B]; hostile/permissive [C]; and hostile/controlling [D]. Each of these, if consistent, is thought by many psychologists to produce a different kind of personality: [A] a friendly dominant child with high self-esteem; [B] one more dependent, less friendly, less creative; [C] an aggressive child with poor self-control; [D] a shy withdrawn child with feelings of insecurity.

Emotional development

From the moment of birth newborn babies differ widely in level of activity, degree of irritability, and general responsiveness to their environment [5]. Today, emotional development—how people come to feel about themselves and others—is seen as being largely the product of early relationships and learning experiences both in the home and in the wider society.

A child's first emotions

The difficulty of gauging just what emotions the newborn child is experiencing is twofold. First, because he cannot communicate in words we must rely on such nonverbal signs as frowns, grimaces, and smiles, which are all open to misinterpretation. Second, our reading of the child's emotional state at any particular moment is strongly influenced by how we would expect to feel if we were in the same situation.

In 1917 the American psychologists J. J. B. Morgan and J. B. Watson proposed that babies are born with three distinct and unlearned emotions—love, fear, and rage—and that all others are refinements and elaborations of these. But it is now widely believed that there are no clearcut distinctions in the emotional responses of newborn infants and that it is only after a month or so that their emotions can begin to be divided into positive and negative. Emotions such as elation, pride, anger, and distrust gradually gain coherence over the next two years.

The evolution of the emotions is clearly shown in the child's response to strangers. Until he is about six months old the infant reacts positively to any friendly face. But, as his ability to differentiate between people increases, this indiscriminate response diminishes. By the time he is a year old the child will often react with considerable distress or fear to a stranger.

Fear, pleasure, and first relationships

Intellectual development is significant in emotional development. Different fears, for instance, are characteristic of different ages [4], because to fear something implies the ability to hold it in the mind and be aware of its physical and emotional consequences. Jealousy, especially that prompted by the birth of another baby in the family, commonly surfaces at about 18 months and is at its most explosive for about two years after that. During this period the child may physically assault either the baby or the parents or both. With increasing maturity the outward signs of jealousy become much less direct.

Positive emotions have been much less extensively researched than negative ones. Pleasure is widely associated by psychologists with the gratification of instinctual drives such as hunger and thirst. But even the one- or two-month-old infant will show a positive reaction in situations in which the satisfaction of primary drives is not involved. He is receptive to friendly strangers, for example, and also appears to enjoy solving problems for their own sake.

Studies with the young of the higher mammals, such as the studies carried out with monkeys in the 1950s by Professor Harry Harlow (1905–) and his associates at the University of Wisconsin [1, 2], and with human infants, have focused attention on the complex relationship that

CONNECTIONS

See also
782 Social development
786 Moral development
810 The idea of the person
812 Aspects of human nature
814 Classifying personality types
790 Adolescence
792 Adolescence: sex and independence
776 Human development
778 Thinking ahd understanding
780 Language development
788 The growing child

1

Avoidance of social contact
Normal social responses

1 The importance of family life in developing proper social responses has been shown in experiments with monkeys. Compared to a monkey raised from birth with its mother [1] one kept in total isolation [2] for more than the first six months avoids all contact and appears fearful, clutching himself and crouching. Monkeys brought up with siblings but without a mother [3] lead a normal life but indulge in more hugging than usual. A monkey raised with an imitation mother [4], although behaving normally with her does not show normal social or sexual behavior on growing up. If the mother can move [5], the monkey is less fearful.

2 A

B

C

2 Comfort and shelter are by far the most important factors in the development of an affectionate social bond between mother and baby, as experiments with monkeys conducted by Harry Harlow demonstrate. Monkeys raised in cages, separated from their natural mother but with both a wire mesh and a soft, cloth-covered surrogate mother, spent more time clinging to the cloth mother even though it was the wire mother who provided the food [A]. When these monkeys were confronted with a strange object placed near them, like a noisy, drum-beating toy bear, they reacted with great fear [B]. When the monkeys could cling to the cloth mother [C] this fear soon subsided. The cloth mother eventually came to provide a reasonably secure base from which to explore. The infant monkey would venture out to investigate novel objects but returned frequently.

3

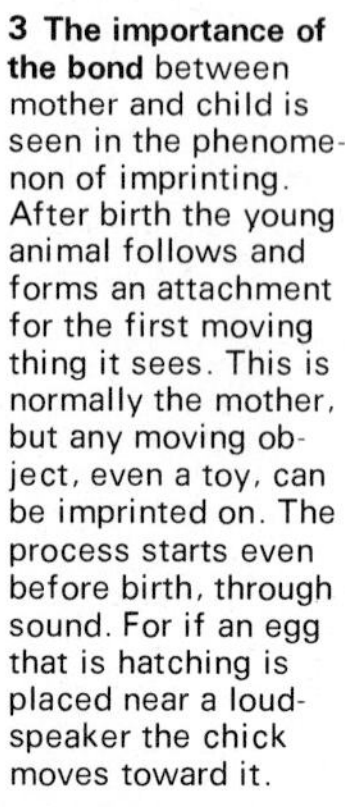

3 The importance of the bond between mother and child is seen in the phenomenon of imprinting. After birth the young animal follows and forms an attachment for the first moving thing it sees. This is normally the mother, but any moving object, even a toy, can be imprinted on. The process starts even before birth, through sound. For if an egg that is hatching is placed near a loudspeaker the chick moves toward it.

develops between the newborn infant and his primary caretaker (usually, but not always, the mother). The future emotional development of the infant is greatly influenced by this relationship. In animals this is also seen in the way that the young form a permanent attachment (imprint) for the first moving object they see, even if it is a human—as in the case of geese that imprinted themselves on the Austrian researcher Konrad Lorenz (1903–) and followed him everywhere [3].

Between the ages of one and three the child is particularly vulnerable to emotional disturbance if the primary tie is disturbed for any length of time—as, for instance, when he is sent to a hospital. This can result in an extremely trying period of crying and clinging and, on occasion, even produces symptoms of depression and despair. Hospitals are gradually changing their rules of excluding parents on the ground that their presence would "disturb" the child. Where prolonged absences are unavoidable, practical experience shows that they ought to be carefully explained rather than ignored and that the child should be surrounded, as far as possible, with familiar objects.

Erik Erikson, the American psychoanalyst, stated that it is in his initial relationship that the child must first learn how to receive and give love, and move from complete dependence to increasing independence [6]. Erikson further noted that the child who experiences feelings of security and love in this primary relationship is more likely to develop a basic trust in the world and in his sense of self.

Learning to control emotion

The child must learn how to express and control the needs he feels. For, as with most areas of human behavior, indiscriminate expression of the emotions is rarely permitted in the developing child. Aggression, a conspicuous feature of childhood behavior, is an important example [7] of this. In infancy aggression is an immediate and shortlived response to the frustration of wants. But as children learn that violence is not acceptable, aggression and anger becomes less physically evident and more internalized.

KEY

The family environment is crucial in guiding the child's emotional development. A fearful child, for instance, is frequently an unconfident one who feels that he will not be able to meet successfully the challenges he is faced with. Stressing his limitations aggravates the situation.

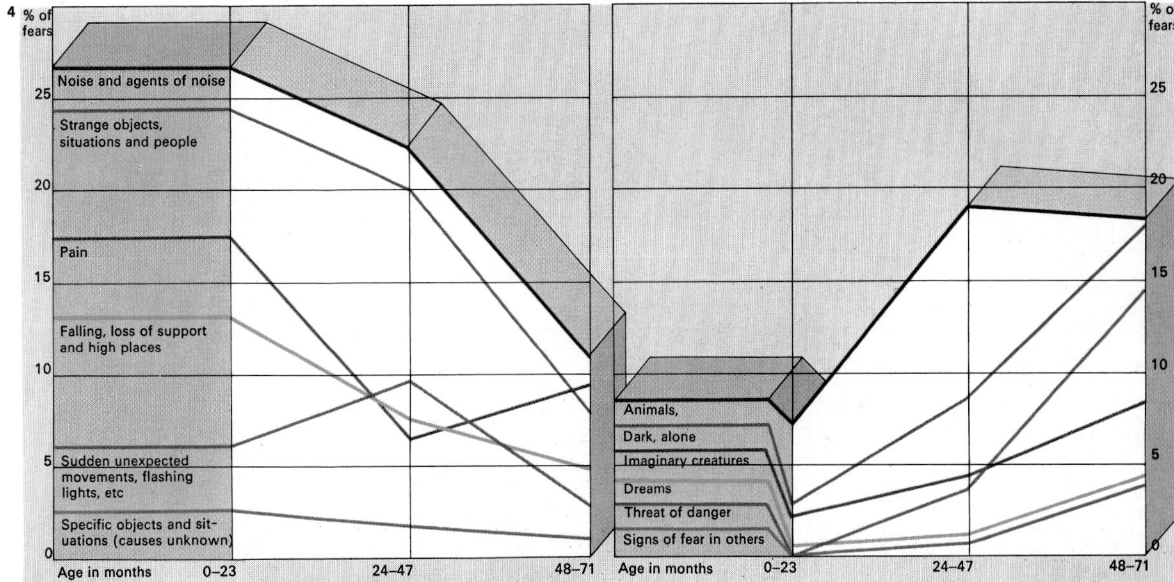
4
% of fears
25
20
15
10
5
0
Noise and agents of noise
Strange objects, situations and people
Pain
Falling, loss of support and high places
Sudden unexpected movements, flashing lights, etc
Specific objects and situations (causes unknown)
Age in months
0–23
24–47
48–71
Animals,
Dark, alone
Imaginary creatures
Dreams
Threat of danger
Signs of fear in others

4 The nature of children's fears changes as they gain experience. Their emotional reactions to different situations and objects reflect developmental shifts in their understanding and knowledge. Children from four to six years of age are more likely than those below two years to be afraid of animals, bodily harm, dangerous situations, being alone in the dark, imaginary creatures, or dreams. These fears depend on imagination and generalization from past experience—unlike those that are more likely to occur in younger children, such as a fear of sudden loud noises and strange situations, people, and objects.

5

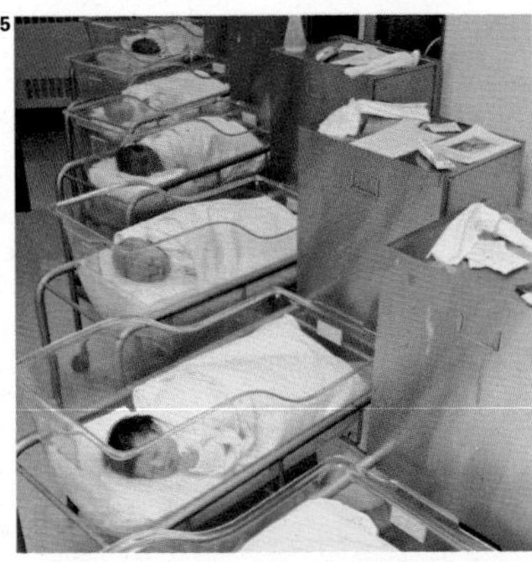

5 Marked differences in temperament or behavioral style are evident in babies only a few hours old. Such characteristics as tempo, adaptability, energy expenditure and mood, in existence from birth, have been found to persist relatively unchanged into adulthood. Where a child's innate style is compatible with the attitudes and expectations he meets in his environment, his development is likely to be healthy; where it is not there may be behavior disturbances.

6

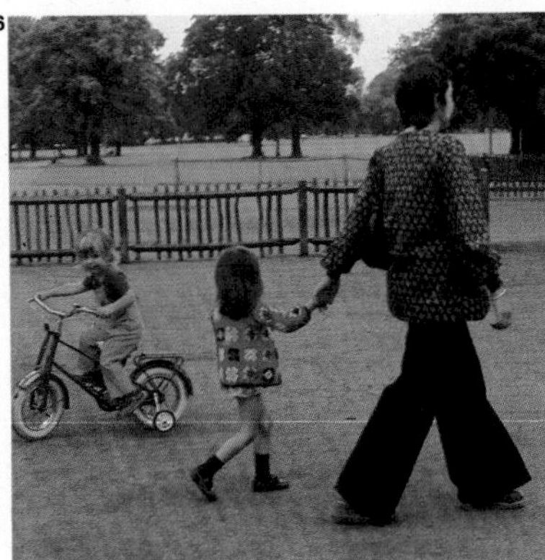

6 Independence is a sense of active mastery of the world, and starts as soon as the infant first discovers that he can influence his surroundings by twisting and turning. Later, crawling, walking, and talking all add to his feeling of self-assertion. Dependence is the need for support in untried, uncertain, or unexpected circumstances. Children tend to remain dependent if they are overprotected and not taught to follow some independent urges and activities on their own.

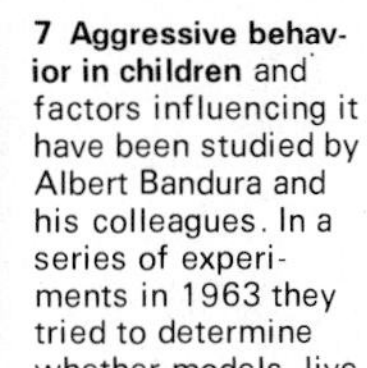

7 Aggressive behavior in children and factors influencing it have been studied by Albert Bandura and his colleagues. In a series of experiments in 1963 they tried to determine whether models, live or filmed, acting aggressively toward an inflated rubber doll, had a greater impact on the children's later expressions of aggression in similar situations. Regardless of whether the children saw live or filmed aggression, they generally imitated the behavior they had observed. They were also appreciably more aggressive than children with either a nonaggressive model or no model at all.

7

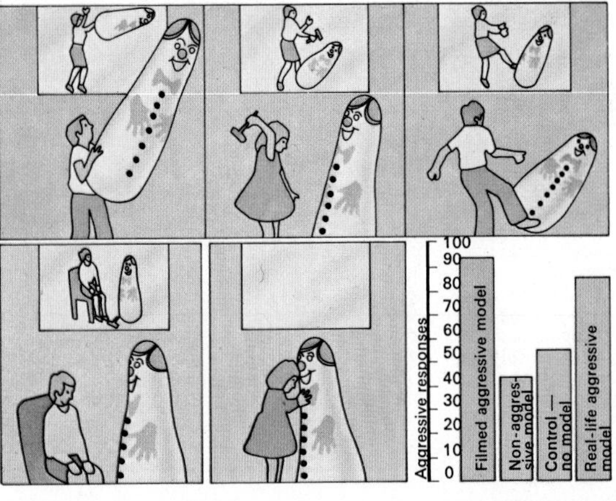
Aggressive responses
100
90
80
70
60
50
40
30
20
10
0
Filmed aggressive model
Non-aggressive model
Control — no model
Real-life aggressive model

Moral development

Learning to judge the rightness or wrongness of conduct is crucial to a child's ability to adapt to society. But it is not easy either to give a universal definition of morality or to say how moral values are acquired. Some people have put forward the theory that there is an absolute morality to which everyone should aspire, whereas others adhere to the view that each culture simply sets its own rules and induces children to conform to them.

Inconsistent values

In the teachings of many religious and ethical systems, morality is sharply defined; right and wrong are presented as polar opposites and the assumption is made that a person who is moral tends to act consistently in accordance with high principles when dealing with other people. But a study conducted during the late 1920s in the United States by H. Hartshorne and M. A. May suggests that most people have flexible moral standards [Key].

Everyone begins as an amoral infant who, as an active learner, acquires his first moral standards from his parents. These early standards are quite rigid and are tied to specific situations. The child often adopts them out of a wish to be obedient and avoid punishment or displeasure. The period between the ages of five and eleven is one of rapid moral development, with friends and teachers becoming significant influences on the standards of conduct adopted—largely through the effort to win their approval.

Although there are several ways of studying these changes in moral development, one of the most productive was that of the American psychologist Lawrence Kohlberg. In face-to-face interviews, children were asked to respond to a number of moral dilemmas and the thinking behind their answers was then investigated [2]. Studies carried out in various societies indicate three basic levels in the development of moral reasoning. Kohlberg classified these as premoral, conventional, and principled.

Steps in progress

Each progressive step is considered to consist of a more complex and balanced way of understanding and thinking about the moral-social world. Premoral reasoning is characterized by primary concern with one's own needs and self-interests. Conventional reasoning includes concern for others and an almost unquestioning acceptance of established authority. Principled reasoning takes into account the welfare of others and reflects self-chosen standards that are based on universal ethical principles. Law is respected but viewed as a human invention that can be changed as circumstances alter.

Higher-level moral concepts are acquired only in late childhood or adolescence, apparently because they require an extensive foundation of intellectual growth and social experience. It appears that levels of moral reasoning may develop in a similar way in all children, regardless of their culture and their religious background [1].

The fact that an individual is able to reason on a principled level does not mean that he will always do so. Different moral situations evoke different responses drawn from all levels. Systems of morality may

CONNECTIONS

See also
782 Social development
888 Structure of societie
892 The individual in soci ety
784 Emotional development
812 Aspects of human na ture
908 Rule of law
808 Questions of life and death
914 Nature and causes o criminality
776 Human development
778 Thinking and understanding
780 Language development
788 The growing child
1282 The foundations of 20th-century science

1

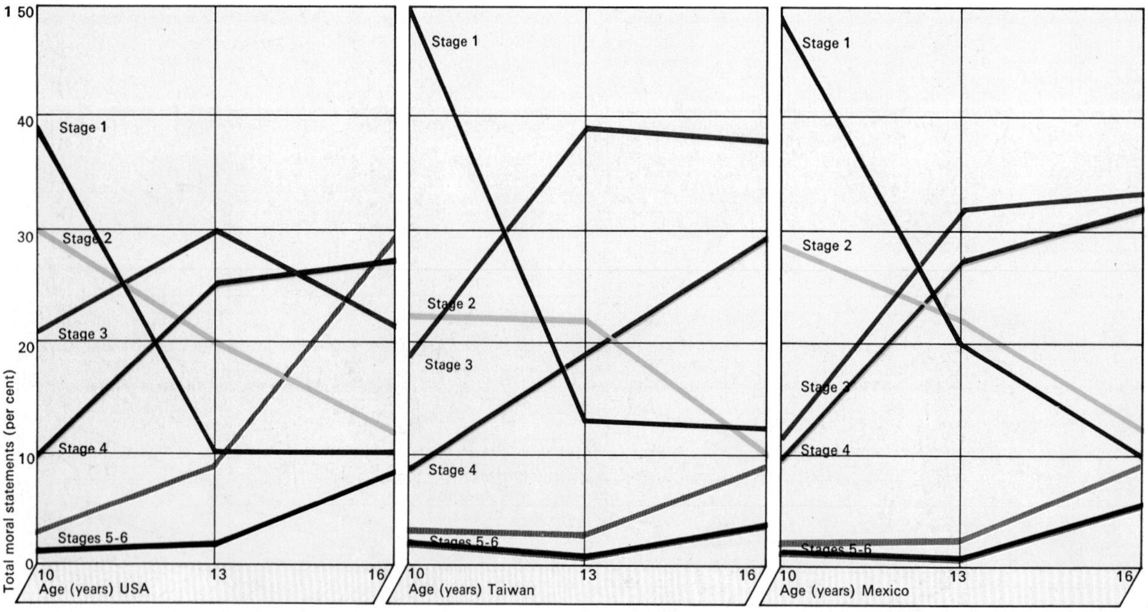

Total moral statements (per cent): 0, 10, 20, 30, 40, 50

Stage 1 / Stage 2 / Stage 3 / Stage 4 / Stages 5-6

Age (years) USA: 10, 13, 16 — Age (years) Taiwan: 10, 13, 16 — Age (years) Mexico: 10, 13, 16

1 Kohlberg's theory that moral reasoning develops in rising stages is shown in three different types of society. As the tested children grew older they provided fewer reasons for action at a premoral level [stages 1 and 2] and more at conventional [stages 3 and 4] and principled [stages 5 and 6] levels. The graphs also indicate that moral reasoning seems to develop in a similar way in different cultures, since the pattern of changing values is basically the same in each of the three graphs. The tests were conducted among groups of middle-class boys of various ages living in urban areas of the United States, Taiwan, and Mexico.

2 A child's level of morality is classified by Lawrence Kohlberg according to the response made to the following story: A woman is dying of cancer. One drug can save her. A druggist sells the drug for 10 times what it cost him and the woman's husband has only half the asking price. He tells the druggist his wife is dying, but the price is not lowered. The desperate husband breaks in and steals the drug. Ignoring the druggist's morality, should the husband have done so and why? Answers both for and against are grouped in six stages. In classifying these it is the reasons that the individual gives for his action that are important.

2

PREMORAL		CONVENTIONAL		PRINCIPLED	
Stage 1	**Stage 2**	**Stage 3**	**Stage 4**	**Stage 5**	**Stage 6**
If you let your wife die because you have not given her the drug, then you will get into trouble. Everyone will blame you for not spending the money to save her and there will be an investigation of both you and the druggist for your wife's death.	If you do happen to get caught, you can always give the drug back and then you will not get much of a sentence. It will not be too great a hardship for you to serve a short jail sentence and it will be worthwhile as long as your wife is still alive.	No one will really think that you are bad if you steal the drug, but your family will certainly blame you and think that you are an inhuman husband if you do not. If you let your wife die, you will never be able to look anybody in the face again.	If you have any sense of honor you will not let your wife die just because you are afraid to do the only thing that can possibly save her. You will always feel guilty that you were the cause of her death if you do not do your duty to her, whatever the consequence for you.	You will lose other people's respect, not gain it, if you do not steal the drug. If you let your wife die, it would be because you were afraid, not because you had worked out that it was a wrong act. So you would lose your self-respect as well as that of others.	If you do not steal the drug and thus let your wife die, you would always condemn yourself for it. No one would ever think of blaming you and you would have lived up to the letter of the law, but you would not have lived up to your own standards of conscience.
Contrary	**Contrary**	**Contrary**	**Contrary**	**Contrary**	**Contrary**
You should not steal the drug because the druggist will know that you were the thief and so you will be caught and sent to prison. And even if you do get away with it, your conscience will bother you and you will always be worrying that the police will catch up with you.	You may not get much of a jail sentence if you steal the drug but your wife will probably die anyway before you get out of jail and so it will not do you much good in the end. If your wife dies you should not blame yourself, because it was not your fault that she got cancer.	It is not just the druggist who will think that you are a criminal; everyone else will as well. After you steal the drug, you will feel bad when you think about the dishonor that you have brought upon yourself and your family. You will not be able to face anyone again.	You are desperate and you may not know that you are doing wrong when you steal the drug. But you will know that you did wrong after you are punished and sent to jail. You will always feel guilty about your dishonesty and the fact that you have broken the law against stealing.	You would certainly lose your standing and the respect of others in your community as well as violating the law if you stole the drug. You would also lose respect for yourself if you allowed yourself to be carried away by emotion and forgot the long-range point of view.	If you stole the drug, you probably would not be blamed by other people, but all the same you would condemn yourself because you would not have lived up to your own conscience and the standards of honesty by which you have always lived in the past.

reflect several levels of reasoning. Traditional Christianity, for instance, preaches right actions both because they are in themselves ethical and because the jaws of hell yawn for those who transgress (exemplifying both principled and premoral levels).

Formal moral values

As children develop their own moral reasoning, the way in which parents and friends react to their ideas becomes particularly important. Parents who take seriously their children's opinions on moral issues are more likely to have children who reason at a conventional level than at the premoral level.

What parents, friends, and others who serve as models actually do has a powerful influence. While words are likely to influence the development of a child's moral reasoning, they do not necessarily result in changes in moral conduct. In general, children copy what others do rather than what they say and are likely to develop consistent moral values only if the actions of influential people do not conflict with their words.

How a child feels about his thoughts and deeds plays a pivotal part in moral development. Typically, a sense of guilt and self-regulation develops gradually and so has an increasingly important role in behavior monitoring. As this occurs the child starts to regulate his own moral conduct. The child behaves morally to avoid guilt.

One of the clearest ways in which parents and others contribute to the development of a child's self-control or sense of guilt is through discipline for disapproved acts. Some research indicates that the most effective discipline is a brief withdrawal of affection combined with a detailed explanation. The latter encourages the child to see things from the perspective of another person and promotes the ability to form independent standards. The timing of discipline may be decisive. It is likely to be most effective if it occurs just before or just as the child begins to do something that is forbidden. When this is not possible, it is helpful if the situation can be carefully recreated by talking with the child and describing the action.

KEY

The American researchers Hartshorne and May tested the moral values of thousands of children during the 1920s by means of games and contests in a wide range of situations. They found that if a child cheated in one situation it was not possible to predict whether or not the same child would do so in another situation. They showed also that a child who cheated on one occasion was not necessarily the child who lied; nor was a child who lied to an adult necessarily the child who lied to a friend. The question in the end is probably not whether children or adults will behave morally or immorally, but rather in what situations they will do so.

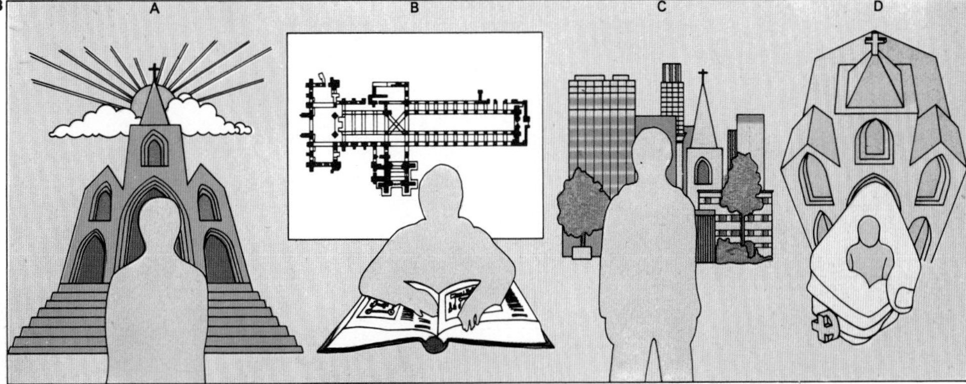

3
A
B
C
D

3 Our perception of the world is radically affected by our moral values. The sight of a church, for instance, will evoke quite different responses in different people. To a priest [A], it is the sacred house of God, while to an architect [B] it may be merely a construction. An atheist [C] may not distinguish it in any significant way from surrounding buildings, yet to a Marxist [D] it may represent oppression.

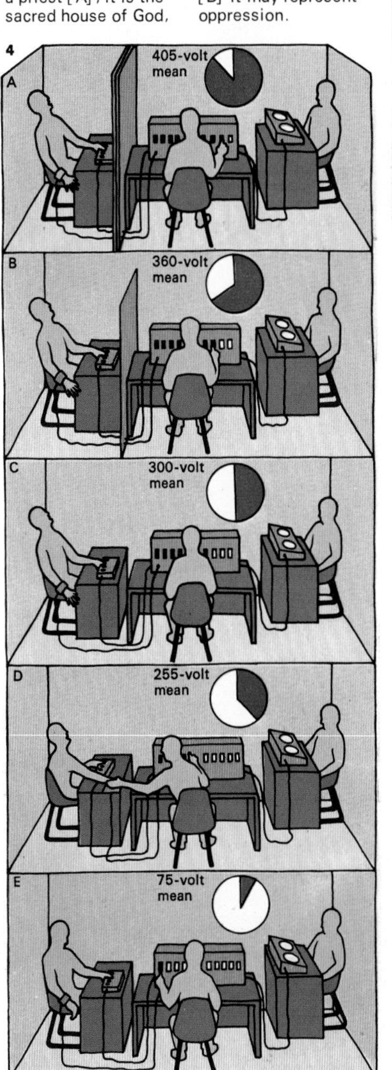

4
A
405-volt mean
B
360-volt mean
C
300-volt mean
D
255-volt mean
E
75-volt mean

4 Individual scruples and the demands of authority are often at odds. A soldier in uniform will kill but the same man in civilian dress might not. To test response to authority, US psychologist Stanley Milgram devised an "experiment" in which volunteers were required to give increasingly severe electric shocks (from 15 to 450 volts) to a protesting man (really an actor who was never actually shocked) to correct mistakes in a learning test. Authority in the guise of a "scientist" told volunteers they must go on despite a rising crescendo of protest. Where the "learner" was remote [A], 26 out of 40 people went to 450 volts, the mean being 405. Willingness to obey orders declined as the "learner" was brought closer [B, C, D] but it was not until the choice of maximum shock was left to the volunteer that the level fell to 75 volts [E]. Control groups predicted they would disobey.

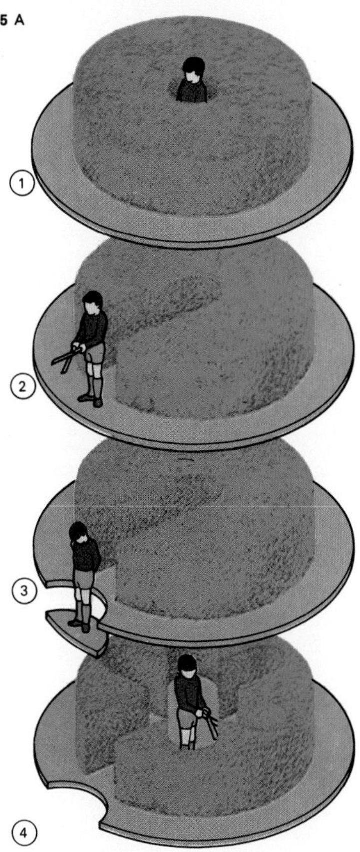

5 A
1
2
3
4

5 The development of a conscience is explained by behaviorist psychologists as the outcome of rewards and punishments [A]. A child starts with no model of how to behave [1]. When he commits a forbidden action [2], the outside world punishes him [3] by at least withdrawing support. Thereafter, in theory, he modifies his behavior to avoid the mental scar of the action and its result [4]. In contrast, Freudian theory [B] explains guilt as the interaction of the id, ego, and superego. The id, present from birth, conflicts with society by trying to satisfy the infant's basic needs. The ego then develops as a mediator to help satisfy these needs. Finally, the superego emerges as internal representative of social values. It inhibits sexual and aggressive impulses of the id while urging the ego to socially approved goals.

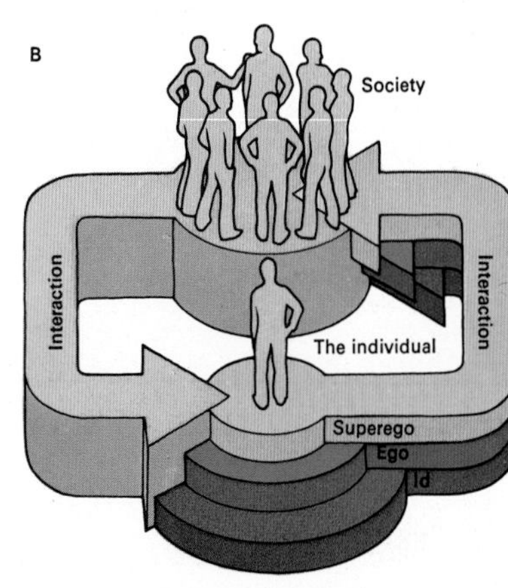

B
Society
Interaction
Interaction
The individual
Superego
Ego
Id

The growing child

Bringing up a child is not like a laboratory experiment—calm and controlled with all inputs carefully measured and predetermined. It is, like all other aspects of life, exciting, varied, and thoroughly unpredictable, and is subject to all sorts of unplanned influences and events, many of them almost totally outside the parents' control. Improvisation within a reasonably established framework is the best that can be hoped for.

Nature and nurture

Psychologists have explained and clarified the process of development. Their experiments and extensive researches have pinpointed a number of factors that contribute to the physical and psychological growth of the individual from newborn child to adult. The insight they give can be used in building the framework, but parents are largely on their own in supplying the improvisations.

There is nothing that parents can do about the hereditary factors they pass on to their children—at least not at the moment. But the behavioral psychologists particularly have highlighted the importance of the learning experiences provided by the child's environment. These both modify and accentuate the child's genetic potential.

It has been shown that the quality of the first relationship the child forms with his mother or whoever takes care of him is crucial in setting the pattern of the child's approach to the world in general and personal relationships in particular. There is also strong evidence that there are particularly sensitive periods in a child's life when the effects of the environment seem to be more readily absorbed and longer lasting. In the first three years, for example, growth in stature is most rapid and diet exerts most influence on eventual adult height.

If this seems to place a heavy burden on parents for the successful development of their children—and many parents suffer from a feeling that they may not be doing the "right" thing—there is equally strong evidence for the natural and striking durability of children. Certainly, single bad experiences rarely have a lasting effect. It is a chain of mistreatment that sets up personality problems. The occasional loss of temper by parents is of little consequence and indeed may be beneficial in showing a child that people are not made of wood. Children can weather anger without damage, but not persistent brutality.

Finally, there is the fact, pointed out by the US psychologist Arnold Gesell (1880–1961) and his colleagues, that children brought up in vastly different circumstances often grow up to be reasonably similar, fully functioning adults, irrespective of the advantages or disadvantages of their environments. Human growth tends to follow a consistent, natural course.

Changing child care practices

Specific child care practices differ widely both from culture to culture and from generation to generation within a single culture. Some North American Indian babies, for example, spend most of their time strapped firmly to a cradle board, but they begin to walk at about the same time as children from other environments who are painstakingly encouraged to walk. There are widely differing views—some of them directly

CONNECTIONS

See also
776 Human development
778 Thinking and understanding
780 Language development
782 Social development
784 Emotional development
786 Moral development
790 Adolescence

1

	At birth	**Up to 2 months**	**2–4 months**	**4–6 months**	**6–8 months**	**8–10 months**	**10–12 months**
Body	Almost totally immobile, but with many primitive reflexes, like sucking, foot extension if the sole is tickled, and finger grasping.	Able to focus eyes and coordinate stare. Can begin to lift chin when lying on stomach.	Can begin to raise head when lying on stomach. Many early reflexes are beginning to be lost (and grasp is no longer automatic). Can turn head and eyes to speaker.	At 20 weeks baby can open hand in anticipation of contact with an object. At end of period can grasp things using palm and fingers but no thumb.	At seven months can sit alone without support for a short time. At end of period can stand with minimum help. Can grasp using forefinger and thumb.	Can crawl by the end of the period and pull self upright to standing position. More adept at using tips of forefinger and thumb. Can hold feeding bottle.	Can walk with help. Begins to stop putting objects in mouth. Bowel movements start to become regular.
Senses	Even at three to four days old a baby is able to follow sound from side to side and to tell a buzzer from a bell.	Hearing may be particularly acute for short period, making loud noises painful. *Face recognition test* Dots and angles on picture of face are enough to elicit a smile.	Signs of recognizing things and of losing interest in stimuli. Depth perception. *Face recognition test* Needs first eye section alone, then nose as well to elicit a smile.	Increasing coordination between hand and eye. Explores objects by bringing them to mouth. *Face recognition test* Mouth helps on picture. Motion helps to elicit a smile.	*Face recognition test* Attention begins to focus on expression rather than features.	Depth perception is further developed. Child will avoid a visible drop from a surface.	No longer likely to be upset by sudden unexpected disappearance of an object.
Mind	Reflexes only, though rapidly learns to turn head to left or right to find food in response to either bell or buzzer.	Up to two years is the time to explore physical dimensions of things. Baby cannot remember existence of object if blocked for more than 15 seconds.	Can follow the trajectory of a ball even when it is out of sight for part of its flight. Can tell mother from others but no conception that he has only one mother.	Child distressed when shown optical illusion presenting three mothers.	Begins to develop the understanding that hidden or out-of-sight objects continue to exist. Will search for them.	Increasing realization that objects continue to exist even when not seen. Child will search for objects in many different locations.	With first words begins to create and use symbols toward end of period.
Speech	Crying or gurgling are the only sounds.	The first three months is usually the period of maximum crying.	At beginning of period cooing starts; it is sustained for 15–20 seconds. Soon baby will definitely respond to human voice and smile when talked to. Sometimes chuckles.	Cooing becomes more vowellike and consonants also appear, but all vocalization sounds very different from the mature language.	Cooing begins to turn into babbling. Most common sounds are *ma, mu, dar,* and *di.* At end of period repetitions of heard sounds become frequent.	Increased imitations of sounds heard but results inaccurate. Child begins to differentiate between words heard by making adjustments to position or behavior.	First words, often nouns which serve multiple uses (ie, "dog" means any four-legged animals). Shows signs of understanding commands.
Social	Can be divided into active, moderately active, and quiet babies.	Has often established a distinct pattern of crying and sociable behavior. Starts smiling at his mother at four to six weeks. Child is in Freud's oral stage.	Starts to play with objects—rattles, etc., if placed in his hand. Beginnings of differential response to people in his environment.	Beginnings of real differentiation between adults at end of period.	Increasing differentiation between faces. Beginnings of serious play but rarely with other children. Definite pattern of mutual interaction between mother and baby.	Beginnings of preference for play with other people rather than alone. Receives social support for trying to walk. Starts using imitative gestures.	May show dramatic decrease in excitability and in attention and response when mother is present. Begins to imitate parents' actions (combing hair, smoking, etc).
Emotional	Feelings are almost undifferentiated. Babies are either awake or asleep, active or inactive.	Beginning of the differentiation of feelings into positive and negative.	At beginning of period first clearly defined signs of pleasure (smiling, chuckling, etc.), and negative emotions.	Pleasure responses to others become selective. Fear and anger begin to emerge as separate emotions. First signs of self-satisfaction.	Up to 12 months is period when fear of unknown becomes marked. Attachment to known adults and relationships focused.	Consciousness of social roles evidenced by timidity toward strangers who are too intrusive. Smiles at own image in a mirror.	Differences between boys and girls begin to show in way they assert themselves and in readiness to touch toys and others.
Moral	Newborn is amoral, having no values, no attitudes, and no beliefs for the first six or seven months.	–	–	–	–	May show signs of withdrawal when admonished for bad conduct.	Understanding of parents' commands remains primitive and tied to immediate situations.

contradictory—on many of the most ordinary problems of child rearing. These include whether a child should be breast fed or bottle fed, whether a child should be strictly disciplined or never thwarted, and whether toilet training is necessary or not.

The question of whether to feed on demand or according to a rigid schedule is a good example of these problems. At the turn of the century it was common to feed babies only when they were hungry.

Then it became fashionable to use scientifically determined feeding schedules. The child was fed every four hours regardless of whether he had to be awakened or left crying until the proper time. This technique was viewed as character building because it instilled a sense of discipline and a feeling that the child was part of a world bigger than that of his own desires. Then, perhaps as a result of the emphasis that Sigmund Freud (1856–1939) placed on the dangers of thwarting the child's impulses, demand feeding again became popular. Today the question is not considered one of great importance, since it has been shown that babies are capable of suiting their food intake to match their needs.

Perhaps as important as anything else to healthy development is the general atmosphere in the family, generated by the interaction of the temperaments of the parents and the child. Some parents prefer active children, some passive. If a child does not conform to his parents' preference problems may arise.

Charting a child's development

There are approximate ages at which a child might be expected to pass some of the milestones of growing up and these are shown in the chart below. These timings are not a prescription nor are they norms that every child has to achieve to be a successful adult. Boys tend to be physically more adventurous than girls, who start speaking earlier. Allowance must be made for a premature baby particularly in the first year. Instead of beginning to smile at his mother at four to six weeks, for example, a two-month premature baby might be expected to start doing so at 12 to 14 weeks.

KEY

It is encouraging for parents who feel they bear a heavy responsibility for the development of their child that the results of very different systems of child rearing are quite similar.

	12–18 months	18 months–2 years	2–3 years	3–5 years	5–7 years	7–11 years	11–13 years
Body	Unaided walking at about 13 months. At beginning of period begins to cooperate in dressing self and in feeding self. Creeps backward down stairs.	During this period control over sphincter muscles begins to develop. Can run but falls often. Climbs up stairs holding rail. Girls reach half adult height just before two, boys just after.	Growth begins to be controlled more by hormones than by genetic inheritance. Control over sphincter muscles allows toilet training. Self-feeding reasonably controlled.	At end of period girls are slightly ahead of boys in skeletal development. Five-year-old's brain is 75% of its adult weight.	At six years child's brain is 90% of its mature adult weight. Nerve fibers, etc. are almost complete.	Significant increases in strength, speed and coordination. Child moves from fundamental skills, like running and hopping, to ones that need instruction and practice—skiing, etc.	Girls put on sudden growth spurt and by end of period they average two-and-a-half years ahead of boys. Menstruation begins.
Senses	Rapid increase in ability to use characteristic features of objects for identification purposes.	Can recognize displacement even though has not seen object moved.	Shows ability to distinguish between primary body parts and features; developing skill at drawing them.	Child finds it difficult to distinguish between open and closed letters. Confuses *b* and *d*, *p* and *q*. Ignores straightness, so confuses *D* and *O*.	Attention is more fixed on significant features of object or event. Increasingly able to discriminate between letters of the alphabet. At end of period can begin to read.	—	Increasingly perceives non-obvious relationships among apparently unrelated events and objects.
Mind	Up to seven years increasingly links image of object with thought about it. Lacks ability to imagine that dimensions are fixed. Piaget's preoperational stage.	Thinks everyone has same view of object as he has (ie. when he covers eyes and cannot see you, you cannot see him). Inability to describe journey, though he can find his way.	Progress in ability to classify many sorts of objects according to one or more shared characteristics.	Although child realizes apparent change in object is not real change (water to ice), unlikely to understand how or why this is so.	This is Piaget's concrete operational stage. Child can use concepts and rules, but deals almost exclusively, at the beginning at least, with here and now.	Can now conserve and see parts of the whole. Can represent a series of actions, like going to school, and can arrange objects according to size, weight, etc.	Child able to think around a subject, mentally testing many solutions. Use of abstract rules to solve problems. This is Piaget's formal stage.
Speech	Repertoire of 3–50 words. Shows no frustration at not being understood. Vocabulary divided by sex (man-lady) and size (man-boy). Telegraphic speech—"all-gone-food."	Repertoire of more than 50 words at end of period. Can string two words together (noun and qualifier). Grammatical use of articles, plurals, etc. Use of passive confuses.	Over period child able to put 3 or 4 words together. Structuring of language begins, use of tenses, plurals, order, etc.	Sentences become longer and more complex. Increasing grasp of basic grammar, like active-passive.	Masters irregular endings (ie. *mice* rather than *mouses*). Vocabulary becomes more complex and school-related.	By end of period has almost complete mastery of complex grammatical rules.	Ever widening vocabulary of more technical and specialized words. Greater range of concepts and terms to describe phenomena.
Social	At end of period fighting and jealousy over toys emerges. First signs of guilt at not living up to rules. Pleasure derived from particular events or people.	At end of period solitary play declines. Parallel play with little contact between children in one room is more common. Beginning of Freud's anal stage.	By 30 months will be helping with domestic chores. Rise in co-operative effort between children when playing together. End of Freud's anal stage, beginning of phallic.	Beginning of importance of peers in shaping behavior. Identification with same-sex parent is at its strongest.	Child's world is now dominated by peers rather than adults. Play teaches social roles and individual limits. End of Freud's phallic stage, beginning of latency.	Social interactions strongest with the same sex; minimal social interaction between sexes.	The sharing of possessions, feelings, and plans is still primarily with same-sexed peers. End of Freud's latency period, beginning of genital.
Emotional	Fear of strange objects and people declines. At end of period shows jealousy over newborn siblings.	At end of period fear of imaginary creatures and dark begins. More sensitive to ridicule.	Boys show increase in expressions of physical assertiveness and anger; these decrease in girls. Attempts at more independence.	Increased satisfaction at accomplishing a self-set task. Rising sensitivity to feelings and responses of others.	Child activity engaged in testing self-image.	Becomes less physical and more verbal in relationships with peers.	Alternating periods of withdrawal and gregariousness. Sexual feelings start to emerge.
Moral	Behavior up to six or seven years is primarily shaped by threat of punishment or satisfaction of needs.	Child's comprehension of parents' moral code consists of simple good/bad distinction.	Child likely to show substantial guiltlike reactions, though still situation-specific.	Still highly egocentric but beginning to show marked guilt and self-regulation.	Child's judgment of "right" changes. Respect for, rather than fear of, law.	Child does things to win approval or because the rules say so. Reasoning is more inclusive.	Actions are guided according to universal ethical principles.

Adolescence

The beginning of adolescence is marked by physical changes brought about by the sex hormones [1]. These physical changes are accompanied by psychological changes of great importance. Before adolescence, most children are primarily interested in relationships with their own sex. Boys form gangs with boys, girls whisper and giggle with girls. As adolescence advances, each sex becomes more interested in, and more tolerant of, the other. But both boys and girls tend to continue to have attachments to older members of their own sex whom they admire. "Crushes" on teachers, or the hero worship of athletes or pop stars [Key], also serve a valuable function; for such people act as models that growing boys and girls can imitate, thus learning how to become fully adult members of their own sex [4]. In this way, older people from outside the family can serve as substitutes for the parental models that governed early childhood.

Physical changes in early adolescence

Early adolescence is a time when both sexes may have anxieties about the changes taking place in the body. Girls are sometimes self-conscious about their figures or bothered by menstrual irregularities [2]. Boys often worry about their developing genitals, believing themselves less well endowed than their contemporaries. Because both boys and girls develop at different rates and different ages, those who are late developers easily become anxious that there is "something wrong" with them. This anxiety is often masked by hypochondriacal fancies, and many adolescents seek reassurance that they do not have heart disease, tuberculosis, cancer, or some other complaint.

In both sexes one unpleasant side effect of the influx of the sex hormones is the development of acne. This unsightly skin disorder, which can affect the chest, back, and face, increases self-consciousness, especially if it appears on the face. Sufferers not only feel, quite rightly, that contemporaries will find them less attractive, but also sometimes believe that acne is a sign of, or punishment for, their early sexual experimentation. Acne is one adolescent complaint that requires expert medical attention.

Another is the obesity that often afflicts both girls and boys at this period of their lives. Obesity should never be regarded as just "baby fat" that will be outgrown. For one thing, it often becomes permanent. For another, it is sometimes the result of compulsive overeating, a symptom of anxiety.

Social awkwardness and exhibitionism

Adolescence is in any case a time of social awkwardness. To be neither child nor grownup is a difficult situation. Some adolescents become intensely shy, avoiding social contacts. Others become aggressively exhibitionist, flaunting the start of emancipation with outrageous clothes and outlandish hairstyles [5].

Now that adolescents in Western cultures have more money they have become a mass market and the target of advertisers. Many advertisements exploit the adolescent's natural anxiety about physical appearance and social acceptability. The result is that many adolescents overspend on

CONNECTIONS

See also
792 Adolescence: sex an
independence
796 Adulthood from
20 to 30
810 The idea of the perso

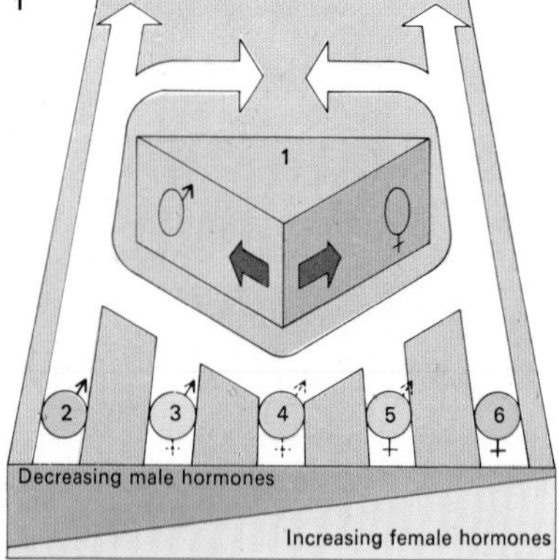

1
1
2
3
4
5
6
Decreasing male hormones
Increasing female hormones

1 Levels of sex hormones in the blood before birth affect gender development. Lack of balance in the sex hormone level may result in a person being in an intermediate state between male [2] and female [6]. Such a person may come up against a social block [1] and have to choose one role. Later in life intermediates [3, 4, 5] may return to emotional states and life styles more appropriate to their own nature.

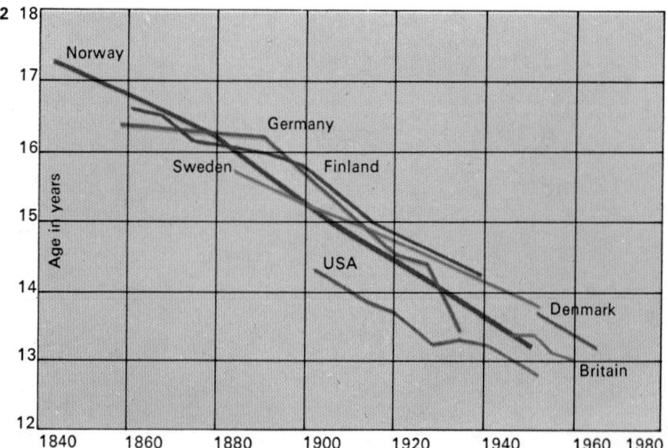

2
18
17
16
15
14
13
12
Age in years
Norway
Germany
Sweden
Finland
USA
Denmark
Britain
1840
1860
1880
1900
1920
1940
1960 1980

2 Over the last century menstruation has begun at an increasingly early age. All girls should be prepared for its onset by being given a straightforward account of its function and purpose. If this is properly done, menstruation can come to be looked forward to as a sign of being grownup rather than as a "curse" to be concealed and moaned over. Usually most girls experience little discomfort.

3
1
2
3
4
5
6
7
8
Parental authority
Adult social values
Peer relationships
Peer activities
Self-identity

3 Adolescence is a period when the individual tries to develop a sense of his own identity and define his position in the world. As a result, parental values [1] are often rejected and acceptance by peer groups becomes of great importance. Through increasing experimentation with the opposite sex [2] and strong attachments to boys of his own age [3], the adolescent boy widens his social world and learns social skills. His dress and attitudes often change to conform more closely with the group [4]. By participating in social activities such as sports [5], talking, drinking and smoking, [6] and parties [7], the adolescent learns to adopt different roles in different social situations. The individual passes through this learning process, which is an aid to his maturity, before joining the adult community [8] and accepting the adult world and its responsibilities.

4

4 Adolescents want to leave childhood behind and become "grownup." It is natural for them to find heroes and heroines on whom they can model themselves and about whom they can have fantasies. Society does not take enough trouble to make use of the idealism of adolescence by providing models of the right kind. Very often the adolescent heroes are themselves hardly more than teenagers and may lend a spurious glamor to such activities as drug-using.

clothes, makeup, deodorants, and hairdressers, feeling that they must match artificially created social expectations.

Search for identity in the young adult

Adolescence is essentially a time of search for identity [3]. Uneasily poised between childhood and adulthood, the adolescent finds his central problem in the question "Who am I?" In primitive societies, the transition from being a child to being grown up is generally clearly marked by initiation rites, often a painful kind. But when these ordeals are over, the individual at least knows where he is and exactly what is expected of him. In Western societies, although such confirmation ceremonies as bar mitzvah [7] may serve something of the same function, the adolescent has no clear picture of his role in society. This is partly because while some adolescents leave school at 16 and have to work, others stay in the more "childish" position of being a student until well into their twenties.

In complex societies, it is much more difficult to define roles in terms of age, since different things are expected of different levels of intelligence and background. At what age should adolescents be allowed to vote, to drive cars and motorcycles, to marry, to have bank accounts? Different countries have different rules [8], and within the same country an adolescent may be put in charge of a potentially lethal machine on the roads, yet not be allowed any political say in the running of his country or home town. Deprived adolescents who feel themselves to be undervalued or unwanted turn to vandalism and violence, a problem in all "advanced" cultures. If they cannot make themselves felt in constructive ways, they may consider violence acceptable [6].

Aggressive self-assertion is an inescapable part of adolescence for most people. For how is an adolescent to define himself unless he has some standards against which to rebel, some way of demonstrating that he is an individual in his own right, a different person from his parents? Discovering identity implies discovering difference; and differences between the adolescent and the parents often lead to conflict.

KEY

5

5 Clothes are one of the most obvious ways of expressing individuality, rebelling against parental standards, and demonstrating that the adolescent is now ready for sexual encounters. Hence, many adolescents dress in ways that are exaggerated and that tend to emphasize their growing sexuality. Girls may use elaborate makeup and boys may wear tight jeans.

6 Rebellion against parents, teachers, and other authorities is a necessary part of growing up. But often it goes too far. Vandalism, gang warfare, and the fights that occur at football games are predominantly teenage affairs. Western society is conspicuously inefficient at providing enough constructive outlets for normal adolescent energy and physical aggression.

6

7

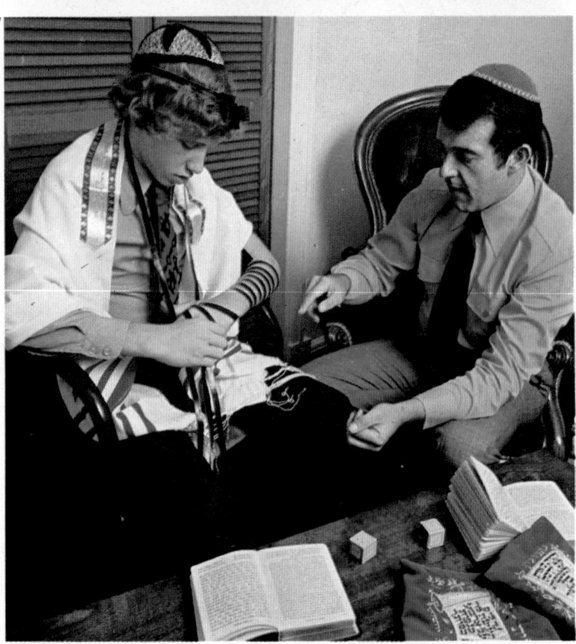

7 Bar mitzvah, one example of a ritual marking the transition from child to adult, is reached by a Jewish boy of thirteen. All the commandments, such as the use of phylacteries (the boy has put them on and is discussing them), symbolizing the covenant, become incumbent on him.

8

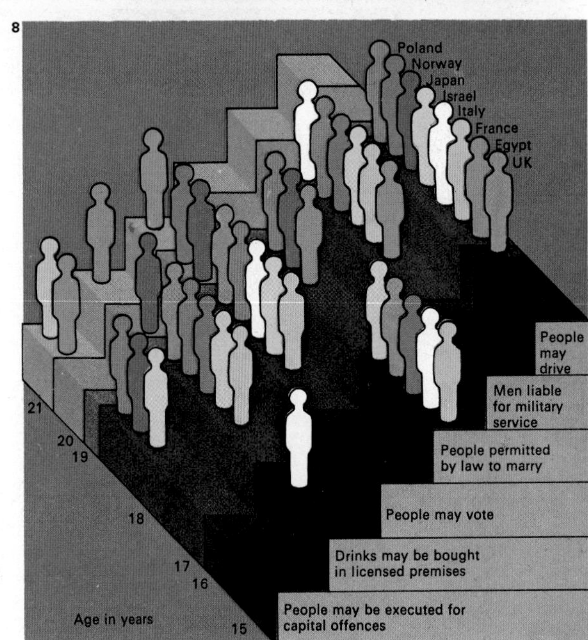
Poland
Norway
Japan
Israel
Italy
France
Egypt
UK
People may drive
Men liable for military service
People permitted by law to marry
People may vote
Drinks may be bought in licensed premises
People may be executed for capital offences
Age in years
21
20
19
18
17
16
15

8 The age at which adolescents can take on adult privileges or burdens varies from country to country as the chart shows. Teenagers are often confused because they are expected to behave like children in one setting and adults in another. In the United States, laws differ from state to state, so expectations vary widely.

Adolescence: sex and independence

Sex and independence are indissolubly linked. Sex is the biological force that compels an adolescent to look for a mate, and the incest taboo ensures that this mate comes from outside his or her own family circle. The taboo on incest, which operates in almost every culture, has more than one kind of significance. First, it removes a dangerous source of disharmony within the family by excluding the possibility of sexual rivalry. Second, it links different families and thus encourages social cohesion. Third, it spurs the adolescent to become independent by forcing him or her to look for sexual experience outside the family circle. Those adolescents who, for one reason or another, stay at home may remain dependent and immature. Lying behind these social and psychological considerations is the biological fact that incestuous unions may concentrate genetic defects in the family and produce serious abnormalities.

Sexual experimentation

The sexual experimentation of adolescents, which often causes parents such anxiety, is in fact a biological necessity that is as much a stage in the development of independence as it is a means of sexual discovery [3].

During adolescence some boys and girls may experiment with both solitary and mutual masturbation and the latter may be with their own sex or the opposite one. Transient homosexual encounters are common and should not be taken as meaning that the adolescent is permanently oriented in a homosexual direction. Nor, in most instances, should such encounters be thought to have any lasting effect. Experts believe that those who become permanently homosexual do so partly because of genetic predisposition and partly because of emotional influences that operated upon them during early childhood.

The changes of partner so characteristic of adolescence are also biologically and psychologically healthy. How are adolescent boys or girls to learn what their real preferences and requirements are if they are given no choice and no opportunity at all to experiment with different partners? Parents may be content if their son "goes steady" with, and then marries, the girl next door; but psychiatrists who have seen many such marriages break up in middle age are more confident of the future security of a marriage when both boy and girl have had more experience with different partners.

The need for privacy

The essential privateness of sex is also valuable in encouraging independence in the adolescent. Parents are often overanxious because their adolescent children do not confide in them, and some go as far as to read their children's diaries and letters. Other parents become hurt and try to force their children to tell them everything, as they used to do when they were much younger. But secrets are a necessary part of growing up and should be respected as such.

Most adolescent secrets are in any case harmless, and those that are not are often best dealt with by adults other than the adolescent's parents. Privacy is the right of every human being, whatever his or her age; forced confidences lead only to re-

CONNECTIONS

See also
790 Adolescence
690 Glands and their hormones
700 Reproduction
916 Changing patterns of crime
816 Freedom and individuality

1 Some parents complain when their children are small that they see too much of them. When the children become teenagers, the parents complain that they hardly see them at all. It is, of course, perfectly natural for teenagers to spend most of their time with their contemporaries. There is bound to be a divergence of interest between parents and teenagers, leading the teenagers to form a subculture of their own. The group bond comes from shared interest and from a need for reassurance. Adolescents are unsure of themselves, and it is comforting to find others as uncertain as they are.

2 James Dean (1931–55) epitomized the often bitter confrontation between the adolescent and adult worlds in his films *East of Eden, Rebel without a Cause*, and *Giant*. He revealed the mental turmoil of a youth attempting to come to terms with himself and the conventions of the adult world and his inability to communicate this inner struggle. As the champion of alienated youth, he highlighted in his roles the gap between the generations and reminded his audience of the problems of self-doubt, frustration, and resentment that youth suffers on the way to adulthood. In his own life he exemplified the gulf that exists between parents and their children.

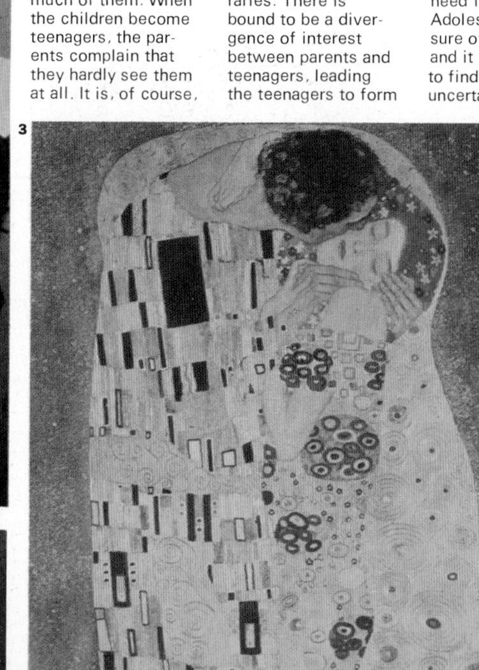

3 "The Kiss" by Gustav Klimt (1862–1918) typifies the romantic aspects of sexual involvement. Sexual potency in the male is at its height during adolescence and the urge to find sexual release is a direct, insistent force that often expresses itself in direct ways. Such expressions of passion do not preclude a more complete emotional involvement, which is commonly expressed by an unselfish preoccupation with the needs and wishes of the beloved. "Commercial sex" (such as prostitution) does not afford any opportunity for the development of emotional involvement. Adolescent interest in pornography is common, but it does not affect the normal capacity to form loving relationships.

sentment. On the other hand, adolescents also need to be understood and so may feel the need to confide in some adult—although preferably not in their parents. It is usual, if a little disconcerting, for parents to find the adolescent children of their friends and acquaintances much easier to get along with and much more polite than their own teenage children.

Adolescents typically find themselves torn by conflicting impulses. Their wish to be private vies with their need to be understood. Their wish to run their own lives is opposed to their need to ask advice about many aspects of life that they have not yet encountered. In practical terms it is difficult for them to be independent if they have to ask adults for money. And managing their own finances is a problem if they are not familiar with the intricacies of budgeting and opening an account at a bank. It is difficult to maintain secrecy about a social engagement or "date" if advice and reassurances about what to wear and how to behave are desperately needed. Dependence upon parents imposes unwelcome restrictions and often results in frustration, but independence involves equally unwelcome anxiety. Only tolerance on both sides, from parents and adolescents, sees people through this difficult stage without incessant conflict [1, 2].

In place of parents

A possible solution to this inevitable and necessary tension between parents and adolescent children is the organization of society and family life in such a way that adolescents always have some known and trusted adults outside the family to whom they can turn at any time for support and advice. As an adult it is much easier to be tolerant and understanding toward the adolescent who is rebelling against parents when one is not directly involved. In the extended families of some cultures the adolescent will often be friendly with a number of adults who are concerned about him but who are not his parents. This probably makes life much easier for both parties. In the days when godparents were a significant force, they could play the part of adviser and confessor.

KEY

The story of Romeo and Juliet, members of two warring families in Verona, Italy, who defied social conventions, expresses the value of love as a force for independence.

4

5

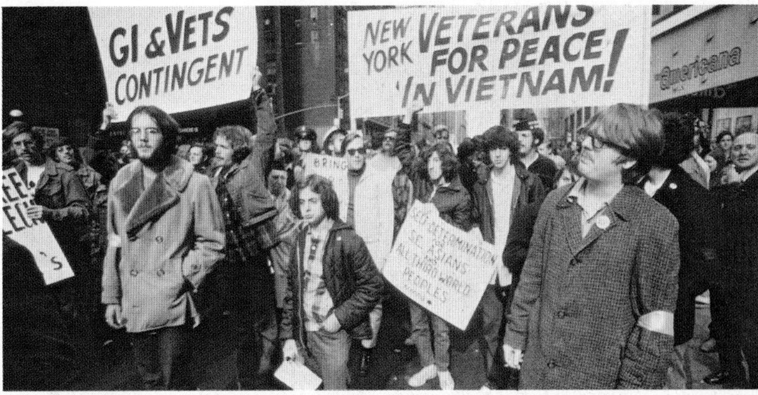

GI &VETS
CONTINGENT
NEW YORK VETERANS FOR PEACE IN VIETNAM!

4 Romantic and cynical attitudes to love have been conflicting elements in society since time immemorial. The romantic view is expressed in this 19th-century Indian picture of a girl yearning for the return of her lover, while Mozart's opera *Cosi fan tutte* is a tale of mutual deceit. Two girls whose lovers pretend to go into the army take substitutes who turn out to be their own lovers in disguise.

5 Opposition to the Vietnam War became a focus for young people's dissent in the 1960s and 1970s not only in the United States but all over the world. Perhaps prompted by the United States' apparently aggressive role in the war, there was evasion of compulsory military service on an unprecedented scale and widespread peace demonstrations that were joined by returned veterans, as here.

6

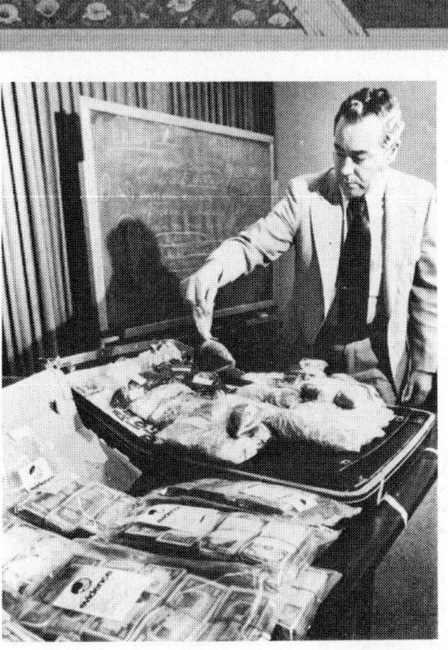

6 Greater affluence and a longer period of education have contributed to the emergence of an alternative mass youth culture. The wide use of illegal drugs by Western youth has been countered by drug raids by legal authorities.

7 Clothes are a sure pointer to the profound social change that has occurred in this century. In the early 1900s adolescents seem to have tried to emulate their parents' dress. Today the reverse is true.

7

Adulthood: marriage

Throughout most of human history marriage, even when it was monogamous, was socially less concerned with sexual companionship than with kinship—the movement of men and women of marriageable age between and within extended family groups, the acquisition of kin, and often the disposal of property [1].

The romantic ideal and its flaws

In Western cultures this pattern of marriage began to change with the general acceptance of the romantic idea of marriage in the nineteenth century, which, in theory at least, ignored dynastic [2] and financial considerations (as some marriages always had done). Instead it substituted complete mutual absorption of the kind common among people much in love—the difference being that this "peak experience" was supposed to be lifelong. In practice, this change was slow to take place. A governess, for example, as a member of the middle class who had to earn money, was not eligible for marriage to a gentleman. Since she usually would not consent to marry "below her station," she remained a spinster. The romantic concept was an advance psychologically in many ways: it recognized the woman as a person with equality of choice; it based marriage on love rather than policy [3]; and it put more value on the sexual relationship. Again, however, it took a long time to become fact. Indeed, it is only recently that women have begun to break away from their stereotype as fragile, passive, submissive, and essentially asexual.

The romantic concept worked well as long as the variety of social relationships provided by the older kinship system and the relatively stratified society it generated continued to be present. Its inherent weakness, however, is that the isolation sought by lovers becomes burdensome for married couples and for their children who are grossly overexposed to each other's society.

This rather negative side of the development of romantic marriage in the twentieth century has determined the forces for further change, although many have found satisfaction in the opportunities for development and mutual respect provided by the romantic-monogamous pattern. Other factors placing strains on the existing system are a drastic reduction in early mortality, leading to longer marriages, and the advent of reliable birth control. In societies where population growth is static, the recreational and relational aspects of sex become more important than its reproductive use. Thus the compelling ethical and practical argument in favor of marital permanence—that children need a stable, two-parent setting—can be countered by not having children.

Serial polygamy and adultery

Romantic marriage has reacted to these processes by a change of practice, most marked in Scandinavia and North America but reflected even in Roman Catholic countries where religion reinforces the institution. The professed attitude of the marriage ceremony, the law, and convention, is one of exclusive, lifelong monogamy. The actual practice of many couples is to indulge in serial polygamy [5], where marriages end-

CONNECTIONS

See also
796 Adulthood: from 20 to 30
798 Adulthood: from 30 to 40
800 Adulthood: middle age
782 Social development
784 Emotional development
876 Origins of human society

1 Dynastic considerations were uppermost in the marriage of Eleanor of Aquitaine (*c.*1122–1204) to Henry II of England (1133–89). Women then were important not only as sexual partners and mothers but also as ambassadors between clans and bringers of inheritances. Henry, who had just succeeded to the duchy of Normandy through his mother, won control of much of southwest France by this fateful marriage.

2 The abdication of Edward VIII (1894–1973) of Britain in 1936 to marry a divorced American, Wallis Simpson, epitomized the romantic concept of "giving up all for the woman you love."

3 "Arranged" marriages, here portrayed by the English painter William Hogarth (1697–1764), are evidence of the practical side of marriage. Wealth, power, and influence are traded off or exchanged for youth and beauty.

4

Number of divorces per 1 million inhabitants
USA
Denmark
Japan
Norway
UK
2,500
2,000
1,500
1,000
500
0
1900 1910 1920 1930 1940 1950 1960 1970

4 Divorce rates are rising as the law becomes less restrictive (in response to public acceptance) and as people become less tolerant of difficult home situations. The increasing ability of women to achieve financial independence has removed one barrier to successful separate existence. To what extent this signals the decline of marriage is unknown, since far more Victorian marriages ended with an early death than modern marriages are ended by divorce.

ing in divorce occur one after another (since marriage is still "required" to sanction intercourse). Adultery may be tolerated when it is not "serious," is for sex only, and is not carried on in too open and flagrant a manner.

Secondary relationships of this kind are not a new feature of monogamy; they were equally common in upper-class Victorian England or in Catholic countries where divorce was barred. Adultery may now be changing its role somewhat—chiefly through a growing dissatisfaction with the idea that monogamy must be an emotionally exclusive relationship with secondary relations thereby devalued or deprived of humanness and openness.

Contemporary marriage is thus in a state of flux. Most couples still enter marriage with the expectation of exclusive lifelong monogamy and start a family. But since divorce has been made less difficult, many resort to it as a way out of marital difficulties [4]. In addition, the mutual-sufficiency, mutual-ownership stereotype of marriage is changing as a growing percentage of younger couples practice trial marriage to test compatibility. (This was an old expedient in rural areas where it was used to test fertility or the economic viability of the couple as farmers.) People's expectations, too, are becoming more realistic. There is considerably less of the "happily-ever-after" conception of marriage.

Contemporary marriage

A legally recognized primary relationship seems unlikely to be supplanted as the focus of most man-woman relationships, and there is no sign that the prevalence of traditional marriage is declining. But the tendency in some societies is for it to become more open, with childbearing recognized both legally and socially as a chosen life-style that imposes limits on the freedom to dissolve a relationship. With this exception, a far wider range of life-styles is becoming accepted—and acceptable without guilt or blame [6, 8]. The moving of sex out of the field of "morals" and the substitution of morals based on responsibility, especially to children, is a logical outgrowth of the change in the family's importance.

KEY

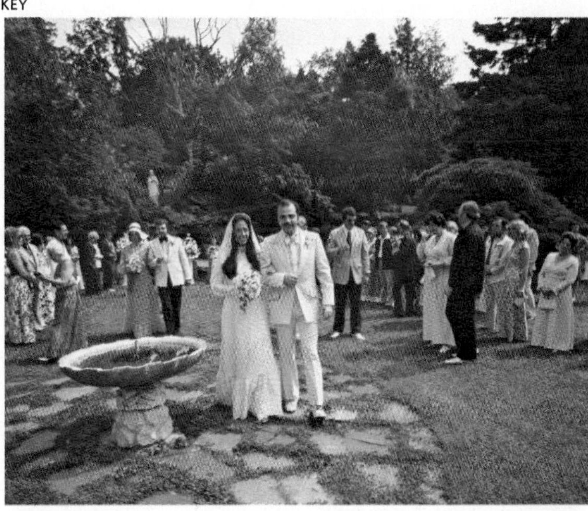

Marriage has been a pragmatic alliance throughout most of history. Families formed primary economic units especially in rural areas. Rural communities, being more interdependent than urban ones, have coped better with the potential isolation of married couples in romantic marriages where love is the foundation. Today, marriage is changing, in part because people have more realistic expectations in marriage.

5

5 "Tommy" Manville (1894–1967), who married 13 times, is a notable example of serial polygamy (repeated marriages and divorces)—one answer to the problem posed by romantic marriage. The most frequent casualties are children, whose experience may be as disturbing as its Victorian equivalent—the death of a parent and arrival of a stepparent.

6

6 Experimentation with different life-styles is a feature of youth culture, which values unpossessive love and rejects ownership as an index of love. It also compensates for shortage of kin by eroticizing friendship as do these members of a commune.

7

7 Polygamy (marriage with several spouses at the same time) is common in many societies, expecially in Asia and Africa. It usually takes the form of one man with many wives (as here in New Guinea), but the reverse occurs (depending on the definition of husband) among Eskimos, Aborigines, some groups in India and Tibet, and others. The number of wives a man may have usually depends on his finances, but it may be limited by law (Muslims may have only four) or reserved for kings and nobles (King Mtessa of Uganda is said to have had 7,000). Sometimes all the wives have similar status; in other groups the first is above the others.

8

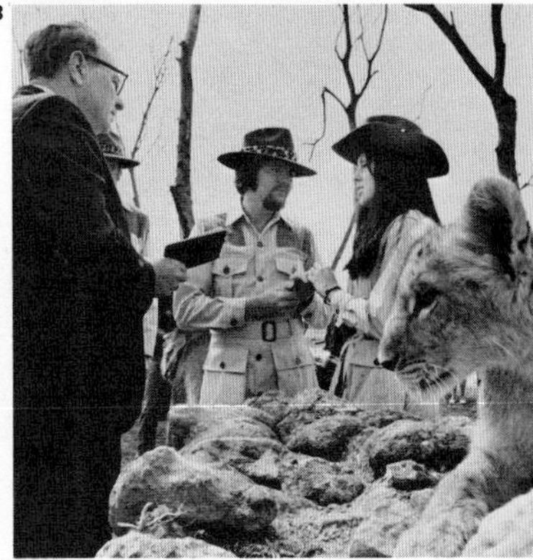

8 Many contemporary marriage ceremonies are performed under unusual circumstances because the engaged couple wants an individualized wedding. The ceremony itself may be written by the couple or the location of the ceremony may be unusual. Here a couple is married in Lion Country Safari in Grand Prairie, Tex.

Adulthood: from 20 to 30

The decade from 20 to 30 is hard to characterize because there are marked differences between the roles of men and women, between the married and the unmarried, and between those with children and those without. Ideally, it is a time of hope and increasing confidence. With the tribulations of adolescence behind them, and many exciting possibilities ahead, young men and women start the road toward maturity impatient to prove themselves and certain that they will do better than their seniors.

The bonds of matrimony

Yet, for the newly married with a young and growing family, financial difficulties are common and, particularly for women, the adjustment to a life centered around the home is difficult to make. Whereas a husband can escape to his work, his wife is often tied all day to the house. For many mothers this leads to a drastic loss of confidence and of self-esteem. Current research indicates that one-third of working-class women with children under six who are at home full time are clinically depressed. Some women find it difficult to cope with the sudden release from parental control and the new responsibilities of running a house and budgeting.

Both husband and wife may find themselves torn between the attention their partner expects and demands and their own wish to remain loyal to the group of friends with whom they spent time before getting married. It takes time for couples to form new patterns of relationships in society as a pair; and as a result some newlyweds, however infatuated and mutally absorbed, feel isolated and cut off from family and friends.

For many newlyweds money becomes an important issue for several reasons. During adolescence, young people, at least in Western society, are often still living in their parents' home and yet have begun to earn their livings. Before marriage, they have few financial responsibilities and become accustomed to spend what they earn on themselves without thought for others. After marriage, their financial horizons become sharply restricted. The couple may soon acquire a home of their own, but they may have the prospect of many years of regular repayments.

The arrival of children

The situation may become more complicated after the arrival of children because they add to expenditures and because after the birth of the first child many women give up their jobs. This reduces the family's income and at the same time promotes a feeling of dependence in the wife. The fact that the money she spends is earned by her husband may seem to her to be irksome and degrading, particularly as she makes such a contribution to the quality of the home life—a contribution that some women think is taken for granted or undervalued. This can become a focus for resentment and bickering. Equally, some men feel heavily the burden of being the sole supporter.

In addition, children impose financial strains and there is evidence that they may also precipitate problems of communication, particularly for low-income families. While husband and wife both have jobs, they share many preoccupations. But as the

CONNECTIONS

See also

798 Adulthood: from 30 to 40
800 Adulthood: middle age
932 Uses of leisure
916 Changing patterns of crime

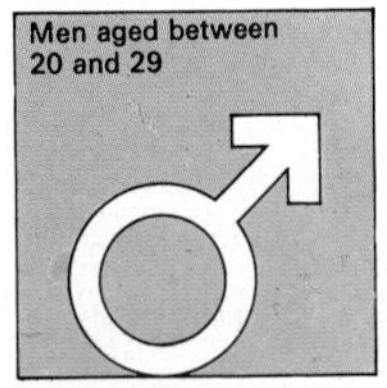

Men aged between 20 and 29

1 The average single man [A] in the United States and Western Europe spends a quarter of his leisure time participating in physical recreation. Popular European sports are swimming, soccer, table tennis, and tennis. In the United States bowling, basketball, football, and baseball are particularly popular. Once married, he adopts more sedentary pursuits, centered on the home. Salaried workers [B], who are often in training in their early twenties, on average earn less than their manual worker counterparts although they have greater earning prospects in the future. Men between the ages of 20 and 30 committed more than a quarter of all crimes in 1975 [C]. Of their offenses, those related to abuse of drugs, including alcohol, and theft were most common. The overwhelming majority of deaths in this age group is caused by accidents or violence. Cancer is the major medical cause (leukemia and cancer of the testes particularly); heart disease ranks second.

Age Group	% of all arrests involving this age group
20–29	26.5
30–39	
40–49	

Age Group	% of all deaths in this age group
20–29	.7
30–39	
40–49	

1 Leisure activities
A

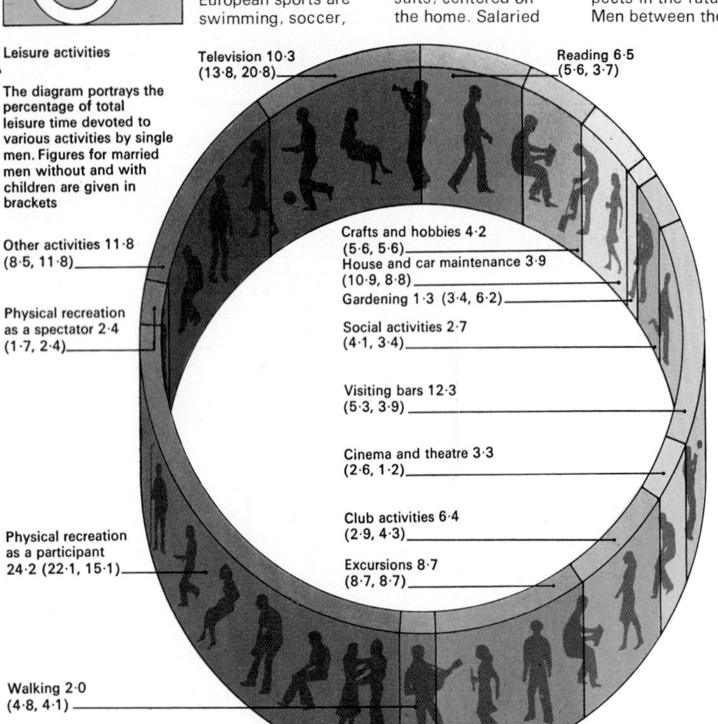

Television 10·3 (13·8, 20·8)
Reading 6·5 (5·6, 3·7)
Other activities 11·8 (8·5, 11·8)
Physical recreation as a spectator 2·4 (1·7, 2·4)
Crafts and hobbies 4·2 (5·6, 5·6)
House and car maintenance 3·9 (10·9, 8·8)
Gardening 1·3 (3·4, 6·2)
Social activities 2·7 (4·1, 3·4)
Visiting bars 12·3 (5·3, 3·9)
Cinema and theatre 3·3 (2·6, 1·2)
Club activities 6·4 (2·9, 4·3)
Excursions 8·7 (8·7, 8·7)
Physical recreation as a participant 24·2 (22·1, 15·1)
Walking 2·0 (4·8, 4·1)

The diagram portrays the percentage of total leisure time devoted to various activities by single men. Figures for married men without and with children are given in brackets

B

C Crime – arrests

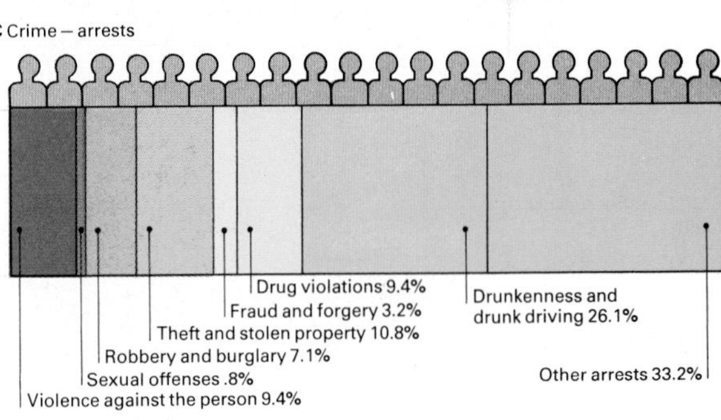

Drug violations 9.4%
Fraud and forgery 3.2%
Theft and stolen property 10.8%
Robbery and burglary 7.1%
Sexual offenses .8%
Violence against the person 9.4%
Drunkenness and drunk driving 26.1%
Other arrests 33.2%

D Causes of death

Infectious diseases 1·3%
Cancers 13·4%
Endocrine and metabolic diseases 1·0%
Diseases of the nervous system 4·5%
Diseases of the circulation 7·1%
Respiratory diseases 4·8%
Diseases of the digestion 2·2%
Urogenital diseases 1·2%
Congenital abnormalities 2·1%
Other medical causes 2·5%
Accidents, poisonings and violence 59·9%

wife becomes absorbed in her work in the home and the husband in his work outside these common experiences largely disappear and there is often little to talk about of mutual interest. For many couples this is an important factor in marital disharmony.

The constraints of the period

Western societies do not make a clear enough demarcation between being a child and being a grown-up, with the result that the adolescent often does not know what society expects of him. This problem continues in the decade from 20 to 30. A particular difficulty is that although at the peak of their powers (albeit with necessarily limited experience) young men and women find difficulty in expressing their full potential. In a society that is still controlled by the middle-aged they cannot usually gain any position of power. In the medical profession, for example, a doctor aiming at specialist training may not have completed that training by the age of 30 and may not have attained a position of eminence until he reaches middle age. In societies where hunting and fighting are the main occupations of younger men, maximum potential and maximum achievement coincide. In Western society youth often does not have the opportunity to use its ability.

This dilemma may be particularly acute for women. The pressure that society exerts on them to measure their success in terms of the children they produce is at variance with their growing wish to participate in the world on an equal footing with men. Their traditional goals clash uncomfortably with their new ones. As a symptom of this there is a shortage of job opportunities and of such facilities as day-care centers for preschool children suited to the needs of women who wish to combine having a job outside the home with caring for their children. Part-time jobs that are stimulating and fulfilling are rare.

In spite of these disadvantages, this decade of life is primarily one of ebullient hopefulness. Career, marriage, and children all seem to contain possibilities as yet unrealized, and limitations are either unknown, shrugged off, or considered conquerable.

KEY

Women aged between 20 and 29

2 The most popular forms of physical recreation [A] for women between 20 and 30 are dancing, swimming, tennis, table tennis, horse riding, and ice-skating. The amount of leisure time spent on these activities declines with marriage and the arrival of children. As with men, activities then center on the home and hobbies and such crafts as knitting and sewing. The earning potential [B] of manual and nonmanual women workers varies little as few nonmanual workers undergo long training. There is still a wide difference between the earnings of men and women. Women aged between 20 and 30 [C] commit less than a fifth of the number of crimes committed by men of the same age group. Shoplifting comprises about 20% of offenses, but violence is increasing. The death rate [D] for women of this age is less than half that for men, and deaths caused by accidents are considerably lower. Relatively more women die of leukemia and certain heart diseases.

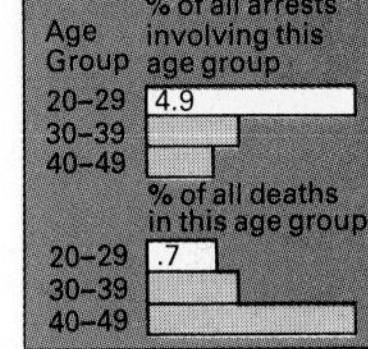
Age Group
% of all arrests involving this age group
20–29 4.9
30–39
40–49
% of all deaths in this age group
20–29 .7
30–39
40–49

2 Leisure activities

A

The diagram portrays the percentage of total leisure time devoted to various activities by single women. Figures for married women without and with children are given in brackets

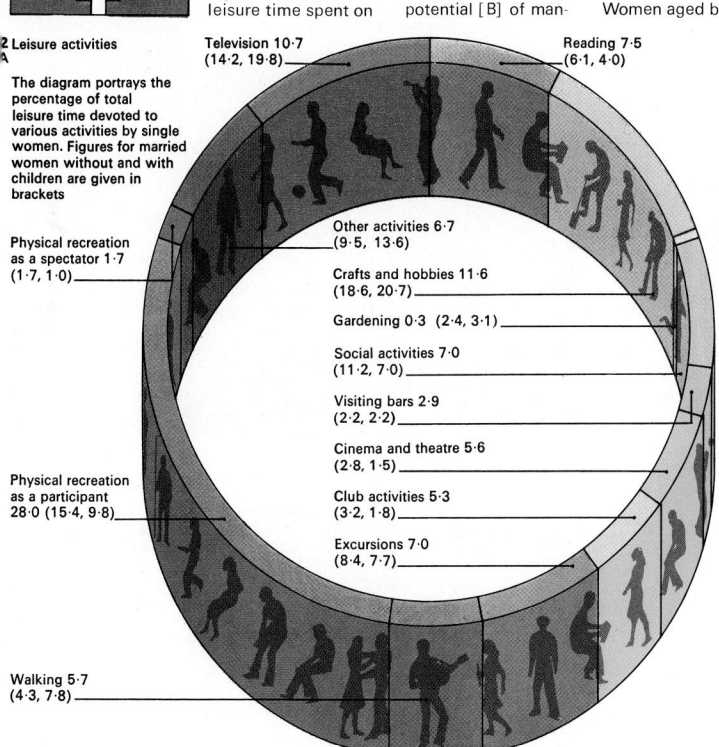

Television 10·7 (14·2, 19·8)

Reading 7·5 (6·1, 4·0)

Physical recreation as a spectator 1·7 (1·7, 1·0)

Other activities 6·7 (9·5, 13·6)

Crafts and hobbies 11·6 (18·6, 20·7)

Gardening 0·3 (2·4, 3·1)

Social activities 7·0 (11·2, 7·0)

Visiting bars 2·9 (2·2, 2·2)

Cinema and theatre 5·6 (2·8, 1·5)

Physical recreation as a participant 28·0 (15·4, 9·8)

Club activities 5·3 (3·2, 1·8)

Excursions 7·0 (8·4, 7·7)

Walking 5·7 (4·3, 7·8)

B

C Crime – arrests

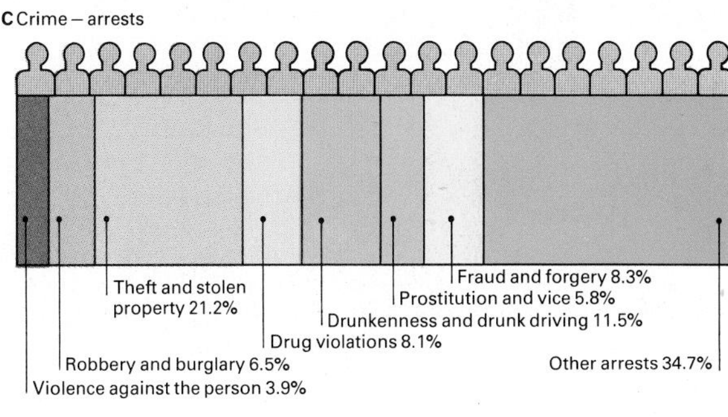
Theft and stolen property 21.2%
Fraud and forgery 8.3%
Prostitution and vice 5.8%
Drunkenness and drunk driving 11.5%
Drug violations 8.1%
Robbery and burglary 6.5%
Other arrests 34.7%
Violence against the person 3.9%

D Causes of death

Infectious diseases 1·9%
Cancers 21·6%
Endocrine and metabolic diseases 2·4%
Diseases of the nervous system 5·5%
Diseases of the circulation 11·5%
Respiratory diseases 7·6%
Diseases of the digestion 3·0%
Urogenital diseases 2·1%
Complications of childbirth 2·5%
Congenital abnormalities 3·4%
Other medical causes 3·8%
Accidents, poisonings and violence 34·7%

Adulthood: from 30 to 40

During their thirties, most people become firmly established in their adult roles. The direction in which a person is going and the probable range of his or her achievement will be settled, although surprising changes of direction can still occur. A married couple will know how many children they want, and their social life will have been established, although this is largely dependent on the age of their children. Many older people look back on this decade as a time of particular happiness. The uncertainties of youth are past; the problems and upheavals of middle-age are still in the future. Asked what age they would like to be, many older people of either sex, will answer: "Thirty-five."

Friendship and love

Although friends can be made at any age, by 35 to 40 most people will have a number of established friends, people whom they know so well that they can be completely at ease and relaxed with them. This is partly the result of having overcome the social anxieties of earlier decades and partly because many friendships do not fully mature for some years after the first encounter.

Nevertheless, this decade may present problems. Married couples usually find that the initial delight of being "in love" has worn off. Being in love is a curious condition, which Sigmund Freud (1856–1939) called "the psychosis of normal people." Most young people carry within their minds a somewhat idealized picture of the opposite sex, derived in part from parents and in part from the images presented by television, movies, novels, advertising, and so on. When they fall in love, the beloved person seems to correspond exactly with this idealized picture. Psychologists would say that the idealized image is "projected" upon the other person. Living with another person day in day out means, however, that each becomes aware of all the ways in which the image and the reality fail to correspond. Real people are not like creatures of the imagination but are human beings with faults and foibles as well as the attractions that first gained their partner's interest.

Being in love, therefore, must be replaced by learning to love the other as a real person. For some this is not an easy transition since they miss the thrill of being in love and may sometimes become disillusioned or bored with the person they once adored. This is the prime reason for what is called the "seven-year itch," the tendency to look for sexual partners outside the marriage. Infidelity, a major reason for divorce, is now recognized as a symptom of marital disharmony rather than a cause, and transient infidelity should lead to a reexamination of the marital relationship, perhaps including counseling, rather than to its immediate break-up.

Psychological maturity

In Western culture, the years from 30 to 40 are commonly regarded as those in which "maturity" is reached. But this prized maturity is hard to define. Both men and women reach their physical peak in their early twenties or earlier. Yet psychological maturity often seems to be a goal that recedes the nearer one approaches it.

CONNECTIONS

See also
796 Adulthood: from 20 to 30
800 Adulthood: middle age
932 Uses of leisure
916 Changing patterns of crime
776 Human development

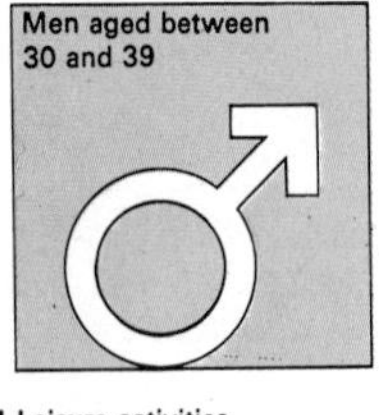

Men aged between 30 and 39

1 The average married man in the United States and Western Europe spends 60 percent of his leisure time [A] pursuing activities in and around the home. Television, gardening, decorating the house, and maintaining the car are main forms of relaxation. Time spent in physical recreation drops to only 10 per cent and favorite sports include swimming, hiking, fishing and golf. Going out in the evening is of minor importance. Earning comparisons [B] show non-manual male workers earning considerably more than their manual counterparts, reflecting the earning potential of qualifications gained earlier. Far fewer crimes [C] are committed by men in their 30s than by those in their 20s. Destructive crimes give way to more offenses of other types but only some kinds of sexual crimes rise absolutely. Male deaths [D] in the 30 to 40 age group are virtually the same as for younger men. Accidental deaths drop. Heart disease and cancer are major causes of death.

Age Group	% of all arrests involving this age group
20–29	
30–39	11.3
40–49	

Age Group	% of all deaths in this age group
20–29	
30–39	1.5
40–49	

1 Leisure activities

A The diagram portrays the percentage of total leisure time devoted to various activities Figures for married men with children

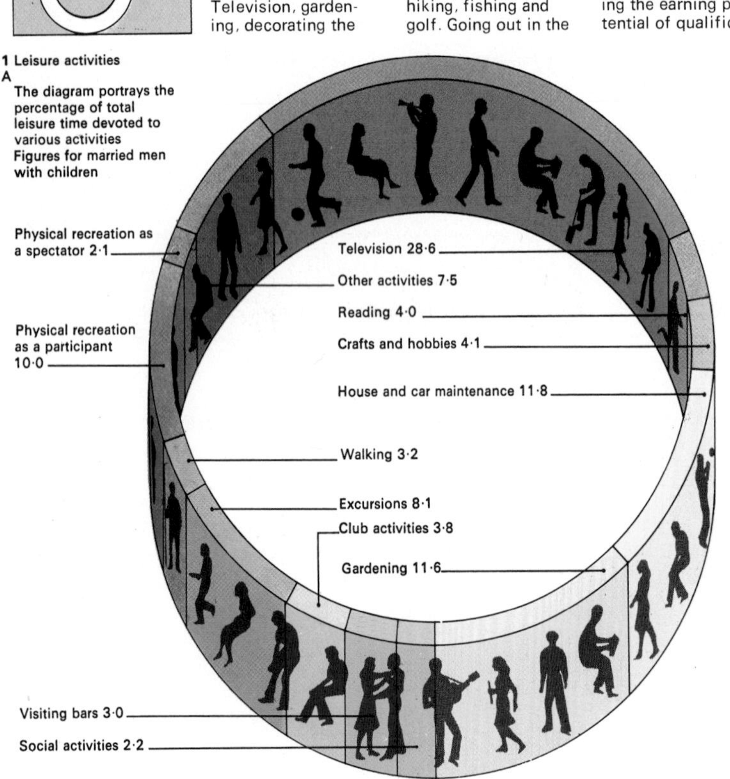

Physical recreation as a spectator 2·1
Television 28·6
Other activities 7·5
Reading 4·0
Crafts and hobbies 4·1
Physical recreation as a participant 10·0
House and car maintenance 11·8
Walking 3·2
Excursions 8·1
Club activities 3·8
Gardening 11·6
Visiting bars 3·0
Social activities 2·2

B

C Crime – arrests

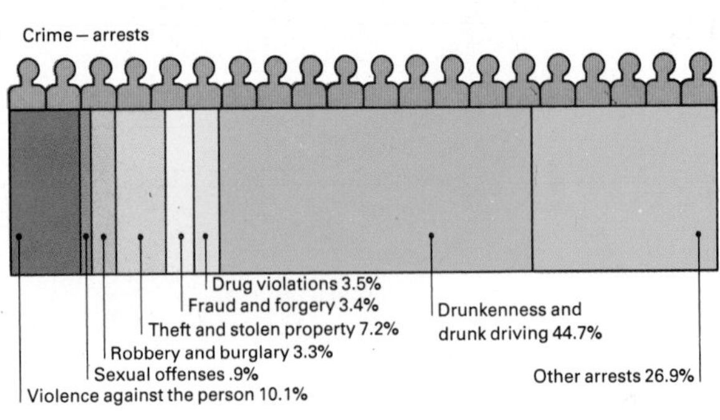

Drug violations 3.5%
Fraud and forgery 3.4%
Theft and stolen property 7.2%
Robbery and burglary 3.3%
Sexual offenses .9%
Violence against the person 10.1%
Drunkenness and drunk driving 44.7%
Other arrests 26.9%

D Causes of death

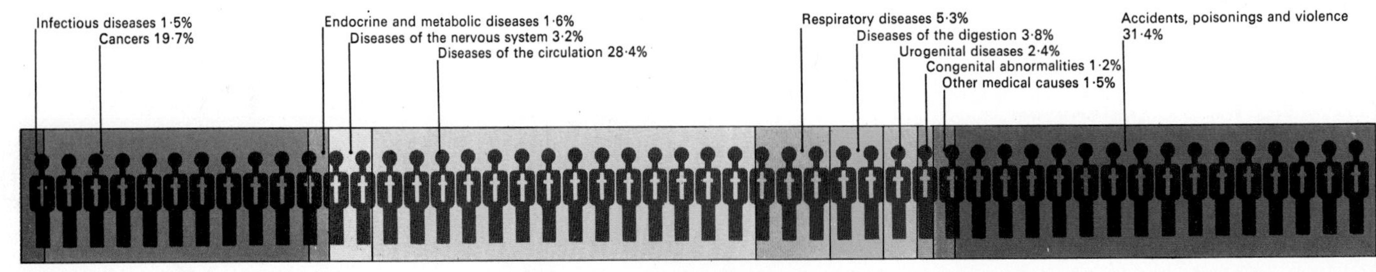

Infectious diseases 1·5%
Cancers 19·7%
Endocrine and metabolic diseases 1·6%
Diseases of the nervous system 3·2%
Diseases of the circulation 28·4%
Respiratory diseases 5·3%
Diseases of the digestion 3·8%
Urogenital diseases 2·4%
Congenital abnormalities 1·2%
Other medical causes 1·5%
Accidents, poisonings and violence 31·4%

What is maturity in psychological terms? Since man is a social being, maturity of personality cannot be defined except in terms of relationships. A person without relationships with other persons cannot be defined as an entity, just as it is meaningless to ask what size an object may be if there is nothing with which to compare it. Although there are many attributes of maturity, one that is obviously important may be singled out: the ability to make fruitful, loving relationships with other people on equal terms, without either being dominated or dominating. This achievement implies an acceptance of the other person as he or she is, without any wish to alter, to direct, or to submit; a recognition of the other person as a separate entity and therefore of oneself as a separate entity also.

Importance of self-criticism

Maturity also demands that a person be realistic, without abandoning the capacity to use imagination. It implies self-control, but combined with the ability to "let go" when this is appropriate. It implies having arrived at some fairly coherent point of view about the universe and the place of man within it, but excludes dogmatism and fanaticism. It implies firmness without rigidity; love without infatuation; decisiveness without being dictatorial; tolerance without a facile permissiveness.

In fact, such maturity is beyond the reach of most, although this ideal state may be approached more nearly by the habit of vigilant self-criticism. Few human beings in modern cultures become mature by the age of 40. Indeed, the extension of the human life span beyond the reproductive period has necessitated the extension of psychological development beyond middle age well into the second half of life.

Statistics [1, 2] show that people in the 30-to-40 age group are usually healthy, socially stable, and spend much of their spare time within the family circle. The material rewards of having gained higher educational qualifications become more evident. In both physical and psychological terms, adults of this age are most likely to store up future trouble by developing false complacency.

KEY

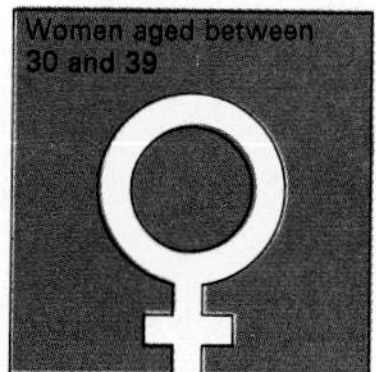
Women aged between 30 and 39

2 Married women in the 30 to 40 age group [A] spend little time on physical recreation, apart from dancing. As with men, more than 60 per cent of leisure time is spent in the home and going out is confined mainly to places the children appreciate. Television, reading, knitting, sewing, other hand crafts, and gardening are the major activities. Women workers [B] in nonmanual occupations have higher wages in the 30 to 40 age group, while women manual workers earn about as much as those in the 20 to 30 age group. Women's crime rates fall in the 30s [C] compared with the 20s. Larceny-theft accounts for 15 per cent of offenses, of which shoplifting, the only offense committed more often by women than by men, is a large part of the total. The death rate of women in their 30s rises faster [D] than it does among men. Cancer of the breast, ovary, or cervix, together with cerebrovascular and rheumatic heart disease, are by far the main causes of death.

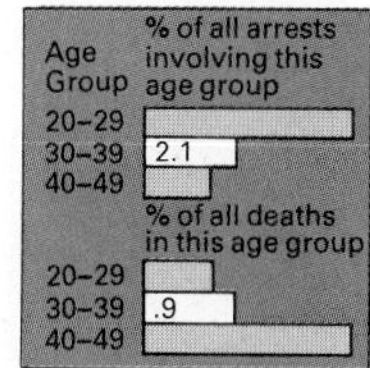
Age Group
% of all arrests involving this age group
20–29
30–39
2.1
40–49
% of all deaths in this age group
20–29
30–39
.9
40–49

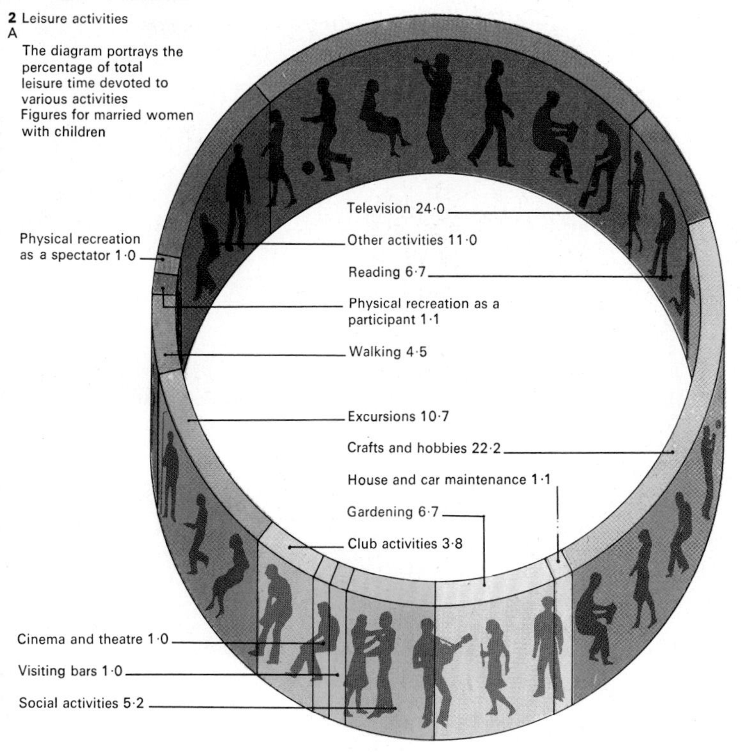
2 Leisure activities
A
The diagram portrays the percentage of total leisure time devoted to various activities
Figures for married women with children
Television 24·0
Other activities 11·0
Physical recreation as a spectator 1·0
Reading 6·7
Physical recreation as a participant 1·1
Walking 4·5
Excursions 10·7
Crafts and hobbies 22·2
House and car maintenance 1·1
Gardening 6·7
Club activities 3·8
Cinema and theatre 1·0
Visiting bars 1·0
Social activities 5·2

B

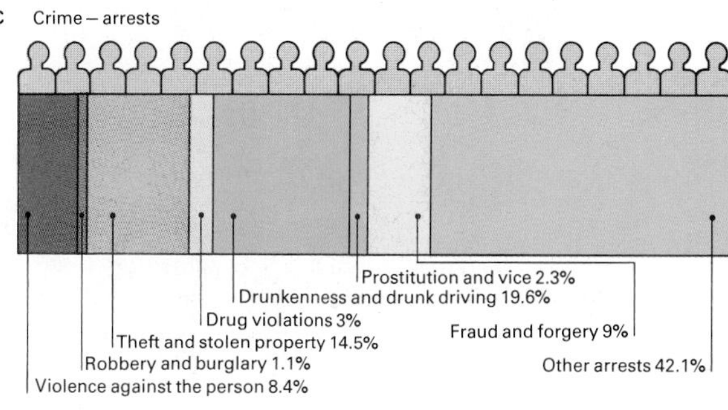
C Crime – arrests
Prostitution and vice 2.3%
Drunkenness and drunk driving 19.6%
Drug violations 3%
Fraud and forgery 9%
Theft and stolen property 14.5%
Robbery and burglary 1.1%
Other arrests 42.1%
Violence against the person 8.4%

D Causes of death

Infectious diseases 1·5%
Cancers 37·1%
Endocrine and metabolic diseases 1·8%
Diseases of the nervous system 4·1%
Diseases of the circulation 18·8%
Respiratory diseases 6·3%
Diseases of the digestion 3·7%
Urogenital diseases 2·6%
Complications of childbirth 1·4%
Congenital abnormalities 1·8%
Other medical causes 2·3%
Accidents, poisonings and violence 18·6%

Adulthood: middle age

In modern culture there is a growing awareness of middle age as a period of change and development. It was once assumed that after the age of 40 both men and women were so fixed in their ways that little change could be expected, and to an extent this is borne out in statistics [1, 2]. But it is increasingly recognized that middle age can and should be a time in which new interests are begun and pursued, and new departures are undertaken.

Mid-life crisis

Emotional disturbances in middle age are so common that psychiatrists often refer to the "mid-life crisis." This was once thought to be the result, at any rate in women, of the "change of life" or menopause. While it remains true that a few women do experience unpleasant physical symptoms at this time and may become irritable and moody, modern treatment with hormones, although controversial, is able to alleviate most of the symptoms. Moreover, the widely held belief that after the menopause women lose most of their sexual desire is demonstrably false. In fact the opposite is often true, since many women experience an increase in sexual desire when pregnancy is not any longer a possibility.

Although men often go through a mid-life crisis, this is no longer generally believed to be the result of some male equivalent of the menopause. It has been shown that diminution in sexual desire and performance is very gradual in most men, so that the emotional upheaval through which some pass cannot be attributed to any sudden decline in sexual potency. What, then, is the cause of the mid-life crisis?

The name itself suggests one reason. At the midpoint of life, both men and women are at the stage when they should have realized their ambitions. If things have gone well, the traditional goals (for a man, of establishing himself in a job or profession; for a woman, of rearing a family) will have been achieved. Many women, however, feel there is nothing left for them once their children are no longer dependent and that years of child care and housework have left them unqualified for work outside the home. And many men regard the effort they have put into "getting ahead" as misplaced.

Inevitably, not all of a person's dreams will have been fulfilled. Some persons become depressed because they have to come to terms with the reality of what their life is. A restless dissatisfaction afflicts many people, often showing itself in transient infidelities, increasing consumption of alcohol, and changes of occupation. People of this age often feel that the future holds nothing but decline into old age and death.

Creative turning-point

A study of the lives of creatively gifted men and women shows that their work often undergoes a change of style at the mid-life period. Some, like the English novelist George Eliot (1819–80), did not begin their really creative production until this time in their lives. Others, like Ludwig Van Beethoven (1770–1827), demonstrated an increase in profundity that distinguished their late work sharply from what had gone before. Sigmund Freud (1856–1939) published nothing of striking originality until he was

CONNECTIONS

See also

802 Aging and longevity
804 An active old age
796 Adulthood: from 20 to 30
798 Adulthood: from 30 to 40
716 Diseases of the circulation
932 Uses of leisure

Men aged between 40 and 49

1 Leisure activities [A] of average middle-aged fathers in the United States and Western Europe continue to center around the home, although children are likely to be more independent. Gardening now takes precedence over the house. Less energetic sports are taken up and watching spectator sports (often with sons) is very popular. In employment [B] earnings of male manual workers may drop because of declining productivity, but the nonmanual worker increases his earnings and his relative prosperity. Crime rates [C] for men aged 40 to 50 show that they commit fewer impetuous offenses than younger men. Most of the crimes in this age group are committed by professional thieves. Men of this age group are responsible for only 8 percent of crimes. Typical causes of death [D] in an affluent society – heart disease and cancers – account for more than one-half of all deaths of middle-aged men. Mortality rates begin showing a rise between the ages of 40 and 50.

Age Group	% of all arrests involving this age group
20–29	
30–39	
40–49	8

Age Group	% of all deaths in this age group
20–29	
30–39	
40–49	3.6

1 Leisure activities
A

The diagram portrays the percentage of total leisure time devoted to various activities
Figures for married men with children

Television 30·6
Other activities 8·6
Physical recreation as a spectator 2·4
Reading 2·8
Crafts and hobbies 3·2
Walking 3·0
Excursions 7·2
House and car maintenance 10·8
Club activities 5·2
Gardening 13·6
Physical recreation as a participant 6·8
Cinema and theatre 0·4
Visiting bars 3·4
Social activities 2·0

B

C Crime – arrests

Drug violations 1.1%
Fraud and forgery 2.1%
Theft and stolen property 5.1%
Robbery and burglary 1.5%
Sexual offenses .7%
Violence against the person 8%
Drunkenness and drunk driving 60.8%
Other arrests 20.7%

D Causes of death

Infectious diseases 1·0%
Cancers 23·7%
Endocrine and metabolic diseases 1·2%
Diseases of the nervous system 1·6%
Diseases of the circulation 48·8%
Respiratory diseases 6·3%
Diseases of the digestion 3·5%
Urogenital diseases 1·0%
Other medical causes 1·4
Accidents, poisonings and violence 11·5%

39; the work that he continued to regard as his most penetrating, *The Interpretation of Dreams*, did not appear until he was 43.

Creative geniuses show in their work that they suffer from the same conflicts as other people. Their ability to cope with this, sometimes by changing their style, is something that others might emulate according to their own talents.

Discovering new goals

Often the midpoint of life is a time to rediscover interests and aspects of the self that have been dropped because there has not been enough time to pursue them. Most middle-aged people have had enthusiasms in adolescence that they were unable to follow up—for painting, music, literature, gardening, or bird-watching. The great Swiss psychologist Carl Jung (1875–1961), who specialized in the treatment of middle-aged patients, said that culture was the goal of the second half of life and that what we needed were schools for 40-year-olds. It was a perceptive and perhaps prophetic suggestion. Middle-aged people sometimes fear that they cannot learn anything new, but this is wrong. At this time, most people are more realistically aware of their strengths and their weaknesses and are much more able to apply themselves systematically to whatever they undertake.

The great mistake is to think that in middle age it is too late to continue searching for anything new. For a while, psychologists thought that the human being was always driven by a need to discharge tension and achieve the peace that comes when instincts are satisfied and hungers temporarily assuaged. Now it has become clear that such an idea is quite inadequate. The brain works best when it is given a variety of different, novel stimuli. New problems are a vital part of living, and if they do not exist it is necessary to invent them. Men and women who have achieved, at the midpoint of life, the goals of youth, must find new problems to wrestle with and other interests to engage them. Discovering these fresh challenges is largely a matter of the person having the right attitude.

KEY

Women aged between 40 and 49

2 Leisure patterns [A] among middle-aged women show a slight fall in television watching and handcrafts. The extra time is spent in and around the home, in gardening or in reading. With a greater degree of freedom from children there is an increase in physical recreation. Women engage more in social activities than men. Women who work [B] maintain much the same level of earnings in middle age as they did in the decade 30 to 40 but they are still consistently less that a man receives for the same work. Few crimes [C] are committed by middle-aged women. Shoplifting and other petty thefts account for an overwhelming percentage of their offenses. Drunken driving is the only offense more common here than among younger women. The death rate [D] among middle-aged women climbs steeply. Cancer and heart disease cause more than 6 percent of deaths at this age. Of these, breast and cervical cancers predominate. Mortality rates begin showing a rise during this period.

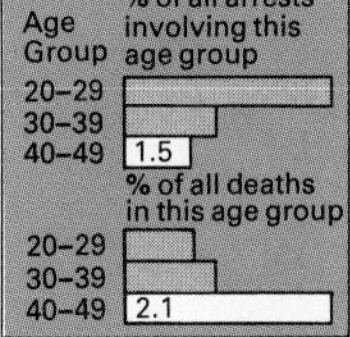
Age Group
% of all arrests involving this age group
20–29
30–39
40–49 1.5
% of all deaths in this age group
20–29
30–39
40–49 2.1

2 Leisure activities

A

The diagram portrays the percentage of total leisure time devoted to various activities
Figures for married women with children

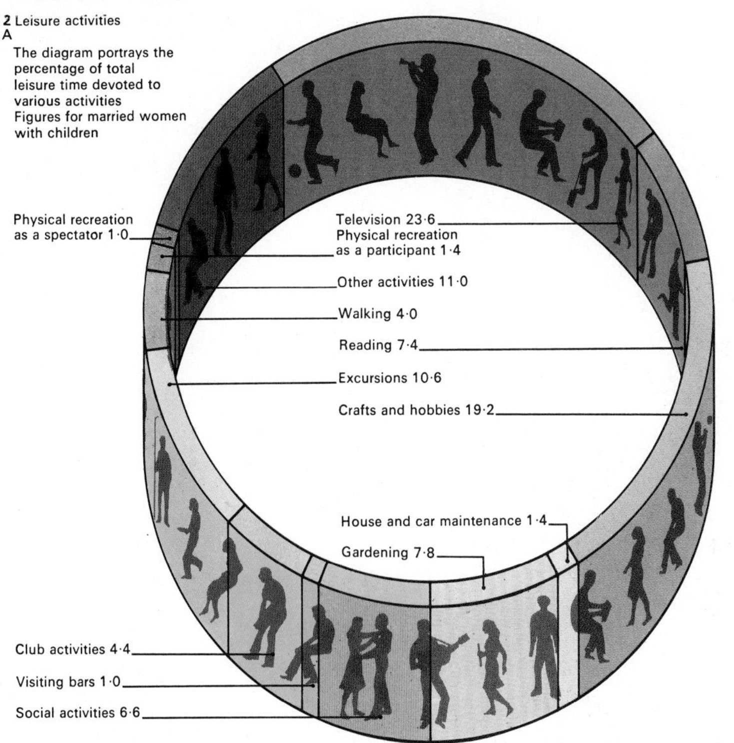
Physical recreation as a spectator 1·0
Television 23·6
Physical recreation as a participant 1·4
Other activities 11·0
Walking 4·0
Reading 7·4
Excursions 10·6
Crafts and hobbies 19·2
House and car maintenance 1·4
Gardening 7·8
Club activities 4·4
Visiting bars 1·0
Social activities 6·6

B

C Crime – arrests

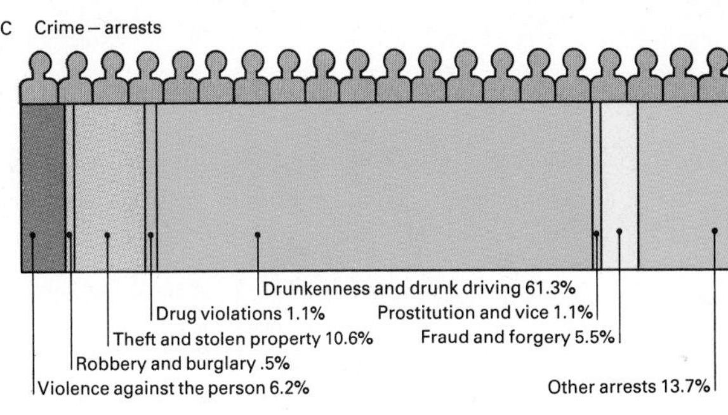
Drunkenness and drunk driving 61.3%
Drug violations 1.1%
Prostitution and vice 1.1%
Theft and stolen property 10.6%
Fraud and forgery 5.5%
Robbery and burglary .5%
Violence against the person 6.2%
Other arrests 13.7%

D Causes of death

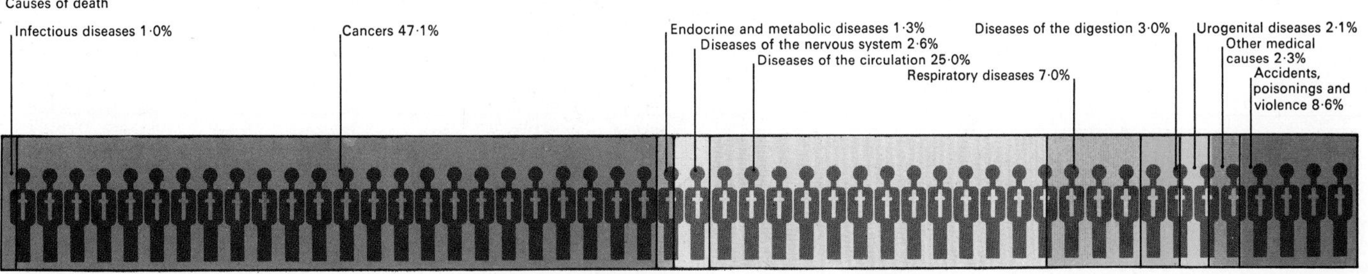
Infectious diseases 1·0%
Cancers 47·1%
Endocrine and metabolic diseases 1·3%
Diseases of the nervous system 2·6%
Diseases of the circulation 25·0%
Respiratory diseases 7·0%
Diseases of the digestion 3·0%
Urogenital diseases 2·1%
Other medical causes 2·3%
Accidents, poisonings and violence 8·6%

Aging and longevity

The rate at which human beings age has not changed since prehistory. Civilized man lives longer [2, 4] because his chance of survival to the age of natural death has improved, not because aging itself has been postponed. Aging is the term for the process that causes organisms to become more likely to die the longer they live. With time, the capacity for self-repair and resistance to damage decreases, and the force of mortality increases [Key]. This leads to a characteristic life span.

Longevity, size, and inheritance

The life spans of animals [1] tend to correlate both with their size and, more closely, with excess brain capacity (as calculated by the information capacity carried in the nervous system) in relation to size. The human life span is often quoted as the biblical "three score years and ten," although certified ages well above 100 are documented. In several localities there is a popular belief, recently widely publicized that people live to great ages. The best known of these are Hunza-land, Abkhaz, in the Georgian Republic, USSR, and Vilcabamba in Ecuador. Abkhazian life spans, some of them up to 140 or 160 years and more, have been much investigated and much disputed. They can neither be accepted nor rejected out of hand. The Vilcabamban records, better authenticated than most, have been under study. There are claims of high ages elsewhere, chiefly in mountain areas where they are linked with "simple life," isolation from disease, and an absence of reliable documents.

If such longevity is true, the causes are likely to be in the first place genetic, with social and possibly dietary factors playing a part. Longevity in humans is heritable, but less so than is stature. What is inherited is not so much longevity as the absence of factors for "shortevity." In most known genetic systems, hybrid vigor (the inheritance of a varied genetic repertoire) outranks any other heritable factor in increasing life span.

Most multicellular organisms age, the probable exceptions being those such as large trees and sea anemones in which all of the component cells propagate clonally by splitting into two exactly similar cells. Aging occurs in mixed organisms such as mammals, which contain both renewable and unrenewable cells, and in organisms in which no cell division is possible.

The process of aging

The nature of the aging process or processes is unknown. One question to be settled is whether in man and other mammals the accumulation of damage is sited primarily in nondividing cells such as neurons; in dividing cells, which may develop faults with successive divisions; in structural materials such as collagen (a protein in fibrous connective tissue); or in the programming of our physiology. No one of these processes can be pinpointed as aging's "cause."

Fixed cells accumulate both viruses and waste materials and are irreplaceably lost with time, although the widely cited notion of massive brain cell loss with aging is erroneous. Dividing cells accumulate mutations and errors but, except when they escape from normal controls, as in cancer,

CONNECTIONS

See also
804 An active old age
800 Adulthood: middle age
806 Death, grieving, and loss
712 The causes of illness 2
698 Keeping fit

1

1 The only mammals comparable in longevity to man are the elephant and the rhinoceros. Small rodents live one year in the wild but may survive two to four years in captivity. Dogs seldom reach more than 20 years, cats possibly longer. About 30 years is the maximum age for most medium or large mammals. Whales are the only possible exception. Ages of up to 80 years may be reached by some species. Birds live longer than mammals. Small species, normally annual in the wild, may live 12–20 years in captivity. Large flying birds (parrots, geese, ravens) may be capable of living 60–70 years. The fish with the longest potential lives are sturgeon (100 years). The animals are listed with their maximum life spans in years. [1] seahorse 1–2; [2] mouse 3; [3] guppy 5; [4] guinea pig 7+; [5] queen bee 7+; [6] silverfish 7; [7] large beetles 5–10; [8] earthworm 5–10; [9] swallow 9; [10] bat 10–15; [11] sponge 15; [12] rabbit 12; [13] sheep 15+; [14] frog 12–20; [15] starling 19; [16] giant spider 20; [17] dog 24+; [18] seal 20–25; [19] cat 27+; [20] cow 30+; [21] snakes, lizards 25–30+; [22] oyster catcher 27; [23] pigeon 35; [24] lion 30–35; [25] newt 35; [26] toad 36; [27] zebra 38+; [28] chimpanzee 39+; [29] ostrich 30–40; [30] horse 40+; [31] hippopotamus 54; [32] carp 50+; [33] lobster 50; [34] pelican 40+; [35] mussel 50–100; [36] goose 47+; [37] crocodile 50–60; [38] sea anemone 60–70; [39] Indian elephant 77+; [40] cockatoo 70–85; [41] golden eagle 80; [42] sturgeon 80–100; [43] man 112; [44] vulture 117; [45] big tortoise 100–150.

countervailing mechanisms operate to censor mismade cells. It was once believed, from faulty experiments of the French biologist and surgeon, Alexis Carrel (1873–1944), that cells grown outside the body were "immortal," being capable of indefinite division. Recent work indicates that this is not so, but that normally they are able to undergo only some 50–60 doublings before the accumulation of defects in their chemical machinery kills them. Major changes also occur with time in the body's immune defense mechanisms. The probability here is that divergence in cell structure causes some cells not to be recognized as "self"—and so they are destroyed.

Aging in most animals can be readily modified by the simple process of limiting caloric intake [5]. This limitation need not be so severe as to affect growth; feeding rats two days in three has little effect on growth but increases life span by 60 percent or more. Such observations suggest that the rate of aging in man could be retarded.

Since mechanisms in the brain probably monitor dietary intake and serve as controllers of cellular aging rates, the study of these, rather than of lifelong dietary modification, seems a likely course for research aimed at making it "take 70 years to reach 60." Human life can probably be prolonged little by overcoming single diseases, with the possible exception of arterial disease.

Towards longer life

Lifetime dietary or other experiments on man or long-lived animals could be useful, but in practice this kind of experiment is confined to rats and mice. High priority in research on aging is therefore given to tests of short duration. Such tests were first applied to Hiroshima survivors in an attempt to find whether aging is accelerated by radiation. Some animal studies designed to discover whether antiradiation drugs delay aging have prolonged life in mice, but it is likely that changes in food intake or liver chemistry have played a part. A technique to alter the human aging rate is, however, almost certainly attainable [3], and much research is being done under the title of gerontology.

KEY

"You start dying the moment you are born" is a favorite saying caught in this artist's impression of man assailed by death. If we dodge the rocks, arrows, blunderbuss, or rifle of death, the bridge itself stops halfway across the river.

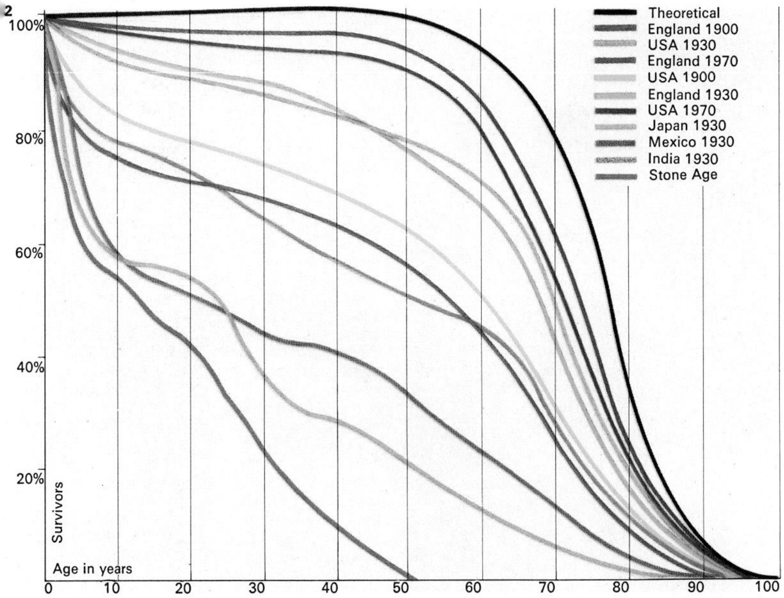

2 Human survival curves show the effect of improvements in living conditions on the lengths of time that people could expect to live in different cultures and at different times. The shape of the curve is revealing. A rapid plunge at the start as in Stone Age man (an estimate), Mexico (1930), and India (1930) indicates high infant mortality. The top line is the theoretical optimum, a situation in which almost everyone lives to be about 70 years old. The curves for modern industrial nations are approaching this point. Current research on aging is aimed at achieving the optimum, where active life is prolonged to the limit. The object is not to produce a population that will live to the age of 120, but to develop one that will retain vigor up to a natural life span of about 80.

3 Many interlinked factors probably contribute to the aging process. Certainly no single common factor has been isolated. Consequently the research that is being carried on is aimed at testing many different areas that are thought to be implicated. Listed below are some of the most important. Generally, tests are carried out on such animals as mice, and positive results that can be applied to humans are years away.

Agents	Effects	Examples
Antioxidants	Prevent cell damage by groups of atoms called free radicals. Many antioxidants affect appetite (so cutting down food intake) and liver enzymes	BHT (butylated hydroxytoluene), selenium, ETQ (ethoxyquine)
Radioprotectants	Prevent chemical changes that are similar to those produced by radiation	SH (sulphydryl) groups
Immunosuppressants	Prevent the body's immune system from declaring war on the body itself	Azathioprine (Imuran: used in prevention of organ transplant rejection), ALS
Cell or lysosome stabilizers	Prevent cell damage caused by enzyme leakage within the cell itself	Prednisolone (synthetic steroid, induces same effects as adrenal gland), aspirin
Enzyme inducers	Cause the liver to produce enzymes that affect the body's metabolism	DDT, phenobarbitone, BHT, Dilantin
Antiappetants	Reduce food intake and thus restrict calories	BHT
Hormones	No one hormone controls ageing, but many are able to affect it via different physiological processes	
Patent medicines	Most are wholly inactive although high claims are made	Gland extracts, embryonic cells, queen bee jelly, etc

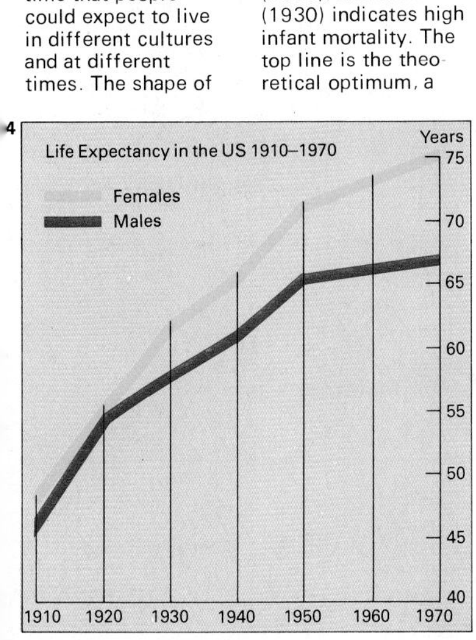

4 Life expectancy at birth has risen markedly in the United States in the last 60 years, due to better nutrition, advances in medical science, smaller families, and improved health and hygiene measures. Total births of boys normally exceed those of girls by about 6 percent. However, birth and mortality rates at almost all ages are higher for men; so women typically live longer and outnumber men in total population (by 100 to 94.8 in 1970 in U.S.).

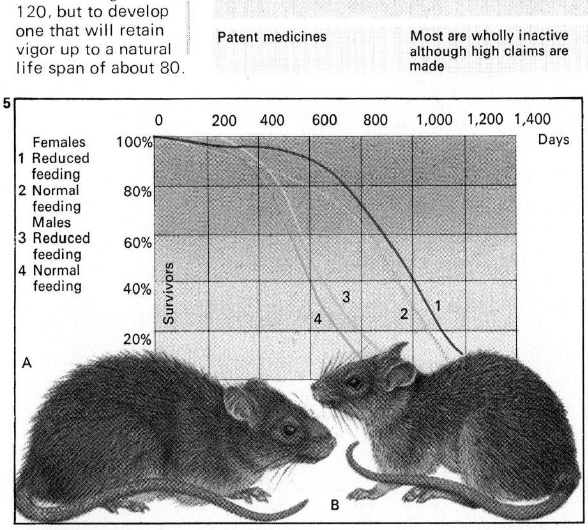

5 Overeating seems to be one cause of aging, judging by a series of experiments carried out on rats. One group was raised on a restricted but nutritionally adequate diet, others from the same litter were fed normally. After 24 months the normally fed ones [A] had effectively reached old age after only two-thirds of their lives, the "retarded" ones [B] when re-fed were as fit at 39 months as the normal rats were at 24. The survival curves reflect this.

An active old age

In preindustrial societies the old were considered to be repositories of wisdom. Because they had seen it all before, and had practical experience of how recurring situations had been effectively dealt with, they were a valued and valuable resource to the community. In societies characterized by large, extended families of mixed ages, the old had vital functions, not only as guardians of experience but also as those who taught the children.

Cultural prejudice toward the aged

In many contemporary societies families are smaller, their range of activies has contracted, and jobs have become more specialized. Money has taken the place of skills, and general functions have been usurped by specialists. Increasingly, in societies that have made youth an obsession, the old have found that ordinary dignities and privileges as equal human beings have been denied them. In the East both life and death are considered to be part of the whole life cycle and so the older a person gets, the wiser he is thought to be [4]; in the West attitudes are different. The tendency, particularly since the 1960s, has been to downgrade the importance of experience, to question the authority of those with seniority in professional or political life, and to inflate the value of youthfulness as a physical attribute and a mental attitude.

While physical changes in aging, such as graying, wrinkling, and muscular weakness, are undeniable [1, 2], much of the picture of "old age" in western cultures is based on social attitudes. Old age is a role imposed by a convention that assumes "the old" to be infirm, unemployable, uneducable, asexual, and dependent. All of these assumptions depend on old people playing the expected role. Too often people equate retirement from a job with retirement from life and treat others and themselves accordingly. But many of the supposed disadvantages of age have been shown to be imaginary [3]or to arise from the expectation that they will occur. Although old people are not so readily aroused, sexual function persists lifelong in normal individuals of both sexes. The rate of learning a foreign language for the first time is identical in 15- and 80-year-old subjects if those with impaired brain circulation or other overt diseases are excluded. The "dependency" of the old is a product of prejudice, not a fact.

The existence of a large population of aged is really a twentieth-century problem since until recently most people did not live past 65. In the United States, for example, only 3 percent of the population was over 65 in 1900; today the figure is 10 percent, and it may soon approach 20 percent. This is a pattern that is evident in all societies with zero population growth, and it is now precisely these societies that exclude older persons from full participation and cultivate negative attitudes to their usefulness and worth.

Planning for the aged

There are some signs that the body of prejudice toward older people may change before long. Even without the probability that the rate of aging can eventually be slowed, so that it takes, say, 70 years to reach the equivalent of 60, society is beginning to

CONNECTIONS

See also

802 Aging and longevity
670 Memory and recall
676 Hearing and balance
712 The causes of illness 2
720 Diseases of the skeleton and muscles
716 Diseases of the circulation
800 Adulthood: middle age
806 Death, grieving, and loss
698 Keeping fit

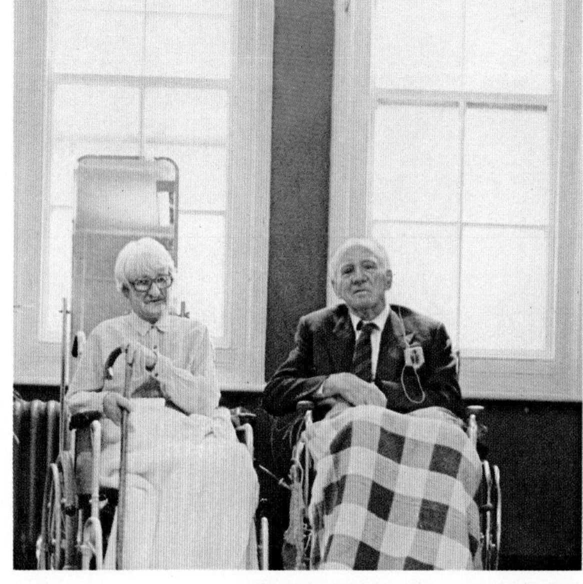

1 Certain physical changes are characteristic of the aging process. Hair grays or writens as a result of hereditary factors. On the head, both men and women start to lose hair, although the process is more marked in men. Facial hair may increase, especially in women, but body hair thins or disappears. Height is reduced as spinal disks atrophy, leading to a sagging posture. Vision weakens at about 45 and a white or gray semi-circle may later develop around the iris. Changes in the inner ear cause a loss of high-tone hearing. Smell and taste also become less sensitive. In men, a bulbous nose may develop due to faulty gland action. Dilation of blood vessels gives a spidery effect at the root of the nose. Teeth that are not looked after may be lost, leading to shrinkage of the jaw. Under the chin and in the breasts soft skin sags as a result of loss of the elastic protein collagen. The top layer of skin thins out all over the body so that blood vessels stand out, especially on the wrists. Skin also wrinkles and becomes discolored. Senile freckles on the back of the hands and warts or raised red blood vessels on the body are common. Hand grip weakens and women may develop a swelling of the top finger joints. The heart is less able to respond to extra work, its valves grow more rigid, and the body is more prone to illness because bloodmaking capacity is reduced. Artery walls thicken. Lungs function less well because of reduced respiratory muscle power and distortion of the rib cage. The lungs' air spaces enlarge, and breathlessness increases. Cellular units in the nervous system do not reproduce, so that nerve cells decline in number and the brain may lose bulk. The functions of the gastric juices, kidneys, spleen, and pancreas deteriorate in effectiveness. Ovaries cease to function at the menopause. In men the testes atrophy, although sperm formation may continue to a late age. The prostate, a male gland, enlarges, tending to cause bladder trouble. Muscles lose bulk and become weaker. Bones grow lighter and more porous. Weight-bearing joints, particularly knees and ankles, may swell and become deformed. Osteoarthritis, a degenerative joint disease, is also common in spine and hips. Stiffness and loss of flexibility are increased by calcification in cartilage and ligaments. The shins may become tender and irritated as a result of the dryness of the skin that comes with old. age Corns and callouses thicken.

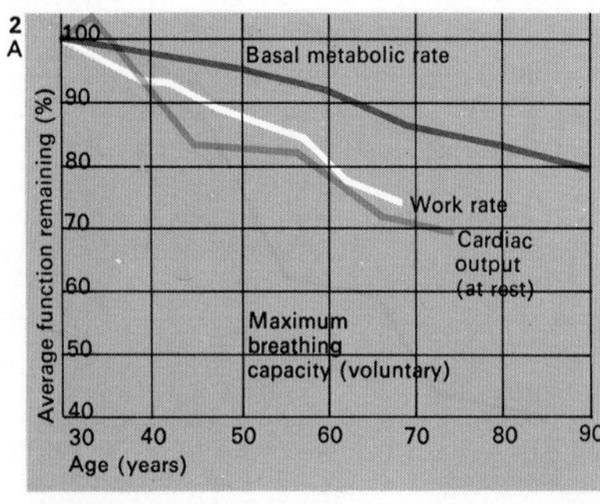

2
A
Basal metabolic rate
Work rate
Cardiac output (at rest)
Maximum breathing capacity (voluntary)
Average function remaining (%)
100
90
80
70
60
50
40
30 40 50 60 70 80 90
Age (years)

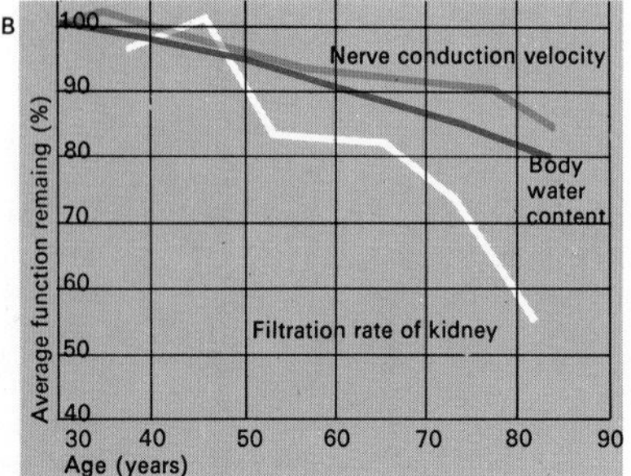

B
Nerve conduction velocity
Body water content
Filtration rate of kidney
Average function remaing (%)
100
90
80
70
60
50
40
30 40 50 60 70 80 90
Age (years)

2 Behind the outward signs of aging, several physiological processes [A, B] start to decline.

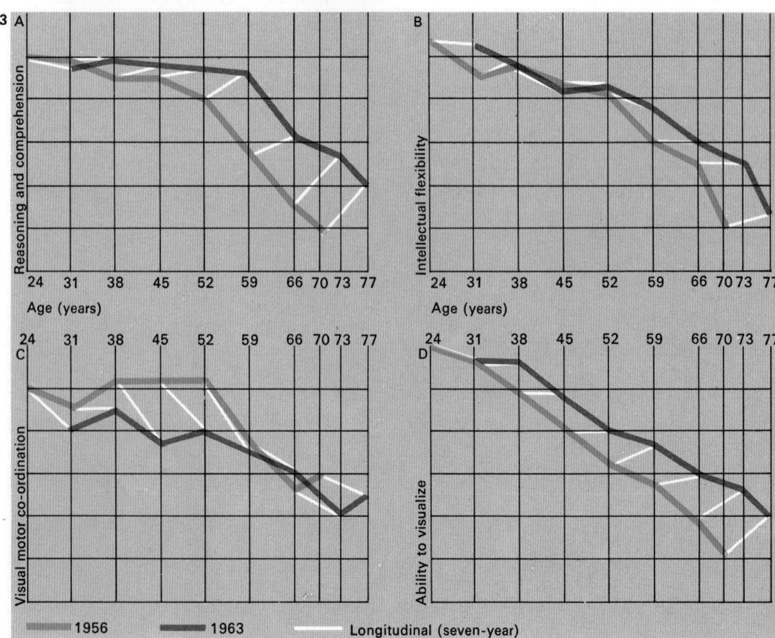

3 A
Reasoning and comprehension
24 31 38 45 52 59 66 70 73 77
Age (years)
B
Intellectual flexibility
24 31 38 45 52 59 66 70 73 77
Age (years)
C
Visual motor co-ordination
24 31 38 45 52 59 66 70 73 77
D
Ability to visualize
24 31 38 45 52 59 66 70 73 77
1956
1963
Longitudinal (seven-year)

3 The popular belief that intelligence declines with age is challenged by recent research. When adults were tested at the same point in time the aged fared worse [red and blue lines]. But generational differences may account for this because tests at different times on the same people revealed another picture [white lines]. In reasoning and comprehension [A], intellectual flexibility [B], and ability to organize visual material [D] the same adults did better in 1963 than in 1956. Only visual motor coordination [C] declined.

move toward the acceptance of two successive life-styles, with a renewal of education in middle and late life and a recognition of "senior citizens" as a political force.

Many people of both sexes already undergo an identity crisis very similar to a second adolescence at about the age of 45–50 in which they reassess their goals and achievements. This is because they can expect to live to the age of 70 to 80. Our ancestors dreamed of rejuvenation [5, 6] but seldom lived long beyond 70. With the dissipation of myths about the inability of older people to learn or acquire new skills, senior education aimed at updating skills may be given higher priority. Destructive retirement practices that expect the retired to be idle, and legislation penalizing pensioners who earn, may come under increasing attack.

Aging does involve an increase in the incidence of illlness, which may impair learning power and efficiency. Planning to meet the needs of old people must accommodate both the vigorous who want to remain fully engaged and a small but increasing proportion of those unable to do so, who need social and medical support. A similar range of options is needed in housing; some older people like to live in a mixed community, others with their contemporaries. The aim of social planning should be to make society "age blind" as well as color blind so that status as a person is no more affected by age than by sex or race. While age inevitably lessens physical efficiency it does not as inevitably bring helplessness, dependence, foolishness, or senility in its train.

Psychological problems

Of all the psychological problems that face the aged, the most difficult are perhaps isolation and the need for adaptability. In addition to physical handicaps and the diminishing number of social roles that are commonly available to the old, the aged have to cope with loss of the familiar—career, standard of living, surroundings, and, above all, people. The death of a spouse is often a blow from which the aged do not recover. The ability to come to terms with these changes is vitally important.

KEY

Creative power in old age has been demonstrated by many artists, including Pablo Picasso (1881–1973). His longevity as a painter was surpassed only by that of Titian (*c.* 1487–1576), who produced some of his finest work in his 80s. Arturo Toscanini (1867–1957) was a vigorous conductor until the age of 87, while at 87, Konrad Adenauer (1876–1967) was chancellor of West Germany.

4

4 A Taoist believes that life can be prolonged by attaining the state of *hsien.* This can be reached by a combination of respiratory, dietary, sexual, and gymnastic techniques. Man must inhale deeply when the earth breathes in, during the day. Grain and meat are impure so consumption is regulated. While sexual intercourse is not forbidden, it involves a loss of vital body fluid.

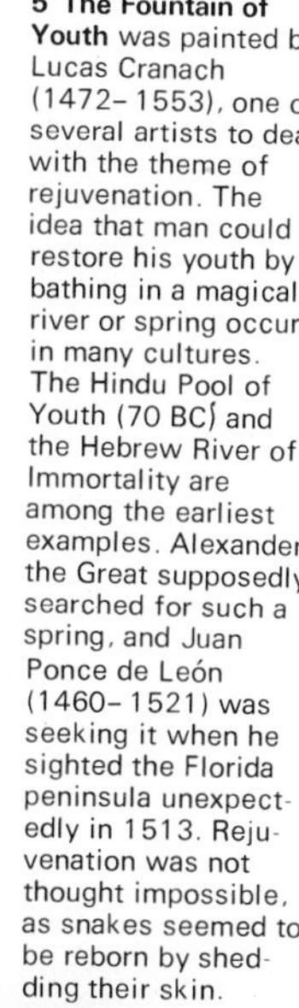

5 The Fountain of Youth was painted by Lucas Cranach (1472–1553), one of several artists to deal with the theme of rejuvenation. The idea that man could restore his youth by bathing in a magical river or spring occurs in many cultures. The Hindu Pool of Youth (70 BC) and the Hebrew River of Immortality are among the earliest examples. Alexander the Great supposedly searched for such a spring, and Juan Ponce de León (1460–1521) was seeking it when he sighted the Florida peninsula unexpectedly in 1513. Rejuvenation was not thought impossible, as snakes seemed to be reborn by shedding their skin.

5

6

6 Satirizing hopes of rejuvenation, an 18th-century artist envisaged a windmill that could grind up old women and reconstitute them as ladies of fashion. The most serious attempts to find an elixir of youth were made by alchemists who sought to gain power over nature through science. One of the basic themes of their search was that man could become eternal through association with things eternal. It was this theory that led Chinese alchemists to recommend that food should be eaten off golden plates. For in this way the patient would take in a little of the metal each time he ate, and since gold was incorruptible he would gradually achieve a higher state of being.

7 Plastic surgery, a drastic means of "rejuvenating" the face, has grown in favor in recent years. Sagging and wrinkled skin, brought about by a decline in the elasticity of muscles, is stretched back from the face and neck by a surgeon, who then removes the excess and stitches the gap beneath the hairline. The process leaves the skin tauter but often has to be repeated.

7

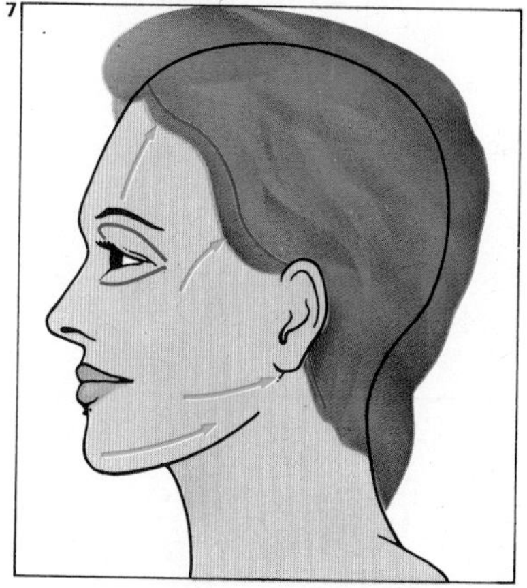

Death, grieving, and loss

From the moment of birth each of us begins to develop a model of the world in our imagination. This model includes everything that we know, or think we know, of the world around us; it includes our own bodies and minds insofar as we can view these ourselves; it includes the things and the people we know, and our plans, expectations, and hopes [1]. Sometimes events will occur that invalidate a part or parts of our world model—the unexpected loss of a loved one, for example—and we may be faced with the need to abandon many of our assumptions and painfully to rebuild the world it has taken so long to create. The experience of a change of this kind has been termed a "psychosocial transition" or crisis period.

Reactions to change and loss

Periods of crisis are both time and energy consuming, and they follow a more or less consistent sequence [2]. At first, particularly if the change is sudden or massive, there is likely to be a stage of shock, denial, or disbelief. The individual is unable to take in the reality of what is happening and tends to behave as if no change were occurring.

Before long, however, realization begins to dawn, and there is a period of striving in the course of which the person bitterly tries to recover the world that he or she is losing and to preserve the old model. Repeated frustration causes him or her to abandon the struggle, and a period of disillusionment, apathy, and despair sets in. Finally, little by little, the appetites of life return and new beginnings are made so that the final phase is one of reorganization and recovery.

Death and bereavement

The most devastating and overwhelming type of change is possibly that which occurs when a previously healthy individual develops a fatal illness. Death implies so radical a change that not only is the dying person likely to avoid facing the prospect of his or her own death, but everyone around tends to collude in the pretense that the illness will disappear. Remarkably, given emotional support and the relief of pain and other symptoms, many people do eventually express a wish to be told the full facts of their illness. They will often arrive at a stage of acceptance in which they fully realize the implications of the illness and can reorganize and enjoy to the full the life that remains [7].

Coping with death implies the possession of a philosophy of life that includes death as a valid part of the world model. In modern Western society this is rare, and death has taken the place of sex as a taboo topic. In the United States Dr. Elisabeth Kübler-Ross has brought the subject into the open, writing extensively of her work with dying patients and their families.

It would be fair to assume that once a person had died his or her troubles are over. For those who remain, however, a fresh stage of adjustment may be just beginning. They may be helped or hindered in this adjustment by the rituals and social events that, in all societies, mark the transition from life to death. The survivor is faced with the need to undertake a major change in his or her model of the world. It is hard to deny

CONNECTIONS

See also
830 Types of ritual
838 Myths of autumn
840 Myths of winter

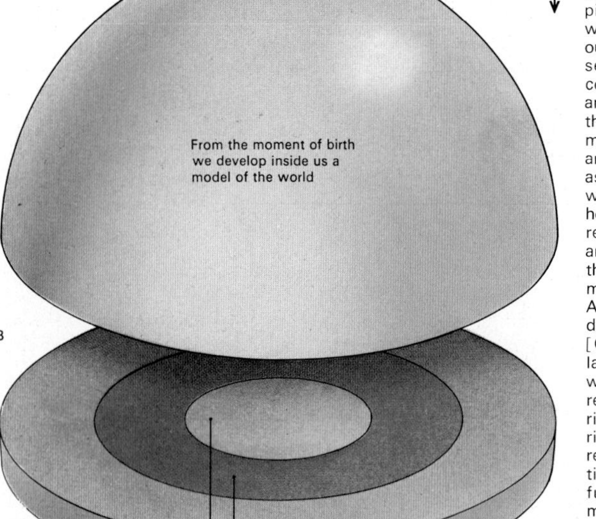

1 A
Time
From the moment of birth we develop inside us a model of the world
B
My body
My wife, car and house
My friends, job and country
Loss of job, workmates, etc
Lost ability to control and relate to one's familiar world
Body image
C
Social and/or psychological crisis
Lost expectations and plans
The rebuilding, reorganization and recovery after loss

1 The model of the world that we contain within us can be pictured as an onion whose center point is our view of ourselves. Around this core are our bodies and those parts of the world that are most intimately ours, and beyond them aspects that are more widely shared: the horizontal slice [B] representing "now" and the upper part of the figure "the remembered past" [A]. Any event, such as a disabling accident [C], which renders a large part of this world model incorrect or useless gives rise to a difficult period of crisis. As a result of this transition a major and painful restructuring of many layers of the onion is necessary.

2 Death, the most fundamental period of transition in our lives, is a crisis that many people in Western society face unprepared. This lack of preparation is reflected in the way that, all too often, relatives, doctors, and nurses try to hide the fact of death and maintain the pretense that a dying person is not very ill [A]. When a person dies those closest to him pass through the grief [B] that for a while will disorganize their lives and make it hard for them to support each other. If they face up to their grief and receive encouragement and understanding from others they will be able to cope better with the successive losses and griefs of old age [C].

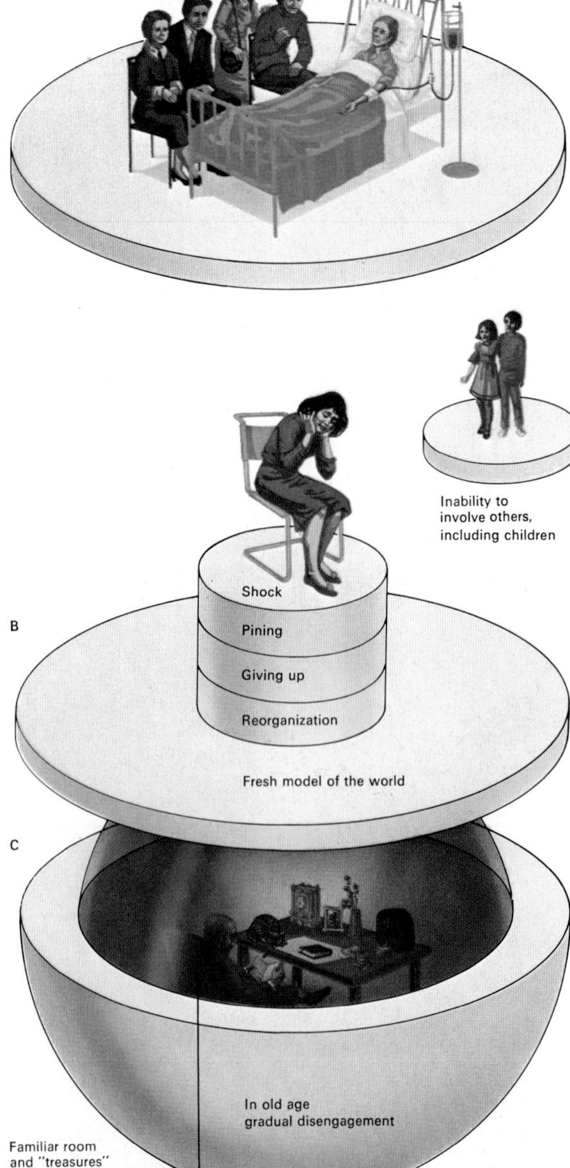

2 A
Inability to involve others, including children
B
Shock
Pining
Giving up
Reorganization
Fresh model of the world
C
In old age gradual disengagement
Familiar room and "treasures" become important – people and world affairs less so

the fact of death for long, and soon the phase of shock is replaced by the pangs of grief—characterized by intense pining.

Some people report an illusory sense of the continuing presence of the dead person that may be retained for many years, but in time the facts are accepted, and if all goes well, the bereaved person discovers a fresh identity. In other types of loss, such as that following divorce, there may be a similar sequence of reactions, but these are more likely to be complicated by anger and self-reproach.

Disablement and old age

Illness and accident may give rise to physical disablement. The patient is then faced with the need to grieve not only for the lost ability but also for those aspects of life that went with it. Thus the person who loses a limb grieves for the job that he or she can no longer carry out, for the lost sports and other activities, and for the future prospects that seem to have disappeared.

Disabled people need time and emotional support if they are to come through the grief that must be expressed for the real losses they have undergone. They may be reluctant to learn the skills appropriate to their disability until this process of realization is complete.

Old people tend to suffer a succession of bereavements and disablements. They often attempt to cope with these by narrowing their horizons and disengaging themselves from many of the people around them. But at the same time they become vulnerable to changes in the small environment that is all they have left. It is important to recognize that an old person's room and its familiar objects are more important than they would be to a younger person.

Periods of grief and loss are times of danger, but they are also times of opportunity. Those who come through them may emerge more mature and secure than before. Those who succumb—by excessive avoidance or by "caving in"—may find future losses even harder to take. The loving support and care of close friends and relatives remain the most valuable consolation available to those facing death or loss.

KEY

The expression of grief in the human face reflects a deep-seated need to cry. This has a "signal" function and evokes support in others. But knowing that it is useless to search for the lost person, efforts are often made to inhibit grief, with varying degrees of success and inner tension.

3

3 The rituals attending death have actually been seen as support to the dead, but most of them also have a psychological function for the living. The provision of food, drink, and familiar possessions, as in this Bronze Age Danish burial, comfort the survivors as well.

4

4 In the former Indian tradition of "suttee" the widow of the dead man joined her husband on the funeral pyre. In this culture she was treated as one of the familiar possessions that accompanied him into the next world. It was also assumed, perhaps, that life for the survivor would, or certainly should, be intolerable.

5

福

5 Societies vary greatly in the ritual expression of mourning. In this Chinese funeral the mourners wear white, and the colorful coffin seems to reflect the hope of a contented future for the deceased. The sarcophagus bears the inscription "good luck" in Chinese characters. But this does not prevent grief from being expressed, and professional wailers may be employed by the family to give social sanction to the shedding of tears among relatives and friends.

6

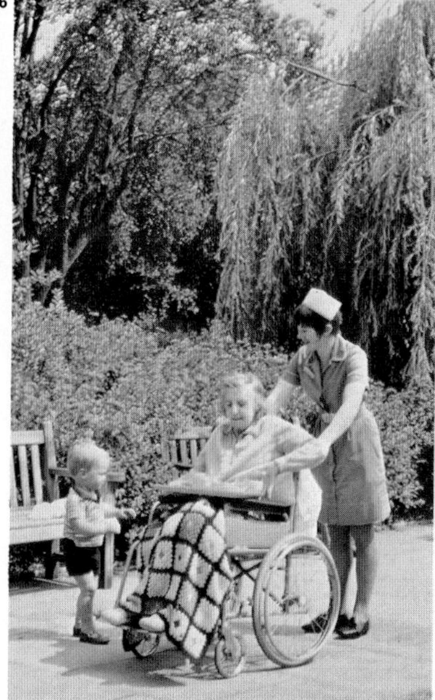

6 In facing the prospect of his or her own death a person can come through the grief and become free to enjoy the life that remains to him or her. This woman, knowing that she may have been within a few days of death, was yet able to enjoy a ride in the garden of a hospital.

7 A

B

7 These pictures were drawn by a woman with terminal cancer. Her feelings when she entered the hospital [A] contrast sharply with her outlook a few weeks later [B]. The pictures reflect a remarkable transformation from all-consuming pain to a balanced, peaceful frame of mind even though the staff made no attempt to conceal the facts of her fatal illness.

Questions of life and death

Humans have always asked questions about what they ought to do, where duty lies, and what rights the individual possesses or grants to others. Humans are moral beings because they cannot evade choices. Since these choices are often difficult to make, humans have evolved systems of principles or morals—usually expressed by a religion or philosophy—in order to help make choices and measure actions. In this way humankind has some concrete and shared idea of what good and evil mean.

The question remains, particularly in a largely secular society, as to whether these principles are absolute—given, as it were, by some external and superior force—or whether they are created by the society. Fyodor Dostoevsky (1812–81) asserted that "if God does not exist, everything is permitted," but it may be that our principles represent a consensus of rules that make living in a group possible.

Attitudes toward moral systems can be classified broadly into two types. Moral principles (for example, "Thou shalt not kill") can be formulated and then applied whatever the consequences and regardless of the specific individual case. (Few if any values, however, have been so applied—men have been encouraged by many churches to kill in war, for instance.) In contrast to this "absolutist" approach to morality, "situationist" or "utilitarian" approach to moral values is more usual today, whereby all the circumstances of the case are considered.

Science and morality

There is nothing really new about any present-day moral problems, but perhaps they are now more pressing than in previous ages because modern science has greatly increased the scope and range of the consequences of human decisions.

This is most obvious in modern warfare. Combatants can now be far removed from each other and, in the process, distanced from the consequences of their actions. War is also no longer simply a combat between armies; the humane distinction between combatants and noncombatants has been obliterated. This raises the question of whether there can be any "innocent bystanders" in modern conflicts.

The problem is at its most extreme with the atomic and hydrogen bombs [1]. Many people have questioned the development and production of these bombs, let alone their use, both because their destructiveness outweighs any justification for their use and because of the probable long-term effects of radiation. Does the end of "saving" lives justify the horrible means of attaining that saving? Even the peaceful use of nuclear power carries the risk of lethal pollution of the atmosphere for many generations. Behind the practical problems of using it peacefully is the moral one of whether it is possible to balance the benefits, however great, against the risk, however small and remote.

Dilemmas in medicine

Advances in medical science pose problems in unusual guises, from the morality of using animals in experiments [4] to the question of exactly when organs for transplant surgery [3] may be removed from "dead" donors.

CONNECTIONS

See also

860 Philosophy and ethics
786 Moral development
888 Structure of societies
908 Rule of law
1746 Nuclear, chemical, and biological warfare
738 Preventive medicine
706 Birth control
752 Development of surgery
922 Changing patterns of punishment
772 Behavior therapy
1340 The home front in World War II

1 The first atomic bomb was dropped on Hiroshima on August 6, 1945. Within a week Nagasaki had been destroyed. (This photo is from a 1965 test.) President Harry S. Truman explained that if the bombs had not been dropped, the war would have dragged on for 18 months longer, at a probable cost of two million Japanese and one million American lives. Ending war swiftly and saving lives are unquestionably moral intentions, but this situation may have been a prime example of the way in which moral dilemmas defy reduction to practical terms. The "equation of suffering" on which Truman based his argument does not necessarily provide a moral justification for his action.

2 Poison gas was used in World War I against the Allied Forces, but it proved to be an unreliable weapon. Other chemical methods have since been used, although germ warfare has not. In many instances, although by no means all, there fortunately seem to be "natural sanctions" that set limits to human behavior.

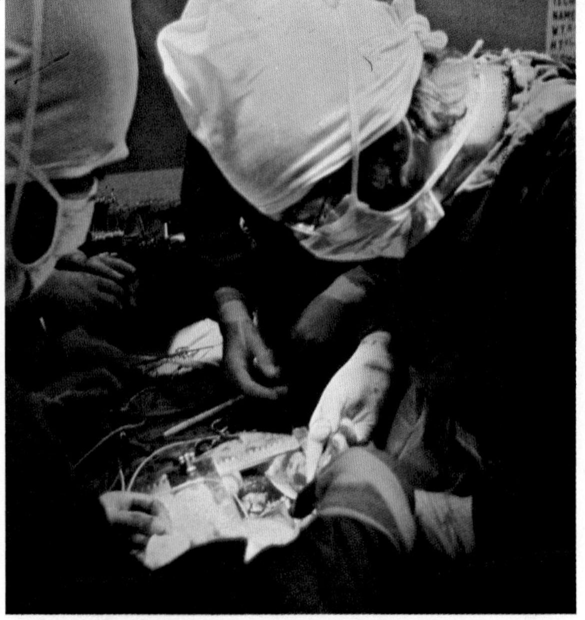

3 The first heart transplant was done by Christiaan Barnard in 1967. Although a great feat, the problem remains whether large sums and rare skills should be used to save a few lives while less spectacular operations are neglected. Some argue that without such pioneering operations, medical knowledge cannot advance.

Another area of medical research—increased control over reproduction—has given new dimensions to one of the most intractable of moral questions: who has the right to decide in matters of life and death? The broad question of social responsibility and individual rights is also relevant to another area of birth control—"genetic engineering" and eugenics. The scientist could be faced with the morality of "improving the breed" at the expense of a couple's right to produce their own children.

The morality of preventing life—by birth control, sterilization, or abortion [5]—is closely linked with that of taking life. Voluntary euthanasia (mercy killing), for example, in the face of intolerable and incurable pain or because life has been reduced to vegetable existence, has been claimed as a fundamental human right. In such cases the conflicting moral arguments of the "absolutists" and "relativists" are thrown into sharpest relief.

Sometimes moral problems arise because the state wants to impose its will on the individual. Even if it stops short of executing undesirables [Key], has society the right to order the sterilization of a mentally retarded girl whose children are likely to be handicapped? Should it reform habitual criminals by aversion therapy or, more radically, by a brain operation that makes them irrevocably? The possibility of such methods being used by an unscrupulous or frightened state in order to control political dissidents is a fearful one.

The root of morality

All moral traditions, both religious and secular, find such radical measures repugnant because these traditions make humans the norm of morality and hold that one may not abuse the dignity of another person without harming oneself. The whole of humanity is ultimately interdependent and interrelated, and humans are responsible for each other and for future generations. In borderline situations there will always be conflicts of duties, but love and respect for other human beings and honesty in relationships provide, if not final answers, starting points on which to base any moral system.

KEY

Capital punishment, here summarily administered in Manchu China, raises the fundamental question of whether life should be taken for any reason at all. Is it an effective deterrent? What sort of crimes should it be imposed for: treason, premeditated murder, acts of terrorism? Because the questions are so difficult and provoke such emotion, most societies invest the power over life and death not in the individual but in "justice," "God," or "the people."

4

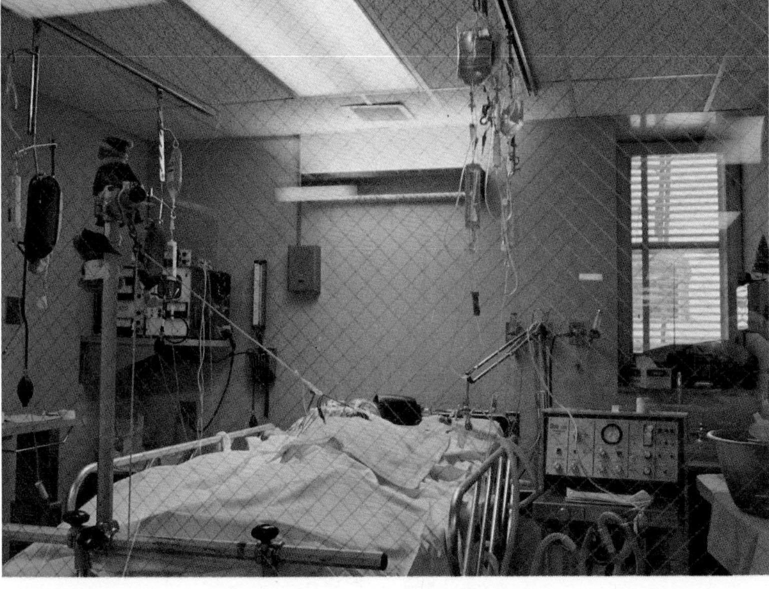

4 Life-support systems are able to keep the heart and respiratory system working even though the brain has stopped functioning. This has raised some questions. Does death occur when the heart stops or when the brain stops functioning? Is it murder to disconnect the life-support system of a "brain-dead" patient? Should a patient be put on life-support if recovery is hopeless?

6 Law and order are necessary in all societies, but in theory, force should be used only to prevent a major breach of the peace. The aim of these riot policemen, once they have been called in, should be to disperse the crowd without causing injury. The right of assembly and peaceful demonstration is basic to free societies, and the erosion of that right is one of the first signs of repression.

6

5 Human characteristics are obvious in a 12-week-old fetus. Its genetic coding has already dictated the color of its eyes and the pattern of its fingerprints, but it is still totally dependent on its mother for oxygen and nourishment. These conflicting factors invite opposing arguments: either that the fetus is simply a part of the mother's body; or that the fetus is a separate human life. Abortion thus becomes, by the first argument, justified if the mother wishes it; and by the second, an indefensible act of murder.

5

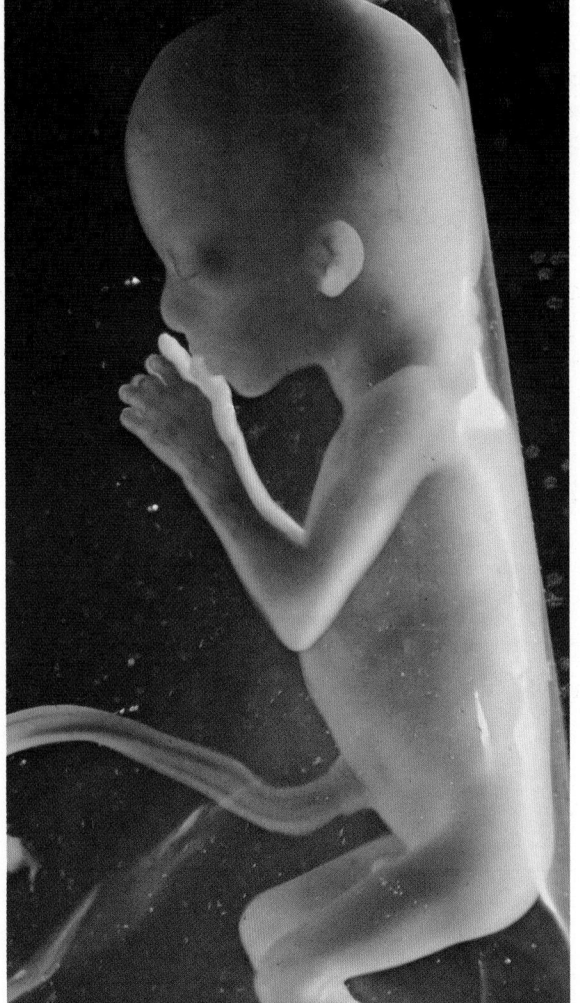

The idea of the person

One of the distinguishing marks of humanity is that whereas other living creatures merely act, men and women can reflect on their ability to act. They are (after they have ceased to be infants) creatures capable of self-consciousness. Since each individual has his or her own consciousness, each one is unique, not only in physical appearance but also in possessing a continuous thread of conscious being that is not shared in its entirety with anyone else.

Self-consciousness

In the Bible story of the Garden of Eden [1] the acquisition of self-consciousness is symbolized by Adam's eating the apple and falling from grace, thus implying that self-consciousness is not an unmixed blessing. It makes an individual likely to be self-conscious on occasions when it would be more enjoyable to be spontaneous, and likely to be led by his own individual interests into actions that others may condemn and that may make him feel guilty. As a result, humans' capacity for self-awareness, which marks them off from all other creatures, also gives rise to morality and the emotions of guilt and remorse, from which other animals appear to be free. Another facet of the story is the belief that people were once innocent, incapable of crime, and free from knowingness and guile; hence the religious idea of original sin and the primal fall from grace. The story also suggests that in the future, either in this or another world, men and women will be able to achieve a state of blessedness in which they are purged of self-consciousness and selfishness.

The unique capacity of humans to be conscious of themselves and of their relation to the world, which enables them to know about and control the environment to an extent other animals could never approach, has resulted from an awareness not only of their individual beings but also of the fact that these beings are only transient. Hence the unique interest of humans in their past, which leads them to create myths and write histories, and in the future, which leads them to create memorials that will, they hope, survive death [4]. They are also driven to pursue fame and to crave descendants who will carry on their lines and names into the remote future. Religion, history, patriotism, nationalism, ancestor worship, time-honored ceremonials—all seem to derive at least some of their vitality and appeal from the fact that they help to decrease our disquieting awareness of the fact that we personally are not eternal.

Loneliness and self-awareness

Since each individual's consciousness is in many ways unique, each one's recognition of himself as an individual carries with it the knowledge that he can be alone and isolated [5], even if there are now companions with whom he can share experiences. The more any individual becomes aware of his individuality, the more aware he will become of being alone and lonely.

In modern Western civilization education and culture set high value on self-awareness and individuality, and society is conceived of as a collection of separate individuals and not as an organic community. Hence techniques of communication have

CONNECTIONS

See also
812 Aspects of human nature
814 Classifying personality types
816 Freedom and individuality
776 Human development
844 Judaism and Christianity
818 Body image and biofeedback
820 Meditation and consciousness
842 The nature of religion
792 Adolescence: sex and independence

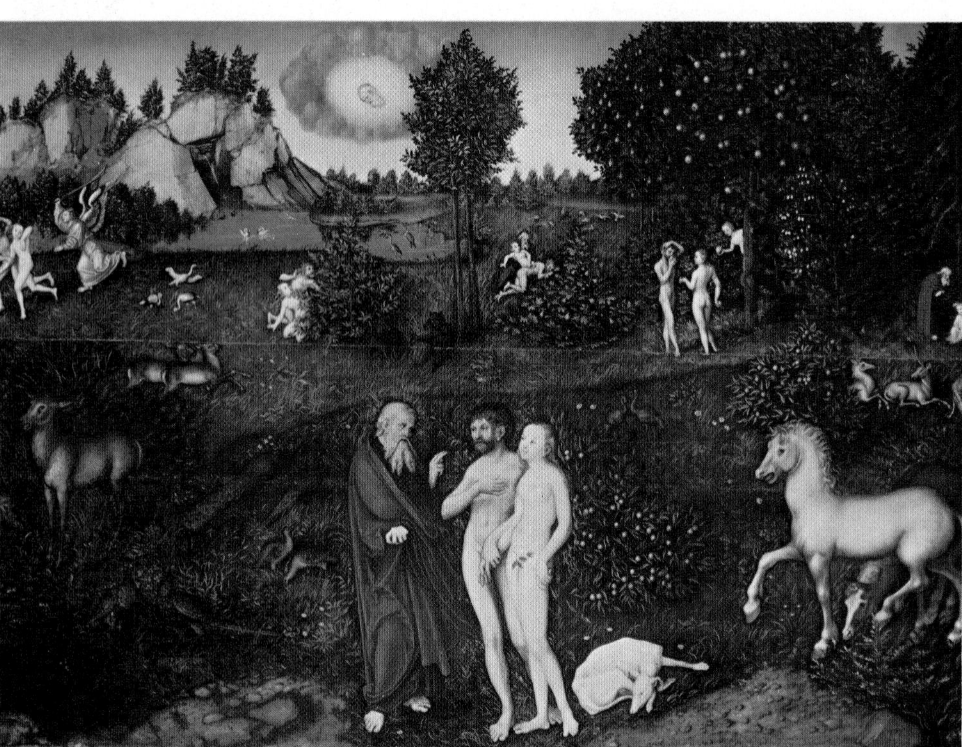

1 The fall of man as seen by the German painter Lucas Cranach (1472–1553) begins when God sternly enjoins Adam and Eve not to eat of the Tree of Knowledge. When they do eat the forbidden fruit, after being tempted by the serpent, God expels them from Eden. This story symbolizes humanity's loss of innocence, the discovery of shame, and the acquisition of a moral sense.

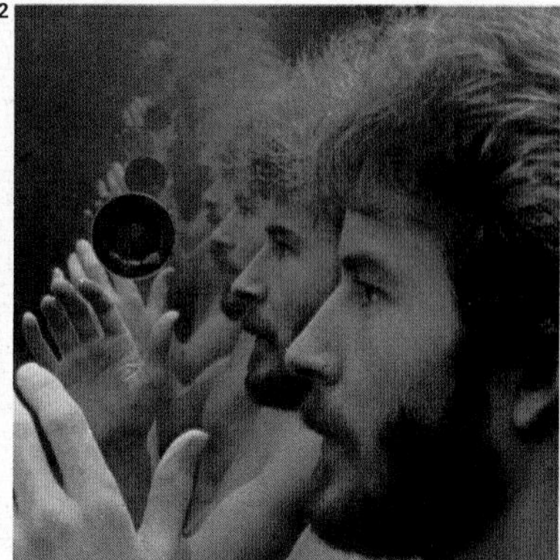

2 Humans, unlike other animals, can reflect upon their actions and recognize their mirror images. Some psychologists believe that invention of cheap mirrors (*c.* 1700) has profoundly affected human consciousness by making people aware of themselves as visible objects.

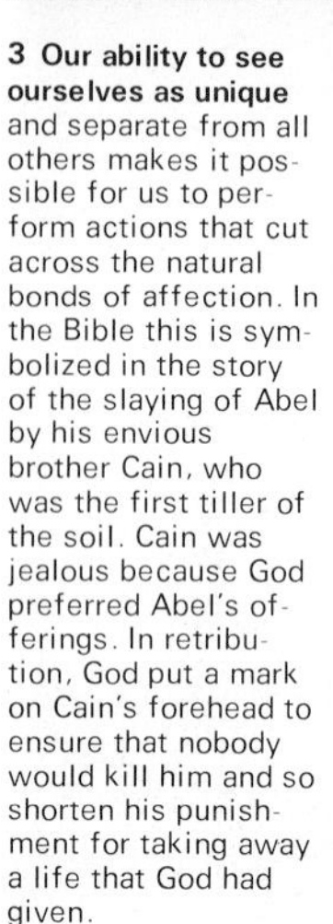

3 Our ability to see ourselves as unique and separate from all others makes it possible for us to perform actions that cut across the natural bonds of affection. In the Bible this is symbolized in the story of the slaying of Abel by his envious brother Cain, who was the first tiller of the soil. Cain was jealous because God preferred Abel's offerings. In retribution, God put a mark on Cain's forehead to ensure that nobody would kill him and so shorten his punishment for taking away a life that God had given.

4 Our awareness of our mortality impels us to create objects that will be remembered after we die. Those with wealth and power often build triumphal arches, palaces, pyramids, or cities in the hope of constructing permanent memorials. The Taj Mahal, shown here, is an example of this striving for immortality, but in one respect it is exceptional. It was built to immortalize not its builder, Shah Jahan (1592–1666), but his favorite wife, Mumtaz Mahal. The mausoleum took 20,000 men 11 years to complete.

become an important object of scientific study. For example, the state of being in love [6], in which the boundaries between selves seem to be miraculously dissolved, has become the most eagerly desired form of experience. In other cultures people rarely fall in love, and when they do their feelings are held to be a threat to social life.

Many people feel that their self-awareness does not include the whole of themselves and that what they do is also directed by other mysterious forces. Sometimes these other forces are conceived to be inside the self but inaccessible to consciousness. These forces have in the past been described as spirits or demons. In contemporary psychological language they are regarded as instincts, which impel the individual from within and which he can never completely know or control. A person, in this view, is like the rider of a horse of which he or she has only imperfect knowledge and control. At times the rider and the horse may proceed smoothly, sometimes the rider may force the horse to go in a direction in which it is reluctant to go, but sometimes the horse may carry the rider off. In other words, sometimes we behave spontaneously and feel at one with ourselves, sometimes we practice self-control, and sometimes we impulsively do things that we do not really want to do.

Fate or destiny

Where these other forces are conceived to be outside the self, they are either viewed in the abstract as Fate [7] or the influence of the stars, or more personally as gods who directly interfere with and control the destiny of individuals. More rationally, human nature may be seen to be determined by historical and social forces that mold it from without [9].

One of the great divides is between those who believe that people are impelled by forces within themselves and those who believe that they are molded by external circumstances. Those who hold the first view are attracted to psychological explanations of behavior. Those who hold the second view prefer historical and sociological explanations.

KEY

Robots can simulate human actions, and computers can simulate human thoughts, but robots cannot themselves decide what actions to perform and have to obey the person who operates them; and computers, despite being able to perform rapidly the mathematical tasks that the human mind performs slowly, must be designed by a person and can only "think" about whatever problem they have been programmed to think about. They also differ from persons in lacking feelings about what they are doing and in being incapable of reproducing themselves. Robots with intelligence and feeling exist only in science-fiction stories.

5

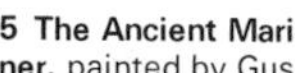

5 The Ancient Mariner, painted by Gustave Doré (1833–83), depicts loneliness–the awareness of isolation from others. But this is not the loneliness of someone whom chance has separated from his fellow men, but of someone who has committed a crime for which he believes there can be no forgiveness–the slaying of the albatross.

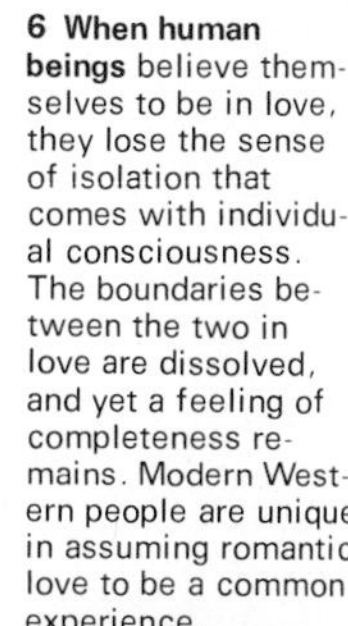

6 When human beings believe themselves to be in love, they lose the sense of isolation that comes with individual consciousness. The boundaries between the two in love are dissolved, and yet a feeling of completeness remains. Modern Western people are unique in assuming romantic love to be a common experience.

6

7

7 The Moirai or Fates of Greek mythology presided over human birth, destiny, and death. Clotho spins the thread, Lachesis decides how long it is to be, and Atropos cuts it. Even the gods could not alter such a destiny.

8

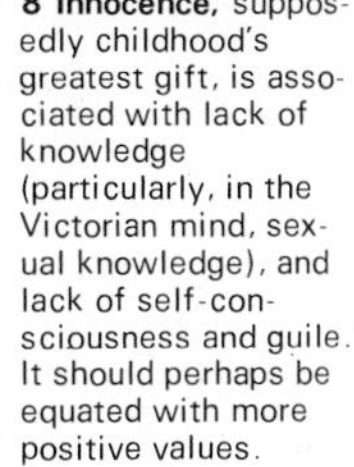

8 Innocence, supposedly childhood's greatest gift, is associated with lack of knowledge (particularly, in the Victorian mind, sexual knowledge), and lack of self-consciousness and guile. It should perhaps be equated with more positive values.

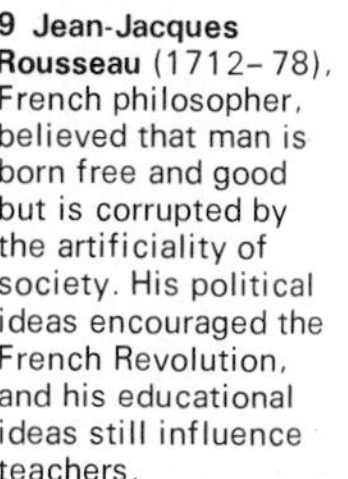

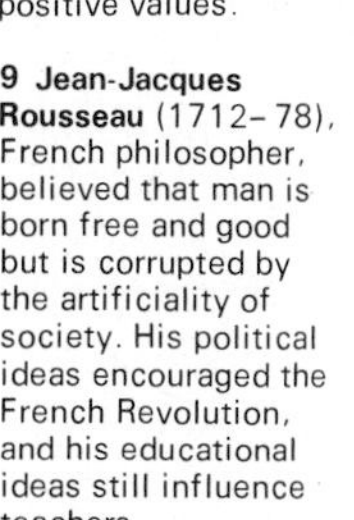

9 Jean-Jacques Rousseau (1712–78), French philosopher, believed that man is born free and good but is corrupted by the artificiality of society. His political ideas encouraged the French Revolution, and his educational ideas still influence teachers.

9

Aspects of human nature

There are two contrasting ways of looking at human nature [Key]. One conceives people to be impelled by forces, drives, and instincts acting on them from within; the other conceives people to be molded by environmental, historical, and economic forces from without. Philosophy, psychology, history, and sociology are to a large measure attempts to define precisely what these internal and external forces are.

Aspirations and instincts

Philosophers and psychologists who have attempted to define the internal forces that actuate humans can themselves be divided conveniently into two groups: those who believe people have innate aspirations and those who believe they have inborn instincts. The former, Platonists or idealists, hold that we are born with innate ideas or ideals and that the prime motive and reward in life is to realize these ideals [1, 2, 7]. The latter, Aristotelians, materialists, or realists, hold that we are born with innate cravings, passions, or instincts that demand enactment or satisfaction. According to the former, there exists somewhere, perhaps in the mind of God, a perfect Idea of Goodness or Beauty or Truth, which each individual has an innate aspiration to become or achieve. According to the latter, the physical nature of humans impels them to behave in ways that ensure physical survival and the continuation of the race; these impulses are usually called instincts.

Although these two ways of looking at human nature are most easily stated as incompatible opposites, so-called dualist philosophies attempt to reconcile them by asserting, for instance, that the spiritual part of human nature aspires toward realization of the ideal, while the physical part is driven by instinct and the pursuit of pleasure. In medieval times, when humans were imagined to be part angel and part animal, the angelic part was thought to aspire toward God, while the animal part was thought to pursue pleasure and bodily gratification.

Since the Renaissance, and more particularly since Charles Darwin (1809–82) and Sigmund Freud (1856–1939), this dualistic view of human nature has been abandoned by the nonreligious in favor of the rationalist view that even the "spiritual" aspects of human nature have evolved from instincts and are, in the last resort, pleasure-seeking and not the effects of divine purpose and grace. Freudian psychology [5], which asserts that "higher" mental activities are functions and "sublimations" of infantile sexual and aggressive drives, is the outstanding modern example of a theory of human nature based on the assumption that we are ultimately pleasure-seeking organisms. The idealist, purposive view of human nature is represented by the work of Carl Jung (1875–1961).

Love and hate

Some biologists and psychologists have assumed the existence of two instincts or groups of instincts: the self-preservative [3]—hunger, aggression, and fear—and the reproductive—sexual and maternal impulses. Some psychologists, including Freud, abandoned this classification in favor of the idea that the two basic instincts are love (or sex) and hate (or aggression).

CONNECTIONS

See also
810 The idea of the perso
814 Classifying personality types
816 Freedom and individuality
786 Moral development
784 Emotional development
888 Structure of societie
892 The individual in society
914 Nature and causes c criminality
668 Mind and brain
924 Work: curse and plea sure
1282 Foundations of 20th-century science

1

1 Captain Lawrence Oates (1880–1912) is depicted walking out into the snow to certain death, so as not to be a burden to other members of Robert Scott's expedition to the South Pole (1911–12). His act exemplified the ideal of self-sacrifice, which is, in Horace's phrase, a "sweet and noble thing to die for one's country," one's cause, or one's team. Oates's heroism is not diminished by the fact that the other members of the team died before reaching base camp.

3 The fate of the 147 people who escaped on a raft from the French frigate *Meduse* when she sank in the Atlantic (1816) dramatizes the instinct of self-preservation. After 12 days only 15 remained to be saved (here portrayed by Théodore Géricault [1791–1824]). The rest had been thrown overboard or killed and eaten by the strongest survivors. In such circumstances life becomes, in the words of Thomas Hobbes, "nasty, brutish, and short."

3

2

4

2 According to the ascetic ideal, not only the renunciation of all pleasures, but even the mortification of the flesh, by fasting and self-flagellation may be virtuous and pleasing to God.

4 In the Indian tradition, high value is placed by some sects on the body and on eroticism, as shown by this temple sculpture. This is a striking contrast to the ascetic, anti-erotic ideal that has until recently pervaded the Christian West.

An interesting sidelight has been shed on the view that people have innate ideals by the animal psychologists, or ethologists, such as Konrad Lorenz (1903–) and Nikolaas Tinbergen (1907–). They have produced evidence of the existence in animals of at least one instinct that is group- or species-preservative and that has been associated with "finer feelings." This is the instinct, in some social species, for an individual animal to shelter or protect from attack the group of which it is a member.

Behavior patterns

In some scientific circles the word *instinct* has become unfashionable, having been replaced by the concept of "behavior patterns," some of which are innate and some of which are learned. According to behaviorist psychologists, such as Ivan Pavlov (1849–1936) and J. B. Watson (1878–1958), and learning theorists, such as B. F. Skinner and H. J. Eysenck, human nature should be explained without using subjective concepts, such as mind, or assuming the existence of inner forces of any kind, but solely in terms of observable patterns of behavior.

Those philosophers, historians, and economists who believe that human nature is largely molded by external forces can again be divided into two groups: those who stress the physical environment and those who stress social forces [8]. The former emphasize the importance of geography and climate in molding character and explaining national differences.

Those who stress social forces are either empiricists or ideologists: the first maintain that individuals or groups are molded by the history of the particular society in which they have grown up; the second, the ideologists, include those Nazi historians who saw history in terms of the predestined rise of the Aryan race to world domination. Also included are Marxists, who see history as a struggle between social classes, which will inevitably end in the victory of the working class. Skeptics and empiricists view these and other theories of history as attempts to impose order and pattern on events that have none.

KEY

The two contrasting views of human nature are summarized here: the first, innate endowments, or those instincts and forces driving us from within; the second, the environmental forces of climate, geography, and social structure acting on us from outside. According to idealists, we strive to achieve some moral or religious perfection, but according to materialists, we strive always to satisfy our innate instincts for physical survival and for preservation of the species.

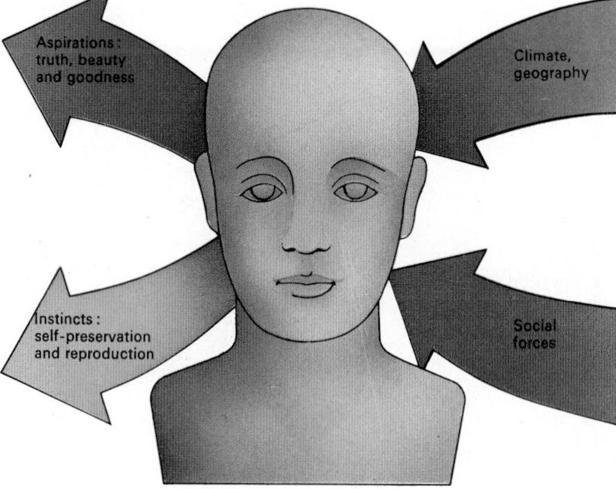
Aspirations:
truth, beauty
and goodness
Climate,
geography
Instincts:
self-preservation
and reproduction
Social
forces

5
A
B
C
D
E

5 Psychoanalytical theory describes how the newborn child does not differentiate between himself and the world [A]. Then he learns to differentiate himself from his parents and other important people [B]. With the development of sexual pleasure zones [C, D] the child passes through oral, anal, and genital stages, followed by a period of latency before puberty and the adult genital stage. The personality has three parts [E]. The *id* contains primitive drives such as sex and hunger, which the *ego* attempts to satisfy without incurring the world's hostility. The *superego* represents values instilled by parents and society.

6 Konrad Lorenz has shown that most animals display submission signals that prevent continued aggression by a stronger animal against a beaten rival. Humans have submission signals, such as avoidance of eye contact. One explanation for the fact that humans kill members of their species is that use of weapons has diminished the ability to respond to such signals.

FAITH

7 John Bunyan's Pilgrim's Progress (1678) is an allegory of spiritual progress. It tells of the pitfalls and battles that a Christian faces in his journey from the City of Destruction to the Celestial City.

8 Differences in class and income play an important part in forming personality. The "Two Nations," a phrase coined by Benjamin Disraeli (1804–81) to describe the classes in Britain, have gradually grown closer together.

Classifying personality types

Although each individual is unique, people do, of course, resemble one another in such characteristics as physique, character, temperament, and susceptibility to disease. Since time immemorial attempts have been made to classify people into groups based on these resemblences.

The four humors and modern versions

For centuries the most generally accepted classification of human beings was Hippocrates's "humoral" theory, as elaborated upon by the Greek physician Galen (*c.*AD 130–*c.*200) [1]. According to Galen there were four different types of temperament —sanguine, phlegmatic, choleric, and melancholic. Each was produced by the preponderance of one or another of the four bodily fluids or humors. If blood predominated, the individual possessed a sanguine or optimistic temperament; if phlegm predominated, he was phlegmatic or unexcitable; if yellow bile predominated, the individual possessed a choleric temperament and was quick to anger; and if black bile predominated, he had a melancholic temperament.

The humoral theory of temperament was generally accepted by both doctors and the general public until well into the nineteenth century and has left its mark in such descriptive terms as sanguine and choleric. Although no one today seriously believes that blood, phlegm, and bile play any role in determining temperament, the theory has had a curious revival in recent years. According to the British psychologist H. J. Eysenck (1916–   ), whose ideas are based on statistical research, human personality can be measured by two different yardsticks, one measuring stability-instability, the other measuring introversion-extraversion. (The latter terms were earlier used by the Swiss psychiatrist Carl Jung [1875–1961].) Extraversion is the tendency to be "outgoing" and interested in what is going on outside oneself; introversion, the tendency toward introspection and interest in one's own responses to outside events.

If both yardsticks are used [3,4], four groups of people emerge—unstable introverts, unstable extraverts, stable introverts, and stable extraverts. Here, says Eysenck, the four personality types correspond fairly precisely with Galen's four temperaments—unstable introverts resembling Galen's melancholics, unstable extraverts resembling his cholerics, stable introverts resembling his phlegmatics, and stable extraverts being sanguine. Further research by Eysenck suggests that most neurotics are melancholic unstable introverts, that most criminals are choleric unstable extroverts and that most healthy, law-abiding citizens are either phlegmatic or sanguine.

Although the remarkable aspect of this system of classification is the way in which it bridges a centuries-old gap between classical and medieval ideas and modern scientific thought, there is a difference between Eysenck and Galen. Galen asserted that a person was one of the four types, while Eysenck proposes that a person can be two, but not three of them at once. For instance, if one is marginally unstable, one is either melancholic-phlegmatic or choleric-sanguine, depending on whether one is intro-

CONNECTIONS

See also

- 766 Personality defects and neuroses
- 826 Astrology
- 776 Human development
- 784 Emotional development
- 810 The idea of the person
- 812 Aspects of human nature
- 816 Freedom and individuality
- 1032 Early Oriental and Western science

1 A

B

C

D

1 Character and temperament were for many centuries thought to be the result of the four humors. These paintings present a medieval view of the sanguine [A], phlegmatic [B], choleric [C], and melancholic [D] man. Excess or deficiency of any humor led to neuroses.

2 A

Sensation
Feeling
Thinking
Intuition

B

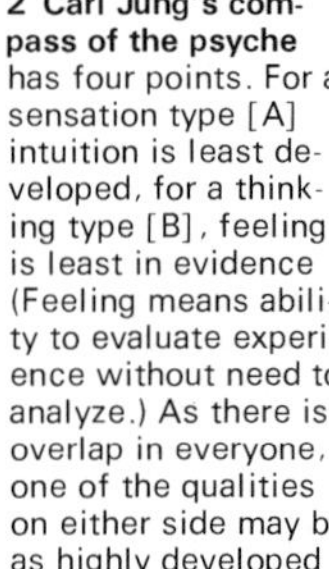

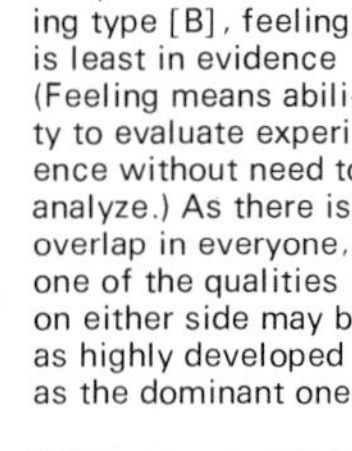

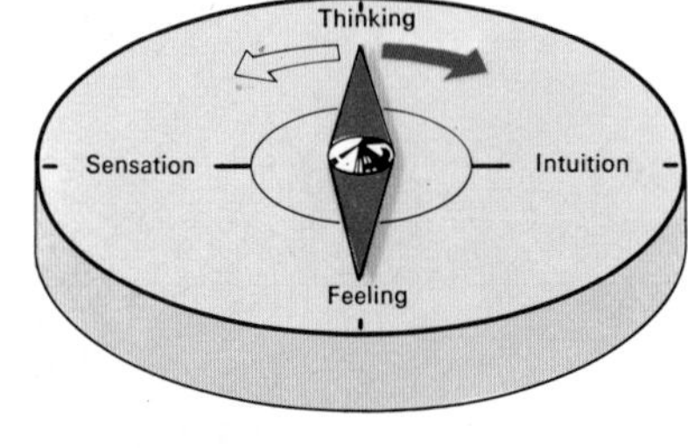

Thinking
Sensation
Intuition
Feeling

2 Carl Jung's compass of the psyche has four points. For a sensation type [A] intuition is least developed, for a thinking type [B], feeling is least in evidence (Feeling means ability to evaluate experience without need to analyze.) As there is overlap in everyone, one of the qualities on either side may be as highly developed as the dominant one.

3

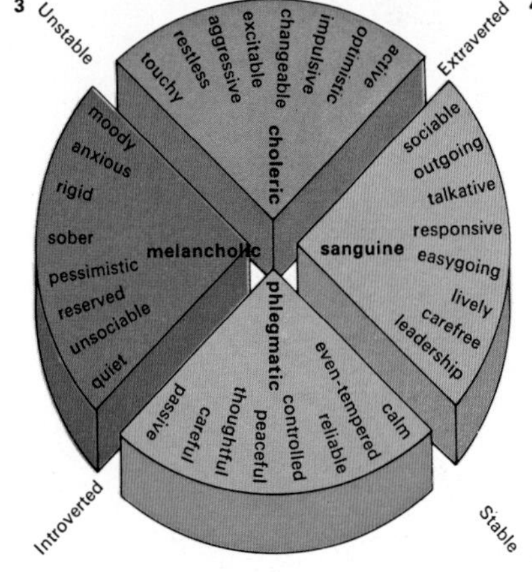

Unstable
Extraverted
Introverted
Stable
choleric
touchy
restless
aggressive
excitable
changeable
impulsive
optimistic
active
melancholic
moody
anxious
rigid
sober
pessimistic
reserved
unsociable
quiet
sanguine
sociable
outgoing
talkative
responsive
easygoing
lively
carefree
leadership
phlegmatic
passive
careful
thoughtful
peaceful
controlled
reliable
even-tempered
calm

3 According to H. J. Eysenck, every personality can be measured along two scales—one measuring introversion-extraversion, the other measuring stability-instability—and assigned a position in one of the four quadrants of a circle. This classification resembles closely that of the traditional four humors or temperaments, in which everyone is categorized as being either sanguine, phlegmatic, choleric, or melancholic.

4

Extravert traits

1 Impulsiveness
2 Hyperactivity
3 Dominance
4 Attention-seeking
5 Verbal expressiveness
6 Gregariousness
7 Leadership
8 Friendliness
9 Active helpfulness
10 Conscientiousness

Introvert traits

1 Irritability
2 Emotional fluctuation
3 Suspiciousness
4 Self-consciousness
5 Withdrawal
6 Submissiveness
7 Depression
8 Calmness

Extraversion
Neuroticism
Stability
Introversion
100 75 50 25 Introversion 25 50 75 100
100 75 50 25 25 50 75

4 The answers given to a series of questions on an Eysenck personality inventory help to locate the individual's place on the extravert–introvert and neurotic-stable dimensions.

verted or extraverted. The reason for this difference is ultimately mathematical; Eysenck's findings and theories are based on statistical theory and coordinate geometry, neither of which existed in the first century.

Although Eysenck's theory of personality types is based on massive research, it is not universally accepted, largely because it leaves unresolved the question of whether personality is innate and unchanging or the result of individual development and experience. For if the latter were so, it would be possible for a person's personality type to change over the years in response to circumstances, thus reducing the value of assigning anyone to a particular type.

Other personality types

The Eysenck-Galen theory of personality and temperament is far from being the only one. Jung, in his book *Psychological Types*, divided people into eight groups, four groups of extraverts and four of introverts, with the divisions in each case based on thinking, feeling, sensation, and intuition [2]. Here also the classification has limited value since Jung held that we are unconsciously of the opposite type to that of our consciousness and that the fully integrated or "individuated" person transcends types. Sigmund Freud was not a classifier, but some of his followers have classified people according to the kind of mental illness their personality most resembles—and which they would presumably develop if they ever did become mentally ill.

Reactions to classifications

People vary enormously in their emotional attitude toward classifications of people. Some are fascinated by them and others find them morally offensive. Any classification that really worked would be of great practical value in medicine and vocational guidance. The German Ernst Kretschmer (1888–1964) claimed that tall, lightly built people were susceptible to one range of illnesses and were introverts, while short, heavily built people were prey to another range of illnesses and were extroverts. But such claims have not been proven.

KEY

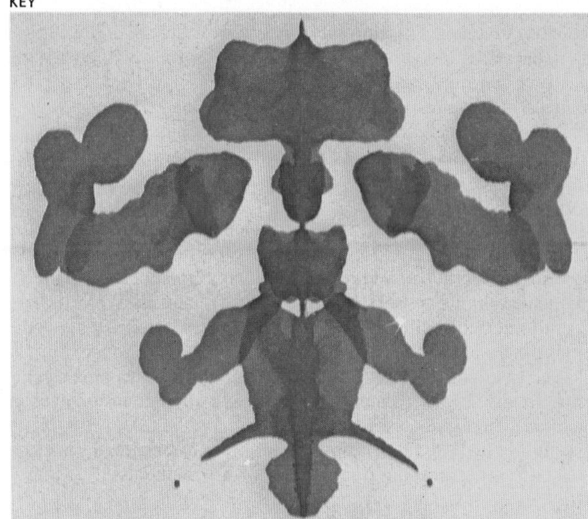

The Rorschach test, invented by Hermann Rorschach (1884–1922), invites a person to describe what he can see in a series of ten standardized ink blots, similar to the one above, his answers being used as evidence of his fantasies, personality, and psychological state.

5 Thematic Apperception Tests are often employed to measure personality improvement during psychiatric treatment. They comprise a series of 20 ambiguous pictures and drawings about which the subject has to make up dramatic stories. He is asked to indicate what the people are thinking and feeling, the events that have led up to the situation and the outcome. A man standing by a lamp post, for example, might be seen as waiting to meet his girl friend before they go out for a drink [A], or as just having been shut out of his fiancée's house after an argument [B]. The stories are then analyzed, for it is assumed that the subject identifies negatively or positively with characters that he makes up and so will reveal something about his own inner conflicts and sources of threat.

A

B

6

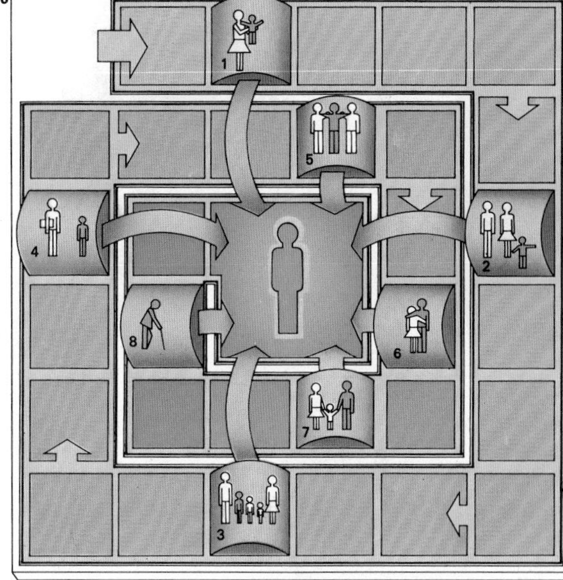

1
2
3
4
5
6
7
8

6 E. H. Erikson, the US psychiatrist, has theorized that we go through a series of psychosocial developments. Each stage is characterized by an identity crisis that strengthens the ego or self.

1 The development of hope in infancy.
2 The emergence of will, and the determination to have independence and free choice with the exercise of self-restraint.
3 A secure family gives purpose and initiative to pursue valued goals.
4 The development of competence, casting aside infantile inferiority.
5 The adolescent develops fidelity and loyalty to the self and others.
6 The crisis of young adulthood — love — encourages mutual devotion.
7 Adulthood brings responsibilities and teaches care.
8 In old age wisdom grows.

7

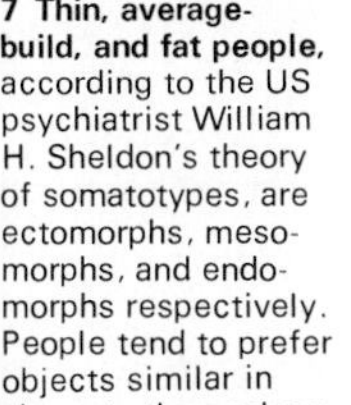

7 Thin, average-build, and fat people, according to the US psychiatrist William H. Sheldon's theory of somatotypes, are ectomorphs, mesomorphs, and endomorphs respectively. People tend to prefer objects similar in shape to themselves.

8

8 Three distinct types of people, according to Kretschmer, are the pyknics (broad, fat, short, and tending to mood swings); asthenics (thin and tending to unsociability); and athletics (muscular and intermediate in personality).

Freedom and individuality

Freedom involves a compromise between the rights of the individual and the rights of society. Each individual is unique, in that he or she is in some respects unlike any other person. But society binds individuals together on the basis of the things they have in common, such as domicile, language, race, or religion.

In liberal democratic societies, individuals possess moral and legal rights deriving from recognition of and respect for their uniqueness; limits are set on the right of the state to interfere in the lives of individuals and on the extent to which individuals are allowed to encroach on one another's freedom. In the United States, for instance, each individual possesses the right to privacy in his own home. The police are not allowed to insist on being granted entry without a search warrant, and they must have good reason for seeking it. Other people may be guilty of trespassing if they enter without the occupant's permission.

In totalitarian countries the right of the individual to privacy is not respected, and the police may enter someone's home whenever they wish; they may also make an arrest without giving a reason.

In some countries, such as South Africa, one class of persons, the whites, has rights that another class, nonwhites, does not have. A similar division existed in the United States before the abolition of slavery [2]. And in the classical civilizations of Greece and Rome there were two classes of human beings, a slave-owning class whose members were individuals with civic rights, and a slave class, which had few rights and whose members could be bought and sold.

Although Christianity has always held that all human beings are individuals and unique in the eyes of God, it is only in the last 200 years or so that there has been widespread practical recognition of human individuality, regardless of color or way of life.

Freedom and dignity

The concept of individuality is closely linked with that of freedom, the right of each individual to pursue his own happiness in his own unique way, with a minimum of interference from the state or from others [Key].

The fact of individuality forms the moral basis for the idea that all human beings possess a dignity that must be respected. Since each individual is unique, each is irreplaceable; no other person can be a true and complete substitute. Therefore, each person has a value that derives simply from being himself or herself. As a result, each has a dignity deriving from individuality and uniqueness, rather than a price deriving from what it cost to produce him or her or what it would cost to replace him or her. The German philosopher Immanuel Kant (1724–1804) stated: "A thing has a price if any substitute or equivalent can be found for it. It has dignity or worthiness if it admits no equivalent."

Individuality as a scientific fact

The idea that each member of the human race is unique is not only a legal and moral assumption but also a scientific and biological fact. The police can identify an individual by fingerprints since no two people

CONNECTIONS

See also

908 Rule of law
894 Prejudice and group intolerance
896 Prejudice and personal choice
660 Family of man: how peoples differ
888 Structure of societies
892 The individual in society
810 The idea of the person
812 Aspects of human nature
814 Classifying personality types
864 Communication through speech: 1

1 Jews destined for Auschwitz, victims of the most complete disregard for the dignity of humanity ever experienced, were collected and herded into cattle cars. In 1940 the Nazi government of Germany, which had from the beginning persecuted the Jews, instituted the policy of the Final Solution—the mass extermination of Jews in the gas chambers and execution yards of Auschwitz, Belsen, Buchenwald, and other camps. Millions of Jews died as a result of this policy, which the Nazis tried to justify by claiming that the Jews were a "lesser race," not fully human, and so were not entitled to human rights.

3 Apartheid in South Africa separates blacks from whites. In public facilities there is a rigid division between those reserved for whites and those for blacks. The white minority rules the country.

2 Slavery, by which a person is bound to work for a master without recompense of freedom, is older than civilization. The Egyptians, Greeks, and Romans all used slaves. The discovery of America gave the slave trade a new impetus. The Spanish, Portuguese, British, French, and Dutch all imported slaves from Africa to work on plantations. Britain abolished slavery in its possessions in 1833; in the United States it was abolished after 1863.

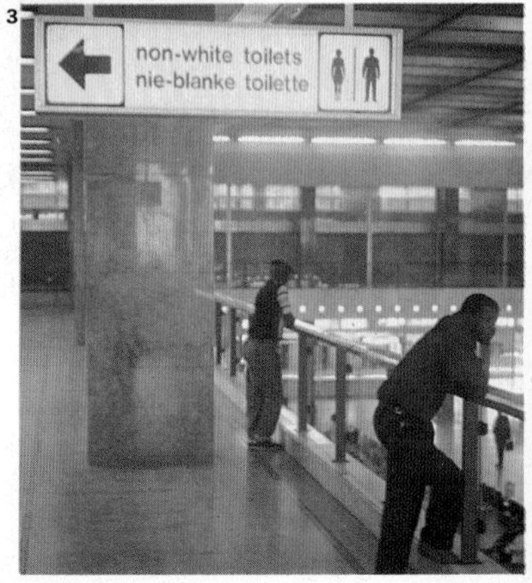
non-white toilets
nie-blanke toilette

have exactly the same pattern. It seems probable that the human voice is similarly unique. Phonetic recordings show voice patterns that are characteristic of each individual and are unaffected by the language being spoken or the accent being adopted. It appears, too, that the arrangement of genes on the chromosomes in the nucleus of each cell in the body is unique for every individual.

Furthermore, since human beings have more genes than any other animals, the possible range of genetic differences is greater than in any other animal. This wide range of innate differences is enhanced by the enormous variety of social circumstances in which men and women grow up and which mold their personalities. People are capable of surviving in a very wide range of climatic conditions and have constructed ways of life enabling them to live in the Arctic, in deserts, marshes, mountains, plains, and valleys. The unique capacity of humans for symbolic thought, expressed in language [6], has created subtleties of psychological "development" that do not exist in any other creature. Since all humans have different bodies, grow up in different environments, and have minds that develop in different ways, all are different and unique.

Identical twins come nearer than anything else to being exceptions to the uniqueness of humans; hence the uncanny effect twins can create and the myths and superstitions that exist about them. But even identical twins have different fingerprints and birthmarks. Within a few weeks, they have recognizably different personalities as well.

Cloning

In insects and plants that reproduce asexually, one generation may be exactly like the previous one. Many plants are not individuals in the literal sense of the word since they can be divided, as they are when a cutting is taken; what was originally one plant can become two or more separate, but not individual, ones. These groups are called clones. The idea of producing human clones—regiments of identical people analogous to worker bees—remains a remote if horrifying possibility.

KEY

OURS...to fight for

Freedom of Speech

Freedom of Worship

Freedom from Want

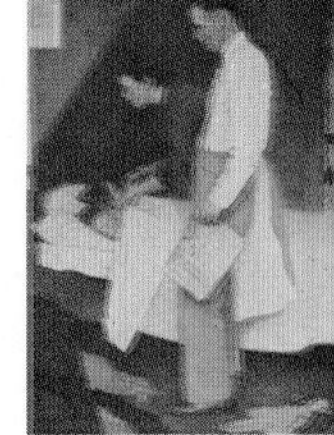

Freedom from Fear

Every person in a democratic society has the right to be treated as an individual and to be free. In a speech made some months before the United States entered World War II in 1941, President Franklin D. Roosevelt (1882–1945) made what has come to be regarded as a classic statement of democratic principles—envisioning a world founded on four essential freedoms: the freedom of speech and expression, the freedom of each to worship in his own way, the freedom from want, and the freedom from fear. These ideals were represented in a series of paintings entitled *"The Four Freedoms"* by US artist Norman Rockwell (1894–) in 1941.

4

4 The Coldstream Guards, trooping the color in London, exemplify the ability of humans to suppress one of their most important qualities—individuality—and achieve a rigid uniformity. This machinelike discipline and obedience implies at least a partial surrender of personality, which, though in the interest of efficiency, may be dehumanizing.

5

5 The seeming contrast between the regimentation of the guardsmen and the relaxed informality of these youths in an Amsterdam square masks a similarity. Nonconformity can take forms that are almost as rigid in their conventions as those of troops.

6

6 In the story of the tower of Babel, here painted by Pieter Breughel the Elder (*c.*1520–69), God punished his people by "confounding their language." Language is both a powerful source of social cohesion and expression of the individual's personality.

7

7 The story of the Good Samaritan symbolizes the need for people not to pursue their own ends selfishly but to be aware of their responsibility to others in need. Jesus told of a Good Samaritan who helped a man left half-dead by thieves after supposedly more worthy people had "passed by on the other side." Modern "Samaritan" groups offer help to people in trouble.

Body image and biofeedback

Body image is our view of the physical aspect of our personality, the image we believe we present to the world. We are so used to experiencing our bodies as if we were observers sitting inside our own heads [Key] that when the letter E is drawn on the forehead of a person whose eyes are closed he commonly reads it as the number 3—that is, he sees it from behind.

Our view of ourselves may be wrong. We may "see" ourselves as bigger, smaller, less or more attractive than we are, and such mistakes can in turn affect our bodies. A timid person fails to "walk tall," for example, and the process of "seeing" our bodies can almost certainly alter functions by subtle processes, sometimes predisposing our bodies to malfunction or disease.

Changing the self-image

The body image grows gradually with child development, and misconceptions can grow with it. The transsexual, for example, finds sexual identity to be at variance with the male or female body he or she possesses.

In an obese person overeating may arise from a false body image either at the physical level or, more often, at the self-valuing level. Moreover, humans love to manipulate the body image symbolically. They are the only animals that choose their own "plumage," and they may do so by decorating [7], deforming [2, 3, 4, 6], or surgically altering their bodies, or by using clothing to signal mood, life-style, status, and other things. Some clothing affects physical stature (such status symbols as crowns increase height; shoes are a more common way of achieving this). Other clothes emphasize features that a particular culture values; genital bulge may be exaggerated [5] or hidden in an extravagant way, and women's bodies have been molded into many biologically unnatural shapes by addition and disguise [1].

Control through biofeedback

Self-image can affect the body physically, for example, when the posture of a timid person leads to backache. A significant recent development is the recognition of the extent to which the body can also be manipulated favorably, giving a person control of physical processes normally regarded as uncontrollable. This is called biofeedback.

Body functions have long been divided, both popularly and scientifically, into the voluntary and the involuntary—those we monitor and control, such as muscular movements of the limbs, and those that are largely self-regulating, such as bowel movements, heart rate, and blood pressure. The latter are affected by an individual's state of mind, but usually on an unconscious level. It is now generally recognized that a great many of these so-called involuntary processes can be controlled by "willing" in the same way that we initiate movement of a leg or a finger, although less precisely. Yogis, with their traditional awareness of the body and its numerous functions (which they have achieved through meditation), have recognized this for centuries and, to some degree, can regulate blood pressure, heart rate, and other such processes at will. This helps to explain how some yogis have survived being buried underground.

CONNECTIONS

See also
892 The individual in society
810 The idea of the person
820 Meditation and consciousness
748 Nonmedical healing

1 A

B

C

1 Fashion has dictated that women regularly alter not only their clothes but also their shape. Women have followed trends set by fashion designers with and without the aid of such extensive undergarments as the whalebone corset and the padded bustle. Variously, shoulders, busts, waists, and buttocks have been emphasized at different times. The first 50 years of this century witnessed a remarkable series of revisions. The century started with the celebrated S shape [A], switched to the boyish bottomless, waistless, bustless style of the 1920s [B], and changed in the 1940s to a broad shouldered, tailored look [C].

2

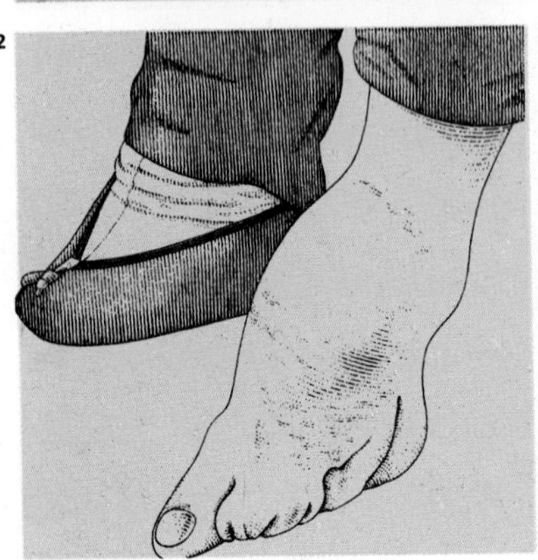

2 Small, delicate feet have been traditionally admired in women. In China, in the past it was customary to bind young girls' feet to limit their growth. This ensured a higher marriage price at the cost of deformity of the foot bones.

3

3 The giraffe look, traditionally admired by some peoples in Burma and East Africa, is achieved by adding year by year to a collar of brass rings. If the collar is later removed, the woman's weakened neck may not support her head.

4

4 Alteration of the natural shape of children's heads in an attempt to improve the aesthetic qualities of the skull has been practiced since ancient Egyptian times. The pliability of the cranium in childhood makes this possible. In different cultures the head has been elongated, broadened, or flattened, initially by pressing by hand and then by a variety of headboards. In France, as recently as the last century, such head deformations took place. Although elongated, broadened, or flattened heads were thought to be beautiful, another aim was to "shape the brain" so that the child would develop the qualities of bravery, moral uprightness, sincere feelings, and intellectual capacities.

In recent years simple machines have been developed that provide a short cut to such body awareness. These so-called biofeedback machines [9] record changes in a person's physiological processes by moving a needle, lighting a bulb, or making audible clicks. The subject, by playing "hotter, colder" with the display (attempting to extinguish the light, move the needle, or make the clicks louder), can acquire the knack of regulating the hitherto involuntary function concerned.

The biofeedback machine has been shown to work for a wide range of involuntary processes including control of brain alpha rhythms, blood pressure, heart rate, and skin blood flow. In fact it appears that almost any involuntary motor process that can be recorded by the machine can be controlled voluntarily.

The medical uses of biofeedback are just being developed and are potentially vast. Biofeedback control of brain rhythms has already been used to fight drug-resistant epilepsy by warning patients of the onset of an attack. The chief potential of the technique is as a drugless method of modifying hypertension, physical expressions of anxiety, and psychosomatic disorders for which drugs are heavily prescribed. It is theoretically possible that not only motor processes but also chemical and hormonal shifts, biological "clocks," and even long-term regulation by the hypothalamus over aging or growth may be controlled by a combination of biofeedback and learning-therapy methods.

Character armor

The importance of body image, including its effect on the body and its control mechanisms, was first stressed by the Austrian psychologist Wilhelm Reich (1897–1957). He saw the posture and organ functions of the individual as a kind of armor ("character armor") that reflects anxieties, rigidities, and negative feelings toward the body and the self, especially in its sexual context. Reich based his therapy on the removal of these rigidities, claiming that this would improve both bodily function and self-esteem.

KEY

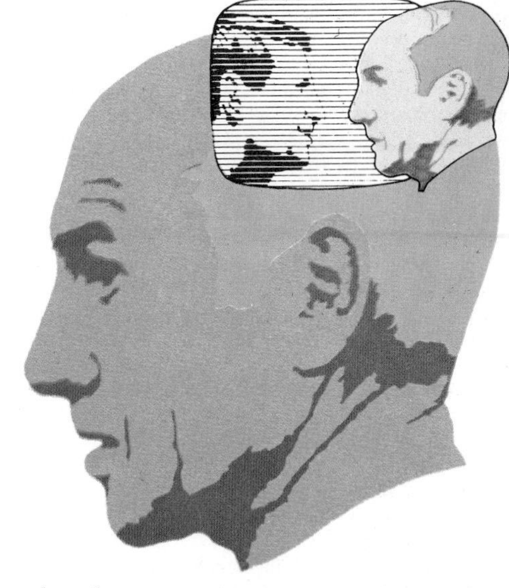

We experience the outside world at second hand and even experience our bodies as if we were sitting inside our heads looking at a TV screen. This is called "body image."

5

5 Male manipulation of the body image is most strikingly exemplified by the codpieces once used to accentuate masculinity. Lodovico Capponi wears one in this portrait by Bronzino (1503–72).

6

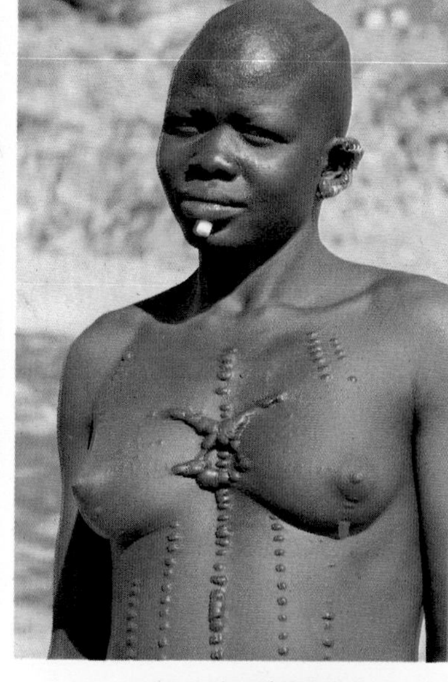

6 Scarification to increase the aesthetic value of the human body is common among some African tribes (here, a Nubian woman from Sudan). Intricate patterns are produced by cutting into the skin and then rubbing charcoal or other substances into the incisions to form permanent designs on the skin.

7

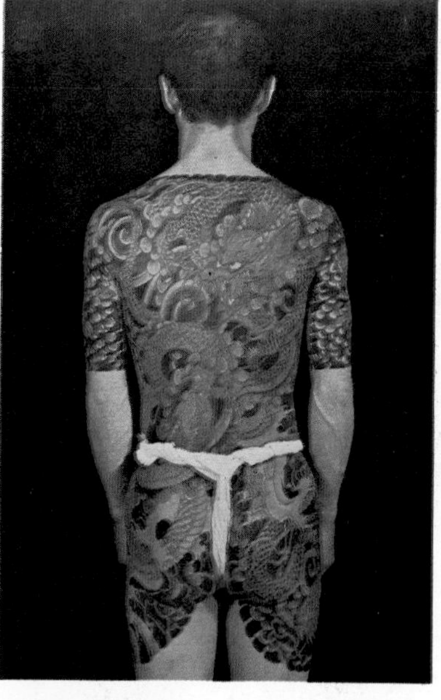

7 Tattooing has been a popular form of body decoration in many cultures. The designs are achieved by pricking or cutting the skin and then injecting colored dyes. Perhaps because its permanence is less appealing now, tattooing is not as common as it was. The Japanese are the greatest exponents of the art.

8

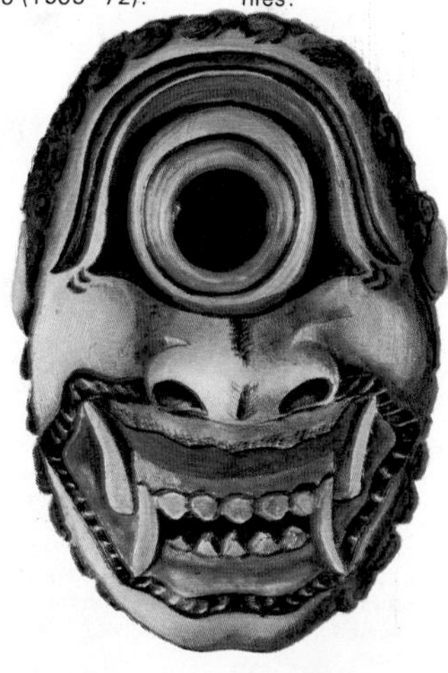

8 Distorted demon masks of intricate design, like this one from Sri Lanka, were used to terrify enemies in battle and to symbolize the forces of evil and darkness in religious ceremonies.

9

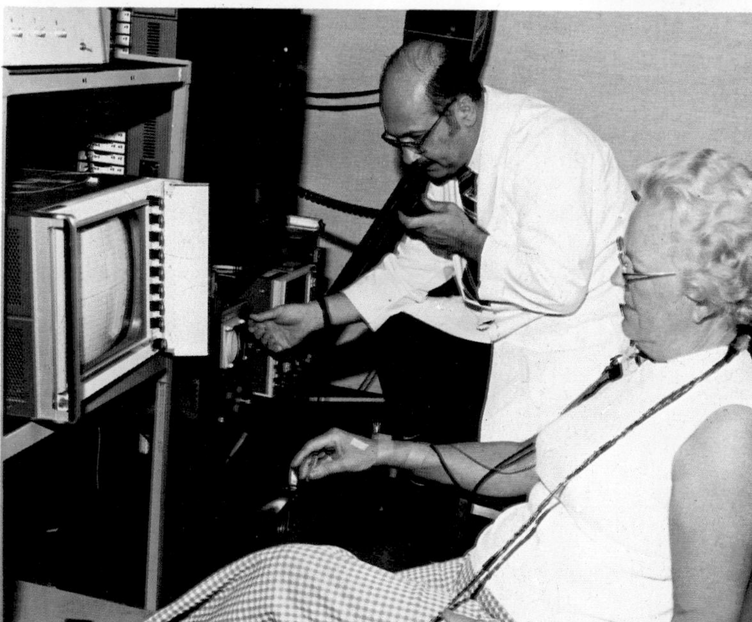

9 Biofeedback relies upon the minute electrical impulses produced when the body performs involuntary processes. These electronic potentials can be picked up by means of electrodes that are placed on certain parts of the anatomy according to the particular body function to be treated. The signal is then amplified, filtered, and rectified so that it can be monitored in the form of an oscilloscopograph, a digital display, or a series of sound frequencies. The patient then concentrates upon the level of activity and tries to reduce it below a certain point. By this method the intensity of a headache and such functions as blood pressure can be controlled.

Meditation and consciousness

Meditation is an ancient inward or spiritual discipline dating back at least to 1000 BC when it was practiced in India. Meditation involves deep thought or contemplation, often helped by postures, sounds, or images that concentrate the mind [1]. The object of meditation is not to heighten reasoning powers but to allow intuitive perception of spiritual truth, usually by excluding distracting physical sensations or intellectual activity. Meditative techniques have also been used, particularly in Western countries during the past several decades, as a means of relieving mental and physical tension.

Altered states of consciousness

Mystics of all major religions believe that God must be approached by inward illumination rather than through reason, logic, or outward forms of worship. As a way to enlightenment, meditation has been used in Western as well as Eastern religions for many centuries. But whereas it has a minor place in Christianity and Islam, meditation lies at the very heart of Hinduism and its great offshoot, Buddhism. In most forms of Hinduism the aim of meditation is to discover the inner self as a means of purification. Yoga, the most widely known Hindu technique, is based on the theory that by training both body and mind, centers of psychic power can be tapped.

Buddhism, dating from the sixth century BC, is a more self-effacing religion, teaching that with strict discipline and study a happy few can reach a state of pure consciousness, transcending body and mind, in which the ultimate reality, nirvana (nothingness), can be understood. Tantric Buddhism evolved more accessible methods of achieving this perfect wisdom and spiritual freedom through the practice of certain rituals and by using body positions (mudras), sacred phrases (mantras), and universal designs (mandalas).

Drugs, herbs, and alcohol also have a long history of use as aids to inward vision, sometimes in combination with meditation. In the 1960s many young people in the West, who felt alientated from the materialism of their own society, turned to drugs or to Eastern meditative techniques in an attempt to expand their consciousness and achieve a sense of spiritual harmony. Hallucinogenic experiences with drugs such as LSD often had adverse effects. But meditation seemed to produce physical benefits that could be measured.

Physiological changes

In 1960 studies made on Zen Buddhist priests showed that distinct electroencephalographic (EEG) brain wave patterns [2, 3] were associated with states of meditation. Practiced meditators slipped quickly into an "alpha" brain wave rhythm, indicating a state of serenity and peaceful alertness later bordering on the "theta" rhythm of trance [5]. The priests and monks who acted as test subjects could maintain this state of deep, yet alert, rest for hours without entering the "delta" rhythm or cycle of full sleep. More experiments showed that meditation was associated with other physiological changes including decreases in heart rate and oxygen consumption (about 20 percent lower) and reduced output of carbon dioxide, indicating a general slowing of metabolism [4].

CONNECTIONS

See also
850 Religion and the plight of modern man
818 Body image and biofeedback
678 Touch, pain, and temperature

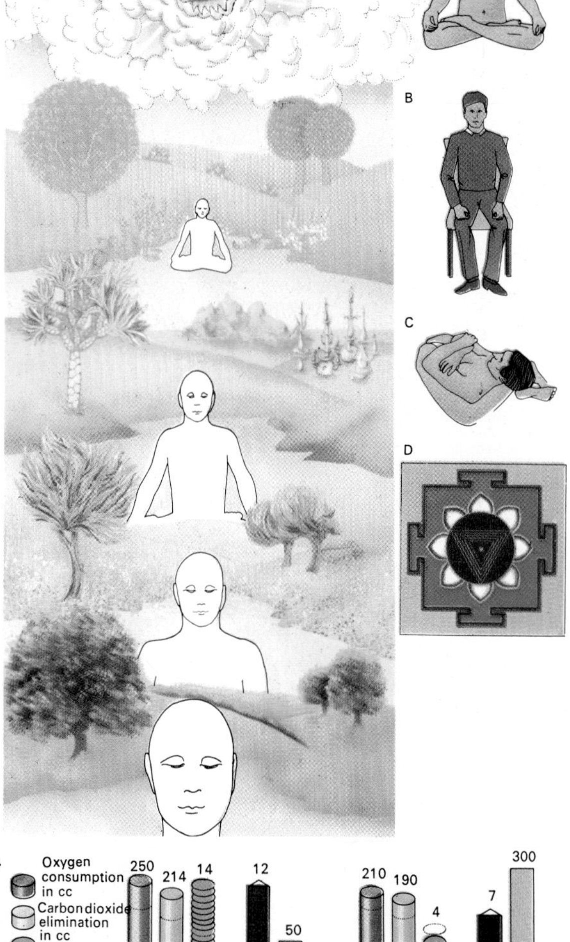

1
A
B
C
D

1 Five levels of consciousness are generally associated with meditation. Although these can be described only in subjective terms, many mystics have attempted to put them in ascending order as a guide to students. At the first level the body is relaxed and the mind stilled. Ordinary wakefulness is then transcended by a state of deep rest but alertness in which the mind is more intensely aware of itself. This state of personal awareness is transcended by cosmic consciousness, a sense of illumination beyond the boundaries of self and time. The next stage is God consciousness, or the sense of inseparability of creator and creation. Finally, at the highest level of all, consciousness itself is transcended in a unity with the whole, or oneness. There are many positions and devices used to help achieve a meditative state. The basic position is the lotus of yoga in which the legs are crossed, the back is erect, and the hands lie loosely on the knees [A]. Westerners may modify this to a comfortable upright position on a chair with open eyes gazing straight ahead [B]. Practiced yogis achieve difficult postures [C] in the belief that control of the body by the mind is the first step to salvation. Beautifully designed mandalas [D] provide aids to concentration.

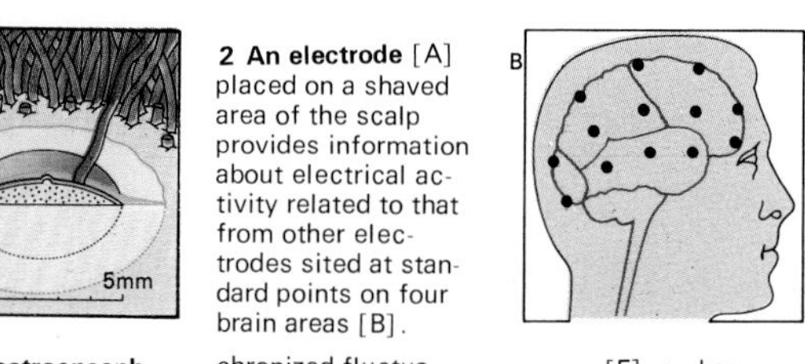

2
A
0
5mm
B

2 An electrode [A] placed on a shaved area of the scalp provides information about electrical activity related to that from other electrodes sited at standard points on four brain areas [B].

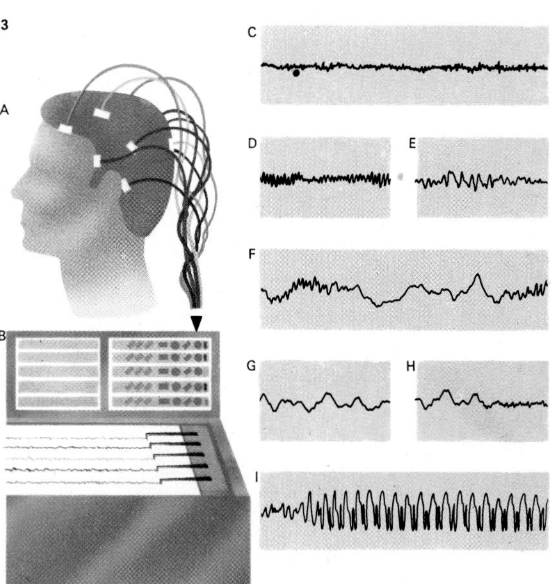

3
A
B
C
D
E
F
G
H
I

3 An electroencephalograph [B] records background electrical activity from the cells of the brain cortex through electrodes attached to areas of the scalp [A]. In the alert state only slightly unsynchronized fluctuations are detected [C]. A dominant alpha rhythm with regular waves appears in an eyes-closed state of relaxation [D]. With the onset of sleep, slower, more irregular waves occur [E], and as sleep deepens [F] large delta waves appear [G] with periodic irregularities [H], apparently related to dream activity. The EEG patterns of epilepsy [1] provide a comparison.

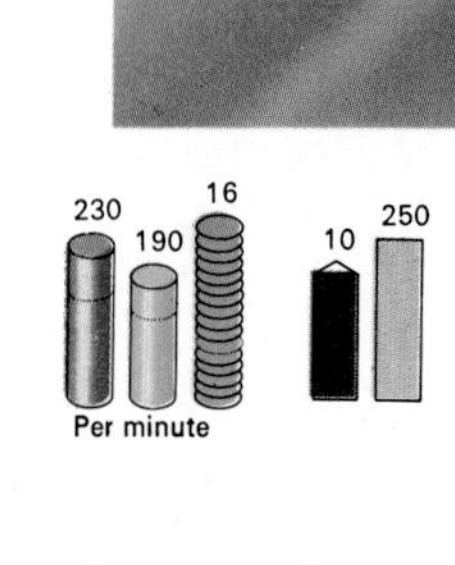

4
Oxygen consumption in cc
Carbon dioxide elimination in cc
Respiration
Blood lactate milligrams/100cc
Skin resistance milliohms
Critical level
Per minute
Sitting
250 214 14 12 50
Per minute
Meditating
210 190 4 7 300
Per minute
Sleeping
230 190 16 10 250

4 A variety of physiological changes takes place during meditation. There is a marked decrease in the rate of respiration and consumption of oxygen, a decline in the concentration of blood lactate (linked with relaxation of muscle activity in rest), and a rapid rise in the electrical resistance of the skin. In sleep, skin resistance normally rises but not so much or at such a rate. There are distinct physiological differences between sleep and meditation.

When control subjects, unpracticed in meditation techniques, adopted the crosslegged "lotus" position of Eastern meditation and were wired to the same instruments, they registered nothing but "beta" rhythm, the state of ordinary wakefulness. But in the early 1970s further studies at Harvard Medical School indicated that the physiological state associated with meditation could be achieved without years of training or self-discipline. In 1972 a report was published in *Scientific American* on tests carried out on 36 people using a simplified technique known as transcendental meditation (TM). The subjects had all achieved, after only a few sessions of training, similar (EEG) brain wave patterns to those of meditating monks.

Benefits of meditation

The discovery that meditation could be instrumentally measured created interest among both scientists and psychologists. The effects of achieving certain EEG patterns cannot be equated with the objectives of spiritual meditation, and physiological changes convey little information about the mind, but the significance of the Harvard results is that meditation, even at a simple level, appears to have benefits for societies with a high degree of stress in daily life. Since Maharishi Mahesh Yogi [7] brought the TM technique to the West in 1957, it has become a popular form of relaxation, particularly in America, where some large claims have been made for its social as well as its individual benefits [8]. The TM technique involves two daily sessions of 15–20 minutes during which the subject sits in a comfortable position with his eyes closed and repeats a sound without a special meaning chosen to keep his wandering mind in tow. No intense concentration or special discipline is required nor is any specific religious belief or philosophy. More rigorous yoga techniques have also attracted many Westerners willing to study and practice meditation and sometimes to travel to the East in search of gurus (teachers) and ashrams (retreats). The question of whether there is a special area of the mind that can be reached by such methods remains open.

KEY

The practice of meditation takes many different forms but, as with this Buddhist monk, it is usually aimed at achieving a higher plane of consciousness in which physical needs are negated and the spirit of man perceives essential truth. To aid transition to this plane some Eastern methods of meditation use an object such as a mandala—a geometric design often symbolizing the cosmos. Other methods include forms of rhythmic breathing and concentration on a point between the eyes or on a mantra (sound), the most famous being "Om," a derivation of the Sanskrit "Aum." Mantras are often phrases that sum up ancient wisdom.

5 Alpha-Theta state. Inner stillness. Decreased self-awareness Pleasant feeling of freedom

Alpha state. Feeling of transcendence. Alert, calm, elated. Sense of insight

Alpha-Beta state. Wakeful, calm, creative, perceptive. Sensitive, investigative, intellectual thoughts

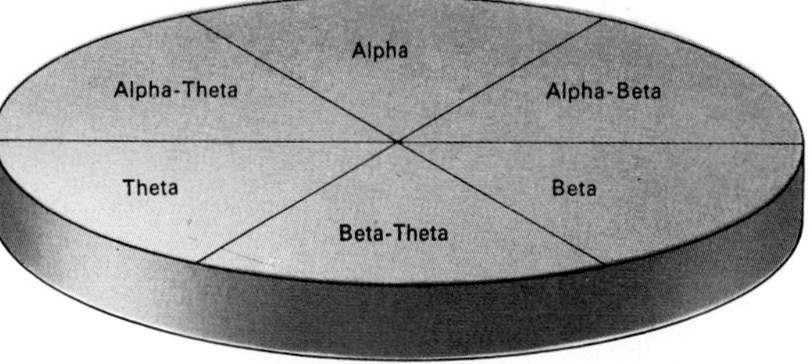

Alpha
Alpha-Theta
Alpha-Beta
Theta
Beta
Beta-Theta

Theta state. Dreamlike trance state. No self-awareness

Beta-Theta state. Disturbed and negative. Feeling of unhappiness

Beta state. Subject to anger, excitement, tension

5 States of feeling may possibly be linked with differing amounts of alpha, beta, or theta rhythm as shown in EEG brain wave patterns. Any interpretation of these relationships is necessarily highly subjective, but a generalized chart can be based on research with numbers of meditators including both Zen monks and yogis of long standing and recent practicers of transcendental meditation.

6

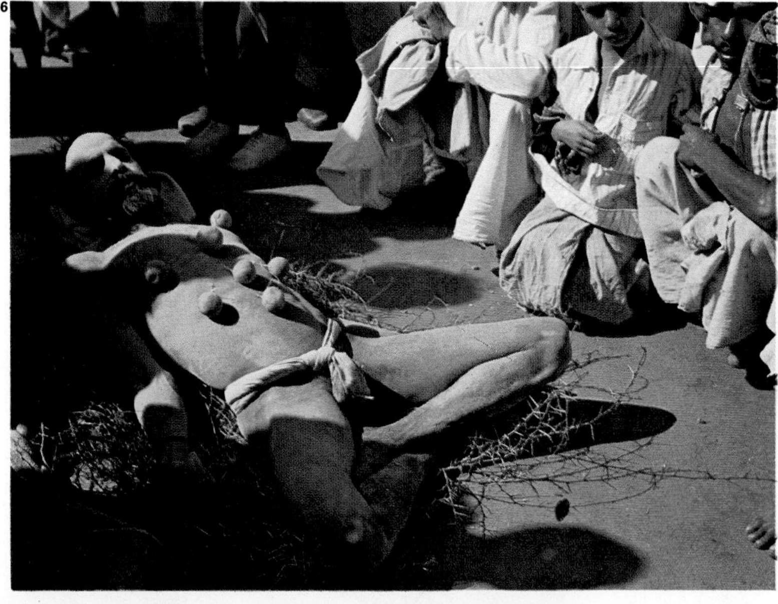

6 An Indian fakir demonstrates his ability, in the meditative state, to negate the pain caused by lying on a bed of thorns, showing how the mind can be trained to control the body.

7

7 Maharishi Mahesh Yogi surrounded by some of his followers) is the best known of a number of Eastern gurus who have influenced Westerners to take up the practice of meditation during the past few years. A physics graduate of Allahabad University, India, the Maharishi studied with yogi master Swami Brahmananda Saraswati for 13 years before teaching transcendental meditation in the West.

8

SCI
HAS ARISEN

8 The benefits of meditation are evaluated somewhat differently in the East and in the West. Eastern mystics see relaxation as a prerequisite for spiritual insight. In the West more emphasis is placed on physiological or social advantages. Considerable claims are made for transcendental meditation by those who practice it. TM researchers report improved physical and mental coordination, reduced depression and irritability, fewer stress disorders, and a reduction in crime rates in cities where it is practiced by 1% of the population. Although most experts agree that TM appears to be an effective method of relieving stress, they are somewhat skeptical about its more ambitious claims.

The occult

People have often felt that there might be hidden forces around them, secret sources of knowledge and latent powers within themselves. The term "occult" describes beliefs about this mysterious "other world" and the means by which people have tried to contact it. Occult beings have varied from culture to culture, changing with the advance of science. But although science explains that gravity makes an apple drop from a tree, it does not attempt to say why the apple struck a particular man passing beneath. Occult lore has been concerned less with explaining events than with trying to predict, forestall, or induce them.

The historical background

For the occult believer, the supernatural dimension includes a variety of gods and demons that were—and sometimes are—thought to influence weather, crops, and procreation. People believed their very survival depended on the good will of these powers. Linked with this was the almost universal belief in life after death and in spirits and ghosts.

Recognizing the power of suggestion or autosuggestion, holy men such as the magi (Persian priests from whom the word *magic* comes) devised rituals and symbols to concentrate the mind. Pagan cults based on some of these rituals survived the growth of such major religions as Christianity, but from about the fourteenth century occult practices began to be condemned by the church as evil. Persecution of sects that held that the material world was created by the Devil was followed by witch hunts throughout Europe, England, and later America. Witches were said to be able to take any form they pleased and create an infinite variety of havoc with magical practices.

Torture and burning of those identified as witches created a climate of hysteria that actually encouraged sorcery and that lasted until the eighteenth century. Tales of people turning into wolves (lycanthropy) and dead bodies remaining fresh by preying on the living (vampirism) flourished, along with belief in less malign spirits such as fairies and elves. Prayers, rituals, and talismans were used to invoke assistance or ward off bad luck. A residue of such folk superstitions as knocking on wood remains today, and exorcism is still occasionally practiced to drive "devils" out of a person said to be possessed.

Prophecy and fortune-telling

Predicting the future has always been a common preoccupation ranging from inspection of the sky or of animal entrails to interpretation of apparently random patterns of coins, cards, dice, or sticks, as in the ancient Chinese book of wisdom, the *I Ching* [7]. The most notable of European seers was Nostradamus (1503–66), a French physician and astrologer who wrote more than 600 obscure verses that can be interpreted as a remarkably accurate forecast of the French Revolution and some other major events. By the eighteenth century more bizarre, older methods of reading the future such as kephlomancy (the crackling made by a burning donkey's head), hydromancy (the noise of running water), and onychmancy (reflections in a virgin's oiled fingernails) had fallen into disuse. But the

CONNECTIONS

See also
826 Astrology
824 Parapsychology
762 How mental illness has been treated
748 Nonmedical healing
968 China to 1000 BC

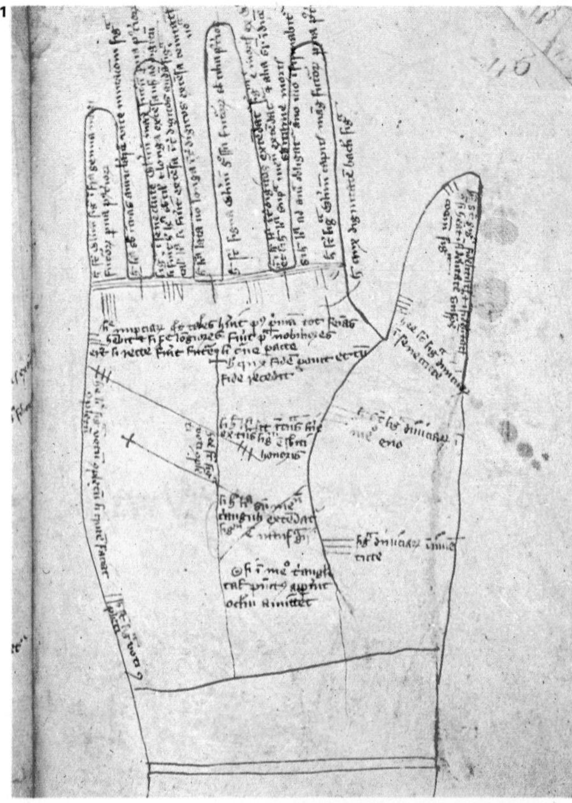

1 Palmistry, the attempt to infer human characteristics and foretell the future from the lines and the shape and size of the palm, is an art of great antiquity. In the 15th century the main features of the palm were related to the planets and signs of the zodiac. The art is sometimes called cheiromancy after an expert modern seer, the Irishman Count Louis Hamon, who called himself "Cheiro."

2 Raising a spirit was among occult feats claimed by John Dee (1527–1608), the most celebrated English psychic experimenter of the 16th century. With his friend Edward Kelley, Dee recorded long conversations with various angels. An inventor and astrologer, Dee was a shrewd politician and was an adviser to Elizabeth I. He inspired scholars to study astrology and alchemy.

3 Seeing the human being as a microcosm of the universe is a Greek concept. From it sprang several occult arts including metoscopy—the interpretation of lines on the brow or moles on the body. In this 17th-century print the subject's characteristics were inferred from a series of circles, perhaps implying a reflection in man of the planets' circular paths around the sun. Adherents of metoscopy believed lines and moles were "stars of the body."

use of Tarot cards [9] and other traditional methods [3] continued. Some gypsies made a business of interpreting cards, dreams, crystal balls, tea leaves, or the palms of hands [1].

The mid-nineteenth century brought a revival of interest in the age-old belief that spirits of the dead could sometimes be seen or heard. The idea that ghosts were lost souls trapped between this world and the next was given impetus after the invention of photography, when exposed film sometimes showed what appeared to be ghostly forms [6]. Spiritualists believed a psychically sensitive person, called a medium, could go into a trance state and, while in this state, receive messages from the departed.

The Spiritualist movement

The Spiritualist movement spread after the teenage Fox sisters in America in 1848 claimed that their home was besieged by rapping noises and that objects fell or were hurled off shelves as if pushed by a poltergeist, a mischievous spirit. Evidence that they had "communicated" with this spirit was later discredited, but a number of mediums soon emerged who appeared to have paranormal abilities. Among them were Helena Blavatsky (1831–91), who founded the Theosophical Society, and Daniel Home (1833–86), who impressed European royalty and baffled skeptics with phenomena ranging from sudden temperature drops to floating tables and the elongation or levitation of his own body [5]. It became fashionable to hold seances, meetings for the purpose of contacting the dead. Answers to participants' questions were either spelled out on a planchette or given in a "yes" or "no" form according to the number of raps on or tilts of the table. Exposure of charlatans who exploited the gullibility of bereaved people led to a declining interest in spiritualism.

During the twentieth century, however, both in the East and the West, scientists are slowly turning their attention to the explanation of "psychic" and "clairvoyant" forces. The result of their studies will, perhaps, be the exposure and full explanation of some of those mysterious elements.

KEY

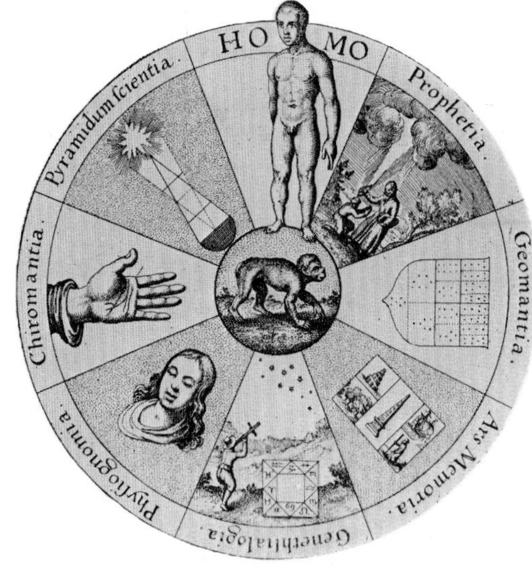
HOMO
Pyramidum scientia.
Prophetia.
Geomantia.
Ars Memoria.
Genethlialogia.
Physiognomia.
Chiromantia.

Divinatory arts that tried to glimpse man's fate through occult means were grouped in a 17th-century diagram by Robert Fludd (1574–1637). They included prophecy, geomancy, astrology, physiognomy, and palmistry.

4

4 A planchette was a popular device at the end of the 19th century for producing "automatic writing," supposedly prompted by a spirit. Hands were placed on a free-moving board that held a pencil.

5

5 Levitation was one of the most astonishing feats performed before critical audiences by D. D. Home (1833–86), a medium whose powers neither were fully tested nor proved fraudulent.

6 "Spirit" photographs were produced by some Victorian mediums, but most of them could be easily faked by parlor magicians. Several mediums were caught using assistants or various mechanical methods to produce the illusion of a spirit substance called ectoplasm. Spirits have been more shy of infrared photography in the dark.

6

7

7 Fortune-telling of the kind practiced in China before 1949 was usually based on the use of coins or sticks like those on this Canton street stall. The classic *I Ching* method dates back to 1000 BC.

8 Jeane Dixon, an American clairvoyant who uses a crystal ball reputedly predicted several election results and the deaths of Dag Hammarskjöld, Marilyn Monroe, and Robert and John F. Kennedy.

8

9

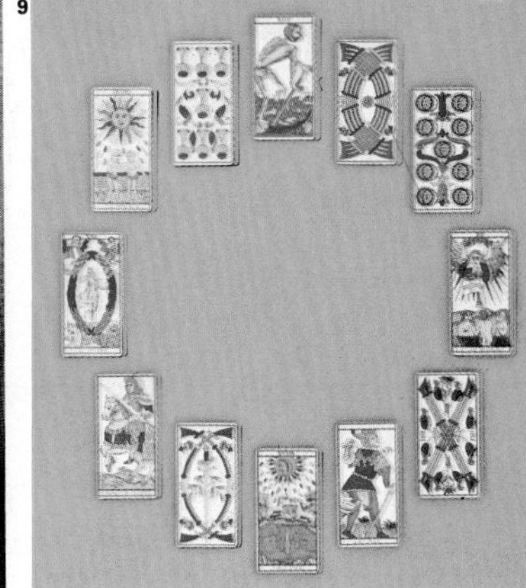

9 The Tarot pack contains 78 cards in four suits – Wands, Cups, Swords, and Pentacles. The picture cards carry symbols that in some cases date back to ancient Egypt and are among the oldest known to man: the Sun, the Moon, the Lovers, the Devil, the Tree of Life. Each suit has an underlying theme. Chosen and laid out by one of several systems, each card is said to moderate and influence its neighbor. Tarot readers use much intuition.

Parapsychology

Parapsychology is scientific research into psychic phenomena such as extrasensory perception (ESP). ESP is the apparent ability of a person to communicate with some entity, or to become aware of something, without using the normal sense organs.

Classification of phenomena

The psychic phenomena that concern parapsychologists are usually divided into four kinds [Key]. Telepathy is communication between one mind and another in some unknown way. It involves the sending or receiving of messages, thoughts, or feelings and is often called "thought transference." Clairvoyance is the awareness of some event, object, or person not known to anyone else, such as the presence of a letter in a secret drawer or a fire in an empty house. Precognition is the ability to foretell future events. Psychokinesis (mind-movement or PK) occurs when a person causes physical objects to move without apparent contact with them [2].

Other odd or unexpected events such as the alleged seeing of ghosts, voice communication with "the dead," the production of "ectoplasm" (a foam-like substance supposedly taking the shape of a disembodied person), and other inexplicable manifestations of the "beyond," in general lie outside the mainstream of parapsychological research.

The first attempts to examine claims about paranormal events scientifically were initiated in 1882 when the Society for Psychical Research was set up in London by a group of interested intellectuals headed by Henry Sidgwick (1838–1900), later professor of moral philosophy at Cambridge University. The society was concerned with investigating and classifying anecdotal evidence. It was not until some 50 years later that J. B. Rhine (1895–   ) at Duke University, North Carolina, began the first controlled laboratory experiments into extrasensory perception [2].

Parapsychology and J. B. Rhine

J. B. Rhine's initial work was the study of clairvoyance by means of written records of so-called spirit communication and by tests with mediums. He hoped to confirm the existence of disembodied spirits.

By 1934, despite exhaustive work with mediums, including Eileen J. Garrett (who was later to found the Parapsychology Foundation in New York), Rhine felt there was no irrefutable evidence possible and turned his efforts to a duller but more tangible form of research with a system of card-guessing experiments using Zener cards [3]. These are a pack of 25 cards, bearing five different symbols such as a circle or a cross, each symbol having its own color. To test clairvoyance, for example, the subject of the experiment tries to name the colors or symbols on the cards, one at a time. No one knows what symbol or color will come up.

The laws of chance would produce five correct answers out of 25. If the subject consistently scores higher than that it could be said that he has some clairvoyant ability.

Rhine's experiments indicated that there were people who clearly had extrasensory perception. He published his findings in *Extrasensory Perception* (1934), a book that aroused both considerable in-

CONNECTIONS

See also
822 The occult
672 Potential of the mind
850 Religion and the plight of modern man
1476 Odds and probability

1 **Levitation of chairs** by a medium is portrayed in this contemporary artist's impression of a seance in Germany in the late 19th century. The well-dressed people around the table indicate the fashionable interest in psychic phenomena at that time. Although early experimental research was concentrated on the alleged powers of mediums, charlatanism soon turned parapsychology toward the laboratory.

2 **Joseph Banks Rhine,** pioneer of scientific inquiry into psychic phenomena, is seen here in his laboratory engaged in research into psychokinesis (PK). The machine spills dice randomly onto the board. As they fall the subject tries to influence which side of the line they will land on. Any discrepancies between the statistically expected results and those of this experiment are ascribed to extrasensory powers.

3 **The Zener cards** are the basic equipment for card-guessing experiments. They have clear geometric designs (a square, circle, star, cross, or waves) and are used as a pack of 25. A score of more than one in five is considered "above chance." Seen here [A] are the results of experiments conducted over several years by Rhine. The cards can be mixed in three ways: they may be shuffled by hand by the experimenter; they may be put in a box and rotated for a predetermined length of time; and they may be run in a machine [B] that rotates them for an arbitrarily chosen length of time. In all cases the subject must guess in what order the cards will appear after they have been shuffled. In modern laboratories at parapsychology institutes the cards may be shuffled and randomly sorted for selection by electronic means.

3A

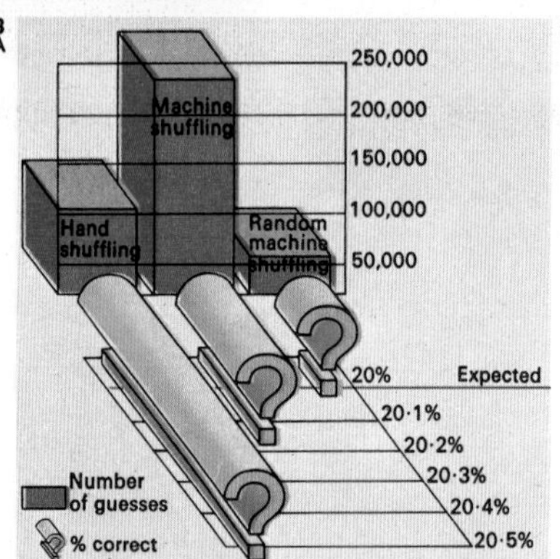

250,000
200,000
150,000
100,000
50,000
Machine shuffling
Hand shuffling
Random machine shuffling
20%
Expected
20·1%
20·2%
20·3%
20·4%
20·5%
Number of guesses
% correct

3B

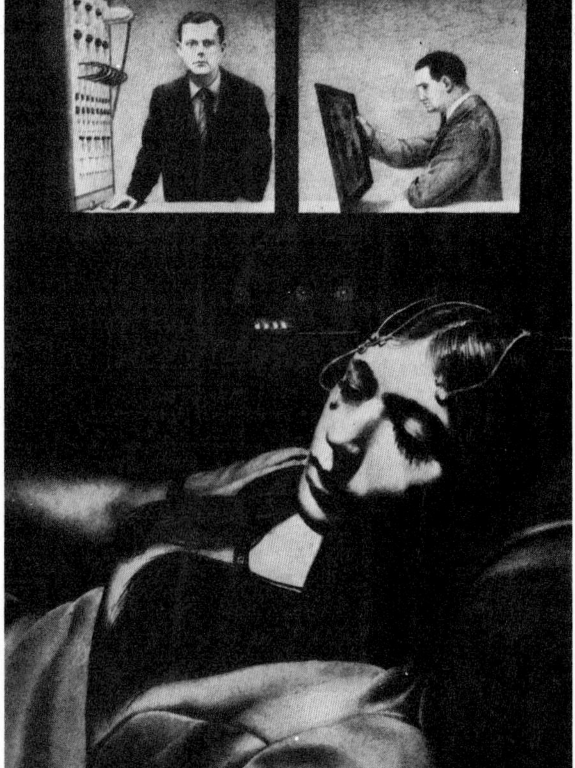

4 **At the dream laboratory** of the Maimonides Medical Center, New York, experiments are carries out on an isolated sleeping subject with electrodes attached to her scalp to show the rapid eye movements of dreaming (REM). An experimenter concentrates on a randomly selected art print in an effort to communicate it by telepathy to the sleeper. The subject is awakened from time to time to describe her dreams and the results are analyzed.

terest and a great deal of criticism over the mathematical validity of his tests. Rhine responded by tightening test controls.

New Frontiers of the Mind (1937), Rhine's next book, became a bestseller; his statistics were pronounced valid by the American Institute for Mathematical Statistics. A separate parapsychological laboratory was then set up at Duke University.

More and more varieties of tests followed, and during the 1940s Rhine was no longer trying simply to prove the existence of ESP, but looking for the various reasons and conditions that favored its production. He discovered that mood and attitude were important factors, as was the relationship between experimenter and subject, and that extremely low scoring was just as indicative of ESP as extremely high (because those who said that they did not believe in ESP had scores *lower* than chance).

Debate about ESP

From the 1950s onward there followed more specialized and sophisticated experiments involving an increased use of electronic instruments for both randomizing and computerizing the test material. Psychokinesis, in particular, was being studied at this time.

In 1969, after long, hard resistance, parapsychology won a place in the American Association for the Advancement of Science. Since that time the exploration of ESP has become associated with many other fields of research under the inclusive title of psi. Parapsychology conferences are now held in many countries.

While some advances have been made toward establishing the fact of the paranormal, its nature or what range of energy or force engenders it has not yet been explained. Only about 10 percent of psychologists believe in the fact of ESP: 10 percent dismiss it totally, and the remaining 80 percent believe that more evidence is necessary before they can wholeheartedly accept its existence. The main problems with the evidence are the difficulties of verifying findings that have often been established by those most eager for positive results and of ruling out cheating.

KEY

Clairvoyance

PK-MT (eg dice)

Precognition

PK-LT (eg healing and growth)

Telepathy

PK-ST

Psychic phenomena are divided into four kinds: telepathy, clairvoyance, precognition, and psychokinesis (PK). PK is subdivided into PK-MT (PK on moving things); PK-LT (PK on living things); and PK-ST (PK on static things).

5 A

B

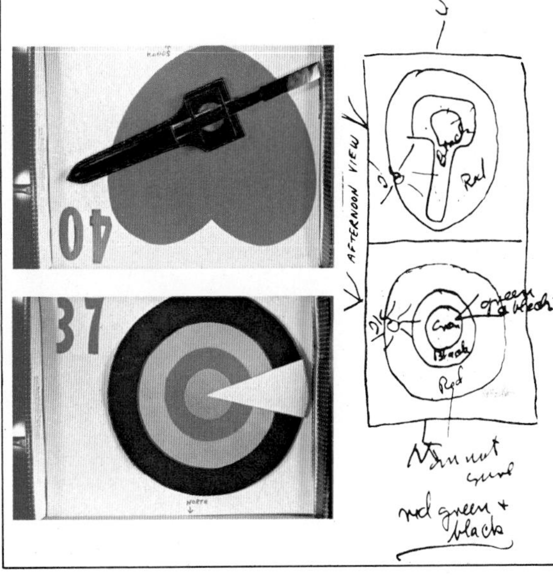
40
37
AFTERNOON VIEW
Red

5 Ingo Swann, a gifted psychic, took part in experiments to test out-of-body perception. Especially drawn art "targets" were laid on a platform placed high above his chair and well out of sight [A]. When he was in a "relaxed state of mind" he began to draw what he could "see." The results were compared [B] and analyzed. He completed many of these drawings with remarkable accuracy.

6 Madame Kulagina of the Soviet Union, famed for her power to move objects by mental force alone (psychokinesis or PK), concentrates in a scientifically monitored experiment and gradually causes matchsticks to move [A], alter their direction [B], and finally bunch together [C]. In other experiments she has moved objects of many different materials and caused compass needles to rotate.

6 A

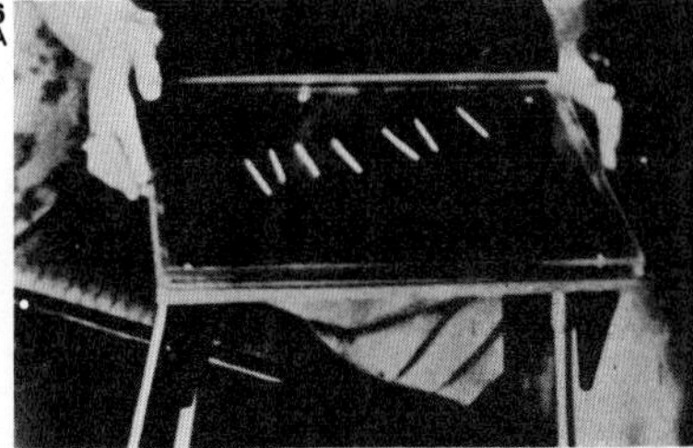

B

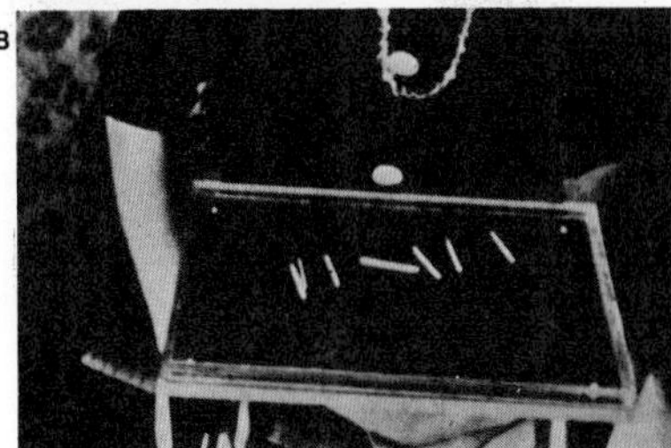

C

7

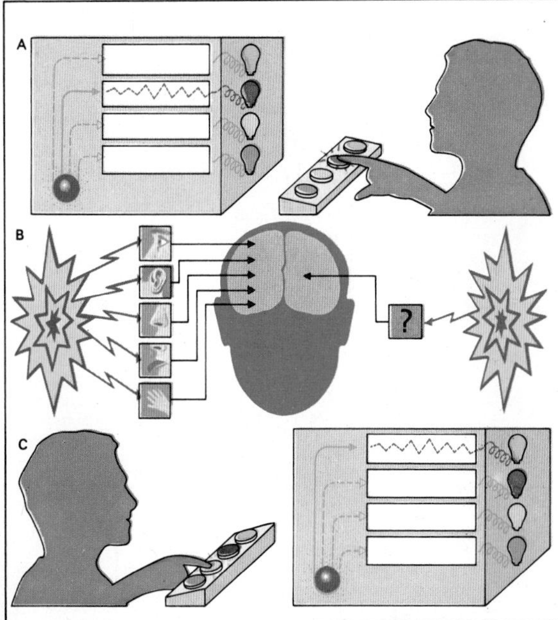
A
B
?
C

7 We normally assume all information received by the brain comes through the senses, but many experiments point to the existence of extrasensory perception [B]. In recent trials four colored lights were lit randomly and the subjects had to indicate either which would light up [A] or which would not [C]. Correct prediction in over 83,000 trials (both tests) were higher than expected.

8

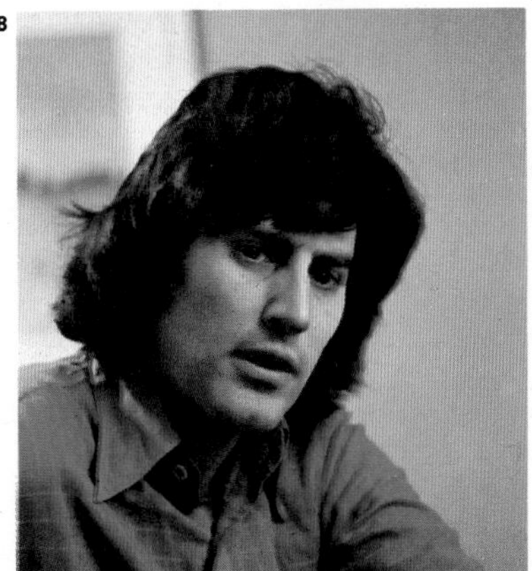

8 Metal bending by mental power has attracted a great deal of attention since the public demonstrations given since 1971 by the Israeli Uri Geller. He claims to be able to bend a variety of objects including nails, spoons, keys, and clock hands, apparently just by mental force. Many others have claimed this power, and they can be classified according to their individual strengths. In the top category there is an unusual preponderance of children.

Astrology

Astrology states that the Sun, Moon, and planets play a vital role in human affairs. For centuries astrology was virtually inseparable from the study of the universe, which we now call astronomy. In technically advanced countries astrology has generally been dismissed as worthless or fraudulent. Still, many Westerners retain an ardent interest in it, and astrology is still highly valued in some Eastern countries. There has also been a more general revival of interest in astrological lore, and the possibility of a link between it and biological rhythms detected by scientific investigation is now being more seriously and systematically pursued.

The aims of astrology

Columns in some newspapers and magazines foster an impression that astrologers attempt to predict the future. But true astrology has little to do with "what the stars foretell." Serious astrologers claim to do no more than indicate trends that may be averted—or promoted—by taking appropriate action.

Astrologers base their deductions on the apparent positions of the bodies of the Solar System and use the stars only as reference points. The Earth is taken as the central point. This geocentric view is reasonable enough since astrologers can make their observations only from the Earth. No modern astrologer really believes the Earth to be the true center of the universe.

Because the planets (and the Moon) move in roughly the same plane, they seem to keep to a certain region of the sky, making up a belt known as the Zodiac [Key]. The Zodiac is divided into 12 equal sections or signs, each named after a constellation. These constellations are Aries (the Ram), Taurus (the Bull), Gemini (the Twins), Cancer (the Crab), Leo (the Lion), Virgo (the Virgin), Libra (the Scales), Scorpio (the Scorpion), Sagittarius (the Archer), Capricorn (the Sea-goat), Aquarius (the Water-bearer), and Pisces (the Fish). The names have no significance, and neither have the star patterns themselves, except as reference points. Moreover, the "vernal equinox," or First Point of Aries—the point where the apparent path of the Sun, or ecliptic, cuts the celestial equator—is no longer in the constellation of Aries as it was in ancient times; it has shifted into the adjacent constellation of Pisces. But this so-called "precession" makes no difference to the astrological signs.

When casting a horoscope, astrologers work out the positions of the Sun, Moon, and planets at the exact time of an individual's birth; for this, it is also important to know the place of birth. The celestial pattern that emerges is supposed to determine, in ways unspecified, the personal characteristics of an individual born under its influence, rather like the Moon's effect on the tides. Although nobody would claim that all Libras, for instance, are similar in personality, some statistical studies would seem to indicate general trends in line with astrological lore.

Historical background

Western astrology may have arisen in Mesopotamia. The earliest known planetary tables date from the mid-seventh cen-

CONNECTIONS

See also
708 An introduction to illness and health
822 The occult
50 Members of the Solar System
128 Mapping the constellations
224 Gems and semiprecious stones

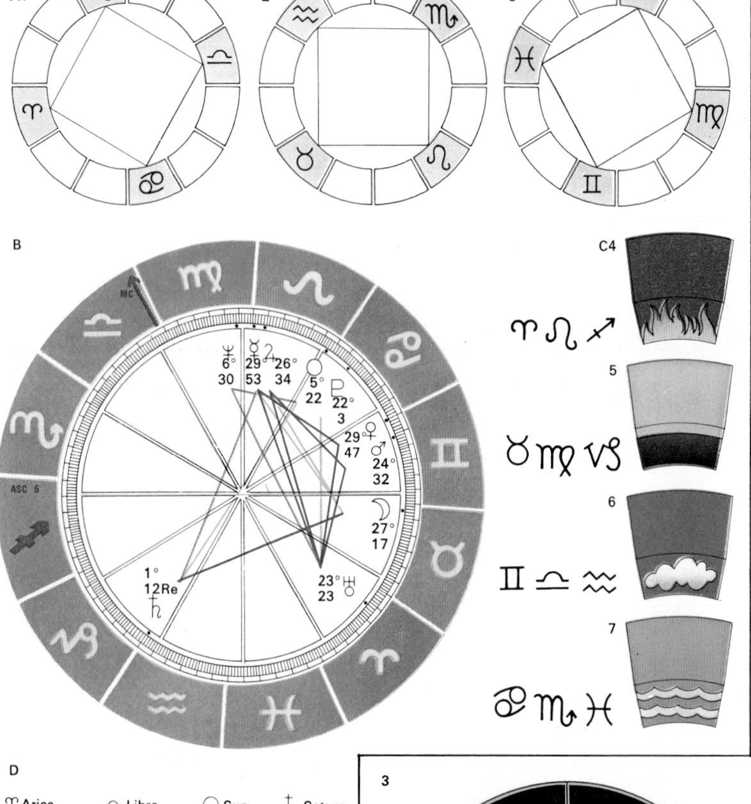

1
A1
2
3
B
MC
ASC 5
C4
5
6
7
D
Aries
Taurus
Gemini
Cancer
Leo
Virgo
Libra
Scorpio
Sagittarius
Capricorn
Aquarius
Pisces
Sun
Moon
Mercury
Venus
Mars
Jupiter
Saturn
Uranus
Neptune
Pluto
Earth

1 A birth chart or horoscope [B] is a map of the heavens at the moment and from the place of an individual's birth. The Earth is taken as the focal point. Around it, the 12 signs of the Zodiac form an encircling band. The inner part of the chart is similarly divided into 12 segments called houses which represent various spheres of life, such as marriage, career, or health. On this chart Sagittarius is the sign in ascendant (ASC), coming over the horizon [blue line] at the moment of birth. It is represented by a traditional sign called a glyph, as are all the signs, the Sun, Moon, and planets [D]. The letters MC in Libra stand for Medium Coeli, the center point of the heavens. The planets pass at differing speeds out of one sign of the Zodiac and into the next in a never-ending circuit. At the birth point, the angles formed with the Earth are measured in degrees [figures]. When there are specific angular relationships between them they are in Aspect [green, red, and orange lines]. From the Aspects, astrologers interpret the subject's potential personality and motivation. A predominance of planets in certain signs is significant since each sign is assigned one of three qualities [A]. The quality of enterprise belongs to Aries, Cancer, Libra, and Capricorn [1]. Taurus, Leo, Scorpio, and Aquarius are fixed or steadfast [2]. Gemini, Virgo, Sagittarius, and Pisces are mutable or adaptable [3]. The signs are also allotted one of four elements [C]. Aries, Leo, and Sagittarius correspond to Fire [4], Taurus, Virgo, and Capricorn to Earth [5], Gemini, Libra, and Aquarius to Air [6] and Cancer, Scorpio, and Pisces to Water [7]. Signs with the elements of Fire and Air are masculine or positive; those of Earth and Water feminine or negative.

2 A baby's first cry is usually taken by astrologers to signify the moment of birth. Accurate timing is crucial, as shown by this medieval woodcut of astrologers charting the celestial bodies at that particular moment. If the time of birth is not known an astrologer will use the planetary positions at noon on the birthday as an approximation. This, however, will restrict the astrologer's conclusions.

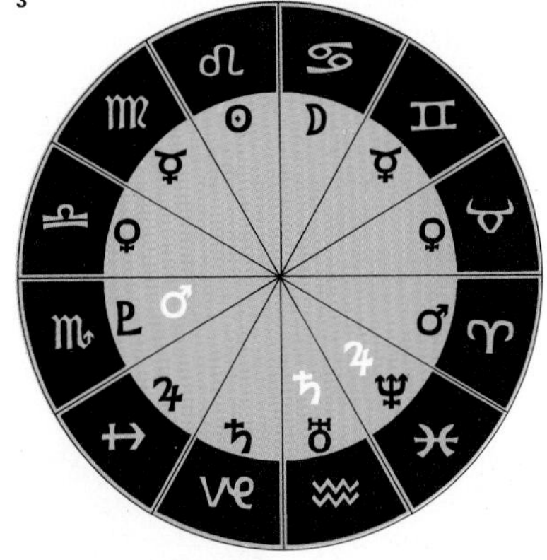

3 The rulership of the signs springs from the fact that traditionally the planets of the Solar System have had special relationships with certain signs of the Zodiac. The Sun and Moon ruled one sign each, with Mercury, Venus, Mars, Jupiter, and Saturn ruling two. This remained the case until the discovery of the so-called "modern planets" (Uranus in 1781, Neptune in 1846, and Pluto in 1930). Astrologers studied many thousands of birth charts to discover what effect this would have. Eventually the new planets were allotted joint rulerships with the old. Uranus now shares the rulership of Aquarius with Saturn, Neptune the rulership of Pisces with Jupiter, and Pluto that of Scorpio with Mars. Modern astrologers consider the effect of Uranus on Aquarius to be stronger than that of Saturn, and that of Neptune on Pisces stronger than that of Jupiter. Pluto's influence is still a matter of debate.

tury BC. Early Babylonian astrology was not directly personal. It was concerned with large-scale events such as the advent of wars, floods, and eclipses and their possible effect on the king, who embodied the affairs of the state and its well-being. The Mesopotamian tradition may have been transmitted to Egypt and through the Middle East to India and then to China and the rest of Asia. In about the fourth century BC, the Greeks began recasting astrological lore in terms of their own traditions. It was they who popularized a method of working out individual destinies based on the moment of birth. Ptolemy is credited with the first astrological textbook composed in the West—the *Tetrabiblos*. The planets, houses, and signs of the Zodiac were rationalized and set down in a way that has changed little since.

With the splitting up of the Roman Empire, the Arabs became the chief exponents of astrology and astronomy. To calculate their horoscopes and other charts they needed to know the positions of the stars and movements of the planets with great accuracy. This led them to draw up tables of planetary motion, together with star catalogs, which surpassed anything that the Greeks produced. But after the rediscovery of the Hellenic tradition in Europe during the fifteenth and sixteenth centuries, astrology was ranked as one of the foremost sciences in all European universities.

From Copernicus to the space age

A gradual ebbing of interest began with the great astronomical discoveries made from the time of Nicolas Copernicus (1473–1543), who showed that the Sun, not the Earth, was the center of the planetary system. The invention of the telescope was followed by the work of Isaac Newton (1642–1727), whose book *Principia* laid the foundations of modern astronomy. But although the Earth was no longer regarded as all-important in the universe, the basic principles of astrology remained unchanged. In an age when men have been to the Moon and sent messages out toward the planets it may be significant that interest in astrology is reviving rather than being eclipsed.

KEY

N

S

The Zodiac [1] follows the Sun's apparent path [2].

4

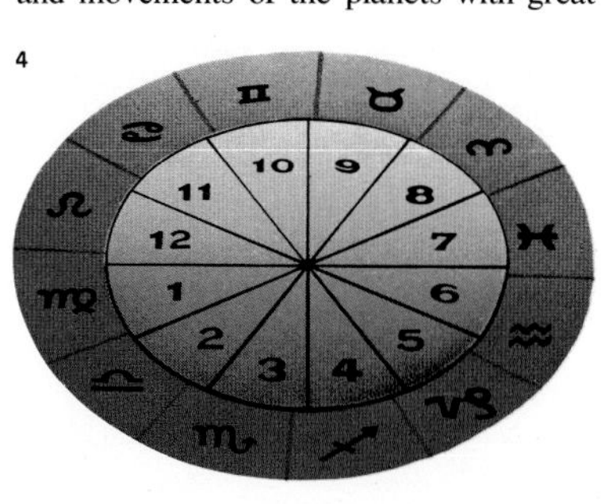

4 The 12 houses occupy the central section of a birth chart. They are associated with everyday activities, some of which are listed below. The influence of the planets and signs that fall within a particular house is focused on those activities. If a house has no planet within its segment of the chart, this does not mean that the sphere of life that the house is normally concerned with is of no importance to the subject. In this case the astrologer will consider the Zodiac sign that is on the cusp or starting point of the house. Each of the houses has its partner across the chart, the first relating to the seventh, the second to the eighth, and so on. The houses are believed to show a relationship between the Zodiac signs and the turning of the Earth on its axis. The symbolic nature of the houses was originally worked out by the Greeks.

1st house: Aries
personality
health
temperament
7th house: Libra
emotional life
business partners
marriage

2nd house: Taurus
possessions
worldly resources
income
8th house: Scorpio
inherited money
life-forces
insurance

3rd house: Gemini
family ties
education
communication
9th house: Sagittarius
further education
long-distance travel
languages

4th house: Cancer
home
family commitments
start and end of life
10th house: Capricorn
career
social standing
personal image

5th house: Leo
creativity
love affairs
children
11th house: Aquarius
societies
friends
intellectual pleasures

6th house: Virgo
physical well-being
subordinates
work hobbies
12th house: Pisces
service to others
escapism
the unconscious

6A B C

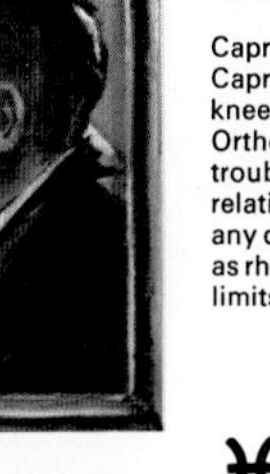

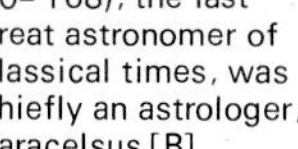

6 Ptolemy [A] (*c*. AD 90–168), the last great astronomer of classical times, was chiefly an astrologer, Paracelsus [B] (1493–1541), a pioneer of medical chemistry, was interested in the interrelationships between man and the planets. Louis de Wohl (1903–61) was employed by the British to predict what astrological advice was being given to Hitler.

5 Astrological medicine was, until the eighteenth century, an important part of conventional medical practice. The various parts of the body were regarded as being under the rulership of specific signs and planets, which were also associated with specific diseases. More recently, astrologers have stressed relationships between the signs and the glandular nervous systems. They hold that this relationship is often one of polarity; an Aries, for example, may be affected by ailments of parts of the body ruled by the opposite sign, Libra. Astrological anatomy thus divides the body according to the ruling signs and their opposites.

5

Gemini-Sagittarius
Gemini rules the lungs, nerves, arms and shoulders. Geminians are, therefore, prone to break collarbones.

Leo-Aquarius
Leo rules the heart, spine and back. This makes Leos prone to heart attacks.

Libra-Aries
Libra rules the kidneys. Any disturbance of the usually well-balanced Libran way of life, through accident or argument, is soon reflected in a serious kidney upset.

Scorpio-Taurus
Scorpio rules the sexual organs. Scorpians are the most highly sexed of all the signs and, with their tendency to do nothing by halves, any frustration or suppression of this sexual energy can lead to unpleasant or cruel behaviour.

Capricorn-Cancer
Capricorn rules the knees, bones and teeth. Orthopaedic and dental troubles are accordingly relatively common, as is any disease, such as rheumatism, that limits movement.

Pisces-Virgo
Pisces rules the feet. Pisceans do not respond well to drugs so these must be administered carefully.

Aries-Libra
Aries rules the head and as a result Arians often suffer from headaches. Aries also controls the supply of adrenalin.

Taurus-Scorpio
Taurus rules the throat and neck, which makes Taureans vulnerable to colds and chills.

Cancer-Capricorn
Cancer rules the stomach and the alimentary canal. Indigestion and ulcers are fairly common, giving Cancerians a reputation for delicate health.

Virgo-Pisces
Virgo rules the nervous system and intestines. Virgoans tend to worry so suffer from indigestion.

Sagittarius-Gemini
Sagittarius rules the liver, hips and thighs. Being active by nature, Sagittarians stagnate if they do not get a considerable amount of physical exercise. They tend to put on weight easily, which in women particularly goes to the hips and thighs.

Aquarius-Leo
Aquarius rules the circulation, so Aquarians suffer from varicose veins and hardening of the arteries.

The meaning of ritual

Ritual involves behavior that cannot easily be explained by what the participants hope to achieve. This indirect connection between actions and results is a striking aspect of ritual, whether seen in the elaborate courting dances of birds [1], in great state occasions such as the July 14 parade in France [Key], or in formal greetings [3, 4]. It is not immediately clear, for instance, how the dancing of grebes facilitates mating or how the movements and words of a witch doctor achieve a cure.

Human and animal ritual

Ritual behavior is displayed by humans and animals. The common factor is that the elaborate way in which an action is performed is as important as, or more important than, the action itself. In both human and animal ritual repetition is equally essential. Rituals follow an intensely detailed program that specifies the movements and sounds that should be made and their order, so that the ritual is always the same.

Although the rituals of animals and men share these characteristics, they nevertheless differ fundamentally. Most animal rituals are instinctive [2], while human rituals have to be learned. Birds whose courting involves complex rituals, for example, display the same kind of male or female behavior throughout the species. But in man, ritual surrounding a similar occasion varies extensively from one social group to another and also within groups; some tribes, for example, prescribe certain ritualistic roles for initiated youths that are entirely different from those for the uninitiated youths of the tribe.

There are two different kinds of human ritual. On the one hand, ritual may be simply an aspect of an activity that is not itself ritual—a cultural "frill." For example, in all cultures the essential activity of eating is accompanied by ritual embellishments that are given great importance and that are called table manners. On the other hand, some entire activities are rituals. In the Masonic ritual, for example, the Freemasons express their system of morality by allegorical acts in which the tools of a working mason are used as symbols.

The nature of ritual can be seen most clearly by comparing the everyday use of language, gestures, and signs with their use in ritual. Ritual language tends to be more formal than everyday language and may preserve old-fashioned speech. Indeed, rituals are often carried on in a totally different language from the ordinary, such as Latin. Ritual speech may be more ponderous or may take on a singsong character. Frequently, ritual uses singing and chanting rather than plain speaking. Ritual gestures are also characteristic. They tend to be both stylized and expressive, often verging on dance, as in military or some religious rituals; indeed dance itself is a common element of the most sacred and important rituals [5].

Religious and secular aspects

A third characteristic of human ritual is the use of objects as symbols [6] displayed on special occasions or used to give meaning to the actions. The flags in military parades are an obvious example; more complicated but no less typical is the symbolic use of water in baptism or the use of animals and plants

CONNECTIONS

See also
830 Types of ritual
848 Varieties of worship
530 How birds reproduce
536 How birds behave

1

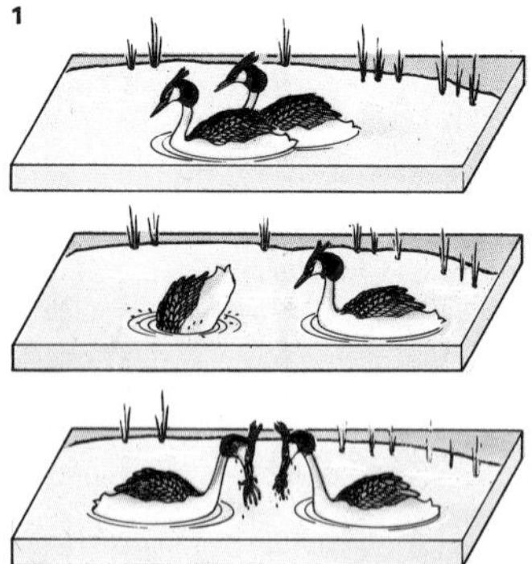

1 Animal ritual is more fixed than human ritual. These great crested grebes have not learned their complicated courtship movements from watching other birds but know what to do instinctively. The similarity with human ritual lies in the fact that the sequence of actions is predetermined, repetitive, and only indirectly related to the end in view—in this particular example, mating.

2

2 Many animals, such as the hartebeest of Africa, establish dominance in the herd by regular stylized combats; the boundary between ritual and purposeful behavior is often indistinct.

3

3 Shaking hands and raising hats are examples of the sort of ritual that pervades all human life, sometimes unconsciously. Elaborate procedures of greeting and leave-taking are characteristic of human societies throughout the world. In one sense, they appear meaningless because they seem to convey no information. But the significance of such rituals—once they are established in a society—appears when they are omitted and cause grave offense.

4

4 Maoris in New Zealand rub noses in a greeting ritual that performs much the same function as the French custom of kissing on both cheeks. One of the interesting aspects of human ritual is that although the use of ritual on similar occasions, such as greeting someone, is extemely widespread, the particular form it takes can vary considerably from culture to culture. In contrast, animal ritual shows little variation within a species.

5

5 Zulu war dances and many other tribal dances have strong elements of ritual. The arts of both theater and dance originated in religious rituals, and many secular rituals also involve dancing or its equivalent—highly stylized gestures or words following in fixed order according to recognized rules and often performed in unison by the group. The use of the body in a more stylized way is characteristic of many forms of ritual behavior.

in fertility rites to represent the various forces of nature.

Activities that are associated with ritual behavior have some remarkably similar aspects in all cultures, whether in remote parts of New Guinea or in New York, and they fall into two categories. Rituals such as initiation ceremonies, church services, or invocation of ancestors are clearly of a religious character. Others, such as formal government receptions for visiting dignitaries, are clearly secular. Often, however, it is not clear which element dominates. The Chinese New Year ceremony [9], for instance, combines secular elements marking the passage of the seasons and the settling of debts with such religious aspects as ancestor worship and purification.

Greetings are perhaps the most common secular rituals. When people meet in all cultures, they usually perform a series of set phrases in a given sequence, accompanied by equally formal gestures and postures. Greeting rituals are significant because they are a convenient way of establishing or acknowledging personal relationships and giving order to social life. They express the degree of familiarity between people or their differences in rank. It is not surprising that the greater these differences, the more elaborate the ritual aspects of greetings, so that a dignitary, for example, is greeted with more ritual than a friend. What is begun by a greeting is continued by other ritual aspects of social behavior, such as rules of politeness, and is ended by a ritual sequence of leave-taking.

Defining relationships

Even relationships between equals may have ritual aspects, although these take various forms. In Madagascar, for instance, brothers-in-law go through standardized, obligatory routines of joking with each other and fixed, reciprocal insults. It is hard to see the practical value of many social rituals, but they help to define relationships and give a sense of predictability. Instead of every new social encounter having to be treated differently, ritual offers routine forms of behavior so that circumstances do not have to be evaluated instantly.

KEY

A ritual such as the laying of a wreath to commemorate a nation's dead unites the whole community. Here Charles de Gaulle leads the French people in an observance of Bastille Day. All ritual stresses the importance of the group. The continuation of rituals after they have lost their significance has led many to reject ritual as meaningless.

6

6 A 15th-century stained glass window represents the four evangelists symbolically rather than literally. Such symbolism depends on social conventions. Rituals of all kinds characteristically refer to objects, people, events, and emotions or abstract concepts by symbols that often seem to be chosen quite arbitrarily. Here John is represented by an eagle, Matthew by an angel, Mark by a lion, and Luke by an ox. Another example is the use of a lamb to represent Christ, although the symbolism of this is clear. The reason why symbols and ritual usually go hand in hand is complicated. Ritual uses stylized language, song, and dance in a generalized way to evoke wide agreement. Symbols contribute to the remoteness and vagueness of ritual while adding depth to its meaning and purpose.

7 Right and left, as in being right-or left-handed, have ritual meaning in many cultures. The lists show ways in which right (green) is associated with good and left (blue) with evil.

7

1 Turn right to pray.
2 A holy place should be entered right foot first.
3 Offerings are made to the gods with right hand.
4 Gifts from gods are received with right hand.
5 In marriage ceremonies, the right hands are joined.
6 Sovereigns wear emblems of royalty on the right.
7 Oaths are sworn with the right hand and people shake hands with the right.
8 Women in Niger cook only with their right hands and Arabs eat with their right.
9 In Indonesia, a well-brought-up child could not use the left hand because it was bound up

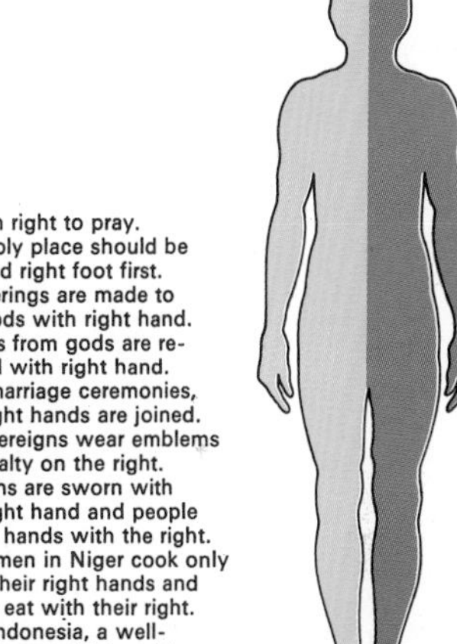

1 If greedy spirits of the dead need placating by a gift it is always given with the left hand.
2 Sinners leave the church by the left door.
3 Guinea Coast tribesmen believe they have the power to kill by putting the left thumb in an enemy's drink.
4 Left-handedness marks a possible sorcerer.
5 Some Christian saints are supposed to have refused as babies to suckle their mother's left breast.
6 In the Arabic world, toilet cleaning is done with the left hand.
7 Left is the hand of perjury, treachery and fraud

8

8 The coronation of Queen Elizabeth II of England as monarch in 1953 was a spectacular example of the use of elaborate ritual to transform a person from one role to another. Wedding and consecration ceremonies serve a similar purpose. Ritual is a way of saying that there is more to people than is immediately obvious.

9

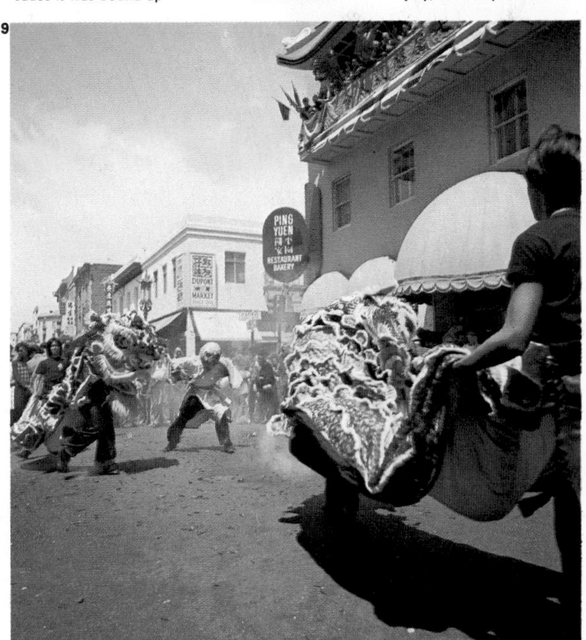

9 The dragon procession mounted at New Year's in San Francisco's Chinatown is one of countless festivities that mark the passing of the seasons. Rituals have always been used to organize time and to attempt to give meaning to its passing by dividing it into units given special significance.

Types of ritual

One of the major functions of ritual is to define situations and people's roles in them according to set routines. This is clearly shown in such rituals as initiation into tribal societies, marriage, and installation ceremonies. These are called rites of passage because they are the public declaration of the change of status of an individual [2, 3, 4].

Rites of passage

The number of rites of passage and their significance vary widely. An East African Samburu man [1B] would traditionally go through complicated rituals at birth, at initiation, on becoming a warrior, at marriage, on becoming a junior elder, on becoming a senior elder, and finally at death, whereas a European Christian would probably go through elaborate rituals only at baptism, confirmation, marriage, and death. The latter might also go through less universal rituals associated with entering a club, a school, or an association or on the occasion of becoming a public official.

Despite their variety, rites of passage usually follow a similar pattern: first they consist of a phase marking separation from the old status, then an intermediary phase, thought to be particularly significant, then a phase marking acceptance of the new status. In the traditional Western marriage, for example, the bachelor's party marks separation from the old status, the intermediary phase consists of the marriage ceremony; acceptance of the new status is represented by such traditions as the groom's carrying the bride across the threshold of their new home.

The same general features are found again and again in the three stages of rites of passage. Separation is marked by ritual acting out of the status that is being lost—being a young man with "the boys," for instance. This is often accompanied by ritual violence, especially the revenge of the group being left toward the individual who is in some sense betraying it. A parallel violence from the group that is being joined may take the form of an endurance test. The intermediary stage is always a period set apart from ordinary life and is sacred, solemn, and sometimes dangerous. The final period of reintegration is usually a happier affair, expressing relief that the mysterious process is finished.

Seasonal rituals

Rituals that mark certain times of the year and the passage of the seasons have been called rites of intensification because they intensify general group solidarity. Nearly everywhere the beginning of growing seasons is marked by rituals associated with fertility and rebirth. Similar rituals accompany the harvest. Sometimes the beginning of the harvest and gathering of the first fruits is chosen as the occasion for ritual, as in much of Asia. Alternatively, rituals may mark the end of the harvest, as in the harvest festivals of Europe. All these rituals embody the same idea—the public recognition of natural changes in the lives of people and seasons and the coordination of activities associated with them.

Other common occasions for rituals arise when a community feels that order has been disturbed and needs to be restored. The most universal examples are rituals of

CONNECTIONS

See also
828 The meaning of ritual
848 Varieties of worship
806 Death, grieving, and loss

1 A
1
2
3
4
5
B
6
7
8
9

Birth — Circumcision — Ilmugit of the Arrows — Ilmugit of the Name — Ilmugit of the Bull — Marriage — Ilmugit of the Milk and leaves — Burial

Age in years — Junior moran 15 — Senior moran 20 — Junior elder 30 — Firestick elder 40 — Senior elder 55

1 Rites of passage, which mark the movement of an individual within society, vary widely between communities and cultures. In most Western societies [A], people do not pass through any set pattern of stages. A man may be baptized [1], become a boy scout [2], graduate from college [3], get married [4], and become a judge [5]. Many of these stages involve little ceremony, and none is obligatory for all members of the society. In contrast to this pattern, in a society such as that of the Samburu of East Africa [B] every male member of the tribe goes through each stage, which is accompanied by elaborate ritual. The birth of a son is marked by the gift of cattle. Until he reaches puberty, the boy grows and braids his hair [6]. At the age of 15 he is circumcised and joins a group of other youths as an initiate. A month later he becomes a junior moran (warrior) by going through the Ilmugit (ceremony) of the Arrows, during which he slaughters an ox and vows to his mother to keep certain laws. To mark his status he first wears red ochre [7] and then cuts his hair [8]. When he reaches the age of 20 he attains senior moran status through the Ilmugit of the Name. This is the most important ceremony and is repeated a month later. A senior moran may father children but may not marry. The Ilmugit of the Bull, at about 26, is the first of a number of ceremonies that lead to marriage and elderhood, culminating in the Ilmugit of the Milk and Leaves at the age of 31. Once a man is an elder [9] he moves steadily upward within this social order as new groups of boys are introduced at the initiate stage.

purification. Throughout the world there are rituals to restore purity after contact with death, often involving a ceremony of washing or stepping over fire. Many of the rituals that follow battles also contain this element. Rituals are common in many groups to purify women after childbirth, menstruation, and even sexual intercourse. selves after involuntary contact with innumerable polluting substances. One such substance is leather because it is associated with dead animals.

Other important restorative rituals are those involved with curing. Disease, whether physical or psychological, is a threat to the order emphasized by ritual, so particularly complex rituals are needed to "heal" a patient. For example, among certain tribal peoples of Southeast Asia disease is thought to involve loss of the patient's soul, and prolonged rituals act out the process of re- Perhaps nowhere are purification rituals so elaborate as in India [5] where, for example, high-caste Hindus have to purify them- capturing it and making the sick man whole once more. In some religions, restorative rituals of this type are believed to be regularly necessary. Because disease or sin is thought of as inevitable, "curing" is always needed. Christian, Judaic, and Muslim weekly worship can be seen as instances of such ritual.

Rituals of sacrifice

A recurring theme of rituals is sacrifice [6], a form that important rituals take throughout the world irrespective of culture or religion. Sacrifice is basically the giving up of something, whether the killing of an animal or a human being or material offerings. By this means a short period of communication is established with the supernatural or life-giving power. In restorative rituals pollution, disease, or sin can then be taken away so that order may be restored.

Ritual colors all aspects of life from the most commonplace to the most sacred and is present in differing degrees in all known cultures. The function of ritual is always to give the appearance of order, security, and meaning to the unpredictable sequence of events that characterizes human life.

KEY

Ritual, in one sense of the word, is an element of almost all human actions in the form of symbolic elaboration. But there are occasions when this symbolic elaboration predominates and the relationship between means and ends is different from that found in everyday behavior. Here, in a High Mass in Jerusalem, the Last Supper is reenacted to include the congregation in Christ's sacrifice, but no attempt is made at realism. Instead, the ceremony involves gestures laid down by church tradition and symbols whose power is allusive. These elements of symbolic enactment and the establishment of authority characterize ritual.

2 Christian baptism is an example of one of many similar ceremonies that in some communities mark the social beginnings of the individual in the world. Such ceremonies nearly always occur at a different time from the person's actual birth. In nearly all cultures of the world the passage through life and the bodily changes that accompany this are marked by ritual (eg, confirmation, marriage, and death).

3 The Circumcision ceremony in Madagascar parallels baptism in other cultures. Here, the banana tree symbolizes the bountiful fertility of nature that the ceremony bestows on the child.

4 A funeral procession in Bali is an instance of the elaborate rituals that surround death, expressing separation of the dead from the living and defining the social status of the dead person.

4

2

3

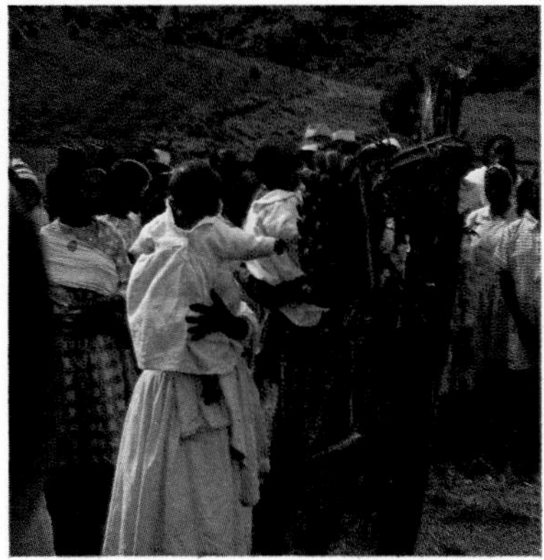

6

6 The supreme religious ritual often involves a sacrificial gift that establishes a moment of communication between men and gods. One gift considered potent in some religions is the life of an animal, as seen here with the sacrifice of a camel by Turkana tribesmen in Kenya, which may take away a god's displeasure from the sacrificer or alternatively enhance the life-giving power of the god.

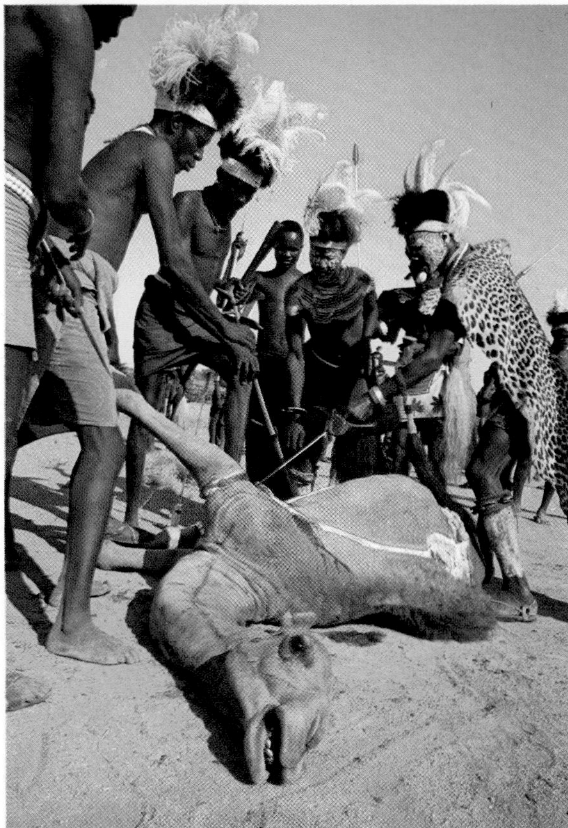

5

5 Ritual bathing by Hindus in the holy waters of the Ganges River is typical of rituals that are seen as having a restorative function, purifying the participants of their failings and allowing them to regain their proper place in the scheme of the universe. The same symbols often recur in different cultural traditions. Water is a symbol of purification and incorporation for Hindus, as it is for Christians in the baptism ceremony.

The meaning and function of myth

Myths are tales or traditions that seek to explain the place of humans in the universe, the nature of society, the relationship between the individual and the world, and the meaning of natural phenomena. Today we tend to draw a sharp line between facts that can be proved scientifically and beliefs and ideas that cannot be proved. The latter are often lumped together and dismissed as "imagination," "inventions," or "myths." This contrast between myth or fantasy and facts conceals and distorts the value and significance of myths as guides to life.

Myth, science, and religion

Myths are found in every part of the world, and despite their bewildering variety, they share certain common characteristics. These similarities arise because people everywhere face the same basic problems and ask the same questions [4,8]. They want to know why they are what they are, why nature behaves as it does, and how cause and effect are linked.

Although science has now answered many of the "how" questions, the reasons "why"—the human race's relation to the cosmos and the nature of the life force within the person—remain basically unanswered and unanswerable.

Myths have in common with religions the fact that both offer explanations of motivations as well as causes—both the "how" and "why" of the universe. In comparison with many world religions, however, most myths are less concerned with direct guidance. They contain an implicit moral, but their main aim is not to impose it. They explain the unquantifiable aspects of existence and deal with both common human experiences and the doings of superhuman divine and demonic beings.

From the mythological standpoint the world we experience directly is not the only world. The phenomenon of birth can be understood as a physical process, but that does not exclude it from also being regarded as a supernatural event (for example, as a reincarnation). Indeed, most people will admit, if they are truthful, that they actually experience life on two levels—the scientific and the mythological. But in our increasingly literal-minded, science-dominated society it is only in extreme situations—where the rational fabric of our existence breaks down and mechanistic explanations are unable to answer the question "why"—that our mythological consciousness surfaces.

The mental processes behind mythology

The step-by-step logical thinking required for the acquisition of scientific knowledge is slow and laborious. It is much easier to arrive at conclusions by comparisons and analogies where "just as . . . so in" are the key words.

For instance, myths explain the phenomena of nature by drawing parallels between simple known things and those that are harder to grasp. Fire has something in common with the sun, the source of heat and energy. Gold is shiny and resembles the sun in color. It also does not rust, therefore signifying immortality. Thus, out of common physical characteristics, symbolic equations are made, and one thing takes on the qualities of another.

CONNECTIONS

See also
834 Myths of spring
836 Myths of summer
838 Myths of autumn
840 Myths of winter
842 The nature of religion

1

1 2 3 4 5 6 7 8 9 10 11 12 13 14 15 16 17

1 Fantastical creatures play an important part in many myths, probably because they appeal to people's awe of the forces around them. The fire-breathing Chimera [9], for instance, expresses the power of the volcanoes it inhabits. The creatures and events of myth may also be shadows of actual events. Hercules' struggle with the Hydra [4] may mirror the draining of the marshes by some former king; while the Centaurs [15], half-horse, half-human, may have originated with the famous horsemen of Thessaly. Others pictured are Hippocampus [1], the Mermaid [2], the winged Lamassu of Babylon [3], the Gryphon from Asia [5], the Satyr [6], Sirens [7], Medusa [8], the Sphinx from Egypt [10], Minotaur [11], Pegasus [12], Cerberus [13], the Unicorn [14], La Tavasque [16], and the Dragon [17].

2

A
B
C
D
E

2 Myths create gods in human form. This anthropomorphism was at its height in ancient Greece where the gods expressed in extreme form such human qualities as beauty, anger, and love. Shown here is part of the Greek pantheon. Hermes [A] was the messenger of the gods, Apollo [B] was patron of music, and Zeus [C] was the ruler of all the gods. Athena [D] was protector of Athens and guardian of crafts. Demeter [E] was a fertility goddess.

3

3 The snake or dragon that eats its own tail forms a circle signifying the cyclical nature of all things (a common mythological theme). This illustration is from a 15th- century European alchemy text. Such taileating dragons are found in myths from all over the world. A Japanese map shows a tail-eating snake whose movements under the surface of the earth are said to be the cause of the earthquakes that periodically afflict Japan.

As the egg originates life, so the world was created out of an egg [5]. Mountains are often inaccessible and inspire awe, as do the beings that people credit with having more power than themselves. Thus the proper habitation for the gods may be a mountain, such as Mount Olympus, home of the Greek gods. Thunder and lightning inspire fear as do outbursts of anger; hence a person killed by lightning must have offended Zeus, the chief Olympian. [2c]. Sometimes one characteristic is made use of in the equation, sometimes another. As thunder ushers in rain, so where rain is scarce, thunder may symbolize fertility. Rivers, trees, and animals, whether monkeys or snakes, mice or lions, all have their characteristics, expressed in terms of such human values as cunning and fertility, destructiveness and courage. In addition, the supernatural beings have their favorite animals or can take on the appearance of animals [6,7].

But myths are not just explanations of why men and women and the world in which they live are as they find them. This view of mythology would be inadequate. Image-making is one of the most distinctive human characteristics. The telling of myths becomes a vital necessity not simply to placate or propitiate superhuman powers, but to stimulate the very same creative and spiritual gifts that made people invent myths. Without meaning and purpose beyond the satisfying of daily physical necessities, no people and no culture can flower. By the same token, humans need an understanding of defeats and victories, of birth and death, in order to stave off the despair that the complexities of life might induce. Accordingly, there is a myth to answer almost every human mood and every question.

The necessity of myths

Myths are timeless when compared with historical events. They are also timeless in the sense that the human need to live in harmony with nature by means of guidelines (which some now call psychological) is as great as ever. Myths provide a bridge between outer "realities" and the hopes and fears of our dreams.

KEY

This 1790 Italian map shows the stars visible from the Earth's northern hemisphere grouped together by constellations whose symbols date back to a time when observations were influenced by the concepts of Greek mythology. The periphery is formed by the Zodiacal signs, which indicate months.

4 This 13th-century Hindu wheel at Konarak, India, symbolizes the circular nature of the universe. The unending cycle of birth and death is a stock element in mythology. The couple, male and female, will always be creating new generations. The idea of no birth without death signifies the eternal cycle to which Hinduism and Buddhism subscribed—the former aiming at the perfection of life, the latter at its renunciation.

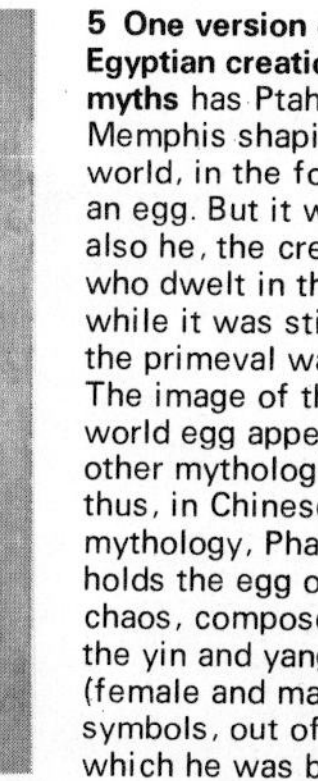

5 One version of Egyptian creation myths has Ptah of Memphis shaping the world, in the form of an egg. But it was also he, the creator, who dwelt in the egg while it was still in the primeval waters. The image of the world egg appears in other mythologies; thus, in Chinese mythology, Phan-ku holds the egg of chaos, composed of the yin and yang (female and male) symbols, out of which he was born.

6 This Roman relief of Leda and the swan depicts one of the love stories in which Zeus mates with mortal women. The transformation of gods as well as mortals into animal form is a common mythological theme. Swans are sacred in many places; killing them is believed to bring misfortune.

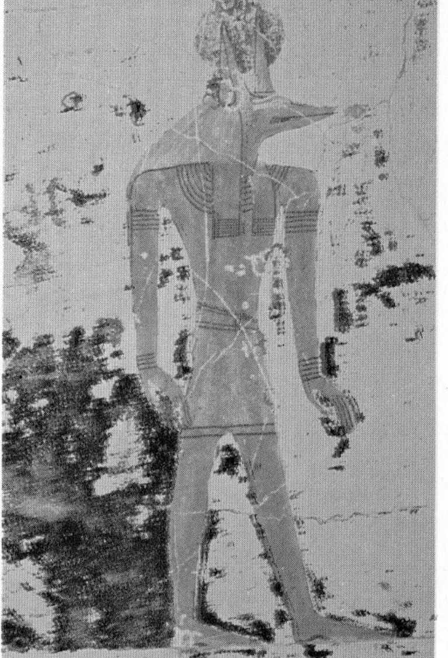

7 Anubis, the jackal-headed Egyptian god, like the Greek god Hermes, conducted souls into the underworld. Here they were judged by Osiris while Anubis assisted by weighing the heart. He was guardian of cemeteries and may have been deified to prevent jackals from devouring the dead. After Osiris had been dismembered by his adversary Seth, Isis enlisted the help of Anubis (as embalmer) to reassemble her husband's body, thus creating the first mummy.

8 Hermaphroditic statues, such as this ancestral Nomo figure from Mali, are found the world over as part of the common preoccupation with fertility. Fertility rites may take the form of a sacrifice to ensure new life or, as here, may be fundamentally magical; bisexual figures can fertilize themselves, thus guaranteeing offspring. The worship of such statues was expected to result in the fertility of land, animals, and humans. Some carvings show a male and a female half.

Myths of spring

Myths can be divided either regionally, corresponding to the centers of civilization from which they originate, or according to their major themes. As some themes are common to all regions, albeit with varying emphasis, it is convenient to take one, the motif of the four seasons, and look at its mythological counterparts. Creation and hero myths (also called epics) correspond to the spring phase, representing the beginnings of mankind.

The myths of creation

Creation myths deal with the origins of the world and presuppose that in the beginning there was something uncreated. This is usually presented as the Abyss or Chaos, vast and dark like Egyptian Nun, the primordial ocean in which lay the seeds of everything before the creation.

The creator is invariably regarded as divine. But in some traditions, notably the Judeo-Christian, he is a nonhuman abstract "Father" and is eternal. In others, such as the Greek or Egyptian, the emphasis is intensely biological. This has two consequences. First, there are several versions, and second, the ruling deity lives under the challenge of rivalry and death. One explanation for the succession of gods that characterizes almost all mythologies is that it reflects invasions of an area by people with other gods, who are set above those of the conquered.

The Egyptian god Atum (later known as Re) is usually described as a human male, but he is also referred to as bisexual, "that great He-She." Nevertheless, this ruler felt lonely and desired a companion. Atum created by masturbation the first creatures Shu, who was male and represented air, and Tefnut, who was female and represented moisture. In another version he spat out Shu and Tefnut. To both he imparted a vital essence, Ka, which may be regarded as the soul. This compares with the Jewish version of God breathing His divine life into Adam. In an earlier Egyptian myth, Atum is a serpent living in the dark waters of the Abyss, his outer coils forming the limits of the world. In subsequent versions, the creator was a mongoose that killed the snake (that is himself), then a primeval goose, and then an egg. All this took place in darkness, before heaven and earth were separated and before light was created (the reverse order from the Creation in the Bible).

This Egyptian creation myth demonstrates two general principles. First a mythology consists of several layers, comprising older and later versions that may coexist and be combined. Second, myths of various regions share common elements [2], for instance, the breath- and soul-giving and the fashioning of man out of earth, and tree symbolism, which is an important part of Scandinavian mythology.

The origins and functions of the hero

With the beginnings of the world and cosmos accounted for, people have to explain themselves and their culture. How did they learn to make fire, fish, hunt, rear domestic animals, cultivate the earth, discover medicines, and, later, write?

Inventions of such extraordinary importance for survival were ascribed to cult heroes who had obviously been endowed

CONNECTIONS

See also
832 The meaning and function of myth
836 Myths of summer
838 Myths of autumn
840 Myths of winter
48 Evolution of the Solar System
126 The expanding universe
406 Life and its origins
408 Evolution of life

1 **The giant Ymir** was the first living being in Scandinavian myth; he was born from the melting ice and suckled by the cow Audumulla. After dying his body became land, his blood the seas, his skull the heavens, his bones mountains.

2 **Trees play a large part in mythology,** from the Indian Asvattha, or tree of life and knowledge, to this Scandinavian world tree Yggdrasil. This represents the entire world as a tree. The branches reach to the sky, the roots down to Niflhel, the underworld. Near the roots gushes the fountain Hvergelmir, the source of the rivers, while the middle world is encircled by a snake.

3 **The phallus or lingam is a holy motif** in India. The female counterpart is yoni. They symbolize all creative energy—antagonistic yet cooperative forces of sex, Father heaven and Mother earth.

4 **Izanagi and Izanami** were brother and sister, the last of seven generations of Japanese gods. Standing on the floating bridge of heaven they created the island of Onokoro by stirring the ocean. Descending to the land, Izanagi walked around it from the left, Izanami from the right. When they met, Izanami spoke to her future husband first, expressing her pleasure at their sexual differences. So did Izanagi, but he was angry that the woman had spoken first. They then produced two children, who turned out to be a leech and a foam island and were both disowned. The gods said that the disaster was caused by Izanami's mistake of having spoken first. So they went back and performed the ritual correctly and produced the many islands of Japan. This myth illustrates the importance of ceremony in Japan and suggests a traditional Japanese view of how the sexes should relate.

5 **Tangaroa,** a creator and sea-god, appears in many Polynesian myths. In Tonga and Samoa he existed alone above a vast expanse of water and then threw down a stone that became land. His bird messenger planted a vine, but it rotted and in the decomposing matter a swarm of maggots became men and women. In the Society Islands he is pictured as existing in an egglike shell that revolved in endless space with no sky, land, or sun—a common mythological idea.

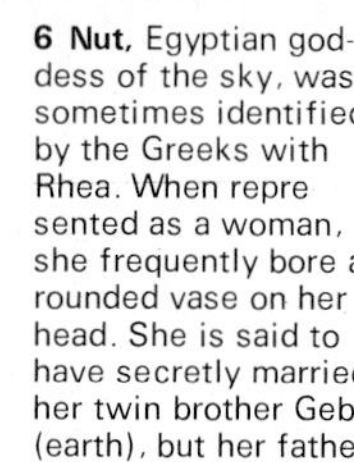

6 **Nut,** Egyptian goddess of the sky, was sometimes identified by the Greeks with Rhea. When represented as a woman, she frequently bore a rounded vase on her head. She is said to have secretly married her twin brother Geb (earth), but her father Shu (air) brutally separated them. This is an example of the theme of separation from a previous state of existence in creation myths. The daily birth of the Sun out of the sky goddess is the next step in the creation myth.

with unusual talents. These heroes were generally the illegitimate sons of gods who were persecuted by their fathers' offended spouses. The heroes' deeds and inventions benefited mankind both materially and spiritually. They served as models for people who had to live and struggle, suffer defeats, enjoy some triumphs, and die. Thus each epic forms a cycle analogous to the rise, zenith, and sinking of the sun each day.

The dawn (or birth) phase of the hero's life, illustrated by Hercules [11], foreshadows the object of his existence. His purpose, as illustrated by the myths of the Babylonian Gilgamesh [9] and by St. George [10], is the preservation of life by saving the realm from an oppressive ruler, the founding of civilization, and the renewal of human spiritual potential.

Trickery and stealth

Another version of the opening phase may be seen when the heroic deed is accomplished by stealth (notably trickery or theft) [8]. As usual, the ruling powers are offended, in this case with Maui, a hero of Pacific cultures. But despite the punishment the gods inflict, the deed is done and mankind has progressed one step nearer equality with the gods.

Among the best-known hero-thieves in Western civilization is Prometheus, who stole the fire that had been the privilege of the Olympians. Not only could people now cook formerly inedible foods and keep warm, but they also had light—an analogy for an increase of human consciousness. Zeus punished Prometheus and also offset the benefit that Prometheus had brought to mankind by creating the beautiful Pandora (all-giving). She was sent to Epimetheus, Prometheus' stupid brother, who married her. She took the lid off a box out of which flew all the diseases and sufferings of mankind. Comparison with the paradisiacal story of the Fall—embracing the view of woman as the dangerous temptress—is obvious. To overcome the woman's power was one of the hero's tasks. When this was accomplished, she could become his indispensable helper.

KEY

Spring, the time when the fields are prepared for the seed, parallels the myths of the creation of the earth. In myths the plow is portrayed as phallic, the furrows represent woman.

7

7 According to an Australian myth, daylight is created when the morning star is blown into the heavens by the east wind. Observation of the sky gave Aborigines the idea of time as an eternal cycle.

8

9

8 Maui, a hero from Oceania, achieved his deeds through trickery. He lassoed the sun to give man a full day and stole fire from the gods. A clown, he expresses man's need to poke fun at the gods.

9 Gilgamesh, a hero of Babylonian myths, fought and overcame monsters. In this seal, *c.* 2200 BC, he and Enkidu, who is still close to the animal stage from which heroes evolve (reflecting the evolution of man from brute creation), fight a bull that was sent against Gilgamesh by Ishtar. Among the hero's functions is the conquest of instinct-driven nature and the establishment of civilization.

10

10 St. George, seen here in a 17th-century Ethiopian painting, has been the subject of famous legends since the 3rd century and may have originated in a historical figure who lived in Palestine at that time. His task was to overcome evil in the form of the dragon and free the maiden. The Greek hero Perseus likewise rescued Andromeda from a dragon.

11 Hercules, portrayed here by Antonio Pollaiuolo (*c.* 1429–98), rescued the Greeks from many dangers. The Lernaean Hydra was ravaging the country. Every time one of her heads was cut off, two sprang up in its place. Hercules solved the problem by burning them with red-hot brands.

11

Myths of summer

Summer, with the sun at the height of its power, is understandably associated with images of the hero's achievement and female receptiveness. The myths of this season embody the idea of the union and the fruit of sky and earth on the sexual and reproductive planes as well as on the spiritual plane.

Woman as goddess

There can be little doubt about mythology having been recorded and told from a man's point of view. Woman is regarded as the second sex, a newcomer to creation and a definitely inferior and possibly evil one. Myths describing the transformation and psychological development of the individual rarely have a heroine as the centerpiece. The story of Eros and Psyche is one of the few. Woman is usually shown to play diametrically opposed roles—as a source of life, on the one hand, and as dangerous temptress and ruthless destroyer on the other.

Given that on one level myths reflect human emotions and attributes, there are several possible explanations of this equivocal attitude. One is that men view women as different sexually, and intolerance for what is different is a consistent human characteristic. When this "other" is also desired, then it may be loathed and feared as well as loved and idealized. Another explanation stems from a baby's experience of its mother. This earliest and most formative relationship seesaws (erratically as far as the baby is concerned) between a warm protective love and anger and punishment. Consequently, men develop an ambivalent attitude toward women. Women and the goddesses who represent them come to symbolize the dread aroused by the unpredictable hazards of man's life.

Mother goddesses around the world are seen equivocally as givers and takers of life, as personifications of the Earth, as creators of animals and vegetation, and as goddesses of love, marriage, and maternity. They appear, with some or all these characteristics, under many names: as Kali (India), Inanna (Sumeria), Ishtar (Babylon), Astarte or Anat (Canaan), Aphrodite, Demeter, and Artemis (Greece), Cybele and Venus (Rome), Isis (Egypt), Ma (Anatolia), and Freya (Scandinavia). Their rites range from the decorous to the orgiastic and are sometimes associated with temple prostitution.

The hero and women

The hero's encounters with women reveal man's attitude toward women and also embody lessons about how man comes to terms with the conflicting urges in his nature. There is an initial theme of separation from the dangerous (or incestuous) union with the mother. Subsequently, woman, in the form of the fair maiden or the king's daughter, becomes a hard-won prize, either as the goal of the hero's quest or as a helper, inspiring him to accomplish his mission, as Ariadne did when she fell in love with Theseus.

Theseus had come from Athens to King Minos of Crete to pay the yearly tribute of seven youths and seven maidens whose fate was to be devoured by a monster bull, the Minotaur, which lived in the labyrinth. Without the thread that Ariadne gave him,

CONNECTIONS

See also
- **832** The meaning and function of myth
- **834** Myths of spring
- **838** Myths of autumn
- **840** Myths of winter
- **846** Islam, Hinduism, and Buddhism

1 Surviving myths almost invariably portray the supreme deity as male. But extremely old objects such as this "Venus" (*c.* 30,000 BC) suggest that in earlier times the Earth—the most revered of the gods, giver and taker of life—was represented as a woman and mother. This crude figure is hardly beautiful, unlike the Venus of the Romans, yet it suggests an awe-inspiring strength

2 Diana of Ephesus (not to be confused with the Roman huntress Diana) was probably of ancient Asiatic origin, although the Greeks found her temple and worship established in Ionia. Her prodigious power to suckle infants is portrayed by her many breasts. Multiplication of an attribute to suggest prowess is seen also in the Hindu pantheon, whose gods often have several arms, legs, or even heads.

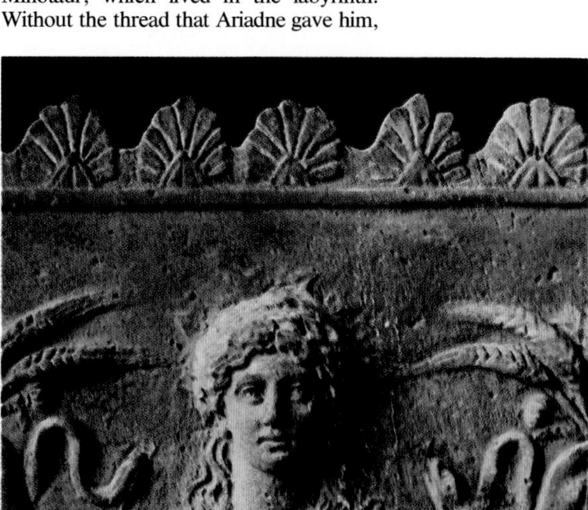

3 Demeter, identified by the Romans with Ceres, was the Greek goddess of the fruitful earth and protectress of marriage and social order. This terracotta head shows her with her attributes of corn, poppies, and snakes. Demeter was especially the goddess of corn; wheat and barley were sacred to her, and she presided over the harvest and all things associated with it. In her capacity as goddess of marriage, she was regarded as a beneficent lawgiver to mortals. But in some parts of Greece her primitive nature was emphasized; there she was represented by a horse's head. In her hands were a dove and a dolphin.

4 Female figures, often holding children, are commonly kept in Bakongo ancestor cult shrines in Angola, to commemorate the founders of the family. From the viewpoint of union and fertilization, birth is the harvest; from the viewpoint of the newborn infant the cutting of the cord separates one state of existence from the last. The cycle leads from unity through separations to final reunification. Familiarity with birth does not destroy a sense of awe.

5 Medusa was the only one of the three Gorgons, the daughters of the ancient sea gods Phorcys and Ceto, who was mortal. Her head (from a 3rd-century Roman mosaic) was covered with snakes in place of hair, and struck such terror in the beholder that it turned him to stone. Perseus, armed with the cap of Hades to make him invisible and guided by Athena, succeeded in cutting off her head by sighting it in a shield and striking it with a sickle.

he would not have found his way out of the labyrinth. Ariadne got little thanks for her help, however, and Theseus at last abandoned her on a small island. Easy victories had spoiled him, and thus he had further trouble with women. His capture, marriage, and subsequent repudiation of the Amazon Antiope led to the invasion of Athens, as did his treatment of the young Helen, whom he carried off from Sparta.

This story may be interpreted as a cautionary tale. Manhood is not easily acquired, and without it woman remains a threat, a devouring, dangerous creature, whether in human form or, as often classically portrayed, as a monstrosity that must be slain [5].

Other elements of this theme are contained in one of the oldest epics recorded, that of Gilgamesh. The story of his partnership with Enkidu, a wild, barely human creature, their killing of a ferocious giant and the "bull of heaven," and Enkidu's death at the hands of the angry gods, contains among other themes allusions to an incomplete development of heterosexuality. In psychological terms, the message is that fear of the other sex is overcome not by contempt (killing the monster), not by tributes and worship, but by recognizing the common humanity of the opposite sex.

The pendulum of mythology

Mythological thinking, like man's nature itself, may be compared with a pendulum that swings between the earthy or biological [8] and the more abstract or spiritual. Myths surrounding fertilization and childbirth show this wide spectrum particularly well. Zeus coupled with Leda in the form of a swan. When he fertilized Danaë (who gave birth to Perseus, slayer of Medusa) he did so as a shower of gold leaking through the roof of her prison. The next step is to represent conception by means of a shaft of light, symbolizing the divine spirit. As the pendulum swings back, man's mythological thinking has matured, and he accepts images of ordinary sexual intercourse, although perhaps under somewhat unusual circumstances, as the symbolic union of opposite qualities in general.

KEY

Summer is a time of ripeness and the full power of the Sun's energy. Grape harvesting is associated with Dionysus, god of wine, who represents the intoxicating power of nature.

6

6 Psyche is one of the few women to have the key role in a myth tracing psychological growth. In Greek mythology, Venus, jealous of Psyche's beauty, sends Eros (Cupid) to make her fall in love with something ugly, but Eros becomes her lover. Forbidden to look upon Eros because he is a god, Psyche disobeys, is deserted, and performs numerous difficult tasks in her search for Eros. Finally, she becomes an immortal and joins him.

7

7 The branches of the Tree of Jesse, in this 12th-century French version, support his descendants, David, the Virgin Mary, and Jesus. Like Sarah before her, Anna, mother of Mary, was barren for 20 years until "the Lord took mercy." The symbol of a tree as axis of the world is not unusual. Adonis, the Greek god of vegetation, was said to have been born from a myrtle.

8

8 The yogic posture known as Yab-Yum (Father-Mother), seen in this 18th-century Tibetan bronze, unites the Hindu male god or "absolute reality" with his female counterpart, Shakti. No greater contrast can be imagined than that between this and the denial of sexuality in Christian mythology, although Mary is often called the consort of God. The female emanation of the Hindu god is called Lakshmi (in the case of Vishnu) or Parvati (in the case of Shiva). As the latter, she is portrayed as a beautiful young woman sitting close to her husband. The imagery of sexual union is also expressed in a linear design of interlaced triangles, which is called ShriYantra.

9

9 Pan, son of Hermes, with the legs, horns, and beard of a goat, was a phallic shepherd-god of the pastures and woods who made the flocks prolific. He was worshiped originally in Arcadia, although his cult spread throughout Greece in the 5th century BC. His revels, depicted here by Nicolas Poussin (1594–1665), were similar to those of Bacchus. Pan frolicked with nymphs at night but liked to frighten travelers, hence "panic."

The myths of autumn

Autumn, when the fertility and vigor of summer give way to the death of crops and the failing strength of the sun, is associated in mythology with the dying god or hero [2, 5, 7], the destructive power of the mother goddess [3, 6], and the death or peril of the earth and the creatures it supports.

The cycle of the seasons

The Greek story of Demeter and her daughter Persephone shows how myth tries to answer the central questions of life—in this case why the earth annually loses its fertility and nature apparently dies. The god Zeus was both the father and uncle of Persephone. Without Demeter's knowledge he promised Persephone to his brother Hades (king of the underworld). While the girl was gathering flowers in the fields of Nysa, the earth suddenly opened and Hades carried her off. When she learned what had happened, Demeter, angry with Zeus, left Olympus. As a result, since she was the goddess of fertility, the earth was barren, and nothing grew. Famine would have destroyed all creatures had not Zeus sent Hermes to retrieve Persephone. Hades consented, but he had already given her a pomegranate to eat. Because she had eaten in the underworld she would have to spend a third of the year below the earth. The rest of the year she could spend happily reunited with her mother, who consequently allowed the earth to bear fruit again.

In this myth of fertility and death, Persephone in Hades is the seed in the ground; Persephone rejoined with her mother is the sprouting seed that nourishes humans and animals. To mark the annual cycle, to make sure that it continued, and to propitiate the goddess, a festival, the Eleusinia, was celebrated in Athens, as harvest festivals are in other parts of the world.

In addition to explaining the succession of the seasons, myths attempt to explain such shorter cycles as the rising and setting of the sun [1] and the phases and eclipses of the moon. In Indo-European myths the orbits of the sun are often interpreted in terms of a horse and chariot. Surya, the Hindu sun god, for instance, drove across the heavens in a flaming chariot, as did the Greek Helios and the Slavonic Dazhbog. A Nordic version explains that the sun and moon move because they are being pursued by ravenous wolves.

In India the moon represented the cup from which the gods drank Amrita, the elixir of immortality. When the gods first extracted Amrita, by churning the Milk Oceans, the monster Rahu stole the first sip. Vishnu immediately cut off his head, which began to pursue the moon. Eclipses happened when Rahu succeeded in swallowing the moon, but because he had no stomach the moon reappeared, and the chase was resumed.

Myths of the flood

Floods as periodic events that destroy the world occur so universally in myths that they may reflect actual events, although it is probable that many local inundations were interpreted as world events. The bare bones of these myths are the same. A great flood drowns all the inhabitants of the world except one man or family whose escape in a boat is made possible by advance warning.

CONNECTIONS

See also
832 The meaning and function of myth
834 Myths of spring
836 Myths of summer
840 Myths of winter
846 Islam, Hinduism, and Buddhism
806 Death, grieving, and loss
52 The Moon
222 Climates

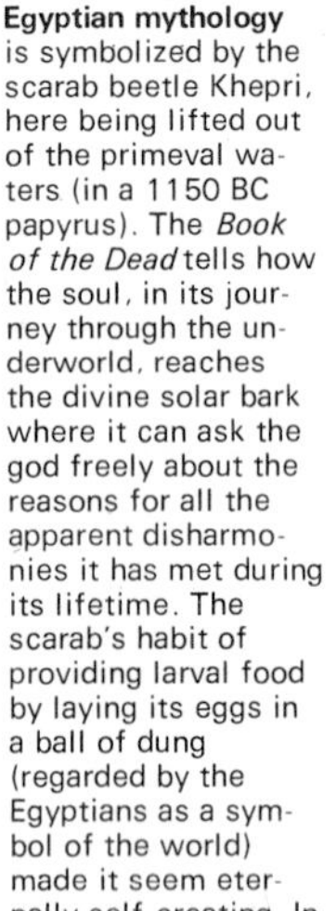

1 **The rising sun in Egyptian mythology** is symbolized by the scarab beetle Khepri, here being lifted out of the primeval waters (in a 1150 BC papyrus). The *Book of the Dead* tells how the soul, in its journey through the underworld, reaches the divine solar bark where it can ask the god freely about the reasons for all the apparent disharmonies it has met during its lifetime. The scarab's habit of providing larval food by laying its eggs in a ball of dung (regarded by the Egyptians as a symbol of the world) made it seem eternally self-creating. In its cyclic decline, the sun god was known as Re-Atum, or "the completed."

2 **Mithraism** was practiced as a religion in Asia Minor centuries before Christ and was taken up as a cult by the Romans about AD 75. It was Christianity's competitor for some 200 years. An important element is the bull sacrifice demanded by the sun god, Mithras, who is also the bull–slayer and slain. The sacrifice marks a state of transition similar to seasonal changes. It ensures fertility and purifies the human soul. The bull suffers; even the god has to avert his eyes. But from the various parts of the newly sacrificed animal a whole renewed cosmos is miraculously created.

3 **As life feeds on life,** so the beautiful young maiden Parvati changes into the death-dealing Hindu goddess Kali. Depicted here is her marriage to Shiva, carved 9th-10th century AD in India. What the goddess has bestowed, she will take away. She is the Black One, usually adorned with a necklace of skulls. Sometimes she is depicted as having large fangs. Often she is shown brandishing a sword as well as scissors with which to cut the thread of life. This Hindu goddess of death is also the embodiment of her husband Shiva's dynamic energy. The word Kali is the feminine for "time" and is a reminder of the brief life span of everything that lives.

4 **Demeter,** the Greek goddess of fertility and the mother of Persephone by Zeus, is shown here in a Roman sculpture. When Persephone was carried off by Hades to the underworld, Demeter was so grieved that the Earth became barren. Searching for her daughter, Demeter went to Eleusis where the Eleusinian Mysteries were begun in her honor. Later Persephone was allowed to spend 8 months of every year with Demeter.

Eventually the gods are appeased, the waters recede, and life reappears.

But there are interesting variants. In the Hindu version Manu, unlike the biblical Noah [8], was the only survivor. He had been warned of the flood by a fish [9]. When it was all over he felt lonely and wanted a wife, and the gods duly created her out of Manu's sacrifices of sour milk, butter, and curds. In the Mesopotamian *Epic of Gilgamesh* the survivors of the flood, Utnapishtim and his wife, had similar experiences, but their relationship with the gods was not as personal as that between Noah and Yahweh. For one thing Utnapishtim was warned only by a subterfuge of Ea, lord of the waters and wisdom, who by doing so gave away a secret plan of the council of the gods. Nor did the gods promise that such a disaster would not happen again.

The coming of death

It is not surprising that death, the ultimate mystery of life, should be a universal theme in mythologies. Death is consistently seen as an intruder, not existing at the beginning when humans repeatedly renewed their lives. Usually, death appears as a result of an error, as a punishment, or by agreement after discussion.

The idea of death as an error often centers around a message that goes astray. In Africa, for instance, God sends the chameleon to tell the first men that they are to be immortal. But because it dawdles on the way it is overtaken by the lizard, who is the messenger of death. Death as a punishment (often through the fault of a woman, as in the biblical story of Adam and Eve) is a common motif. The Algonquin Indians of North America, for instance, held that the Great Hare gave man immortality in a parcel that he was forbidden to open, but his curious wife looked in and let immortality fly away. Death by agreement appears in some parts of the world. A myth of the Greenland Eskimos states that in the beginning there was no death but also no sun. One old woman insisted that if it were not possible to have one without the other, it would be preferable to have both, as life without light was worthless.

KEY

Mythological themes of death, mourning, and dismemberment are represented in this medieval hunting scene by the death of the stag and the trees' colorful autumn foliage.

5

5 The cycle of life and death does not spare the gods of Scandinavian mythology, who are destroyed by monsters at the end of their rule. Here Odin is being devoured by the wolf Fenris. The twilight of the gods reflects the onset of the Nordic winter. But the gods are avenged by their sons. The wolf is slain by Odin's son, and a new generation of men and women arise from the world tree, Yggdrasil.

6

6 Odysseus's encounter with the Sirens (from a Roman mosaic) during his return home after the fall of Troy is typical of threatening myths about women. The Sirens were beautiful maidens whose singing so enchanted sailors that they swam ashore and died miserably. Odysseus filled his rowers' ears with wax and had himself bound so that he could hear the sweet singing without diving to his death.

7

7 The Greek myth of Actaeon being killed by hounds reveals a goddess in a savage mood. Actaeon was hunting a stag when he caught sight of Diana (or Artemis) bathing with her maidens. In anger, she transformed him into his own quarry to be torn to pieces. It is superficially the story of a virago punishing a man's lust. But the stag was a sacred animal, and Actaeon's ritualistic dismemberment perhaps implied an autumnal sacrifice to ensure the next harvest.

8

8 This multistoried ark, from an 18th-century Ethiopian text on Noah, carries all the creatures needed to repopulate the world when the flood finally subsides. Central to the flood myth is a warning to humankind not to be too proud.

9

9 Vishnu, the great Hindu god, can take on whatever incarnation (*dvatas*) is required. Three of the best known are in animal form: fish, tortoise, and boar. During the flood, man's ancestor, Manu, was saved by a fish whose life he had spared (Vishnu in disguise). The motif of a grateful animal saving the hero's life is well known in Western fairy tales and is perhaps as universal as the story of the flood among the various myths of destruction.

Myths of winter

Death as the end of everything is unacceptable to most human beings. Myth's function is, therefore, to explain that life in its known form must come to an end as inevitably as the arrival of winter [Key] but also to point to a future that is not accessible to our senses. It is in this void of unknowability that myths are most needed.

Continuation or transformation?

Seeking to avoid the inevitable, man has created many myths about life-preserving remedies such as magic potions, elixirs of immortality or rejuvenation. In the *Epic of Gilgamesh,* for instance, the hero plunges into the cosmic sea with stones tied to his feet. At the bottom he finds the prickly herb of immortality, plucks it, cuts loose the stones, and surfaces. But his triumph is short-lived, for while he is bathing a serpent eats the herb. Shedding its skin periodically, it is the snake that becomes a symbol of rejuvenation and immortality.

Other semidivine beings have tried to cheat death and its messengers. The Polynesian trickster Maui even tried to kill the goddess of death herself. With his friends the birds he crept up while she was asleep, intending to crawl into her body between her thighs, kill her, and escape through her mouth. When a bird saw only his legs sticking out, however, it chuckled and woke the goddess, who closed her thighs, entombing Maui.

Another widespread motif is the attempt to rescue a loved one from the underworld. Thus Izanami, who according to Japanese myth had, with her husband Izanagi, created the world out of the ocean, dies giving birth to fire. Izanagi follows her to a castle in the Land of Darkness. He persuades her to return, but she delays because she has already eaten food there (as did Persephone in a similar Greek myth). Impatiently Izanagi uses a light and sees that she is already in an advanced state of decay. So angry is she at being seen in a humiliating state that she tries to kill him, and Izanagi barely escapes.

A variation on this story is found in the Greek myth of Orpheus, who, finding that Eurydice has died of a snake bite, decides to follow her to Hades. Such is the quality of his music that Eurydice is permitted to return with him on condition that he does not look back at her until they reach the upper world. His anxiety overcomes him, however; he looks back, and she is lost. (This fatal mistake is echoed in the biblical story of Lot's wife, who looked behind her on the way from Sodom and was turned into a pillar of salt.) The moral of these myths seems to be that man must learn to accept the inevitability of separations, of which death is the most irrevocable.

Beyond death: heaven and hell

Man's difficulty in accepting death as final is reflected in the universal theme of a world after death [1,3,6]. In many traditions this is somewhere on the Earth, often in the west (Eden [8] is an exception), and separated by water from the known world. Examples are the Celtic Avalon, the Greek Islands of the Blessed, and the American Indian Happy Hunting Grounds. In some it is below the Earth, like the realms of Tumbuka (Malawi), and in still others it is in

CONNECTIONS

See also
832 The meaning and function of myth
834 Myths of spring
836 Myths of summer
838 Myths of autumn
842 The nature of religion
126 The expanding universe

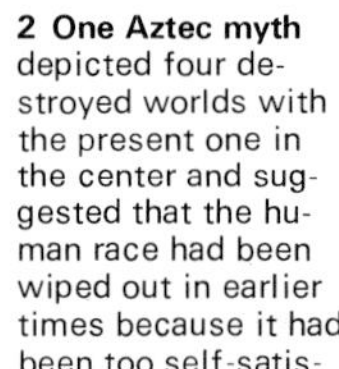

1 **After death,** the Egyptians believed, life continued in the underworld. Each person had a double, or Ka, representing the divine essence. Here it is shown as a strange creature with human head and falcon's body. Although Ka is as spiritual as any Christian soul, a concrete explanation was needed for its ability to fly across the underworld with the corpse to which it belonged.

2 **One Aztec myth** depicted four destroyed worlds with the present one in the center and suggested that the human race had been wiped out in earlier times because it had been too self-satisfied. If men became too proud, the present world would itself be destroyed by means of an earthquake. The ending of a universe and the beginning of a new era was predicted in many other traditions. Greco-Roman mythology, for example, spoke of a descending order of world eras from a "golden" to an "iron" age, the baser metals indicating a progressive worsening of the human condition.

3 **The other world,** according to the Egyptian *Book of the Dead,* was a realm in which the blessed dead lived much as they had always done, only in a state of more perfect happiness, farming the Elysian fields. Osiris, the supreme ruler and judge of the dead, is here attended by his wife-sisters, Isis and Nephthys. His insignia are agricultural. There were no spiritual occupations or heavenly choirs as there were in Semitic religions.

4 **The myth of Jonah and the Whale** represents a Hebrew variation of the theme of death and resurrection. On the surface it is the miraculous story of how the Lord sent a whale to Jonah when he had been cast out into the sea and of how he lived three nights and days in its belly before being delivered to dry land. At a deeper level it is an allegory of how Jonah atoned for disobeying God's command and as a result was delivered from guilt.

5 **Implications of sacrifice** underlie the Hebrew story of how Samson's hair was treacherously shorn by Delilah. A connection between cutting the hair and losing physical strength is widespread, and some Fijian chiefs ate a man as a precaution before cutting theirs. But the theme may also imply a transition from outer to inner strength, in keeping with the sacrifice of hair by nuns and Orthodox Jewish women as a preparation for sacred marriage.

the sky, as in the Judeo-Christian heaven and the Buddhist and Hindu paradises.

Some realms admit all the dead regardless of merit, while others restrict entry to those who have earned it. The Greek Hades, for instance, accepts the souls of all who are ferried across the River Styx by Charon, if they have the fare. But in the Judeo-Christian religions the soul is assigned to heaven or hell according to divine judgment of the person's life on Earth; in Egyptian myths the hearts of the dead are weighed by Anubis.

But merit is not always measured in moral terms, and "heaven" often reflects inequalities on earth. In the Leeward Islands only aristocrats are sent to "sweet-scented Rohutu," while commoners go to "foul-scented Rohutu." The mansions of the Sun were open only to the Incas and nobles of Peru, while the Norse Valhalla was the prize of the mighty in war. Even the Christian Heaven is not always gained by a pure life. John Calvin (1509–64), the Swiss theologian, held that salvation was through arbitrary divine choice. Generally "heavens" are portrayed as beautiful parks filled with earthly delights, where youth is eternal.

The end of the world

A final mythological theme is that of the end of the world and a return to chaos. The gods imposed order on the world and they may well revoke their patronage. It is for this reason that festivals are celebrated, rituals performed, and sacrifices made. But almost every mythology envisages a time of eventual destruction heralded by wars, famines, floods, hurricanes, and earthquakes.

Traditions as separate as those of the Mexican Aztecs [2] and the Indian Hindus and Buddhists incorporated several world ages characterized by decreasing moral standards and piety. The Aztecs believed that when the last age had finished, the world would be destroyed by fire. But almost always such myths contain a motif of reconstruction in an unending wheel of life. For as winter contains the seeds of spring, so the end of one great cycle stimulates the beginnings of the next.

KEY

In dead midwinter, nature rests under a blanket of snow, no sap rises, and trees are being felled. But life lies underground in waiting seed and burns in the Promethean fires of man.

6 **In Chinese mythology,** hell was run like a well-ordered bureaucracy, reflecting the importance of administrative efficiency in China. Here, Yama, king of the Seventh Hell and supreme master of the law courts, dispenses a form of justice in which exact punishment is prescribed for each offense. Misers and dishonest mandarins, for example, have to swallow melted gold, while cannibals and desecrators of graves are chased by demons into a river. Investigation of souls takes place in the first of 10 courts, which assigns each soul to 1 of 18 hells designed to fit various crimes.

七殿泰山王

7 **Shou-Lao,** symbol rather than god of longevity, holds a golden peach. These ripened only once in 3,000 years in a celestial garden, a Chinese parallel to the paradisiacal Tree of Life elsewhere.

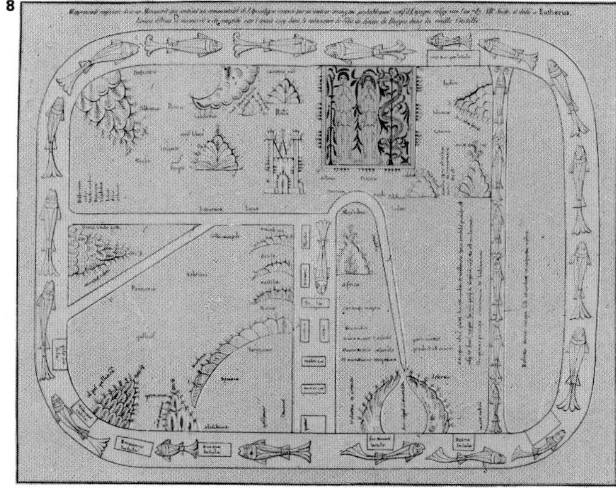

8 **Myths are maps to guide** and stimulate the imagination and orient the individual in life. This 8th-century map by a Spanish priest, Beatus, divided the world into three continents inherited by the sons of Abraham. The surrounding ocean was not to be explored. Paradise was located in the east (top).

9 **In "Resurrection"** by the English painter Stanley Spencer (1891–1959), the Last Judgment has come for the good people of Cookham. Just like people coming up from a cellar, folk are climbing out of their graves, quite uncorrupted after the winter sleep of death. The picture is a literal and earthly allegory of the sophisticated idea that souls can be reunited with their bodies in the building of a New Jerusalem. In many religions, emphasis on heaven or hell is waning, as is the importance of past or future lives. It is conceded that corresponding states of mind can exist here and now.

The nature of religion

For an individual searching for the secret of how to live, the fundamental message of the religious traditions is that man does not know himself. He knows neither the extent of his weaknesses nor the possibilities of his greatness. Thus, at the heart of all the sacred traditions of the world there are ideas and disciplines that seek to acquaint man with both the "animal" and the "divinity" within him [Key]. The early Christian, for example, meditating in the desert of North Africa and practicing the specifically Christian method of continuous inner prayer ("prayer of the heart"), directly experienced the extent to which his mind was distracted and filled with illusions about himself. Facing and accepting this, he also discovered that he was the vehicle for the most divine energies of the universe.

The common spiritual factor

When used wrongly, as a manipulative device to gratify egoistic aims, all the methods and practices of sacred traditions lose their real religious purpose. Thus the prophets of Israel condemned even the most sacred rituals when they were performed externally without an inner recognition of personal helplessness and obligation to the source of life. Thus too, the powerful meditative practices of Mahayana Buddhism, to take an example from Eastern traditions, are said to have a liberating effect only when used to benefit all aware beings.

In its most intensive form, religion offers man even more than the perception of his two opposing natures. When carried far enough, the practices of a great tradition are intended to bring about an actual transformation of human nature at the deepest level. The name given to this state of transformed being varies from tradition to tradition and also from one gradation or aspect of transformation to another. In the Western world it is spoken of as salvation, immortality, the attainment of the kingdom of God, and so on. In the East it is nirvana, liberation, enlightenment, or God-consciousness. Often the terms "wisdom" or "freedom" are used. But whatever words are used to describe the state, the idea of transformation is the common factor in all religions.

The possibilities of human development envisaged by religious tradition are very great indeed. A human is understood as a potential microcosm [4], a being who contains in himself all the forces of creation and destruction that operate in the great universe. This concept of the microcosm forms the backbone of all ancient teachings, Eastern and Western.

Restoration of unity

The traditional teachings see the misery [5] and confusion of human life as rooted in our failure to see, accept, and live by the universal order of reality that is contained within ourselves. In our "fallen" state, the divinity within us is completely cut off from the animal. Thus divided within ourselves, we live our lives governed by impulses that were meant to be servants rather than masters. These "false masters" within us are desires, which are condemned not as such but only because we wrongly identify ourselves with them and obey them blindly and uncomprehendingly. To become a microcosm, that is, a mirror of the whole reach of

CONNECTIONS

See also
844 Judaism and Christianity
846 Islam, Hinduism, and Buddhism
848 Varieties of worship
850 Religion and the plight of modern man
852 What is philosophy?
856 Philosophy and religion
832 The meaning and function of myth

1 The phoenix is a perennial symbol of immortality. In legend, this beautiful bird lives in the wilderness of Arabia and is the only one of its kind. About every 500 years it burns itself on a funeral pyre, but rises from the flames reborn, (as in this 13th-century English manuscript). The central message of many religious traditions is that it is only when we "die" ourselves that a spiritual transformation (e.g. the birth of the Christian "new man") can take place. On a universal scale, the phoenix symbolizes the cosmic dance of birth, destruction, and renewal in which humanity and all of nature are involved.

2 Kilimanjaro, the Tanzanian mountain sacred to several African peoples, is one of many peaks throughout the world that are regarded as places of communion with the spiritual world or as the kingdoms of deities. Some of the most extensive sacred traditions surround Mount Meru in the Himalayas, the symbolic golden mountain of Hindu mythology. It stands at the center of the universe as the axis of the world and abode of the gods. Extending both upward to the heavens and downward to the nether regions, it is a bond both between earth and sky and man and god.

3 Shinto – meaning "way to the gods" – is Japan's oldest religion. Like other animists, Shintoists worship many gods, or *kami*, which are the forces in mountains, rivers, rocks, trees, and other parts of nature. Shinto emphasizes rituals and moral standards but does not stress life after death. One of the most compelling and unanalyzable human experiences is that of identity – that "I am I." Many religions (so-called exotheic religions), like Shintoism, turn upon a relation between Self and That – environment, fellows, and a deity external to and governing the universe with whom dialogue may be had and by whom duties are imposed. Along with such an approach, or in its place, may occur the feeling that the Self is not a citadel private to the person. In these so-called endotheic religions the Self is a microcosm, and the That with which we experience dialogue is not outside but inside ourselves. It is in fact the Self of Selfhood.

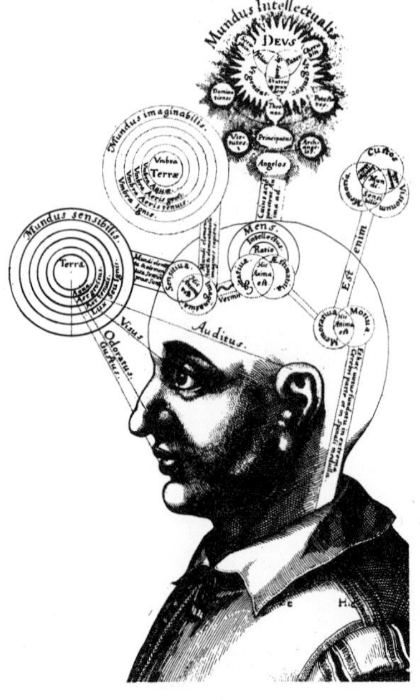
Mundus Intellectualis
DEVS
Mundus sensibilis
Terra
Mens
Auditus

4 Man as a microcosm of the universe is depicted in this diagram by the English alchemist Robert Fludd (1574–1637), harmoniously integrating cosmic principles. All the great traditions teach of the exalted cosmic status of man, if only implicitly. Hinduism has the idea of Primal Man, whose dispersal created the universe. The Judeo-Christian tradition speaks of man being made in the "image of God." But these are conceptions of man in a state of perfection. Fallen man is neither microcosm, nor mirror of God, nor Primal Man. The work of spiritual discipline is to recover or reconstitute the latent microcosmic nature of the human self.

the divine cosmic order, there must be forged within human nature a right relationship between the desires and the spiritual power with which all human are born.

The transformation of an individual (called the "second birth" in the Christian tradition) consists of the tangible establishment within the self of this right relationship, this extraordinary inner unity. Thus transformed, man may take his central place within the whole scheme of creation. He is then the Great King of the Chinese tradition, the Cosmic Man of Hinduism, the All-Containing Void of Buddhism, and the image of God of Judaism and Christianity. He both reflects the whole of cosmic nature and becomes the conscious instrument of the creator within it.

The cosmic pattern

In a general sense, the ideas, symbols, and rituals of the traditions are meant to serve as instruments to help us experience what is taken to be our exalted cosmic destiny, both on an individual and on a social level. Thus the structures of ancient society (called "theocracies") were designed to make human life conform to a cosmic pattern that is outside the range of modern scientific methods. Teachings about life after death [1], the "animistic" view of nature (a belief that all things are filled with life and consciousness), the role of shaman [7] and priest, the symbols of so-called "polytheism," and the function of "magic" may all be approached and studied from this point of view rather than from a conventional perspective, which sees them as expressions of intellectually inferior cultures. It is especially revealing to study the rich and complex social orders of ancient India and ancient Egypt on this basis.

Sacred tradition, whether Eastern or Western in origin, whether "primitive" [3] or "monotheistic," may therefore be defined as a means of transmitting ideas and ways of living that can guide individuals to pierce through the illusions that have become second nature to them and to realize in fact, and not just in fantasy, both the terrors of their present situation and the greatness of their possible inner evolution.

KEY

Janus, the Roman god of beginnings, custodian of the universe, was always depicted with two faces looking in opposite directions – an apt symbol of the duality of human nature. Many sacred traditions see man as being composed of two divergent elements: divinity and animal, spirit and body.

5

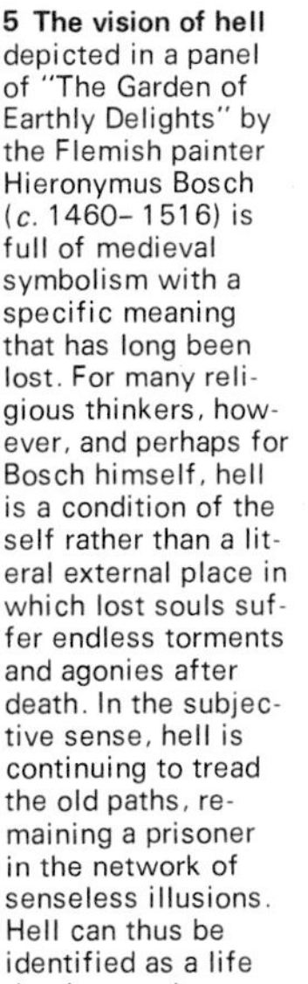

5 The vision of hell depicted in a panel of "The Garden of Earthly Delights" by the Flemish painter Hieronymus Bosch (*c.* 1460–1516) is full of medieval symbolism with a specific meaning that has long been lost. For many religious thinkers, however, and perhaps for Bosch himself, hell is a condition of the self rather than a literal external place in which lost souls suffer endless torments and agonies after death. In the subjective sense, hell is continuing to tread the old paths, remaining a prisoner in the network of senseless illusions. Hell can thus be identified as a life that has not been transformed.

6

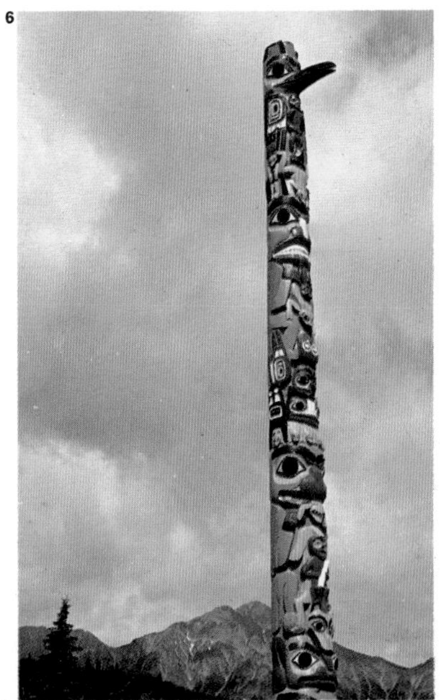

6 A North American Indian totem pole, like much of the symbolism of what used to be called "primitive" religions, expresses a vision of man and his relation to the universe that is extremely subtle and sophisticated. For one to grasp the meaning of these symbols it is necessary not only to have accurate information about the particular tradition in question, it is even more important to be able to see and hear with the intelligence of the heart.

7

7 Shamans, as shown in this 15th-century Turkish painting, are faith healers. Found in many cultures, they are believed to have links with the forces of the cosmos.

Judaism and Christianity

The fundamental message of Judaism is expressed by the prayer: "Hear, O Israel, the Lord our God, the Lord is One." This prayer is named by its first word—*Shema* ("hear"). It calls men to hear the truth that has been revealed, to take it to heart, and to live by it, in order to realize the unity of God in a relationship that demands of a man that he unify his own being.

The Jewish covenant and what it means

Judaism is the religion of a covenant between Yahweh (God) and the descendants of Abraham, who was prepared, when tested, to sacrifice his own son to Him. From the Covenant radiates the mystery of an agreement between man and God. It is in the actions that make up the history of the chosen people that the teachings of the Jewish faith are set forth. The Lord appears both in all the transcendence of His absolute power and in the immediacy of personal concern for His people. He brings Israel out of slavery in Egypt [4] and into the promised land. For the Jew, the "choosing" of his people parallels the mystery of man's being created in God's image. As Israel is called to realize its covenant, so man is called to fulfill the promise of his being. The Jewish philosopher Martin Buber (1878–1965) writes: "Man must liberate himself because man is a microcosm, and there is in him Pharaoh and Egypt; he is enslaving himself."

In Jewish mysticism, the symbolism of exile and return finds another, cosmic, level of interpretation. Medieval Kabbalists, interpreters of the Torah—the law God gave to Moses [Key]—and its rabbinical commentaries, saw in the failure and exile of cosmic man—"Adam Kadmon"—the scattering of the sparks of the divine *Shekinah*, the presence of God in the whole of creation. The redemption of man is thus intimately bound up with the redemption of creation.

This conception of man being responsible for the whole of creation had its greatest modern influence on Judaism in the communities of Hasidim ("the pious"), which arose in Poland in the eighteenth century. In the Hasidic way of life, there is no separation between sacred and profane. Everything that exists contains within it a divine spark waiting to be liberated. Therefore, there is in man a divine energy through which divine sparks that are present everywhere can be attracted and set free. All depends on intention, the condition of a man turned to God with his whole being. For the Hasid, everything is holy, and through his life according to the Torah everything can be brought to union with God.

Christianity and divine love

The whole of Christian religion is centered around the mystery of divine love. Man's task is to respond to that love. From the very source of Christianity come the words of Jesus addressed to the Jews in terms of their own tradition: "Thou shalt love the Lord thy God with all thy heart, and with all thy soul, and with all thy mind. This is the first and great commandment. And the second is like unto it, Thou shalt love thy neighbor as thyself. On these two commandments hang all the law and the prophets" (Matt. xxii: 37–40).

Later the Christian faith came to include people who lacked the common basis of

CONNECTIONS

Read first
842 The nature of religio

See also
846 Islam, Hinduism, an Buddhism
848 Varieties of worship
850 Religion and the plight of modern ma
982 The Hebrews 1200–322 BC
1026 Christ and the Apostles
1388 Modern Christianity and the New Beliefs

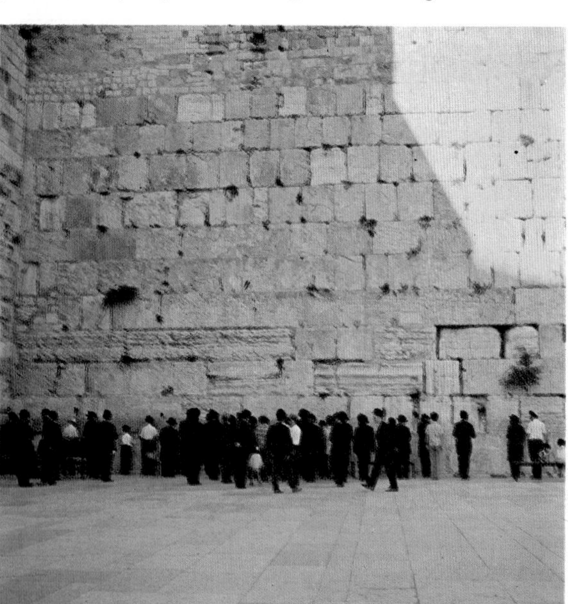

1 The Western Wall (also called the Wailing Wall) in the Old City of Jerusalem is a place of prayer and pilgrimage that is sacred to the Jewish people. According to rabbinical belief, the divine presence never departs from it. It is all that remains of the Second Temple, built in the 2nd century BC and destroyed in AD 70.

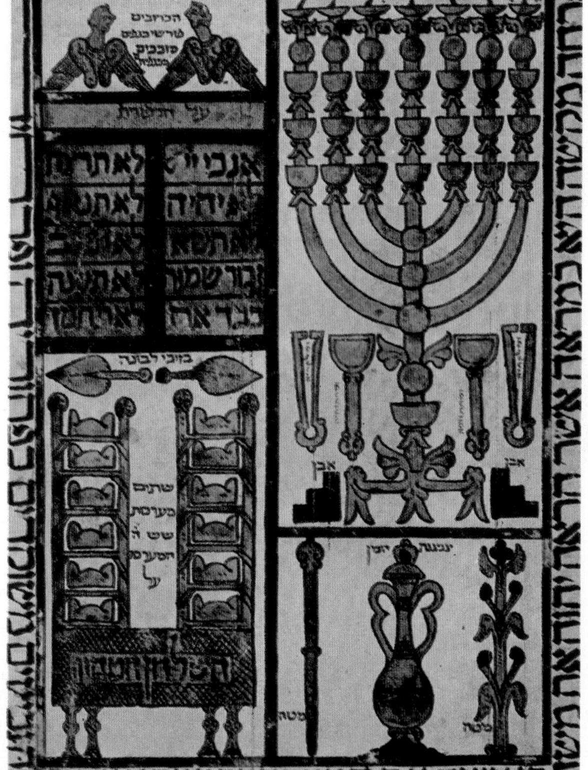

2 The original golden menorah, or ritual candelabrum, was shaped by Moses according to the pattern of the almond. Its branches symbolize the seven days of creation. The middle cup signifies the Sabbath. A nine-branch candelabrum is used in the eight-day Chanukkah festival.

3 Obedience to the Lord—the keeping of the Covenant—is fundamental to Judaism. The Ark of the Covenant is a gold-plated chest that housed the two tablets given by God to Moses. Originally kept at Shiloh and brought out during battles (as depicted here in a 13th-century French manuscript), it was put by Solomon in the Holy of Holies in the Temple at Jerusalem. After that it was seen only by the high priest on Yom Kippur, the Day of Atonement. Its eventual fate after the destruction of the Temple in 586 BC is completely unknown.

4 During the festival of Passover, Pesach, the Jews commemorate their deliverance from Egypt, the prelude to the forging of their eternal covenant with God. The family gathers for the *Seder* night service to retell the events from the *Haggadah* and answer children's ritual questions. Foods symbolizing the hardships of slavery are prepared, and only unleavened bread, *matzo*, is eaten. Each person tries to feel as if he personally were saved by God.

Judaism. In response to their need and in the face of the claims of then-current systems of thought, Christianity began to develop an organized theology.

In its unique perspective, everything that exists was brought into being as an expression of divine love and is moved by that love to "be what it is," to fulfill its own nature as the plant reveals the secret contained in the seed. But in the order of creation, it is man, made in the image of God, who stands out as the element of uncertainty, the risk undertaken by God so that His love might be freely returned.

In Adam's fall [5], the limited and separate existence of the natural world apart from its Creator asserted itself. Yet this failure is sometimes called "the happy fault" because it led on to the greatest act of divine love. The father's sacrifice of his son was fulfilled in a new covenant. The Son of God became man [6]. In the person of Christ, the way was reopened. The Incarnation mysteriously united in Christ the two natures—human and divine—and the passion and death of Jesus demonstrated this unification in the perfect submission of human will to divine will. Finally the resurrection of Christ [7] promises the fruit of sacrifice, the "new man" in whom limited nature is transformed by divine life. "Unless the grain of wheat falling into the ground dies, itself alone remains; but if it dies it brings forth much fruit" (John xii:24). And again: "He that findeth his life shall lose it; and he that loseth his life for my sake shall find it" (Matt. x:39).

The search for God through contemplation

A deep and serious response to this call can be found in the Christian contemplative tradition. To the modern person the idea of contemplation may suggest daydreaming or sentimental ramblings. This is far from the contemplative's understanding of his activity and its demand for a quality of awareness and impassioned searching that can bring him to the core of his being, there to discover his true need for God. Confused and alienated as a result of Adam's fall, man must struggle to find the central impulse of love that calls him to "be what he is."

KEY

Moses, the great lawgiver of the Jews, is depicted here by the French artist Gustave Doré (1833–73) with a sternness that is reflected in Mosaic law itself and that represents the absoluteness of God's word to man. According to Hebrew scriptures, Moses led his people out of bondage in Egypt (probably between the 14th and 12th centuries BC), and it was to him that Yahweh revealed the Ten Commandments in the Sinai wilderness. These laws, which the Israelites carried with them to the promised land, are the epitome of the demand for righteous action that characterizes the entire tradition of Judaism.

5

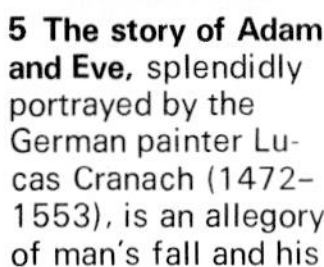

5 The story of Adam and Eve, splendidly portrayed by the German painter Lucas Cranach (1472–1553), is an allegory of man's fall and his anguished sense of separation from cosmic unity. What was the sin of Adam and Eve in eating fruit of the Tree of the Knowledge of Good and Evil? The Trappist monk Thomas Merton (1915–68) saw it as an act whereby man tried to appropriate for himself that which God would give out of his own love. The "original sin" is thus an act of pride stemming from lack of trust in the goodness of God.

6

6 God's divine love, expressed in Botticelli's "Nativity" (1500), was translated by St Paul into ethics in the spiritual life. The result was *agapê* or *caritas*—the concern for the well-being of others.

7 This resurrected figure of Christ by Piero della Francesca (1420–92) conveys the promise of rebirth after death. The suffering of Jesus on the Cross is an indictment of man's inherent drive to crucify or murder the Truth that can save. But the resurrection demonstrates God's loving forgiveness and the rebirth possible for those who can face their own corruption and accept the help of God.

7

Islam, Hinduism, and Buddhism

Islam, the youngest of the major world religions, sounds again the message of God's unity—"There is no God but God." Recognition of this truth constitutes the act of submission by which a man becomes a Muslim—"one who submits." Conscious of his dependence, man acknowledges "I am not the Absolute." Yet one who is called to the inner path of Islam also comes to recognize, "I am nothing separate from or other than the Absolute." Unity is reflected everywhere, drawing itself out like a beautiful arabesque [1] that baffles the eye as it continually turns back on itself.

The basis of Mohammed's teaching

In the Islamic perspective, man needs divine revelation to remind him of the One Reality, which is never directly manifested in the world. Judaism and Christianity are recognized as founded on authentic revelations; Islam offers the final revelation.

Mohammed, the founder of Islam (born in Mecca between AD 570 and 580), denounced the prevailing Arab worship of many gods. Confronted by powerful opposition, Mohammed and his followers became a social and political as well as a spiritual force. Following the teaching of the Koran, Islam developed laws to guide a religiously oriented community as well as a way for the individual to unite with Allah (God).

Traditionally in Islam there is no separation between the sacred and the secular. There is no priesthood, no day reserved for worship. Instead, the law itself offers direction and an ideal of life that meets man's need. In the Islamic perspective, man sins not by willful rejection of God, but by heedlessness or distraction. The required observances of Islam act as reminders of the relationship between everyday life and the Absolute.

The teachings and practice of Hinduism

For a Westerner the Hindu religion of India may be puzzling. In place of God and creation, he finds that Brahman (ultimate reality) is probably utterly impersonal, and the phenomenal world is ultimately unreal. Even the idea of historical progression is overshadowed by the sense of a cyclic world drama of creation, preservation, and destruction. Instead of precise doctrines, the Westerner finds a variety of methods and beliefs. For while Western monotheism seeks to protect the truth from distortion, in Hinduism the truth is left to protect itself [3].

The simplest—and the most difficult expression of the spirit of Hinduism is "Thou are That," which may be understood as a response to the deepest question men can ask. Looking at the world around them, men saw in the sudden flash of lightning, in the invisible power of the wind, signs of energies beyond their control and asked: What is behind all this? Another form of the question concerns the mystery within man: Who am I? In a single discovery comes the answer to both questions: The true Self (Atman) is the same as the ultimate ground of reality, Brahman—"Thou are That" [4].

The Hindu revelation is not the focus of a historical event like the revelation given to Moses, and it does not mark a unique bridging of the gap between God and man like that provided by the incarnation of Christ. It says that the Truth is in each person waiting

CONNECTIONS

Read first
842 The nature of religio

See also
844 Judaism and Christianity
848 Varieties of worship
850 Religion and the plight of modern ma
984 The Persian Empire o the Achaemenids
1058 Mohammed and Islar
962 India: prehistory to 500 BC
836 Myths of summer
838 Myths of autumn
988 Buddha and Buddhism

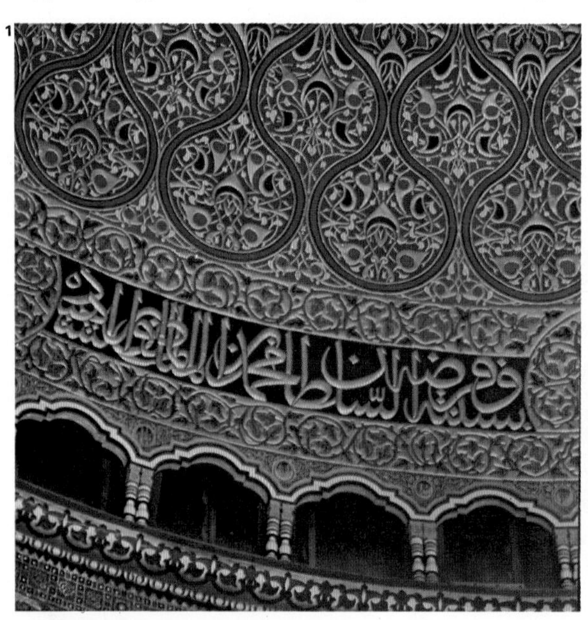

1 The arabesques inside a mosque represent to the Muslim divine unity in a symbol that is at the same time logical and rhythmic, mathematical and melodious. For a Sufi, one who has reached the goal of Islam's inner way, divine unity means much more than that there is only one God rather than several. It is also a key that opens the meaning of creation as a revelation of the Absolute, like white light diffused through a prism. As a microcosm, man gathers up all the attributes reflected separately by other creatures. His greatest potential is to reunite all the colors of the spectrum into a spark of divine light.

2 Prayer at specified times, five times a day, is one of the fundamental practices prescribed by Mohammed and known as the Five Pillars of Islam. The other four are declaration of faith in Allah, almsgiving, fasting during the month of Ramadan from dawn until sunset, and making a pilgrimage to Mecca in one's lifetime. Even fulfilling the law in an external way can help a Muslim understand his condition in life. A Muslim does not seek to go beyond the basic requirements by "doing more" in an external sense but, more importantly, to realize more deeply what it is that he is doing.

3 The many-armed Hindu god, Shiva, symbolizes the many modes of divine energy. The apparent polytheism that many Westerners see in Hinduism is in fact adaptability. Hinduism is monotheistic in a massive way, for in it all creation and experience are one. Judeo-Christian monotheists would be asked by a Hindu: "Who are we to limit the forms in which Brahman may manifest itself?" A devotee may take hold of any of the forms, which are in fact generated only by our partial perception, to arrive at the One. He may use any method from asceticism to orgiastic abandon or from ritual poverty to industrious prosperity if it leads him to God-realization.

4 The AUM symbol (OM) is a ritual and sacred Hindu syllable, rendered in Sanskrit calligraphy, that is understood as the fundamental sound of the universe. It is chanted both for the effect of its vibration on the worshiper and as a tangible symbol of the one fundamental Reality: Brahman, the Absolute. One interpretation of its three sounds, (A, U, M) is that they represent the trinity of Vishnu, Shiva, and Brahma.

to be realized. With this promise comes the warning "Neti, neti" ("Not this, not that"). One cannot identify either the Self or the Absolute with any particular thing. Belief in a separate self or ego is like an assumed identity that keeps us from realizing our true Self. In final wisdom the identity is laid aside and selfhood merged in an oceanic experience of That (Samadhi).

Fundamentals and precepts of Buddhism

Buddhism is more urgent and direct in its teaching than Hinduism, from which it grew. It sees ordinary existence as a nightmare that is not the less painful because its threats are unreal.

In the fifth century BC, Gautama Siddhartha, the son of an Indian king, woke from the nightmare. As the Buddha ("the awakened") [5], he was forever released from suffering and was filled with compassion for those still in darkness. The Buddhist believes that suffering is a universal fact of existence because of man's fundamental ignorance about himself and the world. The world is a process of continuous interaction of unstable compounds in which nothing lasts. Whatever a man may take to be himself—body, mind, feeling, perception—is an obstacle in the form of the assertion "This is mine; this am I; this is my ego," which makes him the center of an imaginary drama of loss and gain, pleasure and pain, good and bad [7].

Some have seen in the Buddhist denial of the ego and emphasis on transience a pessimistic rejection of all values. What is negative in Buddhism, however, is not its truth but its way of presenting that truth. The goal is defined negatively (and practically) as release from suffering, ignorance, and selfishness; indifference to suffering is one way of acquiring deliverance from it.

Whatever has been shaped through the law of cause and effect can be reshaped by the same law. Codes of moral behavior serve principally as a preparatory discipline, a method of purification for the most important task of cultivating "mindfulness" [8]. Direct insight into the workings of the causal law in oneself strikes at the root of the illusions of the ego and its suffering.

KEY

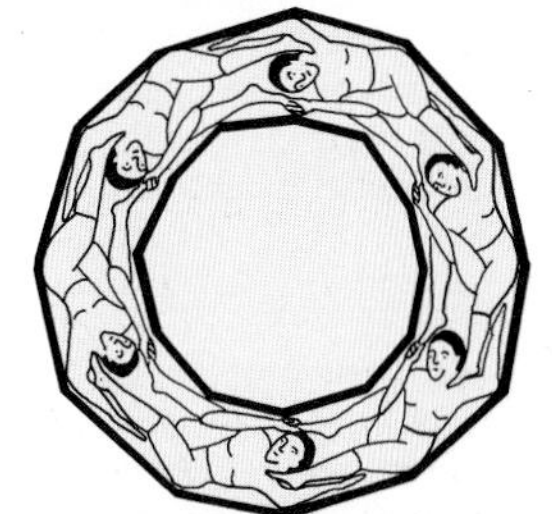

Hindu, Muslim, and Buddhist symbols, reading from top to bottom, respectively, represent sacred aspects of their faith for a devoted following of nearly 1.3 billion people. The vast majority of these are to be found in North African and Asian countries. The syllable AUM *(top)* is a mystic sound representing the Eternal Essence, and uttered by Hindus during the most solemn moments of worship. The arabesque *(center)* is a rhythmically designed pattern of oneness in which no animate objects are represented. The Wheel of Life *(bottom)* means for Buddhists the continuing cycle of death and rebirth that traps mortals with worldly longings.

5 The teaching of Gautama Buddha was directed solely to one point: the extinction of suffering. He saw people everywhere making themselves miserable through deluded belief in the reality of the ego. Rejecting displays of miraculous powers and speculations about metaphysical questions, he urged his followers not to rely on the achievements or the understanding of others, as this might simply be woven into their own fantasies. "Be ye a refuge unto yourselves. Betake yourselves to no external refuge. Hold fast to the Truth as a lamp. Look not for refuge to anyone besides yourselves."

6 Buddhism is split into two main streams—Mahayana and Theravada. Devotees of the latter revere the personality of the Buddha, his teachings, and the order he founded. They hold that the ideal Buddhist is a faithful follower of the Eightfold Path. Mahayana Buddhists regard the Buddha as one of many who have appeared. They hold that the ideal Buddhist is a Bodhisattva, one committed to becoming a Buddha through the six virtues—generosity, morality, patience, vigor, concentration, and wisdom. The Tibetan Buddhists, here ready for the Tsam dance, hold to a mixture of Mahayana and Bönism.

7 The Wheel of Life, the great Buddhist symbol of *samsara*, is the endless round of birth and death in which all beings are trapped who have not pierced through the illusions of the ego and stilled its cravings. In other versions, the hub of the wheel depicts three animals representing lust (dove or cock), hatred (snake), and delusion (pig). These impulses generate a universe of conditioned existence.

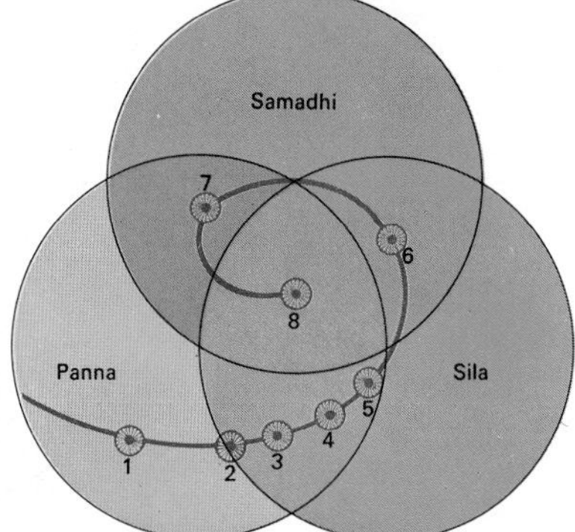
Samadhi
Panna
Sila
1
2
3
4
5
6
7
8

8 An Eightfold Path offers the Buddhist the only way to the blissful state of nirvana—release from the eternal cycle of rebirth. It is based on the fundamentals of Sila (morality), Samadhi (concentration), and Panna (wisdom), and its steps are right views [1], right intentions [2], right speech [3], right action [4], right livelihood [5], right effort [6], right mindfulness [7], and right concentration [8]. Several lifetimes are needed to reach nirvana.

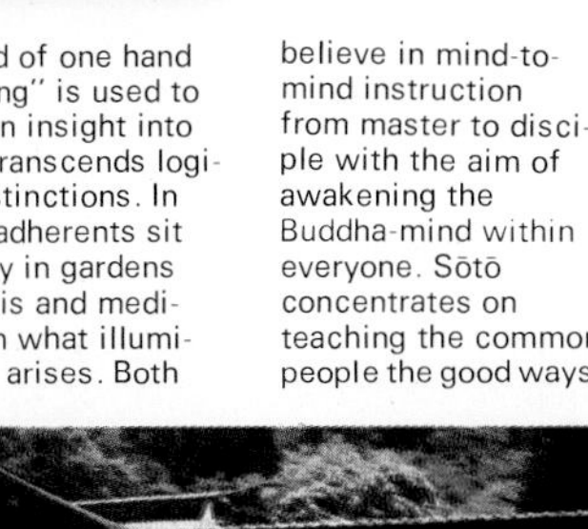

9 Zen Buddhism first flourished in China in the 7th century AD and then spread to Japan in the 12th. There are two main branches—Sōtō and Rinzai. In the latter, meditation on such paradoxes as the "sound of one hand clapping" is used to awaken insight into what transcends logical distinctions. In Sōtō, adherents sit silently in gardens like this and meditate on what illumination arises. Both believe in mind-to-mind instruction from master to disciple with the aim of awakening the Buddha-mind within everyone. Sōtō concentrates on teaching the common people the good ways.

Varieties of worship

Prayer might be defined as the method of communication with what is sacred in belief in an external or transcendent God [1] and meditation as the method appropriate to a religion such as Hinduism or Buddhism directed toward realization of the divine principle within [3]. The Hindu, however, prays before his chosen image of the Lord, and the Christian contemplative engages in an activity that is as much meditation as the "sitting" of a Buddhist monk.

Request, usually for oneself or for one's family or community, is one of the elements of prayer and the one that predominates among primitive peoples. While not denied in other religions, asking for favors in prayer is treated as subordinate to adoration, which is the offering of the whole being before God as well as confession of wrongs committed.

The nature of prayer and meditation

In the Islamic tradition, prayer [Key] is the fundamental right and responsibility of man by virtue of his central place in the cosmic scheme. By his profession of faith—"There is no God but Allah"—the Muslim directly affirms the truth of which all creation is an indirect expression.

In the Judeo-Christian tradition, prayer is the meeting of man and God. According to Hasidism, the Jewish mystical movement: "The people imagine that they pray before God. But this is not so, for prayer itself is the essence of divinity." Similarly, in the Christian tradition, prayer is an effort to find the place where a man is most himself, which is, by the mystery of love, the place where he is most related to God.

Each of the religious traditions presents man with the startling claim that he is not really what he takes himself to be. For example, Christianity has the parable of a rich man's son who squanders his inheritance but remains unchanged in the eyes of God. Hindu sages declare that the true Self is the infinite changeless Witness. Buddhism points to belief in a personal identity as the fundamental illusion that produces all suffering.

Traditionally, meditation is the "laboratory work" in which a man can come to know himself as he is. A relaxed awareness is regarded as a necessary condition of study, and the influences of the body that contribute to it are carefully taken into account. The Bhagavad Gita, one of the greatest texts of Hinduism, recommends a balanced posture for meditation—and the support of a balanced way of life. "Yoga is a harmony. Not for him who eats too much, or for him who eats too little; nor for him who sleeps too little, or for him who sleeps too much."

The inner mystery of scripture

Jewish mystics studied the Torah [8], the five books of Moses, to discover the divine law. Regarded in its mystical essence as the Name of God, the Torah was thought to serve as the instrument of creation. In Christianity it is Christ, the Word, who embodies the truth [9]. "Through Him everything came into being and without Him nothing that exists came into being" (John 1:3). The link between existence and revelation is found also in the Hindu conception of the Vedas, which, as scripture, record what ex-

CONNECTIONS

1 **An American Indian** at prayer exposed himself to the power of the Great Spirit in "crying for a vision." For this, he needed courage and determination. Guided by a wise man through preparatory rituals, he faced his vigil alone. All depended on his recognition of the depth of his need.

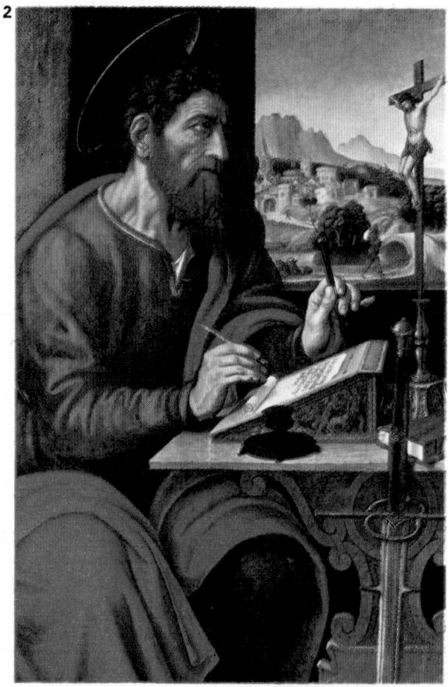

2 **A monastery** is like a laboratory where the conditions of life are arranged in such a way as to enable a man to face more directly the limitations of human nature and the need for supernatural help. Monasteries differ in their character and degree of asceticism, but communal discipline is vital in all.

3 **Hindu meditation** (the lotus posture is shown here) depends on an approach as impartial as that of any scientist making an investigation—"master of his mind, hoping for nothing, desiring nothing." Working in this way a seeker may witness in himself the operation of cosmic laws that govern the play of nature and, by knowing their true forces, disentangle himself from their control.

4 **The weighing of the soul** in the Egyptian *Book of the Dead* is connected with the idea of an exact science of man. Much Egyptian sacred art attempted to express in a statue of a god or goddess an impersonal cosmic principle, guiding the observer past idolatry to a deeper and truer understanding of himself.

5 **A Tibetan thanka,** or sacred temple banner, represents deities in precise postures, expressions, and coloring that will show the viewer a particular kind of awareness. In each painting there is an entire world, a subtle teaching and a benevolent influence for one who studies it. Yet in every case it is nothing other than the awareness of the viewer himself that is being discovered.

ceptional men have seen of the unchanging cosmic laws that govern all transformations of matter and energy. But the "eternal Vedas" are these universal laws themselves, to which the written record provides a key.

Yet, if there is in scripture a mystery corresponding to the mystery that is in man, it is not on the surface. According to tradition, scripture responds to a person's preparation and the level at which he experiences his need for transformation. When the disciples asked Jesus why he spoke in parables, the answer was a paradox: "For whoever has will receive abundantly, but whoever has not will be deprived of whatever he has" (Matthew xiii:12).

An indirect communication, scripture conceals and reveals its truth at the same time. Commandments and special regulations guide a person in all conditions of life, directing his energies and reminding him of God. According to the great medieval Jewish philosopher Maimonides (1135–1204), even the apparent contradictions found in the Bible are intended to lead the reader to search for a deeper meaning and understanding of religious truths than appears on the surface.

The value of sacred symbols

In the Koran [10], the sacred scripture of the Islamic faith, the phonetic and symbolic qualities of the Arabic language itself guide the seeker. Like all ancient sacred languages of revelation, Arabic is inherently symbolic. A single word can convey several levels of meaning. For this reason the Koran is considered untranslatable, since any rendering limits the meaning to whatever interpretation corresponds to the translator's level of understanding of the sacred writings.

Sacred art is a still more symbolic way of embodying truths that can make a deep impression on the inner man. Sometimes the artistic object is designed to embody a cosmic quality [4], sometimes to attract a spiritual influence [6], and sometimes simply to open the observer to a particular kind of awareness [5], as in a Tibetan temple banner.

KEY

The muezzin's call from the tower of a mosque reminds Muslims of the obedience they owe to Allah. Prayer involves a sequence of postures in which the individual stands, bows, and prostrates himself, so that his body shares the act.

6 The sacred art of black Africa has unusual qualities of mystery and power. A characteristic example is this altarpiece from an ancestral shrine of the Yoruba people of Nigeria. In most African sculpture the proportions of a figure are carefully determined by the artist but apparently without any attempt at a naturalistic representation of the human body. The aim of the traditional African artist is not to make an accurate likeness but to capture a quality so accurately that the figure or carving can attract the corresponding cosmic influence or house the spirit of an ancestor.

7 Miraculous power was attributed by many Christians to religious objects such as this 15th-century icon of the Russian Orthodox Church, depicting Jesus and his mother, Mary. According to an Orthodox writer, "An icon or a cross does not exist simply to direct our imagination during our prayers. It is a material center in which there reposes an energy, a divine force, which unites itself to human art." Unlike Western religious painting, which eventually developed individualistic forms of expression, icon art remained largely unchanging, its painters merging their identity with the sacred tradition.

8 The Torah, or book of Mosaic law (a rare Middle Eastern style is shown), and the religious observances it prescribes underlie Jewish life. The ancient scripture is regarded as sacred transmission from a higher source of a teaching that explains to man his covenant with God.

9 A portrait of St John from the illuminated manuscript the Irish Book of Kells probably dates from the 8th century. The medieval artist approached the scriptures with reverence, regarding them in their essence as revelation—an expression of the same creative intelligence that brought forth man and the universe itself.

10 The Koran may appear to the casual reader a confusing collection of stories, religious and social regulations, and enticing images of heaven. But the faithful Muslim can read in the Koran the historic struggles of his religion as a symbolic account of an inner war against the forces of dispersal in his own being.

Religion and modern man

CONNECTIONS

Read first
842 The nature of religio

See also
844 Judaism and Christianity
846 Islam, Hinduism, and Buddhism
848 Varieties of worship
1388 Modern Christianity and the New Beliefs
820 Meditation and consciousness
748 Nonmedical healing
818 Body image and biofeedback
824 Parapsychology

In recent years there has been evidence of renewed interest in the religious dimension of life. Some observers even speak of a twentieth-century "spiritual renaissance in the West." Much of this rebirth is, however, taking place outside the structures of the historic religious institutions. This new religious activity stems partly from efforts to bridge the gap between modern science and ancient spiritual world views, and partly from an eruption—particularly in the United States—of "new religions," most of them influenced by the religions of the Orient.

Knowledge and belief

The conflict between religion [1] and Western science [2] is exemplified by the debate over the theories of Copernicus (1473–1543) and Galileo (1564–1642) concerning the movement of the earth around the sun [Key]. The popular view is that the church regarded the Copernican-Galilean picture of the cosmos as a threat to the biblical conception of the earth as the unmoving center of the universe and that from then on the quest for knowledge of nature was at loggerheads with the demands of faith. Eventually the explanatory power and pragmatic successes of science overwhelmed the teachings of the church, and the scientific view prevailed.

According to this interpretation of events, the ideal of reason and knowledge triumphed over mere belief. In recent years, however, helped along by an influx of Oriental teachings, both the knowledge component of religion and the belief component of science have emerged more clearly.

Psychologists, for example, now generally recognize that the great mystics understood aspects of human nature that have eluded the vision of modern science. As a result, the whole idea of states of consciousness is becoming an increasingly important subject of research among Western psychologists [3]. The emphasis of inquiry is shifting away from pathological or hallucinatory states toward the study of states of consciousness characterized by increased general intelligence, moral power, and freedom from egoistic emotions. In the light of these studies, "normal" consciousness appears limited. Such a perspective is truly revolutionary, for a person's ability to perceive and explain is itself understood to be relative to his or her state. This challenges the orthodox scientific conception of reality much more decisively than any arguments from literal interpretations of the Bible. The point is that only by passionately embracing an inferior state of consciousness could mankind have arrived at its present dangerous predicament.

The key question

Other scientists are seeking to learn from the East. Some physicists are turning to Oriental conceptions of cosmic order, and medical scientists are studying ancient systems of healing, like Chinese acupuncture, that are rooted in a spiritual conception of human nature and a nonmaterialistic view of the universe. At the same time, many Westerners are practicing meditation—some within the Buddhist framework, others within the framework of Hinduism.

1

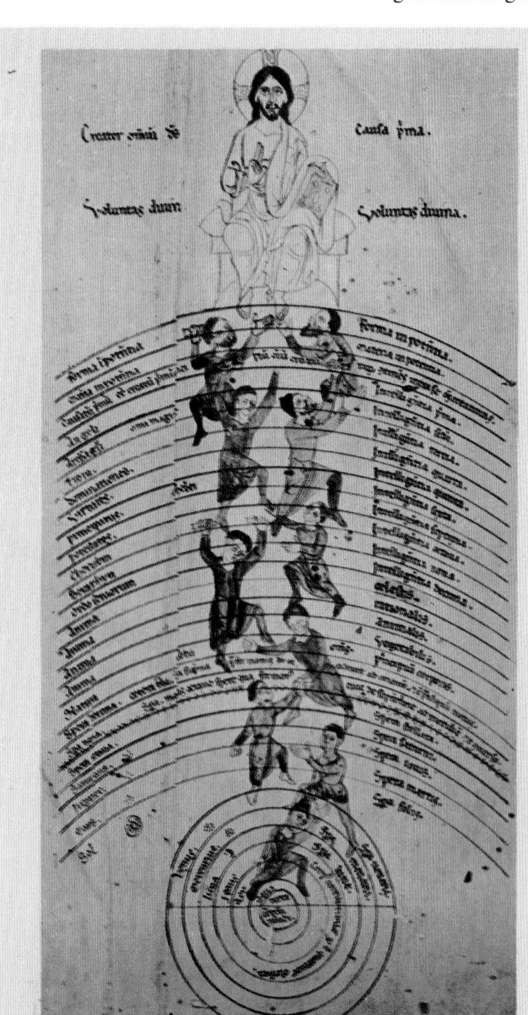

1 The ascent of the soul, as depicted in this 12th-century alchemical manuscript, shows a spiral progress toward God enthroned above the world. Reversing the original process of creation, the soul must pass through stages of gradual enlightenment as it travels outward from the material world. The view of a universe with the world at its center was not necessarily a naive astronomical theory. It was also, and mainly, a symbol of the idea that human life proceeds under the sway of many cosmic influences, both good and evil. Humans must master these to realize their divine destiny.

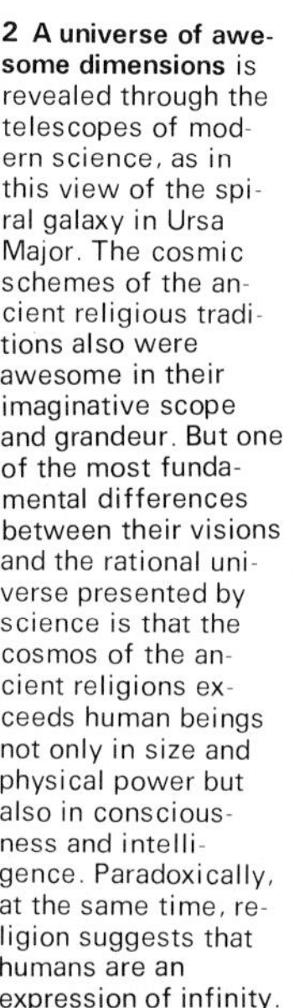

2 A universe of awesome dimensions is revealed through the telescopes of modern science, as in this view of the spiral galaxy in Ursa Major. The cosmic schemes of the ancient religious traditions also were awesome in their imaginative scope and grandeur. But one of the most fundamental differences between their visions and the rational universe presented by science is that the cosmos of the ancient religions exceeds human beings not only in size and physical power but also in consciousness and intelligence. Paradoxically, at the same time, religion suggests that humans are an expression of infinity.

2

3

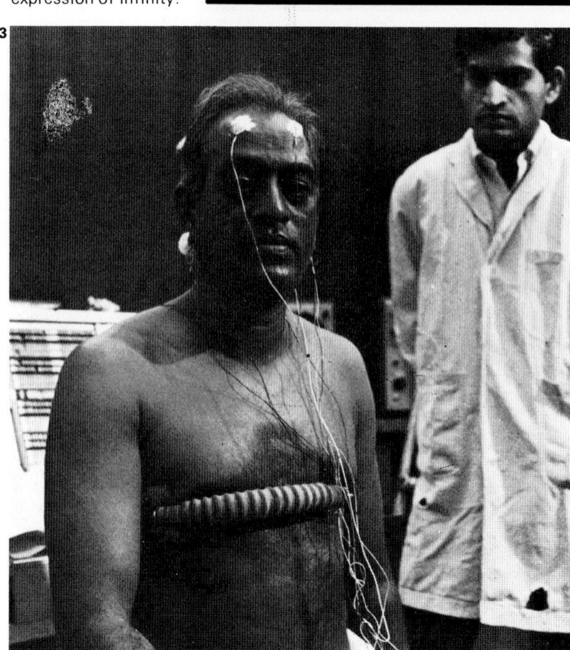

3 Experimental research is now being carried out to study the effects on the human organism of meditation techniques as practiced by experienced yogis. Many Western scientists now practice meditation. Their interest is an acknowledgment that mysticism may contain a knowledge of the human psyche that has eluded Western science. Yoga is an aid to meditation with a view to acquiring enlightenment. It involves attainment of a resting state of mind by the help of manipulation carried out not on the anatomical body alone but also on the inner perception of it in the brain. Paranormal changes in self-perception occur as a result.

Transcendental Meditation, for example, is a radical adaptation of certain aspects of the Hindu Vedanta system.

The question of critical importance is whether modern people can turn to meditation with the same intent as those who were helped by innumerable aspects of traditional culture, such as codes of morality that nourished the spiritual emotions. Will modern men and women make use of these fragments of ancient traditions in the same egoistic way that has characterized their use of the great modern scientific discoveries about the external world? Will they relate to their "inner environment" in the same way they have related to their outer environment?

The "new religions"

The ambiguities of the current "religious renaissance" are strikingly apparent in the "new religions" that have taken root in the past decade, particularly in North America and Great Britain. Thousands of groups, small and large, throughout the Western world have formed around one or another teacher who has migrated from the East [5, 6]. At the same time there has been a pervasive revival of Fundamentalist Christianity [4] that emphasizes emotional commitment to the person of Christ.

The followers of the "new religions," however, tend to accept only those parts of traditions that seem "relevant" or attractive. Can part of a tradition lead to a result that once required the complete tradition?

In the spiritual history of mankind, the tendency of the mind to select out of a teaching only those aspects that it likes, thereby creating a subjective religion out of a carefully interconnected totality, has always been a problem. It is one of the most fundamental meanings of the term "idolatry" in the Judeo-Christian teachings: man must not create his own god. Many of the teachers who have come to the West from Asia are wrestling with this question now. No one yet can say whether they will succeed in transmitting to modern people the workable essence of religion, while adapting the outer aspects to the modern temperament.

KEY

The church's battle with Galileo ended when he retracted his belief that the sun was at the center of the universe. The church's basic conservatism, revealed by its reaction to an issue that was largely irrelevant to religion, may have contributed to the gradual decline in organized religion.

4

4 Billy Graham (1918–) is typical of modern Fundamentalist Christian preachers, with his mixture of modern media methods and a simple Gospel message. He offers followers a form of intense religious experience that until recently was limited geographically and socially in advanced Western societies.

5

5 The Hare Krishna sect is one of the better known examples of "new religions" that have attracted many young Western people. Most US cities also have centers for the practical pursuit of Zen Buddhism. Lamas from Tibet have their followers and so has Islamic mysticism, or Sufism.

6

6 The Divine Light Mission, led by the Guru Maharaj Ji, is one of the "new religions" inspired in varying degrees by the ancient teachings of the Orient. The translation of an Eastern-style, endotheic religion, with all its strong cultural traditions, into the context and social environment of the Western industrialized world poses problems. For instance, are the forms by which truth was once transmitted applicable to modern life?

7

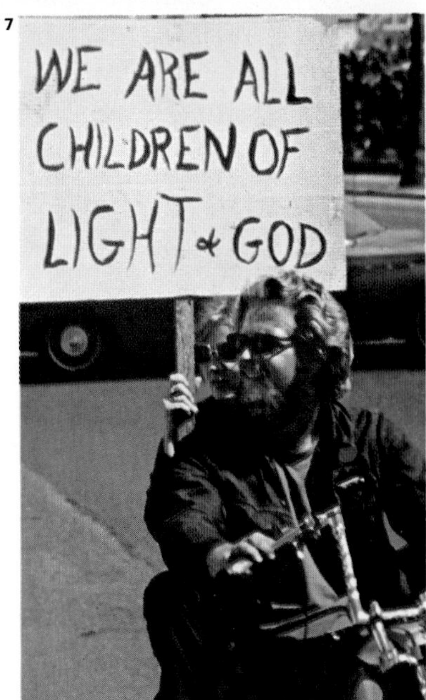
WE ARE ALL
CHILDREN OF
LIGHT & GOD

7 Rejecting the established structure of organized religion and returning to the essentially personal message of love and brotherhood has become one of the growth areas of religion in the West.

What is philosophy?

The word philosophy has almost as many meanings as there have been philosophers. In its broadest sense, every man or woman who exists is a philosopher and has evolved a philosophy: a point of view, an opinion of the world and of how life should be lived. By extension the word philosophy has come to include the personal qualities—calm, balance, the capacity for reflection or detachment—that laymen expect of a philosopher or sage.

In the strict meaning of the word, however, philosophy is a technical study of human thought and knowledge. The word has its roots in a Greek expression meaning "love of knowledge," and students who wish to become "lovers of knowledge" are required to embrace a discipline as rigorous as its subject is potentially vast.

The fields of philosophy
Because philosophy is concerned, directly or indirectly, with almost everything in the known universe, its practitioners have found it necessary to break it down into a number of smaller, although often overlapping, studies: epistemology, or the study of the origins, nature, and limitations of knowledge; metaphysics, the search for reality beyond what we know from our senses; ethics, the study of how men should behave toward each other; and logic, the study of the rules and methods of correct reasoning.

Thus, philosophy stands between the sciences and religion. Like science it appeals to reason rather than authority, whether traditional or revealed, but is not solely concerned with a knowledge of the facts. Like theology, it consists of speculations on matters about which definite knowledge is not—at least so far—possible.

Philosophical method
In the primary, technical sense, philosophy is essentially argumentative, and it is concerned largely with abstract questions that may often seem tiresomely hair splitting and of little practical value. For example, is the world divided into mind and matter, and, if so, what are they and how do they differ? What is "good," and must it be eternal to be valued? Are there laws of nature, or do we invent them to satisfy our innate sense of order? Concern with questions of this kind is what preoccupied those philosophers who are considered important in the European tradition, such as Plato (*c.* 427–*c.* 347 BC); Aristotle (384–322 BC); Thomas Aquinas (*c.*1225–74); René Descartes (1596–1650); Gottfried Leibniz (1646–1716); David Hume (1711–76); Immanuel Kant (1724–1804); G. W. F. Hegel (1770–1831); and in our own day, Bertrand Russell (1872–1970) and Ludwig Wittgenstein (1889–1951). The same concern is shared by the Persian Avicenna (980–1037), the Arab Averrhoës (1126–98) [7], and the Indian Sankara (*c.*800).

Socrates (*c.*469–399 BC) [Key] in Europe and Confucius (*c.*571–479 BC) in China were both outstanding teachers of a philosophical way of life. But Socrates was also a philosopher in the technical sense. He spent his life arguing and teaching in the market place of Athens. Characteristically, in his dialogues he raised and pressed questions about virtues or values, such as "What is justice?" He introduced the idea

CONNECTIONS

See also
854 Logic and the tools of philosophy
856 Philosophy and religion
858 Fields of philosophy
860 Philosophy and ethic
842 The nature of religio
1040 Confucius and Confucianism

1 **Plato,** in the *Republic*, compares those who live by conventional wisdom and who are dominated by their senses and appetites to prisoners living in an underground cave, chained since childhood, so that they can see only what is directly in front of them. A fire behind them throws the shadows of objects on to the wall. Our knowledge of ultimate reality is as incomplete as those prisoners' would be. It is only through philosophy and intelligent reflection that we can escape from this world of shadows of puppets and see true realities. Anyone returning to the cave to describe such realities would be ridiculed.

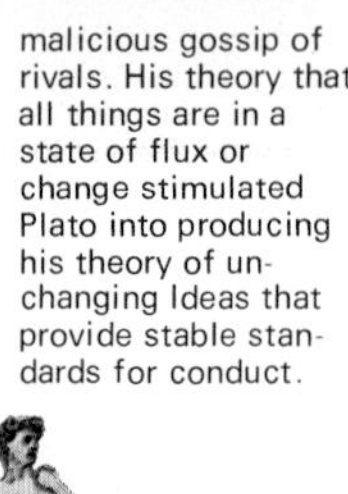

2 **Heraclitus** flourished about 500 BC in Ephesus. As with all other Greek pre-Socratic philosophers, any knowledge of his ideas has to be squeezed from a few surviving fragments and the often malicious gossip of rivals. His theory that all things are in a state of flux or change stimulated Plato into producing his theory of unchanging Ideas that provide stable standards for conduct.

3 **Plato's One-Over-Many Argument** applies to every general word, whether material such as tree or abstract such as piety. "Tree" may describe a number of different examples. These change, and none of them is perfect, but still we recognize the general class. The Form or Idea is eternal, unchanging, incorruptible, and immaterial. It is somehow simultaneously both more real and more ideal than any particular manifestation. These perfect Forms can never be attained in the everyday world and can only be known by the intellect, not the senses. True knowledge is therefore the knowledge of Forms. Plato is not clear as to whether particular examples are caused by the Forms or are a shadowy likeness.

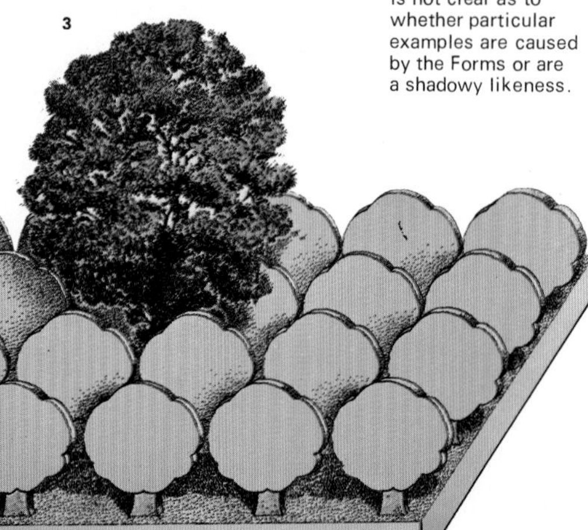

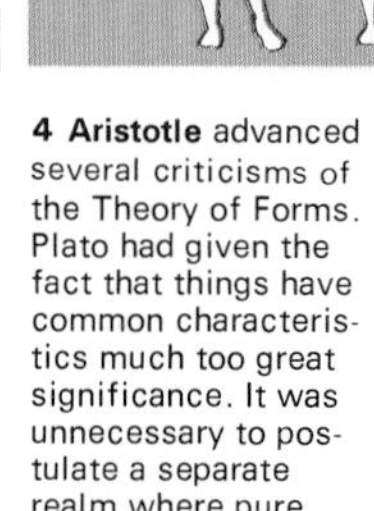

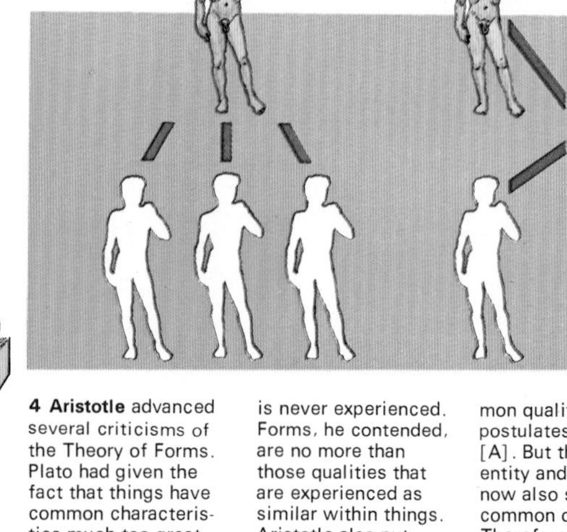
A
B

4 **Aristotle** advanced several criticisms of the Theory of Forms. Plato had given the fact that things have common characteristics much too great significance. It was unnecessary to postulate a separate realm where pure being exists and that is never experienced. Forms, he contended, are no more than those qualities that are experienced as similar within things. Aristotle also put forward the well-known Third Man argument. Wherever two entities are discovered with a common quality, Plato postulates a Form [A]. But the original entity and the Form now also share a common quality. Therefore, we have to postulate yet another Form in which they both share [B]. This process can be extended infinitely.

of universal definitions that could be arrived at by arguing from particular examples. Often there are no definite conclusions from his dialogues, but the aim remains the same —to arrive at answers about meaning and logical presuppositions and implications through the medium of argument.

The gap between appearance and reality

The search for universal definitions is triggered by the need to discover what things, if any, we can know with absolute certainty. Generally, people are aware that there is a gap between appearance and reality. In a world where one of the most salient characteristics is change or flux, how do we gain knowledge of the "real"?

Plato, a pupil of Socrates, identified flux with appearances or what we "know" through our senses, appetites, and emotions. Reality, then, is something other than that which is perceived by our senses—the so-called Theory of Forms, or One-Over-Many Argument.

Plato argued that what is common to things described by the same name, such as *trees,* is their Form or Idea [3]. The Form represents being, the particular examples of that form represent becoming, and these two realms are separate. Plato's arguments are illustrated by curiously haunting imagery. His four ultimate levels of existence (and therefore of knowledge) constitute a hierarchy. These levels correspond to the four sections of what Plato called the Line, which he divided first into two unequal parts with each then subdivided in the same proportions. At the top are Ideas and the knowledge of them; immediately underneath, the purest of pure mathematics. For Plato this ideal world is alone truly real. A long way below falls our everyday world: physical objects on top and, under these, shadows. To move from lower to higher is to pass from shadow to substance.

Yet any such move, up or down, is disturbing. To be confined to the nether region is to be like a prisoner in a cave [1], seeing nothing but shadows cast by artificial light. For the released prisoner it hurts at first to look at things in the sunlight, and still more to confront the sun itself.

KEY

Socrates frequented the market place in Athens, spending his time—to the annoyance of his wife—arguing and challenging the conventional wisdom of the day rather than earning a living. Few could stand up to his style of cross-examination and he made many enemies. Eventually, he was convicted of corrupting youth and being irreligious and was sentenced to death. He could have escaped but argued that it would be inconsistent with all that he had taught. He drank poison hemlock and died comforting his friends.

5 The problem of universals, or words like "man" that apply to many examples, has three differing explanations. For the Realists, like Plato, universals are entities called Forms or Ideas [A], that exist independently of the instances of them. The universal idea of man is more real than the particular men who exist in the world. For Conceptualists [B] universals are purely concepts in the minds of men, so the universal idea of man comes after and is based on particular men. The Nominalist [C] holds that every concept is a specific individual concept—there is nothing in its nature that makes it general.

5

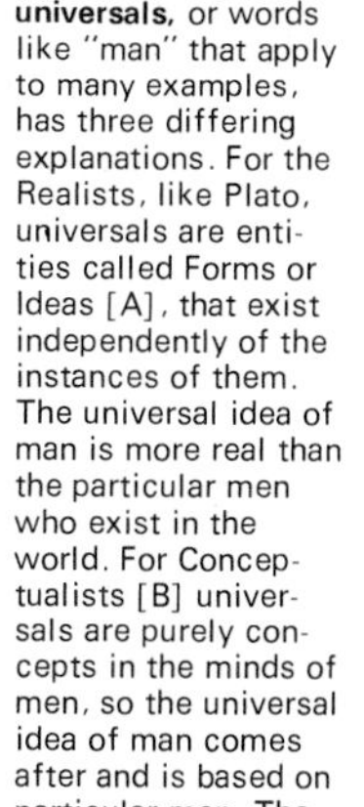
A

B
C
MAN

6

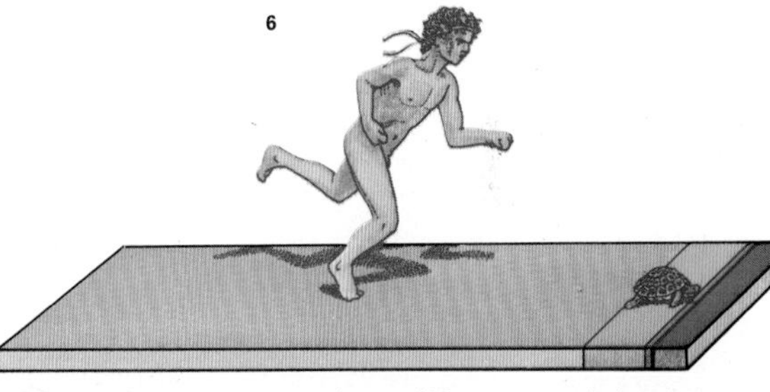

6 Zeno of Elea (*fl.* 475 BC) questioned the notions of time, motion, and change. Achilles can run ten times as fast as the tortoise, who has a ten-unit start. When Achilles has run his first ten the tortoise will be one ahead. When Achilles has run that one the tortoise will be one-tenth ahead. And so on. Logically, Achilles cannot win, despite our senses, because Zeno defines the race mathematically.

7

A

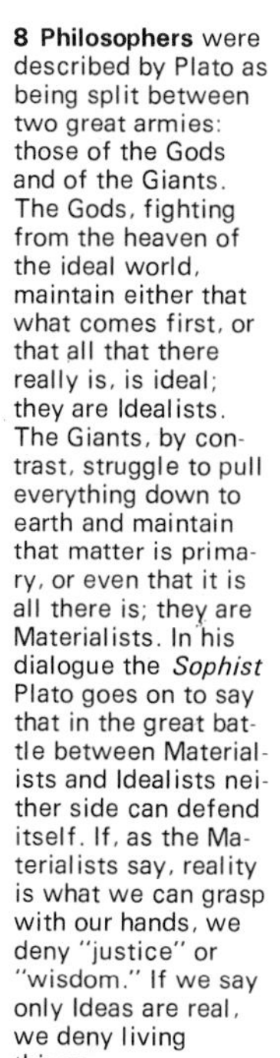
B

7 Avicenna (980–1037) [A] and Averrhoës (1126–98) [B] were Islamic philosophers. Two centuries before Aquinas, Avicenna attempted an Islamic scholasticism, a synthesis of the best of ancient Greek philosophy with the teachings of Mohammed. Some of his work was attacked as heretical, but later both the Jew Maimonides and the Christian Aquinas adopted Avicenna's suggestion that in God essence and existence are one. Averrhoës, born in Moorish Spain, became best known in Christendom for commentaries on Aristotle. Translations of these were at one time regularly bound up with Latin versions of Aristotle's *Works.* He founded the Muslim philosophy of religion.

8

8 Philosophers were described by Plato as being split between two great armies: those of the Gods and of the Giants. The Gods, fighting from the heaven of the ideal world, maintain either that what comes first, or that all that there really is, is ideal; they are Idealists. The Giants, by contrast, struggle to pull everything down to earth and maintain that matter is primary, or even that it is all there is; they are Materialists. In his dialogue the *Sophist* Plato goes on to say that in the great battle between Materialists and Idealists neither side can defend itself. If, as the Materialists say, reality is what we can grasp with our hands, we deny "justice" or "wisdom." If we say only Ideas are real, we deny living things.

Logic and the tools of philosophy

Logic as a discipline was invented by Aristotle [Key]. No doubt people had been reasoning in logical and consistent ways long before Aristotle, but he seems to have been the first to attempt to spell out and formalize the rules of valid inferences [1].

Logic is concerned less with truth or falsity as such than with the transmission of truth or falsity from one set of statements (the premises) to another (the conclusion). Its central concepts are logical consequence and valid inference. If some statement *q* is a logical consequence of a statement *p*, then if *p* is true, so is *q*; if *q* is false, so is *p*. An inference is valid if the conclusion is a logical consequence of the premises from which it was inferred.

Invalid inferences

In the classical form of the syllogism, with two premises and a conclusion, one example of an invalid inference is known as "the fallacy of undistributed middle": All cows are animals, all herbivores are animals; therefore all cows are herbivores. Here the premises are true, and so is the conclusion, but only accidentally, not by logical necessity. That the inference is invalid can be shown by choosing replacements for each of the descriptive terms in such a way that although the premises remain true, the conclusion is false. Thus: All men are mortal, all gorillas are mortal, leads to a false conclusion—all men are gorillas.

Some famous proofs in the early development of mathematics were *reductio ad absurdum* proofs, in which a proposition is proved by showing that its denial, combined with other true propositions, would lead to an absurd conclusion.

As late as 1787, Immanuel Kant declared that since Aristotle's time "logic has not been able to advance a single step and is thus to all appearance a closed and completed body of doctrine." But in the nineteenth and twentieth centuries there were many developments in mathematical logic.

Aristotelian logic could handle only very limited kinds of deductive reasoning. For instance, Euclidean geometry had long been regarded as a superb example of deductive reasoning; yet Aristotelian logic could say almost nothing about its validity.

Kant had endowed mathematical knowledge with a special status essentially different from that of both physics and of logic. Since Kant's view implied that no alternative to Euclidean geometry was conceivable, it became untenable when non-Euclidean geometries were developed. John Stuart Mill (1806–73) tried the alternative of interpreting mathematics as a part of empirical science, but there were overwhelming objections to this interpretation. A remaining alternative was to interpret it as a branch of logic. It was Gottlob Frege (1846–1925) who first undertook the task of showing that all pure mathematics is deducible from premises that contain only logical terms and are logically true. (This program is known as logicism.) Bertrand Russell (1872–1970) [2] discovered, however, that the logical foundations of mathematics contained paradoxes.

Paradox and truth

Logic requires an adequate concept of truth

CONNECTIONS

See also
1088 European learning in the 13th century
1458 Sets and groups
852 What is philosophy?
856 Philosophy and religion
858 Fields of philosophy
860 Philosophy and ethics

1 In Aristotelian logic, propositions containing two terms are classified into four kinds (A, E, I, and O) and displayed in a Square of Opposition. Propositions labeled A are universal and affirmative (All men are brave); E are universal and negative (No men are brave); I are particular and affirmative (some, meaning one at least, men are brave); O are particular and negative (Some men are not brave). Specific relationships of truth and falsehood follow from the positions in the square of statements referring to the same two entities. Thus, if proposition A (All men are brave) is false, then its contradictory, O (Some men are not brave), must be true; while A's contrary, E, could be either true or false and is undetermined, according to Aristotelian logic, in these relationships.

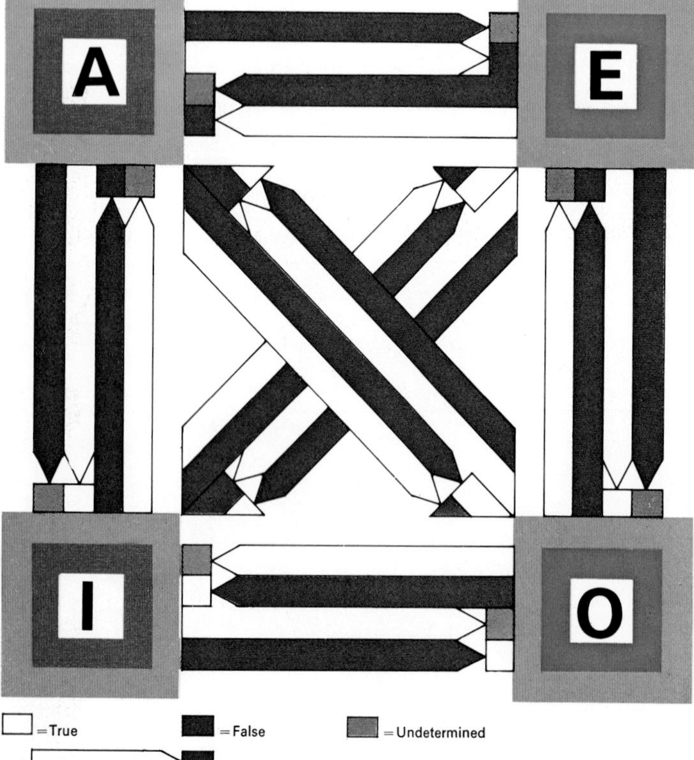
A
E
I
O
=True
=False
=Undetermined
A
E=When A is true, E is false

2 Bertrand Russell (1872–1970) was joint author with Alfred North Whitehead (1861–1947) of *Principia Mathematica.* Their main aim was to show that mathematics was ultimately reducible to logic. That is, every true mathematical statement should be shown to be deducible from premises containing only logical concepts and that are logically true. Their logical system dissolved the traditional Aristotelian distinction between subject and predicate. Russell's theory of descriptions translates the subject-predicate sentence "The King of France is bald" into: "There is an *x* such that *x* is King of France and for all *y*, if *y* is King of France then *y* is *x*; *x* is also bald."

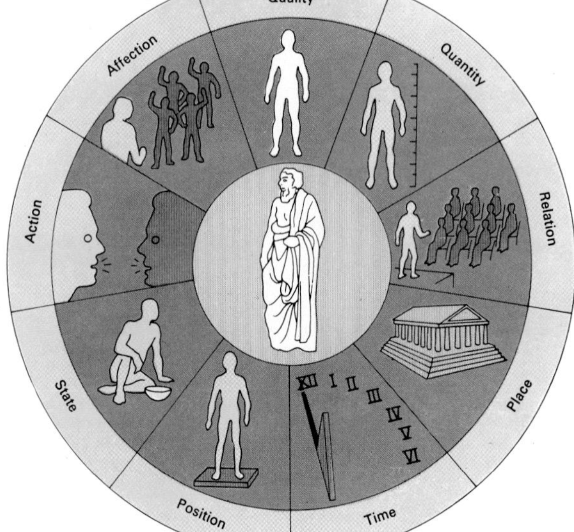
Quality
Quantity
Relation
Place
Time
Position
State
Action
Affection
XII I II III IV V VI

3 "Category" is a key word in philosophy. Aristotle introduced it first as a label for ten items he took to be fundamental and irreducible in human discourse. These items are first, substance (what any statement is about) and next, the nine kinds of statement that can be made about it. For example, Socrates, the central substance in the diagram, can be discussed in terms of quality (he is wise), quantity (he is short), relation (he is the teacher of his students), place (in the Agora), time (at midday), position (he is standing up), state (he is poor), action (he is arguing), and lastly, affection (he is being verbally abused by some of the students). The study of language was an important philosophical pursuit for Aristotle, and his attempt to define its component parts in this way has been followed by many other logicians concerned with the nature and relationships of substances.

[6] since it deals with the transmission of truth. But the traditional theory of truth had paradoxes. One of these, the Cretan Liar, had been known in antiquity. The statement "This statement is false," if true, is false, and if false, is true. A similar paradox arises as follows. Some adjectives (for example "polysyllabic" and "short") possess the property they denote. These are called "homological." Others (for example, "monosyllabic" and "long") do not. These are called "heterological." Is the adjective "heterological" itself heterological? If it is, then it is not; if it is not, then it is.

Alfred Tarski (1902–   ) eliminated such paradoxes with his semantic theory of truth, which involved a sharp separation between an object-language (the language that speaks directly about objects) and a meta-language (the language in which the object-language is spoken about).

But when such difficulties can be found in mathematics and logic, the problems of establishing a coherent system of thought and then using it to establish scientific truths become obvious. For argument from experience is very different from valid inference, in which the truth of a conclusion can be proved to be logically necessary because denial would involve a contradiction. David Hume (1711–76) pointed out that since the conclusion of a valid inference can contain no information not found in the premises, there can be no valid inference from observed to unobserved instances. Thus many laws of science, and nearly all common sense beliefs, are logically unjustified. This is the essential problem of induction faced by philosophers.

Testing scientific hypotheses

One attempted solution, associated with Karl Popper (1902–   ), is to abandon any sort of justifying inference from evidence and to ask of scientific hypotheses that they be subjected to searching attempts to falsify predictions derived from them. If such attempts are successful, the hypothesis has to be rejected. If the hypothesis withstands testing, we may not conclude that it is true (the fallacy of affirming the consequent) but we may nonetheless retain it.

KEY

ΑΡΙΣΤΟΤΕΛΟΥΣ

Aristotle (384–322 BC), one of the greatest philosophers, founded logic as an academic discipline. For a time he tutored the boy who was later to conquer the known world, Alexander the Great. Aristotle directed the first program of research in comparative political science. He both systematized and advanced biological studies. He founded and led the Lyceum (the second university) after withdrawing from the first—Plato's Academy. Medieval scholars spoke of Aristotle as "the master of those that know." So in the 1500s and 1600s his name became for all the pathfinders of the new science the epitome of traditional conservative thinking.

4

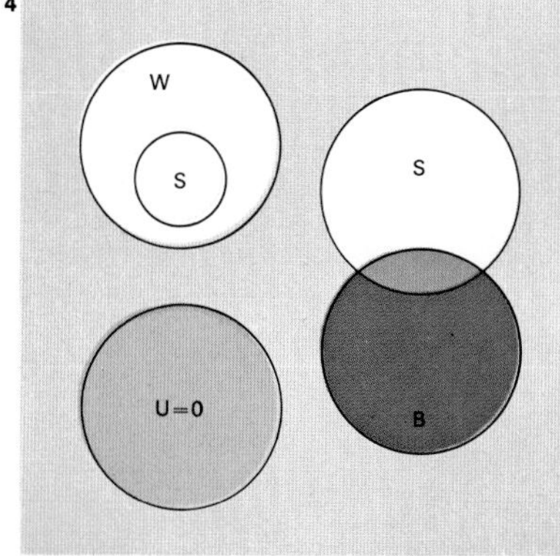
W
S
S
U=0
B

4 Venn diagrams are devices for the visual representation of logical relations. If all swans [S] are white [W] and not all white things are swans, the S circle must be wholly within the W circle. If some swans [S] are black [B] and not all black things are swans, the S circle must overlap the B. If all unicorns [U] are one-horned [O] and all one-horned creatures are unicorns, then the U and O circles must coincide exactly.

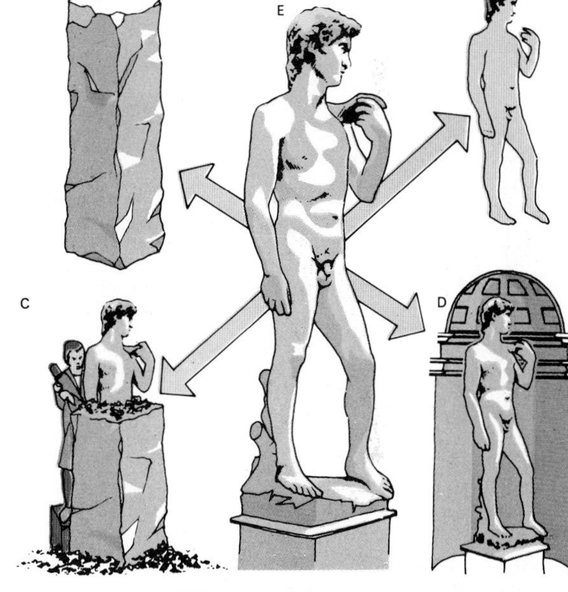
5 A
B
C
D
E

5 A Doctrine of Four Causes was proposed by Aristotle as a means of framing fundamental questions about material and form, means and end. He labeled these four Material, Formal, Efficient, and Final. Of a statue [E], for example, the Material cause is stone [A], its Formal pattern is that of a man [B], its Efficient cause is a sculptor [C], and its Final end is as part of a decorative frieze [D]. In Aristotle's terminology, the Final Cause is not necessarily someone's conscious intention. The Final Cause of a fetus, for instance, is to achieve its intrinsic end by developing into an adult organism.

6 A

B

6 A necessary condition of knowledge is that the statement expressing it be true. There are a variety of theories concerning the ways that the truth of a statement can be verified, of which coherence and correspondence are two. In the coherence theory [A] statements are judged to be true if they form a coherent system in conjunction with other propositions—like the pieces of a jigsaw that one knows to be "right" because they interlock to form a whole. In the correspondence theory [B], a proposition is judged to be true only if there is a fact such as the proposition asserts. Hence the meaning of truth is correspondence with fact—each part of the jigsaw matches part of the known whole.

7 A

B

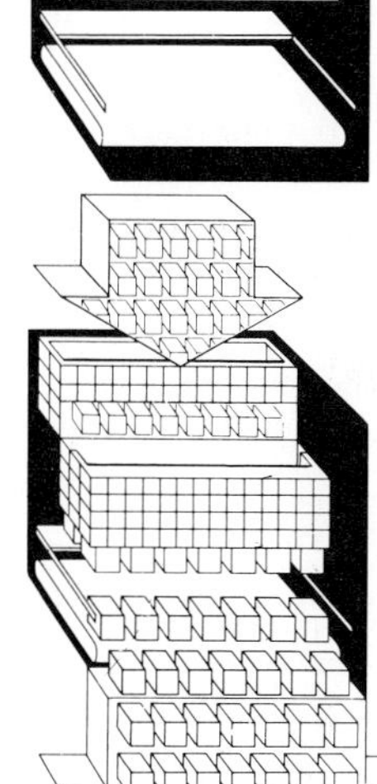

7 The mind was seen by empiricist philosophers such as John Locke (1632–1704) as rather like an empty box [A] "void of all characters, without any ideas." According to this view, human knowledge has to be derived from whatever experience comes flowing in, and the box develops an internal structure only gradually. Against this picture of open mindedness, Immanuel Kant (1724–1804) held that the mind brings a prior system of categories to the organization and interpretation of sensory data. Kant's box [B] therefore has its own structure, imposing order on the intrinsically unknown or disorderly materials of experience though influenced by it.

Philosophy and religion

Religion and philosophy are not the same thing. Nor are they rivals fighting to occupy the same ground, although philosophical conclusions may support or deny religious claims and philosophical questions can arise from religious beliefs.

The impact of St Thomas Aquinas

The philosopher and theologian St Thomas Aquinas (*c.*1225–74) [Key], claimed that the existence of God could be proved in five ways. He was responding to the challenge of newly-revived Aristotelian studies, with their underlying question: "Is there any need to go beyond whatever may be the most fundamental laws of nature?" Aquinas started from broad and uncontentious premises: that in our universe we find causation, motion, order, and so on. He argued that these presuppose that there must be a "first cause," a "Prime mover," a "great orderer," which men call God."

His "first cause" was not defined as that which started things off "in the beginning." Rather it was the ultimate sustaining cause, operating now and for as long as causation continues [2]. Aquinas maintained that it was not possible to prove by philosophical argument that the universe did in fact have a beginning. That was something to be accepted simply on faith, as being taught by the Holy Catholic Church. He argued that philosophy is based on reason and that there is no conflict between faith and reason.

Aquinas's argument that God's existence is demonstrated by familiar general facts took no account of distinctions that were set out later by David Hume (1711–76) [7]. Hume attacked the whole idea of natural (as opposed to revealed) theology: that is, the attempt to reach conclusions about God and the soul through philosophy.

A popular argument, based on human experience, holds that there cannot be order without design. But Hume argued that even if this were true to the facts of, say, biology, the universe as a whole was by definition unique; and so man could have no experience of the origin of the universe. So why not say that its observed order is the order of the universe itself and not one imposed upon it by an outside Power?

Descartes and the Cartesian philosophy

Where Aquinas held the existence of God to be implied by general facts about the world, René Descartes (1596–1650) [3] inverted the argument. He believed that these facts could not be known without a knowledge of God. In order to find unshakeable foundations for knowledge, Descartes began by systematically doubting everything he could. This left him certain only of his own existence as a being incapable of doubt: "I think, therefore I am" ("*Cogito ergo sum*"). Accepting that the idea of God was so perfect that only a perfect God could have caused it to arise, he concluded that his own God-given senses would not deceive him provided they were properly employed. This is the Cartesian answer (Descartes' philosophy is known as Cartesian) to how we can know that there is an external world.

For one of his proofs of God's existence, Descartes drew on an argument that attempts to move directly from the definition of the word "God" to the conclusion that this definition must have its appropriate ap-

CONNECTIONS

See also
1088 European learning i[n] the 13th century
1184 The Enlightenment
852 What is philosophy?
854 Logic and the tools o[f] philosophy
858 Fields of philosophy
860 Philosophy and ethic[s]
842 The nature of religio[n]

1

2

1 Scholastic philosophy was the preserve of monks and priests in medieval times. This 12th-century manuscript shows Bede at work. The teaching was subject to the authority of Christian theology.

2 To explain why the light is burning, something needs to be said both about switching it on and about the continuing flow of current. The former is the initiating, and the latter the sustaining, cause.

The five ways of Aquinas were intended to prove that the universe has a Creator, in the sense of a sustaining cause: without His support all creation must collapse into nonexistence.

3

3 René Descartes is considered the philosopher who ended the medieval period and initiated the modern period of philosophy. He created analytic geometry and did innovative work in physics. Descartes broke the hold that theology had on philosophy by beginning systematically to doubt everything he had been taught in school. He then resolved to believe nothing that was not logically necessary, regardless of the prestige of any belief. He noted that it was not always possible to perceive things clearly and that one must never rely on empirical knowledge. Yet he was certain that he existed, and so his philosophy is based on knowledge of the self.

4
A

B

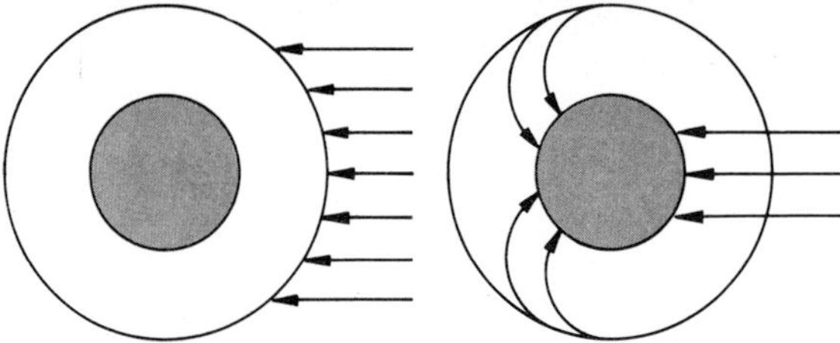

4 From his own consciousness Descartes then proceeded to contend that he was just an immaterial object of consciousness and to discover how such a being knew what was going on around him. As all other animals were to be regarded as machines, he had to ask how it was proved that human machines were inhabited. His answer was their ability to think [A]. From this Descartes argued that the external world (arrows) included not only that which lay outside the body, but also the body itself [B]. Man was, therefore, essentially not the body but the spirit inhabiting it (shaded). Gilbert Ryle (1900–) characterized this view as "the ghost in the machine."

plication. God is defined as embracing all perfections; existence is a perfection; therefore God must exist.

If it were valid, this "ontological argument" would provide the foundation for which every philosophical Rationalist has longed. The three classical Rationalists—Descartes, Leibniz, and Spinoza—made the most of it. Rationalism in this sense is contrasted with Empiricism [5]. The Rationalist hopes to produce a deductive system consisting, like pure geometry, of logically necessary truths—but truths that, unlike those of pure geometry, tell us about the universe and ourselves. The Empiricist believes this is a will-of-the-wisp, insisting that there can be no real knowledge that does not refer to actual experience of the world.

Philosophy of religion

The philosophy of religion deals mainly with questions of how religious beliefs can be both coherent and significant. Thus Gottfried Leibniz (1646–1716) in his *Theodicy* (1710) tried to solve the problem of evil by showing that it is not inconsistent to say that evil exists and that God is perfect. His key idea was that some virtues logically presuppose some evils [6]. For example, it is impossible, both as a matter of fact and of logic, to forgive unless there is an injury to be forgiven. And since there is a perfect God (assuming the validity of the ontological argument) actual evils ultimately must have a justification. It therefore follows logically that this is the best of all possible worlds. Existentialism [8] sees human "essence" controlled by existence.

Some religious philosophers have urged that the idea of personal survival and immortality is senseless. Followers of Plato and Descartes believe that men are composed of two elements, body and soul, of which the immaterial soul is truly the person. But followers of Aristotle insist that words like "mind" and "personality" refer to the qualities and capacities of a unitary organism. To suggest, therefore, that the mind or the personality might survive the death and dissolution of the organism is absurd.

KEY

Thomas Aquinas was born in Italy. Against the objections of his family he entered the Dominican Order, in which his whole life was devoted to study and teaching. Canonized in 1323, he was proclaimed a Doctor of the Church in 1567. By the papal bull *Aeterni Patris* (1879) of Pope Leo XIII his works were given special status in the training of priests. Of these works the most important are the *Summa contra gentiles* and the *Summa theologica*. Aquinas was always concerned with the relations between faith and reason and with assimilating into a new Christian synthesis the then recently rediscovered works of Aristotle.

5 A

B

5 Rationalists, in the technical sense of the word, see all sound knowledge as an inverted pyramid [A]; everything else depends on and is to be deduced from a few fundamental, self-evident, and necessarily true principles. Their Empiricist rivals favor instead a structure built upon a broad base of observations of how things actually are; each truth rests on a wide foundation [B].

6

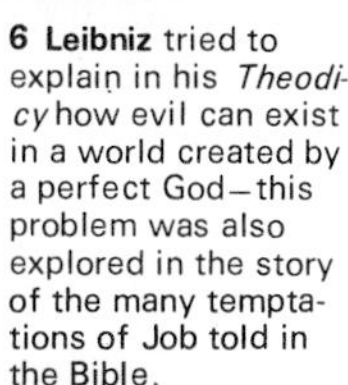

6 Leibniz tried to explain in his *Theodicy* how evil can exist in a world created by a perfect God—this problem was also explored in the story of the many temptations of Job told in the Bible.

7

7 David Hume was most famous in his own time for what was then the best-selling *History of England*. His *Treatise of Human Nature* was the first comprehensive radical work of philosophy written in the English language; however, it was the later *Inquiry concerning Human Understanding* and the posthumous *Dialogues concerning Natural Religion* that so strongly influenced Kant.

8 A

B

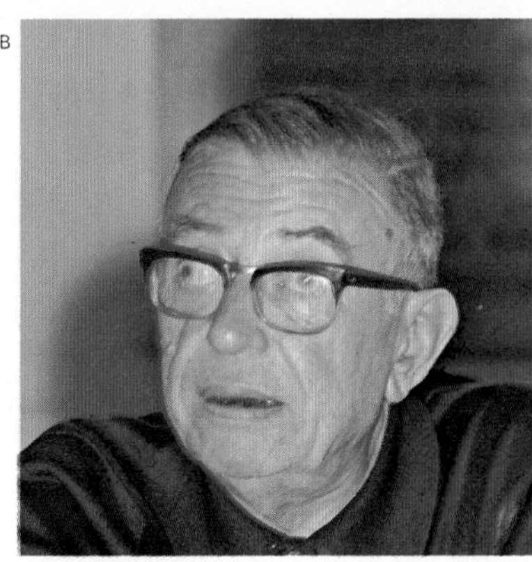

8 Two of the most influential Existentialists were Sören Kierkegaard (1813–55) [A] and Jean-Paul Sartre (1905–) [B]. A main feature of Existentialism is that it sees human essence, or what we are, as being determined by our existence, or what we do. Implicit in this attitude is the notion that existence is always prior to essence and therefore what we make of our lives is always and absolutely determined by our choices. The Existentialism of Sartre has been atheistic.

Fields of philosophy

Philosophy is classically divided into the major fields of logic, the theory of knowledge (epistemology), metaphysics, ethics, and aesthetics. Each of these fields has a set of concepts that constitutes its subject matter [Key].

Elements of metaphysics

Some important concepts discussed in metaphysics are existence, essence, space, time, self, God, cause, event, change, permanence, determinism, and free will.

The question of free will and determinism is a battleground shared by the philosophies of many disciplines. Because the issues are so easily clouded, this is an area where the philosopher is needed and can make a significant contribution. The genuine issues are, as always, issues of meaning, presupposition, implication, compatibility, and incompatibility. How far are the apparently deterministic presuppositions and implications of work in this or that specialist field compatible or incompatible with everyday common sense assumptions about action and choice?

Ordinarily we do not think the world changes randomly. We think that some kinds of events are regularly followed by other kinds. One we call the cause, the other the effect. A law states a causal relation; for example, that mercury expands when heated.

Determinism and free will

Determinists, such as Baruch Spinoza (1632–77), say that every event has a cause, including choices, decisions, and human actions. It follows that man does not have free will. Libertarians, such as Henri Bergson (1859–1941), argue that moral responsibility is not possible in a wholly determined universe. We cannot blame or praise a person for an act if they could not have done otherwise. Libertarians must, therefore, try to show that the will is not invariably predetermined and that there is an element of self-determination in our actions, choices, and decisions.

The views of David Hume (1711–76) are particularly relevant to the problem of causation and of free will. His criticism of the idea of necessary causal connections is one of the landmarks of the history of philosophy. Hume's thinking can be illustrated by the example of one billiard ball striking another. Hume denies that there is a power in the first ball that causes the second ball to move and says that our idea of such a causal relation is only the projection on to the billiard balls of a subjective feeling produced in us by experience of the repeated conjunction of events. Objectively, a causal law is just a matter of regular succession.

The theory of knowledge

Some important concepts discussed in epistemology are knowledge, truth, theory, method, evidence, and analysis.

Knowledge and truth (and falsity) are two concepts intimately interconnected. We can be said to know something only if what we believe is true. I cannot say that I know 5 + 7 = 11 because that equation is false and because the idea of false knowledge is self-contradictory. It would seem, then, that I cannot say I know anything unless I can also say that I know that what I

CONNECTIONS

See also
852 What is philosophy?
854 Logic and the tools of philosophy
856 Philosophy and religion
860 Philosophy and ethics

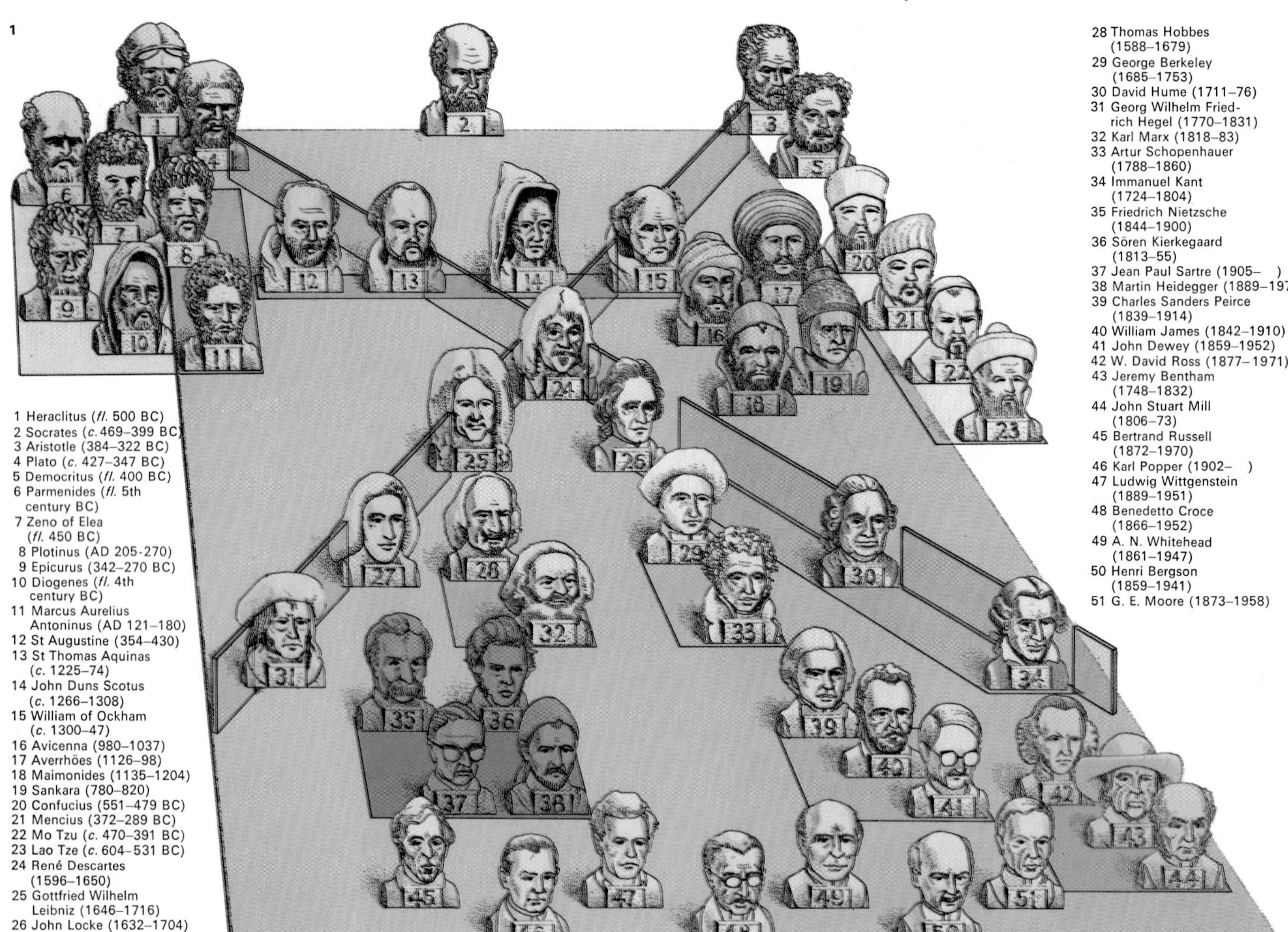

1
1 Heraclitus (*fl.* 500 BC)
2 Socrates (*c.* 469–399 BC)
3 Aristotle (384–322 BC)
4 Plato (*c.* 427–347 BC)
5 Democritus (*fl.* 400 BC)
6 Parmenides (*fl.* 5th century BC)
7 Zeno of Elea (*fl.* 450 BC)
8 Plotinus (AD 205-270)
9 Epicurus (342–270 BC)
10 Diogenes (*fl.* 4th century BC)
11 Marcus Aurelius Antoninus (AD 121–180)
12 St Augustine (354–430)
13 St Thomas Aquinas (*c.* 1225–74)
14 John Duns Scotus (*c.* 1266–1308)
15 William of Ockham (*c.* 1300–47)
16 Avicenna (980–1037)
17 Averrhöes (1126–98)
18 Maimonides (1135–1204)
19 Sankara (780–820)
20 Confucius (551–479 BC)
21 Mencius (372–289 BC)
22 Mo Tzu (*c.* 470–391 BC)
23 Lao Tze (*c.* 604–531 BC)
24 René Descartes (1596–1650)
25 Gottfried Wilhelm Leibniz (1646–1716)
26 John Locke (1632–1704)
27 Baruch Spinoza (1632–77)
28 Thomas Hobbes (1588–1679)
29 George Berkeley (1685–1753)
30 David Hume (1711–76)
31 Georg Wilhelm Friedrich Hegel (1770–1831)
32 Karl Marx (1818–83)
33 Artur Schopenhauer (1788–1860)
34 Immanuel Kant (1724–1804)
35 Friedrich Nietzsche (1844–1900)
36 Sören Kierkegaard (1813–55)
37 Jean Paul Sartre (1905–)
38 Martin Heidegger (1889–1976)
39 Charles Sanders Peirce (1839–1914)
40 William James (1842–1910)
41 John Dewey (1859–1952)
42 W. David Ross (1877–1971)
43 Jeremy Bentham (1748–1832)
44 John Stuart Mill (1806–73)
45 Bertrand Russell (1872–1970)
46 Karl Popper (1902–)
47 Ludwig Wittgenstein (1889–1951)
48 Benedetto Croce (1866–1952)
49 A. N. Whitehead (1861–1947)
50 Henri Bergson (1859–1941)
51 G. E. Moore (1873–1958)

1 Classifying philosophers is not an easy task, but this chart does bring out a few major similarities and dissimilarities, as well as a few major lines of development. The Chinese [20–23] are shown as peripheral if only because their work is not, in the strict sense, philosophical. The Greeks are placed first and at the top because they created the Western philosophical tradition. Aristotle [3] and Plato [4] stand out from the rest in both influence and achievement. After the collapse of the old pagan world, thinkers labored for centuries to reconcile its philosophical achievements with, and to put them at the service of, religion: Christians such as Augustine [12], Aquinas [13], Duns Scotus [14], and Ockham [15]; and also Maimonides [18] in Judaism and Avicenna [16] and Averrhöes [17] in Islam. Descartes [24] is at the center as it was he who, in philosophy, made the modern world. Descartes made the epistemological problem fundamental: Do we know, and if so how, anything of the universe? One line of development then passes through Locke [26], Hume [30], and Kant [34] with the emphasis on discovering the nature and limitations of our learning apparatus. Another line, by way of Leibniz [25], Spinoza [27], and Hegel [31], takes up Descartes's Rationalism. The Existentialists [35–38] can be seen as reacting against a rationalist picture of the world, as can the Pragmatists [39–41], who were concerned with practical bearings. Of the 20th-century group Wittgenstein's [47] works are perhaps most discussed by philosophers. Russell [45] was most in the public eye, but it is Popper [46] whose ideas are most influential.

say is true. What do I have to know in order to know that some proposition is true? Three major theories of truth are correspondence, coherence, and pragmatic certainty.

One view is that what I am thinking—that the apple before me is red, for example—is true because it corresponds with the fact of the apple's being red. There are two difficulties with this view. The first is that I only experience the sensory effect that the supposed red apple has on me, never the red apple itself.

Since there are no observable facts to correspond with $7 + 5 = 12$, this equation's truth has to be explained in another way. The coherence theory would do so by calling attention to the logical relation it has to other equations. Thus, since $5 = 3 + 2$, and $7 = 3 + 2 + 2$, and $(3 + 2) + (3 + 2 + 2) = 12$ all cohere, and because $5 + 7 = 12$ coheres with them, we may take $5 + 7 = 12$ to be true.

The American pragmatists Charles Peirce (1839–1914) and John Dewey (1859–1952) held that our knowledge of truth is acquired through a process of verification. Our thought about the redness of the apple enables us to anticipate its ripeness, and so, further, to anticipate its sweetness. Verification of truth is accomplished when a future experience is in accord with what we predicted.

Other sets of concepts that philosophers study can be classed under the heading of "philosophy of" such as the philosophies of art, of language, of politics, of history, of science, of law, and of mathematics.

Philosophy has links with both arts and sciences, influencing them and being influenced by them. Pure mathematics, for example, inspired the Rationalists. Of these, René Descartes (1596–1650) and Gottfried Leibniz (1646–1716) were themselves also major creative mathematicians; while Plato (*c.*427–347 BC) stimulated generations of philosophers to think of mathematical entities, such as numbers and geometrical relationships, as timelessly existing. Both Newtonian physics and Darwinian evolution have been major influences on philosophical thinking.

KEY

Logic
argument
validity, proof
definition, consistency

Epistemology
knowledge, truth
theory, method
evidence, analysis

Metaphysics
existence, essence
space, time, self
God, cause

Ethics
good, right, duty
responsibility
utility

Aesthetics
beauty, art, taste
standard, judgment
criticism

The traditional labels for branches of philosophy are all more or less unsatisfactory because what earns its place under one heading will often serve under another. Metaphysics is defined as the search for fundamental categories. Ultimately what sorts of things are there? Epistemology asks whether we know, what we know, and how we know. Answers to general epistemological questions are thus in one aspect metaphysical or have metaphysical presuppositions and implications. Logic is the study of valid and invalid forms of argument. Philosophical ethics investigates basic characteristics of moral action. Aesthetics deals with appreciation of beauty. Shown here are some of the concepts examined.

2
Medieval scholastic
Materialist
Idealist
Monist
Dualist
Determinist
Chinese philosopher
Empiricist
Libertarian
Existentialist
Stoic
Hedonist
Utilitarian
Deontologist
Teleologist
Sceptic
Pragmatist
Rationalist

2 Philosophers can also be divided according to where their strongest interest lies. Within the field of metaphysics, materialists believe that matter is all that exists, in contrast to idealists who hold that matter is an illusion. Monists believe that only one kind of ultimate stuff exists, while dualists maintain there are two kinds—mind and matter. Determinists hold that events are caused by other events and are predictable according to laws; libertarians believe that there are uncaused events—human free will. In epistemology, the study of knowlege, the empiricists trace the truth of propositions to observations and experience; positivists are extreme empiricists, claiming that anything that is neither a part of logic and mathematics nor of empirical science is meaningless. Rationalists claim humans have innate ideas that are prior to experience and necessarily true. Pragmatists claim that knowledge comes from practical action. Skeptics deny that any knowledge is possible because our senses and reason are so misleading. In ethics a teleologist maintains that the concept of good is more basic than right (a right action is determined by its consequences). The deontologist holds the opposite—an action is right or wrong regardless of the value of the consequences. Utilitarians measure the goodness of an act by its utility. Hedonists maintain the only thing good in its own right is the experience of pleasure or the absence of pain. Stoics emphasize the practical aspect of philosophy as a guide to living. Existentialists maintain that man's existence precedes his essential nature, which is not given to him but is made by him in the choices he makes.

Philosophy and ethics

Philosophical ethics is concerned with how men should behave and involves consideration of such concepts as good, right, duty, responsibility, and punishment.

The concepts of good and right

There are many definitions of what constitutes "good." Naturalists identify the concept of good with the concept of some natural, psychological feature. Hedonists say this feature is pleasure, others that it is the object of desire, and still others that it is the satisfaction of a need. Non-naturalists dispute these definitions. Plato (*c*.427–347 BC) pointed out that there are morally bad pleasures and that if pleasures and good were identical we would have the self-contradictory notion of a bad good.

In discussing "right" some philosophers assert that the concept of good is more fundamental than the concept of right. To say of an act that it is right is to say that it is productive of a greater balance of good over evil than any other act open to the agent. Typical of those who hold this view are the Utilitarians [4].

Opposed to this view are those who say that right cannot be defined in terms of good. Otherwise it would be possible to judge the punishment of an innocent person as right because by deterring crime it produced a balance of good over evil.

The characteristics of moral discourse

To be genuinely moral, discourse must have several characteristics. First, it is prescriptive as opposed to descriptive [1]. That is, it contains statements about what ought to be rather than what is. From the confusion of these two comes the Naturalistic Fallacy of invalidly deducing an "ought" statement from an "is" statement. One popular form of this fallacy is the move from saying that something is natural (in the sense that it happens or tends to happen) to the conclusion that anything else would be unnatural and wrong, in the sense not that it *will* not happen, but that it *ought* not to happen.

This seems obvious once clearly stated. But it is quite another thing to see all the implications of this ought/is dichotomy. Obviousness is essentially relative to time, place, and person. It was not obvious to Aquinas (*c*.1225–74) when, if only temporarily, he overlooked the crucial difference between those Laws of God that are the scientists' Laws of Nature and cannot be "disobeyed," and those Laws of God that are prescriptive laws that rule human conduct but are at times ignored or breached.

Not all prescriptive utterance is moral. Immanuel Kant [Key] distinguishes the Hypothetical from the Categorical Imperative. The former may suggest a course of action in certain cases but is never absolutely categorical, in contrast to a moral imperative such as "Thou shalt not kill."

Kant further suggested that there are two other conditions that distinguish the authentically moral. The first of these two conditions is universality. If anything is to count, not necessarily as a correct moral principle but as genuinely moral, it has to be a principle applicable universally and impartially. If one claims that the use of chemical weapons or torture is immoral, this claim must be universally applied; to protest

CONNECTIONS

See also
852 What is philosophy?
854 Logic and the tools of philosophy
856 Philosophy and religion
858 Fields of philosophy
1040 Confucius and Confucianism
808 Questions of life and death

1 A prescriptive law states that some action ought or ought not to be done. Transgression of such a law, for which the woman taken in adultery was condemned to be stoned [A], does not prove that the law itself is invalid. A law of nature, by contrast, claims to be a description of a state of nature and stands or falls by whether or not it is "transgressed." The stargazer [B] who observes something that confounds a law of nature must record that the law does not, after all, hold true. He is the spectator, speaking a language of non-participatory description, whom Kant, in his examination of practical reason, contrasts with man as active agent. He says that when we abandon the role of spectator our language ceses to be neutral, and we begin to ascribe values to what we see.

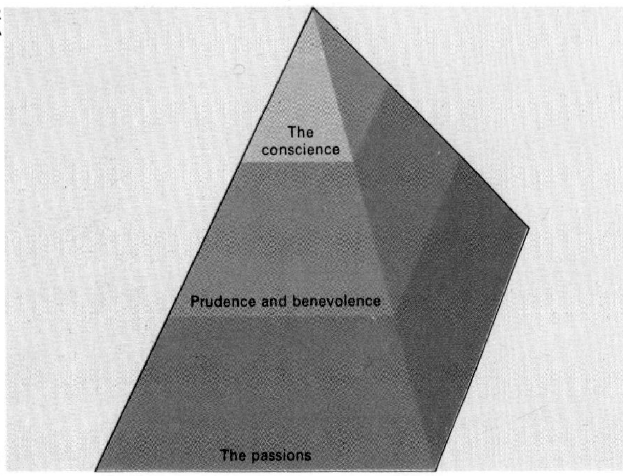

The conscience
Prudence and benevolence
The passions

2 Joseph Butler (1692–1752) appealed to the notion of a self-evidently authoritative hierarchy in the principles of our nature [A]. Just as the passions are subordinate to prudence and benevolence, so these in their turn must be subordinate to the rational and reflective control of conscience. By comparison, Plato's *Republic* represents the Man of Reason [B], controlling (with assistance from the Lion of Self-assertion) the Monster of Passion.

against offenses by those regimes to which one is politically opposed, while remaining silent about those regimes that one favors politically, is not to voice an authentically and sincerely moral protest.

Kant characterizes the second of his two formal conditions for rating discourse as moral rather awkwardly. He maintains that moral discourse has to be autonomous as opposed to heteronomous. The idea is that each person must somehow impose his own moral principles on himself in contrast to external laws, which are imposed from without. It is often rightly remarked, however, that all such legislation is also in principle subject to the moral assessment of the individual: "I know that this is the law, but is it right, ought it to be the law?"

The problems of subjectivism

The problem is to retain this notion of autonomy without succumbing to some form of subjectivism. In the strictest sense, a moral subjectivist holds that moral words do no more than express the reactions of the person who is using them. But the social "subjectivist" may also, by extension, be one who defines moral words in terms of the class or tribe to which the speaker belongs.

Clearly, any moral argument between two strict subjectivists is impracticable, just as it is between two people, one of whom says "I like chocolate" whereas the other says "I don't like chocolate." The more social subjectivist, who has extended the principle of autonomous moral discourse to groups, can at least argue that a group dispute may be settled by a simple vote. If the subjectivist were right the ought/is distinction must collapse.

These conflicting approaches, if rigidly held, would make effective moral argument impossible. Any universal moral principle, however, unless susceptible of modification by the proposer, will have consequences unforeseen by him, and it is this fact that makes moral argument possible. One of the major purposes of a critical moral discussion is to expose such unacceptable consequences and thus persuade the proposer to amend or abandon the offending principle he supports.

KEY

Immanuel Kant (1724–1804) lived in the East Prussian city of Königsberg (Kaliningrad). He was raised in the traditions of Leibnizian rationalism, and his own distinctive "critical philosophy" was a response to the challenge of Hume's radically skeptical Empiricism. Kant's three main works *(Critique of Pure Reason, Critique of Practical Reason,* and *Critique of Judgment)* set out to find the nature and limitations of human capacities or knowledge. Kant emphasized the contribution of the knower to knowledge, whereas Locke and Hume spoke of materials from the external world impressing themselves upon an originally blank mind.

3 Friedrich Nietzsche (1844–1900), seen with his mother, was a philologist who broke with the established conception of ancient Greek culture in his first book *The Birth of Tragedy. Thus Spake Zarathustra,* his most famous work, argues that the "will to power" is the primary human drive. Anti-Christian polemics become progressively more central in his books, in which critics discern signs on his madness.

4 John Stuart Mill (1806–73) was an intellectual leader of the Philosophical Radicals. Active in all liberal causes, he produced the libertarian classic *On Liberty* and works on economics, logic, and ethics. Following Jeremy Bentham (1748–1832), he argued for ethical Utilitarianism–a moral doctrine governed by the idea of the "greatest happiness of the greatest number."

5

5 Jonathan Edwards (1703–58) was the first major philosopher born in North America. Just as Aquinas had seen his mission as the incorporation of the best of ancient Greek philosophy into a new Catholic synthesis, so Edwards labored to incorporate Newton and Locke into a revived Calvinism. In philosophical psychology his *Religious Affections* anticipated much of William James' *Varieties of Religious Experience.*

3

4

6 Mencius (372–289 BC) was both in his life and thought extraordinarily similar to Confucius. Born in the same province, both lived as professional moral teachers. Both shared concerns for filial piety and for established rites, and both respected the Sage Kings. Both agreed that "Once the ruler is rectified, the whole kingdom will be at peace," a statement from the *Book of Mencius.* It was Mencius alone, however, who made explicit and defended his conviction that human nature is essentially good. Apart from his teaching, urged many practical reforms.

6

7 Confucius (551–479 BC) was born in what is now Shantung. His ideas became the greatest single force shaping traditional Chinese civilization, though his thought was not philosophical in the Western sense. When, for example, Tzu Kung asked him whether the True Way could be epitomized in a word, Confucious replied: "Is not reciprocity the word? Do not to others what you do not want them to do unto you." But he never made an attempt to show that this is an essential element in what distinguishes some categorical imperatives as moral.

7

Communication without words

People communicate with each other—talk without words—in many ways other than by speaking or writing. Animals build complex societies by means of nonverbal communication, and humans reveal a surprising amount about themselves through gesture, posture, facial expression, and other behavior. Several thousand pieces of information can be exchanged within seconds.

Ways of expressing emotion

In addition to outward facial and bodily signals, including the use of costume and adornment, there are less obvious means of communication—a person's use of time and space, for example. Touching [5] and distance or nearness of approach can reveal much about a relationship. Punctuality may convey eagerness. On the other hand, a person who keeps someone else waiting may convey an impression of busyness that may be either genuine or false.

It seems likely that nonverbal communication preceded speech, and probably a nonverbal system of expression was important to human cultural and social development in prehistoric times. More than a century ago Charles Darwin (1809–82) suggested that emotions help a species to survive and that feelings such as happiness, sadness, fear, anger, surprise, and disgust all have unique forms of display.

While the expression of these emotions looks similar in all humans [2], cultures differ in the degree to which emotional displays are encouraged or discouraged. In many Western societies, for example, men are not supposed to cry, and women are discouraged from showing extreme anger.

Accurate reading of emotion from the face is complicated by the human ability to control expressions by masking some feelings and fabricating the appearance of others [1]. In addition, many facial displays last only an instant. Displays may also be partial—occurring on only one area of the face [3]—or they may combine two or more emotions in one expression [4]. People differ in ability to decode expressions.

Specific emotions are even more difficult to read from body posture. But overall attitudes, positive or negative, are easily recognizable [Key, 6]. Interest or disinterest is shown by whether the body is erect or slouching, leaning backward or forward. Attraction or dislike is revealed by approach or avoidance. Status is indicated by the assumption of a higher or more dominant position in a group.

The significance of gestures

Gestures can be classified in a number of ways. According to one classification system, adaptors are movements that, at least originally, helped man to adapt to his environment. Scratching, wiping, and fondling are examples. Regulators are movements that guide the flow of speech or contact between people; nods and eye signals are used, for example, to encourage a speaker to continue or to indicate a wish to interrupt. Conversation without regulator gestures (as when someone does not react at all to what is said to him or her) can be disconcerting. Illustrators are movements that help to elaborate, punctuate, and clarify speech. Emblems have specific wordlike meanings and often replace words and phrases.

CONNECTIONS

See also
818 Body image and biofeedback
864 Communication through speech: 1
464 Principles of animal behavior

1

1 Facial expressions in both humans and primates show many similarities. The smile is usually a sign of happiness. But it is also one of the easiest expressions to "put on" and may be used to conceal real feelings of fear, anxiety, or dislike. The tense grin adopted by a chimpanzee when approaching a more dominant male chimpanzee closely parallels the nervous smile a person may wear in a stressful social situation [A]. In both, the expression is meant to demonstrate lack of hostility. When aggressive or angry [B] both primate and human display a stare and, at least initially, a firmly closed mouth.

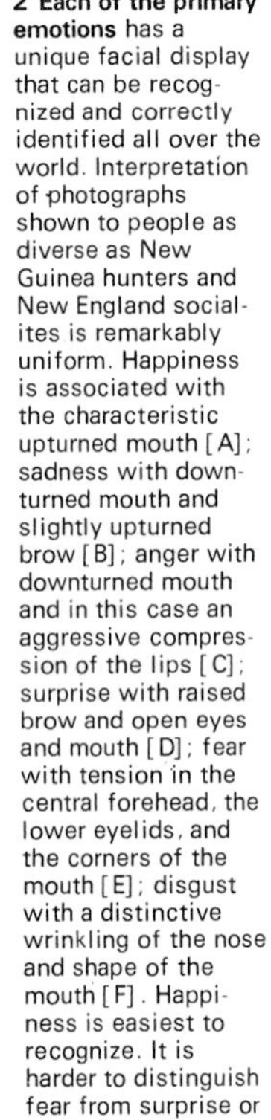

2

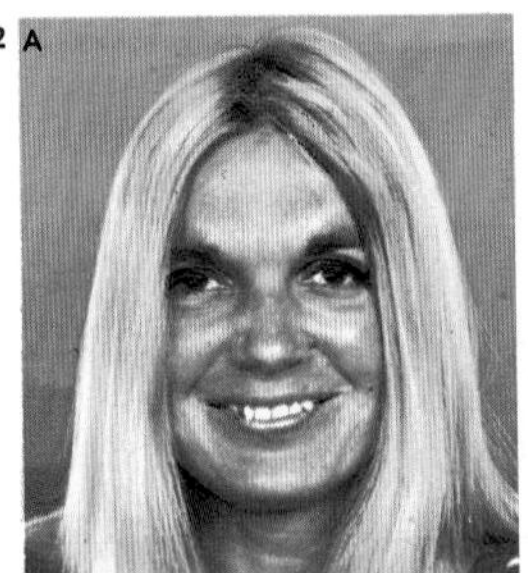

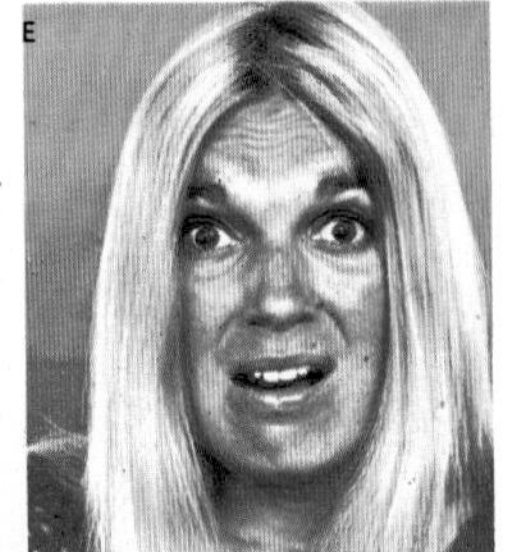

2 Each of the primary emotions has a unique facial display that can be recognized and correctly identified all over the world. Interpretation of photographs shown to people as diverse as New Guinea hunters and New England socialites is remarkably uniform. Happiness is associated with the characteristic upturned mouth [A]; sadness with downturned mouth and slightly upturned brow [B]; anger with downturned mouth and in this case an aggressive compression of the lips [C]; surprise with raised brow and open eyes and mouth [D]; fear with tension in the central forehead, the lower eyelids, and the corners of the mouth [E]; disgust with a distinctive wrinkling of the nose and shape of the mouth [F]. Happiness is easiest to recognize. It is harder to distinguish fear from surprise or to distinguish anger from disgust.

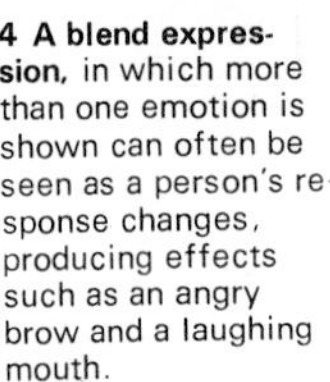

4

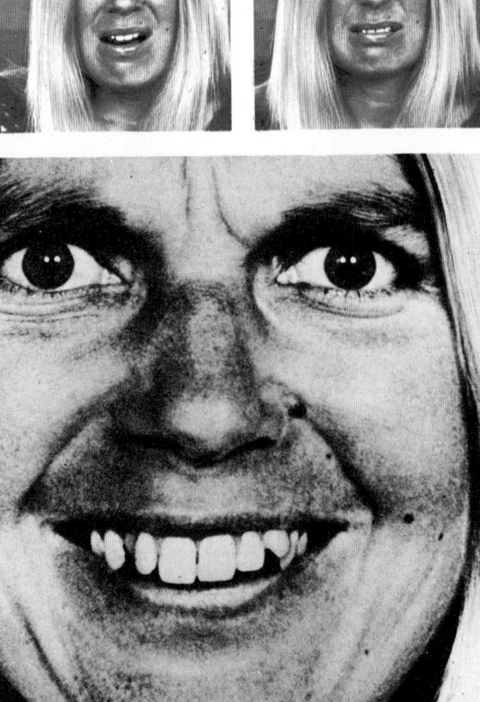

4 A blend expression, in which more than one emotion is shown can often be seen as a person's response changes, producing effects such as an angry brow and a laughing mouth.

3

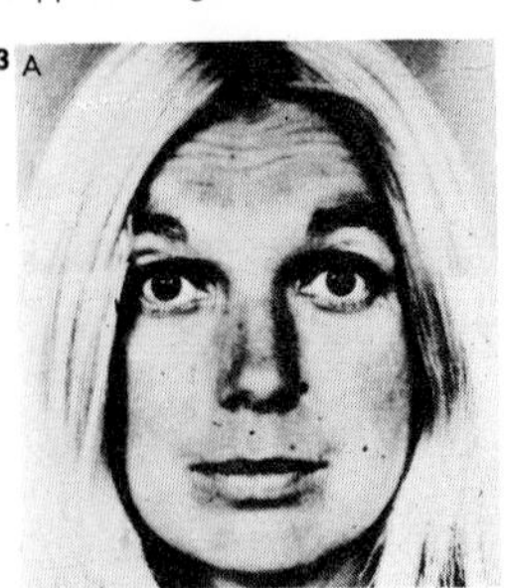

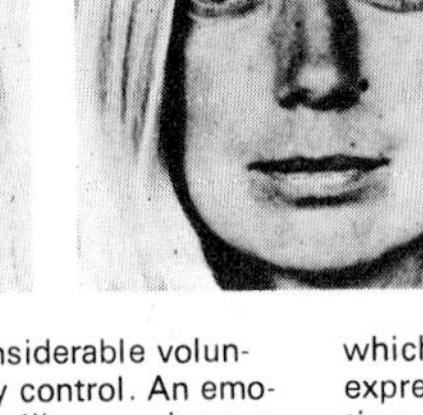

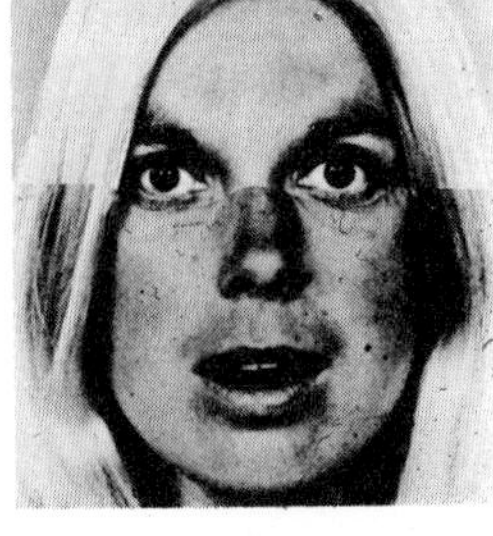

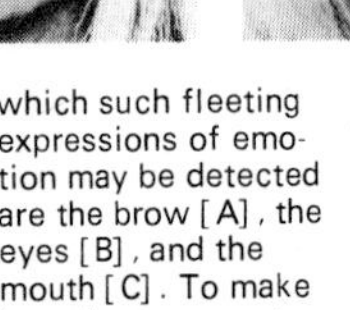

3 Partial expressions are more difficult to interpret than full-face displays of emotion. The human face is tremendously flexible and is under considerable voluntary control. An emotion like surprise may thus appear in only one part of the face and then only briefly. The main areas in which such fleeting expressions of emotion may be detected are the brow [A], the eyes [B], and the mouth [C]. To make it easier to separate the characteristic signs of surprise, each feature is here superimposed on a neutral face (compare illustration 2D).

Adaptors are often used unconsciously with no intention of communicating anything, although an observer may find them informative. A psychotherapist, for instance, may notice that a person fiddles with his hands when a troublesome topic is broached.

Regulators are also used with little awareness. In many cultures gestures of greeting serve as more conscious regulators. The appropriate bow, handshake, hug, or kiss must be delivered before conversation can take place. In societies in which rigid forms of social behavior exist greeting rituals are usually elaborate.

Illustrators are classified into subcategories such as pointers, indicating which object is being discussed; spatials, indicating size or space relationships; batons, used for punctuation or emphasis; pictographs, outlining or portraying an object; ideographs, tracing the flow of an idea; and kinetographs, reenacting some bodily movement. It was once argued that illustrative gestures were innate. A pioneering work by David Efron in New York showed that gestures did differ between eastern European Jews and southern Italians. But it showed also that these gestures changed in second-generation immigrant groups. Thus illustrators, like language, are learned.

Emblems are usually employed consciously to communicate. Examples include the direction-indicating thumb of the hitchhiker and the two-finger "V" for victory (or peace) signal. The significance of emblems differs sharply from one language to another [7, 8]. The American "A-OK" gesture, with forefinger and thumb forming a circle, for instance, has vulgar, derogatory connotations in many parts of the world.

Advances in modern technology have made nonverbal messages increasingly important, especially in visual media such as television and films. There has been a corresponding increase in research into the ways in which these communication patterns have evolved and are used in different cultures today. The term kinesics has been applied to the study of body movement, and efforts have been made to analyze it in the same way as linguists analyze language.

KEY

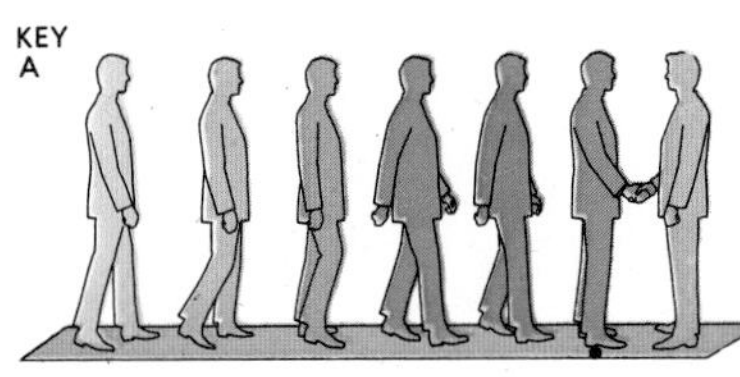
A

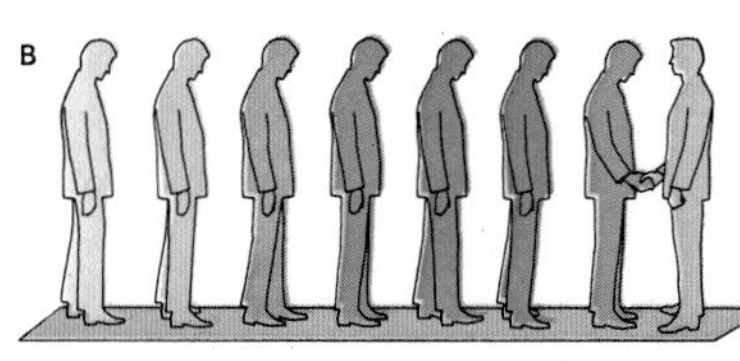
B

C

When people meet their posture and movements can reveal a great deal about their emotional state. Usually, when a man walks across a room to shake hands, he holds himself erect, swings his arms, and remains balanced and in control [A]. If he is depressed, on the other hand, he tends to bend his head forward, taking shuffling steps and holding his arms by his sides [B]. When a man is elated and excited his body may lose its natural balance and erectness, his arms swing widely, and his gait becomes erratic [C]. These movements are often seen when old friends meet. They can also be associated with a manic state of mind.

5

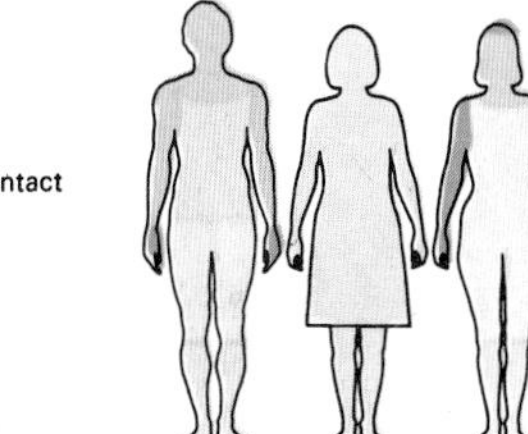
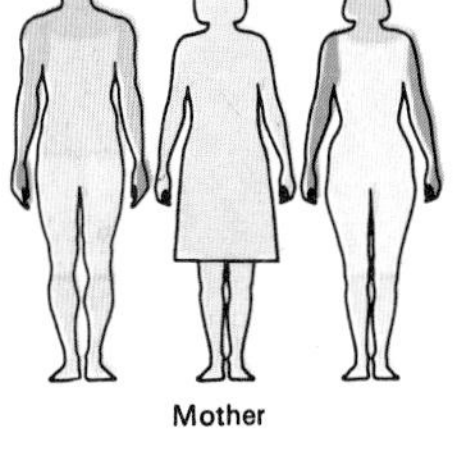
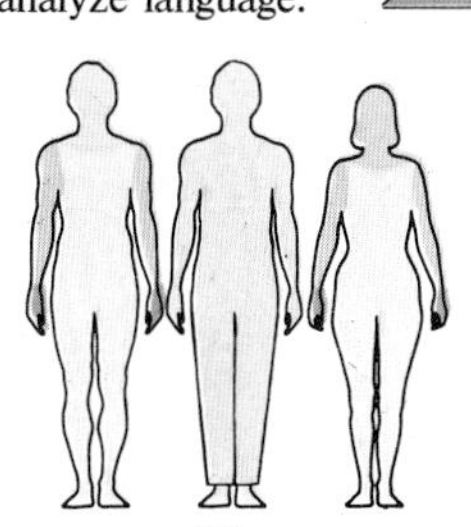
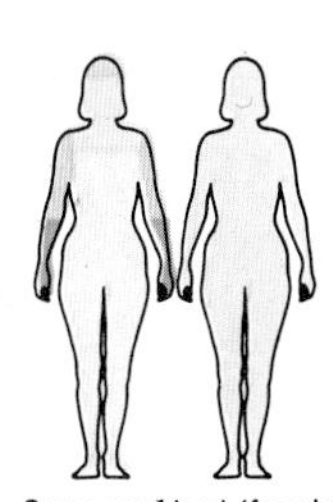
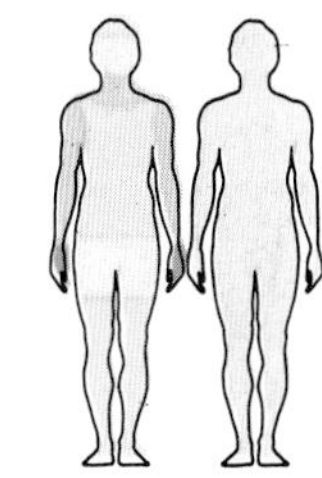
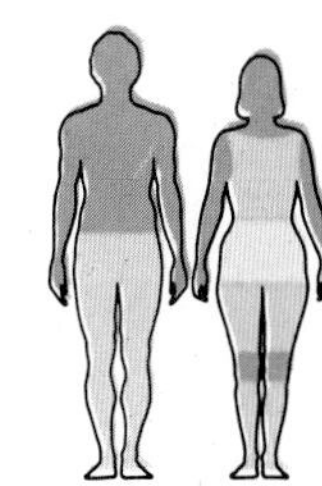
Percentage contact
0–25
26–50
51–75
76–100
Mother
Father
Same sex friend (female)
Same sex friend (male)
Opposite sex friends

5 The extent to which people touch each other varies widely according to culture and relationship. A US study showed where students were touched most often by parents and friends.

6

1
2
3
4
5
6
7
8
9
10

6 Posture and gesture make up a fundamental part of the repertoire of nonverbal communication. One look at a collection of people reveals much about their characters and moods. A man with head in hands and drooping eyes [1] is shut off from the group and does not hide his boredom or sadness. Another [2] shows self-confidence or smugness by forming a steeple of his hands while the open hands of 3 suggest sincerity and warmth. Sorrow or shame are typified by the way that 4 hides his face. The erect posture with hands on hips of 5 conveys assertiveness. An attentive posture is taken by 6, who sits on the edge of his seat leaning forward with hands on mid-thighs. The fact that 7 has chosen the highest place may show that he is the most dominant of the group or simply that he is aloof. Touching or rubbing the nose [8] is associated with doubt, while the arm-gripping, defense posture of 9 suggests that he is nervous (or perhaps sitting in a draft). A nervous person may wrap his fingers around his biceps so hard that the knuckles show white. Finally 10, shows lack of interest by turning away from the group.

7

"Excellent" USA, Europe, Levant, Iran

"Excellent" Sicily

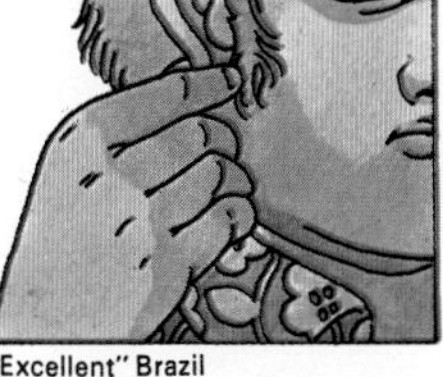
"Excellent" Brazil

"Beautiful" Italy

"Beautiful" Latin countries

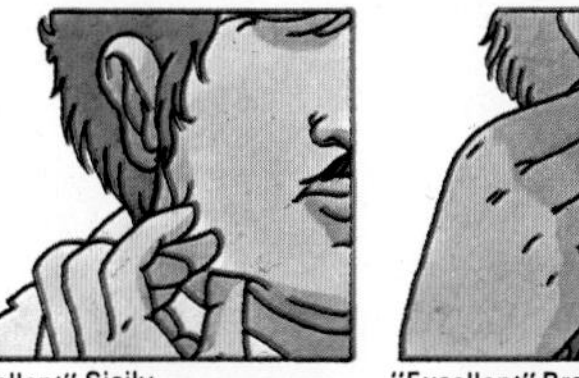
"What a smasher" Brazil

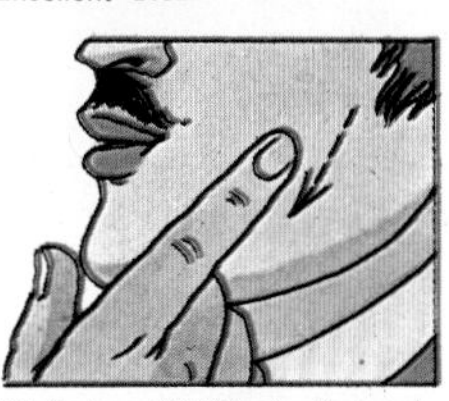
"Hello beautiful" Spain, Portugal

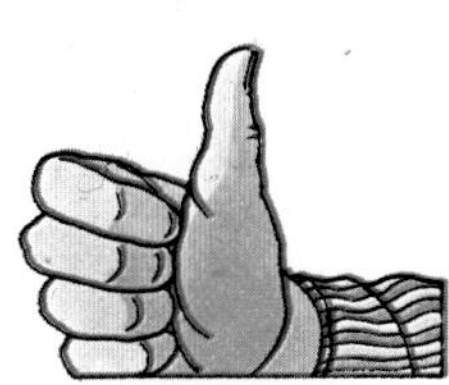
"Excellent" Anglo-Saxon

7 Gestures can convey a common emotion like approval in many ways.

8

A

B

8 An insult to one person may be a compliment to another. Tucking a thumb beneath the forefinger [A] is a good luck charm in Brazil but a jeer or obscenity in some other countries. A raised forefinger, which means "Wait, I have an idea" to Italians and Austrians and "God is my witness" to gypsies, may be seen by other peoples as a vulgarity.

Communication through speech: 1

Any system used by a social group to communicate information, whether drum beats, smoke signals, or finger movements, may loosely be called a language. But of all language forms that exist by far the most flexible and expressive is human speech.

Origins of speech

Language and thought are so intertwined that it is sometimes forgotten that humans originally had to learn to talk to each other by inventing arbitrary vocal symbols for a whole world of nameless objects, actions, and emotions. The idea of naming things is assumed to have evolved from more simple forms of communication such as gestures, facial and bodily movements, and the kind of cries, grunts, snorts, whistles, or clicks uttered by animals or birds [1]. Experiments with animals ranging from apes to dolphins have shown that some are capable of imitating human speech or of responding to a limited number of sounds [2, 3]. One important difference between speech and the communication system of any animal is the human ability to cope with complicated ideas, particularly ideas separated in time and space.

It seems certain that language and thought evolved together, one stimulating the other. Man's ability to perpetuate and extend his knowledge gave him the power of swift cultural development, increasing his dominance over other animals. The idea that language was a divine gift appears in many mythologies.

Although the different shape of their vocal organs allows humans to make more varied sounds [5] than the hominoid ape, this linguistic superiority is primarily intellectual. Every normal child appears to be born with the capacity to learn a language simply by watching and listening to people around him. Since few sentences are ever repeated precisely, this achievement implies an innate faculty not only to learn words and their meanings but also to grasp the complexities of grammatical structure.

The question of whether all languages descend from one common source language or rather evolved among separate groups independently in different parts of the world is impossible to answer. The transitory nature of early cultures and the superimposition of later tongues through trade or invasion have permanently obscured the origins of languages.

Linguistic studies, however, have shown that one historic language, Indo-European has been the parent of existing languages spoken by about half the world's population. In Western Europe only one regional tongue, Basque, is not descended from it. Nevertheless, it is in no sense the "first" language. Indo-European is thought to have originated on the Russian steppe, near the Black Sea, or in Central Asia, and to have spread westward about 4000–3500 BC. Other investigations, including a study of a small group of words for plants and animals that had a common origin [6], have suggested that the geographical origin of the proto-language was a small area of northern Europe from which invaders began to spread out in about 2000 BC, mingling their language with those of lands they reached. As yet, these theories have not been confirmed.

CONNECTIONS

See also
866 Communication through speech: 2
780 Language development
862 Communication without words
552 Whales, porpoises, and dolphins
816 Freedom and individuality
868 Codes, ciphers, and secret messages
870 Communication through writing: 1
872 Communication through writing: 2

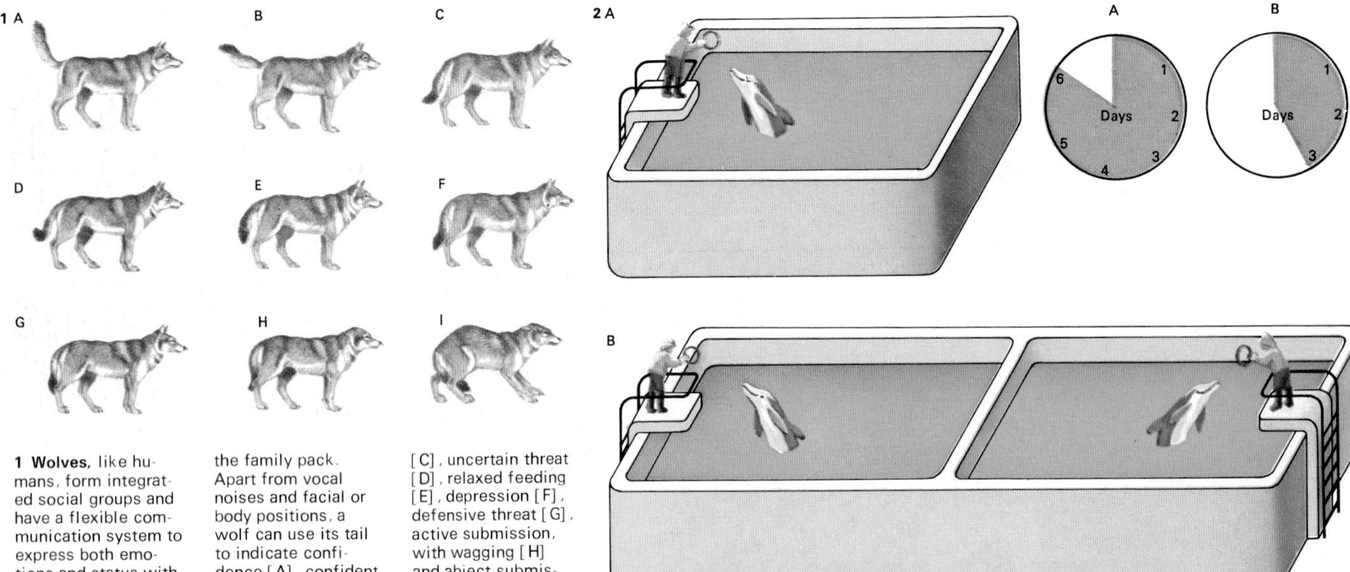

1 A
B
C
D
E
F
G
H
I
2 A
B
A
B
Days
1
2
3
4
5
6
Days
1
2
3

1 Wolves, like humans, form integrated social groups and have a flexible communication system to express both emotions and status within the hierarchy of the family pack. Apart from vocal noises and facial or body positions, a wolf can use its tail to indicate confidence [A], confident threat [B], relaxation [C], uncertain threat [D], relaxed feeding [E], depression [F], defensive threat [G], active submission, with wagging [H] and abject submission [I].

2 Dolphins communicate with each other by a system of distinct sounds ranging from clicks to whistles. These highly developed marine mammals can also locate small objects over relatively long distances by sending and receiving echolocating pulses. To test the ability of dolphins to communicate information through sound codes, scientists noted the time a dolphin took to learn a trick [A]. The skilled dolphin was then placed in a tank alongside an unskilled one that could hear but not see it [B]. In all tests the second dolphin learned to perform the trick much faster, apparently because it was being prompted by sound messages from the skilled dolphin.

3 A

B

C

3 Chimpanzees have been taught a rudimentary vocabulary as a result of experiments conducted in the United States since the early 1950s. In attempting to find out whether animals could be taught to communicate directly with humans, scientists chose the chimpanzee both because its physical and mental capacities are closest to those of humans and because it is able to form strong emotional ties with them. In early experiments efforts were made to teach spoken words to a chimpanzee reared from birth with a family. But it managed to learn only four words. More recent experiments have used systems of geometric shapes or hand signs. Having noticed the use of gestures by chimpanzees in the wild, one researcher adopted a year-old animal into his family and began teaching it American sign language, a system used widely by the deaf. By instruction through play the chimpanzee steadily amassed a vocabulary of signs. Seen here are the signs for listen [A], ear [B], and toothbrush [C]. After four years of study it knew about 150 signs and began to use them in combinations. Signs for bird and water were used to represent a duck, for instance. The sign for dirty, previously used for soiled objects, was combined with monkey when the chimpanzee described a macaque that threatened it. Researchers are now investigating whether chimpanzees will use learned sign language with each other.

Limitations and resources

Each particular language conditions a speaker's way of seeing the world and of feeling and acting in it. The limitations of language have preoccupied many twentieth-century writers and thinkers. At the same time, the film image has become, through movies and television, an important supplement to language as a cultural tool. Yet the influence of spoken language on development remains fundamental. If computer and other logic-based languages are far more precise than speech, speech has the flexibility that they cannot match. Thus it is speech that provides the basis for our complex cultural systems.

Vocabulary itself is only one of an armory of speech resources. Variations in word selection and sentence structure, intonation, and emphasis, can convey infinite nuances. When supplemented by facial expression and gesture, language becomes more expressive still. The Russian actor-manager Konstantin Stanislavsky (1865–1938) used to ask his students to say the word "tonight" in 50 different ways, ranging from inquiry, surprise, jealously, shyly, and doubt to rage, fear, relief, and excitement.

The analysis of language

The study of meaning at its deepest level is the most complicated aspect of language study, not only because of the diversity of human thought and experience but also because the vocabulary of a living language may change rapidly. However, grammatical and phonetic changes, and acceptance of them, evolve slowly.

Linguistics, the scientific study of language, differentiated itself from the older approach, philology, in the mid-nineteenth century. Linguistics stresses spoken language at a certain time without reference to its earlier history. Its subdivisions are phonetics (the study of the sounds of speech); morphology (the study of meaningful combinations of sounds); syntax (the study of the arrangements of words); semantics (the study of meanings of language); and etymology (the study of the history, development, and origin of words).

KEY

International organizations are the modern Towers of Babel. At the UN every speech, no matter what its original language, is simultaneously translated into the five official languages – Chinese, English, French, Russian, and Spanish.

4

A
abcdef
ghijkl
mnopq
rstuv.

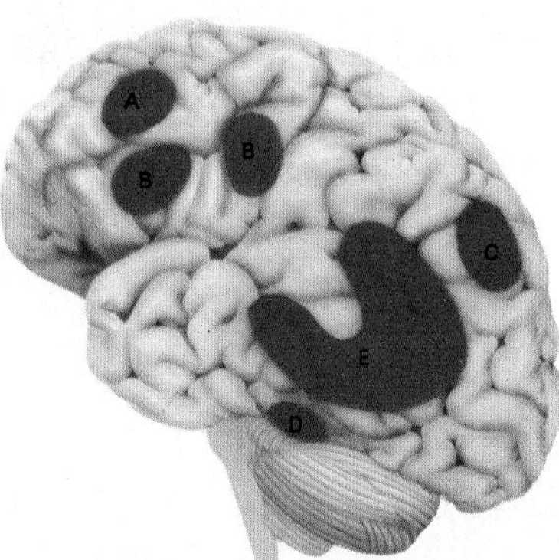
A
B
B
C
E
D

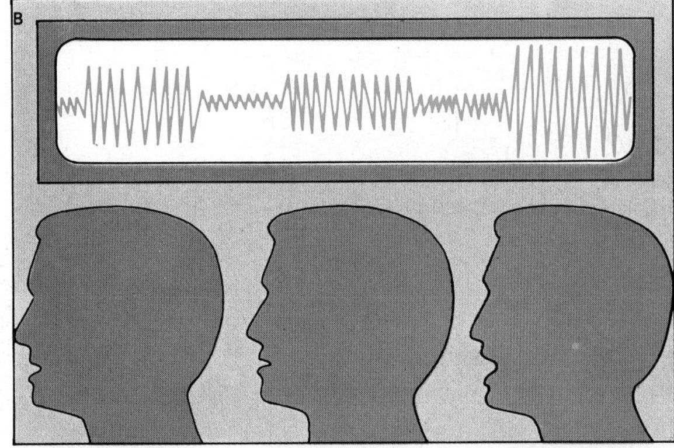
B

C

ALEXIAE
SAWORD
IBLINDNE

D

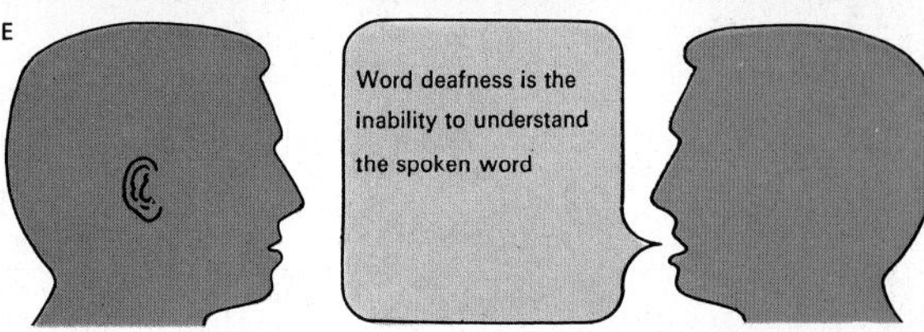
E
Word deafness is the inability to understand the spoken word

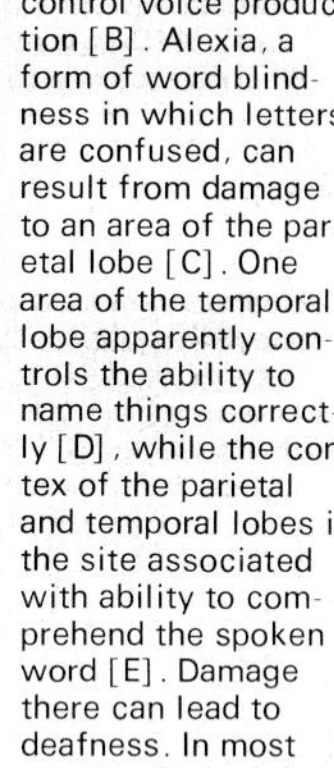

4 Language control areas in the brain are vital for several different functions. Writing ability is located in the frontal lobe [A], together with two areas that control voice production [B]. Alexia, a form of word blindness in which letters are confused, can result from damage to an area of the parietal lobe [C]. One area of the temporal lobe apparently controls the ability to name things correctly [D], while the cortex of the parietal and temporal lobes is the site associated with ability to comprehend the spoken word [E]. Damage there can lead to deafness. In most people, the brain's left hemisphere controls language.

5

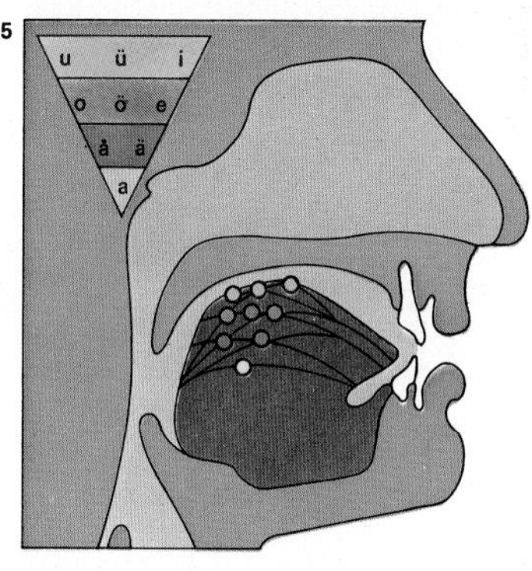
u ü i
o ö e
å ä
a

5 Vowel sounds are controlled largely by the position of the tongue in the mouth. A triangle diagram named after the scientist who originally formulated it, Hellwag, represents the limits of the tongue positions for the major vowels, although these vary slightly for different languages. Depending on their vertical position, vowels are classified as front, central, or back, while the horizontal classification is closed, half-closed, half-opened, and open.

6 Language detective work by scholars and scientists has led to the theory that an area of northern Europe was the place of origin for all the languages of the vast Indo-European group. The names of a small group of plants and animals are similar in all these tongues. But fossil-dating techniques indicate that before 2000 BC only one area, close to the shores of the Baltic, provided a habitat for all four species – wolf, salmon, terrapin, and beech tree. The theory is that a race of people who spread out from this area imposed their own names for these species on other tongues, but adopted various local names for species with which they were unfamiliar.

6

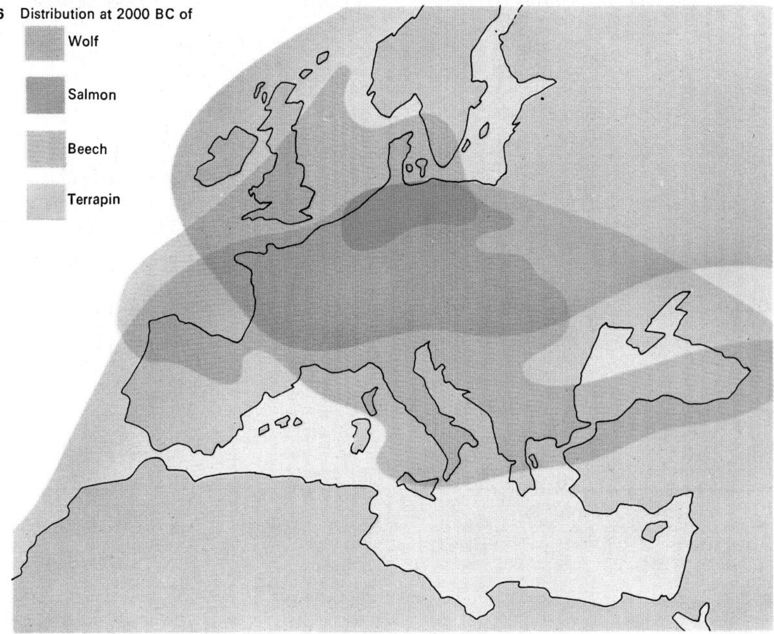
Distribution at 2000 BC of
Wolf
Salmon
Beech
Terrapin

Communication through speech: 2

More than 4,000 languages, living or dead, have been identified. The migration of early nomadic peoples produced an astonishing diversity of speech forms as each group experimented with language, discovering new things to be named, borrowing words from other tribes, and slowly changing its own language forms in so doing.

How languages are classified

Nearly half the population of the world speaks one of the Indo-European group of languages [Key], all of which derive from a common tongue spoken in northern Europe about 5,000 years ago. But the language divided into eight major branches, five of which split and resplit as words were shortened, lengthened, coined, or swapped; as syllables were added or dropped and as vowels and consonants changed. Because people who spoke Balto-Slavic languages, for example, were not accustomed to pronouncing the Aryan sound "k," they altered it to "s" or "sh" when invaders from the west settled among them. As grammatical changes were made, the original links became unrecognizable except to academics and other scholars.

A few languages, called isolates, seem unrelated to others; Basque and Burushaski are examples. But some features of grammatical structure are common to all forms of speech, and many languages are historically related. Classification of the difference between them is of two kinds: genetic and typological. Genetic classification is based on word derivation, common history, and literary traditions and on sociocultural factors. Within the Indo-European family of languages genetic classification identifies such subfamilies as the German, English, Dutch, Swedish, and Danish groups.

Typological classification groups languages according to their structure as isolating, agglutinating, and inflecting types. An isolating language is one that indicates grammar mainly by word order with each word being a single grammatical unit called a morph. Vietnamese is an example. An agglutinating language is one in which individual words can be composed of several morphs glued together, as in Turkish. An inflecting language is one in which there is no specific correspondence between particular segments of a words and particular grammatical functions. An example is the English word "mice" in which plurality is indicated by a syllable change instead of an added morph. English, like many languages, combines all typological features.

Differences within languages

Adding to the enormous diversity of language are the subtleties of accent and tonal change that can be produced by the speech organs [2]. Even within a single language there are subdivisions, or dialects, based on regional, social, or occupational differences. There are American, Australian, and Scottish dialects of English, for example. They contrast with Gaelic, which is quite a different language from Scottish English. The point at which dialects become separate languages is not always clear. The Dutch-German speech community, for example, spans a continuous area of intelligibility from Flanders (Dutch) to Styria (German), but speakers of Flemish and

CONNECTIONS

See also

864 Communication through speech: 1
862 Communication without words
868 Codes, ciphers, and secret messages
870 Communication through writing: 1
872 Communication through writing: 2

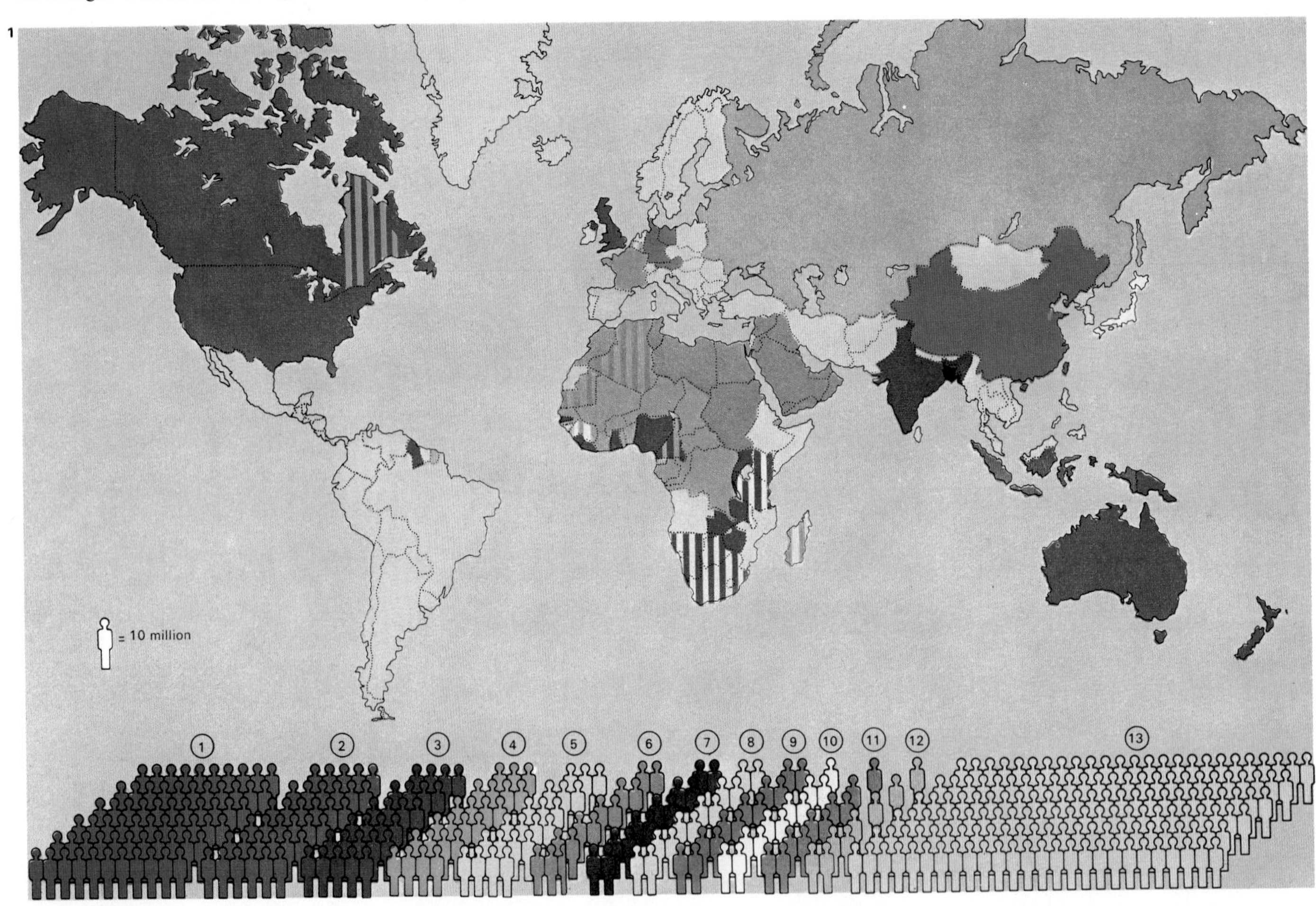

1
= 10 million
1
2
3
4
5
6
7
8
9
10
11
12
13

1 Each of the world's 4,000,000,000 people belongs to a speech community, a group speaking the same language. About 1,500 different languages are spoken, the largest block being Mandarin Chinese, spoken by more than 650,000,000, but this does not include those speaking Wu (70,000,000), Cantonese (47,000,000), and other Chinese tongues. The map shows the principal official languages throughout the world. These 12 take in almost 2,500,000,000 people. The rest of the world is split into smaller language blocks such as Italian (60,000,000) Tamil (55,000,000), Korean (50,000,000), Punjabi (50,000,000), Dutch and Flemish (19,000,000), and Greek (10,000,000). About 100 languages have more than 1,000,000 speakers. A multiplicity of other languages are each spoken by a smaller number of people than this. Superimposed on the thousands of local languages and dialects around the world are the six major international languages of the historic colonial powers: English, Spanish, Russian, Arabic, Portuguese, and French. Easy communications may increase the dominance of some of these languages, and of Japanese and Chinese, as mediums of commerce, education, and cultural exchange. The Indo-European group of related languages is the most widespread. More people now speak these languages outside Europe than inside it. North America has the biggest English-speaking population, and South America has most speakers of Spanish. A growing number of people can speak one of the major international languages as well as their native tongue. At the same time, the number of speakers of minority tongues is dwindling. Efforts to establish an artificially created language have been limited because such languages lack a cultural base.

1 Mandarin Chinese
2 English
3 Hindi and Urdu
4 Russian
5 Spanish
6 Arabic
7 Bengali
8 Portuguese
9 German
10 Japanese
11 Indonesian
12 French
13 Other languages

Styrian dialects cannot understand each other.

Social groups may use speech differences to heighten group identity, to exclude others speaking the same language, or to underline social divisions by the snobbery of a preferred accent. When extended to political or international rivalry the divisive aspects of language can be dangerous. In India, for example, the end of British rule led to rioting over whether Hindi (an Indo-European tongue) or one of the earlier Dravidian tongues, such as Tamil, should become the country's official language.

The potential of language as a unifying force was recognized by the Romans, who used Latin in the west and Greek in the east to weld together the peoples they controlled. Latin provided scholars throughout medieval Europe with a *lingua franca* (common language) and survives today both in such professions as law and medicine and as a source for new scientific words. The prestige of France and the clarity of its language made French the diplomatic language for many years, while in the twentieth century the dominance of English-speaking peoples in technology and commerce has led to increasing acquisition of English as a second language.

Improving communication

Simplified language forms called pidgins facilitated trade and communication between several European nations and the peoples they colonized. At a more sophisticated level, there have been at least 300 attempts to invent a universal language. Of these, Esperanto alone (with more than 750,000 speakers) has made some headway.

A whole range of "languages" has also been developed for computers. These codes are made up of unambiguous words and symbols. The message is first translated into the special language. A typical example in COBOL (Common Business Oriented Language) might read "Multiply hours-worked by rate-for-job giving wage-payable." This is fed into the machine, which translates it into basic instructions that trigger further commands to the machine and produce the result.

KEY

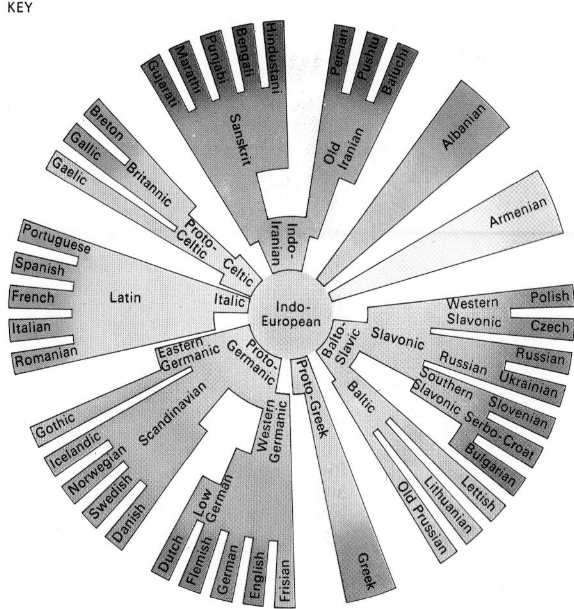

Indo-European
Gujarati
Marathi
Punjabi
Bengali
Hindustani
Sanskrit
Persian
Pushtu
Baluchi
Old Iranian
Indo-Iranian
Albanian
Armenian
Breton
Gallic
Gaelic
Britannic
Proto-Celtic
Celtic
Portuguese
Spanish
French
Italian
Romanian
Latin
Italic
Eastern Germanic
Proto-Germanic
Gothic
Icelandic
Norwegian
Swedish
Danish
Scandinavian
Dutch
Flemish
Low German
German
English
Frisian
Western Germanic
Proto-Greek
Greek
Balto-Slavic
Baltic
Old Prussian
Lithuanian
Lettish
Slavonic
Western Slavonic
Polish
Czech
Russian
Ukrainian
Southern Slavonic
Slovenian
Serbo-Croat
Bulgarian

2

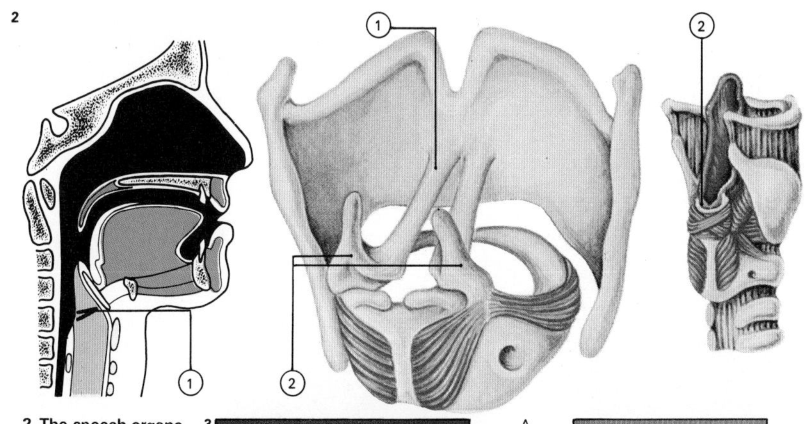

1
2

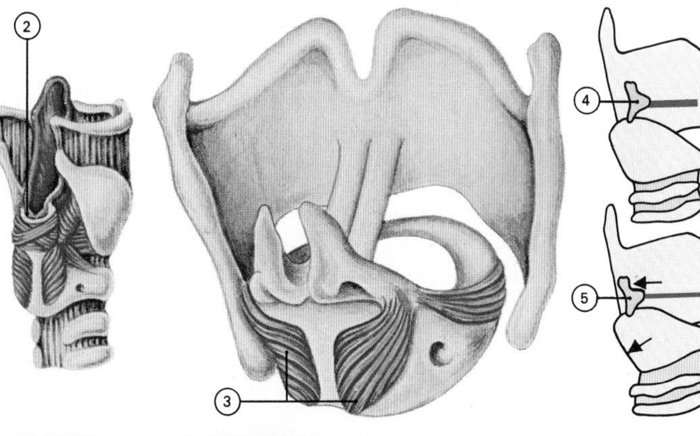

3
4
5

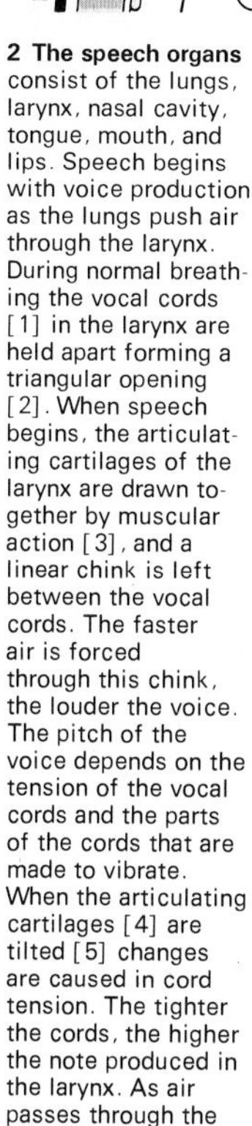

2 The speech organs consist of the lungs, larynx, nasal cavity, tongue, mouth, and lips. Speech begins with voice production as the lungs push air through the larynx. During normal breathing the vocal cords [1] in the larynx are held apart forming a triangular opening [2]. When speech begins, the articulating cartilages of the larynx are drawn together by muscular action [3], and a linear chink is left between the vocal cords. The faster air is forced through this chink, the louder the voice. The pitch of the voice depends on the tension of the vocal cords and the parts of the cords that are made to vibrate. When the articulating cartilages [4] are tilted [5] changes are caused in cord tension. The tighter the cords, the higher the note produced in the larynx. As air passes through the mouth the voice is modulated and broken up by changes in the shape of the other organs.

3

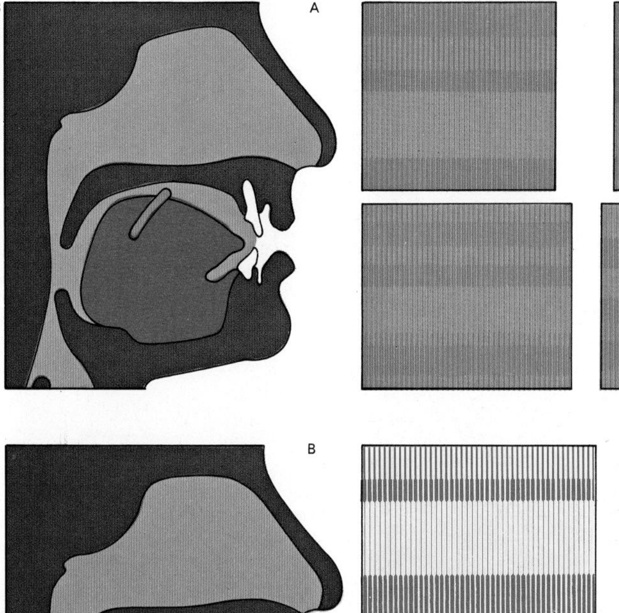

A
B

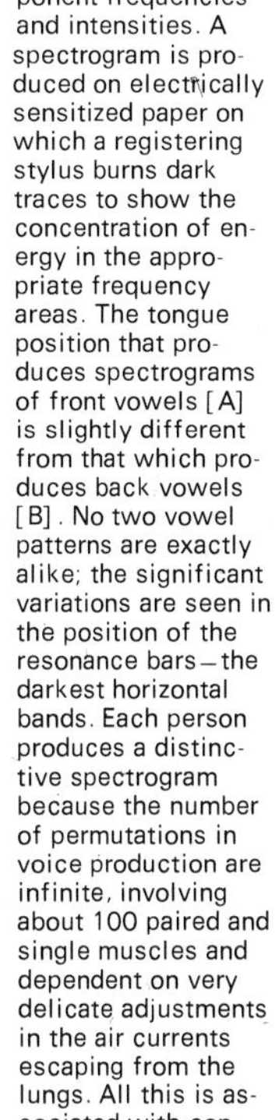

3 The sound spectrograph analyzes the sound waves made by speech into component frequencies and intensities. A spectrogram is produced on electrically sensitized paper on which a registering stylus burns dark traces to show the concentration of energy in the appropriate frequency areas. The tongue position that produces spectrograms of front vowels [A] is slightly different from that which produces back vowels [B]. No two vowel patterns are exactly alike; the significant variations are seen in the position of the resonance bars – the darkest horizontal bands. Each person produces a distinctive spectrogram because the number of permutations in voice production are infinite, involving about 100 paired and single muscles and dependent on very delicate adjustments in the air currents escaping from the lungs. All this is associated with contraction of internal and external muscles of the larynx to maintain the margins of the glottis at the right degree of elasticity. The complex sound wave produced by regular vibrations of the glottal folds consists of a basic vibration (called the fundamental, related to our perception of pitch) and a series of overtones. The relative pitches and ranges of these overtones determine the quality and the character of the eventual voice. In speech and song, sounds (usually initiated by lung air, with or without glottal vibration) are modified by the shape of the resonators provided especially by the pharynx, the nasal cavities and the mouth, which is particularly flexible and important in "molding" the emerging stream of air. An individual spectrogram is unique, as is a fingerprint, although perhaps more variable, opening the way for the use of "voice-prints" as identification.

Codes, ciphers, and secret messages

There are many ways of communicating besides speech and writing. Any system of symbols used for communication can be called a code. The science of codes is known as cryptology. Some codes are meant to be secret, but others, such as Morse [5], are open codes intended only to make communication easier.

Concealment and disguise

There are many ways of concealing messages, but they can all be reduced to two basic strategies. The first conceals the very existence of the message by writing it in invisible ink [1] or by reducing it photographically to a microdot about the size of a period or to a micropulse (by transmitting it at super-speed). A message can also be arranged in such a way that it is effectively concealed in the innocuous text of another message.

The second way to disguise plain text is to transform it in one of two fundamental ways: by transposing the letters of the message in a prearranged order to make a cipher [9]; or by substituting for the letters of the plain text other letters, numbers, or symbols to form a code.

Ciphers and secrecy

To encipher the message "tanks will move tomorrow at dawn" by a simple letter-for-letter substitution cipher based on the following key:

Plain text abcdefghijklmnopqrstuvwxyz
Cipher text monseratbcdfghijklpqzyxwvu

substitute a cipher text letter for each plain text letter as below:

Tanks will move tomorrow at dawn
qmhdp xbff giye qigillix mq smxh

Substitution ciphers afford little protection, however. Each time *o* appears in the plain text above, *i* appears in the cipher version, and so on. Anyone with a knowledge of how frequently letters occur in English would have little trouble in unscrambling the message.

The diagraphic Playfair system provides a better disguise for secret messages. In this system one begins with the letters of the alphabet arranged any way one likes in five columns of five letters each (*I* and *J* taking only one space). Here is one possible key-square:

M S N O E
R A T B C
D F G H IJ
K L P Q U
V W X Y Z

Now the message is broken up into groups of two letters. The tank message would look like this: TA NK SW IL LM OV ET OM OR RO WA TD AW NX. Three rules govern how the cipher is made. (1) If the two letters of a group both occur on the same row, one substitutes the letter immediately to the right of each one (so TA in the message becomes BT in the cipher). (2) If the two letters can be seen as corners of a rectangle (that is, if they are neither on the same row nor in the same column), then the two letters at the other corners of the imaginary rectangle are substituted for them (thus NK becomes MP). (3) If the two letters are in the same column, then the letters immediately below are chosen (SW in the example will become AS, because all columns and rows are considered to connect

CONNECTIONS

See also
1790 Communications: telegraph
862 Talking without words
864 Communication through speech: 1
866 Communication through speech: 2
870 Communication through writing: 1
872 Communication through writing: 2
158 Worlds of many kinds

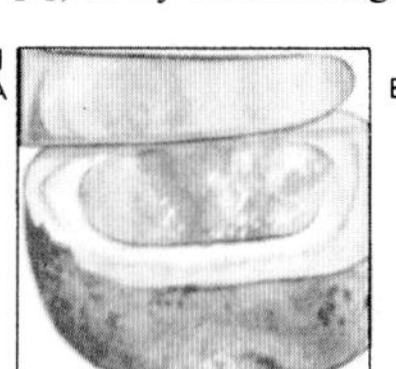

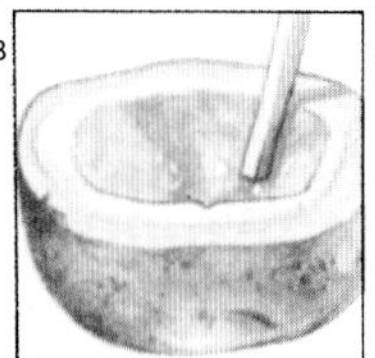

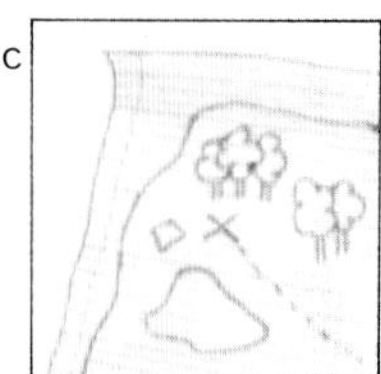

1 Secret inks can be made from many substances ranging from potato juice to the most sophisticated chemical compounds. To make a potato inkwell, scoop out the center of a potato and scrape juice into the hole [A]. A message written with this juice [B] will be invisible but can be read when the paper is heated [C]. If paper is waxed by rubbing it with a candle and laid wax face down on plain paper, then a message written on the plain paper will be impressed as a waxen line and become legible after powdered coffee, soot, or some other dark dust has been scattered on it.

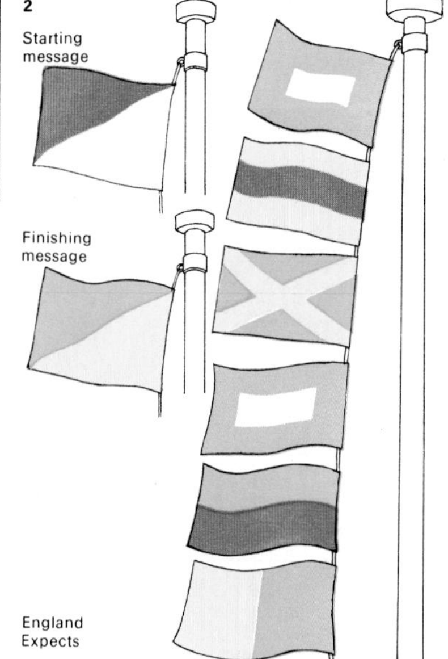

Starting message
Finishing message
England Expects

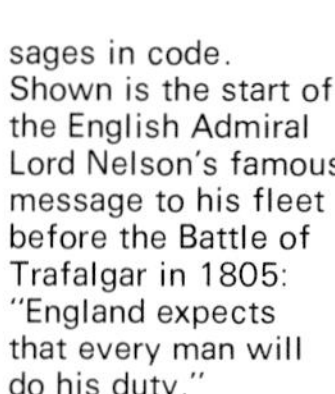

2 Single colored flags are used by ships to send specified messages. A yellow flag means "quarantine." Navies use 24 different designs related to the letters of the alphabet to send messages in code. Shown is the start of the English Admiral Lord Nelson's famous message to his fleet before the Battle of Trafalgar in 1805: "England expects that every man will do his duty."

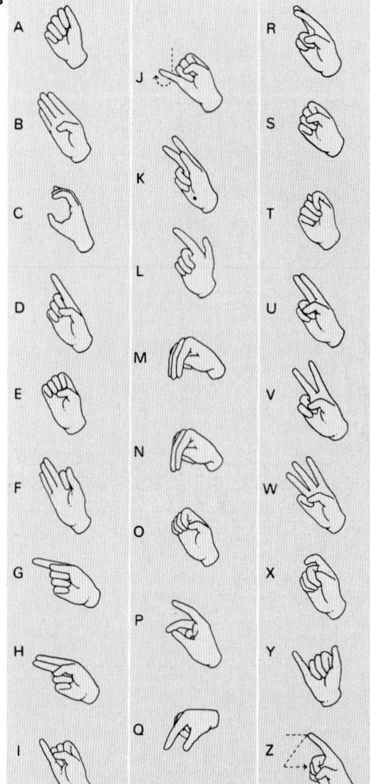

3 The manual language of the deaf is a code in which the fingers and hands are used to illustrate the letters of the alphabet. The one-handed system is the most common one, and a conversation in sign language goes about as fast as careful speech does (about the speed of a television newscaster). Normally, however, the deaf use a mixture of signs, gestures, and lip-reading, which is as fast as normal speech, reserving the formal signals for problems.

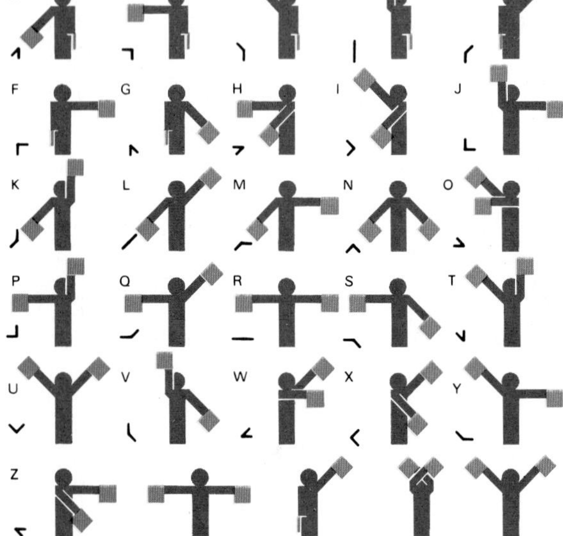

End of message
Ready
Made a mistake

4 Semaphore makes use of two flags or lights to send messages and is based on the circular movement of the two hands of a clock. The angle of the flags, which should be held with straight arms, stands for a letter of the alphabet. B=6:45, D=6:00, F=6:15, and so on. Semaphore was originally designed to communicate over a short distance where the sender and recipient could see each other but were out of earshot. It was used extensively during the 19th century before radio made it largely unnecessary. It is still used at sea and when radio silence prevails. Rail signals have semaphore markers to enable engineers to tell at a glance the way the switch points are set.

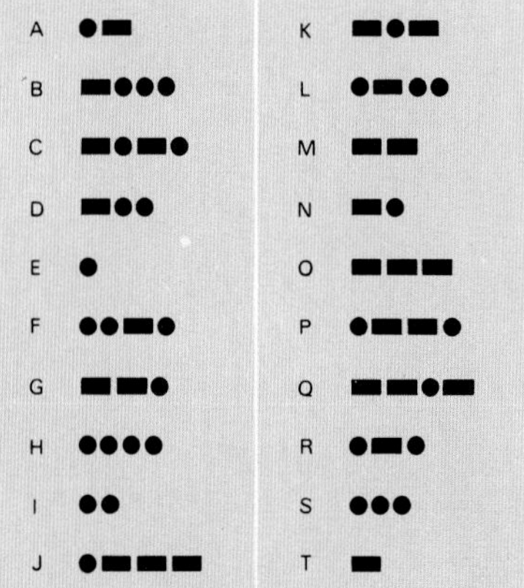

5 In International Morse code letters are represented by combinations of dots and dashes. It was invented by Samuel F.B. Morse in about 1837.

with themselves). The enciphered message now becomes: BT MP OY FU XO MY ES MB BM SF RG FS TN.

Forms of codes

A code, as distinct from a cipher, involves the substitution of prearranged code words, code numbers, or code groups for words, phrases, or syllables. The trilingual international commercial code in English, French, and Spanish, for example, has five-letter groups representing useful words in each language (UVYDU = railroad tie, *traverse, traviesa*). The groups are recorded in a dictionary and are used to save telegram costs. Military and diplomatic codes based on this principle have to be disguised to make them secure. The British used such a code during World War II.

To send that message about the tanks, the sender would look up the basic code, which contains a list of words and phrases commonly used in military messages, thus: "Tanks will move = 9835; Tomorrow = 4439; At dawn = 7463." It would not be safe to send this message as 9835;4439;7463, because frequent repetitions of such phrases as "tomorrow at dawn" would soon be identified and the code cracked. It is therefore necessary to disguise these four-figure groups. The safest way of doing this is for both sender and recipient to have what is known as a one-time pad, on each page of which are columns of four-digit groups printed at random. The sender indicates the page, column, and line where the message is to start, thus; "1549," (which would mean page 15, column 4, line 9). If the next three groups beginning on page 15, column 4, line 9 are 7628;5016;4881, the code text to be sent (9835;4439;7463) is written down and to each group are added the figures taken from the one-time pad, like this:

9835 4439 7463
7628 5016 4881
(1549) 7463 9455 2344 (10s are dropped)

In order to decode the message then, the recipient must first subtract the one-time pad groups from the groups he receives and then look up the numbers in his code "dictionary."

KEY

Giovanni Battista Porta (1535–1615), an Italian physicist-inventor, produced one of the earliest substitution ciphers. He used symbols to replace letters and figures. The symbols were chosen by turning the pointer in the center to the necessary letter or number in the two outer rings, then reading off the corresponding symbol in the inner ring. The cipher could be changed at any time by rotating the disks themselves relative to one another, according to a prearranged schedule. The lines of symbols below the disk spell out the inventor's name. A somewhat simpler version was invented by Leon Battista Alberti (1404–72).

6 Thomas Jefferson (1743–1826) devised a wheel cipher consisting of 36 wheels that can be assembled in any order. Upon each of them the letters of the alphabet are written in jumbled order, and the number of different combinations this gives amounts to many millions. It was by far the most advanced cipher of its day and was adopted by the American army almost at once.

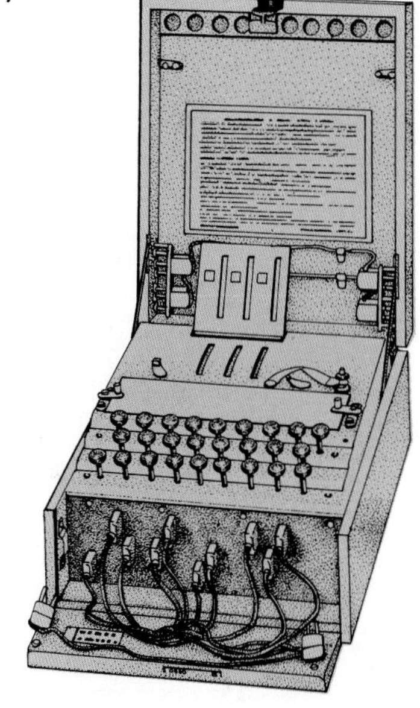

7 The Enigma cipher machine, invented in the 1920s by Arthur Scherbius, handled the Germans' most secret information during World War II. It had a keyboard like a typewriter's but the keys were interconnected electrically so that by pressing a *b*, say, it printed an *x*. This coupling was changed constantly, so there was never any consistency of relationship between key hit and letter produced. First the message was typed and scrambled by Enigma and then sent by Morse. The British broke the Enigma cipher and used the information they got from German secret messages to defeat the Axis. This was the Ultra secret.

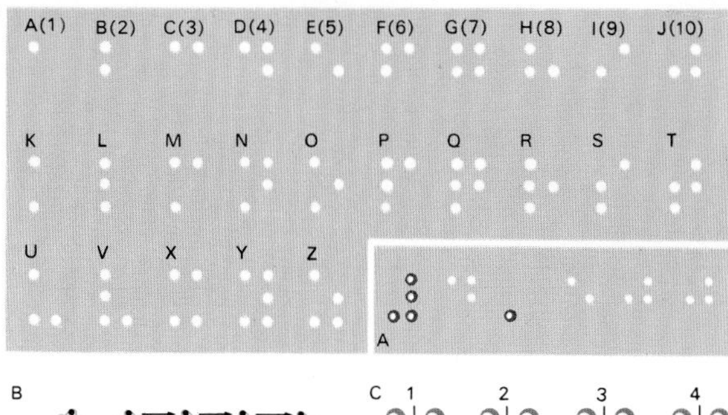
8
A(1) B(2) C(3) D(4) E(5) F(6) G(7) H(8) I(9) J(10)
K L M N O P Q R S T
U V X Y Z
A

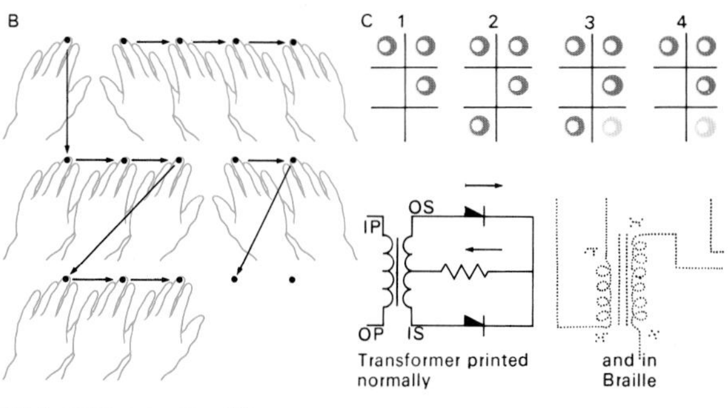
B
C 1 2 3 4
OS
IP
OP IS
Transformer printed normally
and in Braille

8 Braille consists of a different pattern of raised dots for each letter. Both hands are used to read it. The right hand picks up the message, the left feels for the beginning of the next line [B]. All the dots fit into a six-space "domino" pattern. [C1-4] shows the difference among D, N, Y, and TH. Like TH, W is also a special combination. Numerals correspond to the letters A–J, preceded by the numeral sign [A].

10 A pencil or a pen can be used to make a simple cipher machine. Write a message on a strip of paper wound around a pencil or pen. Unwound, it is nonsense, but anyone with a tube of the same diameter can decode it instantly.

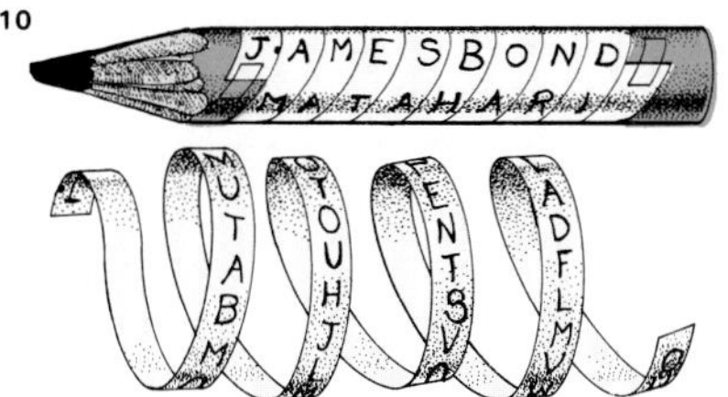
JAMESBOND
MATAHARI

9 "The king is dead, long live the king" is the English for this French plain text [A]. It is enciphered by writing it in rows [C] beneath a code word [B], then numbering the letters of the code word sequentially according to their position in the alphabet (SPECTRUM-CEMPRSTU) [D]. The message is written in the order of the numbered columns [E]. To decipher, the recipient needs only to know the code word and to reverse the process.

9
A LE ROI EST MORT VIVE LE ROI
B S P E C T R U M
C L E R O I E S T
M O R T V I V E
L E R O I X X X
D 6 4 2 1 7 5 8 3
E OTO RRR TEX EOE EIX LML IVI SVX

Communication through writing: 1

Although it is not universal, as spoken language is, writing is an essential ingredient in almost all cultures. Indeed, the presence of written records is usually held to mark the watershed between prehistory and history.

The earliest known scripts

Paleolithic cave paintings may have been an attempt to convey ideas; communication by means of pictures is a recurrent feature in primitive societies [1]. From this it is only a short step to picture-writing, in which a circle, for example, may represent the sun. The next advance is the ideogram, in which the circle that originally stood for "sun" now represents related ideas such as "light" and, eventually, "day."

Ideograms form a recognizable feature of such diverse writing as Mayan "glyphs" [2] and the mysterious script of Easter Island in the Pacific Ocean [3]. They can still be recognized in much more sophisticated writing systems such as Egyptian hieroglyphics [4]. Of its 600 signs some are words ("man," "look"), some determinatives that indicate how the preceding signs are to be understood (for example, as an abstract idea), whereas still others are used for syllables and single sounds, thus foreshadowing a true alphabet.

The earliest known script that can properly be called writing was devised by the Sumerians in the fourth millennium BC. The cuneiform (wedge-shaped) script derives ultimately from ideograms, but soon became a system of conventionalized characters, each having a distinct phonetic (sound) value [5].

Most important of the nonalphabetic scripts is Chinese. Each of its characters, which are derived from ideograms, represents a complete word, with the result that the Chinese scholar must be conversant with about 9,000 different symbols, whereas everyday writing uses as many as 1,500 to 2,000 characters [6]. Most characters are compounded from a radical element, giving the meaning, and a phonetic element indicating the pronunciation. The phonetic "fang" when compounded with the radical "tree" gives the character for "timber"; whereas when compounded with the radical "word" it produces the character for "to inquire." Traditionally Chinese was written right to left in columns, but today it is usually in written in lines from left to right.

The development of the alphabet

Picture-writing and ideographic scripts arose independently in different parts of the world. In contrast, the alphabet was probably invented only once, by the inhabitants of the Syria-Palestine area in the latter part of the second millennium BC. This first alphabet (North Semitic) consisted of 22 characters, each representing a consonant, written right to left [7]. It had two main branches, one of which led directly to classical Hebrew and Aramaic and, indirectly, to Arabic. In its present form Arabic consists of 28 letters and is the most widely used alphabet in the world apart from the Latin alphabet [9]. All these alphabets are consonantal and written right to left.

In the spread of the alphabet eastward, the role of Aramaic, the *lingua franca* of the Middle East for several centuries from the

CONNECTIONS

See also
872 Communication through writing: 2
862 Communication without words
864 Communication through speech: 1
866 Communication through speech: 2
868 Codes, ciphers, and secret messages

1

1 The wampum belts used by North American Indians conveyed messages through pictures. This one represents an Indian and the President of the United States; it shows that the tribe offers friendship and negotiation. These belts are better classed as "mnemonics," that is aids to the speaker, than as writing in the form of pictures.

2

2 The Mayas had a highly developed writing system, but almost all their manuscripts were destroyed by the Spanish invaders.

3

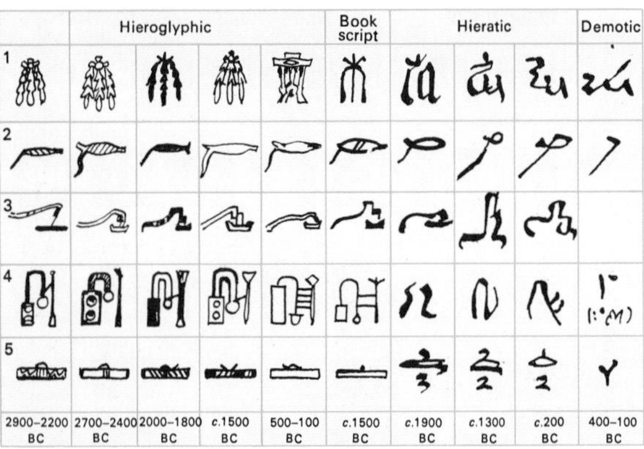

3 The script from Easter Island (as yet undeciphered) has carved characters incised on wood with a shark's tooth.

4

	Hieroglyphic					Book script	Hieratic			Demotic
1										
2										
3										
4										
5										
	2900–2200 BC	2700–2400 BC	2000–1800 BC	*c.*1500 BC	500–100 BC	*c.*1500 BC	*c.*1900 BC	*c.*1300 BC	*c.*200 BC	400–100 BC

4 Hieroglyphics, "sacred carvings" familiar from temples and pyramids, is the earliest form of Egyptian writing, first used in 3000 BC. It underwent no substantial modification in the three thousand years of its history, but a more cursive (rapidly written) form was soon developed for writing on papyrus; this is known as hieratic. A highly cursive form of the same language, known from 600 BC, is demotic (of the people), but the derivation of most of its signs cannot now be deducted. Shown here are the changes in five hieroglyphs and their equivalents in book script, hieratic, and demotic. The first two are just phonetic, *ms* and *mh* respectively; 3 means "to write"; 4 "to choose"; and 5 "abstract idea."

5

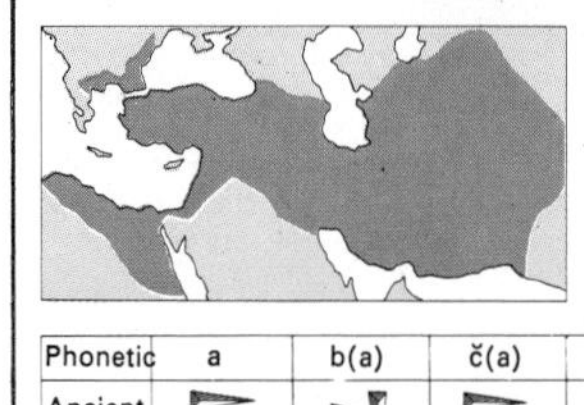

Phonetic	a	b(a)	č(a)	d(a)	d(i)	d(u)	f(a)
Ancient Persian							
Phonetic	g(a)	g(u)	h(a)	h(a)	i	j(a)	j(i)
Ancient Persian							
Phonetic	k(a)	k(u)	l(a)	m(a)	m(i)	m(u)	n(a)
Ancient Persian							
Phonetic	n(u)	p(a)	r(a)	r(u)	š(a)	s(a)	t(a)
Ancient Persian							
Phonetic	t(u)	t(a)	u	v(a)	v(i)	y(a)	z(a)
Ancient Persian							
Phonetic	tr(a)	Word divider	King	Country –	two forms	Divine name	Earth
Ancient Persian							

5 The wedge-shaped writing known as cuneiform was developed because of the ease with which such strokes could be imprinted on wet clay, the normal writing material used for this script. This example is of a relatively late cuneiform script developed in the ancient Persian empire in 500 BC. The external form of the script is the sole connection with the earlier ideographic cuneiform writing of Mesopotamia. The 42 signs shown were created from the Neo-Babylonian model: 36 of these have the value of either a vowel or a vowel plus a consonant; four signs are true ideograms and two are word dividers. The script was written from the left to the right.

sixth century BC, was crucial. It is from this, most scholars now believe, that all the various alphabets used in India and Southeast Asia ultimately derive, both the angular forms such as Devanagari and Sanskrit and the round forms such as Burmese [8].

The other main branch of the alphabet was brought to the West by the Phoenicians, reaching the Greeks by about the ninth century BC. It is certain that the Greeks derived their alphabet from North Semitic; for example, in the Semitic alphabet each letter was given a name: aleph "ox," beth "house," and so on. These were taken over by the Greeks as alpha, beta, etc. (thus giving us our word "alphabet"), although they have no meaning in Greek. The Greeks made one fundamental innovation: the introduction of vowels. Their alphabet came to consist of 17 consonants and seven vowels [7]. Eventually the Greeks changed the direction of writing to left to right.

The classical Latin alphabet

The Greek alphabet reached the Romans through the Etruscans and resulted in the classical Latin alphabet of 23 letters, the parent of the present-day Western alphabet. Subsequent changes have been limited to the introduction of w and of separate forms for i and j, and for u and v. The important part played in the dissemination of this alphabet by the Roman Catholic Church is clearly shown by the scripts of the Slavonic peoples; those converted to Roman Catholicism (Poland) use the Latin alphabet, whereas those converted to the Greek Orthodox religion (Russia) use the Cyrillic alphabet. Cyrillic, invented in the ninth century and traditionally ascribed to St Cyril of Byzantium, consists of 24 letters taken over from Greek uncial to which 19 new characters have been added.

An ideal alphabet should consist of symbols that are distinct and easy to remember, but at the same time capable of representing all significant speech sounds. In our alphabet the first requirement is admirably fulfilled but the second much less so. In English, for example, five vowel symbols must represent 12 vowel sounds and eight diphthongs.

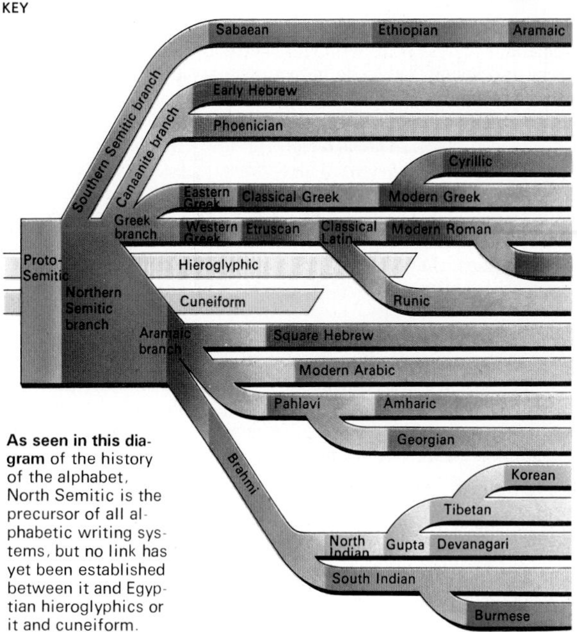

KEY
Sabaean
Ethiopian
Aramaic
Southern Semitic branch
Canaanite branch
Early Hebrew
Phoenician
Cyrillic
Eastern Greek
Classical Greek
Modern Greek
Greek branch
Western Greek
Etruscan
Classical Latin
Modern Roman
Proto-Semitic
Hieroglyphic
Northern Semitic branch
Cuneiform
Runic
Aramaic branch
Square Hebrew
Modern Arabic
Pahlavi
Amharic
Georgian
Brahmi
Korean
Tibetan
North Indian
Gupta
Devanagari
South Indian
Burmese

As seen in this diagram of the history of the alphabet, North Semitic is the precursor of all alphabetic writing systems, but no link has yet been established between it and Egyptian hieroglyphics or it and cuneiform.

6

6 It is generally accepted that Chinese characters are composed of eight basic strokes, all of which are to be found in the character "yung," meaning eternity. The diagram shows the sequence of strokes by which the character evolves (with the arrows giving the direction of the strokes) and how Chinese writing is painted with a brush, often on silk or a similar material. It is said that Wang Hsi-chih, the 4th-century calligrapher, took 15 years to perfect this character.

7

North-Semitic		Greek		Etruscan	Latin		Modern caps
Early Phoenician	Phoenician	Early	Classical	Classical	Early	Classical	Roman
𐤀	𐤀	𐌀	A	A	A	A	A
𐤁	𐤁	𐌁	B			B	B
𐤂	𐤂	𐌂	Γ	𐌂		C	C
𐤃	𐤃	Δ	Δ		ᗡ	D	D
𐤄	𐤄	𐌄	E	𐌄	𐌄	E	E
𐤅	𐤅	𐌅		𐌅	𐌅	F	F
						G	G
𐤆	𐤆	I	Z	𐌆			
𐤇	𐤇	𐌇	H	𐌇	𐌇	H	H
𐤈	𐤈	⊗	θ	⊙			
𐤉	𐤉	𐌉	I	I	I	I	I J
𐤊	𐤊	𐌊	K	𐌊	𐌊	K	K
𐤋	𐤋	𐌋	Λ	𐌋		L	L
𐤌	𐤌	𐌌	M	𐌌	𐌌	M	M
𐤍	𐤍	𐌍	N	𐌍	И	N	N
𐤎			Ξ	⋈			
O	O	O	O		O	O	O
𐤐	𐤐	𐌐	Π	𐌐	Γ	P	P
	𐤑	M		M			
	𐤒	Ϙ		𐌒		Q	Q
𐤓	𐤓	𐌓	P	𐌓		R	R
W	W	𐌔	Σ	𐌔	𐌔	S	S
+	+X	X	T	𐌕		T	T
			Y	V	V	V	U V W

7 The development of the modern alphabet from North Semitic, to Greek, Etruscan, and Latin is illustrated here.

8

Russian

Л Идея использования квантовых систем для ге
радиоволн оказалась весьма плодотворной и
недостижимые для обычной радиотехники резу.

Burmese

ကြ ပစ္စည်းကရိယာများ ရှိပြီးဖြစ်လေသည်။ အလယ်
ပိုင်ရာ ပုဂ္ဂိုလ်များအတွက် အထူးသင်တန်းများ

Greek

λ Ὁ Ὀδυσσεὺς καὶ οἱ σύντροφοι αὐτοῦ
πλοῖα, τὰ ὁποῖα ἦσαν πλήρη λαφύρων, ἀπ
Τρῳάδος, ἐπιθυμοῦντες νὰ φθάσωσιν ὅσο

Hebrew

ת יְהוּדִים שֶׁמָּרְדוּ בָּךְ. כֵּן שֶׁהִגִּיעַ לְאַנְטִיפַּטְרִס :
כֵּן שֶׁרָאָה אֶת שִׁמְעוֹן הַצַּדִּיק יָרַד מִמֶּרְכַּבְתּוֹ וְהִשְׁתַּחֲוָה :

Chinese

是
帶所及，使英國人的生活習慣也起了變化。
館子吃一頓的，現在大多數改爲吃自助餐，
習慣，一星期中，挑了幾天牛油麵包或三文
被迫產生的節約風氣所造成的後果是帶來不
至殃及學生們在假期中找臨時工作的出路。
貶值以來，英國的經濟衰退情形更嚴重。人
情況都還不錯的華僑們所開設的中國
停業。光是倫敦一地，過去一年來停

Sanskrit

प संस्कृतं नाम दैवी वाग् अन्वाख्याता महर्षिभिः । तद्भवस् तत्समो देशीत्य् अनेकः
प्राकृतक्रमः ।। आभीरादिगिरः काव्येष्वपभ्रंश इति स्मृताः । शास्त्रे तु संस्कृताद्
अन्यद् अपभ्रंशतयोदितम् ।। श्लेषः प्रसादः समता माधुर्यं सुकुमारता । अर्थव्यक्तिर्

8 Six different scripts used today are: Russian, the most important alphabet of the Cyrillic family; Burmese, perhaps the most beautiful of the rounded scripts used in SE Asia; modern Greek print, essentially a derivative of Byzantine minuscule; modern Hebrew, which is written right to left; Sanskrit, derived like Burmese from Aramaic (Devanagari, shown here, is similar in form to Sanskrit and is widely used to write Hindi); and classical Chinese.

9

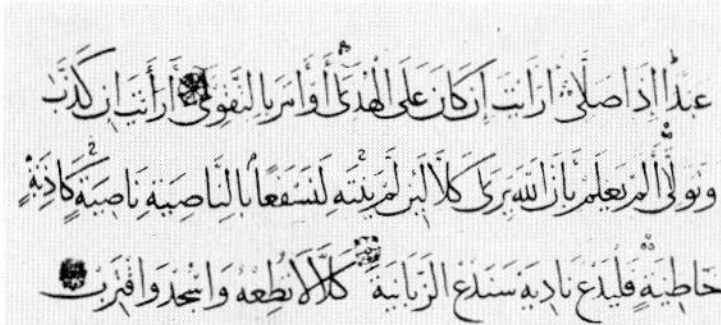

9 Classical Arabic is a consonantal script that is written left to right.

10

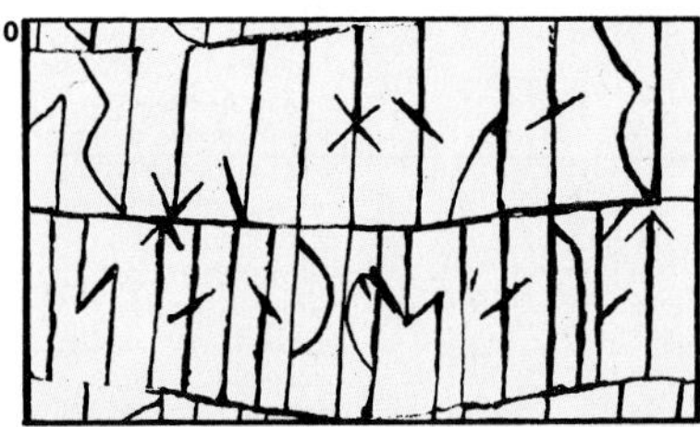

10 Runic writing, found on artifacts in Britain and Scandinavia, dates from the 3rd to the 16th centuries. Its origins are obscure, but it can be deciphered because of manuscripts giving the phonetic value of its 24 characters. Some are regularly found in English medieval writing—in "ye olde Englishe" the letter y is the Runic "thorn" pronounced th.

Communication through writing: 2

Over the centuries man has employed a tremendous variety of writing materials. Stone and metals had to be incised with a hard instrument. The softer but almost equally bulky clay tablets of Mesopotamia [1] and the wax-covered tablets of the Greeks and Romans [4] were also incised. More flexible materials, which were written on with pen and ink or painted on with a brush, included leaves, bark, and textiles, but the most important were papyrus, parchment, and paper.

The earliest materials

The Egyptians were writing on papyrus as early as 3000 BC and it remained in use as a writing material for 4,000 years. Papyrus was made out of strips cut from the stem of the papyrus plant, one set being laid with the fibers running vertically and a second set placed on top with the fibers running horizontally. Pressure was applied to bond the two sets together to form a sheet, and a number of these sheets were then glued to one another to form a long strip that could be wound into a roll.

During the first four centuries AD the roll was gradually superseded by the codex. In this format several leaves of writing material ("folios") were folded down the middle and then sewn to other sets or gatherings, in much the same way as most modern books are produced. The new form began to predominate at the same time as parchment began to replace papyrus as the most common writing material. Animal skins could be prepared for writing by tanning, which produced leather [3], or by tawing (soaking in a solution of alum and salt), which produced parchment or vellum.

Paper is traditionally supposed to have been invented by the Chinese in the first century AD. The earliest paper was made of rag (paper made from wood dates from the latter half of the nineteenth century). The earliest pens were made from reeds, and the ink was carbon-based, using lampblack, for example.

Deciphering early scripts

The decipherment of ancient scripts is obviously most difficult when the language is unknown, and it generally depends on the discovery of a bilingual document with one text in a known language. Thus the Rosetta Stone [Key], inscribed in Egyptian and Greek, enabled Jean Champollion (1790–1832) to penetrate the mysteries of Egyptian hieroglyphics and restore knowledge of a language that had been lost for 1,500 years. Similar bilingual texts made it possible to decipher Sumerian cuneiform. Even when such convenient documents do not exist, ingenuity can sometimes triumph. In the 1950s, Michael Ventris (1922–56), using techniques learned while code-breaking during World War II, deciphered the Minoan syllabic script known as Linear B [5].

Even when the language is known, considerable problems of decipherment remain, especially with examples of writing on soft materials extending over several hundred years. Styles of writing naturally tend to change, sometimes radically. (An exception is Chinese calligraphy, which has remained essentially unaltered for some 2,000 years.) In Greek, for example, the development from monumental capitals to

CONNECTIONS

See also
870 Communication through writing: 1
862 Communication without words
864 Communication through speech: 1
866 Communication through speech: 2
868 Codes, ciphers, and secret messages
1624 Making paper
1770 History of printing
1776 Newspapers and magazines
1778 Books and publishing
1780 Reference books
1782 Information retrieval

1 The 7th century Babylonian tablet is a calendar listing the lucky and unlucky days of the year. Cuneiform writing was originally inscribed on clay with a specially cut reed stylus.

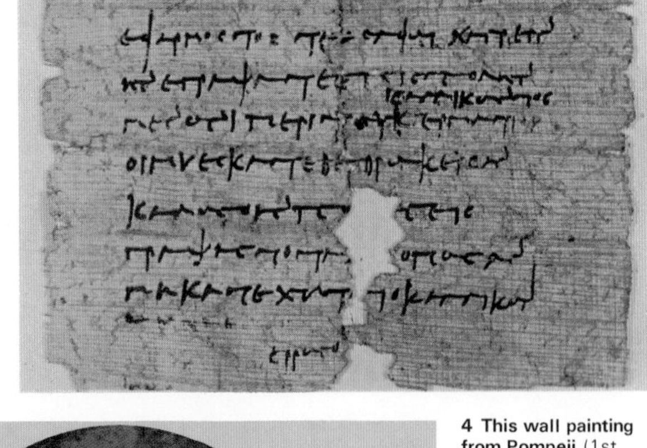

2 The papyrus roll was the usual writing material in the eastern Mediterranean area for 4,000 years. This letter on papyrus (3rd century BC) complains that a previous letter has been eaten by mice. Many works of Greek literature are extant only on papyrus, and it is the material on which the earliest manuscripts of the New Testament survived. It is found only in Egypt and in the Near East.

3 The Dead Sea Scrolls, discovered in the Qumran area in the 1940s, have stimulated considerable interest, principally because of the close relationship between the language and the ideas to be found in the scrolls and those in the New Testament. It is now accepted that the scrolls antedate the Christian era and that they belonged to a sect of Essenes. Many of them contain books of the Old Testament; others regulate the sectarian discipline of Essenes. A few are written on papyrus, but most are written on leather and nearly always in the Hebrew language.

4 This wall painting from Pompeii (1st century AD) represents a lady holding wooden tablets and a stylus. The tablets were covered with wax, then incised with a sharp-pointed stylus and finally all bound together. The codex form, which at about this time began to replace the roll for works written on papyrus and parchment and which resembles the pages of a modern book, may have developed from this.

5 Linear B, the archaic Minoan script, was deciphered by Michael Ventris using a grid [a] on which, according to known or supposed phonetic values, the different symbols used in the Minoan clay tablets were plotted in squares, each symbol being assumed to represent a syllable, consonant plus vowel. After many trials, the language turned out to be Greek. This fragment of one of the inscribed tablets (*c.* 1400 BC) [B] includes vertical strokes representing numerals.

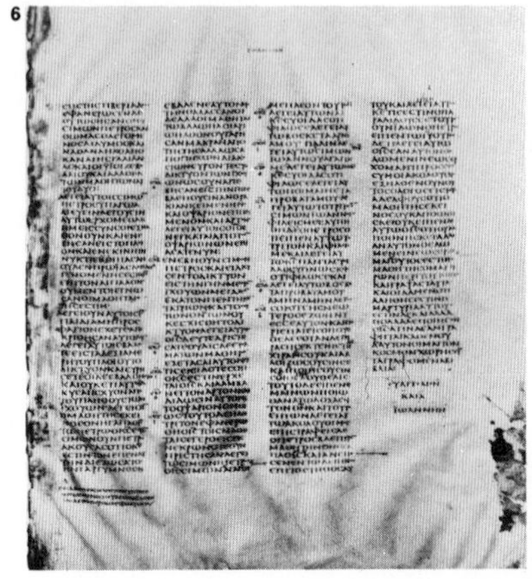

6 Codex Sinaiticus, a 4th-century manuscript of the Bible, is written in Greek uncial or biblical majuscule script, which is a rounded form of the capital script used in inscriptions and the source of the Cyrillic alphabet. The manuscript was found in the nineteenth century in a monastery on Mt Sinai by Konstantin Tischendorf (1815–74) and was eventually purchased by the British Museum. It is written on fine quality parchment.

the uncial (rounded characters) of the early biblical manuscripts [6] is readily detectable. But it is difficult to see any connection between these scripts and the cursive script with its typical flowing characters employed in a papyrus of the third century BC [2], or between the latter and the minuscule, or small letter script, used in a Byzantine manuscript 700 years later [7].

Development of writing styles

Development of writing styles is to be seen at its most diverse in Latin script [10]. In majuscule (capital letter script), the lettering of inscriptions of the classical period shows a clear connection with modern capital letters, a connection still easily seen in the rounded version (uncials) used in parchment manuscripts from the fourth century [9]. However, the everyday Latin cursive writing found on papyrus, wood, and wax tablets from the first two centuries AD [8] bears little apparent resemblance to our own alphabet, or to the more formal minuscule in use about 300 AD. A direct descendant of this minuscule, Carolingian minuscule, because of its simplicity and clarity became the accepted hand used to transcribe books throughout Latin-speaking Europe. Written with increasing angularity as time passed, by the thirteenth century it had developed into Gothic or black-letter script.

When printing was invented in the West, Gothic was the script employed for the first books. In Italy, however, fifteenth-century humanists reverted—in conscious reaction to Gothic—to a script based on ninth-century Carolingian, and this was ultimately to become the universal script of Western Europe (although in Germany this did not occur until the twentieth century). A Carolingian hand, therefore, is immediately recognizable as being in essence the script of modern print.

With the invention of printing the history of manuscript books ends, but styles of writing used in documents and letters continue to develop. The increasing literacy throughout the world has meant that today there are not just one or two recognizable styles of writing but countless individual and idiosyncratic variations.

KEY

The Rosetta Stone was found by Napoleon's Egyptian expedition in 1801 and is now in the British Museum. The stone contains the text of a priestly decree (*c.* 197 BC). The stone provided the key to the decipherment of Egyptian hieroglyphics and opened the way for scientific Egyptology. The top part is written in hieroglyphics, the middle in demotic, a popular Egyptian script, and the lower part in Greek. Comparison of the Greek with the hieroglyphic eventually enabled the latter to be deciphered. A major step was the recognition that characters inside circles, known as "cartouches," represented the names of the rulers of Egypt.

7

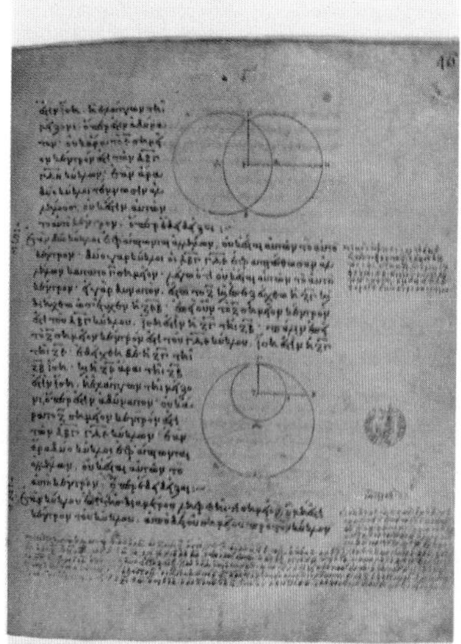

7 This Byzantine manuscript, dating from the 9th century AD, is written in Greek minuscule script, which ultimately derives from the cursive writing on the 3rd-century BC papyrus [2].

8

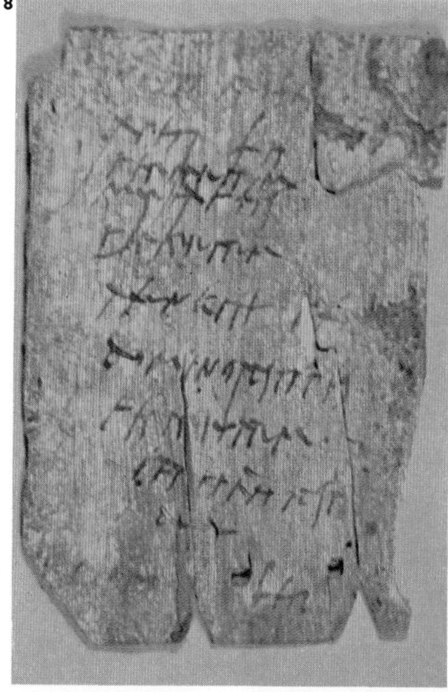

8 A Latin writing tablet from Vindolanda, a Roman fort in the north of England, records a list of military stores. It is part of a remarkable archeological discovery of wooden tablets written in ink, the first of which were unearthed in 1973. The script is the normal everyday Latin writing of the 2nd century AD, descended from monumental capital but written much more fluently and rapidly.

9

9 This manuscript is an example of Latin uncial writing and dates from the 6th century AD. The script is a rounded form of the capitals found in inscriptions; it was also adapted for writing on parchment manuscripts. It was in regular use from the 4th to the 8th centuries, but remained generally popular for headings and titles for considerably longer than this.

10 A B C D

10 Monumental capital [A] is the type normally found in inscriptions and resembles capital letters. It is from minuscule cursive [B], of the 4th century AD, that small letters originally derive. Carolingian minuscule [C] was a deliberate innovation of the period of Charlemagne (*c.* AD 800). Its clarity and simplicity won it acceptance as the script in regular use throughout western Europe. Twelfth-century Gothic minuscule [D] is sometimes known as black letter. The letters are in basically the same form as in Carolingian minuscule but have become more angular over the centuries with a considerable loss of clarity.

11

11 Chinese is not an alphabetic or syllabic script; it employs a different character for each word and therefore a special typewriter has to be used. This consists of a tray, which contains the 2,000 characters in regular use, and a normal typewriter roller. Both parts are movable, enabling the roller to be positioned over the character required, which can then be typed. It is necessary to move the roller along the rows and columns to the next character required and so on. Additional characters are contained in separate trays and must be picked up individually and positioned beneath the roller as required. The apparatus resembles a primitive printing machine.

The study of man

The "discovery" of primitive or tribal peoples has occurred repeatedly. Ancient societies, such as those of the Greeks, Romans, and Chinese [1], "discovered" them in conquering the less developed societies on their frontiers. But tribal customs and institutions were of less interest to them than the military or administrative problems, and any judgments were made in the light of their own cultural values.

For the emergent group of anthropologists of the nineteenth century the ways of life of people whose appearance was strange and who practiced unfamiliar customs became subjects of scientific investigation. Initially, the objective was to use facts concerning simple cultures to determine the broad outlines of history. This gave way to the goal of modern anthropology—the description and explanation of differences and similarities in human culture.

European expansion

The geographical explorations of the Portuguese, Spanish, English, French, Dutch, and others, begun in the late fifteenth century, generated a flood of knowledge concerning the diverse ways of life of non-Western and "uncivilized" societies. Navigators, explorers [Key, 3, 6], traders, fur trappers, soldiers, and missionaries all contributed their observations. Much of the information that accumulated was incidental to other purposes: the pursuit of trade routes, riches, possible missionary settlements, and lands for conquest and colonization. Particularly important in the pre-anthropological era were the observations of trained naturalists and scientists [7], who, while they seldom penetrated the inner workings of native life, offered accounts that were far richer in detail and more objective in perspective than the typically superficial travelers' tales [2].

In the latter half of the nineteenth century the growing knowledge of so-called primitive societies in Africa, the Pacific, and Asia paralleled the course of European imperialism as much of the non-Western world was partitioned into the colonial domains of a few European countries. Knowledge of the life-styles of subject peoples was sought and applied by the administrators of the newly founded colonies in varying degrees. To some, natives were natives, all destined for conversion to "civilization" and Christianity, and a cheap labor supply for the mines and plantations owned by Europeans.

The science of anthropology

By the 1860s knowledge of mankind's diverse cultural manifestations was sufficiently detailed to call forth an organized scientific enterprise—anthropology—to bring some order to the mass of detail. What meaning could be assigned to such strange customs as a man's taking to his hammock during his wife's pregnancy, uttering an oath when a companion sneezed, or referring to his wife's sister as "my wife"? If tribes in different parts of the world practiced the same custom did this prove there was a historical connection? These were among the questions posed by the first anthropologists. Some of them, such as Edward Tylor (1832–

CONNECTIONS

See also
1360 20th-century sociology and its influence
894 Prejudice and group intolerance
876 Origins of human society
878 Stages of social evolution
880 Simplest human societies
882 Prestate societies
884 Origins of civilization
886 Ancient states and empires
658 Family of man: today's peoples

A 人

B 犬

C 虫

1 The Chinese of Han times (206 BC–AD 220) knew of many less developed societies on their borders. Their view of these "barbarians" was expressed in the way they rendered their names. People held in high esteem were honored by having their names written in combination with the radical form of the character *jen,* meaning human being [A]. The names of people on poor terms with the emperor, or held in low esteem, were combined with *ch'uan,* meaning dog [B]. Peoples whose cultures differed greatly and whose customs were repellent had affixed to their names a form of the character *ch'ung,* or insect [C].

2 The ancient Scythian nomads living north of the Black Sea had much in common with the central Asian nomadic peoples observed by Europeans 2,000 years later. Herodotus (*c.* 485–425 BC) left an extensive account of the customs and institutions of the Scythians. Such writings were rare among the ancients, and this one is valuable although partly based on second-hand information obtained from Greeks living in the Black Sea town of Olbia. The Scythians appear to have been cultured people who traded with the Greeks. The decorations on the jewelry seen here showed Greek influences. Typical of the ancients, however, were the tales Herodotus reported of races of men beyond Scythia: some had only one eye, others hibernated for half a year, still others had the feet of goats.

3 Captain James Cook (1728–79) commanded three voyages of exploration in the Pacific Ocean that resulted in the discovery of many islands and their societies. Among the most politically developed and warlike of these societies was Hawaii, where Cook was killed in 1779, while he was on his third voyage. Cook's pioneering voyages in the Pacific opened the way to scientists and collectors, and the records that were kept of them later proved an invaluable source of information on island cultural life for anthropologists. The reports of Cook and his men included notes and observations on peoples from Easter Island to Tahiti, New Zealand, and Australia.

4 The English philosopher Thomas Hobbes (1558–1679) characterized primitive life as "nasty, brutish, and short." Although extreme, the Hobbesian view could have helped to correct the equally one-sided conception of the "noble savage." Hobbes perceived that if all men were equal by virtue of the conditions of life, then every man was a law unto himself. With no power to keep him in awe, life would be a constant state of war—real or potential.

1917), were largely content to sift through the recorded observations of explorers, missionaries, and travelers. Others examined primitive life at first hand. Lewis H. Morgan (1818–81), for example, produced the first systematic account of a primitive culture, namely the Iroquois Indians.

In posing questions concerning the meaning and interconnections of primitive institutions and in devising methods and theories to answer their questions, Morgan, Tylor, and others opened the way for the genuine discovery of primitive peoples.

Anthropologists had clearly gained an idea of man as a species, possessed of differing cultures, and they offered various schemes outlining a universal history of mankind. These showed that throughout most of his history man had lived in small, kin-based or primitive societies of a kind that can still be observed in the contemporary world. What was lacking as a firm basis for generalization, however, was sufficient "ethnography," that is, detailed accounts of the culture of particular primitive societies. Morgan's study of the Iroquois was ethnographic, but most other amassed data on primitive life consisted of scattered observations colored by a variety of European view points. While careful comparison could extract meaning from such facts, it was clear that anthropologists must henceforth collect their own data if understanding of primitive cultures was to advance.

Ethnography, the long-term analysis

The method of ethnography is as simple to describe as it is exacting in application. It calls for intensive, long-term study of native cultures through the medium of the native language and through the participation, as far as possible, in native life in order to gain an understanding of the culture from the point of view of its own members. This method of intensive ethnography was pioneered by the Polish anthropologist Bronislaw Malinowski (1884–1942) in his study of the Trobriand Islanders more than 50 years ago. Our present understanding of primitive man rests upon the many hundreds of ethnographies carried out since then in all parts of the world.

KEY

African explorations by Henry Morton Stanley (1841-1904) were some of the most successful of the 19th century. He traveled partly in boats that could be dismantled for easy portage and partly on foot. During his first journey, on assignment to the *New York Herald* (1871–72), he found David Livingstone (1813–73) living by Lake Tanganyika. His later trips included a trans-Africa expedition in 1874–77.

5

5 The "noble savage," an idealized image exemplified in this romantic portrait of King Kamehameha of Hawaii, was part of the European reaction to the new knowledge concerning tribal societies. Jean Jacques Rousseau (1712–78), influenced partly by travelers' accounts, thought of primitive man as uncorrupted by civilization and conceived of an original "state of nature" in which all men were equal (inequality being the prime source of evil). In 18th-century Europe the noble savage concept entered into philosophical and political debates about the relationship of the individual to society and to government.

6

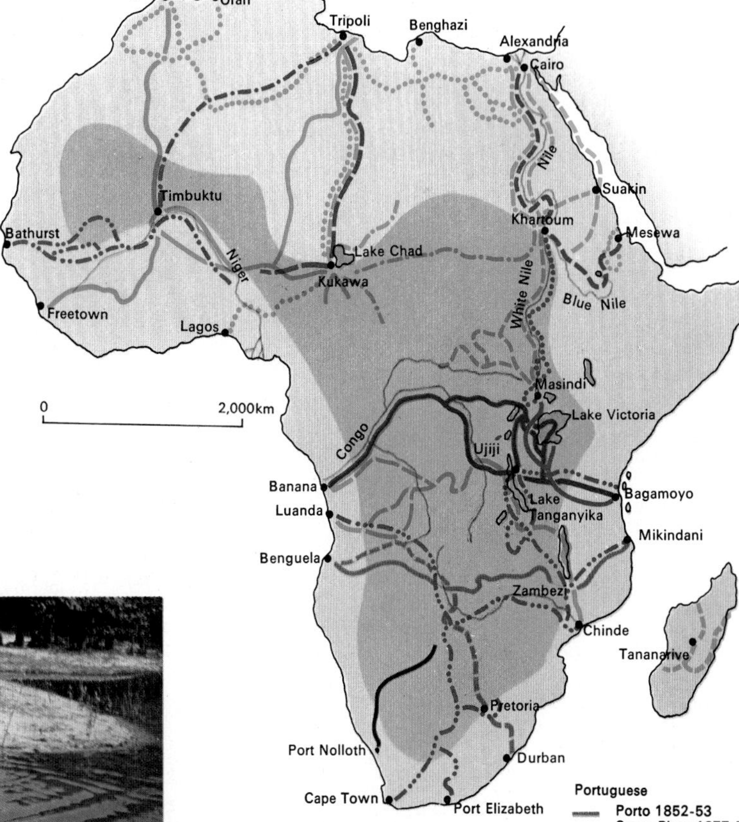
Tangier
Oran
Tripoli
Benghazi
Alexandria
Cairo
Nile
Suakin
Timbuktu
Khartoum
Meséwa
Bathurst
Lake Chad
Niger
Kukawa
White Nile
Blue Nile
Freetown
Lagos
Masindi
0
2,000km
Lake Victoria
Congo
Ujiji
Banana
Luanda
Lake Tanganyika
Bagamoyo
Mikindani
Benguela
Zambezi
Chinde
Tananarive
Pretoria
Port Nolloth
Durban
Cape Town
Port Elizabeth

British
- Baker 1862-65
- Bruce 1769-72
- Burton, Grant, Speke 1851-59, 1860-63
- Clapperton, Denham, Oudney 1822-25
- Laing 1825-26
- Livingstone 1840-73
- Mungo Park 1795-97, 1805-06

French
- Caillié 1827-28
- Grandidier 1868-70

German
- Barth 1850-55
- Junker 1875-8 '79-86
- Nachtigal 1869-74
- Rohlfs 1861-9 '73-80
- Wissmann 1880-87

Portuguese
- Porto 1852-53
- Serpa Pinto 1877-79

Swedish
- Andersson 1851-53

American
- Stanley 1871, 1874-77, 1887-89

Area little explored before the beginning of the nineteenth century

6 Observing and recording the tribes and cultures they discovered were not important aims for the 19th-century explorers of Africa. A notable exception was Richard Burton (1821–90), who published 43 volumes about his travels in Africa, India, the Middle East, and the Americas. With John Speke (1827–64) he led two unsuccessful expeditions to discover the source of the White Nile. On the second (1857–58) they found Lake Tanganyika. For most explorers survival and public acclaim for some important "first," such as finding the source of the Zambezi and opening up territory for colonization, was most important. By the time the trained anthropologists arrived many primitive cultures had already been destroyed through the shattering impact of European civilization.

7 Many South American tribes, with the same life-styles as these Kamairu Indians on a tributary of the River Xingu in Brazil, were observed by the German scientist and explorer Alexander von Humboldt (1769–1859), whose work is an example of the contributions of trained observers during the pre-anthropological era. Between 1799 and 1804, with his French colleague, the botanist Aimé Bonpland (1773–1858), Humboldt traveled thousands of miles on foot, on horseback, and by canoe in Central and South America. He collected scientific data on these previously unknown tribes.

7

Origins of human society

According to various theories, human society is anywhere from a few million years to a scant 50,000 years old. But whereas knowledge of the earliest societies will forever remain fragmentary, their general character is no longer a mystery.

Changing theories

The origins of human society became a subject of scientific scrutiny with the speculations of social evolutionists of the eighteenth and nineteenth centuries, among them Adam Ferguson (1723–1816), Lewis H. Morgan (1818–81), J. J. Bachofen (1815–87), Edward Tylor (1832–1917), Andrew Lang (1844–1912), and J. F. McLennan (1827–81). These scholars focused on fundamental and universal institutions like the family, the incest taboo, and kinship; and they constructed models of early human society.

Morgan was perhaps the most influential classical evolutionist. His *Ancient Society* (1877) contributed to the development of Marxist theory, and his discovery of classificatory kinship (calling by the same name people of the immediate family and more distant relatives), which is the principal basis of organization in tribal society, greatly affected the anthropological investigations of his successors.

Tylor also made important contributions. Seeking an explanation for the universal practice of exogamy, or prohibition of marriage within the immediate group, Tylor argued that marrying out created wider circles of cooperation and mutual aid. Rather than relying upon its own numbers and resources, a local group or band that was tied to others through marriage and kinship could call on them for assistance in time of need.

Modern theories have rejected some of the assumptions of earlier anthropologists. For example, it was thought that social evolution could be explained as an intellectual process in which early man "reasoned out" social rules and customs and that the family evolved from lower to higher, or from simple to complex forms (the Victorian monogamous family being regarded as the "highest" form). Actually, the family does not so evolve, and may even become simpler as other institutions take over what were once its functions. Factual knowledge has also increased enormously, through ethnographic reports on the simplest human societies of hunters and gatherers; field studies of the social life of monkeys and apes; and the archeological and fossil records, which can tell us what early man probably looked like, what tools he used, and what foods he ate.

Basic human institutions

These studies have shown that even the simplest human society, as typified by the hunting and gathering cultures of, for example, the Bushmen of the Kalahari Desert or the Australian Aborigines [2], is a complex system of universal and perhaps primeval human institutions. These are the incest taboo, the prohibition of marriage or sexual relations within the immediate family; exogamy, rules ensuring marriage outside a certain group, usually larger than the primary group; kinship, the recognition of various categories of kin who behave to-

CONNECTIONS

See also
558 How primates behave
556 How mammals behave
794 Adulthood: marriage
646 Primate to hominid
648 The first hominid
650 The first men
652 From ancient to modern man
1582 Early technology
1586 The Stone Age
1588 Fire and bronze
1592 The Iron Age
874 The study of man
878 Stages of social evolution
880 Simplest human societies
882 Prestate societies
884 Origins of civilization
886 Ancient states and empires

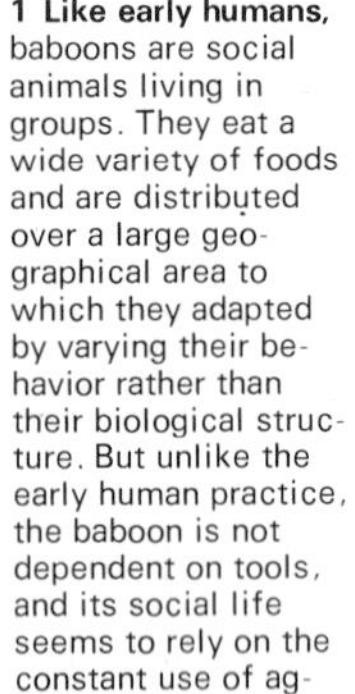

1 Like early humans, baboons are social animals living in groups. They eat a wide variety of foods and are distributed over a large geographical area to which they adapted by varying their behavior rather than their biological structure. But unlike the early human practice, the baboon is not dependent on tools, and its social life seems to rely on the constant use of aggression within the band.

2 Certain tools used by such hunting and gathering peoples as the Aborigines (as here) and Bushmen appeared within the last 50,000 years. The rapid development of technology has led some anthropologists to propose that human society emerged, together with new tool traditions and anatomically modern man, 50,000 years ago. This contradicts the view that humans appeared a million or more years ago.

3 Since marriage is a universal human institution, all humans would appear to be the "marrying kind" (seen here is a French wedding party). Although varying in form, the functions of marriage seem to vary little, even if the marriage practices of complex human societies are included. In all known societies, the incest taboo decrees that of the four cross-sex relationships inherent in a nuclear family—husband-wife, brother-sister, mother-son, father-daughter—only the first is allowed to involve mating. The universality of these proscriptions leads to the assumption that they are of fundamental importance because they remove the inevitable disruption of sexual jealousy. Since early human societies were composed of family groups interrelated by kinship, then marriage, the incest taboo, and marriage rules in general can be viewed as foundations of society.

ward one another in prescribed ways; marriage [3], which universally (in known societies) legitimizes offspring and creates affinal (in-law) relationships; the family, which is the basic economic unit; a division of labor based on sex and age; reciprocity, the sharing of food and other commodities; and the notion of territory, including concepts of property.

The classical evolutionists thought of early humans as mating promiscuously, only later evolving rules governing marriage. If we examine mating patterns among monkeys and apes, it appears that our human precursors might indeed have lived in "promiscuous hordes." Whatever the mating behavior of subhuman primates, however, it does not correspond to the human pattern in which all or many of the most accessible females are off limits because they are thought of as "mothers," "daughters," or "sisters" because of the incest taboo. In this way the potential disruptiveness of sexual relations among groups of parents and offspring was dealt with in early human societies.

An equally serious problem was the threat of conflict over both women and resources among different groups in society. Marital alliances through exogamy did not eliminate such conflict, but they did mitigate it. The simplest form of alliance is that of groups of men exchanging sisters generation after generation. In more complicated systems one group does not give wives to the same group from which it receives wives; a larger number of groups is required for exchange, and thus a larger system of alliances is maintained [4].

Social origins

Human social origins are found in these basic and interrelated institutions. Many forces contributed to their emergence, including the prolonged dependency period of human children; developments such as tool-using, which long antedated the first human societies; and such basic needs of social life as sharing food, providing for attack and defense, and transmitting technical and social knowledge from one generation to the next.

KEY

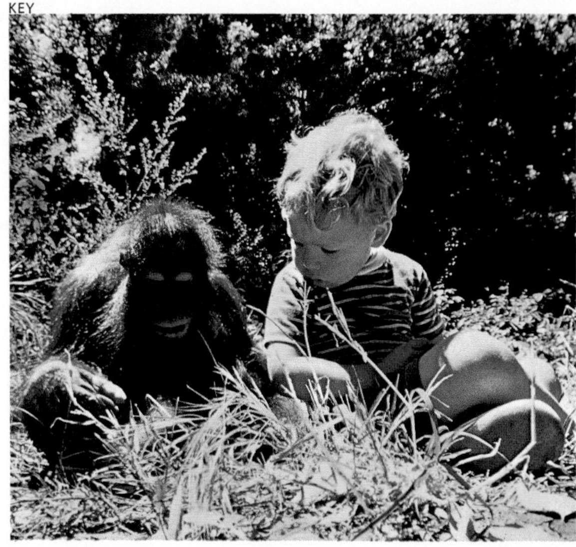

Speculating about which of the great ape species our ancestors might have resembled is an intriguing guessing game. This picture shows a child playing with an orangutan.

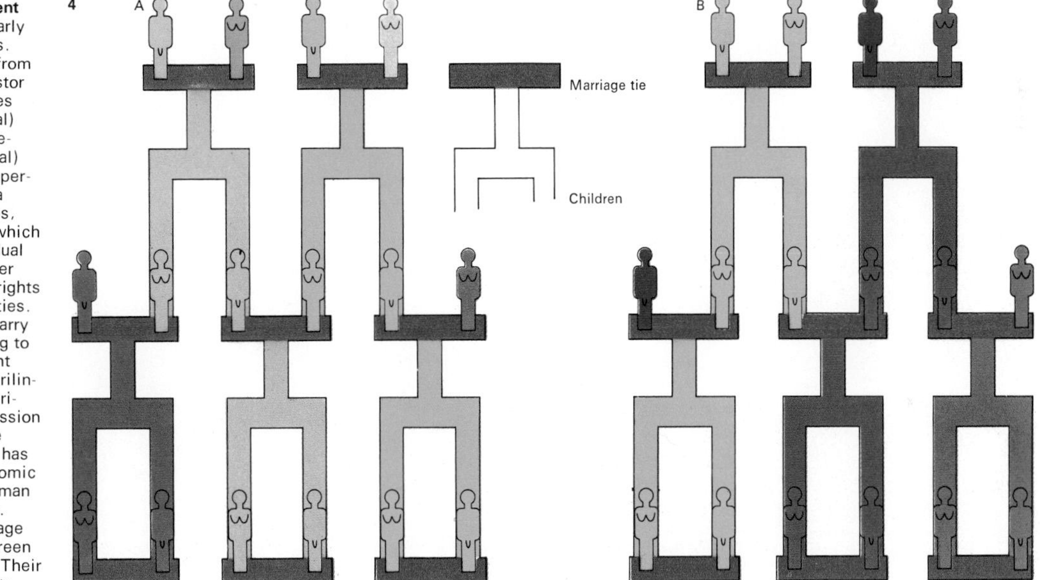
4
A
B
Marriage tie
Children

4 Rules of descent were probably early social inventions. Descent traced from a common ancestor through the males (called patrilineal) [A] or through females (matrilineal) [B] places each person into one of a number of groups, membership in which gives the individual many of his or her most important rights and responsibilities. People do not marry anyone belonging to the same descent group. In the patrilineal system, inheritance and succession pass through the man. A husband has sexual and economic rights over a woman and her children. Here a blue lineage man marries a green lineage woman. Their children belong to the blue lineage. In a matrilineal descent system, membership in the group is inherited through the mother, but this does not imply a matriarchy or rule by women. The maternal uncle is usually the key figure. J. J. Bachofen believed that matrilineal societies represented a simpler stage of social development that predated the emergence of patrilineal societies, because, he reasoned, only maternity could be determined with any certainty. Later anthropologists have rejected this. Patrilineal and matrilineal descent are alternative organizing principles. Patrilineality is common, but both are found in nonindustrial societies.

5

Hunter

Elder sister

Younger brother

Younger sister

Father (tail and part of backbone to his parents)

Elder brother

Mother (part of thigh and shin to her parents)

5 Australian Aboriginal customs show that real rights and duties are associated with kin statuses. A hunter who kills a kangaroo is obliged to give particular portions of the animal to specified relatives. It is presumed that rules governing the sharing of food were among man's earliest cultural inventions.

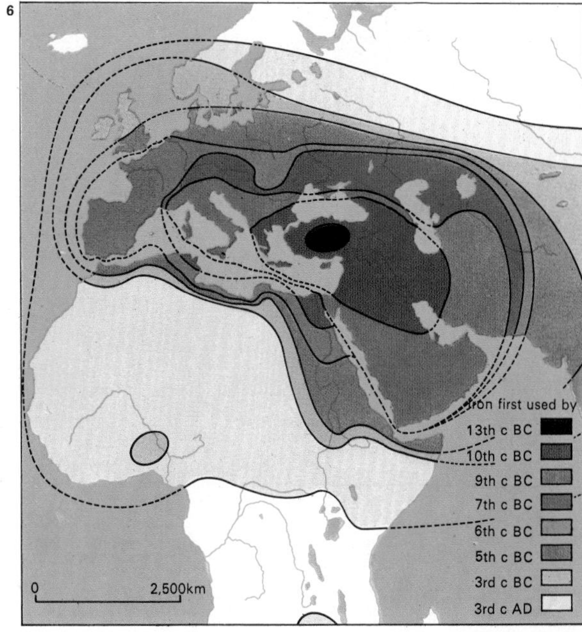
6
Iron first used by
13th c BC
10th c BC
9th c BC
7th c BC
6th c BC
5th c BC
3rd c BC
3rd c AD
0
2,500km

6 Diffusion, through borrowing or by cultures expanding into new areas, is a pervasive influence in social evolution. The spread of iron working from the ancient Middle East made better tools and weapons available. These gave the peoples who possessed them advantages over their neighbors. The resulting invasions brought many social changes.

Stages of social evolution

History is a record of past events or the interpretation of those events. But history alone will not enable one to understand the past. It is also necessary to study social evolution, the process by which societies change their form of organization.

Types of human society

The historian's arrangement of events into periods or ages does not necessarily coincide with a classification of societies into stages of social evolution. A division of European history into ancient, medieval, and modern periods, for instance, would not correspond to the stages of its social evolution. While ancient Europe, or that part of it under Roman rule, exemplified the stage of ancient state-organized society, the succeeding medieval societies were merely smaller and more rudimentary versions of the same stage. Modern European societies, however, beginning with the emergence of industrial capitalism, exemplify an emergent general type, that of the industrial nation state. Different stages of social evolution are really based on distinctive features of organization rather than on time periods, regions, or specific events. Hence, evolutionary stages are not necessarily marked off by, nor identified with, specific technologies. Pastoral nomads, for example, can belong to small tribes or centrally organized chiefdoms [2]. Nor do societies invariably follow a set progression of stages [7].

The evolutionary process is thus "opportunistic," with societies adapting in response to the challenges of their environments, including both their physical settings and their relationships to neighboring societies [5]. Occasionally, however, adaptation to an environment has led to a "higher" form of organization, one in which a society is organized in a more complex fashion. This happened, for example, in northern Europe when a new kind of society formed as a result of the Industrial Revolution, or in the ancient Middle East when agriculture first appeared. Thus, while evolution is mainly a process of diversification as societies adapt to different environments—producing variations on the same organizational themes—on occasion there have been changes involving new organizational themes.

The purpose of distinguishing between stages or types of societies is to locate these major changes in the course of social evolution [Key] and to isolate their causes. Yet anthropologists have often disagreed on these points. One such disagreement concerns the Neolithic period. Since the researches of the British archeologist V. Gordon Childe (1892–1957), it has been widely held that the "Neolithic Revolution" constituted a major evolutionary transformation of society.

The advent of the Neolithic period, when agriculture began, did involve major changes. Through domestication of various plants and animals (the technical breakthrough underlying agriculture) man's relationship to the environment was radically altered. In addition agriculture permitted an increase in human population, perhaps a twenty-fold increase over average population levels of the cultures of foragers and hunters. Yet Neolithic societies, though

CONNECTIONS

See also
880 Simplest human societies
876 Origins of human society
882 Prestate societies
884 Origins of civilization
886 Ancient states and empires
874 The study of man
304 History of agriculture
322 Plant genetic resources
370 Farm stockbreeding and management

1A

B

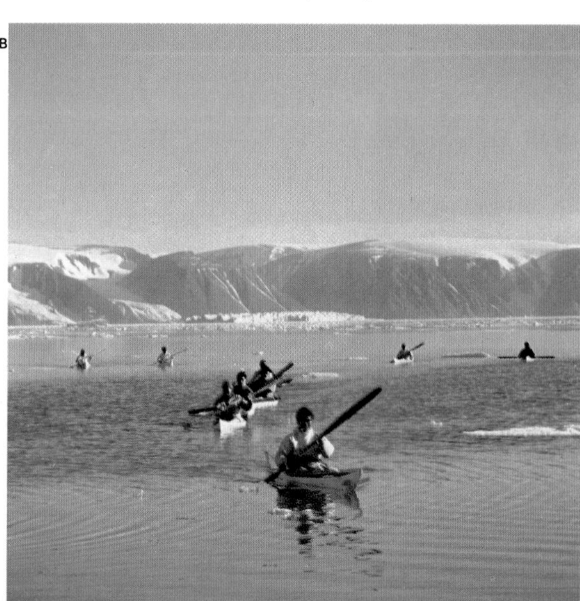

1 Hunting–gathering or fishing peoples, like the Bushmen [A] of the Kalahari Desert in southern Africa or the Eskimos [B] of Greenland, are among the last remnants of the simplest and earliest form of social organization. The harsh environments that they live in are unsuitable for the growth of more complex tribes or chiefdoms because they are unable to support a large or settled population.

2

2 Nomadic pastoralists, like these in Afghanistan, once inhabited the great African-Asian belt of desert and steppe, subsisting on the products of their herds but also raiding oases and agricultural communities. Many herding societies, such as the Tuareg of North Africa and the Mongols of Asia, were organized as chiefdoms whose mobility could make them effective militarily.

3

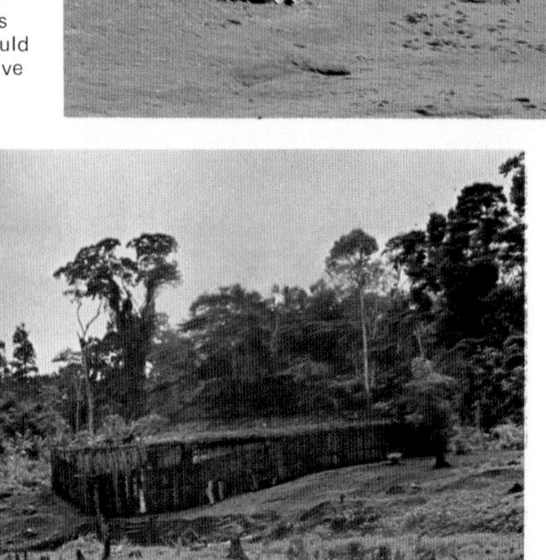

3 Shifting horticulture, in which gardens are annually or frequently moved to newly cleared plots, was probably man's earliest system of cultivation. It survives in tropical areas of Africa, Asia, the Pacific, and the Americas. While sometimes regarded as wasteful of land, it has served as the productive basis of societies ranging in complexity from the tribal Jivaro of South America to the ancient Maya civilization of Yucatán and Guatemala.

4

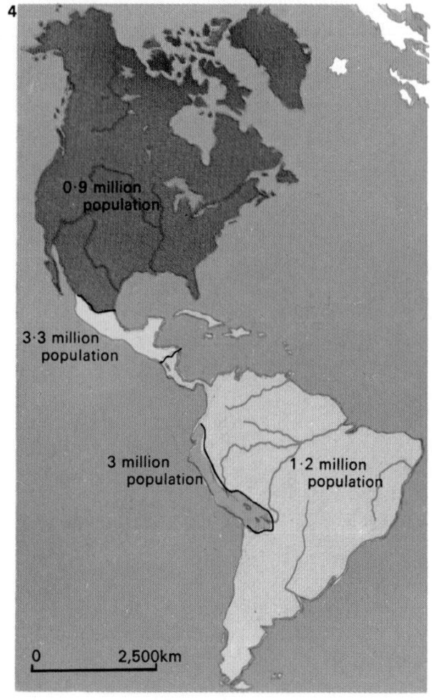

0·9 million population
3·3 million population
3 million population
1·2 million population
0
2,500km

4 Relative densities of population in the New World at the time of the Spanish conquest indicate the significant role played in population growth by the existence of a state-organized form of society. In the areas that were dominated by the Aztec and Inca empires in Central and South America, the population per square mile was much greater than in the larger areas—North America and the vast expanse of South America east of the Andes. This difference reflects the superior economic system made possible by state organization.

often larger and less nomadic than their predecessors, did not necessarily display any new means of organization.

Chiefdom societies

In time, however, and in certain localities, Neolithic technology and economy did give rise to more advanced or complex societies based on a chiefdom or hierarchy. What distinguished chiefdoms from the tribal, egalitarian societies was a measure of institutional centralization. The critical development was the emergence of hereditary chieftainship in place of the rather ephemeral leadership of tribal societies (indeed, chieftainship has been compared in importance to the development of the central nervous system in biological evolution). Chiefdoms were larger, more complex, and more firmly integrated than tribal societies. For the first time, persons, families, and larger subgroupings became differentiated in political and economic power.

Chiefdom societies had the potential for expansion and increasing centralization. Presumably, such societies were the immediate precursors of the first state-organized societies in ancient Mesopotamia and other areas. Such states continued the line of evolutionary advance initiated by chiefdoms by substituting for ruling families a government or ruling group with a monopoly of coercive force. This development of a powerful means of integrating diverse groups, allowing population growth [4] and centralization, initiated a new stage and led to the displacement or absorption of simpler societies.

The nation-state

In terms of evolution, therefore, during most of human history societies were of one type: small-scale egalitarian societies integrated by ties of kinship and marriage and by tribal leaders who, in most societies, were scarcely distinguished from their fellow tribesmen. In favored environments, particularly after the invention of agriculture, chiefdoms developed, some evolving further into true states. Later, nation-states emerged in Western Europe to become the universal type of social organization.

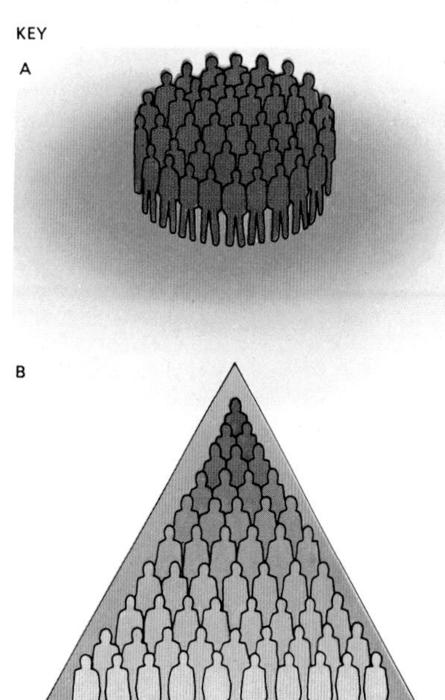
KEY
A
B

The change from egalitarian, kin-based societies [A] to hierarchical chiefdoms [B] was an extremely significant advance in social evolution. By improving and so enormously extending social cohesion, the chiefdom encouraged population expansion by making possible effective social organization. The social mechanisms of eqalitarian societies are not strong enough to hold in check the conflicting needs of large numbers of people. Egalitarian societies are therefore limited to areas of kinship influence, whereas chiefdoms and state societies have definite physical boundaries and a sovereign government set above the population.

5
A
B
C
D
E

5 The cultural evolution of a particular society is usually the result of invasions by societies that are at higher stages of development. Consistent growth within the society is seldom so important. By at least 1,000 years ago in the southeastern United States, the region south of the Ohio River and east of the Mississippi River, tribal Indian societies [A] gave way to more complex chiefdoms, partly the result of cultural influences from Mexico [B]. European colonists then erected the slave-based agrarian society of the Old South [C]. Beaten by the industrial North during the Civil War, the South was not transformed into an industrial urban society until after World War II [D]. In the 1960s the South provided sites for launching the United States to the space age [E] and so became a part of what may develop into a postindustrial electronic society.

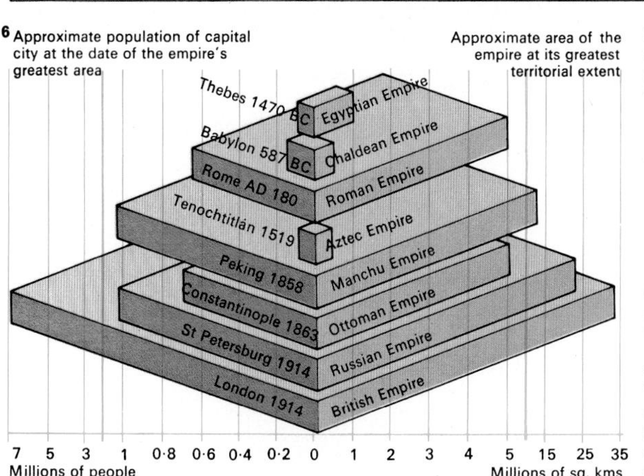
6
Approximate population of capital city at the date of the empire's greatest area
Approximate area of the empire at its greatest territorial extent
Thebes 1470 BC
Egyptian Empire
Babylon 587 BC
Chaldean Empire
Rome AD 180
Roman Empire
Tenochtitlán 1519
Aztec Empire
Peking 1858
Manchu Empire
Constantinople 1863
Ottoman Empire
St Petersburg 1914
Russian Empire
London 1914
British Empire
7 5 3 1 0·8 0·6 0·4 0·2 0 1 2 3 4 5 15 25 35
Millions of people
Millions of sq. kms

6 Effective central control plays an important role in controlling the size of an empire. This, in turn, is reflected in the size of the imperial capital.

7 "Ethnical periods," listed by Lewis H. Morgan in *Ancient Society* (1877), were based solely on technological criteria, implying that all societies progressed through each stage. This idea of unilinear evolution is no longer accepted, and stages are now based on social criteria.

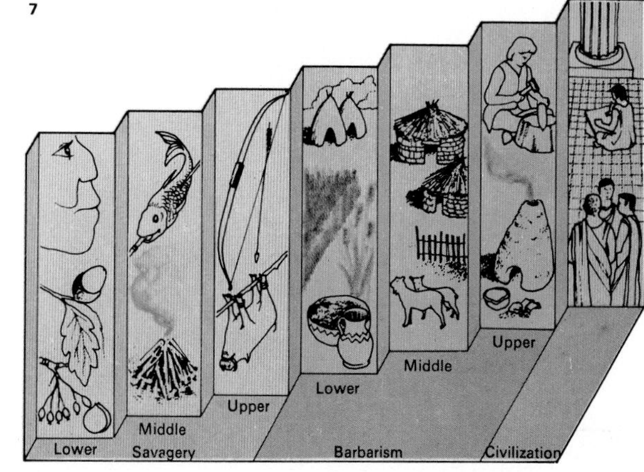
7
Lower
Middle
Savagery
Upper
Lower
Middle
Upper
Barbarism
Civilization

Simplest human societies

Much of human history is the history of primitive cultures. As recently as five centuries ago, on the eve of European expansion, such cultures were spread over a large part of the world—in Africa, northern Eurasia, Australasia, the Pacific Islands, and most of the Americas [1]. Knowledge of man's way of life during most of his existence is derived principally from the study of representatives of primitive cultures that have survived until "modern times."

If anthropologists refer to the simplest cultural adaptations as primitive, this is not an attempt to disparage them. Rather, "primitive" refers to cultures that are simple technologically, small in population, based on kinship ties, egalitarian, and unspecialized institutionally.

Family units in early cultures

Primitive technologies are directed primarily to securing food by collecting wild foods, fishing, horticulture, or herding. Men and women normally perform different tasks, but each family has the required skills, tools, and resources even though some tasks involve the cooperation of people from several families.

Primitive cultures are small, averaging only a few hundred members. A lower limit of two to three dozen people is set by the requirements or advantages of cooperation in economic activities, sharing of food, and caring for the sick. An upper limit is determined by food supply and also by the fact that this way of organizing people cannot cope with more than several hundred people without great strain. Primitive communities that grow too large to function effectively usually split in two peacefully.

Primitive cultures are family cultures [Key]. The so-called nuclear family of parents and children is often part of a larger unit, the extended or three-generation family. Beyond the family, social relationships still center on kinship. Indeed, the society as a whole is often conceived as a body of kin. Prominent as a focus of ceremonial life are individual "life crises" or rites of passage: birth, puberty, marriage, and death.

Primitive cultures do not lack social distinctions: men have more favored social positions than women; older people have an advantage over their juniors; the successful hunter or industrious cultivator is accorded prestige. But primitive societies are egalitarian in that there are as many positions of prestige as there are people with the characteristics needed to fill them.

Multiple roles within kinship groups

The family-based character of primitive societies is the key to their simple organization. For the family is not only at the center of economic life but is also a member of larger groups of kin. It has a social, political, economic, and ritual role to play.

While it is correct to think of primitive cultures as lacking special-purpose institutions, all cultures are more or less specialized in the way they adapt to the environment in order to survive. Specialization of some sort is the invariable outcome of adaptation to specific challenges or opportunities. Primitive cultures are distinguished by their dependence on a narrow range of resources, or even upon a single resource. The acorn, for example, was vital

CONNECTIONS

See also
- 882 Prestate societies
- 874 The study of man
- 876 Origins of human society
- 878 Stages of social evolution
- 884 Origins of civilization
- 886 Ancient states and empires
- 654 Spread of man: 1
- 656 Spread of man: 2
- 888 Structure of societies
- 890 Conflict, power, and social inequality
- 898 Fundamental political ideas

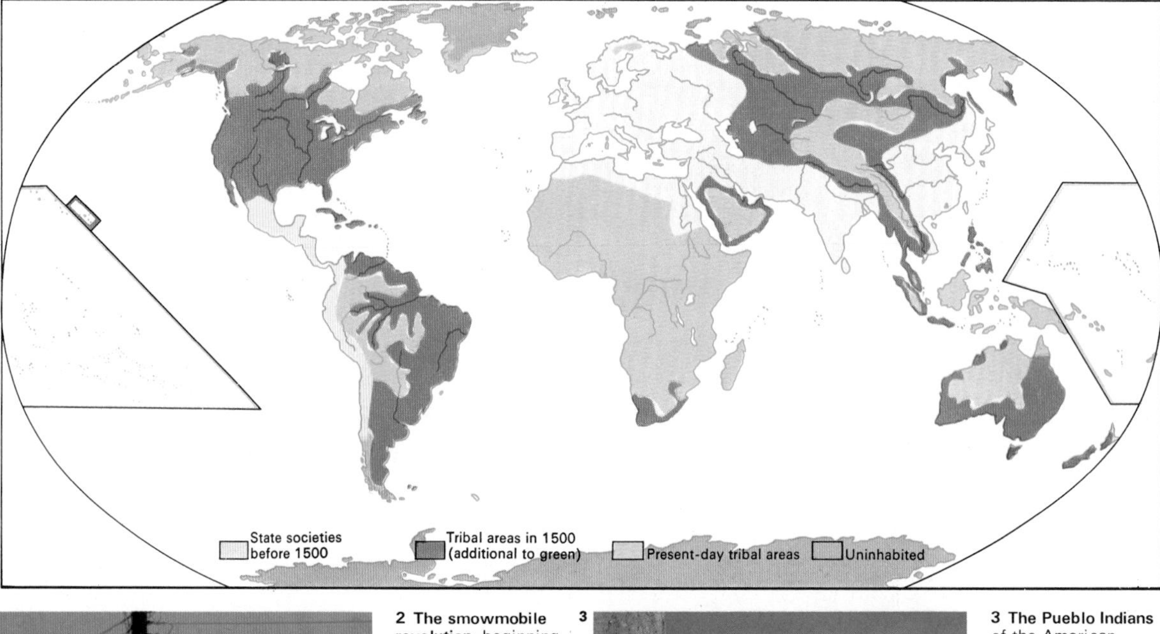

State societies before 1500
Tribal areas in 1500 (additional to green)
Present-day tribal areas
Uninhabited

1 Tribal cultures reigned supreme in the world of 5,000 years ago. They were challenged by the spread of the ancient civilizations, which converted tribal people into ethnic groups within a more complex social organization. This process took place when the Romans conquered and Romanized the tribal Britons, for example. The contraction of the tribal world was greatly accelerated by Western exploration and colonization, particularly during the past four centuries. Tribal peoples now make up less than 1% of world's population. The map compares their settlement today with areas of tribal culture in 1500.

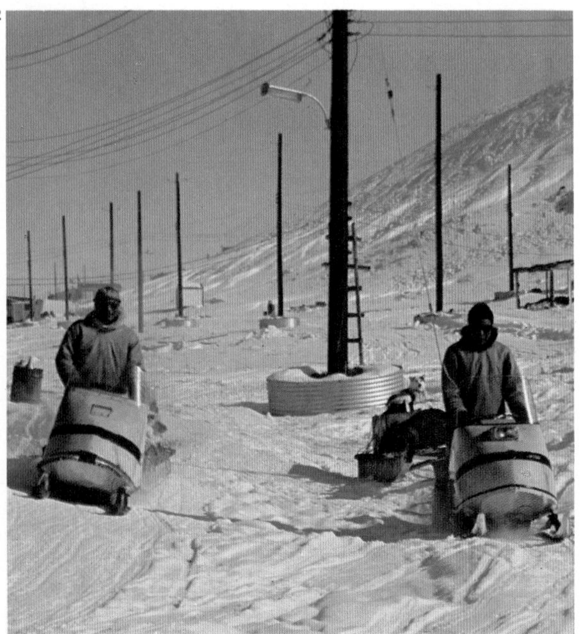

2 The snowmobile revolution, beginning in the 1960s, has already had a significant impact on the way of life of Arctic peoples, including the North American Eskimos and the Laplanders. The range and speed of the snowmobile allow the Eskimos to reach their hunting grounds more quickly. This permits compact settlements and more frequent visiting among people still living in widely scattered groups. Under the impact of Western materialism, the distinction between "rich" (snowmobile owners) and "poor" (dogsled people) has become important. Such a distinction between rich and poor is seldom made and has little significance in tribal cultures.

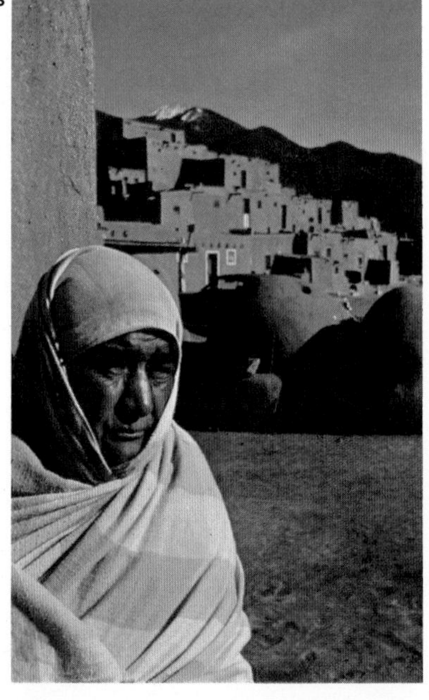

3 The Pueblo Indians of the American Southwest practiced flood-water farming, growing the crops of the Amerindian complex—corn, beans, and squash. They developed an elaborate ceremonial life in which the needs of agriculture and the harshness of their desert habitat were central themes. Although long ruled by the Spanish, the Mexicans, and the United States, the Pueblos have retained much of their traditional culture in modern times. Seen here is a Taos Indian from New Mexico. In spite of the need for a degree of centralized organization to make their type of farming successful, the Pueblos never developed a hierarchical structure or chiefdoms.

to California Indians, as were reindeer to Siberian hunters and pastoralists.

Specialization may prove limiting when environmental change decrees the need for social change. A frequent cause of change is the advent of new relationships with neighboring societies. Widespread change of this kind followed the invention of agriculture. Agricultural societies, more populous and powerful than most hunting-and-gathering societies, became dominant over a large part of the earth because their new skills permitted more effective use of many environments. As a result, hunting-and-gathering peoples retreated to such "marginal" areas as deserts, tundra, the arctic wastes, and other habitats rejected by primitive agriculturalists. For most of human history, of course, wild food was the only means of subsistence, and it allowed humans to survive, if not always thrive, in almost every conceivable habitat.

Impact of the Europeans

The expansion of Western culture in the sixteenth century posed a challenge that primitive cultures could not meet. If Europeans wanted their territories, they were pushed aside—decimated by a combination of introduced diseases and force of arms. Surviving remnants were finally confined to tribal reserves on marginal lands. European exploitation of newly conquered territories was achieved partly through recruiting native populations, initially by force, to supply labor for European plantations, farms, and mines. Primitive societies harnessed to European economic enterprise were thus doubly penalized. They lost territories and resources as well as the services of many of the active men who became wage earners [9].

European trade had far-reaching effects even upon societies that had no direct contact with Europeans. For example, the fur trade in North America led to an increase in Indian warfare as some societies formed tribal confederacies to strengthen their position in the trade. Modification of primitive cultures has been rapid during the past century, and they have ceased to exist in all but a few remote areas.

KEY

Social organization in the simplest cultures centers on the family, such as this Zulu group. Tribal societies, never more than a few hundred strong, are closely bound together by marriage. Leadership is not the preserve of any one person but rotates among the most talented in each tribal activity.

4

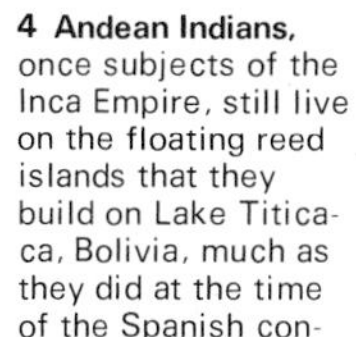

4 Andean Indians, once subjects of the Inca Empire, still live on the floating reed islands that they build on Lake Titicaca, Bolivia, much as they did at the time of the Spanish conquest in 1533.

5

5 Argentinian gauchos are descended from nomadic Indians who began hunting on horseback when the Spaniards introduced horses. Their way of life resembled that of the American Plains Indian.

6

6 Australia was colonized by hunting-and-gathering people at least 30,000 years ago. Bands of a few dozen people had contact with others during their annual wandering across the arid continent. Seasonal abundances of food in certain localities enabled groups numbering in the hundreds to assemble for ceremonial activities like the dance for which these Aborigines have liberally painted their bodies.

7

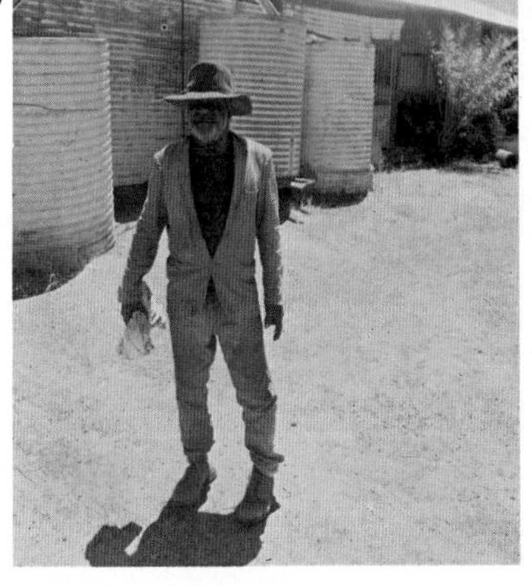

7 Aborigines today frequently live in poverty on the fringes of Australian society, both in urban areas and in the outback, in spite of an official policy of assimilation. Aborigines numbered about 300,000 when the white settlement of Australia began during the eighteenth century, but only a few thousand, mainly in dry inland areas, still carry on a semi-traditional way of life based on the tribal culture developed and practiced by their ancestors.

8

8 The Bantu peoples of Africa are descended from tribal groups that began to expand from a probable base in the Cameroons a few centuries before the birth of Christ. They spread their language, agriculture, and iron tools over much of Africa south of the Sahara. Some Bantu developed chiefdoms that in turn evolved into primitive states under the pressures of the slave trade and European colonization. Prominent groups are the Zulu, Swahili, and Kikuyu.

9

9 A Zulu working as a rickshaw boy in Durban, South Africa, illustrates one of the sadder aspects of the way in which African villagers have been drawn into towns, mines, plantations, and farms to work for wages or to prostitute their original culture for the amusement of tourists, particularly as white settlement has pushed their tribes into poorer, more marginal land. Bantu working for whites during the early phase of European settlement kept strong tribal ties.

Prestate society

Primitive man has been pictured as both an individualist and a rigid conformist—a "slave to custom." These characterizations are not, however, completely opposed. In a society lacking a formal legal system backed by state power, people must adhere strictly to rules of custom lest the conflict of individual interests lead to violence and anarchy.

In modern society, the state can either be seen as simply providing security for people and possessions or as an instrument for constraining individual freedoms. Whatever viewpoint is adopted it is difficult to conceive of orderly social life in the absence of a supreme political authority, yet primitive, prestate societies lack such an authority. To understand their organization is to appreciate what British anthropologist Mary Douglas has called the "miracle of social order in the absence of radio police cars."

The egalitarian, tribal society

Every organization is a system of integrated parts. In these terms, prestate societies exhibit two kinds of organization, which differ in size, in the nature of their parts, and in the means of integrating them.

The first type, the tribal egalitarian society, is built on a segmental plan. The segments—such as families, lineages [1], and clans [2]—are unspecialized, basically equal, and linked together by kinship, marriage, and descent [Key, 3]. Within the segments the male head of a family household wields authority over women and children, lineage elders have a greater say than junior members in family affairs, and yet no leader or group coordinates the activities or relationships of one segment with another.

Men and women in their respective spheres of work engage in the same pursuits; hence each family is involved in the same round of economic activities [4]. People have a common style of housing, dress, and personal adornment. They use the same kind of tools, eat the same foods, observe similar rituals, and worship the same gods. The cultural sameness of a number of such social segments helps to produce a social unity based on likeness, or what the French sociologist and anthropologist Emile Durkheim (1858–1917) termed "mechanical solidarity." The weakness of this system, however, is that it is not really integrated because the social segments are so self-sufficient, yet it has strength in that the loss of one or more segments does not impair or destroy the society.

Segmental societies are not wholly without leaders, but the tribal leader generally lacks the authority to give commands or, if he has this authority, it is limited by context and duration; he may, for example, exercise it only during a hunt or a war party. Because the tribal leader's influence does not extend beyond his own social segment—perhaps a kin group or hamlet—leaders of other segments are likely to be his rivals.

Hierarchical society and the family

The second type of prestate organization, the chiefdom or hierarchical society, achieves a measure of "organic solidarity" because specialized parts depend on each

CONNECTIONS

See also
884 Origins of civilization
874 The study of man
876 Origins of human society
878 Stages of social evolution
880 Simplest human societies
886 Ancient states and empires
890 Conflict, power and social inequality
898 Fundamental political ideas

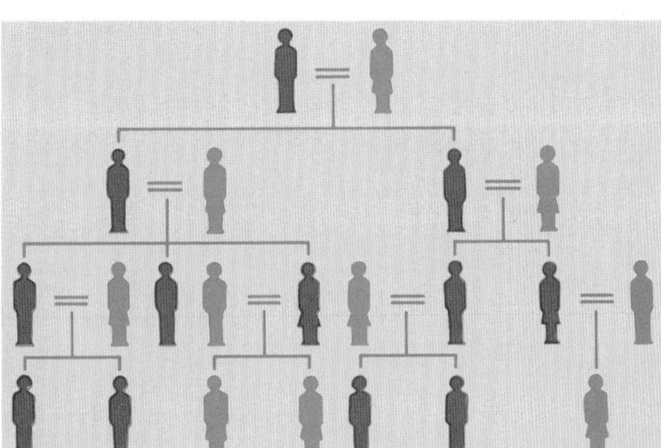

1 Lineages are descent groups. Membership is determined by descent from a common ancestor through lines of either males (patriliny) or females (matriliny). Lineages comprise a common type of social grouping in prestate societies. Since lineages are exogamous—mates must be acquired from other groups—a society must be composed of more than one lineage. Some prestate societies consist of a number of interrelated lineages. Illustrated here are the interconnections between two lineages, brown and green, in a patrilineal society, where children belong to the father's lineage.

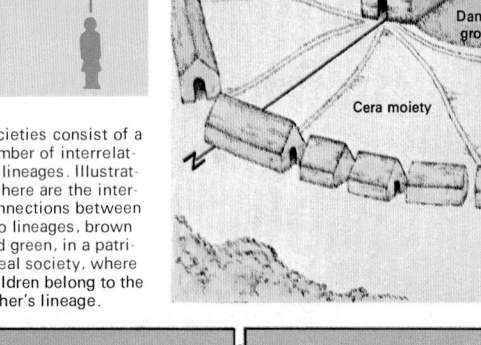

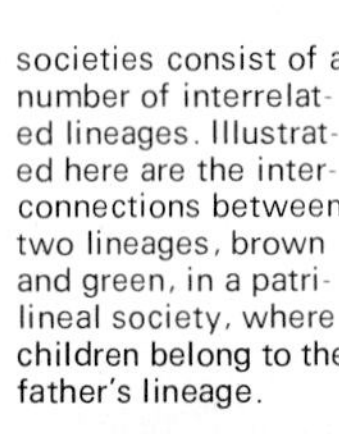

Tugare moiety
Upstreamers
Men's house
Dancing ground
Downstreamers
Cera moiety
S
N

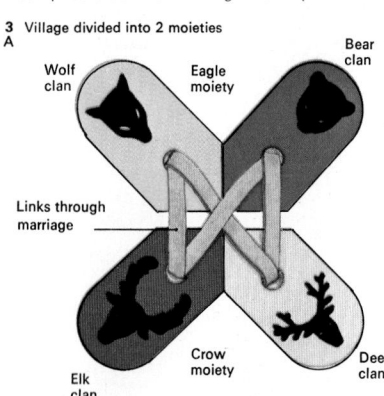

2 In a Bororo village in central Brazil, the men's house and dancing ground are surrounded by a circle of smaller huts for women and their husbands. The unmarried men sleep in the men's house. A line running east-west divides the circle of huts into two halves or moieties. The huts are arranged in clans. Those on the east side of the circle are called upstreamers, those on the west downstreamers, following the direction of the river. Each person belongs to the same divisions—clan and moiety—as his mother and must marry a woman of the same class but opposite half, or moiety, of the village.

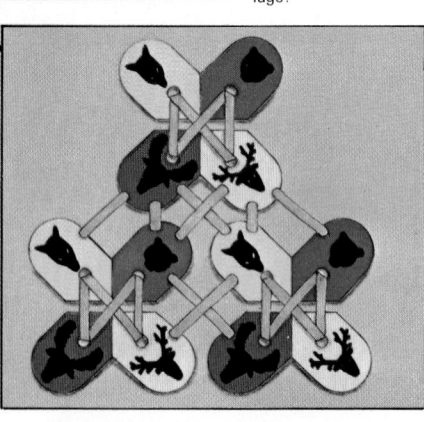

3 Village divided into 2 moieties
A
Wolf clan
Eagle moiety
Bear clan
Links through marriage
Elk clan
Crow moiety
Deer clan
B

C

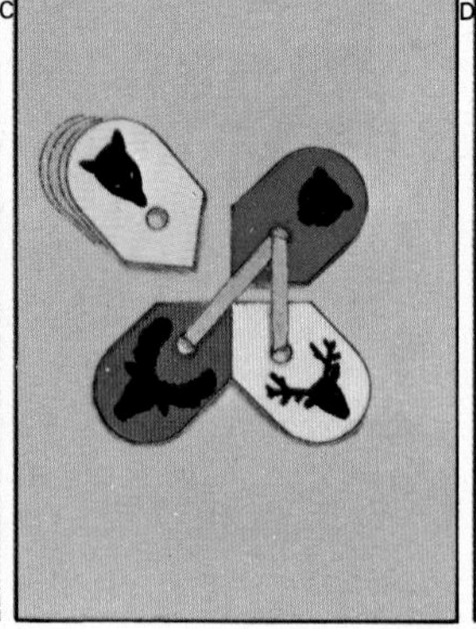

D

3 Tribal societies consists of various kinds of social segments interrelated through kinship, marriage, traditions of common descent, exchange, and perhaps a division of labor in ceremony. This American Indian village contains local segments or lineages of four clans, which are arranged in two intermarrying halves, or moieties, the Eagle and the Crow [A]. Lineage is a system of actual blood ties. A clan is more of a cultural grouping with a common interest such as war, or religion—that cuts across lineage, providing other than family ties for its members. The Wolf and Bear clan people have a tradition of common descent; since they regard themselves as too closely related to marry, they must obtain their spouses from either of the paired clans (Elk and Deer) of the Crow moiety. As local groups of clanspeople increase in population, they break up and some of their members go off to colonize a new village [B]. In time they are joined here by segments of other split lineages. The clan and moiety organization is thus duplicated in the new settlement [C]. Through growth and breakup, members of the four clans are distributed over the tribal territory. Marriage is between men and women of opposite moieties, whether of the same or different villages [D]. Intermoiety marriage and crosscutting clanship are the ties that unify the tribe. A Wolf clan member has fellow clansmen and men of a brother clan in other villages. From these people he can expect hospitality, protection, and assistance in time of need. In addition, he is a relative of Elk and Deer clan people, who have married his clan sisters. Thus the relationship between clans is strong.

other. The same kinds of segments are present, but they differ in rank or status and in their political function and economic role. Some families and groups rank as chiefs and others as commoners. In addition, individuals, families, and village communities begin to specialize their pursuits—some are craftsmen, others are fishermen, still others farmers. This specialization reflects in large part the administrative role of the chiefs [5].

In prestate society social activity takes place predominantly or exclusively between people who are kin. All the men of the elder generation of one's own band or lineage are "father," and all their wives are "mother"; all the clan members of one's own generation are "brothers" and "sisters"; the women of one's wife's group are all "wives," and their brothers are "brothers-in-law," and so on. Relationships are direct or face-to-face among people whose behavior is governed by rules of kin etiquette. Breaches of etiquette—for example, the failure to treat a "father" with proper respect, an allusion to sexual matters in the presence of a "sister," the refusal to share food with a clan "brother"—are immediately seized on and punished by ridicule, withdrawal of support, or ostracism.

Dealing with wrongdoing

Prestate societies, though lacking a formal law-enforcing body, do have means of dealing with social wrongdoing. An obvious approach is for the injured party to take it upon himself to recover stolen property, punish an adulterer, or exact restitution. This is termed "self-help." Often, however, people turn to their kin group for assistance.

Feuding of some kind is universal in prestate societies, whereas the feud is not condoned in state societies, nor are most forms of individual self-help. When feuding escalates as revenge and is met by counter-revenge, a serious threat is posed to the social order. In segmental societies, social ties between different groups and the efforts of those who are outside the fray (but who risk injury themselves if the conflict widens) exert pressure on the parties to settle their differences.

KEY

A tribal village, like this one in North India, although outwardly one unit, is in fact divided into different clans and lineages, whose formal interrelationships are essential to the smooth functioning of the whole tribal society.

4 A

B

4 The division of labor in simple societies [A] is based on age and sex, but since each family household contains this division of labor, families are structurally identical and largely self-sufficient. Larger social units, such as lineages and clans, also have identical functions. The institutions of complex societies [B] are specialized and thus functionally interdependent, like assembly line tasks.

5

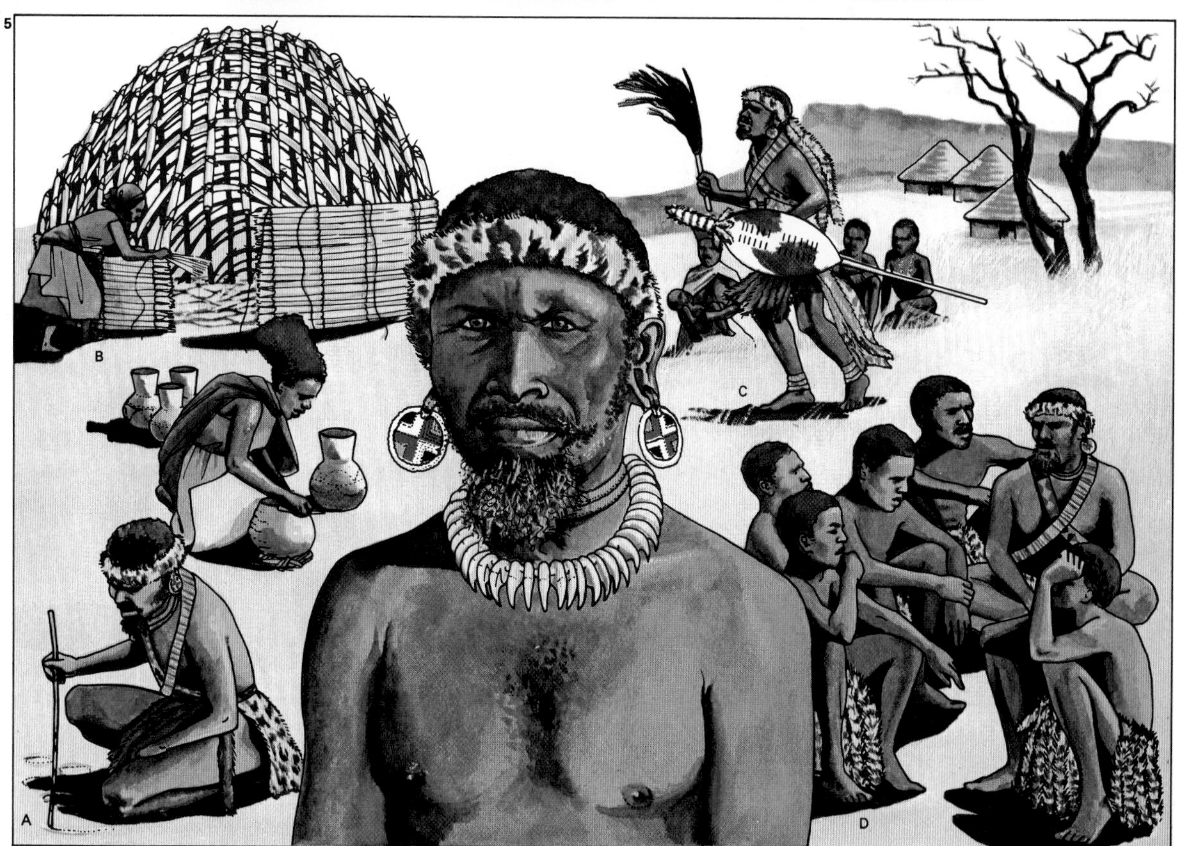

B
C
A
D

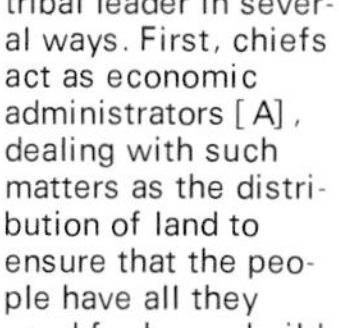

5 A chief's power differs from that of a tribal leader in several ways. First, chiefs act as economic administrators [A], dealing with such matters as the distribution of land to ensure that the people have all they need for house building, cultivation, and pasture; enforcing seasonal taboos on the use of certain resources; and organizing collective hunts. The chiefs can also subsidize the work of specialist artisans [B] by redistributing the taxes and so on. They also have religious power [C], since their ancestral spirits are elevated to the status of gods. This supernatural power was reflected in the custom of carrying the paramount chiefs of Hawaii so that contact with their bodies would not make the land taboo to its owner. Finally, chiefs play an important judicial role in mediating and adjudicating between disputants [D], although they do not have total power.

Origins of civilization

Civilization is often viewed as a complex of elements that include writing, government, law, cities, monumental architecture and art, metallurgy, science, craft specialization, commerce, and large-scale warfare. The problem of the origin of civilization would therefore appear to demand the study of the origins of these elements.

Examining the evidence

Scholars have tended to focus on just one or another of these as being critical. Examples are metallurgy, by which the earliest Old World civilizations are classified as "Bronze Age," and writing, as suggested by the distinction between literate (civilized) and nonliterate (primitive) societies.

From a comparative viewpoint, however, neither metallurgy nor writing nor urbanism can serve as a defining criterion of civilization. Metalworking preceded the development of civilized societies in some areas, while in others, such as the Americas, it never attained great technological importance. Writing was a feature of some early states such as Sumer, but ancient Peruvian civilization lacked a writing system, and the role of writing in Central America and the Indus Valley has not been fully determined. Nor was urbanism an inevitable part of the earliest civilizations. In early Egypt and Central America ceremonial centers appeared rather than cities, and they were probably characteristic of the first phase of development in Mesopotamia and India as well.

There is growing agreement that political organization was the active element in the formation of civilization. This organization—the state—was a powerful new means of regulating the affairs of large and complex societies. It was the state that built cities, pyramids [7], temples, and irrigation systems; organized commerce; carried on wars of conquest; subsidized craftsmen; provided for the discovery, extraction, and smelting of metals; and made use of scribes to keep records.

Ancient or modern, the political state involves a governing group that monopolizes the legitimate right to use force. The relationship of the state to society, however, has long been debated. The issue is probably best resolved by examining the original state-organized societies. States did not spring directly from a tribal milieu. Rather, they resulted from the evolution of hierarchical societies that already had hereditary chiefs, class divisions, and central direction of economic life. In such societies chiefs did not possess a monopoly of the right to use force—they were not yet kings.

Theories of states

A number of theories exist that seek to isolate the key factors in the emergence of the state. The conquest theory, one of the earliest, attributes state formation to the conquest of one society by another, the conquering group forming the governing class [8]. Historically, however, either the conquering group or both the conquerors and the conquered were already complex societies. In other words, this explains the formation of secondary states rather than original ones.

The crossroads theory takes trade as the principal factor in the development of the

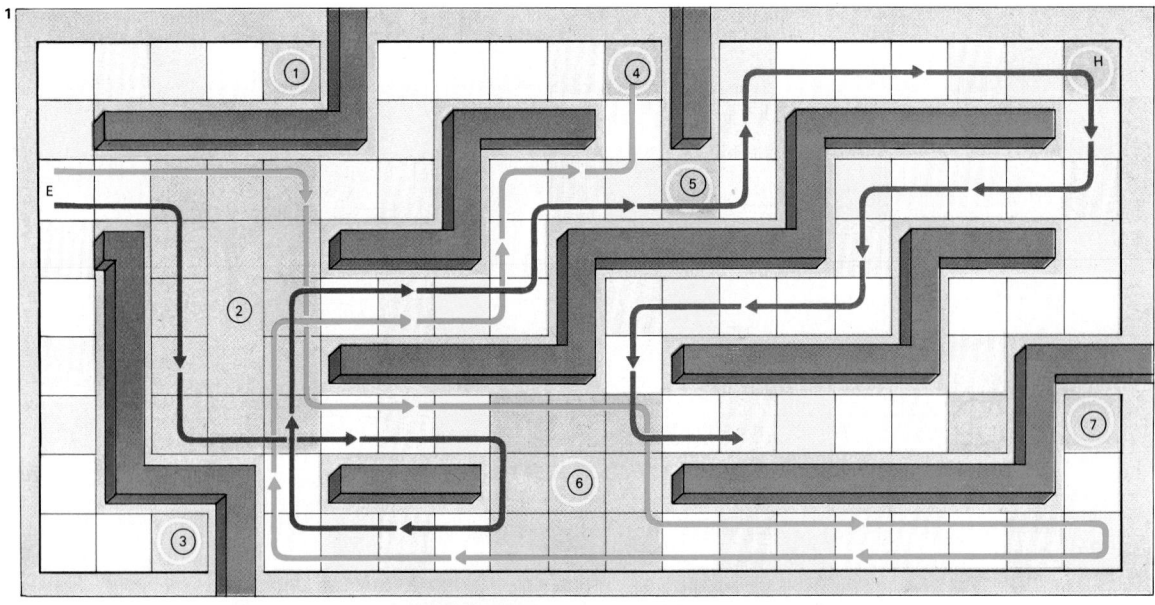

CONNECTIONS

See also
882 Prestate societies
886 Ancient states and empires
952 Beginnings of agriculture
314 Water and irrigation
322 Plant genetic resources
370 Farm stockbreeding and management
1592 The Iron Age
874 The study of man
876 Origins of human society
878 Stages of social evolution
880 Simplest human societies

1 The transition from a simple egalitarian society [E] to a complex hierarchical one [H] is the key to the origin of the state. In theory, the type of environment favoring this transition is a circumscribed area with agricultural potential. With egalitarian societies as a starting point, the numbered areas represent various intermediate or final phases of development suggested by the history of societies. Most egalitarian societies reached a dead end in areas 1, 3, 4, or 7. The blue pathway shows the development of tribal societies of Highland New Guinea, which reached area 4 via population growth, intensified production and warfare. In different circumstances egalitarian societies reaching areas 2, 5, or 6 might emerge as hierarchical societies. This is shown by the red path, relating to certain Polynesian chiefdoms.

1 Potential for agricultural development not realized.
2 Increased agricultural production leads to population growth.
3 Surplus production used to sustain social, ceremonial and artistic activity.
4 Population stabilizes at higher level.
5 Resources scarce as population increases.
6 Agricultural production intensified to meet needs. New population increase.
7 Agriculture intensified by new methods, eg irrigation, requiring formation of hierarchy.

2 Karl Wittfogel, German-born historian and anthropologist, has presented the most systematic version of the theory relating the origins of civilization to irrigation. In his view, the first civilizations were bureaucratic and despotic in response to the requirements of constructing and maintaining large-scale hydraulic works. Criticisms of this theory include the fact that the extent of despotism in ancient societies is exaggerated.

3 Ancient Chinese civilization, in common with other early civilized societies, was irrigation based. Irrigation agriculture, by permitting two or perhaps three crops a year, produced the surplus food needed to support the non-agricultural classes. Moreover, it has been argued that the first centralized state bureaucracies developed to mobilize and coordinate the masses of laborers required to build and maintain large-scale irrigation and flood-control systems. But, as with the development of Mesoamerica and Mesopotamia, archeologists have found no clear evidence of large-scale hydraulic works associated with the early civilizations.

state. At the intersection of major trade routes, communities of traders developed who were drawn from diverse societies. Because they lacked a common culture and common social institutions these internally different communities needed an authority —the state—to regulate their affairs. But since long-distance trade was carried on only by established state societies the theory presupposes the existence of the very institution it is trying to explain.

The hydraulic theory [2] of origins is based on a correlation between certain forms of government and arid or semiarid river valleys. In the valleys of the Yellow River of China [3], the Indus, the Tigris-Euphrates, the Nile, and coastal Peru, irrigation and flood control had to be carried out on a large scale. Thus an organization was required to supervise and supply mass labor. This organization was the state.

While there is no doubt about the importance of irrigation in the early civilizations, hydraulic works may have depended upon, rather than caused, state formation, for it appears that large irrigation systems could have resulted from the linking of smaller systems whose construction was within the capabilities of tribal communities.

The circumscription theory

The circumscription theory [1] combines a number of factors—agricultural development, growth of population, and conflict—to account for the origin of the state. The distinctive feature of the theory is its insistence that areas bounded by geographical barriers such as deserts, mountains, or seas, or areas in which resources were concentrated, were favorable for political evolution. In such areas agricultural production permitted an increase in population [4], which in turn led to intensification of production and a further increase in numbers. Eventually population pressure led to competition for resources in the form of economic warfare. The vanquished chose to submit to the victors and thus the major evolutionary step was taken: the formation of multi-village organizations or chiefdoms. Further warfare led to formation of states and their ultimate expansion into empires.

KEY

The power to organize and direct the work of society is an important advance toward the establishment of a state society. These Samoan chiefs are more powerful than chiefs of egalitarian tribes whose power is not institutionalized.

4

4 The British archeologist V. Gordon Childe (1892–1957) viewed the origin of civilized society as the automatic outcome of agriculture, which permitted the production of a surplus and hence a division of society into food producers and nonfood producers. His theory did not explain why tribal agricultural societies did not develop further, or what made the cultivators give up surpluses.

5

5 The energy theory of cultural development held by American anthropologist Leslie White maintains that societies evolve as the energy harnessed and put to work increases. At the bottom of the scale is human energy, then that of domesticated animals, then wind and water power, then fossil fuels such as oil and coal, and then atomic energy. State-organized societies can realize this potential.

6

6 Julian Steward, (1902–72) US anthropologist, drew attention to the parallels in development of the early civilizations of Mexico, Peru, Mesopotamia, Egypt, China, and the Indus valley. Such parallel patterns of evolution suggest that similar factors, primarily environmental, were at work and that comparisons among the six areas would reveal uniform causes of the origins of civilization.

7

7 The sizes of ancient monuments do not indicate the kind of organization required to build them, since their construction could have been achieved with different combinations of time and labor—small labor forces working over two or three generations or large labor forces working for a shorter period. The Egyptian pyramids were built by large numbers of workers, and their construction periods overlapped one another. This, and the fact that the large pyramids were built during the early phase of Egyptian civilization, suggests that pyramid building was an important factor in consolidating the new state's control over labor and revenue.

8

8 Wars of conquest, as depicted in this scene from the tomb of the Egyptian pharaoh Tutankhamen (*r.* 1361–1352 BC), aimed at capturing territory, population, and resources. Some theorists have argued that conquest was a primary factor in the formation of societies with formal government and social classes. The earliest civilized societies, however, had small populations and territories and were peaceful, so it is doubtful they were born in war.

Ancient states and empires

Civilizations are often judged by their technological inventiveness, and in that light ancient civilizations may appear uninventive, even stagnant; however, the civilizations of the past were based on the greatest innovation of all: the organization of a political state. The political ideologies, social institutions, and means of organization evolved by these civilizations include democratic and totalitarian forms of government, bureaucracy, class and caste systems, cities [7] and municipal government, professional armies [4], the census, taxation, writing, science [2], codified laws [5] and law courts, police, money [8], and "world" religions. Indeed, modern technological civilization has added little radically new to the inventory of the sociopolitical institutions of ancient states.

The development of early states and empires

The first ancient states, some of them taking the form of city-states, such as Sumer and Akkad, comprised relatively small populations and territories. They were theocratic, the business of government being largely controlled by a powerful priesthood [3]. The gradual emergence of civil rulers—whose power was based on the leadership of armies and the command of resources to feed, arm, and equip them—led to military expansion. The first empires were individual states joined by conquest. This was true of the forming of the Assyrian, Hittite, Egyptian, and Persian empires.

Ancient empires tended, however, to be weakly integrated. Conquest, imperial administration, and a thin overlay of imperial culture did not erase deeply ingrained ethnic and regional divisions. Furthermore, the political organization of these empires tended to reinforce this inbuilt bias against centralized government. Beyond a core area surrounding the seat of central government were subject territories ruled by provincial governors who, in command of local revenue systems and armies, might even be able to defy the authority of the central ruler. Outside the provinces, imperial authority trailed off into uncertain border areas of unconquered territories that were often inhabited by tribal nomads.

These forces of disintegration eventually led to parts of an empire either breaking away, challenging the center, or simply fragmenting to the point at which the whole empire was vulnerable to conquest.

In addition to developing a central bureaucracy, ancient rulers devised a number of partial solutions to the problem of "creeping decentralization": these included rotation of provincial officials; alliances through marriage between the royal family and families of provincial governors; the keeping of hostages as pledges for an official's loyalty; systems of inspection, auditing, and spying; concessions to merchants, cities, the priesthood, or other special groups in return for political support; and the development of roads, canals, and messenger systems to facilitate administrative communication [1].

The way of life of the peasants

Written records of ancient civilizations tend to focus on the activities of kings and emperors, priests and philosophers, artisans and city dwellers. Most of the people of past

CONNECTIONS

See also
884 Origins of civilization
956 The Sumerians 4000–2006 BC
960 Egypt: the Old and Middle Kingdoms
962 India: prehistory to 500 BC
970 Preclassic America to AD 300
908 Rule of law
890 Conflict, power, and social inequality
898 Fundamental political ideas
874 The study of man
876 Origins of human society
878 Stages of social evolution
880 Simplest human societies
882 Prestate societies

1

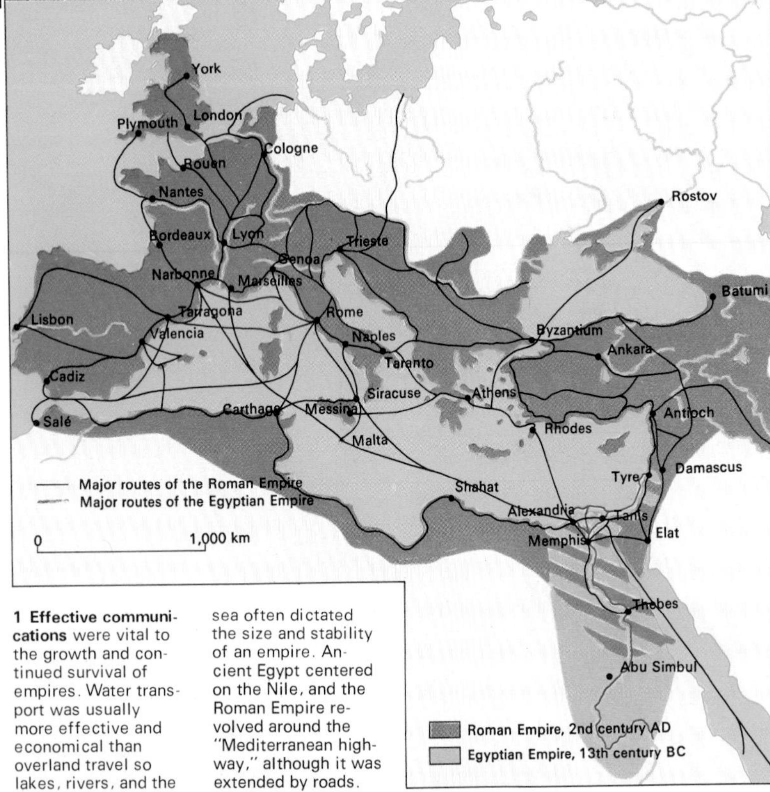

York
Plymouth
London
Cologne
Rouen
Nantes
Bordeaux
Lyon
Trieste
Genoa
Narbonne
Marseilles
Lisbon
Tarragona
Rome
Valencia
Naples
Taranto
Cadiz
Siracuse
Carthage
Messina
Salé
Malta
Rostov
Batumi
Byzantium
Ankara
Athens
Rhodes
Antioch
Damascus
Tyre
Shahat
Alexandria
Tanis
Memphis
Elat
Thebes
Abu Simbul
Major routes of the Roman Empire
Major routes of the Egyptian Empire
0 1,000 km
Roman Empire, 2nd century AD
Egyptian Empire, 13th century BC

1 Effective communications were vital to the growth and continued survival of empires. Water transport was usually more effective and economical than overland travel so lakes, rivers, and the sea often dictated the size and stability of an empire. Ancient Egypt centered on the Nile, and the Roman Empire revolved around the "Mediterranean highway," although it was extended by roads.

2 Early scientists, such as the astronomer and geographer Ptolemy (*c.* AD 90–168), were encouraged by the state because much of their work was useful to the central government in planning and administration. The discovery of the solar year's 365-day cycle by the ancient Egyptians resulted from their observations of Sirius and the time intervals between the annual floods of the Nile. The Egyptians' primary concern was to measure the floodwater level annually. From this, land inundation could be estimated and thus grain production and revenue predicted.

3

3 The role of the priest was important in ancient civilizations, with priest-kings acting as mediators between man and god. Such theocracies were very efficient; the populace was bound with a minimum of coercion to a round of religious duties and rituals that worked to the benefit of society. Civil obedience and service to the state were thus assured. Here Aztec priests conduct a ritual sacrifice. Captives were the usual victims.

4

4 The cultural diversity and territorial extent of ancient empires meant that professional armies were as necessary for maintaining internal order as they were for the purposes of defense and external conquest. The Roman Empire was particularly successful at integrating the subjects of its diverse territories and client kingdoms. As well as instilling a sense of collective identity in their soldiers, the Romans were also adept at using their armies for the control of strategic resources and the improvement of communications. Cohesiveness and mobility were the results of this policy and made the Roman army a formidable policing and fighting instrument throughout the Roman Empire.

civilizations, however, were peasant farmers whose lives might be only slightly affected by long-term political developments, but whose surplus production was the basis of the achievements of the nonagricultural specialists. In return for such benefits as state-organized irrigation and flood control systems, military defense, and perhaps government relief in time of famine, the peasant committed a large part of his land and labor to the support of others [9]. In addition, he or his sons might be conscripted into the army.

The peasant's way of life, as far as material standards and much of his daily routine were concerned, did not differ greatly from that of the agricultural tribesman who preceded him. Yet the peasant was a creation of the ancient state. With permanent fields, irrigation, and animal-drawn plows, he worked in a more advanced agricultural system requiring more disciplined labor. Unlike the tribesman, he produced some food and goods for sale in local markets and purchased in turn exotic goods and specialized services. Through resident officials and priests, and by his contributions of labor and part of his crops to state revenue, he was linked to a political and economic system far larger than his village community. And he shared, in some degree, in the "high" culture produced in the urban centers by the priests and writers.

The citizen enters the social order

The peasant, however, remained a subject with little involvement or interest in the larger forces that helped shape his life. He was both expendable and politically impotent, as was his unskilled compatriot in the city. But in the cities, and among the higher social strata, there emerged another new type of man, the citizen. The citizen was a person with legally defined rights and capacities in relation to the government. Even though ancient law was generally more concerned with protecting the power of the state than safeguarding the rights of citizens, the latter enjoyed a measure of protection because of the simplicity and comparatively small scale of ancient bureaucracies.

KEY

The Great Wall of China was first built in 214 BC by Emperor Shih Huang Ti (259–210 BC), the first monarch of a united China under the Ch'in dynasty. The wall, 1,500 miles (2,400km) long and 30ft (9m) high with watchtowers at regular intervals, protected China's northern boundary against the raids of nomadic tribes.

5

5 Codification of law was one result of the invention of writing. The most complete ancient law code is that of Hammurabi of Babylonia, which was devised in the 18th century BC.

6 The census was an important feature of ancient states. It determined government collection of revenue (usually taken in the form of agricultural produce or labor). The Domesday survey of 1086, shown here, ordered by William I, was England's first census.

6

7

7 The cities of ancient civilizations were generally different in function as well as character from modern cities. Most were small, as even the so-called city-states had predominantly rural populations. In early Egyptian and Central American societies, most cities seem to have been ceremonial centers with small resident populations of officials, priests, and craftsmen. Since ancient societies were agrarian, their cities could seldom become manufacturing, commercial, and financial centers of any size. Ancient cities such as Machu Picchu, the Inca city shown here, were primarily political and administrative centers.

8

9

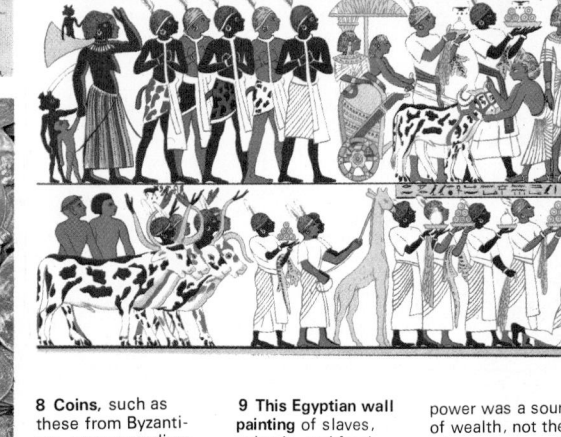

8 Coins, such as these from Byzantium, were a medium for commerce. The Lydians, in the 7th century BC, may have used coins first.

9 This Egyptian wall painting of slaves, animals, and food being brought to the pharaoh reflects the fact that in ancient societies political power was a source of wealth, not the other way around. Power and class were determined by political affiliation. Broadly, the population was divided into the governing class—sometimes including the merchant class—and their dependents who were mostly laborers and peasants.

Structure of societies

Sociology is the study of the way in which relationships among people are organized. The organization of social relationships produces social structures that range from the small group, like the family, through larger groups, like the peasant community or industrial corporation to national states and empires. The social structures of societies are characterized by mechanisms that integrate their members, but they usually contain social divisions, conflicts of interest, and inequalities of power. Social structures have characteristics that are independent of their members, but their workings must be understood in terms of the way these members experience them.

Understanding sociology

Although sociological theories and research findings are often complex and sophisticated, the basic principles of sociology are easily understood on a superficial level. This is because everyone who is aware of his membership in a human society is, in a sense, a sociologist. In order to cope with everyday life we must all have some understanding of social structure, our position within it, its rules, divisions, and hierarchies, and the way that other people will interpret situations in which we are involved. In this sense sociology is as old as human society. Its emergence in Western Europe in the nineteenth century as a distinct academic discipline can be seen as a facet of the increasingly complex division of labor in developing capitalist society.

The pioneer work of the French sociologist Emile Durkheim (1858–1917) showed that explanations of social behavior were to be found within the nature of society. Uniformities in the behavior of individuals, together with constant variations in behavior among societies, may be seen as products of the structure of societies rather than of the specific natures of their members. Durkheim's views of society are revealed by his studies of a very individual act, suicide. He believed that variations in the suicide rates of societies could be explained by the strength of social bonds. Although these views have been disputed, Durkheim did bring out the influence of social groupings on behavior. An individual's religious and political beliefs, his moral values, the type of house he lives in, the type of food he likes and how he eats it, the clothes he wears—all these can be viewed as products of the influence of society [1].

Social rules and social roles

Society influences and controls its members through their acceptance of its social rules (norms) and their occupancy of preordained social positions (roles) together with their willingness to act as expected in these positions. While some societies are more repressive than others, people are generally unaware of the extent to which their actions are socially controlled. In conforming to social rules and acting out the roles assigned to them they usually believe they are exercising freedom of choice.

The rules of society to which the individual member is required to conform include not only codified laws and written rules of organizations, but also a multitude of unwritten rules regulating minute social details. These include knowing when to

CONNECTIONS

See also
686 Skin and hair
914 Nature and causes of criminality
916 Changing patterns of crime
918 Crime prevention
922 Changing patterns of punishment

1

1 The individual is presented by sociologists, at one extreme, as wholly determined by the society in which he lives. He is pressured to conform to social norms through the variety of social institutions and organizations to which he is attached, such as the family, the educational system, the work place, the church, or even the local social club or lodge. This is an extreme characterization and represents only one side of an individual's relationships.

2

2 While people are born into society and both the norms of society and the roles into which they must fit are there before them, it is also true that social structures are initially created and continually changed by people's actions. Protest and other forms of social movement may bring about changes in social norms (eg, compaigns for abortion law reform and homosexual law reform) and changes in social roles (eg, campaigns to change the role of women in society).

3

3 Ferdinand Tönnies (1855–1936) claimed that industrialization and urbanization brought about major changes in social relationships. He depicted the trend as being away from personal, communal (*Gemeinschaft*) relationships characteristic of the pre-industrial rural community toward impersonal, formal, bureaucratic *(Gesellschaft)* relationships. *Gemeinschaft* relationships are based on shared values and sentiments; *Gesellschaft* on self-interest.

4

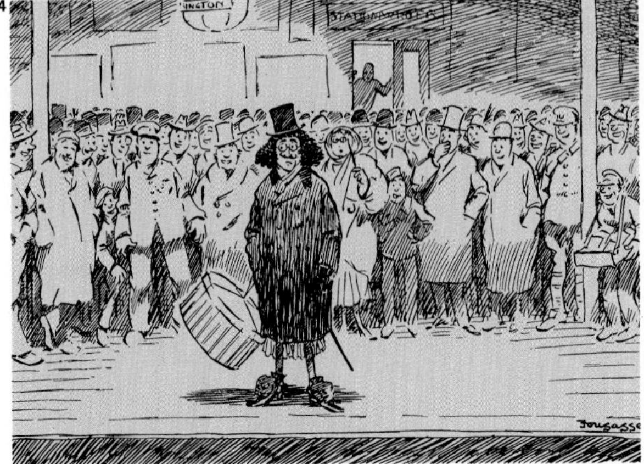

4 Uniformities in social behavior usually imply the presence of social norms. Norms are known to be present only when sanctions ranging from social disapproval to more severe forms are applied to deviants. Often we become aware of social norms only when someone breaks them. In the cartoon all are aware that the central character has broken a norm by wearing the wrong clothes. They are applying their sanction by laughing at him.

speak, how to address people (Sir, Mr Smith, or Joe), when to laugh, when to stand up or sit down, and when to leave.

The process of socialization

Through the process of becoming social beings (socialization) people learn the norms of their society and those of the diverse social groups in which they may participate during their lives—the family, the school, the factory workgroup, the sports club, the professional organization, and so on.

People learn, through socialization, to accept social rules as their own standards of right and proper behavior, so that they may be controlled as much through their own moral sense and avoidance of guilt feelings as by an external coercive force. But external pressures to conform to norms are also present in the form of sanctions applied to deviants, which may range from legal penalties of death or imprisonment and loss of job or position, to the social disapproval of one's fellows [4]. The severity of sanctions generally depends on how far common sentiments are offended by nonconformity.

People know their place in society through the variety of social roles that they occupy. Each person normally plays many roles in his daily life, work, family, community, and other social activities. Old roles are continually cast off and new ones assumed. Social roles are not so much descriptions of what people generally do in the positions they occupy, but rather what they are expected to do. While these expectations may include the performance of tasks, they are mainly requirements of behavior in the social relationships that acting out the role involves. Some roles, such as that of husband, may involve a relationship with only one other person. Others, such as those of waiter [7] or social worker, may require relationships with several types of people.

Role expectations are expectations of behavior toward other people, but they come from the norms of society rather than from the opinions and desires of the individual participants. The structure of societies thus may be seen as based on organized sets of roles.

KEY

Auguste Comte (1798–1857) saw sociology as a science of social life that would discover the laws of social behavior akin to the laws of the natural sciences. His belief that sociologists should be the priests of the new scientific social order has a contemporary relevance in that today critical sociologists are increasingly becoming the conscience bearers of advanced Western societies. While Comte saw sociology as providing justification for the prevailing social order, modern sociologists are more likely to be moral critics of their societies and tend to reject Comte's belief in progress through the application of science.

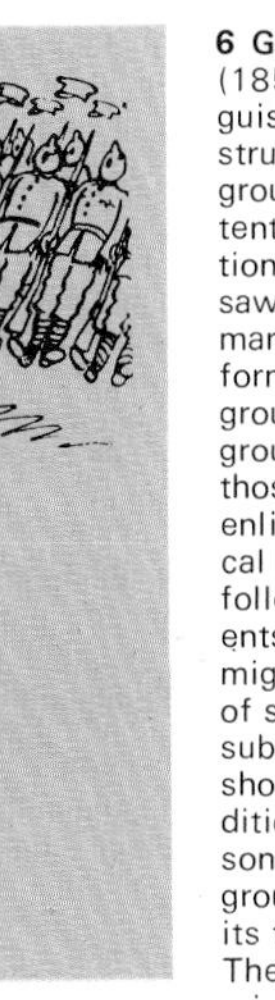

5 Different roles will often bring out very contradictory qualities in the individual. Effective performance of the different roles may be jeopardized if those involved with him in one such role are able to observe his performance of another. The cartoon general's military performance might be undermined, for example, if the soldiers in his command observed him in his role as husband.

6 Georg Simmel (1858–1918) distinguished the formal structures of social groups from the content of social interaction within them. He saw sociology primarily as the study of forms of social groups: a variety of groups, such as those of officers and enlisted men, political leaders and their followers, and parents and children, might share the form of superiority and subordination. He showed how the addition of a third person to a two-person group would change its form radically. The third person might act as a mediator between the original two or exploit the differences of the original two for his own ends.

7 While the individual usually plays several social roles, any one of these roles may involve relationships with a variety of different sorts of people. In a large restaurant the waiter may have to relate to customers, his supervisor, wine steward, chef, busboys, and other members of the staff. When roles involve several relationships it is sometimes found that the demands of one relationship conflict with those of another. The customer wants the waiter to attend to his order promptly while the chef in the kitchen does not want to be rushed with orders. The waiter must keep them both happy. Such roles require social skill and may be stressful.

Conflict, power, and social inequality

The mechanisms by which society integrates and controls its members are never completely successful. All societies have deviants and criminals, and nearly all are subject at times in their histories to serious forms of social disorder, revolts, and revolutions. Many sociologists believe that such occurrences are not just the result of failure of the social structure. Instead they contend that conflict and social division are inevitable in all social structures. Societies are unequal in their distribution of power and of material and social rewards, and it is these inequalities that generate social divisions and conflicts of interest. If uncontrolled they may produce extreme forms of social strife.

The exercise of power

In all societies some social groups are able to exercise power over others [Key, 8]. Their power may result from their control over means of coercion [4]—military or police forces—or control over material resources and social rewards. The German sociologist Max Weber (1864–1920) showed that the ability of groups to maintain their power depended on their success in persuading those subject to it that they had authority; in other words, that their exercise of power was legitimate. Acceptance of the existing power structure by the population may be based on tradition, as in the case of a traditional monarchy [1]; rational laws, as in a constitutional parliamentary system [3]; or personal loyalty to a leader, as in the case of Benito Mussolini [2].

When the exercise of power is accepted as being legitimate it usually complies with prevailing social norms. A result of this is that the norms of society tend, in varying degrees, to serve the interests of powerful groups rather than the common interests of all. For example, in societies where the powerful groups are owners of private property, the norms tend to emphasize respect for private property. The exercise of power always tends to generate resistance on the part of the powerless, who challenge its legitimacy. Just as people may be unaware of the extent to which their actions are controlled by the forces of society, so they may not notice the power that others exercise over them. They may have been socialized to want to act in ways that are in the interests of the powerful. Where power is based on control over material resources and the means of production, as in nineteenth-century Western Europe, then power is exercised by a dominant social class. Where power is based on control of the bureaucratic and military apparatus of the state, then that power lies in the hands of a ruling elite.

Social class structure

Social classes are groups of people sharing common social and economic interests. Where these interests are recognized, class consciousness develops, which may be the basis for social strife in forms ranging from strikes to full-scale revolutionary movements. Political parties often draw support on the basis of class membership, although parties may also be based on religious, regional, tribal, or ethnic divisions. In nineteenth-century capitalist societies, the chief social class division was between

CONNECTIONS

See also
888 Structure of societi
892 The individual in society
898 Fundamental politic ideas
902 Types of political sy tems
894 Prejudice and grou intolerance
896 Prejudice and personal choice
1286 Russia in the 19th century
1288 Political thought in the 19th century
1248 The revolutions of 1848
1156 The English revolution
882 Prestate societies
884 Origins of civilizatio
886 Ancient states and empires

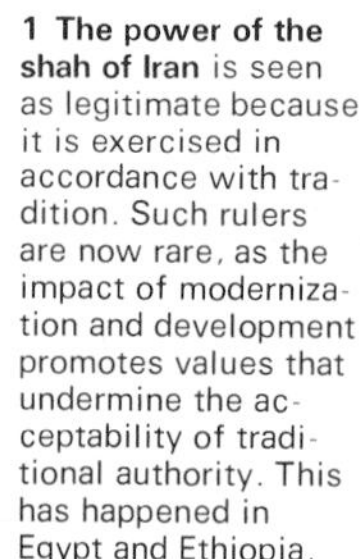

1 The power of the shah of Iran is seen as legitimate because it is exercised in accordance with tradition. Such rulers are now rare, as the impact of modernization and development promotes values that undermine the acceptability of traditional authority. This has happened in Egypt and Ethiopia.

2 Charismatic leaders, such as Benito Mussolini (1883–1945), are seen as legitimate by their followers by virtue of the extraordinary personal qualities—their magnetism—which they are believed to possess. Such leaders often break with both established tradition and codified laws.

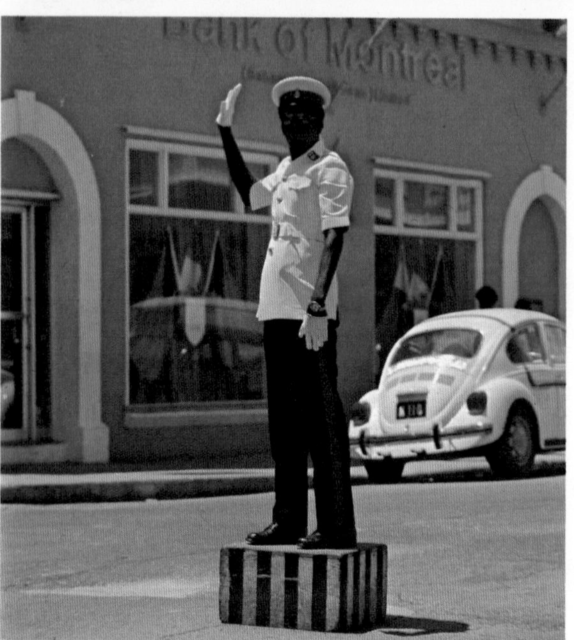

3 The policeman on traffic duty exercises rational-legal authority—power that is seen as legitimate because it is in accordance with rational laws. His authority is vested in the office, not in his person, and its scope is strictly defined by law. The authority of elected parliamentary governments is also rational and defined by law.

4 Tanks in the street as here in Prague in 1968, show the exercise of power based solely on violence. If the power-holders lack legitimacy in the eyes of their subjects, they must rely on coercion. All forms of political domination use force to some degree, although they may try to achieve legitimacy.

property owners and the workers without property whom they employed. In modern advanced capitalist societies, this division has now been overshadowed by that between professionally qualified and managerial workers (the middle class) and manual workers (the working class).

Social classes must be considered in relation to the historical development of each society [5], but there is some evidence that the dominance in advanced capitalist societies of the middle classes is spreading to a number of developing countries. The class structure may often be the key to the distribution of power, but social class membership can also help determine expectations. [7] In societies where in theory there is equality of education, for example, educational opportunities for middle-class children have been shown to exceed those for working-class children.

Ruling elites and their power

Ruling elites are groups that actually control the instruments of power [6]. They may act in the general interest or simply in their own interests. If their power is not sustained by a dominant class, then it is maintained by control of the police, armed forces, and propaganda. The state bureaucracies of the Soviet Union and the military regimes of several Latin American countries are examples of such ruling elites.

The US sociologist C. Wright Mills (1916–62) argued that in the United States in the 1950s, power in matters of national importance rested in the hands of leading businessmen, top politicians, and soldiers.

Power is often exercised by ruling elites in a democracy through their ability to choose the issues on which the majority may vote. If a new urban transportation system is proposed, for example, information and debate on the advisability of having a system at all and the effects that it will have on the area may not be much in evidence. What usually will be presented are several alternative technological schemes. The elite, often businessmen or trade unions in a city, have made the most important decisions, and the majority has a choice only on secondary issues.

KEY

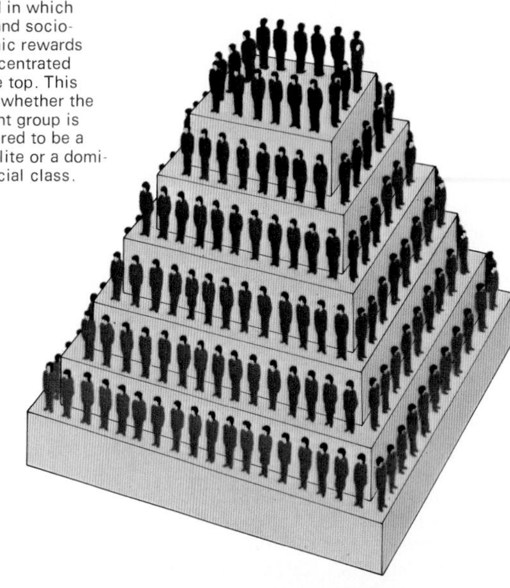

Society can be represented as a human pyramid in which power and socioeconomic rewards are concentrated near the top. This applies whether the dominant group is considered to be a ruling elite or a dominant social class.

5

5 The Indian caste system is a unique form of social stratification representing the most extreme form of social hierarchy. People are born into a caste membership, and castes are segregated: for members of high castes to come into contact with people like these low-caste women collecting dung for fuel, involves ritual pollution. Although in modern India the caste system is officially outlawed, many features remain.

6

6 Vilfredo Pareto (1848–1923), the Italian engineer, economist, and sociologist, argued that people's actions are often based on sentiments rather than on rational thought. Political elites, he believed, maintain their power by manipulation and coercion requiring appeals to sentiment rather than to rational interests. Elites, he claimed, are liable to be overthrown unless they are also prepared to use force.

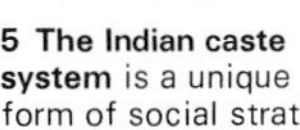

7

7 The British sociologist Basil Bernstein (1924–) has studied how people's use of language is related to their social class. He has distinguished the use of a simple "public" language from a more complex or "formal" language.

8

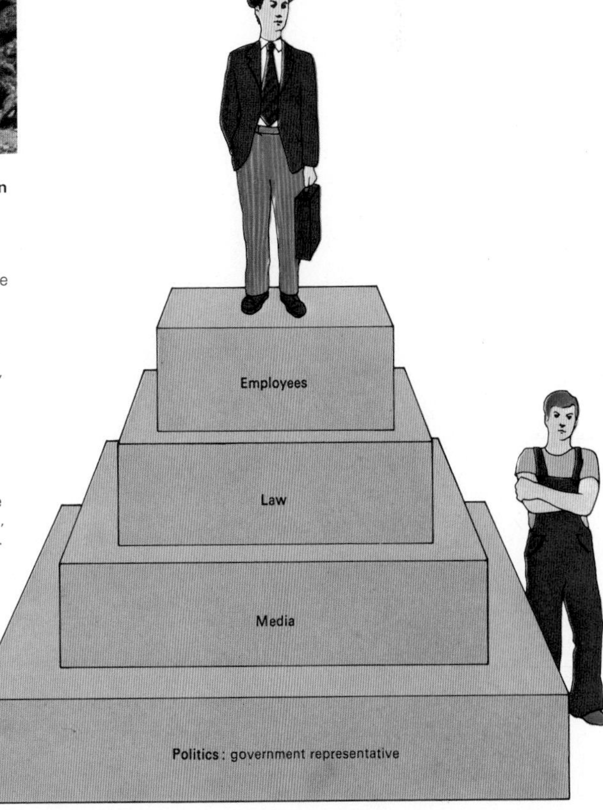

Employees
Law
Media
Politics: government representative

8 A person's position in society largely determines not only his level of material and social rewards, but also the power he has over others and the extent to which others have power over him. A member of a dominant group, in this case an employer, will have direct power over his employees. He also exerts more influence over local and national politics, the operation of the law, and the mass media.

The individual in society

Classes and groups in society are not concrete entities: they exist only insofar as they are accepted as real by the individuals who compose them. Social structures cannot therefore be fully understood without examining their meaning for the participants.

Defining social situations

It has been shown that in social situations people will act according to the way in which they define that situation. Different people may well define the same situation differently [4]: as an extreme example, whether or not the authorities order troops to open fire on an angry crowd will depend on whether they define the situation as a riot. The way people choose to define social situations is not a matter of personal whim but depends largely on social influences.

People may define situations by unconsciously imagining how other people who are significant in their lives would define them. These significant influences, which constitute the individual's reference groups, may include his family, his neighbors, the people he works with, and his church, political party, age group, social class, and sex. He takes his moral standards from his reference groups and through them is influenced by social norms.

Reference groups also provide an individual with a basis for evaluating his social position. Although they are not actual social groups, but constructions in the mind of the individual using them, it is through them that the individual is subject to the influences of society. If, for example, a doctor's reference group is the medical profession, it is his idea of his profession rather than the actual behavior of its members that influences his professional actions.

The social self

The eminent US sociologist and social psychologist G. H. Mead (1863–1931) showed how the individual's very conception of himself, and of how he appears to others, is a product of social interaction [1]. In his work Mead stressed the constant tension in social life between the assertion of individuality and the pressures of social conformity. He distinguished two components of self, the "me" and the "I." The "me" (the social component) is the impression we think we make on other people whose opinion matters to us. We gather these impressions by putting ourselves in the place of these others. The individual's reference groups are therefore important for the development of the "me." The "I" (the individual component) consists of the individual's actual response to the attitude of others. It is the creative element of self, spontaneous, uncertain, and unpredictable. People's actions are never fully socially determined.

Social roles are laid down by the norms of society, but this does not mean that people cannot express their individuality in the roles they play. The various devices that people use to express themselves and convey impressions of themselves have been explored by US sociologist Erving Goffman (1922–   ) in a number of studies. He has shown, for example, that it is normal for people to distance themselves from the roles they are playing, so conveying to others that their real selves are not wholly

CONNECTIONS

See also
888 Structure of societies
890 Conflict, power, and social inequality
1360 20th-century sociology and its influence
812 Aspects of human nature
782 Social development
818 Body image and biofeedback
914 Nature and causes of criminality

1 The different impressions of a young woman that are held by her employer, her mother, her boyfriend, and herself, are portrayed here [left to right]. These views all correspond to the different roles she plays—employee, daughter, girl friend. In these various roles she is not seen by others merely as a player of a particular role but as a whole person. The impression the young woman has of herself derives in part from her idea of the impressions that others have of her and of her actions in social encounters with these others. It is therefore a mistake to think of the individual as having a "true self" that is independent of the impressions that others have. At the same time, the individual's self-image is no mere mechanical reflection of others' impressions. This young woman can, for example, consciously influence these impressions. This may be done not only through choice of speech and action in social situations, but also through the clothes she wears, her hairstyle, body posture, facial expressions, and gestures. Sometimes people try to convey to others impressions of themselves that they do not themselves believe in. This may take the form of presenting an idealized version of the self that the individual believes he or she falls short of—like the teacher who tries to show that she is more knowledgeable than she really thinks she is. In the case of the confidence man, a deliberately false impression of self is conveyed to others.

1

involved in any one particular role. Goffman's work has shown how people's spontaneous individuality in social situations can itself be the subject of sociological study.

The sociology of everyday life often appears to deal with rather trivial things like conversations in bars, but sociologists have shown how an understanding of social rules in everyday situations may illuminate the processes governing the structuring of society [3]. The routine, everyday activities of policemen (how they react to and treat people of various classes and races), for example, are relevant to the explanation of criminal behavior.

Trends in sociology

In many major universities the establishment of sociology dates only from the 1940s, although much important work had been carried out before then. The 1940s and 1950s were dominated by two types of American sociology. One was rather abstract theorizing in attempts to develop models applicable to all societies; the other was the large-scale collection of information about social life through social surveys, questionnaires, and statistical analysis. These surveys were characterized by a rigorously scientific approach in the technical sense. During this time sociologists commonly insisted that they were disinterested scientists and that it was not for them to make policy recommendations or moral judgments on the societies they were studying. Since the end of the 1950s theory and research have been brought closer together. Sociologists have been less inclined to emulate the natural sciences in a narrow technical sense and have paid more attention to understanding people's experiences and the meaning of their lives.

Sociologists today are less likely to proclaim themselves disinterested academics and more willing to advocate policies and to criticize societies. In this they come closer to sociology's founding fathers, whose aim was to produce better societies. By revealing the oppressive elements of social structures, sociologists hope to liberate humans from them.

KEY

A theme of much sociological thought is the tension between the social and individual aspects of humans. The individual is a product of society, but society itself is produced by human actions. The individual, represented by the cut-out figure, fits into the roles that society provides. But at the same time the person continually asserts his or her individuality in the various roles that he or she is called upon to play.

2

2 Alfred Schutz (1899–1959), a sociologist, believed in the importance of the "common sense" beliefs of the mundane world. He used this reality as the point from which to begin examining society.

3

I am bidden to the War Office

I depart for it

I approach it

I enter

I am not observed

I am still not observed

I am observed

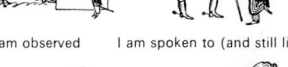

I am spoken to (and still live)

I continue to be spoken to

I am spoken to quite nicely

I am shaken hands with

I take my leave

3 Our images of ourselves are continually being modified to fit our expectations and experiences in social encounters, like this one between a British gentleman and an army bureaucrat.

4

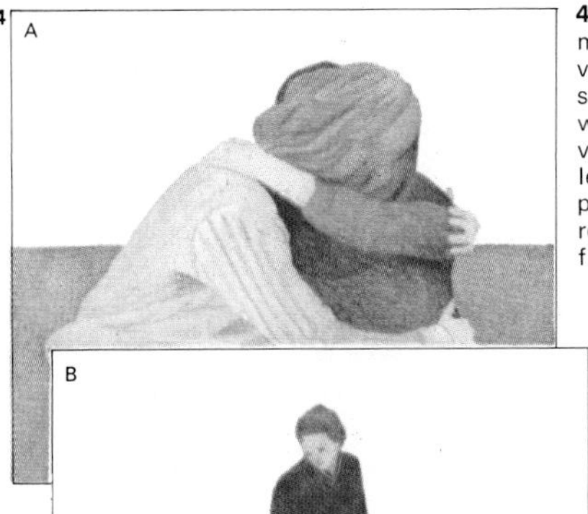

A
B
C
D

4 Different people may have different views of the same social situation in which they are involved. In part at least, these different perspectives are the result of their different reference groups. One person will see a party as a romantic interlude [A], another as empty and boring [B], a third as a drunken get together [C], a fourth may see it as a chance to renew old friendships [D].

Prejudice and group intolerance

Prejudice is a preconceived opinion, usually unfavorable, about a category of people or about individuals thought to belong in such a category. It is likely to lead to discrimination, which involves treating differently people who belong to particular social, ethnic, or religious groups.

Aspects of prejudice

People in groups tend to share preconceived opinions. People learn the prejudices of their parents, teachers, and friends, and often accept their judgments without question. This sharing of opinions is a leading feature of human cultures. Patterns of prejudice are associated with different societies, but they change over time, thus showing that prejudice has a cultural component.

While prejudice may be widely shared within a group, it is manifested in the speech and actions of individuals and has to be understood in relation to their personalities and to their positions in society. The fact that people brought up in the same society at the same time display prejudice and practice discrimination in different degrees indicates that prejudice has a personal aspect as well as social aspects.

Ethnocentrism and racism

There are two types of cultural prejudice, feelings of superiority based on pride in cultural and social achievements and feelings of superiority based on supposed inherent, genetically fixed characteristics. The latter type can be called racism and is characterized by the feeling that members of a particular group are in some way subhuman. This is a crucial element in man's inhumanity to man [Key].

In every known society people tend to prefer those of "their own kind" as friends, fellow workers, and marriage partners. They tend to see international affairs from the standpoint of their own society or nation and devalue the people and customs of other societies. This inclination to prefer peoples and things with which they identify themselves is called by sociologists "ethnocentrism" and necessarily implies a bias against those seen as different [4]. Ethnocentrism has existed throughout history. But international contacts diminish it by making individuals of different groups aware of their common heritage rather than their specific outward dissimilarities.

Within a single society such feelings of preference and suspicion are reinforced by the way that people of similar backgrounds tend to congregate both for company and for protection in the distinct residential zones that are a feature of all towns.

The history of prejudice shows no simple pattern. Although prejudice and discrimination have been evident in most societies, in the ancient world the motivation was ethnocentric rather than racist. This can be said even of the Hindu caste system, which reflects the cultural split between the ancient, conquered Dravidian peoples and the invading Aryans. By way of contrast were the kingdoms that have now become Rwanda and Burundi in central Africa. Here the preeminence of the Tutsi (who made up only 15 percent of the population) over the Hutu (83 percent) and the pygmoid Twa (2 percent) was based largely on the Tutsi's physical characteristics.

CONNECTIONS

See also
896 Prejudice and personal choice
816 Freedom and individuality
658 Family of man: today peoples
874 The study of man
1334 The rise of fascism
1330 Indian nationalism
1380 The question of Israe
1314 Ireland and independence
1262 European imperialisr in the 19th century
1270 The opening up of China

1 Few animals act as aggressively toward members of their own species as man does. And when they do fight (over territory or a mate, for example), they will automatically cease in response to a submission signal. Man has similar submission signals (e.g. avoiding eye contact) but seems to be able to ignore them. This is made easier by the development of long-range weapons.

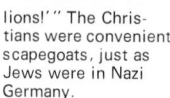

2 The fighting between young supporters of soccer teams in Britain suggests that these games are also often ceremonies in which opposing supporters stimulate each other to more violent expression. As members of groups emotionally committed to "different sides," people are capable of extreme behavior. Friend may even turn against friend, as in the conflict in Northern Ireland.

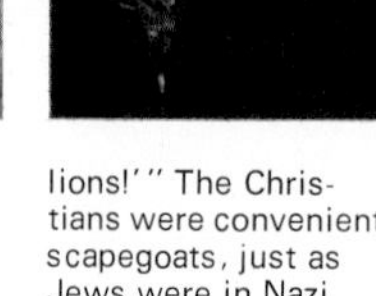

3 The government of ancient Rome had an effective way to divert popular anger when things went wrong. "If the Tiber floods or the Nile fails to flood, if the sky is darkened, if the earth trembles, if famine, war, or plague occurs, then immediately one shout goes up: 'the Christians to the lions!'" The Christians were convenient scapegoats, just as Jews were in Nazi Germany.

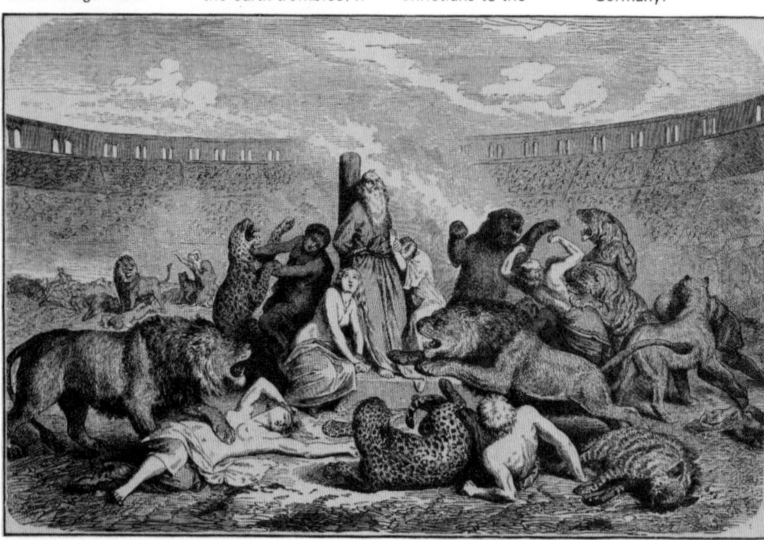

4 Chinese ethnocentrism was evident in 1793 when the Emperor Ch'ien Lung instructed the British envoy to tell George III that he saw no reason to open diplomatic relations. "Even if your envoy were to acquire the rudiments of our civilization you could not possibly transplant our manners and customs to your alien soil . . . we possess all."

One explanation for the absence of racism in ancient socieities is that they were much smaller and so people were more likely to know each other as individuals rather tham to view them as representatives of categories. Furthermore, contact between peoples of different societies was generally limited.

Slavery and prejudice

Colonization and the African slave trade across the Atlantic created a new set of relations between peoples and stimulated the growth of a new kind of prejudice. The chattel slavery of the Americas [5] (in which the legal status of slaves resembled that of domestic animals and nonhuman property) was different from the personal slavery of ancient Rome and medieval Spain (in which the law accorded a slave a human status, the right to marry, and some protection against abuse). To understand this difference it is necessary to consider the demand for labor. In the New World, land was abundant. If a landowner imported a free white worker to labor on his estate, the workman was inclined to go off and establish his own farm. So the landowner found it best to bind laborers to indentures whereby they promised to work for him for seven years in order to pay off the cost of their passage. The move to outright slavery was an easy one to make. Europeans had for centuries regarded blackness unfavorably, but when it became associated with slavery and, indeed, guilt about white maltreatment of blacks, it received a new emotional charge.

When, in the nineteenth century, scientists speculated about classifying mankind into types, just like flowers and fishes, they were quick to describe blacks as a distinct and inferior racial type. Up to the end of that century the understanding of man's physical nature was confused. Thus these early speculations were easily built up into pseudo-scientific theories of race. In later generations these theories have been used to justify people's prejudices and to serve their interest in relegating certain groups of people to a separate (and purportedly inferior) category.

KEY

A Jewish youth is forced by the Nazis to parade through Nuremberg with a placard that reads "I shamed a Christian maiden"—an example of discrimination in the 1930s.

5 Slave families were often broken up when a slaveholder died and his estate was divided. In law slaves were treated like farm animals and other possessions, as shown by this picture of a sale in New Orleans, where household effects are auctioned at each side and the slaves in the center.

6 British rule over India came to an end in 1947, and the subcontinent was divided into India and Pakistan. Both Muslims and Hindus were attacked in areas in which they were minorities. This picture shows Muslims crowded onto the roof and hanging on to the sides of a train in an attempt to escape from New Delhi to Pakistan. Shortly before, a similar train had been attacked by Sikhs, and estimates at the time were that 1,200 refugees were killed and 400 injured.

7 An episode in one of the popular Fu Manchu films shows a sinister-looking Oriental abducting an innocent-looking Western heroine. Hollywood films of the 1920s and 30s developed popular stereotypes of black people as stupid and subservient and of yellow people as inscrutable, evil, and dangerous.

8 An anti-American parade through the streets of Peking was a protest against US involvement in the Vietnam War. A grotesque Uncle Sam is being pulled by mock US soldiers. Governments use psychological warfare techniques not only to confound the enemy but also to persuade their own citizens to hate people on the other side.

Prejudice and personal choice

The frequently heard accusation that men are prejudiced against women provides an insight into the nature of prejudice. No one could allege that most men are against the existence of women. But many men are prejudiced against the upsetting of traditional roles by women's claims to social equality [1]. Society has developed stereotypes of "femaleness" and has attributed such qualities to women as weakness, mildness, and passivity, which are presented as being "natural." In fact they are culturally determined insofar as they exist at all.

Social roles and prejudice

Prejudice thus often occurs in connection with particular social roles and expectations. When blacks are at the bottom of the social scale, some whites wish to keep them there because they get emotional satisfaction from the belief that someone is beneath them, or because they obtain an economic advantage from the restraint upon competition from blacks, or because they have come to regard this state of affairs as natural. Racial prejudice rises to the surface when members of the subordinated category appear to challenge the social pattern.

One way of examining patterns of prejudice is to measure degrees of social distance. In the traditional Hindu caste system social distance was actually translated into physical terms. If a member of a lower caste did not keep a certain number of yards away from someone of higher caste [2], the high-caste Hindu had to perform a ritual to decontaminate himself. Though Europeans saw themselves as occupying the highest positions in British India, Brahmins made their calls on Europeans as early in the day as possible so they could ritually cleanse themselves before the morning meal. Other kinds of social distance are just as real. In some racially mixed societies, whites are much more reluctant to accept blacks in some relationships than in others. Interracial marriage, for example, provokes the greatest resistance [3]. Acceptance of someone as a fellow worker is very much easier because the personal relationship is much more distant.

People's behavior, however, often does not reflect their attitudes. A survey in New York showed that of those white people who objected to black sales clerks, one in four did not notice when a black clerk waited on him or her. When interviewed, the others said they did not mind black clerks in the department in which they had just been served, but they might not like it elsewhere. Such findings reveal the essential irrationality of prejudice.

Attitudes and customs

People tend to accept the customs of their community and to adopt the attitudes that justify those customs. Attitudes and customs influence one another.

A classic study that points to this conclusion was reported in 1934 by a white US sociologist who with his wife and a Chinese couple took a trip in the western United States. Together they stopped at 184 restaurants and 66 hotels and were refused service only once. The sociologist later sent questionnaires to the places he had visited, asking each proprietor if he would accept

CONNECTIONS

Read first
894 Prejudice and group intolerance

See also
782 Social development
890 Conflict, power, and social inequality
816 Freedom and individuality

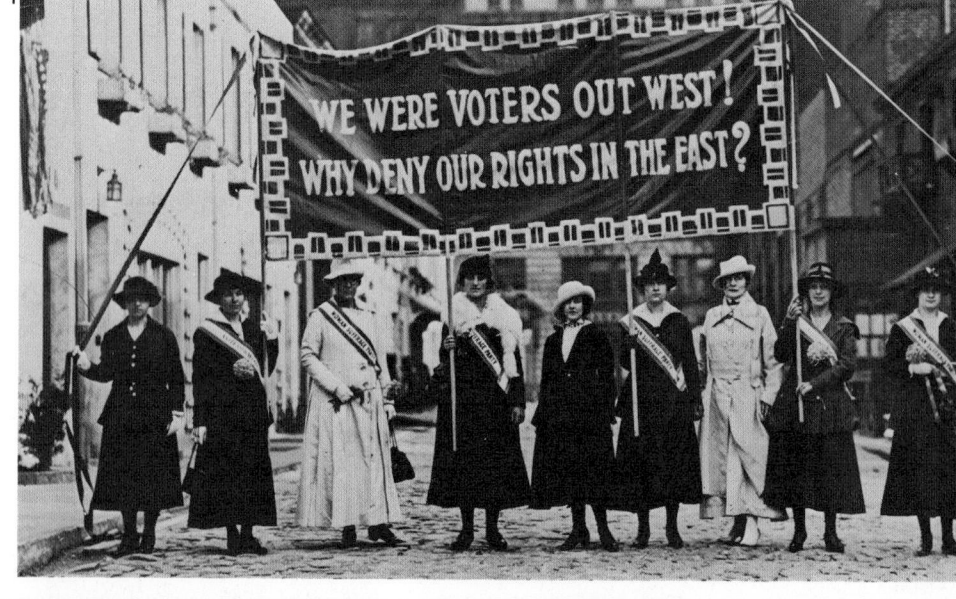

1 The fight to win women's rights centered first on the struggle for the vote. In the US women first achieved the vote in Western states: Wyoming (1890), Colorado (1893), Utah and Idaho (both 1896). By 1918 women had acquired equal suffrage with men in 15 states. The US Constitution was finally changed in 1920. The right to vote in national elections was given to women in New Zealand in 1893, Australia in 1902, Finland in 1906, Norway in 1913, the USSR in 1917, Britain in 1918, and China in 1947. There are still a few Arab countries where women are not allowed to vote.

Nambudiri Brahmin
Nayar
Iravan
Cheruman
Nyadi
Nyadi
2
10
20
23
38 meters

2 A study of Hindu caste in South India published in 1947 stated: "a Nayar must keep 7 ft (2.13m) from a Nambudiri Brahmin, an Iravan must keep 32ft (9.75m), a Cheruman 64ft (19.5m), and a Nyadi from 74 to 124ft (22.6 to 37.8m)." The Brahmin was polluted if a Nayar came closer than 7ft (2.13m) and the Nayar if an Iravan came within 25ft (7.6m). Anyone who was polluted by the proximity of a less pure person was supposed to undergo a ritual of purification. The Indian government has outlawed caste discrimination, but prejudice against intermarriage remains.

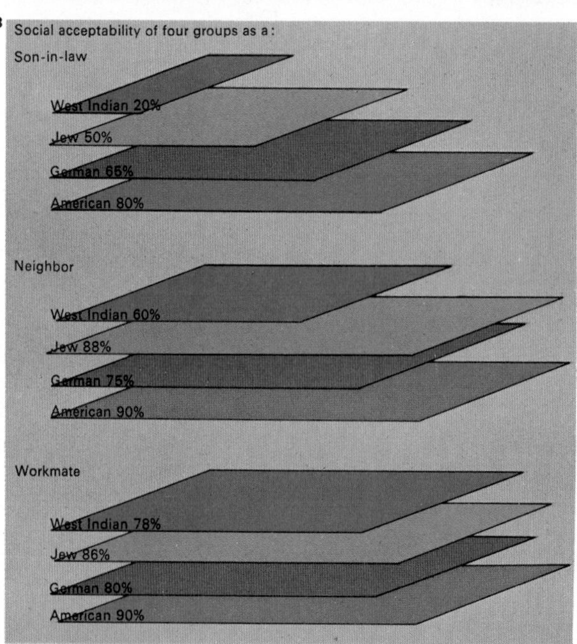

Social acceptability of four groups as a:
Son-in-law
West Indian 20%
Jew 50%
German 65%
American 80%
Neighbor
West Indian 60%
Jew 88%
German 75%
American 90%
Workmate
West Indian 78%
Jew 86%
German 80%
American 90%

3 One social study discerned a three-step pattern of social acceptability in Great Britain in the early 1960s. On the first step, nearly 8 Britons out of 10 were inclined to accept black West Indians as fellow workers. This figure compares favorably with ratings given to Jews (just over 8 out of 10), Germans (8 out of 10) and Americans (9 out of 10). Britons were more inclined to reject West Indians as neighbors than other groups because their presence suggested that the neighborhood had a lower social status. As might be expected, rejection was highest in respect to marriage because it involves close sexual and family relations.

someone of Chinese ancestry as a guest in his establishment; 92 percent said they would not.

Other studies, at children's camps, have shown that arranging children in rival teams evokes prejudice, while placing them in cooperative relationships reduces it [7]. People overcome mutual suspicions when they have a common goal to work for, as in times of war and crisis. To an important extent, then, prejudice is a product of social organization.

Psychological origins of prejudice

Prejudice is often expressed in irrational behavior that has a psychological origin. Research has shown that the people who express the strongest prejudices are hostile toward all strange groups that they consider socially inferior, even fictitious groups. One of the great contributions of the psychoanalyst Sigmund Freud (1856–1939) was the interpretation of the dynamics of personality, which suggests why some people need to display prejudice in order to make up for their own deficiencies. Such people show in extreme form a tendency present in everyone, the inclination to relieve frustrations by displacing them. Like the ancient Jews, who loaded their sins onto a scapegoat and drove it out into the wilderness, people often have a psychological need to find a scapegoat. Complex and conventional societies impose many restrictions on their members, who consequently seek to release their stored-up emotional energy. Groups that look different are often selected as targets.

Prejudice can maintain itself because people often have little personal acquaintance with those they use as scapegoats. Beliefs that are oversimplified in content and unresponsive to the objective facts are called stereotypes. People who believe that all blacks have strong sex drives, all Jews are grasping, and all Englishmen are snobbish select the evidence to suit themselves. They avoid situations in which they might be forced to recognize their error. Their attitudes influence the way they participate in society and so the personal and social aspects of prejudice reinforce each other.

KEY

SHOP
WHITE POWER
WHITE POWER
WHITE POWER

The members of this white anti-civil rights group in the United States chose the swastika as a symbol for their banner. This recalls the Nazi movement in Germany and its emphasis on the superiority of the white races. As such it would probably appeal mainly to aggressive extremists.

4 School bussing to achieve racial integration has been a volatile US social and political issue. Some cities have integrated schools peacefully through bussing, while others, such as Boston, have been the scene of violence. Opponents of bussing have been labeled as bigots but have cited the importance of neighborhood schools. Supporters have been accused of ignoring childrens' education but have defended the necessity of integration.

5 South Africa, with its *apartheid* system, rigidly defines racial roles and reinforces existing prejudices. Blacks are excluded from good jobs and are limited to lower-level positions that make life easier for whites. Blacks cannot participate in many activities open to whites, and the facilities offered them, as in this park, are often inferior to those for whites.

6 The struggle to enroll James Meredith at the University of Mississippi in 1962 was solved when federal law forced the university to accept him as its first black to attend classes.

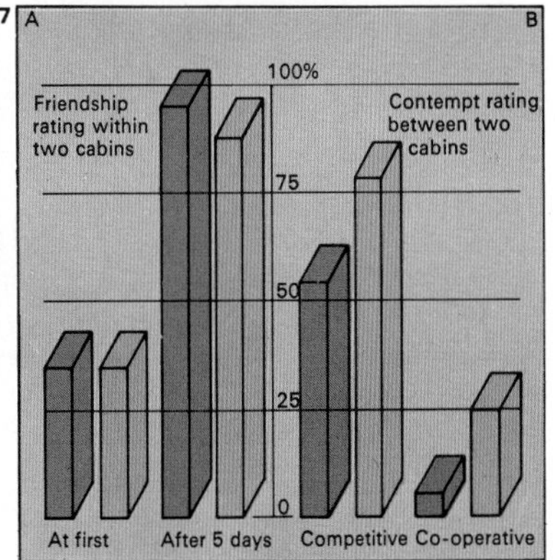
A
B
100%
Friendship rating within two cabins
Contempt rating between two cabins
75
50
25
0
At first
After 5 days
Competitive
Co-operative

7 Several experiments with groups of boys in US summer camps have shown that, although at first suspicious of each other [A], after only 5 days those in the same cabin had become friends. Two similar groups [B], who met only in competitive situations, regarded all members of the other cabin with contempt. After cooperative activities, however, the percentage who felt such contempt fell dramatically.

Fundamental political ideas

Political thought considers the nature and the validity of government. For political thinkers, the perennial questions are: What purpose does government serve? Why and by what right do some persons rule over others? Under what conditions and to what extent should one obey the state? To what degree should political authorities tolerate opposition?

The method of political thought ranges from generalizations and maxims derived from history to philosophical and theological analysis. Political thought is wider than political science in that it has a strong ethical content—it studies not only different forms of government but also the kind of government that is best and the way in which it can be achieved. Above all, it is concerned with the question of political legitimacy and of the circumstances under which a person should obey the state or defy it [Key].

The Greek concern with justice

The Greeks believed that the city-state of the Athenian type [1] arose from a quest for justice that their previous anarchic or tribal arrangements could not satisfy. Plato (*c.*427–*c.*347 BC) in his *Republic* contrasts the view that justice is the rule of the strong over the weak (which being "natural" must therefore be right) with the rival Greek view that justice is the majority of the weak collectively imposing their rule upon the strong. He saw justice as a universal concept that consists of the right relationship of the individual parts to the harmony of the whole. Those he considered fit to rule were an intellectual elite, able to penetrate the nature of truth and reality. Such a view was far from the Athenian practice of democratic election, which appeared to Plato and to Aristotle [2] as the rule of ignorance, likely to lead to strife.

The Roman concept of sovereignty

Roman thought was less speculative and more practical. The major theoretical contribution was the notion of *imperium,* or sovereign authority. When the yoke of the first alien Etruscan kings was thrown off, the Roman people declared that they alone had the right to rule themselves. Although the concept of sovereignty's residing in the people was not always followed in practice, Rome prided itself on a balanced class system whereby patricians (the Roman aristocracy) had preponderant power and authority in the Senate and plebeians (the common people) had their own assembly and officers (called tribunes) as a necessary balance [3]. The Romans saw politics in terms of practical interests that needed protection. The Roman citizens' keen sense of legal rights developed into an elaborate legal system that included principles of law still in use.

Modern political thought has been haunted by the memory of the decline from the "golden age" of the Roman Republic to the decadence of imperial autocracy (rule by one man) backed by military might. This memory has added a strain of pessimism to the modern political idea that human reason makes political progress inevitable.

Political order during feudal times was based on a political hierarchy of kings, vassals, and serfs and a Roman Catholic Church hierarchy of pope, bishops, and priests. Inequality within these orders was

CONNECTIONS

See also
900 Political science
1288 Political thought in the 19th century
996 Classical Greek society
1184 The Enlightenment
908 Rule of law
890 Conflict, power, and social inequality
902 Types of political systems
904 Political participation
906 Machinery of government
880 Simplest human societies
882 Prestate societies
886 Ancient states and empires

1A

B

1 The Greek political heritage is dominated by the idea of democracy, exemplified by the Athenian state [A], a fluid and flexible system that embodied the principle that citizens should rule and be ruled in turn [arrows] by means of annual election to governmental office. But the philosopher Plato distrusted democracy and preferred the militaristic system of another Greek state, Sparta, with subordination of many tribes to one [B]. Cohesion of the governing elite in Sparta resulted in an inflexible system, but Plato disapproved of the extreme libertarian constitution of Athens, believing it could lead to disorder and tyranny.

2

2 Aristotle (384–322 BC) disliked extreme Athenian democracy and held that justice meant giving virtue its due by electing the best to office. The best constitution lay somewhere between oligarchy (rule by the few) and democracy (rule by the many). Extremes of either kind were unjust and led to conflict. A liberal elitist, Aristotle advocated a balanced constitution and a strong middle class.

3A

4A

B

B

3 Attempts to base political order on a hierarchy have met with varying success. The Roman republican system [A] involved a class balance within a unified sovereign system. The two main classes, patricians and plebeians, cooperated in the activity of government. Believing in the dignity of leadership, the Romans gave patricians an influential role in the Senate with safeguards for the plebeians. A fundamental conflict was thus contained in a stable system. The medieval system [B] involved a conflict between two separate hierarchies, spiritual and temporal, whose powers could not easily be separated. Disputes arose about the extent and limits of each.

4 The issue of sovereignty came to a head early in the modern era when people began questioning the ambivalence of the medieval theory that power came from God and was at the same time based on the popular consent from the people. Kings such as Louis XIV of France claimed that as power came from God, kings were responsible to God alone, not to their people. This theory of Divine Right [A] began to lose popular support when discontent grew over the autocratic mismanagement of public affairs. Opponents revived the Roman theory that sovereignty resides in the people and that governments must therefore hold themselves responsible to those from whom their power is derived [B].

generally accepted as the necessary hierarchical order of God. Chaos would result from any blasphemous attempt to challenge it. Monarchy based on election, acclaim, or hereditary right was considered the best form of government because it was thought most likely to preserve unity, a prized ideal in an age of strife [7].

Government by consent

As nation-states gradually claimed independence from the church, kings also tried to claim sovereignty over their people by asserting that they were responsible to God alone for the affairs of the realm [4]. A protracted struggle over this point led finally to an acceptance that governing authority derived from the people and had to be exercised with their consent [6]. As feudal theory was replaced by an assumption of the natural equality of individuals, political thought became more secular and rational.

Despite a stress on individual rights, property owners were long considered to have the sole right to decide the general affairs of the whole community. The question soon emerged as to how men could be free and equal if they were ruled by others. In the view of Jean Jacques Rousseau (1712–78), the individual could be free only if he actively participated in formulating the laws by which he was governed. Socialist thought in the nineteenth century began to question the belief that the rich had a right to govern the poor and that the rights of individuals should be put before the welfare of the state as a whole. To Karl Marx (1818–83) all systems seemed class dictatorships based on exploitation. He believed political freedom was meaningful only if the economic system prevented some men from controlling others.

Marx's dictum: "From each according to his abilities, to each according to his needs" also moved away from the concept that political justice is based on absolute equality. An optimistic theory of evolutionary progress in the twentieth century has assumed that injustice will disappear eventually, but there is no consensus on whether this will come by revolutionary conflict or by peaceful reform [9].

KEY

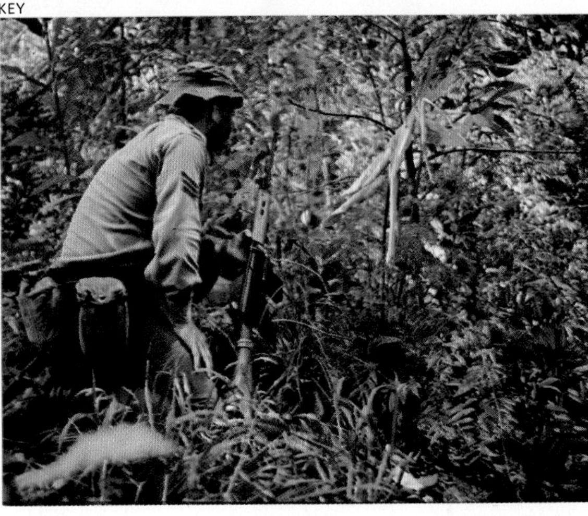

Guerrilla warfare aimed at the overthrow of an established political order raises fundamental issues of political thought. When do people have a right or duty to rebel against a government? Is revolution essential for progress, and does it involve unnecessary violence and chaos? How can freedom and order be balanced, and what is the origin and nature of legitimate governing authority?

5

5 The violence of the French Revolution brought a reaction against Locke's rational theories, which had been used by the 18th-century Enlightenment to attack the irrational basis of church and state. Conservative thinkers like Edmund Burke (1729–97) and Joseph de Maistre (1753–1821) concluded that society was based not on rationalism but on custom, prejudice, and tradition, which preserved necessary harmony and mutual class respect. They believed that religion was the bulwark of civilization and that excessive social criticism resulted in a disturbance of society's equilibrium, leading to uncontrollable violence.

6

6 The return of Juan Perón to Argentina in 1973 illustrates the idea that popular support (in this case for an exiled strongman) is the basis of political power. The answerability of government to the people was established by the English philosopher John Locke (1632–1704), who put more stress than Hobbes on man's natural rights and asserted that if a government set up to protect these rights betrayed its trust it could legitimately be removed, if necessary by revolution. Many of Locke's ideas were enshrined in the American Constitution under which men were entitled to "life, liberty, and the pursuit of happiness."

7

7 Niccolò Machiavelli (1469–1527) was the most original political theorist of Renaissance Italy, advocating ruthless measures to maintain authority. Popularly misjudged as the incarnation of evil, he in fact admired the civic patriotism and the sense of duty of the Roman Republic. Yet in circumstances of corrupt politics, leaders were justified in doing what was necessary to uphold the strength and unity of their kingdom, even if it was contrary to private conscience.

8 Leviathan, written in 1651 by the English philosopher Thomas Hobbes (1588–1679), depicts the state as combining the wills of all men into one sovereign body with a single head to guide it. Hobbes approved of autocracy but not one based on Divine Right. He thought men were too quarrelsome to conduct their own affairs. To avoid constant strife they must rationally agree to a social contract with a powerful coercive authority to make laws and keep the peace. Social freedom could thereby be maintained even at the expense of political freedom.

8

9

9 Freedom of political thought and expression, exemplified by the soap box orators at Speakers' Corner in London, is the idea of modern liberalism. Its most influential political theorist was John Stuart Mill (1806–73), who held that, while harmful actions should be curbed, no opinions should be, as an open society led to truth. With Jeremy Bentham (1748–1832), Mill believed government should be based on the greatest happiness of the greatest number.

Political science

The science of politics seeks to acquire knowledge of the nature of politics and to reach general conclusions about it. Political scientists work on the assumption that political phenomena have certain general causes and consequences, and the theories of political scientists are usually statements about the connection between two or more aspects of politics. The statement that representative democracy is the most stable form of government is, for example, a theory whose truth a political scientist might try to refute or prove by comparing societies that have representative democracies with those that have other governmental systems.

Development of political science

Politicians (those who practice politics) seek to promote or balance sectional interests in finding solutions to political problems. Political scientists (students of politics), on the other hand, try to establish and analyze what the problems are, rather than attempt to solve them. But the knowledge gained by political scientists may well have practical implications for those who rule. Equally greater insight into the nature of politics by all the members of a society may enable all to participate in and influence political decisions [Key].

The focus of interest among students has changed since political science was established as an independent discipline in universities at the beginning of this century. The various approaches to and conceptions of politics that exist today have been influenced by this development.

Initially, political scientists concentrated mainly on the study of constitutional problems. (A constitution is made up of basic laws and rules—written or unwritten—according to which other laws are made and a state is governed.) The assumption was that political life was carried on in accordance with a society's constitution. Typically, the political scientist was interested in such questions as: How can the constitution guarantee civil liberties? Is a two-house legislature better than a one-house legislature? Thus, the object of study was the various state institutions (the legislature, the executive, the judiciary) and the laws regulating the relations between them [2]. This kind of political science, especially in Great Britain, was closely connected with organized politics. It was directed toward those who framed the laws and put them into effect, the civil servants, the politicians, and the judiciary rather than toward people in general.

Constitutional problems [1] are still of considerable interest to political scientists, but they are now only one branch of a wider study. The realization that political science should cover a broader field than constitutional questions first appeared in the writings of US political scientists, who, in the 1920s, began to study other political phenomena.

A broader approach to political science

The mere study of state institutions is inadequate to political understanding because it throws little light on the way political decisions are made or on attempts to influence these decisions by such pressure groups as trade unions, business and man-

CONNECTIONS

See also

1 Devising new political systems is a difficult art, as British political experts found in Africa during the period of decolonization. Arrangements were made for 12 states to start out, as did Kenya on Independence Day, with two-party democratic political systems. Very few of these states still have such a system. This high failure rate was the result of the British seeing their own constitution as a model for the new states, despite considerable social and economic differences. It was soon realized that the problems involved in creating a new state went beyond those of working out a constitution and required broader analysis.

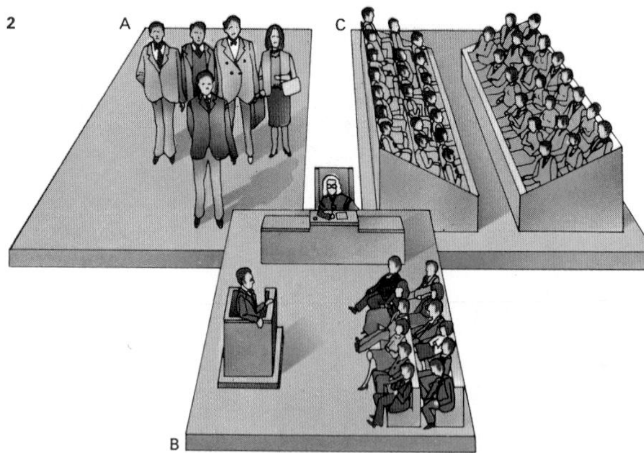

2
A
C
B

2 Early political scientists focused on the relationships among the major institutions of the state—the executive [A], judiciary [B], and legislature [C]. In doing so they reflected the dominant ideas and preoccupations of the time. In the 18th and 19th centuries it was believed that human behavior could be changed by altering laws. Consequently reform efforts, both in the United States and Europe, centered on a fight for written constitutions that could protect basic human rights. The emphasis was on ideal systems, not merely on description and explanation of politics.

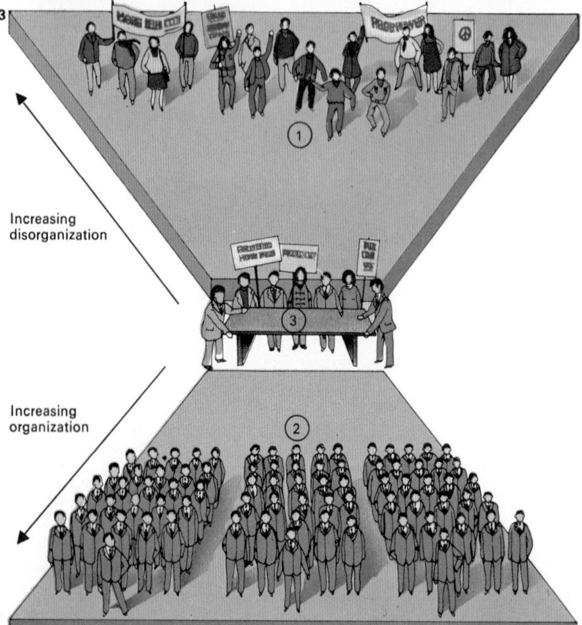

3
1
Increasing disorganization
3
Increasing organization
2

3 In modern political science politics is often viewed as the resolution of a conflict between the inherent forces of violence and revolution in society [1] and the existing institutions—government, law and bureaucracy [2]. By means of consensus and compromise, or the use of power and force, a balance is achieved. The point along the spectrum at which this happens [3] governs the character of the state—increasingly disorganized or institutionalized.

4 A political system [1] can be seen as a machine that must produce a certain number of goods, that is, decisions and actions [2]. The demands [3] made on the system are raw material the machine must process; political support for the system [4] is the fuel that powers the machine. Thus, a political system needs a certain amount of support to cope with demands. A feedback mechanism [5] ensures that if the right decisions are made support will follow.

agement, and political parties. Second, since political science aims at producing generalizations about politics in all kinds of societies, a framework of analysis is needed that can be widely applied.

Another general approach to political problems is systems analysis [4]. In this kind of analysis politics is defined not in terms of what goes on in specific institutions, but in terms of all behavior connected with decisions that affect most members of society. Instead of talking about the legislature, the executive, and so on, systems analysts talk about the political system—by which they mean all of the political interactions in a society. Their main interest is in how political systems persist under changing circumstances; how, for instance, a system will adapt to a situation in which certain groups make greater demands than the system can immediately satisfy.

Sectional interests and practical politics

Many political scientists, rather than concerning themselves with the stability of any political system, view politics as dealing basically with struggles for power [3]. The powers of trade unions [6], for example, can be studied in relation to political parties, as can the powers of trade union leaders in relation to members [7]. Such studies examine not only who takes part in decisions but also the consequences of the decisions made and whose interests are being satisfied. In Western industrial societies political scientists are at variance in their views or theories about power relations. Some contend that their societies consist of a range of groups whose powers balance each other, whereas others hold the view that specific elites or classes rule society [5].

Another important branch of political science is concerned with the motives behind political policies and the effect of these policies and of other factors on electoral support for particular politicians or parties. The analysis of voting trends and statistics is called psephology. Political scientists are often able to throw revealing light on the methods, performance, and future prospects of candidates for political office and on the reasons behind electoral results.

KEY

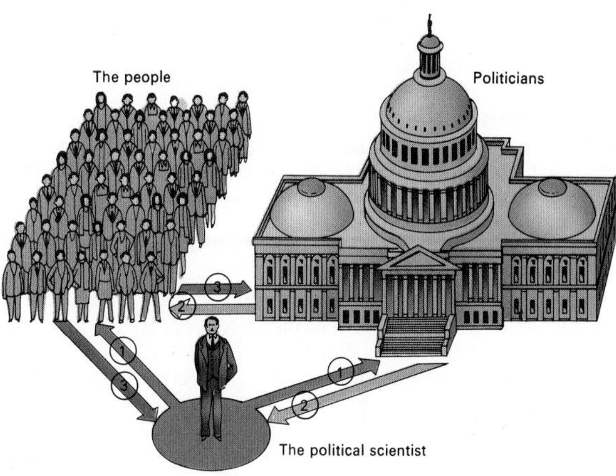
The people
Politicians
The political scientist

Problems studied by the political scientist [1] are considerably influenced by what the rest of society regards as important and relevant. The informed ideas of political scientists may have the practical consequence of increasing the power of the politicians [2] or may enable the people to exercise greater influence [3]. Whether they do one or the other depends largely on the goals of the society and the power relationships within it. In a democratic society political science tends to aim at wide participation in political life.

5

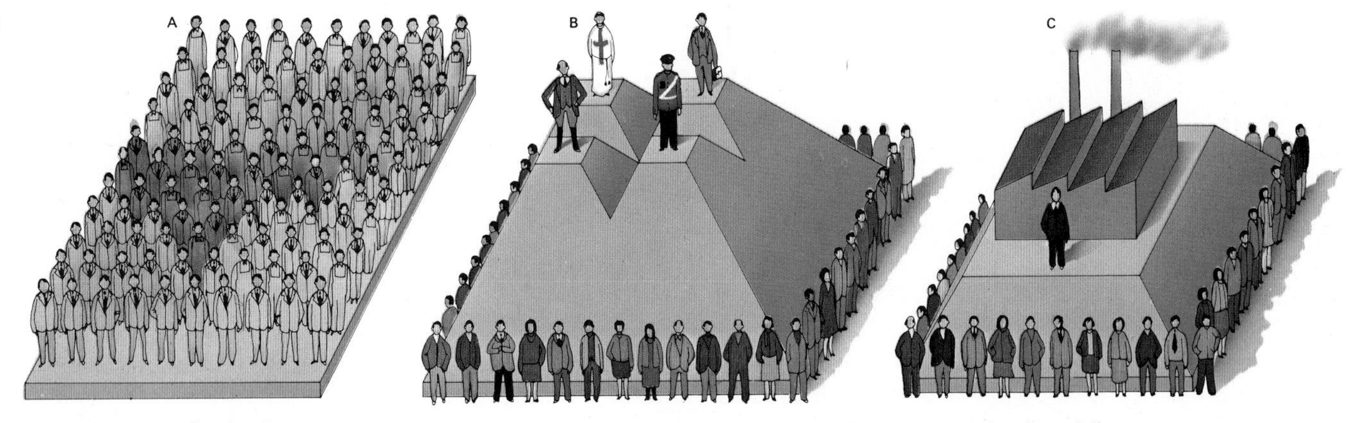
A
B
C

5 The power structure of Western societies has been interpreted in three different ways. Some political scientists hold the theory that in liberal societies such as the United States, Britain, Sweden, France, and West Germany, everybody has a say in the ruling of society. According to this pluralist theory [A] society is viewed as consisting of a number of pressure groups, such as political parties, trade unions, and business organizations, which compete on an equal footing to promote the interests of their members. Some critics of the pluralist view claim that Western societies only appear to be ruled by the people and are, in reality, run by a limited number who form elite groups [B]. Who constitutes these elites is open to question, but one influential theory is that put forward by C. Wright Mills. He identifies three elites that make important decisions together—politicians, military leaders, and the owners of big industry. In the past priests and nobles often formed elites, and today trade unions are beginning to form another. Finally, there is the Marxist view that the state exists to serve a single ruling class, which in Western societies is made up of capitalists or owners of capital [C]. In this view economic forces are decisive in shaping politics, and the apparent freedom of democratic societies merely masks the reality of power.

6

HEATH OUT
WE WANT WORK

7 A C

B

6 Public demonstrations and strikes are among the powerful weapons available to modern trade unions in seeking to sway political decisions in the interests of their members. In Western industrialized societies, the growing strength of unions and their ability to promote sectional interests are important areas of study for political scientists. Industrialization has brought an obvious shift in the power relationships within Western society in favor of the workers.

7 Internal power relations within trade unions have been an important field of study ever since workers' organizations were first formed. A key question is whether trade union leaders [A] take care of the real interests of the workers [B] or whether they have their own goals that are more in accord with those of groups outside the union [C]. Do trade union leaders identify with the workers or with political parties and outside pressures?

Types of political systems

Political systems can be classified in different ways, for example in terms of their political institutions. Western systems of representative government, for instance, can be differentiated according to the way in which the legislature or lawmaking body is elected, the main difference being between single-member systems and proportional electoral systems [1,2].

The basis of elections

In single-member systems, each geographical area or constituency elects one representative on the basis of a simple majority within that area. Proportional electoral systems try to give greater weight to the proportion of votes given to each party, a method adopted by most continental European countries. Either districts elect several representatives on the basis of each party's percentage of the overall vote or, in other systems, where no one candidate has an absolute first-ballot majority, a second ballot is held between the top candidates.

Yet another way of classifying political systems is in terms of how the executive arm of government is chosen. The two major Western systems are the parliamentary and presidential systems. In a parliamentary system [3] the head of government (the prime minister) is appointed on the basis of the distribution of power in parliament. The majority of the members of parliament must consent to the choice of the prime minister, who then decides the composition of his government (his ministers). According to the "parliamentary principle" a government must resign if the majority of parliament votes against it on an important issue. In a presidential system [4] the head of government (the president) is elected directly by the people independently of the election of the legislative body. This means that the president and the government he chooses do not necessarily have a majority in the legislature.

Democracy and dictatorship

The term "democracy" usually refers to a political system in which the people are involved in some way in the ruling of society. A dictatorship is a political system in which the few or one person rule the many. The notion of equality is central to democracy in the sense that in an ideal democratic society all people are supposed to have an equal say in the making of important decisions. But in characterizing existing political systems there is considerable disagreement as to what is the most democratic type of rule. Western liberal societies contend that the most democratic system is the one with regular free elections for which any political party may run a candidate. Socialist societies, on the other hand, claim that there can be no democracy unless all are economically equal and have an equal say in determining the pattern of production.

In view of this conflict of terms political scientists often use other categories to classify political systems. Three types of systems can be differentiated, for instance, according to the ways in which they try to solve conflicts of interest among the various groups in society [5]. Autocracy is a system in which one person or small group rules society and enforces his or its own interests without systematically consulting

CONNECTIONS

See also
898 Fundamental political ideas
900 Political science
994 Classical Greece
1180 Enlightened despotism
1312 The Soviet Union under Stalin
1334 The rise of fascism
1348 China: the People's Republic
1356 Postwar evolution of Western Europe
1358 The United States: postwar development
890 Conflict, power, and social inequality
904 Political participation
906 Machinery of government

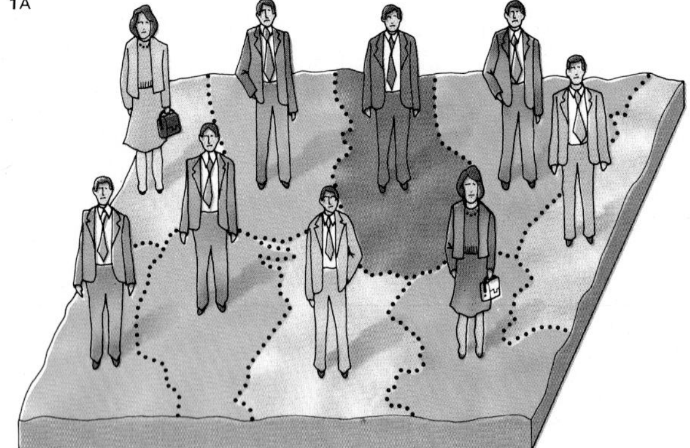

1A
B
22%
33%
45%
Percentage of total number of votes

1 The electoral principle of the single-member system [A] is that each geographical area must be represented by the candidate winning the most votes. The principle of proportional representation [B] is that each political party should be represented according to its share of the total vote. Alternatively, minorities can be given a voice by some system of distributing their second preferences.

2 The same voting support can produce different legislative representation under single-member and proportional representation systems. A country with five constituencies, each with 1,000 votes distributed among three parties, might elect under a single-member system, 3 Red, 2 Yellow, and no Green candidates, while the same vote under proportional representation elected 2 Red, 2 Yellow, and 1 Green. Single-member systems restrict smaller parties. As an example, the British Liberal party, with 19% of votes in February 1974, gained only 14 seats, not the 125 possible under a proportional system.

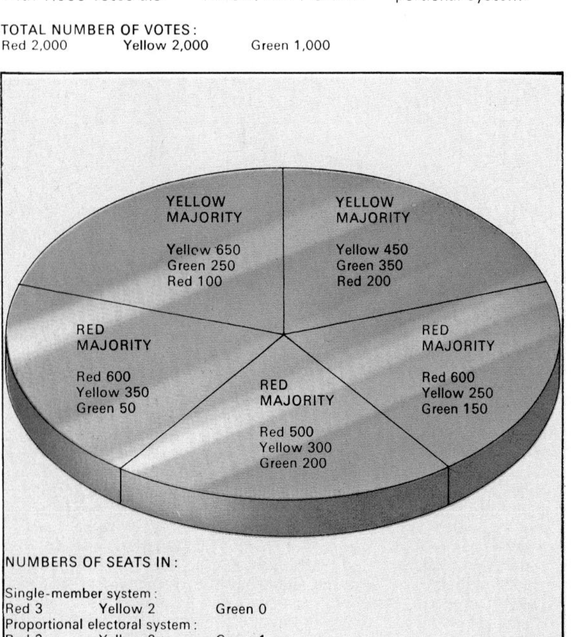

2 TOTAL NUMBER OF VOTES:
Red 2,000 Yellow 2,000 Green 1,000
YELLOW MAJORITY
Yellow 650
Green 250
Red 100
YELLOW MAJORITY
Yellow 450
Green 350
Red 200
RED MAJORITY
Red 600
Yellow 350
Green 50
RED MAJORITY
Red 500
Yellow 300
Green 200
RED MAJORITY
Red 600
Yellow 250
Green 150
NUMBERS OF SEATS IN:
Single-member system:
Red 3 Yellow 2 Green 0
Proportional electoral system:
Red 2 Yellow 2 Green 1

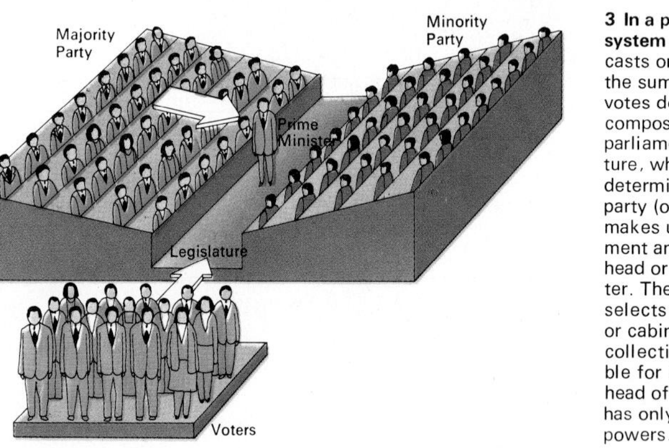

3
Majority Party
Minority Party
Prime Minister
Legislature
Voters

3 In a parliamentary system each voter casts one vote and the sum of these votes determines the composition of the parliament or legislature, which in turn determines which party (or coalition) makes up the government and chooses its head or prime minister. The head then selects an executive or cabinet, which is collectively responsible for its acts. A head of state has only nominal powers.

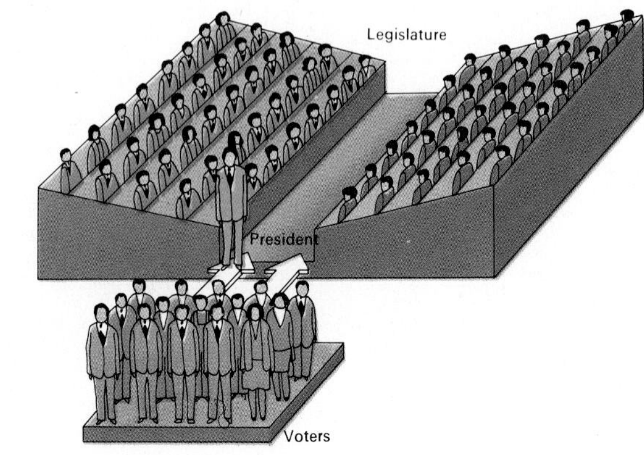

4
Legislature
President
Voters

4 In a presidential system the president is elected independently of the legislative body and is the head of government as well as head of state. He has much more power than the prime minister, president, or monarch in a parliamentary system and usually appoints his own prime minister and executive who are responsible directly to him rather than to the legislature. Legislative control over the passing of laws, or other checks and balances, curbs his power.

other segments of society. Republican government attempts to bring together the different interests by letting all citizens share in government or in the choosing of the government. Totalitarian government attempts to solve the problem of conflict by creating a society in which no major conflicts will arise; the creation of such a society is based upon a system of ideas that is supposed to guide the actions of the people and to mobilize their support for the system. Each of these three categories can be subdivided—to distinguish different types of totalitarian government [6] for example.

Communism, socialism, and liberalism

A common distinction between existing political systems is that between noncommunist, or Western, liberal countries and communist or socialist countries [7]. The difference between these two kinds of societies is basically economic. In the West, the economy is partly capitalist, with the means of production (factories, machinery, and so on) largely in private ownership. In a socialist economy the means of production are publicly owned. The differences in economic systems are to some extent reflected in political systems. Most political systems of the capitalist countries are of the republican type. The state interferes only to a limited extent in production, and all political parties are allowed to compete in all elections.

The political system of Marxist countries is often described as totalitarian. The governments emerged as a result of a revolution, through which the private ownership of the means of production was abolished, and the state, which is seen as representing the interests of the working people, controls production. Only the Communist party is allowed to function; all other parties are considered to be undermining the interests of the working class. The system is based on Marxist ideology, according to which true equality can be achieved only in a society where production is controlled by the working people. Socialism is seen as a transition toward communism, the stage at which the state is assumed to have withered away.

KEY

People, with their capacity for mass loyalty or mass rebellion, are at the heart of any political system. The major differences between systems of government lie in the means by which the will of the people is transmitted to those who govern them and in the methods governments adopt to make decisions on their behalf. Debate about the means and methods of good government is almost as endless as debate about objectives that should be pursued by government.

5

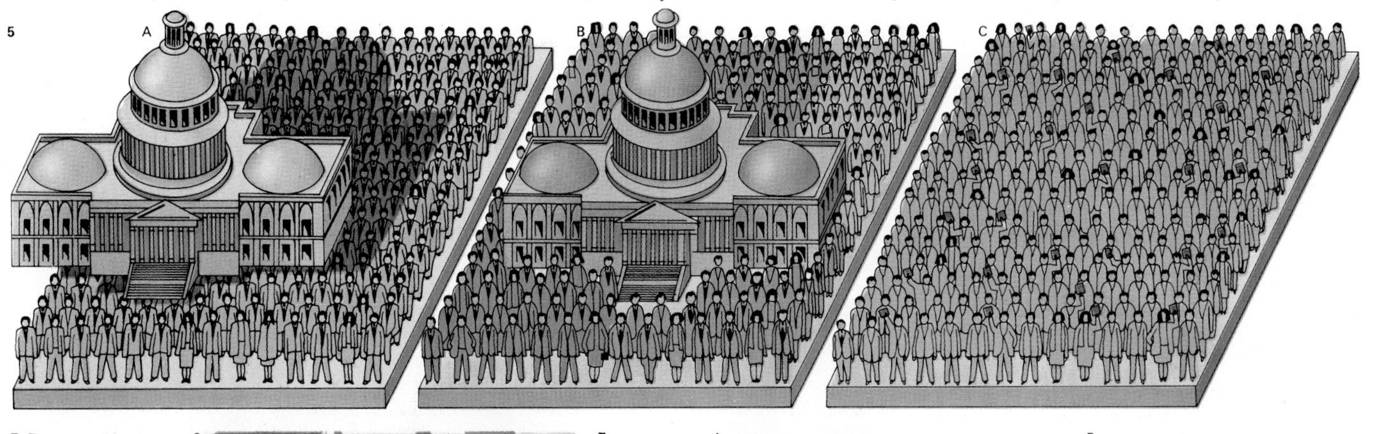
A
B
C

5 Democracies developed from authoritarian systems such as oligarchies [A] in which an elite rule. Modern Western democracy corresponds to republicanism [B]: power derives from the people and is given effect by an executive, legislature, and judiciary. In the 20th century a new political system has arisen [C] where only one party exists; it claims to represent all the people and thus to epitomize democracy.

6

A

B

6 Totalitarian systems governed Germany during the Nazi era of Adolf Hitler [A] and the Soviet Union, particularly under Joseph Stalin [B]. Both mobilized the people in support of the state. But the systems differed in their economic bases and in the ideologies used to mobilize the masses. Germany was economically capitalist and ideologically fascist. The Soviet Union remains economically socialist and ideologically Marxist.

7

A

B

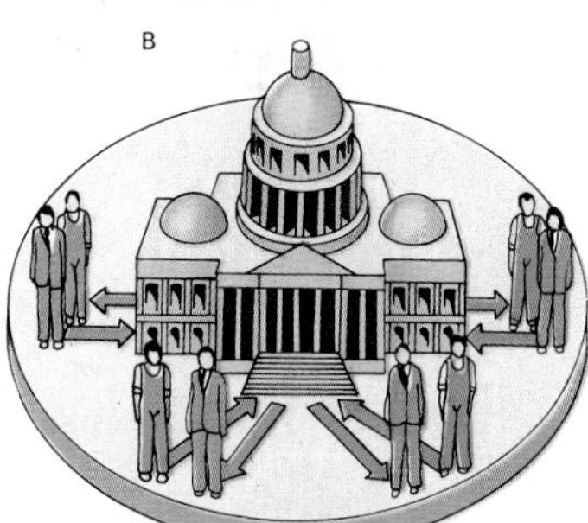

C

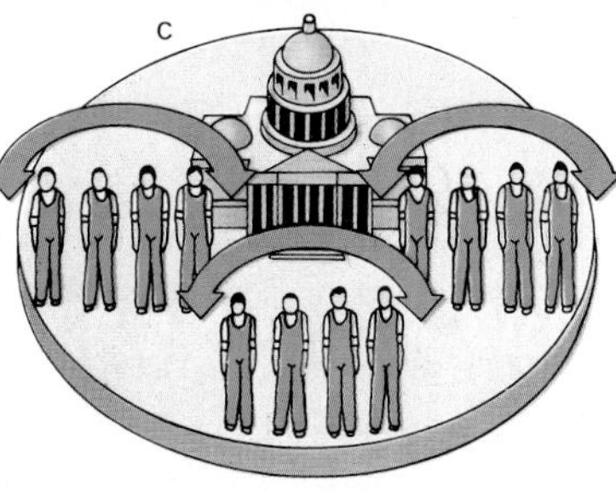

D

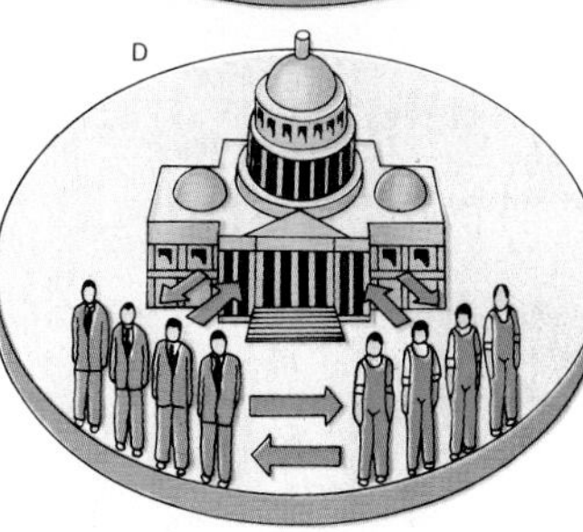

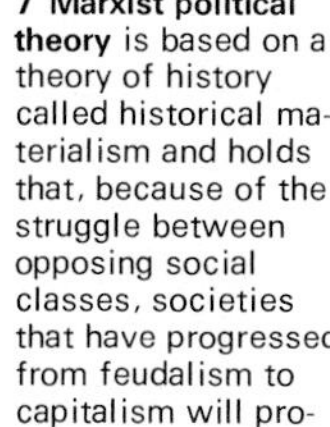

7 Marxist political theory is based on a theory of history called historical materialism and holds that, because of the struggle between opposing social classes, societies that have progressed from feudalism to capitalism will progress from capitalism [A] to socialism [B] and finally to communism [C]. Many Western scholars believe, however, that capitalism and socialism are becoming more and more like each other in the sense of being "mixed economies." Adherents of this "convergence thesis" [D] point to the fact that in many socialist countries, for instance the Soviet Union, some private production has been allowed, to encourage higher output. At the same time, in capitalist countries the state is increasingly interfering to regulate the economy. Therefore many hold that eventually the two kinds of society will become alike with a certain amount of private enterprise and a certain amount of state enterprise.

Political participation

People can take part in politics directly by holding public office or by being active in political parties and pressure groups or indirectly by exercising the right to vote [3,4]. The constitution of a country establishes the institutions through which political power is exercised, the machinery for passing laws and administering policies, the qualifications for public office, the method of election or appointment, and the composition of the electorate. Autocratic or oligarchic systems restrict participation [6], but in a democracy all adults are usually able to participate. Social and economic factors, however, as well as constitutional and legal ones, often determine how real a degree of political participation a society provides.

Parties and pressure groups

Most democracies have representative bodies [Key] whose members are responsible to those who elected them. The more control electors have over their representatives, the more chance they have of real political participation [1]. Frequent elections and the ability to recall representatives give electors greater control. So do committee systems, such as that operated by the US Congress, which expose the policies and actions of officials to public inquiry. An alternative means of control is the establishment of political units small enough to allow citizens to participate directly [2]—a form of democracy that some believe could offset the tendency of government to become too remote and complex for the individual to understand or influence in a practical way.

Organized political parties developed to further the aims of those holding basic common political beliefs. The parties provide a forum for discussion, machinery for political education and propaganda, and a method of achieving political goals by evolving a party policy and supporting candidates to implement it [9]. Participation in parties can range from passive membership and occasional fund-raising and electioneering to membership on policy committees or the holding of public office. While parties further the interests of their members on a broad front and on a permanent basis, pressure groups organize political participation on specific issues or to promote particular interests. When a specific goal has been achieved, such pressure groups often cease to function. Pressure groups cover the spectrum of political activities and may operate behind the scenes or in public campaigns.

Assessing participation

In a democracy, the individual may take part in politics within a party or pressure group or independently by taking an interest in public issues, voting in elections, watching his representatives' actions, and perhaps even running for political office. These forms of activity can take place only under certain conditions. The individual needs the ability and freedom to organize, discuss, publicize, obtain and disseminate information, and criticize or question the existing rulers, policies, and political institutions. Even when such conditions exist it is difficult to assess the amount of political participation. The percentage of the adult population that votes in an election [5], for

CONNECTIONS

See also
898 Fundamental politic ideas
900 Political science
902 Types of political systems
906 Machinery of gover ment
996 Classical Greek society
1326 Socialism in the We
1348 China: the People's Republic
1360 20th-century sociol- ogy and its influenc
1356 Postwar evolution c Western Europe
1358 The United States: postwar developme

1 Ancient Greek city-states provided the first examples of direct democracies. In Athens, all citizens formed the legislature and participated directly in the state's political affairs. They were actively engaged in both decision making and details of administration. Slaves, foreigners, and women were excluded.

2 Direct participation by the people in the making of political decisions works in small-scale units, such as this Chinese commune, or a Swiss canton, or an Israeli kibbutz. It is impractical, however, in societies organized on a larger scale, where a system of elected representatives is much more efficient.

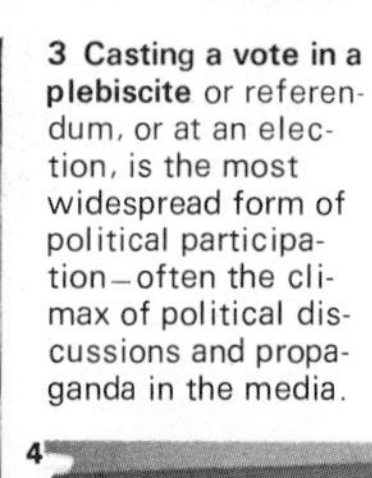

3 Casting a vote in a plebiscite or referendum, or at an election, is the most widespread form of political participation—often the climax of political discussions and propaganda in the media.

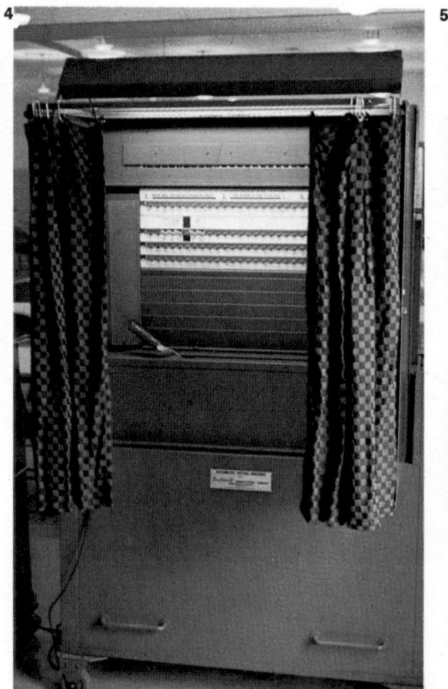

4 Mechanized voting machines reduce the possibility of fraud and improve the speed and accuracy of obtaining election results, particularly when there is a complex voting system. Technical innovation can increase the level of political participation; instant voting machines could reflect public opinion on many issues. But such a "populist" system could undermine representative democracy and the carrying through of wise but initially unpopular policies.

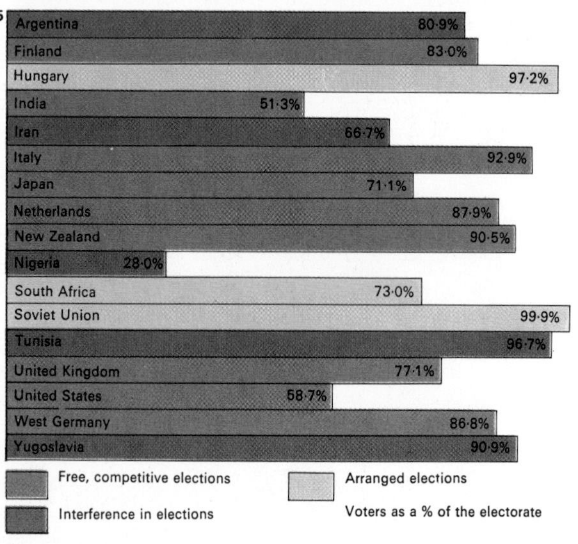

Argentina 80·9%
Finland 83·0%
Hungary 97·2%
India 51·3%
Iran 66·7%
Italy 92·9%
Japan 71·1%
Netherlands 87·9%
New Zealand 90·5%
Nigeria 28·0%
South Africa 73·0%
Soviet Union 99·9%
Tunisia 96·7%
United Kingdom 77·1%
United States 58·7%
West Germany 86·8%
Yugoslavia 90·9%
Free, competitive elections
Arranged elections
Interference in elections
Voters as a % of the electorate

5 Voting patterns in a number of countries indicate formal political participation, but variations in the number of adults who cast a vote do not necessarily measure political apathy or enthusiasm. They are often affected by a legal requirement to vote or limitations on freedom to do so.

example, is an indicator of participation, but voting may simply be a formality or a compulsory obligation. A low poll might indicate widespread apathy, or it might be the result of an organized boycott demonstrating opposition to that particular election. Membership strengths of political parties may be equally misleading if party membership is socially desirable or merely a consequence of labor union membership. Such indicators of political participation must be treated with particular care.

Political frustrations

Democratic institutions of government and a free political system do not themselves guarantee wide and effective participation in political decisions. For this, people need a certain level of political knowledge, leisure time, a consciousness of their political rights, and a belief that their participation is worthwhile.

In modern industrialized societies government institutions are often complex and inaccessible. Political issues that are not straightforward are often obscured by jargon and presented as matters best left to "experts." Political parties, as governments themselves, tend to become bureaucratic and to hinder new ideas. The business of government and the policies of public officials may be difficult for political representatives or the public to understand or influence. In such circumstances even qualified individuals may be reluctant to participate in politics.

Political participation is lower among the illiterate and less well educated. People who believe that political power is the prerogative of superior groups or classes tend to be apathetic about politics. In some countries such apathy may be officially encouraged. This kind of situation has often led to a reaction, however. When existing political institutions and channels are inadequate, the people may resort to direct action [10]. Popular revolts, revolutions, or other forms of mass political action [7] may lead to the establishment of more democratic forms of government and a higher level of genuine political participation by a better-educated community.

KEY

The British House of Commons, the "Mother of Parliaments," has been a model for many other legislative assemblies, providing a forum for the elected representatives of the people to frame new laws and to put the running of government to the test of open political debate.

6

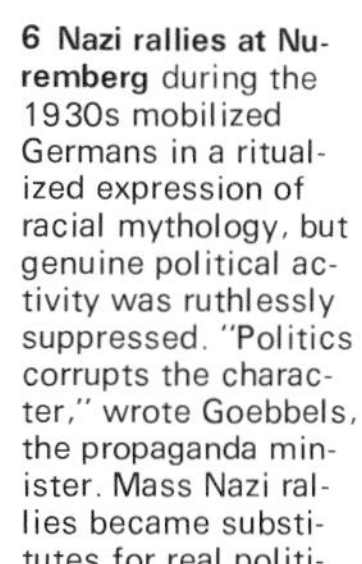

6 Nazi rallies at Nuremberg during the 1930s mobilized Germans in a ritualized expression of racial mythology, but genuine political activity was ruthlessly suppressed. "Politics corrupts the character," wrote Goebbels, the propaganda minister. Mass Nazi rallies became substitutes for real political activity.

7 Lenin, in leading the Bolshevik party to power in Russia in 1917, showed how a popular revolution can overthrow an existing government and change the social and political nature of the state. The tsarist autocracy gave way to elected soviets that soon lost power to the Bolshevik party.

7

8

8 Suffragists in Great Britain fought successfully for the right of women to vote and participate in politics. The women's movement of the 1970s sought to extend women's participation.

9

ABC NEWS

10

9 The Democratic Party Convention in New York City in 1976 was an example of a party organization working through established channels to frame a policy for an election and to choose candidates for high office to implement it.

10 Political demonstrators who clashed with police outside the Democratic Convention in 1968 were dissatisfied with established channels of political participation. Direct action of this kind is often the result of frustration brought on because formal institutions are responding to an unpopular situation too slowly or not at all. The 1960s saw an eruption of worldwide protest movements in opposition to government policies and were met with varying degrees of repression.

Machinery of government

In every political system there is a central body called government that is responsible for the essential functions of the state. It must make provision for external defense and internal order, see that laws are administered, and collect the revenue needed to pay for these state activities.

The modern state

In the modern state, governments are usually responsible for a wide range of activities, including the provision of social services in education, health, and housing. Even under a capitalist system based on private enterprise, the government regulates general economic trends, encourages export industries, helps low employment areas, aids research, controls international trade, and adjusts the money supply. In a socialist state with a "command economy," government activity extends to running all major industries as national enterprises.

The structure of government usually reflects a division of responsibility between national and regional government or federal and state government (federalism) and between the legislative, executive, and judicial areas of government (separation of powers). In the United States these distinct spheres of power may work together in some policy making [6, 7, 8, 13]. This interrelationship can be seen in the development of a highway construction program, where both the national and state governments share in the decision-making process. However the government machinery is organized, a central authority is needed to give coherence to government policy as a whole and to coordinate the activities of individual departments. Each department may be responsible for a particular government function, or for the supervision of a particular group of citizens, and will have its own administrative structure. Departmental activities may be coordinated through a central agency responsible to the head of government, or through a complex of interdepartmental committees also responsible to the head of government [3].

Members of the political executive are each made responsible for a particular area of government activity by the head of the government. In the United States these departmental officers, sometimes called cabinet secretaries, are answerable for their department's policy and its shortcomings. To a great extent, the machinery of government is staffed by nonpartisan civil servants who are employees of the state. Little decision making will be required of civil servants engaged in purely clerical or low-level administrative routines of government work. Similarly, much technical and scientific work may be merely routine testing, done to enforce government standards. But at the highest levels civil servants work with political heads and suggest ways in which political decisions can be carried out and government policy implemented. The satisfactory functioning of government depends on the quality of its civil servants, especially at the higher decision-making positions.

Executive administration

In many countries permanent high-level civil servants administer governmental programs. These individuals are often recruited from institutions that provide train-

CONNECTIONS

See also

898 Fundamental political ideas
900 Political science
902 Types of political systems
904 Political participation
910 Sources and divisions of the law
928 Work: management and organization
938 Industry and economics

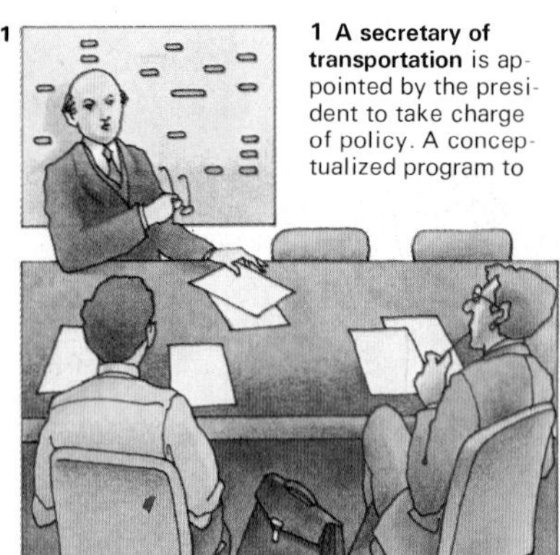

1 A secretary of transportation is appointed by the president to take charge of policy. A conceptualized program to sponsor aid for highway construction is developed. The process involves the research and analysis of various individuals, such as Congressional staff, executive agency employees (Department of Transportation, or DOT), and interest groups (truckers, Chambers of Commerce, etc.) Then the staff of the House Committee on Interstate and Foreign Commerce and of DOT develop proposed legislation.

2 The proposed legislation now passes through two distinct examination periods. First, Congressional hearings (shown here) are held in both the substantive (interstate and foreign commerce) and the appropriations committees. Discussions are held on the legislation's feasibility. Input is also received from the executive agency (in this case DOT), Congressional interests, and outside interest groups.

3 The second examination period takes place in the executive branch of government. The proposed legislation in the executive branch moves to the Office of Management and Budget (OMB) where it is reviewed with all other executive programs and receives clearance on the basis of cost and priority.

4 A vote on the proposed highway construction legislation is then taken by the members of the House of Representatives and Senate, the legislative branch of government in the United States.

5 Passage of the bill by Congress places the burden of approval or disapproval (power of veto) on the president. Advisors from the DOT, OMB, and Treasury indicate their views on the legislation, and the president signs the bill.

6 State government officials are consulted about the impact that the new road is likely to have in their area.

7 A state monitoring system advises the commissioner and staff of the state DOT of the federal program and availability of federal funds to begin construction of a new interstate highway.

8 The state commissioner and staff of the state DOT then develop a proposal for a highway program to utilize federal funding. The proposed legislation of the state DOT will be reviewed by the state legislature and by the governor.

ing in government management and organization theory. In some countries, however, notably the United States, key public service posts are more closely linked to political affiliations and may reflect electoral change. US department heads are appointed by the president, often with the consent of Congress, and are expected to reflect the philosophies of both the president and their departments [1].

In addition to advocating the views of the president and his agency, department heads are charged with representing government activities before the public and special interest groups. National programs are defended, revisions made, and new policies are initiated under conditions of rapid change in response to the desires of society [15].

Control and accountability

Governments spend vast amounts of money, make decisions that affect large numbers of individuals, and offer appointments that bestow power and prestige. It is therefore necessary to safeguard against corruption and dishonesty within the government machine. The task of ensuring honesty, efficiency, and fairness may be undertaken both internally and externally. The machinery of government usually has its own unit to monitor efficiency and promote improvements in standards of administration and personnel. Occasionally, special commissions may be appointed to survey the machinery of government, in part, or as a whole. The US government, in accordance with the Constitution, was organized with a separation of powers. This was to serve as a check on each branch of government [Key].

Members of the public may be protected against arbitrary or illegal administrative action through the courts. Many countries appoint an independent ombudsman who may investigate charges of maladministration and provide relief. Investigative committees of a legislature may bring to light misuse of the government machine. Similarly, public exposure of government processes by the mass media can play an important part in controlling bureaucratic excesses.

KEY

A
B
C
D
Defense
Transport
Industry
Environment
Education
Economics

In a typical representative democracy the legislature [A] passes laws administered by the judiciary [B] and monitors the actions of the executive [C], which governs the country through departments [D]. The story below shows how these relationships work within a government machine.

9

9 Research and extensive geological surveys are done in the area to be under construction. Environmental studies may also be undertaken by the state.

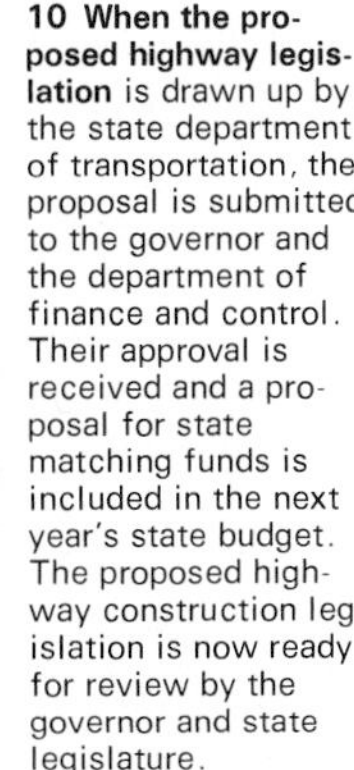

10 When the proposed highway legislation is drawn up by the state department of transportation, the proposal is submitted to the governor and the department of finance and control. Their approval is received and a proposal for state matching funds is included in the next year's state budget. The proposed highway construction legislation is now ready for review by the governor and state legislature.

10

11

11 The bill is reviewed by the state legislature following a pattern similar to the Congressional process. Examination periods are held by the state legislature's highway, bugdet, and environmental protection committees. Public hearings are held before a vote is taken by the legislature.

12

12 Passage of the bill by the state legislature places the authority for approval or disapproval (power of veto) on the governor. The governor's signature on the bill provides the state executive agency, the state department of transportation, with the authority to apply for federal funds for the state department of transportation to begin work on the new highway. The state DOT requests matching federal funds.

13

13 The federal Department of Transportation reviews the application and approves funding for the highway construction project. A grant is then sent to the state to begin construction.

14 After months of government preparation and legislation, the highway construction project is begun. Ninety percent of construction costs on the Interstate Highway system come from the Highway Trust Fund. Although underway, the project may run into some difficulties. Appropriations for the project may not be enough because of inflation; environmentalists may object to the effects on the countryside; residents may be upset at the thought of their neighborhoods changing; and labor strikes might delay construction.

14

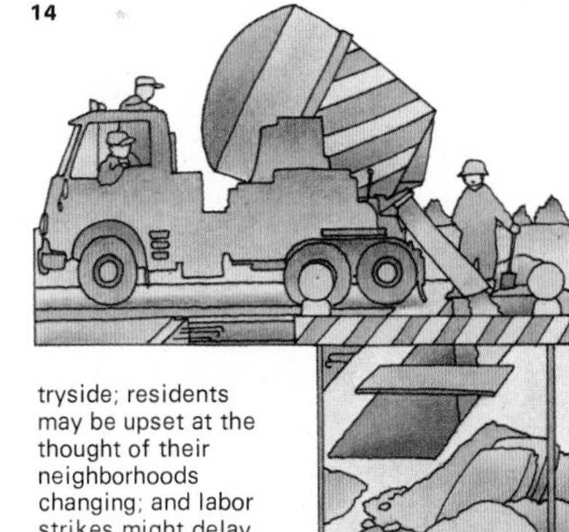

15

15 At this stage the highway project is "ripe" for court action, especially environmental protest over road construction. In a democratic society the public has the potential to influence policy.

16 The interstate highway is now complete. The machinery of government has worked from the federal and state levels to bring a highway construction project from the drawing board to completion. Working within their power areas in the policy-making process, the national and state (local) governments provided for the planning, funding, and construction of an interstate highway. Over 30,000mi of road are in the Interstate System.

16

Rule of law

It is said that "the law and the courts are often in error, but they are never in doubt!" The law demands to be obeyed, and its sanctions can be unpleasant: a fine, imprisonment, or some other social disability. We are not usually conscious of the penalties the law can impose [1], however; we accept and support the law because it upholds our way of life.

Law and justice

There are many arguments about the source of legal authority. The eighteenth-century French philosopher Jean Jacques Rousseau (1712–78) felt that to merit obedience the law must have the status of a social contract freely agreed to by free citizens. In contrast the English jurist John Austin (1790–1859) argued that laws are basically nothing more than a series of commands from the ruler to the ruled. At the same time in Germany Friedrich von Savigny (1779–1861) described law as a thing that grows naturally out of a nation's spirit, environment, and history. And there is something distinctive in each country's legal system.

Although laws vary, certain concepts are basic to almost all legal systems. Perhaps the most important is the idea of justice: the desire to balance fairly the needs of the individual against the needs of society, plus the desire to find a fair balance between the interests of one individual and those of another. The border between these two endeavors is, broadly speaking, the line of distinction between public and private law.

One difficult problem in the search for justice was epitomized by William Blake (1757–1827): "One Law for the Lion and Ox is Oppression." The law that is fair to the lion may be unfair to the ox, and vice versa. But lawmakers cannot produce individual laws for each member of the community [3]. They have to legislate for the whole society. Many legal systems have felt the need for mechanisms to remedy the injustices that result. In medieval Europe the church courts applied a system of equity to protect individuals from legal unfairness. And in imperial China judges were allowed to apply the law flexibly. A simple everyday example of equity in action is that fire engines and ambulances may break speed limits and other traffic laws in emergencies but may not in other circumstances.

Law in ancient times

Legal systems seek certainty. Once early humans learned to write they tried to make their laws certain by writing them down. Later they constructed codes—systematic collections of legal rules—which had the advantage of making the community's laws clear and easy to find.

One of the earliest legal codes known is the Code of Hammurabi (*c*.1792–*c*.1750 BC), a king of Babylon. Its 300 laws deal in a matter-of-fact way with exactly the same kinds of legal matters that exist in modern society, such as sale and purchase, inheritance, employment, marriage, theft, and manslaughter.

A legal code of a different type is the one that—as the Bible recounts—Moses brought down from Mount Sinai in about 1200 BC as a law for the Israelites [2]. The Ten Commandments are essentially a body

CONNECTIONS

See also
910 Sources and division of the law
912 Law in action
888 Structure of societie
898 Fundamental politic ideas
900 Political science
886 Ancient states and empires
996 Classical Greek society
1014 Rome: the organization of the republic
1066 Charlemagne and th Carolingian Empire
1088 European learning i the 13th century
1226 Napoleonic Europe
808 Questions of life an death
816 Freedom and individuality
914 Nature and causes c criminality

1
A
B
C

2

3

1 Why do we obey the law? One powerful reason is the wish to avoid the sanctions by which the law is enforced [A]. Another is that it is customary to obey [B]. For many it is morally right [C].

2 Moses was given the tablets of law on which, according to the Bible, the Ten Commandments were inscribed. The law can be seen as based on fundamental moral principles

3 Mr. Bumble, in *Oliver Twist*, declared, on being told that he was answerable for his wife's actions: "If the law supposes that, the law is a ass—a idiot." This statement has been echoed by many litigants and is the basis of the principle of equity, which seeks to avoid wrongs resulting from strict adherence to the letter of the law. The process of lawmaking and judgment attempts to make the unfair fair.

4

4 Solon the Lawgiver, an Athenian statesman and poet (*c*. 640–559 BC), tried to create a just society. Given power to change the law, he reorganized the community, canceled unfair debate, and carried out many other reforms to improve the lot of the people. The dilemma of balancing the rights, duties, and conflicting needs of all members of society is seen in his lack of success. In the end, Solon managed to please few Athenians.

of principles. They enshrine ideas of morality that subsequently helped to shape law in almost every part of the world.

The ancient Greeks tried to humanize law. They developed the idea that rules should be changed when they ceased to meet the needs of the community. This idea seems commonplace today, but in early society laws were seen as God-given, fixed, and immutable. The great thinkers of ancient Greece, including Socrates, Plato, and Aristotle, also concerned themselves with the quality of law and its standards.

Some Greek ideas were adopted by the Romans. But the Roman genius was essentially practical. The lawmakers were interested primarily in order and efficiency in the administration of their territories. Henry Maine (1822–88), writing of Roman law, said: "The most celebrated system of jurisprudence known to the world begins, as it ends, with a Code." He meant that it began with the rudimentary Law of the Twelve Tables in 450 BC and ended with the *Corpus Juris Civilis*, the complex collections of laws and doctrines made by Emperor Justinian I in the sixth century AD. But Roman law did not really end there; much of its substance still exists in law today.

Modern legal systems

The modern world has hundreds of legal systems, but many of them have drawn principles and methods from the same sources, and for this reason can be grouped together. The two largest groups are those legal systems with a major civil law component and those with a major common law component [7].

Civil law systems utilize the experience and ideas of Roman law. They are found in most of Western Europe, in Latin America, Asia, North Africa, South Africa, and the Soviet Union. Common law systems derive from the common law of England and are found in most English-speaking countries, including the United States.

Contemporary systems draw from innumerable other sources too, and are shaped by such influences as the teachings of Islam and political or economic theory such as Marxian socialism.

KEY

Justice, with her sword and scales, represents the power and impartiality of the law. Often she is shown blindfolded to indicate that she is blind to prejudice. Legal systems may strive to give effect to the principles of reason and morality that constitute justice, but pure justice is unattainable.

5 "We the People," the famous opening words of the Constitution of the United States indicated that the legal authority in the new country derived from its citizens, not from kings or other rulers. The Constitution was signed on September 17, 1787 and, after ratification, became the supreme law of the United States. It has been a model for the constitutions of many other countries. In most countries that have written constitutions, constitutional laws are specially protected. They can be changed only by procedures stricter than those employed for changing the other laws of the land, thus protecting the country's citizens.

6

6 Napoleon I (1769–1821), who is remembered chiefly as a military genius, ordered the compilation of the French code of law called the *Code Napoleon* or *Code Civil*. Promulgated in 1804, it was the first of the great modern legal codes. Based on existing French law and Roman law, it contains the civil as opposed to the criminal law of France and was a compromise between the customary law of the north and the Roman traditions of the south. Pre-revolutionary elements coexist with post-revolutionary innovations. The Napoleonic Code has strongly influenced the legal systems of much of Europe, Asia, Latin America, and Africa.

7

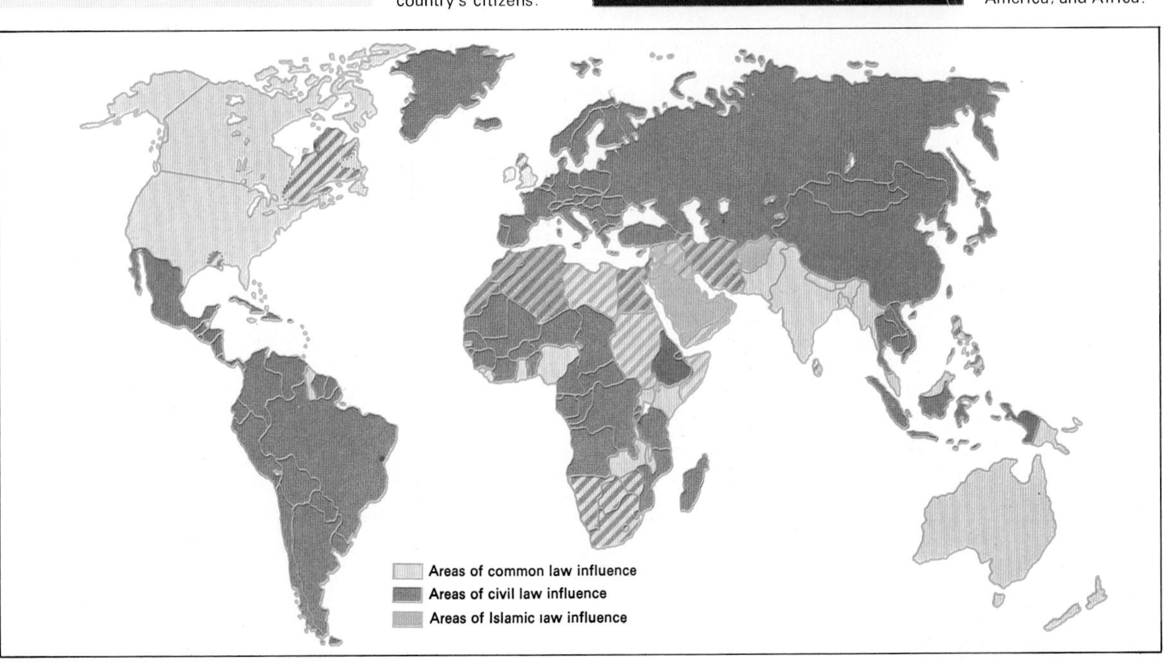

Areas of common law influence
Areas of civil law influence
Areas of Islamic law influence

7 Legal systems of various nations show different influences. Civil law systems derive from Rome. Their roots can be traced through the *Code Napoléon*, the law schools of Bologna and other ancient universities, and the Canon Law of the Christian Church to the *Corpus Juris Civilis*. In common law judges were bound by certain civilized assumptions, such as the principle that all men were equal before the law. They also had recourse to precedent—the recorded reasoning of other judges in similar cases. For these reasons, over the years, judicial decisions were fused together to form a coherent system. There is much cross-pollination between the two systems.

Sources and divisions of the law

In a democratic country, the legislature—the central law-making body, such as the Congress in the United States, or the Knesset in Israel—has power to make almost any law it wishes, and to abolish or change any existing laws. The only major restriction on legislative power is where the fundamental laws of a country's constitution are especially protected. In federal countries the legislative power is shared between a number of law-making bodies. In the United States it is shared between the federal Congress and the legislatures of each state.

The lawmakers

In practice, the legislature is directly concerned in the making of only a small proportion of the laws by which people live. The life of a modern community is so complex that the legislature could not possibly find the time—even if it had the knowledge—to make all the rules needed for orderly existence. Usually, it has to confine itself to making laws, called statutes, on only the most important matters or on broad issues. To deal with the great bulk of day-to-day matters, it delegates some of its powers to government agencies and to other bodies.

Important examples of this delegated legislation are the local laws made by local authorities in many countries relating to such activities as traffic control, education, and the sale of food and drink. Similarly, in the United States, regulatory authorities may make laws about water supplies, electricity supplies, and safety. Taxation, social insurance, labor relations, air travel, and agricultural marketing are among numerous other matters that come within the scope of delegated legislation. The laws made by these various bodies have just the same force and authority as laws made by the legislature directly.

Many laws have their origin in judicial decisions—that is, in decisions made by judges when presiding over trials in court [1]. In countries where trial judges are obliged to follow precedents set by earlier judges, these decisions become part of the established law. But judge-made rules can, of course, be altered by acts of the legislature.

Another important source of law is custom, the rules that have "always" been followed, but whose origins are obscure. As legal systems develop, customary rules tend to be incorporated in statute law or judge-made law. The writings of jurists—that is, legal scholars—are also an important source because they have an influence on judges and can therefore have an impact on their decisions.

Classification of laws

The ancient Romans divided their rules of law into public law and private law. This method of classification is still a convenient one today [Key]. Broadly speaking, public law includes all rules relating to matters in which the state or the community is directly involved. Private law—again broadly speaking—relates to private persons; that is, it deals with the relationship between one individual and another. There are occasions, such as in cases of contract and tort, when corporations (artificial persons) and even state institutions can be sued as if they were private individuals.

CONNECTIONS

See also
908 Rule of law
912 Law in action
906 Machinery of government
900 Political science

1

Constitution
Statutory law
Delegated law
Precedent
Custom

1 As society becomes more complex, rules and regulations increase in number. To some critics it seems that modern man lives in a torrent of lawmaking. The rules that apply to any particular situation may come from one or more of many sources. They may belong to a written constitution as do many US laws, or they may be part of a systematic legal code, such as the *Code Napoléon* in France. They may also be among the tens of thousands of laws in Federal or State statute books, or the even greater number of by-laws, orders of regulations made by delegate bodies such as regulatory agencies. They may be found in reports of judicial decisions, as in the American system of case law whereby a judge's decision, if it creates a precedent, may create a rule of law. Such rules may also be derived from custom.

2

2 Criminal and noncriminal acts are distinguished by the legal procedures they set in motion. Some noncriminal acts are more harmful than others that society punishes as criminal. But, despite juristic arguments about the nature of crime, the position of the criminal has always been clear: most members of society dislike and fear him. Today, because of the pressure of living and increased regulation, traditional attitudes are modified. A large number of acts, such as minor traffic offenses, that are treated as criminal, do not incur the disapproval of members of society in general.

3

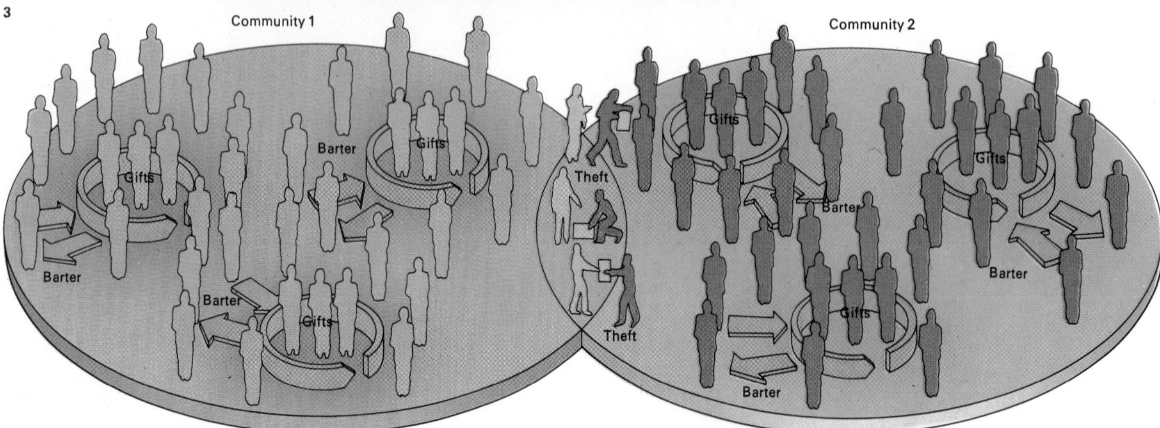
Community 1
Community 2
Barter
Gifts
Theft
Gifts
Barter
Barter
Gifts
Theft
Gifts
Barter
Gifts
Barter
Gifts
Barter

3 Any human act may have several levels of significance, each of which has to be comprehended by the law and custom and each of which requires its own rules. The transfer of property from one individual to another may be regarded as a gift when the relationship is close. At a greater distance it may be an exchange or a sale. In a remote relationship, where there is no mutual awareness of bond between the individuals, robbery or cheating may occur.

The major branches of public law are constitutional law, administrative law, and criminal law. A country's constitutional law consists of the fundamental principles underlying its life, such as the equality of all citizens before the law and the right to free speech and liberty of conscience. It also includes the laws that regulate the various organs of government. In this respect it overlaps to some degree with administrative law, which deals with the day-to-day administration of the country. Criminal law is concerned with actions (or failures to act) that are considered harmful and that are punishable by law.

The rules of international law [5], dealing with relationships between countries, are also included in public law. So are the rules affecting the conflict of laws [4] that occurs when legal issues are affected by the laws of more than one country.

Private or civil law

Private law is sometimes called civil law, a term that is used in a different sense to indicate legal systems derived from Roman law. The chief branches of private law are the laws of property, of domestic relations, of contract and of tort. Contract and tort are sometimes grouped together as the law of obligations. The law of property deals with the ownership and possession of land or buildings and with related rights. It also deals with inheritance and with rights over such things as trademarks, patents, or copyrights.

The laws of domestic relations regulate such relationships as marriage, parenthood, and guardianship. The law of contract is basic to modern society. It governs agreements entered into "for money or money's worth;" such agreements are legally enforceable. And the law of tort (called delict in some countries) deals with wrongful actions for which the injured party can claim money to compensate for personal injury. Examples of tort are defamation of character and physical injury caused by another person's negligence. In substance, there is often little or no difference between the type of injurious action that is treated as a tort and the type treated as a crime.

KEY

The law can be roughly divided into two parts – public and private. Public law deals with matters in which the state or community has an interest, while private law regulates the actions of individuals toward each other.

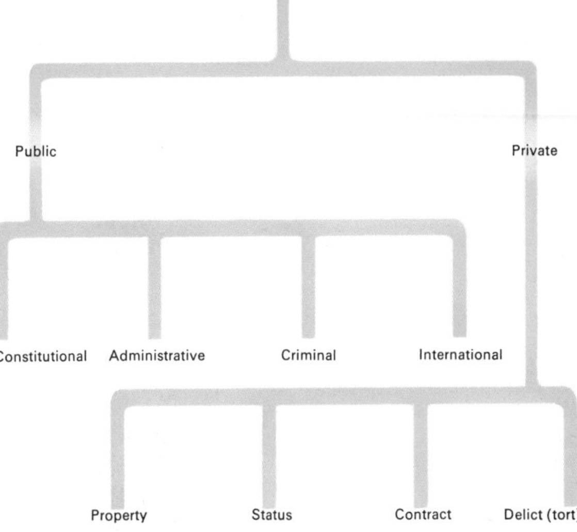
Law
Public
Private
Constitutional
Administrative
Criminal
International
Property
Status
Contract
Delict (tort)

4 A conflict of laws arises whenever an occurrence subject to litigation is affected by the laws of more than one country. An example is a collision at sea between ships of different nationalities, possibly within the territorial waters of a third country. Most of the larger countries have reached some kind of international agreement about responsibility for the effects of such incidents.

5 International law is a flimsy and piecemeal structure painfully inadequate to deal with the circumstances of the modern world. Ease of travel and increasing contact between peoples have brought new problems, one of which is hijacking. One such incident, in September 1970, ended with Palestinian hijackers blowing up three planes in Amman, Jordan.

Galaxie

6 The breakdown of social cohesion in a country leading to continuing street violence and a state of "undeclared civil war" can put a strain on the legal system. One such example was the student rioting in the streets of Paris in 1968.

7 Space-age travel has added a new dimension to legal imponderables: who owns space? The US astronauts who landed on the moon in July 1969 planted their country's flag on the surface. It can be assumed that the astronauts were not asserting American ownership of the moon or even the portion of the surface on which their spacecraft landed. International treaties are currently being drafted in an attempt to formalize some policies in this regard. Areas of sovereignty and "spheres of influence" may be vaguely defined, but the real test will come when some country feels obliged to demonstrate its ability to protect the rights to which it lays claim, possibly by the use of military force.

Law in action

The French author Voltaire (1694–1778) complained that the law comes to life only when something goes wrong. The ultimate test and expression of the law is a trial in court—a contest between two parties, only one of whom can win [Key]. The trial may be a criminal one involving a prosecutor who acts on behalf of the community and an alleged offender who faces punishment if found guilty. Or it may be a civil trial between two private persons, one of whom claims compensation for some injury said to have been caused by the other.

Finding the facts

Every trial has two essential elements. The court has first to establish the facts of the case and then find the legal rule that applies. If the court consists of a jury as well as a judge, the jury decides questions of fact and the judge decides questions of law.

The most difficult problem is establishing the facts—discovering what actually occurred or what was omitted that should, legally, have been done [1]. The court depends on evidence given by the parties to the case and by witnesses who have information concerning the points at issue. A distinction is made between direct evidence, the testimony of an eyewitness, and circumstantial evidence, evidence of fact from which the facts in dispute may be inferred [6]. A witness who says: "I saw the accused throw a bottle through the window" is giving direct evidence. A fingerprint expert who says "I found the accused's fingerprints on the bottle that was thrown through the window" is giving circumstantial evidence.

Some people feel that the value of direct evidence is greater than that of circumstantial evidence. But witnesses, even the most convinced witnesses, are sometimes inaccurate in identifying people they have seen and in describing events they have observed [7]. Moreover, unknown to the court, an eyewitness may be drawing entirely false conclusions from mistaken ideas. One such witness, a bystander at a traffic accident, stated positively that she had seen the accused drive his car through a crowded street at 50 miles an hour. No amount of persuasive questioning could shake her testimony. But eventually it occurred to the accused's lawyer to ask: "How fast do you walk?" To which the witness replied with complete assurance: "About 20 miles an hour." Such inaccurate "evidence" can sometimes be more difficult to disprove.

Rules regarding evidence

Most legal systems have rules governing the types of evidence that may be given in court and the way in which evidence is to be presented. In criminal cases, for example, precautions are taken to insure that a confession by the accused is voluntary and not the result of threats or promises of leniency. A witness may not be allowed to express an opinion—as distinct from explaining a fact of which he or she has knowledge—unless it is an expert opinion, such as a doctor's on medical facts. If a document is used, its authenticity must be established before its contents are admissible as evidence.

There are also rules regulating procedure in court, the purpose of which is to insure that both parties are fairly treated and

CONNECTIONS

See also
922 Changing patterns of punishment
908 Rule of law
910 Sources and division of the law
914 Nature and causes of criminality
916 Changing patterns of crime

1

A
B
C
D
E

1 Establishing the real facts of a case with certainty is a problem that has baffled people for thousands of years. In the past, torture [A] was widely used to extract confessions from accused persons. Sometimes, champions [B] fought as representatives of the parties to a trial; it was supposed that God would not permit the just to lose. The contemporary method is to put a witness on his solemn oath or affirmation to tell the "whole truth" [C]. The decision may be left to a jury [D] on the assumption that ordinary citizens should recognize the facts when they hear them. In technical cases, expert witnesses [E] may be called in to assist the judge and jury in arriving at conclusion.

2

2 The attorney's task is to put his client's case in the most favorable way possible within the law: as the client would put it for himself were he familiar with the law's technicalities. He also seeks – by cross-examination, for example – to show weaknesses in the opposing side's case. In a criminal case, the attorney need not consider whether his client is innocent or guilty. That is the function of the court. But he should not argue the innocence of a client who has privately admitted his guilt.

3

3 A committee of the US Senate met in the early 1970s to investigate allegations of wrongful conduct by White House and other governmental officials involved in the Watergate scandal. Such investigative committees are usually convened in circumstances involving grave issues. Their purpose is purely exploratory. They often follow trial procedures, but have wider discretion than an ordinary court. Unlike courts they can be televised.

4A
B

4 Judges discharge their duties in ways that vary from country to country. In common law countries the judge's role is more that of an umpire insuring fair play between parties [A]. But he may question witnesses. In civil law countries he acts as an impartial inquisitor [B], whose task is to uncover the truth. Thus he has to take a more active part in presenting and sifting evidence.

meet on equal terms. Again, judges in civil law systems are generally allowed more freedom than common law judges, but the purpose is the same: each side is to be allowed to state its case in its own way—within the rules—and to have a chance to answer the argument put forward by the other side.

Finding the rules that apply

Because of the volume and complexity of modern law, finding the correct legal rules to apply is sometimes only slightly less difficult than finding the facts. The statute book—the record of legislation—in any developed country today contains tens of thousands of rules; and to these must be added the mass of indirect legislation emanating from such delegate bodies as local authorities. Even when the relevant rules have been identified, their precise significance may still have to be established, because few statutes are indisputably clear in their meaning when applied to human situations of the kind that occupy the lawcourts. "Interpreting" legislation—deciding its meaning—is one of the functions of the judge. He will look to earlier legislation on the same topic and will seek to discover what the legislators had in mind in modifying the law. He will also have to study their choice of words with great care.

The judge also has a creative role when he finds "a gap in the statute," that is, when there is no existing rule relevant to the points in dispute. He then has to devise a rule that is in accord with the principles of the law. In common-law countries, the grounds on which he decides a case—called the *ratio decidendi*—form a precedent that is binding, in certain circumstances, on judges trying similar cases in the future. In civil-law countries precedents are not binding, but judges often tend to follow them for practical reasons. One strong reason is the desire for achieving certainty and consistency in the law. Another is the reluctance of a judge in a lower court to insist on formulating a principle that he suspects may have a chance of being rejected by judges of higher courts on appeal.

KEY
Judge
Witness
Recorder
Clerk
Jury
Defense Attorney
Prosecuting Attorney
Public

The dramatis personae of a trial include the judge, who presides; the clerk bailiff; the recorder; the plaintiff—the person bringing the action—and his attorney; the defendant and his attorney; the jury to decide the facts; the witnesses; and the press and public.

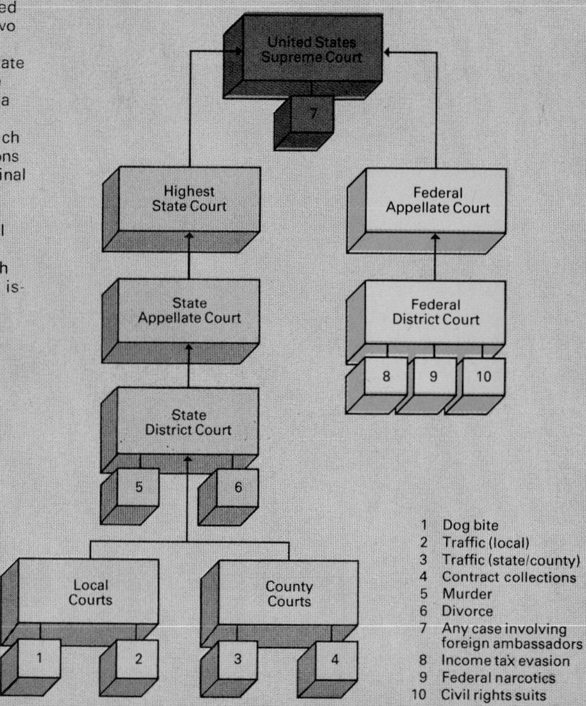
United States Supreme Court
7
Highest State Court
Federal Appellate Court
State Appellate Court
Federal District Court
8
9
10
State District Court
5
6
Local Courts
County Courts
1
2
3
4
1 Dog bite
2 Traffic (local)
3 Traffic (state/county)
4 Contract collections
5 Murder
6 Divorce
7 Any case involving foreign ambassadors
8 Income tax evasion
9 Federal narcotics
10 Civil rights suits

5 Most countries have a hierarchy of courts. In the United States there are two separate systems, one within each state and one within the federal system as a whole. The state systems handle such matters as violations of the state's criminal laws. The federal system handles matters of national concern, such as federal law. In both systems important issues reach higher courts by appeal.

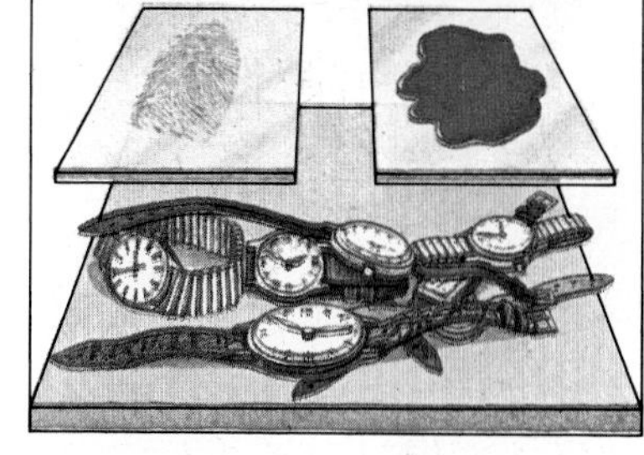

6 The police and courts rely on two types of evidence to establish the actual facts of a case—the testimony of an eyewitness and circumstantial evidence. In different countries and legal systems different emphasis is placed on these two elements. In a smash-and-grab theft prosecution, for example, an eyewitness's claim to have recognized the criminal, although seemingly reliable, may be distorted, or countered by a strong alibi for the time of the crime. Circumstantial evidence—the fingerprints of the accused on the shop window, matching blood types, the stolen property being found in the accused's possession, and so on—often form a stronger case.

7 In a dispute about the facts the testimony of eyewitnesses can be seriously misleading. Eyewitnesses frequently "see" what they expect to see. Few people will clearly observe or make mental notes of the details. A simple road accident [A], for example, will often produce radically conflicting evidence from the various eyewitnesses [B, C, D], although each of the witnesses believes his version is true.

A

B

C

D

Nature and causes of criminality

Criminal behavior takes many forms—from murder to petty theft, from treason to misappropriation of funds. Obviously, there can be no single explanation for such a wide variety of human actions, just as there is no single reason why people are law abiding.

Theories of crime must explain two quite different facets of the crime problem: first, why certain forms of behavior are defined by society as crimes and second, what are the causes that entice or compel certain persons to adopt such behavior.

Crime and its causes

Theories about what constitutes criminal behavior have varied from the ancient belief that the criminal code represents the embodiment of God's law and is independent of the will of man, to the modern radical idea that the criminal law is simply the instrument by which the ruling class maintains its economic and political power.

Explanations of the cause of crime are also varied. There is the theory that assumes that an individual chooses immoral (or criminal) conduct of his own free will and is therefore responsible for his actions [Key]. Other theories portray the criminal more or less as the helpless pawn of biological, psychological, or social forces beyond his reason or control.

Traditional explanations of criminal behavior have tended to focus upon the individual and on particular attributes of his or her personality that supposedly cause the criminal behavior. Moralistic explanations emphasize such "evil" qualities as greed, envy, corruption, revenge, or the like and assume that the individual "gives in" to such feelings of his own free will—that he deliberately chooses to behave criminally. But, at the same time, it is recognized that in some cases criminal acts are performed by the insane who therefore cannot be held responsible for their actions. This tradition has been incorporated into modern legal systems by the acceptance that psychological stress or disturbance can diminish the guilty party's responsibility for his actions. Included are states caused by brain damage, psychotic states such as schizophrenia and manic depression, neuroses such as hysteria, and various psychopathic personality disorders.

Modern theories of crime rely more on statistics than on firmly established causal relations. For example, burglary and assault are most associated with the poorer areas of large cities.

Crime, class, and circumstance

Not all crime can be accounted for by unfavorable socioeconomic factors. "White collar crime"—crimes such as fraud, embezzlement, and tax evasion—committed by people of respectability and high social status [5] in the course of their jobs, is on the increase. Murders of passion and jealousy occur within all social classes and in rural as well as urban areas. Vandalism, drunken driving, forgery, and counterfeiting are evenly spread over all population groups. Sexual crimes may be the result of economic necessity, as with some prostitution, or they may be associated with mental abnormality, as in the case of the exhibitionist or the child molester. Drunkenness is one of the most common causes

CONNECTIONS

See also
786 Moral development
812 Aspects of human nature
888 Structure of societies
892 The individual in society
916 Changing patterns of crime
918 Crime prevention
920 Crime detection
922 Changing patterns of punishment

1 Statistical studies to determine which areas have the highest crime rates in cities, and to identify the conditions of life that are most typical of those areas, have been conducted for over a century in Europe and for many years in the United States. The findings of these studies and the picture that they draw are remarkably and depressingly consistent. Over and over again it is seen that burglary, robbery, and serious assaults occur most frequently in those areas with low income, buildings that are tumbling down or in very bad repair, and concentrations of several different races and cultures. The houses are often extremely overcrowded, with few facilities. Owner-occupation is rare and population density high. The people generally have little or no formal education and are mostly unskilled laborers. There is a high proportion of single males and unemployed persons. Families are often broken up with the parents either divorced or separated. Consequently, the mothers have to go out to work and leave their children behind. Health is generally poor, with high rates of tuberculosis and infant mortality. It is not surprising that such conditions, still common even in the most affluent countries, are associated with crime, although to what extent removing these conditions would eradicate crime is open to question. Criminologists have put forward several explanations for the fact that once such an underprivileged area is established with a criminal subculture it readily encourages crime. By a process called "dissociation" the potential criminal becomes part of an already established group and adopts their often antisocial values and standards.

of criminal behavior, for excessive alcohol produces faulty judgment and impulsive behavior—significant factors in many crimes. Drug addicts often steal—and in the course of that commit crimes of violence—to obtain money for narcotics.

The "training" of the criminal

Crime is one of a large variety of nonconforming patterns of behavior. As such, it cannot be explained solely by the failure of social control over man's innate urges, although many theorists investigating the causes of crime believe this. Rather, as observed by Robert K. Merton, society and its values exert a definite pressure upon some people to be nonconforming rather than conforming. In this view deviant or criminal behavior is regarded as a symptom of a gap between the aspirations that society encourages and socially acceptable ways of realizing these aspirations. Many individuals, in response to pressures or frustrations or because of discrepancies between ambitions and possibilities, break the laws of society and commit crimes.

Yet certain forms of crime represent a special type of professional career. In common with members of other, more acceptable, professions, the professional criminal requires special training and recognition by others in his profession. In this way criminal behavior is learned behavior and is acquired in a process of social interaction. The environment of the correctional institution, where first-time offenders are often thrown in with hardened criminals, is looked upon as a major producer of the professional criminal.

Criminal behavior may, on the other hand, be a successful conformity to the values of a delinquent subculture. Such a subculture group becomes a collective enterprise in crime, opposed to the institutions and values of the greater society [4].

It is clear that criminal behavior, as all behavior, is caused by, or correlated with, a vast number of social, psychological, economic, political, legal, and moral factors. It is as futile to search for the one cause of crime as it is to account for all law-abiding behavior with a single explanation.

KEY

The Devil was traditionally seen as an almost physical force, as shown in this 14th-century French manuscript of the temptations of a nun. Criminal behavior was thought to be the result of a deliberate choice between the individual's good and evil instincts. Modern theories stress various forces that explain criminal acts. Whether society can afford to allow for such mitigating circumstances is still hotly debated.

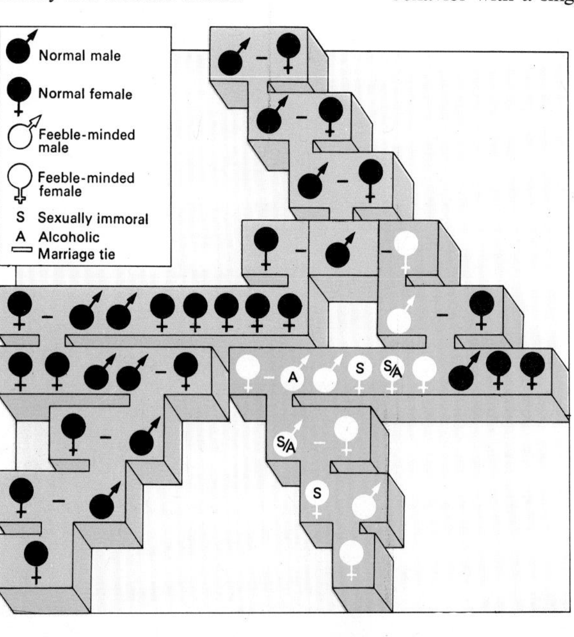
Normal male
Normal female
Feeble-minded male
Feeble-minded female
S Sexually immoral
A Alcoholic
Marriage tie

A
B
C

3 Various psychological theories have been advanced to explain why some people commit crimes and others do not. One such theory is that the criminal is the victim of a "crime neurosis" [A]. He suffers from great internal conflict and in committing the crime he is acting out that conflict. One US psychologist has put forward the thesis that juvenile delinquency is the result of the offender acting out the forbidden wishes of his parents [B]. In Freud's theory of personality [C] the individual follows the dictates of his id (his fundamental drives and desires) if his superego or conscience is not properly developed.

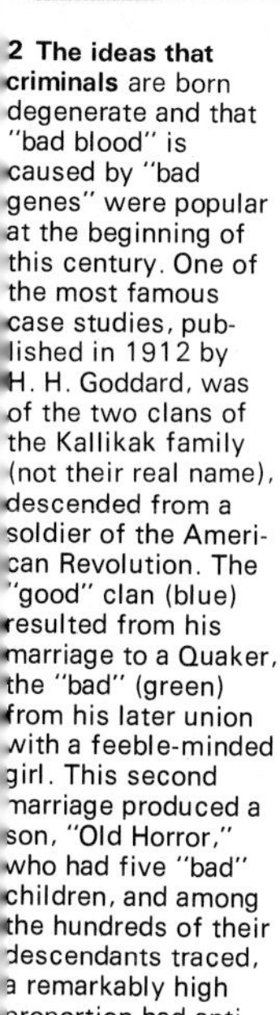

2 The ideas that criminals are born degenerate and that "bad blood" is caused by "bad genes" were popular at the beginning of this century. One of the most famous case studies, published in 1912 by H. H. Goddard, was of the two clans of the Kallikak family (not their real name), descended from a soldier of the American Revolution. The "good" clan (blue) resulted from his marriage to a Quaker, the "bad" (green) from his later union with a feeble-minded girl. This second marriage produced a son, "Old Horror," who had five "bad" children, and among the hundreds of their descendants traced, a remarkably high proportion had antisocial tendencies.

YO 508

4 Antisocial behavior can be defined as the breaking of social rules or norms. It can also be the strict adherence to the norms of a delinquent subculture. These motorcyclists, as a group, solve their individual problems of adaptation.

5 White-collar crime generally involves a betrayal of trust. Horatio Bottomley (1860–1933), British politician and financier, is an example. During a career that included starting nearly 50 companies with a total capital of $100,000,000 and raising money for various enterprises during World War I, he faced three charges of fraudulent conversion and was served with nearly 70 bankruptcy petitions. Such professional people do not see themselves as ordinary criminals.

Changing patterns of crime

Every known community has found it necessary to declare certain actions criminal—and to enforce the ban by punishing anyone who performs them. There has been a remarkable consistency in the areas of behavior regulated in this way—killing, extramarital sexual activity, property ownership, keeping the peace, and so on. Yet in detail the definition of what is regarded as criminal and how seriously it is treated varies so widely that it is difficult to find a single absolute universal prohibition.

Crime and the law

Crimes can be classified in various ways. Perhaps the most widely used divisions are crimes against people (rape, kidnaping, murder, assault); against property [2] (theft, arson, forgery, embezzlement, vandalism); and against public order or morality (drunkenness, gambling, prostitution).

Attitudes, and hence laws, change; thus what once was criminal may cease to be so. Attempted suicide was a crime in Britain until 1961; in the United States, some jurisdictions once had laws against miscegenation, but they were declared unconstitutional in 1967. Such laws are still enforced in South Africa. Crime is not something fixed, but a feature of any one society, evolving and changing with it.

Although most people regard certain activities—murder for example—as invariably criminal, it is the definition of such activities as crimes by the law that is crucial. There is argument, for example, about whether the law should concern itself only with antisocial behavior and leave private "immoral" activities alone. Debates about prostitution, homosexuality, and pornography have highlighted this problem. Most communities control or ban the use of violence, robbery, and antisocial sexual activities; but they have also developed an increasing corpus of law to regulate automobile driving, drug use, the use of credit, and business transactions. These have been the "growth points" of modern crime.

The statistics of crime

Despite the existence of highly organized crime syndicates, especially in the United States, most people arrested and convicted as criminals have committed relatively minor offenses such as small-scale thefts. Successful criminals are either never arrested or never convicted because of skillful defense lawyers.

Discovering hard facts about trends in crime is extremely difficult [1,5]. Reliable statistics have only relatively recently been compiled. In the United States, the FBI has been keeping national statistics only since 1930. There are many types of crime that often are not reported at all to the police, notably rape and blackmail, because they are embarrassing to the victim, and those in which organized crime is involved. The latter tend to concentrate on illegal service activities—narcotics [6], prostitution, loan sharking, and illegal gambling. In such crimes the injured party is usually a willing participant.

Statistics are therefore confused, but certainly the number of crimes committed rises inexorably every year (serious crime rose 144 percent in the United States from 1960 to 1970) but this may be the result in

CONNECTIONS

See also

- 914 Nature and causes of criminality
- 786 Moral development
- 792 Adolescence: sex and independence
- 796 Adulthood: from 20 to 30
- 798 Adulthood: from 30 to 40
- 800 Adulthood: middle age
- 730 Alcoholism and drug abuse
- 908 Rule of law
- 888 Structure of societies
- 918 Crime prevention
- 920 Crime detection
- 922 Changing patterns of punishment

1 A

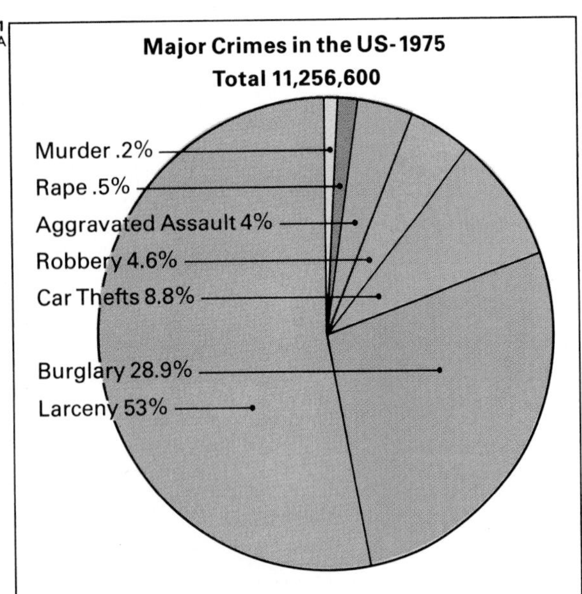
Major Crimes in the US-1975
Total 11,256,600
Murder .2%
Rape .5%
Aggravated Assault 4%
Robbery 4.6%
Car Thefts 8.8%
Burglary 28.9%
Larceny 53%

1 Statistics about crime have only recently been regarded as reliable. US figures suggest that the level of crime per capita depends in part on the ratio of young to old, since 45% of all major crimes are committed by persons under 18. Crimes against property make up a large proportion of all serious crimes and the trend has been for numbers of these crimes to rise faster than crimes against people.

2

2 Vandalism by some groups, such as rioting sports fans, are branded as mindless destruction by a delinquent subculture. These actions may, however, be partly due to unemployment and racial frustration.

3

THE GREAT TRAIN ROBBERY

HOW BALACLAVA AND HIS 40 THIEVES HIT THE UNDERWORLD'S GREATEST-EVER JACKPOT

The biggest robbery of all time

3 The "Great Train Robbery" in England in 1963 was a classic, well-planned crime in which over £1,000,000 (in used bills) was stolen by a large gang after months of planning. Most of those involved were soon arrested—the leaders being sent to prison for 30 years—but an alleged mastermind was never found. In fact probably only a fraction of crimes committed ever comes to the notice of the police. In one US study almost 90% of students who were asked to check off a list of serious crimes admitted committing at least one, yet none had been caught. The chances of a crime's being solved vary considerably. Ninety percent of murder cases, for example, are solved, whereas small thefts are hard to trace.

4

4 Cold-blooded violence has been a feature of 20th-century crime. Terror was widely used to enable gangs to extort payment from potential victims and to scare off rivals. This was the motive for the 1929 St Valentine's Day Massacre in which seven men of the Bugs Moran gang were gunned down in a Chicago garage by Al Capone's men. Capone (1899–1947) controlled the Chicago underworld in the 1920s but retired after being convicted of tax evasion in 1931 and spending eight years in prison. Crime syndicates grew initially to provide liquor during Prohibition (1920–33). After World War II they concentrated on gambling, loan sharking, and drugs.

part of more efficient police reporting procedures. Crimes of violence [8], although they attract most attention and outrage, are not rising faster than other crimes, nor do they account for the majority of arrests. "Minor" offenses such as drunkenness, disorderly conduct, and vagrancy account for up to a third of all arrests. In the ten years 1955–65, crimes against property rose 100 percent in France, Great Britain, Italy, and Norway; almost 200 percent in the United States, and more than 200 percent in Finland, The Netherlands, Sweden, and West Germany.

Levels of crime seem to be linked with the proportion of city dwellers to country people, the degree of racial, social, and cultural tension, and the proportion of young to old people.

Contemporary criminal trends

It was confidently believed that with the expanding affluence of the postwar era crimes associated with poverty and deprivation would disappear. But in fact all advanced societies experienced an upsurge, particularly of violent crimes, notably among youths such as the Teddy Boys in Britain and *stilyagi* in the USSR. Later, in the 1960s, there was violence on university campuses and generally a greater willingness to use force for political ends. By the 1970s urban guerrillas, whether hijacking planes, bombing strategic targets in cities, or holding hostages for ransom, became almost commonplace [7].

While most offenders seen by the courts in most countries are still the routine petty traffic and property offenders, certain changes can be discerned. Young offenders are more prevalent and more violent in cities. Fashions play their part in crime as they do everywhere else in modern society, aided by the impact of the mass media, which bring these acts into the home. It is thus sometimes difficult to say when a "real" change of behavior is taking place and when imitation is producing a temporary wave after some notorious event. A feature of crime in the 1970s, especially urban guerrilla acts and terrorism, has been the increasing prominence of women [9].

KEY

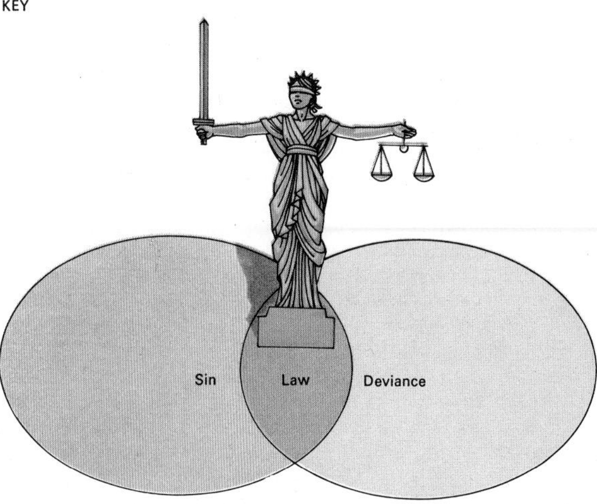
Sin
Law
Deviance

Most of us distinguish "right" from "wrong" and teach our children to do so. We recognize the idea of "sin." We also recognize nonconforming or deviant behavior, although this may be more a matter of taste or practicality. At different times and in different countries criminal law covers parts of both categories and omits parts. Adultery, for instance, may or may not be recognized as a crime.

5 A

5 The image of industrialized societies as being submerged in a wave of serious crime, such as bank robbery [A], is not borne out by statistics that show that minor offenses make up a substantial portion of all crimes committed. Different countries have differing patterns of violence [B]. In the United States there are four times as many murders per million inhabitants as in Canada.

B

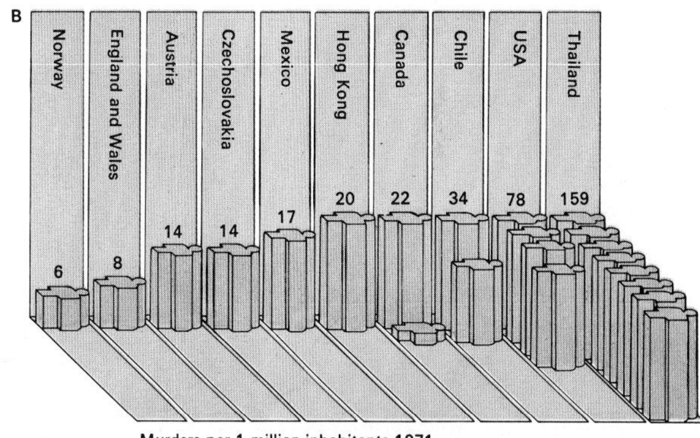
Norway
England and Wales
Austria
Czechoslovakia
Mexico
Hong Kong
Canada
Chile
USA
Thailand
6
8
14
14
17
20
22
34
78
159
Murders per 1 million inhabitants 1971

6

6 Policemen receive special training to handle narcotics cases. Drug abuse is seen as a major modern problem, although the use of narcotics is an ancient practice. What has changed is the group that now uses these drugs – young people in the West. Drug-linked crimes in which addicts steal to pay for their supplies have increased. Most countries ban drug production and sale, but these laws are flouted, and illicit trade continues despite arrests.

7

7 Political crimes are often defended by their partisans. What most people regard as a senseless outrage – such as this bombing that killed 12 people on a bus carrying army families – is to a few a blow for freedom. Political crimes are an increasingly disturbing modern phenomenon, if only because they demand unacceptable countermeasures. The crimes include hijacking, robbery, kidnaping, and terrorism.

8

8 The brutal murder of Sharon Tate and others in 1969, by the "family" of Charles Manson stresses the problems of predicting and preventing motiveless crimes by people who not only work outside society's rules but reject its whole basis.

9 Leila Khaled, a Palestinian liberationist, was involved in the unsuccessful hijacking of an El Al aircraft in 1970, during which her accomplice was killed. Women have become increasingly prominent and ruthless members of several modern liberation fronts and have been featured in political crimes. This contrasts with their traditional criminal image as "bad" girls with hearts of gold or as gangsters' molls who never initiated crime themselves.

9

Crime prevention

Law enforcement, once the responsibility of Jonathan Wild, Eugène Vidocq, and other "thief takers" who did their business out of sight in a *demimonde* of felons and miscreants, is now the daily work of millions of people throughout the world. In efforts to become "modern," agencies of law enforcement often find themselves the center of controversy with their needs and prerogatives often in direct conflict with the rights of the individuals they protect.

History of police power

Some nations, such as France, where the paid informants and *agents provacateurs* of Louis XIV (1638–1715) were to be found in the back alleys and boudoirs of Paris, created their police forces from the center outward. But it was not until 1829 that an act of parliament established Great Britain's first paid, uniformed police force. The "bobbies" of London (at first called "bobby peelers" after their founder Robert Peel) were armed only with wooden truncheons and functioned in an atmosphere hostile to police power.

In the United States law enforcement grew up even more haphazardly, with order being maintained by vigilante groups in the West and police forces under the control of big city political machines in the urban centers of the East. Police not only were corrupt and incompetent but also were hindered by jurisdictional conflicts that allowed criminals to evade arrest by crossing city, county, and state lines.

This situation encouraged Allan Pinkerton (1819–84) to leave his job with the Chicago police force in 1850 and open his own investigation business. Using a wide open eye (hence the term "private eye") as his symbol, Pinkerton helped to carve out a permanent role for the private investigator in law enforcement practice.

While the problems of policing a modern metropolis such as Rome or Tokyo are not the same as those in Micronesia, the spread of industrialization has produced the same enforcement problems and common solutions. All national police forces (those of most Western nations are members of Interpol, originally founded in 1923 to facilitate international investigation of crimes and criminals) tend to look to technology to solve their problems. After the civil disturbances of the 1960s, for example, there was emphasis on the development of nonlethal weapons for crowd control and riot suppression [6].

Most major metropolitan police forces now have helicopters to aid in tactical work, and special weapons units and specialty teams trained to deal with specific crises such as bomb alerts or kidnapings. Computers store information and speed its recall and transmission between cities and also between nations [3].

Detective agencies

The growth of crime has increased the number of detective firms, which were in something of an eclipse after national police forces such as the Federal Bureau of Investigation (FBI, created in 1908) took over most of the semi-official crime-fighting functions once held by Pinkerton's and its imitators. Private detectives still have many investigative functions—negligence cases

CONNECTIONS

See also
920 Crime detection
1668 Electronic devices
808 Questions of life and death
816 Freedom and individuality
914 Nature and causes of criminality
916 Changing patterns of crime
922 Changing patterns of punishment

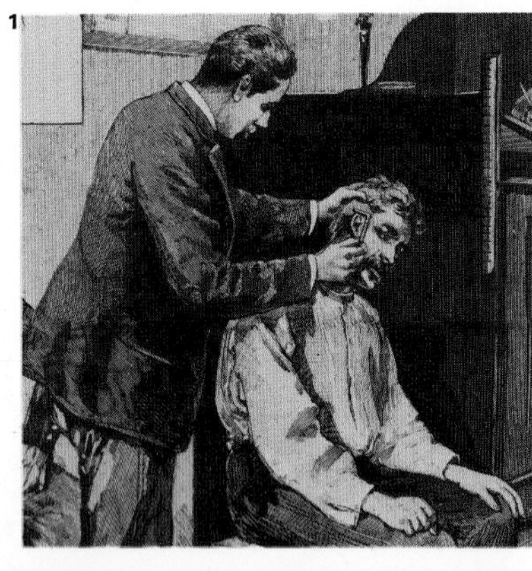

1 **Alphonse Bertillon** (1853–1914), of the Paris police headquarters, devised a system of identifying suspects in 1882 known as anthropometry, or Bertillonage. By a series of careful measurements of the head, body, and limbs of the criminal, he acquired a detailed portrait for his filing system. This system was superseded years later by the discovery that every individual's fingerprints are unique.

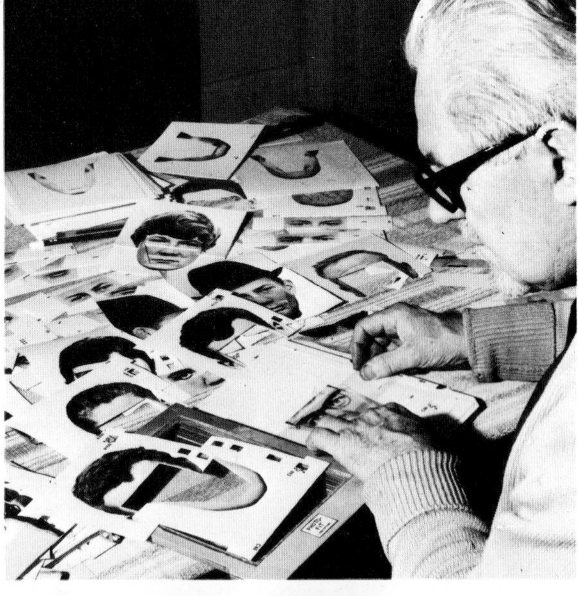

2 **The composite portrait** permits the police to communicate the physical description of a wanted person to the general public and to other police forces. From an eyewitness, an image can be built up by selecting facial characteristics from an existing bank of material (either hand-drawn or photographic) by placing transparent films of a head shape, nose, eyes, and mouth over each other. One such system has 550 variables and from these many millions of combinations can be produced. The witness can also construct a picture by briefing an artist, who constructs a portrait of the suspect.

3 **The arrest of Dr. Hawley Crippen** (1862–1910) on board the liner *Montrose* at Quebec in 1910 marked the occasion on which wireless telegraphy first played a role in crime detection. Crippen had poisoned his wife and fled with his mistress. A search of his house revealed his wife's remains and the news was telegraphed across the Atlantic. The police now use a variety of communication services such as radio, television, the teletype, computers, and picture transmitters. Two modern developments are computer terminals in police cars and communications centers that process all calls from the public, monitor police resources over a wide area, and dispatch police.

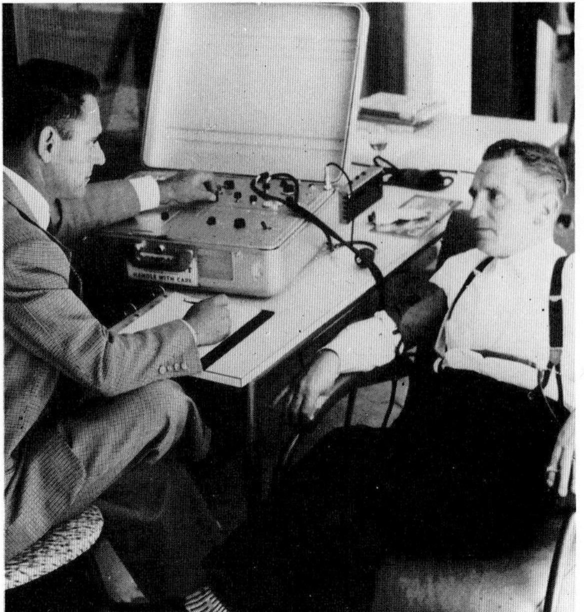

4 **Interrogation** still plays a central part in any investigation but poses problems of assessing the truth, accuracy, and perspective of the witness's memory. The polygraph, or lie detector, is an attempt to assist this evaluation scientifically by measuring body changes said to be caused by a person's emotional state. The first was constructed by John Larson in the United States in 1921, and it recorded blood pressure, pulse, and respiration rate. Later versions recorded "psychogalvanic skin reflex," the flow of current between two different parts of the body. Under stress a witness sweats more and so conductivity rises. Lie-detector evidence is rarely admissible in courts.

concerning property and cars, missing persons, insurance fraud, and the investigative groundwork for civil and criminal defendants that attorneys once performed themselves. But the primary thrust of private investigative firms is now security and guard work [7].

Big business and invasion of privacy
By 1975 individuals and corporations were spending some $4 billion a year on private security and crime prevention in the United States alone, with another $1 billion going into closed-circuit television monitors, burglar alarms, and other security equipment. Crime prevention had become big business.

There are areas of potential friction between private detective firms and public police agencies. Existing licensing procedures do little to lessen police suspicion of private investigators' qualifications since they tend to certify only that an investigator has a minimum level of professional competence. Other countries are carefully watching the Swedish example of requiring clearances for detective firms engaged in sensitive work such as industrial espionage.

The growth of public and private police bureaucracies has surrounded law enforcement with new problems. Many private investigators, for instance, have adapted to their trade the advanced electronic surveillance equipment developed and used by the intelligence services in the postwar era [5]. When used in sensitive areas such as industrial espionage and counterespionage, this equipment has caused controversy. But the debate over its use has certainly not been as heated as that concerning its invasion of individual privacy.

Yet the surveillance practiced by individual private investigators is minimal compared with the data collected by such clandestine organizations as the Central Intelligence Agency (CIA) and national police forces all over the world. In their attempt to grapple with the complexity of modern life and its institutions law enforcement agencies have sought constantly to increase and centralize their own powers.

The James gang was founded by Jesse (1847–82) and Frank (1843–1915) in 1867 after Jesse, a Confederate guerrilla in Missouri, was declared an outlaw at the end of the Civil War. They plundered and murdered, specializing in bank and train holdups. Law enforcement at that time depended largely on posting rewards to attract bounty hunters who bore a grudge or simply wanted the money. Jesse was shot in the back of the head by Robert Ford, a gang member, for the bounty. Frank surrendered and was tried but twice acquitted, spending the rest of his life on a Missouri farm. Their exploits have been romanticized in films and ballads.

KEY

REWARD

$15,000 REWARD
FRANK JAMES
DEAD or ALIVE
$25,000 REWARD FOR JESSE JAMES
$5000 Reward for any Known Member of the James Band
SIGNED
ST. LOUIS MIDLAND RAILROAD

5 Technology has enormously increased the risks and opportunities of industrial espionage. There is a large choice of devices – cameras, microphones, transmitters, and tape recorders – that are widely available. They can be readily hidden under clothes and their range is prodigious: most microphones can pick up sound at 20 feet (6m). Weapons are also more sophisticated. The Swiss produce a pen gun that writes as well as firing a bullet.

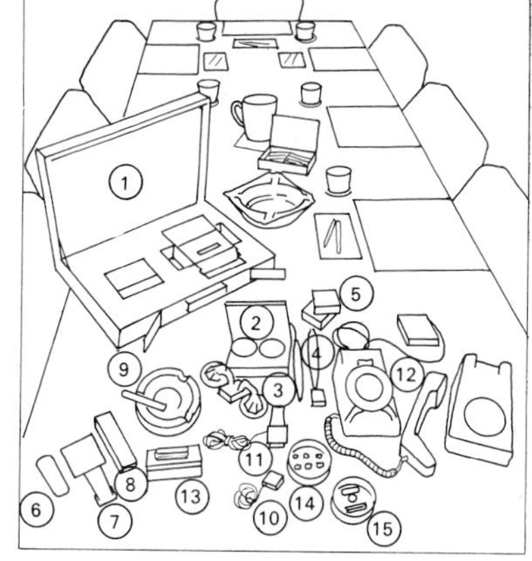

1 Briefcase with tape recorder, switch, microphone and volume control
2 Miniature tape recorder for holster or pocket
3 Pen microphone connected to tape recorder
4 Pen transmitter with built-in microphone
5 Transmitter with built-in microphone to fit in a cigarette case
6, 7 Silent motorized camera that can be worn as a wrist watch
8 Automatic 16mm camera
9 Ashtray with microphone and transmitter
10 Transmitter
11 Microphone watch
12 Telephone transmitter
13 Cigarette lighter with transmitter and microphone in base
14 Tiny transmitters
15 Subminiature microphone and amplifier

6 Civil disturbances of the 1960s caused many police forces to equip themselves with new protective clothing as well as nonlethal weapons for crowd control. Research contractors have developed irritants such as Mace and "pepper fog" (a dense concentration of tear gas from a mobile unit); tranquilizer dart guns similar to those used by big game veterinarians and "stun guns" to shoot rubber bullets at high velocity; chemical dye to be sprayed on demonstrators to facilitate later identification; and a "banana skin" foam that makes it impossible for a crowd to maintain its footing.

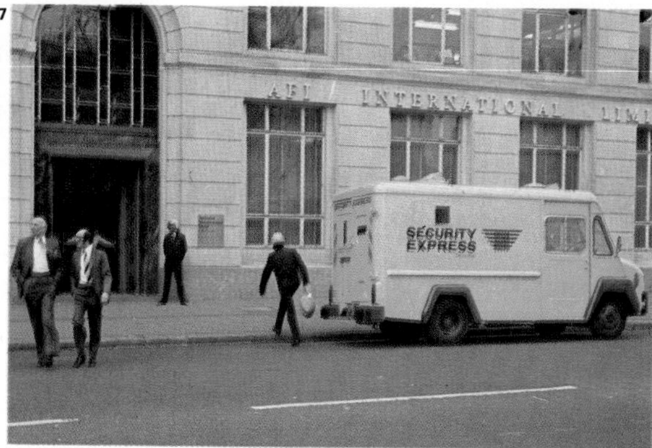
SECURITY
EXPRESS

7 Private security firms have increased in number and size because the hard-pressed police are unable to provide adequate protection for industrial premises or the transportation of valuables or money. Such firms are also hired to prevent espionage between companies and pilfering of goods by customers and employees. The relationship between security firms and police forces poses certain problems. Firms can be infiltrated by criminals, staff wear uniforms that are misleadingly like those of the official police, and their activities in such areas as checking the creditworthiness of potential customers are liable to abuse. In Great Britain security men may carry weapons not available to police.

Crime detection

Whenever a serious crime is committed the police can call on the assistance of a variety of experts to bring the offenders to justice. These are the police surgeons, pathologists, toxicologists, chemists, biologists, ballistics experts, and other highly-trained specialists who provide a service in forensic science or criminalistics—the application of medical, scientific, and technological skills to the investigation of crime.

The most widely used of these behind-the-scenes services is the fingerprint collection. Fingerprints [8] were first used to solve a crime almost a century ago. To aid the speed and accuracy of detection, fingerprints are now compared with central records by computer.

Introduction of forensics

Forensic medicine has its roots far back in history. Among the earliest evidence of the use of medical knowledge to combat crime is a thirteenth-century Chinese treatise, *The Washing Away of Wrongs*, which includes helpful hints on how to tell if a drowned person had been strangled. More recently, there has been a tendency for forensics to be divided into two categories: the examination of the living (sometimes both victims and suspects) and the pathology of the dead.

Forensic pathology is the cornerstone of homicide investigation. Here the doctor called to examine a body found in suspicious circumstances uses his knowledge of the patterns of violent or unexpected death to decide first whether the case is one of murder, suicide, or accident. The actual cause of death is established at an autopsy.

Forensic science as such is a much more recent innovation. Before the turn of the century laboratory science played very little part in the detection of crime. Even in a case of murder it was left to the policeman to make his routine inquiries and to the doctor to examine the body and make a few simple medical tests. It was not until the early 1900s that forensic science, a product of police work and medicine, began to take on a separate identity and to emerge as a new service to the police and the courts.

Today the forensic science laboratory offers a range of specialties that includes chemistry, physics, biology, pathology, metallurgy, ballistics, and document examination. Much of the daily routine is taken up with blood-alcohol analysis in driving-while-drunk cases and with drug offenses. But the laboratory can also call on almost any branch of medicine, science, or technology in the fight against crime.

The workload of individual laboratories varies with geographical location. In the United States, where there are many more shootings than in most countries, the examination of firearms is a major preoccupation. Clearly, too, there are more breaking-and-entering cases, requiring fingerprinting comparisons, in cities than in the country. In general, the three types of offense most often calling for examination of contact traces [14] (clues left at the scene, on the person, or in vehicles) are breakins, assaults, and hit-and-run cases.

Features of scientific investigation

Detectives are taught during their training that every contact leaves a trace—that the criminal leaves some clue, however micro-

CONNECTIONS

See also

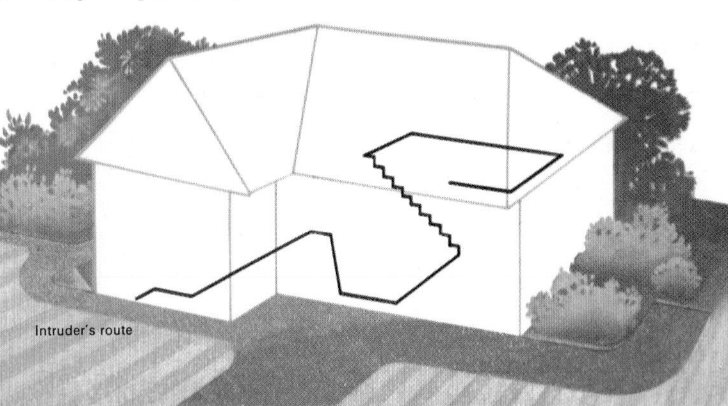

1
Intruder's route

1 In this imaginary crime a casual intruder has broken into a house to steal. After wandering from room to room (the black line traces his route), he then disturbs a woman who has been asleep upstairs and strangles her. Unlike the average homicide—most are so-called "domestic" murders usually solved within two or three days—this could mean lengthy investigations because the killer has no previous connection with the victim. In addition to the regular police, specialists are called in: a police photographer to record details before anything is disturbed; a police surgeon to certify death; fingerprint experts; a forensic pathologist who examines the body before it is taken away for post mortem; and a forensic scientist to gather evidence (although collection of evidence is often the job of especially trained policemen).

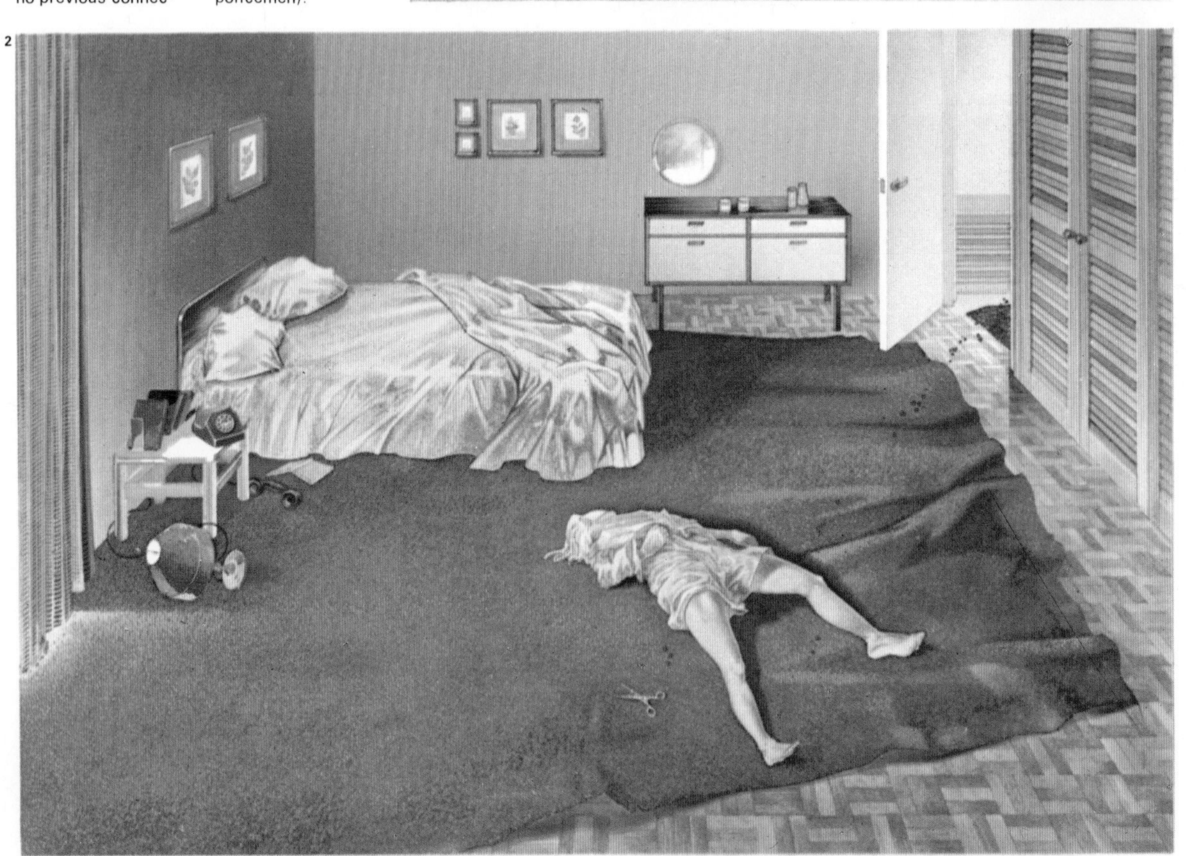

2

2 The experienced investigator gradually pieces together his own interpretation of events from the physical evidence found at the scene. To preserve an accurate record, the scene of the crime must be photographed and sketched in minute detail as soon as the police arrive. The victim was apparently strangled with a knotted nylon scarf. On the floor detectives find blood stains and the dressmaking scissors used by the victim to stab wildly at her assailant. The bedroom is in disarray, indicating a possible line of struggle from the bed to the dressing table and then across to the body's final resting place. The forensic pathologist has the difficult task of estimating time of death, a calculation based mainly on the rate of cooling of the body and the degree of rigor mortis. The position of the bedclothes and the overturned furniture indicate the violence of the struggle, during which the victim tried to defend herself with scissors. The rumpled carpet suggests that the body was dragged away from the area of maximum disturbance, the space between the window and the door. Clues to the identity of the attacker include one or two hairs on the pillows, partial fingerprints on the dressing table and door knob and, leading out to the bathroom, traces of blood from a wound caused by the scissors.

scopic, at the scene of the crime [3–13]. At the start of an investigation the police look to the scientists for what is sometimes called inceptive evidence—information on which to base the search for the offender. As the case progresses corroborative evidence may emerge linking a suspect with the crime.

A feature of some scientific evidence is what is known as "inferred uniqueness"—an overwhelming statistical probability that the item in question incriminates the suspect. Fingerprints are a case in point. Since nobody has ever fingerprinted the world's population, there is no way of knowing that no two people have identical prints. But because, in all the many millions of prints on record, no two sets ever correspond, it is reasonable to assume that each person's prints are unique.

More satisfactory, however, is "proof positive," and here the best example is the "jigsaw fit." This is the matching of fragments of the same article found at the scene and elsewhere. Cloth and paper are most likely to feature in a jigsaw fit, although it may also involve wood, glass, and metals. It is by no means rare for a housebreaker to be caught by the forensic matching of a piece of metal left at the scene of the crime with a broken tool edge found in his possession [5].

Importance of forensic science

Ultimately, the value of forensic science lies in providing objective physical evidence—that, unlike some witness testimony, will withstand close scrutiny in a court of law. It is for this reason that crime laboratories bristle with increasingly elaborate hardware for microscopic examination and analysis of the most minute particles of trace material.

A major attribute of forensic work, therefore, is its inevitable mystique—not least because the average criminal can never be sure what the experts can do. There is, in theory, no limit to the application of science to the detection of crime. This prospect is particularly reassuring because criminologists claim that the most powerful deterrent to criminal behavior is not so much punishment as the certainty of discovery.

KEY

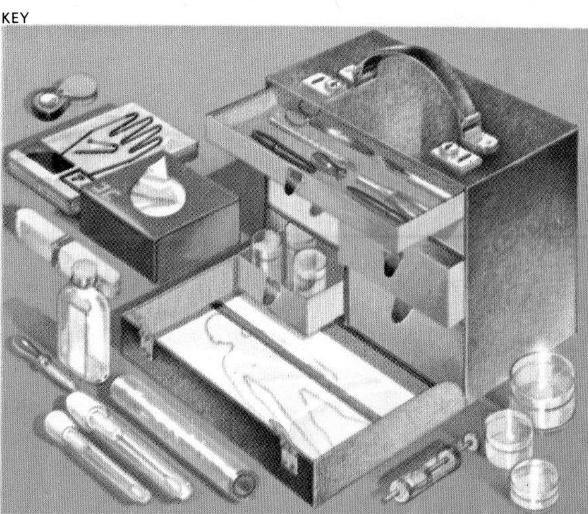

The pathologist's case contains medical paraphernalia and other items needed for forensics. Particularly vital are outline diagrams to record details of the scene and the position of wounds on the body; plastic bags in which to protect the victim's head and hands; a special thermometer used to take the temperature, an aid in estimating the time of death; and containers to hold evidence samples.

3 When a window is broken from outside about two-thirds of the glass goes inside. The rest flies backwards and may lodge in an intruder's clothes, to be matched for type at a later stage.

4

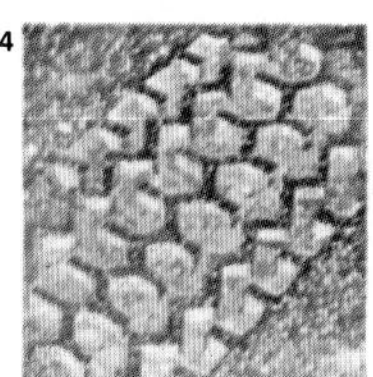

4 Tire marks are photographed and casts taken. Tread pattern may indicate the make of car, and worn tread could lead to identification. Many laboratories have indexed collections of tire treads.

5

5 Entry damage to woodwork may leave a clear impression, identifying the tool by its pattern of scratch marks. The tool and a section of wood are scanned using a comparison microscope.

6

6 Often an intruder will eat on the premises; some cook a meal. As few people have perfectly regular teeth, impressions left in food such as cheese, chocolate, or fruit can be compared, by casting or photography, with a suspect's bite. Bite marks on victims' bodies are also matched with their assailants' teeth. Forensic dentistry (odontology) is a valuable resource in identifying bodies.

7

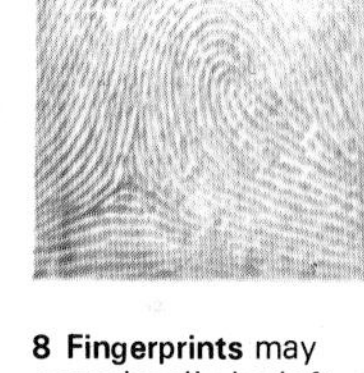

7 Shoe impressions reveal the sole pattern and size. Characteristic wear and defects may pinpoint an actual shoe. Prints may be revealed by scattering tiny plastic beads that adhere to tread marks.

8

8 Fingerprints may occasionally be left by indentation on soft surfaces, or by transfer of materials such as blood or grease. More common are latent prints—faint impressions left by transfer of sweat or natural oil. These are dusted with powder and photographed. Barring tissue damage, fingerprints remain the same throughout life, and no two people have exactly the same fingerprints.

9 When blood falls vertically it produces a star-shaped splash; but if a wounded man is moving the tailed splash reveals the direction he took. This information is useful in dismissing the false confessions that often follow a murder.

10

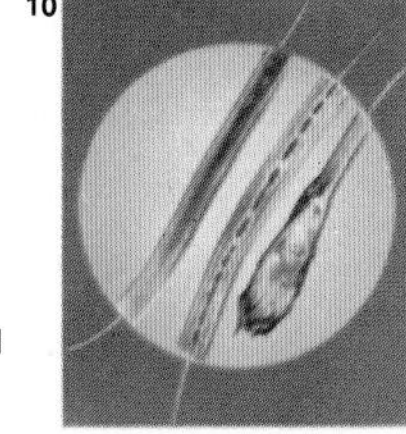

10 The microscope can reveal whether hair is human or animal and whether from the head or elsewhere, but it cannot identify the owner. In the future, metallic deposits derived from diet and environment may help identify hair.

11

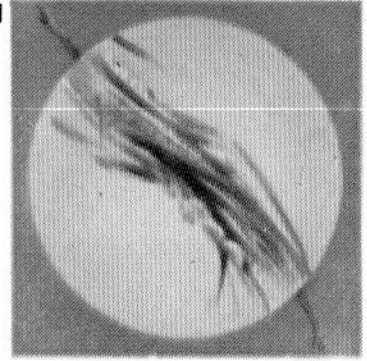

11 There is some transfer of fibers in practically any indoor crime. These strands of cloth caught on a splinter will be examined under the microscope for fiber type, color, and weave.

12

12 The pathologist protects the head and hands of the victim with plastic bags to preserve any clues that may help identify the assailant. Blood or skin fragments, for example, may be trapped under the fingernails of the victim.

13

13 The ligature is always cut off well away from the knot in cases of strangulation, then labeled and tied off so that the cut ends do not unravel. It is important that the knot, which may be of special significance, be kept intact.

14

14 Random murder is often difficult to solve because the killer, often mentally disturbed, is an unknown quantity, someone who has no links with his victim. In this case the police already have a rich haul of clues from the scene. In addition, valuable trace materials such as the glass from the window of entry, will have transferred to the killer's clothing. When an arrest is made, the two sets of clues will be matched to make a watertight case against the suspect.

Changing patterns of punishment

In simple, small-scale societies the obvious way of righting a wrong is for the victim (or his relatives and friends) to exact vengeance or seize compensation. As societies grow and become more complex such a procedure threatens social stability. Offenses come to be seen as wrongs against the community rather than against the individual, and the right to punish is taken over by the state. Punishment is imposed as a retribution for an offense, to deter would-be offenders, and as a means of reforming those who have broken the legal or moral code. The balance among these objectives has varied in different societies, as have the methods adopted to achieve them. These fall into four categories: compensation, humiliation, mutilation, and elimination.

Methods of punishment

The usual punishment for minor offenders was either compensation (including various forms of fine) or public humiliation [1–4], the latter being abandoned in most countries by the early nineteenth century. For more serious or persistent criminals mutilation—such as flogging, cutting off a limb, slitting the nose, cropping ears, or branding—was used. Torture was largely abolished by the mid-eighteenth century in Europe. The law's final sanction against offenders, however, was elimination. This could be exile, as when Great Britain and France, for example, transported prisoners [Key] to distant penal colonies, such as Australia and Devil's Island. But the most drastic method was execution. There are many forms including beheading, drowning, stoning, beating, electrocuting, strangling, gasing, [11], shooting, and hanging.

As a means of enforcing the law, capital punishment presents problems, particularly if it is imposed for a wide range of offenses. (In eighteenth-century England death was decreed for several hundred offenses, mostly against property.) Offenders are not likely to be deterred if they are to suffer the same penalty for large and small, violent and nonviolent crimes. Legislators tried to find a solution by making the process of execution increasingly more terrible for graver offenses.

Hanging, drawing, and quartering, for instance, was introduced in the Middle Ages. The prisoner was hanged until almost dead, removed from the gallows and then disemboweled. Finally the corpse was cut into four pieces and displayed as a warning to others. Until the seventeenth century in many European countries breaking on the wheel [9] and crucifixion were also used.

The development of the prison system

A milder form of elimination is imprisonment. Early prisons were generally squalid and intended solely as retributive deterrents. The notion of reformatory imprisonment grew chiefly through the efforts of John Howard (1726–90) and other penal reformers. Their belief in the beneficial effects of hard labor [10] and strict rules is reflected in the regimes of the Auburn prison in New York (1825) and Cherry Hill prison, Pennsylvania (1829). The first was based on complete separation of prisoners, the latter on preventing communication through a rigid silence regulation. Both ideas influenced later European practice.

CONNECTIONS

See also

762 How mental illness has been treated
912 Law in action
914 Nature and causes of criminality
916 Changing patterns of crime
918 Crime prevention
920 Crime detection

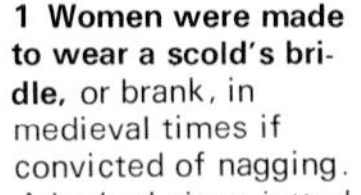

1 Women were made to wear a scold's bridle, or brank, in medieval times if convicted of nagging. A barbed piece jutted into the mouth.

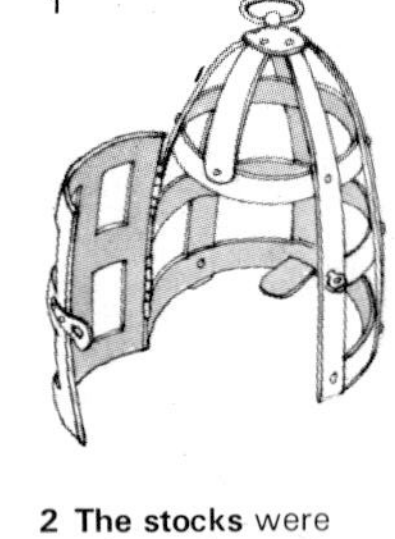

2 The stocks were an alternative to the pillory, which held the head and hands. Offenders had to spend up to six hours in them.

3 Jougs were padlocked iron collars used mainly in Scotland and Holland to punish blasphemers and breakers of the peace in church.

4 The drunkard's cloak, a barrel with holes top and bottom, used throughout Europe, neatly fitted the punishment to the crime.

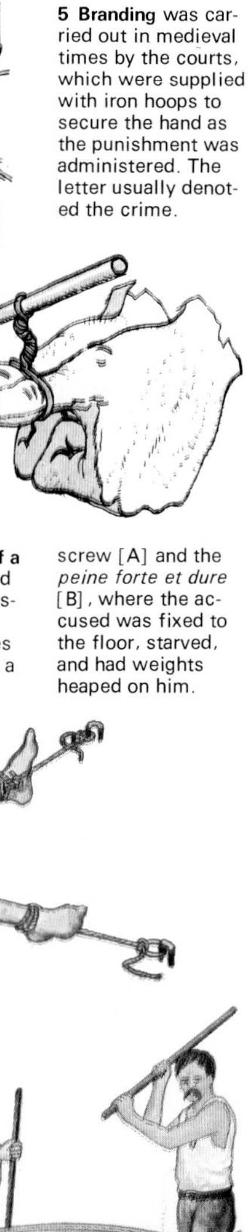

5 Branding was carried out in medieval times by the courts, which were supplied with iron hoops to secure the hand as the punishment was administered. The letter usually denoted the crime.

6 Those accused of a felony often refused to plead to avoid losing property if convicted. Two tortures were used to force a plea: the thumbscrew [A] and the *peine forte et dure* [B], where the accused was fixed to the floor, starved, and had weights heaped on him.

7 The Iron Maiden was a coffinlike iron chamber with spiked doors that impaled the victim when closed.

8 The rack dislocated a victim's joints. It was banned in England in 1628 after being in use since 1447. It was also used by the Spanish Inquisition.

9 Breaking on the wheel was carried out by the executioner, who smashed each of the limbs with an iron bar, before killing with a blow to the heart.

During the past hundred years, ideas of how best to reform prisoners have become more liberal. These have led to the introduction of less brutalizing labor, more emphasis on occupational training and education, better living conditions, and the possibility of earning early release. Recently, psychiatric methods have been adopted to treat offenders individually or through group interaction sessions. But pressure on resources, lack of trained personnel, and a generally unsympathetic public attitude toward "softer" treatment have meant that in many jurisdictions commitment to reform is only token.

The effectiveness of imprisonment

Prisons, although differing in their degrees of security, visiting privileges, recreation, and so on, are generally repressive, with total regulation of the prisoners' lives and few opportunities for constructive activity. The result is that for the inmate a prison sentence means loss of many material goods, loss of heterosexual relationships, loss of individuality, and withdrawal of support by society. Such conditions are unlikely to encourage prisoner reform.

As a result, in recent years many people have begun to doubt that prison experience does prevent individuals from returning to crime on release. Although more than two-thirds of those imprisoned for the first time do not return to prison, there is little evidence to suggest that being behind bars has contributed to their "going straight." Experience suggests that young offenders and those imprisoned more than once are particularly likely to repeat their offenses.

In some countries, therefore, the trend is away from imprisonment and toward supervision in the home and community settings, where it is thought that many of the pressures resulting in criminal behavior arise. In the United States, for example, two-thirds of all offenders are under supervision outside prisons. Probation, parole, and suspended sentences conditional on good behavior—particularly for juvenile and first offenders—are increasingly being adopted because they are both cheaper and more effective than imprisoning.

KEY

Ships or hulks were used as prisons in the 18th and 19th centuries. Felons were kept in them to await transportation to penal colonies. If the sentence was short it would all be served aboard in cramped conditions. Hulk prisoners were employed in dock construction, river dredging, and other public works that required the use of heavy manual labor.

10 The treadwheel was adopted widely in the 19th century to solve some of the prison labor problems, for it meant that a fixed quantity of punitive work could be extracted from each prisoner individually. A period of 15 to 20 minutes hard effort was followed by a short rest. The mental and physical effects were hotly debated. In some prisons the wheels were used to grind corn or raise water. Elsewhere the prisoner's effort was deliberately not harnessed so that its very futility would act as a deterrent. The treadwheel was eventually abandoned because it brutalized rather than deterred or reformed.

B
A

11 The gas chamber was used until recently in the United States. This one is in San Quentin prison in California. The condemned person was strapped into a chair, and globes of cyanide were dropped into acid held in the cylinder, bottom right. This released lethal hydrocyanic acid gas. Unconsciousness was almost instantaneous, and death usually occurred within five minutes. Like most modern forms of capital punishment, it was meant to minimize the suffering that such penalties necessarily involve. This is in clear contrast to the ancient methods of execution where protracted pain was deliberately inflicted.

12 Prisoners lined up in their striped uniforms in the exercise yard at Sing-Sing prison, Ossining, New York (*c.* 1895). Even today prisoners may spend more than 22 hours a day in their cells. Good behavior is rewarded with privileges. Parole can be applied for after serving only a third of the sentence.

13 Minimum security prisons with community involvement and the use of half-way houses to facilitate the return to their communities of former inmates are slowly developing procedures that give some hope of developing a penal system that is corrective rather than brutalizing and self-perpetuating.

Work: curse and pleasure

In societies with slaves, such as ancient Greece, work was a necessary material evil that the elite avoided [2]. The Hebrews considered work a painful necessity but added the belief that it resulted from Adam and Eve's expulsion from the Garden of Eden. Protestantism, and particularly the Puritan followers of John Calvin (1509–64), established work in the modern mind as "the base and key of life": the best way to serve God was to do most perfectly the work of one's profession. Conversely, idleness began to be seen as sinful.

Why people work

Utopian socialism of the nineteenth century was also influenced by religious ideas about the dignity of labor and the value of work. Karl Marx (1818–83) believed that production should be carried on for use rather than for profit so that men would "live to work" rather than "work to live"—thus acknowledging that satisfaction could be found in labor, apart from any economic reward.

In the nineteenth century and the early twentieth, when it was customary to seek wholly biological explanations of human behavior, psychologists tended to think in terms of instincts or drives to explain why people might "live to work." Sigmund Freud (1856–1939) implied that hidden sexual satisfactions must lie behind any pleasure derived from working. Other psychologists believed that people worked out of an instinct for self-preservation, or that an "instinct of mastery" accounted for the human effort to control the environment.

Later theories insisted that humans were so largely social animals that the question of why and how people work must be investigated from a cultural and social viewpoint. Studies of what work means to people in modern societies suggest that a complex mixture of economic, social, and psychological factors is involved [Key, 1]. People may work primarily for money, prestige, or power. They may be motivated by a sense of social purpose or simply by the need to establish wider personal relationships. Their satisfaction may be intellectual, physical, or a mixture of the two.

The degree of emphasis now placed on the material rewards of work is a comparatively recent development. Initially, the central driving forces of Western industrial society were survival and the Protestant work ethic. But as the religious justification for hard work waned and as mass consumption of the goods produced by work became economically important, monetary rewards in excess of bare requirements were increasingly offered as an incentive. One result of this was that the interest of those who worked began to turn from production to consumption; in other words, work became for many a tedious means by which to acquire what in earlier eras would have been called luxuries.

Job satisfaction

Evidence of widespread job dissatisfaction has led in recent years to numerous investigative studies covering many occupations (although mostly factory and office work). Satisfaction with work for its own sake is more likely to be found among skilled factory workers and craftsmen if the job in-

CONNECTIONS

See also
926 Work: motivation and performance
928 Work: management and organization
932 Uses of leisure
888 Structure of societies
812 Aspects of human nature

1 A

B

1 In simple societies with a domestic mode of production people work directly to provide for the needs of themselves and their families. If a house is too much for one man to provide, then his family or tribal members will help and vice versa. In money economies (which include most socialist and communist societies as well as capitalist ones) people work to obtain the means to purchase what they need.

2 Many societies have ascribed a low status to individuals who work. Chinese nobles, for example, traditionally let their nails grow long to indicate that they were not obliged to work.

2

3 The meaning of work varies among occupation groups. Studies show that unskilled workers are likely to see their work as having no other meaning than that of earning money. Skilled craftsmen emphasize work as a source of self-respect. Physicians stress the public service aspect of their jobs. Salespeople value friendship and sociability. Coal miners often have a personal sense of struggling against their environment to conquer it.

3

volves completion of a whole project [4]. Assembly line workers like to be able to control, to some extent, the pace and methods of their work. Variety is important to both factory and office workers, as is the friendliness of the other members of the working group.

Of other factors that influence satisfaction, social relationships seem to be most important, although freedom to make independent decisions and take responsibilities is valued. Satisfaction is also linked with tactful and flexible supervision and leadership and with being consulted in advance about changes in work methods. In general, jobs that involve dealing with people are seen as more satisfying than those that do not.

People's attitudes toward work are influenced by their age, sex, personality, and cultural expectations, which change over time. Women, for example, were assumed to be more satisfied than men with their work even when their jobs gave them less authority, status, and income. As women redefined their roles, their expectations and satisfactions changed. People are usually happier at work as they grow older, if work provides congenial social surroundings, while young people tend to be more concerned about the nature and mission of their job. Professionals may find high satisfaction only if their job meets their complex goals. Menial workers are less dissatisfied if their culture does not equate their job with their self-image. A sharp recession will reduce the variables for everyone and focus attention on survival or maintaining economic well-being.

Working conditions

Studies of job satisfaction [5] are unreliable because there are so many variables and because admission of dissatisfaction may be seen as an admission of personal failure. Automation is radically altering the work environment as it displaces unskilled labor, creates unemployment, and demands subservience to computerized technology. How to reap technological benefits and create a more human environment is an unmet challenge.

KEY

People work for a variety of reasons that are not always easy to separate. First and foremost perhaps, they work to provide the necessities for themselves and their families, including a measure of security. They may work to increase their standard of living and to buy luxuries. They may also work because they enjoy what they do in itself. Work allows them to realize their potential and gain recognition as individuals. Finally, they may work to achieve power and status.

4 A

B

4 The traditional ways and working conditions of the artist and craftsman are still found, even in our highly industrial society. Some products, such as musical instruments, do not lend themselves to large-scale machine production [A], and even where this is possible there is still a market for more expensive handmade products. Hand craftsmen experience fewer of the dissatisfactions felt by routine workers [B]; they make the whole of something, instead of a small part, they feel secure in the exercise of specialist skills, and they can be left to themselves to do the job.

5

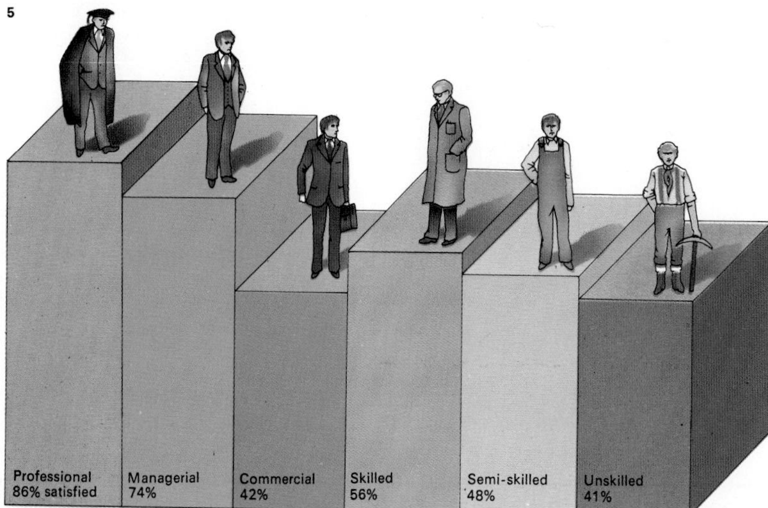
Professional
86% satisfied
Managerial
74%
Commercial
42%
Skilled
56%
Semi-skilled
48%
Unskilled
41%

5 One American study of job satisfaction indicated that levels of satisfaction differed widely in both white-collar and blue-collar workers. In an equivalent British study ninety percent claimed to be satisfied with their work. This proportion, which appears unrealistically high, may be the result of a reluctance to admit dissatisfaction because it would appear to be a confession of failure. It may also be that "satisfaction" is no more than acceptance of the status quo.

6 Occupation confers status in every society. In the industrial United States [blue] the relationship between job and status is less ritualized than in the agrarian Swat region of Pakistan [yellow]. Ranking in both cases is roughly equivalent, as is occupation.

6

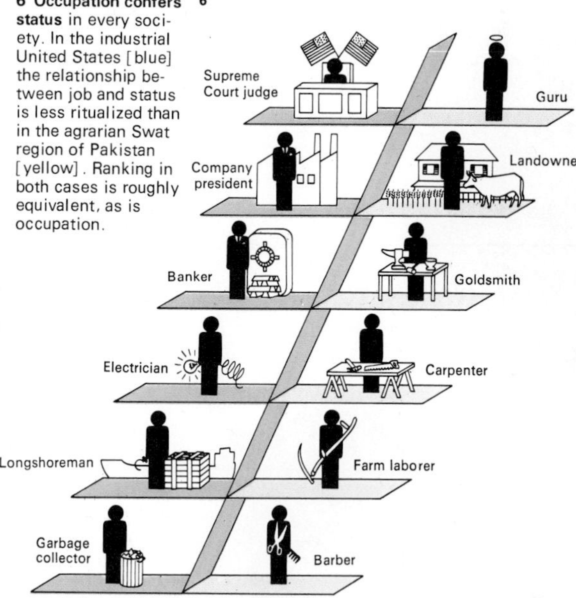
Supreme
Court judge
Guru
Company
president
Landowner
Banker
Goldsmith
Electrician
Carpenter
Longshoreman
Farm laborer
Garbage
collector
Barber

Work: motivation and performance

The first efforts to study work behavior scientifically were focused on work merely as an input in the process of production. The criterion used in those early studies, which began at about the turn of the century, was purely and simply that of mechanical efficiency. An American, Frederick W. Taylor (1856–1915), pioneered what has become known as time-and-motion study [1], and another early investigator working in America, Frank B. Gilbreth (1868–1924), coined the term "therblig" to describe the smallest time-motion units into which any job can be divided.

Workers as machines

The central aim of these early studies was to make the worker as much like a machine as possible. While Taylor and his followers were not chiefly concerned with comfort or fatigue, they were aware that a tired worker is an inefficient producer. Thus a by-product of Taylorism was some reduction in the discomforts of manual labor. Workers, however, have always tended to look askance at the efficiency engineer.

Subsequent studies of work performance have been more concerned with the most efficient deployment of workers and machines and the organization of the relations between them. Consequently, there is now as much interest in adapting the machine to the worker as in adapting the worker to the machine [2, 3]. The attitude and involvement of the worker in what he or she is doing are now seen as significant.

Apart from the importance of avoiding a poor physical environment—noise, temperature, overcrowding, and so on [6]—work efficiency is also affected by the cohesiveness of the group. In one study it was found that absenteeism was highest where people had a low opinion of other group members. Close-knit groups have about a quarter of the average absentee rate. Cohesiveness is affected by the amount of communication among workers. Some jobs demand frequent interactions, while the technology of others restricts communication or makes it unnecessary.

More lighthearted but nonetheless perceptive approaches to work performance are those of Professor C. N. Parkinson (1909–) and Dr Laurence Peter. Parkinson's Law (1965) consists of the basic proposition that work expands to fill the time available for its completion. Parkinson also suggested that the total number of people employed in bureaucracies rises whether the volume of work increases or diminishes. An official wants to multiply subordinates, not rivals, and officials make work for each other.

The Peter Principle (1969) states that in a hierarchy every employee tends to rise to his level of incompetence. The actual work is done by those employees who have not yet reached their level of incompetence.

Aspects of supervision

An important element in the quality of work performance is the amount and the style of supervision. A foreman or first-level supervisor's job differs from that of other managers because the group he or she works with is different. He or she is seen in one of five basic roles: as a key representative of management, sitting astride the chains of author-

CONNECTIONS

See also
924 Work: curse and pleasure
928 Work: management and organization
932 Uses of leisure

1

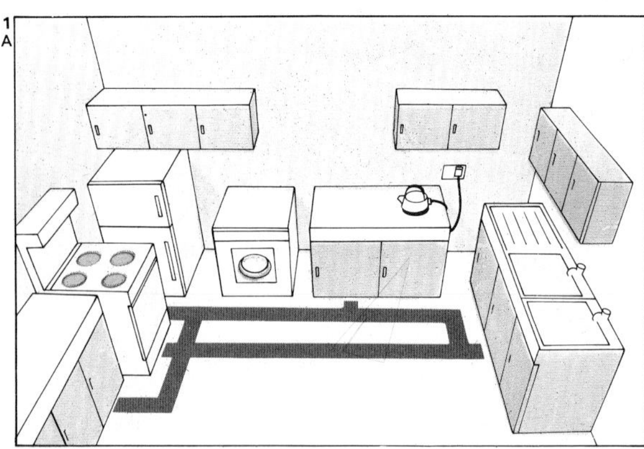
A

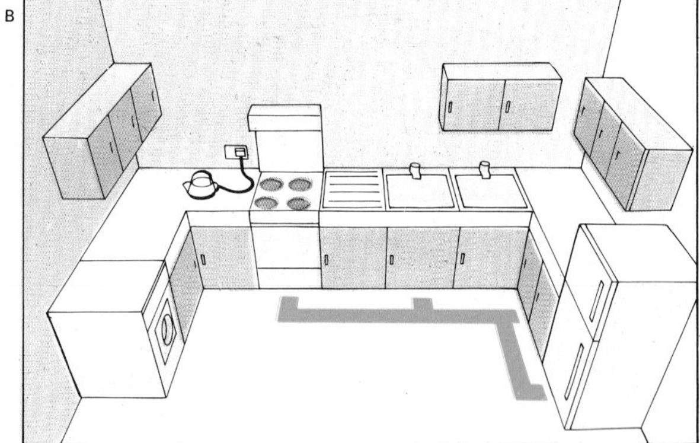
B

1 A time-and-motion study seeks to minimize wasted time and effort. Its principles can be as easily applied to the home as to the factory. Kitchens [A] are often badly laid out so that every job entails a large amount of unnecessary movement [red], between stove, storage, refrigerator, sink, and work surface. In remodeling [B], these units can be regrouped so as to minimize effort [green].

2 In the traditional assembly line method of producing cars the bodies move along a conveyor belt and each worker performs a specific operation on each car. The job cycle usually has to be completed in less than two minutes, and individuals have to keep up with the speed of the line. Although theoretically efficient, the resulting physical and mental strain may promote inefficiency over a long period.

3 Using modern planning methods some automobile companies have organized a system of small work groups. The members of each group are responsible for the entire car, except for some preassembly work. During the assembly work there is no mechanical control of flow. The maximum job cycle time is increased to 30 minutes. The system makes the work more interesting, and vulnerability to disturbances is drastically reduced. The disadvantages are that more floor space is needed and more material is tied up, but work efficiency apparently reaches the same level as on machine-paced lines.

2

3

035 6

4

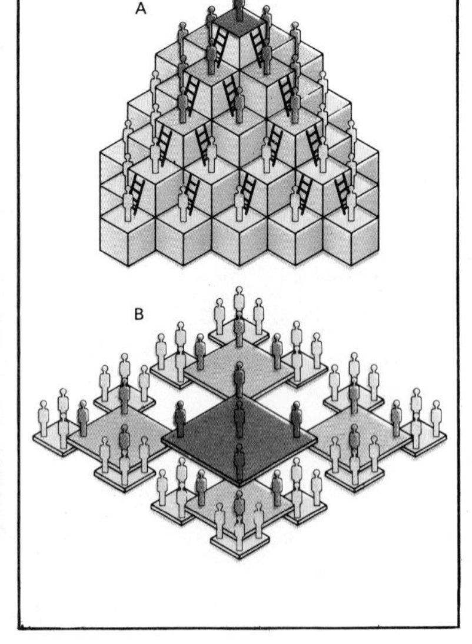
A
B

4 Efficient communication is vital to the success of an organization. In the traditional pyramid model [A] nearly all contacts take the form of orders, with each subordinate receiving instructions from one boss. In this way an individual has contact only with the supervisor above and the subordinates below. The link-pin concept [B] emphasizes social contact and cooperation between groups. At least one member of each group is also a member of the unit immediately above.

ity and communication and with the power to block anything going upward or downward; as a worker in the middle, pressed between opposing forces of management and workers; as a marginal employee, left out of or on the margin of the main relationships between management and workers; as another worker who is regarded as lacking authority because real decisions are made by others; and as a human relations specialist.

Work potential

The role of worker is only one of several roles for people in modern industrial society, and this can lead to difficulties in changing roles. The same man may have to be compliant on the job, the "father figure" at home, and outgoing with his friends.

In an effort to fit square pegs into square holes various methods of assessing work potential have been developed [7]. Four of them are: mental testing, which consists basically of intelligence tests; job analysis, which concentrates more on the type of work than on the personality of the worker; the work-sample approach, which incorporates both of these other methods by setting up simulated industrial operations; and the situational approach, which also involves simulation but is based more on work behavior.

One way of training people is the system of apprenticeship. In the Middle Ages this consisted of a paternalistic relationship between the craftsman and the trainee and formed an integral part of the guild system. Today the paternalism has largely vanished, but many of the associated customs remain. Apprenticeships are served, often for four or five years, and are a mixture of on-the-job and back-to-school training.

New methods of training differ from earlier methods in several ways. They try to operate on an emotional was well as an intellectual level; they concentrate on the group rather than just on the individual; they attempt to make people more aware of the needs of others; and the training program is conducted on a long-term basis so that eventually the whole organization will share these new values.

KEY

Workers relate to their job environment on four different levels. First there are the broad rules, regulations, and purposes of the organization [1]. Next there are the goals of the organization, those of the worker's specific job, and his actual achievement [2]. At the same time the worker has a set of informal relations with his colleagues [3] through which he gains status from his personal characteristics. Finally, there is the worker's direct skill at the job itself. The well-adjusted worker operates on all four levels at his job.

5

1 hour
1 day
1 week
1 month
1 year

5 A worker's level of responsibility can be measured by the amount of time between successive reviews of his performance. Elliott Jaques suggested in 1961 that the time span during which a member of an organization makes decisions at his own discretion defines his position. For a production worker it may be an hour, for the company president as long as a year.

6 A

B

C

D

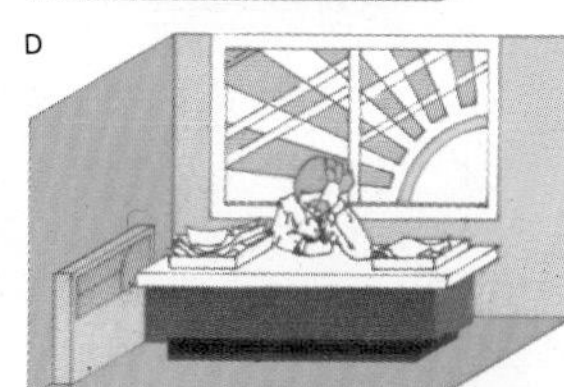

E

F

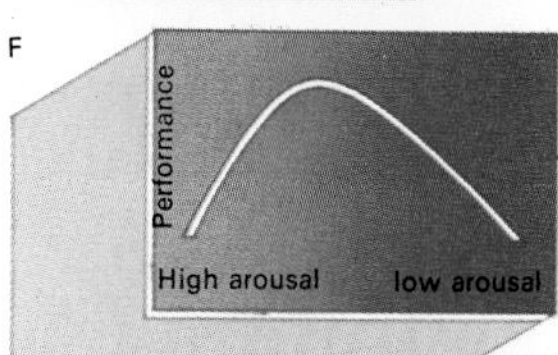

Performance
High arousal
low arousal

6 Alertness and efficiency can be influenced by stress. If an individual is continually told he is failing [A] the stress makes his performance fall off. Other reasons for inefficiency are having too much to do at once [B], a noisy environment [C], hot conditions [D], and lack of sleep [E]. The drop in efficiency [F] in the first three is caused by too high a level of arousal, in the last pair by too low a level.

7 A

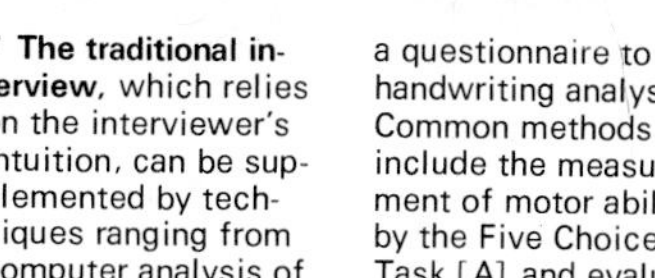

B

C

D

7 The traditional interview, which relies on the interviewer's intuition, can be supplemented by techniques ranging from computer analysis of a questionnaire to handwriting analysis. Common methods include the measurement of motor ability by the Five Choice Task [A] and evaluation of educational skills by written tests [B]. Social ability can be gauged by videotaping the interview [C], while the stress interview [D] indicates how a person reacts in difficult circumstances such as when table tennis balls are being thrown at him by the interviewer.

8

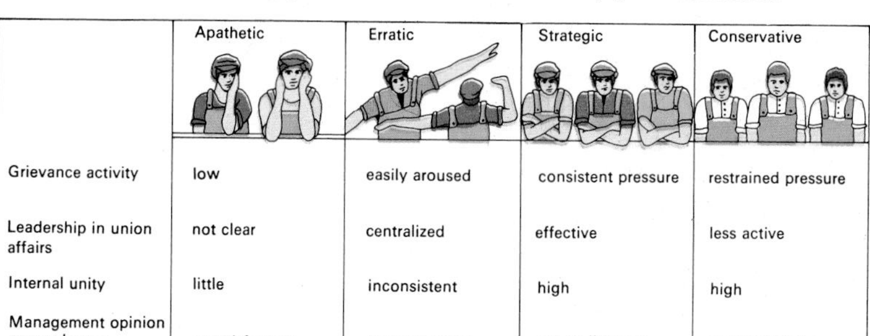

	Apathetic	Erratic	Strategic	Conservative
Grievance activity	low	easily aroused	consistent pressure	restrained pressure
Leadership in union affairs	not clear	centralized	effective	less active
Internal unity	little	inconsistent	high	high
Management opinion as employees	unsatisfactory	unsatisfactory	generally good	most satisfactory

8 Work groups vary according to the level and type of their complaints, their union leadership, their own internal unity, and the opinion management has of them as employees. The illustration shows the characteristics of the four types of work group distinguished by Leonard Sayles (1958): apathetic (many unskilled workers), erratic (automobile assembly line workers), strategic (welders), and conservative (garment cutters and toolroom personnel).

9

9 Many types of workers could technically do their jobs from home seated in front of their television sets. The Canadian sociologist Marshall McLuhan (1911–) proposes that companies feed all their information into central computers, which can be linked to individual terminals in the home. All the information that employees are likely to want could be instantly available and their reactions and decisions quickly relayed back. People would have to retrain for computer work, but they would save time, money, and the nervous energy involved in traveling to and from work in overcrowded conditions. The loss of social contacts could in many cases prove to be counterproductive, however.

Work: management and organization

In modern societies most work is done within the framework of an organization. In addition to allowing specialization by allocating tasks and resources, organizations satisfy the needs of various groups. They provide employees with jobs and wages, shareholders with a return on capital, and the public with products. Analysis of how an organization functions can be based on two contrasting ideas of how society works: as a natural system or as a sphere of individual rational action.

Consensus and individualism

The "system" view of organizations regards them as having a life of their own and existing above and beyond the people who compose them. It assumes that each part of an organization contributes to and receives something from the whole; that organizations are governed by needs, which they must satisfy to survive; and that actions can be attributed both to organizations and also to their individual members. The "individual" view maintains that organizations are the ever-changing product of the self-interest of individual members. It also maintains that the policies of organizations are determined more by power conflicts than by agreement on common goals.

Two major aspects of the controversy over organization theory are bureaucracy and the relationship between the individual and the organization. To most people bureaucracy means red tape and procrastination, but the word also has a technical meaning—the administration of organizations. The German sociologist Max Weber (1864–1920) distinguished in bureaucracy a number of classic features, including the distribution of official duties, an authority structure based on graded ranks, and formal rules and regulations. Despite its shortcomings, an effective bureaucracy may be preferable to other methods of control—for example, administration dominated by a single leader.

The question of the relationship between the individual and the organization sometimes takes the form of asking what type of organization will best meet human needs. An American sociologist, Chris Argyris, considers an organization good if it encourages loyalty and enables its members to be creative, flexible, and productive.

Organizations differ in the types of power on which they are based. Coercive power is the use of threats and sanctions to force cooperation. It often alienates participants, who see the organization as an oppressor. Examples are prisons and some mental hospitals. Remunerative power means that people are paid to cooperate; they exchange effort for money. Cooperative power is achieved when people work willingly because they value the organization's goals.

The nature of management

Management is an important feature of an organization [4] and can be looked at in three ways: as a unit whose significance is mainly economic; as an elite social group, perpetuated by selective education and entry; and as a system of authority within which individuals pursue personal goals.

The increasing scale of economic operations and technical complexity during the

CONNECTIONS

See also
924 Work: curse and pleasure
926 Work: motivation and performance
932 Uses of leisure
888 Structure of societies
1660 The factory and assembly line
906 Machinery of government

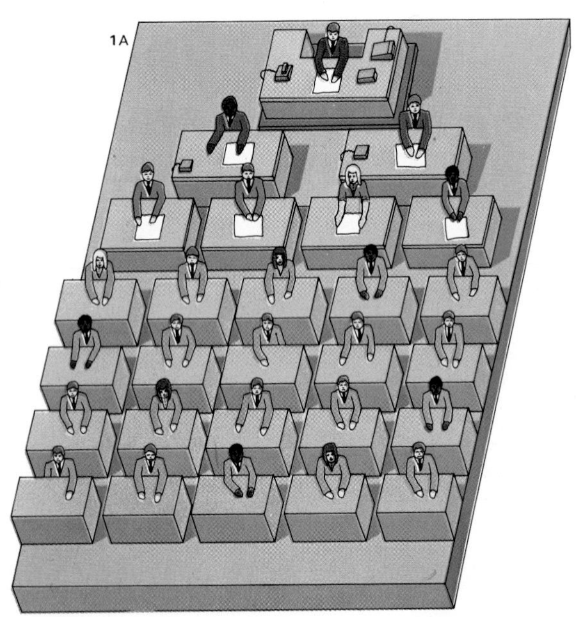

1A
B

1 In management theory the "span of management" refers to the number of persons a manager controls directly. Many factors determine the number that he or she can effectively manage. Too many subordinates may mean wasting time dealing with their problems, but a manager with too few may do too much low-level work. His or her own skill, that of subordinates, the stability of operations, and the type of work managed are other factors influencing the span of management. Organizations with a small span of management [A] have closer coordination and control because each manager works with fewer people; but the communication chain is long. In a larger span [B] there is a shorter communication chain, although each manager controls more people.

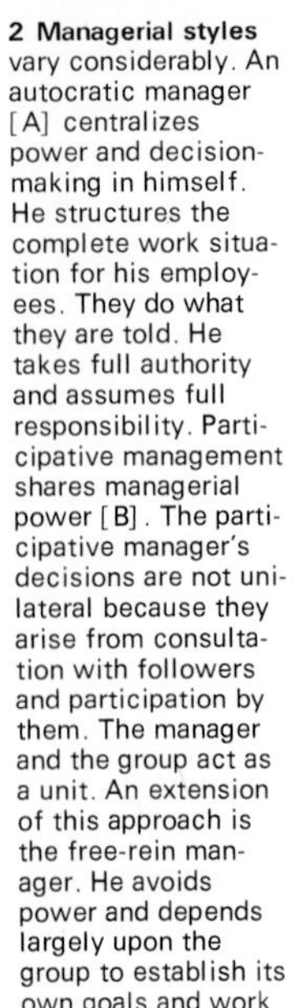

2A
B

2 Managerial styles vary considerably. An autocratic manager [A] centralizes power and decision-making in himself. He structures the complete work situation for his employees. They do what they are told. He takes full authority and assumes full responsibility. Participative management shares managerial power [B]. The participative manager's decisions are not unilateral because they arise from consultation with followers and participation by them. The manager and the group act as a unit. An extension of this approach is the free-rein manager. He avoids power and depends largely upon the group to establish its own goals and work out its own problems.

twentieth century has meant that a higher level of administrative and technical competence is required of managers. Management has become an elite group, increasingly differentiated both from other employees and from business owners.

Management attitudes

Although the term "management" is often used to denote a group of high-level employees who share common interests and a common social identity, the assumption of common interests is open to challenge. Research into managerial attitudes and actions demonstrates that managers differ among themselves. Within a company, for example, research personnel and marketing managers have been found to be more willing to take risks and retain open minds about the solutions to problems than are financial and quality control managers.

In popular usage the term "organization man" implies a lack of individuality and independence. But the need to conform has been exaggerated. Struggles for power form as essential a part of behavior in organizations as the planning and execution of work. In one study older managers without further promotion prospects were found to have formed protective cliques to counter values of the organization that were not to their advantage. Younger managers identified with these values and formed cliques of their own to promote their interests.

Underlying management techniques are two basic approaches [2]. In the traditional, autocratic approach to management those in command have the power to demand that an employee follow orders. The other approach is more democratic. Those in command depend on leadership instead of power. Management provides a climate that helps all employees in the organization accomplish as much as they can with the talents they have. The leader assumes that workers will take responsibility and be motivated to contribute to the organization and to improve themselves if management gives them the chance. The approach is designed to support the employee's performance and to diminish the sense of estrangement from the goals of production [3].

KEY

A

B

One source of conflict between workers and management arises from their different appreciation of the role of work. To management the worker is just one among many inputs [A] (often troublesome and unreliable at that). Buildings, machinery, materials, and services are all interwoven parts of the single process of production. For the worker [B] his or her investment of time and effort requires a respect for individuality, which management may ignore.

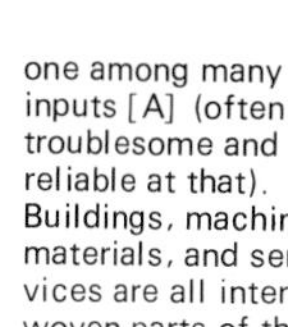

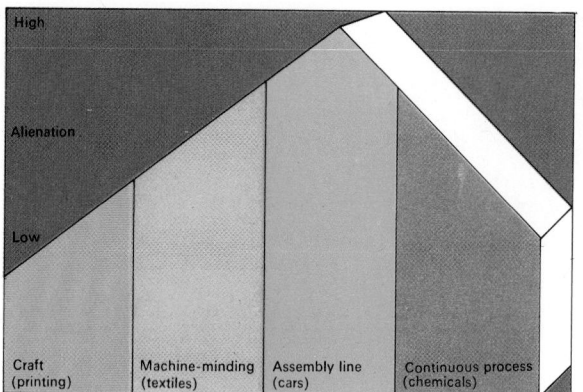

3

High

Alienation

Low

Craft (printing)

Machine-minding (textiles)

Assembly line (cars)

Continuous process (chemicals)

3 A person who feels powerless and useless in his job tends to withdraw from its realities. The term describing this reaction is "alienation," and it is more typical of some types of work than others. Research shows that in craft industries such as printing, which have no standardized product, alienation is usually low. It is higher in machine-minding industries such as textiles, and much higher with assembly lines, where work is fragmented and products standardized. In continuous-process industries, where workers control a whole process, alienation is reduced.

4

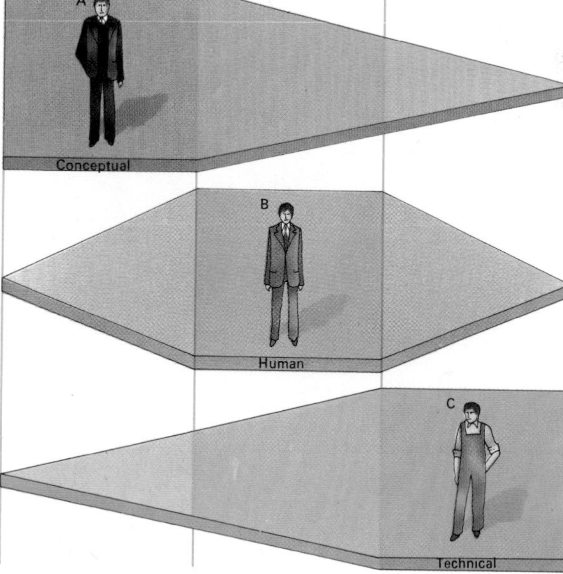
A
Conceptual
B
Human
C
Technical

4 A leader in an organization uses three separate skills; conceptual (green), human (yellow), and technical (blue). Different levels of management are called on to use different combinations of these skills. For top-level managers [A], conceptual skills are crucial, enabling them to deal with abstractions, to set up models, and to devise plans. In middle management [B], human skills – the ability to interact effectively with people – are of paramount importance and conceptual skills less needed. Finally, a foreman [C] relies heavily on his technical skills. For he must know all the processes that he has to supervise.

5

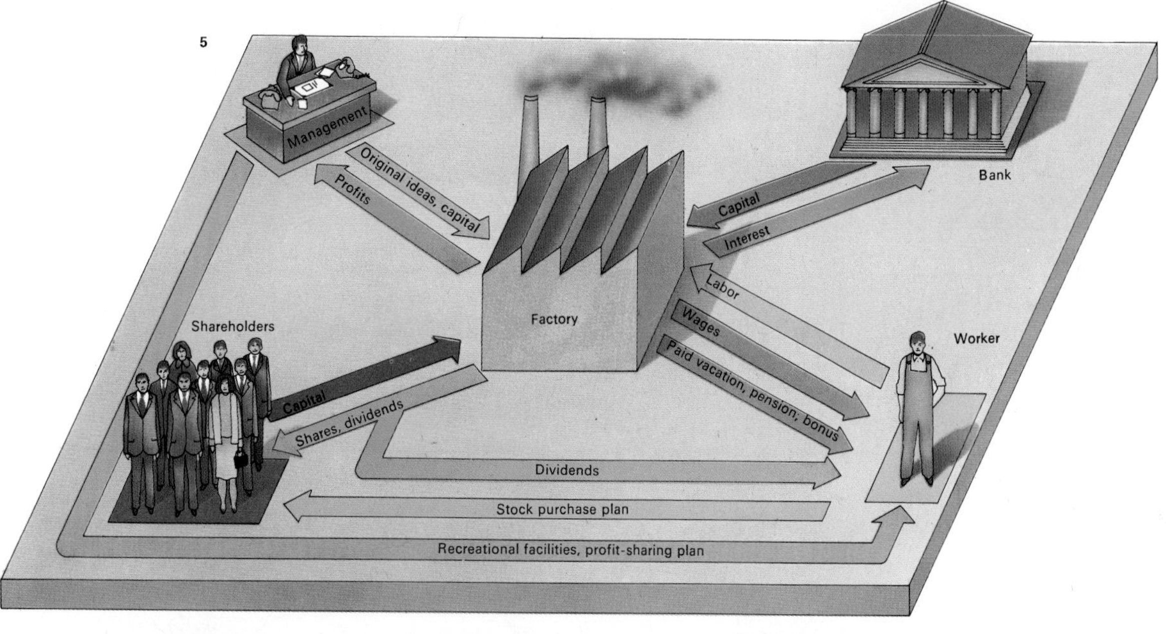
Management
Original ideas, capital
Profits
Bank
Capital
Interest
Labor
Wages
Paid vacation, pension, bonus
Factory
Shareholders
Worker
Capital
Shares, dividends
Dividends
Stock purchase plan
Recreational facilities, profit-sharing plan

5 The rewards of work have risen remarkably during the last 100 years as a result of changing social attitudes and growing union power. Traditionally the worker was given a fixed wage in return for a certain number of hours worked. Management and stockholders (private and institutional) reaped all the benefits of the organization's profit. Increasingly, workers have shared in the profits, seeing theirs as the most significant (and laudable) contribution. Paid vacations, pension and insurance plans, profit bonuses, and stock options are part of this pattern. A parallel development has been worker participation in management, with joint committees.

Play and sports

Play is an almost universal activity of higher animals but one that is hard to define. In essence it consists of two main ingredients—activity for its own sake and experimentation with types of behavior that will be subsequently carried out in earnest (such as hunting, fighting, and hiding).

Animals at play

In animals both of these kinds of play are carried out by the young and are clearly a part of the learning process. Experimental activity familiarizes the young animal with its capabilities. Among adult animals, by contrast, it is the first or exuberant type of play that predominates, particularly in such social and highly active species as the dolphin and otter. In adults play is normally transformed into ritual and serves a social function (as in courtship).

It is debatable how far the concept of "play" can be extended to include ritual social behavior and whether behavior such as grooming in primates (which increases group cohesion) can be described as play. Human play clearly originates in the same two classes of behavior but is enormously extended and complicated by human self-awareness and sociability. The earliest child play, as in animal behavior, takes the form of exploration and experimenting with bodily skills. Then interaction with others becomes important, involving role playing and fantasy enactment. As in monkey play, for example, the "pretend" element in play sometimes involves learning what roles the individual is expected to adopt later. It is through play, too, that children learn that a functioning society is based on rules and values, and also what specific rules and values are current.

Fantasy enactment, the use of play to explore dreams, may be uniquely human or not, but it is important. Where the physical side of play (running, jumping, throwing) develops physical coordination, fantasy play serves much the same purpose for emotional development. Play violence, as in cowboys and Indians, far from encouraging violent, aggressive instincts, may teach the child that his aggressive fantasies do not destroy others.

The real difference between animal and human play is the persistent importance of play in the life of the human adult. For one thing, human playfulness leads to organized sports and games. These may be intellectual (such as chess), or physical (such as tennis), group oriented (such as ice hockey), or solitary (such as skiing). But whatever form these games take they are an important point of social contact for many people and provide relaxation and adventure.

The psychology of games

There are several psychological theories about games. It has been suggested that through them the players release their aggressions in a socially acceptable way. The fact that retired athletes sometimes suffer from a variety of personality disorders suggests that the absence of this means of release may be part of the problem. It has also been found that some people (from gamblers to racing drivers) deliberately put themselves at risk both for the intense emotional arousal that it gives and for the relief afterward [8]. They may become dependent

CONNECTIONS

See also
782 Social development
932 Uses of leisure

1 Sailing is now a sport practiced at various levels, from dinghy racing to single-handed circumnavigation of the globe. But like most sports based on the idea of transport, its origins lie in work skills. Its rise as a sport, boosted by modern technology and such new materials as fiber glass, occurred as its practical function declined.

2 Fishing, like hunting, evolved from the necessary search for food and pelts for clothing in early societies. Although hunting and fishing were undoubtedly pleasurable, they were nevertheless work until technological change supplanted their role.

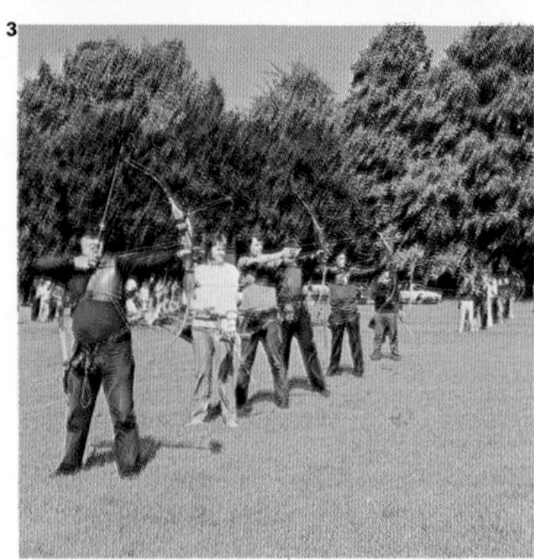

3 Archery is a good example of play with a military origin. Although of no practical use in industrial societies, it was once of prime importance; Richard II banned soccer because it distracted the English people from their archery.

4 Japanese wrestling has arguable origins in combat. Like many of the Eastern martial arts such as ju-jitsu and kendo, it shows a feature prominent in most games – extreme ritualization and a tightly formulated set of specific rules.

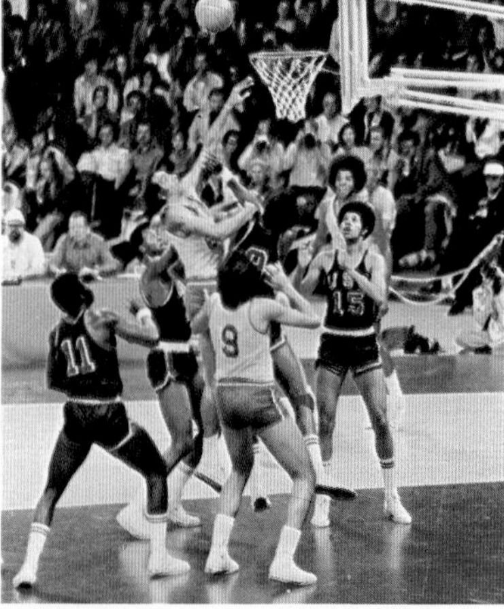

5 Basketball, like most team sports, reflects the values of the mass society that supports it and is involved in its organization; its popularity is second worldwide only to soccer. Unlike most team sports, it was an invention (in 1891 by Dr. James Naismith) rather than a development from an older game.

on this pain-pleasure combination. Games are also a natural expression of human competitiveness.

As far as spectators are concerned, sport is one way of achieving a sense of belonging to a group, but whether they also burn off their aggressions vicariously, in a kind of catharsis, or purging of pent-up emotion, is open to question. Violence sparked by football games suggests that the reverse may be true.

Another form of play that pervades adult life is the play-use of sexuality. Sexuality has a wide range of functions connected with pair-bonding, gender learning, dominance, and fantasy enactment.

Puritan communities have sometimes opposed play in its dramatic, sexual, and non-serious aspects, distrusting the whole notion of pleasure—the emotion generated by effective play. Hindu philosophy, by contrast, makes playfulness a part of reality in that the real world reflects the playful activity of the gods. For modern psychiatry, free and spontaneous playfulness is a good index of a healthy person who has no difficulty in giving and accepting pleasure and in interacting creatively with others.

Games and society

Play, especially in the form of sports and games, is also important for what it can reveal about society. Forms of sport reflect the nature of society [10], as do forms of art, theater, and literature.

In preindustrial societies sports often developed from necessary work and other activities of contemporary life. Jousting, archery, and other martial sports [3, 4] once provided useful practice for the real thing. Hunting, rowing, sailing [1], and skiing evolved naturally from the demands for food and means of transport.

In industrial societies two main influences on sports can be seen. Technological advances have led to the invention of new sports such as automobile racing [8] and skydiving [7] and to the professionalization of team games [6]. Team sports and their values—working as a group, group competitiveness—reflect and reinforce the values of mass society.

KEY

Child play, far from being inconsequential or trivial, serves many useful functions. It is in play that children develop their personalities as well as their physical skills. They also learn many of the written and unwritten rules of their society, reinforcing social and cultural roles. For American youngsters Little League baseball not only mimics major league baseball, but also involves role playing within a tight web of community and family relationships.

6

7

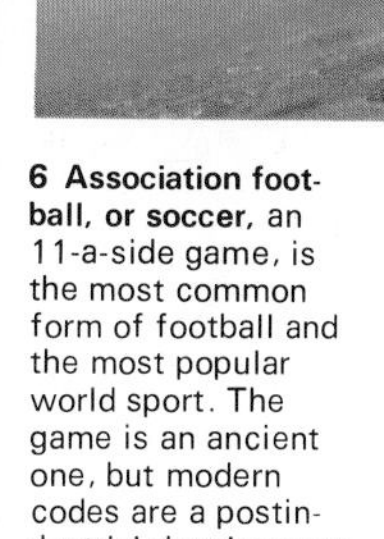

6 Association football, or soccer, an 11-a-side game, is the most common form of football and the most popular world sport. The game is an ancient one, but modern codes are a postindustrial development. Massed spectators and modern communications are essential for its current organization. Equally, the size of its following and the financial investment in the game have made it crucial to the leisure of some societies.

7 Skydiving, or free-fall parachuting, is another sport with military origins. More than 40 nations compete in the biennial world championships. The ceiling for jumps is 12,000 feet (3,657 m) with a free fall of 9,500 feet.

8

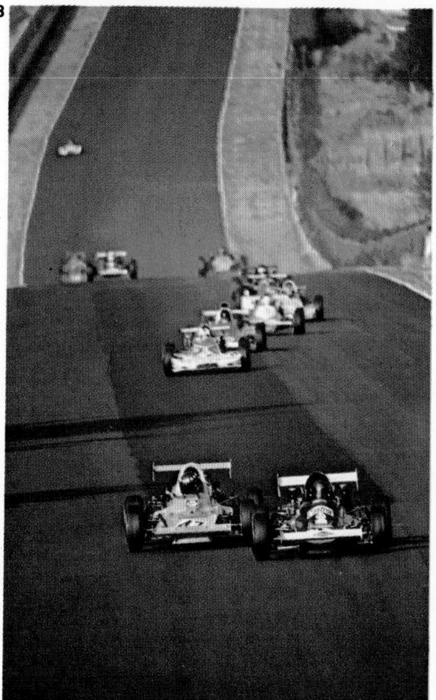

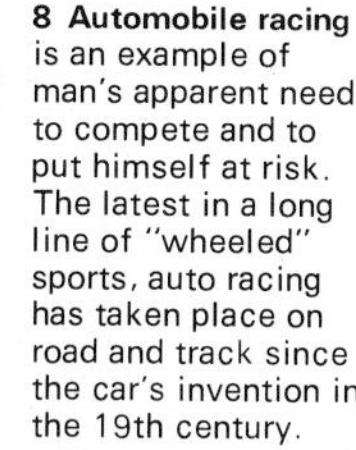

8 Automobile racing is an example of man's apparent need to compete and to put himself at risk. The latest in a long line of "wheeled" sports, auto racing has taken place on road and track since the car's invention in the 19th century.

9

9 The natural competitiveness of humans makes racing a feature of all ages and all cultures. Human beings have raced frogs, snails, dogs, pigeons, balloons, aircraft—anything that moves. Horse racing, the so-called sport of kings, has adherents of all classes and illustrates well the competitive instinct. Numbers directly involved in the sport—competing, organizing, or watching at the track—are minute compared with those who "compete" by betting.

10

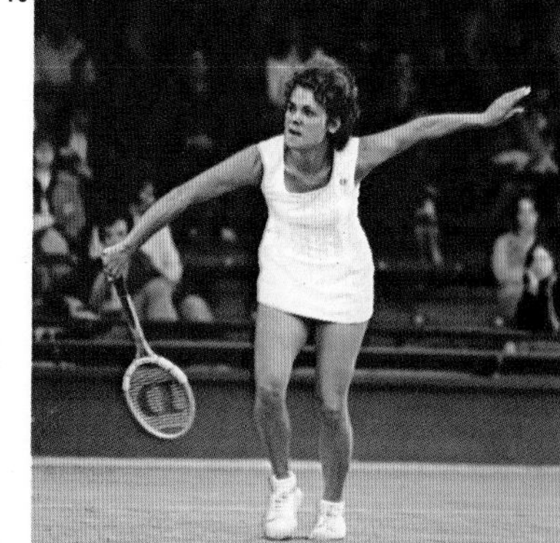

10 Tennis is perhaps the best example of sport as a barometer of social change. Five centuries ago, court, or royal, tennis was an indoor sport for the aristocracy. In the 19th century it was taken out of doors and, although in a radically different form, was played on grass, primarily by the upper middle class. Even today, the most famous tennis clubs are found in the wealthier suburbs, although the spread of professionalism has done much to democratize tennis.

Uses of leisure

Leisure is really a state of mind. As such it can be experienced while lying on a beach, or while vigorously exercising, or even while doing what others look upon as labor (eg, cooking, gardening). It describes a person's attitude toward what he or she is doing and the quality of the time spent doing it. The advantage of such a broad and unspecific definition is seen when two people take the 24 hours in the day and attempt to subtract from them periods they do not consider to be leisure, such as working, sleeping and eating [Key]—no two people are found to agree fully about what periods should be taken out and what periods should be left in.

However defined, leisure is certainly important both in the life of the individual and for the society of which he or she is a part. For the individual it may provide relaxation from daily pressures and routines, creative experience such as education or volunteer work that helps to liberate and develop the personality, or entertainment as an antidote to boredom or drudgery. This last element is reflected in the fact that many employers provide leisure facilities such as baseball fields, piped music, and recreation rooms, because they believe that these will produce fitter and happier workers. Equally, in many countries government agencies provide facilities for certain types of leisure for the "good" of people generally.

Leisure and work

In many ways leisure is bound up with work. It is easy, although misleading, to think of leisure as the opposite of work, or to define it as time left over after work. But not all human societies make the distinction. Rural life has always tended to integrate the two. The tradition of the artist and the craftsman is also one in which there is less division between work and play.

In assessing our lives we may give priority to work or to leisure, or equality to both. Those who say that work is the most important thing in their lives are not necessarily saying that their lives are devoid of leisurelike experiences; usually they obtain from work some of the satisfaction others get from leisure. Those who value leisure highly may be in arduous, dull, or otherwise unsatisfying jobs.

Leisure activities and expenditure

People today generally have more free time than they did a few decades ago, although the actual gain (bearing in mind increased time spent traveling to work and so on) is sometimes overstated. Equally, there are now more diverse ways of spending leisure time: more facilities, indoor and outdoor, provided by both private enterprise and public authorities. Television, sports centers, and foreign travel (other than for the wealthy) were unknown a few years ago. Leisure is now big business, although it is impossible to estimate accurately the total annual expenditure on leisure because of the difficulty of knowing what to include. In recent years leisure spending has increased, although it is difficult to know how much of this rise is the result of inflation. Certainly money spent on the purchase and running of motor vehicles has increased faster than most other expenditure, even accounting for inflation.

CONNECTIONS

See also
924 Work: curse and pleasure
930 Play and sports
796 Adulthood: from 20 to 30
798 Adulthood: from 30 to 40
800 Adulthood: middle age
804 An active old age

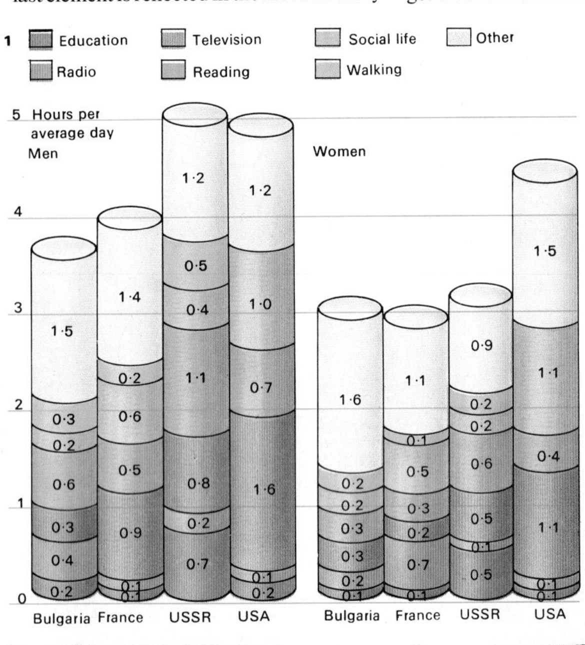

1
Education
Radio
Television
Reading
Social life
Walking
Other
5 Hours per average day
Men
Women
4
3
2
1
0
1·5
0·3
0·2
0·6
0·3
0·4
0·2
1·4
0·2
0·6
0·5
0·9
0·1
1·2
0·5
0·4
1·1
0·8
0·2
0·7
0·1
1·2
1·0
0·7
1·6
0·1
0·2
1·6
0·2
0·2
0·3
0·3
0·2
0·1
1·1
0·1
0·5
0·3
0·2
0·7
0·1
0·9
0·2
0·2
0·6
0·5
0·1
0·5
1·5
1·1
0·4
1·1
0·1
0·1
Bulgaria
France
USSR
USA
Bulgaria
France
USSR
USA

1 A multinational survey (1972) compared the amount of time men and women have for leisure in different countries. Men in France and Bulgaria had less leisure than men in the United States and the USSR, and women had most leisure in the United States. The share of leisure devoted to television was greatest in the United States. Differences in time spent on reading were generally small, except in the USSR, where more time was spent in this way. Most time was spent on social life in the United States. Within the "other leisure" category a higher percentage of time was spent by the French and Bulgarians on "resting."

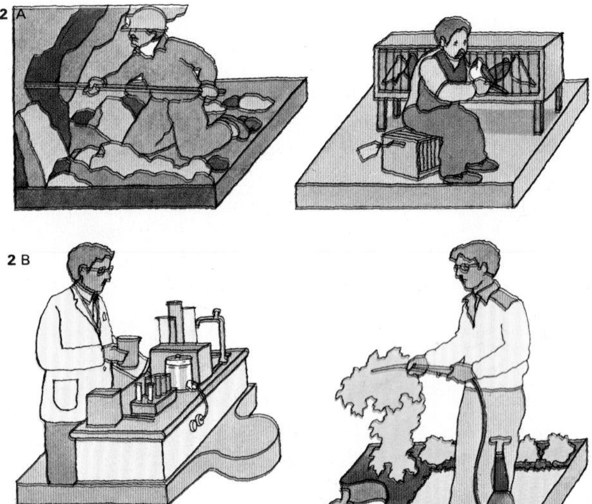

2 A
2 B

2 The ways in which people choose to spend their leisure are often related to the type of work they are engaged in. Research suggests that there are three main patterns of work and leisure. There may be said to be opposition between the two [A] when leisure is deliberately different from work—as when a miner trains and races pigeons or greyhounds and the factory worker races a motorcycle. On the other hand, work can extend into leisure [B] when the leisure activity bears some similarity to the work done. A chemist, for example, may experiment with fungicides in his garden, or the professional social worker may take part in a volunteer project in her spare time. Finally, there is neutrality where passive work is matched by passive leisure [C] and when the person concerned is a spectator rather than an active participant. An example is the clerical worker who plays bingo or watches television for most of the time.

3 A

B

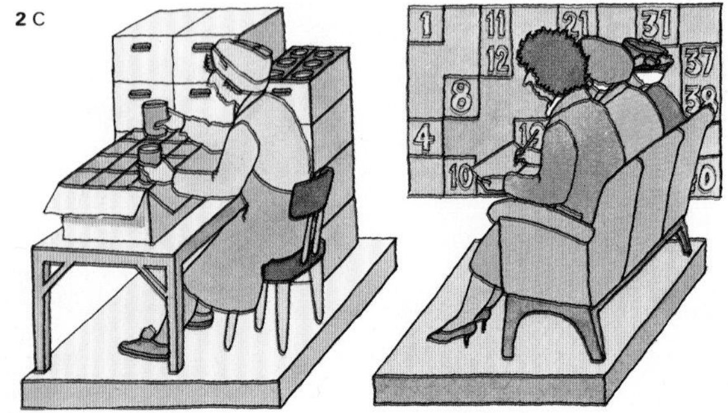

2 C

3 People can take an active part in the way their leisure is used, or they can simply "consume" something produced by others. A sportsman [A] may also be on the committee that organizes the sport. The mass leisure industries, and particularly TV [B], do not lend themselves to participation in policy decisions.

Despite the growth of commercialized leisure, there are still many forms of recreation enjoyed in the home, most especially television viewing and listening to recorded music. There are conflicting views on the effect of television on family life, but these do suggest that we need to distinguish different stages in the growth of television viewing. Until the immediate postwar years, recreation and entertainment outside the home had been steadily gaining ground, resulting in less time being spent in the family circle. In the 1950s television brought families together again. But in the 1960s in the United States, and increasingly in the 1970s in Western Europe, families were acquiring two or more sets, with the consequent separation of family once again.

Leisure and national resources

Many ways of spending leisure involve the use of natural resources—land for parks and golf courses, water for swimming and boating, and so on. Planning is necessary to make the best use of these resources, although there might seem to be a basic paradox in planning for the freedom that leisure ought to mean. Some leisure activities—usually the more artistic ones—are catered to by public or local authorities and require subsidies to exist and flourish. Traditional live arts such as opera, ballet, and classical music would have great difficulty surviving without some form of patronage. Public libraries and art and scientific museums have been traditionally supported, at least in part, by public funds.

There are two important questions about the future of leisure—what form will it take? How much time will be devoted to it? Longer life spans—and earlier retirements—have created a larger population of retired persons with full leisure time. The confident predictions that by the end of the twentieth century the average working week will be less than 30 hours and the average annual vacation several months rather than weeks seem less justified in the slumping 1970s than they had seemed in the booming 1960s. And if the United States is an indicator, "anti-leisure"—a competitive, frenetic approach to leisure—may spread.

KEY
A
B

Leisure for some people is a completely separate part of life [A] – the only part that makes life worth living. They see work as a means to enjoy leisure. For others, leisure is more integrated with the rest of life [B]. They make no rigid separation between work and leisure in their life.

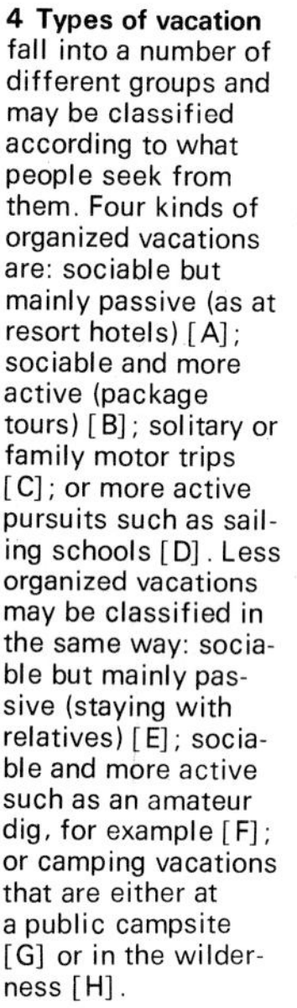

4 Types of vacation fall into a number of different groups and may be classified according to what people seek from them. Four kinds of organized vacations are: sociable but mainly passive (as at resort hotels) [A]; sociable and more active (package tours) [B]; solitary or family motor trips [C]; or more active pursuits such as sailing schools [D]. Less organized vacations may be classified in the same way: sociable but mainly passive (staying with relatives) [E]; sociable and more active such as an amateur dig, for example [F]; or camping vacations that are either at a public campsite [G] or in the wilderness [H].

4
A

B

C

D

E

F

G

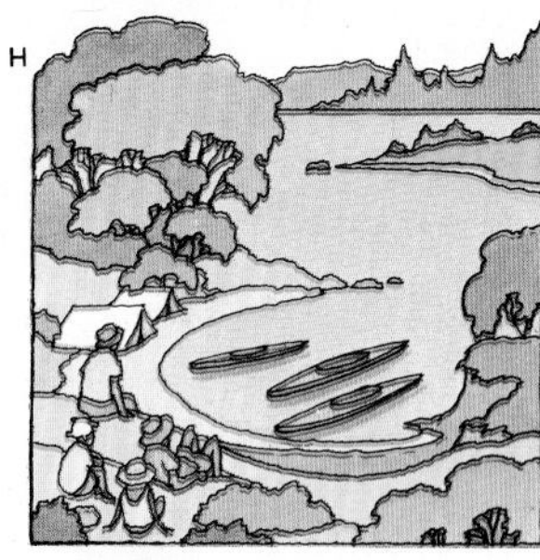
H

5 Retirement presents a major leisure problem because work had filled so much of a person's time. How people adjust to retirement may depend on how interesting their work had been and how much they had been involved in it. People who had been highly involved with creative work will probably continue to do something similar in their retirement [A]. Those who had been accustomed to divide their lives into separate compartments of work and leisure may be able to expand the leisure portion to fill most of their time [B]. Perhaps the biggest problems face those who had been involved in routine work, because they may have fewer inner resources to fill their leisure [C].

Money and capital

People today use money in a wide variety of forms [Key, 1], offering various degrees of liquidity, risk, and return. We use cash to cover a diminishing number of our needs. Most of these needs are met by checks or, increasingly, by a wide variety of types of credit cards.

Where our grandfathers kept a gold coin or two to tide them over rainy days, we use the savings bank, savings and loan association, government bonds, and other deposits as our first line of reserve. These are called "liquid assets," because they can quickly be changed into cash. Other assets, like insurance policies, partly paid mortgages, and stocks and bonds can, if necessary, be turned into cash with varying degrees of notice and cost.

The banking system

A modern banking and monetary system has several constituent parts. Commercial banks, either small or large, which may have many local branches, deal with the general public, holding deposits and dealing with everyday transactions. Above the commercial banks stands the central bank—a government institution that is a banker's bank and "lender of last resort." In the United States, the central bank is the Federal Reserve Bank; most commercial banks belong to the Federal Reserve System as "member banks." The certainty that the central bank will ordinarily support any member bank in difficulties has eliminated the occasional crises of confidence and "runs on the bank" that so disrupted business, both in the United States and in Europe, from the eighteenth century to the Great Depression.

Managing the economy

The relationship between the central bank and the commercial banks is a crucial part of economic management as practiced by modern governments. Governments use the banking system to influence the balance between monetary demand and supply. They may when necessary require the commercial banks to increase the proportion of their liquid funds deposited with the central bank. This forces the commercial banks to call in some loans so that their liquid assets are adequate to cover any normal claims on them.

The central bank can also influence the monetary situation by changing its "discount rate" or "minimum lending rate." As the rate of interest at which commercial banks can borrow money from the central bank, it forms a logical base for all other interest rates. So, if this rate is raised or lowered, other interest rates follow. The central bank can influence the money supply by "open market operations" in which it buys or sells government bonds and so competes in the money market for available funds.

Banks are only part of the complex interlocking system of financial institutions that characterizes the modern monetary economy. New York City has a discount market—a small group of firms that deal in government and commercial short-term paper and form a buffer between the central bank and other financial institutions. There are also the investment banks, which provide specialized banking services to busi-

CONNECTIONS

See also

1126 The rise of banking
936 Man as an economic being
938 Industry and economics
940 International trade and finance
942 International cooperation and development

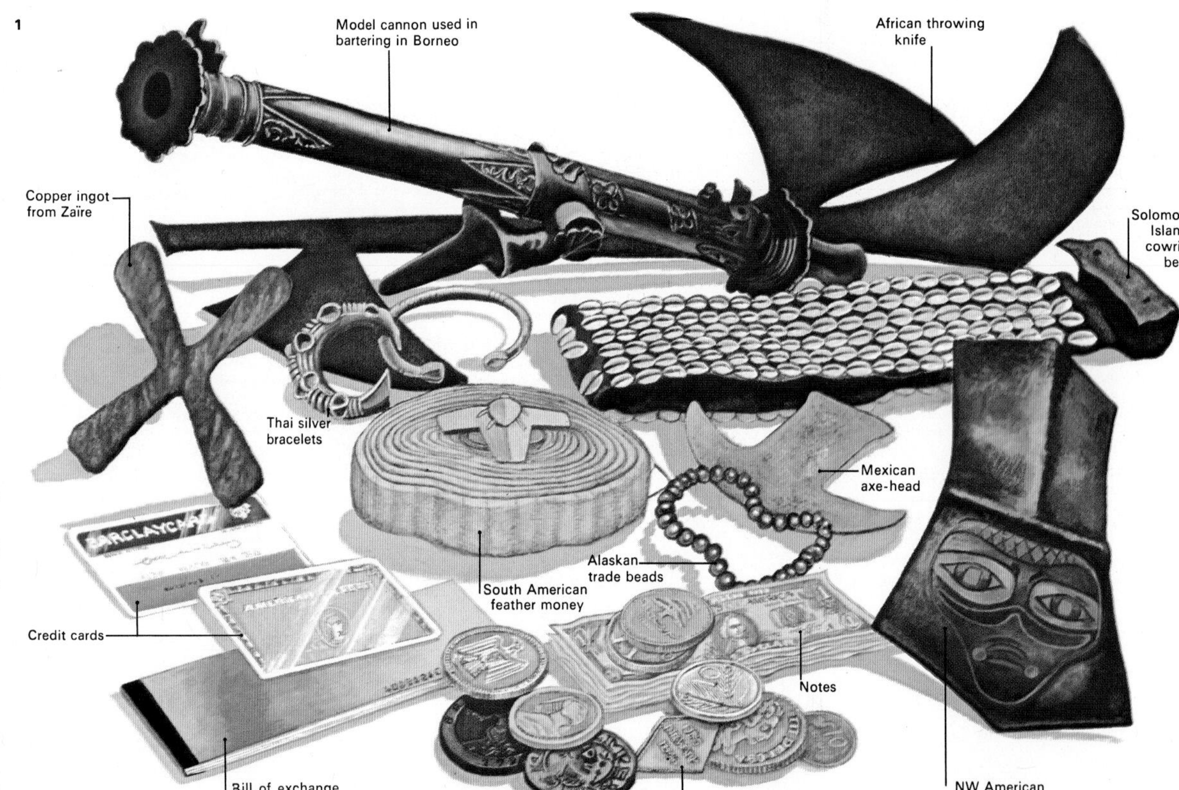

1
Model cannon used in bartering in Borneo
African throwing knife
Copper ingot from Zaïre
Solomon Island cowrie belt
Thai silver bracelets
Mexican axe-head
Alaskan trade beads
South American feather money
Credit cards
Notes
Bill of exchange
Checks
Coins
NW American coast copper

1 Money is, at root, really a matter of confidence. It is anything that a society generally accepts as having value. Once that confidence is destroyed money reverts to its intrinsic value. Throughout history money has assumed many forms. Apart from those shown here, precious stones, fish hooks, nails, compressed tea (the original "cash"), livestock, special stones, and, in prison camps, cigarettes and canned food have been used. Man needs money as a store of wealth, a medium of exchange, and a unit against which to value other goods. To be adopted as money an article needs to be relatively scarce, durable, easily stored, and portable. It is for this reason that gold and silver have formed the basis of many coinages. That confidence is vital is seen by the gradual development of paper money, which has no intrinsic value.

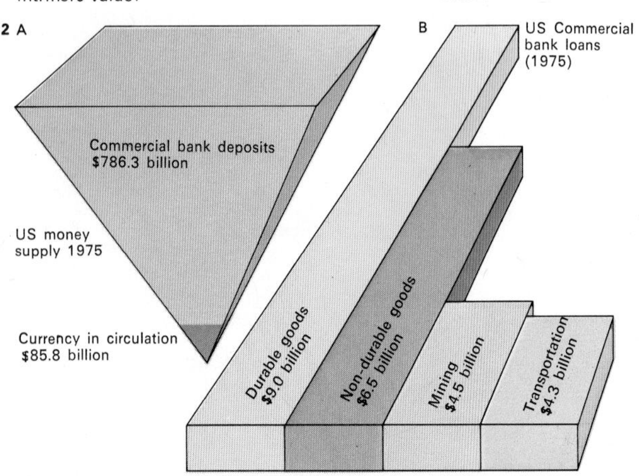

2 A
B
Commercial bank deposits $786.3 billion
US money supply 1975
Currency in circulation $85.8 billion
US Commercial bank loans (1975)
Durable goods $9.0 billion
Non-durable goods $6.5 billion
Mining $4.5 billion
Transportation $4.3 billion

2 Cash makes up only a small part of the total money supply [A], averaging 11% of 1975 commercial bank deposits. Credit [B], in the form of commercial bank loans, totalled $24.3 billion in four major categories.

3 Currencies such as the dollar and pound are "reserve currencies." Other countries hold part of their reserves in New York or London as deposits or investments in government securities so they can be cashed easily.

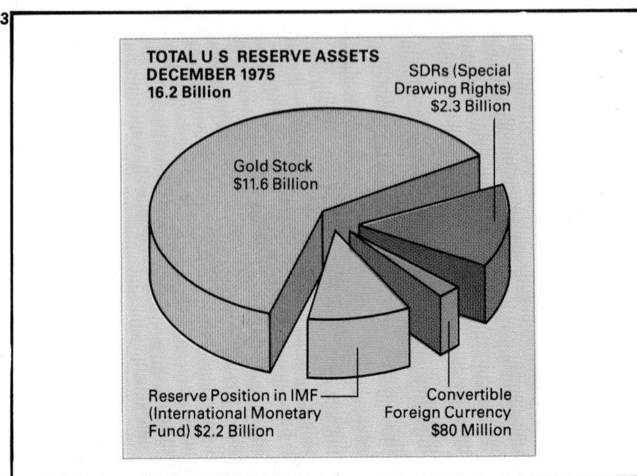

3
TOTAL U S RESERVE ASSETS DECEMBER 1975 16.2 Billion
SDRs (Special Drawing Rights) $2.3 Billion
Gold Stock $11.6 Billion
Reserve Position in IMF (International Monetary Fund) $2.2 Billion
Convertible Foreign Currency $80 Million

ness. They engage in the financing of trade (particularly of commodities) and are active in company development and flotation as well as in organizing the issue of new companies' shares to the general public (as issuing houses) [5, 6].

Significance of the stock exchange

Another key financial institution in the money market is the stock exchange, where stocks and bonds, which represent the physical wealth of the community, can be traded. The stock exchange makes a market through stockbrokers—firms that buy and sell shares on behalf of investors [7]. In the United States the market is made by specialists ("stock jobbers" in London) who are wholesalers of stocks and shares. They hold a "float" of shares at any time, and daily prices are set as they mark prices up and down as they balance shares offered with shares demanded. Stock exchange transactions occur within a complex network of law, government regulations, and the internal rules of the individual governing bodies.

Stock markets throughout the world have become increasingly institutionalized in the last 30 years. Although small savings have expanded greatly, they have in general been used to boost the great growth in personal insurance and pensions. Hence the main supply of funds to the stock market both for existing and new issues is now through insurance companies, pension funds, private universities, and other institutional fund sources.

Another important development has been the mutual funds, called unit trusts in Britain. These buy groups of shares so that the investor in the fund can spread his risks over a wide range of companies even though his investment is relatively small. The financial scene also includes institutions to finance house building and purchase. In the United States savings and loan associations, as well as banks, perform this service. The last 50 years have also seen a dramatic rise in other institutions specializing in the provision of short- and medium-term credit to individuals and also to industry.

KEY

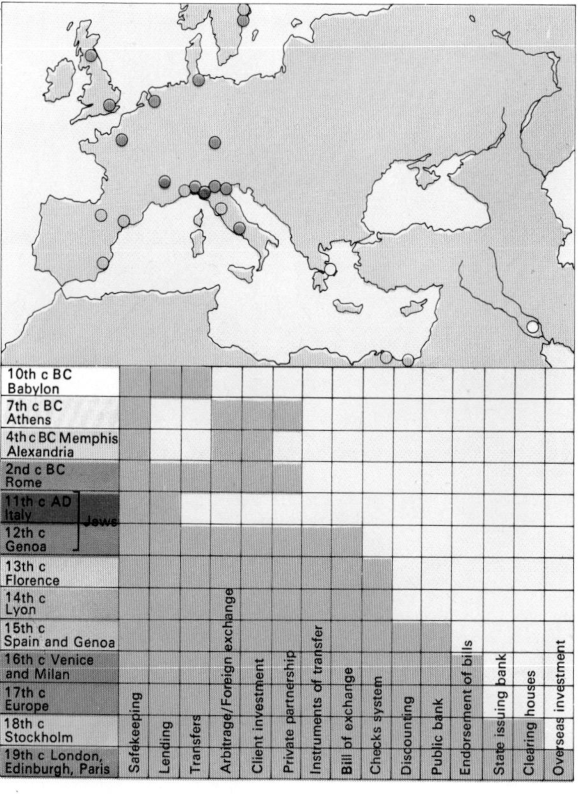
4
10th c BC Babylon
7th c BC Athens
4th c BC Memphis Alexandria
2nd c BC Rome
11th c AD Italy
12th c Genoa
Jews
13th c Florence
14th c Lyon
15th c Spain and Genoa
16th c Venice and Milan
17th c Europe
18th c Stockholm
19th c London, Edinburgh, Paris
Safekeeping
Lending
Transfers
Arbitrage/Foreign exchange
Client investment
Private partnership
Instruments of transfer
Bill of exchange
Checks system
Discounting
Public bank
Endorsement of bills
State issuing bank
Clearing houses
Overseas investment

4 Banking first appeared about 1000 BC in Babylon in the form of safekeeping, lending, and transfers. Modern banking began with Italian merchants and London goldsmiths who gave credit to depositors. The formation of the Bank of England (1694) marked the realization that a central bank was needed to underpin the country's banking. Brown squares indicate services.

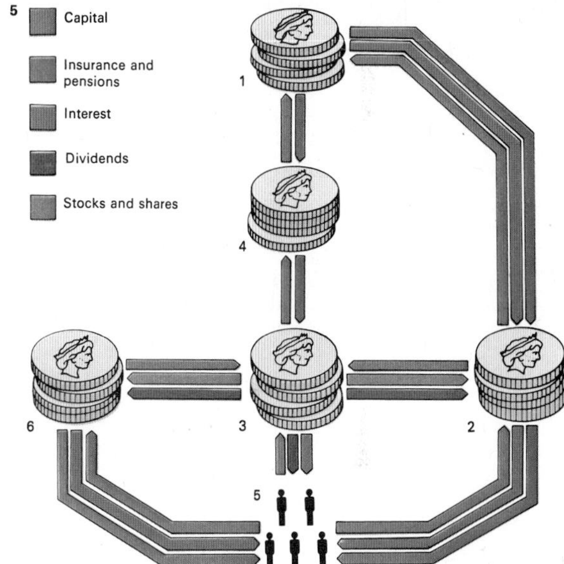
5
Capital
Insurance and pensions
Interest
Dividends
Stocks and shares
1
4
6
3
2
5

5 A business [1] can raise capital either through a bank [2] or by selling a new issue of shares on the stock market [3] through a guarantor, the investment bank [4]. The public [5] and institutions [6] can then invest.

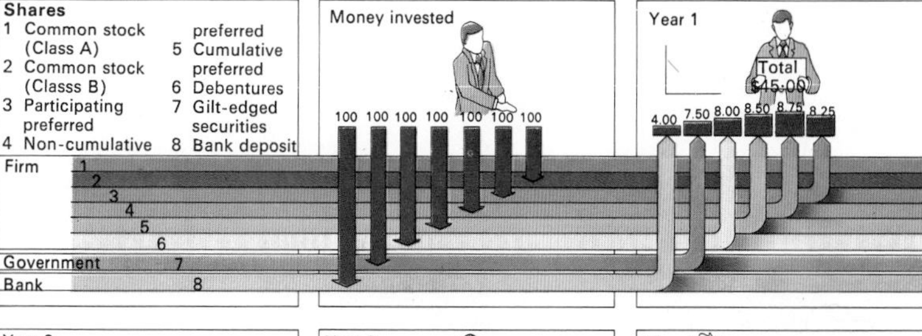
7 Shares
1 Common stock (Class A)
2 Common stock (Classs B)
3 Participating preferred
4 Non-cumulative preferred
5 Cumulative preferred
6 Debentures
7 Gilt-edged securities
8 Bank deposit
Money invested
100 100 100 100 100 100 100
Year 1
Total $45.00
4.00 7.50 8.00 8.50 8.75 8.25
Firm
Government
Bank
Year 2
Total $20.50
5.00 7.50 8.00
Year 3
Total $59.50
17.00
5.00 7.50 8.00 8.75 8.25 5.00
Year 4
Total $72.00
10.25 2.00 12.00
5.00 7.50 8.00 8.50 8.75

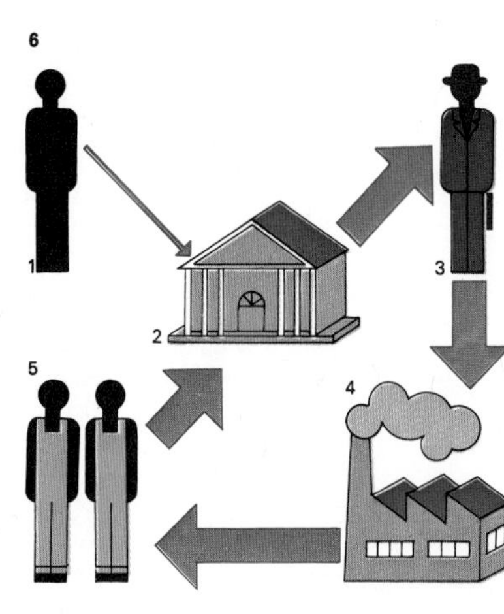
6
1
2
3
4
5

6 The public [1] deposits savings with the banking system [2], which in turn advances money to entrepreneurs [3]. This money is spent on plant [4], materials, and wages and returns to the bank via the recipients' accounts [5]. Since the public does not draw on all the money at the same time, the banking system can safely expand the money supply in the form of loans, which usually equal about five times the amount of its cash reserves.

7 Different types of investments have different interest rates and degrees of risk. The illustration shows the fortunes of a man who divides $700 equally among a bank deposit, government bonds, and company stocks. The red boxes show the interest he receives over a four-year period. Bank deposit, government bonds, and debentures are the most reliable. Preferred stock has first call on dividends over common stock, and both carry the chance of an increase in value.

Man as an economic being

Choice is one of the fundamental ideas in economic thought, and scarcity is another. Man is seen as rationally choosing between alternatives—between different goods, between material benefits and leisure, between present and future consumption, and between alternative uses for the scarce or limited production resources. Limited resources include such items as land, labor, skills, and capital that he uses to achieve his standard of living.

What is economic man?

Economic man is a term for a series of generalizations and abstractions that have been developed over two centuries to determine the essence of "economic life." Economic theory is concerned with three areas: the way in which people's demands are generated; the behavior of organizations that supply these demands; and the behavior of groups within the economy and of national economies interrelated in the world economy. On this substructure rest more detailed theories about the monetary system, taxation, and monopolistic bodies like trade unions, cartels, and multinational corporations.

Economic man is a maximizer. As a consumer, according to his own preferences and the prices that confront him, he adjusts his spending so as to make the best use of his money [2]. This balancing act is performed by adjusting personal consumption of various goods until a given amount spent on any one of them will yield him equal satisfaction [1].

Resources are put into production to the point where they no longer generate additional profits and where no change in their proportionate use would improve the producer's profits. The "marginalist" character of economic theory derives from the Law of Diminishing Returns—the general rule that as more money is spent on a good or on a resource, the return (utility or profit) from each successive expenditure decreases.

The standard of living

Although economic man is a maximizer, he may not always choose to maximize his consumption of material goods. Workers in unpleasant jobs frequently react to a raise in pay by working less, and absenteeism rises. In the mid-twentieth century a small but significant minority has opted out of the competitive pressures and material benefits of industrial society [6]. If, as living standards rise in the world, leisure and peace of mind take precedence over material goods, economic life could be fundamentally affected.

As a general rule, the standard of living in any country is fixed by the average output of each person [7]. The opulent few in a community have virtually no impact on the standard of living of their fellow citizens. That standard is determined by the efficiency with which the community as a whole works. This is as true in the "advanced" countries as in peasant economies, even though the complex organization of the former and their access to capital tends to confuse the issue. Since the eighteenth century many countries have achieved a rapid rise in per capita output and hence in their standards of living.

CONNECTIONS

See also
934 Money and capital
938 Industry and economics
940 International trade and finance
942 International cooperation and development
924 Work: curse and pleasure
926 Work: motivation and performance
932 Uses of leisure

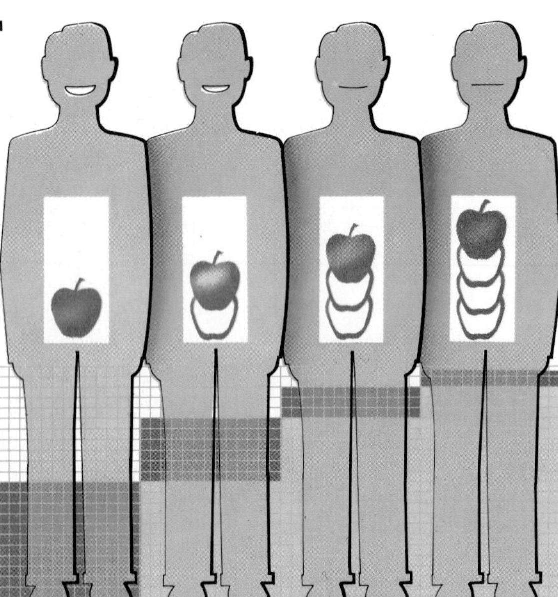

1 "Ravenous, hungry, nearly full, full" illustrates a basic law of economics—diminishing marginal utility. As the most urgent needs are met, additional consumption gives less satisfaction or utility (dark area on graph) until the point is reached when we gain no additional satisfaction from anything more consumed.

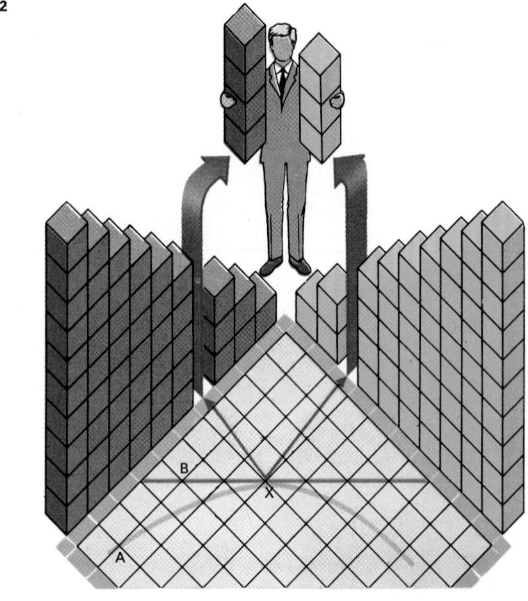
B
X
A

2 Indifference curves [A] and budget lines [B] show how a person will get the most use from consumption with a given income and relative prices. The optimum occurs where line A touches line B at X. Here the marginal utility of the last unit of income spent on each item is equal.

3

Quantity bought at original price

Quantity bought after price falls

1

2

3

3 Demand is elastic [1] when a given percentage fall in price (yellow columns) produces a higher percentage rise in quantity demanded; unity when they balance [2]; inelastic when a smaller percentage rise in quantity demanded results [3].

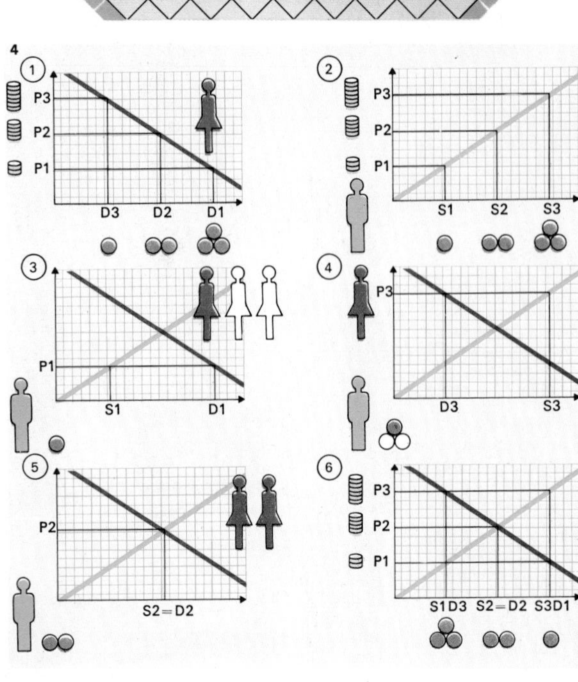
4
1
P3
P2
P1
D3
D2
D1
2
P3
P2
P1
S1
S2
S3
3
P1
S1
D1
4
P3
D3
S3
5
P2
S2=D2
6
P3
P2
P1
S1D3
S2=D2
S3D1

4 In a simple market, quantity demanded [D] changes inversely with prices [P]—as prices rise, quantity demanded decreases [1]. Quantity supplied [S] increases directly with prices [2]—when prices rise, more goods are produced. Excess of demand over supply leaves unsatisfied customers [3]. Excess supply leaves unsold goods [4]. Equilibrium means demand equals supply [5, 6].

Welfare economics grew out of a realization in the early 1900s that competitive economic individualism did not necessarily bring about, in a phrase used by Jeremy Bentham (1748–1832), "the greatest happiness of the greatest number." Poor parents might seek to relieve their misery with liquor rather than feed milk to their children. Exploitation of resources led to large-scale destruction of the landscape. Some people felt that a degree of government intervention was preferable to the largely untrammeled competition experienced in Western Europe and Russia in the period 1850–1900. From this has developed the concept of "cost-benefit analysis" whereby the benefits and costs of an irrigation scheme, chemical factory, food subsidy, indirect tax, or whatever are calculated for the community as a whole and are judged in that framework.

Statistical sampling of economic man

Knowledge is more useful and complete when it can be quantified. Therefore population, trade, output, and money are counted and compared over periods of time. It is usually physically impossible or prohibitively expensive to make a total count, so statistical sampling techniques are used. When a total population is counted and classified, "sampling" is used to collect data about a few thousand representative people (selected in relation to age, social class, or income level), and the results can then be projected for the total.

Statistical indexes are a particularly effective way of describing changes over time. They also give meaning to such ideas as "changes in the price level" and changes in "the volume of industrial production," which, because they are composed of myriad changes relating to a wide range of products, are virtually impossible to discuss without indexes.

"Cost of living" indexes [9] are familiar enough. A representative quantitative collection of goods is priced in the base years. Developments in the successive years are related as a percentage change to the base year, and thus indexes usually show the base year as 100.

KEY

Advanced countries generate their high standard of living through sophisticated selling methods – here epitomized by the Ginza, the hub of Tokyo's commercial life.

5

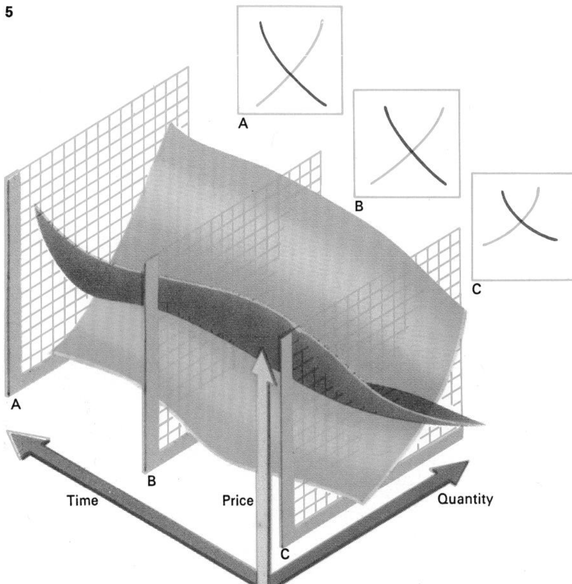
A
B
C
A
B
C
Time
Price
Quantity

5 Economists use simplified models of actual economic situations, which may be either dynamic (tracing changes over time) or static (presenting a single situation). The diagram illustrates both models. A, B, C show the static relationship between supply [green curve] and demand [pink curve] and are three points charting change from A to C with time.

6

6 Drop-out communities are a luxury afforded only by high-pressure wealthy economies. Those disenchanted with stressful urban life seek simpler ways – but their "poverty" may include such things as cars, TV, alcohol, and modern medicine.

7

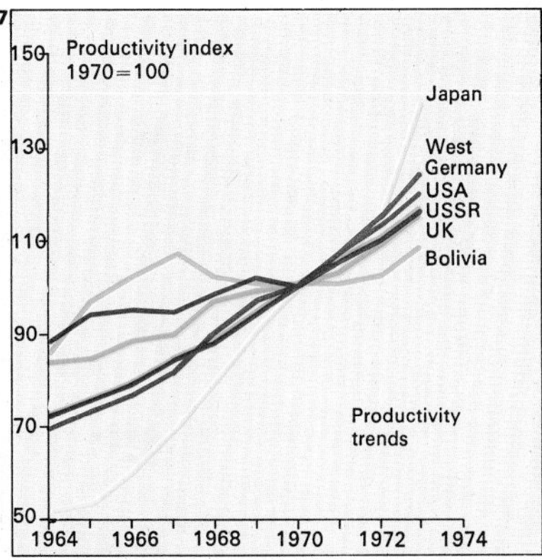
Productivity index
1970=100
150
130
110
90
70
50
Japan
West Germany
USA
USSR
UK
Bolivia
Productivity trends
1964
1966
1968
1970
1972
1974

7 Productivity depends on many factors – efficiency of both management and workers, hours worked, investment levels, and degree of industrialization. Comparing figures between countries is difficult because of special local conditions, but it is possible to monitor trends in productivity within a country. Here the output per person in 1970 is taken as 100 and productivity before and after compared to that. The steeper the line, the faster the standard of living can rise.

8

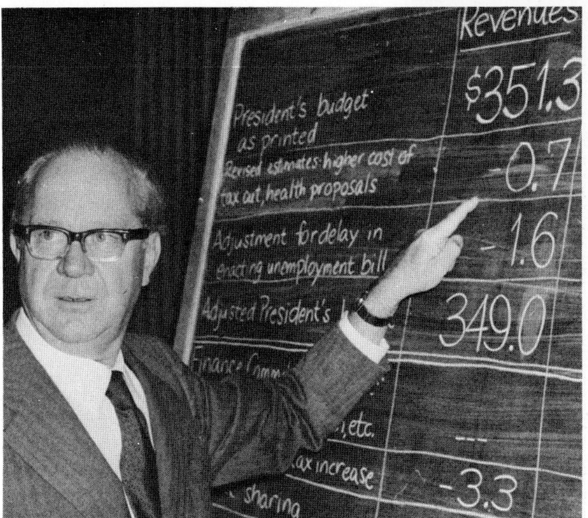
Revenues
President's budget as printed
$351.3
Revised estimates: higher cost of tax cut, health proposals
-0.7
Adjustment for delay in enacting unemployment bill
-1.6
Adjusted President's
349.0
etc.
tax increase
sharing
-3.3

8 All governments, whether federal, state, or local, must work within an economic budget. Here Senator Russell Long, chairman of the Senate Finance Committee, discusses various aspects of the federal budget during hearings in Washington.

9

A

B

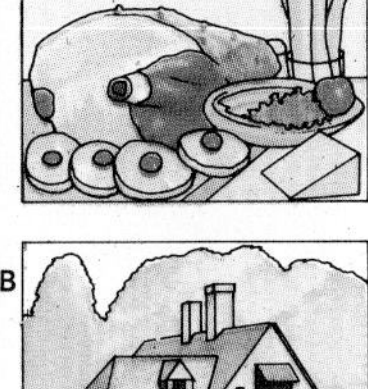

C

D

9 One important way of gauging a country's economic health is to measure shifts in the cost of buying a standard range of common goods. This so-called cost of living index is based, in the United States, on the average price of numerous individual items ranging from grape jelly to mortgage interest rates. Items are listed under various headings.

	Number of items	% of total cost
A Food, drink and tobacco	156	41·6
C Consumer durables	113	14·7
B Housing and heating	12	18·1
D Services and transport	67	25·6
Total	348	100·0

Industry and economics

Economic analysis is applied both to the individual and to group or aggregate situations. Microeconomics deals with the problems of the individual consumer, household, or company and uses supply and demand as its basic model, whereas macroeconomics studies communities or countries and uses the overall flow of money as its basis. This division is largely one of convenience. Each is a different aspect of the same picture, and any understanding of economics requires an appreciation of both.

Behavior of organizations

The behavior of companies is analyzed generally in terms of perfect competition and monopoly. These two extreme forms probably do not exist, and real-life situations form a spectrum between them. Perfect competition assumes a world in which everybody knows what is happening and in which production freely responds to changes in demand. Above all, it requires that individual companies be small in relation to the total market so that they cannot affect price levels by changing their volume of supply, but equally they can always sell as much as they want at the given price [1].

In a monopolistic situation, a company is large enough to affect the market price offered for its wares by withholding or increasing supplies. Under conditions of monopoly [2], the greatest profit is achieved when the volume of sales or output is such that the additional revenue resulting from selling one more unit equals the cost of producing it—that is, when the marginal revenue equals the marginal cost. If a monopoly could be forced to sell that volume of output at which price just equals its average cost per unit, it would sell a much larger volume, and the consumer would pay a lower price.

Control over company activities

Monopoly, oligopoly, and imperfect competition are names for situations in which, because of relative market size or because of product branding and publicity, a company can to some extent control the price at which it sells. In the last 100 years governments have exercised more and more control over the behavior of companies. Corporation law is the chief means of control. It determines the way in which companies are established, how they are controlled by their stockholders, and how they are financed. It also makes them accountable to the community by forcing them to publish certain financial information.

Other laws, covering, for example, safety, health, and pollution, also affect the company. Among the most important are laws, such as the US antitrust laws, that restrict or break up monopolistic companies. Much of this governmental concern is a reaction to the concentration of economic power within industrial and financial corporations where the few largest in an industry may well control more than 60 percent of the total assets.

The boom/slump cycles of the 1920s [7] and the slump of 1931–33 spawned the theoretical work of the British economist John Maynard Keynes (1883–1946), who argued that governments can take countercyclical action (deflation and reflation) to regulate the level of economic activity. Par-

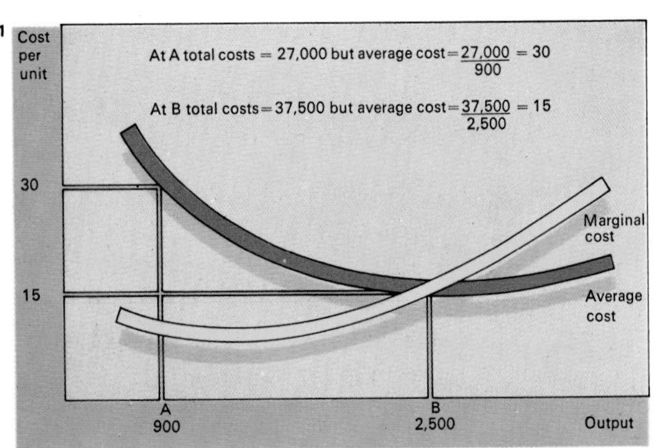

1
Cost per unit
At A total costs = 27,000 but average cost = 27,000/900 = 30
At B total costs = 37,500 but average cost = 37,500/2,500 = 15
30
15
Marginal cost
Average cost
A 900
B 2,500
Output

1 Unit costs depend upon volume of production. At its designed capacity a plant achieves minimum costs. If output is pushed higher, costs tend to rise through machine breakdown, congestion, and so on. Under perfect competition, firms enter or leave an industry until market price and marginal cost coincide with the minimum average cost. Below this price, firms are forced out of production.

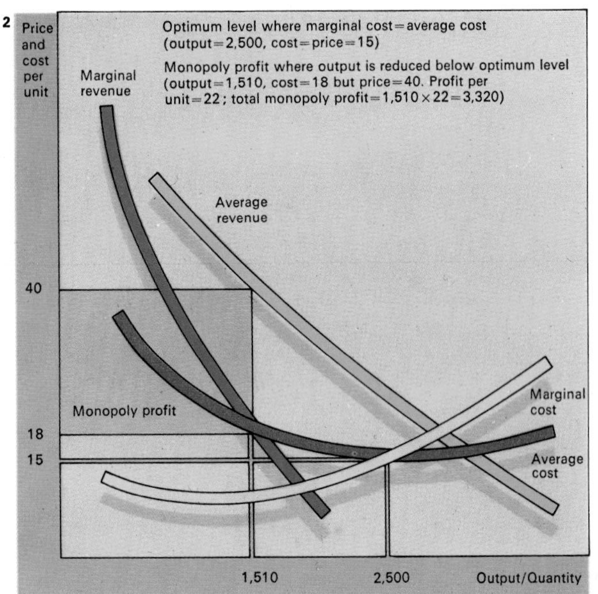

2
Price and cost per unit
Marginal revenue
Optimum level where marginal cost = average cost (output = 2,500, cost = price = 15)
Monopoly profit where output is reduced below optimum level (output = 1,510, cost = 18 but price = 40. Profit per unit = 22; total monopoly profit = 1,510 × 22 = 3,320)
Average revenue
40
Monopoly profit
18
15
Marginal cost
Average cost
1,510
2,500
Output/Quantity

2 A dominant supplier or monopolist can exploit its customers. By restricting output, for example, it can force the price up and increase profit. The consumer pays a higher price but consumes less.

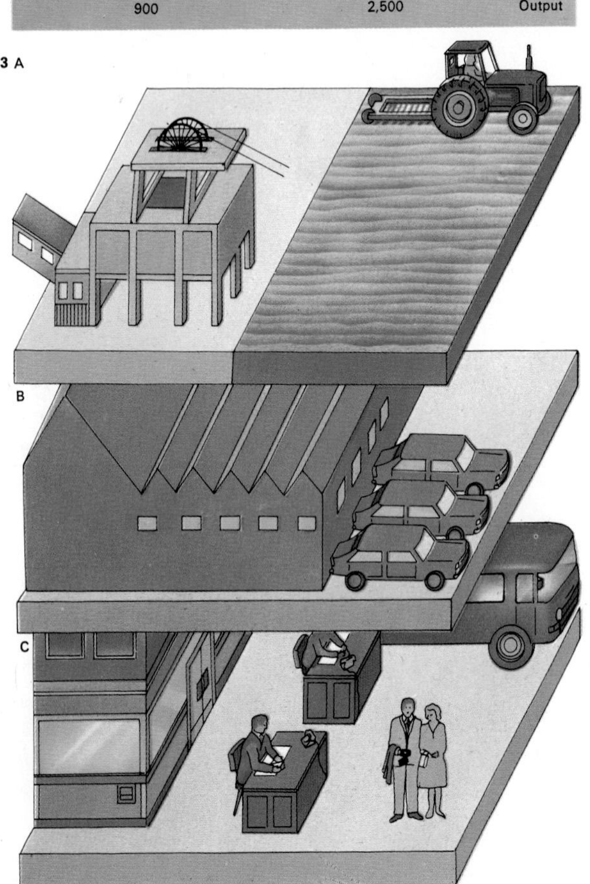

3 A
B
C

3 Primary industry [A] produces food, oil, wood, steel, aluminum, and energy. These materials are worked into higher forms of manufacture by secondary industry [B], which produces chemicals, coats, cans, cars, and so on. Shops, warehouses, and banking facilities are forms of tertiary industry [C]. This service, sector, which also includes credit-card firms and the professions, is growing in advanced economies.

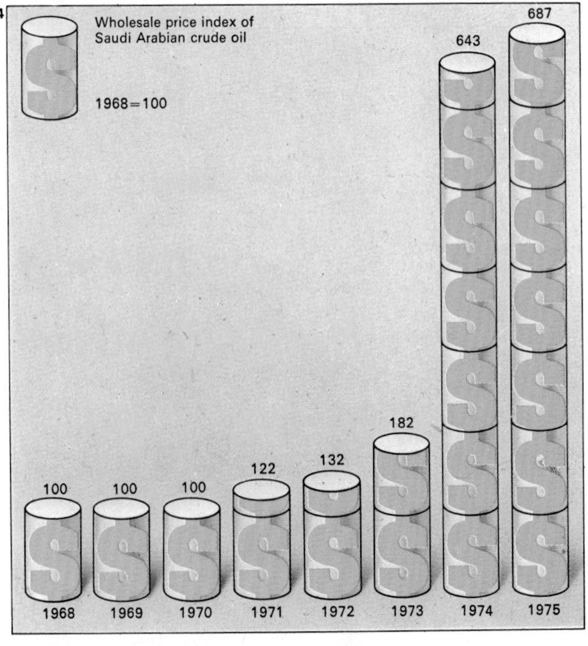

4
Wholesale price index of Saudi Arabian crude oil
1968 = 100
100
100
100
122
132
182
643
687
1968
1969
1970
1971
1972
1973
1974
1975

4 By acting in concert, the main oil producers of the world in OPEC were able to triple the world price of oil in 1973–74. This was monopoly in action. Cartels are not new, however, and they have proved unstable in the past.

ticularly since 1945, governments throughout the world have been expected to follow full employment policies. Gradually it has become clear that creeping—and certainly galloping—inflation limits even the most powerful government's ability to maintain a high level of employment without occasional recessions and resultant increases in unemployment.

Inflation and modern society

Inflation shows itself usually as a persistent rise in prices or fall in the value of money and has long been simply summed up as "too much money chasing too few goods." But inflation is an extremely complex process; its results are obvious, but the reasons are myriad [6]. Prices have risen persistently and with relatively few interruptions throughout recorded human history—and nobody knows why. It has required a major catastrophe (the collapse of a civilization, for example, or the plague in fourteenth-century Europe) to check rising prices.

Many causes are suggested for inflation: governments spending more than they have the courage to collect in taxes; optimistic expectations produced by decades of full employment; growing trade union or industrial monopoly power; international cartels such as those that typify the oil industry [4]; exhaustion of world raw materials; the growth of world population; the side effects of mass communications; and so on.

Modern industrial society is creating great unease among its members. Giant firms that seem uncontrollable; giant trade unions that are sometimes controlled by criminals; sliding ethical standards—all have produced a demand for more and more governmental intervention. The fundamental issue is probably whether the earth with its finite resources can support perpetually growing industrial output. Modern technology may have lightened the human physical labors (at least for a minority), but in subtle ways it may have enslaved the human race to the giant institutions, complex administrative systems, and mass media manipulation that are necessary to use this technology on the increasingly large scale that it demands.

KEY

Production requires the assembling and coordination of capital [A], labor [B], and materials [C]. These are divided into fixed or overhead costs (like rent) and variable costs (materials, overtime), which relate directly to the level of output. The greater the level of output, the lower are fixed costs per unit. Variable costs per unit first tend to fall as work is subdivided and waste reduced, but they rise later when additional costs do not produce an equivalent rise in output.

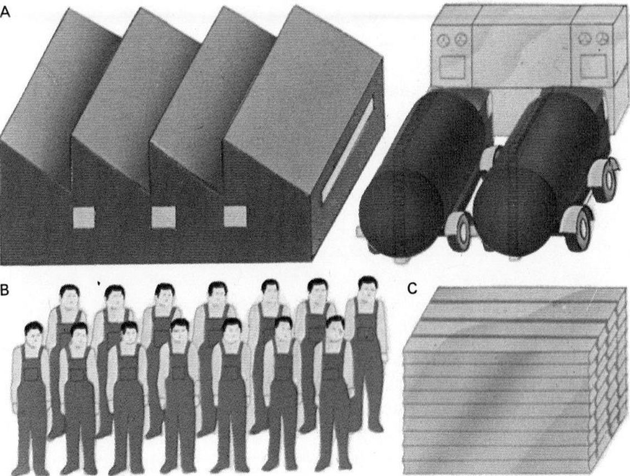
A
B
C

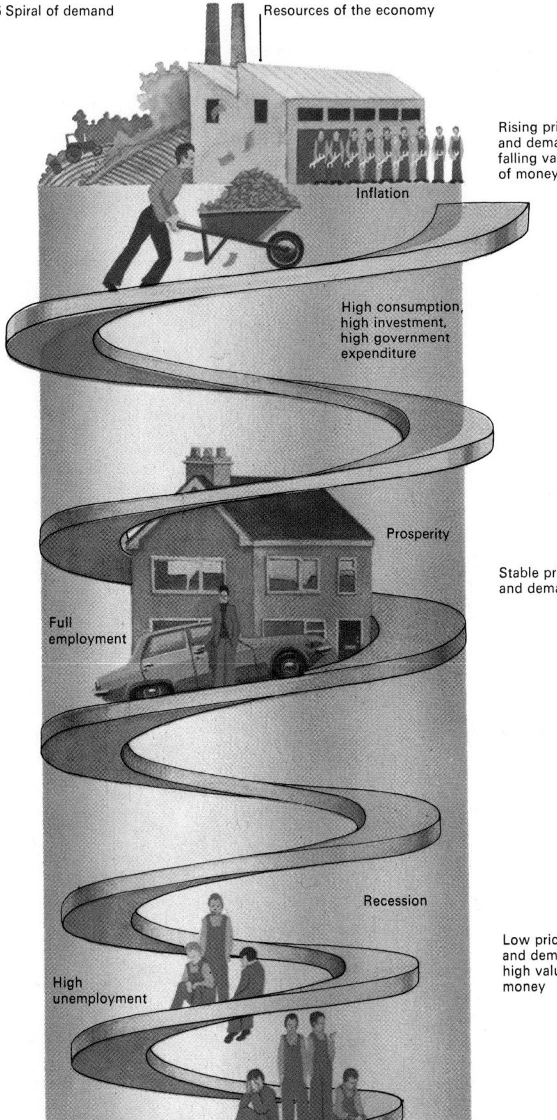
5 Spiral of demand
Resources of the economy
Inflation
High consumption, high investment, high government expenditure
Prosperity
Full employment
Recession
High unemployment
Low consumption, low investment, low government investment

Rising prices and demand; falling value of money

5 "Demand-pull" inflation is used to explain price changes. Inflation is seen as a result of rises in demand pulling on the limited resources of an economy and forcing prices up a self-perpetuating spiral. Changes in consumption, investment, or government expenditure can cause changes in demand. Any increases have an inflationary effect as demand increases, whereas a fall in their levels causes a downward movement on the spiral. At the bottom of the spiral, in a recession, demand for resources is low, production and employment fall and with them income and expenditure. The downward movement has its own momentum.

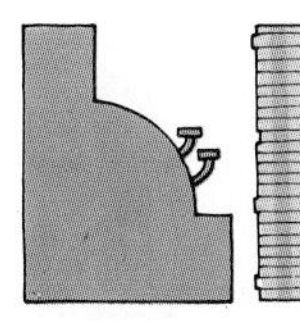

Stable prices and demand

Low prices and demand; high value of money

6 Increased costs of any or all of the three factors of production is the basis of "cost-push" inflation. Raw materials [A], capital [B], and labor [C] may all increase in price, thus pushing upward the cost of goods produced. World shortages, trade union wage increases that exceed productivity, or monopoly profits are examples of cost-push. In a modern interdependent economy, price rises in any one area lead to increases in many other sectors, the multiple effect of a particular increase developing its own momentum, such as the effect of the increase in the price of oil.

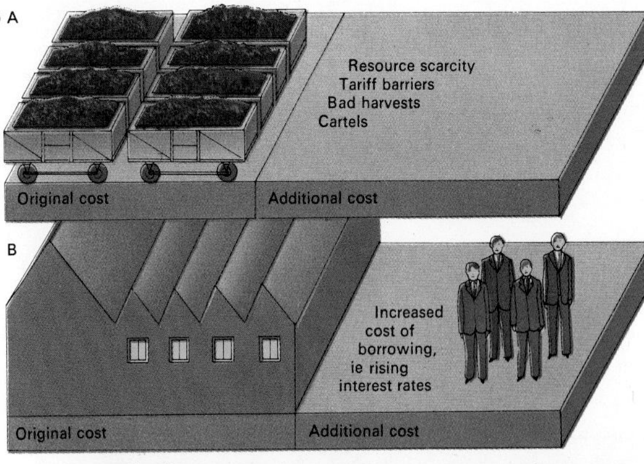
6 A
Resource scarcity
Tariff barriers
Bad harvests
Cartels
Original cost
Additional cost
B
Increased cost of borrowing, ie rising interest rates
Original cost
Additional cost

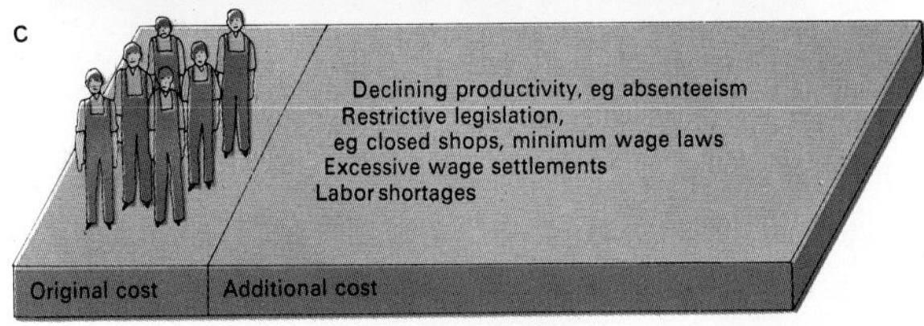
C
Declining productivity, eg absenteeism
Restrictive legislation,
eg closed shops, minimum wage laws
Excessive wage settlements
Labor shortages
Original cost
Additional cost

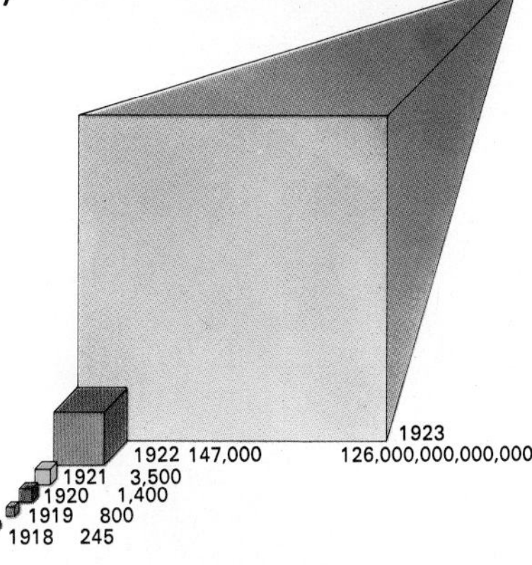
7
1923
126,000,000,000,000
1922 147,000
1921 3,500
1920 1,400
1919 800
1918 245

7 Runaway price inflation was experienced by several European countries immediately after World War I, but Germany was hardest hit. Between 1918 and 1925 wholesale prices rose a trillion times. German wholesale prices tripled in 1919, doubled in 1920, redoubled in 1921, and finally took off in 1922 with a 40-fold increase. In 1923 prices and money wages grew so high that a wheelbarrow was needed to carry a worker's pay.

International trade and finance

Trade, or the exchange of goods between parties, is one of the major wealth-creating activities [Key]. This is so even if the people of a country or region are the most efficient producers in every conceivable field of production: they are still better off if they exchange goods with countries whose pattern of relative efficiencies is different from their own. This is called the theory of comparative advantage [1].

Free trade and tariff barriers

It is easy to see the sense of manufacturing producers and primary producers exchanging their goods, but it is less obvious why the United States, Germany, Japan, and Great Britain are able to profit by importing and exporting similar products among themselves. Yet it is a fact of world trade that the biggest and most rapidly growing markets for manufacturing countries are not the primary producers but other industrial nations. Trade between low-wage and high-wage countries is another source of controversy. While Americans do not suggest putting a duty on shirts imported from low-wage Tennessee into high-wage Detroit, they may think it reasonable to put a duty on textiles from South Korea.

The theory of comparative advantage requires that goods be able to move freely between the trading areas. This raises few problems within a country, but it may be a different matter if boundaries of politics, language, and culture have to be crossed. Similarly, free trade is a wonderful idea if everybody plays the same game, but for various political reasons tariff quotas, levies, and similar restrictions may be more popular than totally free-trade policies.

Governments impede trade in many ways, usually by tariffs but sometimes by nontariff barriers [2] and quotas. In the years 1950 to 1970 tariffs were substantially reduced throughout the world, and today other barriers are more important as limitations on international trade.

A country's trading position vis-à-vis the rest of the world is summed up in its balance of payments [4]. The net result of all transactions on both current (basic flow of goods and services) and capital accounts (loans or debts to other countries) will be seen as a change in the country's international reserves (gold, dollars, sterling, or other convertible currency).

National economic policy and the state of a country's balance of payments are closely linked. Good-neighbor behavior dictates that no country should run a persistent surplus or deficit in its balance of payments. After a year or two of surplus a country should stimulate demand for imports by reflation (for example, by tax cuts or public works); similarly, it should deflate after a year or two of deficit [5].

Exchange rates of currency

An exchange rate is simply the price of one currency in terms of another. This is determined on foreign exchange markets, which exist in such major financial centers as New York, London, Frankfurt, and Tokyo. When the gold standard was used, the currencies of participating countries were all tied to one another by their gold content. The gold standard was largely abandoned during the 1920s because it was thought to

CONNECTIONS

See also
1384 The world's monetary system
302 World food resources
934 Money and capital
936 Man as an economic being
938 Industry and economics
942 International co-operation and development

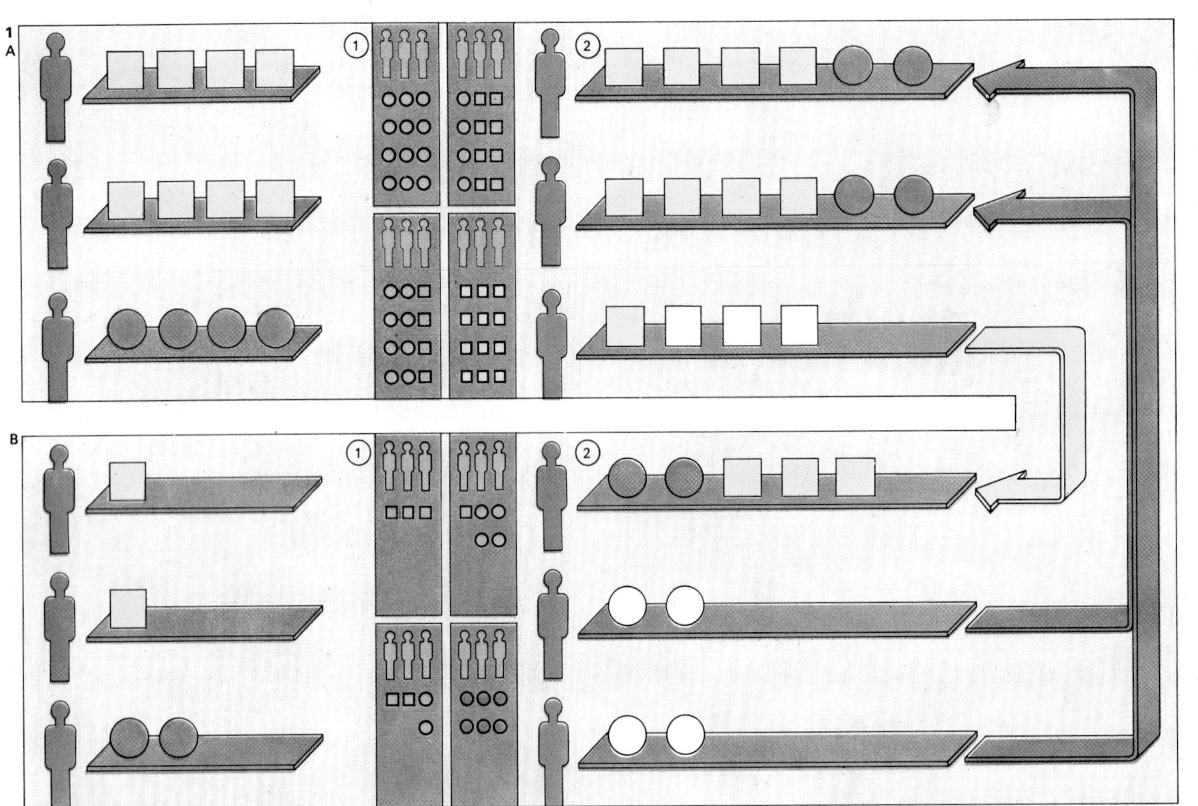

1
A
B
1
2

1 The theory of comparative advantage explains how benefits arise from trade. In the pretrade situation in country A, two persons produce four crates of lemons each and one person produces four bags of corn. In country B two persons each produce one crate of lemons and one produces two bags of corn. Each country can produce various combinations of lemons and corn by transferring labor between the activities [1]. When trade takes place, each country specializes in producing the commodity in which it is relatively more efficient. (Of the various possible combinations [2] the best is in color.) A produces only lemons; B only corn, and they trade four bags of corn for three crates of lemons. Each country now consumes an extra crate of lemons so that both have gained from specialization and trade.

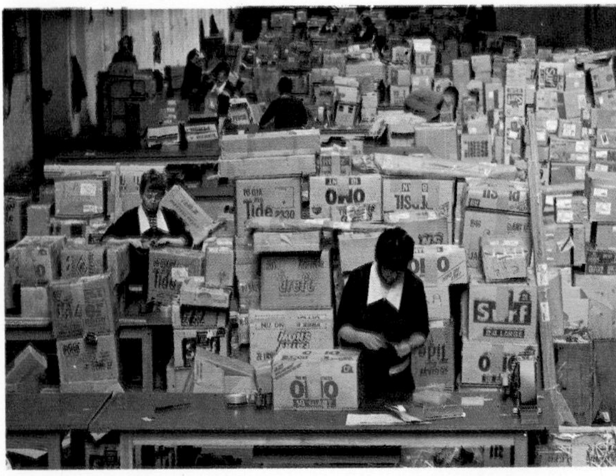

2 Stringent checks on incoming products, food hygiene laws, labeling requirements, and electrical safety regulations are examples of the various kinds of controls that can be greater barriers to trade than tariffs.

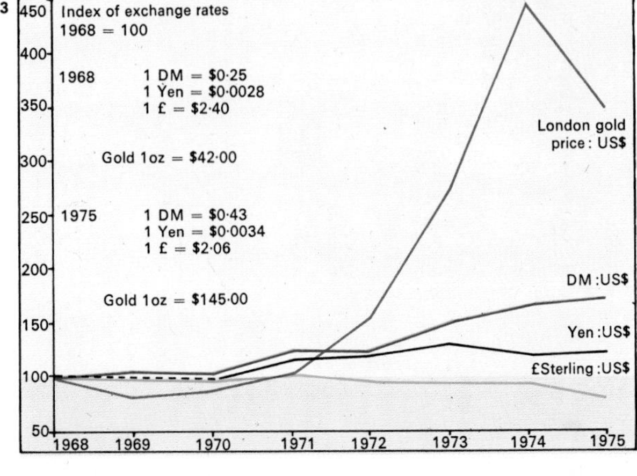

Index of exchange rates
1968 = 100
1968 1 DM = $0·25
1 Yen = $0·0028
1 £ = $2·40
Gold 1oz = $42·00
1975 1 DM = $0·43
1 Yen = $0·0034
1 £ = $2·06
Gold 1oz = $145·00
London gold price: US$
DM:US$
Yen:US$
£Sterling:US$
450
400
350
300
250
200
150
100
50
1968
1969
1970
1971
1972
1973
1974
1975

3 Floating exchange rates gradually replaced fixed exchange rates so that by the early 1970s most major currencies were responding daily to foreign exchange market movements.

e too inflexible and too limiting. Thereafter he major trading currencies became international standards of value.

In the decades after World War II this ystem came under pressures that resulted artly from structural weaknesses in the vorld economy, partly from side effects of ther policies such as the United States' ommitment to massive economic and nilitary aid, and partly from institutional igidities such as fixed exchange rates and he fixed value of the US dollar in terms of old. Both of these were maintained somewhat pointlessly for many years. The result vas a flurry of foreign exchange speculation recipitating devaluations and revaluations f dollars, marks, pounds, yen, and finally old. This led in 1970–71 to a position where here was effectively no agreed international standard of value.

This situation produced the "Smithsoian parities" in which each major currency vas priced against a "basket" of other curencies weighted in relation to their imporance in world trade, and thereby provided a onventional standard of value against which future movements in exchange rates could be judged.

Floating systems in world currency

The world has moved slowly from a regime of fixed exchange rates to one in which most currencies are "floating"; that is, their value in other currencies is allowed to fluctuate from day to day on the foreign exchange markets [3]. Systems have been introduced that allow a currency to float within certain fixed limits so that most major currencies now have two fixed values instead of one—the upper and lower limits of the float—at which points the monetary authorities will intervene to sell or buy the currency. Systems have also been introduced in which short-term and relatively minor market fluctuations are permitted in the value of the currency but in which the fixed limits are sporadically moved up and down, adapting the nominal value of a currency to long-term relative movements in other currencies and to the balance of economic forces that ultimately determines their relative values.

KEY

Trade within a country and trade between countries (typified by thriving ports) have similar economic causes and results. Differences in climate and resources produce different regional patterns of efficiency in the production of goods, hence making trade between countries worthwhile..

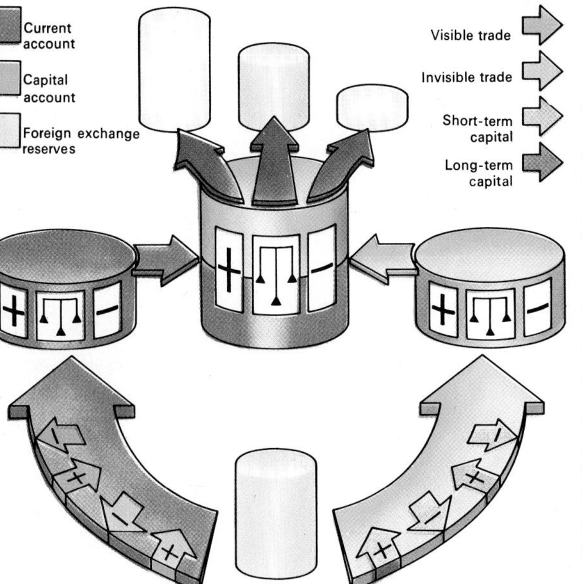
Current account
Capital account
Foreign exchange reserves
Visible trade
Invisible trade
Short-term capital
Long-term capital

4 The balance of payments is the combined net surplus or deficit of current and capital accounts and records the flow into [+] and out of [−] a country. Current account covers visible and invisible (shipping, insurance, etc) trade; capital account includes long- and short-term capital. A surplus will add to the reserves of foreign exchange, a deficit reduces them.

5 Deficits are corrected by deflation, devaluation, or direct controls, whose purpose is to decrease imports [A/D], increase exports [A/C], attract short-term capital [B/C] and reduce capital outflow [B/D]. All three policies add to reserves.

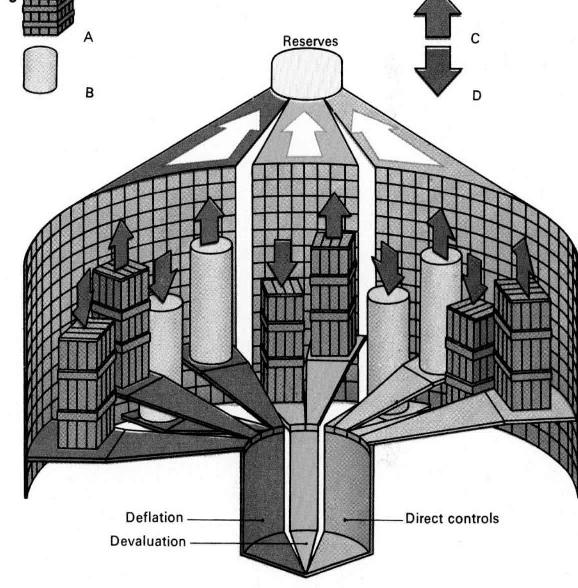
5
A
B
Reserves
C
D
Deflation
Devaluation
Direct controls

	Belgium	Denmark	Eire	France	W. Germany	Italy	Luxembourg	Netherlands	UK
Belgium		163	9	25,000	9,568	539	7,200	22,127	13,500
Denmark	400		24	1,000	3,062	248		180	2,000
Eire	200	414		1,000	930	300		180	470,000
France	15,000	907	184		45,821	4,145	7,100	1,700	20,000
W. Germany	4,500	5,270	297	25,000		7,190	3,800	12,753	20,000
Italy	90,000	809	216	230,000	297,079		10,400	9,000	121,000
Luxembourg	1,400	5		2,000	1,244	32		60	500
Netherlands	13,500	985	85	5,000	52,488	1,146	600		6,000
UK	5,000	4,298		11,000	21,449	4,500	200	3,800	
Spain	34,000	714	18	265,000	129,817	2,006	1,900	8,929	30,000
Greece	6,000	451	6	5,000	203,629	768		828	50,000
Yugoslavia	3,000	4,627	4	50,000	418,745	4,103	600	7,926	4,000
Portugal	4,000	204	12	475,000	70,520	631	11,800	2,534	5,000
Turkey	10,000	5,639	40	25,000	553,217	317		22,203	3,000
Algeria	3,000	179		440,000	1,407				600
Morocco	30,000	824		130,000	16,298			11,835	2,000
Tunisia	2,000	83		70,000				854	200
Others	8,000	15,574	1,032	145,000	245,461	18,205	1,700	10,591	918,205

6 Labor migration has been an important stimulus to world economic developments. The opening up of the United States, Canada, Australia, New Zealand, and Argentina in the 19th century drew millions of migrants from Europe. In the 1960s and 1970s the booming heartland of Europe drew migrant workers as shown from the less economically active peripheral countries. The chart shows foreign workers employed in the nine member countries of the European Economic Community in 1974. Nearly 1,500,000 of West Germany's workers, for example, came from Italy, Greece, Yugoslavia and Turkey. The total number of migrant workers in all of Europe in 1974 was 15 million.

International cooperation and development

The booms and slumps that scarred the interwar years clearly revealed the need for international economic cooperation. One result has been the establishment of two key institutions. The International Monetary Fund (IMF) provides temporary help to member countries that are having balance of payments problems, tries to stabilize exchange rates, and provides an adequate monetary base for trade. The International Bank for Reconstruction and Development (the World Bank) provides long-term loans and technical expertise to aid economic development. Other world bodies [Key] include the Food and Agriculture Organization (FAO), which was set up to improve world standards of nutrition by promoting agricultural development. The General Agreement on Tariffs and Trade (GATT) provides a framework for multilateral reductions in trade barriers.

Cooperation in regional groupings

Regional groupings of countries because of their close cultural, political, and geographical links, have achieved much practical economic cooperation. Undoubtedly the most fruitful so far has been the European Economic Community, or Common Market, closely followed by COMECON (the economic organization of the Soviet Union and the East European countries). Also successful have been the European Free Trade Area (EFTA), the Organization for European Economic Cooperation and Development (OECD), and the Latin American Free Trade Area (LAFTA).

Cooperation in international finance has concentrated on arrangements to finance balance of payments deficits and surpluses and to regulate international liquidity. Controversy has arisen over whether the IMF should have more power to deal with countries that persistently run surpluses or deficits, thus upsetting the world's financial equilibrium, and over the role of gold, its relationships with the dollar, and the wisdom of replacing it with some form of "paper gold" like the IMF Special Drawing Rights (SDRs).

After successive rounds of multilateral tariff-cutting negotiated by GATT, worldwide tariffs are at a historic low. The United States, for example, has moved from tariffs averaging 45 percent to tariffs of less than 10 percent in 1974. The international community is now beginning to focus attention on nontariff barriers to trade—national food hygiene laws, labeling requirements, or weights and measures rules that are sometimes unfairly invoked to exclude foreign goods.

Basis for economic success

Geographical, cultural, psychological, and religious phenomena play a part in explaining the past growth and decline of great civilizations, but a comprehensive theory explaining how growth starts has yet to be formulated. Nevertheless, modern economic theory has greatly extended our understanding of the interrelated parts of the economic growth process once it has started. The world has experienced an exceptional growth of wealth since 1950, but the gap between rich and poor countries has widened. Helped by the World Bank and national aid programs the poor have become

CONNECTIONS

See also
1386 Underdevelopment and the world economy
1330 The Commonwealth
1352 Nonalignment and the Third World
1382 The United Nations and its agencies
940 International trade and finance
934 Money and capital
936 Man as an economic being
938 Industry and economics

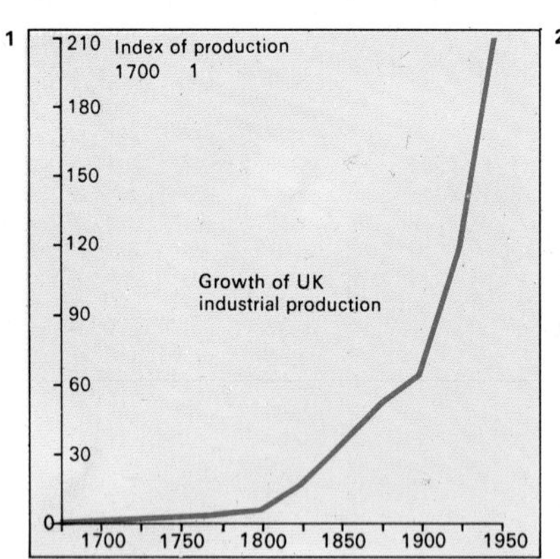

Index of production
1700 1
210
180
150
120
90
60
30
0
Growth of UK industrial production
1700
1750
1800
1850
1900
1950

1 Until the mid-18th century, human population and wealth increased very modestly. Then the application of power to industry, particularly noticeable in Britain, increased productivity. This produced capital surpluses that, when applied to farming, mining, and transportation, diffused the rise in productivity. Population increases followed improved hygiene and living standards.

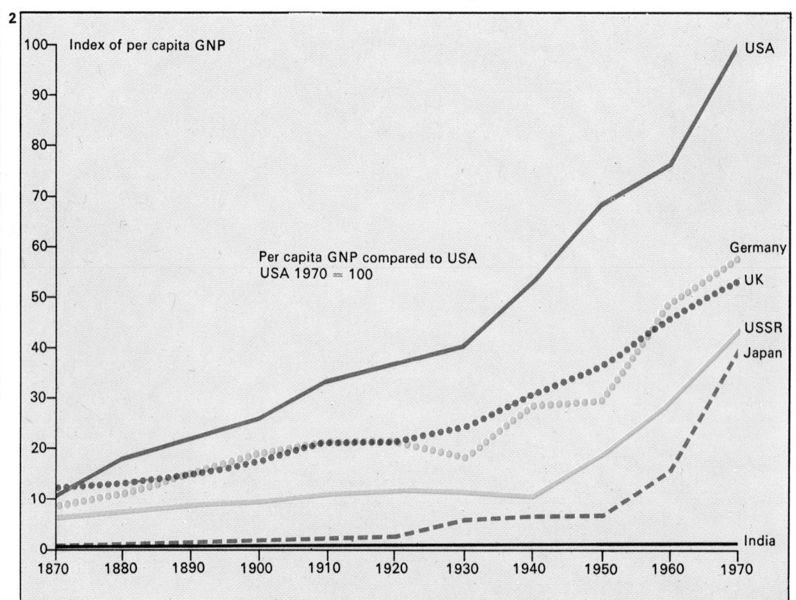

Index of per capita GNP
Per capita GNP compared to USA
USA 1970 = 100
USA
Germany
UK
USSR
Japan
India
100
90
80
70
60
50
40
30
20
10
0
1870
1880
1890
1900
1910
1920
1930
1940
1950
1960
1970

2 Rates of growth vary widely between nations. A mature, relatively wealthy economy may not show the same rate of growth as a poor but emergent one, but in absolute terms its growth may be much greater. Since 1950 the additional income available each year to the United States has been greater than the total national income of India. In the 20th century, growth rates have ranged from the slow climb of India and Brazil to the spectacular increases in Germany, Japan, and the USSR, but the hardships imposed on the peoples of totalitarian states to attain growth would be unacceptable in democratic societies.

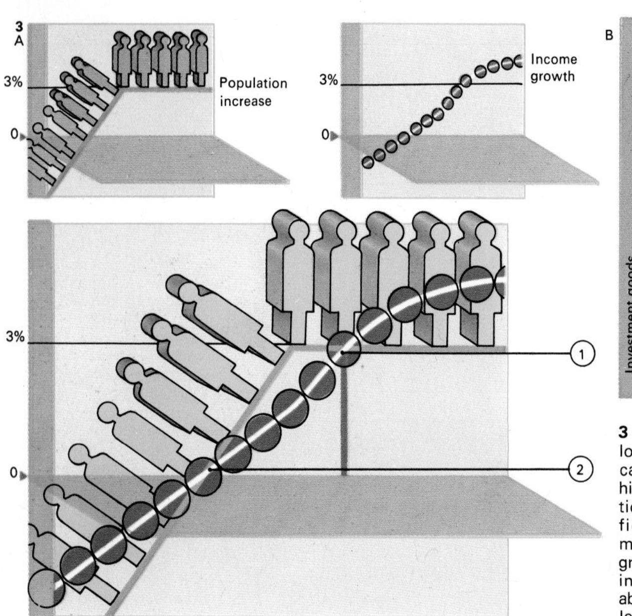

3
A
3%
0
Population increase
Income growth
1
2

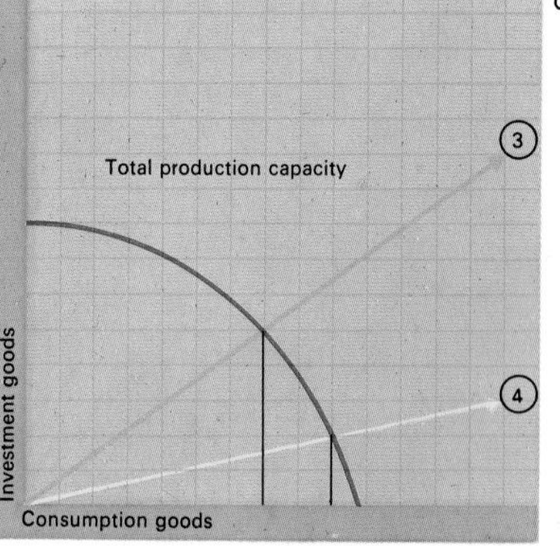

B
Total production capacity
Investment goods
Consumption goods
3
4

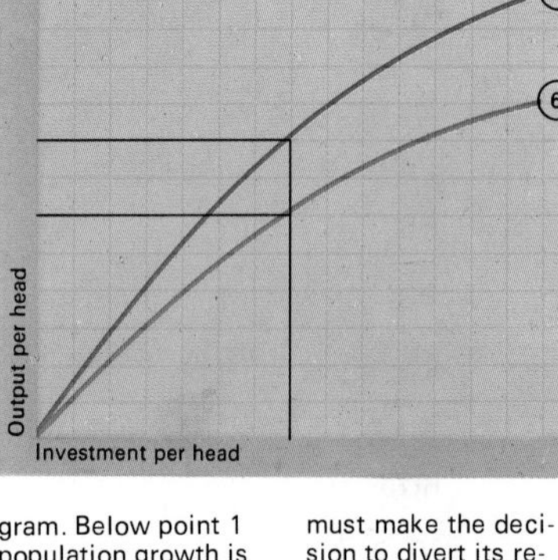

C
Output per head
Investment per head
5
6

3 Poor countries with low levels of per capita income and high rates of population growth face difficulties in development. Population growth [A] rises as incomes increase above subsistence level [2] up to an average high rate of 3% where it becomes steady. To close the widening gap between population increase and the per capita income curve, growth in total income has to be accelerated to point 1. This can be achieved by a massive saving and investment program. Below point 1 population growth is faster than income growth, and per capita income will fall back to subsistence. Beyond point 1 there can be a continuing increase in per capita income. To move to a higher rate of growth a country must make the decision to divert its resources [B] so as to produce more investment goods [3] at the cost of consumption goods [4]. The effect of technology [C] is to increase the output achieved per head [5] at each level of investment [6].

somewhat better off—but less so than have the richer countries giving the aid [2]. It is estimated that even now less than 10 percent of world income accrues to the poorer half of the world.

The attempt to create higher economic growth in low-income areas involves the transfer of both capital and technology—the one helping the other [4].

With the best of intentions, an advanced country giving aid tends to offer its highest technology. As the result, the underdeveloped world is dotted with large-scale plants that are difficult to link with general economic development. More "intermediate" technology that can be grafted into less developed economies should be applied [7]. But this is not necessarily available, because the techniques may have been abandoned by the more advanced countries 50 years before. The dramatic rise in petroleum prices in the early 1970s created new difficulties for the poorer nations. Despite these problems, per capita incomes have been rising at 3 or 4 percent per year in the less developed world.

Growth in population and production

Since the mid-eighteenth century the world has experienced growth in both population and production, principally as a result of the discovery and application of better technology [1]. At the beginning of the nineteenth century economic ideas, especially those put forward by the English economists Thomas Malthus (1766–1834) and David Ricardo (1772–1823), suggested that the world was destined to become a stationary economy with population growth limited by disease and malnutrition among poorer peoples, and capital investment limited by falling profit rates and an upward surge of rents. These views overlooked technology, the application of which has enabled man to increase income levels and provide profit to pay for increasing capital investment, and which has raised the productivity of labor and expanded resources of usable land and available minerals. Perpetual exponential growth is impossible, however, and there are signs that technology has only postponed the appearance of the spectre of Malthus's ideas [8].

KEY

INTERNATIONAL MONETARY FUND
GATT
ILO
UNESCO
F A O
FIAT PANIS
ITU

Economic cooperation has flourished since the end of World War II. International organizations like those whose symbols are depicted here provide its institutional framework.

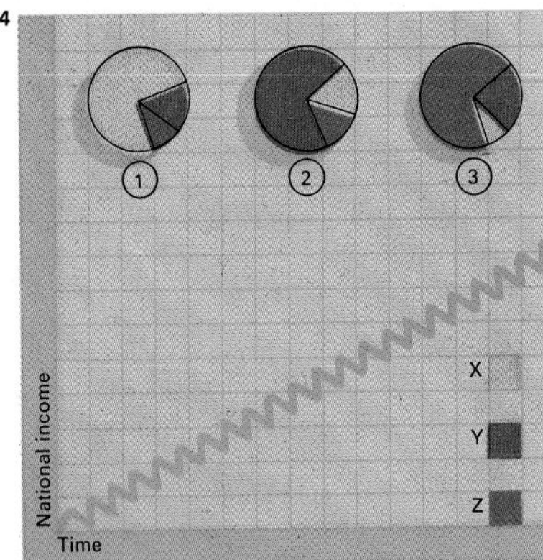
1
2
3
X
Y
Z
National income
Time

4 As a country's national income grows steadily over time, the economy passes through three stages. In underdeveloped societies [1] agriculture [X] is the dominant activity and source of income. As the economy develops [2] manufacturing industry [Y] grows. Finally [3] the service industries [Z], which include such activities as entertainment, social welfare, and transportation, become more important.

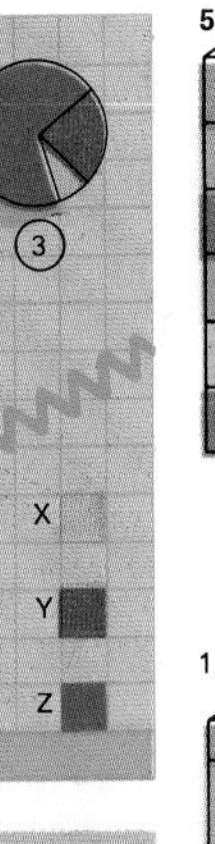
Agriculture
Industry
Construction
Trade
Transport
Others

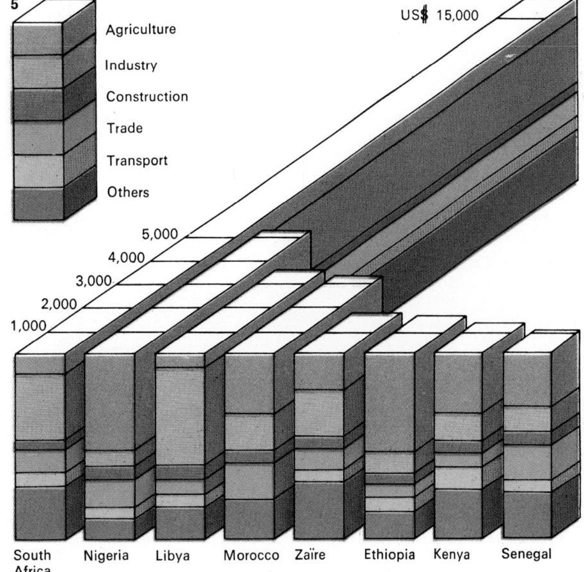
US$ 15,000
5,000
4,000
3,000
2,000
1,000
South Africa
Nigeria
Libya
Morocco
Zaïre
Ethiopia
Kenya
Senegal

5 The output of goods and services produced internally by a country (the gross national product) is indicative of that country's economic state. Shown here is the composition of the gross national product for eight representative African countries and the value of their GNP expressed in millions of dollars. The countries have been chosen to represent different areas of the continent: oil-rich Libya and less-developed Morocco in North Africa; Nigeria and Senegal in West Africa; Zaïre in Central Africa; Ethiopia and Kenya in East Africa; and, of course, the very wealthy country of South Africa.

6 Abu Dhabi shows the ironic contrast between a sterile desert surface and the fabulous wealth of buried oil that has transformed the minute population of herdsmen in the oil sheikhdoms into some of the wealthiest citizens of the world. The question now is whether the technology of oil exploitation can be developed to provide an adequate living for the citizens after the oil has been exhausted. Will they become within 50 years a series of Middle East Switzerlands, earning their living by providing services? Or is it possible that these countries will become nations of investors living on the huge dividends from other countries' industry that they will have amassed by 2050? Their wealth poses new questions.

7 The need in developing countries is for technology that is appropriate to local conditions. An example of such "intermediate" technology is this pedal-operated cassava grinder in Nigeria, made from old bicycle parts. Although less prestigious than expensive imported machinery, it is ideal for countries where labor is plentiful and spare parts, trained personnel, and foreign exchange are scarce.

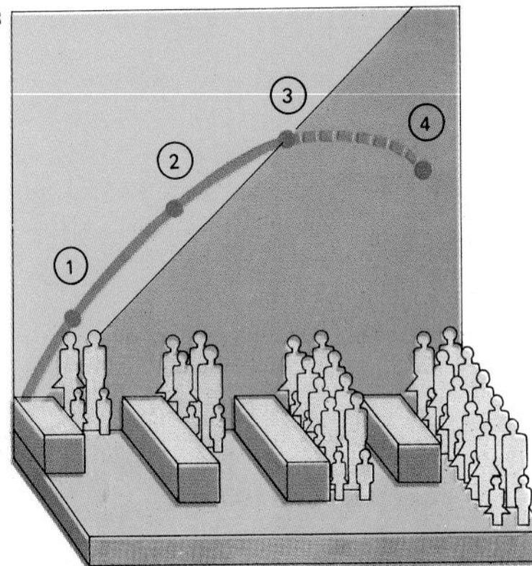
1
2
3
4

8 The Malthusian theory of population attempts to explain the relationship between the size of population [horizontal axis] and the level of output [vertical axis]. As output rises [1, 2] above subsistence [light blue], so does the population. But as more marginal land is brought into production, output falls [4] below subsistence [dark blue]. At 3 equilibrium is reached. The boxes represent the total amount of goods to be shared by the population.

HIC HAROLD MA

HISTORY AND CULTURE

HISTORY AND CULTURE

by Professor Christopher Hill

The word "history" is ambiguous. On the one hand, it means everything that has ever happened in the past; on the other, it refers to what has been written about what is known of the past. History in the first sense is unknowable in its totality. A man living in a small village does not know what goes on behind its hedges; most of what has happened to most of humanity is irrecoverable. We could argue about how much this matters, but the fact is surely indisputable.

History is, therefore, an uncertain discipline. The survival of evidence is often quite haphazard. If we study the distant past, the evidence of archeology seems random although it may be true that artifacts like the pyramids and Stonehenge were built to survive and so tell us a good deal about the aspirations of those who planned their erection. But this does not help us to knowledge of those who actually built them, who may or may not have shared the ideological concerns of their social superiors. In later centuries, as we get written or printed evidence, we appear to know more about what life was like. But writing may be used to conceal or distort as well as to reveal; printing has thoughout most of the history of most countries been subject to censorship. And again, what happens to survive may give a very lopsided view.

Historians of the present generation are increasingly conscious of their ignorance and of the possibility that much of written history is misleading and superficial. The vast bulk of our surviving evidence, until the last few centuries, derives from ruling-class and governmental sources. No sociologist would feel that he could express useful views on what the United States was like after talking only to a Treasury official and a professor of art history. Yet much of the evidence from which we write the history of the last 2,500 years is as flimsy as that. Consequently, all historians have to guard very carefully against falling for "the illusion of the epoch," against accepting at face value the assumptions of ruling classes and intellectuals of the past. The reason why we think of the Middle Ages in Western Europe as "an age of faith" may be only that those who knew how to write were almost exclusively ecclesiastics.

Master of Balliol College, Oxford University (England); Honorary Member of the American Academy of Arts and Sciences; author of *God's Englishman: Oliver Cromwell and the English Revolution; Lenin and the Russian Revolution; Intellectual Origins of the English Revolution; The World Turned Upside Down,* etc.

In our century of the common man we have become embarrassingly aware of how little we know about the lives of ordinary people until relatively recently. About women and children—three-quarters of the human race—we are even more ignorant. We can know a few members of the ruling class as individuals in classical Greece or Rome, in Chaucer's or Shakespeare's England. It is virtually impossible to achieve such knowledge about the bottom 80 to 90 percent of the population until we approach very modern times. So if we are not merely to repeat historical mythology—the self-selected, self-justifying legends of past ruling classes—we are up against great difficulties.

It is not a matter only of ignorance; there is probably a great deal of real distortion in many of our sources. Most of what we know about ancient and medieval heresies and witchcraft, for instance, comes from men so prejudiced against heretics and witches that they were prepared to torture and burn them to death. Most surviving accounts of slave revolts in antiquity and of peasant revolts in the Middle Ages come from men utterly devoid of sympathy with the rebels' causes. Nor is it only a matter of literary sources, in which the bias is often so obvious that it can be allowed for. Historians of an earlier generation cherished the view that if we could only get behind literary sources into the archives, to government documents, then we should be on firm ground. There is, of course, a sense in which this is true. A tax is a tax: government archives can tell us how much was collected and when. But the more that governmental archives are opened up, the more aware historians become of the truth in William Blake's dictum: "Nothing can be more contemptible than to suppose public records to be true." Their apparent objectivity is frequently spurious. Contemporary civil servants, aware that their archives will soon be opened up to the historian, naturally take steps to remove any evidence that they do not wish posterity to see; anyone who has worked in the government can give examples of this.

But it is not only a matter of deliberate suppression. What is involved is also the unconscious assumptions and prejudices of the administrators, who are no more immune from national and class bias than the authors of "literary sources." Professor G. R. Elton's *Policy and Police: The Enforcement of the Reformation in the Age of Thomas Cromwell* gives a mass of fascinating evidence about what ordinary people thought and said in the 1530s—but it is ordinary people seen by those trying to govern them. We have little reason to suppose that the lower classes had any more sympathy with the objectives of their governors than the latter had with theirs; the lower we go down the social scale, the less confidence the central government had in its subjects. The events of 1640 to 1660 in England showed how justified this lack of confidence was, but it should make us skeptical of the views of government officials.

Similarly, a historian has argued recently that, since there is no evidence in ecclesiastical archives that the Pilgrim Fathers were persecuted, the Mayflower Pilgrims must have had some other reason for braving the terrible journey across the Atlantic to unknown shores in 1620. There are many stories of atrocities, or alleged atrocities, in the present century where the official version suggests that the victims and eyewitnesses grossly exaggerated. We smile at the story of the French general who was discovered amid scenes of catastrophic retreat in March 1918 dictating a dispatch describing his successful advance. When questioned, he replied, "Mais—c'est pour l'histoire." But suppose his dispatch happened to be the only document that survived? His side won the war, after all, and throughout most history the defeated leave little evidence.

Whatever we think about the specific examples I have cited, it is clear that official documents are no more going to tell us the whole story than diaries, private letters, and other unofficial sources. Edward I of England circulated to monasteries his own version of his controversy with Scotland in order to get it into the chronicles. Official handouts about the deposition of Richard II deceived eminent 19th-century historians of medieval England. Under Mary I the records were weeded out in order to eliminate evidence of heresy. Almost any official document arising from any government department is engaged in making a case. It therefore omits some facts and arbitrarily emphasizes others. What it leaves out is no doubt well known to contemporary readers, less so to the historian.

The historian's job is to piece together the bits of evidence that happen to survive and to make what sense he can of them. He must approach all his sources with a great deal of skepticism: the fact that a document is official does not mean that it is impartial; the fact that a document has remained unpublished for 500 years may simply mean that it was not worth publishing. Superstitious belief in manuscripts, in archives, can be as misleading as naïve acceptance of accounts of historical events written by participants in order to justify themselves in the eyes of posterity.

What I am saying is perhaps less alarming than it may appear. The factual background of most written history is secure enough. No future discovery is likely to shake our belief that a Norman invading army defeated King Harold's troops near Hastings in 1066, that the American colonies declared their independence in 1776, or that Napoleon lost the Battle of Waterloo. But what the Normans were doing there, what ordinary people thought in 1066, 1776, or 1815—these are matters on which we are still largely ignorant.

Some progress has been made. Application of anthropological and sociological techniques has enabled the *Annales* school of French historians, and historians like K. V. Thomas and E. P. Thompson in England and Eugene Genovese and Alfred Young in the United States, to cast light on hitherto dark and mysterious areas. We are becoming aware that until the coming of industrialization—and perhaps later—magical beliefs and practices dominated the lives of the population. Religious and other beliefs about which we hear a great deal in traditional sources may in fact have mattered very little to the mass of the people. Historians no longer speak glibly about "ages of faith," are no longer surprised that the bastardy rate was higher in Puritan England than in the Catholic France of the 17th century.

Too many historians who believed they were being "objective" were merely ignoring the distorting lenses through which they observed past history. It is easier for a present-day academic to enter into the mode of thought of a bureaucrat in ancient Egypt or 18th-century England than it is for him to imagine how ancient Egyptian peasants or 18th-century American farmers felt. For this reason there was a short-lived reaction against some of the great trail-blazing writers who opened up the history of ordinary people—R. H. Tawney, G. D. H. Cole, and the Hammonds in England, Carl Becker and Vernon Parrington in the United States. The pioneers made mistakes, but these can be corrected. More important, they wrote with imagination and they were skeptical of official attitudes, and this remains of permanent value.

Here we come up against the question of the historian's commitment. He is likely to write better history if he thinks it matters. He may be able to avoid reproducing the illusions of past epochs—mainly ruling-class illusions—if he asks questions that derive from his own society. (He may, of course, introduce the illusions of his own epoch, but, since it is very different from most past epochs, the danger, although real, can be avoided.) What is important is that the historian be aware of what he is doing and make clear to his readers what he is doing. This seems better than thinking one is being objective when one is merely blinkered. The historian must be skeptical of his sources—*all* his sources. He must learn to live imaginatively in the society about which he writes.

History, it has been well said, offers a series of answers to which we do not know the questions. The historian's difficult job is to reconstruct the questions from the recorded answers. This is easier to do when the questions are obviously brash and new—the French Revolution was a question for British radicals; Darwin's *The Origin of Species* was a question for Victorian evangelicals. But historians still argue about the nature of the questions to which the French (or English, or American, or Russian, or Chinese) Revolution was the answer. Most difficult to reconstruct are the questions that were taken for granted by those who answered them or the questions whose novelty is obscured by later events. If a man becomes or stays a Baptist or a Quaker today, for example, the questions include his conviction of the truth of the doctrine of the sect and may include his desire to please or to shock his parents and friends. In the later 17th century we should have to add a question about readiness to endure persecution. But it is much more difficult to be certain what questions George Fox and John Bunyan were answering, even though they wrote so much about themselves, for in their case there was no clearly agreed body of doctrine to be taken or left; and, since each of them was the first of his family to be converted to his faith, there was no question of pleasing his family or friends—although there may have been a question about displeasing them. It is hard to reconstruct the questions that faced men in the 1650s, to which they produced answers deceptively similar to the answers which 18th-century Quakers or Baptists gave. But the initial answer, that of Fox and Bunyan, presupposes a very special type of question; the later answers are to different, perhaps simpler questions.

Any serious history, it seems to me, deals with questions. The answers, the narrative, are known. The narrative can be rearranged, but the true originality of the historian lies in

identifying questions that seem new to us because they approximate the questions men and women were originally answering.

If I am right in so defining the historian's job, this would help to explain why history has to be rewritten in every generation. New bits of experience in the present open our eyes to questions that men had to answer in the past. Consider the attention recently given by American historians to the history of blacks, Indians, women, and children, as well as to the popular "neutralism" in the American Revolution. His experience in the present helps the historian to sharpen and refine his account of the questions being answered in the past. If history has any use, it is in deepening our awareness of the process by which society sets questions that men and women, willy-nilly, have to answer.

Today—by contrast with most of the past—the questions set are not wholly out of our control. The more we comprehend the question-setting process, the greater the hope of our being able to change the questions so as to get the right answers. For we ourselves participate in setting the questions, even if only by passivity, by allowing the present questions to be set.

The English philosopher R. G. Collingwood adjured historians to "think the thoughts of the past." A better, if clumsier, way of expressing it might be to identify the questions that were set to the men and women of past ages. This is less idealistic (in the philosophical sense), for the questions are set by society—or by the historical process, if you like. The historian is not primarily interested in the random thoughts of the past; he has to be selective. His concern should be to identify the major questions that men were in fact answering when, for instance, they executed Charles I, established the protectorate of Oliver Cromwell, and restored Charles II.

The sort of thoughts that Collingwood believed to be important were those that passed through Caesar's mind when he crossed the Rubicon. Crossing the Rubicon has, however, become rather a dangerous obsession for philosophers of history. What matters is not what was actually passing through Caesar's mind at that moment, for this is surely unknowable. The important question is the one to which the act of crossing the Rubicon was an answer, the question posed by the political and social setup of Roman society, which Caesar and his armies were about to recast. The question is vastly complex, and only a historian who knows a great deal about Roman civilization in the 1st century BC can even approximate formulating it correctly. It may be that Caesar never consciously asked himself the question to which crossing the Rubicon was the answer, but his actions answered it nevertheless. "Reasons and opinions concerning acts are not history," Blake observed. "Acts themselves alone are history."

The historian's task, then, is to discover the questions that men and women of a past age were answering and to formulate them in the closest possible approximation of the way in which contemporaries would have formulated them if they had been conscious historians. It would have sounded quite boring and pretentious if I had started with that sort of definition of history, but I hope it makes sense now. The good historian must above all be a questioner. He must question the assumptions of the past and of previous historians; he must question his own assumptions and prejudices; and he must force the past to yield up the questions that were being asked, the problems that were being set, as they were experienced by the person who lived in the period he is studying. The broader his sympathies, the more he is likely to succeed in this imaginative task.

The art of prehistory

The human aesthetic sense seems to have developed recognizable forms of expression about 30,000 years ago, as the modern human form annihilated, displaced, or absorbed Neanderthal Man. The detectable differences between these two sub-species of human being are confined to a heavier bone structure in the Neanderthal. But other differences in behavior and adaptation to the environment can be guessed at from archeological evidence; a predisposition to create art is one of them.

The "childhood of art"

With few exceptions, all of the world's earliest art is associated with the hunting economy of *Homo sapiens sapiens* [Key]. Neanderthal man had developed ritual, perhaps religion, and the practice of ceremonial burial of the dead, but not a way of expressing himself pictorially that has survived. Nevertheless, the earliest art, which is found in caves in southwestern France and northeastern Spain, is of some sophistication. When the art of this Upper Paleolithic period (35,000–10,000 years ago) was first discovered in 1875, it was received with incredulity—"It is the childhood of art, but not the art of a child," said one eminent French archeologist—and until 1900 many regarded it with suspicion. Marcelino de Sautuola (died 1888), the discoverer of the great halls of Altamira in northern Spain, was charged with having forged the paintings and it was not until other paintings were discovered in the French sites of Pair-non-Pair and La Mouthe, concealed beneath Paleolithic cultural deposits, that the skeptics were forced to recant.

The man who finally demonstrated the antiquity of Paleolithic art, and who became the doyen of the subject for the succeeding half century and more, was the Abbé Henri Breuil (1877–1961). He proposed an evolutionary scheme for the development of the art, but current archeological evidence suggests that its appearance was more sudden and full-flowering.

The evidence for Paleolithic art is more or less confined to western Europe, although isolated sites such as Kapova in the Urals of Russia, Levanzo in Sicily, and Beldibi and Belbasi in Turkey exist; and there is a lively tradition of rock-art in northern and Saharan Africa at places such as Tassili [5,6]. Paleolithic art is divided by archeologists into two major categories—parietal, consisting of paintings, engravings, and sculptures on the roofs, walls, and floors of caves from which they cannot be removed; and mobiliary, consisting of small portable objects. To the archeologist each type has its advantages and its frustrations; cave art, while often undatable, is in its original position and context, while mobiliary art is often in well-dated archaeological layers but without any context that might shed light on its use. Mobiliary art consists of single isolated figures, cave art of many adjacent figures, sometimes related to each other.

Distribution of cave art

Cave art is confined to a small area of France and Spain: the Dordogne valley, the high Pyrenees, and the Cantabrian mountains. More than 100 caves are known, including such famous sites as Lascaux [1],

CONNECTIONS

See also
952 Beginnings of agriculture
956 The Sumerians 4000–2006 BC
652 From ancient to modern man
1812 Color chemistry
1586 The stone Age

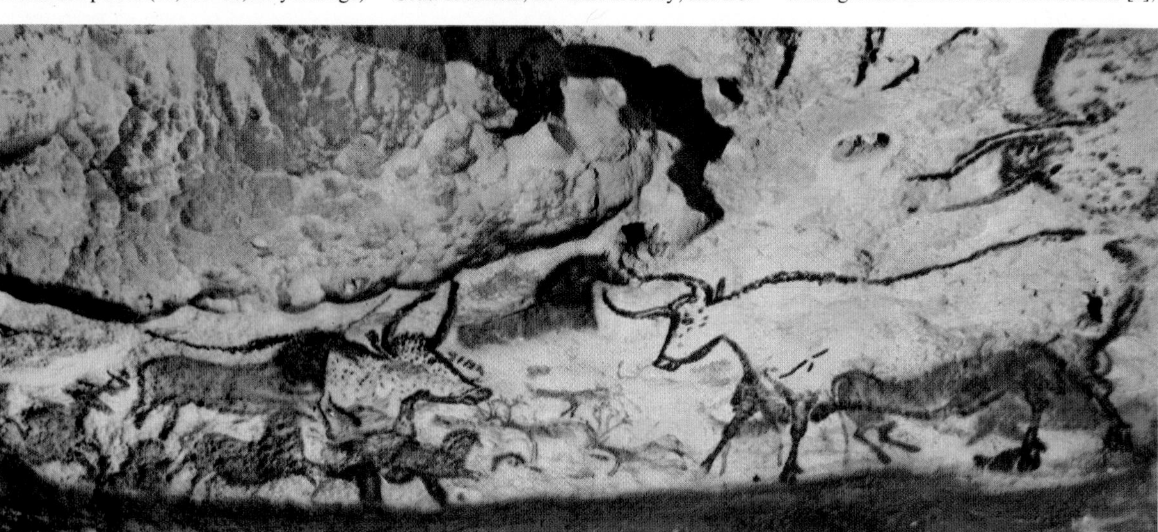

1 **The famous animal paintings** in the cave of Lascaux are in a style similar to the parietal art found at many other sites in the Dordogne district of France. The cave was found accidentally in 1940 by a group of boys and is one of the most recent of Paleolithic cave art finds. Most of the animals in this portion of the Lascaux paintings are aurochs, or European bison *(Bos primigenius)*, which became extinct in Poland in the 17th century. They are drawn so that all four legs and both horns are visible.

2 **A wall of the cave of Pech-Merle** in France shows two spotted horses with more spots surrounding them and heads and necks in solid color. The bodies are full, the limbs attenuated, a feature of much Paleolithic art. The two horses overlap and were clearly painted at different times, but whether hours or centuries apart is not known. There are also handprints made by blowing powdered pigment around a hand.

3 **The small limestone figurine** known as the "Venus of Willendorf" from a Gravettian site in Austria is 20,000 to 25,000 years old. The large breasts, belly, and buttocks are typical of this form of mobiliary art.

4 **Engraved figures** from the cave of Addaura in Sicily show humans in a variety of poses; overlapping suggests that they were not all done together. Engraving, with painting and low relief sculpture, is typical of the Upper Paleolithic.

Altamira, Les Trois Frères, Montespan, and Font de Gaume. In few of these, however, has the art been firmly dated except by its style, and the art at Rouffignac has often been challenged as fraudulent.

On present evidence the earliest dated site is that of La Ferrassie, where painted blocks were found in Aurignacian culture levels dating from about 29,000 years ago. Other paintings and engravings and bas-relief sculpture were found in higher Aurignacian levels, and thus the three major techniques of parietal art are all found from the earliest period onward. Sites such as Pair-non-Pair may date from the late Aurignacian or the early Gravettian period about 25,000 years ago, while Gargas in the Pyrenees has been identified as definitely of the Gravettian period.

The brief Solutrean culture, confined to the same area as the cave art and noted for its superb flint work, has art at Le Roc de Sers. A reindeer-hunting final Paleolithic phase in western Europe, the Magdalenian, gave birth to the astonishing polychrome paintings of Altamira.

Mobiliary art is also found from the Aurignacian onward, as an adjunct to the increasing use of bone and antler for toolmaking. The best-known class of object is that of the so-called Venus figurines, stylized females with the buttocks, breasts, and belly overemphasized and the head and legs reduced to stumps. The Willendorf Venus [3] is more individual than most. The Venuses date mainly from the Gravettian and like it are distributed through eastern Europe, even as far east as Siberia.

Art or magic?

A number of explanations have been advanced for cave art, the simplest of which is that it is "art for art's sake." The theory of Breuil, accepted for many years, was that it was connected with obtaining magical power over the animal hunted by drawing it and also with the totemic association of humans and animal species. Some scholars are using comparisons with the more recent rock art of the Kalahari and the Australian Aborigines to cast light on the prehistoric human mind.

KEY

A group of warriors, hunters, or dancers ornament a cave called Cingle de la Mola Remigia in the Gasulla Gorge of Castella province, Spain. The naked figures of running men are painted in a monochrome grey-black. Each man carries a long bow and a sheaf of arrows – standard hunting (and presumably also fighting) equipment during the late glacial period when this cave was decorated.

5

6

5 These striding men are painted on rock in the Tassili plateau of Algeria in the heart of the Sahara. The figures themselves are shown in solid color and attention is focused on the decoration covering their limbs and bodies, probably representing body-painting with natural pigments, a practice continued today by the Nuba of Sudan. Body art may well have existed in the Paleolithic period.

6 Tassili art persisted into the Neolithic period or later, after the camel had been domesticated, as is shown by this painted scene on the wall of a cave in the Tassili Plateau at the site of Ir Itinen in Algeria. The figures in solid red depict a camel caravan and its drivers, and the camels include both loaded adult animals and, lower left, what appear to be younger camels.

7

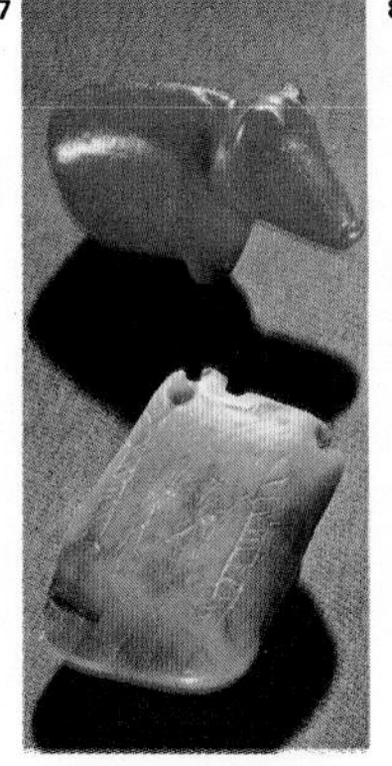

8

9

10 A

B

7 These small amber carvings, including a stylized rendition of a bear, are from Siberia. Amber, a fossil resin found mainly on the shores of the Baltic Sea, was used by people from the Mesolithic period of 10,000 years ago onward.

8 A shrine dating from 6000 to 7000 BC has been reconstructed at the Anatolian Neolithic site of Catal Hüyük in Turkey. This site has claims to being one of the world's earliest towns, with a population of thousands. During excavations, many animal shrines dedicated to the herds on which the economy depended were found, decorated with elaborate paintings and modeled reliefs. The shrines and houses seem to have been entered through the roof.

9 Rock engravings found in the Val Camonica, northern Italy, date from the Bronze Age. Some of these open-air carvings, which are pecked into smooth glaciated rock surfaces, show elaborate scenes, including chieftains in procession. This example (filled with colored pigment to assist photographic visibility) depicts three reindeer and two schematic human figures. Their significance is unknown, and the variety suggests many motives.

10 Scandinavian rock engravings from Bohuslan and Grēvenvaenge in Denmark are similar in technique to the Val Camonica carvings and are of a later date. They depict a long ship [A] with three human figures and perhaps a mast and steering oar as well; and two warriors [B] in great horned helmets brandishing battle axes. The presence of a smooth rock surface presented an irresistible challenge to prehistoric artists throughout Europe and in Asia Minor.

Beginnings of agriculture

Until the Neolithic or New Stone Age the domestication of plants and animals was little practiced. Agriculture developed at different times and rates in different places, and took various forms: plant cultivation, pastoralism, and mixed farming. Although the switch from total dependence on food gathering to the beginnings of food production was a gradual evolution, its long-term effects were nothing short of a revolution. Every food plant and animal of importance today was domesticated during the Neolithic Age.

The first farmers and herdsmen

Early in the eighth millennium BC, cereals were cultivated and animals herded between latitudes 30° and 40° N, over an area stretching for a thousand miles from Anatolia to Iran [1]. This region offered a variety of wild plants and animals that could be domesticated. Early inhabitants found wheat and barley growing on the uplands and goats [4] and sheep grazing on the slopes. Indeed, the wide variety of ecological zones and natural resources would have enabled hunters, fishermen, and food-gatherers to live a semi-sedentary life after the end of the last Ice Age, about 8000 BC.

Initially, the growth of agriculture and herding was slow and haphazard. Wild grain would have been collected and dropped around the settlement, and hunters probably captured young animals and brought them home. In these early stages of farming it is not easy to distinguish between wild and domesticated flora and fauna. Animals evolved smaller forms, and there were gradual changes, for example in the size and shape of horns. From the number of bones unearthed at Zawi Chemi Shanidar in northern Iraq, it seems that sheep may have been herded on the Iranian plateau as early as 8500 BC and goats not long after.

Evidence of cereal cultivation is harder to prove; cereals are preserved only in exceptional circumstances. Grain carbonized as a result of fire, or impressions left in clay ovens or storage pits, are often the only clues that remain. It is known, however, that selection, promoted by some significant mutations, resulted in higher-yielding grain. Some of the evidence provided by Neolithic sites may be purely circumstantial—the discovery of sickles need not necessarily imply cultivation; sickles could have been used to gather wild grain. Using stone-bladed reaping knives [5], one family would have been able to collect enough wild wheat in three weeks to last it a whole year.

Early Neolithic settlements

Most of the early Neolithic sites were located near springs and were occupied for thousands of years. Enormous mounds or "tells" accumulated from the remains of mud-brick houses and generations of rubbish provide archeologists with a rich store of information. One of the most thoroughly investigated sites is Tell es Sultan at Jericho, which must have housed as many as 3,000 people during the "Pre-Pottery" Neolithic period around 7000 BC. Catal Hüyük in Anatolia, the largest known trading center, was four times the size of Pre-Pottery Jericho by 6000 BC and may have been a sizable settlement much earlier, although

CONNECTIONS

See also
950 The art of prehistory
956 The Sumerians 4000–2006 BC
884 Origins of civilization
304 History of agriculture
370 Farm stockbreeding and management

1

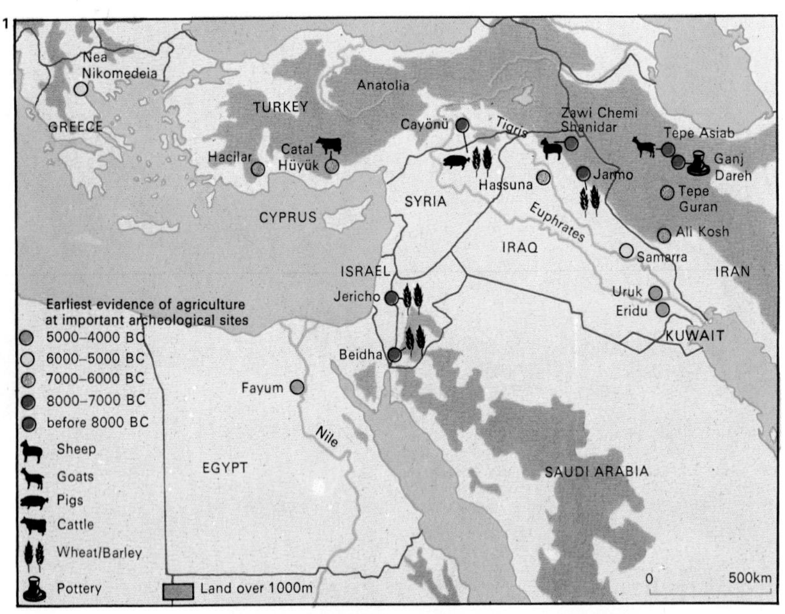

Nea Nikomedeia
GREECE
TURKEY
Anatolia
Hacilar
Catal Hüyük
Cayönü
Tigris
Zawi Chemi Shanidar
Tepe Asiab
Ganj Dareh
Jarmo
Hassuna
Tepe Guran
SYRIA
CYPRUS
Euphrates
Ali Kosh
IRAQ
Samarra
ISRAEL
IRAN
Jericho
Uruk
Eridu
KUWAIT
Beidha
Fayum
Nile
EGYPT
SAUDI ARABIA
Earliest evidence of agriculture at important archeological sites
5000–4000 BC
6000–5000 BC
7000–6000 BC
8000–7000 BC
before 8000 BC
Sheep
Goats
Pigs
Cattle
Wheat/Barley
Pottery
Land over 1000m
0
500km

2

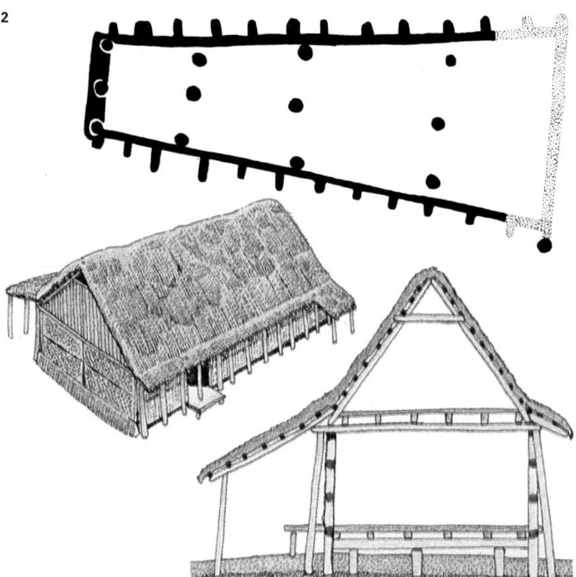

1 The main area of food production stretched from the Zagros mountains in Iran to the Taurus mountains of Anatolia and down the Jordan Rift. Earliest signs of herding are in Iran *c.* 8500 BC. Irrigation was carried out in the Tigris/Euphrates basin *c.* 5000 BC.

3

3 Tassili N'Ajjer, in Algeria, a 500-mile (800-km)-long eroded sand-stone plateau in the Sahara, contains tens of thousands of rock paintings and engravings. The cattle and wild animals that flourished in the equable climate about 3000 BC are superbly depicted, but no other evidence exists to help identify the ancient inhabitants.

2 The long houses of central Europe and Scandinavia are known of from the first half of the 5th millennium BC. The one shown here is a reconstruction of an excavation at Deiringsen-Ruploh in West Germany. It was over 52ft (16m) long, about 26ft (8m) wide, and the same in height. Long houses were normally rectangular, but the trapezoidal shape (as here) seems to have been a recognized variant. Many long houses appear to have been divided in two, but whether this was to separate living quarters from storage is not known. They were constructed on a timber frame.

4

4 The bezoar *(Capra hircus aegagrus)*, the wild ancestor of domesticated goats still lives in the mountains of south-western Asia. Goats and sheep were kept in herds before 8000 BC, the first animals to be domesticated.

5

5 Grain was first harvested with sickles made from stone insets in a bone or wooden shaft. This example comes from Egypt.

the earliest levels have not yet been excavated. It probably had a monopoly of nearby sources of obsidian, the chief material for tool-making; copper and marble were also obtained from the mountains and shells from the Mediterranean. Pottery, weaving, and other arts and crafts reached a high standard. Religious beliefs centered on the worship of a fertility goddess, depicted in plaster reliefs, and a cult of the dead: wall paintings show vultures hovering over headless human corpses. The dominant theme in the shrines, however, was the bull, symbol of virility.

Reasonably secure in their settlements and supported by an agrarian economy, Neolithic populations increased rapidly. With irrigation—which may have been introduced at Jericho—it was possible to expand into the lowlands of Mesopotamia. A settlement at Hassuna in the north dates from before 6000 BC, and a thousand years later the alluvial plains of the Tigris/Euphrates were being exploited at Eridu in the far south. Mesopotamia became the center of Neolithic culture, laying the foundations for Sumerian civilization.

Meanwhile, food production spread from Anatolia to Greece and on into Europe. Land cleared by slashing and burning enabled agriculturalists to exploit the fertile soils of the Danube basin; and at the same time the megalith builders [12] were moving around western European coasts.

The staple crops of different cultures

The civilizations of western Asia and Europe were founded on wheat and barley, which are adapted to temperate climates and the sub-tropics, while millet and rice are better suited to the tropics. Rice was cultivated in India earlier than in China, where millet was the main crop (and the pig the main domesticated animal) until about 2000 BC. In sub-Saharan Africa edible tuber cultivation may have preceded that of cereals (millet and sorghum), although there is no conclusive archeological evidence. The evidence of numerous rock paintings shows that about 3000 BC pastoralists were able to find grazing all over the Sahara [3]. In Mexico corn was cultivated by 5000 BC.

KEY

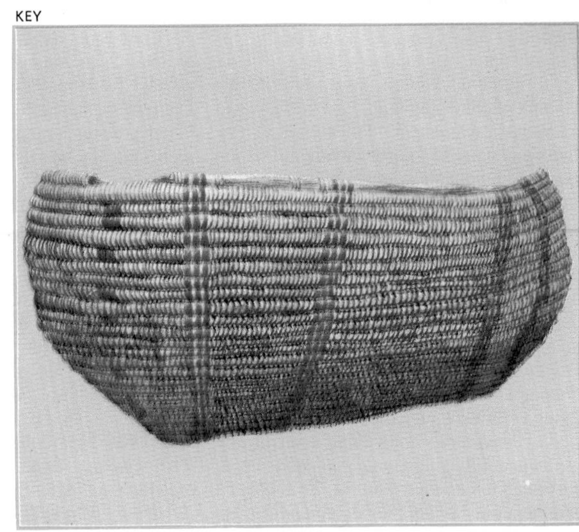

Wheat and barley were the staples of Neolithic economy in the Middle East. By about 4500 BC these cereals had spread from there to Egypt. This 16-in (40-cm)-long basket is made of coiled flax and may have been used for sowing. It was discovered in a grain storage pit in the Fayum, Egypt.

6 Skara Brae, in the Orkney Islands, was occupied by herding and fishing people around 1800 BC. As there was no wood on the island, houses and furniture were made of stone. One village included eight connected huts, each with a hearth, two slabs for beds, and a bureau and wall cupboards.

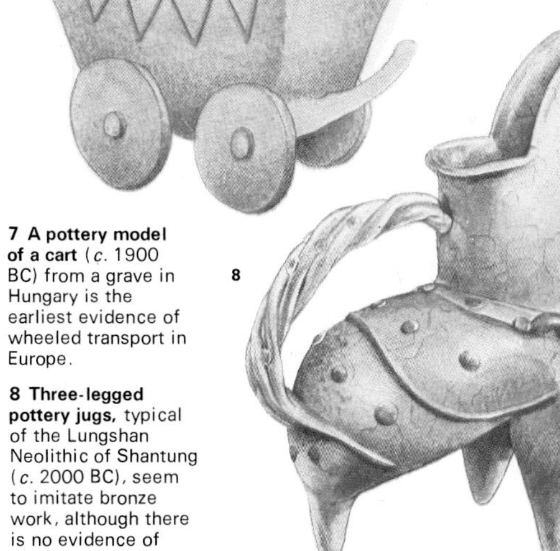

7 A pottery model of a cart (*c.* 1900 BC) from a grave in Hungary is the earliest evidence of wheeled transport in Europe.

8 Three-legged pottery jugs, typical of the Lungshan Neolithic of Shantung (*c.* 2000 BC), seem to imitate bronze work, although there is no evidence of earlier bronze pieces.

9 This beaker from Siyalk, Iran, was made about 4000 BC, by which time the potter's wheel was in use. The earliest Neolithic settlements in western Asia have no pottery, the first appearing about 7000 BC. In Japan Jōman pottery predates agriculture by several millennia.

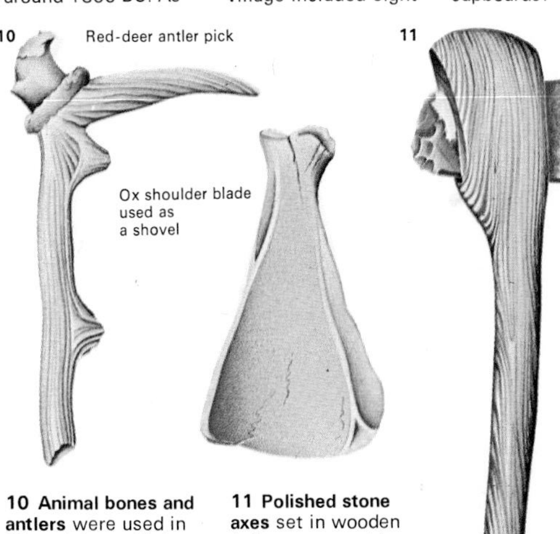
Red-deer antler pick
Ox shoulder blade used as a shovel

10 Animal bones and antlers were used in flint mining, which was an important Neolithic industry in western Europe. At Grime's Graves, England, shafts were sunk through the chalk and galleries tunneled to reach the flint layers.

Neolithic flint axe

11 Polished stone axes set in wooden hafts were used for forest clearance and carpentry. The flints and other rocks used for these highly efficient tools were shaped in "ax factories." Their provenance tells us much about trade routes.

12 Mnajdra, one of the many fine megalithic temples in Malta, is trefoil-shaped and dates from the early copper age (*c.* 2800 BC). The first colonists of the island arrived from Sicily about 4000 BC. A thousand years later, collective burials in rock-cut chambers eventually gave rise to elaborate temples unique to Malta. Built of huge upright slabs surmounted by corbelled blocks, they are often decorated with carvings. There was a cult of the dead, with altars for animal sacrifices; corpulent female statues indicate the worship of a mother-goddess. The megalithic tradition extended from the Mediterranean around the coasts of western Europe.

Early western Asia

The term "Western Asia" is applied to the area occupied by modern Turkey, Syria, Lebanon, Israel, Jordan, Iraq, and Iran; the Arabian Peninsula; and sometimes Afghanistan. In antiquity the center of the stage was occupied successively by Sumerians, Babylonians, Assyrians, and Persians. The Hittites, Hebrews, and Phoenicians also played their part; and Elamites, Hurrians, Urartians, and Arameans—to name only some of the best known—were in the wings. Their civilizations were mostly lost to knowledge after their fall; their recovery was long delayed by restricted access to and exploration of their lands.

The development of writing

Rapid advances in knowledge came in the mid-nineteenth century AD, very much as a result of the decipherment of the Old Persian cuneiform script [Key], which through trilingual inscriptions (Old Persian, Babylonian, and Elamite) provided the key to the immeasurably greater bulk of Assyrian, Babylonian, and Sumerian texts in cuneiform writing of a more difficult kind.

Cuneiform developed from the pictographic script first used by the Sumerians in southern Mesopotamia late in the fourth millennium BC. The Sumerian language fell largely into disuse early in the second millennium, but the cuneiform script in which it had been written was used by the Sumerians' political and cultural heirs, the Babylonians, to express their own Semitic language, known as Akkadian, although it was entirely different from Sumerian. Other speakers of Akkadian, in particular the Assyrians, also used cuneiform. The same script, with relatively minor variations, was used elsewhere in western Asia to express other quite different languages, such as Hittite, Elamite, Hurrian, and Urartian; and the same principle—varying groups of cuneiform (wedge-shaped) impressions—was used for the simpler Old Persian script of the Achaemenid Empire and for the alphabetic script of the Phoenicians, which was the ancestor of the Western alphabets.

The excavation and study of the cuneiform-inscribed clay tablets and of similar inscriptions on stone and other materials were stimulated by the announcement in 1872 of the decipherment of an Assyrian version of the biblical story of the Flood on a tablet found at Nineveh in northern Iraq. Understanding other cuneiform inscriptions was made easier by the Semitic character of the Akkadian language in which many were written—it was related in varying degrees to such known languages as Hebrew, Aramaic, and Arabic. The information provided by the inscribed material (nearly all in cuneiform, but with additions particularly from Old Testament Hebrew, Aramaic, and hieroglyphic Hittite) has been supplemented by surface discoveries and, particularly for the prehistoric (generally pre-writing) periods, by excavation.

The geographical background

There are significant geographical variations in the territories covered by the ancient civilizations of western Asia. The coastlands of the Black Sea and the Mediterranean give way more or less steeply to the Anatolian plateau of central

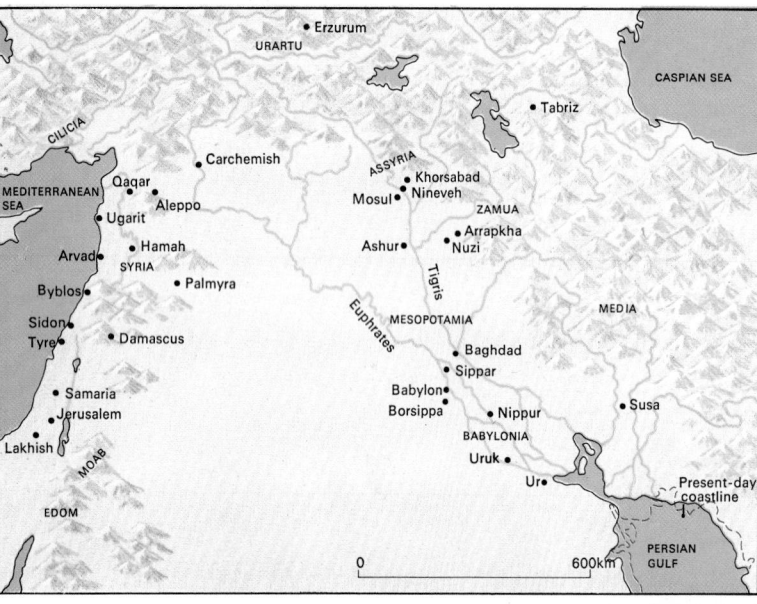

CONNECTIONS

See also
956 The Sumerians 4000–2006 BC
958 The Babylonians 2000–323 BC
976 The Hittites 1700–1200 BC
978 The Phoenicians 1500–146 BC
980 The Assyrians 1530–612 BC
982 The Hebrews 1200–322 BC
984 The Persian Empire of the Achaemenids

Erzurum
URARTU
CASPIAN SEA
Tabriz
CILICIA
Carchemish
ASSYRIA
Khorsabad
Nineveh
Mosul
MEDITERRANEAN SEA
Qaqar
Aleppo
Ugarit
ZAMUA
Arrapkha
Nuzi
Ashur
Hamah
Arvad
SYRIA
Byblos
Palmyra
Tigris
Euphrates
MEDIA
Sidon
MESOPOTAMIA
Tyre
Damascus
Baghdad
Sippar
Samaria
Babylon
Borsippa
Jerusalem
Nippur
Susa
BABYLONIA
Lakhish
MOAB
Uruk
Ur
Present-day coastline
EDOM
PERSIAN GULF
0
600km

1 **The drama of ancient western Asia** was centered on the riverine plains and adjacent hills and mountains between the Mediterranean and the Caspian seas and the Persian Gulf. The area was dominated by the Tigris and Euphrates, the land between them being Mesopotamia, but the term is used loosely for a wider area around the rivers. The silt they and their tributaries produced and the water diverted from them by irrigation helped the growth of the towns and later that of the capitals of Babylonia and Assyria, whose power and conflicts provided the framework for the history of their decline in the 7th and 6th centuries B.C.

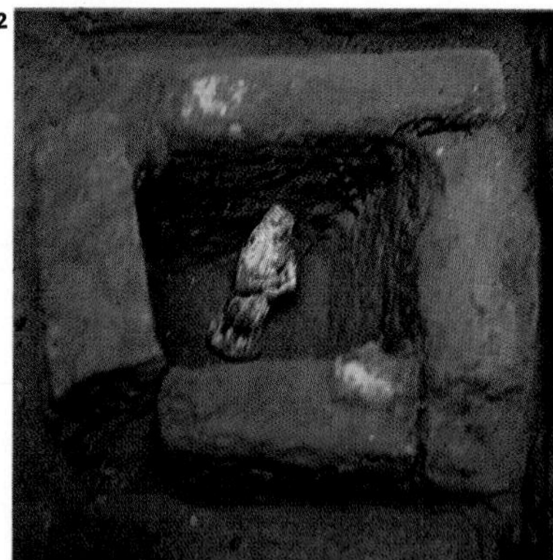

2 **A sun-dried clay figurine** from a ninth-century BC palace at Nimrud in northern Iraq bears the inscription, impressed in the clay on the back in Assyrian cuneiform, "Come in, favorable demon; go out, evil demon." Such figurines lay in the brick-built foundation-boxes that are commonly found in the corners and beside the door jambs of important Assyrian buildings of the first millennium.

3 **A main route** from Trabzon and the eastern Black Sea coastal area of Turkey leads southward up the 6,560ft (2,000m) Zigana Pass, which is open for most of the year. The route continues through high, mountainous country to Erzurum, Tabriz, and Teheran, thus serving as a northwestern gateway to Armenia and Persia. It also provided a trade route between those lands and places accessible by ship from Trabzon. The Persian "Royal Road" between Susa in Persia and Sardis in the west used a more southerly route through Diyarbakir and Ankara, where the going was easier. The lands south of Trabzon are typical of much of eastern Anatolia.

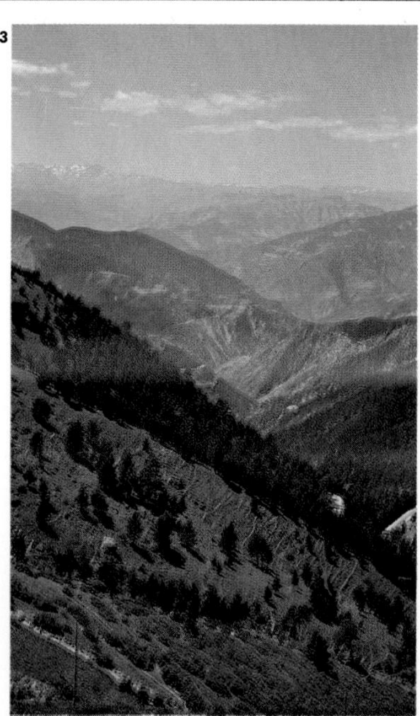

4 **The wheel** was probably invented in Mesopotamia during the fourth millennium. At that time it was constructed not of rings with spokes but of solid circular disks of planks clamped together, with a "tire" of broad-headed nails driven into the outer rim. Spokes came later. The earliest type of wheel still survives in remote areas; this one, for example, is found in a small village in eastern Turkey near Lake Van. Although many notable monuments, including the pyramids, had been built without the wheel, its introduction greatly facilitated farming and transport and proved central to the spread of Mesopotamian civilization.

Turkey, mainly watered—around its central desert—by rivers flowing toward those two seas. The Hittite capital, Hattusas, lay within the bend of the Kizil Irmak River in north central Anatolia.

In the south, the Taurus range impedes the way up from the Cilician plain, while in the extreme east and northeast, high ranges—including Mount Ararat, 16,945ft (5,165m) high—restrict movement and cradle the sources of the Euphrates and Tigris. These two rivers, after flowing westward initially, both turn southeast to form most of the Fertile Crescent, watering the plains of Mesopotamia where the capital cities—notably Babylon, Ashur, and Nineveh—of major empires were built [1]. To the west of Mesopotamia lies the desert, and still farther west are the Jordan and Orontes valleys and eventually the Mediterranean coastland. East of Mesopotamia, valleys wind through the harsh mountains of the Zagros [3] to the dry Iranian plateau where the Elamite capital Susa and the Achaemenid Persian capitals Pasargadae and Persepolis were located.

Early man in western Asia

Excavations have shown that the settlements of prehistoric man in some of these areas date back to as early as 9000 BC. Agriculture began sometime later. The cultivation of grain assured a steady food supply, which led successively to expanding populations, release of labor for pursuits other than food-producing, specialization in craft, trade, government, and religion, and so to the development of civilized societies.

Wild cereal plants grew over much of western Asia, and their cultivation seems to have come first in the highland zones, notably in the Zagros mountains of eastern Iraq and western Iran and on the south Anatolian plateau. But as the grain-producing capacity of an inhabited area was bound to be a major factor in accelerating or retarding human development, the fertility of the Tigris and Euphrates valleys, particularly with the addition of artificial irrigation from those rivers and from their main tributaries, gave the predominant prosperity in western Asia to the civilization of the Mesopotamian and southern plains.

KEY

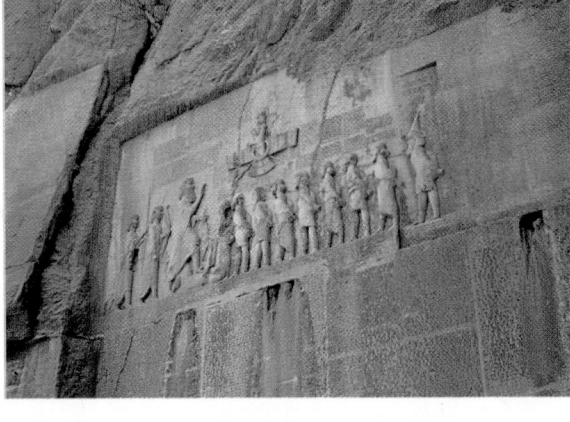

The Bisutun Inscription, carved on the face of a rock in western Iran, was deciphered in 1835 by the English archeologist Henry Rawlinson (1810–95). It is in three languages: Old Persian, Babylonian, and Elamite. Its decipherment offered the key to all cuneiform texts. The bas-relief sculpture shows Darius the Great of Persia (*r.* 521–486 BC) receiving homage from the nine chiefs he defeated to become king of Persia. The adjacent rock faces bear 11 short cuneiform inscriptions identifying Darius and his foes, with a long trilingual inscription.

Original c. 3500 BC	Simplified c. 3000 BC	Archaic Sumerian	Old Babylonian	Assyrian	Neo-Babylonian	Meaning
						Fish
						Ox
						Donkey
						Grain
						God/ heaven
						Sun/ day/ light
						To till/ plough
						House
						Man

5 Sumerian writing probably evolved from the needs of public commerce and administration. As the Sumerian city-states developed, records were needed of goods moving in and out of the towns. Clay or gypsum tags were originally attached to objects and bore a seal-impression identifying the owner; line drawings of the objects followed. Drawings were gradually simplified to signs. Later the sign for a common word such as *ti* (arrow) was used for "ti" sounds generally. (*Ti* also meant "life.") The shift to phonetic representation led to written symbols for entire languages.

6

6 Fragments of ivory boards were found covered by sludge at the bottom of a well in a royal palace at Nimrud. The boards usually had a raised margin around a recessed portion that probably contained a mixture of beeswax and pigment as a base for a cuneiform text. This unrecessed board carries Sargon's name and the title of the "book" of omens taken from celestial observations.

7

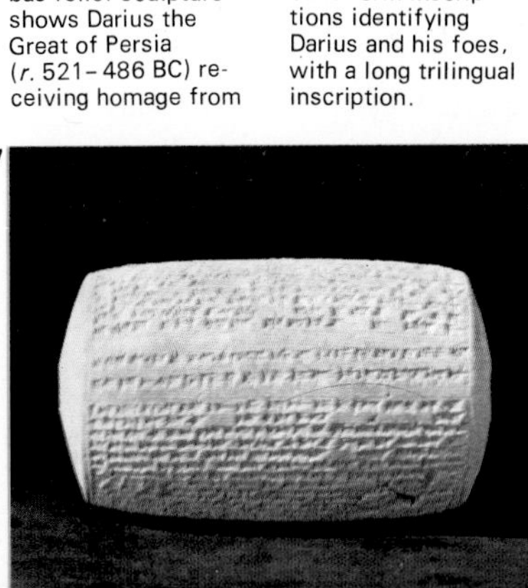

7 Hollow "barrel cylinders" of clay were sometimes used by the Assyrians for recording texts in cuneiform. This one, about 6.7in by 4in, refers to Esarhaddon and gives a general summary of his conquests and achievements. It also tells of a new palace with beams of cedar from the Amanus mountains and "doors of sweet-smelling cypress wood." It dates from about 670 BC.

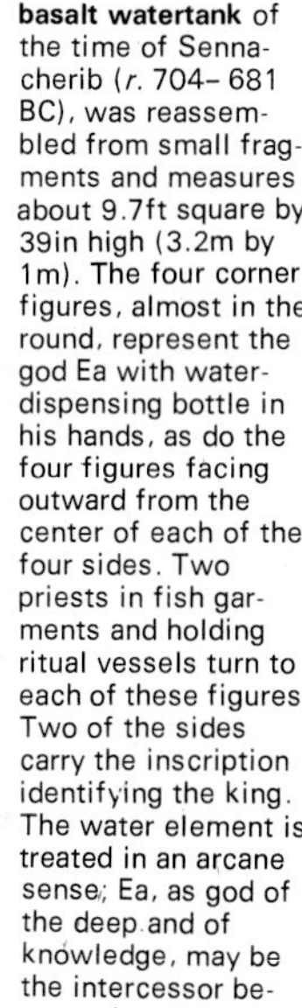

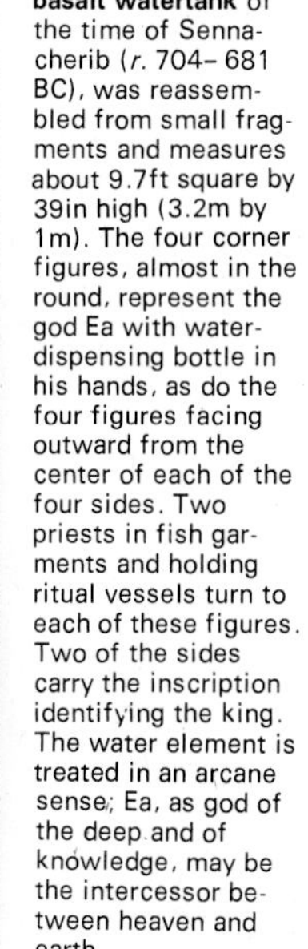

8 This monolithic basalt watertank of the time of Sennacherib (*r.* 704–681 BC), was reassembled from small fragments and measures about 9.7ft square by 39in high (3.2m by 1m). The four corner figures, almost in the round, represent the god Ea with water-dispensing bottle in his hands, as do the four figures facing outward from the center of each of the four sides. Two priests in fish garments and holding ritual vessels turn to each of these figures. Two of the sides carry the inscription identifying the king. The water element is treated in an arcane sense; Ea, as god of the deep and of knowledge, may be the intercessor between heaven and earth.

The Sumerians 4000–2006 BC

The partial excavation of the city of Eridu, about 12mi (19km) southwest of Ur of the Chaldees, the biblical home of Abraham, has produced the earliest settlements so far discovered in Sumei, vindicating the Sumerians' tradition of the antiquity of Eridu—they thought of it as the first of the five cities that existed before the Flood. Subsequent predynastic periods of settlement, spanning more than the fourth millennium BC, are named after the relevant sites: Ubaid, Uruk, and Jamdat Nasr.

The earliest dwellings at Eridu apparently consisted of reed huts and of mud-brick houses. The subsequent predynastic periods produced, successively, painted pottery, boats for fishing and slings for hunting, flint-headed hoes and hard-baked sickles, writing and the potter's wheel, the plow and the chariot, sculpture in the round, and vessels of silver, copper, and lead.

Cuneiform writing appeared in the Uruk period, a little before 3000 BC. Whether the Sumerians brought it with them or developed it in Sumer is not certain; but there is no doubt that they invented the art.

The coming of the Flood

The list of Sumerian kings includes a number of monarchs before the flood, although their position in the archeological framework and their history are unknown. Whether the Flood of Sumerian and Hebrew tradition is represented by the barren strata of silt found at Ur, Kish, and Shuruppak is far from certain. One Ziusudra of Shuruppak, whom we are told survived the Flood, is famous from the *Epic of Gilgamesh* as the man who preserved the seed of living things and was immortal; but it was at Kish that "kingship was restored to earth" after the Flood. Semitic names appear for the first time in written history among the kings of Kish.

Little else is known of these kings. Leadership passed after a struggle to the famous Gilgamesh of Uruk [8] and from his successors there to the First Dynasty of Ur. The names of some verified monarchs belong to this period, as does probably the splendid royal cemetery. Of two vaults at the bottom of a deep shaft, one (partly plundered) presumably contained the king's remains and the other those of a Queen Shub-ad (or Pu-abi) lying on a bed, magnificently adorned and accompanied by female attendants. Charles Woolley (1880–1960), the excavator, thought that the attendants had been buried alive, taking poison from little bowls in the shafts.

Priceless treasures survived in these and the other major graves: golden harps, bull-headed lyres, a golden dagger with lattice sheath, gold and silver florally decorated combs, golden bowls, huge boat-shaped earrings, thousands of beads in gold, silver, and carnelian, and much more; as well as the so-called royal standard of Ur [5].

Early Dynastic period

Very little reliable information survives about the history of the period following the First Dynasty of Ur, except at Lagash, where the royal line was inaugurated by Ur-Nanshe, whose power is attested by buildings, works of art (some archaic and crude), and inscriptions (including references to cargoes of timber arriving from the Persian Gulf) that give the impression of

CONNECTIONS

See also
958 The Babylonians 2000–323 BC
952 Beginnings of agriculture
960 Egypt: the Old and Middle Kingdoms
968 China to 1000 BC
954 Early western Asia
886 Ancient states and empires

1 Mount Ararat, on which, according to the book of Genesis, Noah's Ark came to rest after the Flood, appears also in Sumerian tradition. The name is probably more correctly vocalized as Urartu, the name of a Sumerian kingdom to the south of the mountain during the earlier part of the first millenium BC. The armies of this kingdom pressed long and hard on parts of the northern frontier of Assyria.

2 Most of the Fertile Crescent was made up of the lower reaches of the Euphrates and Tigris rivers. In the northern parts of this region there was some rainfall and natural fertility, and in the plains of Sumer and Akkad in the southeast crops were encouraged by the silt of the rivers and by elaborate irrigation works. The need for these was early recognized by the area's civilizations.

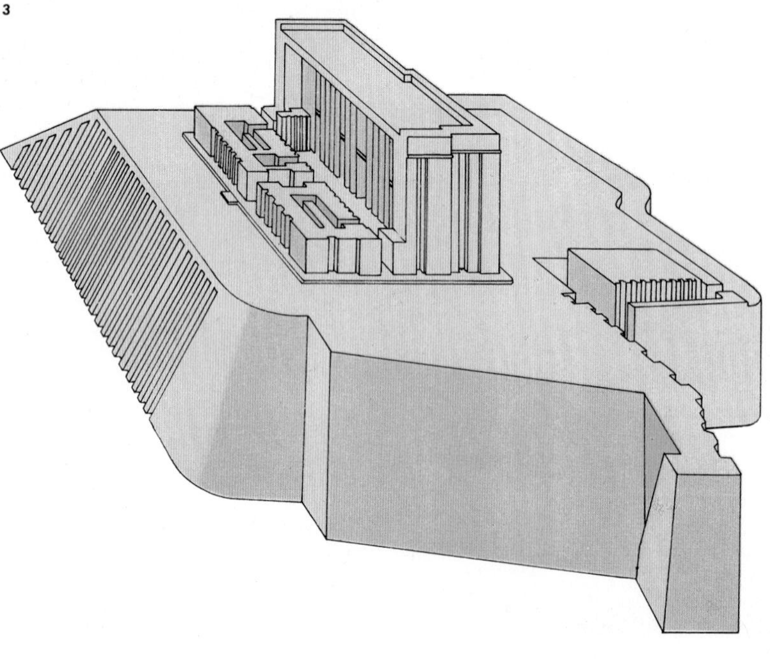

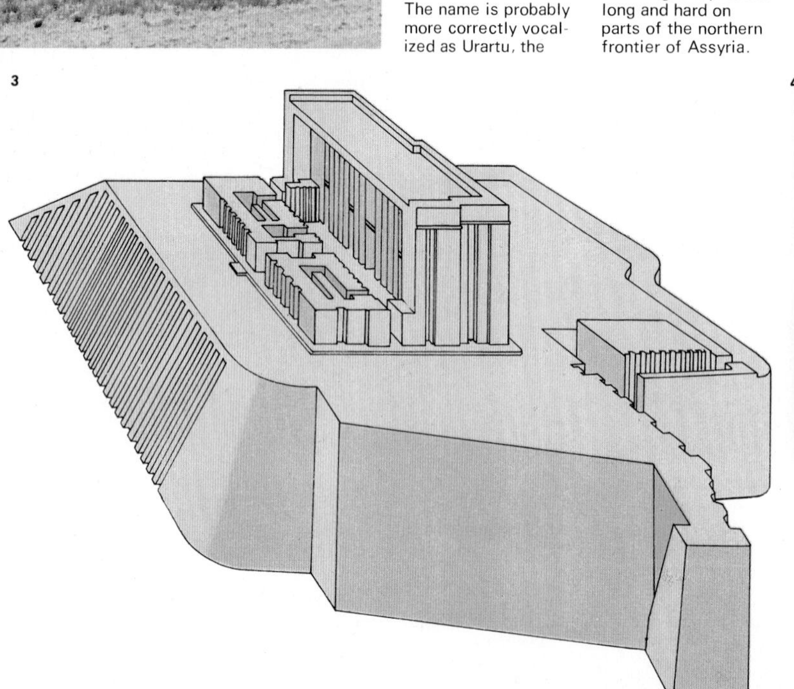

3 Temple architecture dating from about the end of the fourth millennium is best represented by the White Temple at Uruk, an irregular mound shrine that was probably an ancestor of the later, more regular ziggurats. The White Temple, approached by three ramps, was built of sun-dried bricks, whitewashed and buttressed. It had an altar inside; the building's corners pointed to points of the compass. The ziggurat, a many-staged temple tower, may have been an attempt to bridge the gulf between man and the gods. It was strongly felt that man should offer residence to a deity. The tower may have bolstered belief in contact with such superhuman powers.

4 Gudea of Lagash, shown here, was the son-in-law of Ur-Baba, who brought to his city enough wealth to undertake extensive public works. He also patronized a school of sculptors who soon began to produce masterpieces in hard stone. Gudea himself left cuneiform inscriptions describing the religious observances and daily life of his time. He also enumerated the timbers and ornamental stones used in rebuilding the house of his god Ningirsu.

inexperience in the use of writing. His grandson Eannatum rose to a supreme position in Sumer and defeated Mari, on the Euphrates in the northwest, and Subur, perhaps in the north.

The history of the rest of the Early Dynastic period in Lagash, and indeed in the whole of Sumer, is largely poorly attested, except for Urukagina (reigned *c.* 2378–*c.* 2375 BC), who with a surprising political maturity instituted social reforms—some apparently intended to lighten burdens imposed on the population by governors and priests. He fell to Lugalzaggisi of Umma, who in turn fell, after a successful reign, to the great Sargon of Akkad (reigned *c.*2360–*c.*2316 BC) [7].

Sargon the Great, King of Akkad

Sargon rose from obscurity to overthrow Lugalzaggisi and to subdue the rest of Sumer, Syria, perhaps part of Asia Minor, and much, apparently, of the mountain area of southwestern Iran. Revolt followed, but his grandson Naram-Sin ruled for 37 years. Sargon's empire fell *c.*2218 BC to the Gutian tribes from the north or northeast, whose sovereignty left little mark on history and few monuments (although Lagash emerged to a period of great prosperity about that time under Ur-Baba and Gudea [4]) and who were expelled by Utu-khegal of Uruk. His deputy at Ur, Ur-Nammu [6], seems to have overthrown him, and so founded a new dynasty at Ur.

The dynasty of Ur-Nammu

Ur-Nammu took the title King of Sumer and Akkad. His reign was a time of considerable wealth and power, as shown by his many great building works, including the restoration of direct communication by water with the Persian Gulf. His successor Shulgi (reigned *c.*2095–*c.*2048 BC) extended his territories in the northeast and east, dealing among others with the Gutians and the Hurrians. Shu-Sin (reigned *c.*2038–*c.*2030 BC) had to face the threat of western incursion; Ibbi-Sin (reigned *c.*2029–2006 BC), who claimed victory over these Amorites (under Ishbi-Erra of Mari), later saw his city fall to the Elamites.

KEY

The Mesopotamian harvest was won only after a long struggle against fierce heat. Fertility, celebrated on this seal, took on a central religious significance, and the actions of nature were believed to be ruled by the gods.

5 A

5 The royal standard of Ur, dating from about 2600 BC, was found in one of the greatest tombs at Ur. It was apparently carried by an attendant wearing a peculiar bead headdress. One side of it [A] shows fully-manned four-wheeled chariots, perhaps referring to victory; the reverse [B] depicts domestic scenes. If it was a standard it was very small—18.5in by 7.9in—for a public display of royal wealth and success.

B

8 King Gilgamesh of Uruk had more legends told about him than any other hero of Mesopotamian history. The surviving Assyrian *Epic of Gilgamesh* was based on a much larger body of legend in Sumerian. This was so muddled that the king's career is quite unclear, although some of the stories may have been based on fact. He probably repaired a lost sanctuary at Nippur and built the city wall of Uruk.

6

6 Ur-Nammu (*r.c.* 2113– *c.* 2096 BC), King of Ur, to whom this Sumerian seal was dedicated, was probably not a great conqueror. But he did publish certain laws dealing, among other things, with sexual offenses and wrongs committed in connection with the lands of others.

7

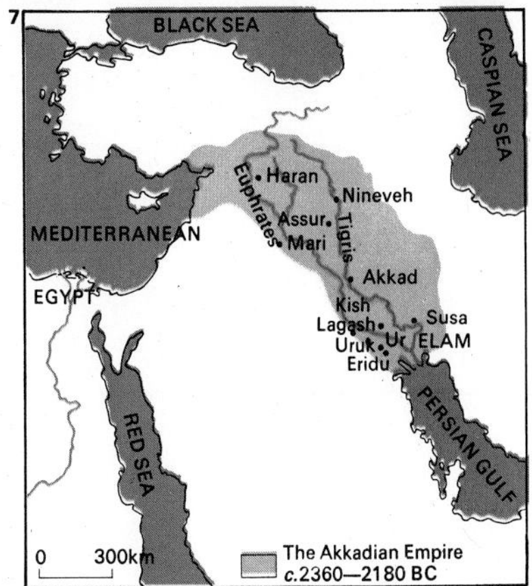
BLACK SEA
CASPIAN SEA
MEDITERRANEAN
EGYPT
Euphrates
Tigris
Haran
Nineveh
Assur
Mari
Akkad
Kish
Lagash
Uruk
Ur
Eridu
Susa
ELAM
PERSIAN GULF
RED SEA
0
300km
The Akkadian Empire
c.2360—2180 BC

7 The world's first great empire, under Sargon of Akkad, extended so far that rebellion was almost inevitable, and this occurred even before his death.

8

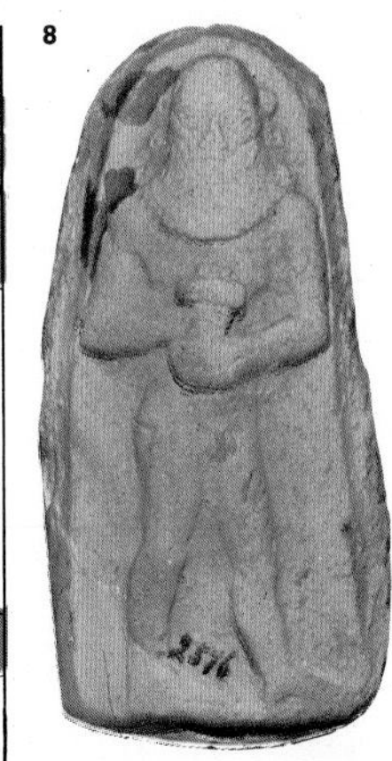

The Babylonians 2000–323 BC

The fall of Ur in 2006 BC to the Elamites allowed Semitic-speaking Amorites under Ishbi-Erra to establish a strong, independent dynasty at Isin. A few years earlier another Semitic-speaking dynasty had arisen at Larsa. The two dynasties dominated Babylonia for a century until a third power was established—unopposed by them—consisting of more Semitic-speaking Amorites at Babylon. Lipit-Ishtar of Isin (reigned *c.* 1934–*c.* 1924 BC) carried out social reforms and issued a code of civil law. A contemporary, Gungunum of Larsa, won military glory in Elam. Early in the eighteenth century BC Larsa, under Rim-Sin "the true shepherd," overcame Isin and became the sole major contender with Babylon for the domination of the land [5].

Hammurabi and his laws

The first five kings of the new dynasty at Babylon were mainly preoccupied with defensive and religious building and by canal-clearing, with little extension of territory. It was left to Hammurabi (fl: 1792–1750 BC) to engage in victorious campaigns that extended his empire from Mari on the Euphrates in the northwest to Elam in the southeast [5] and, by defeating Larsa, to succeed to the traditional kingship of Sumer and Akkad.

Apart from his achievement of this relatively ephemeral empire, Hammurabi's fame rests mainly on his code of laws [8].

No evidence has yet been found for the application of or appeal to Hammurabi's laws in contemporary documents. Their standing and function are therefore unclear. They were written in Akkadian, a Semitic tongue that had by then become the principal language of Mesopotamia. Sumerian was retained for religious use, although the civilization it expressed was absorbed by the Semites and continued to flourish.

The reigns of Hammurabi's successors were long and undisturbed and, although in the later eighteenth century BC mention was made in Babylon of the alien Kassites (probably from the Iranian plateau to the northeast, and possibly Aryans), it was evidently an attack by the Hittite king Mursilis I in or soon after 1595 BC that brought the long-remembered destruction of Babylon and the downfall of Hammurabi's dynasty. But Mursilis can hardly have contemplated permanent conquest; the void was filled by a Kassite dynasty that ruled for over 400 years.

The dark ages of Babylon

Babylonia absorbed the Kassites, and during a dark age of more than 200 years little was heard of the Babylonians. In the mid-fourteenth century BC the Kassite king married the daughter of the king of Assyria. But the alliance led to wars that resulted in the temporary conquest and occupation of Babylonia by the outstanding Assyrian soldier-king Tukulti-Ninurta I in 1235 BC. The Kassites retained Babylonia, but their dynasty fell to the Elamites in 1157 BC.

The Elamites lost political control of Babylonia before the end of the century; it passed to a second dynasty of Isin that, under Nebuchadrezzar I (reigned 1124–1103 BC), ended Elamite interference. The Isin dynasty fell after little more than 100 years of political stability. The ensuing age

CONNECTIONS

See also

956 The Sumerians 4000–2000 BC
976 The Hittites 1700–1200 BC
980 The Assyrians 1530–612 BC
954 Early western Asia

1 A

1 The great ziggurat of the moon god at Ur[A] was begun, according to King Nabonidus (*r.* 555–539 BC), by Ur-Nammu (*r.* 2113–2096 BC), but may well conceal the remains of an older tower from as far back as the predynastic period. Nabonidus says it was continued but left unfinished by Ur-Nammu's son Shulgi; Nabonidus himself improved the stairways with new treads 3 feet above the old and raised the level of the terrace. Different from the Mesopotamian ziggurats, and the largest known—328ft (100m) square—is Dur Untash in Elam [B], near Susa.

B

2

2 Lilith, with talons and feathered legs, was a Babylonian-Assyrian goddess who survived in Jewish lore into the Christian era. Traditionally a sinister bringer of death, in this clay relief she holds what may be a measuring rope to indicate the span of human life. She is mentioned in an early fragment of the *Epic of Gilgamesh,* which also gives some independent corroborating evidence for the biblical flood. The profile used in narrative reliefs was less suited to representing the deity in actual rites; and reliefs over the altars of shrines show the goddess in a front view, perhaps to confront those who approach.

3

3 This Babylonian tablet, not yet fully understood, appears to be concerned with theoretical geometry. Most Babylonian mathematical texts are contemporary with the dynasty of Hammurabi; the rest are datable to the last three centuries BC. The earlier history of Old Babylonian mathematics is not known, beyond the evidence of innumerable economic texts from the earliest periods of Mesopotamian writing, whose numbering system based on 60 was retained by the Old Babylonians. But, although the content of Old Babylonian mathematics reached a level that has been compared with that of the early Middle Ages, it was elementary compared to the Greeks.

of uncertainty and civil disturbance was relieved by the inauguration of the eighth dynasty of Babylon in 977 BC.

Shalmaneser III [Key] of Assyria (reigned 858–824 BC) was called upon to help quell a rebellion in Babylonia; at the time the powerful Chaldaean tribes of southern Babylonia were first making their appearance. Wars with Assyria and anarchy at home preceded the emergence of Tiglath-Pileser III (reigned 744–727 BC) as a strong king of Assyria who at length assumed the Babylonian crown. His successor Shalmaneser V (reigned 726–722 BC) ruled both countries for five years, but Sargon II (reigned 721–705 BC) and Sennacherib (reigned 704–681 BC) both found a strong antagonist in the Chaldaean Merodach-Baladan II. Babylon's fortunes varied widely in the seventh century, until the rise of the unknown "son of a nobody" Nabopolassar (reigned 625–605 BC) inaugurated a great age of Babylonian civilization—this is the period of the hanging gardens—under the neo-Babylonian or Chaldaean dynasty.

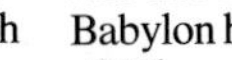

The neo-Babylonians

Babylon helped the Medes in the overthrow of Nineveh and the Assyrians in 612 BC. Nebuchadrezzar II (reigned 604–562 BC), son and successor to Nabopolassar, destroyed Jerusalem and carried off its inhabitants and erected great monuments and buildings, which made Babylon the greatest city of the ancient world. In devotion to the god Marduk he restored and beautified the Processional Way [4] along whose causeway of limestone slabs Marduk passed in effigy in the great New Year festival.

Nebuchadrezzar's son was murdered, and the decay of Babylonia accelerated under the pious antiquarian Nabonidus [1]. Babylon fell without a fight before the military genius of the Achaemenid Persian king Cyrus the Great (c.600–529 BC), who entered the city in the autumn of 539 BC. Xerxes (c.519–465BC) partly destroyed it in 482 BC. It might have been restored by Alexander the Great (356–323 BC) had he not died there. Thereafter, although its cult survived for a time, the population declined, and Babylon passed into history.

KEY

The throne-base of Shalmaneser III found at Nimrud has an inscription on the horizontal surfaces. It includes a separate section referring to the king's campaigns of 851 and 850 BC in Babylonia, in which he helped the Babylonian king defend his throne against a rebellion. This relief carving on the western vertical face shows Shalmaneser [right center] and probably the Babylonian king [left center], each with an attendant, under a canopy. They are shaking hands—a unique representation in Mesopotamian art. Whether it implies equality, Babylonian subservience, or neither, is unknown.

4 Relief bricks from Babylon, some showing bulls and mythical creatures, once formed part of the Processional Way. Like most excavated Babylonian remains, they are of the neo-Babylonian period.

5

BLACK SEA
HITTITES
CASPIAN SEA
Carchemish
Haran
HURRIANS
Aleppo
Chagar Bazar
Qatna
ASSYRIA
Assur
MEDITERRANEAN SEA
Byblos
Mari
Euphrates
Tigris
Hazor
Eshnunna
EGYPT
Babylon
BABYLONIA
Susa
Memphis
Isin
Larsa
SUMER
ELAM
RED SEA
PERSIAN GULF
0
300km
Hammurabi's Empire c. 1695 BC

5 Babylon, on the lower course of the Euphrates River, attained its greatest geographic dominance under Hammurabi, but its influence extended far beyond its borders for over 13 centuries.

8

8 The diorite stele of Hammurabi was carried off from Babylon by an Elamite invader, perhaps in the 12th century, and taken to Susa, where it was found in the winter of 1901-02. The text is topped by a bas-relief showing Hammurabi receiving the commission to write the laws from Shamash the sun god, god of justice. The Elamites apparently chiseled off parts of the text, but most of these survive on copies. It has a prologue and an epilogue in semi-poetic style.

6

6 Early clay tablets reveal the importance of sheep and goats in the economy of early Sumerian communities; they also use the signs for merchant, cattle, and donkey. The Akkadian period improved on the quality of the early tablets in the first-ever recording of a Semitic language – Old Akkadian. Their development into the tablets of Babylonia (those shown are Old Babylonian) and Assyria culminated in the calligraphy of the scribes of Assurbanipal's library.

7

7 Naram-Sin (c. 2254-c.2218 BC) of Akkad is portrayed on this stele triumphing over the eastern Iraqi king of Lullubi. The Semitic line of Naram-Sin was an interlude in Sumerian history presaging the supremacy of the Semitic Babylonians.

Egypt: the Old and Middle Kingdoms

Successive prehistoric cultures designated by the names of Badarian, Naqada I, and Naqada II have been identified from archeological remains in Upper Egypt, but remains from Lower Egypt are so scanty as to make any sound historical judgment difficult. It would appear that two distinct kingdoms evolved in Lower and Upper Egypt [1] and that the unification of the country was brought about by the victory of Upper Egypt over Lower Egypt in about 3100 BC.

The divine kings of Dynasty I

Traditionally, the first ruler of Dynasty I and the conqueror of Lower Egypt is known as Menes [2], and he is credited with the foundation of the national capital of Memphis, just south of the Nile Delta. The reigning king was regarded as the living embodiment of the falcon-god Horus and hence divine. During dynasties I and II farmers began to use the plow extensively, and irrigation was probably introduced. A national government evolved, and writing was developed.

With Dynasty III began the period known as the Old Kingdom (*c.*2686–2181 BC). The most prominent ruler of Dynasty III was Zoser, for whom the Step-Pyramid complex was built [Key]. Under Snofru, the founder of Dynasty IV, the first true pyramid was constructed; the technique of building pyramids was perfected under his successors Khufu, Khephren, and Menkaure. The construction of the pyramids [4] entailed enormous expenditure and organization, and as Dynasty IV weakened the more expensive building techniques were abandoned.

During Dynasty V the cult of the sun-god Re (Ra) regained national preeminence, and the rulers undertook the construction of solar temples. At the end of Dynasty V magical texts were inscribed in the royal burial chambers to ensure the safe passage of the ruler's spirit to the afterworld. During Dynasties IV to VI periodic campaigns were undertaken against tribesmen in the Sinai peninsula, and large-scale expeditions were dispatched to Nubia to obtain ivory, gold, and other precious materials.

At the end of Dynasty VI the growth in power of the provincial governors, the nomarchs, led to the steady weakening of the control of the Memphis hierarchy. Rival dynasties appeared in Heracleopolis and Thebes, and the country was plunged into civil war. The disorder was compounded by the infiltration of Asiatic tribesmen from Sinai into the fertile regions of the Delta.

A period of confusion ends

This chaotic and ill-documented era is known as the First Intermediate Period (*c.*2181–*c.*2050 BC). Montuhotep II of Dynasty XI, prince of Thebes [7], overcame his rivals and reunited Egypt under his rule, although the many nomarchs retained considerable power. He expelled the Libyan and Bedouin raiders, inaugurating the Middle Kingdom in Egypt (*c.*2050–1786 BC). Montuhotep II had a mortuary temple and tomb built for himself at Deir el-Bahari, opposite Thebes. Montuhotep II's descendant Montuhotep IV was succeeded by his vizier Amenemhat I, who founded Dynasty XII in about 1991 BC.

CONNECTIONS

See also

972 Egypt: 1570 BC to Alexander the Great
976 The Hittites 1700–1200 BC
980 The Assyrians 1530–612 BC
956 The Sumerians 4000–2006 BC
886 Ancient states and empires

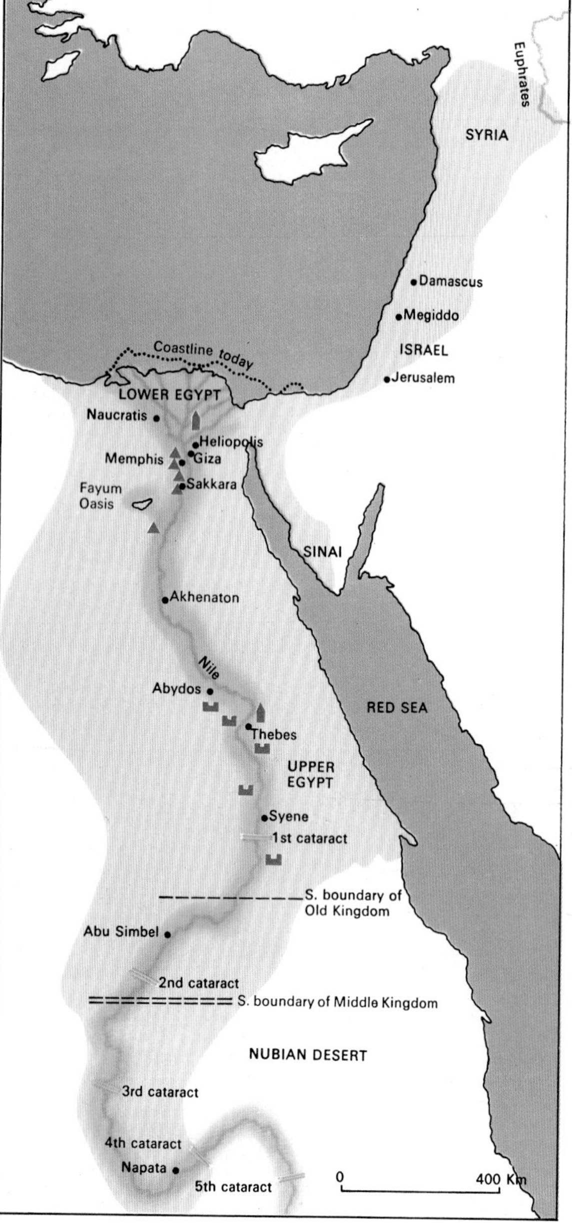

Pyramids
Obelisks
Temples
Maximum extent of Egyptian Empire (New Kingdom, c. 1450 BC)
Fertile region
Euphrates
SYRIA
Damascus
Megiddo
ISRAEL
Jerusalem
Coastline today
LOWER EGYPT
Naucratis
Heliopolis
Memphis
Giza
Sakkara
Fayum Oasis
SINAI
Akhenaton
Nile
Abydos
RED SEA
Thebes
UPPER EGYPT
Syene
1st cataract
S. boundary of Old Kingdom
Abu Simbel
2nd cataract
S. boundary of Middle Kingdom
NUBIAN DESERT
3rd cataract
4th cataract
Napata
5th cataract
0
400 Km

1 Egypt divides naturally into two areas—Lower Egypt, which consists of the Nile Delta region, and the long, narrow strip of Upper Egypt, which is confined on both sides by desert. The annual flooding of the Nile brought water for land irrigation and also deposited a rich topsoil. Egypt's agricultural prosperity was based on the river's unfailing predictability.

2 Egypt's unification was brought about by war. Victories of the early rulers are commemorated on slate palettes, such as this one depicting Menes, the first ruler of all Egypt.

3A

B

3 The monarch's public image in the Old and Middle kingdoms was widely different, a change reflected in the royal statuary. The figure of King Menkaure of Dynasty IV with his queen [A] is an idealized portrait of the god-king. The aftermath of the First Intermediate Period saw the development of a more realistic style, as in the statue of Senusret III [B].

Amenemhat I founded a new capital at Lisht south of Memphis, because Thebes was too far south to serve as an efficient capital. To strengthen his hold on the throne he circulated a spurious prophecy concerning his rise to power and appointed his son Senusret I as co-ruler. Despite these precautions Amenemhat I was assassinated after 30 years of rule, but his son managed to secure the throne. Amenemhat I had begun the conquest of Nubia, and this expansion was completed under Senusret III, who fixed the southern border at Semna. Apart from one incursion into southern Palestine no steps appear to have been taken to exercise direct control in Palestine or Syria, but strong trade links were maintained. A line of fortifications was built by Amenemhat I in Sinai to deter possible invasions. The rulers of Dynasty XII sponsored a vast land reclamation project in the Fayum area adding a new fertile province. During their reigns civilization reached a new height. A uniform system of writing was also developed at this time. The dynasty came to an end after more than two centuries of rule.

The Second Intermediate Period (*c.* 1786–1570 BC) was marked by a decline in the power of the central government. During Dynasty XIII, Asiatic invaders, known as the Hyksos, broke through the Egyptian defenses. The Hyksos eventually secured control of most of the country, with the aid of new weapons, such as chariots, and were the founders of Dynasty XV (*c.* 1674–1570 BC), although it is unlikely that they ever exercised direct control over Thebes and the south. More probably, Thebes was forced to acknowledge the supremacy of the Hyksos ruler in his new capital of Avaris in the Delta.

The invaders are expelled

The Hyksos did not rule as foreigners but adopted Egyptian titles and Egyptian culture. As their power weakened, the princes of Thebes of Dynasty XVII openly rejected Hyksos rule, and after several campaigns Kamose and his brother Ahmose, his successor, succeeded in taking Avaris and expelling the remaining invaders from the country.

KEY

King Zoser's Step-Pyramid at Sakkara, Memphis, was the first major Egyptian building in stone. It was supposedly designed by his vizier Imhotep, who was later deified.

4

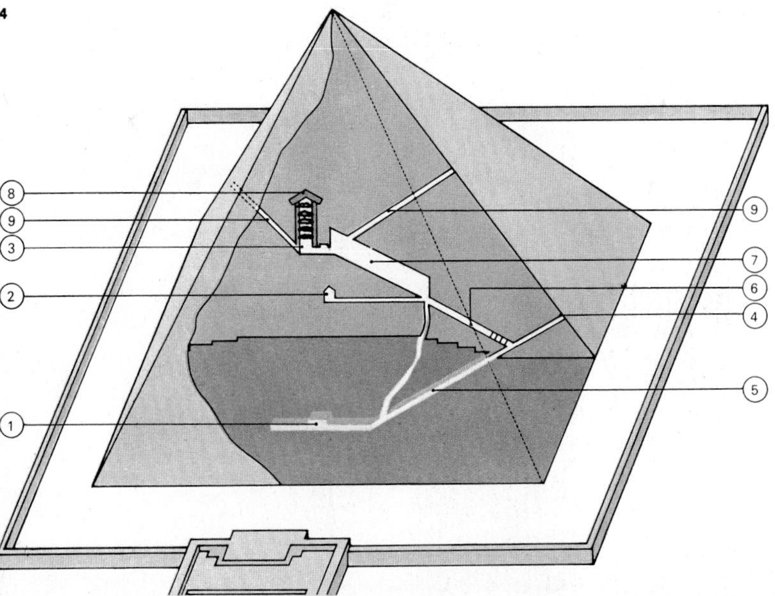

1 Subterranean chamber
2 Queen's chamber
3 King's chamber
4 Entrance
5 Corridor
6 Corridor
7 Grand chamber
8 Vault
9 Shafts

4 The Great Pyramid erected at Giza by Khufu, second ruler of Dynasty IV, is a splendid example of the art of the pyramid builder. It is built of limestone blocks and was originally faced with fine white limestone. It was approximately 480 feet (146m) in height. After two changes in plan the final resting place of the body, known as the King's chamber, was constructed of granite and approached via the Grand chamber. The sarcophagus is still in place.

5

5 Scribes, such as this one depicted in an Old Kingdom statue, were the key to the smooth functioning of the Egyptian administration. Papyrus was used for the recording of daily accounts, but few pieces have survived from this period.

6 In the afterlife the same things were felt to be required as in this life. Everyday items, even down to models of retainers like these soldiers, were therefore placed in tombs.

7

8

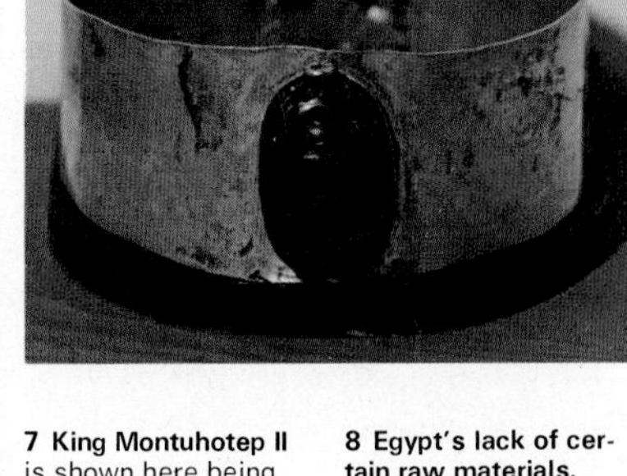

7 King Montuhotep II is shown here being embraced by Re, the sun-god, in a painted relief from the king's mortuary temple at Deir el-Bahari. The king also prepared tombs for Nefru, his sister and queen, and for several of his concubines. Later rulers of Dynasty XI built similar temples opposite Thebes on the Nile's west bank.

8 Egypt's lack of certain raw materials, notably timber, resulted in the growth from early dynastic times of a flourishing trade between Egyptian and Syrian ports. Egypt's influence in Syria and Palestine during the rich period of the Middle Kingdom is reflected in the Egyptian statuary and jewelry found in these regions.

India: prehistory to 500 BC

The earliest evidence of a literate culture in India dates from about 2300 BC, when the Indus civilization emerged from the prehistoric age. This Indus, or Harappan, civilization (named after the town of Harappa) had its principal centers in the Indus River Valley, now mainly in Pakistan, but extended west to the present Iranian border, east to beyond Delhi, and south to the Gulf of Cambay. [1]. Its main cities were at Harappa in the Punjab and Mohenjo-daro in Sind, but there were a number of smaller towns, including the port of Lothal.

The nature of settlements

The cities show advanced town planning, and the remains testify to a high and diverse material culture [2, 3]. A large part of the now fairly arid Indus valley must have been brought under cultivation to yield the surplus crops with which to feed the urban populations.

Such a sophisticated civilization required a form of writing, and thousands of steatite (soapstone) seals [Key] have been discovered. In addition to representations of animals, men, and gods these seals have brief inscriptions in pictographic script, which first responded to attempts to decipher it in 1969. The seals, some of which have been discovered as far away as Syria, were probably attached to goods by merchants.

The fall of the Indus civilization

Even less is known about the end of the Indus civilization than about its origins. After flourishing for several centuries (*c*.2300–1750 BC) with little change, it experienced a brief decline and then completely disintegrated. Although natural calamity cannot completely be excluded as a cause, it now seems that the Indus cities were ravaged by invading nomadic horsemen in the eighteenth century BC. These nomads are usually identified as Indo-Aryans. There is, however, no reliable evidence for their presence until about two centuries after the end of the Indus valley civilization. It is therefore more likely that the Indus cities were conquered by tribesmen from the mountains who later gave way to the Indo-Aryans. By the thirteenth century BC, the Indo-Aryans—now split into numerous tribes who fought each other fiercely—had occupied the Punjab. They subsequently spread into the Ganges valley and southward into Gujerat and Maharashtra.

A vast collection of religious hymns written in archaic Sanskrit, the *Rigveda,* dates from this early phase (*c*.1200–1000 BC). Apparently preserved by oral tradition, the hymns are addressed to many different deities whose help is implored in military and agricultural pursuits. The four Vedic texts, of which the *Rigveda* is the foremost, spawned expositions and commentaries, of which the *Upanishads* are the most celebrated. The gods, such as Indra, are usually conceived of as anthropomorphic, but some features—for example speculation about the true nature of the sacrifice—which were to become characteristic of Hinduism, are already distinguishable.

During the later Vedic period (*c*.1000–550 BC) the Indo-Aryans, by then using effective iron tools, spread over most of northern India including the Ganges valley, burn-

CONNECTIONS

See also
986 India 500 BC–AD 3C
1036 Indian art to the Moguls
988 Buddha and Buddhism
846 Islam, Hinduism, ar Buddhism
886 Ancient states and empires

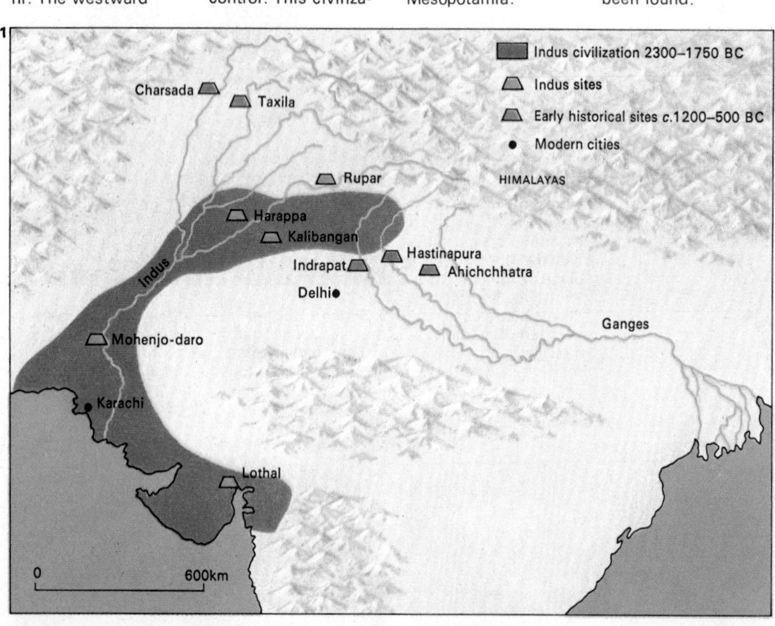

Indus civilization 2300–1750 BC
Indus sites
Early historical sites c.1200–500 BC
Modern cities
Charsada
Taxila
Rupar
HIMALAYAS
Harappa
Kalibangan
Indrapat
Hastinapura
Ahichchhatra
Delhi
Indus
Mohenjo-daro
Ganges
Karachi
Lothal
0
600km

1 The brown areas on the map show the extent of the Indus civilization, stretching southeast down the coast to beyond the Gulf of Cambay and eastward far beyond present Delhi. The westward expansion into Baluchistan is not shown. All over this vast area—Rupar and Lothal are about 1,000 miles (1,600 km) apart—the civilization was uniform, implying centralized control. This civilization thrived in relatively dry areas, which would indicate the existence of a sophisticated irrigation and flood-control technology. Merchants may have traded as far west as Mesopotamia.

2 The ancient Indus city of Mohenjo-daro was built according to a systematic plan with streets crossing at right angles and houses opening onto the streets. Elaborate granaries have also been found.

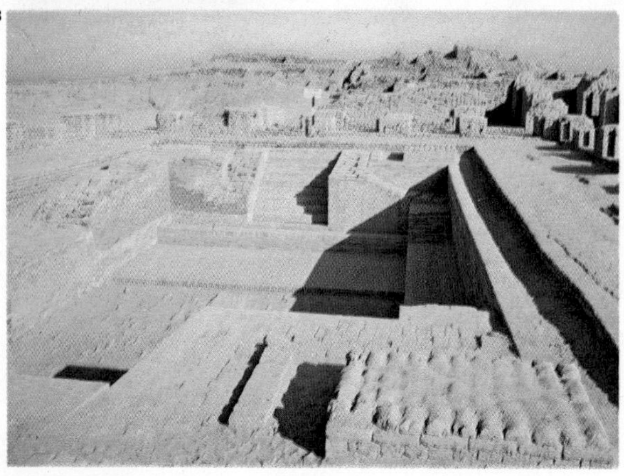

3 The Great Bath in the citadel of Mohenjo-daro was built of fine brickwork and presumably used for ceremonial ablutions. One of the most striking features of the Indus civilization was the importance attached to good water supplies. Well built bathrooms have been found in almost all houses, and most houses also had proper drainage. Each house also had its own water supply, a deep well, the shaft of which was lined with terra-cotta for support.

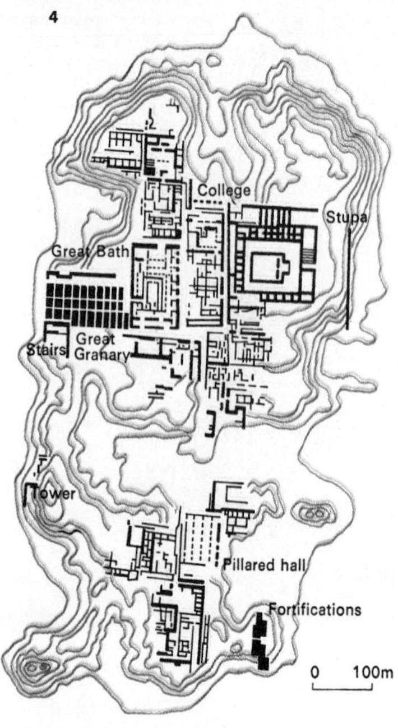

College
Stupa
Great Bath
Stairs
Great Granary
Tower
Pillared hall
Fortifications
0 100m

4 The larger Indus cities all consisted of a citadel mound and a lower city complex stretching eastward from the citadel. The citadel was the site of most of the large public buildings such as, in Mohenjo-daro, the Great Bath, the Great Granary, and a building whose floor plan (several courtyards, corridors, rooms, and compartments) suggests the tentative conclusion that it was a college. The lower city was the residential area. This ground plan of Mohenjo-daro shows the grid of the citadel and the lower part of the city. The houses vary a great deal in size. Some consist of only a single room, while some large residences have more than 20 rooms used for various purposes.

ing down the forest to cultivate the fertile land. The gradual progress of this expansion can be traced with the help of a distinctive type of pottery, Painted Gray Ware. These people were not urbanized as the Harappans had been. During their expansion they mixed with earlier established forest tribes, introducing them to the horse, and their mode of life changed from seminomadic cattle breeders to settled agriculturists.

This change had important political and cultural implications. The tribal units gave way to kingdoms based not on kinship but on territory. The kingdoms were controlled by warrior classes *(kshatriyas)* headed by the king, and assisted by the powerful class of hereditary priests *(brahmins)*. These two ruling classes controlled the free peasants, traders, and craftsmen who constituted the third class *(vaisyas)*, as well as the semiservile laborers, hunters, and fishermen who formed the lowest class *(sudras)*, who were in part descendants of forest tribes. Some of these, especially those whose way of life was considered unclean or repulsive by the Indo-Aryans, were assigned the status of untouchables. This was the beginning of the caste system.

The rise of major cities

During this period major cities developed for the first time since the decline of the Indus cities. The most important were Hastinapura on the Ganges, east of present-day Delhi and, in about 500 BC, Rajgir in southern Bihar, with its impressive walls. In the same period most of the basic concepts of Hinduism took shape: not only caste, but also the belief in the transmigration of the soul, in nonviolence, and in the holiness of the cow. These have all become lasting features of Indian civilization. While the Vedic sacrifice persisted and became more complicated, there was also a reaction among those who felt unsatisfied with formal religion and sought higher values in meditation. People of the ruling classes were encouraged to withdraw to a life of contemplation in the forest. In this environment the great teacher Siddhartha Gautama (*c.*563–*c.*483 BC), known as the Buddha, instituted the precepts of Buddhism.

KEY

Three Mohenjo-daro casts from seals supply valuable data about the Indus civilization, revealing, for example, that cattle had already been domesticated. These seals represent a bull feeding from a manger, an elephant, and a rhinoceros. The writing is pictographic and was not successfully deciphered until 1969.

5 The earliest true history of the Indo-Pakistani subcontinent began when, after the middle of the third millennium BC, a high civilization emerged in and around the Indus valley. Once established, the Indus valley civilization thrived for about six centuries without undergoing any significant change. Its sudden end may have been due to Indo-Aryan invasions, but it seems more likely that these invasions took place when the Indus civilization had already disintegrated. The Indo-Aryans settled in villages in the Punjab and were divided into tribes. The *Rigveda* describes their society. Between *c.* 1000 and 500 BC, Indo-Aryan civilization gradually spread over most of northern India and the Ganges valley, as can be confirmed from later Vedic literature, and early Hinduism took shape.

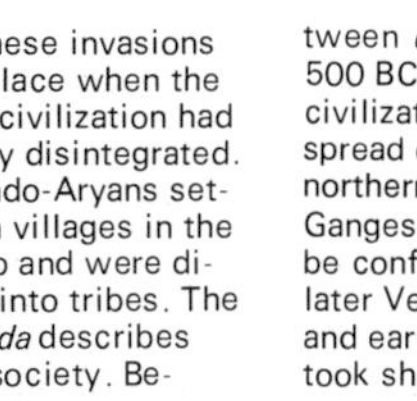

5

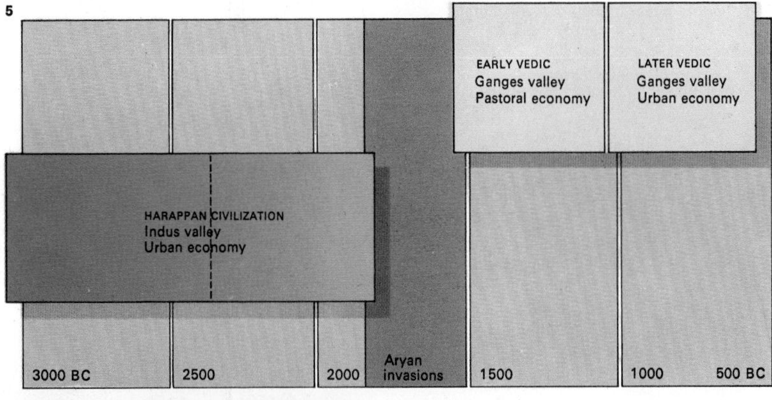
EARLY VEDIC
Ganges valley
Pastoral economy
LATER VEDIC
Ganges valley
Urban economy
HARAPPAN CIVILIZATION
Indus valley
Urban economy
3000 BC
2500
2000
Aryan invasions
1500
1000
500 BC

6

6 This limestone sculpture is one of the few surviving stone sculptures of the Indus civilization. It is 7 inches (19cm) high and is apparently the portrait of a real person. The sculpture is the product of excellent craftsmanship, and, despite its stylized form, it undoubtedly provides the viewer with some impression of the physical appearance of the ancient people of the Indus valley.

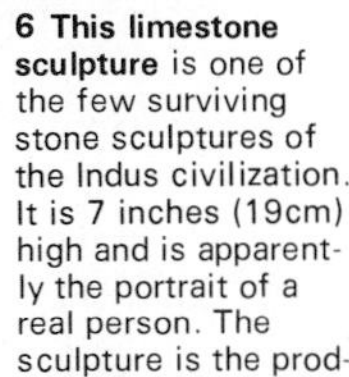

7

7 Most seals from Mohenjo-daro show representations of animals, sometimes natural, sometimes composite or fantastic. This seal shows a horned deity seated in an attitude that is reminiscent of the yoga *āsanas* of later times. The god is surrounded by a number of animals. This, among other features, recalls later representations of the god Shiva. The deity has therefore been identified as a precursor of the Hindu Shiva.

8

8 The modern inhabitants of the Mohenjo-daro area, like their predecessors, still use the river as their lifeline. The river was not only important for irrigation of the fields in the vicinity of its banks, but it was also essential for communications. The striking uniformity of the Indus civilization would have been impossible without adequate communications. Representations of boats have been found on stone and terra cotta at Mohenjo-daro.

Minoan civilization 2500–1400 BC

Arthur Evans (1851–1941), the British archeologist, excavating at Knossos on the island of Crete from 1900 to 1936, uncovered a richly decorated palace, an architectural masterpiece that indicated civilization more distinctive and sophisticated than any other early European culture hitherto discovered [4]. Similar Cretan palaces have since been revealed—by the Italians at Phaestos, by the French at Mallia, more recently by the Greeks at Zakro—and a balanced picture begins to emerge.

Beginnings of Minoan civilization

The Minoans (from the name of the legendary King Minos of Knossos), as Evans called the people who lived in Crete, appeared suddenly on the island at the start of the Bronze Age, about 3000 BC, perhaps as immigrants from Anatolia or, as recently argued, from Palestine. The contents of their circular tombs, most frequent on the plain of the Mesara, show that overseas contacts were maintained, contacts that gradually built up into a great trading network across the eastern Mediterranean.

By about 2000 BC, economic and social advance had spurred architecture to impressive achievements—the Old Palaces. Their details are much obscured by later additions and alterations, but enough survives at Knossos, at Mallia, and particularly under the west court at Phaestos to show that building on a lavish scale was already being carried out. The implications for the social organization are even greater than for the technical abilities of the builders. The Minoans had achieved civilization.

One of the most obvious criteria of this is the use of writing. The earliest brief inscriptions in Crete are found on seals, where picture symbols appear to belong to a hieroglyphic script. Clay tablets found in the early palace at Phaestos show that by then a simpler syllabic writing had been devised for general use. It may well have been employed mainly for writing on some sort of paper or parchment. No convincing translation of these texts, called Linear A, has yet been proposed.

The exact nature of the island's political organization is difficult to discover. The extensive storage capacity of the palaces for commodities such as olive oil, grain, and wine suggests that they were economic as well as administrative centers, controlling territories within the island. Yet these territories had apparently nothing to fear from each other—there are no walled defenses and few signs of weapons or soldiers. Knossos clearly held a leading position.

Height of Minoan culture

Demonstrated by finds of Minoan pottery as far away as Egypt, by colonies on several Aegean islands, and by the permeation of the mainland culture, overseas trade goes far to explain the wealth of Crete at this period. But Minoan civilization cannot be explained as simply imported from abroad: it is far too individualistic for that.

After apparently natural disasters—most likely earthquakes—in about 1700 BC, the palaces were lavishly rebuilt; it is the ruins of these that can be seen today. Building was in limestone, within a timber-frame construction. This added a useful, if not always effective, resilience against earth-

CONNECTIONS

See also
966 The Greek mainland 2800–1100 BC
176 Volcanoes

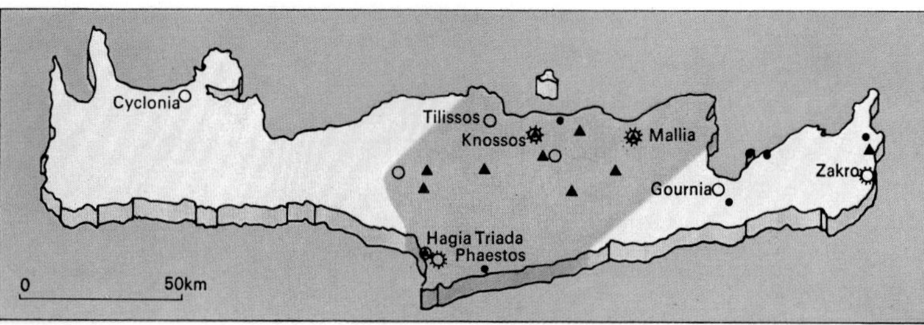

1
Probably dominated by Knossos c.2000–c.1400
Town
Town with palace
Great palace
Cult center
Cyclonia
Tilissos
Knossos
Mallia
Gournia
Zakro
Hagia Triada
Phaestos
0
50km

1 The long narrow island of Crete was the home of Minoan civilization, the first in Europe. With much of the interior mountainous, Mt Ida topping 7,873ft (2,400m), and the rugged south coast broken only by the plain of Mesara behind Phaestos, there seems little to explain civilization here. But the north coast has a gentler relief and is rich in olives and vines, and the surrounding seas encourage trade and contact over wide areas. The Minoans actively developed their agricultural wealth and foreign commerce into a great trading network.

2

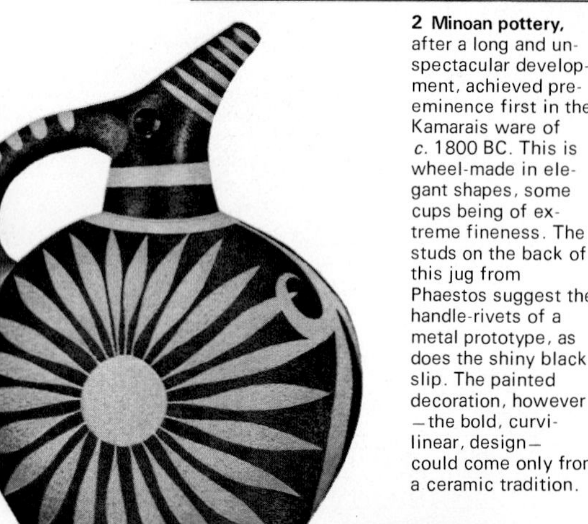

2 Minoan pottery, after a long and unspectacular development, achieved preeminence first in the Kamarais ware of *c.* 1800 BC. This is wheel-made in elegant shapes, some cups being of extreme fineness. The studs on the back of this jug from Phaestos suggest the handle-rivets of a metal prototype, as does the shiny black slip. The painted decoration, however—the bold, curvilinear, design—could come only from a ceramic tradition.

3

3 Elegance in shape is even more marked in the late Minoan period from 1500 BC. The fashion changed at this time to painting in red on yellow and much greater use was made of naturalistic motifs, although some abstract elements remain. Favorite decorative subjects were flowers and sea creatures, such as octopuses, nautiluses, and shells among rocks and seaweed.

4

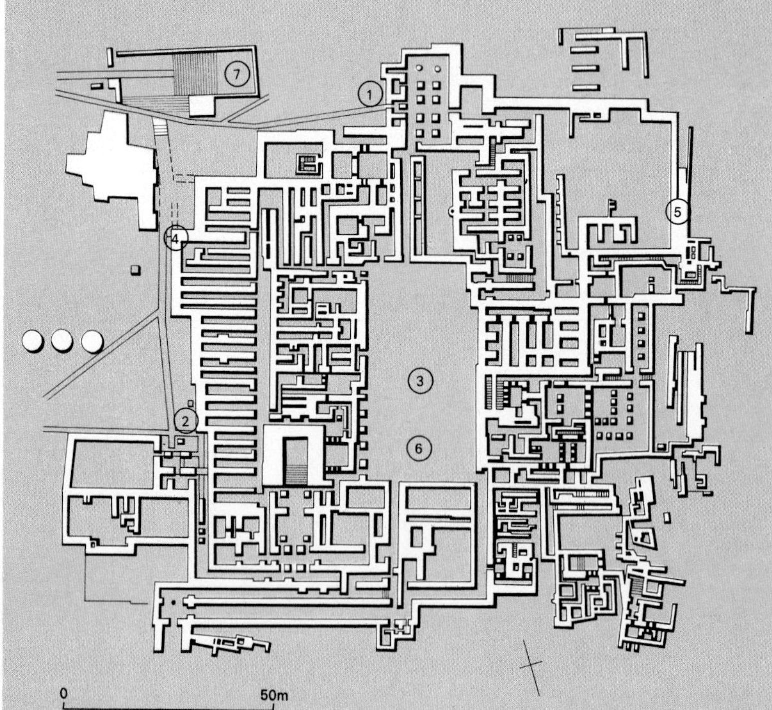

1
2
3
4
5
6
7
0
50m

4 The Great Palace of Knossos had a long history. The plan shows it after its rebuilding *c.* 1550 BC. The main entrances [1 and 2] lead by long corridors to the central court [3]. Beneath this, deposits have been found going back to 6000 BC. Storerooms for oil, wine, and other goods [4] and for pottery [5] hint at the wealth that poured into the building, which controlled at least all of central Crete. The administrative block fronted the court on the west and faced the great staircase to the domestic quarter on the east [6]. Outside the palace to the northwest, a processional way led to a theater [7].

quake shock, to which Crete is prone, but it also added to the fire risk. Ranges of rooms opened on to the great central courts, with well-planned light wells to illuminate inner suites. Internal walls were plastered and often gaily decorated with elaborate and colorful frescoes [9]. Floors were frequently paved with alabaster slabs. But it is perhaps the drainage system, as advanced as any before the eighteenth century AD, that causes the most surprise. The overall impression is a convincing one of light, air, and freedom—so different from that of the contemporary civilizations farther east and so much closer to modern ideals.

The art fully bears this out, whether it is a life-sized figure painted in the frescoes, decoration on the magnificent pottery and earthenware [Key], or minute detail on the carved seal stones [7,8]. The color and naturalism hold an immediate appeal for the modern world.

Decline and conquest

The end of this great civilization is even more hotly debated than its origins, if only because there is so much more evidence on which to base the story. The most widely accepted version, but by no means the only one, would start from the cataclysmic eruption of the volcanic island of Thera, a little over 63 miles (100km) from the north coast of Crete, about 1450 BC. Much of Crete would have been covered with poisonous ash, shattered by the shock waves generated by the explosion, and pounded by enormous tidal waves.

Of the major sites, only Knossos appears to have recovered from this destruction and here there are many signs of a profound change. The new rulers were warriors and used the Linear B script, which is now recognized as an adaptation of Linear A for writing an early version of the Greek language. This would all seem to point to a conquest of the island by mainlanders, Mycenaeans, who had seized the opportunity given them by the eruption of Thera to oust the Minoans from their control of the profitable sea routes. Metropolitan Minoan was replaced by provincial Mycenaean, and the palaces were lost to sight and memory.

KEY

This earthenware figurine displays a courtly elegance typical of the Minoan civilization of Bronze Age Crete. It is 11.6in (29.5cm) high and was found in the Temple Repositories at Knossos, where it was buried *c*. 1550 BC. The tightly-fitting bodice, open to expose the breasts, the embroidered apron, and the long flounced skirt are shown frequently on seals and in frescoes. The lioness, if such it is, on her hat and the snakes in her hands are less usual and more sinister. She is probably the earth mother, whose worship is widely attested in shrines and pillar crypts on Minoan sites and in caves and hilltop sanctuaries throughout Crete.

5

5 This magnificent stone libation vase comes from the palace at Zakro, destroyed *c*. 1450 BC. It shows a sanctuary (left) with wild goats on the roof. A bird flies past two pairs of horns used at consecration.

6

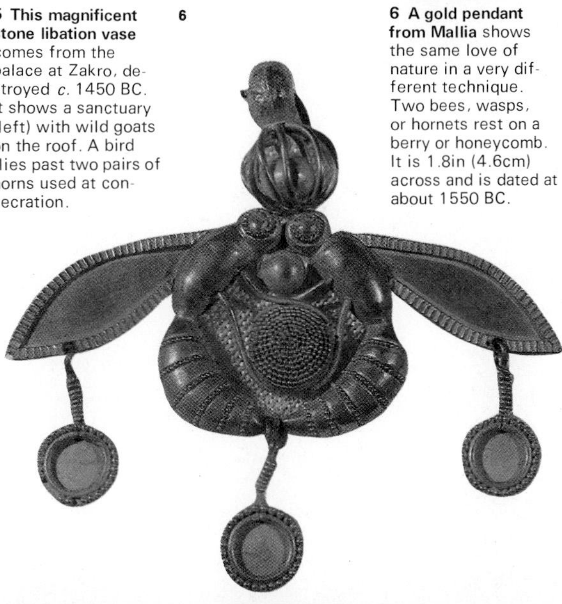

6 A gold pendant from Mallia shows the same love of nature in a very different technique. Two bees, wasps, or hornets rest on a berry or honeycomb. It is 1.8in (4.6cm) across and is dated at about 1550 BC.

7

8

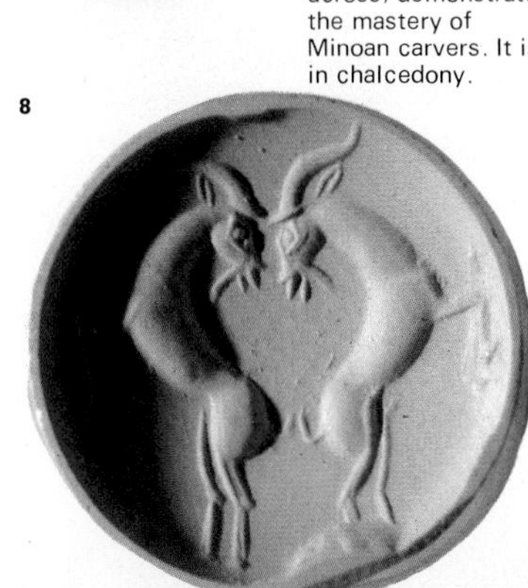

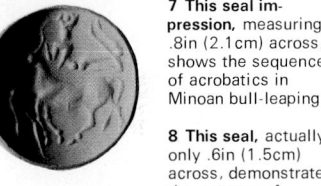

7 This seal impression, measuring .8in (2.1cm) across, shows the sequence of acrobatics in Minoan bull-leaping.

8 This seal, actually only .6in (1.5cm) across, demonstrates the mastery of Minoan carvers. It is in chalcedony.

9

9 Fresco painting was another spectacular art of the Minoans, although it normally survives only in small fragments. This scene of dolphins and fish decorated the so-called Queen's Megaron in the domestic quarter at Knossos. Other frescoes show birds, flowers, plants, animals, and people.

The Greek mainland 2800–1100 BC

Homer's *Iliad* and *Odyssey,* written between about 800 and 700 BC, record the exploits of legendary Greek heroes around the time of the Trojan Wars. For centuries the fact that this heroic age ever existed about 1800–1100 BC was in doubt, until Heinrich Schliemann (*c.*1822–90), a German archeologist, recovered at Troy and Mycenae (from 1874) relics that supported the legends.

Bronze Age beginnings

The Greek Bronze Age, centered on the Greek mainland, began with the introduction of metal, important both for stimulating trade and for the acquisition of visible wealth. About this time, too, the grain economy of the plains of Thessaly and the north was replaced by one based on grain, olives, and the vine, which flourished better in the south. By 2500 BC this economy supported a palace, the House of Tiles, at Lerna in the Plain of Argos. About 2200 BC, however, Lerna and many contemporary settlements were destroyed by invaders from the northeast. These were probably the first inhabitants to speak a language recognizably Greek. At this time the first potter's wheel and the megaron, a hall with pillared porch, were introduced. Soon after, Greek mainland civilization showed signs of influence from Minoan Crete [2].

In time strong towns grew up, such as Mycenae. The first real evidence of the flowering of the mainland civilization appears in the shaft graves of Mycenae, dating largely from the sixteenth century BC. They contain real solid wealth, in gold, silver, and bronze, and artifacts in crystal, alabaster, and clay. We can assume that these were the resting places of a princely, or even royal, family ruling a rich and integrated society. The objects [6,8] reveal a contrast between polished and sophisticated craftsmanship, patently Cretan, and a very un-Cretan emphasis on weapons, armor, and military scenes [7]. The owner of the stern gold mask [Key] was no soft courtier but a warring hero, an ancestor of those whom Homer portrayed.

These early Greeks also became seamen. A few of the objects from the shaft graves may be Egyptian work acquired through trade, rather than Cretan or Greek. Desirous of more trade goods from abroad and supported by local agricultural wealth, the Greeks began overseas ventures.

Expansion of Mycenaean civilization

Their opportunity came when the power of the Minoans was destroyed, perhaps by a cataclysmic eruption of Thera *c.*1450 BC. This freed the rich trade routes of the Mediterranean that the Cretans had hitherto controlled. The mainlanders, comparatively untouched by the disaster, made the most of the new situation. Their pottery, valued both for its own sake and for the perfumed oil exported in it, rose sharply in price in both the Levant and Egypt. It was prized, for example, in Akhnaton's newly built Egyptian capital Tell el Amarna about 1350 BC. Cypriot copper was carried in Greek ships. A great westward trade port grew up at Taranto in southern Italy, bringing more copper from Sardinia and the eastern Alps. Amber was imported from the distant Baltic. Crete itself was occupied by

CONNECTIONS

See also
964 Minoan civilization 2500–1400 BC
992 The Greeks to the rise of Athens

1

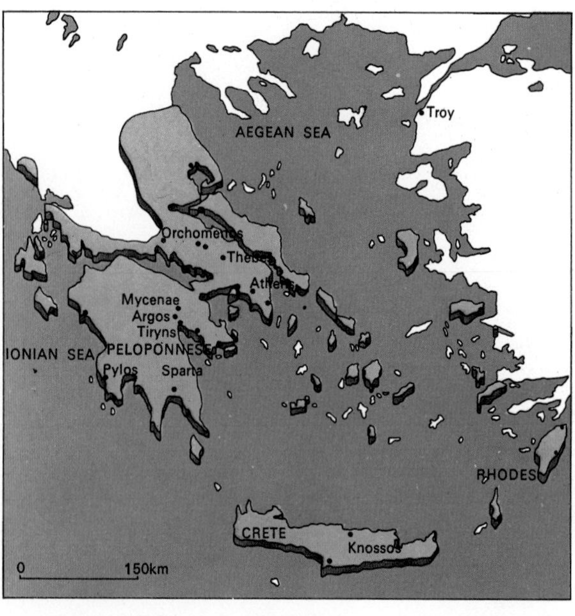

AEGEAN SEA
Troy
Mycenae
Argos
Tiryns
IONIAN SEA
PELOPONNESE
Pylos
Sparta
RHODES
CRETE
Knossos
0
150km

1 The Mycenaeans' homeland was the Peloponnesus and adjacent parts of Greece, centered on the Argolid and Mycenae itself. Here they built their distinctive version of the civilization already flourishing in Crete. When they took over the Minoans' sea trade, their influence spread to the islands and coasts around the Aegean and beyond. This vast territory was never a unified state but a collection of allied kingdoms.

2

2 The Mycenaeans were strongly influenced by the Minoans. This gold cup from Vaphio, near Sparta, if not made in Crete itself must at least have been the work of a mainland craftsman trained in the Minoan tradition.

4

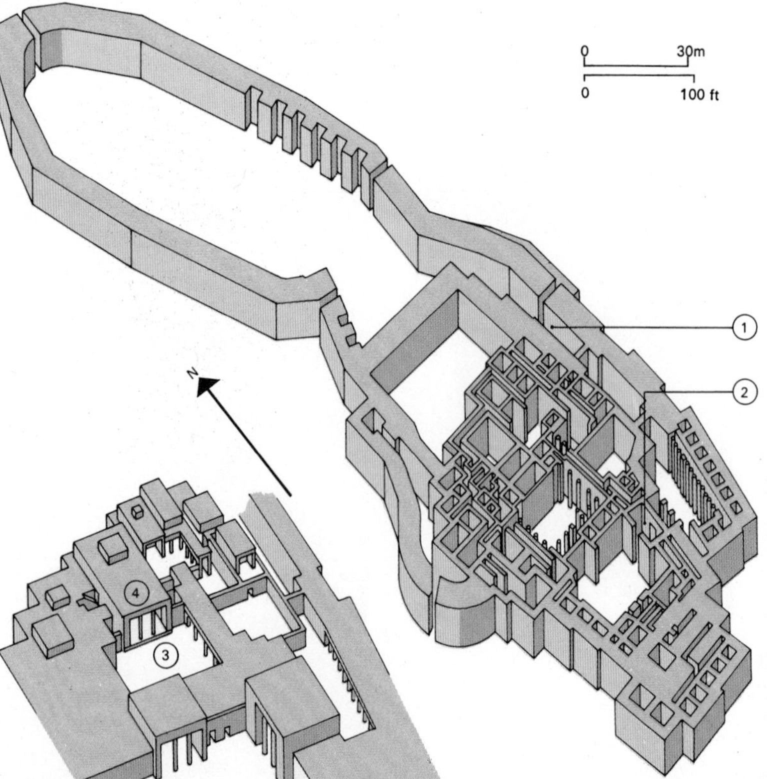

0
30m
0
100 ft
N
1
2
3
4

3

3 The syllabic script came from Crete. Linear B script was extensively used for business documents, such as this stock list of herbs from Mycenae. The language was an early Greek form.

4 The fortified citadel of Tiryns, *c.* 1330 BC, typifies mainland architecture in the Bronze Age. A tortuous entrance passage [1] leads through the massive walls; an inner portico [2] leads to the first court. The adminstrative center was the inner court [3] and the megaron [4] opening on to it. This was a hall with a porch and a great central hearth. The main structural fabrics were wooden framework and columns and sun-dried bricks.

the Mycenaeans, and the palace at Knossos was rebuilt as the seat of a new dynasty.

In the towns of Greece, craftsmen carried out their trades, producing fine metalwork, pottery, and perishable goods. The towns themselves grew larger, stronger, and better appointed. Walls were heightened and extended, with devices to ensure a safe water supply. The palaces, still based on the traditional megaron plan, were now elaborately decorated with frescoes. The richly equipped tombs, now great corbeled *tholoi* (circular buildings first developed at this period) such as the Treasury of Atreus [5], show the architectural skill of their builders.

Writing was needed to facilitate such a level of trade, craft, and administration. The Minoans on Crete had developed a syllabic script of their own, still undeciphered. This is found inscribed on tablets. Archaeologists have called it Linear A. The Mycenaeans adapted it, rather clumsily but adequately, for their Greek tongue (Linear B) [3]. In 1953 the English architect Michael Ventris deciphered Linear B and established beyond doubt that the Mycenaeans, Homer's Achaeans, were linguistically at least the true ancestors of the classical Greeks.

Mainland civilization declines

The closing stages of Bronze-Age Greece are difficult to understand. By one account hardy frontiersmen from the northwest, the Dorians, overran the cities of the south and sacked all of them except Athens. By another account, the Mycenaeans lost their expansionist drive around 1200 BC, engaged in civil war—the siege of Troy exemplifies this—and in effect destroyed themselves. About this time there was certainly great unrest over a wide area, and the bands that attacked Egypt in 1225 BC and again in 1191 BC included Aegean peoples.

In mainland Greece, the succeeding age knew little of what had gone before. Shabby villages replaced the flourishing towns, simple pits the great tombs, and common pots the masterpieces in clay, silver, and gold. The one advance in this dismal period was the introduction of ironworking.

KEY

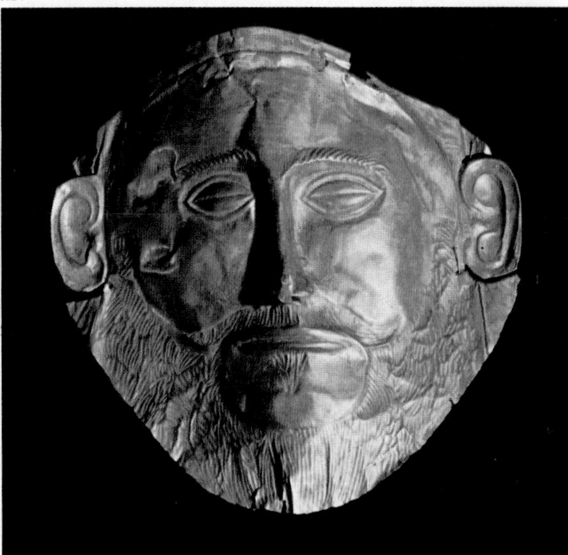

This gold mask recovered by Heinrich Schliemann in 1876 shows a proud Mycenaean of *c.* 1550 BC.

5

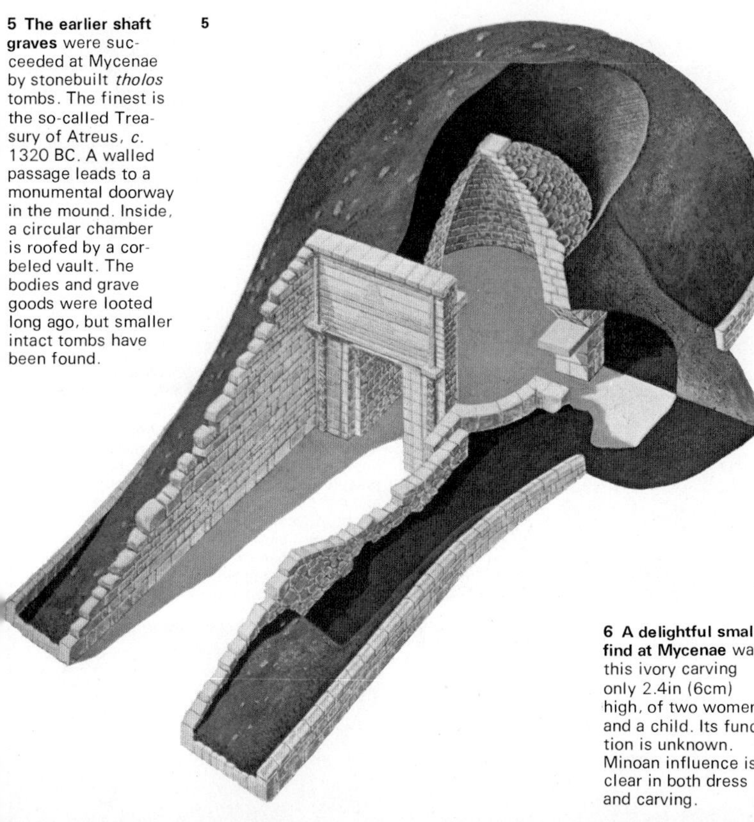

5 The earlier shaft graves were succeeded at Mycenae by stonebuilt *tholos* tombs. The finest is the so-called Treasury of Atreus, *c.* 1320 BC. A walled passage leads to a monumental doorway in the mound. Inside, a circular chamber is roofed by a corbeled vault. The bodies and grave goods were looted long ago, but smaller intact tombs have been found.

6

6 A delightful small find at Mycenae was this ivory carving only 2.4in (6cm) high, of two women and a child. Its function is unknown. Minoan influence is clear in both dress and carving.

7

7 These Mycenaean warriors may have a comic flavor to our eyes, but the discovery of fortifications, weapons, and armor shows that warfare was an important factor in life at the time.

8 Bronze daggers from shaft graves of *c.* 1550 BC reveal great artistic skill in their gold, silver, and niello inlay. Some show sea creatures; one shows a hunting cat in Minoan style, but this one has a more robust mainland subject. A lion is attacking a deer while two more deer escape. The dagger is 9.25in (23.5cm) long and is one of the treasures found in Shaft Grave IV in Mycenae by Schliemann, the German archeologist.

China to 1000 BC

The Chinese have a unique place in history caused largely by the natural barriers that protected their great land mass (the size of Europe) and their relative lack of contact with the outside world until the nineteenth century AD. Their ancient culture did not come to an end like the cultures of ancient Egypt and Greece but has evolved unbroken from 1500 BC to the present.

Earliest human remains

The earliest human remains so far discovered in China are those of the Peking and Lan-t'ien men, dating back well over half a million years. They were among the first humans to make tools, and evidence of their descendants has been found in caves in the hills near Chou-K'ou-tien, which contained scraping and cutting stones. These early people were followed by Upper Cavemen who lived about 50,000 years ago. They were able to make fire and lived by hunting, fishing, and gathering fruits and edible roots. In the Neolithic Age (*c.*7000–1600 BC) people made needles, bows and arrows, and fine pottery [2, 3, 7]. They fashioned antlers into sickles and saws and ground sharp edges on stones and shells. An agricultural and pastoral society arose.

The first agriculturists lived in beehive-shaped huts that were sunk into the ground for additional warmth and security and covered by thatched roofs supported on wooden posts. Agriculture was helped by the existence of a thick deposit of loess, a very fine soil that is thought to have been blown from the northwest. In some places in the Central Plain it is more than 200ft (60m) deep and, being exceptionally fertile, provides some of the finest agricultural land in the world. Like the Nile mud it is an excellent material for building rammed-earth walls or for making bricks. At this time the region had a moderate climate and supported wild horses, buffalo, deer, wild hogs, sheep, and even rhinoceros.

The Central Plain [1] lies between two great rivers—the Huang Ho in the north and the Yangtze in the south. These rivers flow from west to east and carry loess through the region. It is here that the Bronze Age culture of the Shang, or Yin, dynasty was born. By tradition, it ruled from *c.*1766 BC to *c.*1122 BC; modern scholars date it from *c.*1600 to *c.*1030 BC.

The writings of early historians

There is so far little evidence to support the earliest history of China as related by Chinese historians of the second century BC. They held that the country was first ruled by two groups of three and five emperors, who were followed by the Hsia, Shang, and Chou dynasties. The existence of the Hsia dynasty is still in doubt, but archeological evidence has proved the existence both of the Shang dynasty and of a central authority, with a capital city, Great Shang near An-yang in north Honan. The Shang were mainly agricultural, but they are known for their mastery of bronze casting [Key]. Their bronze ritual vessels, bells, and axes exhibit an unsurpassed quality of craftsmanship [5, 9].

Sacrifice played an important part in Shang culture, and people as well as animals were slaughtered to commemorate royal burials and to mark the erection of impor-

CONNECTIONS

See also
1038 China 1000 BC–AD 618
1044 Chinese art to 1368
650 The first men
822 The occult
1588 Fire and bronze

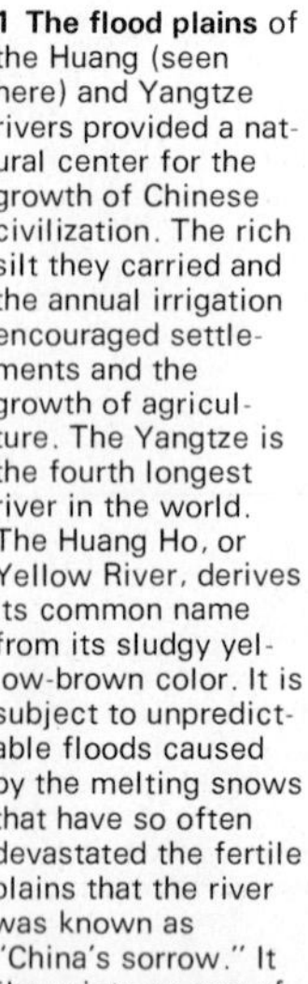

1 The flood plains of the Huang (seen here) and Yangtze rivers provided a natural center for the growth of Chinese civilization. The rich silt they carried and the annual irrigation encouraged settlements and the growth of agriculture. The Yangtze is the fourth longest river in the world. The Huang Ho, or Yellow River, derives its common name from its sludgy yellow-brown color. It is subject to unpredictable floods caused by the melting snows that have so often devastated the fertile plains that the river was known as "China's sorrow." It flows into an arm of the Yellow Sea. The river has changed its course many times.

2 This black pottery tripod vessel is known as a li. It represents the final and most developed phase of Neolithic pottery and comes from Lung-shan in the central Huang Ho basin. The three legs are hollow and have the practical advantage of holding the pot upright on the embers and of offering a larger surface to the fire. Pots of this area are characterized by dark burnished surfaces.

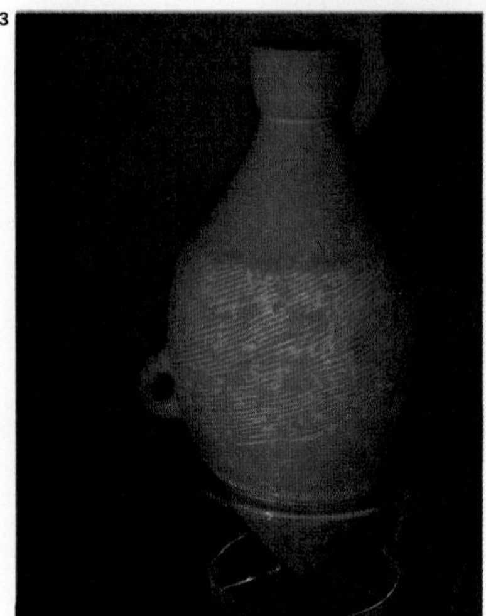

3 This red pottery amphora was excavated from the Pan-p'o village site in Shensi province and is an excellent example of the red pottery ware of the Yangshao culture. The pots were often painted with designs based on fish.

4 Oracle bones, usually made from the shoulder blades of oxen or the carapaces of tortoises, were used for divination. Questions in the form of pictures were scratched on the surface of the bone and a red-hot iron applied. The heat resulted in cracks radiating from the burn, and these enabled the diviner to read the answer to the question. Pictograms were the earliest form of Chinese writing; the symbols are direct ancestors of the modern Chinese script.

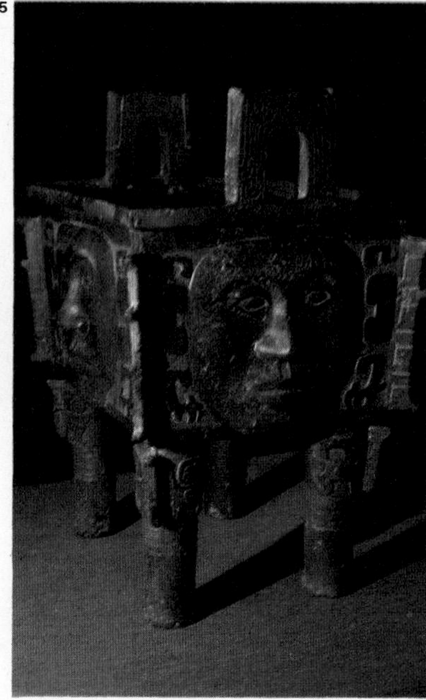

5 The inscription and the human faces on this bronze ritual food vessel or *ting* (14th-11th centuries BC) allude to human sacrifice; the vessel may have been used in the rites. The sacrifice would have been an offering to an ancestor.

tant buildings. One building excavated at An-yang disclosed guards outside the gates armed with halberds and others along the outside walls. Dogs were distributed along the walls, and five chariots with charioteers and horses were buried in the central court.

The royal tombs were even more exacting in their needs. Ramps led down to the pit [8] containing the coffin, which lay in the center of the deepest part, usually over a smaller grave containing the body of a dog. The pit contained the bodies of people, horses, and dogs as well as chariots and all the furniture and household goods needed for the occupant in the next world. Some people had been beheaded and lay in groups of ten with their heads carefully laid in a separate place. Slaves were occasionally buried alive, and in one tomb 70 living people had been buried with the dead.

The Shang dynasty prospered. The new bronze tools made a variety of trade possible, and exchange of foods became necessary. To facilitate trade, money was introduced in the form of cowrie shells, already one of the world's most popular currencies because of their valuable qualities of size and durability and because they were impossible to forge.

Calendars and cities

The Shang were a fairly sophisticated people, and their astronomers produced an accurate calendar, based on the lunar month, which was corrected by the addition of seven extra lunar months over a period of 19 solar years.

Shang culture spread over central China, and traces of it have been found in the Yangtze valley 400 miles (640km) to the south [6]. The Shang method of planning towns in squares can still be seen in Peking. The Shang regarded themselves as the center of civilization. The name for China derives from Chung-kuo, meaning the Middle Kingdom.

Frequent wars and the oppression of the people by the last Shang ruler, Chou Hsin, finally drove the slaves into revolt. Chou Hsin perished in the flames that destroyed his palace, and with this the Chou dynasty began *c.* 1030 BC.

KEY

During the Shang dynasty a highly skilled bronze metallurgy was developed, much later than in the West, although it was still the earliest bronze work in East Asia. The two principal weapons of the Shang people were the bow and the halberd. This bronze ritual halberd blade from the Shang dynasty dates from the later part of the 11th century BC.

6

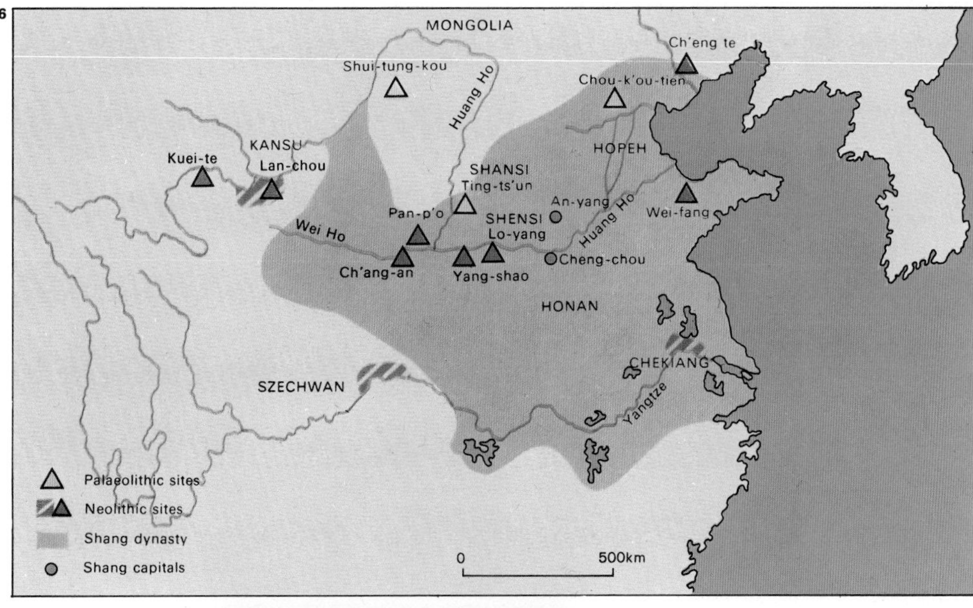

MONGOLIA
Ch'eng te
Shui-tung-kou
Huang Ho
Chou-k'ou-tien
HOPEH
KANSU
Kuei-te
Lan-chou
SHANSI
Ting-ts'un
An-yang
Pan-p'o
SHENSI
Wei-fang
Wei Ho
Lo-yang
Ch'ang-an
Yang-shao
Cheng-chou
HONAN
CHEKIANG
SZECHWAN
Yangtze
Palaeolithic sites
Neolithic sites
Shang dynasty
Shang capitals
0
500km

7

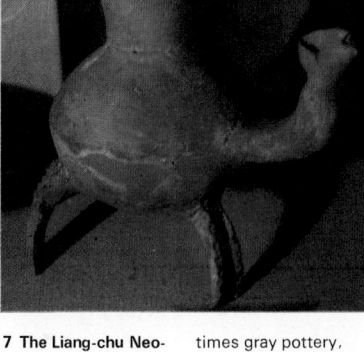

7 The Liang-chu Neolithic culture flourished within a relatively confined area in the region of Shanghai in the northern Chekiang province. It is characterized by a coarse brick-red or sometimes gray pottery, such as this pottery kettle *c.* 4000 BC, which frequently employed curious shapes and forms of a type more usually associated with vessels made from bronze.

6 Neolithic China centered around the fertile plains of the Huang and Yangtze rivers. The Shang dynasty ruled first from Cheng-chou but later moved to Anyang.

8 Ramps lead down to the center of this burial chamber (*c.* 1100 BC). The coffin was placed over a depression containing the body of a dog. Bodies of funeral sacrifice victims were carefully positioned on the ledge surrounding the coffin. Nothing was left to chance: furniture, clothes, household equipment, food, and drink—everything that was needed on earth for the comfort of the deceased was buried with him in order to fill his continuing needs in the next world.

8

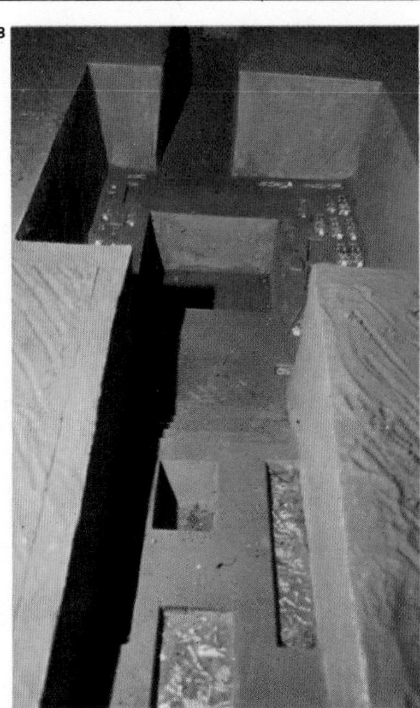

9 Shang dynasty bronzes were mostly discovered at Anyang, the Shang capital; their uses were ceremonial and funerary. Of the food vessels, *chiu* [A] cauldrons had flat bases; the *ting* [B] had three or four legs and handles. Wine beakers of the *chueh* type [C] had tripod bases, handles, and spouts; the *ku* [D] was a deep cup with a flaring rim. Of the wine and water jugs, the *hsi-tsun* or *tsun* [E] had animal or bird forms; the *kuang* [F] had a lid in the back of the animal. The *hu* [G], *yu* [H], and *chih* [I] were wine or water jugs. Raised and depressed decoration with animal motifs, *t'ao-t'ieh*, was at first representative and later geometrically stylized.

9

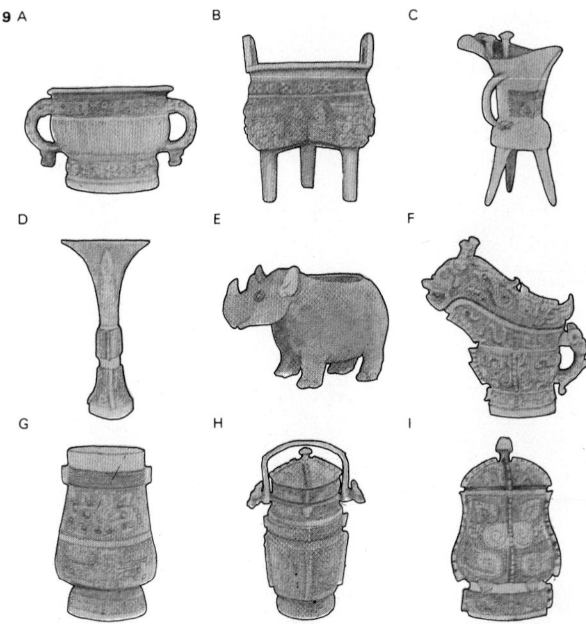

A
B
C
D
E
F
G
H
I

Preclassic America to AD 300

The period between 2200 BC and AD 300 saw the rise of the first civilization in both Mexico, where it is known as the Formative or Preclassic, and Peru. By 1500 BC agricultural villages in both Mesoamerica and South America were developing crafts with specialization in such fields as ceramics; society was also moving toward a stratification, which was expressed in the first public architecture. The first truly complex society, the Olmec culture, based in the tropical lowlands of the Mexican Gulf Coast, had appeared by 1200 BC. The earliest of its great ceremonial centers was San Lorenzo Tenochtitlán.

Spread of Olmec culture

During excavations at San Lorenzo Tenochtitlán, numerous pieces of monumental sculpture in volcanic stone were found, including giant heads deliberately defaced and buried [Key]. The stone itself came from the Tuxtla Mountains many miles away, and the presence of the sculptures—and their sophistication—indicates an organized labor force, a body of specialist sculptors, and a powerful government whose patronage was extended to lapidaries and potters as well as sculptors.

Olmec traders penetrated far into the highlands of Mexico. Oaxaca was a source for various minerals, and the valley of the Río Balsas beyond Mexico City may have been the origin of the blue jade favored by the Olmec—another possible source, in Costa Rica, is even more distant. Rock carvings and cave paintings in Olmec style are known from western Mexico, and the carvings continue eastward into El Salvador. Whether diffusion of this artistic stimulus was commercial, religious, diplomatic, or military, it has a good claim to being the first pan-Mesoamerican style. There is some evidence that the Olmecs possessed a system of numerical notation and perhaps other forms as well, but whether it can be described as "writing" is still a matter for argument.

After about 1000 BC a similar diffusion of a style known as Chavín occurred in Peru. The style involves both birds of prey and feline-human compounds [1] with serpent attributes, and is full of arcane allusion. The style is named after the site of Chavín de Huantar, about 9,750ft (3,000m) high and just below and east of the crest of the Andes in central Peru, where a complex of massive stone buildings with subterranean galleries surround formal courtyards. Some of the galleries contain sculptures, such as the Lanzón that stands in a cruciform chamber in the deepest part of the main structure, a column of rock portraying a mythical being.

Chavín influence on arts and crafts

Examples of Chavín-style pottery are known from as far north as Ecuador, while in textiles Chavín influence is found in the Paracas region [4] in southern Peru. Chavín influence continued until about 200 BC, and may have continued in a provincial form in the sculptures of San Agustín in southern Columbia. The sites at San Agustín cover a wide area on the hills around the modern town and consist of megalithic chambered monuments and feline, fanged sculptures. They are dated from about the time of Christ to AD 500.

CONNECTIONS

See also

1118 Mesoamerica 300–1521

1120 Colombia and Peru 300–1534

886 Ancient states and empires

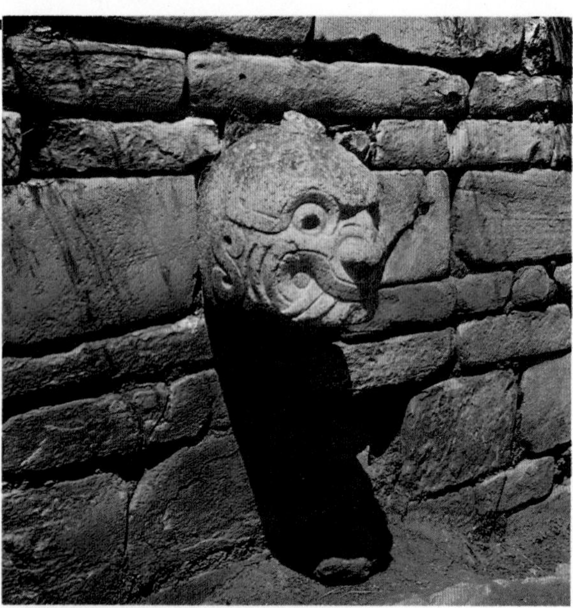

1 Human and feline characteristics are combined in a sculpture of a monstrous head projecting from the wall of the Castillo, the main structure at Chavin de Huantar. The undressed but neat masonry contrasts with the sophistication of the carving. The site lies in a high valley in the upper Amazon basin.

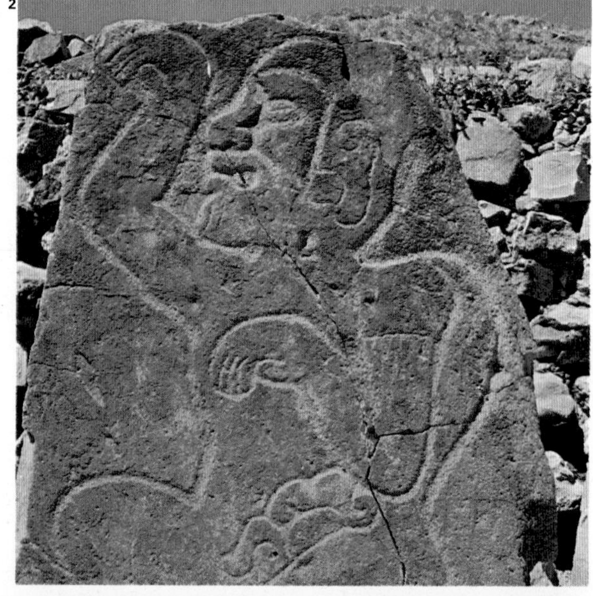

2 Figures of danzantes (dancers) at the Zapotec center of Monte Albán, Oaxaca, Mexico, date from about 500 BC and resemble Olmec art of the same period and earlier. The abandoned poses, closed eyes, and various details on the bodies suggest that the figures depict slain warriors.

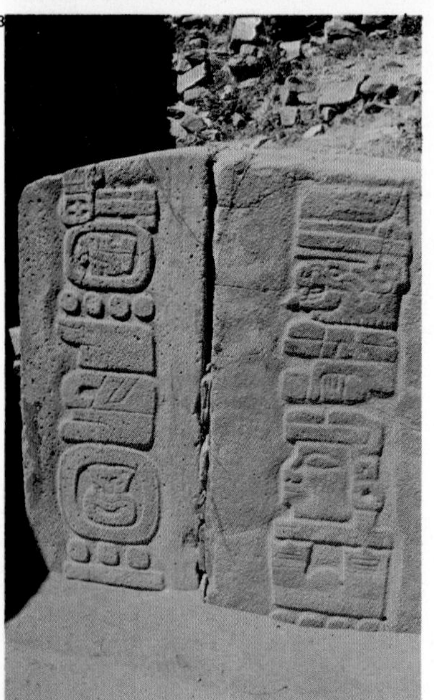

3 Two sculptured stone slabs, or stelae, at Monte Albán bear short inscriptions in a form of hieroglyphic writing, including long bars and disks that probably denote numbers, a bar equaling 5 and a disc 1. These stelae, dating from about 500 BC, are the earliest dated writing in the ancient Americas.

4 Part of a richly decorated textile from the desert cemeteries of the Paracas peninsula, on the coast of south central Peru, shows a complex design that is repeated similarly on each of the many panels. These textiles have been preserved by the dry climate of the Peruvian coast and provide some idea of what may have been lost elsewhere.

Elaborate gold work of the Chavín period is found in the Lambayeque valley and other regions of northern Peru. It initiated a tradition of working precious metals that continued until the Spanish conquest. In the Virú valley, south of Trujillo on the Peruvian coast, major centralized settlements developed during the early centuries AD, apparently in response to population pressure and competition for resources. Pucará in southern Peru was an important cultural center, quite unrelated to Chavín.

From about 500 BC the rise of Zapotec culture [2] in the Valley of Oaxaca in southern Mexico accelerated. The first monumental inscriptions in hieroglyphic script from the New World [3] are found at the great hilltop center of Monte Albán, which also contains large stone buildings and low-relief carvings of humans. Another structure, known as Mound J, could have been an astronomical observatory. By the end of the Preclassic period, Monte Albán already possessed the spacious formal layout, the huge open plazas, and the massive platforms that mark its further development in the Classic.

The Valley of Mexico, after a period of Olmec influence, saw the rise of a number of independent political units around the margins of its broad, shallow lakes. Among these was Cuicuilco, which was destroyed about the time of Christ by an eruption [5].

Teotihuacán, a rival state in the northeast of the valley, grew in the next century into a centralized, planned urban settlement [6], which by AD 150 covered almost 8sq mi (20 sq km). Teotihuacán trade reached far to the east, to the Maya area by AD 400.

The beginning of the Maya culture

The Maya provide the rationale for formally beginning the Classic period at AD 300, because that is roughly when they started to erect monuments bearing inscriptions [8] in the so-called Long Count, a complex calendar that enables Maya monuments [7] to be dated to within a day. It now seems that Maya culture acquired most of the essential attributes of civilization during the late Preclassic period.

KEY

This giant head of the Olmec period, found at San Lorenzo Tenochtitlán near the Gulf Coast of Mexico, dates from about 1200–900 BC. Several such heads were found at the site, and others are known from La Venta and a number of smaller sites, including the early Laguna de los Cerros. They are thought to depict the Olmec rulers and are made of volcanic rock brought at least 60mi (100km) from the Tuxtla mountains, which gives strong evidence of Olmec social control. The Olmec culture is the first complex society in Mesoamerica to attain a level that can be described as a civilization, and it stimulated subsequent developments in other areas.

5

5 The circular and stepped pyramid at Cuicuilco in the Valley of Mexico on the outskirts of Mexico City was the main structure of a city that flourished about the time of Christ. It was overwhelmed by an eruption of the volcano Xitle and buried under lava, but it has recently been excavated and restored.

6

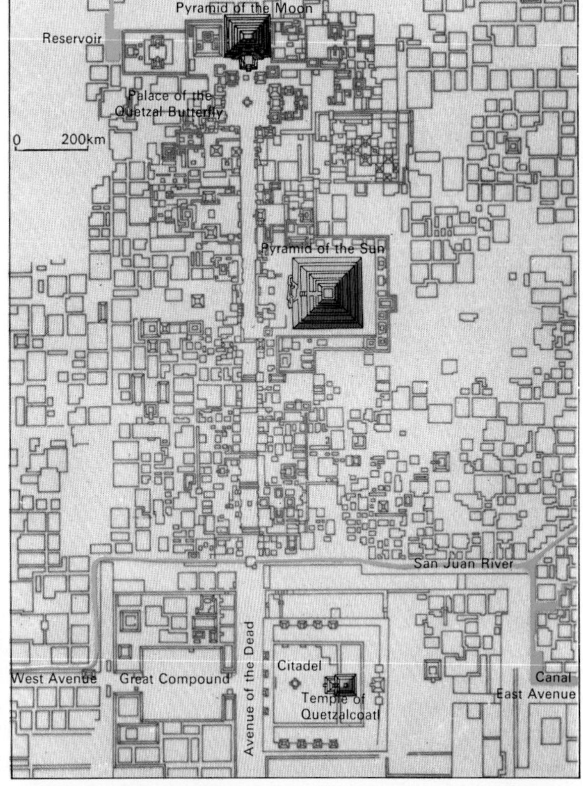
Pyramid of the Moon
Reservoir
Palace of the Quetzal Butterfly
0 200km
Pyramid of the Sun
San Juan River
Citadel
Temple of Quetzalcoatl
West Avenue
Great Compound
Avenue of the Dead
Canal
East Avenue

6 Teotihuacán, a great city in the northeastern basin of Mexico, began its dramatic rise about 100 BC and from AD 100–700 had a population approaching 200,000. The long Avenue of the Dead runs south from the Pyramid of the Moon to the citadel and market compound in the center of the city.

7

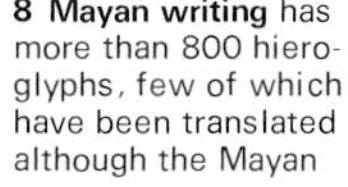

7 Reconstruction of Pyramid E-VII-Sub shows a Pre-classic temple of about AD 200–300 at the Maya site of Uaxactún, Guatemala, which archeologists found beneath a later structure.

8

8 Mayan writing has more than 800 hieroglyphs, few of which have been translated although the Mayan calendar is understood. This is part of an inscription on one of the stelae at Quiriguа, Guatemala.

Egypt: 1570 BC to Alexander the Great

The New Kingdom in Egypt (*c.*1570–1085 BC) dates from the victory of Theban forces over the Hyksos rulers of Egypt. New Kingdom Egypt was an empire extending from the northern Sudan to Syria and was one of the major powers of the ancient world. The god of Thebes, Amun (Amon), was elevated to the rank of principal deity of the realm and was identified with the sun-god Re (Ra) in the form Amun-Re (Amon-Ra), king of the gods [1].

The consolidation of Egyptian power

The early kings of Dynasty XVIII were primarily engaged in keeping Egypt safe from any further incursions by Bedouin tribes in the east or by the Nubians in the south. After stabilizing the eastern frontier, the Egyptian rulers undertook a series of campaigns to conquer the kingdom of Nubia and to seize its gold mines. The chronic lack of male heirs to the throne led to the increasing importance of the royal heiresses, one of whom was Hatshepsut (Hatshepshut, reigned *c.*1503–*c.*1482 BC), wife and half sister of Thutmose II, who bore her husband no sons. On Thutmose's death the child of one of his concubines, Thutmose III (reigned *c.*1504–1450 BC), was placed on the throne and was presumably destined to marry his half sister. Hatshepsut seized the throne, however, and ruled jointly with Thutmose III.

On Hatshepsut's death, Thutmose III assumed effective control of the government and immediately embarked on a series of campaigns to subjugate the petty kingdoms in Palestine and most of Syria. He also completed the conquest of Nubia as far as Napata. His immediate successors continued his expansionist policies, but eventually an agreement was reached with Mitanni, the other major power in the region, as to their spheres of influence.

Under Amenhotep III (reigned *c.*1417–1379 BC) the Egyptian court reached the height of its prestige, receiving tribute or trade goods from Syria, Mesopotamia, Anatolia, Crete, and even Greece. His son Amenhotep IV, or Akhenaton (Ikhnaton) (reigned *c.*1379–1362 BC), inaugurated a change in the Egyptian religion through his worship of the sun-god in the form of Aton, the sun's disk, and moved the capital to the new city of Akhetaton (the modern Tel el Amarna). Akhenaton's policy encountered the opposition of the priesthood of the old gods and led to domestic anarchy and the weakening of Egypt's prestige. His successors abandoned his beliefs, and order was finally restored in the reign of Horemheb, the last ruler of the dynasty. Upon Horemheb's death the throne passed to his vizier Ramesses (Ramses) I (reigned *c.*1320–1318 BC), who founded Dynasty XIX (*c.*1320–1200 BC).

Confrontation with the Hittites

The aim of the rulers of this period was to restore Egypt's power and prestige abroad and to confirm Egypt's dominant position in Palestine in the face of the growth of the power of the Hittite Empire. This rivalry led to a major clash early in the reign of Rameses II (reigned 1304–1237 BC) [Key] at the town of Kadesh, where both the Egyptians and Hittites claimed victory. Peace was eventually concluded in 1280 BC and sealed

CONNECTIONS

See also
960 Egypt: the Old and Middle Kingdoms
974 Africa: Kush and Axum
984 The Persian Empire of the Achaemenids
966 The Greek mainland 2800–1100 BC

1 The ancient cult of the sun-god Re had been eclipsed by the rise of the god Amun, until Akhenaton tried to suppress the worship of all gods except Re. The sun-god was represented in the form of the sun disk, adored here by Nefertiti.

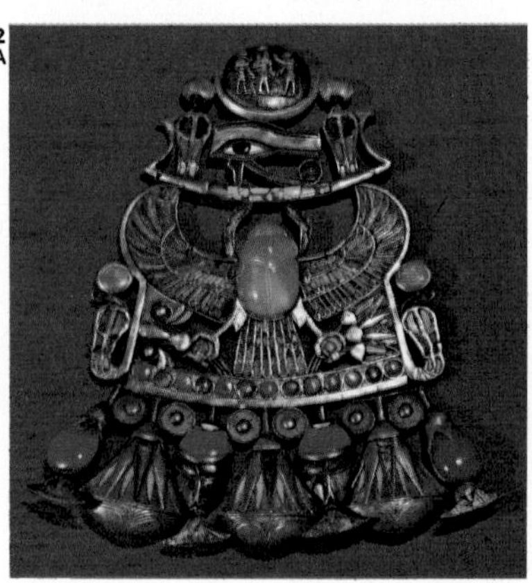

2 This treasure, a pectoral with solar and lunar emblems [A] and a necklace of the rising sun [B] is from the pyramid tomb of Tutankhamen, who succeeded to the throne through his marriage to Akhenaton's daughter and heiress. Bowing to political pressures, he renounced Akhenaton's religion and abandoned Akhetaton, returning to Thebes and restoring the worship of Amun and other gods. He died *c.* 1340 BC. His pyramid tomb was the only one left intact. Persistent robberies ended the system of pyramid burials. Instead, cliff tombs were cut in the well-guarded Valley of the Kings.

3 Egyptian temples conformed to a common plan. This can be seen clearly in the small temple of the god Khons within the temple complex at Karnak in Thebes. The entrance to the temple was through a pylon (gateway) [1] into an open court [2] with a colonnade along the sides. Off this court, along a straight axis, lay a hypostyle (pillared hall) [3] leading to the sanctuary [4] where the image of the god rested. Service and storage rooms surrounded the sanctuary. Because each Egyptian ruler was determined to create an enduring reputation through his buildings, most major temples were continually being enlarged and remodeled by the addition of rooms.

in 1267 BC by the marriage of Ramesses II to a Hittite princess. His successors were threatened by Libyan tribesmen and piratical "sea-peoples," but these dangers were contained by Ramesses III (reigned *c.*1198–1166 BC) of Dynasty XX [6].

Under Ramesses III's successors, who were all named Ramesses, the power of the crown steadily declined in the face of increased Libyan incursions and the growth in the power of local governors, especially that of the high priest of Amun at Thebes. Egypt's possessions in Palestine and Nubia were lost by the end of the dynasty, and Egypt itself fell under the control of foreign rulers. Under Dynasty XXI, Thebes was virtually independent under its high priests. The unity of Egypt was restored by the Libyan general Shoshenk I (reigned *c.*935–914 BC), founder of Dynasty XXII. He installed his son as high priest of Amun and attempted to restore Egypt's position as a great power by embarking on a major campaign in Palestine. Under his successors the unity of the country was broken by civil wars, and Egypt was partitioned into city-states under independent rulers, mostly of Libyan origin. An independent kingdom had emerged in Nubia in the south, and the Nubian kings conquered Egypt in about 712 BC and founded Dynasty XXV.

Nubian rule was terminated by a series of Assyrian invasions that led to the nomination of the prince of Sais as puppet ruler of Egypt. With the help of Greek mercenaries, Psamtik I (reigned *c.*664–610 BC) of Dynasty XXVI managed to impose his authority on the whole country and eventually repudiated his allegiance to Assyria.

Defeat by Babylonia and Persia

The rule of Dynasty XXVI (670–525 BC) marked a period of renewed prosperity, but Egypt's hopes of restoring its position as a great power were smashed by the Babylonians at the Battle of Carchemish in 605 BC. Ultimately, in 525 BC, Egypt was absorbed by the Persians, and although subsequent revolts reestablished Egyptian independence briefly between 404 and 343 BC, the Persians reasserted their domination until the advent of Alexander the Great in 323 BC.

KEY

Ramesses II ensured that his name would be remembered by his extensive building projects. He added the hypostyle hall to the temple of Amun at Karnak and made additions, including his colossus of himself, to the temple of Luxor. On the west bank at Thebes he built his mortuary temple—the Ramesseum. For his favorite queen, Nofretari, a tomb decorated with superb paintings was constructed in the Valley of the Queens. In Nubia he erected the great temple of Abu Simbel, as well as other temples elsewhere in Egypt. He also constructed the city of Pi-Ramesse, his northern capital, possibly using the labor of Hebrew slaves.

4

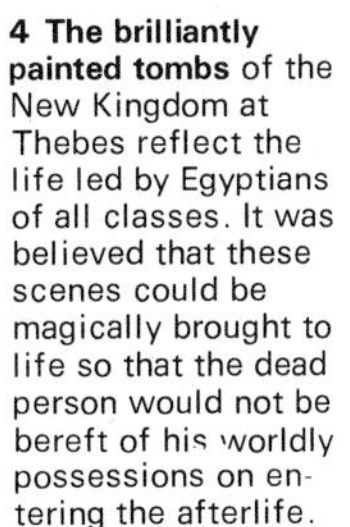

4 The brilliantly painted tombs of the New Kingdom at Thebes reflect the life led by Egyptians of all classes. It was believed that these scenes could be magically brought to life so that the dead person would not be bereft of his worldly possessions on entering the afterlife.

5

5 The economy of Egypt was agrarian, with most of the population working on the land. In theory all land was held by the crown, but in practice large estates were also held by the official classes and the temples. A limited number of peasant proprietors also owned land.

6

6 The invasion of the "sea-peoples," including the Philistines and possibly Sicilians, was repulsed by Ramesses II at the end of the New Kingdom.

7

7 Most tombs in the New Kingdom include a Book of the Dead containing spells intended to guarantee the safe passage of the deceased.

Africa: Kush and Axum

During the course of ancient Egyptian history, the armies of the pharaohs pushed the frontier of their empire ever farther south, along the lifeline of their civilization, the Nile, toward tropical black Africa. By the time of the New Kingdom (*c.* 1500 BC) all the riverine lands as far as the Fourth Cataract—that is, in the middle of the great "S" bend of the Nile—had been conquered and to some extent settled by Egyptians. This country, which was later called Nubia, was known to the Egyptians as Kush.

The emergence of the Kushite kingdom

By about 1000 BC the New Kingdom had fallen, and Kush had emerged as a state that was not only politically independent from Egypt but also increasingly culturally independent. Two hundred years later its rulers had grown so powerful that in 725 BC they were able to march down the Nile and conquer the whole of Egypt, where they formed the 25th dynasty of pharaohs [2].

Kushite control of Egypt, however, was brief. Between 676 and 663 BC, Assyrian armies invaded and devastated Egypt—first under Esarhaddon and later under Ashurbanipal. The Kushite pharaoh Taharqa retreated southward to Kush. What had made the mighty Assyrian armies almost invincible over much of the Middle East was their possession of iron weapons, which were much superior to the bronze weapons of their foes. The leaders of Kush had learned a hard lesson and took with them the Assyrian knowledge of working with iron. This technology was to form the basis for the future stability of of Kush.

After the withdrawal from Egypt, the rulers of Kush expanded southward, keeping to the valley of the Nile. The country on both sides of the great river was more fertile than it became subsequently and could support large herds of cattle. By the sixth century BC the frontier of Kush had reached just to the south of presentday Khartoum.

Dominance of the Meroë civilization

The power center of the empire swung to the south, from the old capital of Napata (near the Fourth Cataract, where the surrounding land had become overgrazed) to Meroë, south of the Atbara's confluence with the Nile. From this time, the empire is often referred to as Meroë, rather than Kush. Whereas some of the inhabitants of the northern part of Kush were black people, now nearly all the people in the country around Meroë were black, and the empire became a black state.

Meroë had abundant iron ore and wood to use in smelting it, and the empire developed a large-scale iron industry. Immense slag heaps still litter the landscape. The well-armed horsemen of the Meroë army were able to defend the settled lands from attacks of desert nomads. A flourishing trade was maintained with Ptolemaic Egypt, Arabia, and even India.

By the beginning of the Christian era, however, the civilization of Kush/Meroë had begun to decline as the state became impoverished, especially as a result of the drying up of once rich grazing and agricultural lands. Attacks by nomads became more difficult to contain, and the empire finally collapsed when an army from neighboring Axum invaded it in AD 350.

CONNECTIONS

See also
1116 African empires 500–1500
1214 African art
972 Egypt: 1570 BC to Alexander the Great

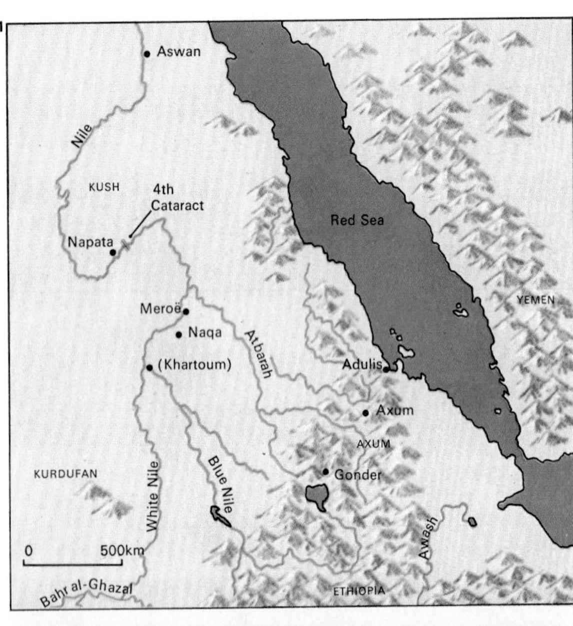
Aswan
Nile
KUSH
4th Cataract
Napata
Red Sea
YEMEN
Meroë
Naqa
Atbarah
(Khartoum)
Adulis
Axum
AXUM
KURDUFAN
White Nile
Blue Nile
Gonder
Awash
0 500km
Bahr al-Ghazal
ETHIOPIA

1 Civilizations of Kush/Meroë and Axum occupied the northeast corner of Africa: Kush/Meroë in the middle Nile valley south of Egypt and Axum on the high mountain escarpment of northern Ethiopia. Axum was the founding state of the Christian empire of Ethiopia, begun in the king's court.

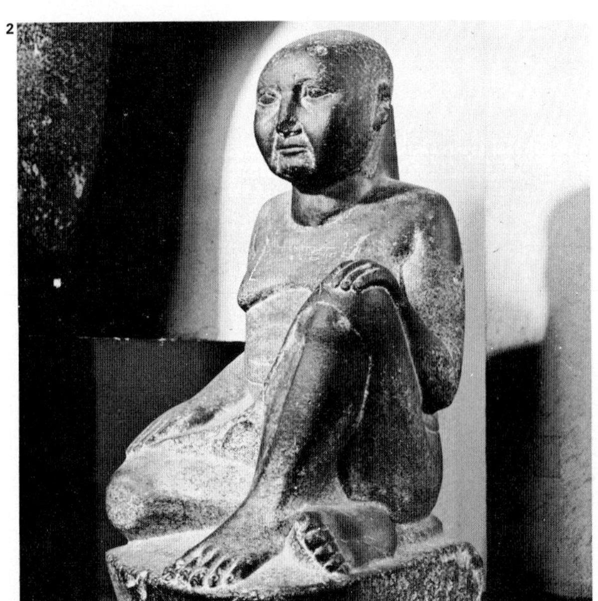

2 Narwa was governor of Thebes during the reign of one of the Kushite line of pharaohs in the 8th and 7th centuries BC. The Kushites had moved north and ruled Egypt until they were defeated and driven back to their old lands by a new invader—the "iron armies" of the Assyrians, equipped with iron weapons.

3 The Lion God of Kush was engraved on a temple wall at Naqa (100 BC–AD 100), a center south of Meroë. The carvings show an Indian influence.

4 An elephant and enemy captives form a frieze from a 1st-century AD temple near Meroë. Elephants had military and ceremonial uses at Kush/Meroë.

The empire of Kush/Meroë had been in existence for over 1,000 years, and its cultural achievements were rich and vital [3, 4]. They represented far more than an Africanized form of Egyptian culture. The inhabitants of the empire took their Egyptian heritage, borrowed from the Hellenistic world and India, and fashioned something unique, including their own form of writing, a cursive script that has yet to be deciphered [Key].

Axum, the rival empire in Ethiopia

Axum, Meroë's rival, had its origin not on the African continent, but in Arabia. A number of small but prosperous states grew up in the Yemen early in the first millennium BC, one of which, Saba, was probably the Sheba of King Solomon's time. By about the seventh century BC, Semitic-speaking people from overpopulated Yemen crossed the Red Sea to the Horn of Africa, settling as farmers on the northeastern edge of the high plateau of Ethiopia. There they prospered and were able to dominate the indigenous Kushitic-speaking peoples, many of whom gradually accepted the culture and the Semitic language of the newcomers. One such group, called the Habashat, established a kingdom in the third century BC. Its capital was Axum [6, 7].

Hellenistic Greeks at the court of the kings of Axum prepared the way for Christianity. The missionary responsible for the conversion of the kingdom in the fourth century AD was the Syrian St Frumentius (*c.*300–*c.*380). He was made bishop of Axum by the patriarch of Alexandria, and within a few decades Christianity had become well established. The rulers of Christian Axum conquered parts of southern Arabia in the sixth century AD. They were eventually driven out by Persian forces however, and Axum went into gradual decline. The Muslim Arab conquest of Egypt disrupted its Red Sea trade, and when the kingdom was devastated by nomads its power withered. Nevertheless, its political, religious, and cultural traditions survived to be revived in the Middle Ages in the Ethiopian heartland. The modern Axum is the holy city of the Coptic Christians.

KEY

A

B

The mysterious Meroitic script [A] is still undeciphered. The Sabaean script [B] of Axum is the forerunner of modern Amharic, the principal language of present-day Ethiopia.

5 Christian art from vanished Christian kingdoms survived in a church at Faras, near Wadi Halfa, which has now been engulfed by the waters of the Aswan dam. Christian kingdoms succeeded the civilizations of Kush/Meröe after the empire collapsed in the 5th century AD shortly before Egypt became part of the realm of Islam.

6 Rich in products that attracted Greek, Arabian, and Indian merchants, Axum was a land of soaring crags. The highest, Rāsdajan, is 15,158 feet (4,620m) tall. Because it was a difficult land to survive in or invade, Kush became part of European mythology as the home of the legendary Christian king Prester John.

7 The tallest surviving stele, or obelisk, at Axum, is one of the many splendid monuments erected by the rulers of the kingdom of Axum as they became wealthy as a result of their trade with Arabia, Egypt, and even India via the Red Sea.

The Hittites 1700–1200 BC

Until the nineteenth century knowledge of the Hittites was derived only from the Bible and Mesopotamian records, but then discoveries were made in Turkey of monuments and massive fortifications that were obviously the work of a flourishing civilization—quickly identified as Hittite. The Hittites were finally brought to vivid life by the discovery (in 1906–07) at Boğazköy, the site of the Hittite capital Hattusas, of more than 10,000 cuneiform tablets. The tablets, found in the state archives, were written primarily in the Hittite (or Kanesian) languages, but other languages included Akkadian, Khattian, Hurrian, Luwian, and Sumerian.

Origins of Hittite civilization

Little is known about the earliest period of the Hittite civilization before contact with Mesopotamia. The Hittites came into Asia Minor before 2000 BC from Europe or southern Russia. In the mid-seventeenth century BC, King Hattusilas I seems to have united a number of small states and established his administrative center at Hattusas. Hittite power evidently grew rapidly, for in the early sixteenth century BC Mursilis I was able to occupy Syria and to march on Babylon, sacking the city. The last king of the so-called Old Kingdom was Telepinus (reigned *c.* 1525–1500 BC), who is best known for rules of conduct for the king and nobles. After a period for which few records survive, the Hittite Empire began about 1460 BC. The first king of the new dynasty was apparently Tudhaliyas II, who is said to have captured Aleppo. Mitanni, a Hurrian state in northern Mesopotamia, checked further Hittite expansion.

The situation changed radically when Suppiluliumas seized the throne about 1380. He fortified Hattusas and in a brilliant campaign conquered Mitanni and its Syrian satellites. Carchemish, which commanded an important crossing point on the Euphrates, remained independent, but in a second campaign Suppiluliumas captured this fortress and occupied all of Syria between the Euphrates and the sea. The Hittite Empire was becoming a threat to Egyptian influence in the area.

Suppiluliumas died about 1346 BC; his son and successor Mursilis proved equally capable, defeating the kingdom of Arzawa to the west and suppressing a revolt in Syria. The next king, Muwattalis, inherited a secure and prosperous empire. But Egypt, led by Ramesses II (reigned 1304–1237 BC), was determined to regain the possessions and influence it had lost in Syria. The two armies met at Kadesh [7] on the River Orontes. Although Egypt claimed an overwhelming victory, the Hittites seem to have held their own and maintained their ascendancy in Syria. Relations between the two powers improved as Assyria became more of a threat, and in about 1284 BC they signed a treaty of friendship and nonaggression, copies of which have been found in Boğazköy and in Egypt. A royal marriage later sealed the alliance.

The end of the Hittite Empire

The records of the Hittite Empire end abruptly in the late thirteenth century BC, when Indo-European invaders known as the "sea peoples" poured into the area from

CONNECTIONS

See also
978 The Phoenicians 1500–146 BC
980 The Assyrians 1530–612 BC
982 The Hebrews 1200–322 BC
1592 The iron age

1

1 The impressive sanctuary of Yazilikaya is open to the air and is cut from the rock outside the walls of Hattusas, the Hittite capital. Spectacular reliefs are carved on the sides of two chambers, which are approached through an elaborate gateway. They depict processions of gods, goddesses, and kings. Many of the deities are shown with their cult animals, weapons, and symbols. Some of the gods are the patrons of Hittite cities, and all are named in hieroglyphic script. The principal scene shows the weather god Teshub standing on deified mountains; facing him are his consort and his son, and beneath him are the gods of the Hurrian pantheon. During the later years of the empire, Hittite religion came under strong Hurrian influence, as the carvings here illustrate.

2

2 The rock carving at Ivriz in the Taurus Mountains exemplifies the Aramaean style in Hittite sculpture, as is shown in particular by the god's cap and by the ringlets and profiles of both figures. But while the king wears an Assyrian cloak of a kind familiar from the royal statue from Malatya, parallels to most details of the god's clothing, including the clear curved seam above the knees, can be found in purely Hittite sculptures. The combination of relief and script facilitated the grouping (in 1880) of similar monuments reported from elsewhere in Asia Minor, notably at Boğazköy and Yazilikaya, as Hittite. The inscription names the king as Warpalawas (about 730 BC).

3

A
B

3 Among the chief deities in the Anatolian pantheon were the weather god Teshub [A] and the Sun goddess of Arinna [B]. Teshub is shown in a ninth-century statue in his customary pose, wielding a lightning bolt. (Unlike Mesopotamia, Anatolia is a land of cloud and storms.) To the Sun goddess, shown in a pendant of the empire period, the king appealed for help in times of war and danger; she was the supreme patroness of the Hittite state.

4

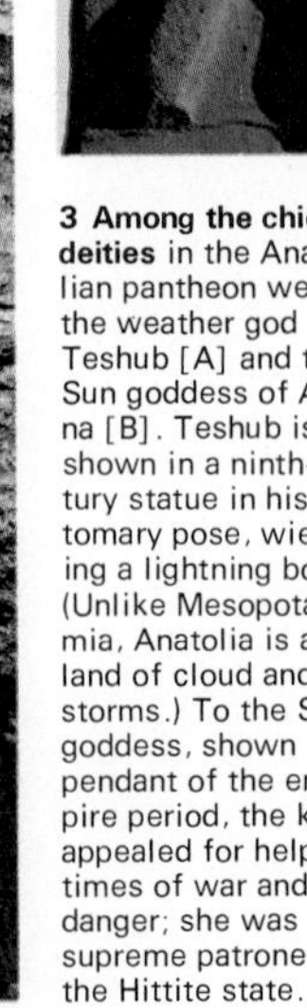

4 Most surviving Hittite sculpture is in the form of monumental bas-reliefs in stone, often with inscriptions in hieroglyphic (as distinct from cuneiform) Hittite. Although almost no sculpture in the round remains, there are a few beautiful miniature figures like this 1.7in(4.2cm) gold statuette of a man, perhaps a king, wearing a full tunic with short sleeves. It was found at Yozgat, near Boğazköy, and dates from about the 14th century BC.

Europe. The Hittites fled southward as the Phrygians overran Asia Minor. But although they lost their homeland, the Hittite way of life survived as the refugees established city-states in northern Syria, an area long under Hittite control. The Hittites may not necessarily have formed the majority of the population, and some southern areas were overrun by Aramaeans about 1000 BC.

Structure of Hittite society

The neo-Hittite city-states, which were often isolated geographically, were unable to unite effectively against the growing power of Assyria. After exacting tribute for many years and putting down occasional rebellions, Assyria, under Tiglath-Pileser III (reigned 744–727 BC), decided to incorporate the Syrian kingdoms into its empire, and by the end of the eighth century BC the Hittite Empire was only a memory.

During the period up to the end of the thirteenth century BC the Hittite king, although perhaps not quite such a dominant figure as in Mesopotamia, made the final decision on military, religious, and judicial matters [4]. On his death he joined the gods—indeed "he became a god" was a euphemism for the death of a king. The queen was also important, playing a role in state affairs. Nepotism was institutionalized and most of the highest offices were allotted to the king's relatives. There seems to have been an exclusive caste of privileged nobility and landowners. The common people worked as farmers, craftsmen, and laborers; members of the servant class were little better than slaves.

The brutality that characterizes the history of Assyria was apparently lacking among the Hittites. A city captured in war suffered grave retribution in that it was generally destroyed and its inhabitants enslaved, but the Hittites are not known to have indulged in the mass killings or systematic torture that the Assyrians favored. Similarly, punishment for crime was generally based on restitution to the injured party or his relatives, even in murder cases. Execution was prescribed only for rape, bestiality, and rebellion or treachery, and even then the king might exercise mercy.

KEY

A double-headed eagle is carved on the back of a sphinx at Alaja Hüyük in Turkey, a city of the empire period. It is clutching in its talons two hares with their faces turned outward like the eagle's heads. A figure, now badly damaged but perhaps a goddess, stood on the eagle's back. The same double-headed eagle motif appears also as a base for two standing figures among the sculptures of Yazilikaya. A double-headed bird appears elsewhere in the ancient world, for example on an early Spartan ivory and on a shrine at Taxila, Pakistan. It was also the symbol of imperial Russia.

5

6

5 In the sphinx gate at Alaja Hüyük in central Turkey, the sphinxes—unusual for Hittite art—are sculpted partly in the round. Many reliefs were found in the ruins, depicting animals, musicians, jugglers, and a shepherd with his flock. Pre-Hittite tombs of the third millennium were also discovered there and contained silver and bronze animal figures, and golden jugs, goblets, and ornaments.

6 The excavation of Karatepe, northeast of Adana, revealed a bilingual inscription, one text in hieroglyphic Hittite and the other in Phoenician, which confirmed the decoding of the Hittite.

7 Use of the light war chariot, shown in this drawing of an Egyptian relief, accounted in part for the Hittites' military success, particularly at the battle at Kadesh (*c.* 1300 BC). Hittite chariots, unlike those of Egypt and other nations of the same period, carried three men—one driver and two fighters—instead of the usual one driver and one fighter. The main tactical aim of the Hittites in battle was to draw the enemy into the open where the chariots would be most effective. But their planning was not based solely on that maneuver. A clever ruse, for example, caught the Egyptians by surprise at Kadesh, and only bad luck prevented an overwhelming victory.

7

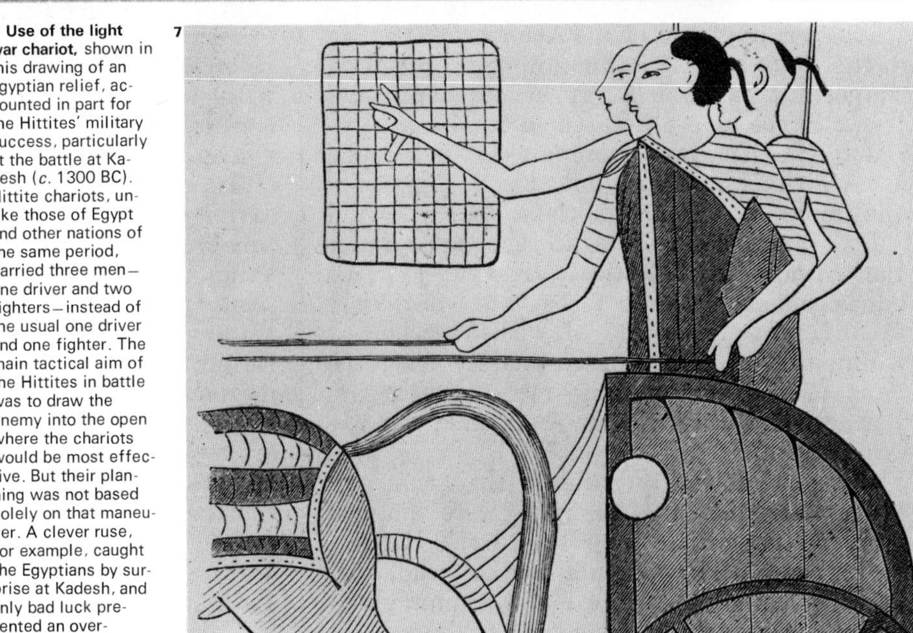

8

8 This basalt carving of a lion from Malatya, dated probably about 1000 BC, is fairly typical of the sculpture of the neo-Hittite period. The use of stone lions to flank entranceways was fairly common.

The Phoenicians 1500–146 BC

The ancient land of Phoenicia covered primarily the coastal strip of modern Israel and Lebanon. Its prosperity depended on the waters of the Mediterranean. Phoenician trading ships sailed remarkable distances, opening up new markets and protecting existing routes by establishing trading stations and colonies. The history of Phoenicia is the history of its great cities and their colonies, particularly Byblos, Tyre, Sidon, Berytus (modern Beirut), Ugarit, and Carthage.

Foreign influence on Phoenicia

Phoenician cities, like the city-states of classical Greece, maintained their independence from each other, but independence from their more powerful neighbors was less easy to sustain. In the early sixteenth century BC, Egypt exacted tribute from the cities and then brought them totally under its control. Egyptian influence [4,6] remained strong in Phoenicia, but the cultural and physical presence of Mesopotamia became increasingly dominant. After a period of Hittite control the Assyrian king Tiglath-Pileser I (reigned *c.*1115–*c.*1093 BC) received tribute from the Phoenician cities. Phoenicia then regained its independence of action. A period of great prosperity followed and with it a remarkable expansion of power throughout the Mediterranean.

As Assyria's power approached its peak, however, the Phoenicians again became a tributary people, in thrall first to Ashurnasirpal II and his son Shalmaneser III in the ninth century and then to Tiglath-Pileser III in the eighth century. In the following century the armies of Esarhaddon overran most of Phoenicia. Tyre held out but eventually fell to the Babylonians in the reign of Nebuchadnezzar II (604–562 BC). Phoenicia then became part of the Persian Empire of Cyrus the Great. It remained an important sea power, but the powerful contingent that it contributed to the fleet that Xerxes (*c.*519–465 BC) led against Greece shared heavily in the defeat at the Battle of Salamis in 480 BC. Alexander the Great (356–323 BC) incorporated Phoenicia into his empire after his victory at the Battle of Issus in 333 BC and his capture of Tyre the following year. Carthage, however, remained strong and independent.

From the earliest days of commerce with Egypt and Mesopotamia, the Phoenician economy relied on trade, importing gold, ivory, livestock, and wheat; it exported timber, metals, cloth, glass, and ships. Its trading vessels often carried the produce of the Asian hinterland to Egypt, Greece, and Cyprus and later to North Africa, Spain, and the Mediterranean islands. Flourishing Phoenician industries included dyeing, which was centered in Sidon and Tyre, metalworking [2], glass-making, pottery, and carvings in ivory [Key] and bone.

Phoenicia as a colonial power

Phoenicia's colonizing era began in the twelfth century BC. It had already planted settlements in Cyprus, but it is likely that contacts about this time with the Mycenaeans sparked the imagination and the commercial acumen of Phoenician merchants. In the Aegean, Rhodes and probably Crete had Phoenician settlements, but there is only literary evidence of a Phoeni-

CONNECTIONS

See also
976 The Hittites 1700–1200 BC
980 The Assyrians 1530–612 BC
984 The Persian Empire of the Achaemenids
982 The Hebrews 1200–322 BC
1012 Early Rome: the kingdom and the republic

1 The Temple of the Obelisks at Byblos (the most powerful Phoenician city in the Egyptian period) dates from the middle Bronze Age. These open-air sanctuaries were dotted with stelae, or pillars, erected in honor of the gods or to mark cremations or the burial places of important objects.

2 The Phoenicians were skilled at working gold, an art they learned from the Mycenaeans and Egyptians. This gold ring dates from the 6th or 5th century BC and was found at Tharros in Sardinia. The scarab on the ring depicts Bes, the Egyptian dwarf god.

3 This limestone coffin dates from the 13th century BC, but was reused by King Hiram of Byblos in the early 10th century. The king is shown seated on a throne and flanked by winged sphinxes. He has a drooping lotus in his hand that indicates he has died. Before him is a food-laden table, and a procession of servants is approaching him. Above this scene is a typically Egyptian lotus frieze. Below are four lions, which are more reminiscent of Assyrian or Hittite reliefs. On the lid is one of the earliest examples of Phoenician script.

4 King Eshmunazar II of Sidon, who perhaps reigned in the 6th century BC, was buried in this black basalt coffin of wholly Egyptian style. A Phoenician inscription warns against disturbing the body and tells how Eshmunazar extended Sidon's dominance south to Joppa.

5 The tree of life, fertility symbol of the Babylonians and Assyrians, and the lotus of Egypt are combined on this Phoenician ivory plaque from an Assyrian palace. It shows both the extent of Phoenician trade, and the resultant diverse influences on their culture.

cian presence on the Greek mainland. No more concrete evidence of Phoenician colonization in Italy exists, although there were close trading ties. But in the central and western Mediterranean, the Phoenicians established a chain of colonies, which made them dominant in the area. Colonies flourished in western Sicily, Malta, Sardinia, the Balearic islands, and Spain.

Phoenicia also founded several colonies on the North African coast [9] at an early period, including Utica, Hadrumetum (modern Sousse, Tunisia), and Leptis Magna (near modern Tripoli). But the most distinguished of all the settlements, eventually surpassing its mother city Tyre in power, was Carthage [7], which fell to Rome in 146 BC. Carthage dominated—although it did not rule—the Phoenician colonies in the west. The most important of these were Gades (modern Cadiz); Ebesus (Ibiza), which Carthage founded in the middle of the seventh century BC; and Carthago Nova (Cartagena), founded by Hannibal's brother-in-law Hasdrubal in 228 between the first and second of the Punic Wars.

A policy of colonization is often accompanied by an impulse toward exploration, and the Phoenicians appear to have been enthusiastic explorers. The Greek historian Herodotus, perhaps skeptically, reports a story that Phoenician ships circumnavigated Africa, returning in three years to Egypt. The details Herodotus gives make it possible that the remarkable voyage did take place. According to a much later Roman geographical work, the Carthaginian Himilco sailed from Spain up the Gallic coast to Brittany. There is a possibility, although no archeological evidence, that he reached Cornwall.

The legacy of a rich literature

Much light has been shed on the mythology and beliefs of the area in pre-Iron Age times by the discovery and deciphering of the cuneiform texts of Ugarit. Although few inscriptions or documents have survived of the once rich Phoenician literature, these relics are important because the Phoenicians' Semitic alphabet of 22 consonants was the basis of the Greek alphabet.

KEY

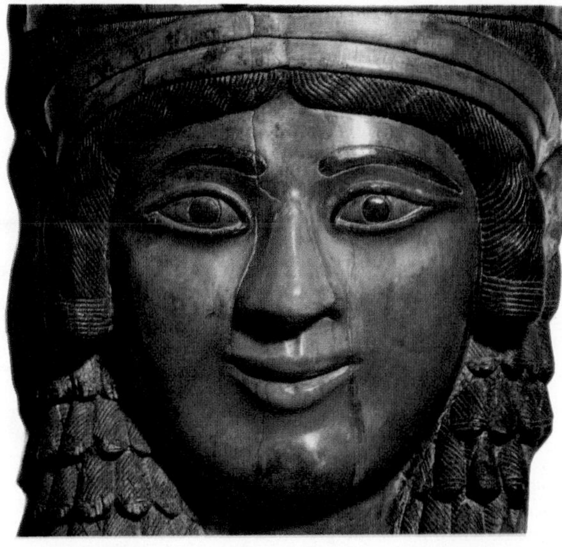

This ivory carving may be Astarte, the Phoenician fertility goddess. In Babylonia she was called Ishtar. The carving was found in a well at Nimrud (Calah), in northern Iraq.

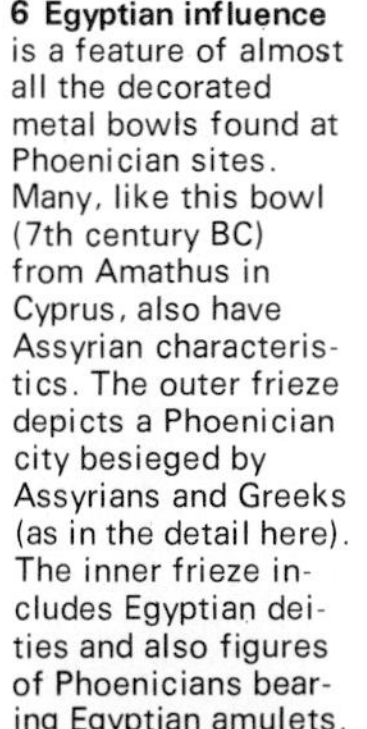

6 Egyptian influence is a feature of almost all the decorated metal bowls found at Phoenician sites. Many, like this bowl (7th century BC) from Amathus in Cyprus, also have Assyrian characteristics. The outer frieze depicts a Phoenician city besieged by Assyrians and Greeks (as in the detail here). The inner frieze includes Egyptian deities and also figures of Phoenicians bearing Egyptian amulets.

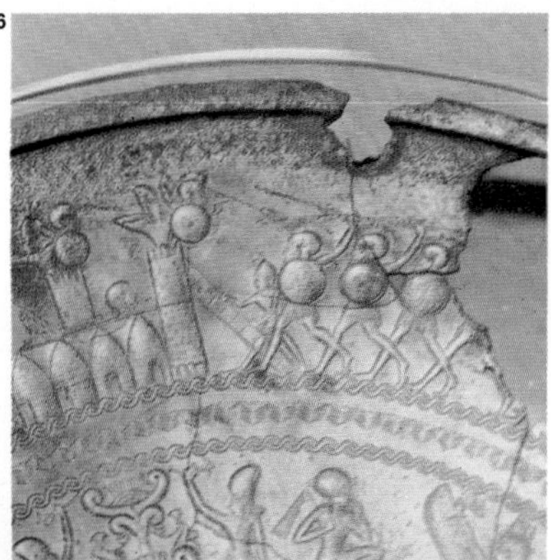

7 The precinct of Tanit at Salammbo was used throughout Carthage's history. Tanit was another name for Astarte, the chief female deity of the Phoenicians. Many stelae with symbols of Tanit and dedicatory inscriptions have been discovered in the precinct, but the most sensational finds were thousands of urns containing the ashes of cremated babies—clear evidence of infant sacrifice in Carthage.

8 Luli, the king of Tyre and Sidon, fled to Cyprus in 701 BC. During his reign he formed alliances with Egypt and Judah and resisted, as far as he could, continual Assyrian aggression. Eventually, however, Sennacherib (*r.* 704–681 BC), king of Assyria, forced the departure depicted in this detail of a relief (which is now lost) from Nineveh. The relief shows two kinds of ship. The larger ships, forerunners of the trireme, were used for war and exploration and had a double bank of oars, with sails, a ram at the prow, and a high stern. The round ships, used for trading, also had two banks of oars but were sailless, with stern and prow of equal height. Both types of ship had steering oars on each side of the stern. The upper decks were hung with shields for protection.

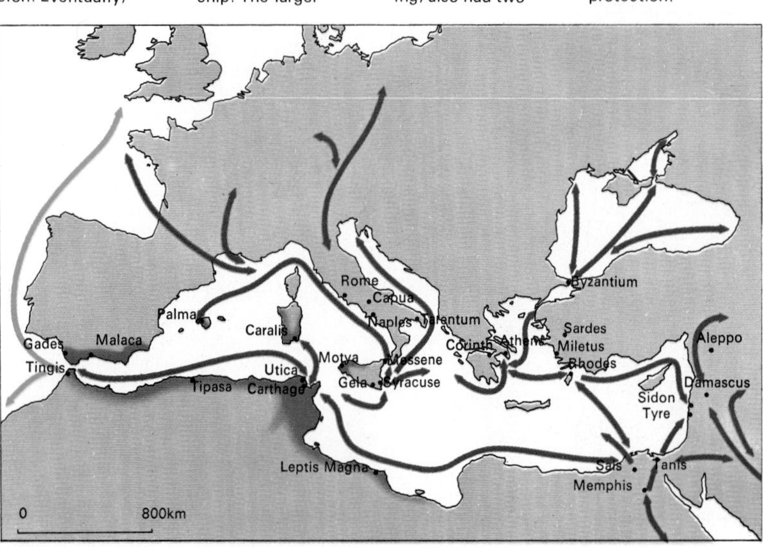

Rome
Capua
Palma
Caralis
Naples
Gades
Malaca
Tingis
Motya
Utica
Tipasa
Carthage
Gela
Syracuse
Corinth
Sardes
Miletus
Rhodes
Byzantium
Aleppo
Damascus
Sidon
Tyre
Leptis Magna
Sais
Tanis
Memphis
0
800km

Carthaginian sphere of influence *c.* 323 BC
Mediterranean trade routes *c.* 375 BC
5th-century Phoenician exploration

9 Carthage extended Phoenician influence in Spain, Sardinia, and North Africa. The Phoenicians had several footholds in western Sicily, and in 480 BC the Carthaginians made an abortive invasion of the north to aid Xerxes. At the end of the 4th century they waged an unsuccessful war against Syracuse.

The Assyrians 1530–612 BC

The Assyrians, a Semitic people in northwestern Mesopotamia, enjoyed a material culture in the third millennium comparable to that of the Sumerians and briefly emerged as a military force under Shamshi-Adad I early in the eighteenth century BC. But for the next four centuries the strongest kingdoms in Mesopotamia were those of the Kassites, who came from the Zagros Mountains to take over Babylonia in the south, and of the Hurrians, who established the state of Mitanni in northwestern Mesopotamia. In the fourteenth century BC, Ashur-uballit led the revived Assyrians into Mitanni after that state had been shattered by Hittite invaders from Anatolia.

The empire established

Adadnirari I (reigned 1307–1275 BC) pushed Assyria's frontiers up to the Euphrates, and Shalmaneser I (reigned 1274–1245 BC) advanced northward and finally crushed the Hurrians. The first of the great Assyrian monarchs was Tiglath-Pileser I (reigned *c.* 1115–*c.* 1077 BC), who came to the throne after a period of instability in western Asia. By a succession of military campaigns that combined brilliance and brutality, he extended Assyria's authority far into the north and northwest, overrunning Syria and exacting tribute even from the rich trading cities of Phoenicia.

Tiglath-Pileser succeeded, although with difficulty, in keeping back incursions by Aramaean peoples from the western desert. But after his death Aramaeans and Chaldaeans overran almost the whole of Mesopotamia, where a kind of Dark Age lasted for more than 150 years. When Adadnirari II came to the Assyrian throne in 912 BC, his kingdom was a strip little more than 100 miles long and 50 miles wide. Yet by the middle of the seventh century BC, Assyria was the largest and most powerful state in the civilized world. Its rulers were insatiable for empire, leading campaigns of conquest almost every year.

Ashurnasirpal II (reigned 883–859 BC) [5] was mainly responsible for the restoration of Assyrian dominion. He built the army into an irresistible fighting unit and led it to the shores of the Mediterranean. At his new capital at Calah (Nimrud) he built a vast palace, the doorway flanked by winged bulls. The glory of Assyria was paid for by the sufferings of its enemies; many inscriptions testify to the tortures inflicted on soldiers and civilians alike. Ashurnasirpal's son Shalmaneser III (reigned 859–824 BC), his father's equal in brutality, continued to conduct annual campaigns [2], but with less success.

The surge of imperialism

A series of weak rulers and the growing power of the kingdom of Urartu to the north made Assyria's position precarious. The situation demanded a decisive and intelligent personality to meet the threat, and the Assyrians were fortunate to have such a man in Tiglath-Pileser III (reigned 745–727 BC). He reasserted Assyrian authority and established a uniform administration. He transformed conquered lands into provinces, each under its own governor and paying tribute, taxes, and duties to the central authority. Although the governors had considerable authority, they were supervised

CONNECTIONS

See also
976 The Hittites 1700–1200 BC
982 The Hebrews 1200–322 BC
978 The Phoenicians 1500–146 BC
972 Egypt: 1570 BC to Alexander the Great

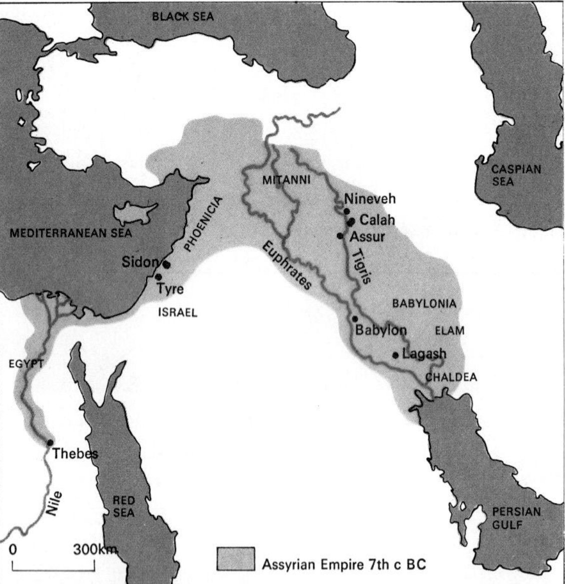
BLACK SEA
CASPIAN SEA
MEDITERRANEAN SEA
MITANNI
PHOENICIA
Nineveh
Calah
Assur
Euphrates
Tigris
Sidon
Tyre
ISRAEL
BABYLONIA
Babylon
ELAM
Lagash
CHALDEA
EGYPT
Thebes
Nile
RED SEA
PERSIAN GULF
0
300km
Assyrian Empire 7th c BC

1 Assyria's empire reached its greatest extent in the 7th century BC, during Ashurbanipal's reign. He subjected its people to merciless repression inflicted by his army, in whose ruthlessness he gloried, and ruled through an efficient administrative system supervised by the central government. Assyrian hegemony collapsed and was followed by a brief resurgence of Babylonian rule.

2 Jehu, the king of Israel, is shown bowing to Shalmaneser III (*r.* 859–824 BC) on this panel from the gates of Balwat. The panels record many of Shalmaneser's campaigns– against Babylon, northern Mesopotamia, and Syria, which after several wars he failed to subdue entirely. But he was able to force Tyre and Sidon to pay tribute to him, and in 841 BC Israel became a tributary.

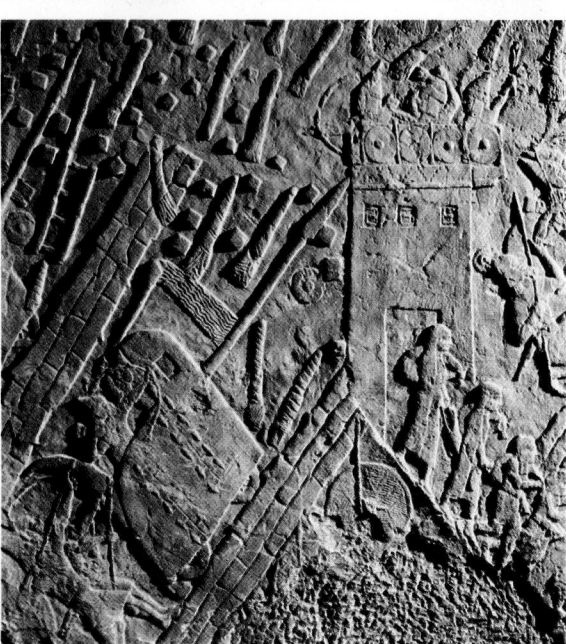

3 Sennacherib's siege of Lachish (701 BC), a Judaean city, is portrayed on stone panels from Nineveh. The city's fall was followed by the submission of King Hezekiah of Judah. Various siege machines developed by the Assyrians are represented on stone panels such as the one shown here.

4 A skin boat on the Tigris carries perhaps building materials for Sennacherib's palace. Herodotus tells how circular hide boats floated down the Euphrates, carrying one or more donkeys in addition to the cargo. On arrival at Babylon, the boats were broken up and loaded on the donkeys for the return journey overland to Armenia.

by the central government, to which they sent regular reports. Tiglath-Pileser initiated a policy of mass deportations of defeated or rebellious peoples. By the end of his reign Urartu was no longer a threat, and Babylonia, Palestine, Syria, and Phoenicia were completely under Assyrian control.

Babylonia, however, was coming increasingly under the influence of the Chaldaean tribes that dominated the surrounding country and were bitterly hostile to the Assyrians. Sennacherib (reigned 704–681 BC) reacted with characteristic vigor, installing his son on the Babylonian throne. But in 694 BC the Babylonians revolted and invited the help of the king of Elam, who carried off the Assyrian prince to his own country. The brutal war that followed lasted five years and ended with the leveling of of Babylon by Sennacherib in 689 BC. He made his capital at Nineveh and initiated a vast program of public works.

Sennacherib was murdered and his son Esarhaddon (reigned 681–669 BC) [Key] at once began the task of rebuilding Babylon. He was an able statesman who knew when to temper strength with mercy. Assyrian authority in the east remained supreme, and the Mannaean buffer state in the northeast was under Assyrian control. A revolt in Phoenicia was settled by deporting the inhabitants of Sidon and executing its king. But Esarhaddon's most spectacular success was against Egypt. The ruling dynasty there had been fomenting trouble in Phoenicia, and Esarhaddon decided to subdue them.

The fall of the empire

Ashurbanipal (reigned 668–*c*. 627 BC) quelled a rebellion in Egypt and again subdued that country, but as it was too large and too distant an area to occupy permanently [1], its administration was left to local princes. Eventually, Ashurbanipal was forced to withdraw from Egypt since he was involved in a large-scale rebellion headed by his brother, the king of Babylon, in alliance with Elam. Victorious in 648 BC, Ashurbanipal could not survive the alliance of Napopolassar, who was installed king in Babylon in 625 BC, with the Medes. Ashur soon fell, and in 612 BC Nineveh was destroyed.

KEY

Esarhaddon, the great imperialist Assyrian ruler, is shown on a stele found at Zenjirli, which lies northeast of the Gulf of Alexandretta and northwest of Aleppo. The king towers over two supplicant prisoners, held by cords through their lips. The standing prisoner may be Ba'alu, king of Tyre, although in that case the stele represents Esarhaddon's wishes rather than the facts, for Ba'alu rejected his terms, and the siege was probably concluded only under his successor. The kneeling figure probably represents either Tarku of Kush or his son Ushanakhuru, who was carried off with his family to Assyria; Tarku also retained control of his land.

5

5 Two figures, one of them (to judge from clothing and inscription) perhaps representing the 9th-century king Ashurnasirpal II of Assyria, stand on both sides of a tree of life. This motif, common in art throughout western Asia, is a symbol of fertility conferred by the goddess Ishtar.

6

6 Ashurnasirpal's son Shalmaneser III built this dais for the throne in his palace at Fort Shalmaneser, Nimrud. Its vertical faces show relief carvings of tribute. The upper surface has shallow, round recesses to house the feet of the throne and footstools and is covered with inscriptions telling of his reign.

7

7 Painted decoration survived in parts of the palaces at Fort Shalmaneser, including the above figure dressed in a fish cloak and holding a pine cone in the fertilization gesture common in the reliefs of Ashurnasirpal.

8

8 Hunting dogs are exercised by servants in the royal park in this relief from the north palace of Ashurbanipal II at Nineveh. The Assyrians believed that the king was fulfilling a sacred duty in hunting wild animals, and lions were brought to the country so that the king could show his skill in lavish hunts. Like Nimrod, Assurbanipal was a "mighty hunter before the lord"; and in his day the lions that infested thickets along the Euphrates ravaged flocks, herds, and people.

9

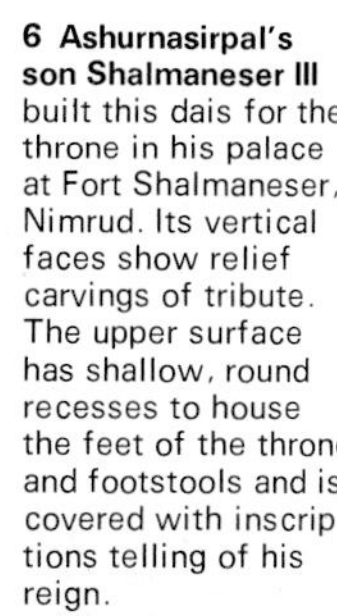

9 The valley of the Zab River in western Iran, a tributary of the Tigris, is typical of the terrain covered by much of the Assyrian Empire. In much of the region the mountains ensured that life was centered in the river valleys.

The Hebrews 1200–322 BC

The name *Hebrew* is of uncertain origin and meaning. The similar name *Habiru* appears in documents of the fourteenth century BC describing certain people, perhaps semi-nomads, who inhabited the northern fringes of the Arabian desert. Eber (Gen. 10.21), the grandson of Shem, may be the eponym of the Hebrews.

The twelve tribes of Israel

The early Hebrews were nomads, and tradition tells of the migration of Abraham from Mesopotamia into Canaan, an area later called Palestine, on the borders of Egypt. Abraham's grandson Jacob, renamed Israel ("striver with God") had 12 sons from whom descended the biblical 12 tribes of Israel. The Bible tells how Jacob's sons sold their brother Joseph into slavery in Egypt. When famine broke out in Canaan, Joseph, who had found favor in Egypt, received his father and his brothers there, and they prospered for many years. Much later, their descendants were enslaved.

Both Moses and the Exodus, in which he led his people out of bondage in Egypt, remain in the consciousness of the modern Jewish people [3]. The name *Moses* is Egyptian, and legend tells of his youth at the royal court, so whether he was of completely Hebrew origin is debatable. Moses was told by God in a vision to deliver the children of Israel from Egypt and lead them into Canaan.

The date of this Exodus is uncertain, but it may have taken place in the thirteenth century BC. The captives escaped across the northern end of the Red Sea into the desert and went to Mount Sinai, or Horeb. The Law, revealed to Moses on Sinai according to the Bible, consisted of the Ten Commandments, or Decalogue, inscribed on stone and later kept in an ark, or chest. The longer Law, or Torah, of "five books," the Pentateuch, is attributed to Moses and comprises the biblical books of Genesis, Exodus, Leviticus, Numbers, and Deuteronomy. In their present form much in these books suggests a settled agricultural community as well as a nomadic existence.

Moses was followed by Joshua (*c.* 1200 BC) and a series of judges and warriors who led the invasion and gradual occupation of Canaan, the Promised Land. The prophet Saul was anointed as first king of the Hebrews. He was successful in defeating some tribes, such as the Amalekites.

David, Israel's greatest king

David, who succeeded Saul, has always been regarded as an ideal Hebrew, second only to Moses. He was more successful than Saul in uniting the tribes and was an able administrator [1] as well as a poet—many of the Psalms are attributed to him. David captured Jerusalem from the Jebusites (*c.* 1000 BC) and made it his capital. The Ark of the Covenant, which had been housed in different places since the desert wanderings, was brought to Jerusalem; when Solomon inherited this united kingdom he built the Temple in Jerusalem [2, 5] for the Ark and a larger palace for himself.

Discontent boiled over after Solomon's death, and the kingdom was irreparably divided. His weak son Rehoboam managed to hold only the southern country around Jerusalem, in a kingdom that came to be

CONNECTIONS

See also
976 The Hittites 1700–1200 BC
978 The Phoenicians 1500–146 BC
980 The Assyrians 1530–612 BC
984 The Persian Empire of the Achaemenids
844 Judaism and Christianity

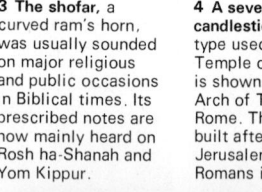

Ancient Israel
Phoenicia
Philistia
Assyrian Empire

1 Biblical tradition holds that the ancient Tribes of Israel escaped from slavery in Egypt in the 13th century BC under Moses. After conquering parts of Canaan in the 12th century, Israel reached its peak under David (*c.* 1000–960 BC), who took Jerusalem and subjugated the surrounding nations [A]. This empire divided after Solomon's death into two smaller and weaker nations, Judah in the south and Israel in the north [B], both declining in the face of Assyrian rule [C].

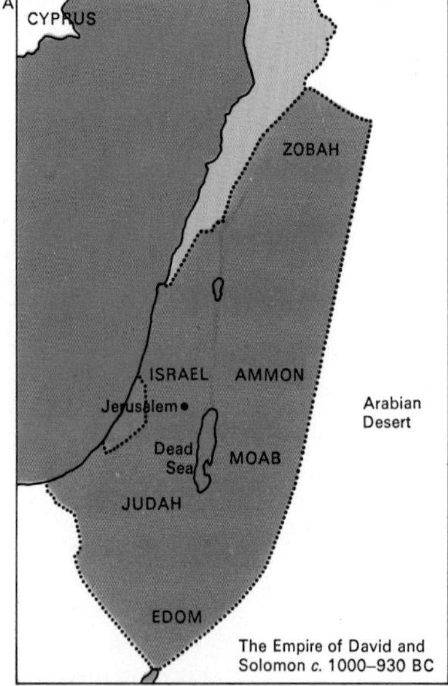

A
CYPRUS
ZOBAH
ISRAEL
AMMON
Jerusalem
Arabian Desert
Dead Sea
MOAB
JUDAH
EDOM

The Empire of David and Solomon *c.* 1000–930 BC

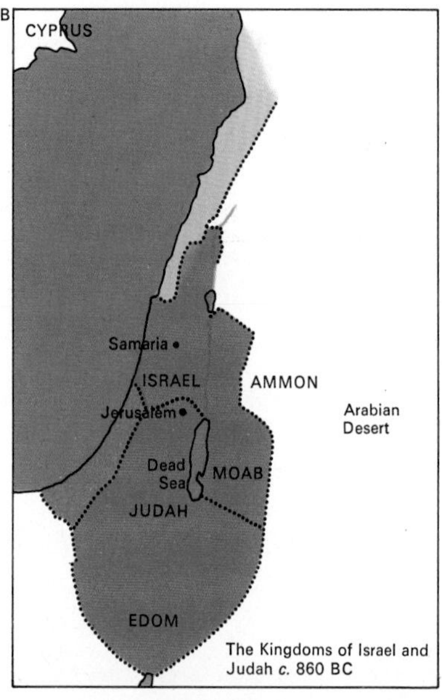

B
CYPRUS
Samaria
ISRAEL
AMMON
Jerusalem
Arabian Desert
Dead Sea
MOAB
JUDAH
EDOM

The Kingdoms of Israel and Judah *c.* 860 BC

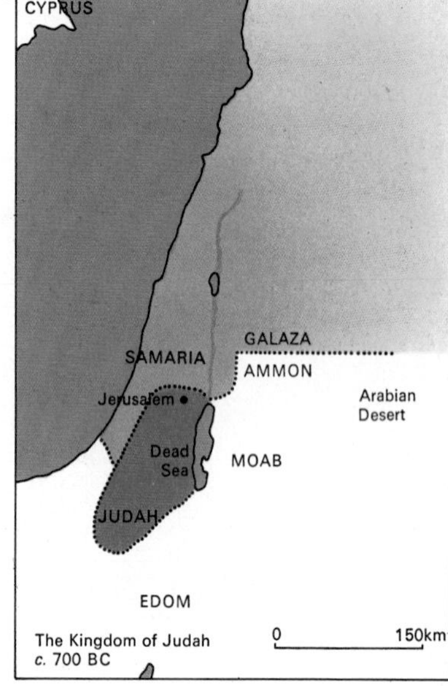

C
CYPRUS
GALAZA
SAMARIA
AMMON
Jerusalem
Arabian Desert
Dead Sea
MOAB
JUDAH
EDOM
0
150km

The Kingdom of Judah *c.* 700 BC

2 The Dome of the Rock, a Muslim shrine on the spot where Mohammed is believed to have risen to heaven, stands on Mount Zion, the site of the Temple of Jerusalem. The Wailing Wall is the western wall of the second Temple.

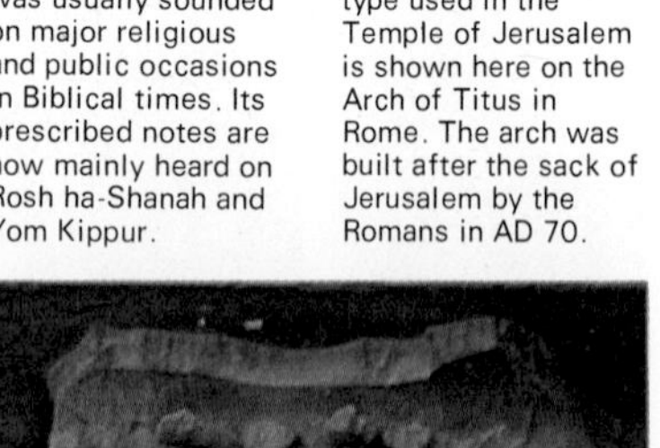

3 The shofar, a curved ram's horn, was usually sounded on major religious and public occasions in Biblical times. Its prescribed notes are now mainly heard on Rosh ha-Shanah and Yom Kippur.

4 A seven-branched candlestick of the type used in the Temple of Jerusalem is shown here on the Arch of Titus in Rome. The arch was built after the sack of Jerusalem by the Romans in AD 70.

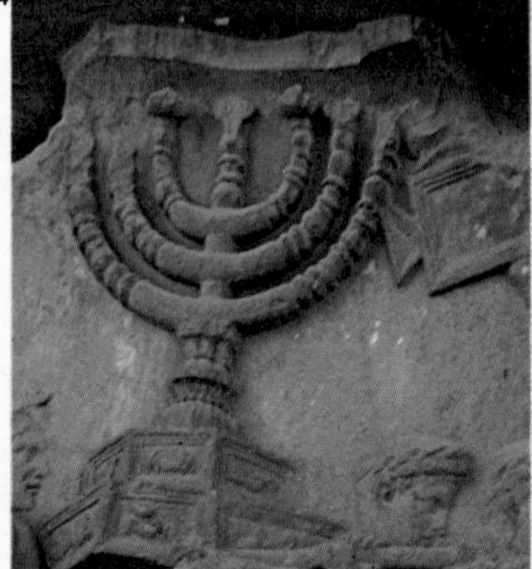

known as Judah (Judea). Jeroboam I, an Ephraimite, broke away with ten tribes to form a northern kingdom called Israel. The following centuries saw the rivalries of Judah and Israel and the destruction of Israel by the Assyrians in 721 BC. [7].

The small kingdom of Judah survived in semi-independence for more than a century, but it finally fell in 586 BC. Thousands of its leading figures were taken as prisoners to Babylon, thus beginning the period known as the Babylonian captivitiy. The northern tribes of Israel had been scattered and lost (the ten lost tribes), so when the leaders of Judah returned from exile after 538 BC, the terms *Judaism* and *Jews* became appropriate.

The Hebrew prophets and monotheism

More important for world religion than these political events was the work of the Hebrew prophets. These were inspired men who were sometimes associated with, but often critical of, the official religion of their time. One of the first, Samuel, was priest, prophet, seer, and kingmaker. He chose Saul to be the first king of Israel and also selected David as Saul's successor. Elijah and his servant and follower Elisha both denounced the prophets of Baal, and as a result were hounded by the rulers.

They were followed by a number of other prophets between the eighth and sixth centuries, whose messages were written down. Amos and Hosea preached in Israel, and Micah and Isaiah preached [6] in Judah. These men declared the unity of God and his demands of just behavior from the people, a teaching that is termed "ethical monotheism." During the reign of King Josiah, the book of the law (probably the biblical Deuteronomy) was found (621 BC). Its exhortations—to put down small shrines and concentrate worship at Jerusalem—was promulgated by Josiah and religious reforms were instituted. Jeremiah preached in Jerusalem before its fall in 586 BC and then went to Egypt, while Ezekiel went to Babylon. Ezekiel denounced heathenism and planned the rebuilding of the Temple, whereas Jeremiah taught a more inner religion of a new covenant with God.

KEY

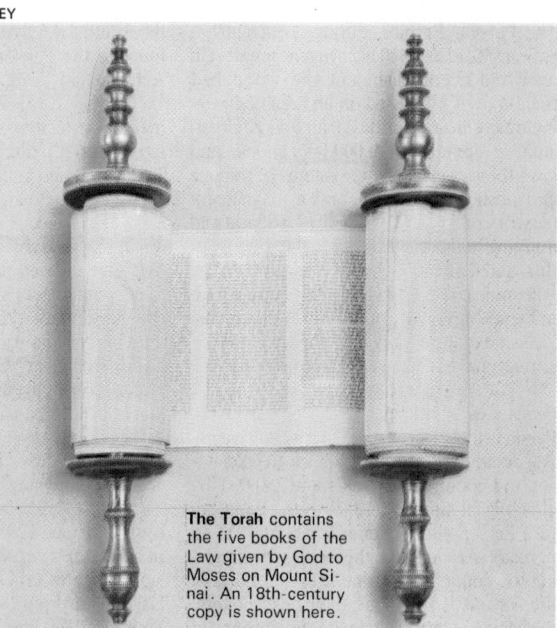

The Torah contains the five books of the Law given by God to Moses on Mount Sinai. An 18th-century copy is shown here.

5

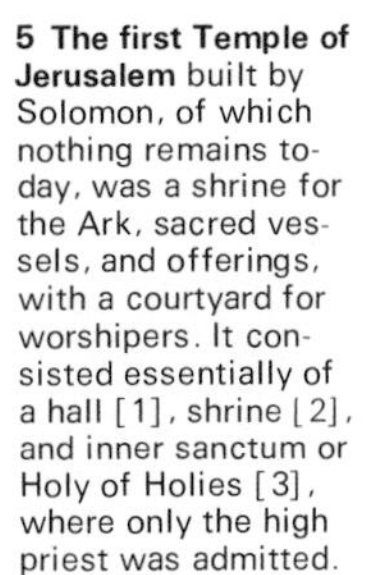

3
2
1
0
10
20m

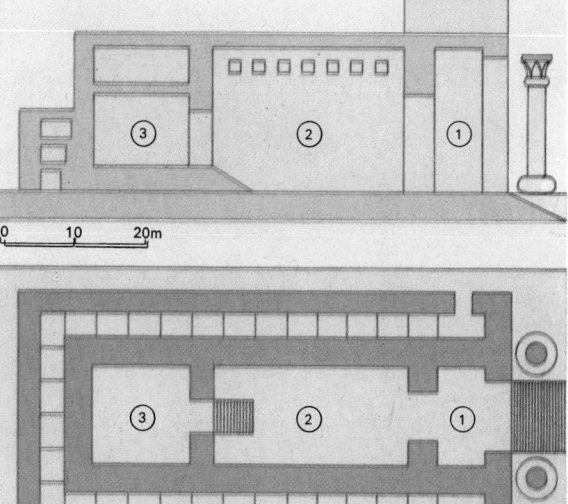

5 The first Temple of Jerusalem built by Solomon, of which nothing remains today, was a shrine for the Ark, sacred vessels, and offerings, with a courtyard for worshipers. It consisted essentially of a hall [1], shrine [2], and inner sanctum or Holy of Holies [3], where only the high priest was admitted.

6

6 In Hebrew history a number of prophets arose who commented on society and rebuked the insincere practice of religion. Like Isaiah, depicted here by Michelangelo, the prophets taught belief in one God, who was just and merciful and who required similar qualities from his followers.

7

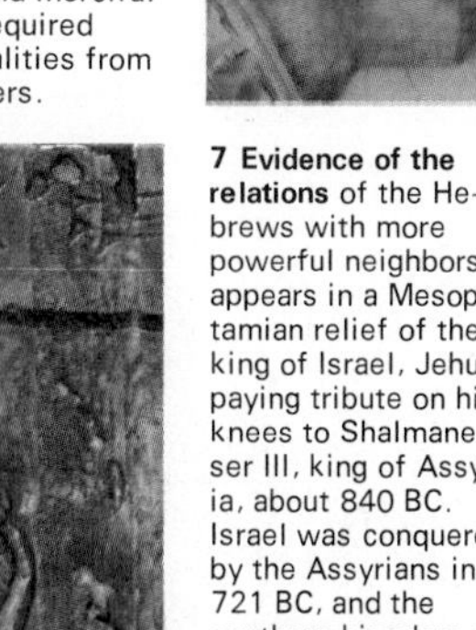

7 Evidence of the relations of the Hebrews with more powerful neighbors appears in a Mesopotamian relief of the king of Israel, Jehu, paying tribute on his knees to Shalmaneser III, king of Assyria, about 840 BC. Israel was conquered by the Assyrians in 721 BC, and the southern kingdom of Judah eventually fell in 586 BC.

8

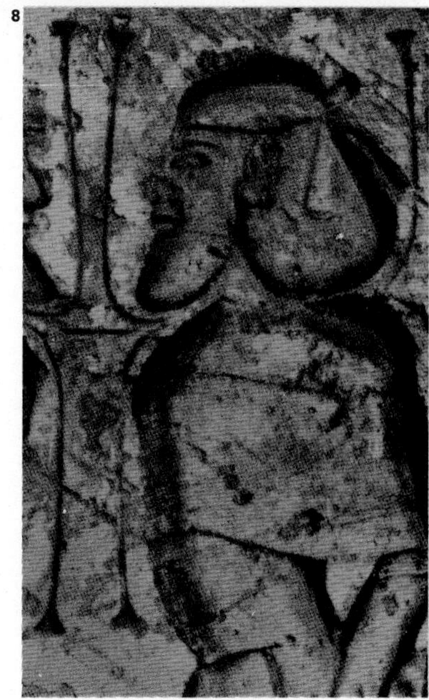

8 A Canaanite captive being led before the pharaoh was depicted in a temple of Rameses III in Egypt. The Canaanites resembled the Hebrews in appearance, since both were Semites and the men wore their hair long and were bearded. They were finally conquered by the Israelites in about 1200 BC.

The Persian Empire of the Achaemenids

The Persian Empire, during its height between 550 BC and 480 BC, was the greatest in area and accomplishment the world had then known. Centered on an area comprising much of present-day Iran and Afghanistan, it contained 40,000,000 people and gave them common law, systems of coinage and postage, irrigation, and a magnificent network of roads [1], as well as a liberal and unifying religion. Although the power of the Achaemenid dynasty was broken by Alexander the Great in 330 BC, Persian influence revived under the Parthian and Sassanid empires and gave way to the Muslim empire in the seventh century AD.

Persia's early history

Persia is the natural bridge between Europe and Asia. Its history dates back to 6000 BC, and the country contains some 250,000 archeological sites [2], 1,000 in the plain before Persepolis [5] alone. In about 1500 BC nomadic Aryans from the north arrived, giving the country the name Iran or "Land of the Aryans." In 549 BC their descendants, the Medes, were united with the Persians in the south by Cyrus the Great, who thus founded the Persian Empire, calling it the Achaemenid Empire after an ancestor.

Cyrus [Key] based his empire not merely on territorial conquest but also on international tolerance and understanding. The rights and religions of all the subject states were upheld, and their laws and customs respected. After his victory in Babylon in 539 BC, which ended the Jewish captivity, he ordered the Temple in Jerusalem to be rebuilt, and more than 40,000 Jews left Babylonia and returned to Palestine. His army added the former realms of Assyria, Lydia, and Asia Minor to the Persian Empire, making it the largest political organization of pre-Roman antiquity. The conquests of Cyrus had been carried as far as the Mediterranean in the west and the Hindu Kush (east) when he was slain in 529 BC.

Cyrus was followed by his son Cambyses II (ruled 529–522 BC), who had none of his father's virtues but inherited his occasional vice of cruelty. Cambyses II began his reign by putting to death his brother Smerdis; then, lured by the wealth of Egypt, set out to capture that country. Some 50,000 of his soldiers perished in the campaign, and Cambyses unsuccessfully tried to put down the Egyptian religion. In a final outburst he killed his sister and wife Roxana, slew his son Prexaspes, and buried 12 of his nobles alive. He died returning to Persia.

The reign of Darius

Darius the Great (548–486 BC), who won a battle for the succession, had been the commander of the Ten Thousand Immortals, the elite of the Persian forces [7, 8]. His succession was marked by revolts among the conquered states, which he rapidly quelled. In Babylon, 3,000 leading citizens were crucified. Realizing how vulnerable the vast empire was to any crisis, he reduced military control in favor of wise administration and reestablished his realms in a way that became a model of imperial organization.

Agriculture based on both grain and livestock was the mainstay of the country. Artificial irrigation was introduced by means of tunnels [3] many miles long. The result was a generation of order and pros-

CONNECTIONS

See also
982 The Hebrews 1200–322 BC
978 The Phoenicians 1500–146 BC
972 Egypt: 1570 BC to Alexander the Great
994 Classical Greece
314 Water and irrigation
846 Islam, Hinduism, and Buddhism

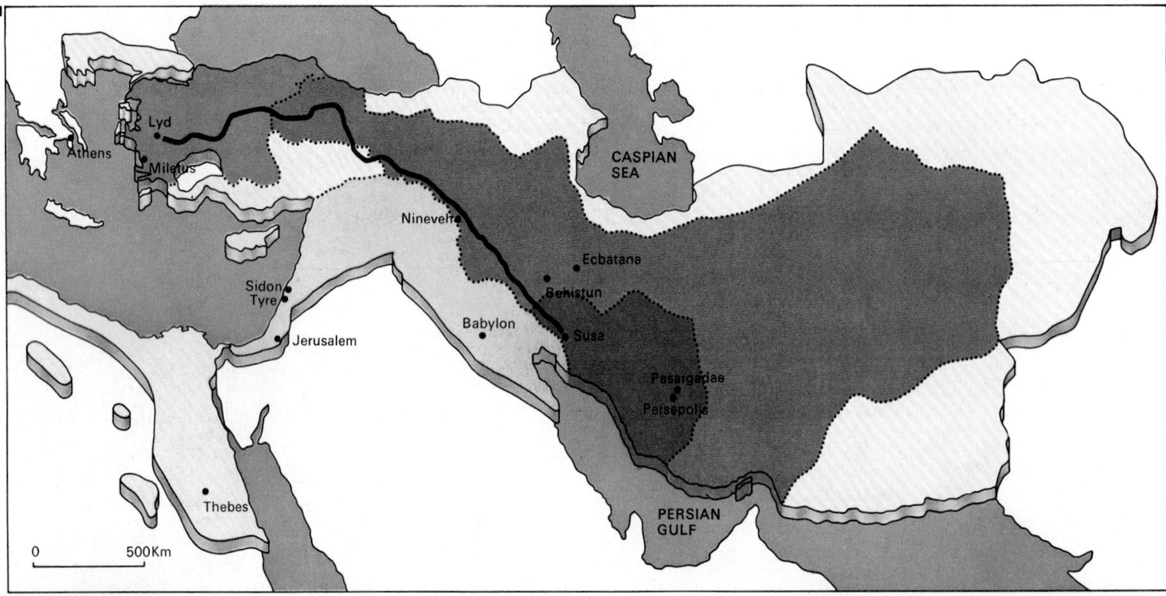

Lyd
Athens
Miletus
CASPIAN SEA
Nineveh
Ecbatana
Behistun
Sidon
Tyre
Babylon
Susa
Jerusalem
Pasargadae
Persepolis
Thebes
PERSIAN GULF
0
500Km
Kingdom of Persia
Median Empire annexed 549 BC
Lydian Empire annexed 546 BC
Chaldean Empire annexed 538 BC
Egyptian Empire annexed 525 BC
Later conquests to 479 BC
Royal Highway

1 The Persian Empire in the Achaemenid period was administered through satrapies. To maintain contact with these provinces Darius created roads whose combined length was 1,680 miles (2,700 km.). At 111 staging posts fresh horses awaited the king's envoys, who could thus traverse the whole system in a week; it took caravans 90 days.

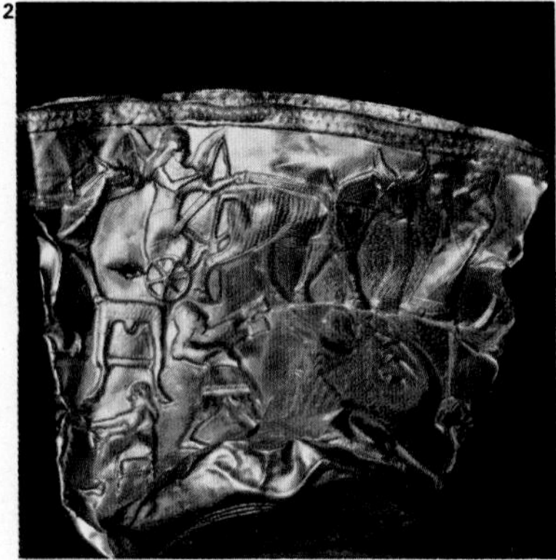

2 The crushed bowl of Hasanlu, exquisitely made in gold, shows a weather god in a chariot drawn by a bull, and a battle with a monster. It was found in 1958 during excavations of the citadel of Hasanlu at the northern end of the Solduz valley and was clutched in the hands of a man's skeleton. He was probably trying to escape from a palace that collapsed in flames when the citadel was attacked in 800 BC. The bowl is now in the Teheran Museum Treasure Room.

3 Underground water tunnels, called *ghanats,* first introduced to Persia in Achaemenid times, carry mountain water across miles of desert safe from evaporation that would deplete surface canals. A one-man windlass is used to reach the tunnels through shafts sunk at intervals of about 30 feet (10m). A digger had to work alone in a tunnel only 2 by 3 feet (60 by 90 cm) in height and width, keeping the channel straight and accurately gauging the amount of fall needed to enable the water to flow steadily to its point of use. This unique water system contributed as much to the progress of the Persian Empire as the wise administration of its rulers.

4 A coin of Xerxes I depicts him in an aggressive pose. Xerxes inherited the empire from his father, Darius I, in 486 BC. In 484 he suppressed a usurper in Egypt in savage fashion and went on to quell a revolt in Babylonia with similar ruthlessness. After early successes in Greece, he lost the Persian fleet to the Greeks at the Battle of Salamis (480 BC); the Achaemenid decline dates from that point.

perity. Having gained peace and stability at home, Darius led his armies first across the Bosporus and the Danube to the Volga, then into the Indus Valley; achieving the Persian Empire's greatest extent.

The original religion of the country had been the worship of Mithras, identified with the sun, and of Anahita, goddess of water and fertility. This religion was later combined with the worship of a supreme being, Ahura Mazda [9], "the wise lord" of the sixth-century prophet Zoroaster, or Zarathustra. As creator and ruler of the world, Ahura Mazda clothed himself with the firmament; the sun and moon were his eyes, and all forms of nature were his: earth, fire [6], wind, and water. To avoid polluting these natural elements, Parsees (who still follow Zoroastrian beliefs in India) expose the bodies of their dead to be devoured by vultures.

The invasion of Greece

Persia's monarchical form of government was supported by its people, who believed that the sovereignty of individuals was best maintained by an individual sovereign, the "king of kings." On the other hand the city-state of Athens propounded the idea of democracy, except for slaves, women, and foreigners. Darius considered the Greek city-states and their colonies a danger, and when Ionia revolted and received aid from Sparta and Athens, he crossed the Aegean but was defeated by an Athenian force at Marathon. In the midst of preparations for another attack on Greece he died in 486 BC.

Xerxes I (519?–465 BC), son of Darius, crossed the Hellespont with a vast army and defeated the Spartans at Thermopylae. But he was driven out of Europe in 479 BC after incurring the lasting hatred of the Greeks by burning the Acropolis at Athens. The Achaemenid Empire then declined until Alexander the Great (356–323 BC) from Macedon defeated the last of the dynasty, Darius III, at the Battle of Arbela (also called the Battle of Gaugamela) in 331 BC. He routed a huge Persian army and burned Persepolis, possibly to avenge the destruction of the Acropolis. Thereafter, Persia formed part of the empire of Alexander.

KEY

The tomb of Cyrus the Great at Pasargadae commemorates an outstanding leader who united the Medes and Persians to form an empire that played an important intermediary role between the civilizations of East and West. Few kings have left such a reputation of tolerance for subject peoples.

5 The Palace of Persepolis was begun in 518 BC by Darius and was built mainly under Xerxes I in 486–485 BC. It owes much to its location, with its back to the mountain from which the great terrace was partly carved. The magnificent staircases leading to the terrace were wide enough for eight horsemen to ride abreast up the shallow steps. A procession of immortals carved in stone decorates the sides of the staircases, followed by lines of courtiers—Medes and Persians—and subject peoples bearing tribute. Iron clamps filled with molten lead lock together some of the blocks of stone of which the terrace is built.

6 The so-called Fire Temple at Naqsh-i-Rustam near Persepolis stands in front of a cliff in which the four tombs of Darius and his successors are carved. It is about 36 feet (11m) high with blind windows [1] of black limestone and a door [3] leading to an empty room [2]. Some authorities believe it to be a Zoroastrian temple for the sacred flame or for holding religious objects.

7 A
B

7 Persian warriors owed much of their success to their skill with bows. The arrows were carried in a quiver by the bowman [A] who wore leather shoes and cap and carried a short sword. A bodyguard of Darius the Great [B] wore long robes and carried a long spear with a cutout shield. Such men, known as the Ten Thousand Immortals, were commanded by Darius during the campaign against Egypt and were the mainstay of his military achievements as emperor.

8 Depicted in color on enameled brickwork from the palace of Susa, one of the two capitals of the empire of Darius, is a soldier of the Ten Thousand Immortals holding a spear and carrying his bow and quiver. Darius rewarded his loyal bodyguard by having them portrayed on the walls of each palace he built.

9 Artaxerxes I (reigned 465–425 BC), a king of the Achaemenid dynasty, is shown enthroned in the Hall of a Hundred Columns at Persepolis. Above him is the winged Ahura Mazda, supreme god in the religion of Zoroaster, who was believed to direct the actions of the king as his viceroy, protecting the earth and its ruler.

India from 550 BC to AD 300

The age of the Buddha (*c.*563–*c.*483 BC) [3, 4] marked the beginning of a world religion and of important political and socioeconomic developments. It was an age in which different religions (such as Jainism) emerged and established values were questioned.

Trade and political change

In the political field large and expansionist states developed; four were preeminent by 500 BC. The most powerful of these was Magadha in southern Bihar with its capital originally at Rajgir, later at Pataliputra (Patna). The main economic asset was iron, but power was also the result of energetic rulers who eliminated their rivals.

Cottage industries, such as textiles, pottery, and metalcraft, flourished and were organized in guilds. Their produce, as well as agricultural surplus, was traded among various north Indian centers and with the Achaemenid (Persian) Empire to the west. Most trade was financed by bankers, who supplied the means of transportation and took the risks. Such activities favored the rise of a prosperous class that included many who felt dissatisfied with the rigid divisions of Hindu society. Such people often became enthusiastic patrons of Buddhism and other non-Hindu religions.

These developments were temporarily disturbed by the invasion in 327 BC of Alexander the Great (356–323 BC), who, after conquering the Persian Empire, set out to occupy its Indian provinces. Attracted by the legendary wealth of India, he advanced farther and managed to penetrate the Punjab. Alexander was forced to retreat, however, soon to be followed by the governors whom he had appointed to rule [5].

The glorious Mauryan age

The retreat of Alexander left behind a strong sense of Indian unity that found a leader in the young warrior Chandragupta (*c.*321–*c.*297 BC). First he liberated the western provinces, and then he marched against Pataliputra, where he defeated the Nanda king of Magadha and founded the Mauryan dynasty in 320 BC. In his bid for the throne, Chandragupta was assisted by his able and cunning minister Kautilya.

The Mauryan age (320–185 BC) was one of the most glorious periods of Indian history. Chandragupta controlled northern India from the Hindu Kush mountains to Bengal and probably parts of southern India as well. The kingdom was largely centralized, partly because of a network of highways. In 305 BC, Chandragupta concluded a treaty with the Greek Seleucus (*c.*355–281 BC), who sent Megasthenes (*c.*350–*c.*290 BC) to the Indian court as an envoy to grant Chandragupta formal rights over Alexander's conquests in India.

The Mauryan Empire [1] reached its zenith under Chandragupta's grandson Ashoka (*c.*274–*c.*236 BC), the mightiest king of ancient India. At first Ashoka followed traditional expansionist policies, but after a cruel campaign against Kalinga (Orissa) he renounced further conquests by force. Instead he substituted conquest by religious missionaries. At about that time Ashoka was converted to Buddhism and became one of its most fervent supporters.

To propagate his ideas Ashoka had edicts engraved on rocks and pillars [Key].

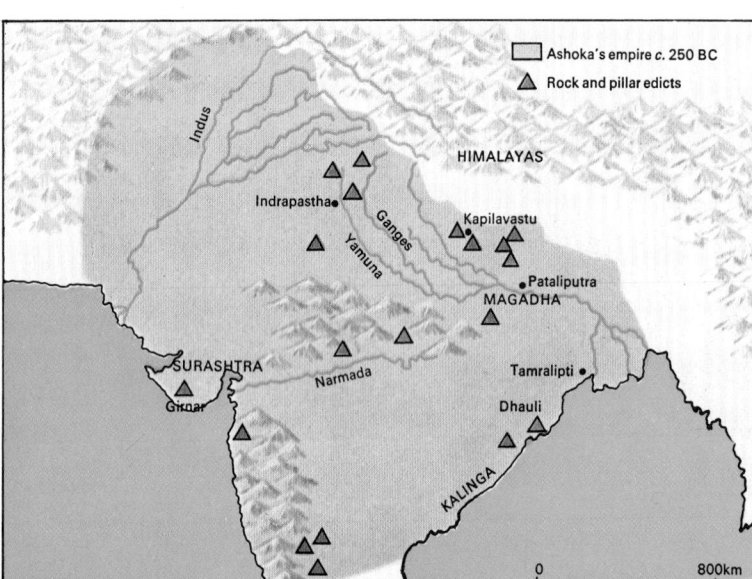

CONNECTIONS

See also
1034 India 300–1200
1036 Indian art to the Moguls
1004 Alexander the Great
988 Buddha and Buddhism
846 Islam, Hinduism, and Buddhism

Ashoka's empire c. 250 BC
Rock and pillar edicts
Indus
HIMALAYAS
Indrapastha
Ganges
Yamuna
Kapilavastu
Pataliputra
MAGADHA
SURASHTRA
Girnar
Narmada
Tamralipti
Dhauli
KALINGA
0
800km

1 The Mauryan Empire was the greatest of the states of ancient India. It comprised most of the subcontinent, except its southernmost portion, and most of Bengal and Sind. It also included significant parts of present Afghanistan, thus controlling the all-important overland communications with the Middle East. The size can be accurately established on the basis of the sites of the Ashokan rock and pillar edicts. Centralized administration of this vast empire was simplified by a network of highways connecting Pataliputra with the provincial centers.

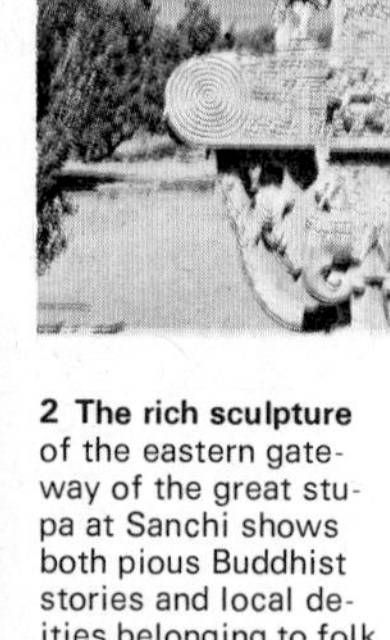

2 The rich sculpture of the eastern gateway of the great stupa at Sanchi shows both pious Buddhist stories and local deities belonging to folk religion but accepted by Buddhism. The Buddhist stories concern either the important events in the life of Lord Buddha or stories relating to his earlier existences as a man or an animal. Popular religion is represented by various deities such as yakshas (female tree spirits).

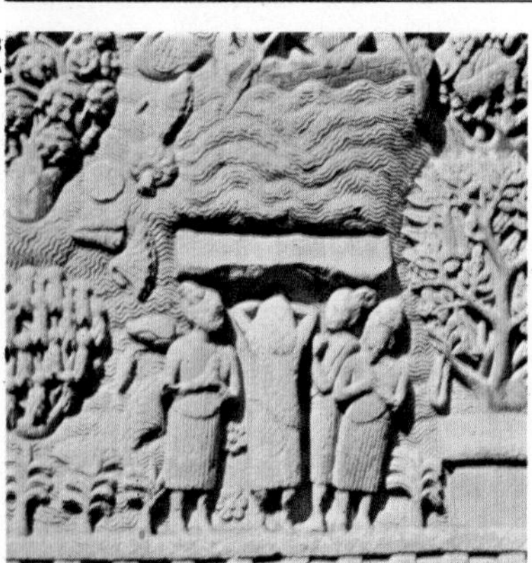

3 The Buddha is said to have converted people by performing miracles such as walking on the water, depicted here [A] in the carvings on the gateway at the Sanchi stupa. The presence of Lord Buddha, who is not represented in this early period, must be inferred. Another scene [B] shows Buddha's father paying homage to the tree under which Lord Buddha attained enlightenment. The presence of the Buddha in the scene has to be inferred from the presence of the pipal tree.

4 The great stupa (dome-shaped shrine) at Sanchi was built in Ashoka's time, but the railings and the richly sculptured gateways were added during the following two centuries. Sanchi, situated in the center of India where the main highways from east to west and north to south crossed, was one of the principal Buddhist centers from at least the time of Ashoka to the 10th century AD; it also gave its name to a school of sculpture.

These edicts enjoined upon the population a common ideology based on the Buddhist concepts of loyalty toward one's elders and those in authority, such as Brahmans and ascetics, and of justice and mercy for all.

The Indo-Greeks and the Kushan dynasty

The Mauryan dynasty continued to rule over vast areas of India until 50 years after Ashoka's death, but during that time its authority declined. In about 185 BC the army commander Pushyamitra, in one of the earliest recorded military coups, overthrew the last Mauryan king and founded the Sunga dynasty. The center of the state was moved from Bihar to central India. Pushyamitra was a powerful ruler, but his successors could not prevent incursions by the Bactrian Greeks, descendants of some of Alexander's generals. Some were repulsed by the Indians, while others founded short-lived kingdoms in the Punjab and elsewhere. Many of these were influenced by Indian culture and are called Indo-Greeks.

The Indo-Greeks were soon followed by invaders from central Asia, and in AD 78 most of northern India was under the control of Kanishka (died *c.* AD 100) [6] of the Kushan dynasty of Scythian origin (from central Asia). Like other Scythians, Kanishka was a pious Buddhist.

A century later, however, the Kushans had been expelled from India, and a Hindu reaction followed. Sanskrit, the language of the sacred texts, developed into a medium of communication among the upper class, in administration, and, above all, in literature. The great Sanskrit epics, the *Mahabharata* and the *Ramayana*, although incorporating much older tradition, were probably written down during this period, as were the *Laws of Manu*, the basic code of Hinduism. These three texts together incorporated the basic values of Hinduism and laid the foundations of the classical age of India in the Gupta period (*c.* AD 320–550).

In the northern Deccan the Satavahana, or Andhra, Empire (*c.* 30 BC–AD 200) extended at its peak from Maharashtra in the west to Andhra Pradesh in the east. In this way it succeeded in controlling the important trade routes crossing the peninsula.

KEY

The Ashokan pillars are among the oldest and most splendid monuments of Indian art. They are built of sandstone with a special bright polish and rest on solid foundations below ground level. They are crowned with animal sculptures; this one at Lauriya Nandangarh in northern Bihar has a heraldic lion. Many pillars are also inscribed with Ashokan edicts proclaiming the emperor's authority. This pillar is inscribed with six edicts of the last phase of Ashoka's reign. Earlier scholars have emphasized foreign, especially Persian, influences, but recent research has established the pillars in the Indian tradition.

5 A

Diodotus

B

Menander

5 After Alexander left India in 325 BC, several of his governors founded small independent principalities in Bactria and northwestern India. Some of these Greeks were strongly influenced by the Indians. For example, the coin of Diodotus [A] (*fl.* 3rd century BC), compared with the coin of Menander [B] (*c.*150 BC), shows Indian influence, particularly in the use of an Indian script.

6

6 Kanishka I, the greatest of the Kushan kings, ruled over vast areas of central Asia and also controlled most of northern India eastward as far as Bihar. This modern illustration is based on a torso of Kanishka (as indicated by the inscription), to which the head has been added from one of Kanishka's coins. The Scythian mantle and boots convey a strong impression of power and authority.

7

7 According to Buddhist tradition, caves have been used by the community of Buddhist monks since early times, especially as shelters during the rainy season. Although they were gradually replaced by structural monasteries, the tradition was continued in parts of India where numerous caves were excavated between 100 BC and AD 900. The *chaitya* cave at Karli, Maharashtra, (*c.*50 BC), seen here, was not used as a dwelling but as a place of worship, as well as for monastic ceremonies. It consists of a long pillared hall with a small stupa, enshrining relics of Lord Buddha, at the end. The rich sculpture of the capitals of the pillars presents a striking contrast to the sober lines of the rest.

8

8 Another richly decorated part of the caves at Karli, Maharashtra, is the façade, which includes the space between the three entrances. In addition to traditional Buddhist scenes, there are usually representations of the pious donors of the caves and especially of the land that was given for the needs of the monks. The donors are usually couples, thus illustrating the high status of women in this period in western India.

Buddha and Buddhism

By the sixth century BC the seminomadic tribes of northern India had developed into settled agricultural communities ruled by oligarchies or royal dynasties. It was a time of social change and of new ideas. Chief among these—evolved in opposition to the rituals and hardening caste system of Hinduism—were the philosophical and ethical teachings of Buddhism.

The life of Buddha

There are many differing accounts of the life of Buddha, but the main outline seems clear. Siddhartha Gautama (*c*.563–*c*.483 BC), who was later to become Buddha ("the Enlightened One"), was the son of Suddhodana, king of the Sakyas, and his queen, Maya. His birthplace, Lumbini (now Paderia) is located in southern Nepal near Kapilavastu, where he spent his early years. After an uneventful childhood the prince, struck by the problem of human suffering, decided to break with the past to seek the supreme truth in meditation. He left home secretly [1] and eventually, after years of seclusion, attained enlightenment seated under the Bodhi tree at Bodhgaya near Gaya in southern Bihar [4]. This subsequently became one of the holiest places of Buddhism, and cuttings from the tree were taken to different Buddhist countries where they grew into new trees. Soon afterward Buddha delivered his first sermon in Sarnath [5] near Varanasi (Benares) "setting the wheel of the Law in motion" [Key].

Buddhist doctrine was a "middle way," avoiding the extremes of mortification and indulgence. It accepted the basic concepts of Hinduism—rebirth and the law of karma, that a man's actions directly control his destiny—but concentrated on ethics as a means to salvation. For Buddha suffering was caused by desire. The abandonment of desire could be achieved by following the "noble eightfold path" of right living and actions. As a result nirvana, the state of bliss in which rebirth ended, would be attained. The ideal of nirvana [3] could best be attained by monastic discipline.

Buddha himself preached all over eastern India and received support from the rulers and the emerging merchant class. When at an advanced age he "entered nirvana," he left a well-established monastic order but no written instructions.

Expansion of Buddhism

For two centuries Buddhism slowly expanded despite difficulties, such as the animosity of the Hindu Brahmins who feared for their own privileges. When the Indian king Ashoka (reigned *c*.269–232 BC) was converted to Buddhism his powerful patronage greatly favored its expansion. The oldest extant stupas, domed monuments built to enshrine relics, belong to this period. Through Ashoka's influence Buddhism was also introduced into Sri Lanka (Ceylon), where it has remained the established faith for 22 centuries.

For the next few centuries Buddhism spread farther into India, with centers in central India, Maharashtra, and Andhra Pradesh, where Buddhist art and architecture flourished. In Maharashtra numerous caves were excavated to serve as monasteries or halls for worship (the *chaiyta* halls). Great stupas (Amaravati and Na-

CONNECTIONS

See also

986 India 500 BC–AD 30
1038 China 1000 BC–AD 618
1040 Confucius and Confucianism
846 Islam, Hinduism, and Buddhism

1 The departure from Kapilavastu, shown here at the Sanchi stupa, is often represented in Buddhist art. The future Buddha left secretly at night, but sculptors usually show a royal procession.

1 Avijja
Ignorance
2 Sankhara
Longing to live
3 Vinnana
Consciousness
4 Nama-rupa
Development of the psycho-physical organism
5 Satayatana
Development of the senses
6 Phassa
Contact of the senses
7 Vedana
Sensation
8 Tanha
Desire or craving
9 Upadana
Clinging or attachment
10 Bhava
Subconscious process of becoming
11 Jati
Rebirth
12 Dukkha
Decay, old age suffering and death
Past
Present
Future

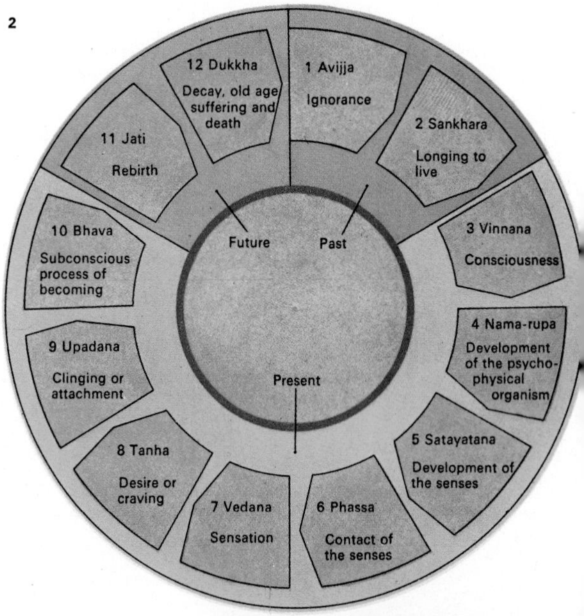

2 In Buddhist philosophy, the Wheel of Existence consists of 12 spokes, each constituting a link in the ever-repeated cycle of life and death. The wheel will revolve as long as ignorance lasts.

3 The fourth great event in Buddha's life is nirvana, which is neither eternal life nor annihilation but an incomprehensible state of utter bliss. Here Buddha is shown in a symbolic representation of the state of nirvana. This huge sculpture at Gal Vihara, Polannaruva, Sri Lanka (Ceylon) dates from the twelfth century.

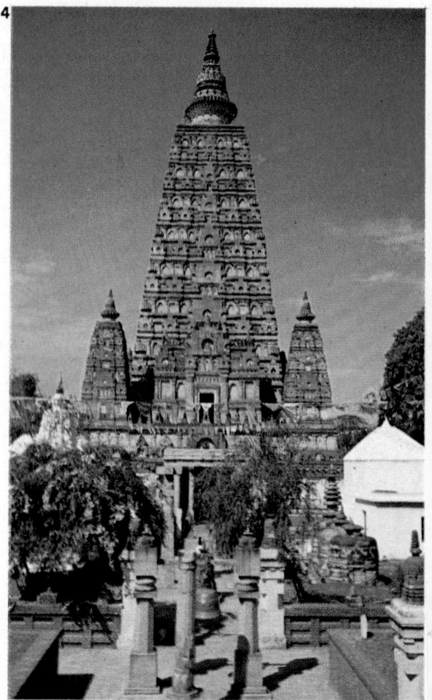

4 The Mahabodhi Temple, Bodhgaya, Bihar, marks the spot where Lord Buddha attained enlightenment seated under the Bodhi tree. This is perhaps the most hallowed spot in the Buddhist world. The present temple, which replaces an older foundation at the site, was built in the Gupta period (*c*.320– *c*.550) but has been restored.

garjunakonda) also arose in the Andhra country.

Buddhism was always prone to divisions, and councils organized to promote unity often had the opposite effect. Early in the Christian era there developed a fundamental division between the adherents of the Mahayana ("great vehicle") and those of the Hinayana ("lesser vehicle"). The former had monks but emphasized the ideal of the pious layman assisting his fellowmen by his wisdom and compassion. The historical Buddha and previous Buddhas were worshiped as deities and so were other beings who had taken the vow to become Buddhas (Bodhisattvas). Buddhas and Bodhisattvas were worshipped in the form of images, thus providing a strong incentive to Buddhist art, which soon included the image of Lord Buddha. Hinayana, however, kept closer to the older teachings.

The spread outside south Asia

From the beginning of the Christian era Buddhism spread outside south Asia [9]. Buddhism entered China in the first century and subsequently spread to Korea and Japan. In Tibet it took root in the eighth century and developed into Lamaism.

In Southeast Asia, too, Mahayana influence, mainly from Bengal, inspired great monuments such as Borobudur in central Java (ninth century) [7] and Ba-yon in Cambodia (twelfth century), but the great expansion of the Theravada school (the monastic version of Hinayana) gained momentum in the eleventh century when the Burmese king Aniruddha (reigned 1044–77) established Theravada as the official religion. In the thirteenth century it was adopted as the official religion of Thailand and spread to Laos and Cambodia.

Although it has not always guaranteed harmony among these countries, Buddhism has provided Sri Lanka and mainland Southeast Asia with a firm ideology and a high standard of education. It has also contributed to great achievements in art and architecture—the astounding temple complex of Pagan (Burma) and the splendid pagodas of Mandalay, Bangkok, and Thailand (Ayutthaya).

KEY

In the life of Lord Buddha the first sermon is the third great event (after his birth and enlightenment). Buddhists call this event the "turning of the wheel of Law"; the wheel represents the cosmos; the Law is the Lord Buddha's philosophy, which aims at providing a rational explanation of the mysteries of life. The presence of the wheel is suggested by the position of the hands. The sculpture of Sarnath belongs to the Gupta period (*c.* AD 500). The perfection of the physical shape reflects perfect knowledge; the elongated ears and almond-shaped eyes suggest profound concentration, and the monastic robe reveals the perfect body.

5

5 The wheel of Law and two deer on this seal suggest the Deer Park of Sarnath. The seal was recovered from the ruins of Nalanda, a great Buddhist monastery in Bihar. Founded in the fifth century, Nalanda became one of the great centers of Buddhist learning, attracting students from Indonesia and China and enjoying the patronage of numerous kings. The Muslims largely destroyed it *c.* 1200.

6

6 One of the oldest known Buddhist images in Southeast Asia is this bronze Buddha from Vietnam, dating back to the fifth century. Its style was influenced by Buddhas from Amaravati.

7

7 Borobudur, situated in the heart of Java, is often described as a stupa (dome-shaped shrine), but although a stupa crowns it, the rest of the structure predominates. It is a marvelous storehouse of sculpture with five lavishly decorated galleries exhibiting pious stories in 1,500 relief panels. It was built by the Sailendras, a Buddhist dynasty in Java from about 750 to 850.

8

8 The Mons of southern Thailand and the Thais of central Thailand became Buddhists by the third century. Despite the Khmer occupation, Buddhism continued to flourish. This Buddha head comes from Lopouri. Although conforming to Buddhist norms, it was modeled to correspond to the aesthetic ideals of the Thais.

9

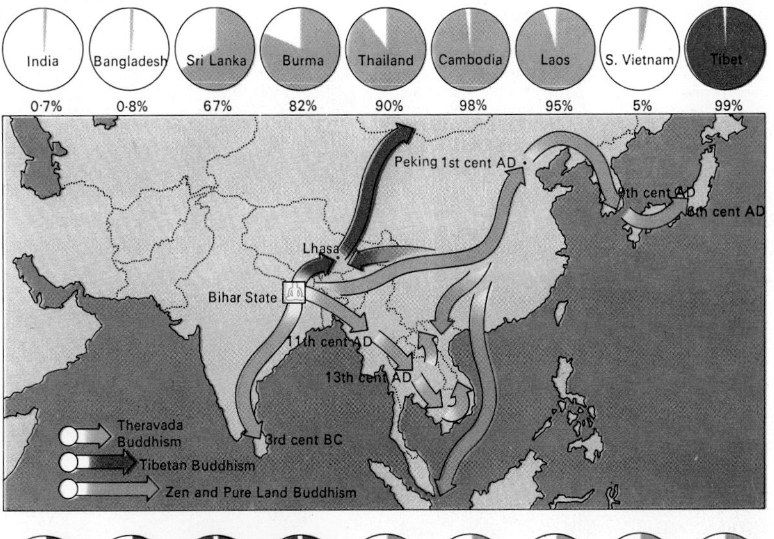

India 0·7%
Bangladesh 0·8%
Sri Lanka 67%
Burma 82%
Thailand 90%
Cambodia 98%
Laos 95%
S. Vietnam 5%
Tibet 99%
Peking 1st cent AD
th cent AD
th cent AD
Lhasa
Bihar State
11th cent AD
13th cent AD
3rd cent BC
Theravada Buddhism
Tibetan Buddhism
Zen and Pure Land Buddhism
Nepal 40%
Sikkim 35%
Mongolia 98%
Bhutan 98%
Japan 78%
Korea 70%
China 40%
N. Vietnam 80%
Malaysia 25%

9 The expansion of Buddhism outside India was a complicated process extending over many centuries. Here the broad outlines of its spread are shown, together with the percentage of Buddhists in various countries today. Buddhism was spread by monks who sometimes acted as advisers to kings.

Europe 1200–500 BC

By 1200 BC the Bronze Age was fully mature among the Urnfield people, who lived north of the Alps and belong to the prehistoric phase of European evolution; their name was given to them by archeologists because they introduced a new burial rite into Europe. Cremation replaced burial in barrows, and the burned bones were placed in an urn. These urns were interred in large flat cemeteries, or urnfields.

Technological revolution

With some exceptions—Basques, Finns, Iberians—the Europeans were of Indo-European origin and thus had linguistic and cultural traditions in common. The Urnfield people, who were farmers living in villages or large homestead complexes, may have spoken some form of Celtic dialect since the distribution of their monuments corresponds with the oldest recognizable Celtic place-names. The Urnfield people are generally regarded as being proto-Celtic, and there seems to be little difference between them and their immediate descendants, the Celts of the Hallstatt culture.

The Urnfield period saw improved agriculture and metalworking in Europe. It was a time of expansion and warfare, and archeological evidence shows that the central Europeans possessed quite sophisticated bronze weapons. Toward the end of the period, in about 800 BC, Europe experienced a major technological revolution initiated by the Celts. They introduced the use of iron into Europe north of the Alps, and with it all the superiority in weapons and edge tools the use of that metal made possible. The areas of initial development coincide closely with Urnfield settlements in the Danube and Rhine regions. By 800–700 BC the Celts had become the dominant and most progressive element in Europe.

Apart from some evidence of contact with people from the steppes in the form of improved types of horse gear, and perhaps the actual import of horses and superior techniques of animal husbandry, there is no evidence of invasion or of changed ethnic type; everything suggests a continuity of the indigenous population enriched and strengthened by the discovery of iron and the richer and wider trade contacts that the new iron-based wealth made possible. This first phase of Celtic culture is known to archeologists as Hallstatt.

The Hallstatt site has provided comprehensive evidence about the early Iron Age in Europe. The community there derived much of its wealth from large salt mines. Both the preserving and healing powers of salt were recognized at an early stage. It became a valuable trading commodity, and it may have been the chief export from the Hallstatt Celts to the Greco-Etruscan world, through Greek colonies in the northern Mediterranean. A leading colony was Massilia (Marseilles), which was founded in about 600 BC.

Workers and aristocrats

The equipment, dress, foods, and eating habits of workers are all too often unknown in societies that were solely concerned with their aristocrats, whose wealth is affirmed by the richness of the burials. At Hallstatt, however, leather helmets, gloves used by miners, and even parts of their clothing

CONNECTIONS

See also
1008 The Celts 500 BC–AD 450
1048 Japanese art

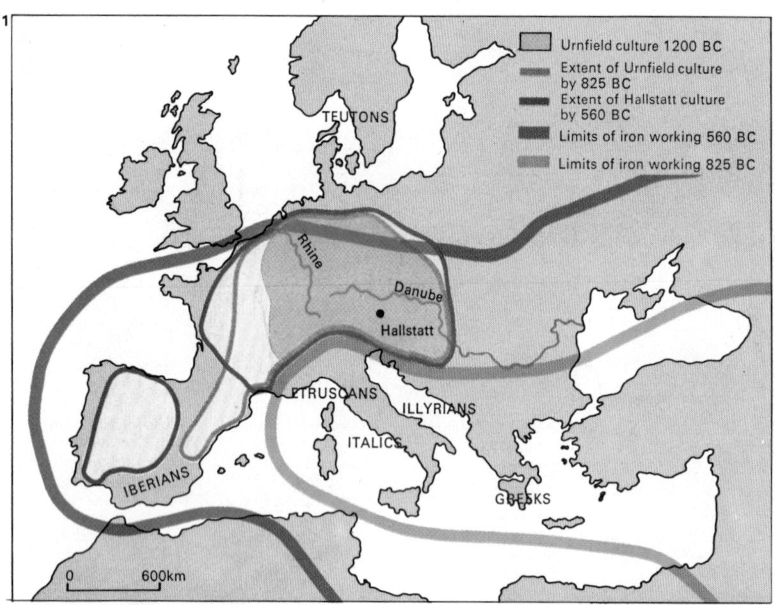

Urnfield culture 1200 BC
Extent of Urnfield culture by 825 BC
Extent of Hallstatt culture by 560 BC
Limits of iron working 560 BC
Limits of iron working 825 BC
TEUTONS
Rhine
Danube
Hallstatt
ETRUSCANS
ILLYRIANS
ITALICS
IBERIANS
GREEKS
0
600km

1 The Urnfield Culture developed around the Danube and Rhine rivers and by 825 BC had reached Spain. The Hallstatt culture, which began in the same place and superseded the Urnfield, had by 560 BC covered most of Spain and Portugal. By that date also, iron working, introduced from the east, had spread through most of Europe. The Hallstatt culture is named after a key archeological site in Austria.

2 In Irish tradition this stone with its spiral designs marked an entrance to the otherworld. It dates from *c.*2500 BC, foreshadowing Celtic designs of 2,000 years later.

3 Hallstatt ceramic skill and restrained decorative elegance are shown in this painted pottery urn from Burrenhof, Germany, dating from about 620 BC.

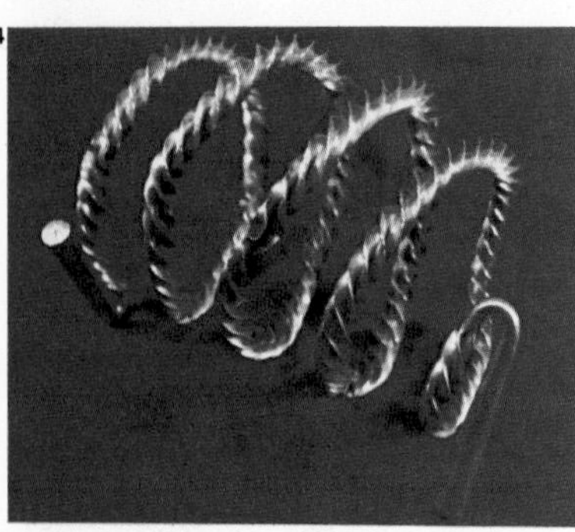

4 A gold neck ornament from Dover, *c.*1000 BC, anticipates Celtic torques.

5 Irish goldsmiths made this gold-plated lead pendant in about 800 BC.

6 Later Celtic symmetry is seen in a gold-plated Irish ring of about 1000 BC.

have been preserved. Their wooden bowls and other eating utensils have remained intact, and numerous seeds and fruit pits indicate something of their diet.

Information about the aristocrats comes from a vast cemetery that bears witness to the great changes in burial customs and personal equipment coinciding with the development of a culture based on iron, a more abundant metal and cheaper for practical purposes than bronze. Chieftains were no longer cremated and placed in humble urns but were buried with much pomp.

Burial ceremony

The richest graves consisted of a wooden chamber, usually of oak and covered by a mound decorated by a commemorative stone figure [Key], sacred tree, or stone pillar. The deceased was placed under his status symbol, a four-wheeled wagon. Horse trappings were included, but there seems to be no evidence for the burial of the horses themselves; perhaps they were sacrificed to the gods and ritually eaten or burned. All the warrior's fine military equipment was placed in the tomb with him—his sword and spear, helmet, and neck and arm ornaments. Drink and food were laid beside him to sustain him on his journey. According to the Old Irish tales, once the actual burial rite was completed, feasting and funerary games followed.

The Hallstatt period lasted until about 500 BC and laid the foundations for the full flowering of Celtic culture in Europe. There must have been some intermarriage with the Teutonic peoples to the north—both "Teuton" and "German" are Celtic names—and the Celts were probably overlords, making up the aristocracy of these closely related peoples. The Hallstatt phase of the Celts was manifest deep in the interior of Spain. Hallstatt art [3,7,8,9] tended to be linear, influenced by Greek Geometric, the naturalism of Urnfield bird and animal art, and old indigenous motifs. It was to become an important element in the magnificent magico-religious art [11] of the La Tène period that followed and the splendid contribution of Irish art [4,5,6,10] to the Western Church in early Christian times.

KEY

This stone statue of a Hallstatt warrior or deified hero dates from the end of the 6th century BC. The figure was found on a Hirshlanden burial mound, broken where it had fallen. The cult of graves and ancestors was strong among the Celts, and this commemorative figure links the prehistoric world with that of the historical Celtic world in all its flourishing vigor. Much present-day knowledge about Celtic life derives from archeological evidence from burial mounds. The Hallstatt peoples had close trade links with the Etruscans, another important bronze-using culture.

7 Warfare, whether as necessity or as an aristocratic sport, dominated most aspects of Celtic culture. Emphasis was placed not only on efficient weapons but also on the appearance of the warriors. Although not commonly worn into battle, helmets were a favored headgear. This bronze helmet from Italy probably dates from the Hallstatt period and is a fine example of Celtic work.

7

8

8 A Greek bronze crater for mixing wine, weighing 460 pounds (208kg) was found in the burial of the priestess at Vix. It shows that as early as the 6th century BC the Celtic and Mediterranean worlds were in close contact. It may have been a peace offering or trade good.

9 The Celts were skilled metalworkers. They introduced iron into northern Europe by 800 BC but continued to use bronze with exquisite results. This detail of a bronze bowl handle from the 6th century BC gives some indication of the sophisticated Hallstatt craftsmanship.

9

10 This gold dress fastener from County Galway, Ireland, dates from about 700 BC and is 11 inches (28cm) across. Such objects not only provide proof of Celtic pride in personal ornamentation but also reveal the exquisite skill and harmony of Celtic craftsmen and their predecessors in their use of various metals as a medium of their art.

10

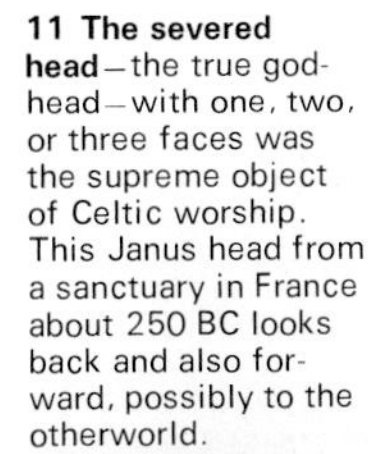

11 The severed head—the true godhead—with one, two, or three faces was the supreme object of Celtic worship. This Janus head from a sanctuary in France about 250 BC looks back and also forward, possibly to the otherworld.

11

The Greeks to the rise of Athens

About 1200 BC, Greek civilization underwent a major change. Dorian tribes moved through the peninsula from the north and settled mainly in the Peloponnesus. The existing peoples were assimilated or confined to smaller areas, and Ionians and Aeolians were pushed across the sea to found cities in Asia Minor.

The development of institutions

Major social changes must have accompanied this upheaval, but little detail is known about the next 400 years; much of what is known comes from Homer's *Iliad* and *Odyssey*. It is possible, however, to identify several developments that were of major significance for subsequent Greek civilization. The use of iron became widespread for tools and weapons [2]; a phonetic alphabet was developed; and a feeling of national consciousness arose—a racial and intellectual identity bound up in the use of the word *Hellas* to describe the whole Greek world. At the same time, a pantheon of gods that appear in Homer's poems was formed, religious ceremonies developed, the importance of shrines such as Delphi became generally accepted, and the city-state was adopted as the most important political, economic, and social unit.

The rugged geography of Greece played a major part in making the inhabitants of each valley regard themselves as a separate entity, and Greece became a patchwork of small states—some of them with fewer than 5,000 inhabitants—that guarded their independence jealously [3]. They varied greatly in size: Athens succeeded in subduing Attica, and no other states developed there; but Thebes failed to overcome Boeotia, and at least 12 states existed there. Writing in the fourth century BC, Aristotle mentions the existence of at least 150 states.

The size of the city-state was important for Greek political development because a belief developed that a satisfactory political unit must be small and totally independent. A Greek had a series of loyalties—to *Hellas,* to his city-state, and to his tribe within the state. Loyalty to the city was the most powerful, and the idea of a larger political unit was never developed. During this period the Greeks also evolved the belief that government must be based on a known constitutional and legal framework.

Agriculture, trade, and politics

Economically, agriculture was all-important [Key], and as the cities developed, the link between them, and the country remained strong. Some states became increasingly involved in trade and industry [6], and a definite class of traders and craftsmen evolved. Politically, by the mid-seventh century BC most states had moved away from monarchies and were ruled by oligarchies of the richest and most powerful citizens. A privileged or noble class held all political, military, and religious power, and there was usually tension between them and the common people.

This tension was made worse by increasing population, and a safety valve was found in colonization [4]. States organized expeditions to found new cities overseas, but once founded these new cities became completely independent, although they retained close links with their mother cities.

CONNECTIONS

See also
966 The Greek mainland 2800–1100 BC
994 Classical Greece
996 Classical Greek society
998 Greek literature and theater
1000 Greek art 1100–450 BC

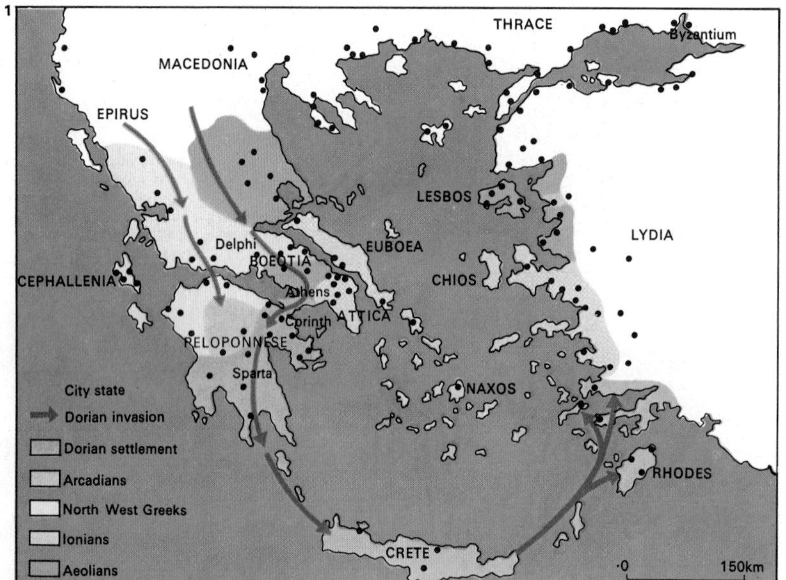
THRACE
Byzantium
MACEDONIA
EPIRUS
LESBOS
LYDIA
Delphi
BOEOTIA
EUBOEA
CEPHALLENIA
CHIOS
Athens
Corinth
ATTICA
PELOPONNESE
Sparta
NAXOS
City state
Dorian invasion
Dorian settlement
Arcadians
North West Greeks
Ionians
Aeolians
RHODES
CRETE
0
150km

1 Little is known of the history of Greece between the arrival of the Dorians (*c.* 1200 BC) and the dawn of the archaic period (*c.* 800 BC). Homer describes a society of small agricultural communities grouped around citadels and led by kings and aristocrats. These communities still retained many of the features of Mycenaean civilization and had little trade or commerce. By the time of Hesoid (8th century BC), whose narrative poems give a description of the early archaic period, trade and commerce were increasing, monarchy had generally been replaced by oligarchy, and the city was becoming the focus of political life.

Helmet (Argos)

Earliest Corinthian helmet

Illyrian helmet

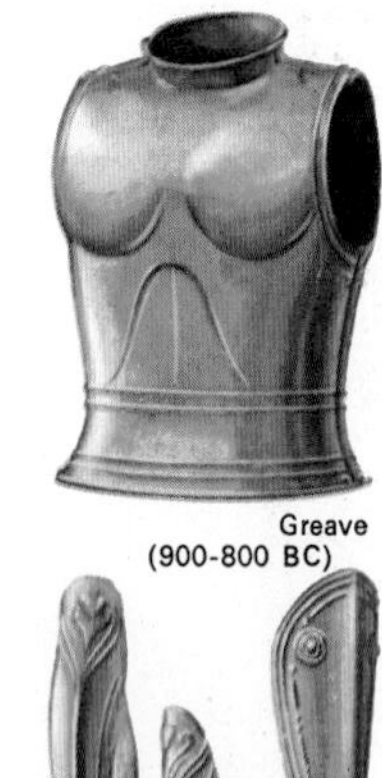
Bell corset

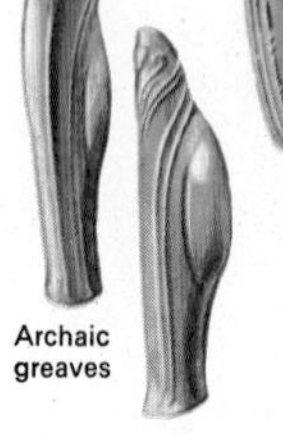
Greave (900-800 BC)
Archaic greaves

3 The landscape of Greece, with its limited fertile plains and harsh mountains, became a significant factor in the rise of small communities such as Corinth (shown here). Travel was difficult, and economic and political life tended to be concentrated in confined areas. The Greeks were convinced that these small independent units were the most natural size for a satisfactory political life. This attitude, combined with constant diplomatic and military maneuvering between states, meant that wider unity was never attempted, although the idea of a distinct Greek identity and a feeling of cultural superiority to outsiders did exist from earliest time.

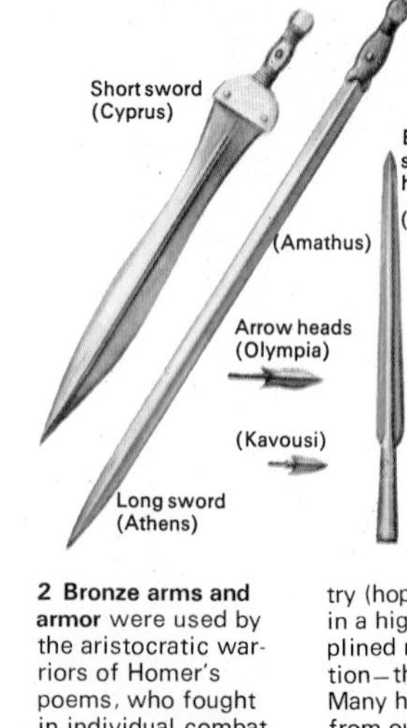
Short sword (Cyprus)
(Amathus)
Arrow heads (Olympia)
(Kavousi)
Long sword (Athens)

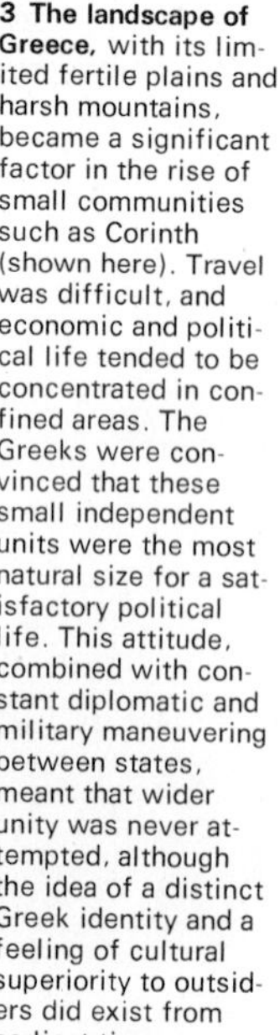
Bronze spear heads (Olympia)

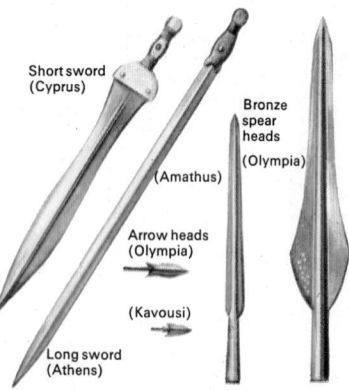

2 Bronze arms and armor were used by the aristocratic warriors of Homer's poems, who fought in individual combat. But iron began to supersede bronze before 700 BC, and tactics changed fundamentally, with heavily-armed infantry (hoplites) fighting in a highly disciplined mass formation—the phalanx. Many hoplites came from outside the aristocracy (although they had to be able to provide their own equipment), and this helped to weaken the old social order.

From about 750 BC migration established Greek cities throughout the Mediterranean to the Black Sea.

Colonization did not solve the problem of class struggle. The archaic Greek world (Greece between 800 and 500 BC) saw the widespread appearance of tyrants, a word originally applied by the Greeks to men who seized power unconstitutionally and ruled without legal backing.

New political systems

In Athens attempts were made by Solon (*c*.640–*c*.559 BC) to solve the economic problems that lay at the root of the class struggle and to make legal reforms to protect the weak. Power was seized in 545 by Pesistratos (*c*.600–527 BC), who increased the rights of the common people and brought the nobility under the rule of law. These developments formalized the democratic system that was to rule Athens for the next two centuries.

The same pattern was followed in other states; tyrants rarely lasted long. Some states, such as Sparta with its special constitution and Corinth with a strong oligarchy, avoided the tyrannical stage completely.

Until the mid-sixth century BC the Greeks were largely unaffected by outsiders, apart from trading contacts [5]. The situation altered when the Lydians extended their power over the Greek states of Asia Minor and were succeeded in 546 BC by the Persians. Neither overlordship was oppressive, but *c*.500 the Greek colonists in Asia Minor rose in revolt and succeeded in temporarily reasserting their independence. In 499 the Persian emperor Darius was able to crush the revolt. He followed this by reimposing his power in Thrace and Macedonia and then in 490 by launching a major invasion of Greece itself.

Athens, as the largest state, was his immediate target. Athens called for help from the others, but before aid could arrive its troops, who were significantly outnumbered, met and decisively defeated the Persians at Marathon. Darius' army withdrew, leaving the Greeks still disunited but convinced of their superiority.

KEY

Greek agriculture, represented by the olive harvest shown on this 6th-century BC amphora, was always faced with the difficulty of providing sufficient food from the relatively small area of fertile land. The natural consequence of an expanding population faced with a limited food supply was emigration, first across the Ionian Sea and then throughout the Mediterranean. But overpopulation was only part of the reason for emigrating: the nature of aristocratic control of land resources meant that the distribution of agricultural land was by no means equitable. The resulting social tensions naturally encouraged emigration.

4 Colonization was used to send surplus and disaffected populations to found cities in new regions. The first phase began about 750 BC with expeditions to the west, where the Greeks found the Phoenicians already well established in many areas. They were able to settle in Sicily, southern Italy and France, and Libya. About 650 BC the Greeks began to move into the Black Sea region until there were colonies around almost all of its shores. By the 6th century BC, the colonies were sending enough food back to Greece to feed the expanding population and thus reduce emigration.

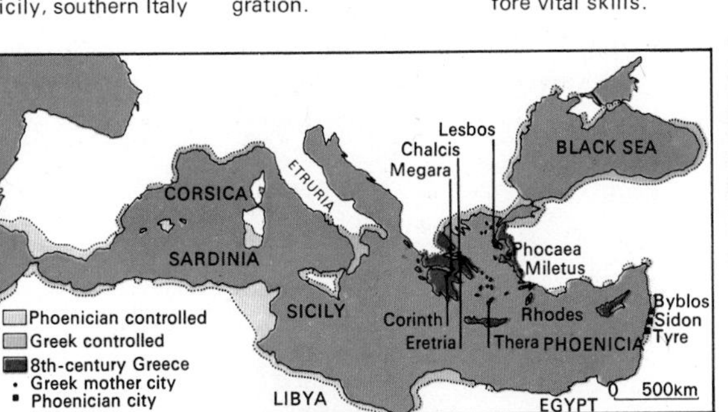

Lesbos
Chalcis
Megara
BLACK SEA
ETRURIA
CORSICA
SARDINIA
Phocaea
Miletus
SICILY
Corinth
Eretria
Rhodes
Thera
PHOENICIA
Byblos
Sidon
Tyre
LIBYA
EGYPT
500km
Phoenician controlled
Greek controlled
8th-century Greece
Greek mother city
Phoenician city

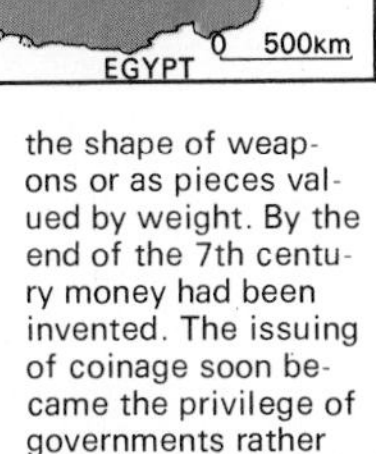

5 The Greeks traded with the Phoenicians, the Egyptians, and the people of the Middle East, as well as between colonies and mother cities. In states bordering the sea, such as Athens and Corinth, trade became an important source of wealth. Shipbuilding and navigation were therefore vital skills.

6 Trade and commerce were free to develop after the city-states had been established, and the system of barter was replaced by more regulated methods. Various systems of weights and measures were developed (such as this one on an Attic black-figure amphora, showing men using a balance scale), but no single system became dominant. Precious metals were used for exchange, either in the shape of weapons or as pieces valued by weight. By the end of the 7th century money had been invented. The issuing of coinage soon became the privilege of governments rather than of individuals.

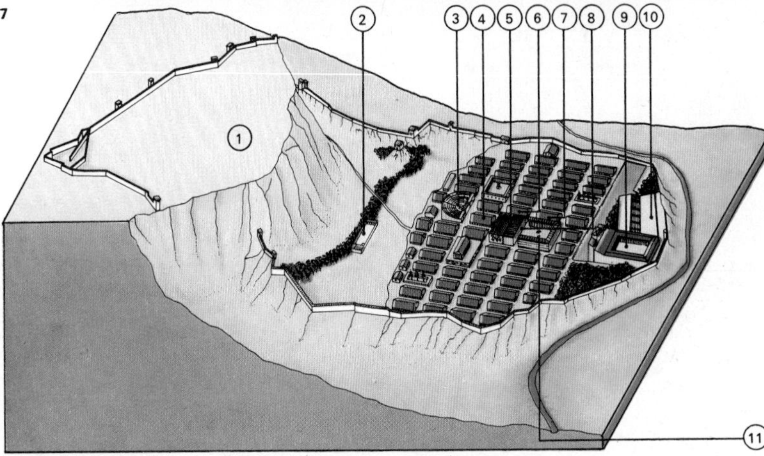

1
2
3
4
5
6
7
8
9
10
11

7 Priene in Asia Minor was a model of Greek town planning. Most cities grew haphazardly, but Priene was well planned and showed clearly the essentials of a small city-state with about 4,000 inhabitants. The citadel, or acropolis [1], stood at the top of the cliff with the main city below it. The principal features were the sanctuary of Demeter and other gods [2]; the huge theater [3], possibly the oldest Hellenistic example, which could accommodate an audience of 5,000; housing units [4], each with four to six dwellings; buildings for the council and courts [5,6]; the agora [11], or marketplace adjoining the main street [8]; the sanctuary of Zeus [7]; gymnasium [9]; stadium [10].

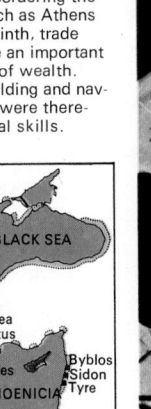

Classical Greece

In 480 BC the Persians under Xerxes I launched a second invasion of Greece. A large army advanced across the Hellespont and down the peninsula; it was briefly halted by the heroism of 300 Spartans under their king, Leonidas, who held the narrow pass at Thermopylae until outflanked. They died to the last man. Athens was occupied, but shortly afterward its fleet, led by the statesman Themistocles (*c*.528–*c*.460 BC), annihilated the Persian army at Salamis [1]. Xerxes' army fell back northward and in 479 BC was defeated at Plataea by a largely Peloponnesian army under the Spartan Pausanias. If the Greeks had not defeated the Persians, the development of Europe might have been very different under the influence of the Persian civilization of the Middle East.

The golden age of Athens

The Persians withdrew but their threat remained, and the Delian League, a defensive alliance of many of the Aegean islands and Greek states in Asia Minor was set up in 478 BC under Athenian leadership, with its headquarters at Delos [4]. A navy was established, maintained by contributions of money or ships.

Athens, as the most powerful Greek state, soon dominated the Delian League, and under the guidance of its statesmen Cimon (died 449 BC) and Pericles (*c*.490–429 BC) became a maritime empire in all but name. The democratic system was refined under Pericles, and the great buildings and cultural achievements that were to make Athens famous grew from its trading wealth.

Inevitably, the power of Athens aroused jealousy and fear, particularly in Sparta, which continued to dominate the Peloponnesian states, and Corinth, the other great trading state. There was sporadic warfare during the mid-fifth century BC, and Athens built up a land empire in Megara, Boeotia, and Achaea, but this was abandoned in 445 BC after Athens concluded a truce with its rivals. Hostilities broke out again in 431, and Athens, secure behind the Long Walls linking it with its major port of Piraeus [5], allowed the Spartans to invade Attica and instead concentrated on using its maritime power to wear down the resistance of its enemies. The conflict, known as the Peloponnesian War, lasted—with interludes of peace—until 404.

Pericles died of plague in 429, but his strategy was continued by Cleon (died 422 BC). Neither side could decisively defeat the other, and a peace was reached in 421. This lasted only two years before fighting broke out again; in 415 the militants in Athens led by Alcibiades (*c*.450–404 BC) persuaded the people to launch a major expedition to invade Sicily and capture Syracuse. The venture was a disaster, and in 413 the bulk of the Athenian army and navy was destroyed. Despite this Athens fought on, although its enemies were now being financed by the Persians, and several of its allies revolted. In 405 the remainder of the Athenian navy was surprised and destroyed at Aegospotami by Spartans under Lysander (died 395 BC) who then besieged the city. When it surrendered in 404, an oligarchy replaced democracy, and the Spartans took over the Athenian Empire.

CONNECTIONS

See also
992 The Greeks to the [...] of Athens
996 Classical Greek so[...]ety
1000 Greek art 1100–450 BC
1002 Greek art 450–31 [...]
1006 Greek science
782 Social developmen[...]

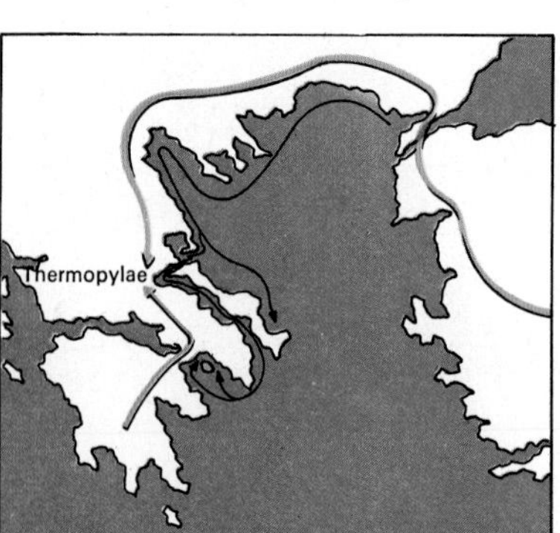

Thermopylae
0 175 km
Route of Persian army
Route of Greek army
Route of Persian navy
Island of Salamis

1 After the Persians overran Athens, the refugees fled with the Greek navy to Salamis. There the Greeks trapped the Persians and destroyed an entire corps as well as 200 Persian ships, with a loss of only 40 of their own.

2 An Athenian trireme was the type of warship that defeated the Persians at Salamis and was the mainstay of the powerful navy built up under the direction of Themistocles at the beginning of the 5th century. The navy was significant in the democratic system, for it was largely manned by the poorer citizens and provided them not only with a livelihood but also with a source of pride and power. Since much of the wealth and power of Athens came from trade and its maritime empire, the common people could assert that they were the backbone of the state and should play a major part in its political life.

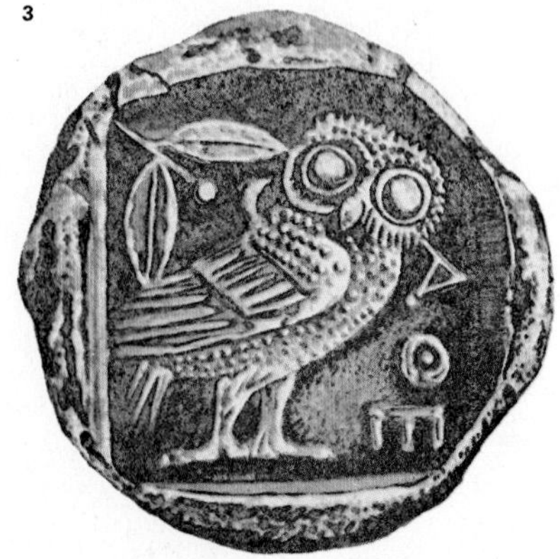

3 This Athenian four drachma coin shows the owl of Athena, who was the patron goddess of the city. Athens' naval and trading domination of the Aegean gave the city great wealth, which was lavished on fine buildings and the arts and which allowed its citizens the leisure to participate in the democratic system or to make contributions to philosophy and literature. Even during its decline, Athens remained the acknowledged intellectual and artistic leader of Greece.

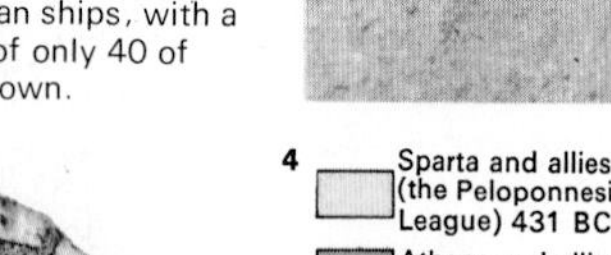

Sparta and allies (the Peloponnesian League) 431 BC
Athens and allies 431 BC
Neutral Greek states 431 BC
Revolts

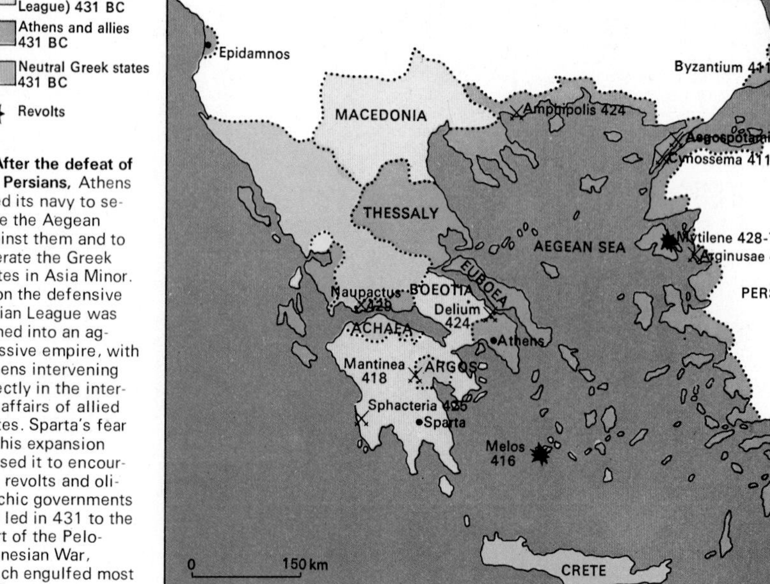

Epidamnos
MACEDONIA
Amphipolis 424
Byzantium 411-408
Aegospotami 405
Cynossema 411
THESSALY
AEGEAN SEA
Mytilene 428-7
Arginusae 406
PERSIAN EMPIRE
EUBOEA
Naupactus
BOEOTIA
Delium 424
ACHAEA
Athens
Mantinea 418
ARGOS
Sphacteria 425
Sparta
Melos 416
CRETE
0 150 km

4 After the defeat of the Persians, Athens used its navy to secure the Aegean against them and to liberate the Greek states in Asia Minor. Soon the defensive Delian League was turned into an aggressive empire, with Athens intervening directly in the internal affairs of allied states. Sparta's fear of this expansion caused it to encourage revolts and oligarchic governments and led in 431 to the start of the Peloponnesian War, which engulfed most of Greece.

Decline of Spartan rule

This Spartan supremacy was short-lived: spurred on by the exploits of Xenophon's Ten Thousand—Greek mercenaries who made an epic march across the Persian Empire—a crusade was launched to regain the freedom of the Greek states in Asia Minor, but the Persians encouraged the Spartans' allies to turn against them, and the attempt had to be abandoned in 387.

The next 50 years saw the worst features of the Greek political system of the Classical age, with petty jealousies and continual military rivalry preventing the emergence of any wider unity. Athens recovered quickly, democracy was restored in 403, and by 377 it was again leading a naval confederacy against Sparta. Thebes became the next dominant power when it destroyed the Spartan army at Leuctra in 371. After a decade Thebes also began to decline, and Phocis enjoyed a temporary mastery.

The Hellenistic age

Interstate rivalries continued and prevented the Greeks from realizing that a new threat was growing in the north. The Macedonians had hitherto been a loose confederation of tribes, but in 359 Philip II (382–336 BC) became king. A fine organizer, general, and diplomat, he unified the tribes in his own kingdom and then went on to annex Thessaly in 352 and Thrace in 342.

The Athenians were the first of the Greeks to become aware of this new danger, for Philip's power threatened their lucrative trade routes to the Black Sea. But years of relative peace had made the people of Athens apathetic. A few orators such as Demosthenes (died 322 BC) tried to arouse them to the danger to their trade and to their city and to exhort them to end traditional city-state rivalries and unite against this new peril. Eventually the Delian League was reactivated, but in 338 Philip routed its armies at the battle of Chaeronea and occupied Thebes. Athens prepared to continue its resistance, but there was little support elsewhere. At the Congress of Corinth a new league of Greek states was set up under Macedonian leadership. The independence of the free city-states was at an end.

KEY

A Greek hoplite (infantryman) is shown killing his Persian enemy on this vase. The Greek Classical age is usually defined as beginning with Pausanias' defeat of the second Persian invasion in 479 BC and ending with the establishment of Macedonian power over all of Greece in 320. Many of the great achievements of the Greeks flowed directly from the feeling of security and superiority that followed the Persian defeat, but with their devotion to the small city-state and their obsession with political and military maneuvering, the Greeks failed to develop the wider political unity that could have resisted the rising power of Macedon.

5

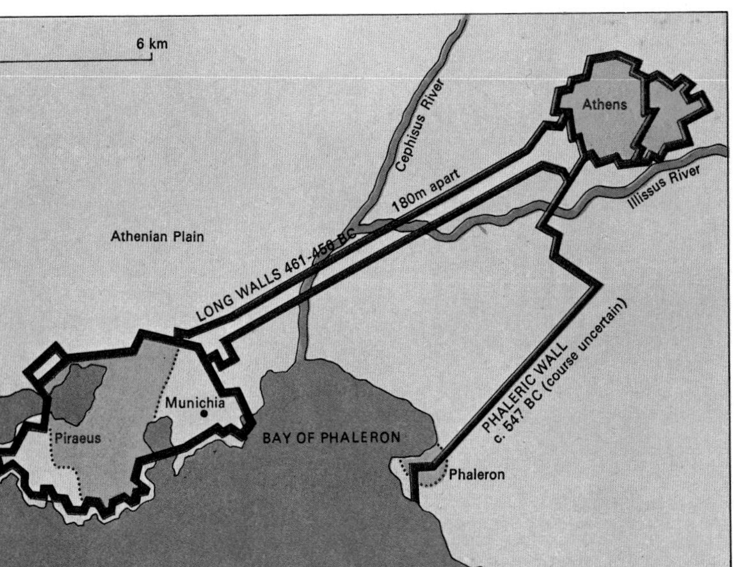

0
6 km
Athens
Cephisus River
Illissus River
180m apart
Athenian Plain
LONG WALLS 461-456 BC
PHALERIC WALL
c. 547 BC (course uncertain)
Munichia
Piraeus
BAY OF PHALERON
Phaleron

5 Themistocles began the development of Piraeus as the base for Athens' navy and its vital trading and commercial port. The Long Walls were built to link it with the city and to give Athens the means to maintain its maritime power even when its territory was invaded. It was symbolic that when Athens was defeated in 404, the Spartans insisted on the immediate demolition of the walls.

6

6 The hoplites were heavily armed infantrymen trained to fight in a highly disciplined phalanx (a solid formation). They were usually citizens recruited from the merchant class, which thereby won great political power.

7

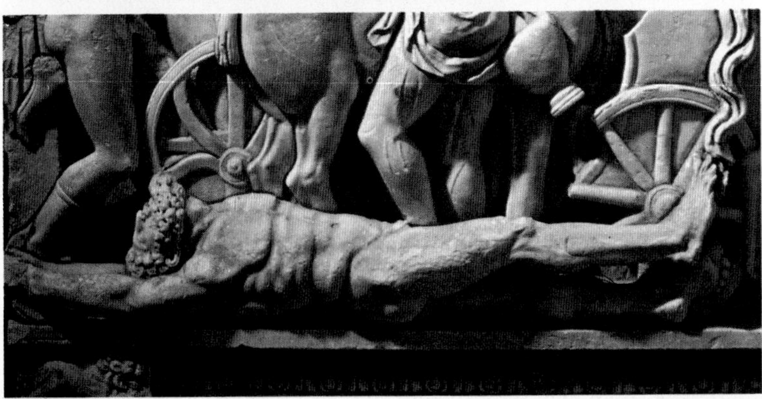

7 This wounded warrior is carved on the pediment of the Temple of Aphaia in Aegina. Throughout the Classical age there was almost continual fighting between city-states. This weakened the Greeks politically but did not prevent a flowering of the arts, literature, and philosophy. The achievements of Athens tend to overshadow the fact that many other states, both on the Greek mainland and in Asia Minor, also produced great artists and outstanding writers.

8

8 The Temple of Athena at Delphi, whose oracle was presided over by Apollo, was part of the widely respected shrine in ancient Greece. Religion in the Classical age was a ritual of sacrifices and ceremonies by the state or individual that gave little moral guidance or mystical experience. A belief in the same gods and legends did, however, promote the feeling of a common culture, which was reinforced by semireligious festivals such as the Olympic Games.

Classical Greek society

Classical Greece was the birthplace of many of the most influential Western ideas in art, literature, philosophy, and science. Its other great contribution was in politics, for it was there that the ideals of democracy were first developed. In all these areas Athens was preeminent, a fact recognized by its contemporaries. In two centuries Athens produced a succession of superb writers, artists, scientists, and philosophers. Many non-natives were attracted to the city, and there are few important figures in Greek cultural life who were not associated with Athens for at least part of their careers.

Athens and democracy

The city-state of Athens, with an area of about 1,000 square miles (2,500sq km), was the largest of the many city-states into which Greece was divided. Its population at its peak was about 260,000, of which about 45,000 were male citizens and about 70,000 slaves. The rest were women, children, and resident foreigners, or *metics*. Corinth may have had a population of 90,000; Thebes, Corcyra, and Acragas about 50,000 each; and other states as few as 5,000.

Politics in all these city-states was a very intimate affair, and this profoundly affected the Athenian concept of democracy [1]. It was based on direct participation, rather than representation, with every citizen having an equal opportunity to hold high office. In common with many other Greek states, Athens went through the transition from oligarchy (a small number of individuals holding power) to tyranny (a single all-powerful ruler) with struggles between rich and poor, before the reforms of Cleisthenes in 508 BC established a democratic framework.

The essence of this democracy was the citizen body, or demos. Citizenship was a jealously guarded right, rarely given to foreigners and never to women [3, 5]. All power was vested in the demos, which met in public assembly about every ten days [2]. There, any citizen could put forward proposals for laws or action that were discussed and voted on, and the civil and religious officials were chosen. There was no hierarchy among the officials, and they were responsible only to the assembly. Juries were selected from volunteers, and the business of the assembly was prepared by a council of 500 citizens, or *boule*, elected by the ten tribes into which the citizens were divided.

Rights and duties

Every Athenian citizen had the right and duty to serve the state, but because there were more than 1,000 offices to be filled each year, the system could work only if there were enough men with both the time and inclination for public service. At no time was Athens short of able men to serve with little or no reward, and it was only during the fourth century BC that a small payment was introduced to help the poorest citizens to participate fully.

Athenians gained their wealth from land, trade, and commerce. In Athens, in particular, a definite class of capitalists and an urban proletariat developed. Their leisure resulted from the widespread use of slaves for many of the most basic jobs [3]. Despite this influence of the wealthy, it is

CONNECTIONS

See also
994 Classical Greece
998 Greek literature and theater
1000 Greek art 1100–450 BC
1002 Greek art 450–31 BC
1006 Greek science
902 Types of political systems
904 Political participation

1 The hub of Athenian democracy was the Pnyx, where the assembly of citizens gathered for its regular meetings. Public and social life was a gregarious open-air affair with informal discussion, theater, and sports providing the most common interests.

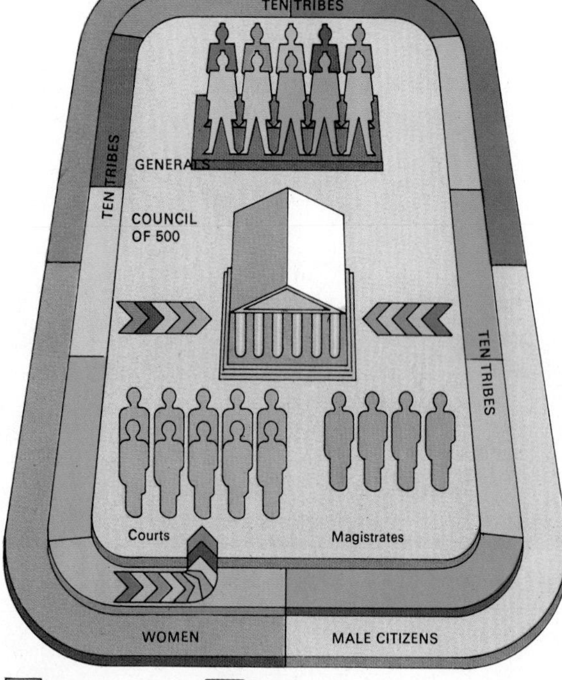

SLAVES
FOREIGNERS
TEN TRIBES
GENERALS
COUNCIL OF 500
Courts
Magistrates
WOMEN
MALE CITIZENS
Assembly
Direct election
Nomination and lot

2 Fifth-century Athenian democracy was based upon the power of the assembly of citizens to vote on all major decisions. All public officials were responsible to the assembly and were chosen by the 10 citizen tribes for limited terms; only the 10 military commanders, or *strategoi,* were elected and could serve for more than a year. Popular control over both the magistrates and the law could also be exercised through the courts, where the large citizen juries had legislative as well as judicial powers and could try a law as unconstitutional.

3 A black slave follows a member of the leisure class. Athenian democracy, with its large number of official jobs being filled by unpaid or low-paid citizens, depended on a plentiful supply of men with the inclination and leisure to take them. Athenian civic responsibility and pride in the system meant that there was never a lack of volunteers, and this was helped by the wealth from land and commerce that flowed into the city. The large-scale use of slaves freed citizens for public service. Athenian thinkers saw no contradiction between the individual rights and freedom on which their system was based and the slaves upon which this system depended.

4 A heifer is led to sacrifice in a religious ceremony. Religion was an affair of the state—the correct prayers and sacrifices were carried out by elected priests or private individuals—but there was little of the moral certainty and interference in private affairs that characterized later religions. The gods were irrational and arbitrary and had to be placated, but their conduct provided little guidance for men in their ordinary, day-to-day affairs.

also remarkable that Athenian democracy saw few of the direct confrontations between rich and poor of the kind that caused continual unrest in most other city-states.

All citizens and *metics* were liable for military service, but usually only the wealthy were called up because troops were expected to equip themselves. By the early seventh century BC, the typical Greek soldier was a heavily—and expensively—armed hoplite (infantryman) [6]. At the height of the Peloponnesian War, Athens put about 16,000 hoplites into the field; few other states could manage as many. In Athens the navy was an unusually important and elite force. It was recruited from the poorer citizens, and gave them an important source of power, money, and pride.

Sparta: a military state

No other state reached such a fully developed system of democracy as Athens. Its main rival for much of the period was Sparta, whose political and social system is remembered as representing the opposite of democracy. By 600 BC, Sparta had become a unique military state; Laconia and Messenia had been conquered and their populations either enslaved *(helots)* of deprived of political rights and forced to support the Spartans through taxation and food and manpower supplies.

To prevent revolt or secession, Sparta became a military camp. The citizen body was not large—probably never much more than 5,000—but every citizen was a professional soldier devoted from childhood to absolute discipline and the art of war. Two hereditary kings commanded the army in the field and were members of the ruling council of elders, who were elected for life from citizens over 60. Five elected magistrates, or *ephors,* had civil and judicial functions. No other Greek state approached Sparta in exclusiveness or xenophobia. A total refusal to admit new citizens led to a declining population and eventual defeat.

Sparta has remained the model of a closed and totally disciplined society, but it was Athens whose pursuit of individual freedom and democracy gave the world two of its most precious and lasting ideals.

KEY

Pericles (*c*.490–429 BC) was the great Athenian statesman under whose leadership Athens became the richest and most powerful Greek state. He was responsible for the building of the fine temples and monuments on the Acropolis.

5

5 Women in classical Greece were the other great "slave" class; they had no political or legal rights and were excluded from all public affairs. Their place was in the home with the children. Their absence from much social life probably contributed to the widespread practice of male homosexuality and the institution of the *hetaera,* a class of highly cultivated courtesans.

6

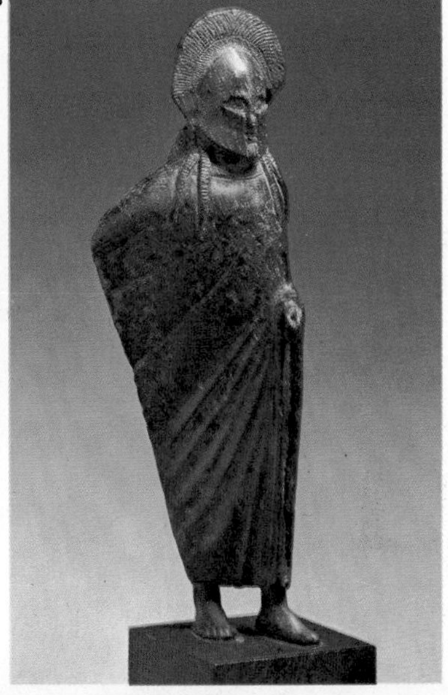

6 Spartan infantrymen (hoplites) were normally well and expensively equipped. The Spartan political system of a totally mobilized citizenry devoted to military service (boys were sent to barracks at the age of seven and not allowed other interests) was unique in Greece and gave Sparta far greater importance than its relatively small size justified. Most other states relied upon temporary conscription to fight the frequent wars that were endemic to Greek life. But a class of professional mercenaries did grow up during the 4th century, possibly as many as 50,000 in all, some fighting for the Persians.

7

8

7 Gods and goddesses, with Athena holding a shield inscribed with an owl, are shown on this Greek vase. The pantheon was featured in the epics of Homer and was the basis of the religion of classical Greece. The gods were conceived of in human form with human emotions. They often interfered in human activities and could be invoked or calmed by prayer and sacrifice. There was little belief in an afterlife; religion was strictly temporal and devoted to a pleasant life.

8 Athletic competitions and the cult of the well-trained and healthy body played an important part in everyday social life; the gymnasium and stadium were popular meeting places where men could talk and hold political or philosophical discussions. The Greeks dated their history from the first Olympic Games in 776 BC, a festival that had contestants from all over the Greek world, providing the opportunity for Greeks to gather together as a nation.

Greek literature and theater

Only a fraction of the literature of ancient Greece has survived, but what remains is unsurpassed in its diversity, strength, and lyricism. Its influence on later European writers, both directly and through Latin literature, has been enormous.

The poets

Homer [Key], one of the greatest names in world literature, still remains a shadow. Whether his works are a compilation of songs, the writings of two or more minstrels, or the masterpieces of one towering genius, although the last seems unlikely, is uncertain. What is indisputable is that the *Iliad* and the *Odyssey* are among the greatest of literary achievements. Composed probably in the eighth century BC, they describe semi-legendary characters and events 500 years earlier.

The *Iliad* portrays events toward the end of the Trojan War. The story has a substratum of fact, although basically it is a marvelous feat of poetic imagination. The shorter *Odyssey* [1] describes Odysseus' experiences on his return journey from the war. A little later than Homer, Hesiod wrote two epic poems with strong didactic elements, *Works and Days* and *Theogony*.

The Greek poets in general preferred the greater freedom of meter and expression offered by the lyric form. Lyric poetry, developed from songs sung to the lyre, reached its height during the seventh and sixth centuries BC, but only fragments have survived to demonstrate the passion, charm, and vigor of the work of such poets as Terpander, Sappho, and Alcaeus [5] of Lesbos, Aleman of Sparta, Anacreon of Ionia, and Simonides of Ceos. Stesichorus, credited with the invention of the choral hymn celebrating the heroes of epic poetry, was a strong influence on Pindar (*c*.522–*c*.440 BC), most of whose surviving poems are odes celebrating athletic victories.

The dramatists

Western literature's debt to the Greeks is perhaps most marked in the field of drama. The 32 tragedies that have survived have moved audiences and inspired writers for more than 2,000 years.

The three giants of Greek tragedy are Aeschylus (*c*.525–456 BC), Sophocles (*c*.496–406 BC), and Euripides (*c*.480–405 BC). Each has his own particular genius—Aeschylus his grandeur, Sophocles his ability to convey moral dilemmas, and Euripides his insight into human nature. Greek tragedies were performed at festivals; three tragedies plus one satyr play—a grotesque parody of ancient legends—were given at a sitting.

It is uncertain exactly how tragedy developed its sophistication. It seems likely that it grew out of choral songs performed at religious festivals. A semi-legendary poet named Thespis (hence "thespians," meaning actors) is reputed to have introduced a character who responded to the comments of the chorus. True drama involving conflict of character began when Aeschylus introduced a second actor. Sophocles used three actors and injected a greater degree of naturalism. Euripides offended many people by his cavalier treatment of the old subjects and the comparative realism of his themes. The motivation of his characters is

CONNECTIONS

See also
996 Classical Greek society
1028 Roman literature

1 In the Odyssey Homer tells of the dangers and trials that beset the unfortunate Odysseus on his way home to Ithaca after fighting with the Greeks against Troy. Vase paintings show many incidents such as his encounter with the Sirens. He ordered his crew to stuff their ears with wax so that they would not be lured onto the rocks by the Sirens' song; Odysseus was tied to the mast so he could safely listen.

2 This terracotta statuette of the 4th century shows two actors playing the roles of drunken old men. As was customary in Greek comedy, the actors wore grotesque masks and weird costumes, in this case padded jackets and tights. Like tragedy, comedy had three actors and a chorus, and the plays were performed at festivals. Also like tragedy, comedy probably came from choral songs.

3 A season of Greek tragedy is presented annually at the magnificent theater of Epidaurus, dating from the 4th century BC. The various parts of the theater may be discerned. In front is the circular *orchestra* on which the chorus danced and sang. Behind it is the stage on which the actors stood. At the back of the stage is the *skene*, or permanent background, made of wood in early times and later of stone. The performance shown is of Sophocles' *Electra*, the story of Orestes, son of Agamemnon and brother of Electra, who revenged his father's death. The actors are to the right, the chorus center and left. Of Sophocles' work, seven complete tragedies survive with several hundred fragments of others. Immensely successful in 5th-century Greece, he remains admired for the skill with which he structured his plays, but even more for his characterization.

convincing, and his portraits of such women as Medea, Hecuba, and Electra are particularly memorable.

Greek comedy is virtually synonymous with the 11 plays by Aristophanes (*c.*450–*c.*388 BC). The comedy is broad, the characters ludicrous, but the satire of the life, ideas, and leading figures of the time is often sharp. Aristophanes was not afraid to lampoon even the gods. Menander (*c.* 342–292 BC) wrote urbane comedies of manners that lacked the exuberance of Aristophanes; however, they influenced such later writers as Shakespeare and Molière.

The historians

The two greatest historians of ancient Greece had very different approaches to their craft. Herodotus (*c.*485–425 BC) took as his overriding theme the struggle between Greece and Persia. His work is part history and part entertainment.

The first scientific historian was Thucydides (*c.*460–*c.*400 BC), who actually lived through the events that he described in his account of the Peloponnesian war. He clearly had questioned participants and eyewitnesses on both sides, related cause to effect, and presented the facts in a concise, direct style. Among other Greek historians of note was Xenophon (*c.*430–*c.*354 BC), whose *Anabasis* describes the retreat of 10,000 Greeks across Asia Minor.

Orators and philosophers

The two remaining branches of Greek literature are oratory and philosophy. Speeches were written to be read as literary works as much as to be spoken. Of the leading orators, who included Lysias, Isocrates, and Aeschines, Demosthenes (*c.*383–322 BC) was by far the greatest. An active politician, he is best known for his eloquent speeches against Philip of Macedon and the speech in his own defense, "On the Crown." Of the philosophers, Aristotle and Plato wrote the most polished prose. Most of Aristotle's work is lost, although the theories of literature enunciated in his *Poetics* have been extremely influential. The *Dialogues* of Plato (*c.*427–*c.*347 BC) [7] show Greek prose at its best.

KEY

Homer is regarded as the father of Greek literature. His importance can be judged by his appearance on this 4th-century coin from Ios. The *Iliad* and *Odyssey* probably evolved from singers' tales rather than from Homer alone, but scholars do not know how they reached their present form.

4

4 The chorus in a Greek tragedy is depicted on this vase dancing to the meter of the verse and singing to the accompaniment of a flute. Particularly in its early period, Greek tragedy incorporated two styles. Dialogue between the actors, or the actors and chorus, was spoken in iambic rhythms. Choral odes were based on complex meters that reflected the emotions of the poetry.

5

5 A wine cooler of the 5th century shows the lyric poets Alcaeus and Sappho. Little remains of Sappho's nine books of verse except for one ode, but there is enough to show the unequalled passion and tenderness of her love poems. The poems of Alcaeus, her contemporary and friend, are also known only by fragments, which express political thoughts and outpourings of love and hate.

6

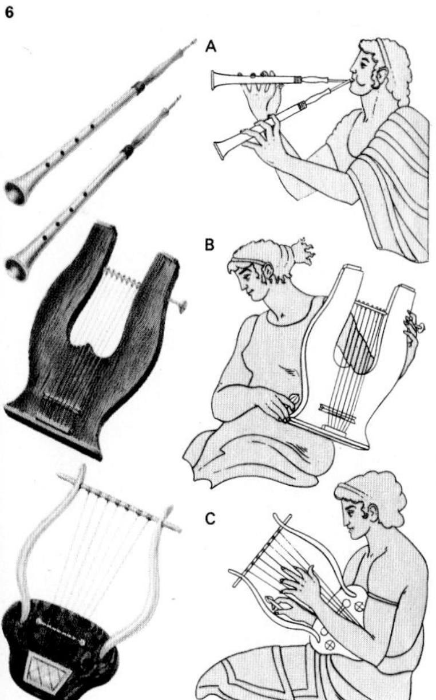

A
B
C

6 No Grecian musical instruments have survived, but from vases and paintings it is known that the main instruments were the *aulos*, or flute [A], and two types of lyre, the *cithara* [B] and *lyra* [C]. *Auloi* were usually played in pairs, sometimes joined by a mouth band. The *cithara* was heavy and was used by paid musicians to accompany epic songs. The lighter *lyra* was used by amateurs.

7

7 This Roman mosaic from a villa near Pompeii shows the olive grove, dedicated to the Greek hero Academus, where Plato founded the Greek school of philosophy, called the Academy, in *c.*387 BC. Plato, third from left, is shown teaching at the Academy, which lasted until AD 529 when it was suppressed by the Romans. Plato was a master stylist. The tone of his *Dialogues* (ostensibly with Socrates) range from casual conversation to dramatic confrontation, and his work provides us with the prototype of the philosopher—questioning, wise, and humble. His thought has been a major influence on western philosophy into the twentieth century.

Greek art and architecture underwent in seven centuries a gradual but profound change, from a primitive phase to a high level of refinement on the brink of the Classical period—the period that has exerted an enduring aesthetic and technical influence on the art of our own era. The objectivity and naturalness achieved in the Greek image of the human figure has remained the norm of later societies in the West. But it should be realized that because of the disappearance of textiles and woodwork and the paucity of early metalwork, the bare stone of ruined temples and the weathered surfaces of sculptures convey no impression of the original color and variety of Greek art.

The origins of Greek art lie in the Mycenaean culture of the sixteenth century BC. Following its overthrow in the twelfth century there was a "dark age." The only examples of its material culture are vases bearing simple linear devices in a style known as protogeometric [1]. The real birth of Greek art, however, was effectively a rebirth—the renaissance of the ninth and eighth centuries BC, by which time the development of trade and the demands that a settled society made on its craftsmen produced a range of functional and aesthetically pleasing objects (for to the Greeks there was no distinction between the beautiful and the useful) such as votive offerings for the new shrines of Delphi and Olympia.

The zigzags and other motifs of the geometric art that flourished between *c.*900–700 BC became progressively bolder and more elaborate, and gradually figures of men and animals were included. Stylized figures were presented in a purely conceptual manner, with no attempt to depict perspective or movement. These early scenes of funeral processions and battles were a breakthrough; they were the first steps toward the narrative art that marked the work of Greek artists who drew on the heroic tales of the *Iliad* and *Odyssey*.

The High Archaic period

The High Archaic period of 725–600 BC saw an oriental influence, developing particularly out of the trade with the Phoenicians. Craftsmen from Cyprus and Syria worked in Crete and Attica, and their innovations were assimilated by the Greeks.

Athens, originally the acknowledged center of geometric painting, engaged less in trade and colonization and for a time was eclipsed artistically. But as a result of imported Egyptian ideas, this period saw the first major works of Greek architecture. Based on the temple design of Egypt, wooden columns and other features were progressively replaced by their equivalents in stone, and the "orders" of Greek architecture emerged, beginning with the Doric in the second half of the century. Sculpture also developed under Eastern influence—originally employing molds to cast small stereotyped images for shrines. By about 640, larger statues, derived from Egyptian models, were being manufactured. Plentiful domestic supplies of marble and ancillary materials, such as emery, were exploited. During this time the tradition of the *kouros* [2] was established.

Although owing much in stance and manufacturing technique to Egyptian

CONNECTIONS

See also
992 The Greeks to the r[…] of Athens
994 Classical Greece
996 Classical Greek soc[…]ety
1002 Greek art 450–31 B[…]
1022 Roman art 27 BC–[…] 117
1024 Roman art 117–550
1198 Neoclassicism

1 Protogeometric pottery, decorated with simple circles and wavy lines, probably originated in Athens before the end of the 11th century. As the potter's craft evolved, these motifs, often based on patterns of woven baskets and produced on a massive scale (up to 5ft [1.5m] high), became more complex with the introduction of zig-zags, friezes, and stylized figures.

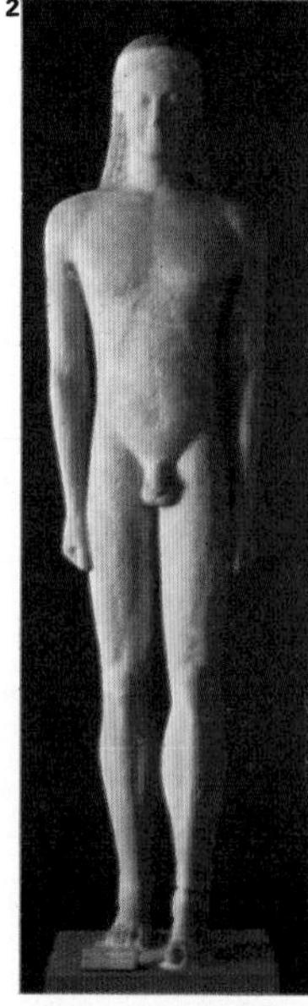

2 Kouros are figures of naked youths that are derived from Egyptian examples. They are often used as grave markers and are typically elegant, with clenched hands and one foot advanced.

3 A masterpiece of black-figure painting, this amphora was made and decorated by Exekias (*fl. c.* 550BC–525BC), the greatest painter of his time. It marks the resurgence of Athenian painting. It captures the drama of the moment of death when, according to legend, the eyes of the Amazon queen, Penthesilea, met those of her slayer, Achilles, and she realized that he loved her.

4 From earliest times the Greek architects' chief concern was with temple building. Based on the traditional house plan, and originally constructed in wood, their designs evolved until in the 6th century BC stone superseded wood. Many of the elements from carpentry, such as the adze-formed grooves in columns, were retained. Originating in mainland Greece, the first and most persistent of the orders—the Doric—was established. Although somewhat modified by western Greek colonists, the temple of Hera I at Paestum, Italy, retains all the classic Doric attributes and is one of the best surviving examples of the style.

works, a distinctive Greek style emerged. The Greek preoccupation with athletics meant that figures of youths were characteristically naked and because of the requirements that this form imposed, sculptors were compelled to study anatomy in greater detail—an important factor in the development of Greek sculpture.

Corinth, a center for pottery

By about 700 BC, Corinth had taken the lead as the great Greek pottery center, and the black-figure technique [3] pioneered and perfected there persisted for over 200 years. During the Archaic period, Greece was experiencing a newfound prosperity. Its colonial expansion was virtually complete, and the development of stable cities provided the patronage that encouraged a wide range of artistic endeavors. Temple building increased, and the Ionic order was introduced; temples became more elaborate, and they were decorated with sculptured friezes of increasingly great artistry. An ever-growing understanding of human anatomy was applied both to a more naturalistic style of sculpture in the round and in relief and to the establishment in vase painting of a set of formal gestures and an iconography on which many masterpieces of black-figure painting were based.

Athens and red-figure painting

By 530 BC, red-figure painting had been invented [5] and Athens had become the chief center of the style which, as a result of its superiority in allowing greater attention to detail, soon ousted the black-figure technique. The artistic feeling of the Early Classical period (*c.*500–450 BC) was profoundly affected by the devastating consequences of the Persian Wars (490–478 BC). The most striking examples of this are seen in the dramatic abandonment of the "Archaic smile" expression and its replacement by a more sober and objective rendering of faces. As the most sudden change in artistic outlook for many centuries it was to contribute greatly to the humanistic "detached calm" that characterizes the art of the subsequent Classical period.

KEY

One of the finest examples of the sculpture of the Attic period is the so-called "Mourning Athena." The blending of full and three-quarter profile views is boldly executed, and the facial expression and relaxed, natural posture of the subject vividly convey a pensive mood appropriate to the purpose. It was once thought that the relief showed Athena mourning by a grave marker, but it is now held that it is a votive offering by a games victor and that the goddess stands beside a *terma*, the starting point of the race. The craftsmanship anticipates the perfection of the sculpture of the Classical age.

5

5 Red-figure vase painting, in which the scenes are portrayed in sharp relief in red against an inky black background, began to supersede black-figure painting about 530 BC. This *krater*, (a bowl for mixing wine and water) is a fine example of this stylistic evolution and depicts a scene from the Trojan Wars—Achilles and Hector in mortal combat. It marks a development that led to the mastery of draftsmanship.

6

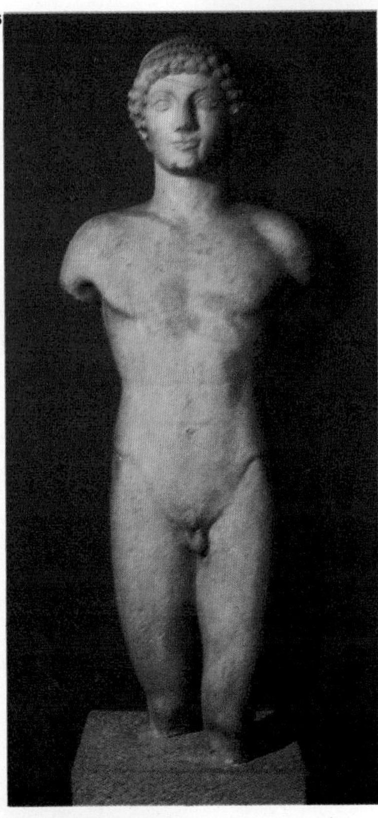

6 An outstanding example of free-standing sculpture from the late Archaic/early Classical period, the "Strangford Apollo" (after its former owner, Lord Strangford) marks the consummation of over a century in the evolution of *kouros* sculpture. The early stiffness and formality of style was replaced by an increasing awareness of anatomical accuracy.

7

7 The "Ludovisi Throne" of the transitional late Archaic/early Classical period is remarkable for the fine quality of its modeling, particularly the effect of the clinging wet hair and clothes. Once in the collection of a Roman cardinal, it is of obscure origin and use but it was perhaps part of an altar. The work of a western Greek artist, it shows the birth of the goddess Aphrodite from the sea, aided by two attendants.

8

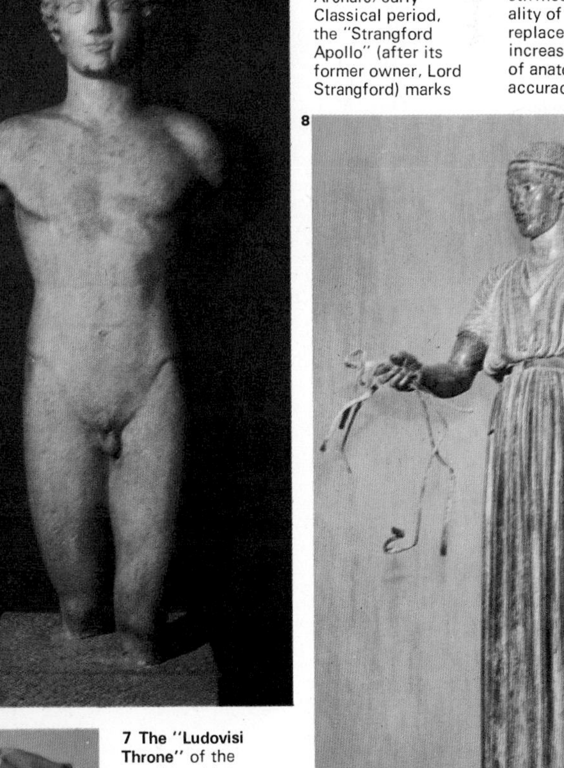

8 The life-sized bronze statue of a charioteer, commissioned *c.* 470 BC as an offering in celebration of a victory by a Sicilian tyrant, Polyzalos of Gela, is of exaggerated proportions because it was designed to be viewed from below and partly concealed by the coach-work of the chariot in which it once stood. Although superficially architectural, the modeling and stance of the figure are brilliantly conceived, making it a classical masterpiece.

Greek art 450–31 BC

After about 450 BC Greek art entered a phase regarded by succeeding generations as its great Classical period. It built on experience, took in new influences (especially from the East), and sought higher goals. Trends that had previously been evident, such as the concern with naturalism in sculpture, reached their peak in the work of such masters as Phidias, who is now regarded as the father of Greek classical art.

Classical formality

Yet, throughout the art of the High Classical period (*c.*450–400 BC), and allied with its technical virtuosity, there is restraint in emotion and a lack of extremes. The art is formal, with few representations of childhood or old age and virtually no depictions of anger or pleasure. The concern of the Greek sculptor for an ideal, a perfection of form, led him to a style that has been described as impersonal.

The High Classical period saw the resurgence of Athens as a great artistic center, particularly under the ruler Pericles (*c.* 490–429 BC). After the destruction of the Persian Wars, a rebuilding program of unsurpassed vision produced some of the world's most remarkable buildings—the Parthenon [3] and Erectheum on the Athenian Acropolis especially stand out for their magnificence. The sculptures of the Parthenon offer a realism and grandeur of concept that have few rivals in the history of art [Key]. Similarly splendid architectural sculpture, reliefs, votive statues, and cult figures also date from this period.

Although the heroic male figure remained the most typical, sculptors turned increasingly to representations of females, paying particular attention to draperies, for example, in Nike (the goddess of victory) figures [7]. This shift from the idealized portrayal of the nude male to the stylized draped female is an important element in the unformalizing process that was to alter Greek art. Among other arts, wall painting is known to have flourished in the High Classical period and indeed to have taken precedence over vase painting, but material evidence is lacking. Die-engraving, especially in Sicily, was developed as a fine art and coinage design became increasingly decorative.

Portraiture develops

In the Late Classical period (*c.*400–323 BC), increased prosperity and patronage led to a shift from the unemotional conventions of the earlier period. Encouraged first by the prestige-seeking rulers of the western Persian Empire, true portraiture developed as a rival to idealized representations of divinities. Similarly, monumental tomb sculpture was introduced as a celebration of status—it is no coincidence that from this period comes the superb sculptured tomb of King Mausolus of Caria at Halicarnassus, from which the word *mausoleum* is derived. This work, like that of the Alexander Sarcophagus [5], was produced by Greek craftsmen working on the fringes of the empire; their work and that of mainland Greek artists—Praxiteles [4], Scopas, and Lysippus in particular—mark the transition from Classical idealism to Hellenistic realism. Lysippus, for example, Alexander the Great's official sculptor, produced works

CONNECTIONS

See also
1000 Greek art 1100–450 BC
996 Classical Greek society
1022 Roman art 27 BC–AD 117
1024 Roman art 117–550
1134 Florentine art 1400–1460
1138 Italian art 1450–1490
1140 Florence and Rome: the High Renaissance
1198 Neoclassicism

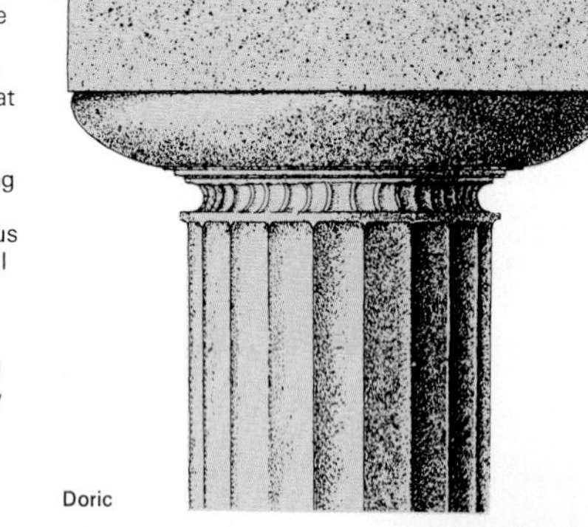

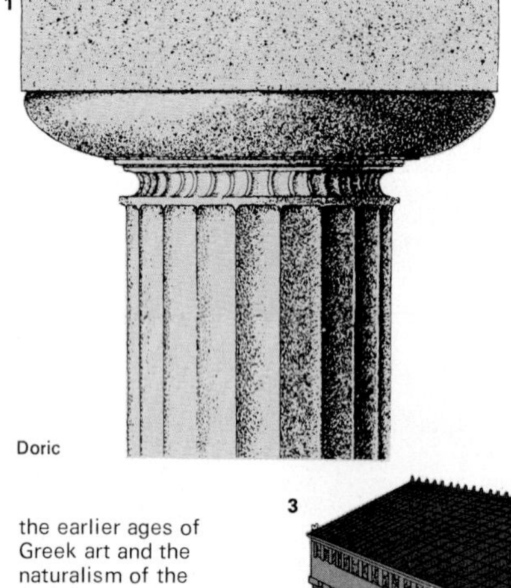
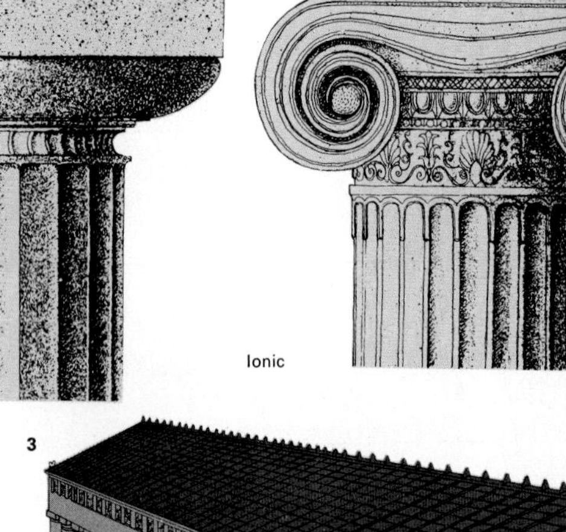

1
Doric
Ionic
Corinthian

1 The three main Greek orders are the Doric, the earliest, whose capital has a deep abacus (the flat slab at the top) and wide-spreading echinus (the molding beneath); the Ionic with a thinner abacus and projecting spiral scrolls with rich carvings; and the Corinthian, deeper, more elaborate, and until its adoption by the Romans, less popular than the other two orders. It was used in the Hellenistic period.

2 "Poseidon of Artemisium" – a representation of one of the most revered gods of the seafaring Athenians – represents an artistic bridge between the somewhat stylized portrait sculpture of the earlier ages of Greek art and the naturalism of the Classical era. He is among the most splendidly modeled of all surviving bronze statues with his muscular body and fine head.

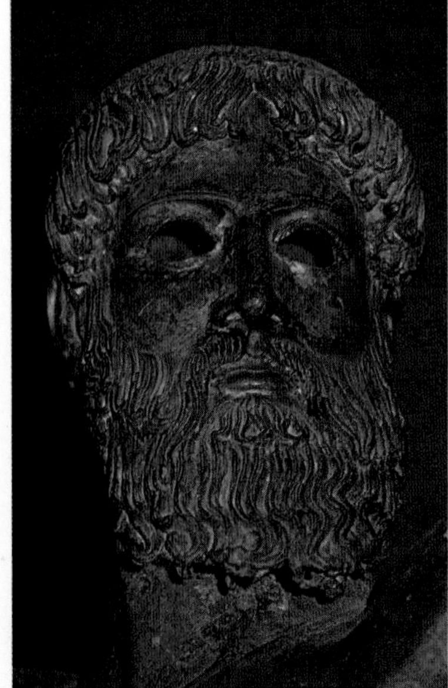

2

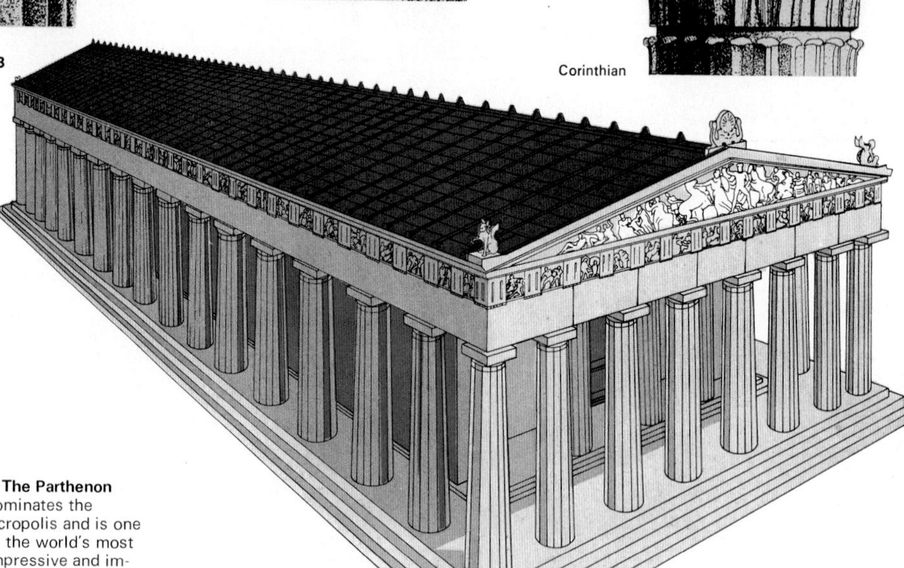

3

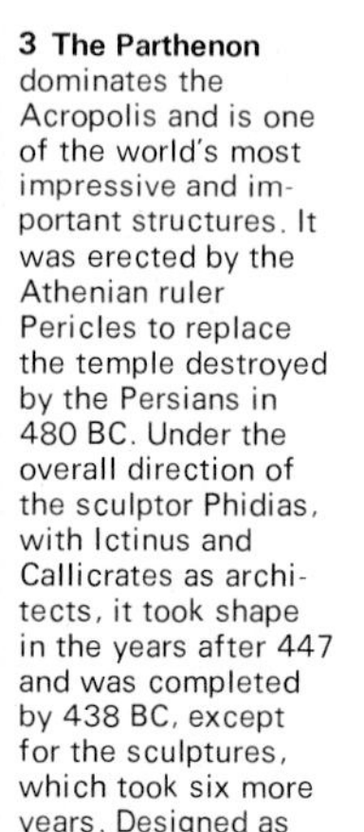

3 The Parthenon dominates the Acropolis and is one of the world's most impressive and important structures. It was erected by the Athenian ruler Pericles to replace the temple destroyed by the Persians in 480 BC. Under the overall direction of the sculptor Phidias, with Ictinus and Callicrates as architects, it took shape in the years after 447 and was completed by 438 BC, except for the sculptures, which took six more years. Designed as an expression of Athens' supremacy and civic pride, it was Greece's largest and most costly building and a fitting center for the display of Phidias' ivory and gold statue of Athena. The Parthenon embodied many bold architectural innovations and the most cherished artistic conceptions of the day. Entirely of the Doric order, it has 8 frontal columns instead of the usual 6, and 17 in the peristyle. The entasis or bulging effect of the columns counters the optical illusion of concavity that would otherwise occur, and their slight inward leaning, coupled with the outward tilt of the upper works, calculated to the most minute degree, ensure its harmonious proportions. The frieze and metopes, which were originally richly painted, were more refined, spectacular, and skillfully executed than any predecessors and stand out among the greatest works of sculpture to be found in the world, both in relief and in the round.

that, unlike some formal groups of earlier Classical times, could be viewed satisfactorily from virtually any angle. He also produced lifelike portraits of his patron. In response to the newfound wealth of the Greek Empire, both painting (known only from Roman mosaic copies) and jewelry of high quality flourished.

Realism in the Hellenistic period

The Hellenistic period (from the death of Alexander in 323 to the Battle of Actium in 31 BC) was the last phase in the history of Greek art. The development of court life stimulated a wide range of arts; Pergamon was established as a leading center of architecture and sculpture, while distinctive local schools emerged in the Seleucid Empire and in Alexandria and Rhodes. Athens alone preserved the Classical traditions.

The aspirations of the rulers of the Alexandrian Empire led to a greater emphasis on portraiture, which often attempted to convey the quasi-divine status of its subjects. For the first time, representations of men predominated over those of gods, and the original religious and mythological flavor of Greek art declined and was replaced by accurate—if still sometimes idealized—depictions of notable people. Both public and domestic architecture became increasingly grand while large-scale temple building declined. The more elaborate Ionic order was generally adopted in preference to the austere Doric, and the Corinthian order was used for the first time in exterior construction, as part of a move to this greater elaboration [1].

Works of sculpture such as the reliefs from the altar of Zeus, Pergamon, the Nike of Samothrace [7], and the Laocoön group depicted vigorous action and emotion [6]; femininity was portrayed in such works as the Venus of Milo; while physical suffering, anguish, old age, and extreme youth were represented for the first time.

Near the end of the Hellenistic period, a trend toward copying earlier, Classical works can be observed. Through this process and the Romans' large-scale absorption of its chief elements the continuity of Greek art was assured.

KEY

The theme of the friezes from the Parthenon—the battle between the Lapiths (people from Thessaly) and centaurs at the wedding of the Lapith king Pirithaus—symbolizes the triumph of order and civilization over barbarism. This was a recurring motif in High Classical art, 5th century BC.

4 **"Hermes carrying the infant Dionysus"** is possibly the only surviving original work by the Athenian master sculptor Praxiteles, who was regarded as one of the greatest craftsmen of his age. This work displayed a refinement of technique seldom encountered before the Hellenistic period. The idealized classical beauty and proportions of the figure of Hermes were enhanced in the original by the impression of a graceful curving upward line as he playfully offered a bunch of grapes to Dionysus. This statue was discovered in Olympia's Temple of Hera in the year 1877.

4

5

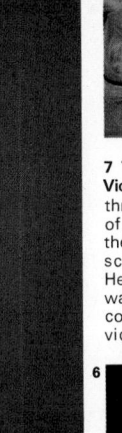

5 **The "Alexander Sarcophagus"** was commissioned by the last king of Sidon, who owed his position to Alexander the Great. It was both a tomb and a monument in praise of Alexander's achievements. It depicts scenes from his life, including a battle against the Persians and a spirited hunting scene. Its style is greatly influenced by the work of Lysippus, greatest of all 4th century sculptors, particularly in the modeling of the figures. It nevertheless conveys the vigor and dynamism with which Hellenistic art was inspired. It is also a fine example of Greek sculpture showing traces of original paintwork.

7 **The Nike (Winged Victory)** of Samothrace—an example of the superb work of the Rhodes school of sculpture from the Hellenistic period—was probably made to commemorate a sea victory over Antiochos III of Syria and originally depicted Victory alighting on a ship's prow. The powerful yet light movement of the figure is expressed by the swirling of the draped garment around it.

6

7

6 **The famous statue** depicting the death struggles of the Trojan prince Laocoön and his two sons was produced in Rhodes by Greek artists who specialized in compositions conveying violence and anguish—emotions that became characteristic of Hellenistic art. Like many Greek works of the time, it was much admired by the Romans and was taken to Rome by the Emperor Titus in AD 69, where it was described by Pliny the Elder as "superior to anything produced in painting or sculpture." In 1506 the statue was rediscovered in the Baths of Titus and bought by Pope Julius II for the Vatican, where it was studied by such artists as Michelangelo, Bernini, and Rubens for its anatomical detail and vigorous action.

Alexander the Great

Alexander, the son of Philip II of Macedon and Olympias, princess of Epirus, was born at Pella in Macedon in 356 BC and died in Babylon in 323 BC. The pupil between the ages of 13 and 16 of the philosopher Aristotle, Alexander succeeded to the Macedonian throne in 336 BC on the assassination of his father, whose cavalry he had commanded two years earlier at the battle of Chaeronea. That battle had established Macedonian hegemony over Greece. It also marked the victory of the soldier over the rhetorician, for it had been Demosthenes, the Athenian orator (*c*.383–322 BC), who had most scathingly attacked the Macedonians and their king.

Securing the frontiers of Macedonia

During the 13 years from 336, Alexander was to establish the greatest empire the ancient world had ever known [4], stretching from the Libyan frontier to the Punjab.

Upon his accession he marched south into Greece and, asserting Macedonian supremacy, had himself elected by the league of Greek city-states as a leader of an Asian expedition. The oracle of Delphi hailed him as invincible. In 335 BC he campaigned toward the Danube, to secure Macedonia's northern frontier. On rumors of his death, a revolt broke out in Greece with the support of leading Athenians: Alexander marched south, covering 240 miles (386km) in two weeks. When the revolt continued he sacked Thebes, killing 6,000 people and enslaving the survivors, sparing only the temples and the house of the poet Pindar (*c*.522–*c*.440 BC). His base thus secured, he prepared for the campaign for which his father had raised him and which was supported by Aristotle's teaching on the political superiority of the Greeks. He also needed the riches of Persia to pay his father's debts to the Macedonian army.

The victory over Darius

Alexander crossed the Hellespont in 334 BC, with 30,000 infantry, 5,000 cavalry, and a corps of specialists. He paid a visit to Troy and at the Granicus River fought a battle that opened Asia Minor to his southward drive. He defeated Darius III, the Persian king at the Issus [2] in 333 BC and continued south until his advance was held up at Tyre, which did not fall until July 332 BC.

After the sack of Tyre, Alexander went to Egypt, where he founded the city of Alexandria. On visiting the shrine of Amon at Siwah Oasis, he was greeted as pharaoh, son of Amon, a precursor to his later claims of divine origin. In 331 BC, he marched eastward to the Euphrates and fought another battle at Gaugamela, but Darius once again escaped; Alexander received the surrender of Babylon and Susa with their enormous riches. In 330 BC he captured Persepolis, where he burned the royal palace. At this point he sent the Thessalians and Greeks home, apparently planning a Persian-Macedonian empire. While he was campaigning eastward, Darius was assassinated.

Alexander next (329–327) marched into Afghanistan and Sogdiana (Transoxiana), and then to Samarkand and Alexandria Eschate (modern Leninabad). There were further revolts until 328 BC, the year of his marriage to Roxana, daughter of the king of

CONNECTIONS

See also
978 The Phoenicians 1500–146 BC
982 The Hebrews 1200–322 BC
984 The Persian Empire o the Achaemenids
986 India 500 BC–AD 30
972 Egypt: 1570 BC to Alexander the Great

1 The battle of the Hydaspes (Jhelum) in the Punjab, shown here on a coin, was one of Alexander's most skillfully planned and executed victories, greatly extending his empire. His tactics were influenced by the horse's natural fear of the elephant. The defeated Indian ruler Poros became an ally. At this battle Alexander's famous charger Bucephalus died and was given a full imperial funeral.

2 This mosaic from Pompeii, copied from a painting by Philoxenus of Eretria, shows Alexander commanding his army against the Persians under Darius at the battle of Issus, 333 BC. Darius fled, leaving his queen and family, together with a vast amount of wealth, to the Macedonians.

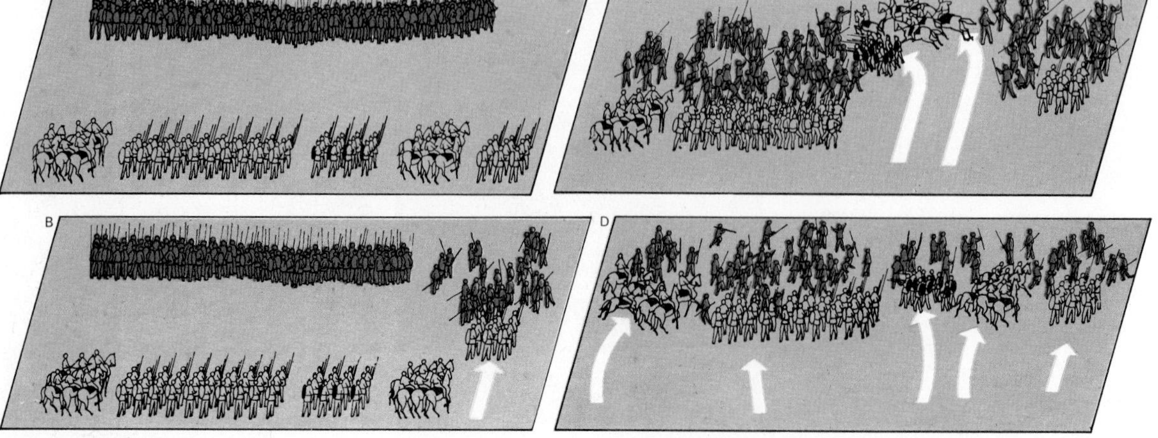
A
B
C
D

3 Alexander placed the phalanx (the large body of foot soldiers shown here in black and white) at the center of his battle order [A]. Fighting was initiated on the extreme right [B]. Alexander would then lead his cavalry, supported by the household infantry, in a charge through the gap in the enemy line [C]. As the enemy ranks broke, he wheeled his cavalry to take the flank and relieve the left and center of his army. He pressed his advantage with his phalanx and cavalry [D]

Bactria, a marriage that seems to have been symbolic of East-West fusion. At the same time his absolutism increased. His murder of his commander and friend Cleitus in a drunken brawl angered the Macedonian troops.

In 327 BC he led his men into India, one army marching through the Khyber Pass while the other, which he commanded, fought its way through Swat. The final battle was fought on the Hydaspes (Jhelum) [1]; after the defeat of Poros, an Indian prince, Alexander's soldiers refused to go farther into India.

Return from the East

On his return to Susa, Alexander found a state of corruption and oppression. He set out on a ruthless campaign of punishment. This was followed by a plan for settling Greeks and Macedonians in Asia and Asians in Europe as part of a plan for fusing the two regions. A more immediate project was the marriage of Alexander and Hephaestion (his closest friend and lover) to two of the daughters of Darius, while another 80 Macedonian officers married daughters of Persian nobles.

Asian soldiers had already been trained in Macedonian military methods and were now admitted to the army; others were recruited for the cavalry and Persian officers for the royal bodyguard. In 324 BC, Alexander's 10,000 Macedonians, already disturbed by the new army policy, mutinied. Alexander ordered 13 of their leaders executed on the spot, appointed more Persians and Medes to Macedonian posts, and transferred regimental names to what the Europeans considered barbarian regiments. The Macedonians relented and set off on the return march to Europe. Plans were now made for a campaign into Arabia, but Alexander developed a fever and on June 13, 323 BC died, not yet 33 years old. His empire began to disintegrate almost at once as the various regional commanders assumed the titles of kings in their own right. Although Alexander was renowned primarily for his military conquests, his most enduring achievement was to extend Greek influence to a vast area of the ancient world.

KEY

Alexander is wearing the ram's horn headdress on this coin.

4

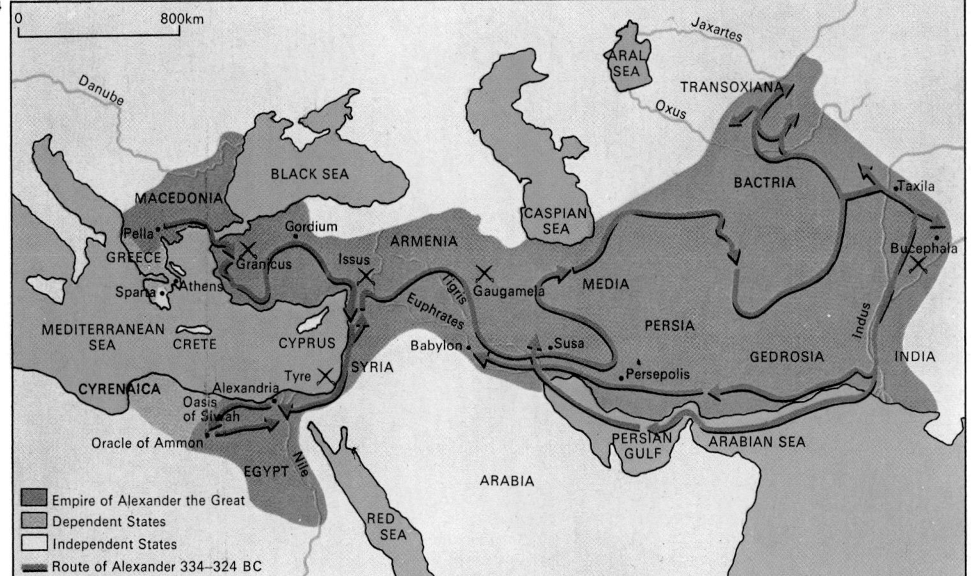

0
800km
Jaxartes
ARAL SEA
Danube
TRANSOXIANA
Oxus
BLACK SEA
BACTRIA
Taxila
MACEDONIA
CASPIAN SEA
Pella
Gordium
ARMENIA
GREECE
Granicus
Issus
Bucephala
Sparta
Athens
Tigris
Gaugamela
MEDIA
Euphrates
MEDITERRANEAN SEA
CRETE
CYPRUS
Susa
PERSIA
Indus
Babylon
GEDROSIA
INDIA
SYRIA
Tyre
Persepolis
CYRENAICA
Alexandria
Oasis of Siwah
Oracle of Ammon
PERSIAN GULF
ARABIAN SEA
Nile
EGYPT
ARABIA
RED SEA
Empire of Alexander the Great
Dependent States
Independent States
Route of Alexander 334–324 BC

4 The extent of Alexander's campaigns over 13 years explains the rapid collapse of his empire after his death. There was no consolidation, and the vast distances precluded real integration.

5 A picture from the Flemish *Alexander Romance* (a 13th-century legend cycle) shows Alexander preparing to fly in a basket attached to two griffins, which are to be lured upward by a lump of meat on a stick. Another illustration from the same source shows him in a glass "submarine," an idea that occurs in a Malay story depicting Alexander. Both portrayals imply Alexander's universal dominion.

6

6 The Alexander legend is told in many languages, from Middle English to Malay, in most countries of Europe, the Middle East, and Asia. He is depicted in many forms—Burgundian king, Armenian horseman, Persian prince. (One sultan in the 15th century had his own features depicted as Alexander's.) In the Muslim world he was held to be a pious follower of Islam, who fought pagans and spread the faith. Almost a thousand years after his death, he was identified with the Two-horned One mentioned in the Koran. In this Persian painting (1595–96) he is being asked to spare pagan idols.

Greek science

The earliest stirrings of Greek science are found in the eighth century BC in the Homeric poems with descriptions of the stars and an unusual concept of the universe as a sphere [1]. Other civilizations had been content with hemispherical skies; the Greek love of symmetrical shapes led them to the concept of a spherical universe.

Greek studies of the universe

The first Greek scientific men whose names are known—Thales, Anaximander, and Anaximenes—came from Miletus on the eastern seaboard of the Aegean and lived during the sixth century BC. Thales accepted the spherical universe and believed that water was the basic substance from which everything was formed. Anaximander, who thought some indefinable substance (not water) was the basic material, taught that the earth was cylindrical in shape. Like Anaximenes, he believed the heavenly bodies were holes in a dark sky through which shone a surrounding fiery zone. The most important sixth-century scientist was Pythagoras—best known for his proof of the relationship between the sides of any right-angled triangle—and his followers, the Pythagoreans. They also investigated musical harmony, which led them to suggest a divine relationship between numbers, music, and the universe.

Significant developments in the fourth century BC followed the establishment by Plato (*c.*427–347 BC) of his Academy in Athens, where he stressed the mathematical nature of the universe. His pupil Aristotle (384–322 BC), the greatest ancient scientific philosopher, set up his own academy, the Lyceum, also in Athens. He adopted the theory, formulated by Empedocles in the fifth century BC, of the four elements—earth, air, fire, and water—as the fundamental components of all matter. Astronomically, Aristotle discussed whether the Earth moved in space but he tended to favor a fixed earth in the center of the universe. Aristotle also discussed the nature of change and especially of motion, as well as teaching that there was a fundamental difference between celestial and terrestrial bodies. The former were eternal and changeless; all change, he believed, must occur below the moon, the nearest body to the earth. He also rejected the idea, proposed in the fifth century BC by Democritus and Leucippus, that the universe is composed of separate and indestructible atoms.

Investigations in the pure sciences

Although it was Aristotle's views about the physical universe that exerted the most profound influence on science for the following 2,000 years, he was at his best in the biological field. He carefully described the compound stomach of such ruminants as the cow and the habits and diseases of bees; he studied the placental dogfish that reproduces its young alive, and made a general study of sexual reproduction [2]. He also studied plants, although it was his friend and disciple. Theophrastos (*c.*372–*c.*286 BC), who is credited as the founder of botany.

Following the claim by Eudoxos of Cnidus (*c.*408–*c.*355 BC) that heavenly bodies moved in circular orbits round the Earth, the third-century astronomer Aristarchos of Samos (310–230 BC) suggested

CONNECTIONS

See also
1032 Early Oriental and Western science
996 Classical Greek society
1438 Prehistoric and ancient science
1444 Mathematics and civilization
38 The restless sky
408 Evolution of life
752 Development of surgery
1732 History of artillery

1

1 A Victorian illustration of the Homeric universe shows a disk-shaped earth with Greece as its center, floating on water and surrounded by the sphere of the universe. The Sun is rising in the east, and the Moon is shown high in the sky. Most Greek philosophers thought that the Sun, Moon, and planets all orbited the earth: their innovative idea was that the heavens were an all-embracing sphere, a more perfect shape than a dome or hemisphere. This was adopted purely for aesthetic reasons. But the belief that the earth was at the center of the universe remained until Copernicus' work in the 16th century.

2

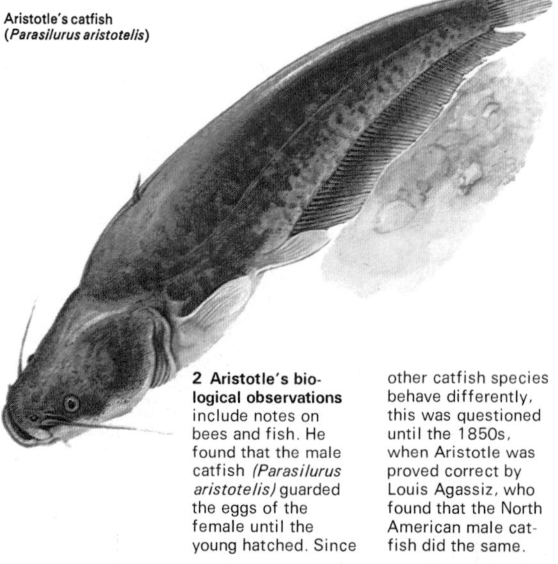

Aristotle's catfish
(*Parasilurus aristotelis*)

2 Aristotle's biological observations include notes on bees and fish. He found that the male catfish *(Parasilurus aristotelis)* guarded the eggs of the female until the young hatched. Since other catfish species behave differently, this was questioned until the 1850s, when Aristotle was proved correct by Louis Agassiz, who found that the North American male catfish did the same.

3

4

3 Archimedes in his bath tub (from a 16th-century engraving) is a reminder of his discovery that a body displaces fluid equivalent to its volume. This means that, regardless of shape, objects of equal density and weight displace the same quantity of fluid. Archimedes used the new principle to determine if a crown was of pure gold. The crown displaced more water than the same weight of pure gold, proving that it contained other metal.

4 The Archimedean screw for raising water may have originated before Archimedes but was attributed to him. Driven by a handle or foot pedals, the spiraling screw rotates in a cylinder, drawing the water upward.

that the Sun, not the Earth, was the center of the universe and discussed the sizes of the Sun and Moon. But his theory of the universe proved unacceptable. A century later, Hipparchos (190–120 BC), the greatest observational astronomer of antiquity, discovered the precession of the equinoxes, compiled a catalogue of stars, calculated solar eclipses, and had an advanced theory of the Sun's motion. The third century BC is notable also for the mathematical physics of Archimedes (*c.*287–212 BC) [3] and the establishment of the library and museum of Alexandria. There, for the next 500 years, advanced research was carried out; mathematics flourished with Euclid (*fl.* *c.*300 BC) [Key] and Appolonius (*fl.* 250–220 BC), who was noted for his work on astronomy and conic sections. There, too, Eratosthenes (*c.*276–194 BC) estimated the circumference of the Earth to within 250 miles (400km).

In the second century AD the astronomer Ptolemy (*c.*90–168) produced his remarkable *Almagest,* a digest of Greek astronomy, and his *Geography,* using longitude and latitude and his own stereographic map projection [7]. The medical lore of Hippocrates of Cos in the fifth century BC was developed by Herophilos and Erasistratos in Alexandria two centuries later [6]. They dissected the human body, distinguishing veins from arteries, sinews from nerves, and generally laying the foundations of anatomical knowledge.

Applied sciences and the study of machines

The compound pulley was known in Aristotle's time and the screw for raising water was invented in Syracuse by Archimedes. Much Greek technology, however, was also developed at Alexandria where, about 200 BC, Ctesibias designed clepsydras, or water clocks [5], and a force pump, and in the first century AD Hero not only developed the study of machines and pneumatic devices (without finding practical uses for his inventions) but also improved surveying techniques. The discovery of a device [8] for astronomical and calendrical calculations suggests that Alexandrian technology had wide influence.

KEY

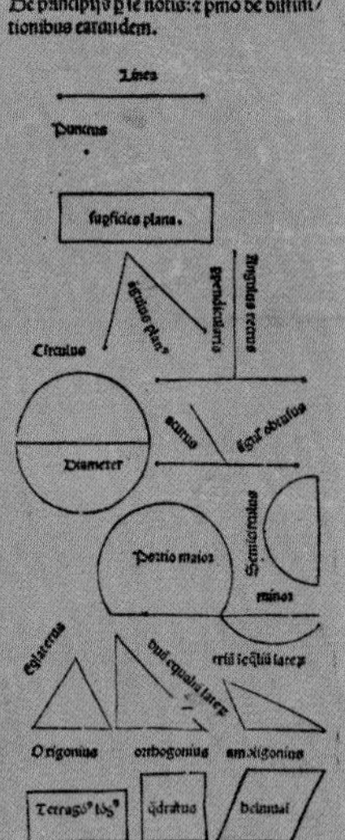

Linea
Punctus
superficies plana.
Circulus
Diameter
Portio maior
Semicirculus
minor
Tetrago⁹ lōg⁹
q̄dratus

The great basic text on Greek geometry was Euclid's *Elements.* This page is from the first printed edition, 1482.

5

5 The tower of winds in Athens is surrounded at the top by sundials. It once held a large clepsydra (water clock), based on a design by Ctesibias. This had an elaborate siphoning system to maintain a constant water pressure so that the clock was reasonably accurate.

6

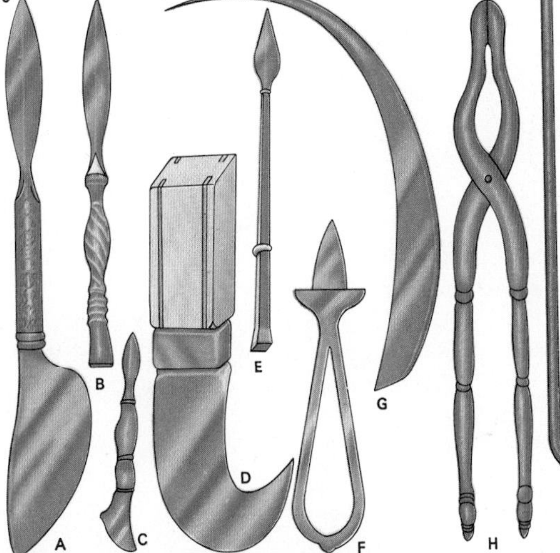

A
B
C
D
E
F
G
H
I
J
K

6 Greek medicine had a long and notable history. Psychological medicine was practiced in healing temples, as was herbal treatment and surgery. A collection of Greek surgical instruments shows, among other tools, forceps and scalpels.

- A Surgical knife with decorated handle and spatula.
- B Small knife with spiral band of silver inlay.
- C Bellied surgical knife made of bronze.
- D Bistoury knife with ivory handle and steel blade mounted in bronze.
- E Phlebotome used as a blood-letting knife.
- F Lancet knife with steel point and guard.
- G Fistula knife with curved blade cutting on one side and blunt end.
- H Uvula forceps.
- I Cautery used to burn away infection or stop bleeding.
- J Drill driven by thong attached to the shaft and used to remove a weapon lodged deeply in the bone.
- K Steel chisel used to divide distorted bone.

7

AFRICA
MARE INDICUM
ETHIOPIA INTERIOR
PRASODUM
MARE

8

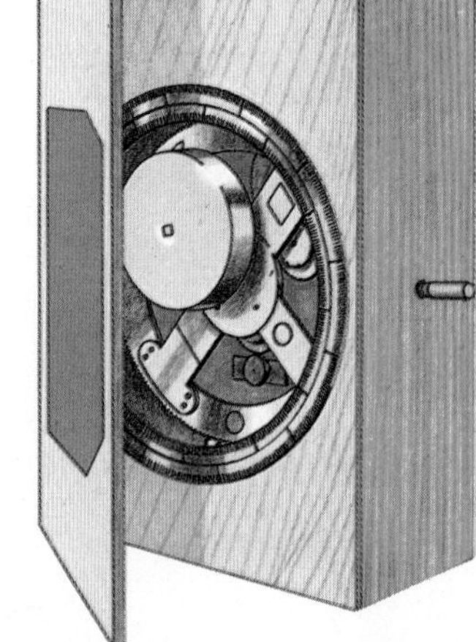

7 This map of the world, published in 1486, was based on one drawn by Ptolemy in Alexandria some 1,200 years earlier. That map drew on evidence from travelers, especially the Greek explorer Pythias of the 4th century BC.

8 A Greek astronomical "computer" was discovered in 1900 in a wreck dating from about 65 BC off the island of Antikythera and is shown in reconstruction here. It contained an extremely elaborate system of internal gears.

The Celts 500 BC–AD 450

From the beginning of the second phase of Celtic culture, known to archeologists as La Tène, knowledge of the Celts becomes much more detailed. Gaps in the archeological record are filled in by written accounts that give a clearer picture of peoples previously distinguished by the remaining artifacts of their material culture alone. For the first 500 years of this period of European history, the story is basically that of the astonishing growth and development of the Celtic world, followed by its gradual decline as Rome began to grow in power and establish its empire.

The development of Celtic culture

The term La Tène is applied to the period of Celtic culture that began in about 500 BC. This is the period of the culture's greatest attainments. Like Hallstatt for the first phase of *c.* 700–*c.* 500 BC, the name La Tène is taken from the name of a major archeological site. In the nineteenth century a large variety of religious offerings [3] were found at La Tène on the shores of Lake Neuchâtel in Switzerland, and these findings, like the discoveries at Hallstatt, testify to the changes in the Celts' equipment and way of life. As with Celts of the Hallstatt culture, the La Tène Celts' lifestyle developed more or less simultaneously, and with great rapidity, over much of Europe.

The Celts still possessed a very aristocratic social organization; kingship was common among the tribes, and below the king were the warrior aristocracy and freemen farmers. The Celts had a highly evolved religion [5, 6] with a powerful priesthood—the Druids—that formed another major class. In addition there were slaves, but little is known about their lives or status.

The La Tène Celts used a light two-wheeled war chariot pulled by two small ponies, and the artistic skill of their craftsmen in metalwork, always remarkable, advanced to new heights. At the same time, a revolution had taken place in their art style. The old Urnfield and Hallstatt patterns, the fine animal art of the Scythians, Greek foliage motifs, and elements from styles formed much farther east had been merged into a brilliantly original art—subtle and full of magical significance. From 500 BC this new aspect of Celtic culture spread rapidly, and by 300 BC it was dominant from the Baltic to the Mediterranean and from the Black Sea to the Atlantic.

Celtic society and warfare

The early Celts did not keep written records; they recorded their history orally. Unlike the earlier Hallstatt culture, however, that of La Tène is well documented; much of our knowledge about the social institutions and daily life of the Celts has been provided by contemporary Greek and Roman writers. The Greeks and Romans described the Celts as tall, muscular, and fair-skinned, qualities most attributable to the warrior class.

Warfare was an essential part of the Celtic life. Armed with highly efficient iron weapons, the Celts swept through central Europe in the fourth and third centuries, overcoming their Etruscan neighbors in about 400 BC, sacking Rome in 390, and plundering the shrine at Delphi in 279.

CONNECTIONS

See also
1050 The Celts and Christianity
1010 The Etruscans
1592 The Iron Age

1

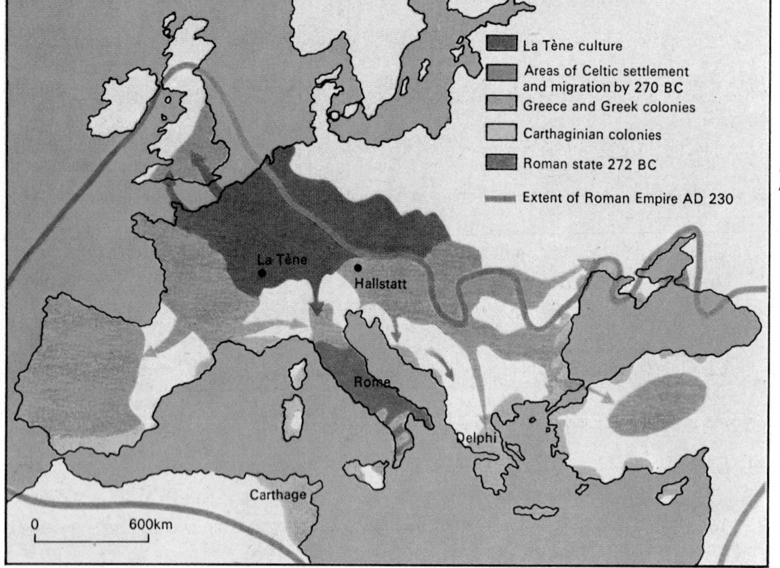
La Tène culture
Areas of Celtic settlement and migration by 270 BC
Greece and Greek colonies
Carthaginian colonies
Roman state 272 BC
Extent of Roman Empire AD 230
La Tène
Hallstatt
Rome
Delphi
Carthage
0
600km

1 La Tène, a key archaeological site in Switzerland, gave its name to the period of Celtic culture in Europe that lasted from approximately 500 BC until the time of Roman expansion during the 2nd and 1st centuries BC. As the map shows, by about 270 BC the Celts had migrated into France and the Iberian peninsula, parts of the British Isles, and to some extent eastward into central Europe. From this time, however, they gradually lost ground to Rome. By the mid-1st century BC, Roman dominance was assured.

2

2 This bronze wine flagon is one of a pair from Basse-Yutz in Lorraine. Inlaid with coral, it demonstrates elements that contributed to the subtlety and charm of La Tène art. The wolflike animals forming the handles and on the lid link this piece with the Bronze Age cult of water birds.

3 This silver-covered iron votive torque (bracelet) weighs about 13lb (6kg). Both ends have sacred ox heads, each with its own twisted necklace. Too heavy to be worn, it was probably hung on a stone or wooden divine image. It comes from Trichtingen, Württemberg, in West Germany.

3

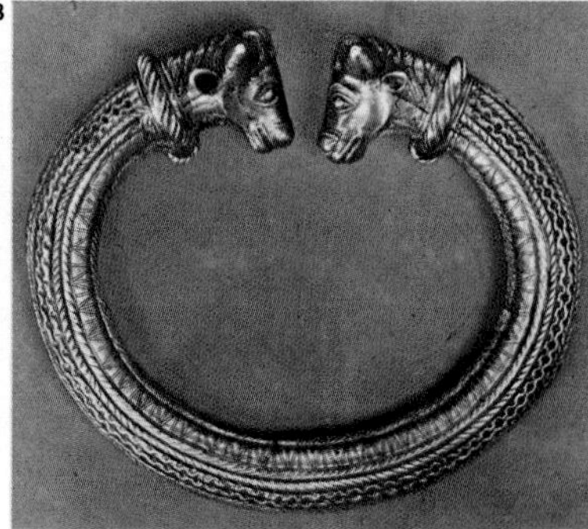

4 A, B

4 Warfare was the main influence on Celtic architecture. Fortified dwellings built for defense were common. One such was the *crannog* [A]. Found mainly in Ireland, crannogs were artificial islands built of timber, clay, peat, and brushwood. Dwellings were constructed on top of the island. This *crannog*, from the La Tène period, is in County Antrim. The most famous Celtic fortifications were the hill-forts *(oppida)* [B]. This hill-fort, seen from the air, is in Somerset, England.

But the Celts were not only warriors. They achieved a high level of material civilization by using their mastery of iron-working to open up new land and develop agriculture. Their economy was based on mixed farming—the cultivation of grains and vegetables, and cattle raising—and on trade. These two aspects—expansionist warfare and domestic settlement—can best be seen in their hill-forts *(oppida),* the remains of which are scattered throughout Europe. Originally built as forts for defense, some developed into major towns.

The rise of the Roman Empire

It was the rise of Rome—a little town on the bank of the Tiber—into a great, organized civilization that ended Celtic domination. By 225 BC, and after bitter fighting, Rome defeated the Celts at Telamon in Italy and took the first major step toward subduing them forever. Even after they were subjugated, the Celts' traditions and language survived, although in forms modified to fit the needs of Roman institutions. Ireland and much of Scotland escaped Roman domination in the British Isles, and there the old Celtic traditions and way of life survived and were eventually written down by the scribes of a Celtic church, established in the fifth century AD and deeply sympathetic to the heritage of its own people.

Although the Roman Empire lasted into the fifth century, it was endangered by increasingly powerful "barbarians" from the third century on. It was these barbarians from the north, from east of the Rhine, and from the vast eastern steppelands of the continent who, during the fifth century AD, eventually wrecked the Roman Empire and laid the foundations of feudal Europe. The people of the Roman Empire had become used to living in towns and obeying a single, absolute government. The barbarians knew no such control, living in tribes without towns and led by chieftains who gained their power through the dictates of tribal custom and tradition. These pagan peoples struck deeply at the growing Christian Church in Europe, a Church to which Celtic missionaries from Ireland were to make a profound contribution.

KEY

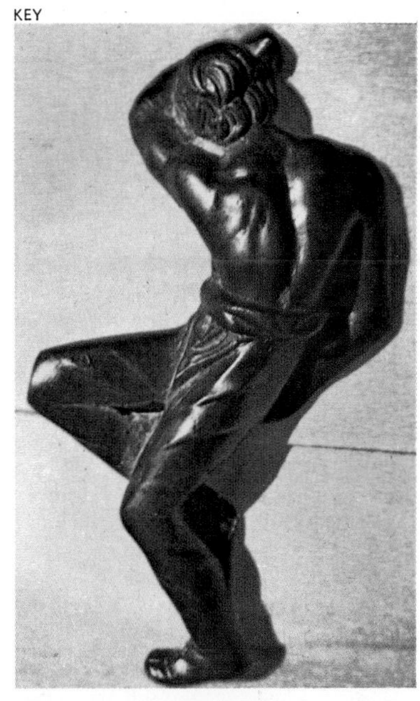

A bronze figure of a dying Gaul was recovered from the hill-fort at Alesia, Alise-Ste-Reine, where Vercingetorix, the young Celtic leader, king, and commander of all the Gallic confederates, made his last great stand against Julius Caesar in 52BC. For a time he managed to repulse Caesar and cause him heavy losses, but after a final bloody battle he was defeated. In spite of the dignified and noble way he surrendered in order to save his fellow-countrymen, Caesar held him prisoner in Rome for six years and ordered his belated execution.

5

5 The god Cernunnos "The Horned One," figures as the Lord of the Wild Beasts on one of the inner plates of the great votive silver cauldron found at Gundestrup, Jutland, Denmark. He wears the antlers of a stag.

6 The rooster [A] was believed to avert evil with its crowing, and thus in Britain it was considered unlucky to eat it. The peculiar three horns on the bull [B] conveyed an idea of its supernatural qualities as the number three had religious meaning.

7

7 Belief in the "Evil Eye" goes far back in Celtic times. The eye on this stone figure of a boar god dates from about the 1st century BC.

6 A

B

8

8 An early example of La Tène art style is shown here. The bronze plaque from a double burial at Waldalgesheim (*c.* 325 BC) shows a masklike face, a torque around the neck, and, on the head, traces of a leaf-crown, which is a token of divinity. The hands are raised in the Celtic attitude of prayer. This is one of a pair.

9

9 Bronze decorated mirrors are among the most splendid pieces of Celtic art. This example, found in a woman's grave in Great Britain, is pre-Christian.

The Etruscans

Far less is known about the Etruscans than about their contemporaries, the Greeks and Romans. The reason lies mainly in the total loss of their literature, which leaves them from a historian's point of view inarticulate. Although their extant writings consist almost solely of brief funerary inscriptions, other material remains offer great scope for archeological research.

Origins of the Etruscans

The long-standing controversy over this people's origins seems at last to be dying down. Ancient records began it: Herodotus declared that the Etruscans sailed from Lydia in Anatolia to colonize a new territory in the west; Dionysius of Halicarnassus argued that they were natives of Italy. Today both views are regarded favorably, and both are at least partly right.

Certainly the argument for continuity between the Villanovan settlements in northern Italy (*c.* 1100–700 BC) and cemeteries of the ninth century BC and the Etruscan cities and cemeteries of the early seventh century BC on the same sites is stronger than ever. Most of the population and much of the culture can be traced back even further, to the Bronze Age. Conversely, at several stages new ideas and cultural traits from abroad could well have arrived with bands of new immigrants. Etruscan civilization was thus the product of a rich native Villanovan culture entering a period of innovation and invention under the stimulus of overseas contacts through trade and immigration.

The result, in the seventh and sixth centuries BC, was a great flowering of culture. It built on local foundations that were supported by the wealth of the metal resources of Etruria (present-day Tuscany) [1], but it was strongly influenced by Greece and other east Mediterranean lands. Indeed, this variety provides a strong argument against Herodotus' simple story of a homeland in Lydia.

Etruscan civilization as a whole is puzzling. The general impression is very Greek. Only on closer inspection of the details does it become apparent that, however Greek in inspiration, everything has been transmuted and absorbed. This, and their adoption of other Asiatic ideas, like divination and burial mound building, and the development of purely local traits, such as the high-quality black *bucchero* pottery, enable historians to think of an Etruscan civilization in its own right, not merely as a provincial version of the civilization of Greece. Yet, politically the two peoples appear to have been bitter enemies, Etruscan history having as its constant theme the attempt to bar the Greeks from the Tyrrhenian Sea. As a result of one sea battle, the Greeks were expelled from the island of Corsica in 535 BC, at the height of Etruscan political domination of the region.

The Phoenicians played a part in this story too, acting as intermediaries between Etruria and the Orient. Here political relations were more cordial, and Etruria and Carthage were often in alliance against Greece. At Pyrgi, a port of Cerveteri, a dedication was found to Uni (Juno)—the goddess Astarte—engraved on gold plates in parallel texts, one in Phoenician, one in Etruscan.

CONNECTIONS

See also
1012 Early Rome: the kin dom and the Repub
1008 The Celts 500 BC–A 450
992 The Greeks to the ri of Athens
994 Classical Greece
978 The Phoenicians 1500–146 BC

1 The Etruscan home territory lay between the Arno and the lower Po. It was there that the distinctive civilization arose and reached its highest development. At its peak, *c.* 535 BC, Etruscan power extended to the Alpine foothills and south to the Gulf of Salerno. But this was not an empire; instead it was a loose federation of independent city-states with no common government.

0
300km
ALPS
Po
Melpum
Spina
Felsina
Arno
Volterra
ETRURIA
Populonia
Perugia
Vetulonia
Chiusi
Vulci
Tarquinia
Veii
Caere
Rome
APENNINES
TYRRHENIAN SEA
Etruscan power at its greatest extent *c.* 540 BC
Etruscan sphere of influence

2 Bronze cists (caskets) held women's personal possessions, jewelry, and toiletries. They were engraved with mythical scenes and were fitted with cast feet, handles, and ornaments. This fine example from Palestrina (*c.* 300 BC) shows an engraving of Bellerophon holding Pegasus.

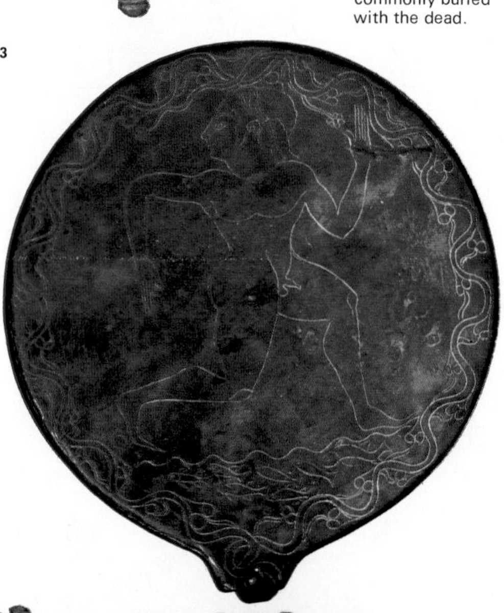

3 Mirrors of polished bronze were used by fashionable Etruscan ladies. The reverse side of mirrors such as this (*c.* 540–530 BC) was often engraved with mythical scenes – in this example Orion is crossing the sea – in incised drawings. Mirrors were objects commonly buried with the dead.

4 Jewelry reached a high level of development with the Etruscan civilization. The Etruscans were particularly skilled goldsmiths, and a number of superb pieces decorated with fine granulation have survived. This fibula, or safety pin, dates from between 700–600 BC. It is an exquisite piece, demonstrating the quality and originality achieved by the Etruscans in their artwork.

5 The Apollo of Veii, together with figures of Mercury, Hercules, and Latona, strode along the roof ridge of the Portonaccio temple at Veii. The sculptor was Vulca, who modeled Apollo in terra-cotta about 500 BC. Apollo has a frightening aspect, not in the least softened by his smile, and is different from the Apollos left by the Greeks. The Etruscans clearly owed much to the Greeks, but they translated any borrowings into their own idiom.

Clues to language

The tablets found at Pyrgi proved of great help in advancing knowledge of the Etruscan language, the most important unifying link between the Etruscan peoples. Since they had adopted the Greek alphabet with little change, there has never been any great problem in deciphering their writings. Translating them has proved much more difficult because all attempts at identifying the language with a known one have failed. It seems to have been the only survivor of those tongues spoken before Indo-European was introduced into the area. Little by little, however, the scholarly competence in translation has increased, beginning with such tomb inscriptions as "x, son of y, aged z years." But the few longer texts are obscure ritual documents, and so far yield little more than the general drift.

Etruscan culture

United by language, the Etruscans were less uniform in culture. There are clear differences (for example, in tomb architecture) between the Etruscan cities, a reflection of their political independence. All, however, give a picture of an energetic, happy people with a bold and attractive art. Although much of the evidence comes from tombs [6,7,8], it is by no means a somber picture. Their temples and cities were also architecturally exciting. Their civil engineering was of a high order, as demonstrated by a ship canal at Cosa, the channeling of streams below ground to prevent soil erosion, and the practice of tunneling rivers below roads instead of building bridges over them.

What survives from Etruscan civilization is to be found in romantic ruins and cemeteries, and vast museum collections looted from these sites. The end of the Etruscan cities probably came in the fourth century BC. They had failed to present a common front and so fell individually to the Romans. The Romans owed much to their rich and powerful neighbors and enemies. What was non-Greek in Roman life was often pure Etruscan; for example, the realism of their portraiture and their religious practices. Many leading Roman families were proud of Etruscan origins.

KEY

This married couple (life-size figures) is part of the lid of a terra-cotta sarcophagus from Cerveteri (Caere).

6

6 The Tomb of the Reliefs at Cerveteri is carved in the solid rock to represent a room in a house, with raftered ceiling supported by pillars, proto-Ionic capitals, and bed niches in the walls. A series of funerary beds, each with two pillows, some even with a footstool and slippers awaiting their owners, was then added in stucco. Above the niches are displayed pieces of armor and weapons in relief—shields, helmets, leg armor, swords. The central pillars are decorated with a wide variety of tools and implements used in daily life. This tomb is the only one of its kind and is very revealing of the customs and habits of the Etruscans.

7

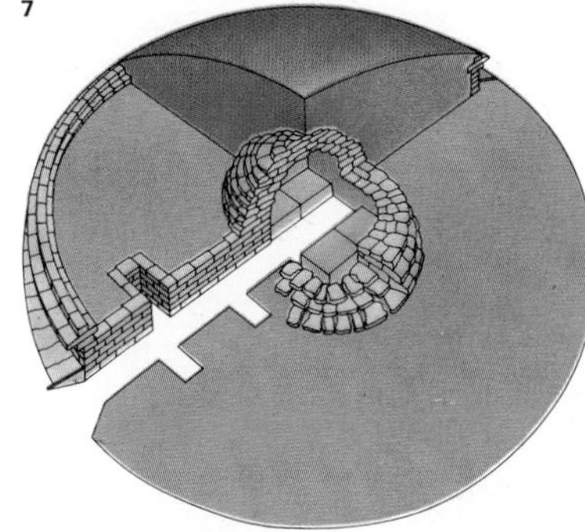

7 Types of tombs differed from city to city. At Populonia, a corbel-vaulted chamber of stone was covered by a hemispheric mound inside a stone retaining wall. The Tomb of the Chariots, shown here, contained two chariots fitted with bronze and iron decoration on ivory and a bronze trumpet, as well as gold jewelry and fragments of weapons and armor. The tomb dates from the 7th century BC. Many such tombs were also erected at Cerveteri.

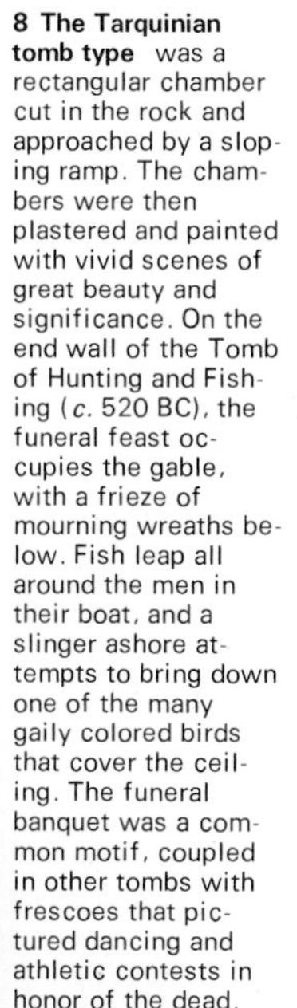

8

8 The Tarquinian tomb type was a rectangular chamber cut in the rock and approached by a sloping ramp. The chambers were then plastered and painted with vivid scenes of great beauty and significance. On the end wall of the Tomb of Hunting and Fishing (*c.* 520 BC), the funeral feast occupies the gable, with a frieze of mourning wreaths below. Fish leap all around the men in their boat, and a slinger ashore attempts to bring down one of the many gaily colored birds that cover the ceiling. The funeral banquet was a common motif, coupled in other tombs with frescoes that pictured dancing and athletic contests in honor of the dead.

Early Rome: the kingdom and the republic

The origins of the city that founded the mighty Roman Empire are obscure. The traditional account, recorded by the Roman historian Livy, is that Romulus and Remus [Key] founded a city on the Palatine Hill [2] on April 21, 753 BC. The date is supported by archeological evidence, which shows that shepherds settled on the Palatine about the middle of the eighth century. This community joined with others in the early sixth century to establish a city around a site that later became the Roman Forum [1].

Of the six kings said to have followed Romulus, the first three were almost certainly legendary, but the fourth, Tarquinius Priscus, was Etruscan. His reign marks the beginning of a period of Etruscan control during which the low-lying marsh areas were drained, temples erected, and the first city walls built.

Expansion under the republic

Etruscan rule and the monarchy ended simultaneously with the expulsion of King Tarquinius Superbus, traditionally in 509 BC. Two elected consuls and a senate, composed entirely of wealthy aristocrats known as patricians, controlled Rome's affairs. During the next 200 years Roman policy in Italy was directed toward expansion, conquest, and consolidation. Within the city the major issue was the political position of the plebeians, the ordinary people.

Soon after the foundation of the republic Rome played a leading part in the formation of the Latin League, an alliance of the cities of Latium, the western region of central Italy. In 390 BC the Celtic Senones and other Gallic peoples overran northern Italy and captured all of Rome except the Capitol. They left after Rome paid a ransom, and the city built the Servian Wall, which made it the best fortified city in Italy.

From this secure base Rome engaged confidently in a number of wars and as a result obtained undisputed mastery over all of Italy from the Po valley southward. In 340 BC the cities of the Latin League rose against Rome but found themselves no match for their powerful partner. Rome imposed separate terms on each vanquished city, awarding some Roman citizenship, some partial citizenship, and punishing others, but in each case it stipulated that the city should trade only with Rome. The next struggle, against the Samnites in the south, was much harder, but by 290 BC the war was won. Next, victory over the Greek cities gave Rome control over the whole Italian peninsula, a position it consolidated principally through threat of force but also through alliances and the establishment of citizen colonies [4].

By this time the plebeians had had many of their grievances rectified. They had their own council, the *concilium plebis*, and their own officers, the tribunes. In 445 BC they received the right to marry into the patrician class, and in 366 BC the first plebeian consul was elected. From 287 BC measures passed by the *concilium plebis* had the force of law. Although these changes muted social conflict, they did little to alleviate the poverty of most of the plebeians.

The Punic Wars

Rome's advance into the south of Italy had brought it face to face with the Carthagi-

CONNECTIONS

See also
1014 Rome: the organization of the republic
1016 Roman life
1010 The Etruscans
1018 From the civil wars Caesar's empire
1020 Rome: the expansion of the empire
978 The Phoenicians 1500–146 BC

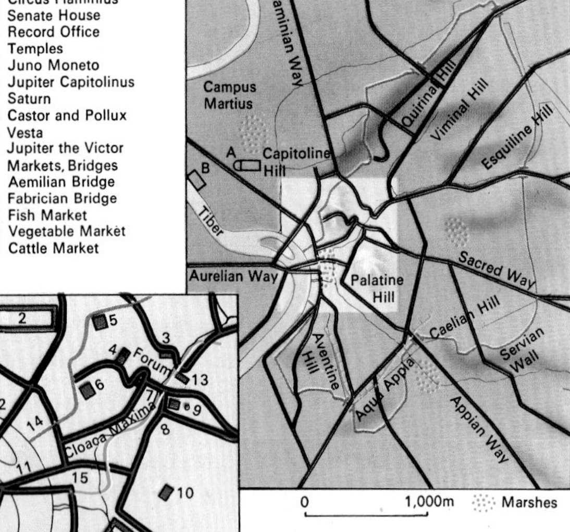
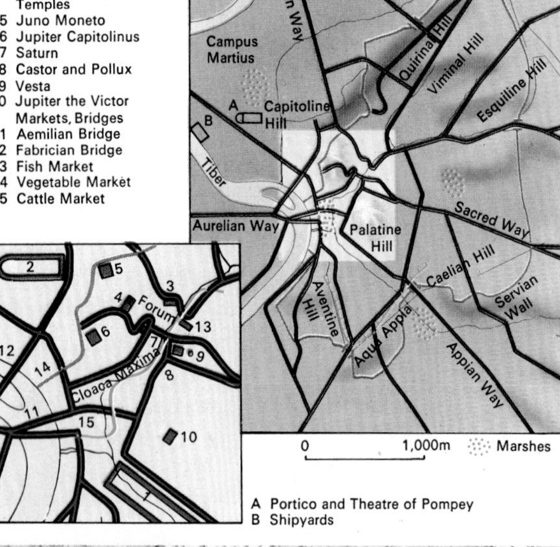

1
1 Circus Maximus
2 Circus Flaminius
3 Senate House
4 Record Office Temples
5 Juno Moneto
6 Jupiter Capitolinus
7 Saturn
8 Castor and Pollux
9 Vesta
10 Jupiter the Victor Markets, Bridges
11 Aemilian Bridge
12 Fabrician Bridge
13 Fish Market
14 Vegetable Market
15 Cattle Market
Flaminian Way
Campus Martius
Quirinal Hill
Viminal Hill
Esquiline Hill
Capitoline Hill
Tiber
Sacred Way
Aurelian Way
Palatine Hill
Caelian Hill
Servian Wall
Aventine Hill
Aqua Appia
Appian Way
Forum
Cloaca Maxima
0
1,000m
Marshes
A Portico and Theatre of Pompey
B Shipyards

1 The Seven Hills of Rome are flat-topped spurs rising from a low, formerly marshy plain. The Palatine, Quirinal, and Esquiline were the first to be settled, the Capitoline and Aventine the last. A unified city began to emerge when villages on the Palatine, Esquiline, and Caelian came together in the early 7th century BC. The first city wall was built, according to tradition, in the 6th century, which was apparently a period of great building activity under the Etruscan kings. The Cloaca Maxima, a sophisticated drainage system, and the temple of Jupiter Capitolinus both date from this early Etruscan period of development.

2 A village of huts on the Palatine, one of which is shown here in reconstruction, was discovered after World War II. They date from the mid-8th century BC and so seem to support the legendary date of the founding of Rome (753 BC). Crude in construction, these huts were the homes of the farmers and shepherds of Latin origin who are the earliest known inhabitants of the city. There is now archeological evidence that Latium, the area surrounding Rome, was colonized in the 12th century BC by Late Bronze Age people who came from the East by sea, thus reinforcing the legend handed down by Livy that Rome's environs were settled by refugee Trojans under the leadership of Aeneas.

3 Aeneas, who fled Troy after the Trojan war ended, was said to have founded Rome. This legend was enshrined in the *Aeneid* by Vergil (70–19 BC). This 4th-century manuscript vividly illustrates the dangers of his voyage.

4 A new Roman colony was officially recognized when the founder guided a bronze plow, drawn by a bull and a cow, around its boundaries. Colonies were useful as a means of garrisoning vulnerable areas and also for relocating and employing surplus population. A few colonies were created as early as the 5th century, but the number increased as Rome's dominions spread because citizen colonies could be founded only in Roman territory.

nians *(Poeni),* who were ensconced in western Sicily and appeared to have designs on the eastern part. In the First Punic War (264–241 BC) Rome, after several near disasters, captured Sicily in 260 BC and Corsica and Sardinia the following year [7]. The ostensible cause of the Second Punic War (218–201 BC) was an attack by the Carthaginian general Hannibal on the city of Saguntum, an ally of Rome on the eastern coast of Spain. With 40,000 men and a train of elephants Hannibal made a remarkable march through Gaul and over the Alps [6]. He inflicted severe defeats on Roman armies at Trebbia, Lake Trasimene, and Cannae, but then the delaying tactics of Fabius and the loyalty to Rome of most of its Italian allies began to show results. A crucial blow was the defeat at the Metaurus River in 207 BC of Hannibal's brother Hasdrubal.

Rome opened a second front, and the young and brilliant Scipio (later given the title of Africanus Major) captured Carthago Nova and then drove the Carthaginians out of Spain. In 204 BC, Scipio led an invasion force from Sicily into Africa. Carthage recalled Hannibal from Italy, but his army was annihilated at Zama, ending the war. The Third Punic War (149–146 BC) began when Carthage attacked Rome's ally Massinissa, king of Numidia. After desperate resistance, Carthage was captured and razed, and its inhabitants were enslaved.

Influence of the Gracchi

During the second century BC, Rome controlled almost the entire Mediterranean area, but storm clouds gathered at home. The patricians and rich plebeians kept a stranglehold on government and monopolized productive land. A champion of the poor arose in Tiberius Gracchus, who was elected tribune of the plebeians in 133 BC and introduced a land bill intended to reduce drastically the size of the large estates. Rioters incited by apprehensive senators murdered Tiberius, but in 123 his brother Gaius became tribune and tried to break the power of the senate. His proposals to extend the citizenship to all Rome's Latin allies, however, brought him political ruin and death.

KEY

According to legend a she-wolf suckled Romulus and Remus, the mythical founders of the city of Rome. This famous bronze in the Capitoline Museum is of the late 6th century BC, the period of Etruscan kings. The figures of the twins were added later, during the Renaissance.

5

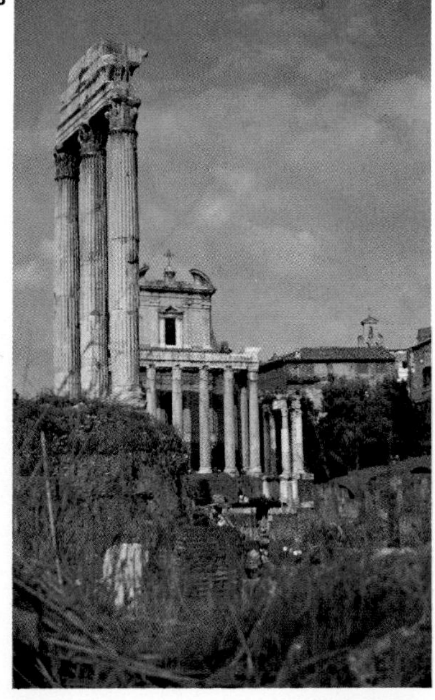

5 The three surviving columns of the Temple of Castor and Pollux in the Roman Forum were once part of a colonnade that enclosed a shrine to the divine twins, who were also known as the Dioscuri. The tradition was that the temple was built following a battle between the Romans and the Latins at Lake Regillus in 499 or 496 BC. The twins fought on the Roman side and carried the news of the Romans' victory back to the city. The temple may, in fact, have been built much earlier, in the misty period of the kings. It lies within the boundary of the early Palatine villages. It was restored in the 2nd century BC and once again in the 1st century AD.

6 This Spanish coin shows Hannibal on one side and an elephant on the other. The elephants that formed part of the force that Hannibal led over the Alps were African forest elephants, which at that time lived near the Atlas Mountains, along the Moroccan coast, and in the oasis of Ghadames in Tunisia. They were much smaller than bush elephants and were better suited to the kind of forced march they had to undertake. They terrified primitive tribes.

6 A

B

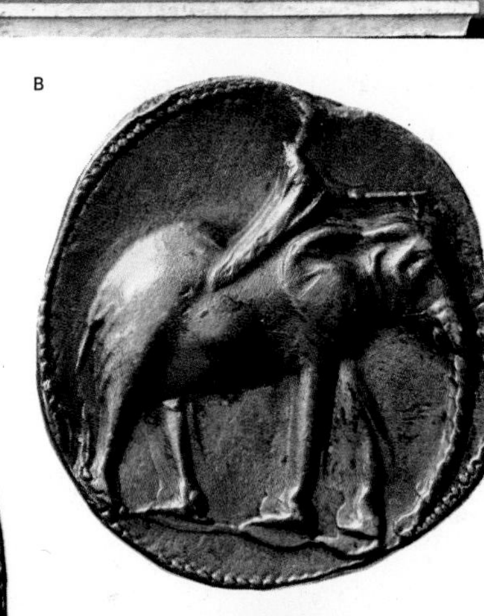

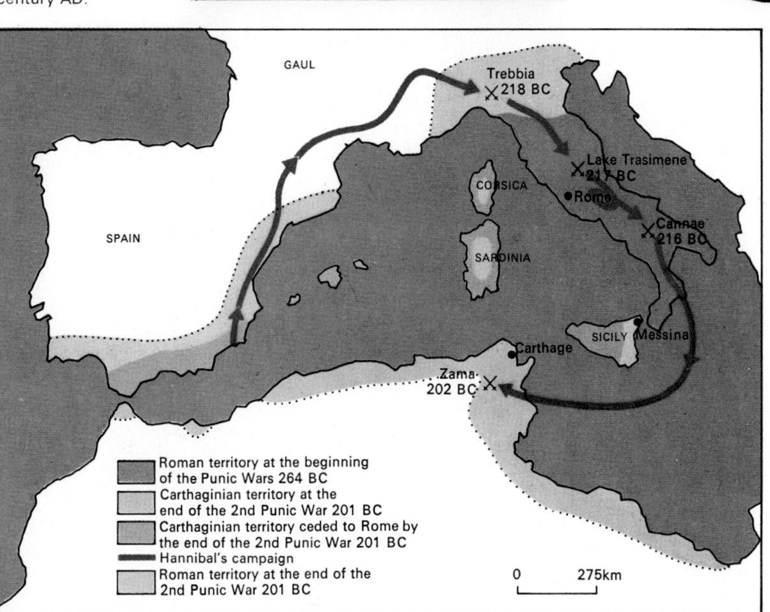
GAUL
Trebbia 218 BC
Lake Trasimene 217 BC
CORSICA
Rome
SPAIN
Cannae 216 BC
SARDINIA
SICILY
Messina
Carthage
Zama 202 BC
Roman territory at the beginning of the Punic Wars 264 BC
Carthaginian territory at the end of the 2nd Punic War 201 BC
Carthaginian territory ceded to Rome by the end of the 2nd Punic War 201 BC
Hannibal's campaign
Roman territory at the end of the 2nd Punic War 201 BC
0 275km

7 To pose an effective threat to Carthage's domination of the western Mediterranean, Rome had to become a naval power. A large fleet was constructed and, after initial reverses, Rome inflicted naval defeat on Carthage in the First Punic War. As the map indicates, the first two Punic Wars ended with the expansion of Rome into northern Italy and into Spain.

8

8 This Roman soldier of the 6th century BC has a breastplate, helmet, sword, and spears. Up to about 400 BC soldiers received no pay and only the rich could afford to do military service. A professional army was set up about 100 BC.

Rome: the organization of the republic

Republican Rome (509–27 BC) is often regarded as a democratic state. Certainly later Roman writers looked back nostalgically on what seemed a golden age of political and social order and agreed morality. There was a theoretical balance between the powers of the magistrates, the Senate, and the plebeians. But in fact most of the early republican period was an age of bitter conflict between the nobles of the Senate, determined to keep their privileges, and the plebeians, equally determined to have a share of the benefits. It was not until the third century that the plebeians were able to make laws on their own account. Their admission to all the magistracies only created an alliance of the nobility and rich ambitious plebeians, forming an oligarchy as exclusive as the former patrician nobility had been.

The political structure of the republic

The Senate and the *concilium plebis* (people's assembly) formed the legislative branch of the republic and the magistrates [1] formed the executive. The 300 senators [5] were chosen from ex-magistrates by the censors (those who watched over public morals). The Senate was basically an advisory body with overriding financial control. It initiated legislation and in practice made the vital decisions on war and peace and foreign policy in general. It also assigned provinces to senior magistrates at the end of their year of office. The *concilium plebis,* which represented the plebeians, was able to initiate legislation, its resolutions having the force of law after 287 BC, but usually it merely accepted or rejected legislation placed before it.

The chief executives during the Roman Republic were the two consuls. They were elected (from candidates proposed by the Senate) by the *comitia centuriata,* an assembly in which wealthy citizens had disproportionate voting strength. The consuls had immense power, presiding over the Senate and acting as supreme commanders in war. Beneath them were the praetors, whose numbers varied from two to eight and whose main duties concerned the administration of the law. Four quaestors were in charge of the state finances. The two censors supervised state contracts and public morals and, during the late republic, checked and if necessary expelled members of the Senate.

Streets, temples, public works, the grain supply, and the public games were the responsibility of individual *aediles*. Twelve *lictors* preceded consuls and two preceded praetors, clearing the way and carrying bundles of rods known as *fasces*. The ten tribunes were entrusted with the defense of the plebeians, having the power of veto against actions of magistrates and against laws. In the second century BC they became entitled to sit in the Senate.

The power of the consuls

At the end of their year of office the *imperium* (power) of the consuls and praetors was transferred from Rome to one of the provinces. The Senate decided which provinces should be consular and which praetorian; to avoid corruption this decision was taken before the election of the magistrates. The actual province each magistrate received was decided by lot. *Imperium* did

CONNECTIONS

See also
1012 Early Rome: the ki dom and the repu
1016 Roman life
1018 From the civil war Caesar's empire
902 Types of political s tems

1
Civil
Quaestors
Tribunes
Aediles
Censors
Praetors
Consuls
Generals
Pontifex maximus
Flamines (priests)
Military
Religious

1 Most of the civil officers of Rome had legal functions as well as administrative. The generals had military responsibilities only. The *pontifex maximus* was head of the state religion.

2 The basilica at Pompeii, measuring 185 × 70 ft (56 × 21 m) was built in the first century BC and was the center of economic life. Most Roman cities had one of these rectangular roofed halls where business transactions were concluded. They generally stood near the Forum. Some basilicas included arcades and galleries; their design influenced later basilicas erected by Christians.

2

3

3 The demobilization of Roman soldiers is portrayed on this relief (*c.* 1st century BC). The scribe on the left takes down details from a discharged soldier who holds his certificate, while others wait their turn.

4

4 The tabularium or record office [center left] was built in 78 BC to the plans of Sulla (138–78 BC). It housed the state archives and was probably an annex of the Treasury. The upper part is a palace (*c.* 1500).

not extend beyond the province's boundaries, as was shown when Julius Caesar, by crossing the Rubicon in 49 BC, in effect declared war on the Senate. Governors might keep their provinces for only one year or by the process of *prorogatio* might have their command extended.

The most important religious figure was the chief priest, the *pontifex maximus*. He was the elected head of the college of priests, which also included the vestal virgins [7] (who kept the sacred fire burning in the Temple of Vesta) and the *flamines*, each of whom was responsible for the cult of one of the gods. Outside the college were the augurs, who from certain signs, such as the behavior of birds, decided whether a particular course of action was advisable.

The Romans worshiped many gods, most of them originally Greek. The chief god was Jupiter, to whom a temple was founded on the Capitol at the time of King Tarquinius Superbus (reigned 534–510 BC). Religious festivals were held throughout the year [6], among the most important being the Lupercalia, held on the Palatine on February 15, and the Saturnalia on December 17.

The security of the republic and its steady expansion into a great empire depended on the discipline and courage of its army. Only citizens with certain property qualifications were eligible, although allies also served. The quality of commanders and centurions must have been high. Not until the reforms of Marius (157–86 BC) was a professional volunteer army formed.

Taxation and tax-collecting

Most Roman taxation was indirect and included customs duties and a number of special taxes, such as that on the freeing of slaves. The *tributum*, a direct tax, was levied mainly in time of war. The censors decided which taxes were applicable to the various classes, while the quaestors administered their collection. But more and more, tax-collecting in the provinces was farmed out to *publicani*. They were closely associated with the wealthy *equites*, the second social class, who became rich from the proceeds.

KEY

The magistrates of Rome had great power and influence. Civil lawsuits were heard first by a magistrate, such as the one shown here, before going to a judge for settlement. In the late republican period criminal cases were tried before special courts, where the penalties were generally exile, loss of citizenship, or hard labor. The most important achievement of the Roman legal system was the classification of its code in order to clarify citizens' rights. The laws were published in 450 BC at the instigation of the plebeians. The body of Roman law, many of the principles of which are still very much in use, vastly influenced the West.

5

5 The Senate was the principal advisory body of Rome. This 19th-century painting by Maccari shows Appius Claudius persuading the Senate to reject peace proposals from Epirus in 280 BC.

6 In the Temple of Vespasian at Pompeii there are sacrificial scenes on an altar dedicated to the Roman imperial cult. Ritual sacrifice of animals such as pigs, sheep, and bulls to encourage divine beneficence was an ancient element in the complex of religious cults of the Romans.

7 The six Vestal Virgins lived in the House of the Vestals in the Forum. They began their service as children and could retire after 30 years. If they allowed the sacred fire to go out, they were whipped by the *pontifex maximus*, the official under whose authority they came.

6

7

Roman life

In Rome, as in all societies, the life the people led depended very much on the social class to which they belonged. In general the class system was based on wealth rather than birth, although the two criteria often merged. The highest class was composed of members of the Senate, who for most of the republican period were *nobiles,* or nobles. The second class, the *equites,* or knights, derived most of their considerable wealth from such business activities as banking. Members of the upper classes wielded authority over their own families and, as patrons, over a number of semi-dependents known as *clients.* The third class of full citizens, the plebeians, after a long struggle won complete political equality. Once they were permitted to hold the magistracies they could move into the highest social class, since former magistrates were *ex officio* members of the Senate.

The Roman slaves

At the base of the social pyramid were the slaves. The settled order of Roman life depended on the toil of slaves, who might well make up half the population of a town. A slave was under the absolute control of his master, who under the republic could inflict on him any hardship and punishment he chose. A slave had no legal rights. He could not marry, and any children he had joined his master's household as slaves.

During the imperial period the treatment of slaves improved somewhat, some protection being given to them against cruel masters. More important, slaves were able to look forward more confidently to eventual manumission, or freeing. Many freedmen became extremely wealthy and influential, and their sons became full Roman citizens. The life of slaves varied greatly. In the country they were likely to work long hours carrying out arduous tasks on *latifundia,* or estates, and on farms or in mills, while in the towns they might be comparatively well treated as servants in the family circle, or as craftsmen.

Law: the respectable profession

The son of a rich upper-class family might well have political ambitions, but he would generally start by training as a lawyer and become either an advocate in the courts or a legal consultant. Other professions were not thought equally respectable. For much of the republic most doctors, architects, and dentists were slaves or freedmen. Writers could expect to make little money from their work unless they could rely on some wealthy patron to encourage them, as Maecenas encouraged Vergil. But most Romans were far from rich or influential. Although manual labor was thought unworthy of citizens, they struggled to make a living as bakers, shopkeepers, and craftsmen of all kinds, generally employing one or two slaves to assist them. Some young men might enter the army, which, after the reforms of Marius, the consul at the end of the second century BC, was a professional force manned by voluntary recruits who received a small landholding on retirement.

Education and sports

Most children of Roman citizens received some formal education, although only boys could expect to go beyond the primary

CONNECTIONS

See also

1014 Rome: the organization of the republic
1018 From the civil wars t
Caesar's empire
1020 Rome: the expansio
of the empire
1030 Rome: soldier emperors to Constantin
1012 Early Rome: the kingdom and the republic

1 The ruins of Pompeii were preserved beneath ashes after the eruption, described by Pliny the Younger, of Vesuvius in AD 79. Excavations revealed a unique record of Roman daily life.

2 This poultry market was located in Ostia, once the port of Rome. Cicero regarded shopkeeping as near the bottom of the list of employments suitable for people of taste – but better than dancing.

3 Every upper-class Roman visited baths – like the Stabian baths of Pompeii – daily with his oil flask, towels, and other toiletries. He progressed from the tepid to the hot bath, from the sweat room to the cold bath. Refreshments and massage were available. Women bathed in separate sections or at different times.

4 All baking was apparently done at home until the 2nd century BC. The exhausting work of turning the grinding mills was done by slaves with the help of donkeys. A bakery like this one was uncovered at Pompeii. The oven in it contained a large number of loaves, still intact and weighing about 2lb (900g).

stage. Under the empire some education was provided free for poor students, but generally parents paid a small fee. Between the ages of seven and twelve, children received a somewhat rough-and-ready grounding in reading, writing, and arithmetic from a *litterator*. They could then, if they chose, move on to a *grammaticus*, under whom they studied Greek and Latin literature and received an introduction to geometry and advanced arithmetic. The third stage in schooling was study under a *rhetor*, or orator, to learn the principles of effective public speaking, ability in which was important for success in politics and in the law courts. Finally, the more ambitious and wealthy students might progress to the equivalent of university level. They either studied law, under an established lawyer or at a law school, or Greek oratory and philosophy, which involved attendance at one of the great centers of Greek learning, the most popular of which were at Athens and Rhodes.

Sports among the Romans were in two categories, spectator sports and participatory sports. In the first group were the public spectacles staged in the amphitheaters, the "bread and circuses" of which the satirist Juvenal contemptuously wrote. These included musical performances, readings of verse, and theatrical performances, which were sometimes staged with extraordinary lavishness. What really drew the crowds were gladiatorial contests to the death between men or between men and beasts, and also the thrilling and dangerous chariot races, which might be run between individual charioteers or between teams of chariots.

The Romans did not place the same emphasis on physical exercise as the Greeks, but many young men of the upper classes were enthusiastic riders and hunters. Many also enjoyed boxing and wrestling, and there were several ball games, such as *harpastum* and *trigon*, the details of which are obscure. Children played many of the games that children have played through the ages—hoops, tops, marbles, hide-and-seek, and leap-frog. In general, the adult Roman preferred gambling games.

KEY

Roman shopkeepers worked long hours. Their products were brought into the city at night to avoid the traffic congestion of the day. This relief of a produce market in Ostia includes illustrations of various vegetables displayed for sale.

5

5 The life of Herculaneum, a residential town between Naples and Pompeii, was revealed only after arduous excavations; the eruption of Vesuvius in AD 79 covered it with a thick layer of mud. The mud, however, preserved much of the original town. Here a mosaic shows a man and woman served by a slave.

6

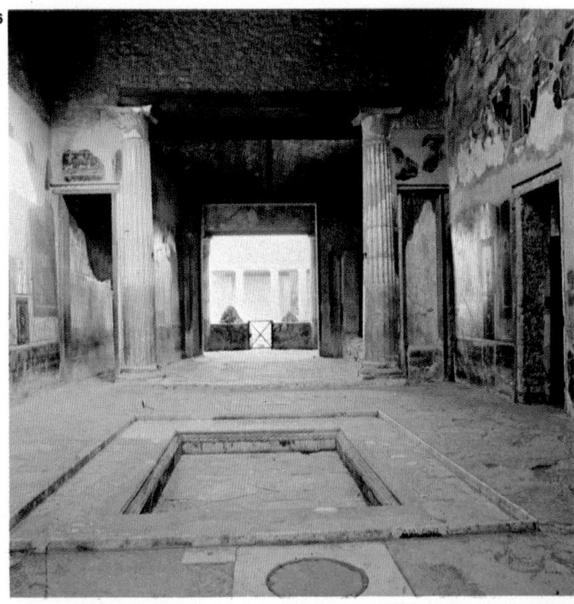

6 The house of Menander at Pompeii was more a country villa than a town house. The main reception room in the center of a Roman villa was the *atrium*, which was luxuriously furnished with tiles, marbles, and fresco paintings. In the floor was a rainwater pool.

7 A number of houses at Herculaneum have kept their second floors. The house shown here, the Càsa del Graticcio, still contains its original beds in two small rooms on the upper floor, together with other furnishings. The house was clearly divided into many small apartments; large apartment houses were a common feature of towns and cities in imperial times.

7

8

8 This sandstone relief from Gaul shows a school scene: A teacher is seated between his two pupils, who are opening their scrolls for the lesson. Discipline was severe and corporal punishment was frequent. Sons of wealthy families were escorted to and from school by a household slave or freedman (known as a *paedagogus*), who was sometimes also a tutor. The children wore warm cloaks and thick shoes to protect them against the rigors of the northern climate.

9

9 Many Roman houses had a lararium, a private chapel to *lares*, spirits of the hearth to whom offerings of food and flowers were made. Closely related was the worship of the *penates*, the guardians of the cupboard.

From the civil wars to Caesar's empire

The period between about 100 BC and 42 BC, leading up to the fall of the Roman Republic and its replacement by the Roman Empire, was one of disorder and disunity in which ambitious men used ruthless methods in their efforts to secure or maintain dominance. Julius Caesar (100–44 BC) was the outstanding figure but Marius, Sulla, and Pompey all contributed to the end of the old form of government.

Political conflicts

In 108 BC, Marius [4], champion of the popular party against undue senatorial power, was elected to the first of his seven consulships. An outstanding general, he proved less skillful as a politician and his influence began to wane. In 90 BC a new popular leader, Drusus, revived advocacy of an extension of citizenship to all Italians. His murder precipitated the Social War in which Rome triumphed by conceding its allies' demands.

The popular cause was left in some disarray. When most of the Eastern Empire rebelled under the lead of Mithridates (*c.* 133–63 BC), king of Pontus [3], command of the campaign of suppression was given to Sulla (138–78 BC), an aristocrat [5]. The popular party had the command transferred to Marius but Sulla forthwith marched on Rome, forcing Marius to flee. He pushed through measures directed against his opponents and then left for the East. Marius returned and began slaughtering enemies.

Sulla returned to Italy from the East in 83 BC and with the help of two powerful commanders, Pompey (106–48 BC) and Crassus (*c.* 115–53 BC), fought his way to Rome. There he began a reign of terror, massacring his opponents and making himself dictator. He drastically reduced the powers of the tribunes and the consuls and increased those of the Senate, but after he resigned in 79 BC the inability of the Senate to use its powers effectively was revealed. Corruption grew, particularly in the provinces. In Spain, Pompey fought a long campaign against Sertorius, a supporter of Marius. Meanwhile, Spartacus (died 71 BC) led a slave uprising crushed by Crassus.

Pompey and Crassus joined forces to gain control of Rome, securing their illegal election as consuls in 70 BC. They soon swept away Sulla's legislation favoring the Senate and asserted their advocacy of populism. Pompey demonstrated his military and organizational ability by speedily clearing the eastern Mediterranean of the growing menace of piracy. In 66 BC he was sent to the East, where he routed Mithridates and reformed the administration.

The First Triumvirate

On his return Pompey received a cold reception from the Senate, and he joined with Crassus and Julius Caesar [Key], who had returned from governing Spain, in forming the First Triumvirate. They forced through legislation by appealing to the Assembly over the heads of the Senate. Pompey received approval of his Eastern settlement, and Caesar, after his consulship in 59 BC, was granted command in Gaul.

In 55 BC, Pompey and Crassus were consuls while Caesar received a five-year extension of his command. Crassus disappeared from the scene when an ill-

CONNECTIONS

See also
1012 Early Rome: the kingdom and the republic
1014 Rome: the organization of the republic
1016 Roman life
1020 Rome: the expansion of the empire
1030 Rome: soldier emperors to Constantine

1 Jugurtha, grandson of Masinissa, seized the throne of Numidia in 112 BC, killing several Romans in the process. Rome sent an army against him but the war dragged on in spite of some Roman successes. Marius, who became consul in 108 BC, led an army enlisted from the poor of Rome to Africa and defeated Jugurtha. After being exhibited as part of Marius' triumph, Jugurtha was strangled to death.

2 A relief from the Temple of Fortuna Primigenia at Praeneste shows a warship of the 1st century BC with soldiers prepared for hand-to-hand fighting.

3 Mithridates VI, king of Pontus, controlled the Crimea and much of southern Russia. In 88 BC he began a struggle against Rome that was to last for 25 years. He occupied Asia Minor and invaded Greece before making peace with Sulla. A second war in 83 BC was soon ended but a third Mithridatic war lasted from 74 to 66 BC, when Pompey made Pontus and Bithynia a Roman province. Mithridates committed suicide when his son Pharnaces led an uprising against him in 63 BC.

4 Pompey the Great (Gnaeus Pompeius Magnus) lacked the military genius of Caesar and was less skillful politically. He was, however, a brilliant administrator and ruthless general who achieved power less by creating opportunities for himself than by waiting for situations to arise in which he would be called upon to lead.

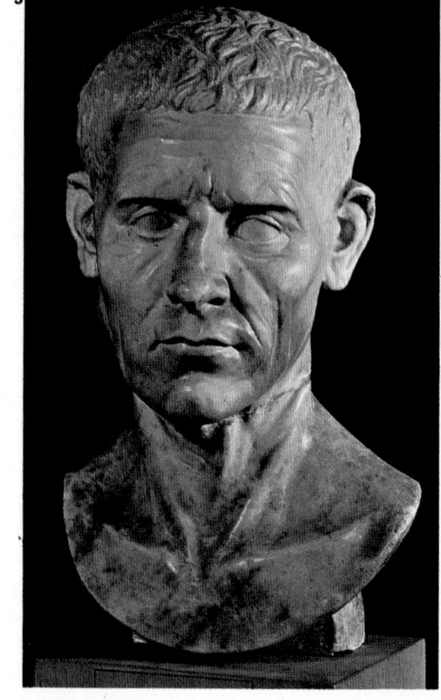

5 Lucius Cornelius Sulla made his military reputation in the Social War. Elected consul in 88 BC, he received the command against Mithridates. Later he used the office of dictator to massacre his opponents and force through pro-Senate legislation. He reformed the criminal law setting up *quaestiones* (new courts for particular crimes).

conceived attack on Parthia ended with his death at the disastrous Battle of Carrhae. Pompey received Spain as his province but preferred to stay in Rome, intriguing with his supporters against Caesar, whose successful campaigns in Gaul [6, 8] were proving an embarrassment. Caesar, having conquered the whole of Gaul and having made two exploratory invasions of Britain, was now ready to return to Rome.

After fruitless attempts to reach a compromise or reconciliation, the Senate in 49 BC ordered Caesar to disband his army. Caesar at once crossed the Rubicon, the river dividing his province from Italy, and marched on Rome, thereby plunging Italy into civil war. Pompey hastily left for Greece, hoping to mobilize the resources of the East. Caesar soon mastered Rome and went on to crush forces favorable to Pompey in Spain, to defeat Pompey himself at Pharsalus in Thessaly in 48 BC, and finally to pursue him to Egypt, where Pompey was murdered. Delaying his campaign, Caesar began his celebrated affair with the Egyptian queen, Cleopatra VII (69–30 BC) [9]. But within two years he had gained control of Roman Africa. Finally, he quelled an insurrection by Pompey's sons.

End of the republic

The main basis of Caesar's authority was the office of dictator, which he held twice before receiving it for ten years in 47 BC. He packed the Senate with his supporters, nominated some of the magistrates, and although denying any ambition for kingship, finally accepted the dictatorship for life. Brutus (85–42 BC) and Cassius (died 42 BC) organized his assassination at a Senate meeting on March 15, 44 BC. They hoped to save the republic but it had been fatally weakened: the only question was who would be Rome's first emperor. Mark Antony (*c.* 83–30 BC), Lepidus (died 13 BC), and Octavian (63 BC–AD 14), Caesar's heir, were the three contestants. In 43 BC they formed the Second Triumvirate, issuing proscriptions for the deaths of many. Caesar's death was avenged when Octavian and Antony defeated Brutus and Cassius in 42 BC. Octavian soon became sole ruler.

KEY

Julius Caesar, born in 100 BC, was the son of a leading patrician family. His aunt was the wife of the popular leader Marius, and his wife, Cornelia, was a daughter of Cinna, Marius's successor. These connections displeased the conservative Sulla and Caesar left Rome. On Sulla's death he returned and made a reputation as a lawyer and political orator. Moving up the political hierarchy, he became quaestor in Spain. After Cornelia died, he married Sulla's wealthy granddaughter Pompeia and set out to become a popular party leader. His election as praetor for 62 BC provided a springboard for his swift rise to absolute power in Rome.

6

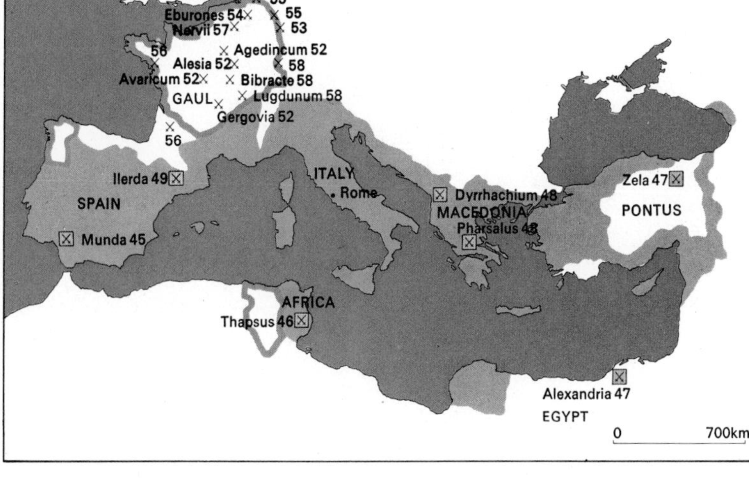
BRITAIN
54
55
Eburones 54
55
Nervii 57
53
56
Agedincum 52
Alesia 52
58
Avaricum 52
Bibracte 58
GAUL
Lugdunum 58
Gergovia 52
56
Ilerda 49
SPAIN
Munda 45
ITALY
Rome
Dyrrhachium 48
MACEDONIA
Pharsalus 48
Zela 47
PONTUS
AFRICA
Thapsus 46
Alexandria 47
EGYPT
0
700km

6 Successful campaigns were waged by Julius Caesar between 58 and 51 BC against the Helvetii, Belgae, Veneti, and the Aquitani. He conquered the whole of Gaul and made it a new province, Transalpine Gaul. He twice landed in Britain, near Walmer or Deal in 55 and near Sandwich in 54 BC. The second expedition was on quite a large scale, and Caesar penetrated northward beyond St Albans.

Roman dominions in 63BC
Conquests of Julius Caesar
Campaigns in Gaul and Spain
Civil war campaigns

7

7 Standard equipment of a legionary in the later Republican period was a *gladium* (short sword) and a *scutum* (shield).

8 The triumphal arch at Orange, France, is the third largest extant Roman arch. It commemorates Caesar's victories over the Gauls with reliefs of prisoners-of-war and captured armor. The capture of the port of Massilia is commemorated by such designs as anchors, prows, and ropes on the arch.

8

9 Cleopatra, Queen of Egypt, was the mistress of Caesar and Antony. She bore Caesar a son and followed him to Rome. After Caesar's death, she returned to Egypt, marrying Mark Antony in 37 BC.

9

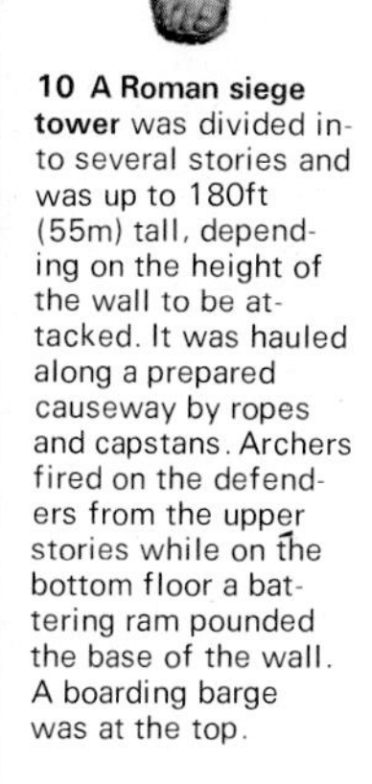

10 A Roman siege tower was divided into several stories and was up to 180ft (55m) tall, depending on the height of the wall to be attacked. It was hauled along a prepared causeway by ropes and capstans. Archers fired on the defenders from the upper stories while on the bottom floor a battering ram pounded the base of the wall. A boarding barge was at the top.

10

Rome: the expansion of the empire

Octavian became the undisputed master of the Roman republic and empire following his victory over Mark Antony at the Battle of Actium in 31 BC. There is no doubt that he intended to establish a personal dynasty, but he was too clever a politician to ignore the strength of republican feeling in Rome. When he returned from the East in 29 BC he ostensibly restored the republic and set out to establish absolute power within it.

Augustus: "first among equals"
The Senate voted Octavian the honorary titles of "princeps" (first citizen) and "augustus", by which he was known thereafter [Key]. Additionally, he received consular status and the power of a tribune with the right to summon the Senate, introduce business, veto decisions, nominate candidates for elections, and issue edicts. This was the basis upon which Augustus was able to influence the government of Rome and Italy and begin massive development programs.

The government of the empire was divided between the older, settled provinces, governed by proconsuls elected by the Senate, and the newer, military provinces that were ruled through legates appointed by Augustus as a proconsul with special powers over all others [1]. The army was reorganized under the emperor's direct control into a force of 28 legions of professionals recruited for 20–25 years. It was drawn from Roman citizens plus an equal number of auxiliaries enlisted from provincial territories. This system, of emperors ruling with the Senate, was to endure for more than 200 years.

The most important immediate task was to restore order to the empire and secure its frontiers. Augustus's first expeditions were to Gaul and Spain, each of which was reorganized into three provinces. The Danube River line was secured with a series of military provinces garrisoned by large legionary forces [3], and attempts were made from 12 BC to push forward across the Rhine to the Elbe. But the annihilation of three legions under Varus by the Germans in AD 9 forced Augustus to accept the Rhine as his boundary. In the east, peace was made with the Parthian empire, and a buffer state was established in Armenia. Internally, taxation and the administration of Roman law were put on a uniform basis.

Augustus died in AD 14, and under his successor, Tiberius (reigned 14–37), his policies of establishing order were continued so well that the incompetence of Caligula (reigned 37–41) caused little lasting harm. Under Claudius (reigned 41–54) the conquest of Britain was begun and Mauretania (now Morocco and Algeria) was occupied.

Problems of succession
A major weakness of the Augustan imperial system was that the succession was never formulated, and when in AD 68 the last of his direct house, the unstable Nero, was killed, four rival candidates for emperor were put forward by different sections of the army. Following a terrible civil war, Vespasian (reigned 69–79) was successful and developed a system whereby each emperor "adopted" his successor.

Under Trajan (reigned 98–117) the frontiers of the empire were again extended and

CONNECTIONS

See also
1018 From the civil wars Caesar's empire
1030 Rome: soldier emperors to Constant
1012 Early Rome: the ki dom and the repub
1054 The barbarian invasions

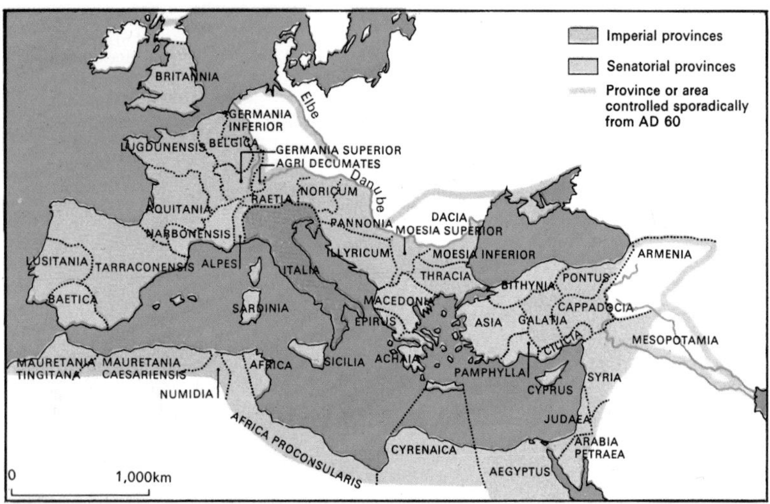

Imperial provinces
Senatorial provinces
Province or area controlled sporadically from AD 60
BRITANNIA
GERMANIA INFERIOR
Elbe
LUGDUNENSIS
BELGICA
GERMANIA SUPERIOR
AGRI DECUMATES
Danube
NORICUM
RAETIA
AQUITANIA
NARBONENSIS
PANNONIA
DACIA
MOESIA SUPERIOR
LUSITANIA
TARRACONENSIS
ALPES
ILLYRICUM
MOESIA INFERIOR
ARMENIA
ITALIA
THRACIA
BITHYNIA
PONTUS
BAETICA
SARDINIA
MACEDONIA
CAPPADOCIA
EPIRUS
ASIA
GALATIA
MESOPOTAMIA
CILICIA
MAURETANIA TINGITANA
MAURETANIA CAESARIENSIS
AFRICA
SICILIA
ACHAIA
PAMPHYLIA
SYRIA
NUMIDIA
CYPRUS
JUDAEA
AFRICA PROCONSULARIS
ARABIA PETRAEA
CYRENAICA
AEGYPTUS
0
1,000km

1 The Roman empire, at its height in the 2nd century AD, was theoretically divided into provinces controlled by the Senate and the emperor. In reality, the emperor had the power to intervene in senatorial provinces. Italy itself was ruled according to a modified version of the republican constitution by emperor and Senate.

2 The Roman Forum (now in ruins) was the center of the government of the empire. Augustus and his successors symbolized their power in a series of impressive public buildings. The administration of all parts of the empire remained almost entirely in the hands of native Romans, who held both governorships and lesser posts until well into the 2nd century. Yet an increasing number of provincials succeeded in working their way up the administrative ladder, first from the western provinces and then from the eastern. By AD 200, fifty-seven percent of the Senate was from the provinces.

3 Legionaries and Germans were often at war in the 1st century, as seen in a contemporary relief. The empire failed to find secure frontiers, and barbarian invasions played a major part in its collapse. In the relatively remote east a client state in Armenia usually provided a reasonable buffer against the Persian and Parthian empires, but in the west, far closer to the heart of the empire, constant vigilance was needed. Of the 28 legions established by Augustus more than half were always stationed in the provinces bordering on the Rhine and Danube. Augustus attempted to gain the more easily defensible Elbe-Danube river line, but failed to secure it.

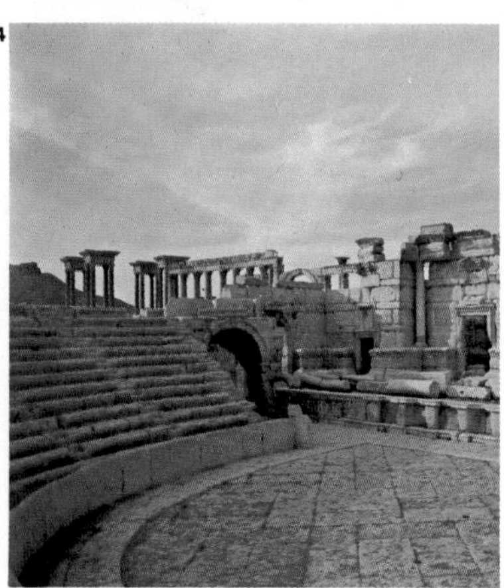

4 The theater at Palmyra in Syria is typical of the fine buildings—temples, amphitheaters, aqueducts and baths—that were built in all the provinces of the empire. Just as they tolerated other religions, the Romans took care not to interfere with the social customs of the peoples they conquered. The civilizations of Greece and the east continued to flourish, but provincials were inevitably influenced by the example of Roman culture in their arts and ideas.

Dacia, Armenia, and Mesopotamia were added [8]; but the last two were abandoned by Hadrian (reigned 117–138). Hadrian concentrated on improving existing imperial defenses—building a wall across northern England and a fortified line between the Danube and the Rhine—and traveled continually throughout the empire inspecting the imperial administration.

Peace and prosperity

Under the Antonine emperors (so called because of the family name of Hadrian's successor Antoninus) the empire was at its most peaceful. A man could travel in safety from Britain to Arabia along superb roads and secure seaways [5]; trade flourished [6], and a single culture, two languages—Latin and Greek—and a single system of law and administration covered the whole empire. Great cities with fine public buildings grew up in the provinces [4], where the people copied Roman education and fashions and strove to become Roman citizens.

There were, however, underlying weaknesses. Rome had grown rich in booty and taxation from the provinces, and economic activity tended to be one-way, with wealth and produce flowing to Rome but little produced in return. This caused jealousy in the provinces and an increasing idleness within Italy [7], problems made worse by the widespread use of slaves for all productive labor and a steady decline in the population. It became more and more difficult to find native citizens to undertake the many administrative and military duties on which the government of the empire depended.

Under Marcus Aurelius (reigned 161–180) [9] the peace ended. In the east a Parthian attack was defeated, but the returning troops brought back a terrible plague, which devastated the whole empire and further reduced its manpower. On the Rhine and Danube frontiers the barbarians were being forced forward by a massive migration of Goths in central Europe, and in 167 several tribes crossed the Danube and Alps and swept into Italy. Dacia was also overrun, and Marcus spent the rest of his reign fighting to restore the frontiers.

KEY

The Emperor Augustus is shown here as Pontifex Maximus (High Priest). The state religion of the Roman Republic continued under the empire. The emperors were deified after their deaths and sometimes they were worshiped during their lifetimes by people in the Roman provinces. Other religions were tolerated as long as they accepted the divinity of the emperor, and many Eastern cults such as Mithraism or the worship of Isis, which provided greater mysticism and color, became popular. Only Judaism and Christianity, because they denied the divinity of the emperor, were in disfavor, but there was little direct persecution.

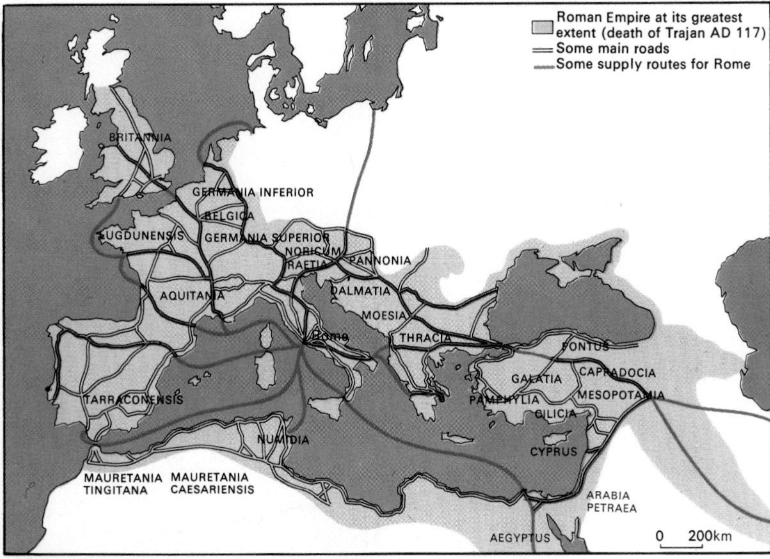
Roman Empire at its greatest extent (death of Trajan AD 117)
Some main roads
Some supply routes for Rome
BRITANNIA
GERMANIA INFERIOR
BELGICA
LUGDUNENSIS
GERMANIA SUPERIOR
NORICUM
RAETIA
PANNONIA
AQUITANIA
DALMATIA
MOESIA
Rome
THRACIA
PONTUS
CAPPADOCIA
GALATIA
PAMPHYLIA
CILICIA
MESOPOTAMIA
TARRACONENSIS
NUMIDIA
CYPRUS
MAURETANIA TINGITANA
MAURETANIA CAESARIENSIS
ARABIA PETRAEA
AEGYPTUS
0 200km

6

5 The network of roads and sea routes that held the empire together was built to enable troops, tax collectors, and administrators to travel swiftly. But the great roads also allowed traders to cover the whole empire easily, and the Roman world became an economic common market with goods from one area available throughout the empire.

6 The loading of a Roman grain ship is depicted in the painting shown above. Egypt and North Africa were the granary of the empire, and the importance of the grain trade, which provided a free ration for every citizen in the capital, was recognized by placing the trade directly under the personal control of the emperor.

7 Races—especially chariot races—and gladiatorial games became increasingly popular and important under the empire. Thus the emperor and rich patricians courted the popularity of the Roman mob by providing ever more lavish spectacles. The distribution of free bread and the frequency of free entertainments helped to insulate the Roman people from economic and political reality and played a major part in dissolving civic responsibility among the citizens.

8 Legionaries and their captives are shown here on Trajan's column, a memorial in Rome to the emperor's victories in Dacia. Trajan brought the empire to its largest extent with legions crossing the Danube into Dacia and down the Tigris and Euphrates to the Persian Gulf. But these areas were never fully pacified, and their defense was a drain on the empire's military and financial resources.

8

9

9 Marcus Aurelius, shown here addressing his troops, was a civilized, highly educated man and a staunch follower of the Stoic philosophy. He was fated to spend most of his reign struggling against the first great onrush of barbarians that threatened to overwhelm the empire. For the first time in centuries a foreign invader swept over the Alps into Italy, and Aquileia was besieged. Only by conscripting every fit man, including gladiators and brigands, was Marcus able to drive back the barbarians, restore the Danube River line and begin the work of reconquering Dacia. His reign marked the end of the enduring imperial peace and the start of Rome's fall.

Roman art 27 BC–AD 117

Until recently, Roman art was regarded as the bridge between the art of Greece and that of the Middle Ages. Largely decadent, it provided a continuity of tradition, but, because it was derived almost entirely from Hellenic models, it offered few original contributions. Now it is widely accepted that, while assimilating Greek styles and techniques, Roman art greatly modified and developed them. Rome remodeled Hellenic art to express imperial ideals—the power of the ruler and his role as patron, benefactor, and protector of an ordered society.

Greek art and artists in Rome

The Romans themselves acknowledged the superiority of Greek art and architecture, and a steady flow of sculptors, architects, and craftsmen in all fields entered the Roman Empire from the east in order to satisfy the increasing demands of its citizens. As early as 268 BC, Greek artists had designed the Roman coinage, while as Rome conquered the Greek world huge quantities of booty, from small decorative objects to almost entire buildings, were taken to Rome. In 187 BC, Marcus Fulvius Nubitor adquired 285 bronze and 230 marble statues during his conquests in Aetolia, while in 168 BC Aemilius Paulus seized no fewer than 250 wagon loads of art treasures from Macedonia. Greek artists were employed to copy art objects.

Different aesthetic attitudes and techniques separated Greek art from Roman. Greek art was produced by individuals whose names are recorded—Phidias' Parthenon, for example. Roman art was almost always anonymous because the patron who commissioned it was more important than the artisan who created it; so it is that we have the Arch of Constantine, the Baths of Caracalla, and Hadrian's Wall.

By the age of Augustus (63BC–AD14) Greek (and to some extent Etruscan) influences had been assimilated, and most architectural forms were established. Roman architecture offers an immense diversity of types and regional styles using a rich variety of local materials. Among its chief characteristics are the development of the columnar and trabeated (post and lintel) design of the Greeks and continuation, with modifications, of the three Greek orders (sometimes all in the same building, as in the Colosseum [6]). To these the Romans added the Tuscan, a variant of the Doric, and Composite, a combination of Ionic and Corinthian. All the orders were used decoratively rather than structurally, and the elaborate Corinthian, the least popular with the Greeks, became the Roman favorite.

Similarly, interior decoration using marble and alabaster, paintings, and mosaics was highly developed by the Romans, who placed a greater emphasis on interiors than did the Greeks. Added to this increased visual richness was a far greater variety of forms—Roman urban life prompted the demand for such structures as baths, theaters and amphitheaters, bridges, viaducts and aqueducts, and multistoried domestic buildings. Many of them were on a massive scale, and their size and rapidity of construction was facilitated by the Romans' introduction of concrete and brick.

The political bias of Roman art was especially obvious under Augustus who, in

CONNECTIONS

See also
1024 Roman art 117–550
1000 Greek art 1100–450 BC
1002 Greek art 450–31 B
1020 Rome: the expansic of the empire

1 The unsurpassed richness of the reliefs of the Ara Pacis symbolizes, through a synthesis of propaganda and art, the Augustan ideals of victory, piety, and peace. They combine a decorative pattern with a narrative frieze, depicting Augustus, members of his family, and officials.

2 This powerful representation of the Emperor Augustus shows him in a cuirass decorated with images commemorating a victory over the Parthians. Although based on a Greek statue, its modified stance and the forcefulness of the head mark it as a truly Roman creation in both conception and style.

3 In the Corinthian-style Maison Carrée, Nîmes, Hellenistic architecture is modified to accommodate the special requirements of the Roman religion, which placed emphasis on the interior rather than the exterior of a temple. The top two of a broad flight of steps form a threshold below the *cella* (the enclosed portion), the width of which equals the length of the portico. The colonnade is continued around the outside of the *cella* but, unlike that of a Greek temple, is embedded in solid walls. Modeled on prototypes in Rome it is one of the best preserved examples of the Augustan age.

4 Augustan art was employed as a propaganda tool. In this cameo the ageless Augustus is represented as the revered messianic leader of a cultured and refined society—Rome as he wished it to be.

5 Roman portraiture developed out of the custom of producing wax death masks for funerary processions. Both this patrician and the busts of his ancestors show clearly identifiable individuals.

keeping with his role as the ruler who brought peace and prosperity to the empire, was portrayed as a pure, magnanimous, handsome, and ageless ruler [4]; the serene formality and diverse imagery of Augustan art is summarized in the reliefs of the Ara Pacis ("the altar of peace") [1]. In his program of urban expansion he restored numerous buildings (82 temples in Rome alone) and built many others, including the magnificent temple of Mars Ultor, the Forum Augusti, and the Maison Carrée, Nîmes [3].

Imperial patronage

The Augustan age had established the range of Roman architectural styles. Subsequent trends reflected the individual preferences of rulers and emphasized the intimacy of the link between the imperial patron and the objects he commissioned. Under Nero and the Flavians, for example, artists were given a freer hand and many extravagant works such as buildings with exotic octagonal, circular, or oval rooms were constructed. Nero's sumptuous Golden Palace in Rome was a notable example. After this flamboyant interlude the more practical Trajan instigated a reaction in which utilitarian structures predominated.

Realism in portraiture

Portraiture, one of the major achievements of Roman art, developed throughout this period. It moved away from the idealism seen in the official propaganda portraits of Augustus toward a remarkable, almost brutal, realism under such later rulers as Claudius and Nero. Greek artists sought to transcend the individual in a quest for universal truths, while the Romans were concerned with accurate likenesses [2,5]. The contrast between idealism and realism is seen particularly in portrait busts and also in the narrative reliefs on the Arch of Titus [7] and Trajan's Column.

Roman painting, known chiefly from examples at Pompeii [8], was largely derived from Greek. Urban Romans maintained their traditional connection with their rural background by favoring landscapes, often combined with new architectural and *trompe l'oeil* motifs.

KEY

A bronze head of Augustus, first emperor of Rome, was found in Meröe, Sudan. One part of a colossal statue, it characterizes the politically significant art of portraiture during the Roman Republic and after. In some ways idealized, it depicts Augustus in the prime of life. In fact it was made at the time of his death at the age of 76. It departs from Greek portraiture in conveying the strength of the man who symbolized the power and unity of the empire. Julian, in his letter to Theodorus, explained the correct attitude toward imperial portraits: "He who loves the emperor delights to see the emperor's statues."

6

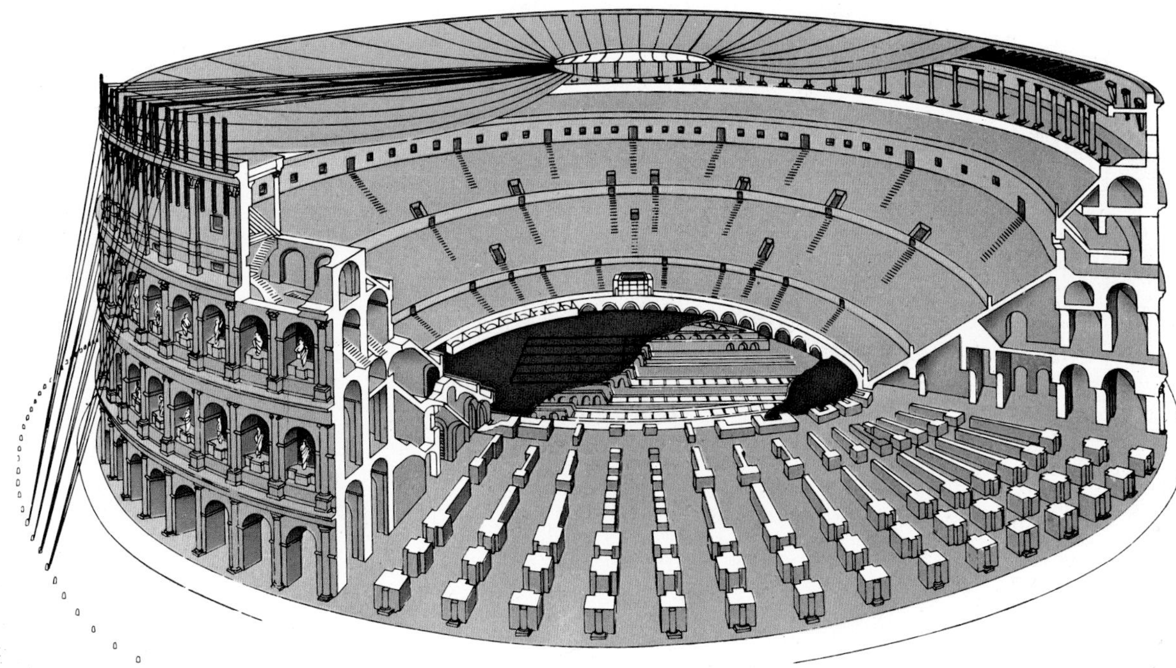

6 The Flavian amphitheater in Rome – the Colosseum – was conceived by the Emperor Vespasian and constructed between AD 72 and 81. It was one of the greatest Roman architectural achievements and served as a model for amphitheaters throughout the empire. Its outer framework and basic interior structure were composed of gigantic blocks of travertine (a kind of hard limestone), the remainder being built of softer stone and concrete, largely faced with marble. Rising 150 ft (45.7m) in four stories, the arcaded façade included columns of all three orders – Doric, Ionic, and Corinthian – the upper part being decorated with numerous statues. As many as 45,000 spectators, who gained admittance through 80 entrances, sat on tiers of marble seats arranged by class. They were protected from sun and rain by a movable awning.

7

7 Titus' military achievements are commemorated on the reliefs of the Arch of Titus, which depicts his triumphal return from the sack of Jerusalem in AD 70. The arch was built by Domitian.

8

8 This Pompeian fresco (detail shown) demonstrates a mastery of color, of perspective, attention to detail, and appreciation of architectural interiors. These were the hallmarks of the painter's art in the 1st century AD.

Roman art: 117–550

In the time of Trajan there was a revival of interest in the art of earlier periods, which reached its apogee under his successor Hadrian (AD 76–138). The unprecedented economic prosperity of the empire, coupled with the emperor's personal patronage, led to a veritable Hellenic renaissance that persisted through Hadrian's reign and beyond, determining to a large degree the character of Roman art in the second century AD.

Hadrian's architectural revival

Hadrian's villa at Tivoli [3], described as "probably the most beautiful collection of ruins on Italian soil," was the most remarkable of all Roman architectural complexes. He made lavish use of multicolored marble and of diverse ornamental architectural features, including such circular forms as the curved architraves that were popular in the Eastern Empire.

These and the innumerable Greek and Greek-influenced masterpieces of sculpture with which Hadrian surrounded himself introduced many new and important elements into the Roman artistic repertory. The great range of his taste created such emphatically Roman works as his Pantheon—the most important domed structure of the age [1].

Under the Antonine emperors who succeeded Trajan, architecture was predominantly Greek in inspiration. Much use was made of the three orders, and many massive works, such as large temple complexes, were built, especially in the Eastern Empire. A number of new architectural devices were employed, including ostentatious façades, exotically decorated (but detached and functionless) columns that visually fragmented interiors, niches in which works of sculpture were placed, and a profusion of surface decoration.

During the rule of the Severan emperors in the third century, the rise of status and wealth of citizens in the Roman provinces in particular was asserted in lavish architectural works. In an attempt to vie with the achievements of earlier emperors, such rulers as Caracalla (176–217) embarked on a number of grandiose building schemes. These were most notable for their monumental and impressive size.

Among them one may include the Baths of Caracalla in Rome, the best preserved of all imperial baths. It accommodated 1,600 bathers and its central hall *(tepidarium)* was roofed by a vault soaring to a height of 180 feet (54.8 meters), decorated with colored marble and priceless statues. But in keeping with the Roman preference for interior rather than exterior elaborateness, it was largely undecorated on the outside.

The later emperors of the third century, because of their preoccupation with the defense of the empire, did not encourage major building programs other than those involving military works. The fortified palace of Diocletian (245–313) at Spalato (Split) in Dalmatia (completed 305) stands out as the major military building of the late period and symbolizes the swing toward pure functionalism.

Sculpture to the third century AD

Through Hadrian's influence, the earnest majesty of the sculpture from Trajan's era was replaced by Greek works in which sensual beauty predominates.

CONNECTIONS

See also
1022 Roman art 27 BC–AD 117
1000 Greek art 1100–450 BC
1002 Greek art 450–31 BC
1030 Rome: soldier emperors to Constantine
1198 Neoclassicism

1

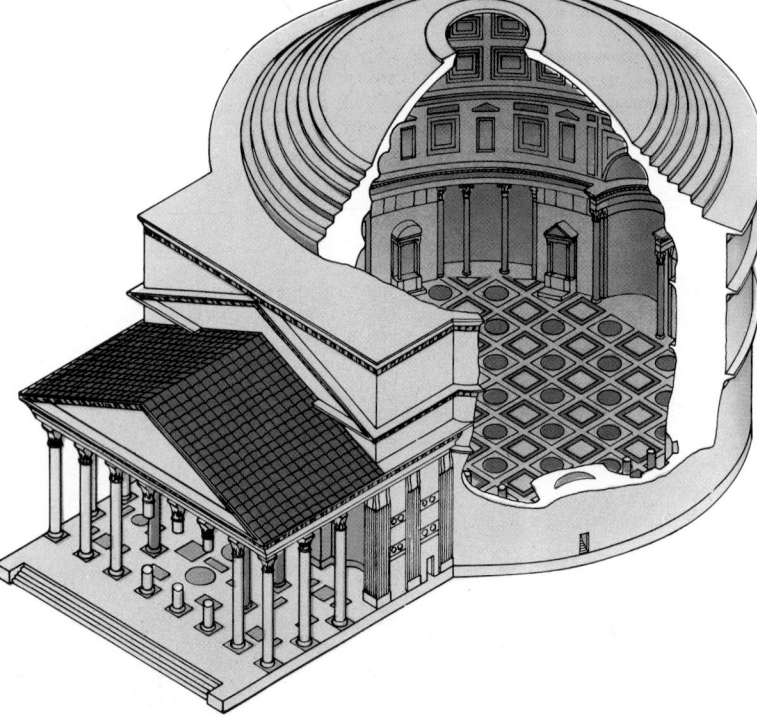

1 The Pantheon, Rome, (*c.* AD 118–*c.* 125), one of the most influential buildings in the history of architecture, has been described as the first major monument to be composed entirely as an interior. Rebuilt completely by Hadrian, it remained the world's largest domed structure until modern times and is the oldest building with its original roof intact. The portico, supported by 16 granite columns, is grandiose but conventional. The dome, however, a perfect hemisphere, is remarkable not only for its size—142 ft (43.2 m) in diameter—but for its apparent lightness, an illusion skillfully created by the use of coffering, once stuccoed and gilded, and a single central light source. The actual method of construction involved a highly sophisticated understanding of concrete technology.

2

2 The Portonaccio Battle Sarcophagus depicts Romans in a violent struggle with barbarians and captures the moment when victory is unquestionably the Roman commander's. The Emperor Hostilian (*d.* 251), detached from the mass of bodies, completely dominates the scene. The craftsmanship represents a theatrical example of mid-3rd century art.

3

3 Hadrian's villa (*c.* AD 130), the most extravagant of all Roman country palaces, represents the eclectic tastes and restless architectural experimentation of a Roman ruler with unlimited resources. No single building is on a grand scale, but the whole—an immense variety of courtyards, fountains, statues, pillars, pools, mosaics, and individual buildings—covers 7 sq miles (18 sq km) of country-side on the edge of the Roman Campagna and is skillfully blended into the landscape.

4

4 This bronze equestrian statue of Marcus Aurelius in Rome dates from the Antonine period, when idealized figures began to displace the realism found under Trajan. Once gilded and with a figure of a barbarian under the horse's raised hoof, it was preserved, while other Roman bronzes perished, in the mistaken belief that it depicted the Christian Emperor Constantine. The statue influenced the work of such Renaissance masters as the great Florentine sculptor Donatello (*c.* 1386–1446).

From *c.* AD 100, for reasons that are not fully understood, burial began to replace cremation throughout the Roman Empire. Tombs became more elaborate and the art of making decorated sarcophagi was developed. In the late empire, battle scenes became particularly popular on the sarcophagi [2] of military leaders.

In the Antonine period statues became more massive and elaborate. The use of chisels for carving stone was steadily superseded by the skillful use of a drill, making possible the achievement of more decorative effects in drapery and hair. These were frequently embellished by gilding. Fine bronzes, such as the powerful equestrian statue of Marcus Aurelius (121–80) [4], were produced, but few have survived.

Two particular types of relief coexisted from this period—a primitive, almost folk-art style, as used on the column of Marcus Aurelius, and the persistence of Greek classical elements—two streams of artistic endeavor that characterize the variety of Roman art and that come together in the Arch of Constantine [5].

Under the Severan emperors massive statues and reliefs were often so elaborate that they virtually obscured entire architectural surfaces.

Sculpture of the turbulent third century was of variable quality—reliefs became cruder, and there was a trend toward mannerism and abstract symmetry, which involved reintroduction of the chisel in place of the drill. This resulted in the angularity found in such stark and impressive works as the colossal head of Constantine [Key].

Painting and crafts

Painting apparently did not develop beyond the so-called Fourth Style identified at Pompeii. Mosaic, originally a flooring technique, developed rapidly in the second and third centuries and virtually replaced painting as a method of decorating walls [8].

Despite several imperial decrees against personal extravagance, fine jewelry, splendid ivory-inlaid furniture, and metalwork, such as the silverware found at Mildenhall, England [6], were popular throughout the empire.

KEY

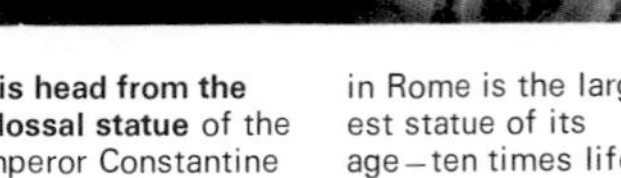

This head from the colossal statue of the Emperor Constantine in Rome is the largest statue of its age—ten times life size. It was sculpted *c.* AD 313 and was the peak of imperial art.

5

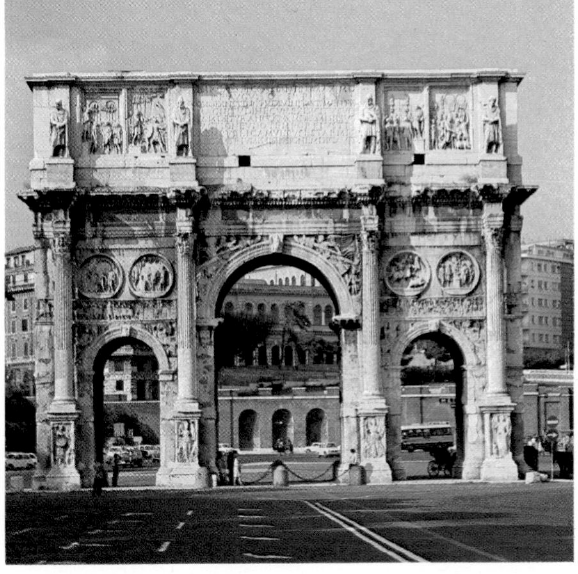

5 The Arch of Constantine is decorated with a rich variety of panel reliefs and statues, many of which were plundered from earlier public monuments. It thus summarizes the major artistic styles of Rome. The reused materials in the arch are from the reigns of emperors Domitian, Trajan, and Hadrian.

6

6 This great dish, part of the Roman silver hoard known as the Mildenhall Treasure (4th century AD), measures almost 2 ft (60 cm) across and weighs 18.3 lb (8.3 kg). The outer frieze represents the triumph of Bacchus, god of wine, over Hercules. Other mythological figures, including Neptune, also appear.

7 In this gold medallion minted at Thessalonica, the Emperor Constantine appears in a portrait that echoes those of Augustus. The restoration of order to the Roman Empire under Diocletian and Constantine prompted the standardization of Roman coinage. While achieving a high degree of craftmanship, representations of rulers became stylized with religious overtones—a typical aspect of late Roman art, foreshadowing that of the Byzantine style of art to come.

7

8 The technique of mosaic, invented by the Greeks, was readily adopted by the Romans, who perfected it and applied it on a large scale. Many local styles emerged in both Italy and such provinces as Britain and Tunisia. Among the subjects employed were stories from classical mythology, interpretations of classical Greek paintings, landscapes, portraits, elaborate decorative motifs, and particularly scenes of vigorous action—chariot racing, hunting, and gladiatorial spectacles. By the 3rd century mosaic work had, in many instances, superseded the three-dimensional representations of gods and cult figures, as in mosaic portraits.

8

Christ and the Apostles

Jesus Christ was an orthodox Jew. Born in about 4 BC, he was crucified outside the walls of Jerusalem in about AD 30. He certainly gave Christianity its original impetus, but it is less certain that he meant to found a new church. His disciples came to think of him as the promised Messiah (the Hebrew equivalent—meaning "the anointed"—of the Greek "Christ"), and then gave to him the value and honor they reserved for the one God alone.

The figure of Jesus and his teaching still dominates Western imagination nearly 2,000 years after his death. Today about 1,000,000,000 people in many parts of the world describe themselves as Christians.

When Jesus lived there were within Judaism several controversial emphases and interpretations. The evidence of the Dead Sea Scrolls and other contemporary sources suggests that Jesus's teachings had much in common with those of some of the sects—for example, the Essenes—current during his lifetime.

According to the gospels he was crucified on the orders of Pontius Pilate, the Roman procurator, at the insistence of the Jewish religious establishment. The gospels suggest he was condemned to death for blasphemy because he claimed to be the Messiah, although such a claim was not technically blasphemous in Jewish law.

The historical Jesus

The only detailed records of the life of Jesus are the gospels. What were believed to be sayings of Jesus and stories about him circulated first by word of mouth and were later collected and written down. It was from such oral and written sources that the four gospels were compiled. They were written in Greek, although Jesus spoke in Aramaic. The first of the gospels, St Mark's, was written in about AD 62. The gospels present highly interpreted history, and it has been impossible to disentangle fact from interpretation.

The earliest records (St Paul's epistles and St Mark's gospel) do not describe Jesus's birth. According to the later accounts of St Luke and St Matthew, Jesus was born at Bethlehem of a virgin mother, Mary, and his conception in her womb was a result of the creative power of God's spirit. Jesus's hometown was Nazareth in Galilee [1].

Jesus was baptized in about AD 26, when he was about 30, by his cousin John the Baptist [5]. Immediately after his baptism he went into spiritual retreat in the desert. Then he began teaching in Galilee, healing those sick in body and mind and proclaiming the imminent arrival of the kingdom (more accurately the kingly rule) of God.

For many, the essence of Jesus's teaching is the Sermon on the Mount—a compilation of his sayings masterfully arranged. It emphasizes the need for spiritual rebirth and describes the heroic goodness that follows as a result. He called men away from the letter of the Jewish law to its spirit. This led him to criticize severely the Jewish leaders of his day.

Arrest and crucifixion

Jesus was marked down by the religious authorities as a public enemy. The civil (Roman) authorities were concerned be-

CONNECTIONS

See also
1050 The Celts and Christianity
1052 The rise of medieval Western Christendom
960 Egypt: the Old and Middle Kingdoms
844 Judaism and Christianity
988 Buddha and Buddhism
1040 Confucius and Confucianism
1058 Mohammed and Islam

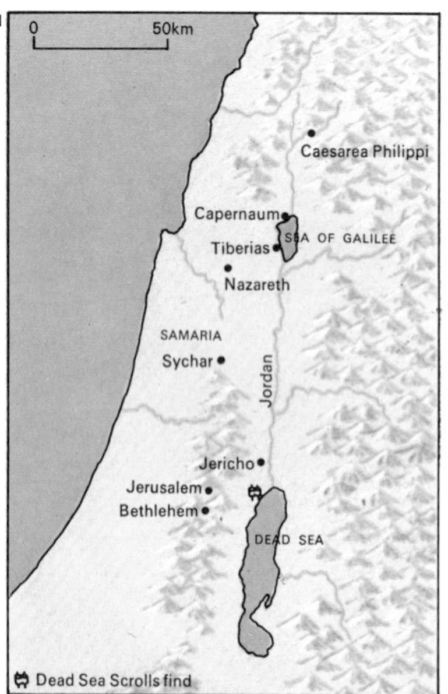

0
50km
Caesarea Philippi
Capernaum
SEA OF GALILEE
Tiberias
Nazareth
SAMARIA
Sychar
Jordan
Jericho
Jerusalem
Bethlehem
DEAD SEA
Dead Sea Scrolls find

1 Christianity began in the northern Jewish province of Galilee, away from the religious center of Jerusalem, and Jesus spent most of his ministry among simple country people. Tradition states some Apostles traveled as far as Persia and India. The most widely traveled Apostle, Paul, was a Jew and a Roman citizen, born at Tarsus, in what is now Turkey. He took the gospel both to Asia Minor and to Greece.

2 Capernaum, where the remains of this synagogue still exist, is at the north end of the Sea of Galilee. Capernaum is mentioned several times in the gospels in connection with Jesus's mission.

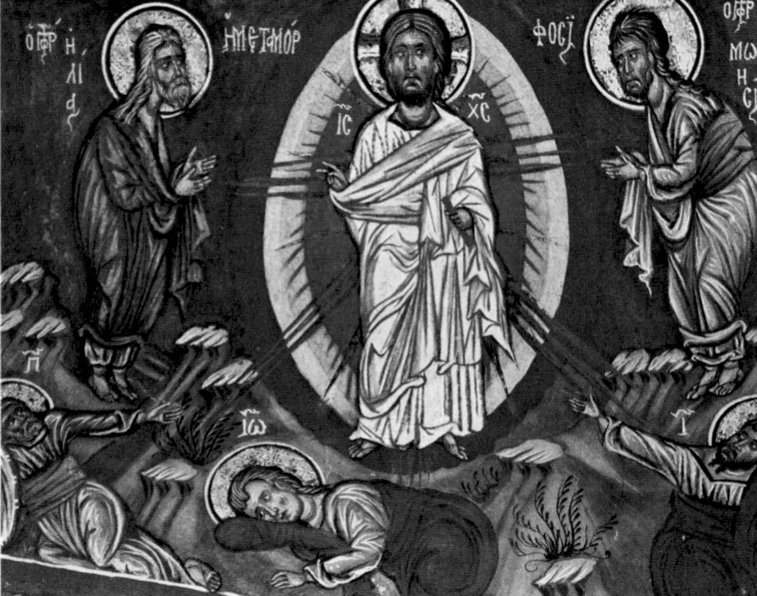

3 Christ is transfigured with Elias and Moses, who represent the Prophets and the Law, and John, Peter, and James recoil from the light in this painting from a 12th-cent. church in Cyprus.

4 The Dead Sea Scrolls were discovered between 1947 and 1956 in caves at the northwestern end of the Dead Sea. They contain most of the books of the Old Testament and some hitherto unknown Jewish writings in Hebrew and Aramaic from a monastic community at Qumran. Most of the manuscripts, made of leather and papyrus, are kept at the Israel Museum in Jerusalem.

cause his wide popular support might lead to disturbances. He probably realized that his life was threatened. On a visit to Jerusalem in about AD 30 to observe the Jewish Passover he provided his enemies with an occasion to arrest him by physically assaulting the money changers and traders in the Temple. He was eventually arrested by the temple guard while he was praying in the Garden of Gethsemane—Judas Iscariot no doubt leading them to the place and betraying the identity of Jesus by kissing him. The Jewish leaders handed him over to Pontius Pilate, who ordered his crucifixion (a Roman form of execution reserved for slaves and low criminals).

The early church

From the third day after the crucifixion the followers of Jesus became utterly convinced that he was alive and had appeared and spoken to them as recognizably himself although now glorified. Slightly later, the news spread that certain women had gone to his tomb to anoint his dead body and had found the tomb empty [7].

At the harvest festival of Pentecost, some five weeks after the crucifixion, the disciples believed themselves visited by the spirit of God sent down by the exalted Jesus. From then on they went about preaching that Jesus was the Messiah crucified and raised from the dead and that through him eternal salvation was offered to all people.

Paul became the chief Apostle to the Gentiles (non-Jews) after a dramatic conversion to Jesus's teachings on the road to Damascus. A Greek-speaking Roman citizen, he began the transformation of Christianity into a world religion. Paul traveled extensively, preaching in Asia Minor and Greece [8]. Eventually arrested in Jerusalem, he used his right as a Roman citizen to appeal to Caesar; he is said to have been executed in Rome at the same time as St Peter, about AD 60.

According to legend, St John, "the disciple whom Jesus loved," lived to an old age in exile. The gospel according to St John is a profound meditation on the life and teaching of Jesus.

KEY

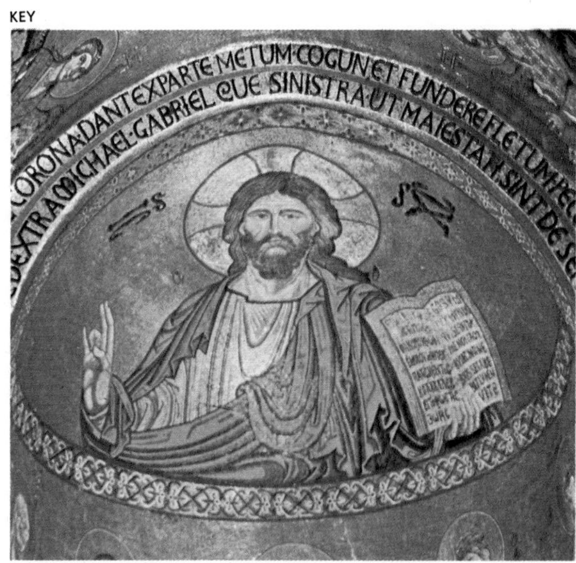

The image or name of Jesus Christ and the gospel open at the words "I am the Light of the World" appear in many mosaics, including this 12th-century ceiling work in Palermo, Italy.

5 Jesus was baptized in the River Jordan by John the Baptist. In this 6th-century mosaic from Ravenna, the figure on the left represents the river god of the Jordan. The dove above the head of Christ represents the Holy Ghost.

6 Jesus celebrated his Last Supper with his disciples on the night before his death. This meal is the distinctive Christian ceremony called the Lord's Supper, Holy Communion, Eucharist, Liturgy, and Mass. This sixth-century mosaic at Ravenna shows 11 disciples reclining with Christ. The two fish recall the miraculous feeding of the multitude.

7 A 5th-century ivory carving depicts the women who went to the rock-hewn sepulcher of Jesus at dawn on Easter Sunday and found that he had risen from the dead.

8 Paul went on his first preaching tour to Asia Minor. A second visit continued over into Greece, and a third journey covered much the same ground. The last journey touched upon Crete, Malta, and Sicily, and ended in Rome.

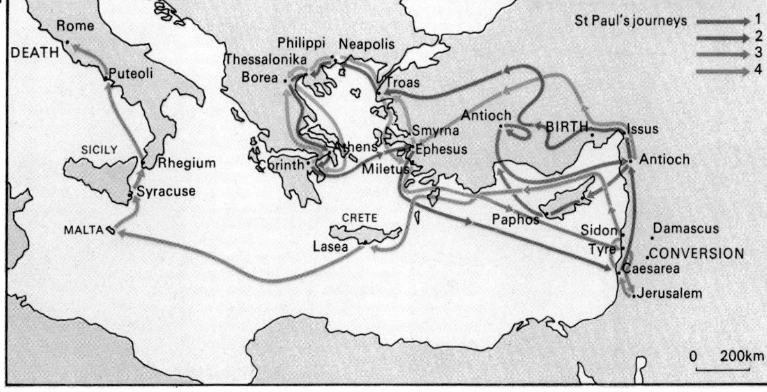
St Paul's journeys
1
2
3
4
Rome
DEATH
Puteoli
Philippi
Neapolis
Thessalonika
Borea
Troas
Antioch
BIRTH
Issus
Smyrna
Athens
Ephesus
Corinth
Miletus
Antioch
SICILY
Rhegium
Syracuse
CRETE
Paphos
Sidon
Damascus
MALTA
Lasea
Tyre
CONVERSION
Caesarea
Jerusalem
0 200km

Roman literature

In the first three centuries of Rome's development the influence of captive Greece on Roman literature was all pervasive. The Romans themselves regarded their literature as having been founded by a Greek, Livius Andronicus (*c.* 284–*c.* 204 BC). He wrote tragedies and comedies based on Greek originals and translated Homer's *Odyssey* using a native Italian meter, the Saturnian.

The Hellenistic influence

The end of the First Punic War (241 BC) marked the beginning of literary work in Rome. Although the epic on the war by Naevius (*c.* 270–*c.* 201 BC) was in the Saturnian meter, Ennius' (239–169 BC) introduction of the hexameter—the meter of Greek epic—in his epic poem the *Annales* laid the foundations for later Latin poetry.

The elder Cato (234–149 BC), to whom Ennius is said to have taught Greek, opposed this Hellenizing movement, writing his works in as basic a Latin as possible.

The greatest writer of Latin comedy was Plautus (*c.*255–*c.*184 BC). He based his plays on Greek originals but added vigorous humor and a brilliant Latin style. The refined style and deep interest in character of his successor Terence (*c.* 190–159 BC) [1], a freed African slave, were less successful on the stage. Drama never became established in Rome as it had been in Greece; Terence was the last significant Latin author to write for the theater. The tragedies of Seneca (*c.* 4 BC–AD 65) were written to be read, not performed.

Satire, which the Romans considered to be the only genre they had not borrowed from the Greeks, was developed from Ennius' foundations by Lucilius (*c.*180–102 BC), a prolific but rather crude writer. He established the hexameter as the regular meter for satire.

The greatest literary figures

The first century BC, the last era of the Roman Republic, produced some of the greatest figures in Roman literature. The huge output of Marcus Tullius Cicero (106–43 BC) [Key] included speeches and works on rhetoric and philosophy. His friend and later enemy Julius Caesar (*c.* 100–44 BC) [3] wrote an important work on grammar, but only his historical works survive.

Contemporaries of Caesar were the poets Lucretius (*c.*99–55 BC) and Catullus (*c.*84–*c.*54 BC) [2,4]. Lucretius' hexameter technique in his didactic poem *De Rerum Natura* forms a link between Ennius and Vergil. Catullus was a member of a coterie that took Hellenistic poetry as its model for the cultivation of elegy and epigram, predominantly on the theme of love and in a variety of Greek meters.

In Vergil (70–19 BC) Latin literature at last acquired its Homer. His last and greatest work, the *Aeneid,* represents a fusion of the epic tradition with the newer, more subjective poetical ideas of the Hellenistic age. His friend Horace (65–8 BC) also rose from humble origins to enjoy the patronage of Emperor Augustus. His *Satires* lifted the genre to a high literary level, while his *Epistles* were an original development from it. His *Odes* are a successful attempt to adapt lyric poetry to Latin.

CONNECTIONS

See also
998 Greek literature and theater
1012 Early Rome: the kingdom and the republic
1014 Rome: the organization of the republic
1016 Roman life
1018 From the civil wars to Caesar's empire
1020 Rome: the expansion of the empire
1030 Rome: soldier emperors to Constantine

1 A twelfth-century illustration shows Terence's comedy *Andria:* as Simo's slaves prepare for his son's wedding, he tells his freedman that the "wedding" is a trick being played on his son, who is in love with a girl from Andros.

2 Ariadne, daughter of Minos of Crete, wakes on the island of Naxos to find that she has been deserted by Theseus, son of the king of Athens, whom she has helped to enter the labyrinth and kill the Minotaur. The myth was a popular subject for wall paintings in the houses of the well-to-do of Pompeii. The myth of Ariadne forms a principal subject of Catullus' longest and finest poem, the *Peleus and Thetis,* and was later treated by Ovid in his masterpiece, the *Metamorphosis*.

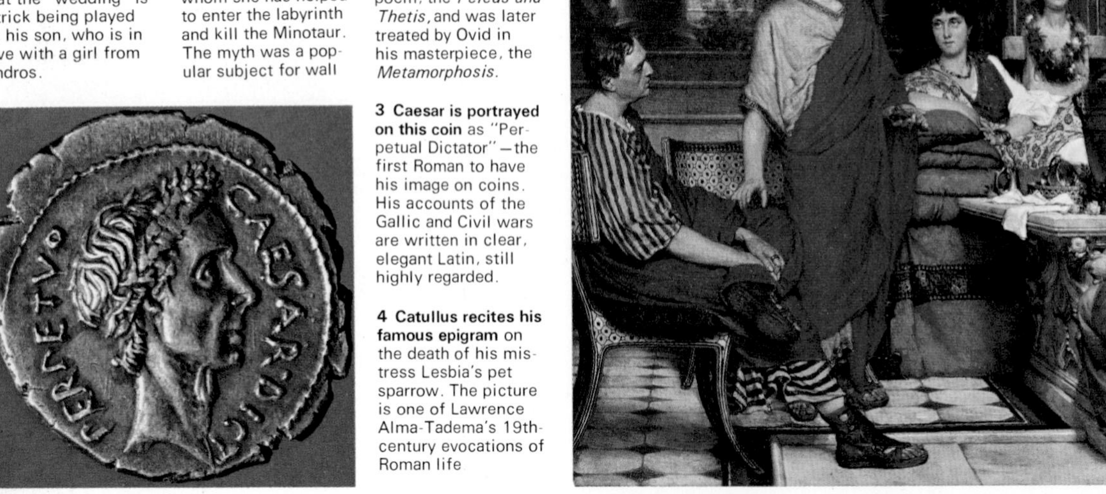
CAESAR DICT
PERPETVO

3 Caesar is portrayed on this coin as "Perpetual Dictator"—the first Roman to have his image on coins. His accounts of the Gallic and Civil wars are written in clear, elegant Latin, still highly regarded.

4 Catullus recites his famous epigram on the death of his mistress Lesbia's pet sparrow. The picture is one of Lawrence Alma-Tadema's 19th-century evocations of Roman life

Livy (59 BC–AD 17), the most notable historian of the age, extolled the glories of the departed republic in his *History of Rome*. Ovid (43 BC–AD 17) carried on from Catullus in the writing of love-elegy; his exuberant talent also produced the *Metamorphoses*, the chief source of mythology for the Renaissance.

Literary decline and transformation

At the end of the first century AD Latin literature in its classical form began to decline. The prose of Seneca, a Roman born in Spain, represents a reaction against Ciceronian fulsomeness in favor of brevity and point [5]. His writings and the epics of his nephew Lucan (AD 39–65) and Statius (*c.* AD 45–*c.* 96) typify a period in which both the Latin and Greek masters were imitated. Among the more original poets and prose writers was Petronius (died *c.* AD 66), whose *Satyricon* is a discursive "novel" written with immense verve and style. Another Roman born in Spain, Martial (*c.* AD40–104), concentrated on the epigram, setting the standard for future attempts in the form.

Tacitus (*c.*55–120), with his inimitable style and powerful personality represents the peak of Roman historical writing. The polished letters of his colleague Pliny the Younger (*c.*62–114) throw a vivid light on contemporary society, as also—less favorably—does the mordant wit and lurid hyperbole of the satirist Juvenal (*c.*55–*c.*140).

Prose authors of the second century tended to favor a style in which archaic and colloquial elements are mixed. A striking case is the rhetorician and philosopher Apuleius (born *c.*125), who is best known for his *Metamorphoses*, written in an ornate and colorful style.

From the third century onward it is Christian authors such as Tertullian (*c.*160–*c.*230), St Augustine (354–430), and St Jerome (*c.*347–420) who are most significant. It was as the language of the Roman Church, no longer of the Roman Empire, that Latin was to remain alive and vigorous up to the Middle Ages, when it was superseded as the standard literary language of the West.

KEY

Cicero rose from obscure origins to become a leading if ambivalent political figure in Rome, chiefly through the power of his matchless rhetoric, which was as effective on the political platform as in the law courts. His published works represent the summit of Latin prose.

5

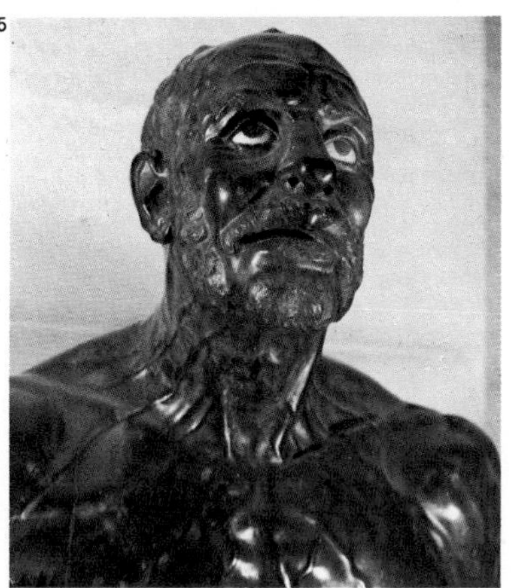

5 Seneca, statesman and philosopher, was rich, vain, and often accused of hypocrisy for failing to live up to the ascetic ideals he professed. He attempted to realize Stoicism in practice by acting as Nero's adviser but toward the end of his life, when his influence over Nero began to wane, he devoted himself to expounding the Stoic philosophy in numerous treatises and in his *Moral Letters.* His philosophy was derivative but influenced later ideas.

6

6 A palimpsest, a parchment reused after the original text has been removed, is the only surviving source of Cicero's *De Republica*, a dialogue concerning the best form of government. It was found in 1882. The original text, dating from *c.* AD 400, was partly obliterated when the parchment was used again for a commentary on the Psalms by St Augustine in the seventh century, but Cicero's text could still be read, fortunately, from this reused parchment.

7

7 Vergil is seated between the Muses of Tragedy and History in this third-century mosaic discovered at Sousse, in Tunisia. He holds a papyrus roll of the *Aeneid,* showing the words from the first book, in which the poet begs the Muse to reveal to him what caused Juno to drive Aeneas "to traverse so many perils," in his journeys to Carthage and Rome.

8

8 St Ambrose, (*c.*340–97), a German-born layman who was elected Bishop of Milan in 374, is enshrined in an early fifth-century mosaic at the Milan basilica that he founded and that is named after him. A great preacher, he wrote a wide range of prose works and is regarded as the father of the Latin church hymn. His hymns, still in use, are written in four-line verses in a simple style to appeal to ordinary Christians, and are arranged antiphonally.

Rome: soldier emperors to Constantine

After the murder of the Roman Emperor Commodus in AD 193, four rivals disputed the imperial succession. There was a costly civil war in which several major cities, including Antioch, Byzantium, and Lyons, were sacked before Septimius Severus (reigned 193–211) was successful. Order was restored, but the military basis of imperial power then became more obvious, and the power of the Senate was reduced.

Political anarchy and religious persecution
Septimius was succeeded by a family dynasty but, because a settled system of succession was lacking and because the legions increasingly realized that they had the power both to elect and to destroy emperors [1], there was continual unrest. In the 74 years from the death of Septimius to the accession of Diocletian (245–313) in 284, there were 27 emperors and many usurpers; all but four died violently.

This political anarchy came at the worst possible time, for the barbarians were again pressing on the empire's frontiers. In 236, Alemanni and Franks crossed into Gaul, and Goths poured over the Danube in 247, raiding the Balkans and killing Emperor Decius (200–251). The Romans were forced either to allow the barbarians to settle within the frontiers or to buy them off.

In the East, a new Persian dynasty, the Sassanids, invaded Syria and Asia Minor and then captured Emperor Valerian (193–260) in 260 [2]. His son and co-regent Gallienus (reigned 253–268) had to put down five rivals before recovering the lost eastern provinces. Aurelian (reigned 270–75) finally abandoned Dacia but began restoring the Danube and Rhine frontiers. The work was completed by Probus (reigned 276–82), who repulsed the Alemanni.

The unrest was accompanied by a breakdown of civil order and a collapse of the economy. Inevitably, men searched for scapegoats and the most obvious ones were the Christians. The Romans had always been highly tolerant of religions provided they accepted the divinity of the emperor, and many oriental cults, including the worship of Mithra and Isis, had become widely popular. But the Christians, who refused to sacrifice to the emperor, were an easy target. Great persecutions took place under Decius and were extended by Valerian (reigned 253–60) [3]. Despite all the disasters, the third century saw the work of some of the greatest commentators on Roman law—Papinian, Paulus, and Ulpian.

Division of the empire
There was a desperate need for reorganization, and in 285 Diocletian established a totally new governmental system [Key]. The empire was divided into eastern and western parts, each ruled by an "augustus" with a "caesar" as his deputy. The augusti were to resign after 20 years and be succeeded by their caesars. The imperial court moved away from Rome [4], and the provinces were replaced by dioceses ruled by a massive new bureaucracy and a reformed army. The system established by Augustus was totally abandoned, and the emperors became absolute monarchs.

Diocletian's reforms did not solve the succession problem, and when he and his co-augustus Maximian (reigned 286–305)

CONNECTIONS

See also
1056 The Byzantine Empire
1054 The barbarian invasions
1052 The rise of medieval Western Christendom
1020 Rome: the expansion of the empire
1018 From the civil wars to Caesar's empire
1014 Rome: the organization of the republic

1 The Praetorian Guard were the elite bodyguards of the emperors. They were the first body of Roman soldiers to realize that they had the power to make emperors and, if need be, to break them—and during the third century their example was followed by troops in the provinces. Anarchy ensued as local garrisons set up their own emperors and tried to dominate the empire.

2 Emperor Valerian was forced to kneel to the Persian ruler in the worst disaster that befell Rome in the third century. The internal chaos of the empire coincided with renewed pressure from barbarian tribes in the west and from the Persians in the east. The cohesion of the empire was further weakened as threatened areas took action independently of Rome to defend themselves.

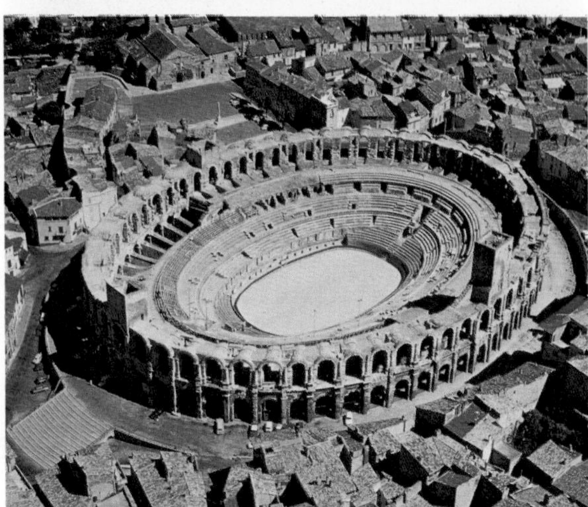

3 Roman persecution of Christians (A), which reached its height under Decius and Valerian, contrasted with general religious toleration. Provided the adherents of a religion paid homage to the divine emperor, they were free to worship and make converts. Many eastern cults—such as the worship of the Persian sun god Mithra, shown here slaying the cosmic bull—flourished, but the exclusiveness of Christians and their refusal to do homage caused them to be treated as a treasonable sect.

resigned in 305, chaos followed. In 312, Constantine (c. 285–337) emerged victorious in the Western Empire in a battle at the Milvian Bridge, during which his armies fought under the Christian cross. In gratitude he made Christianity the official religion of the empire. In 324, on the death of the Eastern emperor Licinius (reigned 311–23), Constantine reunited the empire and moved his capital to Byzantium, which was rebuilt as a totally Christian city with the name Constantinople.

Constantine's death in 337 led to a division of the empire between his two sons; fighting followed until it was briefly reunited in 353. In 355 the Western Empire was placed under Julian, who briefly reunited the empire between 361 and 363. Thereafter, the split became permanent. The difference between the two halves was steadily being emphasized by the presence of barbarians in the West [6], as more tribes were settled within the frontiers, and by the development of a Christianity-dominated absolute empire in the East. In the West the army was by then almost entirely recruited from barbarians; as a result, its ability to resist further incursions was reduced.

Major barbarian invasions

Toward the end of the fourth century renewed major invasions came; in 376 the Visigoths were allowed to cross the Danube to settle, but they were so badly treated that they revolted in 378 and killed Emperor Valens (*c.*328–78) at Adrianople.

Other groups also crossed the frontiers. The Vandals moved through France and Spain to set up an independent kingdom in North Africa; Jutes, Angles, and Saxons occupied Britain; Franks and Burgundians settled in northern France; and Ostrogoths settled in Italy. By the middle of the fifth century the Western Empire had been almost completely occupied by barbarians, although a Romanized administration and culture survived. It came as no great surprise when German troops in Italy elected Odoacer the Ostrogoth (reigned 476–93), as king and he deposed Romulus Augustulus (reigned 475–76) announcing that the West had no more need of emperors.

KEY

Representing Diocletian's tetrarchy, this statue from St Mark's in Venice shows two augusti clasping their caesars, the deputies who would succeed them after 20 years. The chaos and disasters of the 3rd century forced Diocletian to impose major changes on the empire. His reforms, which were the first alterations to the system established by Augustus, can be seen as formalizing the practices of the years of anarchy when emperors reacted on an *ad hoc* basis to barbarian invasion and civil strife. The emperor and his deputies became full-time military leaders, and the whole system was supported by stringent new laws.

4

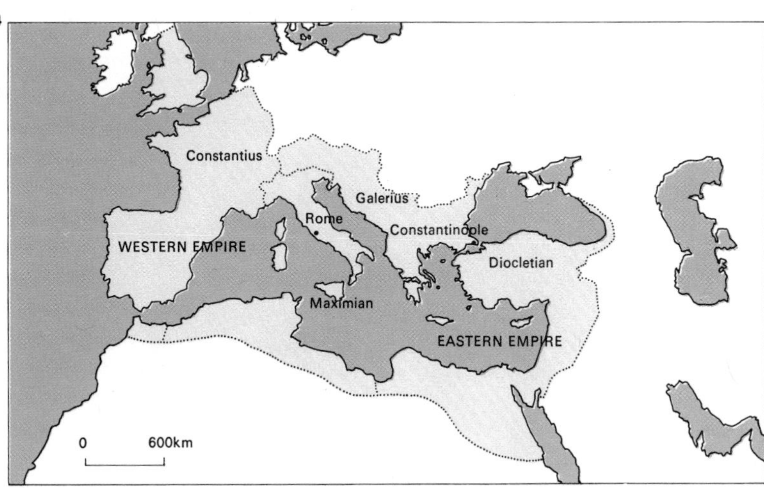
Constantius
Galerius
Rome
Constantinople
WESTERN EMPIRE
Diocletian
Maximian
EASTERN EMPIRE
0
600km

4 The reforms of Diocletian fundamentally altered the empire, splitting it into two almost-independent halves. He and his caesar Galerius were in charge of the crucial Danube and Eastern provinces, while Maximian and Constantius ruled the West. The emperors moved their headquarters nearer to the frontiers. Diocletian ruled from Nicomedia, near Constantinople.

5

5 Constantine the Great made the momentous decision that Christianity was to be the official religion of the empire. He also reunited the empire and moved the imperial capital from Rome to the strategically placed city of Byzantium, or Constantinople, which he had rebuilt as a purely Christian city. Constantine identified with his new faith and put the entire weight of empire behind it.

6

7

6 This detail from a sarcophagus shows Roman soldiers subduing barbarians. Some fighting emperors during the third century were able to hold the frontiers and push back invaders, but generally the barbarians were allowed to enter the empire, settle, and infiltrate the army and administrative structure. During the fourth and early fifth centuries in the West the barbarian kingdoms took shape, and their rise merged almost imperceptibly with the decline of the empire.

7 The influence of the Roman Empire continued as a civilizing force long after its fall. The massive grandeur of its structures, such as the Arles amphitheater (2nd century A.D.) in France, remained as a visible reminder of this influence.

Early Oriental and Western science

Modern scholarship has made it clear that in Roman times there was considerable cross-fertilization among different civilizations. The Roman Empire itself, with its emphasis on foreign trade, provided regular links among the diverse civilizations of Europe, Africa, India, and even China.

The extent of Roman technology

The vastness of the empire posed immense problems in peacekeeping and in government and administration. In all these areas the Romans excelled. They developed military technology by constructing large mechanized catapults, mechanical arrow ejectors and crossbows (originally invented by the Chinese in the third century BC), elaborate battering rams, and wheeled siege towers (Assyrian inventions of the ninth century BC).

Roman roads stretched throughout the empire. Most were graveled or of stone set in concrete with curbstones and drainage channels. Since the empire extended into climates much colder and damper than that of Rome, forms of central heating and damp-proofing were common, at least in the houses built for Roman officials. Heated baths were also common in cities and army camps all over the empire. For their shipping, the Romans constructed huge lighthouses at many ports [1].

Yet, expert though the Romans were in the art of running an empire and in using up-to-date technology to help them, they made little progress in pure science. Such science as they knew they obtained from the Greeks. In the first century AD, Pliny the Elder (23–79) had written his *Historia naturalis*, a vast compendium on all known science, but this was primarily a compilation of Greek science. Galen (*c*. AD 130–200) [2], the greatest medical man of Roman times, was a Greek national. As a physician and surgeon to the gladiators, Galen obtained valuable knowledge about wounds and various internal organs; when he became personal physician to Emperor Marcus Aurelius (121–180), he took many pupils and promoted his interpretation of the operation of the human body, based on the idea that the liver was the main organ of the venous and arterial systems. Galen also developed a simple system of psychological medicine founded on the four humors (blood, phlegm, yellow bile, and black bile) of earlier Greek medicine.

Advances in other centers

It was not until the third century AD that there was a turn away from the Greek concentration on geometry. Then, in Alexandria, the mathematicians Diophantus and Pappus recommended the study of numbers and evolved a kind of algebra. Their work was extended by later generations and particularly in the Muslim world, where algebra became highly developed. The "arabic" numerals [Key], which had originally been devised in India, were adopted.

Arithmetic and a form of algebra also characterized Chinese mathematics. It was in China that the abacus was invented, although the Romans had calculating boards. The abacus became such a useful calculator that it is still in use today.

In the West, some 1,800 years before the Roman conquest, astronomical observa-

CONNECTIONS

See also
1006 Greek science
1038 China 1000 BC–AD 618
1042 China 618–1368
1440 Asian and medieval science
1442 Alchemy and the Age of Reason
1452 Finding unknown quantities: algebra
814 Classifying personality types
1726 Early weapons and defense
1732 History of artillery
1658 Machines for measuring time
1596 Metals and their uses

1 A Roman lighthouse, built at Dover, England, was one of many such aids to shipping, a typical use of technology by the efficient Roman administration. Lighting was by means of a fire, usually of wood and tarry substances, at the top of the building. The lighthouse was built in a stepped form after the pattern of the famous Pharos at Alexandria (3rd century BC), which was built by Sostratus.

2

3

2 Trajan's Column was erected in Rome by Emperor Trajan (*c*. 53–117) to celebrate his victories. Built of marble and more than 100 feet (30 m) high, the column was set up in the Forum of Trajan in 113. This section shows Roman legionaries being treated on the battlefield. It was here and in gladiatorial combat that Galen and other surgeons gained a basic knowledge of anatomy.

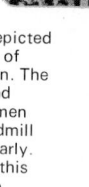

3 A crane is depicted on this section of Trajan's Column. The pulley block and ropes and the men inside the treadmill can be seen clearly. Cranes such as this were found into medieval times.

5

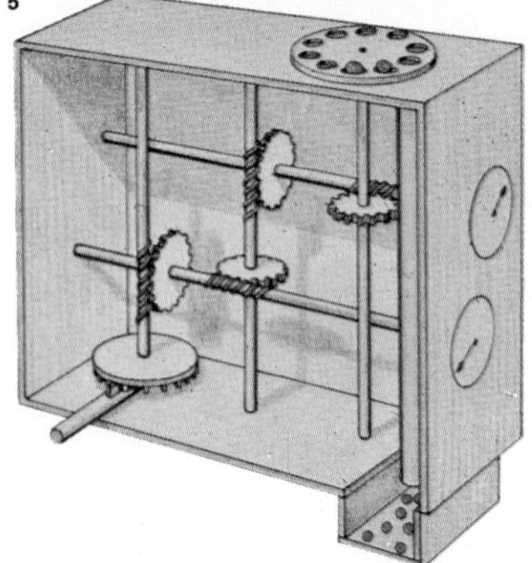

4

C.

4 A euthytonon was a mechanical crossbow so large it had to be mounted on a stand; it was fired by a trigger mechanism. This improvement is usually credited to Philo, who worked at Byzantium (on the present-day site of Istanbul, Turkey) sometime between 200 and 250 BC. This engraving is taken from *Poliorcefi-con,* a book by Justus Lipsius (1547–1606), which was concerned with Roman armaments and was published in Antwerp in Belgium in 1605.

5 Roman taxi meters were operated by the wheels of the carriages. Worms and gear wheels reduced the rotations until dials and a counter could be run at a convenient speed. The dials had pointers that indicated the distance traveled by the carriage. The counting disk (at the top of the taxi meter) allowed pebbles to drop into a holder at the bottom of the meter. By counting the number of pebbles in the holder the fare could easily be worked out by the carriage driver.

tions were being made with great accuracy in Britain by using stone circles, of which Stonehenge is probably the greatest example. The Chaldeans (flourished 1000–540 BC) had discovered that eclipses occurred in cycles. Yet it was not until the early second century AD in China that accurate eclipse predictions and studies of the Earth and heavens were regularly made. However, during that period other technological advances were accomplished—Chang Heng invented a seismograph for recording earthquake shocks, and the art of papermaking was established [7]. By the eighth and ninth centuries AD the Chinese had also invented gunpowder [6] and block printing as well as the first clock ever to be made with an escapement—the large water clock in Sian [8]. Moreover, Chinese technology brought in the first efficient form of horse harness, the sternpost rudder for ships, the manufacture of silk, and most importantly the compass, which was in widespread use by the twelfth century.

Alchemy, the forerunner of chemistry, was an ancient art of obscure origins that sought, among other things, to transform base metals, such as lead, into silver and gold. Carried westward, it was developed in Alexandria particularly by Zosimos in the fourth century AD, along with the important process of distillation.

Medicine and the Chinese influence

Medicine, too, was not free of mysticism and superstition, but herbal drugs were discovered and used by the Chinese, who had drugs against malaria and bronchial diseases, while in India more than 500 drugs came into use, including an early form of tranquilizer. It was in China that the technique of acupuncture evolved.

After the Greeks the development of science was slow and erratic, in the West at least, and seems virtually to have halted for some 600 years. Fortunately, the Muslims collected and collated all knowledge of Greek science, and, with additions from India and the Far East, all this information filtered through to the West from the twelfth century AD, thus laying the foundation for the great scientific revival 400 years later.

KEY

Pythagoras [right], using an abacus, apparently competes against Boethius (475–524), using arabic numerals.

6

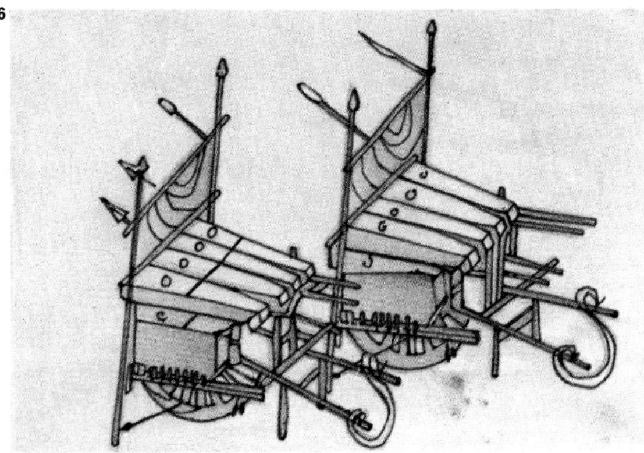

6 Gunpowder, first invented by the Chinese, was originally used for fireworks and only later adapted for war. Shown here are early, wheelbarrowlike, rocket launchers. Gunpowder was first mentioned by Chinese Taoist alchemists about five centuries before it appeared in Europe (*c.* 13th century AD). The development of the gun is more obscure, as for some time gunpowder was used only in rockets.

7

7 Paper was another Chinese invention that only gradually reached the West over many centuries. Known in China in the 1st century AD, the manufacturing technique did not reach even the Muslim world until the 8th century, and it was 400 more years before knowledge of it penetrated to Spain and southern France. Once in the West, it took 200 years more to reach Germany and another 100 to reach England.

8

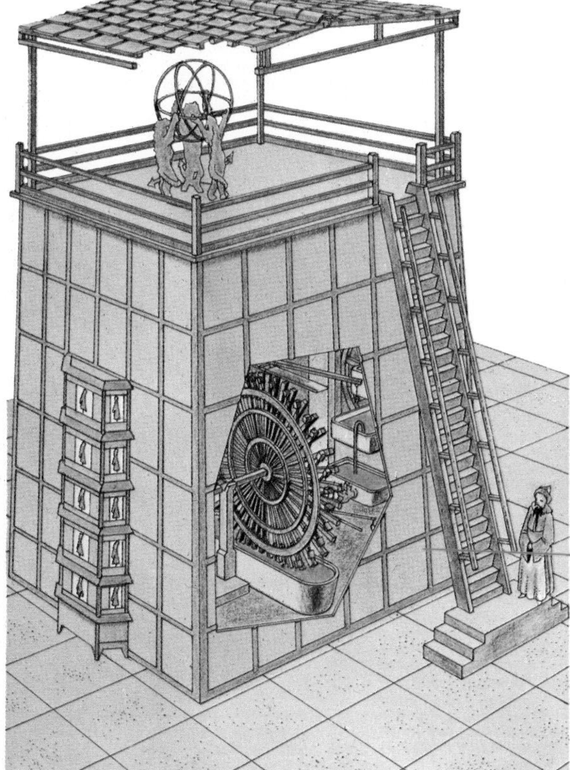

8 The first mechanical clock was Chinese, invented in the 8th century AD by I-Hsing. It was driven by an elaborately engineered water wheel that acted as an escapement—the essence of all mechanical clocks. This clock was built by Su Sung about 1050. The clock was probably known in the West in the 9th century. The first European clocks with mechanical escapements were made in the 13th century.

9

9 Scientific chemistry developed slowly. Practical chemistry, on the other hand, was part of everyday life—as epitomized here in this copy of a 12th-century Arabic manuscript showing the preparation of perfumes. Attempts were made by the Greeks and the Muslims to classify natural substances and build chemistry into a science, but success did not come until the growth of science in the 17th century.

India 300–1200

After centuries of political fragmentation and foreign domination, northern India was once more united under the Gupta dynasty (*c.* AD 320–550)—India's Classical Age. In southern India another great state arose under the Pallavas.

The Gupta dynasty and its empire

The Gupta kings, especially Samudra Gupta (reigned 330–75), Chandra Gupta II (reigned 375–415) and Kumara Gupta (reigned 415–55), founded and maintained, both by conquest and diplomacy, a great empire controlling nearly all of northern India. Good communications, security, and relative prosperity created an atmosphere in which Indian culture attained unequaled heights. Thus the works of the poet and dramatist Kalidasa (flourished fifth century AD) achieved such a degree of perfection that they were often imitated but never surpassed. In art and architecture Indian genius also revealed itself in its most accomplished refinement and symbolism.

The material prosperity of India in this period is emphasized in the accounts of a Chinese Buddhist pilgrim, Fa-hsien (flourished 399–414), who visited India in the fifth century. It is confirmed by the discovery of large numbers of gold coins of the Gupta Empire [5].

At the beginning of the sixth century the White Huns invaded India from the northwest and penetrated as far as central India. This invasion has often been described as the main cause of the downfall of the Guptas, but it can be argued that the White Huns would never have succeeded in invading India if the Gupta Empire had not been divided internally.

The expulsion of the White Huns from India

Although the White Huns were expelled after 30 years, northern India became divided between rival powers in Surashtra, Uttar Pradesh, and Bengal. There were also important changes in southern India (in the present states of Madras and Kerala). A prosperous and cultured society, as reflected in classical Tamil literature, flourished in this area at least from the beginning of the Christian era. In the fourth century AD, the Pallavas made Kanchi (Conjeevaram) the center of a large kingdom. Although much smaller than the Gupta Empire in the north, it was still of great importance. The Pallavas established a successful form of power-sharing between central and local government. The east coast of southern India remained under Pallava control until about 880 and from then until 1200 was under the Cholas.

The Pallavas patronized the Brahmins who, in their turn, provided excellent educational facilities. In art and architecture a particular Dravidian style (named after the language spoken in central and southern India), culminating in the monolithic sanctuaries and rock reliefs of Mamallapuram (the "Seven Pagodas"), was developed [2]. The Pallavas contributed more than any other Indians to the expansion of Indian civilization into Southeast Asia.

The influence of Harsha of Kanauj

Most of northern India was temporarily united by Harsha of Kanauj (606–47), whose career, admirably described in Sanskrit by

CONNECTIONS

See also
986 India 500 BC–AD 300
1036 Indian art to the Moguls
1004 Alexander the Great
1202 India from the Moguls to 1800

1 **On the relief panel** of this temple of the Gupta period, Vishnu is represented during his cosmic sleep on the coils of the seven-headed Naga. His consort, Lakshmi, is the small figure at his feet.

2 **The greatest temple foundation** by the Pallava dynasty of Kanchi, southern India, is the complex of Mamallapuram or Mahabalipuram, popularly known as the Seven Pagodas, south of Madras. The complex, built in 625–74, comprises a number of caves, a group of beautiful monolithic structures (the so-called *rathas*), and this splendid Shore Temple, dedicated to the Hindu god Shiva.

3 **Frescoes depicting beautiful maidens** are painted on the side of a huge rock at Sigiriya, Sri Lanka, where a royal residence was built in the fifth century.

4 **One of the most striking forms** of the god Shiva is that of the four-armed Nataraja, dancing on top of a demon and surrounded by a halo with flames destroying the world at the end of an eon. This is one of the finest bronzes of the Chola period (eleventh century).

5 **The numerous gold coins** of the Guptas (the Bayana hoard alone contains 1,021 specimens) are an important source for the history of the period. Their distribution gives an idea of the areas controlled by various Gupta kings, and the frequency of the minting reflects economic activity. The representations show how the Gupta kings wished the world to see them. This king appears as a fearless hunter slaughtering a lion with a bow and arrow.

his court poet Bana and by a Chinese pilgrim, Hsüan Tsang, reflects high standards of government and a reasonable level of prosperity.

After Harsha, northern India showed progressive political fragmentation with larger states tending to split into smaller units that at first paid homage to the central authority but gradually became independent. Harsha's capital, Kanauj, was made the capital of the Pratihara dynasty in 750. The latter ruled over the present states of Uttar Pradesh, Punjab, and Rajasthan; but before the end of the ninth century their effective authority was limited to parts of the Punjab and Uttar Pradesh while different Rajput dynasties ruled in Rajasthan. Bihar and Bengal were under the control of the Buddhist Pala dynasty (*c.*750–1150), but from the tenth century they shared authority with several minor dynasties.

During such divisions the emperor of Afghanistan, Mahmud of Ghazni (971–1030), invaded and plundered northern India many times between 1000 and 1026 [7]. Although Mahmud was a staunch Muslim, these were primarily destructive raids, carried out for booty. Although many Indian armies fought bravely, their resistance proved ineffective. Further political, but not cultural, decline led to new Muslim invasions, and by the end of the twelfth century most of northern India was under the control of the Muslim sultanate of Delhi.

Sanskrit literature of the post-Harsha period offers many excellent works, although few of the quality of the earlier periods. The most important historical text of ancient India, the *Kashmir Chronicle*, belongs to the twelfth century. In art and architecture some of the greatest achievements, such as the temples of Orissa and Khajuraho, belong to this late period.

There was no decline in southern India, where the Cholas established one of the greatest Indian empires. Their kings invaded Sri Lanka and Bengal and even undertook a great maritime expedition to Southeast Asia. While northern India suffered political fragmentation and Muslim invasions, the Chola kingdom established conditions in which Hinduism flourished.

KEY

Vishnu, one of the principal gods of Hinduism and the supreme deity for the Vaishnava sect, some of whom find a close analogy between religious experience and sexual love, has revealed himself as a savior of mankind in many different forms, in particular in ten descents or incarnations (avatars), as a man or as an animal. His most celebrated avatar was as Krishna, the divine shepherd and king-philosopher. Of the animal avatars, the Boar shown here with elaborate ornamentation is most frequently represented. In Hindu mythology the god is believed to have descended in this form to rescue the Earth, which had sunk in the ocean.

6

6 An older Shiva temple at Orissa shows the typical shape *(shikhara)* of a southern Indian temple. It is built on a platform in front of a pool that is used for ritual ablutions in the Hindu religion.

7 A

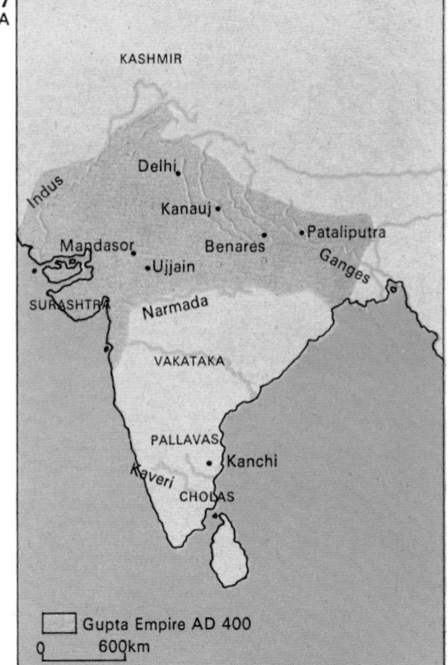
KASHMIR
Delhi
Indus
Kanauj
Mandasor
Benares
Pataliputra
Ujjain
Ganges
SURASHTRA
Narmada
VAKATAKA
PALLAVAS
Kanchi
Kaveri
CHOLAS
Gupta Empire AD 400
0 600km

B

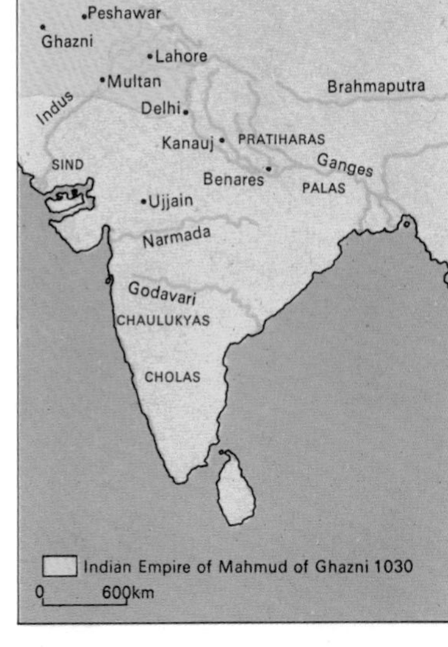
KASHMIR
Peshawar
Ghazni
Lahore
Multan
Brahmaputra
Indus
Delhi
Kanauj
PRATIHARAS
SIND
Ganges
Benares
PALAS
Ujjain
Narmada
Godavari
CHAULUKYAS
CHOLAS
Indian Empire of Mahmud of Ghazni 1030
0 600km

7 Although the Gupta Empire [A] represented the peak of classical Indian culture, its influence hardly reached the south. After its fall, the north was rarely united, while the Pallava and Chola dynasties brought continuity to the south. Despite the lack of cohesion, the north easily resisted Muslim attacks until the growth of Mahmud of Ghazni's empire [B] as a powerful and aggressive neighbor. Mahmud was not impelled by religious motives, but Muslim raids continued until the establishment of the Muslim Sultanate of Delhi in 1206, marking the start of permanent Muslim influence in India.

8

8 Puri is one of the great religious centers, attracting countless pilgrims from all over India during the annual festival of Jagannath (Juggernaut). The god was once a tribal deity.

9 Although they were meant for monks, the Buddhist caves of the western Deccan show little trace of puritanism. This relief, probably of the sixth century, depicts Taras, a kind of female savior, who is performing a devotional dance.

9

Indian art to the Moguls

The beginnings of Indian art can be traced to the Indus valley culture of Harappa and Mohenjo-daro (Pakistan) dating from about 2300 BC. At these two sites small examples of rather naturalistic as well as stylized sculpture in stone and in bronze were found that show a considerable understanding of the human figure.

Mastery of sculptural technique

In the historical gap between the Indus valley culture and the Mauryan era (320–185 BC), the Indian craftsman achieved complete control of his medium. The Ashokan pillar capitals, such as that from Sarnath adopted as the national emblem of India, show both stylized lions and a more naturalistic treatment of animals carried out in polished sandstone. This technique is a characteristic of Mauryan sculpture and it continued into a slightly later period. The *yakshi* [Key], although not a Mauryan piece, also has a polished stone surface. This was probably intended for worship but it is remarkable for its unspiritual treatment of the female figure. This combination of the religious and the sensuous is found throughout Indian art. Similarly, it is not unusual for sculptured pairs of embracing figures *(maithuna)* to be found in a religious context in cave temples or in erotic postures adorning the outsides of temples.

It is likely that major deities were not personalized but represented by symbols until the first two centuries AD. An important development then took place as a result of the cult of *bhakti* (worship of a personal god), in which images became the main icon. The change seems to have occurred in two places simultaneously and with a certain amount of interaction, in Gandhara (now northwestern Pakistan and northeastern Afghanistan) [5] and Mathura (southeast of Delhi).

Hellenistic influences on sculpture

In Gandhara, as a result of latent Hellenism remaining after the eastern extension of Greek culture, a style of sculpture arose that was deeply influenced by Hellenistic ideas. These concerned not only interest in the human figure and the treatment of drapery but also the physical idealization of the deity. Whereas in Gandhara the religion served by sculpture was almost entirely Buddhist, at Mathura Hinduism and Buddhism existed side by side. Here also the style of the images was more Indian, and the stone used was frequently a mottled red or fawn sandstone instead of the gray schist in which most Gandhara stone sculpture was executed. The later (Gupta) Mathura Buddha figures [2], in which the robes appeared to stick to the torso smoothly or in ridges as if they were wet, later became the exemplar of many other statues of Buddha that were made wherever Indian Buddhist culture spread.

Although brick and stone buildings were constructed, most of the remaining architecture from the first few centuries AD comprises caves and formalized Buddhist burial mounds (stupas) [3,4]. The caves, such as those at Karli, Ellora, and Ajanta, were cut from natural rock strata mainly between the second century BC and the ninth century AD for the worship of all three of the main Indian religions, Hinduism,

CONNECTIONS

See also
1034 India 300–1200
986 India 500 BC–AD 300
1204 Indian art: the Mogul age

1

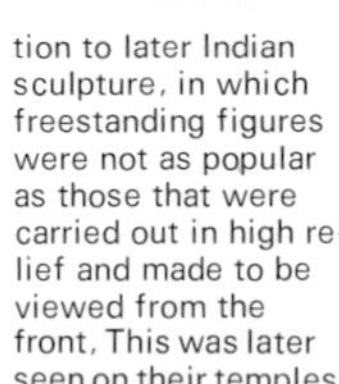

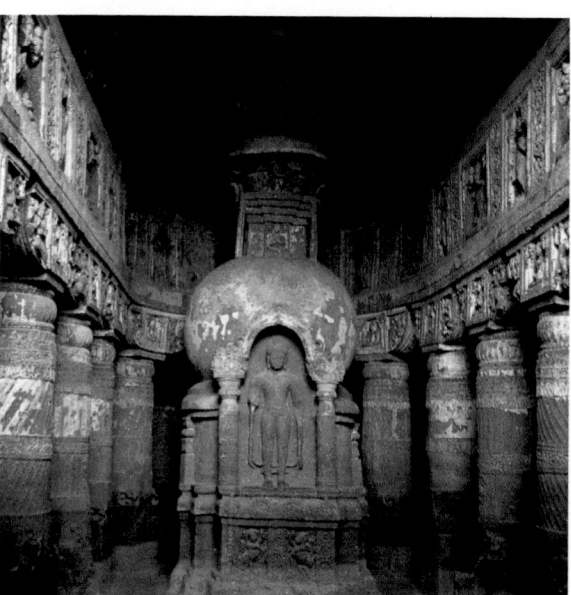

1 The figures of tree-spirits on this 1st century BC railing pillar from Bharut have a low relief and more formalized design than some of the later representations of tree-spirits. They made their contribution to later Indian sculpture, in which freestanding figures were not as popular as those that were carried out in high relief and made to be viewed from the front. This was later seen on their temples.

2

3

2 This elegant sandstone Buddha figure from Mathura was made in the Gupta period, about the 5th century AD. It expresses serene contemplation with a feeling for form and decorative style.

3 In the famous Ajanta caves every detail was cut from solid rock that forms part of a hillside. They were made between the 2nd century BC and the 9th century AD. The construction of the 7th century Buddhist worship hall shown here can be compared with a church, having a nave, aisles, and apse; the stupa and seated Buddha figure on the form make up the focal point of the design.

4

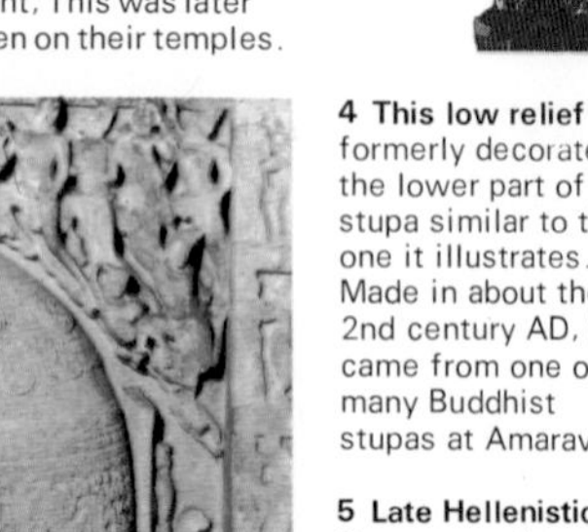

4 This low relief formerly decorated the lower part of a stupa similar to the one it illustrates. Made in about the 2nd century AD, it came from one of the many Buddhist stupas at Amaravati.

5

5 Late Hellenistic influence can be seen in the style of this 2nd-4th century AD image of a Bodhisattva (Buddha-to-be) from Gandhara. Many conventional motifs in later Buddhist art originated in the sculpture of this period.

6

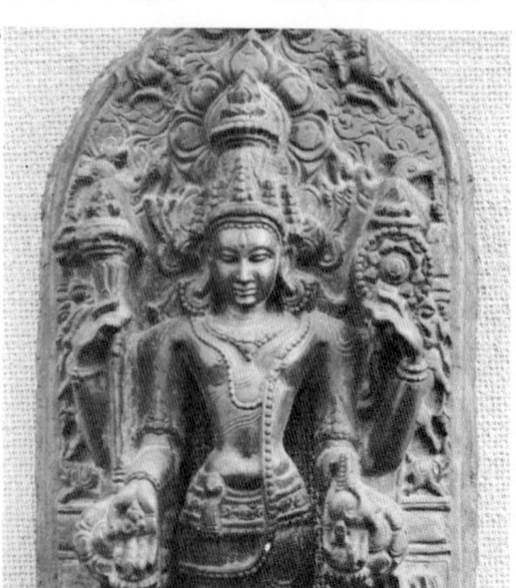
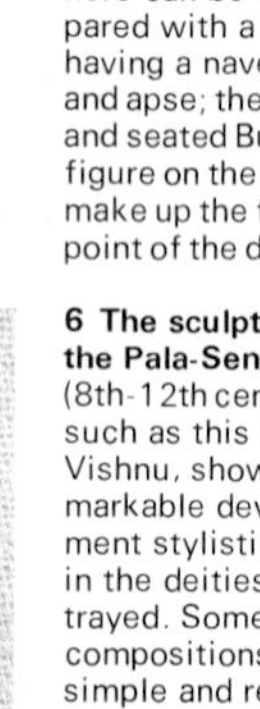
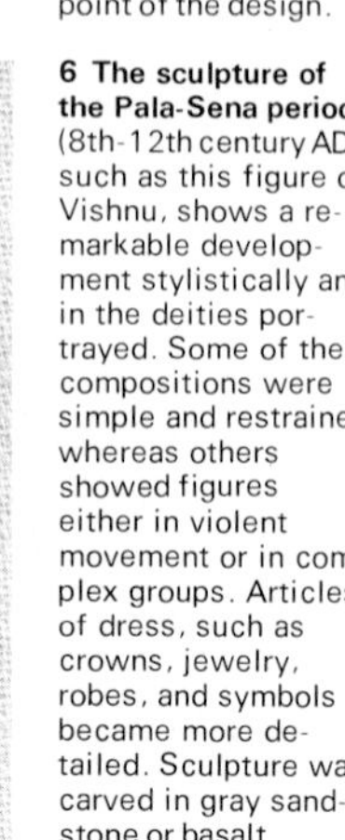

6 The sculpture of the Pala-Sena period (8th-12th century AD), such as this figure of Vishnu, shows a remarkable development stylistically and in the deities portrayed. Some of the compositions were simple and restrained whereas others showed figures either in violent movement or in complex groups. Articles of dress, such as crowns, jewelry, robes, and symbols became more detailed. Sculpture was carved in gray sandstone or basalt.

Buddhism, and Jainism. Some were unadorned but others were decorated with sculpture and painting.

Some impressive freestanding rock-cut temples were also built both in the western and southeastern Deccan. The shore temples at Mahabalipuram are the finest [10]. At the sites shared by more than one religion (as at Ellora) there is no difference in the artistic style adopted, which tends to be regional rather than sectarian.

The theory and practice of sculpture and architecture were recorded in texts *(silpa sastras)* that probably had wide distribution. In spite of this, Indian art is remarkable for the variety and sensitivity of its treatment of religious subjects. This is particularly noticeable if its bronze sculpture is compared with the stone sculpture of Orissa belonging to the eleventh and twelfth centuries [7]. In contrast, an elaborate and agitated style grew up in Mysore during the Hoyshala dynasty (late twelfth to fourteenth centuries), which is attractive in its unrestrained exuberance [9] and treatment of subject matter.

A little earlier, in Bengal and Bihar prior to the Muslim invasions, the art of the Pala-Sena period (eighth to twelfth centuries) flourished under generous royal patronage and religious fervor. Bronze and stone sculptures were produced in great variety and quantity [6]. It was at that period that many of the forms of Indian deities, later accepted as conventional, were created.

Surviving examples of Indian painting

Painting also achieved high standards of skill, as the wall paintings of the cave temples of the western Deccan (such as those at Ajanta) bear evidence. They suggest a long period of development, and it is almost certain that there were other forms of painting that have now disappeared. Those on birch bark were especially susceptible to decay, although a few examples have survived. Others, including illuminated palm-leaf manuscripts [8], remain and exhibit a mastery over line and brilliant color that was to influence early Nepalese and Tibetan painting.

KEY

This fly-whisk bearer of polished sandstone comes from Didarganj (Bihar) and is of the 1st century AD. From its resemblance to figures at Sanchi and Bharut it is likely that this is a statue of a tree-spirit deity *(yakshi)*. The fly-whisk is a symbol of power and is the only visual indication that this figure is not an ordinary mortal. In sharp contrast to later sculpture, it shows figures that leave no doubt as to their status as deities. This image, although early, shows something of the significance with which female deities were eventually to be invested in Indian religion.

7

7 Orissa produced a characteristic local sculptural style, shared by all sects. It is illustrated by this 11th-century Jain figure of the mother-goddess Ambika that continues early traditions.

8 These palm-leaf illuminated manuscripts of the 12th century are some of the earliest examples of Indian painting other than wall painting. It is likely that there were earlier examples that have not survived, as these show evidence of mature development. Unlike later Indian miniatures, which developed from them, they did not necessarily illustrate the text but added to its sanctity as a religious object.

8

9 The Hindu art of Mysore in the 13th century is exemplified in this impressive sculpture. It originally formed part of an elaborate scheme decorating the outside of a temple. It is executed with characteristically meticulous treatment of details such as jewelry, costume, and ornamental motifs. It shows a form of the goddess Durga overcoming the buffalo-demon Mahisha. Like many Indian deities she has several arms—they are necessary to hold the attributes ascribed to deities, partly to symbolize their powers, partly to distinguish them from other deities. Durga holds the symbols of several gods who combined to defeat the demon.

9

10

10 Freestanding temples were also carved in India out of natural rock outcrops, such as the Kailasanatha at Ellora. In southeastern India in the 7th and 8th centuries, a series of temples and huge reliefs, such as this one showing the descent of the Ganges, were hewn from granite rocks near the seashore at Mahabalipuram. They show a masterly control of form and design, especially when carried out in such a difficult medium as granite.

China 1000 BC–AD 618

The Shang dynasty (*c.* 1600–*c.* 1030 BC), the first in the recorded history of China, was overthrown in about 1030 BC by a group of tribesmen from west China called the Chou. Their dynasty was to be China's longest, and its notable contribution to Chinese history was that it was witness to the birth and also the consequences of Confucian philosophy.

The Chou and the Ch'in dynasties

The Chou period (*c.* 1030–221 BC) saw many important developments. The realm was extended to the sea in the east, the Yangtze River in the south, and the borders of Szechwan in the southwest. As this expansion continued, semi-independent states emerged that were more connected by culture and religion than by authority. The delicate balance of power between the emperor's vassal states finally collapsed and the "Warring States" period began (475–221 BC).

During these periods of expansion and struggle, philosophical and moral thought flourished. Chief among the philosophers was Confucius (551–479 BC), whose teachings emphasized duties to the family and society rather than preoccupation with the dead. The influence of his thought signaled the decline of the old feudalism and began a long tradition of close association between philosophical thought and political practice in China.

This was also a period of great technological change. Iron superseded the use of bronze, especially in weaponry; irrigation improved harvests.

Gradually, the smaller and weaker states were absorbed by the militarily and economically stronger states, until the chief contenders were the Chou in the south and the Ch'in in the west. Eventually the Ch'in became supreme rulers, and China was in 221 BC for the first time unified under Shih Huang Ti (259–210 BC), known as the First Emperor. He abolished the political system of the Chou and returned to the old feudal system, dividing the country into 36 provinces over which he set officials directly responsible to himself. He conceived and strengthened the Great Wall [1], today stretching 1,500 miles (2,400km) from southern Kansu province to the coast east of Peking. The written language was simplified and unified over the whole country. Weights, measures, and coinage were standardized. Shih Huang Ti is remembered as a despotic but practical emperor who burned existing literature, exempting only works on agriculture, medicine, pharmacy, and divination. After the First Emperor's death, the structure soon collapsed under the feeble rule of the second emperor, who was murdered in 207, ending the Ch'in dynasty.

The Han dynasty: education and wealth

Out of the chaos that followed emerged a successful candidate for the throne, Liu Pang (247–195 BC), who founded the Han dynasty in 206 BC [2]. Initially the Han endeavored to rule with the Ch'in system. But after about a century the principle of hereditary local power was curtailed, and candidates for local government were selected by examinations [4]. In 124 BC an Imperial University was set up for the study of Confucian classics; its students were

CONNECTIONS

See also
968 China to 1000 BC
1042 China 618–1368
1044 Chinese art to 1368
1040 Confucius and Confucianism
1032 Early Oriental and Western science

1

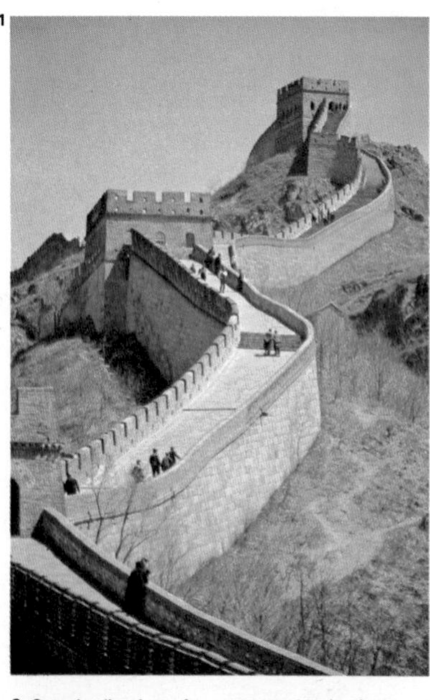

1 The Great Wall of China was commenced under the Chou dynasty in the fourth and third centuries BC. It was designed to protect the Chinese people from attacks by the nomadic tribes who occupied the steppe lands in the far north and west. Building went on under ensuing dynasties; various sections of the wall were connected until, during the Ming dynasty (1368–1644), it extended for 1,500 miles (2,400km).

2

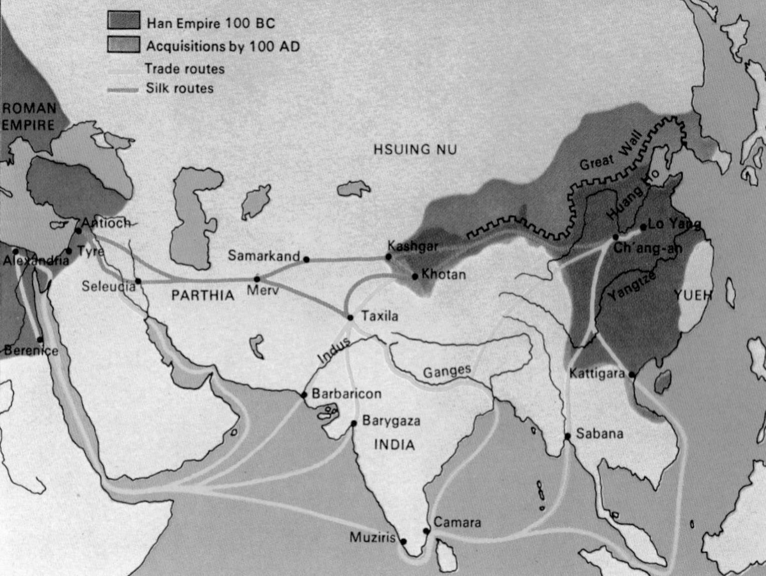
Han Empire 100 BC
Acquisitions by 100 AD
Trade routes
Silk routes
ROMAN EMPIRE
HSUING NU
Great Wall
Huang Ho
Lo Yang
Ch'ang-an
Yangtze
YUEH
Antioch
Tyre
Alexandria
Seleucia
PARTHIA
Merv
Samarkand
Kashgar
Khotan
Taxila
Indus
Ganges
Berenice
Barbaricon
Barygaza
INDIA
Kattigara
Sabana
Camara
Muziris

2 China expanded under Han rule, after unification by the Ch'in. The growing silk trade had to be made secure, but central Asia remained vulnerable to barbarian threats.

3 Standardization of weights and measures was first ordered by Shih Huang Ti, the First Emperor. It was one of a number of measures to consolidate his rule, including standardization of the language, instituting censuses, and the construction of a defensive road system. After his death taxation and the forced labor system led to peasant revolts and the eventual collapse of the dynasty.

3

4

4 A Han official in his carriage is drawn by slaves. His attendant follows in the rear. During the Han dynasty a large bureaucracy was established to implement the growing powers of the state. The officials, usually nobles, were the product of the Confucian training of the official class. The Confucian ethical code required that the official class should possess wisdom, integrity, righteousness, conscientiousness, loyalty, altruism, love, and humanity. Confucius insisted on the importance of education and training expecially for the official class: "By nature men are pretty much alike; it is learning and practice that set them apart."

5 A bronze axlecap dating from the mid-Chou period (7th century BC). The linchpin that held the wheel in place is decorated with a tiger's head. Chariots from which such axles came would probably be ceremonial, or for state use. Although chariots were also widely used in warfare, they were reduced to an auxiliary role as the raids by the mobile, northern horsemen increased.

5

trained for government and grew rapidly in number until by the end of the dynasty there were 30,000 of them. Provincial schools were also established from this time. Education and the growth of the civil service was greatly assisted by the introduction of paper made from rags or bark, and ink and brushes replaced sharp writing tools.

Under state patronage the arts revived, and the early wealth of the Han dynasty can be seen from their rich tombs [6]. Most of the attainments of this period reflect the needs of a growing state bureaucracy—engineers developed irrigation methods and water clocks, and sundials and seismographs were also invented [9].

Until then there had been little contact between China and the outside world, but under Han rule the empire was extended. Caravan routes were opened up, including the Old Silk Road, which followed a chain of oases skirting the foothills of the Tarim basin. China sent ambassadors abroad along with its ever-popular silk, and products were exchanged as far afield as the outposts of the Greek world. Ideas traveled with the trade, most notably Buddhism [10] which was introduced from India under the Han and by the seventh century had become a major force in China.

Under the Ch'in and the Han, China for the first time became a great state. But the mandarins, so carefully picked by scholarly examinations, became corrupt and sided with the great landlords in their oppression of the peasants. The Han dynasty ended in widespread revolt in AD 220.

Disintegration of the empire

During the next three and a half centuries there was a succession of short-lived ruling houses. It was not until AD 581 that the country was at least reunited under the Sui dynasty. Prosperity increased, taxes were reduced, irrigation improved, and public lands were distributed so that each family had some land of its own. But the extravagant second emperor increased taxation, demanding ten years' tax in advance. In AD 618 he was assassinated by one of his officers, LiShih-min, the second T'ang emperor as T'ai Tsung.

KEY

A rubbing from a Han stone relief shows a mounted barbarian archer at full gallop. The reins are looped on the horse's neck, leaving the archer's hands free to operate the bow and arrow. Firing from the saddle he had great speed and mobility. Such raiders were a constant threat to the Han.

6

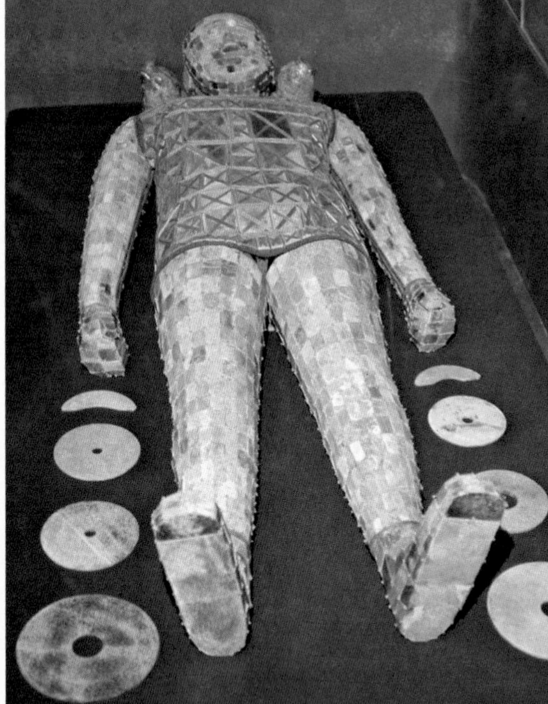

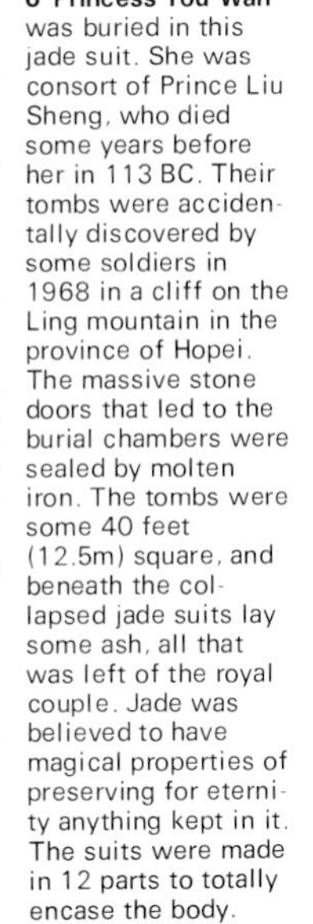

6 Princess Tou Wan was buried in this jade suit. She was consort of Prince Liu Sheng, who died some years before her in 113 BC. Their tombs were accidentally discovered by some soldiers in 1968 in a cliff on the Ling mountain in the province of Hopei. The massive stone doors that led to the burial chambers were sealed by molten iron. The tombs were some 40 feet (12.5m) square, and beneath the collapsed jade suits lay some ash, all that was left of the royal couple. Jade was believed to have magical properties of preserving for eternity anything kept in it. The suits were made in 12 parts to totally encase the body.

7

7 A celestial horse of the Han dynasty was excavated in 1969 from a tomb at Wu-wei in Kansu province. Flying horses were a recurrent motif in art of the Han dynasty.

8

8 The bridge at An-chi, built in AD 610, shows the remarkable sophistication of Chinese engineering, long predating Western achievements. The building of canals and roads, needed for the transport of grain and the maintenance of central control, was fostered under Sui rule. The Grand Canal, built by forced labor, linked the Huang and Yangtze rivers and connected the political centers of the north with the economically important Yangtze region.

9

9 The earliest known Chinese seismograph depicts eight dragons, each holding a ball in its mouth. Around the base of the vessel sit eight toads with open mouths. An earthquake at any point of the compass causes the dragon facing that direction to drop the ball it is holding into the mouth of the toad below, thus indicating the direction of the tremor. This instrument was invented during the Han period by Chang Heng, a famous astronomer, mathematician, and writer.

10

10 The Buddhist school of sculptors produced this white marble stele in the early part of the fifth century AD. It shows the Buddha Sakyamuni in a posture denoting him as the bestower of fearlessness. The Buddha is seated under some sal trees surrounded by his disciples and Bodhisattvas, including Ananda, his favorite disciple, and Mahakasyapa, who became leader after his death. Above the Buddha Sakyamuni float goddesses holding garlands of flowers.

Confucius and Confucianism

Thousands of oracle bones [1] surviving from the Shang dynasty (*c.* 1600–*c.* 1030 BC) give archeologists clues to the form of religion in ancient China. From texts incised on these bones, a picture emerges of a world regulated by spirits of *ti* ("deceased kings,") ancestors, nature gods, and guardian spirits. The Shang dynasty was overthrown by the Chou (*c.* 1030–221 BC), who believed that their dynasty had a mandate from heaven to rule the land. *T'ien* ("heaven") or *Shang Ti* ("supreme ancestor") was believed to govern the universe, fix the seasons, give fertility to humans and animals, and order the cycle of death and renewal.

The life of Confucius

Documents have survived from the Chou period, which are quoted, and may even have been edited, by Confucius. They form part of the ancient tradition, which includes the complementary forces of yin and yang [Key] and reverence toward heaven and ancestors [5], that Confucius inherited. Elements of Chou religion were transmitted by later Confucian teachers. Confucius is the latinized form of K'ung Fu-tzu, or Master K'ung, who was born in the city-state of Lu in northern China in 551 BC and died in 479 BC. Confucius came from an aristocratic family but grew up in comparative poverty and, being disappointed in a political career, found his true work in training young men for public service [2].

Confucius founded his own private school, one of the first in China, and taught what he considered to be the best of ancient wisdom. He discussed the arts of life in a city state, the study of old documents, and the Book of Poetry, which included ritual hymns of early Chou rulers. But while claiming to preserve or restore earlier tradition, Confucius interpreted the documents in his own way and formulated an ethical and moral system that influenced China thereafter. His ideals for a government based on the well-being of all its citizens made little appeal to the rulers of his day, but he trained pupils who eventually came to influence society.

When he was about 50, Confucius was given office in the state council—but he was dissatisfied and later traveled. He returned home a disappointed man and spent his last years in teaching and study.

The literature and teachings of Confucius

Confucius is traditionally credited with authorship, or at least editorship, of the Wu Ching (Five Classics"): of the Shih Ching (Book of Poetry), the Su Ching (Book of History), the I Ching (Book of Changes), the Ch'un Ch'iu (Spring and Autumn Annals), and the Li Chi (Book of Rites). Few of these writings can be safely attributed to him, however. His true teachings are contained in the Analects, a small book of his sayings recorded by his pupils. Modern specialists consider that some of these chapters are not authentic, but they are traditionally held to be the words of the Master. The Analects teach the way of *jen* ("goodness"), which includes courtesy, loyalty, and unselfishness. Rulers should seek it, but it is almost a saintly quality. The ideal prince should rule by goodness and govern his conduct by *li* ("ritual"). This ritual is not confined to religious worship but is con-

CONNECTIONS

1038 China 1000 BC–AD 618
860 Philosophy and ethics
1042 China 618–1368
988 Buddha and Buddhism
1026 Christ and the Apostles
1058 Mohammed and Islam

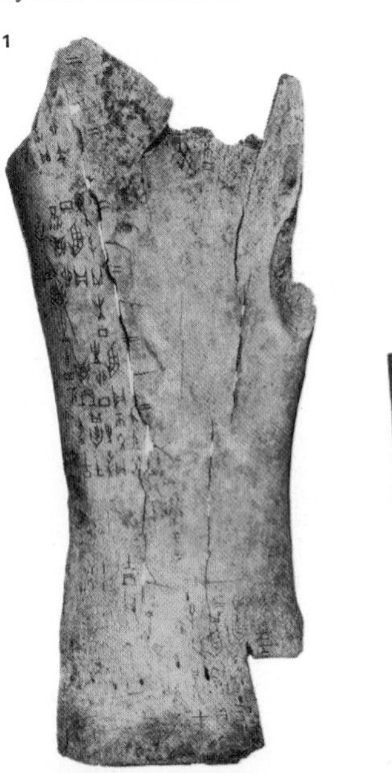

1 Oracle bones, from pre-Confucian China, were inscribed with questions about the future. The bones were heated, and the cracks were "read."

2 This painting on silk from the Ming dynasty (AD 1368–1644) shows Confucius as the ideal teacher, the "uncrowned king." During his life he was a tutor to the sons of aristocrats and wandered from state to state, hoping to find some rulers who would put his teachings into practice. But he met only with indifference and on occasion hostility. Indeed, Confucius was unrecognized in his own lifetime as a moral teacher except by his small band of disciples.

3 The tomb of Confucius can still be seen at Chufu, in the province of Shantung. In front of the tomb stands a stone tablet and altar. The tablet bears the simple inscription: "Ancient Most Holy Teacher."

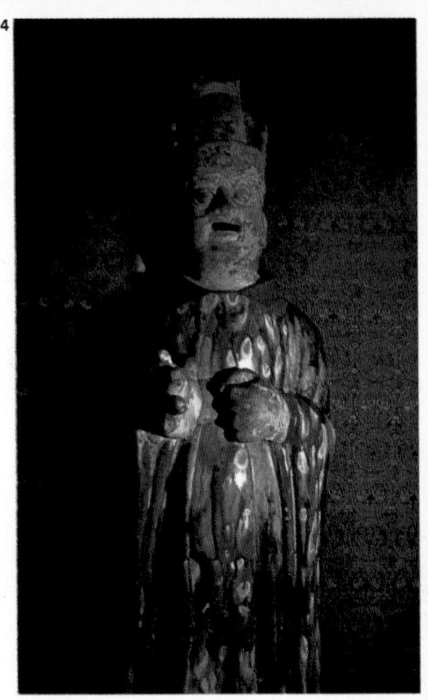

4 Court officials in China, such as this mandarin, even before the beginning of the Christian era were appointed to specialize in the study of the Confucian classics. Eventually the study of these works became universal among the educated classes, and examinations in them had to be passed before service to the state could be undertaken. Eventually a large Confucian-trained bureaucracy developed.

cerned with dress, good manners, and personal morality. Confucius described this as the Way of the True Gentleman, and it is his ideal. He also advocated *hsiao* ("filial piety") and proposed a hierarchy of relationships: ruler and subject, father and son, older and younger brother, husband and wife, and friend and friend. Confucius believed in the Supreme Being, but held that service to God is meaningless if service to man is neglected.

Confucius and his contemporary Lao Tze (*c*.604–531 BC) were teachers rather than founders of religions, but their supposed writings became the sacred scriptures of Confucianism and Taoism respectively, and part of the whole culture of China [8]. The teaching of Confucius was continued and extended a century later by Mencius (372–289 BC) and Hsun Tzu (*c*.298–212 BC). Within a few centuries Confucian teachings became cherished as the orthodox doctrines of the state and the guiding lines of the official classes [4]. Commentaries were written on the classics, careful scholarship expounded Confucian ideas, and examinations for public service were held on the Confucian classics until the beginning of the twentieth century.

The role of Confucius in history

Confucius was neither a god nor a prophet, and it is often asserted that Confucianism is not a religion, but this statement should be qualified. Before the Christian era, emperors offered sacrifice at the tomb of Confucius [3]—a practice that continued for centuries. Yet Confucius was not a god with images but an ancestor or great sage, revered as the Teacher of Ten Thousand Generations. Nevertheless, the Chinese tradition of ancestor veneration and Confucius' own emphasis on filial piety led to ancestral ceremonies being associated with Confucianism. The role of the emperor, and his performance of rituals on behalf of the people [6], added to the complexities.

In modern times Confucius has been alternately attacked as a feudal aristocrat and revered as the greatest teacher of ancient China. The dead are still venerated and temples [7] and graves are preserved.

KEY

P'an Ku, a mythological figure, here holds the symbols of yin and yang, which appear in Confucianism.

5

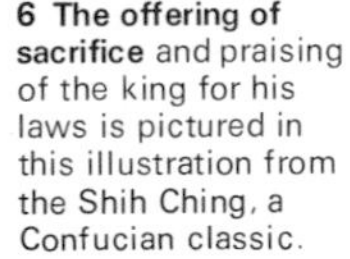

5 Bronze sacrificial vessels were used in sacrifices and ceremonies from ancient times. These vessels, grouped on or around the altar, bore stylized designs and masks. Their inscriptions describe royal or religious ceremonies, traditions that influenced Confucian thought.

6

6 The offering of sacrifice and praising of the king for his laws is pictured in this illustration from the Shih Ching, a Confucian classic.

7 The Temple of Heaven in Peking, with its three roofs, gold-capped shrine, and blue tiles, is one of the finest buildings in China. Here the emperor himself acted as high priest for the people.

8

8 This fanciful picture illustrates the meeting of three ways of thought in ancient China. Confucius, left, as a scholar, may never have met Lao Tze, shown, right, as an old man; and the Buddha, center as a monk, may never have been to China. But Confucian morality and ceremony, Taoist nature mysticism, and Buddhist ascetism and devotion all played formative parts in the traditional structure of Chinese religion, art, and social life.

China 618–1368

Emperor Li Yüan, who founded the T'ang dynasty (618–907), was followed by his son, Emperor T'ai Tsung (reigned 627–49), under whose rule China became the world's most powerful and largest empire. The security China enjoyed in this position encouraged it to trade with the outside world and brought in a rich bounty of goods. The trade also carried scientific ideas westward beyond China [8].

Art, commerce, and religion

Chinese arts flourished during the T'ang dynasty, [3, 4] which was a classical age, particularly for poetry; it produced such poets as Wang Wei, Li Po, and Tu Fu. The earliest known printing also commenced, and paper money was first issued [1]. Moneylenders thrived in the numerous markets, and the growth of commerce generated wealth for the merchants, who brought wares from Japan, Central Asia, Arabia, Turkey, and the Mediterranean.

T'ai Tsung was as tolerant of the religions that the foreigners introduced as he was of the merchants themselves. Although a Taoist by inclination, he supported Confucianism for reasons of state and treated Buddhists with great respect.

Wu Tse-t'ien—an efficient empress

The peace and prosperity that T'ai Tsung brought to the empire was continued by his former concubine, Wu Tse-t'ien, who usurped the throne in 683 and ruled China with ruthless ability until she was forced to abdicate in 705 at the age of 82. She was a profound believer in Buddhism and was the first and only female "Son of Heaven." The progress and stability of the country resulted in part from the selection of civil service officials [2] by means of examinations held under well controlled procedures. The empress also permitted women to sit the state examination, and some were selected for government posts.

The main function of the government was the collection of revenue and the promotion of agriculture. For this purpose the country was divided into districts controlled by magistrates. The people were divided into three groups mutually responsible for each other's conduct and for tax payments—encouraging a sense of collective responsibility that is still a feature of China today.

T'ang influence spread far afield, to such an extent that the Japanese capital of Nara was modeled on Ch'ang-An. In the west it clashed with Islam. Muslim armies had advanced, bringing their faith as far as Samarkand and Bokhara. Eventually they conquered central Asia, severing the overland route between China and the West. Trading continued by sea, but the power of China began to wane, and as it weakened the Chinese became less tolerant of foreigners and their religions. In 845 all foreign religions were proscribed and a ban was placed on Buddhists and their rich but unproductive monasteries [9]. Disastrous revolts and invasions decimated the population, and in 907 the T'ang dynasty ended.

Five Dynasties and the Mongols

The T'ang dynasty was followed by a period called the Five Dynasties, between 907 and 960, when, as a Chinese poet said, "States

CONNECTIONS

See also
1206 China from 1368 to c.1800
1112 Asian empires of th Mongols
1044 Chinese art to 1368
1038 China 1000 BC–AD 618
1032 Early Oriental and Western science
1040 Confucius and Confucianism
1440 Asian and medieval science

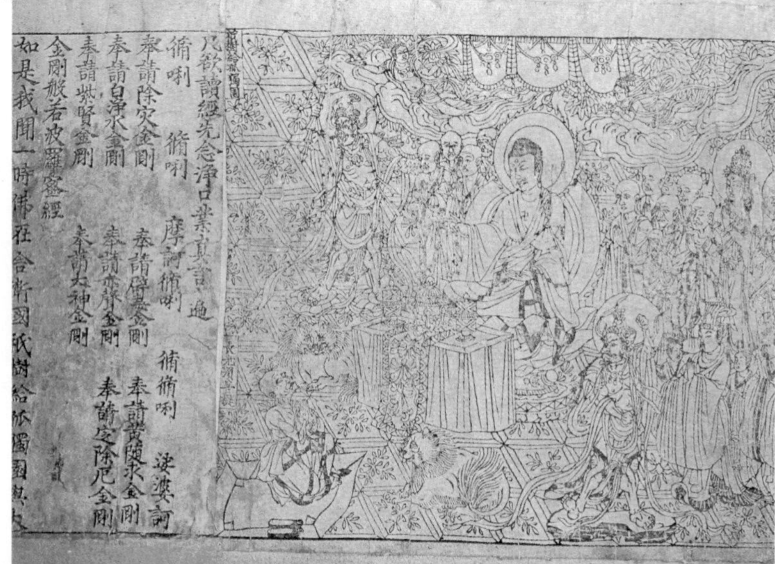

1 **The Diamond Sutra,** the world's oldest printed book, dates from AD 868, nearly six centuries before the first printing in Europe. With gunpowder and the magnetic compass, printing was one of the revolutionary inventions developed by China long before the West. The consequent growth in literacy meant that increasingly the civil service (for which, in theory, recruiting had always been democratic) was drawn from a wider circle of families. Printing facilitated the great expansion of the economy that characterized the Sung dynasty by making possible the introduction of paper money and credit notes into the economic system.

2 **This T'ang mandarin** was one of the highly educated, privileged, and wealthy elite who made up the mandarinate, or civil service. The continuity and resilience of the large state bureaucracy from earliest times was one of the more remarkable features of Chinese history. Its officials, selected by public examination, collected taxes, supervised state projects and the nationalized salt and iron industry (under state control since the Han dynasty), and administered local areas. They also supervised the merchant communities and foreign trade, a despised business largely in the hands of immigrants, but controlled by the state.

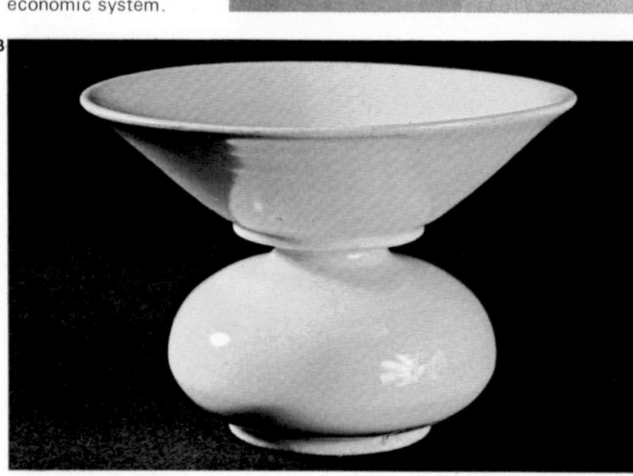

3 **A fine example of the elegant work** that was produced in the classical period of Chinese civilization is this white T'ang porcelain spitoon of the late 9th century. It comes from Hsing-chou in the modern province of Hopei and exemplifies the best of the high-fired ceramic ware produced there. Under the T'ang, Ch'ang-An (present-day Hsi-an) was a thriving capital, one of the cultural centers of the East. Its wealth came partly from the prosperous western trade—Chinese goods were much in demand along the Silk Route. The T'ang is often seen as the artistic complement to the great scientific and technological achievements of the preceding Sui dynasty: the T'ang literary achievement remains unsurpassed.

4 **This silver wine flask** of the T'ang dynasty is a typical piece of Chinese metalwork displaying strong foreign influence. Under this dynasty the capital, Ch'ang-An, was probably the most cosmopolitan city in the world, and as the empire expanded merchandise arrived from all quarters. The flask is modeled on a type of leather water bottle widely used by traveling merchants.

5 **Gunpowder was discovered by Taoist** alchemists in about the 9th century but was not at first used for war. By AD 1000 simple bombs, grenades, and rockets were being made, but it was the Mongols who first exploited gunpowder for military ends. They probably used a type of cannon in their campaigns against the Sung troops and certainly employed Chinese engineers. The Mongols captured the Sung fleet, which was armed with trebuchets for firing bombs. Although gunpowder was a Chinese invention, it did not have the revolutionary effects on Chinese society that it had in Europe. Illustrated is a Chinese rocket developed in the Sung dynasty.

rose and fell as candles gutter in the wind." In 960 the Sung dynasty was founded by Chao Kuang-Yin. The war-weary country was glad to accept established rule and welcomed the new emperor, who took the title Sung T'ai Tsu (from which the dynasty took its name). China was still threatened from the north, and in 1044 an indemnified peace treaty was concluded with the Hsia, a former tributary kingdom. Gunpowder, which had been discovered during the T'ang period, was now used to produce the first military rockets in history [5]. The loss of the northern part of the country was partly offset by sea trade, spurred by the Chinese discovery of the compass. Large ocean-going junks [6] were able to take cargoes of tea, silk, and porcelain, and works of art to the East Indies, Africa, and India. They returned with spices, gems, timber, and ivory. Another useful invention was the abacus [Key], the first calculating machine.

The Sung dynasty ended in much the same way as the previous empires had. Corruption at court and discontent among the people permitted the ascendancy of the Mongols, the nomad empire of the north. The Mongol invasion started in the thirteenth century when the great general Genghis Khan (1167–1227) entered northern China [7]. By 1223 he had conquered most of the country north of the Huang Ho and defeated the Hsia, killing about 90 percent of the population [10]. It was not until 1264, however, that his grandson Kublai Khan (1215–94) was able to move his capital from Mongolia to Peking, and in 1279 he finally defeated the southern Sung, former allies.

Mongol rule or, as it was officially known, the Yüan dynasty (*c.* 1264–1368), was successful in uniting the Chinese and Mongol empires, and Mongol power reached its peak under Kublai Khan. But the invaders were eventually overcome. Kublai Khan's successors did not have his ability, and the oppression of the Chinese by foreign officials led to the formation of secret societies and revolts. In 1356 Nanking fell to a peasant movement led by a monk, Chu Yüan Chang, who finally became the first emperor of a new and purely Chinese dynasty, the Ming, in 1368.

KEY

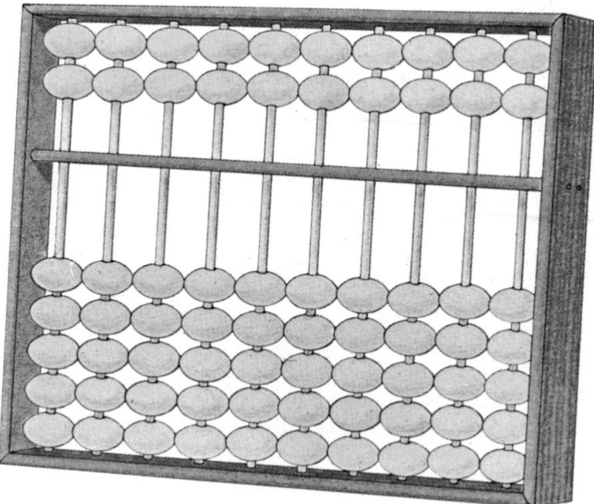

The abacus, a simple counting device introduced during the Sung dynasty, is still widely used. Under the T'ang and Sung the economy underwent a rapid expansion, similar to the one that occurred in 17th-century Europe, but despite this, Chinese society remained essentially feudal.

6

6 Maritime commerce expanded greatly during the Sung dynasty. Seagoing junks, similar to the porcelain model shown, carried cargoes of silk and porcelain to the East Indies, India, and the east coast of Africa. Undoubtedly, improvements in navigation (which was greatly aided by the invention of the floating compass in AD 1021) contributed to these ambitious trading expeditions.

7

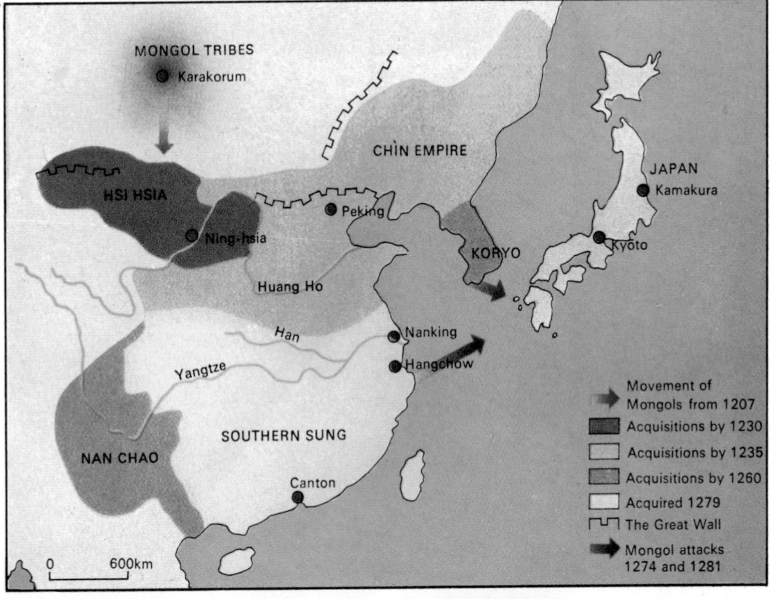

MONGOL TRIBES
Karakorum
CHIN EMPIRE
HSI HSIA
Ning-hsia
Peking
JAPAN
Kamakura
Kyoto
KORYO
Huang Ho
Han
Nanking
Hangchow
Yangtze
SOUTHERN SUNG
NAN CHAO
Canton
0 600km
Movement of Mongols from 1207
Acquisitions by 1230
Acquisitions by 1235
Acquisitions by 1260
Acquired 1279
The Great Wall
Mongol attacks 1274 and 1281

7 The Mongol conquest of China was finally completed in 1279. The Sung had previously allied with the Mongols against the Chin in the north, but were eventually encircled by Mongol conquests.

8

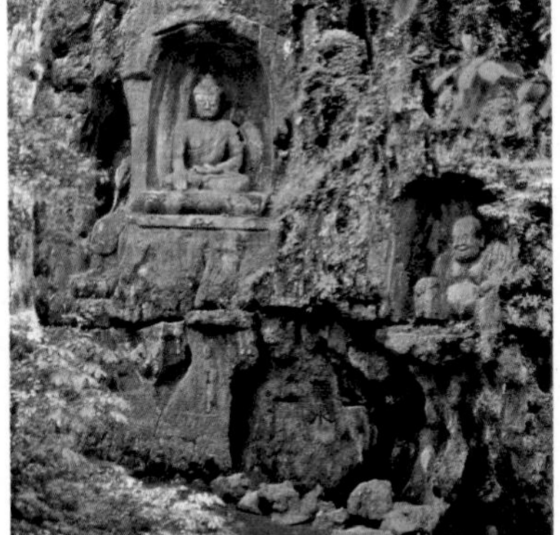

8 This medical drawing from a Persian textbook of the 14th century is in fact of Chinese origin and shows the widespread influence of Chinese science.

9

9 Buddhist temples carved from rock caves were features of the Yun-kang and Lung-men periods (in the 5th and 6th centuries AD). The last of them (like the Fen-lai-feng cave temple near Hangchow, of which a detail is shown) were carved in the late 13th century (in the Yüan dynasty). Buddhism in China reached its peak in the middle of the T'ang dynasty, but thereafter the faith was gradually absorbed into traditional Chinese customs and beliefs.

10

10 Genghis Khan's army capturing a Chinese town is recorded in this painting. The Mongols came to rule almost all of eastern Asia as part of an empire stretching across Asia to Hungary and the Black Sea. After the conquest of the Sung in the south, China was for the first time ruled by foreign invaders. The Chinese-style Yüan dynasty ruled China for just over 100 years. Under the Mongols trade routes across Asia were safeguarded, and a variety of religions, including Christianity, were permitted. Kublai Khan was the first Yüan emperor; after his death Mongol rule was short-lived, ending in a series of rebellions and finally expulsion by the Chinese.

Chinese art to 1368

Neolithic Chinese society (*c.*7000–*c.*1600 BC) was centered around the Yellow River and organized in village communities. The potters made coil pots, which they burnished and painted with black, white, and red slip (a thin liquid clay) in striking animal, flower, and abstract spiral designs. The shapes of later Neolithic pots were elegant and complicated; they appear to be related to the bronze vessels of the first historic dynasty (Shang *c.*1600–*c.*1030 BC).

Early art forms

The ritual vessels of the Shang, a slave society ruled by a god-king, were magnificently designed and cast. The shapes varied and the rich decoration was based on animal motifs [1]. As society changed and the rituals lost their significance, bronzes became more decorative, richer in appearance, and often gilded. Decoration included floral motifs and was achieved by inlay and inserts of gold, silver, and semiprecious stones.

Pottery had always been of great importance to the Chinese, and through the centuries potters were developing the stoneware clay indigenous to eastern China, perfecting the throwing of the clay, glazing, and firing to a high temperature. Lacquer painting was an early invention that also gradually evolved, particularly in the south, into an art form. With the invention of the brush and paper, written calligraphy as opposed to the incised character became a major art from which painting evolved, at first for ritual purposes. By the second century BC, however, there is evidence of painting as a medium of artistic expression.

The great Ch'in (221–206 BC) and Han (206 BC–AD 220) dynasties saw the unification of a country of differing cultures. The newly evolved art of painting with color on cloth or paper was used to express the many myths and legends of this rich heritage [3]. Some of the most lively painting came from the southern area, the old kingdom of Ch'u (present-day Hunan, Anhui area) and from the west in present-day Szechwan, where stamped brick and relief carvings were also used to portray the mixture of everyday life and mythological scenes.

Buddhism was introduced to China during the first century AD but did not appear in the arts until the fourth century. Between that time and the ninth century great temples were built or cut from rock, decorated by rock carvings or massive wall paintings and hangings [4], and furnished with images of gilt-bronze or stone. Unfortunately, periods of anti-Buddhist destruction have obliterated much of this huge output, with only the great rock temples of north China remaining.

The art of the T'ang dynasty (618–907)

The T'ang dynasty is famous as one of the finest artistic periods in China. It was a time of cosmopolitan vitality and metropolitan splendor that encouraged all the minor arts; a taste for extravagance led workmen to produce colorful work ranging from jewelry to bronze mirrors inlaid with carnelian and gold, beautiful silks, and exotic inlaid musical instruments. Great religious paintings are recorded although they have not been preserved. The two major artists were Wu Tao-tzu (mid-eighth century), a majestic

CONNECTIONS

See also
1208 Chinese art 1368 to the 20th century
1038 China 1000 BC-AD 618
1042 China 618–1368
968 China to 1000 BC

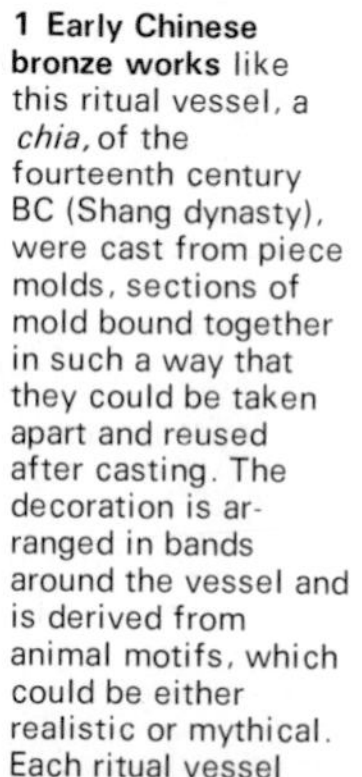

1 Early Chinese bronze works like this ritual vessel, a *chia,* of the fourteenth century BC (Shang dynasty), were cast from piece molds, sections of mold bound together in such a way that they could be taken apart and reused after casting. The decoration is arranged in bands around the vessel and is derived from animal motifs, which could be either realistic or mythical. Each ritual vessel had its function.

1

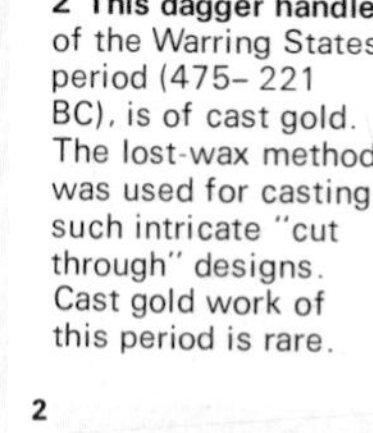

2 This dagger handle, of the Warring States period (475–221 BC), is of cast gold. The lost-wax method was used for casting such intricate "cut through" designs. Cast gold work of this period is rare.

2

3 A painted banner from a tomb of the early Han dynasty depicts both upper and lower world mythology. In the center is a portrait of the occupant, who was buried at Ma Wang Tui.

3

4

4 A meditating Buddha in Paradise is portrayed on this painted hanging, which displays the richness of T'ang painting. The influence of Buddhism in China reached its peak under the T'ang; the textiles, silver, and pottery that were produced mark this as a classical period in Chinese art. The hanging comes from Tun-Auang, a large Buddhist monastic center in northwest China where hundreds of cave temples were decorated with wall paintings.

5

5 A winged lion of the Sung dynasty (960–1279), inlaid with silver and gold, was executed in the style of the late Chou dynasty (*c.* 1030–221 BC). It typifies one aspect of Sung taste. The decoration is similar to that of the Chou but on a larger scale. In contrast to the preceding T'ang dynasty, when external influences such as Buddhism affected much of Chinese civilization, the Sung was a period of self-conscious reassertion of traditional values.

figure painter who used flowing brush line expressing volume and vitality, and his contemporary, Wang Wei (699–759), a poetic landscape painter and the originator of ink painting of hand scrolls in which the tonality of ink expressed depth and atmosphere.

A tradition of landscape painting

It was landscape painting that was developed by major painters through the succeeding four centuries [Key]. The Classical period of the tenth and eleventh centuries saw the painting of monumental mountain hanging scrolls, in which man is shown as a tiny inhabitant of a grand overpowering landscape. This concept gradually gave way to a study of the beauties of the smaller details—a single bird, a flower, or an incident on the banks of a river—in which the painter became interested in style and the niceties of surface composition.

The scholarly taste of this period was expressed in all the crafts—the stoneware tradition of the celadons of Chekiang [7] and the court wares of Kai-feng, jade carving, gilt-bronze [5], and ceramics. At the same time, however, particularly in the north, a robust taste for flamboyant decoration was displayed in the wares of Tzu Chou.

The great flowering of decoration on ceramics with the introduction of cobalt underglaze painting techniques and the painting of lacquer in gold and red to produce rich boxes and small furniture seems to mark a sharp change of taste but perhaps is more an underlining of the added riches and complementary character of the north and south of this huge country. During the early and mid-fourteenth century there was another great flowering of painting. Declining to serve the foreign Mongol court in the traditional role of bureaucrat, gentlemen scholars gave their time to painting comparable with the activity and gravity of the production of the tenth and eleventh centuries. The Four Great Masters, Ni Tsan (1301–74), Wang Mêng (*d.*1385), Wu Chên (1280–*c.*1354), and Huang Kung-wang (1269–1354) [9], painted in traditional but entirely personal styles to lead the way for the next three centuries in the highly honored tradition of landscape painting.

KEY

"Travelers among Streams and Mountains" is a hanging scroll of the early eleventh century by Fan K'uan. Painted in ink and slight color on silk, it is one of the early great masterpieces of landscape and shows the Classical style of construction. The foreground, in which tiny figures wend their way, is a little remote from the viewer. The horizon beyond them is defined by a cloud, a device used to express the space between the midground and the towering mountain up which the eye travels to arrive at a third and fourth eye level. The painting is unselfconscious and has great dignity and serenity.

6

6 This hand scroll of the thirteenth century was done in ink on paper by an anonymous artist. It depicts the preparations for the Spring Festival, when families gather to visit the graves of ancestors. It is a genre scene of great detail, the style being complementary to the decorative romantic work of the same period.

7

7 Fine quality gray stoneware with a thick blue-green glaze was produced by the kilns of the upper Tung River valley. It was known in Europe as celadon ware. This mallet-shaped vase is of Lung Ch'uan celadon ware from west Chekiang (late twelfth or early thirteenth century). Typically, it is simple in shape and decoration and depends for its quality on the exceptional texture of the glaze. Some of the world's most elegant ceramics were produced at that time, and this represents one of the classic wares of China, appealing to the refined Southern Sung taste.

8

8 Liang K'ai was a famous Ch'an (Zen) Buddhist priest-painter of the mid-thirteenth century. This hanging scroll of a walking priest is typical of his style. He used his ink and brush with the bravura of the academic Southern Sung masters but added to this the Ch'an directness. The priest's personality is expressed simply.

9

9 One of the most revered paintings in China is "Fu Ch'un Mountains" by Huang Kung-wang. This ink on paper scroll was painted over the space of about three years, when the artist, one of the Four Great Masters, was an old man. It typifies the character of the scholar-artist with its direct simplicity of technique, which is based on the old masters, and the evocation of a peaceful mountain landscape.

Japan 200 BC–AD 1185

By the first century AD successive waves of settlers from the Asian mainland, coming mostly through Korea, had brought three crucial skills to Japan. The casting of iron and bronze produced more effective tools and weapons. The potter's wheel speeded the production of earthenware. But more important than these was knowledge of irrigation, which permitted rice farming, thereby replacing hunting and fishing with settled agriculture. The resulting Yayoi culture was based on farming villages [2], which had little large-scale political organization.

Unification of Japan

In the third century AD a Chinese chronicle *Wei Chih* described Japan as a country of more than "100 communities" that had been unified by Queen Pimiko. One family claimed descent from the Sun Goddess, and emerged as the political and religious head of a loose confederation of powerful clans.

By the sixth century this embryonic Yamato imperial house [Key] had organized Japanese intervention in Korean civil conflicts. This brought contact with Chinese ideas and skills that swept down the Korean peninsula, leading to a second and more radical transformation of Japanese politics and society.

Buddhism [3], Confucianism, medicine, astronomy, Chinese-style architecture, and the Chinese script all entered Japan in the sixth and seventh centuries [1]. Scholars traveled to China [5], and soon Japan's central rulers sought to model their state upon the bureaucracy of China's T'ang Empire. In 592, Shotoku Taishi [4] became regent and began a program of spreading Buddhism and widening the power of the Yamato clan. The court gave generous support to temples and monasteries and encouraged priests and students to study in the Chinese capital.

In 646, measures known as the Taika Reforms included imperial control of rice land, systematic taxation, and a nationwide network of imperial officials. At the center of the new state was to be a Chinese-style capital with palaces, temples, and broad, straight avenues linking public buildings. Powerful provincial families remained remarkably independent. Yet the legal codes of 702 were detailed and far-reaching, and Heijo (Nara) contained impressive structures that still survive. Pioneering land surveys influenced the pattern of holdings for centuries.

At the close of the eighth century the political influence of Buddhism had become so great that one priest, Dokyo, attempted to capture the imperial throne. Partly in response to this acute danger the court abandoned Nara and in 794 established a new capital at Heian Kyo (Kyoto).

Rise of Fujiwara

After 50 years of stable administration, events at court produced new threats to imperial authority. The Fujiwara family had been loyal state servants throughout earlier centuries, but now they used intermarriage and masterly intrigue to dominate palace appointments. In 857, Fujiwara Yoshifusa became grand minister. Soon after, his grandson was made child-emperor with himself as regent. Later Fujiwara remained regents after young emperors reached

CONNECTIONS

See also

1038 China 1000 BC–AD 618

1042 China 618–1368

1210 Japan 1185–1868

1

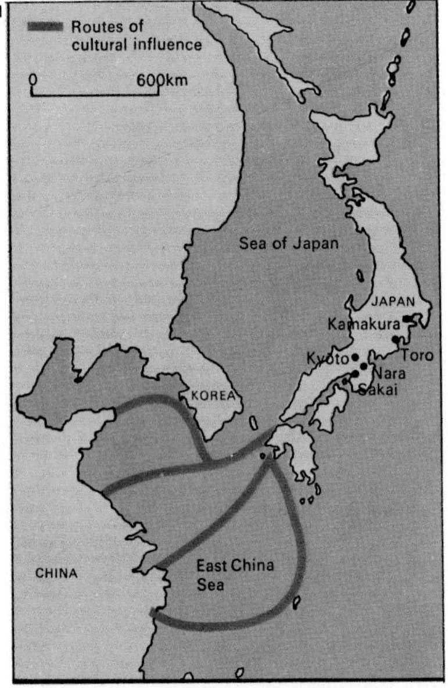

Routes of cultural influence
0
600km
Sea of Japan
JAPAN
Kamakura
Kyoto
Toro
Nara
Sakai
KOREA
CHINA
East China Sea

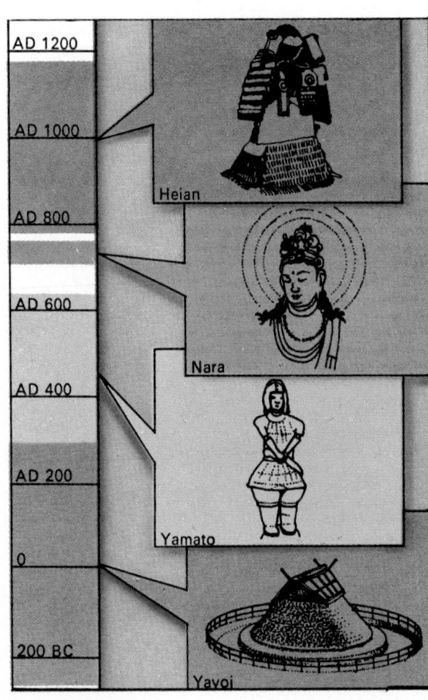

AD 1200
AD 1000
Heian
AD 800
AD 600
Nara
AD 400
AD 200
Yamato
0
200 BC
Yayoi

1 Routes by which Chinese culture and Buddhism entered Japan were well established by the 9th and 10th centuries. Contacts dated from *c.* AD 400 when the king of Paekche, a Korean kingdom, sent scholars to Japan with Confucian writings. Koreans brought Buddhist writings and sculptures in the 6th century. Yayoi, Yamato, Nara, and Heian periods each mark a cultural epoch.

2 A house of the Yayoi period (250 BC–AD 300) was reconstructed at Toro in the suburbs of Shizuoka where the foundations for 11 houses and granaries exist, as do ancient irrigation channels.

3 A mural painting of a Buddhist diety in the Kondo of Horyuji temple, Nara, is in the style of contemporary T'ang painting of the 7th or 8th century and reveals the Indian origins of T'ang and Korean Buddhism. Only fragments of these murals remain, and, unfortunately, in China no similar works survive at all.

4 Shotoku Taishi (574–621) made a profound study of Buddhism and founded such important temples as Horyuji in Nara. He also tried to introduce Confucian ideas into the Japanese state and proclaimed a code of government in 604. The painting shows him in Chinese-style robes and is in the manner of a Chinese imperial portrait.

maturity, and throughout the eleventh century they wielded overwhelming power.

The Heian capital was the scene of outstanding cultural achievements. Whereas the dominant arts of Nara had been in the Chinese T'ang style, the new regime severed links with the continent and developed Japanese artistic styles. Architecture became less flamboyant and more refined. Vivid picture scrolls illustrated historical and literary themes. A new phonetic script supplemented Chinese characters and permitted more supple forms of expression [7]. *The Tale of Genji* (c. 1010–20), Japan's most famous novel, was written by Murasaki Shikibu, a lady of the Heian court.

Warrior families and court life

Parallel with the weakening of imperial authority came the rise of provincial families with new sources of power. To maintain law and order and combat northern aborigines, these lords increased their armies; they became increasingly oblivious of imperial control. Their independent estates *(shoen)* paid little to the capital but stimulated the economic development of outer territories. These new centers produced leaders with a military ethic indifferent to court life.

In the eleventh century courtiers recognized the might of this new class and invited the powerful Taira and Minamoto families to aid them in suppressing rebellions. The Fujiwara may have hoped to control these robust warriors [6], but soon the Taira had replaced them as the effective masters of palace and throne. Taira Kiyomori overpowered his rivals and in 1180 made his six-year-old grandson emperor. After 20 years in dominance the Taira appeared unchallenged in the capital, but military power was now the only determinant of politics and the Minamoto rebelled against the new overlords of Kyoto.

From 1180 to 1185, these two families and their coalitions were embroiled in nationwide warfare. By 1184 the land forces of the Taira were annihilated, and a year later their navy was destroyed. The Minamoto [8] were now masters of Japan. Warriors ruled as shoguns from their capital at Kamakura.

KEY

Haniwa are hollow pottery figures, designed to house a spirit, that were often placed on the burial mounds of clan leaders and members of the imperial family. This figurine of an armored warrior comes from the Yamato period (*c.* AD 300– *c* 625); *Haniwa* exist in the form of human figures, animals, buildings, and boats. The concept of an anthropomorphic tomb figure was native to the Shinto tradition; when Buddhist craftsmen came to influence the Japanese artists, they brought refinements, but not the basic idea. Japanese *haniwa* differ from Chinese statues by having a hollow "eye," supposedly the entrance for the spirit within.

5

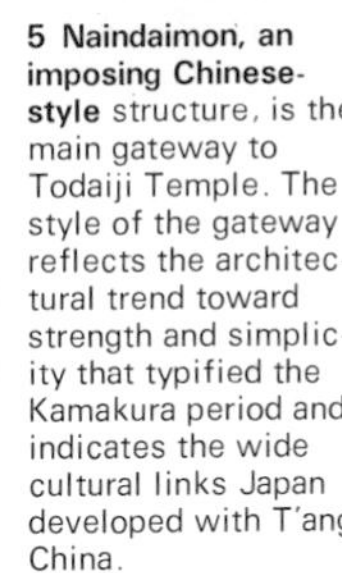

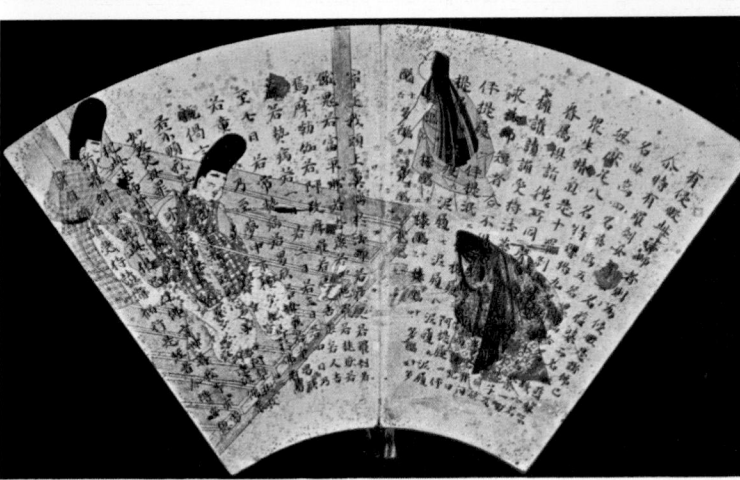

5 Naindaimon, an imposing Chinese-style structure, is the main gateway to Todaiji Temple. The style of the gateway reflects the architectural trend toward strength and simplicity that typified the Kamakura period and indicates the wide cultural links Japan developed with T'ang China.

6

6 Japanese armor from Kamakura shows the artistry associated with the late Heian period and the rise of the shogunate, a provincial military class that demanded very high skills of workmanship. Warriors often donated fine armor to important shrines. Their personal code emphasized simple dignity and courage.

7

7 This hand-painted copy of a sutra (Buddhist scripture) dates from the late Heian period. It was believed that copying sutras by hand was one way to gain rebirth in Paradise. Such a practice was a feature of *Jodo Shinsu*, or Pure Land Buddhism, that arose in the late 12th century and laid great stress on afterlife.

8

8 Minamoto Yoritomo (1147–99), the first shogun, led the armies that destroyed the Taira family's power in 1185. This conflict, immortalized in *The Tale of Genji*, inspired many important works of literature. Shown here in formal dress, Yoritomo set up his capital at Kamakura, far from the imperial capital at Kyoto.

Japanese art

Japanese art since the introduction of Buddhism in the sixth century owes much to mainland China and Korea [1]. Therefore it is sometimes dismissed as derivative. This is far from the truth; although the Japanese are always ready to absorb new influences, they use these imported techniques and ideas for their own purposes and in their own ways to create new styles.

Early Japanese art

Until the sixth century Japanese art had been relatively simple, but under the tutelage of craftsmen from Korea, and later China, there was a burst of development in the arts and in government that led to the art of the Nara period (710–94). Much of its architecture and sculpture in wood, bronze, and dry lacquer survives in temples to this day. In the eighth-century treasure-house in Nara, the Shoso-in, quantities of lacquer, pottery, and leather work, as well as painting and embroidery, give us a good picture of the arts and crafts of the period.

In the succeeding Heian period (794–1185) the Buddhist arts took on a more national flavor. The elegant court of the period, immortalized in the novel *The Tale of Genji,* is depicted in a famous scroll [4] in Yamato-e style ("the Japanese style"). The Yamato-e style differs fundamentally from Chinese styles in its lack of interest in the brushstroke and in its use of flat areas of opaque color.

In the thirteenth century there was a revival of the Nara styles in Buddhist sculpture, led by the Kaikei school. Painting diversified into several groups according to the separate Buddhist sects. Secular art continued in the form of handscrolls depicting histories or satires; the handscroll format (originally a book) was also used by Buddhist artists.

Innovations from China and elsewhere

The arts flourished under the rule of the Ashikaga family during the Muromachi period (1333–1573), in spite of civil wars. Renewed contacts with China enabled painters from the Zen Buddhist monasteries to visit China and Korea and learn the art of ink painting from Chinese painters [5]. At first the painters' academy was exclusively filled by monk-painters. As interest in mainland culture spread, two secular schools of painters arose, the Ami school and the more important Kano school.

The Kano school, which later became the "Classical" school in Japan, employed a basic Chinese style but added to it a decorative quality alien to Chinese scholar-painters' ideals. When in the Momoyama period (1573–1616) Kano Eitoku [6] invented the use of gold leaf as a background to screen painting in opaque color, an unparalleled richness was introduced to Japanese art, which retained the brush stroke of Chinese convention but added Yamato-e color. This decorative effect was ideally suited to the tastes of the new military leaders who succeeded the Ashikaga; where the Ashikaga rulers had encouraged the elegance and simplicity inherent in the aesthetics of the Tea Ceremony, Oda Nobunaga and his successor Toyotomi Hideyoshi wanted grandiose display. During this period the minor arts flourished as never before: lacquer, pottery, and metal-

CONNECTIONS

See also
1046 Japan 200 BC–AD 1
1210 Japan 1185–1868
1044 Chinese art to 1368
1322 Modern architecture after 1930

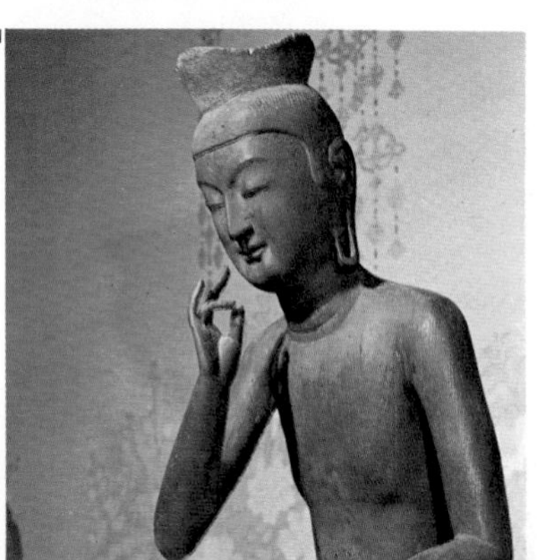

1 A 7th-century bodhisattva (future Buddha) carved in wood in the Korean style.

2 The Phoenix Hall of the Byodo-in, near Kyoto (11th century), was so called because it is said to resemble a phoenix settling with outstretched wings. This beautiful building demonstrates how Japanese Buddhist architects interpreted Chinese ideas and retained Chinese construction methods.

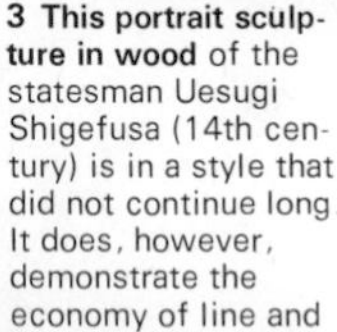

3 This portrait sculpture in wood of the statesman Uesugi Shigefusa (14th century) is in a style that did not continue long. It does, however, demonstrate the economy of line and feature common to most later styles of Japanese portraiture. Portraits of laymen first appeared in the 14th century, following posthumous Buddhist portraits of sages.

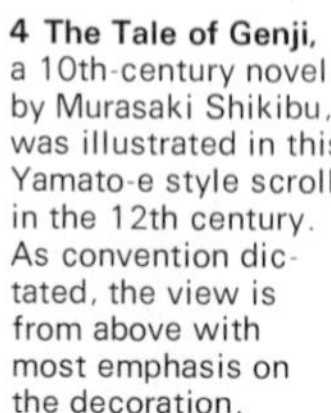

4 The Tale of Genji, a 10th-century novel by Murasaki Shikibu, was illustrated in this Yamato-e style scroll in the 12th century. As convention dictated, the view is from above with most emphasis on the decoration.

5 Sesshu (1420–1506) was a painter who had visited China, where he learned the art of ink painting. This vigorously painted autumn landscape illustrates how he gave a distinctive Japanese flavor to the Chinese style.

work, particularly that associated with the sword and its fittings, all reached a peak of excellence. Military men prided themselves not only on their bravery and skill with the sword, but also on their ability to write verse and paint in ink.

Influences in recent times

Hideyoshi's successors, Tokugawa Ieyasu and his family, ruled Japan until 1868. The Edo, or Tokugawa, period was one of rigid exclusion or control of contact with the outside world in order to maintain internal peace. Trade flourished within Japan and brought with it prosperity for a new merchant class. This in turn brought new styles of painting and decorative arts.

The porcelain industry [9] began in Kyushu and in the middle of the seventeenth century started exporting to Europe and the Near East via the Dutch.

The declining standards of the Kano school assisted the rise of a new, popular school, Ukiyo-e, the school of the print artists, who produced printed books and broadsheets, theater posters, and ephemera for the Edo dynasty: their subjects were the "pop heroes" of the day—courtesans and actors—dramatic moments of plays, and erotica.

New contact with Chinese painting introduced the scholar's style, Nanga, and subsequently two partial offshoots from this, the realist style of Maruyama Okyo and the controlled yet dashing Shijo style of Matsumura Goshun.

With the intrusions of the West into Japan in 1868 this activity changed abruptly. Western fashions became the rage, and only the intervention of such enlightened men as Ernest Fenollosa (1853–1908) prevented neglect or even wholesale destruction of Japan's artistic and architectural heritage. In the present century there has been not only a swing back to native ideals in many of the arts and crafts but also a serious expansion into Western materials and methods, so that Japanese artists are, for instance, among the leading print makers, while such architects as Kenzo Tange are among the leading exponents of a wholly international style.

KEY

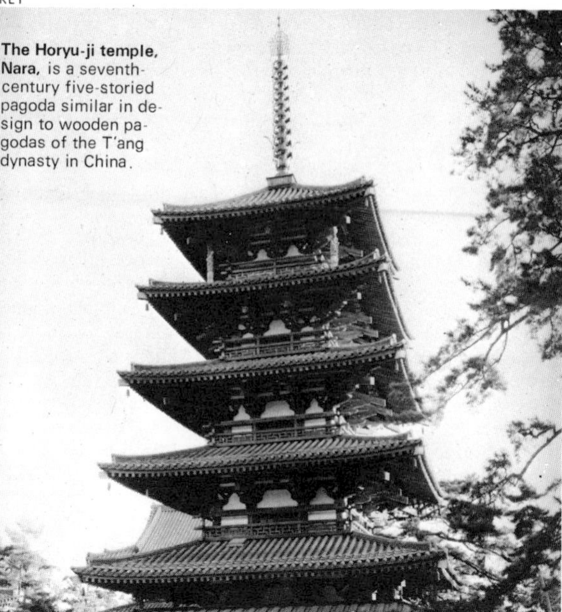

The Horyu-ji temple, Nara, is a seventh-century five-storied pagoda similar in design to wooden pagodas of the T'ang dynasty in China.

6

6 These lion dogs are attributed to Kano Eitoku (1543–90), one of the greatest painters of the Kano school.

7

7 A screen of pine trees in a mist is one of a pair by Tohaku (1539–1610), one of the contemporary rivals of the Kano artists. It shows how skill in ink was retained by artists who otherwise used brilliant color and gold leaf in their work.

8

8 These screens are called "Red and White Plum Trees" and were painted by Ogata Korin (1658–1716). They are supreme examples of the Rimpa or "Decorative" school of painting, and they show the characteristic abbreviation of natural objects, treating them in a conventional way in a layout that is wholly original. Yamato-e was used as a basis for simplified decorative effects in paintings of this period.

10

9

9 Porcelain was exported to Europe via the Dutch from 1650 onward. Enameled wares like this Kakiemon vase of the late 17th century inspired Meissen and other factories, while blue and white wares influenced earthenware design in Delft and elsewhere.

10 "The Hollow of the Deep Sea Wave" is one of a series of 36 Views of Fuji in woodblock color prints by Hokusai (1760–1849).

The Celts and Christianity

Before the Roman conquest, much of western and central Europe was dominated by Celtic tribes of Indo-European origin. Skilled in the use of iron, which they introduced into northern Europe, the Celts flourished from about 700 BC. They achieved a high level of material culture and also developed a highly complex religion and mythology. Celtic art reflected the importance of religion, and geometrical or magic symbols and cult animals are repeated on objects from all periods of Celtic history.

The finest phase of Celtic culture

Celtic culture reached its finest achievements during the La Tène period, which began in about 500 BC and, on the Continent, lasted until its absorption by Rome. Information about the Celts of this period is obtained both from archeological evidence and from Greek and Roman authors. They have recorded details of tribes, kings, nobles, and place names, all of which give important information about the Celtic languages, which have survived in a modified form in Britain, Ireland, and Brittany.

The Celts did not commit their religious beliefs and traditional learning to writing until after the arrival of Christianity in Ireland in the fifth century. The comments of the classical writers at the time Rome's armies destroyed the Celtic world in Europe therefore have a unique importance. Almost fanatical in their religious fervor, the pagan Celts were dominated by powerful, highly aristocratic priests, the Druids, who often combined the role of king with their priesthood. Tribal in social organization, the Celts also possessed the oldest and most complex legal system in Europe. Every man had his rights, and crimes from murder to the smallest wrong were listed and categorized. Correct atonement, specified by the law, was made not to the state but directly to the person who had been wronged, or to his family. Some Christian rites of penance for sins are believed to be based on the old pagan legal system.

Celtic spiritual tradition

The Celts were very conservative in matters of tradition. Nonliterate, they had a complex oral tradition, a deep admiration for intellectual power, and a passionate love of words. The beauty of nature is depicted in somé of their richest poems.

It is understandable, then, that Christianity had such an early and widespread success in Ireland, the only country in western Europe untouched by Roman might. Ireland fell in the fifth century, not to disciplined Roman soldiers, but to the equally disciplined Roman Church. All the Celtic fervor for religion was now transferred to the service of Christianity—a very Celtic type of Christianity, noted for its austere devotions. The detailed and sophisticated laws were now transformed for Christian purposes; the glorious art once used to adorn the pagan warriors and their shrines and to honor the gods now served to praise God in the form of superbly illuminated manuscripts [2, 3], in which the old pagan symbolism of spirals and circles took on a new meaning.

In a Europe torn by invasion and disaster, Ireland remained a haven of peace and learning, far from the terrible ravages of the

CONNECTIONS

See also

990 Europe 1200–500 BC

1008 The Celts 500 BC–AD 450

1052 The rise of medieval Western Christendom

1

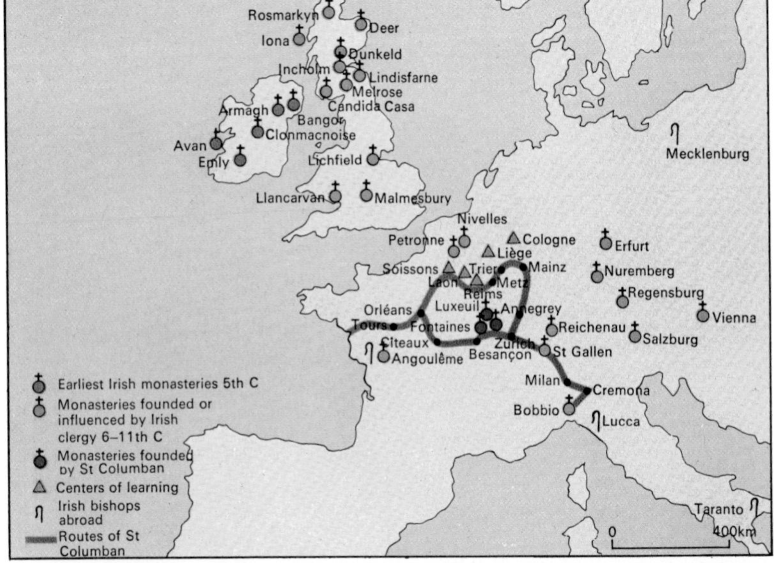

Rosmarkyn
Deer
Iona
Dunkeld
Incholm
Lindisfarne
Melrose
Candida Casa
Armagh
Bangor
Clonmacnoise
Avan
Emly
Lichfield
Mecklenburg
Llancarvan
Malmesbury
Nivelles
Petronne
Cologne
Erfurt
Liège
Soissons
Trier
Mainz
Nuremberg
Laon
Metz
Reims
Regensburg
Orléans
Luxeuil
Annegrey
Vienna
Tours
Fontaines
Reichenau
Salzburg
Cîteaux
Zurich
St Gallen
Angoulême
Besançon
Milan
Cremona
Bobbio
Lucca
Taranto
0
400km
Earliest Irish monasteries 5th C
Monasteries founded or influenced by Irish clergy 6–11th C
Monasteries founded by St Columban
Centers of learning
Irish bishops abroad
Routes of St Columban

1 St Columba founded his monastery in Iona in AD 563. He was the first of numerous missionaries and scholars who, as shown on the map, established centers of sanctity and learning in western Europe. The movement was represented by such figures as St Aidan in England (635), St Columban in France, Switzerland, and Italy (from 590), Feuillen in Belgium (*c.* 650), Kilian in central Germany (martyred *c.* 689), and Fearghal in Austria (mid-8th century). Many of the Irish exiles were monks who sought to evangelize the pagan tribes who had recently overrun the Roman Empire.

2

3

2 Illuminated manuscripts are one of the great glories of European art, as this page from the 7th-century *Book of Durrow* shows. Because Ireland remained untouched by Rome, its art retained its original style.

3 The great period of Irish manuscript illumination was from the late 7th to the early 9th centuries. In these unique works, vitality in the design is combined with austere representations of divine figures, showing by their elongated, somber faces their strong link with the Celtic past. In the *Book of Kells*, St Matthew is surrounded by decorated panels and motifs, which were familiar from the art of Ireland's pagan days.

northern barbarians who, beginning in 406, were burning the churches and the towns of Europe and desecrating and destroying all that was sacred and beautiful. The early Irish Church favored the monastic system, and during the fifth and sixth centuries monasteries sprang up throughout Ireland.

The Age of Saints

This long period of tranquility and learning was known as the Age of Saints. It was a time when the churchmen and their guests were occupied in studying the Gospels and illuminating the manuscripts. Meanwhile, the scribes were busily committing to writing the old pagan oral traditions and poems of their country for, although Christians, they were also Celts, and loyalty to the archaic traditions was strong.

Only the coming of the Vikings at the end of the eighth century broke the spell that had made Ireland the cultural center of the Western world. In the sixth and seventh centuries many Irish churchmen, such as St Columba (521–97), St Aidan (died 651), and St Columban (543–615) traveled in Europe, founding monasteries and churches, converting the heathen, teaching in the courts, establishing their own schools, and inspiring all who came into contact with them by their austere devotion to their calling [1]. Following the Viking invasion, exiled monks continued to travel throughout Europe.

The rich literature of the Irish and that of their neighbors, the Welsh, profoundly influenced the evolution of medieval literature and provided new and thrilling themes that enriched the troubadours' repertoires for the entertainment of the rich courts of later medieval Europe.

The Celtic story in Europe does not end in the romances of the courts of Eleanor of Aquitaine and her contemporaries in the twelfth century. In the eighteenth century the famous Ossianic controversy fascinated Europe. Although the poems of the legendary Gaelic bard Ossian were subsequently proved to be a mixture of traditional Gaelic folk poetry and poems attributed to James Macpherson (1736–96), they nevertheless inspired a fresh interest in the Celts.

KEY

This two-faced stone figure from Boa Island in County Fermanagh dates from the first century BC. It forms a link with the old pagan world of the Celtic past and the flowering of Celtic religious and artistic genius in the Christian era. It is impossible to say how long paganism lingered in Ireland after the arrival of Christianity. As Roman law and administration never interrupted the traditions of tribal life and religious awareness, the transition from pagan gods to the Christian God was complicated by the survival of some elements of Celtic paganism. By the 5th century, however, Christianity was firmly established.

4 A

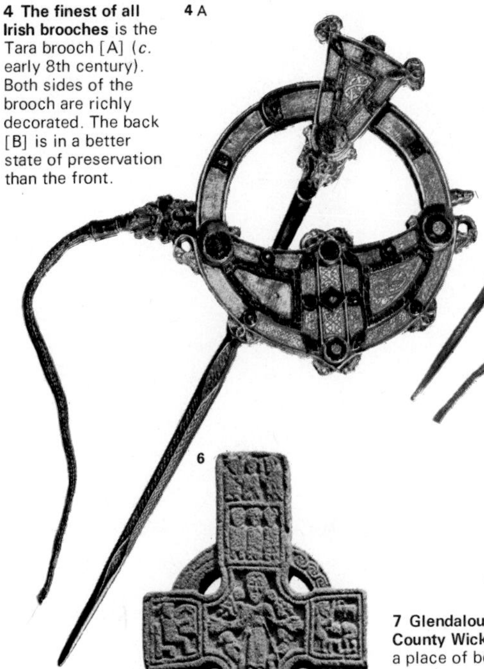

B

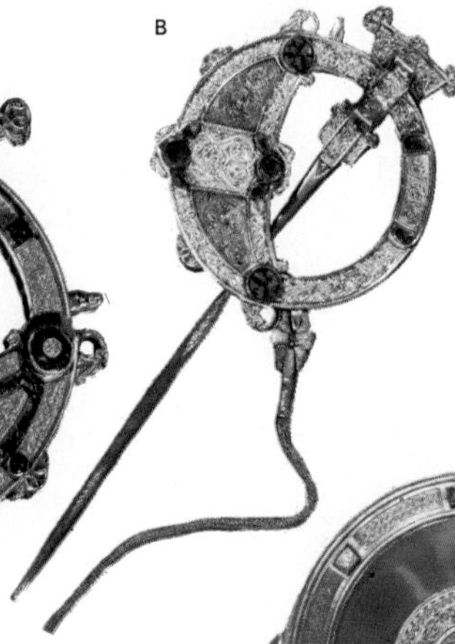

4 The finest of all Irish brooches is the Tara brooch [A] (*c.* early 8th century). Both sides of the brooch are richly decorated. The back [B] is in a better state of preservation than the front.

5 A

5 B

5 The Ardagh chalice [A] was found in County Limerick, Ireland. The contrast of plain surface (silver) with decorative studs and gold filigree makes a striking impact. One of the more beautiful details is on the underside [B] of the foot.

6

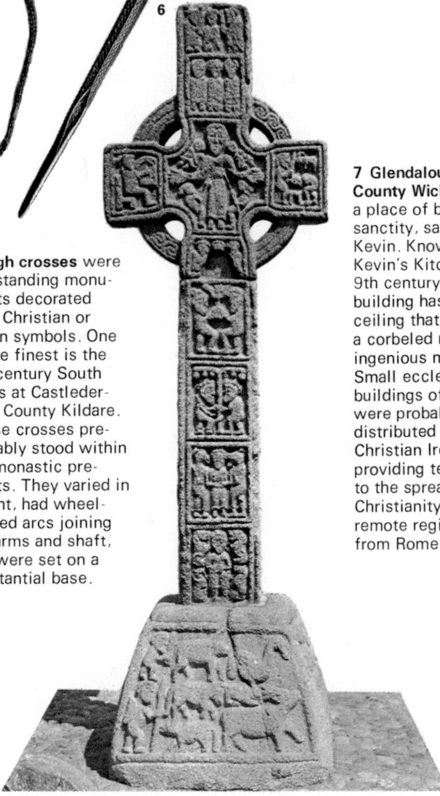

6 High crosses were freestanding monuments decorated with Christian or pagan symbols. One of the finest is the 9th-century South Cross at Castledermot, County Kildare. These crosses presumably stood within the monastic precincts. They varied in height, had wheel-shaped arcs joining the arms and shaft, and were set on a substantial base.

7

7 Glendalough in County Wicklow was a place of beauty and sanctity, sacred to St Kevin. Known as St Kevin's Kitchen (*c.* 9th century), the building has a vaulted ceiling that supports a corbeled roof in an ingenious manner. Small ecclesiastic buildings of this kind were probably widely distributed in early Christian Ireland, providing testimony to the spread of Christianity in that remote region, far from Rome.

The rise of medieval Western Christendom

The barbarians who destroyed the western empires in the fifth and sixth centuries were either pagans or Arian heretics who denied the unity of God the Father and Son and violently rejected Roman Christianity. By the sixth century Europe began to be reconverted. Missionary activity from Rome followed the growth of Benedictine monasticism and a rejuvenation of the papacy. St Benedict (*c.* 480–*c.* 547) lived in Italy when it was ruled by the Arian Ostrogoths. About the year 500 he had begun a hermetical life at Subiaco with emphasis on the performance of the liturgy and on a community life of moderate self-denial. He founded (*c.* 529) the Abbey of Monte Cassino, one of the bulwarks of Christianity and civilization in early medieval Europe. He also wrote a Rule for his monks that was reasonable and humane and ensured the durability of his ideas and institutions [Key].

The papacy—spiritual and temporal

The medieval papacy was founded by Pope Gregory the Great (*c.* 540–604) [2], who was a firm supporter and propagator of monasticism. He became pope in 590, a time when the power of the Byzantine governors of Italy was rapidly declining and the Arian Lombards threatened to reduce the papacy to little more than a Lombard bishopric. Gregory himself managed the Church estates in central and southern Italy, organized the defenses of Rome, appointed governors of the leading Italian cities, and in 592–93 made peace with the Lombards without reference to the eastern emperor.

The Franks were the first of the barbarians to be converted, after Clovis (465–511), influenced by his Christian wife, offered to become Christian if God helped him win a great battle with the Allemanni. Clovis won the battle and was baptized, probably in 496. Gregory dispatched St Augustine to England in 597 with monks from his own Roman monastery to begin the reconversion of Britain. But Britain was reconverted from two different directions because the Irish, who had remained Christian after the mission of St Patrick in 444 [7], had sent St Columba to Scotland *c.* 563 to found the monastery of Iona and convert the Picts. St Aidan went from Iona to Lindisfarne *c.* 635 to convert the English in Northumbria. There the Roman and the Irish traditions met to form the most advanced culture in Europe [3].

Anglo-Irish influence

The Irish also penetrated deep into mainland Europe [4]. In 590 St Columbanus established monasteries at Anagratum and Luxeuil in the Vosges. Expelled from Burgundy for criticism of the behavior of the court, he went to Italy to found the monastery of Bobbio, which set an example that was the most important impetus to the conversion of the Lombards. These and other Irish monasteries reintroduced the Catholic faith into areas where it was unknown and in addition brought with them their libraries, both classical and Christian, which had remained safe in Ireland.

Frisia and Germany were converted from Britain in the eighth century. Willibrord (*c.* 658–739), the apostle of the Frisians, was a Northumbrian who had joined a monastery in Ireland. Boniface (*c.* 680–

CONNECTIONS

See also
1054 The barbarian invasions
1056 The Byzantine Empire
1058 Mohammed and Islam
1062 Arabs and the rise of Islam
1066 Charlemagne and the Carolingian Empire
1072 The Holy Roman Empire
1074 European expansion to the east
1080 Romanesque art of the 11th century

Majority are Christian by 600
+ Patriarchates
······ Eastern Roman Empire

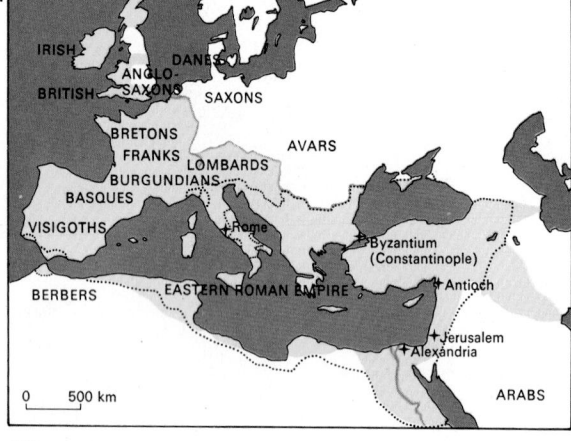

1 Orthodox Christianity in the later Roman world reached its greatest extent *c.* 600. North Africa, Rome, and Ravenna were reconquered from the Arian Goths by Justinian in the mid-6th century. In the north, the Irish had been converted about 430, the Franks in 496, the Burgundians in 516, and the Visigoths in 589. The Anglo-Saxon missions began in 597. The new Christian unity of the Mediterranean, however, lasted only until the Arabs in the 7th century conquered an empire from Syria to Spain including three original patriarchates, Antioch, Jerusalem, and Alexandria.

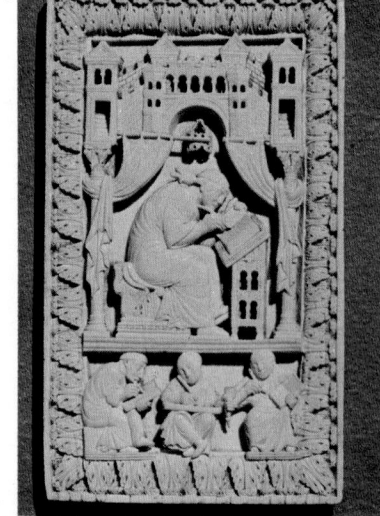

2 Gregory I (center) was elected pope at a time when Rome was under strong pressure from the Arian Lombards. But his energy, dedication, and grasp of administration enabled him to give the Roman Church a status it had never previously enjoyed. He established the principle of papal authority in temporal affairs both by his diplomatic initiatives and by asserting control of the "patrimony of Peter," which later grew into the papal states. By sending Augustine to England in 597, he made sure that the Church in Britain would look to Rome, not Byzantium. Gregorian chant is named after him.

3 The Ruthwell Cross, possibly either a Mass or preaching cross, is the finest monument of Northumbrian art from the British cultural renaissance of the 7th century.

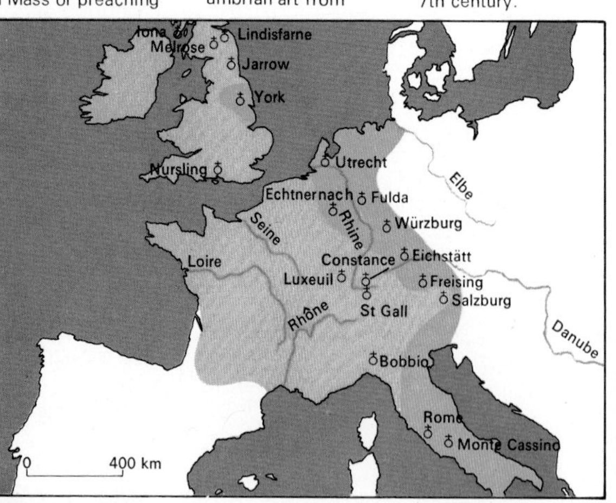
Iona
Melrose
Lindisfarne
Jarrow
York
Nursling
Utrecht
Elbe
Echternach
Fulda
Würzburg
Seine
Rhine
Loire
Constance
Eichstätt
Luxeuil
Freising
Salzburg
St Gall
Rhône
Danube
Bobbio
Rome
Monte Cassino
0
400 km
Celtic monastries and their influence
Anglo-Saxon monastries and their influence

4 Many European monasteries were founded by missionaries from Ireland, where Christianity and classical learning were preserved. Others were founded by Anglo-Saxon converts.

5 The Gatehouse of Lorsch Abbey, in Hessen, West Germany, is an example of Charlemagne's impressive program of new church building in his empire.

754), an Englishman, continued the Frisian mission in 716 and in 719 was appointed by Gregory II to convert the Germans. He laid the foundations for the Carolingian Church but was killed by heathens in 754 [6].

The Arian Visigoths in Spain were converted to Christianity at the Third Council of Toledo in 589 (although Muslim invaders were soon to dominate the country). In northeastern Europe, conversions were delayed longer. Sweden and Denmark were only temporarily converted by St Anskar in the ninth century, Poland and Hungary in the tenth, and Norway in the eleventh.

In the meantime, the emperor of the Franks, Charlemagne (742–814), had imported Anglo-Irish missionaries to establish the basis of Carolingian Christianity, backed by energetic church building [5]. The late eighth century also saw an alliance between the pope and the Frankish emperors against the Lombards and the creation of the idea of the Holy Roman Empire. Anglo-Saxons, Germans, and Franks all visited Rome, accepted the lead of the papacy, and bought relics for their native dioceses. This was the great period of the relic trade when every new church needed an "authentic" relic [8] and when the primacy of the papacy was in part based on the possession of the remains of St Peter.

The rise of the Holy Roman Empire saw a grave decline in the standards of the Church. There was widespread simony (the selling of ecclesiastical appointments, often to laymen), monasteries became rich and lax, and the papacy itself was corrupt.

Church reform

Reform of the Church began at the house of Cluny, a Benedictine monastery in Burgundy [9]. Under Abbott Odo the Benedictine Rule was strictly enforced. The spirit of Cluniac reform permeated all aspects of Western European Christianity, culminating in the pontificates of Leo IX [10] and Gregory VII (1074–85).

In 1054, the last year of Leo IX's pontificate, the Western church broke with the Eastern. The Patriarch of Constantinople would not accept the universal supremacy of Rome, nor liturgy and practice.

KEY

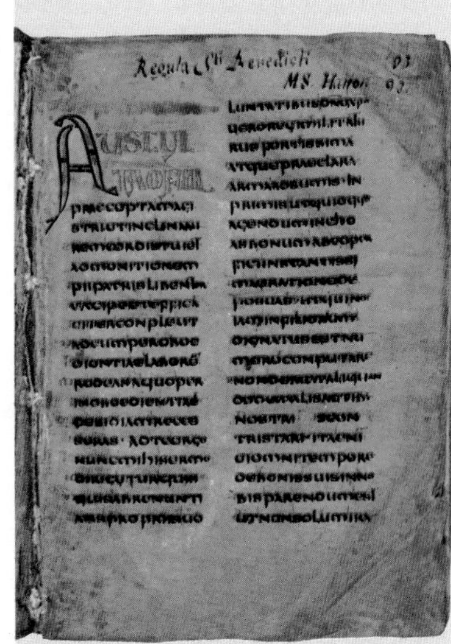

The Benedictine Rule was the cornerstone of the early medieval Church. It contained strict yet reasonable regulations for monastic life, in contrast to the ascetic excesses of Eastern monasticism. The Rule stressed the value of religious community life, humility, self-denial, and the performance of the liturgy. For 600 years after Benedict's death in 543 there was no other monastic rule in the West. Its followers have included 20 popes and many pioneer missionaries. The learning and education of Benedictine monasteries in the early Middle Ages provided the only training for administrators faced with increasingly complex state problems.

6 The story of the martydom of St Ursula is the most famous of the martyrdom legends from the barbarian period. The saint, together with her companions, was murdered by the Huns in Cologne in 454 still protesting her virginity and her faith. Her triumphal funeral is shown in a painting by Vittore Carpaccio (1490). The cult of local martyrs became increasingly important during the reconversion period, at which time the supposed number of St Ursula's companions was increased to 11,000 by a clerical error. A notable missionary martyr was St Boniface, who went to Frisia and was murdered at Dokkum in the mid-8th century.

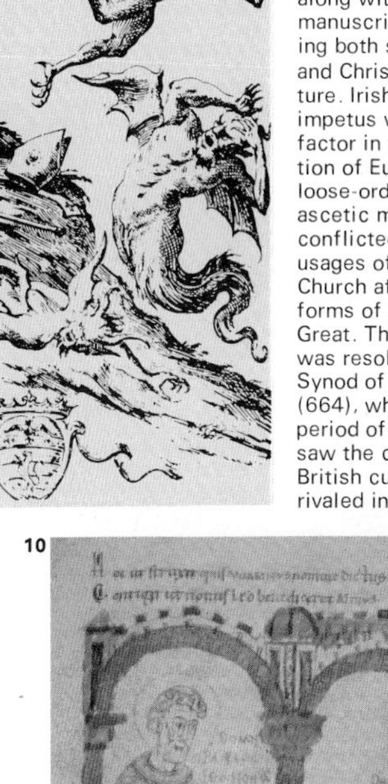

7 St Patrick, a Romano-Briton from Cumbria, converted Ireland between 430 and 461. Ireland was the only country to escape the invasions of the 5th and 6th centuries. Christianity was preserved, along with many manuscripts containing both secular Latin and Christian literature. Irish missionary impetus was a prime factor in the reeducation of Europe but its loose-ordered yet ascetic monasticism conflicted with the usages of the Roman Church after the reforms of Gregory the Great. This conflict was resolved at the Synod of Whitby (664), which led to a period of peace that saw the creation of a British culture unrivaled in Europe.

8 Relics became an essential part of the furnishings of every church in the 9th century. They were housed in the greatest magnificence, as in the High Altar of St Ambrose, Milan, decorated by the German Volfinius.

9 The Abbey of Cluny under St Odo (927–42) reformed the Benedictine system with a strict adherence to the Rule and stress on the splendor of the liturgy. This is the third church at Cluny dedicated to these ideals.

10

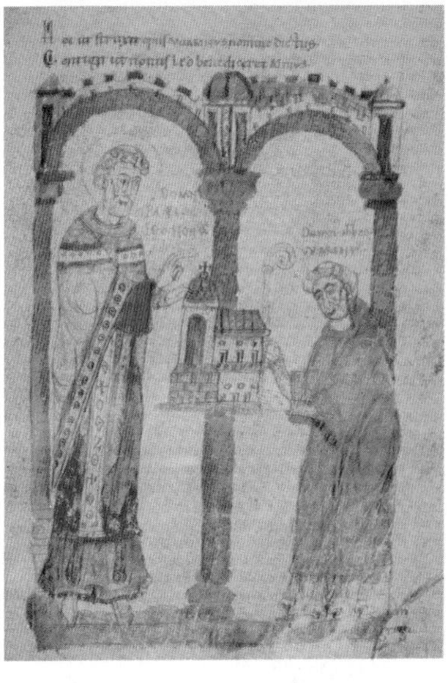

10 Pope Leo IX (1049–54) was an ardent supporter of Cluniac reform. He began to improve papal standards.

The barbarian invasions

"Barbarian" was a term of abuse used by the Romans to describe anyone outside the Mediterranean civilization of Greece and Rome. Since the time of Caesar the frontiers of the Roman Empire had been menaced by invading Germanic peoples, many of whom were conquered, after which they settled as fairly peaceable—though armed—colonists.

The frontier that extended from the North Sea to the Black Sea via the Rhine and Danube was under renewed pressure in the fourth century from a fresh wave of hostile German peoples: Franks, Saxons, Burgundians, Visigoths, Ostrogoths, Sueves, Alans, Vandals, and Gepids [Key]. Their societies were based on the clan and their tribes were relatively small in number, ranging from about 25,000 to 120,000. All able-bodied men were soldiers; farming was done by slaves. Their armies, supported by a powerful cavalry, proved too strong for the last of the Roman legions. The westward pressure of these peoples at the end of the fourth century was due to overpopulation and shortage of food as well as the arrival of the Huns, a fierce nomadic Mongol people who came to pillage rather than to settle.

Eastern Roman Empire

The Eastern Roman Empire was threatened by barbarians on all fronts [2]. In Asia Minor it was under pressure first from the Sassanian Persians and later, after 622, from the rapid expansion of Islam. On the Danube and in the Balkans the threat of the Germans and Huns was ever present.

After the death of Theodosius the Great in 395 the Visigoths rose in Lower Moesia under Alaric (*c.* 370–410). The Eastern emperor Arcadius persuaded them to move west, where Alaric was made Master of the Soldiers in Illyricum (coastal region of modern Yugoslavia); it was therefore as a Roman general that Alaric led a German invasion of Italy in 401–03. He invaded Italy again in 408 and in 410 captured Rome.

In 406 vast armies of Vandals, Sueves, and Alans crossed the Rhine into Gaul, which was already troubled by internal conflicts in the imperial administration. External attack and internal conflict led to the withdrawal of the last legions from Britain, where the Angles, Saxons, and Jutes were now free to invade. The Vandals ravaged Gaul, moved into Spain in 408 and, in 429 under the leadership of Gaiseric (*c.* 390–477), accomplished the most crippling blow of all to the Western Empire—the invasion of Africa. In 442, Gaiseric was recognized as the independent ruler of North Africa.

The first German empires

By 416 the Burgundians in Gaul had established the first German kingdoms within the old imperial frontiers, and with the Franks scattered across northern France the pattern of post-Roman Western Europe was beginning to emerge. But any hopes of peace were shattered by the Huns, who for nearly a century had been stable in what is now Hungary, threatening east and west alike and building up an enforced alliance of subject German peoples. In 450 the empire refused to buy off the Huns with any more gold, so, led by Attila (*c.* 406–53), they invaded Gaul. The Huns, with their powerful horses and incredible stamina, were

CONNECTIONS

See also
1052 The rise of medieva Western Christendo
1030 Rome: soldier emperors to Constanti
1056 The Byzantine Emp
1066 Charlemagne and t Carolingian Empire
1068 The Vikings

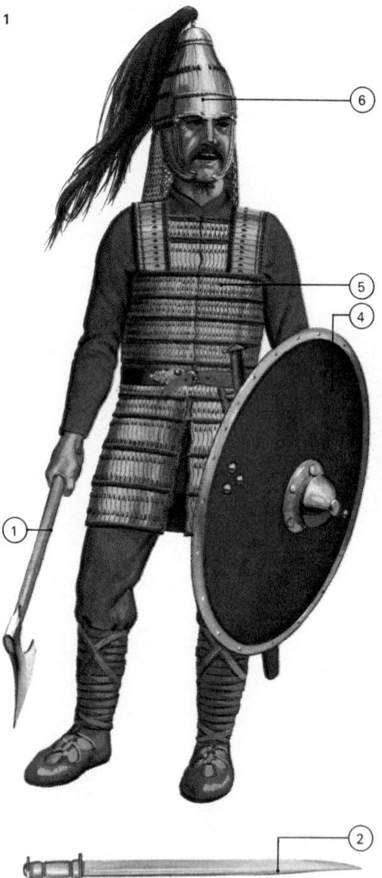

1
6
5
4
1
2
3

1 At the time of their invasion of Gaul in the 5th century, all freemen within the Frankish tribe were warriors. The Frankish army was mainly infantry rather than cavalry. Their most redoubtable weapon was the battle axe, the *francisca* [1], although they also fought with a cutting sword [2] and bows and arrows [3]. Because metal was scarce the round-shield [4] was made of wood covered with stretched hide. They wore close-fitting tunics [5] and leather helmets. [6].

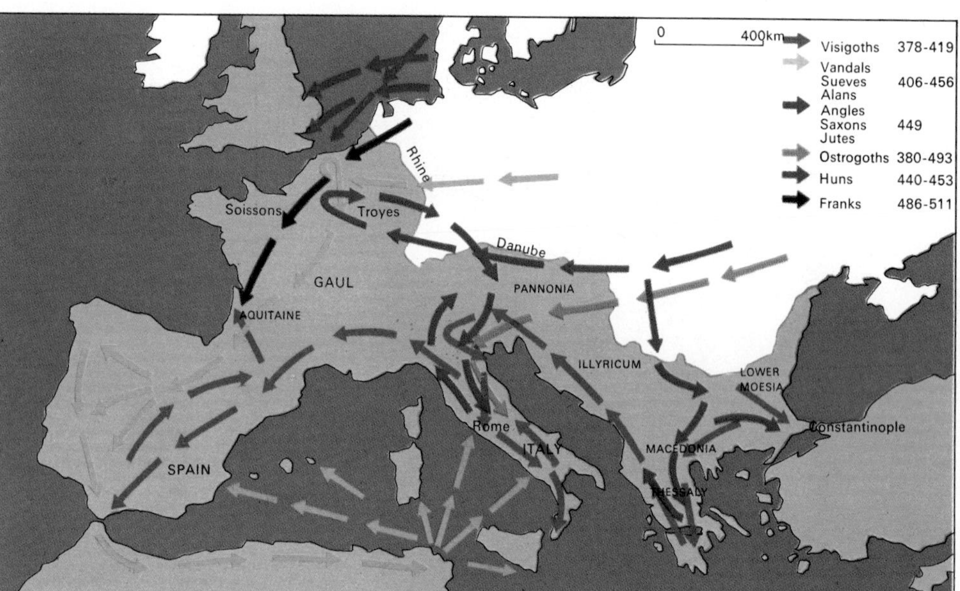

2
0 400km
Visigoths 378-419
Vandals Sueves Alans 406-456
Angles Saxons Jutes 449
Ostrogoths 380-493
Huns 440-453
Franks 486-511
Rhine
Soissons
Troyes
Danube
GAUL
PANNONIA
AQUITAINE
ILLYRICUM
LOWER MOESIA
Constantinople
Rome
ITALY
MACEDONIA
THESSALY
SPAIN

2 A chaotic wandering of barbarians within the confines of the Western Empire followed the collapse of the Rhine and Danube frontier. The barbarians had four main targets: Constantinople, Macedonia, and Thrace; Italy; northeastern Roman Gaul; and North Africa, the granary of the Western Empire. Without any preconceived plan of attack, the citadels of the empire fell according to a "domino" pattern. Westward pressure was intensified as more tribes arrived from the east, in particular the Huns. The crucial blow to the empire was the Vandal invasion of Africa, which, by 429, left Rome surrounded and the Vandals controlling the western Mediterranean.

3
0 200km
PICTS
SCOTS
BRITONS
ANGLES
SAXONS
SAXONS
Rhine
THURINGIANS
Cologne
Metz
Danube
Paris
Orleans
Tours Catholic
Rhône
Arian
LOMBARDS
GEPIDS
Catholic
Milan
Ravenna
Toulouse
EASTERN ROMAN EMPIRE
SUEVES
Arian
Barcelona
Rome
Toledo
Arian
Carthage
Arian
Kingdom of Visigoths
Kingdom of the Franks
Kingdom of the Burgundians
Kingdom of the Ostrogoths
Kingdom of the Vandals

3 The barbarians gradually formed independent kingdoms in the west. They expropriated some property but left much of the Roman landed aristocracy and administration intact. Roman and Teutonic societies existed side by side in an uneasy balance, the military strength of the invaders bringing the defensive capacity that defeated the Huns in 452. The Huns remained nomadic and never founded a lasting kingdom. The barbarian kingdoms were the origins of the national boundaries of Western Europe.

considered almost invincible and were only halted near Troyes in 452 when the Franks and the Visigoths joined forces with the Romans. Attila turned south and menaced Rome, but died in 453 [7]. The destruction was widespread but the Germans had saved the legacy of Roman civilization in the west.

The Franks gradually consolidated their power in Gaul. Under Clovis I (465–511) they created a united and nonheretical Christian Gaul (Council of Orleans, 511), and Clovis was recognized by the Eastern emperor as the ruler of a country that roughly corresponds to modern France. His baptism resulted from a promise that he would adopt Christianity if he won a certain battle with the Alemanni.

After the deposition of Augustulus, the last Western emperor, in 476, the German soldier Odoacer (died 493) became the ruler of Italy. Meanwhile the Ostrogoths had left the Black Sea area and, after the downfall of the Huns, had moved into Pannonia and then to Illyricum. Led by Theoderic from 471, they ravaged Macedonia and Thessaly and in 487 marched on Constantinople. Theoderic was bought off by Emperor Zeno, who persuaded him to go to Italy and overthrow Odoacer. Theoderic defeated Odoacer on the River Adda in 490 and after the three-year siege of Ravenna Odoacer gave in. Theoderic assassinated him and established the Ostrogothic kingdom in Italy [8].

The Eastern Empire

The Eastern Empire averted most dangers from the Germans and the Huns by passing them over to the west, but the Balkans were ruined and depopulated, and the Bulgars were able to threaten Constantinople in 493 and 499. In the east Emperor Justinian (*c.* 482–565) fought for 35 years against the Persian King Chosroes (reigned 531–79). The balance of power in the Mediterranean was temporarily reversed by Justinian's reconquest of Africa (533–4) and Italy (536–54); yet all this effort was wasted when, in the following century, the Arabs overran all imperial lands from the Middle East to North Africa, besieging Constantinople annually until their fleet's defeat there in 718.

KEY

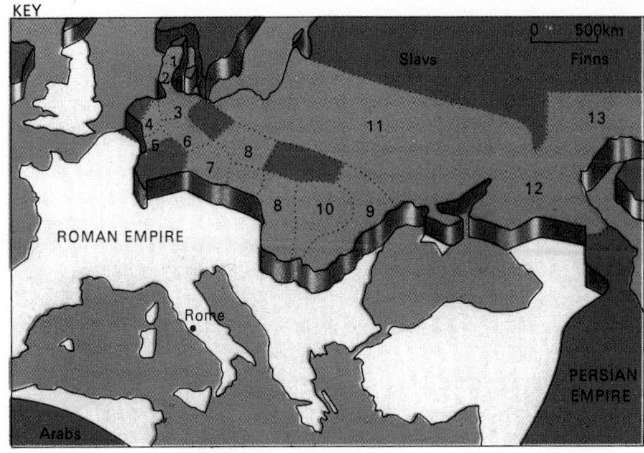

0 500km
Slavs
Finns
1
2
3
4
5
6
7
8
8
9
10
11
12
13
ROMAN EMPIRE
Rome
PERSIAN EMPIRE
Arabs

1 Jutes
2 Angles
3 Saxons
4 Franks
5 Burgundians
6 Thuringians
7 Sueves
8 Vandals
9 Ostrogoths
10 Visigoths
11 Gepids
12 Alans
13 Huns

Barbarian tribes *c.*395
Tribes not invading the Roman Empire 395-511

The positions of the barbarian tribes to the east of the Roman frontier along the Rhine and Danube rivers changed constantly. The pressure on Rome's increasingly ill-defended northeastern frontier was kept up by the arrival of new warring peoples who were impelled relentlessly westward from central Asia by hunger and other barbarians. The Huns invaded Italy in 452.

4 The highest achievement of barbarian art was in its metalwork. The 6th-century silver-gilt dish from Sassanian Persia [B] was the equal of any contemporary east Roman metalwork. In the west work ranged from the sternly Teutonic Visigothic crown [A] to the Anglo-Saxon Alfred Jewel [C]. This is made of continental cloisonné enamel and has classical motifs and a figure of Spring (or Christ).

5 The Mausoleum of Theoderic is the tomb of the first king of Ostrogothic Italy. It was built about 530 and is circular in shape, surmounted by a monolithic dome of Istrian stone weighing 477 tons.

6 The Breviary of Alaric II, king of the Visigoths, an illuminated detail of which is shown here, is a collection of Roman law. Alaric's capital was Toulouse and his kingdom stretched into Spain. The Breviary, which was completed in 506, is an important source of late Roman law and is the result of an established Arian German barbarian king seeking to codify and reconcile his native tribal law with that of the lands of the old Roman Empire over which he ruled.

7 Raphael's fresco of "The Repulse of Attila" (1513) shows Attila and his Huns confronted by Pope Leo I, protected only by the miraculous intervention of St Peter and St Paul. Attila, repulsed by the Romans and Visigoths near Troyes in 452 and by Leo in Italy, retired to Pannonia where he died suddenly a year later on the eve of a new invasion of Italy and was buried in a secret grave.

8 German barbarians, when converted to Christianity, adopted the Arian heresy that denied the divinity of Christ. Theoderic, having established the capital of his Italian kingdom at Ravenna, built an Arian cathedral and baptistry. The mosaics in the baptistery show the formalized presentation of the Baptism of Christ with the Apostles moving toward an altar-throne; a scene, the Etimasia, taken from the fourth chapter of the Apocalypse. The existence of Arian and Catholic buildings side by side in the same city exemplifies the spirit of coexistence that prevailed in Theoderic's Italy.

The Byzantine Empire

In AD 293, Emperor Diocletian decided, for military and administrative reasons, to shift the center of the Roman Empire to the east.

The new state, known as the Byzantine, or Eastern Roman, Empire, became a vital trade and cultural link between Europe and Asia and a bastion within which Greco-Roman civilization developed new and magnificent forms. Byzantium later found itself in doctrinal and political conflict with the western popes and emperors but, as a Christian empire, it resisted Arab, Slav, and Turkish invaders for more than 1,100 years, bequeathing a rich heritage to the peoples of later centuries.

The founding of Constantinople

Both Diocletian (245–313) and Constantine I (*c.*285–337) sought a better base than Rome, one closer to Anatolia and the Balkans, the areas from which they recruited most of their troops. Constantine's choice fell upon a town on the Bosporus that had been the site of an ancient Greek city, Byzantium. Constantinople, as the new capital was called, had a fine harbor, and its military position was almost unassailable [Key]. The scale on which it was conceived surpassed anything in the ancient world. Constantine was determined to found an urban center to which men throughout his empire could direct their loyalties. He believed a common religion could also provide a powerful cohesive force. Converted to Christianity in 312, in 330 he dedicated Constantinople to the Virgin Mary.

After the death of Theodosius (349–95), the gap between the Eastern and Western Empires widened. Rome, the Western capital, fell to the barbarians in 476, and Germanic peoples would thereafter play an important part in the history of the region. The Eastern capital, however, was nearly impregnable, and Byzantium successfully defended its Balkan frontiers against attacks by the Visigoths and Ostrogoths.

Church and state were closely associated in Byzantium. Greek Orthodox Christians were very interested in theological debate, combining in their arguments the philosophical traditions of the Greeks and the spirituality of Christian revelation.

Religious questions often had political implications. The Christological controversy, which came to a head in the fifth century, was concerned with the relationship between the human and divine aspects of Christ's nature. The followers of Nestorius, Patriarch of Constantinople, stressed Christ's humanity while the Monophysites, based at Alexandria, stressed his divinity. A still more bitter controversy, which reached its height in the eighth century, was Iconoclasm—opposition to the veneration of images.

The Justinian era

The empire reached its apogee under Justinian the Great (*c.*482–565), a brilliant administrator with wide-reaching military ambitions [6]. His general, Belisarius, reasserted Christian-Roman authority over large areas of the former Western Empire. Justinian greatly expanded the capital and built Hagia Sophia [8], which was intended to provide a center of worship for all Christendom. Perhaps Justinian's greatest achievement was the codification of Roman

CONNECTIONS

See also
1060 Byzantine art
1030 Rome: soldier emperors to Constanti
1108 The Ottoman Empi to 1600
1062 Arabs and the rise Islam
1054 The barbarian invasions
1084 The Crusades

1 A

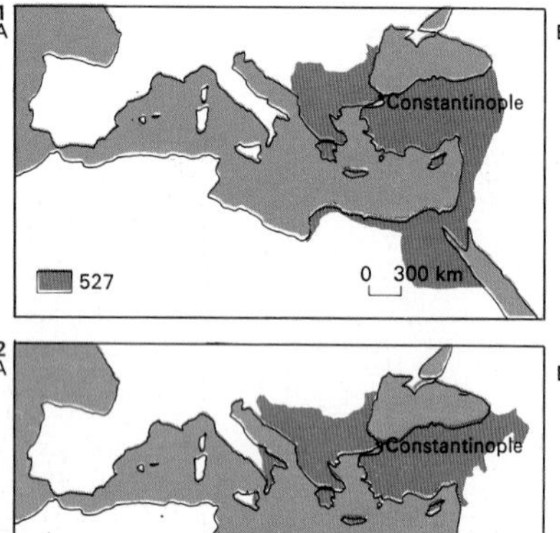

Constantinople
0 300 km
527

B

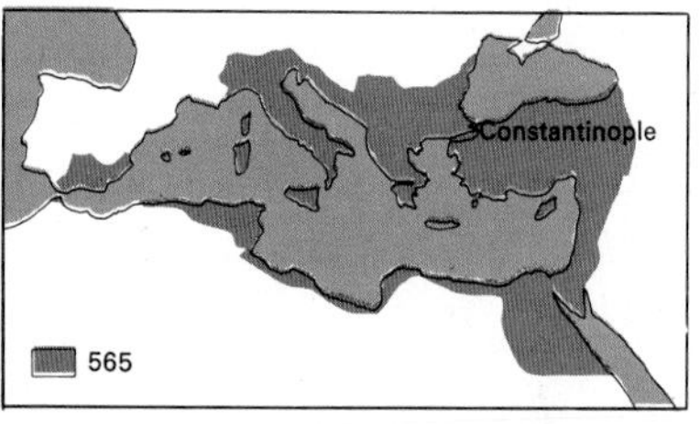

Constantinople
565

1 The Byzantine Empire under Justinian I grew from an exclusively eastern power in 527 [A] to an empire that by 565 ruled many former territories of imperial Rome [B]. Germanic invaders were ousted from many areas.

2 A

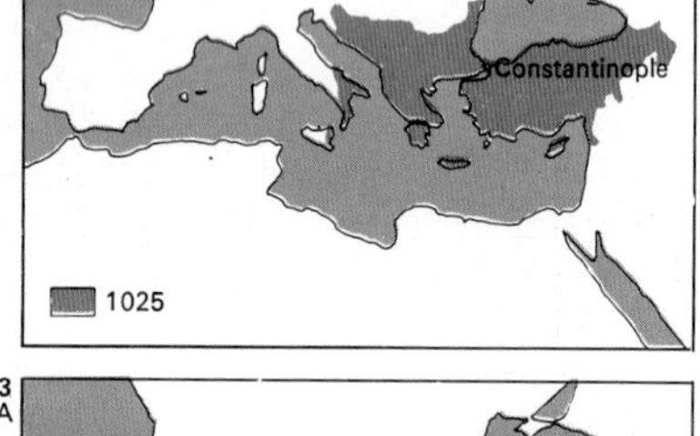

Constantinople
1025

B

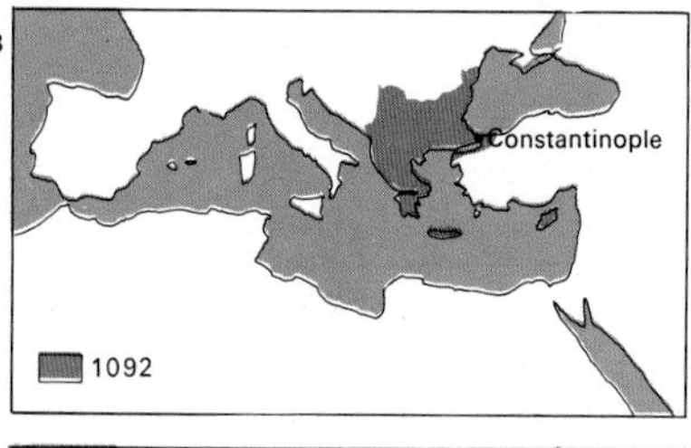

Constantinople
1092

2 The recovery of many areas that the empire had lost to the Slavs, Germans, and Arabs in the 7th and 8th centuries was completed by the conquests of Basil II [A]. But Normans and Turks had made large inroads by 1092 [B].

3 A

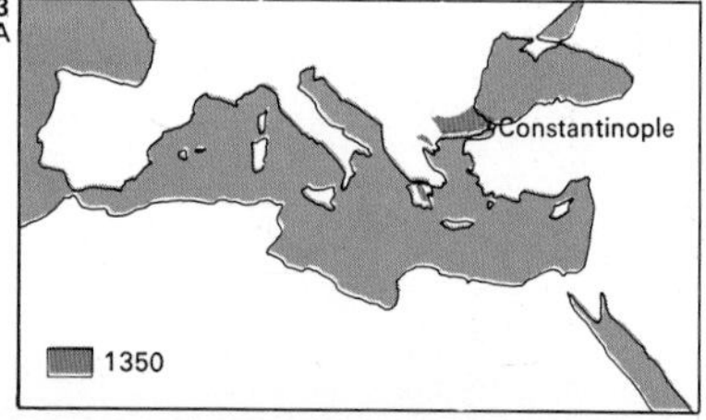

Constantinople
1350

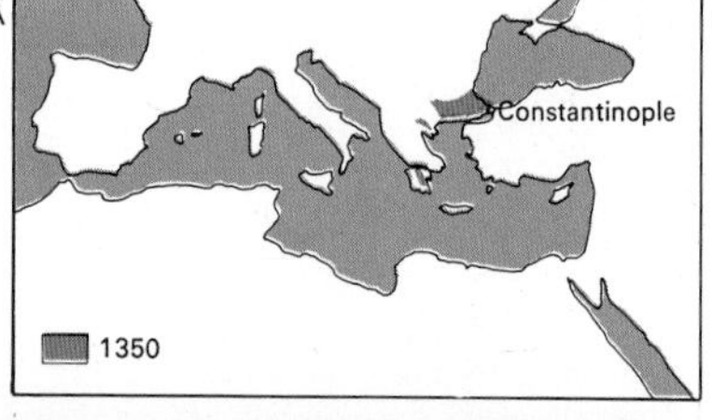

B

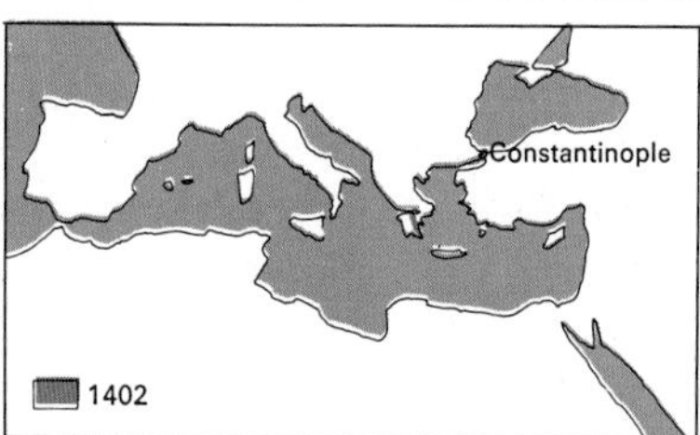

Constantinople
1402

3 Dismembered by the Turks and split by internal feuds, the empire had shrunk in 1350 to a corner of the Balkans and some land in Greece [A]. By 1402 even the Balkan territory was lost [B], and Constantinople was soon to fall.

4

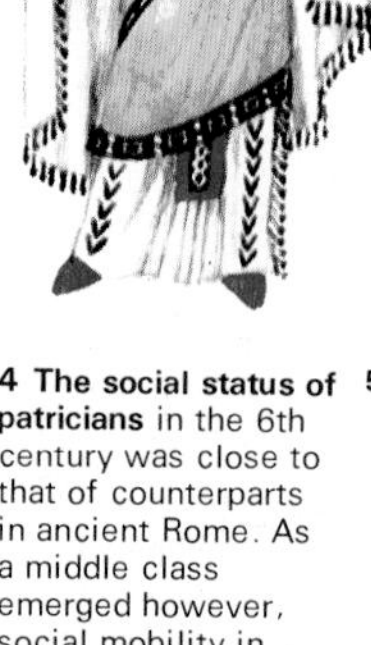

4 The social status of patricians in the 6th century was close to that of counterparts in ancient Rome. As a middle class emerged however, social mobility in Byzantium was higher than in Rome.

5 A

B

5 Byzantine coins reflected a change to a predominantly Greek culture after the 7th century. The Latin inscription on the gold solidus [A] gave way to one in the new official language, Greek [B].

6

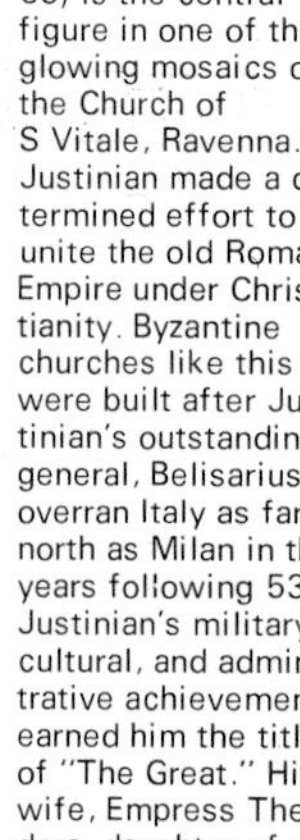

6 Justinian I (r. 527–65) is the central figure in one of the glowing mosaics of the Church of S Vitale, Ravenna. Justinian made a determined effort to reunite the old Roman Empire under Christianity. Byzantine churches like this were built after Justinian's outstanding general, Belisarius, overran Italy as far north as Milan in the years following 535. Justinian's military, cultural, and administrative achievements earned him the title of "The Great." His wife, Empress Theodora, daughter of an animal keeper, was influential in Byzantine court politics.

7

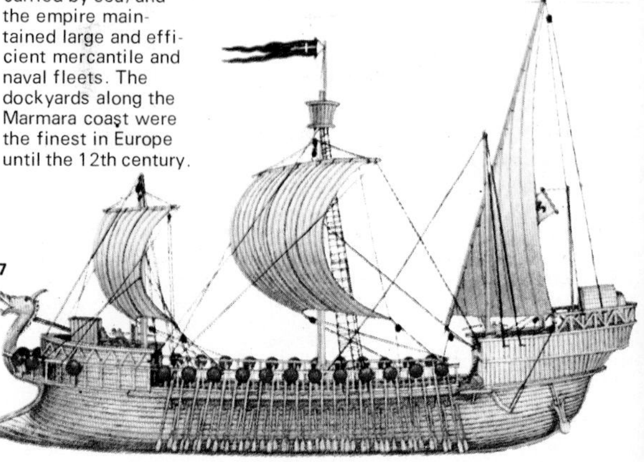

7 The dromon was a Byzantine adaptation of the traditional Greek galley. Much Byzantine trade was carried by sea, and the empire maintained large and efficient mercantile and naval fleets. The dockyards along the Marmara coast were the finest in Europe until the 12th century.

law. His *Codex Justinianus* remained throughout the Middle Ages the principal legal source book in Europe.

Byzantium became increasingly Greek in character after the reign of Justinian, and Greek replaced Latin as the official language [5]. The conquests in the west were short-lived, and the ravages of plague weakened the empire's ability to resist Persian attacks in the east. Aided by dissident Monophysites, the Persians occupied most of Egypt, Syria, and Palestine by 615. A greater menace appeared in 637 when the Arabs, five years after the death of the prophet Mohammed, overran Syria and Palestine. Later they took north Africa, Sicily, and the important grain lands of Egypt, while their fleets secured Cyprus, Rhodes, and other islands.

Revival and decline (867–1453)

As its boundaries shrank, the empire regained its ethnic unity and acquired renewed strength. From 867, under a Macedonian dynasty, it took the initiative against the Muslims, and by the time of the death of Basil II (958–1025) its borders reached from the Danube to Crete and from southern Italy to Syria [2]. Trade flourished [9], and missionaries spread Christianity throughout the Balkans and into Russia.

The Turks were soon to bring the empire to its knees, however. The defeat of Romanus IV at Manzikert by the Seljuks in 1071 and the subsequent capture of Anatolia were the beginning of the end. From then until 1453 the empire was steadily eroded by bureaucratic intrigues, external attacks, and religious conflicts [3]. The Crusaders, whose help was enlisted against the Seljuks, fell out with the Byzantines, took Constantinople in 1204, and set up a number of semi-independent Latin states. Religious schisms and trade rivalries prevented any concerted western effort against the Ottoman Turks. Although only Constantinople and a few outposts along the Sea of Marmara remained by 1453, it took Sultan Mehmet II (1431–81) [10] nearly two months to capture the great city itself. With his final victory the old Byzantine world came to an end.

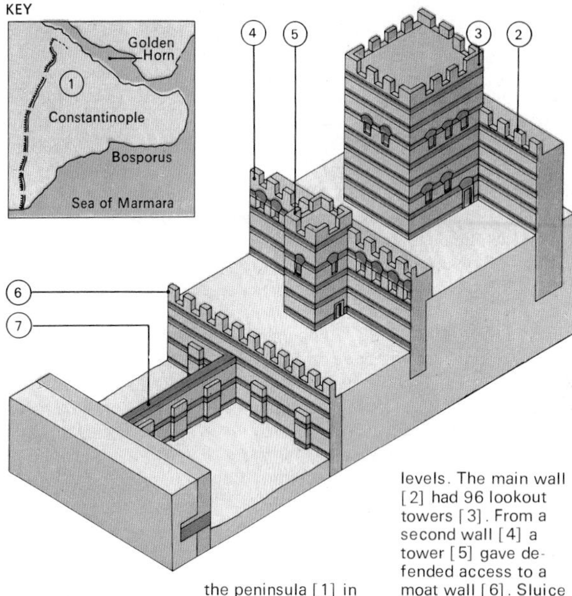
KEY
Golden Horn
1
Constantinople
Bosporus
Sea of Marmara
4
5
3
2
6
7

Constantinople's walls, built across the peninsula [1] in the 5th century, were defensible at varying levels. The main wall [2] had 96 lookout towers [3]. From a second wall [4] a tower [5] gave defended access to a moat wall [6]. Sluice gates [7] controlled water in the moat.

8

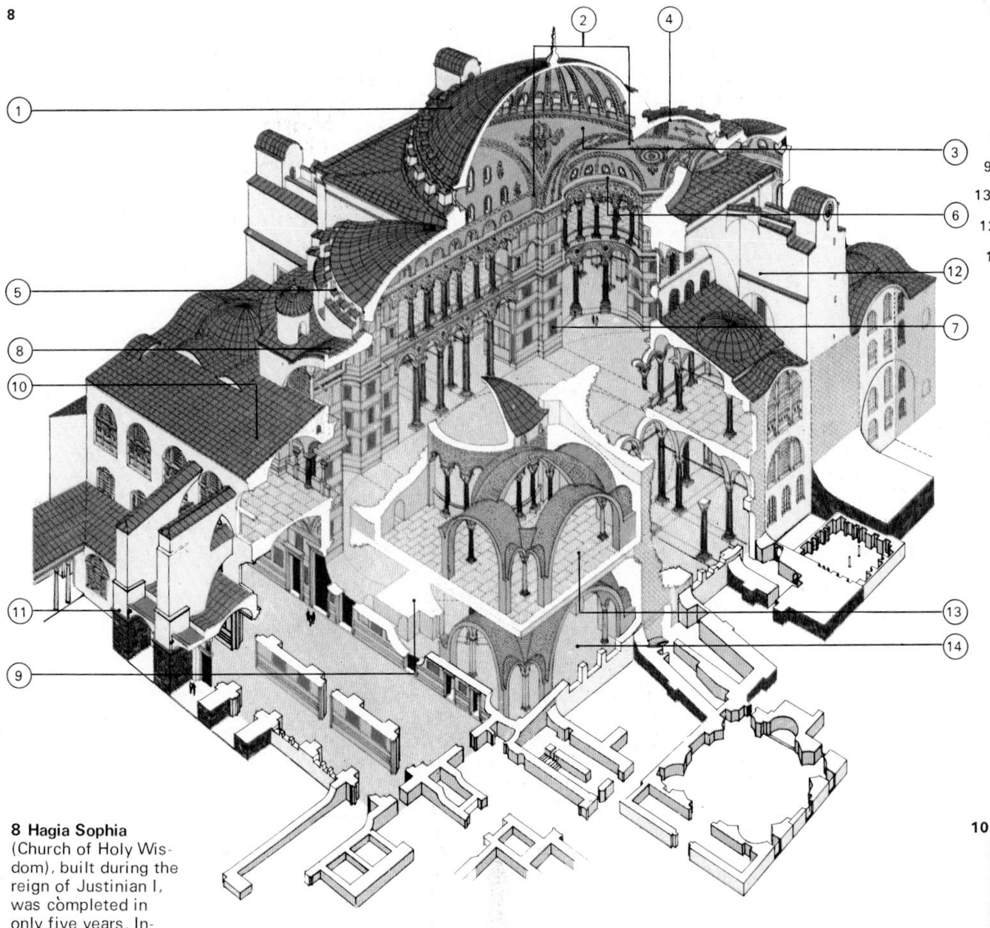
1
2
3
4
5
6
7
8
9
10
11
12
13
14

8 Hagia Sophia (Church of Holy Wisdom), built during the reign of Justinian I, was completed in only five years. Intended to provide a spiritual center for the empire, it was the largest Christian church in the eastern world and was exceeded in splendor only by St. Peter's in Rome. The most famous of many architects who worked on the project were Anthemius of Tralles and Isidorus of Miletus. The overall design shows little classical influence, although Justinian despoiled classical buildings in Athens, Ephesus, Rome, and Baalbek for marble. Technically, the most striking feature is the massive central dome [1], which measures 100ft (31m) across. Its thrust is borne by four arches [2], joined by pendentives [3], which separate the semidomes [4 and 5]. Subsidiary semidomes [6] flank the main piers [7]. The thrust from [5] is taken at the west by an arch [8] supported on piers [9]. Vaulting [10] transfers the outward thrust to a series of flying buttresses [11]. Buttresses [12] support the dome's north and south thrust. By building domes on arches [13 and 14], large areas could be spanned. The exterior brickwork is plastered. Brick domes and semidomes are leadcovered. Interior walls, piers, and floors are clad in various marbles and vaults and domes in rich mosaics. The church was used as a mosque after 1453 and has been a museum since 1933.

9

Buda Pest
Venice
Kaffa
Cherson
Naples
Constantinople
Hieron
Salonika
Abydos
Trebizond
Messina
Aleppo
Damascus
Jerusalem
Alexandria
Cairo

Byzantine Empire in 1045
Trade flow
Customs houses

1	Amber	9	Timber
2	Ivory	10	Spices
3	Gems	11	Salt
4	Minerals	12	Weapons
5	Gold	13	Slaves
6	Textiles	14	Wax
7	Cotton	15	Furs
8	Silk	16	Dried fish

9 Major trade routes of the 11th century reached a natural junction at Constantinople, and the city became a great east-west market. An imperial duty of 10% was levied on imports reaching Hieron from the Black Sea, Abydos from the Mediterranean, Trebizond from Asia, and Salonika from the Balkans. Byzantine craftsmen were famed for their working of gold, silver, amber, and ivory.

10

10 Sultan Mehmet II ("the Conqueror") gave the Ottoman Empire a European outlook when he took Constantinople in 1453 and made it a center of learning and religious tolerance. Although autocratic, he was a gifted administrator. Gentile Bellini, who painted this portrait, was among the Italian artists he patronized.

Mohammed and Islam

Mohammed (Mahomet) was born in Mecca in west central Arabia *c*.570. He had an unhappy childhood: his father, mother, and grandfather died before he was eight and left him in the care of an uncle. At the age of 25 he married a wealthy widow, Khadija, who bore him six children, and for 24 years they lived happily together. Only after her death in 619 did Mohammed take other wives, to strengthen ties with important families and to seek—unsuccessfully—a male heir.

The visions of Mohammed

When he was 40 years old Mohammed, who loved solitude, was in a cave on Mount Hira outside Mecca when he had visions of the angel Gabriel calling him to "recite" in the name of God the creator. He received revelations that were to become the first parts of the Koran ("recitation"). Mohammed conveyed these teachings to a group of friends who believed with him in the unity of God.

At first the little group, which met for prayers to God (Allah), was ignored or scorned, but as their numbers grew they were persecuted. Some took refuge for a time in Christian Ethiopia. They were called Muslims (Moslems)—"surrendered men"; in the religion of Islam they had "surrendered" or submitted to the one God. Early converts were made from Yathrib, a town 120 miles (200km) north of Mecca, and Mohammed was invited to go there. In 622 the *hegira* (migration) took place, with Mohammed and his followers moving from Mecca to Yathrib, henceforth called Medina, the "city" of the prophet. The Muslim year is dated from this *hegira*.

At Medina, Mohammed built a mosque and a house and sent his followers on raids to provide funds and ensure protection against armies from Mecca. There were battles at Badr and Uhud, and finally Mohammed's armies and influence grew, so that in 630 he was able to capture Mecca almost without loss [1]. He rode around the Kaaba [4] and had its idols destroyed.

After the death of the prophet

The death of the prophet in 632 was sudden, but after some hesitation his friend, the elderly Abu Bakr (573–634), was appointed as caliph—successor to the prophet and vicegerent of God. Arabian tribes that had been bound to Mohammed by oath began to break away, but Abu Bakr sent armies to establish Muslim rule. They were so successful that his forces broke out of Arabia into the rest of southwestern Asia. Abu Bakr died two years after his appointment, but under his successors, the caliphs Omar and Othman, Arab armies rapidly conquered Mesopotamia and entered Persia, while others entered Syria. Jerusalem surrendered to them, and Omar visited the Christian churches there and the site of the ancient Jewish temple. Later a great shrine, the Dome of the Rock, was built on the site. Arab armies went to Egypt, where Alexandria surrendered; after some delay they traveled along north Africa and in 711 crossed into Spain and Portugal at Gibraltar. They even penetrated into the heart of France, where in 732 the Muslim armies were defeated by the Frankish forces under Charles Martel.

They remained in southern France for some years and longer in Portugal. Spain

CONNECTIONS

See also
1062 Arabs and the rise Islam
1064 Islamic art
846 Islam, Hinduism, ar Buddhism
988 Buddha and Buddhism
1026 Christ and the Apos tles
1040 Confucius and Con fucianism

1 This painting is from a copy of *Siyar-i Nabi* (Life of the Prophet) and shows Mohammed and Abu Bakr on their way to Mecca from Medina. The prophet, here shown faceless with a flaming halo, is rarely depicted because of religious taboos. Islamic art is unique in that historical events take a secondary place to the intensity of religious feeling. This work is an example of the style of the 16th-century Ottoman court.

2 Mohammed was a "warner," calling men to turn from idols to worship the one true God (Allah). There are no contemporary pictures of the prophet because of the taboo on images. Later he was pictured as a holy man.

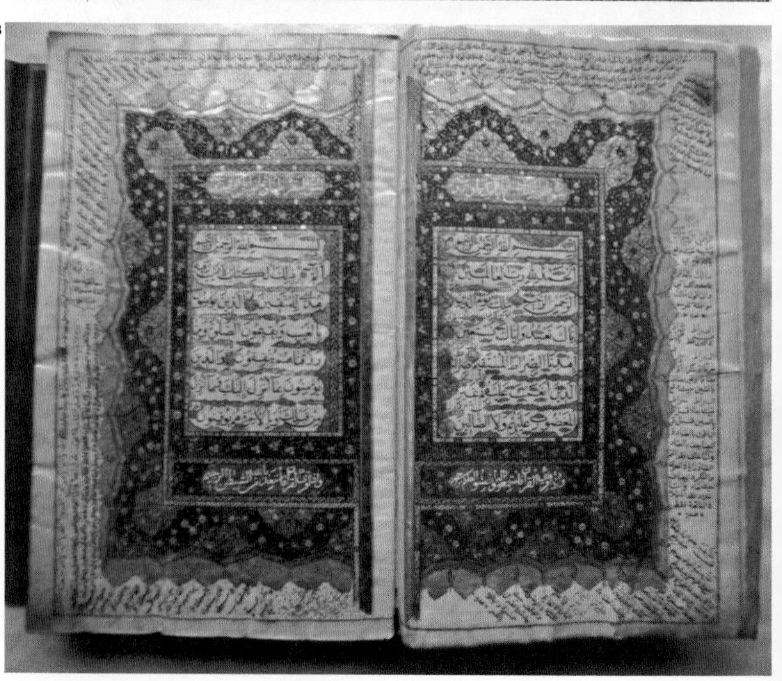

3 The Koran is the sacred book of Islam. All Muslims know some of its verses by heart and use them in daily prayers. Illuminated copies of the Koran in gold and bright colors were painstakingly handwritten by skilled scribes.

was their major conquest and there the Moors, as they were known, remained until the fall of Granada in 1492. In the east, Persia came completely under Muslim rule, as did a large part of India. The Muslims preserved much of the cultures they encountered and transmitted them, taking Indian numerals as Arabic numerals to Europe and preserving Greek medicine, astronomy, and philosophy during the Dark Ages of the west. The last caliph was deposed in Constantinople in 1924.

The importance of the Koran

Mohammed, who is said to have been illiterate, passed the Koran, the divine word, to his followers, and it was written down by scribes at his recitation or from memory [3]. The final official version was completed under Othman, about 20 years after the death of Mohammed. The Koran is in Arabic, in 112 *suras* (chapters), the first of which is always recited in daily prayers. Most of the early chapters are long and deal with religious and social matters, while the later ones are short and challenging.

The Koran teaches faith in God, the coming judgment against unbelief, and the ideas of heaven and hell; it also describes duties appropriate to marriage, the family, and social life. Many stories in it parallel ones in the Old and New Testaments, and Adam, Abraham, Moses, and Jesus appear as prophets. The religious duties of Islam are taught in five pillars: confession of faith in one God and Mohammed as his apostle; prayer five times a day [5, 7]; alms-giving of a proportion of one's income; fasting from all food and drink during the daylight hours throughout the whole of Ramadan (the ninth month of the year); and pilgrimage to Mecca at least once in a lifetime.

All men and women are bound to perform these religious and social duties, with exemptions for the young, sick, and old. Islam is an international religion, with perhaps 500 million followers, mostly in Asia and Africa. The Arabic language prevails in the southern Mediterranean and many Middle Eastern countries and is used by all Muslims in reciting the Koran and in making formal prayers.

KEY

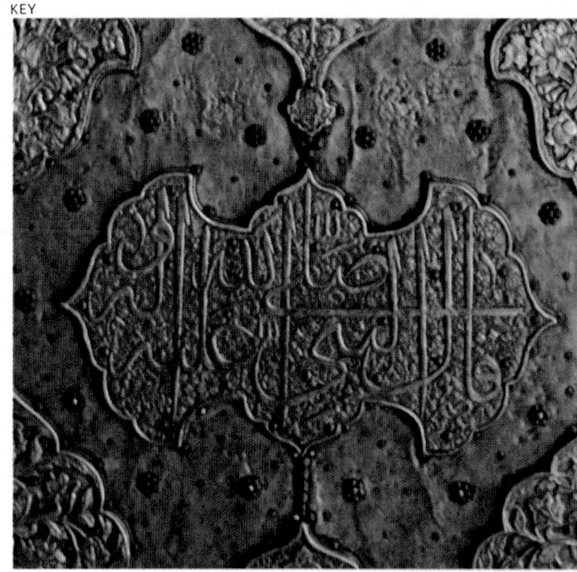

"Praise be to Allah," the first words of the Koran, is a favorite text inscribed on the walls of mosques around the world.

4

4 In the center of Mecca stands the Kaaba (cube), a stone building covered with a black cloth, toward which Muslims turn in prayer and around which they go at times of pilgrimage to Mecca.

5

5 Five times every day Muslims are called to prayer from a mosque or minaret tower. The *muezzin* calls "God is most great; there is no god but God; Mohammed is the Apostle of God; come to prayers; come to salvation."

6

6 The Royal Mosque Masjid-i-Shah, in Isfahan, Iran, was built in the 17th century for Shah Abbas the Great. It is composed of porches, halls, domes, and minarets covered with blue tiles and mosaics. Long friezes of elegant lettering proclaim the glory of God.

7

7 Prayer rugs, such as this eighteenth-century Persian example, are famous products of Muslim artisans. Larger ones cover mosque floors.

Byzantine art

The small proportion of Byzantine art that survives is mostly "official" art—the aesthetic visualization of either Christian "truth" or imperial authority, or a combination of both as the Christian Roman state. Such art was the dominant product of this society. The term "secular art" has little application to Byzantine art, which began with the foundation of the imperial capital Constantinople in 330 and ended with its fall to the Turks in 1453.

"Official" art

The new capital on the site of Byzantium brought Roman art back into the geographical setting where many of its traditions, forms, and media had originated. Yet Byzantine art was no mere continuation of Greco-Roman art in the service of the Orthodox Church. When fourth-century Constantinople emulated Old Rome by erecting two cochleate (spiral) columns, their sculptured reliefs (known from drawings) were developed far beyond Trajan's classical forms; they do not merely abound with Christian symbols but convey imperial triumph with an endless procession of stiff figures. The style reflects the hierarchy of the state. This new art developed in the rich cities of the eastern Mediterranean—for example, in the cupola mosaics of St George in Thessaloniki (450), where a superficially Hellenistic style portrays the place of Christian martyrs in the heavens.

The first great achievements of Byzantine art belong to the reign of Justinian (527–65), whose patronage ranged from St Sophia in the capital to the remote mosaics of Mt Sinai [1]. The "Dark Ages" after Justinian, when Byzantium was under constant threat of invasion, saw a rise in the production of icons for the cult of images or saints as the mediators for personal salvation. The Iconoclast emperors from 726 until 843 tried to impose a nonfigurative religious art, comparable to medieval Muslim and Jewish societies.

After Iconoclasm, the Macedonian emperors (867–1065) celebrated the "Triumph of Orthodoxy" with the redecoration of churches, starting with the apse of St Sophia. It was not a period of stylistic revolution. The period of Justinian was recreated; progress in Byzantium customarily meant regress to past ages.

New patrons

More art survives from the Comnenian dynasty (1081–1185) than from the Macedonian. Under the Comnenes, the wealth of Byzantium significantly shifted from the emperors and bishoprics into the hands of aristocratic landowners and monasteries. The affluence of these patrons is reflected in numerous church decorations and in many other artifacts. Taste for gold and saturated colors stimulated an unrivaled mosaic expertise. Cubes of glass (colored or fused with gold or silver leaf), marble, even precious stones were pressed one by one into lime plaster beds on church vaults. Each could be tilted to reflect light from windows or lamps. Vast mosaic figures in an ethereal gold glow surrounded the Byzantine worshipers.

From the point of view of the artists, the twelfth century was a period of refinement and sophistication of earlier forms, accom-

CONNECTIONS

See also
1056 The Byzantine Empire
1030 Rome: soldier emperors to Constantine
1108 The Ottoman Empire to 1600
1022 Roman art 27 BC–AD 117
1024 Roman art 117–550
1000 Greek art 1100–450 BC
1002 Greek art 450–31 BC

1 This mosaic medallion of St John the Baptist is from the basilica founded around 550 by Justinian on the Burning Bush site on Sinai (now St Catherine's Monastery). Its great expressiveness suggests that the decorators were from Constantinople and were able to transform a classical tragic mask into mosaic.

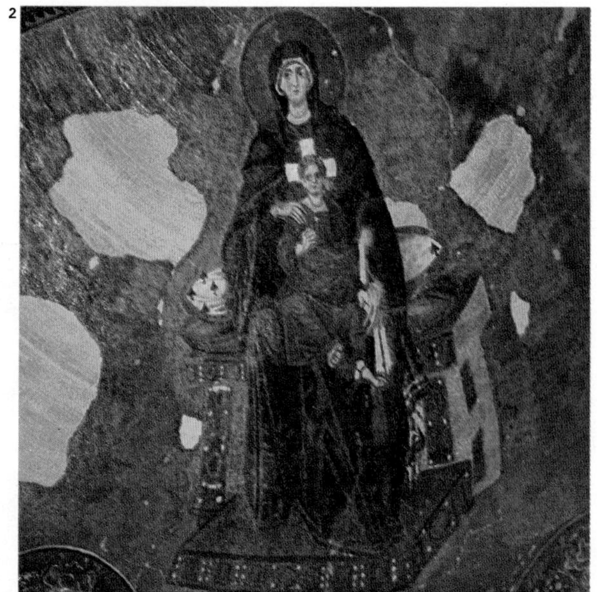

2 The mosaic of the Enthroned Madonna and Child in the apse of St Sophia, Constantinople, was probably unveiled by Patriarch Photius in March 867. The patriarch claimed in a celebrated sermon that the painting seemed so lifelike that Mary is "not incapable of speaking."

3 David fighting a lion is one of seven portraits opening the *Paris Psalter*. The atmospheric setting and female personification assisting David are devices of classical art, suggesting the artist was an antiquarian.

4 This Crucifixion is in the monastery of St Luke of Stiris, central Greece. Luke's relics attracted pilgrims and so financed the 11th-century church. The saints here express piety, and the scene has a direct style.

5 The mosaics of the Crucifixion in the Monastery of Daphni, near Athens (*c.* 1100) suffered extensive restoration in the 1890s. The style is more narrative than at St Luke's Monastery and is also more emotional.

panied by a growing self-consciousness: artists began to sign their works in this century. Two major mosaic decorations in Greece illuminate the middle centuries of Byzantium. The Crucifixion in the Monastery of St Luke, of the Macedonian period, delineates Christ's death as a stark episode in church history [4]. The Comnenian Crucifixion at Daphni [5] still forms one unit in a dogmatic cycle, but the artist emphasizes the human aspects; the mosaic is more consciously "art."

Individuality within conformity

Since Comnenian artists normally decorated standard architecture (the cross-in-a-square cupola church) with a standard repertory (life of Christ and Mary), this may paradoxically have stimulated individuality within conformity. In Monreale the mosaicists brought to Sicily adapted their repertory to a large scale [6]. The challenge was to their technical expertise rather than to their inventiveness with subject matter.

The Latin occupation of Constantinople (1204–61) did permanent damage to the Byzantine economy, and Paleologan art (1261–1453) is on a reduced scale. The last great mosaic decoration was that of the Kariye Camii, where an aristocrat provided himself with a mortuary chapel [7, 8]. Icon production increased in this period, especially for church sanctuary screens. Paleologan artists absorbed earlier styles and made further developments. Late Byzantine art influenced Western European art; it is harder to see what it derived from Western contacts. Did Byzantium stimulate, reject, or fail to understand the Western developments? Late Byzantine compositions become increasingly complicated; clarity of expression was seldom considered a merit by Byzantines.

After the middle of the fourteenth century there was little money left for art in Constantinople, and such outstanding artists as Theophanes the Greek left to find work elsewhere. Though the consequence was to disseminate the Byzantine tradition, the destruction of imperial Constantinople in 1453 terminated the society and creative Byzantine art.

KEY

The frontispiece of a luxurious psalter (detail) painted in Constantinople (1018 to 1025) commemorates the victory of Basil II over the Bulgarians. The triumphant emperor, crowned by Christ, armed by archangels, and assisted by military saints, tramples his conquered enemies underfoot. The picture both declares the power of the Byzantines and expresses their conception of sovereignty, with their emperor as representative of Jesus Christ on earth.

6 A

B

6 Monreale Cathedral [A] near Palermo, Sicily, was founded by William II (*r.* 1166–89) to rival the cathedral of Palermo. It is a Latin basilica, with a Greek cross-in-square sanctuary. The intricate polychrome east façade dominates the hill seen from Palermo. Christ Pantocrator is the focus of the vast mosaic interior [B]. The dramatic style was the fashion in Constantinople.

7 The Kariye Camii, Istanbul with minaret belonging to its Turkish conversion into a mosque, is now a museum. This was the 11th-century Chora Monastery, which was refounded in 1315–21.

7

8 The Chora (Kariye Camii) was decorated by its 14th-century refounder Theodore Metochites with mosaics, except in the south chapel, which held his tomb in a frescoed setting. The apse (detail here) contained the Anastasis Christ at Easter rescuing Adam and Eve from Hell. Metochites justified his greed by his use of wealth; this decoration eased his guilt by promising an afterlife.

8

9

9 The Annunciation is one side of a double-sided icon in the National Museum, Ohrid, Yugoslavia. The icon also portrays the Virgin, Savior of Souls. Once a furnishing of the Peribleptos Church (now at St Clement's), the icon was perhaps sent from Constantinople and was probably painted around 1300.

10

10 In this 14th-century miniature mosaic icon of the Annunciation the minute glass cubes are set in beeswax. Such portable mosaics became fashionable among the few rich families of Paleologan Constantinople and were collected by Renaissance popes. This was virtually the only form of Byzantine art appreciated in the West.

Arabs and the rise of Islam

Arab expansion was a tribal conquest of civilization. Such conquests are commonplace in history, but the Arabs are the only people who started a new civilization as a result of their conquest. This came about by a combination of two special circumstances. First, on the side of the conquerors there was a unique fusion of religious conviction [2] and tribal military force. The Arabs conquered the Middle East [4] in the name of a monotheism that sanctified their tribal heritage over and against the conquered civilizations, and their conquests were so successful that they had no need to come to terms with those civilizations. The Arabs were thus well placed to avoid being culturally absorbed by the peoples they had conquered.

Second, on the side of the conquered peoples there prevailed in Egypt, Syria, and Iraq a unique type of provincial culture. Having lost their own civilizations some 1,400 years before, when they first came under the rule of alien empires, these provinces had not yet been fully assimilated by Byzantium and Persia, later Iran. As a result, they were less committed to these civilizations, and the Arabs were exposed only to a culture filtered through a provincial milieu and language.

The strength of the Arab position as against the weakness of provincial culture is the keynote of early Islamic history politically, culturally, and ethnically.

The political influence

Politically, the strength of the Arab position determined the evolution of the Arab conquest society. With the Umayyad dynasty [4] (661–750) the capital was moved from Medina to Syria, where a tribal confederacy formed the basis of the caliphs' power; in the provinces the tribal armies were placed under tribal leaders in a system of indirect rule. Within some 40 years the erosion of kinship ties had rendered the system obsolete, and the tribal armies gave way to professional soldiers and civilians.

Normally, the loss of the tribal organization means that the conquerors must borrow the political organization of their subjects or suffer political disintegration; either way the conquered civilizations eventually win. But among the Arabs the sanctity of the tribal past meant that neither of these eventualities came to pass, and the obsolete organization was retained until the third civil war (744), which was followed by the Abbasid revolution. It was thus that the Abbasids (750–1258) [3] had to govern an Islamic empire as opposed to an Arab conquest society without losing the link with the tribal past, a problem that eventually proved insoluble. Although the Arabs attempted in various ways to foster an imperial ideal and aristocracy within Islam on the Iranian model, the fourth civil war (811–13) meant the failure of such attempts, the adoption of slave armies [5] as the instrument of government, and, soon afterward, the dissolution of the unitary state. The delay, however, allowed Islamic civilization to develop sufficiently to survive.

Islamic culture and learning

Culturally, Arab strength accounts for the character of Islamic learning. The core of Islam is a revealed law, actually created in

CONNECTIONS

See also
1064 Islamic art
1058 Mohammed and Islam
1108 The Ottoman Empire to 1600
1078 Islam in Europe
1066 Charlemagne and the Carolingian Empire
1070 Western European economy 800–1000

1 Mohammed designated Ali as his immediate successor according to the doctrine of the Shiites, and by the evidence of this miniature. But members of the Sunni sect accept Ali as the third caliph.

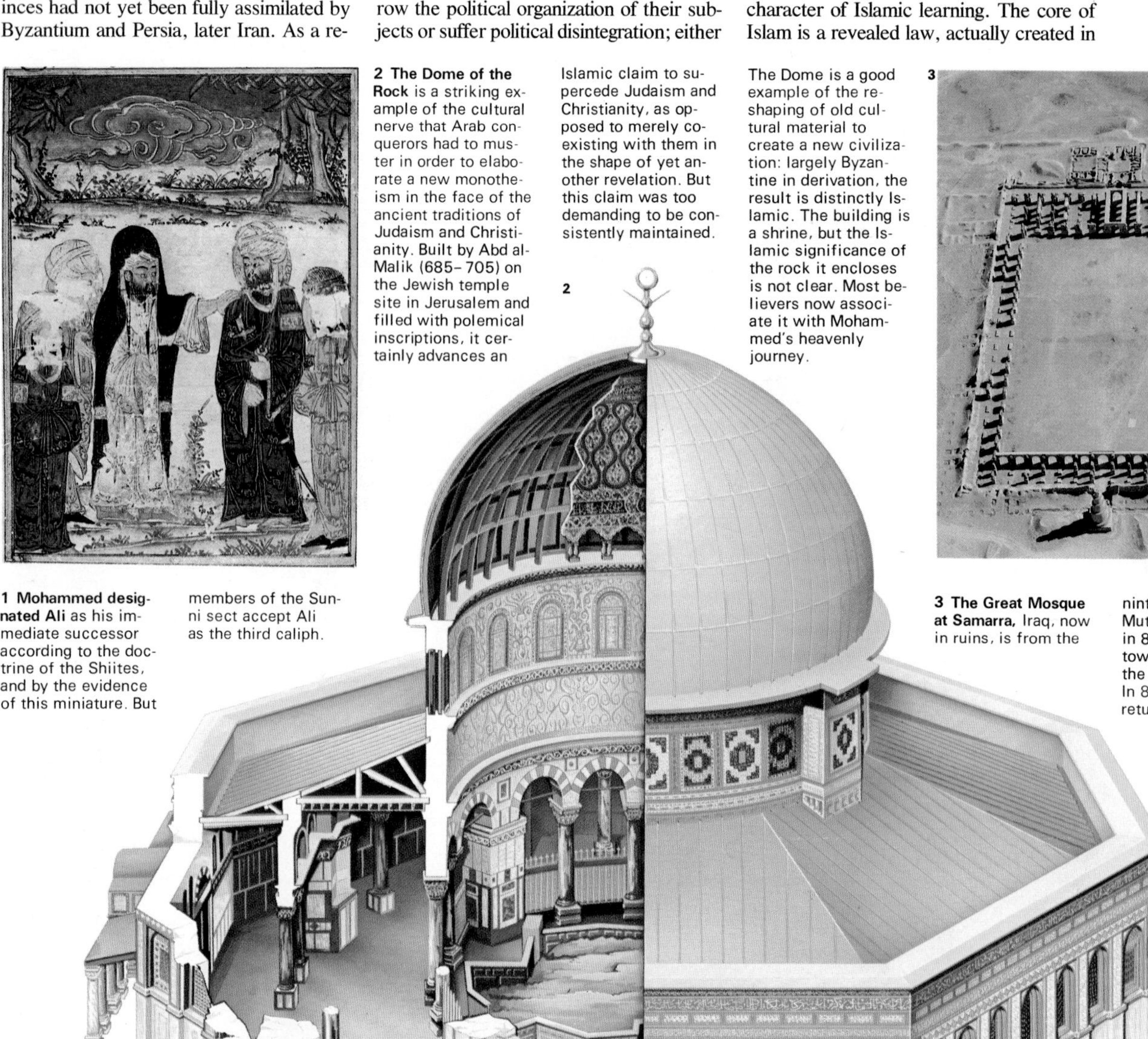

2 The Dome of the Rock is a striking example of the cultural nerve that Arab conquerors had to muster in order to elaborate a new monotheism in the face of the ancient traditions of Judaism and Christianity. Built by Abd al-Malik (685–705) on the Jewish temple site in Jerusalem and filled with polemical inscriptions, it certainly advances an Islamic claim to supercede Judaism and Christianity, as opposed to merely coexisting with them in the shape of yet another revelation. But this claim was too demanding to be consistently maintained. The Dome is a good example of the reshaping of old cultural material to create a new civilization: largely Byzantine in derivation, the result is distinctly Islamic. The building is a shrine, but the Islamic significance of the rock it encloses is not clear. Most believers now associate it with Mohammed's heavenly journey.

3 The Great Mosque at Samarra, Iraq, now in ruins, is from the ninth century when Mutasim (*r.* 833–42) in 836 made the town the capital of the Abbasid Empire. In 892 the caliphs returned to Baghdad.

Iraq in the eighth and ninth centuries from a variety of foreign materials, but in theory based exclusively on the Koran and the Prophet's sayings and doings. It was the learned laity studying Islamic law who came to be seen as the legitimate heirs to Mohammed's preaching.

It follows that it was not difficult to create an Islamic scholarship, overwhelmingly Arab in orientation, but it was not so easy to create an Islamic philosophy and science. The Arabs did inherit Greek philosophy from the conquered provinces but, being neither Arab nor Islamic, such teaching met with stiff resistance from the learned laity to whom it was ungodly wisdom. Although philosophy continued to be cultivated, it was gradually relegated to marginal and heretical circles.

Ethnic development

Ethnically, the weakness of provincial culture explains the overwhelming Arab influence on the Middle East. Islam began as a religion for Arabs, but could not remain so when the non-Arabs began to convert to it. From being an ethnic faith on the Judaic model it had to become a universal belief on the Christian model, but the transition was never quite completed. Mohammed was an Arab who, unlike Jesus, had never ceased to be honored in his own community, and in his name the Arabs had conquered a kingdom that was very much of this world [Key]. The notion that a Muslim was in some sense an Arab, and Islamic civilization in some sense Arabian, therefore proved extremely tenacious. In the ninth and tenth centuries non-Arab converts, especially Iranians, attempted to disentangle Islam from its Arab origins, insisting that Islam was a faith that could be combined with any identity and culture; but the success of these so-called *shuubis* was limited. The three provinces—Egypt, Syria, and Iraq—all became Arab countries, while Iran, not a province but an empire, retained its Iranian identity but largely lost its Iranian civilization. Only where Islam spread peacefully, as in parts of black Africa and Java, has it proved flexible enough to combine with a local culture.

KEY

Camel-breeding Bedouin tribesmen roamed over most of Arabia before the days of oil. South Arabia had sufficient internal resources to maintain stable state structures, while in the north external resources were often available in the form of commercial revenues or imperial subsidies. But most of the peninsula was too poor to support a non-tribal organization. Here Mohammed was the first, but not the last, to create a state in the name of a religious doctrine. By uniting the tribesmen as believers and calling on them to wage war against the unbelievers, he provided a rationale for a conquest of the fertile lands that would form a vast empire.

4 The unification of Arabia is traditionally credited to Mohammed and was accomplished before his death in 632. Egypt and Syria were taken from the Byzantines and Iraq, and the Iranian plateau from the Sasanids between 632 and 656, when civil war broke out. The first Umayyad caliph, Muawiya (661–80), resumed Arab expansion in North Africa and eastern Iran, while a second thrust under Walid I (705–15) pushed the Arabs into Spain and India; but a last attempt to conquer Constantinople in 715–16 failed. At the end of the Umayyad period (750) the limits of Arab expansion were the Pyrenees, the Sahara, the Caucasus, and Turkestan. Further expansion became the work of local dynasties, missionaries, and merchants, and continued far beyond 945.

4

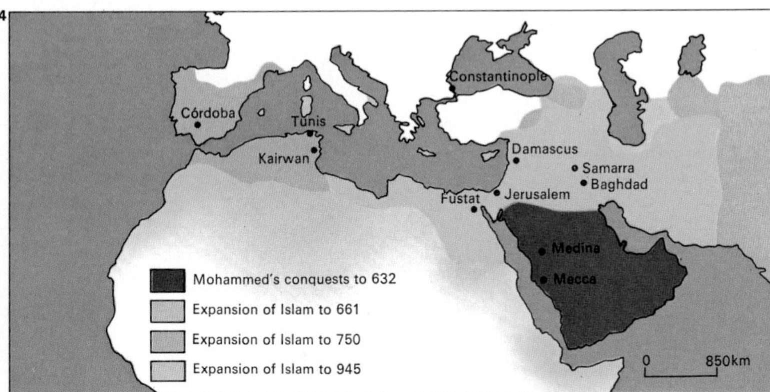
Constantinople
Córdoba
Tunis
Kairwan
Damascus
Samarra
Baghdad
Fustat
Jerusalem
Medina
Mecca
Mohammed's conquests to 632
Expansion of Islam to 661
Expansion of Islam to 750
Expansion of Islam to 945
0
850km

5

5 A mounted archer (detail from a Palmyra fresco) typifies the kind of Turkish slave soldier from Transoxania who swelled the ranks of the Islamic armies. Transoxania, which was once the western frontier of Iran, is now wholly Turkish. Divided into well entrenched principalities, it was a difficult place for the Arabs to conquer. As a result, Iranian culture survived and it was in this marginal province that the revival of Iranian literature in Islam took place from the 10th century onward. Transoxania was exposed to Turkish tribes and after several invasions eventually became Turkish.

6 A hoard of Arab coins from a 10th-century Viking grave in Sweden represents payment for the slaves, fur, and honey that were exported to the Muslims by the Vikings who colonized Russia.

6

7 Harun al-Rashid is one of the few caliphs to have fired western imagination, thanks to *The Arabian Nights' Entertainments*. His reign (786–809) fell in the period following the transfer of the capital from Syria to the culturally richer Iraq, but politically his days were troubled. Faced with revolts and sectarian discontent, he divided his lands between his sons; this provoked a fourth civil war that, disastrously for royal continuity, was won by a provincial army.

7

8 Kairwan, in Tunisia, was founded as a garrison city for the settlement of Arab soldiers. It soon became a center of learning and orthodoxy in North Africa, which was at that time inhabited overwhelmingly by Berbers. On conversion, the Berbers repeatedly made use of the program of tribal state formation and conquest enshrined in the Prophet's career, in the name of a doctrine that was sometimes reformist, sometimes heretical. Although North Africa is extensively Arabized today, it still has a substantial Berber population. But Arab or Berber, Islam among North African tribesmen is distinctive, centering on holy men often identified as descendants of the Prophet.

8

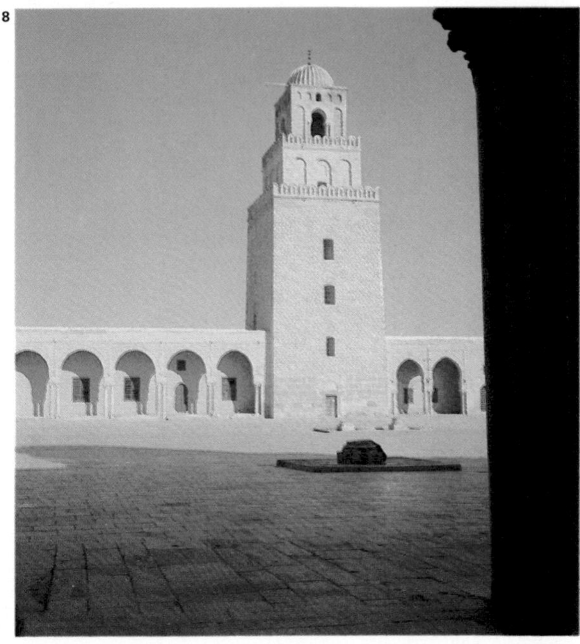

Islamic art

Architecture and its decoration best illustrate what is known as Islamic art. But the glamour of the great religious buildings has also tended to obscure the importance of Islamic secular art, which expressed itself most readily in painting, pottery, metalwork, and textiles.

The extent of Islamic art

Geographically, Islamic art extended from Spain in the west to Indonesia in the east. It flourished from the seventh to the seventeenth centuries and thereafter gradually declined. Despite this wide range in space and time it has an instantly recognizable cachet. This is most apparent in Islamic decoration, which displays unequaled resource and virtuosity. The ban on the representation of living figures in a religious context—a ban that did not apply in secular art—directed the imaginative energy of the artist toward geometric, floral, and epigraphic ornament such as the ubiquitous and aptly named arabesque (winding stems and leaves) and numerous varieties of Arabic script. In religious buildings Koranic inscriptions predominated, and calligraphy was given special reverence [Key].

In architecture the characteristic Islamic building is the mosque [1]. In its primitive form it derived from Mohammed's house in Medina, which had an open enclosed courtyard with a roofed area facing Mecca. Many mosques had a minaret—a tall tower for the call to prayer. Other characteristic Islamic buildings include the *caravansary* for accommodating travelers, the *madrasa* or theological college, and the *ribat*, a kind of fortified monastery. Palaces and tombs [5] abound. These various building types differ considerably from one country to the next, but most have a number of domes; lengthy arcades with pointed or horseshoe arches; complex vaulting; open courtyards as an integral part of the design; and large expanses of flat wall surfaces decorated with carved stucco, polychrome tilework, or inlaid marble.

Early Islamic art was produced mainly in Syria under the Umayyad dynasty (661–750). Umayyad religious buildings clothed Byzantine forms in glittering mosaics, while palaces used chiefly Persian motifs within a basically Roman structure. Such eclecticism remained a constant feature of Islamic art.

Stylistic variations in Islamic art

By the ninth century a classical Islamic art had developed under the Abbasid caliphate in Iraq and spread widely throughout Islam [7]. Its prime feature was carved or molded stucco using geometric and rigorously stylized vegetal motifs, endlessly repeated.

As the power of the Abbasid caliphs waned, new political groupings generated five distinctive regional styles: Hispano-Moorish, Syro-Egyptian, Turkish, Persian, and Indo-Muslim. In Spain the establishment of an anti-Abbasid Umayyad caliphate gave Syrian art a new lease on life, inspiring a distinctive style that spread through northwest Africa. It was marked by an extreme, mannered delicacy of ornament applied to basically simple structures [8].

The Syro-Egyptian tradition produced a notable variety of religious buildings with

CONNECTIONS

See also
1062 Arabs and the rise c
Islam
1108 The Ottoman Empir
to 1600
1056 The Byzantine Empi
1060 Byzantine art
1036 Indian art to the
Moguls

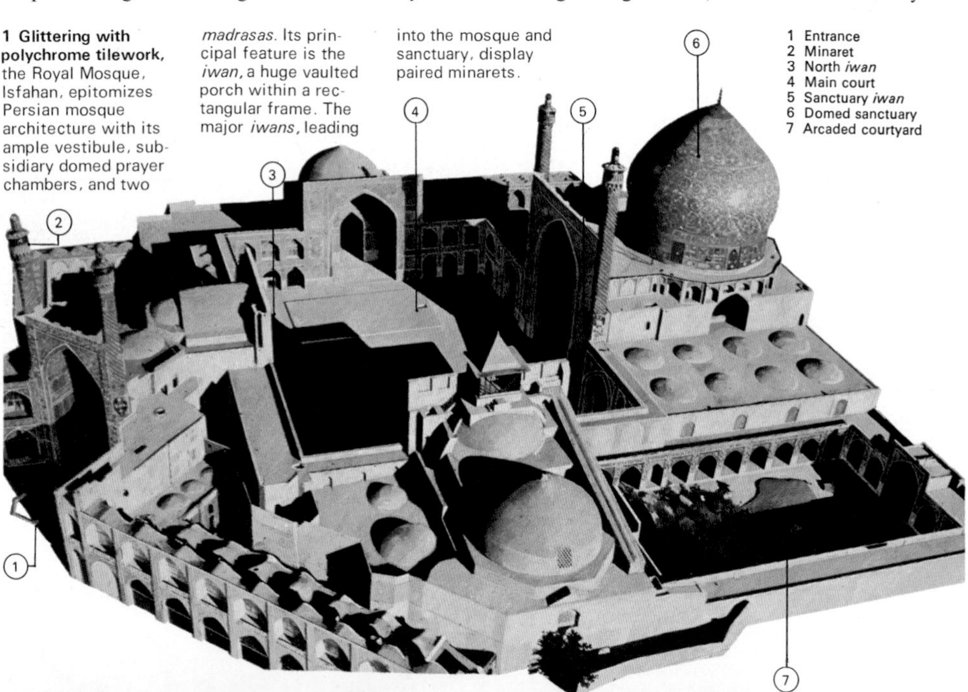

1 Entrance
2 Minaret
3 North *iwan*
4 Main court
5 Sanctuary *iwan*
6 Domed sanctuary
7 Arcaded courtyard

1 Glittering with polychrome tilework, the Royal Mosque, Isfahan, epitomizes Persian mosque architecture with its ample vestibule, subsidiary domed prayer chambers, and two *madrasas*. Its principal feature is the *iwan*, a huge vaulted porch within a rectangular frame. The major *iwans*, leading into the mosque and sanctuary, display paired minarets.

2 The Ardabil carpet (1539–40), signed by Maqsud of Kashan, is 637 sq ft (61.85 sq m), ample room for its complex design.

3 Painted in Iran in 1296, this bestiary page reflects the rule of the Mongols. Through their pan-Asiatic empire, numerous Chinese motifs were introduced into Persian painting–in this case the phoenix and the conventions used for feathers, plants, and border around the page.

4 This ceramic bowl with luster-painted decoration (*c.* 1300) depicts a Coptic priest swinging a censer. The design was scratched with a stick and is essentially a pattern of rhythmical reciprocating curves. The double-fired technique and decoration reflect Mesopotamian influence.

carved stone exteriors and rather cramped interiors. Turkish architects, at first greatly influenced by the neighboring Arab and Persian styles, later responded to the challenge of Hagia Sophia in Constantinople, the greatest of Byzantine churches, by perfecting the Ottoman type of mosque. This has a great central dome visually (but not structurally) shored up by tiers of half-domes and slender, pencil-shaped minarets at the corners.

Pottery, metalwork, and painting

Among the minor arts, which occasionally borrowed from China and also from Europe, Islamic pottery displays technical virtuosity of a high order, especially in lusterware. The accent was always on color and decoration (which could be figural, epigraphic, geometric, or vegetal) rather than on shape or body [4]. The major centers of these arts were successively Mesopotamia, Egypt, Persia, and Turkey.

Islamic metalwork, mainly bronze, was technically extremely diverse, used a variety of shapes, and favored scenes of courtly life framed by bands of stately inscriptions. Its heyday was in Persia and the Arab Near East from the twelfth to the fourteenth centuries [9]. Metalwork was usually cast or engraved; niello, a black metallic composition, was used to fill engraved lines.

Islamic textiles fall naturally into two groups. Silks were used mainly for ceremonial and funerary purposes; most date from the ninth to the twelfth centuries and bear heraldic beasts and inscriptions. For carpets [12] the golden age flowered in sixteenth- and seventeenth-century Persia. Hunting scenes and floral motifs of a complex symbolism abound.

Islam has never had a tradition of easel painting, and frescoes and mosaics are also rare, but book painting has always been popular [6]. Arab painting delights in animal fables, scientific treatises, and genre scenes of an unexpectedly humorous quality. The mature Persian tradition [3], which influenced both India and Turkey, favored scenes from narrative poetry. Indian painting modified this by a more naturalistic approach (a rarity in Islamic art).

KEY

These drawings of angular inscriptions dating between 790 and 1543 are part of the rich repertoire available to the Islamic designer. Often several scripts were used in a monument for added contrast. Extraneous ornament makes some virtually illegible, thus emphasizing their decorative function.

5

5 At Gunbad-i Qabus this tomb of a minor prince, whose sarcophagus was apparently suspended from the roof, is the first and greatest of a series of tomb towers built from the 11th to the 15th centuries for rulers or saints and found throughout northern Iran and Anatolia. Their form probably originated in central Asia and was later modified by the influence of nomad tents and Caucasian churches.

6

7

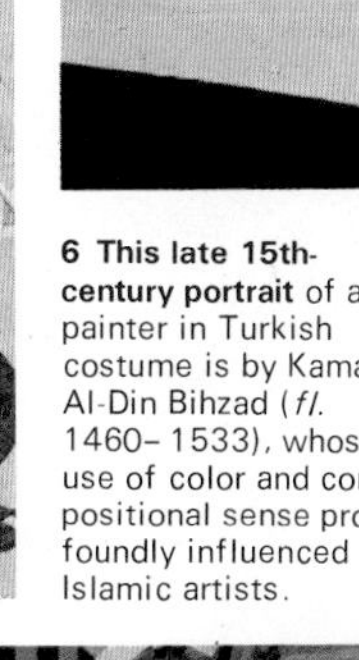

6 This late 15th-century portrait of a painter in Turkish costume is by Kamal Al-Din Bihzad (*fl.* 1460–1533), whose use of color and compositional sense profoundly influenced Islamic artists.

7 The Mosque of Ibn Tulun, Cairo (876–79) with its huge scale, enclosed and empty precinct, crenelated walls, spiral minaret, brick piers, and abstract stucco ornament, carried into Egypt the style of Abbasid Iraq. The arcaded courtyard with a deep sanctuary is always found in early Arab mosques. The mosque's uncluttered spaces are in deliberate contrast to the busy city outside.

8

8 The frequent extensions to the interior of the Great Mosque of Córdoba, Spain (begun 785–86), finally resulted in a sanctuary disproportionately deep in relation to the courtyard. Endless diminishing vistas of horseshoe arches open on every side. A pitched roof covers each arched bay. To gain the requisite height, the architect either placed columns one above the other or built special piers over them. This was a classical device.

9

9 Inlaid with gold and silver, this bronze basin, the "Baptistère de Saint Louis" (Egypt or Syria *c.* 1300), celebrates the technical virtuosity and iconographical resources of early Mameluke metal-workers. Externally narrow animal friezes frame a broad central band with monumental scenes of courtly life; insignia of rank and heraldic emblems identify the main notables.

Charlemagne and the Carolingian Empire

The Carolingians, a dynasty named after Charles Martel ("the Hammer") and his grandson Charlemagne, became the leading aristocratic family among the Franks in the seventh century. The family's power and prestige were greatly increased during the rule of Charles Martel (*c*.688–741), who united the Frankish kingdom, halted the advance of the Arabs at the Battle of Poitiers in 732 [1], and began a political relationship with the papacy that led to the foundation of the Holy Roman Empire. Charles Martel's son Pepin (*c*.715–68), the father of Charlemagne, ruled from 747 and was anointed king with papal approval in 754. In 753, Pope Stephen sought the aid of the Franks against the Lombards, who had taken much of Italy and were threatening Rome. The king of the Franks became a regular ally of the pope, and the Carolingian house was invited to divide Italy with the papacy.

The Frankish dynasty

The Franks traditionally considered their kings as being of divine origin and saw the tribe as the possession of its royal family. The Frankish state as such only existed under strong kings such as Clovis (*c*.466–*c*.511) and Pepin who eliminated their rivals. On Pepin's death his sons Charlemagne (742–814) and Carloman succeeded. When Carloman died in 771, Charlemagne seized full control [Key]. In 773 he answered the papacy's call and defeated the Lombards. From 774 he was ruler of Italy by conquest and swore an oath of mutual assistance with the pope.

The papacy was now as frightened of the Franks as it had been of the Lombards and sought a way of restraining Charlemagne. The solution came in 800 when Leo III crowned Charlemagne [4], creating the Holy Roman Empire and giving rise to the claim that the emperor held his power from God bestowed upon him by the pope.

The reign of Charlemagne

Charlemagne was a warrior king. Wars were fought against the Lombards in Italy and against the Agilolfing dukes of Bavaria; in addition there was a constant succession of campaigns against the barbarians on the borders of the kingdom: Arabs, Avars, Slavs, Saxons, and Danes. War was carried out not only for political reasons but also for plunder. Charlemagne was often poor in the early years of his reign, and a Frankish king's power rested on his ability to reward his followers. Booty taken in war was his single most important revenue.

Charlemagne fought the Arabs in Spain in 778, a campaign that ended in the ignominious defeat of Count Roland at Roncesvalles [7] at the hands of the Basques. In the south he defeated the Lombards and overthrew Tassilo of Bavaria in 788, making Bavaria for the first time an integral part of the Frankish Empire [8]. From 772 to 804 he waged a bloody and almost continual war against the Saxons, led until 785 by Widukind, and he conquered Bohemia in 805–06.

Charlemagne's military prowess recreated a centralized European government that needed an administration more complex than any known to the Franks. Charlemagne created a new court at Aachen [3], with a palace and cathedral built on an im-

CONNECTIONS

See also
1054 The barbarian invasions
1052 The rise of medieval Western Christendom
1072 The Holy Roman Empire
1070 Western European economy 800–1000
1078 Islam in Europe

1 A battle of crucial importance for the future of Europe was fought at Poitiers in 732 when Charles Martel and the Franks finally put a stop to the advance of the Arabs, who threatened to destroy the Christian west completely. The Franks had already been successful in defeating the German tribes east of the Rhine. Frankish expansion under Charlemagne was therefore based on 300 years of strength.

2 Charlemagne's military leadership was the basis of his power. Frankish custom, based on a tribal levy, made every freeman liable for military service and for equipping and feeding himself at war. Later, middle-class freemen gave up their lands to local lords and fought in the lords' own retinues, saving themselves expense but destroying the unity of the army on which Charlemagne had built his power.

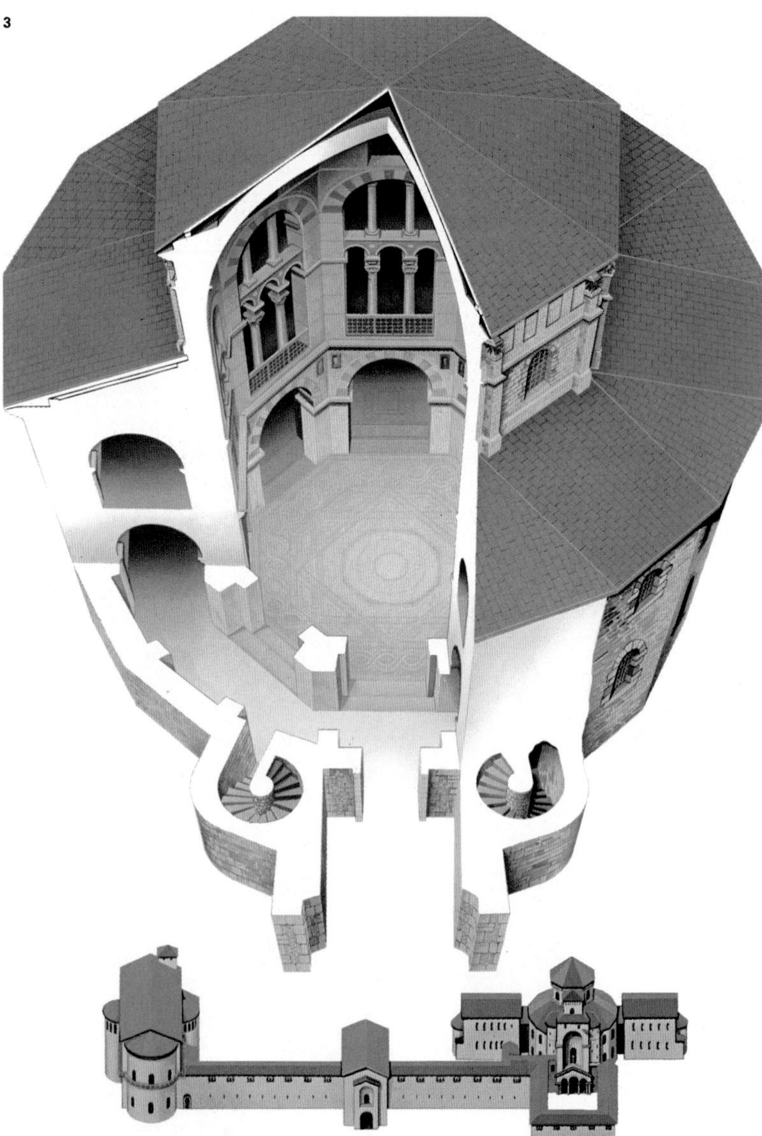

3 Charlemagne's Palace Chapel at Aachen was the architectural masterpiece of Carolingian Europe and a symbol of imperial power. It was based on the design of St Vitale in Ravenna, capital of the empire in Italy after the fall of Rome, and was designed as a chapel to house Charlemagne's throne as Holy Roman Emperor.

perial model. He employed a circle of scholars, including Alcuin from Northumbria and Theodulf from Spain, to educate a new literate class of administrator, to produce a new and legible script, to reform the practice and liturgy of the Church, and to produce a theory of empire to accompany the reality of imperial power. Alcuin, above all, formulated the role and responsibilities of the Christian emperor, thus justifying the imperial side of the relationship with the papacy.

Organization of Frankish society

Charlemagne ruled his lands through local counts, of whom there were more than 200. Many were of royal blood, and their appointment by Charlemagne created the beginnings of an international aristocracy that long outlived the Carolingian Empire. He employed stewards to carry out the business of government and special traveling agents, the *missi dominici,* to keep the counts in line with imperial policy and to raise troops when necessary. The royal will was expressed in a series of imperial charters that were lucid and authoritative. The Church played a central role in administration, both through the services of educated bishops and clerics and through the unification of doctrine and practice.

Frankish society had earlier been based solely on personal loyalty to the king. Gradually, Charlemagne insisted on a new oath of fidelity, initially only in times of crisis. These oaths were the beginning of a feudal monarchy based on the sworn allegiance of a landed nobility.

Charlemagne intended to leave his empire divided among his sons, but Louis' reign, which began in 814, was marred by bitter family rivalry; in addition, the Church was increasing its control over secular affairs. A new wave of external attack further weakened the empire. Louis died in 840, and after three years of feuding the Treaty of Verdun divided the empire in three.

Carolingian rule had disintegrated by the end of the ninth century, but Europe had been given an imperial ideal, an international landed aristocracy, and a series of social bonds that were soon to be revitalized.

KEY

Charlemagne was the most powerful ruler in early medieval Europe. Standing 6 ft 3.5 in (193 cm) tall with broad shoulders, he was physically impressive. His character was enigmatic and his personal religion erratic, although he oversaw the consolidation of Christianity throughout his realm. He was politically ambitious, appointed able ministers, and understood the importance of education. He unified western Europe and recreated an equivalent of the old Roman Empire. But he regarded his lands as private property and willed them to his sons. It is hard to know whether he saw himself as an international leader or simply as a successful tribal chief.

4

4 The coronation of Charlemagne by Pope Leo III in St Peter's on Christmas Day 800 was depicted in a 15th-century miniature by Jean Fouquet. Charlemagne, who had just restored Rome to the pope after an insurrection, needed a sacred seal on his de facto position as emperor. The coronation made him legally heir to the western Roman emperors. It was more the culmination of Carolingian expansion than a papal claim to select rulers, but it gave new authority to the papacy.

5 The Lothair Crystal, a solid piece of rock crystal delicately engraved with biblical scenes, made in the 9th century, was owned by Lothair II of Lorraine (*r.* 855–69). The quality of the carving demonstrates the continuing artistic achievements of the Carolingian Empire despite the political decline of the 9th century. The classical motifs show how Rome was used as an example by the Franks.

5

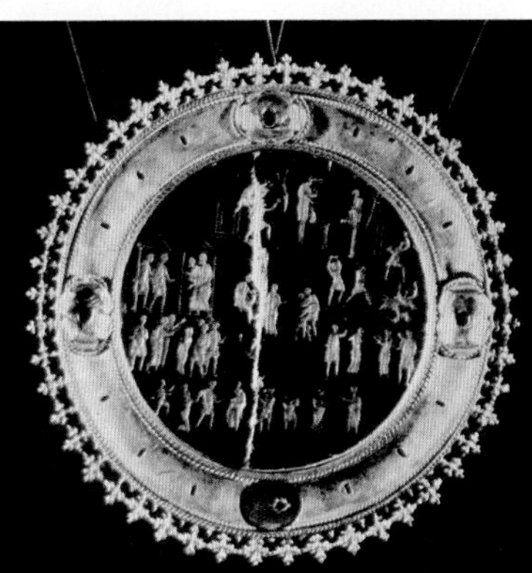

6 This page from the Sacramentary of Charles the Bald (823–77) shows the coronation of a Frankish prince – possibly Charles himself. He is flanked by two clerics and appears to be being crowned by God in person handing a crown down from heaven; the Church's role in supporting the throne and the royal sense of divine mission are thus illustrated together. The *Sacramentary* was written and illustrated in 869–70 and was the height of achievement of the last great school of Carolingian illumination, which had developed around the Court School at Aachen and spread to Rheims and Tours before St Denis.

6

7

7 The death of Roland at the Battle of Roncesvalles in 778 gave rise to one of the great epic poems, the *Song of Roland.* It epitomized Charlemagne's knights as chivalrous defenders of Christianity against the Saracens. In literature, as in politics, the Carolingians thus laid a foundation of medieval lore. During Charlemagne's retreat across the Pyrenees to put down a Saxon rising in the north, the rear guard of his army was in fact annihilated by a Basque force.

8

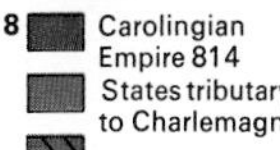

Carolingian Empire 814
States tributary to Charlemagne
Byzantine Empire

Partition of Carolingian Empire at Treaty of Verdun 843:
(1) To Charles
(2) To Lothair
(3) To Louis

8 The size of Charlemagne's empire at his death in 814 contrasts with the partitions ratified at Verdun in 843 after 30 years of squabbling among his successors. The poet Theodulf wrote: "The wall, so firm and artistically decorated in the days of my youth is showing cracks. . . . Everything sweet has fled from the aging world and nothing is left of its former strength."

FINNISH PEOPLES
NORTHMEN
PICTS
SWEDES
ESTONIANS
SCOTS
DANISH KINGDOMS
ANGLO-SAXON KINGDOMS
WALES
FRISIA
SAXONY
SERBS
SLAVIC PEOPLES
KHAZARS
Aix-la-Chapelle (Aachen)
CZECHS
NEUSTRIA
BRITTANY
AUSTRASIA
MORAVIANS
AVARS
ALLEMANIA
AQUITAINE
BAVARIA
BURGUNDY
CARINTHIA
MAGYARS
KINGDOM OF ASTURIAS
Roncesvalles
LOMBARDY
CROATS
KINGDOM OF ITALY
SERBS
SPANISH MARCH
BULGARIANS
Rome
THRACE
EMIRATE OF CORDOBA
DUCHY OF BENEVENTO
SICILY
0
500km

The Vikings

In the late eighth century the pagan Scandinavians, known as Vikings, attacked the rich kingdoms of western Europe. Improvements in ship design and overpopulation at home were two reasons for Viking expansion at this time. The Vikings burst upon undefended monasteries, plundering their treasures and killing and enslaving the priests. The attack in 793 on St Cuthbert's monastery at Lindisfarne in Northumberland, England [2], was the first and thus the most shocking of these raids; but many more followed, affecting the European coast from northern Scotland to Spain.

Colonization of Britain

Some of those who came from Scandinavia turned their attention to colonization. Graves in western Scotland, the Hebrides, the Shetlands, Orkney, and the Isle of Man, furnished in the pagan Scandinavian manner with weapons and household goods, tell of the gradual settlement of these areas [1]. In England, raids gave way to settlement in the late ninth century and after several campaigns against the English kingdoms the Scandinavians—by treaty with Alfred the Great in 878—settled as conquerors to the east and north of a line from the River Lea north of London to the Dee in northeast Scotland. Here they established at least one kingdom (based on York) as well as political groupings in East Anglia and the Midlands. By the middle of the tenth century the English had reconquered these areas, although in the early eleventh century the Scandinavians conquered all of England, and a Dane, Canute (994–1035), became king of England for a short time.

The Scandinavian settlements in Scotland and the Isle of Man [8] continued until the thirteenth century. The Scandinavians in Ireland did not attempt to conquer the whole country but founded several towns (of which Dublin was the most important) through which they could influence the trade of the western European seaboard.

In other western European countries the Scandinavians were less successful as colonists or conquerors. Only in Normandy did they succeed. There in 911 a Scandinavian, Rollo, by treaty with the French king, was given the right to settle and govern much of that corner of France. The Scandinavians also sailed the North Atlantic looking for plunder and farmland. They settled the virtually unknown Faroe Islands and Iceland and reached Greenland, where they founded two major settlements. They also landed along eastern North America.

Eastern Europe

The Scandinavians were also influential in eastern Europe. Beginning in the Roman period they had used the rivers of Poland and Russia to trade spasmodically with the eastern Mediterranean. In the eighth century a larger and more organized commercial traffic developed. The Swedes founded trading stations and collected tribute from Finno-Ugric, Balt, and Slav tribes in the east Baltic. In the ninth century the Scandinavians contributed to the growth of Russian trading towns at Staraja Ladoga, Novgorod, and Kiev. The river route along the Volchov and the Dnieper was largely controlled by the Scandinavians from the ninth to the eleventh centuries.

CONNECTIONS

See also
1070 Western European economy 800–1000
1176 Medieval Russia 900–1600
1076 Norman and Angevin England
1054 The barbarian invasions

1 The Scandinavians of the Viking age used these major routes in their search for wealth and land to settle. In the east are the riverside towns they established as centers, such as Kiev and Novgorod. South along these rivers, the Scandinavians reached the rich trade and wealth of Asia and the Byzantine Empire. In the west the chief areas of settlement were the northern and western islands of Britain, northern and eastern England, northern France, and the Irish ports (which they also founded). By the western sea routes they reached North America, but failed to establish any settlements on this continent.

2 This carved stone provides a Christian view of the Viking invasion of Lindisfarne. An inscription reads: "793. In this year dire portents appeared over Northumbria, the ravages of heathens destroyed God's church on Lindisfarne."

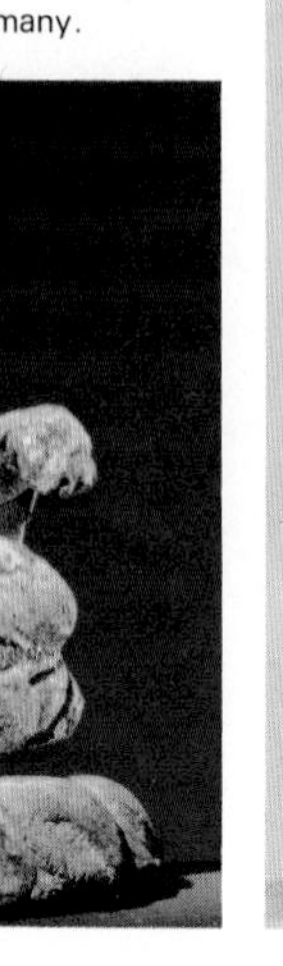

3 This bronze figure of the Buddha was imported from Afghanistan or India to Sweden in the early Viking age, presumably as a souvenir. Other objects imported into Scandinavia and found during excavation include Arabic, Byzantine, English, French, and German coins, as well as silks and foreign animal skins, metalwork from Britain, and pottery and glass from northern Germany.

4 Thor, the Scandinavian god of thunder, agriculture, and war, is usually symbolized by a hammer. In this 2.5 in (6.7 cm) bronze, his beard is developing into a hammer. This symbol was often used in amulets to protect a wearer against evil.

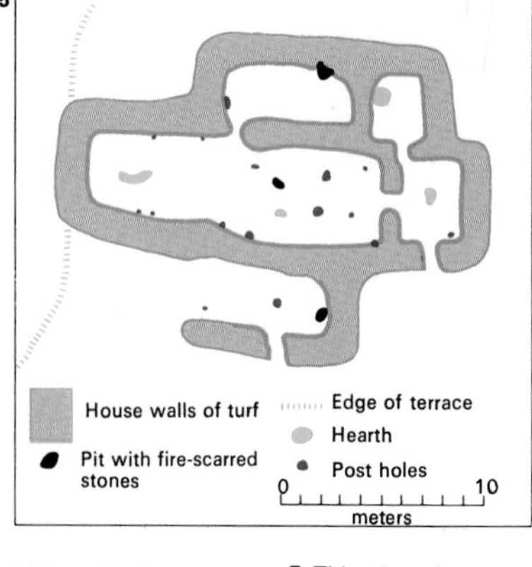

House walls of turf
Pit with fire-scarred stones
Edge of terrace
Hearth
Post holes
0
10
meters

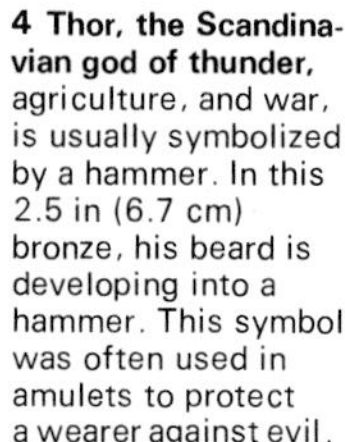

5 This plan of a house, excavated at L'Anse-aux-Meadows in Newfoundland, can be dated to the 11th century. It has many of the structural features of houses built by the Vikings in their colonial settlements in Iceland and Greenland.

Trade and economic organization

The main exports of the Scandinavians were furs, honey, and slaves; the main imports were silver, spices, and other luxury goods. The volume of this eastern trade is demonstrated by the fact that about 40,000 Arabic coins have been found in Viking Age sites in Gotland and Sweden.

These eastern adventures are also reflected in long inscriptions carved in runic characters on Swedish stones. Some refer to merchant expeditions and imply a fairly peaceful Scandinavian presence in Russia. Others tell of more warlike episodes—a military expedition to Arabia, for example, or Scandinavian mercenaries in Russia or Byzantium: Greek literary sources provide ample evidence of the presence of Scandinavians serving in the bodyguard of the emperor. At least one runic stone has been found in Russia and there are runic inscriptions, scratched by Scandinavians, in the church of St Sophia, Istanbul, and on a marble lion from Piraeus in Greece.

The raiding, colonization, and trade of the Vikings were supported by a settled domestic economy based on agriculture. The economy expanded in the Viking age as marginal land was developed in Scandinavia and towns that functioned as major trading stations were founded—towns such as Birka in Sweden and Hedeby in Denmark [7] (now in northern Germany). These towns provide clear evidence of the international contacts of the Scandinavians, both in excavated material and in the written descriptions of travelers. The Scandinavian of the Viking age was, however, basically a farmer—even traders and pirates traveled abroad mainly in summer. The pattern of rural settlement of present-day Scandinavia had largely been formed by the Viking age, that is, by the eleventh century.

The image of the Vikings as marauders and pirates is influenced by the chronicles of priests who remembered the pillaged monasteries. The fact that the Scandinavians were pagan compounded any offense. But in the tenth century the Scandinavians were gradually converted to Christianity, making them more of a kindred and less of an alien culture.

KEY

This richly carved ship's prow is part of a complete Viking longship found in a woman's grave of the 9th century at Oseberg in Norway. The ship itself, built of oak, was 75 ft (23m) long. It was basically a sailing vessel, but it could also be propelled by oars. It is one of the larger examples of Viking longships and was probably used for raiding and longer voyages of discovery and colonization. Much smaller ships were used for coastal and river warfare and trading. The prow here is decorated with intertwining animals and is shaped in the form of a serpent, a style that is characteristic of the final pre-Christian period of Viking art.

6

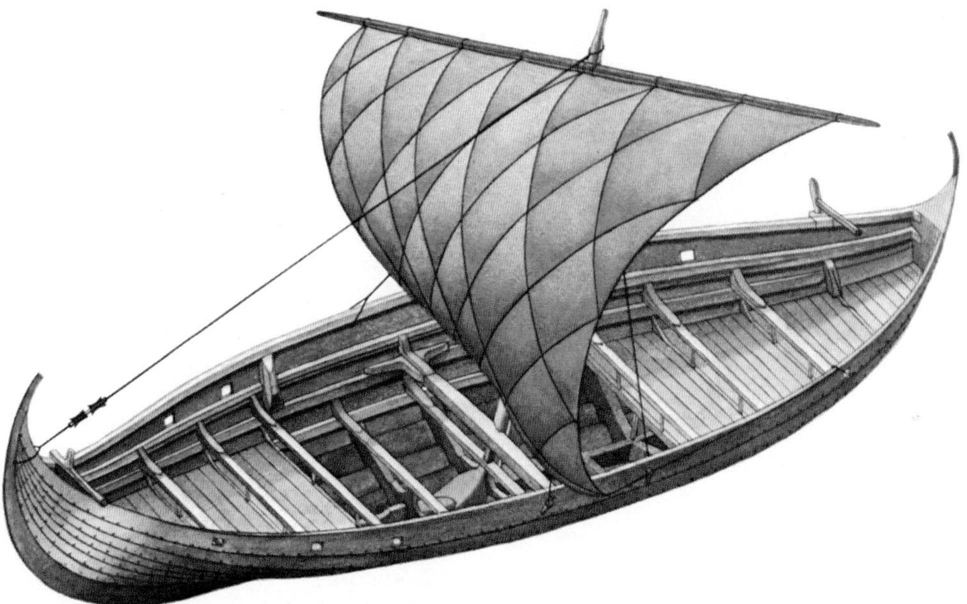

6 The hull of a small cargo vessel, 44 ft (13.5m) long, was raised from the bed of Roskilde fjord in Denmark and reconstructed. As this illustration shows, there is decking fore and aft with a hold in the center. The mast is seated on the keel, and the one large sail is supported by a single transverse spar. When not in use the spar could be lowered and stowed away. The vessel could also be rowed by means of oars inserted through the square holes in the gunwale plank. The vessel was steered by a paddle attached aft on the starboard quarter ("starboard" being old Norse for "steering side"). The ship could make long journeys.

7

7 The open fire in the center of this house, a reconstruction from the town of Hedeby in South Jutland, provided heat for the room and for cooking. The family would sit on the earth benches at the sides of the room. The food was placed on low tables. The wattle and daub walls may have been covered with hangings. There was a room at each end.

8

8 The annual ceremony at Tynwald on the Isle of Man is descended from the assembly established there by the Scandinavians in the Viking age (the Norwegians finally surrendered Man in 1266). Such assemblies acted as a combination of town meeting, law court, and fair and were held in various places throughout the Viking world.

9

9 The craftsmanship of the Vikings is well demonstrated by this early 11th-century weather vane. Made of gilt bronze, it may originally have graced a Viking ship. The Scandinavians were fascinated by contorted animal ornament. Throughout the Viking age, craftsmen produced distinguished objects decorated with animal ornament largely free from the influence of contemporary European art. Objects like this vane demonstrate the brilliance of the ornamentation and workmanship.

Western European economy 800–1000

Western Europe in the ninth and tenth centuries was the poor relation of both the Arab and the Byzantine worlds. It was poor in the exploitation of its natural resources, in technical ability, in political cohesion, and cultural achievement. Europe's social and economic backwardness was further threatened by Magyar hordes from the east and incessant raids by Vikings who swept southward from Scandinavia.

The growth of self-sufficiency

The temporary political unity and economic regulations of the Carolingians (Charlemagne and his successors) throw little light on actual conditions of life in the ninth century. Charlemagne attempted to stabilize and centralize the coinage throughout his empire, centered on France, to avoid exploitation in times of scarcity by regulating prices, to facilitate trade by keeping down internal customs dues, and to introduce a universal system of weights and measures. But the regularity with which his instructions were issued indicates their ineffectiveness; the actual unit of production and consumption remained the great estate [1], a legacy of the Roman "villa."

The economy of the Roman world in the invasion period was based on the great estates of the old landowning aristocracy. The decline of easy communications and trade forced these social units to become more self-sufficient. Alongside the estates, some of which passed into the hands of the invaders, there remained a free peasantry that still existed in the ninth century. But its decline was hastened by the centralization policies of Charlemagne and the obligations imposed by the government on all free men. It became preferable to surrender individual land rights to the local lord in order to escape the fiscal liabilities of freedom.

The Church, trade, and commerce

The decline in personal freedom benefited the great estates of the aristocracy and the Church. Most available records of ninth-century estates are monastic and show a pattern of organized growth indicating that the Church played a crucial role in maintaining a degree of economic stability.

The growth of European towns was based both on the old Roman cities (especially in Italy and the south) and on the garrisons and royal residences of the Carolingians and their predecessors, the Merovingians, such as Aachen, Nijmegen, Worms, Frankfurt, and Ratisbon. Other cities, and mercantile suburbs of older cities such as Paris, grew around the monasteries.

The uncertainty of statistics of trade and commerce after the fall of the Western Empire has given rise to much theorizing by historians. It fostered especially the belief that the economy of the Western world survived the Germanic invasions but was brought to a halt by the Islamic conquests of the seventh century. The loss of the Mediterranean, it was argued, destroyed the movement of merchandise both between East and West and also internally within the West, reducing trade to mere barter. In fact trade continued, although on a much reduced scale. The centers of commerce initially switched from Provence and Languedoc to the north of Europe—Frisia, the Low Countries, northern France, and

CONNECTIONS

See also
1090 Western European economy 1000–1250
1062 Arabs and the rise of Islam
1066 Charlemagne and the Carolingian Empire
1068 The Vikings
1056 The Byzantine Empire
618 Wetlands: marshes and swamps
620 Salt marshes and coastal swamps

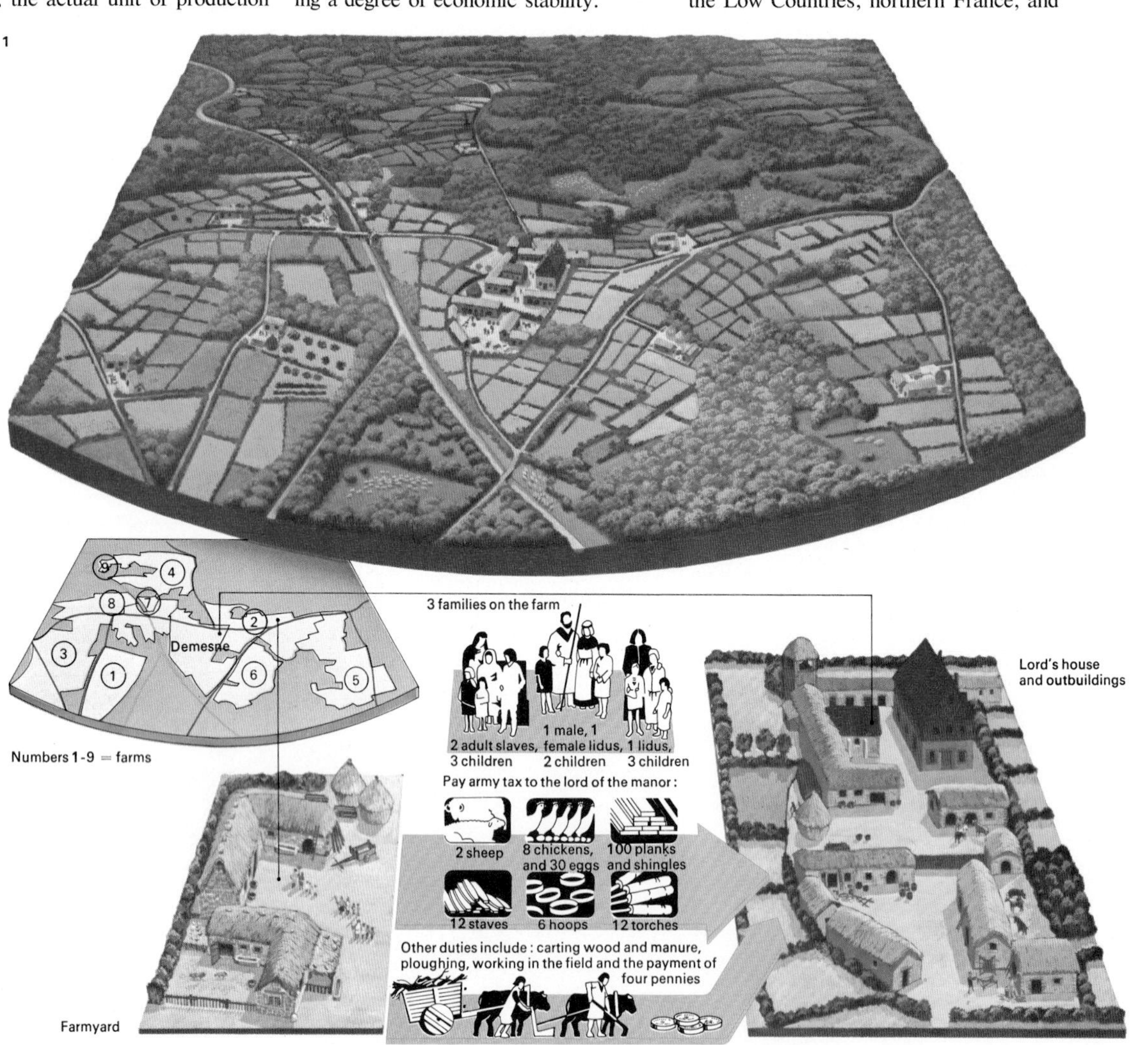

1
Demesne
Numbers 1-9 = farms
3 families on the farm
2 adult slaves, 3 children
1 male, 1 female lidus, 2 children
1 lidus, 3 children
Pay army tax to the lord of the manor:
2 sheep
8 chickens, and 30 eggs
100 planks and shingles
12 staves
6 hoops
12 torches
Other duties include: carting wood and manure, ploughing, working in the field and the payment of four pennies
Lord's house and outbuildings
Farmyard

1 A typical "villa" or rural social unit in Carolingian Europe is here illustrated and its population and composition shown. This organization was the result of the fusion of the old Roman "villa" with the customs of the invading Germanic peoples. The social status of the peasants varied: some were free; some owed various degrees and types of service to the lord. An estate was divided into the demesne land, the property of the landlord cultivated by forced labor, and the land cultivated by his tenants as "mansi." The return for the latter's tenancy was calculated in various burdens of service; these could be increased if the tenant exchanged his military obligations for service to the lord. Carolingian peasants were divided into "coloni," free men still obliged to till their own land; "lidi," half-freemen owing certain legal obligations; and "servi," who had no legal rights at all but who, although outside the law, could hold property. The total population of the estate was known as the "familia" and was supervised by the landlord or his agent. Slaves in principle worked the demesne land for three days a week while "coloni" and "lidi" performed set tasks throughout the year. Estates such as the one illustrated were centralized units of production on land carved from the surrounding forests. They were also early centers of rudimentary industrial organization for weaving and cloth production. Finally, they were the basic unit of the rural feudal society that provided both the stability and the opportunity for oppression in early medieval society. Totally self-sufficient, these great estates formed the foundation of the medieval economy for many years.

the Rhineland. The old route to the north from Ostia (the port of Rome) to Provence and then by land gave way to a land route over the Alps. Italian ports such as Amalfi [4] and Gaeta maintained a precarious commercial liaison with the East, and in the tenth century the emergence of Venice [3] began a new era in Mediterranean trade.

Charlemagne sought to create a stable coinage but never succeeded in making the minting of money a royal monopoly, which was one possible way of avoiding constant debasement. Charlemagne did understand the need for a coinage to be used as a medium of exchange, rather than barter, and his silver denarius, or penny, became one of the standard coins of the medieval West. But Carolingian coinage supplied only the small change of the West, whereas the international trading currency of the Middle Ages became the Byzantine gold nomisma and the Arab gold dinar [2].

The population of Western Europe expanded very slowly after the ravages of the invasion years. Stagnant economies could not support cities of 50,000 to 100,000 people such as those of the Arab world at Cairo, Antioch, and in Spain at Córdoba. Under the manorial system, towns had completely lost their importance, and as a result many had been abandoned.

Industry and agriculture

Industry, such as mining and weaving, was only in its infancy in the ninth century and was mainly centered on monastic properties. Comprehensive rotational systems of agriculture barely survived on the old Roman estates. Agricultural technology gradually improved with the introduction of heavy wheeled plows for northern soils. The harrow and the flail were probably introduced at that time, and the decline of slavery made the extended use of the watermill for grinding corn an economic necessity. Yet, production was too low to support any great increase in population, and trade was too ill-organized to offset local effects of crop failure and plague [Key]. The technological knowledge of the Romans was never wholly lost, however, and new inventions gradually appeared.

KEY

Early medieval life was primarily agricultural. Harvest time was the crucial part of the year. Cereals were the staple of life, meat being a luxury. Limited productivity and trade meant that a successful harvest was the only insurance against famine and its constant attendant, plague.

2 Medieval currency problems were twofold; to preserve a coinage acceptable to all trading partners and also to enable transactions to be performed through a monetary medium rather than by barter. The Clovis II coin [A] shows the Merovingian attempt to maintain a prestige form of Roman coinage, but debased both in design and metallic content. Coins such as the gold solidus [B] of Louis the Pious (778–840) were minted in many towns, although under the control of the king. No Western economic system at this time could support such reliable coinages as the Byzantine nomisma [C] of Justinian II or the Arab gold dinar [D]. These coins were the basic tender of medieval international trade until the Florentine florin was minted in the 14th century.

2

A
B
C
D

3

3 Trade in the Mediterranean was sharply curtailed by the pirates who followed in the wake of Arab conquests. Yet gradually the need for raw materials from the West and for luxury goods and spices from the East ensured that increasing numbers of vessels, as this one portrayed in a Venetian mosaic, plied the Mediterranean.

4

4 Amalfi, with its natural harbor, was one of the key commercial links between the Western world and Byzantium before the rise of Venice. The revival of Western Mediterrean trade came from Italian towns such as Amalfi, Naples, Salerno, and Ravenna that had the closest links with the Byzantine world for the exchange of goods.

The Holy Roman Empire

The Holy Roman Empire sought to recreate the united Christian West that had existed in theory during the last years of the Roman Empire. It was holy because it was based on the theory that the pope was supreme in ecclesiastical affairs, the emperor being the secular arm and the defender of the Church. It was Roman—despite the fact that the emperor was first a Frank and than a German—because Rome had for so long been the political center of the world that imperial rule was unthinkable in any other terms.

Power struggle

The theory that the pope represented the spiritual authority of God on earth and the emperor temporal authority was rarely a reality. In practice there were strong emperors and strong popes, and power fluctuated. From the mid-eighth century the papacy had looked increasingly to the Franks for protection against the Lombards, a dependence that culminated in 800 when Leo III crowned Charlemagne first Holy Roman Emperor in Rome. The tenth century was dominated by the political success of the Ottonian emperors (936–1024), a Saxon royal house [Key 1, 2, 3]. Otto the Great (912–73) was crowned German king in 936 and Holy Roman emperor in 962 [4]. Otto and his dynasty ruled at a time when the papacy was in a very poor state.

The Salian dynasty (1024–1125) saw the height of imperial power at a time when the papacy was also powerful. The Salians were a Frankish family. Their empire under Conrad II (990–1039) included Germany, Burgundy, and Italy, and Conrad saw himself as ruler of the city of Rome.

The Investiture Contest

But a new reforming spirit within the papacy made a major issue of the problems of investiture: who should appoint bishops, the pope or the secular ruler? The quarrel was essentially about the great wealth and power of the benefices at stake. No ruler could afford to relinquish control over appointments to the wealthiest positions in the land.

The so-called Investiture Conflict culminated in a complete breakdown of imperial-papal relations that damaged the theoretical justification and the effective power of the Holy Roman Empire. The conflict reached its height in the reign of Henry IV (1050–1106), who found that there was no possible compromise on this issue with Pope Gregory VII. Accordingly he called an imperial synod at Worms in 1076 and deposed Gregory. Gregory retaliated, deposed and excommunicated Henry, and began to build up a strong anti-imperial coalition. Henry, realizing the seriousness of his position, spent three days in a hair shirt at Canossa [6] awaiting papal forgiveness. Gregory then withdrew the excommunication but not the deposition. Henry had his revenge in 1084 when he marched on Rome and drove Gregory to a bitter death in exile. The Investiture Conflict was solved by a compromise: the emperor was allowed to invest a bishop with his scepter before consecration by the ecclesiastical authorities.

The religious and political pretensions of the empire reached their height under the Hohenstaufens (1138–1254). Frederick I "Barbarossa" (1123–90) and Henry VI

CONNECTIONS

See also

1066 Charlemagne and the Carolingian Empire
1086 The power of the Church: 1073–1309
1074 European expansion to the east
1084 The Crusades
1030 Rome: soldier emperors to Constantine
1128 The politics of Europe 1450–1600
1158 Europe 1500–1700
1226 Napoleonic Europe

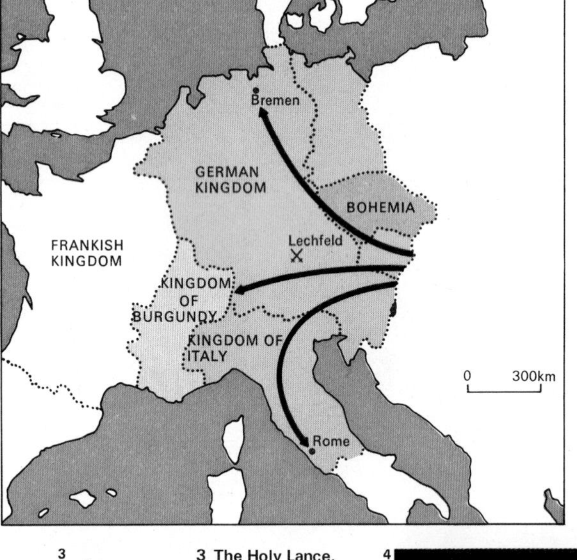

Empire of Otto I 962
Dependent state
Tributary province after 950
Invasion by Magyars until 955
Bremen
GERMAN KINGDOM
BOHEMIA
FRANKISH KINGDOM
Lechfeld
KINGDOM OF BURGUNDY
KINGDOM OF ITALY
Rome
0 300km

1 Expansion of the empire followed the crowning in 936 of a Saxon, Otto I (912–973), as supreme leader of the five German tribal duchies—Saxony, Franconia, Bavaria, Swabia, and Lotharingia. His attempts to increase his power led to constant strife and to his papal coronation as emperor in 962. He became King of the Lombards in 951, and in 955 his victory over the Magyars at Lechfeld began the westward expansion of the empire.

2 St Michael's at Hildesheim in Saxony, destroyed in World War II, was built in the early 11th century under the supervision of Bishop Bernward. It was later decorated with fine bronze ornaments and a magnificent flat, painted ceiling entirely covered with a representation of the Tree of Jesse. The plan of the church referred back both to early Christian and to Carolingian architecture but its internal rhythms were made more subtle by the inclusion of two transepts and an apse. An example of the Ottonian renaissance, it exemplified the supremacy of German art.

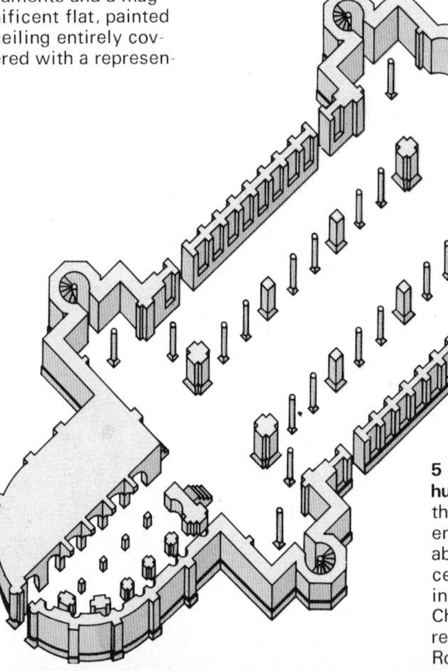

3 The Holy Lance, which pierced the side of Christ, was politically the most important relic. In legend given by St Helena to Constantine, it passed to Otto I, who bore it in battle.

4 The imperial crown of Otto I was made for his coronation by the Pope in 962. With the Christian cross in front, it is octagonal to represent the heavenly Jerusalem, with a semicircular strip above to represent world dominion. Two panels back and front each contain 12 stones representing the tribes of Israel. On the sides are biblical kings. The crown symbolizes the functions of the wearer as temporal ruler and regent of Christ on earth.

5 "Charlemagne's hunting horn," one of the treasures of the emperors, was probably made in the 11th century. It had nothing to do with Charlemagne, the revered first Holy Roman Emperor.

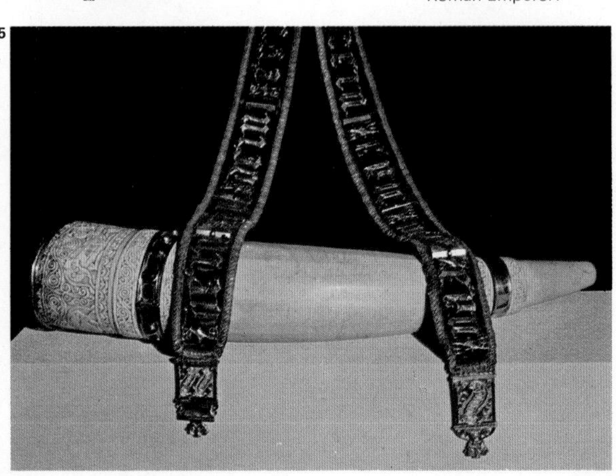

(1165–1197) saw themselves as the holy leaders of a God-given German empire. Frederick I's power was based on an alliance with Henry the Lion of Saxony against the Normans and the Romans, and the opposition of the pope in 1159 led him to appoint his own pope, Victor IV.

The papacy thereafter backed the Lombard League—an association of northern Italian cities that opposed Frederick—and forced him to make peace after the battle of Legnano in 1176.

A dream shattered

Henry VI claimed all the lands of the Normans, especially Sicily [9], and dreamed of capturing Tunis and even Constantinople. He built the first imperial fleet, and defeated a hostile coalition between northern Germany and Britain when he made Richard the Lionhearted his prisoner. His son Frederick II (1194–1250) had been brought up in Sicily and was more Mediterranean than German. He was the mortal enemy of the papacy and achieved the greatest expansion of imperial influence [7].

Sicily under the Hohenstaufens was culturally a mixture of Italian, Arabic, Greek, Norman, and German influences and was part of a larger culture that spread from Mesopotamia through Moorish Spain. Frederick saw politics as an art, government as a bureaucratic skill. He patronized the arts and sciences and founded the university of Naples to rival Bologna. He saw the empire as a German federation and in 1231 was prepared to recognize the territorial claims of the princes. In 1235 he published the Landfrieden of Mainz, the first German law written in German, which defined the empire as a league of princes within a monarchic framework. His negotiations with the Muslims scandalized the Christian West but enabled him to be crowned at Jerusalem without fighting a crusade. At the Council of Lyons in 1245 he was condemned and deposed. When, on his death, the papacy broke the power of his family, the future of the international empire of which he had dreamed was shattered. It remained a more or less spectral organization until the arrival of Napoleon in Germany in 1806.

The imperial seal of Otto III (980–1002) epitomized his ambition with the inscription *Otto Imperator Augustus Renovatio Imperii Romanorum*—Emperor Otto Augustus, the Renewal of the Empire of the Romans. The grandson of Otto I, who founded the dynasty, Otto III was crowned at age three. His education was designed to produce an emperor who combined German strength and tradition with the new Arab, Greek, and Latin learning. To identify himself with Charlemagne, Otto opened his tomb at Aachen and stole a tooth, nail clippings, and clothes. On feast days his clothes were decorated with lions, eagles, and dragons and hung with bells.

6 Canossa was the most humiliating episode in the history of the empire. Although the political results ultimately favored Henry IV, the spectacle of a penitent emperor begging for the intercession of Abbot Hugh of Cluny and Matilda of Tuscany in seeking the pope's pardon was one that injured German pride so much that even Bismarck's 19th-century conflict with the papacy was based on a desire "never to go to Canossa again," as had Henry.

KEY

- Sole Hohenstaufen duchy 1152
- Empire of Frederick I
- Allied with Empire 1184
- Tributary under Frederick I
- Ruled by Henry VI and Frederick II
- Papal states 1152
- Papal states from 1213
- Towns of Leagues of Lombardy and Verona

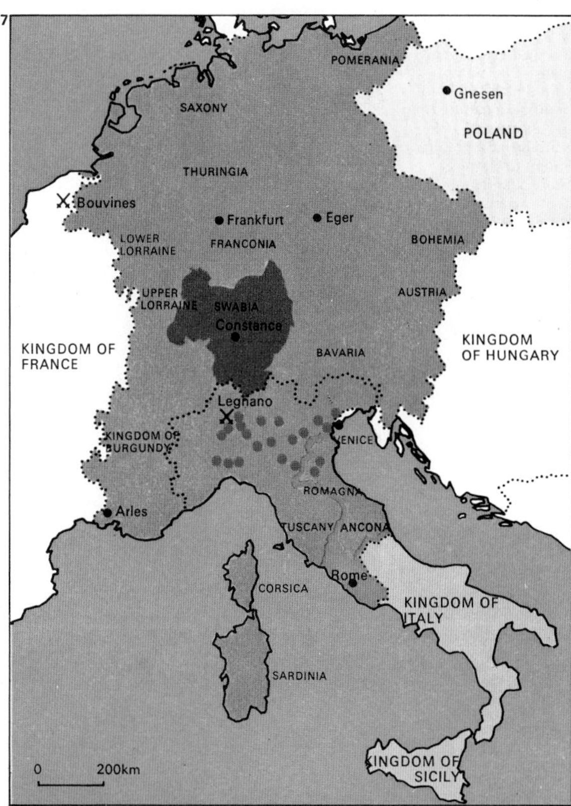
POMERANIA
Gnesen
SAXONY
POLAND
THURINGIA
Bouvines
Frankfurt
Eger
LOWER LORRAINE
FRANCONIA
BOHEMIA
UPPER LORRAINE
SWABIA
Constance
AUSTRIA
KINGDOM OF FRANCE
BAVARIA
KINGDOM OF HUNGARY
Legnano
KINGDOM OF BURGUNDY
VENICE
ROMAGNA
Arles
TUSCANY
ANCONA
CORSICA
Rome
KINGDOM OF ITALY
SARDINIA
0
200km
KINGDOM OF SICILY

7 The territorial achievements of Frederick II (1194–1250), culminating in the Battle of Bouvines (1214) at which he defeated his last remaining opponents, were the fulfillment of German imperial ambition. Frederick inherited his Sicilian kingdom and his southern ambitions from his father, and his lands completely surrounded the papal state. He achieved the federation of Germanic countries and an administration imbued with Mediterranean culture that had been the dream of Otto III.

8 The final humiliation of Henry IV, portrayed in this contemporary illustration, came in 1105 when he was forced to surrender his imperial regalia to his son. Some of Henry IV's family had disagreed with his deposition of Gregory VII and installation of a new pope. His heir, Henry V, joined them after becoming co-ruler in 1099 and soon overthrew the emperor.

9 Peter of Eboli's illumination of the siege of Naples (1191) shows the army of Henry VI attempting to enforce his wife's claim to the south Italian Norman kingdom. Despite his early successes, Naples, aided by the failure of the imperial naval allies and by plague in the besieging army, did not fall. Henry VI was crowned King of Sicily only in 1194.

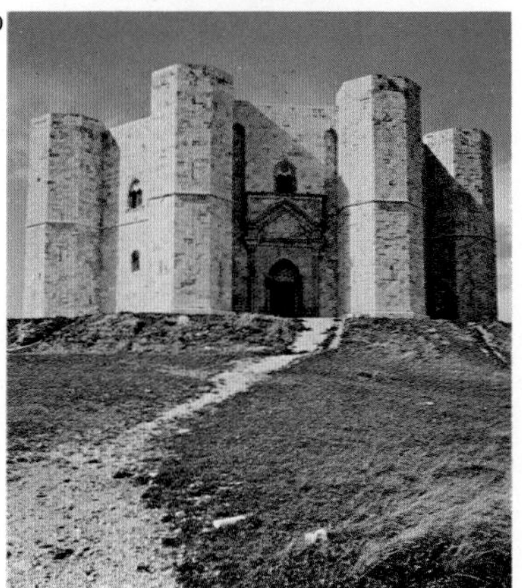

10 Castel del Monte, in southern Italy, is the finest of a chain of strategic fortifications designed in a novel and functional manner by Frederick II. He built up in Sicily and Apulia a system of defense and administration that was the most thorough and rational in Europe. As fortifications the castles shielded Frederick from attack by the Papacy. As architecture, they were part of the flowering of the arts during Frederick's reign.

European expansion to the east

In the centuries before AD 1000, while a lively, enterprising society was emerging in the villages and towns of western Europe, eastern Europe was a land of sparsely occupied forests, grasslands, and low, easily-crossed mountains through which passed at random a variety of peoples. The roaming shepherds of the Carpathians, the nomads from the south Russian steppe who settled in the Danube basin, and the forest peoples of the Vistula (ancestors respectively of the modern Romanians, Hungarians, and Poles) traveled up and down the region between the Baltic and the Danube, the Pripet Marshes and the Elbe. They were untouched either by the political or the religious allegiances of the settled lands to the west and south and were impervious even to the cultural influences of each other.

The forest peoples, Polish and Czech Slavs, seem to have been divided into numerous tribes. Many of their fortified settlements have been uncovered. The middle Danube grasslands were the haunts of successive nomadic peoples who lived by raiding neighboring lands. The last to arrive, the ferocious Magyars of mixed Finnish and Turkish origin, crossed the Carpathians by the late ninth century.

The spread of German influence

To the west of these peoples were the Germans, whose national identity was also recent. Their relations with the Slavs were close, sometimes hostile but often peaceful; their society of well-organized communities and their Christian civilization, contained within the Holy Roman Empire, exercised a constant and fruitful pressure. Under the powerful Ottonian kings (919–1024; emperors from 962) the German advance was rapid and for the first time there is evidence that the tribes, in their turn, were beginning to unite: by 1000 the Magyars (whose raids were checked by the German victory at the Lechfeld in 955), the Bohemians, and the Poles [1] had each united under single, independent dynasties. The earliest sign of the evolution was the advance of Christianity [7]. Already in the ninth century Byzantine missionaries converted the Moravians, whose mushroomed empire was annihilated by the Magyars; in its place, under German influence, there grew up the Czech duchy of Bohemia.

Under German auspices Bohemia was the focus for the rapid development of all eastern Europe. Duke Boleslav I (reigned 929–63) was the father-in-law of the first Polish duke, Mieszko I (reigned 963–92), who received Christianity at his hands; while the influence of St Adalbert, Bishop of Prague [3], caused the Hungarian Duke Stephen (reigned 997–1038) to be baptized. But German influence was ambivalent: the Slav and Magyar dukes seized on the slightest sign of German weakness to assert their independence and to receive directly from the papacy autonomous national Churches. In AD 1000 the Polish duke Boleslav the Mighty (*c.* 966–1025) received a crown from the emperor and Stephen, who ended the influence of Eastern Christianity in Hungary, received one from the pope.

The emergence of national identities

In the eleventh century the Bohemians, Poles, and Hungarians held their own, and

CONNECTIONS

See also
1072 The Holy Roman Empire
1086 The power of the Church: 1073–1309
1176 Medieval Russia 900–1600

1 Boleslav the Mighty was the founder of the first Polish monarchy. His reign resulted in 30 years of internal consolidation for his country, the building of a national Polish Christian church, and significant expansion abroad. All of these developments changed Poland from an alliance of Slav tribes into a powerful, centralized monarchy. Alliances with Bohemia, Hungary, and Kiev enabled the king to make the Oder and the Vistula virtually Polish rivers and also allowed him to declare war on Emperor Henry II (973–1024) between 1004 and 1008. The emperor finally recognized the Polish state and Boleslav was crowned in 1024.

2 St Wenceslas, Duke of Bohemia and an enthusiastic Christian convert, became the patron saint of Hungary, Poland, and Bohemia. As duke he failed to resist the aggression of the German King Henry I (*r.*919–36), who was determined to subdue the Wends and Slavs as well as the Bohemians. Bohemia became a German fief (owing nominal allegiance to the emperor), and Wenceslas, who was blamed for the defeat, was murdered by his brother, Boleslav, who succeeded him.

3 The cathedral of Gniezno (Gnesen) was the center of the Christian religion of the new Polish state. It housed the relics of St Adalbert of Prague, one of the apostles of eastern Europe. Gniezno, an ancient Polish center, was the most important of the castle towns of Boleslav the Mighty. These towns were thriving garrisons that gradually fostered local trade and finally became centers for the export of grain to the west. The towns continued to grow and become more important.

they acquired a sense of national identity under native dynasties. The Premyslids of Bohemia did not receive the royal title until 1198, but although they were included in the German Empire they retained intact their Slavonic language and customs.

The Polish dynasty of Piast was more aggressively anti-German and their court at Gniezno became the focus of resistance to the ambitions of the Salian emperors. But the unity of their vast territories was superficial and from 1079 to the end of the thirteenth century the country was ruled jointly by, and then divided among, several Piast princes. Throughout this period the unity of the Poles was maintained chiefly by a national Church and a common culture.

The Hungarian house of Arpad was more fortunate in maintaining its unity in close relation with the German emperors and Hungary flourished as a bridge between Byzantium, Russia, and western Europe.

Later German migration

The eastward advance of the Germanic peoples had been checked after 1002 short of Pomerania, Poland, and Hungary [Key]; after 1100 it resumed. Slavonic and Magyar rulers welcomed the Germans as cultivators of the sparsely inhabited soil. First came merchants, to swell the Wendish, Polish, and Bohemian towns, especially Lübeck and Danzig on the Baltic. A massive migration of farmers followed in the twelfth century: they occupied the fertile lands of Silesia, spread through Bohemia and parts of Hungary, and pioneered the opening up of Transylvania. Finally came the knights, ostensibly to convert the pagan Lithuanians to Christianity, but also to carve out new territories along the Baltic.

Several military orders in 1237 united as the Order of the Teutonic Knights of Livonia [5]. This heralded German domination of the Baltic, and the maritime communities soon founded an association, the Hanseatic League, or Hansa [4]. The Hansa dominated the culture and politics of northeastern Europe. But the extension of German rule did not accompany the migration; relations with the new settlers were generally friendly and mutually profitable.

KEY

North Sea
Baltic Sea
Oldenburg
Danzig
BILLUNGS
FRIESLAND
Hamburg
Bremen
POMERANIA
SAXONY
NORTH MARCH
Osnabrück
Hildesheim
Brandenburg
Minden
Münster
Magdeburg
Halberstadt
LAUSITZ
Gniezno (Gnesen)
Posen
Aix-la-Chapelle
Paderborn
POLAND
Merseberg
THURINGIA
Meissen
Cologne
WEST
LOWER
EAST
Erfurt
MEISSEN
Breslau
FRANCONIA
LORRAINE
Frankfurt
Mainz
Bamberg
Prague
UPPER
Würzburg
BOHEMIA
Olmütz
Worms
NORDGAU
MORAVIA
Brünn
Toul
Ratisbon (Regensburg)
Strasbourg
Ulm
AUSTRIA
ALSACE
Augsburg
Freising
Passau
SWABIA
Salzburg
Presburg
Constance
BAVARIA
Gran
HUNGARY
Brixen
Holy Roman Empire c. 1000
Main towns c. 1000
CARINTHIA
0
200km

4 Bremen, on the Weser, is one of the great north German trading ports. Founded in the 9th century by Charlemagne, its merchants set up the city of Riga in 1158 and in 1358 joined the Hansa.

5 Marienburg, with its famous castle, was the capital of the Teutonic Knights in Prussia. The Knights, founded as a noble military, charitable, and missionary organization in 1190, abandoned work in the Holy Land and settled on the Baltic coast to enforce the conversion of the pagan Prussians. In 1309 they established their headquarters at Marienburg to carry out these efforts.

6 Pope Sylvester II gave St Stephen the upper part of the crown of St Stephen, symbol of Hungarian nationhood, in 1000. In 1075 the circlet below was given by the Byzantine emperor Michael VII.

7 The advance of Christianity in eastern Europe (1000–1250), and the conversion of the Slavs and Magyars, was quick but superficial; thorough Christianization of these peoples took centuries. First came the German or Byzantine missionaries, whose real purpose was to convert the rulers and establish bishoprics; only later, in the 12th century, did Christianity begin to reach the rural communities.

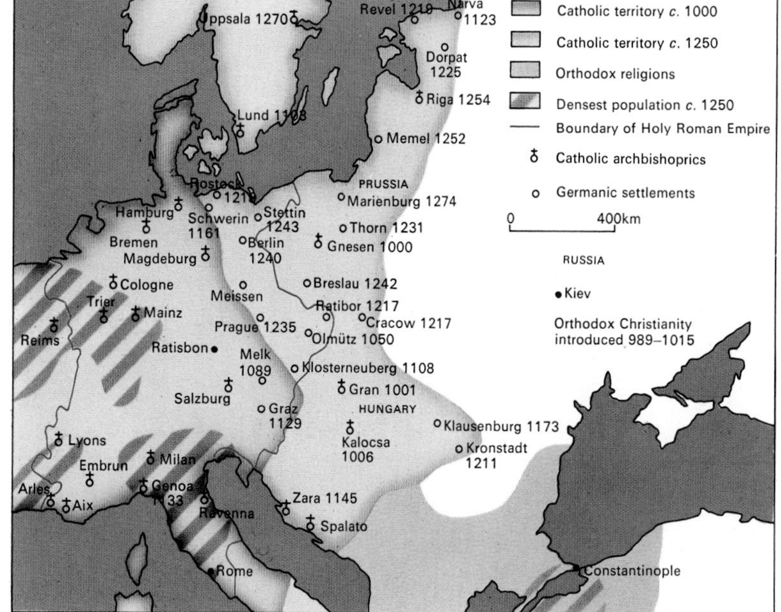
Uppsala 1270
Revel 1219
Narva 1123
Dorpat 1225
Riga 1254
Lund 1103
Memel 1252
PRUSSIA
Marienburg 1274
Rostock 1218
Hamburg
Schwerin 1161
Stettin 1243
Thorn 1231
Bremen
Berlin 1240
Gnesen 1000
Magdeburg
Cologne
Meissen
Breslau 1242
Trier
Mainz
Ratibor 1217
Cracow 1217
Reims
Prague 1235
Olmütz 1050
Ratisbon
Melk 1089
Klosterneuberg 1108
Gran 1001
Salzburg
Graz 1129
HUNGARY
Klausenburg 1173
Lyons
Kalocsa 1006
Kronstadt 1211
Embrun
Milan
Arles
Aix
Genoa 1133
Ravenna
Zara 1145
Spalato
Rome
Constantinople
Catholic territory c. 1000
Catholic territory c. 1250
Orthodox religions
Densest population c. 1250
Boundary of Holy Roman Empire
Catholic archbishoprics
Germanic settlements
0
400km
RUSSIA
Kiev
Orthodox Christianity introduced 989–1015

Norman and Angevin England

Between 1050 and 1100 Europe was transformed by the conquests of the Normans, a warrior people from a section of the north French coastlands. They overran England and southern Italy and settled in Scotland, Wales, the Byzantine Empire, and (after the first Crusade) the Levant. They developed the art of cavalry warfare further than any of their contemporaries. These extraordinarily successful people were a closely interrelated group of families, several of them related to the Viking-descended dukes of Normandy. They crystallized as a distinct group under William I (*c.* 1027–87), also known as William the Conqueror.

The conquest of England

The Normans' greatest achievement was the conquest of England, which because of its distinctive civilization, advanced organization, and great wealth was the richest prize in Europe for soldiers of fortune. Normans had begun to settle there before 1066, but the transformation of England into a Norman kingdom required the ambition of William, an adventurer like the rest. The invasion of 1066 was a corporate enterprise, ostensibly to establish William as the true heir of King Edward the Confessor, but really to win the Normans new fortunes. The narrow victory of Hastings, the slow advance from Canterbury to York, and the rewarding of his companions with wide estates was only just successful. His success created in the midst of living society an uneasy circle of adventurers [1].

Forging the Anglo-Norman nation

Although William hoped to rule like an Anglo-Saxon king, his enemies—King Philip of France, Malcolm of Scotland, Canute of Denmark, in league with dissident Englishmen and rebellious Normans—imposed a state of virtual siege on his dominions and forced him to adopt expedients critical for the future. These included the elaborate system of military service in return for land, out of which the striking solidarity of the Anglo-Norman state was born [4], the series of mighty castles—at the Tower of London, Wallingford, Oxford, and Colchester, in which the grandeur of Norman ambitions can still be seen [5]—and the detailed survey of English wealth made by his order in 1086: the *Domesday Book* [2]. The Normans transformed England, not least by reordering the diocesan structure of the church. When William died, in 1087, England and Normandy were ruled separately by his sons William Rufus (*r.* 1087–1100) and Robert of Normandy, but within a few years they were once more governed by a single ruler.

The Norman Empire, ruled by Rufus's successor and Robert's supplanter Henry I (1068–1135) and his descendants, held together until 1204. For the great Norman families, England was a colonial El Dorado, but Normandy was "home." Rarely have English and continental history been so intertwined: Englishmen such as Adelard of Bath and John of Salisbury contributed to the European revival of learning and science; the great English cathedrals, from Durham at the beginning of the twelfth century to Canterbury at the end, were designed by the most advanced French builders; an English scholar, Nicholas

CONNECTIONS

See also
1068 The Vikings
1098 Feudalism
1096 The emergence of France
1090 Western European economy 1000–1250
1082 Romanesque art of the 12th century

ODO:EPS
WILLELM
ROTBERT

1 The Conqueror and his companions, as portrayed in the Bayeux tapestry, demonstrate the esprit de corps of the Norman leaders, which was one of the secrets of their success. Bishop Odo of Bayeux (on the Conqueror's right), half-brother to William, was probably depicted prominently because he commissioned the tapestry.

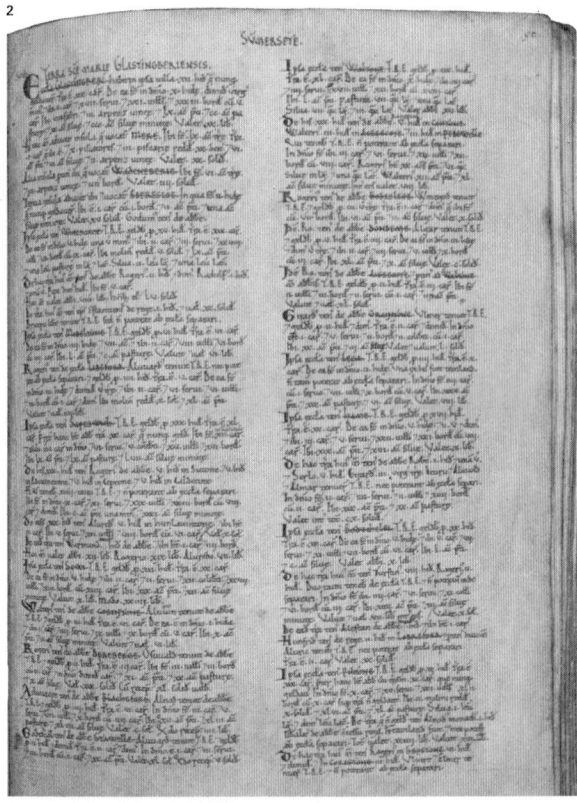

2 The Domesday Book is an astonishing monument to masterful and inventive rule. The survey was ordered by William in 1085 and completed in six months. Its precise purpose is uncertain, but it constituted a record of the wealth of the king and his principal subjects, of stock, of the land, and of the condition of the peasants who cultivated it. Teams of commissioners gathered the necessary information from jurors. This particular page describes a manor in Somerset.

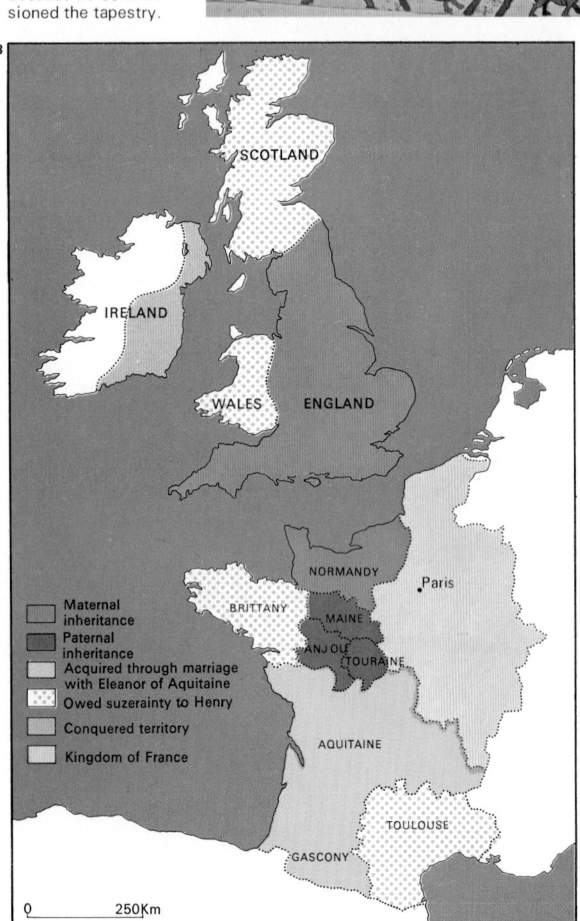

SCOTLAND
IRELAND
WALES
ENGLAND
NORMANDY
BRITTANY
MAINE
ANJOU
TOURAINE
Paris
AQUITAINE
TOULOUSE
GASCONY
Maternal inheritance
Paternal inheritance
Acquired through marriage with Eleanor of Aquitaine
Owed suzerainty to Henry
Conquered territory
Kingdom of France
0
250Km

3 The Norman Empire spread farthest under Henry II, partly because of the union of Norman and Angevin domains via his mother Matilda, but largely through his marriage to Eleanor of Aquitaine.

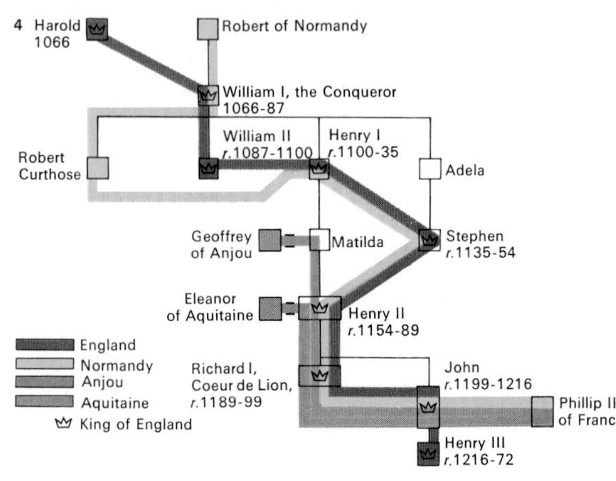

Harold 1066
Robert of Normandy
William I, the Conqueror 1066-87
Robert Curthose
William II r.1087-1100
Henry I r.1100-35
Adela
Geoffrey of Anjou
Matilda
Stephen r.1135-54
Eleanor of Aquitaine
Henry II r.1154-89
Richard I, Coeur de Lion, r.1189-99
John r.1199-1216
Phillip II of France
Henry III r.1216-72
England
Normandy
Anjou
Aquitaine
King of England

4 The network of Norman power was gradually extended by linking powerful families in marriage alliances, although civil war was needed to bring the Angevins to the English throne. England alone was acquired through conquest.

Breakspear, was the first and last Englishman to become pope (as Adrian IV from 1154 to 1159); and Norman French became and remained for three centuries the language of the English royal and legal courts and of polite society.

England's growing prosperity

It was also a period of unprecedented prosperity for England, based primarily on sheep: England was the main supplier of wool to the Flemish textile industry. Many English towns [6] such as Norwich, Oxford, and Salisbury developed rapidly, usually around existing episcopal seats and castles. Flourishing markets for agricultural products needed special protection, and for the first time there is evidence of a growing civic patriotism and a slow but definite movement toward self-governing guilds for the various trades.

Norman England was also remarkably advanced in the arts of government, and a series of monarchs (broken only by the disputed succession between Henry I's daughter Matilda and his nephew Stephen of Blois) sought to marshal England's resources rationally. On Stephen's death, Matilda's son Henry II of Anjou (reigned 1154–89) became king, thereby establishing the Angevin or Plantagenet dynasty. He governed with professional skill, using men who were prepared to experiment with new legal and administrative forms. The English exchequer, jury, and common law courts began during his reign [7].

Their significance, however, lay in the future. At the time there were many signs that the now unwieldy empire was breaking up [3]. Its French inhabitants increasingly looked to the king of France, and the last years of Henry II's reign were disrupted by rebellions, in which his sons joined. After his death the empire was held together by the sheer military genius of his son Richard I (reigned 1189–99); but Richard's brother John, who was no general, lost it forever in only five years [8]. By 1204, England had once more become a separate kingdom, but now it was a kingdom that had been irreversibly enriched and transformed by a century and a half of Norman and Angevin rule.

KEY

Orford Castle in Suffolk, built by Henry II, was typical of the many stone castles that were constructed in every part of England. Control of these castles was the first requirement of effective authority; they could be captured only with the expenditure of much effort. The earliest of these buildings was the Conqueror's wooden prefabricated castle set up on the beach at Hastings before the battle. Henry II showed characteristic inventiveness in the design of Orford, built between 1166 and 1172 to control the Alde estuary and the Suffolk hinterland. Its keep (chief tower) is polygonal outside and cylindrical within; its services are in the outer shell.

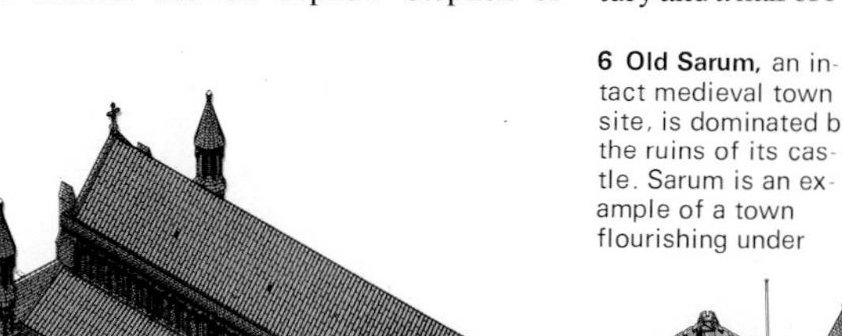

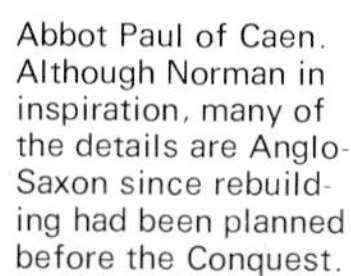

5 The Abbey Church of St Albans is one of the greatest Norman buildings. Its immensely long nave and elaborate east end, which was later rebuilt, are characteristic of the Anglo-Norman style. The Norman part (the central tower and most of the nave) was built (1077–93) under the direction of Abbot Paul of Caen. Although Norman in inspiration, many of the details are Anglo-Saxon since rebuilding had been planned before the Conquest.

6 Old Sarum, an intact medieval town site, is dominated by the ruins of its castle. Sarum is an example of a town flourishing under royal patrons: Norman kings often resided there, and William I made it a bishopric. It declined from 1222 when the bishop moved.

7 The Great Seal of Henry II bears a warlike image even though it was used mostly in the orderly life of the realm. With the aid of capable ministers, Henry transformed the existing customs into a systematic body of law and an efficient administrative procedure.

8 King John was buried at Worcester Cathedral after a reign that provoked hatred and distrust among most of his subjects, principally because he presided over the dissolution of the Angevin Empire. After 1204, when he lost most of his continental possessions, he devoted himself to their recovery. Most of the troubles of his reign were caused by the need for heavy taxation when prices were rising sharply. Abortive campaigns ended with the rebellion of the barons and the imposition on him of the Magna Carta (great charter) at Runnymede in 1215. After the sealing of the charter the Norman Empire had to make way for an emergent English nation.

Islam in Europe

The overthrow of the Visigothic state of Iberia in AD 711 by Berber forces, or Moors, recently converted to Islam was an event unforeseen by the Arabs of the East. The distance of Spain from Damascus was so great that neither the material wealth nor the exploitation of an enormous trading potential proved fully possible and contributed to the fragmenting and then the erosion of Muslim conquests.

Independence from the East

In the early years the governors of al-Andalus, as the Muslim-controlled area of the Iberian Peninsula was called, were nominated by the caliphs in the East, and tax money did find its way across the Mediterranean. No such benefits were forthcoming after AD 756 when the Umayyed family came to power. This family retained supremacy in Córdoba [2] for nearly 300 years, maintaining from the outset political independence from the East. The Umayyads of Córdoba could seldom command the loyalty of all Spanish Muslims, however. It was only in the tenth century, under Abd ar-Rahmān III, who declared himself caliph in AD 929, that hitherto semi-autonomous regions acknowledged, sometimes after protracted conflicts, the supremacy of the Umayyads. The ensuing unity gave al-Andalus a strength that enabled the state to brush aside sporadic forays by the kingdoms of the north and even, on occasions, to arbitrate in the dynastic disputes of these kingdoms. Profitable treaties were struck with some of the small North African dynasties, and trading relations were established with the German and Byzantine empires.

Importance of Córdoba

Córdoba became the undisputed capital of western Islam and a magnet for scholars [9], poets, and artisans who assembled there from throughout the Islamic world. A palace was built in the cooler foothills of the nearby Sierra Nevada where the caliph resided and conducted affairs of state, while in Córdoba successive additions imparted increasing splendor to the Great Mosque.

Unity in al-Andalus proved, however, to be difficult to maintain, and as a result the caliphate was formally dissolved in AD 103. The subsequent fragmentation of al-Andalus into some 30 city-states, all jealous of their own independence and covetous of the territories of their neighbors, occurred in the eleventh century when Christians from beyond the Pyrenees, encouraged by the pope, became involved in the internal affairs of the northern Spanish kingdoms.

The reconquest of Muslim Spain

The reconquest [6] of Muslim Spain may be considered in two phases, before and after the capture of Toledo in central Spain in 1085. Before this date there is scant evidence from Latin or Arabic chronicles that the gradual occupation of territories to their south by the Christian states was either premeditated or concerted. Some Asturian kings of the eighth and ninth centuries implemented a deliberate policy of settling sparsely populated areas with immigrants from all parts of the peninsula and, in this way, laid permanent claim to tracts of land in the frontier zones.

CONNECTIONS

See also
1062 Arabs and the rise of Islam
1066 Charlemagne and the Carolingian Empire
1084 The Crusades
1088 European learning in the 13th century
1058 Mohammed and Islam
1452 Finding unknown quantities: algebra

1 Attributed to Alfonso the Wise (1221–84), the *Cantigas de Santa Maria* is a collection of 400 songs recounting a variety of miraculous and legendary incidents connected with the Virgin Mary. This miniature from a contemporary manuscript depicts three events: the salvation from a storm of merchants bound for trade in Acre, their successful business transactions, and the homage they paid to a Marian shrine.

2 The Great Mosque of Córdoba, begun in the 8th century, was later enlarged and embellished and is a lasting testimony to the magnificence of Islamic civilization in Spain. By 1031 the city had been devastated by civil strife and lost its place of eminence. The mosque survived, was consecrated to Christianity after the reconquest (1236), and had the cathedral built in its center in the 16th century.

3 A commentary on the Apocalypse of St John the Apostle by Beatus of Liebana shows one remarkable side of the culture of Islamic Spain. Christian manuscripts were still copied and studied in monasteries, but their style shows Islamic influence. Thus in this illumination to the text (which was done at Gerona in about 975) Jerusalem becomes a Mozarabic (Spanish-Muslim) city with the horseshoe arches to the second-floor windows that are the hallmark of the style.

4 Rodrigo Díaz de Vivar (*c.* 1043–99), left, known as "El Cid," was a Castilian knight estranged from the king, Alfonso VI, and banished (*c.* 1081). His bloody exploits, such as one depicted here, are enshrined in Spanish legend. Supported by a force of faithful Castilians he moved freely in Muslim-held territory. His crowning achievement was the capture of Valencia in 1094, which effected his reconciliation with the Castilian king.

5 El Cid was born at Vivar, Burgos, where these monuments mark the site of his ancestral home. The Spanish epic *Poema de Mio Cid* portrays him as a noble Christian hero, loyal to his king despite being banished from Castile. Arabic sources emphasize his cruelty. Many ballads celebrate his achievements as an invincible knight, and it has become difficult to distinguish the Cid of Spanish history from the Cid of legend and literature.

Lack of any effective political cohesion among the Christian states was the main obstacle to territorial expansion at the expense of the Muslims. The Duero and Ebro valleys remained the approximate boundaries until Alfonso VI's definitive occupation of Toledo in 1085 altered the map of the peninsula by placing a permanent Christian wedge in al-Andalus in central Spain. From this time the reconquest gathered momentum, and the religious factor, hitherto largely dormant, now emerged. The confrontation between the military-religious Christian order of Santiago and Muslim warriors was evident in the clashes between the Muslim Almoravids and Almohads, Berber tribes from northern Africa, on the one hand, and the Christian forces of Castile and Aragón on the other.

After suffering reverses, notably at the battle of Alarcos in 1195, the forces of Castile, Aragón, and Portugal—usually acting independently of each other—reduced the power of al-Andalus to some 250 miles (400km) of coastline from Gibraltar eastward. The Nasrid kingdom, with its capital at Granada, lasted 250 years by dint of shrewd diplomacy, judicious alliances contracted from time to time with both Castilians and Muslims from North Africa, trading links with Genoese and Catalan merchants, and geographical barriers, such as the Sierra Nevada, that discouraged assaults. The Alhambra, built in the fourteenth century, is the major monument of this bastion of Islamic civilization in a Spain whose political orientation was by then the same as other Western European powers.

Hostility toward the Muslims and reverence for the Islamic cultural tradition were not incompatible in the new Spanish state. While wars were being waged in frontier zones, Toledo, like Norman Sicily [8], became a center from which Greek and Arabic learning was transmitted to Western scholars. Churches in ornate styles were built by Muslim craftsmen, in the style known as Mudejar. Yet the power of Islam in Spain and Sicily was dead. The reconquest was a major political achievement, but the vestiges of nearly 700 years of Islamic presence in Spain were indelible.

KEY

The castle of Manzanares el Real, to the north of Madrid, was constructed near the site of an earlier fortress during the second half of the 15th century in the elaborate Mudejar and late Gothic styles. It was the residence of the Mendoza family, whose members were granted the marquisate of Santillana and the dukedom of Infantado for distinguished political and military service. This brought them material enrichment and prominence in Castile's affairs.

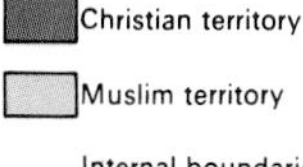
Christian territory
Muslim territory

.... Internal boundaries

6 The boundaries between Christian and Muslim Spain altered little until the capture of Toledo (1085). The reconquest achieved its greatest momentum in the 12th and 13th centuries, when the crusading zeal was at its height. The small kingdom of Granada survived until 1492.

6 A

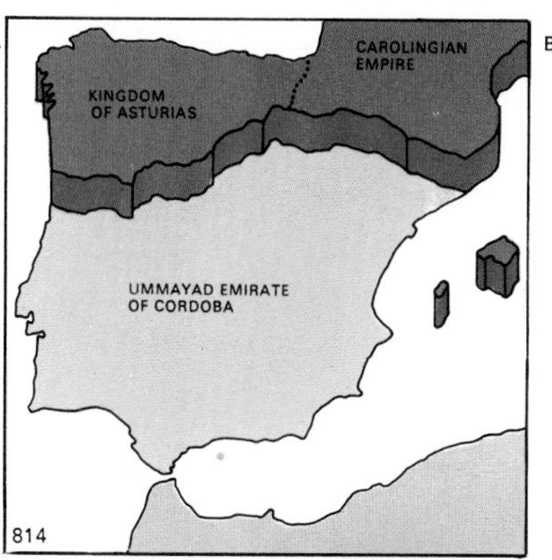
CAROLINGIAN EMPIRE
KINGDOM OF ASTURIAS
UMMAYAD EMIRATE OF CORDOBA
814

B

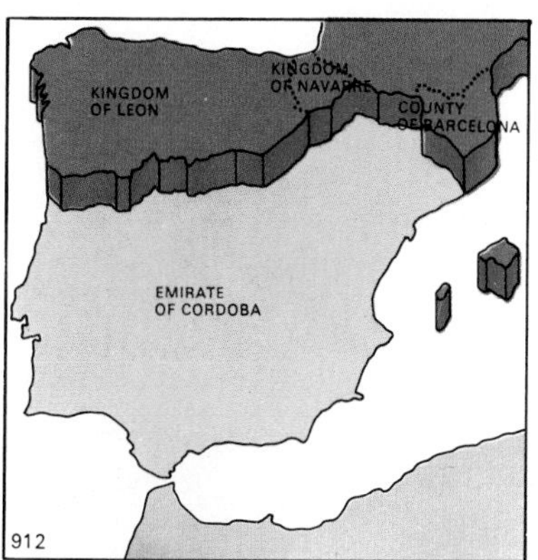
KINGDOM OF LEON
KINGDOM OF NAVARRE
COUNTY OF BARCELONA
EMIRATE OF CORDOBA
912

C

KINGDOM OF NAVARRE
KINGDOM OF ARAGON
KINGDOMS OF LEON AND CASTILE
COUNTY OF BARCELONA
INDEPENDENT MOORISH STATES
MOORISH STATES
1037

D

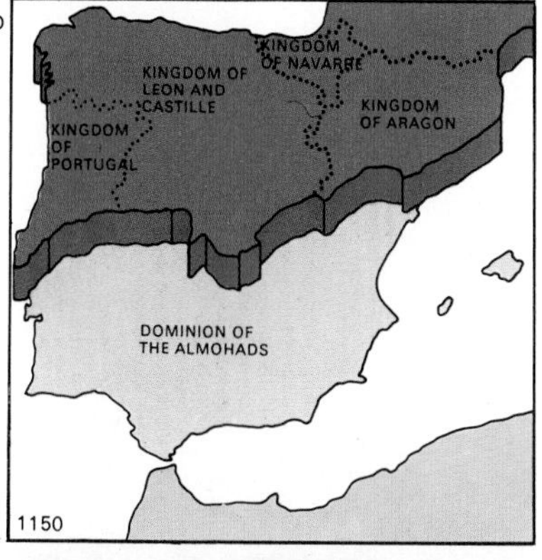
KINGDOM OF NAVARRE
KINGDOM OF LEON AND CASTILLE
KINGDOM OF ARAGON
KINGDOM OF PORTUGAL
DOMINION OF THE ALMOHADS
1150

E

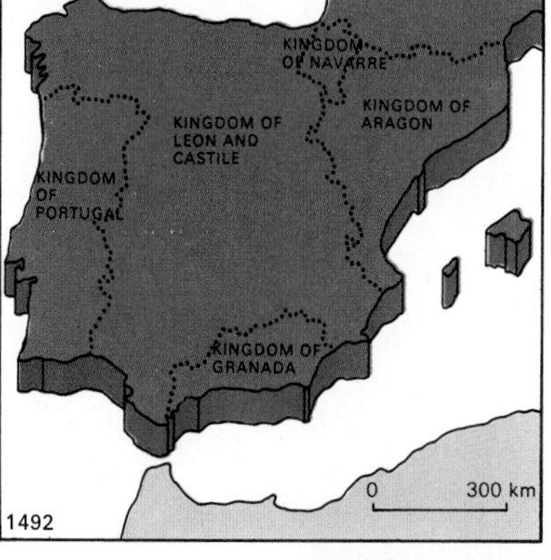
KINGDOM OF NAVARRE
KINGDOM OF LEON AND CASTILE
KINGDOM OF ARAGON
KINGDOM OF PORTUGAL
KINGDOM OF GRANADA
0 300 km
1492

7 St James the *Greater* (d. *c.* 44), or Santiago, is the patron saint of Spain. His body was miraculously discovered in the 9th century in Galicia, where the city of Santiago de Compostela now stands. The shrine became a center of pilgrimage for Christians, thus opening Spain to European influences, and the Spanish Christians acquired a warrior saint who would lead them into battle against the Muslims.

7

8

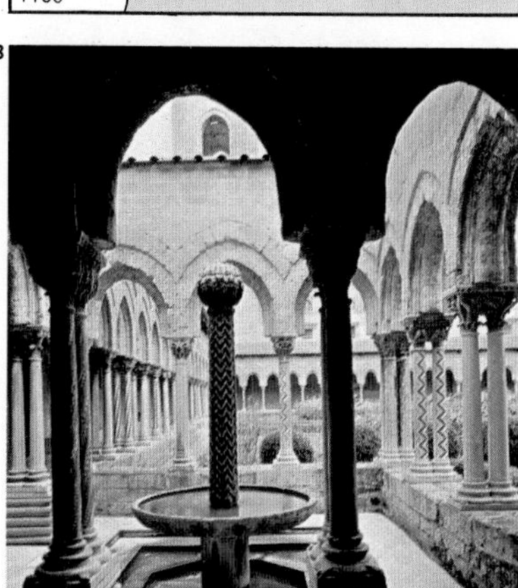

8 Byzantine and Arabic features are prominent in Monreale Cathedral, built by the Norman William II (1154–89), who challenged Muslim political and religious supremacy in the Mediterranean.

9 During Raymond of Toledo's archbishopric (1125–51), large numbers of Arabic works were translated into Latin by scholars from all over Europe. Scientific and philosophical treatises were thus introduced to the West.

9

Romanesque art of the 11th century

The term "Romanesque" was borrowed from literary sources by nineteenth-century antiquarians to describe pre-Gothic architecture, implying that it reflected that of Rome. Today it is applied to the art, and more especially the architecture, of the eleventh and twelfth centuries. The political and economic instability of Western Europe after the abandonment of the Western Roman Empire accelerated the decline of widespread patronage of the arts. Despite the artistic revival under Emperor Charlemagne and his successors, and personal patronage in more localized centers, it was only the reestablishment of strong governments and the parallel reforms within the Church about 1000 that caused the arts to revive throughout Europe.

Patronage of the arts by the Church

Land was the primary source of income in the Middle Ages, and the power of the landowners was supreme. The Church readily accepted gifts of land and became a great feudal landowner, owning as much as a third of France in the eleventh century. Another source of income came from the offerings of the faithful at saints' shrines [7].

Although Rome and Santiago de Compostela in Spain were the major destinations, visits to many other centers were encouraged. The shrines contained holy relics that were believed to have great powers of physical and spiritual healing. To display them in safety was an incentive for rebuilding a church. The creation of monastic orders—particularly the Cluniacs—to protect these relics and the founding of monasteries to administer both spiritual and temporal affairs also encouraged building.

The Church therefore became the greatest patron of the arts, building religious houses, decorating them with paintings [5] and hangings, and filling them with altars, candelabra, and screens made of wood or iron. As religious services grew more elaborate, more manuscripts and religious artifacts were acquired. Stone castles and houses from this period are rare, which may indicate that they were not built in great numbers or, more likely, were soon replaced by better and more comfortable structures. The creation of a church that could serve both pilgrim and monk was the builder's main problem.

Romanesque churches of two forms

Two basic church types were current in Western Europe: the wooden-roofed, aisled basilica, and the vaulted small-scale martyrium (erected on a site of religious significance). The former had been taken up by the early Christians in Rome and continued to flourish with little development in central Italy up to the Gothic period. When Charlemagne and his successors sought to revive the Roman Empire from about 800, it was this type of church they copied in Germany. It gradually evolved into an exclusively north European basilica.

These churches had apsidal choirs, sometimes at both ends; west fronts forming multistoried masses, called *westwerks;* and towers crowning each end. Linking these complex elements was the long nave, with expanses of flat wall between the ground-floor arcades and upper windows. These areas were painted or hung with em-

CONNECTIONS

See also
1082 Romanesque art of the 12th century
1086 The Power of the Church: 1073–1309
1096 The emergence of France

1 The nave of St Michael's, Hildesheim (1000–33) (looking west) has a 12th-century wooden ceiling and the original suspended candelabrum to light the eastern crossing. The church has no vaults, in the Carolingian tradition, and so is wide and well lit. The solid walls of the elevation are now dull and monotonous, but they were once brightly painted, probably to emphasize the width of the nave.

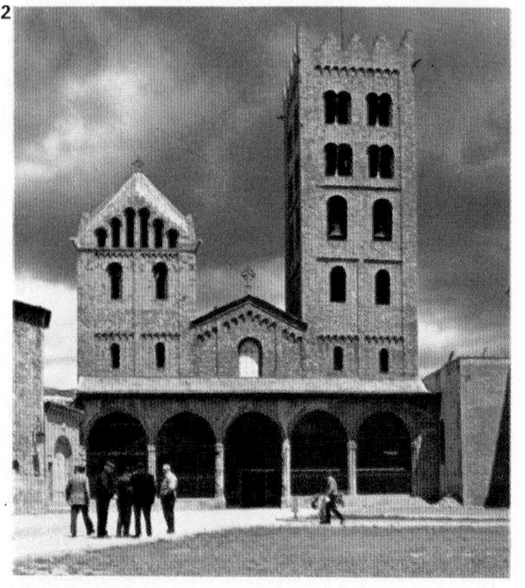

2 The west façade of the monastic church of Sta Maria at Ripoll, near Gerona, was rebuilt between 1020 and 1032 by Abbot Olivia. This style of church can be seen throughout southern Europe and is distinguished by the use of small rubble building material, the covering of all interiors with vaults, and, particularly, by the arched corbel-table running around the summit of all external walls—seen here on the towers and gable of the church's west facade.

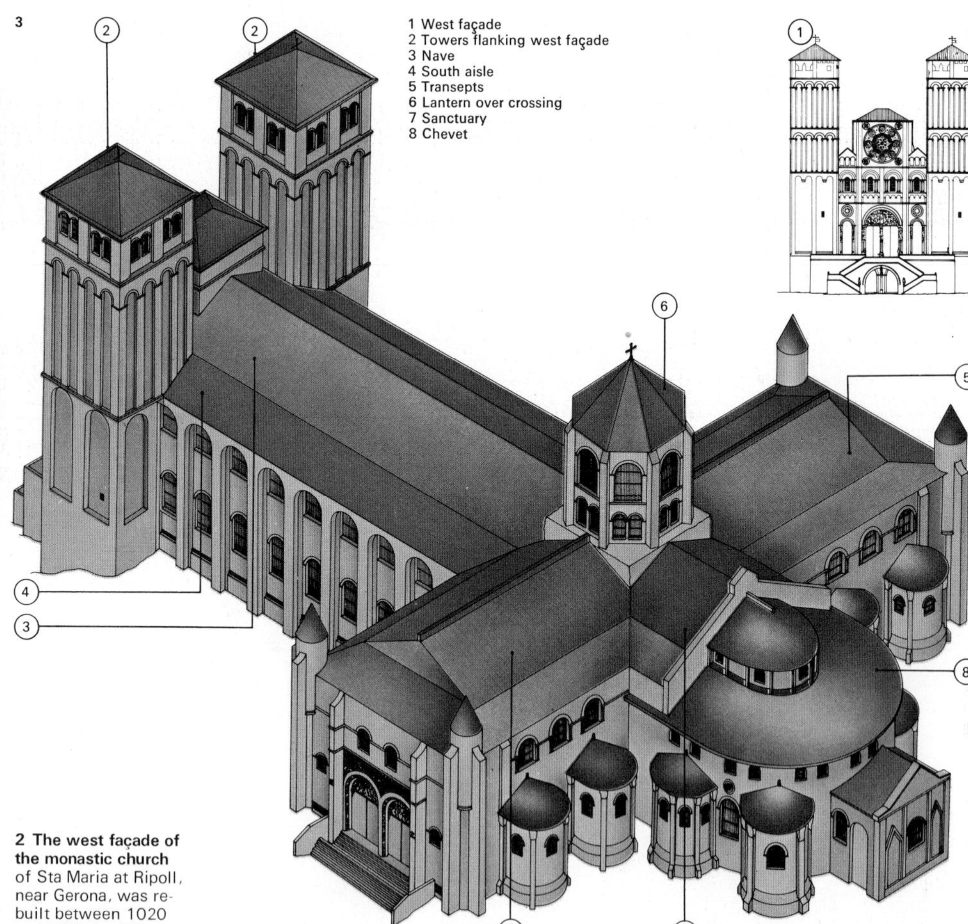
1 West façade
2 Towers flanking west façade
3 Nave
4 South aisle
5 Transepts
6 Lantern over crossing
7 Sanctuary
8 Chevet

3 The cathedral of Santiago de Compostela in Spain is the reputed burial place of the Apostle James, and was the goal of vast numbers of pilgrims from throughout Europe during the Middle Ages. Four main "pilgrimage roads" from France fed a single route through northern Spain, each road being marked by an important shrine. The five greatest churches built between 1050 and 1100 were at Tours (St Martin), Limoges (St Martial), Conques (Ste-Foy), Toulouse (St Sernin), and Compostela. They have similar plans and were influential in spreading the concept of the great Romanesque church—a large, cross-shaped building with a towered main western entrance [1,2], galleries running around the interior at an upper level, and emphasis on the east end with many protruding apses for altars. The nave [3] had altars, but served mainly as a congregating area. Each altar was dedicated to a different saint and had a reliquary on or within it. Candelabra, screens, and hangings were placed around the altar. (It was this profusion of fittings that fed accidental fires.) This is the third church on the Compostela site, probably built by French masons and finished *c.* 1125, although many alterations have since been made on various parts of the church.

broideries. All Romanesque churches were a mass of color, now lost through rebuilding or whitewashing.

In central Italy, no such evolution took place. Marble panels were often used instead of wall paintings in Tuscany, as at San Miniato al Monte, Florence, and bell-towers and baptisteries were usually completely detached, as at Pisa.

The martyrium type is not so easily identified as the Roman, although its distribution corresponds to the extent of the fifth century Roman Empire—that is, north and east Spain, the southern half of France, north Italy, Yugoslavia, and Asia Minor. Its roots lay in the provincial Roman buildings, built of small, local stone or brick rather than the faced stone blocks of imperial monuments. Although limiting size, this material facilitated the vaulting of the narrower spans, in contrast to the open wood roofs of the wide basilica church.

As a consequence, however, the mason became a craftsman in stone rather than a sculptor, and any architectural sculpture, such as capitals, was often crude and carved in relief rather than deeply cut into the stone. Apart from the materials used, the decorative system of thin pilasters (ornamental rectangular columns) rising to a corbel-table (a line of projections running under the eaves) distinguishes this work.

Romanesque churches in provincial France and Spain

These two church types merged, and after much experiment (especially in France), two basic plans evolved, which were modified in each region to suit local conditions. The great pilgrimage churches [3] are typical of the "ambulatory" plan, which allowed pilgrims to see the relics behind the high altar without disturbing the monks at their worship [Key].

Churches associated with the Cluniac order, especially in Burgundy, used parallel apses, that is, a series of semicircular or octagonal recesses of varying heights and depths flanking the main monks' choir. Unlike the ambulatory layout, this plan encouraged masons to vault the main areas, as solid walls were available for support.

KEY

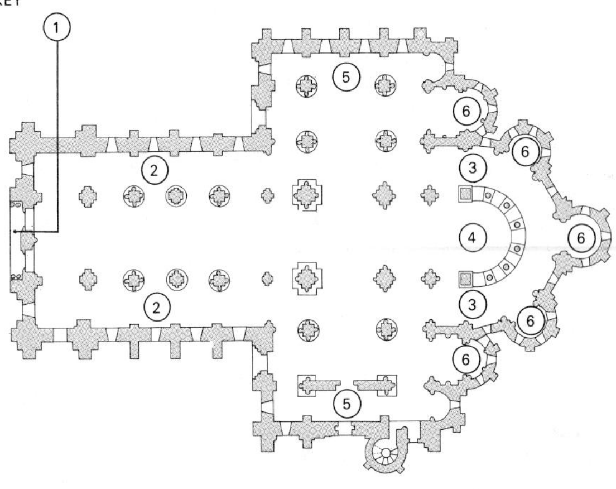
1
2
2
3
3
4
5
5
6
6
6
6
6

This floor plan of Ste Foy, Conques, France (*c.*1050–1110) allowed for the needs of pilgrim and monk alike. The former would enter at the west [1], and go along the aisles [2] to the ambulatory [3] to look at the principal shrine in the sanctuary [4]. The monks would enter the church by the transepts [5] from the cloister (around which the monastery was grouped), and then go in procession to their choir behind screens or to minor altars [6] behind the sanctuary.

4 The nave at St Etienne, Nevers (*c.* 1070), looking east toward the high altar, is made narrow and dark by the need to support the stone barrel vaults. Behind the middle range of arches a half-barrel links the main elevation, helping to support the main span and allowing for small upper windows. The wall shafts divide the elevation into vertical bay units.

5 In the church of S Angelo in Formis, near Capua (rebuilt after 1072), this picture shows Christ touching the eyes of the blind man, who then washes at the well and sees again. Spots on the cheeks and angular drapery patterns show the Byzantine influence. The paintings illustrate scenes from the Old and New Testaments and cover the whole interior of the church. Such a complete cycle is rare today.

6 A

B

6 The marble lintels at St Genis-des-Fontaines, French Pyrenees (1020–21), show the enthroned Christ [B] supported by angels. Saints [A] flank the figure. It is one of the earliest known pieces of monumental medieval stone sculpture. The layout and the light chip carving indicate that the sculptors had studied earlier stone reliefs and contemporary metalwork such as the Basle altar-frontal.

7 The gold-covered cult-figure of Ste-Foy was originally made in the 10th century, but pious visitors to her shrine at Conques have, over the centuries, encrusted this reliquary with precious stones, cameos, and crystals. Although other figures were made, a statue was considered idolatrous, and most reliquaries are casket- or shrine-shaped and contain the saint's relics. Sometimes a representation of a particular part of the holy body is on top.

8 This large altar frontal of beaten gold was given to Basle Cathedral by the German emperor Henry II (*c.*1019). The central figure of Christ is flanked by the archangels Gabriel and Raphael on the left and Michael and Benedict on the right. Few such large precious-metal objects have survived from the early periods. Their value as metal tempted later generations to melt them down for reuse.

Romanesque art of the 12th century

The huge churches built toward the end of the eleventh century placed great emphasis on the east end, where the main altars and relics were sited. Outside, the layered walls and roofs of the apsidal chapels, ambulatory, clerestory, and galleries culminated in mighty towers; inside, the increased use of sculptural decoration and sumptuous church furniture emphasized the respect owed to the shrines in the sanctuary. On entering, usually at the west front, the pilgrim often had to pass under evocative, carved tympana, dominated by a central Christ figure surrounded by the Heavenly Host, or scenes from the Last Judgment.

Interior decoration by secular artists

The increased use of ashlar (cut stone) had led to greater skill in stone-cutting. Because the walls were now divided into arcades and piers, the didactic and decorative functions of the large-scale wall paintings were transferred to sculptured capitals and portals (which were then painted) or, in some regions, to stained glass. These capital designs had to follow the lines of the particular structure, but a tympanum over a door, or a panel inserted into the wall, had no structural function, so only the shape was determined by architectural factors. Animal and human figures, therefore, had to be reinterpreted and traditional iconography amended to fit these new shapes. For subject matter, the sculptor looked to the older arts of metalwork and manuscripts to supply an endless variety of suitable iconography. But for figurative techniques, surviving Roman sculpture was influential.

This divergence from the original and the different treatment of stone help to explain the many styles that emerged, often with little connection to regional variations. It must be remembered that workshops were composed of itinerant masons, sculptors, and painters hired by ecclesiastical patrons, and not of resident monks. Some, such as Gislebertus at Autun and Wiligelmus at Modena, even autographed their work. Although a man might specialize in designing secular buildings such as castles and town houses, his workmen would probably also have built and embellished abbeys, cathedrals, or parish churches. Decorative details are therefore common to all types of structures.

Reactions to ostentation

An enormous increase in the demand for church furnishings led to a concentration of lay craftsmen in places where patronage or raw materials were most readily available. Products from centers such as Cologne or Liège (metalwork) or Limoges (enamels) [4] and sometimes master craftsmen, too, were sent throughout Europe. Similar methods probably applied to the production of illuminated manuscripts [5], particularly the lavish "picture books" for the personal use of abbots and bishops. Everyday service books, however, were most likely copied out within the cloisters of major monasteries. Such ostentation produced inevitable reactions. In particular the Cistercian order, led by Bernard of Clairvaux (1090–1153), returned to the monastic ideals of poverty and purity that they felt had been betrayed by painted sculpture and the liberal use of precious metals and jewels.

CONNECTIONS

See also
1080 Romanesque art of the 11th century
1086 The power of the Church: 1073–1309
1096 The emergence of France
1076 Norman and Angevin England

1

2

3

1 The nave of Durham Cathedral, England (finished in 1133), is a tentative application of rib-vaults to a main span, but clearly shows the advantages that such a coordinated vault type could bring. The emphasis is still on strength and solidity; the cylindrical piers cannot hide their size behind the simple surface patterns. The chevron or zigzag was a popular motif with Norman builders in 12th-century England.

2 The medieval builder was as dependent on resources of wood as of stone because huge scaffolds were essential for the construction of vaults and arches. The arch stones (voussoirs) were placed on wooden centering, the last keystone locking the radiating voussoirs together. Once the mortar had set, the centering was lowered and moved on. Exact workshop practices, however, are difficult to ascertain.

3 This is the massive central keep of the Tower of London (1078–97), one of the earliest Norman castles in Britain. Few stone castles existed in western Europe before 1000, but by the end of the 12th century hundreds had been constructed to house noblemen's families and defend their dependents in time of attack. The Crusades gave rise to more sophisticated and expensive techniques.

4

4 The life of Ste Valerie, the patron saint of Limoges, is illustrated on this enameled casket (*c.* 1170). According to legend, she was engaged to a prince, who found on his return from war that she had dedicated her life to God and so could not marry. The prince then had her beheaded (lower right). This is one of many ornately embellished copper casket reliquaries with attached panels decorated with figures enameled in blue, red, and turquoise on golden backgrounds. Most surviving medieval enamelwork is on church accessories, the medium lending itself to delicate work. Many surviving pieces have been found in Limoges, France, which was the center of enamelwork production.

5

5 The Bury Bible is an illustrated English manuscript of about 1140. On the left, a large painted panel depicts the scene of the prophet Jeremiah lamenting the imminent fall of Jerusalem. On the right, a decorated initial heads the text. The rich palette is evidence of the high quality of the manuscript.

In order to display treasures to their best advantage, the vogue throughout Europe for stone-vaulted churches had to be reconciled with another factor, that of natural, direct lighting. Dark, mysterious interiors were rivaled by open, well-lit spans, the light sometimes being filtered through stained glass. In barrel-vaulted churches the half-cylinder of stone that makes up the roof exerts an even, outward thrust along its entire length, requiring continuous support. Building windows into these walls therefore compromised the stability of the vault.

In Poitou, the barrel-vault rises directly from the top of an arcade of very tall columns. Large windows in the aisle wall flood the central space with light. This technique was efficient only in narrow, single-aisled buildings and left the upper half of the church dark. A more practical system shed light from both aisles and clerestory: to achieve this, vaulted galleries above the aisles were used to buttress the main elevation just below the "springing" level of the main span. This assured stability and allowed small clerestory windows to be made. The problem could only really be solved by dispensing with the need for continuous support, and this meant new concepts of vault design.

The development of new vault types

In western France, about 1100, great domes were built on huge arches over the main span, which concentrated pressure on the four corners. These were then heavily buttressed. This solution was admirable for the traditionally aisleless churches of that area, but elsewhere, especially in the Anglo-Norman region, aisles surmounted by open galleries as high as the main arcade were considered necessary. Over aisles and around ambulatories, "groined" vaults (formed by two simple tunnel vaults intersecting at right angles) had been used. Again, the four corners provided support so that the walls could be pierced for windows.

In northern France, from about 1140, such a system evolved, later to be called Gothic. But elsewhere, Romanesque wall architecture continued to flourish until the thirteenth century.

KEY

In this detail of a capital from the narthex at Vézelay, St Paul (on the left) is praying for the redemption of the world. The function of the capital is to make a smooth transition between the round shaft below and the square or rectangular-shaped masonry above. The Romans used a number of capital types, employing stylized acanthus leaves and scrolls. When figurative scenes were carved out of capitals the sculpture had to conform to the architectural shape and not interrupt the gently splaying lines. Here, St Paul's leg, back, and head continue the capital's contours, although the actual pose of the figure appears unnatural.

6

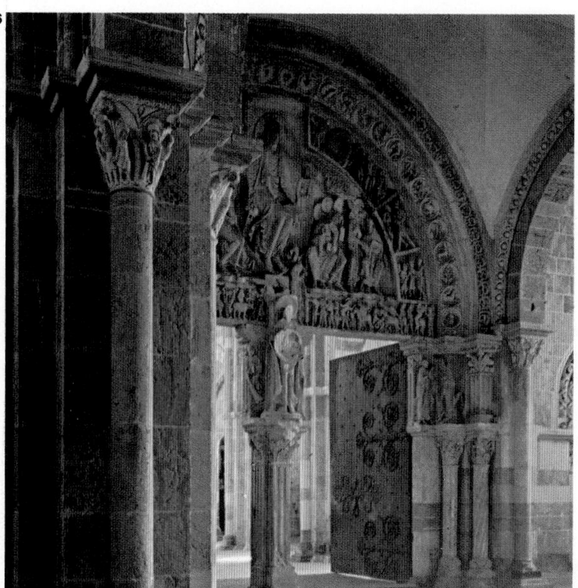

6 Originally the west doors at Vézelay fronted the hilltop church. But a large towered narthex or porch was added in about 1150 to protect this vulnerable sculpture from the weather. It is one of the greatest ensembles of Romanesque carving, full of energetic figures in ample and swirling draperies.

7

7 The existence of many Roman monuments in Autun influenced the architectural decoration of the 12th-century cathedral there; flat fluted pilasters, for example, were used rather than the usual round shafts. Among Autun's Roman ruins are an amphitheater and the gates of SS André and Arroux.

8 The painted apse of the chapel at Berzé-la-Ville is thought to have been commissioned by Abbot Hugh of Cluny before his death in 1109 and to be a smaller version of the main apse painting of his great abbey church at Cluny. Directly above the altar Christ sits in glory within an almond-shaped panel surrounded by the Heavenly Host. Below the windows there is a range of saints. Originally all great churches had such scenes over the altar, often illustrating the life and martyrdom of the saint to whom the altar was dedicated.

8

9 The west façade of Notre-Dame-la-Grande, Poitiers, (*c.* 1140) is considered to be one of the finest in western France, an area noted for its copious use of external sculpture. Also typical of the area are the corner turrets faced by shafts and topped with scalelike stone roofs. Although there is only one central entrance, the vogue for inserting three or more deep decorated portals within a grandiose façade was popular in the Middle Ages.

9

The Crusades

The immediate cause of the First Crusade—and the starting point for a major stage of European expansion—was the threat to the Byzantine Empire created by the Seljuk Turks. These Muslim tribesmen had conquered the empire's richest province, Anatolia, and farther east had dispossessed the caliphs of Antioch, Tripoli, and Jerusalem. An attack on Constantinople seemed inevitable.

In 1095, Emperor Alexius I Comnenus (reigned 1081–1118), an able soldier and diplomat, asked Pope Urban II (1042–99) for assistance, baiting his request for a contingent of mercenaries to retake Anatolia with the suggestion that they could then travel on to liberate Jerusalem. Urban responded [1] and for the first time the papacy sanctioned a "holy war."

The First and Second Crusades

The four separate armies of the First Crusade [3] converged on Constantinople in the winter of 1096–97: men from Lorraine, the Norman kingdom of Apulia, Provence, Brittany, Normandy, and Flanders. The Franks took Nicaea and Dorylaeum; Antioch fell, and the crusaders stormed Jerusalem in July 1099 [2].

With the holy places conquered, territorial motives now became paramount. Four Frankish states [5], defended by the castles and garrisons of the Templars and Hospitalers [6], survived increasing Muslim pressure until 1144, when Edessa fell. A crusade was called for by Pope Eugenius III (died 1153). Emperor Conrad III (1093–1152) and King Louis VII of France (1121–80) incompetently led the armies of the Second Crusade (1147–49) to disaster in Anatolia.

Jerusalem falls to the Turks

A further revival of Islam and the empire's final loss of Anatolia to the Seljuks in 1176 left the Latin states in danger. Saladin (Salah ad-Din, 1137–93), the brilliant Kurdish vizier of Egypt, united Islam from the Nile to the Tigris and in 1187 invaded the Latin Kingdom of Jerusalem and overran the Frankish states.

The armies of the Third Crusade (1189–91) came to their aid and Emperor Frederick I (Barbarossa) (1123–90) took the Seljuk capital of Iconium. Philip II Augustus of France (1165–1223) and Richard I of England (1157–99) joined the ex-King of Jerusalem, Guy of Lusignan (1140–94), in besieging Acre, which surrendered after a two-year siege. Richard then set out for Jaffa, the port of Jerusalem. He won the coast from Tyre to Jaffa, but was prevented from attacking Jerusalem.

The Fourth Crusade (1202–04), supported by Pope Innocent III (*c.* 1160–1216) to restore the kingdom of Jerusalem, resulted in the debasement of the ideal: war was now made against other Christians for gain. Venice, which controlled most of the eastern Mediterranean, forced the army to accept a price for transport to Egypt that it could not pay. The Doge of Venice agreed to forgive the debt only if the troops were diverted to repossess Zara on the Adriatic, a former Venetian city taken by the Magyars in 1186. The army was then persuaded to intervene in a Byzantine dynastic quarrel and besiege Constantinople itself. The presence of a Frankish army exacerbated

CONNECTIONS

See also
1086 The Power of the Church: 1073–1309
1062 Arabs and the rise of Islam
1078 Islam in Europe
1108 The Ottoman Empir to 1600

1 Pope Urban II's appeal to the Council of Clermont (1095) launched the First Crusade and was an attempt to reconcile Church and state. The reply to his call, a shout of "Deus vult" (God wills it), later became the battle cry of crusader knights in the Holy Land. His appeal led to the spontaneous and ill-disciplined People's Crusade (1096). The pope's appeal to biblical images of Jerusalem, the heavenly city, made the idea of freeing the earthly city one of great splendor and power. The pope reinforced his appeal with calculated references to western overpopulation.

2 Crusaders besieging Jerusalem in June and July 1099 faced fortifications more complex than any in northern Europe. A quick assault was necessary as the defenders had poisoned the wells for 6 miles (10km) around the city. Wood had to be brought by sea for the scaling ladders, mangonels (beams that hurled boulders), giant catapults, and trebuchets (slings worked by counterweights). Three wooden "castles" on wheels, to make possible attacks on the upper levels of the walls, were hung with hides to ward off arrows and "Greek fire" (a blazing naphtha-based mixture very difficult to extinguish). The knights cared for their horses before they looked after themselves: heavy war-horses, trained to charge against infantry and able to carry a man wearing a third of his own weight again in armor, were irreplaceable in the East. Loss of his horse reduced the knight to the ranks of the foot soldiers.

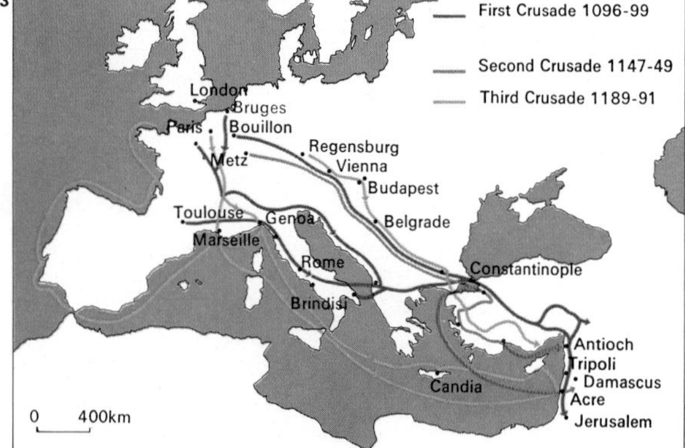

First Crusade 1096-99
Second Crusade 1147-49
Third Crusade 1189-91
London
Bruges
Paris
Bouillon
Regensburg
Metz
Vienna
Budapest
Toulouse
Genoa
Belgrade
Marseille
Rome
Constantinople
Brindisi
Antioch
Tripoli
Damascus
Candia
Acre
Jerusalem
0 400km

3 The recovery of the holy places and the maintenance of the subsequently established Frankish states were the aims of the early crusaders. The separate armies of the first Crusade (1096–99), from France, Provence, Normandy, Flanders, and Apulia, assembled at meeting-points throughout Europe, marched through Magyar territory to Constantinople and fought their way across Asia Minor. Those of the Second Crusade (1147–49), led by the kings of France and Germany, also went overland, but their refusal to adapt to conditions of Eastern warfare led to their destruction by the Seljuks. By the Third Crusade Western naval strength had improved, and Richard I chose a sea route to Acre.

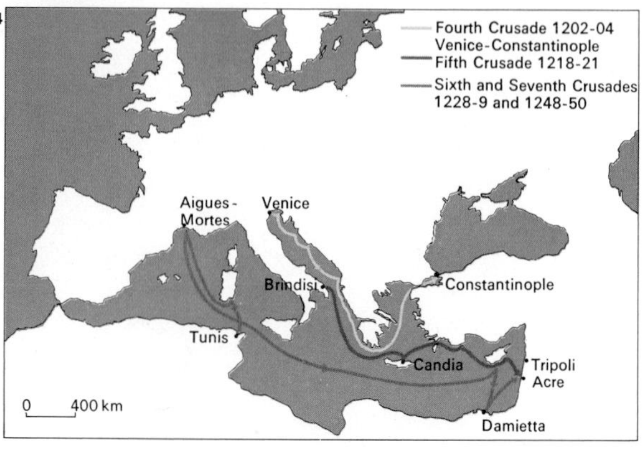

Fourth Crusade 1202-04
Venice-Constantinople
Fifth Crusade 1218-21
Sixth and Seventh Crusades 1228-9 and 1248-50
Aigues-Mortes
Venice
Brindisi
Constantinople
Tunis
Candia
Tripoli
Acre
Damietta
0 400 km

4 Directly concerned with saving Jerusalem, the 4th-7th Crusades aroused far less enthusiasm in the West than had their predecessors. Greed and hatred for fellow Christians in the East made the army of the Fourth Crusade easy prey for Venice's manipulations. In later crusades, personal magnetism and negotiating skill led to the meager victories of Emperor Frederick II and King Louis IX of France.

hatred between Greek and Latin Christians. In April 1204 the crusaders seized and looted the city. Consequent dismemberment of imperial territories gave Venice absolute control of the sea route between Venice and Constantinople and established the "Latin Empire" in the east.

The crusaders finally defeated

After the failure of the Fifth Crusade (1218–21), the last in which the papacy was actually involved, the pope's Hohenstaufen enemy in southern Italy, Holy Roman Emperor Frederick II (1194–1250), conquered Jerusalem by political means. He claimed its throne through his wife and sailed on the Sixth Crusade (1228–29) while actually excommunicate. Supported by the Teutonic Knights, he negotiated a ten-year truce that restored Jerusalem (except for the Temple and Muslim holy places) to the Franks. In 1229 Frederick crowned himself king of Jerusalem. After the truce ended, however, quarrels over territory between Templars and Hospitalers so weakened the kingdom that it fell to the Turks in 1244.

Louis IX of France (St Louis, 1215–70) made another attack on Cairo in the Seventh Crusade of 1248–50, but was taken prisoner. Freed by ransom, he rebuilt Jaffa and Acre and conciliated Muslim leaders. His return to France, however, left the kingdom of Jerusalem exposed to the effects of renewed rivalry of the military orders. Baibars, Mameluke Sultan of Egypt from 1260 to 1277, took advantage of this division; in 1268 he seized Jaffa and Antioch and in 1271 the castle of Krak des Chevaliers [Key]. Louis IX, mortally ill, set out on the Eighth Crusade (1270) but died in Tunis; Prince Edward (later Edward I of England, 1239–1307) reached Acre in 1271 and negotiated an 11-year truce, but in 1289 Tripoli fell to the Mamelukes and in 1291 they captured Acre, the last stronghold.

The territorial and spiritual triumphs of the crusades were short-lived. Urban's vision of a united Christendom degenerated into papal autocracy; the division between Latin and Orthodox Christians, still tentative when the two churches split in 1054, became absolute.

KEY

Krak des Chevaliers, best-preserved of crusader castles, guarded the north-west flank of the County of Tripoli. Begun in 1142 by the early crusaders, it defied 12 sieges, falling to Baibars in 1271 when its garrison of 2,000 was reduced to fewer than 200. Frankish forts were first built by the Templars to protect the pilgrim route to Jerusalem. Later whole chains of castles guarded the frontier and ports.

5

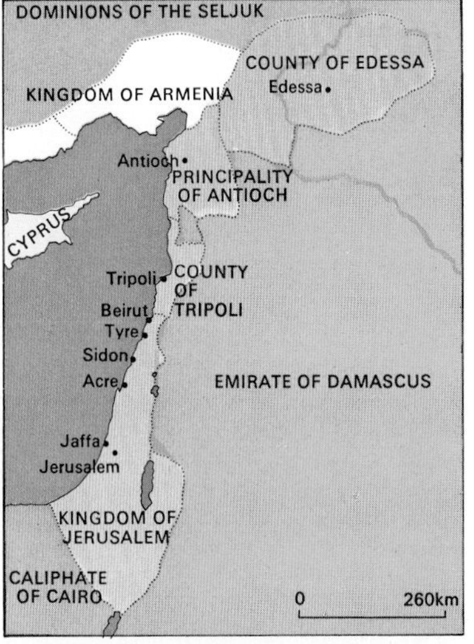
DOMINIONS OF THE SELJUK
COUNTY OF EDESSA
Edessa
KINGDOM OF ARMENIA
Antioch
PRINCIPALITY OF ANTIOCH
CYPRUS
Tripoli
COUNTY OF TRIPOLI
Beirut
Tyre
Sidon
Acre
EMIRATE OF DAMASCUS
Jaffa
Jerusalem
KINGDOM OF JERUSALEM
CALIPHATE OF CAIRO
0
260km

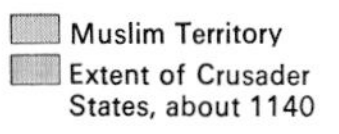
Muslim Territory
Extent of Crusader States, about 1140

5 The four crusader states comprised the County of Edessa (founded 1098), the Principality of Antioch (1098), the Kingdom of Jerusalem (1099), which claimed the overlordship, and the County of Tripoli (1109). Tripoli, the smallest and weakest, had an unexpected ally in the Assassins, heretical Muslim sect that supported the Franks against Damascus for 200 years. The states were feudal, had their own coinage, and traded with Europe and the Levant.

6

Hospitaller
Teutonic Knight
Templar

6 The Military Orders' offer of a life of religion and battle brought recruits from England, France, Portugal, Spain, and Italy. The Hospitalers began in the 11th century as guardians of the pilgrim hospice of St John in Jerusalem. The first Templars, given their rule by Bernard of Clairvaux in 1128, lived in the palace of the King of Jerusalem, the "Temple." Membership in the Order of Teutonic Knights, founded in 1198, was limited to Germans. The military orders, which were answerable only to the pope, had the only standing armies in the East.

7

7 The fortified cathedral of Albi in southern France, founded in 1277, was a deliberate symbol of the Church Militant's triumph over the Cathar heresy, which denied the reality of Christ's incarnation. The Cathars were brutally supressed by Simon de Montfort l'Aumary (1160–1218) in a crusade of 1209, inspired by Innocent III, who introduced the idea of crusades against Christian heretics and enemies of the papacy.

8

8 The sixth-century Quadriga of Lysippus, four splendid bronze horses taken during the sack of Constantinople (1204), still stand over the portal of St Mark's, Venice. A less tangible result of the Fourth Crusade was the flow into western Europe of Greek scholars seeking refuge from the Turks, which gave impetus to the Renaissance. Earlier crusades brought new goods to the West: damask, muslin, carpets, rice, sugar, lemons, spices, dyes; and the Arabic numerals that revolutionized mathematics.

9

9 Saladin, a chivalrous and courteous enemy, was taken as an ideal by many Frankish knights. This 13th-century drawing from the *Chronica Majora* of Matthew Paris shows him wresting a relic of the True Cross from Guy of Lusignan, King of Jerusalem, at the battle of Hattin (1187).

10

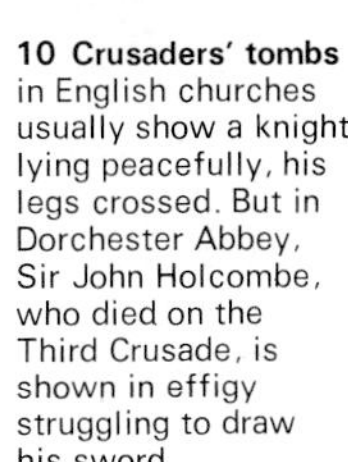

10 Crusaders' tombs in English churches usually show a knight lying peacefully, his legs crossed. But in Dorchester Abbey, Sir John Holcombe, who died on the Third Crusade, is shown in effigy struggling to draw his sword.

The power of the Church: 1073–1309

The years from the accession of Gregory VII in 1073 to the removal of the papacy to Avignon in 1309 saw the highest achievements of the medieval Christian Church in all its spheres of activity. Western Christendom could genuinely be seen as a unified whole with about 500 bishoprics all working as part of an international papal system. Roman Christianity laid the ground rules for everyone in European society. The twelfth and thirteenth centuries also saw the triumph of Gothic architecture and decoration, an achievement paralleled by the complete codification of law, knowledge, and philosophy in a Christian theological context by the scholastic philosophers, in particular Thomas Aquinas (1225–74).

The eleventh-century papacy had been inspired by the example of Cluniac reform, demonstrated best in the Lenten Synod at Rome in 1074, which laid down strict rules for the appointment and behavior of the clergy. The following year Gregory VII formally prohibited lay investiture [8] (the appointment of bishops by a secular ruler), an action that not only antagonized Emperor Henry IV (reigned 1056–1106), but generally inspired violent hostility throughout Germany, France, and England. The resulting battle made it necessary for the papacy to indulge in extensive legal justification of its position and led eventually to an institutionalized papacy.

Papal supremacy

The pope claimed to be the supreme judge and moral arbiter in temporal disputes. Only in this period could Emperor Henry IV have been humbled at Canossa by Gregory VII; could so powerful an English king as Henry II have appeared at Canterbury in a hair shirt to atone for the murder of Thomas à Becket; could King John (reigned 1199–1216) have been forced to submit himself (and the English crown) as a vassal of Pope Innocent III [Key].

The most imposing instrument of papal government was the ecumenical council, a decision-making body of all the bishops of Western Christendom. There were no fewer than seven such councils during the years 1123 to 1312 [1].

The growth of the Curia, the administrative focal point of the Vatican, also led to its increasing use as an international court of law. By the thirteenth century the ecclesiastical nature of the papacy was at times overshadowed, and such popes as Innocent IV (reigned 1243–54) seemed to function more as lawyers and administrators.

Religious reform

In contrast to the growing complexity of papal administration there was a wave of reform within the religious orders, all of which were based on piety, simplicity, and austerity. Despite the Cluniac reforms, the Benedictine Order had lost its pious intensity by the early twelfth century. The constitution of the Cistercians, the *Charter of Love,* written by St Stephen Harding in 1119, was an adaptation of the Benedictine Rule based on a denial of ostentation and an austere life located away from centers of population. The response to this call for a rigorous life of prayer was overwhelming, and 530 Cistercian houses had been established by 1200. Another austere offshoot of

CONNECTIONS

See also
1052 The rise of medieva Western Christendc
1084 The Crusades
1080 Romanesque art of the 11th century
1082 Romanesque art of the 12th century
1072 The Holy Roman Er pire
1074 European expansio to the east
1078 Islam in Europe

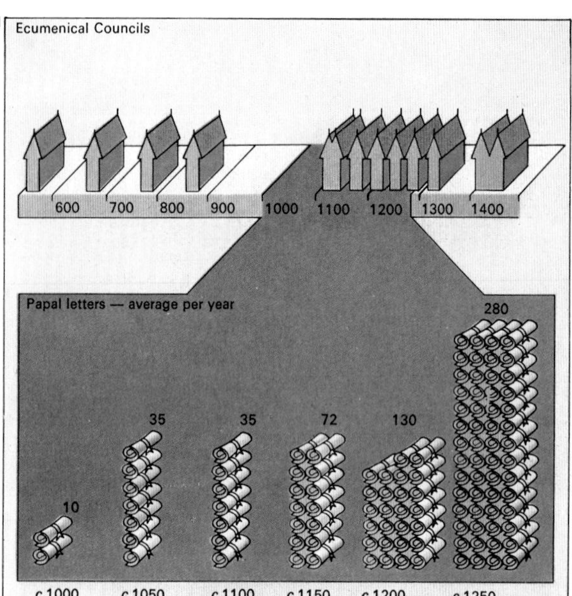

Ecumenical Councils
600
700
800
900
1000
1100
1200
1300
1400
Papal letters — average per year
10
35
35
72
130
280
c.1000
c.1050
c.1100
c.1150
c.1200
c.1250

1 Ecumenical councils, meetings of representatives of the whole Church, reached a peak in the 12th and 13th centuries. As the Roman church established its role as religious authority and arbiter of political affairs, its administrative function developed. The ecumenical council grew, and litigation at the Roman courts increased, as did the Roman Curia (the juridical, legislative, and administrative offices of the papacy). Papal correspondence, a record of ecclesiastical intervention, grew from 130 letters under Adrian IV (1154–59) to 3,646 under John XXII (1316–34).

2 This miniature of St Bernard of Clairvaux (1090–1153) being nourished by milk from the breast of the Virgin Mary is taken from a 15th-century Venetian Cistercian breviary. It exemplifies one of the chief tenets of St Bernard's teaching, an almost sentimental devotion to the mother of God. Reverence of Mary was one of the new and striking elements of popular piety in the 12th century.

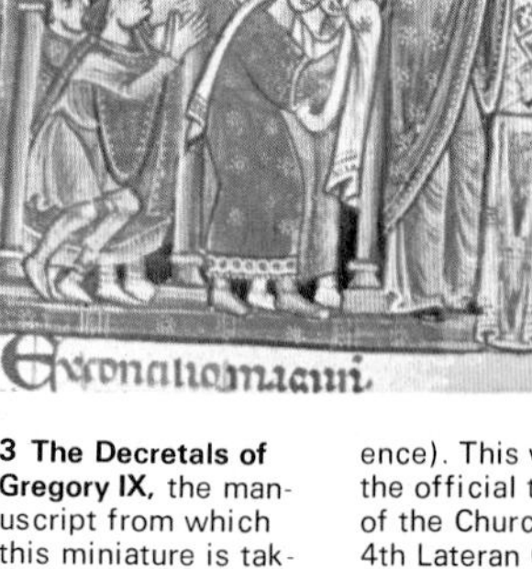

3 The Decretals of Gregory IX, the manuscript from which this miniature is taken, show the importance attached in the 13th century to transubstantiation (the doctrine of Christ's Eucharistic presence). This was made the official teaching of the Church by the 4th Lateran Council (1215), which also prescribed annual confession. Pope Gregory IX also patronized the new monastic orders.

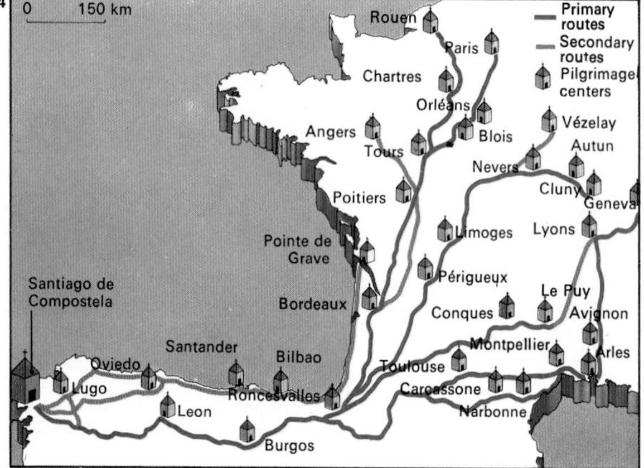

0 150 km
Primary routes
Secondary routes
Pilgrimage centers
Rouen
Paris
Chartres
Orléans
Angers
Tours
Blois
Vézelay
Autun
Nevers
Cluny
Geneva
Poitiers
Limoges
Lyons
Pointe de Grave
Santiago de Compostela
Périgueux
Le Puy
Bordeaux
Conques
Avignon
Santander
Montpellier
Arles
Bilbao
Oviedo
Toulouse
Lugo
Roncesvalles
Carcassone
Leon
Narbonne
Burgos

4 The pilgrimage was the "package tour" of the Middle Ages; pious Muslims tried to go to Mecca just as devout Christians sought to go to Rome, Compostela, or Canterbury. The pilgrimage was at once the fulfillment of an active religion and the experience of a lifetime. In the early Middle Ages the focus of Christian pilgrimages was Rome; but the gradual appearance of famous relics around the Western world led to a proliferation of provincial shrines, the most famous of which was that of the body of the Apostle James at Compostela in Spain. The pilgrimage route to Compostela became a thoroughfare along which many famous Romanesque churches were built.

5 The Dance of Death or *danse macabre* shows death in the role in which it appeared in late medieval popular mythology. It was seen to be an immediate tangible threat, a malevolent joker. Although many of the precepts of Christianity that are emphasized today appear to have been ignored in the early Middle Ages, it was the common religion of all in the West, and death for the Christian was the consummation of life. Death was therefore prominent in contemporary hagiography and was personified in the popular religious mystery plays. Awareness of death was intensified by the various catastrophes of the 14th century, especially the Great Plague of 1348, which depopulated Europe.

the Benedictine system was that of the Carthusians, founded by St Bruno in 1084.

There were many other new orders in the twelfth century—Augustinian canons, Hospitalers, crusading orders, Templars, and organizations for the visitation of the sick and the imprisoned. The ultimate in clerical reform was the foundation of the Friars [7]. St Francis of Assisi (1181–1226) and St Dominic (*c.* 1170–1221) both stressed that their followers should take vows of complete poverty and that neither individuals nor the order as a whole should possess any property. Friars were by definition to live by the work of their hands and, if necessary, by begging. They were to preach and exhort and to set a visible example of self-denial. By the fourteenth century, however, the orders were holding property and becoming part of the structure of the Church.

The twelfth and thirteenth centuries were also ages of secular piety and involvement with the Church. The Crusades were central to religious activity, as were pilgrimages to Rome, Compostela [4], Canterbury, and local shrines.

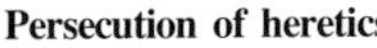

Persecution of heretics

The ugly side of the universality of papal pretensions and the increasing extremes of the religious life was the persecution of heretics [6]. The Jews, as nonbelievers, were largely left alone at this time, but heretics, as deserters from the true faith, had to be reconverted, by force if necessary. The most celebrated heretics were the Albigensians, whose beliefs in the need for absolute perfection stemmed from the same sentiments as those that inspired the Cistercians and the Franciscans. They went further, however, and proclaimed all material things and social life to be evil, thus presenting a challenge both to the Church and to the stability of society.

Removal to Avignon

The power of the Church seemed absolute until Pope Boniface VIII (reigned 1294–1303) confronted Philip IV (1268–1314) of France. Boniface died a prisoner of Philip and in 1309 the papal court was pressured to remove to Avignon, France, where it remained until 1377 [10].

KEY

Pope Innocent III (*c.* 1160–1216), a brilliant jurist, studied at Paris and Bologna. His ambition and administrative gifts brought the medieval papacy to an unsurpassed height. Through the legislative power of the papal Curia, his tight control of ecclesiastical affairs throughout Europe, and his influence in imperial elections, Innocent fulfilled for a time the papal ambition of directing the entire secular European world.

6

6 Some followers of Amalric of Chartres were burned at the stake in the early 12th century for believing that those in love with God partake in his perfection and are proof against sin. Traditionally it was the business of the Church to preserve orthodoxy. The ecclesiastical authorities, the Dominicans and Franciscans in particular, investigated heresy; the secular powers punished it.

7 A B C D

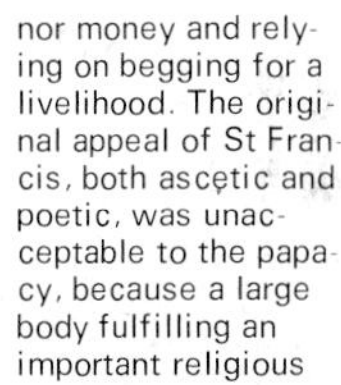

7 The religious orders increased greatly in number as a result of popular piety and the growing complexity of Church organization. The Cluniac reformers of the 10th century had merely tightened the Benedictine rule. The Carthusians [A], founded by St Bruno in 1084, and the Cistercians, the "white monks" [B], lived according to new rules that emphasized the virtues of self-denial and the strictest religious observance. The orders of friars, the Dominicans [C] and Franciscans [D], were a new kind of wandering priest who traveled Europe preaching, possessing neither property nor money and relying on begging for a livelihood. The original appeal of St Francis, both ascetic and poetic, was unacceptable to the papacy, because a large body fulfilling an important religious function needed corporate property if it was not to become socially subversive. Despite opposition from loyal followers, the friars soon obtained property and became an integral part of the Church.

8

8 The dispute over who invested bishops was not resolved in the popes' favor until late in the 11th century. This bronze depicting Emperor Otto I investing Bishop Adalbert of Magdeburg in 962 demonstrates the earlier power of secular rulers. Secular leaders did not willingly give up this right to reward or bribe subjects with the wealth and power that went with the office of bishop. In 1075 Pope Gregory VII formally prohibited the practice of lay investiture in Europe.

9

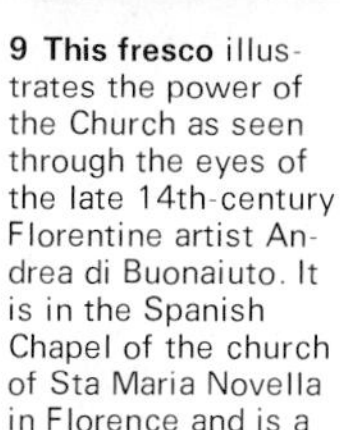

9 This fresco illustrates the power of the Church as seen through the eyes of the late 14th-century Florentine artist Andrea di Buonaiuto. It is in the Spanish Chapel of the church of Sta Maria Novella in Florence and is a contemporary commentary on the growth of the structure of the Church into a vast international organization with a role to play in administration and religious teaching. Sta Maria Novella is a Dominican church, and the picture emphasizes the role of the Dominican friars, many of whom had been made permanent commissioners for the extermination of heresy, as agents of the Holy Inquisition, under Gregory IX. Dominican friars are here shown as the *domini canes*, "hounds of the Lord."

10

10 The Papal Palace in Avignon was a more efficient center of papal government than Rome, and it is testimony to the wealth, success, and culture of the papal court in captivity. After two centuries of great power, the papacy endured a period of submission to temporal rulers when from 1309 to 1377 it was forcibly removed to Avignon. Ostensibly the move was to avoid the unsettled conditions in Rome, but the influence of the French monarchy over the papacy increased.

European learning in the 13th century

The medieval papacy reached the height of its power, wealth, and cohesion in the thirteenth century. During the same period St Thomas Aquinas (1225–74) finished his *Summa Theologiae* (1266–73), the greatest work of scholastic philosophy.

The genesis of Scholasticism

The highest achievement of medieval Christian thought, Scholasticism was an intellectual system that employed the logic, or dialectic, method of inquiry [Key] of Aristotle. In the course of the twelfth century, as Aristotle's works became available to western scholars in Latin translation, his analytic method was applied in all fields of inquiry. The result was a revolution in the methods and content of learning that produced a coherent system of philosophy and theology and a new science of jurisprudence. It also laid the first fragile foundations of experimental science.

As a growing number of Greek and Arabic philosophical and scientific texts became available, the centers of learning were no longer monasteries and episcopal schools but academic organizations of a new kind—the universities [1]. Universities were associations or corporations of masters and students that arose in urban centers where the new learning was available. The first of them appeared early in the thirteenth century at Bologna [5], Paris, Montpelier, Naples, Oxford, Cambridge, Toulouse, and Salamanca. It was these schools that gave Scholasticism its name (the teaching of the "Schoolmen").

Training at a medieval university was long and arduous. It usually took six years to become a Master of Arts, studying logic, grammar, rhetoric, arithmetic, geometry, astronomy, and music. The doctorate of theology, the highest academic achievement, required about eight more years of study. Learning was through lectures and set disputations. Students were often rowdy and not infrequently idle.

This was the age of translation, both from the original Greek and from Arabic and Hebrew texts and interpretations. Much classical cosmology, mathematics, and philosophy was derived from the writings of Arabic scholars such as Al Farabi (died 950), Avicenna (980–1037), and Averroës (1126–98). Gradually, through the works of Aristotle, Ptolemy (90–168), Averroës, and Avicenna, the knowledge of Greek cosmology and medicine became available, but above all the ideas of Aristotle [2] influenced the thought of the early universities. Aristotelian thought was opposed to the emphasis on divine grace in early scholastic thought and thus incurred the wrath of the conservatives.

Reconciling faith and reason

The crux of the Scholastic controversy was the relationship between revelation and reason. Aristotle's writings challenged the primacy of theology by asserting that rationality was the basis of knowledge, and the greatest works of this period were devoted to reconciling this apparent contradiction between faith and reason. A group of arts masters at Paris, the leader of whom was Siger de Brabant (*c.* 1235–81), adopted Averroës' view that reason and philosophy were superior to faith and to knowledge

CONNECTIONS

See also
1078 Islam in Europe
1052 The rise of medieval Western Christendom
1442 Alchemy and the Age of Reason
856 Philosophy and religion

1 Cino da' Sinibaldi was a famous Tuscan lawyer and poet who died in 1336. His tomb is one of many Italian funerary monuments for academics showing the university classrooms of the later Middle Ages. The magnificence of this tomb is an indication of the importance that Italians were beginning to accord to teachers of civil law in the Italian cities. Cino had studied at the great university of Bologna and had worked at Pistoia, Rome, Treviso, Florence, Siena, and Perugia. He was a link between the Scholastic academics of the 13th century and the humanist scholars who were to establish the intellectual framework for the Renaissance period.

2 This 13th-century French miniature shows Aristotle teaching the Emperor Alexander as a child. The illustration is from the *Treasury* of Brunetto Latini (*c.* 1210– *c.*1295), a compendium of history, philosophy, and legend completed in 1265. Philosophy was thought indispensable in training a ruler.

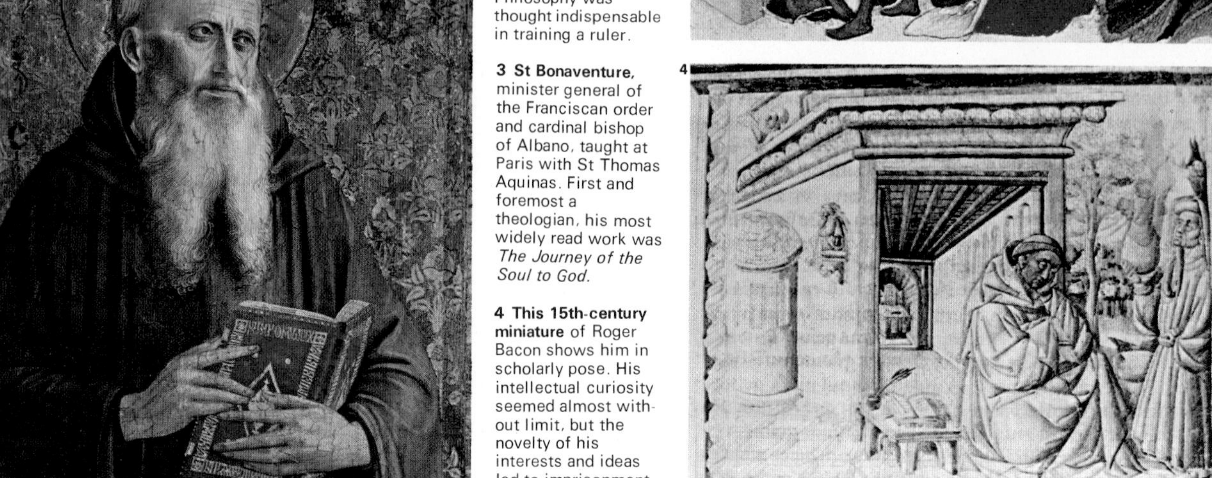

3 St Bonaventure, minister general of the Franciscan order and cardinal bishop of Albano, taught at Paris with St Thomas Aquinas. First and foremost a theologian, his most widely read work was *The Journey of the Soul to God.*

4 This 15th-century miniature of Roger Bacon shows him in scholarly pose. His intellectual curiosity seemed almost without limit, but the novelty of his interests and ideas led to imprisonment.

from faith. This provoked a fierce controversy, in the course of which Aquinas composed his famous apologia for revealed religion—the *Summa contra Gentiles*.

A more conservative defender of theology against the rationalist philosophers was St Bonaventure (1221–74) [3], a friend of Aquinas, who was prepared to concede that some knowledge could be gained from philosophy alone without the need of faith. Like St Thomas, Bonaventure held that a philosophical proof of God's existence could be found in the need for an original cause or motion to begin the chain of events in the universe. He believed, however, that philosophy could neither explain the details of revelation nor provide a moral framework for life.

Roger Bacon (*c.*1212–92) [4], an Englishman who taught at both Oxford and Paris, was a complex thinker. He inherited from Robert Grosseteste (*c.*1175–1253) an interest in empirical observation that epitomized the growing belief in man's powers of investigation and understanding. Following the Scholastic tradition, he saw in the behavior of material things, including the commonsense behavior of man, a "natural law" that manifested divine insight. Consequently, Bacon believed that science was a natural and harmonious basis for religion. But he was also a firm believer in alchemy [9] and in astrology.

The development of Aquinas' thought

Albert the Great (1193–1280) incorporated the new knowledge of Aristotle within an encyclopedic formula that embraced Platonism, Neo-Platonism and Arabic theology. Thomas Aquinas, his pupil, inherited this breadth of reference and consciously set out to provide a logical Aristotelian substructure for Christian thought. Aquinas took faith as the starting point and argued that all discoveries from reason could be interpreted in the light of it. If there appeared to be a conflict between reason and faith, then the reasoning was wrong. He acknowledged that human knowledge depended on sense perception, and in his theory of "natural law" provided the basis for a purely rational system of ethics.

KEY

DIALETIC

This 15th-century figure is an allegory of dialectic. Christian vices and virtues, portrayed in human form throughout medieval times, were joined in the 13th century by figures representing the disciplines of the philosophers. Dialectics, the branch of logic concerned with the rules of reasoning, was first formulated in Greece by Aristotle.

5

5 Bologna, one of the earliest and most famous of European universities, was noted for its law schools. The 12th century saw the emergence of student guilds, which gradually became independent of the law of the city. By the 14th century, Bologna University had an organized collegiate system.

6

6 St Thomas Aquinas was the greatest doctor of the medieval Church and the greatest exponent of Scholasticism. His *Summa Theologiae,* the best known philosophical treatise of his time, attempted a comprehensive synthesis of reason and revelation that established him as the Church's foremost theologian. Whereas initially his Aristotelian analysis was criticized, his statements have come to be regarded as a wholly Christian interpretation of man's being.

7

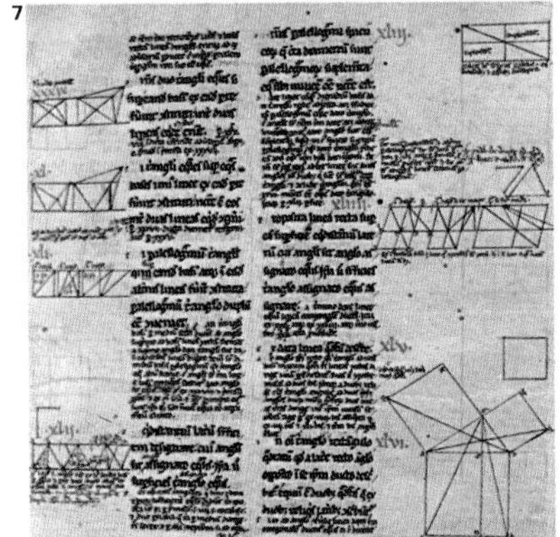

7 Mathematics, like logic, played a part in the curriculum of the Scholastic philosopher, revealing through the human intellect the divine plan for the universe. Medieval mathematics consisted almost completely of a rediscovery of Greek knowledge in the field, preserved and transmitted by Islamic scholars. These Pythagorean theorems are from a typical 13th-century treatise.

8

8 Notations on this 13th-century manuscript of the Roman writer Lactantius indicate textual criticisms common to a generation aware both of the ambiguities of classical texts and the textual corruptions that had developed over the centuries. Greek and Latin works had been translated into Syriac, then Arabic, and back into Latin. Careless transcription created more inaccuracy, but greater care ushered in a new era of classical scholarship.

9

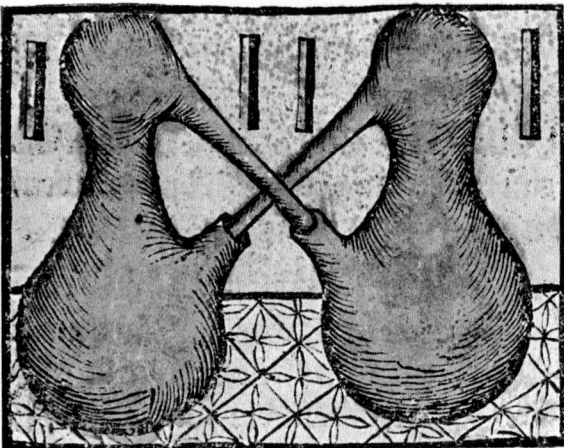

9 Alchemy was a pseudo-science of the Middle Ages. Although much effort went into improbable experiments (like this one, which uses a double still) and into vain attempts to transmute base metals into gold, many alchemists were able chemists whose work laid the foundations of later knowledge. Like astrology, alchemy had its roots in classical antiquity and flourished in the 13th century alongside more fruitful work on mathematics and astronomy.

Western European economy 1000–1250

Between 1000 and 1250 the economic foundation of Europe shifted to the north. The new wealth came from a rapidly developing agriculture in the northern European plain [2] between the Loire and the Elbe. Under the Romans this had been a sparsely populated forest area; now it was the Mediterranean that became a frontier zone.

An era of expansion

In this new world all the energy and enterprise of the pioneer were yoked to clearing the forests, establishing villages, and marking out the routes, largely independent of the Roman system, that bound the plain together. Here and there the directing force of some powerful family or monastic community could be detected, but almost certainly most of the work was done by small family groups and peasant communities. In the progressive draining of the marshes of Lincolnshire, Flanders, and the Po basin—among the most remarkable achievements of these centuries—the lead may have been given by abbeys like Ramsey or Les Dunes, but the fiercely independent spirit of the subsequent peasant proprietors suggests that many drained the land themselves.

Intensive settlement of the soil implies an increasing population. In this period, without records of taxation, there is no direct evidence to measure population growth; but an indication that numbers increased rapidly comes from the twelfth-century migrations of both peasants and knights from France, Germany, and Flanders to eastern Europe, Spain, Sicily, and Palestine.

Within the bounds of western Europe the few surviving monastic estate documents give glimpses of the slow development of a farming expertise geared specifically to northern climates, such as the use of the heavy-wheeled plow *(carruca),* the harnessing of draft animals in columns, and the development of the watermill for grinding corn, which gradually came into use between 1000 and 1250. By 1200, horses were shod and harnessed with a shoulder collar. More had been learned about spring and autumn crops: wheat and rye for standard autumn-sown cereals, but other varieties for the more rigorous climates.

Social and economic organization

The social structure of this developing agrarian society is difficult to determine and probably varied dramatically from area to area. Where seigneurial and monastic landlords took an interest in developing their lands (and many did, especially the new order of Cistercian monks), it was common to attract landless laborers with the promise of heritable tenures, on condition that they bound themselves and their heirs to the soil. Serfdom was one way of organizing labor for cooperative work, but it is a mistake to see it as universal. The peasant communes of the open-field system in France and England, with their periodic redistribution of holdings, the independent holdings *(allods)* of Aquitaine, and the farmsteads *(casalia)* of Italy all resulted from peculiarities of local custom and circumstance. What is reasonably certain is that the number of such communities increased sharply during the eleventh and twelfth centuries.

CONNECTIONS

See also

1070 Western European economy 800–1000
1098 Feudalism
1102 European society 1250—1450
1086 The power of the Church: 1073–1309
1126 The rise of bankin
300 Land uses
634 Destructive man
304 History of agricultu

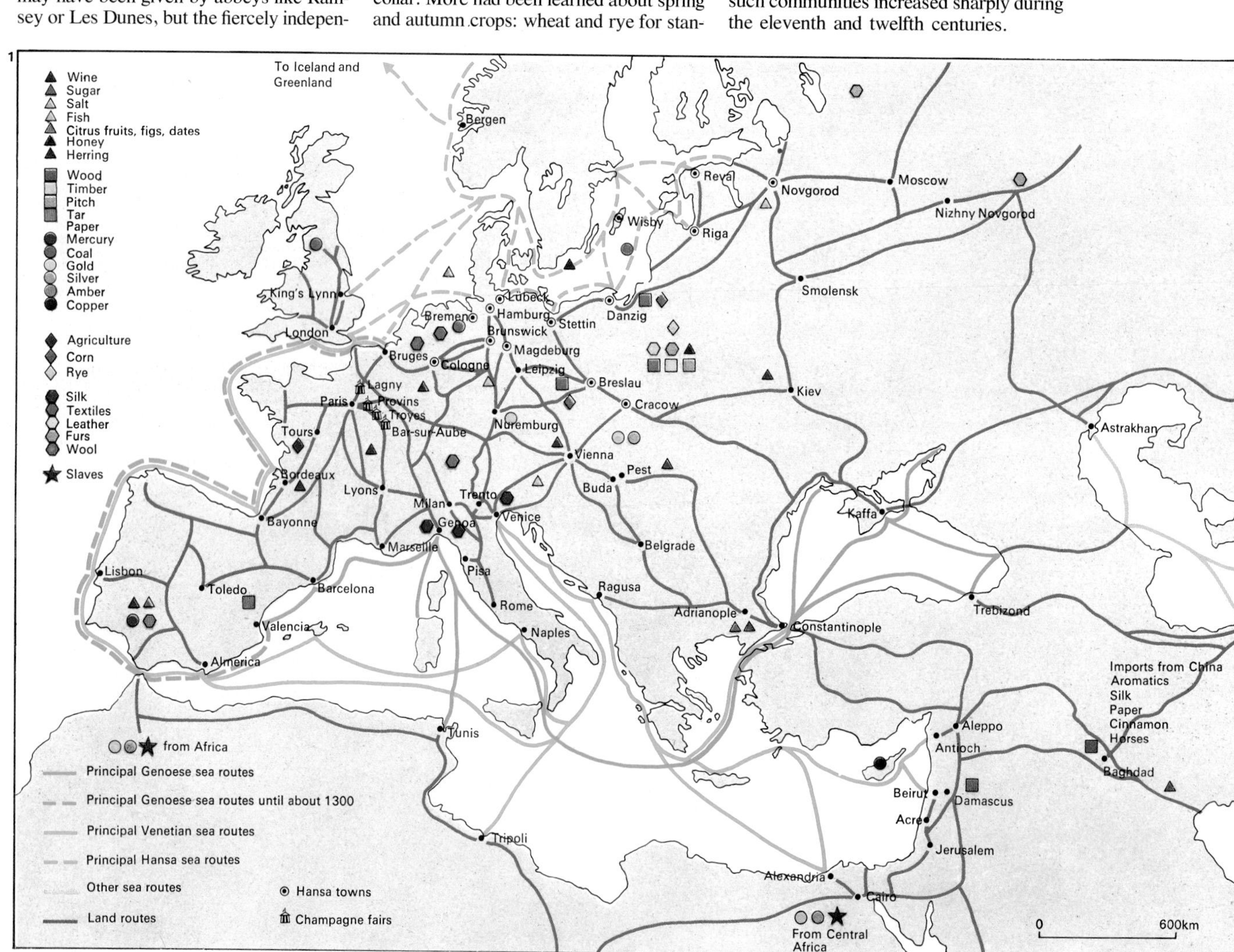

1
Wine
Sugar
Salt
Fish
Citrus fruits, figs, dates
Honey
Herring
Wood
Timber
Pitch
Tar
Paper
Mercury
Coal
Gold
Silver
Amber
Copper
Agriculture
Corn
Rye
Silk
Textiles
Leather
Furs
Wool
Slaves
To Iceland and Greenland
Bergen
Reval
Novgorod
Moscow
Nizhny Novgorod
Wisby
Riga
King's Lynn
Lübeck
Hamburg
Bremen
Stettin
Danzig
Smolensk
London
Brunswick
Magdeburg
Bruges
Cologne
Leipzig
Breslau
Lagny
Paris
Provins
Troyes
Bar-sur-Aube
Cracow
Kiev
Tours
Nuremburg
Vienna
Astrakhan
Bordeaux
Pest
Lyons
Buda
Trento
Milan
Bayonne
Genoa
Venice
Kaffa
Marseille
Belgrade
Lisbon
Pisa
Toledo
Barcelona
Ragusa
Rome
Adrianople
Trebizond
Valencia
Naples
Constantinople
Almeria
Imports from China
Aromatics
Silk
Paper
Cinnamon
Horses
Tunis
Aleppo
Antioch
from Africa
Baghdad
Principal Genoese sea routes
Principal Genoese sea routes until about 1300
Beirut
Damascus
Principal Venetian sea routes
Acre
Tripoli
Principal Hansa sea routes
Jerusalem
Other sea routes
Hansa towns
Alexandria
Cairo
Land routes
Champagne fairs
From Central Africa
0
600km

1 The number of trade routes, by both land and sea, increased during the High Middle Ages. The most popular form of bulk transport in the early Middle Ages was by river. In the 11th and 12th centuries land transport became much easier, partly because the routes were safer, partly because of the increased use of pack animals. The trade of the carrier, often a native of the high Alps, had by 1250 become an integral link in Italian commerce with northern Europe. The routes primarily linked importing centers such as the Italian and Hansa towns with the centers of production and exchange—the fairs of northern Europe and Flemish towns. But links were also forged through Poland and Hungary with the ancient Asiatic routes. Sea routes developed dramatically during the 12th century. Mediterranean ships of the period were small, rarely more than 100 tons. They usually traveled in convoy and with enterprising crews from Venice, Pisa, and Genoa to most Mediterranean ports. Some Levant towns had Italian quarters as early as 1110. Subsequently, the Venetians established themselves at Alexandria, and their attempts to control the trade of Constantinople culminated in their conquest of that city in 1204. The northern seas had their own Viking tradition of seamanship. The trade in furs originally carried by Scandinavians from Novgorod to the Baltic fell into the hands of merchants from the north German towns in the 12th century. The merchants soon organized themselves into a protective league, or Hansa, to provide needed security for trade.

The rise of towns

The other consequence of population increase was the growing importance of towns as centers both of exchange and production. The origins of towns varied, but most of them grew up to serve local needs, as fortified towns (the *burg*) to which agricultural markets were attached, or as ports importing and exporting goods. The more intensive the settlement of the land, the larger and more numerous were the towns. The number of cities in Flanders and northeastern France—Bruges, Arras, Valenciennes, and others—reflects a dense agricultural population. The burgeoning cloth production of Bruges depended, in the twelfth century, on the farming of sheep in the Flemish salt marshes. The towns' specialized way of life needed independent institutions: the earliest guild of merchants known, that of Tiel in Holland, existed earlier than 1000, but the merchant guild as an instrument of communal government became common only in the twelfth century. The towns flourished, however, because of the vast consumer market that had developed by 1200. The early medieval ideal of local self-sufficiency, evident in the monastic *polyptyques* or inventories, was being superseded by the habit of buying goods that were often of distant origin.

By 1000 western Europe was in sporadic but persistent contact with the East through the Baltic and Russia, and with the decline of Saracen piracy in the Mediterranean the Italian ports developed strong links with Egypt and (after 1098) the Crusading states, which enabled Oriental silks and spices to reach the West. Mediterranean trade [1], necessarily large scale and risky since goods bought abroad were never presold, gradually led Venetian merchants to develop a "capitalist" system of investment [3].

The High Middle Ages was a period of almost universal expansion in western Europe, an underdeveloped continent ready for sustained exploitation. As conditions changed, however, the warning signs of overpopulation and overuse of the land went unnoticed until persistent famine and plague brought a general recession in the fourteenth century.

KEY

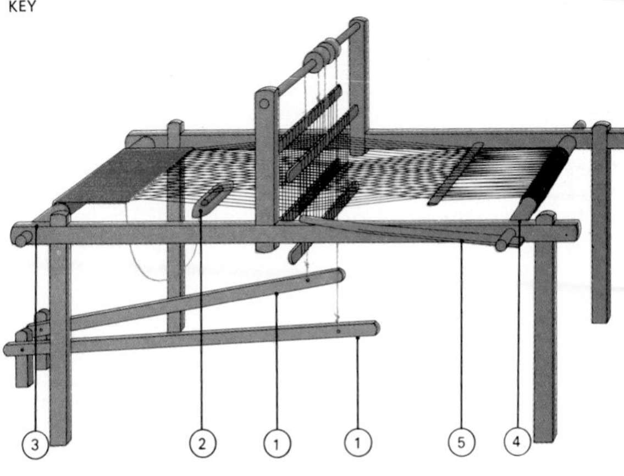
3
2
1
1
5
4

Horizontal treadle looms, introduced in the 13th century, stimulated textile manufacture, the medieval industry that employed most urban craftsmen. The less efficient vertical loom was replaced by a machine using treadles [1] to raise or lower the lengthwise threads as the shuttle [2] passed through them. Cloth was wound onto the cloth beam [3] as thread was released from the warp beam [4] by depressing a lever [5]. About two-thirds of all trade was in textiles. Most weaving was done in the Low Countries, partly by urban industry and partly by cottage labor.

2

2 Drainage and land reclamation was one of the most spectacular aspects of the clearing of the northern European plain in the 11th and 12th centuries. This area near St Omer, France, was reclaimed in the early Middle Ages; lowlands diked, marshy land made fit for grazing, and a system of waterways constructed. Cultivation of new lands led both to a larger population and gave greater freedom to farmers, who paid for pioneer lands in fees rather than in services, two vital factors for the commercial and industrial expansion of the Low Countries during this period.

3

3 The Fondaco dei Turchi (Turkish warehouse) on the Grand Canal in Venice was built in the late Romanesque style in the 13th century. Although it takes its name from a later period of the city's mercantile development, the building exemplifies Venetian power in the first era of its commercial success. From the 11th century, Venice dominated European trade with the East, and its Arsenal and dockyard comprised the biggest industrial unit of this mercantile period.

5

4 A

B

C

4 Illustrated calendars of seasonal activities provide the best visual evidence of medieval costume and methods of agriculture. Shown here are May, a shepherd, and his flock [A]; June, cutting wood [B]; and July, haymaking [C].

5 The grape harvest depicted in an Italian calendar shows the method of pressing the grapes with the feet, a tradition that survived in parts of rural Italy until after 1945. Wine was produced in quantity throughout southern Europe, in most of France, and in the Rhine and Moselle areas of Germany. Production methods had changed little since the days of the great Roman villas; and viticulture was, throughout the Middle Ages, still the economic prerogative of the big landowner or entrepreneur. By the 13th century a genuinely international wine trade had developed along a north-south axis, with large quantities of wine being shipped in barrels by water transport to foreign posts.

Gothic art 1140–1200

The term "Gothic" was coined during the Italian Renaissance for a style of architecture then considered so barbaric that it could be ascribed only to the Goths, the fifth-century ravagers of classical Rome. Gradually the word "Gothic" has ceased to be pejorative. Its application to sculpture and the graphic arts is a fairly recent development.

Beginnings of Gothic in France

In the early Gothic period, as in the early Middle Ages, the principal artistic enterprises were the great abbey and cathedral churches and their decoration. No new form of church was evolved by early Gothic masons, but both architectural style and building techniques underwent a complete transformation. Indeed, the Gothic style is, of all architectural styles before the twentieth century, the one most completely independent of the classical traditions of antiquity.

For the first 30 years of its existence, Gothic architecture was an exclusively French development, but by about 1250 it had displaced the local Romanesque styles of most regions of western Europe. This expansion may well have been due to the aesthetic and technical advantages of the style, but it must also have been connected with the rise of France as a major political force and its acknowledged cultural superiority. It is therefore highly appropriate that the first mature example of Gothic architecture should be the choir of the Abbey of St Denis [Key], just to the north of Paris, which was to become the principal mausoleum of the kings of France. The Abbot of St Denis, Suger (*c.* 1081–1151), was a passionate believer in the natural superiority of all things French.

The choir of St Denis (begun in 1140 and consecrated 1144) is a building whose extraordinary originality is matched by consistency of execution. The qualities that distinguish it from previous buildings, however, all stem from a single technical innovation, the combination of rib-vaulting with pointed arches. Both of these features were derived from earlier buildings: rib-vaulting from Norman churches such as Lessay (begun *c.* 1100) and pointed arches from the Burgundian Abbey of Cluny (begun *c.* 1090) or a derivative.

Rib-vaults and weight-bearing buttresses

Rib-vaults had several advantages over other types of vault [4]. Their diagonally crossed pairs of arches (ribs) provided a framework allowing the cells of the vault to be filled in afterward. Centering (curved scaffolding on which vaults were built) was thus required only for the ribs, not for the whole vault. Rib-vaults were also relatively light, being made of carefully shaped stones rather than rubble embedded in mortar. The use of geometrically regular arches made them easier to fit over variously shaped spaces. The disadvantage of semicircular ribs as used at Lessay and elsewhere was that their height (radius) was required to be half their span (diameter). This meant that in an oblong vault diagonal ribs and wall ribs required rather clumsy adjustments to make them equal in height to transverse ribs.

By combining rib-vaults with pointed arches, whose height can be kept constant

CONNECTIONS

See also
1094 Gothic art of the 13 century
1104 Gothic art of the 14 century
1106 Gothic art 1400–15

1 Senlis Cathedral is the earliest surviving French cathedral (begun in 1153) based on St Denis. Pointed rib-vaulting is used throughout and is mostly carried on slim columns with foliage capitals. This view shows the ambulatory looking northeast with one of the semicircular chapels in the distance at right.

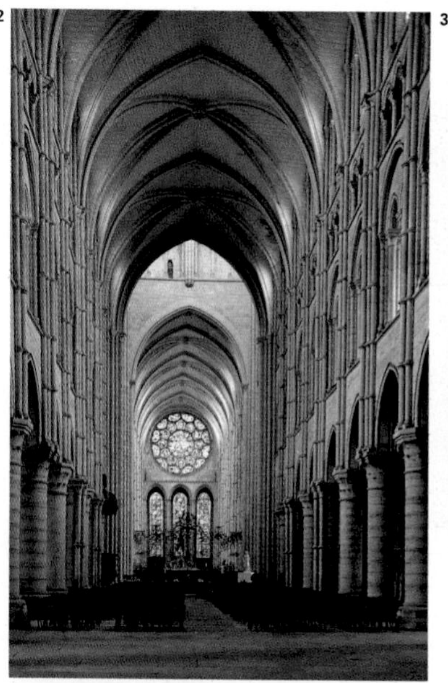

2 Laon Cathedral remains largely unaltered except that the original ambulatory was replaced in the early 13th century by a flat east end lit by a rose window. In the nave there was an attempt to extend the alternating rhythm of the vaults downward by adding extra shafts to every other column of the arcade.

3 A simplified version of Gothic architecture had been evolved by 1160 in the Cistercian abbeys of northern England, but the adoption of Gothic started with the rebuilding of Canterbury choir *c.* 1175 by the French architect William of Sens. The design has several features not usual in France, notably the dark marble shafts. These became standard in English Gothic for a century afterward.

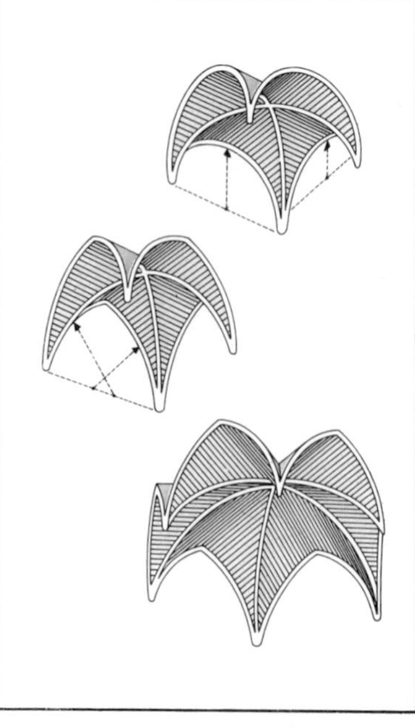

4 Vaults using semicircular ribs appeared in England and Normandy about 1090. The main problem with semicircular ribs was that the wide diagonal ribs had to be depressed and the narrow wall-ribs raised as vertical pieces in order to rise to the same height as the transverse ribs. Gothic architects solved this problem by using pointed ribs. These are struck from two centers, which means that their height is no longer dictated by their width. Pointed arches were adopted for aesthetic rather than structural reasons. Sexpartite vaults (so called because they have six compartments) were used over paired rectangular bays at Laon in the late 12th century.

5 The jamb figures at Chartres Cathedral (central west portal) probably represent Old Testament personages. The Christ in Majesty above the doors has a calm nobility different from the terrifying Judging Christs of the Romanesque portals.

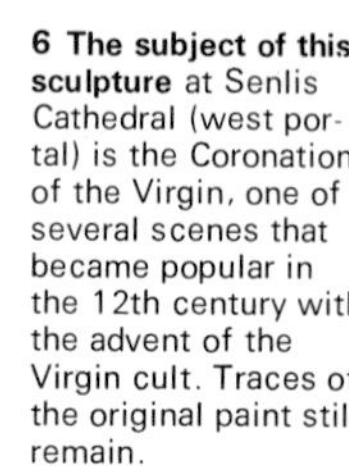

6 The subject of this sculpture at Senlis Cathedral (west portal) is the Coronation of the Virgin, one of several scenes that became popular in the 12th century with the advent of the Virgin cult. Traces of the original paint still remain.

whatever the span, the St Denis mason put vaults of even height over a complicated series of spaces of various sizes and shapes. He emphasized the lightness of the vaults by setting them on single, slender columns. He also extended the skeleton principle of rib-vaults to the outer wall of the choir. Realizing that rib-vaults did not exert a continuous outward thrust that needed to be absorbed by massive walls, he placed deeply projecting buttresses only at those points where the thrust was concentrated. The walls, relieved of their load-bearing function, opened up as an almost continuous band of windows. It was the brilliant lighting of the St Denis choir that most impressed Abbot Suger.

Laon Cathedral

St Denis immediately became the inspiration for a whole series of northern French cathedrals, of which Laon [2], begun *c.*1160, is in many respects the classic example. The internal elevation is of four stories, including an ample gallery, or tribune. The vault is in six sections with shafts arranged alternately singly and in threes. The narrow proportions of churches of this period, regarded as typically Gothic, are no less than those of some major Romanesque churches, such as Cluny or the churches on the pilgrim route to Santiago.

The smooth exterior contours of twelfth-century Gothic churches were generally enlivened by towers, ranging from the usual two at the west end to the seven projected at Laon. West fronts were pierced by large portals in which high-relief sculpture was used not only on the tympana (the area between the top of the door and the arch above it), as in the Romanesque period, but also on the framing arches (archivolts) and on the jambs (the sides of doors and archways). These large-scale jamb figures [5] became a hallmark of the Gothic style.

Apart from foliage capitals, early Gothic interiors contain little carved decoration beyond the molded arches, ribs, and shafts of the buildings. Their austerity was offset by lavish use of stained glass and a restricted use of painted color.

KEY

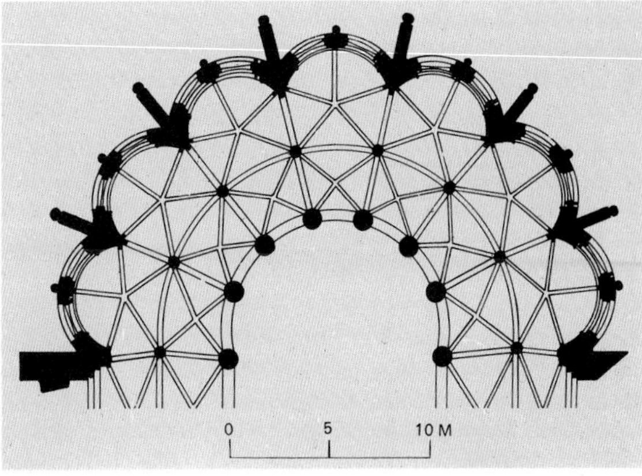

0
5
10 M

The east end of the 8th-century church of St Denis was demolished and replaced in the 12th century by this complex structure in which the semicircular processional path or "ambulatory" enabled visitors and pilgrims to see the shrine of St Denis without disturbing the services there. Opening out of the ambulatory are seven chapels partly contained in shallow round apses. Their windows form a continuous band separated only by small stretches of wall and thin, deep buttresses. Crossed lines indicate the position of the vaulting ribs. St Denis inspired a series of cathedrals.

7

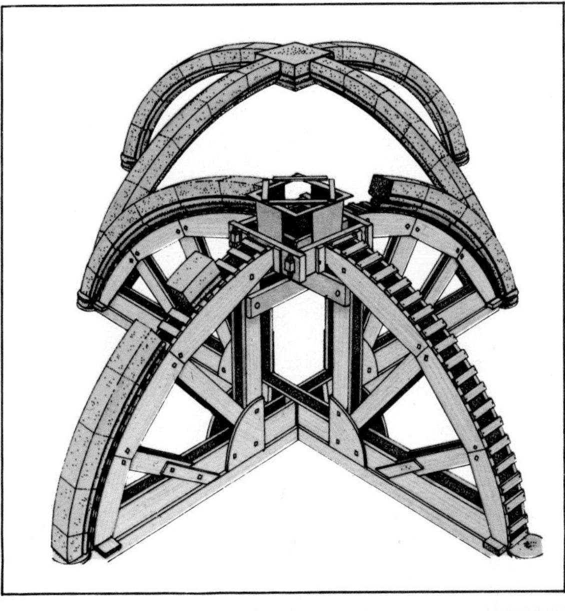

7 The south choir aisle at Exeter Cathedral (*c.* 1300), England, was bombed in 1942 and rebuilt in 1949. This view shows the wooden arched scaffolding or "centering" used to build up the ribs. Some of the ribs are in position, but none of the sculpted keystones ("bosses") at the intersections has yet been replaced. After the completion of the ribs the next stage is to fill the curved triangular spaces in between with horizontal courses of stone. No scaffolding is required for this process because the ribs serve the purpose adequately. By this stage the wooden protective roof would already have been built.

8

9

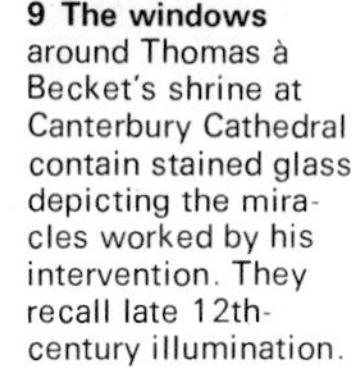

8 The Jesse tree window at Chartres Cathedral shows the ancestry of Christ, beginning with Jesse, who lies in the lowest panel with the tree growing out of his loins. Christ sits in the top panel.

9 The windows around Thomas à Becket's shrine at Canterbury Cathedral contain stained glass depicting the miracles worked by his intervention. They recall late 12th-century illumination.

10 Church metalwork was among the most esteemed forms of art in the Middle Ages. Abbot Suger of St Denis wrote long descriptions of the treasures that he collected for his abbey, but made no mention of the stone sculptures of the new west portals that are now regarded as the starting point of Gothic sculpture. The Klosterneuburg altarpiece (1181) was originally made as a pulpit, which explains why more precious materials were not used. Most unusually, the artist, Nicholas of Verdun, was allowed to sign his name. These classical figures are invested with a 3-dimensional solidity unlike the linear exaggerations of most Romanesque art.

10

IT·REDIMAT·GENT EM·DVX·SVBPHARAONE·GEMTE
MOYSES·IT·IEGIPTV
RA·VIMPERO

11

11 Like metalwork, manuscript illumination was a major art form. Many fine manuscripts were produced in monastic scriptoria, but there are good grounds for thinking that leading artists—of whom this Winchester, England, master was one—were professional laymen. The figures in this initial to the Book of Isaiah (*c.* 1170) in the Winchester Bible achieve in one way what Nicholas of Verdun did in another, that is the effect of solidity and a respect for the proportions and articulation of the human figure. The Winchester style derives from Sicilian mosaics of provincial Byzantine style. The same artist may have executed some wall paintings in Winchester Cathedral.

Gothic art of the 13th century

In their plans and in the disposition of their internal spaces the twelfth-century Gothic cathedrals adhered largely to Romanesque precedent. But in a number of churches begun toward the end of the century, of which the most important was Chartres Cathedral, the middle story (the gallery or "tribune") was omitted to make room for very high arcades and clerestory, separated only by a low triforium (a passage along the wall).

The immense enlargement of the clerestory windows necessitated extra support to resist the thrust of the high vaults; this was provided by flying buttresses, which henceforth became a feature of French cathedral design.

Externally, the flying buttresses effaced the simple contours of the early Gothic churches and substituted the complex, restless silhouette now regarded as characteristically Gothic. The grandeur and simplicity of the interior at Chartres were enhanced by the plain quadripartite rib-vaulting, supported by piers consisting of a column with four attached shafts, thereby bringing the vertical lines of the vault shafts down to the ground.

Chartres, like St Denis 50 years earlier, became the prototype of a whole series of northern French cathedrals [7]. Rheims, begun in 1210, followed Chartres closely but made an important advance in window design. Instead of the groups of three openings, two pointed and one circular, that made up the Chartres clerestory, the Rheims mason treated all windows as one unit, but with subdivisions built up as an interdependent series. This innovation, known as "bartracery" or simply "tracery", was taken up by other masons and became an enduring characteristic of Gothic architecture.

European developments

In the reign of Philip Augustus (1165–1223) France was established as the leading power in Western Europe, and in the reign of his grandson Louis IX (1215–70) it became the arbiter of European taste. As a reresult, there are major churches outside France, such as León Cathedral in Castile (begun *c.* 1250) and Cologne Cathedral (begun 1248), that are practically indistinguishable from French work. The same cannot be said of Westminster Abbey (begun 1245), even though it has more French features than any other thirteenth-century English church.

Among the most impressive examples of this so-called "Early English" style is Lincoln Cathedral (begun 1192). The proportions are broad, and the walls are of Romanesque thickness, although any effect of heaviness is offset by the use of fine moldings on the arches and marble shafts on the walls and supports. This English predilection for complicated linear pattern is remote from the austerity and single-mindedness of contemporary French designs. During the second half of the thirteenth century the English masons learned all they wanted to know of French Gothic, but their enthusiasm for elaborate decoration remained undiminished. English window tracery, for instance, was the most inventive in Europe—English vaulting even more so.

CONNECTIONS

Read first
1092 Gothic art 1140–120

See also
1104 Gothic art of the 14 century
1106 Gothic art 1400–15

1 All the important Gothic churches in northern France, beginning with St Denis, were intended to have two-tower west façades. Here at Rheims, as well as at Laon and Chartres, towers were also intended over the transept facades but they were never completed. The portals are exceptional in substituting rose windows for sculpted tympana.

2 The influence of Chartres on the cathedral at Soissons is apparent in the high arches and clerestory; however, the overall proportions are taller and piers are simple round columns with only one shaft attached, as opposed to the four at Chartres. The extreme lightness of the interior is caused by the destruction of the original stained glass windows.

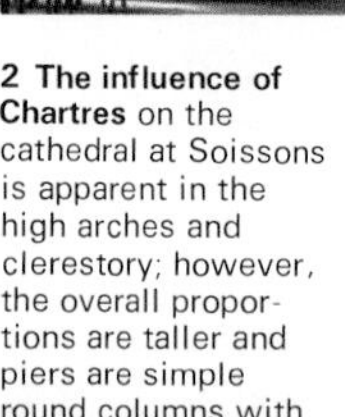

3 The foliage on the chapter-house door (late 13th century) at Southwell Minster (left to right: buttercup, vine, oak) achieves a fine balance between the natural and the ideal while still respecting the architectural function of the capitals (the tops of columns). Sculptors at Rheims in about 1230 were the first to carve leaves that corresponded closely to forms found in nature.

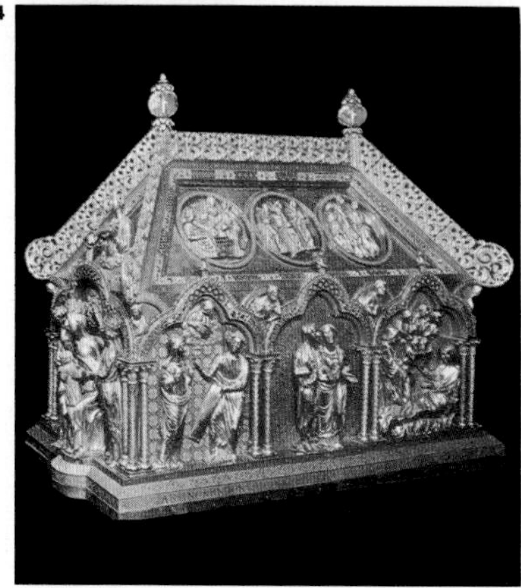

4 The Reliquary of our Lady at Tournai Cathedral has been attributed to Nicholas of Verdun, who finished the Klosterneuburg altarpiece in 1181. The figures have ample, fluid draperies anticipating those of some of the stone sculptures at Rheims. The reliefs show the Annunciation, the Visitation, and the Nativity. More important shrines such as Thomas à Becket's at Canterbury had the same shape but stood on tall bases.

5 The sole surviving large exterior sculpture at Notre Dame, Paris, this Virgin stands on the *trumeau*, or central pillar, of the north transept portal. Her pose, with the weight on the left leg, serves to draw attention to the infant Christ on her arm and is accentuated by pointed, hanging folds. Her air of mannered refinement became typical of 14th-century sculpture. Like most Gothic sculpture this figure was colored.

6 The broad proportions and elaborate decoration at Lincoln Cathedral are in complete contrast to contemporary French cathedrals. The arcades are so wide that the aisles merge with the central space. Most available surfaces are enlivened by brownish-gray polished shafts from Purbeck (Dorset). The vault is the earliest in which additional decorative ribs are introduced to blur the divisions between bays and create an effect like a series of palm fronds.

Master masons

Unfortunately, little is known of the organization of thirteenth-century masons because of the scarcity of contemporary documents. But it seems clear that master masons performed much the same role as architects in later periods although, unlike architects, they were promoted from the ranks of the working masons and not trained purely as designers [Key]. Master masons were generally well paid and often the owners of extensive property. The working masons were divided into "cutters," who carved the architectural components, and "setters," who actually put up the building.

The masons' tools were extremely simple. Stone was given various degrees of finish by using finer or coarser chisels. Simple lifting tackle was used. A primitive wooden crane remained in position at Cologne Cathedral until the building was finished in the nineteenth century. The vast front of Cologne was completed then with the aid of the original designs on parchment, which were probably made as presentation drawings for the approval of the design by the cathedral authorities. Working drawings were usually drawn full-size on boards or on a plaster "tracing floor" in the masons' lodge. A surviving example of such a floor at York, England, has many layers of partly erased drawings underneath the most recent set, which is late fourteenth century.

Decorative features

Stained glass remained the principal form of internal decoration, but by about 1250 the deep blues and reds of the early thirteenth century gave way to a wider range of color.

Thirteenth-century sculpted portals retained the basic twelfth-century format but, like the cathedrals they adorned, were much larger than those of the preceding century. There was an increased emphasis on the Virgin, and even in Last Judgment scenes she and St John appear interceding with Christ on behalf of mankind. A certain humanizing of religious subject matter was achieved in the opening decades of the century by the increasing depiction of character types.

KEY

Hugues Libergier was master mason of the important church of St Nicaise in Rheims, which was destroyed in the French Revolution. He appears holding a model of his church with his square and dividers by his feet. His dress is indicative of the professional status of masons in this period. The Dominican friar Nicholas de Biard compared bishops with master masons who, he said, gave orders wearing gloves and holding a measuring rod and who received higher pay although they themselves never set their hands to the work. Often master masons were commemorated by inscriptions placed in "their" buildings.

8 Chapter-houses were used by the ecclesiastical communities for the transaction of secular business. Their central plan was an early 12th-century English invention, although the finest examples are 13th century. At Salisbury Cathedral (shown here) the huge filled windows with bar tracery are of French derivation, but at Lincoln and Wells the vault is more prominent.

8

7

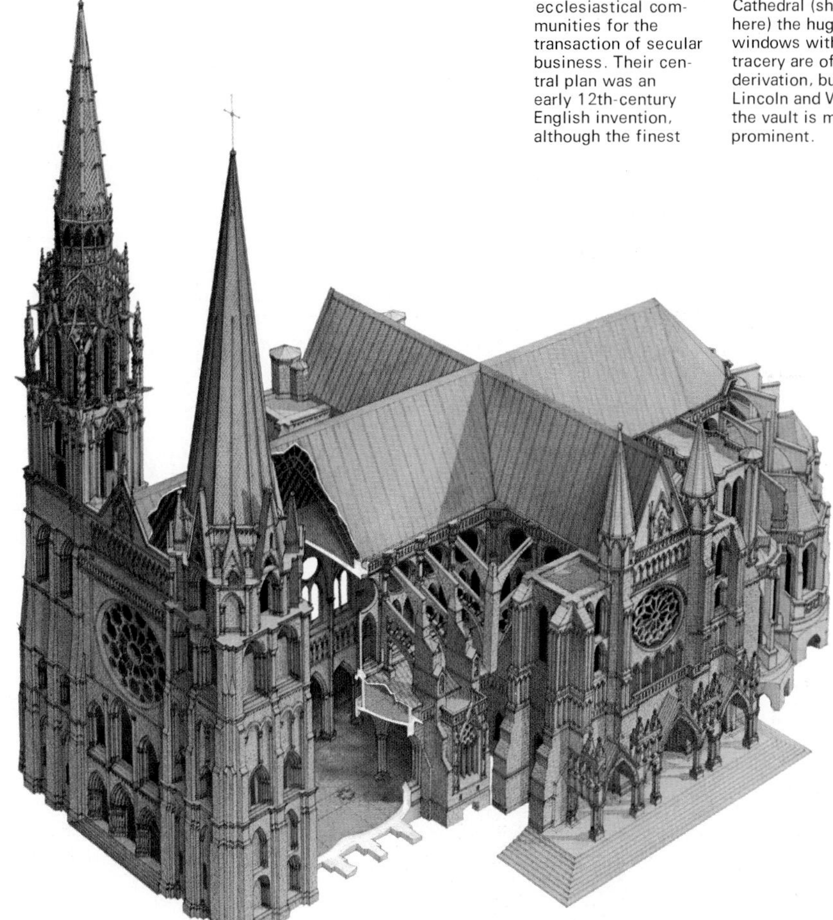

9 This detail at Westminster Abbey shows St Peter and is one of 13 compartments of a wooden panel whose original purpose is unknown. It may have been placed behind or in front of an altar. Despite severe damage, it is still recognizable as the finest panel painting surviving from the 13th century. The thin features and mannered gestures recur in wall paintings at Westminster.

9

7 The west towers of Chartres Cathedral, with the portals and windows, were added to an 11th-century, wooden-roofed basilica in the period 1130–50 and retained after the basilica was burned in 1194. The new Gothic church has the same width as the old basilica but the increased height may be gauged from the rose window added above the west windows. Smaller roses occur in the clerestory windows and more complex ones in the transept fronts. Even the lower tiers of flying buttresses are linked by radiating arches to make them look like segments of rose windows. The niches on the buttresses are the first examples of what became a favorite device of the Gothic designers. The austere interior displays to perfection the medieval stained-glass windows that have been preserved in their entirety at Chartres, alone among French cathedrals. After the decision to retain the old west portals, the transept fronts were decorated with as much sculpture as if they had been west fronts; the similarity would have been complete if their twin towers had been carried up. The total number of towers planned was to have been nine, two more than Laon.

The emergence of France

The beginnings of the French nation can be traced to the medieval house of Capet. Hugh Capet, a feudal lord whose lands centered on the Isle de France region on the middle Seine, was elected king of the west Frankish domains in 987 and reigned until 996, superseding the Carolingians. France was then only a part of Gaul, which stretched from the Pyrenees to the Rhine and had been, since the Frankish invasions of the fifth century, a conglomeration of Germanic, Celtic, and Romance elements. The French-speaking peoples came to the fore and were united only with the slow extension of Capetian authority.

The Capetian kings

The Capetian kings had almost no contact with Aquitaine and the south, while in the north powerful dynasties of the nobility in Normandy, Anjou, Flanders, and Burgundy were their equals in wealth and influence. But the real source of Capetian strength was the popular veneration they were increasingly accorded. The kings, although at first powerless, gradually emerged as sacred figures, consecrated by the holy oil first used by St Remy (*c.* 438–533), the "Apostle of the Franks," *c.* 496 at the baptism of Clovis. This oil was thereafter kept at Rheims in a venerated ampoule [Key].

Gradually the French kings built up their political power too. This had a solid base in the growing prosperity of France—in the thriving city communes, which were actively encouraged by the twelfth-century kings and which became centers of loyalty. A dramatic expansion of authority beyond the royal patrimony took place in the reign of Philip II Augustus (1163–1223); he took advantage of the unpopularity of King John of England to regain English-ruled Normandy and bring his own vast territories, extending to the Pyrenees, under direct royal rule. His son, Louis VIII (1187–1226), introduced royal power into the heartland of southern France (Languedoc) after the Albigensians there had been crushed by a papal crusade against their heretical view of the world as a creation of the devil. The power and prestige of Louis IX (St Louis) (1215–70) were so great that he was able to act as the arbiter of all Europe. The apogee came in the reign of Philip IV (1268–1314), who advanced the eastern frontier and reduced the papacy to subservience.

The change in government

With this advance came a new kind of government. The thirteenth-century kings attracted formerly independent lords into their service and, with the help of educated men from the University of Paris [5], began to establish a "civil service" of local officers who judged cases and collected revenue in the provinces. At the center were the *parlement* of Paris, the highest court of the kingdom, and the Chambre des Comptes, a financial department, staffed by lawyers of high caliber who made French royal justice widely sought. By 1314 the French king was richer, more respected, and better served than any other European ruler.

That his power was nevertheless limited was shown by the crises of the fourteenth century. Until 1314 power had passed uninterruptedly from father to son; but the direct

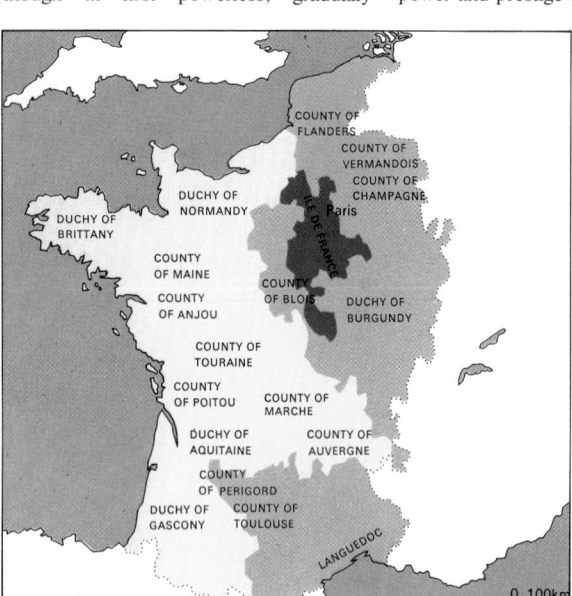

CONNECTIONS

See also
1102 European society 1250–1450
1090 Western European economy 1000–1250
1086 Triumph of the Church
1088 European learning in the 13th century
1098 Feudalism
1104 Gothic art of the 14th century
1106 Gothic art 1400–155

1

COUNTY OF FLANDERS
COUNTY OF VERMANDOIS
COUNTY OF CHAMPAGNE
DUCHY OF NORMANDY
ILE DE FRANCE
Paris
DUCHY OF BRITTANY
COUNTY OF MAINE
COUNTY OF ANJOU
COUNTY OF BLOIS
DUCHY OF BURGUNDY
COUNTY OF TOURAINE
COUNTY OF POITOU
COUNTY OF MARCHE
DUCHY OF AQUITAINE
COUNTY OF AUVERGNE
COUNTY OF PERIGORD
DUCHY OF GASCONY
COUNTY OF TOULOUSE
LANGUEDOC
0 100km

1 By 1180 the map of France included parts of modern Belgium, but excluded Franche Comté, Dauphiné, and Provence, ruled by the Holy Roman Empire. But even within the confines of the Capetian dynasty's formal authority, many provinces were almost wholly beyond royal control. The real center of the king's power was between Paris and the Loire. To the west lay the dominions of his Plantagenet rivals. Almost all of these were gained by Philip II Augustus (r. 1180–1223) in protracted wars.

Royal demesne 1180
Fiefs held by English king 1180
Other fiefs 1180

2

COUNTY OF FLANDERS
COUNTY OF ARTOIS
COUNTY OF PONTHIEU
DUCHY OF NORMANDY
COUNTY OF VALOIS
Paris
COUNTY OF CHAMPAGNE
DUCHY OF BRITTANY
COUNTY OF ANJOU
COUNTY OF BLOIS
DUCHY OF BURGUNDY
COUNTY OF POITOU
COUNTY OF MARCHE
DAUPHINE OF AUVERGNE
DUCHY OF GUYENNE
DUCHY OF GASCONY
COUNTY OF TOULOUSE
LANGUEDOC
COUNTY OF FOIX
0 100km

2 By 1328 France had expanded beyond her borders of 1180, and in 1349 she gained the Dauphine. Internally the Capetian dynasty had established its hold on the former Plantagenet lands, and all the feudatories in Burgundy, Brittany, and Languedoc acknowledged it, as did the English king in Guyenne. But the numerous enclaves and noble houses indicate how shallow were the roots of royal authority, which often did little more than confirm the positions of local magnates. In ensuing wars, many nobles played off the English and French crowns against each other, to gain great independence.

Royal demesne 1328
Territories of royal princes 1328
Fiefs held by English king 1328
Other fiefs 1328

3

Louis VI 1108–1137
Louis IX 1226–1270
Philip III 1270–1285
Philip IV 1285–1314
Louis X 1314–1316
Philip V 1316–1322
Charles IV 1322–1328
Philip VI 1328–1350
John II 1350–1364
Charles VIII 1483–1498
House of Capet
House of Valois

3 The French monarchy descended in the male line from 987 to 1848. The direct succession of son-to-father was carefully preserved until 1316. The elder Capetian line died out altogether in 1328. The Valois line then ruled until 1589.

4

4 The ambulatory of the Abbey of Saint-Denis was one of the earliest inspirations of Gothic architecture, and it represented the cradle of French national sentiment. It was built in the mid-12th century during the reign of Louis VII.

5

5 The seal of the University of Paris was made in 1215. The university began as a corporation of scholars in the 12th century and in the 13th century trained many of the most useful servants of the crown as well as great philosophers.

line of Capetians ended in 1328 with Charles IV's death, and the crown passed to their Valois cousins [3]. The Valois claim was challenged by Edward III of England (1312–77), to whose court flocked all the dissidents of France: in Flanders, in Brittany, and above all in the south, local noblemen hoped to increase their patrimony by playing off Philip VI (1293–1350) against his rival. Edward crushed the French army at Crécy (1346), while France became the prey of war bands who made their fortune from the profits of ransom, pillage, and terror. At Poitiers (1356) [7], King John II (1319–64) was captured by Edward's son, the Black Prince, and released only for an enormous ransom. English successes were not continuous, and there were intervals of peace; but during the disastrous reign of Charles VI (1368–1422) a murderous factional struggle between the rival houses of Burgundy and Orléans exposed France to a renewed attack from England. With the help of the Duke of Burgundy, the Lancastrian King Henry V was able to conquer Normandy, occupy Paris, and induce Charles VI to disinherit his son in Henry's favor. In the popular mind the kings remained sacred figures.

Joan of Arc, the maid of Lorraine

At the lowest ebb of the Valois fortunes, when the English and Burgundians ruled northern France, the popular and religious aspect of kingship reasserted itself in the extraordinary events involving Joan of Arc (*c.* 1412–31) [6]. Joan, a humble girl from Lorraine, went to the court of the disowned heir, Charles VII (1403–61) [10], and by claiming the miraculous intervention of the saints in his cause endowed it with a popular fervor. She herself was killed by the English, but a reconciliation between Burgundy and Charles VII at Arras (1435) made the English position hopeless.

As the English withdrew from France, the monarchy found itself firmly established in the affections of its subjects. Louis XI (1423–83) was able to humble the nobility and bring the remotest provinces under his personal rule; the unity of France was never again in doubt.

KEY

The coronation chalice at Rheims Cathedral is the symbol of a sacred kingship. The French monarchy made up for its lack of physical power by the prestige of its religious sanction. Kings were anointed with the oil said to have been used at the baptism of Clovis, the first king of the Franks; the oil was kept in a phial miraculously refilled for each coronation. The king was regarded by many as a religious figure: the lilies on his shield were said to have first appeared supernaturally on the shield of Clovis; and his banner, the oriflamme, was said to be the mythical flaming lance of Charlemagne, King of the Franks. His touch was said to heal scrofula.

6

6 Joan of Arc was captured at the battle of Compiègne in 1430. She had appeared at the court of Charles VII when his fortunes were at their lowest in 1429. Her adoption of the dress and manners of the mercenaries shocked some but inspired many more, and she eventually turned events in Charles's favor. She was tried as a heretic by the English in 1431, burned at the stake, and then canonized.

7

7 The Battle of Poitiers, 1356 (from a 15th-century manuscript), was a great defeat for the French army. The English, led by Edward, the Black Prince, were heavily outnumbered, but at the height of the battle they launched an attack from behind the French lines and the French king, John II, fled, only to be captured with his son Philip. John was freed in 1360 but returned to captivity.

8

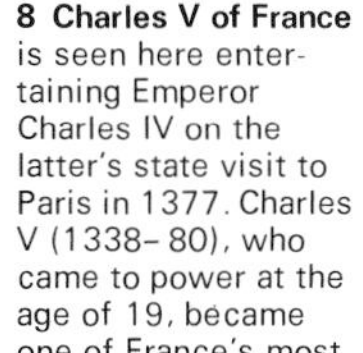

8 Charles V of France is seen here entertaining Emperor Charles IV on the latter's state visit to Paris in 1377. Charles V (1338–80), who came to power at the age of 19, became one of France's most successful kings in her darkest days. After drastically reducing English power in France, he sought European allies to drive his enemies from his country and introduced domestic reforms.

9

9 A miniature by Jean Fouquet (*c.* 1420–80) shows the trial of John, Duke of Alençon, for treason in 1458. The duke fought with Joan of Arc and was loyal to her even during the court intrigues of the time. However, as an outspoken rebel who had made no secret of his loathing for the king, he was still given a fair and formal trial and did not die until 1476. French judicial institutions, which enjoyed a high prestige throughout Europe, had been perfected in the 13th century. They were based on Roman law and ably staffed.

10

10 Charles VII was painted by Jean Fouquet in 1445. This much-abused monarch is among the least understood of French rulers. He overcame appalling misfortunes that began with his disinheritance by his father Charles VI in 1420 in favor of Henry V of England, the victor of the Battle of Agincourt. Yet, Charles became the focus for all enemies of English rule in France and succeeded over 30 years in expelling his opponents from the realm. However, revolts of the nobles disturbed the last years of his reign.

Feudalism

In a civilization like Europe's in the early Middle Ages, with no civil service, police, or legal profession, the only stable institutions were the family group and especially —since wealth and power could result from it—the warrior band with its lord. The bond between lord and warriors was the basis of feudal society in the Germany, England, and France of the eleventh and twelfth centuries. The ethic of the medieval warrior, which demanded fierce loyalty from the retainer and unstinted generosity from his lord, can be seen in the epic literature of the tenth century. For example, in the *Battle of Maldon*: "He broke the board-wall, burst in among them, wrought on the sea-wreckers a revenge worthy his gold-giving lord, before the ground claimed him. . . ."

Land tenure

In time, the language of this personal bond—fief, vassalage, later homage—came also to describe property relations. Absolute ownership was unknown to the Middle Ages: land was granted with definite obligations, often military. The ceremony of homage [1] did not necessarily imply either a permanent or an exclusive tie, and it was common for a knight to owe homage for an estate to several lords, or even to a social inferior. Feudal terminology was therefore simply a way of describing the complexities of land tenure; society was not in any hierarchical "feudal pyramid."

Nevertheless, the period from about 950 to 1250 is properly called feudal because of the dominant position of a warrior aristocracy in Western Europe and in crusader Palestine. This aristocracy shared a common training and fighting technique, that of the mounted knight, and a common code of conduct, the ideal of "chivalry." Its basis was the technological superiority of mounted men over footsoldiers, which emerged about the time of Charlemagne. In antiquity the stirrup and the horseshoe were unknown; introduced about 750 from Central Asia, stirrups in particular had revolutionary consequences: they made it possible to charge effectively with a lance carrying the full impetus of a galloping horse without the rider being unhorsed on impact with his target [2]. This placed great value on mounted warriors [Key] but, before about 950, horses were scarce; the Franks' relative wealth in them partially explains Charlemagne's military successes.

Rise of the knights

There is evidence that the number of horses increased rapidly after 950, and in the next century mounted men everywhere decided the fortunes of war. Their numbers were small, their equipment expensive, and their training long. But this increased their pride and prestige and, by 1100, mounted warriors would symbolize their corporate spirit by the initiation ceremonies of knighthood.

Local society was thus dominated by the knightly classes. They served in various capacities: many, without a permanent master, sold their services as mercenaries to the highest bidder. Others, especially at the start of their careers, took service as the household knights of a great lord. Still others, particularly the Normans, were bound by the conditions of their tenure to

CONNECTIONS

See also

1090 Western European economy 1000–1250
1076 Norman and Angevin England
1066 Charlemagne and the Carolingian Empire
1074 European expansion to the east

1 The ceremony of homage is shown in a metaphorical context in a 12th-century illustration of Theophilus paying homage to the Devil. The Devil carries a charter or written record. But the original ritual of homage was designed to register the contract in public in a memorable way without the need of documentary record. Because few men were literate in the earliest period of feudalism, it was essential to make legal contracts before witnesses whose memories could be relied on. Submission was represented by the lord taking the hands of his man between his own; afterward they kissed to symbolize the bond of friendship.

2 A 14th-century knight, Sir Geoffrey Luttrell, receives his helmet and lance from his favored lady. Knights were regarded as heroes and their combats were considered heroic feats. The thrust of their charge depended on the innovation of stirrups; the high saddle also acted as a lever. The lance, intended to unseat opposing horsemen, could be used properly only with these aids. Few lords had many horses but evidence exists that careful breeding was increasing the number. An important stud at Corvey, Saxony, supplied the German imperial armies with battle horses.

3 Functional armor was characteristic of Norman knights. As the sword [G] and ax [F] became longer, protection had to be increased with heavy shields [D,E], and the 10th-century helment [A] gave way to a helmet with visor [B] and a fitted coif of chain mail [C].

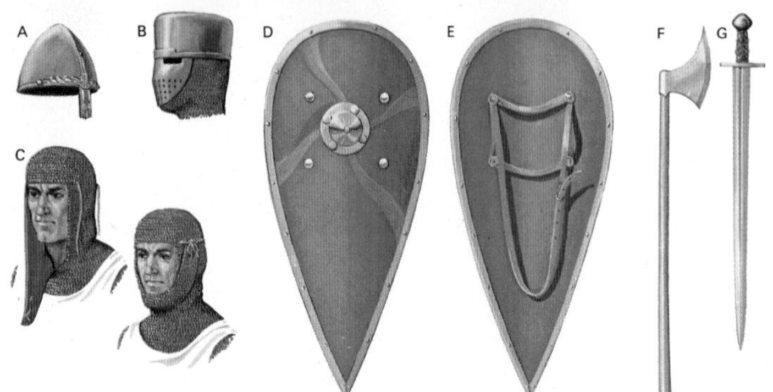

A
B
C
D
E
F
G

4 Langeais castle was one of 13 built by Fulk Nerra, Count of Anjou (987–1040); from them the House of Anjou, which later ruled England, began its formidable rise to power. In each, a castellan and garrison controlled roughly as much country as could be traversed in a day Although fortified towns had existed before, the stone keep, which was the oldest type of castle, was an invention of the 10th century. Keeps, such as that at Langeais, stood on an artifical mound. Internally they might have only one big room and a storehouse, but they were focal points of feudal power and by 1100 had spread throughout Western Europe.

fight at specified seasons; "knight-service" was the most important and usual obligation borne by landowners.

The most formidable of knightly warlike skills was probably the charge in close formation, which was used devastatingly against the Turks in the First Crusade. But as professionals, knights also learned defensive skills, the most spectacular of which was the development of the castle from the simple eleventh-century keep to the elaborate curtain-walled and bastioned castles of the thirteenth century [5].

Chivalry and land owning

The knightly ideal of chivalry demanded that knights should fight to avenge the oppressed, to vindicate the honor of ladies—the theme of romantic love first appears in knightly circles in southern France in the twelfth century—and to advance the Christian religion against the Muslim Saracens [7, 8]. Members of the Orders of the Templars and Hospitallers combined knightly prowess with monastic chastity in the defense of the Holy Land.

A knight's fighting career, unless he became a lord's military official, a marshal, or a constable, was comparatively short, and his ambition was usually to acquire and cultivate an estate. Once on the land most lived simply in keeps with one first-floor room for living and sleeping and, below, a storehouse. Although knights had customary rights over the tenants who held plots by their grant, villagers did not live entirely in the shadow of their lords. The spread of a "three-field system" of farming with its complex organization and the appearance of village communes in France suggest that many villages [6], while paying dues, had an independent corporate life, to which the knight contributed leadership and protection.

Feudalism thus maintained a series of obligations that linked the peasant with his immediate lord and, indirectly, with royal power. Although the dominance of a warrior caste was crumbling by the fourteenth century through the competition of other less military groups, the disappearance of feudalism was gradual, and the knight was to constitute a social ideal for centuries.

KEY

The knight, armed and mounted, was at the center of feudal society. Only an elite could afford the costly equipment.

5

5 Caernarvon Castle, Wales (1283–92), was one of the massive castles built by Edward I after he conquered Wales. By 1300 the primitive keep had developed into a fortified community large enough to house, and strong enough to protect, a provincial government behind thick bastions.

6

6 An English village (center, left), dating from feudal times, created on uncultivated land at Chelmerton, Derbyshire. It shows a pattern implying a planned settlement, either through the enterprise of a lord or simply peasant cooperation. Each house has a garden and narrow strip extending into the wasteland.

7

7 Ekkhard and Uta, a 13th-century crusader and his lady sculpted in Naumburg Cathedral, represent the highest ideal of European nobility—the Christian warrior—toward the end of the feudal period. From the First Crusade (1096–99), warfare found an idealized form in the defense of Christendom against the Saracens. Great numbers took part in expeditions to Jerusalem and enthusiasts banded together in the military orders of the Templars and Hospitallers. Besides the great international crusades, many knights went individually—to win a reputation or expiate an offense—to fight in Palestine, Spain, or pagan Lithuania. The chivalric code required them to fight.

8

8 Chivalry is exemplified by St Louis IX, king of France (1226–70), rescuing a Saracen lady and her child in battle. The feudal knight evolved a code of conduct transcending even his Christian allegiance, and chivalry was a central theme.

Medieval literature and drama

Latin, the common literary language of medieval Europe, was extensively used in works of philosophy, theology, law, history, and even storytelling and romance. Yet the fascination of medieval imaginative literature lies in the evolution of the use of vernacular, or local, language. The invaders of the western Roman Empire brought new cultures, languages, and mythic traditions that in some cases superseded, and in others fused with, the literary traditions and language of Rome.

From epic to romance

The mythology and folklore of the Germans [3] and Norsemen were initially passed on by word of mouth from recitations in the banqueting halls of the great; they were rarely written. Contemporary history was sometimes turned into instant legend, as in the Anglo-Saxon poem *The Battle of Maldon* recording a famous battle with the Danes in 991. In contrast, *Beowulf* (*c.* 700) is the written version of an ancient epic, and the Norse *Eddas* are epics from the same ancient tradition.

By the eleventh century such native and ancestral traditions were being combined with conventions from classical Greece and Rome. Lyrical, allegorical, and epic themes underwent classical revivals, on the one hand, or, periodically, romantic yearnings for a non-classical past. The Arthurian legend [1] pervaded medieval literature though it was not until the fifteenth century that Thomas Malory (died 1471) recorded it in full in the *Morte d'Arthur*.

At the beginning of the twelfth century an influential literary model was the French *Chanson de geste*. One example is *The Song of Roland,* an epic poem in Old French based on a heroic interpretation of Charlemagne's defeat at the Battle of Roncesvalles. Like the *Morte d'Arthur,* the poem involves changing history into legend and legend into literary epic. Another quasi-historical epic is the Spanish *El Cid*.

Epic and narrative poetry of the early Middle Ages gave way to the poetry of courtly love, the most famous exponent of which was the French poet Chrétièn de Troyes (flourished 1165–80). *The Romance of the Rose* [2], a vast thirteenth-century poem of allegory, is really a cynical variation on Latin love poetry, while the Middle English *Sir Gawaine and the Green Knight* is an example of a chivalric romance of the fourteenth century. Meanwhile the troubadour poets of Provence, such as Bertran de Born (*c.* 1135–1207), and the German Minnesänger, such as Wolfram von Eschenbach (*c.* 1170–1270) and Walther von der Vogelweide (*c.* 1170–1220), produced a new and sophisticated poetry of courtly romance that was recited by wandering minstrels and poets [5]. Troubadour and Minnesänger song and poetry marked the high point of medieval courtly culture.

Development of music and drama

Troubadour song also marked a meeting point between developments in medieval literature and music. In the early Middle Ages music had been almost entirely in the service of the liturgy of the Roman Catholic Church and had been dominated by Gregorian chant, or plainsong. The great musical innovation of the eleventh century was

CONNECTIONS

See also
1148 English Renaissance literature
1106 Gothic art 1400–15

1 Courtly love, which centered on the unworldly excellence and beauty of the beloved contrasted with the lover's servitude, is depicted in this early 15th-century painting. Its chief exponent in poetry was Chrétièn de Troyes, who introduced the theme of the Holy Grail into the Arthurian romances.

2 The Romance of the Rose, the greatest—but most ambiguous—13th-century poem, was begun by Guillaume de Lorris as an allegory of love; here Dame Nature confers with the priest Genius in an enclosed garden. Jean de Meun added 17,000 lines to the 4,000 of Lorris, but in so doing obscured the original theme.

3 The capture of the magic ring by Brünnhilde, a Valkyrie maiden, on the funeral pyre of Siegfried, is the dramatic Wagnerian finale of *The Ring of the Nibelungen,* the most emotive epic of the German people. The story is Burgundian-Frankish in origin.

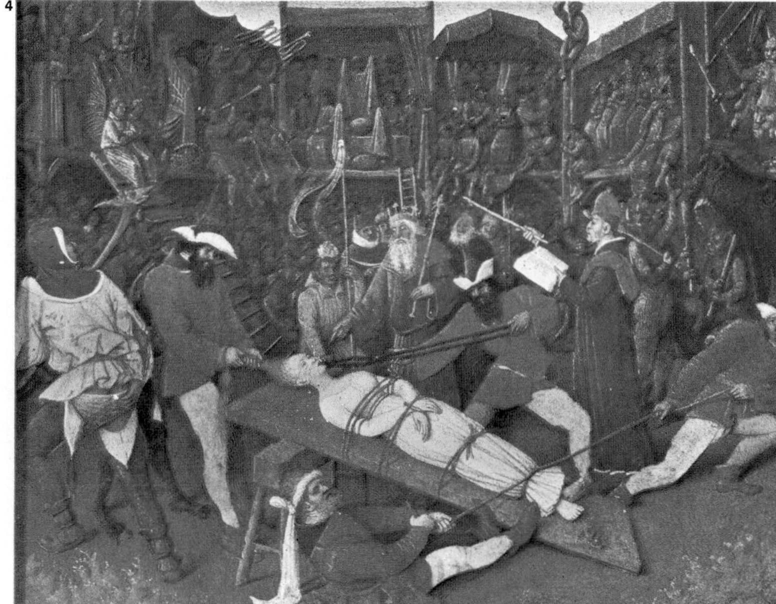

4 A medieval mystery play is recorded pictorially in a detailed miniature by Jean Fouquet (*c.*1420–80). It shows a circular theater surrounded by galleries or scaffolds, with players above and spectators below. The drama has been removed from the church interior, and although the action takes place on the raised central area, the angels, throne, and audience intermingle.

polyphony—the juxtaposition of two or more voice lines harmoniously intertwined. It was exemplified by the musical school of Notre Dame in Paris that in the twelfth century produced such famous composers as Léonin and Pérotin.

Church music also led to dramatic representations of the Easter and Christmas Gospels, performed at Winchester as early as 970. Gradually, other religious cycles were dramatized, at first within the church and later outside; this was the origin of the mystery [4] and morality plays of the late Middle Ages.

Triumph of the vernacular

Medieval song culminated in the thirteenth century in the motet, the expression of sung verse in a polyphonic context that gave musical form to troubadour and Minnesänger poetry. In Italy the lyric flourished at the Sicilian court of Frederick II, where Provençal language and themes were merged into the new Italian language. A parallel movement occurred in Galicia and Portugal in the thirteenth and fourteenth

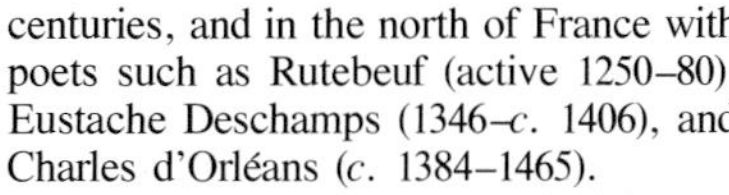

centuries, and in the north of France with poets such as Rutebeuf (active 1250–80), Eustache Deschamps (1346–*c.* 1406), and Charles d'Orléans (*c.* 1384–1465).

The fourteenth century marked the true literary emergence of the languages of modern Europe. Renaissance rediscovery and re-evaluation of Latin and Greek as imaginative literature began at the same time. Poets such as Francesco Petrarch (1304–74) wrote both in Italian and Latin.

Geoffrey Chaucer (*c.* 1345–1400) in *The Canterbury Tales* [7], and Giovanni Boccaccio (1313–75) in *The Decameron* [8], developed the art of storytelling in the manner of the Italian collections of the *Novellino,* the French *Bestiaries,* and the French novel *Aucassin et Nicolette,* adding a new breadth of humor and experience. The masterpiece of late medieval literature was the *Divine Comedy* [9] by Dante Alighieri (1265–1321), an imaginary personal voyage through Hell, Purgatory, and Paradise, guided by Vergil, the sage of ancient Rome. The *Divine Comedy* secured the triumph of the vernacular language.

KEY

The jongleurs, jugglers or tumblers, in this ornamented medieval manuscript initial were traveling entertainers who sang, danced, clowned, and, originally, recited the narrative poems of popular medieval poetry. They brought diversion to the far-flung courts of medieval Europe and carried with them the traditions of popular music, poetry, epic, and drama. Their musical role was gradually taken over by minstrels and troubadours. As part of a tradition of itinerant entertainers, however, ranging from bear-keepers and street buskers to court clowns, *jongleurs* remained common in Europe from Roman times to the 19th century.

5 Adenez, "King of the minstrels," is shown in this manuscript reciting the *Roman de Cleomadès* to the Queen of France. Minstrels, wandering singers, and troubadours sometimes attained exalted status in European courts; Adenez was the employee of Henry, Duke of Flanders. Throughout the Middle Ages minstrels passed on orally the great epic romances of ancient heroes such as Roland.

6

6 The Exultet ("Let the angelic choirs of heaven now rejoice") was one of the great Easter hymns. In its present form it was probably written by St Ambrose of Milan (*c.*340–97), creator of Ambrosian plainsong, which was the forerunner of the Gregorian chant. The words of the Exultet were written on special scrolls, often lavishly illustrated with scenes of contemporary life as in this 11th-century Italian example.

7 The Canterbury pilgrims are shown setting out in this illustration from *The Canterbury Tales.* Each pilgrim entertained the others with a story in this poem, the first major work of English literature. Chaucer incorporated ancient tales in a new, medieval setting and also produced a complete and highly entertaining account of 14th-century manners, customs, and morals in England.

7

8

8 Giovanni Boccaccio ranks with Dante and Petrarch as one of the great 14th-century writers. His major achievement was the narrative realism of *The Decameron* (*c.* 1348–53), a loosely knit series of engrossing and often bawdy tales of contemporary manners and morals. But writing in Italian was for him an indulgence and his weightiest works, such as *De claris mulieribus,* were in Latin. He was a mixture of medieval poet and Renaissance theorist.

9

9 The topography of Hell, as described by Dante Alighieri in his *Divine Comedy,* was drawn by Bartolomeo de Fruosino about 1420. Though it had a high theological and philosophical theme, the poem gave the most graphic account of the tortures undergone by sinners, particularly those Dante himself most disliked. The characterizations change from the descriptive in Hell, to the lyrical in Purgatory, to the mystically rapturous in the voyage in Paradise.

European society 1250–1450

By 1250 the material basis of Europe as it is now known was established; most of the towns and villages that exist today were already inhabited. Although forests were more extensive, the area under cultivation had passed the period of most rapid expansion. The next 200 years were characterized by crises of population and production, alternating boom and slump, and by the development of the techniques of finance [Key, 3], business, and trade. The underlying crisis was probably the large population of the thirteenth century. Tax records show that in southern England and Provence the number of inhabitants doubled during the century. Older towns such as Florence [2] pushed out beyond their walls and multiplied their parish churches, while new towns were founded in every part of Europe.

The increase in urban populations

In 1250 the population of Europe had reached about 70 million, and evidence from several sources suggests that the rate of increase was about one percent a year. As a result, the food resources of the continent were stretched. Migration from Germany into central and eastern Europe reached its height in the thirteenth century, while the poor soils and marginal lands of the alpine and Apennine uplands came under the plow [1] for the first time. Longer life expectancy combined with a higher birthrate to push European society into a slowly maturing demographic crisis.

This process created new social forms, above all the large towns that profoundly modified European civilization. Since classical times, probably no town with more than 40,000 inhabitants had existed; now Venice, Naples, Barcelona, Bruges, Paris, and some others far exceeded this limit. Immigrants, often from distant places, crowded into them, to work in the textiles of Bruges or Florence, or the more diversified trades of London and Paris. Two great ports, Venice [4] and Genoa, provided Europe with the products of the East, and among the first Europeans to visit China was the Venetian merchant Marco Polo. The Baltic trade was monopolized by the Hanse—a league of North German cities.

In the urban centers, more specialized ways of life developed. The skills of the accountant and the banker (first notable in Pisa and Florence) and the practice of marine insurance (a Venetian speciality) made possible the first international companies; the Bardi of Florence, through their agents in London and Bruges, were the greatest creditors of the English crown, for instance. Courtiers, patrons of art, and people of fashion flourished in the midst of a new, degrading poverty. The friars adapted religion for the urban masses, while poverty and disease were mitigated by burgeoning charities. Whatever the crises of the European economy, the cities continued to grow.

A century of catastrophe

Undernourishment left the teeming population of the thirteenth century susceptible to a worsening climate, hunger, and disease. In 1315 persistent rain inaugurated a series of harvest failures and two years of famine throughout northern Europe. The high prices and booming business of the previous century now proved unstable; the economy

CONNECTIONS

See also
1090 Western European economy 1000–1250
1128 The politics of Europe 1450–1600
1096 The emergence of France

1 This twelfth-century plow, shown in a medieval manuscript of Gregory the Great's *Moralia* on Job, shows the colter (cutter) and moldboard, which sliced and turned over the sods. The moldboard and colter were fixed to a beam drawn by oxen. The design and function of farm implements changed little before the beginning of the sixteenth century.

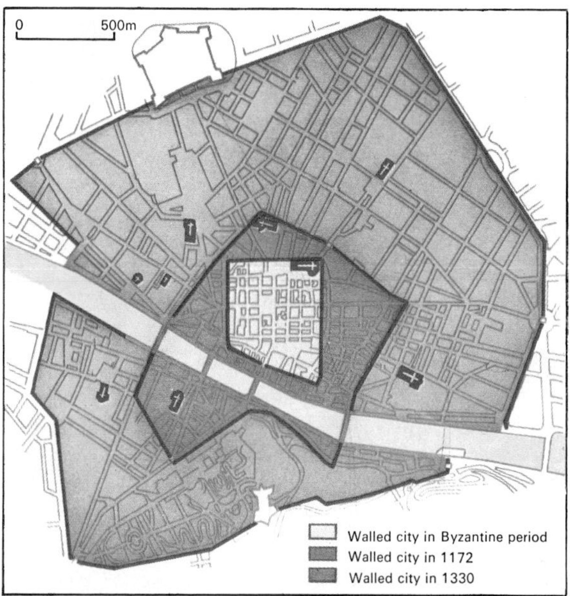

0
500m
Walled city in Byzantine period
Walled city in 1172
Walled city in 1330

2 The fortified Roman town of Florence was reduced during the stagnation of the Dark Ages but grew rapidly in the twelfth and thirteenth centuries. Its expanding size and power were marked by the wider walls of 1172 and 1284–1330. In spite of internal factional struggles the city's position as a center of cloth-making and the wool trade led to an era of prosperity and cultural achievement, particularly after the rise of the Medici merchant family in the early 1400s. Florentine bankers were the most influential in Europe, and the florin, minted in the thirteenth century, became a monetary standard throughout the West.

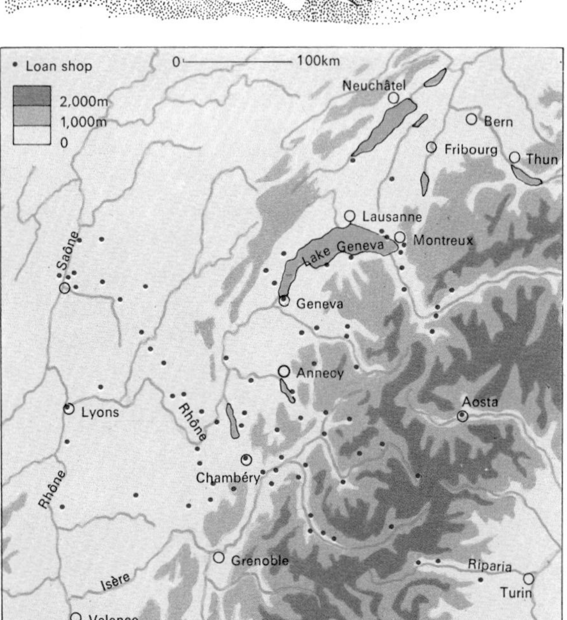

Loan shop
0
100km
2,000m
1,000m
0
Neuchâtel
Bern
Fribourg
Thun
Lausanne
Montreux
Lake Geneva
Geneva
Saône
Annecy
Aosta
Lyons
Rhône
Chambéry
Rhône
Grenoble
Riparia
Turin
Isère
Valence

3 Loan shops, or *casane*, of Lombard moneylenders were a feature of the alpine valleys of Savoy in the thirteenth century. In many parts of Europe country life was transformed by money at this time, especially in Italy. The rise in the population made necessary the rapid development of different soils. Peasants obtained the required capital to a large extent from loans. Moneylenders operated from shops set up in rural areas to accommodate the peasant population.

4 Venice at the time of Marco Polo's departure for Asia in 1271 (depicted in this imaginative book illustration) was the busiest port in the world. The city was also a center of shipbuilding and a leader in ship design for the rest of Europe.

had advanced too fast. The boldest venturers, the Italian bankers, were hit hardest of all, and in 1343 repudiation of the English royal debt precipitated a crash.

In 1348–50 came the terrible Black Death, the first of the recurrent bubonic and pneumonic plagues that were to beset Europe until the 1730s. Carried by both rats and humans in ships from the Crimea, the plague was immediately fatal and spread rapidly from southern to northern Europe. Its effects were catastrophic: probably about 50 percent of the total population died; some towns in Provence lost four-fifths of their inhabitants, and many villages were completely abandoned. In many parts of Europe there was some recovery but the plague returned in 1361, 1369, and 1379, and by 1400 the population had shrunk to about a half or two-thirds of its total a century before. The impression made by the catastrophe is reflected in the all-pervading theme of Death in late medieval art [6].

One of the effects of these calamities was social disorder, in the towns and in the country. For the first time peasants and townsmen took violent action against bad government, in the Jacquerie rising [7] of northern France (1358) and peasant rebellions in England (1381) and Catalonia (1409–13). Governments everywhere were fearful of such movements and tightened their control wherever they could. These revolts were led by men of enterprise, peasants, farmers, or artisans who resented the legal limits on their status and freedom. The fall in population led to a demand for labor and laborers demanded the right to sell their services to the highest bidder.

The standard of living

The revolts reflected the rising expectations of the peasantry; in England, wage rates doubled while prices remained stable between 1350 and 1415, a sign of the vitality and independence of humbler men [8]. For them, the demographic decline meant a higher standard of living and the opportunity to turn peasant holdings into small farms. After a century of catastrophe, the peasant followed the bankers and merchants into a measure of prosperity.

KEY

A
B
C
D
E
F

Coins proliferated in the late Middle Ages with the development of economies based on trading. A gold coinage, almost unknown since the seventh century, was restored in the thirteenth. Pioneers of the new money were the republics of Venice with the ducat and Florence with the florin. These coins are of roughly standard appearance and were issued in 1357–67 by Pedro I of Castile [A]; in 1399–1413 by Henry IV of England [B]; in 1419–34 by Conrad III of Mainz [C]; in 1368 by the republic of Florence [D]; in 1350–64 by John II of France [E]; and in about 1420 by Tommaso Mocenigo representing the Venetian republic [F], all gold coinage.

5

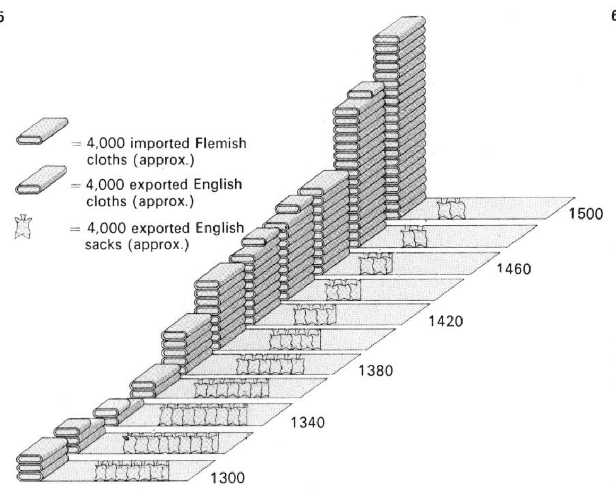
= 4,000 imported Flemish cloths (approx.)
= 4,000 exported English cloths (approx.)
= 4,000 exported English sacks (approx.)
1500
1460
1420
1380
1340
1300

5 The English wool trade expanded rapidly after 1200. Raw wool was at first sent for processing to the established cloth-makers of Bruges, Florence, and other centers in France, Flanders, and Italy, but their monopoly was broken by the increasing export of cloth made in England.

6

6 "The Triumph of Death" by Andrea Orcagna (*c.* 1308–68) was painted shortly after the Black Death of 1348. It depicts with terrifying realism the sufferings of the sick who beg to be released from the torments of plague. The theme of death and instability of human fortune pervades the literature and art of the later fourteenth century, and it is likely that this was an effect of the dramatic carnage of the plague. "No one wept for the dead," wrote a Sienese chronicler, Agnolo di Tura, "because everyone expected death himself." Survivors surveyed their shrunken world in a somber mood.

7

7 The Jacquerie, a peasant uprising that engulfed the Paris region in 1358, resulted from the disorder in France after the English captured King John II in 1356. The main grievance arose from attempts by landowners to keep down wages in a time of labor scarcity. All of the fourteenth-century peasant rebellions had similar causes.

8

8 The shepherds in "Nativity" by Hugo van der Goes (*c.* 1440–82), clearly drawn from peasant life, show a marked individuality characteristic of the confident peasant culture of the age and exemplified also in the popular art of the woodcut. Compared with the animal skins of three centuries earlier, the clothes worn are luxurious.

Gothic art of the 14th century

Building and the decorative arts from the end of the thirteenth century to the end of the fourteenth century combine grace with naturalism. The source was French Rayonnant, the radiating style, best seen in rose windows, but by the end of the period a style known as International Gothic had developed.

At the beginning of the period, buildings became larger and more elaborate. In England the rebuilding, on a grand scale, of the east end of Old St Paul's, London (1256–*c.*1328), inspired the square-ended Angel Choir of Lincoln Cathedral (1256–80) and the new Exeter Cathedral (*c.*1280–1375). Towers with spires became popular—for instance Salisbury (1330) by Richard Farley. Capitals (heads of columns), bosses (ornamental knobs), and corbels (stones that support wall shafts) were richly ornamented; hence the name "decorated."

The use of wood

Many impressive effects were achieved by using wood instead of stone. The overall weight was less, and therefore less buttressing was needed. The nave of England's York Minster (1291–1345) was given a wood vault that may have been the model for later Continental net vaults. The idea may have come from the Chapter House at York, which contrived to do without the traditional central column—an innovation taken further at Ely [Key], near Cambridge.

Gradually, wood was recognized as a building material in its own right. Elaborate roofs were built, such as that of Westminster Hall (1390s) commissioned by Richard II, although even here stone construction provides details such as the tracery "paneling" above the arches. Tracery had been a favorite type of decoration throughout Europe since 1240, when complicated patterns first appeared in windows. Tracery was first applied to walls in France about 1250, but it was not taken up in England until the building of St Stephen's Chapel, Palace of Westminster, in about 1310. English "panel" tracery then developed and fitted well with the simplified lines of perpendicular architecture as exemplified by York choir and Canterbury nave [3]. It was even applied to vaults: probably first at Tewkesbury [1], then as fan vaulting in the cloister at Gloucester (after 1357).

European innovations

European architecture followed the Rayonnant style of the thirteenth century, increasing in scale: Beauvais—the tallest cathedral of all—had a choir vault of 157ft (48m), which collapsed in 1275. Cologne incorporated five aisles.

After the middle of the fourteenth century, France did not rival the inventiveness of Germany and Bohemia. The dominant German architects were the Parlér family, the eldest of whom had worked at Cologne. His design for Schwäbisch Gmünd [6] became a model for the great town churches of southern Germany in the later Middle Ages in which, with nave and aisles of equal width and height, greater prominence was given to the windows and vault. These are known as hall-churches.

Italian architects tried to graft northern Gothic ideas of scale and ornament on to a Romanesque tradition. The results were

CONNECTIONS

Read first
1092 Gothic art 1140–120
1094 Gothic art of the 13t century

See also
1106 Gothic art 1400–155
1258 Architecture in the 19th century
1222 Origins of romanticism

1 The additions at Tewkesbury Abbey in the early 1300s transformed a plain Norman choir into a sumptuous burial chapel for members of the Despenser family. The church was also vaulted.

2 The stained-glass program in the clerestory windows of Tewkesbury included a series of armored knights, counterparts of the effigies on the canopied Despenser tombs in the chancel.

3 The nave of Canterbury Cathedral 1378–1405) followed the new fashion for a greater delicacy of line. Originally it had stained glass throughout, but little is left of its splendor.

4 A new interest in nature was shown in the graceful decoration (largely by Italian artists) of the Papal Palace, Avignon. The papacy had retreated there from Rome in 1309, transforming a fortress into elegant apartments.

5 The Angers tapestries were used for interior decoration. Their subject was religious, for they were based on an apocalypse manuscript owned by the French King Charles V, who commissioned seven tapestries in 1377.

6 At Schwäbisch Gmünd in Germany, the Church of the Holy Cross was built as a "hall-church" by Heinrich Parlér. Although influential, the design was not original, being based on St. Elizabeth, Marburg. The choir was begun 1351.

picturesque, but often structurally overambitious. Work on the new Florence Cathedral, begun in 1296, had reached the crossing in 1367 when it was realized that no one knew how to vault such a space. Brunelleschi finally solved the problem in the 1420s and 1430s. Siena Cathedral reflects the aspirations of its citizens [7, 10].

A greater contribution was made by Italy in the field of sculpture. Although everywhere this remained closely connected with architecture, figures were conceived more and more in the round. In the thirteenth century Nicola (*c.* 1225–*c.* 1284) and Giovanni Pisano (*c.* 1250–*c.* 1320) and Arnolfo di Cambio began this trend toward sculpture as a work of art in its own right.

Developments in painting

In contrast to architecture, little northern European painting survives. Some English panel paintings are of high quality, but whether they were done by English or French artists is uncertain. For example: faces on the retable (altar shelf) in Westminster Abbey (late thirteenth century), the Wilton Diptych, and the portrait of Richard II in Westminster Abbey (both fourteenth century) are of uncertain origin.

In contrast, illuminated manuscripts of high quality survive in large numbers. Perhaps the first to combine naturalism and grace was the *Douce Apocalypse* of the early 1270s. Religious texts began to show scenes from everyday life as well as traditional subjects. For instance, the late thirteenth-century Windmill Psalter is full of accurate portraits of birds.

Italy has been much luckier in the survival of its pictures, which show a similar progression. Coppo di Marcovaldo's Madonnas at Siena (1260) and Orvieto (*c.* 1265), still in the Byzantine tradition, are now seen as seated human beings. Cimabue's Santa Croce crucifix (1283) [8] shows an understanding of anatomy and a delight in transparent drapery. A developing understanding of depth and form is very clear in the portraiture of Ambrogio Lorenzetti, as shown in the fresco of the martyred Franciscans from the Chapter House of San Francesco, Siena [11].

KEY

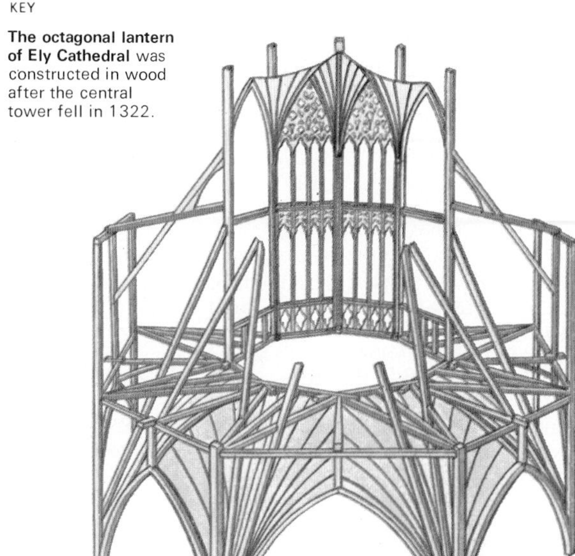

The octagonal lantern of Ely Cathedral was constructed in wood after the central tower fell in 1322.

7

7 The figure of the prophet Isaiah, now in the Cathedral Museum at Siena, was one of the large figures sculpted by Giovanni Pisano for his west front of Siena Cathedral (1284–1300).

8 The realism of Cimabue's Santa Croce painted crucifix provided a challenge for contemporary painters. A departure from Byzantine tradition, it brought new freedom to Italian painting.

8

9

10

10 Siena Cathedral had later Gothic additions to the west front. Aisle and clerestory windows received tracery, the vault was raised and the choir built out over the precipice (with a baptistery below). Finally a gigantic new nave was to have been constructed southward from the hexagonal crossing, for which the existing nave and choir would have been merely transepts. Insufficient buttressing made this unsafe, and the project was abandoned, but the new aisle walls and vaults remain embedded in a later building.

11

9 The Arena chapel at Padua was entirely decorated with frescoes by Giotto (1266–1337) about 1305. Enrico Scrovegni, a moneylender (here presenting a model of the chapel), paid for the work.

11 Ambrogio Lorenzetti brought new realism to portraiture in his frescoes in the church of S Francesco, Siena (*c.* 1329). Except for scenes from the life of St Francis, as in the Basilica at Assisi, near-contemporary events did not usually appear in frescoes. This scene shows St Louis of Toulouse (canonized 1317) being received at Avignon by the pope, who is seated to the left.

Gothic art 1400–1550

Art in Europe during the late Middle Ages can be seen as a further development of the International Gothic style. Delight in the colorful, courtly, and complex is found in all branches of art and architecture, with regional variations.

Gothic art at its height

In Italy the love of Gothic decoration and rich materials persisted in the work of Gentile da Fabriano (*c.*1370–*c.*1427) and Benozzo Gozzoli (*c.*1420–97). In the north of Europe, International Gothic had no rival. On the whole, there was a redoubling of decorative detail in parallel with increasing realism. For example, the animals, birds, and plants that surround the principal figures in the tapestries of the "Lady with the Unicorn" [5] stand out in lifelike detail. This is probably helped by the novel use of red instead of the usual blue for the ground. As a result, blue and green could be used for modeling without spoiling the overall effect.

Almost everywhere, panel paintings were a popular art form for use as altarpieces, but few have survived other than Flemish or German ones. Illuminated manuscripts have suffered much less, and Books of Hours [1, 8] seem to have been extremely popular. These were service-books for wealthy laypersons, especially ladies, and they appear to have been objects of prestige and pleasure. The *Bedford Hours*, for example, was given to King Henry VI for Christmas when he was a boy.

Not all patronage came from the aristocracy, however; the "Lady with the Unicorn" tapestries were commissioned by a family of the high bourgeoisie rather than of the nobility. The patronage of this section of society was extremely important during the period. Many outstanding English manor houses were owned by merchants; for example, Hever Castle in Kent was bought by Sir Geoffrey Boleyn, a textile dealer, in 1462. The house of Jacques Coeur in Bourges [3] is a French example of property being accumulated by the merchant classes. Merchants founded charitable institutions such as hospitals, and in England they also financed the building of many great "wool-churches" in East Anglia. In Europe generally, and especially in central Europe, this was the great age of the parish church, usually paid for by the local trading community but often built on a cathedral scale.

Late Gothic architecture

Late Gothic architecture tends toward the exotic. For the French version, with its flamelike tracery rippling over walls as well as in windows, the term "flamboyant" is appropriately used. Examples can be seen at Rouen (St Maclou), Caudebec in Normandy, and Notre Dame de l'Epine near Nancy. In the Iberian Peninsula plantlike decoration was popular, as at Alcobaça and Batalha abbeys in Portugal. In Germany and Bohemia architects designed ingenious new patterns for vaults. Net vaults were extremely popular: instead of the ribs splaying out from the supports and crossing at various angles, the whole area was covered by a fretwork of parallel ribs. Sometimes nave and aisles are treated together; but often there is a different pattern for each area, and at Nördlingen in Bavaria there are three patterns for the nave alone.

CONNECTIONS

Read first
1104 Gothic art of the 14th century

See also
1092 Gothic art 1140–120(
1094 Gothic art of the 13t century
1144 The German and Netherlandish Renaissance
1258 Architecture in the 19th century
1222 Origins of romanticis

1

1 Mehun-sur-Yèvre, the favorite castle of the Duc de Berry, was made even more fantastical in this illustration to his manuscript, the *Très Riches Heures*, than it ever appeared in reality.

2

2 The ruins of the Château of La Ferté Millon, built for a cousin of the Duc de Berry, give some idea of how fantasy castles really looked, even though it has now lost most of its ornamentation.

3

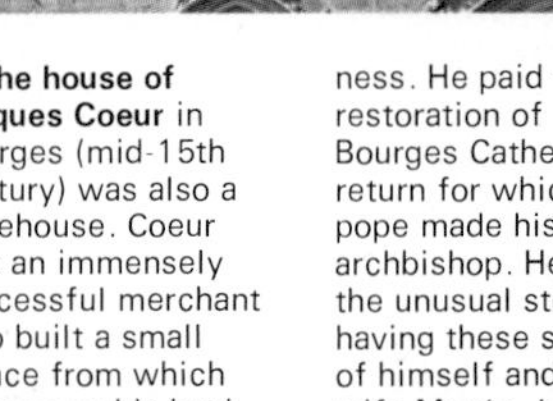

3 The house of Jacques Coeur in Bourges (mid-15th century) was also a warehouse. Coeur was an immensely successful merchant who built a small palace from which to carry on his business. He paid for the restoration of Bourges Cathedral, in return for which the pope made his son an archbishop. He took the unusual step of having these statues of himself and his wife Macée, leaning from behind stone balconies, added to the façade of the building. It was at this time that merchants throughout western Europe were having more influence on the arts as their wealth grew.

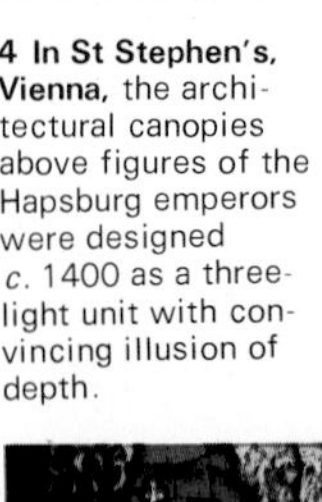

4 In St Stephen's, Vienna, the architectural canopies above figures of the Hapsburg emperors were designed *c.* 1400 as a three-light unit with convincing illusion of depth.

5 The six French tapestries of the "Lady with the Unicorn" in the Musée de Cluny, Paris, were made a little after 1500 for the Le Viste family. The tapestries show a new realism in the figures.

4

5

6

6 Little is known of medieval masons and builders, and portraits are rare. Adam Kraft (*c.* 1450– *c.* 1508) carved himself holding a mallet and chisel as one of the "Atlas" supports in the Sacrament House of the Church of St Lorenz, Nuremberg (1493). In sculpting this church he took the opportunity to invent architectural forms that did not have to bear any weight and that would writhe right up to the vault. He introduced a new restraint into late Gothic sculpture.

An alternative to the net vault is to make the ribs curve sinuously across the surface of the vault. This makes flowerlike effects, as at Wasserburg in Germany, and invites such excesses as making the rib appear to jump diagonally across the space of a window, as at Kutna Hora in Czechoslovakia. Similar artistry was lavished on the small structures that make up church furnishings: fonts, pulpits, and especially containers for the sacrament. These architectural motifs were repeated in the stained glass, which was often provided to add color to the interiors [9], and especially in the wooden altarpieces, which are such outstanding works of art of the period. Tilman Riemenschneider and Veit Stoss are justifiably the most famous carvers and sculptors. Their figures are so lifelike as to appear portraits, yet they are stylized in order to fit into the narrative subjects.

English architecture

English architects created a style known as Perpendicular, lavishing their efforts on vaults, with elaborate wooden angel-roofs as a substitute in smaller structures. Many vaults are variations of the lierne design (a system of smaller connecting ribs) of Canterbury: for instance, York Minster choir (*c.* 1400). Others like Bath Abbey, Sherborne Abbey (*c.* 1430 to *c.* 1500 in stages), St George's Chapel, Windsor (begun 1481), and Henry VII's chapel at Westminster, develop the idea of "fan" vaults [Key] first initiated in the cloister at Gloucester during the previous century.

In most Gothic decorative forms of the fifteenth century there is less variety than in the fourteenth, a trend that led, for example, to numerous instances of the same cartoon being used for stained glass in different churches. The figure of St John the Evangelist in Sherborne Almshouse, England, is repeated at East Brent in Somerset. Such repetition, both in art and architecture, reduced the original freshness and inventiveness of the Gothic style, permitting a readier acceptance of the Renaissance in northern Europe, where the Gothic and Renaissance styles were intermingled, especially in architecture.

KEY

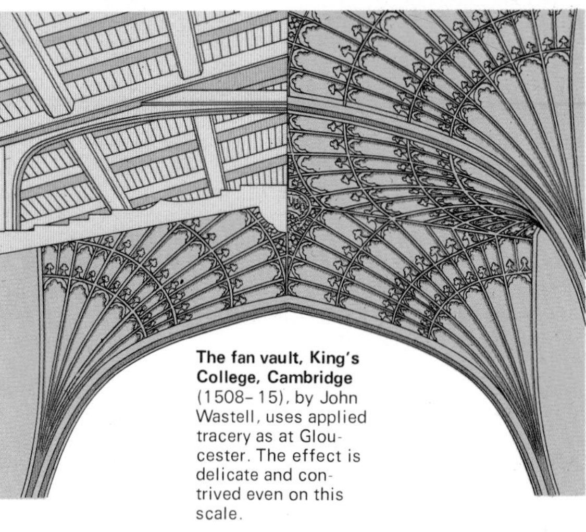

The fan vault, King's College, Cambridge (1508–15), by John Wastell, uses applied tracery as at Gloucester. The effect is delicate and contrived even on this scale.

7 The Royal Pew in St Vitus' Cathedral, Prague, demonstrates a different illusionism from that of the Church of St Lorenz. At Prague the normal stone rib construction is carved to imitate wood with its knots and forks. Benedict Ried's Vladislav Hall (1487–1502) and stairs in Hradčany Castle nearby have ribs that intersect and overshoot each other as if they were single branches.

8 The Hastings Hours (*c.* 1480), which includes a portrait of Edward V, contains detailed studies of wild and garden flowers and this picture of the royal barge on the River Thames.

8

9 The Beauchamp Chapel (*c.* 1447) of St Mary's Church, England, was a religious enterprise financed by lay patronage. No expense was spared over the sculpture of the Warwick tombs or the stained glass that fills the windows on three sides of the chapel. It includes a series of angels holding a continuous scroll of the Te Deum and magnificent figures in the east windows.

9

7

10

10 The Great Hall of Hampton Court Palace was built by Henry VIII in 1531–36 after the fall of Cardinal Wolsey. As at Warwick, all details were planned together to produce a rich effect. The hammer-beam roof, with elaborate pendants, was carved by Richard Rydge of London. Armorial glass filled the windows, and imported tapestries lined the walls of this domestic interior.

11 The cones of ribs in the vault of Oxford University Divinity School (1483) are designed to hang free as pendants. On a small scale this is the principle of the fan vault in Henry VII's chapel at Westminster Abbey (1503–19). The panels of tracery "ribs" there are merely carved on the surface of the stone slabs of which the vault is constructed. This is a measure of development of vaulting – that the load-bearers could be treated as ornament.

11

The Ottoman Empire to 1600

The Ottoman Turks or Osmanlis (so called after their founder Osman, who died in 1326) began as Muslim warriors who patrolled the eastern Byzantine borders. Osman's military genius raised them from nomadic tribesmen lacking any political institutions and a national consciousness to become the formidable potential masters of a great empire by the mid-fourteenth century.

Osman's son and successor Orkhan (ruled 1326–*c.*60) defeated a Byzantine army sent against him in 1329 and went on to capture Nicaea (Iznik) and other Greek cities. He annexed the neighboring Turkish principality of Karasi. But his success in the holy war against the Christians attracted numerous other Turkoman warriors voluntarily to his lucrative service. Before 1453 the emerging Ottoman state held more lands of greater extent in eastern Europe than its considerable provinces in Asia Minor.

An era of expansion

By the time Orkhan's son Suleiman had set himself up in Gallipoli in 1354, the Ottomans commanded a large enough army to begin major campaigns against Europe. Murad I, Suleiman's brother and Orkhan's successor, took Adrianople and by 1365 had made it his European capital, thus establishing a pattern of conquest whereby the Turks took over a Greek capital and with it the machinery both of government and Church administration; they employed the local clergy as tax collectors and held them responsible for the behavior of their charges. The average peasant was allowed as much freedom as he had enjoyed under Greek rule, if not more. Ottoman society was very flexible, and the success of the Turks was in part due to the greater opportunities they offered to the peasant class.

The move westward was halted momentarily during the latter part of the fourteenth century by the incursions into Anatolia of the Tatar ruler Timur (Tamerlane). Timur set up independent Turkoman emirates and although these did not survive long, their existence demonstrated the weakness of the empire. As long as the Ottoman objective remained the conquest of European territory (and the militarist structure of the state made constant expansion a necessity), Anatolia, so vital to the survival of the empire, would be vulnerable to Tatar and Persian attacks as well as to internal revolt.

The golden age

The golden age of Ottoman power occurred under Murad II (ruled 1421–51) and his son Mohammed II (ruled 1451–81). Murad was responsible for the creation of the Janissaries [Key], a corps of troops and administrators conscripted from among the Christians of the Balkans and raised to unquestioning obedience. This levy, called the *devşirme*, created a new social class whose fortunes were identified with the sultanate.

Mohammed II, called "The Conqueror," was responsible for the demise of the Byzantine Empire. In 1453, after a prolonged siege, he took Constantinople (now Istanbul), [3, 4], thus giving the empire the cultural and administrative center it had lacked. Mohammed's achievement was to reunite the old Eastern Empire under a single sovereign. The relocation of the sultan and his court to the new capital finally

CONNECTIONS

See also
1062 Arabs and the rise of Islam
1084 The Crusades
1122 The age of exploration
1064 Islamic art

1 The major east-west trade routes were taken over by the Ottoman Empire as it absorbed the old Greek world. Trading stations in the Peloponnesus, along the Sea of Marmara, and also in Cyprus, came under attack. But commercial interest was only one motive for Turkish aggression, and trade profits were sometimes sacrificed to serve the Ottoman economy's overriding need for military expansion into the non-Islamic countries of Europe to maintain control.

Sea trade routes 15th century
Land trade routes
Ottoman Empire 1480
Ottoman Empire 1600

2 Caravansaries were built as staging inns for the camel caravans that carried trade for the Ottoman Empire over a vast network of overland routes to and from the East. These routes declined when trade with India began to go by sea. The traditional caravansary, following the Persian model, consisted of a two-tiered building with a lower floor that consisted of stables built round an open courtyard. The oldest of these buildings still standing dates back to about 1080.

3 When Constantinople (seen here on a 15th-century map) fell in 1453, a new phase of Ottoman history began. The great city had long been the focus of Turkish ambition, but repeated attempts to overcome it had failed. When at last the old Byzantine capital was taken it became the Ottoman Empire's cultural and administrative center.

Stone frame around glazed brickwork
Glazed tiles
Stairs
Arcade

4 The Topkapi Sarayi or Old Palace was built by Mohammed II, the conqueror of Constantinople, on the site of the old Acropolis. One of the earliest Ottoman buildings in the new capital, it was the sultan's official residence and also housed the harem. It was built around a series of courtyards and was conceived on a grand scale.

brought about the triumph of the *devşirme* faction over the old Turkoman nobility, but it also removed the center of power from Anatolia.

The next major period of expansion occurred under Suleiman I, "The Magnificent" (ruled 1520–66) [5, 6], who extended the empire still farther into Europe. The main force of the attack fell on Hungary, which in 1526 became a vassal state of the sultan. But the need to maintain a strong presence in Anatolia and the problems of supply and transport over such vast areas meant that no farther westward expansion was feasible. The siege of Vienna in 1529 [6] was a failure. The struggle by sea, however, continued, for the shipbuilding yards at Constantinople had made the Ottoman Empire a major sea power. It was the Battle of Lepanto in 1571 [8] that finally drove the Turks back into the eastern Mediterranean.

Decline and fall

Throughout the late fifteenth and the sixteenth centuries the two superpowers, the Ottomans and the Hapsburgs, faced each other menacingly. But by 1600 Ottoman power began to decline as a result of internal discord, factional struggles, and harem politics at the center, as well as constant pressure on the eastern frontiers. A mid-seventeenth-century revival ended when the second siege of Vienna failed in 1683.

The Ottoman Empire remained throughout its long history essentially tribal in structure. The divan, the sultan's administrative body, had only slight powers, and although after the reign of Suleimān the Grand Vizier came increasingly to rule the empire, his position was always tenuous and provided no means for an easy succession if he died or fell from favor. The distribution of land in *timars,* quasi-feudal grants, never created a landed nobility that could identify itself with the sultan, and although the *devşirme* gave the sultan a strong military power base, they also alienated him from the Turkoman nobility and became themselves in time a threat to his security. Despite internal weaknesses, the Ottoman Empire succeeded in knitting into a single people a group of scattered nomads.

KEY

The Janissaries were recruited from Balkan Christians originally taken at the capture of Adrianople and reared as Muslims with unquestioning obedience to the sultan. They were not only the army's best soldiers, but after they had received *timars* (land grants), they formed a social class. Because they had no links with any of the traditional tribal groups, they became the sultan's chief defense against the Turkoman nobles, who resented attempts to curtail their autonomy. After the 17th century the sultanate declined, and the Janissaries, like the barbarians in the Roman army in the 3rd century, came to manipulate rather than uphold the government.

5

5 Suleiman I, called "The Magnificent," brought the empire to the height of its power. Here is a scene depicting daily life in Egypt—a mark of the extent of his military power and authority over his empire.

6

6 The first siege of Vienna, undertaken by Suleiman the Magnificent in 1529, marked the limit of Ottoman expansion in the West. Ottoman supply lines already stretched too far from Istanbul.

7

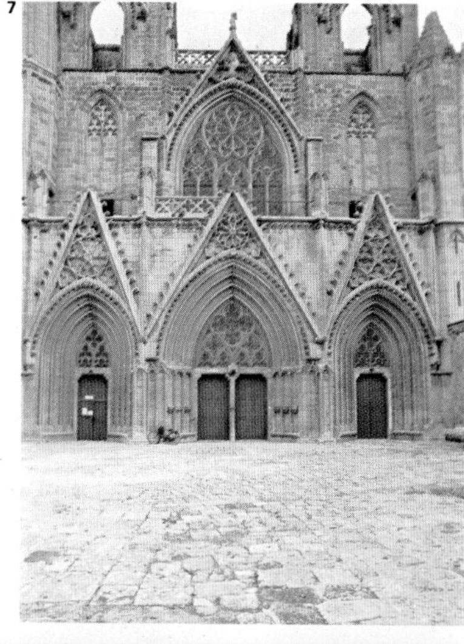

7 The Cathedral at Famagusta symbolized the magnificence of Cyprus under Venetian rule. In the 1500s it had become the wealthiest island in the Mediterranean. The Ottoman conquest of the island in 1570 was the main event in the reign of Sultan Selim II, an otherwise unworthy successor of Suleiman the Magnificent. It marked the beginning of a new phase of hostilities between Christians in the West and the Turks. The war was fought largely at sea and culminated in the Battle of Lepanto in 1571, lost by the Turks.

8

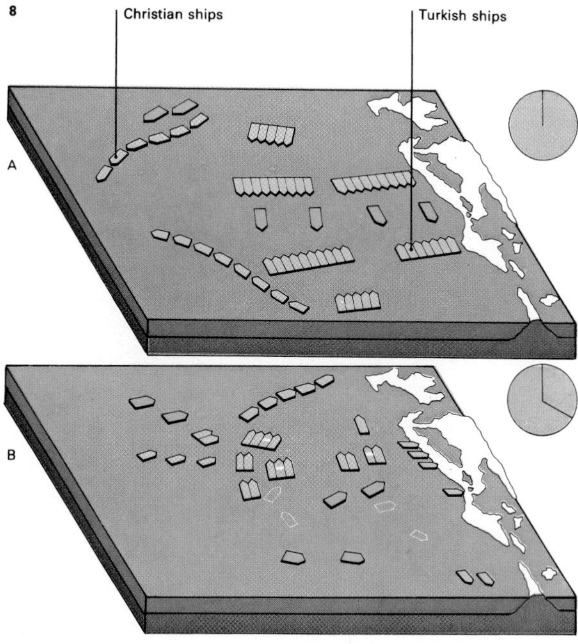
Christian ships
Turkish ships
A
B

8 The Battle of Lepanto, between the allies (Spain, Venice, and the papacy) and the combined Ottoman fleet was fought off the Greek coast. At the start [A], both navies were grouped in two advance lines and one rearguard. The Christians had both galleasses (dark blue) and galleys (light blue). Four hours later [B] the Turkish fleet lay scattered with most of its ships beached, sunk (white outlines), or boarded (white-barred vessels between blue).

9

9 A miniature painting of Suleiman from the mid-1500s shows the borrowing of foreign styles typical of Turkish art. The Turks adapted the skills of their subjects. There is little original Turkish art.

The world Europe set out to explore

At the end of the fifteenth century Vasco da Gama (*c.*1469–1525) sailed around the Cape of Good Hope to India and Christopher Columbus (1451–1506) stumbled upon the Americas, beginning an age of discovery in which Europeans were to navigate the seven seas, make their landfall in most of the inhabited regions of the globe, and come to think of the world as a whole. The voyages east, however, took new routes to reach places already, if imperfectly, known.

Alexander the Great had marched Greeks through Persia into India; Rome had bought Asia's goods and had bequeathed Ptolemy's geography to medieval Europe; Byzantium had long been a bridge between Europe and Asia. But the hostile crescent of Islam had hemmed in Christian Europe, cutting it off from the outside world until the conquests of Genghis Khan (*c.*1167–1227) [4] gave it respite from Islamic pressure.

The achievement of Marco Polo

The Mongol empires, stretching from Russia to China, straddled the land routes between Europe and Asia and allowed the two continents to trade directly. In 1271 Marco Polo (*c.*1254–*c.*1324) traveled with his father and uncle via Bokhara to Kublai Khan's court at Peking [2], and in the mid-fourteenth century an Italian handbook for merchants, *La Practica della Mercatura,* described the 140-day journey from the Black Sea to China [3] and listed 288 spices and drugs that could be bought in Asian markets. But the tenuous links established by traders and missionaries were once again snapped by the hordes of Tamerlane (*c.*1336–1405) and the dynasties that succeeded the Tartar (Tatar) empires. Thus, finding a way of sailing directly to the East became very important for Europe.

The importance of China

At the end of the long journey east lay China, where the native Ming dynasty (1368–1644) expelled the foreign Mongols, cultivated its own empire, restored its economy, and refined its bureaucracy. Threatened by offshore rivals and by the scourge of Japanese piracy, the Ming withdrew into partial isolation, broke off relations with some of China's old tributaries, forbade its people to travel overseas, ejected foreign traders, and prohibited private foreign trade. But the first Ming emperor had established relations with 17 neighboring states, and in 1502 more than 150 self-styled rulers from Central Asia traded with China under the cloak of tribute relations. The maritime expeditions of Cheng Ho [6] hinted at a vast Chinese potential for expansion by sea that was never to be realized.

Its self-denying ordinance prevented Ming China from fully exploiting the valuable interport trade of the Indian Ocean, with its hub in the archipelago. This was left to the merchant principalities of the East Indies and to Arab, Persian, and Indian traders. Since the time of the Cholas, India's mainland empires, expanding from their bases in Hindustan, were more concerned with defending their northern frontiers and acquiring territory in the south than with probing overseas. Babur (1483–1530) the first of the Moguls, began his conquest of India soon after Vasco da Gama reached Calicut. But the empire he founded

CONNECTIONS

See also

1122 The age of exploration
1112 Asian empires of the Mongols
1042 China 618–1368
1206 China from 1368 to c.1800
1118 Mesoamerica 300–1521
1120 Colombia and Peru 300–1534

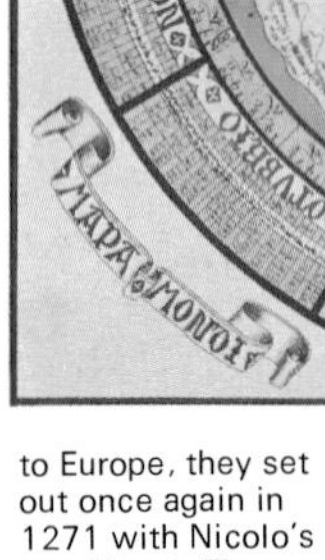

1 This Venetian map of 1448 shows how the typical medieval "wheel" map of the world was beginning to change. The medieval *mappamundi* was biblically inspired, with Jerusalem at the center, the terrestrial paradise at the top and systematically disposed continents. By the mid-15th century the conventional medieval map was showing the influence of contemporary marine charts and was being enriched by incorporating information from travelers. It was also modified by the recovery of classical writing about the outside world, in particular the geography of Ptolemy and Fra Mauro, as evidenced by the execution of this map.

2 Marco Polo traveled to Peking in 1271 and served the Mongols in the East for about 20 years. Returning to Venice in 1295, Polo gave Europe its first detailed account of China and its neighbors in *The Description of the World.* It was the most comprehensive account of the East produced before 1550, full of details about cities, canals, rivers, ports, and industries. A practical administrator and merchant, Polo took little note of religion and civilization, but his accounts are factual and relatively free from the fantasies that characterized contemporary travel literature. He thus revised the European picture of Asia.

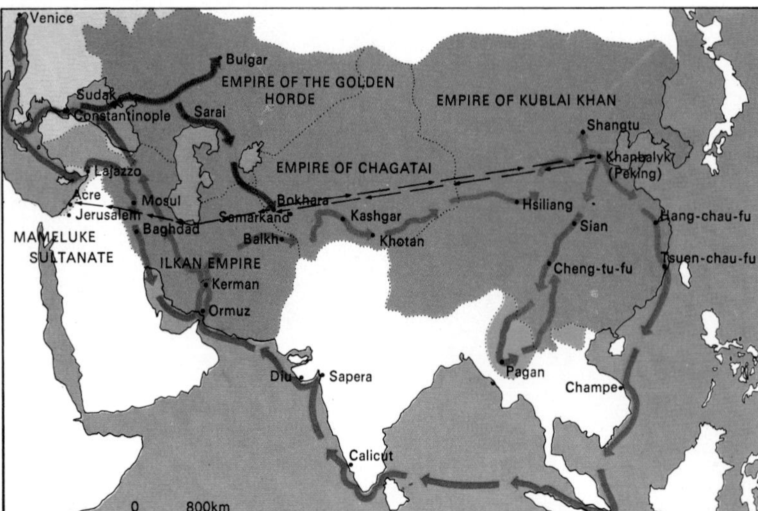

Venice
Bulgar
EMPIRE OF THE GOLDEN HORDE
EMPIRE OF KUBLAI KHAN
Sudak
Constantinople
Sarai
Shangtu
Khanbalyk (Peking)
EMPIRE OF CHAGATAI
Lajazzo
Acre
Mosul
Jerusalem
Bokhara
Samarkand
Baghdad
Kashgar
Hsiliang
Sian
Hang-chau-fu
MAMELUKE SULTANATE
Balkh
Khotan
Tsuen-chau-fu
ILKAN EMPIRE
Kerman
Cheng-tu-fu
Ormuz
Diu
Sapera
Pagan
Champe
Calicut
0 800km

3 In 1260 the Polos, Nicolo and Maffeo, traveled from the Crimea via Bokhara to Peking. Returning to Europe, they set out once again in 1271 with Nicolo's son Marco. The return trip, from 1292–95, was via Malaya, Sumatra, and India. These journeys revealed how Mongolian rule had helped to connect Europe with Asia and enabled Europeans to learn about the East.

Mongol Empire late 13th century
Mongol tributaries late 13th century
Christian world late 13th century
Polo's known first journey 1260-69
Unknown portion of first journey.
Polo's second journey 1271–95

4 Genghis Khan, the Tartar conqueror, dealt harshly with the civilized Chinese, selling many people into slavery. The Chinese resented the khan; and they did not appreciate the links that their conqueror forged for them with the outside world. For China, the imposition of Mongol rule meant that the continuity of its traditions had been broken. The Mongols were looked upon as foreign overlords and were finally expelled by the native Ming dynasty in the 14th century.

remained land-based, regarding with tolerance the activities of traders at its ports.

Europe's deadliest enemies were also its closest neighbors—the Ottoman Turks. By capturing Constantinople in 1453 [5], the Ottomans took possession of the gateway between Europe and Asia; by taking Mameluke Egypt in 1517 (the Mamelukes, originally foreign slaves, had controlled Egypt since 1250) and Syria (1516–17), they destroyed the European trade route east and wrested much of the eastern trade from the Venetians and Genoese.

The Ottomans move into Europe

Perhaps the most fateful decision in modern times was the Ottoman resolve to push westward into Europe. The Ottoman armies marched across the plains of Hungary to the gates of Vienna and maintained their navy in the Mediterranean. By establishing themselves throughout the Balkans, the Black Sea region, and the Levant, the Ottomans sealed off these areas from European expansion and gave the Iberian powers on the far western tip of Europe the incentive to find new outlets, whether by sending their ships creeping eastward around Africa or by making their landfall in America.

In Asia, Europe once again came into contact with great oriental despotisms, many of them Muslim, which it did not dare to challenge and which it could not hope to penetrate. In their journeys to the east by the new sea routes, Europeans only touched upon the western and eastern edges of Africa, a continent whose northern territories had long been influenced by Islam but whose interior was long to remain unknown to the rest of the world.

In the New World the story was different. Here the Europeans actually discovered a continent that was out of touch with the rest of the world. There were remote, isolated civilizations that had wondrous monuments and elaborate customs, but their technologies lagged far behind those of Europe or Asia. America's discovery by Europe opened it swiftly to the full blast of European influence: conquest and exploitation, disease and religion. The result was a clash of two wholly different cultures.

KEY
Until Marco Polo's return to Venice, Europe knew little about mainland Asia, which was thought a continent of monsters and demons. In the 12th century, Christians debated whether the dog-headed men of India might be converted, and even as late as the 14th century Western manuscripts showed Indians with dog heads, fantasies that the discovery of direct sea routes to the East were at last effectively to dispel.

5

5 The siege of Constantinople in 1453 illustrates the fact that Europe in the 15th century was contracting, not expanding. The Ottomans had triumphed against the last Crusade from Europe. The capture of Constantinople meant that the Ottomans were in Europe to stay.

6

6 Cheng Ho's seven maritime expeditions, (the first began in 1405) visited over 30 countries and were remarkable feats of seamanship. The largest of his ships was 400 ft (121m) long and 180 ft (54m) wide, with four decks and watertight compartments. The 62 ships on his voyage to India carried 28,000 men.

7 Nicolas Deslien's "upside-down" map of the world of 1567, based on lost Portuguese originals, shows how radically the European view of the world was changing as exploration continued. Whereas maps in the Ptolemaic tradition had often been drawn with east at the left and Jerusalem at the center, this has north at the bottom and, as nearly as possible, France at the center. Its accurate description of known parts of the world reflects the growing precision of navigational techniques, but when describing unknown parts—the land mass to the south of Java, for example—it is still inaccurate.

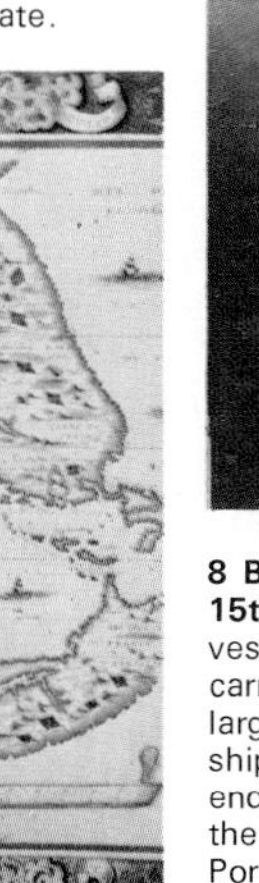

7

8

8 By the end of the 15th century, the vessels known as carracks were the largest merchant ships, at the other end of the scale from the small caravels. Portuguese carracks could be from 600–1,000 tons, and were heavily built, with large castles, commonly three-masted with square-rigging on fore and main and with lateen mizzens. The castle structures became more elaborate (as this 16th-century picture shows), and they were more often incorporated into the bull. These were the ships whose size, capacity for goods and men, and solid construction made them the vessel most often chosen by the Portuguese in their eastern reconnaissance and trade, even though their bulk made them less well suited than smaller ships to carrying out the more detailed tasks of exploration.

Asian empires of the Mongols

The Mongol Empire, at the height of its power in the thirteenth century, was the largest land empire in history. It stretched from the Yellow Sea in the east to the Danube in the west and included areas of what is now the modern Soviet Union, China, and Iran.

The origins of the Mongols are obscure. They were traditionally nomadic tribes who lived in felt tents called *yurts* and followed their herds of horses, cattle, camels, and sheep on an annual round of pasturage in the areas that are now Manchuria, Mongolia, and Siberia. The numerous, loosely organized, and constantly feuding Mongol tribes were first brought together as a unified nation under Genghis Khan (*c.* 1162–1227), who, because of his successes in tribal warfare, was proclaimed ruler of all the Mongols in 1206 [2].

Genghis Khan and the Mongol Empire

Genghis Khan's first move was to reorganize the major tribal groups in Mongolia as well as those on the Siberian borders. He then turned his attention to China. In 1211 he launched an attack on the Chin Empire, in northern China, an attack that continued until the whole of China came under Mongol domination on the surrender of the last of the Sung in 1279.

But China was not the only target: the previously unknown Mongols raided the west also. In 1219–20 Genghis defeated Mohammed Shah of Khwarizm and as a result acquired Transoxiana and Persia. Two of his generals defeated successively the Georgians, the Kuman-Turks on the Volga-Don steepe—later to provide the manpower reserve of the Mongol Golden Horde that dominated Russia—and the Russian armies themselves on the Dnieper. The Mongols then withdrew to Central Asia.

Campaigns of Genghis Khan's successors

Ogodei (1185–1241), who succeeded to the khanate after the death of Genghis in 1227, resumed the western offensive, and Persia, Georgia, and Armenia were overrun as far as the Black Sea. At the same time, the eastern campaign led to the defeat of the Chin in 1234 and pressure against the Sung dynasty in South China increased.

Batu (died 1255), Genghis's grandson, drove north of the Caspian and the Caucasus into Europe, defeating the Bulgars on the Volga and capturing many cities, including Kiev, before splitting his army into two and initiating attacks on Poland and Hungary. Cracow and Breslau were captured, and a German and Polish army was defeated at Legnica in 1241. Batu himself devastated the Hungarian army at the Sajo, captured the towns of Pesth and Gran, and then led his forces to the Adriatic.

Another grandson, Hulagu (1217–65) [6], the founder of the Persian Ilkhan dynasty (the title recognized subordination to the Great Khan), campaigned to the southwest. The Isma'ili sect, the Assassins, lost their great stronghold of Maymundiz in 1256; Baghdad fell in 1258 when the Abbasid Caliph was killed. The conquest of Aleppo and Damascus followed, but in 1260 the Mongols met their first defeat, at Ain Jalut at the hands of the Mamelukes under Baibars (1233–77).

CONNECTIONS

See also
1176 Medieval Russia 900–1600
1056 The Byzantine Empire
1210 Japan 1185–1868
1114 The empires of South-east Asia

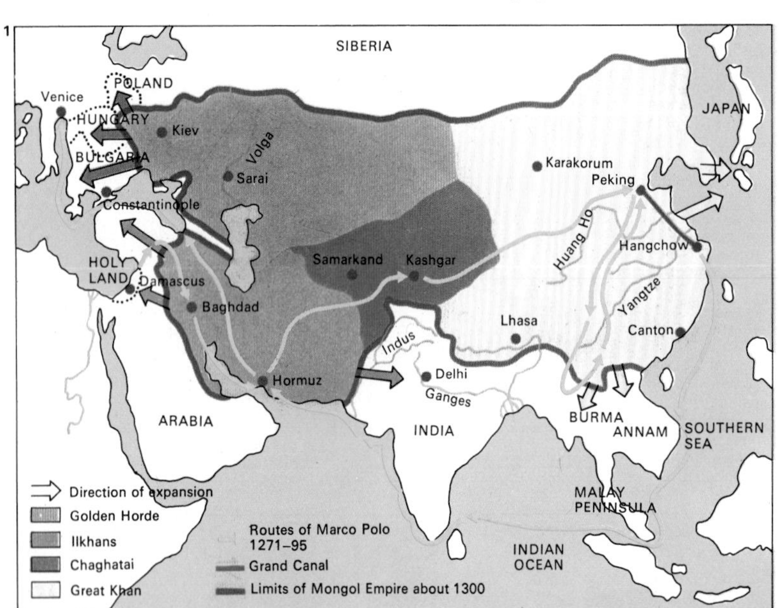
SIBERIA
POLAND
Venice
HUNGARY
Kiev
BULGARIA
Volga
Sarai
Constantinople
JAPAN
Karakorum
Peking
Huang Ho
Hangchow
HOLY LAND
Damascus
Samarkand
Kashgar
Baghdad
Yangtze
Lhasa
Canton
Indus
Hormuz
Delhi
Ganges
ARABIA
INDIA
BURMA
ANNAM
SOUTHERN SEA
MALAY PENINSULA
INDIAN OCEAN
Direction of expansion
Golden Horde
Ilkhans
Chaghatai
Great Khan
Routes of Marco Polo 1271–95
Grand Canal
Limits of Mongol Empire about 1300

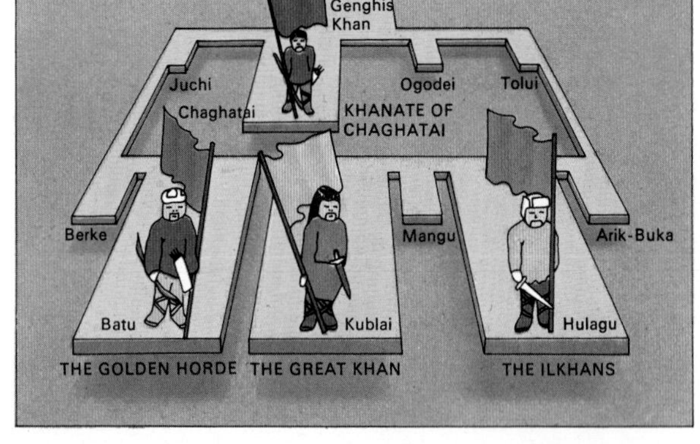
Genghis Khan
Juchi
Ogodei
Tolui
Chaghatai
KHANATE OF CHAGHATAI
Berke
Mangu
Arik-Buka
Batu
Kublai
Hulagu
THE GOLDEN HORDE
THE GREAT KHAN
THE ILKHANS

1 Despite the terror that the Mongols inspired, their domination of large areas of Asia and parts of Europe led to the development of trade routes used by traders of many nations in the 13th century. The Venetian Marco Polo set out for Peking in 1271. It was more than 20 years before he returned to Europe to describe the wealth and splendor of the Khan's court, increasing interest in Asia.

2 Genghis Khan united the Mongol tribes in 1206 under his leadership. After his death in 1227, the growing Mongol empire was divided into four among his descendants, with Ogodei as chief.

3 Genghis Khan, portrayed here by a Chinese artist, was a politician as well as a warrior. He skillfully used patronage and alliances to further his aims.

4 A Yuan empress (from the dynasty founded by Kublai Khan) wears a medieval Mongolian headdress. Similar headdresses were worn in this century.

5 Mongol troops are shown attacking a town with the aid of siege engines. These engines, called mangonels, were made by a German in China in the year 1273.

The Mongol army in this battle was commanded by the Christian Kitbogha, which illustrates the wide range of religions accepted by the Mongols [8]. Shamanism, Buddhism, Islam, and Nestorian Christianity were all practiced, but in general the Mongols themselves were Shamanists. This tolerance explains the presence of various Christian priests at the Mongol court, and encouraged Marco Polo (1254–1324) to travel to China with his uncle and father.

Kublai Khan conquers China

In 1260 Kublai (1216–94) became Great Khan, moving his capital from Karakorum to the site of present-day Peking in 1264. From there he conducted the campaigns that led to the annexation of all China.

Although the campaign did not finish until 1279, the Yuan dynasty that Kublai founded is generally considered to run from the foundation of the new capital until the last ruler fled before the Ming armies to seek refuge in the Mongol homeland in 1368. But the unified Mongol empire of which Kublai was the last ruler had broken up earlier, for by 1295 the western khans had accepted Islam and were no longer willing to submit to the overlordship of a non-Muslim khan.

Nor did all Kublai's campaigns prove successful. In the north he was never able to subdue Kaidu (died 1301), the grandson of Ogodei. To the south, Burma surrendered but was not occupied, while in northern Vietnam disease forced a withdrawal. A sea-borne campaign against Java was defeated, as was an attempted invasion of Japan. After Kublai's death there were nine rulers up to 1368. The dissolute rule of the last emperor, Togan Timur, saw revolts and chaos develop into open rebellion in 1348 and eventual defeat by the Chinese.

In the Middle East and in Russia, Mongol dynasties continued to rule until 1502, although by that time they were little more than nominally Mongol because their various conquests had diluted the original Mongol groups to an enormous extent. The time when a trader might travel from Tana on the Black Sea to the coasts of north China in substantial safety by day or night had come to an end.

KEY

The horsemen who formed the elite of the Mongol armies were the key to their military success. They were trained to use the bow or sword while at full gallop, inspiring great fear.

6

6 Hulagu invaded Iran in 1256, captured Baghdad, and later defeated the Assassins, but was himself defeated by the Mamelukes in Syria. This was a turning point in the Mongols' history.

7

7 The Gur Emir, the tomb of Tamerlane (1336–1405) at Samarkand, was finished in 1434. This is one of the many magnificent buildings that this Mongol ruler, who was a great patron of the arts as well as a warrior, had constructed in Turkestan, his favorite region, and elsewhere. With his nomadic Tatar supporters, he temporarily reunited the original empire of Genghis Khan.

8

8 The Prophet Jeremiah is illustrated in Rashid-al-Din's *History of the World* (1306). The author, a physician in the court of Abaga-Khan, the mongol ruler of Persia, included biblical themes in his world history – an indication of Mongol tolerance of alien religions. This illustration also shows Chinese cultural influences – another indication of Mongol absorption of foreign ideas. Khans invited religious debate.

The empires of Southeast Asia

The lands that lie along the maritime route between the Indian subcontinent and China [1] have been strongly influenced by both these regions. Except in Vietnam, the major cultural influence has been from India in the west, but during most of the Christian era the kingdoms of Southeast Asia have recognized, to a greater or lesser degree, the political suzerainty of China in the north.

The first centuries AD

The involvement of India and China in the affairs of this complex region seems to have been the largely accidental result of a need to find an alternative route between them when the land journey was made difficult by political instability in central Asia. But Southeast Asia had already achieved a considerable degree of technological, economic, and political development by the time it came under the influence of its larger neighbors in the first centuries AD.

Lin-i, with its capital near Hué, and Fu-nan, in the Mekong Delta are two of the best known states that existed to the south of China in the early Christian era. Lin-i became the kingdom of Champa, which dominated central Vietnam and parts of the south until the fourteenth century. Fu-nan grew into a substantial empire that dominated the greater part of the northern and eastern shores of the Gulf of Siam and their hinterland until the center of power shifted, about the middle of the sixth century, to a former vassal state, Chen-la, probably in the vicinity of the Tonle Sap. From this kingdom the Khmer Empire or Cambodia [Key] developed from the beginning of the ninth century onward. To the west, in the seventh century, lay Dvaravati, near present-day Bangkok, and farther west again, in Burma, lay the Pyu kingdom of Shrikshetra, with its capital at Prome.

Southward in the Indonesian archipelago, and on the Malaysian peninsula (parts of which seem to have been dominated by Fu-nan), a number of small kingdoms flourished due at least in part to the development of trading routes between China and the West. These routes brought Buddhist pilgrims through the region and traders whose posts seem to have attracted teachers of Hinduism as well. These two faiths, originating in India, were to become the state religions of Southeast Asia, a role that Buddhism has retained until the present. But Hinduism [5, 7] has, except in Bali, almost disappeared.

Buddhist and Hindu influences

By about the seventh century AD a Chinese Buddhist traveler, I-ching, was advising his fellows to spend some time in Sumatra studying Sanskrit and Buddhism before going on to India. He himself spent almost a decade there translating Buddhist texts into Chinese. The rise of this center in western Indonesia, the beginnings of a state known as Shrivijaya which exercised commercial control in western Southeast Asia for several centuries, followed a shift of power from the coast to the interior on the mainland. Meanwhile, elsewhere in the archipelago, in west Java (Taruma) and Borneo, Indian influences began to be detectable, and a major dynasty—the Shailendras, Lords of the Mountain, who may have had links with Fu-nan—came to power in

CONNECTIONS

See also
1038 China 1000 BC–AD 618
1042 China 618–1368
988 Buddha and Buddhism
1062 Arabs and the rise of Islam
1112 Asian empires of the Mongols

1

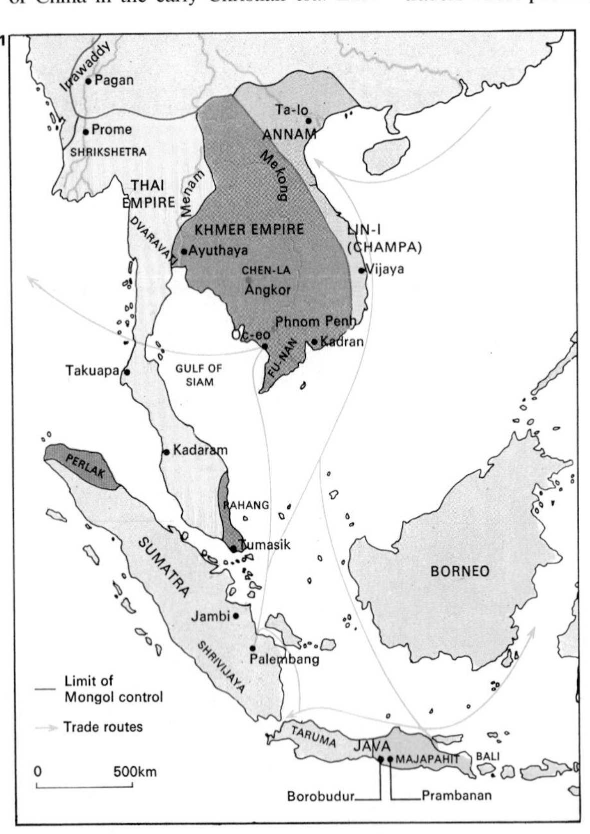
Irawaddy
Pagan
Prome
SHRIKSHETRA
THAI EMPIRE
Menam
DVARAVATI
Ta-lo
ANNAM
Mekong
KHMER EMPIRE
Ayuthaya
CHEN-LA
Angkor
LIN-I (CHAMPA)
Vijaya
Phnom Penh
Oc-eo
FU-NAN
Kadran
Takuapa
GULF OF SIAM
Kadaram
PERLAK
PAHANG
Tumasik
SUMATRA
Jambi
Palembang
SHRIVIJAYA
BORNEO
TARUMA
JAVA
MAJAPAHIT
BALI
Borobudur
Prambanan
Limit of Mongol control
Trade routes
0 500km

1 The geographic position of Southeast Asia, lying between India and China at the center of a monsoon system that facilitated sailing to and from both these countries, explains much of its cultural development and historical importance. The thriving commercial trade, carried inland along the great river systems, also brought a diversity of religious, political, and cultural influences to the area.

2

2 Chandi Plaosan in central Java is a large Buddhist complex built about the mid 9th century. Two apparently symmetrical groups have central shrines framed by rectangles of temples. Each main building is two-storied and houses a pantheon of Buddhas and Bodhisattvas. Inscriptions say that the images "shine forth the Doctrine," and windows were evidently arranged to create a radiant effect.

3

4

3 Borobudur, one of the world's greatest Buddhist shrines, was built in Java during the 9th century to a unique plan involving colossal resources—two million cubic feet (570,000 cubic meters) of stone were moved from a riverbed, dressed, positioned, and carved with countless spouts, urns, and other embellishments. The walls are covered with reliefs relating to Buddhist doctrine, and there are altogether 504 shrines with seated Buddhas at each one.

4 Chandi Mendut, a small temple of the Borobudur group, probably served as an antechapel. This relief, on the north wall of the porch, shows Kuvera, god of wealth, often associated with the merchant class who supported Buddhism.

central Java. There, from about the eighth to the ninth centuries, Buddhism [2] appears to have flourished, its culmination being seen in the shrine of Borobudur [3, 4], with its miles of reliefs expounding the faith.

Hinduism was not neglected, however, and it was perhaps from this setting that Jayavarman II (*c.* 770–850), "returning from Java" as an inscription says, established in Cambodia the kingdom that dominated the central mainland from about the ninth to the fourteenth centuries. Hinduism, centered upon a lingam (phallic) cult located in a temple at the center of the capital, was the state religion. The temples were of ever-increasing complexity, culminating in the magnificent structure of Angkor Wat [8] and the enigmatic Bayon in the center of Angkor Thom. The economic strain of these ostentatious building programs contributed to the fall of the Khmer Empire under attacks from both the Thai and the Vietnamese.

Eastern Java, also perhaps for socio-economic reasons, saw the rise of a state whose maritime power enabled it to repel a Chinese fleet in 1293—the kingdom of Majapahit. Its influence extended as far west as central Sumatra, and its blending of Hinduism and Buddhism was the culmination of a trend that can be detected in central Java as early as 782. The end of this kingdom seems to have been linked with the coming of Islam, which, already established in northern Sumatra at the time of Marco Polo's visit in 1291, became important on the coast of Java a century or so later, although Majapahit's fall is traditionally dated to 1480.

Developments on the mainland

On the mainland, the Mongols, although unsuccessful in Java, had intervened with limited results in Vietnam. In Burma, the kingdom centered upon Pagan on the Irrawaddy, where some thousands of temples built over a period of two centuries testify to the power of Buddhism. It fell to the Mongols in 1287. At about the same time, Rama Khamhaeng consolidated Thai power in what had been the western part of the Khmer Empire to found the present state of Thailand.

KEY

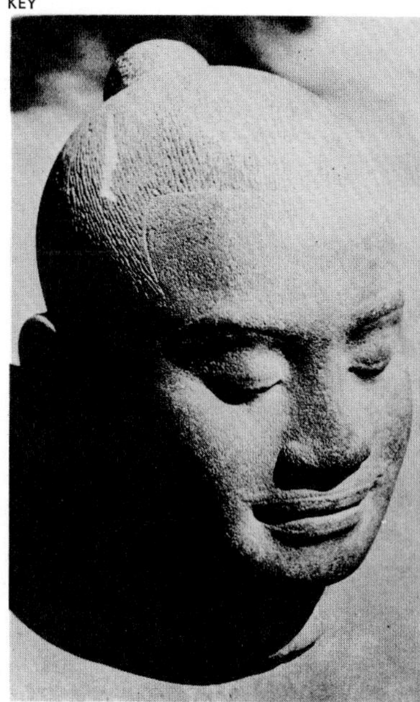

Jayavarman VII (*c.* 1120–1215) became king of Cambodia in 1181 after driving out Cham invaders. Following his father, Suryavarman II, who built Angkor Wat, he embarked on an enormous building program. In addition to temples and associated buildings he created hospitals and resthouses for travelers and improved roads, with many stone bridges still in use today. Most of his predecessors were Hindu, identifying themselves with Hindu gods; Jayavarman was a Buddhist who seems to have had a special relationship with the god Lokeshvara (shown here), whose carved head dominates the towers and gateways of his buildings.

5

5 A terra cotta head from southern Thailand depicts a manifestation of Shiva's wrath—a creature that ate its own body to satisfy its hunger after the demon it was born to eat had been pardoned.

6

6 The Lake Pavilion at the Summer Palace, Bangkok, with its elaborate carving and gilding, is a reminder that bamboo and wood have been used as the materials for most buildings in Southeast Asia during the past millennium (as they are today). Even shrines and their images were often wooden, so that much of the past has been lost from the archeological record.

7

7 Garuda, vehicle of the god Vishnu, was a magic bird and enemy of snakes. In Southeast Asia it became a divinity in its own right and was the center of cults of salvation of various kinds.

8

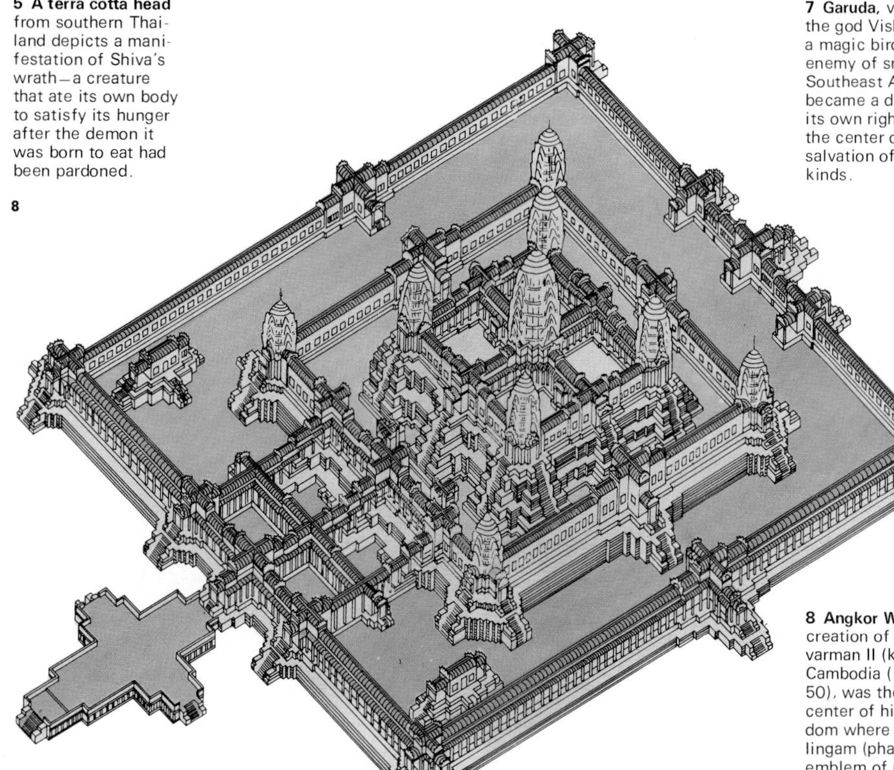

8 Angkor Wat, the creation of Suryavarman II (king of Cambodia (*c.* 1113–50), was the ritual center of his kingdom where the royal lingam (phallus), emblem of power, was housed. The outer cloister, 4,529 × 3,733ft (1,380 × 1,150m), enclosed a complex of buildings, the main group arranged as a square of four at the corners and one in the center. All were covered in exquisite low relief with divine dancers, plants, birds, and animals. The many towers housed images. The walls of the central group were covered with reliefs depicting Hindu stories and battle scenes. In two, the king was shown. It was to be his shrine after death when he became identified with the god Vishnu.

African empires 500–1500

The most obvious sign of Africa's emergence from the primitive status of a "prehistorical continent" was the growth of political states [1]. The 1,000 years from AD 500 to 1500 saw the gradual emergence and then the great flowering of the black kingdoms that created such a rich and varied culture. By the beginning of the sixteenth century, much of the continent had entered this stage, evolving organized political societies with rulers, armies under their direct command, and stratified social classes. These states were economically supported by the tribute that could be exacted from the mainly agricultural peoples considered to be their subjects. In many instances, rulers also controlled important trade routes.

The first black empires

The most ancient black African states were the empires of Kush/Meroë in the middle Nile valley (*c.*800 BC–AD *c.*400) and Axum in northeastern Ethiopia (first to fifth centuries AD). These were shaped by the influence of Egypt and south Arabia, respectively, and although they had considerable effects upon later societies, were rather special cases. These empires apart, the main African empires were in the Sudanic belt, that is, in the area to the south of the Sahara and north of the tropical forests, running from Senegal in the west to the Nile valley in the east.

The earliest of these Sudanese empires was Ghana, which was founded by the West African Soninke people. By AD 800 it had emerged as a powerful trading state, ruling the whole of the country between the Senegal and Upper Niger rivers. The prosperity of Ghana was based largely upon its control of the gold trade. The gold fields of West Africa lay well to the south, and Ghanaian traders obtained the precious metal by a strange process known as dumb barter, in which the gold producers never met these traders face to face. The Ghanaians then sold the gold to North African merchants, who gathered in the southernmost oases. These oasis communities on the edge of the Sudanic belt served as the terminal points for the famous caravans that plied the trade routes across the Sahara [3].

Sometimes the fierce Berber nomads who usually guided these caravans turned upon the settled trading empires. In the middle of the eleventh century, the Almoravids, a Berber confederation, broke out of the western desert and led a great Muslim holy war to the north and to the south. In 1056 they invaded Morocco (later conquering the Umayyad Moors in Spain) and in 1076–77 seized the capital of Ghana.

The growth of the desert empires

Although the Ghanaian Empire fell, many smaller kingdoms survived; one of these grew into the spectacular empire of Mali [2]. Three great kings (who ruled between *c.*1230 and *c.*1340)—Sundiata, Mansa Uli, and Mansa Musa—so expanded Mali that it became one of the greatest empires in the world. It covered much of the western Sudan, and included the famous city of Timbuktu. The rulers had become Muslim, and in 1324 Mansa Musa made the pilgrimage to Mecca, taking so much gold that he upset the Cairo money market en route. The successor state to Mali was Songhay, which

CONNECTIONS

See also
1212 Subsaharan Africa 1500–1800
974 Africa: Kush and Axum
1214 African art

1 The empires of Africa

Timbuktu
Ghana
Gao
Mali
Niger
Lake Chad
Nile
Benin
Congo
Zambesi

The languages of Africa

HAMITO-SEMITIC
NILO-SAHARAN
NIGER-CONGO
BANTU
KHOISAN

Axum: 5th cent AD
Ethiopia: 14th cent
Ghana: 11th cent
Mali Empire: 14th cent
Songhay Empire: 15th cent
Berber dynasties: 11th–13th cent
Almoravid *c.* 1050–1140
Almohad *c.* 1125–1269
Hausa states: 14th cent
Oyo and Benin: 15th cent
Monomatapa Empire: 15th cent
Kanem-Bornu 14th cent

1 The population of subSaharan Africa is mostly Negroid, though the Khoisan, in the south, are smaller peoples of different origins. The inhabitants of Africa north of the Sahara are paler—often Caucasoid in origin. Three main features distinguished the development of African languages: the long evolution of western African languages; the fairly rapid spread, after about 2000 BC, of an offshoot of them, the Bantu languages, over all of Africa south of the equator; and the imposition of Arabic on the much more ancient Semitic languages, such as Berber, still spoken in northern Africa.

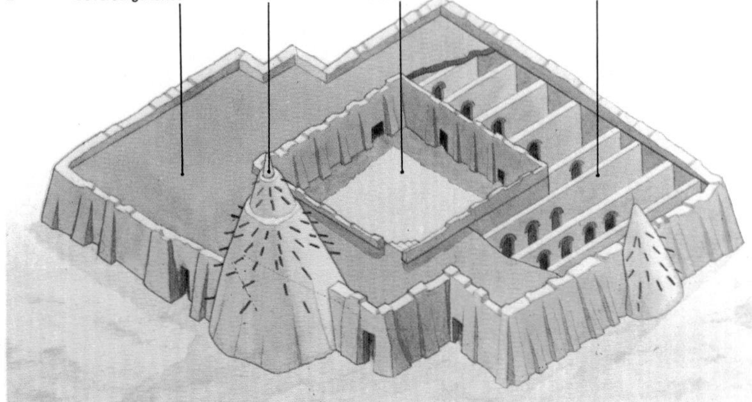

2
Covered galleries
Tower
Court
Vaulted arcades

2 The great mosque at Timbuktu was designed in the 14th century by As-Saheli, one of the Egyptians brought back to Mali by Emperor Mansa Musa after his pilgrimage to Mecca in 1324. Timbuktu grew to be an important center of commerce, religion, and learning, producing many fine Muslim scholars.

3 Trade routes across the Sahara had developed in Greek and Roman times, but first came into their own with the introduction of the camel to Africa around AD 100 and the growth of the Islamic states six centuries later. This thirteenth-century picture shows a Muslim merchant of the kind that engaged in this hazardous commerce. He would have traded in West African gold, ivory, kola nuts, slaves, and leather wares in exchange for salt, weapons, and luxury goods. Control of the southern end of these trade routes enriched the great Sudanic states of Ghana, Mali, Songhay, Hausa states and Kanem-Bornu.

had its center on the middle Niger. The great rulers of Songhay at the height of its power were Sonni Ali (reigned 1464–92) and Askia the Great (reigned 1493–1528).

To the east of Songhay were the Hausa states, such as Kano and Katsina, whose origins are traditionally traced back to the eleventh century. By the fourteenth century they had become the domains of powerful kings and prosperous merchants, centers of population, crafts, and trade. They were particularly famous for their leather work, which was exported north across the desert. Europeans obtained it in North Africa and knew it as Moroccan leather. In the central Sudan, surrounding Lake Chad, was the great state of Kanem-Bornu. From as early as the eleventh century its rulers had been Muslims. Kanem-Bornu was one of the oldest and largest African states, retaining its independent existence until over-thrown by European invaders at the end of the nineteenth century. In the mountains at the eastern end of the Sudanic belt, the Christian empire of Ethiopia [6] was the successor of ancient Axum.

In the woodland and forest areas to the south of the Sudan, kingdoms made a somewhat later appearance [4], but many, including Benin and the Oyo empires of Yorubaland (both of which produced some of the world's great sculptures) were in existence before the coming of the first Europeans in the fifteenth century.

The kingdoms of the Bantu nations

In other parts of Africa, especially in the vast regions south of the Equator over which the Bantu language family had spread rapidly during a few thousand years, states were beginning to be established. A cluster of kingdoms came into existence between the great lakes of East Africa, including Ruanda and Buganda. Another group, the Luba-Lunda kingdoms, grew up south of the Congo (Zaïre) forests, and the Kongo kingdom also emerged south of the river estuary that in colonial times bore its name. Much farther to the south were Great Zimbabwe and the empire of Monomatapa [7], on the Zimbabwe/Rhodesia plateau, which traded gold on the East African coast.

KEY

This bronze head with ivory headdress portrays an *Oba* (king of Benin). The splendor of the great African states was epitomized in the persons of their rulers. The headdress is carved with pictures showing the power of the *Oba*, which in the case of most African rulers was circumscribed; they were seldom absolute monarchs, being regarded instead as fathers of their people and personally responsible for their welfare. Many African kings were considered to be divine—their function in the world being to mediate between man and the gods. This high concept of leadership did not, however, prevent corruption in ambitious rulers.

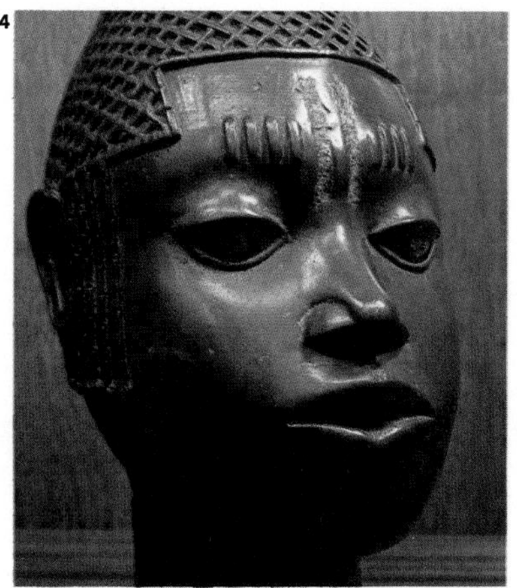

4 Powerful kingdoms had grown up in the forest regions of West Africa by the 1400s and were in trading contact with the older Sudanic states to the north. The former had a rich and ancient artistic tradition, especially in sculpture—Ife terracotta and bronze heads and Benin bronzes have achieved world renown. This detail of a bronze head from Benin lacks the finesse of very early Benin workmanship but, though heavier, still exhibits considerable skill.

5 Knowledge of iron technology for producing tools and weapons was important in the development of African cultures and political systems, contributing to the ascendancy of many kingdoms that later became great empires. The spread of iron-working occurred over West Africa before the end of the first millennium BC and is linked south of the Equator with the rapid expansion of the Bantu. This picture shows the processes of smelting, forging, and trading.

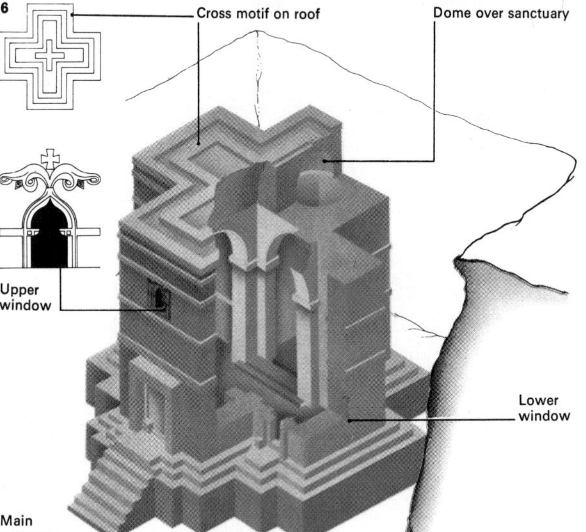
Cross motif on roof
Dome over sanctuary
Upper window
Lower window
Main entrance

6 This church at Lalibela in Ethiopia was one of several hewn out of solid rock during the thirteenth century. The Middle Ages was a time of great church building and of general revival and expansion for this ancient Christian empire.

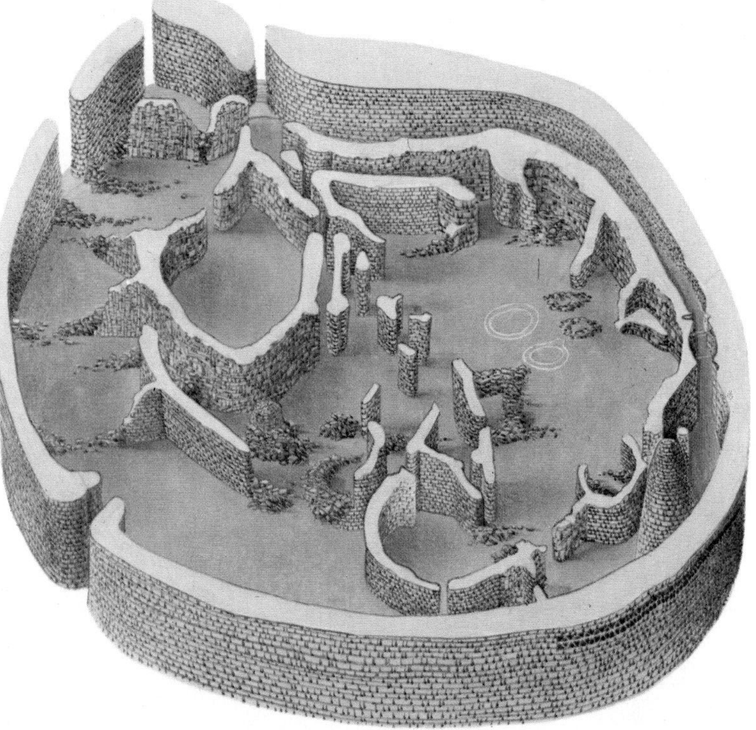

7 The Great Enclosure at Zimbabwe was built mainly in the fourteenth and fifteenth centuries on a site used for ritual purposes since *c.* AD 1000. The plateau area of Zimbabwe (modern Rhodesia) supplied gold to Arab traders at Sofala, a coastal outpost of the rich trading city of Kilwa in East Africa. To the north of Great Zimbabwe, the Monomatapa kingdom was formed probably in the 15th century. By 1500 the Portuguese were supplanting the Arab trading links.

Mesoamerica 300–1521

During most of the 1,500 years after Christ there was a definable Mesoamerican, or Middle American, civilization. The term "Mesoamerican" was coined to describe the very similar cultures that occupied what are now southern Mexico, Belize (British Honduras), Guatemala, Honduras, and El Salvador. They extended eastward through Nicaragua into Costa Rica between AD 1000 and 1500. These cultures shared temple-pyramids as religious centers; the sacred ballgame called *pok-ta-pok* by the Maya and *tlachtli* by the Aztec; a pantheon of deities including sun, wind, and rain gods; and an iconography with a grisly emphasis on death.

Classic and Preclassic cultures

Many of these features appeared first in the Preclassic cultures, and in the succeeding Postclassic period (AD 900 to the Spanish conquest in 1519) they attained their most complex form and widest distribution.

The first important Classic culture was that of Teotihuacán, based on the great city of that name in the central Valley of Mexico. From AD 300–600 the city was at its maximum size, which is estimated to have contained about 200,000 people.

One of the surrounding cultures was that of the Maya. These people occupied the Yucatán Peninsula and the adjacent highlands of Guatemala, and their area can be divided into three regions: the southern, consisting of the volcanic highlands and the short, steep slope down to the Pacific; the northern, the arid plateau of northern Yucatán; and the central, the jungle basins of the Usumacinta, Belize, and Hondo rivers. It was in this central area, in spite of its oppressive climate, that Classic Maya civilization emerged and flourished.

The appearance of this civilization is defined by the erection of stone stelae (upright slabs) with inscriptions in the complex calendar known as the Long Count, which combined three different calendars in one; by the building of massive stone temples and other public buildings in civic and religious complexes normally described as "ceremonial centers"; and by the appearance of decorated polychrome pottery.

Oaxaca, a highland valley in southern Mexico, has one of the longest histories in Mesoamerica. The apogee of the culture of the Zapotec Indians who lived there came between AD 300 and 600 and was focused on the great hilltop city and ceremonial center of Monte Albán [3], which overlooks the colonial city of Oaxaca.

The site has one enormous plaza created by leveling the hilltop. All four sides of the plaza are lined by large buildings approached by broad sweeps of steps. The working of precious stones and metals was one of the most notable characteristics of the Zapotec and of the Mixtec, their successors as rulers of Oaxaca. After Classic Monte Albán was abandoned in the seventh century, some tombs were reused by the Mixtec nobility [7]. Mixtec expertise also extended to architecture, and their capital at Mitla [6] has walls decorated with long, formal, repetitive mosaics.

The Gulf Coast

No such spectacular manifestation of architectural brilliance existed along the Gulf

CONNECTIONS

See also
1120 Columbia and Peru 300–1534
970 Preclassic America to AD 300
1124 Americas: conquest and settlement

1 **The Pyramid of the Moon** at Teotihuacán is one of two massive structures that dominate the heart of this great city, the first major planned settlement in Mesoamerica. It flourished from about 100 BC until AD 700 in a small valley branching off from the Valley of Mexico. Its population may have reached 200,000. The pyramid and the great plaza in front close the Street of the Dead.

2 A

MEXICO
Tula
Teotihuacan
Cholula
Chichén Itzá
YUCATAN PENINSULA
BELIZE
Palenque
Uaxactun
Tikal
Piedras Negras
GUATEMALA
HONDURAS
Copán

B

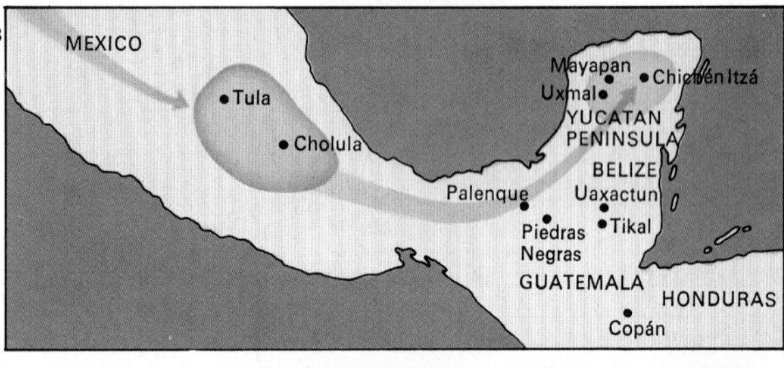
MEXICO
Tula
Cholula
Mayapan
Uxmal
Chichén Itzá
YUCATAN PENINSULA
BELIZE
Palenque
Uaxactun
Piedras Negras
Tikal
GUATEMALA
HONDURAS
Copán

C

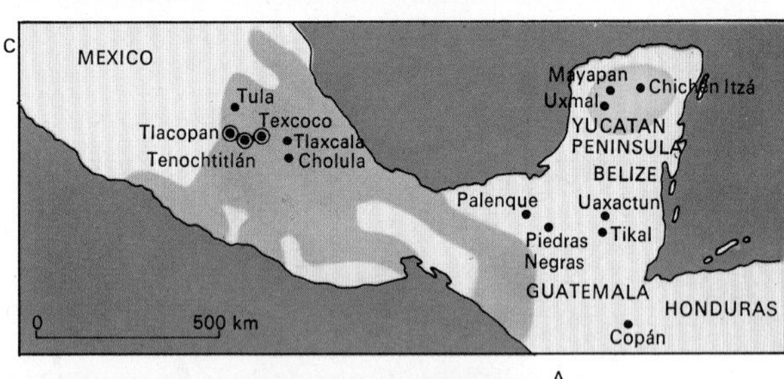
MEXICO
Tula
Texcoco
Tlacopan
Tlaxcala
Tenochtitlán
Cholula
Mayapan
Uxmal
Chichén Itzá
YUCATAN PENINSULA
BELIZE
Palenque
Uaxactun
Piedras Negras
Tikal
GUATEMALA
HONDURAS
Copán
0
500 km

A
- Maya Empire c.300-630
- Maya Empire by 960
- Teotihuacan c.300
- Toltecs by 960

B
- Maya Empire 960-1200
- Toltecs 960-1200
- Toltec-expansion 10th-12th centuries
- Aztec migration 12th century

C
- Maya Empire 1200—c.1450
- Aztec Empire by 1519
- Aztec city alliance by 14th century

2 **There were three stages** in the prehistory of Mesoamerica. [A] The great cities of Teotihuacán and Cholula dominated highland Mexico (AD 500). [B] Toltec influence from Tula reached Chichén Itzá in the Maya lowlands. The Maya civilization began to collapse in about AD 1000. [C] The Aztecs ruled the highlands, and the Yucatán Maya sites eventually were abandoned (AD 1500).

3 **The great plaza** forms the core of the main Zapotec ceremonial center of Monte Albán, on the hills overlooking the Valley of Oaxaca. The building in the foreground, Mound J, lies on a different orientation from the rest of the site and has been identified as an astronomical observatory; it is also adorned with carved panels depicting the towns conquered by the lords of Monte Albán. A large population lived nearby.

Coast, the home of the Olmec. But the cultures of Veracruz, and to the north that of the Huasteca, had their own distinctive characteristics. Veracruz sculpture is marked by panels filled with complex designs, many of them concerned with sacrifice, the ball-game, or both. The best known site is El Tajín [Key], where five ball courts have been uncovered. These panels are close in conception to those on the great court of Chichén Itzá in Yucatán.

Chichén Itzá is a Maya site in origin. Its most spectacular ruins mark the occupation of Chichén and the domination of northern Yucatán by the Toltec, a warrior people from highland Mexico north of Mexico City. Many of the buildings at Chichén are derived from the architecture of the Toltec capital, Tula. The most spectacular are the Castillo, a massive temple-pyramid with steps on all four sides, and the Temple of the Warriors [5]. The most impressive feature of the site is natural—the great circular Cenote (Well) of Sacrifice, more than 60ft (18m) deep, into which victims, mostly children, were flung to bring rain.

The civilization of the Aztec was in full flower when it was destroyed by the European invaders and was the only Mesoamerican high culture to be observed.

The cities of the Aztec

The Aztec had taken Teotihuacán [1] and Tula as models in making the central highlands of Mexico their base and like them had extended into the coastal lowlands. Their capital, Tenochtitlán, was on islands in Lake Texcoco and had a population estimated at 300,000. It comprised two cities, the second being Tlatelolco to the north of Tenochtitlán, which acted as the commercial center. Parts of the marketplace and temples of this city have been excavated and restored, whereas the major part was demolished by the Spaniards during the conquest; the center of the colonial capital of Mexico City was built on its ruins. Most of what remains of Aztec culture consists of grim lava sculpture, delicate turquoise mosaic work, and a number of manuscripts in picture writing, often with notes in European script added after the conquest.

KEY

The Pyramid of the Niches at El Tajín is a large ceremonial center on the Gulf of Mexico and one of the best known sites of the Classic Veracruz civilization. It flourished through the first millennium AD, contemporary with the Maya to the southeast and Teotihuacán to the south. There are 365 niches on the pyramid. They have been interpreted as reflecting the days of the solar year in another aspect of the Mesoamerican obsession with the calendar and the passage of time. El Tajín also had a number of ballcourts decorated with sculptures showing sacrifice, possibly of an earlier date than Chichén Itzá.

4

4 Famous for its stucco sculptures is the temple at the western lowland Maya site of Palenque. This was one of the first Maya sites to be explored in the eighteenth and nineteenth centuries, and work has continued there since. The most spectacular discovery came in 1952 when a stairway was found leading to a buried vault where a great stone sarcophagus contained the jade-laden body of a ruler. Recent study of the hieroglyphic tablets that give this Temple of the Inscriptions its name identify him as Pacal, first and greatest ruler of Palenque.

5 The great ballcourt at Chichén Itzá was the largest in Mesoamerica. This huge structure, about 270ft (83m) long, was erected by the Toltec conquerors of Yucatán in AD 1000. Stone rings in each wall were targets for the ball. Sculptures along the base of the walls depict the decapitation of a ballplayer, perhaps the punishment of the captain of the losing team. A small temple stands at the end.

5

6

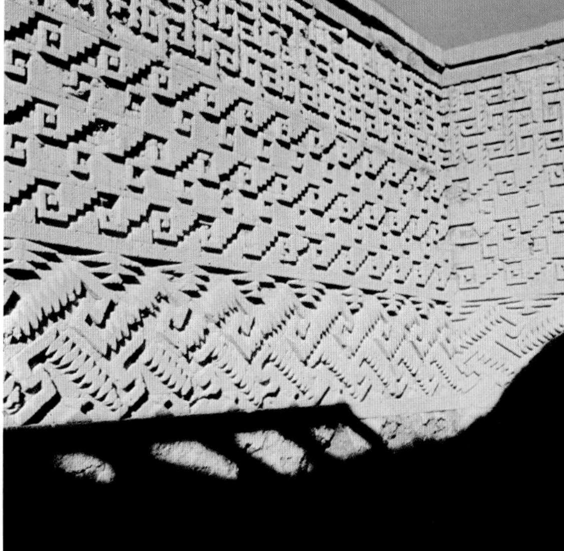

6 A room in the Mixtec palace at Mitla shows the complex stone mosaic decoration based mainly on the step-fret motif and built up of thousands of individually shaped stone blocks. The rooms, which were roofed in timber, lie around a series of closed courtyards accessible through narrow passages. There is also a pillared hall and tombs that lie below the level of the courtyard.

7

7 This head is one of the superb pieces of Mixtec gold work discovered in 1932 in the excavation of Tomb 7 at Monte Albán. This was a Zapotec tomb of an earlier period that had been reused for the burial of a Mixtec lord. The tomb also contained carved bones, rock crystal, turquoise, mosaics, and jades. This piece was probably worn on the chest and reveals a complex symbolism. The goldworking technique came from South America.

Colombia and Peru 300–1534

In South America one area led the rise to civilization—the Andes region from Lake Titicaca northward to Panama, including both the eastern (Pacific) and western (Amazon) slopes. There the earliest pottery, the first signs of agriculture, and the first settlements and public buildings have been found. From AD 300 onward, after 1,500 years of increasing momentum, numerous regional cultures arose. The fact that their art had such strongly regionalized features suggests separate and competing political units. The existence of strongholds attests to warfare among them.

The arts of Colombia

In the far north of South America in present-day Colombia, a gold-working tradition of great technical competence and artistic originality emerged [7]. Pendants and nose ornaments of sheet gold with added detail are often discovered, but other finds include magnificent gold vessels for holding coca leaves and such unique items as a model raft with a god and his attendants. Techniques extended from the simple hammering of sheet metal to granulation, lost-wax casting, and the creation of a gilt surface on a gold-copper alloy.

In southern Colombia the monumental art of San Agustín [1] flourished. The mounds in the area contain stone megalithic chambers, apparently both tombs and shrines, entered by stone tunnels decorated with painted designs. Huge blocks of the volcanic rock andesite were worked into box-like sarcophagi, and shafts of rock were turned into menacing statues of warriors and demons that combined the features of men and jaguars; some were double figures, with an animal alter ego looming over the man's head; others represented birds of prey wrestling with serpents. In the nearby Tierradentro region there are rock-cut tombs with domed roofs and stepped entrance shafts.

At the time of the Spanish conquest, Colombia was occupied by large populations living in palisaded settlements. Religion centered on sun worship, and the economy was based on potatoes and corn. Trade was in salt, gold, and emeralds.

The principal center in northern Peru was the basin of the Moche River, the seat of Mochica, Chimú, Inca, and Spanish colonial rulers. Moche civilization dates from about AD 200 to about 700, and its resources are demonstrated by the colossal Temple of the Sun [2], a terraced pyramid 741ft by 442ft (228m by 136m) high, made entirely of 133ft (41m) adobe bricks, and the nearby Temple of the Moon, a palace complex adorned with wall paintings, as well as irrigation canals cutting across the desert. Some Moche cemeteries have been excavated, many others looted. The most notable furnishings are the stirrup-spouted jars [4], some with painted scenes of warfare and daily life, others modeled into three-dimensional portrait heads or scenes of death and sexual activity.

Palaces for life and death

From about AD 1000 onward, the Moche valley was the site of the capital of the kingdom of Chimor, the great city of Chan Chan, which covers more than 6 square miles (15.5sq km) [8,9]. The center of the

CONNECTIONS

See also
1118 Mesoamerica 300–1521
970 Preclassic America to AD 300
1124 Americas: conquest and settlement
354 Coffee, tea, and cocoa

1 Enigmatic and massive carvings are scattered on the hills around the present town of San Agustín in southern Colombia. Many depict men with spirit alter egos in the form of animals sitting on their heads and others combine human and feline features, with long fangs. There are megalithic chambers—possibly tombs—that are similar to those of prehistoric Europe, with rock-cut basins and carved boulders.

2 Millions of mud bricks were used to build the Temple of the Sun (or Sun Pyramid) and the neighboring Temple of the Moon at Moche, on the north coast of Peru. The Temple of the Sun formed the ritual heart of the Mochica state during the first thousand years AD. Both palaces have suffered greatly from erosion and looting, and the original form of the Sun Pyramid is now hard to discern.

ECUADOR
PERU
Cajamarca
Moche
Chavin
Paracas
Nazca
Machu Picchu
Cuzco
Lake Titicaca
Tiahuanaco
BOLIVIA
CHILE
ARGENTINA
Inca roads
Inca Empire c. 1200–1400
Acquisitions 1438–71
Acquisitions 1471–81
Acquisitions 1493–1525
0 650km

3 The Inca Empire at the height of its power reached from northern Ecuador to the center of Chile, a distance of more than 1,000 miles (3,200km). The capital was at Cuzco, in the homeland of the conquering Inca nation. From there the Inca himself was linked to the distant parts of his empire by a network of roads and way stations and messengers in foot relays.

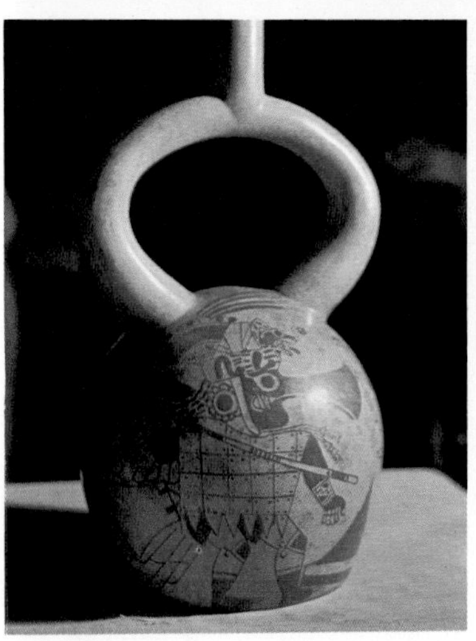

4 Stirrup-spouted pottery vessels were characteristic of the Mochica period in the first thousand years AD. These vessels were made by specialist potters. One type took the form of portrait heads while another (an example of which is shown here) had plain, smooth bodies with painted designs. These often took the form of scenes from Mochica life and warriors in action. The spout shape changed in subtle ways as centuries passed.

5 Nazca potters, renowned for the strong blocks of color that give their work a cartoon-like effect, made this lifelike figure of a drummer. Nazca culture flourished in Peru at the same time as Mochica in the north.

city consists of ten similar walled enclosures, each with a maze of rooms and open courtyards and once rich but now looted tombs. It has been suggested that these were the palaces of the Chimú rulers and that each king built a new compound while his predecessor's was maintained in perpetuity as a funerary shrine. The tombs are known to have contained gold and silver vessels and jewelry, pottery, and textiles.

On the central coast of Peru the "Lima style" of pottery suggests a state similar to Moche with ceremonial centers such as Aramburu, near present-day Lima. The most spectacular pottery style, however, was undoubtedly that of Nazca on the south coast, with polychrome vessels [5], often in four or five colors, and a dominant motif of a cat demon.

The most influential culture in southern Peru was based on Tiahuanaco, south of Lake Titicaca. Vast areas of ridged fields along the lake indicate a large agricultural potential and the labor to exploit it. Tiahuanaco is noted for its monolithic stone carving, including the Gate of the Sun [6], which stands on one side of a large enclosure, and tall column statues in a stiff but detailed relief style. Tiahuanaco was preceded in the Andes by Pucará as a cultural center and passed on some of its features to Huari, north of the lake.

Rise and fall of the Incas

Inca grandeur lasted for less than a century, from 1476 to 1534. Expansion began under the ruler Pachacuti Inca Yupanqui (reigned 1438–71) and continued under his successor Topa Inca. At its peak it reached from Ecuador in the north into what are now Chile, Bolivia, and Argentina, running along the *cordilleras* of the Andes 2,000 miles (3,200km) [3] and leaving Inca military power severely overextended. Much is known of Inca social and political organization, including its system of recording information on knotted string *quipus* [10], its professional army, its communications by relays of runners, and the supreme authority of the Inca himself—the source of the empire's strength and ultimately its downfall.

KEY

Inca stone walls in the Peruvian Andes were constructed with quite remarkable skill, the hard stone blocks fitting closely together even though their outlines are irregular. One block in a Cuzco street has 12 angles; such intricacy is not unusual. In Cuzco itself many Inca structures survive, including part of the Temple of the Sun. It now forms a section of a Dominican monastery. On the hills above Cuzco the great fortress of Sacsayhuaman presents its multiple ramparts to an enemy. Similar stonework exists at the mountaintop city of Machu Picchu, and a version was used for agricultural terracing.

6

6 The Gateway of the Sun, Tiahuanaco, Bolivia, is carved from a single block of stone and formed part of a great ceremonial enclosure. The lintel is adorned with low-relief carving.

7

7 The art of gold ornamentation was highly developed in South America. The main centers of innovation were in Colombia and Ecuador, and it spread northward from there into Mexico.

8 A restored panel of decoration in adobe – mud brick – forms part of the outlying temple of El Dragon at the site of Chan Chan, the ancient city north of Trujillo in the Moche Valley of northern Peru. Moche was an early focus of civilization in this valley, preceding Chan Chan, which was in turn succeeded by colonial and modern Trujillo. The site contains a series of great walled enclosures containing a maze of rooms and courtyards, altogether covering some 11 square miles.

8

9

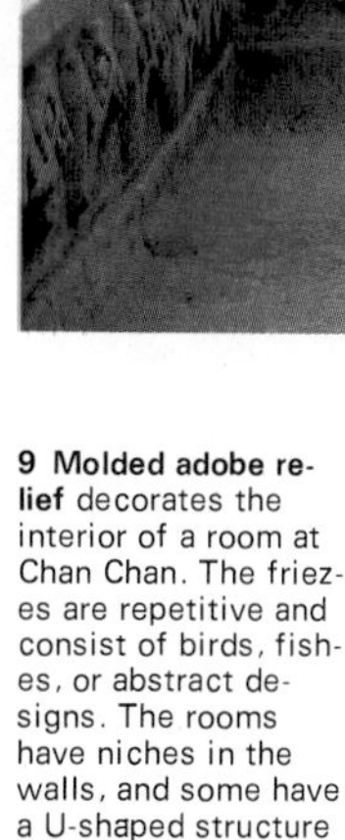

9 Molded adobe relief decorates the interior of a room at Chan Chan. The friezes are repetitive and consist of birds, fishes, or abstract designs. The rooms have niches in the walls, and some have a U-shaped structure called an *audiencia,* which is thought to have been the seat of a clerk, who checked goods in and out.

10

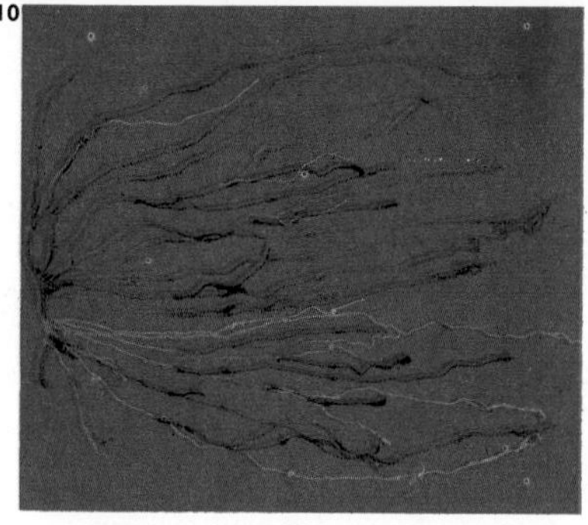

10 A quipu, a series of knotted cords, was used by the Incas as a counting and memory device. The knots were of different colors to denote different kinds of numerical information and are an eloquent testimony to the bureaucratic structure of the Inca Empire. For recording the constant payments of incoming tribute they were indispensable.

The age of exploration

The late fifteenth and early sixteenth centuries make up one of the most momentous periods in the history of Europe. In 1492, Christopher Columbus (1451–1506) sailed west across the Sea of Darkness and stumbled upon the Americas. In 1497, Vasco da Gama (*c.*1469–1525) embarked from Lisbon, sailed down the west African coast and around the Cape of Good Hope, up to Mozambique and Mombasa, and then across to Calicut in India. In 1519, Ferdinand Magellan (*c.*1480–1521) [3], seeking the route to the Orient that Columbus had failed to find, led a Spanish expedition around the southern extremity of South America and across the Pacific to the East Indies. Magellan himself was killed, but the survivors of his expedition, returning by way of the Cape of Good Hope, circumnavigated the globe for the first time.

The voyage of the Portuguese

Vasco da Gama's [2] expedition eastward was less a voyage of discovery and more an armed embassy determined to open up Portuguese commerce with the East. It was the culmination of almost a century of tentative, hesitant exploration by the Portuguese in which their frail caravels (light Mediterranean sailing ships) had groped their way along the west African coast and finally rounded the Cape. Lured by the gold and ivory of Africa and the Eastern trade that awaited Europeans who could reach India by sea, the captains of Henry the Navigator (1394–1460) [1] paved the way for da Gama by voyages to Madeira (1418) and the Azores (1431); rounding Cape Bojeador (1434); discovering the mouth of the Senegal (1444); and eventually by Bartolomeu Diaz's (*c.*1450–1500) discovering the Cape of Good Hope in 1488.

The motives of the explorers

The motives behind these early explorations, whether Portuguese or Spanish, were a combination of acquisitiveness and religious zeal. Barred by the Italians from the large profits of the Mediterranean trade and deprived of the profits of the luxury commerce in Eastern goods that Muslims and Venetians controlled, the Iberians sought new routes to the sources of supply. At the same time, they were spurred on by their crusading zeal: by the hope of outflanking Islam and of finding the legendary Christian kingdom of Prester John, as well as by the chance of making converts to Christianity. But not all the voyages during this period were by Iberians. Under Spanish patronage the Genoan Christopher Columbus sailed in search of a westward sea route to the Indies trade and in October 1492 landed in the Bahamas, believing them to be an Asiatic archipelago.

By 1504 Columbus had made three more voyages to the Caribbean but had come no nearer to finding Asia. Meanwhile, from England, the voyages of John (*c.*1450–*c.*1500) and Sebastian Cabot (*c.*1476–1557) along the northeast coast of America, and the explorations of the Florentine Amerigo Vespucci (1454–1512) along the north coast of South America and Brazil on behalf of the Spanish led to the belief that there was an uncharted land mass to the west between Europe and Asia, a New World [4].

CONNECTIONS

Read first
1110 The world Europe se out to explore

See also
1260 Colonizing Oceania and Australasia
1206 China from 1368 to *c.*1800
1210 Japan 1185–1868
1128 The politics of Europe 1450–1600
1118 Mesoamerica 300–1521
1120 Colombia and Peru 300–1534
356 Seeds and spices
214 Winds and weather systems

1 Prince Henry of Portugal, "the Navigator," was the most important of the precursors of the Age of Exploration. Placing gentlemen of his own household in command of his ships, Henry developed a systematic if intermittent program of African exploration beyond Cape Bojeador. By the time of his death his ships had advanced south by 1,500 miles.

VISOREIE
COMDE

2 Vasco da Gama's voyage by which he reached Calicut, India, in 1498 was an event of great significance, but his achievement cannot be ranked with those of Magellan and Columbus. He completed what had been begun by others—Diaz had rounded the Cape of Good Hope in 1488 and in fact accompanied da Gama part of the way to India.

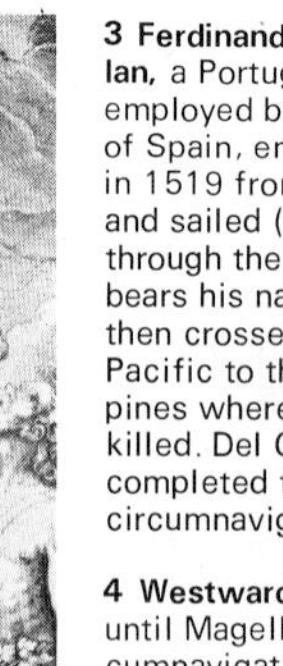

3 Ferdinand Magellan, a Portuguese employed by the king of Spain, embarked in 1519 from Seville and sailed (1520) through the strait that bears his name. He then crossed the Pacific to the Philippines where he was killed. Del Cano completed the circumnavigation.

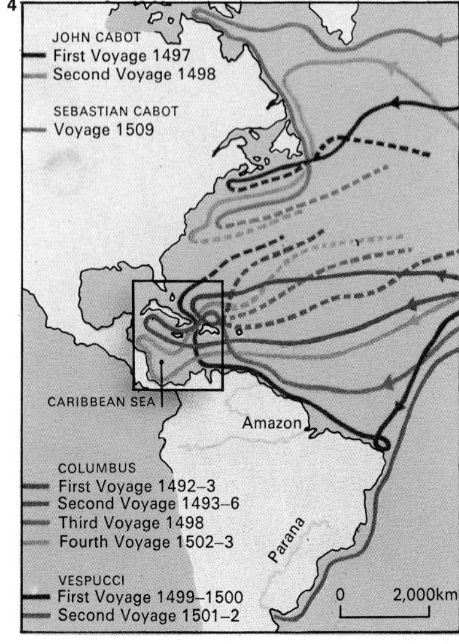

JOHN CABOT
First Voyage 1497
Second Voyage 1498
SEBASTIAN CABOT
Voyage 1509
CARIBBEAN SEA
Amazon
COLUMBUS
First Voyage 1492–3
Second Voyage 1493–6
Third Voyage 1498
Fourth Voyage 1502–3
Parana
VESPUCCI
First Voyage 1499–1500
Second Voyage 1501–2
0
2,000km

4 Westward voyages, until Magellan's circumnavigation, gradually led to the realization that an uncharted continent lay between Europe and the Indies. While the Portuguese sailed eastward for the spice trade, Spain and England were eager to find a quicker, westward route.

The Portuguese had many advantages over other European rivals in the exploration of Africa and Asia. Portugal possessed a large fleet, a seafaring population, a well-organized system of marine insurance and investment, and a royal family ready to back these enterprises.

Portuguese dominance in the spice trade
By finding a direct route to India by sea the Portuguese were able to gain an advantage in the spice trade. The architect of Portuguese supremacy in the Orient was Alfonso Albuquerque (1453–1515). In 1510 he seized the island of Goa; in 1511, Malacca. From the East Indies Portuguese ships went on to China and sailed annually between China and Japan. Their twin commercial aims were to monopolize the spice trade with Europe and to get as large a share as possible of the valuable inter-port trade of the Indian Ocean.

But in fact the Portuguese commercial empire of the sixteenth century—the result of the Age of Exploration—achieved less than its architects had hoped. The Portuguese succeeded in overawing but not in controlling their Asian competitors at sea. Until the coming of the Dutch the Portuguese retained a monopoly of the sea route around the Cape that they had pioneered. But they never achieved a monopoly of the spice trade between Europe and Asia. The Venetians, supplied by the old land routes, continued to sell some spices in Europe, and the Portuguese never did achieve control of all the spice-producing islands. Like every European in Asia until the nineteenth century, they found there was much they wanted to buy and little they had to sell. Their Estado da India [7], a set of fortified trading posts clinging sometimes precariously to the coast or to islands, never penetrated and certainly did not dare to challenge the great empires of mainland Asia.

The explorations in the East were initially more important to Europe than to the countries explored. They indicate a shift in the center of gravity of European trade from the Italian states to the Atlantic. The new routes to the East by sea permanently changed the mercantile map of the world.

KEY

The astrolabe, together with the quadrant, was one of the chief navigational aids that made exploration possible.

5

5 Lisbon in the late 16th century was the largest and most important city in Portugal. It was the nerve center of the Portuguese seaborne empire where the spices of Asia were distributed to the Mediterranean and Atlantic worlds in exchange for their goods. In the next century Portugal was to lose its commercial dominance in Asia and its political independence in Europe.

6

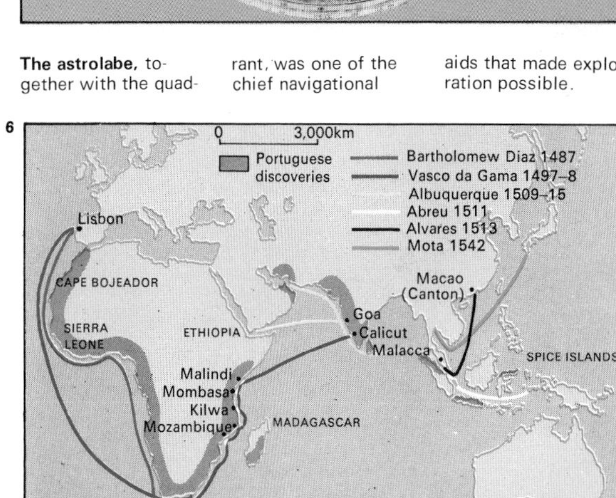

0
3,000km
Portuguese discoveries
Bartholomew Diaz 1487
Vasco da Gama 1497–8
Albuquerque 1509–15
Abreu 1511
Alvares 1513
Mota 1542
Lisbon
CAPE BOJEADOR
SIERRA LEONE
ETHIOPIA
Goa
Calicut
Malacca
Macao (Canton)
SPICE ISLANDS
Malindi
Mombasa
Kilwa
Mozambique
MADAGASCAR
CAPE OF GOOD HOPE

6 The route to the Indies took the Portuguese 50 years to develop from the time that Diaz rounded the Cape of Good Hope in 1488. The greatest single step was da Gama's crossing of the Indian Ocean, but it was the later venturers who gained for Portugal its central position in the Far East trade.

7

8

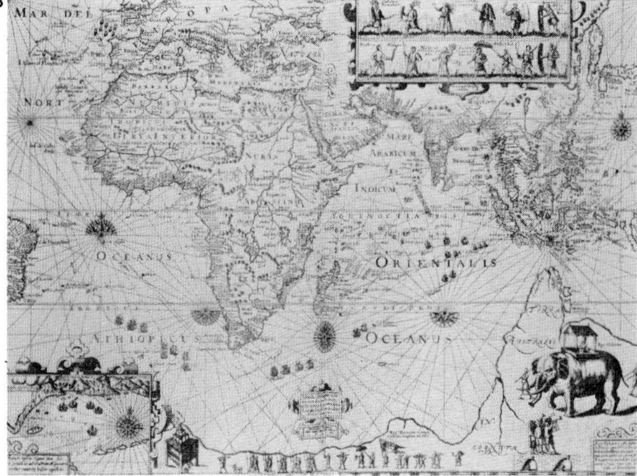

7 The Portuguese empire in the East consisted of a string of fortified trading posts all the way from Sofala in east Africa to Macao in the China Seas. The headquarters of the Estado da India was Goa, on the western coast of India. The grand forts such as this one, that the Portuguese built in Goa were meant to overawe rivals from the sea and to dissuade attack from the hinterland.

8 The Dutch began to sail eastward in 1595. Their innovation in getting to the East Indies was to leave India on their flank and sail directly from the Cape across open water (see map) to the Sunda Strait and then turn north to Java. This new route had the advantage of bypassing Goa and Malacca, but it also meant that they had to carry European goods directly to Indonesia, without being able to trade locally.

Americas: conquest and settlement

By the early sixteenth century the Spaniards had established colonies in the Antilles and the Isthmus of Panama. The mineral resources of these colonies, however, proved disappointing, and, despite the name Golden Castile, the area had little to offer. Trading expeditions along the coast of Yucatán revealed a likelihood of greater wealth in the interior. In 1519, after two preliminary expeditions, the governor of Cuba, Diego Velázquez (1599–1660), sent a fleet under Cortés to settle the region [1A].

The major conquests

Hernán Cortés (1485–1547) [2] and his expedition of 550 men landed on the coast of Mexico and founded the settlement of Veracruz [1B]. Cortés then overthrew Velázquez' authority and placed himself directly under the crown. By a series of adroit diplomatic moves and superior military technology, Cortés took formal possession of the Aztec capital of Tenochtitlán (Mexico City). He was welcomed by its ruler, Montezuma, whom he promptly imprisoned. According to Cortés, Montezuma made a willing donation of his empire to Charles V in the mistaken belief that Cortés was the emissary of the god Quetzalcoatl. This story is almost certainly a fable.

The conquest of Peru in 1532 by the adventurer Francisco Pizarro (*c.* 1470–1541) [4] was the result of the search for gold. When the Spaniards arrived on the Peruvian coast at Tumbez, the Inca Empire was divided by a civil war. Atahualpa emerged victorious shortly before Pizarro caught up with him at the fortress of Cajamarca [3]. Here the Spaniards succeeded in killing most of Atahualpa's retinue and capturing the Inca himself. Atahualpa offered to fill his cell with gold in exchange for his freedom. Pizarro accepted, but although Atahualpa kept his part of the bargain he was not released. The value of his ransom has been estimated at about $20,000,000.

Pizarro lacked Cortés' powers of leadership, and after the subjugation of the Inca Empire, the conquerors began to fight among themselves. The civil war lasted until the death of Pizarro in 1541 and the execution of his brother Gonzalo in 1548.

With the conquest of Peru, the attention of the European explorers turned elsewhere. Expeditions were sent to Texas and Florida, and some settlements were established. The colonization of New Mexico was slightly more determined, but the area became little more than a military outpost.

Administration

The Spanish crown, fearful that the more successful *conquistadores* (conquerors) would set up independent feudatories, rapidly took control of the government of the new colonies. The administration was complex. At the top was the viceroy, responsible only to the crown. The distance between Spain and the Indies and the slowness of communication between king and viceroy inevitably placed great power in the viceroy's hands.

To maintain the balance of power within the colony, a separate court of appeal, the *audiencia*, was established. This had the right of direct representation before the crown and could suspend crown officials from their duties; it also served to represent

CONNECTIONS

See also
1118 Mesoamerica AD 300–1521
1120 Colombia and Peru 300–1534
1128 The politics of Europe 1450–1600
1158 Europe 1500–1700
1164 Baroque art: patronage and development

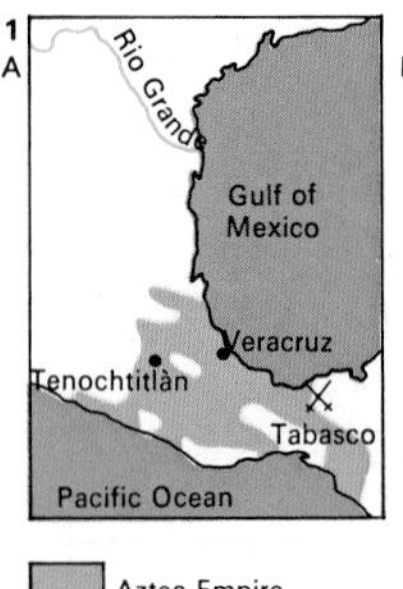

Rio Grande
Gulf of Mexico
Veracruz
Tenochtitlán
Tabasco
Pacific Ocean

Aztec Empire
Route of Cortés 1519–20
Route of Cortés 1521
Tribes who allied with Cortés
Marshland
4,500 meters
4,000
3,500
3,000
2,500
2,000
0

1 Cortés landed at Veracruz [A] on April 22, 1519. By forming alliances with the peoples of Cempoala, Jalapa, and Tlaxcala, he maintained his supply line with the coast [B]. After some skirmishes, he persuaded the powerful independent state of Tlaxcala to join him, thus obtaining the much-needed base from which to launch his attack on the Aztec capital of Tenochtitlán. After the retreat of the "Sorrowful Night" on June 30, 1520, Cortes fled to Tlaxcala. With the help of local workmen he built a fleet of brigantines to harass the defenders of Tenochtitlán from the lake. These were carried in pieces and assembled on the lake shore, while the army, composed largely of Tlaxcalans, attached the towns that seemed sympathetic to the beleaguered Axtecs in Tenochtitlán.

2 Hernán Cortés was born in the province of Estremadura in Spain. He sailed for Hispaniola in 1504, and as Velázquez' lieutenant, he took part in the conquest of Cuba. His career subsequent to the conquest of Mexico was, like that of so many *conquistadores*, spent largely in an effort to secure from the crown due recognition of his achievements. He died in Spain in 1547, neglected by the court.

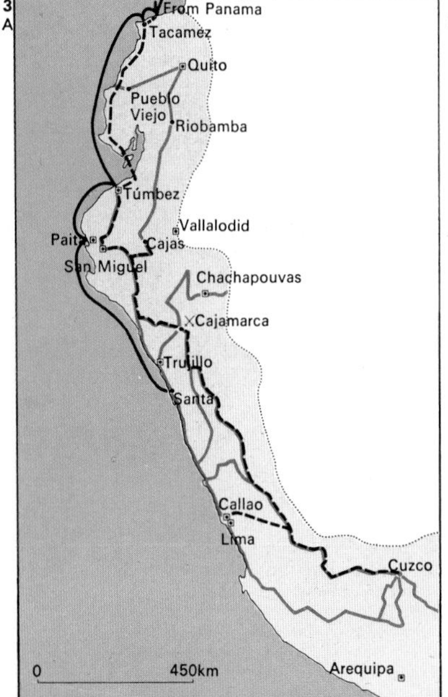

From Panama
Tacamez
Quito
Pueblo Viejo
Riobamba
Túmbez
Vallalodid
Paita
Cajas
San Miguel
Chachapouvas
Cajamarca
Trujillo
Santa
Callao
Lima
Cuzco
Arequipa
0 450km

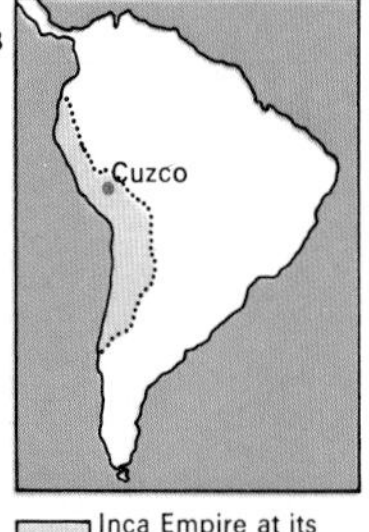

Cuzco

Inca Empire at its greatest extent in1525
Inca roads
Pizarro's expeditions 1524–8
Pizarro's expedition 1531–3
Spanish settlements
Capital of Inca Empire

3 A superb network of roads helped Pizarro to conquer Peru. Reaching Tumbez in 1531, he then marched inland to Cajamarca to find the Inca ruler Atahualpa. Following a surprise attack, the city fell; Atahualpa himself was eventually executed. Pizarro founded a new capital at Lima, thus shifting the center of Inca society from Cuzco to the coast.

4 Charles V gave his support in 1523 to Pizarro's third expedition to Peru. Pizarro had accompanied Balboa on his march across the Panama isthmus in 1513 and later formed a partnership with Diego de Almagro and Fernando de Luque to settle Peru and seek out the riches of the Incas. The first expeditions (1524–28) were unsuccessful. In 1531, Pizarro and his brothers left Panama for Peru, joined later by Alamgro. Pizarro, lacking the diplomatic skills of Cortés, was unable to control his followers. Shortly after the subjugation of the Incas, Almagro broke away, and during the ensuing civil war Pizarro was murdered in 1541. Pizarro's brother Gonzalo was executed in 1548.

the Indians before their overlords and to administer justice. The crown also imposed the system of *residencia*, whereby a crown official was examined at the end of his term of office and any misconduct punished. These institutions were often ill-equipped to deal with the American situation.

The Indians were "granted" to settlers under the *encomienda* system. Theoretically this provided the colony with a salaried labor force; each settler was given a number of Indians (but not their lands) from whom he took tribute or labor. The position of the Indian was therefore rather like that of the European serf, and the power that this appeared to give to the colonists forced the crown to make several efforts to abolish the system. By the Laws of Burgos of 1512–13 and subsequent royal decrees, the number of Indians held in *encomienda* was limited and their duties lightened.

The wealth of the Americas

The great wealth of America lay in its silver deposits. The mines of Potosí in Peru and of Zacatecas, Guanajuato, and the other Potosí in Mexico were all discovered during the 1540s, and their output soon came to dominate the European silver market. The colonists benefited little, however, and were forced to subsist on agriculture and trade in lesser commodities, such as silks, with the Philippines. Precious metals were shipped via Seville, which enjoyed a monopoly on America's trade and where a clearinghouse, the *Casa de la Contratación*, had been set up as early as 1503. The Americas had always been a Castilian venture and the crown benefited directly [6].

The impact of Spanish colonization on the New World was considerable [9]. The introduction of European crops and livestock destroyed the domestic life of the Indians and altered the ecological balance of central Mexico. The disruption of old tribal divisions and of the hierarchy of Aztec society produced an alienated, enfeebled community that easily succumbed to European diseases; as a result, populations declined rapidly during the sixteenth century. Latin America thereafter was a mixed culture dominated by that of the Spanish settlers.

KEY

This 17th-century Inca wooden beaker shows Peruvian Indians and a European together. At first, the Spaniards tried to preserve the Indian social structure, using local chieftains as justices and tax collectors. Over the course of the 17th century, however, the native nobility intermarried, and the Spaniards took Indian women as concubines, producing a racially mixed group known as mestizos. The Indian culture declined and was supplanted by that of a white society.

5

5 The Spanish crown rapidly replaced the *conquistadores* with its own officials, who set up a complicated government machine providing checks and balances to prevent any single individual from growing too powerful. There was also the *audiencia*, a court of appeal to which every citizen had recourse and which was responsible directly to Spain. This former governor's palace is in Morelia, central Mexico.

6 Silver bullion from the Indies provided Castile especially with great wealth during the 16th century, but the influx slowed as the mines were worked out in the 17th. The massive inflation of 17th-century Europe may have derived from these imports of American silver.

6

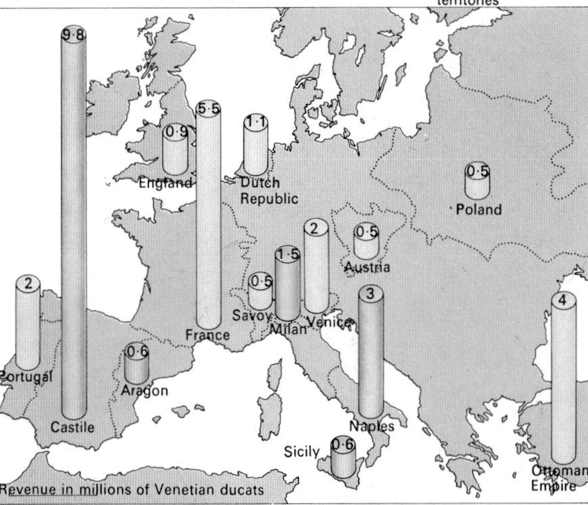
Spanish territories
Other European territories
9·8
5·5
1·1
0·9
England
Dutch Republic
0·5
Poland
2
0·5
1·5
0·5
Austria
3
4
Savoy
Milan
Venice
France
2
0·6
Portugal
Aragon
Castile
Naples
Sicily
0·6
Ottoman Empire
Revenue in millions of Venetian ducats

7

7 Spanish cruelty toward the Indians was notorious. *Brief Relation of the Destruction of the Indies* by Bartolomé de las Casas, which became a best-seller during the 16th century, fostered and disseminated this "black legend." The book's popularity, however, was due more to fear and hatred of Spain than to love of the Indians. This anti-Spanish illustration by De Bry appeared in the Netherlands.

8

8 The conquest of America by Europeans in the 16th century meant that the indigenous cultures were almost wiped out. Because of the Spaniards' desire to convert the Indians to Christianity, the traditional features of the native way of life were absorbed into the dominant culture. Although this process was uneven, the tribes that survived were the least developed. The highly developed civilizations of the Aztecs and Incas wholly disappeared.

9

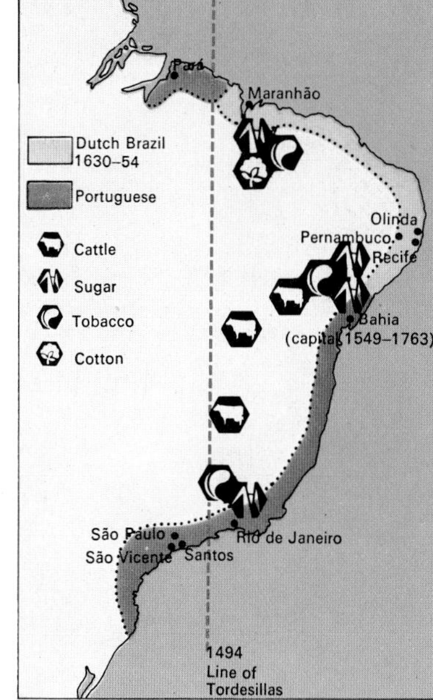
Pará
Maranhão
Dutch Brazil 1630–54
Portuguese
Cattle
Sugar
Tobacco
Cotton
Olinda
Pernambuco
Recife
Bahia
(capital 1549–1763)
São Paulo
Rio de Janeiro
São Vicente
Santos
1494
Line of Tordesillas

9 By the Treaty of Tordesillas of 1494 the Spaniards and the Portuguese – at the instigation of Pope Alexander VI – agreed to a demarcation line between their territorial claims. When Brazil was discovered in 1500 by Pedro Alvares Cabral, Portugal therefore claimed it but did not seriously colonize it until 1530. Spain and Portugal were united between 1580 and 1640, so that Brazil was open to attack by Spain's enemies. In 1630, the Dutch seized a rich area in the north, which they kept until 1654 when they were driven out. The Brazilian economy developed rapidly in the 17th century, based on sugar, tobacco, cotton, and cattle. Coffee was not important until the 18th century.

The rise of banking

Between the twelfth and the fifteenth centuries Italy exercised a European supremacy in commerce and finance and was responsible for most innovations in business and banking. By the sixteenth century that supremacy was being eroded. In twelfth-century Genoa banks accepted deposits, exchanged foreign coins for local currency, and engaged in bullion dealing. Later the Florentines became the leading Italian bankers. Throughout this period banking and trade were invariably combined, and the commercial contacts of the Italians throughout Europe necessitated the regular international transfer of money. The simple but commercially important bill of exchange [Key] was evolved in the fourteenth century, doing away with the problems and dangers of transporting gold and silver coins between towns.

Activities of medieval bankers

Largely as a consequence of the Church's ban on usury (lending money for interest), medieval bankers made exchange operations a key activity. Although the bill of exchange did involve an element of credit until the money was paid out at a later date in another place and in another currency, it was not classified as a loan.

The banker's profit came from the exchange rate—the Medici averaged 15 percent. The prohibition on charging interest may also have impeded the evolution of the basic banking activities of borrowing and lending at interest, although deposit banks did exist, mainly in Italy, but also in Bruges [1]. They offered non-interest-bearing current accounts and the facility of making transfers between customers' accounts. These were for fixed periods, and the interest, although not guaranteed, was disguised as a gift or bonus from profits.

From the fourteenth century on, some towns allowed written orders (the distant ancestor of the check) to make payments or transfers. These orders replaced the original requirement that such orders had to be made orally by the depositor. In the later Middle Ages the making of loans to rulers and towns became another area of operation for some bankers.

A decline in private banking in the Low Countries and Italy in the fifteenth century is illustrated by the decrease of large Florentine banks from 80 to 8 between 1330 and 1526. Because the emerging money economy was unstable, medieval banking had its hazards. By 1585, 96 out of 103 Venetian banks had failed, often through incautious loans to merchants and governments. Deposit banking recovered in the late sixteenth century, often in the form of municipally controlled public banks, as in Venice and later in Amsterdam [9], both of which accepted deposits and made transfers.

Small banks and moneylenders

More widespread than the handful of great Italian merchant banks such as the Medici [6] were small local banks. These shared many of the functions of their large counterparts but avoided exchange and transfer operations.

Throughout Europe there were also the reviled but necessary moneylenders and pawnbrokers [3]. They made small short-term loans to the poor, who comprised the

CONNECTIONS

See also

1066 Charlemagne and the Carolingian Empire
1070 Western European economy 800–1000
1090 Western European economy 1000–1250
1134 Florentine art 1400–60
934 Money and capital

1

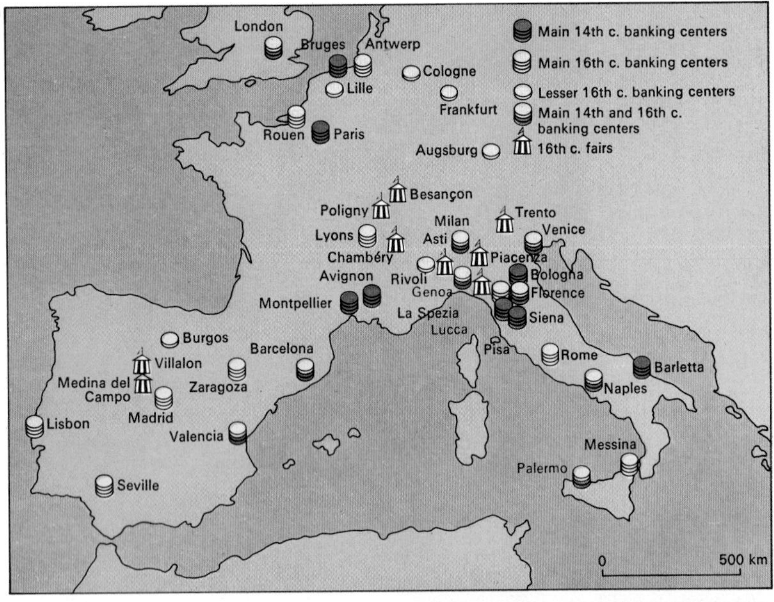

London
Bruges
Antwerp
Cologne
Lille
Frankfurt
Rouen
Paris
Augsburg
Main 14th c. banking centers
Main 16th c. banking centers
Lesser 16th c. banking centers
Main 14th and 16th c. banking centers
16th c. fairs
Besançon
Poligny
Trento
Milan
Venice
Lyons
Asti
Chambéry
Piacenza
Avignon
Rivoli
Genoa
Bologna
Florence
Montpellier
La Spezia
Lucca
Siena
Burgos
Barcelona
Pisa
Rome
Barletta
Villalon
Medina del Campo
Zaragoza
Naples
Lisbon
Madrid
Valencia
Messina
Palermo
Seville
0
500 km

1 Bruges, whose financial activities were dominated by Italians, was the only permanent medieval banking center outside Italy. The late 15th century witnessed the rise of the south German houses. The major 16th-century centers were Antwerp, Lyons, and the seasonal fairs of Castille and Besançon. The Genoese controlled the Besançon fairs, which soon left and reconvened in Piacenza by 1579.

2

2 The papacy received dues and taxes from all over Europe. Heedless of the usury prohibition, the papacy also borrowed at interest from bankers. The great basilica of St Peter's, begun in the early 16th century, was partly financed by the proceeds from the sale of indulgences conveyed by the Fuggers, who had broken the Italian monopoly on banking.

3 Aaron, a noted Jewish moneylender, built this house in Lincoln, England, in about 1170–80. He conducted business with the greatest families and financed part of the building of Canterbury Cathedral. On his death a special department of the exchequer had to take over his huge financial assets. The Jews were expelled from England in 1290, as the king hoped to take over their assets.

3

4

4 Jacques Coeur (*c.* 1395–1456), French merchant, moneylender, and government financier, built this palace in Bruges during his spectacular career. He lost his fortune in 1453 and was exiled.

5

5 This painting by Quentin Massys (*c.* 1465–1530) shows the money changer and his wife at work. For a small fee they exchanged gold for silver coins or the coins of one currency for another.

mass of the population. Even in a largely subsistence peasant economy, money was needed to pay taxes and the poorest might seek a loan in hard times. Some of these moneylenders were Christians, but most were Jews, to whom the usury laws did not apply. Some, such as those in Florence in 1437, were officially invited to set up licensed pawnshops so Christian souls would not be jeopardized through usury, although Christian moneylenders were not above charging disguised interest.

In mid-fifteenth-century Italy churchmen established non-Jewish pawnshops, the *Monti di Pietà*, to meet the needs of the poor. The original charitable purpose of these shops was perverted, when governments and the rich turned to them for loans.

Sixteenth-century banking

The sixteenth century saw no major innovations in banking practices, but as the European economy expanded, the scale of operations increased, credit became more extensive, and other nationalities, especially the south Germans, adopted Italian methods. Methods of obtaining credit became more flexible as a result of the increasing use of endorsement and discounting. Interest rates fell, and some Protestant states adopted a more liberal attitude toward usury. Expanding trade was facilitated by the evolution of an unofficial system of settling international trading debts and balances during the great seasonal European trade fairs.

The most spectacular development was the mid-sixteenth-century boom in government borrowing to meet the escalating costs of war. The French kings raised money in Lyons, the English and Spanish [8] rulers in Antwerp, the greatest center for long distance trade of the era. Fortunes were lost as the kings of France and Spain defaulted on their debts, just as Edward III of England had ruined two Florentine banks in the 1340s. Small operations as well as great banks such as the south German Fuggers [7] were hit, and by the end of the sixteenth century the era of the international financier was over, although more mundane forms of banking prospered.

KEY

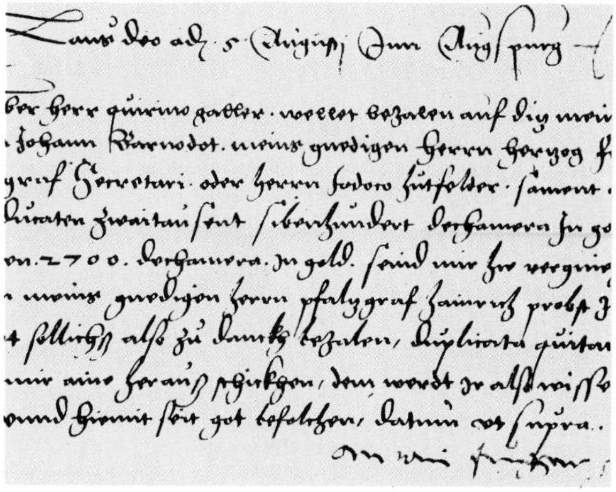

The form of the bill of exchange altered little from its evolution in the 14th century. To avoid the Church's prohibition on usury it had to instruct the recipient in another country to make payment in another currency to the person specified. Usually the rate of exchange was given. This bill, signed by the south German Anton Fugger, required the Fugger agents in Rome to pay 2,700 ducats to the Dean of Elwagen.

6

6 The Medici family were the greatest of all 15th-century Italian bankers, with branches in France, England, the Low Countries, and throughout Italy. Under Cosimo de' Medici (1389–1464), like his successors a patron of the arts, they reached the peak of their influence and wealth. Already in serious financial trouble, the firm finally foundered when the Medici were expelled from Florence (1494).

7

7 In the early 16th century the Europe-wide commercial and financial empire of the Fugger family in Augsburg was the largest the western world had ever seen. It rested on lucrative mining monopolies, extensive trade, and loans on a vast scale. The most spectacular period occurred under the guidance of Jakob Fugger the Rich (1459–1525) (here painted by Albrecht Dürer). He learned the banking trade in Italy.

8

8 Jakob Fugger's most famous loan was made to the Hapsburgs: 543,585 florins that helped to buy the votes of the imperial electors who made Charles V of Spain Holy Roman Emperor in 1519. The fortunes of the Fuggers and the Hapsburgs were thereafter closely linked. Charles V had to borrow unprecedentedly large sums from foreign bankers living in Antwerp to pay for his wars with the French, the Turks, and the German Protestants.

9

9 The Amsterdam Exchange Bank (1609) was one of the most famous and successful of the municipally supervised banks set up after the financial recovery of the late 16th century. It received cash deposits of over 300 florins, transferred money between customers' accounts, traded in bullion, and handled all bills of exchange over 600 florins. Like other municipal banks the Amsterdam Bank did not make loans, grant overdrafts, or discount bills.

The politics of Europe 1450–1600

Medieval Europe was the *respublica christiana,* the universal world of Christendom ruled by two swords—the spiritual wielded by the pope, the secular by the emperor. But in the sixteenth century this ideal disintegrated and the monarchical states were strengthened at the expense of the church and the nobility. The process was clearest in France [Key], where the crown gradually succeeded in expanding its holdings through accommodations with the papacy and the nobility.

Popes and kings

Disputes over the papal succession from 1378 to 1417 damaged the position of the pope as head of Christendom and the rival candidates became the puppets of secular rulers. Later popes played Italian politics, while the princes of Europe exploited their weakness to gain control of the church.

Monarchs of the sixteenth century attempted to increase their control over the nobility. The medieval king's real power rested ultimately on his wealth and the military strength that he could command. Toward the end of the Middle Ages a few noble families in many parts of Europe greatly extended their own power and fortunes. The Percy family, for example, had as much power in the north of England as kings. When kings were weak, this situation produced civil war in France, Spain, and England (the Wars of the Roses, 1455–85). But the disorder of war threatened the privileged classes as a whole, and they looked to a strong king to restore stability. The princes set about re-erecting the former effective monarchical rule based on financial resources, powerful adherents, the centralization of the administration, and the neutralizing of the power of the independent nobles.

In England the Lancastrian Henry VII (reigned 1485–1509), who won his crown in battle, attempted to establish personal control of government. Henry enjoyed the forfeited lands of the vanquished and was financially stable. He administered the affairs of the realm from his own household and was able to discipline a nobility weakened by wars, and to reduce the numbers of their military retainers. By marrying into the House of York he minimized the possibilities of dynastic rivalry. Henry rebuilt a strong personal monarchy in a realm that had seen nothing like it since Edward I (reigned 1272–1307). His son, Henry VIII (reigned 1509–47) [5], incorporated Wales within the kingdom and gathered the wealth and authority of the church into his hands.

Francis I and Charles V

Francis I (reigned 1515–47) came to the throne after France had been rent by war. Noble families like the Bourbons were powerful, and the kingdom was large and divided. Francis exploited the royal rights of direct taxation, centralized the treasury, and attempted to impose uniform Roman law codes. He controlled the representative assemblies and distracted the nobility by foreign wars and life at his glorious court.

A degree of unity and centralization seemed possible in Spain when the kingdoms of Aragón and Castile were both inherited by the Hapsburg Charles V (1500–58) in 1516 [1]. Charles suppressed the

CONNECTIONS

See also
1102 European society 1250–1450
1158 Europe 1500–1700
1096 The emergence of France
1124 Americas: conquest and settlement

1

From Mary of Burgundy (1506)
From Ferdinand of Aragon and Isabella of Castile (1516)
From Maximilian of Austria (1519)
Charles V's Empire 1518
0 400km
HOLY ROMAN EMPIRE
NETHERLANDS
FRANCE
FRANCHE-COMTE
CHAROLAIS
AUSTRIA
TYROL
NAVARRE
CATALONIA
ARAGON
PORTUGAL
CASTILE
VALENCIA
BALEARIC ISLANDS
SARDINIA
NAPLES
GRANADA

1 The empire of Charles V was the product of dynastic accident. He succeeded his father Philip as duke of Burgundy in 1506, and his grandfather Ferdinand as king of Aragón and of Castile in 1516. The territories of the Holy Roman Empire came with his election to the title in 1519. There was no logic to the empire, and problems of communication made imperial rule almost impossible. Charles resolved these problems by handing over the Netherlands (1555) and Spain (1556) to his son Philip II and the rest of his empire to his brother Ferdinand (1556).

Disputed areas in Italy 1519-59
Held by Francis I of France
Under Spanish (Hapsburg) rule
States under Spanish influence 1559

2 The warring Hapsburgs and Valois dominated early 16th-century politics. Charles V, of the Hapsburgs, inherited disputed claims to parts of Burgundy and Italy [A]. Francis I, consolidating Valois rule in France, feared encirclement by the Hapsburgs. The focus of conflict was Italy, important for its wealth and a vital hub of communications for the Hapsburg possessions in Spain and the empire. The route through the Italian passes was the only alternative to the Channel route. Most of the disputed areas came under imperial control by the Peace of Cateau-Cambrésis [B].

3

3 The life of Niccolò Machiavelli (1469–1527) coincided with the rise of the nation-state and the beginning of the art of statecraft. Machiavelli outlined a guide for princes in *The Prince* (1532) and in his *Discourses* (1531) on the first ten books of Livy, the Roman historian. The appearance of *The Prince* shocked Christian Europe and earned for its author a reputation for devious and treacherous statesmanship. He became a leading figure of the Renaissance.

4 The "Field of the Cloth of Gold" is a painting that commemorates the historic meeting of King Henry VIII of England and King Francis I of France in June 1520 near Calais, in France, to conclude a long awaited peace. The encounter was marked by great festivity and elaborate preparation. Henry had built a temporary palace, all tents were embossed with gold and velvet, and the royal interviews were occasions for jousting and other contests of chivalry, ceremonial banquets, and fireworks displays. As each king tried to outdo the other in pomp and splendor, the occasion turned into a trial of strength. No alliance resulted from the meeting, and open war had broken out by 1522.

4

"Comuneros" revolt and sent royal officials *(corregidores)* to enforce his will. But the powerful nobility guarded their privileges, and the two kingdoms remained separate. Charles was distracted by his imperial duties (he was also Holy Roman emperor) from consolidating his position in Spain. In order to obtain Castilian money, he recognized the privileges of the nobles. Philip II (1556–98) continued to rely on Castilian bullion for his campaigns and neglected Aragón, which voted little money to the crown. The kingdoms of Spain were never centralized, and in the seventeenth century Aragón and Catalonia revolted.

When he became emperor in 1519, Charles V tried to centralize his lands through imperial institutions and constant visits, but the task was impossible. Large cities like Nuremburg were proud of their independence, the princes were trying to assert themselves, and powerful families like the Wittelsbachs were anxious to stop the Hapsburgs from becoming too strong. The Reformation [8] finally divided the empire. In the late sixteenth century the Hapsburgs gained control over their hereditary lands, but only in order to provoke resistance in Bohemia.

Attempts by both Charles V and Francis I of France to increase control of their kingdoms led them into more than 40 years of war over disputed claims in Italy [2], but the result was a completely fragmented country that ceased to be a major European power.

The need for a strong monarchy

Although more powerful monarchies emerged in Western Europe during the sixteenth century, there were serious limitations on their control. Without a paid civil service, kings still depended on the nobility. Men thought of Catalonia or Provence before they thought of Spain or France; allegiance to family, locality, or lord could still overcome allegiance to the king. In the late sixteenth century religious divisions threatened the monarchy in England and encouraged a return to separatism in France. But war once again convinced the ordinary nobles that a strong monarchy was needed to maintain order.

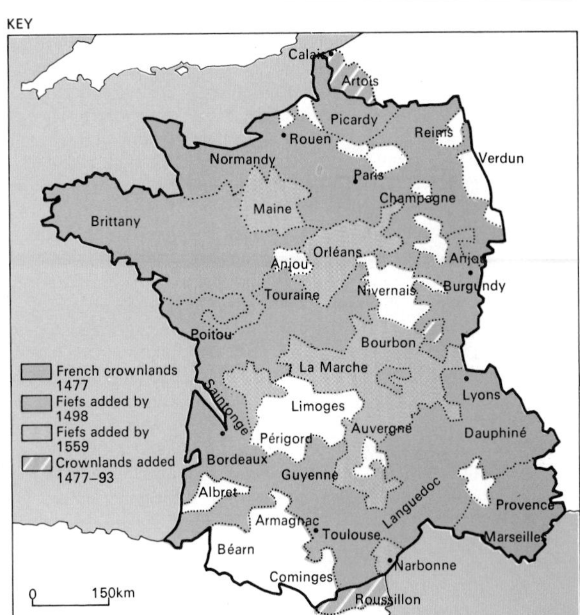

KEY
French crownlands 1477
Fiefs added by 1498
Fiefs added by 1559
Crownlands added 1477–93
Calais
Artois
Picardy
Rouen
Reims
Normandy
Paris
Verdun
Champagne
Maine
Brittany
Orléans
Anjou
Anjou
Touraine
Nivernais
Burgundy
Poitou
Bourbon
La Marche
Saintonge
Limoges
Lyons
Périgord
Auvergne
Dauphiné
Bordeaux
Guyenne
Languedoc
Albret
Provence
Armagnac
Toulouse
Marseilles
Béarn
Narbonne
Cominges
Roussillon
0
150km

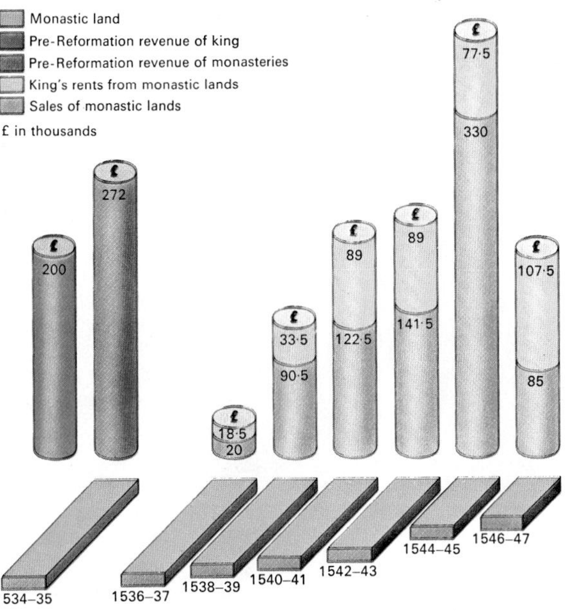

Monastic land
Pre-Reformation revenue of king
Pre-Reformation revenue of monasteries
King's rents from monastic lands
Sales of monastic lands
£ in thousands
200
272
18·5
20
33·5
90·5
89
122·5
89
141·5
77·5
330
107·5
85
1534–35
1536–37
1538–39
1540–41
1542–43
1544–45
1546–47

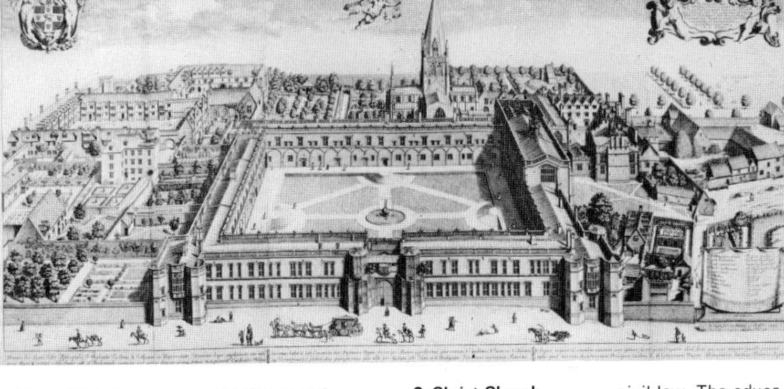

5 Henry VIII's increased revenue from his dissolution of the monasteries, with the proportion received from the rent and sale of the lands, is shown here. Henry took this action four years after his break with Rome and claimed that he did it to put an end to corruption. But another motive was to acquire extra income for the financing of wars to further his dynastic ambitions in Europe.

6 Christ Church (Cardinal's College), at Oxford was founded by Cardinal Wolsey (*c.* 1475–1530) in the 16th century. Its purpose was to train young scholars in philosophy, rhetoric, humanities, and civil law. The educational foundations of the period owe much to the humanist belief in the important relationship between education and the nobility of rendering service to the realm.

7 Lisbon, central market for the spices of Asia, was the heart of a Portuguese empire that expanded east to the Indian Ocean and the Moluccas and west to Brazil. The population of this cosmopolitan city increased from about 50,000 in 1500 to more than 100,000 by the end of the century. Similar developments in the important cities of Amsterdam, Madrid, Antwerp, London, and Paris were integral to the rise of the modern states. Capital cities, already centers of trade, also became the bases of administration and government and of court life.

8 Political propaganda in Reformation Germany is typified by this woodcut of a figure brandishing the banner of freedom. The development of printing, the growing respectability of vernacular languages, and a period of religious and political conflict gave rise in the early 16th century to cartoons and broadsheets as a means of persuasion. Pictorial representation had the widest appeal in an age of limited literacy. Monks were depicted as wolves, and the enemies of Martin Luther were caricatured. The method of contrasting woodcuts in juxtaposition was employed frequently. In one, the Ascension of Christ was shown next to the descent of the pope into hell.

Renaissance humanism

It is impossible to assign precise dates to the Renaissance. The traditional picture of a rebirth of creative thought and learning after the dark years of the Middle Ages has rightly been discarded. The new learning was not wholly original, and there was no dearth of creative thought in the Middle Ages. But this modification does not detract from the importance of the Renaissance, which from the fourteenth to the late sixteenth centuries produced a more secular spirit, a new interest in classical civilization, and increased respect for literature.

The classical revival

Interest in the classics was promoted by Francesco Petrarch (1304–74), who worked on classical texts and wrote poetry in Italian and classical Latin. The prosperous towns of fifteenth-century Italy became the centers of classical scholarship, which was pursued outside the universities and under the patronage of urban patricians interested in the civilization of the pre-Christian world. Florence became famous for Greek studies during the residence of a Byzantine scholar, Manuel Chrysoloras (*c*.1350–1415) and Marsilio Ficino (1433–99) established an academy for the study of Plato's philosophy. The concentration on classical texts owed something to the medieval interest in Arabic translations of the ancients, but the textual scholarship of men like Lorenzo Valla (1407–57), who used philological investigation to discover pure texts of the classics, was completely original.

In Italy, burgher patronage and the casual acceptance of a worldly church meant that the new learning was predominantly secular. Patrons and scholars were fascinated by the human achievement and came to believe that humankind had real power to shape its own destiny. They looked back to a time in which human achievement had reached its peak—to the past of classical Rome. The new learning received the name *humanitas* (humanism) from Leonardo Bruni (1370–1444), who wrote a *History of the Florentine People* inspired by classical models.

Since Italy was the crossroads of the Mediterranean trade routes, the movement soon spread. Frenchmen who fought in the Italian wars took back books to the court of Francis I (1494–1547), who encouraged the new scholarship. By the mid-sixteenth century the influence of Italian humanism on French scholarship was evident. French humanists such as Lefèvre d'Etaples (1455–1536) and Guillaume Budé (1468–1540) [5] embarked upon etymological and philological studies of Greek and Roman texts and of their own institutions and codes of law.

The growth of printing

The printing press was another factor encouraging the rapid northward spread of Italian scholarship. Venice became a major center for the printing of Greek and Latin secular and theological classics. In conjunction with the scholars of Germany and the Netherlands, printers produced new editions of the classics [7] and works by the Italian humanists. The growth of universities and interest in education in fifteenth-century Germany guaranteed printers a market and scholars communication.

CONNECTIONS

See also
1088 European learning the 13th century
1132 Renaissance music
1148 English Renaissanc literature
1128 The politics of Euro 1450–1600
1770 History of printing

1

1 The woodcut shows a lecture being delivered by Cristoforo Landino. Landino was one of the most widely read commentators on classical literature and a professor at Florence. His principal work was a study of Vergil and Dante; he also translated the works of Aristotle. Landino was much interested in politics. One of the circle of Lorenzo de Medici, he believed in the freedom of the citizens. In his *Disputationes Canaldulenses* (1475), he discussed one of the central questions of philosophical speculation, namely the relative advantages of the active as opposed to the contemplative life style.

2

Machiavelli
Leonardo da Vinci
Michelangelo
Verrochio
Amerigo Vespucci
Savonarola
Donatello
Francesco Guicciardini
Angelo Ambrogini
Lorenzo di Medici
Botticelli

2 Prominent figures of the Florentine Renaissance, pictured here, often worked in many cultural and political fields. Lorenzo de Medici combined diplomatic activity with art patronage; Guicciardini (1483–1540) was a politician and historian; Michelangelo was a poet, painter, sculptor, and architect.

3

3 The rich library of Lorenzo the Magnificent (1449–92), grandson of Cosimo de Medici (who built the Bibliotèca Marciana in St Marco, Florence), became a public library in 1571, in a building by Michelangelo.

4

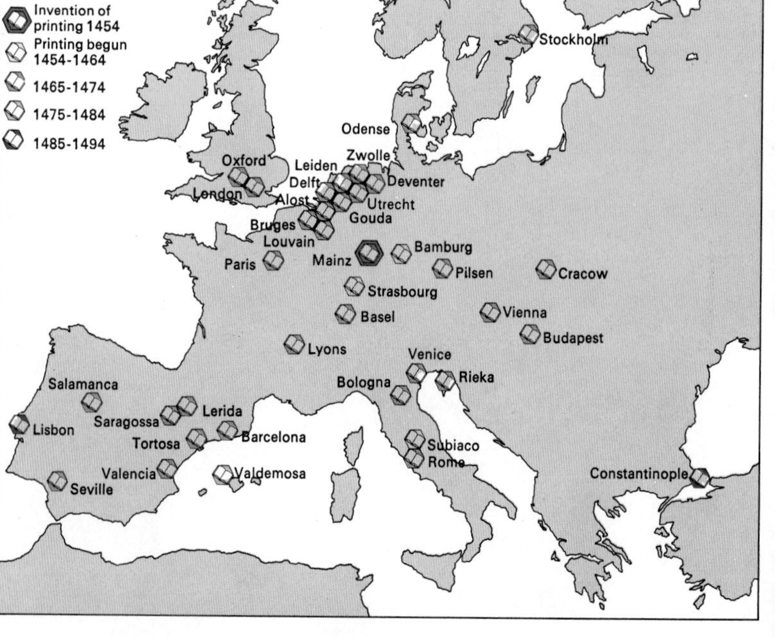

Invention of printing 1454
Printing begun 1454-1464
1465-1474
1475-1484
1485-1494
Stockholm
Odense
Oxford
Leiden
Zwolle
London
Delft
Deventer
Alost
Utrecht
Gouda
Bruges
Louvain
Bamburg
Paris
Mainz
Pilsen
Cracow
Strasbourg
Basel
Vienna
Budapest
Lyons
Venice
Rieka
Bologna
Salamanca
Lerida
Lisbon
Saragossa
Tortosa
Barcelona
Subiaco
Rome
Valencia
Valdemosa
Seville
Constantinople

4 The new humanist learning of the centuries of the Renaissance would not have had so much impact without the invention of printing in the mid-15th century. The map shows those European cities that had sizable printing presses between 1454 and 1494. By 1500 Italy had 73, Germany 50, France 45, and England only 4. Although the printing press was of immense importance, secular literacy was not common until the spread of education in the Reformation.

In the Netherlands and Germany, however, the influence of Italian humanism was tempered by the new devotional movements like the devotia moderna. Gradually, new ideas were admitted into the structure of medieval scholasticism and the Christian philosophy of St Thomas Aquinas. The interests of the northern humanists were less secular than those of their Italian counterparts—although their concern with a pre-Christian culture and more personal religion led to some clashes with the Church. Their philosophy is best exemplified in the work of Desiderius Erasmus (*c.* 1466–1536) of Rotterdam [6 B]. Erasmus applied the new textual scholarship to the production of a pure Greek text of the Scriptures [6A] and by 1516 he had published a translation of the New Testament, based on the Greek texts that he had collected.

In England, Humphrey, Duke of Gloucester (1391–1447), was a patron of the New Learning. After 1490 the teaching of William Grocy (*c.* 1446–1519) made Oxford a center of Greek studies, and Thomas Wolsey (*c.* 1475–1530) built a college at Oxford (now Christ Church) to be devoted to the new humanism.

In large part the new learning was sponsored by laymen and by the princes of Europe, who were growing in power and building brilliant courts as monuments to their prestige and authority. It is not suprising that many of the questions with which scholars were concerned were those of the ideal state, the model ruler, the best laws.

Politics and humanism

The humanists believed that people could improve their condition and so encouraged speculation about politics, a speculation evident even in Erasmus' writings and more obvious in those of Thomas More (*c.* 1478–1535) [8], Claude de Seyssel of France, and Niccolò Machiavelli (1469–1527). Scholars who regarded the classical past with interest and who employed new critical skills in evaluating evidence looked to the new learning to build the future. It was that spirit of optimism, that belief in the potential achievements of men, that endowed the Renaissance with its unique vitality.

KEY

Renaissance intellectual life was characterized by a desire to emulate the scholars of Greece who had embraced all philosophical and rhetorical knowledge. The Florentine academies were often modeled on those of Plato and Aristotle, who are pictured here in a relief by Giotto (1266–1337) from the campanile of the Duomo in Florence.

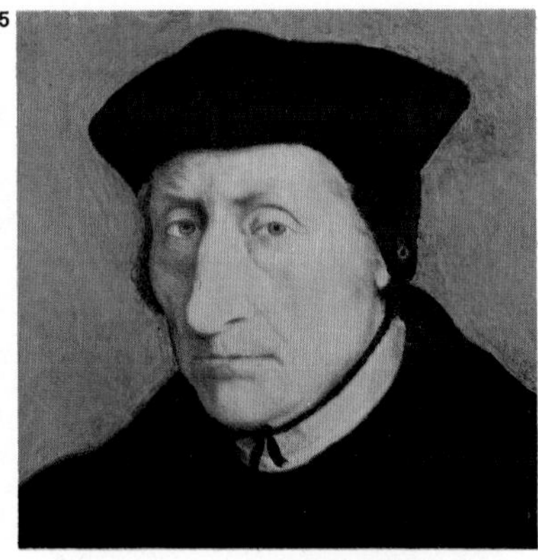

5 Guillaume Budé was the father of Greek studies in France and introduced the new sciences of philology and etymology. His critical study of Justinian's *Digest*, a compendium of Roman civil jurisprudence, showed how the text had become corrupted over the centuries. Budé was instrumental in demonstrating to the French humanists how language and law were affected by time and change.

6 Erasmus of Rotterdam [B] more than any other scholar represents the humanist scholarship of northern Europe. He combined the Italian interest in the classics and textual scholarship with religious movements of the Netherlands. To return to the Church of the Apostles he worked to produce a pure Greek text of the New Testament [A] in the hope of ending theological dispute.

ΕΥΑΓΓΕΛΙΟΝ ΚΑΤΑ ΜΑΤΘΑΙΟΝ.

ΒΙΒΛΟΣ γενέσεως ἰησοῦ χριστοῦ, υἱοῦ δαβίδ, υἱοῦ ἀβραάμ. ἀβραὰμ ἐγέννησε τὸν ἰσαάκ. ἰσαὰκ δὲ, ἐγέννησε τὸν ἰακώβ. ἰακὼβ δὲ, ἐγέννησε τὸν ἰούδαν, καὶ τοὺς ἀδελφοὺς αὐτοῦ. ἰούδας δὲ, ἐγέννησε τὸν φαρές, καὶ τὸν ζαρά, ἐκ τῆς θάμαρ. φαρὲς δὲ, ἐγέννησε τὸν ἐσρώμ. ἐσρὼμ δὲ, ἐγέννησε τὸν ἀράμ. ἀρὰμ δὲ, ἐγέννησε τὸν ἀμιναδάβ.

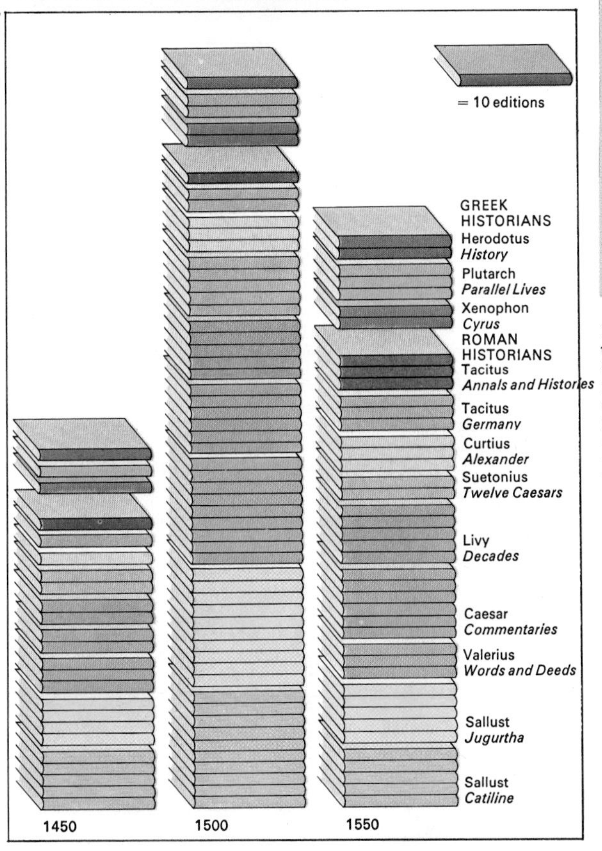

= 10 editions
GREEK HISTORIANS
Herodotus
History
Plutarch
Parallel Lives
Xenophon
Cyrus
ROMAN HISTORIANS
Tacitus
Annals and Histories
Tacitus
Germany
Curtius
Alexander
Suetonius
Twelve Caesars
Livy
Decades
Caesar
Commentaries
Valerius
Words and Deeds
Sallust
Jugurtha
Sallust
Catiline
1450
1500
1550

7 Editions of classical texts were produced in great numbers following the reemergence of interest in the classics and the invention of printing. The diagram shows a survey of classical book production, 1450–1600. Beginning in Italy, the editing of texts spread to France, Germany, and England by the 16th century. That century's interest in Livy and Caesar gave way in the 17th century to a greater interest in Florus and Tacitus. Two million copies of classical texts circulated in Europe between the invention of printing and 1700.

8 A blueprint for the perfect republic—Utopia—was presented by Sir Thomas More in 1516. It described the communal ownership of land, the education of men and women alike, and religious toleration. As a humanist More believed that people could by their own endeavors improve the quality of their lives. In particular, humanists thought that learning would teach citizens how to govern and serve the commonwealth. Often they wrote to advise rulers: at the court of Henry VIII "commonwealth men" advised on social policy.

Renaissance music

The Renaissance in music was very largely the work of Flemish composers—some six generations of them in all, between 1400 and 1570—who spurred musical development in France, Italy, Germany, Spain, and England.

Rise and spread of Flemish music

It is surprising that such a small country should have produced such an enormous amount of talent, but at a time when its larger neighbors were engaged in long and disruptive wars or suffering the effects of plague, Flanders—part of the dukedom of Burgundy—had a stable, highly developed, and thriving middle-class society that was relatively free, fond of the arts, and ready to patronize its artists. Musical education in the cathedral choir schools of Flanders and northern France was one of the chief factors that contributed to this wealth of talent. Musical composition was taught as well as singing, and every chorister therefore had the opportunity to emerge as a composer.

For this reason Flemish singers were highly sought after throughout Europe. The career of Orlando di Lasso (*c.*1532–94) [6] illustrates extremely well the possibilities open to choristers. As a child he had a beautiful voice, and was taken into the service of the viceroy of Sicily, with whom he traveled to Milan and Sicily. As a result of his talent as a composer he was given a patent of nobility by Emperor Maximilian in 1570, and made a knight of the Golden Spur by the pope in 1574.

Orlando's career demonstrates vividly two important aspects of Renaissance music. First, the social status of the musician had changed dramatically. In the new appreciation of art of all kinds that the Renaissance brought, creative talent was at a premium. A musician was no longer simply a servant or artisan to be employed. If his music won favor and esteem, there was virtually no limit to what he might aspire to. Second, but more far-reaching in its effects, the Renaissance saw a secularization of music. Musicians emerged from a tradition that had hitherto been centered on the cathedrals and monasteries and joined the music establishments of kings.

Secularization of music

Inevitably this new patronage had its effect on written music. Gregorian chant had been the thematic base for writing music of the mass, but now secular tunes were used by such composers as Josquin des Prés (*c.*1450–1521), chapel master to Lorenzo de'Medici, Louis XII, and Maximilian I, who took the tune "L'Homme armé," and John Taverner (*c.*1494–1545) in England who used the "Western Wynde." Gradually composers began to turn to secular forms, and this was of crucial importance for the evolution of Western music. Composers turned to poets for lyrics, the madrigal was born, and the *chanson* (which corresponded in France to the madrigal) received further stimulus to its development.

According to Baldassare Castiglione's manual for courtiers, *Il Cortegiano* (1528), singing was permitted as an aristocratic accomplishment for the perfect gentleman. Castiglione went on: "Harmonious too are all keyed instruments; and with ease many things can be performed on them which fill the soul with the sweetness of music." It is

CONNECTIONS

See also
1100 Medieval literature and drama
1174 The origins of oper
1196 Baroque and classic music
1244 Development of the orchestra

1 Royal and noble courts offered regular employment to musicians, whose duties included taking part in entertainments staged for visiting dignitaries. The court ballets or masques, of which the entertainments often consisted, were of Italian origin and included singing, dancing, mime, and elaborate staging, usually on an allegorical theme. One such was the *Ballet des Palonais*, represented in this tapestry. It was given at the French court in 1573 in honor of Polish ambassadors, and the music was written by Orlando di Lasso. A group of musicians is shown here seated on a stage machine. They are playing an antique lyre (top), cornett, lute, and viols. Violins were also used, and three singers took part.

2 John Day (1522–84) published his *Psalter* in 1560 containing this illustration of musical instruction in the home. It was issued after the requirement of 1559 that music in the reformed church be "a modest and distinct song . . . as plain understanded as if it were read without singing." Day was an exile during the reign of Mary Tudor and, while abroad, studied printing.

3 Jean d'Okeghem (*c.* 1430–95) was one of the most important Flemish composers. His 36-part motet was held to be one of the wonders of the world. He was master of the king's chapel in Paris in the reign of Charles VII (1403–61), the choir of which he is directing here. Josquin des Prés was a pupil.

4 Music for the lute was commonly written in tablature, instead of staff notation, between the 14th and 17th centuries. In tablature there is no indication of pitch, either between notes or the strings themselves, although there was a conventional tuning of the instrument. The horizontal lines show the string courses of the instrument, the figures (sometimes letters were used) indicate which finger is to be used for stopping the string, and the notes at the top indicate rhythm. Another form of tablature existed for keyboard music. The piece shown is from the music of John Dowland (1563–1626), one of the greatest exponents of the lute. Lutenist to Christian IV of Denmark and then to James I of England, Dowland is chiefly remembered as the composer of exquisite songs with lute accompaniment.

5 The rackett was a double reed instrument that preceded the bassoon. It was an attempt to compress the necessary length of tube for an instrument of the bassoon's compass into the smallest possible space; but it gave a muffled sound.

not surprising that one of the stringed instruments of the time, a *lira da braccio* [10C], made by Giovanni d'Andrea of Verona in 1511, has a Greek humanistic inscription on its back which runs: "Song is doctor to the pains of Man."

Instrumental music was similarly developing. Lute [4], harpsichord, organ, viols [7], and many kinds of wind instrument [5] were in common use and with aristocratic encouragement began to be further exploited. Wind instruments were thought unsuitable for gentlemen to play, for as Castiglione wrote, they were instruments "disdained by Minerva," though even that was to change. Wind bands were, however, an essential feature of ceremonies and festivities in aristocratic circles.

Italian and English Renaissance

The Flemish migrants dominated the places to which they went for only a few years, but acted as stimulants to the native musicians. In Italy, for example, the Flemings can be said to have founded the Roman classical tradition, the Venetian choral tradition, and the madrigal: but it was the Italians themselves who brought them to their full development.

With the music of Palestrina [Key], Italy became the center for sacred music. Using plainsong themes and sacred motets and working in the spirit of the Council of Trent reforms, Palestrina emphasized strict polyphony and clear delivery of the choral words in such works as *Song of Solomon* (1584). He represented the Golden Age of the Renaissance—the balance between the north and south of Europe, between polyphony and melody, between words and music, between what had gone before and what was to come. Printing [2] gave impetus to this music, and the upheavals of the Reformation and the Wars of Religion influenced its development along new paths.

Although the Renaissance arrived late in England, Thomas Tallis (1505–85) showed great contrapuntal skill in setting English words to music for the Church of England and William Byrd (1543–1623), his student, was a pioneer of keyboard music.

KEY

Giovanni Pierluigi da Palestrina (1525–94) summarized in his work the achievements of polyphonic music—the art of combining two or more voices in harmony with one another—and brought to a climax a tradition that had begun in the 9th century and was never improved subsequently. He also represented the rise of native Italian talent in Rome, which had previously been dominated by Flemish musicians. Indeed, almost the entire musical foundation of St Peter's was, at one stage, Flemish. Palestrina wrote about 100 masses; one of the most beautiful is that dedicated to Pope Marcellus II, seen here receiving the music.

6

6 Orlando di Lasso, (left, foreground) was born in Mons, traveled as a young man to Sicily and Milan and was choirmaster at St John Lateran, Rome. He returned home and settled in Antwerp in 1555. Soon afterward he entered the service of Duke Albrecht of Bavaria and spent the rest of his life there and in the service of Albrecht's successor, Duke Wilhelm. He is seen here directing a concert at the Bavarian court. He contributed to all the sacred and secular vocal forms of his time, and ranks with Palestrina and Byrd for the quality, variety, and sheer quantity of his output. As such, he was undoubtedly one of the greatest composers and practicing musicians of his day.

7

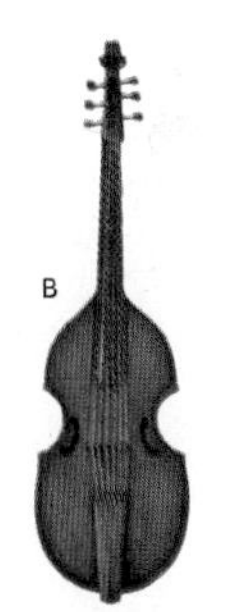

A
B
C

7 The viol family, of which the bass—or viola da gamba—[A], tenor [B], and treble [C] are examples, succeeded the medieval fiddles. The viols emerged during the 15th century and survived into the 18th, when the family as a whole was displaced by the violin family. The viols had movable frets of gut on the fingerboard, and usually six strings, although the number varied. The most important difference from the violin family was the way the bow was held underhand resulting in a rather soft, unaccented sound. The more incisive quality of the violin family made the viol obsolete.

8

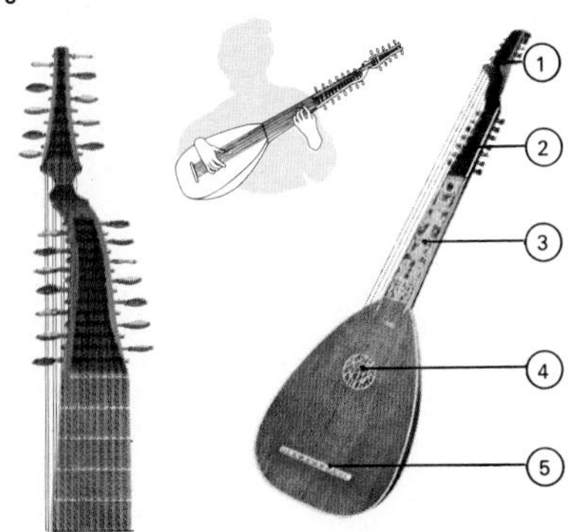

1
2
3
4
5

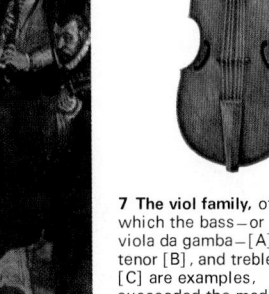

8 The theorbo was a bass lute, shown here sideways, in the playing position and front view. Five pairs of bass strings were fitted to the extra pegbox [1] and seven to the main one [2]. There were frets [3] spaced down the fingerboard, an elaborately carved soundhole or rose [4], and a bridge [5] to which the strings were attached. The performer was unable to play the theorbo at any great speed, so it was more suited to accompaniment work than for solo use.

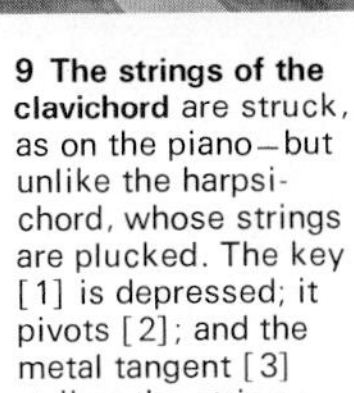

9

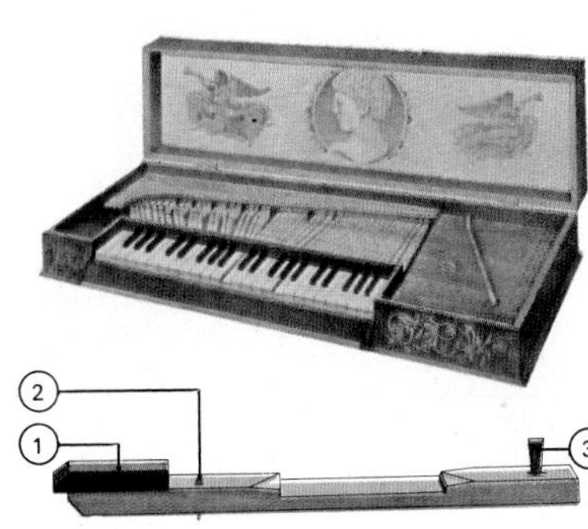

2
1
3

9 The strings of the clavichord are struck, as on the piano—but unlike the harpsichord, whose strings are plucked. The key [1] is depressed; it pivots [2]; and the metal tangent [3] strikes the string. Because of its small size and intimate sound the clavichord long remained a favorite domestic instrument, although it was replaced by the harpsichord and eventually by the piano.

10A

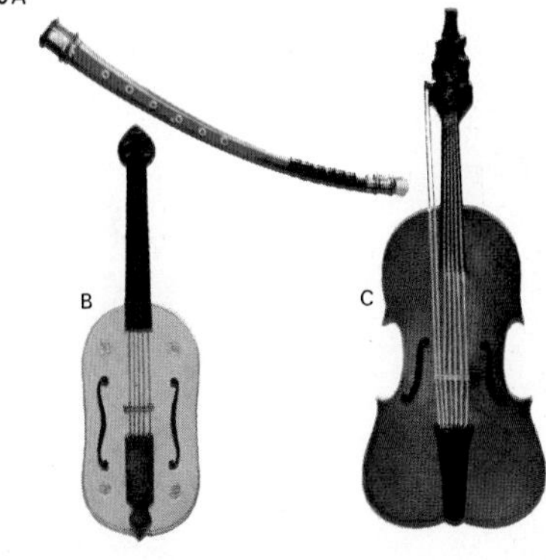

B
C

10 The cornett [A] was made of wood or ivory and was a cross between a woodwind and a brass instrument, because although it had fingerholes it also had a cupped mouthpiece that was vibrated, "reed" fashion. The Renaissance fiddle [B] and the *lira da braccio* [C] were two forerunners of the violin. The fiddle usually had five strings, as did the *lira*, but in addition the *lira* had two open strings off the fingerboard, which could be bowed for a drone effect, or plucked.

Florentine art 1400–60

The opening years of the fifteenth century in Florence were marked by costly and alarming wars, which the city survived somewhat luckily, and by political upheaval. These circumstances led to high taxation, the ruin or exile of several prosperous families, and a great decline in the city's absolute wealth; but they also provoked a resurgence of patriotism, a consciousness of the city's cultural traditions and supposed Roman origin, and public competition among patrons.

The cathedral dome

The construction of the dome [1] of the cathedral by Filippo Brunelleschi (1377–1446) symbolized the new condition of Florence; it seemed the realization of an impossible civic dream, it was achieved by the study of medieval and Roman engineering, and inevitably it was compared with the greatest triumphs of antique architecture.

The dome is not classical in detail, except in its latest elements—the lantern and the four semicircular exedrae that act as buttresses around its drum. It is characteristic that even these, formed as they are out of classical pilasters, capitals, entablatures, scrolls, and shell-niches, are not classical in function. Brunelleschi solved with extraordinary confidence the problem that remained fundamental to most later Renaissance architecture—that of applying the antique formal vocabulary to building types of a new age. To some extent he was helped by the example of Florentine Romanesque architecture, notably the Baptistery and SS Apostoli. His determined use of traditional local materials, a dark grey stone known as *pietra serena,* brick, and whitewashed stucco, even colored-marble facing, also meant that in their colors his buildings were much more closely related to the vernacular than to antiquity. The strong contrasts inherent in these materials gave his buildings very distinct articulation of their parts [8].

Florentine sculpture

Clarity of structure and evidence of intensive study of the antique also characterize the mature sculpture of Donatello (1386–1466), whose "Saint Mark" (*c.* 1412) [Key] made the first forceful statement *all'antica* (in imitation of the antique)—a statement about the nobility and gravity of man such as Cicero might have made and in a language that revived that of Roman sculpture [2]. It was followed by a long series of saints and prophets that peopled the public buildings of Florence with heroic, alert, and intensely personal beings, each an embodiment of a virtue.

Donatello's work is not dependent for its expressiveness on the beauty of craftsmanship and rich materials; in this respect he exemplifies an aesthetic revolution enunciated in Alberti's essay *On Painting* (1435), which advocated a revival of the antique standards of simplicity, even austerity, and eloquence. But Donatello's contemporary Ghiberti (*c.* 1381–1455), a much less radical individual, found an elegant compromise between Gothic ideals of beauty and the new style. A matchless craftsman, he won for this reason the competition (1401–02) for the first set of gilt bronze doors for the Baptistery. Their design and details owed practically nothing to antiquity. His second set, however, the

CONNECTIONS

See also
1138 Italian art 1450–149
1140 Florence and Rome: the High Renaissan
1142 The High Renaissanc in north Italy
1136 The Flemish Renais sance
1146 The French Renaissance
1144 The German and Netherlandish Renaissance
1130 The Renaissance: humanism

1 The Cathedral, Florence, was begun by Arnolfo di Cambio *c.*1300. By the early fifteenth century construction had reached the octagon. Advice was sought in all directions for covering the 130-ft (40-m) opening before, in 1420, Brunelleschi's solution was accepted: a dome of double herringbone brick shells and stone ribs that could be built without scaffolding. This dome was completed in 1436.

2 "David" by Donatello was made for the Medici *c.*1435. Sensual and pagan, it was the first convincing revival of the canons of the classical nude. The head derives from a Roman "Antinbus."

3 "Tribute Money" (*c.* 1427) by Masaccio is the dominant scene in a cycle of frescoes in the chapel of the Brancacci, S Maria del Carmine, Florence, detailing the story of Peter. The series was begun *c.* 1424 by an older artist, Masolino. The subject was interpreted by theologians as one of the proofs of the supremacy of the pope as Vicar of Christ.

4 "Tarquinia Madonna" by Filippo Lippi was an early work (1437), painted in tempera on panel, after a period of close imitation of Masaccio and a journey to north Italy. A knowledge of Flemish painting accounts for the informal, domestic treatment of the subject and the dark, rich colors.

"Paradise Doors," are much more lucid in design and participate in the revival in many ways; and in the conspicuous use of mathematical perspective, effectively a rediscovery of Brunelleschi's, they show where his new allegiance lay [7].

Florentine painting

Perspective was very quickly exploited by the youngest of the pioneers, the painter Masaccio (1401–28). It allowed him to place objects in apparently rational relationships in space; but he saw that the visual laws it expressed, when applied consistently, controlled not only the boundaries and intervals of space but also the drawing of forms to suggest three dimensions. The result was realism in a new sense, the realism of structure. But the same way of thinking, about space and form as unities, also led him to the first true pictorial light, unified and rational to the extent that shadow was its inevitable companion. In his "Tribute Money" [3] light as much as linear perspective produces a convincing reality. Like Brunelleschi, he was inspired by Tuscan tradition, particularly Giotto, and by antiquity, in his case a repertoire of realistic and expressive forms. His art has the same tone of austerity and moral seriousness as Donatello's.

No painter changed the course of his art as Masaccio did in so short a life. He had simplified formal problems to make them amenable to laws, and some of his followers, such as Paolo Uccello (1397–1475) continued in this way; most, however, applied his discoveries to complexities more in line with both Gothic traditions and natural appearances. Fra Angelico (*c.* 1387–1455), indeed, owed as much to the example of late Gothic painters such as Lorenzo Monaco (died 1424). Filippo Lippi (*c.* 1406–69) [4] and Domenico Veneziano (*c.* 1410–61) further modified the new style toward a descriptive naturalism, the former by responding to Flemish art, the latter by an intensified study of reality and especially of light. Domenico's "Saint Lucy Madonna" [9] represents the most advanced stage reached in Florentine painting by the mid-fifteenth century, and it exemplifies the dominant type of altarpiece.

KEY

"Saint Mark" by Donatello was made (*c.*1412) for the Weavers' Guild for their niche on the guild hall, Orsanmichele. Donatello imitates antique statues not only in details, such as drapery folds, but also in the whole design. The balanced movement of the figure's structure *(contrapposto)* is expressed with clarity through and by the superimposed drapery, and there is no trace of the swinging posture and elegantly curved forms characteristic of late Gothic sculpture. The solemnity and intensity of expression is typical of Donatello, but his rugged simplicity is now exaggerated by the loss of gilt details and weathering over the years.

5

5 The Palazzo Medici-Riccardi was built (*c.*1444–60) by Michelozzo for Cosimo de'Medici, who had rejected a design by Brunelleschi for being too ostentatious. Michelozzo's design conforms superficially on its exterior to the traditional Florentine merchant's house, although a heavy classical cornice replaces the projecting eaves. Inside it has a splendid Renaissance arcaded court.

6

6 San Lorenzo by Brunelleschi was begun *c.*1418 with the Medici Sacristy, attached to the left transept. The church was largely funded by the Medici family (Cosimo is buried under the central dome). Michelangelo added the New Sacristy to the right transept.

7 Jacob and Esau by Lorenzo Ghiberti, from the "Paradise Doors" of the Baptistery (1425–47) (gilt bronze) is one of 10 Old Testament reliefs from the third set of doors (his second), all commissioned by the guild of businessmen who had responsibility for the Baptistery. The reliefs were modeled in wax and cast separately, chased to a very high finish, and then set into a massive framework. A rich leafy border frames the opening. Ghiberti, one of the most notable figures of the early Renaissance, left Florence in 1400 but was recalled to take part in a competition that led to his casting the Baptistery's second pair of doors.

7

8

8 The Pazzi Chapel, Santa Croce, Florence, was designed by Brunelleschi *c.*1430 to be both the private chapel of a wealthy family and a chapter house. The plan, a lateral domed rectangle with a smaller domed chancel, is a development of Brunelleschi's earlier sacristy in San Lorenzo (1420–28). But the elevations, articulated characteristically in dark *pietra serena* on white stucco, are so much more logically composed that it is generally considered his best building. It shows him to be a master of construction as well as a designer of beauty and elegance.

9

9 "Saint Lucy Madonna" by Domenico Veneziano (*c.*1445) is an alterpiece of the type known as a *sacra conversazione,* which implies a close and informal relationship, spatially and psychologically, between the Madonna and the saints. The single panel generally supplants the polyptych, but its hierarchical division is often preserved, as here, by painted architecture. The perspective construction is of extreme sophistication and the color and light are exceptionally unified. A *predella* with five narratives of the lives of the saints had been attached.

The Flemish Renaissance

In the years just before 1400 the two most vital artistic centers in northern Europe, Paris and Prague, were far apart, but the distance made strangely little difference because of a widespread style in court art known by two unsatisfactory but descriptive titles, International Gothic or the Soft Style, which was also to be found in London and Lombardy. A new beginning sprang from a dynastic event of great importance, the union under Philip the Bold of the duchy of Burgundy with Flanders. This north-south (Bruges-Dijon) axis brought together artists from Flanders, Holland, and Germany to form a school that is conventionally called Flemish.

From naturalism to realism

The first phase of the patronage of the dukes of Burgundy was centered on Dijon. Philip the Bold (1342–1404) brought the painter Melchior Broederlam (died *c.*1410) from Ypres and the sculptor Claus Sluter (died *c.*1406) from Haarlem and Brussels. The main surviving work by Broederlam is the painted part of a very large altarpiece at Dijon. It is of a kind found all over northern Europe in the fifteenth century, from Burgundy to Poland, and quite distinct from Italian traditions: the main part is polychrome and gilded wood sculpture with a highly-wrought Gothic frame, which is enclosed by wings with painted narratives.

Sluter's greatest work is his last, the so-called "Well of Moses" (a Calvary group) in the Charterhouse at Dijon [1]. He developed a strikingly massive and lifelike style that characterized Burgundian sculpture for a generation.

Philip also employed the most brilliant miniaturists of the time, the Limbourg brothers (from Nijmegen, trained in Paris); but it was for Philip's brother, Jean de France, Duc de Berry, that they made their most celebrated manuscript, the *Très Riches Heures*. The narratives in this book reflect the cosmopolitan, especially Italianate, nature of French art at the end of the fourteenth century, but the calendar pages have a startling naturalism that is quite new. It is on a firm tradition of panel painting, newly inspired by the discoveries of sculptors and miniaturists, that the "Flemish" style is based.

The second phase of Burgundian patronage is centered on Bruges, the northern commercial and banking capital, where Philip the Good (duke from 1419) and his chancellor Rolin employed Jan van Eyck (died 1441) [2] from 1426, the year Jan's brother Hubert died. The enormous painted polyptych "The Adoration of the Lamb" in the Cathedral of St Bavon, Ghent, seems to have been begun by Hubert and finished by Jan in 1432, and it was commissioned by a merchant; Jan also painted for churchmen, the bourgeoisie, courtiers, and visiting Italians. His style, still more naturalistic than the Limbourgs' or Sluter's, was technically the most sophisticated and luxurious of its period [3]. While not the first to use oil, he put it to great effect in obtaining strength and transparency of color, closely observed descriptions of light and texture—as in the sheen on a pearl—and minuscule detail. A contemporary artist of almost equal importance, Robert Campin (*c.*1375–1444), worked mainly in Tournai in a tougher, less

CONNECTIONS

See also
1134 Florentine art 1400–1460
1144 The German and Netherlandish Renaissance
1138 Italian art 1450–149[0]
1140 Florence and Rome: the High Renaissanc[e]
1142 The High Renaissanc[e] in north Italy
1146 The French Renaissance
1106 Gothic art 1400–155[0]
1130 The Renaissance: humanism

1 **Claus Sluter's** "The Prophet Zachariah" (*c.* 1401), begun in 1395 for Philip the Bold, is one of six prophets around the base (commonly called the "Well of Moses") of a Calvary group of which only fragments survive. The figures were painted by Jean Malouel; such collaboration between major painters and sculptors was common in the 15th century, when unpainted sculpture was the exception to the rule

2 **Jan van Eyck's** "The Madonna of Chancellor Rolin" (*c.* 1435) was in the Cathedral of Autun, the home town of Nicholas Rolin, who was also one of the patrons of Rogier van der Weyden.

3 **In "The Arnolfini Wedding"** (1434) by Jan van Eyck, the signature states "Johannes de Eyck fuit hic," meaning "Jan van Eyck was here"—that is, was witness to what is clearly a marriage. It is believed that the couple are Giovanni Arnolfini, a merchant from Lucca, and Giovanna Cenami. The picture is filled with appropriate symbolism: the marriage-candle a reminder of Christ's presence; the mirror, signifying purity; the dog, fidelity. The statuette at the rear is of St Margaret, patron saint of childbirth.

refined style with strong expressive and realistic effect; and this style was developed by his pupil Rogier van der Weyden (1400–64) [5], who established in Brussels the most important mid-century workshop.

Enrichment of tradition

Exchange of artistic ideas between Italy and the Low Countries in the fifteenth century left the Flemings richly rewarded. The three founders of the Flemish school were followed by a host of painters operating in the Low Countries in the second half of the century who enriched the tradition and maintained its prestige; but the Flemish "rebirth" also revitalized German painting, which for the first half of the century was in general an independent development from the Soft Style. The decisive change here came through the influence of Rogier, particularly upon Martin Schongauer (*c.*1450–91), who worked mainly in the upper Rhine around Colmar. Schongauer was not only, as painter and draftsman, the principal inspiration for Dürer, but also the first great engraver (from *c.*1470) [Key].

German sculpture, by the end of the century the liveliest of northern schools, was also transformed by Dutch influence, mainly through the activity in several German centers of Nicholas Gerhaert of Leyden, (flourished 1463–73), who brought to the Gothic style a richer variety of surface through strong undercutting. The masters of this final quasi-Baroque stage of Gothic sculpture were the exuberant Veit Stoss [4] (*c.* 1440–1533), who worked as much in limewood and boxwood as in stone, and the more restrained Tilman Riemenschneider (*c.*1460–1531).

Virtuosity in architecture

Architecture was far from conservative in this period. Builders pursued virtuosity and enormous scale in their work, as in a number of Netherlandish town halls, notably Brussels (begun 1402). The most inventive results were in spectacular vaulting systems, above all in England, especially by delicate fan vaults [7], which sometimes had pendants, and in Germany by rib patterns of increasingly complex geometry.

KEY

Martin Schongauer's engraving of "St Michael" (*c.* 1475) is closely related in style to contemporary German woodsculpture. Schongauer is the earliest northern engraver known by name. His work formed one of the major channels of northern influence on such Italian painters as Giorgione, while one of the earliest works by Michelangelo, the "Temptation of St Anthony" (*c.* 1490), was a painted copy of a similarly spiky, fantastic design. Schongauer published more than 100 prints, covering a wide range of sacred and profane subjects; their combination of rich invention and disciplined clarity makes them particularly attractive.

4

4 Veit Stoss's "The Archangel Raphael and Tobias" (1516–18), was commissioned for the Carmelite church in Nuremberg by a Florentine silk merchant, who undoubtedly chose the subject because in Florence Raphael was popularly the guardian angel of travelers. In this sculpture the natural beauty of the material is revealed and not covered by the usual polychromy and gold. It is one of the latest, most vivacious works of Veit Stoss.

5

5 Rogier van der Weyden's "The Magdalen" (*c.* 1451) is the right wing of a triptych, with Christ in the center flanked by the Virgin and St John, painted for Jean de Braque. The triptych was made immediately after Rogier's return from Italy, and the simplicity of style and sense of order in the painting may reflect Italian influence upon him.

6

6 Hans Memling (*c.* 1440-94), a German pupil of Rogier, was from 1465 the most successful painter in Bruges, where he enjoyed an international clientele. Several of his portraits were of Italians, such as this one – "Portrait of an Italian" (*c.* 1480) – and these pictures exerted considerable influence in Italy, where his imaginative landscape style was much imitated by others. The subject here may be a medalist but is more probably a businessman and collector.

7

7 King's College Chapel, Cambridge, was begun for Henry VI in 1446; after interruptions the fabric was completed in 1515. The fan vault is the work of Henry VII's mason, John Wastell. Of all English fan vaults this is the most majestic and the most happily balanced between clarity and finesse of design. Although of massive construction, its taut curvature and brilliantly resolved geometrical web of ribs, carved in relief, give an illusion of weightlessness. The screen dates from the 1530s.

Italian art 1450–1490

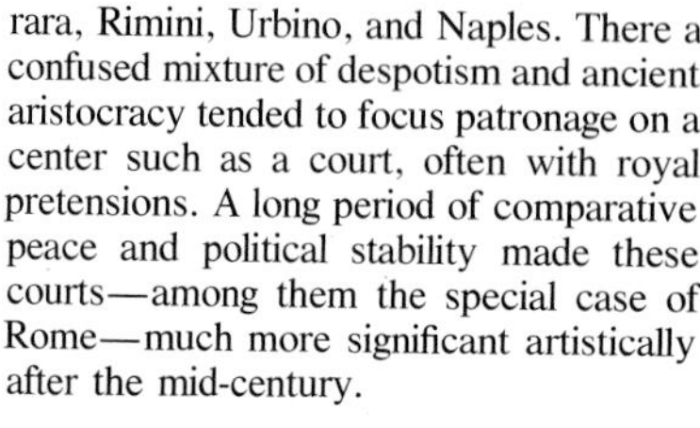

The stylistic revolution in Italy in the second and third decades of the fifteenth century had results that were in two crucial respects different from those that followed Duccio's and Giotto's achievements in the fourteenth century. First, the revolution's effects were quickly felt in almost all centers of any artistic importance; second, a profusion of artists of talent and imagination ensured that what followed was not reassessment, nor merely exploitation, but a continuing ferment of activity with a sustained momentum of invention.

Increase in secular patronage

One reason for this situation was the wider opportunity offered to artists in the second half of the century by a multiplicity of centers of patronage. These may be divided crudely into two types: on the one hand were the old nominal republics, such as Florence and Venice, where a prosperous bourgeoisie with a patrician upper crust offered at least as much patronage as the state; on the other hand were the petty principalities, such as Milan, Mantua, Ferrara, Rimini, Urbino, and Naples. There a confused mixture of despotism and ancient aristocracy tended to focus patronage on a center such as a court, often with royal pretensions. A long period of comparative peace and political stability made these courts—among them the special case of Rome—much more significant artistically after the mid-century.

A change in status

These opportunities for artists were augmented by a slowly, subtly changing attitude toward the status and use of works of art. During this period the battle to promote the visual arts to the level music held among the liberal arts was in general won. And independently of any philosophical change of this kind there was more lavish investment in culture for culture's sake; so if artists were not painting more fresco cycles in churches than before, they *were* producing more paintings and sculpture for private enjoyment. The quantity of artistic objects in domestic settings was significantly higher at the end of the century than at the beginning.

The result of these changes in demand is in harmony with new possibilities of supply that arose from technical and expressive progress; in general terms, there was a wider diversity in the forms and functions of works of art in the second half of the century. The bronze statuette and the portrait-bust, for example, became firmly established in this period. These two types illustrate a general phenomenon: the meeting of new and mostly secular demands by the adaptation of earlier and mostly religious forms. The small bronze of mythological or allegorical subjects followed a long tradition of statuettes of saints, and the composition of the sculptured portraits is best explained by reference to the continuing manufacture of reliquary busts. The evolution of each type was stimulated by the collecting of similar objects from antiquity. Similarly, the new large-scale secular figurative paintings, which decorated princes' palaces and patricians' houses, were made possible by the painters' experience of ecclesiastical art, which is why one is reminded in Andrea Mantegna's Camera degli Sposi in the Ducal

CONNECTIONS

Read first
1134 Florentine art 1400–1460

See also
1140 Florence and Rom the High Renaissar
1142 The High Renaissar in north Italy
1136 The Flemish Renai sance
1146 The French Renais sance
1144 The German and Netherlandish Renaissance
1130 The Renaissance: humanism

1 Antonio Pollaiuolo's "Hercules and Antaeus," a bronze statuette *c.* 1470–80, is similar in design to a small painting by Pollaiuolo (1429–98) on the same subject (Virtue) done for the Medici; the bronze was also most probably in the Medici collection. Although it has a triangular base, it is only intelligible from one viewpoint; the all-round view was first achieved by Verrocchio.

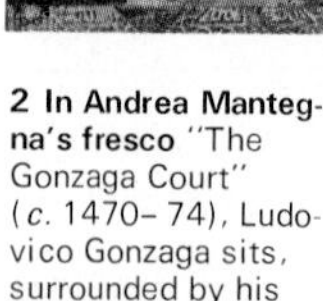

2 In Andrea Mantegna's fresco "The Gonzaga Court" (*c.* 1470–74), Ludovico Gonzaga sits, surrounded by his family and court. He has just received a letter. A second wall fresco has similar scenes, and the ceiling is an illusion of a circular opening to blue sky above.

3 Villa Medici, Poggio a Caiano (Florence), was begun *c.* 1482 by Giuliano da Sangallo for Lorenzo de' Medici and completed for Pope Leo X *c.* 1520. The curved external staircase replaced the original one which comprised two simple ramps. Close to the roads into Florence from the north, the villa was intended for receptions as well as the usual rural and summer pursuits; hence, probably, its unusual size and formality for a villa.

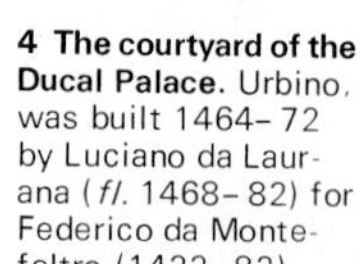

4 The courtyard of the Ducal Palace. Urbino, was built 1464–72 by Luciano da Laurana (*fl.* 1468–82) for Federico da Montefeltro (1422–82), warrior, statesman, scholar, and patron of the arts, later first duke of Urbino. The broad proportions and subtlety of rhythm distinguish it from Florentine courtyards; the whole palace is spacious, most refined in its sculptural decoration, and placed to command a sweeping view.

Palace, Mantua, of religious narrative, and in front of Sandro Botticelli's "Spring" [5] of a madonna and saints. More rarely—but both Mantegna (*c.* 1431–1506) and Botticelli (*c.* 1444–1510) provide examples—their secular compositions are inspired by classical sculpture.

Styles of architecture

Architecture shows that diversification by cross-fertilization works in both directions. Giuliano da Sangallo (1445–1516) and Lorenzo de' Medici (1449–92) designed at Poggio a Caiano [3] the first of the great Renaissance villas, for a life-style inherited from the Middle Ages and fortified by rereading the ancients. Similarly, Giuliano's building is a blend of traditional big farmhouse and selected classical elements—externally, the arched basement and the applied temple-front, a dignifying feature with a great future in domestic architecture. Conversely, the principal source of inspiration for the church designs of Leone Battista Alberti (1404–72) was a secular form, the Roman triumphal arch.

These architectural examples also illustrate the adjustment of newly enriched styles to what were enduring problems, and it is only too easy to overstate the degree of change. Churches, tombs, altarpieces, and so on were of course made as prolifically as before. The diversity of styles was as great as that of art forms and showed similar vigorous continuity and change, so that generalization is unusually difficult. But in architecture it may be said that style was characterized by a more exact, complex, and literate knowledge of antiquity; in sculpture and painting, on the other hand, typically in the work of the greatest sculptor of the period, Andrea del Verrocchio (*c.* 1434–88), or of the greatest painter, Giovanni Bellini (*c.* 1430–1516) [7], the antique was not the overwhelming inspiration it had been for their predecessors Donatello and Masaccio but was replaced by the imitation of nature. Simplicity was superseded by complexity, austerity by refinement, and in these ways late fifteenth-century Italian art reflected the structure and values of its market.

KEY

Filippo Strozzi (1428–91), the most important Florentine patron after the Medici, built a palace grander than theirs. This marble bust of him (*c.* 1485) is by Benedetto da Maiano.

5

5 Sandro Botticelli's allegory, "Spring" (*c.* 1478) was painted to be fixed above a couch in the town house of the young cousins of Lorenzo de' Medici. The earliest secular paintings are generally either wall decoration or on furniture.

6

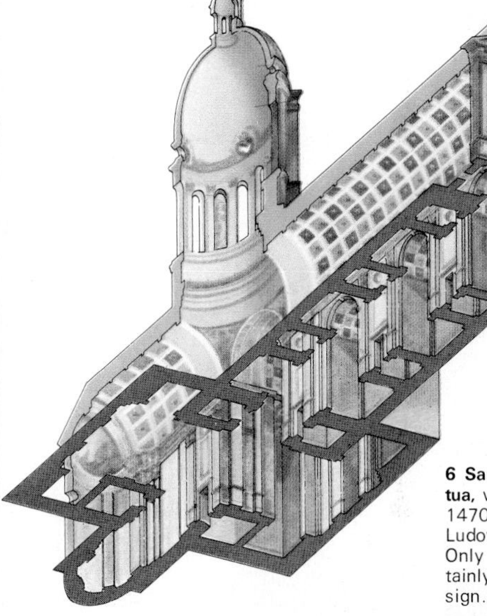

6 San Andrea, Mantua, was designed in 1470 by Alberti for Ludovico Gonzaga. Only the nave is certainly Alberti's design.

7

7 The "Madonna and Saints" of Bellini in S. Maria dei Frari, Venice (1488), is characteristic of the artist's dignity and restraint, with especially refined description of light and resonant color. It was painted when he was turning, in his later work, to simpler, more monumental forms. The classically shaped frame is original.

8

8 Andrea Verrocchio's Colleoni Monument commemorates Bartolomeo Colleoni who was *condottiere* of the Venetians. Verrocchio made his competition model for the monument in Florence and moved to Venice in 1483 to execute it. It was cast, after his death (1488), by Leopardi, who also designed the base.

Florence and Rome: the High Renaissance

Historical events around 1500 seemed in general once again to concentrate artistic activity in Florence, Rome, and Venice and to reverse the earlier tendency toward diffusion among many centers. Foreign invasions and power struggles within Italy clearly had a disastrous effect upon patronage in courts such as Naples, Urbino, and Milan. Indeed, the presence of Leonardo (1452–1519) and Bramante (1444–1514) in Milan, and the ambitious patronage of Lodovico Sforza (1451–1508), might have made that city one of the artistic capitals of Europe but for the French conquest of 1499. Leonardo then returned to Florence, where for six vital years he and Michelangelo (1475–1564) were in direct rivalry; they were joined in 1504 by Raphael (1483–1520) [6, 7] and younger men, notably Andrea del Sarto (1486–1530).

In Florence, too, there had been a political earthquake, but the expulsion of the Medici in 1494 and the formal revival of the republic (until 1512) left a prosperous oligarchy in power, and the new state institutions provided some of the greatest opportunities any Florentine artist had had, especially in the commissioning of two enormous battle-pieces from Leonardo and Michelangelo for the new council chamber (neither was finished).

Bramante and St Peter's

After 1499, Bramante went to Rome. His great opportunity came in 1506, when the energetic Julius II (pope 1503–13) [2] chose him as architect for New St Peter's; this building is unavoidably a symbol of the power and centralization of the spiritual church, and for Julius its rebuilding was not so much a practical necessity as a gesture of regeneration. Bramante's plan [Key] expresses these ideals with majestic clarity, and the piers of the crossing that he constructed established the colossal scale.

Michelangelo had already been in Rome; he returned to work for Julius, first (1506) on a projected tomb of a massive size and prolixity of sculpture undreamed of since the mausoleums of antiquity [4], and next (1508–12) on the painting on the ceiling of the Sistine Chapel [1]. Before the Sistine ceiling was complete Raphael had decorated for Julius the first of the suite of rooms in the Vatican Palace, the Stanze; and the Stanza della Segnatura, painted with ideal examples of the faculties of the mind, was immediately followed by his Stanza d'Eliodoro (1511–44), decorated very differently with dramatic narratives from church history.

Pope Julius made Rome an artistic center as important as Florence. He was succeeded by Leo X (pope 1513–21), son of Lorenzo de' Medici; his taste for the arts was more personal, more refined than visionary, but many projects such as St Peter's and the decoration of the Vatican Palace and Sistine Chapel were continued. And artists enjoyed the patronage of cultivated members of the papal court and their bankers on a scarcely less lavish scale and far above fifteenth-century levels; this was a great period of palace building and urban redesign. The architecture of the High Renaissance was not only Bramante's; the work of the Sangallo family is scarcely less important, and Bramante's position at St

CONNECTIONS

Read first
1138 Italian art 1450–149(

See also
1142 The High Renaissar in north Italy
1134 Florentine art 1400-1460
1136 The Flemish Renais sance
1146 The French Renaissance
1144 The German and Netherlandish Renaissance
1130 The Renaissance: humanism

1 **Michelangelo's painting** on the ceiling of the Sistine Chapel in the Vatican was commissioned by Pope Julius II, who asked Michelangelo to paint the 12 Apostles. The artist, if we believe his account, said this was a poor scheme and was given a free hand. The principal figures (on the supports of the dome) are 7 prophets and 5 sibyls, representing revelation to Jews and Gentiles. Down the center is a sequence of 9 Old Testament subjects, from the Creation (shown here) over the altar to the Drunkenness of Noah, illustrating an epoch of religious history not previously represented in the chapel. The first half was unveiled in 1511; this second a year later.

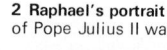

2 **Raphael's portrait** of Pope Julius II was painted between 1511 and 1513.

3 **Bramante's Tempietto** in S. Pietro in Montorio, Rome, was built as a shrine over the traditional site of St Peter's martyrdom. Bramante intended that it should be tightly enclosed in a circular courtyard. The design departs from classical circular temples in its high drum with windows between colonnades and dome.

4 **Michelangelo's** "Moses" (1513–16), in S. Pietro in Vincoli, Rome, was made for the tomb of Julius II. According to the second plan (1513), it was to be set fairly high up on the tomb. Its present setting, at floor level, is in a much reduced monument—a compromise reached, after many frustrations, during the 1540s.

Peter's and the leadership that that almost inevitably entailed were inherited by Raphael; Michelangelo's career as an architect began about 1516. All of these, as was normal in the Renaissance, were trained in some other art, and this fact is yet another cause for variety.

New intensity of feeling

High Renaissance architectural style does exist, however: it is distinguished by total mastery of the language of antiquity, by clean and measured design, by solemnity, mass, and—increasingly—richness of materials. The units tend to be larger in proportion to the whole, the forms denser and more plastic than in the earlier Renaissance, and the same characteristics are found in painting and sculpture. Here, however, because figurative art offers a direct comparison with the norm of nature, the effect is, by artifice, superhuman. Figures move, with violence or deliberation, in postures that far exceed natural behavior; in their heroic and idealized forms they appear a race of supermen. This figure style is eloquent, even rhetorical, and informed by a wholly new intensity of feeling.

In painting, largely through Leonardo's example, a new range of dramatic effects, of action, and of physical presence of form was made possible by discoveries about light and atmosphere and especially by powerful and unified effects of chiaroscuro. In all three arts drawing had a new role (again, this was largely Leonardo's doing); the quantity of preparation in drawing was greatly increased and exploration in drawing much more conscious.

The artist's status

The four principal artists were all personalities that changed definitively the social position of the artist (Raphael lived in a palace designed by Bramante for a cardinal). And the maturity, the apparent perfection of their forms, and the inventiveness of their compositions gave their works the status of classics. These artists earned the title Divine, hitherto reserved for poets, and their style was to be labeled the Grand Manner.

KEY

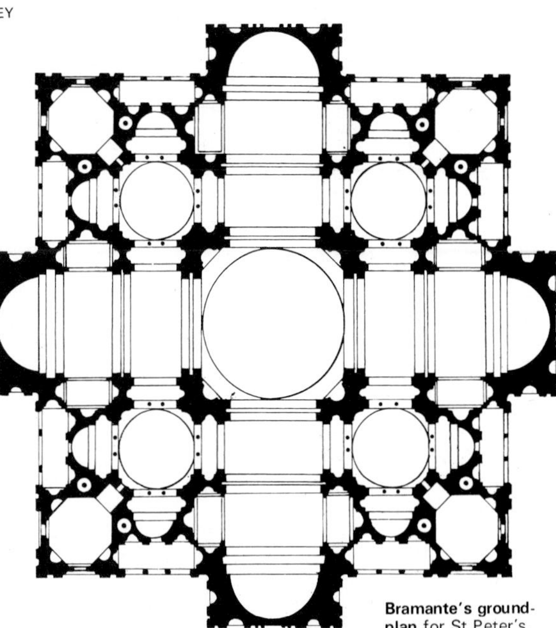

Bramante's groundplan for St Peter's.

5

5 Leonardo da Vinci's "Virgin and Child with Saint Anne" (*c.* 1510) first appeared in a cartoon (now lost) shown in Florence in 1501. The composition was slightly different from this version.

6

6 Raphael's "Paul Preaching at Athens" (1515–16) was one of a set of ten colored cartoons (of which seven survive) for tapestries, made in Brussels, with which Leo X intended to complete the decoration of the Sistine Chapel. The weaving technique required that each scene, from the lives of Saints Peter and Paul, be designed in reverse. The surviving tapestries are now on display in the Vatican.

7

7 Villa Madama, Rome, was designed by Raphael in 1517 for Cardinal Giulio de' Medici. This garden loggia, decorated after Raphael's death by his pupils, particularly the brilliant decorator Giovanni da Udine, is a rare example of form, function, and decoration all imitating the classical forms of art and architecture.

8

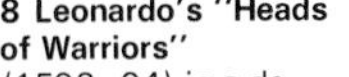

8 Leonardo's "Heads of Warriors" (1503–04) is a detailed study of the expression of horsemen for the "Battle of Anghiari," a mural commissioned by the Florentine republic but never completed. It is representative of the new drawing techniques that were invented by Leonardo as part of an intensive preparatory process.

The High Renaissance in north Italy

Many of the opportunities and interests of Roman and Florentine artists around 1500 were shared by their contemporaries in northern Italy; but there too it makes no sense to think of the High Renaissance in terms of generations. Giorgione (*c.* 1475–1510), with whom a new phase of Venetian painting seems to begin, was outlived by the much older Giovanni Bellini.

Transfusions of style

The legacy of Leonardo's most active periods in Lombardy (1483–99, 1506–08) was an assurance that north Italian artists would be as dedicated as any Florentine to forceful presentation and animation of all subject types, and there were continued migrations, in both directions, that were direct and even intended causes of style transfusions. The feeling that a Roman golden age had passed by the early 1520s dispersed Raphael's pupils, among them Giulio Romano (1499–1546), who attempted to fulfill the ambitions of Federico Gonzaga [1] to make of Mantua a new Rome. Furthermore, the catastrophe of the sack of Rome (1527) benefited several north Italian cities, notably Venice, which acquired Jacopo Sansovino (1486–1570) [Key].

The Gonzaga family in Mantua and the Este family in Ferrara escaped the momentary eclipse that most Italian courts suffered about 1500 and continued their tradition of enlightened, if strong-willed, patronage. In such centers there was much local talent, but it is characteristic of a new situation that the major artists were employed at a distance, Titian (*c.* 1487–1576) in Venice or Antonio Correggio (*c.* 1490–1534) in Parma, which was briefly an artistic center of the first importance not because of peculiarly favorable, if temporary conditions of patronage but rather because of the residence there of Correggio and Parmigianino (1503–40). Andrea Palladio (1508–80) in Vicenza exemplifies best of all the phenomenon of the great "provincial" artist. None of these, however, was provincial in the sense of artistic isolation, partly because distances are short across the roughly triangular area between the Apennines, the Alps, and the Adriatic. In the sixteenth century this area was characterized artistically by a large number of minor centers of activity—such as Bergamo or Bologna—whose fortunes fluctuated and by the continuous dominance of Venice.

Venice offered civic and corporate patronage on an enormous scale in this period, and in all the visual arts; in architecture the new library and mint commissioned from Sansovino [7] are outstanding examples. These new buildings, together with the old Doge's Palace, were decorated lavishly by painters and sculptors.

Sumptuous decoration

In general the style of Venetian decoration is unique in its sumptuousness and harmoniously interwoven complexity, festive as Venetian music of the same period [4]. Personalities have rarely been more important in defining the character of a city's art. Giorgione seems to have worked, immune to market pressures, within a restricted range of his own choice; and by focusing on particular problems, such as transient states

CONNECTIONS

Read first
1140 Florence and Rome: the High Renaissanc

See also
1134 Florentine art 1400–1
1138 Italian art 1450–1490
1136 The Flemish Renaissance
1146 The French Renaissance
1144 The German and Netherlandish Renaissance
1130 The Renaissance: humanism

1 Federico Gonzaga, painted by Titian *c.* 1528, was the son of Isabella d'Este and spent his youth at the court of Julius II. He was an important patron of Titian's and introduced him to Emperor Charles V., whom Titian later painted. The portrait here, in the relatively new three quarter-length format, set a fashion for including dogs: this one is probably a symbol of fidelity.

2 Giorgione's "Tempesta" (*c.* 1507) is one of the few attributions to Giorgione sustained by evidence. The subject has given rise to much speculation: perhaps Giorgione, inspired by the legend of the Greek painter Apelles painting the unpaintable, a thunderstorm, took this challenge as his major theme. The painting counts among the earliest Western landscapes.

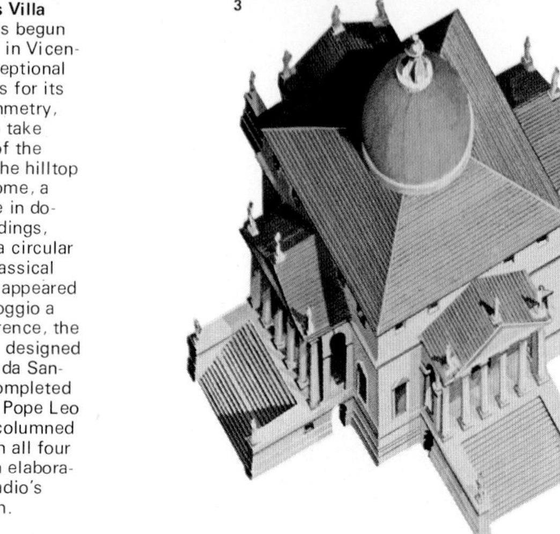

3 Palladio's Villa Rotonda was begun about 1550 in Vicenza. It is exceptional among villas for its perfect symmetry, designed to take advantage of the view from the hilltop site. The dome, a new feature in domestic buildings, surmounts a circular hall. The classical portico had appeared before at Poggio a Caiano, Florence, the Medici villa designed by Giuliano da Sangallo and completed in 1520 for Pope Leo X. The six columned porticoes on all four sides are an elaboration of Palladio's basic design.

4 Paolo Veronese painted the fresco decoration (*c.* 1562) in the Villa Barbaro, Maser (near Treviso), designed by Palladio. The villa is Palladio's most perfect blend of palace and farmhouse. Veronese was his ideal decorator. His illusionism takes amusing but slight liberties with the real architecture. Veronese's brilliant color and realistic observations of landscape make the frescoes quite remarkable. Some have religious subjects—such as the "Marriage of Saint Catherine" seen here. Some are landscapes, and others contain portraits of the owner's family, friends, and servants.

of nature in the "Tempesta" [2] or the description of sentiment in portraits, enlarged rather as Leonardo did the whole notion of what a work of art might be. Then Titian [6]—very different, especially through the universality of his art—by the fame and example of a succession of masterpieces over an immensely long career kept Venetian painting concentrated on problems like atmosphere and color, dramatic expression, and characterization, which were largely neglected in central Italy.

Correggio [5], whom Titian admired, was in some respects an even more original artist, and of all sixteenth-century painters he came nearest to a baroque style. His were the most advanced experiments with movement and emotion and—again following Leonardo's lead—he achieved through naturalism and immediacy a newly intimate relationship between works of art and their spectators.

Palaces and villas

The other great "provincial," Palladio, has European stature for different reasons. Building activity generally gathered pace in north Italy from about 1525, especially in civic and domestic fields. Giulio Romano, Sansovino, and Sanmicheli (*c.*1484–1559)—another transmitter of Roman experience, especially to Verona—built palaces and villas, and Palladio was much indebted to them.

The growth of villa building in the period was extraordinary but natural; the patricians, especially from Venice, tended to put their capital increasingly into land and wanted to live on their estates. Palladio's genius lay in a rare combination of theoretical excellence and flexible common sense; both very practical by temperament and imaginative, he could provide a new clientele with widely varied aspirations and needs a range of building types that became (partly through publication) almost definitive. They ranged from a thinly disguised farmhouse, the wings of which were barns, to an impressively spreading rural palace [3, 4]; and they fulfilled a social need no less perfectly by their evident use of classical styles as a mark of social distinction.

KEY

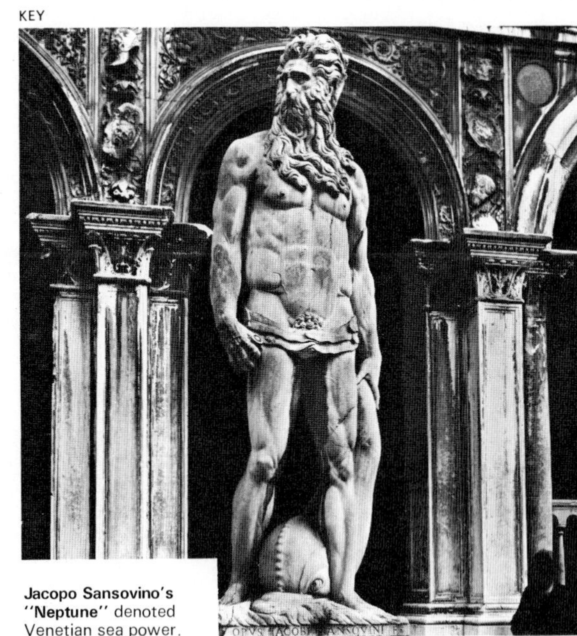

Jacopo Sansovino's "Neptune" denoted Venetian sea power.

5

6

5 Correggio's "Adoration of the Shepherds" (*c.* 1528–30) is the outstanding example of the artist's illusionistic painting of light. The informal, eccentric design of this scene is calculated to make the spectator feel he completes the group.

7

7 Jacopo Sansovino's Library of S Marco, Venice, was begun in 1536. The site required a building filling the whole length of the Piazzetta, incorporating an arcade (as a public amenity and to accommodate shops), reflecting that of the Doge's Palace, which it faces.

8

6 Titian's "The Rape of Europa" (1559–62) is one of a set of mythologies painted for Philip II, king of Spain, Titian's principal patron in the later part of his career. Philip seems to have left the artist free to choose his subjects as he desired.

8 Palladio's S Giorgio Maggiore, Venice, was begun in 1566. This was Palladio's first church. Like many architects working in Venice, he was inspired by St Mark's to use columns in large numbers, but the interior is exceptionally light in color, well-lit, and unadorned.

The German and Netherlandish Renaissance

The tides of stylistic influence flowed northward in the sixteenth century as the prestige of Italian culture compensated for Italy's loss of political power. Albrecht Dürer of Nuremberg (1471 –1528) was one of the first northern artists to digest the Italian Renaissance achievement. He saw its works at first hand, mainly in Venice. The greater part of his work was in woodcuts and engravings [Key], to which he brought immense refinement of technique and capacities for narrative invention that made him the most imitated artist in Europe. The religious series issued for the popular market were more Germanic, more realistic in style, while the prints of humanist subjects, and the later panel paintings (from *c.* 1506), were more clearly of the Renaissance.

Grünewald and Holbein

A painter and draftsman of equal imaginative power, but narrower range, was Mathias Grünewald (*c.* 1480–1528), court artist to the archbishops of Mainz and Brandenburg, who is best known for his prodigious altarpiece for the hospital of Isenheim, now Colmar (*c.* 1512–16) [4]. By expressive distortion, brilliant color and technique, and extraordinary invention Grünewald painted with emotive power.

Cooler and more cosmopolitan was Hans Holbein the Younger (1497–1543), who was born in Augsburg, grew up in Basel [2], and later worked in London. His thoroughly Germanic beginnings were transformed by knowledge, probably firsthand, of north Italian High Renaissance art, and also of French and Flemish art. His later work, especially in England, is largely portraiture, in which he combines an Italian sense of form and composition with dispassionate observation of detail and texture. In England, too, he worked as court artist to Henry VIII and established a tradition of miniature portrait painting; his principal English follower was Nicholas Hilliard (*c.* 1547–1619). German painting at the beginning of the century had another focus along the Danube between Bavaria and Austria; the major master of the Danube school was Albrecht Altdorfer (*c.* 1480–1538) who began, at about the same time as Giorgione (*c.* 1475–1510) in Venice, to make paintings of which the main subject was landscape.

Painting in Flanders was centered in Antwerp, which supplanted Bruges as the commercial capital from about 1490. The founder of the Antwerp school was Quentin Massys (*c.* 1465–1530) who, like his German contemporaries, combined native traditions with Italian ideas. His collaborator Joachim Patenier (died *c.* 1525) was a landscape artist whose panoramic view of the world initiated a Netherlandish tradition.

Rejection of local traditions

Massys had a group of followers whose complicated, neo-Gothic, figurative painting has the dubious label "Antwerp Mannerist." But in Flanders, and still more in Holland, a contrary current impelled by a rejection of local traditions (except technique) in favor of Italian is labeled more sensibly Romanist; chief among these were Scorel (1495–1562, Utrecht and Haarlem) and Heemskerck (1498–1574), and out of this school came a flourishing group of genre painters.

CONNECTIONS

See also
1136 The Flemish Renaissance
1106 Gothic art 1400–1550
1146 The French Renaissance
1142 The High Renaissance in north Italy
1140 Florence and Rome: the High Renaissance
1130 The Renaissance: humanism

1 "SS Paul and Mark" by Albrecht Dürer (1526), was one of a pair of paintings representing the Four Temperaments, which the artist presented to the city of Nuremberg. The other painting showed SS Peter and John. Dürer combined the oil painting tradition of the north, emphasizing realism, with Italian monumental figure style. He was influenced by Bellini, whom he had seen in Venice, and by more recent studies of Raphael (probably via engravings), with whom Dürer corresponded and exchanged works.

2 Hans Holbein the Younger's "The Meyer Madonna" (1526) was painted for the burgomaster Meyer's castle near Basel. It was completed just before Holbein's first trip to England. The painting was later modified (about 1530) when Holbein added Meyer's first wife. Holbein, one of the most accomplished portrait painters of his time, was a close friend of Erasmus and painted three portraits of him. While in Basel, Holbein also worked on designs for wood engravings and illustrated the Luther Bible.

3 "Derich Born" by Holbein was painted in 1533 on the artist's second London visit. Derich Born was a Cologne merchant resident in London. He was one of the many Germans Holbein painted for the Merchants of the Steelyard before his royal service.

4 Mathias Grünewald's "Resurrection" (*c.* 1512–16, detail) is part of a large altarpiece from the Antonite monastery of Isenheim. When closed, it shows the Crucifixion. On the first opening the Annunciation, Nativity, and Resurrection are revealed; on the second opening the hermits Paul and Anthony and the Temptation of Anthony. The wings flank three carved wooden figures of saints. Grünewald rejected Renaissance ideas. The intensity in his work is expressed in Gothic imagery.

Netherlandish painting in the sixteenth century, as in the seventeenth, was practiced by a bewildering array of minor masters, few of whom had any real stature. Two, however, stand out: Hieronymus Bosch (*c*. 1450–1516) and Pieter Bruegel the Elder (*c*. 1528–69). Bosch, who worked in apparent isolation in Brabant, was active well before 1500, but about that date began to enjoy European patronage (one patron was Philip, archduke of Austria). His peculiar fantasies, based on popular proverbs and vernacular visual imagery, are moralistic comments on the human condition [6]; and to him is to be traced a fluid, transparent panel-painting technique that continues down to Rubens. Bruegel was one of the links in this tradition, but he looked still harder at nature and its seasons [5] as well as at social classes, and enriched the content of secular painting.

Sculpture and architecture

A Renaissance style in sculpture began in south Germany around 1520, especially at Innsbruck and Augsburg; the exceptional Apollo Fountain at Nuremberg [8] by Pieter Flötner (*c*. 1493–1546) is clearly part of the legacy of Dürer. Antwerp was the other main center of northern sculpture and the training ground of Gianbologna (1529–1608), who spent most of his career in Florence. Buildings in a true Renaissance style are isolated freaks: they include the Fugger Chapel at Augsburg (1509–18), the Chapel of Sigismund at Cracow (1517–33), and the Castle of Breda (begun 1536), the last two by Italians. Clumsy imitations or superficial applications of Italianate detail are more common. A distinctively northern decorative style, spreading from England to Poland, was based upon the Mannerist engravings of the Antwerp school (particularly Cornelis Floris) (1514–75), with strapwork, scrolls, and grotesque masks. But the most interesting architectural developments were in large, functional, and stylistically unself-conscious buildings with many windows among the civic architecture of German towns (such as the Rathaus at Bremen) and houses such as Longleat and Hardwick [7] in England.

KEY

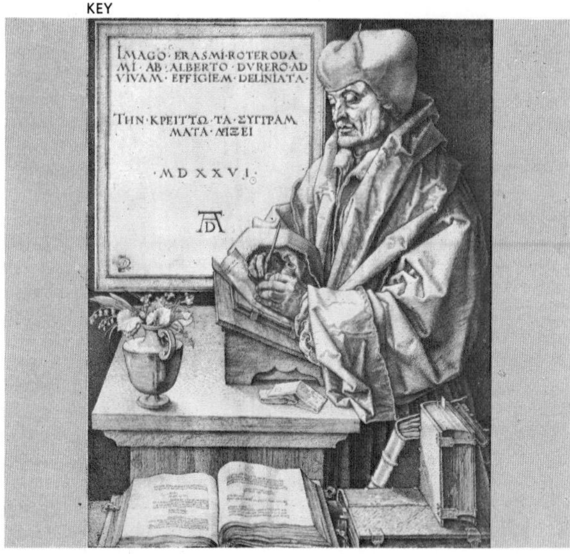
IMAGO·ERASMI·ROTERODA
MI·AB·ALBERTO·DVRERO·AD
VIVAM·EFFIGIEM·DELINIATA·
THN·KPEITTΩ·TA·ΣΥΓΓΡΑΜ
MATA·ΔΕΙΞΕΙ
·MDXXVI·

Albrecht Dürer's engraving. "Portrait of Erasmus" was executed in 1526. Desiderius Erasmus was the most important figure in north European Renaissance humanism.

5

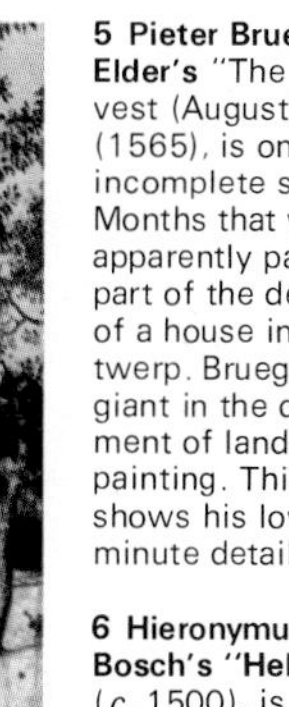

5 Pieter Bruegel the Elder's "The Cornharvest (August)" (1565), is one of an incomplete set of Months that were apparently painted as part of the decoration of a house in Antwerp. Bruegel was a giant in the development of landscape painting. This scene shows his love of minute detail.

6

6 Hieronymus Bosch's "Hell' (*c*. 1500), is the right wing of the "Garden of Delights" triptych. The left panel shows the Creation. With the wings closed one sees, in near monochrome, the Flood. Bosch's macabre fantasies seem to be meditations on man's follies and their results.

7 Bremen Rathaus was built in the 15th century and is mainly Gothic in style. Its facade was later rebuilt, between 1609 and 1614, by a Flemish architect, and it includes many characteristic features of Renaissance civic architecture. The high-pitched roof and the stepped gables show a strong Flemish influence, while the round-headed arcade and the decorative panels are typically Italian. Civic building during the 17th century flourished, illustrating the wealth and pride of the expanding commercial center in Northern Europe.

7

8

8 In the Apollo Fountain (1532) by Pieter Flötner the figure is about half life-size and at this early date is unique in northern sculpture for its classicism. This is partly based on Dürer's research into the ideal proportions of the human body (as in his "Adam and Eve" engraving, 1504), and partly (presumably) upon Flötner's own experience in Italy, where he may have seen the Apollo Belvedere in Rome. Flötner's work precedes all the known Italian examples of this pyramidal type of fountain, with sea monsters and putti positioned around the base.

The French Renaissance

The origins of French painting and sculpture of the fifteenth century have much in common with those of Burgundian and Netherlandish art; indeed, such artists as the Franco-Flemish Jean Malouel (died 1415) and the Flemish Limbourgs worked for both French and Burgundian courts. French painting, however, was rooted in a lively tradition of miniature painting, especially in Paris, which was also one of the main centers of the International Gothic style [1].

Naturalism and simplicity

Inspiration for a new beginning came from two directions, Italy and Flanders, and the most important artist concerned was Jean Fouquet (*c.* 1420–80) [2], who was in fact in Rome *c.* 1446–50. The combination of the new naturalism of the north with the simplification and lucidity of form and space of the south is without parallel in the midcentury. Fouquet, who appears to have been the principal artist of Charles VII (1403–61) and Louis XI (1423–83), worked as a panel painter and miniaturist in Tours and Bourges; and other artists connected with the court, such as the Master of Moulins [3], worked in this part of the Loire valley, then favored by the royal household. There was also, however, a very active school in Provence from about 1440, and the painters there were sometimes more inclined to a Flemish style or to an Italian style.

French sculpture of the fifteenth century was mainly the product of regional schools pursuing the Gothic style into its last naturalistic stages, and the chief new stimulus was provided by Claus Sluter (*fl.* 1390–1406) in Dijon. Michel Colombe (*c.* 1430–*c.* 1512), who shared royal patronage and even commissions with Fouquet, was perhaps as outstanding a figure; almost all his works have been destroyed. Those that survive, such as the transitional Gothic-Renaissance tomb of François of Brittany at Nantes (1499–1507, partly by Italian assistants), are late. Architecture is generally most original in secular genres, châteaux, and such great town houses as the Hôtel Jacques-Coeur at Bourges (1444–51) or the Hôtel de Cluny in Paris (begun 1485); in such buildings there appear elements of planning that were to recur in the great châteaux of the next century: broad courtyards, external staircases, round towers, and rudimentary galleries.

Culture from conflict

The reinvigoration of French art from about 1500 was mainly the result of the successes of Charles VIII and Louis XII in military raids into Italy in 1494 and 1499; culturally the French became subject to Italy, overwhelmed by the cultivated Renaissance they met in Florence, Naples, and Milan. The beginnings of an Italianate court were made under these kings. The earliest well documented (but imperfectly surviving) product is the Château de Gaillon (1501–10) built and decorated, in part by Italians, for the Cardinal-Minister d'Amboise. But this Italianism became a program under Francis I (reigned 1515–47), who also visited and admired Italy and attracted to his court Italian poets, musicians, and artists (among them Leonardo). Thereafter it was secular building that dominated French art for a

CONNECTIONS

See also
1142 The High Renaissance in north Italy
1144 The German and Netherlandish Renaissance
1140 Florence and Rome: the High Renaissance
1138 Italian art 1450–1490
1136 The Flemish Renaissance
1134 Florentine art 1400–1460
1130 Renaissance humanism

1 "The Visitation" from the *Boucicaut Hours* (*c.* 1405) is a narrative scene surrounded by a foliate border. The soft, convoluted drapery typifies International Gothic, but the landscape looks to Van Eyck's naturalism.

2 Jean Fouquet's "Etienne Chevalier and St. Stephen" (*c.* 1452) is the left half of a diptych that stood over the tomb of Chevalier at Melun. The right half of the work shows a madonna with angels; the donor's patron saint was thus seen to be recommending him to the Virgin's mercy. Chevalier was one of the most important of Charles VII's courtiers, and for him Fouquet made a book of hours. This work also reveals the virtuosity of his perspective and classical pilastered backgrounds – clearly the fruits of his recent Italian journey. But few Italians were so advanced, and his realism derives more strongly from Flemish art.

3 Master of Moulins' "Madonna" (*c.* 1490) was influenced by the Fleming Hugo van der Goes as much as by Fouquet. The artist may have been the Dutchman Jean Hey, court painter to the Bourbons in Moulins.

century, as the monarchy and its dependents provided themselves with settings in the new style, adapted, naturally, to social and climatic conditions quite different from those in Italy and retaining such characteristically French features as the gallery.

The earlier of Francis' own surviving buildings—a wing at Blois and the Château de Chambord [6]—are transitional, and Italian detail is grafted onto local forms, sometimes with bizarre results, as among the half-flamboyant, half-Renaissance chimneys and dormers on the fantastic roof of Chambord. But all traces of Gothic have disappeared in the new buildings at Fontainebleau, begun for Francis in 1528 by Gilles le Breton [7] and completed in the 1560s by Primaticcio. The result cannot, of course, be mistaken for an Italian building—its steep roofs and dormers preclude that—but by about 1530 a genuinely French Renaissance style was established, by far the most mature outside Italy. French architecture maintained this position under the leadership in mid-century of Philibert de l'Orme (*c.*1510–70) [4] and Pierre Lescot (*c.*1510–78) [5]; the chaste, cerebral style of the former seems from the standpoint of later centuries the foundation of the French classical tradition.

The School of Fontainebleau

The royal court was so much the focus of activity in painting and sculpture that "the School of Fontainebleau" is a title that adequately covers the most striking developments in these arts. Again the presence of Italians summoned by Francis I was crucial: Rosso Fiorentino (1495–1540) and Francesco Primaticcio (1504–*c.*1570) among the painters, Benvenuto Cellini (1500–71) among the sculptors. As it happened there was far more native talent among the sculptors than among the painters; Jean Goujon (*c.*1515–62) and Germain Pilon (*c.*1535–90) [Key] treat the human figure with grace and competence to match any Italian, excepting only Michelangelo. The School of Fontainebleau, which was also strong in engraving and metalwork, was to become, from 1530, one of the most influential centers of Mannerism.

KEY

"Diana," attributed to Pilon (*c.* 1550), is from a fountain of the Château of Anet.

4

4 The tomb of Francis 1 in St Denis, Paris, was begun in 1547 by Philibert de l'Orme. The form of a triumphal arch symbolizes the triumph of life over death, as in Italian tombs. The couple are presented within the tomb as dead and on top of it as alive, praying. The sculptor was Pierre Bontemps.

5

5 Pierre Lescot's Cour Carrée of the Louvre was begun in 1546. Francis I's rebuilding of the old Louvre (from 1527) was a sign of the return of central power to Paris. Lescot collaborated here and elsewhere with the sculptor Jean Goujon, for whose elaborate reliefs there are Italian precedents.

6

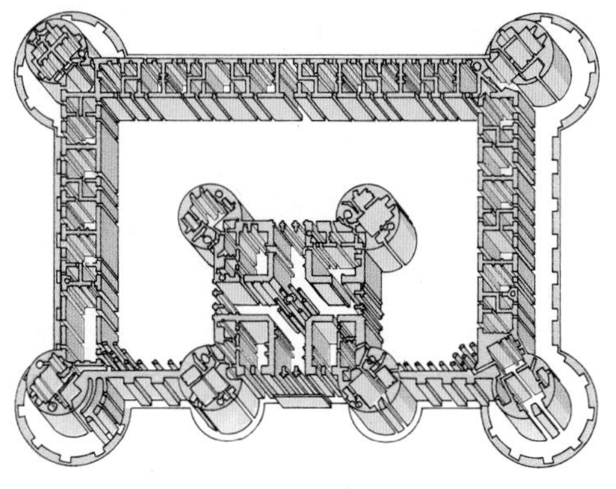

6 Château de Chambord was begun in 1519, and its architect was probably Domenica da Cortona, although the only real traces of Italian planning are in the cruciform keep. Otherwise the overall design is characteristic of French medieval châteaux. It was built for Francis I.

7

7 The Cour Ovale of the Château de Fontainebleau (begun *c.* 1530) was added by Gilles le Breton to the medieval hunting lodge that Francis I was expanding into one of his major residences. The domed gateway was added *c.* 1640. The side wings provided apartments for courtiers.

English Renaissance literature

The new learning of Italy in the fifteenth century rapidly spread northward and was promoted in England by the "Oxford reformers," the humanist scholars John Colet (*c.*1467–1519), William Grocyn (*c.*1446–1519), and Thomas Linacre (*c.*1460–1524). Traditional learning had undergone a change of purpose. It was no longer primarily aimed at elucidating the truths of the Scriptures but, through the study of classical philosophy and history, at training future leaders in the arts of government. This program was first summarized in *The Book Named the Governor* (1531) by Thomas Elyot (*c.*1499–1546).

Latin and Italian influences

The new learning also promoted an outpouring of original works in Latin—from *Utopia* (1516), a tract on ideal politics and government by Thomas More (*c.*1478–1535), to *Novum Organum* (1620), on the ideal of education, by Francis Bacon (1561–1626). Scholarly writing in Latin reached only a small audience, and therefore translations from the classics became common, such as Thomas North's version of Plutarch's *Lives* (1579) [2].

Imitation, in a creative rather than a slavish sense, was another important aspect of the literature of the period. The brilliance of the Italians Francesco Petrarch (1304–74), Giovanni Boccaccio (1313–75), Ludovico Ariosto (1474–1533), and, later, Torquato Tasso (1544–95) was quickly taken as a model; Thomas Wyatt (*c.*1503–42) and the Earl of Surrey (*c.*1517–47) both distinguished themselves in their sonnets based on the pattern devised by Petrarch. It was the beginning of a great age of English poetry that continued through Spenser [Key, C], Sidney, and Shakespeare [A] to the seventeenth-century poets Robert Herrick (1591–1674), Richard Lovelace (1618–57), Andrew Marvell (1621–78), John Donne, and John Milton [B].

All kinds of poetry were produced during this extraordinary period—from long romances such as Spenser's *Faerie Queen* (1589–96) and the great epic *Paradise Lost* (1667) by Milton to brief, gemlike lyrics from French and Italian models that were intended to be sung [1]. The greatest poets of Elizabeth's reign (1558–1603) were Edmund Spenser and Philip Sidney (1554–86). Sidney's collection of sonnets *Astrophel and Stella* (1591) shows great mastery of the Petrarchan form. Spenser's main work, *The Faerie Queen,* contains both allegorical and heroic elements in which the heroic subject matter blends with the Renaissance aim of fashioning a virtuoso nobleman.

Elizabethan drama

In drama the revival of Greek and Latin learning introduced classical elements. The old morality play had culminated in the plays of Christopher Marlowe (1564–93), whose four great tragedies, *Edward II, Tamburlaine the Great, Doctor Faustus,* and *The Jew of Malta,* are studies of heroic power and the vices that such power creates. They foreshadowed the great Shakespearian studies in kingship.

With the new learning, the Latin playwright Seneca (*c.* 4 BC–AD 65) became a favorite model for tragedy. Here were introduced the themes of vengeance and re-

CONNECTIONS

See also
998 Greek literature and theater
1028 Roman literature
1130 The Renaissance: humanism
1132 Renaissance music

1 The lute, a stringed instrument played by plucking with the fingers, characterized music of Elizabethan times. English lutes were prized throughout Europe. Because singing was such a favorite entertainment at court, a normal gentlemanly accomplishment was the ability to write one's own songs—including lyrics—and to perform them while playing on the lute.

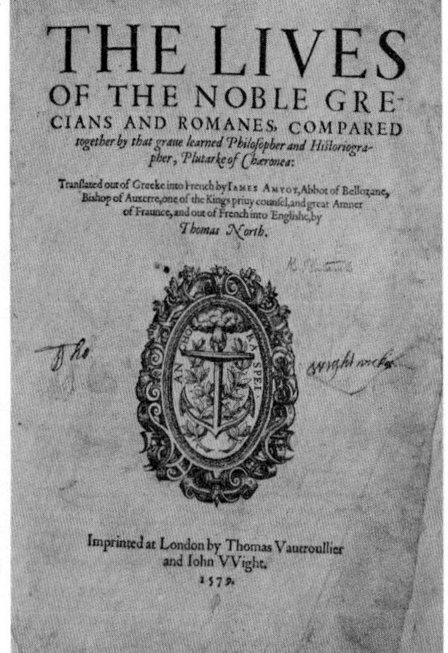
THE LIVES OF THE NOBLE GRECIANS AND ROMANES, COMPARED together by that graue learned Philosopher and Historiographer, Plutarke of Chæronea:

Translated out of Greeke into French by IAMES AMYOT, Abbot of Bellozane, Bishop of Auxerre, one of the Kings priuy counsel, and great Amner of Fraunce, and out of French into Englishe, by Thomas North.

Imprinted at London by Thomas Vautroullier and Iohn VVight. 1579.

2 Plutarch's Lives was translated into English in 1579 by Thomas North (the frontispiece is shown here). It provided one of the main sources for plot and character in the Roman plays of Shakespeare.

THE HOLY BIBLE, Conteyning the Old Testament, AND THE NEW: Newly Translated out of the Originall tongues: & with the former Translations diligently compared and reuised, by his Maiesties speciall Comandement. Appointed to be read in Churches. Imprinted at London by Robert Barker, Printer to the Kings most Excellent Maiestie. ANNO DOM. 1611.

3 The authorized King James version of the Bible, based on earlier work by William Tyndale and Miles Coverdale, was published in 1611. It is one of the great monuments of English literature.

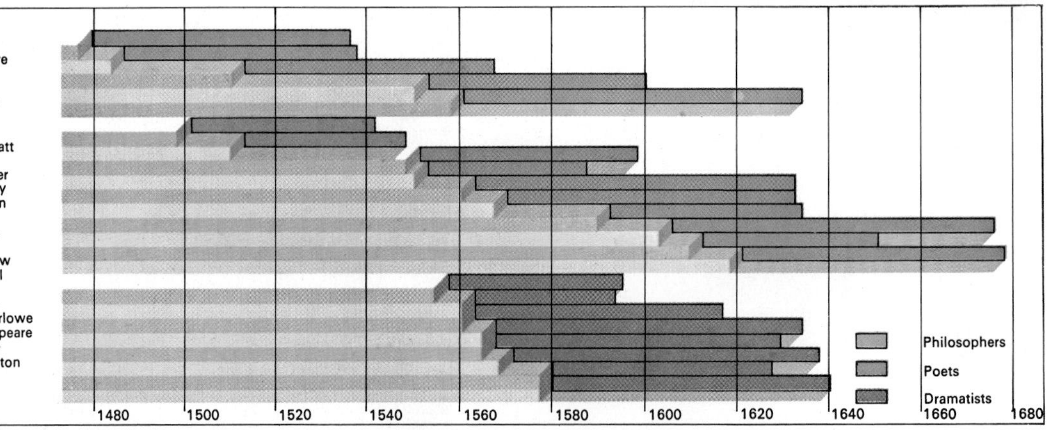

Sir Thomas More
Thomas Elyot
Roger Ascham
Richard Hooker
Francis Bacon
Sir Thomas Wyatt
Earl of Surrey
Edmund Spenser
Sir Philip Sidney
Michael Drayton
John Donne
George Herbert
John Milton
Richard Crashaw
Andrew Marvell
Thomas Kyd
Christopher Marlowe
William Shakespeare
Thomas Dekker
Thomas Middleton
Ben Jonson
John Webster
John Ford
Philosophers
Poets
Dramatists
1480
1500
1520
1540
1560
1580
1600
1620
1640
1660
1680

4 This chronological diagram shows the development of various forms of writing in the golden age of English literature, which embraced the Tudor and Stuart periods. The interpreters of the new learning of the Italian Renaissance predated the dramatists and poets, but all three reached a peak in the late Elizabethan period and continued to dominate the first decades of the seventeenth century. Drama flourished for the briefest time.

tribution, with accompanying horror and violence. Stage mechanics were devised to provide unexpected effects.

The earliest English tragedy in the manner of Seneca was *Gorboduc* (1561) by Thomas Norton (1532–84) and Thomas Sackville (1536–1608). It started a tradition that culminated in *The Spanish Tragedy* (1592) by Thomas Kyd (*c*.1558–*c*.1594), in which the Senecan elements are enlivened by a modern setting, elaborate stage devices, and highly individualistic characters. In comedy the Latin influence of Plautus and Terence was of the greatest importance, as can be seen in two of the best early plays, *Ralph Roister Doister* (*c*.1553) by Nicholas Udall (*c*.1505–56) and *Gammer Gurton's Needle* (1575) by William Stevenson.

English Renaissance literature is dominated by William Shakespeare. His earlier plays are adaptations of models in vogue; later comedies show a greater complexity in character and plot, as do the cycles dealing with kingship. Then come the great tragedies and the complex *Cymbeline, The Tempest,* and *The Winter's Tale*.

Shakespeare's greatest contemporary was Ben Jonson (*c*.1572–1637), who developed a series of characters of outstanding force, especially in *Volpone* (1607). He also wrote masques [6], which incorporated mythology, courtly life, folklore, and satire. In purely literary terms the masque found its zenith in Milton's *Comus* (1634).

The Metaphysical poets

A group of poets who flourished in the seventeenth century are known as the Metaphysical poets. Their language was complex and double-edged; their subject matter contained the pious, the amorous, and the reflective. They included Herrick, Lovelace, Marvell, and Donne [7].

John Milton was the greatest poet of the seventeenth century; his masterpiece was the Christian epic *Paradise Lost* [8]. Divinity, the moral and theological concern of the Church, was thus once again in the forefront of English writing. But it was tempered by the study of man's character in his own right and not merely as the creation of a mighty God.

KEY
A
B
C

The greatest figures of English Renaissance literature were William Shakespeare (1564–1616) [A], John Milton (1608–74) [B], and Edmund Spenser (1552–99) [C]. Spenser wrote lyric and narrative poetry in a sensuous style; Shakespeare is the greatest dramatist in English history; and Milton stands as the unrivaled master of English epic poetry.

5

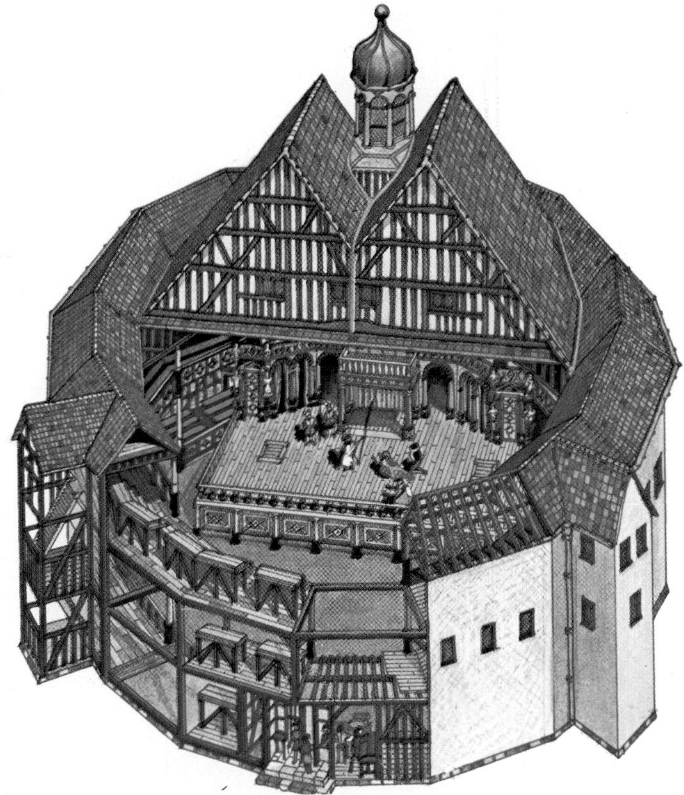

5 The Globe theater was probably the largest in London in the late sixteenth and early seventeenth centuries. This was the great age of English popular drama; the theaters, in total, attracted an estimated weekly audience of 21,000 theater goers. The audiences consisted of ordinary people in the "pit" and the wealthy patrons who sat in the tiered galleries. A protruding stage brought the audience into intimate contact with the action.

6

6 The sets for the Masque of the Augurs (1622) were designed by Inigo Jones (1573–1652). The masque shows the intimacy between architectural design, the theater, and music. It was an aristocratic, exclusive, and purely courtly art form. Of Italian origin, the masque was an ancestor of modern opera and ballet. Even though most of the pageants were not written dramas, they have been preserved in designs, drawings, and music.

7

7 John Donne (*c*. 1571–1631) was the most famous Metaphysical poet. He was a soldier, courtier, lover, preacher of distinction, and, later, dean of St Paul's. A passionate sensualist, his use of language was refined, philosophical, and complex. A world of emotion is pared down and paralleled in images that have reflective origins. His verse also expresses a basic piety: "Nor thou nor thy religion dost controule,/The amouresnesse of an harmonious Soule,/ But thou would'st have that love thy selfe: As thou/Art jealous now,/Thou lov'st not, till from loving more, thou free/My soule..."

8

8 The Battle of the Angels, from an edition of Milton's *Paradise Lost*, reflects his interpretation of life as a struggle between the forces of good and evil that goes back to the first catastrophic fall of the rebel angels. Milton's interpretation was probably fostered by his experience as a supporter of Cromwell in the Civil War. A man very much aware of the attractions of life and nature, Milton evoked both physical and psychological conflict: "A dungeon horrible, on all sides round/ As one great Furnace flam'd, yet from those flames/ No light, but rather darkness visible/ Served only to discover signs of woe..."

Mannerism

The High Renaissance style in Florence and Rome had been in many ways artificial, most obviously in its grace, idealism, and tendency to exaggerated posturing. The achievement of the major artists was a perfect style, or so it seemed; and the pursuit of perfect style was to become an end in itself. The phase so characterized is called Mannerism (from *maniera,* Italian for "style").

Qualities of style

Artifice was not the only quality of style felt worthy of further cultivation; novelty, license, variety, and the esoteric were appreciated in the sixteenth century—in the criticism of Giorgio Vasari (1511–74), for example—as never before. The demonstration of artistic genius was thought a legitimate object in a work of art. This demonstration could become the work's true subject. Mannerism was a late Renaissance style, and it was important that all the beliefs on which it was based could be justified by selective reading of ancient authorities. But the surviving monuments of antiquity were studied in a new spirit, with particular attention paid to license, complexity, and grace. In northern countries the appreciation of similar qualities in late Gothic art facilitated the reception of the new style, but Gothic as such was held in contempt and classical breeding was embraced.

The phenomenon of Mannerism did not occur everywhere—Venice, for example, was almost immune—and its arrival was never marked by a sharp break but by a shift of emphasis. Qualities such as grace, of course, appear in many stages in Renaissance art and were generally subject to inflation throughout the period; in some centers, as art looked inward at itself and not outward at nature, an extra twist of the spiral produced hyperinflation. This first happened in Rome; and perhaps it had already happened by 1520 in the work of Raphael and Michelangelo.

Artistic conditions in Rome soon after 1520 were ideal for the growth of Mannerism. A brilliant group of young artists, the pupils of Raphael, Florentines such as G. B. Rosso Fiorentino (1494–1540) and Benvenuto Cellini (1500–71), and north Italians such as Girolamo Parmigianino (1503–40), were impelled toward the display of virtuosity by their own competitive situation, by the qualities of the last works of Raphael (died 1520), and by the current work of Michelangelo (1475–1564) in Florence—his drawings rich in invention and fantasy, his sculpture suave and turning away from the natural, his architecture increasingly more marked by license than by rule [2, 3]. The dispersal of this group had begun before the sack of Rome in 1527, but that event was directly effective in the spread of Mannerism, through Perino del Vaga (*c.* 1500–47) to Genoa, through Parmigianino to Emilia, and through Rosso, eventually, to Fontainebleau. The Mannerist style was unusually accessible because so much of it appeared in engravings.

Medici patronage

In Italy the most impressive Mannerist in the 1530s, if Michelangelo is excepted, was certainly Parmigianino, first in Bologna and then in Parma. His "Madonna of the Long Neck" [4] is one of a number of religious

CONNECTIONS

See also
1142 The High Renaissan in north Italy
1140 Florence and Rome the High Renaissan
1146 The French Renaissance
1144 The German and Netherlandish Renaissance
1138 Italian art 1450–149

1 Rosso Fiorentino's section of the Galerie François Ier (1535–39) in the Château de Fontainebleau is one of 12 bays in the gallery, each different. In general, the subjects appear to be allegories of the reign of Francis I. The central fresco here—one of those most likely to be by Rosso's own hand—is the "Death of Adonis," which may refer to the death of the dauphin in 1536. The salamander above is the king's personal emblem. A similar mixture of painting and stucco was used by Primaticcio.

2 Michelangelo's Porta Pia, Rome, begun in 1561, is a fine example of Mannerist license. There are no true capitals, merely fragments of an architrave topped by the guttae of a frieze.

3 Michelangelo's "Victory" (*c.* 1527–28) was designed to stand in a niche in the lowest zone of the tomb of Julius II and to be flanked by two slaves. The continuous spiral movement of the figures is known as the *figura serpentinata* (snakelike figure). Movement and largeness of conception typified his work.

4 Parmigianino's "The Madonna of the Long Neck" (1534–36) was painted for Elena Baiardi, for a church in Parma. The subject refers to St Helen's vision of the Cross, represented in the crystal vase. All the figures react to this vision—the Virgin by seeing in the child across her knees a prefiguration of the Passion. The column is a symbol of the Virgin's purity. The content is comparable to that of an altarpiece by Correggio (*c.* 1494–1534) but the ecstasy seems more stylish than expressive.

works whose spiritual message is less obvious than their elegant forms, rhythmic grace, refinement of detail, and airless, unreal color. After 1540, Florence became the most vital Italian center and remained so until the early seventeenth century under the patronage of the Medici dukes. Cosimo I (1519–74) assembled a team of highly talented artists: the painters Salviati (1510–63) and Il Bronzino (1502–72), the sculptors Cellini [Key] and Bartolommeo Ammanati (1511–92), and the architect Buontalenti (1536–1608). To this court and its new nobility was attracted, in about 1560, the one really great artist who worked wholly in the Mannerist style, the Fleming Gianbologna (1529–1608); no sculptor's work has ever been so suavely complex, nor made so purposefully to be admired for its art. He brought the bronze statuette to perfection [5], but worked also on a large scale in marble [8].

It is natural that a style that rested upon technical accomplishment should flourish in metalwork and jewelry; Cellini is the most celebrated goldsmith of the period, but the richest concentration of talent was in south Germany [6].

Northern centers

Centers of Mannerism in the north were mainly, but not exclusively, at courts and the first of these was at Fontainebleau where, from about 1530, the decoration of Francis's new château was emphatically Mannerist, and very influential (for example, in England); the principal artists were Italian—Rosso and Primaticcio—and their main work was the Galerie François Ier, an exuberant mixture of stylized allegorical painting and complex stucco relief [1] of stupefying invention. Here first appeared on a monumental scale the universal hallmark of Mannerist decoration, strapwork (ornamental straplike bands). Around 1600 the last vital centers of Mannerism were in Holland (the school of Haarlem) and at the court of Rudolph II at Prague, where the Flemish painter Bartholomäus Spranger (1546–1611) and the Dutch sculptor Adriaen de Vries (c.1548–1626) produced decadent, erotic art of high order.

KEY
Cellini's bronze bust of Duke Cosimo I of Florence was executed between 1545–47. Cosimo was a Medici who was created grand duke of Tuscany in 1569. He was a great art lover and Cellini's patron.

5 Gianbologna's "Astronomy" (*c.* 1573) is one of the most highly finished of this artist's statuettes and was made to be turned around in the hand so that the brilliance and variety of its composition could be admired. From any angle the forms make a balanced and complicated design, each one different. In his work Gianbologna took a characteristic aspect of the 16th century—making art for connoisseurs—to its logical conclusion. He believed that the subject was of no particular significance, the figures being chosen "to give scope to the science and accomplishment of art" as a first priority.

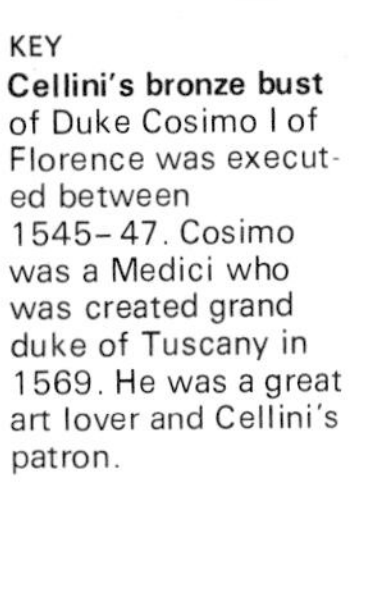

6 Wenzel Jamnitzer's ewer (*c.* 1570) is made of vermeil, enameled and inlaid. Vases of surprising fantasy, in bronze and silver, survived from the Roman Empire. Thereafter, the creation of more witty and complex tableware was a main Mannerist preoccupation. Jamnitzer used casts of real animals.

7 Bartholomäus Spranger's "Venus and Adonis" (*c.* 1590) was characteristic of the taste of Rudolph II and his court at Prague, where there was an unusual interest in all things strange and improbable. Spranger was a cosmopolitan artist, trained in Antwerp, Paris, Parma, and Rome, who exerted great influence in the last stages of Mannerism through his engraver Goltzius. In general he gives the impression, as here, of finding his style as absurd as his subjects.

8 Gianbologna's "The Rape of the Sabine" (1582) seems to have been made without the artist having in view a subject, a site, or a patron, but only the ambition to show the world that, contrary to rumor, he could work as well on a colossal scale in marble as in the small bronzes that had brought him fame. He believed that he had made his task as difficult as possible by multiplying the figures and by varying their age and sex. He titled it after completion.

The Reformation

When Martin Luther (1483–1546) posted his *Ninety-Five Theses* on the door of the Castle Church, at Wittenberg, Saxony, on October 31, 1517, he was initiating a religious debate in traditional fashion. But the consequences were revolutionary and heralded a new historical era: the end of the dominance of the Catholic Church of the Middle Ages; the creation of "reformed" or Protestant churches; a century and a half of "religious" wars that convulsed the emerging nation-states of Europe; and a new understanding of the Christian faith. All these developments are historically grouped as components of "the Reformation."

The original intention

The term *Reformation* precisely describes Luther's original intentions [Key]. His *Ninety-Five Theses* were an attack on abuses within the Roman Catholic Church. He denounced the frivolous uses to which the pope put his vast wealth and, in particular, the way in which he was raising money by the sale of "indulgences" [1], documents that the pardoner Tetzel claimed gave any purchaser automatic remission of his sins and release from purgatory.

The history of the Catholic Church, however, had been for centuries a sequence of "reformations," and for more than a decade before 1517, John Colet (*c.*1467–1519), Erasmus [3], and Thomas More (*c.*1478–1535) had been working to cleanse the church of its abuses. What made Luther more than merely a traditional reformer was the conviction from which his desire to purify sprang, coupled with the accidental political situation in Europe.

Luther's conviction

Luther's complaint against indulgences went beyond distaste of the money involved to a rejection of the whole concept of spiritual bookkeeping with God. Luther felt a sense of infinite personal unworthiness that no amount of good works could ever overcome. As an Augustinian monk, a doctor of theology, and then professor at the University of Wittenberg, he had mortified himself mercilessly but still felt impure, repulsive, sinful—unworthy even to approach God's presence. Only blind faith could save him. From this conviction was born the doctrine of "justification by faith," which was to inspire the spiritual side of the Reformation. It involved great emphasis on the single gesture of faith—conversion—and rejected reliance on the priest as a middleman between the believer and God. This meant unadorned churches, simpler ceremonies, and marriage for ministers if they so chose. Luther himself married a former nun in 1525.

Luther's ideas had a dynamic impact throughout Germany and were given immeasurable help in taking root by a fatal four-year delay on the part of the Catholic authorities. Pope Leo X (1475–1521), who hoped to strengthen his personal power by manipulating the imminent election of a new Holy Roman emperor, adopted the traditional papal tactic of supporting a weak candidate for this position that carried so much influence in Germany. He had already selected as his protégé Frederick the Wise of Saxony (1463–1525), Luther's own protector. Thus Luther's teachings were

CONNECTIONS

See also
1154 The Catholic Reformation
1130 The Renaissance: humanism
1168 The golden age of Dutch painting
1158 Europe's economy and society 1500–1700
1156 The English revolution

1

1 The sale of indulgences was to raise money for the rebuilding of St. Peter's in Rome. An indulgence was originally a remission from punishment for a sin and was conditional on the sinner's sincere repentance. But in the Middle Ages, indulgences came to be granted to sinners who did good works, such as going on crusade or contributing money to the building of a church. This led to the idea that forgiveness could be purchased as a commodity.

2

2 The religious orders of monks, nuns, and friars provoked hostility. To ordinary people and reformers they seemed idle and excessively wealthy, spending their money on their own enjoyment and not in the service of God. They were envied by rulers for their valuable town properties and country estates.

3

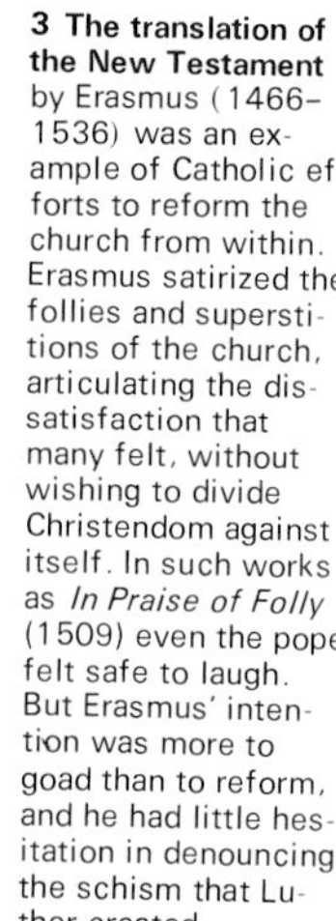

DES· ERASMI RO
TERODAMI IN NOVVM TESTAMENTVM

Apud inclytam Rauracorum Basileam.
AN. M. D. XXII.

3 The translation of the New Testament by Erasmus (1466–1536) was an example of Catholic efforts to reform the church from within. Erasmus satirized the follies and superstitions of the church, articulating the dissatisfaction that many felt, without wishing to divide Christendom against itself. In such works as *In Praise of Folly* (1509) even the pope felt safe to laugh. But Erasmus' intention was more to goad than to reform, and he had little hesitation in denouncing the schism that Luther created.

4

4 Encouraged by Luther's success and sharing some of his ideals, the peasants of the southwest and central German states rose against their rulers in 1524. But Luther denounced their complaints—mainly political and economic—and in the face of stern repression the revolts collapsed.

5

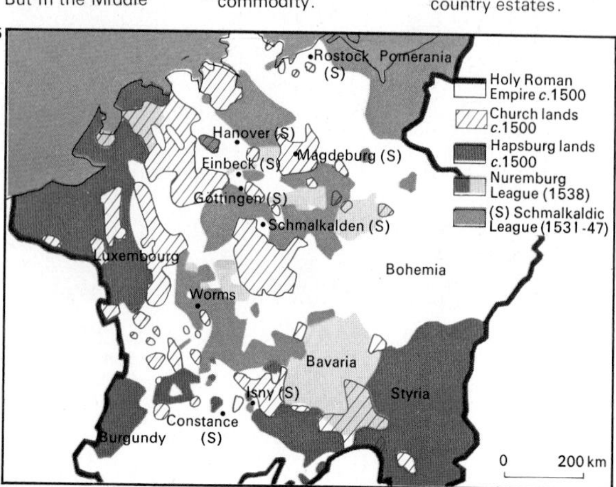

Rostock (S)
Pomerania
Hanover (S)
Einbeck (S)
Magdeburg (S)
Göttingen (S)
Schmalkalden (S)
Luxembourg
Bohemia
Worms
Bavaria
Isny (S)
Styria
Constance (S)
Burgundy
Holy Roman Empire c.1500
Church lands c.1500
Hapsburg lands c.1500
Nuremburg League (1538)
(S) Schmalkaldic League (1531-47)
0
200 km

5 The Holy Roman Empire, in theory the political expression of the Catholic Church, was in practice a grouping of rival German States. The Reformation provided the chance many of them had been waiting for to defy the power of the emperor. The Protestant rulers formed themselves into the Schmalkaldic League in 1531, and the emperor replied with the Nuremberg League in 1538. War seemed imminent, but a compromise was reached in 1539.

not officially condemned until 1521 at the Diet of Worms.

Frederick the Wise then sent Luther into hiding for a year, and the new emperor, Charles V [6], had neither the time nor the power to control this defiance of his authority. In 1520, Luther had urged princes to throw off the unbiblical authority Rome claimed over the church in their states, and rulers were not slow to profit from this invitation. In 1529 all the Lutheran states and towns in Germany put their names to a "Protestation" against the emperor—the origin of the term Protestant—and after more than 25 years of conflict the Peace of Augsburg in 1555 recognized the ruler's right to determine his country's religion.

England and Switzerland

The principle of the rights of a ruler had earlier been practiced by Henry VIII (1491–1547) in his Reformation in England, which was confirmed by the Act of Supremacy of 1534. It was essentially a forcible transfer of the supreme power over the church from the pope in Rome to the English sovereign. As in Sweden in 1527 and Denmark and Norway in 1536–39, there was little attempt to pretend that Thomas Cromwell's dissolution of the monasteries (1536–40) was any more than a crude confiscation of the church's vast wealth [7].

Only in Switzerland was the "purification" of the old church's images and decorations a matter of genuine Christian austerity. In Zurich in the 1520s Huldreich Zwingli (1484–1531) had the church organs destroyed because their sound was profane, while the citizens as a whole were banded into a democracy that contrasted with the princely rulers of Luther's churches.

In Geneva [9] after 1541 John Calvin (1509–64) created a holy city that gave shelter to more than 6,000 refugees fleeing from persecution in France, Italy, Spain, and, during Mary Tudor's reign, England as well. Calvin promulgated the great Reformation theme of "predestination"—that God chooses his own elect. It was the buoyancy of those who felt the assurance of their own election that inspired the Calvinists throughout Europe.

KEY

Martin Luther, an Augustinian monk, was the first great inspirer of the Reformation. On a visit to Rome in 1511 he was appalled by the wealth and spiritual emptiness of the Catholic Church, so different from the ideals of primitive Christianity. These ideals became his watchword as he argued against the church's corruption in his *Ninety-Five Theses* (1517). Luther was not a revolutionary, for he retained vestments and certain Catholic ceremonies, but in his reformed church the communion cup was given to the congregation, saints were no longer objects of special prayers and church wealth went to pastoral and educational activities.

6

6 Emperor Charles V (1500–58) inherited the lands belonging to the Austrian and Burgundian Hapsburgs and also the kingdoms of Aragón and Castile. This provoked the fear of France, which fought throughout his rule to prevent encirclement and encouraged German Protestant princes to defy his authority. Unable to reunite Christendom, he gave his possessions to his brother and son.

7

7 Fountains Abbey was among the finest religious houses destroyed during the dissolution of the monasteries in England (1536–40). The first act (1539) based dissolution on whether a monastery enjoyed an annual income of less than £200. The Act of the Dissolution of the Greater Monasteries (1539) completed the process. Pensions were paid to monks refusing to join the secular clergy, and the crown took the rest. A few lands were kept by the crown, a few given away, but most were sold to gentleman farmers, thus creating a new class of landowners with the strongest reasons for staying loyal to the new order.

8

8 The Bible replaced the priest as the ordinary man's spiritual authority. The scriptures were translated from the Latin and Greek and offered to the people in their own languages—notably German in a translation by Luther, and English in the KIng James version of 1611.

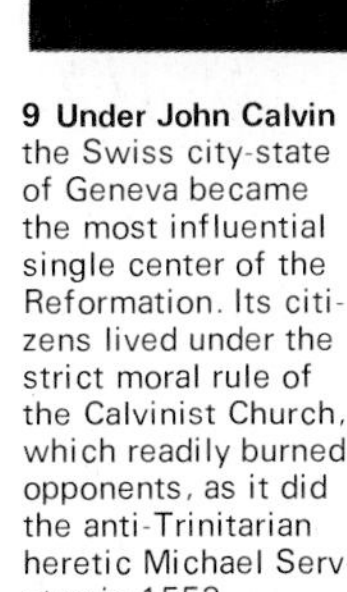

9 Under John Calvin the Swiss city-state of Geneva became the most influential single center of the Reformation. Its citizens lived under the strict moral rule of the Calvinist Church, which readily burned opponents, as it did the anti-Trinitarian heretic Michael Servetus in 1553.

10

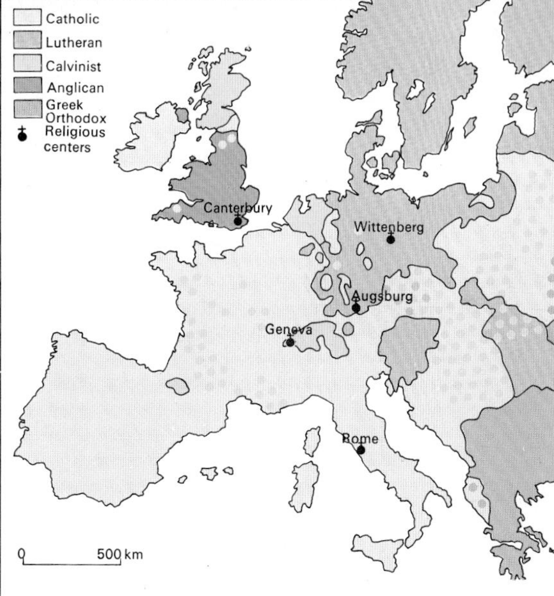
Catholic
Lutheran
Calvinist
Anglican
Greek Orthodox
Religious centers
Canterbury
Wittenberg
Augsburg
Geneva
Rome
0
500 km

10 By 1560 Lutheranism had spread from north Germany to Scandinavia, Poland, and Hungary along German trade routes and among the scattered German communities in the trading cities. After 25 years of religious wars the Peace of Augsburg (1555) had given the Lutheran princes and cities the right to freedom of worship, in effect strengthening the hands of both Catholic and Protestant rulers within their own territories. But it gave no privileges to the followers of Zwingli and Calvin, who were the dominant religious groups in the Netherlands, Scotland, and most Swiss cantons, and who formed a Swiss minority in France, Hungary, and south Germany.

9

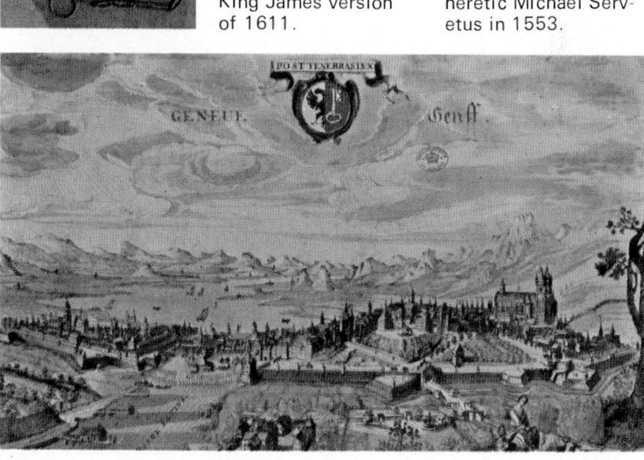
POST TENEBRAS LUX
GENEVE
Genff

The Catholic reformation

CONNECTIONS

Read first
1152 The Reformation

See also
1158 Europe 1500–1700
1162 Baroque art: style and content
1164 Baroque art: patronage and development

The Reformation in the early 1500s divided Europe into the Roman Catholic countries of the south and the Protestant countries of the north. Under the protection of the German princes, Protestantism became established, and the Holy Roman Empire existed in an uneasy state of religious cold war.

Within the Catholic Church, such reformist cardinals as Gasparo Contarini (1483–1542) advocated a conciliatory policy and reform of abuses. But discussions between Catholics and Protestants at the Diet of Regensburg in 1541 revealed only the impossibility of a theological compromise.

Since the Lutheran Reformation a new, formidable Protestantism had assaulted the Catholic Church—the organized church of John Calvin. As Protestants gained ground in Germany and Switzerland, and missionaries went out from Geneva to France and the Low Countries, the Catholic Church realized the need for action.

Between 1536 and 1545, Pope Paul III repeatedly called for a general council but was forced to postpone it for political reasons. The council finally met in Trent on December 15, 1545. Ostensibly this was a council for all Christendom. But the location in the Italian Alps and Pope Paul's successful coup in determining votes by representative rather than by nation ensured an Italian, papal dominance.

The new orthodoxy

Contarini's followers still hoped for reconciliation with the Protestants. Cardinal Gian Petro Caraffa (1476–1559) and his party were in no such mood. Meeting in three sessions (1545–47, 1551–52, 1562–63), the council answered the Lutheran challenge for the first time. On all major points of theological controversy concerning salvation, transubstantiation, and the authority of the fathers, the Catholic position was reasserted with a clarity that late medieval theology had lacked. The council made token reforms of more glaring abuses. Most important, the Council of Trent reinforced the authorities of the church from the bishops to the pope, whose supremacy was not questioned. The defenders of a new orthodoxy were equipped with the weapons of the Inquisition and the papal Index of prohibited books. Trent made the Roman Catholic Church one denomination among many—but a denomination that was ready to fight. Even before the council met, Ignatius Loyola (1491–1556) [2], general of the Society of Jesus from 1541, had provided the pope with his army of missionaries—the Jesuits.

In Spain, a Carmelite nun, Theresa of Ávila (1515–82), founded a powerful order of nuns and so reawakened religious fervor in that country that her influence soon spread throughout Christendom. Her writings, a mixture of practicality and mysticism, became one of the great forces of the Catholic Reformation.

Beginnings of a religious war

The end of a policy of conciliation meant religious war. Where nobles and princes had emerged as the patrons of the Protestant faiths it meant civil war. In France the rival noble factions of Bourbon and Guise, adopting the causes of Calvinism and Tridentine Catholicism (Roman Catholi-

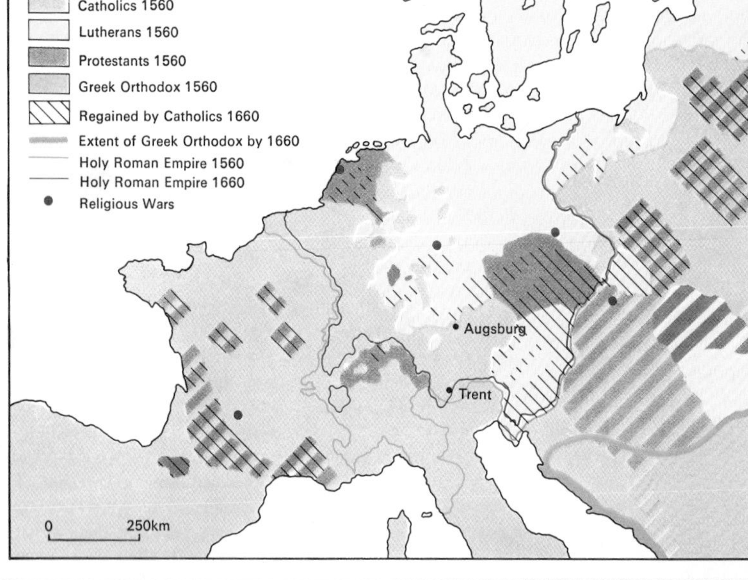
1
Catholics 1560
Lutherans 1560
Protestants 1560
Greek Orthodox 1560
Regained by Catholics 1660
Extent of Greek Orthodox by 1660
Holy Roman Empire 1560
Holy Roman Empire 1660
Religious Wars
Augsburg
Trent
0
250km

1 The Catholic Reformation in the century following the Council of Trent won back much of the territory lost to Protestantism. It was most successful in achieving a popular reconversion in Poland. There the enactment of religious toleration in 1573 led to a sudden growth in Jesuit activity in the field of education. The support of Sigismund III (*r.* 1587–1632) for the Jesuit cause enabled the complete suppression of Protestantism. The Catholic Reformation was often marked by the banning of heretical books, church control of higher education, with support from royal and noble families, and the denial of Protestant rights.

2 St Ignatius Loyola was a Spanish nobleman born in 1491. He underwent a religious experience during his convalescence after being wounded in battle. After studying theology at the Sorbonne in Paris, he formed in 1534 a group of devout men who swore to serve Christ and his vicar on earth, the pope. His religious order, the Society of Jesus, was strictly organized, its members being subject to rigorous discipline. The theology outlined by Loyola in his *Spiritual Exercises* has been described as a "shock tactic spiritual gymnastic." Originally, membership was confined to 60 Jesuits, but in 1540 the pope authorized the order to increase its membership without limit. By 1556 the order was firmly established in Europe, and it grew until the mid-17th century, acting as the principal agent of the Catholic Reformation. It conducted widespread missionary work throughout the world, including China, India, and extensive missions throughout the New World.

3 William of Orange (1533–84), "the Silent," was the largest landowner in the Netherlands. He led the opposition to Philip II's erosion of the aristocratic and constitutional liberties of the Netherlands. During the war William tried to unify the provinces; he was jealous of their individual privileges and promoted religious toleration to prevent a rift between Protestants and Catholics in their defense of constitutional rights. Dutch independence was recognized in 1648.

4 The Massacre of St Bartholomew's Day–Aug. 24, 1572–was a slaughter of French Protestants (Huguenots). Catherine de Medici (1519–89), the French regent, alarmed at the growing Huguenot political power instigated the massacre. The slaughter of Protestants spread throughout France and led to the outbreak of civil war.

5 The rebellious Netherlands were helped in their struggle against Spain in the 1560s and 1570s by Elizabeth I of England. It became increasingly evident to Philip II that Spanish control of the Low Countries could not be secured while the rebels received that aid. In addition, Philip's ambitions in England had been thwarted by the death of his wife, the Catholic Mary Tudor, and he hoped to reestablish himself and Catholicism there. He decided to launch his Armada in 1588. In league with French Catholics, Philip hoped to put in at French ports, while his regent for the Netherlands, the duke of Parma, was to clear the towns along the coast. The great plan was aborted by a rare combination of factors: bad admirals, a storm that worked against the Spanish ships, and the unexpected speed and maneuverability of the English navy. The complete rout of the Armada ended Catholic ambitions toward England.

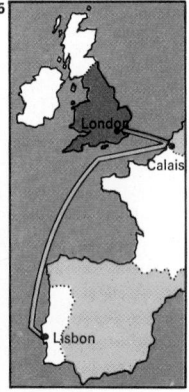

cism as reformed at the Council of Trent), entered into three decades of conflict.

The popes looked to the Catholic princes of Europe to be the secular arm of Tridentine decrees. In particular they looked to the principal heir of Charles V—Philip II of Spain (1527–98) [Key].

In 1555 the Peace of Augsburg had brought a temporary lull to conflict in Germany. For the rest of the century the empire remained in uneasy peace as the Hapsburgs tried to reestablish their authority and the Calvinists (not recognized in the peace) gained ground. The Catholic princes of Germany, acting independently of the emperor, formed their own political league under Maximilian of Bavaria (1573–1651).

Thirty Years War

The signal for conflict was given when the Bohemian subjects resisted the decision of Emperor Matthias (1557–1619) to make the staunchly Catholic Ferdinand of Styria (1578–1637) king of the Bohemians. The Bohemians wanted neither a Hapsburg nor a Catholic. In 1618 they cast two imperial councillors from the window of the council chamber at Prague (the so-called Defenestration of Prague) and called upon the head of the German Protestants, Frederick, the Elector Palatine (1596–1632), to defend their cause [8]. Thirty years of war ensued.

The imperial forces, assisted by Maximilian, crushed Frederick, and Hapsburg power was restored. By 1629, Ferdinand, now emperor, imposed an edict restoring to the Catholic Church all lands secularized since 1552, thereby undermining the territorial strength of the Protestants. But the strengthening of the Hapsburgs and the identification of Spanish and imperial Hapsburgs with Catholicism brought in turn all their enemies against them. The Swedes led by Gustavus Adolphus (1594–1632) [7], then ironically the French, under the Catholic Cardinal Richelieu [9], fought with the Protestants against the weary Hapsburgs. After 30 years of turmoil the weary Emperor Ferdinand III (1608–57) signed the Peace of Westphalia, 1648, at which he was forced to recognize the Calvinist faith within Germany.

KEY

Philip II of Spain dominated European politics in the late 16th century. Philip was looked to as the champion of the Roman Catholic Church. In practice, as more than one pope complained, he defended first and foremost the interests of the Hapsburgs. He complicated the religious and political life of Europe by identifying the Hapsburg interests with the Catholic interest and by his use of the Inquisition in Spain. He was involved constantly in war—against the Turks, the rebellious Dutch, the French Huguenots, and the English. Philip made Spain a great power, but in the process he alienated almost all the states of Europe.

6

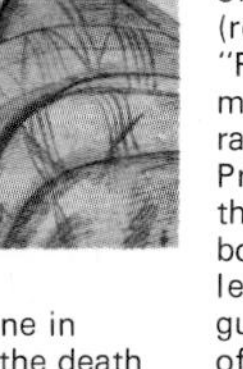

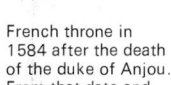

6 The Protestant Henry of Navarre (1553–1610) became heir to the French throne in 1584 after the death of the duke of Anjou. From that date and after more than 20 years of civil war in France the political and religious situation was reversed. Now the Catholics feared repression, and the Guise feared subjection. Catholics, formerly apologists for divine monarchy, penned tracts justifying rebellion. But Henry of Navarre, who became king (as Henry IV) in 1589, finally brought peace to France. Renouncing Protestantism for official Catholicism (reputedly saying "Paris is well worth a mass") he thus separated the cause of Protestantism from the House of Bourbon. By offering toleration to the Huguenots in the Edict of Nantes (1598) he ended the French civil wars.

7 A

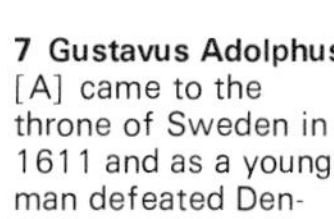

B

Magdeburg 1631
Breitenfeld 1631
Lützen 1632
Steinau 1633
Nuremberg 1632
Nördlingen 1634
Donauworth 1632

The Empire 1630–34
Main areas of war
Sweden enters war
Imperial-Allied victory
Protestant-Allied victory

7 Gustavus Adolphus [A] came to the throne of Sweden in 1611 and as a young man defeated Denmark, Poland, and Russia. He built a fleet and a formidable army that transformed Sweden into a great power. The threat to Sweden was the Hapsburg Catholic control of northern Germany [B]. The Polish war persuaded Gustavus to postpone a defensive war against the Hapsburgs in the Baltic, but growing Hapsburg strength after 1629 threatened Swedish security as well as Swedish Protestantism. The Swedes won resounding victories at Breitenfeld in 1631 and Lützen in 1632, but Gustavus Adolphus was killed in the latter battle, and the Swedes were routed at Nordlingen, 1634.

8

8 The Defenestration of Prague occurred in 1618 when the Bohemian Protestants hurled two imperial regents from a council window. In 1609 they had obtained from Emperor Rudolph II (1552–1612) a guarantee of religious equality and freedom of worship. Rudolph was succeeded by the old and sick Matthias, who was urged to name as his successor the king of Bohemia. Although they disliked Ferdinand of Styria, the Bohemians consented to his election. The crisis occurred after Matthias had visited Prague securing the election. In his absence the ten regents denounced the decree of religious freedom and demolished Lutheran churches.

9

9 The policies of Cardinal Richelieu (1584–1642), minister to Louis XIII, reflected the French conflict of interests at home and abroad. The French saw the Catholic Hapsburgs as their greatest threat. If Philip II and III had established strong controls in both Spain and the Low Countries, France would have been sandwiched between two branches of a hostile power. It was the dilemma of the French monarchy that its interests required Catholic orthodoxy at home but support of the Protestant cause abroad. From 1634, Richelieu joined with the Protestants against the Hapsburgs and brought France openly into war with the emperor and with Spain.

The English revolution

The English revolution (1640–60) was the first of the modern revolutions, and it compares closely in many ways with the later French and Russian revolutions. Each political revolution follows its individual and complex pattern of development, but some common stages can be identified.

The revolutionary pattern

These stages include initial political excitement, with the collapse of the old regime; the emergence of a radical leadership as the political crisis becomes protracted; an eventual halt to the leftward movement; the consolidation of power by an often military-based party and a return towards political stability; and sometimes a formal restoration and a collapse of the revolutionary movement. The causes of the English revolution included religious and class divisions exacerbated by Charles I's heavy-handed Roman Catholicism and a split between ruling courtiers and aspiring gentry who favored freer trade, more religious toleration, and increased parliamentary power. The first stage [2] was the constitutional or "bloodless" revolution of 1640–41. It began in November 1640, when Charles I (1600–49) summoned the Long Parliament to help him out of a financial crisis. Charles, deeply unpopular, was forced to agree to a wide-ranging set of constitutional reforms that gave Parliament a much more prominent and secure place in the constitution, power over taxes, and abolished such arbitrary courts as the notorious Star Chamber. These changes were accompanied by much political debate, especially after the ending of press censorship [4] in July 1641.

The escalation of the crisis

The second stage saw the revolution move leftward, as the political crisis escalated into civil war. The Long Parliament split into rival parties in the autumn of 1641, the Royalists (Cavaliers) forming a King's party in opposition to the Parliamentarians (Roundheads). Charles attempted unsuccessfully to arrest his main opponents in January 1642 and then fled from London. He thus entered the first civil war (August 1642–April 1646) from a weakened position, because the Parliamentarians held London and the machinery of central government. The Parliamentarians were not, however, able to clinch their dominance until the reorganization of their forces into the zealous New Model Army in January 1645. This successfully harnessed militant Puritanism to the Parliamentarian cause. The army, ably directed by Thomas Fairfax (1612–71), won a decisive victory over the Royalists at Naseby in June 1645.

The third stage marked the apogee of the leftward movement of the revolution. The victorious Parliamentarians themselves split at the time of their success in 1646 and 1647. The more conservative group, the Presbyterians and Scots, allied themselves with Charles. The more radical party, the Independents, backed by Oliver Cromwell (1599–1658) [8] and the army, attempted a settlement, failed, and remained hostile to Charles. The brief second civil war (February–August 1648) ended with Cromwell's overwhelming defeat of the Scottish army at Preston in August 1648. It was soon followed by the purge of Pres-

CONNECTIONS

See also
1158 Europe 1500–1770
1152 The Reformation
1154 The Catholic Reformation
1224 The French Revolution
1248 The revolutions of 1848
1310 The Russian Revolution

1 Parliament was a long-established institution in 1640 with its own traditions and privileges. In the House of Commons there were a speaker (center), two committee clerks, the sergeant-at-arms (carrying the mace) and the members.

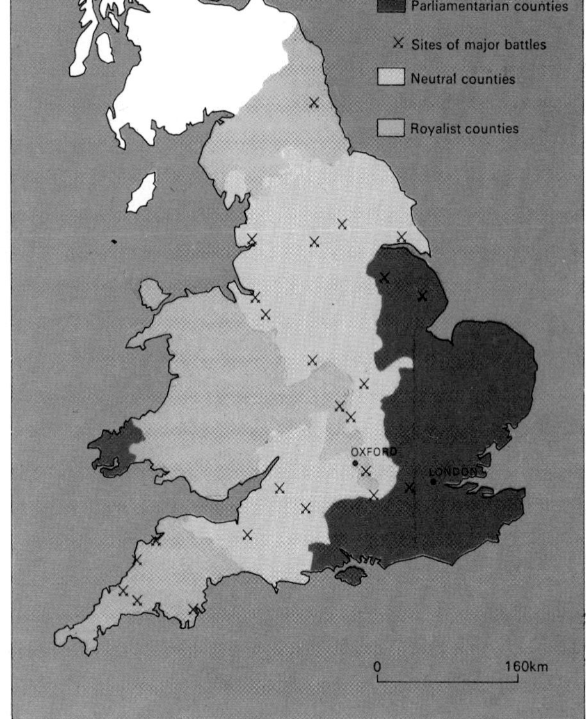

Parliamentarian counties
Sites of major battles
Neutral counties
Royalist counties
OXFORD
LONDON
0
160km

2 In the first civil war the Royalists were strongest in areas remote from London in the north and west, while the Parliamentarians kept the capital, the southeast, and western Wales. Most fighting was for control of neutral areas.

3 The elegant portrait of Charles I by Anthony van Dyck concealed the king's small stature but emphasized his regal dignity and melancholic determination, a characteristic that Charles indulged in dealing with Parliament, thereby losing both crown and head.

Ould Extreame

Goulden Meane

New Extreame

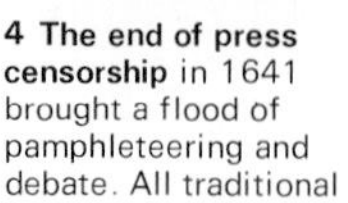

4 The end of press censorship in 1641 brought a flood of pamphleteering and debate. All traditional ideas were opened to discussion and argument. Before long, moderates on the Parliamentary side called for caution in reform, stressing the Aristotelian "goulden meane." They warned of the "new extreame" among radical political and religious groups as much as the "ould extreame."

byterian members of Parliament (Pride's Purge) in December 1648, the trial and then the execution of Charles on January 30, 1649, the abolition of the monarchy and House of Lords in February 1649, and the establishment of the Commonwealth.

At the same time Cromwell and the army leadership broke with the lower-class radical political party, known as the Levelers [6], which pressed for fundamental consitutional changes, including considerable extension of the (male) franchise. In the autumn of 1647 the Levelers briefly challenged Cromwell for control of the army itself. But Cromwell, worried by the Levelers' radical views, decided to crush the movement. A Leveler army mutiny was defeated at Burford (Oxfordshire) in May 1649. The difficulty of Cromwell's position—sandwiched between left and right—was accentuated; he was a regicide, as well as the man who had broken the Levelers.

The fourth stage represented the gradual return to political stability. The New Model Army was, in the 1650s, a force of more than 60,000 men. Its power was shown in the brutal suppression of the Irish rebellion (1649–50) and the routing of a further Royalist uprising (1650–51). Its support was essential to government, although it did not rule directly.

Cromwell and collapse of army rule

Cromwell proved the most successful ruler in those years because he was both a skilled politician and a brilliant general. His regime had some foreign policy successes, such as peace with the Dutch in 1654 and victory over Spain (1658–58), but he failed to find a satisfactory formula to preserve this system after his death in September 1658.

The fifth stage in the revolution therefore saw an initial period of political confusion with the collapse of army rule, followed by the restoration of Charles II (1630–85) in May 1660 at the invitation of the Convention Parliament. The restored monarchy [9] was much weaker than it had been previously, and it was the landowning gentry as represented in Parliament who were the ultimate victors of the English revolution.

KEY

To him pudel.
Bite him·peper

The civil wars marked a breakdown in ordered political and social life, and animosities heightened during the course of the fighting. There were not only political and religious divisions between the Royalists and Parliamentarians in 1642, but also social ones. The Royalists were satirized as courtiers and rakes; the Parliamentarians as low-born moralists. The Royalists drew support from some of the gentry and most of the peerage, who often wore lavish costume and long hair, denoting them as men of social standing and wealth. The Parliamentarians also had considerable backing among landowners, but they derived additional support from urban merchants, tradesmen, and artisans, who were often motivated by Puritan zeal and wore sober clothing.

5

	Royalist	Parliamentarian
Infantry	10,500	12,000
Cavalry	2,800	2,150
Dragoons	1,000	720
Guns	20	37

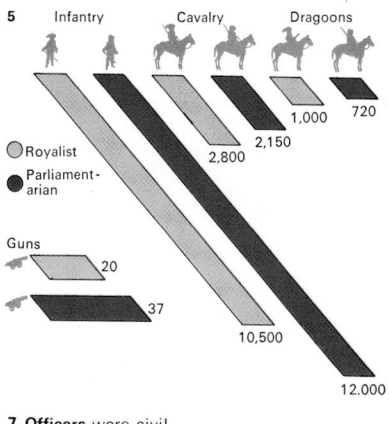

5 Edgehill, in central England, was the first major battle of the civil war (Oct. 23, 1642) and the majority of the troops involved were in action for the first time. The two armies were fairly evenly matched, and in military terms the outcome was indecisive. By the end of the war, the king's forces were only a little more than half those of Parliament. The king set up his capital in Oxford, as London continued in Parliamentary hands.

6

6 A key development in the 1640s was the growth of the first organized, mainly lower-class political party in English history. This group, known as the Levelers, played an important political role in the years 1647–49 before eventually being defeated by Cromwell. The Levelers did not have one party leader, but a dominant part was played by "Freeborn John"—the spirited propagandist John Lilburne (1614–57), shown here. The Levelers called for a considerable extension of the franchise and were suppressed by both king and Parliament.

7

Cuirassier
1
2
3
4
5
6
Captain of infantry

7 Officers wore civilian garb, whereas troopers on both sides wore armor.

1 Beaver hat
2 Gorget
3 Partisan
4 Burgonet with face bar
5 Wheel-lock pistol
6 Pistol holster

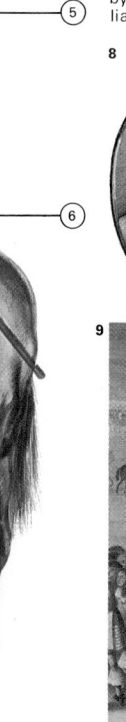

8

8 Oliver Cromwell was a military genius and a pragmatic politician. He ruled 1653–58 as Lord Protector and tried to reconcile discordant factions, staunchly upholding religious tolerance.

9 The restored monarchy in 1660 was much weakened, and power was shared with Parliament. The "Cavalier Parliament" was opened amid much state pageantry on April 22, 1661, with Charles II riding in procession from the Tower of London. The landowning gentry had learned to fear a powerful monarchy and standing armies, and they soon became critical of Charles and his ministers.

9

Europe's economy and society 1500–1700

In the first half of the sixteenth century the economy of Europe was dominated by a steady price rise; in the second, by unprecedented inflation. Price increases were felt first in Spain and resulted from the greatly increased imports of gold and silver from new mines in Mexico and Peru. The effects of this massive importation of bullion [5] were later offset by its export to other parts of Europe, either openly—to liquidate Spain's unfavorable trade balances and to supply the needs of her armies in the Netherlands—or by smuggling across the French border. Before these movements of bullion, prices in the rest of Europe had risen more slowly than in Spain.

Stimulus to international trade

This differing rate of inflation in the European countries gave additional stimulus to the expansion of international trade that had followed the discovery of the New World. The Baltic trade in grain with southern Europe, soon to be controlled and financed by the Dutch, was also promoted by the tendency of food prices to exceed those of manufactured goods. This was because an impressive growth in population in Europe [1, 2]—from 50–60 million in 1450 to nearly 100 million in 1600—increased the demand for food when supply was restricted.

Although industry still focused mainly on providing luxuries to the wealthy, commercial expansion led to a greater use of credit facilities and an extension in public banking, especially in Italy, where Genoese financiers arranged the transfer of Spanish remittances to the Netherlands.

The Dutch "economic miracle"

In the seventeenth century many of these trends were reversed. Inflation was checked in the second decade as imports of bullion from the New World decreased. International trade, which had been supported by the defense requirements of the Thirty Years War (1618–48), later experienced a downturn and then stagnated. Competition between the powers for a preponderant share of world trade led to the adoption by most governments of mercantilism, a protectionist trade system.

The shift of the center of commercial activity from the Mediterranean to the Atlantic seaboard, however, continued. The chief beneficiary, apart from England, was The Dutch Republic, which won virtual great-power status by its preeminence in the carrying trade, exploration, and finance [8]. This "economic miracle," which occurred in a period of general contraction, rested on Dutch control of the North Sea herring and the Newfoundland cod fisheries; on technical expertise in shipbuilding and insurance; on the elimination of the Portuguese from the Far Eastern spice trade and the Spanish from their monopoly of commerce with South America; on the international exchange and credit facilities provided by the Bank of Amsterdam (founded in 1609) [11]; and on the policy of toleration that induced the prosperous victims of religious persecution in Spain and France—the Sephardic Jews and Huguenots—to settle in Amsterdam [Key].

Economic and naval warfare between the Dutch Republic (the United Provinces of the northern Netherlands) and its main

CONNECTIONS

See also
1128 The politics of Europe 1450–1600
1122 The age of exploration
1152 The Reformation
1154 The Catholic Reformation

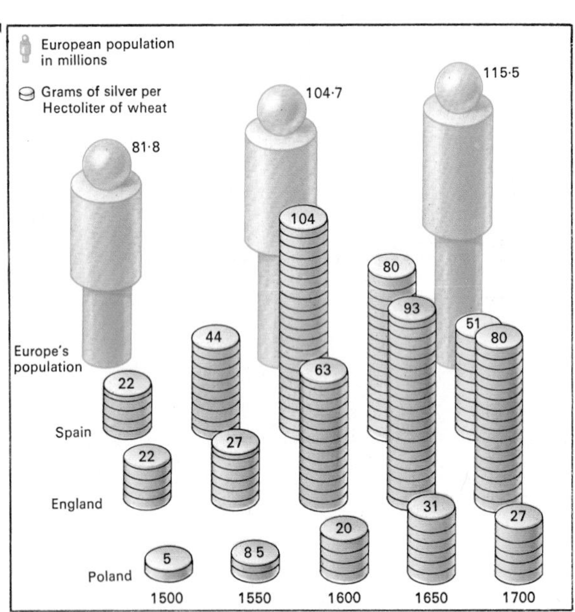
1
European population in millions
Grams of silver per Hectoliter of wheat
81·8
104·7
115·5
Europe's population
Spain
England
Poland
22
22
5
44
27
8 5
104
63
20
80
93
31
51
80
27
1500
1550
1600
1650
1700

1 The rapid rate of inflation illustrated here (prices of all foods soared, not just the price of wheat) had no definitive explanation, but population growth seems to have been a major factor.

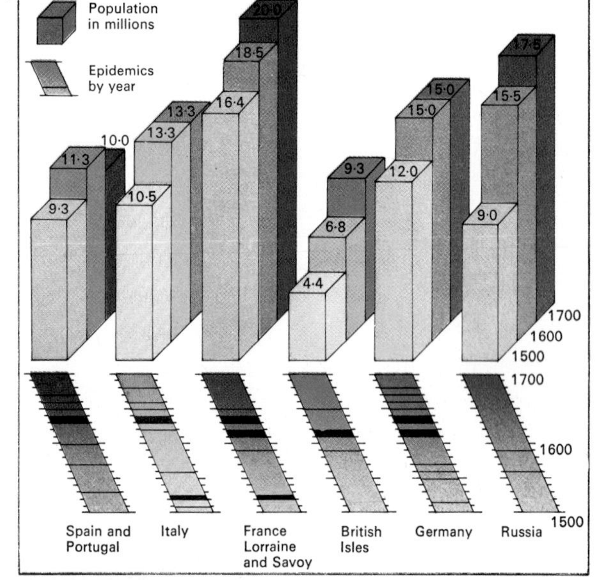
2
Population in millions
Epidemics by year
9·3
11·3
10·0
10·5
13·3
13·3
16·4
18·5
20·0
4·4
6·8
9·3
12·0
15·0
15·0
9·0
15·5
17·5
1700
1600
1500
1700
1600
1500
Spain and Portugal
Italy
France Lorraine and Savoy
British Isles
Germany
Russia

2 The growth of population during the 16th century was considerable. The increase seems to have begun around 1450 and become more rapid after 1500. The recurrence of the plague and the long duration of European wars had, by the mid-17th century, reduced the rate of growth once more. The diagram illustrates the changing population figures of the major European nations (1500 to 1700).

3 Death by plague had been by 1500, common in Europe for almost two centuries. Periodic epidemics were a major check on population growth, but it is difficult to assess accurately the effects of the plague in an age when routine diseases and accidents also made a significant contribution to the high mortality rate. Between a sixth and a third of the population died in each epidemic, although this figure could rise to as much as two-thirds, as it did in Germany in the 1630s. The plague also had long-term effects; unstable social and economic conditions pushed up the age of marriage and thus lowered the birth rate. Worst hit by the plague were the crowded, badly housed, poor of the cities.

4 In early modern Europe life was hard for ordinary people, as depicted by Bruegel the Younger. Beggars were a common sight, and for the laborer the holy days of the church were the only respite from the burdens of day-to-day existence. The church also ordained that periods of abstention from any work or indulgence should be strictly observed. Such decrees were often not followed; archbishop Laud (1573–1645) encouraged sports on the sabbath.

5 Silver mined in the New World and imported by Spain had a considerable influence on political and economic life in Europe. How Spain distributed this bullion between 1580 and 1626 is shown here. Spending in Spain and the Netherlands reflects the huge sums used for defense. The rest of Europe, learning from Spain, looked to trade to provide the wealth necessary for military power.

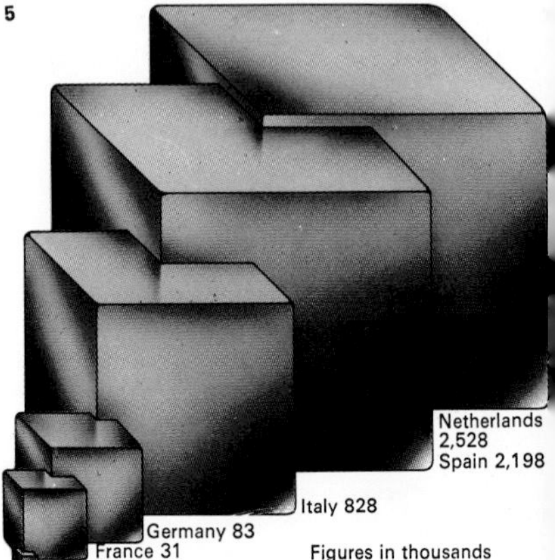
5
Netherlands 2,528
Spain 2,198
Italy 828
Germany 83
France 31
England ·032
Figures in thousands of kilograms

rivals, England and France, worked against Dutch commercial supremacy [6] in the second half of the century; the War of the Spanish Succession (1701–14) finally destroyed it.

European society, 1500–1700

The society of early modern Europe was principally agrarian, with 90 percent of the population deriving a living from the land. Farming was carried out under the jurisdiction of the manorial lord, although the farmer was also governed by various local customs. Inflation, however, was a social solvent that loosened the characteristic rigidity of sixteenth-century society in which status was determined by law and not by wealth. The medieval concepts of a "just price" and a controlled economy also ceased to be valid. Until the end of the sixteenth century the pressure of population on the means of subsistence involved a fall in living standards and in real wages.

The more volatile situation in the seventeenth century enabled the emergent middle classes to consolidate their wealth and to improve their social status. Generally the people who profited most were those who could charge higher prices without in turn having to pay them. These fortunate ones included farmers with secure tenure and noblemen who could evict their tenants and exploit the land. For those who were landless or whose title to their land was insecure, the real effect of the price rises was eviction, vagrancy, and perhaps death by starvation. Because fewer workers were needed for pasture farming, many were condemned to a life as wandering beggars [4]. From the landowners' point of view labor was relatively cheap. This encouraged improvements in agricultural and manufacturing processes, as did the introduction of New World crops (such as potatoes).

The seventeenth century saw the growth of mining, finishing industries (such as dyeing), tobacco-growing, and even market gardening. But the place of "manufacture" in this period was the cottage and not the factory; cloth was distributed piecemeal to be spun, dressed, or dyed by rural laborers or farmers.

KEY

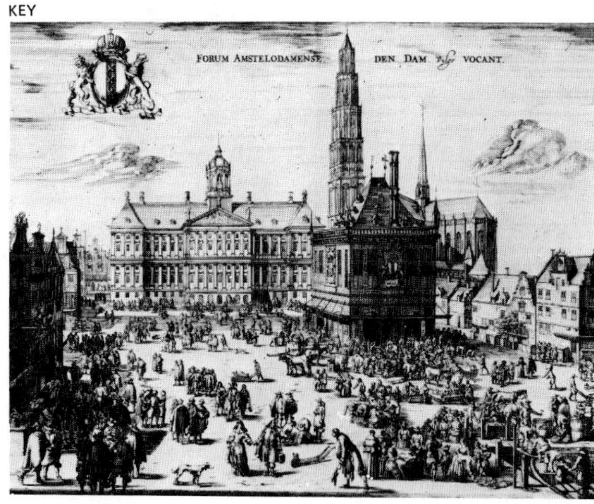
FORUM AMSTELODAMENSE
DEN DAM
VOCANT

Amsterdam, more than any other city, illustrates the revolution in the economic life of early modern Europe. During the 17th century the axis of economic activity shifted north—a concentration on Mediterranean trade gave way to a prevailing emphasis on Atlantic trade. As the center of the Dutch carrying trade, Amsterdam became an economic power—a market, a world bank, and a center of insurance for traders.

6

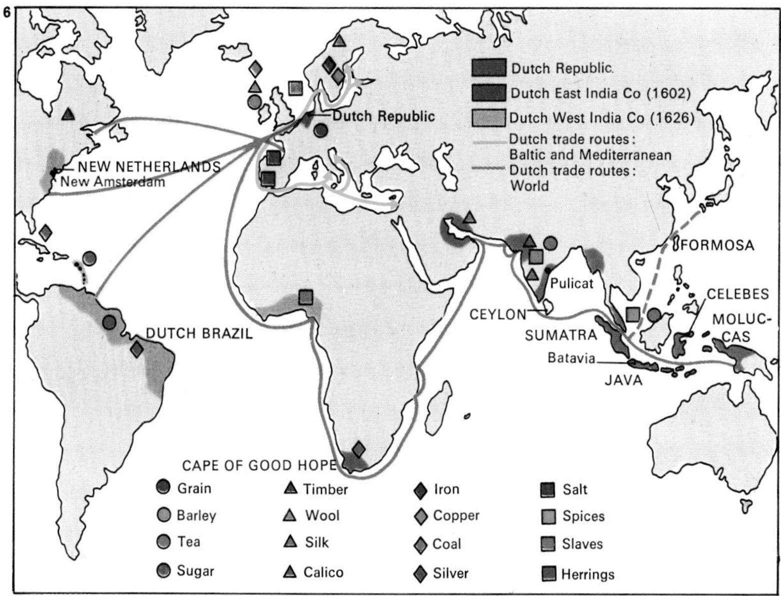
Dutch Republic
Dutch East India Co (1602)
Dutch West India Co (1626)
Dutch trade routes: Baltic and Mediterranean
Dutch trade routes: World
Dutch Republic
NEW NETHERLANDS
New Amsterdam
DUTCH BRAZIL
FORMOSA
Pulicat
CELEBES
CEYLON
SUMATRA
MOLUCCAS
Batavia
JAVA
CAPE OF GOOD HOPE
Grain
Barley
Tea
Sugar
Timber
Wool
Silk
Calico
Iron
Copper
Coal
Silver
Salt
Spices
Slaves
Herrings

7

6 The Dutch held economic sway in Europe principally by carrying the products of other countries. The central areas of the carrying trade were the Mediterranean, the English Channel, and the Baltic. The East Indies were the source of spices and luxury goods for resale in Europe. The West India Company had the more political aim of reducing Spanish trade by privateering.

7 Wealth and culture went hand in hand during the golden age of Dutch trading. Dutch art of the 17th century, for example, Rembrandt's celebrated protraits of Dutch merchants, reflects this alliance.

8 Rich Amsterdam merchants provided most of the backing for the Dutch East India and West India Companies. Both were joint-stock companies in which there were many shareholders, thus dividing the risks as well as the profits involved in colonial trade. The diagram illustrates the sources (in florins) of the capital invested in the companies when they were originally formed.

8

Amsterdam
Zealand
Enkhuisen
Hoorn and Enkhuisen
Delft

Capital in the East India Company 1602 fl6,425,000
fl3,675,000
fl1,300,000
fl540,000
fl470,000
fl267,000
fl173,000

Friesland and Groningen
Hoorn
Rotterdam

Capital in the West India Company 1621 fl7,100,000
fl3,155,555
fl1,577,778
fl788,889
fl788,889
fl788,889

Fl = Dutch florins

9 Cloth was one of the most important 17th-century manufactures. Italian silk damask-weaving techniques of the 15th century (shown) were taken to England from Flanders in the 16th century.

9

10

10 Venice was one of Europe's most important trade centers at the beginning of the 16th century, but the wars in the early part of the century and the colonization of the New World shifted the focus of trade to such Atlantic ports as Amsterdam and Bristol.

11

11 The growth of joint-stock trade over long distances gave rise to the need for more flexible instruments of credit and exchange. Significantly, the Dutch first broke with the tradition of raising money from such private families as the Fuggers, and the Bank of Amsterdam (shown here) was set up in 1609. The Bank of England, opened in 1694, was modeled on it.

Science and technology 1500–1700

By the dawn of the sixteenth century the European Renaissance was well under way, and during the following two centuries the broad basis of modern science was laid. Knowledge of Greek science was widespread, and an inquiring spirit that led to a critical examination of ancient ideas prevailed. Some scientists and philosophers came to believe that nature had no spiritual properties but had to be investigated impersonally.

The revolution in astronomy

The first fruits of this new approach came in astronomy. In 1543 the theory that the Sun, not the Earth, was the center of the universe appeared in *De revolutionibus orbium Coelestium* by Nicolas Copernicus (1473–1543). This theory profoundly affected man's view of himself and his place in nature. In astronomy the Copernican theory stimulated a spate of precise observations—notably by Tycho Brahe (1546–1601)—laying the basis for seventeenth-century discoveries with the telescope. Johann Kepler (1571–1630) used Brahe's observations in his reinterpretation of the planets' motions in terms of ellipses instead of the complex Copernican system of circles. In England, Francis Bacon (1561–1626) advocated the empirical method but denigrated the use of mathematics for the interpretation of results, unlike René Descartes (1596–1650), whose work contains many of the philosophical ideas that were at the root of the new spirit of inquiry. Descartes wanted to lay a rational foundation for religion and science to give them a mathematical validity, proof against skepticism and superstition. He formulated an entire philosophical system that postulated a wholly mechanical universe in space completely filled with fluid matter [1], rejecting the idea of a vacuum.

The Italian astronomer, mathematician, and physicist Galileo Galilei (1564–1642) was the first to use the telescope to study the heavens. Galileo's conclusions about mechanics laid the foundations for later work, particularly Newton's [6], but his belief in a universe governed by mathematically regular laws led to great hostility, not least from the Church. The culmination of this period was the work of Isaac Newton (1642–1727), whose masterpiece *Principia* is one of the most important single works of modern science. In it he defined his laws of motion [Key], developing Kepler's and Galileo's work, and he first formulated the law of universal gravitation. Newton also made important contributions to mathematics, including the invention of the calculus, although it had been formulated independently by Gottfried Leibniz (1646–1716).

Discoveries in optics

Science gained new impetus in the seventeenth century from the invention of the telescope and the microscope. Galileo, using the telescope, was able to observe mountains on the Moon, spots on the Sun, the phases of Venus, and the four larger satellites of Jupiter. Improved instruments followed, Newton perfecting the first reflecting telescope in about 1668. This led to further discoveries, as well as the use of the telescope as a celestial measuring instrument of great precision, and the estab-

CONNECTIONS

See also

1186 Exploration and science 1750–1850
1220 The early Industrial Revolution
1032 Early Oriental and Western science
1282 The foundations of 20th-century science
1442 Alchemy and the Age of Reason
856 Philosophy and religion
38 The restless sky
752 Development of surgery
1770 History of printing
1492 Speed and acceleration
1502 States of matter: gases
1460 Finding changing quantities: calculus

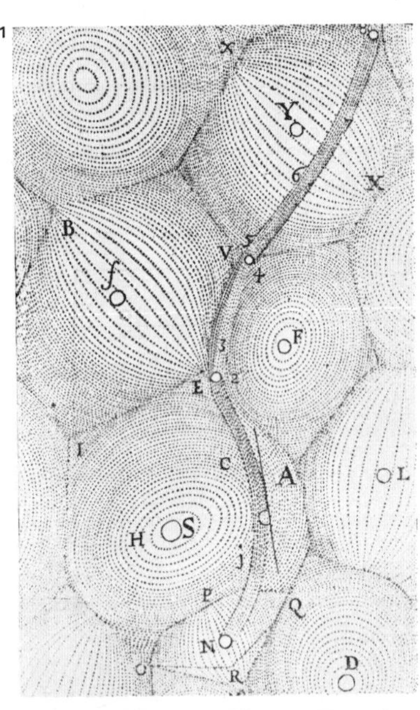

1 Descartes' idea of the universe rejected the theory of the existence of a vacuum and held that matter filling the universe was perpetually moving in vortices with stars at their centers. Some stars became planets with orbits in the vortex of another star. Comets wound their way between and across vortices, as in this engraving.

FACIES SPECULÆ SEPTEN:

2 The Royal Observatory at Greenwich was founded in 1675 to compile a new star catalogue for navigational use. Designed by Christopher Wren, it became an important center for accurate astronomical observations. The meridian of zero longitude still runs through Greenwich, but observation is now done in Sussex.

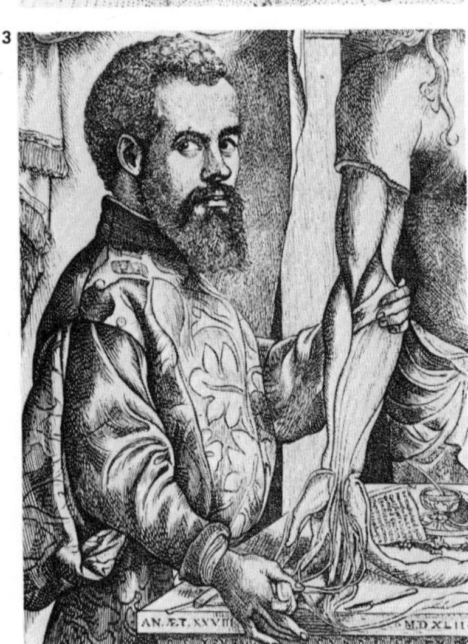

3 Vesalius, the great 16th-century anatomist, is shown holding a partly-dissected human arm. The portrait is taken from his book, *De humani corporis fabrica* (1543).

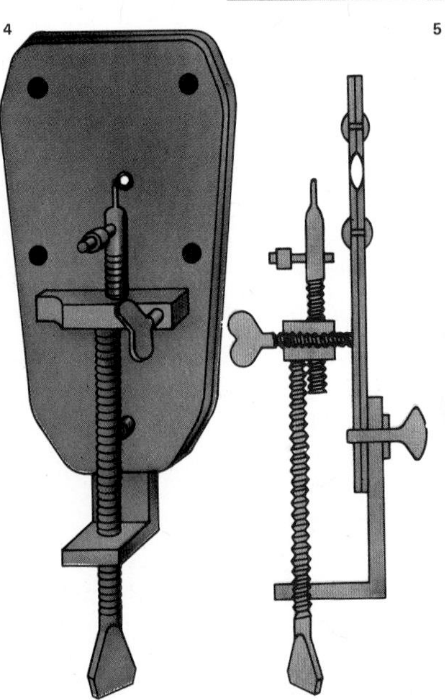

4 The powerful, single-lens microscope was designed in the 17th century by van Leeuwenhoek.

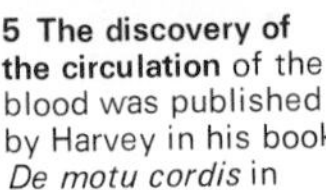

5 The discovery of the circulation of the blood was published by Harvey in his book *De motu cordis* in 1628. Harvey is shown in Hannah's painting demonstrating the principle to Charles I.

lishment of national observatories in Paris and at Greenwich, England [2].

The seventeenth century saw much fundamental work on optics. Willibrord Snell (1591–1626) determined the law of refraction of light. Christian Huygens (1629–95) used this knowledge to improve telescopes, also working with information obtained from Kepler's study of lenses. Above all, Newton discovered that white light could be separated by a prism into components of light of every color.

Developments in medicine

In 1538, André Vesalius (1514–64) [3] produced his immense study of the human body—the first to go against the teachings of Galen (*c.*AD 130–*c.*200). Vesalius' successor at Padua University, Bartolommeo Eustachio (1520–74), discovered the Eustachian tubes of the ears. In the next century Hieronymus Fabricius (1537–1619) laid the foundations of embryology and discovered valves in the veins, a finding that was used by his student William Harvey (1578–1657) [5] who, in 1628, announced his discovery of the circulation of the blood. Marcello Malpighi (1628–94) discovered the capillaries connecting veins and arteries and, like Jan Swammerdam (1637–80) after him, used it also in embryological studies. The microscope greatly helped to advance medical and biological knowledge during a period when it became increasingly based on physiological experiment. In Holland, Antony van Leeuwenhoek (1632–1723) devised his own microscopes to study blood and microscopic life forms [4].

In the sixteenth century botanical encyclopedias became common. In the next century Nehemiah Grew (1641–1711) used the microscope to study the sex organs of plants, and Robert Hooke (1635–1703), John Ray (1627–1705), and others began to reclassify the plant and animal kingdoms. In chemistry, Robert Boyle (1627–91) experimented on the physical properties of air and formulated his law on the relationship between the pressure and volume of a gas. Rationalism and observation now replaced superstition and dogma as scientific guidelines.

KEY

C
T
a
I
E

The third of Isaac Newton's three laws of motion states that to every action there is an equal and opposite reaction. An experiment designed to prove the validity of the theory is shown in this early 18th-century book on Newton's laws. A metal globe emits a jet of steam in one direction and causes the "engine" to react by moving in the opposite direction.

6

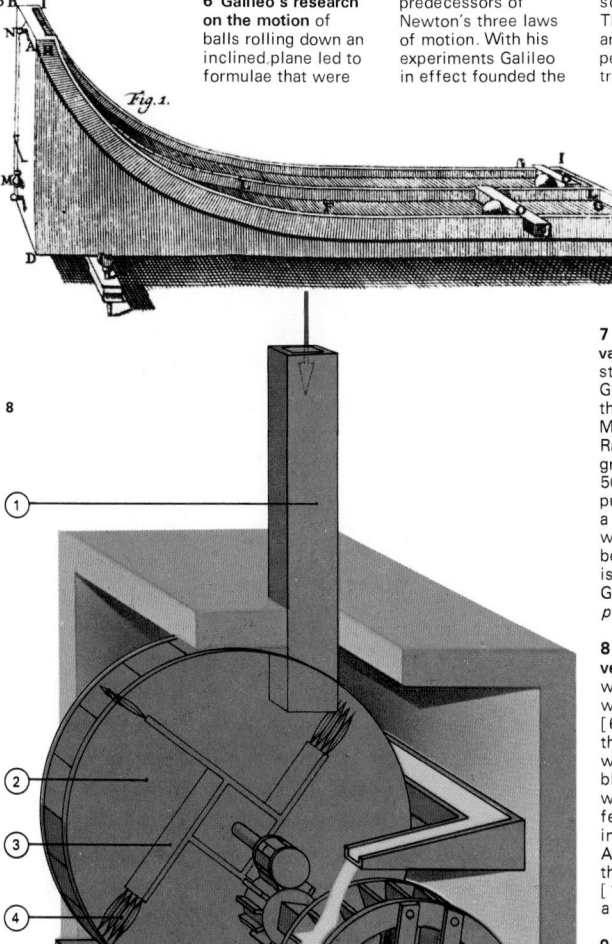

6 Galileo's research on the motion of balls rolling down an inclined plane led to formulae that were predecessors of Newton's three laws of motion. With his experiments Galileo in effect founded the science of dynamics. The illustration is of an 18th-century experiment in the same tradition.

7

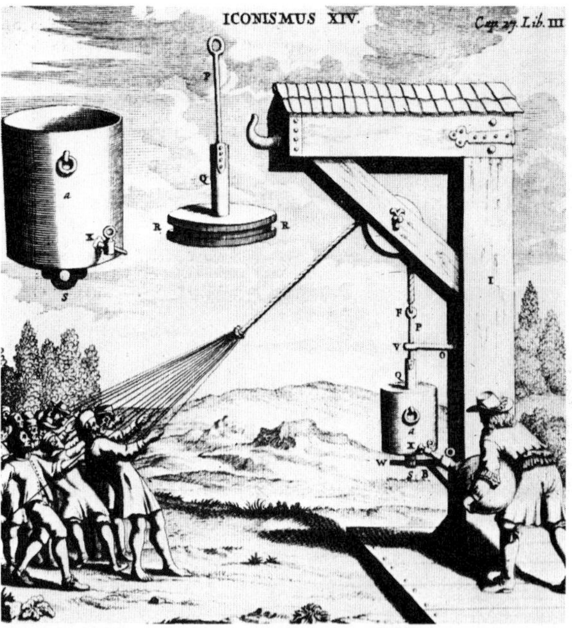
ICONISMUS XIV.
Cap. 27. Lib. III

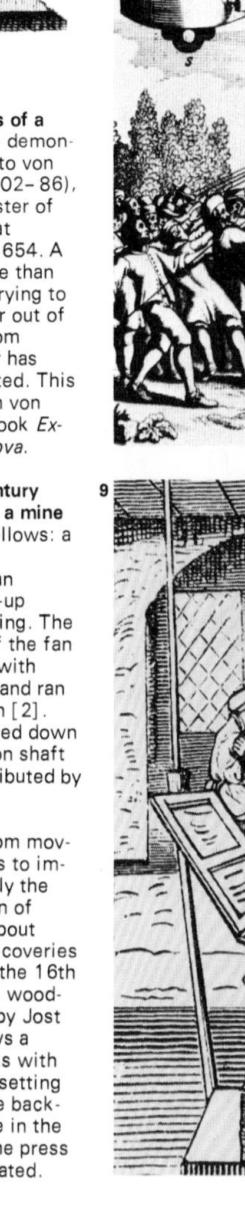

7 The effects of a vacuum were demonstrated by Otto von Guericke (1602–86), the burgomaster of Magdeburg, at Ratisbon in 1654. A group of more than 50 men are trying to pull a plunger out of a cylinder from which the air has been exhausted. This is taken from von Guericke's book *Experimenta nova*.

8

8 A 16th-century ventilator for a mine worked as follows: a water wheel [6] drove a fan through step-up wooden gearing. The blades [3] of the fan were tipped with feathers [4] and ran inside a drum [2]. Air was sucked down the ventilation shaft [1] and distributed by a duct [5].

9

9 Printing from movable type was to improve radically the dissemination of knowledge about scientific discoveries in Europe by the 16th century. This woodcut of 1568 by Jost Amman shows a printing works with compositors setting up type in the background, while in the foreground the press is being operated.

Baroque art: style and content

Baroque was the most dynamic style of art and architecture produced by Western civilization in the seventeenth and eighteenth centuries. Flamboyant and emotional, it arose in Italy shortly before 1600, and by the late seventeenth century had reached most other parts of Europe, taking root especially in Germany and central Europe and spreading to Latin America. All these were Catholic regions with autocratic political regimes, and it is no accident that Baroque flourished more there than in the Protestant and relatively liberal states of northern Europe; its style made it a suitable vehicle for expressing the colorful, assertive doctrines of Catholicism and the political principles of absolute monarchy.

The influence of the Renaissance

Two of the greatest Baroque artists, Peter Paul Rubens (1577–1640) and Gianlorenzo Bernini (1598–1680), were devout Catholics and supporters of absolutism. But it would be wrong to identify Baroque too closely with one particular ideology and social order. It also occurs in modified form, for example, in Britain and the Netherlands. Conversely, in Catholic France under one of the most autocratic governments in Europe there was some resistance to it on both nationalistic and aesthetic grounds.

To understand Baroque as a style it must be seen against the background of the Renaissance, for the Baroque drew heavily on that movement and its successor, Mannerism. On the whole, classical forms were used throughout all three periods, although to a diminishing extent in the final stages of Baroque. ("Classical forms" are primarily the conventions for representing the idealized human body, seen in Greek sculpture, and features of classical architecture such as columns, pediments, and friezes.) Renaissance artists employed classicism with restraint and with the dual aim of achieving clarity and realism. Mannerists abandoned these principles and pursued, instead, extremes of decorativeness, complexity, and artifice. Baroque kept the complexity and some of the decorativeness but returned to the realistic style of the Renaissance.

Realism, space, and movement were expressed in new ways: in painting, by placing at least the main figures in the foreground; in sculpture, by stressing the roundness of forms and the details of their surface modeling; and in architecture, by using massive columns, overlapping pilasters, and elaborate, deeply cut ornament. These features were emphasized in all three arts by dramatic use of light and shade. Everywhere there was a tendency for the barriers between the arts and between them and the real world to be broken down.

A rich and dynamic style

Because of its use of swelling forms, a great deal of ornament, and rich and glowing materials—much marble (often colored), gilt, and bronze—the Baroque is a heavy style. But it is also dynamic. Angels fly, and saints soar up to heaven; men on the ground gesture and struggle; draperies flutter as if they had a life of their own. Baroque painters loved to depict a crowd; it is not surprising that their supreme large-scale achievement was ceiling decoration [5]. In architec-

CONNECTIONS

See also
1164 Baroque art: patronage and development
1154 The Catholic Reformation
1190 The Rococo
1196 Baroque and classical music
848 Varieties of worship

1

1 Bernini, foremost of the Baroque sculptors, first asserted his hold over his patrons and fellow artists by the brilliance of his technique. In his life-size marble of "Apollo and Daphne" (1622–25), for Scipione Borghese, Daphne is changed before one's eyes into a laurel tree as the pursuing god is about to catch up with her.

2

2 Baroque realism was first expressed in a brutal and dramatic way by Michelangelo da Caravaggio, a north Italian painter who took Rome by storm in the 1590s. Although largely untutored, Caravaggio was a man of genius with a fiery temperament; it is well exemplified in his "David with the Head of Goliath" (*c.* 1606).

3

3 The full flowering of Baroque style in architecture as a field for structural even more than decorative ingenuity occurred in Germany in the 18th century. The church of the Vierzehnheiligen, or fourteen saints, (1743–72) in northern Bavaria was designed by Balthasar Neumann with a ground plan of intersecting ovals. Thus there is a constant sense of interpenetrating spaces, a sense enhanced in the vertical plane by endless vaults and arches. The interior appears to be all arches and projecting piers, with jutting curves and no walls. The decoration of the altar is Rococo.

ture, curved façades, oval ground plans as at Vierzehnheiligen [3], designed by Balthasar Neumann (1687–1753), and broken pediments tend to replace the straight façades, square or circular ground plans, and simple pediments of the Renaissance.

Although Baroque artists invented few new forms, they displayed the utmost ingenuity in devising new types of decoration and in twisting traditional forms into unusual shapes. From its reverence for classical art the Baroque derived its erudition and sense of grandeur; from the Renaissance it took its understanding of form and its feeling for color and light and shade; from Mannerism it inherited its love of complexity and decoration. But the mixture was new.

Development and spread of Baroque

The first signs of the new style were a return to realism [2] and a powerful use of light and shade, exemplified by the Italian painters Michelangelo da Caravaggio (1571–1610) and Annibale Carracci (1560–1609). Dynamism and a mastery of glowing color emerged with Rubens [6], who brought the Baroque to northern Europe after visiting Italy from 1600 to 1609. The "high Baroque" in Italy followed, dominated by a trio of artists active in Rome in the second and third quarters of the seventeenth century: the sculptor and architect Bernini [1], the architect Francesco Borromini (1599–1667), and the painter and architect Pietro da Cortona (1596–1669). After this period, the initiative shifted northward through the work of Guarino Guarini (1624–83) in Turin [Key] to central Europe and southern and central Germany, where Baroque architecture reached the ultimate in flamboyance and fantasy. Meanwhile, Baroque painting enjoyed a last, golden revival in eighteenth-century Venice with Giovanni Battista Tiepolo (1696–1770).

In Spain and Portugal, Baroque arrived first in a restrained form in painting and sculpture, achieving both a popular version in religious art and a courtly version in the portraits of Diego de Silva y Velasquez (1599–1660). Spanish and Portuguese Baroque architecture shows a cascade of surface ornament on a basic form [4].

KEY

Ingenuity and boldness in the handling of traditional forms, together with a sense of movement, are the hallmarks of Baroque architecture as seen here in the dome of Guarino Guarini's Holy Shroud Chapel, Turin (1667–90).

4

4 Spanish Baroque architecture commonly has separate units or "blocks" placed on top of each other, and the vertical effect thus created is emphasized by pepperpot domes, turrets, and slender grouped pilasters. The Reloj Tower (1676–80) of Santiago da Compostella Cathedral, designed by Domingo de Andrade, has these features. Its encrusted decoration is also typical.

5

5 In late Baroque, the time-honored Italian ambition to paint a many-figured fresco ceiling decoration was carried out with greatest virtuosity. In the dining room of the Würzburg Residenz, Germany, the 18th-century Venetian painter Giovanni Battista Tiepolo not only worked on an oval field but dispensed with an internal painted architectural framework, so that the whole vast design occupies a single unit of space and spills out onto the white and gilt stucco surround. He received the commission from the prince-bishop in 1751, and took as his subject "Apollo conducting Beatrice of Burgundy to Frederick Barbarossa," completed in 1753.

6

6 Italian inspiration and a degree of Flemish realism are the basis of Peter Paul Rubens' style. To this he added shimmer and fluency and a vigorous dynamic sense. In his paintings, everything—nature, animals, human flesh—is instilled with superabundant life. Significantly, he was the one major Baroque landscapist. His "Judgment of Paris" (*c.* 1632–35) shows all this well. The story is the classical legend of how the goddesses Venus, Juno, and Minerva, arguing among themselves as to which was the most beautiful, allowed Paris to make the decision, and Paris awarded the prize—an apple—to Venus.

Baroque art: patronage and development

The chief patrons of Baroque were kings, popes, cardinals, the higher aristocracy, diocesan councils, and representatives of religious orders. The two latter groups, although neither necessarily cultivated nor wealthy, were more active in their patronage than they had been since the fifteenth century. Baroque thus became the first style since the Middle Ages to develop both a popular and a sophisticated form.

Religious background of Baroque

The popular form is naturally most evident in outlying districts. While each region produced its own variations, the local monastery or parish church [2] with slim bell tower, simple Baroque doorway, and Baroque stucco-work in the interior is a familiar sight throughout the Catholic world from Poland to Peru. Popular Baroque, unless mixed with non-European influences as in Spain and Central and South America, is, however, essentially a coarsened and simplified version of its sophisticated forms, and it is these that must be examined to understand the background of the style.

Baroque arose under the stimulus of the Catholic Reformation. This movement, aimed at reaffirming Catholic doctrine in the face of Protestantism, began in the 1530s, long before the emergence of Baroque art in the usual meaning of the term. During the Catholic Reformation several new, militant religious orders were founded, most notably the Society of Jesus (Jesuits), founded by St Ignatius Loyola (1491–1556).

St Ignatius [5] was, like many of the principal Catholic figures of the period, a Spaniard. In their writings the Spanish religious teachers evolved meditative techniques to turn the mind's eye upon the details of Christ's Passion and so train the soul for its ultimate reward—union with Christ. This reward was achieved through a good death (at its highest, through martyrdom) or through experiencing visions of Christ, the Virgin, and the saints. The realization of these experiences depended on cultivating a heightened emotional state, and the visions and the state of mind required to produce them were well suited to representation by Baroque art [1].

It was many years before Baroque emerged, however. The Catholic Reformation in its early stages was a puritanical movement, and the religious orders were poor and indifferent to the arts. Official policy was confined to ensuring that religious pictures and statues were kept free of indecency and heresy. But in the late sixteenth century a few artistically minded prelates, such as Cardinal Federico Borromeo, began seeing the possibilities of using art not only to demonstrate Catholic doctrine but also as an aid to worship. They believed that vivid and attractive representations of the sacred stories and the visions of the saints would help ordinary Christians to believe in the stories and share the visions.

The use of art as propaganda

Art, in other words, was to be used to reach the mind through the emotions—the fundamental technique of propaganda as it has been revived in modern times (the word derives from an organization founded in this period, the Council for the Propagation of the Faith, the *Propaganda Fide*). Put to this

CONNECTIONS

See also
1162 Baroque art: style and content
1154 The Catholic Reformation
1196 Baroque and classical music
1190 The Rococo

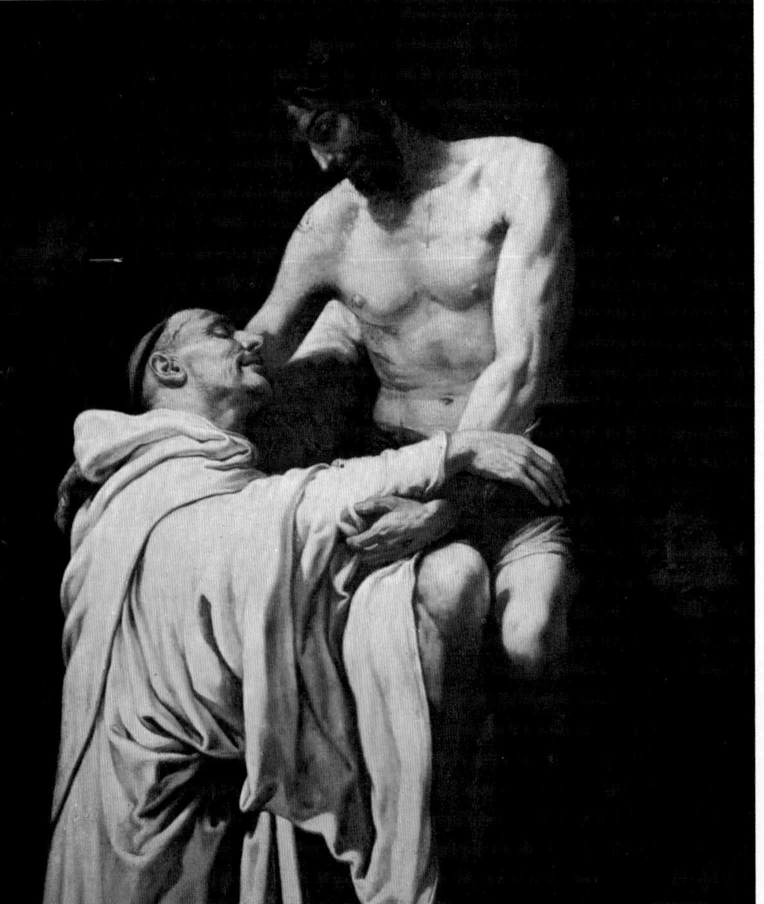

1 The spirit of devotion in the time of the Catholic Reformation is seen at its most extreme in Francisco Ribalta's "Vision of St Bernard" (*c.* 1625, detail). This is typical both of Spanish religion and painting. The saint draws so close in spirit to the suffering Christ that Christ appears to bend down from the cross to embrace him. Such vivid imagining reflects the ideals of Ignatius Loyola's *Spiritual Exercises*, and the painter uses all his art to convey this.

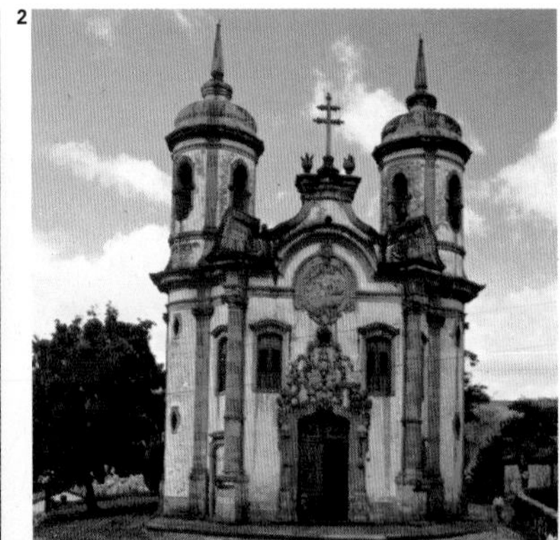

2 S. Francisco at Ouro Preto (1766–94), in the (then) Portuguese colony of Brazil gives some idea of the type of small Baroque church that sprang up in the farthest corners of the Catholic world. More sophisticated than some, with its exquisite decoration and round towers set back from the façade, it is by a Brazilian architect, Francisco Antônio Lisboa, called Aleijadinho ("little cripple")

3 Diego Velasquez, like Bernini and Van Dyck, conceived it his task when portraying royalty—here, Philip IV of Spain (1644)—to ennoble his sitter, but he used more subtle, less flamboyant means. The face is stubborn and guarded rather than beautiful and, although the colors glow, the pose is restrained. Besides Velasquez, who painted many portraits of him and his family, Philip patronized Francisco de Zurbarán (1598–1664) and Rubens.

use, the Baroque style, with its realism and dynamism, proved to be a very effective instrument. It could translate a religion—stirring in its appeal and richly provided with incident and heroic characters—into visual terms and do it with energy and panache. A worshiper entering a church and gazing at the solemn pictures on the altars, the glittering statues against the piers, and the vision of heaven on the ceiling was made to feel almost literally in the presence of God and the saints.

Power and glory of the Catholic Church

Beginning in the 1620s, art was increasingly called upon not only to proclaim the faith but also to demonstrate the power and glory of the Catholic Church. Supported now by art-loving cardinals and some popes, Baroque painters, sculptors, and architects became busily engaged in embellishing and building churches. The greatest single achievement of this kind was the transformation inside [4] and outside of St Peter's, Rome, the principal lifetime task of Gianlorenzo Bernini (1598–1680).

Baroque was also well suited to the purposes of secular rulers, who saw themselves as divinely ordained. In the mid-seventeenth century a group of monarchs—Philip IV of Spain [3] (1605–65), Charles I of England [6] (1600–49), the Archduke Leopold-Wilhelm, regent of Flanders, Pope Urban VIII (1568–1644) (who acted in many ways like a secular monarch)—were all active and knowledgeable patrons of the arts and of artists such as Velasquez (1599–1660) and Van Dyck (1599–1641). All these rulers generally favored the Baroque style.

They were succeeded in the late seventeenth century by the most powerful monarch of all, Louis XIV of France (1638–1715), who turned French classicism toward the Baroque [Key], and in the eighteenth century by the princes of many German states. Where kings and princes led, dukes and lesser nobles followed, dotting the countryside of Europe with magnificent palaces [7] and great houses; eloquent symbols of aristocratic power realized through the agency of Baroque art.

KEY

Louis XIV summoned Gianlorenzo Bernini to Paris in 1665, among other things to sculpt his portrait bust—a meeting of luminaries combining to produce a Quintessentially Baroque work. Chantelou, a Frenchman, noted how Bernini altered nature to bring out the effect of majesty in the king.

4

4 The visual climax of St Peter's, Rome, and hence one of the most sacred monuments of Catholicism, is the *Cathedra Petri* at the west end (unlike most cathedrals, the main entrance of St Peter's is at the east end). Bernini designed it in 1657–66 in the final stage of his transformation of the basilica's interior. The *Cathedra* takes its name from the ancient wooden chair of St Peter, said to be encased in the bronze throne that forms the centerpiece. Below are four Fathers of the Church, also in bronze, and above are gilt angels on white stucco clouds surrounding the Dove of the Holy Ghost set in a colored window. Gilt metal rays extending from this window complete the scheme.

5

6

5 St Ignatius Loyola founded the Society of Jesus in 1534. The Gesù, mother church of the order in Rome, begun in 1568, followed a stark design by Vignola (1507–73). The magnificent chapel to St Ignatius in the Gesu was executed in 1695–99 by Andrea Pozzo (1642–1709), with a silver statue of the saint by Pierre Legros. In 1797 the statue was melted down to pay Napoleon after his Italian campaign. It is now replaced by a partly silver copy, shown here. The long passage of both Baroque art and Catholic Reformation from heroic debut through ostentatious triumph to humiliation shares the chapel's history.

6 Charles I, king of England, joined his fellow European monarchs to become one of the keenest patrons of the age. No other English monarch has rivaled him in this respect. Here he is portrayed in the hunting field as an elegant gentleman—yet every inch a king—by his court painter, Sir Anthony Van Dyck (*c*. 1635).

7 There is a hint of Versailles in the palace of the Upper Belvedere, Vienna, built by Lukas von Hildebrandt for Prince Eugène (1721–24). (No ambitious patron of the period, let alone one who had helped to defeat Louis XIV, could ignore the Sun King's palace.) But the design is more playful and festive.

7

French art in the 17th century

Seventeenth-century French art, like most aspects of French life and thought, was dominated by one special quality: a profound belief in order and reason. There was much talk of "rules," and academies were founded for the first time with the object of setting standards (the Royal Academy of Painting and Sculpture was started in 1648, although it did not become effective until the 1660s). Typical of this approach is the painter Nicolas Poussin's (1594–1665) statement: "Things having the quality of perfection ought not to be viewed hastily but with care, discrimination, and intelligence."

Classical sources

Ancient Greek and Roman forms in architecture and sculpture were regarded above all as models of harmonious organization. They were preeminently creations of a rational mind, fitting together to form wholes with the logic of a mathematical proposition. Harmony in the relationship of parts is the essence of classicism. In France the idea was pursued with vigor. The French were also unusually interested in theory and insisted upon adherence to the rules of proportion in architecture laid down by the Roman writer Vitruvius.

When French artists adapted forms from Greek and Roman art they saw them as possessing even more clarity and order than they contained originally [Key]. French works consequently lack the grace of contemporary Italian art. Seventeenth-century French classicists opposed both the confusion of Mannerism and the license of the Baroque.

Development of architecture

The first major artist of the period was an architect, Salomon de Brosse (1571–1626), and architecture alone has a continuous history in and around Paris throughout the century. Most French architects did not even visit Italy, believing all they needed could be gleaned from books and the work of their sixteenth-century predecessors, some of whom had been trained in Italy. De Brosse introduced symmetry on all four sides of a building and was the first for some time to design in terms of the mass of the building rather than the decoration of its surface. These qualities were inherited by his greatest successor, François Mansart (1598–1666) who, in such buildings as Maisons [1], expressed most purely and completely the principal characteristics of the French classical spirit in this period: clarity combined with subtlety; restraint with grandeur; obedience to a strict code of rules combined with flexibility within them; and the elimination of nonessentials.

Until the 1650s the most important buildings had been executed for the rich bourgeoisie who had amassed fortunes in the new France of Cardinal Richelieu (1585–1642); Parisian town houses are as significant in the architectural history of this period as country châteaux. The patrons of Poussin were also drawn from this class.

After 1660, however, when Louis XIV came of age, developments became increasingly centered on the crown. The first major undertaking to reflect this change was the erection of the east front of the Louvre (1667–70) [6]. Symbolically, the most cele-

CONNECTIONS

See also
1170 The age of Louis XIV
1172 French classical literature
1150 Mannerism
1162 Baroque art: style and content
1164 Baroque art: patronage and development
1140 Florence and Rome: the High Renaissance

1

1 In the 17th century the typical French château consisted of a solid block with frontispiece, short wings, and high-pitched roof. It appears in its most massive and classical form at Maisons, near Paris, built 1642–46 by François Mansart for a Treasury official, René de Longueil. The walls are divided into two nearly equal stories by a heavy entablature running all around the building, and each story is articulated by repeated groups of pilasters. The roof line is varied by chimney stacks and dormer windows.

2 In Nicolas Poussin's "Arcadian Shepherds" (*c.* 1639), gestures are limited to lines parallel to the picture plane, and space is plotted with precision.

3 The serene art of Claude Lorrain conjured up a mood of harmony and repose. In his "Hagar and the Angel" (1646) the angel comforts the servant Hagar.

2

3

brated artist in Europe, Gianlorenzo Bernini (1598–1680), had been summoned to Paris to design it, but his proposals were rejected in favor of those of a French architect, Louis Le Vau (1612–70). Ambition to use an internationally famous architect yielded to French national pride and the desire for Baroque splendor to French classical taste.

Development of painting

French painting meanwhile had found its most interesting and significant expression in two centers remote from Paris: Lorraine and Rome. In Lorraine Georges de la Tour (1593–1652) painted candlelight scenes of religious subjects [4] in the dark manner of Michelangelo da Caravaggio (1571–1610), but he treated them with a solemnity, precision, and restraint that were typically French. In Rome, Poussin [2] and Claude Lorrain (1600–82) [3], who resided there for most of their lives, developed a classicizing style in intimate contact with ancient Roman and Italian Renaissance sources, although Poussin, at least, worked mainly for French patrons and decisively influenced French painting. His saturation in the moral attitudes and visible remains of the ancient world gave a mood of austere gravity to his work. He took great care to arrange his figures in such a way that every gesture and expression would tell.

Claude Lorrain was a more genial artist. His specialty was the ideal landscape of which he was, although not the inventor, the greatest exponent. The principle of ideal landscape is the production of an image of nature more harmonious than nature. To this Claude added a poetic light.

The last quarter of the century is dominated by Louis XIV's creation of the palace of Versailles [5]. It was designed by Le Vau and decorated by a team of painters, sculptors (whose art became important for the first time in the period), and designers under the supervision of the head of the Academy, Charles Le Brun (1619–90). Although the general lines of the buildings and their ornamentation were classical, the need for pomp and splendor at last proved irresistible and turned French art, temporarily, in the direction of the Baroque.

KEY

This plate from a French architectural textbook of 1650 underlines the link between French classicism and its ancient sources.

4

4 Biblical characters were given contemporary reality by the Italian Caravaggio, who painted them dressed in clothes worn by the poor of his time. Georges de la Tour borrowed this idea, perhaps indirectly, for this "Penitent Magdalene" (*c.* 1650), adding a note of French refinement.

5

5 The Salon de Vénus by Charles Le Brun (*c.* 1671) is part of the king's state apartments at Versailles. With it heavy gilt stucco moldings and architectural wall treatment, it shows how French classicism approached the Baroque.

6

6 Louis Le Vau's east front of the Louvre, Paris, 1667–70, which completed the palace (apart from 19th-century additions) is almost a manifesto of the French classicism of its date – the period between Maisons and Versailles. It is clear and regular, yet magnificent.

The golden age of Dutch painting

The flowering of painting in the Netherlands during the seventeenth century is one of the most remarkable events in the history of art. In many ways the Dutch school seems uniquely "modern" in the Europe of its time: realistic, bourgeois, unencumbered by rules, and based on the operation of a free market rather than the system of ecclesiastical and aristocratic patronage prevailing in other countries. But its development, like that of the society it mirrored, was the result of a reshaping of past traditions, as well as of some new forces.

The new republic

Seventeenth-century Dutch realism was rooted in an attitude that was already evident in fifteenth-century Flemish painting. A fondness for minute detail and for narrative, together with a certain popular appeal and an interest in depicting everyday life, remained undercurrents even in the art of the sixteenth century, despite the Italianate forms of the Renaissance.

The whole Netherlands, including Flanders, was under the suzerainty of Spain in the sixteenth century, but the Dutch, many of whom were Protestants, fought a long war against the Spanish army of occupation and by the early seventeenth century had established an independent republic, the United Provinces. The new republic rapidly became what was from many points of view the most progressive nation in Europe, with a flourishing economy, an advanced technology, a powerful merchant class, and a habit of political and even, to some extent, religious toleration. At the same time it was conservative enough to maintain the ancient rights of the individual provinces and towns as well as of the various guilds.

The guild of painters in each town was able to regulate entry to the profession and decide how and where artists could sell their works—normally through auctions at fairs. More broadly, the guild system favored a traditional, craft-oriented approach to art, in contrast to the more intellectual approach fostered in aristocratic societies under Renaissance influence. The association of art with craft in turn encouraged the distribution of pictures over a wide cross section of the community, and prices were generally low.

Society also had some negative effects on art. Since the establishmentof Protestantism as the official faith meant the exclusion of religious art [Key] from churches, the popularity of religious art with private buyers declined. The absence of a royal family also significantly deprived Dutch painters of the opportunity to execute large-scale Baroque decorative schemes. Nor were painters, in contrast to architects, much interested in the classical forms that pervaded art in most of the rest in Europe.

Realism in portraiture and genre scenes

All this left Dutch artists free to concentrate on depicting, with increasing realism, themselves, their possessions, and their surroundings. As in other mercantile societies, the seventeenth century in the Netherlands was a great age of portraiture. The highest category was the group portrait, usually of the officers of some militia company [1] or professional guild; both Rembrandt van Rijn (1606–69) and the Dutch portrait

CONNECTIONS

See also
1158 Europe 1500–1700
1144 The German and Netherlandish Renaissance
1164 Baroque art: patronage and development

1 Militia companies, formed to defend Dutch towns against Spanish troops in the 16th century, became social clubs after the republic was established early in the 17th century. Frans Hals was one of their greatest portraitists. Shown here is his "The Banquet of the Officers of the Company of St George" (1627).

2 When he and they were old, Rembrandt saw the rich Dutch merchants and their wives as Old Testament patriarchs—proud, stiff, and severe, yet with a sense of the pathos that affects all mankind. His portrait of Margareta Trip (*c.* 1661), shows his mastery of light, shade, and brushwork.

3 Low life, a genre inherited from the 16th-century Flemish artist Bruegel, was practiced in Flanders and the Netherlands by Brouwer; his "Boor Asleep" was painted in Flanders *c.* 1635, but is also typical of Dutch painting. Its earthy realism, spiced with wit, is a feature of the first half of the period.

4 After 1650, Dutch paintings of scenes from daily life became more refined and a new pictorial type was invented: the bourgeois domestic interior, the main subjects of which were woman. "Lady and Gentleman at the Virginals" (*c.* 1660), by Jan Vermeer, a masterpainter of daylight, is a subtle example.

painter closest to him in stature, Frans Hals (1581?–1666), made significant contributions in this field. Their single portraits were equally memorable [2]—canvas after canvas of serious-faced, strongly characterized men and women, the somberness of their black clothes relieved only by white collars and cuffs.

The Dutch also loved pictures of themselves at home and at parties or in taverns; these were normally not portraits but genre scenes from daily life ranging from refined interiors showing women alone or conversing with gentlemen or making music [4], by artists like Jan Vermeer (1632–75) and Gerter Borch (1617–81), through the rowdy feasting and drinking scenes of Jan Steen (1626–79), to the tavern brawls of Adriaen Brouwer (*c.* 1606–38) [3] and Adriaen van Ostade (1610–85). One aspect of daily life generally conspicuous by its absence, however, is work, except light domestic employment or the traditionally paintable rural activities of tending herds and fishing.

Material possessions are often prominent in genre scenes but are presented even more blatantly in still-life painting: glass and silver goblets, pottery bowls and jugs, imported Turkish carpets, and flowers, of which the Dutch were so fond, as well as all kinds of food. Still life also gave an unrivaled opportunity for that cool, painstaking realism in the rendering of detail that Dutch painters brought to so extraordinary a pitch [8].

Land and seascapes

Finally, the Dutch invented a method of their own in landscape and marine painting. Gone were the contrived if beautiful conventions of previous ages and other schools. It is true that they introduced other conventions, but these were mere fashions in composition and subject matter rather than systems for creating imaginary visions more varied and more seductive than nature itself. Seventeenth-century Dutch landscapes and seascapes, by artists like Jan van Goyen (1596–1656) and Jacob van Ruisdael (1628?–82), are windows on an actual world [7], a world of dunes, estuaries, and canals, of flat coastal plains and dark inland woods.

KEY

The most typical and most exceptional of Dutch painters, Rembrandt shows the human side of his religious faith in a detail of his etching, "Christ Healing the Sick" (1643–47).

5 Realism in Dutch landscape painting was first achieved by simplification, with concentration on tone and light at the expense of form and color, as in Van Goyen's "View of Emmerich" (1645).

6 Architecture was one field of Dutch art in which classical rules were followed. The Dam Palace of Amsterdam, originally the town hall, was designed by Jan van Campen in the style of Palladio. Begun in 1648, the year in which the republic formally became independent, it has many symbols in sculpture of the maritime and commercial supremacy achieved by the Dutch at this time.

6

5

7 The most powerful and versatile of Dutch landscapists was Jacob van Ruisdael. After an era of grayness and austerity, he brought back color and a sense of form to the treatment of dunes, forests, and windmills. His "Wooded Landscape" (*c.* 1660) suggests a contrast of life and death.

8 The Dutch love of material things is shown in this sumptuous "Still Life" by Willem Kalf.

7

8

The age of Louis XIV

In 1660, France was internally divided, torn by faction. The rebellion of the "officers" and nobles in the Fronde—years of chronic civil unrest from 1648 to 1653—had presented a threat of civil war and driven Cardinal Mazarin (1602–61), the first minister during Louis XIV's minority, from Paris. The work of Richelieu in reestablishing the authority of the monarchy had collapsed. France needed a strong adult king. In March 1661, Mazarin died, and the young Louis, then 23 years old, decided to dispense with a first minister and to rule as well as reign. By that decision he restored to the crown the charisma surrounding it and the obedience owed to a divinely appointed king. He was determined to restore authority and majesty to the Bourbon dynasty in France and in Europe and, further, to end the disorder that affronted a dynasty ordained by God.

The theme of order is important in understanding Louis XIV's policies at home and abroad. Louis' obsession with order is depicted best at Versailles [3]: the architecture of the palace and the plan of the gardens and fountains follow the rules of symmetry; elaborate ceremonial accompanied the king's actions throughout the day. Louis reduced the powers of nobles, *parlements*, and the various provincial and national interest groups, which he felt had swelled beyond their true station. Centralization extended court authority into the provinces. Agents of the central government (intendants) supervised regional affairs while the nobles enjoyed Versailles. Order demanded too the eradication of heresy. By the revocation of the Edict of Nantes in 1685, the French Protestants (Huguenots) were forced to conform or go into exile.

Foreign policy

The same belief in order and justice lay behind Louis' foreign policy. He aimed to restore to France all territories to which it once had a claim and to extend the nation to its "natural frontiers." What Louis saw as rights, the rest of Europe regarded as naked aggression. War characterized the reign of Louis XIV, and campaigns were almost continuous from 1667 onward. The War of Devolution, concerned with Louis' claim to the Spanish Netherlands, was fought from 1667 to 1668; the war against Holland from 1672 to 1678; the War of the League of Augsburg from 1688 to 1697; and the War of the Spanish Succession from 1701 to 1713. The needs of war directed all departments of government to require new taxes and increases in the traditional taille (land tax) and gabelle (salt tax).

Economic policy

The economic policies of Jean Baptiste Colbert (1619–83) were a response to the needs of war. France needed to be self-sufficient if it was not to depend on its enemies, especially the Dutch. Colbert attempted to stimulate the growth of native French industries [5]—iron and textiles—and especially the production of luxury goods, such as silk and lace. When these fashionable goods were acquired from the Mediterranean and the East Indies they were often brought to France by the Dutch and had to be purchased with bullion. As contemporary economic attitudes as-

CONNECTIONS

See also
1158 Europe's economy and society 1500–1700
1166 French art in the 17th century
1172 French classical literature
1180 Enlightened despotism
1182 Europe: economy and society 1700–1800
1178 Early modern Russia

1 A majestic image was a central facet of the absolutism of Louis XIV, well represented in this portrait by Hyacinthe Rigaud, and by Louis' famous maxim "L'état, c'est moi" (I am the state). The preeminence of the king was seen as part of divine and natural order, the establishment of his power a duty to God. Louis described that preeminence in his memoirs: "All eyes are fixed on him [the king] alone; it is to him that all wishes are addressed; he alone receives all respect; he alone is the object of all hopes. . . no one can raise himself but by gradually coming close to the royal person or estimation."

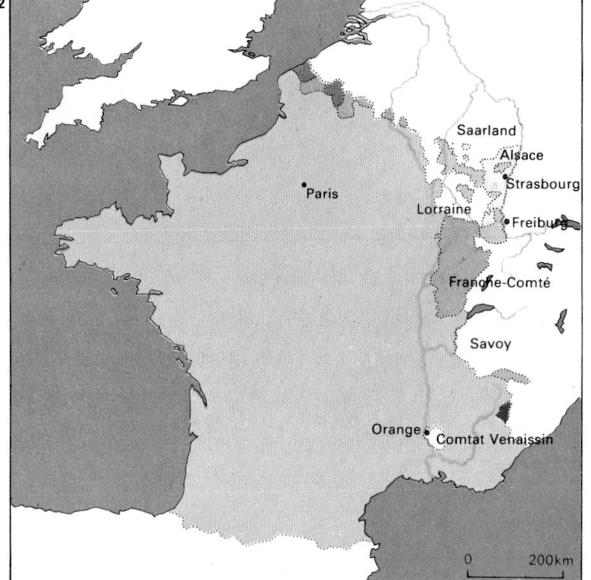

Paris
Saarland
Alsace
Strasbourg
Lorraine
Freiburg
Franche-Comté
Savoy
Orange
Comtat Venaissin
0
200km
France in 1661
Acquired in Treaty of Aix-la-Chapelle 1668
Acquired in Treaties of Nimwegen 1678–9
Ceded to Savoy in 1696
Acquired in Treaty of Ryswick 1697
Acquired in Treaty of Utrecht 1713

2 France's northern and southern defenses were strengthened by the acquisition of various frontier towns by treaties. Louis XIV's foreign policy was directed to annexing to France areas that would consolidate the frontiers. The map shows the territories gained over the course of 50 years.

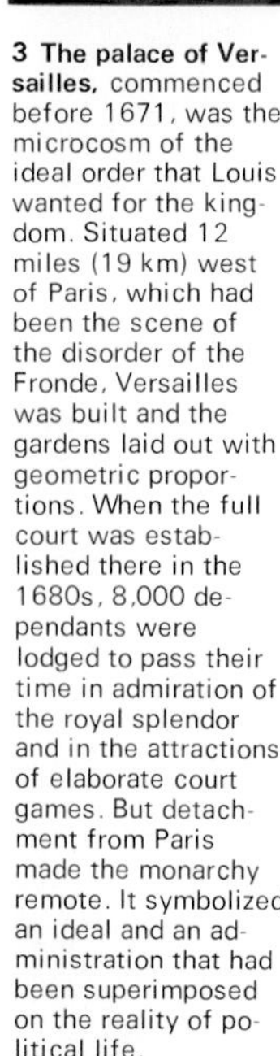

3 The palace of Versailles, commenced before 1671, was the microcosm of the ideal order that Louis wanted for the kingdom. Situated 12 miles (19 km) west of Paris, which had been the scene of the disorder of the Fronde, Versailles was built and the gardens laid out with geometric proportions. When the full court was established there in the 1680s, 8,000 dependants were lodged to pass their time in admiration of the royal splendor and in the attractions of elaborate court games. But detachment from Paris made the monarchy remote. It symbolized an ideal and an administration that had been superimposed on the reality of political life.

sociated power with the possession of bullion, these imports could not be tolerated. More trade and industry meant more power and wealth. Mercantilist economic theory meant economic war, and therefore Colbert embarked upon a tariff policy [6] to hamper the Dutch. The French East India Company was formed in an attempt to wrest trade from the Dutch in the colonies.

For much of his reign Louis appeared to have fulfilled his desires. Order was established at home, territories were conquered and recognized as French possessions by treaty, military victories were won. Colbert's new industries enjoyed some success, and France emerged as a rival to the commercial supremacy of the Dutch and the English. The glory of the Bourbon dynasty was recognized: Versailles and French absolutism became the model for other monarchs.

But the achievements were won at the cost of great strain at home and the enmity of almost every power in Europe. As the cost of war reached unprecedented levels royal finances began to fail. Louis never felt strong enough to tax the nobility, and there was no developed system of credit in France. In 1688, when William of Orange, the stadholder of Holland, became king of England, the might of two naval powers was joined, and the financial resources of the two most advanced commercial nations in the world were placed at the disposal of Louis' bitterest enemy.

Reaction and rebellion

As war continued and defeats mounted, a reaction set in in France. The peasants, who bore the brunt of taxation but who were the least able to pay it, rebelled. Toward the end of the reign, shortages of grain became acute. Poor harvests and high taxes in 1693–94 and 1709–10 forced up grain prices and led to many deaths in rural areas. The nobility reacted against Bourbon ambition and ostentation. Many trumpeted the virtues of the humbler life of pastoral simplicity and rural retreat. Louis' absolutism, centered on Versailles, became remote from the French nation, a symbol of the strength and the limitations of autocratic rule.

KEY

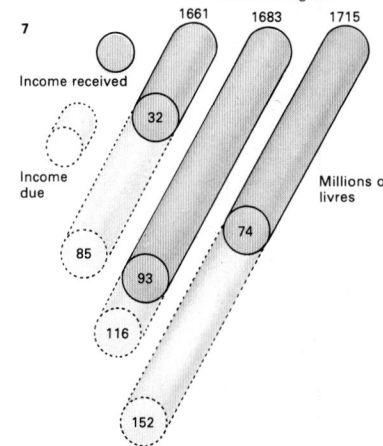

The glory of Louis XIV (1638–1715), the Sun King, is symbolized in his emblem.

4

4 In the reign of Louis XIV fortification methods were improved by Sebastian de Vauban, as demonstrated by Neuf Brisach fortress at Alsace. Situated vulnerably on flat ground, its defenses extended in depth around the whole circuit by detaching bastions [1] from the inner line, filling the gaps with *demilunes*, surrounding *ravelins*. First came the curtain [2], then a moat [3], *tenaille* [4], and second moat [5]. Next a *ravelin* [6], moat [7], *demilune* [8], outer moat [9], covered way [10], and lastly the *glacis* [11], sloping to outer ground level. The inner rampart was commanded by angled "bastion towers" [12].

5

The five major "tax farms"
"Foreign" provinces
Provinces not under French control
• Ports
Canal du Midi
Linen
Cloth
Tapestries
Lace
Shipbuilding
Iron works
Silk

5 The map shows the industries fostered by Colbert as part of his mercantilist policy. It shows too the internal customs areas that resulted from the gradual growth of the French kingdom.

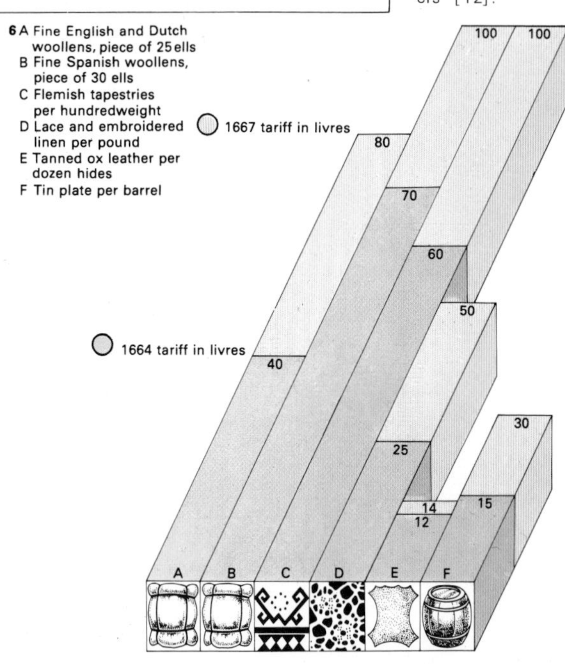

6 A Fine English and Dutch woollens, piece of 25 ells
B Fine Spanish woollens, piece of 30 ells
C Flemish tapestries per hundredweight
D Lace and embroidered linen per pound
E Tanned ox leather per dozen hides
F Tin plate per barrel
1667 tariff in livres
1664 tariff in livres
100
100
80
70
60
50
40
25
30
14
12
15
A
B
C
D
E
F

6 Colbert sought to bring order to the multiplicity of internal and external tariffs that impeded French trade. He also intended to employ a protective tariff to defend newly developed French industries and to hit at Dutch and English competition. The tariff first (1664) was primarily a product of the first aim of consolidation. The second (1667) strongly protected the French textile industry. The tariff brought retaliatory duties against French wine, and economic rivalry brought war with the Dutch in 1672. At the Peace of Nijmegen (1678–79), economic questions were settled in favor of the Dutch, and the customs tariffs of 1664 and 1667 were lifted.

7

7 One of the major financial problems of the monarchy stemmed from the difficulty of collecting taxes and ensuring that the monies due actually arrived at the treasury. Under Colbert the process of tax collection was improved, although taxes increased. Following Colbert's death in 1683 and with growing reaction against the costly wars of Louis, the situation deteriorated. By 1715 more than half the income due failed to arrive at the treasury.

French classical literature

All the French writers of the sixteenth century in one way or another attacked the culture of the Middle Ages. The emphasis was on self-awareness and the development of individualism and innovation, a trend culminating in the critical skepticism of Michel de Montaigne (1533–92) [Key]. Similar qualities are seen in Clément Marot (1496–1544) [1], whose irreverent humor and obstinate insistence on his right to think for himself are also found in the works of François Rabelais (*c.* 1494–*c.* 1553) [2]. John Calvin (1509–64), the Protestant reformer, was equally concise and ironical; his polemic writings showed that the French language could be as effective for argument as for narrative.

The Renaissance in literature

The spirit of Renaissance humanism had begun to permeate French literature. This at first led to the establishment of Greek and Latin writers as the supreme models. There were many translations, and classicism remained dominant until the "Quarrel between the Ancients and Moderns" in the latter half of the seventeenth century brought equal respect to some French writers.

Apart from Rabelais, Calvin, and Montaigne, there were few distinguished prose stylists in the sixteenth century. But in poetry supremely important innovations were made, first by Marot, then by the Lyons poets. Their chief representative was Maurice Scève (*c.* 1510–64), whose complex masterpiece *Délie* (1544) depended to a great extent on Petrarch's example. Scève was regarded as a pioneer by the Pléiade, a group of poets—Rémy Belleau, Jean Antoine de Baif, Etienne Jodelle, Pontus de Tyard, Jacques Peletier, Pierre de Ronsard [3A], and Joachim du Bellay [3B]—who took their name from a constellation of seven stars. The name was also given to the seven most eminent Greek poets of the reign of Ptolemy II in Alexandria in the third century BC.

The Pléiade intended to rehabilitate French poetry and put the French language on an equal footing with Latin, Greek, and Italian. The group's inspiration was obviously classical. Later the court poet François de Malherbe (1555–1628) turned sharply against the aims of the Pléiade because of its excessive complexity and erudition; but its practice had made its mark on him and continued to influence the course of poetry.

French classical theater did not reach its apogee until the seventeenth century, but Robert Garnier (1534–90) wrote humanist (if overly literary) tragedies, such as *Les Juives* (1583), that were performed by itinerant actors. He paved the way for the dramatists who succeeded him and exercised a strong influence in England.

"Ancients" versus "Moderns"

The seventeenth century was above all a period of classicism, although native individualism was by no means entirely suppressed. Individuals were scrutinized against the background of general truths about human nature. The quest for a perfect language continued, resulting in the foundation of the Académie Française [7].

The battle of the Ancients and Moderns developed with Nicolas Boileau (1636–1711) [9] as the chief representative of the former

CONNECTIONS

See also
1170 The age of Louis XIV
1166 French art in the 17th century
1148 English Renaissance literature
1188 The 18th century: the novel and the press

EMENS MAROTVS FRANCVS POETA PRIM

1 Clément Marot was a court poet. He wrote, at first, in the fashionable late 15th-century style but soon abandoned this to become an important innovator. He began to fashion his poems on Latin and Greek models and introduced almost all of the new styles that the Pléiade announced as theirs. In particular, he introduced the sonnet into the language. He knew Calvin and joined him in Geneva. Marot was a witty, graceful, epigrammatic writer—one of the best court poets and an important transitional figure. After being exiled and imprisoned for heresy, he won the patronage of Francis I and Margaret of Navarre.

2 This illustration by Gustave Doré of Rabelais' *Gargantua and Pantagruel* (*c.* 1532–52) shows Gargantua poised above Notre-Dame Cathedral. In 1530, Rabelais abandoned the monastic life and became a doctor. His contemporaries saw him mainly as an eminent physician and humanist. His work changes as it proceeds. The first two books tell a fantastic tale of a family of giants, and also satirize the clergy and educational methods of the times. The third book is more topical and the fourth the most complex. Rabelais was a realist who believed in the equal importance of all human beings. His great work, uneven though it is, anticipated many of the concerns of 20th-century novelists. He has incomparable value as an imaginative writer and as a lucid and commonsensical portrayer of his times, sixteenth-century France.

3 The two most gifted members of the Pléiade group were Pierre de Ronsard [A] and Joachim du Bellay [B]. Du Bellay wrote the manifesto of this group in his *The Defense and Illustration of the French Language* (1549). His advice to authors was this: take Greek, Latin, and Italian models to make French "illustrious;" create new words to enrich the language; use ancient and Italian forms and reject those of the Middle Ages; above all, seek formal perfection. Ronsard's greatest achievement was in his lyrical poetry and his mastery of the ode and sonnet. Du Bellay wrote the first sonnet sequence in French, *L'Olive* (1549), which was influenced by Petrarch's poetry.

4 Mme de La Fayette [left], the novelist; Mme de Sévigné the observer; and La Rochefoucauld, the moralist represent three great strands of French writing in the 17th century. It is significant that all three were aristocrats, for *belles lettres* were almost an aristocratic preserve. Another dominant fact of French literary life was the near equality between the sexes and the markedly social nature of the circumstances of much literary work.

and Jean Desmarets (1596–1676) and Charles Perrault (1628–1703) as champions of the latter. The virtues of fairly rigorous imitation of classical models were set against the merits of exploring modern and progressive ideas. Finally (1700), Boileau acknowledged to Perrault that contemporary French writers could—if they recognized the classical virtues—be as good as any ancient authors.

Drama and prose in the seventeenth century
Poetry flourished in the tragic drama, first in the rhetorical Pierre Corneille (1606–84) and then with Jean Racine (1639–99) [6]. The great tragedians also wrote comedy, which was developed to perfection by Molière (1622–73) [5]. The fable was mastered by La Fontaine (1621–95) [8].

Fiction, a product of the expansion of literacy and the desire (especially among *salon* frequenters) for entertainment, properly begins (even though Rabelais is, with Cervantes, the real father of the novel) with *L'Astrée* (1607–27) by Honoré d'Urfé (1567–1625). *L'Astrée* is a long pastoral story, but with some psychological realism and evident moral intention. One of its admirers, Marie de La Fayette (1634–93) [4], wrote the first great French novel: *La Princesse de Clèves* (1678). This tale of passion is remarkably modern. It is quietly realistic, psychologically acute, and obliquely critical of society. It has virtues of structure and style that Stendhal and others thought supreme.

The picture of the age given by the major writers is completed by the letter writers, moralists, aphorists, and writers on religion. Among these are Marie de Sévigné (1626–96) [4] whose feminine and intelligent letters give an incomparably lively and accurate picture of Paris, the center of culture; François de La Rochefoucauld (1613–80) [4], whose *Maxims* are far more than merely cynical in their exposure of the real nature of motives; and Blaise Pascal (1623–62), the mathematical genius whose *Pensées* (unpublished until after his death) defend the influential brand of critical Catholicism called Jansenism and anticipate the existential tone of modern religious discussion.

KEY

SEIGNEVR DE MONTAIGN

The Essays (1580–95) of Michel de Montaigne contain the purest expression of the spirit of 16th-century France. Montaigne—an aristocrat by birth—invented the essay. Although a skeptic, he would not offend religious orthodoxy and took the conservative side in the religious wars. The curiosity he displayed was a typical feature of those men of his time who were fighting against the stultifying effects of the Middle Ages. In his essays he touches on almost every known subject in a direct and lucid style: on anthropology, morality, judicious behavior, education, and above all on the acquisition of wise and sound judgment.

5

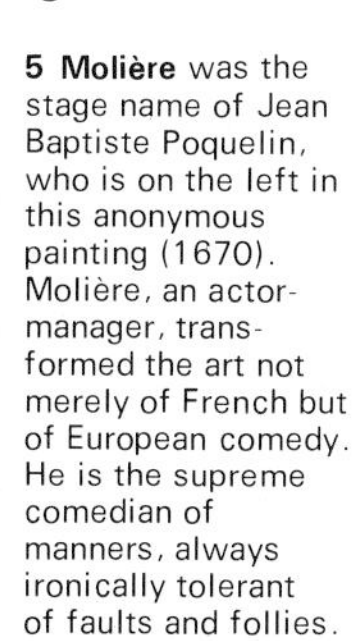

5 Molière was the stage name of Jean Baptiste Poquelin, who is on the left in this anonymous painting (1670). Molière, an actor-manager, transformed the art not merely of French but of European comedy. He is the supreme comedian of manners, always ironically tolerant of faults and follies.

6

6 A scene from Racine's tragedy Phèdre is shown here. Racine achieved classical dramatic perfection, observing Aristotle's three unities of time, place, and action, and yet he sacrificed no psychological power. His plays are deeply moving, with his eloquent verse heightening emotion.

7

7 The Académie Française was established by Cardinal Richelieu after some authors took to meeting secretly (about 1630) to discuss literary questions. Its purpose was to define and thereby to perfect the language.

8

8 Jean de La Fontaine (1621–95), an adherent of the "Ancients" in the famous "battle," drew from many sources, including Aesop, for his *Fables*, an illustration from which is shown here. By attributing human responses and motivations to animals, he created situations that he could use to expose and satirize human failings both large and small. He was not a true moralist, but rather an amused, detached, and subtle observer of human nature and social behavior.

9

9 The influential critic and poet Nicolas Boileau, although not a great poet, was a legendary figure in his own lifetime and the chief advocate of the "Ancients" in their quarrel with the "Moderns." His many associates included Molière and Racine. His *L'Art poètique* (1674) became famous throughout Europe, and his rules were taken as law. by contemporary writers. The poem preaches, in an epigrammatic manner, all the classical virtues of poetry.

The origins of opera

Opera developed from three distinct sources and became established in Italy about 1600. *Sacre Rappresentazioni,* dramas with music, usually presented in the vernacular, were influenced by court pageants mounted to celebrate feast days and royal birthdays during the fifteenth century. Simultaneously, part-songs and madrigals (*i.e.,* polyphonic vocal works) were popular. They were often linked in cycles to tell a story.

Opera takes shape

A sung story, spectacle, and drama were forged into opera by the *Camerata,* a group of artists who were concerned with the role of music in Greek classical drama. The *Camerata* invented the recitative, a declamatory style of singing in which the notes and rhythms were allied to verbal accentuation. This was initially accompanied only by the harpsichord and was designed to enhance the meaning of the words.

The great master of the madrigal, Claudio Monteverdi [Key], adopted the formal recitative but combined it with the madrigal style to provide the basis of arias or set songs that punctuated the recitatives. In addition, Monteverdi employed a small orchestra and decorated the sung melody with runs and other musical devices to increase the expressiveness of the form. His *Orfeo* (1607) is accepted as the first operatic masterpiece with a known score.

By 1637 opera was established as a secular entertainment in Florence; and in Venice the first commercial opera house opened. Early opera houses were equipped with complicated machinery for lavish stage effects [2, 3, 4, 5]. Orchestras became larger and, with the development of their major instrument—the violin—they played an increasingly important part in Italian opera.

The spread of opera

Royal marriages between Italy and France brought opera to France, which then became the center of a controversy about the preeminence of words versus music. Jean-Baptiste Lully (1632–87), a Frenchman, adapted the recitative to the unique cadences of the French language and indulged the court's love of dance and spectacle in his operas [6]. Jean-Philippe Rameau (1683–1764), who succeeded Lully at the French court, used the chorus and orchestra to give opera a new grandeur and dignity [7]. The French approach to opera was essentially literary; drama took precedence over music.

In Italy an increase in musical resources and the advance of vocal technique to a stage where it rivaled the violin in agility concentrated public interest in opera. The works of Alessandro Scarlatti (1660–1725) established the form of the *da capo* aria (in three sections, the last one being a repetition of the first) and the overture.

English opera also derived from court entertainments but was slow to adopt the new musical forms. Henry Purcell (1659–95) set English words to the new "recitative musick," and his *Dido and Aeneas* is regarded as the first true English opera [8].

This germ of a tradition was not further developed. Instead, English opera was dominated by one of the first truly international composers, Frederick George Handel (1685–1759). Born in Germany,

CONNECTIONS

See also
1132 Renaissance music
1194 Early ballet
1148 English Renaissance literature
1256 Opera in the 19th and 20th centuries
1196 Baroque and Classical music

1

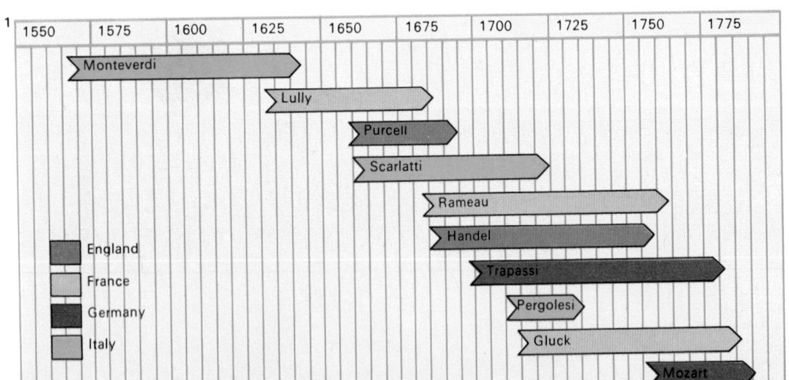

1550
1575
1600
1625
1650
1675
1700
1725
1750
1775
Monteverdi
Lully
Purcell
Scarlatti
Rameau
Handel
Trapassi
Pergolesi
Gluck
Mozart
England
France
Germany
Italy

1 Some of the major composers whose work established or advanced opera are shown here. The chart shows that from its origins in Italy, opera's creative center moved first to France and later seemed to settle in Germany, although Gluck did his most important reformist work in Paris. In the 18th century Europe experienced a period of concentrated activity, a kind of operatic heyday with many composers.

2

Teatro Grimani
a S. Giovanni Grisostomo

2 One of the first opera houses was that of Cardinal Barberini. It was built in his palace in Rome in 1632. The first opera performed there, Landi's *Il s. Alessio,* made several departures from tradition. It dealt with a 15th-century legend rather than a classical subject and also contained comic scenes. The first commercial opera house opened its doors in Venice in 1637 and in the following 60 years at least 16 more opera houses were established in Venice alone. These early houses were extremely lavish and equipped with all manner of ingenious stage machinery.

3

3 "Cloud machines" were used by Giacomo Torelli (1608–78), the leading stage technician of his day. Here, one has been lowered to introduce dancers; the other holds an orchestra.

4

4 A recent revival of Cavalli's *La Calisto* at Glyndebourne, England, recreated in modern terms some of the stage effects used at the time of its first performance. For example, gods and goddesses were always required to float above the stage, to descend from the flies, or heaven, while devils logically entered through trapdoors from below stage. Adherence to these rules in modern productions has helped to revive interest in some neglected works.

5

5 Some of the early stage effects were achieved with great simplicity. In 1638 Nicola Sabbatini, whose inventive devices were widely used, wrote an illustrated treatise on stage mechanics. Despite technical advances, it is doubtful whether modern producers have been able to rival the spectacle of some of these early presentations. Revival of interest in 17th-century music has recently led to a new concern with authenticity in staging the operas.

Handel worked briefly in Italy before moving to England. He was well placed to absorb all of Europe's major musical forms and traditions and brought *opera seria* (opera sung throughout) to its peak. Vienna was the true home of *opera seria*, which used sparsely-accompanied recitatives to tell the usually ennobling story, frequently interrupted by ornately embellished, often repeated arias. The major influence in *opera seria* was Pietro Trapassi (1698–1782), known as Metastasio. This, too, was the age of the singer—for whom arias were conceived primarily as vehicles for vocal brilliance—and especially the *castrato* (a singer castrated in boyhood to preserve the soprano or contralto range of his voice).

From Gluck to Mozart

Christoph Willibald Gluck (1714–87), a Bohemian working in Vienna and Paris, was the major reformer after *opera seria* fell into disfavor. He strove for simplicity and directness, as seen in *Orfeo ed Euridice*.

Comedy had so far played little part in opera, although the practice of inserting comic interludes had long been popular in Italy. *Opera buffa*—full comic opera—emerged in 1733 when Giovanni Battista Pergolesi (1710–36) presented *La Serva Padrona*. *Opera buffa* required a lighter musical touch.

All these forms were familiar to and employed by Wolfgang Amadeus Mozart (1756–91). His great operas, *The Marriage of Figaro*, *Cosi Fan Tutte*, and *Don Giovanni*, are a dazzling amalgam of styles, welded together into supreme musical-dramatic entities. His command of a large orchestra, his perfection of vocal ensemble, his gift of melody, and his sure sense of psychology lifted opera to new eminence. He transformed the popular *singspiel*—a combination of spoken dialogue and sung material—into high art in *The Magic Flute*, and at the end of his life wrote in the older *opera seria* form in *La Clemenza di Tito*.

Mozart's operas provided the basis for late eighteenth and nineteenth century development, when the stylistic division between German and Italian opera became absolute [11].

KEY

The father of opera, Claudio Monteverdi (1567–1643), was born in Cremona, where he served as a choirboy. He wrote more than 250 madrigals that are masterpieces of the form and that employed new, expressive harmonies. His first opera, *Orfeo*, at once indicated his ability to marry the vocal and instrumental traditions of his time with the new recitative. He became a priest in 1632 and wrote much church music, including the celebrated *Vespers*. A few examples of his enormous operatic output have survived; they include *Orfeo*, *Il Combattimento di Tancredi e Clorinda*, *The Return of Ulysses*, and *The Coronation of Poppea*. These works have provided musical scholars with many problems, but the works are now widely known. He spent his last 30 years in Venice where he was deeply involved with commercial opera.

6

DEMIE
ROY
E DE
MUSYQU
ARMIDE

6 Jean-Baptiste Lully was a French musician who was born in Italy. Early in his career he collaborated with the playwright Molière in the production of opera-ballets. His first true opera was performed in 1672; thereafter he wrote 20 more. (The title page of *Armide* [1686] is shown here.) He used accompanied recitatives that acknowledged the supremacy of words over music.

7

7 Jean-Philippe Rameau was Lully's successor, and he continued the formal tradition of French opera. He was a controversial composer who played a leading part in the enduring quarrel about the supremacy of words over music. He was a great theorist, and his ideas brought flexibility to the recitative.

8

8 Henry Purcell, the organist at London's Westminster Abbey, wrote church music and provided music and songs for plays and masques. His only true opera, *Dido and Aeneas*, the first masterpiece of the form produced in England, was written for performance by a London girls' school. Several 20th-century composers, including Michael Tippett and Benjamin Britten, have been influenced by him.

9 George Frederick Handel is universally known for his great English oratorio, *Messiah*. He was, however, a prodigious composer of operas such as *Serse* and *Alcina* and of other music.

10 Carlo Farinelli (1705–82) was the most celebrated of the Italian "male sopranos" or *castrati*. Women are said to have fainted with excitement when he sang.

9

10

11 Wolfgang Amadeus Mozart was a child prodigy who was attracted to the theater early in life. He had already written music for the stage when, at the age of 12 years, he wrote his first *opera buffa*, *La finta semplice*, followed in the same summer of 1768 by the operetta *Bastien und Bastienne*. Much later, his friendship with Emmanuel Schikeneder (1751–1812) led to their collaboration in the singspiel *The Magic Flute*, first performed in 1791.

11

Medieval Russia 900–1600

The first Russian state emerged out of the Slavic settlements northeast of European Byzantium between the sixth and ninth centuries AD. The Russian Slavs occupied a large belt of territory bounded by the Carpathian Mountains, the Baltic Sea, and the headwaters of the Volga, Don, Dnieper, and Dniester rivers. In the ninth century fierce Scandinavian merchant-warriors, called Varangians, conquered the area and established a federation of city-states. Its center was Kiev, and it was ruled by the Grand Prince of Kiev. The existing Slav ruling class assimilated the Varangian princes and established a lucrative trade with Constantinople [1]. In contrast to the barter economy of the medieval West, money and credit systems were widely used, and a prosperous commercial civilization grew up.

Byzantine influence in Kievan Russia

By 1100, bolstered by commercial wealth and contact with the Byzantine Empire, Kievan Russia had become a powerful state and the center of a flowering culture. From its chief trading partner Russia accepted the cultural heritage of Byzantine Orthodox Christianity. Missionaries introduced Orthodox liturgy by means of a language that, using the Cyrillic alphabet, became the basis of modern Russian. Grand Prince Vladimir I (*c.* 956–1015) adopted Orthodoxy as the official religion and a Metropolitan bishop arrived from Constantinople and set up an ecclesiastical organization. Byzantine styles of building [2] and icon painting [3] flourished.

The Russian political and social structures contrasted sharply with their Western counterparts. Three governmental elements managed to coexist—the ruling Riurik dynasty had to share power with a council of noblemen *(duma)* and with town meetings *(veche)* at the local level. The princes and their relations stood at the top of the social order, followed by the boyars [9], a class of merchants, soldiers, and landowners, then landowning peasants, tenant farmers, and slaves.

The emergence of Moscow

During the twelfth and thirteenth centuries Russia was profoundly affected by events beyond its frontiers. The growth of competing Venetian trade routes, raids by Asiatic tribes, the decline of Byzantium, and the rise of Poland-Lithuania and the Mongol Empire all contributed to Kiev's disintegration; there was also internal political and dynastic strife. Russian links with Constantinople loosened, and the economic strength of the Kievan state began to decline. The great city of Novgorod with its mercantile democracy and rich, forested hinterland was able to establish its independence [8], but western Russia fell under Polish-Lithuanian (and hence Roman Catholic) domination, and eastern Russia was overrun by the Mongols, whose empire was expanding rapidly under Genghis Khan (1167–1227) and his successors.

It was under Mongol rule that the principality of Moscow (Muscovy) first became important and then asserted political control over most of what is now European Russia. The Grand Dukes of Moscow, descended from a branch of the Riurik family, were originally the tax collectors of Sarai

CONNECTIONS

See also
1178 Early modern Russia
1068 The Vikings
1112 Asian empires of the Mongols
1056 The Byzantine Empire
1060 Byzantine art

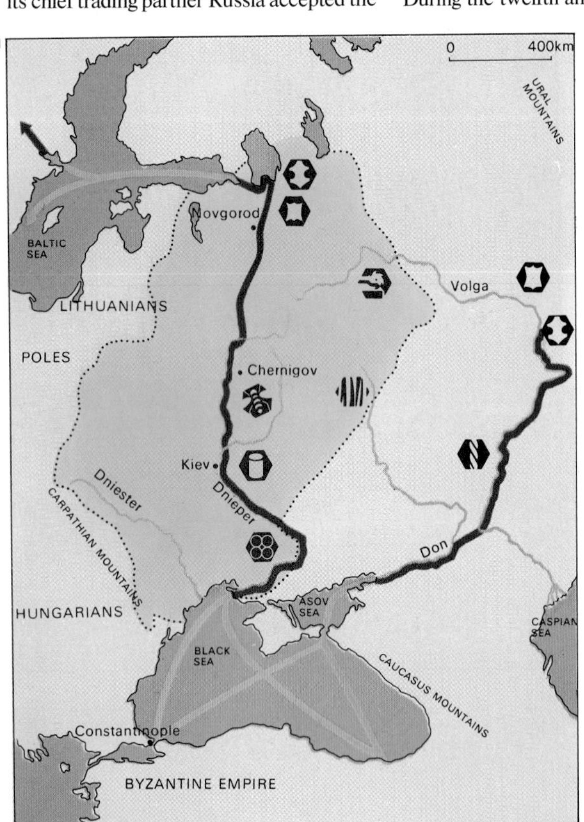

0
400km
URAL MOUNTAINS
BALTIC SEA
Novgorod
Volga
LITHUANIANS
POLES
Chernigov
Kiev
Dniester
Dnieper
CARPATHIAN MOUNTAINS
Don
HUNGARIANS
ASOV SEA
CASPIAN SEA
BLACK SEA
CAUCASUS MOUNTAINS
Constantinople
BYZANTINE EMPIRE

Kievan state
Furs
Honey
Wax
Wood
Slaves
Flax
Hemp
Hides
Sea routes
River routes

1 Trade was essential to the Kievan economy. Kiev owed its importance to its location on the international trade route that connected the Baltic Sea with the Mediterranean—the water road from the Varangians to the Byzantines. Great annual trading convoys floated down the River Dnieper and via the Black Sea to Constantinople. At the Byzantine capital the products of the Russian forests—chiefly furs, honey, and beeswax—were exchanged for spices, wines, perfumes, and weapons. The river route was protected against nomads by soldiers.

Eastern end

2 Construction of Sophia Cathedral, Kiev, began in 1037, during the reign of Grand Prince Yaroslav ("the Wise," *c.* 1036–54). One of the first major Byzantine-inspired churches in Russia, it set an example for innumerable Orthodox churches built during the next nine centuries. A brick, cross-domed basilica, its square plan was based on that of the Hagia Sophia at Constantinople. A striking Russian feature was the arrangement of 13 cupolas—a large central dome surrounded by 12 smaller domes, with each shallow dome set on a tall drum.

3 Christianity penetrated the Russian lands long before it became the official state religion (*c.* AD 988). Kievan Russia remained largely a cultural province of Byzantium, and the icon was part of Constantinople's legacy. Icons were important vehicles for conveying religious truths to the masses. At first, icon painting, represented here by the 12th-century "Virgin of Tenderness" from the city of Byelozersk, followed Byzantine styles.

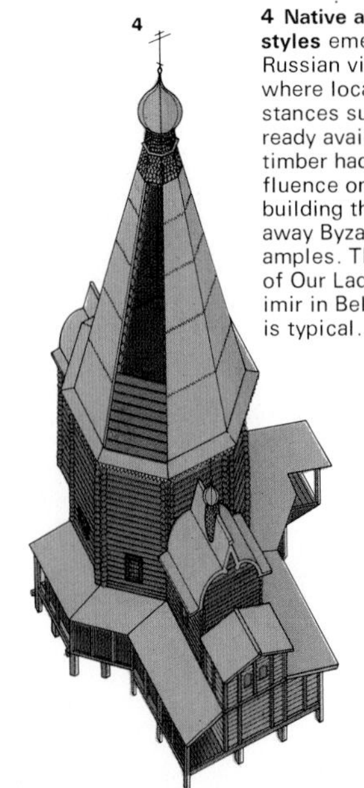

4 Native architectural styles emerged in the Russian villages, where local circumstances such as a ready availability of timber had more influence on church building than faraway Byzantine examples. The Church of Our Lady of Vladimir in Belaya Sluda is typical.

5 Muscovite icon painting reached its peak in the 14th and 15th centuries. The most famous masterpiece of this period, the "Old Testament Trinity," was painted about 1411 by Andrei Rublev (*c.* 1370–1430), Russia's greatest iconographer.

(the Mongols' western headquarters on the lower Volga). By various means—treaty, conquest, purchase, and the strategic marriage of their numerous offspring to the heirs of important principalities—the grand dukes emerged with the largest territory [6] and as the head of a coalition of princes that eventually drove out the Mongols. The grand dukes' nicknames suggest the variety of their methods —Iuri ("Long Arm," reigned 1149–57), Vsevolod ("Big Nest," referring to his fertility, reigned 1176–1212), Ivan I ("Money Bags," reigned 1328–40).

Development of national monarchy

Between 1460 and 1600, Moscow vastly increased in size and strength, and its rulers assumed the trappings of a national monarchy. Ivan III ("the Great," 1440–1505) undertook a series of brilliant diplomatic and military campaigns and dealt the final blow to the disintegrating Mongol Empire in 1481 by forming an alliance with various Mongol confederations. He began to see his newly independent realm as a successor to the recently vanquished Byzantine Empire. He married Sophia, niece of the last emperor, and adopted the Byzantine double-headed eagle as a royal symbol. Ivan IV ("the Terrible," 1530–84) conquered fresh territory and crowned himself "Tsar (Caesar) of all the Russias" [7].

The fall of Constantinople to the Ottoman Turks in 1453 encouraged the establishment of a separate Russian Orthodox Church. The seat of the Church had moved from Kiev to Moscow in the fourteenth century and a distinct Russian style in architecture [4] and painting [5] had emerged there by 1589, when the first Russian Orthodox patriarch was sworn in.

Modern Russia owes its political and social character to Moscow rather than to Kiev. The Russian state was consolidated on the basis of a mercantile economy, but the economy became agrarian. While feudalism was on the wane in the West, the roots of serfdom were being sunk in Muscovy. To compound the problem, no properly articulate class of townsmen or independent farmers emerged to set limits on the power of the crown.

KEY

The crown of Vladimir Monomach (1053–1125) was a gift from the Byzantine emperor. The notion that it symbolically bestowed imperial succession rights on the Russian dynasty gained credence during the national awakening of the 15th century. This bolstered Moscow's claim to be the secular and spiritual successor to fallen Constantinople. Vladimir was one Kievan ruler whose folk-hero status extended into Muscovite times. He married the daughter of Harold of England, who had fled after the Battle of Hastings (1066).

6

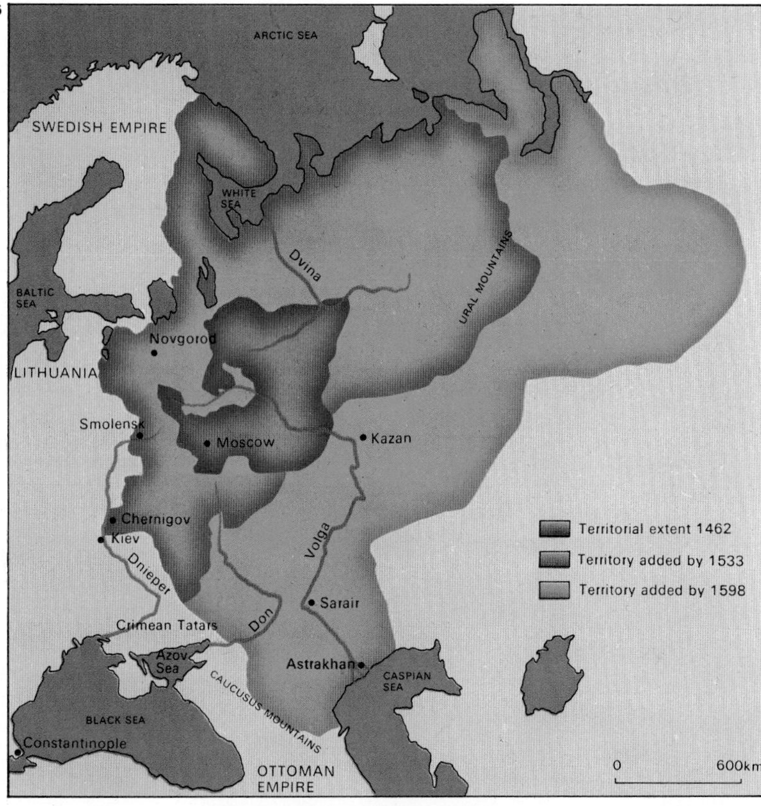
ARCTIC SEA
SWEDISH EMPIRE
WHITE SEA
Dvina
URAL MOUNTAINS
BALTIC SEA
Novgorod
LITHUANIA
Smolensk
Moscow
Kazan
Chernigov
Kiev
Dnieper
Volga
Sarai
Don
Crimean Tatars
Azov Sea
Astrakhan
CASPIAN SEA
CAUCUSUS MOUNTAINS
BLACK SEA
Constantinople
OTTOMAN EMPIRE
Territorial extent 1462
Territory added by 1533
Territory added by 1598
0
600km

6 The expansion of the Muscovite principality (founded mid-12th century) was aided by the absence of mountain barriers within European Russia. By 1452, Muscovy controlled the headwaters of the major rivers leading to the White, Black, Azov, and Caspian seas. Ivan III and Vasily III conquered Novgorod (1478) and Smolensk (1514). Ivan IV established control over areas on the Don and Volga and extended Russian territory east across the Urals.

7

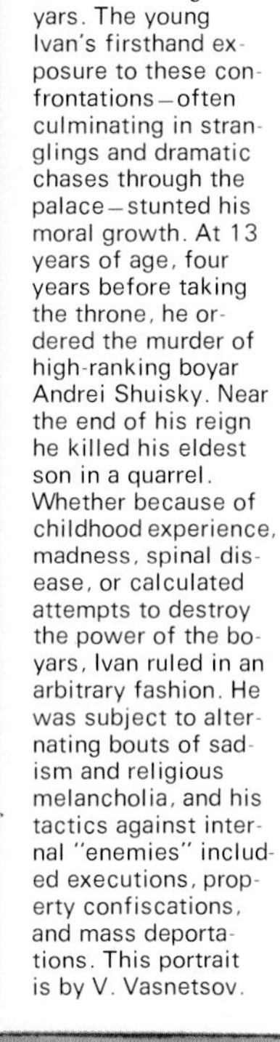

7 Ivan "the Terrible" earned his name. His childhood coincided with a period of court intrigue and open conflict among boyars. The young Ivan's firsthand exposure to these confrontations—often culminating in stranglings and dramatic chases through the palace—stunted his moral growth. At 13 years of age, four years before taking the throne, he ordered the murder of high-ranking boyar Andrei Shuisky. Near the end of his reign he killed his eldest son in a quarrel. Whether because of childhood experience, madness, spinal disease, or calculated attempts to destroy the power of the boyars, Ivan ruled in an arbitrary fashion. He was subject to alternating bouts of sadism and religious melancholia, and his tactics against internal "enemies" included executions, property confiscations, and mass deportations. This portrait is by V. Vasnetsov.

8

8 The city of Novgorod and its province became an independent republic early in the 12th century. Shown is the 11th-century Kremlin with the cathedral of St Sophia (rear center). Novgorod's economic strength was based on a flourishing handicrafts industry and trade in forest products. Its ruling institution, as in other Russian towns, was the *veche*, made up of all free citizens. Novgorod held off the Lithuanians and Mongols for over three centuries, but finally succumbed to the superior force of Muscovy in 1478.

9

9 The Russian boyar class developed in Kievan times out of the intermarriages between the Varangians and the native Slavic aristocracy. Under Muscovy they were given large tracts of land as rewards for military service. Leading boyar families had hereditary access to privileged positions in the state administration. This woodcut by Michael Peterle (1576) shows a procession of boyars and merchants at the Austrian court of Maximilian II.

Early modern Russia

The seventeenth and eighteenth centuries saw the transformation of Russia from a medieval kingdom into a powerful, modern state. Its population more than doubled, from 15 million to 35 million; it acquired territory from Sweden, Poland, Lithuania, and Turkey until, by 1700, Russia was the largest European state [8]. Russia also developed a modern army and navy and a centralized civil service. The two rulers chiefly responsible for this metamorphosis were Peter the Great (1672–1725) [Key] and Catherine the Great (1729–96) [6].

Military and economic expansion

Russia's territorial expansion was achieved with a new army and navy based on compulsory service, equipped with new weapons and led by trained officers. By the 1670s Russia had the largest army in Europe. Military growth and the increasing cost of administering and equipping the armed forces—particularly with artillery—strained both the economy and the administrative structure inherited from the Riurik dynasty. New sources of revenue had to be tapped and repeated attempts were made to make tax-collecting more efficient [2].

To increase taxable wealth and satisfy military and naval needs, Russia's rulers actively encouraged the growth of trade and industry. A nationwide market was formed as local and regional trade barriers were eliminated [7]. Foreign trade—especially with Britain and Holland—increased during Catherine II's reign from 21 million rubles to 71.3 million, thanks to the acquisition of ice-free ports on the Baltic and Black seas. Russian iron and hemp found large British markets, and hemp was also sought after by the fledgling United States. High import tariffs and borrowed French mercantilist doctrines helped Russia's balance of trade, and fewer goods were imported. With European money and technical knowledge, Russia became more self-sufficient.

The new aristocracy

The increasing volume and complexity of state affairs demanded the creation of a modern civil service. Theodore III (1656–82) abolished the Muscovite system of choosing military officers and civil officials according to the positions occupied by their fathers. Peter I ("the Great") accelerated the decline of the upper nobility (boyars) by creating a civil service staffed by career officials recruited from the lesser gentry. Promotion through the military and administrative ranks was achieved according to merit. Anyone advancing halfway up a scale of 14 ranks automatically became a nobleman. Thus, in theory, nobility became a mark of impersonal service to the state.

Peter I set up separate administrative "colleges," based on the Swedish system. The most powerful of these dealt with the army, the navy, foreign affairs, and finance, and reflected his priorities. Alexander I (1777–1825) brought this arrangement into line by introducing ministries. By the beginning of the nineteenth century there were more than 80,000 civil servants, whose upkeep absorbed 10 percent of the budget.

The new service nobility soon grew into an increasingly privileged class (the *dvorianstvo*), whose sons found it easier than those who were not nobles to reach the

CONNECTIONS

See also
1176 Medieval Russia 900–1600
1286 Russia in the 19th century
1180 Enlightened despotism
1190 The Rococo

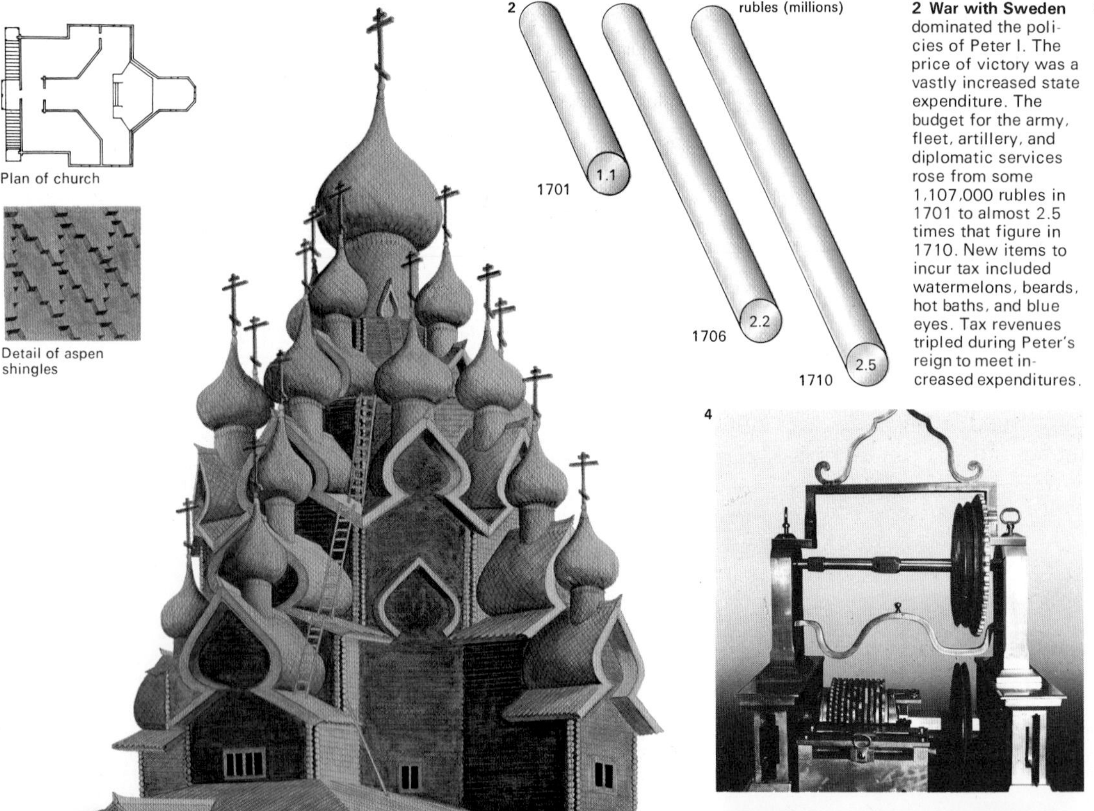

Plan of church
Detail of aspen shingles
rubles (millions)
1701
1.1
1706
2.2
1710
2.5

1 **The cultural gap** between the educated elite and the masses is a theme that has pervaded the history of modern Russia. No more striking contrast could be offered than that between the baroque and rococo buildings of St Petersburg and local, wooden church architecture. The latter could be quite splendid, as in the case of the Church of the Transfiguration on Kizhi Island in north Russia (1714), with its 22 aspen domes and its sculptural unity of composition. Village life could go on for decades and remain largely unaffected by the artistic and literary currents that reached St Petersburg from the West. While Catherine II and her court spoke French and lived in Italianate palaces, the villager spoke Russian and lived in a hut. While culture among the ruling classes became increasingly secular, the Church provided the only example of civilized culture experienced by the masses who lived in small villages unaware of change.

2 **War with Sweden** dominated the policies of Peter I. The price of victory was a vastly increased state expenditure. The budget for the army, fleet, artillery, and diplomatic services rose from some 1,107,000 rubles in 1701 to almost 2.5 times that figure in 1710. New items to incur tax included watermelons, beards, hot baths, and blue eyes. Tax revenues tripled during Peter's reign to meet increased expenditures.

3 **Peter, portrayed as a cat** in this derisive cartoon, inspired much hostility by breaking with tradition and shaving his beard.

4 **Peter's lathe** was one of his many Western acquisitions—his interest in European craftsmanship is legendary. A restless, vigorous person, with great manual dexterity, he became master of dozens of crafts, including shipbuilding, and was as much at home working on the wharves as he was conducting affairs of state. While travelling incognito in Europe he disguised himself as a carpenter.

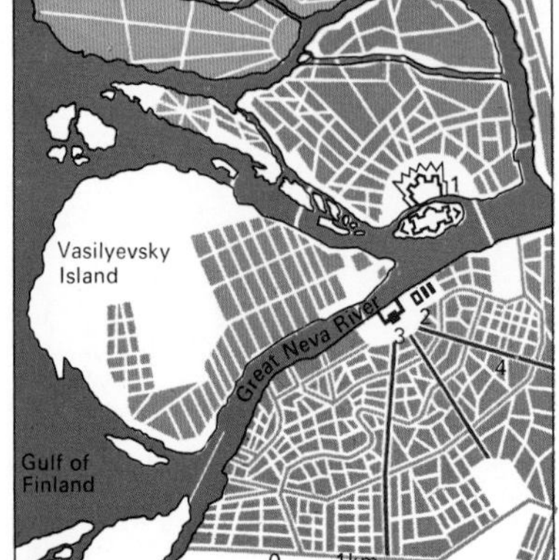

Vasilyevsky Island
Great Neva River
Gulf of Finland
1
2
3
4
0 1km
Central radial avenues
Canals
Gardens
1 Peter and Paul Fortress
2 Winter Palace
3 Admiralty
4 Nevsky Prospect

5 **St Petersburg was** founded in 1703 on Baltic marshlands. Peter mercilessly requisitioned over 100,000 laborers each year to build the city. With its canal system and Western architecture, St Petersburg became known as the "Venice of the North."

top rungs of the bureaucratic ladder. Catherine II ("the Great") confirmed their right to own serf-populated estates and their exemption from taxation, corporal punishment, and even the obligation of service. It was left to the peasants, who formed 90 percent of the population, to bear the brunt of the tax burden. The institution of serfdom, which made them virtual chattels of the landowners, was formally recognized by the law code of 1649 and throughout the eighteenth century landowners gained increasing powers.

There was nothing in the tradition or self-interest of the *dvorianstvo* to prompt them to seek limitations on the power of the crown. Indeed, they depended on its strength to guarantee their position as officers and administrators and their wealth as serf-owners. Nor was any other social class able to challenge the Tsar. The power of the old aristocracy had lessened, the urban middle class remained small and dependent on royal favor, and the clergy's power was further reduced as Russia became more Westernized and secular.

The Church's declining power

The Russian Orthodox patriarchate enjoyed a brief revival during the reign of Michael (1596–1645) when the Patriarch Philaret, Michael's father, ruled Russia as the "second lord" at the side of his weak son. But when Patriarch Nikon tried to assert a measure of independence from Tsar Alexis (1629–76), he was demoted by the Church Council of 1666. Peter I abolished the patriarchate in 1721 because it was largely opposed to his reforms, and replaced it with a Holy Synod of bishops under the chairmanship of a state-appointed layman.

The political humiliation of the Church did not eliminate its cultural influence, particularly in rural areas, but the nobility became more receptive to secular European artistic and literary styles. The eighteenth century saw the emergence of a Westernized elite who spoke better French than Russian and designed new buildings in the current styles of France and Italy [9, 10]. The first secular schools were established and the first universities were founded at Moscow and St Petersburg.

KEY

PETRO
CATHARINA

Peter I, more than any other person, was responsible for the conversion of the medieval tsardom into the modern Russian state. He, with Catherine II, stood out from the rest of the Romanov dynasty because of keen intelligence and determination. Peter's contributions to Russia's modernization were many: he reorganized and Westernized the army, created a navy, reformed the tax system, expanded mining and manufacturing, and remodeled the civil service. Étienne-Maurice Falconet's statue, commissioned by Catherine II and erected in St Petersburg's Senate Square, symbolizes Peter's strength and, significantly, faces west.

6

6 Catherine II was the philosopher and educator of modern Russia. A student of the works of Montesquieu and Blackstone and a friend of Voltaire, she considered herself an "enlightened despot," much like Austria's Joseph II and Prussia's Frederick II. Most of Catherine's good intentions were corrupted by the realities of power, but she did lay the groundwork for the Russian state school system. By the end of her reign (1796) there were 22,210 pupils and 760 teachers in 288 primary and secondary schools. One result of her work was the development of an intellectual class in Russia in the 19th century.

7

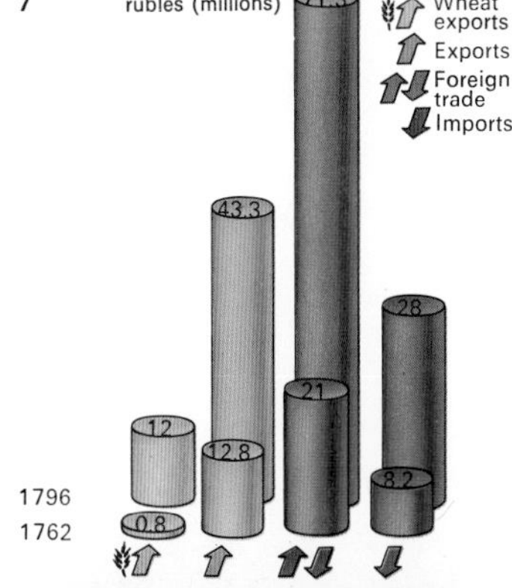
rubles (millions)
Wheat exports
Exports
Foreign trade
Imports
1796
1762
12
0.8
43.3
12.8
71.3
21
28
8.2

7 Catherine's economic policies furthered the expansion of Russian trade and investment. During her reign most internal trade barriers were abolished, and she entered into trade agreements with Britain, Poland, Denmark, Turkey, Austria, Naples, Portugal, and France. In the same period foreign trade grew enormously: the percentage growth in exports was 230, and the percentage increase in imports was 250.

8

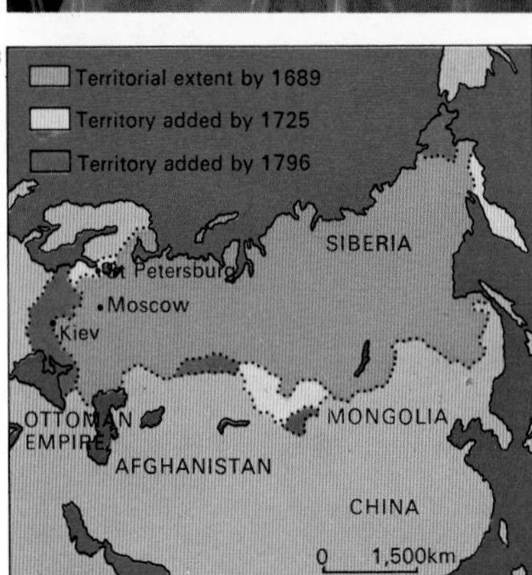
Territorial extent by 1689
Territory added by 1725
Territory added by 1796
SIBERIA
St Petersburg
Moscow
Kiev
OTTOMAN EMPIRE
MONGOLIA
AFGHANISTAN
CHINA
0 1,500km

8 The Romanovs' urge to acquire large new territories was part and parcel of an insatiable desire for new maritime outlets. By 1700, Russia was the largest of the European states. Peter won a length of the Baltic coast after two decades of war with Sweden. Catherine II annexed areas of Poland and Lithuania, giving Russia Austrian and Prussian borders for the first time. War with Turkey yielded a Black Sea coast and rights of commercial passage into the Mediterranean.

9

9 An ornate rococo style was favored for domestic architecture by aristocrats of 18th-century Russia. Illustrated here is the lavish Knight's Dining Room, now restored to its original richly decorated design, in the Great Palace at Pushkin.

10

10 The stateliness of Renaissance and Baroque public buildings complemented the domestic architecture of St Petersburg. The city is still remarkable for its Western feel—the result of its canals as much as of its unity of style.

Enlightened despotism

The wave of new ideas that swept Europe in the eighteenth century and that has come to be known as the Age of Enlightenment had its origins in the scientific and rationalistic movements of the seventeenth century. The spirit of rational inquiry that typified the writers and thinkers of the eighteenth century also had important political repercussions. Radical criticism of existing institutions, values, and practice were the characteristic features. In many European states these ideas influenced powerful monarchs, creating "Enlightened despotism."

The influence of writers

The most common feature of the ideas of the *philosophes,* as this group of thinkers was called, was their faith in reason and their willingness to question the religious, social, and political conventions of their time. Among the most influential writers and thinkers were Voltaire [Key], Charles-Louis Montesquieu (1689–1755), Denis Diderot (1713–84), and Jean Jacques Rousseau (1712–78), whose ideas attracted a large following among the newly educated middle classes of Europe. Although the political theories of such thinkers would in ideal circumstances have led many of them to favor constitutional government [4] and consultative institutions, they were often prepared to act as advisers to such powerful absolute rulers as Frederick the Great of Prussia (1712–86) and Catherine the Great of Russia (1729–96). In this capacity and in their writings they advocated a number of specific reforms, such as the introduction of equality before the law, the abolition of serfdom, religious toleration, and the reduction of noble and clerical privilege. *Laissez-faire* economic doctrines (a minimum of governmental interference) were also widely advocated.

The "enlightened despots," however, did not all share the same ambitions. Many European rulers adopted the ideals of the *philosophes* because they were useful in their own domestic political arrangements. The application of enlightened legislation, therefore, depended upon individual circumstance. For many monarchs the need to increase revenues was a central aim, which made them favor intellectual attacks upon such noble and clerical privileges as exemption from taxation. Similarly, European rulers had a vested interest in the efficient economic exploitation of their lands. Thus, many of the policies of the "enlightened despots" can be explained in terms of the traditional doctrine of *raison d'état* (for the good of the country).

Implementation of Enlightenment ideas

Many European monarchs practiced to some degree the policies advocated by the *philosophes*. Among the most effective was Joseph II (1741–90), Holy Roman Emperor. In his short term as sole ruler (1780–90), a large number of reforms were initiated [8].

Frederick the Great of Prussia, who succeeded to the throne in 1740, was keenly interested in the ideas of the *philosophes* and presented himself as an exponent of their ideals. In practice he was an authoritarian ruler who placed his personal and state interests before the ideals of the Enlightenment. He emancipated his serfs (for military rather than humanitarian reasons),

CONNECTIONS

See also

- **1178** Early modern Russia
- **1184** The Enlightenment
- **1182** Europe: economy and society 1700–1800
- **1188** European literature in the 18th century
- **1196** Baroque and Classical music
- **1170** The age of Louix XIV
- **902** Types of political systems

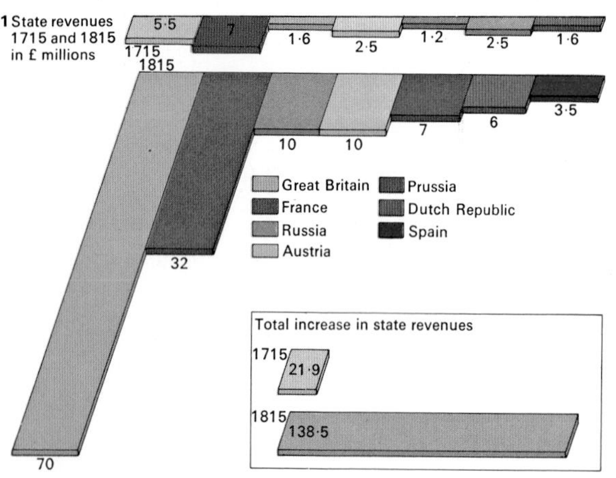
1 State revenues 1715 and 1815 in £ millions
5·5
7
1·6
2·5
1·2
2·5
1·6
1715
1815
70
32
10
10
7
6
3·5
Great Britain
France
Russia
Austria
Prussia
Dutch Republic
Spain
Total increase in state revenues
1715 21·9
1815 138·5

1 The rapid growth of agriculture and industry in 18th-century Europe helped state revenues to rise rapidly. Greater power wielded by the European states also enabled them to exact larger sums from their subjects. Because Great Britain's economic growth outstripped that of other countries, it was able to expand government revenue faster and raise it to higher levels than many larger countries in Europe.

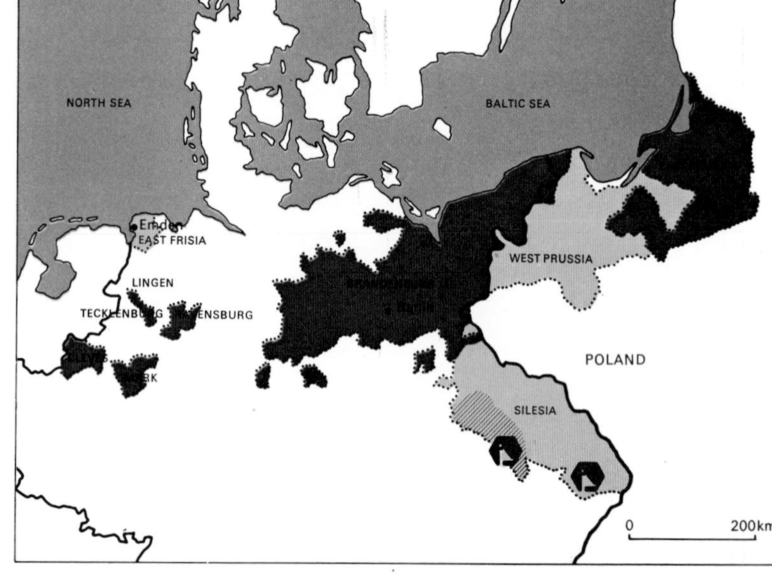
NORTH SEA
BALTIC SEA
EAST FRISIA
LINGEN
WEST PRUSSIA
POLAND
SILESIA
0
200km
Brandenburg-Prussia 1740
Territories gained 1740-86
Coalfields
Textiles
Boundary of Holy Roman Empire

2 Frederick the Great's acquisition of Silesia in 1740 gave him an economically valuable area. The addition of East Frisia in 1744 and West Prussia in 1772 greatly expanded Prussia's borders.

3 Monarchs still played an important part in leading their nations in war. George II (1683–1760), shown here, was the last British monarch to lead his troops in person (during the Battle of Dettingen in Germany in 1743).

4 The "Tobacco Parliament" was an informal gathering of political advisers with Frederick I of Prussia. The idea of such assemblies sprang from the Physiocratic concept of "legal" despotism in which elected landowners would guide the monarch in his deliberations. In spite of support from writers and intellectuals, the tendency toward strong government militated against such elected bodies. The centralizing reforms of Frederick and Joseph II, for example, led to the extinction of provincial administration and institutions. Even where constitutional bodies existed, however, they tended to reflect and represent the interests of the propertied classes (especially landowners and merchants).

but he failed to eliminate serfdom elsewhere in Prussia because to do so would alienate the nobility. He did, however, reform the legal system and establish more humane punishments. His economic policies were strictly mercantilist [2] and drew little from the progressive economic ideas of the Physiocrats (a school of political economists). He used state monopolies and protectionist tariffs to raise extra revenue and to foster industry.

Catherine the Great of Russia was also an admirer of the ideas of the Enlightenment, maintaining correspondence with Voltaire and entertaining Diderot at court. Her most idealistic proposal was a reform of the Russian law code, issued as the "Instruction" of 1767. To discuss it she called together a legislative commission representing the entire nation. The reform, however, was never enacted because of disagreements among the delegates and the outbreak of war with Turkey. In spite of her expressed desire to adopt such enlightened policies as emancipation of the serfs, she was forced to compromise with vested interests. Her "Charter of the Nobility" in 1785 placed the serfs even more firmly under the landowners' control and established the nobility's corporate rights, forging an alliance between the nobles and her dynasty that was to last almost to the Russian Revolution.

Other influences in Europe

Elsewhere in Europe the ideas of the Enlightenment were adopted rather unevenly [6]. In Portugal Sebastião Pombal (1699–1782), chief minister from 1751 to 1777, attempted to strengthen the state and its economy by expelling the Jesuits and attacking noble privilege. He standardized administration, adopted free trade policies, and granted civil rights to the Jews.

Enlightened despotism took many forms and therefore is not a precise description of the great variety of motives and policies adopted by eighteenth-century European rulers. Nevertheless, its legacy of humane and rational legislation, at least in theory, laid the foundations for liberal governments of the post-revolutionary era.

KEY

Voltaire [left] was the pen name of François-Marie Arouet (1694–1778). One of the great French *philosophes*, he was on occasion a guest at the "enlightened" courts of Europe. The degree of respect that he was accorded by Frederick the Great of Prussia is clear in this painting of the two. Voltaire was the greatest playwright of his time, writing more than 50 plays. He was exiled to England in 1726 after an argument with a powerful nobleman. From 1734 to 1749 he lived with Mme du Châtelet, one of the most educated women of the day. After her death he lived in Berlin and Switzerland, returning to France just before his death.

5

5 Maria Theresa's long reign over Austria (1740–80) laid the foundations for the rule of her son Joseph II. She helped to transform the diverse Hapsburg dominions into a centralized nation-state and initiated many progressive reforms in the spheres of education, law, and the Church. Her son completed her work by emancipating the serfs in 1781, imposing administrative uniformity upon the state, and stimulating rapid economic development.

6

6 Enlightened principles also influenced lesser monarchs such as Charles III, king of the Two Sicilies (1735–59) and of Spain (1759–88), seen here (center) entering Madrid. In Naples he sought to bring solvency and order to a poverty-stricken state, while in Spain he provided an enlightened government with the aid of able ministers. Workhouses were used to attack poverty, while schools, roads, and canals were built and education secularized.

7

Kingdom of Poland
Land acquired by Russia
Land acquired by Brandenburg-Prussia
Land acquired by Austria
= 1 million people

1770
LIVONIA
COURLAND
BALTIC SEA
SAMOGITIA
Vitebsk
Danzig
BRANDENBURG
EAST PRUSSIA
GRAND PRINCIPALITY OF LITHUANIA
GREAT POLAND
Warsaw
PODLESIA
KINGDOM OF POLAND
RUSSIA
LITTLE POLAND
Krakow
VOLHYNIA
AUSTRIA
UKRAINE
PODOLIA
KINGDOM OF HUNGARY

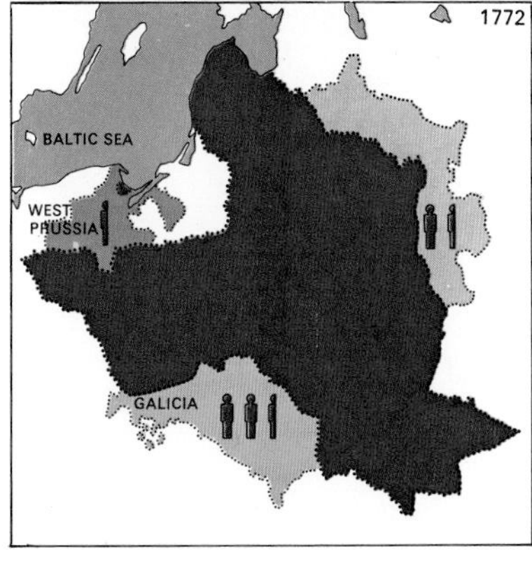

1772
BALTIC SEA
WEST PRUSSIA
GALICIA

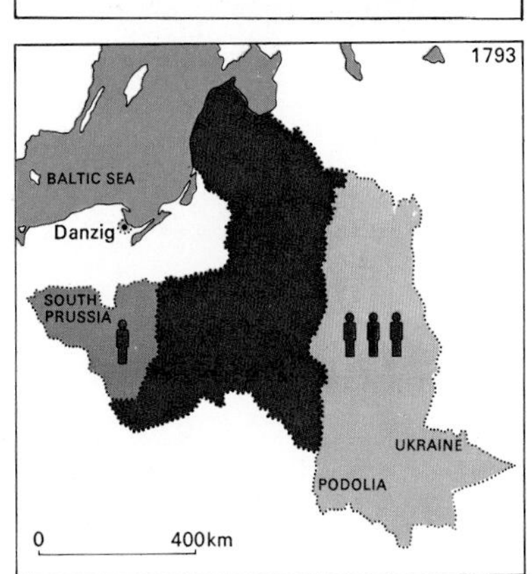

1793
BALTIC SEA
Danzig
SOUTH PRUSSIA
UKRAINE
PODOLIA
0
400km

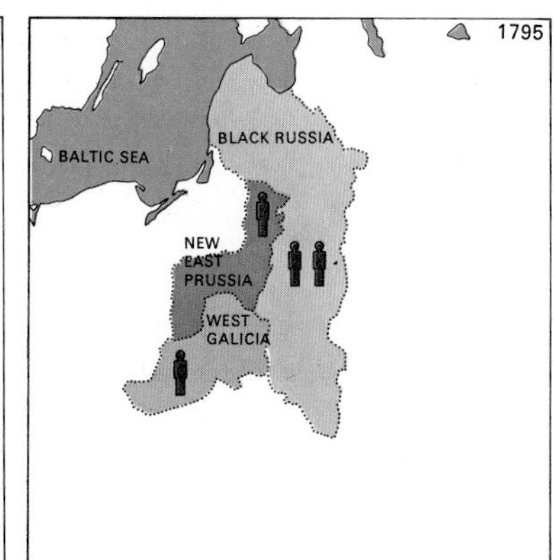

1795
BALTIC SEA
BLACK RUSSIA
NEW EAST PRUSSIA
WEST GALICIA

7 Poland was repeatedly dismembered through partition in the 18th century. Its elective monarchy proved a considerable weakness and led to the involvement of its powerful foreign neighbors in its internal struggles. With a backward economy, a small army, and little revenue Poland was in no position to defend its frontiers. All its monarchs in the 18th century were the nominees of foreign powers. The first partition occurred in 1772, when Prussia, Russia, and Austria took a total of a third of Polish land area and half of its population. In 1793 more was seized, and in 1795 the remainder was divided among the three neighboring powers.

8

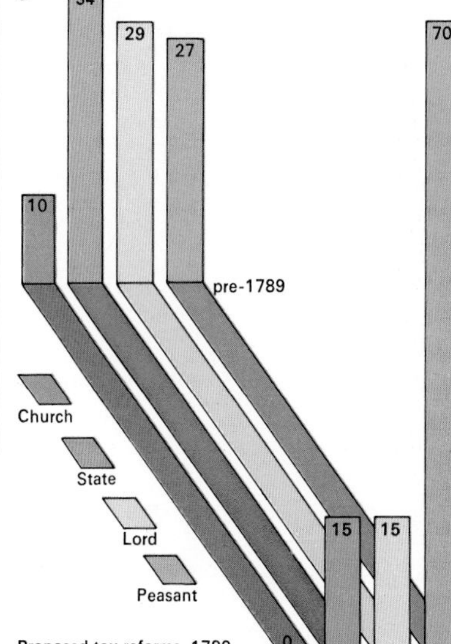

34
29
27
70
10
pre-1789
Church
State
Lord
Peasant
15
15
0
Proposed tax reforms, 1789

8 Joseph II planned to change the feudal labor obligations of the peasants to their landlords, the state, and the Church into a new tax based on a fixed percentage of their gross yearly income. This would form a new land tax that was to apply equally to all his subjects in the empire. This diagram shows the percentage distribution of a peasant's income before and after the proposed scheme. The reform was abolished, however, when Joseph died in 1790, before it became effective.

Europe: economy and society 1700–1800

The most important economic developments of the eighteenth century [2] took place in Britain, France, the Low Countries, and parts of Germany; eastern and southern Europe made much less progress. At one extreme Britain was, by the end of the century, well on the way to becoming the first industrial nation, while at the other, countries such as Russia and Italy retained economic systems little different from those of the medieval period. Socially, too, the most striking developments occurred in the countries of the Atlantic seaboard where the growth of trade, agriculture, and industry created greater wealth and a more rapidly changing social structure.

Population growth and better harvests

One development common to Europe as a whole was population growth, caused chiefly by a declining mortality rate [5]. In the more advanced countries, such as Britain, economic expansion also increased the demand for labor, permitted more children to be supported, and made early marriages economically possible.

Population growth was stimulated by agricultural improvement, and greater agricultural output was in turn required by the growing population [4]. Large tracts of land were brought under cultivation, and new techniques and crops were harnessed to meet the growing demand for foodstuffs. Agricultural yields rose during the century, especially in northwestern Europe. Elsewhere, agriculture often remained backward, at near subsistence levels. Famine continued to afflict many communities in southern and eastern Europe until the nineteenth century, although the adoption of the potato as a subsistence crop helped to increase food supplies. Agricultural practice varied enormously along with different systems of tenure and landholding throughout Europe. In Russia and much of central and eastern Europe, serfdom was still in force. In other areas, a landowning peasantry had emerged, ranging from the relatively prosperous peasants of the Low Countries to the poorer ones of Brittany. In the British Isles the poor tenants of southern Ireland, the landless agricultural laborers of the enclosed counties of southern England, and the semi-feudal crofters of Scotland were in marked contrast with the prosperous tenant farmers and great landowners.

International trade played a vital part in the economy of the advanced states. Trade expanded in the eighteenth century, especially for the Atlantic countries with their easy access to West Indian, American, African, and Asiatic markets. Both Britain and France made large strides in trade, founding a prosperous merchant middle class.

Domestic trade and manufacturing

Internal trade also flourished, aided by improvements in river and road transport [Key]. In many countries agricultural produce, particularly grain, was the major commodity traded.

Growing population and increasing wealth in Britain and other European countries stimulated the demand for a wide range of manufactured goods, but this increased output was still achieved by pre-industrial methods [3]. The domestic system and handworking remained the principal means

CONNECTIONS

See also
1220 The early Industrial Revolution
1158 Europe 1500–1700
1184 The Enlightenment
1186 Exploration and science 1750–1850
1200 International economy 1700–1800

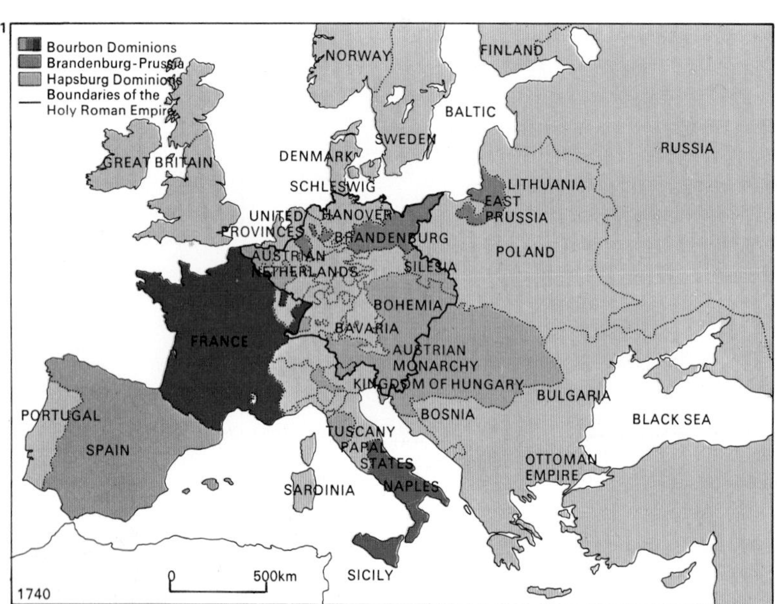
Bourbon Dominions
Brandenburg-Prussia
Hapsburg Dominions
Boundaries of the Holy Roman Empire
NORWAY
FINLAND
BALTIC
SWEDEN
RUSSIA
GREAT BRITAIN
DENMARK
SCHLESWIG
LITHUANIA
EAST PRUSSIA
UNITED PROVINCES
HANOVER
BRANDENBURG
POLAND
AUSTRIAN NETHERLANDS
SILESIA
BOHEMIA
BAVARIA
FRANCE
AUSTRIAN MONARCHY
KINGDOM OF HUNGARY
BULGARIA
PORTUGAL
BOSNIA
BLACK SEA
SPAIN
TUSCANY
PAPAL STATES
OTTOMAN EMPIRE
SARDINIA
NAPLES
SICILY
0 500km
1740

1 Political stability was a characteristic of 18th-century Europe until the French Revolution in 1789. The previous century witnessed the consolidation of a number of powerful nation-states, ruled by well-established monarchies (in Britain, France, Prussia, Austria, and Russia). Despite changing dynasties and disputed successions, political authority had been established in these countries for a long period. Much of Germany and Italy, however, remained a jumble of separate states and kingdoms until the middle of the 19th century. Poland was another unstable monarchy, subject to encroachment and partition by other powers. Europe's political boundary in the southeast was the Ottoman Empire – in decline but still dominant in the Balkans. This instability hampered growth.

1701	1710	1720	1730	1740	1750	1760	1770	1780	1790	1800
100	110	96	95	92	91	99	95	110	114	175

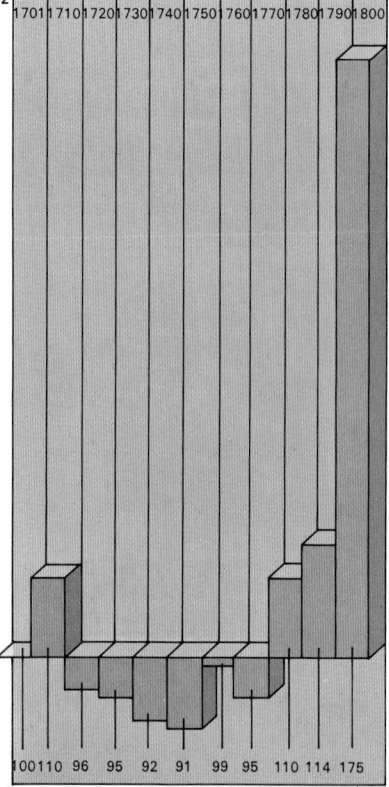

2 Price indexes for a range of goods in 18th-century Britain suggest that the cost of living decreased until the latter part of the century. Favorable economic conditions and an expansive social environment were the keys to political stability. Good harvests made for cheaper food, while early industrial enterprises began to reduce the cost of many everyday items such as clothing, furniture, and domestic utensils, which, together with widely available foodstuffs, make up the bulk of this index. One result of the overall price stability was a better diet, which in turn resulted in a higher birthrate, reduced infant mortality, and provided a longer life expectancy. By the 1790s, strain on food supplies, exacerbated by the effect of war with France and a series of bad harvests, led to much higher prices, which particularly affected the industrial classes.

	1750	1761	1780
Linen	284	184	228
Cotton	81	627	1,018
Silk	292	1,185	2,220
Wool	2,880	3,082	2,286

3 The textile industry in Berlin grew in the 18th century. The number of looms (shown here) in the textile industries increased as domestic production had not yet been replaced by mechanized factory methods. The new silk and cotton industries caused the decline of wool, the main textile since the Middle Ages.

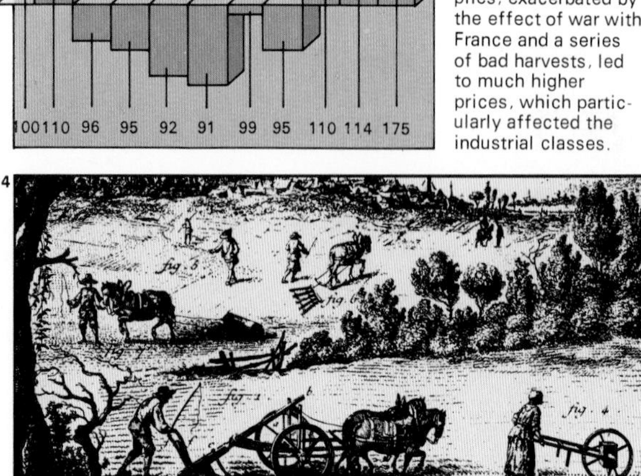
fig. 3
fig. 1
fig. 4

4 Rising demand for food stimulated the adoption of improved techniques, new crops, and better farming machinery. By the 1750s increased production had all but eliminated serious famine in western Europe, but periods of scarcity persisted, especially as population grew toward the end of the century. Scientific farming was encouraged by such enthusiasts as Arthur Young and the French Physiocrats.

of producing a wide range of goods, including textiles, iron, and pottery. In Britain, water power was the most widely used source of energy for manufacturing, as steam power was obtaining a foothold only by the end of the century. The units of production were generally small, domestic organization being by far the most widespread, although the expanding coal mines and textile towns of Britain, France, and Belgium were beginning to concentrate production. Overall, outside Britain, the picture was one of gradual expansion.

Minuets and misery

European society remained essentially traditional in the eighteenth century. Most of the population still lived in a hierarchic, rural society based on agriculture. The village and small market town continued to dominate the social and cultural environment for most people. In these areas, religion still played an important role in everyday life and helped to cement social bonds. Parishes, manors, and guilds remained the typical forms of social organization, and in most of Europe social structure was little affected by economic changes. Although serfdom was attacked in some "enlightened states" and was abolished in the Hapsburg dominions by Joseph II (1741–90), in Russia it was increasing. Peasant revolts and periodic rioting did little to shake the social structure before the French Revolution.

In contrast, capital cities such as London, Paris, Vienna, and St Petersburg continued to grow in size, adding many magnificent buildings and becoming centers of government and major markets. Merchant cities, such as Liverpool and Bordeaux, also grew rapidly, bringing new standards of comfort to the upper and middle classes [7]. For these classes education and prosperity led to the development of a sophisticated urban culture, shown in the demand for literature and art and in the access to wider means of communication such as newspapers and journals. For the poorer urban populations, living conditions were much harsher, with bad housing, poor health, and low incomes [6]. Crime was rife and was usually met by savage punishment.

KEY

Improved travel was one of the most important features of 18th-century Europe. Much easier movement by road, river, and canal greatly stimulated trade and early industrial developments. For the wealthy classes, better communications created the basis for a European culture.

5 European population 18th century

Total (millions)	
1700	115
1750	140
1800	187

= 1 million — 1750, 1800

Population 1750 and 1800

	1750	1800
Russia	19	29
Hapsburg Empire	20	27
France	22	26
Italy	15·5	18
Great Britain	10·5	15·5
Prussia	3·5	6

5 The major factor in population growth was a fall in the death rate. Better diet, an improved climate, the decline of some major diseases, and an increase in personal hygiene (aided by the increasing availability of cheap soap and washable cotton clothing) contributed to lower mortality. Smallpox inoculation and improved midwifery perhaps also played a part. Increased life expectancy in western Europe thus led to a population increase, which had previously been prevented by epidemics and famine. Even in eastern Europe and Russia, where the improvements were less widely felt, the increase was marked.

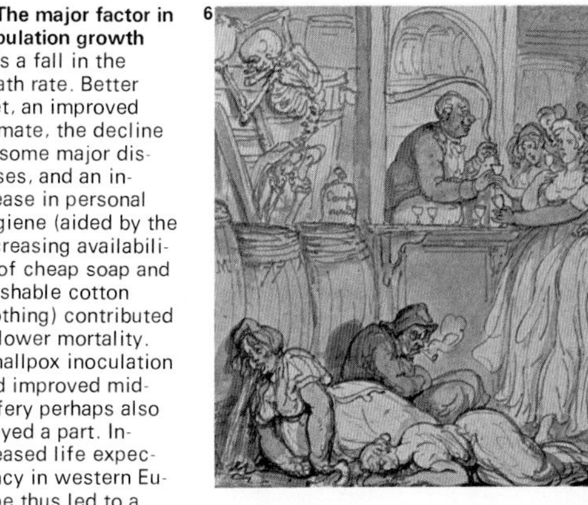

6 Harshness and squalor were still the lot of the poor, even in the age of enlightenment. Cheap liquor became readily available through large-scale distilling and caused widespread drunkenness. Food and drink adulteration by dishonest traders was common, promoting death and disease in the larger urban slums. Moral tracts condemned the "Gin Lane" conditions of the urban poor.

7 Improved living standards among the upper and middle classes led to the building of elegant town houses in many European cities. New squares, like those in London's West End and Edinburgh's New Town, showed Britain's commercial wealth. The merchant cities of the Continent, such as Amsterdam and Bordeaux, and the great governmental centers such as Versailles provided the basis for an affluent urban society. Spas and fashionable resorts such as Bath (shown here) and Dresden provided recreation for the rich, who generated a demand for luxury goods and cultural amusements. The rich also enjoyed improvements such as street lighting and water supply.

British Grenadier
Austrian Infantryman
Soldier of the Spanish Imperial Army

8 Armies in the 18th century were composed of long-service volunteers or conscripts. Harsh discipline, low pay, and bad conditions attracted only the poor and criminals into the ranks. Officers, drawn from the nobility, used influence to gain commissions. Distinctive uniforms were worn. Warfare was formalized, and long-range weapons were inaccurate.

The Enlightenment

The seventeenth century saw the emergence of a belief among European philosophers and writers that the truth about the nature of man and his world could be discovered by the use of reason. "In the search for truth in the sciences," the *Discours de la Méthode* (1637) by René Descartes (1596–1650) led to a more skeptical approach to astrology and history. At the same time, critical interpretation of the Scriptures and an interest in comparative religion brought about a weakening of religious orthodoxy.

In England, the execution of Charles I discredited belief in the divine right of kings, and the revolution of 1688 established a liberal constitution that served as an ideal in continental Europe for a century. This shift in opinion and the continued search throughout the eighteenth century for a rational explanation of human problems was named the Enlightenment.

Scope of the movement

The Enlightenment was a literary and philosophical movement against superstition, ignorance, traditional knowledge, and accepted wisdom. Politically it ran from John Locke (1632–1704) to the French Revolution a century later. Lessing (1729–81) and Goethe (1749–1832) were its representatives in Germany, Franklin [3] and Jefferson (1743–1826) in America, and Algarotti (1712–64), Alfieri (1749–1803), and Beccaria (1738–94), in Italy. It was little known in Spain and eastern European countries, but attempts to Westernize Russia under Peter the Great (1672–1725) and Catherine II (1729–96) owed their inspiration to aspects of the Enlightenment.

Scientific and literary inquiry

Although this movement did not give rise to any particular school, its leaders shared a spirit of scientific inquiry, an acceptance that the universe was regulated by discoverable laws, a belief that knowledge should be widened so that all men could exercise their God-given gift of reason, and a wish to combat the errors of antiquity that led to superstition and had become the pretext for persecution [4].

Literature centered on humane contemporary topics. Works tended to be more cosmopolitan and used non-European settings or characters, as in Defoe's *Robinson Crusoe* [6] and Montesquieu's *Lettres persanes* (1721). Satire, whether in verse or prose, became the principal genre and vehicle for criticism, bringing with it a strong plea for toleration and liberty of conscience.

In religion, the scientific spirit of the age was reflected in a denial of miracles and revelation and an abhorrence of "enthusiasm." Enlightened writers (the *philosophes*), while not usually aesthetic, considered on humanitarian grounds that it was absurd to foist one's religion upon another individual or nation; differences of creed were seen by Voltaire in *Zaïre* (1732) and Lessing in *Nathan der Weise* (1779) as mere accidents of birth and education. Accounts of voyages of exploration turned interest toward the common denominator of all religions: a belief in a God, that could serve as a rational hypothesis to account for existence. As a result, there arose the concept of an honest pagan and of deism, which

CONNECTIONS

See also

1186 Exploration and science 1750–1850
1188 European literature in the 18th century
1180 Enlightened despotism
1222 Origins of romanticism
1224 The French Revolution
1218 The American Revolution
1288 Political thought in the 19th century
1290 Masters of sociology
860 Philosophy and ethics
898 Fundamental political ideas

1 De Rerum Natura by Lucretius (*c*.99–55 BC) was a popular text for Enlightenment writers. Lucretius had attacked religion and favored rational explanation to combat superstitious fears of natural disasters such as volcanoes, earthquakes, or plague (depicted here in a 1725 edition).

2 Alexander Pope (1688–1744), although primarily a satirical poet, was best known in Europe for his *Essay on Man* and *The Universal Prayer*. They summed up what his contemporaries felt about the inflated theories of metaphysics and the possibility of a form of deism that would be universally acceptable.

3 Benjamin Franklin (1706–90)—depicted here in an allegory—was an intellectual whose diversity embodied the spirit of the Enlightenment. Born in Boston, he was an artisan, inventor, journalist, author, founder of a philosophical society and later of an academy that acquired university status, experimental scientist, traveler, civil administrator, and statesman of international repute.

4 The massacre of Huguenots on St Bartholomew's Day (1572) was made an example of religious fanaticism by Voltaire in *La Henriade*. This epic, secretly published in 1723, praised Henry IV for being an enlightened king and granting the Edict of Nantes. Religious tolerance gradually eroded, and the edict was revoked in 1685. The flight of Protestant refugees to Holland, Britain, and the German states was an important impetus to internationalism in the Enlightenment.

5 Göttingen University was founded in 1737 by the Elector of Hanover, George II of England. This hall is a notable example of 18th-century civic architecture. Academic expansion was one of the practical effects of the Enlightenment.

held that, having created a workable universe, God left it running rather in the manner of a clock. Rousseau (1712–78) [7] expounded in *Emile* (1762) a more emotive form of deism.

The *Encyclopédie* [Key] of Diderot (1713–84) and d'Alembert (1717–83) embodied the central idea of the Enlightenment that knowledge is power. A final monument to human endeavor before the days of specialization, this massive encyclopedia concentrated attention largely on the skill of the artisan at a time when literature too was dealing more and more with common people. Jeremy Bentham's Utilitarian plea for "the greatest happiness of the greatest number" was an offshoot of this interest, while the Physiocratic movement in France and Adam Smith's *Wealth of Nations* (1776) also typify the Enlightenment in the attempt to apply rational and natural solutions to problems of land tenure, taxation, and money. Their strong plea for commercial liberty *(laissez-faire)* is the counterpart of the philosophers' plea for liberty in matters of conscience.

Sociopolitical problems provided the most obvious targets for satire, frequently in the form of imaginary journeys, as in Swift's *Gulliver's Travels* (1726). Serious historical writing of the period again shows the desire to reject accepted judgments and to replace them with the kind of critical appraisal of original material undertaken by Bayle and Montesquieu in France, Hume and Gibbon in Britain, and Alfieri in Italy.

The arts and politics

In the arts, there was a trend away from emotion toward order and disciplined form. Civic architecture such as the New Town, Edinburgh, the theater at Bordeaux, or the *aula* (great hall) at Göttingen University [5] clearly embodied Enlightenment ideals. Diderot's *Salons* (1759–79) and Lessing's *Laokoon* (1766) exemplified the new importance given to criticism of the arts.

To ascribe the French Revolution to the direct influence of the Enlightenment is an oversimplification—the leaders of the Enlightenment [8] were optimistic reformers, not revolutionaries.

KEY

The Encyclopédie, published between 1751 and 1772, had this frontispiece by C. N. Cochin sold as a separate item. It captures the semi-poetic, almost religious fervor with which the *philosophes* pursued enlightenment. In the background the obscurity of Antiquity is ruptured by a burst of light. Reason appears emblazoned in the center; at her feet the Sciences and Useful Arts bring their tribute. Nor are the Fine Arts forgotten; in the left foreground silversmiths and goldsmiths bring a luxurious contribution of elegantly wrought plate. The emotive quality of the frontispiece is reminiscent of Rococo church decoration.

6

6 Robinson Crusoe, a work of fiction by Daniel Defoe (1660-1731) based on a real episode and published in 1719, reveals the 18th-century love of discovery. Its high minded moral tone, its practicality, and its attention to the "noble savage" mark it as a foremost novel of the Enlightenment.

7

7 The French Revolution claimed Jean Jacques Rousseau as its spiritual progenitor although his major work, *Le Contrat Social* (1762), was widely read only after 1789. This allegory of the revolution shows Rousseau presiding over the eye of truth, above the tree of liberty and other symbols of the revolution.

8 Madame Geoffrin's salon [A,B] brought together in Paris during the mid-1700s many of the artists and *philosophes* of the time, together with such distinguished visitors as Gibbon, Hume, and Horace Walpole. Marie Thérèse Geoffrin (1699-1777), who appears [7] in the painting, was a wealthy bourgeoise and patroness of men of letters. Le Kain [4] addresses a group that includes Buffon [1], Mlle de Lespinasse [2], Mlle Clairon [3], D'Alembert [5], Helvetius [6], Fontenelle [8], Montesquieu [9], Mairan [10], Turgot [11], Diderot [12], Quesnay [13], Saint-Lambert [14], Rousseau [16], Raynal [17], Thomas [18], Marmontel [19], Marivaux [20], Condillac [21], and Réaumur [22]. Presiding over the assembly is a bust of Voltaire [15], who in a letter to M. Lefebvre in 1732, encouraged such salons.

8 B

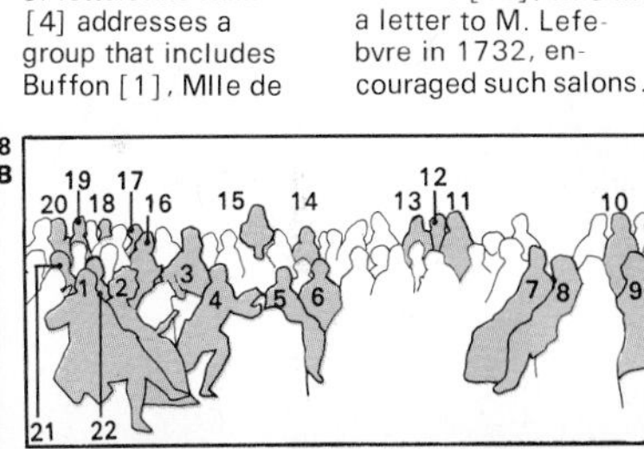

19 17
20 18 16
15
14
12
13 11
10
1 2 3 4 5 6
7 8
9
21 22

8 A

Exploration and science 1750–1850

The advances in exploration and science made in the century between 1750 and 1850 were based upon the scientific movement and overseas expansion of Europe in the years before 1700. Scientists and explorers were assimilating and extending the pioneer exploits of seventeenth-century giants such as René Descartes (1596–1650) and Isaac Newton (1642–1727). Greater knowledge of the non-European world excited interest in its huge range of exotic flora and fauna and its geography; many accepted notions about the physical universe and its origins were being questioned. Scientific inquirers such as Humboldt [4] and Darwin [Key] emphasized accurate observation and recording, which in turn led to the formulation of new theories about the natural world.

Growth of technical knowledge

In part the growth of knowledge depended upon technical innovations: improvements in navigational instruments, such as the sextant and the marine chronometer [1], facilitated scientific exploration. Captain James Cook (1728–79) commanded three voyages of exploration between 1768 and 1776, and the precision of his navigation depended on these new techniques. On his expeditions Cook charted large areas of the Pacific, including New Zealand, and added the islands of Tahiti and Samoa to existing maps.

The use of a greatly improved telescope by William Herschel (1738–1822) led to the discovery of the planet Uranus in 1781. More sensitive balances contributed to chemical discoveries that displaced the phlogiston theory of combustion. In physics the properties of heat were investigated by Joseph Black (1728–99) in Glasgow, where he met James Watt, inventor of the first efficient steam engine. In mathematics, trigonometry and the calculus were greatly advanced by a number of eminent men, among them Johann Bernouilli (1667–1748) and Joseph Lagrange (1736–1813).

Impact of electricity and chemistry

Electricity was one of the principal fields of the physical sciences to be developed. Luigi Galvani [7] discovered "galvanic" (current) electricity, and Alessandro Volta obtained it from his "voltaic pile" or battery, which quickly made electrolysis possible.

In chemistry many natural elements were isolated for the first time. Joseph Priestley (1733–1804) is usually credited with the discovery of oxygen, while Antoine Lavoisier (1743–94) laid the basis for the modern understanding of chemical reactions. In botany the standard classification of plants was devised by the Swedish botanist Carolus Linnaeus (1707–78) [3], while the French naturalist Georges Buffon (1707–88) in his *Histoire naturelle* suggested that the earth had evolved through a far longer time than the 6,000 years of biblical history. Other pioneers included Charles Lyell (1797–1875), whose *Principles of Geology* [5] emphasized the theory that the processes of geological change were long, slow, and uniform, and that this was as true of the remote past as of the present. Many more speculative but competent naturalists such as Erasmus Darwin (1731–1802) and Jean Baptiste Lamarck (1744–1829) were already propounding the notion of organic evolution,

CONNECTIONS

See also
1184 The Enlightenment
1200 International economy 1700–1800
1282 The foundations of 20th-century science
1160 Science and technology 1500–1700
1260 Colonizing Oceania and Australasia
276 Earth's time scale
408 Evolution of life
418 Evolution: classical theories
510 The classification of fish
638 Zoos and botanic gardens
738 Preventive medicine
614 Life on islands

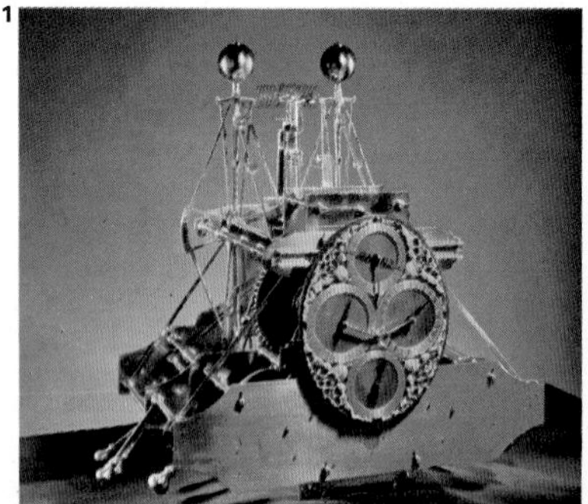

1 The marine chronometer, developed by John Harrison (1693–1776), revolutionized maritime navigation in the 18th century. Latitude had been easy to fix for centuries, but the chronometer made it possible for the first time to establish longitude to within half a degree. Harrison's remarkable invention won him a British prize of £20,000.

2 The paintings of animals by George Stubbs (1724–1806) revealed a deep interest in and knowledge of anatomy. A friend of eminent natural scientists, he published a series of anatomical studies. Among them were reconstructions of animals from material brought by Joseph Banks from the Pacific. Stubbs painted this study for William Hamilton.

3 Carolus Linnaeus, the Swedish botanist, founded modern biological classification with his *Systema naturae*, published in 1735.

4 Alexander von Humboldt (1769–1859) made his name as a traveler to many parts of the world and as a geographer, natural historian, ethnographer, and oceanographer. His main work was the multi-disciplinary *Kosmos* (1845–62), which attempted to synthesize all knowledge of the universe. He is shown here with his close and faithful companion, the Frenchman Aimé Bonpland (1773–1858). He examined wildlife on Mount Chimborazo in the Andes and ascended to record heights in those mountains. At the time vast areas of the world were still unknown. Although the existence of all the continents was known by 1800, there remained large tracts of unexplored land beyond the coastlines of many of them. Settlement was steadily filling the gaps in the Americas, but great areas of the Pacific and elsewhere remained untouched. Original accounts of Africa, South America, and Arabia were also published during the 19th century.

that is, the descent of the present species of animals and plants from antecedent, dissimilar forms.

Many advances in the physical sciences were directly related to and stimulated by economic activity, trade, and industrial processes. Physics played an important part in the rise of the new technologies upon which the Industrial Revolution was based, especially the harnessing of steam power.

The rationalists of the eighteenth century who discovered laws underpinning the physical world were soon joined by economists and philosophers who saw similar laws in politics; thus the scientific movement also gave rise to the "laws of political economy." *Essay on Population* (1798) by Thomas Malthus (1766–1834) produced a theory of demography similar to that accepted by the classical economists Adam Smith (1723–90) and David Ricardo (1772–1823). The concept of immutable laws governing political behavior was adopted by the utilitarian philosophers Jeremy Bentham (1748–1832) and James Mill (1773–1836). Similarly, the scientific movement by the early nineteenth century led to the first works of sociology and comparative law.

Science and religion

Undoubtedly the most important effect of the scientific movement was its impact upon conventional religious beliefs. Clearly the account of the Creation contained in the Old Testament was not literally trùe, and the world was older than the Bible suggested. Fossil evidence was proof of the existence of life on earth at hitherto unthinkably remote periods. Moreover, to some the evidence of geology and of fossils disproved the Old Testament idea of simultaneous creation of all living things. Although these ideas encountered intense hostility and were at first rejected, they provoked profound questioning about the place of revealed religion in the scientific age. *On the Origin of Species by Means of Natural Selection* (1859) by Charles Darwin (1809–82) detonated an explosion of ideas that had been accumulating during the late eighteenth and early nineteenth centuries.

KEY

Lampooned as an ape, Charles Darwin attracted, with other scientists of his time, the wrath of society when his discoveries and arguments undermined the traditional and biblical accounts of human creation. The investigation of foreign cultures, and the new scientific approach to the world of nature, threw Western institutions and conventional thought into sharper focus and led to questions about their assumptions and legitimacy. As a result, Darwin and others who supported his treatise on organic evolution were treated for some time with hostility by their contemporaries who held more orthodox opinions on the origin of species.

5

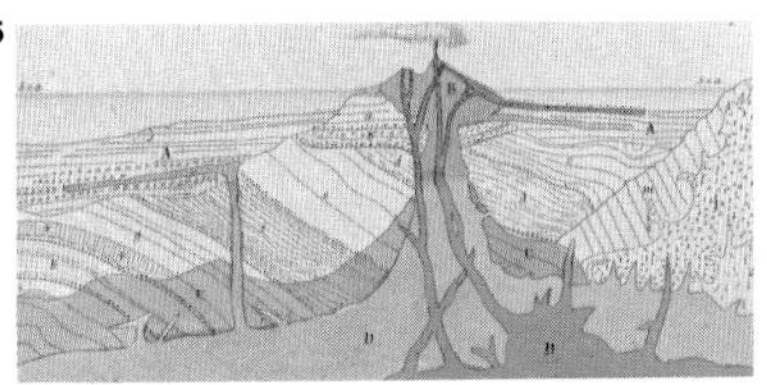

5 The foundations of modern geology were laid down in the 18th century with the study of rock strata and with attempts at geological dating. The frontispiece of Lyell's *Principles of Geology,* (1830–33) is shown here. It formulated an evolutionary theory of the earth and rejected earlier writers who had tried, for theological reasons, to reconcile geological and fossil evidence with literal interpretations of the Old Testament.

6 A

B

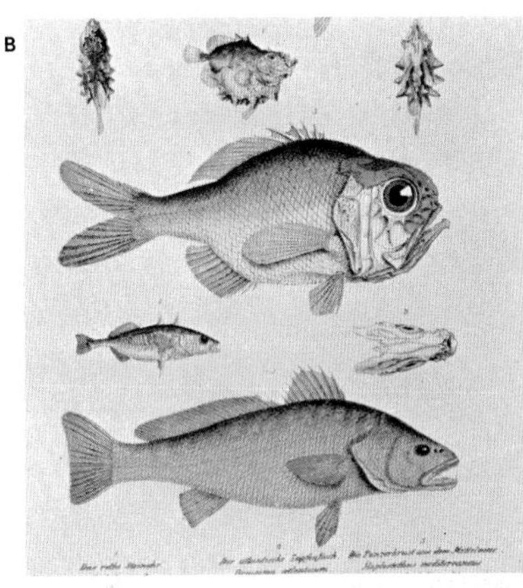

6 Accurate observation of flora and fauna provided one of the most important vehicles of early scientific inquiry. Natural history attracted professional and amateur collectors, and precisely illustrated studies proliferated. This illustration of *Phyllanthus niruriodes* [A] is from a collection called *Hindustan Plants.* The fish [B] formed part of a collection that appeared in a German publication by Schinz (1836). The drawings are quite accurate.

7

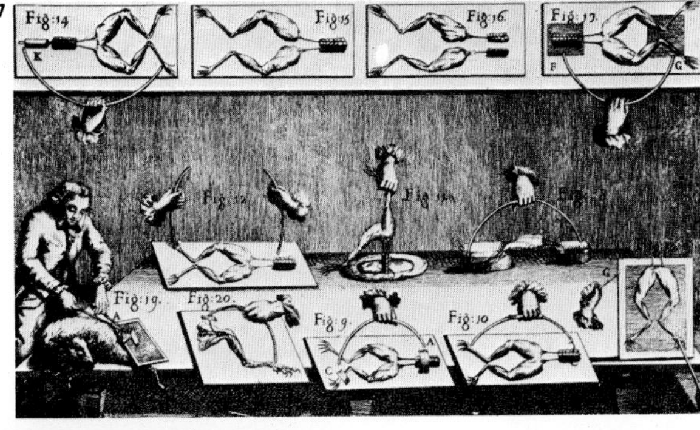

Fig:14
Fig:15
Fig:16
Fig:17
Fig:19.
Fig:20.
Fig:9.
Fig:10

7 In the physical sciènces one of the most important fields of development in the 18th century was electricity. Luigi Galvani (1737–98) here demonstrates the effect of electrical impulses on a frog's nerves. Benjamin Franklin (1706–90), Alessandro Volta (1745–1827), André Marie Ampère (1775–1836) and Georg Ohm (1787–1854) also worked with electricity.

8

8 The academic study of anatomy became accepted by the 18th century. Its teaching was much advanced by the work of Hermann Boerhaave (1668–1738) and by John Hunter (1728–93) and his brother William (1718–83), seen here giving a lecture to the Royal Academy in London. It was not until the advances in chemistry and bacteriology of the 19th century that the causes of diseases were diagnosed accurately and surgery became less risky.

9

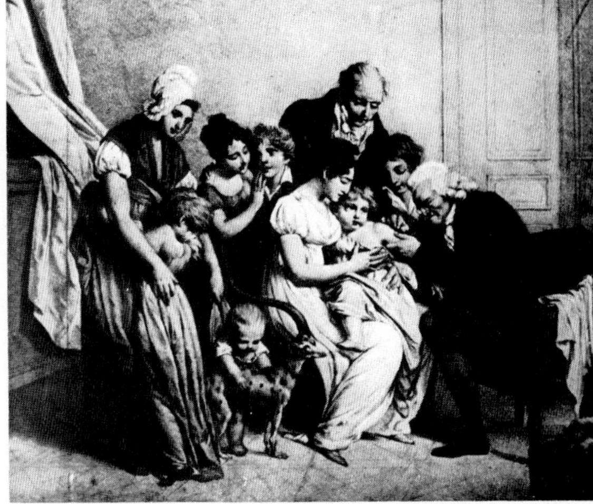

9 The old wives' tale that dairy maids never caught smallpox led to an effective counter to the disease – Jenner's vaccination. Epidemics of the disease were rife and regularly killed or scarred great numbers of people, especially children and young persons. In many countries it had replaced the plague as a major check on population growth. Inoculation using human virus was used among the poor in the 18th century, but it was expensive and dangerous with a high risk of serious infection. Edward Jenner (1749–1823) examined the traditional view, saw that people who had caught the relatively harmless cowpox were immune from smallpox and was able to develop a vaccine that carried a minimum risk of ill effects and could be made widely available. Inoculation remained in use in many European countries even after the development of vaccination, but it was finally prohibited and replaced by vaccination.

The 18th century: the novel and the press

The rise of the novel in the eighteenth century appears paradoxical in that increasingly scientific age. However, the expanding and newly literate middle class with their "enlightened" attitudes learned to accept fiction, first disguised as fact, then in novels of character and predicament, in picaresque romances, in works of sentiment and sensibility, and finally by the end of the century, in the Gothic novel. Samuel Johnson [5] intended to define literary language in his *Dictionary of the English Language*.

Early development of the novel

Daniel Defoe (1660–1731) gave the English novel its vigorous start with *Robinson Crusoe* (1719), *Moll Flanders* (1720), *Colonel Jack* (1722), and *Roxana* (1724). He was a realistic narrator, suited to a credulous public. But the novel demanded the elements of social observation and conversational style that were being developed by Jonathan Swift [2] and by Richard Steele and Joseph Addison [3], whose essays and sketches created lively characters and stressed the morality of a rational social order. The final step toward the true novel was the addition of a coherent plot to a prose narrative dealing with the interplay of human relations. Samuel Richardson (1689–1761) effected such changes with *Pamela* [7], which in turn encouraged the burlesque of novels such as *Joseph Andrews* (1742) and *Tom Jones* (1749) by Henry Fielding (1707–54).

The comic masterpiece *Don Quixote* by Cervantes (1547–1616) probably had the most influence on the European novel. In France, Alain le Sage (1668–1747) published *Gil Blas* (1715–35), a romance of picaresque adventures. His Scottish translator, Tobias Smollett (1721–71), developed the novel of diverse characters and incidents—coarse, realistic, and episodic. His novels—*Roderick Random* (1748), *Peregrine Pickle* (1751), *Humphrey Clinker* (1771)—all lack the subtlety and irony that mark Laurence Sterne's *Tristram Shandy* (1760–67) and *A Sentimental Journey* (1768). Sterne (1713–68) wrote a fluid, surreal fantasy that lies outside the mainstream of the novel, but his success was immense and his imitators many, notably Denis Diderot (1713–84) in *Jacques Le Fataliste* (1796). A more central novel is *The Vicar of Wakefield* (1766) by Oliver Goldsmith (*c.* 1730–74), a delicate stylist who dealt with the trials of virtue and domesticity. With Fanny Burney (1752–1840) and her *Evelina* (1775), a new sensibility was added to the theme of a young girl's adaptation to society.

The change in the novel

At this point the novel, which had seen occasional outbursts of fancy and imagination such as Horace Walpole's *Castle of Otranto* (1764) and *Niels Klim* (1741), a Gulliverlike satire by the Dane Ludvig Holberg (1684–1754), turned almost entirely to Gothic sentimentalism and terror. Matthew Lewis' (1775–1818) *The Monk* (1796) and Mrs. Radcliffe's *The Mysteries of Udolpho* (1794) were widely acclaimed and imitated.

The preeminence of the English novel did not obscure the brilliance of the French authors who chose this form. The Abbé Prévost (1697–1763) was successful with *Manon Lescaut*, the seventh volume of his

CONNECTIONS

See also
1184 The Enlightenment
1222 Origins of romanticism
1172 French classical literature
1180 Enlightened despotism
1182 Europe: economy and society 1700–1800

1 The nocturnal wanderings of Nicolas Restif (1734–1806) among the low life of Paris produced a vast output of moralizing, multi-volumed novels and tracts written between 1767 and 1802. Part fact, part fantasy, often tinged with erotic fancy (as illustrated), his work is a unique but diffuse picture of urban life. The novels focus on the vicissitudes of the human heart and the inevitable corruption of country innocence by the fascinating vices of the city.

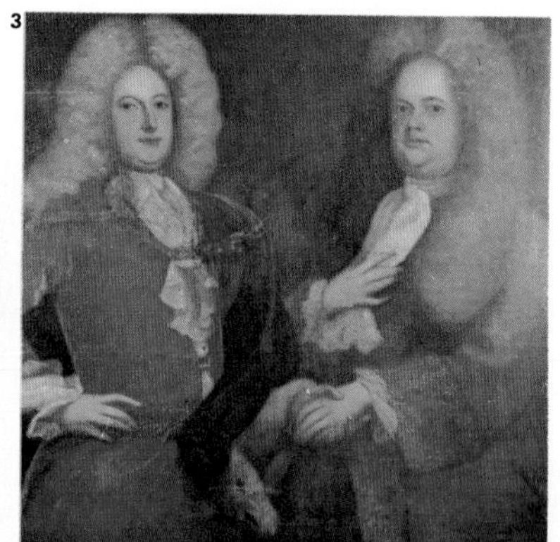

3 The literary partnership of Richard Steele (1672–1729) and Joseph Addison (1672–1719) set the civilized tone of the age in their publications the *Tatler* (1709–11), the *Spectator* (1711–12), and the *Guardian* (1713). Both were among the 48 wits, politicians, and men of letters who were members of the Kit-Cat Club. The *Spectator* embodied middle-class concern with manners, morals, and character.

2 Gulliver's Travels (1727) has outlasted its original political and social targets. This work by Jonathan Swift (1667–1745) has become a landmark in English fiction. Gulliver, the one flesh-and-blood character, moves in a satiric world that disregards the conventions of realism. He is tossed between a world of giants and a world of midgets, meets with nobility and vileness, and is at last returned to his own tragic race, which is incapable of perfection.

otherwise dull *Memoirs of a Man of Quality* (1728–31), and he translated all of Richardson's works into French. Choderlos de Laclos (1741–1803) published *Les Liaisons Dangereuses* in 1782, a novel that analyzed corruption caused by passion just as *Manon* depicted love's degradation. Fiction for Voltaire (1694–1778) [4] was only a device to convey ideas: with the pessimistic *Candide* (1759), the optimistic *Zadig* (1747), and the other philosophic fictions he conveyed his freethinking and rationalism.

The development of the press

Daniel Defoe is one of the pioneers in that other great manifestation of prose in the eighteenth century, the press. His weekly *Review* (1704–13) created a new class of reader, which was also brilliantly served for a while by the *Tatler, Spectator,* and *Examiner*. Such commendable ventures as the *Gentlemen's Magazine* (1731), which ran for nearly two centuries, raised the standards of English journalism.

The first English daily paper, the *Daily Courant,* appeared in 1702 and flourished with six pages until 1735. The *Daily Universal Register* (1785) became *The Times* and began its unbroken run in 1788, by which time there were 40 London and countless provincial newspapers. There were no national papers because road communications were so bad. This was also true in Europe. It was generally late in the century before papers of wider consequence emerged.

The first regular American newspaper (a weekly), the Boston *News-Letter,* appeared in 1704 and was published continuously for 72 years. By 1776 there were about 25 newspapers in the thirteen colonies, including Benjamin Franklin's Philadelphia *Gazette*.

Inevitably, as newspapers began to see themselves as champions of public opinion, a struggle for freedom of the press developed. John Peter Zenger [6] was thrown into prison in 1734 for his attacks against the royal governor in his *New-York Weekly Journal*. His acquittal in 1735 on charges of seditious libel began the American tradition of freedom of the press that was codified in the Bill of Rights (1789).

KEY

English booksellers of the 18th century were entrepreneurs who bought copyrights, commissioned authors, dealt with printers, and sold books over the counter. Samuel Johnson considered them to be "liberal and enterprising," but the popular view was of monopolists, contemptuous of genius, promoters of bad taste, and employers of worthless hacks.

4

4 Voltaire was a prolific writer (he is here dictating as he dresses) who produced in *Candide* a kaleidoscope of the adventures and misfortunes endured by Candide and Dr. Pangloss. Polite irony and cheerful common sense pervade this fine tale, yet beneath the surface the characters are merely instruments of Voltaire's philosophy. Pangloss' motto, "All is for the best in the best possible of worlds" is ironically subverted by the action of the book; an intractable universe defies human attempts to impose reason on it. The author's ironical response to disillusionment is that "we should cultivate our garden."

5 A

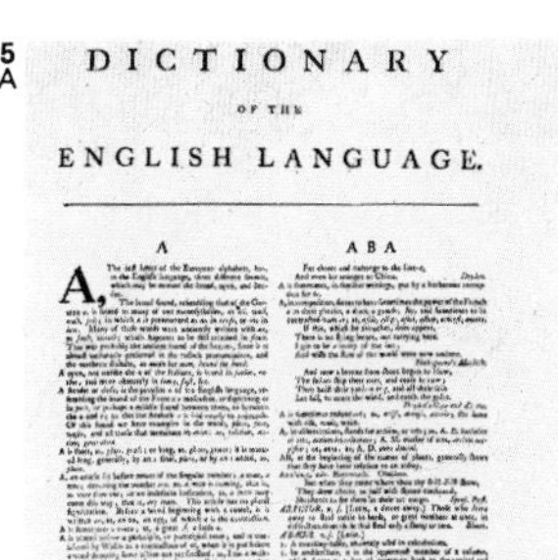

DICTIONARY

OF THE

ENGLISH LANGUAGE.

A ABA

B

5 The Dictionary (1755) of Samuel Johnson (1709–84), commissioned by seven booksellers for £1,575, was a great feat of single-handed scholarship [A]. With his idiosyncratic etymologies, definitions, and quotations, Johnson outdistanced the struggling French Academy, which was engaged on an identical task. The *Encyclopaedia Britannica* began as a Scottish dictionary [B] first issued in parts (1768–71).

6

Le nouvelliste sans argent

7

6 A mass of cheap occasional papers and social journals was published in France in the later 18th century. This cartoon of a penniless columnist getting his news without effort shows how unprofessional a trade journalism was.

7 Pamela, the first work of the London printer Samuel Richardson, captivated the reading public of 1740. The author, a prim, unadventurous man, nevertheless revealed the ways of the female heart. *Pamela* is about a maid exposed to the designs of the son of the house upon her mistress's death. (She is shown here asking her abductor's mercy.) Vivid in dialogue and told in a series of confidential letters, its instant fame encouraged Richardson to produce *Clarissa*, another novel but with a more convincing story. Henry Fielding's parallel, and at times competitive, career yielded more robust novels, including *Jonathan Wild* (1743), *Tom Jones* (1749), and *Amelia* (1751).

The Rococo

The Rococo was perhaps the first purely pleasure-giving style in the history of art. It had no didactic purpose, was not a form of thanks-offering to God, and was not particularly adapted to telling stories or supplying a comprehensive picture of the visible world. Its primary aim was to delight.

The spirit of the Rococo

This is not to say that the Rococo could never be a vehicle for serious feeling, as the paintings of Antoine Watteau (1684–1721) demonstrate, or that it was altogether cut off from reality. On the contrary, Rococo artists were fascinated by nature, especially plants, small animals, and birds, and at least one painter, Jean Baptiste Chardin (1699–1779), was a supreme natural observer. But these considerations apart, the Rococo was essentially playful, decorative, and witty, a style in which taste and ingenuity were pursued as ends in themselves. Unsurprisingly, it was not a style for a wide public or for official monuments. Its sphere was the private apartments and pleasure gardens of a small, sophisticated elite.

In keeping with all this, the Rococo was developed at least as much in the applied arts of furniture, porcelain, silverware, and interior decoration as it was in the fine arts of painting, sculpture, and architecture. Indeed, the term can hardly be used of architecture at all, except in relation to its surface decoration, as Rococo had no role in the field of structures. The applied arts, however, were ideally suited to the style, and it is noteworthy that they reentered the mainstream of stylistic developments for the first time since the Middle Ages.

Historically, Rococo grew out of the Baroque style that preceded it and of which it was in one sense a continuation, although at the same time it represented a reaction against Baroque gravity and pomp. Rococo's dominance coincided almost exactly with the first half of the eighteenth century. It occurred chiefly in France and the German states—in the latter partly under France influence—but it also spread in some degree to Britain, Italy, and other countries on the outer ring of Western Europe. The word "rococo" probably derives from *rocaille* ("rockwork"), meaning the shells and bits of rock used in sixteenth-century decorative schemes; this is appropriate because many characteristics of the style, such as irregular s-curves, wavy spikes, and the quality of asymmetry, are summed up in the elegant, curlicued conch shell [Key].

Rococo interiors

The first Rococo interiors appeared about 1700 in the very citadel of French Baroque: Versailles [1] and its associated royal châteaux. In their various private apartments the style of decoration employed, instead of heavy architectural features, a series of tall wooden panels, painted ivory-white and covered with low-relief carving in gilt. Mirrors, especially over the mantel-pieces, formed an important part of the decoration, and the same principles of style were applied to the furniture and ornaments in the room. The effect was rich and even restless, for there was no break in the scheme, but it was in a sense intimate—the setting for a "private" life.

CONNECTIONS

See also
1162 Baroque art: style and content
1164 Baroque art: patronage and development
1182 Europe: economy and society 1700–1800
1196 Baroque and Classical music

1

1 The Cabinet de la Pendule (1738) forms part of the private apartments created by Louis XV at Versailles. They were deliberately planned to be lighter and more intimate than the state apartments made for Louis XIV and are typical of French Rococo.

2 Watteau, the creator of French Rococo painting, designed for it a new genre, the *fète galante*, in which a kind of game of ideal romantic love is played out by real people clothed in fancy dress. In his most famous painting, "Embarkation for Cythera" (1717), part of which is reproduced here, the lovers are shown preparing to leave for the island, which the Greeks knew as the birthplace of Aphrodite, after a day's pleasure. The style is colorful and the picture charged with an atmosphere of passion and sweet regret that the day had come to an end.

2

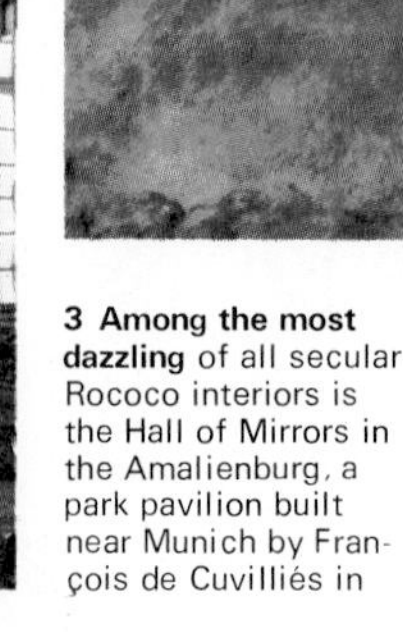

3

3 Among the most dazzling of all secular Rococo interiors is the Hall of Mirrors in the Amalienburg, a park pavilion built near Munich by François de Cuvilliés in 1734–39 for the Bavarian elector, Karl Albrecht. Although it reflects Cuvilliés' French training, the design is developed with a freedom and plasticity typical of Germany. Decorative motifs inspired by an overgrown garden climb up the walls between the mirrors and spill out onto the ceiling across which birds fly.

The style soon spread from Versailles to Paris, where it became even more extravagant, and from there it was carried to the francophile German courts. The designers often came from a north European provincial background (where there were long traditions of craftsmanship), trained in Paris, and either stayed there or moved on to one of the French provincial or German centers of patronage. One who followed this pattern was the Flemish-born François de Cuvilliés (1695–1768) who, after a Parisian training, became court architect to the elector of Bavaria. His Hall of Mirrors in the Amalienburg, an ornamental villa in the grounds of Schloss Nymphenburg, near Munich, is more fantastic in design than anything in France and is perhaps the finest example of Rococo decoration [3].

Besides this French-inspired Rococo, there was in Germany a more native form of the style, particularly in churches. Unlike French Rococo, this emerged by a process of natural evolution from the Baroque, which still flourished in Germany in the eighteenth century. Often a Baroque church, such as Ottobeuren [4], will contain Rococo decoration inside, in a style produced mainly by changing the powerful, dynamic rhythms of the Baroque into the quicker, more playful, and more sinuous ones of the Rococo.

Watteau and Boucher

Rococo painting, on the other hand, was created by a single artist of genius: Antoine Watteau. Basing his style on the Flemish Baroque painter Peter Paul Rubens (1577–1640), Watteau invented a new pictorial genre, the *fête galante*, in which the loves of the classical gods are replaced by the fantasy loves of human beings, as in a ballet or opera [2]. As the nineteenth-century critics, the brothers Goncourt, wrote: "Watteau renewed the quality of grace." His truest successor was Chardin, whose subject matter—still life and scenes of gentle bourgeois domesticity [6]—was real, not ideal; but Watteau also provided the starting point for the decorative painter François Boucher (1703–70), the most erotic and most successful artist of the age [5].

KEY

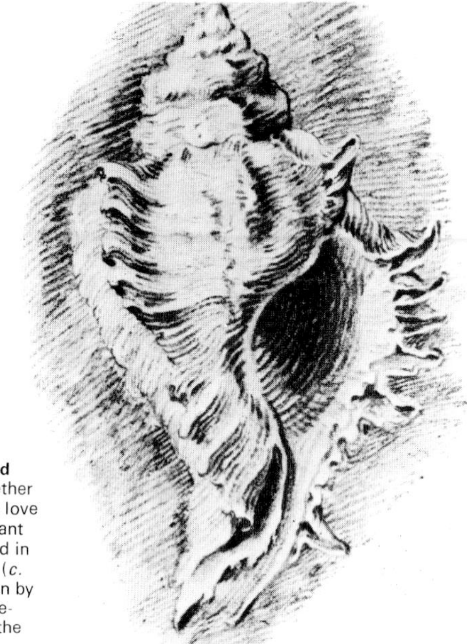

Rococo forms and asymmetry, together with the Rococo love of marine and plant life, are reflected in this conch shell (*c.* 1710–15), drawn by Watteau, the foremost painter of the Rococo.

4 The Abbey Church of Ottobeuren, Bavaria (1737–67), like many German 18th-century works, is by several hands and combines more than one style. The architecture, late Baroque with regularly grouped columns and a heavy cornice, was completed by Johann Michael Fischer (1692–1766). The Rococo ornament—playful, inventive, and brilliant in white, gold, and other colors—was executed by the stuccoist Johann Michael Feuchtmayr (1709–72).

4

5 Eroticism was a favored quality of art at the sophisticated, pleasure-loving court of the French king Louis XV. Its most fluent exponent was François Boucher, whose "Cupid a Captive" (detail) was part of a series painted in 1754 for the boudoir of Louis' most celebrated mistress, Madame de Pompadour. The result is a decorative asymmetrical mixture of forms similar in feeling to a figure group in porcelain or a Rococo silver table ornament of the period.

5

6 Using the themes of the love between a mother and her children and the innocence of childhood, Jean-Baptiste-Siméon Chardin produced, in "Saying Grace" (1740), a remarkably unsentimental picture. He relies on a simple pyramidal composition, balanced yet still with a hint of asymmetry, and restricts his facility with still life to subordinate details, such as the toy drum, the pot in the foreground, and the objects on the table. But while he rejects the Rococo spirit of frivolity he retains its grace.

6

British and American art 1530–1790

Although British art from the sixteenth to the eighteenth centuries was affected by the same stylistic movements as was art on the European continent, it also had a character of its own. In particular, owing to the conditions of patronage, it had an unusual pattern of subject matter. Toward the end of the period, American art, which began as an offshoot of British art, developed its own significant style.

Portrait painting in England

After the Reformation reached England in the 1530s there resulted not only the disappearance of church patronage of the arts but also a general contraction of interest in the visual arts. Popular monarchs such as Elizabeth I spent little on art; conversely when Charles I patronized the best contemporary artists and built up one of the finest picture collections ever seen, his extravagance enraged Parliament as well as the City of London and helped to bring about civil war. From the early sixteenth to the mid-eighteenth centuries there was also a dearth of native talent and, until William Hogarth (1697–1764), almost all the leading painters and sculptors—although not the architects—were foreign born.

Patrons required two main tasks of painters and architects in Britain: painting portraits and building country houses. Hogarth put his finger on the reason for the first: "We are a Trading country whose wealth can buy their curiosities [ie Italian and French pictures and sculptures] ready made, as in fact we do," he wrote. "Selfishness as in Holland more prevails here than vanity. Portrait painting therefore ever has and will succeed better than in any country whatsoever, and where has it been carried higher? The demand be as constant as faces will arise. . . ." The rows of portraits of the British upper classes that still line the walls of country houses today prove Hogarth right. But portraiture could be subtle and imaginative as well as being merely a social art, and great masters of the genre won fame and fortune in Britain. They included such foreigners as Hans Holbein the Younger (1497–1543) and Anthony Van Dyck (1599–1641), the second of whom [1] established an image of elegance for the British aristocracy that lasted nearly 300 years. In the sixteenth and seventeenth centuries, British portrait miniaturists, especially Nicholas Hilliard [3] and Samuel Cooper (1609–72), held a unique position in Europe. Finally, in the second half of the eighteenth century, the native tradition of portraiture came into its own, led by Joshua Reynolds (1723–92) and Thomas Gainsborough (1727–88) [2].

Meanwhile, in the mid-eighteenth century, Hogarth created a new pictorial fashion by which he hoped to improve society through revealing human behavior as a "modern moral comedy" [7].

Architecture: Wren's London

Elizabethan and Jacobean country houses were often huge, stately constructions, to which Renaissance detail was applied without much care for Renaissance proportions. The seventeenth century after the accession of Charles I in 1625 is difficult to characterize, because fewer large houses were built, and the crucial change—the introduc-

CONNECTIONS

See also

1218 The American Revolution
1184 The Enlightenment
1216 Settlement of North America
1166 French art in the 17th century
1148 English Renaissance literature
1412 The American experience: architecture to the 20th century
1416 The American experience: painting

1 Van Dyck brought to Britain the most fluent and up-to-date style of aristocratic portraiture in northern Europe, exemplified in his portrait of the 4th duke of Lennox, painted about 1634.

2 "Countess Howe" (*c.* 1764) was painted in Bath, England, by Gainsborough. He reworked the style of Van Dyck using lighter rococo embellishment with his subjects set in landscapes.

3 The portrait miniature was often a love token. This "Unknown Man" by Nicholas Hilliard (1547–1619) was painted about 1595. It shows the subject consumed by the flames of passion and holding a miniature of his lady love. besides being the first of the great English miniature portrait painters, Hilliard was also carver, goldsmith, and portrait painter under the patronage of Queen Elizabeth I.

4 The Banqueting House in Whitehall (1619–22), by Inigo Jones, shows the beginnings of classical architecture in Britain. Modeled on palaces by Palladio it was built for court masques.

5 Richard Wilson (1714–82), in his "Croome Court" (1758, detail) produces harmony between the picture and its parkland subject. His style was inspired by 17th-century landscape painting, especially that of Claude.

tion of a classical style, eventually with baroque overtones—occurred as a result of the influence rather than the direct participation of leading architects.

The greatest architects of the period, Inigo Jones (1573–1652) and Christopher Wren (1632–1723), worked mainly in cities, particularly London. Jones, who had studied in Italy, designed the first building wholly in the Italian Renaissance style to be completed in Britain—this was the Banqueting House [4], originally part of the royal palace of Whitehall. Wren, a more intelligent, more versatile, and perhaps greater architect, had the unusual opportunity of building the new St Paul's Cathedral [Key] and 51 London churches after the Great Fire of 1666. It was Wren's London, with its skyline of beautiful steeples, that became the symbol and the reality of the great new eighteenth-century city of northern Europe.

The country house in England and America

The eighteenth century was also the heyday of the country house, when wealth, the classical tradition, and a cult of orderly nature came together to produce the grand house set in a landscaped park.

Nowhere was the concept of the country house more successfully exported than to America—once the colonies there had begun to develop. Despite the break with Britain in the late eighteenth century and the influence of ideas taken from the French Enlightenment, the leading citizens of the new United States shared with the British the Protestant heritage and a strong belief in landed property. Their country houses [8] were less sumptuous but often more elegant than those of the British. Scaled-down imitations of Wren's smaller London churches (less ornate than Gibbs's St Martin-in-the-Fields [6]) were built all over New England; and, while two of America's best painters, John Singleton Copley (1737–1815) and Benjamin West (1738–1820), emigrated to Britain and became important members of the British school, a third, John Trumbull [9], after training in London and Paris, returned to America to become the most vivid battle painter of the age.

KEY

The dome of St Paul's Cathedral by Christopher Wren was finished in 1710, and from that date British classical architecture came of age. The dome was the greatest visual symbol of the New London, rebuilt after the Great Fire. It owes something to the domes of Paris and Rome but shows typically English restraint.

6

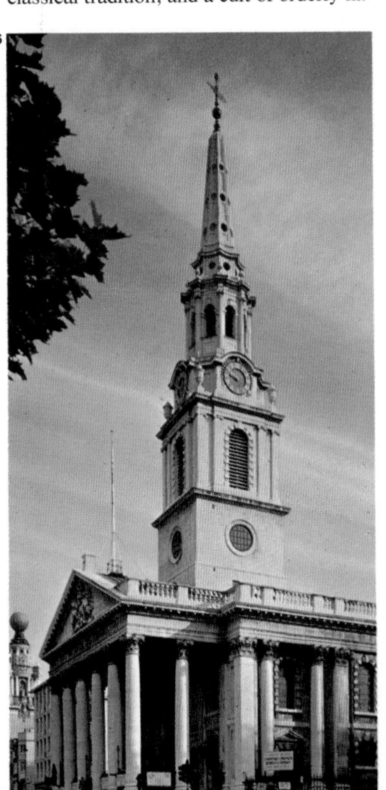

6 James Gibbs (1682–1754) built St Martin-in-the-Fields, London (1721–26), modeling it on Wren's London churches but with more Baroque detail. The interior has Italian Baroque plasterwork.

7

7 "The Countess's Dressing Room" (1745), from William Hogarth's "Marriage à la Mode" series, is a satire on the morals and manners of the time, with hypocrisy as its theme.

8

8 Thomas Jefferson (1743–1826), the third US president, designed Monticello, Virginia, for himself in 1769. It has the intellectualism and elegance appropriate to a man of the Enlightenment.

9

9 The Battle of Bunker Hill, fought near Boston in 1775 at the beginning of the American Revolution, was painted a decade later in London by John Trumbull (1756–1843), a former US colonel.

Early ballet

Ballet was in its infancy at the beginning of the seventeenth century, having been introduced to the French court from Italy by Catherine de' Medici (1519–89). A ballet then consisted of a number of *entrées* by masked dancers in elaborate costumes, and at the conclusion there was a *grand ballet* in which the king and queen generally took part. The *entrées* for the ballets of Louis XIII (1601–43) were related to a theme, which was explained by speech or song.

Court ballet in Italy and France

Two of the most famous court ballets were *La Liberazione di Tirrenio* [1], given in Italy in 1616, and *La Déliverance de Renaud,* performed at the French court a year later. Many of the ballets had political significance; *La Déliverance de Renaud* was typical in that it was intended to reassure the ambassadors of Spain and Austria that the young King Louis XIII was still ardent toward his queen.

For the ballet's presentation seats were erected in tiers along the length of the Grande Salle of the Louvre, with the royal throne at one end facing a stage concealed from the audience by a painted drop curtain. On both sides of the hall musicians were concealed in clumps of trees. After a short opening chorus the curtain rose to reveal a grotto at the back of the stage, with Monsieur de Luynes, the dancer portraying Renaud, lying on the grass. The king and 12 of his gentlemen represented devils left by another character, Armide, to watch over Renaud. Louis, de Luynes, and two other gentlemen came down to the floor of the hall and performed the first *entrée*.

Following further *entrées,* there was a magical transformation on stage, in which a mountain revolved to show a garden with three fountains; a nymph, portrayed by a young boy, rose from a fountain and sang; six monsters appeared and attacked two knights before fleeing; a giant cart, on which there were singers and a small wood, entered the hall, and a choir of 92 voices sang the triumph of Renaud. Finally the king and his gentlemen danced the *grand ballet*.

During the reign of Louis XIV (1638–1715) [Key] ballets attained unparalleled splendor, with dances arranged by Pierre Beauchamps, music by Jean-Baptiste Lully (1632–87), words by Molière (1622–73), and designs by Jean Berain. These ballets sometimes took place out of doors. *Le Carrousel de Louis XIV* was a celebrated horse ballet given in front of the Louvre in 1662. Two years later *Le Palais d'Alcine* [3] was given outdoors at Versailles.

The Royal Academy of Music

The Royal Academy of Music (now the Paris Opéra) was founded in 1669, and three years later Louis XIV authorized Lully to add to this academy a school to educate pupils in dancing as well as in singing and playing musical instruments. In creating the academies, Louis unwittingly helped bring about the decline of ballet at court. The amateur gradually gave way to the professional dancer, and in 1681 the first professional women dancers took the stage.

Ballets at the beginning of the eighteenth century still combined dancing, music, and singing; in other words, they were operas with the dancing subservient to the singing.

CONNECTIONS

See also
1368 Classical and modern ballet
1196 Baroque and classica music
1174 The origins of opera
1170 The age of Louis XIV

1 La Liberazione di Tirrenio was given at the theater of the Uffizi Palace in Florence in 1616 to celebrate the wedding of the duke of Mantua to Catherine de' Medici. The spectators were seated on raised platforms on both sides, with the royal host in the foreground. Divinities were lowered on a cloud machine, and the dancers descended from the stage to join in the *grand ballet* on the floor of the huge hall.

2 This horse ballet was performed in the open air in Florence to celebrate a visit by the duke of Urbino; 42 horse riders and 300 foot soldiers were used in this representation of a battle.

Troisiesme
Journée

3 The island of Alcina appeared in *Le Palais d'Alcine* performed at Versailles in May 1664, on the third day of a series of entertainments. Alcina is shown riding on a sea monster with nymphs perched on dolphins. On both sides are long rocky "islands" where the orchestra sits. On another "island" in the background is Alcina's enchanted palace, which is "destroyed" in a huge fireworks display.

4 Le Triomphe de l'Amour, a ballet by Jean-Baptiste Lully, was presented at St Germain in 1681 with ladies of the court. When the work was given later in public at the Academy of Music in Paris, the part of Mars, originally danced by Pierre Beauchamps, the king's ballet master, was given to a professional dancer. Mademoiselle Lafontaine, the first *premiere danseuse,* led three other *danseuses*. The costumes were designed by Jean Berain, who dressed the men in Roman style, while the women wore theatricalized adaptations of court dress.

It was not until 1717, in John Weaver's *The Loves of Mars and Venus* at the Theatre Royal, Drury Lane, London, that the dancers alone conveyed meaning through movement. In this ballet Weaver made a clear distinction for the first time between the steps given to a man in the *pas de deux* and those given to the woman.

The dancers: teachers and pupils

The eighteenth century saw the rise of many famous *danseuses,* such as Marie Camargo [5], Marie Salle, and Madeleine Guimard, and *danseurs* such as the Vestrises, father and son [7], and Pierre Gardel. Both Gaetano and Auguste Vestris appeared in ballets by Jean-Georges Noverre (1727–1810), one of the most influential men in the history of ballet. Noverre put into practice the theories set out in his *Lettres sur le danse et les ballets* published in 1760. He suggested abolishing the mask (it was actually Maximilien Gardel who implemented this) and replacing the series of conventional dances that then constituted a ballet with the *ballet d'action,* in which dance and story were united. Costume innovations, such as Camargo's shorter skirt and heelless slippers encouraged freer movements.

Noverre's pupil, Jean Dauberval, moved ballet a further step forward in 1789 with the first comedy ballet, *La Fille mal gardée,* in which ordinary people replaced shepherds and shepherdesses.

Charles Didelot [8], who trained in turn with Dauberval, Noverre, and Auguste Vestris, synthesized the contributions of his three teachers. From Dauberval he took ideas for comedy ballet, from Noverre the *ballet d'action,* and from Vestris pure dancing. Didelot's ballet *Flore et Zéphyr,* produced at the King's Theatre, London, in 1796, not only put these ideas into practice but also introduced dancing on *pointe* (on blocked toe shoes). This was probably brought about by improved flying machines that enabled dancers to fly across or around the stage, because the dancer rose onto the tips of her toes before beginning her flight. The development of dancing on *pointe* paved the way for the romantic ballets of the early nineteenth century.

KEY

Louis XIV appeared as the Sun King in *Le Ballet de la Nuit* given in 1653. The ballet's 43 *entrées* symbolically spanned 12 hours, the king appearing in the fourth and last section, covering 3 am to sunrise. Louis, aged 14, was dressed in the male costume typical of the period–short, scalloped skirt and plumed headdress embellished with the sun and its rays. In ballets during his reign Louis represented exalted figures, such as Apollo, Neptune, and Jupiter. His last appearance was in 1669. Louis' ballet master, Pierre Beauchamps, invented the five accepted modern positions of the feet to make the dancers appear more elegant.

5 Marie-Anne de Cupis de Camargo (1710–70), the first famous ballerina, was painted by Nicolas Lancret in this idealized, pastoral setting. In 1730 she created a sensation by shortening her skirt several centimeters to enable her to perform *entrechats* (the crossing and uncrossing of the legs in a vertical jump). Camargo was renowned for her technical brilliance and vivacity, while Marie Salle was more expressive and graceful. Salle appeared in her own creation of *Pygmalion* wearing a plain muslin dress draped like a Greek robe. Two hundred years later Isadora Duncan revived this revolutionary costume.

6

6 The basic costume for the male dancer in the mid-18th century was a plumed helmet and tunic, with a hooped skirt *(tonnelet).* This was adapted by varying the decoration and type of mantle to show different characters. The costume shown here is for a faun and is draped and spotted to suggest an animal's skin, with vine leaves in the hair, at the elbows, and across the tunic and a pan pipe nestling in the leaves on the *tonnelet.* The dancer is wearing buskins on his legs. In 1907 Alexandre Benois was to revive this style in his costumes for *Le Pavillon d'Armide,* which brought fame to Vaslav Nijinsky.

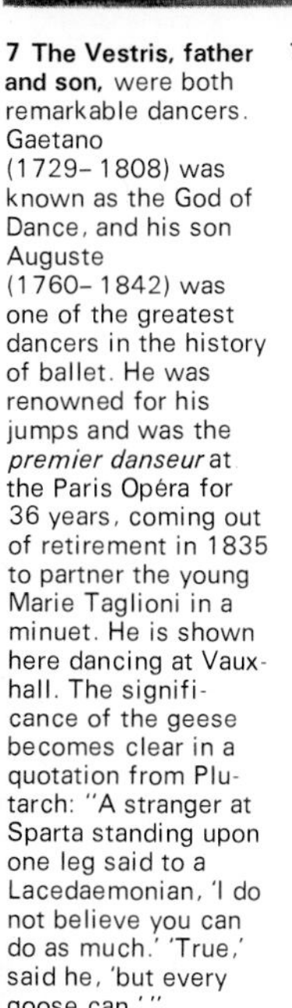

7 The Vestris, father and son, were both remarkable dancers. Gaetano (1729–1808) was known as the God of Dance, and his son Auguste (1760–1842) was one of the greatest dancers in the history of ballet. He was renowned for his jumps and was the *premier danseur* at the Paris Opéra for 36 years, coming out of retirement in 1835 to partner the young Marie Taglioni in a minuet. He is shown here dancing at Vauxhall. The significance of the geese becomes clear in a quotation from Plutarch: "A stranger at Sparta standing upon one leg said to a Lacedaemonian, 'I do not believe you can do as much.' 'True,' said he, 'but every goose can.' "

7

8

8 Charles Didelot and Mademoiselle Théodore appeared in *Amphion and Thalia* at the Pantheon, London, in 1791. Thomas Rowlandson's watercolor shows not only the two dancers but also the musicians and crowded auditorium of a typical theater of the time. The French Revolution two years before had been responsible for alterations in costumes that were adopted by the ballet. Dresses, now modeled on the tunics of ancient Greece and Rome, were shorter, lighter, and slightly transparent. This led to the introduction of tights or *maillots.* Pink tights were worn by Didelot, who also introduced the transparent tunic in *Corisandre* in 1791.

Baroque and classical music

The Baroque era in European music dawned in Italy at the beginning of the seventeenth century with a new expressive style of singing modeled on natural speech and established in the first tentative operas. The genius of Claudio Monteverdi, who was master of music at St Mark's, Venice, for 30 years beginning in 1613, was able to embody both old and new styles in his *Vespers* (1610). The richness of his sacred and secular music (especially his operas) stems largely from his imaginative synthesis of both traditions. In contrast to the older, other-worldly polyphony, an urge to express the feelings came to dominate the music of the Baroque age, a trend that led to excessive ornamentation.

The rise of instrumental composition

The Roman Catholic Church was not slow to sanction the attractive new style in its Counter-Reformation drive, and the Oratory of Philip Neri in Rome was the scene of sacred dramatic works by Giacomo Carissimi (giving music the "oratorio"). Alessandro Scarlatti in Naples contributed brilliantly to a Neapolitan opera style and established the *sinfonia avanti l'opera*, the Italian opera overture, an ancestor of the movements of the classical symphony in its quick-slow-quick movement format. The new operatic convention of emphasis on a solo voice over a bass line was also to have important implications for the development of instrumental music, where small groups of solo instruments separated out, as in the divided orchestras of Alessandro Stradella, in the beginnings of the concerto. Guiseppe Torelli, Arcangelo Corelli, Tommaso Albinoni, and Antonio Vivaldi [1] were important in the development of the instrumental *concerto grosso* (a small instrumental group in contrast and in combination with a larger group) and the solo concerto. The development of violin-making in the great Cremona families of Amati, Stradivari, and Guarneri greatly assisted composers in obtaining orchestral expressiveness.

In small chamber groupings [2], the new style demanded a harmonic "filling." This led to the Baroque convention of *basso continuo* [7], using a harpsichordist to direct a performance from the keyboard while "filling in" the harmonies as indicated in a shorthand notation in the bass part. Music for these small groups formed the core of the popular trio sonata. *Sonata* meant simply a piece played instrumentally, as opposed to *cantata*, to be sung, and only later acquired its specialized use.

The style spreads through Europe

Eventually Italy's dominant influence in operatic and instrumental styles spread throughout Europe. In Germany, Heinrich Schütz—whose Passion compositions influenced J. S. Bach—Michael Praetorius, and Johann Jakob Froberger (1616–67) were leading disciples of the style. In France, Louis XIV's court dictated taste for nearly a century and was served by an Italian-born ballet and opera composer, Jean-Baptiste Lully. Jean Philippe Rameau maintained the independent French tradition in orchestral music and opera.

In England, after the Restoration in 1660, Henry Purcell created vital English music that would be matched only by

CONNECTIONS

See also
1132 Renaissance music
1246 Music: the Roman[tic] period
1180 Enlightened despotism
1256 Opera in the 19th a[nd] 20th centuries
1222 Origins of romanticism
1244 Development of th[e] orchestra

1 Antonio Vivaldi (c. 1675–1741) was a prolific Venetian composer and master of the concerto—a form that emerged in Italy during the Baroque. He was a virtuoso violinist, and his more than 400 works include many for solo violin and for groups of violins with orchestra. He worked as director of a combined music school and orphanage, the Ospedale della Pietà in Venice (1703–40), composing many works for his charges.

2 The collegium musicum, or amateur musical society, was a major support of music in Germany in the 17th century. These institutions reflected the rise in middle-class prosperity and were frequently attached to the universities. They spread to nearby countries and later to America. Many of the societies gave public concerts. The famous Leipzig Collegium was founded by George Philipp Telemann in 1701.

3 King Frederick the Great of Prussia who reigned from 1740–86, was a typical royal patron of his time. An iron ruler of the old Prussian military class, he was also an amateur flute player. His palace in Berlin and summer residence in Potsdam provided employment for several notable musicians including C.P.E. Bach and Johann Joachim Quantz, who was a gifted flutist. Church and aristocratic patronage, which would see its final flowering in the late 18th century, had been the support of music until then. There had been many famous associations of composer and patron: Lully, Couperin, and Louis XIV; James II, William and Mary, and Purcell; Handel and George I; Haydn and Prince Esterhazy are notable.

4 Franz Joseph Haydn (1732–1809) was the major composer of the early classical period and was responsible for giving such structural cohesion and organization to the sonata principle in the symphony and string quartet that the classical forms of these compositions date from his time. The Hungarian Esterhazy family were his employers, but he also twice visited London, where he was greatly admired.

5 The Mozart family portrayed by della Croce. The composer Wolfgang Amadeus is at the harpsichord with his sister Maria Anna. His father, Leopold, is prominent with his violin, while the composer's dead mother, Anna Maria, gazes down from a portrait on the wall. Leopold toured the children as musical prodigies, and the precocious Wolfgang astonished musical Europe with his compositions and performances.

Handel. In the momentous year 1685, Handel, J. S. Bach [Key], and Domenico Scarlatti were born. Of the three, Scarlatti had the least influence, but in his hundreds of harpsichord works one can hear hints of the classical keyboard sonata.

Handel and J. S. Bach are the complementary giants of the High Baroque era. They followed distinct yet not opposed paths. Handel, extrovert and worldly, was at home in the intrigues of the opera house and happy in the massed performances of his English oratorios such as *Messiah* and *Judas Maccabeus*. J. S. Bach was confined to provincial Germany, devotional in his music, an industrious court and municipal composer who always had to fight to maintain the meager musical forces at his disposal. He summarized rather than innovated and contemporaries associated the name Bach more readily with his son Carl Philipp Emanuel, whose dramatic style was more akin to the natural simplicity and passion advocated by the French philosopher Jean-Jacques Rousseau than to the grand, unified, and somewhat rigid expressions that large Baroque forms such as the fugue had become.

The classical period emerges

The classical period, which rose on the foundations of the Enlightenment in response to the overdeveloped, ornamental style of High Baroque and Rococo music, found two masters in Joseph Haydn [4] and Wolfgang Amadeus Mozart [5]. Their classical style distinguished itself from the many-voiced Baroque texture by its greater clarity and simplicity of thematic treatment and chordal accompaniment. The prolific Haydn is considered the father of the classical period. His innovative use of contrasting themes, written in related keys, proved to be the formal perfection of the classical sonata. Mozart, drawing on Haydn, the Italian influence, and his own genius, proved a brilliant exponent of all the forms bequeathed by his predecessors. The last of the era's giants was Beethoven [8], whose epochal Symphony No. 3 *(Eroica)* marked the end of the classical period and the beginning of romantic style.

KEY

Johann Sebastian Bach (1685–1750) brought the great contrapuntal forms of Baroque music to their peak in a glorious summary of the musical development of several centuries. A member of a noted musical dynasty, Bach lived most of his life in the eastern German province of Thuringia, working mainly at the courts of Weimar (1708–17), where much of his organ music was composed, and at Cöthen (1717–23). During this fruitful time his compositions included the *Brandenburg Concertos*. His last post was at St Thomas's Church in Leipzig (1723–50), for which he wrote his great church works, among them the *St Matthew Passion*.

6

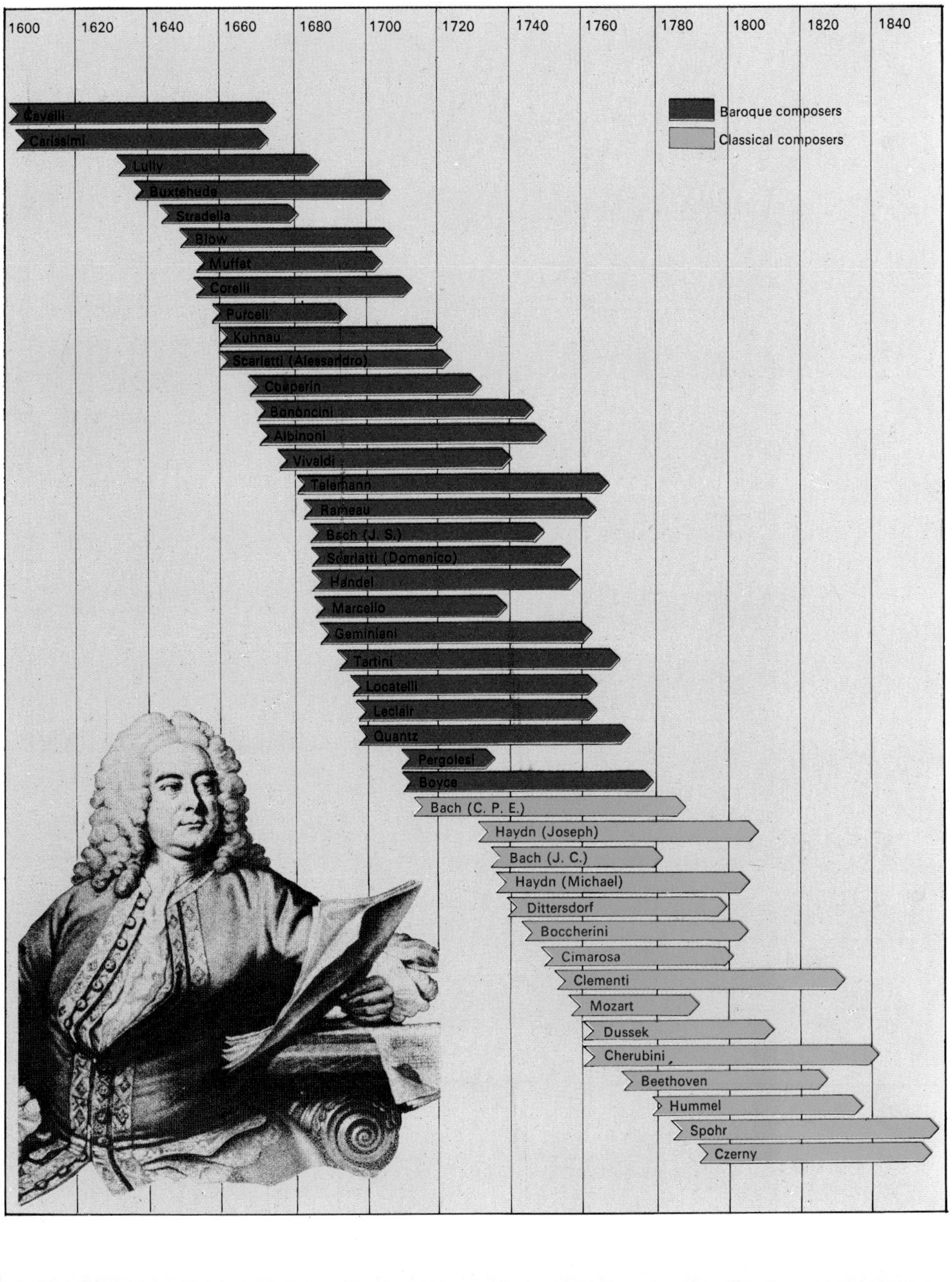

1600 1620 1640 1660 1680 1700 1720 1740 1760 1780 1800 1820 1840

Baroque composers
Classical composers

Cavalli
Carissimi
Lully
Buxtehude
Stradella
Blow
Muffat
Corelli
Purcell
Kuhnau
Scarlatti (Alessandro)
Couperin
Bononcini
Albinoni
Vivaldi
Telemann
Rameau
Bach (J. S.)
Scarlatti (Domenico)
Handel
Marcello
Geminiani
Tartini
Locatelli
Leclair
Quantz
Pergolesi
Boyce
Bach (C. P. E.)
Haydn (Joseph)
Bach (J. C.)
Haydn (Michael)
Dittersdorf
Boccherini
Cimarosa
Clementi
Mozart
Dussek
Cherubini
Beethoven
Hummel
Spohr
Czerny

6 The beginning of the Baroque period is generally dated about 1600 because of the rise of Italian opera at that time. The period effectively came to an end in 1750 with the death of J.S. Bach, who recognized the influence of the classical style of his young contemporaries. Handel, a major Baroque composer, is shown on the left. The classical era centers around the works of Haydn and Mozart.

7

7 An organ built by the celebrated organ builder Gottfried Silbermann at Leipzig (1724) is characteristic of the High Baroque period with its taste for flamboyant ornament. In the 17th century organs were substantially improved and had an important role in the *basso continuo*, or supporting bass, in Baroque music.

8

8 Ludwig van Beethoven (1770–1827) is the key transitional figure between classical and Romantic styles in European music, between the decorum of the 18th century and the free-ranging expression of the 19th century. In his early work one sees influences from Haydn and Mozart but a dynamic originality is apparent.

Neoclassicism

Neoclassicism, a movement of the late eighteenth century, was partly a reaction against the excesses of the Baroque and the Rococo, but more importantly, the fruit of a new age of inquiry into ancient Greek and Roman art.

Knowledge of antiquity

Some classical buildings, especially in Rome, had always been familiar as they were above ground. With the passionate interest in antiquity that inspired the Renaissance, pieces of classical sculpture, including several important ones, were dug up in Italy in the fifteenth and sixteenth centuries. But the very vitality and freedom that characterizes Renaissance art in a sense depended on a degree of ignorance of its sources; the few examples that were known fired the imagination in a way that the thousands of pieces that became available later could not have done. More than this, no distinction was yet drawn between Greek and Roman art or among different periods of either. Although the importance of the Greek contribution was known in theory from texts—this was particularly so in painting, of which almost no examples survived—classical Greek sculpture of the fifth and fourth centuries BC was known only through Roman copies.

This situation altered only gradually in the seventeenth century. The decisive change came in the eighteenth century, when not only were far more classical statues excavated and a museum of them opened on the Capitol in Rome, but whole unknown ancient arts were rediscovered, such as Greek painting at Herculaneum and Pompeii, near Naples, and Greek vases, then paradoxically thought to be Etruscan, in southern Italy. In short, a new science—archeology—was born. Above all, Greece itself was explored, notably by the British architects James Stuart (1713–88) and Nicholas Revett (1720–1804), and by the end of the century a real perception existed of the differences between Greek and Roman architecture. A further revelation was brought about by the arrival of the Parthenon sculptures in London, imported from Athens by Lord Elgin (1766–1841) in the early nineteenth century, for these showed that the art of the greatest Greek sculptor, Phidias, did not conform to the so-called "classical ideal" as it had been previously understood but consisted instead in something at once more primitive and more naturalistic. Scholars and amateurs (who played a key role in the Neoclassical movement) were now concerned to place things in chronological order and against the background of the culture that produced them.

The new conception

Out of this in turn was evolved a new aesthetic on which Neoclassicism was based: art was now austere, simple, static, with clear, hard outlines and, in sculpture and painting, almost without shadows.

One further piece in the jigsaw puzzle remained: the moral element. It was a preoccupation with this that brought the Neoclassicists in France out in full cry against the Rococo. The French reformers were full of admiration for the Roman ideals of civic virtue and the Greek experiment in

CONNECTIONS

See also
1224 The French Revolution
1184 The Enlightenment
1222 Origins of romanticism
1228 Romantic art: figure painting
1242 Romantic art: landscape painting
1192 British and American art 1530–1790

1 This secretaire was made by J.H. Riesener (1734–1806) in 1783 for Marie Antoinette in the "Louis Seize" style. It has Neoclassical lines but a richness of ornament that was typical of the court.

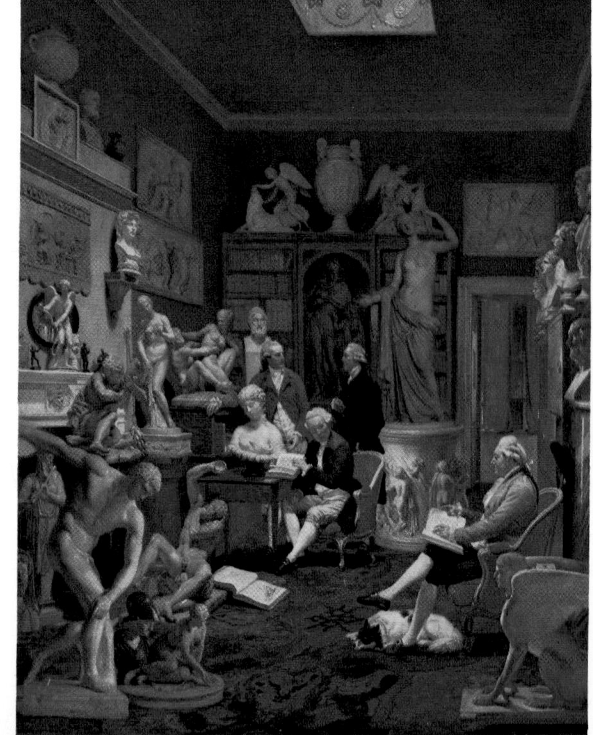

2 Collecting antiques was a central part of the Neoclassical movement. Sometimes it reached absurd proportions as with Charles Towneley and his marbles (1782) painted by Johann Zoffany.

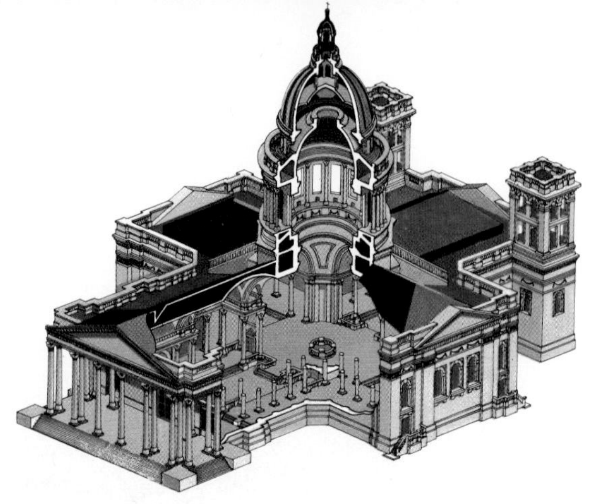

3 Jacques-Germain Soufflot's church of Ste-Genevieve (now the Panthéon), Paris (built 1757–92), was the first large Neoclassical building. It was also influenced by the dome of St. Paul's, London.

4 The revival of Greek poetry as a subject for art is reflected in "Priam Begging Achilles for the Body of Hector" (*c.* 1770) by Gavin Hamilton (1723–98).

democracy. The Rococo began to seem a decadent, frivolous style associated with a decadent, frivolous society. There was a strong move, at least in theory, toward bourgeois rectitude, a wave of moral idealism that carried over into Revolution.

Neoclassicism in France

Consequently, from about 1760 onward there was in all the arts in France, but first in architecture and the applied arts, perhaps last in painting and sculpture, a reaction in favor of straight, simple lines and austere ornament derived from classical and sometimes specifically Greek models.

The first important French building to show this trend was the Panthéon in Paris designed by Jacques-Germain Soufflot (1713–80) as early as 1755–56 [3]; a fuller, more imaginative brand of Neoclassical architecture was developed some years later by Claude-Nicholas Ledoux (1736–1806). In painting it was less easy to depend on classical precedent because surviving examples were few. The solution was to use as an intermediary the greatest seventeenth-century master of classicism, Poussin. His influence was of vital importance for Jacques-Louis David (1748–1825), the first major Neoclassical painter and the interpreter of both the heroic spirit of the Revolution [6] and the imperious genius of Napoleon. His successor, Jean-Auguste-Dominique Ingres (1780–1867), evolved a purer, more refined form of Neoclassicism [7], harking back to Raphael and Pompeii.

Although the grandest Neoclassical paintings and buildings were French, the movement was an international one with public American architecture, especially banks and government buildings, dominated by Neoclassicism until the end of the nineteenth century. By far the greatest Neoclassical sculptor was an Italian, Antonio Canova (1757–1822), but the German architects evolved the most scholarly manifestations of the style in the early nineteenth century. Neoclassicism was by no means a merely backward looking or monolithic phase of art history; on the contrary, it reflected the radical questioning of established values in a period of revolution.

KEY

As with the Rococo, some of the most attractive and ingenious expressions of Neoclassicism are to be found in the applied arts. Devotees of Neoclassical taste liked to own ornaments derived (often rather freely) from objects that once had a practical or symbolic function in antiquity. This "Pedestal and Vase in the Etruscan Taste" (*c.* 1795), by the British architect James Wyatt (1747–1813), has a base like a Roman altar, with Greek decoration and a Greek vase on top. While the curling candle-brackets and lighthearted mood recall the Rococo, the chaste lines and figured details are in the purest spirit of Neoclassicism.

5

5 The American passion for Neoclassical architecture was pursued by Alexander Jackson Davis (1803–92) to include interior design, as in this water-colored drawing of a double parlor in New York City. The rooms, filled with Greek-styled furniture, are divided by Ionic columns. After 1841 Davis turned from Neoclassical designs and became America's leading proponent of Gothic Revival.

6

A MARAT.
DAVID

6 Jacques-Louis David's painting, "The Death of Marat" (1793), is a commemorative monument but with everything concentrated on the individual. David depicts Jean-Paul Marat, the French rationalist writer and demagogue, stabbed at work in his bath by Charlotte Corday, as a revolutionary martyr. Neoclassical touches include the echo in the pictorial treatment of the figure of the deaths of the classical philosophers, Socrates and Seneca, and the clarity and economy of the composition of the painting.

7

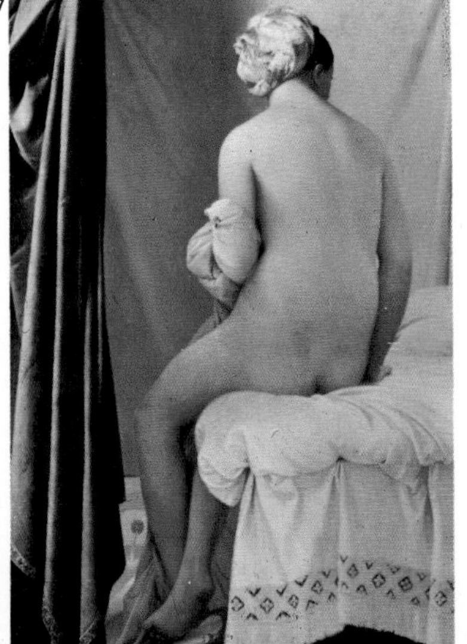

7 A less brutal, less realistic painter than David, Jean-Auguste-Dominique Ingres interpreted Neoclassicism mainly in terms of line. He created an ideal, dignified world of pure contours and clean colors, yet not a world without feeling—all well exemplified in his "Baigneuse" (1808). He was the father of 19th-century academic art in Europe.

8 The founding of public museums in the major European cities was one of the products of Neoclassicism. The Old Museum, Berlin (1823–30), by Friedrich Schinkel (1781–1841), built to house the art collection of the Prussian state, is an important example of Neoclassical architecture.

8

International economy 1700–1800

During the eighteenth century, trading links between Europe and the rest of the world strengthened into commercial bonds that were vital to prosperity. The rise of Great Britain to a dominant position in trade, overtaking the Dutch, Spanish, and French, showed itself in extensive contacts and trading arrangements with the Americas and Asia [5]. There was a general expansion of trade at the same time, particularly in the Atlantic, in which other countries, especially France, shared. Expansion of trade brought with it specialization in shipping and finance and provided a stimulus to the increased production of manufactured goods in Europe helping to promote industrialization in England by the end of the century.

Incentives for trade expansion

The expansion of European influence in the years before 1700 had introduced a wide range of precious and tropical products that became staples of extra-European trade. Gold and silver bullion had provided one major component of the trade of the declining Spanish Empire, but this trade had also included spices, tobacco, coffee, sugar, and cocoa. A growing taste for tropical products gave merchants the incentive to incur the risks of long overseas voyages. Merchants from such countries as Britain and France, relative latecomers to colonial trade, made greater efforts in the eighteenth century to capture part of the trade controlled by the older empires.

Several commercial wars were fought by the other European nations to open up the colonial trade of the declining Spanish Empire to their merchants. In 1715, British merchants obtained permission in the Asiento Treaty to deliver 4,800 slaves annually to the Spanish colonies and for one ship a year to trade with Panama. In all other respects, Spain tried to keep its colonial trade closed. But because Spain was unable to supply all the needs of its colonists, there was much illicit traffic. After the Seven Years War (1756–63), this rigid control was relaxed, and British and French shipping seized a greater part of the Spanish-American trade.

Similarly, British and Dutch ships captured an increasing share of Portuguese trade. In the East, the Dutch had taken over much of the old Portuguese Empire. With stations in Ceylon, Bengal, Malabar, and Batavia, Dutch influence extended as far as Japan and was organized through the Dutch East India Company based on Batavia in Java. By the end of the century, however, they began to feel the effects of British and French competition and Dutch trade stagnated.

French and British power

France had colonies in North America, including Quebec and Louisiana, and in the West Indies, including Guadeloupe and Martinique; France held Senegal in Africa and colonized Madagascar and Mauritius in the Indian Ocean. In India, France maintained important trading positions at Pondicherry and Chandernagore. From these colonies and contacts French trade grew rapidly in the late eighteenth century, especially with the West Indies. After the Seven Years War, however, France lost Quebec

CONNECTIONS

See also
1126 The rise of banking
1182 Europe: economy an society 1700–1800
1186 Exploration and science 1750–1850
1220 The early Industrial Revolution
354 Coffee, tea, and coco
362 Fiber and oil crops

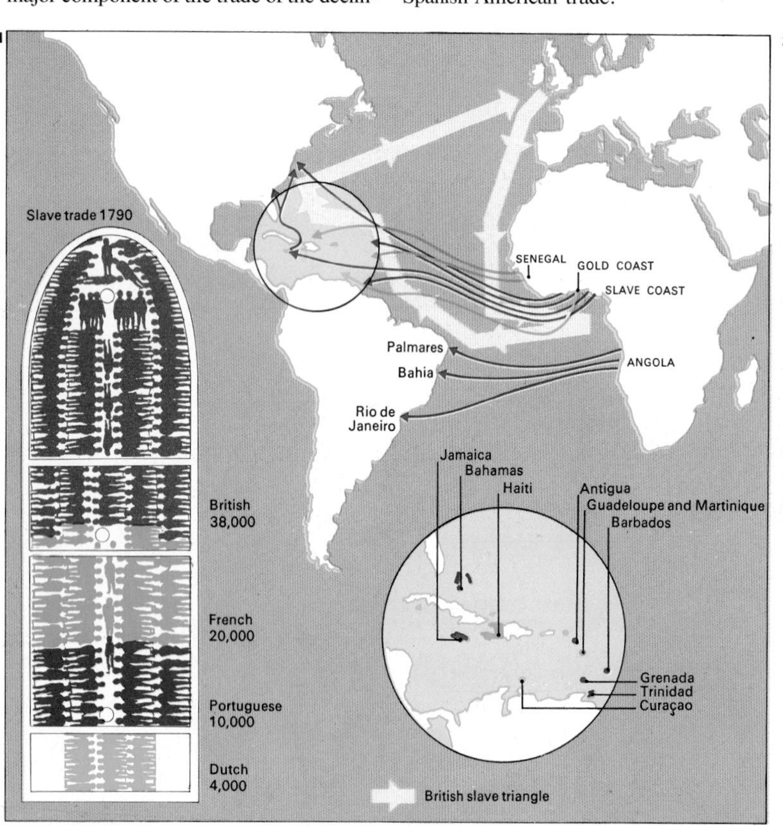

Slave trade 1790
SENEGAL
GOLD COAST
SLAVE COAST
Palmares
Bahia
ANGOLA
Rio de Janeiro
British 38,000
French 20,000
Portuguese 10,000
Dutch 4,000
Jamaica
Bahamas
Haiti
Antigua
Guadeloupe and Martinique
Barbados
Grenada
Trinidad
Curaçao
British slave triangle

1 The triangular route taken by slave ships from European ports such as Liverpool, Bristol, and Bordeaux took them to Africa to collect slaves, across the Atlantic to sell them, and back again with cargoes acquired in exchange. The major share of the slave traffic was carried on by Great Britain by the end of the 18th century, supplying plantations in the West Indies and on the mainland.

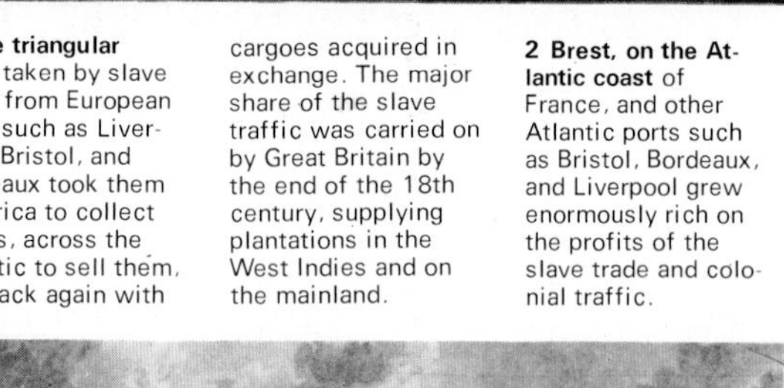

2 Brest, on the Atlantic coast of France, and other Atlantic ports such as Bristol, Bordeaux, and Liverpool grew enormously rich on the profits of the slave trade and colonial traffic.

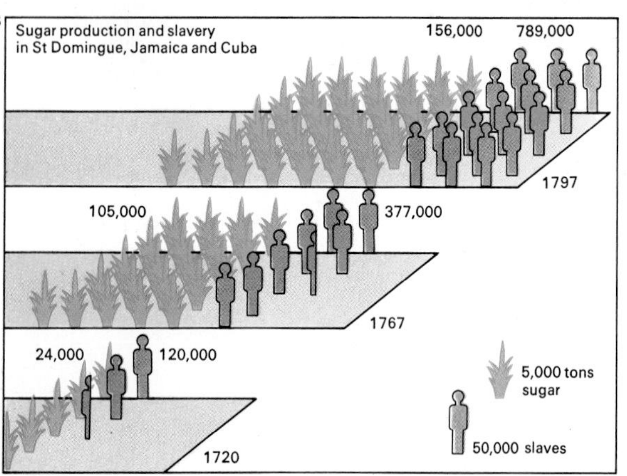

Sugar production and slavery in St Domingue, Jamaica and Cuba
156,000
789,000
1797
105,000
377,000
1767
24,000
120,000
1720
5,000 tons sugar
50,000 slaves

3 Economic development in the West Indies depended on a steady supply of slave labor from Africa. The slave population and sugar production grew to satisfy the European demand for sugar.

4 Smuggling in the 18th century was a common way of avoiding heavy duties on such commodities as liquor, wines, and tobacco. Revenue men waged an intermittent war with smugglers, especially along remoter coastlines.

and much of its influence in India. Nonetheless, its flourishing trade with the remainder of its colonies led to the expansion of ports such as Bordeaux, Nantes, and Brest [2], while Marseilles prospered on the basis of the Levant trade.

The major rising power was Great Britain, which exerted its superiority over the older empires by the middle of the century and conducted all the trade of its colonies in British-registered ships. In spite of the loss of the North American colonies, trade expanded with the Americas both through chartered companies, such as the Hudson's Bay Company [8], and through more open commerce. The vastly profitable slave traffic was primarily British by the end of the century, the "triangular route" [1] among Britain, Africa, and the Americas providing great profits upon which mercantile cities such as London, Liverpool, and Bristol flourished. Second to the slave traffic in importance was the sugar trade [3], which with other tropical produce provided a valuable reexport trade to continental Europe. In the Indian Ocean the British East India Company triumphed over the French and controlled Bombay, Bengal, Madras, and most of southern India; but by the end of the century the company's monopoly was broken.

Stimulus for industrialization

Expansion of trade led to increases in merchant shipping and the development of more versatile credit and financial institutions. Growing trade led to relaxation of the old mercantile ideas of monopolistic companies and favored the adoption of laissez-faire ideas of free trade and open competition among companies.

In many countries industries grew up that refined tropical products and reexported them either to other European countries or back to the colonies as manufactured goods. Thus sugar refining, tanning, distilling, and other processes became early examples of industrial activity. The most striking development in the late eighteenth century was the rapid rise in raw cotton exports from the plantations of the southern United States to the growing British textile industry.

KEY
Worldwide expansion of Europe's trade in the 18th century was carried in ships such as this heavily armed East Indiaman.

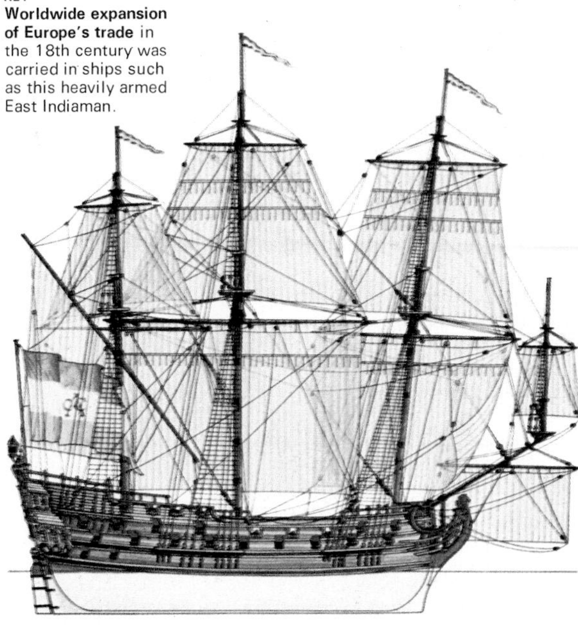

5

5 Trading horizons widened in the 18th century as European contact with hitherto exotic countries became more regular. Tea plantations in China were developed to meet a taste for tea in Britain, and an extensive trade also grew up in silk, porcelain, and spices. Although China limited European influence to specified trading centers, these provided a foothold extended in the next century.

6 Speculation, greed, and dishonesty were caricatured by William Hogarth (1697–1766) in 1720 when the South Sea Company, on which heavy speculation had centered, collapsed and led to a change of government. Financial and credit institutions in the 18th century were often unstable, partly because governments drew on them for credit and partly because investors panicked easily.

6

7

Nº 1422.
ACCION DE LA REAL COMPª DE COMERCIO ESTABLECIDA EN BARCELONA

8

7 Spanish financial institutions, established in the 16th century, shared in the great expansion of European trade in the 18th century. This deposit certificate, dated 1759, is from the Real Compania de Comercio of Barcelona.

8 The Hudson's Bay Company, whose Fort Garry, Manitoba, trading post is shown here, was founded by the British in 1670 to open up a lucrative trade in Canada, supplying Europe with furs, timber and salted fish. Simultaneously, the colonists at Albany and New York City were extending trade with the Indians. France was also active in the Canadian trade but lost its share in 1763 when it was defeated in the Seven Years War and surrendered control of Canada to Britain.

India from the Moguls to 1800

In 1192 Muhammad of Ghur destroyed the Rajput princes at Tarain. In the next ten years the Muslims overran the Ganges plains and founded the Sultanate of Delhi (1206). This marked the beginning of Islam's long dominance over Hindustan (northern India). That dominance survived into the eighteenth century, creating an entity, both Indian and Muslim, that was distinct in the Islamic world.

Islamic rule

The three centuries that followed saw the rise and fall of dynasties—the Turko-Afghans, Khaljis, Tughlaks, Sayyids, and Lodis—under which the Delhi Empire sometimes expanded as far as the Deccan and the south (as it did under the megalomaniac Alaudin Kalji, or under Mohammed Tughlak, the greatest of the sultans) and sometimes contracted into the narrow regions around Delhi and Agra (as it did under the Lodis) [2].

The regions continued to challenge the center; invasions from the north (of which Timur's sack of Delhi in 1398 was only the most ferocious example) still threatened the empires, and Delhi remained unable to dominate the Deccan.

Two new forces, however, were to alter the old patterns: Mogul rule and European expansion. In 1526 Babur (1483–1530), driven from his mountain stronghold in Firghana, crushed the Lodis at Panipat and established the Moguls in Delhi. In 1498 the Portuguese explorer Vasco da Gama sailed into Calicut, the precursor of other seaborne powers from Europe who in time were to be the heirs of the Mogul.

Mogul Empire

The great Mogul rulers—Babur, Humayun, Sher Shah, and, above all, Akbar [3] and Aurungzebe [4]—brought more of India under one empire than any ruler since the time of Ashoka in the third century BC and gave it a more sophisticated administration than it had ever possessed. But the Great Mogul, sitting on his peacock throne, despite his show of pomp and wealth, had built an empire on a fragile base, and Mogul rule could not be sustained by force alone. Despite all the trappings of imperial power, the army, and the centrally controlled military bureaucrats (the *mansabhadars*), the Moguls were forced to come to terms with their Indian subjects. This meant they had to give reasonable freedom to the magnates who actually controlled the land. They had to tolerate Hinduism, and above all they had to avoid meddling too much in local affairs. All this qualified the notion of Mogul power, which was more in the nature of overrule than real empire, and helps to explain the decline of the Mogul Empire [6].

Like all land empires in premodern times, the fundamental difficulty the Mogul rulers faced was how to raise revenues from limited sources, while retaining the cooperation of local notables, the Zomindars. One obvious device was to extend the empire, but, as Aurungzebe discovered, more conquest meant more expense. Another was to try to extract more land revenue from their subjects, but in the end the Moguls lost the cooperation of the Zomindars, who were squeezed from above and resisted by the

Connections

See also
1034 India 300–1200
1266 India in the 19th century
1262 European imperialism in the 19th century
1204 Indian art: the Mogul age

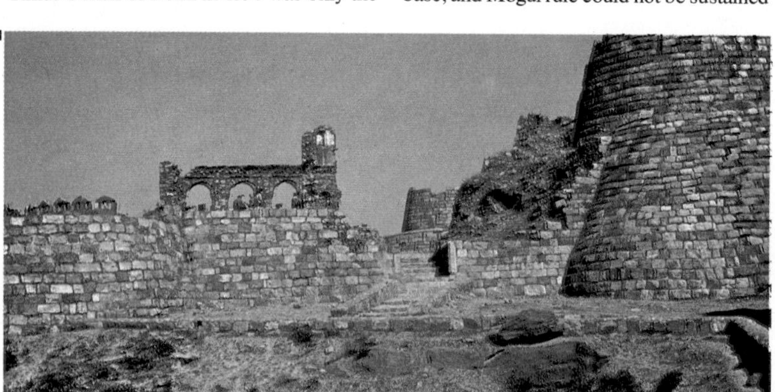

1 The ruins of the fortress and city of Tughlakabad, near Delhi, are an example of the feckless manner in which Indian cities were made and unmade by rulers who sought to commemorate themselves by building new capitals. Constructed 1321–23, Tughlakabad was soon abandoned by Tughlak Shah (*r.* 1321–25) in favor of Deogir, ostensibly because of bad water.

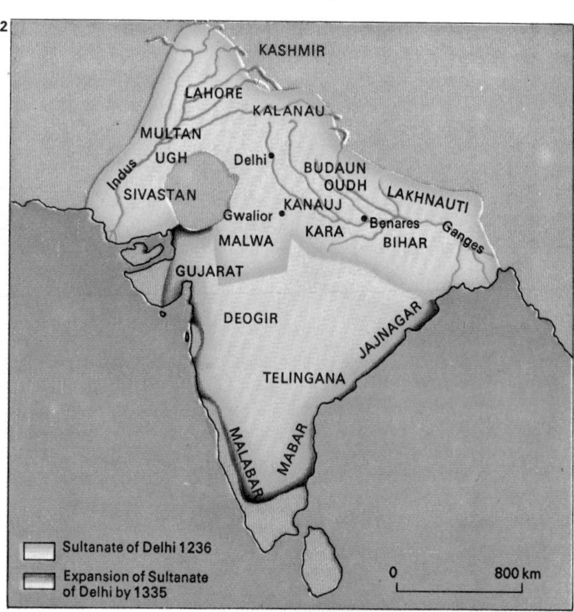

KASHMIR
LAHORE
KALANAU
MULTAN
UGH
Delhi
Indus
SIVASTAN
BUDAUN
OUDH
LAKHNAUTI
Gwalior
KANAUJ
Benares
Ganges
KARA
MALWA
BIHAR
GUJARAT
DEOGIR
JAJNAGAR
TELINGANA
MALABAR
MABAR
Sultanate of Delhi 1236
Expansion of Sultanate of Delhi by 1335
0
800 km

2 The Sultanate of Delhi at the death of Iltumish (1236) and 100 years later under Mohammed Tughlak (*r.* 1325–51), when it reached its greatest extent, is shown on the map. It indicates that Muslim dynasties had dominated northern India for centuries before the Moguls and had made attempts, only temporarily successful, to dominate the Deccan and the south of India.

3 Akbar (*r.* 1556–1605), the most celebrated Mogul emperor, was the almost exact contemporary of Queen Elizabeth I. He vastly expanded the Mogul's territories, gave them an efficient system of government, and tried to encourage new sources of work. In his effort to conciliate his Hindu subjects and to stamp out Muslim bigotry, the Emperor tried, without lasting success, to create for India a new religion reconciling the different beliefs.

4 Under Aurungzebe (*r.* 1658–1707), the Mogul Empire reached its greatest extent: from Kabul to the Cauvery. But the empire he bequeathed did not survive much beyond the five years of his son's reign. The seeds of disruption, always present, were germinated by his religious intolerance; he alienated the Rajputs, the military prop of the empire; at great cost he conquered, but failed to integrate, the Deccan; he neglected Hindustan and fought the Marathas.

5 The Red Fort at Delhi, build by Shah Jehan (1592–1666), was surrounded by massive red sandstone walls 75 ft (22.8m) high and enclosed a complex of palaces, gardens, military barracks, and other buildings. The fort, like many other masterpieces of this reign, including the Taj Mahal, illustrates the magnificent splendor of Mogul rule in India.

peasantry below. These inherent difficulties were made worse by Aurungzebe's religious intolerance, which alienated the Rajput allies and confirmed the Marathas in their hostility. A sequence of ineffectual successors after Aurungzebe reduced the throne at Delhi to the plaything of factions; another round of invasions from the north culminated in Nader Shah's sack of Delhi in 1739.

Rise of the East India Company

With the collapse of Mogul rule, India was parceled out among a set of virtually independent "country" powers—Bengal and Oudh under the Nawabs, Mysore under the Muslim dynasty of an adventurer, Hyderabad under the Nizam, and the Maratha confederacy marauding throughout India from its western base.

This was the background of the territorial rise of the British-owned East India Company. The company had gone to India to trade, not to conquer. Throughout the eighteenth century its directors protested that commerce, not dominion, was their aim. But by the mid-eighteenth century the British, long established in their factories at Calcutta, Madras, and Bombay [8], had a trade (mainly in Indian cotton goods) that was worth protecting both against the smaller but acquisitive French company and against Indian disruption [7].

When Britain and France fought in Europe, the companies in India could not stay neutral. Faced in India by a more powerful British company, Joseph-François Dupleix (1696–1763) of the French East India Council decided, during the Austrian War of Succession, to improve the odds by using Indian allies against his rival.

The British soon adopted the French tactic. Robert Clive (1725–74) used it to win the battle of Plassey (1757) and thereby gain Bengal. Dupleix's idea of using Indian resources to pay for European expansion gave Britain the richest province of India and set it firmly on the road to dominion [9].

By the time William Pitt (1759–1806) and Henry Dundas (1742–1811) began to think of an Indian Empire as part of British expansion, the East India Company had become the heir of the Moguls.

KEY

After the Afghan defeat of the Marathas at Panipat (1761), Mahadaji Sindhia (1727–1794), a bluff but literate soldier of fortune, built a large empire in Hindustan. Acting nominally as the soldier of the *peshwa* (sovereign), he became the master of the Mogul ruler, Shah Alam, and the "actual sovereign of Hindustan from the Sutlej to Agra, the conqueror of the princes of Rajpootana, the commander of an army." But although he modernized the Maratha armies, giving them artillery and recruiting Muslim and Jat soldiers and European officers into his service (one of whom he is seen entertaining here), his power was fragile because his domains lacked the resources to support his armies.

6

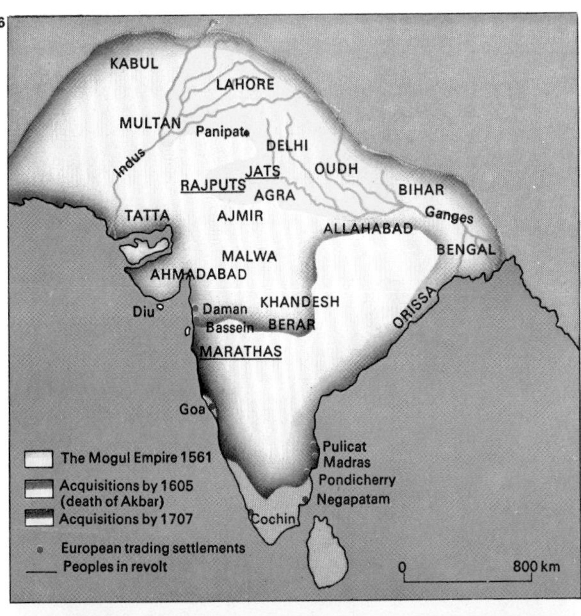
KABUL
LAHORE
MULTAN
Panipat
DELHI
Indus
JATS
OUDH
RAJPUTS
AGRA
BIHAR
Ganges
TATTA
AJMIR
ALLAHABAD
BENGAL
MALWA
AHMADABAD
KHANDESH
Diu
Daman
Bassein
BERAR
ORISSA
MARATHAS
Goa
The Mogul Empire 1561
Acquisitions by 1605 (death of Akbar)
Acquisitions by 1707
European trading settlements
Peoples in revolt
Pulicat
Madras
Pondicherry
Negapatam
Cochin
0
800 km

6 The rise of the Mogul Empire and the early signs of its decline are indicated on the map. By 1561 Akbar had created a unified Mogul Empire in the north of India; by 1707 when Aurungzebe died, the Mogul Empire had reached its utmost limits. But the Rajputs, Jats, and Marathas were already in revolt, and the European seaborne powers who were to be the heirs of the Moguls occupied the coast.

7

7 The English settlement at Fort St. George in Madras was one of the earliest in India, set up in 1639. The struggle with the French for mastery was centered in the south; the fort was crucial.

8

't Engelse Fort Aande stadt in Bombaja zyde.

8 Bombay was ceded by Portugal to the British in 1661 and granted to the East India Company in 1668. Its fort helped to defend British commercial interests on the west coast of India.

9

9 In 1765 Shah Alam made his grant of the right to collect land revenue to Clive, by then the real master of Bengal. The fact that the Mogul, although politically impotent by this time, was still seen as the source of legitimacy in ratifying the East India Company's authority in Bengal shows the conservative nature of Indian politics; it is also indicative of British reluctance to move from trade to dominion that Clive did not demand more power.

10 The East India Company's fortunes in the late 17th and 18th centuries were built upon the export of hand-loom cottons whose thread was spun in villages throughout India, sometimes with the aid of the gharka, or spinning wheel, illustrated here. The 19th century saw the decline of village spinning and weaving, and India became the largest market for Lancashire's cotton goods. In the 20th century Gandhi revived the hand loom.

10

Indian art: the Mogul age

The Muslim conquests in India in the twelfth century brought about a fundamental change in the art of the subcontinent. The invaders imposed a foreign style—Persian—upon the country; the new royal patronage encouraged the survival of secular art; and there was a systematic attack on religious art. Before the invasions the royal court had patronized art from religious establishments. Afterward there was far more secular art, especially from the end of the sixteenth century.

The contrasts with Islam

There could hardly be a sharper contrast than that between the religious monuments of the Hindus, Buddhists, and Jains, with their heavy forms and exuberant figure sculpture, and the light, airy mosques of Islam with arcades, domes, and slender towers [3]. These mosques were without sculptured figures but were decorated with disciplined floral and geometric ornaments carried out in bright colors, either flat or in low relief. The floors were often covered with carpets. This helped to foster the Indian carpet industry, which, as with other crafts, began with a marked Persian influence but eventually developed its own national style. The same architectural idioms that applied to mosques were used in the erection of other buildings. An important technique of surface decoration consisting of patterns of inlaid colored stone [6] is similar to Italian techniques and may have been imported from the West.

The independence of some cultures within the area of Muslim influence is shown by Jain painting, which developed as a form of manuscript illumination [1]. This painting style is quite distinct from the more naturalistic wall paintings at Ajanta that preceded it. The Jains adopted a highly-stylized, flat and decorative form that made use of bright colors, particularly red, blue, and gold. A characteristic trait is the use of wiry, angular figures, each having the head in three-quarter front view with the farther eye protruding beyond the line of the face. The conservatism of early western Indian painting gradually became freer and more sensitive.

A studio system set up

The establishment of the Mogul dynasty in northern India created conditions under which Muslim art was able to flourish. The emperor Akbar (1542–1605), an enlightened monarch, expanded the studio system set up by his father in which Indian painters had worked under the supervision of two Persian painters. This arrangement, together with a prevailing Persian taste, imposed a strong Persian influence on painting at the Mogul court. Under Akbar's patronage, however, a style quickly evolved that was unmistakably Indian, showing a refined naturalism and the use of rich colors [2].

In the early seventeenth century an interest in portraiture and natural history (perhaps under Western influence) was added to heroic and mythological subjects. A sense of serene contemplation took the place of violent motion; it was coupled with a simpler, more subtle sense of composition and deeper psychological insight. This continued into the reign of Shah Jahan (1629–58), [Key and 4]. but while the high standard of technique remained, a stiffness of

CONNECTIONS

See also
1202 India from the Moguls to 1800
1036 Indian art to the Moguls
1262 European imperialism in the 19th century

1 This Jain religious diagram (yantra), of which a detail is shown, was painted in Gujerat in western India in 1447. It makes no attempt at realism because its purpose was not primarily aesthetic; such considerations were subordinated to the stimulation of religious ideas through the use of traditional artistic forms. Jainist paintings often took the form of manuscript illuminations made on palm leaves. This technique continued even after the introduction of paper in the 14th century.

2 The Annals of Akbar (*Akbar-nama*) *c.*1600, illustrates the festivities that marked the birth of Prince Salim at Fathpur Sikri in 1569. Under Akbar, Indian painting absorbed the Persian style and became unquestionably Indian. Attentive to detail, its bright colors and agitated composition produced pictures that were like mosaics but seemed to be in constant movement.

3 The Qutb-Minar at Lalkot, Delhi, was built *c.*1230 with later additions. As well as being a minaret, it also served as a watchtower and war memorial. It is a monument to early Islamic architecture in India, since the minaret is one of the more obvious characteristics of a mosque. In this case the mosque was constructed partly of material from a nearby ruined Hindu temple and was decorated in geometric reliefs.

4 This carved jade wine cup in the form of a gourd bears a legend indicating that it was made for the Mogul emperor Shah Jahan in 1657. It was during his reign that Mogul sumptuousness reached its zenith, represented by the Taj Mahal, built by Shah Jahan as a tomb for his favorite wife Mumtaz Mahal. The naturalism of the cup is entirely Indian, showing the emancipation of Mogul art from that of Persia.

execution inhibited the former supple spontaneity. Under Aurungzebe (1618–1707), Mogul painting began its decline.

In the Deccan, a style similar to that farther north (but somewhat modified by pre-Islamic elements) continued during the eighteenth century and produced, among other subjects, illustrations corresponding to musical modes (scales). To the northwest, in Rajasthan, a large number of schools developed under the patronage of local courts, of which those at Mewar, Bundi, Kotah, Bikaner, and Jaipur are probably the best known. Their style was characterized in the seventeenth century by emotional intensity and in the eighteenth century by the vivid use of bright colors and an acute sense of drama. Under similar patronage, but below the Himalayas in the hill states of the Punjab such as Kangra and Guler, several schools of painting arose that exhibited a marked individuality of style known as Pahari ("of the hills"). These pictures took as their subjects romantic themes found in Hindi and Sanskrit poems such as the *Gitagovinda* of Jayadeva. This epic, dating from the twelfth century, recounts the amorous adventures of the Krishna, such as those describing his love for Radha, his favorite milkmaid. The adventures are admirably illustrated in the Pahari miniatures [5].

The decorative arts

Under the Moguls decorative arts flourished as an aspect of the ostentatious luxury of the court and minor rulers. Intricately wrought gold and silver work was produced as well as jewelry (for men and women) set with diamonds, pearls, rubies, and other precious stones. Vessels and other objects such as rings and dagger hilts were carved in rock crystal and jade [4] and were also sometimes inlaid with gold and gems. In addition to embroideries, sumptuous textiles were woven.

In southern India, Hindu traditions in decorative art generally held their own in spite of Muslim influence from the north, but they did not remain entirely unaffected. This resulted in a style, best illustrated by some superb ivory carvings [7], that made use of tightly controlled organic motifs.

KEY

The Mogul emperor Shah Jahan looks at a piece of jewelry in this portrait (*c.*1618) that reflects most of the characteristics of post-Muslim-conquest Indian art. Opulent, tender, and fastidious, it glorifies the individual. It records also the name of the artist (Abu'l Hassan), who earlier would have been anonymous. Although some attempt has been made to achieve a likeness, the result is formalized and without character. The floral background, in which plants are treated in a naturalistic but gemlike way, reflects the interest in flower painting that was fashionable during this period.

5

5 Divine love as an ideal for human love was a popular theme in Indian art, as seen in the poetic paintings of Krishna and Radha. In this picture from the Punjab hills, their love is depicted with a poignant tenderness. The complete painting follows the Indian convention of showing two or more related events within the same frame; above the lovers' meeting, shown here, there is another picture of their forest walk. Subtle colors were used for a tender effect.

6

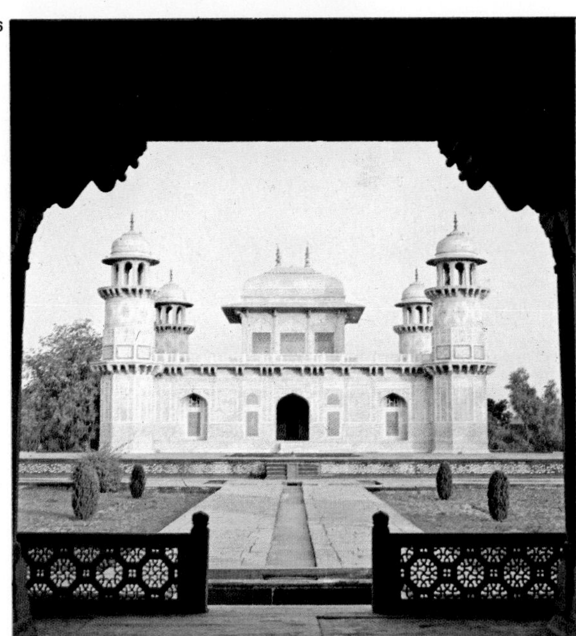

6 A mausoleum at Agra, built in 1628, is constructed of marble inlaid with patterns of colored stone. It shows the Mogul interest in surface decoration and linear movement.

7

7 Ivory carving has had a long history in India. It was probably most fully developed in the south, as this 18th-century comb from Mysore, showing Gaja-Lakshmi, goddess of fortune and prosperity, magnificently reveals.

8

8 Cotton paintings ("chintz") on an 18th-century coverlet combine Indian technique and European designs, such as engravings of ornamental motifs. Hand painted at first, they were later block printed.

China from 1368 to *c.* 1800

The Ming or "Brilliant" dynasty (1368–1644) was founded by a Buddhist peasant who became leader of the rebel bands that overthrew Mongol rule. He made his capital at Nanking and gave himself the title Hung Wu (reigned 1368–98). Under the new emperor the government reverted to the T'ang system of Confucianism, taxes were reduced, and peasants were allowed to keep the land they reclaimed. The empire expanded, taking in vassal states that included Annam and Siam. Maritime expansion also occurred, and under the able command of Admiral Cheng Ho fleets of exceptionally large Chinese vessels made seven expeditions between 1405 and 1433 to places as far away as Sri Lanka, the Persian Gulf, and parts of Africa. The ships carried treasure and merchandise, and Cheng Ho was able to establish trade with about 30 ports.

Protection of the homeland

At home the government was determined to defeat further invasions from the north. The Great Wall was repaired, many towns were fortified, and Nanking was surrounded by a wall 20 miles (32km) long and 60 ft (18m) high. This "closed door" policy of the Ming was similar to that of the early Sung period, which had also re-established Chinese rule over the Middle Kingdom after a period of foreign intervention. In spite of this attitude, the Ming were to see the arrival of Europeans from the south. The Portuguese established a settlement in Macao and were followed by missionaries.

The Ming built numerous palaces and splendid tombs, the most famous being the Imperial Palace in Peking [1] and the tombs of the emperors just north of the city [3]. In 1958 that of the Wan-li emperor was opened to reveal three lacquer coffins containing the bodies of the emperor and two of his wives.

The end of the Ming dynasty

In spite of elaborate security precautions, the Brilliant dynasty reached its end when the northern barbarians, in this case the Manchus, entered north China. They came at the request of the Ming commander, who sought their help to unseat a rebel, Li Tzu-ch'eng, who had made himself master of Peking. Rather than submit to humiliation the last Ming emperor hanged himself, and the rebel emperor in his turn was overthrown by the Manchus, whose leader, Fu-lin (1638–61), proclaimed himself emperor of the Ch'ing or "Pure" dynasty.

For a century and a half the Manchus governed wisely; they provided the country with domestic prosperity and extended its boundaries beyond all previous limits. The emperors ruled as conquerors and skillfully protected themselves against rebellion by instituting a system of banners—military and administrative divisions in which the people were registered, taxed and conscripted during the formation of their own state. The Manchus were unable to read or write and accepted the Ming examination procedure for the selection of civil service officials. They were careful, however, to forbid the Chinese to hold office in their native provinces, and they also divided responsibility in such a way that the officials were obliged to check on one another. The Manchus were more sophisticated than the

CONNECTIONS

See also
1270 The opening up of China
1112 Asian empires of the Mongols
1042 China 618–1368
1208 Chinese art 1368 to the 20th century
1232 European empires in the 19th century
1264 The expansion of Christianity

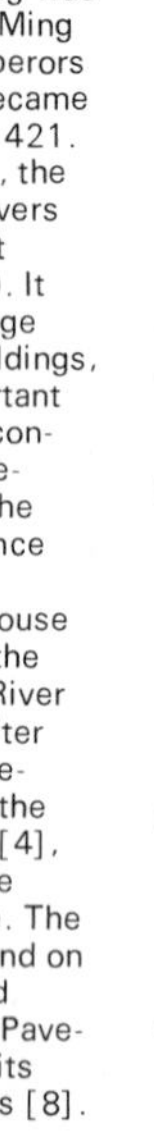

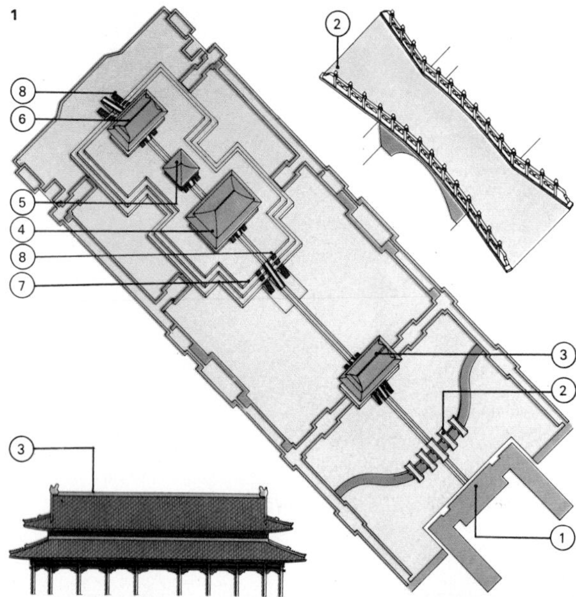

1
2
3
4
5
6
7
8

1 The Imperial Palace in Peking was the seat of 22 Ming and Ch'ing emperors after Peking became the capital in 1421. Begun in 1406, the palace now covers 7,750,000sq ft (720,000sq m). It is an assemblage of imperial buildings, the most important [shown here] containing the ceremonial halls. The principal entrance is through the Meridian gatehouse [1] leading to the Golden Water River bridges [2]. After the second gatehouse [3] lies the first great hall [4], which holds the imperial throne. The halls [5, 6] stand on the three-tiered marble Dragon Pavement [7] with its triple staircases [8].

2 Chinese astronomers were the most persistent and accurate observers of celestial bodies anywhere before the Renaissance. The importance of the calender for a primarily agrarian society and the state interest in astrology meant that astronomy was of central importance in their lives. In contrast with Europe, scientific work was not a private concern, and astronomers often worked from the Imperial Observatory in Peking. Their observations, like the work of scientists in many other fields, were included in large encyclopedias that were compiled and published at state expense.

3 The tomb of the Ming Wan-li emperor (1573–1620) is situated at the foot of rugged mountains to the northwest of Peking. The complex is approached by an avenue lined with stone sculptures. Work on the tombs began in 1584.

4 The throne of the Ming Wan-li emperor from the interior of his tomb. Ming emperors generally enjoyed an unprecedented, although often abused, degree of power. Ultimately, the Ming dynasty fell to the invading Manchus, who seized Peking in 1644. but already during Wan-li's reign internal dissent and foreign attacks threatened Ming power.

Mongols, proved to be neither barbarous nor destructive, and grew to admire Chinese culture. One of their first acts was to request a group of leading scholars to write a history of the Ming dynasty, which was followed by a vast encyclopedia, the *Ssu-k'u ch'uan-shu,* comprising 36,000 volumes, begun in 1772 and completed nine years later.

The influence of the Manchu

Abroad, Manchu authority spread to Manchuria, Mongolia, Tibet, and Turkestan. During the Ch'ien Lung era their armies entered Burma, Nepal, and Annam [6]. As the empire grew in size and wealth, foreigners increased their pressure to trade with this huge untapped territory. The Jesuits, accepted during the Ming dynasty, were now followed by other Catholic orders from Europe, and before the end of the seventeenth century Franciscans, Dominicans, Augustinians, and others had established themselves in several cities in the interior.

European merchants did not penetrate China as readily as did the missionaries, but they persisted in their efforts and eventually limited trading facilities became available for the French, British, Dutch, and Portuguese. In 1784 the first of many ships from the United States arrived. By the mid-eighteenth century British trade, the monopoly of the British East India Company, had outpaced all others [8].

Chinese silk, tea, cotton, and porcelain were in endless demand in Europe; however, business could be carried out only through selected groups of Chinese merchants, the Co-Hung. There were no fixed tariffs, a policy that increased corruption among officials. The Chinese were forbidden to teach the foreigners their language, and foreigners had to submit to Chinese law in Chinese courts, where the Chinese, with their belief in group responsibility, held the foreign communities liable for the misdemeanor of any of their members.

Such conditions soon became impossible. The Western trading countries therefore sent missions to Peking [5], which began the lengthy process of bringing China out of its isolation.

KEY

This Ming imperial crown, decorated with a phoenix, is indicative of Ming wealth and their patronage of art.

5 The first official British mission to China was made in 1792 by Lord Macartney (1737–1806) and came at a time of demands for increased trading rights as foreign powers pressed for a foothold. Already the British East India Company had a monopoly over the trade in tea; however, the mission was treated by the Ch'ien-lung emperor as purely diplomatic.

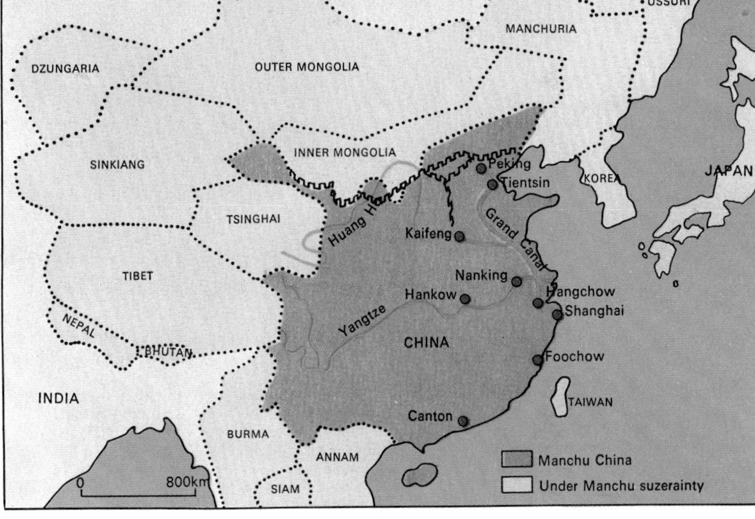
RUSSIAN EMPIRE
AMUR
USSURI
MANCHURIA
DZUNGARIA
OUTER MONGOLIA
INNER MONGOLIA
SINKIANG
Peking
Tientsin
KOREA
JAPAN
TSINGHAI
Huang He
Kaifeng
Grand Canal
TIBET
Nanking
Hankow
Hangchow
Shanghai
Yangtze
NEPAL
BHUTAN
CHINA
Foochow
INDIA
TAIWAN
Canton
BURMA
ANNAM
SIAM
0
800km
Manchu China
Under Manchu suzerainty

6 The Manchu Empire in 1800 covered a large area of central and Southeast Asia, but European and Russian expansion in search of trade already threatened this shaky conglomerate.

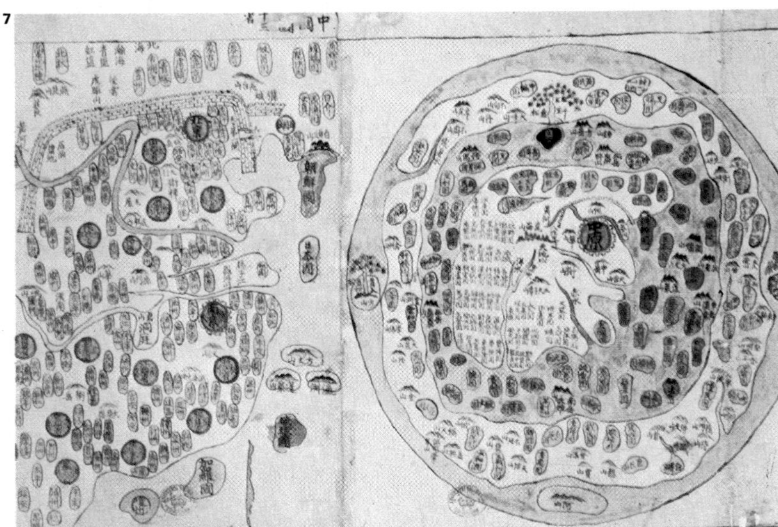

7 This Sinocentric map (*c.* 1800) shows China at the center of the world, both culturally and geographically, as a "middle kingdom" surrounded by barbarians. China was generally self sufficient and pursued a policy of aggressive isolationism, believing that little was gained by contact with others.

8 European ships moored in the port of Canton in the 18th century reflected the West's desire to trade with China. Western merchants regarded the China trade as an immensely rich prospect, but China refused to allow trading. From 1557 the Portuguese had had a monopoly of trade with China from Macao until the Dutch began to trade, but attempts by the British East India Company in the early 17th century failed to gain official approval. The Europeans pressed for greater trading concessions, but from the 1750s all foreign trade had to go through Canton and was supervised by the state. British trade in tea grew, and in the 1780s they began to smuggle opium from India.

Chinese art 1368 to the 20th century

With the establishment of the Ming dynasty, Chinese society, as reflected in the arts, underwent a renaissance. The style of the arts of the succeeding three centuries is reminiscent of that of the T'ang dynasty in its boldness and grandeur. The Imperial Palace (Forbidden City) [7] and the Imperial tombs of Peking, planned and initiated by the emperor Ch'eng Tan (1403–24), embody much of this style. The large scale of the buildings and the use of immense space in the courtyards and processional ways show the designers's confidence and flair.

The arts during the Ming dynasty

The applied arts also flourished, particularly during the earlier centuries of the dynasty. Carved lacquer of beautiful quality was made by masters in small workshops. By contrast, the less personal ceramic industry had grown to considerable production and was by now centralized on the great kiln area of Ching-te-chen, Kiangsi. This area became the center of supply for the rapidly expanding needs of the imperial palaces of the north and the growing wealthy classes.

Added to this home market, the overseas trade in ceramics was accelerating apace. The taste for decorated porcelain led to the development of new techniques. First, the use of underglaze painting in cobalt blue was perfected through various styles [1]; second, by the sixteenth century low-fired colored glazes painted on top of the primary porcelain glaze and refired produced the increasingly popular polychrome decorated wares. Cloisonné enamels on metal bodies also produced rich effects. This technique, of much earlier origin, may have come from the Near East. Eloquent yet simple jade carving was rare and had a stylistic affinity with early Ming lacquer work. In the later years of the dynasty there was a move toward elaboration, exemplified by the use of inlay and onlay of semiprecious stones on both jade and porcelain.

The fine arts of the Ming reflect the tastes and position of the scholar classes. At the beginning of the dynasty several styles of painting were practiced. The court attempted to reestablish an academy along traditional lines. Painters such as Tai Chin (1390–1460) [2] served for a time but soon retired and became the leaders of a group known as the Che School (centered in Chekiang). Using color and broad, wet brushwork, they produced marvelously evocative genre paintings of country people and elegant landscape compositions.

The great rival of the Che School was the Wu School, headed by Shen Chou (1427–1509) [3], a native of Wu Hsi. Painters of this group kept away from court and emulated the great Yuang dynasty masters, living as scholar literati and painting in an eclectic, erudite style. Shen Chou himself never took up official life. He was the first painter to use his own poetry as part of his painting and also to use figures in the composition in such a way as to invite the viewer to identify with the figure.

Wen Cheng-ming (1470–1559) [4], Shen Chou's pupil, showed a certain decorative quality in his work, which typified a movement that eventually caused concern to the purists. These scholars made an analytical and historical study of painting that was intended to rectify what they saw as a

CONNECTIONS

See also
1206 China from 1368 to c.1800
1270 The opening up of China
1044 Chinese art to 1368

1 **White porcelain** was made in a wide range of styles and decorated in cobalt and copper under glaze, as is this large wine jar from the 14th century, which was made at Ching-te-chen, Kiangsi. Cut-through techniques often included an inner decorated vessel.

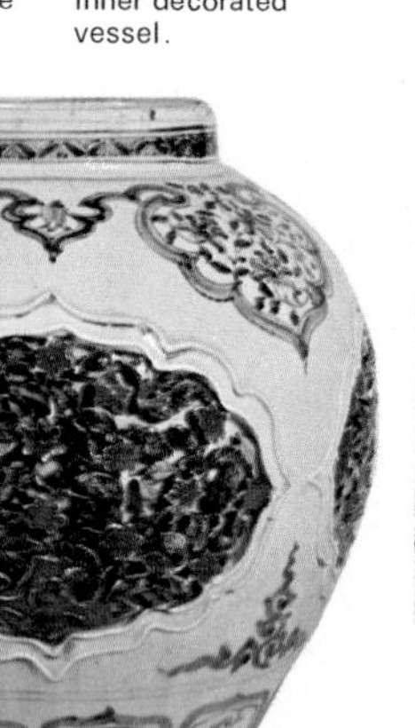

2 **A native of Chekiang, Tai Chin** became a court artist for a short time but he was banished to Hangchow, where he painted his major works. He is regarded as the leader of the Che School. This handscroll in ink color on paper is called "Fishermen on the river."

白雲如帶束山腰
石磴飛空細路遙
獨倚杖藜舒眺望
欲因鳴澗答吹簫
沈周

3 **Shen Chou** came from a scholarly family. At first he followed the Huang Kung-wang but later established his own simple style. This album leaf in ink is called "Poet singing in the Mountain."

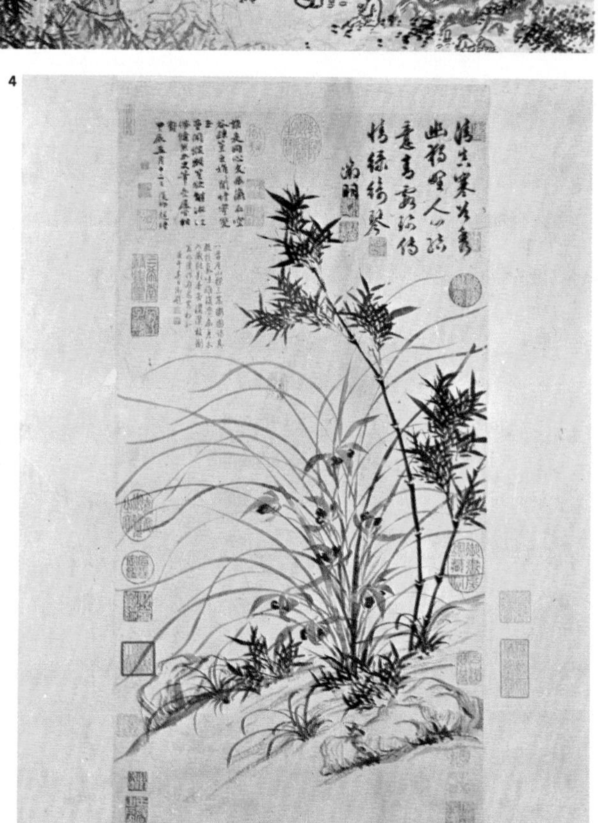

4 **Wen Cheng-ming** was the head of a notable family of painters from Tsang Chou. His style was both elegant and decorative and included the popular subject shown here of "Bamboo and Epidendrum."

trivialization. Their precepts and classification were a great influence on painters and critics of later periods.

From purist to romantic art

The painters of the generation following the purist Tung Ch'i-ch'ang [8] were mindful of his analysis, and the four Wangs (men with the surname Wang but not all related) are often regarded as being the followers of Tung. The two elder Wangs, Wang Shih-min (1592–1680) and Wang Chien (1598–1677), follow Wen Cheng-ming and the later Wu School. They painted large eclectic landscape compositions but were also part of the general movement toward a high Romantic style that flowered in the eighteenth century.

Contemporary with the elder Wangs were Shih T'ao (1641–1720) and Chu Ta (1626–1705), two minor members of the Ming ruling house who retired to monastic life at the fall of the dynasty. Shih T'ao was by inclination a scholar-painter who relied a great deal on literary inspiration. He was an innovator in the use of ink, color, and brush. Chu Ta, eccentric in personal life, was an instinctive Ch'an (Zen) artist.

At this time a generation of Romantic painters appeared. With the establishment of the grand courts of the Ch'ing, K'ang Hsi, Yung Cheng, and Chien Lung, Romantic art was served by the European Jesuit painters led by Castiglione (Lang Shi-ning, 1698–1768), whose curious Italianate Chinese style was true *chinoiserie*.

Chinese art to the present day

The newly wealthy towns of Souchow and Yangchow were the homes in the seventeenth century of innovative painters, known as the Eccentrics, who advertised their wares and painted for money. The eighteenth century saw a strong taste for archaism in all crafts. With the dawn of the nineteenth century painting moved slowly along the old paths of the seventeenth century. Twentieth-century Chinese artists have been unsure of their direction, and they experimented first with European and Japanese styles. Communism redirected the arts to serve political aims.

KEY

An inventive artist in both techniques and subject matter, Shih T'ao was a late 17th-century recluse who corresponded with his contemporaries and was one of the most influential artists in his own and later generations. His quite distinctive use of the surface texture of the paper, as in this landscape in ink and color, is still being explored by artists today.

5

5 Wu Ch'ang-shih (1842–1927) followed the broader ink style of the late 19th century as well as adopting then-current subjects.

6 Carved by Chu San-sung, in the 16th century, this bamboo brush pot was designed to hold a scholar's pens and brushes.

6

7

8

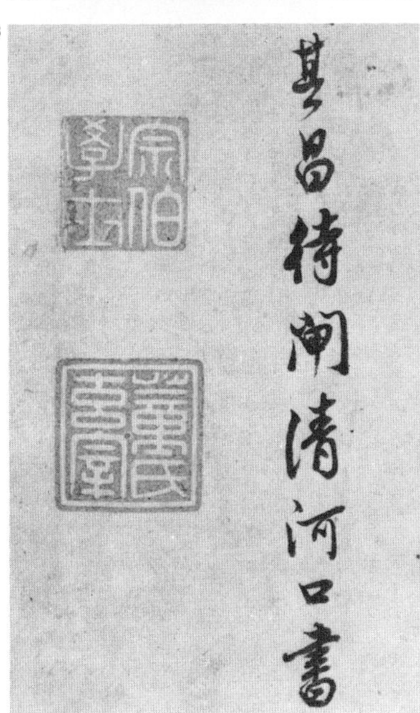
其昌待閘清河口書

7 The Forbidden City, palace of the Ming emperors, is enclosed within a large, rectangular, moated, walled compound. The central north-south axis is marked by a series of huge audience halls, each flanked by smaller halls and surrounded by large courtyards and tiered walks. The buildings are of gaily painted wood with yellow glazed roofs; the surrounding courts are constructed of white marble.

8 This calligraphy by Tung Ch'i-ch'ang (1555–1636) is strong and fine and typifies the Chinese scholar-painter's command of his art form. Tung was a theorist and historian who also painted landscapes.

9

9 Fu Pao-shih (1904–65), one of the major Chinese painters of the 20th century, studied in Japan in the 1930s and was highly influential as a teacher at the Nanking Academy of Arts. This is his "Scholar in his study."

Japan 1185–1868

In 1185, following five years of civil war, Minamoto Yoritomo ruled much of Japan from his headquarters at Kamakura. In Kyoto the emperor reigned, but effective power lay in the Minamoto house.

The new Japanese rulers

In 1192 the emperor recognized this new reality. Yoritomo was made shōgun (general), as head of the military class, and his followers were rewarded with further rights in land at the expense of their defeated enemies. Some became military governors of distant provinces; others supervised tax collection on the estates of imperial courtiers. On these foundations Yoritomo created a practical and efficient administration that gradually eroded the basis of imperial power. When Yoritomo died his widow's family, the Hōjō, became regents.

This new power produced a new spirit and a new culture. Warriors (samurai) rejected the ceremonies of established Buddhists and turned to a simpler religion.

In 1221 this dynamic government defeated an imperial revolt against its authority. Fifty years later it overcame a greater challenge from Asia. In 1274 and 1281 the vast Mongol armies of Kublai Khan [1] invaded Japan, but effective defenses repulsed these expeditions.

In time jealousy and hatred of the Hōjō grew, and in 1333 Ashikaga Takauji joined Emperor Daigo II in destroying their power [3]. The emperor then tried to reestablish his authority, but the Ashikaga house resented their poor rewards, and in 1336, Takauji drove Daigo II from Kyoto. Two years later he became shōgun.

Civil war

By 1467 the rising economic and military strength of the great provincial houses was uncontrollable. As the shōguns grew weaker, civil war broke out and continued for a hundred years. During this unrest, Europeans first reached Japan and began to influence its domestic politics. In 1542 the Portuguese arrived, and soon Jesuits began missionary activities. Some Kyushu lords were attracted by Christianity, but more so by firearms and trade.

When Oda Nobunaga (1534–82) began the task of unification, religious and secular forces obstructed his advance. In 1571 he destroyed the temples of monastic armies and two years later extinguished the power of the Ashikaga line. In 1582 he was assassinated in Kyoto, but his chief commander, Toyotomi Hideyoshi (1537–98), continued his campaign. Soon Hideyoshi dominated Japan and turned his armies against Korea. His death ended these adventures and left Tokugawa Ieyasu supreme at home. Ieyasu officially became shōgun in 1603 and sought to establish a regime that would restore peace throughout Japan [2].

Like his predecessors Ieyasu remeasured lands and regulated taxes. He relegated his enemies to outer provinces and concentrated his allies in central Japan. Lords or their families were compelled to reside at his new capital of Edo (later Tokyo). Confucianism became the official ideology in order to create a comprehensive social philosophy from the Samurai, code of conduct (bushido), and society was modeled on an agrarian ideal. Warriors were a

CONNECTIONS

See also
1046 Japan 200 BC–AD 1185
1112 Asian empires of the Mongols
1272 Japan: the Meiji Restoration
1048 Japanese art

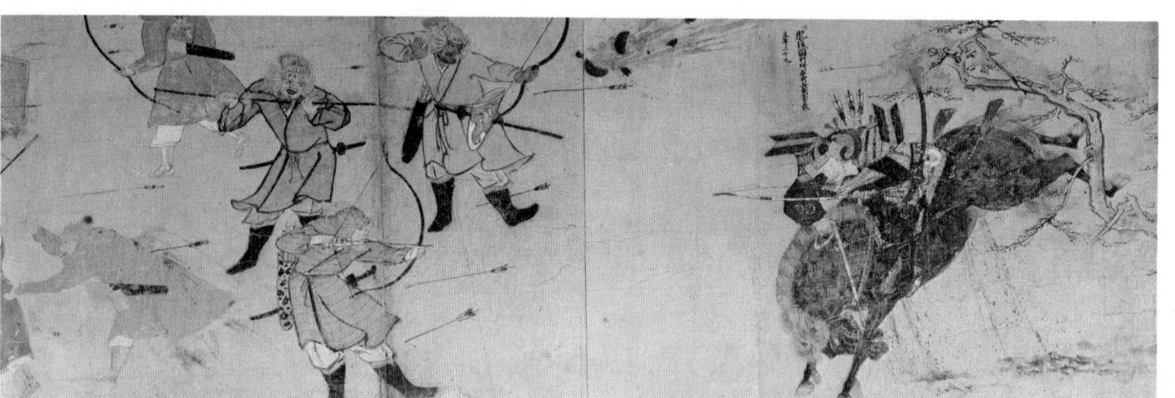

1 In 1274 Kublai Khan launched a force of almost 30,000 troops against western Japan, but violent storms drove his ships back to their bases. Seven years later a second expedition (shown here) landed in Kyushu. Well-organized resistance and gales combined to repel the invaders. There were fears of a further onslaught, but in 1294 Kublai Khan died, and preparations for a third attack were abandoned.

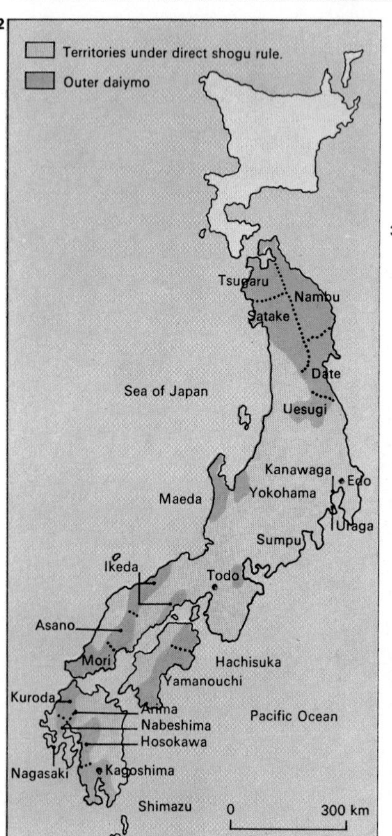

Territories under direct shogu rule.
Outer daiymo
Tsugaru
Nambu
Satake
Date
Sea of Japan
Uesugi
Kanawaga
Edo
Maeda
Yokohama
Uraga
Sumpu
Ikeda
Todo
Asano
Mori
Hachisuka
Yamanouchi
Kuroda
Arima
Nabeshima
Pacific Ocean
Hosokawa
Nagasaki
Kagoshima
Shimazu
0
300 km

2 Following his victory at Sekigahara (1600), Ieyasu redrew the political map of Japan to reduce possible threats to his supremacy. Eighty-seven families lost all their lands. As a result, the territory of Ieyasu and his allies was increased and concentrated in central Japan. Traditional enemies were relegated to outer provinces. With minor adjustments, these boundaries survived until 1868.

3 Ashikaga Takauji (1305–58) supported the Emperor Daigo II in destroying the Kamakura military government. Later he drove the emperor from his capital and made himself shōgun in 1338.

4 Tokugawa Ieyasu (1543–1616) was the son of a middle-rank lord who rose to become political master of Japan. After serving as a successful general under Nobunaga and Hideyoshi, he destroyed his rivals at the battle of Sekigahara. In 1603 he became shōgun and proved to be an astute and determined politician. He limited the emperor's power, and his regime continued until 1868.

privileged elite, farmers next in importance, craftsmen and merchants of lowest esteem. Ieyasu's successors developed his policies [7]. They also suppressed Christianity and restricted foreign trade in the interest of political stability. A few Dutch and Chinese merchants resided at Nagasaki [5], but no Japanese were permitted to travel abroad. The Dutch were tolerated because they had not tried to spread Christianity. These policies brought peace to Japan and preserved the Tokugawa regime.

The nineteenth century

One result of the Tokugawa peace was commercial growth, undermining samurai power. On several occasions after 1700 the shōgun's government tried to halt this development by returning to the principles of Ieyasu. Austerity was encouraged and officials dismissed. More land was cultivated, and townsmen were urged to return to their villages. Merchants made forced loans to warriors, and censorship increased.

Along with this growing domestic crisis, Japan faced increasing threats from the Western powers. At first, foreign ships were driven off and seclusion maintained, but this could provide no lasting solution. In 1853 Commodore Matthew Perry (1794–1858) led a US naval squadron to the Japanese coastline [6] and demanded stores and an opening up of diplomatic relations. After a year's delay his requests were granted, and similar agreements were made with other powers. Commercial treaties followed.

From 1859 the Western powers traded at Yokohama, Hakodate, and Nagasaki, and diplomatic contacts increased. The Tokugawa made more agreements with foreign powers, but many Japanese feared colonization. Foreigners were murdered, and warships brought destructive retribution. A sense of national crisis was felt throughout Japan. The Tokugawa built warships and cannon and began modernization [8]. Yet their measures seemed insufficient for national survival. Many turned to the emperor, long a figurehead, for inspiration. In January 1868 warriors from the western provinces restored his power [Key]. A modern imperial age had begun.

KEY

The Emperor Meiji (1852–1912), aged only 16 at the time of the Meiji Restoration (1868), played an important role in symbolizing its legality. In later years he was a focus for national unity and supported policies of modernization. He moved his court to Edo, which he renamed Tokyo.

5

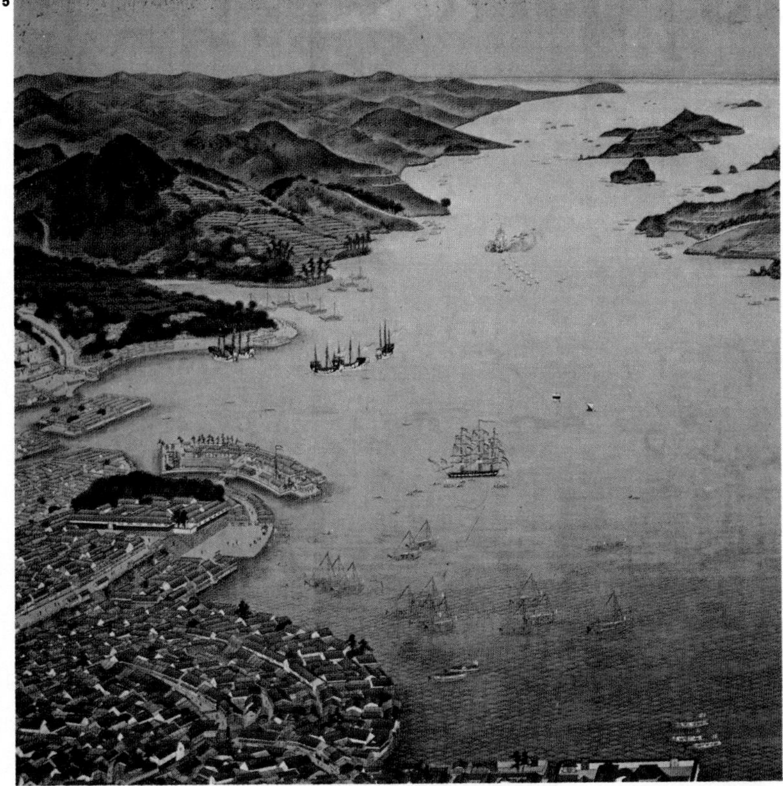

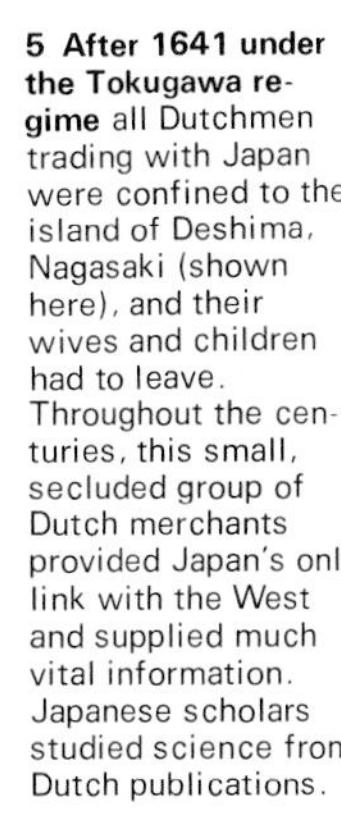

5 After 1641 under the Tokugawa regime all Dutchmen trading with Japan were confined to the island of Deshima, Nagasaki (shown here), and their wives and children had to leave. Throughout the centuries, this small, secluded group of Dutch merchants provided Japan's only link with the West and supplied much vital information. Japanese scholars studied science from Dutch publications.

6

6 In July 1853 Perry's naval squadron arrived off Japan to demand the end of isolation. These first talks were inconclusive, but in 1854 Perry returned to sign Japan's first modern treaty.

7

7 The Tokugawa Period (1600–1868) saw a growth in education and literacy. Village schools, such as this one at Okayama, gave a simple education to children from backgrounds other than samurai.

8

8 Following the forced opening up of Japan in 1854, the Tokugawa government feared a Western invasion and ordered the construction of this furnace at Nirayama to produce European-style artillery.

Sub-Saharan Africa 1500–1800

The appearance of a Portuguese fleet off the west coast of Africa in the mid-fifteenth century marked a new and decisive stage in the history of the continent: the beginning of a long and tumultuous relationship between Africans and Europeans. The Portuguese were followed by the Dutch in the sixteenth century and by British, French, and other Europeans a century later.

Complementary systems of trade

The many coastal trading posts that these Europeans established and linked to the Europe-based worldwide system of trade complemented an existing trans-Saharan commercial network. This network, which had been operating for at least 500 years, was forged between Arabic-speaking people from North Africa and black Africans living south of the Sahara.

As might be expected, these twin commercial presences influenced African development in a variety of ways—some brutally obvious, others subtle and hard to assess. Many Africans in the Sudanic belt had become Muslims in the 500 years of Arab trading in North Africa, and this fact set up stresses in African societies and eventually provoked the Holy Wars of the nineteenth century [7]. These states continued to look north to the Muslim world, just as some of the savanna and forest peoples began to turn to the Christian newcomers to the south for their external contacts. The massive depopulation of some regions and the encouragement of predator states has yet to be fully evaluated. Many peoples in western Africa, and nearly all those of central and eastern Africa, however, were entirely outside the direct influence of Arabs or Europeans until 1800.

The limited impact of the foreigners is illustrated by the history of the East African coast. There Arabs had established trading settlements at favorable harbors on the coast and nearby islands—for example, Mombasa and Zanzibar [3]. These settlements were part of a large and prosperous Muslim trading system in the Indian Ocean, which at the end of the fifteenth century was taken over by the Portuguese. By the end of the seventeenth century the East African settlements had reverted to Muslim control. Neither the Arabs nor the Portuguese in all this time had the least contact or influence with any but the peoples actually living on the coast, except in the Rhodesia/Zambia area, where gold led to inland forays.

Human beings—"a most profitable trade"

When the Portuguese first arrived in West Africa, they, like European adventurers in the New World, were interested in gold and luxury tropical products. But they quickly came to realize, as did the Dutch, British, French, and others who followed them, that the most profitable commodity in Africa was human beings [1]. The lands of South and Central America, the Caribbean islands, and the southern parts of North America required large numbers of laborers to exploit the silver mines and, more important, the tropical crops—sugar, coffee, rice, indigo, lumber, and cotton—grown there. Within a few decades the transatlantic slave trade came to dominate relations between blacks and whites in western and central Africa.

CONNECTIONS

See also
1116 African empires 500–1500
1268 Africa in the 19th century
1214 African art

1

To Europe
Tangier
Ceuta
Fez
Tunis
Tripoli
Cairo
St Louis
To the Americas
Lake Chad
Sokoto
Kano
Freetown
Accra
BENIN
Lake Victoria
Lake Tanganyika
Mombasa
Zanzibar
To India
To the Americas
Mozambique
Capetown
Overland trading routes
Maritime trading routes
Salt
Slaves
Gold
Hides
Ivory
0
1200km

1 Although Africa was a major source of various goods, it was primarily the slave trade that established Africa's link with the outside world, as well as expanding internal trade networks. There was a steady flow of slaves to Muslim lands, but most were shipped from west Africa to the New World.

2 Before they were shipped to the New World slaves were assembled in barracks, or barracooms, where they were treated as prize but unruly animals. The slave trade was so lucrative that European traders made little effort to develop large-scale trade in other commodities until the 19th century.

2

3

3 The great slave market at Zanzibar became the center of Arab trading on the east coast after the Portuguese evacuated it at the end of the 17th century. Here the Arabs traded with the native rulers who raided and enslaved their weaker neighbors, exchanging guns and cloth for slaves.

4 The inhuman packing of a human cargo is shown on this plan of the *Brookes*, a vessel of the late 18th century. The Atlantic crossing, the notorious Middle Passage, took a terrible toll of lives, and the sugar, cotton, and tobacco carried back to Europe was more profitable.

4

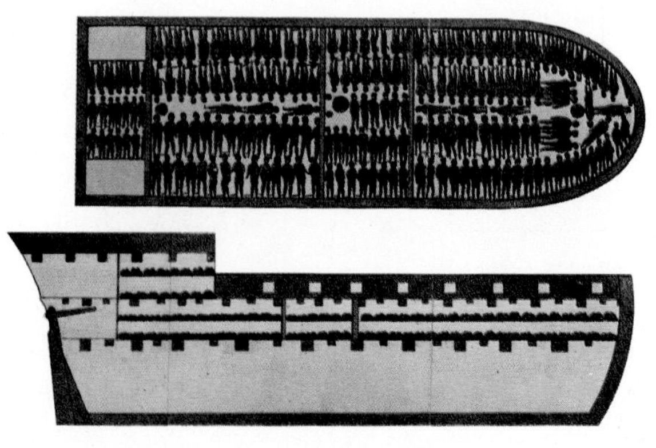

From 1451, when the first cargo in this barbaric trade was shipped across the Atlantic, until the early 1870s, when the slave trade finally came to an end, it has been estimated that almost 10 million Africans arrived in the Americas—one of the largest migrations of peoples in history. The peak of the trade was the 1760–1810 period, by the end of which most European countries had abolished the slave trade; during these years, over 4 million Africans were taken away from their homelands.

Most of the African slaves came from the inland regions—from Senegal around the bulge of West Africa to the Angola region of west-central Africa. The African middlemen, who sold the slaves to the European "factories" on the coast [5], prospered from the trade, as did states such as Asante and Dahomey [6], which grew powerful partly from their raids upon weaker peoples for slaves.

In the area of the Congo estuary and Angola, the Portuguese slavers and their agents ventured inland more actively. In the nineteenth century the East African slave-trading network, which until then had been in Muslim hands, was tapped to supply slaves to Brazil and Cuba, where slavery persisted longest in the New World.

There is no doubt that the slave trade greatly increased the level of violence among many African peoples. This is especially true of the Niger delta region, neighboring areas of southern Nigeria, the interior of Angola, and later in the period, east-central Africa, where Arabs controlled the trade. In a number of instances, the resulting breakdown of social order led to increased interference by Europeans.

Purely African cultures

During the period from 1500 to 1800, in the areas of Africa unaffected by the transatlantic slave trade, societies were developing under their own momentum. New and powerful states emerged—Ruanda and Buganda in the fertile lands between the great lakes of East Africa, and farther south, the states on the plateaus of central Africa. The kingdom of Monomatapa faced the Portuguese in the Zambezi valley.

KEY

Foreign influence—Muslim from the northern interior and European from over the sea—was a striking feature of African history between 1500 and 1800. African societies proved to be flexible but discriminating about these influences, a capacity reflected in their art. The kingdom of Benin, founded about 1400, was richly creative. Its artworks were mostly bronze sculptures. Benin sculpture was based on a tradition that was more than a thousand years older than the kingdom itself, but the artists managed to assimilate influences from western culture (note the rifle here) without abandoning their traditions.

5

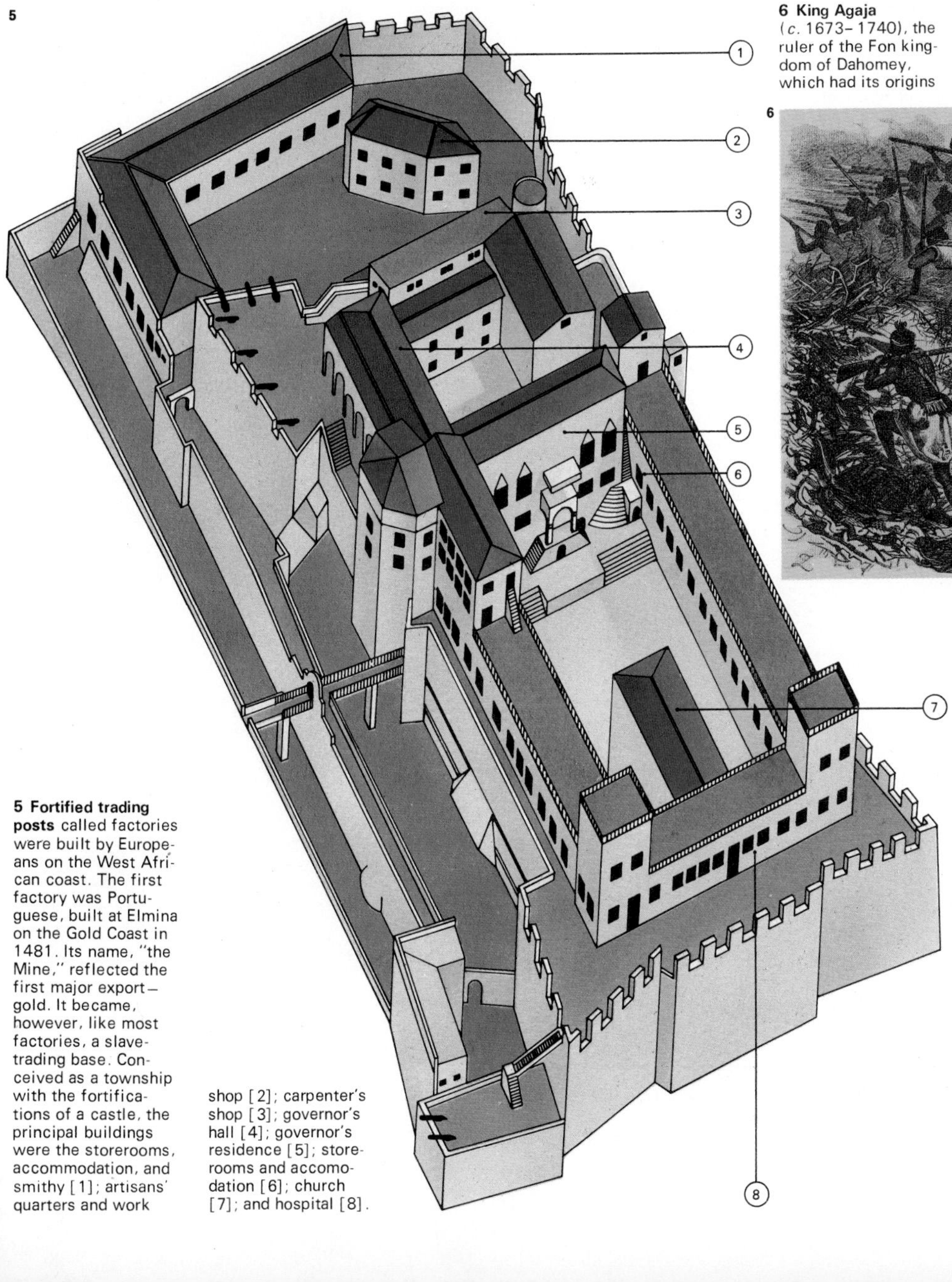

5 Fortified trading posts called factories were built by Europeans on the West African coast. The first factory was Portuguese, built at Elmina on the Gold Coast in 1481. Its name, "the Mine," reflected the first major export—gold. It became, however, like most factories, a slave-trading base. Conceived as a township with the fortifications of a castle, the principal buildings were the storerooms, accommodation, and smithy [1]; artisans' quarters and work shop [2]; carpenter's shop [3]; governor's hall [4]; governor's residence [5]; storerooms and accomodation [6]; church [7]; and hospital [8].

6

6 King Agaja (*c.* 1673–1740), the ruler of the Fon kingdom of Dahomey, which had its origins in the mid-17th century, controlled a powerful state. He was able to press many people into its service, including these famous units of women soldiers, in the drive to establish the state.

7

7 Kano in the north of Nigeria reached the height of its commercial power in the 18th century at the time of a Muslim revival. Usuman dan Fodio, leader of one of the principal Nigerian tribes, the Fulani, founded the Caliphate of Sokoto in 1807 and in 1809 took Kano.

African art

Present knowledge of the genesis and development of art in Africa is fragmentary, and it is often extremely difficult to relate styles even within restricted geographical areas. For example, the bronze castings of Igbo Ukwu in Nigeria bear no stylistic resemblance to the castings of Ife or Benin, despite the proximity of these cultures.

The genesis of Benin art

Benin art of the Niger delta is unique, for it is possible to correlate a vast body of works in brass, pottery, iron, ivory, and wood with traditions recorded and handed down orally, the evidence being provided by present-day local ritual and political forms and European records that go back to the late fifteenth century. By studying these sources, changes in style over the last five centuries can be dated relatively if not absolutely. The Portuguese, for example, who were the first Europeans to reach and trade with Benin, clearly had a profound effect on Benin art, although they certainly did not introduce the technique of brass casting. First, they made available vast quantities of metal in the form of the bracelets with which they purchased pepper, slaves, and ivory. This made possible the enormous expansion of the casting industry in Benin in the sixteenth century. Second, by their very presence, and perhaps by affording Benin artists the sight of "exotic" objects brought from Europe and the Orient in their baggage, the Portuguese traders stimulated them to invent and incorporate new forms and motifs in their art.

Today, as in the past, African art is the work of individual artists. Metalworking is always a full-time specialization, whereas among some peoples woodcarving may be essentially a self-taught spare-time activity at which anyone may try his hand, and which brings a man no special status in the community. Where, however, a woodcarver has been apprenticed to a master for several years, he may belong to a professional guild and work more or less full-time at his art. A talented carver is likely to be recognized in his community.

African sculptors working with wood or metal are always men, whereas pottery sculpture is usually produced by women, except in Benin (and perhaps in ancient Ife) where it is the work of brass casters. In any African community this division of labor between the sexes in the production of art is rigidly adhered to. Thus in Nigeria, for example, men weave as a full-time profession on one type of loom, while women weave for personal use on another type.

Ephemera and the unfinished object

In addition to sculpture in wood, metal, or clay, there are all kinds of less enduring forms in fabric, beads, basketry, feathers, leaves, wax, and so on, which are often ad hoc creations of a completely ephemeral character. Even wooden sculptures are likely to be decorated and redecorated by their owners using beads, seeds, bits of mirror, paint, and so forth. Indeed, the objects can hardly be described as finished when they leave the carvers, being liable to a variety of subsequent subtle transformations. This may perhaps reflect a greater preoccupation with process rather than with static form in art.

CONNECTIONS

See also

1212 Sub-Saharan Africa 1500–1800

1116 African empires 500–1500

1122 The age of exploration

1 The paintings and engravings on rocks all over the Sahara, like this example at Tassili, provide the earliest evidence of African art. They show a continuous development over the past 5,000 years in four main periods. In the earliest, wild animals are depicted, perhaps indicating a hunting way of life. In subsequent periods cattle, horses, and camels are introduced. Rock painting is also found elsewhere, especially in southern Africa, where it is probably the work of Bushmen. Murals are a common feature throughout Africa and are found in the houses and shrines of most tribes.

2 The earliest known sculptures in sub-Saharan Africa are the pottery heads and figures of the Nok culture (*c.*500 BC–AD 200) from the centers of northern Nigeria. Both human and animal figures have been found. Some of the heads are near life-size, broken from correspondingly large figures. The ability to fire large and complex pottery sculptures indicates a fairly high level of technology, which is shared only by the ancient Yoruba town of Ife (11th–14th centuries AD). The Nok culture also provides the earliest evidence of iron working in West Africa.

3 The working of iron follows directly upon that of stone in sub-Saharan Africa. The earliest evidence of bronze casting comes from the Ibo village of Igbo Ukwu, Nigeria, where 9th-century regalia and ceremonial objects such as this cylindrical stand have been excavated.

4 This brass figure was cast in ancient Ife, although it was found far to the north in a village on the Niger. Several heads and figures of brass and pottery in this extraordinarily naturalistic style have been excavated at Ife, together with other artifacts made of stone and glass.

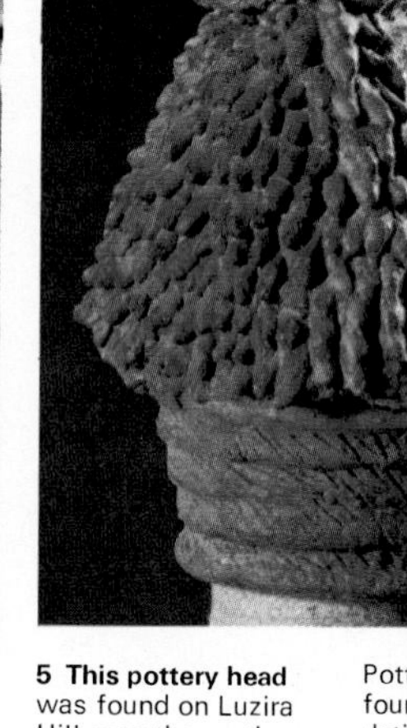

5 This pottery head was found on Luzira Hill near the northern shore of Lake Victoria in Uganda. Nothing is yet known about its age or the people who made it. The unfired mud statuary of the Edo and Ibo peoples may be a related tradition. Pottery sculpture is found all over Africa, dating both from the recent past and from antiquity. Among the many ancient cultures in which pottery sculpting flourished were the Nok culture, Ife, and the Sao culture of the Lake Chad region.

It is often wrongly said that there is no art for art's sake in Africa. Of course a sculpture may represent an ancestor, a god, or one of its devotees, or even some impersonal magical form that is manipulated for curing the sick, but it can just as well be an ornament for a rich man's house. Masks serve to disguise someone impersonating a spirit or an idea, yet while some masked figures are heavily charged with power or ritual significance, others are merely "costumed" entertainers devised for the delight of their owners.

African sculpture is, broadly speaking, concentrated around the two great river systems of tropical Africa, the Niger in West Africa and the Zaire or Congo in Central Africa. This curiously uneven distribution is partly explained by the distribution of the appropriate raw materials. Another factor is the more settled type of economy in these areas, whether agricultural or pastoral. People who are always on the move with their livestock, carrying all their belongings with them, are unlikely to see any need for sculpture. But even among some agricultural communities there are some for whom sculpture is unnecessary within the terms of their culture. In both West and Central Africa there are peoples who produce no sculpture, either because they do not need it or because they are satisfied with the work acquired from neighboring peoples. Equally, although a people may not have any sculpture of the kind that finds its way to a museum or art gallery, they may have a rich tradition of completely ephemeral forms that are dismantled after use.

A multiplicity of art forms

It would be wrong to assume that because people have no sculpture they have no art. Sculpture is, after all, only one among many arts that flourish in Africa, including architecture, mural decoration, textile design, pottery, leatherwork, embroidery, basketry, and, perhaps the most universal art of all, the decoration and adornment of the human body; and to the rich and varied visual arts of Africa must be added diverse types of music and song, dancing, and poetry and other forms of oral literature.

KEY

The art of Benin in Nigeria was created exclusively for the glorification of the king. The main forms of brass casting were memorial heads for the altars of dead kings and rectangular plaques mounted, in the 16th and 17th centuries, on wooden pillars in the palace. The early 16th-century ivory mask illustrated here was worn by the monarch as part of his ceremonial dress. Around the top of it is a tiara of Portuguese heads. The Portuguese first visited Benin in 1486. The clear derivation of Benin artistic tradition from that of ancient Ife disproves the theory that the Portuguese introduced brass casting to the Benin people. Ife long predates their arrival.

6 This pair of wooden doors was carved in 1915 for the palace of the king of Ikere-Ekiti in Yomtaland, Nigeria. Made by a famous sculptor, Olowe of Ise, they show the king receiving his first British administrator around the turn of the century. Wooden objects do not survive for long in Africa, with the result that much of the finest sculpture known now was carved only within the past 100 years.

7 Every king of the Bakuba people of Zaire had his portrait carved in wood during his installation rites, to house his spirit double. This custom was introduced by Shamba Bolongongo, 93rd king of the Bakuba, *c.* 1650, whose portrait is shown here. Shamba Bolongongo was a great innovator; he introduced weaving and textile manufacture to his people as well as initiating the custom of wood portraiture.

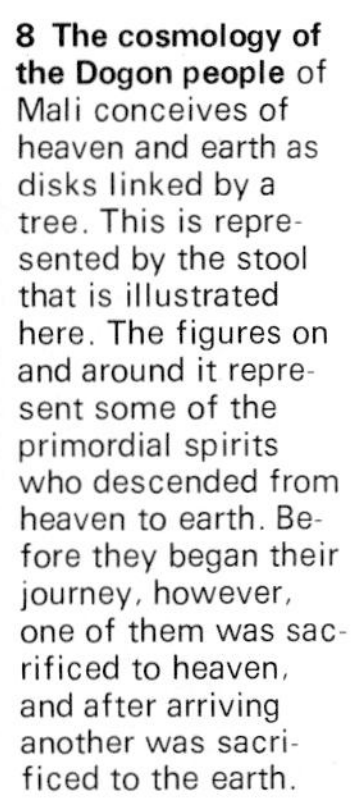

8 The cosmology of the Dogon people of Mali conceives of heaven and earth as disks linked by a tree. This is represented by the stool that is illustrated here. The figures on and around it represent some of the primordial spirits who descended from heaven to earth. Before they began their journey, however, one of them was sacrificed to heaven, and after arriving another was sacrificed to the earth.

9 These masks are worn during initiation rites among the Bwa, or Bobo-Ule, people of Upper Volta. They apparently represent particular animals, birds, and spirits, the symbolic associations of which provide some indication of the meaning and value of the rites themselves. Conversely, masks also derive meaning from the wider context of the performance—which includes costume, movement, sacrifice, prayer, and song—of which they are but a part.

10 The Nuta of southeastern Sudan are one of many peoples with complex systems of body painting. Some patterns are representational, and subjects are chosen if aesthetically worthy of imitation; other patterns, as illustrated, are nonrepresentational. The painting nevertheless follows precise rules and indicates social and physical status. Each clan has its own shade of red or yellow; the differences are slight but visible to the clans.

The settlement of North America

Discovery and settlement were long and often discontinuous processes; at times the English led the way, at others they trailed behind the Spaniards, Portuguese, and French. Eventually the greater part of settled North America was to fall to the English, while Spain held the stronger empire in Central and South America. The growth of the English economy in the late Middle Ages spurred settlement and was achieved through increasing mastery of the seas. Between 1400 and 1600 English seamen penetrated ever deeper into the Atlantic, to Iceland, Greenland, and what is now eastern Canada and northern United States.

The first emigrants from Europe

Settlement of the southern United States began in the sixteenth century: the first permanent city in North America—St Augustine, Florida—was founded by the Spaniards in 1565. They had conquered the densely populated empires of Mexico and Peru (the population of Aztec Mexico when they arrived is said to have equaled that of Western Europe). The English and French in the following century went to the West Indies and North America, where they found vast, sparsely populated lands inhabited by semi-nomadic peoples living at subsistence levels. After 1700 free migration, as distinct from the importation of black slaves, was nearly all into the English colonies of the Eastern Seaboard, although most of these migrants were not English but Scots, Irish, Germans, or Swiss.

The first serious attempt to found a permanent English settlement on North American soil was made by Sir Walter Raleigh (1552–1618) at Roanoke Island off the coast of North Carolina in 1584. This colony had a tragic history, for the first settlers vanished without trace. Raleigh's venture was partly a strategic move in the long sea war between England and Spain and, when his colony perished, the shoreline north of Spanish Florida was left open to competition by the European powers in the early seventeenth century. The next attempt to establish an English colony in the area, the Jamestown settlement—founded by the Virginia Company of London in 1607 [3]—was basically a commercial venture, although it also sought to help to build a strong merchant fleet, train mariners for England's protection, spread the gospel among the heathen in Virginia, and plant a Protestant colony in a land still threatened by Catholic Spain.

Principal reasons for settlement

Trade and religion were the two principal motives for the founding of North American settlements [7]. Religious enthusiasts from the British Isles, hampered at home by the Court of High Commission, were sometimes willing to venture into the unknown. Without the prospect of trade with Europe, however, they could only survive in subsistence conditions. During the 50 years following the foundation of Jamestown, further colonies were established, mostly by the English. Plymouth was established in 1620 by the Pilgrim Fathers, who sought religious and civil autonomy from the English government, and Maryland by Lord Baltimore, for Roman Catholics, in 1632. In 1625 the Dutch founded New Amsterdam,

CONNECTIONS

See also

1218 The American Revolution

1110 The world Europe set out to explore

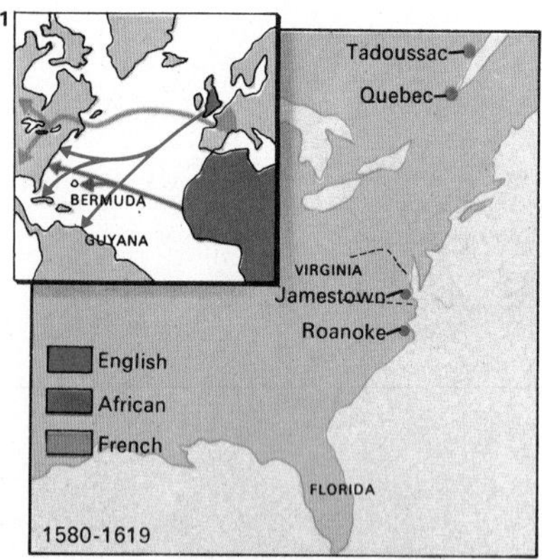

Tadoussac
Quebec
BERMUDA
GUYANA
VIRGINIA
Jamestown
Roanoke
English
African
French
FLORIDA
1580-1619

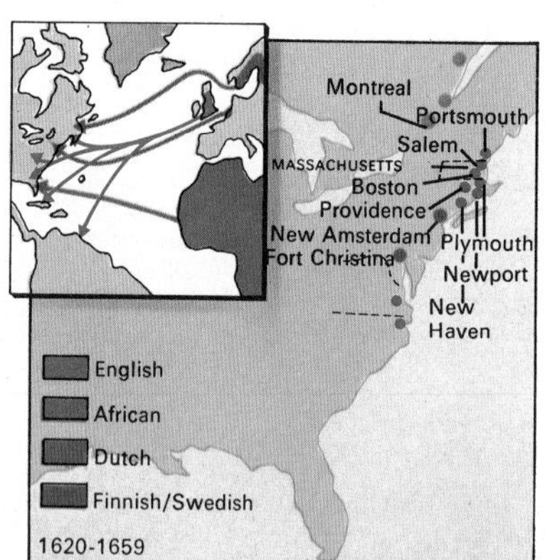

Montreal
Portsmouth
Salem
MASSACHUSETTS
Boston
Providence
New Amsterdam
Plymouth
Fort Christina
Newport
New Haven
English
African
Dutch
Finnish/Swedish
1620-1659

NEW HAMPSHIRE
NEW YORK
PENNSYLVANIA
MARYLAND
CONNECTICUT
NEW JERSEY
DELAWARE
English
African
Charleston
1660-1699

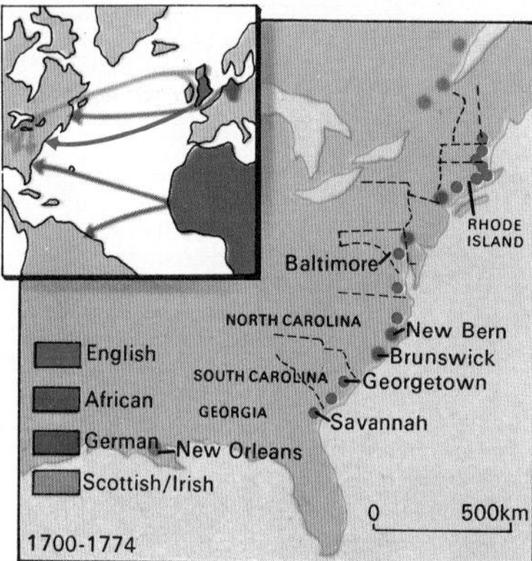

RHODE ISLAND
Baltimore
NORTH CAROLINA
New Bern
Brunswick
SOUTH CAROLINA
Georgetown
GEORGIA
Savannah
English
African
German
New Orleans
Scottish/Irish
0
500km
1700-1774

1 The pattern of migration changed over the years. From 1580 to 1619, England settled the Eastern Seaboard while France established settlements in Canada and down the Mississippi. The next 30 years saw the increase of African slave imports as well as the establishment of New England and the Scandinavian and Dutch colonies. Then England consolidated its hold and the Irish, Scots, and Germans led the march west.

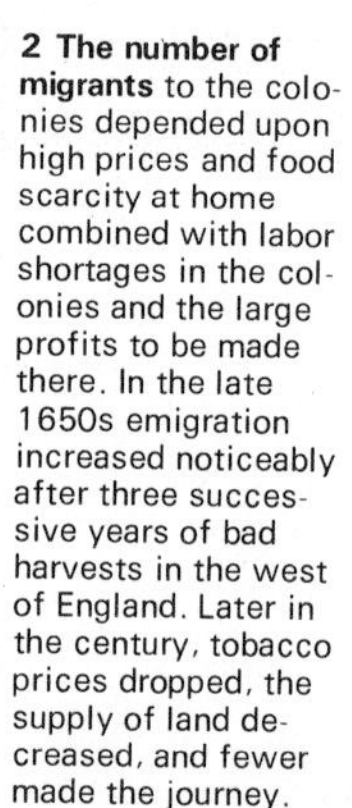

2 The number of migrants to the colonies depended upon high prices and food scarcity at home combined with labor shortages in the colonies and the large profits to be made there. In the late 1650s emigration increased noticeably after three successive years of bad harvests in the west of England. Later in the century, tobacco prices dropped, the supply of land decreased, and fewer made the journey.

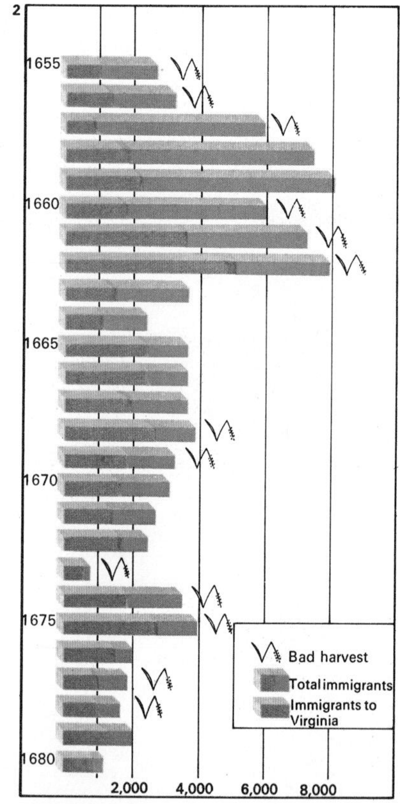

1655
1660
1665
1670
1675
1680
Bad harvest
Total immigrants
Immigrants to Virginia
2,000
4,000
6,000
8,000

3 James I (1566–1623) granted charters to some merchants to colonize the Eastern Seaboard. The Virginia Company of London was allocated what is now Virginia and Maryland; the Virginia Company of Plymouth, the coast of New England. This company's charter was revoked and a royal colony, whose seal is shown, established in 1624.

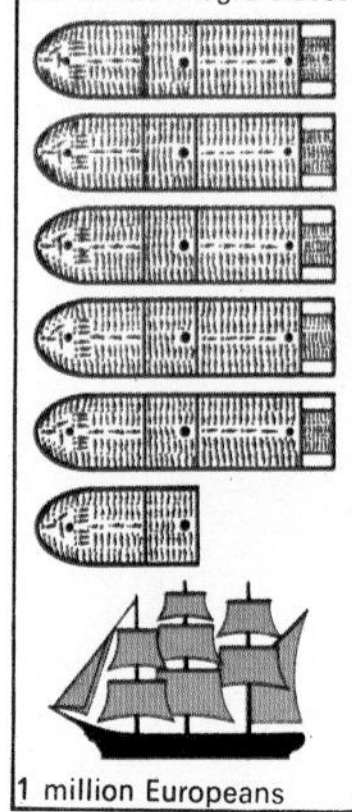

5.5 million Negro slaves
1 million Europeans

4 Six and a half million people had crossed the Atlantic to the New World by the 1770s. One million whites came from Europe—mostly from England, France, Germany, and Spain; the other five and a half million were black slaves from West Africa, who were transported in appallingly cramped conditions on the slave ships. They were chained flat on the decks or in the holds. There they could cause little trouble and needed less food.

BEST
VIRGINIA

5 Tobacco, introduced to Virginia in 1612, became the main export by 1619. Tobacco and cotton were to remain the staple products of the Southern colonies, despite many English attempts during the Colonial period to diversify the Southern economies. The Northern colonies, first a major source of furs and timber, developed their mineral resources, notably coal and iron, early, thus laying the basis for their industrial development.

later renamed New York, as a trading post, and they were soon followed by the Swedes and Finns, who sought to fill the gap that existed between the English to the north (New England) and south (Virginia).

French beginnings in North America stemmed from the trading activities of fishermen and fur trappers who established trading posts along the St Lawrence waterway. Samuel de Champlain (1567–1635) founded Quebec in 1608, and in less than 30 years the French had established posts as far west as Wisconsin. By 1660 a portage route from Lake Superior to Saskatchewan had been located, and by 1720 New Orleans was guarding the mouth of the Mississippi. Thus, by the mid-eighteenth century the French had occupied, if sparsely, the whole of middle America.

Influence of European events

Meanwhile, the Spanish North American empire, which included the whole coastline of the Gulf of Mexico as well as Florida, blocked English expansion to the south. But the Seven Years War (1756–63) [11] weakened France and Spain and allowed the English to fill the vacuum those two nations left in America. When George III (1738–1820) came to the throne of England in 1760, the French were confined to eastern Canada and the Great Lakes, while Spanish territory, vast although virtually unoccupied, stretched from Panama almost to the Canadian border west of the Mississippi. With the Treaty of Paris (1763). France lost all its North American possessions to Britain with the exception of the small island group of St Pierre et Miquelon, while Spain ceded Florida. Fearing a resurgence of French and Spanish power, however, the English set up a buffer zone west of the Alleghenies and east of the Mississippi, which they allocated as an Indian reserve.

Having consolidated their position, the British determined to exploit their possessions in North America, but it was the unwillingness of these colonies, now 13 in number, to submit to taxation without representation in Parliament and their desire to manage their own economies that led to the American Revolution.

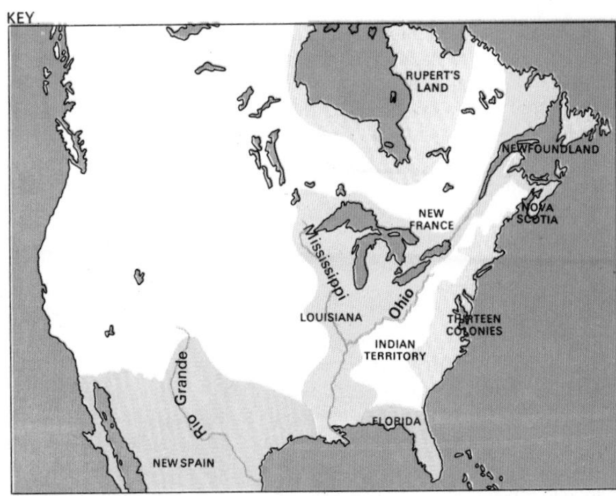
KEY
RUPERT'S LAND
NEWFOUNDLAND
NOVA SCOTIA
NEW FRANCE
Mississippi
Ohio
LOUISIANA
THIRTEEN COLONIES
INDIAN TERRITORY
Rio Grande
FLORIDA
NEW SPAIN
Under British control 1756
Under French control 1756
Under Spanish control 1756

Conflicting claims to the North American continent were the subject of intense rivalries among France, Spain, and Great Britain during the 18th century. By the Treaty of Paris (1763), Britain received all of France's important American possessions; Spain was too weakened to assert its claims to Florida.

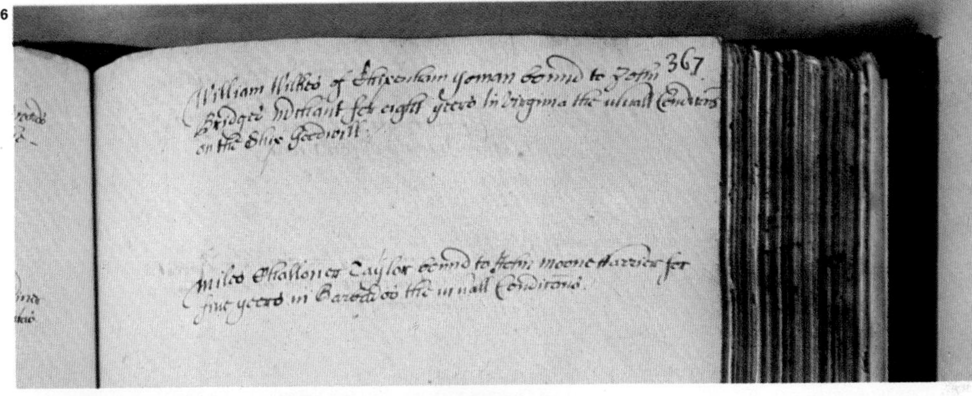

6 Indentured servants made up a large part of the total number of early emigrants. Orphans, petty offenders, political and religious prisoners, younger sons of impoverished landowners, and young men and women who possessed a taste for adventure and a better life bound themselves, or were bound, for a term of years, to work for a planter in Virginia or the West Indies. In theory they were taught to become planters themselves and at the end of their term, usually four or five years, they were allowed to go free and were given 50 acres (20 hectares) of land and other essentials to start their own farms. The indentures shown were recorded at Bristol, July 1660. The first reads: "William Wilkes of Chipenham Yoman bound to John Bridges Marchant for eight years in Virginia the usual conditions on the Ship Goodwill."

7 Many Quakers left England in the late 17th century when they came into conflict with laws passed at the restoration of Charles II concerning worship and freedom from oaths.

8 John Harvard (1607–38), an English clergyman founded Harvard College at Cambridge, Massachusetts, in 1636, within a few years of the establishment of that colony.

9 Pocahontas (*c.* 1595–1617), shown here in English court dress, was the daughter of Powhatan, an Indian chief in Virginia. Her marriage to John Rolfe provided a period of peace.

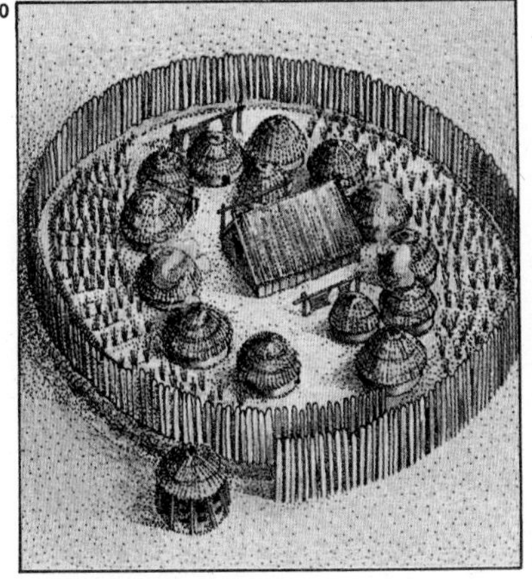

10 Indian villages, the homes of semi-nomadic hunters, bordered the rivers that flow into Chesapeake Bay and the creeks and inlets of New England. The early settlers bartered beads and trinkets for large tracts of land, some of it already cleared for cultivation, thus beginning the relentless process of Indian dispossession. Ports such as Baltimore and Annapolis were established around Chesapeake Bay by the beginning of the 18th century.

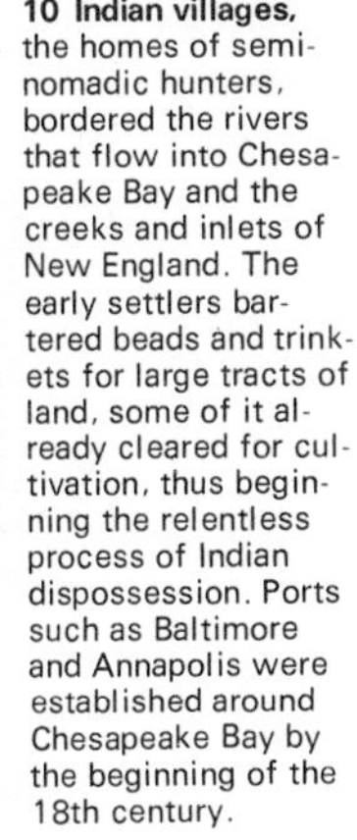
British Dragoon
French Infantryman

11 The British and French clashed in the Seven Years War (1756–63). Both sides adopted uniforms designed for splendor. Shown here is a trooper of the 10th British Dragoons and an officer of the Regiment de Saint Germain. A significant part of the war was fought in North America, where it was known as the French and Indian War. It ended in defeat for the French, and the Treaty of Paris (1763) vastly increased Britain's territory in America.

The American Revolution

The American Revolution was both a rebellion and an act of nation building. It was a political upheaval in which Great Britain's 13 colonies in America gained their independence and formed the United States. The revolution was also the first national struggle in modern times for the rights of the individual and for the establishment of a democratic government.

The British colonies

The Treaty of Paris of 1763, which ended 70 years of colonial wars between Britain and France, gave the British complete victory over the French in North America and control over vast new territories in Canada and as far west as the Mississippi. It caused fundamental changes in attitude both in Britain and in the 13 colonies. The colonists were now rid of the great external threat that had made them rely on Britain for defense. Since Britain was spending large sums to defend the new territories, it felt that the terms of trade with the colonies should be revised so as to improve their profitability and to increase the local contribution to defense. In addition, George III was determined to exercise royal authority.

To achieve these aims a Sugar Act was passed in 1764 and a Stamp Act in the following year; and wider use was made of Admiralty courts in their enforcement [1]. The colonies reacted strongly; demonstrations and rioting broke out. A congress was called in Albany, New York, that defined the major objections: first that the acts had been imposed by the British Parliament, where the colonists had no representation; and second that the colonists—like all British subjects—had the right to trial by jury rather than by arbitrary courts. Such was the opposition that the Stamp Act was repealed in 1766, but a Declaratory Act was added; it asserted that Britain retained the right to legislate for the colonies.

A year later, that claim was put into force with a series of acts—known as the Townshend Acts—taxing glass, lead, paper, and tea. Widespread unrest followed, climaxing with the "Boston Massacre" [4] in 1770. Most of the Townshend Acts were repealed, but in 1773 another Tea Act was passed giving favorable trading terms to the East India Company. The colonists again objected, and at the "Boston Tea Party" a cargo of tea was dumped into the harbor [3]. In Britain, acts were passed—the so-called Intolerable Acts—putting the government of Boston under direct British control.

First Continental Congress

Outraged, representatives of the colonies met in 1774 at the First Continental Congress in Philadelphia [2], where a petition was drafted insisting that there should be no taxation without representation. The congress also prepared an association among the colonies that would regulate their own trade. The British government replied that a state of insurrection existed, and both sides prepared for war.

The first fighting took place on April 19, 1775, when Massachusetts militiamen clashed with British troops at Lexington and Concord. The Battle of Bunker Hill [7] followed on June 17. A Second Continental Congress met and established an army with

CONNECTIONS

See also
1216 Settlement of North America
1236 Britain and the Industrial Revolution
1274 The United States: the opening up of the West
1192 British and American art 1530–1790
1224 The French Revolution

A Total British revenue from the 13 colonies 1763-4 £2,000 pa
B Cost to Britain of maintaining army in the colonies 1764 £350,000
C Expected yield of Sugar Tax £25,000 pa
D Expected yield of Stamp Tax £100,000 pa
E Total actual British revenue from the colonies 1764-8 £30,000 pa
C,D
B
E
A

1 During the 17th century, the British colonies in North America had had the right to tax themselves embodied in their charters and had thwarted attempts by the British to obtain any more revenue from them. But in 1763, faced with heavy debts and the need to support a standing army in North America, Britain tried to relieve some of the burden by imposing a series of taxes on the colonies without consultation. The taxes fell far short of Britain's revenue expectations, but they aroused the colonists in defense of their traditional rights, and "taxation without representation is tyranny" became a rallying cry of the revolutionaries.

Jefferson
Sam Adams
John Adams
Franklin
Hancock
Washington

2 The First Continental Congress, which met at Carpenters Hall in Philadelphia on September 5, 1774, was a gathering of delegates from 12 colonies (Georgia did not attend until 1775) called to prepare a declaration condemning British actions. There was little talk of independence, but the government in Britain reacted strongly, treating the actions of the congress as rebellion. When the Second Congress, some of whose leading figures are pictured here, met a year later, fighting had broken out. Although it had no statutory powers, it managed to maintain its position of leadership throughout the war. It took the vital steps to issue the Declaration of Independence and to move toward a federal constitution.

3 On December 16, 1773, about 50 colonists disguised as Indians boarded three British ships in Boston harbor and dumped their cargoes of tea overboard to discourage enforcement of a tea tax. British reprisals led to the calling of the Continental Congress.

4 The Boston Massacre (1770) was the first clash between colonists and the British. Mobs, angered by the occupation of Boston by British troops, jeered at and finally attacked the soldiers. The troops, acting without orders, fired on the crowd. Five men died as a result.

George Washington (1732–99) as its commander. As royal government collapsed, the Continental Congress became the recognized governing authority.

On July 4, 1776, the congress institutionalized the break with Britain by passing the Declaration of Independence, which gave a valuable boost to American morale but had little immediate effect on the precarious military position of the former colonies, whose coasts and trade were blockaded by British sea power and whose small, ill-trained forces faced the professional British "redcoats." The British commanders made only fumbling attempts to seize the initiative, however, and a force under General Burgoyne (1723–92) was surrounded and forced to surrender at Saratoga in 1777.

Victory for the colonists

This victory was crucial in persuading France to send a fleet to help the Americans and to declare war on Britain in 1778. The British fell back from Philadelphia, and Washington was able to contain them around New York. The British then attempted to switch the center of the war to Georgia and South Carolina. When an expedition led by General Cornwallis (1738–1805) attempted to march from South Carolina to link up with British forces in the north, it was cut off and forced to surrender at Yorktown on October 19, 1781 [6].

The defeat at Yorktown convinced the British that the war must be ended. Negotiations were begun in Paris with an American delegation led by Benjamin Franklin (1706–90) and John Adams (1735–1826), and peace was formally ratified in September 1783.

Beginning in 1781, the 13 states attempted with increasing difficulty a kind of national coexistence under the Articles of Confederation. A federal constitution was drawn up in 1787 and came into operation in 1789. A Bill of Rights was added in 1791 to protect the rights of individuals. The success of the revolution encouraged and inspired democratic and libertarian movements elsewhere in the world during the following decades, particularly in Europe.

KEY

1 New Hampshire
2 New York
3 Massachusetts Bay
4 Connecticut
5 Rhode Island
6 Pennsylvania
7 New Jersey
8 Maryland
9 Delaware
10 Virginia
11 North Carolina
12 South Carolina
13 Georgia

Ticonderoga, Saratoga, Concord, Boston, New York, Philadelphia, Brandywine, Yorktown, Charleston, Savannah

0 200km

The 13 colonies in America were the seeds from which the United States grew. Resentful of British taxes and repressive measures, stirred by the attractions of liberty and independence, they joined in 1776 to declare an independent nation.

5 American
British

5 British "redcoats" were well trained professional soldiers, generally superior in conventional battles to the less well trained American volunteers. It was General Washington who largely kept the patriot armies in fighting trim despite repeated disappointments, and who used the American skill in guerrilla tactics to wear down the British forces until they could be outmaneuvered.

6

6 General Cornwallis' forces surrendered to George Washington's command at Yorktown on October 19, 1781. Cornwallis was trapped between superior American forces on land and a French fleet at sea.

7

7 At the Battle of Bunker Hill, outside Boston on June 17, 1775, the Americans twice drove back British assaults before retreating. The first major battle of the Revolution, it was an expensive British victory, in which the Americans proved that they could fight.

8

8 Scottish-born John Paul Jones (1747–92) took the Revolution to sea by raiding British shipping. Called upon to surrender when his vessel *Bon Homme Richard* was battered by HMS *Serapis,* Jones replied, "Sir, I have not yet begun to fight," and went on to capture *Serapis.*

9 A primary objective of the Constitution was to establish a balance of power among the executive, the legislature, and the judiciary to prevent tyranny. Much power was reserved for the states, represented in Congress by the Senate, whose members were chosen (until 1913) by state legislatures.

9

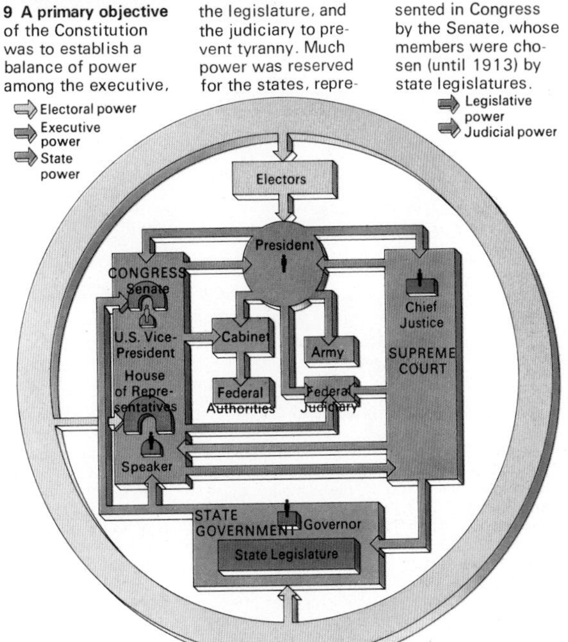

Electoral power
Executive power
State power
Legislative power
Judicial power
Electors
President
CONGRESS
Senate
U.S. Vice-President
House of Representatives
Speaker
Cabinet
Army
Federal Authorities
Federal Judiciary
Chief Justice
SUPREME COURT
STATE GOVERNMENT
Governor
State Legislature

10

10 Thomas Paine (1737–1809) emigrated to Philadelphia from England in 1774 and soon became one of America's most influential revolutionaries. His pamphlet *Common Sense* and his *Crisis* papers profoundly stirred popular sentiment in the country with their impassioned pleas for liberty, condemnation of tyranny, and powerful arguments favoring American independence. His tracts were distributed to American soldiers to bolster morale during the war.

The early Industrial Revolution

Britain was the first industrial nation in the world. By the middle of the eighteenth century there was already a thriving commercial economy, with a growing population, developing agriculture, and expanding trade both at home and abroad.

Population growth

The growth of Britain's population from the mid-eighteenth century was not directly caused by industrialization, although a large work force was an essential factor in the development of industry. A run of good harvests in the first half of the century, low food prices, favorable climatic conditions, the decline of plague, and a number of minor improvements in health all contributed to lower death rates and a consequent rise in population [2]. By the end of the eighteenth century, birthrates also began to rise as people in the industrial towns were able to marry earlier and to have, and keep, more children. Unlike Ireland, where population growth led to impoverishment, Britain's commercial and agricultural prosperity meant that a growing population contributed to increasing demand for all products. Increased consumption was a great stimulus to industrial innovation and improved methods of production.

In the past, periods of expansion had been brought to a halt by harvest failure, over-population, and economic downturn. By the middle of the eighteenth century, the profits of thriving overseas trade enabled landowners to borrow capital to increase agricultural production. With increasing demand and prices for foodstuffs, agricultural expansion followed. The enclosure movement grouped the old open fields and common lands into individual, more efficient units, on which more productive techniques could be applied, such as improved animal husbandry, new root crops, and the first agricultural machines. Enclosure, secured through parliamentary acts, had affected about 20 percent of the area of England by 1845. Capital was required to make the most of enclosure, and it led to many smaller farms being amalgamated into larger holdings. Contrary to common myth, enclosure did not depopulate the countryside but often increased the demand for agricultural labor.

Increased demand

The continued profitability of foreign trade [1], particularly as the colonies grew, provided the capital for increases in production to meet demand at home and abroad. One of the first industries to feel this increased demand was mining, with the need for more domestic and industrial fuel. Output was increased 400 percent in the course of the eighteenth century through the use of steam pumping engines to keep mines from flooding. Coal was an important raw material for many industrial processes as well as the fuel for steam power. Coal and iron together laid the foundations for the development of industry [4]. The iron industry of the early eighteenth century depended on charcoal for smelting and had a relatively small output. The discovery by Abraham Darby of coke-smelting at his Coalbrookdale works in the 1730s revolutionized the production of cheap iron and enabled it to be used in the first machines and iron structures.

CONNECTIONS

See also
1236 The Industrial Revolution
1186 Exploration and science 1750–1850
1284 European industrialization 1870–1914
1182 Europe: economy and society 1700–1800
1200 International economy 1700–1800
938 Industry and economics
1584 Modern technology
1594 The Steel Age

1

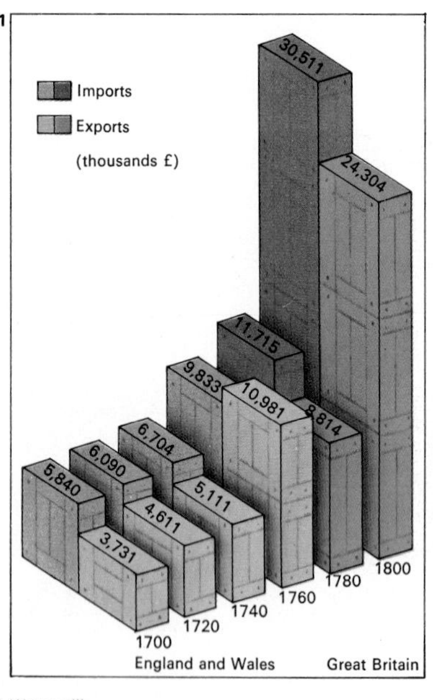

Imports
Exports
(thousands £)
30,511
24,304
11,715
9,833
10,981
8,814
6,704
6,090
5,111
5,840
4,611
3,731
1700
1720
1740
1760
1780
1800
England and Wales
Great Britain

1 British industry was stimulated by growing demand, both at home and abroad. Its overseas trade experienced a rapid expansion from the 1680s, providing new market opportunities and the capital for investment in new techniques. New colonial markets acquired after the Seven Years War proved lucrative, as Britain engaged in the "Triangular Trade," carrying manufactured goods to Africa and the West Indies, transporting slaves across the Atlantic, and bringing back colonial products to Europe. Britain's largest export commodity in the first half of the 18th century was woolen textiles, overtaken later by cotton.

2

2 Europe's population increased from the 1750s, and despite some appalling conditions in towns (here shown at one extreme in one of William Hogarth's Gin Lane pictures), mortality rates declined. The cause of this is not fully understood but may have been related to the end of plague epidemics after 1700 and improvements in hygiene after 1800, such as the availability of cheap soap, easily washable cotton clothing, and improved water supply. Increased population because of earlier marriage and larger families provided a growing market for cheap industrial products and also the necessary ready supply of labor.

3 Water mill

3 Mills driven by water provided the moving force for many processes before the Industrial Revolution, including grinding grain and spinning yarn. A flourishing woolen industry already existed in areas where waterpower was readily available, such as the Cotswolds, East Anglia, and the West Riding of Yorkshire. Many early machines could be driven by water power, and the first phase of industrialization was based almost entirely upon the use of water-driven machinery. Both the cotton and woolen industries developed on the slopes of the Pennines with abundant water power. It was only with the development of efficient steam power after 1776 that industry began to concentrate on the coalfields and was freed from dependence on the hilly regions. The use of coal and invention of coke-smelting enabled industry to grow more quickly, escaping the problems of a critical shortage of wood for fuel.

4

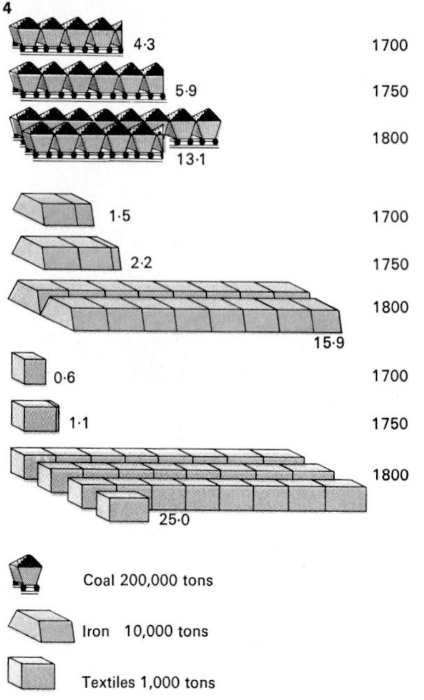

4·3
1700
5·9
1750
13·1
1800
1·5
1700
2·2
1750
15·9
1800
0·6
1700
1·1
1750
25·0
1800
Coal 200,000 tons
Iron 10,000 tons
Textiles 1,000 tons

4 The most striking developments in 18th-century industry were shown in coal, textile, and iron production. Coal mining increased with the rise of steam power, an expanding population, and improvements in communications. Wool output rose to meet domestic and foreign demand but mainly used traditional processes. Cotton production grew dramatically with the use of machinery and steam power until it became Britain's principal export commodity. Iron production also increased rapidly with the introduction of coke-smelting. These developments were evidence of a broad expansion of techniques to meet opportunities presented by rapidly growing markets.

Allied to these developments was a major advance in technological power following the patenting of the improved Boulton and Watt steam engines after 1774. They used much less fuel than earlier models. Besides pumping, Watt's steam engine of 1769 was harnessed to drive machinery. The use of steam power drew industry away from the old sources of water power [3] toward the coalfields.

Labor-saving machinery

After steam power, the most important innovations were associated with the growth of labor-saving machinery. They occurred most dramatically in the cotton industry, which witnessed technical breakthroughs in weaving (Kay's flying shuttle, 1733), then in spinning [Key], and gradually in other processes. The harnessing of steam power to machinery in the cotton industry led to the first factories in which the production processes were concentrated under one roof [7]. Although many factories still relied on water power [3], the development of the factory system in cotton foreshadowed the growth of the factory and the use of steam in other industries. Woolen production, for example, expanded mainly by using traditional methods such as water power. Gradually, however, the introduction of machinery and the use of steam power drew it toward the coalfields of Yorkshire.

Concentration of production needed both capital and cheap transport. Capital was provided out of the profits of agricultural improvement and overseas trade. Country banks, although subject to panics and bankruptcies, provided a basic network of credit for industrial and agricultural development. By 1800 there were about 70 London banks and about 400 country banks, usually issuing their own notes. The Stock Exchange was founded in 1773 and soon became a focus for raising capital.

Land transport remained slow and expensive for bulky products, in spite of the development of turnpikes. With the development of the canal network—by 1815 there were almost 2,000 miles (3,200km) of canals—bulky products could be moved cheaply by water [6].

KEY

The use of machinery during this period greatly increased the production of goods. James Hargreaves' spinning "Jenny" (1764) increased the spun-cotton output.

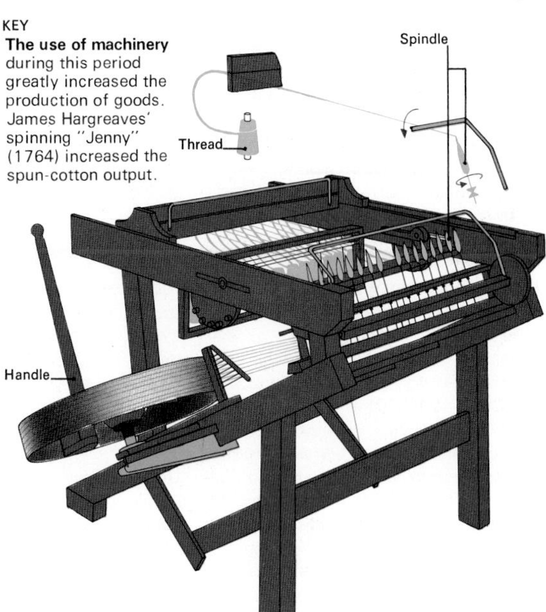
Spindle
Thread
Handle

5

6

7

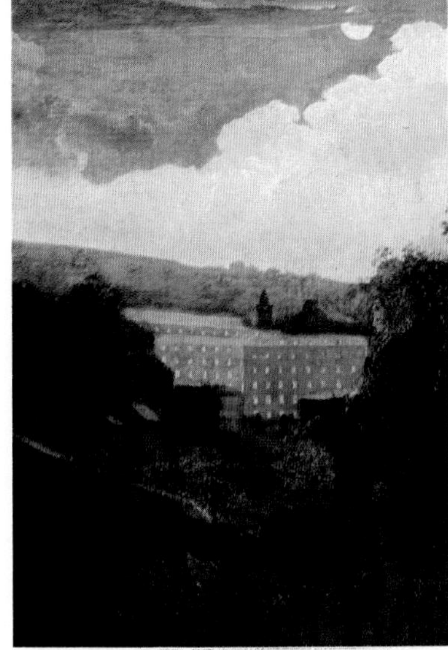

5 Agriculture could be highly profitable in the late 18th century, thanks to a growing population and new techniques, as witness this substantial farmhouse in Gloucestershire, England. Enclosures grouped fields more efficiently, permitting the use of four-crop and other rotations, while selective breeding and inventions such as Jethro Tull's speed drill contributed to increased agricultural prosperity.

6 Transport developments played a vital part in the Industrial Revolution by widening markets and allowing production to be concentrated where goods could be brought by cheap bulk transport. Turnpikes and improved road surfaces increased passenger traffic by road, but the most important advance for industry came with the growth of canals. England's Bridgewater Canal between Worsley and Manchester was built for the Duke of Bridgewater by James Brindley (1716–72), an engineer who remained illiterate until his death. The canal, opened in 1761, halved the cost of coal in Manchester by reducing transport costs. In the "canal mania" that followed, an extensive canal network was built up, giving many early industries access to raw materials and markets.

8 Josiah Wedgwood (1730–95) pioneered the large-scale production of china at his Etruria works near Stoke-on-Trent. He was a self-educated man and typical of those who made the Industrial Revolution.

8

9

7 A pioneer of the factory system, Sir Richard Arkwright (1732–92), built this cotton mill at Cromford, Derbyshire, which Joseph Wright of Derby painted in the 1780s. The first factories were built for the textile industry, where mechanization and the use first of water power, then of steam, made concentration of production essential. Factories increased in size as steam became the principal source of power. The words *factory* and *mill* were long interchangeable.

9 Labor conditions were often bad in the early stages of the Industrial Revolution. Child labor was common, especially in the textile industry, with long hours of work, low pay, and frequent accidents. Women also worked in the textile factories, where they made up half the work force. Although women and children had worked on the land, these new industrial conditions provoked a series of parliamentary inquiries in Britain and by the mid-19th century Factory Acts were passed, restricting hours of work and prohibiting women and children from certain areas of employment, such as work underground. By 1900 most other industrialized countries had also introduced some forms of factory legislation.

Origins of romanticism

The reaction against the Enlightenment began early in the eighteenth century and was evident in many isolated ways that eventually coalesced in the great pre-Romantic period of 1770–98. The Enlightenment had asserted the powers and worth of the individual, laying the philosophical foundations of an individualism that the Romantics elevated to subjectivism. Romanticism rejected rationalism, exalting the emotions as the source of all truth.

Influence of Celtic mythology

One theme is clearly evident in the mid-eighteenth century: a fascination with Scandinavian and Celtic mythology and antiquities. Among many who explored this legacy, Thomas Percy (1729–1811) translated runic poetry from the Icelandic in 1763 and Thomas Gray (1716–71) sought inspiration from Scandinavian sources for works such as *The Descent of Odin* (1761); but the audacious efforts of James Macpherson (1736–96) soon eclipsed all others. His *Fragments of Ancient Poetry* (1760) derived from Irish cycles that had found a way into Scotland and the success of this work led to *Fingal* (1761) and the Ossian phenomenon [6], a timely invention of sublime Celtic lore that lent greater impetus to the European Romantic movement.

Although romanticism quickly spread to painting and music, its origins and first expressions were predominantly literary—German and English. In 1765, Percy's *Reliques of Ancient English Poetry* brought the strength and freshness of the ballad into the literary domain; at about the same time a *cause célèbre* centered on Thomas Chatterton (1752–70), who devised medieval imitations alleged to be by Rowley, a fifteenth-century author, as well as writing his own poems.

Genuine scholarship

While Chatterton indulged in his "pious fraud," genuine scholarship looked into the past to assist the revival of romance. *Letters on Chivalry and Romance* (1762) by Richard Hurd (1720–1808) and Thomas Tyrwhitt's edition of Chaucer's *Canterbury Tales* were influential.

Romantic curiosity was not merely academic. A new feeling for landscape took men on journeys to the wild Hebrides, to unknown mountains, in search of the physically "horrid and sublime" and, later, the picturesque and romantic. These pursuits would have been almost unthinkable at the beginning of the century under rational classicism. The latent awareness of nature was to bear fruit with the Lake Poets of the 1820s such as Wordsworth, Coleridge, Keats, and Shelley. Countries of the mind appeared in works such as *Rasselas* (1759) by Samuel Johnson (1709–84) and *Vathek* (1786) by William Beckford (1760–1844), a potent tribute to the fascination of the Orient.

In 1771, Henry Mackenzie (1745–1831) published *A Man of Feeling*, a slight novel of sentiment that attested the influence of Jean Jacques Rousseau (1712–78), the man of nature and feeling par excellence, who, with Johann Herder [2] (1744–1803), was the great theoretical precursor of European romanticism. Rousseau's early involvement with the *encyclopédistes* turned into a conflict of head and heart, and it is the

CONNECTIONS

See also
1184 The Enlightenment
1228 Romantic art: figure painting
1242 Romantic art: landscape painting
1240 Poetry and theater in the 19th century
1246 Music: the Romantic period
1256 Opera in the 19th and 20th centuries
1104 Gothic art of the 14th century
1106 Gothic art 1400–1550
1190 The Rococo

1

1 Horace Walpole (1717–97) converted a farm at Twickenham into a "little Gothic castle" and for 40 years added architectural detail, armor, and stained glass, largely derived from chapels and cathedrals of Europe. A "Strawberry Hill Committee," consisting of Bentley the archeologist, Walpole and others, was virtually the originator of the revival of Gothic. Because of his influential social position, Walpole was an unconscious instrument of melancholy romanticism and the inspirer of many monastic country houses.

2

2 Johann Herder remains the most significant harbinger of the Romantic movement. His real achievement was the effect he had on Goethe's outlook. The young author's Rococo ideas were replaced by concepts of spontaneity and originality, and he was introduced to popular poetry, to Ossian and Shakespeare. Herder's own important statement of the *Sturm und Drang* movement appears in two essays written in 1773. He particularly sought to establish the *Volkslied* (folk song) as the only valid poetry.

3

3 Thomas Parnell's poem "A Night Piece on Death" (1721) initiated the morbid and Baroque "Graveyard School." Robert Blair's "The Grave" (1743) in this pre-Romantic style was illustrated by the painter William Blake in 1808.

4

4 The new interest in Shakespeare owed much to Herder, whose essay *Shakespeare* (1773) celebrates him as an irrational genius, a philosopher of folk-poetry. This illustration of Lady Macbeth is the work of Henry Fuseli (1741–1825).

5

5 The poetic wonder of Goethe's old age, *Faust* (Part I 1808, Part II 1832) grew from a lifetime of reflection. The ultimate transformation of the medieval alchemist into the troubled Romantic scholar was Goethe's symbol of man in search of experience and salvation.

supremacy of the heart that infuses *La Nouvelle Héloïse* (1761), a novel in letter form that extols simple virtue.

Its enormous success was followed by Rousseau's equally important *Emile* (1762), a novel that revolutionized the concept of education. The child, Rousseau maintained, should grow under the moral influence of nature's laws, protected from ready-made instruction, a theory that still has echoes in modern thought. Rousseau exercised a profound influence on English literature and the French Romantic movement.

The influence of Germany

Germany, however, can be regarded as the first home of romanticism. There it took on its most characteristic forms. Of its theorists, Gotthold Lessing (1729–81) was of prime importance. He dismissed the old classical forms, extolled Shakespeare as a model, and drew attention to the resources of German folk song. Shakespeare [4] was first translated into German by Christoph Martin Wieland (1733–1813), a move that further advanced the *Sturm und Drang* [2] (storm and stress) movement, which embraced a number of young poets, including Goethe, and placed an overwhelming emphasis on intensity of passion.

Rousseau's counterpart, the critic Herder, was also paving the way for German romanticism. His advocacy of a return to nature—and to him Shakespeare was a natural phenomenon—and his precognition of Faust's "feeling of all," guided the young Wolfgang von Goethe (1749–1832 [8]) at Strasbourg into inspirational rather than classical paths. Goethe's multifarious activities and literary achievements, and his fusion of both rational and Romantic elements mark him as the supreme Romantic figure, unsurpassed in European literature.

Many strands were woven into later Romantic attitudes. None equaled the decisive impact of the French Revolution. Where madness and melancholia had been the escape route of the forerunners of romanticism, those who followed were educated to a new freedom.

KEY

George, Lord Byron (1788–1824), was by temperament and tragic destiny an arch-Romantic. His voluminous poetry, reckless in its spontaneity and expressive of his disenchantment, had a hypnotic effect in Europe, beginning with the first two cantos of *Childe Harold's Pilgrimage*.

6

6 The misty Celtic world of Ossian was a rich and enormously influential vein in European Romanticism. Ossian was a semilegendary third-century Irish poet-warrior (here dreaming over his lyre); Macpherson's "translation" of Ossian in 1762 created a cult that spread throughout Europe within a few years. Despite some fierce academic criticism, few suspected that Macpherson had invented freely, with only passing nods to genuine Celtic lore.

7

7 Siegfried, a hero both of Germanic and Norse legend, is a principal figure in the *Nibelungenlied.* The imposing mythology of the Rhineland attracted much attention from early Romantic writers and painters seeking to establish a mystical German tradition.

8

8 Goethe's own disappointment in love was the foundation for his *Sufferings of Young Werther* (1774). The hero's intensity of feeling, dramatic gestures (as in this illustration), and later suicide inspired imitators, thus ensuring Goethe's notoriety.

9

9 The first substantial Romantic, who "lost his native country and conquered Europe," Lord Byron took Spain, Italy, the East, and Greece as a background for his aristocratic individualism. A fervent ally of the Greeks, he died supporting their struggle for independence.

The French Revolution

The prestige and apparent power of the absolute monarchy that Louis XIV (1638–1715) had built up disguised fundamental weaknesses that were to become serious under his successors. French society was increasingly divided into a small aristocracy jealously defending its privileges of wealth and partial exemption from taxation [2]; a growing middle class frustrated by its lack of political power and the incompetence of royal government; and the peasantry, which did not own enough land for security from bad harvests, and which hated the feudal dues it had to pay the aristocracy.

Calling of the Estates-General

During the reign of Louis XV (1710–74), royal prestige was damaged by a series of disastrous wars with Britain, and the government went deep into debt despite a general increase in trade and industry. Even success in helping the American colonists [1] at the beginning of the reign of Louis XVI (1754–93) in 1774 only highlighted the contrast between American ideals of liberty and democracy and repression and privilege in France. An economic slump began in the 1780s, and an attempt was made to tax the privileged classes. They refused to pay, and the king was forced, for the first time since 1614, to call the Estates-General. When this met in 1789, the Third Estate—the bourgeoisie, or middle classes—swiftly tired of the actions of the aristocracy and clergy and on June 17 proclaimed itself a National Assembly [4A].

While this political crisis had been growing, a disastrous harvest in 1788 had brought many peasants and industrial workers close to starvation [3], and riots had broken out in many parts of France. When, on July 11, 1789, Louis dismissed his popular minister Jacques Necker (1732–1804), there was widespread protest.

Antiroyal feeling grows

The people of Paris stormed the Bastille [Key] on July 14 and there was a general breakdown of social order throughout France, with aristocratic property being looted or seized. The National Assembly stripped away the privileges of aristocracy and clergy, and the king was forced to leave Versailles and go to the Tuileries palace in Paris.

The political turmoil continued over the next two years with attempts to establish a new constitution and with antiroyal feeling growing. Confiscation of aristocratic and church land and wealth gave the new government welcome financial help, but an issue of paper currency—the *assignats*—soon led to renewed inflation. In June 1791 the king attempted to flee abroad but was recaptured at Varennes. Popular hostility to him increased when the the Holy Roman emperor, representing Austria, and the king of Prussia issued a declaration calling for the restoration of the ancient rights of Louis. In September a new constitution [4B] was introduced, setting up a legislative assembly and giving the king a strictly limited role. But political tension rapidly developed between moderate constitutionalists and extreme antimonarchists.

In April 1792 war was declared on Austria. As royalist armies backed by Austria and Prussia gathered on France's borders

CONNECTIONS

See also

1226 Napoleonic Europe
1218 The American Revolution
1170 The age of Louis XIV
1184 The Enlightenment
1180 Enlightened despotism
1182 Europe: economy and society 1700–1800
1248 The revolutions of 1848
1198 Neoclassicism

1 The Marquis de Lafayette had become a popular hero when he led the French volunteers who helped the American colonists break free from Britain. With other aristocrats he joined the National Assembly in 1789, presenting a declaration of rights. A moderate reformer, he became trapped between Jacobin extremists and court, fled to Austria in 1792, and was captured.

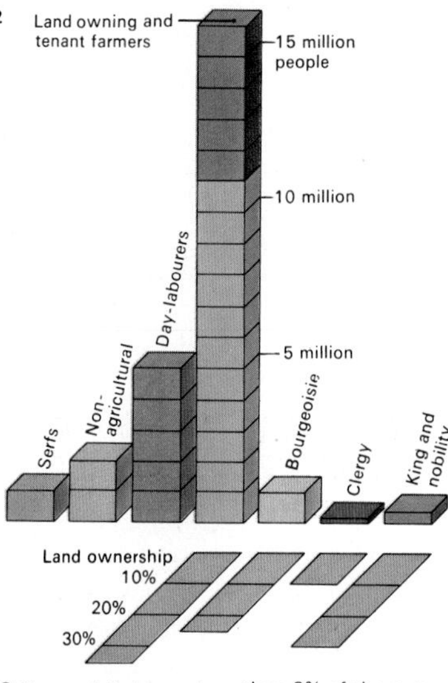

Land owning and tenant farmers
15 million people
10 million
5 million
Serfs
Non-agricultural
Day-labourers
Bourgeoisie
Clergy
King and nobility
Land ownership
10%
20%
30%

2 Unequal division of land, with more than 40% owned by less than 3% of the population, was a major grievance and fundamental problem of French society. As most of the nobility and clergy were largely exempt from taxation, the principal share of the burden fell on the bourgeoisie and the more prosperous of the peasantry.

(8 sous)
Price of 2kg loaf in "normal times"
(15 sous)
Laborer's wage
Amount of wages remaining
1788 July
August
September
October
November
December
1789 January
February
March
April — Réveillon riots
May
June
July — Storming of Bastille
August

3 Prices rose steadily during the 18th century as a result of increases in population (more than 50%) and money supplies and relatively slow expansion of industrial and agricultural production. This had the effect of making the upper classes even more determined to hold on to their privileges, while the lives of the peasantry and industrial workers became even more precarious. In "normal" times, a loaf of bread cost about half a day's wage of a laborer, but bad harvests in 1788 and 1789 raised bread prices to the point where they precipitated the Réveillon bread riots of April 1789.

4A

4B

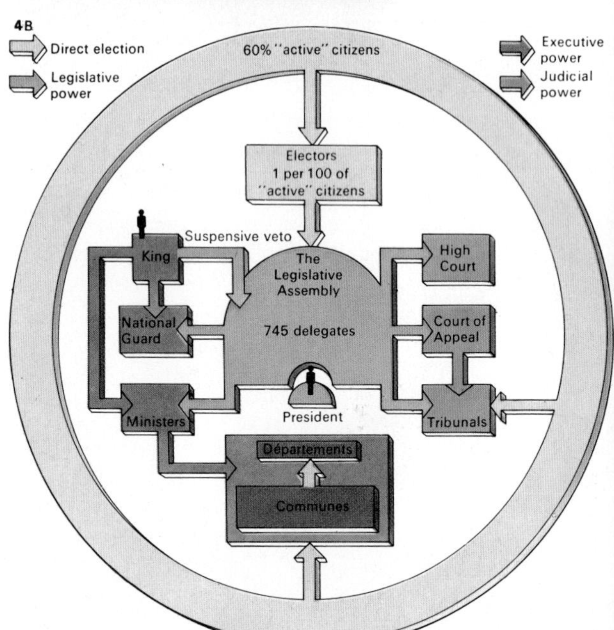

Direct election
Legislative power
60% "active" citizens
Executive power
Judicial power
Electors 1 per 100 of "active" citizens
Suspensive veto
King
The Legislative Assembly
745 delegates
High Court
National Guard
Court of Appeal
President
Ministers
Tribunals
Départements
Communes

4 The meeting of the Third Estate as the National Assembly [A] on June 17, 1789, pledged to end feudal privileges and was the political start of the revolution. The constitution it produced [B] was a limited monarchy, with power residing in a Legislative Assembly elected by active citizens who paid taxation at least equivalent to three days' wages of a laborer per year. The 1791 Constitution also divided France into the local government *departements*.

[6], the mob demanded that the Assembly act against the king. In September, Prussian armies invaded France, precipitating a massacre of captured aristocrats. An unexpected victory over the invaders at Valmy on September 22 relieved the pressure. On the same day France became a republic ruled by a Constituent Assembly elected by the extremist Jacobins, the most radical group to hold power during the revolution.

The king was put on trial and executed [5] in January 1793. In the following months defeats by the *émigré* armies, proroyalist risings in La Vendée and the south, and continuing economic problems prompted the Assembly to appoint a Committee of Public Safety to exercise emergency powers. The Reign of Terror began, during which more than 40,000 "enemies of the revolution" were sent to the guillotine. Organized religion was officially abolished and replaced by worship of the Supreme Being.

By spring 1794 the republican armies had rallied; in June 1794 the counter-revolutionary armies were defeated at Fleurus, and in July the Jacobin leader, Maximilien Robespierre (1758–94), who had been virtual dictator for a year, was overthrown and executed. A reaction set in, with moderates seizing power. In 1795 a basically conservative constitution was set up, headed by a five-man Executive Directorate.

Emergence of Napoleon

The Directorate made peace with Prussia and the Netherlands, but launched a major offensive against Austria by sending a young general, Napoleon Bonaparte (1769–1821), to campaign in Italy [7]. He was brilliantly successful during 1796, forcing Austria out of the war. He then led an expedition to Egypt to cut Britain's communications with India, but was forced to abandon the campaign when Horatio Nelson (1758–1805) destroyed his fleet at the Battle of the Nile in 1798. Meanwhile, the Directorate had become profoundly unpopular with all sections of the population, and when Napoleon returned in October 1799 he was able to engineer a coup that gave power to three consuls [8], of which he was the senior.

KEY

The storming of the Bastille on July 14, 1789 was seen by contemporaries and later generations as the true beginning of the French Revolution. Although the political crisis began more than a year earlier, the rising of the Paris mob against this ancient prison and symbol of absolutism was of fundamental importance. It forced the basically middle-class National Assembly to ally with the people to prevent a royalist counterattack, and it led to uprisings in the provinces in which aristocrats' estates were seized, land deeds destroyed, and officials murdered. It paved the way for feudalism's downfall, transferring political power from the king to the legislature.

5

5 The execution of Louis XVI on January 21, 1793, followed the threat of an invasion of royalist *émigrés*. Popular opinion turned wholly against the king, and the Jacobins were able to seize power and declare France a republic on September 22, 1792. Victory over royalist forces at Valmy gave them the self-confidence to try the king, and his execution symbolized the break with the past system.

6

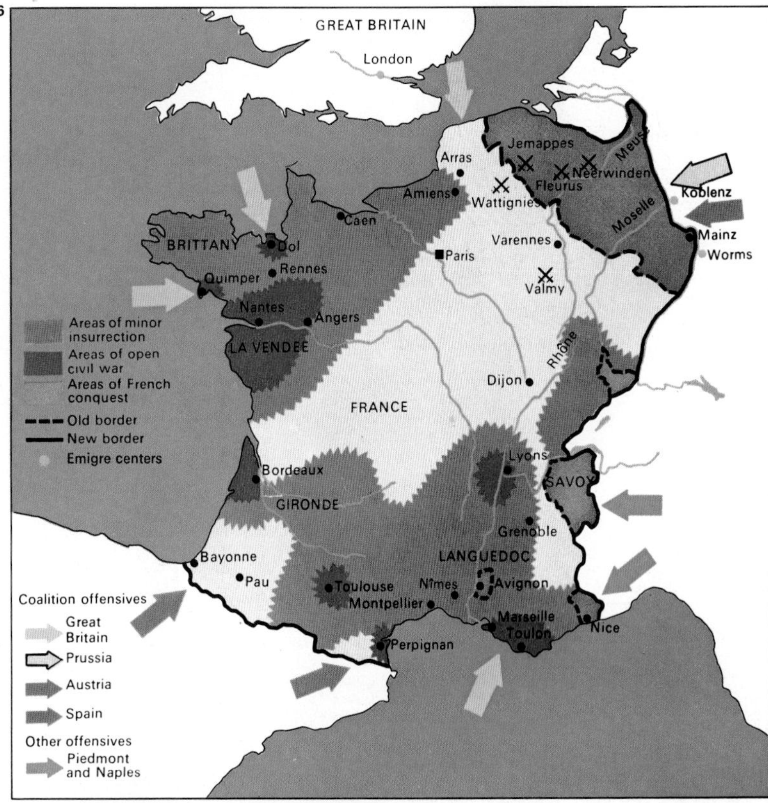
GREAT BRITAIN
London
Arras
Jemappes
Neerwinden
Fleurus
Meuse
Koblenz
Amiens
Wattignies
Caen
Moselle
Mainz
Worms
Varennes
BRITTANY
Dol
Paris
Rennes
Quimper
Valmy
Nantes
Angers
LA VENDEE
Rhône
Dijon
FRANCE
Lyons
Bordeaux
GIRONDE
Grenoble
Bayonne
LANGUEDOC
Pau
Toulouse
Nîmes
Avignon
Montpellier
Marseille
Toulon
Nice
Perpignan
Areas of minor insurrection
Areas of open civil war
Areas of French conquest
Old border
New border
Emigre centers
Coalition offensives
Great Britain
Prussia
Austria
Spain
Other offensives
Piedmont and Naples

6 France's neighbors were antagonized by the gathering forces of the revolution. Aristocratic *émigrés* formed a nucleus of resistance and received support from Austria and Prussia. Their first invasion was halted at Valmy, and the republic then counterattacked, occupying Nice, Savoy, and Belgium after a victory at Jemappes (November 1792), invading the Rhineland states and threatening Holland. After the king's execution, war was declared on Spain, Holland, and Britain, but military reverses followed, with a major revolt in La Vendee and enemy offensives in southern France, Belgium, Alsace, and Britanny. Unprecedented emergency measures put down internal revolts and Belgium and Holland were reconquered. By the end of 1795, France had made peace with all except Austria and Great Britain.

7

7 Napoleon Bonaparte led the French armies to attack Austrian territories in Italy early in 1796. The Directorate intended this to be a diversion while a major offensive was mounted in the Rhineland. But Bonaparte traversed northern Italy in an extraordinary series of victories, forcing the Austrians to make peace. He changed the face of warfare by using shock tactics to harness the revolutionary zeal of armies raised by mass conscription.

8

8 The installation of the Conseil d'Etat on December 24, 1799 made Bonaparte first consul. With the prestige of his victory in Italy and the Egyptian campaign behind him, Napoleon was the most powerful man in the turbulent political scene at the turn of the century. The failure of the Directorate to cope with internal problems had lost it all support, and Napoleon hoped to use his widespread popularity to persuade the assemblies to vote him into power without opposition. But they refused to do so, and he had to use troops to drive them out and allow a small rump of supporters to vote through a constitution. This gave power to a first consul who was assisted by two colleagues and a senate nominated by the consuls. Napoleon then made use of a new device—the plebiscite—to obtain popular support. He announced that 3,000,000 votes had been cast for the new constitution and only 1,562 against.

Napoleonic Europe

In 1799 Napoleon Bonaparte (1769–1821) [Key] became first consul of France, then still menaced by hostile states. His new constitution concentrated internal authority in his own hands. Once in power, he acted swiftly to achieve peace in Europe. After a surprise crossing of the Alps, he shattered Austrian power in Italy at the Battle of Marengo on June 14, 1800, and made peace with Austria by the Treaty of Campo Formio. Russia, under the pro-French Tsar Paul I, (1754–1801), also ceased hostilities against Napoleon and in December joined Prussia, Denmark, and Sweden in a French-inspired League of Armed Neutrality designed to weaken Britain, Napoleon's chief remaining foe.

Although Paul was soon assassinated and succeeded by the pro-English Alexander I (1777–1825), Britain and France ended the French Revolutionary Wars at the Treaty of Amiens in March 1802. Britain agreed to return all overseas conquests except Ceylon and Trinidad, and Napoleon agreed to evacuate Holland and Naples. Napoleon soon aroused British suspicions by looking for new colonies, by remaining in Holland, and by extending French power in Germany. When the British realized that French markets would still be closed, they refused to evacuate Malta. Hostilities broke out again in May 1803, beginning the Napoleonic Wars.

Internal reforms

During the years of comparative peace between 1800 and 1803, Napoleon began the internal reconstruction of France, his most lasting achievement. The Bank of France was established in 1800, and tax collecting centralized; the new local government *départements,* established in 1790, were put under the control of prefects; the law was remodeled and codified, and a centralized secondary school system was set up. Napoleon's concordat with the papacy extended his power. In 1802 he became first consul for life.

The renewal of war identified Britain as Napoleon's most stubborn and dangerous enemy, and at first he tried to defeat Britain by invasion. Gathering a fleet of barges and a large army in the Boulogne area, he planned to use his navy to lure the British fleet away to the West Indies and then slip back to gain control of the English Channel for a successful crossing. The British navy instead blockaded the coasts of France and Spain and then under Admiral Horatio Nelson destroyed their fleets at Trafalgar on October 21, 1805 [2].

Even before this interim defeat of his invasion plan, Napoleon, who had declared himself emperor [3] in 1804, had had to redeploy the Grande Armée to meet a renewed threat from Austria and Russia, who were now joined in a Third Coalition with Britain. In a swift campaign he smashed an Austrian army at Ulm on October 20, 1805, occupied Vienna, and defeated the Russians at Austerlitz [5] on December 26. In the Treaty of Pressburg with Austria, Napoleon gained complete control of Italy and unified much of Germany outside Prussia in the Confederation of the Rhine. Prussia felt obliged to intervene but was defeated at Jena and Auerstadt in October 1806. Napoleon occupied Berlin and defeated the Rus-

CONNECTIONS

See also
1224 The French Revolution
1230 The Congress of Vienna
1232 European empires in the 19th century
1248 The revolutions of 1848
1288 Political thought in the 19th century

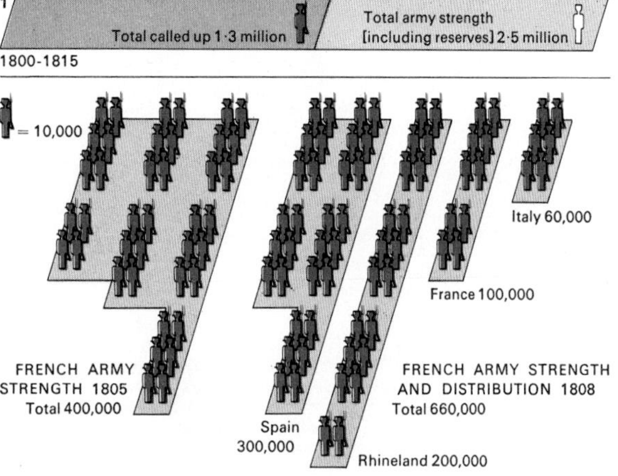

1
Total called up 1·3 million
Total army strength [including reserves] 2·5 million
1800-1815
= 10,000
Italy 60,000
France 100,000
FRENCH ARMY STRENGTH 1805
Total 400,000
FRENCH ARMY STRENGTH AND DISTRIBUTION 1808
Total 660,000
Spain 300,000
Rhineland 200,000

1 Conscription on an unprecedented scale laid the foundation for the armies that enabled Napoleon to dominate Europe. From 1800 to 1812, an average of 85,000 men were called up in France each year. The demand for military manpower grew, especially in 1812 with the costly invasion of Russia. Total deaths during the Napoleonic Wars were about 1,000,000, of which 400,000 were French.

2 Nelson's annihilation of the combined French and Spanish fleets at Trafalgar was the decisive event in the long naval war and convinced Napoleon that direct assault on Britain was impossible. Saved from invasion, Britain used its superb navy to blockade the coasts of Europe and its wealth to organize resistance to France. Napoleon was forced to extend his control of neighboring states to stifle British trade. The resulting hostility finally brought down his empire.

3 As emperor of the French, Napoleon used the trappings of imperial glory to consolidate his new dynasty. Most Frenchmen responded, but some felt he had betrayed the Revolution.

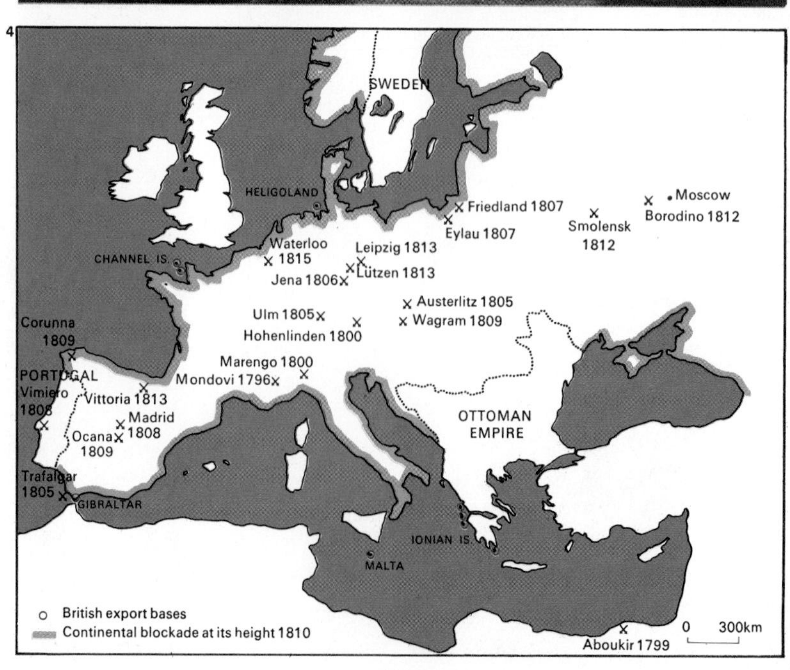

SWEDEN
HELIGOLAND
Friedland 1807
Eylau 1807
Moscow
Borodino 1812
Smolensk 1812
CHANNEL IS.
Waterloo 1815
Leipzig 1813
Jena 1806
Lützen 1813
Austerlitz 1805
Wagram 1809
Ulm 1805
Hohenlinden 1800
Corunna 1809
Marengo 1800
Mondovi 1796
PORTUGAL
Vimiero 1808
Vittoria 1813
Madrid 1808
Ocana 1809
OTTOMAN EMPIRE
Trafalgar 1805
GIBRALTAR
IONIAN IS.
MALTA
British export bases
Continental blockade at its height 1810
Aboukir 1799
0 300km

4 Brilliant victories in an almost continuous series of campaigns enabled Napoleon to establish France temporarily as the main power in Europe. In controlling the "traditional" powers of Austria, Prussia, and Russia by a mixture of war and diplomacy, he enjoyed almost total success. But the need to extend the Continental System led him to become trapped in a guerrilla war in Spain and then to launch the disastrous invasion of Russia.

sians at Friedland in June 1807. Meeting the tsar at Tilsit he persuaded him to enter an alliance with France against Britain.

The Continental System

Napoleon now sought to defeat Britain economically by using force to prevent British trade with any part of Europe. The British continually found ways of smuggling in their goods, particularly through Spain, Portugal, north Germany, and Holland, and Napoleon had to try to extend his "Continental System" ever farther. The military presence [1] and economic hardships resulting made Napoleon's rule increasingly unpopular with his subject nations.

In 1808, Napoleon forced Charles IV (1784–1819) of Spain and his son Ferdinand to abdicate in favor of Napoleon's brother Joseph. The Spanish revolted, and the British sent an army to support them. The Spanish campaign cost Napoleon more than 50,000 men and led to his first defeats on land. In 1810, Napoleon tightened up the Continental System by annexing Holland and the German coast. Europe was thrown into a commercial crisis that persuaded the tsar to end his alliance in December 1810.

Retreat from Moscow

In June 1812, Napoleon launched a massive invasion of Russia with 611,000 men, including forced contingents of Austrians and Prussians. His troops reached Moscow, but lack of supplies and military reverses forced them into an undisciplined winter retreat, which left only some 10,000 men fit for combat [7]. In February 1813, Prussia declared war on France and Austria, and many subject states followed. Napoleon was defeated at Leipzig in October, and the Allies pushed into northern France while the British invaded across the Pyrenees. Paris was occupied on March 30, 1814; Napoleon abdicated on April 11.

On March 1, 1815, Napoleon took advantage of quarreling among the Allies and the unpopularity of the restored Bourbons in France to reestablish his power. But defeat by the Duke of Wellington (1769–1852) at Waterloo [8] on June 18, 1815, led to his exile on St Helena, where he died in 1821.

KEY

Napoleon Bonaparte, the Corsican-born general who made himself emperor of the French, had the military genius to win France a short-lived supremacy over most of Europe. But it was his reforms of French society in codifying the law and rationalizing education and administration that were his greatest achievements. Some of them endure to this day.

5

5 Napoleon's victory at Austerlitz on December 2, 1805, and the campaign that preceded it showed all the qualities of speed and decisiveness that made him one of the world's greatest generals. Having force-marched the Grande Armée from the English Channel to the Danube, he destroyed an Austrian army at Ulm and then pushed a Russian force back until it rejoined the main Russian army at Austerlitz. In the battle he used a combination of devastating artillery barrages and massive infantry assaults to sweep the Russians off the vital heights commanding the field of battle and into a retreat.

6

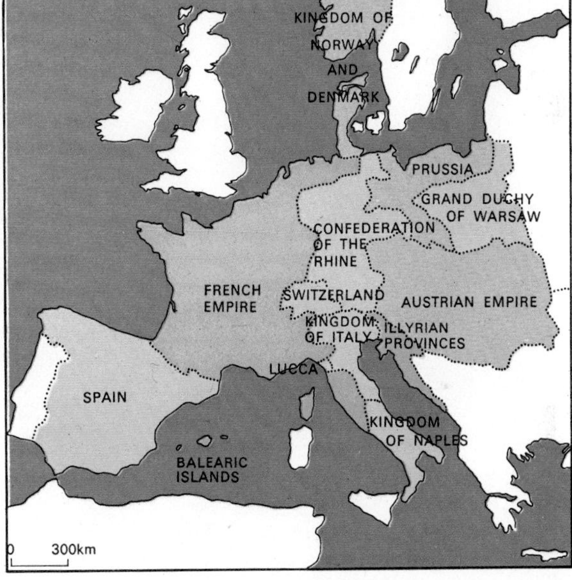

KINGDOM OF NORWAY AND DENMARK
PRUSSIA
GRAND DUCHY OF WARSAW
CONFEDERATION OF THE RHINE
FRENCH EMPIRE
SWITZERLAND
AUSTRIAN EMPIRE
KINGDOM OF ITALY
ILLYRIAN PROVINCES
LUCCA
SPAIN
KINGDOM OF NAPLES
BALEARIC ISLANDS
0 300km
French Empire 1812
Dependent states 1812
French Allies 1812

6 Almost all Europe in 1812 was either ruled directly by Napoleon or members of his family, or was allied with him. At the outset Napoleon had been able to draw on widespread support in Europe for the revolutionary ideals of overthrowing the old order. He furthered his own power by using the desire of neighboring states for freedom, organizing many small states of Italy and Germany into dependent republics and setting up the Confederation of the Rhine that effectively ended the Austrian-dominated Holy Roman Empire.

7

SNUFFING OUT BONEY!

7 The invasion of Russia was Napoleon's decisive error, celebrated by an English cartoon. The Russians refused to make peace when Moscow was occupied and resorted to guerrilla tactics to destroy the invasion armies, thereby encouraging subject states to rise.

8 Napoleon was finally defeated at Waterloo, near Brussels, by British and Prussian troops led by the Duke of Wellington and Marshal Blücher. An alliance of major European powers and conquered states had previously forced Napoleon to abdicate, but he had viewed exile on Elba only as an interlude. When the restored Bourbons had earned the dislike of most Frenchmen and the Allies were bickering among themselves at Vienna, he returned and marched to Paris with popular support. But the shock tactics of the Grand Armée met their match at Waterloo, where the British infantry held firm against cavalry assaults until relieved by the Prussians.

8

European Romantic art: figure painting

In the later part of the eighteenth century, the classical order was coming under attack in one area after another. Its most formidable antagonist, and one who is now recognized as the father of the Romantic movement, was the French philosopher Jean-Jacques Rousseau (1712–78). He argued that feeling, not reason, should be the basis of belief and conduct and asserted, in opposition to classical theory, that art was not the servant of morality. In addition, British and German writers, such as William Blake (1757–1827) and the young Johann Wolfgang von Goethe (1749–1832), identified the unconscious as the source of true art and poetry and made sincerity for the first time a test of artistic value.

Romanticism in French painting

The development of Romanticism in the visual arts is easiest to see in French painting. This is because it was only in France that a tradition of state patronage of grand historical subjects was kept up and because in the treatment of these subjects a gradual progression can be traced, beginning with an almost pure Neoclassicism and leading through a steady undermining of classical principles to a more or less pure, but not undisputed, Romanticism.

The subversion of classicism began in that temple of Neoclassical painting, the art of Jacques-Louis David (1748–1825), especially in his work done around the time of the French Revolution and Napoleon's rule. Not that David abandoned classical qualities of style—clarity, precision, economy, and references to the Antique and to Nicolas Poussin—but in paintings such as "The Death of Marat" (1793) one can feel beneath the formal calm some of the emotions released by Rousseau: a sense of the precariousness of human life and institutions; an awareness of the power of fanaticism and of chance; a morbid fascination with violence. In part these qualities reside in the subject rather than its treatment, but the choice of the former is significant: one solitary man working, as he believed, for society and then being struck down by it. Throughout Romantic art, the image of a man alone defying and being ultimately defeated by some overwhelming force, whether of society, nature, the dark gods of unreason, or in extreme cases the universe itself, is one of the most potent symbols.

The poetry and horror of war

After David, the impulse toward emotionalism increased, stretching, although not yet breaking, the mold of classic form. Antoine Gros (1771–1835) [5] expressed the stirring poetry (as it was regarded at the time) of Napoleonic war, a poetry enhanced by its horror and destructiveness. Théodore Géricault (1791–1824) [6] represents a further stage still, in which the color black becomes eloquent and dark shadows begin to bite into classic outline. With him, the solitary man may be not only the madman, the shipwrecked man, or the man on a wild horse, but also the artist, contemplating in despair the impossibilities of his task.

Finally there was Eugène Delacroix (1798–1863) [7], over whose work there broke out a classic-romantic battle. While he never repudiated classical principles al-

CONNECTIONS

See also
1242 European Romantic art: landscape painting
1222 Origins of romanticism
1252 Realist painting in the 19th century

1 Henry Fuseli's "The Nightmare" (1782) is merely sensationalist by comparison with Goya's subtle comment on the horrors that may visit the mind asleep. It evokes a shudder in the spectator partly by drawing on legends of witchcraft (the incubus) and partly by its stirring of sexual fantasies. Yet, it was a pioneering effort, not only in its theme—it seems to have been the first picture of a nightmare ever painted—but also in its reliance on (then) modern psychology.

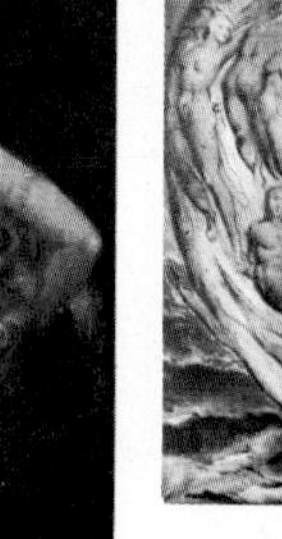

2 In his painting of a vision—the damnation of Paolo and Francesca (*c.* 1824), from Dante's *Inferno*—William Blake treated a moral and poetic theme.

3 The execution of a group of Spanish insurgents in Madrid after their abortive uprising against the French occupying forces was powerfully depicted by Goya in the macabre "The 3rd of May, 1808," painted in 1814.

4 The Nazarenes, an early 19th-century group of German "pre-Raphaelites," were the first systematically to revive late medieval styles, as in Franz Pforr's "Rudolf of Hapsburg and the Priest" (*c.* 1810) (detail).

together, his supporters saw his work as directly opposed to that of his older contemporary, the Neoclassicist Ingres (1780–1867) (who was not immune from Romantic feeling himself). This "battle of the styles" was joined around 1830, and it was then that the word "Romantic" was applied to pictorial art for the first time. Romanticism in painting, as epitomized by Delacroix, was identified with color, movement, breadth of handling, and the uninhibited representation of violence.

It is much more difficult to discuss Romantic figure painting in other countries, as they had no continuous tradition either of patronage or outlook. In Britain there was a growing interest in the irrational expressed by, for example, Fuseli (1741–1825) [1] and Blake [2], and this reached a climax before 1800, earlier than any comparable development in painting elsewhere; however, it was not followed up. In keeping with the date—the late eighteenth century—the style of Fuseli and Blake retains a strong link with Neoclassicism, in the use of forms derived from the Antique and Michelangelo and a dependence on outline. On the other hand, these forms were "pulled out" and given a sort of airy, boneless quality, which was employed by Fuseli to explore the psychological states of terror and nightmare and by Blake to express his "Visions of Eternity." German Romantic painting took a different course in a turning back to the styles and subject matter of the Middle Ages and early Renaissance; this was carried out by a group founded by Johann Friedrich Overbeck and Franz Pforr, who settled in Rome in 1810 and were called the Nazarenes [4].

A portrayer of violence

There was no Italian painting to speak of in this period, owing partly to lack of patronage, but there was one very important artist in Spain: Francisco de Goya (1746–1828) [Key, 3], who is perhaps the hardest of all to classify. Formally, he was no Neoclassicist, yet his print "The Sleep of Reason Produces Monsters" can be interpreted as a warning of what happens when rational—that is, "classical"—order breaks down.

KEY

Reason attacked by the forces of irrationalism and the supernatural and the solitariness of the individual in his journey through life are two leading themes of Romanticism. Both are reflected in Goya's original frontispiece to his series "Los Caprichos" (1799), a set of cryptic satires on contemporary mores. Both the frontispiece and its caption, "The Sleep of Reason produces Monsters," typically reveal only part of the artist's meaning. In a private note he explained that whereas fantasy abandoned by reason produces monsters, united with it she is the mother of the arts.

5

5 Violent action and the sense of "poetry" surrounding it was a major Romantic theme. The sense was that not only the results of conquest are desirable but that the experiences are exciting in themselves; seen in this light defeat may seem as "poetic" as victory. The living embodiment of this ideal was Napoleon, whose military career was charted in pictures by Antoine Gros. In "Napoleon at Eylau" (1808) (detail) the emperor is shown displaying his humanity toward defeated Russians.

6

6 Romantic belief that artistic creation springs from pain and turmoil is depicted in realistic terms in Géricault's "The Artist" (*c.* 1818). Whether inspiration comes or goes, the artist is a lonely, tormented being.

7

7 "The Death at Sardanapalus" (1827) by Delacroix, a huge, sprawling exhibition of sex and violence, taken from an oriental verse-play by the English poet Lord Byron, was the ultimate in French Romantic painting.

The Congress of Vienna

Even before Napoleon's defeat in 1814, the idea of an international diplomatic assembly with the aim of restoring order in Europe was proposed by Prince Metternich of Austria (1773–1859). Intended to ratify decisions made at the first Treaty of Paris, the congress was announced, and from September 1814 delegates from throughout Europe arrived in Vienna [Key]. From the start the congress was dominated by four great powers, Austria, Great Britain, Prussia, and Russia, although Prince Talleyrand (1754–1858) soon gained an equal voice for France. Their decisions were summarized in 1815 by the Paris Treaty, also signed by Spain, Portugal, and Sweden.

The distribution of rewards

A major purpose of the Congress was to prevent any one power from gaining more than its fair share of rewards, and to establish a balance of territorial interests. In fact Russia took the major share and established a dangerous foothold in Europe. From this time until the Crimean War (1854–56), fear of Russia was a dominant theme.

At the Congress of Vienna, however, the immediate fear was that France might cause another European war. Buffer states were created to hinder its expansion eastward. The kingdom of Piedmont was strengthened; Belgium (previously the Austrian Netherlands) was joined with Holland in the kingdom of the Netherlands; and the former Holy Roman Empire became the German Confederation—39 states dominated by an Austrian president.

Yet France was generously treated in the Treaties of Paris of 1814 and 1815. The frontiers of 1790 were restored, and an army of occupation was installed only until France had paid an indemnity to the allies—a condition met by 1818. Although the monarchy was restored in the shape of Louis XVIII (1755–1824), he was obliged to reign under the Charter of 1814.

A new political settlement

In addition to the territorial changes, political settlement was considered essential for future peace. The French Revolution was largely blamed for the upheavals of the previous generation. The best hope for stability seemed to lie in the restoration of legitimate monarchs who had been overthrown. To try to prevent future disturbance in Central Europe, states in the German Confederation were advised to offer constitutions to their subjects—advice largely ignored.

Finally, the Vienna settlement itself had to be maintained; to this end the four great military powers—Austria, Russia, Prussia, and Britain—renewed their Quadruple Alliance and pledged to uphold the settlement for 20 years. Castlereagh [5], the British foreign secretary, in particular saw the alliance as fundamental to the maintenance of the balance of power in Europe.

But the relative cooperation and harmony of views shown at Vienna did not continue in the four congresses held between 1818 and 1822. Austria, Prussia, and Russia had formed the Holy Alliance in September 1815. They rapidly adopted the view that the powers should intervene in the internal affairs of European countries where stability was threatened, a doctrine repudiated by Britain.

CONNECTIONS

See also
1232 European empires in the 19th century
1226 Napoleonic Europe
1248 The revolutions of 1848
1302 Balkanization and Slav nationalism
1304 Causes of World War
1250 German and Italian unification

1

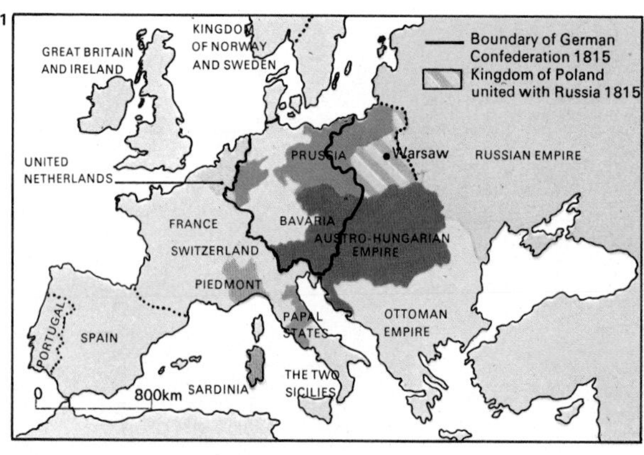

GREAT BRITAIN AND IRELAND
KINGDOM OF NORWAY AND SWEDEN
Boundary of German Confederation 1815
Kingdom of Poland united with Russia 1815
UNITED NETHERLANDS
PRUSSIA
Warsaw
RUSSIAN EMPIRE
FRANCE
BAVARIA
SWITZERLAND
AUSTRO-HUNGARIAN EMPIRE
PIEDMONT
PORTUGAL
SPAIN
PAPAL STATES
OTTOMAN EMPIRE
SARDINIA
THE TWO SICILIES
0
800km

1 The map of Europe had to be redrawn after the 1815 Vienna settlement. The Hapsburg Empire received the Illyrian provinces and the two Italian provinces (Lombardy and Venetia) in return for the former Austrian Netherlands (Belgium). Sweden won Norway, which had been Danish; Russia kept its wartime conquest, Finland, and dominated the new "puppet" kingdom of Poland. Prussia kept Polish Posen and received almost half the kingdom of Saxony and the area of the Ruhr. Britain consolidated its overseas empire and naval routes by holding onto the Cape of Good Hope, Malta, the Ionian Islands, Ceylon, Mauritius, Tobago, St Lucia, and Heligoland. Partly because of these overseas areas, Britain became relatively remote from 19th century European politics.

2 The diplomats at Vienna reached compromises over their territorial ambitions, but there was to be no compromise with the new forces of liberalism and nationalism. Within 15 years unrest in Spain, Portugal, Italy, Germany, and France showed the growing desire for constitutional restraints on the monarchies that had been restored. Nationalists were crushed in the Polish revolt of 1830, but they won independence for Belgium (1830) and Greece (where war with the Turks began in 1821). These threats to the Vienna settlement were the main topics discussed at the four subsequent congresses: Aix-la-Chapelle (1818), Troppau (1820), Laibach (1821), and Verona (1822). Greek independence was a blow, weakening Turkish resistance to the nationalist claims of its other Balkan states.

2

Britain therefore opposed, although not always successfully, intervention in European revolution and ceased to send official representatives to congresses after Aix-la-Chapelle. Finally Britain dealt the death blow to the congress system by forcing acceptance of Greek independence (confirmed in 1832) against Russian interests and Austrian-Prussian protests.

Consequences for Europe

The settlement reached by the Congress of Vienna shaped the following generation in Europe. The Continental powers were committed to upholding the status quo they had created, and they interpreted their obligations with a rigidity that turned the settlement into a straitjacket. Liberal revolts attempting to introduce constitutional limits to the powers of the restored monarchs were crushed almost without exception, although they were successful in France, Switzerland, and Belgium in 1830 because it was neither convenient nor in the interests of all the powers to intervene [2]. The settlement had ignored nationalist feelings, and there were revolts in Belgium and Poland and growing unrest in Italy and Germany. Furthermore, the old multinational empires—the Hapsburg Empire and the Ottoman Empire (Turkey)—had been confirmed.

The Greek revolt of 1821 proved disastrous for the Ottoman Empire. Its success encouraged other Balkan states to push for independence and weakened the ability of Turkey, the "sick man of Europe," to resist. The Hapsburgs had added Croats and Italians to their multiplicity of nationalities. Nationalism anywhere was to be treated by the Austrians as an epidemic that could destroy their empire. Metternich [3] used his skill at the Congress of Vienna, his influence in the congress system, and his authority in the German Confederation and the whole of Italy to wipe out any symptom of nationalism. The Metternich system (secret police, interference with mail, press censorship, control of universities, prohibition of public meetings) spread from the Baltic to Sicily. The main aim of the Congress of Vienna, however, had been to secure European peace, and in a sense it succeeded.

KEY

In 1815, Napoleon was safely on St Helena. The crowned monarchs of Austria, Prussia, and Russia waltz in unison (England is not quite in step, and France is jumping) to celebrate the restoration of their political power and the promise of armed backing by all powers. Five monarchs and the heads of 216 princely families participated in the great congress. Their fear of revolution and desire to restore the political situation of the 18th century meant that France was left intact.

3

3 Prince Clemens von Metternich was foreign minister of the Hapsburg Empire from 1809 until the revolution of 1848. To many he seemed the epitome of autocracy, reaction, and the police state.

4

4 A grand sleigh ride was included in one of the weekly programs issued by the festivals committee responsible for entertaining the visitors. The expenses were paid by the Austrian emperor.

5

5 Viscount Castlereagh (1769–1822) was Britain's foreign secretary from 1812. Regarded as reactionary at home, he proved too liberal for the congress system, which he had hoped would provide a diplomatic arena for peaceful change.

6

6 Frequent liberal and nationalist revolts threatened the settlement but were usually suppressed. Eugène Delacroix (1798–1863) won the Legion of Honor for his painting "Liberty leading the People," after the French revolt of 1830.

European empires in the 19th century

The Austro-Hungarian, Russian, and Ottoman empires were deeply involved in the Balkan states during most of the nineteenth century. The diplomatic and military conflicts among the three powers were caused partly by their own political ambitions and partly by aggressive national independence movements that were developing in the region.

The Serbian struggle for independence

Serbia, one of the Ottoman provinces in the Balkans, was the first subject nationality to challenge the political power of the Ottoman Empire (Turkey). Turkish rule in Serbia (which had been conquered in 1389) had become particularly tyrannical at the end of the eighteenth century. The local military commanders *(dahis)* exercised a largely independent authority. In 1801 they executed the pasha of Belgrade, the sultan's own representative, and in 1804 they ordered the execution of 72 Serbian village elders. The Serbian uprising of 1804 under Karadjordje [3B], a capable military leader, started as a protest movement against the excesses of Turkish rule, but after striking military successes it developed into a movement for full independence.

Russia offered some military and diplomatic support to the Serbs, to whom it was tied through the Orthodox religion and the Slav race, but it was chiefly a combination of Turkish weakness and Serbian resistance that enabled the rebels to remain independent for eight years. The Turks finally crushed the Serbian revolt in 1813, but within 18 months the Serbs revolted again, this time under the leadership of Milos Obrenović (1780–1860), a better diplomat than Karadjordje.

Obrenović worked out an agreement with the Turks under which Serbia remained formally a Turkish province garrisoned by Turkish troops but was allowed to share in the administration of justice, to maintain a militia, and to summon a national assembly in Belgrade. Although Serbia's struggle for independence was fully consummated only in 1878 when the Congress of Berlin [8] recognized it as an independent state, the example of the successful Serbian struggle had a powerful effect on the other Balkan nationalities, especially the other southern Slavs living under both the Ottoman and Hapsburg empires. It reinforced their desires for independence.

The unification of the Slavs

The effect was greatest in the Hapsburg Empire, where many Serbs had fled from the Turks in the seventeenth century. The Orthodox Eastern Church was a powerful link between the Serbs in Serbia and those elsewhere. Fear of being crushed by the twin pressures of forcible Germanization from Vienna and Magyarization from Budapest brought the Croats and other Slavs, notably the Slovenes, closer together.

In the 1848–49 anti-Hapsburg revolution, the Croat general Josip Jelačić (1801–59) fought against the Hungarian revolutionaries with Serbian and Slovene support. But Austria, after successfully crushing that revolution, introduced a centralist, strongly Germanizing rule. The existence of a semi-independent Serbia fired the imagin-

CONNECTIONS

See also
1230 The Congress of Vienna
1248 The revolutions of 1848
1250 German and Italian unification
1286 Russia in the 19th century
1108 The Ottoman Empire to 1600

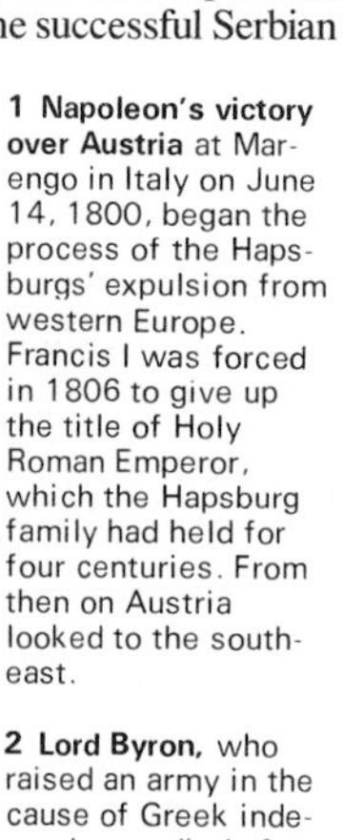

1 Napoleon's victory over Austria at Marengo in Italy on June 14, 1800, began the process of the Hapsburgs' expulsion from western Europe. Francis I was forced in 1806 to give up the title of Holy Roman Emperor, which the Hapsburg family had held for four centuries. From then on Austria looked to the southeast.

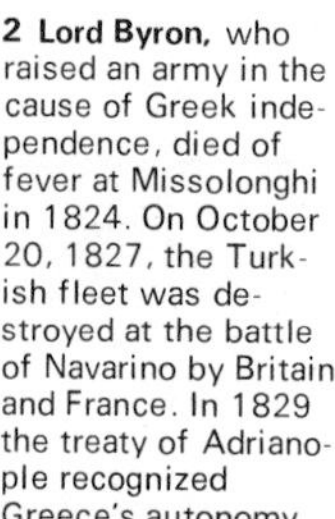

2 Lord Byron, who raised an army in the cause of Greek independence, died of fever at Missolonghi in 1824. On October 20, 1827, the Turkish fleet was destroyed at the battle of Navarino by Britain and France. In 1829 the treaty of Adrianople recognized Greece's autonomy.

3 Two of the most important figures in the Serbo-Croat independence movement were Ljudevit Gaj (1809–72) [A] and Karadjordje (Georgije Petrovic) (1768–1817) [B]. Gaj founded the movement for the emancipation of Croatia from Austria. Karadjordje led the uprising against the Turks in 1804. After the suppression of an uprising in 1813, he fled first to Austria and later to Russia.

4 Montenegro was conquered by the Turks in 1499, but a large area of its forbidding moutain territory remained outside their grip. From there Montenegrins like these raided the towns that the Turks held. After the successful wars against the Turks in 1876–78. Montenegro was recognized as an independent state by the 1878 Congress of Berlin. As a result, Montenegrin territory was increased by 70%, and the population of the country almost doubled.

ation not only of the Serbs but of the Croats and Slovenes as well. Linguistic similarities fostered the idea that all Serbs, Croats, and Slovenes were one nation of Yugoslavs, or southern slavs. This idea was developed further in Pan Slavism, a movement for the cultural and political unity of all the Slavonic peoples.

The effect of Russia's foreign policy

Russia sought to use these movements in its drive toward Constantinople. Meanwhile, with Prussia squeezing Austria-Hungary out of Germany after 1815, Austria developed a renewed commitment to its Balkan role. Because of its mistrust of the new nationalism of the Balkan Slavs, Austria in the first half of the nineteenth century also became a protector of Turkey. In response, Russia stepped up its support for Turkey's and Austria's enemies.

Turkey enjoyed the support of Russia's chief adversary, Great Britain; Britain was joined in the early 1850s by France. After a quarrel over the holy places of Palestine on July 21, 1853, Russia occupied Wallachia and Moldavia, which were still under Turkish suzerainty, as a "material guarantee" for the concessions to its "just demands" in Palestine. On October 4, 1853, Turkey declared war on Russia, as later did Britain and France, believing the integrity of the Turkish Empire to be at stake. Austria stayed neutral but took an anti-Russian stand. The Russian forces were worn down in the Crimea [5] until Tsar Nicholas I died in February 1855. His successor Alexander II sued for peace.

The Crimean War checked Russian ambitions in the Balkans, opened the Danube to international navigation, and neutralized the Black Sea. The Turkish Empire's territorial integrity and independence were guaranteed and so were Serbia's liberties. In 1859 the election of Alexander John Cuza (1820–73) as prince of Moldavia and Wallachia prepared their official union as Romania, which became formally independent in 1878. The Ottoman Empire, however, continued to decline, despite the efforts of the revolutionary movement, the Young Turks.

KEY

Sulayman's mosque still stands in Istanbul, symbolizing the once mighty Ottoman Empire. In decline from the 17th century, the empire was still strong enough in the early 19th to resist Russian expansionism and maintain power in Europe.

5

5 The Battle of the Alma on September 20, 1854, was the first big engagement of the Crimean War between Russia and Turkey, Britain, and France. Following the Treaty of Paris in 1856, Russia's dominance in southeast Europe ended, and Turkey gained a new lease on life under protection of the European powers.

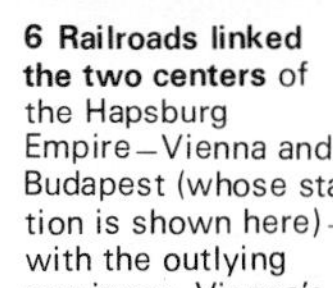

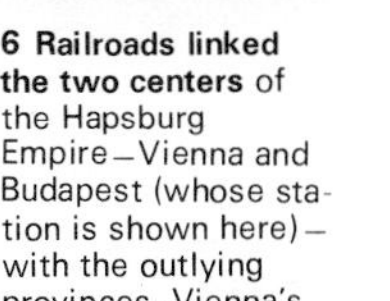

6

6 Railroads linked the two centers of the Hapsburg Empire—Vienna and Budapest (whose station is shown here)—with the outlying provinces. Vienna's railroad to the port of Trieste was built in 1854; Austrian imports in 1869–73 increased by 83%. Budapest was linked to Rijeka (Fiume) in 1873.

7

7 The coronation of Francis Joseph took place in Budapest on June 8, 1867. A dualist empire emerged as a result of a compromise *(Ausgleich)* between Vienna and Budapest in 1867, and Francis Joseph was separately crowned in Vienna as emperor of the Austrian half of the dual monarchy and as king of its Hungarian half in Budapest. A separate agreement *(Nagodba)* was reached with Croatia by the Hungarians in 1868, guaranteeing it special status and some autonomy within the Hungarian half. But Magyar nationalism was resisted by Romanians, Croats, Serbs, and Ukrainians. In the Austrian half the Czechs led the autonomy struggle against pan-Germanism.

8

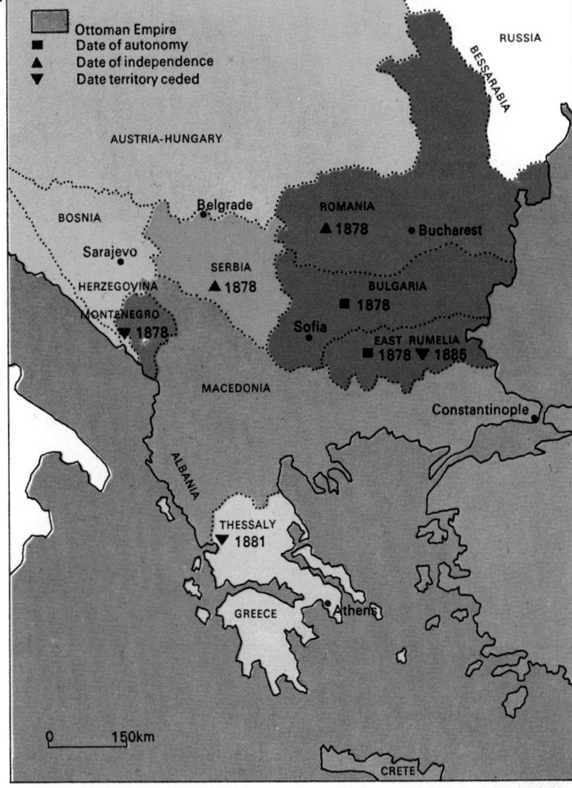

Ottoman Empire
Date of autonomy
Date of independence
Date territory ceded
RUSSIA
BESSARABIA
AUSTRIA-HUNGARY
Belgrade
ROMANIA
▲1878
Bucharest
BOSNIA
Sarajevo
SERBIA
▲1878
HERZEGOVINA
MONTENEGRO
▼1878
BULGARIA
■1878
Sofia
EAST RUMELIA
■1878 ▼1885
MACEDONIA
Constantinople
ALBANIA
THESSALY
▼1881
GREECE
Athens
0 150km
CRETE

8 The Congress of Berlin produced an uneasy compromise that carried the seeds of future conflict. It gave Austria-Hungary control over the strategic province of Bosnia-Herzegovina but not the title to permanent occupancy. Serbia developed large-scale propaganda among its fellow Serbs and other southern Slavs in Bosnia-Herzegovina and other southern Slav-inhabited provinces of the Hapsburg Empire. In 1908, Austria-Hungary decided to carry out the annexation of Bosnia-Herzegovina. Bulgaria, cheated of access to the Aegean and of Macedonia, nursed a grievance against Britain and other powers except Russia and Serbia. Romania had to give up southern Bessarabia to Russia.

Latin American independence

Most of the republics that make up present-day Latin America became independent between 1810 and 1824, the period that began after juntas set up in major cities of Spain's American empire had refused to accept Napoleon's brother Joseph as their ruler. The era ended with the victory of Antonio de Sucre's troops over Spanish forces in the battle at Ayacucho that established Peru's independence.

Haiti had seized independence from France in 1804. The Haitians later imposed their rule upon neighboring Santo Domingo, which did not achieve freedom as the Dominican Republic until 1844. Brazil, the Portuguese empire in America, became independent with very little bloodshed in 1822, and Dom Pedro I, the Portuguese prince regent, was crowned its emperor. Uruguay emerged as a separate state in 1828 after Argentina and Brazil had fought to claim it. Cuba and Puerto Rico remained Spanish possessions until the Spanish-American War (1898). Thereafter Cuba became independent (despite close ties with the United States), and Puerto Rico was ceded to the United States. Panama was a province of Colombia until 1903, when its inhabitants successfully revolted. Its new government leased in perpetuity to the United States (which had assisted the revolt) the strip of land 10 miles (16km) wide through which the Panama Canal, completed in 1914, was cut.

The consequences of independence

Independence meant essentially that men of European stock born in Latin America replaced men from the Iberian Peninsula in positions of power and privilege. The colonial social structure remained virtually intact, typified by the *hacienda*, or great landed estate. The Roman Catholic Church continued to exercise a strong conservative influence [5]. The military, strengthened by the prolonged wars, was another privileged institution and one that discouraged the establishment of effective civilian government in Spanish America.

The vast size of many of the new states, problems of communication, economic dislocation brought about by the wars, the new rulers' lack of experience in administration, and the illiteracy of the masses all contributed to extreme government instability. Few of the heroes of independence were able to govern successfully when peace came. Simón Bolívar (1783–1830) [Key], the greatest of them, died in self-imposed exile; José de San Martín (1778–1850) [6], the other outstanding liberator of Spanish America, decided to withdraw from politics and retired to Europe. The characteristic ruler of the new countries was the *caudillo*, or military dictator.

Relationships among countries

Relations among the Latin American countries following independence were generally neither close nor friendly. While Portuguese America remained intact (as Brazil), Spanish America had disintegrated along the lines of the old imperial administrative divisions, and there were often disputes over ill-defined boundaries, which sometimes led to armed conflict.

Geography and history have combined to separate the countries of Latin America.

CONNECTIONS

See also
1262 European imperialism in the 19th century
1200 International economy 1700–1800
1354 Latin America in the 20th century

VICEROYALTY OF NEW SPAIN
Havana
CAPTAINCY GENERAL OF CUBA
Mexico City
Antigua
CAPTAINCY GENERAL OF GUATEMALA
Panama
Caracas
CAPTAINCY GENERAL OF VENEZUELA
GUIANAS
Bogotá
VICEROYALTY OF NEW GRANADA
Quito
PRESIDENCY OF QUITO
VICEROYALTY OF PERU
VICEROYALTY OF BRAZIL
Lima
PRESIDENCY OF CARACAS
La Plata
Rio de Janeiro
1494 line of Tordesillas
CAPTAINCY GENERAL OF CHILE
VICEROYALTY OF LA PLATA
Buenos Aires
Santiago
Río de la Plata
Spanish
Portuguese
British
Dutch
French
Seats of government
0
1,500km

1 On the eve of the wars of independence (*c.* 1800) Latin America was divided between Spain and Portugal. The newly independent Spanish American states agreed among themselves to keep their national boundaries generally in line with the old colonial administrative divisions. But because these were often not clearly demarcated, territorial disputes inevitably arose. The Banda Oriental (the east bank of the Río de la Plata) had been a particular bone of contention between Spain and Portugal and continued to be one between Argentina and Brazil after independence. Following a war between these countries (1825–28) and diplomatic intervention by Britain, the disputed territory became a buffer state—the new Republic of Uruguay.

2 The Washington Conference (1889–90) convened on Oct. 2, 1889, in Washington, D.C., and was attended by all western hemisphere countries except the Dominican Republic. Political and economic questions were discussed, and the International Union of American Republics established.

3 Joseph Bonaparte (1768–1844) was imposed on Spain by his elder brother Napoleon I after the French invaded the Iberian Peninsula (1807–08). The issue of Latin American independence was forced when the French deposed Ferdinand VII of Spain and then threatened Portugal. Spanish Americans at first pledged loyalty to Ferdinand but later declared their independence. The Portuguese royal family fled briefly to Brazil, and the king's son stayed as regent of Brazil, declaring it independent in 1822.

4 Native Indians generally viewed Latin American independence as no more than a change of masters. Many who had been subject to the old forms of colonial bondage became *peones* (peasant laborers) on the great estates.

5 A church in Quito, capital of Ecuador, with an ornate and richly sculptured structure, reflects the power and wealth of the church in Latin America, both in colonial and modern times. But church-state relations were generally uneasy following independence.

Formidable physical barriers have been a major cause of this isolation; regionalism within individual countries, another. During the colonial era each division of Spain's American empire was linked to the mother country rather than to each other. Since independence, relations with powers outside the region generally have been much more important than those among the Latin American countries themselves, although efforts at regional cooperation continue.

Dependence on other countries

Colonial trading patterns continued after independence. Most countries had to rely on exporting one or two primary products and on importing manufactured goods. The new states of Latin America thus became economically and financially dependent upon powers outside the region. During the nineteenth century Great Britain was the major economic power in Latin America, especially in Argentina. British naval power forced Brazil to acquiesce in efforts to stamp out the slave trade. The eventual abolition of slavery itself was a major cause of the overthrow of the Brazilian emperor, Pedro II, and the establishment of a republic in 1889.

By that time the United States had greatly increased its territory at the expense of Mexico, which it defeated in war (1846–48). Even earlier, in 1823, President Monroe (1758–1831) had enunciated his famous Monroe Doctrine. It warned European powers against incursions or further colonization in Latin America and implied that the United States had a special relationship with Latin America. By the end of the nineteenth century the United States, with military strength, was able to compel respect for the Monroe Doctrine. At the same time it promoted "pan-Americanism," embodying the idea that the countries of the Americas shared a community of interests and a special "system" of international relations. A conference of the United States and almost all of the Latin American countries, held in Washington (1889–90), covered numerous issues of mutual concern and established the International Union of American Republics.

KEY

Simón Bolívar, known throughout the continent as "the Liberator," was the greatest hero of Latin American independence. He played a leading part in winning freedom for his native land, Venezuela, and for Colombia, Ecuador, Peru, and Bolivia, the country named for him. Bolivar brought together the first three of these countries in one state, the republic of Colombia, and he inspired the Congress of Panama (1826) with the principal aim of establishing a league of Spanish-American nations. But the league did not materialize: Greater Colombia dissolved into its constituent states, and Bolívar died, disillusioned, in 1830.

6

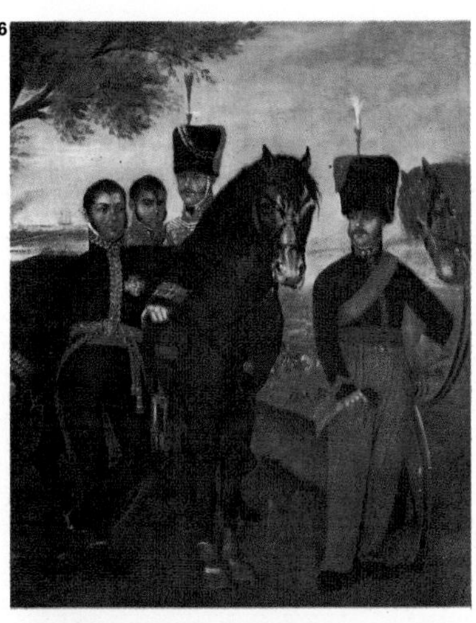

6 José de San Martín (right) was the outstanding liberator of southern South America. He assured independence for Argentina and achieved it for Chile and part of Peru (including Lima, the capital). While the liberation of Peru, the last great stronghold of Spanish power in South America, was incomplete, San Martín had a famous meeting with Bolívar at Guayaquil in Ecuador (July 1822) to discuss the future of Spanish America. San Martin then withdrew, leaving the field to Bolivar.

7

7 San Martín's "Army of the Andes" crossed the moutains through the Uspallata pass at a height of 12,464ft (3,799m)—an extraordinary military achievement. The army was on its way to liberate Chile, in cooperation with the Chilean patriot Bernardo O'Higgins (1778–1842). The Spanish forces in Chile were taken completely by surprise and routed at Chacabuco on February 12, 1817. In the following April another victory, this time at Maipú, ensured the independence of Chile.

8

8 Bolívar (right) **triumphantly** accepts the surrender of the Spanish at the Battle of Boyacá (1819), which assured Colombia's independence.

9

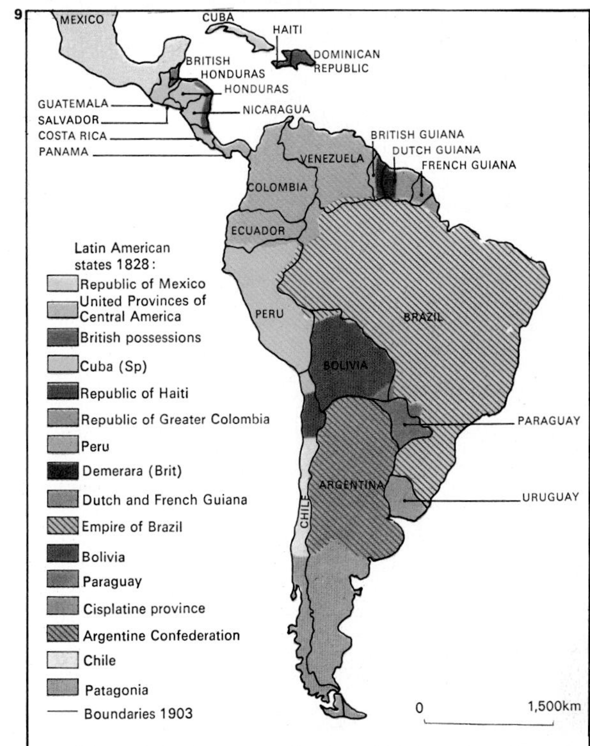

MEXICO
CUBA
HAITI
DOMINICAN REPUBLIC
BRITISH HONDURAS
HONDURAS
GUATEMALA
SALVADOR
NICARAGUA
COSTA RICA
PANAMA
BRITISH GUIANA
DUTCH GUIANA
FRENCH GUIANA
VENEZUELA
COLOMBIA
ECUADOR
PERU
BRAZIL
BOLIVIA
PARAGUAY
URUGUAY
ARGENTINA
CHILE
Latin American states 1828:
Republic of Mexico
United Provinces of Central America
British possessions
Cuba (Sp)
Republic of Haiti
Republic of Greater Colombia
Peru
Demerara (Brit)
Dutch and French Guiana
Empire of Brazil
Bolivia
Paraguay
Cisplatine province
Argentine Confederation
Chile
Patagonia
Boundaries 1903
0
1,500km

9 Latin American in 1903 looked much as it does today. Mexico had long before lost more than half its national territory (the former Viceroyalty of New Spain) to the United States. Cuba and Panama had become nominally independent, although virtually protectorates of the United States, in 1902 and 1903 respectively. Paraguay had declared itself independent in 1842. Bolivia had lost its coastal territory to Chile in the War of the Pacific (1879–83) and was now landlocked. Central America had dissolved into its constituent states (Costa Rica, El Salvador, Guatemala, Honduras, and Nicaragua) as early as 1838.

Britain and the Industrial Revolution

The first 70 years of the nineteenth century saw unprecedented economic development in Great Britain as forces unleashed at the end of the eighteenth century created the first urban industrial society. Population growth and urban development followed an acceleration of industrialization based on a great expansion of trade, the widespread application of the factory system to production, and the harnessing of steam-driven machinery to an increasing range of processes. Steam power was also applied to transport with the development of railroads and the first steamships. Urban life prompted Britain to develop many social and political institutions that were to become standard in other countries as the Industrial Revolution spread to Europe and the United States.

The British lead

Britain's economic development between 1800 and 1870 was startling, even compared with the progress of the late eighteenth century. There were giant increases in production. Output of pig iron grew 60 times, coal output ten times, and total trade by the same amount. Britain maintained and increased its lead over other countries by advances in mechanization and factory production. In a real sense Britain had become the "workshop of the world" by the time of the Crystal Palace Exhibition [Key] in 1851 when industrial expertise was on display.

Britain supplied a large percentage of the world's textiles, iron, and machinery, and a massive increase in its export income was stimulated by the development of "free trade," especially during the 1841–46 ministry of Robert Peel (1788–1850). After 1850 trade expanded even more rapidly than it had in the first half of the century, encouraging further economic development. New industries such as steel and shipbuilding began to balance Britain's dependence on exports of textiles [10] and iron products.

The development of railroads after the opening of the Stockton and Darlington Railway in 1825 gave a major boost to the economy, making it possible to move bulky goods cheaply and stimulating the iron and steel industries. The railroads served to concentrate production still further, as raw materials could be brought long distances and finished goods sent to ports many miles away. During the boom years of "railroad mania in 1845–47 a basic railroad network covering the major towns, industrial areas, and ports had been laid out by such railroad pioneers as George Stephenson, Isambard Kingdom Brunel, George Hudson, and Thomas Brassey. In addition, the development of railroads played an important part in refining investment procedures.

Financial organization

As the pace of industrial expansion quickened, the need arose for a more elaborate banking system. In Britain the less reliable "country" banks were increasingly superseded by "joint-stock" banks after 1826. The Bank Charter Act of 1844 secured the role of the Bank of England as the central note-issuing authority and guarantor of the rest of the banking system. Company finance and formation were regulated by a series of limited liability and company acts in the middle of the nineteenth century. The growth of trade led to the expansion of the

CONNECTIONS

See also
1220 The early Industrial Revolution
1284 European industrialization 1870–1914
1280 The impact of steam
1262 European imperialism in the 19th century
1258 Architecture in the 19th century
1274 The United States: the opening of the West
282 Energy resources: coal
938 Industry and economics
1584 Modern technology
1594 The Steel Age

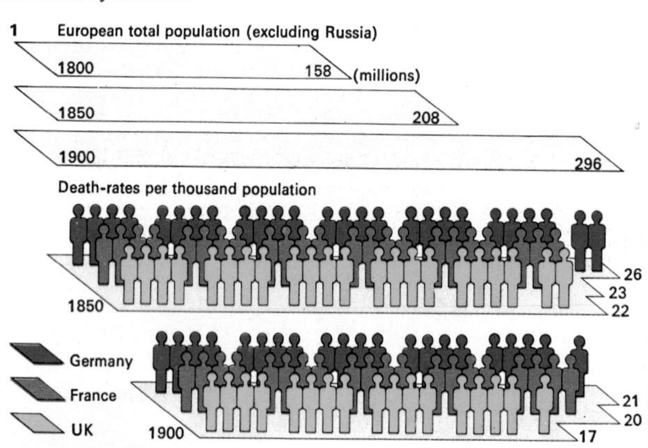

1
European total population (excluding Russia)
1800
158
(millions)
1850
208
1900
296
Death-rates per thousand population
1850
26
23
22
Germany
France
UK
1900
21
20
17

1 Europe's population rose steadily during the century, mainly because of a falling death rate through improvements in medicine, diet, and living conditions. Birth rates also tended to rise with industrialization and urbanization. As a result, the total population of Europe almost doubled in the course of the century, quickening migration from the countryside to the increasingly crowded urban centers.

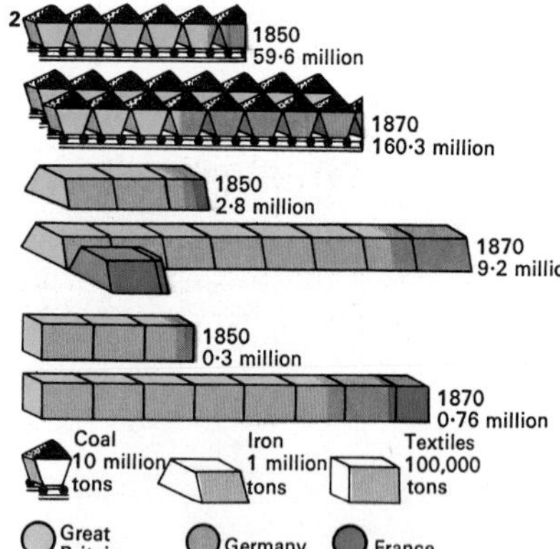

2
1850
59·6 million
1870
160·3 million
1850
2·8 million
1870
9·2 million
1850
0·3 million
1870
0·76 million
Coal
10 million tons
Iron
1 million tons
Textiles
100,000 tons
Great Britain
Germany
France

2 Industrial output was rising in many parts of Europe by the middle of the 19th century. Germany and France began to take a significant share in producing iron, coal, and textiles, and smaller countries such as Belgium and Switzerland were also beginning to develop important industrial sectors. European industrialization still lagged behind that of Britain and was inhibited by Britain's marketing dominance.

3

1 Almshouses
2 Congregational church
3 Washhouses
4 Wesleyan chapel
5 Factory school
6 Factory

3 New industrial towns, such as Saltaire in Yorkshire, England, provided shelter and adequate living conditions for large numbers of workers. By the middle of the 19th century factory owners and municipal authorities began to create some order out of the squalor of early factory towns. Regular gridiron patterns of workers' housing were built, providing the most basic amenities of sanitation, water supply, and mains drainage. Local philanthropy often paid for schools and hospitals.

WEST-GATE

4 Riots and strikes in England during the 1840s accompanied efforts by the Chartist movement to win urban workers the vote. Industrialization brought many such political movements and played a part in the European revolutions of 1848.

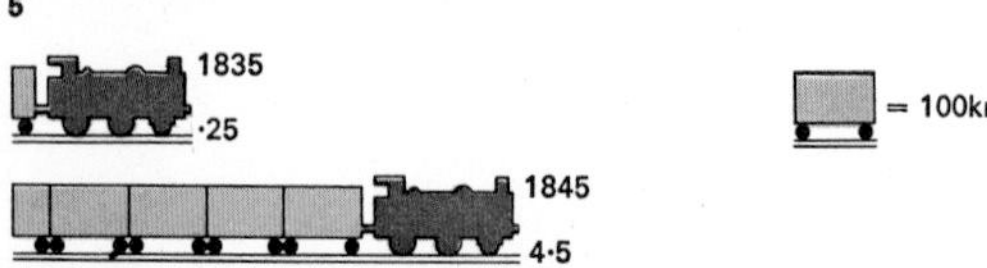

5
1835
·25
1845
4·5
= 100km

1870
31·7

5 Railroad expansion in Belgium between 1835 and 1870 was typical of the rapid developments that took place in Europe in the middle and late century. British engineers, contractors, and equipment were often employed in an effort to overtake the lead Britain had established after pioneering railroad development in 1825. Though railroads developed more slowly on the Continent, Britain had opened a major trunk route system for carrying goods and people by 1847.

Stock Exchange and the rise of provincial exchanges [8] to deal in specific commodities. By 1870, Britain was not only the center of the world's industry and trade but its financial capital. Personal wealth increased rapidly [7].

Population growth

Economic and industrial development was accompanied throughout Europe by population growth [1]. Britain's population increased most rapidly of all, doubling between 1801 and 1851. By the middle of the century Britain was no longer a predominantly rural nation; more than half its people lived in towns [3]. In 1801 there were only 14 European towns with more than 100,000 inhabitants, but by 1870 there were more than 100.

Urban development brought with it a wide range of social and political problems. To deal with these Britain, as the first industrial nation, pioneered many social institutions fundamental to modern life. Measures to regulate public health, provide basic sanitary and housing amenities, and preserve public order through the formation of professional police (the "bobbies") were copied by other countries. Similarly, the introduction of a reliable, cheap postal service [9], the rise of cheap newspapers, and the development of cheap railroad travel did something to offset the human misery that often accompanied urban development and industrial advance.

Factory Acts [6] regulated child and female labor, as well as hours of work, from the 1830s. Under early pioneers such as Robert Owen (1771–1858) and Robert Applegarth, industrial workers began to organize themselves into trade unions, political associations, and the cooperative movement [4].

In Europe the gathering pace of industrial development was shown in the growth of railroads [5], textile industries, and iron and coal production [2] by 1870. Belgium, France, and Germany made the largest strides, and although far behind Britain, both Germany and the United States were poised for rapid industrial development in the latter years of the nineteenth century.

KEY

The Great Exhibition of 1851, in London, marked a high point in Victorian industrialization. Organized to show the progress in trade and manufactures achieved since the first days of the Industrial Revolution, it became a symbol of British manufacturing ingenuity and dominance of world trade, although it exhibited industrial goods from many other countries. It was intended to display the virtues of free trade *(laissez-faire)* as an agent of economic progress. To house it, a revolutionary building of glass and iron was designed by Joseph Paxton and built in only seven months. The Royal Society of Arts sponsored the exhibition with the enthusiastic backing of Albert, the prince consort, and it was attended by visitors from many countries.

6

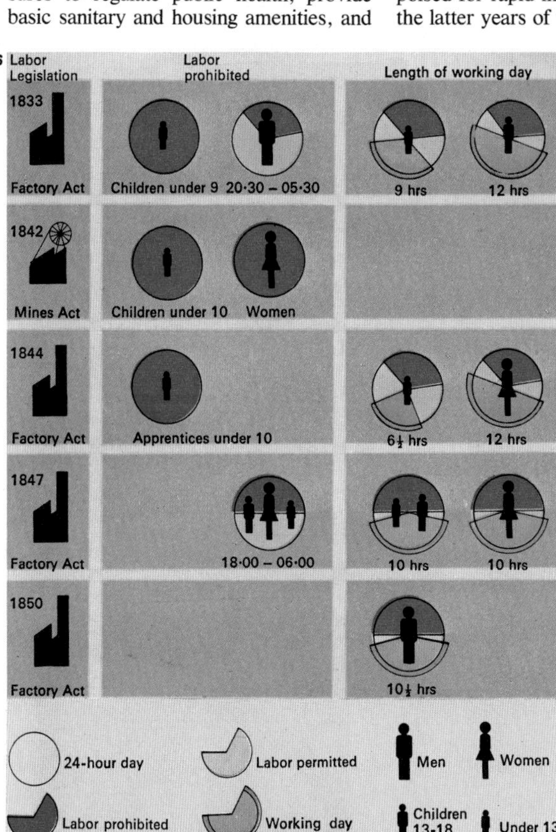

Labor Legislation
Labor prohibited
Length of working day
1833
Factory Act
Children under 9
20·30 – 05·30
9 hrs
12 hrs
1842
Mines Act
Children under 10
Women
1844
Factory Act
Apprentices under 10
6½ hrs
12 hrs
1847
Factory Act
18·00 – 06·00
10 hrs
10 hrs
1850
Factory Act
10½ hrs
24-hour day
Labor permitted
Men
Women
Labor prohibited
Working day
Children 13-18
Under 13

6 Exploitation of child and female labor, with long hours, low wages, and poor conditions, was a major abuse of the Industrial Revolution. In the middle of the 19th century, humanitarian concern in Britain led to the passing of Factory Acts to protect women and children.

7

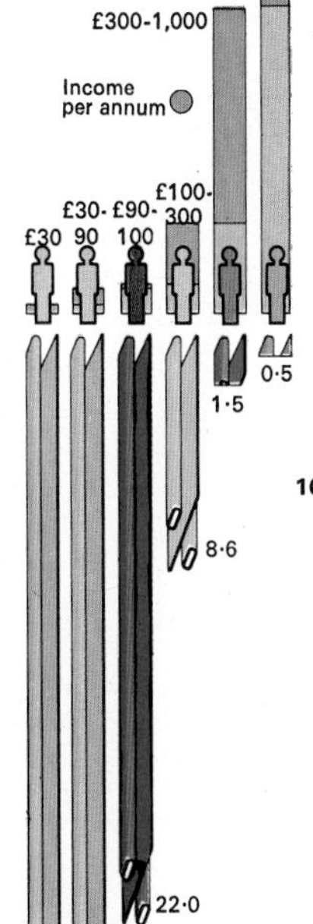

£1,000+
£300-1,000
Income per annum
£100-300
£30-90
£90-100
£30
0·5
1·5
8·6
22·0
27·7
39·7% of population
Less skilled and farm workers
Lower middle-class and skilled workers
Lower middle-class
Middle-class
Upper-class

7 Incomes and social status in Britain changed with the rise of the middle and professional classes and the creation of a new class of manufacturers. But in the mid-19th century the largest group earned less than £30 a year.

8

8 The Cotton Exchange in Manchester was one of a number of major commercial institutions set up throughout Britain to deal in particular commodities. The growth of large-scale industry and the demands of a more complex society forced rapid developments in finance and banking. The Stock Exchange, which had become the center for financial dealings, continued to expand, doubling in size during the 1860s alone.

9 A

POSTAGE
ONE PENNY

B

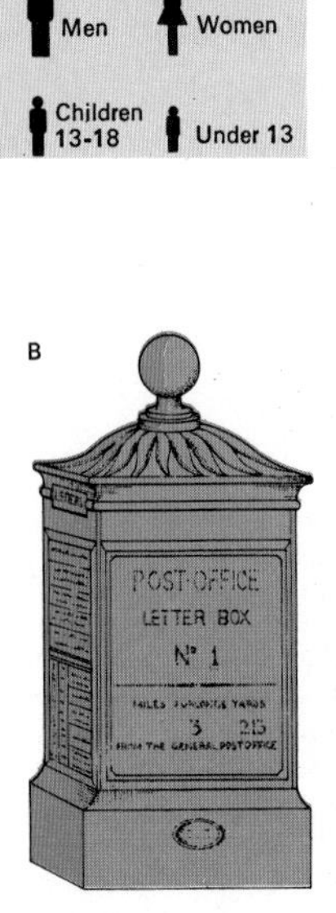

POST-OFFICE
LETTER BOX
No 1

9 A cheap postal system was one of the many new social amenities made possible by growing community wealth and a more ordered urban society. In Britain, the railroad system permitted rapid movement of mail and a "penny post" was introduced by Rowland Hill in 1840 [A]. The British Post Office introduced the first of its distinctive red letter boxes in London in 1855 [B]. A telegraph sytem came into use in the middle of the century, with undersea cables providing the first international means of communication. By 1861, 12,250mi of cable had been laid.

10

10 The cotton mill was the symbol of the 19th-century industrial town. Cotton was the most completely industrialized sector of the economy, being almost entirely mechanized, steam-powered, and factory-based. It was also one of the first industries to develop in Europe. Mills were usually gaunt, utilitarian structures, housing long banks of spinning and weaving machines, tended largely by women and children. Conditions were often dangerous with many accidents; hours were long, even for very young children, and discipline was strict. In Britain by 1851 over half of the population lived in urban areas. Factory conditions improved only slowly.

The novel in the 19th century

There were many technical innovations in printing between 1800 and 1900 that had important effects on the novel. The use of steel engraving, stereotypes, and mechanical presses completely altered the production process. The ability to produce large numbers of books rapidly demanded new marketing techniques. Circulating libraries [Key], conveniently located bookstores, and cheap reprints of successful titles helped to establish and satisfy a market that expanded with the rising population, increased literacy [7], and greater educational opportunities.

The British novel

The first two important British novelists of the nineteenth century, Jane Austen (1775–1817) [2] and Walter Scott (1771–1832) [1], were not much concerned with the problems of industrialization [6] or the new intellectual climate of Europe following the French Revolution. Jane Austen's domestic comedies, carefully structured in her six novels, are at once amusing and deeply serious. Scott, who virtually invented the historical novel, enjoyed a popular success that brought him a fortune.

Popular success was also achieved by Scott's Victorian successors, William Makepeace Thackeray (1811–63), Anthony Trollope (1815–82), and above all by Charles Dickens (1812–70) [3] and George Eliot (1819–80). Dickens built up an intense and astonishingly close relationship with his British and American public in his sentimental but brilliantly funny and sometimes despairing depiction of the distortions and cruelties of city life. George Eliot (born Mary Ann Evans) is provincial in her subject matter but European in the range and discipline of her thought.

The mid-century also saw the publication of the Brontë sisters' novels. Charlotte (1816–55) was the most successful, but Emily (1818–48), author of significant poems as well as of the novel *Wuthering Heights* (1847), has since been more highly regarded. Important later novelists include George Meredith (1828–1909), George Gissing (1857–1903), Samuel Butler (1835–1902), and Thomas Hardy (1840–1928). Hardy's novels about Wessex express a passionate feeling for man's tragic involvement in nature and estrangement from it.

The novel in Western Europe

French fiction in this period was much more urbane and less prudish than British fiction. The realists Stendhal (1783–1842), Honoré de Balzac (1799–1850) [5], and Gustave Flaubert (1821–80) depicted French history and bourgeois life at great length and in minute detail. Romantic experience and attitudes, however, were given vivid expression in the works of Victor Hugo (1802–85) and George Sand (1804–76). Emile Zola (1840–1902) [8], leader of the naturalists, produced frank and painfully pessimistic studies of the workings of heredity and environment in human affairs [6]. The enormous popular success of the historical romances of Alexandre Dumas the father (1802–70) was matched by the success of his son of the same name (1824–95).

The giant figure of Johann Wolfgang von Goethe (1749–1832) overshadows nineteenth-century German literature. In his

CONNECTIONS

See also
1240 Poetry and theater in the 19th century
1188 The 18th century: the novel and the press
1222 Origins of romanticism
1374 American writing: into the 20th century
1376 Emergent literatures of the 20th century
1776 Newspapers and magazines

1

1 Scott's novels are full of dramatic incidents, such as Amy Robsart's death in *Kenilworth*, pictured here. His success with historical romance was huge. He built a country house with the proceeds, went bankrupt, then wrote himself out of debt. Much of his writing is slack, and he is no longer so widely read, but his greatness is unquestionable. His use of famous historical characters is discreet; they are rarely central. His sense of how history bears on the experience of ordinary people has a breadth and humanity declared Shakespearean by his admirers.

2

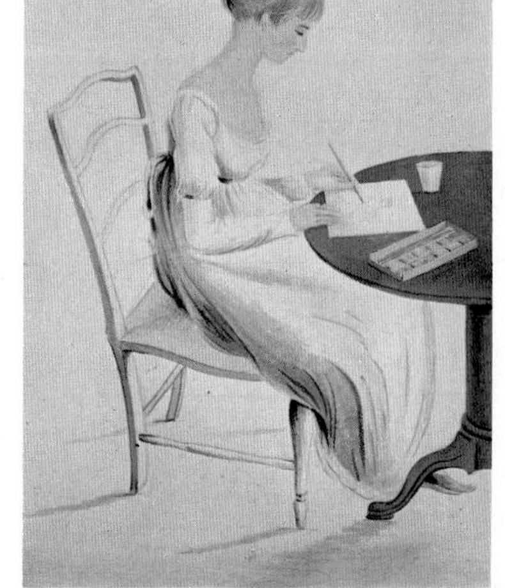

2 Jane Austen (imaginatively portrayed here) concentrated on witty, incisive descriptions of rural English society. Her sense of form had its roots in the classical English comedy of William Congreve. She was the first of a remarkable line of women novelists whose lives were otherwise provincial and obscure. During her lifetime she earned only £250 for six novels, but she is now regarded as one of the great English novelists. Two of her best works, *Pride and Prejudice* and *Emma*, are about ordinary people unaffected by world events.

3

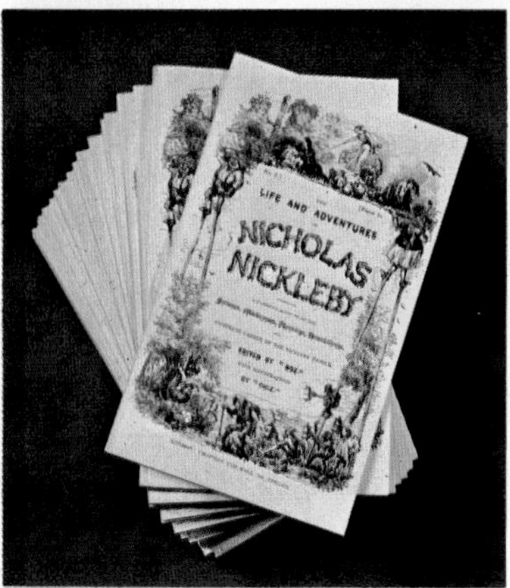

3 Dickens' novels were published in frequent illustrated installments, as with *Nicholas Nickleby*, the parts of which are shown here. Part-publication was common practice. It allowed Dickens to keep in close contact with his public and alter plots if sales fell off. He kept the English-speaking world in agonized suspense over the death of Little Nell in *The Old Curiosity Shop*. He was, however, a serious artist who influenced, many authors.

4 A

LATEST INTELLIGENCE.

THE SIEGE OF SEBASTOPOL.

(BY SUBMARINE AND BRITISH TELEGRAPH.)

VIENNA, MONDAY MORNING.

The *Morgen Post*, which is a paper of no great authority, has the following :—

" CZERNOWITZ, Nov. 11.

" On the 6th the whole garrison of Sebastopol, amounting to 65,000 men, made a sortie.

" A furious battle ensued, which was not ended when the messenger left ; but the allies had the advantage."

We have received, at half-past 4 o'clock this morning, the following despatch, dated yesterday afternoon, from our correspondent at Vienna :—

" The news forwarded this morning relative to the sortie was but too true.

" Reliable information has been given me that the English suffered a very heavy loss, and had three Generals wounded.

" It is said that later intelligence has been received, according to which the Russians had at last been repelled with a loss of 3,000 men."

B

THE MURDER OF
MARIA MARTEN
IN THE RED BARN AT POLSTED.
Containing the whole Account of the horrid Murder,
COMMITTED BY HER LOVER AND SEDUCER WILLIAM CORDER
ACCOUNT OF HIS CONFESSION AND EXECUTION

4 Mass circulation newspapers became possible after the development of new printing techniques and the ending of the newspaper tax in 1855. Serious journalistic innovations, such as coverage of the Crimean War by *The Times* of London [A], had less influence on novels than sensationalism [B].

wake the regionalist antiromanticism of Theodor Storm (1817–88) and Fritz Reuter (1810–74) seems relatively less significant. Italian prose in this period was dominated not by one great man but by one great book, *The Betrothed* by Alessandro Manzoni (1785–1873), a patriotic Romantic who was greatly influenced by Scott. The task of modernizing the Italian novel fell to Giovanni Verga (1840–1922) and Antonio Fogazzaro (1842–1911).

The literary tradition in Russia

In some ways the most surprising national achievement in the development of the nineteenth-century novel was that of Russia. The conflicts between a liberal aristocratic culture, a backward and brutalized peasantry, political oppression, and the Orthodox Church may be part of the explanation. The first major Russian novelists were Mikhail Lermontov (1814–41) and Nikolai Gogol (1809–52). Their successors, Ivan Turgenev (1818–83), Fyodor Dostoevsky, (1821–81), and Leo Tolstoy (1828–1910) [9] were to make a deep impression on Western European culture. Tolstoy's *War and Peace* and *Anna Karenina* are among the greatest of all literary works.

The American novel

While Dostoevsky's intellectual perspectives are significantly "modern," it was Henry James (1843–1916) who introduced "modern" techniques into the novel. The formal complexity and ironic indirectness of his work are also characteristic of Nathaniel Hawthorne (1806–64), Herman Melville (1819–91), and Mark Twain (1835–1910). As a young critic James attacked the seemingly unstructured novels of Dickens, and in his own fiction he abandoned the convention that the author knows everything and selected one or two characters from whose point of view he told his story. This technique led to the writing of shorter, more economical works by others. With the advent of cheap editions, the great circulating libraries began to decline and publishers became less interested in length for its own sake. The age of the Victorian novel was over.

KEY

The Temple of the Muses in Finsbury, London, was a fee supported "public" lending library. Novel reading was widespread in middle- and upper-class households by the middle of the 19th century. In Britain even the wealthy subscribed to circulating libraries. Consequently, a novel's success or failure depended on the good will of these libraries, which had a vested interest in keeping books both expensive and "pure." "Society will not tolerate the natural in our art," complained Thackeray in his novel *Pendennis* (1848). But the influences of the lending libraries were not easily resisted.

5

5 This remarkable sculpture of Balzac by Rodin suggests the bulk and force of Balzac's vision of human society. His 85 novels attempt to characterize life in France between the 1789 revolution and the fall of Louis Philippe in 1848. Although he imagined society as a huge organism, his individual characters are lively and real.

6

6 Germinal, Emile Zola's outspoken novel, described the degrading conditions of life endured by miners working and living in the more animal than human conditions of northern French mines seen here. In a more decorous way, Charles Dickens depicted the moral and emotional consequences of industrialism in England.

7

THE SAVOYARD BOY.

AH! here is a Sa-voy-ard boy, with his or-gan and his dog.

He has come to play us a tune to make us glad.

And what is that mount-ed on the dog's back?

Why, it is in-deed a lit-tle mon-key, the Sa-voy-ard's pet mon-key!

These poor boys come from

THE SAVOYARD BOY. 81

their coun-try a long way off, to gain a few pence.

Their own coun-try is not so rich as ours, and we ought not to de-ny them a few pence.

We may chance, some time or o-ther, to be left friend-less in a strange coun-try, and we shall then feel ve-ry glad if a-ny kind peo-ple take no-tice of us, and give us food, or mo-ney to buy food with.

We should al-ways give to those who are in need, and if we do so, we shall be sure to get help when we our-selves are in need.

You will some-times meet with per-sons who beg, and could do with-out beg-ging, but they like to live an i-dle life.

7 Green's Universal Primer injected heavy-handed moralizing into reading lessons. Urban literacy was fairly high in the 1840s. About three-quarters of the working class was literate by the middle of the century, but total illiteracy ranged between 16% and 25%. Most people read only "novels of the lowest character," and fears were expressed about whether "good" literature could survive.

8 Emile Zola in *Les Rougon-Macquart* attempted to follow the adventures of a family during the 1880s, calling it "a physiological history of the Second Empire." The series has 20 volumes with modern themes: in *The Dram Shop* (1877) the evils of drink; in *Nana* (1880) sex; in *Earth* (1887) brutality of peasant life. Naturalists believed writers should portray the brutality of industrial life.

8

9

9 Tolstoy's funeral was nonreligious, yet he died with the reputation of a saint because of his religious and political devotion to the ideal "simple peasant" life. In *What is Art?* (1897) he had repudiated most of European literature including his own and Shakespeare's works, yet in his own ascetic and prophetic old age he demonstrated the same passion and contradictory idealism with which he had invested his fictional heroes.

Poetry and theater in the 19th century

The Romantic movement in poetry at the end of the eighteenth century stressed intensity of emotion rather than elegance and art, freedom of expression rather than stylistic rules. In England its most important forerunner was William Blake (1757–1827), although Walter Scott (1771–1832) and Thomas Moore (1779–1852) were better known at the time. The rebellious spirit of the movement was epitomized by the life of Lord Byron (1788–1824) who, with Johann Wolfgang von Goethe (1749–1832), towered over literature in the 1820s.

William Wordsworth (1770–1850) and John Keats (1795–1821) better represent the actual changes in English poetry brought about by Romanticism. Wordsworth's ideas about mind and nature [1] forced him to adopt an unorthodox style and subject matter. His creed was to take "ordinary things" and show them in "unusual aspect," he believed that intense joy could arise from deep harmony with nature. Percy Bysshe Shelley (1792–1822) wrote more directly of the power of joy as a reforming influence, while Keats stressed the power of beauty. The lyrical intensity of Keats' poetry deeply influenced later poets.

Lyricism, nature, and the exotic continued to attract Victorian poets. Robert Browning (1812–89) used antilyrical effects, tough rhythms, and difficult meanings but was always drawn to the exotic. Faith in joy and the senses waned, however. Both Alfred Lord Tennyson (1809–92) and Matthew Arnold (1822–88) wrote a more somber verse, and Tennyson had earnest doubts about the relevance of his lyric gift. A reaction against undue moral earnestness came with Algernon Charles Swinburne (1837–1909) and the Decadents, who stressed flagrantly amoral beauty. But the greatest of the later British poets, Gerard Manley Hopkins (1844–89), Thomas Hardy (1840–1928), and W. B. Yeats (1865–1939), retained a moral vision.

Romanticism and anti-Romanticism

The writings of Wordsworth's friend, the poet and critic Samuel Taylor Coleridge (1772–1834), reveal the debt English Romanticism owed to Germany, where Goethe, a champion of the Storm and Stress movement, had established the concept of the suffering hero. But Goethe's work shows the difficulty of arbitrary distinctions between romanticism and classicism. He wrote the classical *Roman Elegies* as well as passionate lyrics to Charlotte von Stein. Similarly, the Romantic *Songs* of Heinrich Heine (1797–1856) are balanced by his more somber later poems. The Byronic mood was recreated with irony as well as sentiment in Russia by Alexander Pushkin (1799–1837) [2] and Mikhail Lermontov (1814–41).

In France, Victor Hugo (1802–85), poet, novelist, and dramatist, led other Romantic anticlassicists including Alphonse Lamartine (1790–1869), Alfred de Musset (1810–57), and the young Théophile Gautier (1811–72). But Charles Baudelaire (1821–67), lyricist of moral decay [5], the boy-poet Arthur Rimbaud (1854–91), and Paul Verlaine (1844–96) are better seen as early Symbolists rather than late Romantics. Stéphane Mallarmé (1842–98) and the Symbolists tried to create a poetry of

CONNECTIONS

See also

1238 The novel in the 19th century
1222 Origins of romanticism
1374 American writing: into the 20th century
1376 Emergent literatures of the 20th century

1 The English Lake District inspired some of Wordsworth's finest work. There, faced with sublimely rugged scenery, he experienced a sense of harmony with nature that he expressed as a moral force. In 1798 he and Samuel Taylor Coleridge (1772–1834) published *Lyrical Ballads*, which included Coleridge's "Ancient Mariner." Coleridge was later more famous as a critic.

2 Pushkin, the first major Russian writer, was exiled for writing epigrams against the Russian government. During his exile he read and imitated Byron, but in his masterpiece, *Eugene Onegin* (1833), a novel in verse, he transformed the Byronic hero. He also wrote popular prose romances and felt the conflict between patriotism and liberalism shared by many Russians later in the century.

3 Riots followed the first performance of Hugo's stage rhapsody *Hernani* (1830), which broke the rules of classicism. Hugo's romanticism was ardently supported by young French poets, but a reaction against emotionalism and looseness of style soon followed as poets turned to subtler themes and more concise imagery.

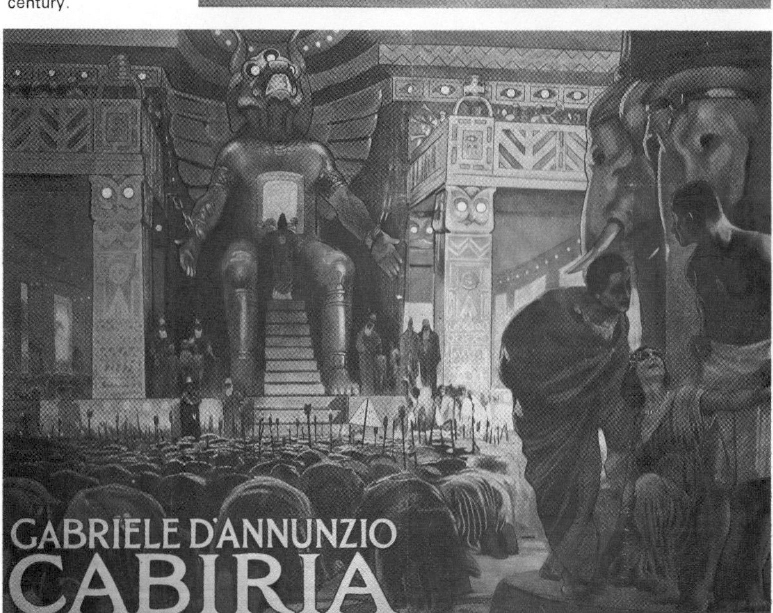

GABRIELE D'ANNUNZIO
CABIRIA
ITALA FILM-TORINO

4 Gabriel D'Annunzio, who worked on the script of the film *Cabiria* (1913), was also a dramatist, novelist, and flamboyant political leader. His later support of Mussolini has tarnished the reputation of the sensuous poetry he wrote in the 1890s during his love affair with actress Eleanora Duse.

emblems to convey the meaning beneath the surface of things. In Italy, Giosuè Carducci (1835–1907) led a reaction against undisciplined verse, but Gabriele D'Annunzio (1863–1938) [4] sounded late in the century the authentic note of Romantic joy.

From melodrama to naturalism in drama
Romantic and post-Romantic drama is generally weak as theater. The plays of Goethe show classical influences, while his masterpiece, *Faust,* transcends categories. Hugo's triumph in France with the Romantic *Hernani* [3] is hard now to understand. Victorien Sardou (1831–1908) and Alexandre Dumas (1802–70) wrote successful comedies and romances. Later Alexandre Dumas the younger (1824–95) produced some solemn social problem plays and Edmond Rostand (1868–1918) poetic dramas. But the dominance of opera and of Shakespearean revivals [8], artificial acting, and massive sets, inhibited convincing representation of contemporary society.

Toward the end of the century, three major dramatists emerged as forerunners of modern theater. The Norwegian Henrik Ibsen (1828–1906) moved from verse plays to a series of controversial and influential social dramas in prose, among them *A Doll's House* [6]. August Strindberg (1849–1912), a Swede, injected an element of psychosexual horror into his work. Like Ibsen, he moved away from naturalism toward symbolism. The Russian plays of Anton Chekhov (1860–1904) are notable for their formal grace, realism of detail, and insight into personal and social insecurities [7].

New directions in the theater
The comedies of the Irish dramatist Oscar Wilde (1854–1900) [9] were old-fashioned in plot and characterization, but Wilde used his scintillating wit to parody cleverly the conventions of melodrama and Romantic comedy. George Bernard Shaw (1856–1950), a champion of Ibsen, used similar techniques in constructing plays of social and moral ideas, at once amusing, humane, and deeply thoughtful. Experiments, however, were pointing toward expressionism and the theater of the absurd.

KEY

Shelley's death by drowning is immortalized in this memorial to him in University College, Oxford. A radical and passionate poet, Shelley connected the health of society with the health of literature and denied that poets had any obligation to express contemporary ideas of morality.

5

5 Charles Baudelaire in *The Flowers of Evil* (1857) foreshadowed Symbolism by searching for significance in all things, not merely the respectable, and finding symbols of hollowness in the beauty that hid corruption. He was responsible for the European vogue for Edgar Allan Poe and was an important influence on English poets, especially Swinburne and the poets of the 1890s.

6

JANET ACHURCH
HELMER
ACT II

6 Nora Helmer, here dancing the tarantella, was the central character of Ibsen's most controversial play, *A Doll's House* (1879), which was seen as a breakthrough in theatrical realism. His audience must have expected this drama of blackmail and wifely loyalty to end in a triumph of domestic virtue. But in a famous final scene Nora leaves her husband and children to seek her own identity.

7

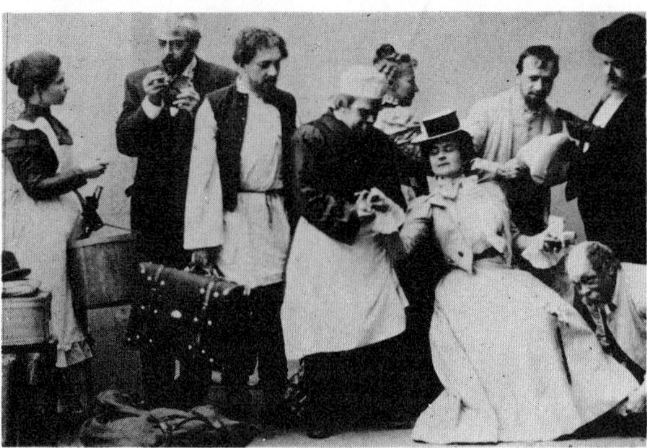

7 Chekhov's The Seagull, as produced in 1898 by Konstantin Stanislavsky, was a landmark in drama. Stanislavsky taught actors to identify with the characters they played, a technique particularly adapted to Chekhov's plays, which concentrated on the unfolding of character rather than on plot development or melodramatic situations.

8

8 Henry Irving (1838–1905), here playing Hamlet, led the idolatry of Shakespeare, who had become an English institution and an important influence in Europe by the 19th century. Shakespeare provided virtuoso actors with great parts. But heavy naturalistic sets led to tediously long intervals and to brutal cutting of the original text.

9

9 Oscar Wilde, who was imprisoned for homosexuality after a famous trial, was the wittiest dramatist of the 1890s and a leading poet of the English aesthetic movement. He was a master of paradox and an apostle of "art for art's sake."

European Romantic art: landscape painting

"Everything is becoming more airy and light than before, everything tends toward landscape," wrote the German painter Philipp Otto Runge (1777–1810) in 1802. His remark, although in one sense exaggerated, was truer than he perhaps realized, as landscape painting had become popular in Britain as well as in Germany at that time. In these two countries especially the genre assumed a new role during the Romantic period. Previously, it had been considered little more than a minor decorative form, given over to the production of pleasing imaginary compositions or topographical views—and this despite its great seventeenth-century practitioners such as Poussin and Claude. Now, however, it was called upon to express feeling, not just for the outward beauty of woods, fields, and skies but for nature's "inner life."

The German approach to landscape

In Germany, where attitudes were more conditioned by philosophy than in Britain, nature was invested with an all-pervading spirit of an almost sacred character, not static but subject to growth and change, analogous to the spirit in man. To represent the changing states of nature as symbols of the varieties of human emotion was therefore the aim of Romantic landscape painting.

Runge's work was insufficiently developed (he died young), especially in landscape painting, to produce more than a fragmentary and eccentric, although highly interesting, reflection of these ideas [3]. With his visionary temperament and boldly original mind, he had something in common with his English contemporary, William Blake (1757–1827), although probably neither knew of the other's existence. The greatest German Romantic landscapist was Caspar David Friedrich (1774–1840), whose art is superficially more traditional, in that he represented natural views seen from fixed points in space and time. But for him, too, nature was only the physical manifestation of an inward life, a continuous process corresponding to the agitation of the artist's mind. He specialized in changing effects of atmosphere and light, depicting them with a refinement and air of gentle melancholy unlike almost anything else in art [4].

The British tradition

If the purest and most studied forms of Romantic landscape painting were produced in Germany, it was Britain that had, in this period, the longest and most varied landscape tradition. (In France, broadly speaking, what was new in landscape was not Romantic and what was Romantic was not new.) Some of the qualities already discussed in connection with German landscape—the emphasis on mood, the concern with nature as a process rather than an order, the awareness of some spiritual entity concealed within nature's visible forms—are present in varying degrees in British painting too. They were intimated first in the calm and serene watercolor views of the Swiss Alps [1] by J. R. Cozens (1752–97) and in Thomas Girtin's (1775–1802) solemn water colors of the Yorkshire dales [2]. They showed more fully in the response of Joseph Turner to the violence of storms at sea [5] and his fascination with the

CONNECTIONS

See also
1228 European Romantic art: figure painting
1222 Origins of romanticism
1226 Napoleonic Europe

1

1 The emotional bond between man and nature is stressed by eliminating figures from the picture. J. R. Cozens's "Valley in the Tyrol, near Brixen" (*c.* 1783) offers the viewer an impression of stillness and of vast space. The innate beauty of Alpine scenery was one of the early Romantic discoveries.

2

2 Stillness and quiet are features also of Thomas Girtin's "Kirkstall Abbey, Yorkshire" (*c.* 1800), but the setting is gentler. Besides exploring new types of scenery, the Romantics turned their attention to Gothic remains. Cozens and Girtin were two preeminent watercolorists.

3

3 Runge's "Morning" (1803), a baby lying in a radiantly lit paradisiacal landscape, symbolizes not only natural morning but also the dawn of the universe and the beginning of each individual life. More than the English, German Romantics dealt with the idea of nature in terms of symbols.

4

4 The symbolism of Friedrich's "The Cross in the Mountains" (1808), an altarpiece for the chapel of Schloss Tetschen, is at once more literal and more orthodox than that of Runge. Friedrich's theme is the impact of Christianity on world history and its gifts of faith and hope in God.

brilliance of sunlight ("the Sun is God," he is reported to have said on his deathbed), in Constable's feeling for the moral and religious values inherent in ordinary nature, and in Palmer's assertion that "bits of nature are generally much improved by being received into the soul."

British landscape painting is, on the whole, less mystically inspired and more empirical than German. Its sense of the divine is diluted by being combined with more mundane preoccupations such as topography and the picturesque, the interaction of the ideal and the real, and the influence of the Old Masters. It is also more involved with the idea of the sketch—that is, both with "sketchiness," in the sense of breadth of handling (where German painting is very smooth and neat in handling), and with working direct from nature in watercolor and oils. The Romantic concern with transience is thus realized by British painters chiefly, although not exclusively, in terms of movement—through clouds being blown across the sky and wind whipping up the waves.

Importance of the sky

In both, indeed all, countries the sky is the focus of Romantic landscape painting; it was, as John Constable (1776–1837) called it, "the keynote, the standard of scale, and the chief organ of sentiment." Constable was the best-known landscapist in this period to make sky studies, with notes on the back stating the date, the exact hour of the day, and the direction of the wind. In his finished landscapes of the Suffolk countryside, in which he was born and brought up, he used the light of the sky to give vitality and poetry to his rendering of simple agricultural scenes [6]. Turner did the same with a much wider range of scenery and phenomena, concluding his career by almost dissolving form altogether in a haze of light and color [8].

The next and final "Romantic generation" produced a type of landscape painting more overtly expressive of feeling, such as the apocalyptic and grandiose fantasies of John Martin (1789–1854) [7] or, at the opposite extreme, the intimate pastoral visions of Samuel Palmer (1805–81) [Key].

KEY

A sense of heightened mood is the chief common factor of Romantic landscape paintings. It is expressed by Samuel Palmer in terms of the pastoral genre, which he saw as partly religious, in "The White Cloud" (*c.* 1831–32).

5

5 The huge output of Turner (1775–1851) embraced the extremes of traditionalism and experiment and of agitation and calm. His early paintings, such as "The Wreck of a Transport Ship" (*c.* 1810) are predominantly dark in tone, acknowledging the Old Masters, but the vital role he always gave to light is evident. Shipwreck, an all-too-common instance at that time of the destructive powers of nature, is a frequent theme portrayed by Romantic artists.

6

6 "Flatford Mill" (1817), one of Constable's best-known paintings, shows him at his most naturalistic. His sheer love of and identification with the countryside he painted, the Suffolk of his childhood, make Constable a Romantic artist. His aim was to achieve truth to nature and its light and to combine this with the practical details of agricultural life at that time.

7

7 Mountain grandeur combined with the theme of the lone man defying his enemies is illustrated in Martin's "The Bard" (1817). The subject is from a poem by Gray lamenting the suppression of the Welsh bards—symbols of freedom and nationhood.

8

8 The ultimate expression of the Romantic concern with light is found in Turner's late work. In "Norham Castle; Sunrise (*c.* 1835–40) his earlier preoccupations—old castles, hills, rivers, the sunlight effects of Claude—remain, but only as traces suspended in color.

Development of the orchestra

Although by the sixteenth century there existed a body of secular instrumental music, it was slight compared with the wealth of church music. The growing patronage of secular works, especially opera and ballet, required accompaniment by instrumental groups.

Various combinations of instruments had been popular from the sixteenth century. In some, called consorts, all the instruments were of one family, such as the viol or recorder families. A "broken" consort might include a few instruments of other families to lend a more lively character to the sound. The development of opera in Italy led composers to more colorful use of instrumental groups. Claudio Monteverdi (1567–1643), in his opera *Orfeo* (1607), used an orchestra consisting of 15 keyboard instruments, brass, strings, and woodwind. He left to the music director the choice of which instruments should play which parts of his music, except for sections where he specified trombones for music associated with Hades. His understanding of orchestral sound was not entirely new. About ten years earlier Giovanni Gabrieli (1557–1612) specified instruments to play parts in *Sacrae symphoniae* (1597).

The string families

The improved quality and brilliant sound of the violin in the second quarter of the sixteenth century overwhelmed the viol family, although one descendant of the viol, the double bass, has survived. The violin family produced the sound that was to be fundamental to the symphony orchestra.

Throughout the seventeenth century, composers used a thorough (through or continuo) bass in writing for orchestra. The continuo instrument, usually a harpsichord or an organ, "filled in" harmonies where there was no instrument free to play a certain part or where the part needed support. The system of thorough bass demanded a creative contribution from players and director that was diminished when composers began to write out parts in full.

By the late seventeenth century the four-part string orchestra—first and second violins, violas, and cellos—was well established. The double bass at first played the cello line an octave lower. The instrument was regularly a part of the orchestra by the mid-eighteenth century but was not a standard form until the Italian model with four strings won general recognition in the late nineteenth century.

The woodwind families

Various instruments were added to the strings until some of them found lasting places in the orchestral establishment. First and second oboes and bassoons added woodwind tone in the seventeenth century. At first the bassoon took a bass role but later came to play tenor parts. From about 1650 oboes "doubled" the violin parts, but virtuoso players soon carried the instrument to a more individual role.

The flute appeared in early orchestras. Its vertical forms, the recorders, were ousted by the oboes and the transverse flute, which owed much to French craftsmen and musicians in improving their mechanics. The final addition to the orchestral woodwind families was the clarinet.

CONNECTIONS

See also
1132 Renaissance music
1196 Baroque and classical music
1246 Music: the Romantic period
1500 Musical sounds
676 Hearing and balance

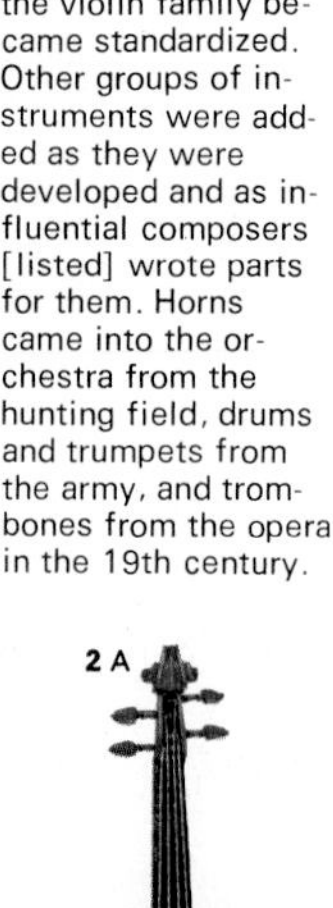

1 Woodwind
Piccolo
Flute
Oboe
Cor anglais
Clarinet
Bassoon
Brass
Horn
Trumpet
Trombone
Tuba
Percussion
Timpani
Celeste, etc.
Percussion strings
Harp
Piano
Strings
1st violin
2nd violin
Viola
Cello
Double bass
1650
1700
1750
1800
1850
1900
1950
Wagner
Britten
Berlioz
Bartók
Stravinsky
Beethoven
Debussy
Handel
Bach
Mozart
Haydn
Strauss
Gluck
Purcell
Scarlatti
Bach's sons
Tchaikovsky

1 The historical growth of the orchestra began in the late 17th century when the nucleus of the violin family became standardized. Other groups of instruments were added as they were developed and as influential composers [listed] wrote parts for them. Horns came into the orchestra from the hunting field, drums and trumpets from the army, and trombones from the opera in the 19th century.

2 A

B
C

2 The string section of the modern orchestra is based on the violin family—violin, viola and cello. The violin role divides into first and second parts, although the instruments played [A] are identical for either part. The larger viola [B] plays a part that corresponds to the alto voice in singing, and the violoncello, or cello [C] as it is usually called, takes the tenor part. The fourth main member of the modern string section—the double bass—is not a member of the violin family but is really a viol. String quartets consist of first and second violins playing different parts, a viola, and a cello.

3

3 Tambourines combine the stretched membrane of drums with a jingle that has elements both of cymbals and of rattle instruments. Percussion instruments, including triangles and gongs, were late additions to the orchestra. For a long time, only timpani represented percussion and were usually combined with trumpets to give brilliance of effect. There are also some early instances of the orchestral use of bells by Bach and Handel.

4
A

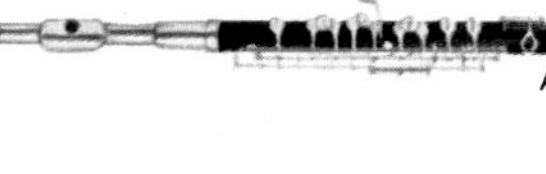

B

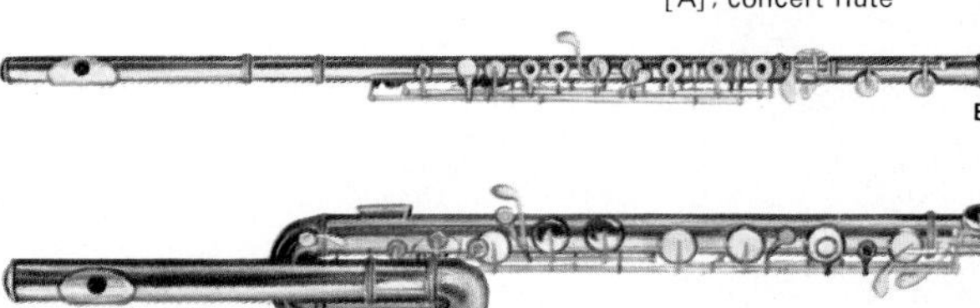

C

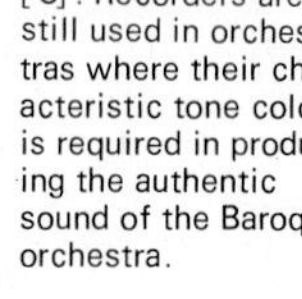

4 Nonreed woodwind instruments in the orchestra were originally of two kinds: recorders, played by blowing vertically into the mouthpiece, and flutes, played horizontally. The second group is a regular component of the modern orchestra. It includes the piccolo [A], concert flute [B], and bass flute [C]. Recorders are still used in orchestras where their characteristic tone color is required in producing the authentic sound of the Baroque orchestra.

The principal woodwind instruments had some variants that gained regular orchestral places: the oboe's cousin, the cor anglais or English horn, with its deeper tone became a popular instrument with Romantic composers seeking fresh tone colors; the bass flute and bass clarinet were used occasionally; and the piccolo added sparkle.

The brass and percussion families

By the time Bach wrote his first *Brandenburg Concerto* (1721), the French horn had joined the orchestra. The trumpet had already won a place, usually playing at the top end of its range. French horns were often grouped in pairs with oboes in a woodwind section. Wolfgang Amadeus Mozart wrote 19 of his first 40 symphonies for orchestras whose wind sections consisted only of oboes and horns. The trombones, used in late eighteenth-century opera, entered the symphony orchestra 50 years later.

The invention in Germany of valves for brass instruments in about 1815, meant that they could produce semitone scales throughout their ranges without fitting alternative lengths of tubing every time the music changed key. More percussion instruments were added as Romantic and post-Romantic composers explored orchestral color, until the section might include over a score of instruments, even blocks, whips, and wind machines.

The discipline of orchestras had not always been as high as the standards established by Johann Stamitz (1717–57) in Mannheim, whose orchestra was compared favorably by Mozart to his "rabble of players." By the early nineteenth century the leadership of orchestral performance was outgrowing the situation where the leader of the violin section controlled a performance. In 1820 Ludwig Spohr surprised orchestra and audience in London when he directed the orchestra with a baton, apparently for the first time. Hector Berlioz (1803–69) and Wagner pleaded for higher standards of performance, and the nineteenth-century middle classes, flocking to the new concert halls, made long rehearsal time and full-time orchestras financially possible.

KEY
STRINGS WOODWIND BRASS PERCUSSION

The pitch range of a symphony orchestra is fairly evenly represented across the various sections – strings [blue], woodwind [green], brass [mauve] – except for percussion [brown].

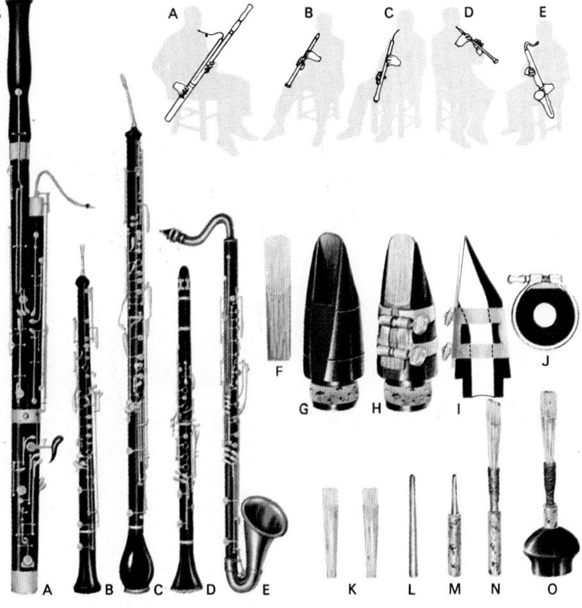
5
A
B
C
D
E
F
G
H
I
J
K
L
M
N
O

5 Reed woodwinds, shown in appropriate playing positions, are the bassoon [A], oboe [B], cor anglais [C], clarinet [D], and bass clarinet [E]. The clarinets have a cylindrical bore and are played by means of a single reed [F] fixed over a chamber in the mouthpiece [G] and secured by a ligature [H], shown in transverse [I] and cross section [J]. The oboe family [A, B, and C] is played by blowing through two pieces of reed [K] fitted around a brass tube [L]. The tube is placed in a cork cylinder [M] with the twin reeds whipped around it [N], as shown in cross section with the complete double reed in position [O].

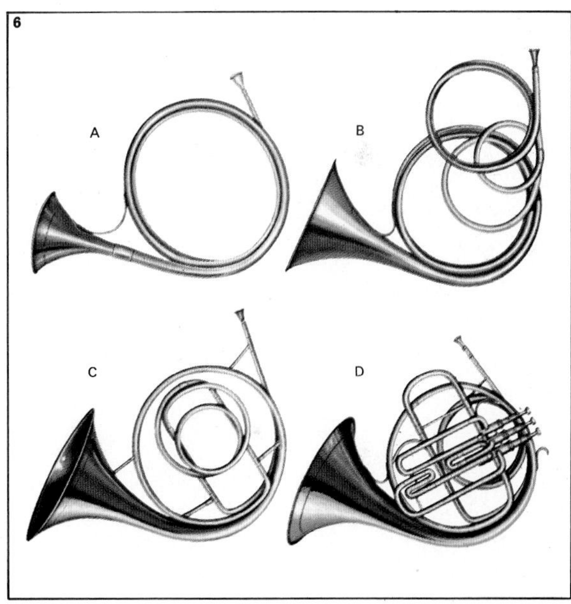
6
A
B
C
D

6 The French horn is a direct descendant of a coiled hunting horn [A] that originated in France about 1660. It changed its form because when it was first used in orchestras, players were obliged to change horns when the music changed key. Crooks, or extra lengths of tube, were introduced [B], and later both crooks and a tuning slide were added [C]. The development of the piston valve [D] early in the 19th century gave the horn a full range of semitones. Other members of the orchestral brass group are the trumpet and trombone, with cylindrical bores, and the tuba, which has a conical bore like the French horn and is at the lower end of the pitch range.

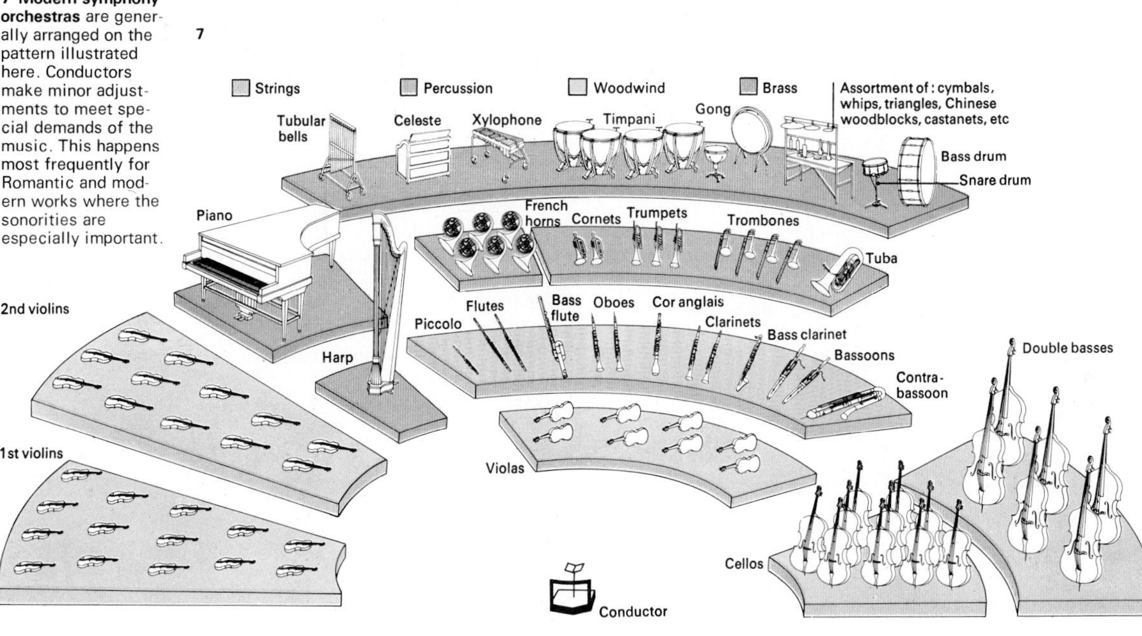
7
Strings
Percussion
Woodwind
Brass
Assortment of: cymbals, whips, triangles, Chinese woodblocks, castanets, etc
Tubular bells
Celeste
Xylophone
Timpani
Gong
Bass drum
Snare drum
Piano
French horns
Cornets
Trumpets
Trombones
Tuba
2nd violins
Flutes
Bass flute
Oboes
Cor anglais
Piccolo
Clarinets
Bass clarinet
Harp
Bassoons
Contra-bassoon
Double basses
1st violins
Violas
Cellos
Conductor

7 Modern symphony orchestras are generally arranged on the pattern illustrated here. Conductors make minor adjustments to meet special demands of the music. This happens most frequently for Romantic and modern works where the sonorities are especially important.

Music: the Romantic period

The nineteenth century saw the birth of the idea in Western music of the composer as an artist instead of merely a craftsman providing music for an employer—usually the church or an aristocratic patron. Beethoven [Key], whose revolutionary stance was one of determined self-expression, was a central figure in the gradual transition from craft to art.

The influence of Beethoven

Having absorbed classical elements from Haydn and Mozart (whose last three symphonies to a degree prefigure romanticism), Beethoven embarked on a course that in music is parallel to the emergence of the Romantic concept of the liberated individual. His third symphony, the *Eroica* (1803–04), is a pivotal work in this respect and revealed a powerful impetus that was to burst forth in his later symphonies, concertos, and piano sonatas. The intense late string quartets are a more intimate expression of similar emotional power.

Virtually all serious European music of the nineteenth century was to flourish under the far-reaching influence of this music, for Beethoven transformed the standard classical forms of sonata, symphony, concerto, and quartet by infusing them with a musically emotional intensity. Many subsequent composers took the liberation of individual emotional expression for their starting point, and at times Romantic music suffered the excesses of self-indulgent feeling and emotionalism of the composers.

The early Romantic giants

Carl Maria von Weber (1786–1826) is generally credited with being the first freely Romantic composer. His often superficial piano music was destined for the increasingly popular public concerts that encouraged virtuoso composers such as the noted Italian violinist Niccolò Paganini (1782–1840) [7].

At the opposite pole were the private musical evenings given by Franz Schubert (1797–1828) [6] in Vienna. They saw in particular the fashioning of the *lied* (song), in which Schubert's accompaniment opened new worlds of melodic and harmonic enrichment of lyrics. Yet songs were just part of the general response music was making to literature in this period, offering a framework for ideas of fantasy and heroism by that time unsuited to the old classical forms.

Felix Mendelssohn (1809–47) [3] made Shakespeare's *Midsummer Night's Dream* the subject of a concert overture, but his fresh-sounding music still drew much charm from traditional eighteenth-century restraint and balance. Hector Berlioz (1803–69) [1], expressed a passion for the works of numerous poets, and they figure in many of his orchestral and dramatic works including his *Symphonie Fantastique* (1830). Robert Schumann (1810–56) also drew characters from Romantic writers. Original melodic and rhythmic invention and an individual harmonic sense contributed to Berlioz' influence on later music, especially on works for the orchestra.

More adventurously, Franz Liszt (1811–86) [7] created the symphonic poem *(Tasso, Mazeppa)* by combining both the narrative and pyschological aspects of a story or

CONNECTIONS

See also

1196 Baroque and classical music

1244 Development of the orchestra

1256 Opera in the 19th and 20th centuries

1364 Twentieth century music—tradition and experimentation

1222 Origins of romanticism

1760·1770 · 1780·1790 · 1800 · 1810 · 1820 · 1830 · 1840 · 1850 · 1860 · 1870 · 1880 · 1890 · 1900 · 1910 · 1920 · 1930 · 1940 · 1950 · 1960 · 1970

Beethoven, Spontini, Paganini, Field, Spohr, Weber, Meyerbeer, Hérold, Rossini, Marschner, Loewe, Donizetti, Schubert, Bellini, Berlioz, Glinka, Mendelssohn, Schumann, Chopin, Liszt, Verdi, Wagner, Offenbach, Gounod, Franck, Bruckner, Smetana, Brahms, Borodin, Saint-Saëns, Delibes, Balakirev, Bruch, Bizet, Mussorgsky, Tchaikovsky, Dvořák, Chabrier, Sullivan, Massenet, Grieg, Rimsky-Korsakov, Fauré, Parry, D'Indy, Humperdinck, Puccini, Wolf, MacDowell, Strauss, Glazunov, Busoni, Reger, Rachmaninov

Germany, Austria, Poland, Hungary, Norway, France, Czechoslovakia, Italy, Russia, Ireland, England, USA

1 Romantic music, initiated by Beethoven, was still finding a powerful exponent in Rachmaninov in the 1930s. The portrait is of Berlioz, who represents the most intense expression of the movement.

2 The Royal College of Organists, established in London in 1864, was just one of the many conservatories and academies of music that proliferated in Europe in the 19th century. They owed their origin to the Italian *conservatorio*, where orphans were taught music. Notable conservatories were founded in Paris (1784), Vienna (1817), London (1822), and Leipzig (by Mendelssohn, 1843).

4 Tchaikovsky stood apart from the self-proclaimed nationalist composers of late 19th-century Russia in his constant use of established European forms such as the symphony, the concerto, and the symphonic poem. Even so, his personal idiom was colored by a Russian emphasis on style, minor keys, and folklike melody. His popularity today is based chiefly on his symphonies, concertos, and ballet music.

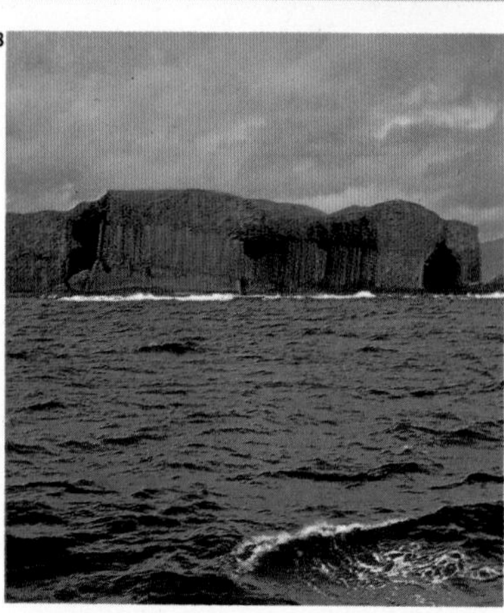

3 Fingal's Cave in the Hebrides inspired Mendelssohn with a theme for a concert overture (1830). Music describing scenery or literary subjects, or program music, was a commonplace of Romantic composition.

5 Johann Strauss the Younger (1825–99), conducting the orchestra, often presided as musical director at Viennese entertainments, such as the one pictured here. Described as the Waltz King because of works such as "On the Beautiful Blue Danube" and "Tales from the Vienna Woods," he composed lighthearted music whose brilliance and gaiety captured the spirit of the Hapsburg capital. He also composed a number of sucessful operettas.

poem in music. Many composers used this format, most notably the German composer Richard Strauss (1864–1949) in his symphonic poems *Don Juan* (1888) and *Death and Transfiguration* (1889).

Nationalism and the Romantics

In 1848 revolutions throughout Europe were crushed but gave new directions to nationalist feelings that were finally to emerge in music. Frédéric Chopin (1810–49) [9] had already used the mazurka and polonaise in exile to express his nostalgia and hopes for Poland. In Bohemia, Antonín Dvořak (1841–1904) and Bedrich Smetana (1824–84) were to emerge as nationalists, as would Edvard Grieg (1832–1907) in Norway, Edward MacDowell (1861–1908) in the United States, and, following the early lead of Mikhail Glinka (1804–57) in Russia, the "Mighty Five," of St Petersburg headed by Modest Mussorgsky (1839–81), Alexander Borodin (1837–1887), and Nikolai Rimsky-Korsakov (1844–1908). Peter Ilyich Tchaikovsky [1840–93] [4], as the head of the opposing Moscow group, did not espouse nationalist causes in his music; he emphasized the melodic and harmonic aspects in his highly emotional and often tragic works, particularly his Fourth, Fifth, and Sixth symphonies.

Tchaikovsky's musical successor was his countryman, Sergei Rachmaninov (1873–1943); a dramatic, even passionate Romantic, his popular works ("Prelude in C Sharp Minor") reflect the brooding pessimism found in Tchaikovsky's music. Wagner's use of native German myth to create a flowing music drama in place of traditional opera was eventually secondary to the pervading influence of his extremely lush, chromatic harmony and inspired use of the orchestra in his operatic works.

The final flowering of Romantic nationalism was seen in England with Edward Elgar (1857–1934) and Frederick Delius (1862–1934), in Finland with Jean Sibelius (1865–1957), and in France where, in 1871, a national society was founded under César Franck (1822–90) and Camille Saint-Saëns (1835–1921) to foster the composition of French music.

KEY

Ludwig van Beethoven (1770–1827) is portrayed as Janus, god of the new year. He looks back to the classical tradition, which he transformed, and forward to the 19th-century music and the Romantic composers whom he inspired.

6

6 Franz Schubert, son of a Viennese schoolteacher, was a prolific composer, writing nine symphonies, much chamber and piano music, and an incomparable body of more than 600 songs. He gained little public recognition during his lifetime–his *C Major Symphony* was not performed until 10 years after his death–and his last years were spent in Vienna, often in real poverty.

7

7 The close links between music and literature are underlined in this group portrait of several Romantic artists by Joseph Danhauser (1805–45). Liszt at the piano is playing to the novelist George Sand, who was Chopin's lover. She is sitting beside the novelist and dramatist Alexandre Dumas the younger. Standing [from the left] are the poet Victor Hugo, the violinist and composer Paganini, and the opera composer Rossini. At Liszt's feet is the Comtesse Marie d'Agoult, with whom the pianist had a lengthy affair. Beethoven's bust is on the piano. Byron's portrait on the wall.

8

8 A silhouette of Johannes Brahms (1833–97) shows him going off to his favorite tavern, "The Sign of the Red Hedge hog." Brahms was a late Romantic composer who revitalized the tradition of classical forms that had culminated in Beethoven. Brahms's use of traditional devices such as the harmonic sequence and counterpoint, his emphasis on colorful harmony in structure and not only for effect, the stringent unity he sought within music, and the independence of his pieces from poetic or literary interpretations all show classical qualities. These, combined with his expansive rhythmic and lyrical Romanticism–as in his songs–resulted in music rich in feeling.

9

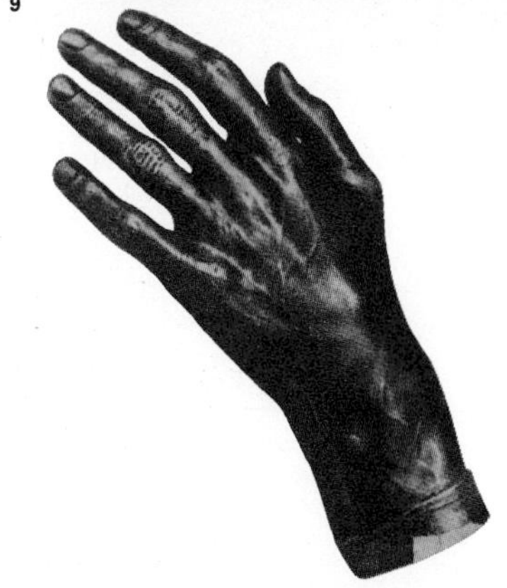

9 A Plaster cast made of Chopin's hand testifies to the public enthusiasm and admiration evoked by his skill and sensitivity as a pianist. Often called "the poet of the keyboard," he was preeminent among 19th-century composers in his command of the modern piano's improved dynamic and expressive possibilities. Early in his career he wrote music for piano and orchestra as showpieces with which to establish his reputation. After leaving Poland and settling in Paris at the age of 21, he concentrated on composing and playing short solo works, mostly for salon audiences. In all he wrote more than 150 such pieces before his death at 39.

The revolutions of 1848

In an age of revolution 1848 was the year of revolution. The governments of France, Italy, and central Europe were all shaken by insurrection. Contrary to the belief of some contemporaries, there was no overall plan, however, and this lack of coordination was fatal for the revolutionaries.

Political reform through revolt

The roots of the uprisings throughout western Europe were remarkably similar. The Industrial Revolution had uprooted traditional patterns of life and had created a new urban proletariat and a much enlarged bourgeoisie intent on political power. Economic and social unrest was exacerbated by the autocratic rule that was a legacy of the Vienna Settlement of 1815, which provided a focus for the intellectuals who were agitating for political reform. People were hungry as a result of crop failures in 1845–47, and desperate mobs demanded change.

Significantly, the centers of unrest were the great cities [2], where thousands had come only to live in squalor and work in conditions of frightening degradation. These people were hit by the second crisis of 1848—an international credit collapse, which led to wholesale bankruptcies and unemployment. The newly unemployed joined the hungry on the streets. Finally, there was a psychological catalyst. The epidemic of revolution was accompanied by an epidemic of cholera [7].

Wave of early successes

The first revolts erupted in Italy [5]. Once Louis-Philippe (1773–1850) had abdicated the French throne in February revolution took hold [3]. In March the resignation of the apostle of European stability, Prince Metternich (1773–1859), chancellor of the Hapsburg Empire, boosted the morale of the revolutionaries. Caught by surprise and overwhelmed by the extent of the outbreak, governments could not call on each other for help. Their only hope seemed to be to make concessions. Liberal constitutions [1] were granted everywhere, and the Hapsburg emperor, the pope, and the kings of France and Prussia fled from their capitals.

Simultaneously with the liberal revolts came an upsurge of nationalism. The Hapsburg Empire with its spheres of influence in Italy and Germany [4] seemed doomed. Hungary declared its independence, the Bohemians formed a nationalist movement, and a Slav Congress met to consider demands for Slavic equality in the empire. In Italy, Giuseppe Mazzini (1805–72) called for an uprising to form a new Italian state. At the same time, King Charles Albert of Piedmont (1798–1849) sent an army to help the Lombards drive out the Austrians, hoping to form a North Italian kingdom. In the German Confederation an assembly met at Frankfurt to decide on a policy to unite Germany. These political moves showed the degree of hostility to the Vienna Settlement of 1815 and its legacy of repression. By 1848 a new generation was not prepared to pay any price for peace.

In spite of all this, by the middle of 1848 the tide of revolution had turned. Early successes proved illusory. The Hapsburg Empire followed its historic policy—divide and rule—by exploiting deep divisions among

CONNECTIONS

See also
1230 The Congress of Vienna
1226 Napoleonic Europe
1224 The French Revolution
1250 German and Italian unification
1288 Political thought in the 19th century
1232 European empires in the 19th century
1286 Russia in the 19th century
1302 Balkanization and Slav nationalism

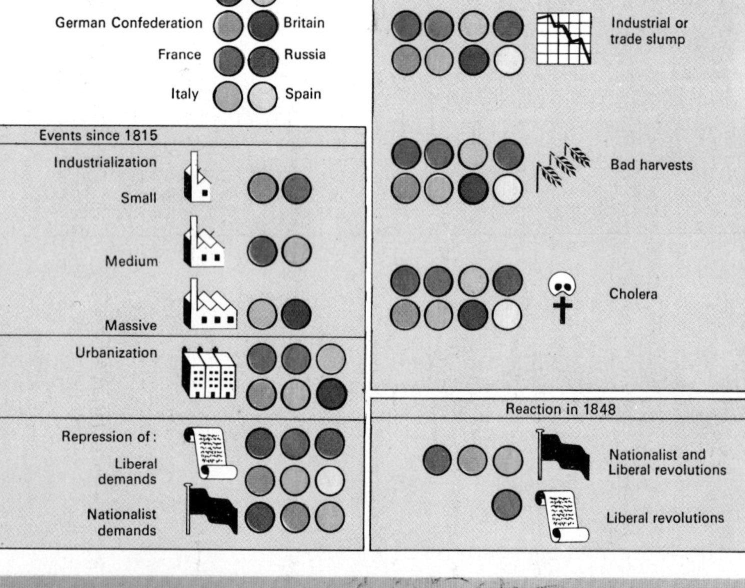

Hapsburg Empire
Belgium
German Confederation
Britain
France
Russia
Italy
Spain
Events since 1815
Industrialization
Small
Medium
Massive
Urbanization
Repression of:
Liberal demands
Nationalist demands
Crisis in 1848
Industrial or trade slump
Bad harvests
Cholera
Reaction in 1848
Nationalist and Liberal revolutions
Liberal revolutions

1 Uprisings occurred in most European countries in 1848, with similar causes but varying in intensity and effect. In Russia and Spain, political dissent lacked the concentrated support of the factory or city, while Belgium and Britain had already made political concessions in the face of heavy industrialization and increasing urbanization, avoiding the violent confrontations of 1848.

2 The revolutions of 1848 were urban; the peasants were apathetic or conservative. Political ideas spread quickly along the new railroads, attracting city intellectuals, workers, and businessmen.

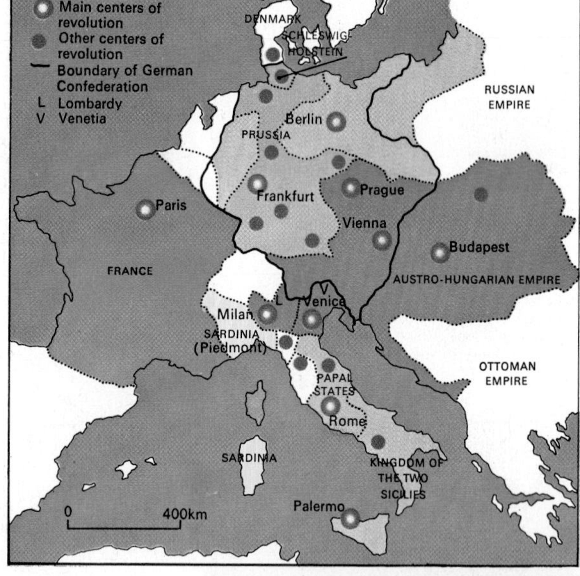

Main centers of revolution
Other centers of revolution
Boundary of German Confederation
L Lombardy
V Venetia
DENMARK
SCHLESWIG
HOLSTEIN
RUSSIAN EMPIRE
Berlin
PRUSSIA
Frankfurt
Prague
Paris
Vienna
Budapest
FRANCE
AUSTRO-HUNGARIAN EMPIRE
Milan
Venice
SARDINIA (Piedmont)
PAPAL STATES
OTTOMAN EMPIRE
Rome
SARDINIA
KINGDOM OF THE TWO SICILIES
Palermo
0
400km

3 Paris barricades in March 1848 were manned by middle-class liberals, working-class socialists, and the unemployed. Shattered by his unpopularity, Louis-Philippe had abdicated in February.

4 Liberal revolts in the 39 German states won constitutions that did not survive the repression of 1849. The impotence of nationalists in the Frankfurt Assembly was shown when they called on Prussian troops to keep order.

the revolutionaries. Croats and Romanians who resented Magyar domination rose against Hungary's new leader, Louis Kossuth (1802–94). Their armies helped to do the Hapsburgs' work for them. In Italy, Charles Albert's forces were smashed by the Austrian army in two campaigns. Traditional loyalty to existing separate states deprived him of wide Italian support. Catholics hesitated to disobey the pope, who had forbidden violence against the Catholic Hapsburgs.

In Germany, at the Frankfurt Assembly, the intellectuals wrangled interminably and failed to decide on a form for the new Germany until it was too late. Everywhere the middle classes, who had provided the impetus and leadership for the revolution, were horrified by the forces they had unleashed. Having seen revolution degenerate into anarchy, they welcomed the restoration of law and order. By 1849 all was quiet again. The forces of reaction seemed triumphant. Disorganized mobs [Key] stood no chance against the professional armies [6] of Austria, Prussia, Russia, and France. The Hapsburg tradition of garrisoning each province with troops from other provinces had prevented any chance of soldiers siding with the revolution. In every area the peasants had proved deeply conservative. There was little hope of successful revolution when most of the population—those living on the land—rejected it.

The legacy of 1848

There were a few significant gains, however. Serfdom was abolished in the Hapsburg Empire. Piedmont and Prussia kept their constitutions and eventually led Italy and Germany to unity in 1871. Governments learned to pay more attention to the material interests of their subjects and to pay lip service to democratic processes.

But nationalists had learned that idealism and enthusiasm are not enough. Their hopes would be fulfilled only if they could match their opponents' military strength. The revolutions of 1848 were followed by a period of cynicism and use of armed force. Bismarck's age of "blood and iron" had begun.

KEY

DU PAIN OU LA MORT
WOMEN ON THE BARRICADE, NEAR THE PORTE ST. DENIS.

Women on the barricades; the tricolor, symbolizing hopes for liberty, equality, and fraternity; the red flag of socialist revolution; the flags of German, Italian, Hungarian, or Bohemian nationalism—all made a heroic display in 1848. But slogans such as "Bread or Death" did not match an army.

5

5 Italian revolts for state constitutions, republics in Rome and Venice, and a North Italian kingdom all collapsed by 1849.

6 Military saviors of the Hapsburgs (caricatured left to right) were Jelačić (1801–59), who led Croats against Magyars in independent Hungary, Radetzky (1766–1858), who successfully ended the Italian revolts, and Windischgrätz (1787–1862), who subdued Bohemia.

6

7

7 The Paris sewers, begun by Baron Haussmann (1809–91) during the 1850s, were a response to criticism of governmental failure to stop cholera from spreading in 1848, when fear of the disease acted as a catalyst in the revolutions. Haussmann also created wide boulevards to facilitate cavalry charges against future revolutionary barricades.

8

8 Karl Marx (1818–83) (shown as Prometheus chained to his printing press) and Friedrich Engels (1820–95) published the *Communist Manifesto* early in 1848. Although this made no contribution to the outbreaks of 1848, fear of socialism inhibited the revolution.

German and Italian unification

Italy and Germany were created in spite of limited popular support, strong communal loyalties to existing units, and the proximity of two powers, France and Austria, whose interests were endangered by their emergence as strong nations. Idealism and courage had failed in the revolutions of 1848. The new nations were the fruit of the ambitions of their strongest components, Piedmont and Prussia, and of two outstanding practitioners of *Realpolitik,* Camillo di Cavour and Otto von Bismarck.

The birth of modern Italy

As prime minister from 1852, Cavour (1810–61) [5] built up Piedmont as a magnet to attract the rest of Italy. He made the new parliamentary democracy work, encouraged up-to-date agriculture and industry, and linked the Piedmontese economy to that of Europe through a railroad network and the modernized port of Genoa. He created a fair legal system and an efficient bureaucracy. With a good army and a king, Victor Emmanuel (1815–98), Piedmont became the focus of national hopes.

Outside help was vital to drive out the Austrians. France became a pawn in Cavour's game. In the Pact of Plombières (1858), the French Emperor Napoleon III (1808–73), promised him help in a future war. Cavour engineered an attack against Piedmont by Austria in 1859, and French troops were sent in. After triumphs at Magenta and Solferino, Napoleon had second thoughts and withdrew his support from Cavour, but his help had been decisive. In the excitement of the victories, Parma, Modena, Tuscany, and the Romagna demanded amalgamation with Piedmont. In return for the acquisition of Nice and Savoy, Napoleon backed plebiscites in Emilia and Tuscany, and Cavour won an overwhelming majority in favor of the formation of a north Italian kingdom.

Matters might have rested there but for Giuseppe Garibaldi (1807–82). When the Sicilians rose in revolt against Naples in 1860, Garibaldi and more than 1,000 men went to their aid. Within weeks the Neapolitan army had been swept out of Sicily, and Garibaldi marched in triumph through Naples itself. Rome was his next objective. But this conflicted with Cavour's plans. If Garibaldi attacked Rome, then France and Austria might intervene to defend the pope, so Cavour sent a Piedmontese army to forestall any further advance. Garibaldi, in a dramatic gesture, handed over the south to Piedmont [6].

Only two areas of Italy now remained unintegrated. Venetia was held by Austria, and Rome and its surrounding territories were held by the pope and a garrison of French troops. In 1866, Victor Emmanuel joined Prussia in the Austro-Prussian war and was rewarded with Venetia. In 1879, France withdrew its troops from Rome to fight in the Franco-Prussian War. At last, the king ruled a united Italy [7].

Prussia and the "Iron Chancellor"

In Prussia, Bismarck (1802–78) had become chancellor in 1862, and he was faced with a Liberal majority hostile to his aims. But he managed to undermine and manipulate them and finally gain their support for unification and his policy of *Realpolitik.*

CONNECTIONS

See also

1248 The revolutions of 1848
1232 European empires in the 19th century
1230 The Congress of Vienna
1284 European industrialization 1870–1914
1300 Europe 1870–1914
1288 Political thought in the 19th century
1262 European imperialism in the 19th century

1 Kaiser Wilhelm I of Prussia was proclaimed German emperior at Versailles in 1871. He called it "the unhappiest day of my life," he had wanted, despite the triumph, even more prestigious titles. He left the room without glancing at the architect of the new Germany, Bismarck. Bismarck [center] had crushed all opposition to German reunification by "blood and iron." It was his skill and vision that had created Germany; as chancellor until 1890 he molded its institutions. Von Moltke (1800–91) [on Bismarck's left], chief of the Prussian general staff, was the strategist of the triumphs against Austria and France.

NORTH SEA
BALTIC SEA
MECKLENBURG
PRUSSIA
Berlin
SAXONY
HESSE-DARMSTADT
THURINGIA
ALSACE-LORRAINE
BAVARIA
WÜRTTEMBERG
BADEN
AUSTRIAN EMPIRE
Vienna
North German Confederation 1867
Joined German Confederation 1871
Ceded by France 1871
German Empire 1871
0 200km

2 A potpourri of 39 states, the German Confederation, was united in the customs-free Zollverein in 1844. The Confederation was further extended by the Austro-Prussian War of 1866. Thuringia and Mecklenburg sided with Prussia, and joined; Hesse-Darmstadt and Saxony were annexed on Austria's defeat.

3 This caricature of Pope Pius IX expresses the disappointment felt at his failure to support liberalism consistently. As papal lands were lost, he increased the spiritual claims of the Holy See. In 1864 he condemned contemporary political doctrines and in 1870 proclaimed papal infallibility.

Together, the customs union, or Zollverein [2], and the growth of railroads had already removed most natural and artificial impediments to German integration and prosperity. Bismarck was determined to remove Austrian influence, and in three wars he succeeded.

Bismarck's diplomatic skill ensured that each war was fought against an isolated opponent. In the Danish war of 1864, he fought ostensibly to free the two German-speaking duchies of Schleswig and Holstein from Danish control. But by setting up joint control with Austria, the principal obstacle to German unification, he could start a quarrel with that country.

The time was ripe in 1866. France's neutrality had been bought by vague promises of territorial concession, and Napoleon III had no time to realize his mistake [Key]. In a war lasting only seven weeks, the Austrian army was smashed at Sadowa (or Königgrätz). In 1867, Prussia dominated a north German confederation. The south German states, not yet included in the confederation, remained disunited.

France woke up too late to the emerging danger on its eastern frontier. Vital reforms to its army had come too late, and Napoleon was outmaneuvered by Bismarck in a diplomatic game over rival candidates for the throne of Spain. The hysterical reaction in both countries to the candidacy of a cousin of the king of Prussia provoked France to declare war on Prussia in July 1870. French aggression provoked massive German support for Prussia, and its army swelled to more than a million men. In September, the French capitulated at Sedan, and all resistance collapsed by January 1871.

A wave of enthusiasm for unity with the north swept the south German states. On January 18, 1871, Wilhelm I was proclaimed German emperor at Versailles [1].

Death of a dream

Before 1848, Italian and German nationalists had dreamed of new states that would free their citizens. The new states of 1871 were created at a price. Liberalism was sacrificed to nationalism; cynicism and opportunism had triumphed.

KEY

Napoleon III, emperor of France, was exploited and outwitted first by Cavour, then Bismarck, in the unification of Italy and Germany. By offering help to Cavour, he hoped to gain Savoy and Nice and create a weak client state. Instead he saw the creation of a unified Italy. He was outmaneuvered by Bismarck, realizing the Prussian threat only after Prussia had defeated Austria. By staking his authority on an attempt to force Bismarck to give up any future plans to put a Hohenzollern on the Spanish throne, he led France into the war with Prussia that led to his capture, bringing his own empire to an end.

4

4 Mazzini's proclamation of a Roman Republic in 1849 left a legend of heroism to Italy. Giuseppe Mazzini (1805–72) had founded "Young Italy" to lead his countrymen toward democracy without outside help or compromise, and he dreamed of a state that would "evoke the soul of Italy."

5

IL CONTE DI CAVOUR

5 Camillo di Cavour was never able to inspire the sense of moral crusade that was brought to the *Risorgimento* by Mazzini and Garibaldi. But he understood politics, grasped the international context, and had the skill to exploit the possibilities. Without the exertion of his skills, Italy could not have been unified.

6

7

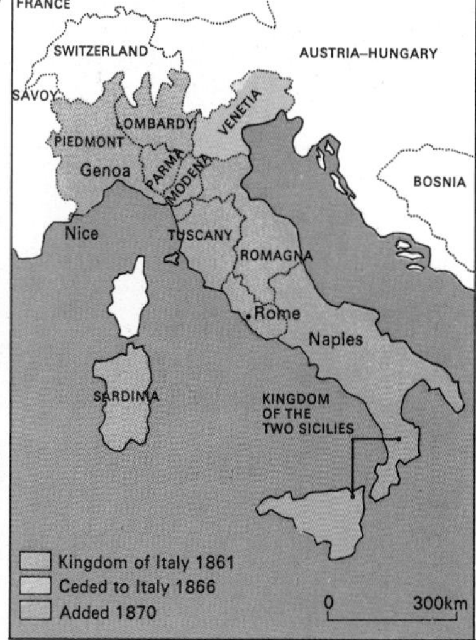

FRANCE
SWITZERLAND
AUSTRIA–HUNGARY
SAVOY
LOMBARDY
VENETIA
PIEDMONT
PARMA
MODENA
Genoa
BOSNIA
Nice
TUSCANY
ROMAGNA
Rome
Naples
SARDINIA
KINGDOM OF THE TWO SICILIES
Kingdom of Italy 1861
Ceded to Italy 1866
Added 1870
0
300km

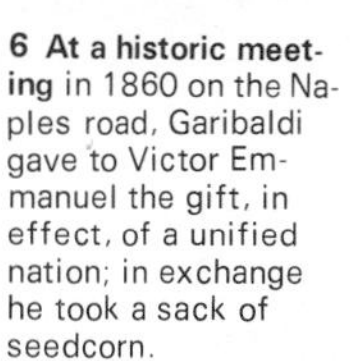

6 At a historic meeting in 1860 on the Naples road, Garibaldi gave to Victor Emmanuel the gift, in effect, of a unified nation; in exchange he took a sack of seedcorn.

7 Although Italy was united by 1870, political and economic development was uneven. Despite Garibaldi's exploits, southern Italy remained backward compared with Piedmont.

Realist painting in the 19th century

Realism is the term used to describe the most characteristic style that arose in painting, particularly in France, between the end of Neoclassicism and romanticism and the beginnings of Impressionism. In Europe it belongs essentially to the years 1840 to 1870, although some paintings with realist tendencies were produced before this date, and the style continued to flourish until almost the end of the century. Closely associated with its more serious developments was the new art of photography [Key].

The social context

Photography as the ultimate in pictorial realism was at once a challenge to painting and an echo of and influence on it. At first it was chiefly painting that influenced photography, but from about 1860 onward the influence began to flow the other way [8]. Realism grew as much from social as aesthetic motives, but the reasons for it were not the same in all countries. In Great Britain, where it began soon after 1800, it succeeded chiefly because, in the nineteenth century, art for the first time became really popular with a mass public. The more traditional styles of painting, which depended for their appreciation on an educated few, fell out of favor. They were replaced by a new, more direct art [6] representing (within contemporary tasteful limits) things as they were, in a style based on the accepted models of seventeenth-century Dutch and Flemish painting and with a strong element of humorous or sentimental narrative that enabled pictures to be "read" like a novel.

The pioneer of popular narrative painting was David Wilkie (1785–1841), who was actually patronized by the aristocracy but whose art reached a wide public through exhibitions and prints. Wilkie was the most popular artist in Britain during the first 40 years of the century, and his approach [1] became the model, more or less, for all subsequent British Victorian artists.

The situation in France was different and Realism began there later. It was not a popular style as it was in Britain; rather, it was serious and committed, even subversive. Whereas in Britain Realism developed within the Academy, the home of official and aristocratic taste, in France it was conceived at least partly as an attack on the official historical art sponsored by the Ecole des Beaux-Arts, then the guardian of academic values.

Influence of Courbet

The leading French Realist was Gustave Courbet (1819–77), whose career ran from the mid-1840s to the early 1870s. He was aggressively bohemian, provincial, and democratic; he founded the doctrine, which became a realist battle-cry, that the artist must be "of his own time." "Painting is an essentially concrete art," he wrote, "and can consist only in the representation of real and existing things."

In contrast to British painters, Courbet played down the element of narrative and, for virtually the first time, represented ordinary provincial and working-class people in everyday terms. This was thought undignified. A picture such as "The Meeting" [2], with its portrayal of the rich bourgeois patron doffing his hat to the journeyman artist (Courbet himself), caused offense because

CONNECTIONS

See also
1284 European industrialization 1870–1914
1228 Romantic art: figure painting
1242 Romantic art: landscape painting
1258 Architecture in the 19th century
1254 Impressionism
1198 Neoclassicism

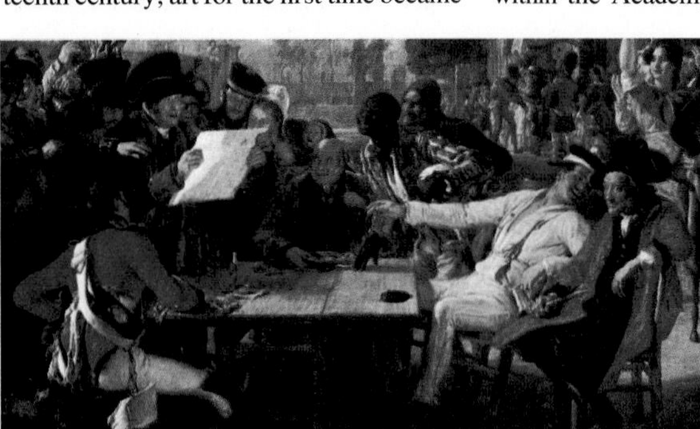

1 David Wilkie's "Chelsea Pensioners reading the Gazette announcing the Victory of Waterloo" (1822, detail), is an example of early "popular" Realism.

2 Gustave Courbet's "The Meeting" (1854), familiarly known as "Bonjour, Monsieur Courbet!", shows the artist being greeted on the road by his friend and patron, Alfred Bruyas.

3 The labors of the fields, previously depicted in pastoral scenes, were treated realistically by Jean François Millet. In "The Angelus" (*c.* 1858) he added an element of religious sentimentality, which made the picture especially popular at that time.

4 The Pre-Raphaelite Brotherhood, founded in 1848, sought to combine fidelity to nature with the purity of spirit of the Italian painters before Raphael. These qualities are reflected in John Everett Millais' "Sir Isumbras at the Ford" (1857).

5 William Holman Hunt (1827–1910) was a Pre-Raphaelite who in "The Awakened Conscience" (1853) turned his attention to personal morality, preaching a sermon to his middle-class audience on the evils and pathos of adultery. The girl starts up from her lover's lap on being reminded of her lost innocence by the tune he is playing and by the sunlit garden outside.

of its reversal of the normal relationship between artist and patron and on account of its apparent lack of any interesting subject.

With Courbet, French Realism began to take on a class-conscious, political tendency and to be identified with what was then thought to be grim and sordid subject matter. Realist paintings from this time onward are often dark in tone and drab in color, resembling contemporary photographs. Although Courbet himself does not seem to have intended his work as social propaganda other painters sought to convey a social message. Jean-François Millet (1814–75) showed the hard life of a depressed French peasantry redeemed only by the consolation of religion [3], and in England a generation later Hubert von Herkomer [9] specialized in painting industrial workers.

Nineteenth-century Realists broke new ground by taking work seriously as a subject for art and treating it not in some symbolic guise, as had been done by artists in the pastoral tradition, but as a dedicated, often grinding and monotonous activity. By painting such shocking and gory subject matter as surgeons at work [7] Thomas Eakins (1844–1916) infused American Realism with an intense interest in the scientific and industrial society.

Morality, mythology, and history

While Realism was usually identified in this period with modern life and dealt with questions of social rather than individual morality, there were exceptions to both these rules, especially in British painting. Pre-Raphaelitism was an English style of the late 1840s and 1850s that applied realistic pictorial aims to personal moral problems [5] and to religious themes [4]. In both cases it produced a sense of shock comparable to Courbet's paintings and for fundamentally the same reason: art was being used to disturb its audience, not to please it. Finally, Realism increasingly invaded the realm of historical and mythological painting, reducing that once noble and intellectual genre to the level of a make-believe voyage into past time, as in the languid reconstructions by Edward Poynter (1836–1919) of the daily lives of the ancient Greeks and Romans [10].

KEY

The symbol of 19th-century Realism in art is, ironically, not a painting but a photograph. Photography, which began to become effective in the 1840s, fulfilled the Realist painter's wildest dreams, yet did so in a medium that was not his own and that dispensed with the arduous process of matching nature by means of brushmarks. In fact, the two arts coexisted in an uneasy but mutually beneficial relationship for the rest of the century. The inventor of the first practical photographic process was a Frenchman, Louis Daguerre (1789–1851), portrayed here in a "daguerrotype" by the English photographer J.J.E. Mayall in 1848.

6

6 "Derby Day" (1856–58, detail), by William Powell Frith (1819–1909) follows Hogarth and David Wilkie rather than either the Pre-Raphaelites or the French Realists. Yet it shows a characteristic side of 19th-century life—its energy and vulgarity—and has the contemporary feel of a magazine illustration. The picture also contains some witty character drawing and is composed with skill.

7

7 The discovery of anesthetics and antiseptics made surgical operations a possible subject for art. In "The Gross Clinic" (1875) American Thomas Eakins (1844–1916) practiced his belief: "Respectablity in art is appalling."

8

8 After 1860, cafés were a popular subject of the Realists, and cropping of the image to produce a casual effect, as in a photograph, became common. "Au Cafe" (1878, detail) by Edouard Manet (1832-83) is an example. It also shows the reintroduction of vivacity and color as the painter's technique moves toward Impressionism.

9

9 "On Strike" (1891), by Hubert von Herkomer (1849–1914), enters the world of the industrial working class. Its style reveals the direct influence of photography, although this is most evident in black-and-white reproduction. As with most life-size Victorian paintings, the original disappoints because of its labored execution.

10

10 "A Visit to Aesculapius" (1880) by Edward Poynter, shows what the grand style of history painting came to in the end. For all the correctness of the drawing, the intrusion of "realism" and the trivial subject—a parade of naked Victorian ladies with imaginary illnesses before a classical faith healer—make the picture embarrassing.

Impressionism

"Impressionism" was initially a derogatory term. A bewildered critic, Louis Leroy, first used the word in the satirical newspaper *Le Charivari* on April 25, 1874 after being outraged by Monet's "Impression—Sunrise" [1], which was hanging in an independent exhibition of 251 paintings. The critics singled out eight painters as a distinct group that had abandoned traditional form and content in favor of subjective impressions.

The Impressionist painters

The "father" of the Impressionist group was Camille Pissarro (1830–1903). Others were Paul Cézanne (1839–1906), son of an Aix-en-Provence banker and childhood friend of Emile Zola; Edgar Degas (1834–1917), habitué of the race-track, theater, and ballet studio; Claude Monet (1840–1926) who was contemptuous of all Old Masters; Auguste Renoir (1841–1919), a former porcelain decorator at the Limoges potteries; Alfred Sisley (1839–99), son of a well-to-do English merchant in Paris; Berthe Morisot (1841–95), pupil and sister-in-law of Manet; and Armand Guillaumin (1841–1927). Edouard Manet (1832–83), "leader" of the group had refused to exhibit outside the official Salon.

Although not recognized as a group until 1874, the Impressionists had met and worked together during the preceding decade. Some of them trained together, and some painted the same scenes side-by-side: Monet, Sisley, and Renoir in the Forest of Fontainebleau in 1864; Monet and Renoir at "La Grenouillère" near Paris in 1869; and Monet and Manet at Argenteuil in 1874 [Key]. These artists also shared the experience of frequent rejection by the Salon, which made it very difficult to sell their paintings. Furthermore, with the exception of Degas none of them had received the Salon-approved training offered by the Ecole des Beaux-Arts. This freed them from current artistic conventions.

Style and subject

The Impressionists refused to paint historical events in the tradition of Jacques Louis David or idealized landscapes in the manner of Claude and Poussin. Instead they chose everyday subjects from the region of Paris and Normandy. Degas painted racetracks [2], Monet views along the Seine or the insides of railway stations, and Renoir figures in dappled shade [3, 4]. Cézanne [6] was the exception with his landscapes of Provence. These subjects could be directly experienced and immediately recorded on the spot by the artist; recourse to imagination was thus made superfluous, and studied composition was impossible. Their paintings were impressions "in the sense that they portrayed not a landscape but a sensation produced by a landscape." This was not entirely innovative. The determined use of everyday subject matter by Courbet (1819–77) was an important precedent. Painting on location had been practiced by such French artists of the eighteenth century as Claude Joseph Vernet and Valenciennes as well as by Corot (1796–1875), Constable (1776–1837), and the nineteenth-century masters of the Barbizon school. The Impressionists differed in that they produced not sketches but finished paintings out of doors.

CONNECTIONS

See also
1228 Romantic art: figure painting
1242 Romantic art: landscape painting
1252 Realist painting in 19th century
1294 Fauvism and Expressionism
1296 Cubism and Futurism

1 Claude Monet's "Impression–Sunrise" provoked a contemporary critic to explode: "Impression–of that I was certain! I had to tell myself that since I am impressed it must contain some sort of impression."

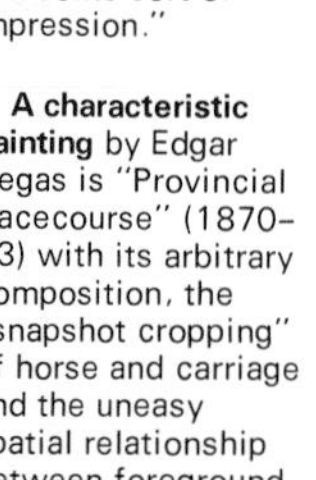

2 A characteristic painting by Edgar Degas is "Provincial Racecourse" (1870–73) with its arbitrary composition, the "snapshot cropping" of horse and carriage and the uneasy spatial relationship between foreground and background.

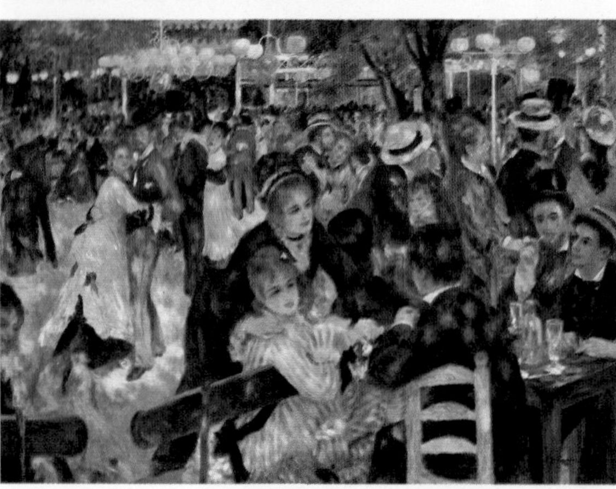

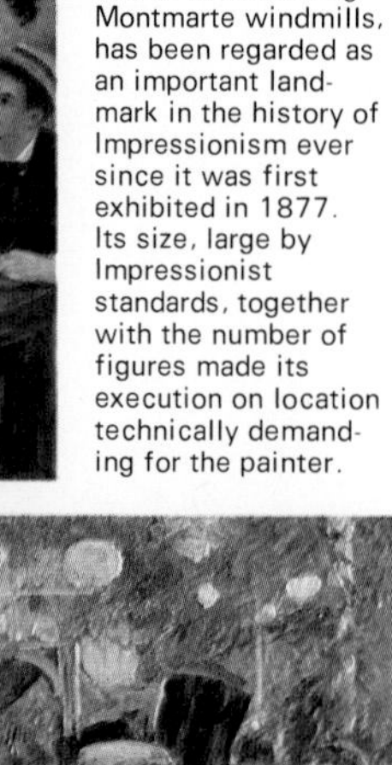

3 Auguste Renoir's "Dance at the Moulin de la Galette" (1876), which shows a Sunday afternoon scene at an outdoor ballroom at the foot of one of the surviving Montmarte windmills, has been regarded as an important landmark in the history of Impressionism ever since it was first exhibited in 1877. Its size, large by Impressionist standards, together with the number of figures made its execution on location technically demanding for the painter.

4 A detail from Renoir's "Dance at the Moulin de la Galette" shows rapidly-placed dabs jostling one another. Black is used not for shadow but only for a top hat; white is placed not for highlights but for a collar; and forms merge with their surroundings to express sunlight filtered through leaves.

5 The first big figure composition Monet painted entirely out of doors and without any preliminary sketches was "Women in the Garden" (1866–67) painted in the artist's garden. His use of black and the harsh divisions between light and shade betray his debt to Manet.

Traditional artists working in studios recorded light as tone. The Impressionists, by working out of doors, came to realize that light, whether ephemeral as for Renoir, or enhancing eternal forms as for Cézanne, was composed of color. In developing this new-found relationship they quickly modified and increased the number of colors on their palettes; they eliminated black from shadow, substituting blue or purple, and adopted the system of complementary colors proposed by the physicist Chevreul in the 1830s. Additionally, they lightened the grounds of their canvases, replacing the traditional brown and biscuit tones with the white and beige of the English watercolorists Bonington (1802–28) and Turner (1775–1851).

Latest developments and changes

The Impressionist style took time to mature. During the 1860s, for example, when Monet painted his "Women in the Garden" [5], extensive use of black and broad brushstrokes hindered expression of the movement of light. By the early 1870s, when Monet painted "Impression—Sunrise" and Pissarro "The Entrance to the Village of Voisins" [7], the Impressionist style can be said to have come of age and featured short, comma-like brushstrokes, the banishment of black from the shadow, and direct confrontation with the subject.

The opening years of the 1880s saw the group's stylistic unity crack. Their early champion, Zola, doubted that "Nature seen through the temperament" could ever provide the recipe for a masterpiece. Sisley, Guillaumin, and Morisot remained stylistically faithful, but Monet sought new subject matter and more intense light on the Côte d'Azur and later embarked on his "serial" paintings [9]. Cézanne, in Provence, began an intense analysis of the relationship between color and form. Renoir rediscovered the formal qualities of the classical nude. Degas reduced his compositions to exercises in two-dimensional patterning, and Pissarro briefly adopted the pointillism of Georges Seurat (1859–91), whose scientific analysis of light lay at the center of Neo-Impressionism [10].

KEY

The Impressionists' working method is amply demonstrated in Edouard Manet's "Monet at Argenteuil" (1874), which shows the spontaneity of his friend's method of work. Monet is sitting with his wife in his improvised studio, working up a finished picture without any preliminary sketches. Manet's picture was painted in a similar manner.

6

6 Cézanne, like his fellow Impressionists, sought to record his "powerful sensations in front of Nature" by working directly in front of his subject. In this photograph he is lifting a half-finished canvas of a favorite subject, the Mont Sainte-Victoire outside Aix-en-Provence, on to his easel ready for work.

7

7 Camille Pissarro, who painted "Entrance to the Village of Voisins" in 1872, had been in self-exile with Monet in London during the Franco-Prussian war. There he developed an admiration for the landscapists Turner and Constable," who obviously shared our aims of *plein-air*, light, and fugitive effects."

8

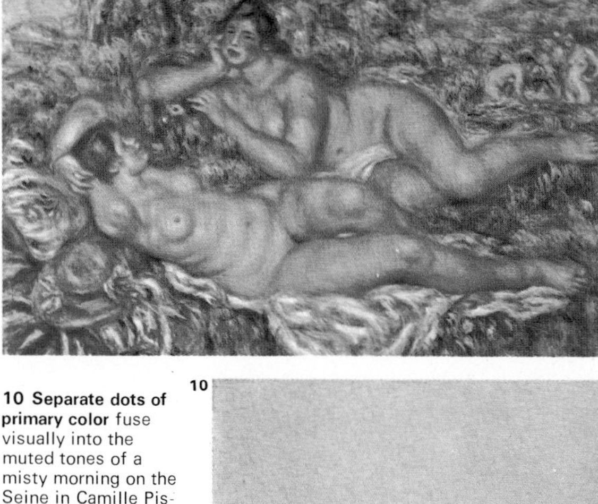

8 "Nymphs" (1918) is part of a series of monumental nudes that Renoir had begun in the early 1880s. Integrity of form has replaced a preoccupation with the dissolution of form by light. During a visit to Italy, Renoir wrote that he had become dissatisfied with the imprecise "blotting" technique of Impressionism and that he had discovered the grandeur and simplicity of Ingres and Raphael, both masters of the idealized nude.

9

9 "Rouen Cathedral—Morning Effect" is one of 40 similar views painted by Claude Monet by 1895. In February 1892 and March 1893 the artist rented a room overlooking the west porch of the cathedral to observe the façade and make notes and sketches in different weather conditions and at varying times of the day. He worked up the finished paintings afterward. As in his other series, Monet's choice of a static subject allowed him to turn his attention exclusively to the formal compositions that were created by the translation of light effects into color.

10

10 Separate dots of primary color fuse visually into the muted tones of a misty morning on the Seine in Camille Pissarro's "Ile Lacroix, Rouen" (1888). In 1885, Pissarro complained that his Impressionist paintings were "poor—tame, gray, monotonous—I am not at all satisfied." His reaction was to adopt the new "divisionist" technique of Georges Seurat, whom he had met through Paul Signac. Although Pissarro's adherence to the style was short lived, he did nonetheless produce some pointillist pictures.

Opera in the 19th and 20th centuries

About the beginning of the nineteenth century the growth of a middle-class, concert-going audience encouraged the practice of giving performances in public opera houses. The resulting demand for new repertory allowed many composers to specialize in opera for the first time.

Serious and comic opera

The traditional streams of serious opera and comic opera remained distinct in the early nineteenth century. Serious operas derived from Neapolitan opera (with recitatives and arias, no chorus) and number opera (arias, duets, ballets, etc., separated by recitative) continued into the 19th century. Essentially showcases for virtuoso *bel canto* singers of the time, these forms were used by Vincenzo Bellini (1801–35) in *La Sonnambula* and *Norma,* Gaetano Donizetti (1747–1848) in *Don Pasquale,* and by Verdi in early works such as *Rigoletto* (1853).

Gluck's eighteenth-century reforms in reaction to *bel canto*—music and drama more closely related and style more continuous—strongly influenced nineteenth-century serious opera. Mozart's later operas (*Don Giovanni,* 1787) began to adopt this style, as did Beethoven in his only opera, *Fidelio* (1805–14). Gluck's heroic opera style finally blossomed into the large-scale grand opera of Rossini's *William Tell* (1829) and Meyerbeer's *Les Huguenots* (1836). Grand opera reached its height in Italy with *Aida* (1871) and *Otello* (1887) by Giuseppe Verdi (1813–1901).

At the same time, comic opera (with spoken dialogue, popular music style, and scenes from everyday life) was developing along several lines. The comic operas (*opera buffa*) of Gioacchino Rossini (1792–1868) [Key] were in great demand; *The Barber of Seville* (1816), *Italian Girl in Algiers* (1813), and *Cinderella* (1817) had crowd-pleasing vocal music.

By the mid-nineteenth century, comic opera began to lose some distinctive characteristics. Some comic operas tended more toward entertainment (the operettas of Gilbert and Sullivan), while others were large-scale and were like serious opera—Wagner's *Der Meistersinger von Nurnberg* (1868). In France, *opera comique* reached its zenith with Offenbach and developed, in the 1850s, into a lyric opera style—a reaction to grand opera. Lyric operas included Charles Gounod's *Faust* (1859).

But the comic opera style that was to have the greatest influence on nineteenth-century opera was the German *Singspiel.* Its elements of mystery, folklike humor, and vernacular dialogue were used by Mozart in his comic operas *Abduction from the Seraglio* (1781) and *The Magic Flute* (1791). This thread was picked up by Carl Maria von Weber (1786–1826), particularly in *Der Freischutz* (1821) [1] and *Euryanthe* (1823). With these works he shaped the German Romantic tradition of combining folk melody and operatic arias, influencing Richard Wagner (1813–83) [4]. Beginning with *Lohengrin* (1847), Wagner united the comic and serious, particularly in *Der Ring des Nibelungen* (1853–74).

By the end of the nineteenth century, reaction began against the overpowering effect of Wagner's works. Some composers took a more realistic approach, as in the

CONNECTIONS

See also
1174 The origins of opera
1246 Music: the Romantic period
1364 Twentieth century—tradition and experimentation
1368 Classical and modern ballet

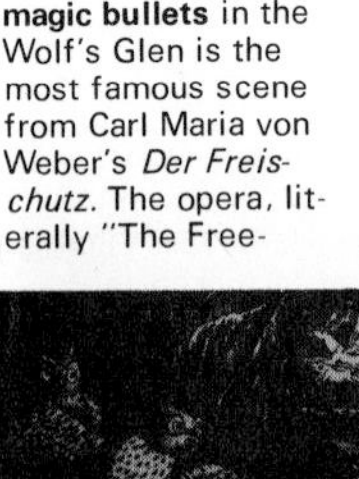

1 The casting of the magic bullets in the Wolf's Glen is the most famous scene from Carl Maria von Weber's *Der Freischutz.* The opera, literally "The Free-shooter," meaning a marksman who uses magic bullets, is regarded as a pioneer work of the Romantic era and is notable for Weber's orchestral effects, particularly during the sinister action in the scene depicted. In *Der Freischutz* Weber reinforced the line of German opera leading from Mozart to Wagner.

2 Adelina Patti (1843–1919), the celebrated Madrid-born coloratura soprano, here in the role of Marguerite in Gounod's *Faust,* enjoyed an operatic career that spanned nearly 60 years. Patti was acclaimed as the last in a great line of prima donnas who were typical of 19th-century opera. She was notable as Rosina in *The Barber of Seville,* and Rossini himself arranged music for her.

3 Fyodor Chaliapin (1873–1938), the great Russian bass, gained world fame in the title role of Mussorgsky's *Boris Godunov,* which he was the first to perform outside Russia. His strong acting performances and resonant voice brought him world premiere roles in Massenet's *Don Quichotte* and Mussorgsky's *Khovantchina.* His success in New York in the 1920s made him as admired as Caruso.

4 The knight Lohengrin arrives in a boat drawn by a swan in a scene from the first production of *Lohengrin* by Richard Wagner, given at Weimar in 1850 under Franz Liszt. *Lohengrin* represents a mid-point in the development of Wagner's music; it is the last in a series of operas with traditional elements from grand opera and set-piece numbers. His later operas—*Tristan and Isolde, Der Meistersinger, The Ring of the Nibelung* cycle, and *Parsifal*—would exemplify his ideas of opera as a continuous music drama of endless melody, bound together by musical motifs representing characters and ideas.

5 Aida, by Giuseppe Verdi (in a production at the Royal Opera House, Covent Garden), London, represents the full flowering of Italian opera in the 19th century, with its spectacle, color, dramatic love triangle, and tragic ending, all enriched by Verdi's dramatically apt music. The opera was commissioned as a festival work by the khedive of Egypt to celebrate the opening of the Suez Canal, and was first performed in Cairo in 1871. Set in ancient Egypt, the story tells of the Ethiopian slave girl Aida's love for the Egyptian army officer Radames.

verismo operas of Pietro Mascagni (1863–1945), Ruggiero Leoncavallo (1858–1919), and Giacomo Puccini (1858–1924), and in George Bizet's *Carmen* (1875). In France, Claude Debussy (1862–1918) produced his single opera, *Pelleas and Melisande* (1902).

Nationalism

The nationalism of nineteenth-century Romanticism also appeared in opera. In Italy, Verdi's operas became identified with the cause of a united Italy.

The Bohemian Bedrich Smetana (1824–84) produced the very popular comic opera *Bartered Bride* (1866), and the Russian school displayed national tradition in *Life for the Tsar* (1836) by Mikhail Glinka (1804–57), *Boris Godunov* (1869–72) by Modest Moussorgsky (1839–81), and *The Snow Maiden* (1882) by Nikolai Rimsky-Korsakov (1844–1908). Tchaikovsky wrote ten operas (including *Eugene Onegin* and *The Queen of Spades*) and, in the twentieth century, Serge Prokofiev (1891–1953) wrote several operas, including *Love for Three Oranges* (1921) and *War and Peace* (1946).

20th-century opera

A wide range of operatic techniques and styles developed in the twentieth century. There was a return to eighteenth-century opera and music forms (number opera; use of sonatas, suites) composed in modern idioms. Paul Hindemith's (1895–1963) *Cardillac* (1926) is in the style of number opera, while Igor Stravinsky's (1882–1971) opera-oratio, *Oedipus Rex*, is sung in Latin. Arnold Schoenberg (1874–1951) and Alban Berg [7] used Stravinsky's 12-tone system and *Sprechstimme* (combination of song and speech) in *Moses und Aron* (1932–51). Jazz operas were written by Kurt Weill (1900–50) and Ernst Krenek (1900–), while George Gershwin (1898–1937) composed the memorable folk opera *Porgy and Bess* (1935).

New operas included Samuel Barber's (1910–) *Vanessa* (1958) and *Antony and Cleopatra* (1966) and Alberto Ginastera's (1916–) *Don Rodrigo* (1964). Benjamin Britten (1913–76) [9] and Gian-Carlo Menotti (1911–) both composed operas for television.

KEY

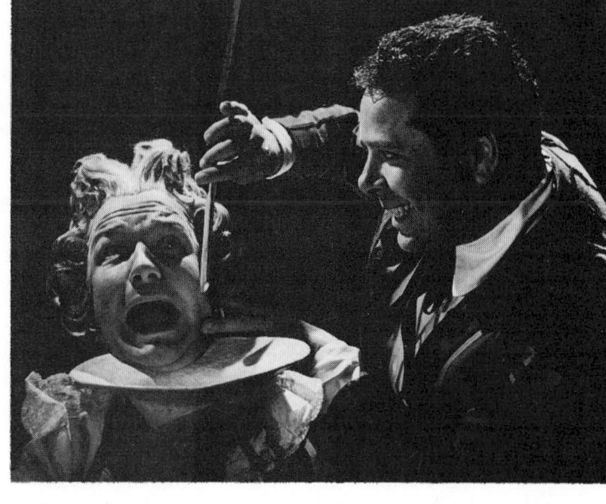

The Barber of Seville is the best known comic opera by Gioacchino Rossini, whose music dominated the world of opera in the early 19th century. In this characteristic scene from Act II the cheerful barber Figaro shaves Dr. Bartolo, who mistakenly believes he will marry the heroine Rosina, while Figaro is scheming another husband for her.

6

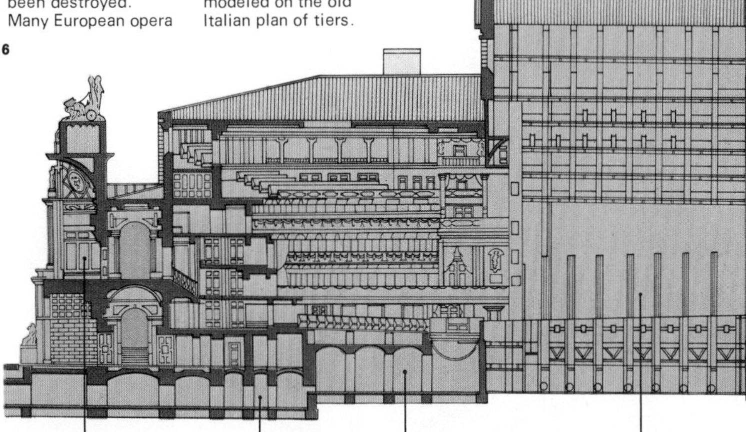

Main foyer
Basement
Auditorium
Stage

6 The Dresden Hoftheater or opera house was designed and built between 1871 and 1878 to replace an earlier building that had been destroyed. Many European opera houses built or rebuilt in the 18th and 19th centuries (La Scala, Milan, 1778; Royal Opera House, Covent Garden, London, 1856) were modeled on the old Italian plan of tiers.

7

LULU

7 Lulu, by Alban Berg (1885–1935), is one of the major operatic works of the 20th century. It tells the story of Lulu, a prostitute who becomes one of Jack the Ripper's victims in a London street. Written in the 12-tone harmony developed by Arnold Schoenberg (1874–1951), Berg's teacher, *Lulu* was unfinished at Berg's death, with only two out of three acts published; it was performed in that state two years later. The opera continues Berg's concern for human beings as victims of persecution—a theme that he first explored in *Wozzeck*, the study of an anti-hero—and is dramatically suited by the often harsh music.

8

8 Beverly Sills (center) the distinguished bel canto soprano of the New York City Opera and an international star, here after her triumphant debut at the Metropolitan Opera, April 1975, as Pamira in Rossini's *The Siege of Corinth.*

9

9 Peter Grimes, by Benjamin Britten, scored a resounding success throughout Europe and America from its first performance in 1945, and started a new interest in British opera. Based on a poem by George Crabbe, its central character is the fisherman Peter Grimes, seen here with Balstrode, a retired skipper. Grimes is an alienated figure in his own community, and the situation is clearly reflected in Britten's spare yet attractively lyrical music.

Architecture in the 19th century

Industrial progress was the touchstone of the nineteenth century. With it came growth in population and prosperity, factors that created a boom in building. More buildings were constructed in this century than in any previous century, modern building types were born, old building types transformed, and new materials employed. Several styles and architectural theories jostled for supremacy. Likewise, a new professional type emerged: the architect.

In the eighteenth century the cataloging of architectural styles began, with the careful recording of Greek and Roman remains. This effort was extended into the nineteenth century to cover Gothic, Italian Renaissance, Northern Renaissance, and Byzantine buildings. George Gilbert Scott could consequently change in 1857 his original Gothic-style design for the Foreign Office building, London [1], to an Italian Renaissance building more to the taste of the foreign minister, Lord Palmerston.

The selection of a style was by no means only a matter of individual taste: styles had associations. Commercial buildings were often of Italian Renaissance style to recall the wealth and power of such families as the Medici. The Houses of Parliament, London, designed by Charles Barry (1795–1860) and Augustus Welby Pugin (1812–52), were built in perpendicular Gothic to reflect the period when the institution began to assume some importance.

Eugène-Emanuel Viollet-le-Duc (1814–79), the French architect, Gothic renovator, and theorist, declared that "to believe that one can create Beauty by lying is a heresy." The moral connection made between beautiful architecture and truthful architecture was one that was enunciated, in particular by Pugin, and by John Ruskin (1819–1900) in books such as his *Seven Lamps of Architecture* (1849).

Truth and honesty

For Viollet-le-Duc, truthful architecture lay in the honest use of materials: "stone must really look like stone; iron like iron; wood like wood"; hence iron pillars must not be clad in stone, but left exposed and incorporated into the design, a point illustrated by his project for a Market Hall [3] and later by Hector Guimard (1867–1943) in his Sacré Coeur School, Paris (1895). Ruskin argued that "good" (that is, beautiful and moral) architecture could be produced only by a "good" architect who reflected in his work a "good" society. The material expressions of this belief can be seen in the extensive building program of High Gothic churches such as George Street's St Paul's, Rome [7].

Finally, it was "good," honest design that played an important part in liberating the plan and elevation of the private residence, pioneered in Great Britain by Norman Shaw (1831–1912), Philip Webb (1831–1915), and Charles Voysey (1857–1941). The ideal of domesticity and "coziness" was allowed free expression in asymetrical ground plans and unostentatious elevations, such as that seen at Broadleys, Lake Windermere, England [10].

New building materials

Industrialization not only provoked concern about the quality of society and its architecture; it also introduced new building

CONNECTIONS

See also
1296 Origins of modern architecture
1236 Britain and the Industrial Revolution
1284 European industrialization 1870–1914
1280 The impact of steam
1192 British and American art 1530–1790
1104 Gothic art of the 14th century

1 Britain's growing prestige in the area of foreign affairs in the 19th century made the need for a new departmental building imperative. In the architectural competition held in 1857, George Gilbert Scott (1811–78) won with this Gothic design, later changed to an Italian Renaissance style.

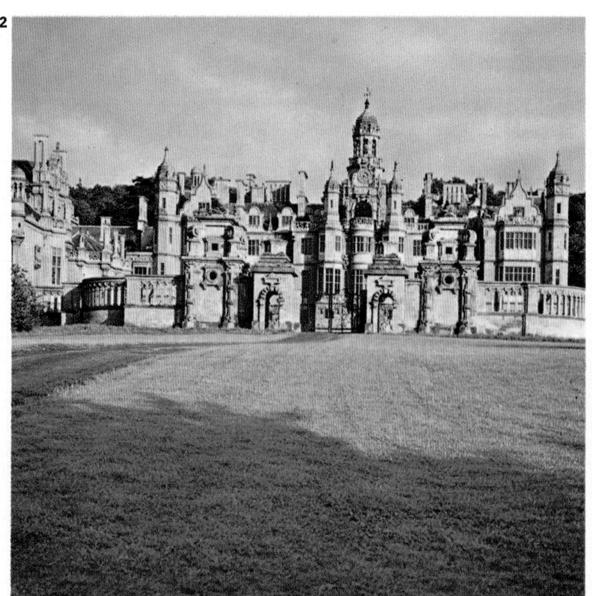

2 New wealth from iron ore financed the building of Harlaxton Manor in Lincolnshire, England. Started by Anthony Salvin (1799–1881) and finished by William Burn (1789–1870), its size was dictated in part by the client's expanding art collection. The mainly Jacobean style was mixed with Elizabethan features.

3 Viollet-le-Duc's project for a market hall was published in his *Entretiens sur l'architecture* (1863–72). There he advocated the use of exposed cast iron for pillars and roof supports.

4 Exposed cast iron was used by Karl Etzel in the Dianabad, Vienna (1841–43) to achieve the barrel vaulted ceiling of the German "round arch." The design of the balcony supports echoes the vault.

RUBBER STAMPS
MERCHANTS VEGETABLES

5 James Bogardus (1800–74) was neither an architect nor an engineer but rather a builder and inventor. In New York in 1848 he built a four-story factory for his own use, made of cast iron that was bolted together on site. This was followed by a five-story pharmacy and the Laing Stores, shown here. Although this building took but two months to erect, it displayed no trace of shabby prefabrication. Cast iron could adapt to different styles such as Gothic, Renaissance, or Grecian with great ease, and when painted the material could give the impression of stone. Bogardus pioneered the idea of bearing loads on cast iron columns rather than on walls.

materials such as cast and wrought iron, steel, plate glass, and lightweight, fireproof, caustic bricks. These innovations permitted the construction of "engineering" monuments such as Isambard Kingdom Brunel's (1806–59) Clifton Suspension Bridge, Bristol, England (1830–64), John A. Roebling's Brooklyn Bridge, New York (1869–83), and Victor Baltard's Les Halles, Paris (1853–58, now demolished). Advanced engineering also pioneered in the construction of such "architectural" structures as Karl Etzel's indoor swimming pool Dianabad, Vienna (1841–43) [4]. Iron also lent itself to prefabrication. Buildings such as James Bogardus' Laing Stores, New York (1849) [5], were precast and bolted together on site.

Changes in society also brought aggrandizement, extension, and specialization of traditional building types. With the increasing complexity and importance of central and local governments, government offices and town halls became monuments on a grand scale. Visconti and Lefuel extended the Louvre, Paris, in an ebullient neo-Baroque style in 1852–57, while across the Atlantic, Alfred B. Mullet was adorning Washington, DC, with his neo-Roman State, War, and Navy Department Building (1871–75). Growing public services required a variety of new buildings. Many of these were gigantic, such as Giuseppe Calderini's Palazzo di Giustizia, Rome (1888–1910) [9]. Most were built after careful investigation of specialized requirements, as in P. J. H. Cuypers' Rijksmuseum, Amsterdam [6].

Railroad stations

Of special significance and interest were railroad stations. Focal points of urban and industrial activity, they rapidly became symbols of and monuments to the new industrial age. In some instances the station would be no more than a dominant shed with forecourt buildings, such as King's Cross, London (Lewis Cubitt, 1850–52). In others the shed was masked by the forecourt structure, which often doubled as a hotel. Such was George Gilbert Scott's Midland Grand Hotel and St Pancras Station, London (1868–73) [8].

KEY

Charles Garnier (1825–98) built the Paris Opéra, at the end of the Avenue de l'Opéra, between 1861 and 1874. It is neo-Baroque in style and one of many examples of wholesale urban improvement carried out in 19th-century Europe as the result of the growth of central government.

6

6 The Rijksmuseum, Amsterdam (1877–85), was erected to house the state collection of art. It was designed by P.J.H. Cuypers (1827–1921), a leading member of the Dutch arts reform movement in the 19th century.

7

7 St Paul's American Church, Rome (1872–76), was built by George Edmund Street (1824–81) to serve the religious needs of the American community. Its Italian Gothic style shows a sensitivity to location and accords with the Ruskinian doctrine that Gothic was the most suitable style for church building.

8

8 Architectural contests held for major 19th-century building projects reflected a faith in excellence that emerged from the workings of a free market economy, a desire for public accountability, and a new professionalism in architecture. In May 1865 architects were invited by the Midland Railway Company to submit plans for a Grand Midland Hotel and station offices at St Pancras Station, London. A complex involved designing a building that would entirely mask a train shed erected two years earlier and also the planning of a type of building that had only recently been created – the grand hotel. George Gilbert Scott won the contest in January 1866 with a grandiose design of monumental proportions (shown here in the background), which was the most expensive plan submitted. Evidently the company wanted to advertise its services by making use of the prestige of Scott and the romance of his architectural conception.

9

9 A new national style emerged in Italy after Rome was established as the capital of a unified nation and new government buildings were needed. Their designs tended to derive from the Renaissance or else the Baroque, a style that was the basis of Giuseppe Calderini's design for Rome's High Court buildings, prominently sited above the Tiber.

10

10 Broadleys, Windermere, England (1898), exemplifies a style of rural domestic architecture evolved by C.F.A. Voysey, who sought to create an organic relationship between his houses and their natural surroundings. At Broadleys the scale is comfortable, with windows along the southwest façade designed for maximum sunlight and view. The service wing of the house is hidden.

Colonizing Oceania and Australasia

The voyage of Ferdinand Magellan across the "Peaceful Sea" in 1520 brought the Pacific Ocean to the attention of Europe. But it was 1565 before the Spaniard López de Legaspi (died 1572), sailing west from the New World, settled the Philippines, where Magellan had died [1]. Spanish rule, although challenged, was uninterrupted until the Spanish-American War of 1898, when the Philippines were ceded to the United States.

The Indies and Australia

Meanwhile, to the southeast, as Portuguese power declined the ships of the Dutch East India Company, founded in 1602, routed the pirates of the Malay Archipelago, seized control of the lucrative spice trade, and paved the way for a Dutch colonial empire extending from Sumatra, Java, and Borneo to Celebes, the Moluccas, and western New Guinea [9]. The prosperity of the new colonies, largely derived from cloves, nutmeg, pepper, and coffee, was set against a background of repression and bloodshed. In Borneo, where gold and diamond mining attracted Chinese immigration, Dutch rule was precarious; and not until 1701 did the British East India Company, formed in 1600, establish a factory or trading post there.

Commissioned by East Indies Governor Anthony van Diemen (1593–1645) to chart the western and southern shores of New Holland (Australia), Abel Tasman [2] in 1642–43 discovered Van Diemen's Land (later Tasmania), skirted New Zealand, and later sailed along the southern coast of New Guinea. More than a century passed before the British admiralty dispatched James Cook (1728–79) [5] to take possession of any land in the south in the course of a scientific expedition to the South Seas. By sailing during 1768–71 from Cape Horn to New Zealand, Cook finally exploded the theory that a great southern continent balanced the land mass of the Northern Hemisphere. He sailed up the east coast of Australia, claiming it for Britain, showed that New Guinea was a separate island, and, in two later voyages, made other significant Pacific discoveries.

Britain was left to colonize the subcontinent of Australia in 1787, first as a penal settlement, later as rich sheep and cattle country. Population was concentrated in the east and south where Brisbane, Sydney, Melbourne, and Adelaide were founded. Sparse settlement spread out as explorers trekked across the vast deserts of the interior [6]. The principal victims of white expansion were the Stone Age culture aborigines, whose clubs, spears, and boomerangs were ineffectual against firearms. Introduced diseases had an even more devastating impact. Guns and epidemics wiped out the native population of Tasmania and sharply reduced that of the mainland. The aborigines were to have no share in new Australian prosperity, accelerated by future gold rushes [7].

New Guinea and New Zealand

Rumors of gold also drew prospectors to the great island of New Guinea in the midnineteenth century. Mineral resources proved negligible, but traders and speculators stripped coastal forests of timber. In the

CONNECTIONS

See also
1186 Exploration and science 1750–1850
1200 International economy 1700–1800
1262 European imperialism in the 19th century
236 Oceanographic exploration
596 Woodlands of Australasia
590 Australian desert grasslands
614 Life on islands

1

ASIA
NORTH AMERICA
(Hawaiian Is.)
Sandwich Is.
Philippines
Ladrone Is. (Mariana Is.)
Andaman Is.
Caroline Is.
Penang
Singapore
Spice Is. (Moluccas)
Sumatra
Borneo
Celebes
New Guinea
Timor
Java
Santa Cruz Is.
Samoa
Marquesas Is.
New Hebrides
Fiji
Society Is.
Tahiti
Cook Is.
New Caledonia
Pitcairn Is.
Easter Is.
New Holland
New South Wales
Boundary 1788
Australia
Lord Howe Is.
Sydney penal colony 1788
Van Diemen's Land (Tasmania)
New Zealand
Legaspi 1564–5
Tasman 1642–4
Bougainville 1766–9
Wallis 1767
Cook 1768–71
Cook 1772–5
Cook 1776–9
British possessions 18th cent.
Dutch possessions 18th cent.
Spanish possessions 18th cent.
Batavia—headquarters of the Dutch East India Co

1 Imperial ambition, commercial rivalry, and the search for a legendary southern continent motivated navigators of the great European maritime nations – Spain, Portugal, Holland, Britain, and France – to explore the Pacific between the 16th and 18th centuries. They included Legaspi, who conquered the Philippines; Tasman, the discoverer of Tasmania and New Zealand; Bougainville, first Frenchman to sail around the world; Wallis, discoverer of Tahiti; and Cook, who opened up most of the Pacific.

2

2 Abel Tasman (1603–69), an employee of the Dutch East India Company, touched on the southern shore of an island he named Van Diemen's Land after the Indies' governor general; in 1865 the island was renamed Tasmania. He was deterred from landing in New Zealand by Maoris. After discovering Tonga and the Fiji Islands he returned to Batavia (Jakarta), where he was rebuked for "having been negligent in investigating the situation, conformation, and nature of the lands and peoples discovered." An equally frosty reception greeted his second voyage along the coast of northern Australia

3

3 William Dampier (1652–1715), formerly an English buccaneer, explored the coasts of Australia, New Guinea, and New Britain, vividly describing the lands.

4

4 Louis de Bougainville (1729–1811) set out on a round-the-world voyage of discovery in November 1766 in the frigate *La Boudause*. He sailed through the Straits of Magellan to Tahiti, which he claimed for France, unaware that Samuel Wallis (1728–95) had found it ten months earlier. He sighted and named islands in the Samoa and New Hebrides groups and would have reached the unknown east coast of Australia had he not been diverted by the Great Barrier Reef. Despite starvation and scurvy, he lost only seven men by the time he returned home in 1769. He also founded a settlement in the Falkland Islands.

5

5 The voyages of Captain James Cook were supplemented by careful and perceptive accounts of lands he visited and by scientific observations of great practical value. During the first voyage in *Endeavour* in 1768–71 he circumnavigated the two main islands of New Zealand, charted and claimed the east coast of Australia, and returned home through the Torres Strait. In the second voyage he took *Resolution* to the Antarctic and discovered or rediscovered many Pacific islands. Finally, he visited Australia and New Zealand again in *Resolution* and discovered Hawaii, where he was killed in 1779.

mountainous interior, inhabited by plumed and painted head hunters, civilizations made little impact even after Holland, Germany, and Britain annexed the island in 1884–85.

In New Zealand the Maoris, more advanced socially and culturally, were treated with more respect by European settlers. Whalers [10] and sealers were initially welcomed by the local population, although disease took a terrible toll. The early nineteenth-century arrival of traders and missionaries in the North Island was followed by British annexation with Maori agreement in 1840 and rapid settlement of both islands. But misunderstandings over tribal rights to sell land to the colonists led to disputes as the Maoris realized the threat to their lands. They resisted in a series of fierce wars, particularly in the 1860s [8] but were defeated and lost most of their land.

The Maoris had left their original homelands in Polynesia several centuries earlier. Other peoples—Micronesians, Melanesians, and Polynesians—still inhabited the island groups of Oceania that were sighted (and sometimes colonized) by Europeans between the sixteenth and nineteenth centuries [3, 4]. Copra (dried coconut), used for animal feeding and later for the extraction of edible oil, was the staple export crop. A few islands were commercially more rewarding—notably British Fiji with its forests of sandalwood; French New Caledonia, where nickel was found; and Hawaii, where a combination of American missionary work and a more developed local rule led to a theoretically independent monarchy as early as 1843; a prosperous economy based on sugar and pineapples developed.

Cultural impact

Elsewhere, repression, missionary conversion, disease, and the forced transport of native labor to work in the sugar and cotton plantations all helped to destroy local cultures and tribal structures as white civilization spread. Colonialism also put a stop to more savage rituals—cannibalism, head hunting, and blood feuds—with a promise of education and a share in economic wealth and political power.

KEY

The Maoris of New Zealand, whose Polynesian ancestors paddled some 2,000 miles (3,300 km) across the Pacific in about the 13th century, were unsurpassed craftsmen of dugout canoes, of which a model is shown here. War canoes, carrying up to 100 men, were elaborately carved by sculptors who also taught their pupils the magical and religious ritual associated with the craft. Paddled at full speed, they could overtake European sailing ships.

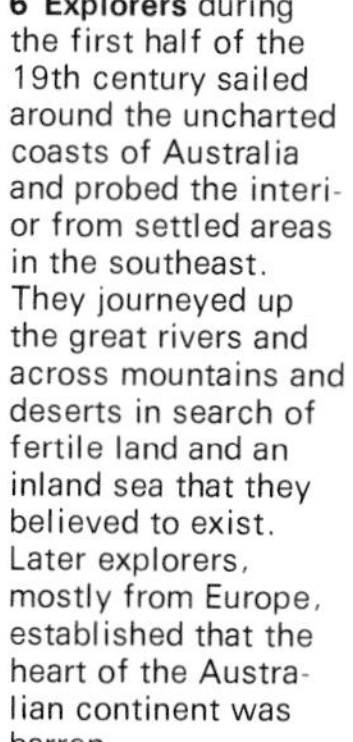

6 Explorers during the first half of the 19th century sailed around the uncharted coasts of Australia and probed the interior from settled areas in the southeast. They journeyed up the great rivers and across mountains and deserts in search of fertile land and an inland sea that they believed to exist. Later explorers, mostly from Europe, established that the heart of the Australian continent was barren.

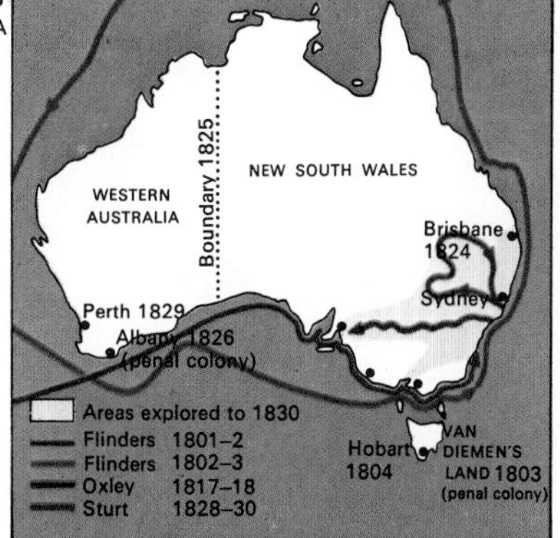

6
A
WESTERN AUSTRALIA
NEW SOUTH WALES
Boundary 1825
Brisbane
1824
Sydney
Perth 1829
Albany 1826
(penal colony)
Hobart
1804
VAN DIEMEN'S LAND 1803
(penal colony)
Areas explored to 1830
Flinders 1801–2
Flinders 1802–3
Oxley 1817–18
Sturt 1828–30

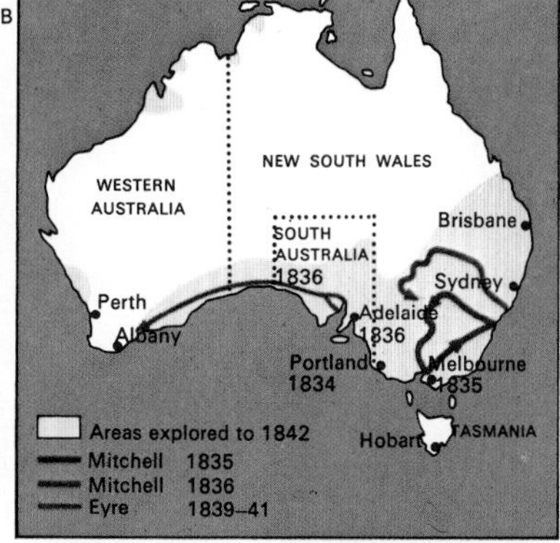

B
WESTERN AUSTRALIA
NEW SOUTH WALES
SOUTH AUSTRALIA
1836
Brisbane
Sydney
Perth
Albany
Adelaide
1836
Portland
1834
Melbourne
1835
Hobart
TASMANIA
Areas explored to 1842
Mitchell 1835
Mitchell 1836
Eyre 1839–41

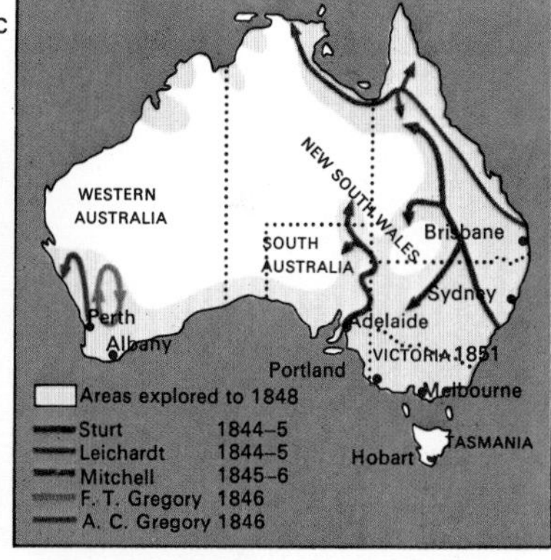

C
WESTERN AUSTRALIA
NEW SOUTH WALES
SOUTH AUSTRALIA
Brisbane
Sydney
Perth
Albany
Adelaide
VICTORIA 1851
Portland
Melbourne
Hobart
TASMANIA
Areas explored to 1848
Sturt 1844–5
Leichardt 1844–5
Mitchell 1845–6
F. T. Gregory 1846
A. C. Gregory 1846

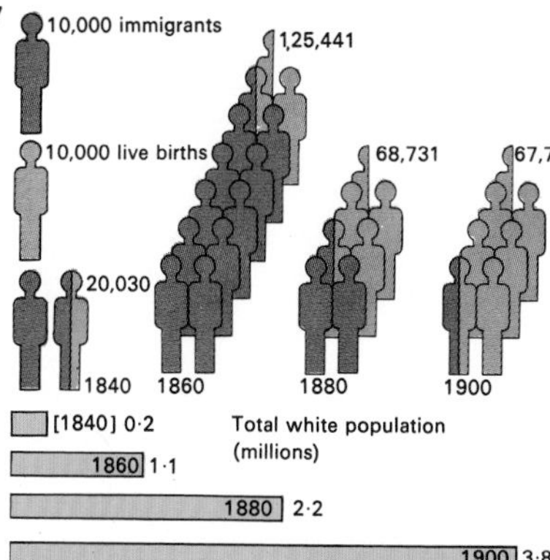

7
10,000 immigrants
10,000 live births
20,030
1,25,441
68,731
67,776
1840
1860
1880
1900
[1840] 0·2
1860 1·1
1880 2·2
1900 3·8
Total white population (millions)

7 Australia relied initially on immigration to build up its population. An assisted immigration program was introduced in 1829 and up to 1860 immigrants accounted for over three-quarters of the population growth. The gold rushes of 1851-56 brought an even greater immigrant surge. Thereafter, the Australian birthrate began to rise and overshadow a reduced inflow of immigrants to the continent.

8

8 Maori gallantry against superior weaponry marked many battles during the 1860s when British attempts to satisfy the land hunger of New Zealand settlers without disrupting Maori tribal rights broke down in bitter disputes over land sales. Maoris defended redoubts such as this one above the Katikara Stream near Mt Egmont. In 1863 the fort was battered by naval guns, and 350 troops routed 600 Maoris.

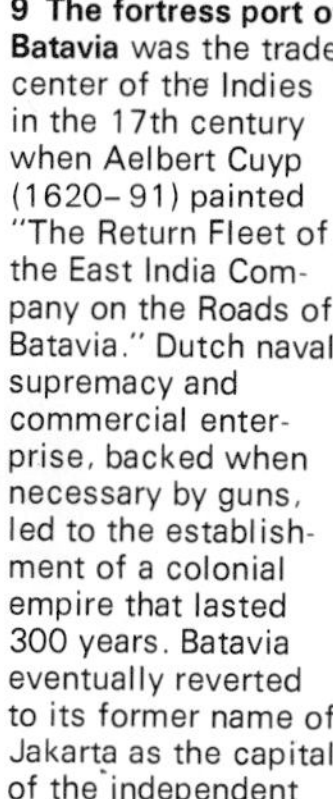

9 The fortress port of Batavia was the trade center of the Indies in the 17th century when Aelbert Cuyp (1620–91) painted "The Return Fleet of the East India Company on the Roads of Batavia." Dutch naval supremacy and commercial enterprise, backed when necessary by guns, led to the establishment of a colonial empire that lasted 300 years. Batavia eventually reverted to its former name of Jakarta as the capital of the independent nation of Indonesia.

9

10

10 Whalers, along with traders and planters, brought guns and disease to many Pacific islands in the 19th century. The profitability of whaling meant that fishing grounds were eventually depleted, although the industry survived for many years. This somewhat fanciful print entitled "The North Cape New Zealand and Sperm Whale Fishery" may exaggerate the density of the whale population but typifies the old-style shore whaling practices carried on by local fishermen.

European imperialism in the 19th century

The nineteenth century saw a major expansion of European control and influence over the rest of the world. Important empires had existed in the ancient world, and the Spanish, Dutch, and Portuguese had established extensive trading empires in the sixteenth and seventeenth centuries. But the nineteenth century was the period of Europe's greatest overseas expansion, during which European influence was felt for the first time by a wide variety of races and peoples [Key]. By 1914 more than 500 million lived under imperial rule [1].

The rise of Britain

In the course of the eighteenth and early nineteenth centuries, the older empires of Spain, Portugal, and Holland began to decline. A series of revolts freed the Latin American republics from Spanish domination and virtually ended the economic importance of the Spanish Empire. After a sequence of wars in the eighteenth century, culminating in 1815 with the defeat of Napoleonic France, Britain emerged as the strongest maritime nation, with substantial colonies in Canada, the West Indies, South Africa, India, Australia, and New Zealand.

During the mid-nineteenth century, colonial expansion was relatively limited; Britain concentrated on consolidating its hold upon the colonies it already possessed, partly by conceding self-government to the most developed and stable, such as Canada, and also by military force [7], as in the suppression of the Indian Mutiny (1857–58). During this period Britain pursued a policy of "informal control," attempting to limit its commitments to those essential to the maintenance of trade, while avoiding large-scale involvements in governing new territories. Thus the characteristic acquisitions of the mid-nineteenth century were positions of strategic or commercial significance, such as trading rights in Singapore, purchased in 1819 from the sultan of Johore, and trade settlements on the African Gold Coast, bought from Denmark in 1850. The British attitude toward India was somewhat anomalous. Although many Englishmen were prepared to contemplate the eventual secession of most of Britain's white colonies, the prospect of India's becoming independent was never actively supported. The maintenance of India as a vital part of Britain's overseas interests became the linchpin of imperial policy.

The scramble for Africa

By 1870 there were stirrings in several parts of the world that had remained beyond European influence. Africa was being opened up by the journeys of the great missionaries and explorers. Technological developments in weaponry and transport and advances in tropical medicine made it easier to penetrate the "dark continent." Once explorers had charted the routes, it was inevitable that European involvement in Africa would expand. The "scramble for Africa" began when, largely for the strategic reason of safeguarding the main route to India, Great Britain occupied Egypt in 1882 [6]. Within 20 years almost the entire continent had been divided up among the major powers. Economic incentives, strategic concerns, and diplomatic rivalry all played a part in the expansion of European influence

CONNECTIONS

See also
1206 China from 1368 to c.1800
1232 European empires in the 19th century
1234 Latin American independence
1260 Colonizing Oceania and Australasia
1264 The expansion of Christianity
1266 India in the 19th century
1268 Africa in the 19th century
1270 The opening up of China
1272 Japan: the Meiji Restoration
1280 The impact of steam
1300 Europe 1870–1914
1332 The Commonwealth
894 Prejudice and group intolerance

1 The colonial empires of the European powers were rapidly extended between 1870 and 1914. The British Empire, which was already vast, expanded in Africa and Southeast Asia; France and Germany acquired large areas. Belgium, Italy, Portugal, and the Netherlands also joined the scramble. Including former colonies in America, European influence extended to 84 per cent of the world's land area by 1914.

1

1914 area of colonies (millions of square miles)
1914 population of colonies (millions)

United Kingdom 12·3 391·5
France 4·0 62·3
Germany 1·2 13·0
Belgium 1·0 15·0
Portugal 0·9 10·0
Netherlands 0·7
Italy 0·6

European or ex-European empires as % of world land surface
1800 55%
1878 67%
1914 84%

2 As trading partners, colonies were usually more important suppliers of raw materials and food than buyers of imperial goods. Some of the territories acquired after 1870 hardly repaid the cost of running them. But Britain's "white" colonies were significant investment outlets and trading partners, particularly after 1900 when the volume of two-way imperial trade rose to more than one-third of Britain's total.

2

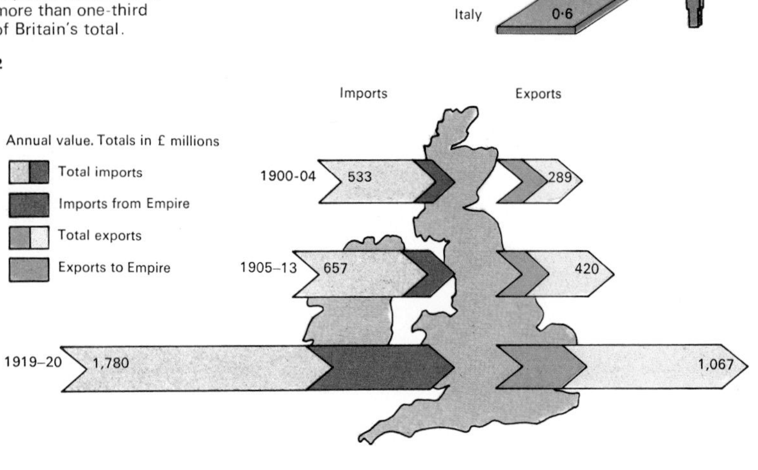

Imports
Exports
Annual value. Totals in £ millions
Total imports
Imports from Empire
Total exports
Exports to Empire
1900-04
533
289
1905–13
657
420
1919–20
1,780
1,067

3 National rivalries for overseas territories (this cartoon depicts the division of China by Britain, Germany, Russia, France, and Japan) were often fanned by attitudes at home. In the 1870s the word "jingoism" was coined to describe a belligerent attitude fostered by the rise of mass-circulation papers. British disputes with Russia on the North West Frontier of India and with France over Sudan in 1898, for example, led to this kind of support for war.

3

both in Africa and in the Far East, where much of Southeast Asia was divided between Britain and France. The degree to which economic motivation accounts for the rapid expansion of the European empires between 1870 and 1914 has often been overstated. In contrast to the earlier phase of European colonialism, trade [2] now tended to follow the flag rather than to act as a direct cause of territorial annexation.

Strategic and political considerations

In 1865 a British parliamentary committee was prepared to concede influence in the economically important area of West Africa in favor of strategic benefits in the economically poorer East Africa, with its ports on the Indian Ocean. In France, colonial development was largely a preoccupation of government officials, a few businessmen, the military, and exploration groups, with little active support from the electorate. Similarly, in Germany, Bismarck pursued a colonial policy for diplomatic and internal political reasons. As a result, the territories acquired after 1870 tended to receive only a limited part of the export of European capital [4] and population and provided a relatively small volume of trade.

Although the new imperialism was motivated primarily by political and strategic imperatives, it was fostered by a climate of approval for the "civilizing mission" of the European races. The benefits of trade, Christianity, and European rule were considered obvious by many educated people in the imperial nations, providing powerful self-justification for the extension of colonial rule over "primitive" peoples. By the late nineteenth century, the glamour of imperial adventure [5] was promoted by the emerging mass-circulation press, which fostered "jingoism" and brought pressure to bear on politicians to support aggressive imperialism [3]. Until 1914, in spite of periods of acute tension and rivalry, the partition of Africa and expansion elsewhere was conducted without a major conflict between European powers. A series of agreements and treaties defined areas of control and spheres of influence, leaving Great Britain with the largest overseas empire.

KEY

Queen Victoria took the title of Empress of India in 1876, symbolizing European supremacy overseas. The greatest imperial expansion, however, took place in Africa.

4

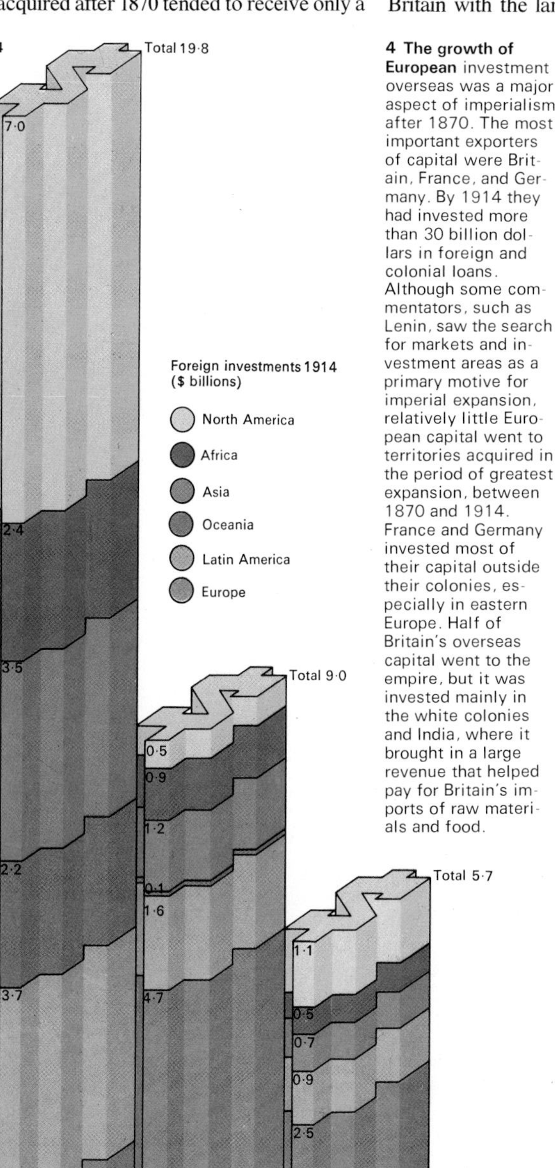
Total 19·8
7·0
2·4
3·5
2·2
3·7
1·0
Total 9·0
0·5
0·9
1·2
0·1
1·6
4·7
Total 5·7
1·1
0·5
0·7
0·9
2·5
Foreign investments 1914 ($ billions)
North America
Africa
Asia
Oceania
Latin America
Europe
United Kingdom
France
Germany

4 The growth of European investment overseas was a major aspect of imperialism after 1870. The most important exporters of capital were Britain, France, and Germany. By 1914 they had invested more than 30 billion dollars in foreign and colonial loans. Although some commentators, such as Lenin, saw the search for markets and investment areas as a primary motive for imperial expansion, relatively little European capital went to territories acquired in the period of greatest expansion, between 1870 and 1914. France and Germany invested most of their capital outside their colonies, especially in eastern Europe. Half of Britain's overseas capital went to the empire, but it was invested mainly in the white colonies and India, where it brought in a large revenue that helped pay for Britain's imports of raw materials and food.

5

5 Charles Gordon (1833–85), a British general, was killed at Khartoum by the Mahdists, a radical Muslim group. His death caused public outrage in England against government bungling. Gordon's rash bravery epitomized the romantic appeal of imperialism, viewed as an outlet for heroism and adventure in exotic parts of the world, whether in seeking new colonies or in protecting existing ones.

6

6 The Suez Canal provided Britain with a reason to add Egypt to its empire in 1882. Constructed by a Frenchman, Ferdinand de Lesseps, the canal was opened in 1869, making a short route from Europe to India. Britain acquired the canal shares in 1875, following the bankruptcy of the Egyptian khedive. A nationalist revolt prompted Britain to intervene and take Egypt under effective control to safeguard the canal.

7

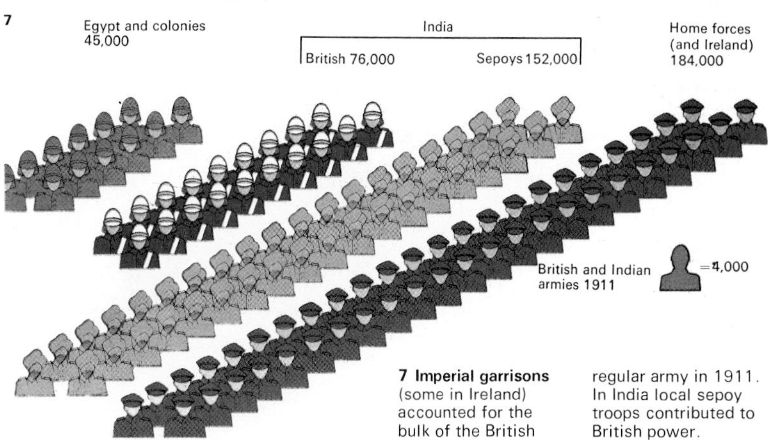
Egypt and colonies
45,000
India
British 76,000
Sepoys 152,000
Home forces
(and Ireland)
184,000
British and Indian
armies 1911
=4,000

7 Imperial garrisons (some in Ireland) accounted for the bulk of the British regular army in 1911. In India local sepoy troops contributed to British power.

The expansion of Christianity

The spread of Christianity across the world has taken place in stages. The first saw the new religion spread during the first centuries of its existence from its birthplace in Palestine into the wider Roman world. The second was the early medieval period when the faith survived the tumult of the Dark Ages, and most of Europe became Christian. The third stage began in the fifteenth century when, held in check by Islam in the Near East, European civilization and Christianity turned to the oceans and lands beyond.

The instrument of conquest

The founding of the Portuguese and Spanish empires in the Americas in the fifteenth century and along the coastline of Africa, the Indies, and the Pacific gave an immense impetus to the advance of Roman Catholicism. The world was divided by papal bull in 1493 into spheres of influence for the Catholic crowns of Portugal and Spain, and the church itself became an instrument of conquest and colonization [2, 3].

In some instances whole populations in the newly discovered lands were forcibly converted, and there were other abuses of colonial power. Often the Catholic missions were outspoken critics of these abuses, none more so than the protector general of the Spanish Caribbean, Bartolomé de las Casas (1479–1566). Catholic advances were not, however, confined to territories formally ruled by Spanish or Portuguese governors. The foremost Jesuit missionary, Francis Xavier (1506–52), was papal nuncio over the Portuguese Indian settlements. He went on to found a mission in Japan and died near Macao in China. Another Jesuit, Matteo Ricci (1552–1610), was responsible for bringing Catholicism to China, where for a time it enjoyed the protection of the emperors and made many converts [6]. Only in the eighteenth century did squabbles within the church bring it into disrepute so that Catholicism was repressed.

The success of the mission to Japan was less impressive. For 50 years from 1587 the church was severely persecuted, and few Christians survived [4].

Protestant forms of Christianity were taken to those parts of the world where large numbers of Europeans settled—notably North America (except in French Canada, where the settlers were Catholics), and later South Africa, Australia, and New Zealand; but the seventeenth and early eighteenth centuries were a time of dormant missionary activity. The main exception to the lack of interest in missions was the work of Moravian and German Pietist groups.

Christianity and colonial activity

The second great spurt of missionary activity took place at the end of the eighteenth century and throughout the nineteenth and was closely connected with the Protestant revival in northwestern Europe. The new Christian advance coincided with the increase of European colonial activity in the generally densely populated, tropical parts of the world, notably India and Africa, and with the ferment of the French and Industrial revolutions. A spate of well-organized and often financially powerful societies was formed—the British Baptist Missionary Society in 1792, which sent missionaries to India; the Nonconformist London Mission-

CONNECTIONS

See also
1262 European imperialism in the 19th century
1388 Modern Christianity and the New Beliefs
1270 The opening up of China
1234 Latin American independence
1266 India in the 19th century
1268 Africa in the 19th century

Missionary activity 1925-26
Intense missionary activity 1925-26

1 Christian missionary work greatly expanded from 1815 into the 20th century. Along with a revival of Roman Catholic missions there was an upsurge of Protestant activity, characterized by a notable degree of cooperation. This culminated in the International Missionary Council set up in 1921, which assisted and stimulated missionary activity throughout the world. This map shows its activity in the mid-1920s. More than one billion people were claimed to be Christians, in 1965 divided as follows: North America, 226 million; South America, 200 million; Europe, 515 million; Asia, 90 million; Africa, 90 million; Oceania, 7 million.

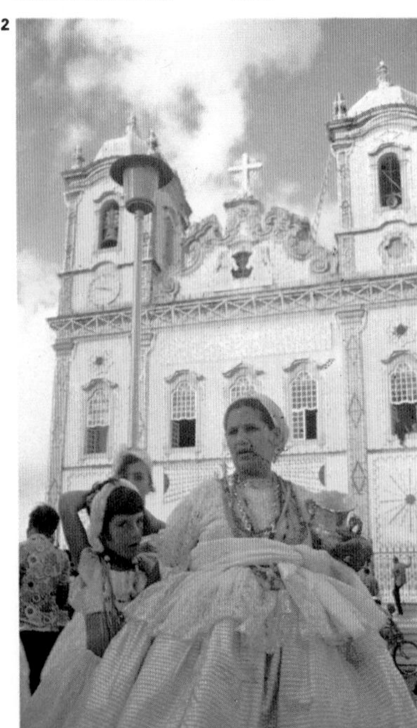

2 The church in Brazil, as in the Spanish colonies, was intimately united with the state despite Rome's influence over the Jesuits. Portuguese churches, such as this one in Salvador, were less opulent than those built by the Spanish.

3 This roadside shrine in Otovalo, Ecuador, symbolizes the assimilation of religion at the grass-roots level. The church, although concerned with Indian welfare, aided their cultural decline by accepting Indian employment in the mines.

4 Christianity in Japan arrived with the Portuguese in the mid-16th century, but its presence became a source of suspicion within a few decades. In 1637 many thousands of Christian converts were massacred. The succeeding isolation of Japan was finally broken in 1858, and missionary work resumed, making notable contributions to education. Hugh Foss, one of the first missionaries, became bishop of Osaka in 1899. He is seen here [left] with native clergy.

ary Society in 1795; the Netherlands Missionary Society in 1797; the Church of England Church Missionary Society in 1799; the American Board of Commissioners for Foreign Missions in 1810; and the Wesleyan Methodist Missionary Society in 1813 (various Scottish Presbyterian societies came together about the same time). The interdenominational Basel Missionary Society, with support from Germany and Switzerland, was founded in 1815. Some of the great names associated with these Protestant missionary societies in Britain were the Baptist William Carey (1761–1834), William Wilberforce (1759–1833), who was also a leader in the successful campaign for the abolition of slavery, and David Livingstone (1813–73), who became a hero both as a missionary and as an explorer.

Catholic revival in the nineteenth century

By the end of the nineteenth century, more than 300 such societies or boards existed. Catholic missionary activity, at first slow to revive, produced an effect as large as that of advances in areas where other religions with claims to universality, particularly Islam, were strong. Indeed, at the same time as the spurt of Christian missionary activity at the end of the eighteenth century, there was a revival of Islam, which made gains on the periphery of the older heartlands of the religion, especially in Indonesia and Africa [5].

Although most of the nineteenth-century missionary societies were rivals, the decline of European imperialism after World War I brought a wider, more international approach. This resulted in the forma- the Protestants—perhaps, in terms of numbers of converts, even larger. One of the foremost Catholic missionary societies was the mainly French White Fathers.

The result of all these remarkable missionary endeavors, which continued from the nineteenth century into the twentieth, was the spread of Christianity over much of the tropical world. It did not make great tion of the World Council of Churches in 1948. This body did not include the Roman Catholic Church, but ties between Catholicism and the council (and its member churches) have grown increasingly close.

KEY

The Ibo of southeastern Nigeria, like a number of ethnic groups in Africa, were receptive to Christianity and education under British colonial and missionary influence in the 19th century. The Christian faith was often assimilated into existing religions, which included belief in a creator god as well as numerous other deities and spirits. The mask illustrated reflects this assimilation. Carved in wood, it depicts Christ on the cross flanked by angels. The Ibo mask is the basis of a long tradition still vigorously maintained. It is employed in various dramas such as the invocation of the gods or initiation, as well as specifically Christian festivals.

5 A mosque in Malawi [A] stands in stark contrast to its Christian counterpart [B] and marks one point where Islam and Christianity competed for the souls of inhabitants in central Africa. The church, built by the Church of Scotland mission in Blantyre in the late 19th century, symbolizes the permanence of its missionaries' work in the conversion of people in the old British central Africa.

5B

5A

7 British dominions in India were the focus of increasing missionary endeavor in the late 18th and 19th centuries, initially centered on the work of medical doctors. After the pioneering work of Alexander Duff (1806–78) in Calcutta in the 1830s, Christianity became a central force in the education system established by the British. But it failed to make large inroads into the native religions, especially after the Indian Mutiny of 1857–58 led to a new realization of the importance of indigenous culture. Here St Thomas' Cathedral in Madras reflects the uncompromising application of Christianity in the Victorian mold.

6 Christian spires dominate the waterfront of Canton, in southern China. It was here that Jesuits arrived in the 16th century after the successful pioneering work of Matteo Ricci. Canton became an important port of entry into China for later missionaries, who were able to establish colleges and hospitals.

6

7

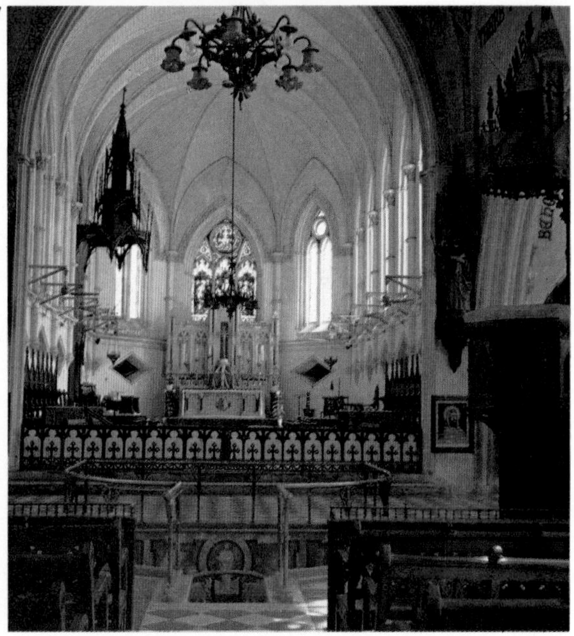

India in the 19th century

By the end of the nineteenth century most Englishmen regarded India as being as indissolubly linked to Great Britain as Yorkshire or Wales. The idea of an independent India was so remote as to be almost unimaginable. The creation of the great Indian Empire was largely accomplished between 1800 and 1860, and many Victorians saw it as Britain's supreme achievement in its rise to world power status [Key].

British territorial conquests

After 1800 the British deliberately set about enlarging the territorial conquests that Clive had begun in the mid-eighteenth century [1]. By 1820 they had greatly expanded their holdings in south India and secured their position against the revival of native princes such as Tipu Sahib [2]. In the north of India the same process was carried on more slowly, but no less relentlessly, culminating in the conquest of the Punjab from the Sikhs in 1849 and the annexation of Oudh in 1856.

These great conquests seemed to follow logically from the efforts of the East India Company (which was the instrument of British power in India until the British government's takeover in 1858) to protect itself against the threats to its trade. For with the decay of the Mogul Empire new states arose more unstable and less friendly to the East India Company, forcing it to rely not on diplomacy but on its own armed strength. Once this expansion process began it was difficult to stop. Raising armies in India required the company to control more land and more people, and to extract more revenue, the main source of which was the tribute traditionally paid by cultivators to their ruler. Thus each new war led to new annexations of land to pay for the company's armies and to ensure that the defeated rajahs and nawabs would not have another opportunity to attack.

Once India was fully under their control the British used the country's resources, and above all its army (paid for by the Indian taxpayer), for their own wider purposes in Asia, compelling the Chinese to open their ports to British trade [3]. Possession of India became indispensable to Britain's position as a great power east of Suez. But in India itself the British had to devise a system that would enable them to govern its vast area and huge population efficiently and cheaply. It was a novel problem: nowhere else had they attempted to rule people so different in language, culture, and religion. And it had to be accomplished using only a very small number of British administrators [5].

The result was that for all the appearance of despotic power the British relied upon the cooperation of Indians: village administration was largely delegated to Indian lesser officials, while the good will of rural notables—upon whom fell the main burden of keeping order in the countryside—was vital. This meant turning a blind eye to minor irregularities and preserving the structure of local power.

Indian Mutiny: causes and effects

The extension of British control was not accomplished without violent reaction on the part of their Indian subjects, most notably in the mutiny of 1857–58 [4]. Although the mutiny arose initially from the refusal of

CONNECTIONS

See also
1202 India from the Moguls to 1800
1330 Indian nationalism
1204 Indian art: the Mogul age
1262 European imperialism in the 19th century
1264 The expansion of Christianity
1236 Britain and the Industrial Revolution

British possessions 1805
British acquisitions by 1858
British acquisitions by 1914
Dependent Indian states 1914
Area of mutiny 1857
KASHMIR
PUNJAB
BALUCHISTAN
SIND
RAJPUTANA
Delhi
OUDH
ASSAM
BIHAR
BENGAL
BURMA
GUJARAT
CENTRAL PROVINCES
HYDERABAD
CARNATIC
CEYLON
0 800km

1 British control of India developed from small beginnings in Bombay, Madras, and Calcutta into an empire that made Britain one of the greatest powers in Asia. Apart from direct administration of the large provinces, Britain supervised nearly 600 princely states that were allowed wide autonomy but were carefully prevented from befriending imperial rivals or threatening the basic authority of the British.

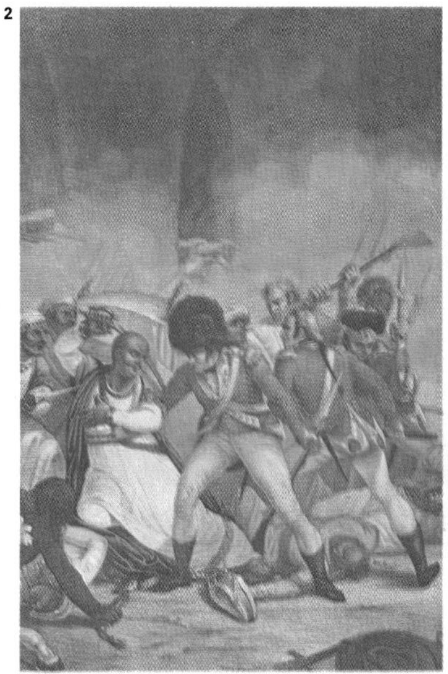

2 Tipu Sahib, Sultan of Mysore, was an aggressive, expansionist ruler who was a thorn in the side of the British in south India, even allying with Napoleon. He died fighting the British in 1799.

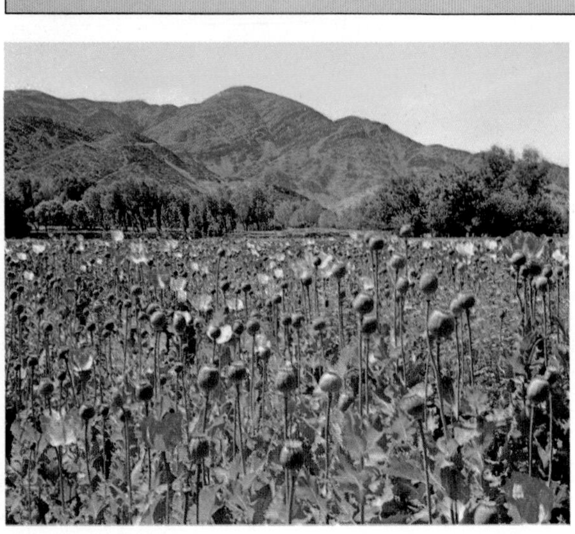

3 Indian opium was bought by the British in exchange for manufactured goods and sold in China for silks, spices, and tea demanded by British consumers.

4 The Indian Mutiny of 1857–58 was marked by several fierce battles before British reinforcements arrived and suppressed the sepoys. Although lack of concerted action caused the revolt to fail, it took Britain completely by surprise. The mutiny disturbed the complacency of British attitudes toward the Indians.

Indian sepoys (soldiers) to bite open cartridges greased with animal fats forbidden to Muslims and Hindus, it swiftly became a much wider rebellion against the side effects of company dominance: heavier taxation, displacement of Indian magnates from positions of authority, and the introduction of laws that abruptly altered the old systems of landholding, rent-paying, and tenancy.

For a time British authority all over north and central India swayed in the balance; Lucknow was overrun and Cawnpore besieged. The British restored their authority through the deployment of a large army, the systematic destruction of the hostile sepoy forces, and savage punishment for those they considered rebels. But they learned their lesson. They realized that the mutiny had resulted from too rough a handling of the Indian gentry, from the anxieties that too much rapid change had aroused in the Indian population, and from Indian fears that the British were planning to attack religious customs and practices.

After the mutiny the British were more careful and administration by the company was replaced by government rule. Headlong changes in law and in the economic character of rural life through new systems of taxation were slowed down or stopped altogether. The wholesale demolition of the remaining princely states was halted, and the rajahs and princes were promised security in return for allegiance to Britain.

Stirrings of independence

By the later nineteenth century the whole spirit of British rule in India had changed. The British gave up the hope that social change and education would quickly and smoothly turn Indians into "brown Englishmen" and India into a modern society. Administrators [7] concentrated on keeping the status quo so as not to risk losing their power. This could not work for long. India had been opened up to the outside world and flooded with British goods and British ideas. In the cities, economic change produced Westernized Indians who wanted a say in government. In 1885 such men founded the Indian National Congress and began the struggle for independence.

KEY

INDIA

Queen Victoria's assumption of the title of empress of India in 1877, at the suggestion of Benjamin Disraeli, marked the eventual achievement of stable British rule in India.

5

5 A British magistrate on tour represented a focal point of authority. Great value was attached to keeping in touch with local headmen and other important Indians in rural districts.

6

6 British and Indian troops on the Northwest Frontier were deployed in large numbers in attempts to check the incursions of mountain tribesmen into the plains of northern India. When the British became rulers of India they resolved to subdue the historically aggressive hillmen. They also feared that their great rivals in central Asia, the Russians, would try to undermine their power in India using Afghanistan as an ally. Desperate rearguard actions like that depicted in W. B. Wollen's painting "Last Stand of the 44th Foot at Gandamuk," followed some Afghan campaigns.

7

7 Lord Curzon, viceroy of India from 1898 to 1905, symbolized the pomp and circumstance of British rule. Although an untiring administrator, he found the task of governing India frustrating, and his autocratic ways were resented.

8

8 Indian economic life continued largely unchanged in villages during British rule. Better communications, however, did help to combat the scourge of famine but also stimulated the growth of large cities such as Calcutta and Bombay.

9

9 Simla became the summer capital of the British central administration in India after 1864. Lying in the Himalayan foothills, its bracing climate was a relief from the heat of the plains. It became a resort where British administrators, army officers, and their families, isolated in their districts for most of the year, could enjoy a wider (and sometimes disreputable) social life. The hilly site provided a status scale—senior officials lived higher up.

Africa in the 19th century

The nineteenth century was a period of great and often rapid change for much of Africa, set in motion either by Africans themselves or by outsiders, especially Europeans. The partition of almost the whole continent among seven European states took place in the last 20 years of the century. In the previous 80 years trends continued that had already been long established. Tiny trading "factories" (or castles) set up by European slave traders dotted the west coast of Africa, from Cape Verde to the Congo estuary [1]. On the southern tip of the continent, Britain had assumed control of the settlement of the Dutch East India Company at the Cape.

Foretaste of expansionism

The extension of European influence was gradual: in 1820–22 the Ottoman dependency of Egypt conquered the Nilotic Sudan; in 1830 the French invaded the Ottoman dependency of Algiers and began the long, costly process of conquering the territory; and in the late 1830s Dutch farmers (known as Boers) trekked deep into the interior of southern Africa, away from British control in the Cape Colony.

With the abolition of the slave trade by most European countries early in the nineteenth century, palm oil and other tropical products became the most important trade goods in West Africa. Only the French on the Senegal River expanded fairly deep into the interior.

Islam had penetrated what is known as the Sudanic belt of Africa for so long that by the beginning of the nineteenth century it was thoroughly "Africanized." Much of this region was swept, from the eighteenth century on, by a wave of religious revival, spearheaded by holy wars *(jihads)* waged against black Muslims as much as against pagans. A *jihad* in 1804 rapidly conquered all the old Hausa city states (such as Kano) and beyond, and led to the establishment of a huge new empire, the Sokoto caliphate, which survived until taken over by the British in Northern Nigeria in 1903. Other Muslim empires were created on the middle Niger and in what is now Guinea and the Ivory Coast, where they offered stubborn opposition to French invaders in the 1880s. South of the Sudanic belt, several great kingdoms, such as Ashanti and Dahomey, continued to expand while others, notably Oyo and Benin, began to disintegrate.

Rise of Ethiopia and the Zulus

In Ethiopia, the ancient Christian Amhara Empire, after a long period of feebleness, slowly and painfully recovered during the reigns of three forceful emperors—Theodore (reigned 1855–68), Johannes IV (reigned 1868–89), and Menelik (reigned 1889–1911). These rulers asserted their power against that of the mighty landed aristocracy and the Coptic Church. Menelik [5] maintained his position against the powerful northern barons and greatly expanded the boundaries of Ethiopia in the south. He also beat off an Italian attempt to conquer his state at the Battle of Adowa (1896).

In 1818 in southern Africa, Shaka (*c.* 1787–1828) became king of a small group known as the Zulu. By revolutionizing the military and social structure of his people, he fashioned a formidable and ruthless

CONNECTIONS

See also
1212 Subsaharan Africa 1500–1800
1262 European imperialism in the 19th century
1264 The expansion of Christianity
1280 The impact of steam

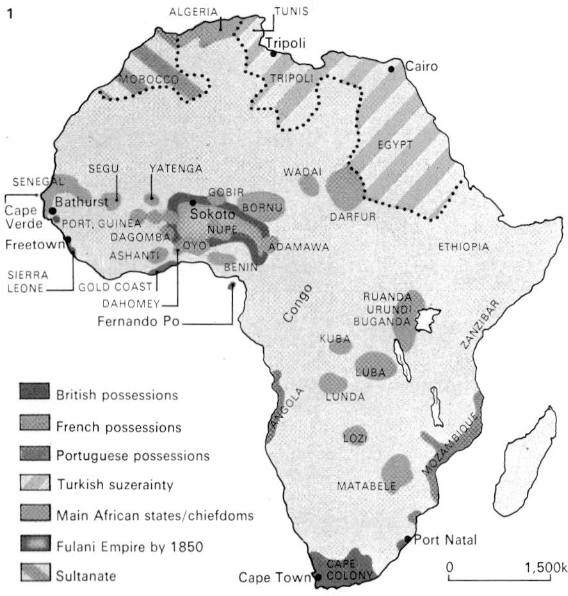

1
ALGERIA
TUNIS
Tripoli
Cairo
MOROCCO
TRIPOLI
EGYPT
SEGU
YATENGA
WADAI
SENEGAL
GOBIR
Bathurst
BORNU
Cape Verde
PORT. GUINEA
Sokoto
NUPE
DARFUR
DAGOMBA
Freetown
ASHANTI
OYO
ADAMAWA
ETHIOPIA
BENIN
SIERRA LEONE
GOLD COAST
DAHOMEY
Fernando Po
Congo
RUANDA URUNDI BUGANDA
ZANZIBAR
KUBA
LUBA
LUNDA
ANGOLA
LOZI
MOZAMBIQUE
MATABELE
Port Natal
Cape Town
CAPE COLONY
0
1,500km
British possessions
French possessions
Portuguese possessions
Turkish suzerainty
Main African states/chiefdoms
Fulani Empire by 1850
Sultanate

1 European possessions in Africa in 1830 were few. France had invaded Algeria (1830), and some Boer (Dutch) settlers were trekking out of the British Cape Colony into the hinterland of South Africa. Britain and France had a few tiny colonies in West African Senegal, Sierra Leone, and Gold Coast. Apart from Europeans in trading posts, only the Portuguese had long-established colonies—in coastal parts of Angola and up the Zambezi valley of Mozambique. Although the Egyptians had conquered the Nilotic Sudan in 1821, the rest of the continent consisted of African empires, kingdoms, and independent peoples.

2 An idealized view of European influence appears in this picture of the British explorer John Speke (1827–64) with King Mutesa of Buganda. Men like Speke, who found the source of the Nile in 1858, played an essential role in opening up Africa to Europeans. Two early Scottish explorers were James Bruce (1730–94), who traveled in Ethiopia and the Sudan, and Mungo Park (1771–1806), who probed West Africa. Heinrich Barth in northern and western Africa, David Livingstone in central and eastern Africa, and H.M. Stanley, who found Livingstone in 1872 and journeyed down the Congo, were prominent.

3 The storming of Magdala, a mountain citadel in Ethiopia, by British forces in 1868 was one of the most extravagant episodes in the history of relations between Europeans and Africans in the 19th century. An expedition under General Robert Napier invaded Ethiopia to punish its emperor, Theodore (or Tewodoros), for briefly holding prisoner a British consul and some Europeans. After Magdala fell, the emperor committed suicide, and the expedition withdrew.

4 This Ethiopian village has hardly changed at all since the 19th century. Then, as a community of peasant cultivators producing little more than what was necessary for subsistence, it would have been typical of rural Africa.

military state that rapidly conquered surrounding peoples. Offshoots of the Zulu, and other groups who copied their techniques, rampaged over much of southern and central Africa in mass population movements and tribal regroupings, known as the *mfecane*, the "Time of Troubles."

Explorers and imperialists

During the middle years of the nineteenth century Africa gradually became better known to Europeans through the efforts of many courageous travelers [2], such as the German scientist Heinrich Barth (1821–65) in the Sudanic regions, and the Scotsman David Livingstone (1813–73), whose travels were partly motivated by his concern over the ravages of the Arab slave trade in central and east Africa. The Welsh-American explorer Henry Morton Stanley (1841–1904) was more concerned with exploitation. In 1877 he completed an epic journey down the Congo River—and then sold his services to the Belgians.

By this time bitter trading rivalries had grown up between Britain and France in West Africa, stimulated by British occupation of Egypt in 1882. Motivated largely by politics, a rush for African colonies began with Britain and France in the forefront, followed by Belgium and Germany, and with Portugal, Spain, and Italy bringing up the rear. There was little appreciation of the economic potential of the lands being taken. In many areas the conquest of Africa met with intense opposition, and vicious wars of "pacification" were mounted. But resistance [3] was seldom unified, and local opposition could be dealt with piecemeal.

In southern and central Africa the main impetus for British expansion was provided by Cecil Rhodes (1853–1902), who, from a base in the Cape Colony, appropriated a vast private empire for himself (as did King Leopold in the Congo/Zaïre). The two independent Boer republics of the Transvaal and Orange Free State were annexed in a war that required fullest use of the British Army (the Anglo-Boer War, 1899–1902). By the turn of the century all of Africa, with the exception of Ethiopia and Liberia, had been conquered by European nations. [9].

KEY

Moshweshwe (*c.* 1786–1870) was the founder of the Sotho nation (Lesotho) in southern Africa, and an example of how African rulers adopted practices and ideas introduced by Europeans. Moshweshwe emerged as the leader of the Sotho, a small group of people who found refuge in the Drakensberg Mountains from the devastation produced in the interior of southern Africa by the Zulu and other warrior kingdoms in the 1820s. He was a man of peace and ensured the protection of his people through wise diplomacy. Lesotho rapidly increased in prosperity. It was a British protectorate from 1868 until 1966.

5

5 Emperor Menelik (1844–1913) successfully maintained the independence of Ethiopia against European encroachment. In 1896 his forces defeated an Italian invasion at the Battle of Adowa.

6

6 Mochudi in Botswana was one of several large towns to develop long before the coming of Europeans – notably in the Sudanic belt, Yorubaland in West Africa, Botswana, and southern Africa.

7

7 Freetown, capital of Sierra Leone, was typical of European coastal towns in tropical West Africa. Its plan included churches, business centers, and separate areas for whites and blacks.

8

8 Johannesburg in South Africa grew from a farm on the veld to a sprawling city by 1900. The discovery of gold in the Boer Republic of the Transvaal in the mid-1880s led to rapid development.

9

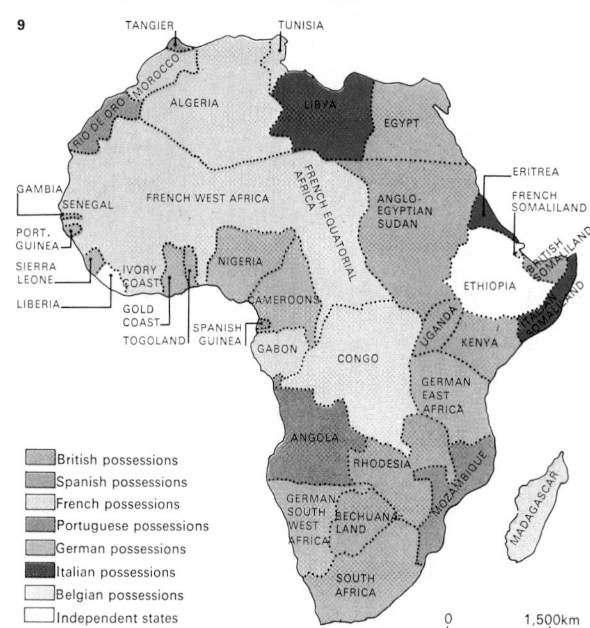
TANGIER
TUNISIA
MOROCCO
RIO DE ORO
ALGERIA
LIBYA
EGYPT
ERITREA
FRENCH SOMALILAND
GAMBIA
SENEGAL
FRENCH WEST AFRICA
FRENCH EQUATORIAL AFRICA
ANGLO-EGYPTIAN SUDAN
PORT. GUINEA
SIERRA LEONE
IVORY COAST
NIGERIA
BRITISH SOMALILAND
ETHIOPIA
ITALIAN SOMALILAND
LIBERIA
GOLD COAST
TOGOLAND
SPANISH GUINEA
CAMEROONS
GABON
CONGO
UGANDA
KENYA
GERMAN EAST AFRICA
ANGOLA
RHODESIA
MOZAMBIQUE
MADAGASCAR
GERMAN SOUTH WEST AFRICA
BECHUANALAND
SOUTH AFRICA
British possessions
Spanish possessions
French possessions
Portuguese possessions
German possessions
Italian possessions
Belgian possessions
Independent states
0
1,500km

9 A map of Africa in 1914 shows how it had become partitioned among seven European countries. This partition was a rapid process taking place during the last 20 years of the 19th century. Only Ethiopia and Liberia remained independent of European rule. Although some territories were termed protectorates (like Uganda and Morocco) rather than colonies, Europeans were firmly in control. The four white-ruled colonies in South Africa had formed a Union in 1910 but remained a British dominion. Colonial boundaries drawn up entirely by Europeans were often arbitrary lines on the map. This caused great problems when Africa regained independence.

The opening up of China

Two changes in China during the nineteenth century sowed the seeds of the revolution that flowered in the twentieth century. One change, hardly novel in Chinese history, was the decay of a dynasty—the Manchu (Ch'ing), founded in 1644. The other, unprecedented, confusing, and finally explosive, was the challenge of Western power and technology.

The "unequal treaties"

The opening up by the West of the closed, Confucian, agrarian society of China began with the first Opium War of 1839–42, during which Great Britain crushed a Manchu attempt to stop illegal trade in opium through Canton, then the only point of contact between China and the West's money economy. The resulting Treaty of Nanking (which also gave Britain a foothold in Hong Kong) was the first of the so-called unequal treaties. They eventually forced China to grant trade and territorial rights to Western powers, legalize the opium trade, and permit missionaries [4] to spread Christianity throughout the country. After pressure by France and Britain in 1856–60, China even had to grant Europeans a diplomatic quarter in Peking, implying their equality with a country whose emperor had been a guardian of civilization for a thousand years.

The disruptive impact of the West on the traditional pattern of Chinese life coincided with a chaotic situation in the countryside. Rural misery was accentuated by the massive population increase of the eighteenth century [1], and the weak and corrupt administration that neglected its duty to maintain grain reserves and irrigation systems. In reaction, China was swept by a series of risings against the Manchus, beginning with the Taiping Rebellion (1850–64). Almost a civil war, this uprising was suppressed only with the deaths of at least 25 million people in the lower Yangtze provinces [2]. Other rebellions soon followed, including those of the Nien in north-central China and the Chinese Muslims in the southwest and northwest, which were suppressed by 1875.

Meanwhile, the Western-administered treaty ports and the foreign missions that spread all over the country steadily eroded Chinese sovereignty. In the 1860s a serious attempt was made to reinvigorate the dynasty. But this "restoration" failed to transform the conservative thinking of a court that was already falling under the influence of the autocratic Tz'u Hsi (1835–1908), the dowager empress.

Slow technological progress

The "self-strengthening movement" of the restoration period began with the construction of arsenals, railroads, and dockyards in the 1860s [3] and continued with early moves for industrialization in the 1870s. But compared with Japan's speedy industrialization, China's was slow and unsure of its direction. Anti-Western feeling grew, often heightened by antagonism to Chinese "rice Christians" who took advantage of the privileges exacted by foreigners. Incidents in which Westerners were attacked embittered relations between the Chinese government and foreign powers. The need to learn from the West and to introduce fundamental changes was widely recognized only in 1895, when China suffered a humili-

CONNECTIONS

See also

1206 China from 1368 to c.1800
1262 European imperialism in the 19th century
1272 Japan: the Meiji Restoration
1286 Russia in the 19th century
1328 East Asia 1919–1945

1 Pop. in 20 millions
1741
1851

1 China's population growth between 1750 and 1850 was immense, although the figures are unreliable. Growing land hunger in peasant economy coincided with laxity in administration.

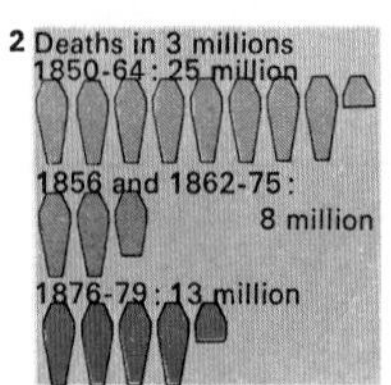

Deaths in 3 millions
1850-64: 25 million
1856 and 1862-75: 8 million
1876-79: 13 million

2 Unprecedented casualties were caused by the Taiping Rebellion (1850–64), two Muslim uprisings (1856; 1862–75) and a north China drought in 1876–79 that led to famine.

3 A "self-strengthening" movement, aimed at increasing military strength to overcome Western power, was launched in 1860. The buildup of armaments and improvement of railroads were continued during the 1870s with moves to lay the foundation for a modern industry run by the mandarin class. Textile mills, a shipping company, and an iron and steel works were established as well as smaller industries.

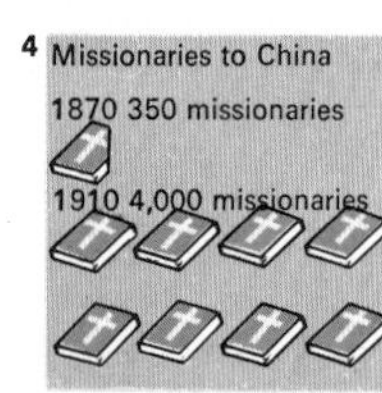

Missionaries to China
1870 350 missionaries
1910 4,000 missionaries

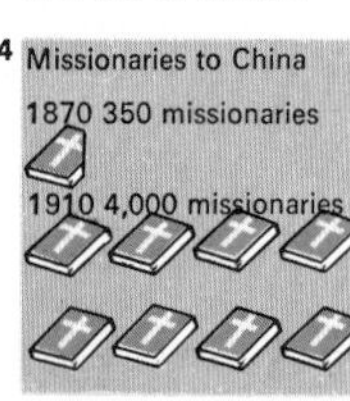
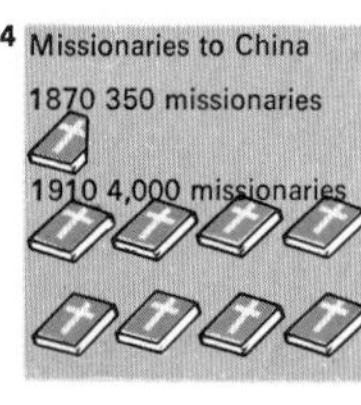

4 Missionaries aroused Chinese hatred and stimulated nationalism. But some, such as Timothy Richard, also brought new ideas and won respect for their dedicated help.

Students to Japan
1900
500
1910
10,000

5 Chinese students began to go to America in 1872, but the real flow to Western universities began only after 1919. Until then, Japan was the source of modern thought for a generation of Chinese.

6 Li Hung-chang (1823–1901) became China's official foreign minister after the "Office for Barbarians" gave way to an office for "foreign matters" in 1861. He made his reputation commanding an army against the Taiping rebels and later revealed a talent for diplomacy that was acknowledged by Western powers, with whom he negotiated from a position of weakness. Founder of the Chinese navy, he advanced China's interests by visiting Europe.

Russian influence
British
French
Japanese
German
Russian possessions
British
French
Japanese
German
The Great Wall
Boxer Rebellion 1900
Railways
First treaty ports 1842
Later treaty ports
Christian missions
1900
RUSSIAN EMPIRE
MANCHURIA
OUTER MONGOLIA
SINKIANG
INNER MONGOLIA
Peking
Tientsin
Lü-ta
KOREA
Niu-chuang
Chefoo
Weihaiwei
Tsingtao
TIBET
NEPAL
BHUTAN
Nanking
Chinkiang
Soochow
Shanghai
Ichang
Hankow
Wuhu
Shasi
Hangchow
Ningpo
Yangtze
Chungking
Kiukiang
Wenchow
Foochow
Tengchung
Hungshui-Ho
Amoy
Formosa
Mengtsz
Lungchow
Canton
Swatow
Pescadores Islands
Szemao
Nanning
Macao (Port.)
Kowloon
BURMA
Pakhoi
Hong Kong
INDOCHINA
Kiungchow
SIAM
Hainan
0 750km

7 Foreign influence never extended to rule over China. But such "treaty ports" as Shanghai, Tientsin, and others inland were administered, policed, and taxed by foreigners. Chinese living in them were outside their government's jurisdiction. The diplomatic quarter of Peking itself was foreign administered until 1947. Toward the end of the 19th century key areas were divided up into "spheres of influence." While the coastal cities prospered, China's peasant economy could not compete with foreign imports. Rural areas were drained of talent, and the exactions of absentee landlords increased.

ating defeat by Japan in a quarrel over suzerainty rights in Korea [8].

The nationalist movement

In the treaty ports a new class of middlemen in foreign trade favored change. Sun Yat-sen (1866–1925), educated in Hawaii and Hong Kong, preached nationalism, and mandarins such as K'ang Yü-wei (1858–1927) backed the young Kuang Hsu Emperor (*r.* 1875–1908) in reform edicts in 1898. But the tyrannical dowager empress imprisoned her son and assumed power.

European imperialists now threatened to partition China—a scramble halted only by a US-inspired "Open Door" policy by which the Western powers agreed to restrain their territorial ambitions in return for open trade. Meanwhile, fierce antiforeign rioting broke out in 1900 when the court diverted the thrust of a rising by the secret society of the "righteous and harmonious fist" against Westerners. Known as the Boxer Rebellion, it cost the lives of nearly 250 missionaries and thousands of Chinese Christians before it was suppressed by an international army made up of troops from eight nations.

The old China was finished, however, outmoded and discredited. The archaic civil service examination system was abolished in 1905, and the Manchu dynasty hastily abdicated after a provincial revolt in 1911. The formula for a workable Chinese Republic did not yet exist. A parliament headed by Sun Yat-sen immediately gave way to rule by a former Manchu commander, Yüan Shih-k'ai (1859–1916). A decade of rule by rival war lords followed.

The intellectual consensus needed for change was emerging, however. Sun Yat-sen [10] refounded his movement as the Kuomintang party, and thousands of students educated overseas [5] or at new universities were influenced by such liberal teachers as Ch'en Tu-Hsiu (1879–1942) and Hu Shih (1891–1962) [11]. When China's weak government accepted concessions to Japan imposed after World War I (in which China had played little part), student protest on May 4, 1919 launched a revolutionary nationalism [11] that set China afire.

KEY

A common Western attitude toward China in the 19th century was summed up in a cartoon of the Western powers shaking the corpulent body of China. After the 1840 Opium War contempt for the China of the Manchu emperors began to replace the admiration held by 18th-century Europe for the achievements of Chinese civilization. By the 1890s, when such nations as Germany, Russia, Japan, Britian, and France were scrambling for territorial rights, most Europeans thought "this rotten old hulk" would break up and be remade by Western enterprise. Few perceived the enduring strength of Chinese civilization beneath the decay.

8

8 The Sino-Japanese war of 1894–95 ended with China suing for peace (as depicted in a Japanese drawing). Joining the Western powers in their demands on China, the Japanese had disrupted China's sphere of influence in Korea. In the war that followed the Chinese were easily beaten and had to cede Formosa to Japan. This aroused Chinese shame and nationalism more than defeats in earlier wars against Britain and France; the Chinese had always looked down upon the Japanese as inferiors who had adopted Chinese culture. After 1868, Japan's modernization sent its military and industry ahead of China.

9 Chinese dislike of foreigners is shown in an 1891 cartoon of a Chinese Christian as a pig and foreigners as goats being slaughtered. Earlier in the 19th century, foreigners were almost unknown; most Chinese lived and died without seeing one. Christianity had little appeal to the Chinese.

9

射豬斬羊圖
一刀斬羊頭問畜牲還想來麼
萬箭射豬身看妖精再敢叫不

10 A B

10 Intellectual leaders played a vital role in changing attitudes toward the structure of government and society after the old China was swept away in the turbulence that followed the death of the dowager empress in 1908. The next decade brought together strands of nationalism, cultural change, and revolution. Sun Yat-sen [A] was an outsider to the Chinese classical tradition and the world of the mandarin. Impressed by Victorian progress, he wanted to modernize China. His magnetic personality attracted a mixed following in the secret societies. Supported in Japan and welcomed in the West, where his Christianity and good English helped, his tenacity finally won mass backing after 1919. Ch'en Tu-Hsiu [B] was a more revolutionary intellectual. When he founded the influential "New Youth" in 1915, he favored "Mr Science and Mr Democracy," but by 1921 he had emerged as the first leader of the rising Chinese Communist party.

11 A revolutionary consciousness was developed in China by the teaching of such men as Hu Shih [A]. Since the use of classical Chinese by writers had set off educated classes from the rest, Hu Shih invented a simplified form of Chinese. A pragmatic thinker who studied in America and was a spokesman for Western liberalism, he still influenced the future communist leader of China, the young Mao Tse-tung [B] (1893–1976), who was snubbed by professors when he went to Peking University. For Mao's generation of students 1919 was the year of revolutionary awakening.

11 A B

Japan: the Meiji Restoration

Until the middle of the nineteenth century Japan had been closed to the outside world for more than 200 years. Only the Chinese and the Dutch were allowed limited trading access to one port, Nagasaki. It was Commodore Matthew Perry in command of a squadron of US warships who, during visits in 1853 and 1854, cajoled a reluctant shogunate—Japan's military government—into opening two ports to American shipping. Other powers soon followed the American lead; Japan's self-imposed seclusion was soon a thing of the past.

Civil war and a new capital

The intrusion into Japan by the Western world fatally harmed the prestige of the Tokugawa shogunate, which, under pressure, signed treaties granting extraterritorial rights and tariff privileges to the foreign powers [1]. The imperial court at Kyoto, universally revered but possessing no effective power of its own, became the focus of loyalty for those samurai (warriors) who called for the expulsion of the alien "barbarians." After some years of complicated domestic strife the shogunate was overthrown in 1868 by an alliance of provincial lords and warriors from domains in southwest Japan. Their successful civil war was fought in the name of the youthful Emperor Meiji—"enlightened rule." Edo, which was renamed Tokyo, was made the new capital.

By this political upheaval, known as the Meiji Restoration, governing powers were restored, although in name only, to the imperial house. It marked the beginning of Japan's transformation from a feudal society to a modern state. The new government, an oligarchy of relatively young samurai, resolved to bring Japan up to the technological level of the West.

Japan's industrial revolution

Foreign teachers and specialists of every kind, skilled in the techniques of Western civilization, were invited to Japan; and Japanese in large numbers went abroad to study [2]. Remarkable progress in modernization was made within two decades [3]. The cotton-spinning industry provides a striking example. In the 1870s annual production, increasing yearly, barely exceeded 2,000 bales, but the figure for 1889 was 142,000 bales; ten years later it was 750,000 bales. Comparable growth occurred in many other sectors of manufacturing industry. The cost of this early expansion fell heavily on the rural areas, the home of most of the rising population.

Japan's industrial revolution was broadly completed by the eve of World War I and within the lifetime of some of the leading figures of the Meiji Restoration. Political change was symbolized by the Constitution of 1889, which established a diet (parliament) of two chambers. But the Meiji constitution was authoritarian in letter and spirit. The upper house of the diet was not elected, and until after World War I members of the lower house were elected on a limited basis. Cabinet ministers were responsible only to the emperor, not the diet, and the war and navy ministers were always generals and admirals representing services strongly imbued with the samurai martial spirit.

CONNECTIONS

See also
1328 East Asia 1919–1945
1286 Russia in the 19th century
1262 European imperialism in the 19th century
1206 China from 1368 to *c.*1800
1210 Japan 1185–1868

1 The first Japanese railroad line, completed in 1872, was built by British engineers and covered the 18 miles (29km) between the capital of Tokyo and Yokohama. Railroads played a particularly important role in the modernization of Japan, for in pre-Meiji days there was very little wheeled traffic along the roads. Commerce between the main centers of the country was mainly seaborne. The growth of the railroad system was very rapid: in 1886 there were 430 miles (692km) of track; in 1896, 2,490 miles (4,007km); and in 1906, 5,278 miles (8,494km). By 1918 the total was more than 9,000 miles (14,480km) of track.

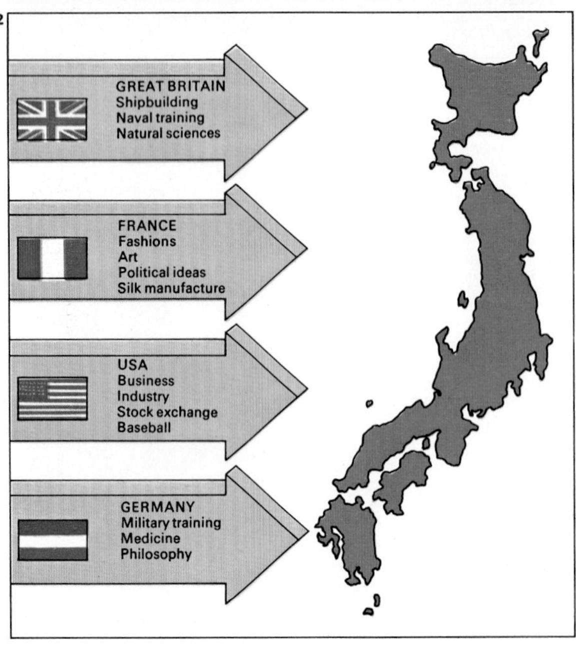

GREAT BRITAIN
Shipbuilding
Naval training
Natural sciences
FRANCE
Fashions
Art
Political ideas
Silk manufacture
USA
Business
Industry
Stock exchange
Baseball
GERMANY
Military training
Medicine
Philosophy

2 The greatest contributions to Japan's modernization were made by Great Britain, the United States, Germany, and France. Britain trained the Japanese navy and influenced other maritime activities. The United States influenced such areas as business and education. France and Germany trained the army and introduced western political ideas.

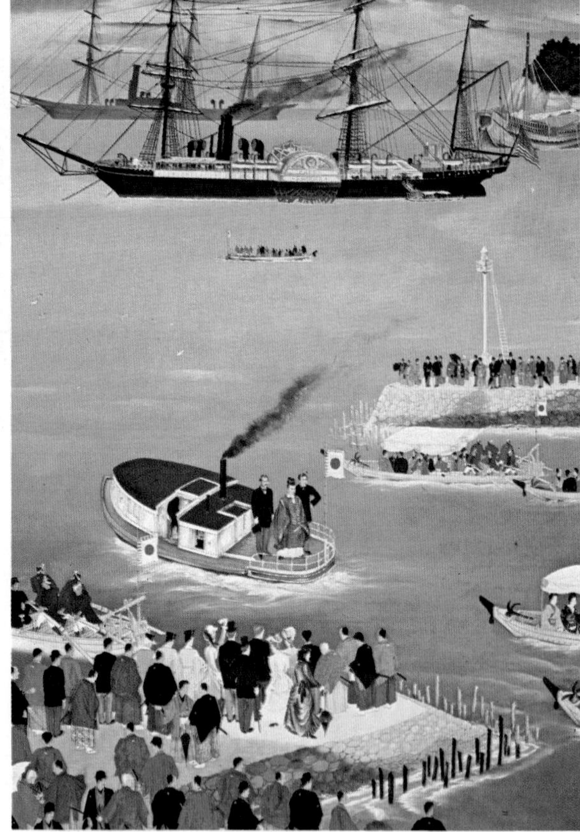

3 Japan's first important diplomatic mission abroad in 1871 was led by Prince Iwakura. In the United States and Europe the aim of the mission was to persuade the Western powers to revise the "unequal treaties" they had signed with Japan. But the Japanese had to wait nearly 30 years before they could secure treaty revision and thereby obtain tariff autonomy and the abolition of extraterritorial privileges. This picture of Iwakura's departure at Yokohama illustrates Japanese society in a state of transition. Some of the men wear Western dress, while their companions still favor the traditional "topknot" hairstyle and carry the samurai (warrior) sword.

The same spirit was also perceptible among the people at large, for the state education system gave great importance to loyalty and patriotism. The effectiveness of such indoctrination was illustrated by the events of the Sino-Japanese War of 1894–95 and the Russo-Japanese War of 1904–05.

Military and naval supremacy

In both struggles the Japanese surprised the world with their victories on land and sea, of which the most dramatic was the destruction of the Russian fleet off Tsushima in May 1905 by Admiral Togo (1846–1934) [5]. This demonstration of naval supremacy won Japan acceptance as a great power.

The Sino-Japanese War had arisen from rivalries in Korea. Japan's victory gave it possession of Formosa and eliminated Chinese influence in Korea. In 1904 the reason for war was again largely Korea. Russia, occupying key points in Manchuria, seemed about to penetrate Korea, still nominally an independent state, although dominated economically and politically by Japan. By the Treaty of Portsmouth (New Hampshire) in the United States, which ended the Russo-Japanese War, Japan acquired south Sakhalin and inherited Russia's lease of Port Arthur and its valuable rights and interests in south Manchuria. This setback for Russian power in the Far East sealed the fate of Korea, which was finally annexed by Japan in 1910 [7].

Emperor Meiji died in 1912 [6]. Due to ill health the new ruler (Taisho) was a mere figurehead. The Anglo-Japanese Alliance, first concluded in 1902 as a gesture of solidarity against Russian ambitions in Asia, brought Japan into World War I on the British side. Japanese forces captured Germany's leased port in China, Tsingtao, and occupied its island possessions in the Pacific. While the European powers fought each other, Japan tried, with only partial success, to extend its influence over a weak and divided China.

At the 1919 Paris Peace Conference, Japan was given a permanent seat on the Council of the newly created League of Nations, which amounted to full recognition of Japan's status as a world power.

KEY

The Japanese battleship Kashima (16,660 tons, four 12-in guns) was built by the Elswick shipyard in England and launched at Newcastle-upon-Tyne in 1905. Until the Russo-Japanese War all Japan's larger warships were built abroad, the majority of them in Britain. The last was the battle-cruiser *Kongo* (27,500 tons, 8 14-in guns) launched by Vickers Armstrong, Barrow-in-Furness, in 1913.

4

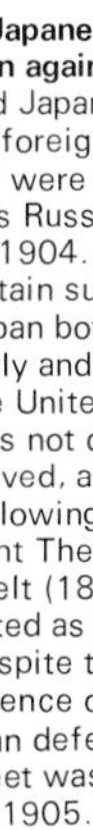

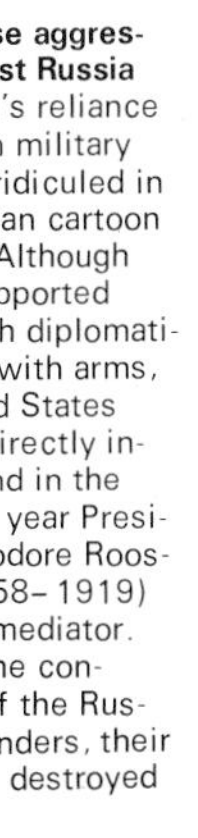

Вася Флотскій.

4 Japanese aggression against Russia and Japan's reliance on foreign military aid were ridiculed in this Russian cartoon of 1904. Although Britain supported Japan both diplomatically and with arms, the United States was not directly involved, and in the following year President Theodore Roosevelt (1858–1919) acted as mediator. Despite the confidence of the Russian defenders, their fleet was destroyed in 1905.

5

5 Admiral Togo Heihachiro, a national hero after his annihilation of the Russian Baltic fleet at Tsushima in 1905, was revered almost as much in Britain as in Japan. Trained in England on HMS *Worcester,* he based his signal at Tsushima—"On this battle will depend the fate of our empire"—on a famous signal of Britain's Admiral Nelson at the Battle of Trafalgar (1805). He was given a title in 1907 and died in 1934, aged 88.

6

二重橋外御大葬之圖

6 The death of the Emperor Meiji in 1912 marked the end of Japan's "Victorian age." The funeral procession in Tokyo took place at night, the coffin being carried on an oxwagon from the palace to Tokyo station. Enormous silent crowds kneeled respectfully as it passed. Interment was at Momoyama near Kyoto. A detachment of British marines took part in the procession.

7

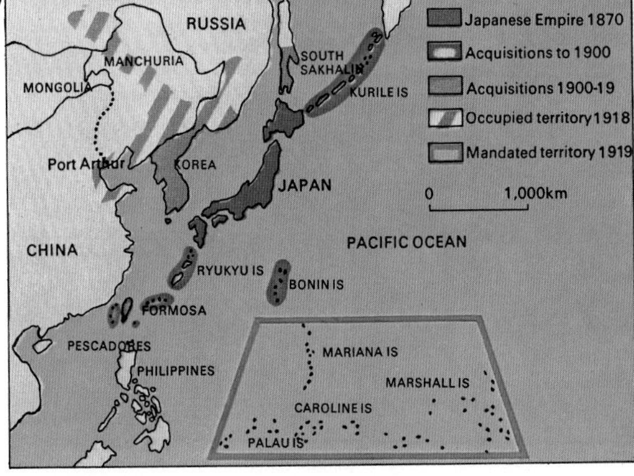

RUSSIA
MANCHURIA
MONGOLIA
SOUTH SAKHALIN
KURILE IS
Port Arthur
KOREA
JAPAN
CHINA
PACIFIC OCEAN
RYUKYU IS
BONIN IS
FORMOSA
PESCADORES
PHILIPPINES
MARIANA IS
MARSHALL IS
CAROLINE IS
PALAU IS
Japanese Empire 1870
Acquisitions to 1900
Acquisitions 1900-19
Occupied territory 1918
Mandated territory 1919
0
1,000km

7 The expansion of Japanese territory at the end of the 19th and in the early part of the 20th centuries was a result of both war and treaties. In 1875 the Kurile Islands were acquired from Russia by treaty in exchange for abandonment of Japanese claims on Sakhalin. Formosa was won in the Sino-Japanese War; south Sakhalin, lease of Port Arthur, and rights in south Manchuria were obtained in the Russo-Japanese War. Korea was annexed in 1910.

8

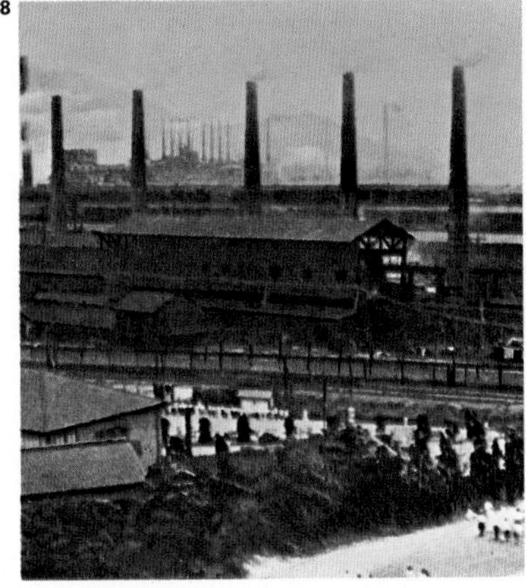

8 The Yawata Ironworks in northern Kyushu (completed in 1901) was for many years the main steel-producing plant in Japan. Production of iron and steel on a large scale began relatively late because Japan was deficient in natural resources such as iron ore and coking coal. The need for these materials, essential to Japan's industrialization, was one of the reasons for Japan's aggressive interest in both Manchuria and China.

The United States: the opening of the West

During the first half of the nineteenth century, the United States grew from a small cluster of 13 states huddled against the Atlantic coast into one of the largest nations on earth, extending from the shores of the Atlantic to the Pacific, and from Canada in the north to Mexico in the south [Key].

Frontiersmen and settlers

The opening of the West began as a scattered penetration by hunters and explorers into the areas adjacent to the coastal settlements. Even before the Revolution, men such as Daniel Boone (1734–1820)—who crossed the Appalachians to scout Kentucky—blazed trails through unknown regions. They and their successors drifted into the Ohio Valley and the Alleghenies. Probing ever deeper inland, frontiersmen reached the Mississippi River, the western limit of the territory won in the Revolution.

Settlers followed, venturing westward in search of land, livelihood, and living space. Their numbers were swelled by migrants from Europe who, in addition, sought religious and political freedom. The settlers—their lives often threatened by the Indians whose land they were appropriating—dotted the new areas with cabins, forts [4], then towns. Gradually the western territories took shape.

To avoid a land scramble among the states Congress promulgated its precedent setting Northwest Ordinance of 1787. This was designed to promote an orderly development of self-government in the newly settled regions. Each "territory" was empowered to elect a legislature when its free male population reached a total of 5,000 and to claim statehood when its population grew to 60,000.

From sea to shining sea

In 1803 the United States, barely two decades old, doubled in area. Napoleon, embroiled in a war with Britain, sold the vast Louisiana Territory—extending from the Mississippi to the Rocky Mountains and from Canada to the Gulf of Mexico—to the US government for $15 million. President Thomas Jefferson (1743–1826) immediately dispatched Meriwether Lewis (1774–1809) and William Clark (1770–1838) to explore this enormous acquisition [1], as well as the Oregon territory to the west. The prospect of the nation's extending "from sea to shining sea" began to materialize.

Pioneers penetrated beyond the Mississippi in ever-growing numbers. Among them were resourceful, independent, nomadic hunters who chose to make the western wilderness their home. Known as "mountain men," they ranged far and wide through the West, often acting as intermediaries between the Indians and white settlers and officials. They also served as scouts for the wagon trains of settlers who had to make long, hazardous journeys across Indian territory to lush fertile valleys in the Far West [2].

To the south, thousands of Americans settled in the Mexican province of Texas. Refusing to accept Mexican authority, they rebelled in 1835 [7] and set up a provisional government. This paved the way for the US annexation of Texas a decade later and the Mexican War (1846–48), as a result of which the United States acquired vast

CONNECTIONS

See also
1218 The American Revolution
1276 The American Civil War
1278 The United States: Reconstruction to World War I
1280 The impact of steam

1

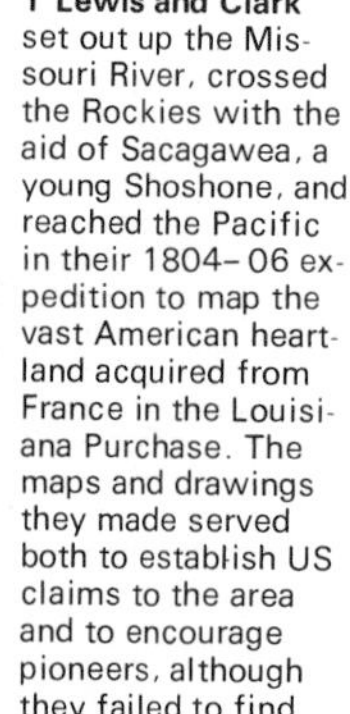

1 Lewis and Clark set out up the Missouri River, crossed the Rockies with the aid of Sacagawea, a young Shoshone, and reached the Pacific in their 1804–06 expedition to map the vast American heartland acquired from France in the Louisiana Purchase. The maps and drawings they made served both to establish US claims to the area and to encourage pioneers, although they failed to find a portage route.

2

2 Covered wagons were the main vehicles used for long-distance travel by settlers penetrating the West. Wagon trains often consisted of more than 100 canvas-draped wood-framed "prairie schooners," which were usually drawn by from two to six yokes of oxen. A journey of migration up the Oregon Trail could take six months or more. Wagons crossed the central Rockies before turning north to reach Portland. Caravans would form in towns on the Missouri and the Mississippi. Seeking safety in numbers to cross dangerous territory, groups would elect leaders to consult with hired scouts about the route and to settle any disputes.

3

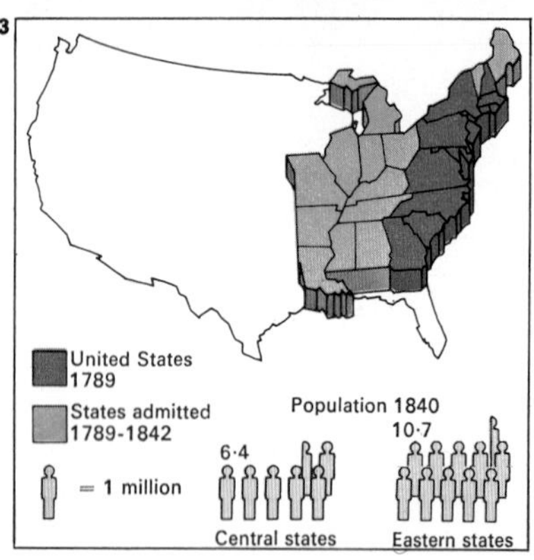
United States 1789
States admitted 1789-1842
= 1 million
Population 1840
6·4
10·7
Central states
Eastern states

3 By 1842 the westward movement was well under way, opening up the fine farmlands of the new states. Meanwhile, a steady stream of European immigrants, particularly from Britain and Germany, converged on the northeast.

4

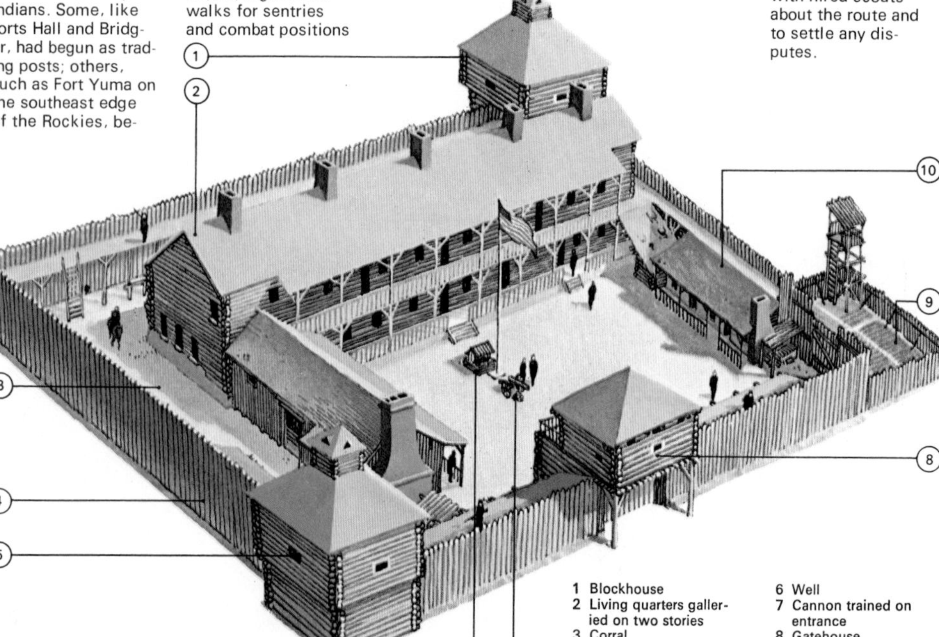
1 Blockhouse
2 Living quarters galleried on two stories
3 Corral
4 Palisade
5 Loophole for small cannon
6 Well
7 Cannon trained on entrance
8 Gatehouse
9 Garden
10 Storehouse and kitchen

4 Forts were built along commonly traversed pioneer routes such as the Oregon Trail to protect travelers and scattered communities and to provide refuge in the event of attack by Indians. Some, like forts Hall and Bridger, had begun as trading posts; others, such as Fort Yuma on the southeast edge of the Rockies, became posting stations for mail routes. Manned by US cavalry, the forts were rectangular enclosures up to 500 ft (152m) long with timber walls up to 18 ft (5m) high. Plank walks for sentries and combat positions were placed 4 ft (1.2m) from the top with loopholes offering protected firing positions. Two block-houses, at diagonally opposite corners provided the main defense against Indian attackers. Some forts became centers of thriving communities in the West as time passed.

5

5 The Mormons, persecuted for their religious beliefs in Illinois, set out in 1847, led by Brigham Young (1801–77), and founded Salt Lake City.

new areas, including New Mexico, Arizona, and California.

Few events provided greater impetus for the opening of the West than the discovery of gold in the Sacramento Valley in 1848. Tens of thousands scurried to California to seek their fortunes [10], and communities sprang up overnight.

Seeking different objectives, 148 Mormons had headed southwest from the Oregon Trail in 1847 to claim the inhospitable area around the Great Salt Lake [5]. There they sought a sanctuary to practice their newly founded faith without harassment. They, and the thousands who joined them, transformed the stark Utah territory into flourishing communities through irrigation.

Dispossessed Indians

Sporadic settlement had left large areas thinly populated. In order to attract settlers to the Great Plains, Congress passed the Homestead Act of 1862, promising farmers free land for cultivation. Within five years of this event the settlement of the American heartland was well under way [6].

The relentless westward expansion was a disaster for the Indian peoples [9]. The 1830 Indian Removal Bill (authorizing removal of eastern Indians to locations west of the Mississippi) merely confirmed the right of settlers to dispossess Indians wherever they found them, including the regions beyond the Mississippi. Some tribes, notably the Creeks, Comanches, Apaches, and Sioux, resisted the invasion, terrorizing isolated communities, attacking wagon trains and battling with the US cavalry. Outnumbered and outgunned, they were swept aside, slaughtered, or pressed back. Tribes were sometimes induced to cede their land for territory farther west—from which, later on, they were also evicted. They were relegated to reservations as farmers, cattlemen [8], and miners moved in.

The coming of the railroads sharply accelerated westward flow and settlement. In 1869 the first transcontinental rail link was completed [11] and the West's open spaces became less remote. The frontier soon passed into history and legend [12].

KEY

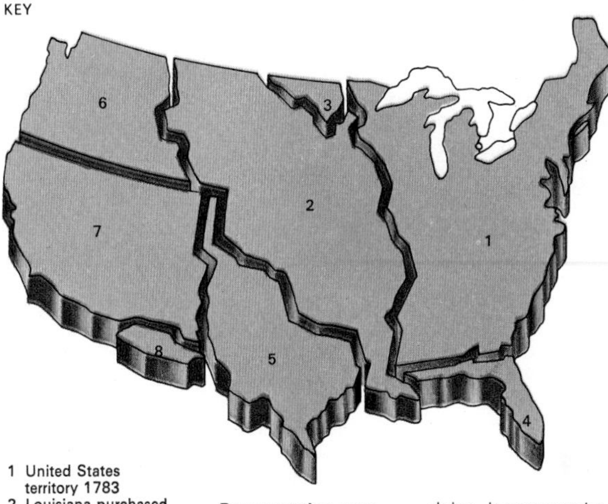

1
2
3
4
5
6
7
8

1 United States territory 1783
2 Louisiana purchased 1803
3 Ceded by Great Britain 1818
4 Florida purchased 1819
5 Texas annexed 1845
6 Oregon Country ceded 1846
7 California, Arizona, New Mexico ceded 1848
8 Gadsden Purchase 1853

By annexation, war, purchase, or treaty, the United States increased its territory to its present boundaries (minus Hawaii and Alaska) in the 90 years between 1763 and 1853. In so doing, it prevented a resurgence of British or French influence and gave force to the Monroe Doctrine of 1823 that America was not to be colonized by any other power.

6

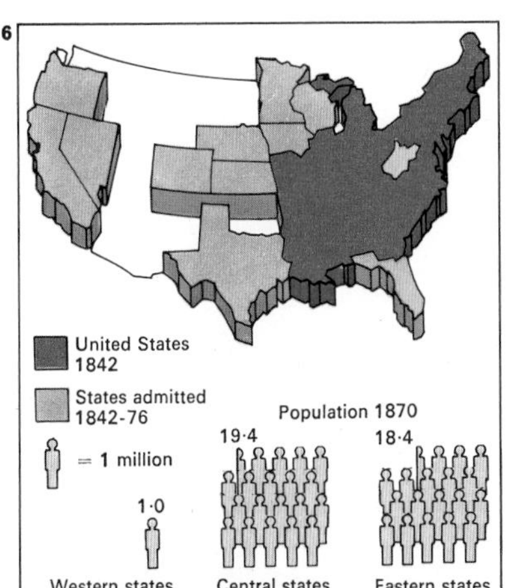

United States 1842
States admitted 1842-76
= 1 million
Population 1870
1·0
19·4
18·4
Western states
Central states
Eastern states

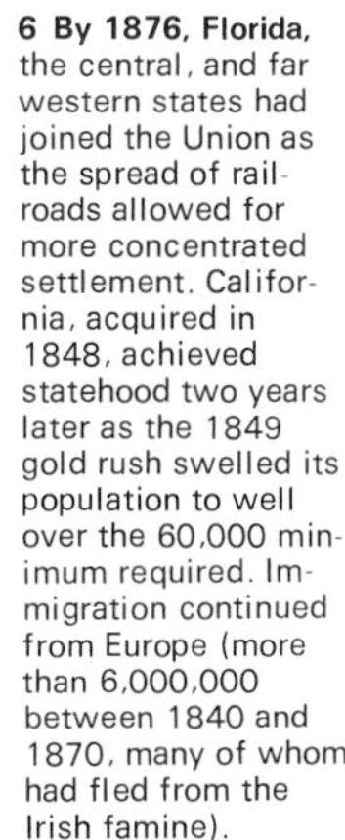

6 By 1876, Florida, the central, and far western states had joined the Union as the spread of railroads allowed for more concentrated settlement. California, acquired in 1848, achieved statehood two years later as the 1849 gold rush swelled its population to well over the 60,000 minimum required. Immigration continued from Europe (more than 6,000,000 between 1840 and 1870, many of whom had fled from the Irish famine).

7

7 The Alamo, an old Spanish chapel in San Antonio, was the fortress in which 187 Texans, rebelling against Mexican rule, held out for nearly two weeks in 1836 until all but two women and two children were killed. The Texans gained formal independence later that year.

8 Cowboys, a hard-riding, hard-working breed, built the Texas cattle empires. Later they opened Wyoming, Montana, and Colorado pastureland.

8

9 A

Mississippi
— Proclamation Line 1763
United States territory 1783
Tribal lands lost by 1784

B

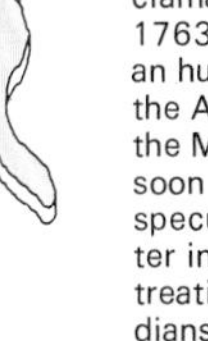

UNITED STATES
Mississippi
Tribal lands lost by 1870

9 Indian land cessions permitted settlers to expand westward. The Proclamation Line of 1763 protecting Indian hunting between the Alleghenies and the Mississippi was soon passed by land speculators [A]. After independence, treaties with the Indians pushed them farther and farther west. By 1890 no Indian titles to land were left and the Indian population had been largely restricted to reservations on poor land [B] or goaded to resistance and suppressed in the many Indian wars. A major campaign, in which George Custer was killed in 1876, followed a Sioux uprising led by Chief Sitting Bull [C], who attacked US cavalry invading his hunting grounds.

C

10

10 The California gold rush (1849) led to a frantic search for "pay dirt," which drew prospectors and then settlers to remote regions of the West. Miners alone numbered more than 5,000 by 1850.

11

11 The continent was spanned by rail in 1869 when the Central Pacific and Union Pacific were linked by a golden spike at Promontory Point, Utah. By 1870, 52,800 miles of rail existed.

12 By 1912 the American frontier which had been so central a feature in the life of the nation, had ceased to exist, and the country had turned from territorial expansion to concentrated industrial and agricultural production, as the mineral deposits of the West stimulated the growth of new towns. Meanwhile, European immigration to the teeming cities of the eastern states reached a record figure of 5,200,000 in the decade 1880–90. By 1910 the total US population was 91,972,266.

12

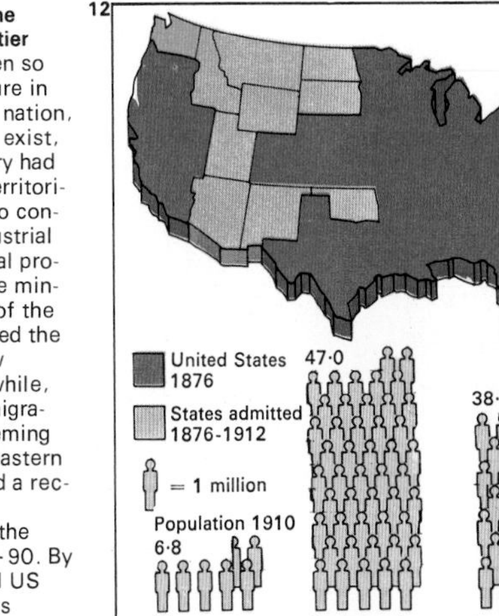

United States 1876
States admitted 1876-1912
= 1 million
Population 1910
6·8
47·0
38·1
Western states
Central states
Eastern states

The American Civil War

The Civil War from 1861–65 was the bloodiest and most bitter conflict the United States has ever experienced. It was, President Abraham Lincoln said, a test of whether the United States could endure. Although the nation emerged from it intact, the "war between brothers" left a legacy of grief and hatred. It was a vital formative influence on one of the strongest nations in the world.

Regional interests

The Civil War was kindled by a conflict of interests between the northeastern and southeastern sections of the country at a time when most of the West was still being settled. The North was a major manufacturing and commercial region while the South was overwhelmingly agricultural, with "King Cotton" providing most of its wealth [2]. The North believed in strong central government to nourish its economic growth; the South insisted on "states' rights" to guard its regional interests. Tariffs, which the North demanded to protect its industries, were opposed by the South because they raised the prices of manufactured goods. Northern industrial expansion was able to accommodate growing numbers of free laborers, despite extremes of poverty and wealth. The South's plantation economy depended on a large, work force of black slaves [1], and it was on the slave question that North-South differences gradually came to focus.

By 1850 slavery had become the most important issue in US politics. The South considered the system proper as well as necessary; many in the North considered it abominable and held it responsible for the South's comparative economic backwardness. Congressional compromises patched up differences and delayed an open break, but the South continued to press for the extension of slavery into western territories. In the North, abolitionists, of whom William Lloyd Garrison (1805–79) was the most eloquent, agitated against the "peculiar institution" of human bondage. The influential novel of Harriet Beecher Stowe (1811–96), *Uncle Tom's Cabin* (1852), dramatizing the brutalities of slavery, won support for the anti-slavery movement. The drift toward a violent resolution of sectional differences gathered momentum as hatred was whipped up by inflammatory speeches on both sides.

Both the Democratic and Whig parties, the two major national political organizations, were badly split over slavery, and the Whigs proved unable to survive the internal divisions. From the ruins of their party there emerged in 1854 a new Republican party, whose presidential candidate six years later was Abraham Lincoln [Key]. Lincoln opposed the spread of slavery and foresaw its eventual disappearance.

A month after Lincoln was elected president, South Carolina seceded from the Union and was followed by Mississippi, Florida, Alabama, Georgia, Louisiana, and Texas. On February 8, 1861, the secessionist states proclaimed the existence of the Confederate States of America.

The war begins

Lincoln refused to recognize the dismemberment of the United States and appealed

CONNECTIONS

See also
1218 The American Revolution
1274 The United States: the opening of the West
1278 The United States: Reconstruction to World War I
1200 International economy 1700–1800

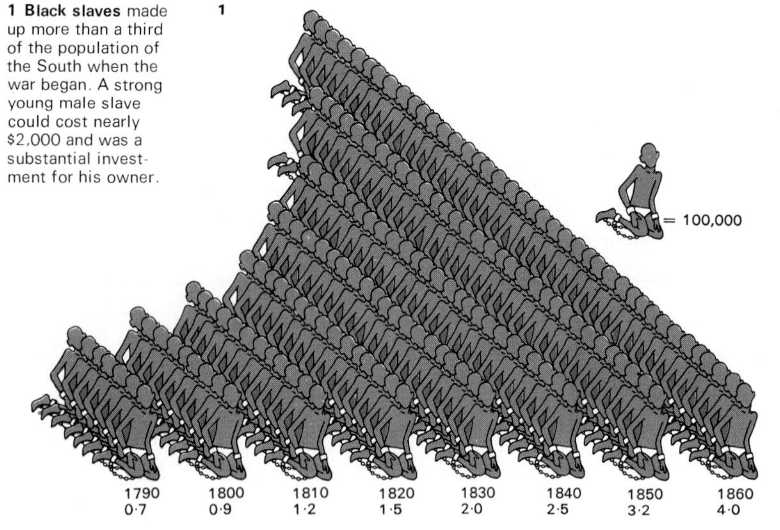

1
= 100,000
1790 0·7
1800 0·9
1810 1·2
1820 1·5
1830 2·0
1840 2·5
1850 3·2
1860 4·0
Totals in millions

1 Black slaves made up more than a third of the population of the South when the war began. A strong young male slave could cost nearly $2,000 and was a substantial investment for his owner.

2

2 A stately mansion with stucco columns and verandas on the first and second floors was the focal point of many Southern plantations. House slaves acted as servants while field slaves tilled the surrounding soil. Although there were fewer than 10,000 plantation owners who had 50 or more slaves in the 1850s, they wielded overwhelming political and social influence in the South.

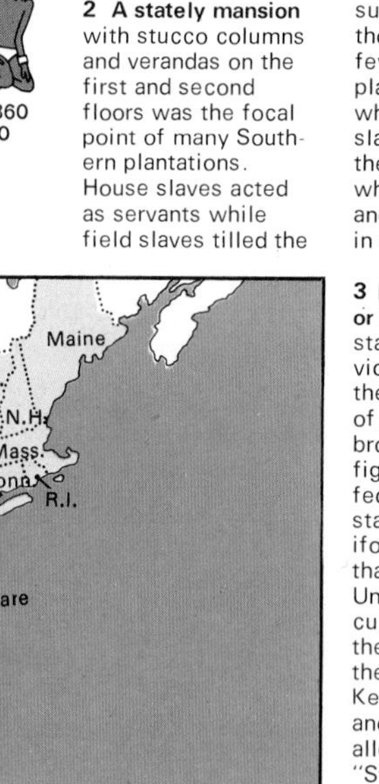

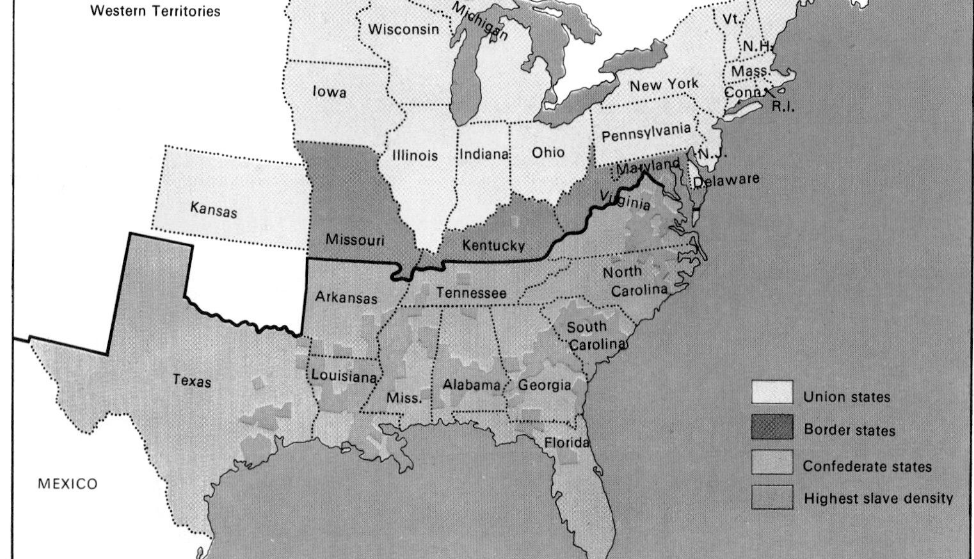

3
Minnesota
CANADA
Maine
Western Territories
Wisconsin
Michigan
Vt.
N.H.
Mass.
Conn.
R.I.
Iowa
New York
Pennsylvania
Illinois
Indiana
Ohio
N.J.
Maryland
Delaware
Kansas
Virginia
Missouri
Kentucky
North Carolina
Arkansas
Tennessee
South Carolina
Texas
Louisiana
Miss.
Alabama
Georgia
Florida
MEXICO
Union states
Border states
Confederate states
Highest slave density

3 Loyalties to South or North crossed state lines and divided families during the Civil War. Three of Abraham Lincoln's brothers-in-law died fighting for the Confederacy. Of the 23 states, including California and Oregon, that were loyal to the Union, the most difficult decision fell to the "border states," the slave states of Kentucky, Maryland, and Missouri. Their allegiance to the "Stars and Stripes" proved to be stronger than their purely regional interests and they remained in the Union. Although the state of Virginia joined the Confederacy, the western part of the state chose the Union instead and gained statehood as West Virginia before the end of the war.

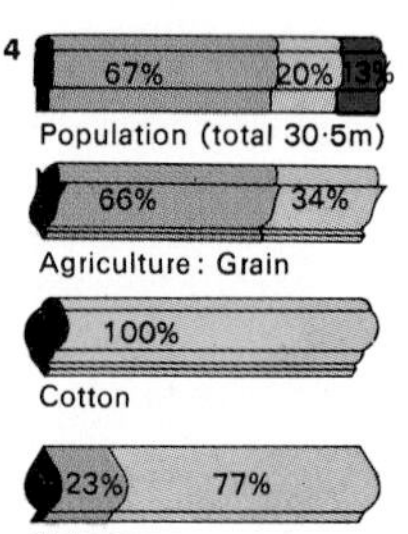

4
67%
20%
13%
Population (total 30·5m)
66%
34%
Agriculture: Grain
100%
Cotton

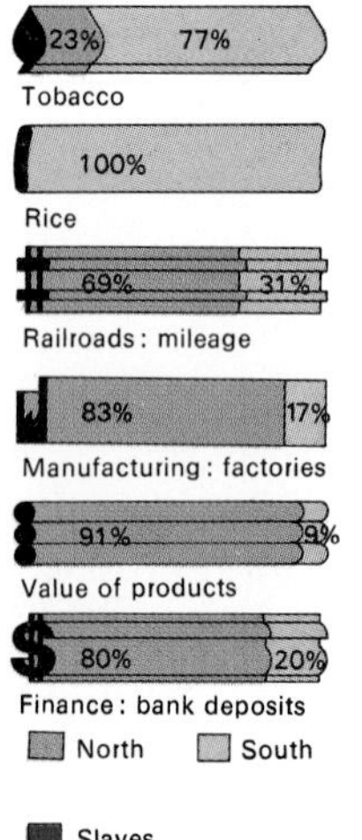

23%
77%
Tobacco
100%
Rice
69%
31%
Railroads: mileage
83%
17%
Manufacturing: factories
91%
9%
Value of products
80%
20%
Finance: bank deposits
North
South
Slaves

4 Outmatched industrially, with a much smaller population, the South counted in vain on a collapse of Northern determination to fight.

to the Confederate states to reconsider. Their reply came at dawn on April 12 when Southern guns opened fire on Fort Sumter, a federal outpost in Charleston, South Carolina. Virginia, Arkansas, North Carolina, and Tennessee soon joined the Confederacy [3]. Both sides mobilized. The Civil War had begun.

The North had distinct advantages because its industrial capacity was far greater. The South's free population was less than a quarter of that of the North. The North controlled the sea and imposed an increasingly effective blockade of the South. The South's only dubious advantage, apart from the quality of its fighting men, was that it was defending its home ground, while the North had to launch an assault.

The first major battle quickly showed that there would be no easy Northern victory. Union troops tried to crash through Confederate lines at the First Battle of Bull Run and were driven back in panic to Washington. But Northern superior numbers and equipment soon began to tell. After a major Northern victory at Antietam, Lincoln issued an Emancipation Proclamation, effective from January 1, 1863, declaring all slaves in the Confederate states free.

Southern attempts to rally to preserve slavery and the Confederacy met with increasingly confident and effective Northern onslaughts [6]. There was no recovery from a devastating Confederate setback at Gettysburg in July 1863 [7, 8]. General William Sherman's (1820–91) "March to the Sea" in Georgia the following year undermined the South's remaining capacity to fight.

Victory and its aftermath

With victory inconceivable and the bulk of his forces cut off, the Confederate commander, General Robert E. Lee (1807–70) surrendered to the Union commander, General Ulysses S. Grant (1822–85) at Appomattox, Virginia, on April 9, 1865.

The Civil War had cost the lives of 360,000 Union and 260,000 Confederate men as well as thousands of civilians. The South was in ruins. Despite Lincoln's plea for "malice toward none," the seeds of enduring bitterness had been sown.

KEY

Abraham Lincoln (1809–65), United States President during the Civil War, believed the country could not survive "half slave and half free" but was determined to prevent the breakup of the Union. A self-taught lawyer of great shrewdness, sincerity, and common sense, he gained national recognition through public debates on slavery and was elected in 1860. Mild-mannered but strong-willed, he led the North with firmness and urged "charity for all" after the South was defeated. He was assassinated by an actor, John Wilkes Booth, in a Washington theater on April 14, 1865, soon after starting his second term of office.

5

5 Jefferson Davis (1808–89), the champion of "states' rights" and the extension of slavery to western territory, was elected president of the Confederacy in 1861 and led the South until its surrender. He suffered from poor health, and his relations with other Southern leaders were often strained. Taken prisoner after the war and indicted for treason, Davis was never tried.

6

A

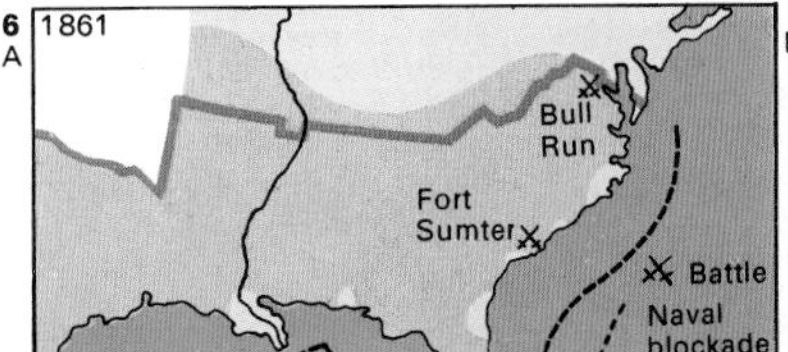
1861
Bull Run
Fort Sumter
Battle
Naval blockade

B

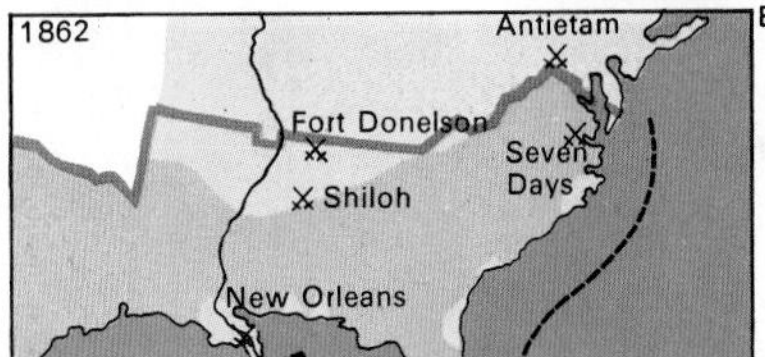
1862
Antietam
Fort Donelson
Shiloh
Seven Days
New Orleans

C

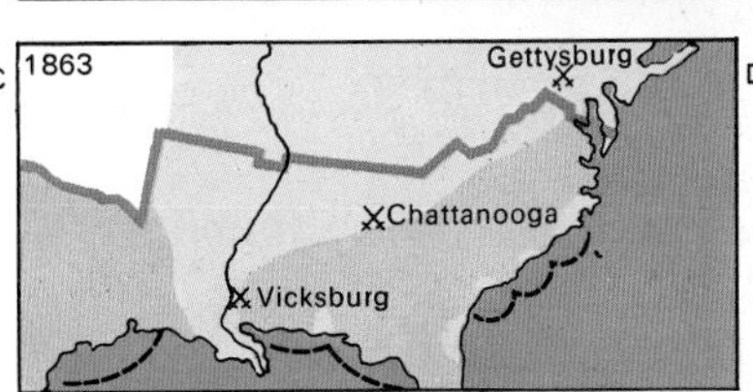
1863
Gettysburg
Chattanooga
Vicksburg

D

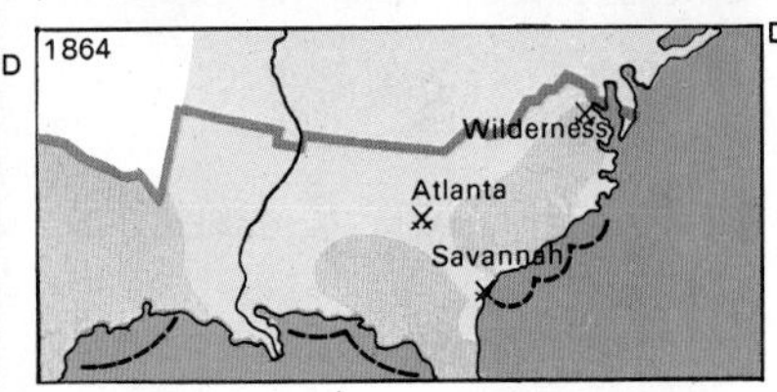
1864
Wilderness
Atlanta
Savannah

E

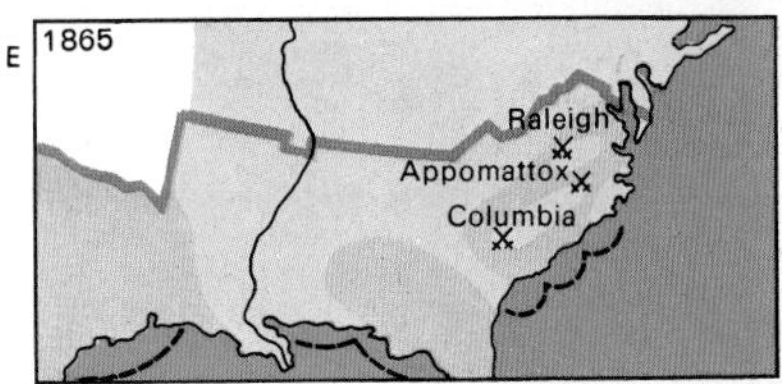
1865
Raleigh
Appomattox
Columbia

6 Erosion of Confederate territory was steady after an initial stalemate [A] in 1861 when the North realized it must blockade the South. In 1862, after western victories, the Union advanced from the north [B]. By May 1863 it controlled the Mississippi [C]. By the end of 1864, Sherman had split the South in two [D]. Surrender became inevitable in 1865 after further Union gains [E].

7

Battle
Union march
Confederate march
Cavalry
Cashtown
Gettysburg
Frederick
Washington
Falmouth
Fredericksburg

7 Gettysburg marked the turning point of the war in 1863 when a daring Confederate invasion of Pennsylvania was blocked in a ferocious three-day battle. General Lee, the Confederate commander, intended to await a Northern repulse near Cashtown. But a chance encounter between rival patrols precipitated the battle near the small town of Gettysburg on July 1. Successful probing assaults on Union positions led Confederate officers to misread the situation, and cavalry that was engaged elsewhere failed to scout the terrain. Finally Confederate troops were sent marching hopelessly into a withering barrage of fire.

8

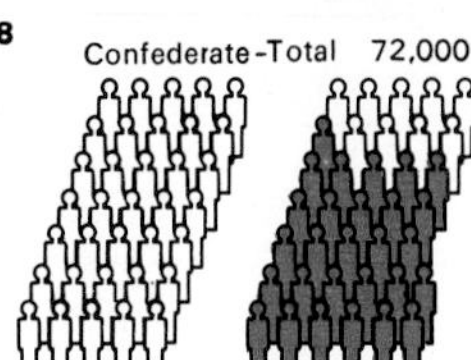
Confederate-Total 72,000

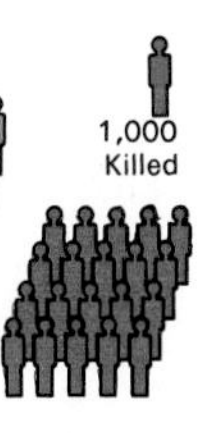
Union-Total 90,000
1,000 Killed

8 Battle statistics at Gettysburg are the subject of controversy, but it is likely that about 72,000 Confederate troops faced nearly 90,000 Union troops. This disparity need not have been decisive in view of earlier Confederate successes. While about 23,000 Union men were killed or died of wounds, the South's losses were about 28,000 (higher than the official figure given at the time). The strength of the Union was not undermined significantly. But although its surviving forces escaped back to the South, the Confederacy had suffered a crippling and irrevocable loss. By 1865, with both sides conscripting men, the North had 960,000 soldiers under arms and the South only 450,000.

9

9 Union troops with a battery of 32-pounders near Fredericksburg were photographed by Matthew Brady (*c.* 1823–96), one of the first war photographers in history. The Civil War was also the first conflict in which telegraphy and railroad transport were used widely and the first in which ironclad naval vessels went into battle. In March 1862 the USS *Monitor* and the Confederate *Merrimac* fought each other at Hampton Roads, Virginia. An early submarine attack was launched by the *Hunley*, which rammed its torpedo into the USS *Housatonic* off Charleston in 1864, with the loss of both ships.

The United States: Reconstruction to World War I

The United States developed from a predominantly rural nation at the end of its Civil War (1861–5) into the world's largest and wealthiest urban industrial power by the time of its entry into World War I (1917). Among the key factors responsible for this major transformation were a huge population increase, discovery and exploitation of enormous mineral resources, consolidation of the settlement of the Great Plains and most of the West, and the construction of extensive railroad networks to service industrial, agricultural, and population growth.

Problems of the South

US development during this period was blighted by serious problems. Reconstruction of the defeated and devastated South after the Civil War was retarded by residual North-South hostility. Northern military units policed some Southern states until 1876, when Reconstruction ended. Carpetbaggers (northerners who migrated southward for opportunistic reasons) sought to govern and control sections of the ravaged South, aggravating Southern animosity and leaving a heritage of dissension that became a part of Southern politics.

In the rest of the country, however, industrial development was rapid. Rich coal veins were worked along the Appalachian mountain spine and in the Monongahela, Ohio, and Allegheny valleys. Iron ore was mined in the Great Lakes region; copper, lead, and other minerals were discovered and hungrily tapped [Key], and the exploitation of oil began.

Industrial growth was further intensified by a host of inventions [8], including commercially viable electric lighting, the telephone, and rubber vulcanizing. The mechanization of agriculture through the invention of the reaper, thresher, mechanical harvester, and other farm machinery enabled farmers to expand land cultivation. Between 1860 and 1910 farm acreage more than doubled and farm production more than tripled.

A complex of railroad networks reached out across the country linking industry and agriculture with their markets. By 1900, 193,000 miles (310,000km) of track crisscrossed the United States—more than existed in Europe at that time. By 1916 the figure was 250,000 miles (425,000km).

The rapid pace of development lent itself to the activities of aggressive entrepreneurs [5]. Men such as Scottish-born Andrew Carnegie (1835–1919), instrumental in consolidating the US steel industry, and John D. Rockefeller (1839–1937), who concentrated on oil, built personal fortunes through huge companies that could overwhelm competition by fixing prices and benefiting from large-scale marketing.

Population explosion

The giant companies [6] played a major role in the surge in the US gross national product. which rose from $7,000,000,000 in 1870 to $91,000,000,000 in 1920, despite economic fluctuations. The country's pool of labor, provided by a rapidly growing population, seemed bottomless. The number of US citizens grew from 40,000,000 in 1870 to 92,000,000 in 1910. A flood of immigrants [3] from Europe

CONNECTIONS

See also
1276 The American Civil War
1274 The United States: the opening of the West
1282 The foundations of 20th-century science
1402 The American experience: the economy since the Civil War

1

1 Members of the Ku Klux Klan, hooded and robed, hold elaborate initiation ceremonies. The society was originally organized by former Confederate soldiers in 1866 at Pulaski, Tennessee, to maintain white supremacy in the Southern states after emancipation of black slaves had been confirmed by the defeat of the South in the Civil War. The Klan attracted many recruits, but its nightriding vigilante violence against blacks and Northerners led to its formal dissolution in 1869. Resurfacing in 1915, its anti-black policies were supplemented by an anti-Catholic, anti-Jewish, and anti alien emphasis.

2

2 In the unsettled years after the Civil War, bands of outlaws roamed across the central states. One of the best known figures was Jesse James (1847–1882), here seated front left. He led a gang of bank and train robbers that included his brother Frank [front right] and four brothers of the Younger family—Coleman [rear left], James, Robert [rear right], and John. Jesse and Coleman had been members of Quantrill's Raiders—a band of Confederate mounted guerrillas—and they had no respect for Northern controlled banks and railroads. The James-Younger gang left a blood soaked trail of robberies across the Midwest. After John Younger was killed in a bank raid, his brothers were captured and imprisoned. Badly shaken, the James brothers went into hiding. Three years later they returned to robbing trains. In 1882, Jesse was killed by Robert Ford, a new member of his gang who was tempted by the $10,000 reward for Jesse.

3

3 Health services were largely superficial for the more than 20,000,000 immigrants who settled in the United States between the Civil War and World War I. At first they came mainly from Britain, Germany, and Scandinavia, and later mostly from southern and eastern Europe, seeking religious or political freedom or escape from poverty. They formed German-American, Scandinavian-American and other ethnic pockets in the agricultural regions of the Great Plains; or they mined the natural resources, chopped down the forests, and built the railroads for the burgeoning US economy. By 1920 one out of every eight US citizens was of foreign birth.

throughout the period contributed substantially to this increase and averaged almost 1,000,000 a year between 1900 and 1910.

Housing was frequently inadequate in congested urban centers, wages were low, and poverty widespread. These conditions gave rise to the US trade union movement. The Knights of Labor, founded in 1869, was superseded by the American Federation of Labor, founded in 1886, which was to become a potent industrial and political force. Agriculture's rapid growth confronted farmers with the problems of overproduction, soil exhaustion, droughts, and dust storms. Farmers formed protective associations, known as Granges, that became the basis for the Populist movement and for the ultimate success in promoting legislation to further farmers' interests.

A burgeoning campaign against social injustice established a tradition of investigative journalism. Lincoln Steffens (1866–1936) exposed municipal corruption. The novels of Theodore Dreiser (1871–1945) and Frank Norris (1870–1902) described the often unsavory machinations of big business. New laws limited the length of the working day, regulated railway rates, and prohibited the sale of "deleterious" foods and medicines. President Theodore Roosevelt (1858–1919) launched the conservation movement aimed at ending the indiscriminate exploitation of natural resources.

War against Spain

The country was already looking outside itself. Aroused by sensational press reports of the brutal suppression of a Cuban revolt against Spanish rule, and provoked by the sinking of the USS *Maine* by a mine in Havana harbor, the United States took up arms against Spain in 1898. It emerged victorious from the Spanish-American War in less than three months; Cuba became independent from Spanish rule. A more far-reaching consequence for the United States was that by annexing the Philippines, Guam, and Puerto Rico, it became a colonial power. By 1900 the United States was an economic giant: by 1914 it had become a full fledged international power.

KEY
Coal in million tons
Steel in million tons
Manufactures in million dollars

Coal and steel production increased phenomenally in the closing decades of the 1800s and the opening years of the 1900s to feed the US industrial boom. Augmented by substantial quantities of other important minerals such as copper, aluminum, lead, zinc, and tin, the ground-work was laid for the major industries that are now the pillars of the US economy. In 1860 the North already had a huge lead over the South in industrialization with, for example, more than 80% of the country's factories; the South was slow to recover from the ravages of the Civil War and so industrial growth was at first confined almost wholly to the North.

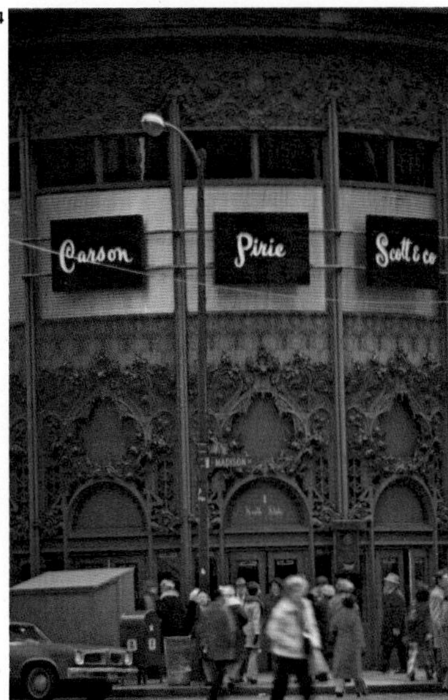
Carson
Pirie
Scott & co

4 Carson, Pirie, Scott Store (1899, 1903–04, 1906) by Louis Sullivan (1856–1924) was one of the most starkly modern buildings constructed in Chicago between the Great Fire (1871) and World War I. The upper floors are devoid of decoration, the large windows framed by only the structural steel skeleton. The interior is flooded with light and free of obstructing columns.

5 Assets: 5 financiers and allies 1901

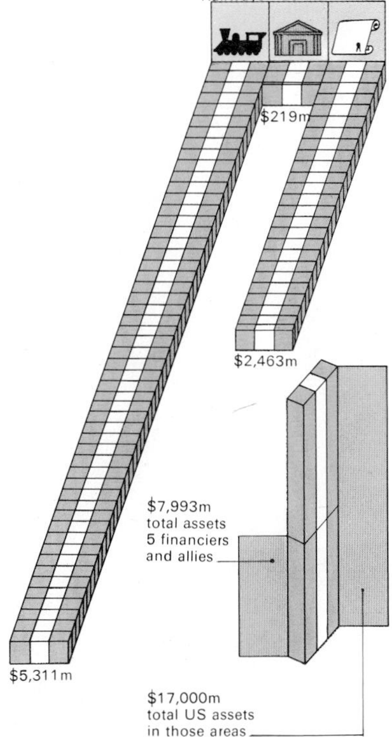
Railways
Banks
Trusts
$219m
$2,463m
$7,993m total assets 5 financiers and allies
$5,311m
$17,000m total US assets in those areas

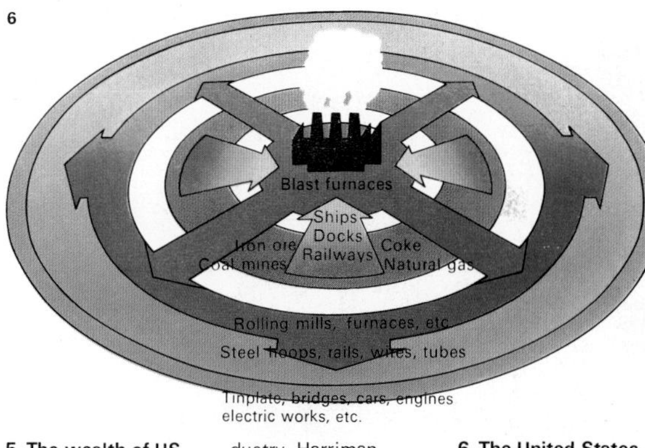
Blast furnaces
Ships
Docks
Railways
Coke
Rolling mills, furnaces, etc
Steel hoops, rails, wires, tubes
Tinplate, bridges, cars, engines electric works, etc.

5 The wealth of US millionaires at the turn of the century is illustrated by a chart showing the assets of five of them in 1901. Together, John D. Rockefeller, Edward Harriman, J. P. Morgan, William K. Vanderbilt, and George Gould had personal assets of $800,000,000 and could control ten times that amount through company directorships. Rockefeller, who started as a bookkeeper, formed the Standard Oil Company to dominate the US oil industry. Harriman (1848–1909) once consolidated most of the rail networks of the western United States. Morgan (1837–1913), founder of US Steel, manipulated investment banking to build his enormous fortune. Vanderbilt (1849–1920) inherited the transport empire of his grandfather, Cornelius Vanderbilt (1794–1877). George Gould (1864–1923) was heir to the immense rail holdings of his unscrupulous father Jay Gould (1836–92).

6 The United States Steel Corporation, founded in 1901, was the first of the giant "vertical" US companies that dominated the entire process of production and distribution through ownership of raw material sources and means of transport. It gained control of smaller firms and integrated them into massive, profitable, corporate structures that were capable of virtually eliminating competition, fixing prices, and completely manipulating markets.

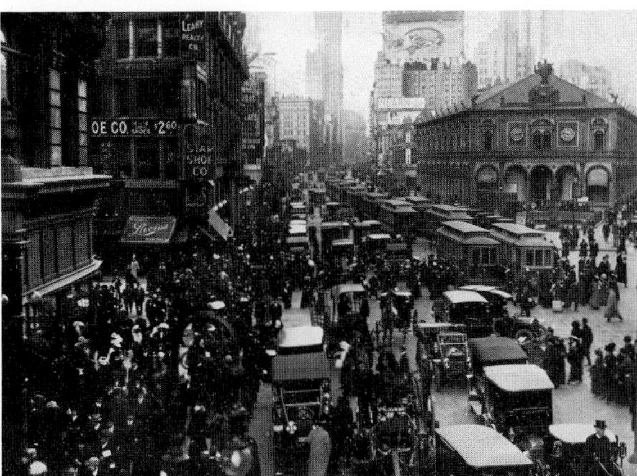

7 New York in 1911 had a population of almost 4,000,000 and was already a sprawling metropolis. It was a major cultural and business center, stitched together by a network of streetcar and subway lines, tunnels, and bridges. Extremes of rich and poor were seen in the contrast between the elegant mansions of "Millionaires' Row" and the grim immigrant slums. The automobile industry rapidly expanded, as the number of cars here in Herald Square indicates.

8 Thomas Alva Edison (1847–1931) became America's most prolific inventor. His formal education amounted to three months' schooling at the age of seven. Edison is credited with inventing the phonograph, the automatic telegraph receiver, and the first commercially viable incandescent lamp. He had over 1,000 patents, and among them was the world's first plant for distributing electric power for lighting, built in New York City, 1882.

The impact of steam

The application of steam power in the course of the nineteenth century to land and water transport [Key] and to manufacturing and agriculture [5] transformed the world trading system. It also enormously increased the mobility and economic dominance of the most advanced Western nations over the economically backward territories of the earth. Of all the agencies of change, railroads had the largest impact.

Nationalism and the railroads

In the first stage of their development, until about 1870, railroads served to strengthen and enlarge national markets and to consolidate national states. The opening of the first transcontinental railroad in 1869 linked with "hoops of iron" the state of California to the rest of the United States. The unification of both Germany and Italy and the growth of their national economies was accelerated by means of the railroad. The condition laid down by the Maritime Provinces (Nova Scotia, New Brunswick, Prince Edward Island, and Newfoundland) for their acceptance of Canadian Confederation in 1867 was that a railroad should be built to link them with the provinces of the interior. A similar condition was laid down by British Columbia when it joined the confederation in 1871.

Later railroad developments had a greater effect on the world economy, especially by increasing the volume of commodity exchange. The extension of railroads into the prairies of North and South America through such agencies as the Canadian Pacific Railway and the Argentine Railroad, the opening of the "Western windows" of Russia—Riga and Odessa—through railroads stretching into their wheat-growing hinterlands, and the construction of lines into the fertile plains of the Punjab and of Bengal, all contributed greatly to the expansion of world markets in such basic commodities as wheat, chilled and frozen meat, cotton, and jute. Before the railroad age national economies were largely self-sufficient, but in the age of steam the importation of vast quantities of basic foodstuffs and essential raw materials by the advanced industrial nations enabled them to concentrate on the large-scale, steam-powered production of standardized manufactured goods. Raising the funds for building steam railroads was one of the most important reasons for the growth of a world capital market, with London as its leading center before 1914.

Emigration and colonialism

Steamship and railroad companies both stood to gain by encouraging the mass migration of labor. Many companies preferred to carry immigrants, who loaded and unloaded themselves, rather than cargo that did not. The steerage fare from Liverpool to New York in the 1880s was only £3. Forty-six million people emigrated between 1831 and 1915.

Without the aid of the gunboat [4] and the railroad, military and political domination of colonial territories by the metropolitan powers would have been impossible [2]. In the 1880s the French sent several military expeditions to Algeria to suppress a serious insurrection under Bu Amama. The uprising was eventually subdued by the building

CONNECTIONS

See also
1236 Britain and the Industrial Revolution
1284 European industrialization 1870–1914
1220 The early Industrial Revolution
1708 Railroad transportation
1274 The United States: the opening of the West
1278 The United States: Reconstruction to World War I
1266 India in the 19th century
1268 Africa in the 19th century
1272 Japan: the Meiji Restoration

1 Small steamboats played an important part in the exploration of Africa between *c.* 1855–85, and thereafter in the policing and administration of colonial territories. In this steam launch; the *Ma-Robert*, David Livingstone explored the Zambezi in 1850. He explored the River Rovina in the steam launch *Pioneer* in 1860. Four years later H. M. Stanley used the steam launch *Lady Alice* to circumnavigate Lake Victoria and help in the search for the source of the Congo. Colonial administrators in West Africa used steam launches between railheads up and down the Senegal and Niger rivers.

2 Steam-powered warships were used by Western powers to drag Japan out of its long sustained policy of isolation. In July 1853, fearing that unless he acted quickly Russia would forestall him, the president of the United States sent Commodore Matthew Perry with four war ships (two were steamers) to Uraga with a letter addressed to the shogunate demanding trade concessions, including coaling stations. In February 1854, Perry returned with seven ships, insisting on a reply. Overawed by the "black ships" in the harbor, the shogunate yielded. The Treaty of Kanagawa, signed in March, opened two ports to US ships.

3 The Great Eastern, 18,915 tons, 685ft (210.9m) long and powered by paddle, screw and sail, was too large for weak contemporary marine engines. In July 1866 she laid the first successful transatlantic telegraph cable.

4 Gunboat Foxhound served in the British Royal Navy from 1877–90. Built to a length of 41.5ft (38.1m), a beam of 8ft (7.16m), and a tonnage of 445, she carried two 60-pounder and two 20-pounder guns and could sail toward trouble faster than major capital ships. Small frigates steamed into harbors and even up estuaries to devastate enemies. It was ships of these relatively small sizes that made Britain mistress of the seas before 1914.

of a railroad through the heart of the troubled area. Following the suppression of an Ashanti rebellion by the British in 1900, the pacification of the Gold Coast was sealed by building a railroad. Once colonial rule was established railroads reduced administrative expenses in the transport of personnel and stores. A train of the 1890s did the work of 13,000 carriers at five percent of the cost.

Before the 1860s steamships had a voracious consumption of coal, which limited their range of economic operations to coastal and short sea routes. (The North Atlantic, with a large passenger traffic, was an exception.) Technical improvement came more slowly to the marine engine than the locomotive. In 1840 the 1,139-ton *Britannia* carried only 90 passengers and only 225 tons of goods because it needed 640 tons of bunker fuel for the Atlantic crossing. But the introduction of the compound marine engine in the 1860s made a 40 percent saving in fuel consumption. In 1914 the 4,556-ton Cunarder *Bothnia* carried more than three times as much cargo as coal and had room for 340 passengers. With the opening of the Suez Canal in 1869 it was profitable to use compound-engined steamships in the Far East trade.

The use of steel in ship construction in the 1880s and the introduction of the steam turbine in the following decade drove sailing vessels off the sea lanes to Australia and New Zealand. These advances also led to the increase of freight carried in the world's steamships from 27 million tons in 1873 to 63 million tons in 1898.

Industry and agriculture

Before 1914 the use of steam power for driving textile machinery was still heavily concentrated in Western Europe and the United States, which together accounted for 80 percent of factory textile production. But its dispersion had produced rapid advances in industrialization in India, Japan, Australia, and Egypt. Steam power was used at all stages in the production of iron and steel, but dispersion of steam power outside the older industrial areas was slow. Steam's biggest impact agriculturally was on the processing of grains, as in threshing.

KEY

The maiden voyage of inventor Robert Fulton's *Clermont* in 1807 sparked widespread use of the steamship in the development of the United States. It took the *Clermont* 33 hours to go the 150-mile (240-km) distance. By the 1830s hundreds of steamships were plying America's rivers.

5

Boiler

Traction engine

Plow

Windlass

Rope

Traction engine

Plow

Anchor

Windlass

5 The agricultural application of steam power is indicative of 19th century enthusiasm for its uses. Steam plowing was never extensively used because it was cumbersome, and the difficulties of fueling with coal added to the cost of its operation. It was most popular in the grain belt of eastern England, where over 200,000 acres (81,000 hectares) were steam plowed during the 1860s.

6 The US Civil War (1861–65) was the first major war in which railroads played a decisive role. Here, a train bringing Union reinforcements to General Johnston has run off the track in the forests of Mississippi (1863). In Virginia, some railroad tracks were blown up and relaid as many as six times during the fighting. The repair gangs worked in sight of the enemy's artillery, thus braving great danger.

7 The Chilean railroad from Valparaiso to Santiago was built between 1853 and 1864 and was the first important South American railroad. Its construction through the Andes represented a great engineering feat, and was financed largely by British investment. Such railroads brought economic development to remote areas, encouraged greater administrative centralization in previously disunited countries, and focused nationalist aspirations.

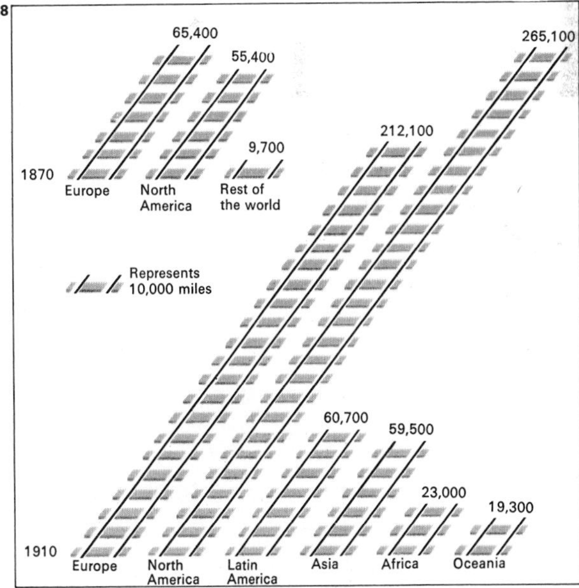
8
65,400
55,400
9,700
1870
Europe
North America
Rest of the world
Represents 10,000 miles
265,100
212,100
60,700
59,500
23,000
19,300
1910
Europe
North America
Latin America
Asia
Africa
Oceania

8 Steam railroads were pioneered by Great Britain and the United States. The world's first fully locomotive powered public railroad, the Liverpool and Manchester (1830), was quickly followed by the Baltimore and Ohio and other lines. For the next 40 years railroad building was mainly concentrated in Europe and North America, where capital and engineering skill were available, linking centers of industry and commerce. From 1832–38 railroads were started in France, Belgium, Bavaria, Austria, and Canada. After 1870, railroads on the American continent were often built to open up new land and to develop its commercial potential. Railroads in Japan and India dominated rail construction in Asia.

The foundations of 20th-century science

Many fields of science in the nineteenth century seemed to be marked by orthodox progress—that is, a series of discoveries that could be fitted into the existing view of nature. Yet in retrospect some of these discoveries were to lead to fundamental changes in the scientific picture. The new fields of thermodynamics and electromagnetism suggested new concepts of energy, and the mathematical work of the Germans Karl Gauss (1777–1885) and Georg Riemann (1826–66), although purely academic in the 1850s, by the 1920s was used to describe the very nature of space.

Biology and medicine

The biological world also seemed straightforward until it was upset by Charles Darwin (1809–82) and Gregor Mendel (1822–84) [4]. When Darwin produced his *Origin of Species* in 1859, placing man among the animals in an evolutionary process that worked by natural selection, a storm of controversy broke that did not completely subside for more than a century. Mendel's work in the 1860s on inheritance factors went unnoticed at the time but was to help lay the foundations of genetics.

Medical science also progressed; Claude Bernard (1813–78) studied the chemical properties of the digestive system, and the treatment of infection improved with the new bacteriological ideas of Louis Pasteur (1822–95) [3]. These studies, together with the introduction of antiseptics and anesthetics, were to lead to advances in surgery and in the understanding of new ways to combat disease. Medical scientists also began to explore the realms of the mind, left virtually uncharted until the late nineteenth century, and in the work of Sigmund Freud (1856–1939) [8] the foundations of psychoanalysis were laid and the important concept of the unconscious and its conflicts introduced.

The atomic theory

Chemistry finally broke its remaining ties with alchemy and its mysticism, becoming a truly practical and scientific study according to the principles laid down by Antoine Lavoisier (1743–94). Its central advance was the atomic theory. Introduced in its modern form at the beginning of the nineteenth century by John Dalton (1766–1844), the theory propounded the view that all chemical changes are merely rearrangements of small basic particles—atoms—that are indestructible.

Acceptance of the theory required accumulation of a considerable amount of independent evidence, yet in the work of Amadeo Avogadro (1776–1856), Stanislao Cannizzaro (1826–1910), and Jöns Jakob Berzelius (1779–1848), the desired correlations and experimental proofs were found, and the theory of the atomic nature of matter became established. Other discoveries followed, notably in the field of organic chemistry. Especially important advances were made by Justus von Liebig (1803–73), who studied agricultural chemistry and fertilizers, and Friedrich Kekulé (1829–96), who discovered the ringlike structure of the atoms in a molecule of benzene and similar compounds. This eventually led to the development of plastics, many other petrochemical products, and modern synthetic drugs and explosives.

CONNECTIONS

See also
- **1186** Exploration and science 1750–1850
- **1160** Science and technology 1500–1700
- **418** Evolution: classical theories
- **416** Principles of heredity
- **1480** What is an atom?
- **1482** Nuclear physics
- **1484** Beyond the atom
- **1524** The idea of relativity
- **1812** Aspects of human nature
- **1628** Steam engines

1 Faraday's "ring" was constructed for a central experiment in the work of Michael Faraday (1791–1867) on the nature of electromagnetism in London in 1831. He knew that electricity flowing along a wire had an associated magnetic field, and he argued that a magnet should create by induction an electric current in a wire placed near it. He showed that this could happen if the magnet was moving, and with this apparatus discovered self induction of an electric current.

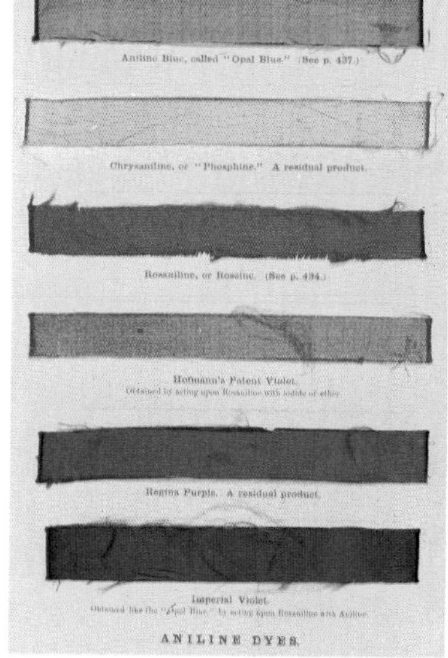
Aniline Blue, called "Opal Blue." (See p. 437.)
Chrysaniline, or "Phosphine." A residual product.
Rosaniline, or Roseine. (See p. 434.)
Hofmann's Patent Violet.
Regina Purple. A residual product.
Imperial Violet.
ANILINE DYES.

2 In the middle of the 19th century William Henry Perkin (1838–1907) carried out research in his laboratory in organic chemistry and in particular into quinine and a substance derived from aniline, a coaltar product. By chance this led him to discover a mauve dye. Previously purple colors could be produced only from an expensive natural product. Other aniline dyes followed—some early samples are shown from an article in the *Popular Science Review* (1864).

T.

3 This illustration of Louis Pasteur is from a cartoon published in *Vanity Fair* in 1887. Pasteur worked on fermentation, on the souring of milk, on putrefaction, and then on a disease in silkworms. He showed that all resulted from the presence of microorganisms and proved that these were airborne. He then studied other animal diseases and devised a method of immunization by inoculating a toxin to raise the host's resistance to more virulent forms of the organism.

4 Gregor Mendel was dissatisfied with current explanations of how the many different changes in, and varieties of, living things occurred. In the 1860s he began experiments in cross-breeding peas and found the existence of dominant and recessive characteristics (now called genes). Crossing tall and dwarf types gave him a tall hybrid, not one half as tall, as current theory predicted. Tallness was the dominant characteristic. The next generation gave a quarter that were short; the recessive characteristic (dwarfness) had returned. Continued breeding showed the dwarf strain interbred as dwarfs. Mendel showed how proportions changed in later generations.

5 James Dewar (1842–1923) could not have given this 1904 demonstration of pouring liquid hydrogen without the 19th century's work on thermodynamics. The law of the conservation of energy and the identifying of heat as energy were vital advances. The idea that the heat of an object depends on the movement of its molecules led to the concept of absolute zero and is basic to the 20th-century idea of matter.

From electricity to the electron

In physics, important advances were made in the understanding of electricity. In 1800 a cell or battery—the "voltaic pile"—was constructed by Alessandro Volta (1745–827), by means of which a continuous flow of electricity was obtained for the first time. Research on electricity engaged others, especially Humphry Davy (1778–1829), on the chemical effects of electricity, and Michael Faraday [1], on the connections between electricity and magnetism. Faraday's ideas were taken up and carried further by James Clerk Maxwell (1831–79), who studied the mathematical properties of the electromagnetic field and predicted the existence of types of electromagnetic radiation other than light.

Maxwell used the theory that light moves in waves, which had been developed by the experiments in interferometry by Thomas Young (1773–1829). Interest in the nature of light was intensified by the invention of spectroscopy by Joseph von Fraunhofer (1787–1826) and its later development by Gustav Kirchhoff (1824–87). Spectroscopy proved to be a delicate means of chemical analysis, and it soon became a revolutionary tool of astronomical research. In the nineteenth century it was generally assumed that light traveled through an invisible substance known as the ether, although no proof of its existence was available. An experiment conducted in 1887 by Albert Michelson (1852–1931) and Edward Morley (1838–1923) indicated that the ether did not exist. This experiment left physics in a state of confusion until the publication in 1905 of the special theory of relativity by Albert Einstein (1879–1955) [9].

In other fields, too, new studies at the end of the nineteenth century brought about important breakthroughs. Work on the discharge of electricity through gases, in particular, led to astonishing results. William Crookes (1832–1919) discovered cathode rays and J. J. Thomson (1856–1940) [Key] the electron. Together with the quantum theory developed by Max Planck (1858–1947), these major discoveries formed the cornerstone of twentieth-century atomic and nuclear physics.

KEY

J. J. Thomson was director of the Cavendish Laboratory at Cambridge University, England. With a brilliant research student, Ernest Rutherford, he found that when a rarefied gas was bombarded by X rays it became able to conduct electricity. From this Thomson considered the nature of cathode rays, and this led him to discover that they were composed of electrons, the first subatomic particles, thus proving that atoms were not the smallest units of matter.

6 Thomas Young revived the wave theory of light, which had been overshadowed by Newton's particle theory. In the 17th century the Dutch physicist Huygens had suggested that light waves pushed outward longitudinally from a source; in 1800–09, however, Young postulated up-and-down (transverse) waves [A], illustrated in his *Course of Lectures on Natural Philosophy and the Mechanical Arts* (1807). Interference patterns [B] were explained by the wave theory.

6

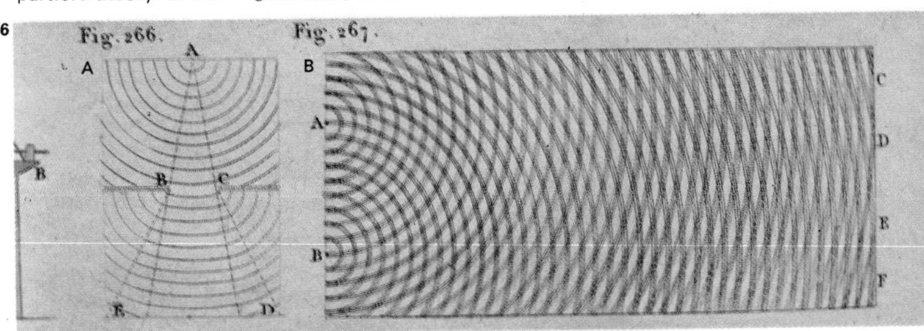
Fig. 266.
Fig. 267.
A
B

7

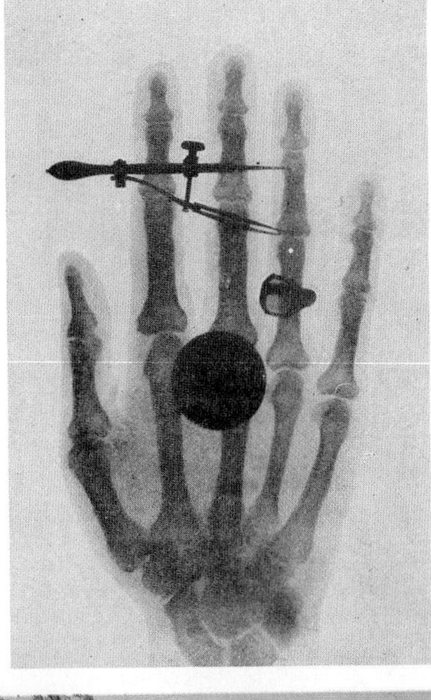

7 In 1896 it was discovered that uranium constantly emitted rays more penetrating than X rays; such rays also made gases conduct electricity. This field was next studied by Marie and Pierre Curie, who found that other heavy substances emitted such rays (gamma rays). They analyzed pitchblende, a uranium compound, and found it contained polonium and radium, the latter being a strong emitter. They realized the emission must be caused by some behavior of the atoms in the materials; they called this behavior "radioactivity." The illustration shows Marie Curie's hand photographed using a gamma-ray source.

8

8 Sigmund Freud, a Viennese, developed a theory of the "psyche," at first through the use of hypnosis in the treatment of hysteria and later through the technique of free association. Both probed the unconscious and its power to affect conduct. He also stressed the sexual motivation behind much human behavior. Freud's ideas, which included the analysis of dreams, were taken up and modified by others, particularly Carl Jung.

10

10 The University of Göttingen, famous for its mathematics and physics faculties, produced some of the leaders in the massive expansion of physical science studies in late 19th-century Germany.

9

9 Albert Einstein's paper in 1905 on special relativity showed that not all physical quantities are capable of absolute measurement, but are relative to the same frame of reference. This did not take account of gravitation. But in 1915 he published his general theory of relativity, which extended the idea to include gravitation and accelerated motion. Einstein's theory profoundly affected modern science.

European industrialization 1870–1914

The most striking feature in Europe during the latter part of the nineteenth century was the growth and spread of industrialization. The rise of industrial economies in Western Europe had profound social and political consequences. With the rapid growth of cities and towns came the development of a more complex political society in which new groups of people—the middle and working classes in particular—began to organize and exert greater political influence.

Spread of industrialization

In 1850 the only country that could be described as having an industrial economy was Britain [3]. But industrial development spread to Belgium, France, and Germany by 1870, and in the last decades of the century was becoming established in countries such as Sweden and Russia.

Belgium industrialized rapidly and by 1870 had one of the leading economies in Europe. French commerce, iron production, and textile output were flourishing by the latter part of the century, and between 1870 and 1890. French technical innovation played an important part in the development of many engineering products, such as the bicycle.

By 1900 the most important industrial economy to emerge in Europe was that of Germany. Its unification by 1871 was accompanied by an accumulation of capital and development of the transport network. From 1850 to 1880, Germany increased coal production tenfold and, with the acquisition of the iron ore fields of Alsace-Lorraine from France in 1871, launched a rapid expansion of iron and steel [1]. Other countries, such as Sweden, Russia, Switzerland, and Austria, began to share in these developments by 1900.

Technology and trade

European industrialization rested upon the application of a technology pioneered in Britain but made use of more advanced techniques. The Bessemer process for making steel, invented in 1856, enabled the cheap production of a material stronger than iron. Steelmaking from the phosphoric ores common in Europe was made possible by the Thomas-Gilchrist process after 1878. Cheap steel could be used for machinery, shipbuilding, and many other items of general use and provided the basis for the rapid expansion of engineering industries. By 1900, with scientific research into chemical and electrical phenomena, other new industries appeared. The first electrical apparatus and industrial chemicals began to emerge, especially in Germany. Development of the internal-combustion engine was well under way by 1900, and refinements in mechanical engineering provided the impetus for a flood of labor-saving products ranging from sewing machines and vacuum cleaners to typewriters.

Trade expanded rapidly during the late nineteenth century, facilitated by the increasing use of iron and steel steamships. Imperialism stimulated the search for new markets and raw materials, but the bulk of trade occurred between European and American markets. Cheap foodstuffs from North America after 1870 played an important part in reducing European food prices while at the same time depressing local ag-

CONNECTIONS

See also

1220 The early Industrial Revolution
1236 The Industrial Revolution
1298 Europe 1870–1914
1278 The United States: Reconstruction to World War I
1280 The impact of steam
1302 Causes of World War I
1262 European imperialism in the 19th century
1286 Russia in the 19th century
1296 Origins of modern architecture

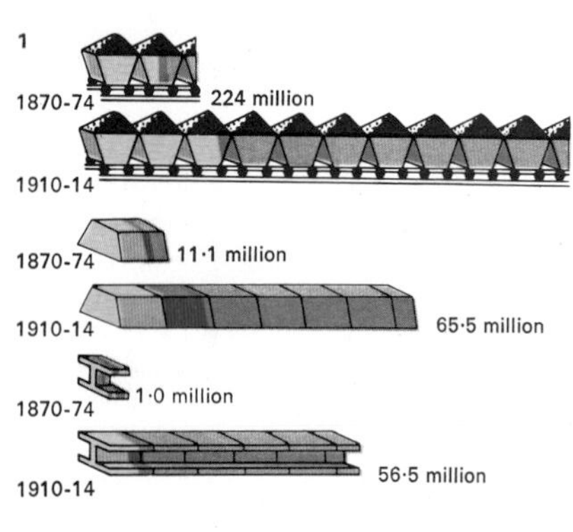

1
1870-74
224 million
1910-14
1,035 million
1870-74
11·1 million
1910-14
65·5 million
1870-74
1·0 million
1910-14
56·5 million
Coal 100 million tons
Iron 10 million tons
Steel 10 million tons
Great Britain
France
Germany
United States

1 Industrial output rose rapidly in the latter half of the 19th century, aided by advances in engineering and financial expertise. The 1878 Gilchrist process to make steel from phosphoric iron enabled France and Germany to base industrial expansion on vast ore deposits. This diagram shows average yearly production in 1870–74 and 1910–14.

2 Opera houses such as that of Vienna were part of an impressive urban culture created by the growing wealth of many European cities, which built concert halls, art galleries, and museums together with municipal buildings and better systems of sanitation, lighting, and street paving. Improved housing for better-off workers and the middle classes led to the first suburbs and mass transport.

3

	1850 Country	1850 Town	1870 Country	1870 Town	1890 Country	1890 Town
Britain	40%	60%	30%	70%	28%	72%
France	75%	25%	69%	31%	63%	37%
Germany	73%	27%	61%	39%	53%	47%

3 A population shift from the country to the cities proceeded rapidly as industrialization spread. In 1850, except for Britain, nearly three-quarters of Europe's people still lived on the land. But as Germany industrialized, its population ratio began to alter in the direction of Britain's—a trend followed by France toward the end of the century.

4 London celebrated the relief of Mafeking in 1900 during the Boer War with an outburst of national pride fueled by widespread reporting of the war in the popular press. The rise of mass newspapers helped to create a powerful and excitable public opinion in the last decades of the century, when widely supported imperial adventures and colonial rivalry gave birth to Jingoism expressed in bellicose literature, spirited demonstrations, and songs.

5 The bicycle was the first luxury consumer product to gain a mass market. Heavily promoted by colorful advertisements such as this 1896 Toulouse-Lautrec poster, it was sold in such numbers that manufacturers realized a huge new market had been suddenly created. Other mass-produced goods developed through advances in engineering and metallurgy, including sewing machines, phonographs, typewriters, and automobiles.

PARIS-BREST
1891
CH.TERRONT

riculture in the "Great Depression" of the 1890s. Established industries were also exposed to fluctuations with the rise of competing industrial economies. To protect their newly established industries, France and Germany imposed tariffs. A more complex economic structure emerged with large trusts and cartels grouping related industries into large combines; joint stock companies supplanted many family firms, and banking and investment institutions became more sophisticated. By 1914, London was the financial center of the world, controlling much of the existing shipping, insurance, and investment.

Far-reaching social changes

Industrial development and the continued growth of Europe's population associated with European urbanization [7] brought fundamental social changes. There was a great increase in middle-class wealth, often derived from investment in stocks and shares [8]. But even the poorest classes benefited from rising real wages. Urban living conditions in Europe were often harsh and difficult but were improving at record rates. Social welfare measures began to be adopted by some states, as in Bismarck's Germany, and philanthropy in countries such as Britain provided some relief for the most deprived. Emigration was widespread from the poorest countries, especially Ireland, Russia, and the Austro-Hungarian Empire. Most migrants went to North America, although some went to British colonies, Australia in particular.

An advance in living standards by 1900 was reflected in the emergence of the first aspects of mass consumer society [Key]. The rise of cheap newspapers, widespread advertising and selling of consumer goods such as bicycles [5], and the growth of mass entertainment in sports, music halls, and vacation excursions showed that the working classes were beginning to enjoy some of the fruits of industrialization. This was certainly the case with the large middle-class families [6] who gave the latter part of the nineteenth century a somewhat staid character that belied the changes at work in society.

KEY

MARKS & SPENCER
ORIGINAL PENNY BAZAAR
ADMISSION FREE

Growing wealth for all sections of society in the late 19th century led to the first mass consumer market with the development of advertising and the growth of chain stores, among them Marks & Spencer, which opened a "penny bazaar" in Manchester, England in the 1890s.

6

6 Victorian families of all classes tended to be large because of a high birthrate and declining mortality due to improved medical care, diet, and general living standards. Among poorer sections of the community infant deaths from infectious diseases continued to be high, and there were usually more pregnancies than surviving children. But upper-class family life was based on large units with many servants as well as children. Two or three servants were a bare minimum for a solid middle-class family. In the aristocratic households of the great country estates it was not unusual to find over 100 house servants, kitchen staff, and gardeners. The rambling Victorian house was often a viable living unit only when it could be maintained by numerous staff.

7

Pankow
Weissensee
Lichtenberg
Charlottenburg
Friedrichsfelde
Wilmersdorf
Schöneberg
Neukölln
Tempelhof
Old town center and villages
Expansion to 1860
Expansion to 1900

7 The growth of Berlin was typical of many 19th-century cities. Up to 1860 its expansion was mainly around the old city center, but with the growth of the German state and the development of Berlin as a capital city and industrial center, it grew into a major European metropolis. As with many other cities Berlin's rising population spread out to create surrounding suburbs, incorporating villages that had once been separate.

8

1% total population over 25 years old
Proportion of total capital

Income below £100	87·2
£100 – £1,000	9·4
£1,000 – £5,000	2·3
£5,000 – £10,000	0·4
£10,000 – £25,000	0·5
£25,000+	0·2

8 Much of the wealth created by the Industrial Revolution was concentrated in the hands of the upper classes. In Britain, in 1911, a tiny group of extremely wealthy industrialists and aristocrats still disposed of a large share of the national income; a growing proportion was held by lesser industrialists and professional men.

Russia in the 19th century

In Russia, since the time of Peter the Great (1672–1725), fundamental reforms have followed in the wake of war. For many years after the Crimean War (1854–56) [1], Russia was not regarded as a friendly power by Britain and France. Despite the fact that Russia had the largest land forces on the continent of Europe, this war showed that it was no match for the Anglo-French alliance and that its effort to insulate itself from the political changes in the rest of Europe had proved to be a source of weakness rather than of strength. Finally, its economy and social order could not withstand the strains of the war. Russia, if it wished to regain its position as a leading European power, had to imitate the Western powers and adopt their forms of government.

The emancipation of the serfs

Alexander II (1818–81), who came to the throne in 1855, was willing to introduce reforms. He warned the nobility that if reform did not come from above it would come from below. In February 1861 the Emancipation Act was issued. The act ensured personal freedom for millions of peasants and introduced the elective *zemstvo*, an organ of local government.

Other major reforms followed: in 1864 equality before the law, trial by jury, and independence of courts and judges were introduced; legislation of 1863 and 1864 broadened the basis of education; the 1870 government act set up new municipal institutions; the 1874 army reforms established the principle of universal military service and reduced actual service from 25 years to six. But the peasants were still subject to customary law and had special courts; their freedom of movement was limited, and they still paid poll taxes.

The emancipation disappointed most of the peasants and their supporters. The population increased from 70 million in 1863 to 155 million in 1913 (excluding Finland and Poland), increasing rural poverty. Migration eased the problem slightly, but the problem of land hunger was exacerbated by the failure to introduce modern agricultural methods, obstructed by the communal system of land ownership. Peasant dissatisfaction also stemmed from the poor land that they were allotted and the high level of repayments they were forced to pay the government to compensate the former owners of the land.

Seeds of revolution

Alexander's reforms were viewed as inadequate by the growing class of educated persons. In their disillusionment these people turned increasingly to nihilism. The nihilists believed that the existing order could not be successfully reformed, and in Russia they contributed significantly to the tradition of revolutionary political movements. During the 1870s a more positive populism [5] or agrarian socialism developed, which glorified the peasant as the repository of pure, untainted wisdom. Those who were educated felt that they owed a debt of gratitude to the toilers who had made it possible.

Agrarian populism was difficult to convert into political action, and the onset of industrialization in the late 1880s and the boom of the 1890s made it less relevant.

CONNECTIONS

See also
1178 Early modern Russia
1310 The Russian Revolution
1312 The Soviet Union under Stalin
1232 European empires in the 19th century
1288 Political thought in the 19th century
1300 Europe 1870–1914
1302 Balkanization and Slav nationalism

1

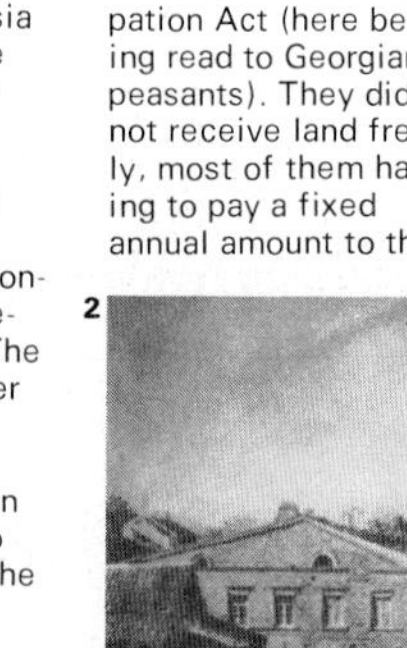

1 Following the capture of Sevastopol and its defeat in the Crimean War, Russia became little more than a second-rate power. Britain and France had turned against Russia and exposed the backwardness of its economy and the brittleness of its army. The new tsar, Alexander II, was convinced that Russia had to imitate the Western powers if it was to beat them, and so he favored reforms.

2

2 Peasants received insufficient land as a result of the Emancipation Act (here being read to Georgian peasants). They did not receive land freely, most of them having to pay a fixed annual amount to the state, which in turn compensated the landlords with state bonds. Repayments were to extend over 49 years and were higher than the market value of the land warranted. The result was that the peasants had less land than before, in fact, about 20% less in total – 23% of this in the black earth lands and 31% in the Ukraine. Former state and crown peasants received the best terms.

3

3 The execution of terrorists who planned the assassination of Tsar Alexander II by a bomb in March 1881, in the hope that the whole imperial edifice would collapse, sums up the impotence of revolutionary politics in 19th-century Russia. The acute disappointment felt by the peasants and intelligentsia after the Emancipation Act led to pessimism concerning the ability of the system to reform itself from above. Many radicals, known as populists or agrarian socialists, believed the peasantry would rise en masse and sweep away the hated autocracy. Some believed in the gradual awakening of peasant consciousness, molded by radical idealists. Others were unwilling to wait and adopted terrorist methods.

4 Georgi Plekhanov (1857–1918), the father of Russian Marxism, started his political life as a populist. He opposed terrorism but had to flee the country to Switzerland in 1880 during a wave of political repression and did not return to Russia until 1917. A brilliant writer, his influence within Russia in the 1890s was immense. He initially supported Lenin, but later opposed him.

5 Populism became the leading philosophical attitude in the 1870s. Its most significant leader was Peter Lavrov (1823–1900). Populism rejected the industrial Revolution and favored rural life.

4

5

Marxism, placing its faith not in the rural worker but in the urban, industrial worker, became a doctrine more in tune with contemporary Russian conditions. The Social Democratic party, the forerunner of the Communist party, emerged, although it still appealed for the most part to intellectuals rather than to the working classes.

After several attempts, the terrorist wing of the populist movement finally succeeded in assassinating Alexander II. But instead of collapsing as expected, the autocracy struck back at its opponents.

The end of the era

Alexander III (1845–94) who came to the throne in 1881, was ultra-reactionary. His policies reversed many of the liberal reforms of his father and began a tradition of conflict between the *zemstvos* and central government that came to a head in the disturbances of 1905. The succession in 1894 of Nicholas II (1868–1918) [8] occurred at a time of rapid economic advance [6]. The dynamic thrust of Sergei Witte (1849–1915), minister of finance from 1892–1903, kept the economy moving until the first years of the twentieth century. Then harvest failures and industrial crises produced civil unrest. The revolution of 1905–06 shook the autocracy to its foundations [10]. It could be suppressed only when the war against Japan had been lost and troops were released for internal duties.

The years 1903–13 were a golden era for industry and agriculture, and this helped the government, led by Peter Stolypin (1862–1911) [9], to resist the growing demands for political and social reforms, which were voiced in the Duma (a parliament forced on the tsar by the crisis of 1905) by the Social Democratic and Kadet (liberal) parties. Thwarted in the Far East, Russia turned after 1906 toward the Balkans where, throughout the nineteenth century, it had supported Slav states against the decaying Ottoman Empire. But the Great Powers stepped in and blocked Russia's progress to the Mediterranean. Austria-Hungary was the main rival power in the Balkans, and therefore Russia felt obliged to support Serbia against the empire in August 1914.

KEY

Servile labor was typical of the life of millions of Russians in the 19th century, but with industrial development and the population explosion, many changes occurred. There were 412,000 barge haulers on the Volga in 1830, but by 1851 this number had been reduced to 150,000. The steamship had gradually replaced them. There were approximately 40 million peasants (80% of the population) in Russia on the eve of emancipation, and about half were in personal bondage to the gentry. Their plight dominated economic life.

6

6 In the 1890s the industrial development of Russia was improved by the opening up of new oil fields, including this one at Baku. Russia was the world's largest producer of oil until 1900, when the United States took the lead. Railroad building was another dynamic force; by 1874 there were 11,320 miles (18,220km) of railroads. A by-product of this was Russia's emergence as a major grain exporter. From the 1880s the state began to play an important role in the economy. Development was concentrated in railroad construction and in heavy industry.

7

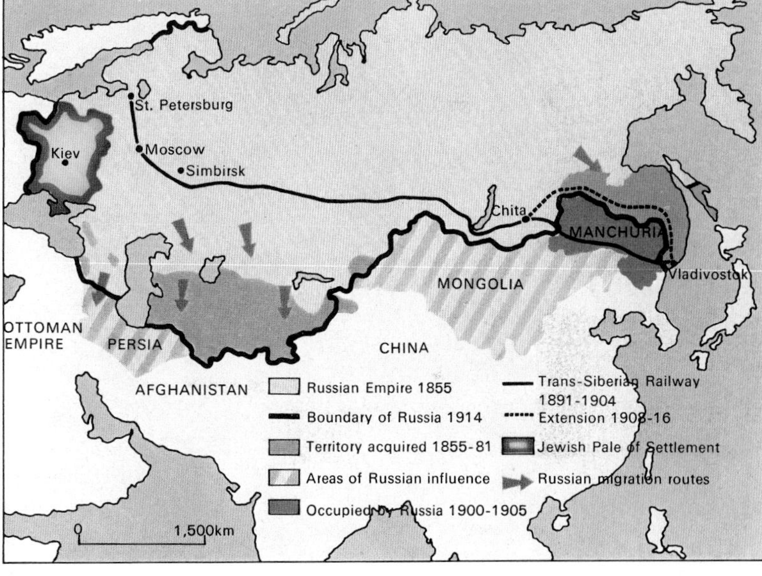
St. Petersburg
Kiev
Moscow
Simbirsk
Chita
MANCHURIA
Vladivostok
MONGOLIA
OTTOMAN EMPIRE
PERSIA
CHINA
AFGHANISTAN
Russian Empire 1855
Boundary of Russia 1914
Territory acquired 1855-81
Areas of Russian influence
Occupied by Russia 1900-1905
Trans-Siberian Railway 1891-1904
Extension 1908-16
Jewish Pale of Settlement
Russian migration routes
1,500km

7 Russia's imperial advance was spectacular in the late 19th century. It colonized central Asia and acquired territory that the Chinese now claim as their own. Russia's population explosion caused seven million peasants to move eastward and cross the Urals. Meanwhile, two million Jews emigrated to the United States and 200,000 more to Britain between 1880 and 1914. The trans-Siberian Railroad (built between 1891 and 1904) made a more active policy feasible in the Far East—that is, toward Japan—with the secondary aim of securing an ice-free port on the Pacific. Russia's eastward push and its influence in Manchuria alarmed the Japanese to the point of their going to war in 1904–5. Russia also greatly extended its influence on its southern borders.

8

8 The last of the Romanovs, Nicholas II, was a reluctant tsar. He came to the throne in 1894 as a very young man. His mind lacked the cutting edge necessary to evolve a coherent policy and to see it through. Although Russia changed rapidly during his reign, he did not move with the times and listened instead to reactionaries. Among them was the monk Rasputin (1871–1916), whose great influence was destructive. Here Nicholas [center left] is seen with the Prince of Wales [far right].

9

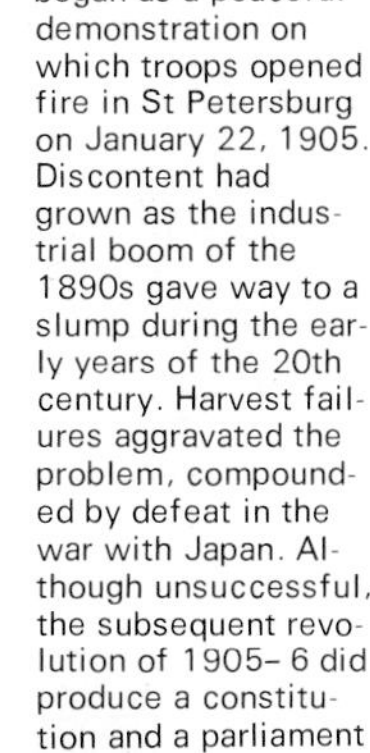

9 An outstanding statesman, Peter Stolypin's main achievement was to introduce agrarian reforms. He swept away the communes and encouraged individual property holdings, but his autocratic methods lost him liberal support.

10

10 "Bloody Sunday" began as a peaceful demonstration on which troops opened fire in St Petersburg on January 22, 1905. Discontent had grown as the industrial boom of the 1890s gave way to a slump during the early years of the 20th century. Harvest failures aggravated the problem, compounded by defeat in the war with Japan. Although unsuccessful, the subsequent revolution of 1905–6 did produce a constitution and a parliament (Duma).

European political thought in the 19th century

In the mid-nineteenth century most people with any political awareness would almost certainly have described themselves as either "liberals" or "conservatives." The conservatives would have had little difficulty in explaining what they were and what they stood for, namely, the established order. They were firmly against radical change and followed the line laid down by Edmund Burke (1729–97) in his *Reflections on the Revolution in France,* published in 1790. This insisted that state and people alike were products of imperceptible, natural, and organic growth and that artificial change based on general theories was self-defeating.

In the realm of practical politics, however, it was not quite so easy to preach and practice conservatism—particularly after the fall of the Austrian statesman Prince Metternich (1773–1859) in the revolution of 1848. Metternich refused to concede that any kind of change was permissible, if only as a tactical maneuver to prevent more radical developments, and was ultimately obliged to take refuge in England.

Metternich's downfall was one of the factors that encouraged the British prime minister, the astute Benjamin Disraeli (1804–81), to present the country with a Second Reform Bill. Meanwhile, in Germany, Prince Otto von Bismarck (1815–98) introduced universal suffrage and limited social welfare legislation. In France, Napoleon III (1808–73) began similar action.

The decline of liberalism

Liberals were distinguished by the belief that progress could be achieved by means of "free institutions." In Britain and France this usually referred to a freely elected parliament, with ministries responsible to it, an independent judiciary, freedom of speech and religion, freedom from arbitrary arrest, and freedom to acquire property.

In Russia a liberal might merely be someone who advocated a strong state council to advise the tsar. But even in France there were liberals, including François Guizot (1787–1874), the statesman and historian, who believed that institutions were already as free as possible.

One of the most interesting themes of nineteenth-century European history is the decline of liberalism as a real political force. The main reason for the collapse was that, although the liberal ideal of making a framework of free institutions was born of the Enlightenment, once erected it became a bastion behind which the propertied classes defended their vested interests. The Continental turmoil of 1848 saw middle-class liberals deserting their ideals when faced with the prospect of sharing power with the lower paid and less educated.

The rise of socialism

The creed that began to appeal to many of those apparently abandoned by liberalism was socialism, and the greatest socialist thinker of the century was without doubt Karl Marx (1818–83) [Key]. The young Marx of the first half of the century drew his ideas from a wide variety of sources, but the foundation of his beliefs was the conviction, derived from the German philosopher Georg Hegel (1770–1831), that history was progressive, had objective meaning, and

CONNECTIONS

See also
1290 Masters of sociology
1184 The Enlightenment
1222 Origins of romanticism
1224 The French Revolution
1236 The Industrial Revolution
1248 The revolutions of 1848
1250 German and Italian unification
1326 Socialism in the West
1302 Balkanization and Slav nationalism
1334 The rise of fascism

1 Appalling social conditions existed in 19th-century Europe as a result of the development and concentration of industry and a boom in population. By 1848 the "social question" was causing concern. Neither governments nor individuals did much to tackle the problem. The Chartism reform movement emerged as a force in Britain, while in Europe the old spirit of revolution was again showing signs of revival. But in the long term, a steady if slow increase in living standards was brought about not by political organization and agitation, but by the unexpected growth of the economy in the following years.

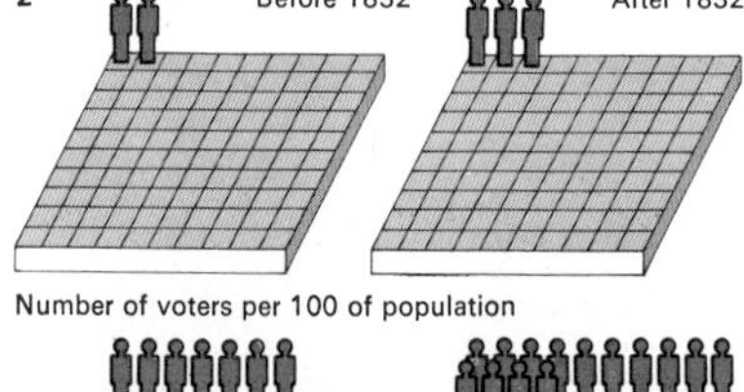

2
Before 1832
After 1832
Number of voters per 100 of population
After 1867
After 1884

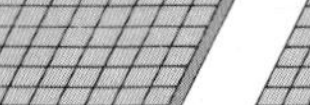

2 A new British electoral system was created between 1832 and 1885, based on a series of Reform Acts. The result was that by 1886 two-thirds of the adult male population in England and Wales, and three-fifths in Scotland, had the right to cast their votes in secret. The measures that brought this about were three Representation of the People acts, a Ballot Act, and two acts to redistribute the seats and prevent corruption.

FRIENDLY SOCIETY OF IRON AND STEEL FOUNDERS
OF GREAT BRITAIN & IRELAND
ESTABD FEBY 6 1809 AT BOLTON-LE-MOORS

3 The world's first trade unions were founded in Britain, where they were legalized in 1825. This was well in advance of other countries—trade unions were first tolerated in France in 1864 but not made legal until 1884, while Germany did not permit them until the 1890s. Membership of the early British unions such as the Friendly Society of Iron and Steel Founders was restricted to local skilled artisans. The first large union was the Amalgamated Society of Engineers, founded in 1851, but it had more interest in social benefits than in trade disputes. By 1875 unions were well established, and the laws on strikes, picketing, and contracts had been clarified.

4 Mikhail Bakunin (1814–76), a Russian aristocrat, resigned his commission in the Imperial Guard to become Europe's leading anarchist. Not surprisingly his life was eventful: he was sentenced to death by the Austrians and the Prussians and was sent to Siberia by his own country. He escaped in 1861 and spent the rest of his life advancing anarchism in western Europe. He believed that society could only be overthrown through individual revolt.

would reveal this meaning through a series of revolutionary jumps.

The *Communist Manifesto* of 1848 reflected Marx's faith in the success of the European revolutions of that year, but with their ultimate failure he laid more stress on the deterministic aspects of his thought. He predicted that bourgeois society would collapse as a result of its own internal contradictions. Capital, he said, would become concentrated in fewer hands until the oppressed workers would be forced to revolt against their exploiters. A "dictatorship of the proletariat" would then emerge, paving the way for such social harmony that the state could wither away. The Paris Commune [7] revived his faith in revolutionary activity, and in the 1870s he even toyed with the possibility of a peaceful overthrow of the social system through the vote of a fully enfranchised proletariat.

The development of nationalism

It was not the thoughts of Marx, however, that dominated the nineteenth century. By far the greatest force was nationalism.

In 1815 nationalism was still weak in Europe, but only 45 years later the philosopher and economist John Stuart Mill (1806–73) was to write that it was "in general a necessary condition of free institutions that the boundaries of government should coincide in the main with those of nationalities."

Meanwhile, nationalism had developed in many ways. The German philosopher Johann Herder (1744–1803) had insisted before the end of the eighteenth century that men's minds were conditioned by their cultural environment and, especially, by their language. Other thinkers took up this theme at the beginning of the new century and subsequently gave rise to many linguistic revivals. European scholars compiled dictionaries and grammars; folk songs and folk poetry were collected; national histories were written. This in turn stimulated political demands, and national wars radically redrew the map of Europe. The rest of the world did not escape: frustrated nationalism led to adventures overseas and the great wave of imperialism.

KEY

Karl Marx was the father of modern socialism. His political views are outlined in the *Communist Manifesto,* his views on political economy appear in the major word, *Das Kapital.*

5 "The Republic," a symbolic painting by Daumier (1808–79), shows the idealism often attributed to such government. Before the French Revolution republics were considered as legitimate as any monarchy, but after 1815 they went out of fashion, and Europe grew more monarchical. As new states such as Belgium, Greece, Romania, and Bulgaria were created, so too were new monarchies. Although monarchy was no longer divine, it was the system of government most comprehensible to the ordinary man. It was argued that only monarchy could unite all groups and all classes. Even France was little different. It was ruled by kings or emperors for most of the century, and the Third Republic was established by one vote in 1875 as the regime that "divided Frenchmen least."

5

6

6 The Geneva Convention of 1864 established the International Red Cross. This was a humane reaction to the suffering of soldiers in the wars of the 1850s but also reflected concern about the problems of war itself. Other aspects of this were the continuing attempts to regulate war by law and the strength of the international pacifist movements. Peace congresses were held frequently from the middle of the century onward. By 1900 there was a belief current in Europe that some genuine progress had been made toward achieving permanent peace.

7

7 Napoleon's statue was overturned in 1871 to signal the founding of the Paris Commune, one of the significant events of 19th-century Europe. Socialists saw it as a vindication of their belief that only by resorting to force could workers hope to overthrow the rule of the bourgeoisie. Yet the truth, in retrospect, is more complex, and it must be conceded that national and sectional interests were involved in the tragedy. Paris had declared itself independent of the rest of France and had to be brought back into line before peace with Prussia was possible. The end of the Commune brought vengeance and bloodshed: 20,000 were killed and 50,000 arrested.

Masters of sociology

The development of sociology in nineteenth-century Europe was stimulated by the need to understand the birth of industrial society [1]. The traditional agrarian social order, apparently based on the squire and the church, was in the process of dissolution. In its place a new order was emerging, whose symbols were the factory and the vast, anonymous urban proletariat [2]. A previously integrated structure of culture and authority was giving way to a series of sharply differentiated economic cultures and to class warfare. In this atmosphere of frightening uncertainty, intellectuals began to search for explanations of what was happening to society.

The British tradition

In Great Britain the path of industrialization generally caused little concern. Until the end of the century most Englishmen felt that the factory represented an unequivocal force for good, which was moving their society toward perfection. This largely unquestioning acceptance of the notion of "progress" meant that Britain produced no original sociological theory. Indeed, the main British theoretical tradition was inherited uncritically from the optimistic Enlightenment of the previous century. Its tenets were that society consisted of autonomous individuals, each of whom was naturally good; that an "invisible hand" lay behind human activity and pushed it toward the level where the individual could express his innate goodness; and that social science should proceed by reason to discover the objective laws by which the hand worked and so facilitate its operation.

The one man who added something new to these ideas was Herbert Spencer (1820–1903) [3C] who recognized that the orthodox interpretation of society assumed but did not explain change. Spencer, however, did not abandon the ideas of the Enlightenment but regarded them in relation to a model of social change owing much to Darwin's *Origin of Species*. He argued that societies were driven forward to more complex and higher forms by the struggle for survival between individuals, and that the struggle had produced in Britain a laissez-faire industrial society, which was as yet the highest social form.

The French tradition

In France, the aftermath of the Revolution produced a reaction against Enlightenment thinking. The vicomte de Bonald (1754–1840) argued that society ought to be seen not as a collection of individuals but as an organic whole. Any individual was bound to upset the entire organism.

The organic tradition was continued by Auguste Comte (1798–1857) [3B], not only to order and control change but also to understand it. Comte held the Enlightenment view that there were objective, discoverable laws of social progress. But he insisted that these laws operated in the context of whole societies and not individuals. People, through their conditioning in society, were made by laws they could not alter; they should see this and accept their place.

Comte's positivism was most highly refined by one of the most influential figures in sociology, Emile Durkheim (1858–1917), who systematically laid out the subject mat-

CONNECTIONS

See also
1288 Political thought in the 19th century
1326 Socialism in the West
1360 20th-century sociology and its influence
1248 The revolutions of 1848
1284 European industrialization 1870–1914
1186 Exploration and science 1750–1850
1184 The Enlightenment
1238 The novel in the 19th century
850 Religion and the plight of modern man
888 Structure of societies
890 Conflict, power, and social inequality

Sources of 19th century social thought

French Enlightenment
Kant
De Bonald
Herder
Hegel
Comte
Darwin
Spencer
Marx
Durkheim
Weber
Reaction against
British
French
German

1 The common origin of European sociology was the Enlightenment. Different national traditions reacted to the Enlightenment inheritance in different ways. The only British innovation was Spencer's adaptation of Darwin's model of biological evolution to provide explanations of social change. In France, however, the conservative reaction to the French Revolution rejected atomistic models of society (centered on the individual) and questioned the validity of empirical inquiry (based on experience). But with Auguste Comte, Enlightenment empiricism was brought back into French sociology. In Germany, Kant and Hegel added new insights to these ideas. Man was no longer seen as an object moved around by impersonal laws and social forces: his own consciousness created the relationships in which he participated.

2 The Industrial Revolution dramatically changed the environment of European society. Millions of people were crowded into filthy, disease-ridden towns and were obliged to move to the new social and economic rhythms of factory labor. The obvious horror of mid-19th century urban life, illustrated by this Manchester, England slum interior, caught the attention of many early sociologists—Frederich Engels (1820–95) for example—and produced some of the first exercises in applied sociology. Sociologists surveyed specific situations in the hope of solving major problems.

3 Major 19th-century sociologists included Max Weber [A], who attempted to combine empiricism and neo-Kantianism in his *Protestant Ethic and the Spirit of Capitalism* (1905). Auguste Comte's [B] doctrine of positivism (the organization of all knowledge into a consistent philosophy) is contained in *Système de Politique Positive* (1851–54). Herbert Spencer [C], amalgamated atomistic sociology and Darwinian evolution in *The Principles of Ethics* (1879–93).

ter of sociology and provided a method for its analysis. The distinctive characteristics of French sociology included "methodological collectivism," which studied only phenomena that would reveal how men and women were conditioned by their society. There were also functional explanations whereby social institutions were described in terms of their functions within the entire social system rather than by their history. Finally, there was an emphasis on the need for order where change was regarded as the result of a malfunction in society.

The German tradition

In Germany the inheritance of Enlightenment rationality was joined by two other intellectual elements. The Kantian philosophical revolution (after Immanuel Kant [1724–1804]) held that the laws of nature exist only in men's minds, and the Romantic movement of Johann Herder (1744–1803) stressed the creative importance of language and culture.

The first great German sociological theorist was G. W. F. Hegel (1770–1831), who saw social change as the product of human reason driven forward by its need to know and overcome the world around it. Hegel's theme was further developed by Karl Marx (1818–83) [4], who is perhaps best seen as a sociological Hegelian. Marx shared Hegel's view that the force behind social change was man's pursuit of rational understanding and control of his environment. But Marx's most important sociology resulted from his belief in the economic basis of social structure and in his suggestion of a sequence of social development.

The third major German theorist was Max Weber (1864–1920) [3A], who complemented Marx by adding an appreciation of the role of cultural values to Marx's work.

The principal achievements of the German tradition were "methodological individualism:" an approach to society from the viewpoint of self-conscious human subjects, a combination of explanations from history and explanations from function, and the development of a theory of knowledge of the social sciences.

KEY

These men on strike in 1889 at the East and West India Company's docks in London symbolize the class and culture conflict produced by industrialization, which sociologists of the period tried to understand. It aggravated the division of culture along class lines and led to strife in every nation.

4

Primitive
Patriarchal
Feudal
Capitalist
Socialist

4 Karl Marx argued that human society developed in response to man's desire to satisfy his material needs. But needs themselves continued to develop. Eventually the prevailing form of social structure would no longer be able to accommodate these growing needs and would break down, giving way to a new structure that permitted the continuation of need satisfaction. The final stage would be reached when bourgeois capitalism succeeded in concentrating wealth in a few hands and in impoverishing the masses. The starving proletariat, whose basic needs were not being met, would rise up and take over the means of production and create a society in which the forces of production and the social structure were no longer in conflict.

5
A

B

PARIS

5 The interpretation of the European revolutions of 1848 and 1870 brought out the different perspectives of French, English, and German sociology. For the French, the revolutions (particularly the Commune of 1870 [A]) represented evidence of a deep-seated malfunction in society. For the British, they represented the just struggle of European society for individual, bourgeois freedoms against the tyranny of anachronistic, feudal governments. For the German Marxists, the revolutions were a sign of the imminent destruction of the whole capitalist order. The cartoon [B] shows French President Thiers (1797–1877) with a Prussian soldier looking down on the boiling cauldron of Paris.

The development of archeology

Man's interest in his remote past began with the Renaissance, although the urge to know about one's ancestors is an ancient one. For instance, Nabonidus, last king of Babylon, excavated the foundation stone of a temple 3,200 years earlier than his reign to find out how old it was.

The knowledge of the Renaissance

During the Renaissance two things stimulated study of the past. The texts of classical authors, such as Lucretius' *On the Nature of Things*, became widely disseminated by the printing press, so that their discussion of earlier ages and of the evolution of society from savagery through barbarism into civilization was firmly implanted in the educated minds of the time. Secondly, the age of exploration revealed the New World of America, where a Stone Age technology was still in active use, where the civilization of the Aztec was just developing bronze.

The Renaissance tradition spread from Italy northward to France and England, and collecting Greek and Roman statues and vases became a fashionable occupation for those wealthy enough to afford it. As the middle classes achieved classical educations in the grammar schools, but lacked the financial resources to collect or go on the Grand Tour, their attention turned to the antiquities of their own region. In the work of such men as John Leland (*c.* 1506–52) and William Camden (1551–1623) [1], the English antiquarian tradition was born in the sixteenth century, continuing to develop through the seventeenth with such notable figures as John Aubrey (1626–97), Thomas Browne (1605–82), and later William Stukeley (1687–1765). These men began to record all local monuments and traditions.

Developments in Scandinavia

In Scandinavia the work of Johan Bure in Sweden and Ole Worm (1588–1644) in Denmark in the first half of the seventeenth century led to a parallel development, with more state involvement and a greater degree of protection being extended to antiquities. Such a systematic attitude appeared in England following the creation of the Royal Society in 1660.

The period of the Enlightenment saw speculation on the social origins of man, and from the stimulus of John Locke (1632–1704) the French and Scottish schools of thought evolved the notion of social typology (the study of types) and the development of society from the family through the band and the tribe to civilized urban groups with kings. This idea, itself a revival of classical thought, was later to prove crucial in the emergence of social anthropology under Edward Tylor (1832–1917) and Lewis Morgan (1818–81) in the late nineteenth century.

In the latter part of the eighteenth century evidence accumulated to show that the earth was very old, much older than the biblical date for its creation of 4004 BC. From the work of the geologist James Hutton (1726–97) in 1785 to the publication of the *Principles of Geology* by Charles Lyell (1797–1875) in 1833, a revolution in thought occurred in which the earth was recognized as immensely old and biblical chronology as wrong [Key]. In 1859 the Royal Society in London heard two of its most distinguished members accept the antiquity of man, and

CONNECTIONS

See also
1160 Science and technology 1500–1700
1184 The Enlightenment
1130 The Renaissance: humanism
1186 Exploration and science 1750–1850
964 Minoan civilization 2500–1400 BC
998 Greek literature and theater
972 Egypt: 1570 BC to Alexander the Great
1120 Colombia and Peru 300–1534
648 The first hominids
874 The study of man

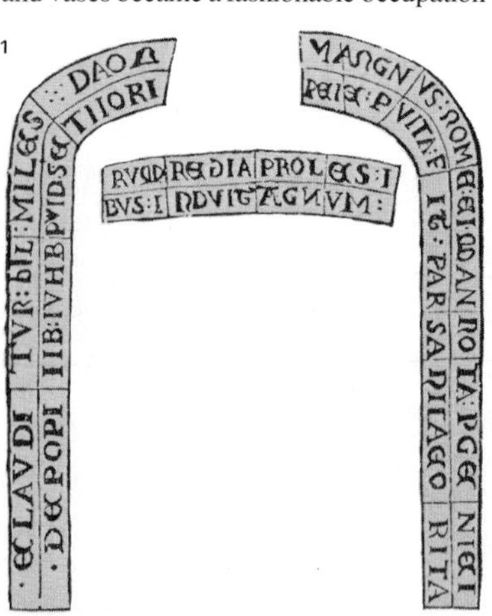

1 The earliest illustration of an archeological monument to appear in a book was a typographical arrangement depicting in a stylized manner the inscription to the hermit Magnus, a prince from Scandinavia. This still exists outside a church in Sussex, England. The illustration appeared in the late 16th century in the second edition of William Camden's famous *Britannia*, the first serious work in English on the subject of antiquities.

2 Stonehenge, in Wiltshire, is an outstanding megalithic monument that has long been one of the most notable and controversial sites in Britain. King James I sent Inigo Jones (1573–1652) to draw plans of it, and Jones's account, describing it as a Roman temple, was published in the 1660s, setting off a violent argument in which it was ascribed by various scholars to the Danes, Saxons, Druids, and ancient Britons. The first of these views shows the influence of contemporary Scandinavian scholars. In the late 17th century it was attributed to the Druids, although it is much older than this.

3 The great mound at Grave Creek, Miss., was excavated in the mid-19th century, more than 50 years after President Jefferson had undertaken a similar excavation in Virginia. A great stimulus to American archeology was the presence of Stone Age Indians.

4 Hissarlik in Turkey was claimed by Heinrich Schliemann as the site of Homer's Troy. Schliemann was obsessed with uncovering the Homeric world and in the 1870s and 1880s excavated at Mycenae and Ithaca as well as Troy. At Hissarlik he uncovered a collection of Bronze Age jewelry, which he claimed was "Priam's Treasure" and which he smuggled out of Turkey. He thought the second of the seven superimposed settlements he excavated was Homer's Troy, but recent work dates it as too early.

in the same year Charles Darwin's *Origin of Species* raised new speculations as to where man had come from.

Discovery in the Middle East

The middle of the nineteenth century was also the period when the great Middle Eastern civilizations were discovered. Mesopotamia saw the work of Austen Layard (1817–94) in the 1840s at Nineveh and the fierce rivalry of French and British archeologists to loot the mounds of Assyrian and Babylonian sculpture. In the 1870s Heinrich Schliemann (1822–90) dug at Troy and Mycenae [4] and brought to the world the glories of Bronze Age Greece, a previously unknown civilization, the ancestor of which was uncovered at Knossos in Crete from 1900 onward.

The increased length of human history and the multitude of new discoveries of the prehistoric period were brought within a chronological scheme of successive Stone, Bronze, and Iron Ages. This was first applied to museum material by Christian Thomsen (1788–1865) in Copenhagen in 1816; it was subsequently proved stratigraphically by his successor Jens Worsaae (1821–85) and elaborated internally by the Swede Oscar Nontelius (1843–1921). The careers of these three men spanned a century, from 1816 to 1917, and Scandinavians were again influential in archeological thought.

A concern for better excavation methods to acquire archeological information was typified by Augustus Pitt-Rivers (1827–1900), who between 1880 and 1900 set a standard still unrivaled for comprehensive recording. At the same time in Egypt, Flinders Petrie (1853–1942) was trying to do the same thing under difficult conditions.

Petrie and Montelius both overlapped the careers of archeologists still alive in the 1970s, such as Mortimer Wheeler (1890–) [7], and in a sense the development of prehistoric studies that began with Gordon Childe (1892–1957) in the 1920s still continues. The ancestry of man has been pushed still further back in time under the impact of the work of Louis Leakey (1903–72) in Africa.

KEY

This flint hand ax, (top and side views shown) came from Suffolk, England. John Frere sent it to the Society of Antiquaries in 1797, suggesting that it had a great age, "even beyond that of the known world." Frere's attitude reflected contemporary speculation about man's antiquity.

5

5 Howard Carter (1873–1939), right, directed the excavation of the tomb of Tutankhamen. In 1922 he located the entrance, cleared it, and discovered "wonderful things" inside after a long and frustrating campaign. Tutankhamen was a boy king who died when he was 18; the construction of later tombs above his own covered the entrance and preserved it from almost certain looting.

6

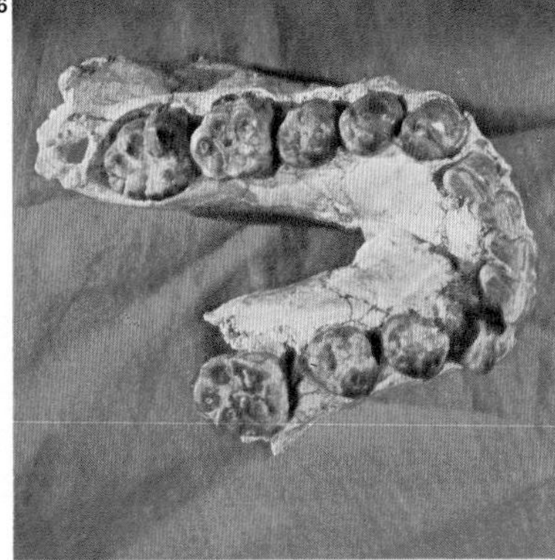

6 The jawbone of one of man's earliest ancestors, *Homo habilis*, was found at Olduvai Gorge in Tanzania by Louis and Mary Leakey. Their work there and the later extension of it to Lake Rudolf by their son Richard has taken the ancestry of man back (in less than 20 years) from under one million to nearly five million years. "Handy man" was found to be nearly 1.75 million years old.

7

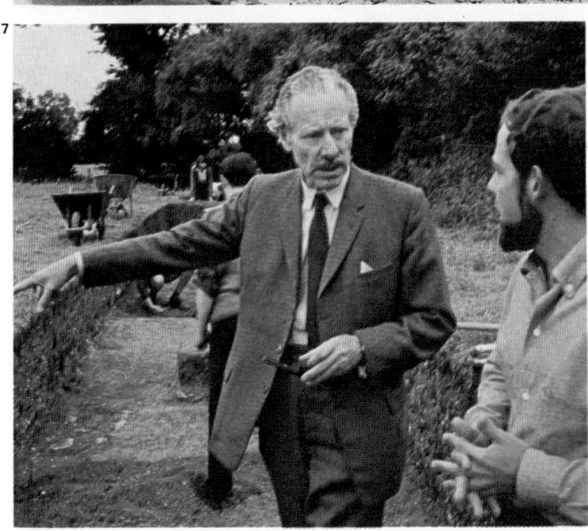

7 Mortimer Wheeler has worked on sites from Roman Wales to the mysterious Indus civilization in Pakistan. He was also the founder of the Institute of Archeology at London University and has done much to make archeology popular.

8

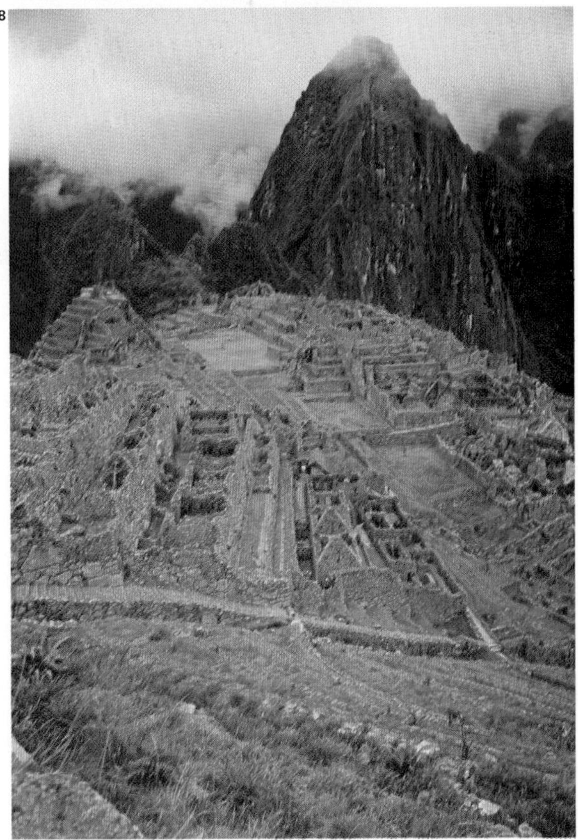

8 The Incan city of Machu Picchu, high in the Andes, was discovered in 1912 by Hiram Bingham (1875–1956) of Yale University. It was the first time that a late Inca settlement in such a good state of preservation had been found by archeologists.

Fauvism and Expressionism

The technique of "divisionism" or "pointillism," meaning the building-up of a composition with a multitude of colored points that merge in the eye of the spectator to produce the required color, was pioneered by Georges Seurat (1859–91). Paul Signac (1863–1935) enlarged each point into a substantial block of paint so that there was no longer any question of such visual combination. In this way color began to lose its representational function.

Liberation of color

A different path to greater freedom of color was taken by the Pont Aven school, whose most important representatives were Paul Gauguin (1848–1903) [1] and Emile Bernard (1868–1941). They evolved a manner known as "cloisonnism," based on the enclosure of forms within black outlines that bore the entire burden of expressing the shape of the object and did away with the need for shading with light or dark.

The complete liberation of color from form, so that it could act autonomously, was the hallmark of the group of diverse French painters known as *Fauves* ("wild beasts") who exhibited together in 1905 at the Salon d'Automne. (This was founded in 1903 to give artists whose work was too radical for the established salons the chance to show their work in a suitably professional setting.)

The most gifted of the Fauves, Henri Matisse (1869–1954), superficially adopted the divisionist technique in his "Luxe, Calme, et Volupté" (1905), which Signac admired and bought. In fact though, Matisse was more concerned with the decorative possibilities of the style than with any scientific analysis of color.

He abandoned divisionism altogether and at the end of the decade received from wealthy patrons commissions that permitted him to work on a larger scale. He then produced compositions dominated by areas of flat, unbroken color of equal intensity [3], emphasizing the picture surface.

The most important of the other members of the group were André Derain (1880–1954) and Maurice Vlaminck (1876–1958). The influence of Signac is apparent in the fragmentation of their brushstrokes [2], although the mood of their paintings owes far more to Vincent Van Gogh (1853–90). At their best, their pictures have an intense emotional force rooted in the immediacy with which the spectator feels he has shared in their creation.

This desire to transmit emotion links these two painters with Expressionism; however, Expressionism is not a historically precise term like Fauvism. It covers a whole range of art that, broadly speaking, is more concerned with expression than beauty and distorts the subject to that end.

The most significant influences on twentieth-century Expressionism were van Gogh and the Norwegian Edvard Munch (1863–1944), with his powerful evocations of the psychological tensions that underlie modern life [Key].

The Brücke ("Bridge") group, founded in Dresden in 1905 and including Ludwig Kirchner (1880–1938) [4], Karl Schmidt-Rottluff (1884–), and Erich Heckel (1883–1970), were influenced by the stark, violent color of Fauvism, but the content of

CONNECTIONS

See also
1254 Impressionism
1294 Cubism and Futurism
1318 Abstract art

1 Paul Gauguin's "Taa Matete" (1893) simplifies reality into a colorful and decorative frieze. While the painter found stimulation in the life of Tahiti as a source of subject matter, this work stems stylistically from Egyptian art.

2 Fauve color is intense in Andre Derain's "The Pool of London" (1906), and its lack of concern for realism is particularly noticeable in the portrayal of a very gray and dull scene. The high viewpoint contributes to the flattening of space; hence the reduction of the picture to a pattern.

3 In Matisse's "Harmony in Red" (1908–09), a large scale decorative painting, the patterns on the wallpaper and the cloth are as important pictorially as the woman on the chair. The flatness of the composition is so extreme that the window has been taken for a picture.

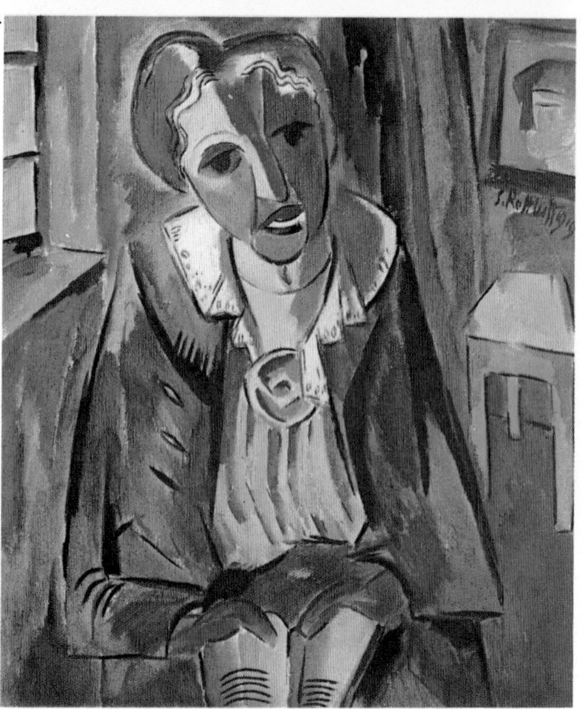

4 "Rose Shapiro" by Karl Schmidt-Rottluff uses certain Cubist conventions, such as geometrical forms and the stylization of facial features, to achieve a direct and pungent image unhampered by unnecessary detail. To suit his expressive purpose he also employs sharp perspective, as in the table. Raw impact is gained by the rough canvas showing through.

their art is fully Expressionist. (Even at their wildest, the French group essentially continued in the Impressionist tradition, transmitting joy in nature and light.) The work of Brücke painters was full of venom against nineteenth-century materialism, and their paintings present a morbid and pessimistic view of contemporary society.

Rejection of materialism

Wassily Kandinsky (1866–1944) and Franz Marc (1880–1916) [5], who were working together in Munich in the years preceding World War I, were motivated by a similar rejection of materialism and pushed the distortion of the object toward total abstraction. Together they published an almanac, *Der Blaue Reiter* (the Blue Rider—blue horses were practically Marc's trademark), to which composers and critics contributed as well as artists.

Kandinsky arrived at a complete dissolution of the object in his work by a combination of Expressionist distortion and an emphasis on the picture surface by methods similar to those used by Matisse.

After the war there emerged in German painting a new tendency that contemporaries called "New Objectivity." While reacting against the strident technique and color of the earlier Expressionists, such painters as Otto Dix (1891–   ) and George Grosz (1893–1959) continued to employ distortions as a means of expressing their protest against the injustices of society. Max Beckmann (1884–1950) is usually classed with these painters, but his work is more private in its imagery [7]. The Swiss Paul Klee (1879–1940) veered between abstraction and fantasy [6].

Modern art comes to America

The rise of Hitler effectively put an end to the development of modern art in Germany until after World War II. American pathbreakers such as Marsden Hartley (1877–1943), Arthur Dove (1880–1946), and Max Weber (1881–1961) were quick to experiment, combining Fauvism, abstraction, and expressionism to their own purposes, thus presaging the later dominance of abstract expressionism.

KEY

Edvard Munch's "Evening on Karl Johann Street, Oslo" (1892) takes an everyday subject that might have appealed to the Impressionists. His concern, however, is not the visual world but the revelation of the anxieties of urban man. Notice how, in the background, the brightly-lit windows have a sinister presence; and the way that the faces acquire a ghostlike quality in the gaslight. Munch's art was the expression of a neurotic personality, but he depicted more than a personal malaise. The oppression of bourgeois city life was a theme in Expressionism.

5

6

KLEE

7

5 Franz Marc's "Fate of the Animals" is not just a forest scene but a comment on all of the most threatening aspects of nature. To depict the particular was not enough for the Expressionists.

6 Paul Klee's picture "Senecio" (1922) is based on a kind of humanized geometry. Klee methodically investigated form.

7 In "The Night" (1918–19), Max Beckmann's art is shown to be Expressionist in its violence, but its power lies in ambiguity. This is far from the robust directness that characterized Brücke painting.

8 Francis Bacon's "Seated Figure" (1974) creates an uneasy atmosphere more by precarious postures and intense handling of paint than distortion or the use of violent colors.

8

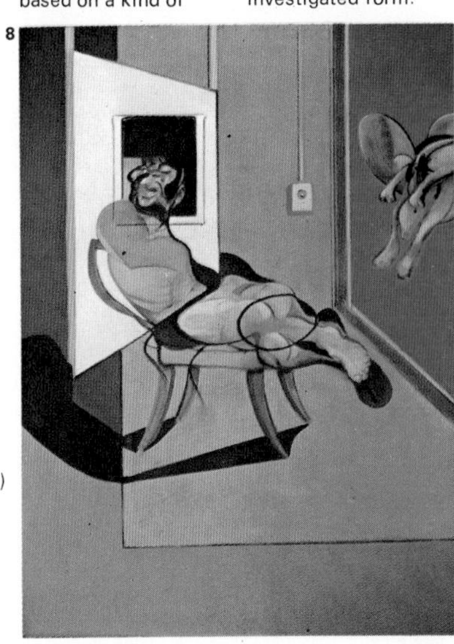

Cubism and Futurism

Cubism was a term of abuse invented without understanding by a disgruntled art critic, Louis Vauxcelles. It came to mean an international movement whose influence is still felt not just in painting but in sculpture and architecture. Pablo Picasso made it possible. He wanted to shock, a desire rooted in the philosophy of Friedrich Nietzsche (1844–1900) and in the demand for an individualistic assault on all conventions. Georges Braque (1882–1963) met Picasso in 1907 and was indeed at first shocked by his work, but later responded positively with an ambitious painting, "The Large Nude" (1908) [1].

The basic features of Cubism are present in this painting. First, the nude is distorted by fusing into a single image more than a single view of its parts. Second, it is treated as an arrangement of forms shallowly modeled in relief and not as a fully three-dimensional figure. Both these features followed from the conviction that painting should not imitate the appearance of things at any one moment (as in Impressionism) but should present the artist's accumulated idea of his subject, and that painting should be itself an art of flattened forms, not of three-dimensional illusions.

Between 1908 and 1911 a further feature was added to Cubist painting. Space was solidified, making the picture a single arrangement of flattened surfaces. Braque was the first to move in this direction, inspired by Paul Cézanne's attempt to treat the world as a mosaic of flat color patches [2], and it was only when Picasso also looked back to Cézanne that he followed suit in 1909 with a series of landscapes whose skies appear as a crystalline structure almost attached to the buildings below them [3].

The invention of collage

The process of fragmentation followed by Picasso and Braque took them to the very edge of abstract art, but they always left recognizable details in their paintings because for them the real point was to create a flexible give-and-take between the spectator's appreciation of structure for its own sake and his or her remembered knowledge of the structure of figures and objects in nature. The invention of collage (material stuck on the canvas) in 1912 made possible both a flatter effect and a clearer reference to the objects of the subject. Although it was first developed by Picasso [5] and Braque, the painter who most clearly used collage to create a conflict between objects and pictorial structure was Juan Gris [4].

Principal painters of Cubism

It was Picasso, Braque, and Gris who developed the central line of Cubism, taking it further after 1918, but each in an increasingly personal way. For them Cubism was never a style with a single "look;" its basic principles lay behind many variations.

These Cubists remained unconcerned with communication to a wide public even when their work began to sell during the 1920s, but as early as 1909 Cubism was taken over by artists actively concerned with communication, who often took their themes from the most popular aspects of emerging industrial society. In Paris there were the painters Jean Metzinger (1883–

CONNECTIONS

See also
1318 Dada, Surrealism and their legacy
1294 Fauvism and Expressionism
1320 Abstract art
1254 Impressionism
1298 Origins of modern architecture
1284 European industrialization 1870–1914

1 The distortion in Georges Braque's "Large Nude" (1908) is almost fully Cubist. The buttock is presented both in profile and from behind, the left side of the back is pulled forward, and the head is swung around far more than it could be in reality. Moreover, the figure is made even more fully Cubist by being treated in shallow relief, its surfaces defined with an angled brushstroke precisely like the equally flattened setting. One of the most important influences on Braque was Paul Cézanne, from whom this "hatched" brushstroke is borrowed.

2 Paul Cézanne (1839–1906) often painted the subject of this 1904–06 oil painting, "Mont Sainte-Victoire." He wanted to show how the mountain's volume and the space around it was revealed by the fall of light on surfaces—warm colors where the sun struck, cool where it did not. This led him to break his paintings down into small dabs of color, creating an effect that is both atmospherically spacious and flat. The Cubists, adopting this technique, also broke their surfaces down into small flat areas.

3 Pablo Picasso (1881–1973) was on vacation in the Spanish Pyrenees when he painted this oil, "Landscape, Horta de San Juan," in 1909. Reversed perspectives flatten the roofs, while the sky is effectively solidified. Braque made similar landscapes in 1908–09. It was these landscapes and the still lifes influenced by Cézanne that prompted the critic Louis Vauxcelles to compare the work to "little cubes," which later became "cubism." This work, however, does not represent a fully-developed version of Cubism in that it still uses traditional forms of pictorial space to denote three dimensions.

4 Juan Gris (1887–1927) achieved a perfect balance between composition and subject in his 1913 collage "Violin and Engraving." He presents the objects aspect by aspect. These fragmentary aspects together form an idea of the objects that is complete. The still life is actually more fully represented than in traditional illusionist painting, yet each fragmentary aspect is firmly contained within a stable composition of vertical strips. Gris thus creates an artificial structure on a flat surface to make another structure in three dimensions—the still life. The tiny framed engraving is in fact a real engraving stuck on. The artist even suggested that a future owner might change the engraving as if it were the decor of a real room.

1956) and Albert Gleizes (1881–1953); the Duchamp brothers, the husband and wife painters Robert (1885–1941) and Sonia Delaunay (1885–), who tried to fuse an interest in color with a Cubist sense of structure, and, most impressive of all, the Norman painter Fernand Léger (1881–1955). It was Léger who successfully adapted the possibilities of Cubist collage and by the firmly tangible modeling of early Cubist painting to the task of communicating the sheer force of city life [6].

Outside Paris, Cubism initiated several avant-garde movements: Vorticism in London; Russian and Czech Cubism; but most important of all, and an influence often the equal of Cubism itself, the Italian Futurism movement.

The development of Futurism

Futurism was invented by the poet Filippo Tommaso Marinetti (1876–1944), who saw life as constant change and individuals as part of a dynamic system of forces caught up in progress. Modern experience heightened this vision—change was so dramatic, the machine capable of such speed. Umberto Boccioni (1882–1918), Carlo Carrà, Luigi Russolo, Giacomo Balla, (1871–1958) and Gino Severini (1883–1966)—the painters whom he sponsored—concentrated on the expression of speed and change, as manifested in modern events and urban scenes [7]. In 1911–12, Cubist distortion and the breakdown of the barriers between solid and space were taken over by the Futurists, so that it is by basically Cubist means that Boccioni binds figures and setting together in his "Matter 1912" [8]. Yet there can be no doubt of the originality of much Futurist art, especially evident in Boccioni's monument to mechanized man [9].

Futurism used Cubist ideas for its own ends. Its success in doing so underlines what was the major legacy of Cubism, the freedom to create the objects and scenes of the world in a fresh way. So infinitely adaptable has it been that it has led to developments as widely divergent as the geometric art of Mondrian and the so-called "pop art" of Robert Rauschenberg.

KEY

In Georges Braque's "Still Life with Fish" (1910) things are so fragmented and so absorbed into the overall linear scaffold that the painting is almost abstract art. The recognizable bottle and fish heads allow one to "read" the still life and also to see how much of the scaffold is the result of the distortion of observed things.

5

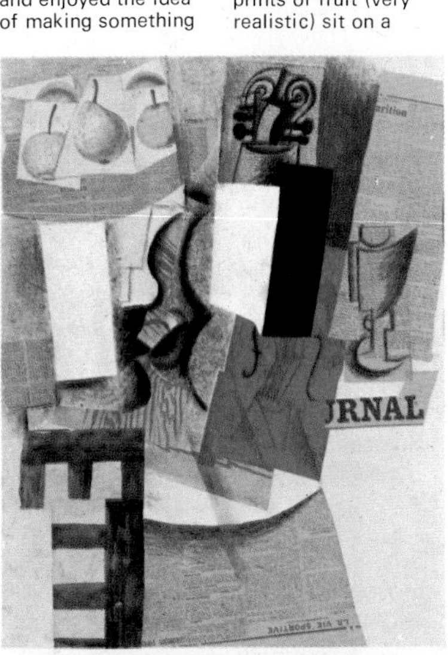

5 Picasso's collages, such as the 1913 "Violin," are less tidy than those of Gris. He collected junk and enjoyed the idea of making something out of otherwise worthless items. Here he pursues a series of paradoxes. The cutout color prints of fruit (very realistic) sit on a piece of newspaper cut to the rough shape of a fruit bowl. The solid violin head tops a body that is utterly insubstantial.

6

6 Léger, in his painting "Discs in the City" (1919–20), focuses on a combination of flat target discs, which appear mechanically geared together, suggesting the potential for movement. On either side there are scattered images from the city—robot men, crane derricks—which create the idea of an urban setting for the energy released by the colors and the whirl of the discs. The use of recognizable fragments is Cubist; the subject and its dynamic interpretation are Futuristic.

7

7 Carlo Carrà (1881–1966) in his oil "Funeral of the Anarchist Galli" (1911–12) combined a riot and a funeral. The use of repeated images to represent the beating arms and legs is typical of Futurist painting at this time and generates a feeling of both psychological unity and violence.

8

8 To the Futurists even an immobile figure could seem dynamic because of its psychological mobility and potential for movement. Thus Boccioni painted his mother in "Matter 1912," shown here in detail.

9

9 Umberto Boccioni (1882–1916) in his 1913 bronze "Unique Forms of Continuity in Space" mechanized the human form, developing the prophecy of Marinetti of a mechanized human type. Boccioni's aim was to define and freeze the forms that are most expressive of the continuity of motion through space of a striding man.

Origins of modern architecture

Modern architecture derived from the Industrial Revolution. Its styles were adapted to the discoveries of the engineers and to the mass production of materials such as iron and steel. The new movement began in France and Belgium; one of the most passionate advocates of a new style was Eugene-Emanuel Viollet-le-Duc (1814–79), who claimed that iron construction must lead to new kinds of support and vaulting, and therefore a new architecture. The Paris Exhibition of 1889, for which the Eiffel Tower [1] was constructed, proved him right.

Art Nouveau in architecture

Toward the end of the century more and more buildings were being constructed in a freer, more naturalistic way. This Art Nouveau style was represented by Victor Horta (1861–1947) in Brussels, Hector Guimard (1867–1943) in Paris, and Antoni Gaudi (1856–1934) in Barcelona, all of whom produced whimsical decorative styles. Horta used decoration to underline the elegance of iron construction [2].

There was another route toward modern architecture, often openly classical, and better attuned to the needs of mechanized production (simple forms capable of repetition). This was the style developed by Louis Sullivan (1856–1924) and the Chicago architects after 1872, by Auguste Perret (1874–1954) and Tony Garnier (1867–1948) in France after 1900, by Adolf Loos (1870–1933) in Vienna, and by Peter Behrens (1868–1940) in Germany.

Perret evolved the basic techniques of using reinforced concrete, and his 1905 garage [3], now demolished, used concrete frames for posts and beams. Sullivan was capable of decorative fancy, but Perret's dislike of surface decoration was shared by Garnier, Behrens, and Loos, and stark simplicity became a feature of this anti-individualist route into modern architecture. The shape of the building became more important than decoration.

In 1907, German craftsmen and designers formed the *Deutscher Werkbund*, an organization that studied the problems and application of design. In 1914 the *Werkbund* held an exhibition at Cologne. There the differences between the two main routes into modern architecture were thrown into high relief. On one side was Henri van der Velde (1863–1957), whose self-expressive style was representative of Art Nouveau, and on the other was Hermann Muthesius (1861–1927), who stood for a functional modern style and a timeless "ideal" beauty. In between was a former pupil of Behrens, Walter Gropius (1883–1969), an extraordinarily inventive architect, capable of designing simply with repeated units. His factory [Key], built for the exhibition, showed an original style that was geometrically simple and that played on the effects of lightness produced by his steel frame construction.

De Stijl and the Bauhaus

Yet, the anti-individualist trend became dominant among those who searched for modern architecture during the 1920s. Headed by the painter Theo van Doesburg, a movement called De Stijl was founded in Amsterdam (1917). By 1923 its leading architect was Gerrit Rietveld (1888–1964),

CONNECTIONS

See also
1258 Architecture in the 19th century
1322 Modern architecture after 1930

1 The Eiffel Tower was designed by Gustave Eiffel (1832–1923) for the 1889 Paris International Exhibition. He was already known as a daring engineer of some superb structures, including the Garabit viaduct. When built, his iron tower was the highest structure ever known. Eiffel was also engineer of the Bon Marché department store in Paris (1876) and of the Statue of Liberty in New York, which was completed in 1886. Both of them use iron structures.

2 The Solvay House, designed by Victor Horta, was built in 1895–96 for a rich Brussels manufacturer. It is a traditional doublefronted town house, but its combination of masonry and exposed iron construction was new, and so were many of its formal qualities. The projecting bays have more glass, used more expansively than was usual, and their thin iron columns are shaped to give the impression of growth and, where they carry weight, of gripping and lifting. Also, the entire stone surface gives the impression of a gentle swell, its flanks and the flanks of the bays curving outward.

51 · PONTHIEU AUTOMOBILES · 51
P

3 Auguste Perret's 1905 garage on the Rue Ponthieu in Paris used a reinforced concrete frame. Perret, almost single-handed, developed the basic techniques for handling this new material. He believed that reinforced concrete should be used like timber for frames and panels. The frame in this garage carried all the weight, as can be seen by the areas of glass. The building's structure was plainly expressed in the simple vertical and horizontal organization of the facade. The classical pillars, the small row of windows like a frieze above, and the projecting cap were all features, however, of the Ecole des Beaux Arts tradition. There was no decoration on the concrete.

whose Schröder House, with its overlapping rectangles, its lack of complex curves, and its living room window that turns a corner at the second-floor level, pulled together many typically modern features [4]. Mies van der Rohe (1886–1969) was active in Berlin, and between 1919 and 1928 Gropius headed the Bauhaus, which produced the first designs for "modern" furniture and fittings to be manufactured on any scale by industrialists. In France Charles-Edouard Jeanneret (1887–1965), known as Le Corbusier, took reinforced concrete architecture beyond the traditional classicism of his teacher, Perret. He eliminated the cornice, invented the horizontal window, and avoided symmetry—as in his Villa Savoye [6].

Toward an "International Style"

Open planning was made possible by the fact that with steel or reinforced concrete construction internal walls were no longer needed to carry roofs, but it followed too from the desire for a more informal way of life coupled with a closer relationship between the house and nature. Frank Lloyd Wright (1869–1959), the most gifted of Sullivan's pupils, stressed the organic nature of architecture. He believed that a building, like a living organism, must "grow" out of its surroundings. Between 1893 and 1911 Wright built a number of small suburban houses (the "prairie houses") which were planned outward from a central hearth. The open planning and flying horizontals of houses like the Willitts House (1902) [5] made a great impression on Gropius, the early architects of De Stijl, and many others when books on Wright appeared in Europe before 1914.

The individualistic modern alternative in architecture was never halted, but during the 1920s the inventive styles of Gropius, Mies van der Rohe, Le Corbusier, and De Stijl characterized by an asymmetrical arrangement of simple geometric forms, by extensive windows, and by open planning gave the illusion of a single modern style. It was this that led to the term "International Style," and the attempt to create a modern international architecture based on shared convictions.

KEY

Walter Gropius' factory, built for the Cologne Werkbund exhibition in 1914, is one of the first wholly modern buildings. The office building with its sheets of glass wrapped around both ends and its sash bars of steel establishes a clear rhythm. The horizontal slabs over the doorway show the influence of Frank Lloyd Wright. Contrasts between transparency and opacity were to become common.

4 A

B

4 The Schröder House on the outskirts of Utrecht was designed by Gerrit Rietveld in 1924. The exterior [A] is brick with steel posts to support the projecting balconies only where necessary. Outside walls were white and gray, creating a neutral ground for the colored horizontals and verticals. In the interior [B] large areas were in primary colors with white.

5 The Ward W. Willitts House in Highland Park, a suburb of Chicago, was built in 1902 by Frank Lloyd Wright. It was one of his "prairie houses." These were low, spreading houses, with open-plan interiors, terraces merging into the landscape, and low, sloping roofs. The construction is traditional wooden post and beam. They were among the early Wright designs.

5

6 A

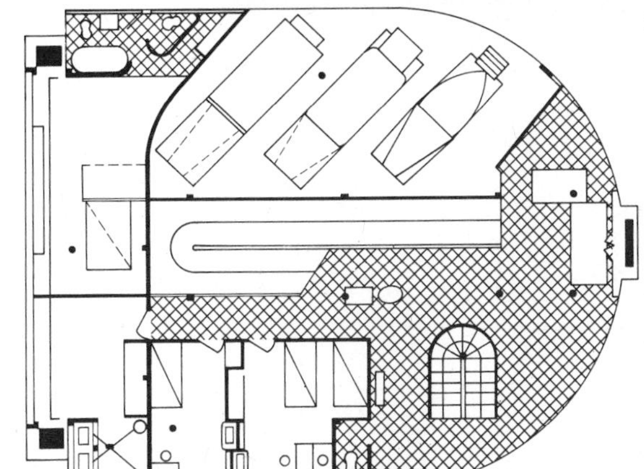

B

6 The Villa Savoye [B] at Poissy, east of Paris, was designed by Le Corbusier in partnership with his cousin between 1929 and 1931. The plan of the first floor [A] shows the curved end of the structure and the way that car space is incorporated into the building to preserve the idea of a self-contained structure. Living quarters are mainly on the second floor, which is largely open plan, together with some services. Four rooms are at ground level.

Europe 1870–1914

The period after the unification of Italy and Germany witnessed the consolidation and growth of the major nation-states. Population increase, growing industrialization, and stronger governments created an immensely dynamic period, marked by intense national rivalry. The rise of democratic institutions in many parts of Europe and the development of trade unions encouraged more social legislation, such as welfare programs. By the outbreak of World War I, socialist parties had appeared in many countries and won seats in representative institutions.

The rise of German power and influence

In terms of population, trade, industry, and armed forces Imperial Germany was clearly the most powerful European state [4]. Its easy conquest of France in the Franco-Prussian War of 1870–71 testified to its military strength [1]. Following the war the German chancellor, Count Otto von Bismarck (1815–98), sought to create a stable diplomatic environment in which a "satiated" Germany would be able to consolidate its gains and build up its international power and prestige. Germany's Dual Alliance with Austria-Hungary (1879) and the Reinsurance Treaty with Russia (1887) were designed to prevent those two countries from clashing in the Balkans. Bismarck's diplomatic system survived recurrent crises over this issue [3], until his resignation in 1890.

The Dual Alliance became the Triple Alliance with the addition of Italy in 1882 and was faced by the Franco-Russian alliance of 1891. Great Britain joined France in the Entente Cordiale in 1904, and an Anglo-Russian Treaty was signed in 1907, forming the Triple Entente. Bismarck's bequest became a dangerous system of alliances that was put under severe strain by imperial rivalry, Balkan crises, and the instability of the Austro-Hungarian Empire.

Domestically, many European states made considerable advances. In Britain extension of the franchise in 1867 and 1884 gave the vote to many working men. France also had a parliamentary democracy. Although still basically an autocracy, Imperial Germany had the façade of constitutional government, and political groups were developing rapidly, including a powerful socialist party. The Scandinavian countries experienced a largely peaceful political evolution, often pursuing progressive social legislation.

In southern Europe parliamentary democracy had only limited success. Italy [8] was threatened by widespread poverty and political instability. The first Spanish republic was proclaimed in 1873, but its ineptness in the savage Carlist civil war caused a group of generals to support return of the monarchy. The loss of Cuba and the Philippines in the Spanish-American War (1898) also weakened Spain. In eastern Europe, Austria-Hungary [5] remained essentially a monarchy, troubled by the disintegrative forces of nationalism.

The conflict between church and state

The growing power of the nation-states and increasing state intervention in public education and welfare brought conflict with the Roman Catholic Church. The church was

CONNECTIONS

See also
1284 European industrialization 1870–1914
1262 Imperialism in the 19th century
1250 German and Italian unification
1304 Causes of World War I
1302 Balkanization and Slav nationalism
1326 Socialism in the West

1 The entry of Prussian troops into Paris at the end of the Franco-Prussian War (1870–71) illustrated the power of the newly unified German Empire under the rule of the Hohenzollern dynasty and the direction of Bismarck. Domination of Europe by France as the greatest continental power was rudely ended by the growing industrial might of Imperial Germany, whose armies made efficient use of the German railroads and artillery built by Krupps. In France defeat toppled Napoleon III's Second Empire and, after the Paris Commune, ushered in the Third Republic.

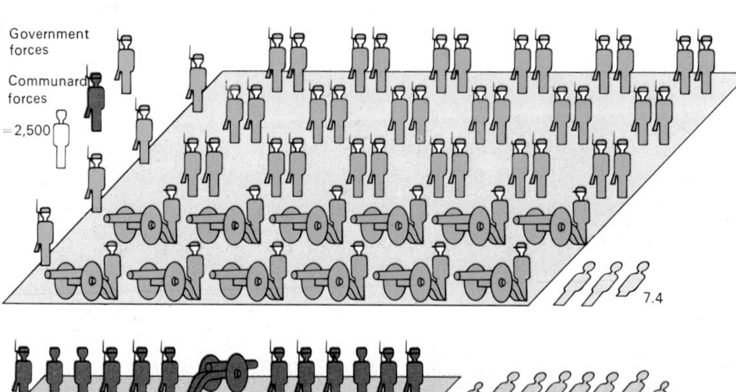
Government forces
Communard forces
=2,500
7.4
Communards sentenced (thousands)
Casualties (thousands)
20

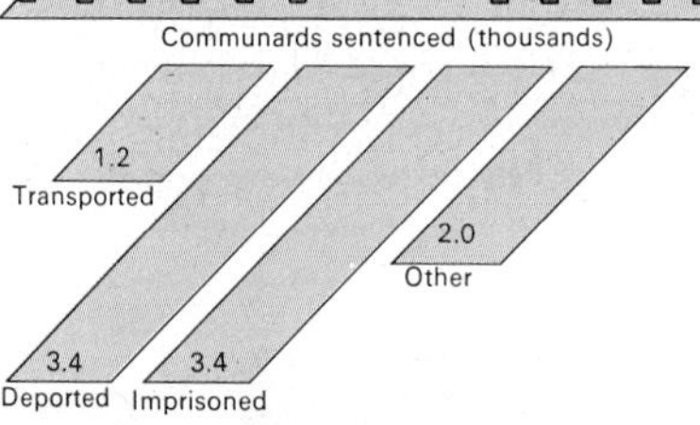
1.2
Transported
2.0
Other
3.4
Deported
3.4
Imprisoned

2 The Paris Commune resulted from the Parisians' sufferings during the Franco-Prussian War. When a new government at Bordeaux removed Paris's municipal independence and levied taxes, the lower middle classes and workers revolted and held the city for two months (March–May 1871). They introduced a semi-socialist regime until savagely suppressed by government troops.

3 The great powers all attended the Congress of Berlin in 1878. A major source of conflict was the fate of the decaying Ottoman Empire (Turkey) and its Balkan dependencies, where Austria-Hungary (represented by Karolyi, wearing cape, far left), and Russia (Shuvalov, right foreground, shaking hands with Germany's Bismarck), were deeply involved. The congress recognized the independence of several Balkan states but denied them some of the territory they had just won from Turkey with Russia's help. Austria was allowed to occupy Bosnia-Herzegovina while France and Britain also made gains. This painting is the work of Anton von Werner.

attacked in many countries for political conservatism and opposition to liberal and national aspirations. In France the conflict mainly concerned education, where the church had great influence. Republican aims were advanced by the French statesman Jules Ferry (1833–93), who secularized education through legislation in 1882 and 1886. In spite of a period of relative amity between church and state in the period that followed, known as the *Ralliement*, in the Dreyfus affair [7] old tensions flared once again and led to bitter anticlerical feeling. As a result, the concordat between the papacy and the state was ended in 1905, and church and state were completely separated.

In Germany, too, between 1870 and 1880, Bismarck waged the *Kulturkampf* in which religious orders were dissolved, civil marriage made compulsory, and other anticlerical legislation introduced [6].

Tariff reform became a pressing political issue in an era of growing rivalry in international trade and an influx of cheap foodstuffs from outside Europe. France protected its manufacturers by the Meline Tariff of 1892, and Germany sheltered its growing industry behind protective barriers. Even laissez-faire Britain witnessed a tariff reform campaign in 1902–05 conducted by Joseph Chamberlain (1836–1914); it failed, however, to secure majority support among the electorate for protection of British and colonial goods.

Appeals to patriotism and nationalism

Several states sought to appease growing working-class demands by social legislation. In Britain, Benjamin Disraeli (1804–81) and later David Lloyd George (1863–1945) introduced social welfare. The latter copied the comprehensive social insurance schemes of Bismarck. In France, politics essentially consisted of safeguarding vested interests, and social legislation lagged. Governments everywhere tended to rally public opinion by stimulating patriotic feeling. Growing literacy, prosperity, and communications also fostered intense nationalism. Conscript armies, equipped with modern weapons, created formidable war machines [Key].

KEY

A growing armaments industry toward the end of the 19th century produced such weapons as this German howitzer, which fired a 100 lb (45 kg) shell. Consolidation of nation-states and the emergence of an intense patriotism was translated by conscription and industrialization into mass armies with which the nations of Europe faced each other in 1914.

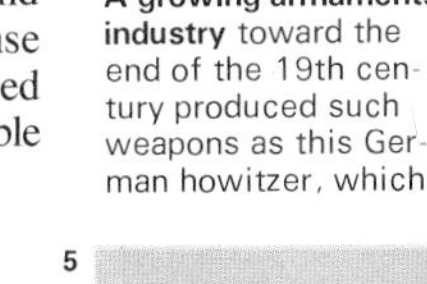

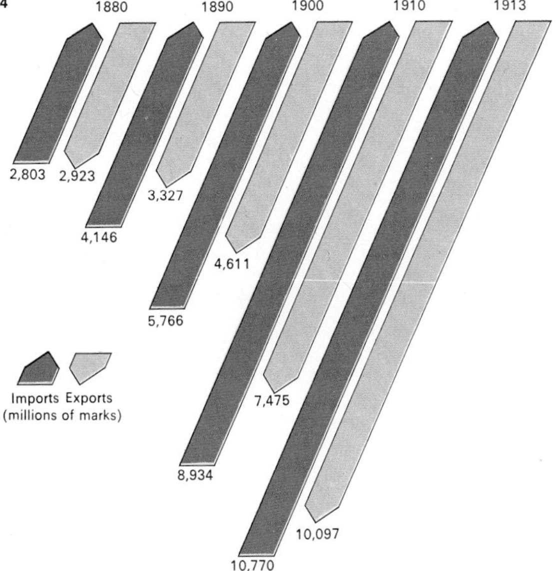

4
1880
1890
1900
1910
1913
2,803
2,923
3,327
4,146
4,611
5,766
7,475
8,934
10,097
10,770
Imports Exports
(millions of marks)

4 The unified German Empire became the greatest industrial power in Europe in the years before World War I, surpassing Great Britain in many branches of manufacture by 1900. After 1880, Germany's trade soared and both imports and exports increased more than threefold by 1913.

5 Elegant women, dashing officers – the outward glitter of "Gay Vienna" at the turn of the century masked a rich, diverse intellectual and artistic life that stemmed not only from the polyglot Austro-Hungarian empire but also from much of eastern Europe. The culture it produced influenced all Europe.

6

7

Musée des Horreurs
N:6
le Traitre!

6 Count Bismarck was a master of diplomatic chess, countering the interdicts of Pope Pius IX (1792–1878) with antimonastic legislation, as shown in this cartoon of the day. Bismarck presided over the unification of Germany, conducting foreign and domestic policy with ruthless cunning until he resigned as chancellor in 1890 after conflicts with the new emperor, Wilhelm II. Groups such as the Catholics and socialists had to submit in the interests of the state.

7 Caricatured as a traitor to France, Captain Alfred Dreyfus (1859–1935) was the center of a bitter controversy after 1896, when it emerged that an army court had unjustly convicted him of spying for Germany. Dreyfus was a Jew, and both anti-Semitic and ultra-conservative groups tried to block a fair retrial. Anticlerical and radical groups supported him with ultimate success, and the issue showed the deep divisions underlying the apparent stability of France.

8 Giovanni Giolitti (1842–1928), five times prime minister of Italy between 1892 and 1921, managed to achieve periods of near stability and considerable industrial progress at a time when Italy was socially and economically backward. Parliamentary democracy was often difficult to introduce in recently unified states, and in Italy political strikes and hunger riots were common before 1914.

8

Balkanization and Slav nationalism

Austria-Hungary and Russia were the chief protagonists in the struggle to supplant the once powerful Ottoman, or Turkish, Empire, "the sick man of Europe" [3], as the dominant power in the Balkans in the second half of the nineteenth century. For Russia, the mastery of the Balkans would have served its historic aim: to gain control of the Bosporus, the Dardanelles, and the city of Constantinople and thus gain access to ice-free seas. Austria-Hungary's main concern was to prevent Russia from establishing itself in the Balkans as the protector of a cluster of small states, some claiming territory within the Hapsburg Empire. The Austro-Hungarian policy of blocking Russia's advance toward the Mediterranean was upheld by Germany and Britain.

Russian hopes dashed

In 1877–78, Russia fought Turkey on the side of Serbia and Montenegro in support of Slav Christians in the province of Herzegovina who had clashed with the Turkish authorities because they refused to pay taxes or to perform the customary labor services. A Turkish force sent against them in 1875 had been defeated with the aid of sympathizers from Serbia and Montenegro as well as from Austria-Hungary's Croat province of Dalmatia. The insurrection had then spread in 1876 to Bulgaria, where an estimated 12,000 to 30,000 Bulgarians were killed by Turkish irregulars in atrocities that aroused European indignation.

Although Russian armies reached the outskirts of Constantinople in 1878, the diplomacy of Britain and Austria-Hungary frustrated Russia's main aim. At the Congress of Berlin [1], Russia secured territorial enlargement for Serbia and Montenegro and independence for Bulgaria. Austria-Hungary (which had stayed neutral) was allowed to occupy Bosnia-Herzegovina, Bulgaria was denied access to the Aegean, and the province of Macedonia, to which both Serbia and Bulgaria [2] aspired, was handed back to Turkey.

Serbian and Montenegrin successes in the war fired the imagination of all Slavs in the Austro-Hungarian Empire, but particularly those in the south: Croats, Slovenes, and Serbs living outside Serbia proper in Bosnia, Croatia, and Hungary. In Serbia itself the government covertly, and various nonofficial bodies overtly, gave money and encouragement to groups working for south Slav union. Serbian nationalists saw Serbia as the nucleus of a greater southern Slav nation [Key].

Revolutionary societies

Croats and other Slavs living in the Hungarian half of the Hapsburg Empire originally viewed the idea of a union with Serbia with suspicion, preferring a south Slav state under Hapsburg leadership. But alienated by Magyar dominance in Hungary, many of them became revolutionary toward the 1900s. Sensing the nationalist threat to their multinational empire, the Hapsburgs redoubled efforts to control and subdue Serbia, in their view the originator of the monarchy's troubles. The annexation of Bosnia-Herzegovina in 1908 was the result. It was an attempt to preempt south Slav nationalism by simply incorporating a disputed area into the empire and thus, it was

CONNECTIONS

See also

1232 European empires in the 19th century
1248 The revolutions of 1848
1250 German and Italian unification
1304 Causes of World War I
1300 Europe 1870–1914

1 The Congress of Berlin in 1878 drew up a Balkan settlement that was to last a generation. Dominant personalities were British Prime Minister Benjamin Disraeli (1804–81) and German Chancellor Otto von Bismarck (1815–98). Under a treaty signed in July, Russia agreed to scrap the Treaty of San Stefano, signed in March, giving it and its Balkan allies huge territorial gains. Under pressure from Britain, Austria-Hungary, and Germany, victorious Russia agreed to limit itself to taking a strip of Bessarabia from Romania, Batum and Kars in the Caucasus, and a part of Armenia. Romania's independence was formally recognized. Bosnia and Herzegovina were handed over to Austria-Hungary to administer. Britain was given Cyprus to keep as long as Russia kept Kars and Batum. Serbia and Montenegro received land that Bulgaria had gained earlier but remained cut off from the Aegean. Macedonia was handed back to Turkey.

2 San Stefano, the name on the woman's flag in this Bulgarian poster, summed up Bulgaria's efforts to regain from its neighbors what it had won in the San Stefano treaty but lost at Berlin. To that end, Bulgaria fought and defeated Serbia in 1885 but was forced to withdraw after Austrian intervention. In October 1915, Bulgaria, allied to Austria and Germany, again fought Serbia.

3 At Constntinople in 1876, Sultan Abdul-Hamid II (1842–1918), the Ottoman emperor, proclaimed a constitution under pressure from his own officials to reform the reactionary Turkish Empire. But he soon abrogated the constitution, and it was only in 1908 that the Young Turk movement forced him to reissue it, summon parliament, and abolish press censorship. When he prepared a countercoup in 1909 he was overthrown and replaced.

4 The German Kaiser, Wilhelm II (1859–1941), seen here visiting Constantinople, played a major role in Germany's moves to acquire influence in Turkey as part of a larger extension of power in central Europe and the Mediterranean. Based on a concession granted in 1899 by Turkey to the German company of Anatolian Railways, a rail system was to be built from Berlin to Constantinople and Baghdad as the key to a new German empire.

hoped, neutralizing it. Russia's weakness after defeat by Japan in 1905 enabled Austria-Hungary to escape retaliation.

The Balkan Wars

The Bosnian annexation initially turned the main thrust of Serbian nationalism south toward Albania and southeast Macedonia, which Serbia, Bulgaria, and Greece all claimed but which the Congress of Berlin had handed back to Turkey. Exploiting Turkey's preoccupation with its war against Italy in 1911–12, the four Balkan states—Greece, Bulgaria, Serbia, and Montenegro—set up the so-called Balkan League and declared war on Turkey in October 1912 [6, 8] (the first Balkan War 1912–13). But the victorious anti-Turkish forces were again frustrated by Great Power diplomacy, notably by Austria-Hungary and Russia.

Germany saw Turkey as the strategic base of its own future thrust into the Middle East and beyond [4] to challenge its greatest rival, Britain. Under Austrian pressure the Serbs were denied access to the Adriatic by the establishment of Albania as a separate state. Serbia in turn quarreled with Bulgaria over Macedonia, and war broke out between them in June 1913 and lasted a month. Bulgaria was defeated by an alliance of all its neighbors, including Romania.

But Hapsburg hopes of the situation's becoming calmer in the wake of the Bosnian annexation were disappointed. Nationalist agitation for a union of all south Slavs was boosted by Serbia's successes in the Balkan wars. Assassinations by members of secret societies in Bosnia and elsewhere became commonplace. The apparent political impasse made Austria-Hungary's leaders think once again of a military solution. The idea was that if only Serbia, the hotbed of nationalistic agitation, could be subdued and neutralized, the rest of Europe would calm down. Germany's enthusiastic backing of Austria-Hungary's policies strengthened the resolve of certain Austrian military and civilian leaders. The assassination of the heir to the Hapsburg throne, Archduke Francis Ferdinand, in the Bosnian capital of Sarajevo in June 1914, gave them the pretext for an ultimatum, then war.

KEY

The spirit of Slav nationalism is captured in *The Illyrian Revival* by a 19th-century Croatian painter, Vlaho Bukovac. Illyria was a hoped-for independent union of south Slavs under Croat leadership. But the Serbs, who managed to free themselves from Turkish rule in 1830 and to become a kingdom in 1882, took the upper hand while Croatia and Slovenia remained part of the Austro-Hungarian Empire.

5 The new Balkan states, formed as a result of Turkey's retreat from Europe, were in dispute with each other: Serbia and Bulgaria over Macedonia; Romania and Bulgaria over Dobruja; and Romania and Austria-Hungary over Transylvania. But the most explosive dispute was between Serbia and Austria-Hungary because of Serbia's support of terrorist activity among Slavs living under Austro-Hungarian rule. This was greatest in Bosnia-Herzegovina, a province of Croats, Serbs, and Slav Muslims, which Austria-Hungary had taken over in 1878 and formally annexed in 1908 in order to prevent Serb agitation. Austria-Hungary also frustrated Serbia's attempt to gain direct access to the Adriatic by encouraging the formation of a separate Albanian state, which was proclaimed in 1912.

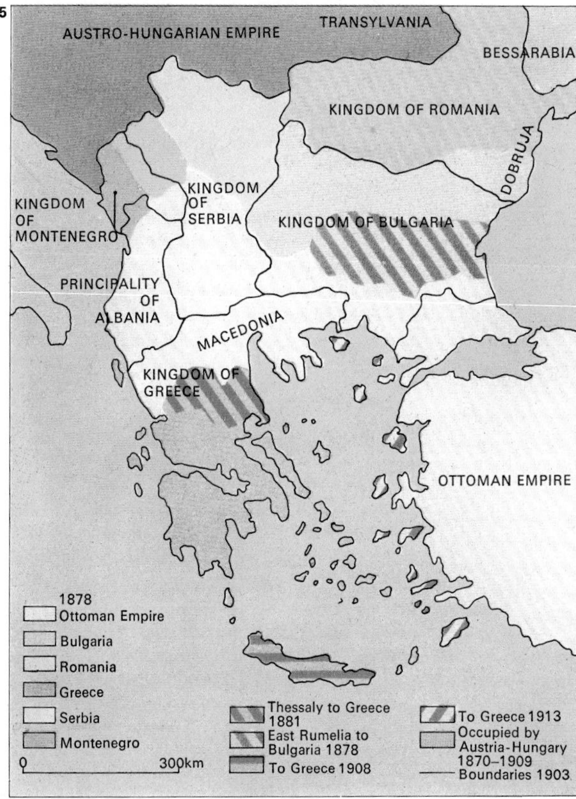
5
AUSTRO-HUNGARIAN EMPIRE
TRANSYLVANIA
BESSARABIA
KINGDOM OF ROMANIA
DOBRUJA
KINGDOM OF MONTENEGRO
KINGDOM OF SERBIA
KINGDOM OF BULGARIA
PRINCIPALITY OF ALBANIA
MACEDONIA
KINGDOM OF GREECE
OTTOMAN EMPIRE
1878
Ottoman Empire
Bulgaria
Romania
Greece
Serbia
Montenegro
0 300km
Thessaly to Greece 1881
East Rumelia to Bulgaria 1878
To Greece 1908
To Greece 1913
Occupied by Austria-Hungary 1870–1909
Boundaries 1903

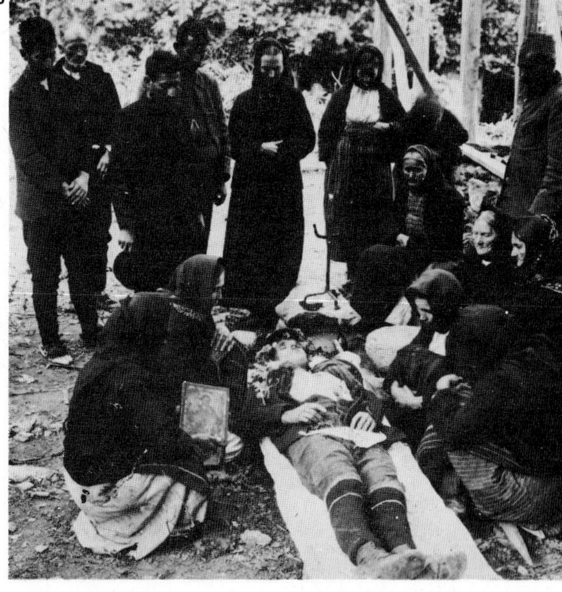

6 The first Bulgarian soldier to be killed in the first Balkan War is surrounded by mourners. Although fighting did not begin until October 1912, the seeds of the conflict were sown in a secret treaty concluded between Serbia and Bulgaria in March. They planned to attack Turkey and divide the spoils between them. According to this, Serbia was to have been given most of Albania. The war started when Montenegro attacked Turkey on October 8. Bulgaria, Serbia, and Greece then joined in, and soon the Turks were reeling under the combined onslaught. They asked for a truce in December.

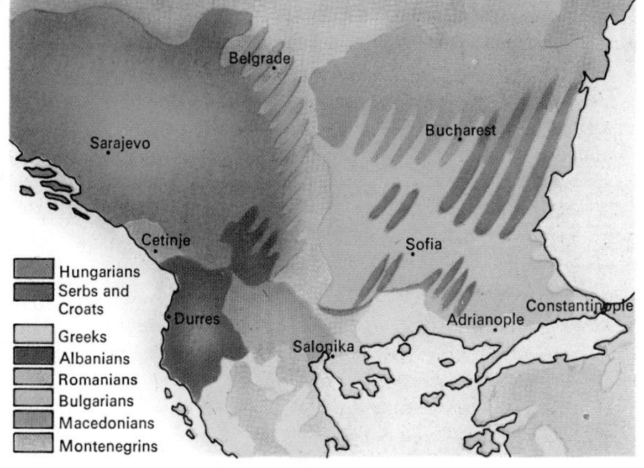
7
Belgrade
Bucharest
Sarajevo
Cetinje
Sofia
Durres
Adrianople
Constantinople
Salonika
Hungarians
Serbs and Croats
Greeks
Albanians
Romanians
Bulgarians
Macedonians
Montenegrins

7 Peoples of many religions inhabit the Balkans. The Croats have a Latin script and are Roman Catholics. The Serbs, Bulgarians, Montenegrins, and Macedonians received their Cyrillic script, Orthodox religion, and political tradition from Byzantium. Under Turkish rule the Orthodox Eastern Church retained its autonomy and was influential in the national revival of the Balkan peoples. Turkey left two enclaves of Islam in Europe: Bosnia and Albania.

8 Bulgarian troops in the first Balkan War (1912–13) gained much territory from Turkey, as did their allies, Serbia and Greece. But Serbian hopes of gaining Albania were dashed when Austria-Hungary blocked this; in compensation, Serbia wanted Bulgaria to give it more territory in Macedonia. Bulgaria attacked Serbia in 1913 and was beaten by an alliance of all its neighbors, with Serbia gaining the most and Turkey winning back some territory.

Causes of World War I

During the 1890s Germany's ruling class, headed by the intelligent but vacillating German Kaiser Wilhelm II (1849–1941), abandoned Chancellor Bismarck's cautious foreign policy in favor of a more dynamic one designed to reflect Germany's industrial and military strength. Germany wanted a large colonial empire for economic reasons and to enhance its prestige. To this end a law to expand the German navy, the first of many such laws, was enacted in 1898. The new navy was designed ultimately to challenge British naval supremacy [1] and to force Britain to collaborate in a reallocation of colonial territory.

German diplomatic setbacks

The first setback to Germany's "world policy" came in 1904 when Britain and France settled their colonial differences. Then, in 1907. Britain resolved its long-standing central Asian disputes with Russia, France's ally since 1894. In 1905, Germany, taking advantage of Russia's defeat by Japan, challenged France's increasing strength in Morocco [2] and coerced it into participating in an international conference in January 1906 at Algeciras to settle the Moroccan question on Germany's terms. Germany suffered a diplomatic defeat however, for its plans for Morocco were supported only by Austria-Hungary. Moreover, Germany's assumption that the Anglo-French entente would be wrecked by Britain's failure to support France proved to be similarly erroneous. Britain cooperated closely with France during the conference and, alarmed by Germany, began Anglo-French military conversations.

Germany next proceeded to alienate Russia. In 1909 it insisted with a veiled threat of war that Russia recognize Austria-Hungary's 1908 annexation of Turkish Bosnia-Herzegovina and abandon support for Serbia's claim for compensation. International tension was further increased when, in a bid to secure colonial compensation from France, now almost in control of Morocco, Germany sent a gunboat to the Moroccan port of Agadir on July 1, 1911. Although during the following months Britain and France came close to war with Germany over the Moroccan issue, a Franco-German colonial compromise was signed in November. The crisis left a legacy of bitterness and hatred in both countries. As a result, Germany in 1912 further increased its naval strength and began to expand its army; it was followed in this by every other continental great power [3].

Instability in the Balkans

The causes of World War I were, however, more directly connected with events in the Balkans. In 1912 the Balkan League (Serbia, Greece, Montenegro, and Bulgaria) drove Turkey out of most of its remaining possessions. In the following year Bulgaria was defeated by its former allies, Greece and Serbia, and lost its Macedonian gains of 1912 to Serbia. Austria-Hungary was thus faced with a greatly enlarged and ambitious Serbia, determined that the Slavs within the Hapsburg Empire should soon be added to the Serbian kingdom.

The cumulative effect of these crises was to increase preparations for war: indeed, Germany had long since devised its

CONNECTIONS

See also
1284 European industrialization 1870–1914
1302 Balkanization and Slav nationalism
1306 World War I
1308 The Peace of Paris

1

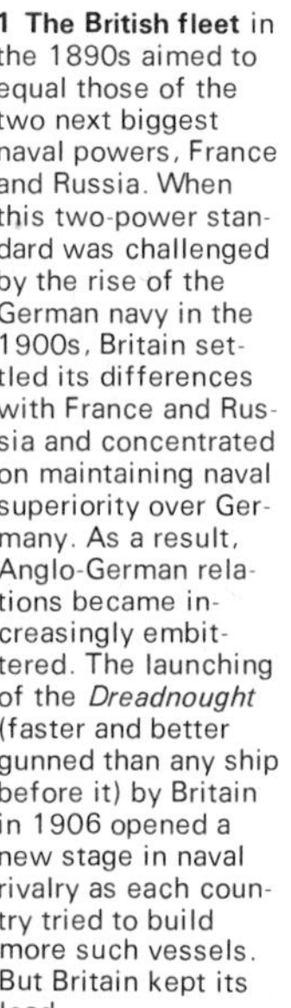

1 The British fleet in the 1890s aimed to equal those of the two next biggest naval powers, France and Russia. When this two-power standard was challenged by the rise of the German navy in the 1900s, Britain settled its differences with France and Russia and concentrated on maintaining naval superiority over Germany. As a result, Anglo-German relations became increasingly embittered. The launching of the *Dreadnought* (faster and better gunned than any ship before it) by Britain in 1906 opened a new stage in naval rivalry as each country tried to build more such vessels. But Britain kept its lead.

2

2 Visiting Tangier in March 1905, Wilhelm II pledged to uphold Morocco's independence. He hoped to protect German interests in that country (rapidly falling under French control) and to force France to recognize that its future lay in alliance with Germany. While the independence of Morocco was thus preserved until 1911, Germany's clumsy diplomacy drove France and Britain closer together.

3

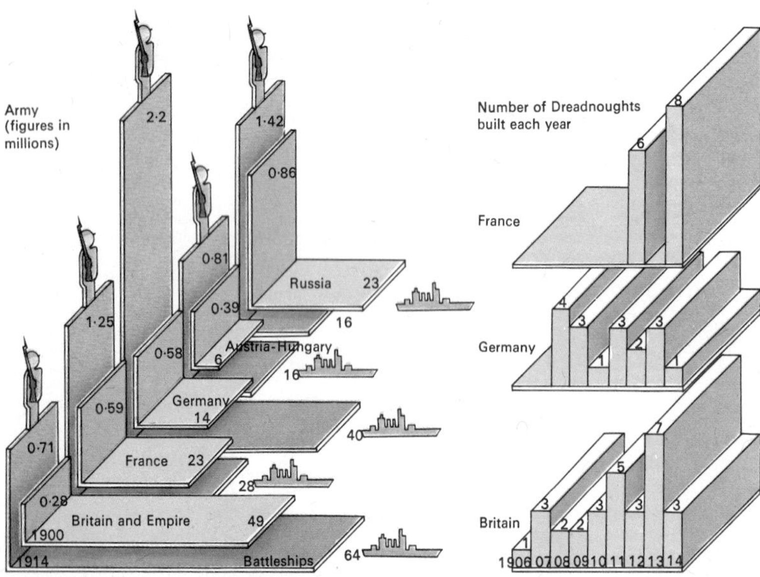

Army (figures in millions)
2·2
1·42
0·86
0·81
0·39
1·25
0·58
0·59
0·71
0·28
Russia 23
16
Austria-Hungary 6
16
Germany 14
40
France 23
28
Britain and Empire 49
64
1900
1914
Battleships
Number of Dreadnoughts built each year
France
Germany
Britain
1906 07 08 09 10 11 12 13 14

3 An armaments race among the Great Powers before 1914 both reflected and heightened European tension. In addition to building a large navy, Germany possessed the most formidable army in Europe. Although its size remained fairly stable from 1900–10, Germany's deteriorating diplomatic situation led in 1912–13 to increases in army strength that provoked the other Great Powers, except Britain (with a volunteer army), to increase their forces.

4

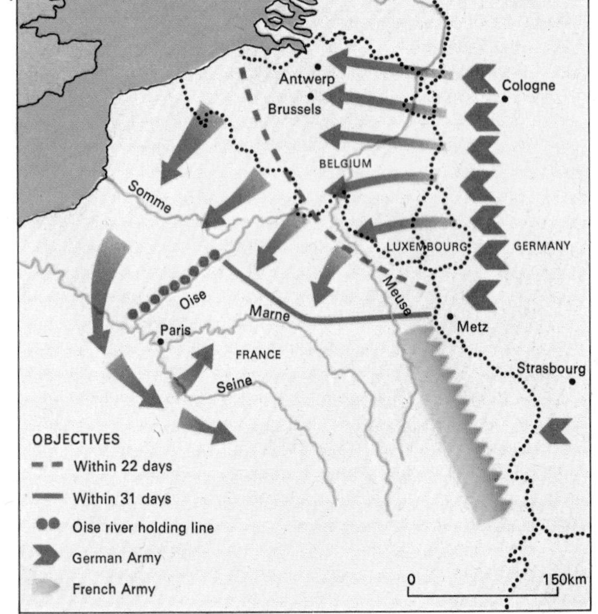

Antwerp
Brussels
Cologne
BELGIUM
Somme
LUXEMBOURG
GERMANY
Oise
Meuse
Marne
Paris
Metz
FRANCE
Seine
Strasbourg
OBJECTIVES
Within 22 days
Within 31 days
Oise river holding line
German Army
French Army
0
150km

4 The Schlieffen Plan was based on a two-front war with Russia and France, which had been allies since 1894. It provided for a massive German assault through Holland (later excluded) and Belgium to outflank the French army. Meanwhile, Austro-German forces would defend the east until the main German army, having knocked out France, could be rapidly moved to meet the Russians. Violation of Belgian neutrality would risk British intervention.

blueprint for victory, perfected by Count Alfred von Schlieffen (1833–1913), chief of staff, in 1905, and amended by his successor, Helmuth von Moltke (1848–1916). The Schlieffen Plan [4] relied on the slowness of Russian mobilization and provided for a rapid thrust through Belgium to defeat France, leaving the German army free to move rapidly east to meet the Russians.

The assassination of the heir to the Hapsburg throne, Franz Ferdinand (1863–1914), at Sarajevo on June 28, 1914 [8], was the climax of a series of Serbian provocations of Austria. Berlin feared that if Austria-Hungary failed to take the opportunity provided by the murder to bring Serbia within its orbit, its multinational empire would collapse, leaving Germany isolated. Thus Austria was under German pressure to act against Serbia, with the promise of German military support should war ensue. Successive German diplomatic defeats, a sense of "encirclement" by Britain, France, and an increasingly strong Russia, and deep divisions within German society all combined in 1914 to convince the German ruling elite of the desirability of war, partly to preserve the idea of a German-dominated *"Mittel Europe."* Although apprehensive, German Chancellor Theobald von Bethmann Hollweg (1856–1921) gambled on both Russian and British neutrality [6] and hoped that the Austro-Serbian dispute could be localized.

The final steps to war

Austria finally presented an ultimatum [7] demanding the right to investigate Serbian terrorists and, when Serbia rejected this, declared war on July 28, 1914. Russia could hardly stand aside and, faced with growing pro-Slav feeling, Tsar Nicholas II (1868–1918) ordered mobilization. British mediation failed to persuade Austria and Germany to compromise. When France refused to leave Russia to fight alone, the Schlieffen Plan was activated and events proceeded rapidly [9] toward a general European war between the Central Powers (Germany, Austria-Hungary, and Turkey) and the Allies (Russia, Serbia, France, Belgium, and Great Britain).

KEY

High-spirited French soldiers marching to the front after the outbreak of war in August 1914 typified the enthusiasm of all the belligerent countries, based on intense nationalism and a belief that the war would be short and glorious.

5 A wartime photograph of the Kaiser (center) and his generals reflects his fondness for military life. Responsible for Germany's foreign policy, the decision to mobilize on August 1 was his alone.

6 Germany's Chancellor Bethmann Hollweg [left] and Foreign Minister Gottlieb von Jagow (1863–1935) misjudged the willingness of Britain to go to war over a "scrap of paper" guaranteeing the neutrality of Belgium. They gambled on diplomatic victory for the Central Powers when, with the promise of German military support, they encouraged Austrian action against Serbia.

7 Count Leopold von Berchtold (1863–1942), the Austrian foreign minister, was convinced that the multinational Hapsburg Empire would collapse unless Serbia was crushed. His opportunity was provided when Franz Ferdinand was murdered but although promised full German support, he encountered considerable opposition to his plans from the Hungarian government. This partly accounted for the delay in presenting the Austrian ultimatum to Serbia.

8 Gavrilo Princip (1893–1918) precipitated the chain of events leading to war when he shot the heir to the Austro-Hungarian thrones, Archduke Franz Ferdinand, and his wife while they were visiting Sarajevo, capital of Bosnia, on June 28, 1914. Princip was one of a group of Bosnian conspirators.

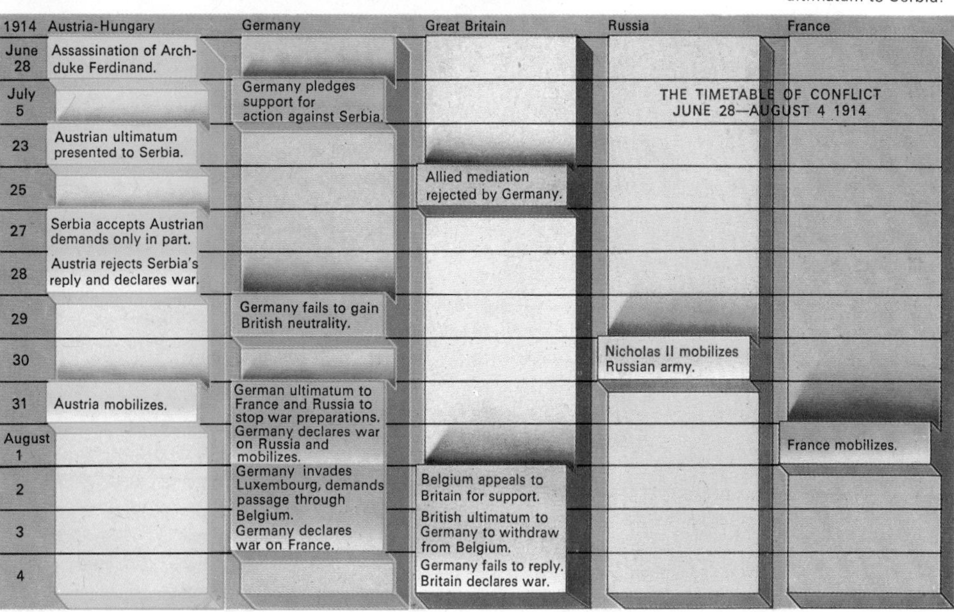

THE TIMETABLE OF CONFLICT JUNE 28—AUGUST 4 1914

1914	Austria-Hungary	Germany	Great Britain	Russia	France
June 28	Assassination of Archduke Ferdinand.				
July 5		Germany pledges support for action against Serbia.			
23	Austrian ultimatum presented to Serbia.				
25			Allied mediation rejected by Germany.		
27	Serbia accepts Austrian demands only in part.				
28	Austria rejects Serbia's reply and declares war.				
29		Germany fails to gain British neutrality.			
30				Nicholas II mobilizes Russian army.	
31	Austria mobilizes.	German ultimatum to France and Russia to stop war preparations.			
August 1		Germany declares war on Russia and mobilizes.			France mobilizes.
2		Germany invades Luxembourg, demands passage through Belgium.	Belgium appeals to Britain for support.		
3		Germany declares war on France.	British ultimatum to Germany to withdraw from Belgium.		
4			Germany fails to reply. Britain declares war.		

World War I

On June 28, 1914, Archduke Franz Ferdinand (1863–1914), heir to the Austro-Hungarian throne, was assassinated in Sarajevo, Bosnia, by a Serbian nationalist, precipitating a chain of diplomatic maneuvers that ultimately led to war. Balkan nationalism had long threatened the shaky Austro-Hungarian Empire, whose collapse would isolate its ally, Germany, in Europe. Russia, Serbia's ally, was also involved in the Balkans, because whoever controlled them controlled Russia's main trade route.

The first battles on both fronts

Germany pressed its ally to take firm action, and on July 28, Austria-Hungary declared war on Serbia. Two days later Russia mobilized, and Germany responded by declaring war on Russia on August 1. Germany's Schlieffen Plan, drawn up to avoid a war on two fronts, necessitated an all-out attack through Belgium to knock out France, Russia's ally, quickly. Germany therefore declared war on France on August 3 and invaded Belgium the next day. In response, Great Britain entered the war.

By September 9, German forces had advanced to the Marne, where the Allies (i.e., the British and French) were able to halt them. At the end of October each side faced the other in trenches running from the English Channel to the Swiss frontier. In East Prussia the vast, ill-equipped Russian army was crushingly defeated on August 20 at the Battle of Tannenberg.

Throughout 1915 the Germans remained on the defensive in the west, allowing the Allies to exhaust themselves in a series of futile attacks, while launching a massive summer offensive in the east that hurled the Russians back more than 300 miles.

Turkey had entered the war on the side of the Central Powers in October 1914. After a costly naval attack by the Allies, 75,000 Australian, New Zealand, British, and French troops tried to open a new front at Gallipoli at the mouth of the Bosporus. The expedition failed miserably and Russia was cut off from Allied supplies.

By the end of 1915 both sides realized that the war was going to be a long-drawn-out struggle, and unprecedented mobilization of civilians into the armed forces and industry began. On February 21, 1916, the Germans assaulted Verdun in an offensive calculated by General Erich von Falkenhayn (1861–1922) to exhaust the French. By July nearly 600,000 men had died in this action, but the French managed to hold on. The Russians under General Alexei Brusilov (1856–1926) launched an offensive that gained some territory with terrible loss of life, and the British under Field Marshal Douglas Haig (1861–1928) attacked on the Somme, suffering 20,000 dead on the first day and gaining less than 5 miles (8km) in five months' fighting.

Naval warfare: effective blockade

At the beginning of the war, the British Navy had begun a blockade of German ports, turning back neutral shipping [6]. The Germans replied with U-boat, or submarine attacks [8], but had little success in 1915 and 1916 because the sinking of neutrals was banned. The two great battle fleets fought only one major action, at Jutland on May 31, 1916. The outcome was inconclusive,

CONNECTIONS

See also
1304 Causes of World War I
1300 Europe 1870–1914
1308 The Peace of Paris
1302 Balkanization and Slav nationalism
1310 The Russian Revolution
1326 Socialism in the West
1324 The twenties and the Depression
1730 Automatic weapons
1732 History of artillery
1736 Armored fighting vehicles
1740 Modern fighting ships
1742 Early military aircraft
1746 Nuclear, chemical, and biological warfare

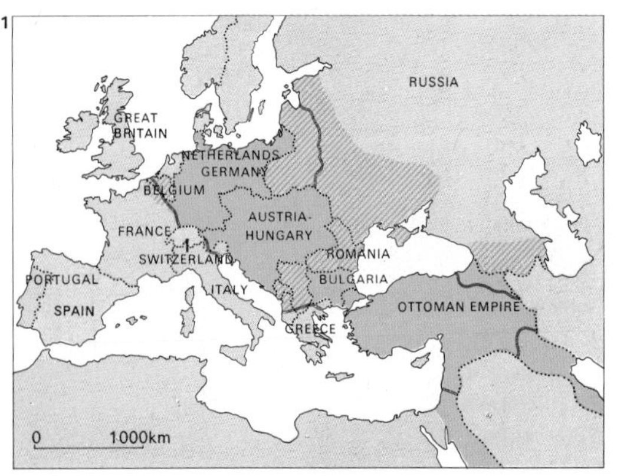

RUSSIA
GREAT BRITAIN
NETHERLANDS
GERMANY
BELGIUM
FRANCE
AUSTRIA-HUNGARY
SWITZERLAND
ROMANIA
BULGARIA
PORTUGAL
SPAIN
ITALY
GREECE
OTTOMAN EMPIRE
0 1000km
Entente powers and allies
Central powers and allies
Neutral powers
Greatest advance of Central powers
Front lines November 1918

1 Most of the fighting took place in Europe; the main battlefields were in northern France and Belgium, Poland, Russia, and Italy. Overseas campaigns were fought in Mesopotamia and the Middle East and in the German colonies in Africa.

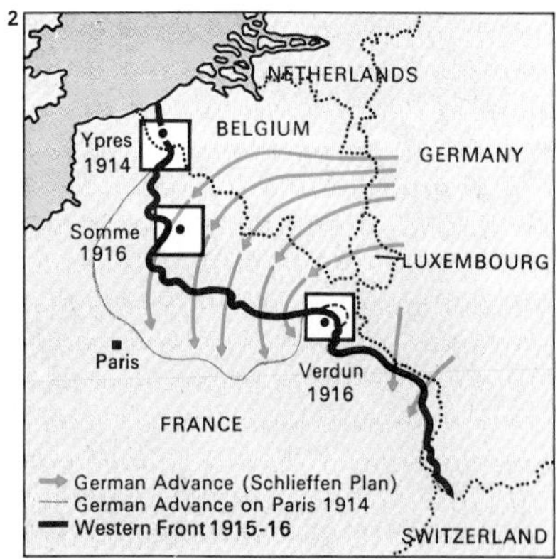

NETHERLANDS
BELGIUM
GERMANY
Ypres 1914
Somme 1916
LUXEMBOURG
Paris
Verdun 1916
FRANCE
German Advance (Schlieffen Plan)
German Advance on Paris 1914
Western Front 1915-16
SWITZERLAND

2 The Western Front was the decisive battleground of the war. Once the Schlieffen Plan had failed to eliminate France, it was here that the bloodiest battles were fought, as both sides poured in men and materials to achieve the vital breakthrough. In 1918 the impetus of a new Allied offensive backed by the fresh US armies convinced the Germans, even before the Allies reached them, that the war was lost.

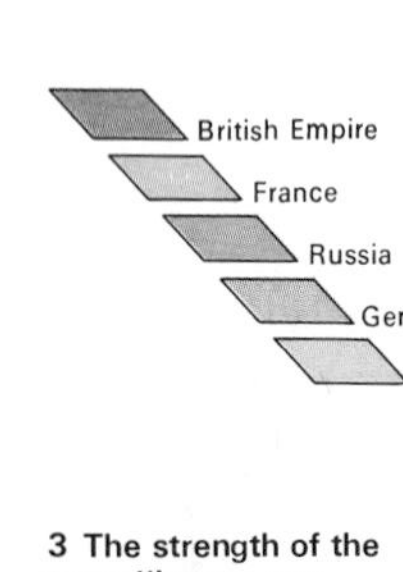

Soldiers (millions)
Battleships
Cruisers
Submarines
British Empire
France
Russia
Germany
Austria-Hungary
0·16
1·2
1·4
2·2
0·8
64
28
16
40
16
121
34
14
57
12
64
29
73
23
6

3 The strength of the two alliances was reasonably well balanced, as what Britain lacked in troops it made up in naval strength. It was this balance that made World War I a war of attrition that was to result in horrific loss of life and massive destruction. Figures quoted here for troops are those of the standing armies. Mobilized forces were approximately: Britain 711,000, France 3,500,000, Russia 4,400,000, Germany 3,800,000 (in emergency a maximum of 8,500,000 could be raised), Austria-Hungary 3,000,000.

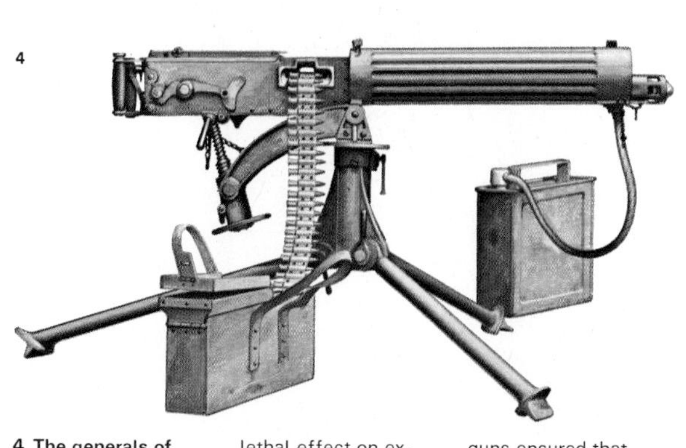

4 The generals of 1914 had been trained to think of mobile offensive warfare, but the relatively new British Vickers medium machine gun with its lethal effect on exposed infantry was among the armaments that upset their view. Once the exhausted armies had dug themselves in, artillery and machine guns ensured that trench warfare would continue. Commanders tried to break the stalemate, but massive infrantry attacks proved hideously ineffective.

5 US soldiers move up to the front line in World War I. Of the 2,084,000 US troops that arrived in France, 1,390,000 took part in active combat, and 112,432 American lives were lost.

but the German surface fleet remained in harbor for the rest of the war. During 1916 the blockade caused severe food shortages in Germany, which led to widespread unrest. On January 31, 1917 the Germans launched unrestricted submarine warfare, and by sinking US ships encouraged the United States to enter the war. The U-boats had great success against British shipping, and only the introduction of the convoy system in May prevented Britain from being economically strangled.

On the Western Front the French launched a series of unsuccessful offensives; elements of their army mutinied in May 1917, but were brought under control during June by Marshal Henri Pétain.

Tanks were used en masse at Cambrai on November 20, but their initial successes were not followed up. Italy had entered the war on the Allied side on April 26, 1915 and fought against Austria-Hungary until defeat at Caporetto on October 24, 1917 effectively removed Italy from the war.

In Russia, the unpopularity of the war led to the overthrow of the tsar in March 1917. A provisional government launched another offensive but, after that had been thwarted, the Bolsheviks seized power in November and sued for peace. The Treaty of Brest-Litovsk in March 1918 gave Germany territorial gains in western Russia.

The final offensives and Allied victory

Aware that they must follow up success in the east with victory in the west before US help could arrive in force, the Germans launched a series of offensives under General Erich Ludendorff (1865–1937) from March to July 1918. They drove the Allies back to the Marne, but were again halted there. Then, strengthened by US troops, the Allies counterattacked during August. A massive offensive of 1,031,000 troops—80 percent of whom were Americans—launched on September 26 convinced the German high command that the war was lost, and they sued for peace. The kaiser abdicated on November 9, and an armistice was signed on November 11. Austria-Hungary also collapsed in November after an Allied offensive in the Alps.

KEY

For future generations World War I was to become a symbol of senseless slaughter and destruction. Not only did more than 10 million soldiers die, but the war affected every level of society in all combatant countries. Wholesale conscription was introduced, and governments took dictatorial powers to control economies and to ration food and supplies. The war radically changed the map of Europe, sweeping away the German, Austro-Hungarian, and Russian empires and setting up smaller states in Eastern Europe.

6

British minefields
German minefields
U-boat routes
Convoy terminals
British blockade
Naval battles

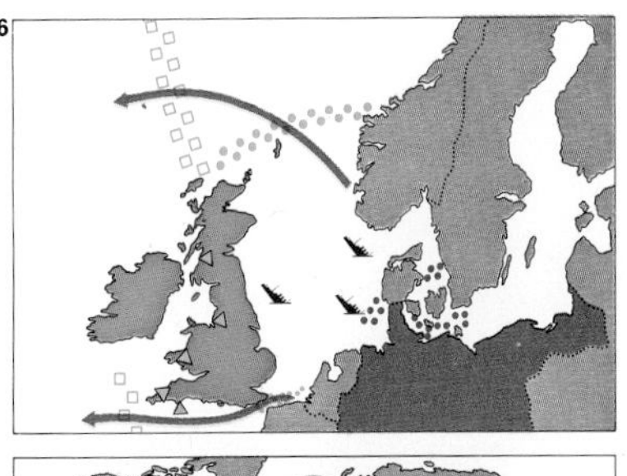

Central Powers
German raider activity Aug 1914-Mar 1915
U-boat attacks February 1917 onwards
Main trade routes

Allied powers
Naval blockade 1914-18
Convoy routes May 1917 onwards
Main trade routes

7

6 The great battle fleets met only once during the war. The Germans used long-range raiders and submarines, while British warships mounted a highly effective blockade of German ports.

7 Cavalry, like this German troop, found few outlets other than the Eastern front, where the trench system never evolved. There cavalry was used chiefly as a reconnaissance screen for infantry.

11

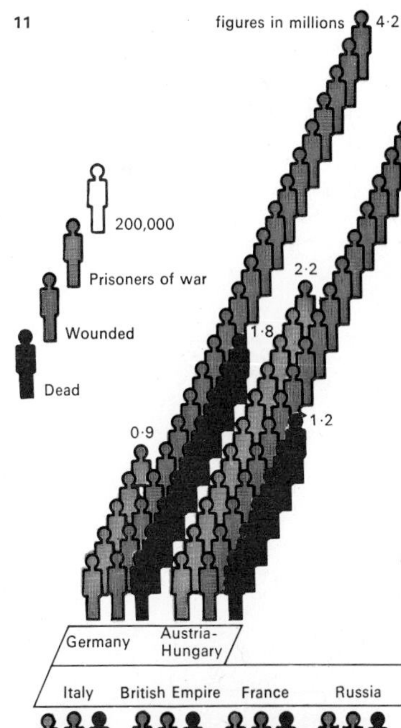

figures in millions
200,000
Prisoners of war
Wounded
Dead
Germany
Austria-Hungary
Italy
British Empire
France
Russia
United States
4·2
3·6
2·2
1·8
1·2
0·9
0·2
0·4
0·5
0·5
0·9
0·9
1·4
1·7
2·1
2·0
2·5
4·9
0·2
0·1

8

8 German submarines were technically superior to those of Great Britain at the beginning of the war. This—a Class 31–37—was 212ft (64.7m) long, and fully submerged it weighed 880 tons. It was armed with 24 20in (500mm) torpedoes fired through four tubes. The attacks on British shipping were relatively ineffective during 1915–16. With the unrestricted warfare of 1917, however, the Germans came close to starving Britain.

9

9 German Gotha IIIs were used for armed reconnaissance over the battlefields as well as for bombing. Developed to take over the Zeppelins' role in bombing English cities, they arrived too late in the war to make a significant difference. After their attacks on England (in which they claimed 857 lives) the Gothas were switched to the French theater.

10

10 Gas was first used in 1915 by the Germans to try and break the trench stalemate. It proved inefficient, difficult to control, and easy to detect. The masks these soldiers wear were early attempts at protection.

11 The military casualties of the major powers were vast. France suffered most heavily in both death and destruction. Never had a war killed so many people in so short a time, removing a whole generation of young men and scarring Europe for the next 20 years.

The Peace of Paris

The Paris peace conference, formally opened on Jan. 18, 1919 [6], was dominated by the five major victorious powers of World War I—the United States, France, the British Empire, Italy, and Japan. The defeated nations and the Soviet Union were excluded.

Conflicting demands

The French delegation, led by Prime Minister Georges Clemenceau (1841–1929), was obsessed with the long-term threat posed to France by Germany's larger population and superior industrial potential. The French therefore demanded the imposition of a harsh treaty that would prevent any further German aggression against France. These aims conflicted with those of US President Woodrow Wilson (1856–1924), who, in his Fourteen Points (accepted with reservations by Britain and France on Nov. 4, 1918), called for a peace settlement based on national self-determination and a League of Nations [2].

Britain's major demands had already been met with the surrender of the German fleet and the British occupation of most of Germany's colonies and the bulk of the Turkish Middle East. Despite pressure from Wilson that these areas should be administered directly by the league, they were retained by the British Empire under a complex mandate system [4]. Thus, British Prime Minister David Lloyd George (1863–1945) was in a position to mediate between France and the United States.

Italy demanded the satisfaction of its claims under the terms of the 1915 Treaty of London to the Tyrol, Trieste, and a large part of the Slav-populated Dalmatian coast, including Fiume. Wilson, however, refused to recognize the Italian claim to Fiume, and it was assigned to Yugoslavia, leaving Italy with Trieste and the Tyrol [1].

Despite strong opposition from Wilson and the Chinese, Japan secured the former German concessions in Chinese Shantung promised to it by the entente in 1917.

Wilson's ideals compromised

The Republican victory in the November congressional elections in the United States undermined Wilson's prestige, and he was forced to compromise on some of the Fourteen Points in order to secure the adherence of the other leaders to his League of Nations Covenant. Neither he nor Lloyd George, however, would accept France's demand for a Rhineland buffer state under French military control. This would have been a clear breach of the principle of national self-determination, and, in Lloyd George's view, was likely to breed lasting German resentment. The French accepted on April 14 a compromise whereby the Allies were to occupy a demilitarized Rhineland, including the Rhine bridgeheads, for 15 years, with an Anglo-American guarantee to protect France against German aggression. The French were also permitted to exploit the Saar coalfields.

Despite Wilson's strenuous opposition, France demanded massive reparations from Germany, not only to compensate for the immense destruction inflicted during the war but also as a means of weakening the German economy [7]. By the end of March Lloyd George was becoming concerned at

CONNECTIONS

See also
1300 Europe 1870–1914
1304 Causes of World War 1
1306 World War 1
1310 The Russian Revolution
1324 The twenties and the Depression
1326 Socialism in the West
1272 Japan: the Meiji Restoration
1328 East Asia 1919–1945
1334 The rise of fascism
1302 Balkanization and Slav nationalism

1 The new East European states emerged from the wreckage of the German, Austro-Hungarian, and Russian empires. Although founded on the basis of national self-determination, they incorporated alien minorities, like the Germans in Czechoslovakia, which were a source of constant unrest after 1919. Britain and France divided the former Ottoman Middle East between them, but both faced rising Arab nationalism and, in Britain's case, increasing Arab-Zionist conflict in Palestine. The harsh Sèvres Treaty of 1920 led to the establishment of an independent Turkey in 1923.

Russian Empire 1914
Germany 1914
Austro-Hungarian Empire 1914
Ottoman Empire 1914
Boundaries 1920
French mandate 1920
British mandate 1920
Emirate under British suzerainty 1923
Serb-Croat-Slovene kingdom created 1918 Name changed to Yugoslavia 1929

2 The Allied leaders—(from left to right) Lloyd George, Orlando, Clemenceau, and Wilson—were bitterly divided by opposing policies and temperamental differences. The peace settlement they eventually imposed on Germany was soon condemned by their countrymen and none remained long in office after it was concluded. The treaty was signed in 1919 by all the great powers except the United States.

3 Germany's losses and gains from 1919 to 1938 are shown on this map. The Supreme Council had endeavored to settle Germany's frontiers on the basis of nationality. Its territorial losses, particularly those in the east, were one reason Germany detested the treaty. Allied disunity and weakness in 1938 enabled Hitler to incorporate Austria into the Reich and to annex the German Sudetenland.

Territory lost by Germany 1919
Demilitarized 1919–36
Territory retained by Germany after plebiscites
Gained by Germany 1938
Controlled by League of Nations 1919–35. Returned to Germany 1935
Free city

German territories mandated by League of Nations after 1919
British mandate
French mandate
Belgian mandate
Union of South Africa mandate
British mandate
Australian mandate
Japanese mandate
New Zealand mandate
Held by Germany until 1914. Occupied by Japan 1914–22. To China 1922–3

4 Germany lost all its colonies at the end of World War I. Woodrow Wilson hoped that the captured German colonies would be administered directly by the League of Nations. This idea was opposed by the British and Japanese, who had conquered them. A compromise was reached by a system of "A," "B," and "C" mandates: "C" was virtually indistinguishable from annexation. Thus Wilson's idealism was again frustrated by the other leaders.

the increasing severity of the Allied demands on Germany, which he feared would hinder Germany's economic recovery and lead to a Bolshevik victory there. Finally, a compromise was reached. The total sum owed by Germany was to be determined by an inter-Allied reparation commission by 1921. Meanwhile, Germany was forced to accept responsibility for causing the war. The Allies also imposed a substantial measure of disarmament on Germany.

The eventual compromise

The Allies could not agree upon the settlement of Germany's eastern borders [3]. France supported granting large territorial gains at Germany's expense to the newly established East European states, especially Poland. After a long struggle Lloyd George managed to reduce Poland's acquisitions by insisting on a league-controlled free port of Danzig, the reduction of the Polish corridor, and a plebiscite in Upper Silesia. Czechoslovakia retained the German Sudetenland. Austria, stripped of its empire, was forbidden to unite with Germany. In 1920, Hungary lost all of its non-Magyar lands to its neighbors and severe peace terms were imposed on Turkey. The Allies presented the draft treaty to Germany on May 7, allowing 15 days for counter-proposals, most of which were then rejected. After further delays Germany signed the treaty at Versailles on June 28, 1919. It was widely regarded in Germany as a dictated peace and a betrayal of Wilsonian principles. Failure to apply the principle of self-determination to the distribution of the German countries of the former Austrian Empire, in particular, was a major German grievance and one that gave the German nationalists and Hitler's Nazi party valuable propaganda against the Weimar Republic in the 1920s.

The US Senate rejected the treaty and the league covenant, and the country retreated into isolationism. France thus lost its Anglo-American guarantee and became even more determined to insist on German compliance with the treaty, especially the reparations clauses. The result was friction with Britain.

KEY

The armistice was signed on Nov. 11, 1918, at the French headquarters in the Forest of Compiègne. Marshal Foch signed for the Allies. Germany agreed to an evacuation of occupied territories and a cessation of all hostilities.

5

5 British troops marched along Whitehall, London, in July 1919 in a "Peace Procession" that marked the signing of the Treaty of Versailles, but disillusionment soon replaced enthusiasm.

6 A quick conclusion to the peace conference was essential, to permit European reconstruction. Although attended by most nations and governments, it was dominated by the US, Britain, and France.

6

11 Nov 1918	German armistice
18 Jan 1919	Paris Peace Conference opens
22 Jan	Council of Ten sets up League of Nations Commission
3 Feb	League of Nations Commission meets
14 Mar	Formation of Council of Four
10 Apr	Council of Four appoints Reparation Commission
22 Apr	Italians withdraw
26 Apr	Conference accepts League of Nations Covenant
6 May	Italians return
7 May	Draft treaty is presented to Germans
29 May	Germans present counter-proposals
16 June	Allies reject most of the counter-proposals
28 June	Treaty of Versailles

7 Germany's reparations payments were a major obstacle to its economic reconstruction and weakened the entire European economy in the 1920s. But after the French invasion of the Ruhr and the dramatic German inflation in 1923 the need for a strong German economy was recognized. This led to increased investment, especially from the US. Many of these funds, however, were spent on public buildings.

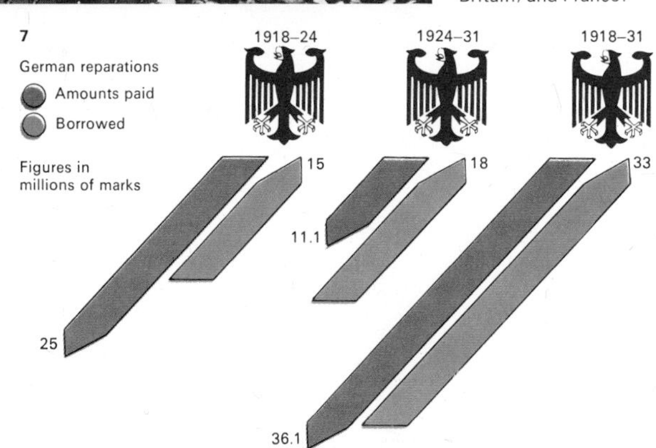
7
German reparations
Amounts paid
Borrowed
Figures in millions of marks
1918–24
1924–31
1918–31
15
25
18
11.1
33
36.1

8

8 The League of Nations was intended by Woodrow Wilson to be the foundation of a new and peaceful world order; however, the refusal of the US to join in 1920 and the exclusion of both Germany and the Soviet Union (until 1934) reduced its effectiveness. After the admission of Germany in 1926, the league was fairly successful until its failure to prevent the Japanese conquest of Manchuria in 1931–32 and the Italian conquest of Ethiopia, 1935–36.

9

9 Hitler's rise to power in 1933 and the Treaty of Versailles are not directly connected, but the treaty was an important element in Nazi propoganda against the Weimar Republic and the Social Democrats in the 1920s. Hitler's appointment as chancellor was the product both of luck and calculation. His opportunity was provided by general discontent and the economic depression, and by the inability of Weimar politicians to cope with either.

The Russian Revolution

Russia went reluctantly to war in 1914. Its army was in no condition to face imperial Germany, and early enthusiasm for the war waned with a shattering defeat by the Germans at Tannenberg within a month after hostilities began. But only the Bolsheviks vehemently opposed the war; and the five Bolshevik deputies in the Duma (Parliament) were banished to Siberia. Their leader, Vladimir Ilyich Lenin (1870–1924), nevertheless saw the defeat of imperial Russia as the surest way of furthering revolutionary goals.

Impact of the February revolution

The longer hostilities lasted, the more incompetent the imperial administration appeared. It was astonished by the revolution in March 1917 (dated as February by the old-style calendar), but then so were its opponents. Power was wrested by hungry peasants, disenchanted aristocracy, and mutinous troops from Tsar Nicholas II (1868–1918) [3], the last of the Romanov dynasty. A provisional government was formed to govern until a Constituent Assembly adopted a constitution and appointed a legal government. The first of four provisional governments fell because it failed to end the war. Popular feeling favored peace and the distribution of more land to the peasants.

Peace and the redistribution of land were closely connected. If Russia left the war, the soldiers (who were mostly peasants in uniform) would descend on the countryside and demand more land; if the peasants were granted land while war continued, the soldiers would desert to seize their portion. The government had also to contend with the emergence of genuinely democratic institutions, the soviets (councils). The most famous of these were in Petrograd and in Moscow, but they sprang up spontaneously everywhere after the revolution. Despite support from the moderate socialists—the Mensheviks and the Socialist Revolutionaries (SRs)—the provisional governments were violently opposed by Lenin and the Bolsheviks. During July armed workers and soldiers tried to seize power in Petrograd [4, 5]. Denounced for accepting German money, Lenin was forced to flee to Finland when the demonstrations were unsuccessful. On July 22, Alexander Kerensky (1881–1970) became premier and tried to restore order in the capital [2, 6]. But Leon Trotsky (1879–1940), a leader in the Petrograd soviet, organized armed insurrection under the cover of soviet legitimacy. Lenin slipped back into Russia, and on November 7 (October 25, old style) he and his Bolsheviks [7] swept away Kerensky.

The October Revolution and after

Some workers hoped that the new Russia would be ruled by the soviets, but events soon dictated otherwise. Given their narrow political base (there were fewer than 300,000 Bolsheviks in November 1917), Lenin and his supporters faced widespread opposition on every front [8]. There were those who advocated a revolutionary war to advance socialism in the rest of Europe; there were Bolsheviks who wanted money abolished and a socialist economy installed overnight; there were the peasants who

CONNECTIONS

See also

1286 Russia in the 19th century
1312 The Soviet Union under Stalin
1326 Socialism in the West
1288 Political thought in the 19th century
1290 Masters of sociology
1306 World War I

1 Russia paid a fearful price in human life for its incompetence in waging a long modern war. More than 15,000,000 men had been mobilized by mid-1917. About 1,700,000 men perished on the battlefield, 4,900,000 were wounded, and 2,400,000 were taken prisoner. Russia was superior in strength to Turkey, Bulgaria, and Austria-Hungary, but was outmatched by their ally, Germany.

2 Alexander Kerensky played a major role in shaping policies of the provisional governments in 1917. He was a minister in the first two provisional governments, prime minister from July onward, and after he had suppressed an army revolt in September he also took over as commander-in-chief. His "failure" to solve the twin problems of land and peace paved the way for Lenin's victory in October.

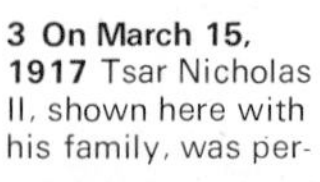

3 On March 15, 1917 Tsar Nicholas II, shown here with his family, was persuaded to abdicate, and the first provisional government was formed.

4 Demonstrations against the war during the "April Days," 1917 led to the fall of the first provisional government and the resignation of Foreign Minister Milyukov (1859–1943). But Russia's war effort continued, and in the soviets support for the Bolsheviks grew at the expense of the moderates. Calling for peace and complete transfer of power to the soviets, further demonstrations in June showed the growing influence of the Bolsheviks and declining support for the provisional government.

5 Clashes broke out in Petrograd on July 16–17, 1917, when armed workers demonstrated for "all power to the soviets" but were suppressed by the government.

6 General L. G. Kornilov (1870–1918), Kerensky's commander-in-chief, marched his troops on Petrograd in August 1917. This was seen by Kerensky as a right-wing attempt to take power, and he turned to the Bolsheviks for help. The plot dissolved, but it emphasized the growing political divisions that Kerensky could no longer bridge and paved the way for Lenin.

7 The Winter Palace was taken by the Bolsheviks on November 7, 1917. Lenin had secretly returned to Petrograd to promote Bolshevik plans for the overthrow of the provisional government, the collapse of which seemed imminent as unrest mounted. With the almost bloodless seizure of the palace Kerensky fled, and other members of the provisional government were arrested.

wanted to be left alone with the land now redistributed; and there were the dispossessed of the former regime.

The treaty of Brest-Litovsk in March 1918 ended the war with Germany; in the summer of the same year civil war broke out between the "Reds" (the Bolsheviks) and the "Whites" (anti-communists). In the autumn, the Allies intervened [9], in an attempt to reestablish the Eastern front, and soon began assisting the Whites. Hostilities lasted until the end of 1920 and revealed two victors, the Red Army and the Communist party. During this time the Bolsheviks murdered the imprisoned tsar and his family. The Reds had the advantage of a claim that they were defending Russia from invasion. The desperate measures needed to secure military victory alienated many workers and peasants. Although desertions from the Red Army were frequent, Trotsky was successful in forging Soviet military might, but democracy was an early victim of the conflict. Lenin fashioned a new force to rule the country, the Communist party of the Soviet Union.

The bloodshed and exhaustion of seven years of war left Soviet Russia torn by revolt. Lenin gave way to the peasants and in 1921 introduced the New Economic Policy (NEP), which temporarily relaxed socialism in favor of some private ownership [10]. The "commanding heights of the economy" stayed in state hands, but agriculture, employing 80 percent of the population, was on a market basis. The economy gradually recovered under the NEP.

The emergence of the new Russia

Soviet Russia had less territory than the old empire. The borderlands—Finland, Estonia, Latvia, Lithuania, Poland, part of the Ukraine, and Bessarabia—were lost. But in the three independent Transcaucasian republics, the British departure in December 1919 cleared the way for the Bolsheviks to take over, and by April 1921 Transcaucasia was under Soviet control.

There remained the problem of succession. Lenin expected Trotsky to succeed him, but ultimately the ruthless Joseph Stalin (1879–1953) prevailed.

KEY

Vladimir Ilyich Ulyanov (known as Lenin) was born in Simbirsk (now Ulyanov) on the Volga. He was usually in exile from 1900 on, but he returned for the Revolution of 1917.

Тов. Ленин ОЧИЩАЕТ
землю от нечисти.

8 "Comrade Lenin sweeps the world of its rubbish" in this early Soviet cartoon. Peace and land were the two major demands Lenin promised to meet, and immediately on seizing power the Bolsheviks put into effect the land policy they had adopted from the Socialist Revolutionaries. Land was later nationalized, but in 1917 most peasants still regarded it as their own. During the civil war grain was forcibly requisitioned to feed the Red Army and city dwellers. Peasants planted less, and there was famine and disease. Finally, Lenin capitulated and introduced the New Economic Policy in 1921.

ДЕНИКИН
КОЛЧАК
ЮДЕНИЧ

9 Civil war divided Russia in 1918–20, threatening Bolshevik rule. In March 1918, Germany had forced Russia to a disadvantageous peace settlement at Brest-Litovsk, but Allied troops then came to Russia to prevent the Germans from occupying key centers. After Germany's defeat they stayed and aided the Whites during the civil war. The Bolsheviks, who had demobilized the imperial army by granting land to the peasants and by seeking a separate peace, had to create a new force, the Red Army. Trotsky, the father of the Red Army, was a brilliant military leader. The Reds had to contend with Greens (anarchists), Poles, and dissident nationalities, and the British, Americans, Japanese, and French scattered around the country. The cartoon shows the Allies—the Americans, British, and French—unleashing the dogs of war: the White leaders Denikin, Kolchak, and Yudenich.

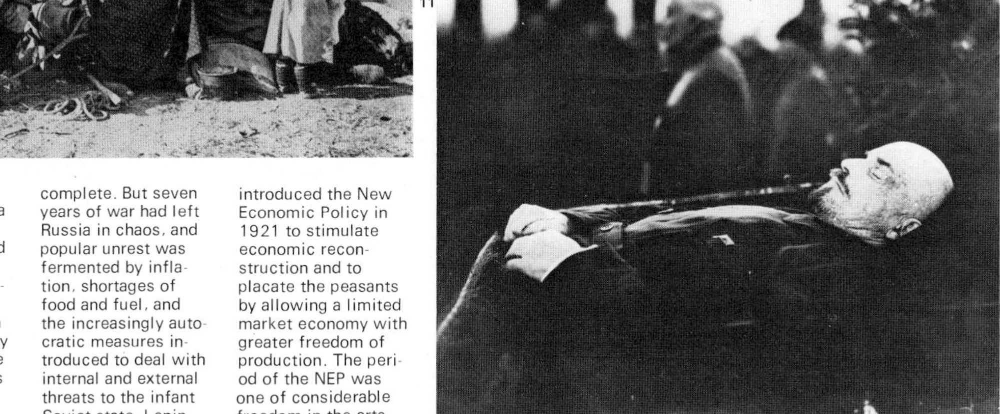

10 The famine that devastated the Volga region in the winter of 1921–22 claimed about 5,000,000 lives and closely followed a virtual collapse of the Russian economy in 1921. By the end of 1920, the defeat of the Whites and the withdrawal of the Allies was complete. But seven years of war had left Russia in chaos, and popular unrest was fermented by inflation, shortages of food and fuel, and the increasingly autocratic measures introduced to deal with internal and external threats to the infant Soviet state. Lenin introduced the New Economic Policy in 1921 to stimulate economic reconstruction and to placate the peasants by allowing a limited market economy with greater freedom of production. The period of the NEP was one of considerable freedom in the arts.

11 Lenin's death in 1924 followed a stroke in 1922, at which time a troika of Zinoviev (1883–1936), Kamenev (1883–1936), and Stalin was established to continue the leadership. Lenin distrusted Stalin, whose main rival for the succession was Trotsky. But by skillfully playing off various factions and by control of the party mechanism, Stalin isolated Trotsky by 1925 and moved toward personal domination and ultimate dictatorship.

The Soviet Union under Stalin

The evolution of the Soviet Union between 1917 and 1953 was dominated by two men, Vladimir Ilyich Lenin (1870–1924) and Joseph Stalin (1879–1953) [Key]. While Lenin was alive he was the main driving force behind events. Nevertheless, there were other important personalities. Leon Trotsky (1879–1940) [1], Nikolai Bukharin (1888–1938) [2], Mikhail Tomsky (1880–1936), Grigorij Zinoviev (1883–1936), and Anatoli Lunacharsky (1875–1933), to name only a few. All made original contributions to Soviet development.

The policies of Joseph Stalin

Lenin realized the importance of consolidating the revolution; Stalin developed and extended the means. He sanctioned the revolutionary violence of the Cheka (secret police) and extended the primacy of the party in state affairs. His doctrine of "Socialism in One Country" meant that all foreign communist parties became subservient to Soviet interests through the Comintern (Communist International). Further, he continued the Bolshevik tradition of show trials of so-called counterrevolutionaries. The first took place in 1922 and were directed at the Socialist Revolutionaries.

Nevertheless, there were major differences between the two men. Stalin was an intuitive anti-intellectual. His intellectual insecurity did not permit him to envisage a policy and then take on his opponents in open debate. Instead, he sought to outmaneuver them in labyrinthine intrigue. Lenin was good at placing labels, often misleading ones, on his opponents; Stalin, however, was a master at the art. Lenin used Marxist theory like a skilled artist. Stalin used it like a laborer. Lenin used the Cheka and the show trials against non-Bolsheviks; Stalin used them against the Communist party as well.

The achievement of power

Stalin built up his power by his administrative skills and filled the leading party bodie with workers, but he did take the precaution of first briefing them on how to vote.

Stalin's journey on the way to supreme power can be divided into three stages, the completion of each marking a significant step forward. The first, terminating in 1928–29, saw him with almost total control over the apparatus of the Russian Communist party, which, because of the events of the immediate post-October period, had inherited the dominant role in the state. Victory over the party was not sufficient to permit Stalin to reach out to every corner of the Soviet Union. This he did during the 1930s when collectivization and industrialization transformed the scene. The peasants, making up about 80 percent of the population, lost their land and their livestock and were brought under complete state control [3]. The foundations of great industrial advance were laid, with heavy industry, vital for defense, receiving top priority [4]. A terrible massacre of real, putative, imaginary, and potential opponents of Stalin's dictatorship took place. No one was secure, whether top party official (a major target were the Old Bolsheviks, who had seized power with Lenin in October 1917), military leader, writer, peasant, worker, engineer, or foreign communist leader living in

CONNECTIONS

See also
1310 The Russian Revolution
1390 The super powers: from confrontation to détente
1352 Non-alignment and the Third World
1342 The division of Europe
1344 The Soviet Union after World War II
1346 Eastern Europe 1948–Present
1336 Causes of World War II
1326 Socialism in the West
1286 Russia in the 19th century
1308 The Peace of Paris

1 An outstanding theorist, Trotsky was, however, a poor politician, ill at ease with the minutiae of government. Although expected to succeed Lenin, he was inept at intrigue and was defeated. It was his failure to perceive the machinations of his fellows that led to his exile and death. He was an unequaled speaker, but his independent, critical attitude was not tolerated by Joseph Stalin.

2 Lenin called Bukharin "the darling of the whole party" and its "most valuable and most powerful theorist." Bukharin was the leading party writer on economic subjects. He sided with Stalin against Trotsky, Kamenev, and Zinoviev and was a leading defender of the New Economic Policy. He was swept aside at the end of the 1920s when collectivization became the new official policy in Russia.

1927
1932
Collective farms 0·6%
State farms 1·4%
State farms 10%
Individual farms 22%
1927 Total peasantry 120,000,000
Total households 25,000,000
Percentage of peasant households collectivized:
Collective farms 68%
Individual farms 98%
0·8% 7·6% 16·9% 57·6% 21% 52·7% 61·5%
1927 Oct
1929 Oct
1930 Jan
1930 Mar
1930 Sept
1931
1932

3 The New Economic Policy was a compromise on the way to socialism. It permitted the blossoming of private farming, and since four out of five Soviet citizens lived in the countryside there was a risk of the capitalist ethic proving attractive. Lenin had preached cooperation, and Bukharin ably elucidated his views after 1924. When agricultural production climbed back after 1924 to the level of 1913, the Soviets were faced with a choice—allow private agriculture to develop and provide the basis for overall economic growth or socialize agriculture and base economic growth on industrial development. They chose to base economic growth on industry out of fear that private agriculture could overturn the socialist state, and Stalin wanted food supplies for the urban worker.

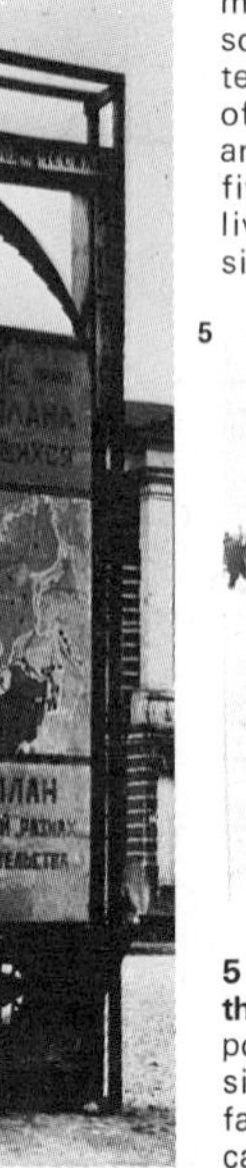

ПЯТИЛЕТНИЙ ПЛАН

4 Soviet power was insecure without a strong industrial and military base. Ambition ran riot as the first Five Year Plan got under way in 1928. Production goals were pushed up in the belief that revolutionary spirit could perform miracles. Heavy industry was favored at the expense of light industry and agriculture. Wonders were performed but at an appalling cost. Enthusiasm waned after the first plan and labor discipline became severe, with saboteurs and counterrevolutionaries unmasked everywhere. Living standards dropped as millions flooded to the cities, where accommodations were primitive. Both food and clothing were also in short supply.

5 The tractor was the symbol of Soviet power in the countryside. The collective farm, or *kolkhoz,* became the dominant enterprise in socialist agriculture after 1928. Much virgin land was brought into cultivation in the 1930s, and *sovhozes,* or state farms, were usually set up in new areas. Collective farm peasants were permitted a small private plot and some animals. These farm peasants received a share of the produce in proportion to the net income of the kolkhoz.

exile in the USSR. More than 10,000,000 people perished.

When this period ended, Stalin was master of Soviet Russia; he controlled the party, the government, and the police. Through the agency of foreign communist parties he could influence the internal politics of other countries. The third phase, which began with the outbreak of World War II and ended with Stalin's death in March 1953, saw Stalinist Russia reach a major position in world influence.

Stalin exhibited great tactical skill in the 1920s in overcoming his competitors one by one. In 1923–24 he allied himself with L. V. Kamenev (1883–1936) and Zinoviev against Trotsky; in 1925 he sided with Bukharin against Kamenev and Zinoviev; in 1926–27, still with Bukharin (who realized too late that Stalin's allegiance was merely tactical), he opposed Trotsky, Kamenev, and Zinoviev; finally in 1928–29 he was strong enough to oppose Bukharin, Tomsky, and Rykov (1881–1938) by himself. By 1929, Trotsky was in exile and the others living on borrowed time. Most were to perish in the purges of 1936–38 [7]. Trotsky, exiled in Mexico, was murdered by Stalin's executioner in 1940.

Industrial and political development

Industrial effort in the 1930s made great progress. The bases of a thriving heavy industry were established and were to prove of vital importance when war came. Stalin took a long time to learn foreign affairs [11]. He indirectly helped Hitler gain power in Germany, then saw the danger and launched the Popular Front, inviting the collaboration of all democratic forces. He again put his faith in National Socialist Germany in 1939 and almost paid with the annihilation of the USSR after the German attack of June 1941.

Stalin's war record, except for the opening days of the war when he lost his nerve, is admirable. He led by example, and his ruthlessness steadied his armies. Stalin played a vital role in the victory of the Allies. But had he allied the USSR with Britain and France in 1939, Germany might not have attacked Poland.

KEY

"Lenin is the Marx of our time" was the slogan when Vladimir Ilyich Lenin was alive. Soon a new slogan appeared: "Stalin is our Lenin." Stalin became the main interpreter of Marx's chief Russian disciple. Those who threatened his supremacy were soon removed from positions of power.

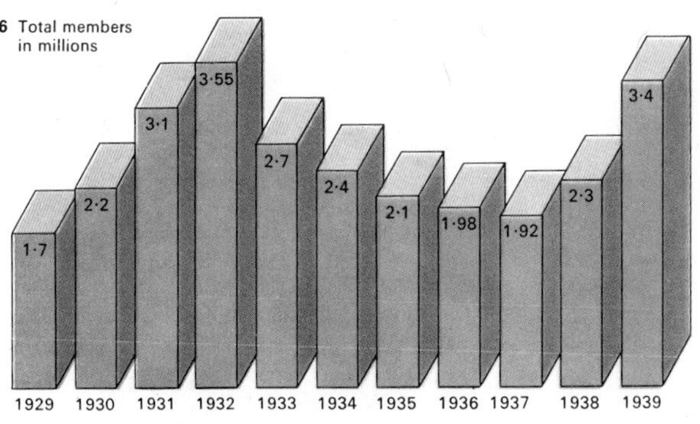

6 Total members in millions
1·7
2·2
3·1
3·55
2·7
2·4
2·1
1·98
1·92
2·3
3·4
1929 1930 1931 1932 1933 1934 1935 1936 1937 1938 1939

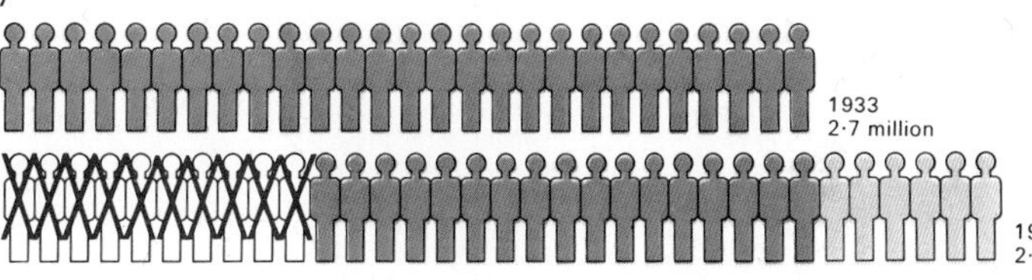

7
1933 2·7 million
1938 2·3 million
Party members
Purged
New members

7 The purges of the 1930s were in fact composed of many different operations; these gathered momentum and reached a crescendo in the "Yezhovschina" (named after Yezhov, the head of Internal Affairs) of 1937–38. The first purge was launched by the party in January 1933. In 1935 a "verification of party documents" was ordered. About one member in five was expelled, including recent worker and peasant recruits. About 9% had been purged before the show trials ushered in the devastating Great Purge of 1936–38, when millions perished in the party and populace alike.

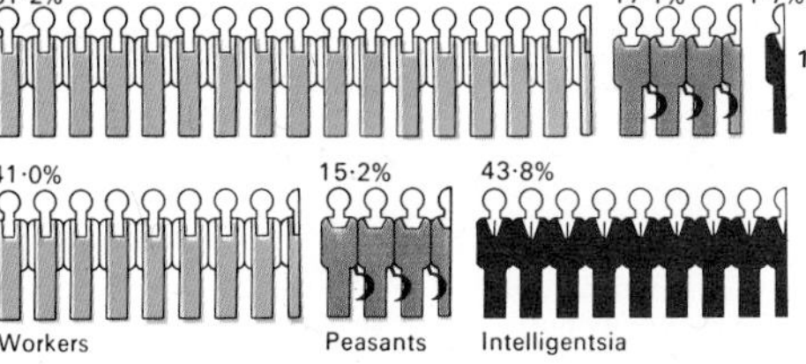

Class composition of recruits 1929
81·2%
17·1%
1·7%
1936-39
41·0%
15·2%
43·8%
Workers
Peasants
Intelligentsia

6 The composition of the Communist party's membership changed markedly between 1929 and 1939. In 1929 four-fifths of party members were workers; ten years later that proportion had dropped to two-fifths. The difference was made up by a massive recruitment of the intelligentsia, partly because of a deliberate campaign to recruit the "best" people, partly because a party card was needed as a qualification for many important posts in industry and the administration. The dramatic change in membership reflects the policy behind the 1933-38 purges as well as their effects.

11

БЕСПОЩАДНО
РАЗГРОМИМ
И УНИЧТОЖИМ
ВРАГА!
Договор о ненападении между СССР и Германией
КУКРЫНИКСЫ-41

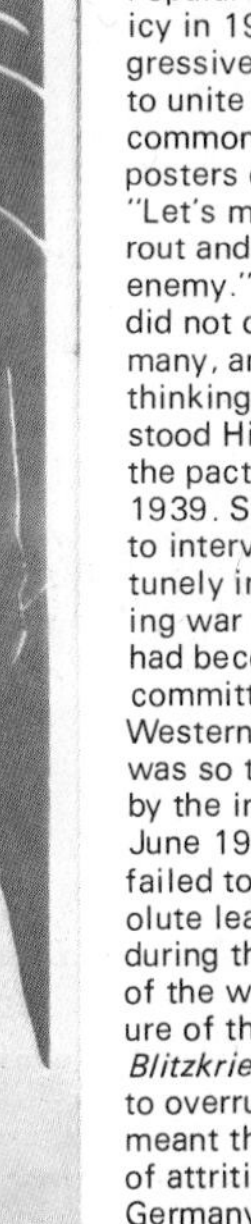

11 Stalin misjudged fascism in the early 1930s, but when he realized the danger he launched the Popular Front policy in 1935. All progressive forces were to unite against the common enemy, and posters declared "Let's mercilessly rout and destroy the enemy." This policy did not deter Germany, and Stalin, thinking he understood Hitler, signed the pact of August 1939. Stalin intended to intervene opportunely in the impending war when Hitler had become overcommitted on the Western Front. Stalin was so thunderstruck by the invasion of June 1941 that he failed to provide resolute leadership during the first days of the war. The failure of the German *Blitzkrieg* in 1941–42 to overrun the USSR meant that the war of attrition, which Germany could not win because of inadequate resources, became inevitable. Major battles were Moscow and Stalingrad.

8

8 Vyacheslav Molotov (1890–) became a full member of the Politburo in 1926. He was instrumental in shaping the nonaggression pact with the Nazis, and he remained a loyal servant to Stalin. He was also involved in party construction.

9

9 Nikita Khrushchev (1894–1971) was on the Moscow party committee between 1932 and 1938, when he took the key post of First Secretary of the party in the Ukraine. He became a member of the Politburo in 1939 where he backed Stalin.

10

10 Lazar Kaganovich (1893–) became a full member of the Politburo in 1930. He headed the Moscow party committee 1930–35 and was minister of transport 1935–44. A loyal supporter of Stalin, he remained in favor 1930–53.

Ireland and independence

On April 24, 1916, Easter Monday, an armed insurrection against British rule broke out in Dublin, the Irish capital. Although in itself it was a small-scale military event, lasting only a week, it represented the culmination of more than 100 years of nationalist agitation in Ireland and was followed six years later by the emergence of a sovereign entity, the Irish Free State [Key]. In the northeast six of Ireland's 32 counties remained part of the United Kingdom, but in the late 1960s a bloody conflict erupted there between the Catholic and Protestant communities in which the British Army intervened. The violent and intractable Irish problem therefore remained unsolved.

English rule in Ireland

Ireland's history is inseparable from that of its powerful neighbor, England, which from the twelfth century established its rule in at least part of Ireland. Comprehensive control was secured in the seventeenth century, and it was in that period that a colonial landownership system emerged, with immigrant Protestant farmers from Scotland in the northeast and Anglo-Irish landowners presiding over an impoverished Catholic peasantry in the rest of the country.

In the eighteenth century rising agricultural unemployment led to the first peasant resistance, and in 1798 the Society of United Irishmen, influenced and encouraged by the French Revolution, staged the first of Ireland's attempts to expel the English from the island. In the 1820s, Daniel O'Connell (1775–1847) led the Catholic Emancipation movement, which resulted in Catholics being granted equal rights in 1829. But the situation in the countryside deteriorated. After potato blight led to the Famine in 1846–47, nearly one million people died, and another two million were forced to emigrate in a single decade [2, 3].

In the 1860s a revived nationalist movement, the Fenians, organized with the assistance of Irish immigrants in the United States, tried to stage another insurrection, and after them the Irish Land League, led by Michael Davitt (1846–1906), and the Irish Home Rule movement pressed for social and political change. The main support for the movement came from the urban middle class, although their most powerful leader was a Protestant landowner named Charles Stewart Parnell (1846–91) [4A]. But it was only in the 1880s that Land Acts began to lay the foundations for a more stable system, one of independent, medium-sized farms. In 1905 Arthur Griffith (1872–1922) founded Sinn Fein ("Ourselves Alone"), an organization that demanded an independent island altogether.

The Loyalist factor

The Protestant population of the industrialized northeast did not want to sever the link with Britain and participate in a predominantly Catholic state; not only were they separated by religion and culture from the Catholic majority, but they also enjoyed a higher standard of living [6]. For them independence presented both an economic and a political threat, and they had opposed the first liberal attempts at Home Rule in the 1880s. On the eve of World War I, both nationalists in the south and Protestant "loyalists" formed paramilitary groups.

CONNECTIONS

See also
1278 The United States: Reconstruction to World War I
1284 European Industrialization 1870–1914
1288 Political thought in the 19th century
1324 The twenties and the Depression

1 Eviction of cottagers was common in the 1870s and 1880s when conflicts between tenant farmers and landlords were at their sharpest. Although death and emigration reduced crowding on the land, there was an agricultural crisis in the 1870s when many families were evicted after being unable to pay their rents. More than 2,000 families were driven out in 1880 alone, and in that year there were nearly 2,600 incidents in which the peasants retaliated by burning haystacks, maiming farm animals, and destroying buildings. Land Acts restored rural order only in the 1890s.

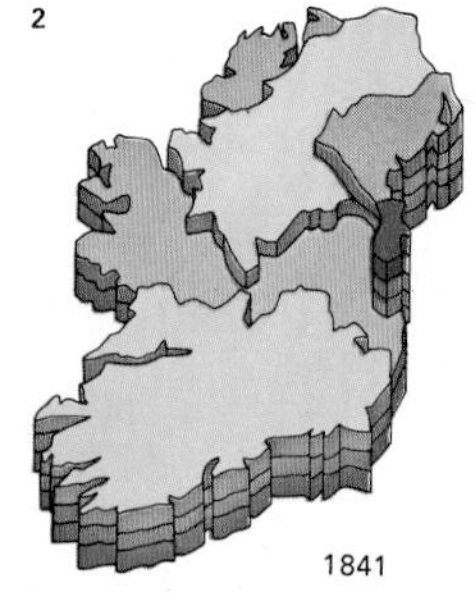

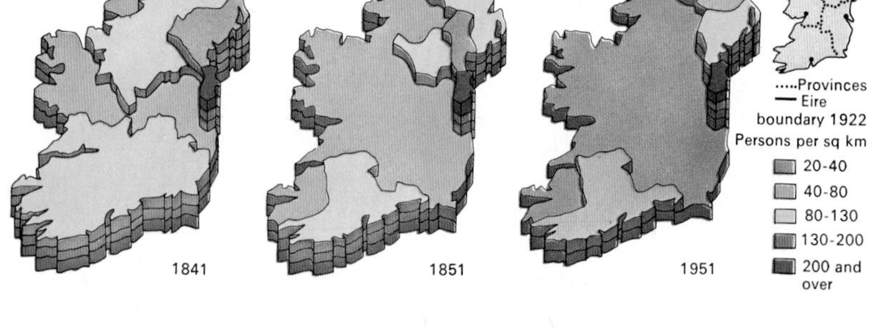

1841
1851
1951
Provinces
Eire boundary 1922
Persons per sq km
20-40
40-80
80-130
130-200
200 and over

2 The total population of Ireland fell by half between 1841 and 1851 – from 8.1 million to 4.3 million. Only in 1971 did census figures indicate that the population was again increasing. Depopulation began with deaths in the Famine of the 1840s and was accelerated by emigration, which continued into the late 1950s. Other reasons for population decline were that fewer people married in the rural areas than in towns, and those who did married later than couples in other parts of Europe – both of these reflecting a shortage of landed property. Overall depopulation was felt far more seriously in the countryside; since Dublin and Belfast are in the east there was a balance shift from the south and west to the north and east. Between 1841 and 1911 the population of the towns rose slightly from 1.2 million to 1.5 million, while that of rural areas fell from almost seven million to less than three. Throughout both the 19th and 20th centuries, visitors to rural Ireland commented on the large numbers of abandoned cottages that were found there.

2·4
1·4
1·2
1·0
0·6
0·7
0·1 million
From 32 counties
From Eire
From N. Ireland
1841-60 1861-80 1881-1900 1901-26 1926-51 1951-71

3 Mass emigration from Ireland dates from the dramatic years of 1846–47, the period of the Potato Famine when 346,000 people left. In the decade 1845–55 nearly two million fled the country. Another agricultural crisis in the late 1870s and 1880s provoked a massive new outflow of more than one million in these two decades. By 1925, about 4.7 million had emigrated to the United States, 70,000 to Canada, and 370,000 to Australia. Although no accurate figure exists for emigration to Britain, it was probably at least half a million. The period from 1914–39 saw a decline in emigration, but the numbers going to Britain increased during World War II, and in the 1960s annual emigration was 15,000.

4 Irish nationalist leaders included Charles Stewart Parnell [A], who led the Home Rule movement from 1879–90 and made it a central issue in British politics. Imprisoned in 1881, he was able after his release to persuade the Liberal leader Gladstone to support Home Rule, a development blocked chiefly by the Conservative majority in the House of Lords. Parnell lost his position of leadership after he was cited in a divorce case that aroused Catholic hostility. Eamon de Valera [B] was a teacher turned soldier who was, by the mid-1920s, the only Republican leader to have survived the battles of the previous decade. As prime minister, then president, he became the dominant figure in Eire after independence. Michael Collins [C], known as "the Big Fellow," was a former bank clerk who in effect commanded Republican forces in the Anglo-Irish war of 1919–21. He led the Treaty faction in 1922 and was killed during the civil war.

The main southern groups organized in this manner were the Irish Volunteers and the Irish Republican Brotherhood, successor to the Fenians, who led the unsuccessful 1916 uprising in Dublin [5]. When World War I was over, the coalition government of Lloyd George tried to solve the problem by offering Home Rule to north and south separately. The nationalists now demanded full independence, however, and from 1919 to 1921 the Irish Republican Army fought a guerrilla war against British forces. In 1921 the British agreed to negotiate with the Republican forces and talks were held in London. While one group, led by Michael Collins (1890–1922) [4C], accepted the terms of the London agreement, which excluded the six northern counties from an independent Eire, another group, led by Eamon de Valera (1882–1975), refused; when the Irish Free State came into existence a civil war broke out between the Treaty and anti-Treaty Republican factions.

Within a year the anti-Treaty forces were defeated, and although de Valera and his followers at first refused to participate in the Dáil Eireann (Assembly of Ireland) because members had to swear allegiance to the British crown, they agreed to do so in 1927. In 1932, de Valera became prime minister, a position he held, with two brief interruptions, until 1959 [4B]. The south broke its ties with Britain, while in the north a Protestant majority, represented by the Ulster Unionist Party, opposed a united Ireland and administered a form of Home Rule through a parliament at Stormont.

Violence in Ulster

Contacts between the Dublin and Belfast governments in the mid-1960s appeared to presage greater cooperation between north and south, but the emergence of a Catholic civil rights movement in the north in 1968–69 was followed by communal violence [7], the resurgence of an Irish Republican Army (IRA), and the entry of British troops into the province in August 1969 [8]. Serious fighting was taking place by 1971, and in 1972 direct rule from Westminster was imposed and Stormont abolished. By the mid-1970s the death toll approached 1,500.

Ireland before partition had 32 counties. During the Anglo-Irish war of 1919–21, in which 752 Irish were estimated to have died, fighting was mainly rural and in the south and west. Except for Cork, there were only "incidents" in towns, such as Dublin and Limerick. When the Irish Free State was established in 1922, 26 counties were included while the other 6 (Ulster) stayed within the United Kingdom with a degree of Home Rule. Partition excluded from the Free State the main areas of Protestant population, and these included the major industries (linen, engineering, and shipbuilding), which were located in the northeast of the country.

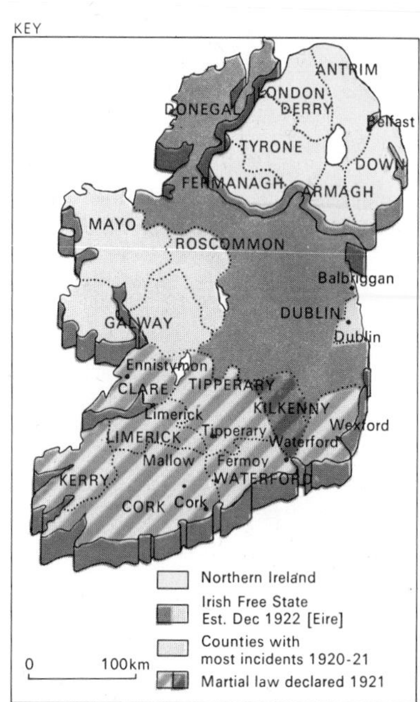
KEY
ANTRIM
LONDONDERRY
DONEGAL
Belfast
TYRONE
DOWN
FERMANAGH
ARMAGH
MAYO
ROSCOMMON
Balbriggan
DUBLIN
Dublin
GALWAY
Ennistymon
CLARE
TIPPERARY
Limerick
KILKENNY
Wexford
LIMERICK
Tipperary
Waterford
Mallow
Fermoy
KERRY
WATERFORD
CORK
Cork
0
100km
Northern Ireland
Irish Free State Est. Dec 1922 [Eire]
Counties with most incidents 1920-21
Martial law declared 1921

5

5 The 1916 Easter Rising was planned by the nationalist Irish Republican Brotherhood (the Fenians) and led by them and the Irish Volunteers, with the more socialist Irish Citizen Army led by James Connolly (1870–1916). With an estimated 1,600 men they seized several public buildings in the center of Dublin and from headquarters in the Post Office building proclaimed a republic. With little support from outside Dublin, they were no match for British artillery and surrendered within a week. Although many Irish people were not in sympathy with the insurrection itself, support for the Republican cause grew after the secret execution of the rebel leaders and widespread arrests of suspects. The rising thus gave the Republican movement a popular base for its struggle.

6

1926
53 | 47 (figures in %)
26 | 74
1951
41 | 59
18 | 82
1971
27 | 73
9 | 91
Eire
Northern Ireland

6 An economic disparity between north and south was clearly established after the partition of Ireland in 1922. The south was dominated by agriculture (53 percent of its labor force in 1926), whereas the north was more industrial (74 percent of its labor force in 1926). Unlike the people of Eire, the people of Ulster were able to enjoy a higher standard of social services provided by Britain. Industrialization in the south made rapid strides only in the late 1950s, when the Republic began to encourage investment of foreign capital. Despite chronic unemployment in the north, per capita income stayed higher than in the south.

7

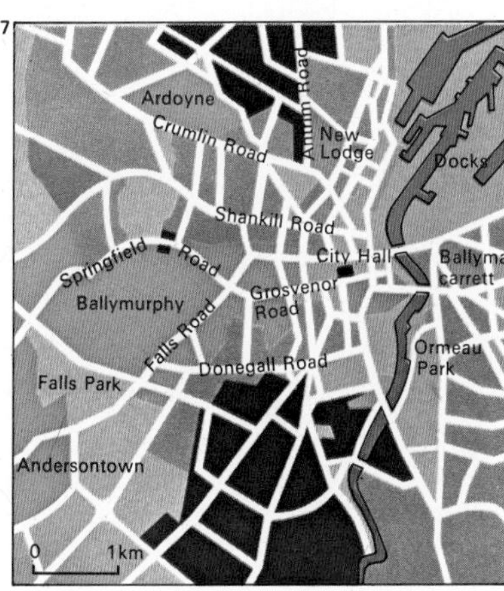
Protestant
Catholic
Mixed
Ardoyne
Crumlin Road
Antrim Road
New Lodge
Docks
Shankill Road
Springfield Road
City Hall
Ballymacarrett
Ballymurphy
Grosvenor Road
Falls Road
Ormeau Park
Falls Park
Donegall Road
Andersontown
0
1km

7 Belfast's growing working-class population partly segregated itself in the 19th century into Catholics living around the Falls Road and Protestants around the Shankill Road. It was in these depressed streets that the maximum violence of the post-1969 period was seen in community clashes and attacks on the British Army.

8

8 The British Army was sent into Northern Ireland in August 1969 to provide the Catholic community with a peace-keeping force not dominated by the majority Protestant community. But by 1971 the main struggle was between the Provisional IRA, based in Catholic areas, and the British Army. An army of 17,000 was soon involved in continual clashes with paramilitary groups from both communities and in attempts to stop terrorist activities.

Origins of film

The inventors of motion pictures were trying to perfect a scientific instrument for studying motion. Not one foresaw the impact that movies would have on the world of entertainment.

The illusion of movement

The motion in motion pictures results from faulty perception. The human eye retains images for a fraction of a second longer than they are actually present. In addition, the human brain perceives motion in short intervals where no motion actually exists. Thus, when a succession of still images is projected at the proper interval, the viewer sees continuous movement.

During the last quarter of the nineteenth century many Europeans and Americans were trying to find the right mechanism for photographing and reproducing motion. But it was probably W. L. Dickson (1860–1935), working for Thomas Edison, who first solved the problem of how to get effective cinematographic reproduction in 1889–92. Then, on December 28, 1895, the Lumière brothers, Louis (1864–1948) and Auguste (1862–1954), first projected movies in public in Paris.

The potential of the movies as an entertainment medium soon became apparent. Georges Méliès (1861–1938) was one of those who developed the techniques of double exposure, fast and slow motion, fades, dissolves, and close-ups [1].

In England the film makers of the Brighton School and in the United States Edwin S. Porter (1869–1941) began to make movie stories out of short sequences of film, just as movies are made today. Porter's *The Great Train Robbery* (1903) [2], one of the earliest and most adept of these films, had a tremendous popularity that insured that the future of the medium lay with the story film.

The early film industries

In the first 10 to 15 years of the movie industry in Europe, the United States, and Japan, magical "trick" films, action chase films, and documentaries (many of them faked) dominated production. The Japanese were among the first to make extensive use of stage drama for more "serious" films. The first feature-length film, *Ned Kelly and His Gang,* was produced in Australia in 1906, although it was not until the success of spectacle films like *Cabiria* [3] that longer films became the norm.

Intolerance (1916), a box office failure, was one of the most influential films ever made. D. W. Griffith (1875–1948) [4] used an impressive battery of movie techniques to explore the theme of his title. He combined the major production trends of his time into one uniquely American synthesis, drawing on social realism, a mark of the early Scandinavian industry and of some Italian films; on the spectacle film from Italy; and on the serious theatrical films of France. His contemporary and one-time associate, Mack Sennett (1880–1960) [7], used the old chase films and elements from burlesque, pantomime, and comic strips to create something else peculiarly American—slapstick comedy.

World War I hurt European film production badly. By 1919 only Hollywood could afford the mammoth investment needed to sustain a healthy movie industry. In spite of

CONNECTIONS

See also
1362 Hollywood
1370 Cinema as art
1364 20th century music—tradition and experimentation

1

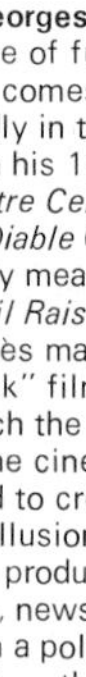

1 Georges Méliès' sense of fun and fantasy comes through vividly in this still from his 1906 *Les Quatre Cent Coups du Diable* (which really means *The Devil Raises Hell).* Méliès made many "trick" films in which the resources of the cinema were used to create magical illusions, but he also produced dramas, newsreels, and even a political exposé on the Dreyfus Affair (1899).

2

2 The Great Train Robbery linked shots together to tell a story in a way few audiences had seen before 1903. In the hands of Edwin S. Porter, the story was able to move across great distances in split seconds. He switched from outdoor shots of the bandits making off with their loot [top] to an interior scene, supposedly miles away, where some western fun is broken up when news of the robbery is brought and the townspeople rush to form a posse [bottom]. Porter's 10-minute Western contained 15 separate shots edited together in this new and effective manner.

3

3 The Italian spectacular, *Cabiria* (1914), was the high point of that nation's production of historical pageantry. The film capitalized on the reputation of novelist Gabriele D'Annunzio (who actually only approved the outline and wrote some titles), but its real power came from director Giovanni Pastrone's massive sets, slowly moving camera shots, and the character of Maciste, the black slave, who became a national hero.

4

4 D(avid) W(ark) Griffith was the "father of modern cinema," although many of his films seem old-fashioned to audiences today. Griffith used movie techniques with a facility that had no equal in his day. He broke up the action within scenes into different shots, controlling the dramatic emphasis of the scene with editing and camera placement and making a decisive break with the contemporary theatrical style of film production.

this, it was in Europe that the major advances of the 1920s originated.

The great national styles of the 1920s

In Germany Expressionism had a profound influence on the cinema. *The Cabinet of Dr. Caligari* (1919) with its distorted sets [5] is probably the most famous movie made in this style. Many of the best-known German directors—Ernst Lubitsch (1892–1947), F. W. Murnau (1888–1932), and Fritz Lang (1890–1976) among them—eventually moved to Hollywood.

At the same time, cinematic naturalism was reaching a high point in the work of Scandanavian directors like Victor Sjöstrom (1879–1960), Mauritz Stiller (1883–1928), and Carl Dreyer (1889–1968), while in France the first movie avant-grade was producing highly stylized work in the films of René Clair (1898–   ) and others.

The second half of the decade, however, was dominated by films from the Soviet Union. Seeing an illustration of the power of Marxist dialectics in the way two shots combine to create meaning, Soviet directors like Sergei Eisenstein (1898–1948), V. I. Pudovkin (1893–1953), and Alexander Dovshenko (1894–1956) created movies based upon the collision of images. Eisenstein's *Potemkin* (1925) is the masterpiece of this revolutionary style [6].

The assured visual and dramatic style of Kenji Mizoguchi (1898–1956) and the haunting images of Teinosuke Kinusage (1896–   ) signaled the maturity of the Japanese silent film in the late twenties. In France the surrealist movement began its long association with the cinema in the shocking short film by Luis Buñuel and Salvador Dali, *An Andalusian Dog (Un chien andalou)* (1929).

Sound

In a desperate gamble to stave off financial ruin the Warner Brothers Studio in Hollywood committed itself to the development of "talking pictures." In 1927 *The Jazz Singer* [8] featured synchronized talking, singing, and music. Audience response was immediate and enthusiastic. By 1930 silent films were a thing of the past.

KEY

Charles Chaplin's little tramp is one of the cinema's most enduring creations. Beginning in 1914, Chaplin touched millions with his funny/sad tales of human resiliency.

5

5 The Cabinet of Dr. Caligari brought something new and unexpected to films, subjective storytelling. Influenced by painting, German Expressionist film makers used distorted sets, lighting, camera angles, and highly stylized acting in films that were meant to show an interior, psychological view of the action in them.

6 The Odessa steps sequence from *Potemkin* creates the experience of a fictional massacre by carefully controlling the movement, rhythm, composition, and order of the fragmentary shots that make it up. It is a landmark in the history of film as art.

6

7 Film stunting and slapstick were born in the Keystone studio of Mack Sennett (1880–1960), who in 1912 got together former music hall comedians, acrobats, cowboys, daredevils, and other uninsurables, put them into policemen's uniforms and sent them on an endless series of surrealistic escapades as the Keystone Kops. Sennett's one-reelers were fast, furious, funny—and dangerous. They invariably ended in a chase sequence with vehicles careering into screen infinity.

7

8

8 Al Jolson, playing a blackface entertainer in *The Jazz Singer*, told audiences "You ain't heard nothin' yet," and the line became immortal as the first dialogue heard in a feature film. Sound had been presented with film as early as 1893, but it was the popularity of the songs and the few lines of ad-lib dialogue in *The Jazz Singer* that persuaded Hollywood businessmen that the cost of reequipping for sound would be recouped at the box office. The first all-talking movie was Warner Brothers' *The Lights of New York* in 1928, but the sound-on-film system which finally became standard was controlled by Fox Films.

Dada, Surrealism, and their legacy

World War I had a twofold influence on the development of twentieth-century art. The centers of activity moved from France and Germany to New York City and neutral Switzerland. Meanwhile, the rejection of established artistic values (postulated by the Cubists and the Expressionists) acquired a new political relevance in the light of the war, which many intellectuals saw as the logical culmination of the whole ethos of the nineteenth century.

Shock the bourgeoisie!

Dada, a complex international movement, was essentially an attack on both artistic and political traditions. There remains some controversy as to the origin of the name, but it was certainly in use by mid-1916 to describe the activities of the Cabaret Voltaire in Zurich, which included performances and recitations intended to outrage the conventional. An early associate was the Franco-German artist Jean (Hans) Arp (1887–1966). A refugee from the war, he was making wood reliefs based on organic forms so simplified as to appear ridiculous; in his own words they were "designed to show the bourgeois the absurdity of his world." Meanwhile, in New York, Marcel Duchamp (1887–1968) [1] was questioning established artistic procedures—and, by implication, the context in which they operated—by exhibiting "ready-mades" such as a bottle-rack or urinal.

After the war Dada spread to other centers. Its varied guises had in common nihilism and a desire to shock.

The collage technique developed by Picasso and Braque was employed by many Dadaists for their own subversive ends. Kurt Schwitters (1887–1948) made art from rubbish [2] and Max Ernst (1891–1976) assembled fragments of photographs and engravings to create irrational compositions. This latter method was to lead Ernst back to the art of painting when, in 1921, he embarked on a series of paintings in an illusionistic academic manner that presented suggestive and disturbing juxtapositions of images [3].

As the Dada manifestations died down, a group of writers and painters including Ernst and Arp assembled in Paris around the poet André Breton (1896–1966). While sharing Dada's disgust for bourgeois values, they rejected its nihilism and adopted a strongly positive philosophy inspired by the psychological theories of Sigmund Freud (1856–1939).

They believed that society repressed man's true nature and that in both life and art it was necessary to give full rein to the imagination. In the *First Surrealist Manifesto* of 1924, Breton defined Surrealism as "pure psychic automatism" and decreed that it was to be achieved by writing without conscious control.

Chance and imagination

When applied to painting, this procedure led Surrealism away from illusionism. Joan Miró (1893–) in his paintings of 1925 laid down highly diluted paint in a fairly arbitrary fashion that simply suggested the lines of a more controlled composition [5]. Ernst sought inspiration in wood grain textures, which he transferred to the paintings by rubbing. Both painters were exploiting

CONNECTIONS

See also
1294 Fauvism and Expressionism
1296 Cubism and Futurism
1320 Abstract art

1 **Marcel Duchamp's "Bicycle Wheel"** (1913) was the first of his "ready-mades," attacking the almost religious reverence given by society to original art works. An artist's choice of object, in this instance reflecting an interest in movement shared with the Italian Futurists, was enough reason to give it artistic status, to place it on a pedestal, here represented by a stool. By 1964 replicas of this work were selling well.

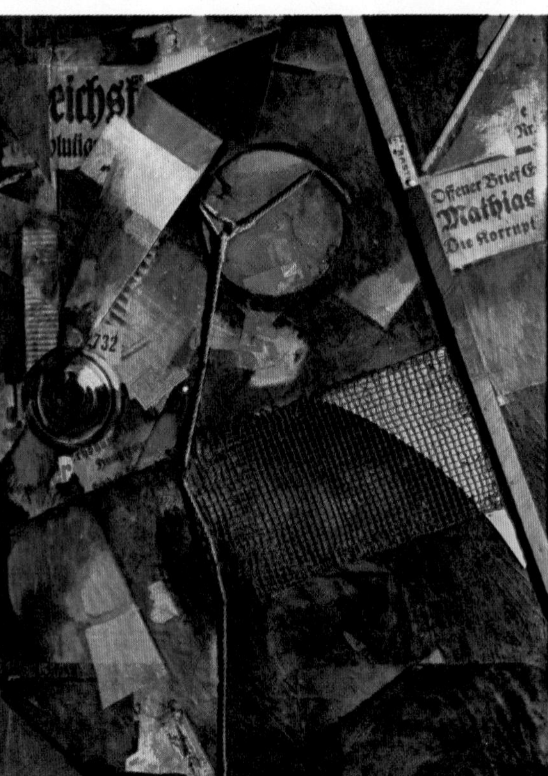

2 **Kurt Schwitters,** a Hanover Dadaist, made his "Merz" pictures, such as "Das Sternbild" (1920), from rubbish. They contrast strongly with the neat collages of the Cubists. Their texture is rich, their design strong.

3 **Max Ernst's** "Two Children Threatened by a Nightingale" is an early (1924) Surrealist attempt to render in paint the experience of dreams. Ernst used both paint and wood relief, the latter breaking out of the illusionist space of the picture surface to spill across the frame, perhaps an analogy for the transition from the nightmare to the waking world. The threat of the nightingale represents here both an external menace and fear at discovery of sexuality.

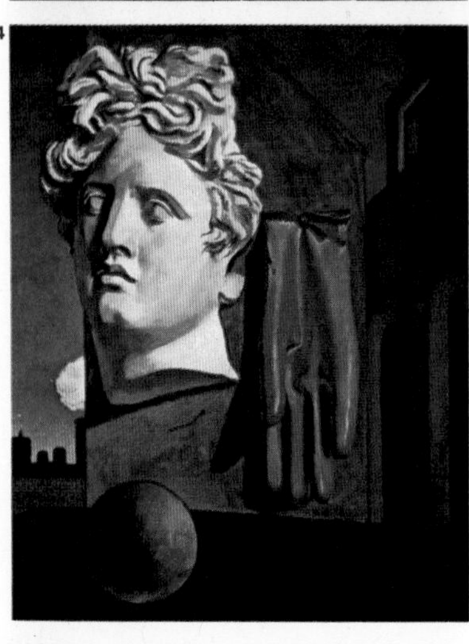

4 **"Song of Love"** (1914) by Giorgio de Chirico (1888–) is one of his mysterious scenes that anticipate the dream pictures of the Surrealists. He rejected their psychoanalytic interpretation of his art, however, and was concerned with creating a heightened "metaphysical" awareness of reality without any desire to shock in the Surrealist manner. Indeed, the surprise at the juxtaposition of the plaster head and the glove stems from the confounding of conscious expectation.

5 **Miró's "Birth of the World"** with its exquisite contrasts of hard-edged shapes and abstract washes shows how effective could be the Surrealist notion that the painter should free his imagination by painting without any idea of the end result.

chance in order to provoke the imagination in new directions.

By the end of the decade Surrealism had returned to the illusionism of the earlier Ernst, largely because of the work of Salvador Dali [Key] (1904–   ), who painted sensational subject matter deriving from psychoanalysis in a highly accomplished academic manner. The Belgian René Magritte (1898–1967) rejected automatism in favor of the presentation of startling visual paradoxes [6].

Generally, the Surrealists of the 1930s tried to express the unconscious by highly conscious artistic means. At the same time they turned increasingly to making "object-sculptures" in order to create disturbing images in a more tangible form than was possible in the most illusionistic painting.

Examples include Miro's combination of a stuffed green parrot, an artificial leg, and a bowler hat, and Maeret Oppenheim's fur-lined teacup. This tendency reached its climax in the Paris Surrealist exhibition of 1938. A total Surrealist environment was created with fantastically garbed mannequins; Duchamp covered the ceiling with coal sacks and the floor with moss.

World War II forced Breton and many other Surrealists to flee to the United States. Young painters there, most notably Arshile Gorky (1905–1948), took great interest in the automatic aspect of Surrealism and the way in which semi-abstract forms could bear a potent sexual charge [8], as in Ernst's and Miró's work. This led Gorky to a highly personal manner of loosely painted, contorted forms that was of considerable importance for Jackson Pollock (1912–1956), whose "action painting" was a form of automatism.

Surrealism today

After the war Breton returned to Paris, but the real heritage of the movement lay elsewhere. The "combine-paintings" that Robert Rauschenberg (1925–   ) [9] began in the mid-1950s had the irrational rightness of the best Surrealist objects, while the Dada assault on art was continued by, for example, the self-destructive machines of Jean Tinguely (1925–   ).

KEY

Salvador Dali's "Rainy Taxi" (1938), had live snails climbing over the face and chest of the mannequin. The disturbing eroticism is characteristic of Surrealism and Dali's particular adeptness here, plus his genius for publicity, marked him as a Surrealist leader long after he had left the movement.

6 René Magritte's "On the Threshold of Liberty" raises paradox to a point where our notions about the way we understand a picture are much undermined (just as Surrealist philosophy threatened established morals by making desire the final criterion of value judgments). The openings in the surrounding space are contradicting. The woman's torso and the cloudy sky cannot both be real. Which, if any, represents liberty? Perhaps they are all just painted panels on an imprisoning wall? The only way to find out for sure would be by firing the cannon.

6

7

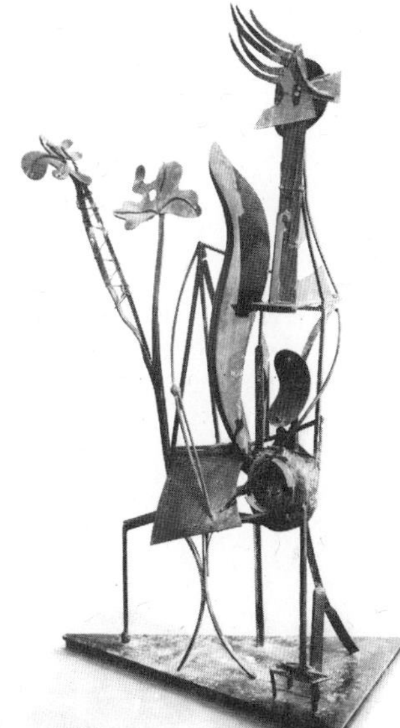

7 Pablo Picasso was never a member of the Surrealist group, but his "Woman in a Garden," unifying as it does images of both flowers and the female body within one structure, was the kind of metamorphosis that appealed strongly to the Surrealists. They were eager to claim him as an antecedent and ally because of his great prestige, his love of visual metaphor, and the strong erotic content of much of his art. These factors became particularly apparent in the late 1920s, when his work turned toward great violence of expression. He had found an ideal vehicle for fantasy in the new sculpture.

8 "Agony" (1947) was painted by Arshile Gorky. Armenian-born, Gorky was strongly influenced by Miró, whom he met as a refugee in New York during World War II. By 1944, Gorky had arrived at a more original style based on automatic procedures (highly diluted paint dribbled down the canvas) while retaining suggestions of organic form. His final works, such as "Agony," were more tightly handled, and brought to abstraction unprecedented emotional force.

8

9

9 Robert Rauschenberg's "Monogram" (1961) is almost a posthumous compendium of Surrealist preoccupations. The unusual stuffed animal was sometimes presented as a "found object" in Surrealist exhibitions; here, as usual, it is given an unexpected context. The accumulation of letters and images on the base suggests the "Merz" pictures of Schwitters, and the Surrealist automatism survives in the vigorous smears of paint. The juxtaposed goat and tire and the red paint make it clear that the subject is a traumatic birth. Veiled presentation of taboo themes was a constant element in the shock tactics of the Surrealist group.

Abstract art

Abstract art is the most dramatic manifestation of the attempt by twentieth-century painters to overturn the assumption that art must represent appearances. By 1900 photography had already begun to replace realistic painting. The developing use of photography, coupled with new ideas about the expressive potential of painting and sculpture, resulted in abstraction.

The beginnings of abstract art

Between 1910 and 1918 abstract art evolved in several places. In Munich, Wassily Kandinsky (1866–1944) achieved almost total nonrepresentational painting in 1912. He had a firsthand knowledge of the work of Gauguin, Van Gogh, and the Neo-Impressionists as well as a profound admiration of "primitive" Bavarian glass painting and Russian icons. His ideas (published in an influential text *On the Spiritual in Art* [1912]) were based on an extensive study of Goethe and theosophy. He worked spontaneously, abstracting from images inspired by landscape, legend, and biblical themes [1]. Artists in Amsterdam and Moscow, however, first made works that were composed of "pure" forms without being consciously abstracted from nature. In Moscow Kasimir Malevich's (1878–1935) "Suprematist" compositions of 1915–19 [2] were the product of an attempt to define an "alphabet" of simple geometric shapes which, set on a white background, seemed to move in infinite space.

At the same time Vladimir Tatlin (1885–1953) launched Constructivism with dynamic constructions of glass, metal, and wire, sometimes suspended across corners. These works were free of any mystical content. They led Tatlin to an art based on the tangible qualities of materials assembled in space. By 1921–22 Tatlin, joined by the Russian painter and typographer Alexander Rodchenko (1891–   ) and others, was making structures directly related to engineering; celebrations of an emerging socialist industrial society. Many of the structures were inspired by Tatlin's own wooden model for a metal structure (which was never built) taller than the Eiffel Tower, his "Monument to the Third International" [3].

Piet Mondrian (1872–1944) in the Netherlands was the other artist to arrive at an abstract art that was not abstracted from natural objects. His friends in the Amsterdam-centered de Stijl movement geometrized observed forms, but Mondrian began to compose works with black lines and color patches 1917 and 1918. His style remained unchanged for nearly 20 years [4].

During the 1920s and 1930s the clear-cut geometrical abstract art of Mondrian, Malevich, and Constructivism developed considerably. After 1922 Russian Constructivism moved in a utilitarian direction, and the mystical art of Malevich was left to die. At the Bauhaus in Germany, Laszlo Moholy-Nagy (1895–1946) backed Constructivist developments, and Kandinsky too moved toward geometry. In France such artists as César Domela (1900–   ) and Jean Gorin accepted the more static line followed by Mondrian, while in London, from 1933, Ben Nicholson (1894–   ) developed a geometric style [5], as did Burgoyne Diller and Fritz Glarner (1899–   ) in New York.

CONNECTIONS

See also
1294 Fauvism and Expressionism
1296 Cubism and Futurism
1322 Modern architecture after 1930
1318 Dada, Surrealism, and their legacy

1 Kandinsky's 1911 "Composition IV" is abstracted from a fairy tale scene. In the center is a blue mountain crowned by the jagged outline of a castle. To the left riders fight, their mounts leaping at each other across a rainbow. Although the forms can be interpreted thus, in 1913 Kandinsky wrote that he meant us to read no narrative into them. The story is merely the starting point for a conflict of abstract elements – yellow against blue, curve against linear action.

2 In 1915 Kasimir Malevich exhibited a simple black square on a white ground. The painting shown here, "Suprematist Painting" (1915), combines geometrical shapes that by their overlappings, their different sizes, and their color, create the illusion of movement in space.

3 This is a reconstruction of Vladimir Tatlin's "Monument to the Third International" (1919), which influenced sculpture and architecture.

4 "Composition I with red, yellow, and blue" is one of the paintings with which Piet Mondrian established his complete abstract style in 1921. Mondrian held that life was change, and that change was created by the reconciliation of opposing forces. He therefore deliberately reduced painting to a conflict of the most basic visual oppositions.

Biomorphic abstract art

Alongside these developments the Alsatian artist Jean (Hans) Arp (1888–1966) introduced organic forms in an abstract style called "biomorphic." He made a series of painted wooden reliefs when he was a Dadaist in Zürich (1916–18). His early Dada truculence led him to give his reliefs and sculptures such comical titles as the 1926 "Navel Shirt and Head" [6], and his links with the Surrealists in Paris after 1924 ensured a strong biomorphic line in Surrealism, with Joan Miró (1893–) and Yves Tanguy (1900–55) as its best known exponents. Henry Moore, in moving from his strongly figurative work of the 1920s to a highly abstracted style (1931 onward), took Arp's direction a step further [7].

Abstract Expressionism

Neither geometric nor biomorphic abstraction died during the 1940s, but in New York there was a further major development in abstract art—Abstract Expressionism. This was not a style but rather a group of individual styles, the most influential artists being Jackson Pollock (1912–56) after 1943 and Willem de Kooning (1904–) after 1947. Behind this development lay the Surrealist emphasis on the creative process itself, coupled with a desire to break with the strictures of geometric abstract art and Cubist structure.

After 1947 Pollock's "drip paintings" [8] focused attention on the movement of the painter's hand and decisively challenged the tight shapes of 1920s and 1930s abstraction, both geometric and biomorphic. Thus an entirely new kind of abstract painting was created. Among the artists to follow Pollock's direction without sacrificing individuality was Franz Kline (1911–62), who in 1950 began to produce black-and-white paintings, for example "Chief" [Key], which were in effect hugely magnified brush drawings. Less explosively exciting, but equally free of the shaping and the spatial structures of Cubism and geometrical abstraction, were the huge expanses of color produced by Clyfford Still (1904–), Barnett Newman (1905–70), and Mark Rothko (1903–70).

KEY

"Chief," by Franz Kline (1950), is one of the artist's earlier large black-and-white abstracts. Until the late 1940s Kline was painting city scenes, but he made a rapid change. The resemblance to Chinese calligraphy is misleading; Kline stated clearly, "I paint the white as well as the black, and the white is just as important." His later experiments with color did not lead him back to a full use of it again.

5 Ben Nicholson carved and painted this "White Relief" in 1935. In 1933 he visited Mondrian in Paris, and the painting's tight geometric forms, its simplicity, and its exact balance are in sympathy with Mondrian. There is, however, a feeling for the wood from which the shapes have been cut, and a pleasure taken in different depths of surface that is peculiar to the work of Ben Nicholson.

6 "Navel Shirt and Head" (1926), a painted plywood relief by Jean Arp, anticipates his later free standing sculpture. The first true three-dimensional work, "Head with Three Annoying Objects" appeared in 1930. Arp wanted to make things that seemed alive and were the product of hand, eye, and intuition, yet that repeated the form of no known living things. He never abstracted from observed forms and disliked the term "abstract art." His connections with the Surrealist movement were made possible by his dislike of reason and calculation and by his spontaneous methods.

7 In 1931 Henry Moore (1898–) began to use bones, flints, and pieces of wood as the inspiration for his sculptures, which were evocative of the human figure. He made sheets of drawings to explore the figurative possibilities in these natural forms, arriving at images that he then carved in stone or, more rarely, as in this small "Figure" of 1931, in wood (beech).

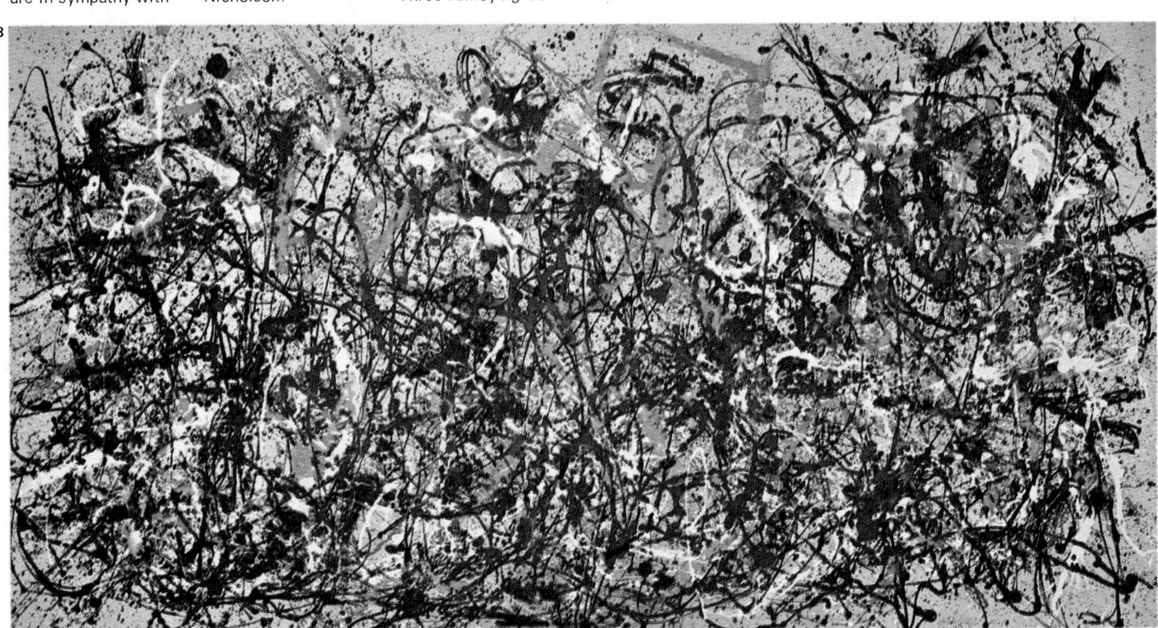

8 Jackson Pollock's first attempts to create "automatically" without the intervention of conscious control, used archetypal symbols from Jung as their starting point. But here in "Autumn Rhythm" (1950) he did not require the impetus of symbolic imagery, producing by the swift action of hand and arm the sweeping trails of paint that cross over one another to form a whirling mesh of movement. For some critics, paintings like these are expressive through the action of the painter's hand they recorded, hence the description "action painting"; for others, they were significant for the new type of abstract composition that they introduced.

Modern architecture after 1930

In 1928 leading modern architects of Europe formed the International Congress of Modern Architecture (CIAM) to share ideas and experiences and to promote their work. They had obtained some success in the 1920s, but official opposition was growing. The Soviet Union, when under Stalin, rejected its earlier interest in modernism. In Italy, Mussolini demanded a "heroic" architecture, and in Germany, Nazi opposition became more strident. Political opposition and, ultimately, war drove many modernists from Europe.

The International Style

In 1932 the Museum of Modern Art in New York City opened an exhibit of modern architecture called the International Style. The main features of this style were man-made, or inorganic, materials, especially steel, glass, and reinforced concrete; cantilevered floors and balconies; free-standing curtain walls; simple, repetitive, geometric forms in open, often asymmetrical plan; and absence of decoration. Henry-Russel Hitchcock and Philip Johnson expanded the exhibit catalog into an influential book, *The International Style*. Thus, when leading modernists arrived in the United States as refugees, their early works were known and respected in academic circles. Walter Gropius (1883–1969) came to lead Harvard's school of architecture, and Mies van der Rohe (1886–1969) became head of the school of architecture at the Illinois Institute of Technology.

Mies van der Rohe

More than any other modern architect, Mies saw his theories realized in all types of buildings—college campus (IIT, basic plan, 1931–41), private home (Farnsworth house, Plano, Ill., 1946–50), apartment buildings (860 Lake Shore Drive, Chicago, 1949–51) [2], office structure (Seagram Building, New York City, 1956–58, with Philip Johnson). In his glass-and-steel buildings he reintroduced formality and classical symmetry into modern architecture. So mechanically precise and fastidious in detail are his buildings that it is doubtful if anyone can improve upon them in their own idiom.

Le Corbusier

Le Corbusier (1887–1965, born Charles-Edouard Jeanneret) was less successful than Mies in seeing his projects realized. His only major project in Europe in the 1930s was the Swiss Dormitory at the Cité Universitaire (Paris, 1931–32). He had greater influence in South America, where he served as a consultant on the Ministry of Health and Education (Rio de Janeiro, 1937–43) by Lucio Costa (1902–). Finally, after World War II, the French government commissioned him to build a residential complex in Marseilles, l'Unité d'Habitation (1946–52) [Key]. This massive building in rough concrete contrasted markedly with Mies' contemporaneous glass-and-steel Lake Shore Drive Apartments. Corbusier's next major contract, a chapel at Ronchamp, France (1950–55) [3], is one of the most individualistic buildings of the twentieth century. In 1951 he received his most important contract, the planning of Chandigarh, the new capital of Punjab, India, and the designing of its administrative complex.

CONNECTIONS

See also

1298 Origins of modern architecture
1296 Cubism and Futurism
1320 Abstract art
1414 The American experience: the skyscraper
1612 Making large buildings

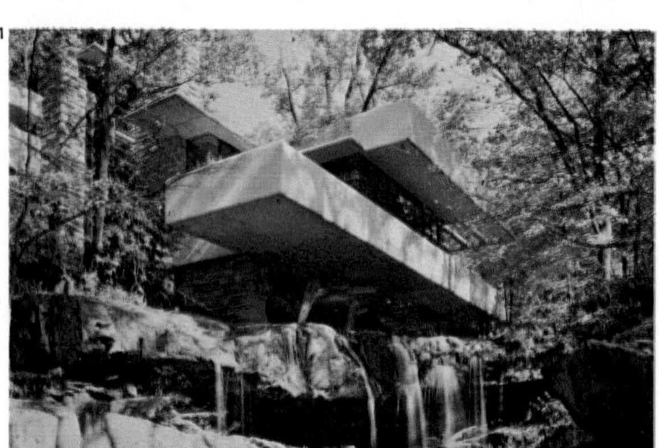

1 Fallingwater by Frank Lloyd Wright is probably the most famous house of the twentieth century. Reinforced concrete balconies cantilever over a waterfall. Inside, the stone ledge on which the house is built forms some of the walls.

2 Two identical towers at right-angles to each other make up the Lake Shore Drive Apartments, Chicago, by Mies van der Rohe. Each building has 26 floors with apartments grouped around a central service core for stairs and elevators. The structure is a load-bearing steel frame fireproofed with concrete and filled in with glass. The black frame and pale blinds behind the windows add interest to an impersonal facade. Of immense significance to postwar architecture was the concept of a home in an anonymous box with flexible planning.

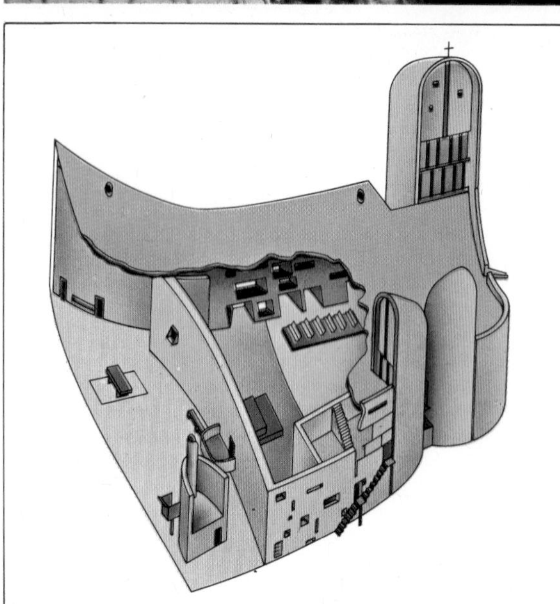

3 In Notre Dame du Haut, a pilgrimage chapel in Ronchamp, France, Le Corbusier took full advantage of the plastic capabilities of reinforced concrete. The chapel defies all rules of geometric proportion in a free flow of self-expression. Irregularly shaped, sized, and positioned windows pierce the double-thick walls providing diffuse, ever-changing streams of light.

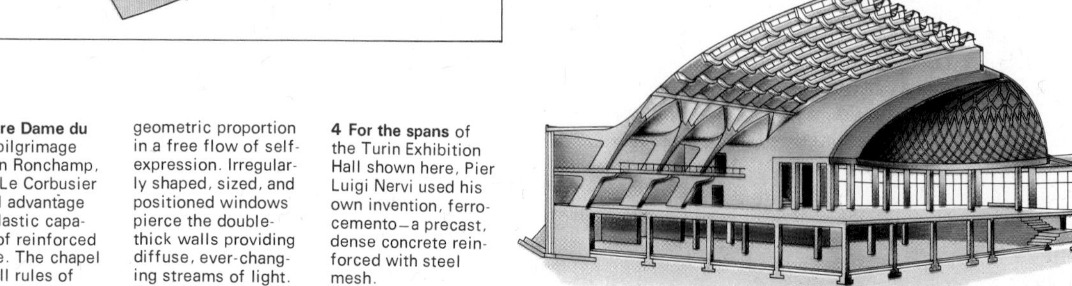

4 For the spans of the Turin Exhibition Hall shown here, Pier Luigi Nervi used his own invention, ferro-cemento—a precast, dense concrete reinforced with steel mesh.

Other trends

Italian architects became especially adept in using reinforced concrete for large public spaces, including the Turin Exhibition Hall (1947–50) [4] by Pier Luigi Nervi (1891–) and the Rome Railway Terminus (1947–51) by Montuori and Associates.

Free from war and welcoming European refugees, Latin America saw the birth of a dynamic modern architecture. The church that Oscar Niemeyer (1907–) built in 1943 for the new town of Pampulha, Brazil, has an undulating concrete roof and a front covered with painted tiles. The University of Mexico library (Mexico City, 1951–53) by Juan O'Gorman (1905–) is a simple concrete slab tower placed over a glass-walled platform, but the slab is decorated with brilliantly colored mosaics based on native motifs. What should have been the triumph of Latin American architecture, the new Brazilian capital at Brasília [9], proved to be a disappointment.

In the United States, Frank Lloyd Wright (1869–1959) continued his distinctive, individualistic work [1, 6], disapproving of the glass-and-steel style but applying the cantilever and reinforced concrete.

"Form follows function," the dictum of pioneer modernist Louis Sullivan (1856–1924), reverberated in many forms in post-World War II architecture. Mies' glass boxes seemed to say "form *is* function"—any function could be carried on inside. Reinforced concrete's adaptability led to free-form buildings, such as the TWA Terminal (New York City, 1956–62) by Eero Saarinen (1910–61), that seemed to say "form follows form." Architecture that followed Sullivan's dictum to a logical conclusion—identifying each element separately by its function—came to be called Brutalism [8]. Constructivism, first popularized by Moshe Safdie (1938–) in Habitat (Montreal, 1967), allows for great variation in the placement of separate functional units with flexibility to add or remove units. The Yamanashi Communication Center (Konju, Japan, 1964–67) by Kenzo Tange (1913–) is an important building in this style.

KEY

The massive l'Unité d'Habitation by Corbusier contains 337 duplex apartments, yet it appears to float above the ground on its inward tapering columns (pilotis). Space underneath is used for parking and a play area. The rough concrete surface shows the imprint of the wooden molds in which it was set. Balcony interior walls are painted in bright colors.

5

5 Lever House, designed by Gordon Bunshaft of Skidmore, Owings and Merrill, was a brilliant solution to New York City's zoning regulations that forced a stepped-backed construction for skyscrapers based on their width, height, and plot density. SOM turned the building so its narrow side faced Park Avenue and raised the tower on a low platform, thus opening up much of the lot while allowing for a much taller building with a flat, curtain wall facade. The low roof serves as an employee garden and outdoor eating area, while the space under the platform is a sheltered public pedestrian mall.

6

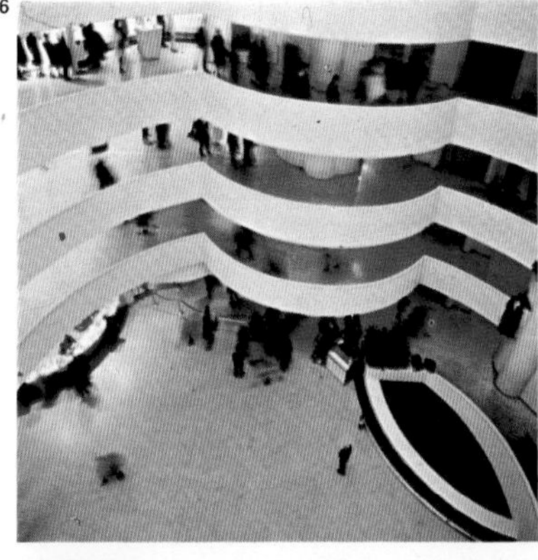

6 The Solomon R. Guggenheim Museum, New York City (1957–59), by Frank Lloyd Wright was designed as a continuous spiral ramp surrounding an open well. The spiral widens in diameter as it rises toward a glass dome 91ft (28m) above the ground. The dome is a main source of natural light on the exhibits. Wright believed, but many disagree, that the curving walls were the best surface for showing pictures. The museum is cast in concrete with a smooth finish. Although, as with Le Corbusier's chapel at Ronchamp, the fluidity of the shape appears to defy rigid industrial values, the building could not possibly have been realized without 20th-century technology.

7

7 Kurashiki Town Hall, designed by Kenzo Tange, is constructed from the roughcast concrete of International Brutalism and incorporates Corbusian features. Japanese architecture, surprisingly, has favored rugged Le Corbusier rather than the clean lines of the Miesian idiom. The Town Hall facade is nevertheless an essentially Japanese interpretation of the Brutalist manner.

8

8 The Palace of the National Congress (Brasília, 1960) by Oscar Niemeyer lacks the innovativeness and vibrancy of his earlier works. The convex Senate chamber and concave Hall of Deputies are static, arbitrary shapes. The double-towered Secretariat looks cramped. The complex lacks unity and human scale.

9

9 The Engineering Building (Leicester University, England, 1959–64) by James Stirling and James Gowan is a prime example of Brutalism. Entrance is up a protruding ramp past an undisguised ventilation stack and between the sharply-angled lecture halls. To the left of the administrative tower are the low, glassed-in workshops with roof panels set at a 45° angle to provide steady indirect light.

The twenties and the depression

The years 1919–38 were dominated by an economic depression that troubled Europe for most of that period but had its greatest impact on the rest of the world in the 1930s. In the aftermath of World War I, the world attempted to return to "normalcy," a term coined by US President Warren Harding (1865–1923). In Britain the years immediately after the war witnessed a boom in industrial production and rising living standards. After 1922, however, trade and industrial activity declined, creating unemployment in Britain's major heavy industries [1]. Germany, the other great industrial economy of Europe, was unable to recover from the effects of the war and the impositions of the peace settlement [2]. The result was to depress the economy of Europe, which needed the prosperity of German industry. Forced to contend with the problems of inflation, political instability and heavy reparations, the German economy did not begin to make a major recovery until the mid-1920s.

The war had left the United States as the major creditor nation, a position once held by Great Britain. A large proportion of the world's gold reserves had accumulated in Fort Knox, Kentucky, providing the basis for a large-scale expansion in US output. The growth in credit and consumption that these gold reserves allowed stimulated a boom in manufacturing output [3].

The United States in the 1920s experienced a wave of prosperity that combined with the release of energies after the sufferings of the war years to create the hectic atmosphere of the "roaring twenties." Europe had some of this feeling toward the end of the decade.

Aspects of social life

Socially, the twenties were a paradoxical decade. On the one hand, the end of the war heralded new freedoms, particularly for women. They had worked in many new occupations during the war and now began to enjoy greater political and social emancipation. Fashions became more practical; there was more knowledge about birth control; smaller families became more common; and the range of job opportunities widened. The twenties in the United States also saw the triumph of Prohibition, the restriction of the sale of alcohol, which created a vigorous trade in illicit liquor.

Crisis and deflation

The optimistic economic climate of the late twenties was brought to an end by the Wall Street crash of October 1929. The US boom had already begun to falter by the summer of 1929 with a downturn in the economic indices. The slide in stock prices that followed became a panic [5]. In the United States, unemployment soared as credit dried up, consumption declined, and bankruptcies multiplied. Compounding the effects of the depression, agricultural prices fell catastrophically, bringing disaster to farmers in many countries. World unemployment doubled within one year.

For two years the depression deepened throughout the industrialized world. By 1932, more than 12,000,000 people were out of work in the United States and whole communities were idle. The Great Crash had an equally disastrous impact on Euro-

CONNECTIONS

See also

1326 Socialism in the West
1334 The rise of fascism
1284 European industrialization 1870–1914
1356 Postwar evolution of Western Europe
1384 The world's monetary system
938 Industry and economics

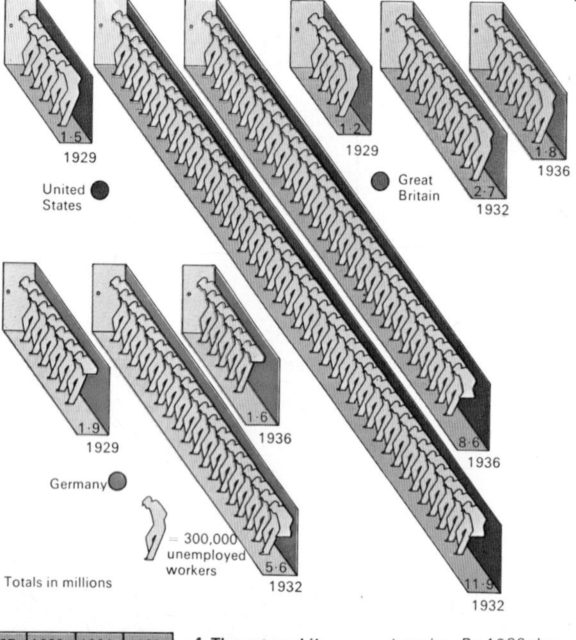

1
1·5
1929
United States
2·7
1932
1·2
1929
Great Britain
1·8
1936
1·9
1929
Germany
1·6
1936
5·6
1932
8·6
1936
11·9
1932
= 300,000 unemployed workers
Totals in millions

1 After World War I, Britain suffered from the decline of its basic industries and the rise of competition, while Germany needed several years to recover from the war and reparations. The United States enjoyed a boom period in the twenties, which was halted by the great crash of 1929 and the decline in investor confidence and world trade. The resulting rise in unemployment in the industrial West is shown here.

2 German paper marks equivalent to one gold mark

16 Jun 1921 · 46 Dec 1921 · 75 Jun 1922 · 1757 Dec 1922

2 The German economy was thrown into severe difficulties by the effects of the war and the peace settlement. Reparations and the loss of major industrial areas depressed the economy and created preconditions for inflation. French occupation of the Ruhr because of German default on reparation payments triggered massive inflation that wiped out all savings, until a loaf of bread cost millions of marks.

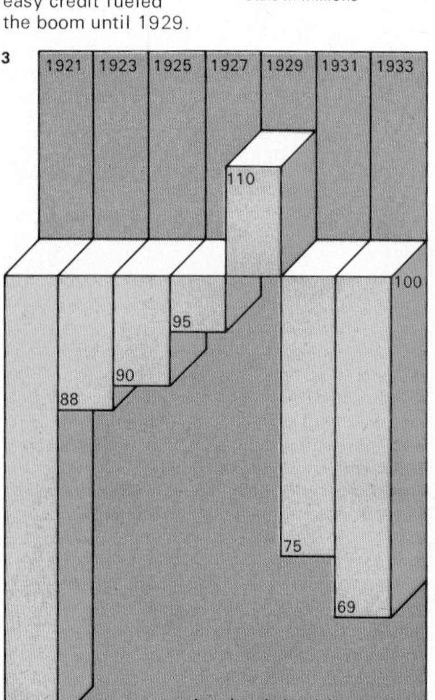

3
1921
1923
1925
1927
1929
1931
1933
58
88
90
95
110
75
69
100
American industrial production

3 The US economy boomed in the 1920s with a rapid growth of heavy industries. The industrial production index here shown is based on an average index of 100 for 1935–39. Rising consumption and easy credit fueled the boom until 1929.

4 The automobile industry grew to major importance in the interwar period. Although invented and produced before 1914, cars had remained expensive luxuries. By 1932 the assembly lines, which had made possible cheap cars for a wider market, had come to a halt, leaving thousands jobless.

5 Thousands rushed to sell their stocks on Wall Street in the panic selling of 1929. In two months stock values had declined by a third and paper losses of millions were registered. The growth in the US economy had been accompanied by a major speculative boom in stock prices, involving small investors and large trusts. By 1929 industrial production began to peak and stocks slumped, causing the panic.

pean economies, many of which depended on the credit offered by the United States.

Current economic thinking decreed that a crisis of this kind could only be cured by a harsh dose of deflation. The storm was to be ridden out by balancing budgets and reducing surplus capacity. In Germany the government of Franz von Papen (1879–1969) applied ever tougher deflationary measures, and this pattern was followed in Britain under Prime Minister Ramsey MacDonald (1866–1937), and in the United States under President Herbert Hoover (1874–1964). Although British economist J. M. Keynes (1883–1946) was formulating alternative policies that would emphasize increased government spending and rising consumption to revive economic activity, his radical views were not generally known or respected.

Political repercussions

The depression had important political repercussions. In the United States dissatisfaction with the performance of President Hoover and his management of the economic crisis led to the 1932 victory of Franklin D. Roosevelt (1882–1945), with his promise of a "New Deal" [9]. In Britain, the effects of the deepening depression in 1930 brought about a financial and political crisis for the Labour government of Ramsey MacDonald. A national coalition government was formed after the 1931 general election. It included Conservatives, Liberals, and Labour members, but MacDonald continued as prime minister. In Germany mounting unemployment and the fears of social breakdown it engendered played an important part in building up support for the Nazi party and in undermining the legitimacy of the Weimar Republic [8]. France was affected later than the rest of Europe because its large agricultural sector disguised unemployment and its industrial base was small.

Although the depression dominated the thirties in Europe and the United States, recovery began in 1933, so that by the outbreak of World War II considerable advances had been made in the living standards of those who had jobs.

KEY

Drought and low prices for farm produce forced many US families to migrate from the Midwest to California. Their hardships, immortalized in John Steinbeck's *The Grapes of Wrath*, symbolized the Depression's ravages.

6

CRUSADE

6 In Britain the depression led to "hunger marches" like this one (1936) when 200 men marched to London seeking work. In the United States unemployed ex-servicemen marched to Washington in 1932. The army's tactics in dispersing them resulted in deaths and public outrage.

7

7 Under Roosevelt's "New Deal" several ambitious projects were started to give work to the unemployed and to stimulate the economy. The Tennessee Valley Authority sought to revitalize the economy and living conditions of that region, and mammoth projects such as the Hoover Dam gave work to many.

8

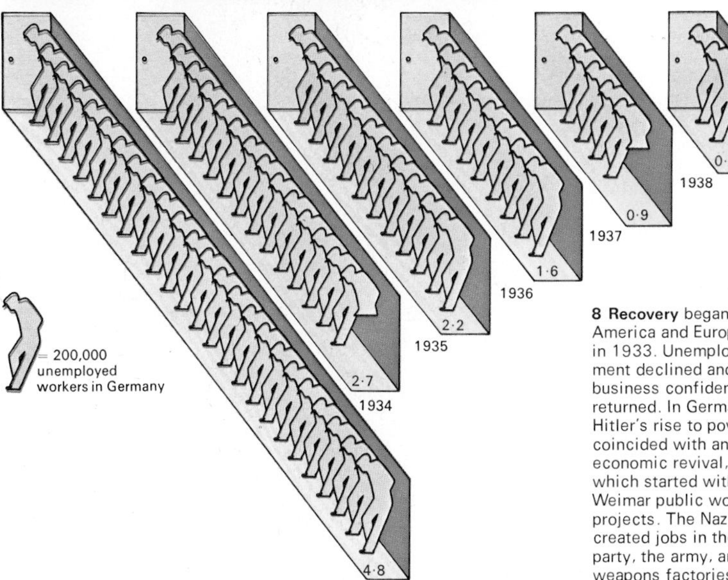
0·4
1938
0·9
1937
1·6
1936
2·2
1935
2·7
1934
4·8
1933
= 200,000 unemployed workers in Germany
Totals in millions

8 Recovery began in America and Europe in 1933. Unemployment declined and business confidence returned. In Germany Hitler's rise to power coincided with an economic revival, which started with Weimar public works projects. The Nazis created jobs in the party, the army, and weapons factories. The drop in unemployment is shown here.

9

9 Franklin D. Roosevelt, here shown with his wife Eleanor, won a landslide victory over Herbert Hoover in the 1932 presidential election on a program for a "New Deal" for the United States, consisting of welfare legislation, public works, agricultural aid and planning, and an end to Prohibition. Roosevelt's confident style was almost as important as his legislation, bringing a measure of optimism and stability to the business world. His "fireside chats" on the radio helped to reassure the public that the government was acting to help the ordinary people. Although economic recovery was sluggish until 1940, he was elected for three more terms, and died in office in 1945.

Socialism in the West

Socialism developed from a group of thinkers, especially Robert Owen (1771–1858), Henri de Saint-Simon (1760–1825), and Charles Fourier (1772–1837), who criticized industrialism because of the suffering and hardship it caused the working class. But it was not until the mid-nineteenth century that socialism developed a mass following as a direct result of the growth of industry in different parts of Europe and the related rise of an urban working class.

Early developments

As the first industrial nation, Great Britain took the lead in the development of workingmen's organizations. Despite legal restrictions and occasional persecution, such as the transportation to Australia of the Tolpuddle Martyrs in 1834 for trade union activity, unions flourished by the middle of the nineteenth century, especially among skilled workers. The political ideas of this "labor aristocracy" were largely Owenite, emphasizing cooperation and reformist political activity. Attempts to establish a Grand National Consolidated Trades Union had failed by 1834, and following this the Chartist movement attempted to enlist the mass of factory operatives in the cause of political rights, which were enshrined in the "People's Charter," presented to Parliament and rejected three times. Significant advances were made, however, in the formation of self-help and cooperative societies. Under reformist leaders British trade unions concentrated on securing gradual political and social concessions during the period of prosperity after 1851.

In Europe the slower progress of industrialization hampered the growth of organized socialist movements. Trade unions remained illegal in France until the middle of the nineteenth century, and socialist support was divided among the followers of revolutionary leaders, reformists, and anarchists. Although workers participated in the overthrow of Louis-Philippe (1773–1850) in 1848, there was no organization to unite them. In Germany, too, the workers who supported the revolution of 1848 remained divided and dominated by middle-class liberals. The German uprisings of 1848 did, however, see the emergence of Marxism in the *Communist Manifesto*. Written by Karl Marx (1818–83) and Friedrich Engels (1820–95), the manifesto provided a coherent intellectual basis for many later socialists.

The First International

Although Chartism was defeated in Britain in 1848 and socialist ideas played little part in the revolutions elsewhere, they marked the emergence of the first important mass movements of workers in Europe. In 1864 socialist groups came together in the First International. Although racked by dissension, the International provided a vehicle for Marxist ideas and encouragement to socialist groups throughout Europe. In France in 1871 the rising of Parisian workers and the lower middle classes in the commune was proof of the growing strength of socialist ideas. The International was liquidated in 1876, following quarrels between the anarchists and Marx. In the less developed parts of Europe, anarchist ideas propagated by Mikhail Bakunin (1814–76)

CONNECTIONS

See also
1288 Political thought in the 19th century
1324 The twenties and the Depression
1334 The rise of fascism
1310 The Russian Revolution
1300 Europe 1870–1914
1306 World War I
1290 Masters of sociology
1284 European industrialization 1870–1914
1356 Postwar evolution of Western Europe
904 Political participation

1 Two British reformers, Sidney (1859–1947) and Beatrice Webb (1858–1943), adapted socialism to the cause of practical social reform, which they sought to achieve gradually via the democratic process. They formed the Fabian Society in 1884. It attracted many middle-class and intellectual figures. The British Labour party adopted the ideals of "Fabianism" for its philosophical basis.

2 In Russia, anarchism inspired the opponents of the tsarist regime in a campaign of terrorism, including the assassination of Alexander II in 1881. Anarchism grew out of the ideas of Pierre Proudhon (1809–65), among others. It rejected all authority in its search for a self-governing ideal in which men could totally fulfill themselves. The most famous 19th-century exponents were Russians, especially Mikhail Bakunin and Prince Peter Kropotkin (1842–1921). In France, anarchism became blended with trade unionism, and in Spain anarchists played a part in the political upheavals of the early 20th century, including the Spanish Civil War.

3 The years before World War I were marked by labor militancy and violent strikes throughout Europe and the United States. In Britain there was a wave of bitter disputes, and troops had to be called out in South Wales during the coal strike of 1912. The trouble was caused by the rise of organized labor, the spread of militant ideas, and a slight downturn in living standards.

4 Jean Jaurès (1859–1914) was an eminent French socialist. A successful politician and moderate Marxist, he brought unity to the fragmented socialist groups in France before being assassinated for opposing the war with Germany.

5 Polish-born Rosa Luxemburg, with Karl Liebknecht, led the Marxist "Spartacist" movement that sought to end the 1914–18 war through revolution. They were both assassinated in Berlin during the revolt of 1918–19.

6 Liberals everywhere protested in 1927 the death penalties imposed on two US anarchists, Nicola Sacco (1891–1927) and Bartolomeo Vanzetti (1888–1927). Many believed their murder conviction was politically motivated.

had a strong appeal and led to risings in Spain and terrorism in Russia [2].

After 1870 the German socialist movement became the most powerful in Europe. In 1890, in spite of laws restricting its operation, the Social Democratic party was the largest in the Reich. Although divided between Marxist and "revisionist" groups, the socialists continued their rise up to 1914. In the aftermath of Germany's defeat, an alliance between the Social Democrats and the army was formed to set up the Weimar government and to frustrate the challenge from the Marxist "Spartacists" led by Karl Liebknecht (1871–1919) and Rosa Luxemburg (1871–1919) [5]. In France the socialist movement remained fragmented. French workers turning aside from party politics were attracted to syndicalist ideas of control being achieved by workers through strikes.

The Second International

The Second International, formed in 1889, was severely divided between reformist and revolutionary groups, and was not strong enough concertedly to oppose World War I. Nevertheless, by 1914 socialism was a powerful political force in Europe and had also spread to Latin America and the United States. Although it was never as strong in the United States as in Europe, labor unions increased in strength [7]. A socialist candidate for the presidency, Eugene Debs (1855–1926), polled 900,000 votes in 1912, while the militant Industrial Workers of the World mounted a series of bitter strikes.

The Russian Revolution led to a revival of left-wing militancy in the aftermath of World War I, but the interwar period saw the socialist parties of Britain, France, and Germany playing a prominent part in parliamentary politics and the triumph of socialist parties in Scandinavia. Although the Depression and the rise of fascism led to suppression, as in Germany, Italy, and Spain, they also led to a revival of socialism in middle-class and intellectual circles. The Spanish Civil War [9, 10] provided a rallying point for the left and the triumph of the Allies in World War II left socialist parties in a prominent position in much of Europe.

KEY

MEMBERSHIP AND ATTENDANCE CARD
UAW
United Automobile, Aerospace and Agricultural Implement Workers of America UAW
1977
Name John Doe
City Detroit, Michigan
S. S. No. 100-10-1000 Init. Dt. Jan. 1, 1977
Local 123 Card No. 4567
F. Secy. James Smith

DUES SPEC'L	DUES SPEC'L	DUES SPEC'L	DUES SPEC'L	DUES SPEC'L	DUES SPEC'L
Jan	Feb	Mar	Apr	May	June
July	Aug	Sep	Oct	Nov	Dec

By 1914 the labor union movement, representing millions of working people, was a growing force in the major industrial countries. The years between 1900 and 1914 saw an increase in the number and intensity of union strikes. Generally, employers still disputed the right to strike and often still challenged the unions' right to exist. Bitterness and hostility underlying strikes often led to open violence. Labor unions were often narrowly sectional in their interests while generally supporting a socialist political stance. Cards, such as this for the United Automobile Workers, are proof of full union membership.

7

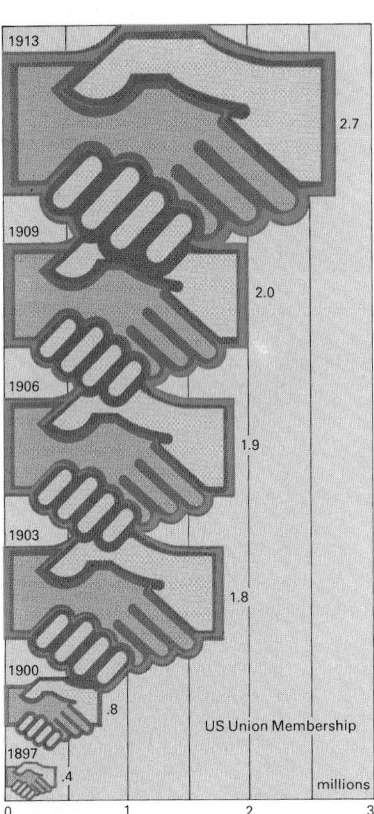

1913
2.7
1909
2.0
1906
1.9
1903
1.8
1900
.8
US Union Membership
1897
.4
millions
0
1
2
3

7 Before 1914 there was a surge in labor union membership because of industrial development. In the United States the number of unionists more than tripled between 1900 and 1913, mainly as a result of the organization of unskilled and semiskilled workers, in addition to the skilled "labor aristocracy" who had created the unions. In Britain in 1893 the Independent Labour party (ILP) was formed, later to become the Labour party (1906).

8

EATON'S

8 The concept of the general strike became widespread in the early years of the 20th century under the influence of syndicalist ideas. In Britain, the reformist character of the Trades Union Congress, formed in 1868, made it reluctant to use the general strike as a weapon, but in 1926 it called a general strike in support of a bitter dispute in the coal industry. After a tense confrontation with the Conservative government of Stanley Baldwin (1867–1947) the strike was defeated. Because of the government's fear that food supplies would be looted, imports were collected from the London docks with army protection.

9

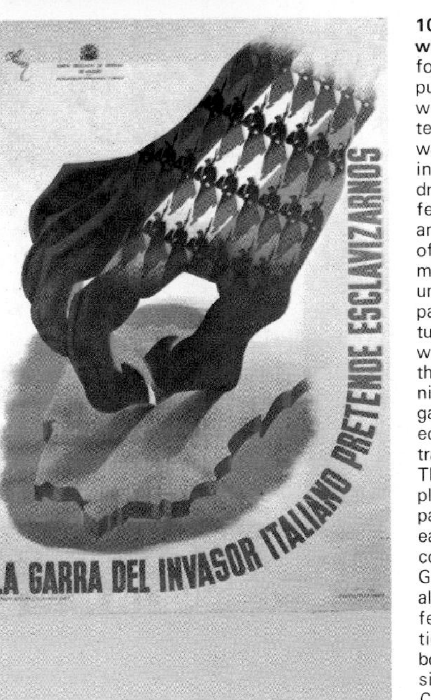

LA GARRA DEL INVASOR ITALIANO PRETENDE ESCLAVIZARNOS

9 The Spanish Civil War (1936–39) was a rallying point for left-wing forces in Europe. The attempt by Franco's Nationalist forces to topple the Spanish Republic with aid from Italy and Germany resulted in cooperation between many divided communist and socialist parties. Although the war was a complex battle between various Spanish groups, it seemed to many socialists to symbolize the threat of fascism and the need for a united front.

10 As a result of widespread concern for the Spanish Republic among left-wing groups, an International Brigade was formed to fight in Spain. It was drawn from many different nationalities and consisted mainly of Communist party members, trade unionists, and sympathetic intellectuals. The Brigade was recruited through the Communist party, which organized training, equipment, and transport to Spain. The volunteers played an important part in preventing an early victory by Franco's forces and his German and Italian allies, but they suffered heavy casualties. Their role symbolized the wider significance of the Civil War.

10

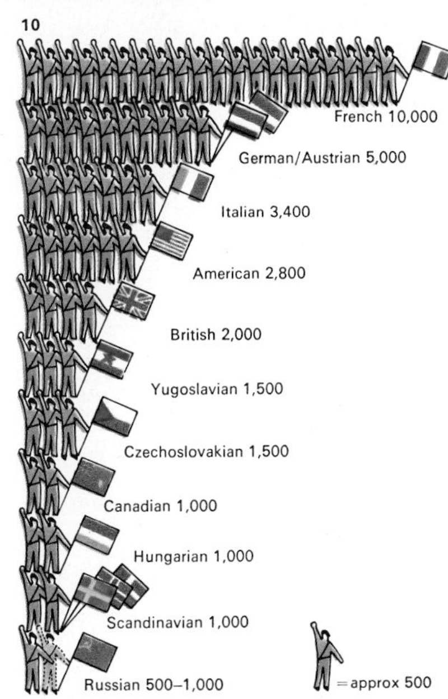

French 10,000
German/Austrian 5,000
Italian 3,400
American 2,800
British 2,000
Yugoslavian 1,500
Czechoslovakian 1,500
Canadian 1,000
Hungarian 1,000
Scandinavian 1,000
Russian 500–1,000
= approx 500

East Asia 1919–45

The history of East Asia from 1919 to 1945 is dominated by two related themes: the rise of Chinese nationalism in the 1920s and the spread of Japanese imperalism after 1931. Both developments were influenced by Western imperialist presence in the region. Chinese nationalism was complicated by the diverging interests of the two major political parties, the Nationalist Kuomintang (KMT) and the Chinese Communist Party (CCP).

Rise of Chinese nationalism

The year 1919 is a watershed in Chinese history. Demonstrations against the Paris Peace Conference's granting of former German concessions in China to Japan—which the Chinese government accepted—developed into an unprecedented national movement [1]. Sensing the revolutionary mood, Sun Yat-sen (1866–1925) reorganized his Nationalist party into the disciplined KMT. With a socialist ideology and a party-dominated army under Chiang Kai-shek [Key], the KMT received help from the Comintern and collaborated with the CCP formed in 1921. Both parties sought to end the division of China into military regions run by warlords and exploitation by privileged powers such as Britain, France, the United States, and Japan.

These privileges were little diminished by the Washington Conference (1921–22), which achieved only partial withdrawal by Japan. Chinese dissatisfaction coalesced with labor unrest, particularly in the treaty ports, culminating in a 15-month strike and boycott of foreign trade in Hong Kong in 1925–26. Against this background, Chiang Kai-shek led a northern expedition to unite China under the national government set up in Canton. In 1927, Chiang clashed with party leftists, especially the Communist bloc within the KMT. Purging the areas under his control [3], he succeeded in reunifying the KMT at the expense of the left and the CCP, setting up his own government in Nanking, and bringing Peking and much of the rest of China under his control in 1928.

By 1930 extension of Nationalist authority put Chinese nationalism and Japanese imperialism on a collision course. Japanese privileges secured in Manchuria after 1905 were threatened by China's reassertion of its sovereignty there. Not only was Manchuria a buffer against Soviet ideology and military power, it also represented a considerable economic investment and had a million Japanese subjects.

Japanese imperialist expansion

Japan of the 1920s was characterized by paternalistic capitalism with limited democracy at home and cooperation with the great powers abroad. But in the 1930s ultranationalism and militarism fostered ideas of an autonomous economic empire as an answer to the Depression. As confidence in politicians waned, popular support grew for the militarists who were close to Emperor Hirohito [5]. Japanese officers in Manchuria used the Mukden Incident of 1931 [4] to create a situation that led to the establishment of a Japanese puppet state, Manchukuo, in 1932. Expansion southward in 1935–36 was designed partly for military reasons to create a subservient North China

CONNECTIONS

See also

1348 China: the People's Republic
1338 World War II
1272 Japan: the Meiji Restoration
1270 The opening up of China

1 The May 4th Incident in 1919 was a demonstration by 3,000 students in Peking, protesting the Paris Peace Conference that left Japan in control of German possessions it had seized in China. Spreading protest forced government changes and foreshadowed a new Chinese nationalism.

2 Japanese naval power grew rapidly in east Asia after 1919 despite the 1922 naval treaty limiting replacement of capital ships by the United States, Britain, and Japan to a 5:5:3 ratio. Ratios for auxiliary ships set in 1930 were: heavy cruisers, 10:10:6; light cruisers and destroyers, 10:10:6; submarines, parity.

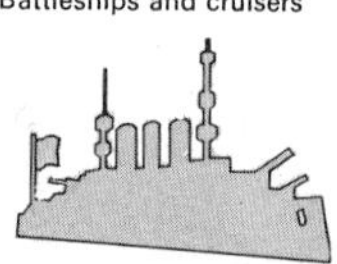

Built by Japan	Battleships and cruisers	Destroyers	Submarines
1919–20	4	17	9
1921–24	12	34	32
1925–28	8	21	19
1929–32	7	17	12

3 Communists were massacred in Shanghai on April 12, 1927, when Nationalist troops, police, and secret agents disarmed workers and pickets and dissolved labor unions. The culmination of a power struggle between the left and right wings of the KMT, the purge spread elsewhere with more massacres of the left wing and communists.

4 Japanese troops marched into Manchuria after the Mukden Incident of September 18, 1931. Acting without the authority of their government, Japanese forces occupied Mukden using the pretext of a bomb on the Japanese-run South Manchurian railway and a skirmish with Chinese patrols. The speedy occupation of Manchuria followed.

to protect Japan's rear in the event of war with the USSR.

Japan's encroachment brought a temporary truce between the KMT and CCP in 1936. Chiang had dislodged the Communists from their southern rural bases and forced them to undertake the Long March [6]. But the CCP leader, Mao Tse-tung (1893–1976), urged on by the USSR, now sought a united front against Japan, and Chiang was obliged to agree. When full-scale fighting broke out in 1937, the powerful Japanese army forced the KMT to retreat to Changking in the southwest. The fall of Nanking in December [7] was followed in 1938 by the announcement of Japan's "New Order" with Japanese army rule in occupied parts of China and a puppet government in Nanking (1940).

Japan's empire in World War II

To secure access to Southeast Asian raw materials and to block Western aid for Chiang, Japanese troops entered Indochina in 1940 and moved southward in 1941. The United States, Britain, and the Netherlands responded with a near total embargo on exports to Japan in July 1941, reducing oil supplies by 90 percent. Japan soon put into operation its contingency plan to achieve economic self-sufficiency by force. Allied to Germany and Italy and envisaging the imminent collapse of Britain and China, it tried to eliminate US interference by sinking part of the Pacific fleet at Pearl Harbor on Dec. 7, 1941. The United States was now at war with Japan.

By August 1942, Japan had seized a vast oceanic and continental empire [8]. It was not until early in 1944 that Allied sea power reversed these successes. While the Chinese Nationalists and Communists tied down large numbers of Japanese troops and Allied supply lines were restored in Burma, US offensives in the Philippines and Gilberts established bases from which air power could be brought to bear on Japan itself. In 1945, after atomic bombs had destroyed Hiroshima (August 6) and Nagasaki (August 9), Japan agreed to unconditional surrender, signed aboard the USS *Missouri* on September 2 [9].

KEY

Chiang Kai-shek (1887–1975) was the leading military aide of Sun Yat-sen by 1919. After Sun's death in 1925 he dominated the Kuomintang and became president of a largely reunited Republic of China in 1928. But his authority was contested by the Communist party and threatened by the Japanese. Recognized by the Allies as China's wartime leader, he secured the abolition of extraterritorial rights in China in 1943 and in 1945 obtained a seat for China in the UN Security Council. Renewed postwar conflict with the Communists led to the military defeat of his government and its withdrawal to Taiwan in 1949.

5

5 Emperor Hirohito (1901–) came to the Japanese throne in 1926, having been named regent in 1921. Under the Meiji constitution his position was both sacred and sovereign, although there is little evidence to show the part actually played by the emperor in Japanese policies.

6

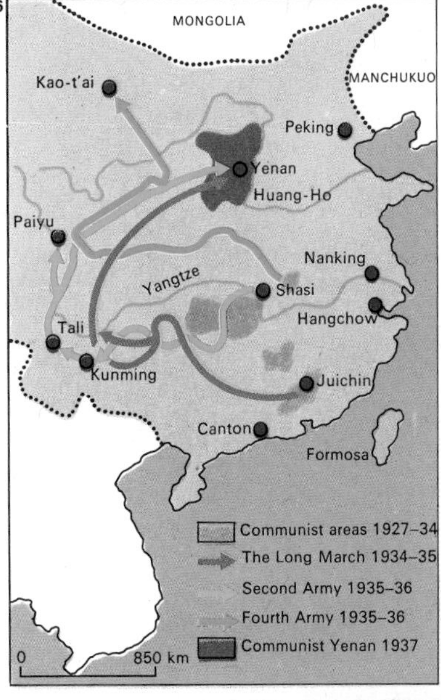

MONGOLIA
MANCHUKUO
Kao-t'ai
Peking
Yenan
Huang-Ho
Paiyu
Nanking
Yangtze
Shasi
Hangchow
Tali
Kunming
Juichin
Canton
Formosa
Communist areas 1927–34
The Long March 1934–35
Second Army 1935–36
Fourth Army 1935–36
Communist Yenan 1937
0
850 km

6 In the Long March, about 85,000 Communist soldiers and 15,000 officials left Kiangsi under pressure from Chiang Kai-shek in October 1934. A year later 30,000 survivors regrouped near Yenan after a march of 5,000 miles (8,000 km). The Communist 2nd and 4th armies also had to regroup in the north.

7

7 The fall of Nanking, Chiang Kai-shek's capital, on December 12, 1937, was followed by the massacre of some 100,000 people by Japanese troops. Known as the "rape of Nanking," this atrocity was revealed at the International War Crimes Tribunal in Tokyo. The city's fall came after three months of stubborn opposition by Chiang's army to the advance of the Japanese.

8

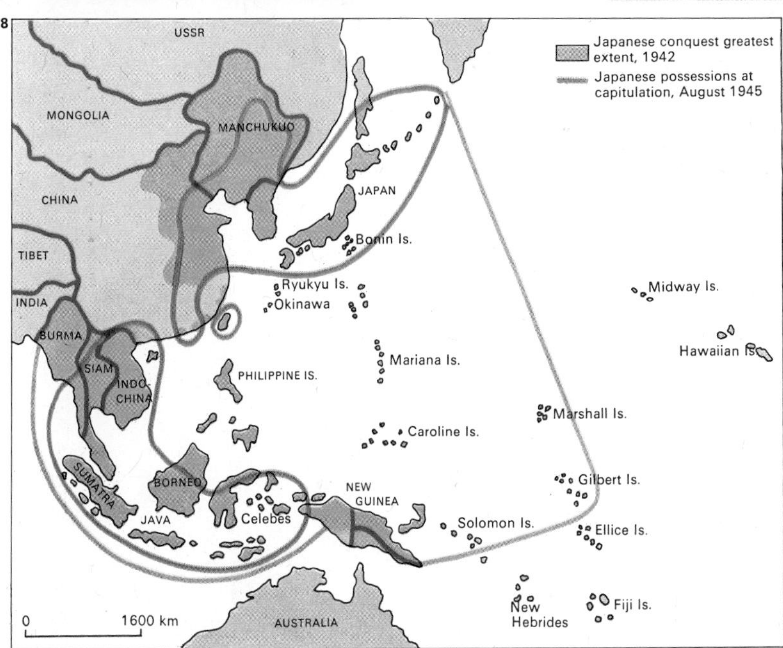

Japanese conquest greatest extent, 1942
Japanese possessions at capitulation, August 1945
USSR
MONGOLIA
MANCHUKUO
CHINA
JAPAN
TIBET
INDIA
BURMA
SIAM
INDO CHINA
Bonin Is.
Ryukyu Is.
Okinawa
Midway Is.
Hawaiian Is.
Mariana Is.
PHILIPPINE IS.
Marshall Is.
Caroline Is.
SUMATRA
BORNEO
Gilbert Is.
NEW GUINEA
JAVA
Celebes
Solomon Is.
Ellice Is.
New Hebrides
Fiji Is.
AUSTRALIA
0
1600 km

9

8 Japan's territorial acquisitions in World War II reflect its initial aims to conquer China before dealing with the USSR and to control the southwest Pacific. Later the military priority shifted to include invading India in preference to defending Pacific islands. Before the Allies entered the war against Japan, China traded space for time. Once deep in Chinese territory, Japanese troops, although controlling most industrial areas, were surrounded by a hostile countryside.

9 Japan's surrender was signed aboard the USS *Missouri* in Tokyo Bay on September 2, 1945, with General Douglas MacArthur representing the Allies. The Japanese decision on August 14, 1945, to surrender came from the emperor.

Indian nationalism

In 1900, British rule in India appeared more secure and more permanent than ever. Lord Curzon's years as viceroy (1898–1905) emphasized Britain's determination to govern India. The greater efficiency of the administration, the maintenance of peace and order, and the spread of railways [3] and the telegraph all seemed to confirm Britain's grip on India, while in the wider world British foreign policy was geared to the retention of the Indian Empire as the second great base (after Britain itself) of British world power. Yet within 50 years the Indian Empire had been split up and the British stripped of all authority in its affairs.

Growth of nationalism

Part of the reason for this reversal lay in the growth of a nationalism that drew support from Indians all over the subcontinent. This nationalism had risen from modest beginnings in the late nineteenth century with the foundation of the Indian National Congress party and was at first approved by the British for its attempt to break through the divisions of caste, religion, and region that stifled efforts to modernize India. But before long they came to see it as a potent threat to British power and a stimulant to disorder. Anti-British terrorism before 1914 made many officials hostile to the call of nationalists for more Indian participation in government. The British believed that the Congress was the tool of ambitious and unscrupulous westernized Indians, seeking not independence and unity but self-advancement, regardless of the true interests of the peasantry.

The first great triumph of Indian nationalism came in the years immediately following World War I when Mahatma Gandhi (1869–1948) [Key] emerged as a charismatic leader pioneering the technique of noncooperation and nonviolent resistance to the government through peaceful demonstrations and refusal to pay taxes. Gandhi was helped in showing the British that many Indians rejected their authority by the effects of India's involvement in World War I. Higher taxation, the recruitment of thousands of Indians for the army, and the use of that army in northern France united Indians of diverse interests in the belief that the British were placing new and unfair burdens on them and breaking the terms on which British rule was accepted. They turned for protection to the Congress party. To the British, Gandhi's campaign was deeply worrisome. Some of them believed a second mutiny was imminent—the first mutiny in 1857–58 had resulted from unrest amongst the sepoys (soldiers) but was suppressed by the British—and it was in a climate of fear that the shooting of unarmed Indian demonstrators—the Amritsar massacre [1]—occurred in 1919.

Divisions among the Indians

For all its successes between 1918 and 1922, Indian nationalism faced enormous problems in trying to destroy British power. Once India had settled down after the war and its aftermath, noncooperation fizzled out. Many Indians were profoundly suspicious of the politicians who ran the Congress party. The rural landowners who wished to keep the social status quo disliked the urban and westernized Indians who

CONNECTIONS

See also
1266 India in the 19th century
1332 The Commonwealth
1350 Decolonization
1352 Non-alignment and the Third World

1

1 At Amritsar on April 13, 1919, British troops killed over 300 unarmed Indians during an illegal demonstration. The Indians were forced to apologize publicly after the riot because the British thought such displays would encourage them to be orderly and respectful. Here a Sikh is arrested after the riot.

2

2 By origin, Gurkha soldiers, still a distinctive element in the British army, were mountain tribesmen from Nepal who were defeated by the British in the Gurkha wars of 1814–16. They became famous for their endurance, loyalty, and courage, and for their *kukri,* deadly broad-bladed knives.

3

SHELABAGH

3 By 1948, India had the fourth largest railroad system in the world. The railroads had originally been constructed to serve British purposes, to help control India's vast expanses cheaply and efficiently, and to open up the hinterland to trade. But they also helped to unify India economically and politically and thus lay the foundations for the spirit of Indian nationalism on the subcontinent.

4 Jawaharlal Nehru (1889–1964) was the first prime minister of independent India. Educated in England, he emerged as a leading figure in the Congress party in the 1930s and as Gandhi's heir.

5 Mohammed Jinnah (1876–1948) was the architect of Pakistan, which resulted from the partitioning of the old unified India into two states. He believed this the only way to protect Muslim interests.

4

5

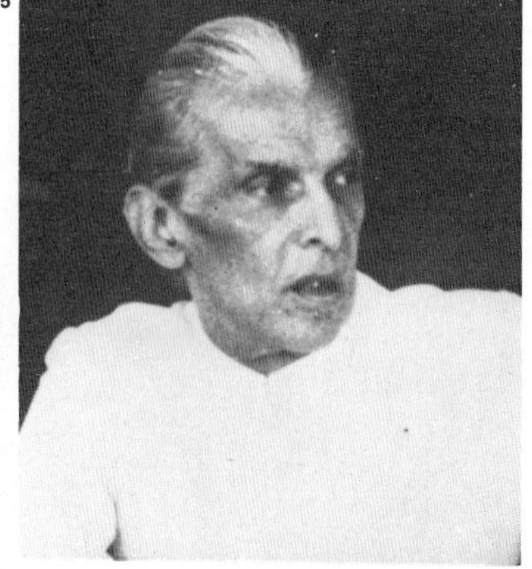

6

6 As well as the provinces which they ruled directly, the British retained ultimate power over nearly 600 autonomous princely states. The Victorians adopted the durbar (traditionally in India a gathering of vassals to do homage to their ruler) to symbolize the allegiance of the Indian princes to the British monarch. The 1911 durbar was attended by King George V of England in person.

dominated the nationalist movement. They feared that if such men became strong enough to throw out the British their next target would be the conservative gentry. And not all Indians wanted democracy and one man, one vote. Hindus living in areas where the majority was Muslim, and vice versa, were fearful that popular government would threaten their interests and perhaps their lives. India remained deeply riven by economic, class, and religious divisions.

This meant that the British still had an advantage. They were willing to give Indians greater internal responsibility so as to avoid trouble, and they found that delegating some power to some Indians was a convenient method of preventing all Indians from uniting against them. They hoped by this to keep India united in a federation that in international matters would still be tightly bound to Britain.

These clever calculations were swept away by two "accidents." The first was the outbreak of World War II—once again involving India—which aroused more resentment among Indians than World War I. Meanwhile, British prestige was undermined by humiliating defeats by the Japanese. The second "accident" was the resolve of the leaders of the large Muslim communities of north India to insist upon partition and the creation of Pakistan (Land of the Pure) as a separate Muslim state.

Independence

Thus India gained independence in 1947 in a way quite unintended by the British. The division of the subcontinent wrecked the delicate mechanisms of federalism through which they had planned to influence India in its international role as a pillar of the Empire-Commonwealth. Deprived of Indian help, the British Empire east of Suez withered away in less than 20 years. In India itself, independence left vast problems unsolved: the overpopulation of the countryside, the failure to increase food production sufficiently, the desperate poverty of village and city alike. The victory won by Indian nationalism in 1947 was, therefore, only a beginning. The building of a modern nation-state lay ahead.

KEY

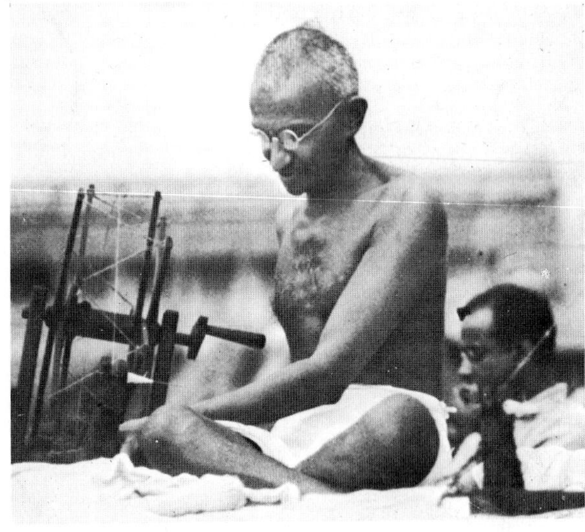

Gandhi adopted the symbol of the spinning wheel in 1920. He believed that India should make its own cloth, thus threatening British textile exports to India and giving Indians the self-confidence necessary for independence.

7

8

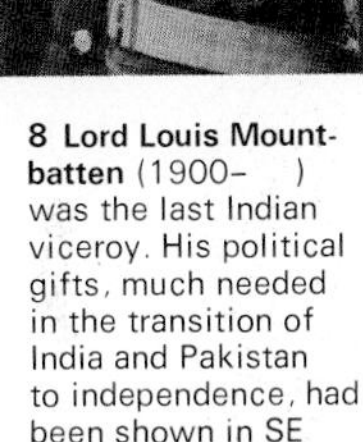

7 The Indian Army was an enormous asset for the British in the defense of their vast empire. In World War I, Indian troops fought on the Western Front, while in World War II they were used in Burma, the Middle East, the Mediterranean, and North and East Africa. The loss of their services after independence in 1947 placed a great strain on Britain's own military resources and strength.

8 Lord Louis Mountbatten (1900–   ) was the last Indian viceroy. His political gifts, much needed in the transition of India and Pakistan to independence, had been shown in SE Asia in World War II.

9 Political democracy in India was extended in the reforms of 1919 and 1935 when the British gave the Indians the right to participate in government. Universal suffrage was achieved in 1947.

10 As independence drew nearer, the tensions among different communities in India became acute. The most serious were those between Hindus and Muslims, especially in areas where their numbers were almost equal and the proposed partition caused great bitterness. The aftermath of bitter riots in Calcutta in 1946, when at least 4,000 people died, is illustrated here.

9

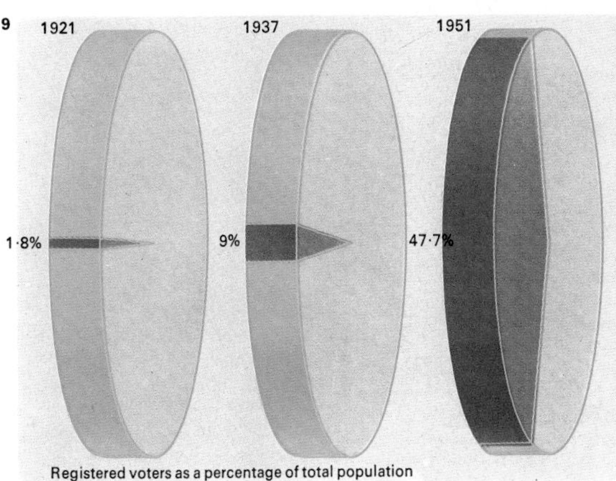
1921
1937
1951
1·8%
9%
47·7%
Registered voters as a percentage of total population

10

BATHGATE & CO · CALCUTTA

The Commonwealth

The Commonwealth [1] is a free association of nations comprising Great Britain and (in 1975) 34 other sovereign states that were once colonies or dependent territories within the British Empire.

The origins of the association go back to Britain's relations with its colonies of European settlement. For these Britain established during the nineteenth century a system in which they would acquire independence by stages [4]. Crown government concentrated power in the governor and council, which might be advisory or executive. Later there might also be a legislative council or assembly that lent itself to constitutional progress as the proportion of elected members grew in relation to the nominated members. Further advances would occur when the executive council, or government ministers, became responsible to the representative assembly, and when the indigenous council and assembly acquired powers of internal self-government over all but special and external matters. Finally, the country would gain full independence.

Perhaps the first significant step in the transition from empire to commonwealth was a report by Lord Durham (1792–1840) [2], in 1839, stating that one cause of unrest in the Canadian provinces was the lack of harmony between the executive and the legislature. The remedy, according to the report, was to choose executive ministers from the majority group in the representative assembly.

From colonies to dominions

Once the principle of such local government had been conceded in Canada, its extension to other colonies of settlement quickly followed. The British government, however, reserved the power to manage foreign relations and external trade, dispose of unoccupied public lands, and amend constitutions.

These limitations were gradually removed, but that on the conduct of foreign relations remained until the twentieth century (by which time the self-governing colonies—Canada, Australia, New Zealand, South Africa, and Newfoundland—were known as "dominions"). The precise status of the dominions was undefined until a committee under Lord Balfour (1848–1930) produced a report (1926) that stated, "They are autonomous Communities within the British Empire, equal in status, in no way subordinate one to another in any aspect of their domestic or external affairs, although united by a common allegiance to the Crown, and freely associated as members of the British Commonwealth of Nations."

In those colonies that were not primarily settled by Europeans, constitutional advance was very much slower. In the 1930s colonial rule in Africa and Asia was assumed to have a long future in view. World War II, however, helped to stimulate nationalist pressures, especially in India, which had already acquired some international recognition as a state. The struggle for independence in India had produced a number of powerful leaders, such as Mahatma Gandhi [3], who acquired worldwide fame for their defiance (usually nonviolent) of imperial authority. In 1947

CONNECTIONS

See also
1330 Indian nationalism
1268 Africa in the 19th century
1262 European imperialism in the 19th century
1350 Decolonization
1352 Non-alignment and the Third World
1356 Postwar evolution of Western Europe
1382 The United Nations and its agencies
1386 Underdevelopment and the world economy
942 International co-operation and development

1

1 United Kingdom	
2 Canada	1867
3 Australia	1901
4 New Zealand	1907
5 India	1947
6 Sri Lanka	1948
7 Ghana	1957
8 Malaysia	1957
9 Nigeria	1960
10 Cyprus	1961
11 Sierra Leone	1961
12 Tanzania	1961
13 Jamaica	1962
14 Trinidad and Tobago	1962
15 Uganda	1962
16 Kenya	1963
17 Malawi	1964
18 Malta	1964
19 Zambia	1964
20 Gambia	1965
21 Singapore	1965
22 Guyana	1966
23 Botswana	1966
24 Lesotho	1966
25 Barbados	1966
26 Mauritius	1968
27 Swaziland	1968
28 Nauru	1968
29 Tonga	1970
30 Western Samoa	1970
31 Fiji	1970
32 Bangladesh	1972
33 Bahama Islands	1973
34 Grenada	1974
35 Papua-New Guinea	1975
36 Seychelles	1976

1 A quarter of the world's land surface is covered by the Commonwealth, which also embraces a huge number of languages and dialects as well as numerous religions. The feature common to all of the members is the historical accident of settlement, annexation, or conquest by Britain; and British institutions and the English language also remain important elements in the modern association. Since 1965 there has been a permanent central secretariat, based in London. But the Commonwealth in no sense acts as a unit in international affairs. The map shows the dates of independence of each country.

2

2 Lord Durham's report in 1839 on the unrest in the Canadian provinces led to the introduction of responsible government in Canada, and later in other colonies of settlement. This report opened the way for the development of independent parliamentary governments linked by allegiance to a single crown.

3

3 The strong moral leadership of Mahatma Gandhi (1869-1948), at center with head bowed, lay behind much of the nationalistic agitation against the British in India after 1918. His asceticism, aura of holiness, and his use of fasting and passive resistance often embarrassed the British government and actively involved the masses in India.

and 1948 independence was granted to India. Pakistan, and Ceylon.

Nkrumah's "self-government now"

The concept of gradual progress was destroyed after Malaya and the Gold Coast became independent in 1957. In the Gold Coast, the nationalist leader, Kwame Nkrumah [5], who became prime minister in 1952, refused to recognize any impediment to the early transfer of power, advocated positive action to cripple the forces of imperialism, and popularized the slogan "self-government now." When the Gold Coast gained its independence, British Togoland joined it to form the new nation of Ghana. In 1960 Ghana became a republic, with Nkrumah as president. The "Wind of Change" speech by British Prime Minister Harold Macmillan (1894–) in 1960 reflected the British government's new attitude toward Africa.

The newly independent countries chose to remain in the Commonwealth because they believed that participation would bring them economic and diplomatic benefits and enhance their international influence. But they did not feel the older members' special attachment to the monarchy, and in 1949 India was the first state allowed to retain its membership as a republic.

All members participate in the Commonwealth system of consultation and cooperation that covers a multitude of governmental activities. Periodically the heads of government meet [8] in conferences organized and serviced by a secretariat that has its headquarters in London.

Expansion and the loosening of old bonds

Nevertheless, the old bonds of commonwealth are no longer as strong and much of the earlier informal intimacy has been lost as the association has expanded. Disillusionment with the Commonwealth has been evident among many members. And several countries have gone so far as to leave the Commonwealth: Ireland in 1949, South Africa in 1961, and Pakistan in 1972. The modern Commonwealth, however, continues to function as a flexible system of cooperation among its members.

KEY

George V was called "King of Great Britain, Ireland, and the British Dominions beyond the Seas, and Emperor of India." His title illustrated the extent of his authority and emphasized India's special position in the British Empire.

4 The character of colonial government varied in detail from one territory to another, but each was expected to follow much the same series of stages on the way to independence. And the advance to dominion status by the old European colonies of settlement became the model. But in the final period of decolonization, the stages were not always as clearly defined as earlier.

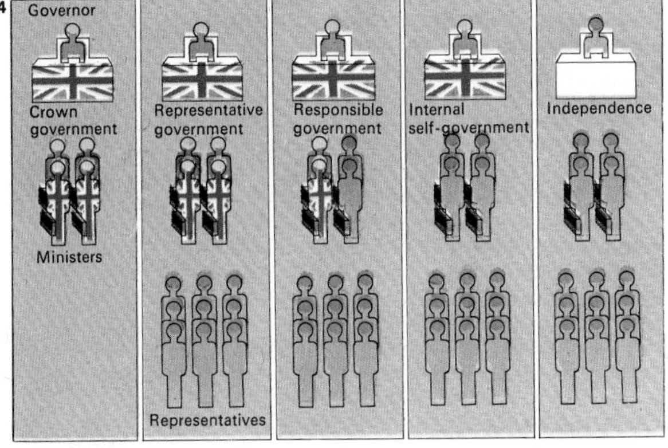
Governor
Crown government
Representative government
Responsible government
Internal self-government
Independence
Ministers
Representatives

5 By campaigning strongly for "self-government now" in the Gold Coast, Nkrumah (1909-72) helped destroy the concept of gradual transference of power in the restive African colonies.

6 Conflict—like this in Bangladesh—sometimes followed independence. National unity could be endangered, and often parliamentary democracy was replaced by one-party rule.

7 Until colonial territories in Africa and elsewhere became independent after World War II, the Commonwealth "family"—here assembled in 1926—was small, subscribing to British traditions and acknowledging one crown.

8 As membership of the Commonwealth grew, the informality of heads of government meetings became more difficult to maintain. But the members still felt that the meetings were valuable for the discussion of problems and improvement of mutual understanding. The offers of other capitals (here Singapore in 1971) to host meetings further emphasized that the modern Commonwealth was no longer "British" but a unique, worldwide association.

The rise of fascism

Fascism developed in the years between World Wars I and II to become a major ideological and political force in many European countries, most notably in Italy and Germany. Expressed as an intense nationalism, often with strong social and collectivist overtones, it had the support of many different groups of people.

Fascist ideology

Although fascism shared many characteristics with reactionary nationalism and the tenets of more conservative, authoritarian regimes, it had its own distinctive characteristics. These were derived from its rejection of the individualistic liberalism that had dominated nineteenth century European political thought.

Fascist ideology embraced many thinkers, often distorting and misapplying their ideas. Indeed, unlike Marxism, fascism never formulated a clear ideology, but remained open to a number of different interpretations, in which the component elements received varying emphasis. Among the most important contributors to fascist ideas were the German Friedrich Nietzsche (1844–1900), who stressed the need for dynamic "supermen;" Henri Bergson (1859–1941), who stressed instinct above reason; and Georges Sorel (1847–1922), who emphasized the moral value of action.

Italian fascism and Mussolini

Italy emerged from World War I disappointed and frustrated by its war losses and the failure of the Versailles settlement to fulfill the treaty promises that had induced it to enter the war. Unemployment, strikes, and violence [1] provided the background to the breakdown of parliamentary government. Right-wing volunteers led by Gabriele d'Annunzio (1863–1938), seized the port of Fiume on the Adriatic coast in 1919 in defiance of the Versailles settlement. In city and countryside riots, estate seizures by the peasants, and sitdown strikes created a revolutionary atmosphere.

In this situation Benito Mussolini (1883–1945) [Key], an ex-socialist schoolteacher, organized anti-socialist *fascios* to combat left-wing groups with strong-arm methods. He received support from diverse conservative elements, and by 1921 there were more than 800 branches of his "blackshirt" organization, the *Fasci di combattimento*. Taking advantage of the disorganization of left-wing forces, he organized a "March on Rome" that ended when he became premier in October 1922.

Mussolini concentrated on liquidating and terrorizing opponents, establishing the Fascist party in power and building up his personal position. Press, courts, and unions were brought under his control, and he established a concordat with the Roman Catholic Church. He inaugurated public works, such as the draining of the Pontine marshes, and mounted a drive for self-sufficiency for Italy. Increasing state intervention marked Musolini's economic policy after 1925 as he tried to create a "corporate state" in which industrialists and workers cooperated for the good of the nation. Combined with his expansionist foreign policy, demonstrated both in the war in Ethiopia and his involvement in aiding Francisco Franco (1892–1975) in Spain,

CONNECTIONS

See also
1336 Causes of World War II
1326 Socialism in the West
1324 The twenties and the Depression
1308 The Peace of Paris

1 A

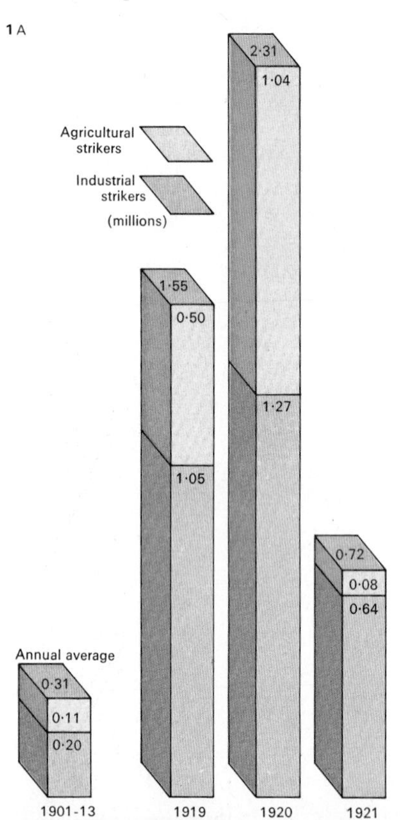

Agricultural strikers
Industrial strikers
(millions)
Annual average
0·31
0·11
0·20
1901-13
1·55
0·50
1·05
1919
2·31
1·04
1·27
1920
0·72
0·08
0·64
1921

B

1919 0·9
1920 20·6
1921 249·0
(totals in thousands)

1 In 1919, Italy was crippled by war losses, inflation, and unemployment. Fascism grew in response to conservative fears of a left-wing revolution, fueled by the mounting toll of strikes [A]. Fascist membership [B] rose from under 1,000 in 1919 to 249,000 in 1921, taken mainly from the middle classes. Aided by industrialists, landowners, and the army, Mussolini took power in 1922.

2

2 Field Marshal Paul von Hindenburg (1847–1934), a hero of World War I, was president of the Weimar Republic from 1925. Under nationalist pressure, he made Hitler chancellor in 1933.

3

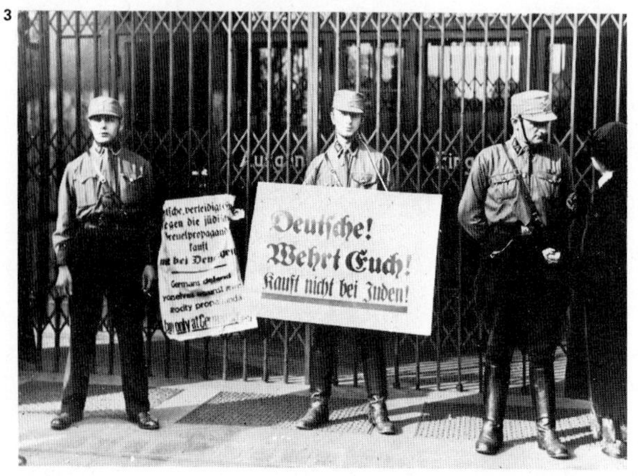

Deutsche!
Wehrt Euch!
Kauft nicht bei Juden!

3 The Nazis based much of their propaganda upon virulent anti-Semitism, in which the Jews were used as scapegoats for Germany's economic difficulties. The Nazis conducted boycotts of Jewish shops, attacked synagogues, and assaulted individuals but were unable to adopt formal measures until Hitler's accession to power in 1933. Anti-Jewish laws promoted emigration and denied civil rights. Many Jews had left or were interned by 1939.

4

Total votes
Nazi votes
(millions)

	May 1924	Dec 1924	May 1928	Sept 1930	July 1932	Nov 1932
Total votes	29·7	30·7	31·2	35·2	37·2	35·7
Nazi votes	1·9	0·9	0·8	6·4	13·8	11·7

4 The fluctuation in votes for the Nazis reflected the economic fortunes of the Weimar Republic. In May 1924 the Nazis gained 1,900,000 votes and 32 seats in the Reichstag. With the recovery of the Weimar Republic from its postwar difficulties and the inflation of 1923, the Nazi vote declined to its lowest point in 1928 when Nazis held only 12 seats in the Reichstag. Under the impact of a renewed depression after 1929, and with the rise in unemployment and the polarization of the middle classes, the Nazi vote rose rapidly. By July 1932 the Nazis were the largest party. Although they lost votes in November, Hitler became chancellor in January 1933.

Mussolini's policies not only antagonized other European countries but also exhausted Italian resources.

Hitler and German fascism

In Germany the Nazi party (National Socialist German Workers' party) was founded in the disillusionment and economic chaos following World War I. Joined by Adolf Hitler (1889–1945) [Key] in 1919, who expanded and transformed it, the party gained some seats in the Reichstag [4]. In 1923, Hitler tried unsuccessfully to overthrow the Bavarian government in a *putsch* in Munich, for which he was imprisoned.

Votes for the Nazi party declined as the Weimar Republic recovered in the middle and late 1920s, but the onset of the worst phase of the Depression after 1929 swelled party ranks with the young, the unemployed, and frightened middle class and conservative elements. For Hitler and some of his followers, anti-Semitism [3] formed an important part of the program. The Jews were made scapegoats for Germany's misfortunes and cast as intruders.

Support for the Nazis, however, seemed to have reached its peak toward the end of 1932 and the party was running into financial difficultes as funds from major industrialists dried up. In January 1933 Hitler was put into office through a coalition with the right-wing Nationalist party, which hoped to control him. After the Reichstag fire [6], Hitler was able to assume dictatorial power. The rule of terror through the Gestapo gave the regime a more vicious character than Mussolini's in Italy. Like Mussolini's fascism, however, Nazism offered an aggressive foreign policy and a solution to unemployment through public works and rearmament [5].

Fascist parties grew up in many other countries. In Spain [7], the Falange provided support for Franco, while in Eastern Europe the Romanian "Iron Guard" and the regime of Admiral Horthy in Hungary had strong fascist elements. In Western Europe the blackshirts of Oswald Mosley (1896–) in Britain and the *Croix de Feu* in France [8] appeared, temporarily, to threaten democratic government.

KEY

By 1934, Italy and Germany were ruled by Fascist dictators. Mussolini (right) assumed power much earlier than Hitler (left), but the latter dominated international politics in the 1930s. The Rome-Berlin Axis was formed in 1936.

5

5 Hitler's flamboyant rhetoric was aimed in part at gaining support from the middle class, which was suffering from unemployment and inflation. He tried to satisfy public opinion by cutting unemployment and creating a prosperous Germany. Public works, such as the building of the *autobahn* (highway) network, provided an advertisement for the regime in reply to domestic and foreign critics and also served the purposes of the military forces. Soon, mass rallies and the obligatory greeting "Heil Hitler" became signs of Hitler's complete dominance of all sectors of German life.

6

DEM DEUTSCHEN VOLKE

6 Hitler's rise to power was only half completed with his accession to the chancellorship. He awaited the opportunity to introduce emergency laws to strengthen his position. His chance came when a young Dutchman, Marinus van der Lubbe, set fire to the Reichstag on February 27, 1933. The Nazis were suspected of starting the fire, but it appears they merely took advantage of it to promulgate emergency decrees, imprisoning opponents, and vesting power in Hitler and the Nazi party. Although the Nazis failed to achieve a majority, they were supported by the Nationalists.

7

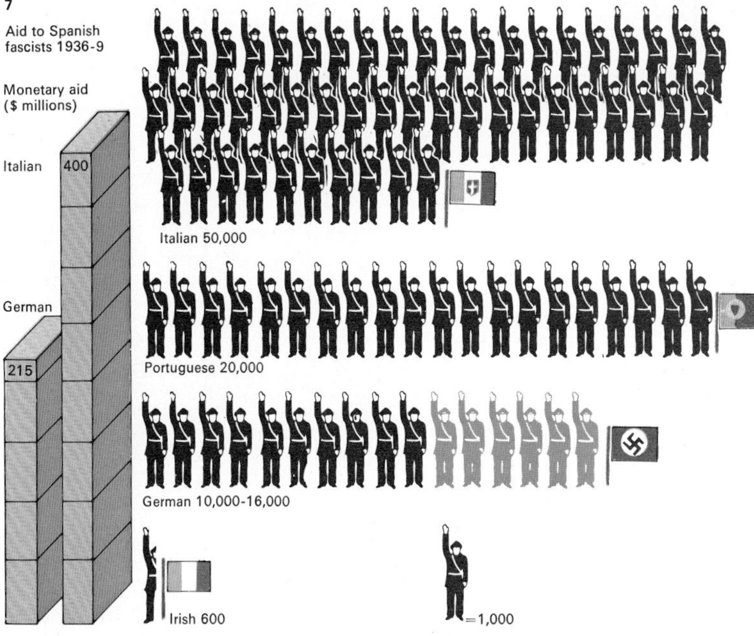
Aid to Spanish fascists 1936-9
Monetary aid ($ millions)
Italian
400
German
215
Italian 50,000
Portuguese 20,000
German 10,000-16,000
Irish 600
=1,000

7 By 1936 both Italy and Germany were expanding their influence in international politics. The outbreak of civil war in Spain provided diplomatic and military advantages for both countries. Mussolini hoped to gain military bases in the western Mediterranean. By 1937, Italian war production was beginning to show signs of strain. Hitler hoped to sow dissension between England and France, while binding Italy closer to him. He used Spain as a training ground for his air force, including the "Condor Legion," a force of 6,500 men consisting mainly of air force units but with a few ground support units. From 1937, Spain could be considered as only a brutal sideshow.

8

PARAIT LE 15 DE CHAQUE MOIS
lisez
LE
CAHIER
JAUNE

8 Political instability in France promoted anti-Semitism, as expressed in such magazines as *Le Cahier Jaune*.

Causes of World War II

The interwar years in Europe were dominated by the rise of the fascist dictators [Key] in Italy and Germany. Their nationalistic and expansionist policies increasingly undermined the credibility of diplomatic negotiation.

The rise of the dictators

World War I had left a bitter legacy in the crippling reparations and arbitrary territorial divisions of the Treaty of Versailles (1919). Its effects were highly influential in the rise to power of Benito Mussolini (1883–1945) and Adolf Hitler (1889–1945). Italy had suffered losses in World War I and disappointments at Versailles, and Mussolini owed a large part of his support to a policy of militant nationalism that was bound to create tensions in the postwar world [6]. Hitler, like Mussolini, based his support upon a policy of extreme nationalism, determined to reverse the penal aspects of the Versailles treaty and to pursue the ultimate goal of territorial unification of all German-speaking peoples in Eastern Europe [4].

The isolationism of the United States meant that the major initiative for peace lay with France and Britain, the two strongest powers. Both nations were fearful of renewed war. They felt that war in 1914 had arisen out of an inability of the diplomatic system to cope with international crises, and both France and Britain believed that they must negotiate with the dictators to avoid accidental war.

During the 1920s faith was placed in the League of Nations and pursuit of disarmament policies—policies that foundered on mutual distrust among the great European powers. By the early 1930s it was clear that the League of Nations was unlikely to act as a guarantor of peace. Japan's invasion of Manchuria and then, more seriously, the Ethiopian crisis (1935–36) and the Spanish Civil War (1936–39) showed that the League was incapable of restricting international aggression.

A policy of appeasement

For much of the 1930s, statesmen in both France and Britain believed that Hitler's policies were designed solely to satisfy Germany's legitimate demands for revision of the Versailles settlement. In spite of Germany's reoccupation of the Rhineland in 1936 [2] and virtual control of Austria [1], Britain in particular maintained the hope that war could be averted by concession. The efforts of both Stanley Baldwin (1867–1947) and Neville Chamberlain (1869–1940) to negotiate with Hitler were supported in large part by a populace worried about another war and resentful of military expenditures during economic depression. Left-wing forces in Britain were convinced that policies of disarmament must be pursued to lessen the risk of war. Chamberlain was operating from a position of weakness when Hitler was busy rearming [3]. France was also beset by weakness; internal political divisions prevented the development of a firm foreign policy and the country's losses in World War I inclined it to follow a defensive policy.

Hitler exploited the confusion and weakness of the Western European powers to reverse Versailles and further his plans

CONNECTIONS

See also

1338 World War II
1308 The Peace of Paris
1334 The rise of fascism
1326 Socialism in the West
1324 The twenties and the Depression
1312 The Soviet Union under Stalin

1

1 Chancellor Dollfuss of Austria was murdered in 1934, on Hitler's orders, as the first stage of Germany's Austrian annexation. Virtual control was achieved in 1936; the takeover came in 1938.

2

2 The Versailles Treaty had excluded German forces from the Rhineland. In March 1936, German troops reoccupied it in defiance of France and Britain; neither was prepared to risk war to prevent this.

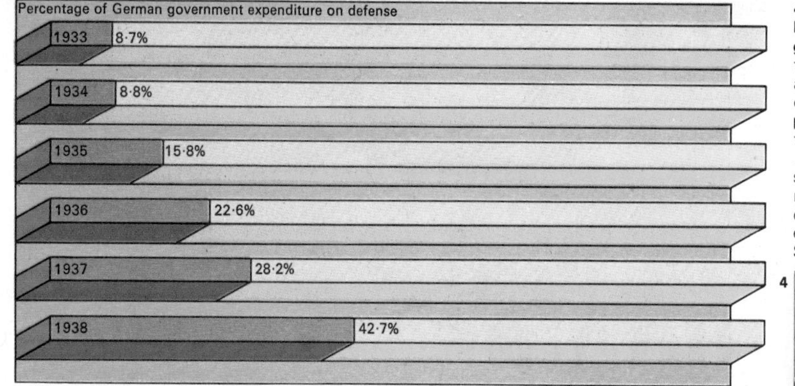

Percentage of German government expenditure on defense
1933
8·7%
1934
8·8%
1935
15·8%
1936
22·6%
1937
28·2%
1938
42·7%

3 Expenditure on defense increased fivefold in Hitler's Germany between 1933 and 1938. Spending reached a peak in the latter stages of World War II. Germany started rearming immediately after Hitler came to power, but this drive became dominant only after 1936. Then the adoption of a Four Year Plan of rearmament directed more of the German economy to war than in any other European country.

4

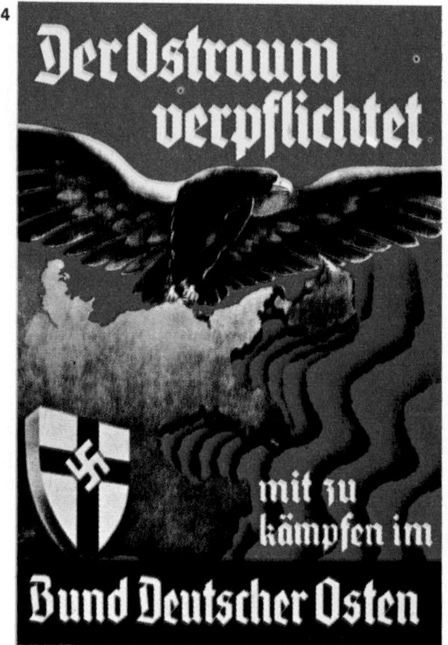

Der Ostraum
verpflichtet
mit zu
kämpfen im
Bund Deutscher Osten

4 In his book Mein Kampf ("My Struggle"), published in two parts in 1924 and 1926, Hitler described his future policy, including the famous demand for *lebensraum* or "living space" for the German peoples in the east. Expansion into eastern European and Soviet territory had long been part of right-wing German thought. Its true place in Hitler's plans is much debated, but his conquests in eastern Europe by diplomacy, by threat—backed by propaganda such as this poster—and ultimately by war fulfilled his publicly stated program.

5

GERMANY
SILESIA
POLAND
Prague
Cracow
Teschen
BOHEMIA
MORAVIA
BAVARIA
Brno
SLOVAKIA
RUTHENIA
Danube
Vienna
Bratislava
HUNGARY
AUSTRIA
Budapest
ROMANIA
0
200km
Czechoslovakia before Munich
Ceded to Germany at Munich
To Poland September 1938
To Hungary October 1938

5 Germany's aim of absorbing German-speaking parts of Czechoslovakia—the Sudetenland—almost plunged Europe into war. At Munich in 1938, Britain and France virtually sacrificed Czech industry and defense in an attempt to appease the Germans.

for conquest in the east at a later date. The reoccupation of the Rhineland was followed by the Austrian *Anschluss* and demands for the cession of the German-speaking Sudetenland from Czechoslovakia [5]. After threatening war, Hitler was placated by an agreement in 1938 that virtually dismembered Czechoslovakia in return for promises not to occupy the non-German speaking areas of the country. Chamberlain's surrender was hailed as a triumph that had avoided war, but it was increasingly seen that Hitler would not be stopped. The occupation of Prague in March 1939 dispelled the illusion that Hitler's demands were limited.

The influence of peripheral powers

Resistance to Hitler had been confused by suspicion of the Soviet Union's intentions. Coming out of isolation in the mid-1930s, the Soviet Union was concerned to prevent an alliance of Western European states against it, but became increasingly fearful of the rise of fascism in Germany with its implied threat to the USSR. The Soviets sought to bring the Western powers more clearly into an anti-fascist alliance but were frustrated by the faith in appeasement and widespread mistrust of the USSR. The actions of Britain and France over Czechoslovakia encouraged the USSR to form a nonaggression pact with Germany in 1939.

In the Far East, the rise of a militantly aggressive Japan provided an additional strain upon peace [7]. Japan's occupation of Manchuria (1931–32) and its war with China from the mid-thirties illustrated the weakness of the League and increased Japanese self-confidence and ambition.

Britain's guarantees in 1939 to Poland and Romania were a last attempt to restrain Hitler's actions. He had agreed with the USSR, however, to dismember Poland on the pretext of annexing the "Polish Corridor" [9]. Hitler probably expected Britain and France to back down once again as they had over Munich. Instead they presented Hitler with demands to withdraw. When the British ultimatum expired on September 3, 1939, Britain declared war on Germany; France followed suit a few hours later.

KEY

Hitler riding into Vienna at the head of German troops symbolizes the domination of Europe by the dictators. While Mussolini was backing Hitler in the West, Japanese economic expansion threatened the stability of the Far East.

6

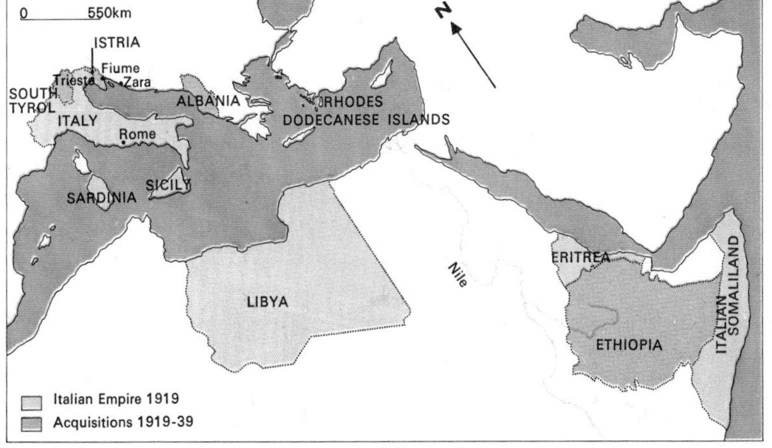

0 550km
N
ISTRIA
Fiume
Trieste
Zara
SOUTH TYROL
ITALY
Rome
ALBANIA
RHODES
DODECANESE ISLANDS
SICILY
SARDINIA
ERITREA
Nile
LIBYA
ETHIOPIA
ITALIAN SOMALILAND
Italian Empire 1919
Acquisitions 1919-39

6 Mussolini's main aim from the time of his appointment in 1922 was to increase Italy's prestige and to consolidate its "Great Power" status by foreign acquisition and aggressive diplomacy. After 1922, Italy tightened its grip on Fiume, the South Tyrol, and the Dodecanese Islands. Protests and sanctions from the League of Nations did not prevent war with Ethiopia in 1935 and the country's rapid annexation. Italy also intervened in Spain in 1936, leading it to a closer *entente* with Germany, which was formalized in 1939 by the "Pact of Steel."

7 Matsuoka [left], the Japanese foreign minister from 1940 to 1941, was largely responsible for Japan's Tripartite Pact with Germany and Italy. Japan had already joined Germany in an Anti-Comintern Pact in 1936. Throughout the 1930s, Japan pursued an aggressive foreign policy. In 1931 it had taken Manchuria, increasing tension in the Far East, where the League of Nations was virtually powerless. In 1937, Japan went to war with China, seizing a large area of the mainland. Europe and the United States failed to resolve the conflict, encouraging Japan to further aggression.

7

8

8 The appeasement policy of Britain and France arose out of fear of renewed war and belief that the dictators' demands could be met by negotiation and concession. But concern grew that such "weakness" provoked more demands.

9

9 German troops symbolically destroyed the Polish frontier when they invaded Poland on Sept. I, 1939. Polish access to the Baltic had been guaranteed by Britain and France, who declared war on Germany on September 3.

World War II

On September 1, 1939, German troops invaded Poland. Britain and France were pledged to support Poland and declared war on Germany two days later. Using revolutionary *blitzkrieg* ("lightning strike") tactics the Germans defeated the outdated Polish army in 18 days, and the country was partitioned between Germany and the Soviet Union, with whom Germany had just signed a nonaggression pact. A British army crossed to France, but the Allies did not attack.

German and Japanese victories

Germany overran Norway and Denmark in April 1940 and then on May 10 invaded Holland, Belgium, and Luxembourg, which had been neutral. As the Allied armies swung forward to meet them, German tanks burst through the "impassable" Ardennes and reached the English Channel. The Allied army to their north was forced back into the Dunkirk region, and 338,226 British and French troops escaped to England by sea between May 29 and June 3. France, except for the southeast of the country under the puppet Vichy regime of Marshal Henri Pétain (1856–1951), was occupied by the Germans.

Germany's leader, Adolf Hitler (1889–1945) expected Britain to make peace, but it fought on defiantly under the leadership of Winston Churchill (1874–1965). The *Luftwaffe* (air force) of Hermann Goering (1893–1946) then attempted to destroy the Royal Air Force (RAF) so that an invasion of England could be launched. But the Germans were unsuccessful in the Battle of Britain, August–October 1940.

Taking advantage of the French Atlantic ports, German submarines intensified their attacks on British sea routes, and in the next two years nearly strangled Britain [7].

Italy entered the war in June 1940, but suffered serious defeats in Greece and Libya. Germany sent forces under General Erwin Rommel (1891–1944) to help the Italians in North Africa and swiftly overran Yugoslavia, Greece, and Crete in April and May 1941.

On June 22, 1941, in a breach of the earlier pact, German troops swept into the Soviet Union [4], achieving total surprise. After five months they were just 19 miles (30km) from Moscow but were halted by bitter winter weather and stubborn Russian resistance. On December 7, 1941, in the second major onslaught of the war, Japan launched a surprise attack on the US fleet at Pearl Harbor in the Pacific.

The first half of 1942 saw the Axis forces (Germany, Italy, Japan, and minor allies) at the height of their powers. In the Pacific the Japanese captured the Dutch East Indies, Malaya, Burma, the Philippines, and many Pacific islands [5]. In the Soviet Union a German offensive advanced on Stalingrad and the Caucasus. In North Africa the British had been driven back to Egypt.

The turn of the tide

A series of crucial battles later in 1942 and in 1943 gave the initiative to the Allies. In the Pacific, Japanese naval power was shattered at the Battle of Midway on June 4–7, 1942, and on August 7, US marines landed on Guadalcanal in the first of the amphibious assaults by which US naval forces

CONNECTIONS

See also
1336 Causes of World War II
1340 The home front in World War II
1334 The rise of fascism
1308 The Peace of Paris
1324 The twenties and the Depression
1312 The Soviet Union under Stalin
1342 The division of Europe
1328 East Asia 1919–1945
1802 Radar and sonar
1730 Automatic weapons
1732 History of artillery
1736 Armored fighting vehicles

1 A

Axis controlled
Allied controlled
Vichy controlled
Soviet controlled
Neutral states
Narvik
Battle of Britain
Dunkirk
Oran
June 1940

B

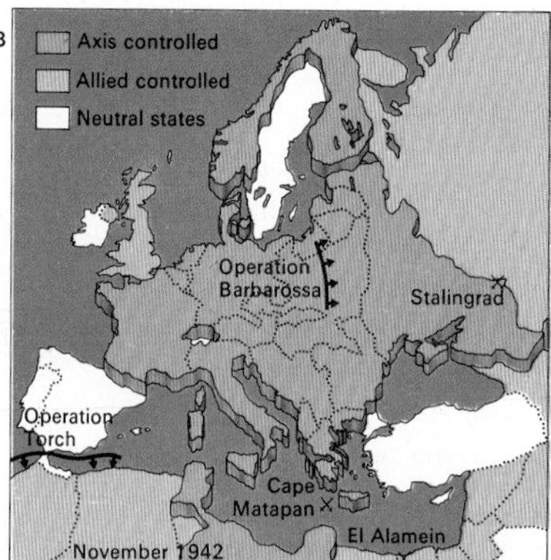

Axis controlled
Allied controlled
Neutral states
Operation Barbarossa
Stalingrad
Operation Torch
Cape Matapan
El Alamein
November 1942

C

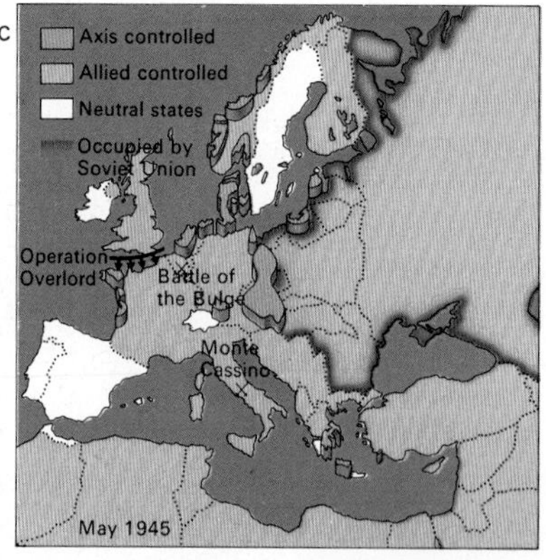

Axis controlled
Allied controlled
Neutral states
Occupied by Soviet Union
Operation Overlord
Battle of the Bulge
Monte Cassino
May 1945

1 The main theater of war was in Europe, as it was in World War I. [A] By June 1940 the Axis powers controlled almost the whole of Western Europe and Germany then broadened the conflict by attacking the Soviet Union a year later. [B] Axis conquests reached their peak in November 1942. [C] By May 1945, Soviet counter-offensives and Allied landings in France and Italy had defeated Germany.

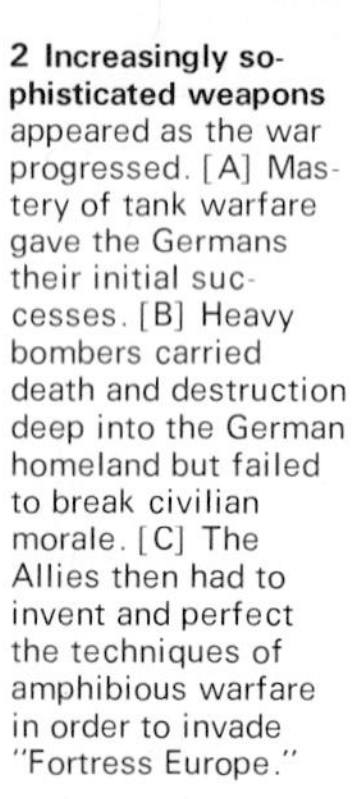

2 Increasingly sophisticated weapons appeared as the war progressed. [A] Mastery of tank warfare gave the Germans their initial successes. [B] Heavy bombers carried death and destruction deep into the German homeland but failed to break civilian morale. [C] The Allies then had to invent and perfect the techniques of amphibious warfare in order to invade "Fortress Europe."

2 A

B

C

3

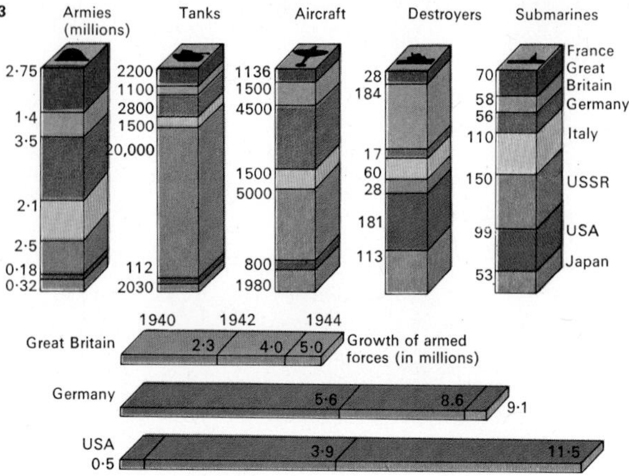

Armies (millions)
Tanks
Aircraft
Destroyers
Submarines
2·75
1·4
3·5
2·1
2·5
0·18
0·32
2200
1100
2800
1500
20,000
112
2030
1136
1500
4500
1500
5000
800
1980
28
184
17
60
28
181
113
70
58
56
110
150
99
53
France
Great Britain
Germany
Italy
USSR
USA
Japan
1940
1942
1944
Great Britain
2·3
4·0
5·0
Growth of armed forces (in millions)
Germany
5·6
8·6
9·1
USA
0·5
3·9
11·5

3 This comparison of military power at the outbreak of war shows that although Germany had the most aircraft in 1939, Britain and France together were in fact stronger in men and equipment. Soviet figures reveal the extent to which the Stalin-Hitler pact helped Germany. The war effort demanded manpower on a massive scale, and the lower half of the diagram shows the growth of armed forces in millions—a remarkably rapid increase.

4

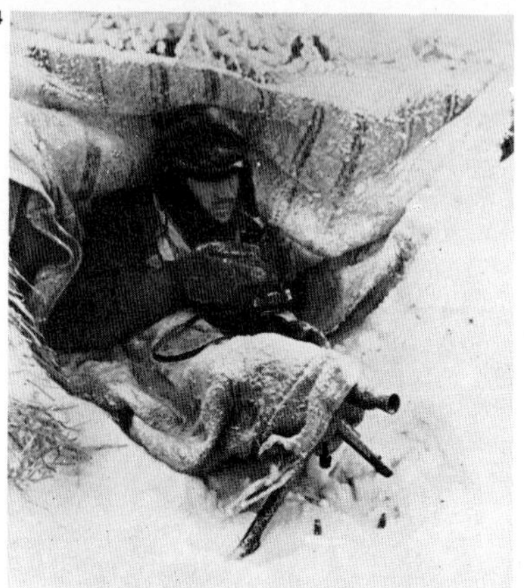

4 The turning point of the war in Europe came when Hitler attacked the Soviet Union in 1941 and failed to deliver a swift knockout blow. The key battle took place at Stalingrad where, after weeks of bitter fighting, the German 6th Army was forced to surrender. Germany was committed to a war on two fronts, with a possible counterattack from Britain in the west and a war of attrition against the vast Russian reserves available in the east.

under Admiral Chester Nimitz (1885–1966) pushed back the Japanese. During the winter in the Soviet Union, 110,000 men of the original German army of 270,000, fighting at Stalingrad, surrendered on January 31, 1943. The remaining 160,000 men had been killed. In North Africa the victory of General Bernard Montgomery (1887–1976) at El Alamein in October 1942, and an Allied landing in Algeria, forced the Axis troops back into Tunisia, where 250,000 surrendered on May 12, 1943. In the Atlantic, Allied sonar and radar developments, more escorts, and long-range aircraft led to increased U-boat losses.

The beginning of the end

The last major German offensive in the Soviet Union was halted at Kursk in July 1943, and the Red Army pushed forward during the autumn and winter. The Allies under General Dwight Eisenhower (1890–1969) invaded Sicily on July 10, 1943, and landed in Italy on September 3. The RAF had made its first "1,000-bomber" raid on Germany in May 1942, and with the arrival of the US Army Air Force in mid-1943, massive raids were mounted into 1945.

On D-Day, June 6, 1944, Allied forces under Eisenhower landed in Normandy, crossed France and the Low Countries to reach the Rhine by November. In Italy, Rome had been captured on June 4, while a Soviet offensive begun in June drove the Germans out of the Soviet Union and swept into Poland and the Baltic states. In the Pacific, US forces destroyed the remnants of the Japanese fleet at the battles of the Philippine Sea and Leyte Gulf and invaded the Philippines in October 1944.

The Allies crossed the Rhine in March 1944 and drove deep into Germany. A Soviet assault under Marshal Georgi Zhukov (1896–1974) began in January 1945 and reached Berlin in April. Hitler committed suicide, and on May 4, Germany surrendered unconditionally.

On August 6, US forces dropped the first atomic bomb on Hiroshima, Japan [8]. A second bomb on Nagasaki three days later forced Japan to surrender on August 14, 1945.

KEY
1914-18 17 total dead (millions)
1939-45 37 45

1939-45 casualties: major powers

Germany 7, 35
Japan 2·6, 12
Italy 0·8, 3·3
USSR 100, 75
Yugoslavia 12·8, 4
France 3·5, 2·5
UK 0·62, 3·26
USA 3

Axis
Allies
Civilian = 100,000
Military = 100,000

World War II was the most destructive and wide-ranging war in history: the total dead may have reached 45,000,000. Military casualties were only slightly higher than in World War I, but massive bombing and German policies against civilians in the occupied territories meant that civilian deaths were far higher.

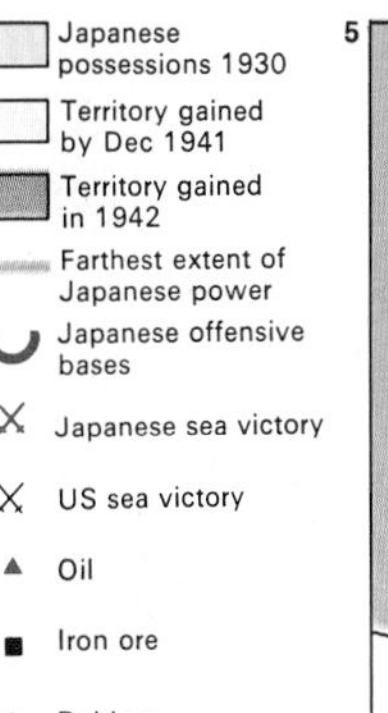

Japanese possessions 1930
Territory gained by Dec 1941
Territory gained in 1942
Farthest extent of Japanese power
Japanese offensive bases
Japanese sea victory
US sea victory
Oil
Iron ore
Rubber
Tin

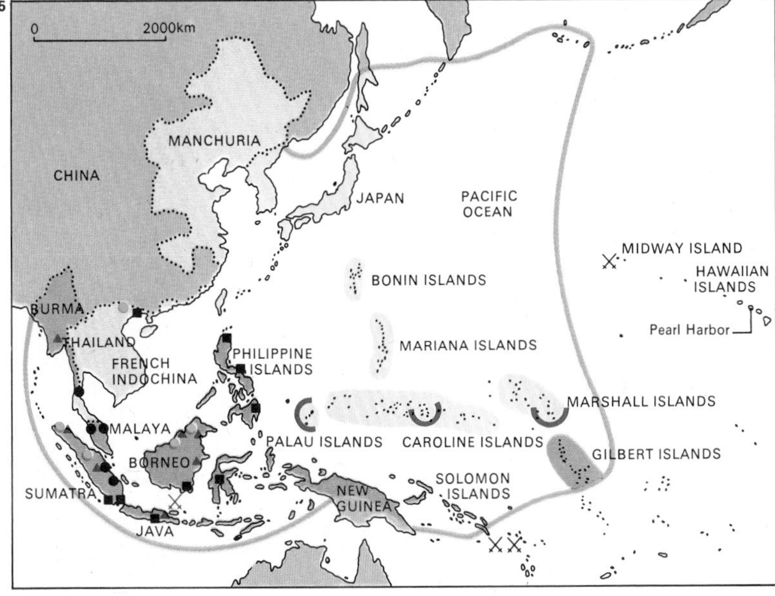

5
0
2000km
MANCHURIA
CHINA
JAPAN
PACIFIC OCEAN
MIDWAY ISLAND
HAWAIIAN ISLANDS
Pearl Harbor
BONIN ISLANDS
MARIANA ISLANDS
BURMA
THAILAND
FRENCH INDOCHINA
PHILIPPINE ISLANDS
MARSHALL ISLANDS
MALAYA
PALAU ISLANDS
CAROLINE ISLANDS
GILBERT ISLANDS
BORNEO
SUMATRA
NEW GUINEA
SOLOMON ISLANDS
JAVA

5 The Japanese expanded into the Pacific in order to secure the oil and minerals of southern Asia and then build a defensive perimeter against Allied counterattacks.

6 The Allied counter-offensive in the Pacific depended largely on a unique naval campaign in which carrier-borne aircraft played a decisive role. Quickly mastering this new type of warfare, the US Navy was able to destroy the Japanese fleet, bypass enemy-held islands, and cut off Japan from its vital supplies. Major land campaigns took place only in Burma and the islands of the Philippines.

7

Allied air cover
Sept 1939—May 1945
Added 1942—May 1945
US air bases
Sept 1939—May 1945
Added 1942—May 1945
U-boat bases
Allied convoy routes

7 The Battle of the Atlantic was a crucial one for Britain once the threat of a German invasion had been removed. The German U-boats hoped to starve Britain into submission, thus eliminating the possibility of a counterattack in the west. In 1941–42 the U-boats almost succeeded in their aim, and it was not until anti-submarine measures had been intensified and improved that the U-boats were eventually mastered.

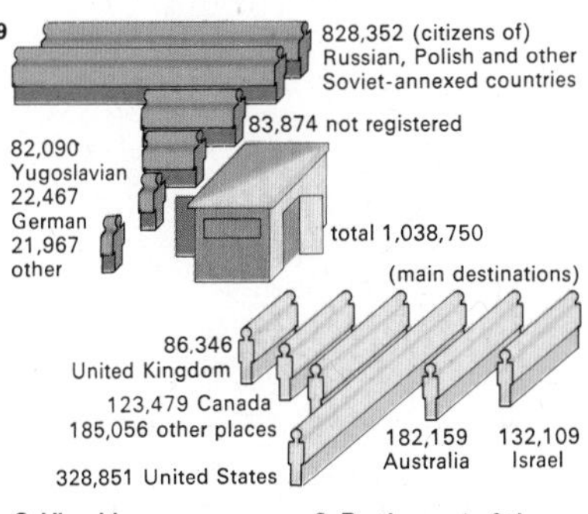

9
828,352 (citizens of) Russian, Polish and other Soviet-annexed countries
83,874 not registered
82,090 Yugoslavian
22,467 German
21,967 other
total 1,038,750
(main destinations)
86,346 United Kingdom
123,479 Canada
185,056 other places
182,159 Australia
132,109 Israel
328,851 United States

8

8 Hiroshima was devastated by the first atomic bomb. By later standards this was a very small bomb of less than one kiloton, but it was enough to obliterate an entire city and kill more than 78,500 people in the space of one minute. A new era of warfare threatening total annihilation had been unleashed on mankind.

9 By the end of the war more than a million displaced persons were living in refugee camps throughout Europe. The majority were Soviet citizens or citizens of countries annexed by the USSR. The diagram shows where the East European refugees came from and where the International Refugee Organization settled them.

The home front in World War II

World War II has been called "The People's War." No previous conflict had so directly involved the civilian populations of the combatant countries or caused them so much suffering through death and privation.

Civilian involvement in war

Even before war had been declared, civilians had become involved through conscription, introduced in Germany in 1934, in Great Britain in June 1939, and in the United States in 1940. Once the war began even those civilians who escaped being called up into the armed forces found themselves in varying degrees directed into home defense [2] or civil defense or into essential work in factories [8] and vital services such as transportation. In every combatant country (except the United States, which could meet about all its needs) the share of resources allocated to civilians was sharply reduced by the end of the war.

Civilians, despite their involvement, were in far less danger than the soldiers. Even in Germany casualties among civilians, including those caught up in military operations, were estimated at no more than 700,000, compared with 3,500,000 servicemen who died. The comparable figures for Britain were 62,000 against 326,000, and for Japan 260,000 civilians compared with 1,200,000 servicemen; the United States had virtually no civilian casualties. But the civilian's life was at risk; although each country claimed at first to be directing its bombers against only military objectives, such restraints were soon abandoned [11]. Bombs were not the principal cause of civilian deaths, however. In the countries occupied by the Germans far more resulted from disease, famine, and mass murder.

Civilian daily life

Even within occupied Europe daily life varied enormously between different countries. In Hitler's "model protectorate," Denmark, the standard of living was far higher than in Britain. In France, if one had access to the black market, it was also possible to live reasonably well. But in Holland by the winter of 1944–45 people were living on tulip bulbs, and in the Channel Islands only the arrival of Red Cross packages prevented starvation. All the occupied countries shared some discomforts. Everyone's life was encompassed by curfews, permits, and the fear of being a victim of the next roundup of suspects or forced-labor.

In the countries still under arms the civilian population was encouraged to believe that a vast gulf separated them from their counterparts in enemy lands. Civilian experience in Germany probably had more in common with life in wartime Britain than in any other country. Both suffered the upheaval of evacuation [Key] and of long nights in shelters. Gasoline in both countries was strictly rationed [5].

Almost all necessities were either rationed or hard to find, and though the German system of control was more complicated and less efficient than the British, there were many similarities between them. Household textiles and clothes, for example, were rationed on a points system in Germany in 1940, and in 1941 the same system was used in Britain. To find consumer goods of every kind, from baby car-

CONNECTIONS

See also
1338 World War II
1356 Postwar evolution of Western Europe
1328 East Asia 1919–1945
1324 The twenties and the Depression
1344 The Soviet Union after World War II

1

1 Pots and pans were collected for aluminum for making aircraft after a British government appeal.

2

2 A volunteer signs up for US civilian defense, aimed against submarine and air attacks.

3
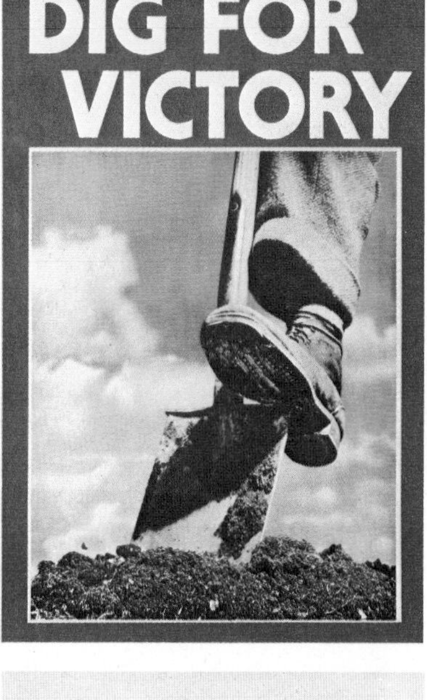

DIG FOR
VICTORY

3 "Dig for Victory" was an early wartime slogan thought up to promote home grown food.

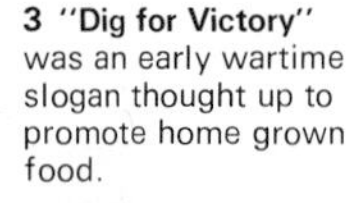

4

5
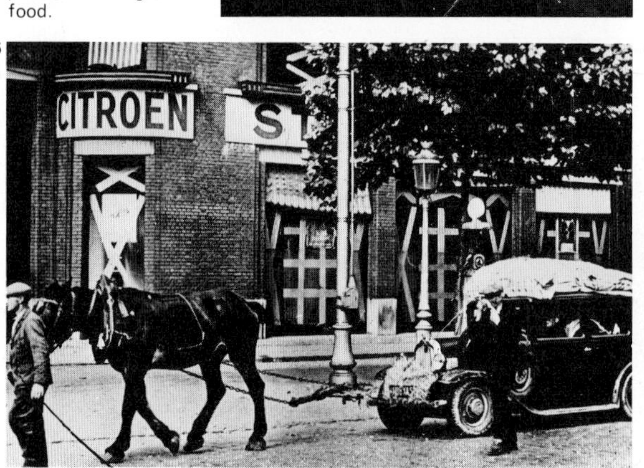

CITROEN

6

4 Air raids on London began Sept. 7, 1940, and lasted until mid-1941. In the opening phase the capital was bombed on 57 consecutive nights. In the first four months, 13,339 people were killed and 17,937 injured.

5 Refugees flooded on to the roads of Europe as the German armies advanced. This Frenchman's horsedrawn vehicle was one way of overcoming the shortage of gasoline; bicycle taxis were also common.

6 Nazi military bands like this one, photographed in the Place de l'Opéra in Paris in June 1941, often played in public in the occupied countries. Ostensibly a goodwill gesture, they also symbolized German strength.

riages to furniture, necessitated a long search; in both countries, as coal was diverted to the war factories, people became preoccupied in winter with keeping warm.

Food rationing made the deepest impact on most people, and here, as in other areas, the Germans probably suffered most. The same basic items were rationed in both countries: meat, butter, fats, bacon, cheese, sugar, jam, milk, and eggs. But in Germany one also had to part with coupons for bread and potatoes, both plentiful in Britain [3], and there were no "lend lease" supplies of American dried egg or canned meat.

American soldiers arriving in Europe readily admitted that "back home they don't know there's a war on." Even in the United States there was some rationing—canned goods, sugar, coffee, shoes, gasoline, meats—but in practice there was no real shortage of any type of goods. The Japanese fuel shortage prevented their indulging in the constant ritual bathing demanded by tradition. Japan also suffered a near-breakdown in the railroad and island-ferry transportation systems, and by 1945 food supplies had shrunk to less than half the normal minimum.

A new prosperity

If the war years brought unprecedented hardship to civilians they also brought many benefits. In both Germany and Britain, because of the fairer apportioning of food supplies and full employment, poorer families lived better than they had ever done before. Everywhere, including the United States, rigid price controls kept the rise in prices within limits; by 1945 the cost of living was only a third higher than before the war.

For factory worker and farmer alike, in every combatant country, these were boom years. The new prosperity masked deeper long-term changes. The drift from country to city was accelerated; there was increased pressure for urban amenities to be extended to the countryside; it was demonstrated that full employment was not an impossible dream, and everywhere the shared sacrifices and wider opportunities led to a demand for a fairer social order after the war.

KEY

In World War II, America became, as President Roosevelt, said, "the arsenal of democracy." US economic might and industrial capacity gave the Allies a decided advantage.

7

UNITED STATES TREASURY
WAR FINANCE COMMITTEE
Know All Men By These Presents:
This is to certify that
is the owner of a War Bond, thereby becoming an investor in this country's fight for human liberty and a contributor in a world struggle to make life free and forever peaceful for all men.
This Bond presented by:

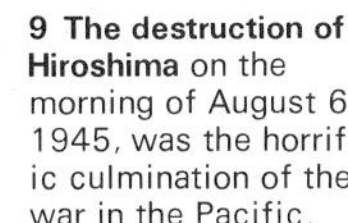

7 War savings were encouraged by all countries to stop inflation. This US Victory Bond was designed by Disney.

8

8 The mobilization of women was greatest in the USSR. Here ammunition is being prepared for the Leningrad siege.

9

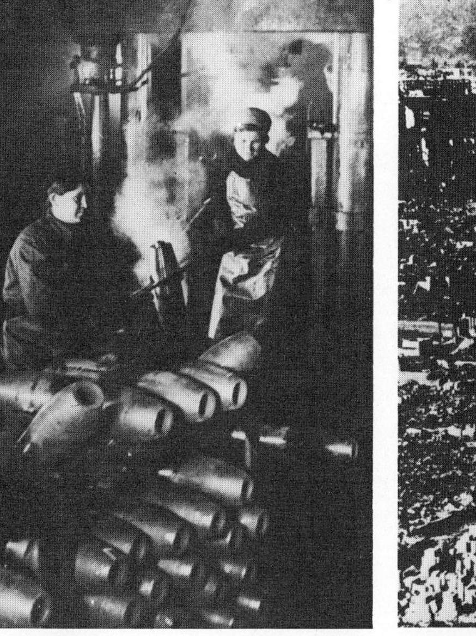

9 The destruction of Hiroshima on the morning of August 6, 1945, was the horrific culmination of the war in the Pacific.

10

pst!
Feind hört mit

11

12

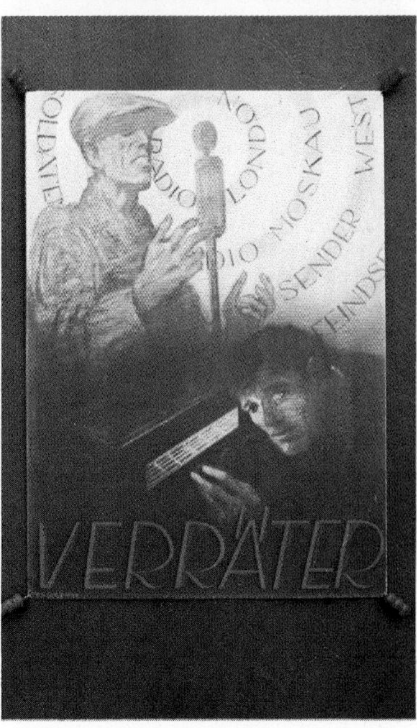

LONDON
MOSKAU
SENDER
WEST
VERRÄTER

10 Propaganda was used by both sides, both offensively and defensively. This German poster warns against careless talk.

11 Allied bombing devastated the non-military city of Dresden. These are the ruins of the church of St Sophia.

12 "Traitor" warns this German poster. German propaganda techniques were more sophisticated than the Allies'.

The division of Europe

The cold war is usually thought of as a global struggle between the two great powers that had emerged by the end of World War II. These two powers, the Soviet Union and the United States, were at first by no means equal; the United States was far superior in terms of economic capacity, air power, and its initial monopoly of nuclear weapons. The Soviet Union had an important advantage, however: the ability to threaten Western Europe with the might of its army. It was because of this Soviet threat that the United States was obliged to help the Western European countries.

East-West misunderstandings

This traditional view of the origins of the cold war derives from an interpretation according to which Soviet troops overran Eastern Europe between 1945 and 1947 and seemed to threaten Western Europe, too. An opposing view is supported by some historians. They argue that the USSR, which had in the past been invaded many times from the west, was still afraid of its titular allies at the end of World War II. In this view, the Stalinist takeover of Eastern Europe was merely a defensive reaction.

Whichever view is correct, it is fairly clear that mutual misunderstanding and mistrust between the Soviet Union and the United States played a large part in bringing about the division of Europe [5]. When Churchill (1874–1965), Roosevelt (1882–1945), and Stalin (1879–1953) met at Yalta in 1945 [Key], Soviet displeasure at the west's plan for a Second Front gave way to western suspicions over Soviet intentions in the east—particularly its plans for Poland. Thereafter the powers failed to reach agreement on Germany.

The division of Germany

At first the US forces had not intended to stay long in Germany, just as they did not expect the Soviet troops to remain there. The victorious powers were supposed to supervise German reconstruction only until they could all agree on its future as a united country. All four administered Berlin equally. But the picture changed, partly because of Soviet dominance in Eastern Europe and in the Soviet zone of Germany, which was rapidly organized as part of the Soviet system. In addition, Soviet reparations demands seemed to threaten the economic ruin of the West by encouraging the total collapse of the German economy [2], whose revival was clearly necessary if western Europe was to recover from the destruction and chaos of the war. Despite meetings of the Big Four foreign ministers—Ernest Bevin (1881–1951), Georges Bidault (1899–   ), Vyacheslav Molotov (1890–   ), and Secretary of State George Marshall (1880–1959), no agreement on the German question was reached.

At first the United States had hoped to include eastern as well as western European countries, and certainly the whole of Germany, in a vast program for European recovery based on US aid. Although this plan, the European Recovery Program, or Marshall Plan, of 1947, was rejected by the Soviet Union, the United States still sought to include western zones of Germany. Applying it there meant the introduction of a separate West German currency.

CONNECTIONS

See also
1338 World War II
1344 The Soviet Union after World War II
1346 Eastern Europe 1948–present
1390 The super powers: from confrontation to détente
1382 The United Nations and its agencies
1312 The Soviet Union under Stalin

1 US and Soviet troops met at Torgau, Germany, on April 25, 1945. But already Russian resentment over delay in the second front, and US distrust of Soviet motives, heralded the cold war.

2 The Soviets dismantled German industry so thoroughly that it caused hardship in the western zones and was halted, despite the fact that the USSR's reperations claims had been accepted.

3 James F. Byrnes (1879–1972) the US Secretary of State, attended the 1946 Paris conference that was to draft peace treaties with Italy, Romania, Finland, Bulgaria, and Hungary. Achieving only part of its aim, the conference also revealed disagreements over Germany.

4 Marshall, Bevin, Bidault, and Molotov made one last futile attempt to agree on the German question at Moscow in 1947.

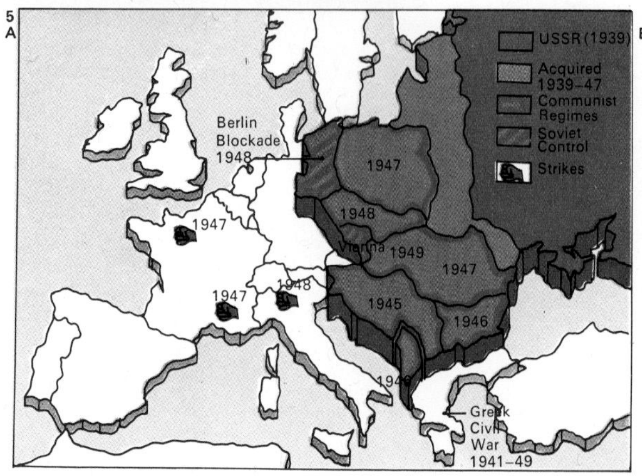

5
A
USSR (1939)
Acquired 1939–47
Communist Regimes
Soviet Control
Strikes
Berlin Blockade 1948
1947
1948
Vienna
1949
1947
1945
1946
1947
1947
1948
Civil War
1941–49

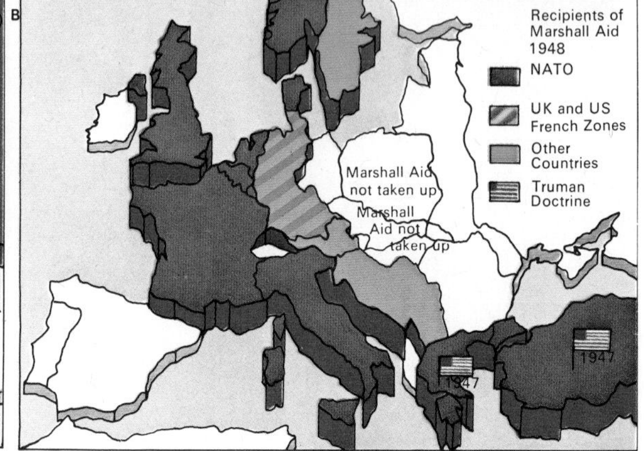

B
Recipients of Marshall Aid 1948
NATO
UK and US French Zones
Other Countries
Truman Doctrine
Marshall Aid not taken up
Marshall Aid not taken up
1947
1947

5 From the Western point of view [A] it appeared that a vast Soviet army had taken over Eastern Europe, subjected it to Stalinist rule, and was poised ready for a westward advance. From the East [B], the Western world, with its superior economic power backed by US nuclear weapons, seemed ready to disrupt the defensive system that the USSR was trying to create. Each seemed to be threatening the other, and so the cold war escalated.

The significance of Berlin

After the currency reform in West Germany the USSR began the blockade of Berlin. The Berlin blockade [6] lasted for nearly a year (July 1948 to May 1949) and was a turning point in the history of Europe. It came when the division of Europe was essentially complete—for in February 1948 the Soviet Union had promoted a successful communist coup in Czechoslovakia.

It was against this background that the decision was made to form NATO (North Atlantic Treaty Organization) [8,9]—a long-term alliance by which the United States was pledged to the defense of Western Europe. The original (1949) members of NATO were the United States and Canada and the principal countries of Western Europe. Greece and Turkey joined in 1951 and West Germany in 1955 [10]. Meanwhile, West European countries began to recover economically and to cooperate. They had already sketched some form of cooperation in defense (in the West European Union before NATO was founded) but equally important was the Organization for European Economic Cooperation (OEEC), formed in 1948. And from 1949 onward the Europeans began to pool their resources in a system that was eventually to lead to the formation of the European Economic Community, or Common Market.

In the East the Stalinist system of almost total control exercised through the Cominform was challenged only by Yugoslavia, although a more cooperative pattern was established after 1949 through the Council for Mutual Economic Assistance (COMECON). But the early contrast between Western cooperation and Eastern dictatorship reinforced the division of Europe and the rigidity of the cold war, even after Stalin's death in 1953.

Before this, in 1950, the outbreak of the Korean War seemed to confirm the necessity of NATO. As a result, by 1955 West Germany was invited to join. West Germany's membership in NATO meant the end of any chance for German reunification in the foreseeable future and solidified the postwar division of Europe, which was ratified by the Helsinki Conference in 1975.

KEY

The three leaders of the Grand Alliance, Churchill [left], Roosevelt [center], and Stalin met at Yalta in February 1945. France was not invited. It has often been argued that Europe was divided into two blocs at this meeting, but the "Big Three" agreed on little beyond the final arrangements necessary for a temporary division of Germany.

6 **The Berlin blockade** was the first great confrontation of the cold war. It arose from restrictions imposed by the Soviets on Western access to Berlin. For months the city was maintained by an airlift. The outcome depended equally on the refusal of West Berliners to accept Soviet economic help in return for political surrender. The blockade divided Berlin and completed the division of Germany.

7 **The Allied Control Council** (shown here in 1948) governed Germany from 1945 to 1948. It did not establish a central government for the whole country but served to resolve disagreements arising among the separate governments of the different zones. When the three Western powers decided to introduce a new currency in West Germany, the Soviets walked out and the council was dissolved.

8 **The foreign ministers** of NATO countries gathered in Washington to sign the NATO Treaty before the Berlin blockade was over. Events in Europe had seemed to confirm the aggressive intentions of the USSR and the need for a firm Western response. Also, the economic recovery of Western Europe depended on a security guarantee. By committing the United States to a long-term defense alliance, NATO superseded European arrangements.

9 **NATO was formed to offset** the Soviet military presence in Europe. The forces committed to NATO were too small to be anything but a stopgap. Their purpose was to buy time until the full resources of all the signatories could be mustered. In 1955, West Germany became a fully independent state and a member of NATO. In May of that year, partly in response to that event, the Soviet Union set up the equivalent defense organization of the Warsaw Pact.

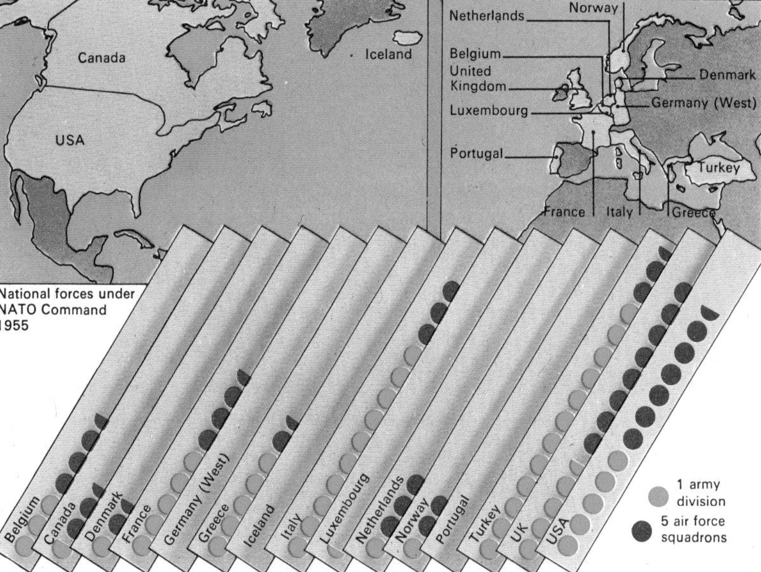
NATO membership 1955
Canada
USA
Iceland
Netherlands
Norway
Belgium
United Kingdom
Denmark
Germany (West)
Luxembourg
Portugal
Turkey
France
Italy
Greece
National forces under NATO Command 1955
Belgium
Canada
Denmark
France
Germany (West)
Greece
Iceland
Italy
Luxembourg
Netherlands
Norway
Portugal
Turkey
UK
USA
1 army division
5 air force squadrons

Belgium
Canada
France
Germany
Italy
Luxembourg
Netherlands
United Kingdom
United States

10 **By 1955, West Germany** had made an amazing economic recovery. At Paris in 1954 the powers met to determine the extent of its entry into the European community. Konrad Adenauer (1876–1967) (seen here with other leaders) had worked for this since election as West German chancellor in 1949.

The Soviet Union after World War II

The USSR at the end of World War II had lost more than 20,000,000 of its citizens and 4,500,000 homes. Some 40,000 miles (65,000km) of railroad track, and thousands of industrial and agricultural machines were destroyed, and countless livestock killed. Reconstruction of the nation was a formidable task. Joseph Stalin (1879–1953) reintroduced five-year planning, and soon he declared many of his targets over-fulfilled.

Costly progress

By the time of Stalin's death in 1953, the USSR had acquired nuclear weapons and had far surpassed prewar production in iron, steel, coal, oil, and electricity. It had made these advances at the cost of great sacrifices by its own people and by Eastern Europeans, whose resources were essentially at Moscow's disposal after 1945. Life was hardest in the countryside. There, underinvestment, low prices for compulsory deliveries, high taxes on private plots, and doctrinaire administrative measures hampered production. By 1953 agricultural output per capita was below that of 1928.

The onset of the cold war and Stalin's attempts to contain the effect of Tito's independent line in Yugoslavia increased tension within the USSR. Stalin's "personality cult" reached its peak in the postwar era when purges were revived. Stalin's paranoia grew as he approached the end of his life. In his last days not even his closest advisers were safe from his secret police.

Collective leadership

After Stalin's death on March 5, 1953 [1], "collective leadership" was proclaimed. Accordingly, the new Premier—Georgi M. Malenkov (1902–)—relinquished the post of senior party secretary ten days after assuming it. Their "plot" exposed as a fabrication, the Kremlin doctors were released. Curbs on secret police power were dramatized by the secret trial and execution of Lavrenti Beria (1899–1953), the reorganization of his Ministry of Internal Affairs, and the progressive release from labor camps of millions of people.

Stalin's successors came into conflict. Premier Malenkov and First Secretary Nikita S. Khrushchev (1894–1971) [2] disagreed over economic priorities and the implications of nuclear warfare, but while Khrushchev exploited their differences to engineer the removal of Malenkov from the premiership in February 1955, he later endorsed Malenkov's repudiation of nuclear war, pleas for more consumer goods, and greater rewards for the peasants.

The trend toward relaxation in domestic and foreign policies alarmed Foreign Minister Vyacheslav Molotov (1890–), especially after the 20th Communist Party Congress in February 1956 at which Khrushchev denounced Stalin and envisaged different roads to socialism. The subsequent turmoil in Poland and Hungary confirmed Molotov's fears. He spearheaded a revolt, culminating in the Party Presidium's vote for Khrushchev's dismissal in June 1957. In the Central Committee meeting that followed, however, Krushchev's opponents were themselves defeated. Nikolai Bulganin (1895–1975) remained, but lost the premiership within a year to Khrushchev himself.

CONNECTIONS

See also
1390 Europe from confrontation to détente
1346 Eastern Europe 1948-Present
1342 The division of Europe
1312 The Soviet Union under Stalin
1352 Nonalignment and the Third World
730 Alcoholism and drug abuse

1 Stalin's funeral, on March 9, 1953, drew crowds of Russians to Red Square in Moscow. Not everyone mourned. Some grieved for the man who had transformed their country into a powerful state, but others abhorred the cost. Without abandoning police control or strict censorship, Stalin's successors eradicated the "personality cult" and the rule of terror. Stalin's body was removed from the Lenin Mausoleum in 1961.

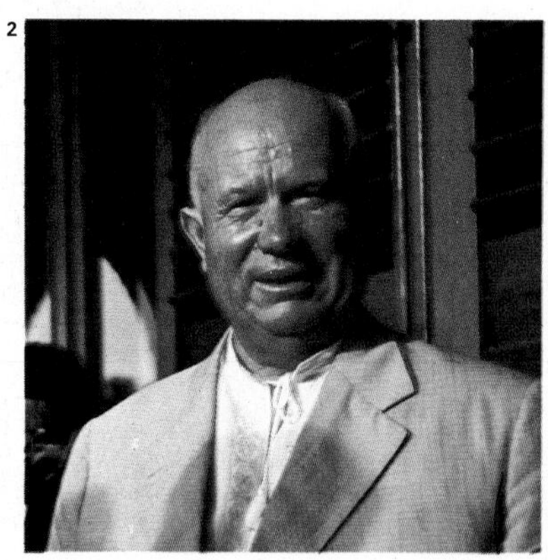

2 Nikita Khrushchev joined the Communist party in 1918 and became a loyal executor of Stalin's policies. As first secretary in the Ukraine in 1938, he administered the purges with fervor. Later, as the party chief, he rejected the cruder forms of terror and moved fitfully toward detente. His caprices and bombast infuriated all, yet his consignment to obscurity in 1964 was widely regretted in the West.

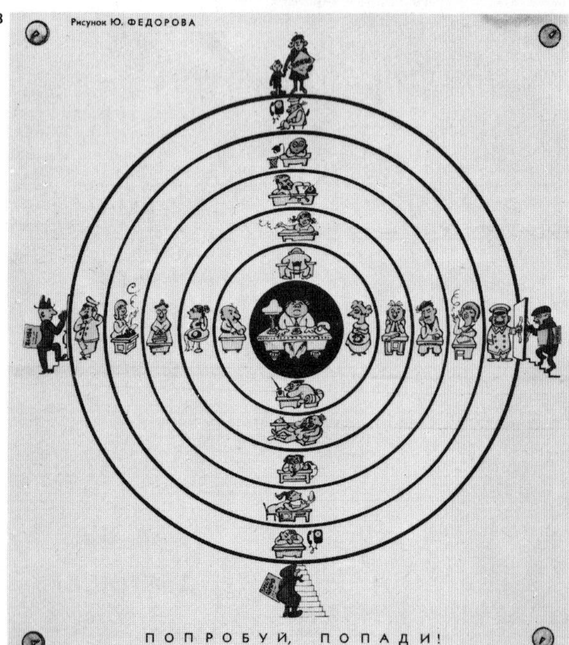

Рисунок Ю. ФЕДОРОВА
ПОПРОБУЙ, ПОПАДИ!

3 This Soviet cartoon satirizes the inadequacy of curbs on bureaucracy. Attacks on officialdom are tolerated, but criticism of higher officials and party policy is banned.

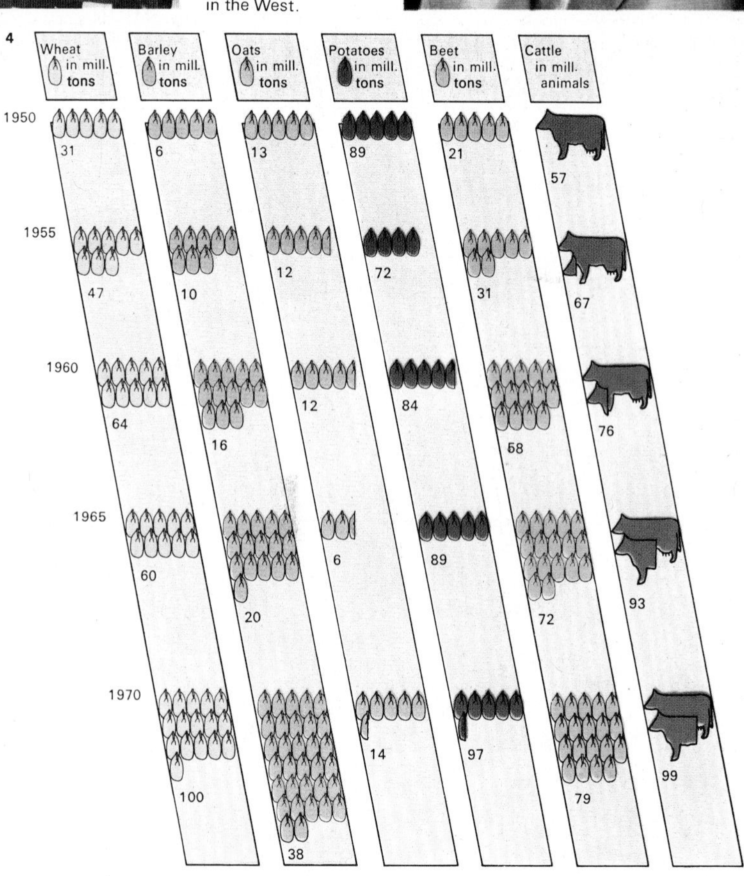

Wheat in mill. tons
Barley in mill. tons
Oats in mill. tons
Potatoes in mill. tons
Beet in mill. tons
Cattle in mill. animals
1950
31
6
13
89
21
57
1955
47
10
12
72
31
67
1960
64
16
12
84
68
76
1965
60
20
6
89
72
93
1970
100
38
14
97
79
99

4 Output of Soviet agriculture has been disappointing since collectivization. Price incentives and doubling of investment in the 1960s raised productivity. Today, with over 500,000,000 acres under cultivation and a quarter of the workforce engaged in farming, Soviet agriculture is still unable to meet the population's demand for a better diet.

Khrushchev's elevation led to improvement in material conditions. He cut the working week, reduced wage differentials, diminished the stringency of Stalin's Draconian labor laws, and gave greater priority to consumer needs. But overcentralized, often incompetent planning plagued economic development. Notwithstanding industrial performance [7] and the Sputniks and the space triumphs after 1957 [Key], agricultural production [4] remained disappointing despite increased investment. Khrushchev's failure to satisfy expectations aroused resentment and, in October 1964, he was dismissed.

A decade of stable government

Despite policy disagreements, the post-Khrushchev leadership was remarkably stable. Leonid Ilyich Brezhnev (1906–) [5], First Secretary of the Central Committee, Alexei Kosygin (1904–), Chairman of the Council of Ministers, and Nikolay Viktorovitch Podgorny (1903–), President, held office for well over a decade. The USSR advanced militarily to achieve virtual strategic parity with the United States, while the rift with China, begun under Khrushchev, widened. Economic progress was less spectacular. Central planners resisted thoroughgoing decentralization, but they permitted a degree of autonomy. In agriculture massive investment and such concessions as relaxation of restrictions on private plots helped to boost production and improve the Soviet diet, although major problems remained. Industrial technology still lagged behind that of the West.

Yet there are signs of strain and nonconformity in the monolithic Soviet society. Alcoholism is one problem, dissidence another. Outspoken intellectuals and writers, such as Solzhenitsyn, Sinyavsky, and Daniel, along with protesters of Soviet political actions such as the intervention in Czechoslovakia in 1968, are dealt with harshly. Nevertheless, administrative measures have not silenced the nonconformists nor stemmed the circulation of *samizdat* (illegal typescripts). And with the USSR's growing stake in détente, the leadership has not reverted to Stalinist repression.

KEY

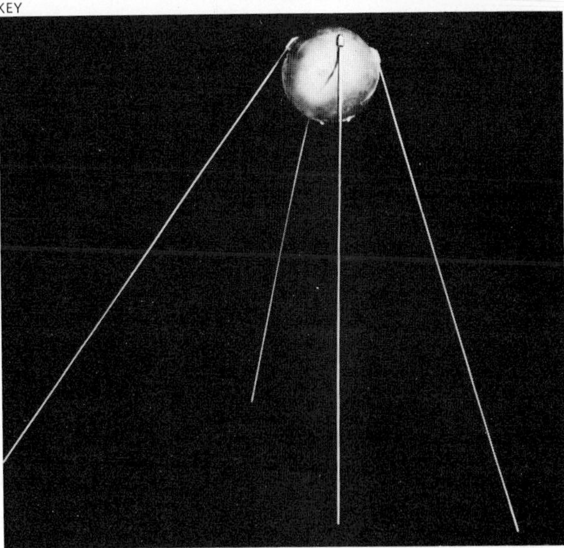

Sputnik I was the world's first artificial satellite. It was launched on October 4, 1957. This success was the first of a series of pioneering space ventures by the USSR.

5 Richard Nixon and Leonid Brezhnev celebrated signing the first agreement on Strategic Arms Limitation (SALT) in 1972. It was designed to stabilize nuclear forces and reduce risks of war. Other agreements on trade and agriculture were signed during the three Nixon-Brezhnev summits. SALT II has been hampered by technical disagreements over balancing the different types of nuclear weapons.

6 Gosudarstveni Universalni Magasin – GUM – is Moscow's biggest department store, selling everything from luxury fur coats to simple hairpins. Lines abound, but, as in shops elsewhere in the USSR, GUM is better stocked than before, reflecting a rise in general living standards.

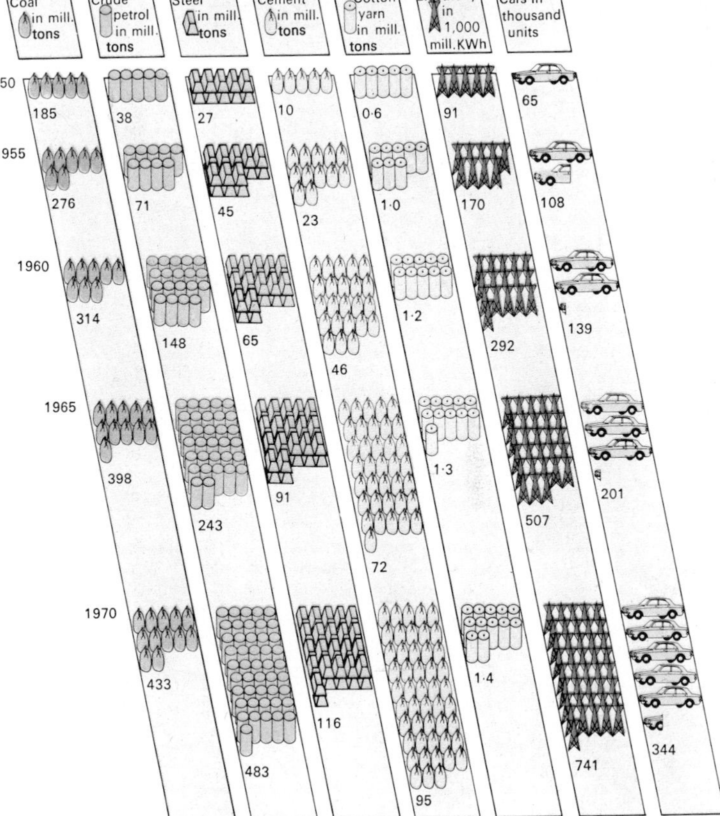

Coal in mill. tons
Crude petrol in mill. tons
Steel in mill. tons
Cement in mill. tons
Cotton yarn in mill. tons
Electricity in 1,000 mill. KWh
Cars in thousand units
1950
185
38
27
10
0·6
91
65
1955
276
71
45
23
1·0
170
108
1960
314
148
65
46
1·2
292
139
1965
398
243
91
72
1·3
507
201
1970
433
483
116
95
1·4
741
344

7 Soviet industrial development since the war has been impressive, even allowing for statistical exaggerations. From 1945 to 1975 output increased tenfold, more than doubling during the 1960s after reforms that gave more scope to individual initiative. Expansion of heavy industry is still stressed, but consumer production is growing in importance. Productivity per man, however, is still lower than in the West, hence the Soviet interest in Western technology.

8 International soccer matches draw great crowds in Moscow. Sports receive generous official encouragement, as part of the view that physical accomplishment makes for healthy, contented citizens and international prestige.

Eastern Europe 1948–present

A successful coup made Czechoslovakia a communist state in February 1948 and extended the area of intensive Soviet influence in Eastern Europe. Each country under communist control became a "people's democracy"—a one-party dictatorship closely modeled on that in the Soviet Union. The characteristic features of these regimes were strict censorship of the press and control of all aspects of culture and religion, central economic planning, rapid and forced industrialization, at least partial collectivization of agriculture, and in foreign policy submission to the line laid down in Moscow. Soviet control of Eastern Europe was guaranteed by the presence of Soviet troops in most of the satellite countries and numerous Soviet advisers, who often reported directly to the Soviet Union's ruler, Joseph Stalin (1879–1953).

After the defection of Tito's Yugoslavia (always the most independent of the satellite countries) from the Soviet bloc in 1948, purges took place in Albania, Bulgaria, Czechoslovakia, Hungary, Poland, and Romania. These purges often culminated in show trials of officials accused of being sympathetic to the idea of the "separate roads to socialism" advocated in Yugoslavia [3]. Non-communists, too, especially senior bishops and other members of the churches, were subjected to persecution and harassment during that period [2].

Hungary—to encourage the others

After Stalin's death some of the most unpopular features of his policy toward Eastern Europe were modified by his successors, and East European leaders were allowed some degree of autonomy in their domestic policies. But in October 1956, Hungary revolted against its communist regime and repudiated its alliance with the USSR [4]. At the same time in Poland leadership of the party was restored to Wladyslaw Gomulka (1905–), who had been dismissed and imprisoned in 1948 for the alleged adoption of an independent line. After a show of indecision, Soviet tanks were used to crush the Hungarian uprising, but the Soviet Union stopped short of more permanent intervention in Poland. Within a year Gomulka renounced the liberal concessions that had been wrung from the regime by the intelligentsia in the autumn of 1956; but Poland kept its system of private agriculture, while other East European countries moved toward full collectivization in the late 1950s.

No action was undertaken against Albania, which defected from the Soviet bloc in 1960 and promptly took China's side in the Sino-Soviet quarrel that was beginning. Romania opted for a more independent foreign policy in 1964, after several years of strenuous opposition to Soviet plans for economic integration within Eastern Europe. But in their domestic policies both Albania and Romania remained one-party dictatorships.

The 1968 invasion of Czechoslovakia

Czechoslovakia, which had been the Soviet Union's model satellite for 20 years, provoked the most serious crisis in postwar Eastern Europe in 1968. Alexander Dubcek (1921–), who had become party leader and president in that year [Key], embarked

CONNECTIONS

See also
1390 Europe from confrontation to détente
1344 The Soviet Union after World War II
1342 The division of Europe
1326 Socialism in the West

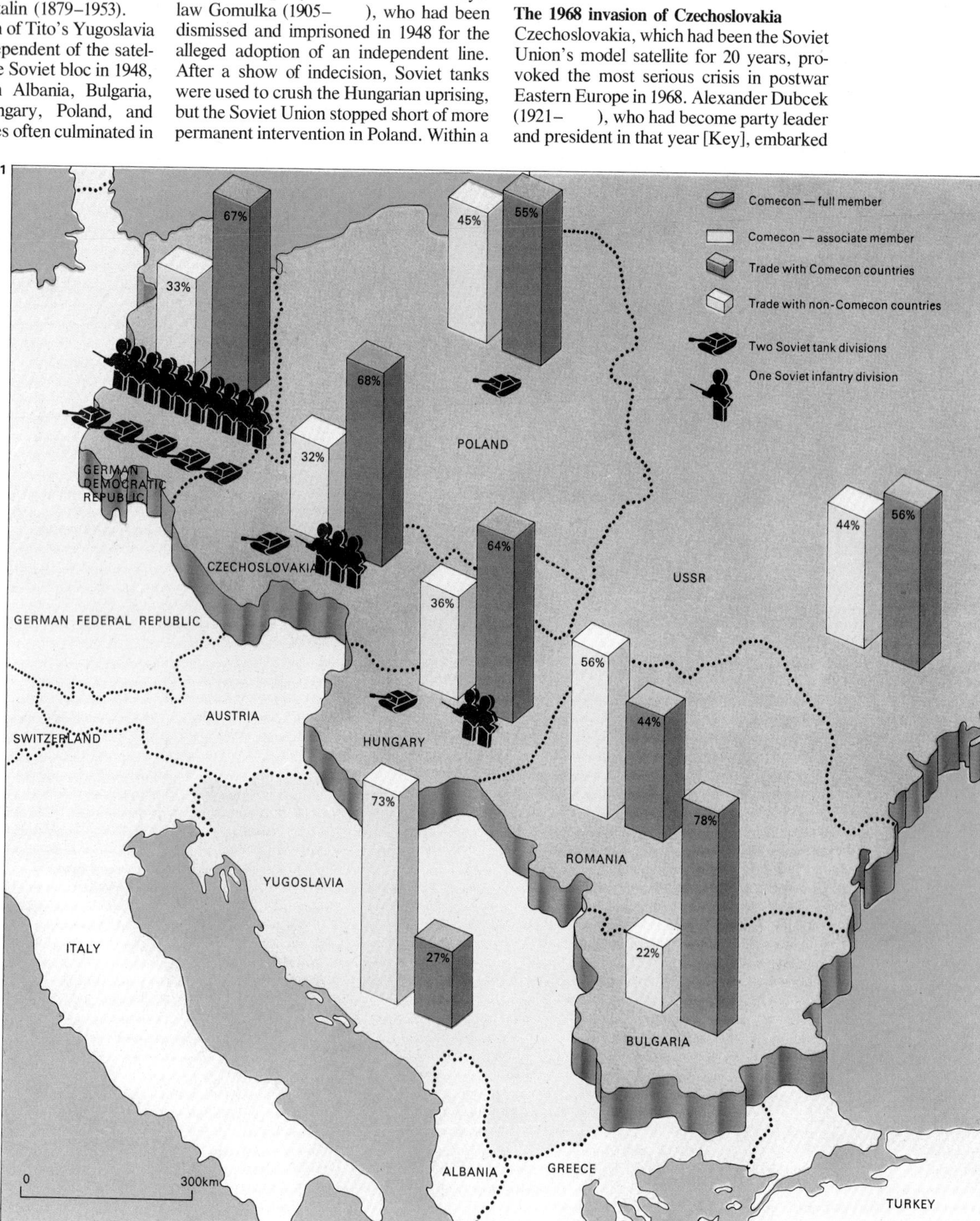

1
Comecon — full member
Comecon — associate member
Trade with Comecon countries
Trade with non-Comecon countries
Two Soviet tank divisions
One Soviet infantry division
33%
67%
45%
55%
32%
68%
36%
64%
44%
56%
56%
44%
73%
27%
22%
78%
GERMAN DEMOCRATIC REPUBLIC
POLAND
CZECHOSLOVAKIA
USSR
GERMAN FEDERAL REPUBLIC
AUSTRIA
SWITZERLAND
HUNGARY
ROMANIA
YUGOSLAVIA
ITALY
BULGARIA
ALBANIA
GREECE
TURKEY
0
300km

1 Comecon, the Council for Mutual Economic Assistance, (which includes Cuba and Mongolia) was founded in 1949 as Stalin's answer to the Marshall Plan in Western Europe. Revitalized in 1958 by Nikita Khrushchev, the Soviet leader, to consolidate Soviet economic control of Eastern Europe, Comecon embarked on a policy of integration adopted at Bucharest in 1971 and further elaborated at Budapest in June 1975. In 1973, Comecon, with 366,000,000 people, accounted for only 12% of world trade (the European Economic Community, by comparison, with a population of 253,000,000, accounted for 40%). Its trade with the West and the EEC in particular, however, is growing fast, with an increasing proportion generated by "joint ventures" between partners from Eastern and Western Europe. Higher costs of Western imports helped to promote more inter-Comecon joint ventures and greater investment in Soviet projects for the exploitation of natural resources. Eastern Europe still needs the West for its advanced technology, however. Yugoslavia, an observer in Comecon, conducts over 70% of its trade with the non-communist world, and Romania deals directly with the European Economic Community. Albania trades with both East and West.

on a course of energetic liberalization, a policy of which the Soviet and some other East European leaders publicly disapproved. Censorship was relaxed, and a higher degree of local autonomy was granted to the national minorities. Reduction in the high level of centralization in economic planning was sought, prices were allowed a closer relationship to market forces, and individual enterprises were given greater freedom. When Dubcek refused to bow to their pressure, Warsaw Pact troops from the Soviet Union, Poland, East Germany, Hungary, and Bulgaria marched in on August 21, 1968 [5]. Czechoslovak leaders were arrested and taken to Moscow, but when no replacements of any stature could be found they were allowed to stay in nominal power for a few months before their final ouster in 1969.

Although Czechoslovakia's experiment was brutally suppressed, Hungary, under its leader Janos Kadar (1912–), was allowed to carry out a relatively successful series of reforms. Kadar's popular shift toward the consumer goods sector was emulated elsewhere in Eastern Europe. Poland's new leader, Edward Gierek (1913–), who had replaced Gomulka after workers' riots in December 1970, made "Kadarization" one of his basic tenets. East Germany too embarked on its own version of "consumer revolution" in 1971, after the dismissal of its conservative leader, Walter Ulbricht (1893–1973).

The Soviet bloc closes ranks

Although agreements were reached that lowered some barriers between West Germany on one side and the Soviet Union, Poland, and East Germany on the other in the 1970–72 period, Eastern Europe generally reaffirmed ideological solidarity. New economic predicaments also helped the Soviet Union to turn Comecon's [1] focus eastward once more. Western inflation had in the mid-1970s made imports from the West suddenly much more expensive; at the same time the Soviet Union raised the prices of oil and the other raw materials that it sells, as a virtual monopoly supplier, to Eastern Europe.

KEY

Alexander Dubcek (front, second right) kept in uneasy step with other Eastern European leaders at their meeting in Bratislava on August 3, 1968. Less than three weeks later, Warsaw Pact troops invaded Czechoslovakia. The Pact was concluded between the Soviet Union and its satellites in May 1955. It forms the cornerstone of Soviet policy in Eastern Europe, bolstered by the presence of over 30 Soviet divisions.

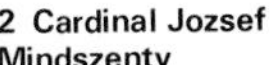

2 Cardinal Jozsef Mindszenty (1892–1975), primate of Hungary (center), and a strong anti-communist, was imprisoned for life in 1949 after a dramatic show trial. Freed by the rebels in the 1956 rising, he remained in political asylum in the US embassy in Budapest until 1971 when he was ordered to Rome by the pope. He was fervently opposed to Vatican attempts to come to terms with communist regimes.

2

3 Nikita Khrushchev (1894–1971, right) Malenkov's successor as Soviet leader, went to Yugoslavia in May 1955 to repair the rift caused by Yugoslavia's assertion of independence in 1948. Khrushchev blamed the quarrel on Beria, the former chief of Soviet police, executed in 1953. Josip Broz Tito (1892– left), the Yugoslav leader, insisted on formal Soviet recognition of Yugoslavia's ideological autonomy.

3

4

4 Stalin's statue was torn down in Budapest on November 2, 1956, in the uprising against Soviet domination and the brutal Hungarian regime. Within two days 150,000 Soviet troops and 2,500 tanks were "pacifying" Hungary. The executions that followed the uprising soon gave way to the more pragmatic policies of Janos Kadar, which tried to improve both living standards and ideological freedom.

5

5 The Warsaw Pact troops who invaded Czechoslovakia in August 1968 faced no military resistance, but the many spontaneous acts of obstruction such as raising roadblocks and setting fire to Soviet tanks were humiliating for the Soviet leaders who, attempting to allay foreign criticism, claimed that intervention had been requested by Czech leaders. In fact, the invasion had little popular support.

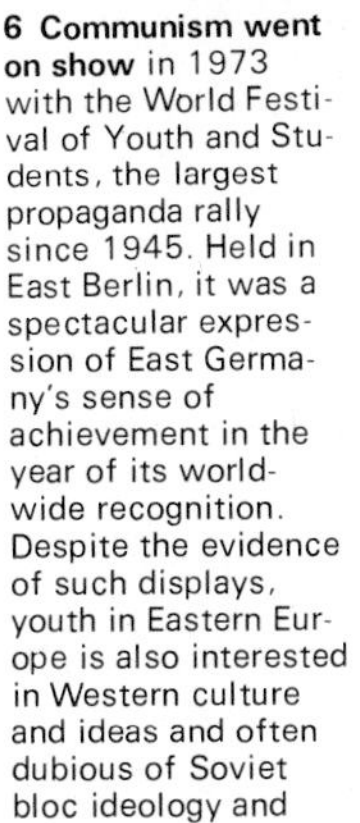

6 Communism went on show in 1973 with the World Festival of Youth and Students, the largest propaganda rally since 1945. Held in East Berlin, it was a spectacular expression of East Germany's sense of achievement in the year of its worldwide recognition. Despite the evidence of such displays, youth in Eastern Europe is also interested in Western culture and ideas and often dubious of Soviet bloc ideology and politics.

6

SCHÜTZT DEN FRIEDEN

7 The Berlin Wall was begun on August 13, 1961, to stop the continual exodus of large numbers of East Germans to the West. Between 1949, when Germany was divided, and 1961, more than 2,700,000 people escaped into West Berlin. Many East Germans still attempt to reach the West despite the dangers. This may change: East Germany now has higher living standards than any other communist country and is the world's seventh largest industrial power.

7

China: the People's Republic

The Chinese People's Republic was established on October 1, 1949 [Key], by a mandate from a constituent assembly convened under the aegis of the Chinese Communist party (CCP). The immediate task of the new government was to rehabilitate the war-ravaged economy inherited from Chiang Kai-shek's Nationalist administration after its forced withdrawal to the offshore province of Taiwan. A gradualist policy was adopted, characterized by the creation of a coalition of the various elements in Chinese society and the avoidance of violent class struggle. The communists did not balk at suppressing their most intractable class enemies, but they were preoccupied with carrying out measures to ensure economic survival.

Major reforms of the 1950s

Mass support gave the new government the authority to take steps to conquer hyperinflation [1]. Land reform affecting over 80 percent of the population was completed by early 1953. As a result, the government gained control over surplus agricultural production and the peasant backing it needed to weaken existing social institutions based on a clan and kinship system dominated by elders [2]. This made it easier to set up new communist institutions in place of the old system. Another major reform was the implementation of the 1950 Marriage Law, which greatly improved the status of women.

From 1953–57 China underwent a transition to socialism as commerce and industry were nationalized and agricultural institutions transformed. These changes were not accomplished without dissent but, as a 1957 rectification campaign showed, the power of the enlarged party machine considerably exceeded that of its critics. Meanwhile, in foreign affairs China was aligned with the USSR, whose aid was crucial to industrialization during the first five-year plan (1953–57) and bitterly opposed to the United States, its major adversary in the Korean War (1950–53) and proponent of the policy of "containment."

Hoping to expand production rapidly by amalgamating collective farms into communes [3] and by adopting a backyard approach to industrialization [4], China launched the Great Leap Forward in 1958, marking the implementation of a Chinese strategy of economic development and the rejection of the Soviet strategy employed in the preceding five years. As a result, an ideological dispute between China and the USSR gathered momentum, leading to a withdrawal of Soviet technicians and their blueprints in 1960. The Great Leap Forward failed, because of dissent, bad weather, and an underestimation of the problems [5]. The outcome was economic crisis and forced retreat from Maoist principles.

The Cultural Revolution

The retreat was only temporary. Once economic recovery had been achieved in 1963, Mao Tse-tung (1893–1976), who had relinquished his post as head of state in 1959 to be replaced by Liu Shao-ch'i (1898–1973), resumed his efforts to realize socialism in China [6]. Foreign affairs remained largely in the hands of Chou En-lai (1898–1976). By now the ideological split between the USSR and China was being

CONNECTIONS

See also
1328 East Asia 1919–194
1270 The opening up of China
1378 The wars of Indochi
1352 Nonalignment and the Third World
1382 The United Nations and its agencies
904 Political participatio

1 Crowds outside banks in 1948 marked a collapse of confidence in China's currency and in the ability of the Nationalists to manage the economy. Inflation set off by the irresponsible issue of banknotes was a problem during the Japanese war, and it accelerated between 1945 and 1948 when the Shanghai price index rose 135,742 times, causing a hyperinflation. This the communist government inherited.

2 Burning of land title deeds and the public condemnation of landlords were common during the nationwide land reform campaign conducted by the Chinese government between mid-1950 and early 1953. The political and social impact of this campaign was as important as its economic effect. Socially, the destruction of the old system was underlined by the public humiliation of landlords and the venting of grievances by peasants led by communist cadres. Politically, the richer classes were isolated; economically, land redistribution among 300 million peasants stimulated their willingness to increase production.

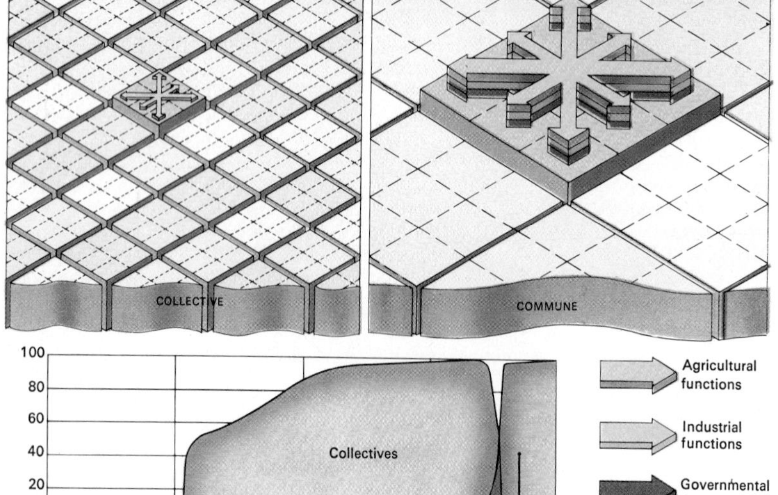

COLLECTIVE
COMMUNE
100
80
60
40
20
Collectives
Percentage of households in collectives and communes
1956
1957
1958
1959
Communes
Agricultural functions
Industrial functions
Governmental functions

3 People's communes were introduced in the summer of 1958. This was to be the culmination of the socialist transformation of agriculture. In 1953–54 peasant housholds had been organized into mutual aid teams. In 1955 these merged to form cooperatives which, in turn, were merged into collectives in 1956–57. About eight times larger than the collectives, communes were also units of government coordinating planning in agriculture, industry, defense, and education.

4 Backyard furnaces and foundries epitomized the Great Leap Forward, a drive launched in February 1958 to accelerate expansion of the Chinese economy. By mobilizing underemployed rural labor in small, labor-intensive industries it was intended to complement the production of urban-based, capital-intensive industries at little extra cost to investment funds. Called "walking on two legs," this strategy of economic development was widely promoted throughout China.

reflected within the CCP, and the specifically Maoist attempts at running the economy had been openly criticized. Mao countered by launching a campaign to reverse a deteriorating ideological situation and a weakening in his personal influence. The campaign, the Cultural Revolution, aimed on the one hand at purging the CCP and on the other at ridding China of aspects of traditional culture incompatible with socialism. Party members were ousted and the state structure usurped by revolutionary committees. Mao's support came from the young people [7] and the armed forces.

During the Cultural Revolution Mao presided over the rebuilding of the CCP and the mass organizations, a restoration of the state system, a restructuring of the education system, and a reassessment of Chinese culture. The spilling over of the excesses of the Cultural Revolution into foreign affairs damaged China's international position for a while. Some 45 divisions of Soviet forces were deployed along the frontier, giving rise to armed clashes in 1969 [8]. China's foreign relations now became marked by alignment with the Third World, friendship with the medium-sized developed countries, trade and diplomacy with Japan and the United States, and continuing confrontation with the USSR.

Admission to the United Nations

The success of China's new foreign policy was characterized by its admission to UN membership in 1971 and by a visit by US President Richard M. Nixon in 1972 [9]. The eclipse of Lin Piao (1908–71?), the defense minister and Mao's heir apparent, who was reported killed during a flight to the USSR, suggests that an accommodation with capitalism at the expense of a reconciliation with the Soviet bloc was not unanimously approved. Nevertheless, China moved to the Fourth National People's Congress in January 1975 (the first for a decade), a new constitution and, for the first time since 1966, a fully manned state structure. The deaths of both Chou and Mao in 1976, however, led to internal political upheaval. Premier Hua Kuo-feng succeeded Mao as communist party chairman.

KEY

Mao Tse-tung, as chairman of the Chinese Communist party and chairman-elect of the government, stood in Tien An Men square in Peking to proclaim the establishment of the People's Republic of China on October 1, 1949.

5

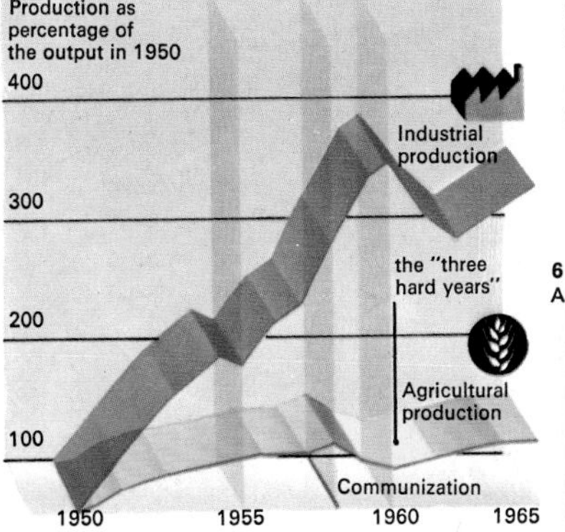
Production as percentage of the output in 1950
400
300
200
100
Industrial production
the "three hard years"
Agricultural production
Communization
1950
1955
1960
1965

5 During the Great Leap Forward agricultural and industrial output dropped. Inadequate planning and accounting led to miscalculation of potential yields and failure to meet the targets set. Lack of experience and disorganization meant that many communes were ill-equipped and badly run. The worst weather for a century in 1959–60 led to economic crisis, and the policies of the Great Leap Forward were shelved.

6 Exemplary production units singled out by Mao Tse-tung in 1964 were the Tachai agricultural brigade in Hsiyang county, Shansi province, and the Taching oilfield in Heilungkiang province. In Tachai [A] peasants transformed a poor environment and increased grain output without state aid or material incentives. In Taching [B] workers created a prototype agro-industrial community developed without foreign aid by reliance on their own technological innovations. Both show the importance attached to self-reliance, hard work, and persistence in Chinese economic development after 1960. Then, as a result of frequent ideological differences, the Soviet Union withdrew its many technicians and canceled all its aid programs to the Chinese People's Republic.

6 A

B

7 The Little Red Book of quotations from Mao Tse-tung became the "bible" of the Cultural Revolution of 1966–68. It was studied on a nationwide basis as a pocket guide for action in any set of circumstances. But it was put to most use in the hands of young people, particularly Red Guards recruited from middle schools, universities, and factories. As "successors to the revolution," they formed a main force in the campaign by Mao Tse-tung and his supporters against Liu Shao-ch'i, then head of state, and aspects of traditional culture standing in the way of Maoist policies.

7

8 Border clashes between Chinese and Soviet forces on the Ussuri River frontier in Heilungkiang in March 1969 showed the extent to which Sino-Soviet relations had worsened in the ideological disputes of the late 1950s. After the worst fighting over Chenpao or Damansky island, China claimed that the Soviet Union had provoked 4,189 incidents.

8

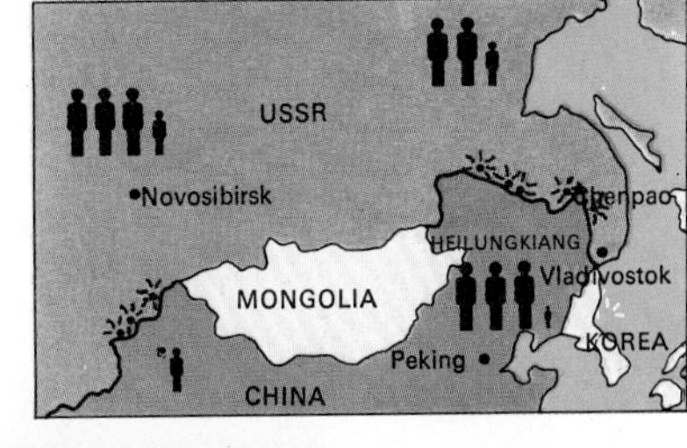
10 military divisions
Border incidents in 1969
USSR
Novosibirsk
Chenpao
HEILUNGKIANG
Vladivostok
MONGOLIA
KOREA
Peking
CHINA

9

9 The visit of Richard M. Nixon, the US President, in 1972, hosted by Chou En-lai, marked a new era in China's foreign relations. Less hostile Sino-US attitudes contributed to the admission of the People's Republic of China to the UN in 1971. It also led to better relations between China and Japan and increasing diplomatic isolation of the Nationalist government of Taiwan.

Decolonization

Decolonization has been one of the greatest transforming processes in the world since 1945. It is a new word in political vocabulary and has achieved widespread usage since 1960, as far-flung colonies have generally achieved independence.

Processes of decolonization

The term *decolonization* covers a wide range of processes by which power is transferred from the departing colonial authority to the newly independent nation. To date, transfer has usually been peaceful and by agreement—for example from Great Britain to Ceylon (now called Sri Lanka) in 1947, Ghana in 1957, and Jamaica in 1962. In a few important instances, strife has been an integral part of the process of decolonization but was not directly connected with the issue of independence—the Mau Mau emergency in Kenya, the *enosis* dispute in Cyprus, and British confrontation with Indonesia over the creation of the Malaysian Federation. In some of the best known examples of decolonization, independence has been won by force from a reluctant colonial power—from the Netherlands to Indonesia in 1949, and from France to North Vietnam in 1954 and to Algeria in 1962 [6]. In the Congo in 1960, the Belgians granted independence to a territory that was wholly unprepared for it and chaos ensued [5]. But there can be two-way effects of decolonization too—as in Portugal in 1974 when internal dissent and colonial unrest resulted in a revolution at home that hastened the independence of its colonies.

The process of decolonization, and the consequent emergence of new states, has resulted in major changes in the political map of the world [1]. In 1914 there were only eight sovereign states in the whole of Asia and Africa, and of these only Japan was regarded as a power in world affairs; almost everywhere else throughout those two continents the rule or dominating influence of Western Europe, the Soviet Union, or the United States prevailed. Only since World War II has the dismantling of the overseas empires of Western Europeans come about, first in Asia in the late 1940s and then only slightly in North Africa in the early 1950s. After that decolonization gathered momentum, was in full force between 1955 and 1965 [3].

Most of the principal overseas empires of the Western European powers were already dissolving when the fifteenth session of the UN General Assembly opened in September 1960. At that session an anticolonialist charter drawn up by 43 African and Asian countries was adopted without dissent. The British Empire was moving into a state of more or less voluntary liquidation: India [Key], Pakistan, Burma, Ceylon, Ghana, Malaya, Cyprus, and Nigeria [4] had become independent. Empire-into-Commonwealth was partially accomplished although the wider problem of the role of the white man remained unresolved in Rhodesia and the apartheid regime of South Africa. In his forthright "wind of change" speech to the South African Parliament in February 1960, British Prime Minister Harold Macmillan (1894–) had rightly predicted that the rate of decolonization was quickening. In the same year France's colonial presence was

CONNECTIONS

See also
1352 Nonalignment and the Third World
1358 Underdevelopment and the world economy
1378 The wars of Indochina
1330 The Commonwealth
1328 Indian nationalism
1262 European imperialism in the 19th century
1266 India in the 19th century
1268 Africa in the 19th century

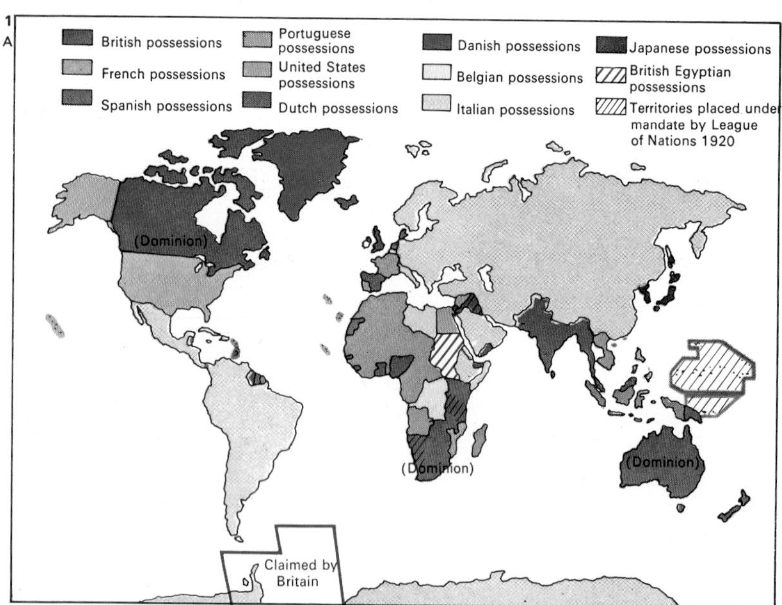

1
A
British possessions
French possessions
Spanish possessions
Portuguese possessions
United States possessions
Dutch possessions
Danish possessions
Belgian possessions
Italian possessions
Japanese possessions
British Egyptian possessions
Territories placed under mandate by League of Nations 1920
(Dominion)
(Dominion)
(Dominion)
Claimed by Britain

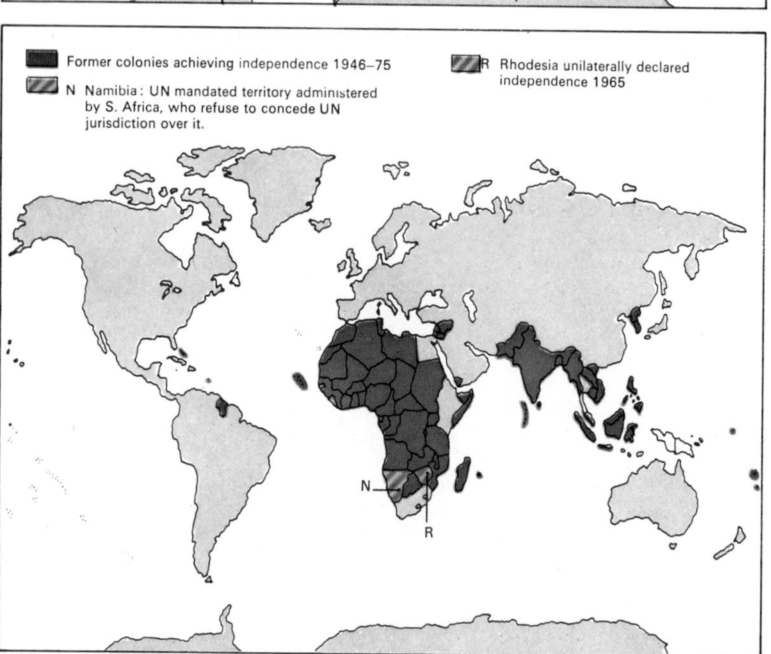

B
Former colonies achieving independence 1946–75
N Namibia: UN mandated territory administered by S. Africa, who refuse to concede UN jurisdiction over it.
R Rhodesia unilaterally declared independence 1965
N
R

1 In 1926 there were more than 80 separate colonies and dependencies [A]. These represented over 33% of the population and land area of the world. Seven western European countries (Britain, France, the Netherlands, Belgium, Portugal, Spain, and Italy), whose total home population was about 200 million, controlled about 700 million people in overseas colonies. The British and French empires were by far the largest. Most of the new states of the post-1945 world [B] have come from these two empires. While the British Empire was worldwide, that of the French was predominantly in Africa and Indochina.

2 The election of U Thant of Burma as UN Secretary General after the death of Dag Hammarskjöld in 1961 symbolized the growing number of voices and votes of new and nonaligned states in UN affairs, especially of Asian and African members. UN membership is valued by all newly independent states as an important symbol of their status and as a platform from which to air their grievances.

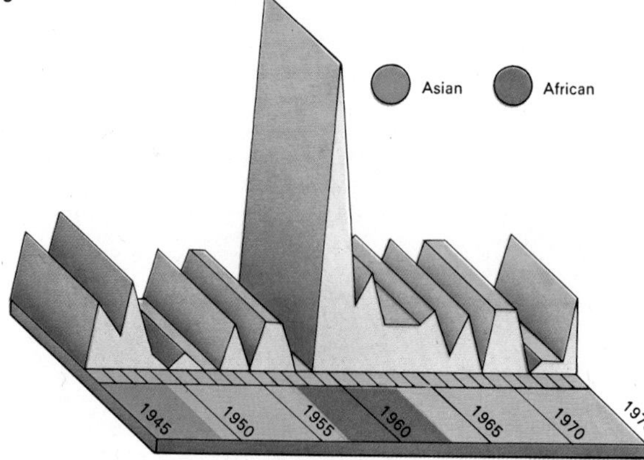

3
Asian
African
1945
1950
1955
1960
1965
1970
1975

3 Decolonization took place in spurts. First, from 1945 to 1949, it occurred chiefly in the flanks of Asia—Israel, Syria, and Lebanon; then India, Pakistan, Burma, Ceylon; and the Philippines and Indonesia. From 1950 to 1957 little decolonization took place. Libya, Morocco, and Tunisia became independent peacefully, and Algerians began the war for independence that ended in 1961. From 1957 to 1963 African decolonization got rapidly under way, with Ghana in 1957 and Guinea in 1958. It reached a peak in 1960 when all the French African colonies plus Nigeria and the Belgian Congo became independent.

to shrink considerably in Africa and soon disappear completely.

Adjustment after decolonization

The whole period of decolonization, now virtually over, has created acute problems of adjustment both for former rulers and ruled. Some former imperial powers—notably Britain—have found the transition to lesser power status and a lower world standing acutely uncomfortable. Only since the decision to stay in the European Economic Community, or Common Market, and with the Commonwealth discussions on world economic issues in June 1975 has Britain begun to find a new role as intermediary and honest broker between rich and poor, developed and developing countries. Most other former colonial powers have experienced domestic difficulties over decolonization—notably France, because of the Indochina and Algeria wars.

The new states themselves have had to evolve political systems appropriate to their new situation and not necessarily those bequeathed by the outgoing authority [7]. Thus the abandonment of parliamentarian constitutions in favor of one-party systems, often dictatorships; the rejection of Soviet or US models of development through industrialization in favor of the Chinese model of concentration on agriculture, "backdoor" industrialization, and self-sufficiency; and the adoption of an independent foreign policy are part of the process.

Neocolonialism

But if colonialism is almost dead, "neocolonialism" is alive. The United States, historically the greatest advocate of anti-colonialism, is also the country most often charged with neocolonialism. It may take the form of economic control through multinational corporations, military influence through arms aid and advisers, or even political "destabilization" as practiced against the Marxist regime of President Allende in Chile. The Soviet Union is accused in similar terms, chiefly by China, which argues that Moscow's "social imperialism" aims to carve out spheres of neocolonialist influence.

KEY

The inauguration of Earl Mountbatten as viceroy of India in 1947 prefaced India's independence from Britain later in the same year. This event symbolized the advent of the age of decolonization, carried out with a formal transfer of power.

4

4 Nigeria achieved independence peacefully from Britain in 1960. Power was handed over to a working federal parliament and government. But six years later, Nigeria suffered two military coups in one year and a bloody, but unsuccessful, attempt to create a new secessionist state of Biafra.

5

5 The Belgians' abrupt departure in 1960 from the Congo (now called Zaïre) led to bitter civil war, much bloodshed, and the attempted, but ultimately unsuccessful, secession of the copper-rich province of Katanga. The introduction of a UN peace-keeping force caused great controversy.

6

ZONE
FRANCAISE

6 Algeria is one of the few countries since 1945 to have won independence by means of a successful war against a colonial power (in this case, France). This lasted from 1954 until 1961–62. Charles de Gaulle, who had returned to power backed by the slogan "Algérie Française," conceded independence in July 1962. Algeria then began to play an active part in Arab League affairs and, later on, as an oil-producing country with limited reserves, within OPEC. A number of important Afro-Asian and nonaligned conferences have been held at Algiers, especially the Afro-Asian meeting of 1965 and the 1973 summit.

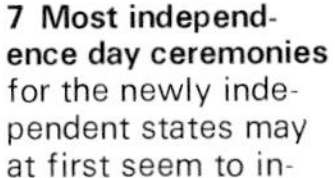

7 Most independence day ceremonies for the newly independent states may at first seem to involve only changes of personnel, who in style and outlook often resemble their predecessors. They may even wear wigs and carry maces. But parliaments, British- or French-style, are not always resilient institutions and often give way to military rule. For most of these new states their sense of community goes deeper than their constitutionalism. Almost all Third World societies are pluralistic, with deep economic and racial differences that may stand in the way of political stability and sustained economic progress.

7

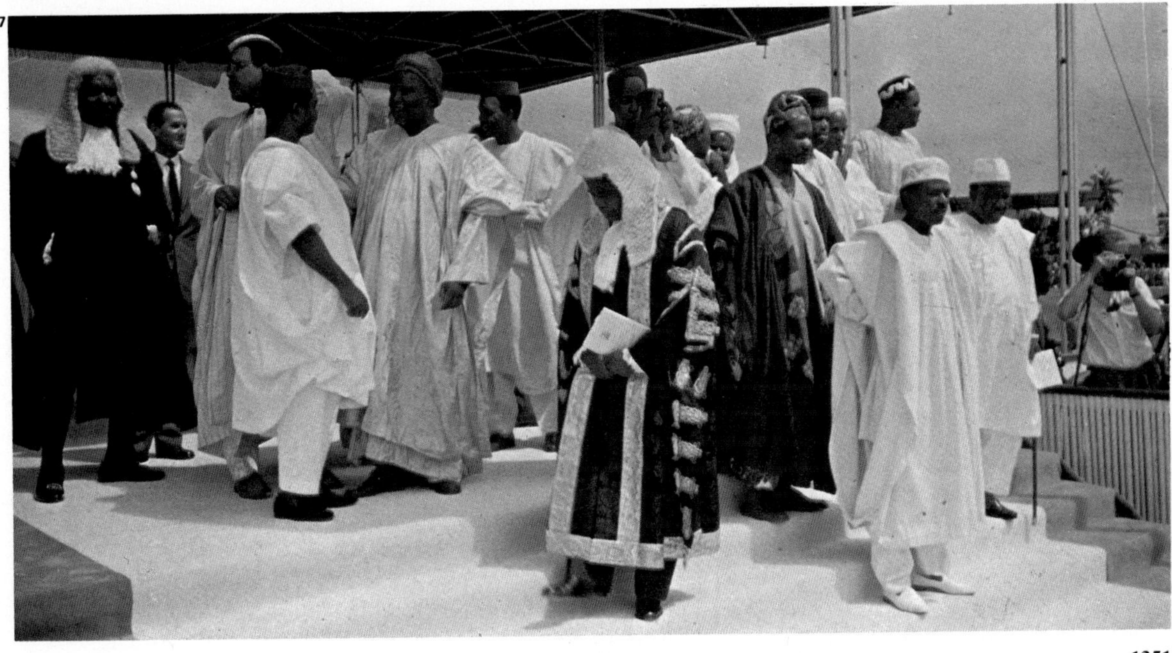

Nonalignment and the Third World

In Europe, Asia, and North Africa in the early 1950s, the term *neutralist* was applied to countries that were outside the alliance systems of the great powers and wished to remain dissociated from the cold war struggle between the United States and the Soviet Union. Leaders such as Jawaharlal Nehru (1889–1964) of India, Gamal Abdel Nasser (1918–70) of Egypt, and Josip Broz Tito (1892–) of Yugoslavia [Key] denied the need to enter alliance, to acquire nuclear weapons [3], or to allow foreign military bases to be set up in their countries.

Motives for nonalignment

A neutralist stance had been adopted by the United States itself during the nineteenth century. But the violation of the neutrality of several European countries in two world wars and the global scope of the power struggle that began after World War II led to a belief, particularly in the United States, that neutralism was a wishful attitude that failed to recognize that effective protection against "international communism" could be obtained only within the shelter of alliance of the "Free World" [5]. For leaders of the militarily weak new nations of Africa and Asia a neutralist stance had three compelling advantages. It allowed them to assert an independence that would have been compromised by their military dependence on one of the great powers. It enabled them, by skillful diplomacy, to draw on aid from both the Western and Soviet blocs. And it gave them the opportunity to attempt objective moral leadership at a time when both power blocs were taking up rigid attitudes.

The neutralist or nonaligned nations, as they more accurately called themselves, emerged as a coherent force in world politics with the organization of the Bandung Conference in April 1955 in Indonesia, a country that played a leading role in the movement against colonialism [2]. The conference was dominated by Premier Chou En-lai (1898–1976) of China, whose moderate attitudes at the conference did much to diminish Asian tensions. Further conferences were held in Belgrade in September 1961[4]; Cairo, October 1964; Lusaka, September 1970; and Algiers, September 1973 [9]. The conferences steadily increased in numbers attending and in importance.

The political label "Afro-Asian bloc" gained general acceptance at Bandung. The more current term *Third World*, or *Le Tiers Monde* [1], was coined in France in the mid-1950s to denote decolonized areas that wished to avoid conscription into US alliances or overseas base agreements. (They were collectively designated by some US strategists, including the later US Secretary of State Henry Kissinger (1923–), as "grey areas.") The voting power of this bloc at the United Nations made it a force that none of the great powers could ignore.

Developments in the 1960s

Events of the later 1950s and 1960s led to significant shifts in the oversimplified tripartite division of the world into communist, Western, and nonaligned blocs. The credibility of India's neutralist stance was reduced by its call for Western aid during its clash with China in 1962. Egypt became heavily dependent on Soviet military aid after the Arab-Israeli war of 1967, and, in

CONNECTIONS

See also

- **1354** Latin America in the 20th century
- **1350** Decolonization
- **1378** The wars of Indochina
- **1386** Underdevelopment and the world economy
- **1382** The United Nations and its agencies
- **942** International co-operation and development

1 The Third World conference in Sri Lanka in 1976 attracted 85 nations. Membership of the Third World has grown with the spread of decolonization and now includes much of Latin America. China also claims membership. *Third World* is a general political label applied to developing peoples.

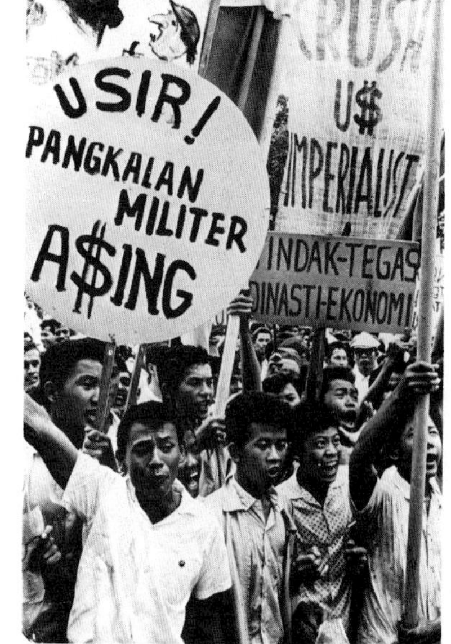

USIR!
PANGKALAN
MILITER
A$ING
U$
IMPERIALIST
INDAK-TEGAS
DINASTI-EKONOMI

2 Demonstrations in Indonesia in the early 1960s against the establishment of Malaysia marked a phase of intense anticolonialism under the feverish leadership of Achmad Sukarno (1901–70), who took Indonesia out of the UN in 1965 and proposed a rival group of New Emerging Forces.

3 The mushroom cloud of China's first nuclear explosion in October 1964 while the Cairo nonaligned summit was meeting also marked the first entry into the "nuclear club" of a member of the Afro-Asian bloc. Nuclear testing, the spread of nuclear weapons, and the possibility of nuclear blackmail by the great powers have been central and recurrent worries of the world's nonaligned nations.

4 The first large meeting of the nonaligned nations at Belgrade in September 1961 drew representatives from 25 countries. Earlier, a number of smaller meetings had been called between Tito, Nehru, Nasser, and some other leaders. Nonaligned nations had also conferred in some larger forums, in particular at the UN General Assembly late in 1960. The 1961 conference and subsequent meetings had to resolve frequent controversy about the admission of new members and whether they were genuinely nonaligned. But the number of nations attending grew steadily, and the conferences provided the opportunity for broad discussions of topical world issues.

the same year, the failure of a communist coup in Indonesia turned that country toward a more Western alignment. At the same time, developing Sino-Soviet tensions and the dwindling of the cold war led to more subtle and complex international groupings [10].

Third World economic policies

In the mid-1970s relations between the great powers became less hostile, the Third World opposition to alliances and pressure against colonialism were subsidiary to economic concerns, particularly the wish to see the emergence of a new international economic order. Nonalignment continued to be a predominantly Afro-Asian movement, but it was the Arab and Latin American members who did most to infuse the nonaligned movement with new vitality.

The Arab nations led the way by seizing the initiative after November 1973 when OPEC, the Organization of Petroleum Exporting Countries, unilaterally quadrupled the price of oil and dealt a major blow to the existing worldwide distribution of wealth. The Latin Americans broadened the base of the attack from oil to natural resources in mid-1975 when Cuba proposed that all countries wishing to protect their natural resources should join the nonaligned [7]. The most important issue on the agenda at the Lima conference of foreign ministers of nonaligned states in August 1975—the statute on foreign investment, multinational companies, and technology—was modeled closely on regulations established in the Andean Pact, Latin America's economic integration movement launched in 1968.

These moves were aimed at retaining control of national development and strategic resources. Foreign investment was viewed as acceptable only so long as it contributed to national goals. The nonaligned movement grew from a negative reaction to the cold war into a positive policy to protect national resources and control foreign investment.

Nonaligned leaders intended to ensure that in the future the rich, industrialized countries would no longer find it easy to negotiate with weak producers.

KEY

Tito, Nehru and Nasser (pictured left to right at the Belgrade Conference, 1961) worked together as leaders and promoters of nonalignment from the mid-1950s. Nehru, spokesman for newly independent India, advanced nonalignment as a positive moral force and advocated non-nuclear "areas of peace." Tito represented independent Marxism resisting the pressures of the USSR. Nasser, leader of the new nationalist government in Egypt and of the larger Arab world, successfully played off cold war competitors with rival aid bids and rid his country of British military bases.

5

UNIT

5 John Foster Dulles, US secretary of state (1953–59), was an unrelenting opponent of communism and the chief advocate of US strategy to contain China and the USSR by military alliances. Announcing in June 1956 that 42 nations were allied with the United States, he achieved some notoriety when he said that "except in very exceptional circumstances, neutrality is an immoral and short-sighted conception."

6

Official nuclear-free zone
Nuclear-free zone proposed by Pakistan
Nuclear-free zone proposed by India
Proposed neutral zone
Proposed Australian zone of peace

6 Nuclear-free zones and zones of peace or neutrality are being proposed, debated, and actively promoted in Southeast Asia, southern Asia, the Indian Ocean, and parts of Africa. A lead was taken in 1967 by Mexico and some other nations when the Treaty for the Prohibition of Nuclear Weapons in Latin America (the Treaty of Tlateloco) was signed. Most other zones have yet to be ratified.

7

HASTA LA VICTORI
SIEMPRE

7 Strident anti-US attitudes emerged in Cuba after Fidel Castro (1927–) came to power early in 1959. A large Cuban delegation attended a turbulent 15th session of the UN in September 1960. Cuba's role as a small country defying a neighboring superpower was further dramatized by an abortive US-backed invasion by Cuban exiles at the Bay of Pigs in April 1961 and a Soviet attempt to arm Cuba with nuclear missiles in 1962. Cuba has campaigned to make Havana a Third World capital linking Afro-Asia and Latin America.

8

8 OPEC, the Organization of Petroleum Exporting Countries, meeting at Geneva in January 1974, represented the most powerful cartel in the world—a position gained through the importance of petroleum in the world economy.

9

9 A World Food Conference sponsored by the UN in Rome in November 1974 and attended by 1,250 delegates from some 130 nations originated with the 1973 Algiers conference of nonaligned countries. The idea was adopted by Henry Kissinger, US secretary of state, with Western backing.

10

10 Commonwealth prime ministers, shown at Kingston, Jamaica, in 1975, make up an international grouping that includes aligned and nonaligned, nuclear and non-nuclear, rich and poor countries. This voluntary association of former members of the British Empire engages in continuous consultation.

Latin America in the 20th century

The history of Latin America in the twentieth century is, above all, the story of attempts to break out of the economic, political, and social patterns of the nineteenth century and of the resistance such attempts have encountered. Developments in Latin America have been increasingly affected by outside influences. The Great Depression of the 1930s brought a collapse of world prices for Latin American exports, and two world wars further stimulated industrialization and modernization by cutting the region off from traditional markets and sources of capital goods. Major cities like Buenos Aires, Mexico City, and São Paulo have experienced rapid growth.

Dictatorships and the military in politics

Industrialization and modernization did not automatically bring fundamental political and social change to Latin America. Trade and industry were dominated by foreign enterprises, increasingly those based in the United States. Nor did the growing middle classes in Latin America play the social role of their counterparts in the United States or Western Europe, and middle-class political parties seldom carried out essential reforms when they gained office. This situation encouraged the emergence of a new kind of dictator—one who sought the support of the urban workers. Such a dictator was Juan Perón (1895–1974) of Argentina [3].

The military has remained a significant element in Latin American politics. Beginning in 1929, military intervention was given considerable impetus by the Depression, which caused political convulsions in most Latin American countries. Intervention was later encouraged by cold war tensions. Often faced by weak and ineffective civilian governments, the military has tended to regard itself as the true guardian of the national interest. Nationalism has always been strong in the Latin American military, and—although the latter has generally been conservative and, in recent decades, strongly anti-communist—this nationalism has sometimes been combined with radicalism, especially among younger officers. As early as the 1920s a military president, Colonel Carlos Ibáñez (1877–1966) [2], carried out a program of social reform in Chile. The most far-reaching of such programs, however, has been that of the Peruvian military government that seized power in 1968. Beginning with the expropriation of a prominent United States-owned oil company, it continued with the United States as one of the prime targets of Peruvian nationalism.

Antipathy toward the United States

Latin American nationalism has for a long time been directed mainly at the United States, which is by far the most important foreign presence in the region. The United States has usually exerted its influence in favor of stability and the status quo and against revolutionary changes that would threaten its interests. Fear of communism has sometimes led the United States to support Latin American dictatorships. When, in 1961, President John F. Kennedy (1917–63) launched the Alliance for Progress—an ambitious program of economic and social development in Latin America involving substantial reforms and the promotion of

CONNECTIONS

See also

1234 Latin American inde[pendence]
1386 Underdevelopment and the world economy
1352 Nonalignment and the Third World
1384 The world's monetar[y] system
1264 The expansion of Christianity
1262 European imperialis[m] in the 19th century
294 Misuse of the land
602 New World tropics

HUELGA

1 The ideology of the Mexican revolution is symbolized in huge murals by Rivera, Orozco, and Siqueiros. The revolution was nationalist, and the murals are a vivid expression of cultural nationalism. They depict great violence: the oppression of the Indians by the Spanish conquerors and the furious reaction of the Mexican peasants and workers. The Indians and their leaders are idealized in these murals; the oppressors grotesquely caricatured. In this mural Marx is exhorting the workers, while the Church and the capitalists are engrossed in wealth. The Mexican revolution took place in 1910–11.

2 Colonel Carlos Ibáñez became president of Chile in 1927 and pursued policies combining nationalism and social reform. His programs, however, were undermined by the Great Depression.

3 General Juan Perón was president of Argentina from 1946–55. Assisted by his wife Eva, he won over the urban masses with social benefits. After Eva's death in 1952 his position deteriorated and he was eventually overthrown by the military. The *Peronistas* remained a key element in Argentine politics Perón was recalled to power in 1973 but he died during the following year.

4 Fidel Castro, the charismatic leader of revolutionary Cuba, seen here addressing one of the countless gatherings at which he explains his policies, is probably the most widely known Latin American figure since Simón Bolívar. Although "Castroism" has not spread to other parts of the continent, Castro's success in defying the powerful United States has profoundly affected the political influence and prestige of the United States in Latin America.

5 Salvador Allende became the first freely elected Marxist head of state when he won the Chilean presidential election in 1970. Although faced with congressional opposition and US hostility, he embarked upon an ambitious socialist program. Both his supporters and his opponents resorted to unconstitutional tactics. Economic chaos and violence culminated in 1973 in President Allende's overthrow by a military coup and his death.

democracy—it met with apathy. Latin Americans have since denounced "aid" as increasing their dependence upon the United States.

Despite United States influence and the durability of traditional social structures there have been three authentic revolutions in Latin America during the twentieth century: in Mexico (1910), Bolivia (1952), and Cuba (1959). The Mexican revolution [1] created a new system of government, redistributed land holdings, and improved the status of the Indians. In 1938 the government asserted Mexican nationalism by taking over the foreign-owned oil industry. The Bolivian revolution (1952), although less far-reaching, destroyed the privileges of the great landowners, nationalized the tin mines (Bolivia's main source of foreign exchange), and raised the status of the Indians. The Cuban revolution (1959) has been the most radical, and Cuba has become an avowedly Marxist state under the leadership of Fidel Castro (1927–) [4].

The Cuban example has not been followed elsewhere in Latin America, although urban guerrilla violence has increased markedly in some countries, notably Argentina. The victory of Salvador Allende (1908–73) [5] in the Chilean presidential election of 1970—even though he was overthrown by a military coup three years later—indicated a significant shift.

Third World cooperation

Meanwhile, the countries of Latin America [6] have come to identify themselves with the developing countries of Asia and Africa and to cooperate with them in endeavoring to obtain better terms of trade from the wealthier industrialized powers. They have also tried to cooperate more closely with each other and to increase their trade outside the Western Hemisphere in order to lessen dependence upon the United States.

Brazil [7], traditionally more friendly toward the United States than the Spanish American countries, has for a long time entertained hopes of becoming a great power. After its considerable economic progress since the mid-1960s, Brazil no longer considers itself a developing nation.

KEY

The Pan-American Union building in Washington, DC, is the headquarters of the Organization of American States (OAS), which links Latin America and the United States.

6

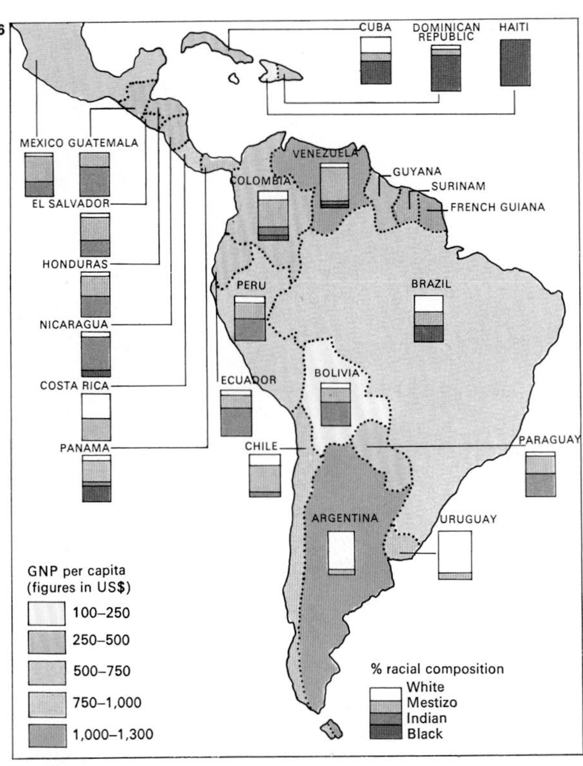
CUBA
DOMINICAN REPUBLIC
HAITI
MEXICO
GUATEMALA
EL SALVADOR
HONDURAS
NICARAGUA
COSTA RICA
PANAMA
VENEZUELA
COLOMBIA
GUYANA
SURINAM
FRENCH GUIANA
PERU
BRAZIL
ECUADOR
BOLIVIA
CHILE
PARAGUAY
ARGENTINA
URUGUAY
GNP per capita (figures in US$)
100–250
250–500
500–750
750–1,000
1,000–1,300
% racial composition
White
Mestizo
Indian
Black

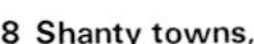

7

6 The identification of Latin America with the Third World is illustrated by this map; the average per capita incomes and racial compositions are similar to those in other developing nations. The gap between rich and poor is often wide.

7 Brazil's Foreign Affairs Ministry building is in Brasilia, the nation's new capital. Brasilia symbolizes Brazil's determination to become a power and to exploit the hitherto largely untapped wealth of the country's undeveloped interior.

8

8 Shanty towns, such as this one in Rio de Janeiro, demonstrate the glaring disparity between rich and poor in Latin America, as well as the population drift into the burgeoning cities from the stagnant countryside areas.

9

9 The Transamazonian highway in Brazil exemplifies modernization in Latin America. When complete, the network of roads is designed to integrate the Amazon basin—vast, underpopulated, but rich in resources—with the more developed coastal regions.

10

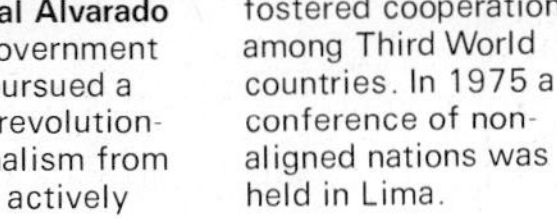

10 General Alvarado head of government of Peru, pursued a policy of revolutionary nationalism from 1968 and actively fostered cooperation among Third World countries. In 1975 a conference of non-aligned nations was held in Lima.

Postwar evolution of Western Europe

World War II left Europe divided into two political camps. Except for Greece, where a communist-led revolt was raging, eastern Europe was under Soviet occupation, including eastern Germany—although the Western allies held part of Berlin. The first task was to put the war-torn countries of Europe on their feet. This was undertaken by the United States through the multi-billion-dollar European Recovery Program [3], otherwise known as the Marshall Plan after its initiator, Secretary of State George Marshall (1880–1959) [2].

Breach with the Soviet Union

The Marshall Plan was designed to redevelop industries throughout Europe on an aid-sharing basis through the Office of European Economic Cooperation (OEEC). The Soviet Union was invited to join but refused in July 1947. At the same time it vetoed the participation of other countries within its sphere of influence, including Czechoslovakia, which was soon to be incorporated in the Soviet bloc by the coup of February 20–25, 1948.

Although it already had complete power over East Germany, the Soviet government wished to exact heavy reparations from West Germany under the arrangements for four-power control. Thus they continued to dismantle factories, preventing the recovery of West Germany that was believed by the other powers to be vital for the economic recovery of Europe. By 1948 the breach between the Soviet Union and its former western allies was complete.

The United States and Great Britain introduced a currency reform into West Germany that had striking success in bringing goods into the shops again and restarting the wheels of industry. But when they extended the reform to their occupation zones in West Berlin the Soviets imposed a blockade on the city (June 1948). The blockade was rendered ineffective by a gigantic airlift, and the USSR ended it in May 1949. Meanwhile, the Western allies oversaw the transition of West Germany to independence as the German Federal Republic in 1949.

A strong wave of idealism, strengthened by Churchill's call for a United States of Europe (Zurich 1947), brought into being the Council of Europe (1949), comprising most countries outside the Soviet bloc. It disappointed many of its promoters, for, because of British policy, it remained a consultative body without power.

Steps to unity

Britain, with its predominant position in Western Europe in the immediate postwar years, had also been able to thwart US hopes that the OEEC could become a supranational body. Promoters of West European unity led by Jean Monnet (1888–   ) accordingly took another initiative. With the aid of Robert Schuman (1886–1963), the French foreign minister [4], and supported by West Germany and Italy, they set out to bring together their countries and others in a supranational organization to administer their coal and steel industries jointly [5]. In May 1950 the Schuman Plan was launched, leading to the creation in 1951 of the Coal and Steel Community of France, West Germany, Italy, Belgium, the Netherlands, and Luxembourg. This act of statesmanship

CONNECTIONS

See also
1390 The superpowers from confrontation to détente
1384 The world's monetary system
1342 The division of Europe
1346 Eastern Europe 1948–Present
1344 The Soviet Union after World War II
1308 The Peace of Paris
1324 The twenties and the Depression
1336 Causes of World War II
904 Political participation

1 The entry to Paris of General de Gaulle at the head of Free French forces on August 26, 1944, marked the beginning of the end of World War II in the west. But the German armies resisted until May 1945. As Soviet forces fought their way across eastern Europe and the Western allies advanced through Italy and across the Rhine, the postwar political division of Europe began to take shape.

2 US Secretary of State Marshall [left], seen with British Foreign Secretary Ernest Bevin (1881–1951), initiated the aid plan named after him in 1947–49 to restore a weakened Europe that might otherwise turn to communism.

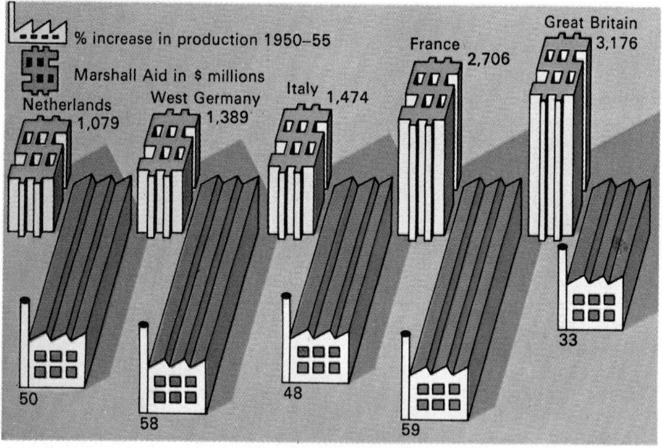

% increase in production 1950–55
Marshall Aid in $ millions
Netherlands 1,079
West Germany 1,389
Italy 1,474
France 2,706
Great Britain 3,176
50
58
48
59
33

3 The European recovery program, set up to administer the Marshall Plan, disbursed $13 billion between 1948 and 1952 in addition to the $9.5 billion already granted for Western Europe since the end of the war and private gifts of food worth $500 million. By mid-1951 industrial production was 42% higher than the prewar level, while agricultural output was 10% higher. Trade had more than doubled. Coal and steel production also made impressive advances.

4 Two Frenchmen initiated the scheme for the European Coal and Steel Community of France, West Germany, Italy, Netherlands, Belgium, and Luxembourg, established by the Treaty of Paris in 1951. Foreign Minister Robert Schuman [A] based this organization on proposals for pooling coal and steel output that were formulated by Jean Monnet [B], in charge of French modernization.

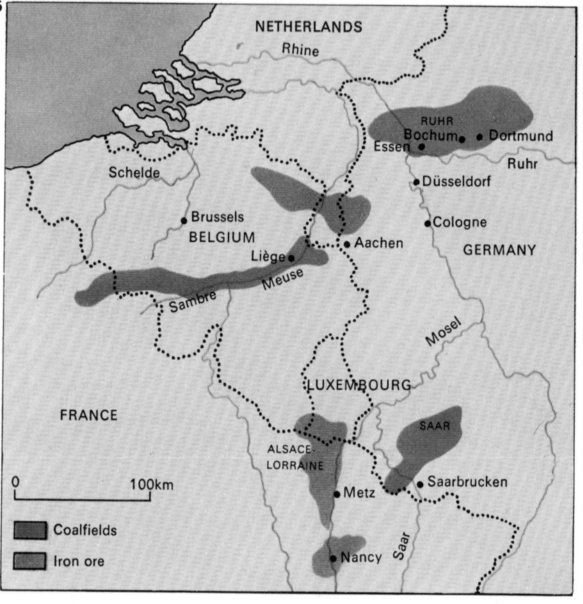

NETHERLANDS
Rhine
RUHR
Bochum
Dortmund
Essen
Ruhr
Düsseldorf
Schelde
Brussels
BELGIUM
Cologne
Aachen
GERMANY
Liège
Meuse
Sambre
Mosel
LUXEMBOURG
FRANCE
SAAR
ALSACE-LORRAINE
Metz
Saarbrucken
0
100km
Coalfields
Iron ore
Nancy
Saar

5 Coal seams cross frontiers in northern Europe, and the ECSC countries saw that they could build up an efficient coal and steel industry only by devising a supranational system. In this way the coal and coke of the Ruhr could supply the steel industry of Lorraine, while the Benelux countries (Belgium, Luxembourg, Netherlands) and Italy could enjoy similar advantages. By combining these industries (vital for armaments) the risk of another European war was reduced.

was made possible by a new climate of opinion that erased wartime hatred [Key].

Belgium, the Netherlands, and Luxembourg had set up a customs union (Benelux) at the end of the war, and in 1957 these countries took the lead in a further step toward the unity of Western Europe, the creation [6] of the European Economic Community, or Common Market, to create conditions of fair trade for manufactured and agricultural products.

Although the EEC Commission, with powers of initiative and supervision, is a supranational body, major decisions are made by a council of ministers of member states. Attempts to increase the powers of the commission as a decision-making body were thwarted by General de Gaulle [1] as president of France, and the council continued as an intergovernmental body with every minister retaining the right of veto.

De Gaulle's position was particularly strong after he returned to power in 1958, settled France's colonial problem in Algeria, and initiated the French Fifth Republic, whose constitution gave impressive powers to the president. He asserted the right of France to leadership of "European Europe" in opposition to US influence. In pursuit of this policy he blocked moves for the United States' close ally, Britain, to join the Common Market. In 1966 he also took France out of the North Atlantic Treaty Organization (NATO), which had been set up in 1949. West Germany joined NATO in 1955, following the unsuccessful attempt to establish a European Defense Community.

Expansion of the Common Market

After De Gaulle resigned in 1969, France's veto on British entry into the Common Market was soon removed [7]. Denmark and Ireland joined when Britain did, in 1973. The countries of the European Free Trade Association [8], an industrial customs union that Britain had set up as a rival to the Common Market in 1956, were given favored relations with the community. Membership in the EEC system of associated states, first given to former French colonies, was extended to many African and Caribbean states in 1975.

KEY

Reconciliation of France and Germany laid the foundation for a new political and economic structure within which the countries of western Europe could be integrated. After more than 80 years of suspicion, tension, and conflict, including three major wars, the two countries joined forces in the Schuman Plan (1950) leading to the European Coal and Steel Community. In January 1963 West German Chancellor Konrad Adenauer (1876–1967) and French President Charles de Gaulle (1890–1970) left and right respectively met to sign the Franco-German Treaty of Friendship.

6

6 The signing of the Treaty of Rome in March 1957 set up the European Economic Community after intensive negotiations under the chairmanship of Paul-Henri Spaak of Belgium (1899–1972). Six member states established a common market for industrial and later for agricultural products, along with plans to "harmonize" regulations affecting such things as working conditions to ensure fair competition.

7

7 Consultations in May 1971 between Edward Heath (1916–), prime minister of Britain [left], and Georges Pompidou (1911–74) president of France, cleared the way for Britain's entry to the Common Market, a step that British governments had attempted since 1961. De Gaulle twice vetoed British entry, but a changed French attitude enabled Britain, Denmark, and Ireland to become members in 1973.

8

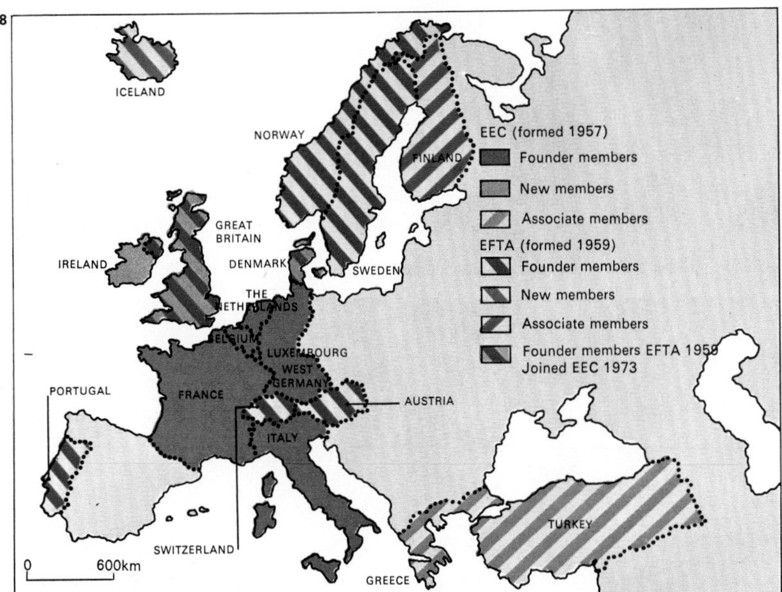

ICELAND
NORWAY
FINLAND
SWEDEN
GREAT BRITAIN
IRELAND
DENMARK
THE NETHERLANDS
BELGIUM
LUXEMBOURG
WEST GERMANY
FRANCE
PORTUGAL
AUSTRIA
ITALY
SWITZERLAND
GREECE
TURKEY
0 600km
EEC (formed 1957)
Founder members
New members
Associate members
EFTA (formed 1959)
Founder members
New members
Associate members
Founder members EFTA 1959 Joined EEC 1973

8 The European Free Trade Association was set up under the leadership of Britain before it entered the EEC to offset advantages the "Six" were gaining. EFTA, a customs union for industrial goods, facilitated trade between its member states, although trade growth was faster within the more powerful EEC. Some countries were associated with the EEC pending full membership. EFTA survived Britain's entry into EEC, and gained special trading links with EEC.

9

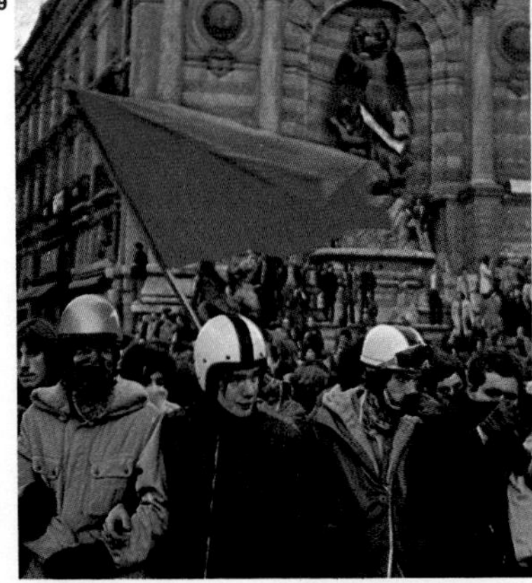

9 Riots in Paris in 1968 were led by students who, in both France and Germany, sought reforms. Sit-ins and violence developed into a general strike in France. De Gaulle's regime recovered after the army pledged support but was badly shaken. Promises of far-reaching educational reforms and generous wage settlements ended the strikes and unrest, although de Gaulle himself did not long remain in office as president.

10

10 Arab representatives appeared unexpectedly at the first summit meeting of the enlarged Common Market at Copenhagen in 1973. The summit closely followed the October Arab-Israeli war and consequent oil embargo. A steep increase in oil prices indicated a fundamental change in the relative positions of oil-producing and industrial nations, particularly affecting Europe. The Arabs arrived in Copenhagen seeking support against Israel.

The United States: the affluent society

The pervasive theme of US society since the end of World War II has been growth, bringing prosperity, innovation, and not least, growing pains. This growth has been most evident in the number of people living in the United States [1]. The population at the time of the 1940 census was 131,000,000; by 1970 the population was 203,000,000, an increase of 72,000,000. The population explosion had been fed domestically—by the baby boom after the end of World War II, by the "second-generation" baby boom of the late 1960s, and by people living longer—rather than by continued immigration from Europe. By 1972 the rate of immigration was about one-sixth what it had been before World War I, and less than six percent of the country's population was foreign born.

The increase in population has meant a vast expansion in the size of urban areas, although typically the city centers themselves have lost population. Those who remain in older cities are often black [6]. Among large US cities nine have populations that are 40 percent or more black, including Washington, D.C. which is more than two-thirds black. The growth in population has been greatest in the so-called "Sun Belt" or southern half of the country extending from the Carolinas south and west in a broad belt to California. In 1940 California had less than half the population of New York; by 1970 it had become the most populous state in the Union.

The rise of the bureaucratic leviathan

The population explosion has been mirrored by an enormous growth in government. The number of public employees has tripled since the 1930s and more than doubled since 1945, and now constitutes nearly 20 percent of the total work force. The expansion of the US military (conscription in various forms was in force from 1941 until the late days of the Vietnam War) is shown by the fact that there were 28,000,000 ex-servicemen in the United States in 1975.

The growth in government was reflected in the creation of three new cabinet departments (Health, Education, and Welfare; Housing and Urban Development; and Transportation). They were a response to the federal government's commitment to expand its capabilities for looking after its citizens.

Superficially, party politics has changed less than society as a whole. The presidency is generally contested by candidates of the Democratic and Republican parties, as it was a century ago. But the voting has been very unstable. Throughout most of the period, the Democratic party has controlled both houses of Congress. In three postwar elections however, the man who won the presidency took less than half the vote, because of divisions within the two parties and the votes received by minor party candidates.

Expanding economy and prosperity

The US government was able to expand activities at home and abroad because of the continued growth of the nation's economy. Between 1950 and 1970 the gross national product almost quadrupled. This growth in total national resources meant that, even without raising tax rates, the flow of money

CONNECTIONS

See also
1378 The wars of Indochin
1384 The world's monetar system
1374 American writing: int the 20th century
1360 20th-century sociology and its influence
1356 Postwar evolution of Western Europe
1344 The Soviet Union afte World War II
1348 China: the People's Republic

1 Rapid population growth in the United States after the war was caused more by a marked increase in the birthrate and life expectancy than by immigration; since 1945 total population has increased by over 50%. Until the mid-1970s growth did not greatly affect population distribution across the continent. But there has been a significant movement of people to new centers of growth, north and south mixing in this internal migration. Sunbelt states such as Florida and California were centers for migration. America's massive manpower and industrial wealth provided the means of a worldwide "defense" effort.

2 A

B

C

D

E

F

G

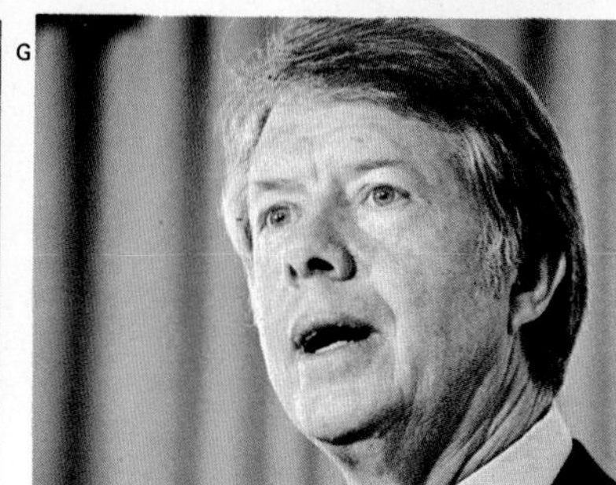

2 Postwar US presidents have been almost evenly divided in party terms, Eisenhower [B], Nixon [E], and Ford [F] being Republicans, and Truman [A], Kennedy [C], Johnson [D], and Carter [G] being Democrats. But all were united in the priority given to foreign affairs. Truman found this compensated for domestic policy setbacks, but Johnson lost by his foreign policy the support that his domestic war on poverty had gained. Nixon found that his success abroad could not bury the Watergate Affair. Of these men John F. Kennedy, the son of a multimillionaire, came from established power and wealth; the others were all from small towns or farming areas.

into the federal treasury increased massively. The amount of money left in the pockets of individual consumers also increased, although by a lesser rate, because a portion of the increase went to looking after the increased number of children and elderly and to employ the larger number of Americans of working age. Until the recession of the 1970s family income rose steadily, even when allowance is made for the effects of creeping inflation. The real income of the average US family doubled from 1947 to 1971.

Higher earnings meant that people could afford to buy more of everything. The great postwar housing boom meant that the proportion of Americans living in substandard houses dropped from nearly two in five in 1945 (many living in old farmhouses) to one in 20 in the early 1970s. The number of cars sold more than doubled from prewar years, totaling more than 8,500,000 in 1970 [5]. Until the mid-1970s Americans also invested more money in education.

One of the most significant changes in US society in the postwar era occurred through the courts and the statute books, with the legal, if not always actual, integration of blacks as full citizens in US society. A series of Supreme Court decisions culminated in 1954 in the declaration that segregation of public education was unconstitutional. Until the mid-1970s, when busing to achieve integration became unpopular, the Supreme Court's order to integrate with all deliberate speed led to major changes in schooling and housing patterns throughout the country.

The raising of black consciousness

In the 1960s blacks began to turn to the streets, protesting peacefully under leaders such as Martin Luther King (1929–68) [4], or rioting as an expression of frustration, as in the Watts area of Los Angeles, in Detroit, Newark, and even in Washington, D.C. Black family income, reflecting generations of discrimination, does not yet equal that of whites. Nonetheless black family income has been rising, as more blacks receive better education and equal opportunity in employment.

KEY

Nassau's
JO-ANN FABRICS

The shopping mall, with its variety and abundance of goods, symbolizes the affluence of postwar America. In the decade following World War II this wealth was highlighted by a profusion of goods unknown to a war-torn world.

3

3 American affluence was based on the unlimited supply of cheap energy, particularly oil. When the Organization of Petroleum Exporting Countries (OPEC) quadrupled the price of oil in 1974, US economic growth was threatened. Formerly an oil exporter, the United States had become a major importer. The search for new sources of energy intensified, the building of the Alaskan pipeline being one example.

4

4 Martin Luther King organized the Montgomery, Alabama, bus boycott of 1955–56, the first great civil rights protest in the South. This spokesman for blacks was assassinated in 1968.

6 The growing black population migrated to cities such as Detroit, Chicago, Los Angeles, and Houston. This influx provoked an outflow of white residents to the suburbs. The whites were partly attracted by suburban life itself and partly fearful of the urban ghettos. As a result the largest US cities have acute social, political, and economic problems intensified by years of racial antagonism.

5

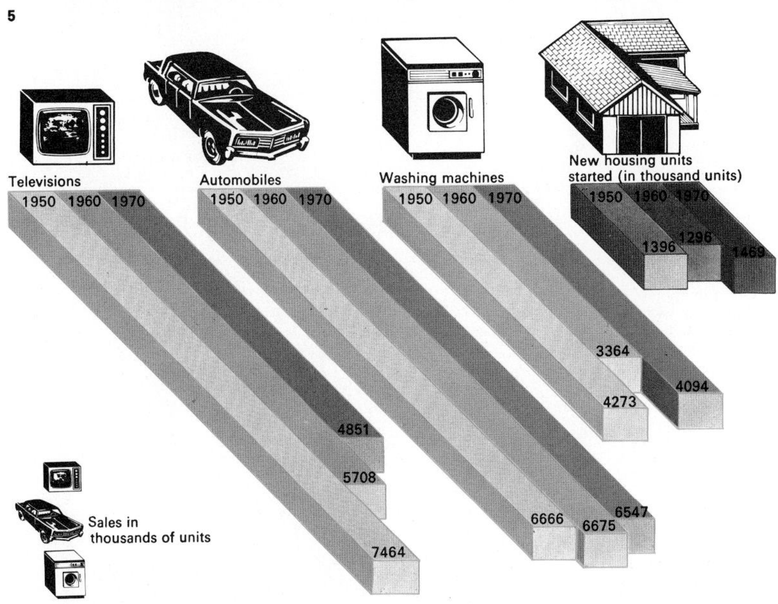

Televisions
1950 1960 1970
4851
5708
7464
Automobiles
1950 1960 1970
6666
6675
6547
Washing machines
1950 1960 1970
3364
4273
4094
New housing units started (in thousand units)
1950 1960 1970
1396
1296
1469
Sales in thousands of units

5 The consumer goods boom in postwar America created a "democracy of consumption": new homes, cars, washing machines, and television sets became the birthright of most Americans. Characteristic of this boom was the demand for television sets, first for black-and-white sets in the 1950s and later for color sets, as technological advance made black-and-white television obsolescent. The boom in house construction brought mass production to the building industry, with economies of scale and standardization of product. A record of building well over 1,000,000 houses a year meant that by the mid-1970s the number of homes built in the postwar era would have been able to provide a new house for almost every US family in 1939. Consumer durables also generated further costs – most notably the automobile. It consumed tracts of land for highways and oil to fuel engines. Until the oil crisis of the 1970s resources seemed boundless.

6 Black population as a percentage of total population

1970
1940
Los Angeles 16·5 6·5
Houston 25·7 22·5
Chicago 32·7 8·3
Detroit 43·7 9·3
Philadelphia 33·6 13·1
New York 21·1 6·4

20th-century sociology and its influence

In the years following the end of World War II, sociology began to change from a theoretical study to a practical tool that could be used by government and industry. But it did not lose sight of its origins. It had begun from a desire to explain—and to counteract—the forces in industrialization that divided people, both economically and socially. Although their means were widely divergent, modern sociologists preserved that desire, concentrating on ways of reducing economic and social inequality and of increasing social integration.

The "good society"

The insecurity and disruption of the 1930s and 1940s had increased the concern of sociologists with the "good society." The good society was seen by some theorists as involving a high level of integration and stability, a common core of values, and an emphasis on community. One such school of thought, structural functionalism, developed a picture of society as a self-regulating organism, in which all the various elements (institutions) perform necessary functions. Functionalism originated with Emile Durkheim (1858–1917) and was developed in the United States by Talcott Parsons (1902–) and Robert Merton (1910–). Bronislaw Malinowski (1884–1942) and Alfred Radcliffe-Brown (1881–1955) were early functionalists who founded British social anthropology with their studies of small-scale "primitive" cultures in New Guinea, Africa, and elsewhere.

The conservative tenor of structural functionalism is apparent in its concentration on moral integration, in its emphasis upon the importance of existing social institutions, and in its tendency to identify their functions with the interests of the more powerful groups in society.

Sociology and "social engineering"

Functionalism provided a theoretical basis for the widespread use of sociologists as "social engineers," dealing with particular problems for industry or government. Many different policies were drawn from functionalist analyses—some, for example, stressed the need for different social levels, others advocated integration. Busing and integrated schooling are examples of government policies adopted to promote equality by bringing together privileged and underprivileged children at school [9]. Delinquency is another problem about which governments have increasingly turned to sociologists. Functionalist analysis underlay the 1958 "Mobilization for Youth" program in the United States, an effort to narrow the gap between the desires of and the actual opportunities offered to the underprivileged—a gap that the program's originators believed to be a cause of delinquency [5]. In their postwar public housing and urban renewal schemes, governments of many industrialized nations have employed sociologists in planning [4].

The pioneering research at the Western Electric Company into the productivity and working conditions found in their factories in 1927 showed the great importance of "human factors" in raising productivity levels. The value of those findings led to the large-scale employment of sociologists by managements of various industries to work

CONNECTIONS

See also
1290 Masters of sociolog
1358 The United States: postwar developme
1282 The foundations of 20th-century scienc
1326 Socialism in the We
830 Types of ritual
874 The study of man
888 Structure of societie
890 Conflict, power, and social inequality.
900 Political science
904 Political participatio

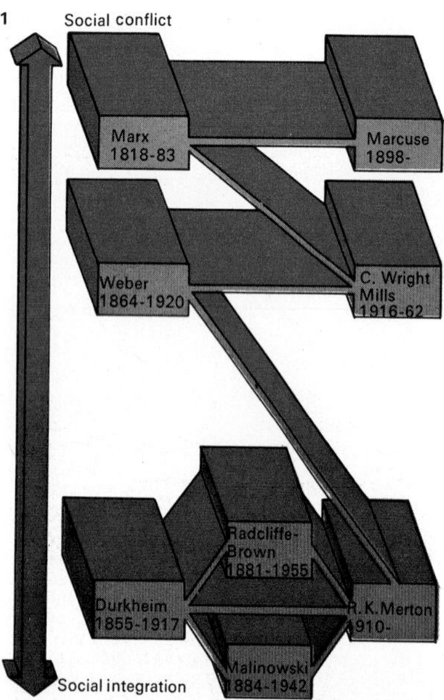

1
Social conflict
Marx
1818-83
Marcuse
1898-
Weber
1864-1920
C. Wright
Mills
1916-62
Radcliffe-
Brown
1881-1955
Durkheim
1855-1917
R.K.Merton
1910-
Malinowski
1884-1942
Social integration

1 Sociological thought in the 20th century is, in many respects, as divided as that of the 19th century when many of its current disagreements began. There is no one sociological theory, but instead a number of different theories, some complementary and some conflicting. One of the most fundamental of these concerns the model of society with which the sociologist starts. Some, such as Talcott and Parsons, define society as a harmonious, self-regulating system. Others, like Marcuse, argue that society is not as harmonious as it may sometimes appear but is deeply divided by vast economic inequalities.

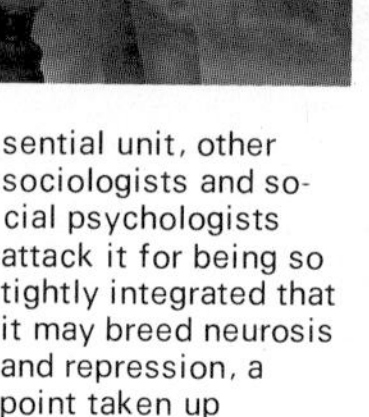

2 The "nuclear family"—consisting of parents and their children only—appears to fulfill the basic function of caring for children and socializing them. Whereas functionalists see it as an essential unit, other sociologists and social psychologists attack it for being so tightly integrated that it may breed neurosis and repression, a point taken up strongly by the Women's Movement.

3 The Israeli kibbutz, one of the experiments in group living in Western society, demonstrates that, contrary to early functionalist thinking, the nuclear family is not the only possible structure that can nurture children. In theory, children on the kibbutz are raised collectively, although some sociologists have pointed out that a strong sense of the family unit remains in the kibbutz.

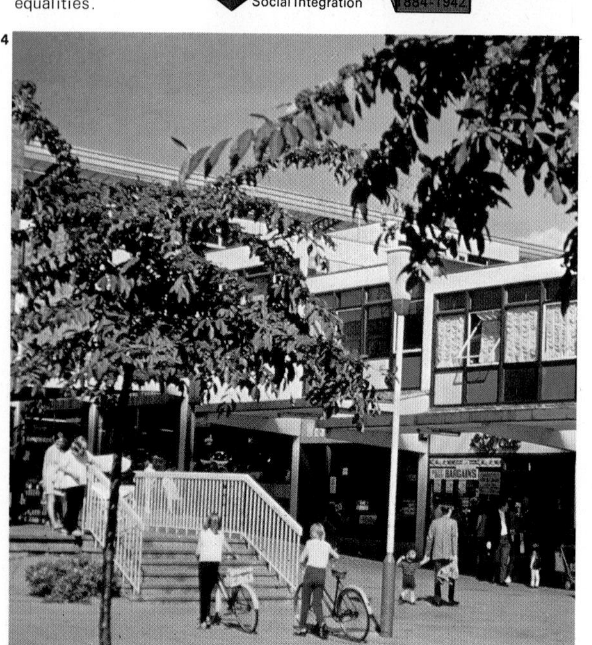

4 Governments have increasingly employed sociologists to assist in social planning. Postwar prosperity and recognition that slums were a source of social problems led to large-scale public housing programs. However, "improvements" were often carried out despite lack of experience on which to predict their effects on the people involved. Established communities with strong, supportive social systems were broken up in the move to well-designed but socially anonymous new towns. Various measures, from the grouping of houses in small units to the location of shops have been tried to recreate a community feeling.

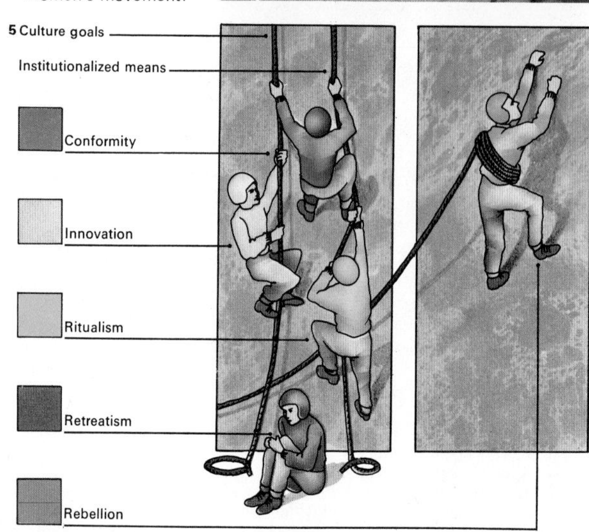

5
Culture goals
Institutionalized means
Conformity
Innovation
Ritualism
Retreatism
Rebellion

5 Individual adjustment within a structure of socially defined goals and means is shown on this diagram by Merton. With this model it is possible to analyze the behavior of the delinquent who may pursue a socially acceptable goal, but who does not follow morally prescribed means of attaining it, and of rebels who seek to change goals and means.

in such areas as marketing and industrial relations.

The legacy of Karl Marx

Structural functionalism was paralleled by another line of argument stemming from the theory of Karl Marx (1818–83). Whereas the structural functionalists stressed the notions of integration and cooperation, those inspired by Marx saw society as composed of conflicting classes divided by their differing economic positions.

Influenced by Marx, C. Wright Mills (1916–62) in his book *The Power Elite* pointed to a threefold power concentration—the corporations, the military, and the politicians—whose interests and actions were closely related [6]. But he argued that the power basis of this alliance could not be explained simply in Marxist, economic terms but required a wider analysis of social organization. Marxist analysis greatly influenced the Black Power movement, whose leaders were disillusioned with the philosophy of integration advocated by the Civil Rights movement, and who questioned whether integration was possible or even desirable. Following race riots across the United States in 1968, black and white politicians and sociologists argued for increased economic aid and social legislation for the ghettos, proposals rejected by the Black Power movement as palliatives for deeper divisions and conflicts.

The Vietnam War and the related rise of student protest also brought to the fore the well-developed and incisive but previously uninfluential Frankfurt School of sociology. It emphasized the control of knowledge through the mass media.

The development of this theme by Herbert Marcuse [7], a founder of the Frankfurt School, gained prominence as the theoretical base of much of the growing student protest movement [10]. According to Marcuse, students, along with marginal and dispossessed groups, are the contemporary revolutionary agents, precisely because they are outside the hypnotic culture of consumer society; however, the Frankfurt School has as yet had little influence in official circles.

KEY

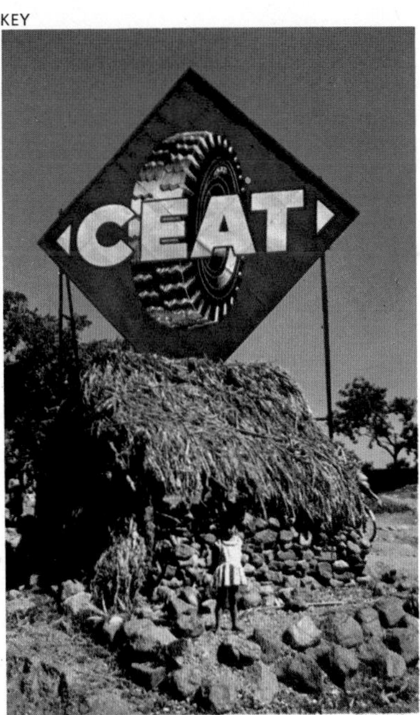
CEAT

The 20th century has been characterized for many by a widening gap between living standards and expectations (developed, for example, through advertising). Sociologists have approached this gap in different ways. Some have seen it as a cause of unrest and social problems; others have attributed the apathy of the underprivileged toward improving their situation to the use of advertising as a palliative and the creation of a "consumer dreamworld." This gap has also contributed to the use of sociology by governments, who have increasingly intervened to reduce inequalities.

6

Senators

6 The basis of power in US society, according to C. Wright Mills, greatly depends on the common social background of the political, military, and business leaders. Educated similarly, attending the same social events, yet careful to maintain a popular image—here President Eisenhower opens the 1960 baseball season—they maintain a common outlook that obviates the need for a conscious conspiracy to preserve rule.

7

7 Herbert Marcuse (1898–), professor of sociology at the University of California, Berkeley, has provided a sharp critique of modern society. His analysis, fusing Freudian ideas of bourgeois repression and Marxian notions of class conflict, characterized modern democracy as "repressive liberalism," in that freedom to dissent was more apparent than real. In the achievement of a truly liberated society, Marcuse allotted a central role to students. His work was an important strand in the ideology of the student movement of the 1960s, as many of those involved in the student unrest of 1968 acknowledged.

8

8 Social science research has undergone a rapid expansion. The methods and findings of sociology have been applied to a wide variety of public and private fields, from military strategy to housing, and from marketing to industrial relations. Leading US sociologists include Talcott Parsons (1902–), *right,* and Robert K. Merton (1910–), *far right.*

9

SCHOOL BUS

9 The policy of busing children encompasses two key sociological ideas. The first is the belief that educational achievement is as much a matter of environment as of heredity (emphasizing the need to equalize opportunities in the classroom). The second is that of racial integration. Public discontent with this policy, typified in Boston's antibusing demonstrations, points to the problems in such attempts at social engineering.

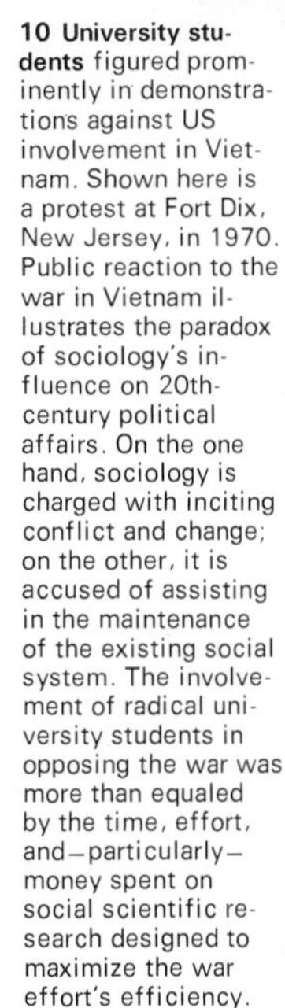

10

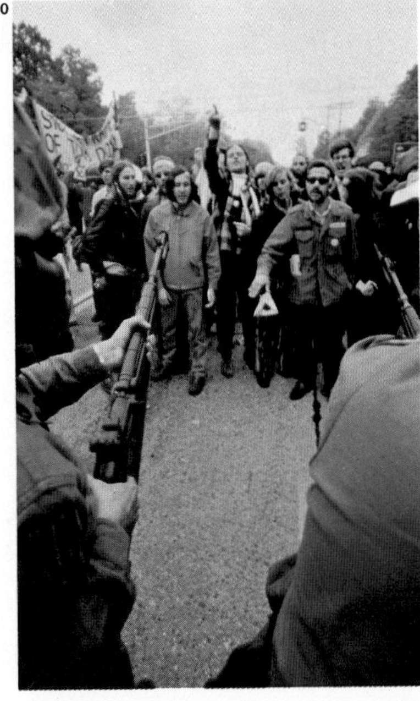

10 University students figured prominently in demonstrations against US involvement in Vietnam. Shown here is a protest at Fort Dix, New Jersey, in 1970. Public reaction to the war in Vietnam illustrates the paradox of sociology's influence on 20th-century political affairs. On the one hand, sociology is charged with inciting conflict and change; on the other, it is accused of assisting in the maintenance of the existing social system. The involvement of radical university students in opposing the war was more than equaled by the time, effort, and—particularly—money spent on social scientific research designed to maximize the war effort's efficiency.

Hollywood

To most people in the world, Hollywood and the movies mean the same thing. For more than fifty years the American movie industry was centered in the area of Los Angeles known as Hollywood, but even today, when the heyday of Hollywood as a production center has passed, Hollywood movies retain a worldwide appeal, and the legend of the glamorous film capital exercises a powerful influence on the world's imagination.

The Dream Machine

The first movie made in Hollywood was finished on October 27, 1911, at the Centaur Company's studio, located on the corner of Sunset Boulevard and Gower Street. California offered independent producers a chance to escape the sometimes brutal attempts of the Motion Picture Patents Company to control the new industry. In addition, there was the area's year-round sunshine—a decisive factor in the days when most movies were made out-of-doors.

By 1917 the Patents Company had been defeated in the courts, and Hollywood was already well on its way to becoming the film capital of the world. Patterning themselves along lines pioneered by Thomas Harper Ince (1882–1924), mammoth production and distribution organizations called studios came to characterize Hollywood film making. Some, like Metro-Goldwyn-Mayer, headed by the authoritarian Louis B. Mayer (1885–1957), turned out a movie geared to what the studio believed to be the public taste. Others, like Paramount, United Artists, and Universal, relied upon the individual abilities of directors, stars, producers, and writers to create works that would capture the public fancy. Whatever the studio's policy, the mass audience was the final judge of what was produced. Profit was the motive, and popular art was the result.

Hollywood's stock in trade was glamour. Its image of a modern Mount Olympus where godlike creatures played and incredible things happened was the inevitable outcome of an industry that catered to the world's fantasies. Movie stars [1, 4, 6, 8] were not-quite-human beings whose larger-than-life activities were reported in daily gossip columns and magazines. The films in which the stars appeared were unveiled in frenzied ceremonies called premieres [Key] and displayed in theaters of exotic design [2]. It is no wonder that Hollywood was periodically called upon to reform itself, most notably in 1922, when Will Hays (1879–1954) was called in to oversee the morals of the industry and its product, and in 1947, when the House Un-American Activities Committee determined to ferret out Communist infiltration into the movies. Nothing that happened in Hollywood—sexual, social, religious, or political—was ever anything less than "merely colossal."

Artists and genres

The movie moguls found that the public liked variations on familiar themes. Hollywood production became conventionalized, grouped around certain types of movie stories to which audiences responded. Musicals [3] and Westerns [6] are among the Hollywood genres that gained worldwide popularity. In some cases, as in the Andy Hardy series [7], the same per-

CONNECTIONS

See also
1316 Origins of film
1370 Cinema as art
1324 The twenties and the Depression
1374 American writing: into the 20th century

1 Rudolph Valentino, shown here in a passionate moment from *Blood and Sand* (1922), was the idol of millions of women. He incarnated the "Latin lover" of the period with a mixture of boyish charm and feline grace. His amazing popularity, culminating in a public orgy of grief after his death (from peritonitis) in 1926, demonstrated the power of women at the box office in the 1920s.

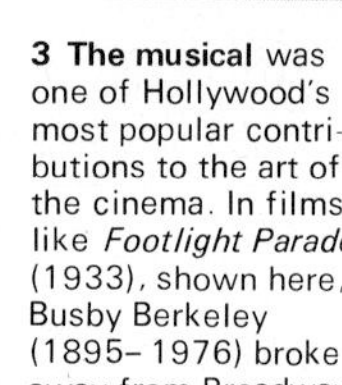

2 The picture palace was a place of escape and enchantment in the 1920s. Fantastic decorative flourishes were featured inside and out. S. L. Rothafel's Roxy Theatre in New York, shown here, was called the "Cathedral of the Motion Picture." It opened in 1927 and is considered the ultimate achievement in this style. John Eberson's design for the Bronx Paradise Theatre in New York City also shows off the style.

3 The musical was one of Hollywood's most popular contributions to the art of the cinema. In films like *Footlight Parade* (1933), shown here, Busby Berkeley (1895–1976) broke away from Broadway production methods, creating stunning sequences of forms in motion and outlandish madcap fantasies. Fred Astaire brought his special buoyancy and charm to the screen in other musicals. In the 1940s, Vincente Minnelli made the genre a vehicle for his personal vision; Gene Kelly and Stanley Donen made the last "real Hollywood" musicals in the late 1950s.

4 The phenomenon of stardom has never been demonstrated more hauntingly than by Greta Garbo (1906–). Her steady gaze into the camera (here from the 1927 film *Love*) had a unique effect on both men and women, and the movies she made in Hollywood between 1926 and 1941 did much to make her a legendary figure. Brought to the film capital by the great Swedish director Mauritz Stiller, she was literally taken away from him as her popularity grew. "Garbo vehicles" were assembled by a special team of craftspeople dedicated to the creation of the star's image.

sonalities appeared in a number of virtually identical films. But in others, it might be a certain type of character—like the ruthless urban gangster—who figured in movies that in all other respects reflected the changing society around them. For example, the 1972 film *The Godfather* [9] is different in almost every respect from the 1930 *Little Caesar*, a classic of the genre, but both are called gangster movies.

Those Hollywood craftspeople who could adapt themselves to the demands of convention and the factory-like working conditions produced some motion pictures of undeniable merit. Perhaps the archetype of all Hollywood movies is *Gone with the Wind* (1939) [5], a film whose glossy production and romantic story reflect the personality of its producer, David O. Selznick (1902–1965), as thoroughly as they typify Hollywood itself. The Hollywood system nurtured and challenged such noted directors' talents as John Ford (1895–1973), Howard Hawks (1896–   ), and Alfred Hitchcock (1899–   ); such writers as Dudley Nichols (1895–1960); and such individual talents as Walt Disney (1901–66) and James Wong Howe (1899–1976).

At the same time the conventionality of Hollywood film production should not be overemphasized. The public demands novelty as much as familiarity, and Hollywood had to be ready with both. Movie genres adapted themselves to the times or, like the classic musical, faded away. Idiosyncratic talents like those of the Marx Brothers, whose anarchic comedy flourished in the 1930s and 1940s, and Orson Welles (1915–   ), whose first film was *Citizen Kane*, had an opportunity to use the film medium because of Hollywood's need for new things to show the public.

End of an era

Economically, television killed Hollywood. By the late 1940s attendance at movies had declined to a point from which it never recovered. The eventual result was the breakup of the studio system, which was replaced by independently arranged "packages" that consist of stories, stars, and film makers.

KEY

GRAUMAN'S
DIETRICH
MOROCCO

Hollywood was never slow to promote its own legend. Here a 1930 premiere of Dietrich's *Morocco* stops traffic at Grauman's Chinese Theatre. "Strip off the phony tinsel," said Oscar Levant, "and you'll find the real tinsel underneath."

5

5 Gone with the Wind has probably been seen by more people than any other film. Produced in color, it runs nearly four hours and boasts a willful heroine (Vivien Leigh), a robust he-man (Clark Gable), a pair of saintly supporting leads (Leslie Howard and Olivia de Havilland), and a story of high passions and turbulent events in the Civil War. It is the epitome of American romance.

6 In the ritual of the Western movie Hollywood found a parable of moral conflict that could be restated endlessly. The Western hero was a man alone who fought for the community, an untamed spirit pitted against the "bad guys." Although many of the cinema's finest artists made Westerns, the heart of the genre was in the humble B-picture where the bare formula alone thrilled audiences all over the world for decades. Stars, like John Wayne (shown here in *Stagecoach*), were the real gods of the Western myth.

6

7

7 The Hardy family was another American myth the movies brought to life. Mickey Rooney became a box-office star partly as a result of this MGM series. The stories of these films stressed honesty, simplicity, and serenity and usually dealt with the conflict between society and the individual in upbeat terms. Television now is the medium for this type of cultural message.

8

8 Marilyn Monroe was at the height of her fame as a sex symbol when she posed in a scene from *The Seven Year Itch* (1955), one of two films she made for comedy director Billy Wilder. But within seven years she was dead. The warmest and most tragic of all Hollywood sirens, she appeared just as the film capital's ambivalent attitude toward sex (long hedged by a "code of decency") was giving way to a less restrictive approach.

9

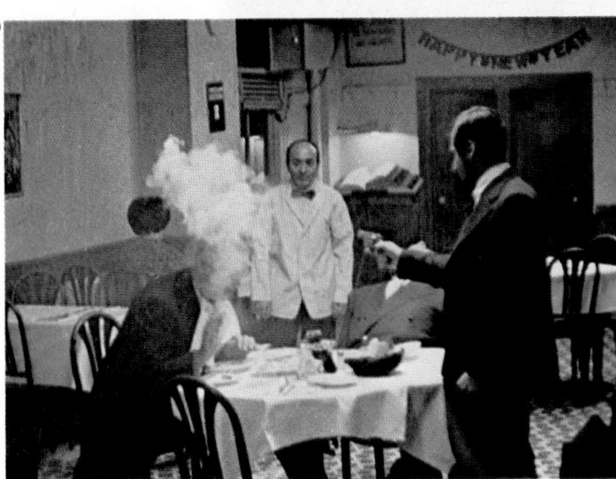
HAPPY NEW YEAR

9 This scene from *The Godfather* could never have been shown in a classic 1930s gangster movie. The old Production Code forbade having a gunshot and its result in the same frame. But that is not the only difference between present-day gangster films and older ones. Contemporary gangster movies have a touch of nostalgia for the "good old days," whereas older films presented those days as times of unrelenting terror, corruption, and violence.

Twentieth century music—tradition and experimentation

The history of Western classical music in the twentieth century has followed two main paths—tradition and experimentation. While existing conventions that had governed Western music for centuries were giving way to the intense search for new expression in sound, as in atonal and electronic music, the traditional eighteenth-century forms and tonality were embraced by an influential group of composers—the neoclassicists.

Experimentation and innovation

Harmony in music began to disintegrate in reaction to the lush sounds of the chromatic music cultivated by Wagner from 1865 into the 1880s. Using a whole-tone scale of five tones, free treatment of rhythm, and subtle dynamics (loudness and softness), Claude Debussy (1862–1918) turned away from Wagner when he composed the atonal and impressionistic *Pelleas and Melisande* (1902). Perhaps the first truly twentieth-century composer, Debussy prefigured the developments in atonality that would soon occur in Vienna. The Vienna school headed by Arnold Schoenberg (1874–1951) [4] and his pupils Anton Webern (1883–1951) and Alban Berg (1885–1935) [9] moved directly to the exploration of sounds in a more abstract sense.

The true pioneer of the post-Romantic era, Schoenberg was committed to the "emancipation of dissonance." In 1912 he produced the classic *Sprechstimme* (speech-melody) work *Pierrot Lunaire* for five musicians and a reciter who loops and slides through the poems rather than sings; Stravinsky called this composition "the mind and solar plexus of early twentieth-century music." Schoenberg then recognized the logical need for new organizing principles, and he eventually refined a 12-note method of composition in which the 12 notes of the chromatic scale are arranged in rows or series (hence "serial music") that replace traditional keys and harmony.

Continuation of traditional music

Against the extremes of the atonal experimentalists, the Franco-Russian school of neoclassicists dominated by Igor Stravinsky (1882–1971) [2] and also including Richard Strauss, Paul Hindemith, Dimitri Shostakovich, Serge Prokofiev, Aaron Copland, Edward Elgar, Zoltan Kodály, Maurice Ravel, and the French group *Les Six* (Poulenc, Milhaud, Honegger, Durey, Tailleferre, and Auric) continued in a more traditional vein in reaction to nineteenth-century Romanticism. Using eighteenth-century musical forms and the tonality of the seven-note scale, the group also drew from ethnic folk tunes, jazz, and polytonal techniques.

The neoclassicist influence has been particularly strong in the United States with such composers as Samuel Barber and Walter Piston.

Developing along with the Franco-Prussian school was a group of individualists not entirely bound to classic tonality. In America, Charles Ives (1874–1954) produced an original corpus of individualistic and entirely American music. His masterpiece is his *Third Symphony*, completed in 1917 but not performed until 1947. In France, Erik Satie (1866–1925)

CONNECTIONS

See also
1246 Music: the Romantic period
1324 The twenties and the Depression
1358 The United States: postwar development
1428 The American experience: music
1278 The United States: Reconstruction to World War I

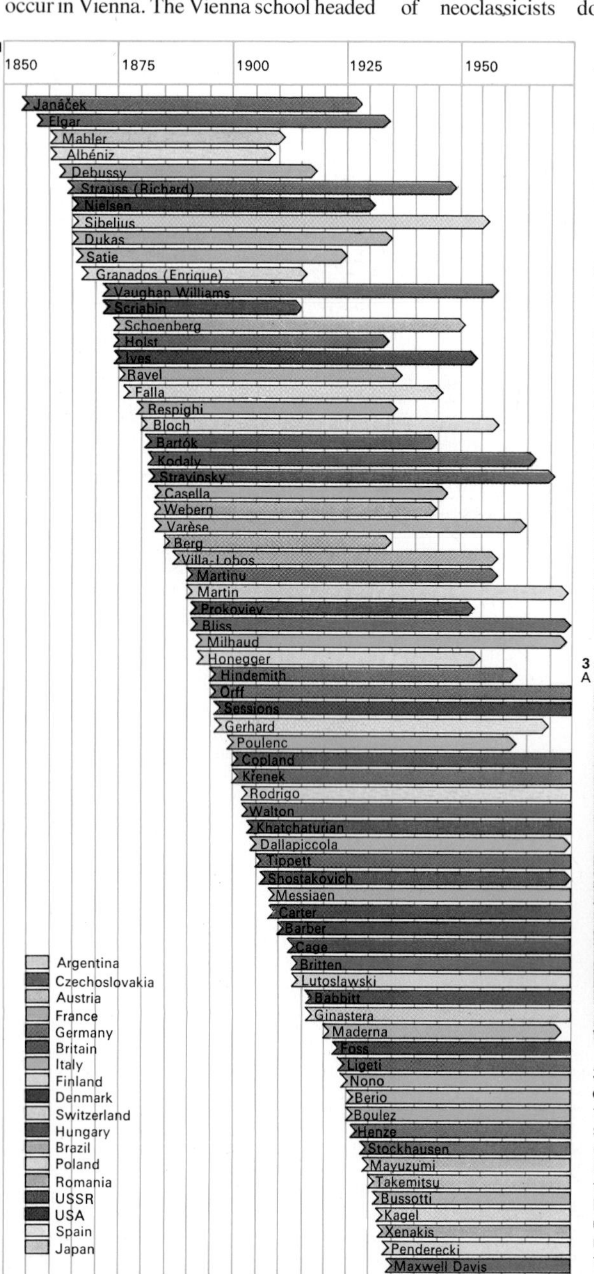

1850
1875
1900
1925
1950
Janáček
Elgar
Mahler
Albéniz
Debussy
Strauss (Richard)
Nielsen
Sibelius
Dukas
Satie
Granados (Enrique)
Vaughan Williams
Scriabin
Schoenberg
Holst
Ives
Ravel
Falla
Respighi
Bloch
Bartók
Kodaly
Stravinsky
Casella
Webern
Varèse
Berg
Villa-Lobos
Martinu
Martin
Prokoviev
Bliss
Milhaud
Honegger
Hindemith
Orff
Sessions
Gerhard
Poulenc
Copland
Krenek
Rodrigo
Walton
Khatchaturian
Dallapiccola
Tippett
Shostakovich
Messiaen
Carter
Barber
Cage
Britten
Lutoslawski
Babbitt
Ginastera
Maderna
Foss
Ligeti
Nono
Berio
Boulez
Henze
Stockhausen
Mayuzumi
Takemitsu
Bussotti
Kagel
Xenakis
Penderecki
Maxwell Davis
Argentina
Czechoslovakia
Austria
France
Germany
Britain
Italy
Finland
Denmark
Switzerland
Hungary
Brazil
Poland
Romania
USSR
USA
Spain
Japan

1 These 70 important composers from the rich, diverse 20th-century world of Western classical music represent many styles. Symphonists in traditions established in the 19th century—Sibelius, Shostakovich, Nielsen, or Vaughan Williams—are contemporary with the 12-note composition school of Schoenberg, Berg, and Webern. Electronic music composers—Stockhausen, Milton Babbitt, or Xenakis—contrast with those rooted in a more traditional nationalism like Casella, Falla, or Khatchaturian. In recent years an international "modern" style that depends on abstract notions of sound has been recognized.

2

1750 1775 1800 1825 1850 1875 1900 1925 1950

Russian | Neo-Classical | Serial

Russian influences
Teacher
Other early influences
Serial influences

Stravinsky
Glinka
Borodin
Mussorgsky
Tchaikovsky
Rimsky-Korsakov
Wagner
Debussy
Glazunov
Scriabin
Schoenberg
Webern
Berg

2 Stravinsky is one of the giants of 20th-century music, largely because his work shows an outstanding originality through his changes of style. The diagram shows which of his predecessors and contemporaries most influenced him and the stages through which he moved. Born in Russia he transformed his native harmony and rhythms in his early scores, especially for the Ballets Russes in Paris; after World War I a restrained neoclassical quality informed his works; and from the 1950s until his death he found "serial" music a dynamic inspiration, as in his *Canticum sacrum* (1956).

3 A

B

3 The impact of recording in general on the appreciation and spread of music this century has been incalculable. From the first commercially successful 3-minute shellac disks made by the Italian tenor Enrico Caruso (in 1903 he received the first-ever gold disk for one million records sold of the aria "Vesti la giubba" from Leoncavallo's *Pagliacci*) to the 4-channel quadrophonic and video reproduction of the 1970s, a vast audience outside the concert hall has been given easy contact with every kind of music and performance through records and tapes. The illustration shows old and new styles of recording: Poland's noted pianist and prime minister (1918–20) Ignace Paderewski (1860–1941) making an acoustic recording at his home in Switzerland in 1911, the sound being cut directly onto a wax disk [A]; and the New Philharmonia Orchestra and chorus under Raymond Leppard recording on magnetic tapes [B].

composed witty, eccentric pieces including his influential *Parade* (1911) using American jazz forms, sirens, and airplane motors. The Russian mystic composer Alexander Scriabin (1872–1915) combined colored lights and free tonality in his fifth symphony *Prometheus: Poem of Fire* (1910).

A group of nationalist composers used traditional forms in composing native compositions. Among these is the Romanticist Jean Sibelius (1865–1957), who put Finnish nationalism into musical form in tone poems like *Finlandia* (1899) as well as in his monumental symphonies. Béla Barók (1881–1945) [5] a Hungarian, collected folk tunes and composed a vividly personal music of strong rhythms and sophisticated modal elements. Ralph Vaughn Williams (Britain) and Manuel de Falla (Spain) also composed in this idiom.

Electronic Music

Another form of experimental music developed in reaction to both 12-tone and traditional music—electronic music. Pioneered by Edgard Varèse (1885–1965), a Frenchman, in the 1920s, this form repudiated the past entirely. There was no pitch, only sound and rhythm; music was considered as "organized sound."

From 1945 experimental music focused even more on the sounds in themselves and the treatment of durations, dynamics, rests, and colors. The piano piece *Mode de valeurs et d'intensites* (1949) by Olivier Messiaen (1908–) [6] became a key work in the evolution of Pierre Boulez (1925–) and Karlheinz Stockhausen (1928–) [Key], whose work gained specific direction from Pierre Schaeffer's Paris radio studio where from 1948 *musique concrete* (using tape recorders and natural sounds) was being advanced [11]. Soon, Stockhausen composed the pioneering *Electronic Study I* (1953), the first piece composed wholly from electronic pure sine waves. Experiments continued in the integration of "theater of the absurd" methods and chance in music into the creation and performance of music by John Cage [10] and in new means of determining the sounds in music by mathematics and computer.

KEY

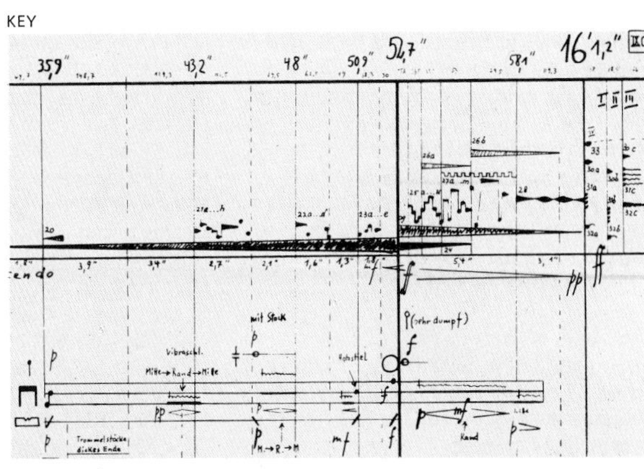

New notation has been a major innovation in music this century. Shown here is a page from the score of Karlheinz Stockhausen's *Kontakte* ("Contacts") for electronic sounds, piano, and percussion (1960). The electronic sounds that issue from loudspeakers (indicated by Roman numerals I to IV) in the four corners of a hall, are described graphically above the thick line, while the live sounds made by the two performers are represented below. Time in seconds is given at the top to enable the players to coordinate precisely with the tape. The percussion instruments are shown by symbols. To encompass the variety of elements, actions, and sounds required, composers also use graphs and drawings.

4

4 Arnold Schoenberg has been as much celebrated in 20th-century music for the dominating influence of his 12-tone method of composition as for his own works. Yet his music, from the early Brahms and Wagner-influenced pieces like *Transfigured Night* (1899) to the late (1949) *Phantasy for Violin* with piano accompaniment, reveals a striking, adventurous imagination not confined by a rigid method.

5

5 Béla Bartók is the most strikingly successful of the modern composers who found folk-music a vivid source of inspiration. Professor of piano at Budapest Academy for nearly 30 years, he began in 1905 to transcribe Hungarian folk songs on field trips with his friend, the composer Kodály. By the end of his life he had noted and recorded about 8,000 tunes, and his music drew imaginatively from their style.

6

6 Oliver Messiaen has been among the most durable, imaginative, and individually poetic French composers of the 20th century since Debussy. From 1931 organist at the Church of the Trinity in Paris, and a teacher at the Paris Conservatory since 1942, he has written music characterized by unusual rhythmic series and influenced by oriental melody and plain chant, birdsong and religious themes.

7

7 Benjamin Britten (1913–76) was for many years the central figure in the development of 20th-century British music. Turning from full Romantic expression, he integrated new sounds and classical techniques (influenced at first by Stravinsky and Gustav Mahler) into the English choral and vocal tradition, always with a concern for directness of expression and melodic clarity in his music.

8

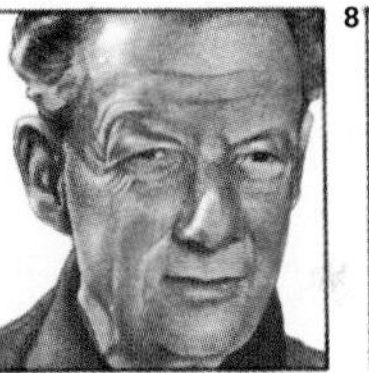

8 Hans Werner Henze (1926–), generally recognized as one of the most outstanding of the younger generation of composers, studied and worked in his native Germany before turning to composition full time. He has produced opera, ballet, symphonic works, chamber music, and music for voices, all of which demonstrate his chief virtue: the constant assimilation of contemporary styles in an original way.

9

9 Alban Berg and Anton Webern were Schoenberg's two most brilliant pupils. Each demonstrated and developed the influence of Schoenberg's ideas and method in his own way, although all three were collectively seen as the Viennese school of early 20th-century composition and were close friends. Webern's very precise music was to have the greater influence later in the century.

10

10 John Cage (1912–) has been a fearless and prolific American explorer of sounds and silences. His "absurd" experiments have had a stimulating influence on avant-garde painting, theater, and multi-media happenings. From early performances (1938) on prepared piano (nuts, bolts, rubbers, etc., between the strings) he has prescribed chance music using several radios, silence—his *4'33"* for silent player(s)—and even funny stories to a piano background.

11

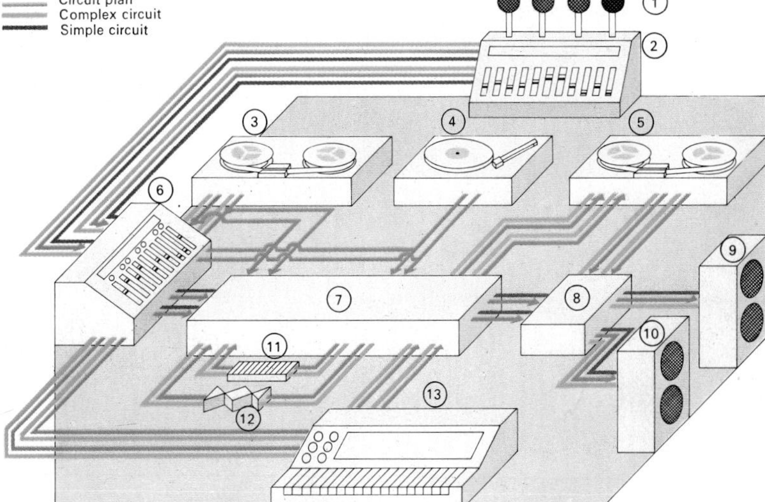

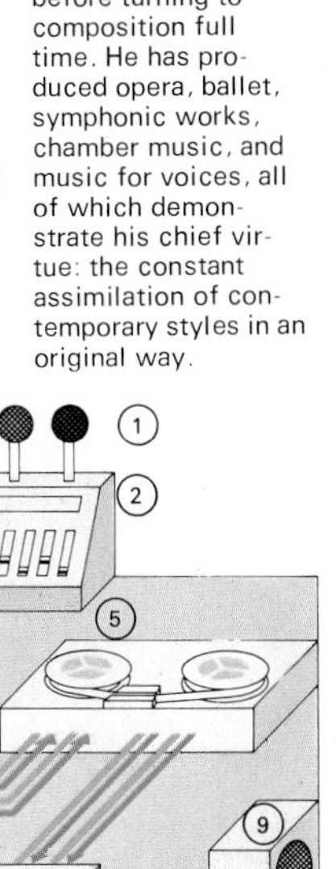

Circuit plan
Complex circuit
Simple circuit
1
2
3
4
5
6
7
8
9
10
11
12
13

11 A small electronic music composition studio, based on a synthesizer [13] is shown here. The synthesizer's waves, together with signals from microphones and mixer [1, 2], tape decks [3, 5], and record player [4] are modified by the use of mixers [6], filters [11], and reverberation units [12]. All outputs go to a patch-board [7] and then through amplifier [8] and speakers [9, 10] as sounds.

Jazz and pop

Western popular music during the twentieth century has been dominated by the United States. Black artists have played a central role, with the folk music of the southern slaves [2] transformed into a new style: jazz. The new sound, a mixture of European and African traditions, was rhythmic, emotional, and vital; it could be played by a full band, a small band, or by a soloist. Above all, it could be danced to.

The stages of jazz

In the period from 1890 to 1917, a new kind of music, known as ragtime, emerged from St Louis, with Scott Joplin (1868–1917) as its principal exponent. Then came a second independent jazz style, the classic blues, sung by such entertainers as Ma Rainey, Bessie Smith [Key], and Billie Holiday.

Around 1910, the syncopation of ragtime and the vocal-type melody of blues combined to form the base from which jazz developed in the following decade. Influential transitional figures of this period were Jelly Roll Morton (1885–1941), and W. C. Handy (1873–1958). New Orleans was the center of jazz during this period, with at least 30 bands playing improvised pieces developed from marches and dirges.

The "jazz age" 1920s produced the symphonic, or sweet, jazz of Paul Whiteman and George Gershwin, and also the hot jazz (with subtle improvisation solos, scat singing, and jam sessions) of Louis Armstrong [3] and Bix Beiderbecke that later led to the swing music of the 1930s.

Swing was big-band music and used large brass sections to provide a tidal wave of sound. Such bandleaders as Benny Goodman (1909–), the Dorsey Brothers, and Glenn Miller (1904–44) achieved a popularity as great as the important black big-band leaders Duke Ellington (1899–1974) [4] and Count Basie (1904–). During the same period, radio, the movies, and the phonograph record were creating a vast audience for commercial popular music, the center of which (known as Tin Pan Alley) was New York. The most popular singers of this kind of pop music were Bing Crosby (1904–) and Frank Sinatra (1915–).

The development of the blues

Meanwhile, a new, cooler jazz style was emerging. One result, in the 1940s, was be-bop or, simply, bop, a musically sophisticated product of such young black musicians as trumpeter Dizzy Gillespie (1917–) and saxophonist Charlie "Bird" Parker (1920–55) [5]. The blues had also been evolving. The "12-bar" style was not only the basis for much early New Orleans band music, but also was used by guitar soloists as the basis for powerful folk blues or country blues.

As blacks moved to the north, their blues changed with the new environments. Rhythm and blues, a more commercial style, emerged. It was played on electric guitars with bass and drum backing, and the sound was now harder and more driving. The white equivalent of rhythm and blues was coming out of Nashville, Tennessee. There was also a handful of extraordinary itinerant white folk singers, such as Woody Guthrie (1912–67), who took interest in what the black soloists (such as Huddie "Leadbelly" Ledbetter) were doing.

CONNECTIONS

See Also
1246 Music: the Romanti[c] period
1256 Opera in the 19th a[nd] 20th centuries
1368 Classical and moder[n] ballet
1362 Hollywood
1428 The American expe[ri]ence: music
1430 The American exper[i]ence: dance

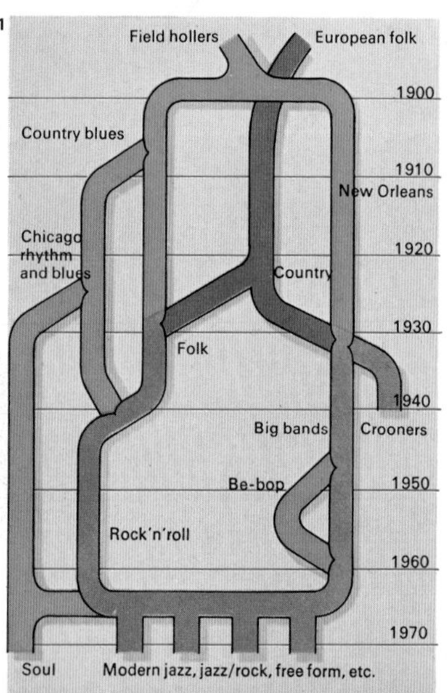

Field hollers
European folk
1900
Country blues
1910
New Orleans
Chicago rhythm and blues
1920
Country
1930
Folk
1940
Big bands
Crooners
Be-bop
1950
Rock'n'roll
1960
1970
Soul
Modern jazz, jazz/rock, free form, etc.

1 The development of jazz and pop has been the result of the interaction of two musical forces: black music taken by the African slaves to America and white, originally European, folk-music. The United States was the cultural melting pot as black music developed through blues into the various jazz styles and then mixed with the urban rhythm and blues to produce rock. By the 1970s it was a free-for-all.

2 The African slaves brought with them songs that had rhythmic complexity and used certain musical patterns. The most characteristic was the "call and response" pattern. In its most primitive form it could be found in functional songs—work songs and "field hollers." Groups working on the plantations eased the work with repetitive songs in which the lead singer was echoed by a chorus reply.

3 Louis "Satchmo" Armstrong (1900–71) [left, foreground] was born in New Orleans and learned to play the cornet at reform school. Later he met the famed King Oliver (1885–1938), who became his teacher. In 1927 he formed his own band. An influential jazz performer, he was the best known exponent of "hot" jazz, scat-singing, improvisation, and virtuoso solos.

4 Duke Ellington (1899–1974) [left], perhaps the most important single talent jazz has produced, was a composer, songwriter, arranger, and pianist. The most masterful exponent of big-band jazz, he developed a unique style by working on the individual sounds of the first-rate instrumentalists in his band. He gave the blues its finest orchestral form, and wrote "composed jazz" that still left room for improvisation. The subtlety of his orchestration was unique.

5 Charlie Parker was as influential in the 1940s and 1950s as Armstrong had been earlier. Born in the slums of Kansas City, he played in big bands, then rebelled against their repetitive styles to become the leading revolutionary of bop. His alto sax playing was complex and tortured, but for all his experimentation his roots were in early blues. An unhappy vagabond and drug addict, he has been called the "Rimbaud of modern jazz."

By the 1950s the big-band jazz era had passed. The new "modern" jazz, or progressive jazz, with complex harmonic forms was played by small groups headed by Dave Brubeck, Dizzy Gillespie, Charlie Parker, Miles Davis, Gerry Mulligan, and Thelonius Monk; a more classical form was pursued by the Modern Jazz Quartet. More experimental jazz was being played by Ornette Colman and Charlie Mingus.

The coming of rock and roll

The emergent postwar youth culture mixed the smoother white country music styles with the energy and aggression of rhythm and blues and the commerciality of straight pop music. In 1954, the white singer Bill Haley recorded "Shake, Rattle, and Roll" with an exaggerated black-influenced beat. Rock and roll was born, and Elvis Presley [7] was its most popular vocalist.

By the late 1950s, folk singing was resurrected by such singers as Joan Baez. New material, often in protest against social or political conditions, was written by Bob Dylan (1941–) [9].

Contemporary rock music

The rock and roll of the 1950s was transformed in the 1960s by the influence of the Beatles [8]. That group progressed from simple clever songs like "Hard Day's Night" to the musical and electronic complexities of their "Sergeant Pepper" album. Developing in a similar vein were the Rolling Stones, headed by Mick Jagger. The psychedelia of the drug culture were reproduced through elaborate lighting and lengthy instrumentals by the Grateful Dead and the Jefferson Airplane (later Jefferson Starship), while a more clean-cut rock was produced by the Beach Boys. The blues was combined with rock in the singing of Janis Joplin and the guitar improvisitions of Jimi Hendrix and Eric Clapton.

During the 1970s, many established groups, particularly the Rolling Stones, continued to dominate rock. Theatrical stage effects and electronics were featured [10] and resulted in such "glitter rock" groups as David Bowie and Kiss and groups, particularly Alice Cooper, featuring bizarre and morbid stage effects.

KEY

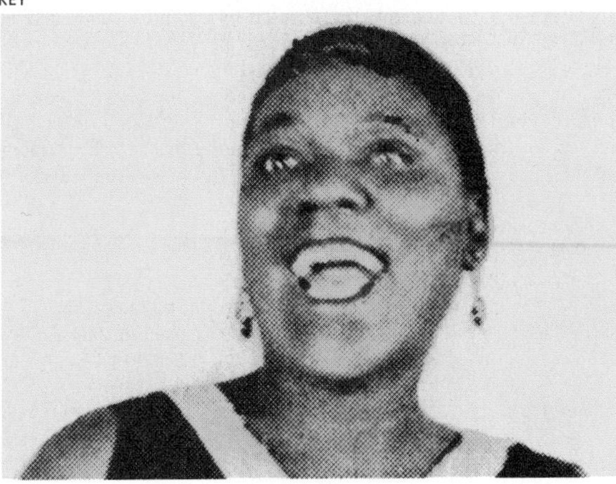

Bessie Smith (*c.* 1898–1937), one of the greatest jazz-blues singers of all time, was born into poverty in Chattanooga, Tennessee. At the age of 11 she began touring the southern states with the Rabbit's Foot Minstrel Show, where she was greatly influenced by Ma Rainey. Bessie was extraordinarily popular during the 1920s, after which the taste for the blues began to wane. Her records continued to sell, however. A large, handsome, lonely woman, she sang about the transitory nature of men, money, and drink.

6

6 Jimmie Rodgers (1897–1933), an important country singer and guitarist, was the first man to be installed in Nashville's Country Music Hall of Fame. The son of a Mississippi railroadman, he himself worked on the railroad as a flagman, brakeman, and baggage man, but left because of ill health and became an entertainer. He wrote his own songs, which were influenced by blues.

7 Elvis Presley was born in 1935 in East Tupelo, Mississippi and moved to Memphis, becoming a movie usher after leaving high school. He came to the attention of a local record company and became a show business phenomenon by being the first white artist to mix the wildness of black rhythm and blues with country music. He has survived because of his mastery of vocal technique.

7

8

THE
BEATLES

8 The Beatles were for eight years—from 1962 to 1970—the most successful group in the history of popular music. From playing in Hamburg and Liverpool clubs they became a legend, transforming rock and roll with their fine melodies and harmonies. They had a truly progressive and experimental attitude to songwriting and record production that developed the more successful they became.

9

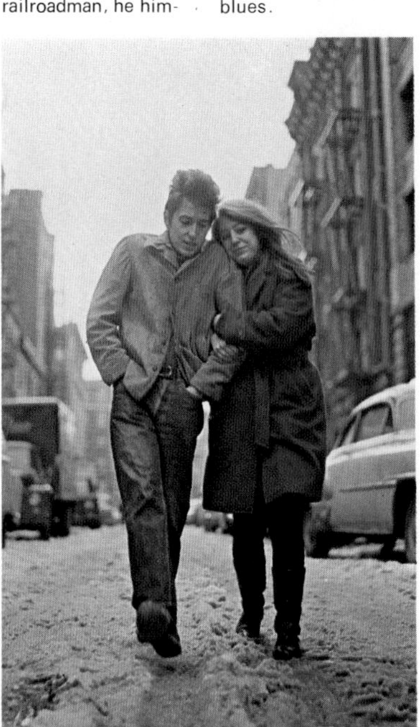

9 Bob Dylan was the leader of the "folk-rock" wave that swept America and Great Britain during the 1960s. His singing was first influenced by Woody Guthrie, in whose style he wrote protest classics such as "Blowin' in the Wind." He later moved to amplified blues styles and has remained a remarkable lyricist.

10 Pink Floyd was originally a London rhythm and blues band, but it soon switched to mixed-media experiments and the use of elaborate light shows. By the late 1960s it was the leading British "underground" band. It has pioneered lengthy rock symphonic works using masses of electronic equipment.

10

Classical and modern ballet

The Romantic movement, represented by the writings of Byron and the paintings of Delacroix, soon spread to ballet. Dancers abandoned masks and began to act the emotions required in the ballet, thereby reducing the distinction between dance and mime.

The first romantic ballets

La Sylphide, the first romantic ballet, was presented in 1832 with choreography by Filippo Taglioni, created for his daughter, Marie Taglioni (1804–84) [2], the dancer most closely associated with the Romantic ballet. *La Sylphide* was the first of many ballets featuring strange and mysterious creatures. Wilis, the spirits of girls who die before their wedding day, appeared in *Giselle* (1841), the romantic masterpiece.

By about 1850 romantic ballet became merely a vehicle for the ballerina's virtuosity and fell into decline. Dancers, choreographers, and musicians turned to Russia, its state ballet school founded in 1735, its artistic tradition kept alive by men such as Marius Petipa (1819–1910), a Frenchman whose long career as both dancer and choreographer was spent in Russia. He created numerous ballets, many in four or five acts. His main objective was to show off the ballerina to the best advantage, using the corps de ballet usually as a mere decorative background. One act was often given over to a series of unrelated dances known as divertissements, highlighted by the pas de deux danced by the two principals.

The importance of Russia

The Sleeping Beauty [3], generally considered to be Petipa's masterwork, was given its first performance at St Petersburg in 1890 with an inspired score by Tchaikovsky. When Petipa fell sick, Lev Ivanov, his assistant ballet master, took over the choreography of *The Nutcracker* and with Petipa created *Swan Lake.*

The elderly Petipa was quick to appreciate the early work of Michel Fokine (1880–1942) [4]. Fokine, however, rebelled against many of the traditions of the Petipa ballets. He abolished the antiquated mime and replaced the classical ballet skirts (tutus) with costumes appropriate to the period in which the ballet was set. So it was not surprising that the impresario Sergei Diaghilev (1872–1929) chose this young rebel to be his ballet master and choreographer when he took the Russian Ballet to Western Europe.

The influence of Diaghilev

During the first season of Russian opera and ballet presented by Diaghilev in Paris in 1909, the Fokine works included *Les Sylphides,* with music by Chopin, and *Prince Igor* (music by Borodin). The company was a tremendous success, and Tamara Karsavina (1885–), Anna Pavlova (1881–1931) and Vaslav Nijinsky (1890–1950) [Key] became famous overnight. Four years later Diaghilev left the Russian Imperial Theaters and formed the Ballets Russes.

Diaghilev felt that ballet was part of a complex spectacle made up of literature, painting, music, and choreography, and he tried to gather together all these elements in the ballets created by his successive choreographers: Fokine, Nijinsky,

CONNECTIONS

See also
1194 Early ballet
1430 The American experience: dance
1246 Music: the Romantic period
1364 Twentieth century music—tradition and experimentation
1296 Cubism and Futurism

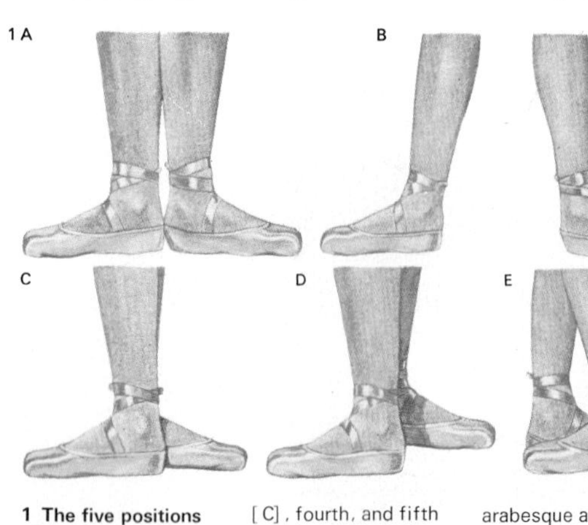

1 A
B
C
D
E

1 The five positions of the feet are the starting points for all ballet steps. In the first position [A], the heels touch; in the second [B] and the fourth [D] the feet are 12in (30cm) apart; in the third [C], fourth, and fifth positions [E] the feet are parallel. Turnout is where the legs are rotated outward from the hips. The arm movements are known as ports de bras. The two most familiar poses are the arabesque and the attitude. Steps can be classified conveniently as either jumps (the jeté), beats (the entrechat) or turns (the pirouette, a full turn on one foot).

2 Marie Taglioni in La Sylphide, the first romantic ballet, danced the part of the sylphide (fairylike being) who falls in love with James, a Scotsman. Taglioni wore a bodice that left the shoulders bare, a mid-calf-length muslin skirt, tights, and pink satin point shoes, and this has become the accepted costume for the romantic ballerina. *La Sylphide,* with different music by Lvenskjold and new choreography by August Bournonville, has been in the repertory of the Royal Danish Ballet since 1836. The leading roles in the ballet are now most closely associated with Margarethe Schanne and Erik Bruhn.

3 The Sleeping Beauty was chosen by the Royal Ballet—at that time the Sadler's Wells Ballet—to reopen the Royal Opera House, Covent Garden, London, after World War II. Margot Fonteyn and Robert Helpmann (1909–), shown here, dance in the last act, sometimes given on its own as *Aurora's Wedding.* Petipa's masterpiece (1890) is the cornerstone of the Royal Ballet repertory. Also frequently performed by the company are works by British choreographers including Kenneth MacMillan's *Manon* and the non-dramatic ballets *Symphonic Variations* (1946) and *La Fille Mal Gardée* (1960) of Frederick Ashton.

Leonide Massine (1896–), Bronislava Nijinska (1891–1972), George Balanchine (1904–), and Serge Lifar (1905–). When he died in 1929 his company disbanded and dispersed, spreading his ideas throughout the Western world. Marie Rambert (1898–) went to London and formed what became the Ballet Rambert, and Ninette de Valois (1898–) formed the company that today is known as the Royal Ballet. Serge Lifar became dancer, ballet master, and choreographer at the Paris Opéra. George Balanchine [6] went to the United States and became director and choreographer of New York City Ballet.

Other companies had a strong tradition of their own. The Royal Danish Ballet in Copenhagen continued to train dancers in the style of August Bournonville (1805–79). The Bolshoi Ballet in Moscow and the Kirov (formerly the Maryinsky) Ballet in Leningrad still present their post-revolutionary works with Soviet themes.

In addition to the traditional ballet of the twentieth century (Ashton [3], Robbins [6]), a freer style also developed—modern dance. Foreshadowed by the mechanical, discontinuous dance styles in the Diaghilev-produced *Petrouchka* (1911) and *Le Sacre du Printemps* (1913), modern dance was pioneered in Europe and America by Isadora Duncan (1878–1927), Ruth St. Denis (1877–1968), and Ted Shawn (1891–1972). Emphasis was on expressionistic, free movement and on ensemble rather than solo dancing. A Denishawn student, Martha Graham (1893–) raised modern dance to an even higher level. Forming her first company in 1926, she created over 150 works featuring dramatic costumes and scenery and sharp, percussive dance movements. Current modern dance groups include those that emphasize ballet training (Alvin Ailey, José Limon) and Graham-trained choreographers who stress dance in any setting (Merce Cunningham, Alwin Nikolais, Paul Taylor). In the 1970s there were some collaborations between classical ballet and modern dance—in 1975 both Rudolph Nureyev and Margot Fonteyn appeared in *Lucifer*, created for them by Martha Graham.

KEY

Vaslav Nijinsky was among the most accomplished male dancers of this century. Fokine created several ballets for him, including *Scheherazade*, but Nijinsky also created several for himself. His performance, shown here, in his own *L'Apres-midi d'un faune* (1912) caused a scandal, and there was a riot at the premiere of his *Le Sacre du Printemps* in 1913. Mental illness ended his eight-year career.

4

4 Michael Fokine's Scheherazade (1910) had Ida Rubinstein as the shah's favorite wife and Vaslav Nijinsky as her slave. This was one of several Oriental ballets given by Diaghilev. Léon Bakst's brilliantly colored sets had a great influence on the fashion and interior design of the period.

5

5 Martha Graham, seen here in her ballet *Hèrodiade* produced in 1944, has created an entirely original style of dancing. The Graham dancer moves according to principles of contraction and release, producing sharp rather than lyrical movements, and concentrates movement on or near the floor.

6

6 George Balanchine, artistic director of the New York City Ballet, has created numerous ballets for it since 1948. His company and the American Ballet Theatre are the two foremost classical companies in the United States. Balanchine's collaboration with Igor Stravinsky produced *Apollo Musagetes* (1928), choreographed for Diaghilev, and *Agon* (1957). *Agon* (shown here) is a plotless one-act ballet danced in black and white practice costume to a 12-note musical score. The American Ballet Theater, directed by Lucia Chase and Oliver Smith, has produced such notable works as Jerome Robbins's *Fancy Free* (1944) and *Les Noces* (1965) and Anthony Tudor's *Pillar of Fire* (1942).

7

7 Margot Fonteyn and Rudolf Nureyev, the defected Russian dancer, became one of ballet's most exciting partnerships. *Marquerite and Armand* (shown here) was created especially for them by Frederick Ashton. It was Ashton's collaboration with Fonteyn during the formative years of the Royal Ballet that produced such masterworks as *Ondine* and *Symphonic Variations*. Nureyev's partnership with Fonteyn resulted in a wonderful pas de deux in *Le Corsaire* and a memorable *Giselle*. He not only dances in a wide range of ballets and styles but also rechoreographed several of the classics, including a sumptuous *Sleeping Beauty*.

Cinema as art

It is as hard to find out what makes a movie "art" as it is to say what makes some music, painting, or writing special and immortal. Fine acting, good stories, beautiful pictures, and interesting ideas—are all artistic elements that have at one time or another been included in the movies. But it is the way all of the different parts of a film are brought together that makes for "cinema," the art of the film. For this reason the cinema is often called a director's art, since it is usually the director who has the responsibility of bringing the film together.

A dream of reality

Movies seem like a dream of reality. The camera faithfully records what is placed in front of it but at the same time makes it unreal. The film's illusion of reality has been exploited by movie makers since the Lumière brothers found that audiences jumped out of their seats when a locomotive seemed to be coming toward them when motion pictures were first shown in 1895.

When Georges Méliès and other film pioneers used movies to create illusions as well as to record them, the cinema had arrived. By 1909, D. W. Griffith (1875–1948) had used the medium to unite two different strands of action thematically in *A Corner in Wheat*. Only the film's theme of the exploitation of farmers and the poor gives meaning and coherence to its separate shots of worn-out land, bread lines, and upper-class revelry [Key].

Audiences sometimes mistake personal visions for documents of reality. In *Nanook of the North* (1922) [1] and other films, Robert Flaherty (1884–1951) filmed his own ideas of how the Eskimo and other traditional cultures once had been, not what he actually found among them. The 3½-hour *Olympiad* [3] made in 1936–38 under the supervision of the Nazis is an astounding record of the games, a deliberate attempt to evoke the "superiority" of Adolf Hitler's Germany, and one of the most beautiful works the cinema has produced.

Personal expression

From the time of Méliès, film makers have made the medium a vehicle of personal expression. Some, like Erich von Stroheim (1885–1957), whose most uncompromising film, *Greed* (1923–25) [2], was cut to a fraction of its original length, could not be accommodated in the mass entertainment industry. Von Stroheim directed no pictures after 1932, but his influence is still felt. An obsessive concern with what the camera shows was von Stroheim's trademark and became characteristic of many of the medium's greatest directors, such as Jean Renoir (1894–) in *A Day in the Country* [4], Orson Welles (1915–), and the Italian director Michelangelo Antonioni (1912–) [9].

Others followed Griffith's lead and began to break with the usual story pattern. Soviet directors and surrealists made exciting and disturbing movies in which the story took second place to political themes or fantastic dream images. In these films one shot was linked to another not because of an action that was continued from shot to shot, but because of ideas that the film maker wanted the audience to relate to one another.

CONNECTIONS

See also
1362 Hollywood
1316 Origins of film
1372 Recent trends in the visual arts

1 Eskimo life with its stark daily battle for survival inspired a film that is generally regarded as the starting point of the modern documentary, *Nanook of the North*. Its director, Robert Flaherty, wanted to show the lives of people in the grip of severe elements, and he had his Eskimo hero recreate old ways of hunting in order to do so. During the 1930s in Britain the documentary movement produced short films that dealt with the ways in which people and institutions work together. *Cinéma vérité* is the name given to modern documentaries that seem like direct records of reality, but represent reality as seen by the producers.

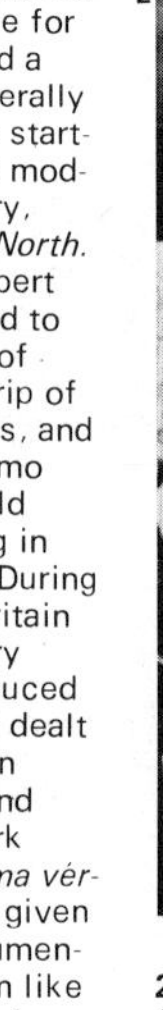

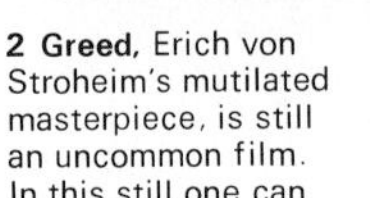

2 Greed, Erich von Stroheim's mutilated masterpiece, is still an uncommon film. In this still one can see much of what it was about: the bride's sly glance, the curly-topped groom's oxlike awkwardness, the intrusion of the man in the striped suit (who will destroy their happiness)—above all, the way the tawdry setting engulfs everyone and the repellent greed of all the participants.

3 Olympiad, made by Leni Riefenstahl (1902–) for the Nazi regime in Germany, is a film of extraordinary beauty. The director's creative editing produced not only a hymn to the human body in motion but also a subtle propaganda film for the Nazi ideals of a strong and heroic elite to lead the masses. Riefenstahl's cooperation with Hitler made her a controversial figure.

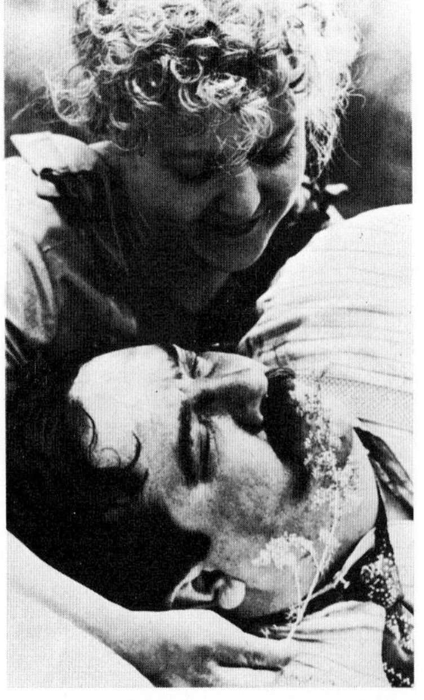

4 Lyrical photography and warm observation of ordinary people distinguish *A Day in the Country*, Jean Renoir's 1936 short film, based on a story by Guy de Maupassant. Renoir, son of the Impressionist painter, has a place among the greatest film artists because of his deceptively naturalistic work. Reacting against the idea that the art of film was in editing, he concentrated on what was shown in the shot.

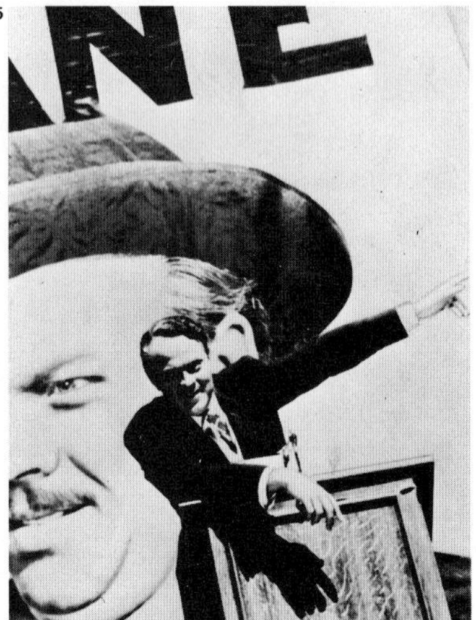

5 Orson Welles starred in his own film, *Citizen Kane*, a devastating study of a business tycoon who bore some resemblance to the publisher William Randolph Hearst. Dispensing with the usual type of story, Welles' movie built up its plot by flashbacks and snatches of key events, creating a kind of film kaleidoscope. He brought together the von Stroheim and Soviet traditions along with some innovations of his own.

Postwar cinema

Orson Welles' *Citizen Kane* (1941) [5] combined the story film with the film of ideas in the most personal movie that the commercial film industry had produced, but immediately following World War II there was little sympathy for personal excess. Instead, the dominant cinematic trend was a return to simple documentary style.

Neo-realism, as this style was called, had its beginnings in Italy with such directors as Roberto Rossellini (1906–) and Vittorio De Sica (1901–74). Neo-realist films had the look of documentaries and were concerned with the social problems of everyday people [6]. Yet the Italian directors managed to find ways of imposing personal points of view on this documentary style. Federico Fellini (1920–) and Luchino Visconti (1906–76) are among the film artists with roots in neo-realism.

In the 1950s the Japanese films of Akira Kurosawa (1910–) [7], Kenji Mizuguchi, and Yasujiro Ozu (1903–1963) displayed a cinema quite different from that of the West. But Japan was only the first of many nations to unveil exciting movies. In this sense, the movies are truly an international art form.

The cinema made its next important stylistic shift in France during the 1960s. Here the work of the New Wave directors combined personal cinema with a "realistic" point of view. At times, New Wave movies had a casual, improvised air; as in the films of Jean-Luc Godard (1930–); but other directors, like François Truffault (1932–) and Alain Resnais (1922–), produced works of studied deliberateness. The New Wave directors were "writing with the camera," that is, using the properties of film as an author uses the properties of language.

Today film artists from Czechoslovakia, Hungary, Brazil, Cuba, Senegal, and Australia make movies in the vivid "camera writing" style. The movies are used for personal expression, even by artists from outside the cinema, such as author Norman Mailer and artist Andy Warhol, each of whom has been responsible for, and appeared in, several films [10].

KEY

Owing to the
advance in the
price of flour
the usual 5cts loaf
will be 10 cts

The use of the cinema as language is apparent in D. W. Griffith's *A Corner in Wheat*, where the rural poor [left] and the urban rich [right] are brought together in separate shots linked not by action or characters but by the idea of economic exploitation that the film illustrates. The meaning of a movie shot comes more from how it relates to the other shots in the movie than from how it appears by itself, just as words are defined by their context.

6

6 Neo-realism gained world acclaim with the release of *Open City* in 1945. In this and later films, Roberto Rossellini used a mixture of trained and untrained actors, fiction and fact. The neo-realists, led by writer Cesare Zavatini, wanted to discard falsehood by taking the camera into the streets and fields to film actual situations that would express the experience of living in a postwar world. Few neo-realist films lived up to these ideals, but many were powerful cinema based on the impact of a documentary visual style and carefully crafted stories of ordinary people in harsh circumstances.

7 Akira Kurosawa's *Rashomon* established a western reputation for Japanese film when it won the Grand Prix at Venice in 1951. The Japanese film tradition is one of the richest in the world.

7

8 In The Seventh Seal (1957), the black-draped figure of Death was one of many powerful images used by the Swedish director Ingmar Bergman to explore the meaning of human life. Bergman set this and other films in medieval Europe, making heavy use of symbolism and allegory and drawing intense contrasts between happiness and suffering. He also made perceptive studies of contemporary life and particularly of marital relationships. Although enigmatic and oppressive, his films have won a worldwide audience.

8

9

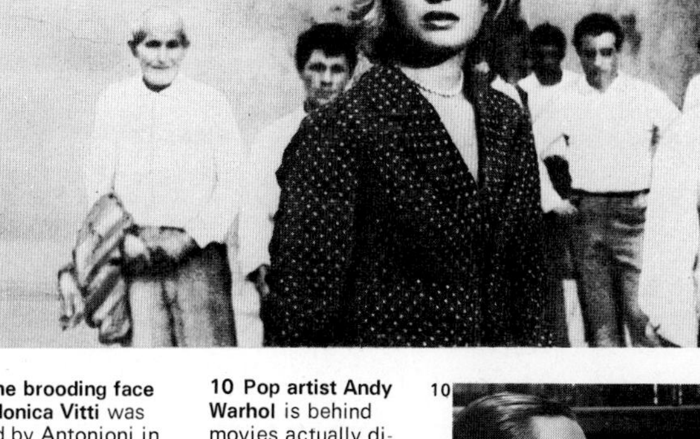

9 The brooding face of Monica Vitti was used by Antonioni in *L'Avventura* (1959) in audaciously slow-paced sequences that explored the thoughts of his characters and the emptiness of their lives.

10 Pop artist Andy Warhol is behind movies actually directed by Paul Morrissey, such as *Frankenstein*. In this case a film by an avant-garde modern artist reached a mass audience.

10

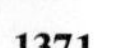

Recent trends in the visual arts

Today, "art is anything you can get away with," according to social thinker Marshall McLuhan. Never before has the idea of art included so many different kinds of activity. A visitor to an art gallery is almost as likely to see a pile of dirt, a typewritten page, or an artist in a box as he is to see paintings and sculpture—and some of what is called art today never reaches the gallery at all [8].

"What is art, anyway?"

The roots of today's mixed-up art scene are in the Dada movement. The Dadaists tried to force everyone to ask the question, "What is art, anyway?" Some made paintings that were deliberately ugly; others did shocking things. The Dadaist Marcel Duchamp (1887–1968) bought a urinal and signed it "R. Mutt," claiming that the signature alone made any manufactured object into a work of art. He called such things "readymades." This "readymade" idea, which also lies behind the impudent Pop art movement [Key], is that art is not what is beautiful or noble but only a certain way of seeing.

Some people find texture painting [3] or abstract expressionism [2] "not artistic." These sorts of paintings emphasize qualities of which we usually take little notice in visual art. Texture painting makes much of the "feel" of what we see. Abstract expressionism is often called "action painting" because of the sense of movement such paintings can transmit. Modern visual arts tend to take just one aspect of experience and stress it—framing it and putting it into a gallery as Duchamp did with his "readymades."

People sometimes complain that all modern art is "weird." Contemporary artists want people to feel that way. One of the aims of art, according to most modern artists, is to "make things strange," and one of the ways in which we know that what we are experiencing is really art is that it appears unfamiliar and foreign to our everyday experience [1].

Art and the art market

Much of the hectic activity in the art world since World War II is the result of society's treatment of the arts as consumer goods. The market for art objects is a large one, and buyers want only what is both up-to-date and genuine. So, the experts—museum directors, professors, critics—wield extraordinary power to say what is really art, what is "significant."

Each new art movement seems to be a response to the one before it. The messy nonrepresentational work of the abstract expressionists was followed by the highly representational art of the Pop art movement; the very clean, "hard-edged" look of Op art, in which optical illusion plays a part [7]; and minimalism, in which simple shapes are the major feature [5]. Pure abstraction veered away from pictures entirely in conceptualism, where descriptions of actions, definitions of words, and other wordplay were displayed in order to stimulate the viewer's mind. Physical action itself has been the subject of much contemporary art. Kinetic sculpture, which moves and sometimes makes noises [4], is one means of bringing motion to works of art. Happenings—events in which artists actually performed

CONNECTIONS

See also

1320 Abstract art
1318 Dada, Surrealism, and their legacy
1296 Cubism and Futurism
1294 Fauvism and Expressionism
1364 Twentieth century music—tradition and experimentation

1

1 Richard Hamilton's "Just what is it that makes today's homes so different, so appealing?" effectively launched British "Pop Art" in 1956. In contrast to the directness of Warhol, Hamilton creates a complex composition using collages to incorporate images from a wide variety of sources including romantic comics and advertising material. A figure from a bodybuilding magazine is the dominant image.

2

2 In his "Veils" series of the 1950s, Morris Louis tried to establish a format permitting the purest possible experience of color. In his later paintings colors were not merged but separated into stripes.

3

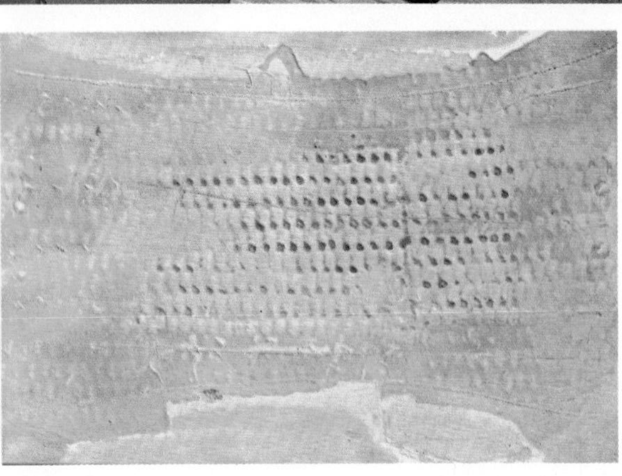

3 Many Spanish painters have specialized in texture painting. Here, in "Composition" (1958) by Antoni Tapies, sand and plaster are used in a way that evokes crumbling walls. The general air of desolation and dilapidation is characteristic of much recent European painting and sculpture. It is a reaction to the over-refined abstraction produced by fashionable painters in the early postwar years.

4

4 Kinetic art is often elaborately programmed but the most satisfying examples tend to be based on simple principles that leave exact movements to chance. Takis' sculptures, for example, merely employ magnetism, which either makes them quiver discreetly in space or, as in this "Telesculpture," swing violently in an arbitrary motion around the electrified coil. In other works Takis added sound by causing magnetic vibrations against wires or gongs. When several of these sculptures are exhibited together and their movement amplified the result is powerful but also demonstrates showmanship.

for onlookers—were a prominent feature of the arts in the 1960s, such as Gilbert and George's "Singing Sculpture" [6]. More recently, artists have risked their lives by offering viewers the opportunity to kill them, or by mutilating themselves.

Some artists have sought to escape the influence of the art market by creating works that will not fit into any gallery. One art museum was even wrapped up by an artist, who later hung a curtain across a river valley [8]. Earthworks use the land as material for works of art. Often these will be created on the land itself by digging trenches in certain patterns or otherwise shaping the landscape; but sometimes the dirt is brought into the gallery, where the unusual setting is meant to force spectators to see it in a new way. There are waterworks, lightworks, skyworks, and many others of this type. Few of these artworks can be sold, and so alternate means of finance have been evolved. Souvenirs of the work are marketed, and sometimes government or industry pays for the project as part of a cultural program.

The new realism, on the other hand, is conventional painting displayed in the conventional manner. The trouble for many viewers is that it is *too* conventional. New realist pictures sometimes look exactly like large color photographs (indeed, many are painstaking copies of such photographs). Everything in these works is taken from the mundane circumstances of our lives: the facades of buildings we see every day, recognizable types of automobiles, ordinary people, even trash and garbage. Making these things into art is meant to make us see them anew.

Where is art going?

No one can say what tomorrow's art trend will be. Contemporary artists are working with space-age materials, with nature itself, with their own bodies, as well as with the traditional paint and canvas. They are making works that range from extremely abstract to intensely realistic. Whatever the experts decide is art—and whatever the public will buy—will decide the content and direction of the art of the future.

KEY

"Marilyn Six-Pack" (1962) by Andy Warhol (1928–) shows the directness with which Pop artists present their material. Warhol's subject matter has usually become a standardized image or a cliché before he gets hold of it. His techniques of printing (often having the actual work done by assistants) remove him farther from the final product. The result is the ultimate in "cool," uninvolved, and impersonal art. The images are presented and always repeated (either in the work, as here, or in the fact that the work itself is reproduced over and over), but nothing the artist does suggests how we are supposed to feel about them.

5

5 "Bird in Arras IV" (1969) is by Tim Scott (1937–), one of a group of British sculptors who gained prominence in the mid 1960s using brightly colored shapes in synthetic material. The group was primarily concerned with creating an abstract sculpture by completely removing any figure conventions and by avoiding mathematical methods of composition.

6

6 Utilizing physical action, some artists have succeeded in merging art and life. Gilbert and George, shown here, did so in a performance of "Singing Sculpture," in which they mimed mechanically for eight hours to music. Their art is a parody of respectability. Perhaps the ultimate attempt to link art and reality is the American artists Alan Sonfist's bequest of his body to the Museum of Modern Art in New York. He proposed that the process of decay will be his final artwork. Some artists in Austria have resorted to disemboweling animals.

7

7 Mathematical systems are the basis of the compositions of many of today's artists. The resulting combination of repetition and change can give rise to a special optical resonance of the kind deliberately cultivated by Victor de Vasarely (1908–) a Hungarian-born painter working in Paris, who is often regarded as the inventor of Op Art. His paintings create sensations of space, movement and volume.

8

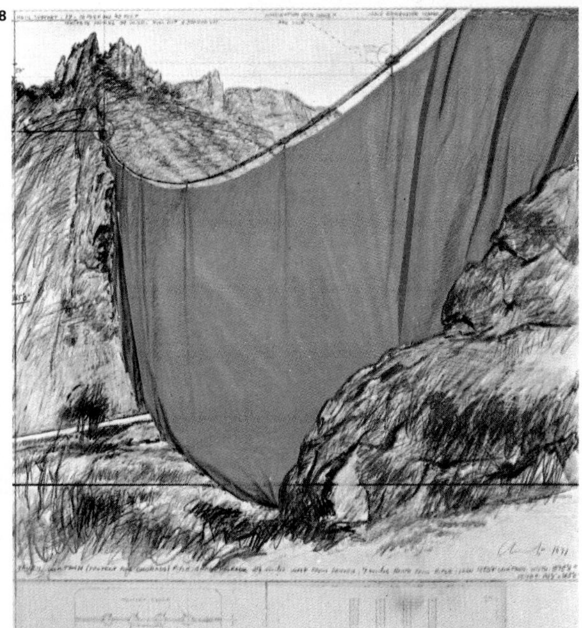

8 Packaging is the one idea that dominates the work of Christo. This idea he has carried out with astonishing consistency and thoroughness, moving from shopping carts, to shop fronts, to part of the Australian coastline. Since such works cannot be exhibited in galleries, they are economically dependent for their very expensive realization on the sale of documentary "souvenirs," such as this drawing of a valley in Colorado which was covered by Christo with an enormous curtain. While the traditional arts have become totally immersed in their own specialized problems, an art such as Christo's perhaps demonstrates a means of escaping some limitations.

American writing: into the 20th century

American literature of the past two centuries has reflected an increasing self-awareness. For some time after national independence, the literature was derivative, but the conflict between American consciousness and European heritage grew steadily.

The early giants

The first great figures of American literature were James Fenimore Cooper (1789–1851) [1], Washington Irving (1783–1859), and Edgar Allan Poe (1809–49). Then came the era of Transcendentalism, led by Ralph Waldo Emerson (1803–82). Emerson and Henry David Thoreau (1817–62) [3], the sage of Walden Pond, believed that only in America could individuality coexist with group harmony.

Nathaniel Hawthorne (1804–64), whose greatest novel is *The Scarlet Letter* (1850), was haunted by the problem of evil, a theme deepened by his friend Herman Melville (1819–91) in *Moby Dick* [2]. Poets Henry Wadsworth Longfellow (1807–82) and James Russell Lowell (1819–91) were dominant figures in the "American Renaissance" centered in and around Boston. One poet of great originality—Emily Dickinson (1830–86)—lived in obscurity apart from her contemporaries. With *Leaves of Grass* (1855) by Walt Whitman (1819–92), the first completely native American poetry emerged.

Realism and experimentalism

Two of the most distinctive characteristics of American writing—humor and directness—came together in the works of Mark Twain (1835–1910) [4], who bridged romanticism and realism. The apostle of realism was the novelist William Dean Howells (1837–1920); its most accomplished writer was his friend Henry James [5]. Edith Wharton (1862–1937) wrote subtle studies of a rapidly changing American society, while Willa Cather (1873–1947) concentrated on her native New England. Stephen Crane (1871–1900) anticipated the naturalists. The naturalists, who pushed realism to the limit in portraying a harsh American life, are epitomized by Theodore Dreiser (1871–1945) in his celebrated novel *An American Tragedy* (1925), and James T. Farrell (1904–). Social criticism is also found in the works of Sinclair Lewis (1885–1951), the first American to win the Nobel Prize for literature (1930); John Steinbeck (1902–68); and Nathanael West (1903–40); as well as the influential experimentalist John Dos Passos (1896–1970). From Paris, Gertrude Stein (1874–1946), influenced many, including Sherwood Anderson (1876–1941), Ernest Hemingway (1899–1961) [9], and F. Scott Fitzgerald [Key]. Pearl Buck (1892–1973) [13] was the first US woman to win the Nobel Prize for literature. Among the regional writers, the major novelist was the complex dissector of the South, William Faulkner (1897–1962) [8]. Faulkner was the leader of the great Southern renaissance that produced Katharine Anne Porter (1890–), Eudora Welty (1909–), Carson McCullers (1917–67), and Flannery O'Connor (1925–64). Thomas Wolfe (1900–38), another Southerner, explored his own and America's consciousness in four semi-autobiographical novels.

American drama first came of age in the

CONNECTIONS

See also
1376 Emergent literatures of the 20th century
1362 Hollywood
1326 Socialism in the West
1324 The twenties and the Depression
1238 The novel and press in the 19th century
1420 The American experience: poetry
1426 The American experience: drama

1 James Fenimore Cooper in *The Last of the Mohicans* (1826) tries to portray fairly the aspirations of both white Americans and Indians. The hero of the native frontier is a shrewd backwoodsman.

2 Captain Ahab in Melville's *Moby Dick* (1851) hunted the white whale that had caused him to lose his leg. Melville was largely ignored until this century, but *Moby Dick* is now well recognized.

3 Henry David Thoreau retreated (1845–47) to Walden Pond, near Concord, Mass., where he devised his philosophy of self-reliant individualism seen in *Walden, Or Life in the Woods* (1854).

4 Mark Twain's gusto concealed a bleak pessimism. *Huckleberry Finn* (1884) is a crucial examination of the "American dream," and of the hypocrisies that undermine it.

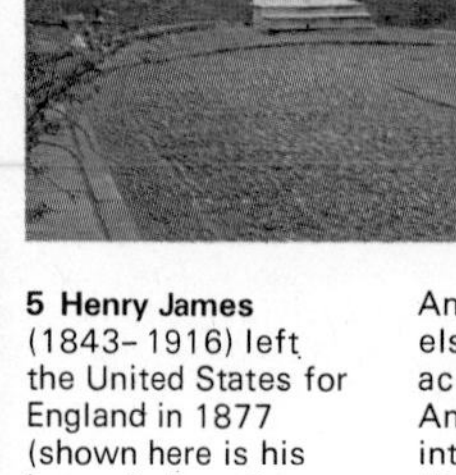

5 Henry James (1843–1916) left the United States for England in 1877 (shown here is his house in Rye, Sussex). His awareness, however, remained American. His novels, universally acclaimed, study American-European interactions, social life, and the interaction of art and morality.

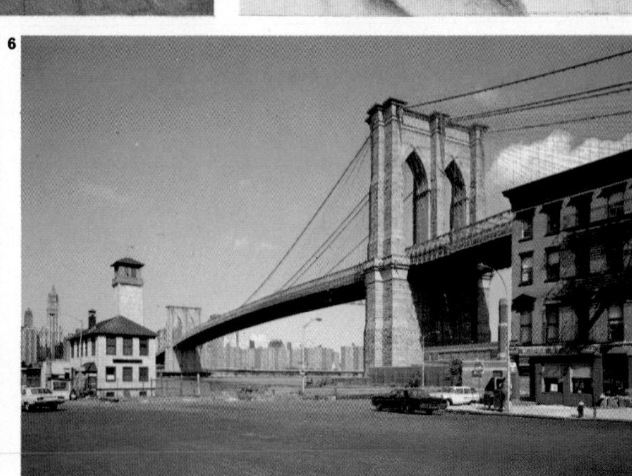

6 Brooklyn Bridge, built between 1869–83, spans New York's East River between Brooklyn and Manhattan. It has inspired poems by Walt Whitman, Marianne Moore, and Hart Crane. In his poem *The Bridge* (1930), Crane made it a symbol of the migration across the continent from the Atlantic to the Pacific. Crane's optimistic vision weaves the heroes of the past with present conditions in a way that shows his awareness of the problems of modern society.

1920s in the plays of Eugene O'Neill (1888–1953). His high standards have been sustained by Tennessee Williams (1914–), Arthur Miller (1915–) [10], and Edward Albee (1928–).

Recent developments

Early in this century a revival of poetry was led by Edwin Arlington Robinson (1869–1935) and Robert Frost (1874–1963). Their traditionalism has persisted in poets such as John Crowe Ransom (1888–1974) and Allen Tate (1899–), while the symbolists Wallace Stevens (1879–1955), Marianne Moore (1887–1972), and Hart Crane (1899–1932) were independent figures. The later group of Robert Lowell (1917–), Theodore Roethke (1908–63), Anne Sexton (1928–74), Sylvia Plath (1932–63), and John Berryman (1914–72) developed freer styles from traditionalist beginnings.

Modernism derived from Ezra Pound (1885–1972) [1] and T. S. Eliot (1888–1965). A more consciously indigenous innovator was William Carlos Williams (1883–1963). Heir to Williams, as well as Whitman and the outspoken novelist Henry Miller (1891–) [11], was the Beat Generation of the 1950s, led by the poet Allen Ginsberg (1926–) and the novelists Jack Kerouac (1922–69) and William Burroughs (1914–). But the most influential novel in the 1950s was *The Catcher in the Rye* by J. D. Salinger (1919–).

World War II provided the subject matter for the first novels of Norman Mailer (1923–), (*The Naked and the Dead,* 1948), James Jones (1921–) (*From Here to Eternity,* 1951), and Joseph Heller (1923–) (*Catch 22,* 1961). A most important development has been the emergence of literature by black and Jewish writers. Major black writers include James Baldwin (1924–), Richard Wright (1908–60), and Ralph Ellison (1914–). The chief exponents of the new Jewish literature are Saul Bellow (1915–), Bernard Malamud (1914–), and Philip Roth (1933–). William Styron (1925–), John Updike (1932–), and Truman Capote (1924–) write elegantly styled, forthright novels.

KEY

F. Scott Fitzgerald (1896–1940) was an archetypal example of the expatriate American writer. He spent much of his time in Europe (here he is with his wife Zelda and daughter Scottie at Annecy, France, in 1931), apparently divided between his fascination with his own country and his need to escape its provincialism and prudishness. *Tender is the Night* (1934) reflects his period in Europe. He helped create the "jazz age" yet he was a horrified critic of it, as *The Great Gatsby* (1925) shows. He returned to America and became a scriptwriter in Hollywood but years of drinking and the pressure of personal problems took their toll, and he died at 44.

7

7 Ezra Pound was one of the most influential and controversial literary figures of the 20th century. His unfinished epic *The Cantos* (1925–59), although often obscure, chronicles the cultural rot and materialism that Pound saw around him. He lived in Italy for much of his life and was a supporter of Mussolini. He is seen here in 1965 at the age of 80, when he attended the memorial service for T.S. Eliot.

8

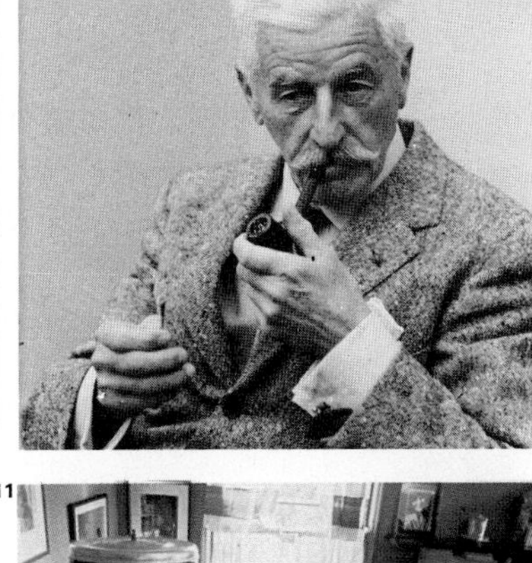

8 William Faulkner spent most of his life in and around north Mississippi, a region he recreated in his fiction as Yoknapatawpha County. He was a regionalist who also elevated the anguish of the South to the status of universal myth. He was awarded the Nobel Prize in 1949.

9

9 Ernest Hemingway wrote about the masculine frontiers of war, bullfighting, big game fishing, and hunting—pursuits in which he found a code of courage and honor to set against the despairs of life. His laconic style was formed during his early years as a newspaper reporter and later as a war correspondent.

10

10 The dramatist Arthur Miller married Marilyn Monroe in 1956. The failure of this union of a cinematic sex symbol and a liberal intellectual was treated in Miller's *After the Fall* (1964).

11

11 The Beat Generation regarded Henry Miller as a prophetic ancestor. In the 1920s he left a good job in New York for Paris to become a bohemian writer of candid sexual autobiography.

12

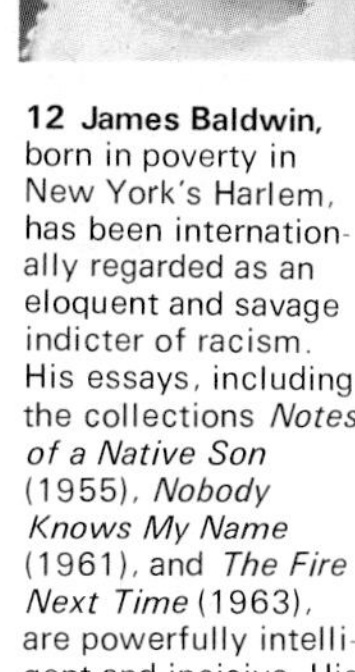

12 James Baldwin, born in poverty in New York's Harlem, has been internationally regarded as an eloquent and savage indicter of racism. His essays, including the collections *Notes of a Native Son* (1955), *Nobody Knows My Name* (1961), and *The Fire Next Time* (1963), are powerfully intelligent and incisive. His most successful novel is *Go Tell it on the Mountain* (1953).

13

13 Pearl Buck (1892-1973) became in 1938 the first American woman to be awarded the Nobel Prize in literature. Her most acclaimed novel, *The Good Earth* (1931), describes the struggle of a Chinese peasant family to obtain land and wealth. Buck had spent most of her early life in China with her Presbyterian missionary family.

Trends in 20th-century literature

In the 20th century, literature is first and foremost a literature of crisis; it both reflects and conditions traumas of modern industrial society. World War I, a central event in the lives of many European authors, was seized on by Thomas Mann, D. H. Lawrence (1885–1930), and others as a primary symbol of the dissolution of the West. This sense of literary crisis and conflict has persisted despite periods of peace, economic recoveries, and political reorganizations. The 20th century also marks the dramatic emergence of non-European literatures within the Western tradition. The rise of the modern novel in Japan and in many of the countries of Latin America is particularly notable.

Exile and engagement

In the 19th century the man of letters was frequently at the center of his culture and society; the author in the 20th century often finds himself at the social periphery. Modern writers are figures of alienation. James Joyce chose exile from his native Ireland; Marcel Proust retreated from Parisian society to a cork-lined room; Franz Kafka (1883–1924) instructed that the unpublished manuscripts of such classics as *The Trial* and *The Castle* be burned after his death. The very different exiles of Vladimir Nabokov (1899–   ) and Aleksandr Solzhenitsyn from the Soviet Union are examples of a less voluntary estrangement. Sometimes it is the radical innovation of the works themselves that produce public indignation rather than acceptance and acclaim.

The alienation of the writer may take an active political form: André Malraux (1901–76) chronicles the fate of men involved in political revolt; Jean-Paul Sartre (1905–   ) calls for a literature of existential and Marxist *engagement;* the "epic theater" of Bertolt Brecht (1898–1956) aims at rousing the audience from its passive acceptance of social oppression. Often, as in the case of William Butler Yeats (1865–1939) and Irish Republicanism or of Thomas Mann and the rise of Nazi Germany, the modern writer is torn between political and artistic commitment.

Everything and nothing

The breakdown of traditional divisions between literary genres and the awareness of the vast array of literary forms from earlier ages began in the 19th century. This trend accelerated and intensified in the 20th century. Indeed, modern literary production has gone hand in hand with the growth of the academic study of literature. The great modern works are often both encyclopedic and eclectic; James Joyce's novel *Ulysses,* T. S. Eliot's poem *The Waste Land,* and Ezra Pound's poem sequence *The Cantos* are prominent examples. They ransack such sources as Renaissance drama, medieval romance, Greek epic, Hindu scripture, and Confucian analects for their materials. Yeats, Lawrence, and Mann used primitive magic, myth, and ritual to relate the individual to deeper patterns of nature and history. This vein of 20th century literature reaches out to include as much as possible in its effort to express the human condition.

An opposite tendency is seen in the novels, plays, and stories of Samuel Beck-

CONNECTIONS

See also
1374 American writing: into the 20th century
1238 The novel and press in the 19th century
1354 Latin America in the 20th century

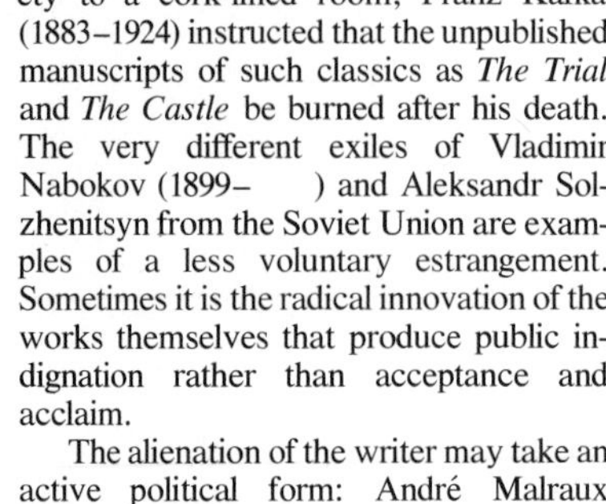

1 James Joyce (1882–1941) was an Irish novelist of major importance. His collection of interrelated short stories *Dubliners* (1914) and the subtly autobiographical *Portrait of the Artist as a Young Man* (1916) were remarkable in their fusion of realism and symbolism. His subsequent novels *Ulysses* (1922) and *Finnegans Wake* (1939) revolutionized the modern novel with their encyclopedic assimilation of history and myth and their radical experiments with style and language.

2 George Bernard Shaw (1856–1950) was a brilliant and iconoclastic Irish dramatist and critic. Influenced by Fabian Socialism and the ideas of Nietzsche and Ibsen, his plays and essays are wittily satiric of the social and political conventions of his age. The best-known include *Man and Superman* (1905), *Major Barbara* (1905), *Pygmalion* (1913), and *Saint Joan* (1923).

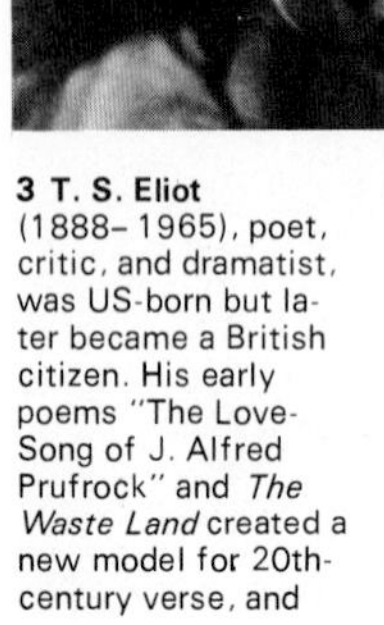

3 T. S. Eliot (1888–1965), poet, critic, and dramatist, was US-born but later became a British citizen. His early poems "The Love-Song of J. Alfred Prufrock" and *The Waste Land* created a new model for 20th-century verse, and his essays on earlier poets like John Donne fixed new standards of literary taste. In the play *Murder in the Cathedral* (1935) and the later poems of *Four Quartets* (1943), Eliot explored a religious vision of modern man.

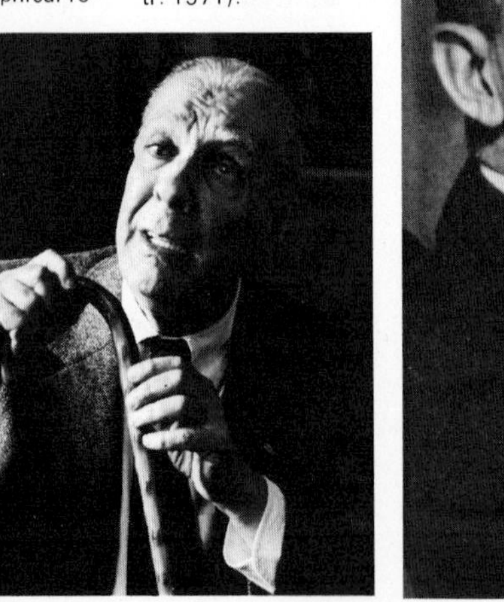

4 Jorges Luis Borges (1899–   ), the Argentine poet, critic, and short story writer, is a master of illusion. His genius lies in deliberately confusing the lines between fiction, reality, and philosophical reflection. His imaginative, lyrical poems too hover between reality and spirituality. Major collections of his work include *A Personal Anthology* (tr. 1967) and *Extraordinary Tales* (1955, tr. 1971).

5 Thomas Mann (1875–1955) was a German novelist who explored in a series of monumental novels and brilliant stories the conflicts and decadence of modern European culture. *The Magic Mountain* (1927) is a symbolic treatment of the sickness of Europe before and after World War I. *Doctor Faustus* (1947) deals obliquely with the tragedy of Nazism. Mann fled Germany in 1933 and lived thereafter in the United States and Switzerland.

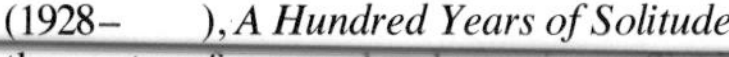

ett (1906–), who refines and excludes all elements foreign to an essential human consciousness pondering itself until literature approaches silence. Radical experimentation with idiosyncratic story telling is not confined to literature, as Alain Robbe-Grillet (1922–), among others, has shown in films like *Last Year at Marienbad*.

Despite such claims to innovation, however, the novelty of 20th century literature should not be exaggerated. It inherits the opposite legacies of realism and symbolism from the preceding century, when authors like Henry James (1843–1916) and Joseph Conrad (1857–1924) began exploring and combining these and earlier traditions.

The decentralization of the West

Non-European authors have further transformed and revitalized traditional European literary forms. Besides the literature of the United States, which has risen to world prominence in the modern period, works of international significance have come from Latin America. The sprawling and fantastic family saga of Gabriel García Marquéz (1928–), *A Hundred Years of Solitude*, the poetry of personal and cosmic conflict in Octavio Paz's *Sun Stone*, and the elliptical, paradoxical fragments of Jorge Luis Borges's *Ficciones* are only several examples of a strong new tradition. From Africa, the novels of Chinua Achebe (1930–) and Amos Tutuola (1920–), the plays of Athol Fugard (1932–), and the poetry of Léopold Senghor have claimed a world audience. Yasanuri Kawabata's (1899–1972) adaptation of the Western novel to Japanese tradition earned him the Nobel Prize in literature in 1968, and the more violent explorations of change in the novels of Yukio Mishima have been especially popular in the West.

Thus the form and theme of crisis in modern literature has two sides. On the one hand there is the fear of fragmentation—of the isolation of images and symbols from their traditional meanings, of individuals from society, and of societies from their historical roots. On the other hand, there is the hope of a new synthesis and a new integrity.

KEY

Lèopold Senghor (1906–), who from 1960 served as president of Senegal, was a major poet and essayist of the principles of *nègritude*. This concept, which he developed with Aimé Césaire in the 1930s, stresses the pride, originality, and vitality of the black African heritage. In addition, Senghor compiled an influential anthology of African poetry.

6

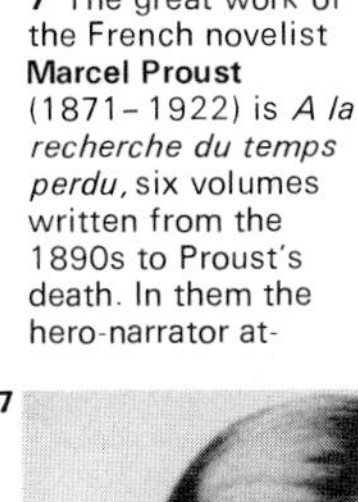

6 The Bengali poet, dramatist and novelist, Rabindranath Tagore (1861–1941) created a literature nearer to spoken Bengali than had ever been written before. He played an important part in the liberation of India, but made himself unpopular by quarreling with Mahatma Gandhi. His work includes the drama *The King of the Dark Chamber* (1910) and several novels, of which *Gora* (1908) provides an outstanding picture of Indian life. But he is best remembered as a poet whose own translation of his *Gitanjali* (1909) was acclaimed by W. B. Yeats and others.

7

7 The great work of the French novelist **Marcel Proust** (1871–1922) is *A la recherche du temps perdu*, six volumes written from the 1890s to Proust's death. In them the hero-narrator attempts to recapture his past life through art. In addition to the profound reflections on writing, music, painting, love, and jealousy, there are brilliant portraits of society at the turn of the century.

8

8 The stories of Yukio Mishima (1925–70) analyze relationships of psychological obsession in a rootless society. The four novels of *The Sea of Fertility* chronicle the decline of traditional Japanese ideals. *Confessions of a Mask* (1949) and *The Temple of the Golden Pavilion* (1956) depict perversion and pathology. Mishima committed suicide to protest Japan's military decline.

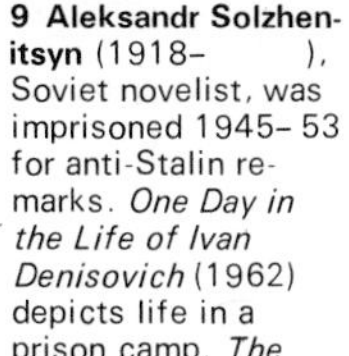

9 Aleksandr Solzhenitsyn (1918–), Soviet novelist, was imprisoned 1945–53 for anti-Stalin remarks. *One Day in the Life of Ivan Denisovich* (1962) depicts life in a prison camp. *The first Circle* (1964), *Cancer Ward* (1966), and *August 1914* (1972) ensured his international reputation. Publication in 1974 of *The Gulag Archipelago: 1918–1956*, prompted his deportation.

9

10

10 Pablo Neruda (1904–73) was a Chilean poet, diplomat, and Communist party leader who received the 1971 Nobel Prize in literature. His early poems use highly subjective imagery. After experiences in the Spanish Civil War, he began to write for the world's "simple people."

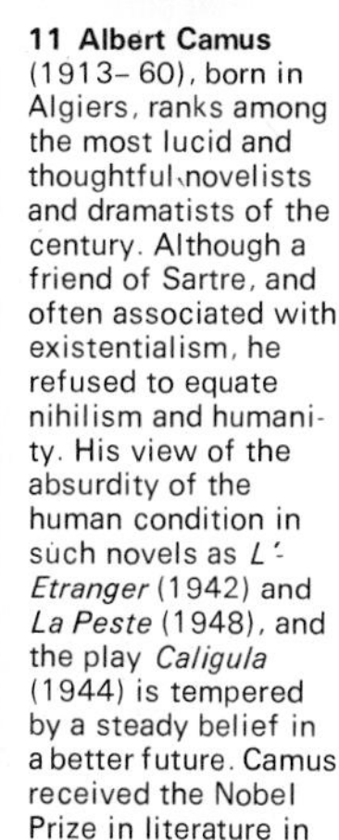

11 Albert Camus (1913–60), born in Algiers, ranks among the most lucid and thoughtful novelists and dramatists of the century. Although a friend of Sartre, and often associated with existentialism, he refused to equate nihilism and humanity. His view of the absurdity of the human condition in such novels as *L'Etranger* (1942) and *La Peste* (1948), and the play *Caligula* (1944) is tempered by a steady belief in a better future. Camus received the Nobel Prize in literature in 1957.

11

The wars of Indochina

In the brief interlude between the Japanese surrender at the end of World War II and the arrival of Allied troops to enforce it in French Indochina, the communist-dominated Viet Minh movement [Key] seized power in Vietnam and proclaimed the country's independence on September 2, 1945. With British support, however, the French returned to Vietnam and as a result the Viet Minh were forced to try to negotiate independence. But their hopes were dashed at the Fontainebleau Conference [2] in 1946, and war broke out [6].

The Geneva Agreements

In spite of heavy US financial support, the French were unable to defeat the Viet Minh, who were backed by China and the Soviet Union, and growing war weariness at home compelled the French to seek a negotiated settlement. An international conference convened in Geneva in 1954 met in the shadow of the Viet Minh victory at Dien Bien Phu [4]. Vietnam was temporarily partitioned and reunification elections were to be held in 1956.

After Geneva the communist regime in North Vietnam concentrated on socialist reconstruction and instructed its followers in the south to restrict their activities to the political sphere. An anti-communist regime in the south, under the leadership of Ngo Dinh Diem (1901–63 [5], had supported peaceful decolonization and did not sign the Geneva Agreements. By 1956 it had consolidated its authority, with US support, and felt strong enough to block reunification elections on the northern regime's terms and to move against communist supporters in the south. In January 1959, faced with the near destruction of its apparatus in the south, the Communists' in Hanoi gave the order for armed struggle.

By the autumn of 1961 President John F. Kennedy (1917–63) felt obliged to send large numbers of military advisers to South Vietnam. These did not turn the tide of insurgency and on February 8, 1965, President Lyndon B. Johnson (1908–73) ordered US bombing of North Vietnam to deter the movement of men and weapons to the south. But the war on the ground [9] continued and the United States was forced to commit growing numbers of its own troops to the fighting from April 1965 onward [8].

US withdrawal

In January 1968 the communists, who now included large numbers of North Vietnamese regular soldiers, launched the Tet or New Year offensive through South Vietnam. It was beaten back, but it weakened the United States' will to fight. President Johnson announced, on March 31, a cutback in the bombing of North Vietnam and his own withdrawal from the forthcoming presidential election campaign.

His successor, President Richard M. Nixon (1913–), pinned his hopes upon "Vietnamization." Although the United States continued to provide air and sea support for the South Vietnamese forces, US combat troops were gradually withdrawn.

Meanwhile, negotiations between the United States and North Vietnam had begun in Paris in May 1968 and after the stalemate of a second major communist offensive in March-May 1972 and renewed

CONNECTIONS

See also
1350 Decolonization
1358 The United States: postwar development
1382 The United Nations and its agencies
1348 China: the People's Republic
1344 The Soviet Union after World War II
1360 20th-century sociology and its influence

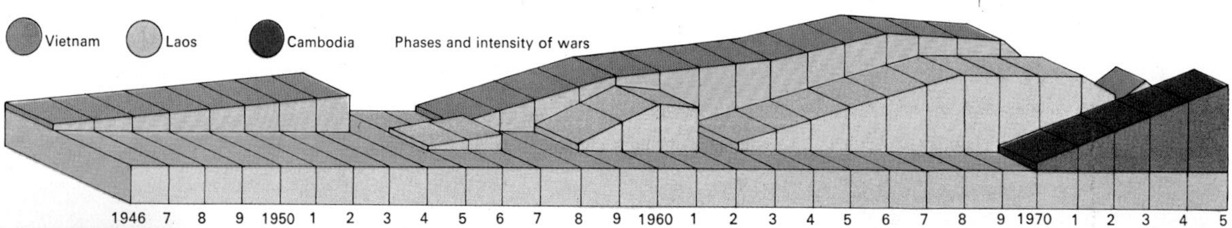

1
Vietnam
Laos
Cambodia
Phases and intensity of wars
1946 7 8 9 1950 1 2 3 4 5 6 7 8 9 1960 1 2 3 4 5 6 7 8 9 1970 1 2 3 4 5

1 The intensity of war in Indochina increased over a 30-year period, spreading from Vietnam first to Laos and finally to Cambodia, although fighting was on a smaller scale in those countries.

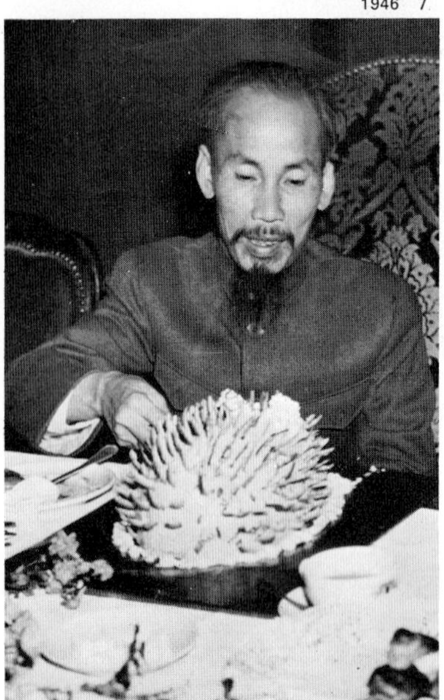

2 At the Fontainebleau Conference in 1946 Ho Chi Minh insisted on the unity of Vietnam, which the French had split into the colony of Cochin China in the south, Tonkin in the center, and Annam in the north. The conference broke down when France made Cochin China a separate republic.

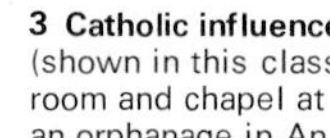

3 Catholic influence (shown in this classroom and chapel at an orphanage in An Loc) was important in the educational system introduced to Vietnam by the French and was a factor in the anti-communism of many in the south. In 1939 about 1.6 million Vietnamese (or 8% of the population) were Catholic.

4 The raising of the Viet Minh flag on the French command post at Dien Bien Phu on May 7, 1954 marked the greatest military setback ever suffered by a European colonial power at the hands of local forces. This French fortress in northwest Vietnam fell to General Vo Nguyen Giap (1912–) after a 55-day siege.

5 Ngo Dinh Diem (1901–63), a Roman Catholic, bitterly opposed both French colonialism and communism. These traits initially won him US support when he became prime minister of South Vietnam in 1954. Gradually, however, nepotism and his authoritarian rule alienated the United States. In 1963 the administration of President Kennedy connived at a coup by dissident South Vietnamese generals. Diem was assassinated in Nov. 1963.

US bombing raids on Hanoi in December of that year, a peace agreement was signed on January 27, 1973.

Communist armed forces from North Vietnam were not obliged by the agreement to withdraw from the south [7], and further fighting began almost immediately. The final collapse of South Vietnam [10] came on April 30, 1975.

In 1976 North Vietnam and South Vietnam were formally reconstituted one nation by the Communist government in Hanoi.

Laos and Cambodia

Laotian nationalists split, in 1949, into pro-communists (Pathet Lao) and anticommunists, and it was to the latter that the French conceded independence in 1953. With the United States striving to preserve an anti-communist government and the Viet Minh supporting the Pathet Lao, a full-scale civil war developed in 1960 and an international conference at Geneva in 1961–62 only temporarily defused the crisis. United States' bombing of North Vietnamese and Pathet Lao positions in Laos that controlled supply routes to South Vietnam increased steadily after 1964, but by mid-1975 the Pathet Lao dominated the country.

Cambodia also obtained its independence from France in 1953. Under its ruler, Prince Norodom Sihanouk (1922–), it managed to maintain a position of neutrality in the Indochina conflict for some years, but with the escalation of the war in Vietnam, Cambodia was forced to serve as the main supply route for arms to the communists and to grant them virtual freedom of action in border areas. On March 18, 1970, Sihanouk was overthrown by a right-wing coup and Cambodia was plunged not only into its own civil war, but also into the wider Indochina conflict [1]. While the United States and South Vietnam attacked the communists in Cambodia, Sihanouk proclaimed a government-in-exile in Peking and allied himself with the left-wing Khmer Rouge rebels who had taken up arms against his own regime in 1967. The US bombing of Cambodia ended in August 1973 and the "Red Khmers" took the capital, Phnom Penh, on April 18, 1975.

KEY

Ho Chi Minh (1890–1969), principal figure in the Viet Minh struggle against the French and leader of North Vietnam after 1954, was born Nguyen That Thanh in north-central Vietnam. He left Vietnam in 1911 and was converted to communism in France after World War I. As a Comintern agent he founded the Indochinese Communist party in 1930 but did not return to Vietnam until 1941, when he set up the Viet Minh front. He returned again in 1944 to organize the Viet Minh seizure of power in August 1945. Ho Chi Minh, whose adopted name means "he who enlightens," is shown here with the premier of Vietnam, Pham Van Dong (1902–).

6

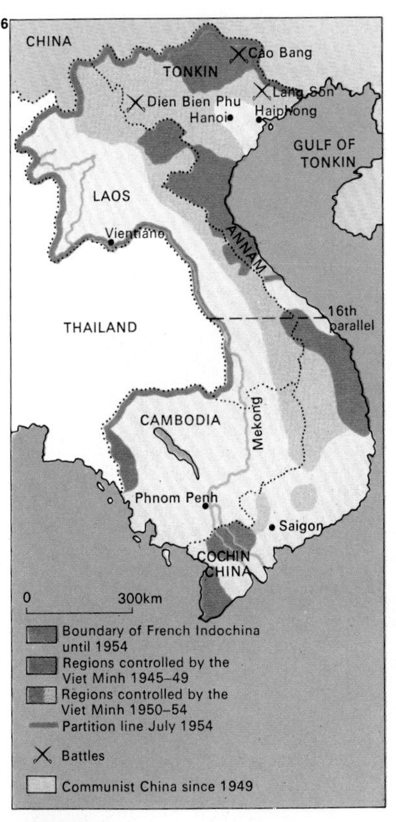
CHINA
TONKIN
Cao Bang
Lang Son
Dien Bien Phu
Hanoi
Haiphong
GULF OF TONKIN
LAOS
Vientiane
ANNAM
16th parallel
THAILAND
CAMBODIA
Mekong
Phnom Penh
Saigon
COCHIN CHINA
0 300km
Boundary of French Indochina until 1954
Regions controlled by the Viet Minh 1945–49
Regions controlled by the Viet Minh 1950–54
Partition line July 1954
Battles
Communist China since 1949

6 The war in Indochina between the Viet Minh and the French leading to the Geneva Agreements of July 1954 had two main phases. A French defeat at Cao Bang and the subsequent loss of Lang Son in October 1950 marked the onset of a more aggressive strategy by the Viet Minh, supported by aid from the newly established Chinese People's Republic. A French recovery followed, but it was short-lived.

7 The ceasefire position early in 1973 left the main prizes of the long Indochina war still to be won. Communist forces held key border areas in South Vietnam, Laos, and Cambodia along the Ho Chi Minh trail carrying military supplies from North Vietnam. The peace agreement, designed chiefly to allow US withdrawal, called for a political settlement, but both sides prepared for a military solution.

7

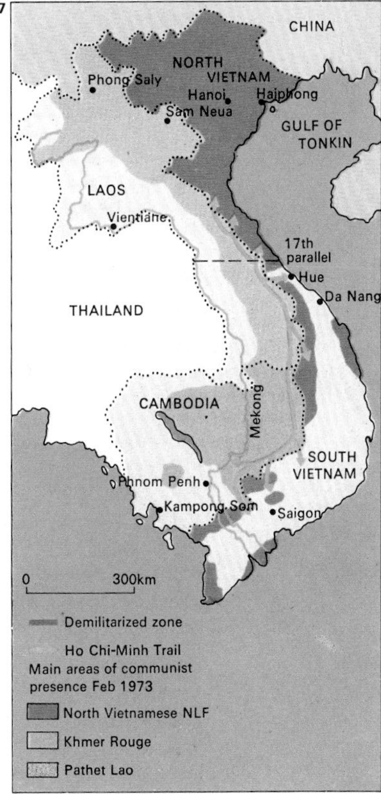
CHINA
NORTH VIETNAM
Phong Saly
Hanoi
Haiphong
Sam Neua
GULF OF TONKIN
LAOS
Vientiane
17th parallel
Hue
Da Nang
THAILAND
CAMBODIA
Mekong
SOUTH VIETNAM
Phnom Penh
Kampong Som
Saigon
0 300km
Demilitarized zone
Ho Chi-Minh Trail
Main areas of communist presence Feb 1973
North Vietnamese NLF
Khmer Rouge
Pathet Lao

8

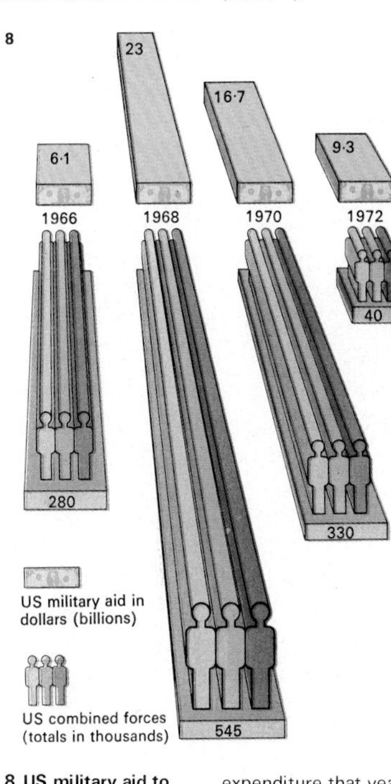
23
16·7
6·1
9·3
1966
1968
1970
1972
40
280
330
545
US military aid in dollars (billions)
US combined forces (totals in thousands)

8 US military aid to South Vietnam rose to a peak in 1968 when US combat troops totaled 545,000. Actual (incremental) US war expenditure that year was $23 billion with $1 billion more in aid. US expenditures gradually fell as this effort produced only stalemate.

9

9 US troops on a patrol in rough country epitomize the problem faced by the United States in Vietnam where sophisticated military technology failed to win the war on the ground. As the fighting went on, an ultimately more important struggle for the allegiance of Vietnam's mainly peasant population was being won by the communists at village level.

10 As Saigon fell US helicopters evacuated their allies on April 29, 1975.

10

The question of Israel

Zionism—the movement to establish a Jewish state in their ancient homeland of Palestine—emerged late in the nineteenth century as a form of the nationalism then sweeping Europe. It represented an attempt to channel the Jewish sense of corporate existence into a secure political entity that would provide an answer to continuing persecution. Among Arabs at about the same time the nationalist concept began to fertilize a deep sense of separate identity.

Origins of the conflict

Zionism and Arab separatism clashed from the beginning. In 1882 the first modern Jewish agricultural settlement was founded in Palestine, where Jews had been a minority for centuries. Muslim and Christian notables of Jerusalem urged the Ottoman administration to prevent further immigration. Nonetheless, the Jewish population of Palestine gradually increased.

During World War I the defeat of the Turks was a vital military objective for the Allies. Great Britain therefore secured the assistance of Hussein Ibn Ali (1854–1931), ruler of the Hejaz and guardian of Mecca, by pledging in vague terms to help realize the independence of most of the Arab world.

On November 2, 1917, Zionist hopes also seemed near fulfillment when the British foreign secretary, Arthur Balfour (1848–1930), declared: "His majesty's government views with favor the establishment in Palestine of a national home for the Jewish people . . . ." But meanwhile, in 1916, the Allies had agreed secretly to a postwar Middle East division of spoils that slighted Zionist hopes; in 1920, Palestine came under British mandate.

Over the next 25 years the conflict in Palestine steadily worsened. The Jewish population increased [1] and so did Arab violence against the Jews, erupting in riots in 1921 and 1929. With the advent of racist persecution in Nazi Germany during the 1930s the Zionists felt that increased immigration was desperately necessary. On the other hand, new and more extremist Palestinian Arab leaders advocated halting immigration by force. Britain finally crushed an Arab revolt of 1936–39 [3], but the White Paper of 1939 restricting Jewish immigration was a political victory for the Arabs.

During World War II, under the stress of Nazism, Zionism became a mass movement, calling upon the US government and public for support. After 1945 US Zionists shipped money and arms to the Haganah, a semi-underground Jewish army, and to more extremist guerrillas. In the face of British refusal to increase immigration, Jewish guerrilla violence and British counterviolence intensified [4]. Finally, Britain referred the problem to the UN, whose Special Committee on Palestine in August 1947 recommended partition. The Zionists accepted; the Arabs rejected it.

The birth of Israel

The British left on May 14, 1948; that same day the independent state of Israel was proclaimed [Key], and the armies of five Arab states attacked it. Armistices in 1949 left Israel holding most of the territory it had been granted together with some of the territory alloted for an Arab Palestinian state

CONNECTIONS

See also
1382 The United Nations and its agencies
1334 The rise of fascism
1306 World War I
1344 The Soviet Union after World War II

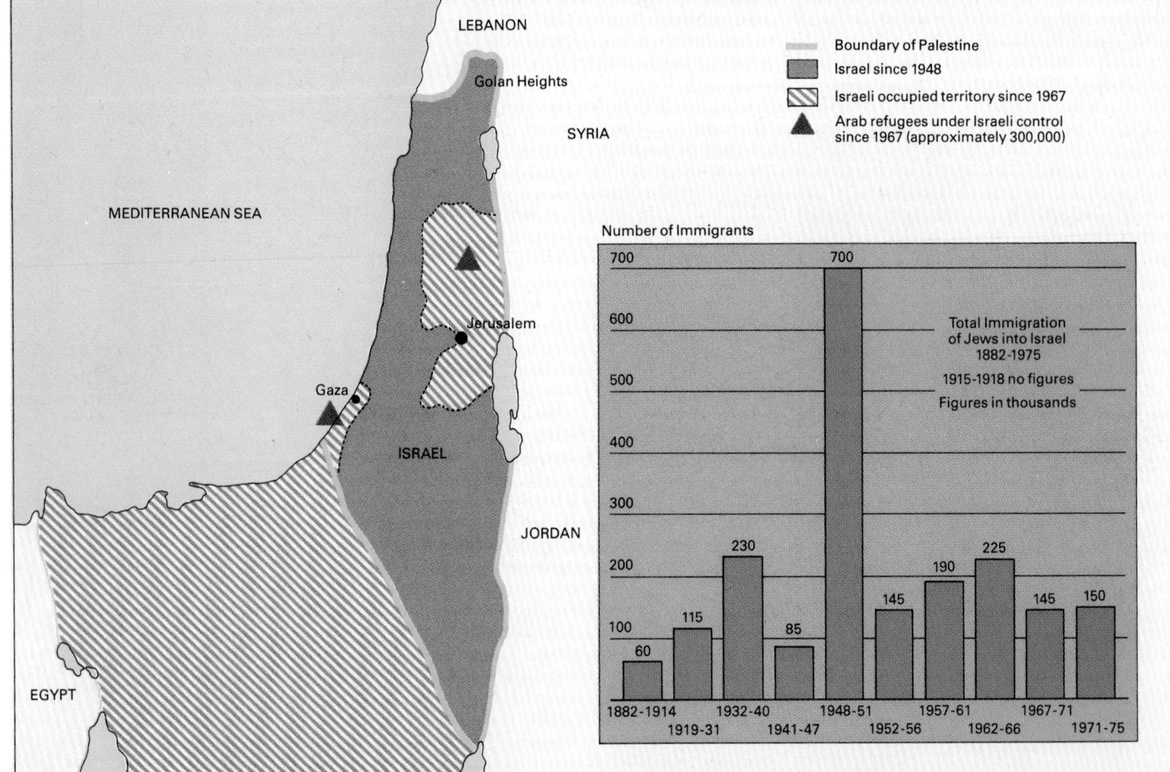

LEBANON
Golan Heights
SYRIA
MEDITERRANEAN SEA
Jerusalem
Gaza
ISRAEL
JORDAN
EGYPT
Boundary of Palestine
Israel since 1948
Israeli occupied territory since 1967
Arab refugees under Israeli control since 1967 (approximately 300,000)
Number of Immigrants
Total Immigration of Jews into Israel 1882-1975
1915-1918 no figures
Figures in thousands
700
600
500
400
300
200
100
60
115
230
85
700
145
190
225
145
150
1882-1914
1919-31
1932-40
1941-47
1948-51
1952-56
1957-61
1962-66
1967-71
1971-75

1 Migration to Palestine began in the late 19th century as groups of Jews sought freedom from persecution and reaffirmation of Jewish dignity by establishing settlements there. After the foundation of the World Zionist Organization by Theodor Herzl (1860–1904) in 1897, larger numbers arrived and bought land for agricultural collectives. During the Mandate (1920–1948) immigration fluctuated, most arrivals being from Europe. After 1948 many Jews living in Arab countries migrated or fled to Israel. The Palestinian Arabs left their homes in two waves, the majority (more than half a million) in 1948 and a second group of between 200,000 and 400,000 during the Six Day War in 1967. Most were settled in UN refugee camps, only Jordan granting them citizenship. After 1967, 300,000 lived in refugee camps run by Israel.

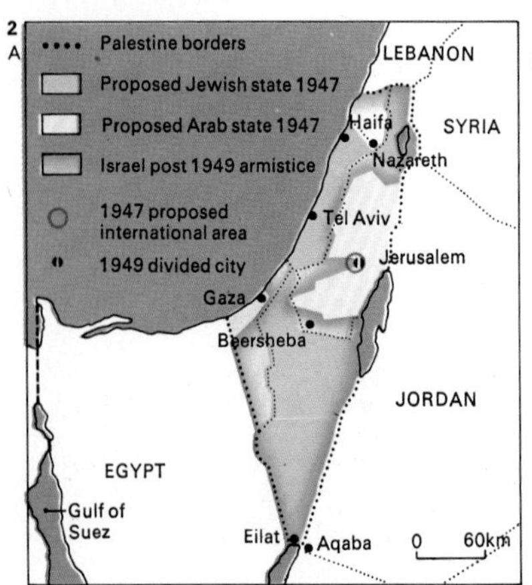

2
A
Palestine borders
Proposed Jewish state 1947
Proposed Arab state 1947
Israel post 1949 armistice
1947 proposed international area
1949 divided city
LEBANON
Haifa
SYRIA
Nazareth
Tel Aviv
Jerusalem
Gaza
Beersheba
JORDAN
EGYPT
Gulf of Suez
Eilat
Aqaba
0
60km

B
Ceasefire lines June 1967
Israeli occupied territories after June 1967
Haifa
Nazareth
SYRIA
Tel Aviv
Port Said
Gaza
Jerusalem
Beersheba
Ismailia
Cairo
Suez Canal
ISRAEL
JORDAN
Suez
Sinai
Eilat
Aqaba
EGYPT
Gulf of Aqaba
SAUDI ARABIA
0
100km
Sharm el Sheikh

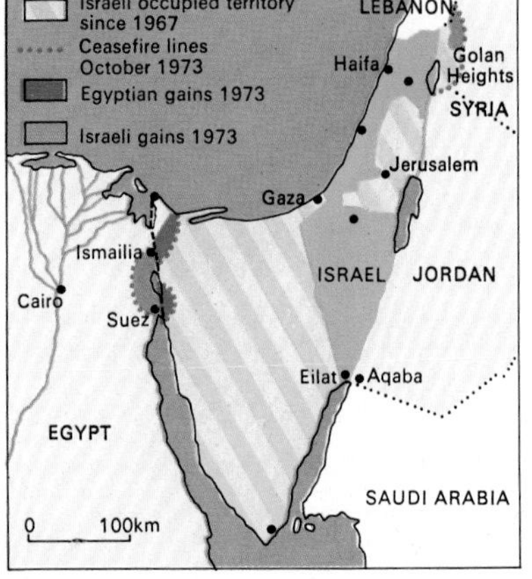

C
Israeli occupied territory since 1967
Ceasefire lines October 1973
Egyptian gains 1973
Israeli gains 1973
LEBANON
Haifa
Golan Heights
SYRIA
Jerusalem
Gaza
Ismailia
ISRAEL
JORDAN
Cairo
Suez
Eilat
Aqaba
EGYPT
SAUDI ARABIA
0
100km

2 Israel's borders at the time of the 1949 armistice were wider than envisaged in the 1947 UN partition plan [A]. Arab Palestine had been largely incorporated into Jordan. After the 1967 war, Israel occupied East Jerusalem, the West Bank, the Golan Heights, and the whole of Sinai [B]. The war of October 1973 and the 1975 Israel-Egyptian agreement returned some of the Golan to Syria and the Suez Canal and part of Sinai to Egypt [C].

[2]. In the absence of such a state, Jordan occupied the West Bank while Egypt took the Gaza Strip. About 600,000 Palestinian Arabs had left their homes.

Israel was left surrounded by hostile neighbors, and Arab humiliation and defeat demanded redress. Open war broke out on three further occasions. In 1956, with its shipping blocked by Egypt, Israel joined in an Anglo-French effort to recapture the nationalized Suez Canal. In a lightning attack the Israelis occupied the Sinai Peninsula on the east bank of the Suez Canal. US and Soviet pressure forced Israel to withdraw from Sinai and a UN buffer force was put in the Gaza Strip.

When Egypt ordered the departure of the UN force in 1967 and on May 22 closed the Strait of Tiran, the Israelis seized the initiative on June 5 by a preemptive strike on the airfields of Egypt, Jordan, Syria, and Iraq. After six days of fighting Israel held all of Jerusalem [5] as well as the Suez Canal; the Jordanian army had been forced across the Jordan, and the Syrian Golan Heights were occupied. This time Israel did not withdraw. On October 6, 1973, the forces of Egypt and Syria attacked simultaneously, Egyptian troops crossing the canal while Syrian troops advanced over the Golan plain. Although soon stopped, Egypt and Syria gained a little territory.

Distant hopes of peace

Settled in camps, the exiled Palestinian Arabs meanwhile had formed desperate guerrilla groups, which eventually united in 1969 under the umbrella of the Palestinian Liberation Organization. In October 1974 the PLO was recognized by all Arab countries as the sole legitimate representative of the Palestinians [6] and was accorded permanent observer status and the right of participation in UN international conferences. But diplomatic failure to achieve an independent Palestine acceptable to the nationalist aims of Israelis and Palestinian Arabs provoked the use of terrorism. Palestinian airplane hijackings, suicide raids, and bombings were countered by Israeli responses, such as the rescue of terrorist-held Israelis in Uganda in 1976.

KEY

David Ben-Gurion (1886–1973), first prime minister of Israel, proclaimed the establishment of the Jewish state in the Museum of Modern Art in Tel Aviv on May 14, 1948, the day on which the last British high commissioner departed.

3

3 Arab revolts broke out in April 1936 against British rule in Palestine, partly as a result of declining prosperity but mainly because of mounting Jewish immigration. Spontaneous and horrifying attacks on Jews occurred throughout the country. At the same time Arab leaders called a six-month general strike in an effort to force the British to suspend Jewish immigration. At first directed against the Jews, the revolt later became anti-British; eventually armed bands of unemployed also attacked Arabs who opposed them. The unrest ended in 1939.

4

4 Martial law was imposed in Tel Aviv in 1945. Jews saw the immigration limits in Britain's White Paper of 1939 as a betrayal, and reaction was muted only by the outbreak of war. Ben-Gurion said: "We shall fight with Britain as if there was no White Paper and we shall fight the White Paper as if there was no war." An unofficial Jewish army, the Haganah, had existed since the 1920s, and in 1937 a more extreme group formed the Irgun (or Etzel). Allied in September 1945, these groups set out to change British policy by increasingly violent attacks on British troops. British military reaction was viewed as counterviolence.

5

5 Jerusalem, a city sacred to Judaism, Christianity, and Islam, was visualized in all external partition plans for Palestine as an international city. In the 1948–49 war it was divided, with the east and Old City held by Jordan and the west by Israel. During the Six Day War of 1967 the city was forcibly reunited by the Israelis. New buildings encircling the whole city (in the distance here) are evidence of Israel's determination to retain control of Jerusalem in its own hands.

6

A

B

C

D

6 Arab opposition to Israel has taken different forms. Under Anwar Sadat (born 1918) [A] Egypt, the main combatant, adopted a new and much criticized course in 1975 by concluding an interim peace agreement with Israel. From a rigidly Islamic standpoint that rejected the idea of any part of the Islamic world under non-Muslim rule, Saudi Arabia used its enormous oil wealth [B] to help "frontline" Arab states like Syria maintain a bellicose attitude. While the PLO [C] aimed politically at a "secular democratic state" in the whole of Palestine, its militant extremist wings [D] captured world headlines with terrorist attacks inside and outside Israel.

The United Nations and its agencies

The name *United Nations* was devised by US President Franklin D. Roosevelt (1882–1945) and was first used in the Declaration by the United Nations of January 1, 1942, when representatives of 26 nations pledged their governments to continue fighting together against the Axis powers. In effect, the new United Nations (UN) was a drastically reorganized and updated version of the old, unsuccessful League of Nations.

The charter of the UN was drawn up by the representatives of 50 countries at the UN Conference on International Organization, which met at San Francisco from April 25 to June 26, 1945. The charter was signed on June 26, 1945, and the UN officially came into existence on October 24, 1945 [1].

Peace and security

In theory, UN membership is open to all peace-loving states that accept the obligations of the charter. In fact, the principle of universality has been accepted, so that apart from Switzerland (which feels that membership would contravene its neutrality) almost all independent nations have joined or are in the process of doing so. By 1976 there were 144 members.

The UN is not a world government or suprastate. All member states are sovereign and equal. The charter provides that the UN will not intervene in the internal affairs of any country, except when it is acting (through the Security Council) to maintain or restore international peace.

In the Security Council the five permanent members (France, the United Kingdom, the United States, the USSR, and the People's Republic of China) each has a veto. But conflicting outlooks—particularly the ideological cold war between the USSR and the West—have meant that one or another of the great powers has been able to frustrate the General Assembly's wishes, although less so since the United for Peace Resolution of 1950 gave the Assembly additional authority to recommend enforcement action in the event of a veto.

The UN has been involved in more than 100 situations where peace has been at stake [2, 5]. For example, the Security Council played an important part in solving the dispute between the Netherlands and Indonesia over the latter's independence in 1949; it prevented a threatening situation from escalating into outright hostilities when foreign troops intervened in Lebanon and Jordan in 1958; it contributed toward the peaceful transition of colonies to independence by organizing plebiscites and referenda; and on numerous occasions the Secretary General of the UN [4] has used quiet diplomacy to prevent conflicts.

The preamble to the UN charter determines to "reaffirm faith in fundamental human rights, in the dignity and worth of the human person, in the equal rights of men and women." Major steps to this end have been the 1946 Convention on the Political Rights of Women, the 1948 Universal Declaration of Human Rights, the 1951 Convention on Genocide, and the 1965 Convention on the Elimination of Racial Discrimination.

Economic and social work

More than 80 percent of the UN's funds are devoted to helping poorer countries de-

CONNECTIONS

See also

1386 Underdevelopment and the world economy
1352 Non-alignment and the Third World
1350 Decolonization
1308 The Peace of Paris
1380 The question of Israel
732 Diseases and the Third World
734 World health
942 International co-operation and development

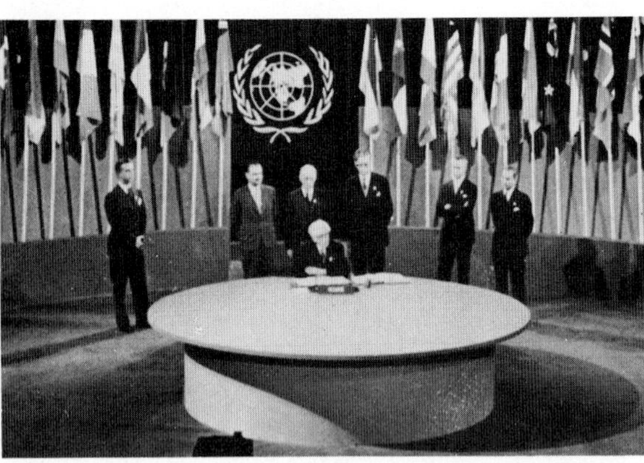

1 Joseph Paul Boncour (1873–1972) signs the UN Charter for France at the first meeting of the organization in San Francisco in 1945. Since the first 50 members appended their signatures to the charter the membership has grown to almost triple that original number. As they have joined, the numerically superior emergent nations have inevitably weakened the great powers' domination of the UN.

2 UN troops cross the Han River in Korea as they move to meet the North Korean invaders of South Korea in 1950. It was the UN's first military intervention in a war—but almost by default. The USSR, at that time boycotting the Security Council, was unable to veto a recommendation that the UN go to the aid of South Korea. Sixteen nations responded to the call to arms, but actually it was the United States that provided the men, equipment, and overall command to drive the North Koreans back across the dividing line of the 38th Parallel.

3

1 UNCTAD Conference on Trade and Development
2 UNIDO Industrial Development Organization
3 UNITAR Institute for Training and Research
4 UNHCR High Commission for Refugees
5 UN Capital Development Fund
6 UNDP Development Programme
7 Trade and Development Board
8 UNICEF Children's Fund
9 UN-FAO World Food Programme

General Assembly
Secretariat
Trusteeship Council
Security Council
International Court of Justice
Economic and Social Council
IAEA Atomic Energy Agency
IMF Monetary Fund
WHO World Health Org.
FAO Food and Agricultural Org.
ILO International Labor Org.
IDA Development Assoc.
UNESCO Education, Scientific and Cultural Org.
IBRD Bank of Reconstruction and Development
IFC Finance Corp.
ICAO Civil Aviation Org.
Universal Postal Union
ITU Telecommunications Union
WMO World Meteorological Org.
IMCO Maritime Consultative Organization
GATT General Agreement on Tariffs and Trade

3 The "political" aspect of the UN is dominated by the General Assembly and the Security Council, but apart from these there are four other bodies. The Economic and Social Council (ECOSOC), under the supervision of the General Assembly, coordinates the UN's economic and social work and that of 14 of its specialized agencies. The Trusteeship Council was established to supervise the affairs of 11 trusteeship territories, of which all but one (the Pacific Islands) have now achieved independence. The International Court of Justice is the principal judicial organ, and all UN members are parties to its statutes and can refer cases to it. It consists of 15 judges elected by the General Assembly and Security Council voting independently. The Judges serve an initial term of nine years. Finally, the Secretariat services all the other organs and administers the programs and policies that are laid down by them.

4

A

B

C

D

4 The chief administrator of the UN is the Secretary General, who is proposed by the Security Council and elected by the Assembly. Since 1946 there have been four: Trygve Lie (1896–1968) [A] of Norway; Dag Hammarskjöld (1905–61) [B] of Sweden, whose term of office ended tragically in an air crash in northern Rhodesia; U Thant (1909–) [C] of Burma, who retired in 1971; and Kurt Waldheim (1918–) [D] of Austria.

velop their own human and economic resources [9]. Under the supervision of the Economic and Social Council, there are seven functional commissions that make studies, issue reports, or draft international treaties relating to such subjects as human rights and control of narcotic drugs. There are also five regional economic commissions—one each for Africa, Western Asia, Asia and the Pacific, Europe, and Latin America. Increased emphasis on direct field activities is reflected in the stepped-up pace of the UN Development Program, a voluntarily financed operation carried out by the UN and 15 related agencies.

The emergence of a new majority

Until the 1960s the balance of power within the UN General Assembly lay with the Western Alliance, partly because of the composition of the Security Council, but as colonial territories acquired independence in the 1960s, new states with traditions and interests very different from those of the United States and the European liberal democracies joined the UN. The influence of these new states became manifest in the General Assembly, where increasing emphasis was placed on the evils of colonialism and on the need for economic development. The numerical majority of present members is from Africa, Asia, Latin America, and the Middle East. By 1970 it was apparent that the balance of power in the Assembly had shifted to a nonaligned group, which did not necessarily support either side in the East/West ideological battle [7]. The Western states found themselves in a minority as resolutions favoring interests of the nonaligned group passed, often with Eastern European backing.

The full effects of this change, however, were not felt until 1974, when a special session of the Assembly adopted a declaration and a program of action on the establishment of a new international economic order. UN members proclaimed their determination to work urgently for "the establishment of a new international economic order based on equity, sovereign equality, interdependence, common interest, and cooperation among all States. . ."

KEY

The "Parliament of the World," the UN General Assembly, has its permanent home in New York City. It can discuss and make recommendations on any subject mentioned in the UN charter, except when the Security Council is discussing it, but it has no power of enforcement. It elects members to the other UN agencies, appoints the Secretary General, and fixes and allocates the budget for UN activities.

5 Potential "powder keg" situations throughout the world have seen the presence of UN peacekeeping forces since the organization moved to back South Korea when it was invaded in 1950. They have been used to separate forces in the Middle East, to control armed conflict, and to keep internal order in the Congo after its independence (1960–64) and in Cyprus, (from 1964 on) where clashes between Greek and Turkish communities erupted into an invasion of the island by Turkey in 1974. Noncombatant observer groups have operated in Indonesia, Korea, Lebanon, Kashmir, West Iran, and the Yemen.

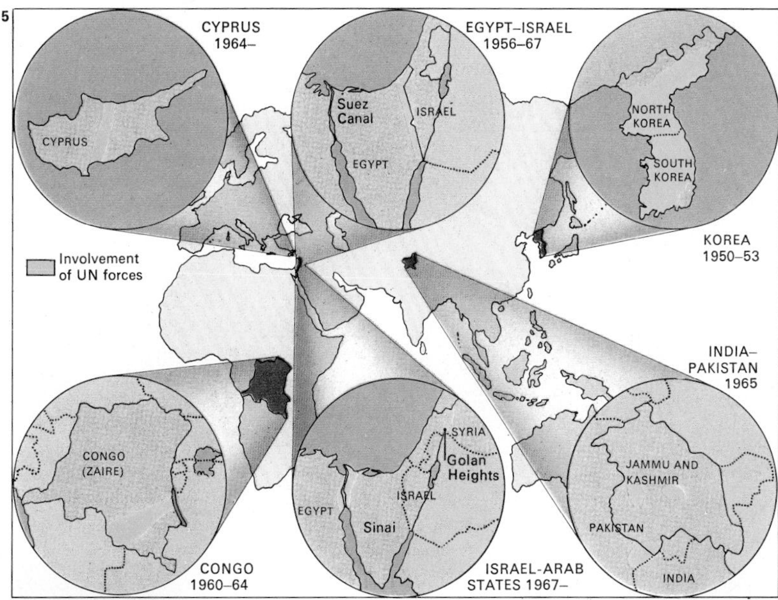
5
CYPRUS
1964–
CYPRUS
EGYPT–ISRAEL
1956–67
Suez
Canal
ISRAEL
EGYPT
NORTH
KOREA
SOUTH
KOREA
KOREA
1950–53
Involvement
of UN forces
INDIA–
PAKISTAN
1965
CONGO
(ZAIRE)
CONGO
1960–64
SYRIA
Golan
Heights
ISRAEL
EGYPT
Sinai
ISRAEL-ARAB
STATES 1967–
JAMMU AND
KASHMIR
PAKISTAN
INDIA

6

6 The giant monuments of Abu Simbel were saved from the waters of Lake Nasser by UN agencies, in particular UNESCO. As yet the UN's cultural work, like its exercises in international diplomacy, has been less impressive than its continuing battle against disease and famine, waged by the World Health Organization and the Food and Agriculture Organization and affiliates such as UNICEF.

7

7 The UN membership consists of sovereign states that accept the obligations contained in the UN Charter. From time to time non-self-governing territories have been allowed to present their cases to the committees of the Assembly, but a precedent was set in 1975 when the head of the Palestine Liberation Organization, Yasser Arafat, was allowed to address the Assembly.

8 After the Arab-Israeli War resumed in October 1973, two cease fire resolutions sponsored by the Soviet Union and the United States were adopted by the Security Council. But the fighting continued, and it was the eight nonaligned members of the Security Council who then proposed dispatching a noncombatant observer force, whose function was to supervise the cease-fire conditions.

8

9

9 The UN's Food and Agriculture Organization helps farmers with new methods and materials. An FAO expert shows Indonesians increased yields from fertilizer.

The world's monetary system

The establishment of a new and more stable international money system was one of the most important tasks facing world leaders as World War II drew to a close. At the Bretton Woods Conference in 1944 negotiators had bitter memories of the 1930s when the breakdown of the gold standard [1] as a semiautomatic system of adjusting imbalances in trade and payments between nations was followed by a period of unstable exchange rates, restrictive trade practices, and deep economic slump in most major countries. It was the aim of the conference to devise a monetary system that would encourage international cooperation and end instability.

The Bretton Woods system

The essential features of the new system were stable, or fixed, exchange rates; the creation of a new central organization, the International Monetary Fund (IMF), to oversee the new arrangements and assist countries in balance-of-payments difficulties [Key, 2]; and assistance, through the newly established World Bank (International Bank for Reconstruction and Development), to poor countries. Stable exchange rates required each IMF member to report to the Fund the value of its currency (in terms of gold). Since all currencies were thus "priced" in terms of a single denominator, gold, this also established rates of exchange between them. These rates were to be regarded as essentially fixed, and a major change in the value of a currency was permitted only when a country was suffering from "fundamental disequilibrium" in its balance of payments. To correct a "fundamental" surplus (exports greater than imports) a country would revalue (making its exports more expensive and its imports cheaper); to adjust a deficit it would devalue.

The US dollar, and to a lesser degree the British pound sterling, came to play a central role in the new system. Sterling had long had an important position as a major trading or "hard" currency [4]. The dollar's preeminence was largely a postwar phenomenon and reflected the economic and political strength of the United States in a world in which most other leading countries were still ravaged by the results of the war. Together with the fact that the US Treasury undertook to convert foreign holdings of dollars into gold at a fixed price of $35 per ounce (thus making the dollar "as good as gold"), this prompted other countries to accumulate holdings of dollar balances on which they could earn interest. The dollar and sterling thus acted as key "reserve currencies," supplementing gold. The Bretton Woods system became fully operational only in 1958 when, after a prolonged period of postwar reconstruction, all major currencies became freely convertible one for another.

Pressure on sterling

The crucial requirement for the smooth functioning of the Bretton Woods system was the willingness of countries to hold the two reserve currencies. In general they did so until 1964, after which a series of currency crises progressively undermined the fixed exchange rate system. Pressure centered initially on sterling. International

CONNECTIONS

See also
1386 Underdevelopment and the world economy
1382 The United Nations and its agencies
1358 The United States: postwar development
904 Political participation
940 International trade and finance

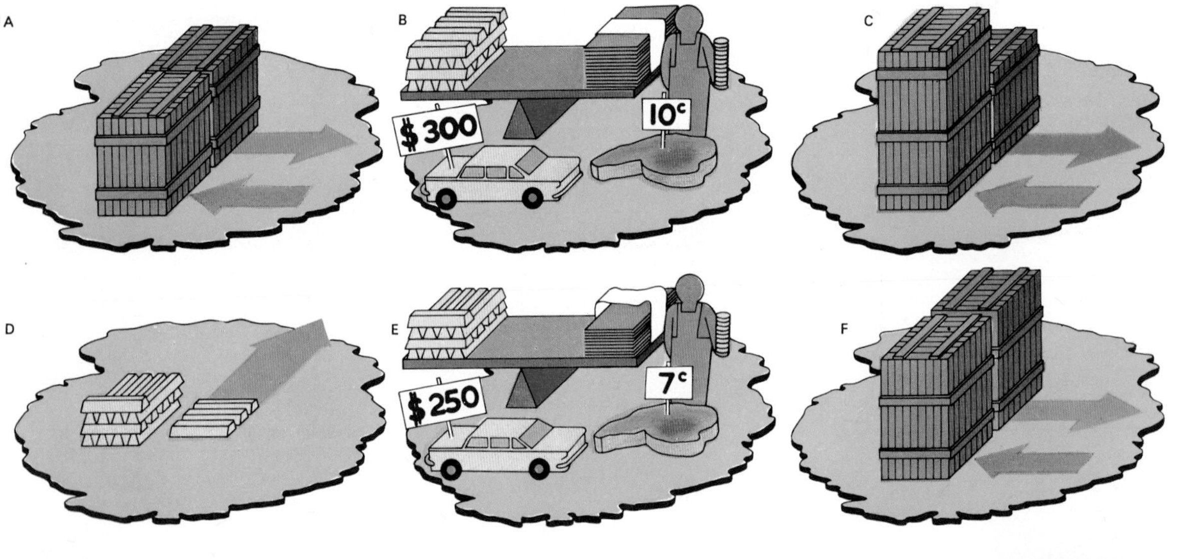

1A
B
$300
10c
C
D
E
$250
7c
F

1 Under the gold standard imbalances in trade are settled by transfers of gold between countries. If the value of exports and imports balances [A], a country neither loses nor gains gold. The value of money circulating in a country is directly tied to its stock of gold [B]. When a deficit arises because imports are greater than exports [C] an outflow of gold takes place to settle the difference [D]. This reduces the volume of money at home, depressing wages and prices [E]. Exports are cheaper, more are sold, and equilibrium is restored with a smaller gold stock [F].

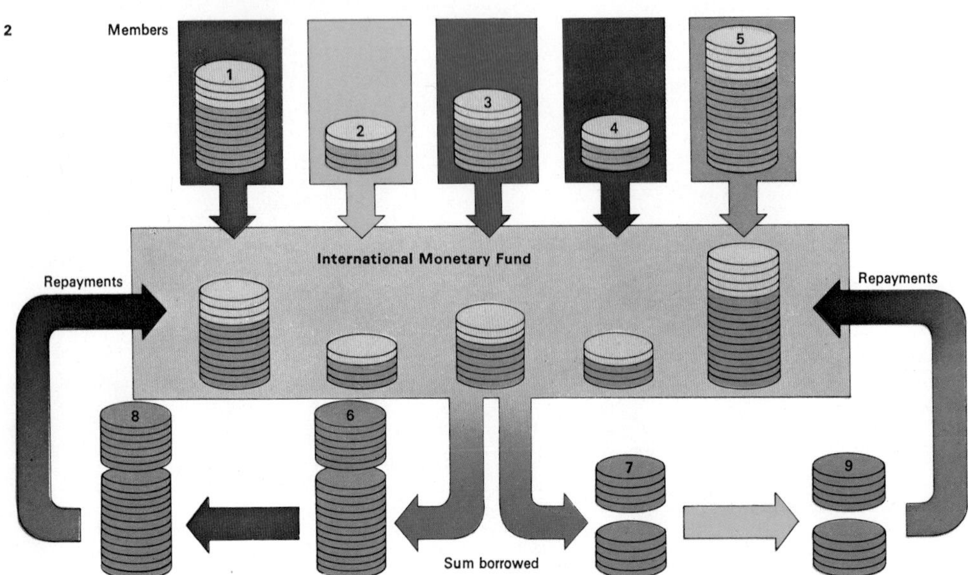

2
Members
1
2
3
4
5
International Monetary Fund
Repayments
Repayments
8
6
7
9
Sum borrowed

2 The resources of the International Monetary Fund come from quotas subscribed by its members [1-5], 25% in gold [yellow] and the rest in their own currency. Any member in balance-of-payment difficulties can borrow from the Fund the currency of other members up to a top limit of 200% of its own quota. Country 1 is borrowing 150% [6] while country 2 draws the full 200% [7]. So that appropriate balance of currencies is maintained, repayments [8,9] must be made within five years in the currencies of members whose money has been borrowed from the International Monetary Fund.

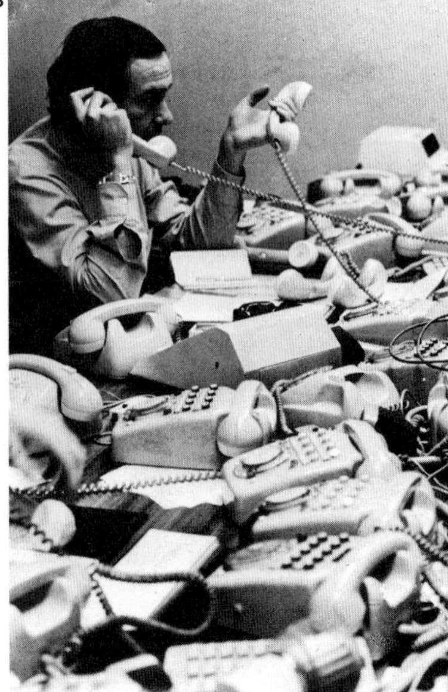

3 The flow of world money is very fast indeed. The foreign exchange rooms of international bankers handle the equivalent of millions of dollars a day.

confidence was eroded by Britain's chronic economic problems at home and overseas. There was heavy selling of sterling by international holders on a number of occasions, facilitated by the gradual buildup of large quantities of easily transferable or "hot" money in the Eurodollar market [8]. Selling could be stemmed only at the cost of the Bank of England's decreasing its own holdings of foreign currency in order to buy up sterling in the exchange markets and thus prevent the exchange rate from falling below its agreed value. Even the provision of additional funds to the Bank of England by other central banks and by the IMF (through loans and by boosting total world reserves through the creation of a new reserve asset, the Special Drawing Right [7]) could not succeed in saving sterling, and in November 1967 the pound was devalued by 14.3 percent.

The crisis of confidence soon spread to the dollar, took the form of persistent demand by holders of dollars for their conversion into gold and resulted in a serious drain on US gold reserves. In August 1971, President Richard M. Nixon took steps to check this outflow and shocked the world by announcing the ending of the longstanding US commitment to sell gold for dollars. This surprise package prompted new international negotiations and resulted in the Smithsonian Agreement of December 1971. It provided for a substantial revaluation of all major currencies against the dollar and was intended to produce a more realistic dollar exchange rate.

Floating exchange rates

The Smithsonian Agreement failed to restore confidence [6], and renewed pressure against sterling early in 1972 culminated in a decision in June to allow the pound to "float" and find its own value in the foreign exchange markets. Early in 1973, Italy, Switzerland, Japan, and eventually all the major European currencies followed suit.

This system of generalized floating [5] still prevails. The authorities, however, do not let the markets freely determine the rate, but intervene occasionally to serve national interests.

KEY

The International Monetary Fund has its headquarters in Washington, D.C. Set up in 1945 to stabilize exchange rates and help finance world trade, it draws its members from all the major non-communist countries of the world.

4

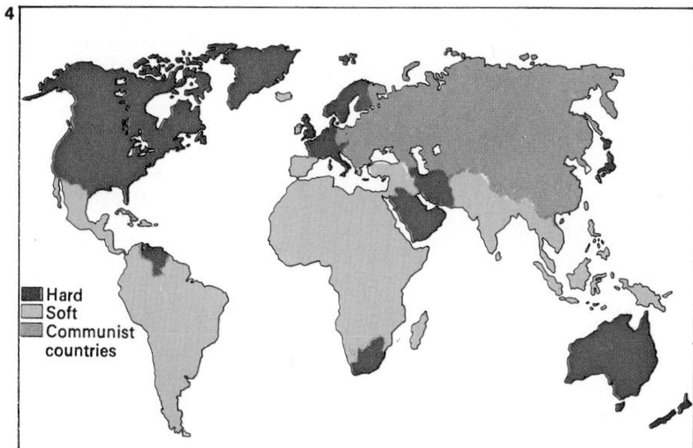
Hard
Soft
Communist countries

4 World currencies can be roughly split into "hard" or "soft," but in some areas these categories are changing, notably as a result of oil revenues. Hard currencies were once those convertible at a fixed rate and much used for trade. Soft currencies included those in limited use or not convertible. With the breakdown of fixed rates the terms now have the more general meaning of strong and weak currencies.

5

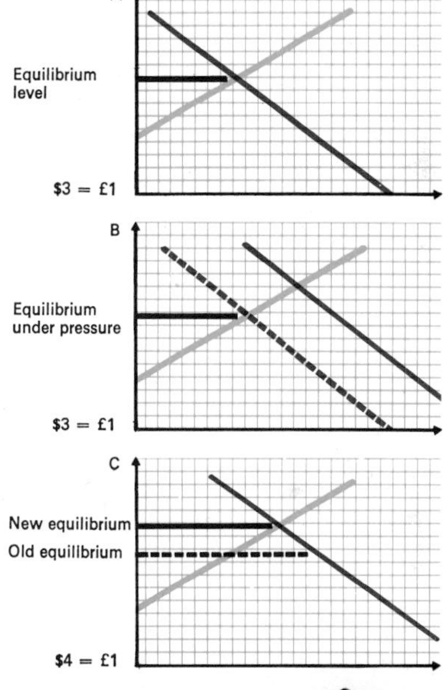
A
Equilibrium level
$3 = £1
B
Equilibrium under pressure
$3 = £1
C
New equilibrium
Old equilibrium
$4 = £1

5 A floating rate of exchange finds its level according to supply and demand in the world's money markets at any given time. Assuming that a home currency is $ and the foreign currency £, the exchange rate settles at a level that will equate demand [red] and supply [blue]. If demand for imports increases, in the absence of countervailing measures demand for foreign currency will exceed supply at the old exchange rate [B]. The price of foreign currency therefore rises or, in other words, the exchange rate of the home currency depreciates [C]. The world has had a system of floating exchange rates since 1972.

6

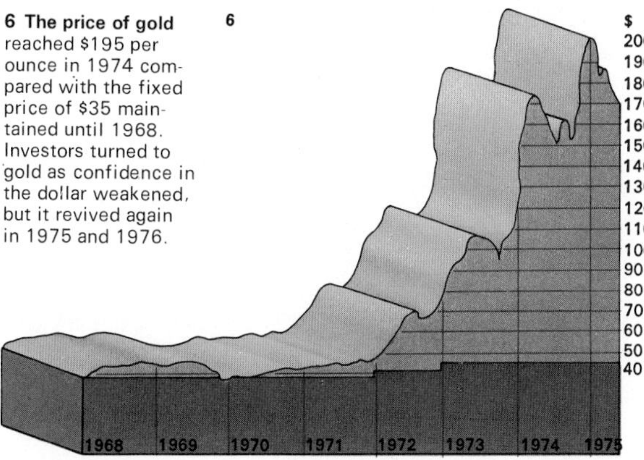
$
200
190
180
170
160
150
140
130
120
110
100
90
80
70
60
50
40
1968
1969
1970
1971
1972
1973
1974
1975

6 The price of gold reached $195 per ounce in 1974 compared with the fixed price of $35 maintained until 1968. Investors turned to gold as confidence in the dollar weakened, but it revived again in 1975 and 1976.

7

Total reserves $222,132 million (1974)

Foreign exchange
$156,628 million
Special drawing rights
$10,977 million
IMF reserves
$10,829 million
Gold reserves
$43,698 million

7 Special Drawing Rights (SDRs), introduced in 1970, were created by IMF to increase the volume of resources for financing world trade. SDR's have two main advantages. First, they are a stable, internationally acceptable form of exchange. Second, they enable the IMF to make transferable loans to those countries that need additional foreign reserves to finance trade deficits. In this way they act as an international system of debits and credits.

8

8 A Eurodollar is created when a dollar passes to a holder outside the United States and, instead of being converted to another currency or deposited within the United States, is deposited with a bank outside the United States. There are other "Euro" currencies, such as Eurosterling. The term signifies that the currency concerned is deposited outside its country of origin. Once a European bank [A] has received a Eurocurrency deposit from, for instance, a French exporter, it can lend it in turn to other banks in need of funds [B,D] and it may finally be borrowed by a British businessman who wants to finance investment. The Eurocurrency market emerged in the late 1950s and constitutes a vast international pool of highly mobile money sometimes used for currency speculation. Estimates put the size of this pool at $200 billion in 1975.

Underdevelopment and the world economy

In the decades following World War II the economic world has been characterized by marked distinctions between the Western industrialized nations where general living standards and prosperity have risen quite rapidly, the Communist-bloc nations, and the overwhelming majority of nations (the Third World) where poverty remains acute [Key, 1]. In the first group are found the highly industrialized countries of North America, Western Europe, Australia and New Zealand, and Japan. The Third World consists of the underdeveloped regions in South America, Asia, and Africa [1].

Patterns of trade

Simultaneously with this steadily widening gap in material standards, dozens of new nations have been created in the process of decolonization. But self-government has not brought economic freedom. The pattern of trade established during the colonial period means that the new nations are still frequently dependent on the old metropolitan countries. Their economic role remains largely one of supplying agricultural goods and industrial raw materials [3], serving as markets for the surplus manufactures of the industrialized nations, and acting as a reservoir of cheap labor. Finally, much of the trade and industry of the former colonies is in the hands of international companies whose bases are in the rich countries and whose profits do not therefore accrue where they are created.

As a result of these traditional ties, the less developed countries have also suffered the booms and recessions of the industrialized world. There have been sharp swings in demand for the primary products sold by the poorer nations, leading to violent fluctuations in commodity prices and therefore in their foreign earnings [2]. This—together with the inevitable unpredictability of agricultural production and high population growth, which has created shortages where surpluses formerly prevailed—makes planning a development program almost impossible because the unpredictable level of export earnings frequently forces planners to curb imports of machinery and capital equipment.

Although the rich countries provide some overseas aid [6], the flow of funds is inadequate, and few of the less developed countries have what economists call "self-sustained growth"—that is, profit levels that are high enough to finance expansion on the scale desired. Indeed, there is much argument about whether the conditions that led to industrialization and economic take-off throughout the 1800s in the countries of Western Europe and North America still exist or could ever exist again, and whether therefore it is even feasible for the less industrially developed countries to attempt to copy the development patterns of the West.

The developing nations and cartels

Nevertheless, if the governments of the Third World countries are to eradicate poverty and maintain social and political stability, they would seem to have no alternative but to follow the road to industrialization [4] in the hope of finding a formula for self-sustained economic growth. This means mechanizing industry and agriculture and has led to demands that the industrialized

CONNECTIONS

See also
1384 The world's monetary system
1382 The United Nations and its agencies
1352 Nonalignment and the Third World
1350 Decolonization
1354 Latin America in the 20th century
1358 The United States: postwar development
302 World food resources
322 Plant genetic resources
634 Destructive man
734 World health
942 International co-operation and development

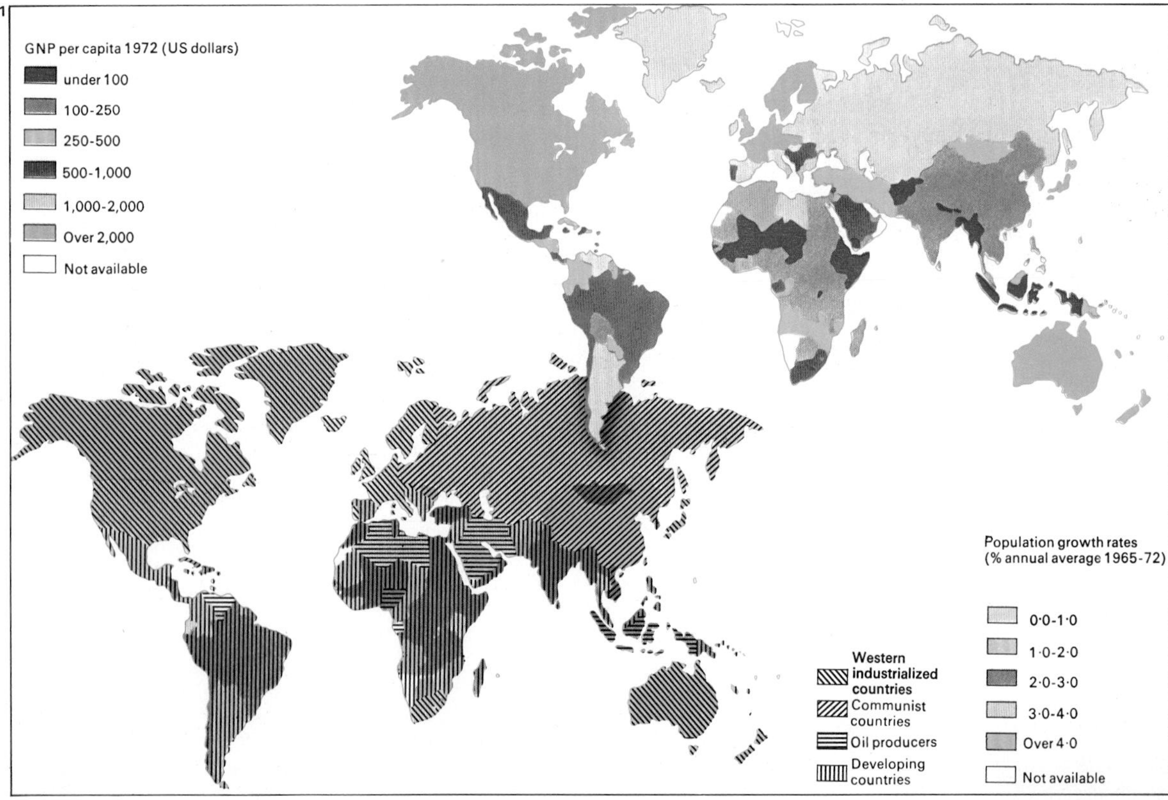

1
GNP per capita 1972 (US dollars)
under 100
100-250
250-500
500-1,000
1,000-2,000
Over 2,000
Not available
Western industrialized countries
Communist countries
Oil producers
Developing countries
Population growth rates (% annual average 1965-72)
0·0-1·0
1·0-2·0
2·0-3·0
3·0-4·0
Over 4·0
Not available

1 Some 600 million people live in countries which in 1970 had per capita incomes of between $2,000 and $3,000 a year; yet 2 billion live in countries where per capita income is estimated at less than $200. In countries where small labor-intensive landholdings predominate, rural population increase often exceeds the ability of the land to support it, encouraging migration to the towns, where the urban labor market cannot support it, either. Indeed, the poorest countries are usually those in which the population growth rate is highest: there were over 538 million people in India by 1970, and the numbers have been swelling at the rate of 2.3% a year. Mexico's annual rate of increase in the 1960s was 3.5%. By contrast, population in many Western European countries is rising by less than 1% per year.

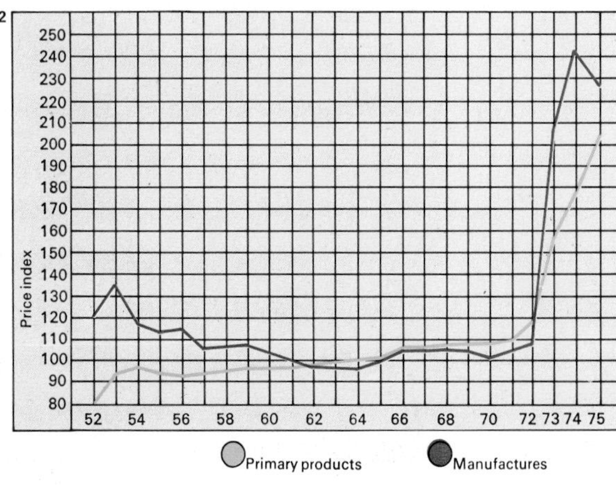

2
Price index
250
240
230
220
210
200
190
180
170
160
150
140
130
120
110
100
90
80
52 54 56 58 60 62 64 66 68 70 72 73 74 75
Primary products
Manufactures

2 World export prices between 1950 (the peak of the commodity boom of the Korean War) and 1970 moved first of all in favor of the products of the less developed countries, but after a period of relative strength this advantage was lost. Some economists blame the weak economic performance of the less developed countries on a deterioration in their "terms of trade"—the fall in the price they get for exports relative to the cost of their imports.

3 Export figures for the 1960s and early 1970s show that developing countries accounted for a relatively small proportion of world trade. This began to change in 1974, but only as a result of higher oil prices. The exports of most developing countries are still agricultural products like coffee or sugar and raw materials for industry like rubber or tin. Only about 25% of the exports of the developing nations are manufactured goods—usually textiles.

nations should provide the requisite funds. For example, it has been suggested that they should lower the present customs duties and quotas they impose on some of the industrialized goods they import from the Third World—such as textiles—which now often encounter high tariffs because they compete with the goods of the industrialized nations. For these reasons political tensions have been increasing between the world's rich and poor countries. Some less developed countries have also attempted to achieve higher prices for their primary products by banding together in associations. One of the most successful of these has been the Organization of Petroleum Exporting Countries (OPEC). Because of its near monopoly in the export of oil, OPEC succeeded in getting a fivefold increase in the oil price during 1973 and 1974. Other groups of commodity producers have not been as successful, and higher oil prices and the resultant higher price of manufactured goods have hurt developing countries, such as India, that do not possess oil. Nevertheless, OPEC has proved an inspiration for other producers of raw materials, although many economists argue that such associations, or "cartels" as they are called, cannot last for long because the free forces of supply and demand will eventually drive the price back down to a sustainable level.

The desire of developing nations for changes in the world trading system has also led to political initiatives such as the United Nations special conference on raw materials in 1974, which adopted a program for a "New International Economic Order." A resolution to this effect was approved by most countries despite opposition from many of the richer nations.

The success of OPEC, possible growth of more such cartels, and fear of political upheaval in the Third World should existing levels of poverty persist have produced statements of willingness on the part of the industrialized group to make at least some concessions. But despite growing concern about Third World problems and sincere efforts by certain countries, the general level of development aid has been dropping since the 1960s [6].

KEY

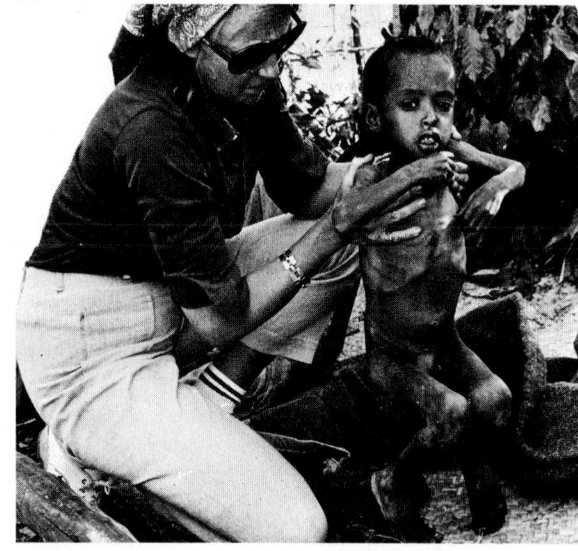

Undernourishment, disease and bad housing are the lot of 80% of the world's 4 billion people, in stark contrast to the affluence of the people of a relatively few nations.

4

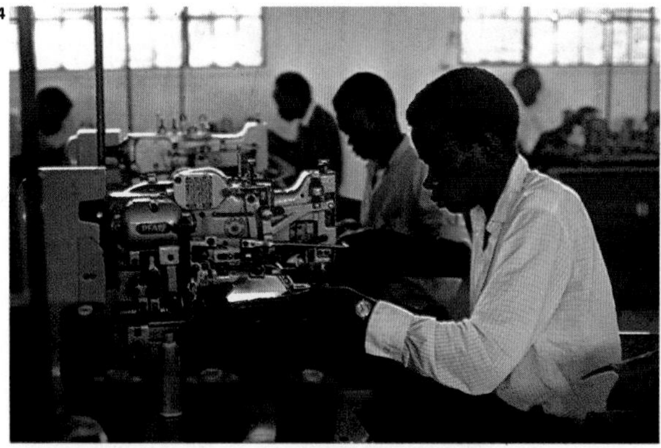

4 Factories set up by many developing countries reflected a belief that poverty could be eliminated by rapid industrialization. But this proved to be overambitious and led to many problems. There is often a lack of skilled manpower, and the industrial programs do not help the rural poor, although they attract unskilled workers to the cities where work is not available for the large number seeking it.

5

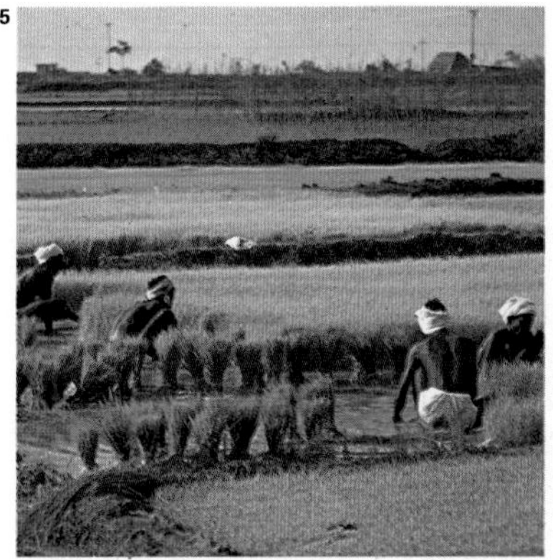

5 Rice-planting in India and elsewhere in the 1960s raised the hope that some less developed countries could become more self-sufficient in food by a Green Revolution. The term referred to the new, high-yielding rice and wheat plants that could greatly increase harvests. Although modestly successful in some areas, the costs involved have proved formidable for peasants borrowing at high interest rates.

6 The rich countries provide foreign aid both in goods and in funds. Here [A] a US helicopter lands supplies. But aid is inadequate when set against the real food shortages and lack of jobs. Some 80% of the money invested in developing nations comes from their own limited resources. Official development assistance from 17 of the world's richest nations in 1974 was just 0.33% of their combined GNP (in 1960 it was 0.53%). Diagram B shows 1972 figures.

6 A

YM
MARINES

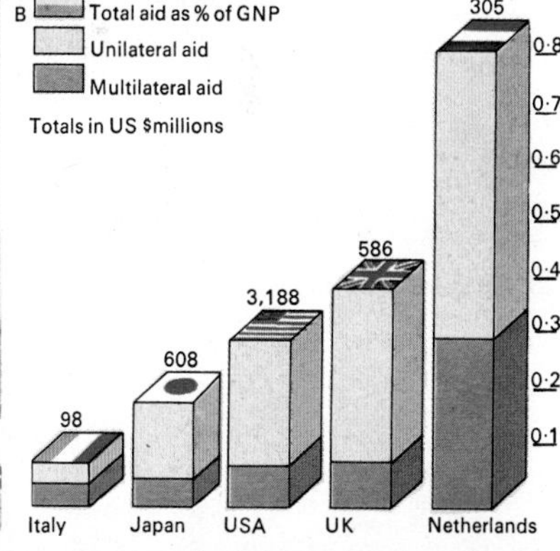
B
Total aid as % of GNP
Unilateral aid
Multilateral aid
Totals in US $millions
98
608
3,188
586
305
0·8
0·7
0·6
0·5
0·4
0·3
0·2
0·1
Italy
Japan
USA
UK
Netherlands

7

7 Shanty towns have grown on the fringes of urban areas such as Bombay, shown here, because poverty in poor countries is less severe in the towns than in the countryside. But such migration increases demands on services and facilities that are already strained.

8 Aid is not spent on welfare alone. Some of it is committed to such prestige projects as the Organization for African Unity building in Addis Ababa.

8

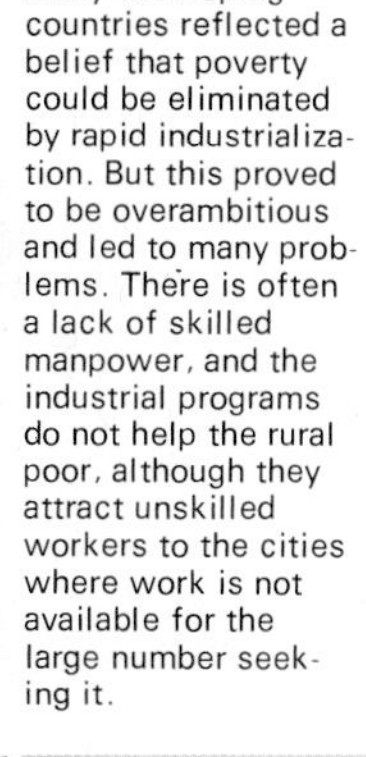

Modern Christianity and the New Beliefs

Developments in the life of the Christian churches during the latter half of the twentieth century have been faster and more far-reaching than at any stage since the Protestant Reformation of the sixteenth century. The main features have been the ecumenical movement (which seeks reunion of the churches), the churches' deeper commitment to the service of the secular world and the cause of world justice, and the dialogue with "unbelief," notably Marxism. Two outstanding events have been the foundation of the World Council of Churches, and, among the Roman Catholics, the important changes brought about by the Second Vatican Council (1962–65).

The work of the World Council

The World Council of Churches [1], formed in 1948, encompasses almost 300 denominations and sects in 90 countries. It is not a union of churches but a forum for the joint study of theology and ecumenism and of Christian insights into the socioeconomic and political problems of society; it also organizes relief and other social services for the deprived regions of the world. The principal churches represented are Anglican, Baptist, Congregationalist, Lutheran, Methodist, Moravian, Old Catholic, Eastern Orthodox, Presbyterian, Reformed, and the Society of Friends (Quakers).

At first the Roman Catholic Church stood apart from the World Council, but soon it began to send observers to World Council meetings and eventually formed permanent links with it in the fields of social theology and action. The new ecumenical climate received dramatic impetus during the pontificate (1958–63) of Pope John XXIII and the visit to Pope Paul VI (pontificate 1963–) in 1966 by the archbishop of Canterbury. The joint theological commission the pope and the archbishop set up has already approached agreement over, for instance, the central doctrine of the Eucharist, an achievement for which few Christians would have dared to hope a decade before. Four major obstacles that remain are the questions of teaching authority in the church, papal infallibility, priestly celibacy, and ordination of women.

Impact of the Second Vatican Council

The Second Vatican Council, known as Vatican II [2], summoned by Pope John and completed under Pope Paul, to some extent narrowed the theological gaps among the churches in regard to revelation (the Bible and tradition), authority (the collegial authority of the bishops), the nature of the church, and the recognition that all Christians are united in Christ by baptism. The council encouraged dialogue between Christianity and the great non-Christian religions, and also between Christians and nonbelievers. The church's commitment to the service of the world was reinforced by Pope Paul's many journeys overseas, especially his visits to the United Nations headquarters and to the developing countries of Asia and Latin America. His first visit to Jerusalem, where he met with Patriarch Athenagoras in 1964 [Key], was seen as the first great step toward healing the breach, nearly a thousand years old, between the papacy in Rome and the Orthodox Eastern Church.

Traditionalists in the Church have ar-

CONNECTIONS

See also
1264 The expansion of Christianity
1290 Masters of sociology
1360 20th-century sociology and its influence
850 Religion and the plight of modern man
844 Judaism and Christianity

1 The World Council of Churches held its first General Assembly in Amsterdam in 1948. The WCC includes all major Christian churches except the Roman Catholic church. It is not an amalgamation of churches but a forum for theological discussion intended to lead ultimately to Christian reunion. It is also concerned with applying Christian teaching to the problems of world justice. It aids development projects in deprived regions but has been criticized for helping left-wing movements and thus "fostering violence." Eventually the Roman Catholic church sent observers to the WCC.

2 The Second Vatican Council was opened in 1962 in St Peter's, Rome, by Pope John. Nearly 3,000 bishops and other Roman Catholic church prelates met to renew the spirit of the church from within. Vatican II, in its theological statements, narrowed the gap between itself and the other Christian communions. It assigned itself a role as "The Church of the Poor," and opened the way to dialogue with non-Christian religions and with the communists, thus ending the period of direct confrontation with the communist powers that had begun after the end of World War II.

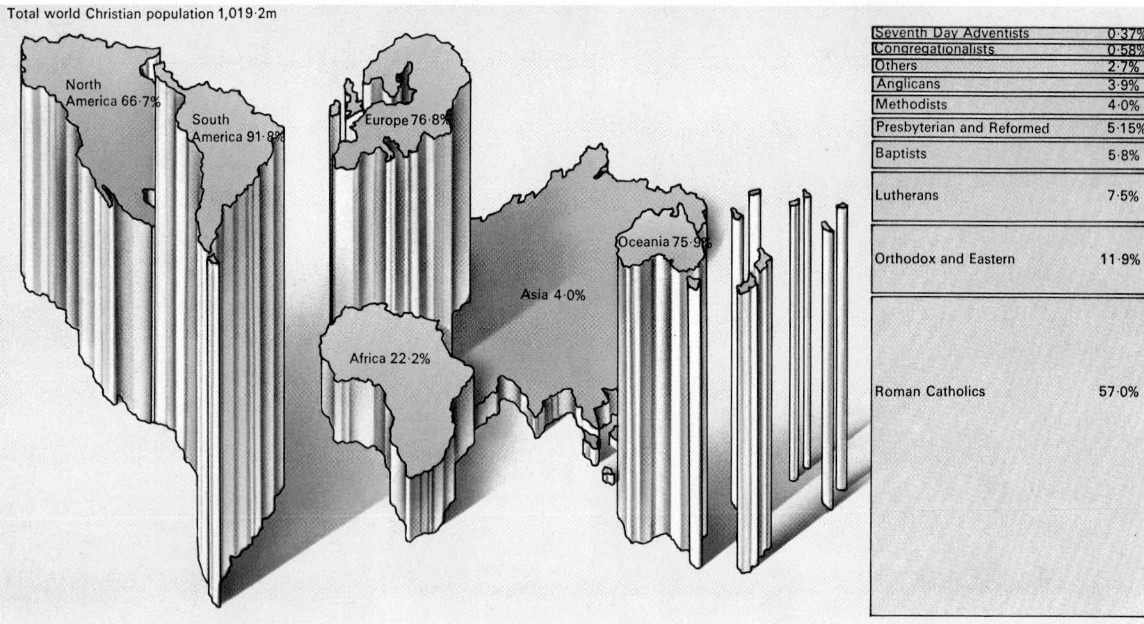

Total world Christian population 1,019·2m
North America 66·7%
South America 91·8%
Europe 76·8%
Asia 4·0%
Oceania 75·9%
Africa 22·2%
Seventh Day Adventists 0·37%
Congregationalists 0·58%
Others 2·7%
Anglicans 3·9%
Methodists 4·0%
Presbyterian and Reformed 5·15%
Baptists 5·8%
Lutherans 7·5%
Orthodox and Eastern 11·9%
Roman Catholics 57·0%

3 The distribution of the world's Christians is the result of several factors. Christianity spread through the Roman Empire in Europe, and was later transmitted throughout the world by European emigrants, colonizers, and missionaries. The Roman Catholic Church still has by far the largest Christian congregation, claiming almost 60 percent of the estimated total world Christian population. World Christianity divides into two main streams: those having an episcopal or hierarchical, organization (Orthodox, Anglican, and Roman) and those that are autonomous in organization. Map figures show the estimated percentage of Christians within each continent.

gued, however, that Vatican II weakened the authority of the church. They blame it for the new independence of Catholic laymen and for their increasing acceptance of such forbidden practices as birth control and divorce.

The new theologies

During the 1960s there was intense interest in the "Death of God" theology identified with such Protestant thinkers as Paul Tillich (1886–1965) [4] and Dietrich Bonhoeffer (1906–45) ("religionless Christianity"). Broadly speaking, this line of thought rejected the traditional "analogous" way of talking about God; God is not "a person" somewhere "out there" but the transcendent "ground of being," grasping the life of each man at its center and manifested to the world in the life of Christ.

Eventually the "Death of God" theology was supplanted by the more positive "Theology of Hope," which owes much to the thought of the Jesuit scientist Pierre Teilhard de Chardin (1881–1955). Described as a "this world" theology, in Latin America it has given rise to what is now called the "theology of liberation" [7]. One of its first practical exponents was the Colombian priest Camilo Torres who, despairing of converting what he looked upon as the rich oppressors of the poor, joined the guerrillas in 1965, and was soon afterward killed by the police. He thus became a martyr to Latin American revolutionaries. A corresponding movement in the Anglican Church has been most notable in South Africa [8], beginning with the championship of the black and colored (i.e., of mixed race) African people by Father, later Bishop, Trevor Huddleston (1913–).

A recent development has been the rise of movements in the Christian communions that lay less stress on intellectual religious experience and more on emotional fervor and "discernment." The popularity of revivalism, such as that of US evangelist Billy Graham (1913–), has been augmented by such youth-oriented sects [9] as the Children of Jesus and the Unification Church of the Korean evangelist, Sun Myung Moon (1921–).

KEY

The meeting in Jerusalem in 1964 between Pope Paul VI and Patriarch Athenagoras of the Orthodox Eastern Church was the first of its kind since the Orthodox Eastern Church broke away from the papacy in Rome in 1054.

4

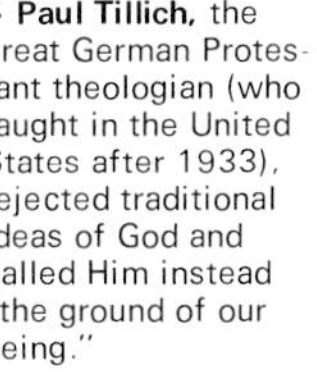

4 Paul Tillich, the great German Protestant theologian (who taught in the United States after 1933), rejected traditional ideas of God and called Him instead "the ground of our being."

5

5 Rudolf Bultmann (1884–) prominent German theologian, became famous for demythologizing the New Testament, stressing Jesus Christ as a spiritual figure rather than a historical figure.

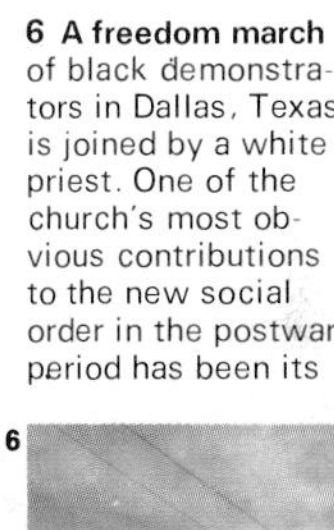

6 A freedom march of black demonstrators in Dallas, Texas, is joined by a white priest. One of the church's most obvious contributions to the new social order in the postwar period has been its active opposition to racial discrimination and its efforts to defend the rights of the black people of North America and oppressed peoples in various parts of the African continent and elsewhere.

6

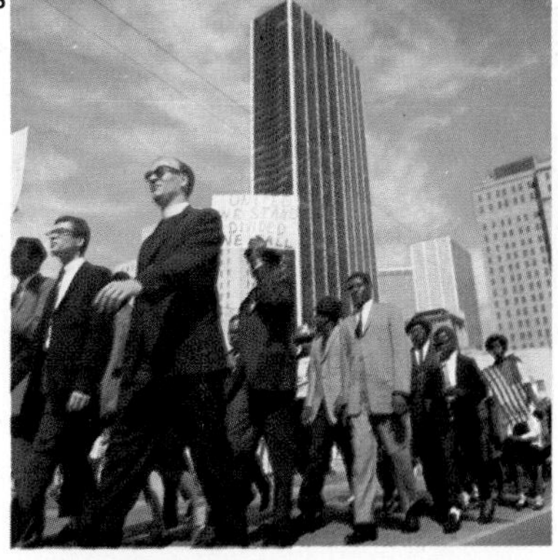

7

RTL

7 Archbishop Helder Camara of Recife, Brazil, is one of the religious leaders of the battle for social revolution in Latin America. The archbishop's methods have remained nonviolent, unlike those of Father Camilo Torres, the priest turned guerrilla. The church's struggle for the underprivileged in Latin America has taken many forms: the constitutional struggle through the Christian Democrat parties and the dialogue between Christians and Marxists, social action via the church's cooperatives and credit union, housing and educational programs, and the proclamation of the theology of liberation. Many committed priests in Latin America have paid a heavy price for their actions.

8 Students in Cape Town demonstrated outside the cathedral in 1972. The meeting was called to support the principle of racial equality in education. The students obtained the permission of the Anglican dean to hold their meeting on church property because street demonstrations were banned, but the meeting was nevertheless broken up by the local South African police.

8

9

9 The Children of Jesus is one of many spontaneous pentecostal groups seeking knowledge of God and Christ through emotional experience. Some of the movements appear to conservatives to be extremist and grounded in emotional instability. Other Christians look upon them to be in the tradition of early Christianity with its blend of Charismatic Renewal, mysticism and "service of the brethren."

The Superpowers: from confrontation to détente

Between 1955 and 1975 the Western powers and the Soviet Union moved from the conflicts of the cold war to the beginnings of cooperation. In a military sense the confrontation continued because both the North Atlantic Treaty Organization (NATO) and the Warsaw Pact nations built up their armed strength and deployed nuclear weapons [1]. Gradually the existence of the confrontation came to be accepted as a guarantor of stability in the relations between the Eastern and the Western powers.

The meaning of détente

Détente, however, took many years to develop. Originally, it appeared that there were two reasons for optimism. The first was the denunciation of Stalin's methods by Nikita Khrushchev (1894–1971) in 1956. De-Stalinization seemed to promise greater liberalism in Eastern Europe and an improvement in East-West relations. The agreement on a neutral and independent Austria through the Austrian State Treaty appeared to confirm this judgment [Key]. The second ground for optimism lay, paradoxically, in German rearmament. When West Germany joined NATO in 1955, the Soviet response was to organize its allies in the Warsaw Pact. While this reaction appeared threatening, the Soviet government clearly expected that each superpower would now recognize the final division of Germany and that this would provide the basis for peaceful coexistence. Both hopes were short-lived. When Soviet control in Hungary was threatened [2], Soviet tanks quickly demonstrated the limits of the new liberalism. At the same time the Western powers refused to recognize East Germany. Khrushchev tried to force them to do so by creating a series of crises over Berlin [3]. These crises, which continued from 1958 to the building of the Berlin Wall in 1961, helped to accelerate the arms race.

The fear of nuclear war

From 1957 onward, nuclear missiles were introduced into the arms race. Crises between the superpowers became increasingly dangerous. The most intense of these crises, which involved the emplacement of Soviet missiles in Cuba in 1962 [5, 7], induced the superpowers to reconsider their relations and move toward détente.

So détente was born from the fear of nuclear war, and the avoidance of such a war remained its chief imperative. But within this general approach there were distinct differences. The two superpowers agreed —tacitly at least—to respect each other's spheres of influence, which implied an acceptance of the alliances as they stood. At the European level, however, there were attempts to change the existing system. In Eastern Europe such attempts arose from a desire to win greater independence from the Soviet Union. In Western Europe they arose from a sense of growing economic power and partly from a wish to see greater liberalization in the East. The most articulate spokesman of this Western European approach was President Charles de Gaulle (1890–1970), who took France out of NATO (but not the alliance) in 1966.

From 1963 onward the two superpowers developed an increasingly better under-

CONNECTIONS

See also
1342 The division of Europe
1356 Postwar evolution of Western Europe
1346 Eastern Europe 1948 —present
1344 The Soviet Union after World War II

1

Armed forces in thousands
Long-range bombers
Ballistic missiles (sea based)
ICBMs (land based)
USSR
USA

3,623
2,514
190
35
32
18
450
1960

3,150
2,723
180
630
120
496
270
854
1965

3,305
3,066
150
550
280
656
1,300
1,054
1970

3,525
2,174
140
437
720
656
1,575
1,054
1974

1 The USSR has a much larger army than the United States, including a greater number of land and sea-based strategic missiles, although the number of nuclear warheads is uncertain.

2 In 1956 there was a popular revolt against communism in Hungary. The rebel government, headed by Imre Nagy (1895–1958), demanded that the Soviet troops leave. Instead, more tanks arrived in November, and during the next two weeks thousands of "freedom fighters" were killed by Soviet troops. The USSR, despite de-Stalinization, refused to let Hungary break up the Eastern bloc.

3 Instead of leading to better relations, the scaling down of the programs of Joseph Stalin (de-Stalinization) and the adoption of a policy of "peaceful coexistence" was a prelude to crisis. Through pressure on Berlin, Nikita Khrushchev tried to force the West to acknowledge the division of Germany. But the two superpowers also tried to manage the crisis through a common understanding. Although at this 1959 meeting Eisenhower and Khrushchev [left] failed to resolve the crisis, it set a precedent for later consultations and suggested that the powers recognize that their interest in avoiding war was more important than any victory from such a conflict.

4 A new crisis arose when a US intelligence aircraft was shot down over Russia in May 1960. The pilot, Gary Powers, was captured. At the Paris conference in May Khrushchev demanded that Eisenhower apologize for the incident; when the US President refused, Khrushchev left the conference, which then broke up. He also withdrew his offer to Eisenhower to visit the Soviet Union. Eisenhower eventually accepted responsibility for the incident.

5 The relationship between President Kennedy and Khrushchev fluctuated over the years 1961–63. They first met in Vienna in 1961 to discuss the future of Berlin. Khrushchev demanded an end to the military occupation but Kennedy did not agree. Not until after their confrontation during the Cuban missile crisis did the Soviet premier begin to respect the young, inexperienced Kennedy.

standing based on the attempt not only to avoid nuclear war but also to control the arms race that might produce it. Their agreements began in 1963 with the renunciation of nuclear tests in the atmosphere or space; they continued through the attempt to halt the spread of nuclear weapons in the nonproliferation treaty of 1968, and they culminated in a series of talks and agreements designed to control the dangerous new weaponry that each was capable of developing—the Strategic Arms Limitation Talks (SALT) [8].

These agreements on controlling the arms race also helped to provide the basis for other agreements, most notably the Berlin Agreement of 1972, to dispose of conflicts that once threatened to lead to war.

Problems in Eastern Europe

Progress toward increased understanding was not uniform. It had seemed at one time that détente in Europe would go hand in hand with détente between the superpowers and that the Soviet Union would show greater flexibility in the East. But the period of relative tolerance ended in 1968 when the Soviet Union and members of the Warsaw Pact invaded Czechoslovakia to end the drive for democratic government led by Alexander Dubcek (1921–).

Thereafter, West German Chancellor Willy Brandt (1913–) [9] helped to restore European détente at about the same time that the two superpowers began the SALT talks. Brandt's *Ostpolitik* brought about West Germany's political and economic agreements with the Soviet Union, Poland, and subsequently East Germany. It was this last agreement that led to the recognition of East Germany by all the Western powers. Since his *Ostpolitik* was also instrumental in bringing about the Berlin Agreement, it laid to rest two of the major causes of tension in the cold war.

Détente was by then firmly established and became the basis of US foreign policy under Henry Kissinger (1923–). At the same time the Helsinki agreements of 1975 covered a wide variety of issues [10]. It was unclear how far détente could lead to cooperation, but the foundations were laid.

KEY

The independence of Austria was restored by treaty in 1955, as the Allies had agreed it would be after Stalin's death. Soviet Foreign Minister seen here signing the treaty in Vienna. The day before, the Warsaw Pact had been set up, enabling Soviet troops to remain in neighboring Hungary. Whether Austrian an independence would lead to the end of the cold war was not known, since agreement on Germany was the more important issue at this time.

6

7

6 By 1961 the refugee flood from East Berlin threatened East Germany itself. The Soviet government hesitated to start a new crisis by sealing the city off but finally began the wall in August.

7 In October 1962 the United States discovered that the USSR had set up missile bases in Cuba, where their proximity would presumably balance US numerical superiority. Through the UN Security Council, President Kennedy demanded removal of the missiles and isolated Cuba with naval forces. Khrushchev offered to withdraw if he was allowed Turkish bases. The USSR backed down.

8 Nuclear arms: US-USSR agreements

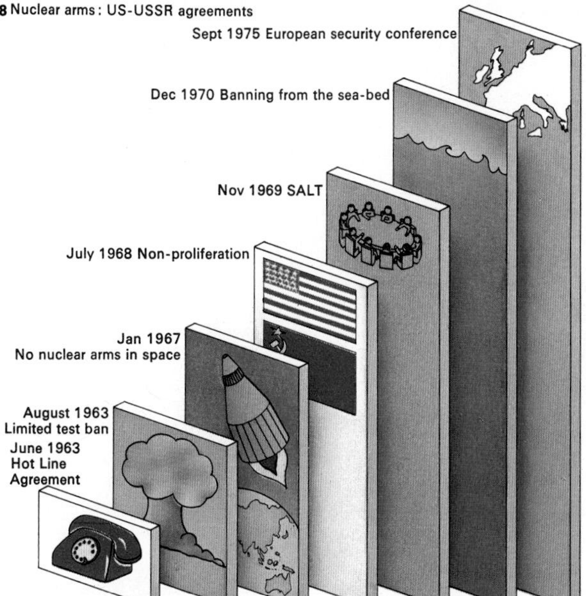

Sept 1975 European security conference
Dec 1970 Banning from the sea-bed
Nov 1969 SALT
July 1968 Non-proliferation
Jan 1967
No nuclear arms in space
August 1963
Limited test ban
June 1963
Hot Line
Agreement

9

10

ATS-UNIS D'AMERIQU

8 After the Cuban crisis, East and West tried to come to agreement on control of the arms race and on forms of cooperation that gave each side an interest in maintaining détente. They substituted agreement for threat of nuclear war.

9 Willy Brandt was German chancellor from 1969–74 when he harmonized the attitudes of détente that had developed in Europe. He established a new relationship with the USSR and improved relations with Eastern Europe.

10 The Conference on Security and Cooperation in Europe, the largest European summit conference, convened in Helsinki on July 30, 1975, and was attended by 33 European nations, the United States, and Canada. The nonbinding declaration of policy intent signed on August 1 committed the signatories to the recognition of the territorial status quo in Europe and called for the free movement of peoples, commerce, information, and ideas as another step in détente.

The American experience: the Indians

The native population of North America—called Indians by Christopher Columbus because he thought he had reached the East Indies—has been estimated as being around 1,000,000 persons at the time of the first colonizations by Europeans. The Indians had inhabited the continent many thousands of years before the arrival of the white men—a fact based on studies of the long-abandoned burial and ceremonial mounds found in the Ohio Valley and further south and east [Key] and of the pueblos in the Southwest [6].

After explorations in the early eighteenth century by the Russians showed that Alaska and Siberia are separated only by the Bering Strait, movement across it was increasingly accepted as the logical migration route of the first Americans. Later it was discovered that during the last Ice Age the sea levels around the Bering Strait lowered and a land bridge emerged, making crossing even easier. During most of the nineteenth century, it was generally believed that the first migrants had arrived in North America about the time of Christ.

In 1926, in Folsom, N. M., a cowboy discovered a large cache of bison bones; interspersed with them were numerous carefully crafted spearheads (named Folsom points). The bones were soon identified as belonging to Taylor's bison, a species known to have been extinct for 10,000 years. Since it was obvious that the bison had been killed by hunters equipped with the Folsom points, it followed that North America had been inhabited far longer than previously believed. Later discoveries have led archeologists to conclude that the ancestors of the modern Indians arrived from Asia at least 40,000 years ago.

The Paleo-Indians were nomadic big-game hunters who followed herds of musk oxen, mammoths, camels, and antelopes all over the continent; some eventually migrated to Central and South America. Ice-Age America was far colder than it is today, and the present-day deserts were grassy plains and woodlands offering ample feeding grounds for the large mammals of the period. As the ice cap receded, the geology of the continent changed. The days of the great mammals ended; most of them became extinct in a relatively short time as the grazing land turned into desert.

But a new source of food for the Paleo-Indians made its appearance around 9000 BC. It was corn, or maize as the Europeans later called it. No wild varieties of corn have existed in historic times, which would allow botanists to reconstruct the steps of its cultivation. Central Mexico is its most likely place of origin. When the white men arrived, corn was being raised in every part of the Western Hemisphere, in varieties that had been adapted to every climate and soil type. It was cultivation of corn—and to a lesser extent of bean and squash—that had turned the nomadic Paleo-Indian hunters into the sedentary agriculturists discovered by Europeans in the sixteenth century.

The clash between Indians and whites

By the sixteenth century the Indians of North America had evolved into widely different cultures, as would be expected of a people who had fanned out over such a large continent [1, 3, 4, 7]. Relations with the

CONNECTIONS

See also
1216 Settlement of North America
1274 The United States: the opening of the West

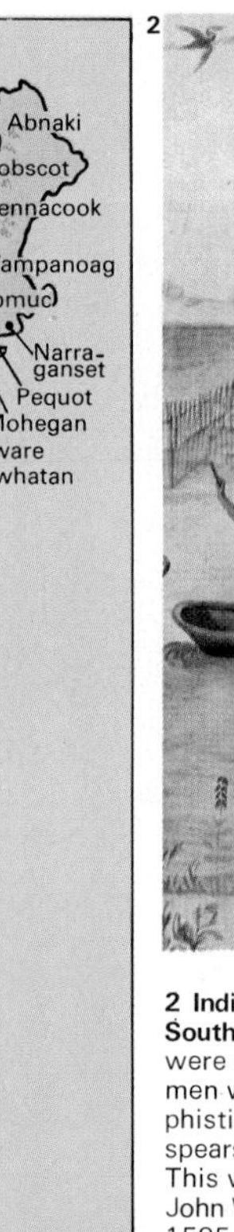

American Indians 1600
0 250 500
Miles
Northwest
Plateau
Great Basin
California
Southwest
Plains
Southeast
Eastern
Alaska
ROCKY MOUNTAINS
SIERRA NEVADA

1 This map only approximates the location of the major Indian tribes at the time of the first arrival of Europeans. Many tribes shifted their home ground more than once to follow game, to find more fertile or less arid land, and to avoid contact with more powerful tribes. Geographic barriers—in particular mountains (the Rockies, the Sierra Nevadas in California) and rivers (the Snake, the Colorado, the Missouri, etc)—defined major regional divisions. One of the well known present-day tribes, the Seminoles of central and southern Florida, did not even exist in 1600. The Seminole tribe evolved about the time of the American Revolution from Creeks, Hitchiti, and Apalachee who had fled southward before encroaching whites and from runaway black slaves fleeing their white masters. The name "Seminole" comes from a Creek word meaning "runaways." Earlier, beginning in 1713, the Tuscarora had begun migrating from North Carolina to New York to join the five tribes of the Iroquois Confederacy. They too were fleeing white encroachment and also the more powerful Catawbas and Cherokees. Further expansion of the Iroquois Confederacy was held in check by the hostile and powerful Huron to the north and west in Canada.

2 Indians of the Southeastern coast were expert fishermen who used sophisticated boats, spears, and traps. This watercolor by John White (fl. 1585–93)—who may be the same John White named governor of Roanoke colony by Sir Walter Raleigh in 1586—shows a nighttime fishing expedition. White's watercolors are an invaluable record of native life, plants, and animals.

3 Bark-covered longhouses were the dwellings of the member tribes of the Iroquois Confederacy, the most powerful political grouping of Indians north of Mexico. Each longhouse held 8 to 10 families, all members of the same clan. The longhouse was also the symbol of the Confederacy: the Mohawk guarded the "eastern door"; the Seneca, the "western door"; and the centrally located Onondaga were "keepers of the council fire."

white men were at first generally friendly, but they quickly worsened as white encroachment upon Indian lands increased. Unfamiliar with European concepts of private property, the Indians readily signed documents deeding their lands to the whites. Bloody wars broke out when the Indians realized that access to their lands was to be denied them by the whites. The superiority of European arms—and Indian susceptibility to such European diseases as smallpox—greatly decreased the Indian population.

The Indians who survived war and disease were steadily and methodically pushed westward onto lands not yet settled by whites. It was a pattern that was to persist for two centuries. It culminated with the Plains wars of the late nineteenth century, remembered most for the Massacre at Sand Creek, Col., 1864; the battle of Little Big Horn, Mont., 1876 [5]; and the battle of Wounded Knee, S.D., 1890. Indian control of any part of the continental United States was effectively ended. The Indians who survived the wars were placed on reservations (with the United States often disregarding treaties made with the Indians).

The modern Indian

Today nearly a quarter-million Indians of the approximately 800,000 total still live on reservations. With some exceptions, they live in poverty; high unemployment, poor education, high infant mortality, and inadequate medical care are common on the reservations. The Bureau of Indian Affairs, which has had the responsibility of protecting Indian interests since 1824, has rarely fulfilled its trust. Often it has allowed the Indians to be exploited or neglected by other Americans. Only in recent years—and mostly because of stands taken by the Indians themselves—has an effective Indian rights movement taken shape. Indian action combines attention-getting militant stands with carefully worked out legal action. Yet despite the efforts of the Indians themselves [8], of the federal government, and of private groups, much remains to be done before most Indians achieve an even minimally acceptable standard of living.

KEY

Mound builders is the general name given to the Paleo-Indians who lived in the Ohio Valley and in the Southeast. This 1/4mi (2/5km) long mound in southern Ohio is in the shape of an uncoiling serpent. It is not a burial mound but is thought to be a totemic shrine—a monument honoring the emblem, or totem, of a clan. Mounds vary in size from less than 1 acre to more than 100 acres.

4

4 The Plains Indians adapted quickly to the horse and the rifle—as illustrated here in "The Buffalo Hunt" by Charles F. Wimar (1828–62). They gave up farming to hunt the buffalo, from which they derived food, clothing, and shelter. Competition over buffalo hunting grounds turned them into warring tribes. The slaughter of the buffalo herds by whites destroyed the Indian economy.

5

5 This hide painting celebrates the Indian victory at the battle of Little Big Horn on June 25–26, 1876. Sioux and Cheyenne troops under the command of Chief Sitting Bull completely annihilated a US cavalry battalion led by Gen. George A. Custer. But the victory only led to more oppression.

6 The Hopi Indians of the Southwest have lived for 1,000 years in large communal buildings, called *pueblos* by the Spanish. This pueblo has been modernized, but baking is still done outside in large beehive-shaped ovens. At first, the Hopi built their pueblos on the desert floors, near their farmlands. But after a revolt against the Spanish in 1680, they built on the more easily defended mesas.

6

7

7 The ceremonial shirt of the Tlingit Indians was woven of the hair of the wild mountain goat and the inner fibers of cedar bark. Decorated with mystical symbols and representations of clan totems, it was worn or given as a gift at potlatch rituals—where gifts were distributed as a means of displaying one's wealth. The Tlingit were introduced to fur trading by the Russians.

8 Sioux Indian women wiring electric circuits at a tribally owned factory on the Rosebud Reservation, S. D., have transferred the manual dexterity needed for traditional beadwork to a modern industry.

8

The American experience: the people

The United States has been called a melting pot so often as to make the term a cliché [Key]. But it has been noted that "melting pot" is not quite accurate as a metaphor; many ethnic groups have tended to hold on to their particular characteristics and have not been totally assimilated into one national type. No "national" religion has replaced the myriad religions, denominations, and sects to which immigrants belonged when they arrived. Ethnic neighborhoods, either by choice or by discrimination, have continued to exist [4, 5, 6]. Marriage within an ethnic group, or at least within the same religious group, continues to be the norm today.

In other important ways, however, the American people have become assimilated. Most obvious is the universal language: English. Despite isolated areas where another language is spoken—and despite the large communities of Spanish-speaking Puerto Ricans, Cubans, and Mexicans [7]—English has quickly become the primary language of all ethnic groups as they settle into the American way of life.

The origins of Americans

Strictly speaking, there is no indigenous American population. The Indians and Eskimos came from Siberia, the Hawaiians originally migrated from other Pacific islands. The whites who began settling in what is now the United States in the 17th century were mostly from northern Europe—England, Holland, and Sweden. The first blacks arrived in 1619 [2]. The first Jews arrived in New Amsterdam in 1654. Many of the early colonists—such as the first Jews who arrived in New Amsterdam in 1654 to escape Portuguese persecution in Brazil—emigrated to North America for religious reasons: Puritans in Massachusetts, Baptists in Rhode Island, Quakers in Pennsylvania, Roman Catholics in Maryland, French Huguenots in South Carolina. But the American population remained small; by 1700 there were still fewer than 250,000 colonists.

The eighteenth century

North America continued to be settled mostly by northern Europeans in the eighteenth century. Most of them came from the British Isles; there were increasing numbers of Protestants from Scotland and Ireland (or Scotch-Irish, as they became known) emigrating to the New World, particularly to Pennsylvania and the southern colonies. Germans immigrated to Pennsylvania in response to the guarantee of religious freedom by its founder, William Penn (1644–1718). By 1776, when the British colonies declared their independence, the population was about 2,000,000. Despite the war, the population continued to rise; by the beginning of the nineteenth century there were 5,000,000 US citizens.

The black slave population rose rapidly toward the end of the century after the invention of the cotton gin increased the demand for cheap labor to produce cotton. In 1790 there were 700,000 slaves in the country; in 1830 there were 2,000,000; the figure rose to 4,000,000 by 1860.

The great tide of immigrants

The nineteenth century was the great age of immigration [1, 3]. Europe's population was

CONNECTIONS

See also
1216 Settlement of North America
1278 The United States: Reconstruction to World War I

1

Where Immigrants Came From 1821-1970
(Thousands/Decade)

	Total	Great Britain	Ireland	Germany	Scandinavia	Other Western Europe(1)	Italy	Other Southern Europe(2)	Central Europe(3)	Eastern Europe(4)	Asia(5)	Africa	Latin America & Caribbean	Canada
1821-30	143.4	25.1	50.7	6.8		12.8		2.6					9.3	2.3
1831-40	599.1	75.8	207.4	152.5	2.3	51.8	2.3	3.0					19.8	12.4
1841-50	1713.3	267.0	780.7	434.6	14.4	95.2	1.9	2.8					20.7	41.7
1851-60	2598.2	424.0	914.1	951.7	24.7	116.9	9.2	10.4	1.2		41.4		15.4	59.3
1861-70	2314.8	606.9	435.8	787.5	126.4	75.1	11.7	9.4	9.8	2.6	64.3		12.7	153.9
1871-80	2812.2	548.0	438.9	714.1	243.0	124.3	55.8	20.6	85.9	39.6	123.2		20.4	383.6
1881-90	4777.0	817.4	655.5	1453.0	656.5	206.3	307.3	24.4	405.5	221.2	68.4			439.1
1891-1900	3687.6	271.5	388.4	505.2	371.5	106.9	651.9	52.3		521.8	71.2			
1901-10	8795.4	526.0	339.1	341.5	505.3	198.2	2045.9	265.7		1769.6	243.4		182.7	179.2
1911-20	5735.8	341.4	146.2	144.0	203.5	162.5	1109.5	350.7		1012.5	192.5	8.4	401.5	742.1
1921-30	4107.2	330.2	220.6	412.2	198.2	122.9	455.3	121.2	442.5	174.7	96.1	6.3	592.2	924.5
1931-40	528.4	29.4	13.2	114.1	11.3	30.7	68.0	20.1	.48.7	12.9	19.8	1.8	50.5	108.5
1941-50	1035.0	131.6	27.5	226.6	26.9	77.2	57.7	22.1	45.8	8.5	31.8	6.2	183.0	171.7
1951-60	2515.5	208.9	64.4	345.5	57.3	115.3	188.0	79.5	374.2	70.6	139.0	16.6	558.9	274.9
1961-70	3321.7	230.5	42.4	200.0	44.9	86.9	206.7	200.0	171.9	36.4	343.7	39.3	1288.8	286.7

(1)France, Benelux, Switzerland
(2)Spain, Portugal, Greece
(3)Austria, Poland, Czechoslovakia, Hungary, Yugoslavia
(4)Russia, Baltic States, Finland, Romania, Bulgaria
(5)Excluding the Philippines

Insufficient Data
Less than 1000/Decade
Greatest Influx/Decade
Second Greatest Influx/Decade

2

Charleftown, July 24th, 1769.

TO BE SOLD,

On THURSDAY the third Day of AUGUST next,

A CARGO

OF

NINETY-FOUR

PRIME, HEALTHY

NEGROES,

CONSISTING OF

Thirty-nine MEN, Fifteen BOYS, Twenty-four WOMEN, and Sixteen GIRLS.

JUST ARRIVED,

In the Brigantine DEMBIA, *Francis Bare*, Mafter, from SIERRA-LEON, by

DAVID & JOHN DEAS.

1 No decade saw a greater influx of immigrants to the United States than the first one of this century. Nearly 8,800,000 people arrived. In that decade alone, more immigrants came from Italy and Eastern Europe than had come previously since the nation began. But Irish immigration was one-half what it had been during the 1840s, and German immigration was one-tenth what it was in the 1880s.

2 Slave ships brought thousands of blacks to the New World from Africa under conditions of unbelievable barbarity. The 94 "prime, healthy Negroes" advertised here were those who survived the journey. The Constitution had disallowed the importation of slaves as of 1810 but did not interfere with the sale of slaves in states where slavery was legal. Slave auctions continued right up to the Civil War's end.

3

3 Immigrants from around the world arrived in New York City during the 19th century. In this idealized 1855 painting by Samuel Waugh (1814–85), Irish immigrants disembark from a three-masted schooner, while, in the background, passengers leave a Chinese junk, (an unlikely occurrence in New York harbor). The round fort to the left, Castle Garden, was replaced by Ellis Island as immigration headquarters in 1892.

increasing faster than the land or the economy could accommodate, causing large numbers to emigrate to the underpopulated continents of America. Movement was made easier by the steamship.

The first great wave of immigrants to reach the United States was the Irish, who were forced to leave their homeland by the potato famine of the 1840s. They were followed in the next decades by Germans and Scandinavians, many of whom settled on the rich farmlands of the Middle West. Chinese laborers were brought in through West Coast ports to build the new transcontinental railroads. Italians, Poles, Czechs, and Russians came later, especially from the 1880s into the 1920s.

The decline in immigration

All together, more than 22,000,000 immigrants arrived in the United States from 1890 to 1930. They came from every country of Europe. Mexicans crossed the border from the South, and Canadians crossed from the North. But the age of massive immigration was ending. Pressures to halt or reduce immigration had begun in the nineteenth century, both from working people who resented the cheap labor offered by the newly arrived and by conservative, established people who considered themselves to be culturally superior. The Chinese Exclusion Act of 1882, which did precisely what its name indicated, was the first federal law to control immigration. The National Origins Act of 1924 limited the total number of persons allowed in the country each year and set up a country-by-country quota system. The quota as established greatly favored northern Europe and the Western Hemisphere countries at the expense of eastern and southern Europe and Asia.

Despite its inequities, the law remained in effect until the administration of Lyndon B. Johnson, when the Immigration Act of 1965 was passed. While keeping the quota system, the new law increased the quota for nations previously discriminated against. Congress, in addition, has from time to time passed special laws allowing easier access to the country by political refugees such as the Vietnamese [8].

KEY

Immigrants have not always been as welcome to the United States as in this cartoon of 1880 entitled "Welcome to All!" Since 1868, Chinese immigrants had been denied the right to apply for citizenship. The Chinese Exclusion Act of 1882 banned the immigration of Chinese laborers. Japanese immigrants were similarly excluded by the Gentlemen's Agreement of 1907. Neither ban was lifted until 1924. Several times in the 19th century Roman Catholic immigrants were the target of organized exclusionary movements, including the notorious American (Know-Nothing) Party (1849).

4

4 The festival of San Gennaro, the largest of the many ethnic religious celebrations held each year in New York City, takes place each September in "Little Italy." Little Italy, in lower Manhattan, was settled around the turn of the century, when the great wave of Italians (mostly from southern Italy) came to the United States. Today, it is increasingly an area of old people as younger Italian-Americans move to the suburbs.

5

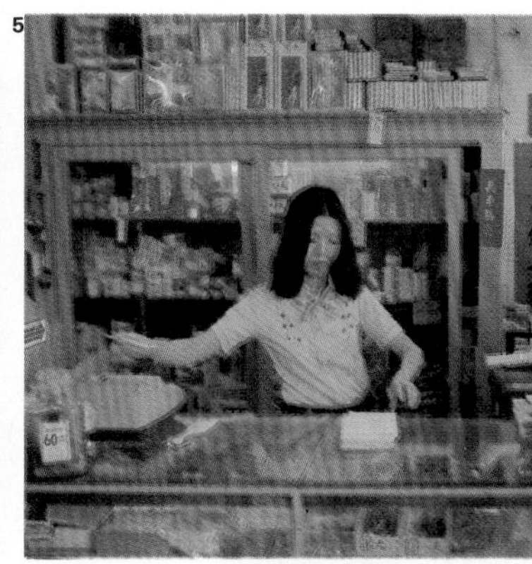

5 Large and thriving Chinatowns are found in San Francisco, Los Angeles, and New York City. This store in Los Angeles' Chinatown serves the community, not tourists, selling both traditional Chinese and modern Western products. Chinese-Americans have tended to remain in Chinatowns, often as a matter of choice. As a result, the larger Chinatowns have remained viable neighborhoods although crowded.

6

6 The Lower East Side of New York City was at the turn of the century a center of Yiddish-language culture. The *Jewish Daily Forward,* founded in 1897 by Abraham Cahan (1860–1951), was the leading newspaper. Along with news and social discussion, it published important fiction writers, including Sholom Aleichem (1859–1916) and Isaac Bashevis Singer (1904–   ).

7

7 The oldest European immigrants to what would become the United States were the Spanish. Yet Spanish-speaking immigrants from Mexico (legal and otherwise) form a large group among the newest immigrants. Latin immigrants as a whole share a common language, but come from diverse cultures. The many Cuban immigrants who have arrived in Florida as political refugees since the early 1960s would find the fare in this Mexican restaurant in Los Angeles nearly as "foreign" to them as it would be to a New England Yankee. One of the largest groups of Spanish-speaking Americans, Puerto Ricans, are not immigrants. They may travel to and from the mainland without passports.

8

8 The end of the Vietman War created a refugee problem. In 1975 US Congress enacted special laws allowing Vietnamese refugees to come to the United States. By 1976, when the program ended, about 145,000 Vietnamese had settled in the United States. Only in California, where 27,000 of them settled, were there enough to form Vietnamese neighborhoods.

The American experience: political parties

The United States has been a two-party country since the eighteenth century. One of those two has always been the Democratic party; the other has been, successively, the Federalists, the Whigs, and, since 1856, the Republicans. Third parties have rarely played a decisive role [1].

Beginnings

The Founding Fathers expected the new republic to be governed without political parties. James Madison (1751–1836) argued (in *The Federalist*, No. 10) that a federal republic, of all forms of government, would offer the best defense against factious rule. The Constitution itself makes no allowance for a party role in the government; the election of George Washington as president was accomplished without any such role.

Political differences quickly arose within Washington's cabinet [2], however. Alexander Hamilton, the secretary of the treasury, was an advocate of strong federal government, of mercantile and financial interests, and of close ties with Great Britain. Thomas Jefferson, the secretary of state, believed that most power should reside with the states and that an agricultural economy was the best basis on which to build a democratic society. He favored French interests over British.

The Federalists and the Jeffersonians

The election of John Adams (1735–1826) in 1796 was a victory for Hamilton's faction, the Federalists. The Jeffersonians (known first as Republicans, then Democratic Republicans, and finally as the Democratic party) opposed the conservative Adams administration with increasing vehemence [3]. Adams retaliated with the Alien and Sedition Acts (1798), which imposed restrictions on freedom of speech and of the press. The Adams administration was unpopular; Jefferson's support grew. He became president in 1800 and was succeeded by two Democratic Republicans, James Madison and James Monroe (1758–1831).

Jacksonians and Whigs

The War of 1812 was unpopular in New England, where Federalist strength was strongest, and gave the Federalists their last major national issue. But the successful completion of the war left the party in disarray. The war also produced the great military hero who was to revitalize the Democratic party and dominate it for the next generation: Andrew Jackson [Key]. When Jackson ran for president in 1824 he assembled what some historians consider to be the first political party in the modern sense. He organized the small farmer in the West, the urban working classes in the East, and the small businessman into a tight political organization. In a four-way race, Jackson won the most votes, but since no candidate had an electoral college majority the election had to be decided in the House of Representatives, which selected John Quincy Adams (1767–1848).

Elected in 1828, Jackson consolidated the strength of the Democratic party. But anti-Jackson sentiment also grew. The opposition, known first as the National Republican party, eventually became the Whig party. Its leaders were Henry Clay (1777–1852) and Daniel Webster [4]. The party's

CONNECTIONS

See also
904 Political participation
1398 The American experience: voting

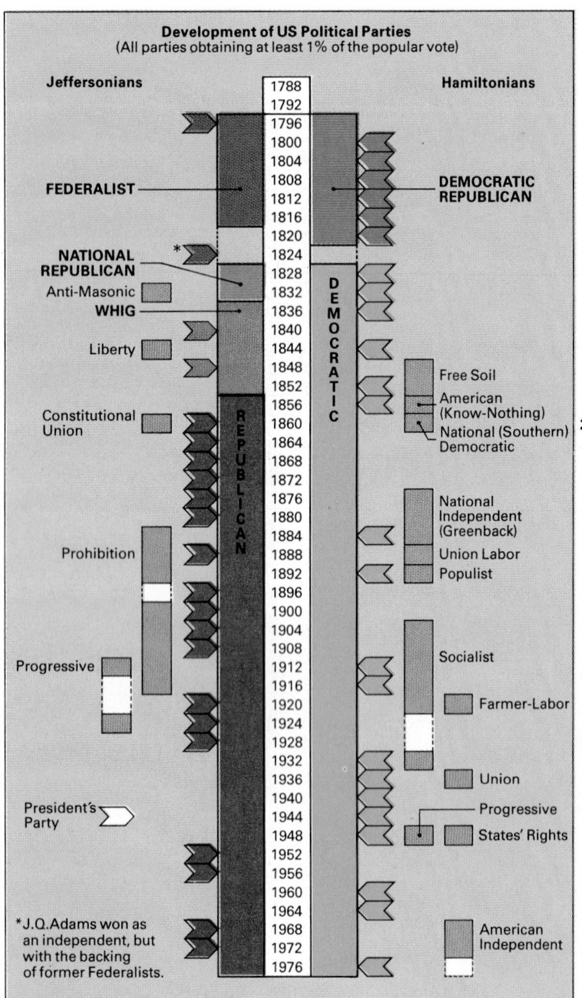

Development of US Political Parties
(All parties obtaining at least 1% of the popular vote)
Jeffersonians
Hamiltonians
1788
1792
1796
1800
1804
1808
1812
1816
1820
1824
1828
1832
1836
1840
1844
1848
1852
1856
1860
1864
1868
1872
1876
1880
1884
1888
1892
1896
1900
1904
1908
1912
1916
1920
1924
1928
1932
1936
1940
1944
1948
1952
1956
1960
1964
1968
1972
1976
FEDERALIST
DEMOCRATIC REPUBLICAN
NATIONAL REPUBLICAN
Anti-Masonic
WHIG
Liberty
DEMOCRATIC
REPUBLICAN
Free Soil
American (Know-Nothing)
National (Southern) Democratic
Constitutional Union
National Independent (Greenback)
Union Labor
Populist
Prohibition
Socialist
Progressive
Farmer-Labor
Union
Progressive
States' Rights
President's Party
American Independent
*J.Q.Adams won as an independent, but with the backing of former Federalists.

1 George Washington was elected president without opposition in 1789 and 1792. The only other candidate to ever run unopposed was James Monroe in 1820. The Federalist party, which had been discredited for its secessionist sympathies during the War of 1812, fared so poorly in the 1816 election that it did not run a national candidate against the Democratic Republicans in 1820. Monroe received 231 electoral votes to 1 for John Quincy Adams cast by William Plummer of New Hampshire. Tradition states that Plummer cast his dissenting vote in order to preserve for Washington the distinction of being the only president selected unanimously, although he may have disliked Monroe.

3 This crude cartoon depicts an actual incident that occurred on the floor of the House of Representatives in 1798. Federalist Congressman Roger Griswold of Connecticut is shown attacking Vermont Republican Matthew Lyon, who defends himself with fireplace tongs. Lyon was the most prominent citizen prosecuted under the Sedition Act. He was jailed for publishing a letter critical of President Adams.

2 The original cabinet of President George Washington is pictured here. Left to right: Henry Knox (1750–1806), secretary of war; Thomas Jefferson (1743–1826), secretary of state; Edmund Randolph (1753–1813), attorney general; Alexander Hamilton (1755–1804), secretary of the treasury; and the president. (Randolph is probably pictured turned away because he was forced to resign his cabinet position because of allegations of scandal.

4 Daniel Webster (1782–1852), whose name was synonymous with the Whig party, began his political career as a Federalist. He was one of three Whig candidates for president in 1836, but the new party, which had run several candidates in the hope of forcing the election to be decided in the House of Representatives, lost to Martin Van Buren, the Democrat. Thereafter, Webster, despite his ambition and his power within the Whigs, was never again its candidate.

choice in 1840, hero of the Indian Wars William Henry Harrison (1773–1841), won; the Whigs retained power until 1852. But the party expired soon after, hopelessly split over the slavery issue. The antislavery Whigs joined the new Republican party; the others joined the Democrats or various minor parties [5].

Republicans and Democrats

The Republican party was founded in 1854 by groups opposed to slavery; in 1860 its candidate, Abraham Lincoln [6], was elected president. The Republicans became indelibly associated with the Union cause in the Civil War. After the war they entered their greatest period of triumph. With the exception of Grover Cleveland (1837–1908), all presidents were Republicans from Lincoln's election in 1860 until 1912 when Woodrow Wilson [7] was elected.

The business prosperity of the 1920s brought the Republicans their second period of success. It lasted from 1920 until 1932, when the Great Depression brought the Democrats back to power. Franklin D. Roosevelt (1882–1945), the Democratic candidate in 1932, put together a potent political coalition. Holding on to the traditional Democratic bases—the South and the blue-collar vote—he added farmers, professionals, and blacks. That coalition elected Roosevelt for four terms. Harry S. Truman (1884–1972) was elected in 1948 despite the Dixiecrat revolt [8].

Dwight D. Eisenhower, the Republican candidate in 1952 and 1956, won by cutting sharply into the Democratic coalition, particularly in the South. But it was the Vietnam War that divided the Democrats most seriously, leaving the party open to defeat in 1968 and 1972 by the Republican Richard M. Nixon (1913–). The Republican triumph crumbled, however, when both Nixon and his vice president, Spiro T. Agnew (1918–), resigned in disgrace. Nixon's appointed successor, Gerald R. Ford (1913–), in his bid for election in 1976 was defeated by Democrat Jimmy Carter (1924–) [9]. In a close election, Carter won most of the South and the industrial Northeast and Midwest.

KEY

Andrew Jackson's progress to Washington, D.C., for his first inauguration reenforced his "man-of-the-people" image. He was met at every stop by enthusiastic crowds. For the inauguration itself, thousands of Jacksonians poured into Washington, and the White House was thrown open to them. More conservative and sedate Washingtonians were horrified at this "Jacksonian rabble." But Jackson saw the political value of the western farmer and the urban laborer and courted them.

5

A SKETCH from
The New Tragic Farce, of "AMERICANS SHALL RULE AMERICA."
as enacted by Mr. SHAM of Baltimore, and his wonderful STAR Company:
Scene, laid in the Heart of the City of Baltimore.

5 Know-Nothing ruffians wandered through the streets of Baltimore during the 1856 election intimidating German and Irish voters. The Know-Nothing movement began as a secret society in the 1840s (its members, when asked about it, claimed to "know nothing"). Its purpose was to keep immigrants, particularly Roman Catholics, out of the country (and to keep those in the country out of political life).

6

Lincoln
and
Hamlin

6 Abraham Lincoln and Hannibal Hamlin, presidential and vice-presidential candidates of the Republican party, won in 1860 with fewer than 40% of the votes cast. The Democrats, badly split over slavery, fielded two candidates, Stephen A. Douglas and John C. Breckinridge, while the Constitutional Union party, a coalition of old-time Whigs and Know-Nothings, ran John Bell.

7 In 1912 former President Theodore Roosevelt, disturbed by the conservatism his hand-picked successor, William Howard Taft, had evidenced in his first term, tried to wrest the Republican nomination away from Taft. After his efforts were blocked and the Republicans renominated Taft, Roosevelt broke away from the party and formed the National Progressive party, otherwise known as the Bull Moose party. Roosevelt won more votes—both popular and electoral—than Taft, but with the Republican vote split, the election was won by the Democratic candidate, Woodrow Wilson.

8 Harry S. Truman brought off a political upset in 1948 when he won the presidency over the supremely confident Republican candidate, Thomas E. Dewey. Truman conducted a nationwide whistle-stop campaign, lambasting the "do-nothing" Republican Congress. Dewey, believing that his victory was assured, conducted a mild, lackluster campaign. Truman defeated Dewey by more than 2,000,000 votes.

9 In 1976 Gerald Ford and Jimmy Carter faced each other in three nationally televised debates. In the only previous such event, the 1960 debates between Richard M. Nixon and John F. Kennedy, it was widely agreed that Kennedy had won. In 1976, however, there was no such consensus. Some observers felt that Carter had gained from the debates, if only because he held his own against the president.

7

NATIONAL
PROGRESSIVE PARTY
ROOSEVELT-JOHNSON

8

9

The American experience: voting

Universal adult participation in public elections is a twentieth-century event; elections in colonial America, as elsewhere, were limited in scope. In the Puritan theocracies of New England, public officials were chosen by the church elders. The Southern colonies were organized after the English county system. The members of Virginia's House of Burgesses were voted into office by the gentry. Democracy evolved in town meetings, however [Key].

The new republic

The US Constitution, as ratified in 1788, stipulated that the president and vice president were to be chosen by the electoral college [1], not by people in a direct election. Senators were to be chosen by the state legislatures. Federal judges were to be named by the president. Only members of the House of Representatives were to be popularly elected. Furthermore, the Constitution left to the states the decision of who should be allowed to vote. Most had property requirements for voting. New Jersey, alone and only briefly, permitted women to vote (if they met the property requirement).

George Washington was twice elected president unanimously by the electoral college in the manner envisaged by the framers of the Constitution. The emergence of political parties during Washington's administration, however, crucially altered the process. The parties accomplished the change in the electoral college by running candidates for the college who were already committed to vote for a specific presidential candidate. The role of the electoral college was reduced to the formality of ratifying the will of the voters (except in 1824, 1876 [3], and 1888 when the candidate with the highest popular vote was not chosen). Since 1796, virtually all US elections have been conducted under the two-party system, and since 1856 those two have been the Democratic and the Republican parties.

The Jacksonian era

The early nineteenth century saw a steady liberalizing of the voting requirements. In 1828, Andrew Jackson, running on the Democratic ticket, won the presidency. His opponent, President John Quincy Adams, was backed by the anti-Jackson coalition that later became the Whig party. The electorate had so grown that more than 1,000,000 votes were cast (as opposed to about 350,000 in the 1824 election). Both sides mounted aggressive campaigns, each side accusing the other of dreadful crimes, not all of them political. There were campaign tours, military bands, and charges of vote buying. That campaign is generally considered the prototype of the modern presidential election.

In 1832 the Democrats convened at Baltimore to renominate Jackson; it was the first national political convention of a major party. That peculiarly American institution—colorful, illogical, and incomprehensible to foreigners—became a vital part of American politics. The party primary election [7] began in the 1840s.

After the Civil War

The Republican party emerged from the Civil War triumphant. The Democrats, as

CONNECTIONS

See also
904 Political participation
1396 The American experience: political parties

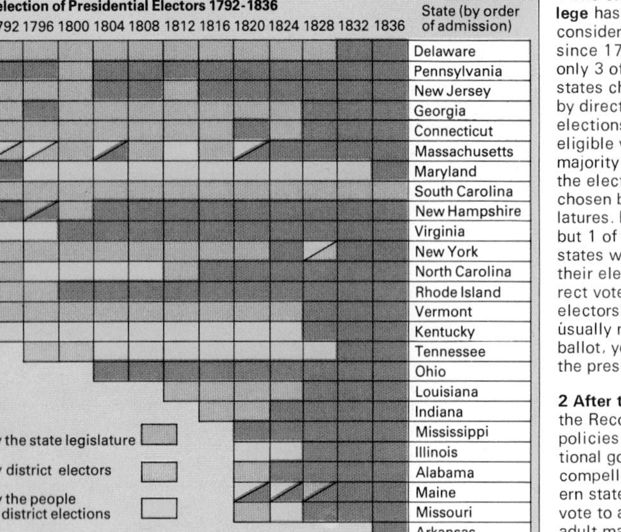
Selection of Presidential Electors 1792-1836
1792 1796 1800 1804 1808 1812 1816 1820 1824 1828 1832 1836
State (by order of admission)
Delaware
Pennsylvania
New Jersey
Georgia
Connecticut
Massachusetts
Maryland
South Carolina
New Hampshire
Virginia
New York
North Carolina
Rhode Island
Vermont
Kentucky
Tennessee
Ohio
Louisiana
Indiana
Mississippi
Illinois
Alabama
Maine
Missouri
Arkansas
Michigan
by the state legislature
by district electors
by the people in district elections
by the people in statewide elections

1 The electoral college has undergone considerable change since 1789. In 1792 only 3 of the 15 states chose electors by direct statewide elections open to all eligible voters; in the majority of states, the electors were chosen by the legislatures. By 1836, all but 1 of the 26 states were choosing their electors by direct vote. Today, the electors' names are usually not on the ballot, yet they elect the president.

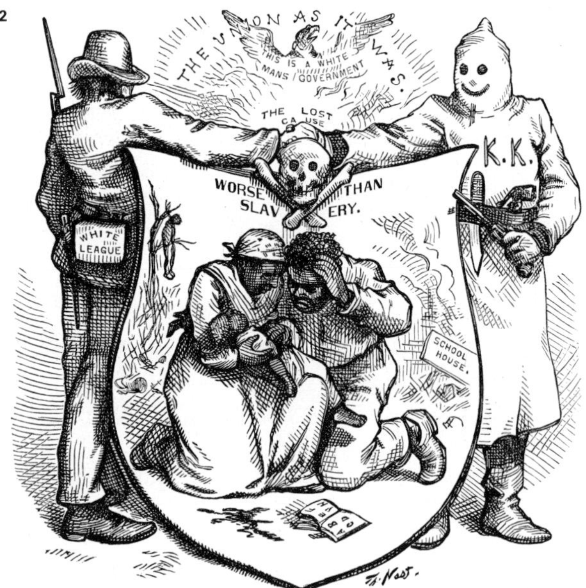
THE UNION AS IT WAS
THIS IS A WHITE MANS GOVERNMENT
THE LOST CAUSE
WORSE THAN SLAVERY
WHITE LEAGUE
K.K.
SCHOOL HOUSE
T. Nast

2 After the Civil War, the Reconstruction policies of the national government compelled the Southern states to give the vote to all former adult male slaves. Within a decade, however, white Southerners had regained control of the state governments and had succeeded in disenfranchising virtually all black voters. They used various methods—as indicated in this 1876 cartoon by Thomas Nast—to do this.

NATIONAL
DEMOCRATIC
SAMUEL J. TILDEN
THOMAS A. HENDRICKS

3 In 1876 Samuel J. Tilden, the Democratic candidate, received a majority of the popular vote and was widely believed to have won an electoral majority. But there were contested electors in three Southern states: Florida, Louisiana, and South Carolina, and one contested Oregon elector. Congress appointed a commission (with a Republican majority) to settle the issue, and it awarded all the contested votes to the Republican Rutherford B. Hayes.

4 Carrie Chapman Catt (1859–1947), president of the National American Woman Suffrage Association, is greeted by Gov. Al Smith (1873–1944) and other well-wishers on her return to New York City after the passage in 1920 of the 19th (Women's Suffrage) Amendment to the US Constitution. The women's suffrage movement began in earnest in 1848, with a national meeting of women at Seneca Falls, N. Y. Various suffrage organizations merged in 1890 to form NAWSA, the prime aim of which was a constitutional amendment giving women the right to vote.

the party of the Confederacy, were in disarray. The Reconstruction plan put forth by the Republicans in Congress called for enfranchisement of former slaves and disenfranchisement of white supporters of the Confederacy. The results were elections in which the Republican party in the South won impressive majorities (to add to their Northern victories). The Republican success in the South was short lived, however. Southern whites reestablished control over the political apparatus (through the Democratic party) and disenfranchised blacks by various methods (including such devices as the poll tax) [2].

Elections in the late 19th century were often decided by well-organized political machines based in the large cities and more often than not Democratic. Tammany Hall of New York City was the prototype. Although often riddled by corruption, these groups were frequently the only political avenues open to new immigrants. The importance of machine politics lasted until well into the second half of the 20th century [5].

Twentieth-century reforms

The tendency toward universal adult participation in elections is reflected in a number of amendments to the US Constitution. The first such amendments—the 13th, 14th, and 15th—went into effect after the Civil War to assure full citizenship, including the right to vote, to former slaves. The 17th (ratified 1913) provided for direct election of US senators. The 19th (1920) gave the vote to women [4]. The 23rd (1961) allowed residents of the District of Columbia to vote in presidential elections. The 24th (1964) outlawed the poll tax. The 26th (1971) lowered the voting age to 18 [6].

These amendments, coupled with the various voting-rights acts passed during Lyndon Johnson's administration, had the effect of assuring the vote to every adult in the country. Despite these assurances, however, the percentage of Americans who actually vote in national elections is dramatically lower than that of most other Western democracies. Attempts to increase voter participation have not met with any great success.

KEY

The New England Town meeting, a political phenomenon going back to colonial days, has been regarded as democracy in its purest form. The voters gather together to resolve town problems and to elect officials. Most modern political units are too large to accommodate the town-meeting type of voter participation. Similar atmospheres often prevail, however, in such small-scale bodies as library boards, boards of education, and block associations.

5

6

6 The 26th Amendment to the Constitution, giving the vote in all local, state, and national elections to those between the ages of 18 and 21, was ratified in 1971. It was approved in record time. Congress proposed the amendment on March 23; by June 30 it had been approved by the required two-thirds of the state legislatures. Despite predictions that the infusion of young voters would radically change American politics, very little immediate effect was felt. First, only a small percentage of young people actually register and vote. Second, those who do vote show voting patterns that are similar to those of older voters.

5 Richard J. Daley (1902–76) was first elected mayor of Chicago in 1955 and, until his death in December 1976, maintained complete control over the government of Chicago and usually over the Democratic party in all of Illinois. Looked upon as the last of the old-time, big-city political bosses, Daley was often credited with running an extremely efficient city government. His reputation for being able to deliver large Democratic majorities in Chicago and in Illinois caused him to be courted by would-be Democratic presidential candidates. He suffered a political setback in 1976 when Illinois went to Gerald Ford and Daley's hand-picked candidate for governor also lost.

7 The practice of choosing presidential candidates by primary elections (rather than by state political conventions) has been growing. Here five Democratic candidates are shown participating in a March 29, 1976, primary debate in New York City sponsored by the League of Women Voters. While the primary system is undeniably more democratic, it creates its own problems. Candidates who choose to enter all the primary contests find it expensive, time consuming, and physically exhausting. Furthermore, since the first primaries are held in March and the election is held in November, many voters are bored with the issues and candidates by election day.

7

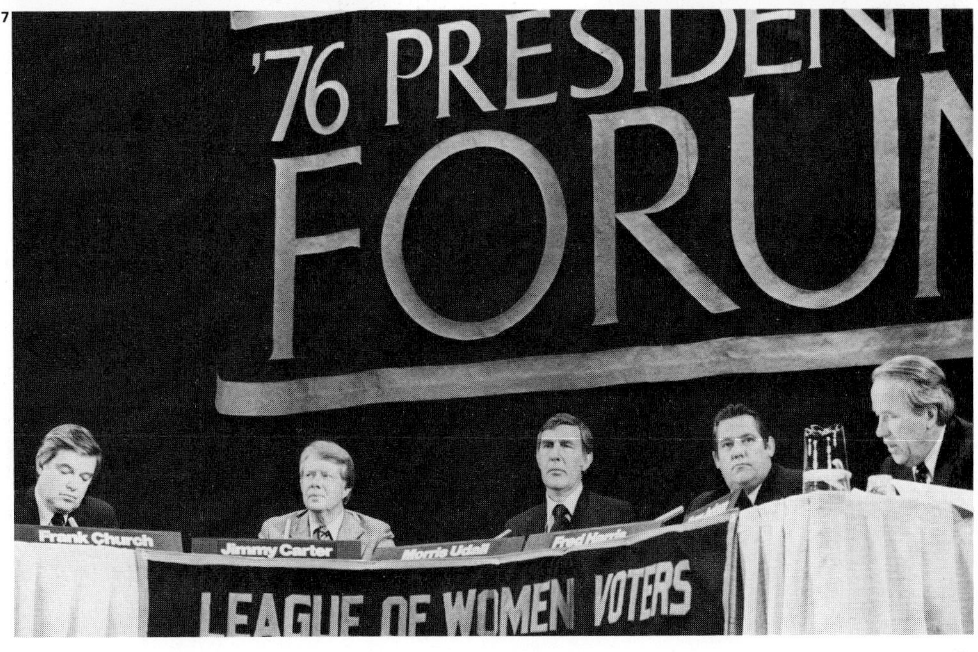
Frank Church
Jimmy Carter
Morris Udall
Fred Harris
LEAGUE OF WOMEN VOTERS

The American experience: the economy 1607–1865

Because of varying geography, climate, and political origins, the thirteen colonies developed individual economies. Although these different economies eventually added to the diverse strength of the United States, economic rivalries also underlay the sectionalism that led to the Civil War.

The climate and rich, open land of the Southern colonies encouraged large-scale agriculture that produced surpluses for export [7]. The products—rice, indigo, timber, naval stores (tar, pitch, turpentine), and most important, tobacco, and, later, cotton—were much in demand in Europe. Black slaves provided the necessary labor. New England farmers—confronted with rocky, poor land and a severer climate—barely subsisted, with no farm surplus to export. But New England had other assets, including abundant fish off the coast, good ships' timber, excellent harbors, and cheap power from numerous rivers. New Englanders turned to fishing, shipbuilding, shipping [4], and manufacturing.

England made sporadic efforts to control the colonial economies, beginning with the first Navigation Act in 1650. But by and large, the colonies developed without undue regulation from London until after the collapse of the French empire in Canada in 1763, when Parliament began more systematic control. Many colonists objected to newly imposed taxes and trade restrictions. Economic causes for the American Revolution were as important as political and social ones.

The new republic

The end of the American Revolution found the former colonies in a precarious economic position. The traditional market, Great Britain, was no longer guaranteed. Merchant ships, without the protection of the British navy, were prey to marauding privateers and pirates. France, America's most powerful ally, soon in its own revolutionary wars, was unable to offer much help, economic or other. Nevertheless, the United States prospered. The Constitution created a stable government under which business and, later, industry would prosper. It also, until the Civil War, protected the institution of slavery, on which the South depended for its economic life.

The first water-powered cotton textile mill opened in 1790 [Key]; 1793 saw the invention of the cotton gin by Eli Whitney [3]. Technological developments often took hold quicker than in Europe; the new nation was readier to try new methods.

The movement to lands west of the Alleghenies opened rich farmlands in western Pennsylvania, the Ohio country, and the Old Southwest. Abundant coal, and later oil [6], was found in Pennsylvania and Ohio, laying the base for Midwest industry.

The Louisiana Purchase of 1803 added vast territories to the United States and secured the Mississippi as a waterway from the heartland of the continent to the Gulf of Mexico. The opening of the Erie Canal [1] in 1825 created a waterway between the Eastern Seaboard and the Great Lakes area.

The intent of the Embargo Act of 1807 had been to use economic means to protect US interests from the rivalries of France and Great Britain, but US businessmen objected to the government's interference

CONNECTIONS

See also
1216 Settlement of North America
1200 International economy 1700–1800
1218 The American Revolution
1274 The United States: the opening of the West
1402 The American experience: the economy since 1865

1

1 The Erie Canal, constructed by New York State from 1817 to 1825 at the urging of Gov. De Witt Clinton (1769–1828), connected Buffalo on Lake Erie and Albany on the Hudson River. Built primarily by Irish immigrant labor, it had 83 locks and 18 aqueducts along its 363mi (585km). Within nine years it recouped its $7,000,000 cost in tolls. It provided a direct, economical link between the Midwest and New York City. This aquatint (*c.* 1830) by J. W. Hill shows the juncture of the Erie and Northern canals. Railroad competition eventually cut into the canal's long-haul traffic.

2

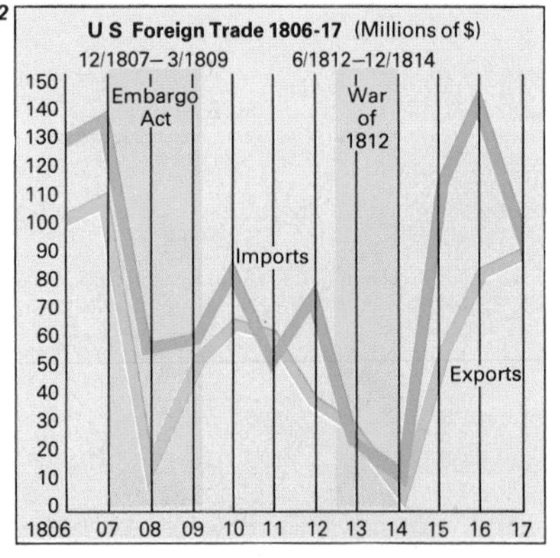

U S Foreign Trade 1806-17 (Millions of $)
12/1807–3/1809
6/1812–12/1814
Embargo Act
War of 1812
Imports
Exports
150 140 130 120 110 100 90 80 70 60 50 40 30 20 10 0
1806 07 08 09 10 11 12 13 14 15 16 17

2 US foreign trade, particularly important to the manufacturing centers of New England, was hard hit in the years immediately following 1806. First the Embargo Act of 1807 curtailed shippers' activities. Vital raw materials could not be imported, nor could manufactured goods be exported for sales. Then the War of 1812 pitted the small US merchant marine against the British navy. US business was crippled.

3

3 Eli Whitney (1765–1825)—shown here in a painting by another prominent US inventor, Samuel F. B. Morse (1791–1872)—attempted to mass manufacture 10,000 rifles for the federal government after his cotton gin was pirated. In his factory at Whitneyville, Conn., he adapted power-driven tools that could be operated by semi-skilled workers to produce interchangable parts. His efforts were the precursor of mass production.

4

Glidden & Williams'
LINE
For San-Francisco!
FROM LEWIS WHARF
CLIPPER SHIP
California!
HENRY BARBER,
Commander,
Is now in berth with one half her cargo on board. This ship was built expressly for the trade, and is in every way a most desirable conveyance. Her engagements are large, and we confidently expect to despatch her at an early day.
Shippers will oblige by forwarding their goods promptly.
FOR FREIGHT.......APPLY TO Glidden & Williams,
NO. 114 STATE STREET, BOSTON.
Agents in San-Francisco......MESSRS. MEADER, LOLOR & CO.

4 The clipper ship, which saw a brief period of glory in the mid-19th century, evolved around 1832 from the Baltimore clipper, a small swift Chesapeake Bay schooner. New York and Boston shipyards soon became the major construction centers. Especially fast ships were needed in the China trade to carry the season's finest tea to America and England and, later, to compete with the land route to California during the gold rush. Donald McKay (1810–80) designed the largest clipper ship, the *Great Republic*, in 1853 and what was probably the fastest, the *Flying Cloud*, which made the New York to San Francisco run in a record-breaking 89 days in 1851.

with free trade. US business suffered far worse than that of the European countries. New England was especially hard hit. The embargo was soon lifted. The War of 1812 created even greater economic havoc for New England [2], so much so that a number of prominent New England Federalists met in Hartford, Conn., in December 1814 to consider suing for a separate peace with England. But the war was soon concluded.

The battle over the Second Bank of the United States (1832–36) was fought along sectional lines. The Jacksonian Democrats looked upon this central bank as an instrument for the control of the economy by conservative Eastern and foreign financial interests. The bank's National Republican defenders saw it as a stabilizing influence upon the nation's economy and an aid to growth. The Democrats won; the charter of the Second Bank was not renewed in 1836. But their sense of triumph was short-lived; in 1837 the nation was hit by the severest depression of the antebellum period [5].

Despite setbacks such as the 1837 depression, the United States vastly expanded its economic sphere in the first half of the nineteenth century. Besides the purchase of Louisiana Territory, Florida was acquired from Spain (1819), Texas annexed (1845), and California and much of the Southwest seized from Mexico (1848). US economic interests vied with British interests for hegemony in Latin America.

Impact of the Civil War

The Civil War (1861–65) demonstrated the superiority of the North's resources. The agrarian South could not stand up to the industrial superiority of the North. The North effectively used its far more extensive transportation system to move men and supplies. The Union navy blockaded Southern ports, which were dependent on the cotton trade with Europe to obtain funds and manufactured goods. The war left the South in economic ruin. Slavery, which had been of great economic importance, was abolished. Reconstruction policies imposed on the South delayed economic recovery by decades. The North, on the other hand, emerged stronger than ever.

KEY

The first US water-powered cotton textile mill was built at Pawtucket, R.I., in 1790–93 by Samuel Slater (1768–1835). To protect its textile industry, England prohibited the export of textile technology and forbade the emigration of textile workers. Slater, a mill supervisor, left England in disguise and arrived in Rhode Island in 1789. With the backing of Moses Brown (1738–1836), Slater directed the building of the plant and all its equipment completely from memory. In 1798, Slater founded his own textile manufacturing firm.

5

GLORY
JULY 4th 1837
CUSTOM HOUSE
MECHANICS BANK
All Bonds must be paid in Specie
SHAVING
SPECIE

6 The first successful oil well, shown here, was drilled in Titusville, Pa., in 1859 by Edwin L. Drake (1819–80) (right foreground). It produced 25 barrels a day from a depth of 69ft (21m). Drake also built the first oil refinery nearby in 1860. Despite his pioneering work in the oil industry, Drake died in poverty because of poor business management. It was John D. Rockefeller (1839–1937) who organized the Standard Oil Company in 1870. The chief commercial use of petroleum at the time was for kerosene lamps. By the end of the century, the full potential of petroleum as an industrial fuel was being realized.

6

5 The panic of 1837, the severest the young nation had experienced, was accelerated by the financial dislocations caused by President Jackson's suppression of the Second Bank of the United States, by rapid exploitation of Western lands, by the collapse of the canal boom, and by international factors. Whig leaders blamed it all on Jackson, the Democratic party, and especially the Locofocos, a radical, egalitarian rump group within the Democratic party. Whig cartoonist Edward Clay mockingly portrayed Jackson as just a top hat and spectacles looking over the results of his policies. The panic cost the Democrats the next election.

7 The development of the cotton gin and the growing demand for cotton by British and New England textile manufacturers made cotton production a highly profitable industry. Cotton quickly surpassed tobacco as the South's major cash crop. Vast new plantations were carved out of the fertile wilderness of the Deep South; swamps were drained and pine lands were cleared to plant cotton. Although slavery was waning in the Old South states of Maryland and Virginia, it was vitally important to the cotton economy of the newly wealthy Deep South states of Alabama, Mississippi, and Louisiana. But the ascendancy of the Deep South was destroyed by the Civil War.

7

The American experience: the economy since 1865

The Civil War left the South in economic ruin [1]; recovery would be long and difficult. The North, on the other hand, had learned from the production buildup of the war and, with its factories all intact, was poised for a great economic boom. Growth came quickly [4].

Railroad building

The superiority of the Northern rail system had been a crucial factor in the triumph of the Union. During the war, in 1862, Congress had chartered two transcontinental railroads. The first was completed in 1869. Vast federal subsidies were put into railroad building [2]. Congress voted railroad builders more than $200,000,000 in direct subsidies, loaned them about $65,000,000, and ceded to them millions of acres of public lands in the West. Such vast riches led to monumental battles for control of railroads, battles involving the great entrepreneurs of the age, including James ("Jim") Fisk (1834–72), Jay Gould (1836–92), J. P. Morgan [Key], E. H. Harriman (1848–1916), and Leland Stanford (1824–93).

Economic growth into the twentieth century

The new railroad network was an impetus for economic growth in all parts of the country. New industries, such as John D. Rockefeller's Standard Oil Company (1870), were developed in the East and Midwest, and the rich agricultural lands of the Plains states and the West were opened to settlement. A brief setback occurred during the economic panic of 1873 and the subsequent depression. But overall economic growth continued except for the harsh depression following the panic of 1893.

Wages for both skilled and unskilled workers rose between 1865 and 1898. Some workers, however—farm laborers in the South, textile workers in the Northeast, coal miners in Appalachia—did not fully share in this earnings improvement. Often they were subjected to intolerable working conditions. Child labor was widespread [3]. Attempts at unionization met with brutal suppression. Multitudes of immigrants crowded into unhealthy city tenements.

As US industry grew, it began looking more and more to foreign markets. The Spanish-American War (1898) added the Philippines, Cuba, and Puerto Rico to the US economic sphere. US sponsorship of the Panama Canal (completed 1914) and the enormous investments of US companies in Latin America made the United States the preeminent hemispheric economic power.

The new century

The coming of the twentieth century saw the rise of an important new industry—that of the automobile. Henry Ford (1863–1947) introduced his Model T in 1908; it was the first automobile successfully mass-produced for the ordinary citizen [5]. Between 1908 and 1910, William Durant (1861–1947) formed General Motors by combining numerous small automobile manufacturing and parts companies. The oil companies found a rich new market in the automobile; the rubber industry came into its own with the great market for tires.

After World War I

At the end of World War I, the United States, in contrast with Europe, was in good

CONNECTIONS

See also
1274 The United States: the opening of the West
1278 The United States: Reconstruction to World War I
1324 The Twenties and the Depression
1358 The United States: postwar development

1 Richmond, Va., the capital and most important city of the Confederacy, was devastated at the end of the Civil War. From June 19, 1864, to April 2, 1865, Richmond was besieged and bombarded by General Grant's Army of the Potomac. After its defenders withdrew, the Union forces marched in to find the city in ruins. Much of the South, urban and rural, was despoiled by the war's end.

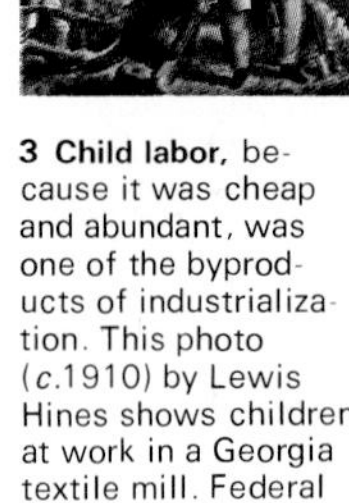

3 Child labor, because it was cheap and abundant, was one of the byproducts of industrialization. This photo (*c.*1910) by Lewis Hines shows children at work in a Georgia textile mill. Federal laws to stop the practice nationwide were declared unconstitutional (in 1918 and 1922) by the Supreme Court. The first effective piece of federal legislation was the Fair Labor Controls Act (1938).

2 New towns sprang up all across the continent as the railroads moved westward. Most of the towns were not so charming as the one shown in this idealized Currier & Ives print of 1868, but they were vital to the economic growth of the heartland of America. Chicago, as the hub of railroad lines spreading in all directions across the United States, became the major city of the Midwest.

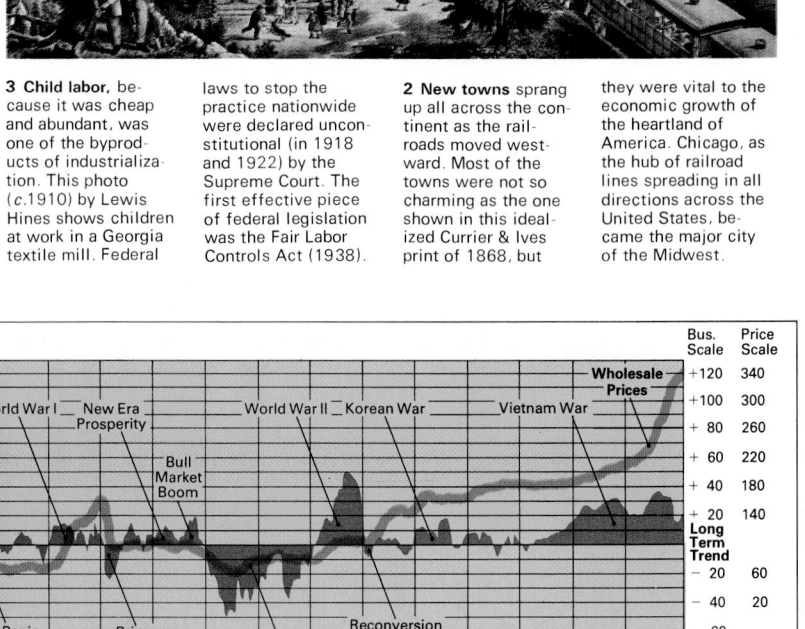

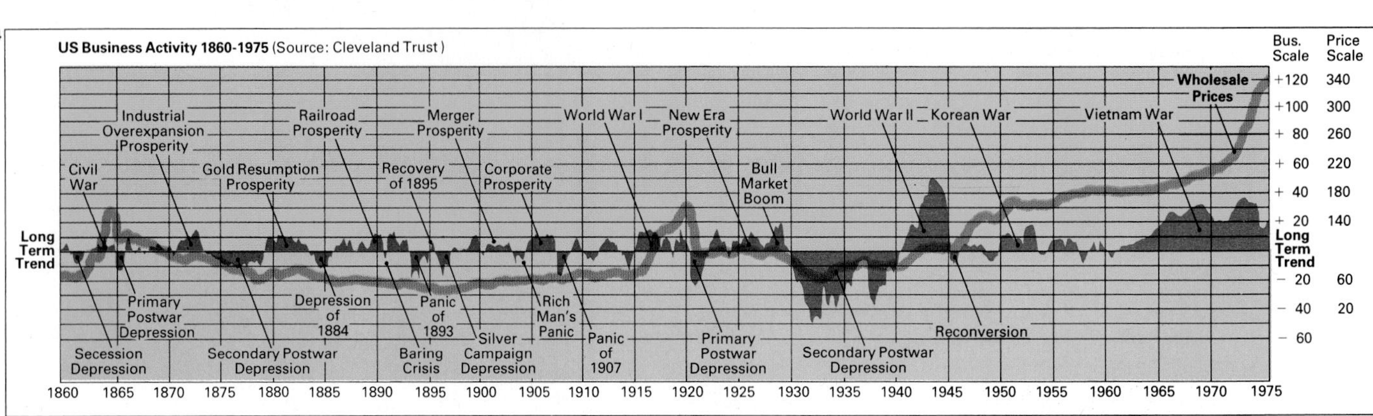

US Business Activity 1860-1975 (Source: Cleveland Trust)
Bus. Scale
Price Scale
Wholesale Prices
+120 340
+100 300
+ 80 260
+ 60 220
+ 40 180
+ 20 140
Long Term Trend
– 20 60
– 40 20
– 60
Industrial Overexpansion Prosperity
Railroad Prosperity
Merger Prosperity
World War I
New Era Prosperity
World War II
Korean War
Vietnam War
Civil War
Gold Resumption Prosperity
Recovery of 1895
Corporate Prosperity
Bull Market Boom
Primary Postwar Depression
Depression of 1884
Panic of 1893
Rich Man's Panic
Silver Campaign Depression
Panic of 1907
Primary Postwar Depression
Reconversion
Secession Depression
Secondary Postwar Depression
Baring Crisis
Secondary Postwar Depression
1860 1865 1870 1875 1880 1885 1890 1895 1900 1905 1910 1915 1920 1925 1930 1935 1940 1945 1950 1955 1960 1965 1970 1975

4

economic condition. The business boom of the 1920s was encouraged by a series of business-oriented Republican administrations. The nation's farmers, however, did not fare well; agricultural prices began falling in 1921 and continued downward. Mortgage foreclosures on farms and bankruptcies followed. More and more farm owners became tenant farmers or sharecroppers. Agricultural economics began to favor large-scale farmers [8].

The stock market soared during the 1920s. Fortunes were made on Wall Street, but many were made on margin (a type of credit). The boom collapsed in 1929. Fortunes vanished when stock prices plummeted. Banks with over-extended credit, unable to meet obligations, began failing. Worldwide economic conditions worsened, and the United States, along with the rest of the world, was plunged into the Great Depression, the worst in modern history. The New Deal administration of Franklin D. Roosevelt that came into office in 1933, with its emphasis on economic reform and social planning, restored basic confidence in the nation's economy. Prosperity, however, was not fully restored until the coming of World War II.

After World War II

The US economy boomed during World War II [6]. At the end of the war, it was the only major economy in the industrialized world that had not been devastated by the war. That advantage helped to turn the US economy into the richest and most productive in history. It provided the rising US population with unprecedented material luxury. It supported such postwar foreign-aid programs as the Marshall Plan and the Point Four program. After the advent of the Cold War, it also supported a vast military establishment, including a worldwide system of defense alliances.

The US economy has retained its premier position despite recessions in the 1950s and 1970s, the Korean and Vietnam wars, the economic competition of rebuilt Western Europe and Japan, and the new economic influence of the oil-producing nations of the Middle East.

KEY

J. Pierpont Morgan (1837–1913) was the most powerful US financier of the late 19th and early 20th centuries. His access to vast amounts of European capital gave him a huge advantage in the financial battles of the period. With his ally, James J. Hill, he fought other financiers for control of the nation's railroads. In 1901, Morgan, Hill, and Harriman set up the Northern Securities Corporation, a vast holding company whose purpose was to eliminate competition among railroad companies. This trust was dissolved by the Supreme Court in 1904. In 1901, Morgan merged several steel companies into the US Steel Corporation.

5

5 A moving assembly line was first employed in the Ford Motor Company's Highland Park, Mich., plant in 1913 to assemble the flywheel magneto. The success of this first effort—time required to assemble a magneto was reduced from 20 minutes to 5 minutes—led Ford to apply the system to all Model T assembly. As other industries quickly adapted the system to their own needs, the era of mass production began. The economic benefits of the assembly line are unquestioned, but many workers complain of the boredom of repeating the same minor operation many times a day.

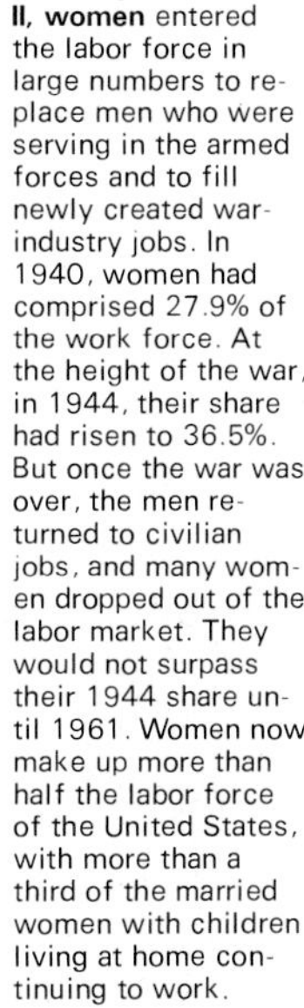

6 During World War II, women entered the labor force in large numbers to replace men who were serving in the armed forces and to fill newly created war-industry jobs. In 1940, women had comprised 27.9% of the work force. At the height of the war, in 1944, their share had risen to 36.5%. But once the war was over, the men returned to civilian jobs, and many women dropped out of the labor market. They would not surpass their 1944 share until 1961. Women now make up more than half the labor force of the United States, with more than a third of the married women with children living at home continuing to work.

6

"THE GIRL HE LEFT BEHIND"
IS STILL BEHIND HIM
She's a WOW
WOMAN ORDNANCE WORKER

9 Many US products are sold worldwide. Shown here are just some of the foreign forms for the trademark of one of the most ubiquitous products—Coca-Cola. The bottle is the same worldwide, but the trademark is rendered in 80 languages to serve markets in 135 countries. In 1975, net sales of foreign operations represented over 40% of total net sales of Coca-Cola.

9

ኮካኮላ
Amharic

Arabic

Cyrillic

ΚΟΚΑ-ΚΟΛΑ
Greek

Hebrew

Bengali

コカ·コーラ
Japanese

โคคา-โคลา
Thai

7

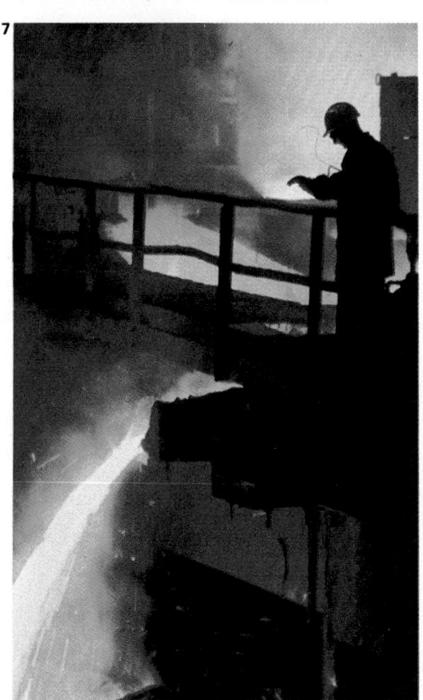

7 Heavy industry, such as the steel casting shown here, has been a hallmark of the US economy since the late 19th century. The railroads and later the automobile industry required vast quantities of steel. The use of the open-hearth process, from the 1880s, led to rapid expansion in steel production. Pittsburgh was the primary eastern steel center, while Midwestern cities such as Gary, Ind., prospered because of their proximity to the Lake Superior iron ore fields. The South's industry—and recovery from the Civil War—was helped by the development of a regional steel industry centered on Birmingham, Ala.

8 The small, self-sufficient family farm is rapidly giving way to the large, highly mechanized farming operation. The huge capital investments necessary for modern farming are usually only possible where thousands of acres are involved. From the time of Thomas Jefferson, the small farmer has been looked upon as the social and economic mainstay of the country. But the economic realities of the 20th century—especially the enormous growth of agribusiness—have threatened the existence of the family farm. Shown here is a grapefruit-processing center in Lakeland, Fla.

8

The American experience: religion

Virtually every religion in the world has adherents in the United States, although Christians predominate [1]. Approximately 40% of the nation's population attends religious services on a weekly basis. All are protected in their worship by the Bill of Rights and a long tradition of separation of church and state. The Constitution forbids the establishment of a national religion, and court decisions have emphasized that government must not show religious partiality.

The early settlements

Among the first white men in America were Spanish Roman Catholic missionaries who, beginning in the early sixteenth century, fanned out over the Southwest to convert the Indians to Christianity [2].

The Pilgrims and Puritans who settled New England in the early seventeenth century had left England to practice their stern religion without being persecuted. This did not prevent them from persecuting their own dissenters. Nonmembers of the church were banished or were prohibited from participating in community affairs. Roger Williams (1603?–83) was forced to flee into the wilderness where he founded Rhode Island (1636), which became the first colony to allow religious freedom.

The Church of England was firmly established in Virginia after 1619 and at least nominally established in North and South Carolina; both the latter also attracted many Methodists, Presbyterians, and Baptists. Salem (now Winston-Salem), N.C., was founded by German Moravians in 1766. South Carolina had settlements of Huguenots—Protestants who had fled France after the revocation of the Edict of Nantes in 1685. Maryland was founded as a refuge for English Catholics, although it later became a crown colony with an established Anglican church. New York and New Jersey were centers of the Dutch Reformed Church. In 1654, 23 Portuguese Jews who had been banished from Brazil settled in New Amsterdam (now New York); four years later, a community of Jews arrived at Newport, R.I. [3]. Pennsylvania, settled by Quakers [4], welcomed other radical Christian groups, especially from Germany, including Amish, Mennonites, Dunkards, and Moravians.

The Great Awakening

A great spirit of revivalism, known as the Great Awakening, emerged toward the middle of the eighteenth century. Begun by dissident Presbyterians and Congregationalists, it eventually brought doctrinal changes to all Protestant denominations. Numerous new sects were established; large numbers of these eventually joined the Baptists. The Awakening spread throughout the colonies. Its leading figures were Theodore J. Frelinghuysen (1661–1748?), William Tennent (1673–1746), his son Gilbert (1703–64), Jonathan Edwards [5], and the English Methodist evangelist George Whitefield (1714–70).

The Great Awakening unwittingly increased religious toleration in the colonies; the very increase in the number of religious sects assured that no one of them could establish itself at the expense of all the others. For example, they all took a unified stand against the belated attempt by the

CONNECTIONS

See also
850 Religion and modern man
1388 Modern Christianity and the new beliefs

1

U S Religious Membership 1975
(In thousands for all membership over 200,000)

Denomination		Total
Armenian Church of America		372
Assemblies of God		785
Baptist		27,706
American Baptist Association	787	
American Baptist Church in U S A	1,579	
Baptist Missionary Association	204	
Conservative Baptist Association	300	
Free Will Baptist	235	
General Association of Regular Baptist Churches	225	
National Baptist Convention, U S A	6,487	
National Baptist Convention of America	2,669	
Primitive Baptist	1,645	
Progressive Baptist	522	
Regular Baptist	225	
Southern Baptist Convention	12,516	
Brethren		233
Church of Christ		2,400
Church of God		676
Church of God in Christ		425
Church of Jesus Christ of Latter-Day Saints (Mormons)		2,208
Church of the Nazarene		430
Disciples of Christ		1,312
Eastern Orthodox		4,070
Greek Orthodox	2,000	
Orthodox Church in America	1,000	
Serbian Eastern Orthodox	350	
Jehovah's Witness		554
Jewish		6,215
Union of American Hebrew Congregations	1,100	
Union of Orthodox Jewish Congregations	3,000	
United Synagogues of America	1,500	
Lutheran		8,678
American Lutheran Church	2,438	
Lutheran Church in America	3,007	
Missouri Synod	2,776	
Wisconsin Evangelical Lutheran Synod	390	
Methodist		13,191
African Methodist Episcopal	1,500	
African Methodist Episcopal Zion	1,025	
Christian Methodist Episcopal	466	
United Methodist	10,063	
Pentecostal		528
United Pentecostal	300	
Polish National Church		282
Presbyterian		3,787
Presbyterian Church in the United States	902	
United Presbyterian Church	2,724	
Protestant Episcopal Church		2,917
Reformed Church		435
Christian Reformed Church	206	
Reformed Church in America	214	
Roman Catholic		48,702
Salvation Army		362
Seventh-Day Adventist		464
Unitarian Universalist Association		211
United Church of Christ		1,841

2

2 Spanish missionaries established presidios – combination missions, forts, and farming manors – all through the American Southwest beginning c. 1539. The missions' primary aim was the conversion of the Indians, but they also were expected to be self-sufficient economically.

3

3 Touro Synagogue in Newport, R. I., the country's oldest standing synagogue, is considered to be a masterpiece of colonial architecture. Designed by Peter Harrison (1716–75) and built in 1763 for Newport's thriving Jewish community, it is a national historic site.

4

4 The Society of Friends, or Quakers, as its adherents soon came to be called, was founded in England in 1650. Its members were widely persecuted for various reasons, especially for their refusal to accept the authority of the king in religious matters and their refusal to pay tithes to the Church of England. Many fled to the American colonies, where they fared little better, except in Rhode Island, where considerable religious toleration existed. In 1681, William Penn (1644–1718) received a royal charter (in payment for a debt owed his father) from King Charles II to found the colony of Pennsylvania as a haven for Quakers. The colony quickly prospered and attracted, in addition to Quakers, numerous other sects.

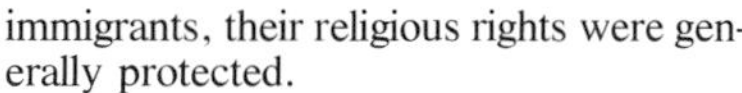

British crown to establish the Anglican Church throughout the colonies. And by associating the crown with the Anglican Church, these colonists found it easier to oppose the crown itself. Thus, the Great Awakening had an indirect but important influence on the American Revolution.

Religion in the new republic

The republic set up after the American Revolution was a product of the eighteenth-century Enlightenment; freedom of religion was one of the cornerstones of the Enlightenment. Consequently, the US Constitution forbade the establishment of a national religion by the government [Key].

Religious freedom in the republic was chiefly concerned with protecting the rights of the various Protestant denominations. The presence of large numbers of Catholics and Jews, who began arriving in the nineteenth century, however, put the ban on religious discrimination to its first practical test. By and large, the Bill of Rights was upheld. Although there was social and economic discrimination against the new immigrants, their religious rights were generally protected.

The first serious religious confrontation occurred after 1831, with the rise of Mormonism. From the beginning Mormon beliefs and practices set them apart. Driven consecutively from Ohio, Missouri, and Illinois, the Mormons eventually settled Utah [8]. Only after they foreswore plural marriages was Utah admitted to the Union.

The twentieth century

The Eighteenth, or Prohibition, Amendment to the Constitution, ratified in 1919, was largely the product of Protestant temperance groups. Because most Catholics opposed prohibition, the issue polarized Protestants and Catholics politically. Alfred E. Smith (1873–1944), the Democratic candidate for president in 1928, was defeated largely because of anti-Catholic sentiment in the country; it was especially strong in the South. John F. Kennedy, however, who was elected president in 1960, was a Catholic and his religion was not deemed to have played a crucial part in the election.

KEY

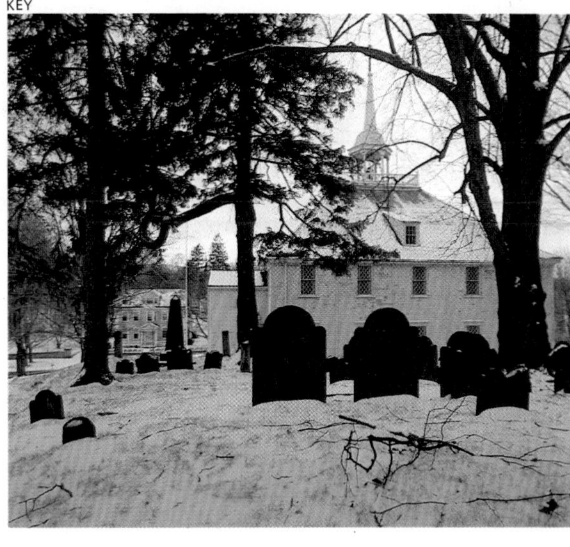

The white clapboard church standing serenely in the center of a New England town has come to be a symbol of the continuing importance of religion in the United States. Religion is not established, but its influence is pervasive.

5

5 Jonathan Edwards (1703–58) preached a rigorous and strict Calvinism. His influence was immense; the Great Awakening was largely the result of his preaching. Eventually his views became so strict (he wanted to limit church membership to those who had experienced a spiritual conversion) that he was turned out of his church in Northampton, Mass., in 1750. He then became a missionary to the Indians of western Massachusetts and wrote his most influential work, *Freedom of the Will* (1754). Shortly before his death, he became president of the College of New Jersey, which later became Princeton University.

6

6 US blacks are overwhelmingly Protestant, with the Baptists and Methodists claiming the largest numbers. The church plays an important role—social and political as well as religious—in the black community. Until recently, in many parts of the country, the church was the only institution blacks controlled without white interference. Ministers were both comforters of and spokesmen for their people. Thus it is not surprising that the leader of the civil-rights movement of the 1960s, Dr. Martin Luther King, Jr. (1929–68), was a leading black minister or that many of his top aides were also prominent ministers.

7

7 Elizabeth Seton (1774–1821), founder of the Sisters of Charity, is the first native-born US Roman Catholic saint. In 1805, after being widowed and left with five children, she became a Roman Catholic. In 1808 she founded a Catholic free school in Maryland. She opened a number of such schools and her efforts became the pattern for the whole parochial school system in the United States.

8

8 The Mormon Temple in Salt Lake City, Utah, constructed in 1853–93, is one of the world's largest religious structures. All streets in Salt Lake City are named and numbered according to their direction and distance from Temple Square. The temple is open only to Mormons and is used for such ceremonies as marriages and baptisms. Regular worship services are held in the nearby Tabernacle.

9

9 The place of women in the clergy surfaced as a major issue in the 1970s. The Episcopal Church formally approved ordination of women as priests in 1976. Shown here are two Episcopal ministers at Cape Cod's oldest Episcopal church. In 1977 the Roman Catholic Church upheld the exclusion of women as priests on grounds that the concept of the priest reflects the male image of Christ.

The American experience: education

American education has changed dramatically and often from its colonial beginnings to the present as it has tried to meet the demands of a changing society [3, 7].

Colonial beginnings

Elementary education in reading was fostered in colonial New England so that by knowing the Scriptures it would be possible to defeat "that old deluder Satan" [1]. Higher education existed primarily to train the ministry. In the South the wealthy planters educated their children by hiring tutors, but they ignored the education of poorer whites and slaves. In 1647, Massachusetts required every township with 50 or more families to hire a teacher to instruct children in reading and writing; larger townships were instructed to have a Latin "grammar school" (high school) to see to it that able older children would be prepared to attend Harvard College.

Two ordinances during the Revolutionary years—the Land Ordinance of 1785 and the Northwest Ordinance of 1787—provided that every township formed in the Northwest Territory reserve land "for the maintenance of public schools." The Constitution, though, did not mention education, leaving the matter up to the states and people locally. In recent years, however, the principle of promoting "the general welfare" has allowed the federal government to become an increasingly active participant in the educational process.

Education in the nineteenth century

Reformers such as Horace Mann [2] attempted to build a comprehensive educational system for a rapidly expanding and industrializing society. Massachusetts became the first state to make public school attendance compulsory (1827) and to create a state board of education (1837).

Until the Civil War higher education was privately sponsored, except for New York State, which in 1787 had founded the University of the State of New York. The Morrill Act of 1862 made large land grants available to states for the purpose of establishing colleges that would emphasize "agriculture and the mechanic arts" as well as military science and other scientific and liberal studies. State universities spread throughout the country.

Curricula of schools and colleges broadened. In 1861 Yale became the first US university to grant the PhD; in the same year the Massachusetts Institute of Technology was founded to concentrate on science and technology. Johns Hopkins established the nation's first separate graduate school in 1876. Although coeducation became a standard feature of public education, private schools and colleges were mostly sex segregated, with women's colleges far fewer than men's. Racial integration was virtually nonexistent. In 1865 the Freedman's Bureau—set up by the federal government to aid former slaves—began the development of black schools; later in the century the first black colleges came into being [6]. The 1896 Supreme Court decision in *Plessy v. Ferguson* ruled that public educational facilities could legally be "separate but equal," thus sanctioning racial segregation and limiting the education of black Americans until the 1954 Supreme

CONNECTIONS

See also

1216 Settlement of North America

1360 20th-century sociology and its influence

1

A In *Adam's* Fall
We Sinned all.

B Thy Life to Mend
This *Book* Attend.

C The *Cat* doth play
And after slay.

D A *Dog* will bite
A Thief at night.

E An *Eagles* flight
Is out of sight.

F The Idle *Fool*
Is whipt at School.

1 This early New England primer taught the alphabet and reading through moral and religious lessons. Learning the letters was aided by woodcut illustrations and rhymed couplets.

2 Horace Mann (1796–1859), as secretary (1837–48) of the first Massachusetts board of education, advocated universal public, nonsectarian education with professionally educated teachers.

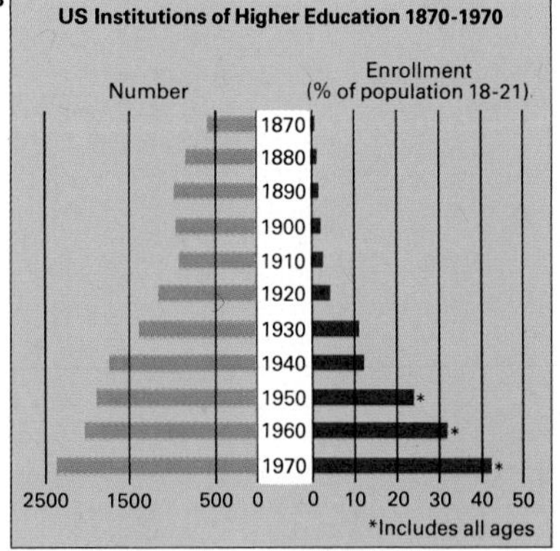
US Institutions of Higher Education 1870-1970
Number
Enrollment (% of population 18-21)
1870
1880
1890
1900
1910
1920
1930
1940
1950
1960
1970
2500 1500 500 0
0 10 20 30 40 50
*Includes all ages

3 Since 1946, with the great influx of adult veterans into colleges, enrollment figures have included all age groups. Today, many adults in addition to those receiving veterans' benefits are enrolled.

4 "Snap the Whip" (1872) by Winslow Homer (1836–1910) depicts a schoolyard scene outside a one-room rural schoolhouse, the most common type in 19th-century America.

5 In 1896 John Dewey (1859–1952) established a separate school of pedagogy at the University of Chicago with a laboratory where educational theory could be tested in practice.

Court decision in *Brown v. Board of Education* declared that separate educational facilities were unconstitutional.

John Dewey and progressive education
By the end of the nineteenth century the question no longer was whether public education should be universal and mandatory, but what its purposes and methods should be. John Dewey [5] emphasized not only the concept of "learning by doing," but, perhaps even more importantly, the idea that schooling was not just a preparation for life, but a period of life itself. Dewey and other progressive educators helped to change elementary education in the direction of following the child's own pace of development rather than imposing an academically prescribed path [10].

Education in the twentieth century
The enormous growth and change in the school-age population through immigration and migration from rural to urban settings made US schools preeminently concerned with successful socialization [Key].

World War II brought the federal government into education, not just by sponsoring the GI Bill of Rights, which gave veterans funds for continuing higher education, but also in making education part of national policy. The concern that the United States had fallen behind its cold-war rival after the Soviet Union launched the space satellite Sputnik in 1957 prompted Congress to pass the National Defense Education Act of 1958, pumping billions of dollars into the upgrading of teaching, especially in the sciences and foreign languages. In 1965, Congress passed the Elementary and Secondary Education Act, which was primarily aimed at strengthening education for children in low-income areas [8].

The slowing of the economy in the 1970s, the subsequent cutback in tax dollars for education, and the ever more complex and technological nature of US society amid growing job-competitiveness caused debate over education to focus on functional effectiveness. The use of busing to achieve racial integration had become a major political issue [9].

KEY

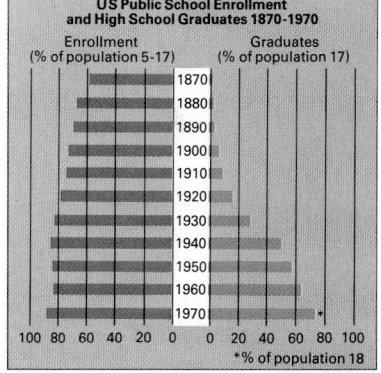

Immigrant children were expected to assimilate quickly into the US educational system. They often learned English and became Americanized long before their parents, in large part because of their schooling. In this late 19th-century photograph, taken by social reformer Jacob A. Riis (1849–1914), immigrant children in a school on New York's Lower East Side salute the American flag.

6

6 Booker T. Washington (1856–1915) became the first head of Tuskegee Institute in Alabama in 1881. Beginning with limited funds, 4 rundown buildings, and only 30 students, he turned it into a model industrial and agricultural school before 1900. Today it is a fully accredited college offering undergraduate and graduate programs. There are schools of nursing, education, and engineering.

7 These encouraging enrollment figures do not take into account the education of native Americans in reservation schools. Enrollments and graduates for those schools are drastically lower.

9 Opposition to the use of student busing to achieve racial balance in public schools has weakened in the face of determined courts and realistic community leaders opposed to violence.

7

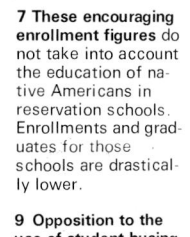

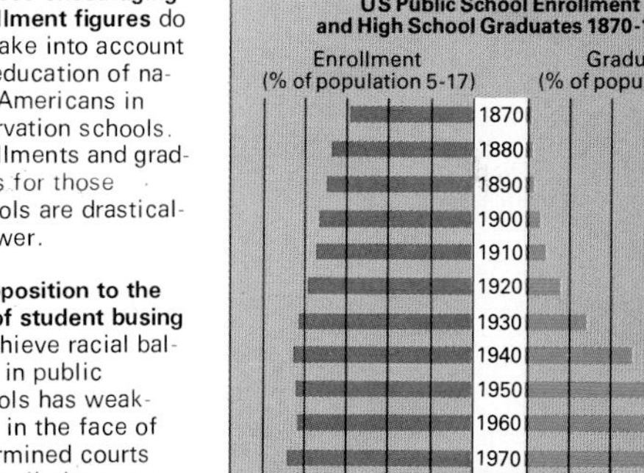
US Public School Enrollment and High School Graduates 1870-1970
Enrollment (% of population 5-17)
Graduates (% of population 17)
1870
1880
1890
1900
1910
1920
1930
1940
1950
1960
1970
100 80 60 40 20 0
0 20 40 60 80 100
*% of population 18

8

9

10

8 Project Head Start was enacted by the federal government in 1964 to provide economically and/or culturally deprived preschool children with a meaningful preliminary educational experience. The program is staffed primarily by paraprofessionals from the communities involved, and classes are held in community centers, such as this church Sunday school room in Albuquerque, N. M. The program began as part of President Johnson's "Great Society."

10 In the open-classroom school each student advances at his or her own pace, moving from one activity area to another as specific assignments are completed. Individual attention is available for areas of study the student finds difficult. Free time can be spent on the student's favorite activities. Each student is appraised for his or her own achievement, not against an arbitrary level. Cooperative group activities are as important as individual tasks.

The American experience: sports

Sports have always played an important part in American life [1, 3, 7, 9, 10]. Baseball is a familiar part of the American scene, as are the traditional rivalries of college football teams, the making of business deals on golf courses, and company bowling leagues.

Baseball

For many years, Abner Doubleday (1819–93) was credited with having invented baseball at Cooperstown, N.Y., in 1839. But it is now known to have an earlier origin. Indeed, such English precursors of baseball as cricket and rounders have been traced back to the fourteenth century. In 1845, Alexander J. Cartwright (1820–92) established the first set of standard rules using a diamond-shaped playing field with three bases and a home plate for the Knickerbocker Base Ball Club of New York City. The first recorded game using Cartwright's rules was played at Elysium Fields in Hoboken, N.J., in 1846. During the Civil War, baseball was played behind the lines and in prisoner-of-war camps. The game was thus introduced to young men from throughout the country, and standardized rules evolved. The Red Stockings of Cincinnati, Ohio, became the first all-professional team in 1869, and the first national professional league was organized in 1871. By the first World Series in 1903, baseball was the national pastime [Key].

Football

American football is also based on old English games—rugby and soccer (the latter of which is called *football* in virtually all parts of the world except the United States). Rutgers University, in New Brunswick, N.J., credited with being one of the organizers of American football, played Princeton in 1869, in the first intercollegiate football game. The game was really a form of soccer with 25 players on each side. Harvard played a game much more like rugby learned from playing with McGill University of Montreal, Canada. The Harvard game, unlike Princeton's version, allowed the ball (which was egg-shaped rather than round) to be carried. When the newly-formed American Intercollegiate Football Association adapted the Harvard rules in 1876, modern American football began to emerge as a distinctive game [2]. Semiprofessional teams began playing as early as 1895, but it was not until the 1920s that organized professional football was firmly established. And it was only after World War II, with the coming of television, that professional football developed a large national following. Since 1967, football's Super Bowl game has surpassed baseball's World Series as the most watched US sporting event.

Basketball

Of all the major sports, only basketball is strictly American in origin. In 1891, Canadian-born James Naismith [4], a YMCA physical-education instructor, invented the game. It spread quickly to high schools and colleges across the country and was played by both males and females. Long one of the most popular amateur sports in the country, it—like football—became popular as a spectator, professional sport after World War II.

CONNECTIONS

See also
930 Play and sports

1

1 Lacrosse was being played by Indians in America when the first European settlers arrived. Called *baggataway* by the Indians, the game was especially popular among the Iroquois. They sometimes fielded teams of 500 players who took part in games lasting two or three days. Broken limbs, even death, from the rough playing were not uncommon. The name lacrosse was given to the game by early French traders because the long stick used reminded them of a bishop's *crosse*, or staff. The painting here, showing Choctaw Indians playing lacrosse, is by George Catlin (1796–1872).

2

2 Early football was played without helmets or special padding. The 15 players on each team scrambled all over the field (longer and wider than today's) in what was often close to a free-for-all. Walter Camp (1859–1925), who coached the Yale football team after 1888, devised many of the rules and strategies that characterize modern football. He also began the practice (1889) of naming all-American teams.

3

3 The Astrodome in Houston, Texas, was opened in 1965, making it the first major fully enclosed, air-conditioned sports stadium. Officially the Harris County Domed Stadium, it seats up to 66,000 spectators on six tiers. The dome, spanning 642 ft (196m), consists of plastic panels supported by steel lattice. The stadium is temperature-controlled at 74° F (23° C) and has its own electric-generating system. Astroturf, an artificial grass, was developed specifically for use on the Astrodome playing surface, and is now widely used on both indoor and outdoor playing fields. The stadium can accommodate virtually any sport, including baseball, football, tennis, boxing, basketball, and rodeos.

4

4 James Naismith (1861–1939) invented the game of basketball in 1891. At the request of the director of the YMCA Training School, Springfield, Mass., Naismith was looking for a game to be played indoors in cold weather. Using a soccer ball and two peach baskets, one hung at each end of a gym, Naismith developed basketball. Most of his original rules are still in use. He was honored in 1936 when basketball was first played as an official Olympic game.

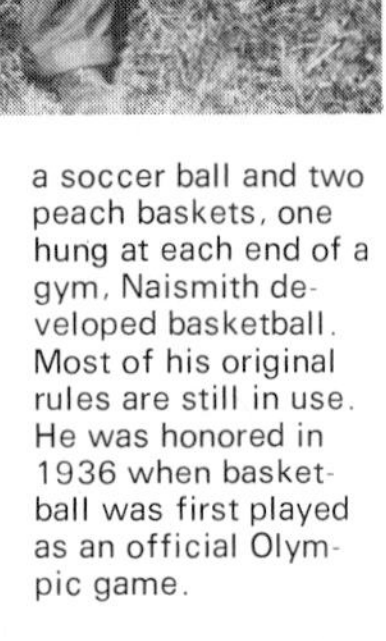

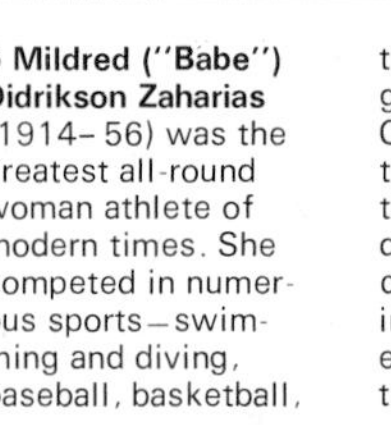

5 Mildred ("Babe") Didrikson Zaharias (1914–56) was the greatest all-round woman athlete of modern times. She competed in numerous sports—swimming and diving, baseball, basketball, track and field, and golf. In the 1932 Olympics she won the javelin throw and the 80-meter hurdles. After 1935 she concentrated on golf, in which she won every major women's title.

5

Tennis

Lawn tennis—or simply tennis, as it is usually known today—was invented in 1873 in Wales (based on older types of tennis games). It was almost immediately taken to the United States from Bermuda by Mary E. Outerbridge, who had a court laid out in Staten Island, N.Y., in 1874 [6]. The US National Lawn Tennis Association, formed in 1881, standardized rules and equipment and established the first nationally recognized tournaments. The first international competition, the Davis Cup, was organized by the American Dwight F. Davis in 1900. Professional tennis finally came into its own in 1968, when the major international competitions were opened to professionals.

Horse racing

Members of Virginia's gentry were racing horses before the mid-seventeenth century. In 1665, Gov. Richard Nicolls of New York laid out on Long Island the first permanent race track in the colonies. Around the mid-eighteenth century, races in which trotting horses pulled a cart and a driver became popular. In 1825, the New York Trotting Club established rules governing trotting races. A special breed of horse, the standardbred, was developed for trotting (or harness) racing, and the breed was first registered in 1867.

Golf, bowling, and ice hockey

Golf, which was played in Scotland in the twelfth century, was brought to the United States in the eighteenth century, but it was not until the 1880s that permanent golf courses were first laid out [5]. Modern tenpin bowling evolved ultimately from the ancient game of ninepins, which was played in New Amsterdam (New York City) by Dutch settlers as long as 350 years ago. In 1841, Connecticut outlawed ninepins because of widespread betting on the game. Other states soon passed similar laws. Players circumvented these laws by adding the tenth pin. The introduction of automatic pinsetters in the early 1950s added greatly to the popularity of the game. Ice hockey, the national sport of Canada, has gained considerable popularity in the United States [8].

KEY

KEY
George Herman ("Babe") Ruth (1895–1948) set or tied 76 pitching and batting records in his major league career (1914–35). In 1936 he was among the first elected to baseball's Hall of Fame.

6

6 Major Walter C. Wingfield (1833–1912), the British inventor of modern tennis, named his game "Sphairistike" (from Greek, meaning "playing ball"). The name did not stick, but the game quickly caught on. In 1880 a tournament was held on courts laid out on Staten Island. The first official US tournament was held in 1881 in Newport, R.I.

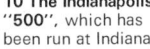

7

7 "Dempsey Through the Ropes" by George Bellows (1882–1925) celebrates the 1923 championship fight between Jack Dempsey and Luis Firpo. Boxing's leading fighters, including John L. Sullivan, Dempsey, Joe Louis, and Muhammad Ali—have attracted great public attention.

8

8 Organized sports for young people are taken very seriously by the players, their parents, and the promoters. Although Little League baseball has by far the most participants, junior ice hockey, basketball, football, and soccer leagues are increasing at a very fast rate.

9

9 The triumphs of US athlete Jesse Owens (1913–   ) at the 1936 Olympic Games in Berlin, Germany, were galling to Adolf Hitler. Owens, a black man, was clearly the outstanding athlete at the games, thereby refuting the Nazi racist claim of Nordic superiority. Owens set Olympic records in the 200-meter race, the broad (now called long) jump, and tied the Olympic 100-meter race record. Here he is shown at the award ceremony for the broad jump. Behind him, with arm raised in the Nazi salute, is the second-place German. In front of him is the third-place Japanese athlete. More recent Olympics have also been marred by political and racial controversies.

10

10 The Indianapolis "500", which has been run at Indianapolis, Ind., since 1911, (except during the world wars) is the best known automobile race in the United States. Specially built racing cars compete by racing 500mi (804km) around the 2.5mi (4km) track. In addition to such racing cars, there are four other major categories of automobiles racing in the United States: stock cars, sports cars, dragsters, and land speed-record vehicles.

The American experience: leisure

Arriving in Jamestown, Va., in 1611 to take over as governor, Sir Thomas Dale was shocked to find colonists idly playing bowls. He immediately outlawed such games and put the settlers to work so they would not end up like the Lost Colony of Roanoke, N.C. In New England, the harsh climate and poor soil made work an even greater necessity—a necessity backed up by the Calvinist work ethic of the Puritan leaders.

Work into pleasure

The settlers nevertheless found ways to turn some of their work into pleasure [Key]. Barn (or house) raisings were occasions for neighbors to gather together. The work—accompanied by gossiping, singing, and courting—was followed by a large meal (often a barbecue) and sometimes by dancing. Cornhusking bees and sheepshearings added contests of speed and agility, railsplitting added tests of strength. This social pleasure in work has disappeared in this century because work has been removed from the family and home environment, even from the community, and it is performed during specific "working" hours. But activities such as hunting and fishing that once were economic necessities have become favored recreational pastimes, as have sailing and horseback riding, which once were everyday means of travel.

The church and social activities

In all the colonies, churches were the centers of the communities. By law Sunday was a day of rest, yet there was pleasure to be found in meeting neighbors at church. The religious leaders of Massachusetts eventually realized that they had been mistaken in establishing a midweek service because, while decorum was still insisted upon in the church, after-church activities on weekdays were free of Sabbath restrictions. Socializing might involve trading or even a visit to the local tavern.

The eighteenth-century religious revival known as the Great Awakening introduced the camp meeting [2]. Families from miles around loaded up their wagons and drove to a central location where they pitched tents and camped around an open-air meeting site. Hunting parties were organized to obtain food, and the women prepared communal meals. No service was complete without the rousing singing of hymns, no preacher a success unless his fire-and-brimstone sermon drove his listeners into a frenzy.

Nineteenth-century church meetings, although more subdued, were equally important to people now living in settled towns. Church suppers, socials, strawberry festivals, and bazaars were often the only "respectable" forms of entertainment and socializing outside the home. Religious centers still play an important role in the social life of many American communities.

Holidays

Americans' love of holidays began early; the first Thanksgiving was a three-day feast and included shooting matches as part of the festivity. Court days became public spectacles, with people flocking to pilloryings and hangings. Cotton Mather lamented that "Training Dayes [when the militia practiced] become little more than Drinking

CONNECTIONS

See also
930 Play and sports
932 Use of leisure
1408 The American experience: sports

1 The Fourth of July, since the early days of the republic, has been a day of celebration, with patriotic speeches, militia reviews, parades, band concerts, fireworks, and picnics. John Lewis Krimmel (1786–1821), one of America's first important genre artists, painted this scene of *Independence Day Celebration in Centre Square, Philadelphia* in 1819. He had painted his first *View of Centre Square on the 4th of July* in 1810, shortly after he arrived in America from his native Germany. The painting shown here—in watercolor, ink, and pencil on paper—measures only 12in (30cm) by 18in (45cm). Yet it abounds with patriotic paraphernalia—flags, portraits of national heroes, and banners celebrating momentous national triumphs. In the background (before the classical pump house designed by Benjamin Latrobe in 1801), the militia drills and parades to the accompaniment of its fife and drum corps. In the 1970s, amateur fife and drum corps, complete with Revolutionary uniforms, were founded or revived in preparation for bicentennial celebrations.

2 The culmination of the camp meeting came when repentant sinners stepped forward to declare themselves for Christ. A mass baptism usually followed. But the camp meeting was also often the first chance that couples already living together had to be married by a minister. And the meeting was an excellent opportunity for couples to meet, court, propose, and marry—often all occurring within a few days. Widows and widowers with children—and there were many—needed to find mates quickly to keep their families together in the face of the harsh conditions on the frontier.

3 Seaside resorts have been popular in America since colonial times. One of the earliest resorts was Newport, R.I. Wealthy planters and traders from the South sailed north to Newport on packet boats to escape the summer heat. Newport has never lost its image as a playground for the wealthy. In this 1869 painting by Winslow Homer, elegantly dressed ladies with tiny parasols stroll along the cliff at Long Branch, N.J., a leading resort of the nineteenth century. Only the most adventurous vacationers went swimming. By the active standards of today's vacationers, the leisurely pace of 19th-century resorts would be considered to be unbearably dull.

Dayes." Although first looked upon disapprovingly by the English, the Dutch Kris Kringle eventually became the American Santa Claus. The nation's most important holiday, the Fourth of July [1], remains a favorite time for celebration.

Crazes and fads

Americans have spent much of their leisure indulging in games, sports, and hobbies that for a time seem to captivate and engage the whole country. The late nineteenth century saw successive waves of enthusiasm for ballooning, croquet, and bicycling. Just before World War I, table tennis became a craze. In the 1920s mah-jongg and crossword puzzles filled many idle hours. Miniature golf was at its height in the 1930s, as were contract bridge and the new board game, Monopoly. The 1950s saw a do-it-yourself craze that developed in the next decade into the more sophisticated crafts movement [9]. Since the 1960s participatory sports such as skiing [8], tennis, scuba diving, and, again, bicycling have gained in popularity.

Increasing mobility and free time

In the nineteenth century, boats plied the Hudson and Mississippi rivers not just for commerce but also as floating entertainment centers offering gambling, dancing, and bawdy shows free from the scrutiny of local laws and moral arbiters. Trains brought the circus to any town with a siding. Trolleys took urban residents to pleasure parks—the first were beer gardens developed by German immigrants—and later to amusement parks such as those at Coney Island in Brooklyn, N.Y.

The automobile became available to the majority of Americans at about the same time that their free, nonwork time was expanding. The Sunday drive became the weekend trip when Saturday also became a free day. Paid vacations made trips to resorts possible for ordinary Americans, not just the wealthy [3]. Once isolated National Parks have become crowded with trailers and other camping vehicles [7]. The manufacture and sale of leisure-use products [6] and leisure resorts have become a major business—the recreation industry [4].

KEY

This oil on wood painting from Western Virginia of a quilting party sometime after the mid-19th century depicts a favorite country social gathering and is itself the product of some anonymous amateur painter's leisure hours. During the colonial period and throughout the 19th century, women often busied themselves with needle art crafts. Samplers were produced by young girls to perfect their sewing skills for use on more practical projects.

4

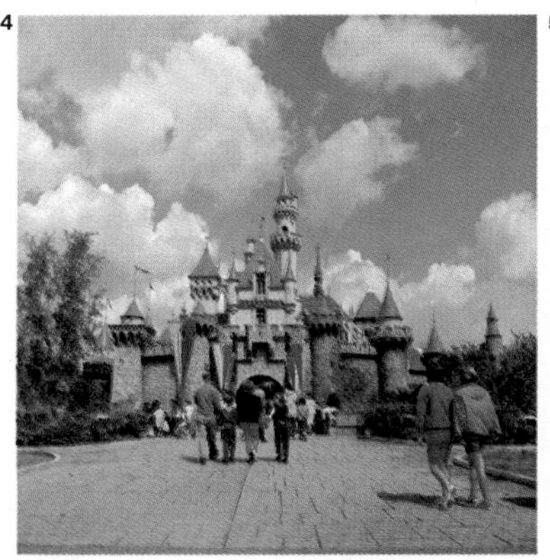

4 Disneyland—created by Walt Disney (1901–66), the pioneer producer of animated films—opened on July 15, 1955, in Anaheim, Calif. Containing four major areas: Adventureland, Frontierland, Fantasyland, and Tomorrowland, it quickly became one of America's leading tourist attractions. Even Soviet Premier Nikita Khrushchev visited it when he came to the United States in 1959.

5

5 Rodeos have been recorded as early as 1847. They grew out of informal contests held by cowboys after the roundup. The standard contests of the modern rodeo are bullriding; bulldogging (steer wrestling); bronco riding, both bareback and saddled; calf-roping; and steer-roping, both singly and in teams. The Wild West Show of "Buffalo Bill" Cody grew out of a Fourth of July rodeo held in 1892.

6

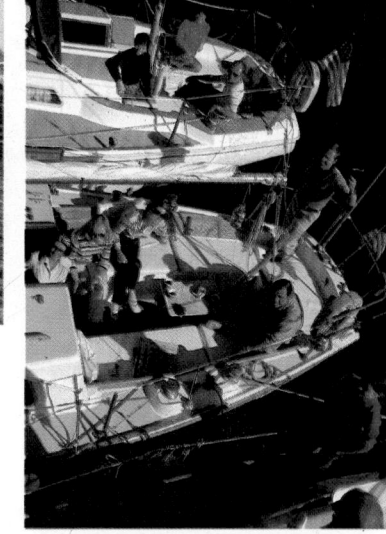

6 Although the United States has extensive, excellent intercoastal and inland waterways for boating, many pleasure boats rarely travel far from dockside. Their owners often gain satisfaction merely from owning and maintaining their boats and in socializing "in port" with other boat owners. Small houseboats have become popular as "floating cottages." Small sailboat use grew rapidly in the 1970s.

7 US National Parks and Recreation Areas have not increased their acreage or facilities sufficiently to meet the increasing demand made upon them by tourists. The quiet, rural atmosphere of some major parks has been destroyed by heavy vehicular and pedestrian traffic. Campsites in many popular areas must be reserved months ahead of time, and vehicle use is restricted in some areas.

8 Cross-country skiing, which waned in popularity once ski tows and lifts were installed at slopes, has seen a recent revival. Many of the cross-country skiers are the same people who have rediscovered the pleasures of hiking and backpacking. Cross-country skiing, unlike downhill skiing, which can be aided by snowmaking machines, is dependent upon ideal, snowy winter weather.

9 Craft fairs, where amateur and/or professional crafts people exhibit and sell their wares, are held in many communities in the open air or under tents. Demonstrations by potters, weavers, glass blowers, and other artisans are often a major attraction. The craft fair also provides an opportunity for craft workers to share ideas with other enthusiasts and to learn about new techniques and materials.

7

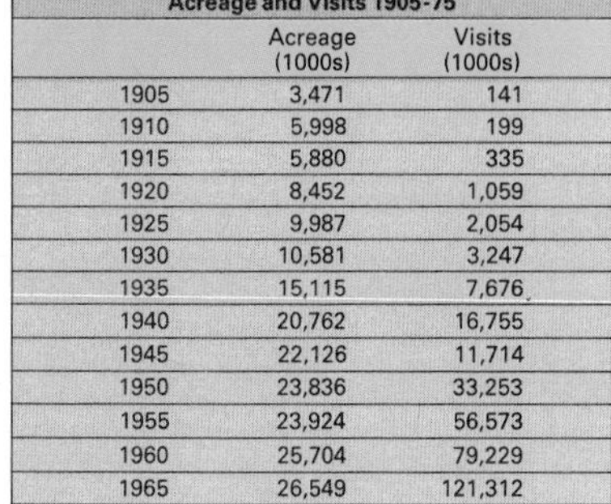

US National Parks and Recreation Areas: Acreage and Visits 1905-75

	Acreage (1000s)	Visits (1000s)
1905	3,471	141
1910	5,998	199
1915	5,880	335
1920	8,452	1,059
1925	9,987	2,054
1930	10,581	3,247
1935	15,115	7,676
1940	20,762	16,755
1945	22,126	11,714
1950	23,836	33,253
1955	23,924	56,573
1960	25,704	79,229
1965	26,549	121,312
1970	28,543	172,005
1975	31,027	238,849

8

9

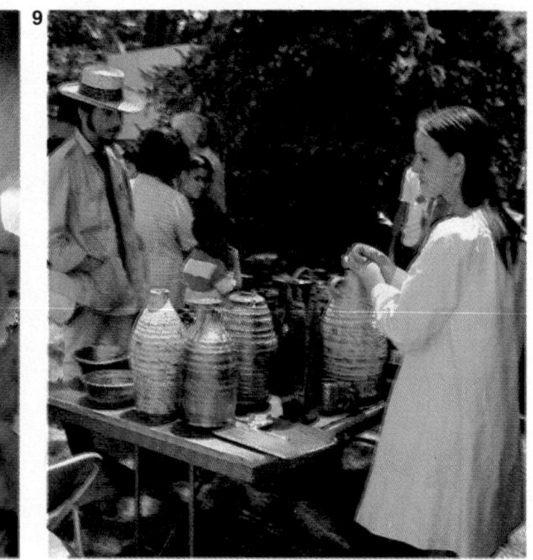

The American experience: architecture to the 20th century

St Augustine, Fla., founded by the Spanish in 1565, is the oldest inhabited US city. The oldest extant Spanish buildings, however, are in Santa Fe, N.M., founded in 1609. The influence of the Zuñi pueblos, first sighted in 1539, is evident in these early Santa Fe structures [1].

The seventeenth century settlers on the East Coast, unimpressed with native dwellings they found, reconstructed, as much as conditions and available materials allowed, the world they had left behind. Their first permanent buildings, such as St Luke's Church (1632), in Smithfield, Va. [2], did not echo the fashionable buildings of Jacobean London but the sturdy late medieval buildings of rural England from where most of the settlers came. The seventeenth century New England house [3] was modeled after the farmhouses of East Anglia.

The Spanish and English were not the only colonists making lasting contributions to American architecture. The Swedes in Delaware introduced the log cabin, which later became a symbol of the American frontier. The French houses in the Mississippi Valley [4] influenced the design of later plantation mansions of the Deep South.

By the eighteenth century the 13 colonies were prosperous. Especially in Virginia, great houses [5] and public edifices were built. Homes in New England were more modest, but they had many improvements over the earlier dwellings. Overhangs disappeared; and the availability of glass allowed large, double-hung windows. Inside, beams were plastered, creating smooth ceilings; walls were paneled or papered. The massive central chimney was replaced by side chimneys, thus opening up the center of the house for a wide hall and handsome staircase.

The Federal period

With independence came a search for an architectural style that could be identified with the new nation. Thomas Jefferson turned from English Palladian design books to Roman examples for inspiration, deciding that the new republic should be identified with the Roman Republic [6]. His Virginia State Capitol (1785–98) copied the Maison Carée, a Roman temple that he had seen restored at Nîmes, France. But it was not the Roman temple that became the prototype of American state capitols; instead it was the State House (1798) that Charles Bulfinch (1763–1844) designed for Massachusetts, combining Roman, Georgian, and Adam elements and distinguished by its impressive dome. Bulfinch was chiefly responsible for transforming the appearance of Boston from a provincial town into a sophisticated city. Only Charleston, S.C., rivaled Boston's Federal homes [7].

Revivalism

In the early nineteenth century a fervor for Greek Revival swept the country, with Philadelphia as the trendsetter. The Second Bank of the United States (1819–24) by William Strickland (1784–1854), modeled after the Parthenon of Athens, became the prototype for banks. Thomas Ustick Walter's (1804–87) transformation of Nicholas Biddle's eighteenth century farmhouse, Andalusia, into a Greek temple (1832) was the model for other homes in the country [8].

CONNECTIONS

See also
1192 British and American art 1530–1790
1198 Neoclassicism
1258 Architecture in the 19th century
1278 The United States: Reconstruction to World War I
1298 Origins of modern architecture

1 The Palace of the Governors (1609), Santa Fe, N.M., combines indigenous and Spanish elements. The thick adobe walls; stark, geometric shapes; and projecting end beams under a flat roof are all reminiscent of Zuñi pueblos. The *portal*—the covered porch shown here—is reminiscent of a medieval Spanish cloister. The rooms open on to a central court, as in both Spanish and pueblo architecture.

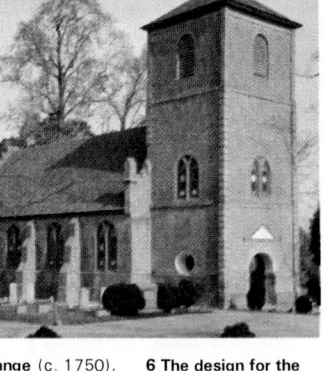

2 St Luke's Church (1632), Smithfield, Va.—the oldest standing church in English America—is a typical late medieval English country parish church. English Gothic characteristics include its buttresses, pointed tracery windows, open porch, square tower, and step-gabled roof. This last architectural element had been introduced into English architecture in the late Middle Ages by Flemish artisans.

3 The Stanley-Whitman House (c. 1660), Farmington, Conn., is one of the finest preserved 17th-century New England farmhouses. The overhanging second story with ornamental drop pendants and small, cross-paned casement windows recalls Elizabethan English architecture. The massive central chimney is rooted in the Middle Ages. The symmetrically placed windows with the door as a focal point show sophistication.

4 Parlange (c. 1750), Pointe Coupée, La., shows Canadian and West Indian influences. The broad front and steep, dominant roof are typical of Normandy, where many of the artisans of New France originated. In Normandy and in Canada the deep porch created by the roof overhang sheltered against rain and snow; in Louisiana and the West Indies, the porch was extended around the house in a *galerie* to provide shade.

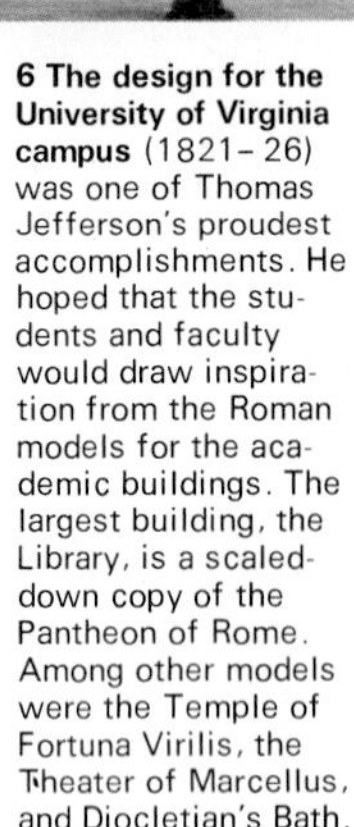

6 The design for the University of Virginia campus (1821–26) was one of Thomas Jefferson's proudest accomplishments. He hoped that the students and faculty would draw inspiration from the Roman models for the academic buildings. The largest building, the Library, is a scaled-down copy of the Pantheon of Rome. Among other models were the Temple of Fortuna Virilis, the Theater of Marcellus, and Diocletian's Bath.

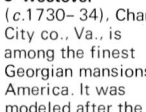

5 Westover (*c.*1730–34), Charles City co., Va., is among the finest Georgian mansions in America. It was modeled after the Governor's Palace (1706) in Williamsburg, but improved upon the verticality and severity of its model by replacing the plain entrance with an elaborate Palladian door reached by elegantly simple pyramid stairs; by spanning the windows with brick arches; and by adding low balancing outbuildings.

Even at the height of its popularity, Greek Revival was challenged by other revivals [Key]. Promoters of Gothic Revival scorned the pagan Greek in favor of their more "Christian" style. Not surprisingly, Gothic Revival predominated for churches, with New York City's Trinity Church (1839–46) by Richard Upjohn (1802–78) its finest example. The most important secular public building in Gothic Revival was the Smithsonian Institution (1839–46), Washington, D.C., by James Renwick (1818–95). Alexander Jackson Davis (1803–92) was one of the most successful architects of the first half of the nineteenth century, perhaps because he could adapt to all styles. His designs included "Etruscan" buildings [9].

The influence of Richardson

After the Civil War American architecture slipped into a period of eclecticism; elements from unrelated architectural styles were combined in an attempt to impress with opulence and monumentality [10]. Out of this chaos, Henry Hobson Richardson (1838–86) restored order and dignity. He designed buildings that fulfilled the Victorian need for monumentality without destroying the integrity of the building itself. His works inspired both the Beaux-Arts school of academic architects epitomized by the firm of McKim, Mead, and White (1879–1906) and the Chicago school of modern architecture pioneered by Louis Sullivan (1856–1924). Richardson's Beaux-Arts followers were impressed by the unity and monumentality of his works. At their best, they produced brilliantly conceived and proportioned buildings with a richness of detail that later ages could not afford to construct [11]. Sullivan and his followers were impressed with the fundamental integrity of Richardson's buildings [12]—the walls were massive because they carried massive weight; the rough stone or heavy timber was not smoothed or concealed. Later architects would translate this functional integrity into steel, glass, and reinforced concrete. At the close of the nineteenth century, buildings in the revivalist-eclectic style and in the emerging modern style were going up side by side.

KEY

The Architect's Dream (1840) by Thomas Cole illustrates how most American architects during the 19th century turned their backs on their colonial heritage. The architect Ithiel Town (1784–1844) is shown receiving inspiration from Egyptian pyramids and temples, Greek and Roman temples, a Roman viaduct, a Byzantine capital, Tuscan arches, and a Gothic cathedral—in nothing native to America. This dependence on classical and medieval models for architecture contrasts with Cole's own inspiration for most of his paintings—the Hudson Valley landscape.

7

7 The Nathaniel Russell house (c. 1803), Charleston, S.C., was one of many elegant houses built in Charleston after the American Revolution. Buildings of the Federal Period defied the flat, rectilinear design of Georgian architecture. Windows and doors might be framed in arched embrasures; different window treatments were often found on the same façade. Walls that curved out created semicircular or elliptical rooms.

8 The Finch-Brooks house (1842), Marshall, Mich., is one of the finest Greek Revival houses in the Midwest. The small portico on the side, not the large porch in front, serves as the entrance.

8

9 An "Etruscan" villa designed by Alexander Jackson Davis in 1835 was somewhat reminiscent of a small, late Renaissance Italian villa. Davis did not know what an Etruscan house looked like.

9

10

11 The Boston Public Library (1888) by McKim, Mead, and White stands across Copley Square from H. H. Richardson's Trinity Church (1872–77). Both Charles F. McKim and Stanford White had worked on Trinity while young architects in Richardson's office. The three arched doors of their library echo the three mighty portals of Richardson's church, but otherwise it is markedly different.

11

12

10 The Connecticut State Capitol (1878–85), Hartford, by Richard Mitchell Upjohn (1828–1903), combines Roman, Gothic, Italianate, Palladian, and French Second Empire elements.

12 The Marshall Field Wholesale Store (1885–87), Chicago, was the H. H. Richardson work most influential on the Chicago school of architecture. It was a simple, direct yet impressive statement in stone of its construction and use.

The American experience: the skyscraper

The dream of constructing tall edifices soaring into the sky is as old as the tower of Babel, but not until the nineteenth century in the United States was the technology developed to make this dream a reality. In 1853, Elisha Graves Otis (1811–61) demonstrated his safe elevator [1], which could carry people beyond the few stories they were willing to climb. In 1857 the first public passenger elevator was installed in the Haughwout Department Store [2] in New York City. This building was also innovative in its cast-iron rather than masonry construction, which added considerable interior space and light by eliminating thick supporting walls. With the development, beginning in the 1850s, of stronger, more heat-resistant metals through the Kelley-Bessemer steel manufacturing process, ever taller buildings could be constructed.

Chicago rebuilds

The Chicago fire of 1871 led to major rebuilding that made Chicago the most important center for skyscraper design. William LeBaron Jenney (1832–1907) built some of Chicago's first skyscrapers; his Rand McNally Building (1890) was the first skyscraper completely of steel construction. But Jenney was an engineer; his skyscrapers were technologically innovative but aesthetically uninspired.

Louis Sullivan (1856–1924) designed some of the first skyscrapers that attempted to state a skyscraper aesthetic. One of his early successes, the Wainwright Building (St. Louis, 1890–91), stressed the verticality of the skyscraper [3A]. It was classical in proportion—with a two-story base, a seven-story shaft, a frieze-decorated top floor, and heavy-cornice roof capital. Concurrently, Daniel H. Burnham (1846–1912) and John W. Root (1850–91) designed the horizontally emphasized Reliance Building (Chicago, 1890–94) [3B].

Gothic and other decorative styles

Skyscraper design was not the exclusive domain of modernists. Traditionalists looked to the past for appropriate styles. Gothic, inspired by the soaring towers of medieval cathedrals, became the most popular style [4]. Many other decorative styles appeared. A Mayan style grew out of the need to step back buildings in decreasing towers to conform to zoning restrictions. The Chrysler Building (New York City, 1929–30), inspired by Art Deco, was one of the most resplendent and original decorative skyscrapers.

Modernism in the 1930s

The first direct influence of the International Style on US skyscraper design was the Philadelphia Savings Fund Society Building (1929–32) [5]. One of its architects, William Lescaze (1896–1969), was born and trained in Switzerland. Raymond Hood (1881–1934), who had designed Gothic towers, turned to distinctly modern designs for the Daily News Building (1930) and the McGraw-Hill Building (1931), both in New York City. The Great Depression prevented the 1930s, which began so promisingly, from becoming a highpoint of modern skyscraper design, but it witnessed the construction of Rockefeller Center [6], the first successful skyscraper complex.

CONNECTIONS

See also

1278 The United States: Reconstruction to World War I

1322 Modern architecture after 1930

1612 Making large buildings

1

1 Elisha Graves Otis, demonstrating his steam-driven elevator, shouts to onlookers "All safe, gentlemen." Although its cord has been cut, safety devices prevent it from plunging to the ground.

2

BROADWAY MFRS. SUPPLY CO.

2 The Haughwout Building, with its highly decorative façade reminiscent of Jacopo Sansovino's 16th-century library in Venice, would not appear at first glance to be innovative. Its large windows and open interior space would have been impossible, however, in a masonry building. Its exterior consists of prefabricated, modular cast-iron panels that were manufactured elsewhere, then shipped to the site.

3A B

3 Louis Sullivan believed that a skyscraper "must be every inch a proud and soaring thing, rising in sheer exultation so that from bottom to top it is a unit without a single dissenting line." To accent the verticality of the Wainwright Building [A], he deemphasized the windows (which would have formed horizontal planes) and stressed the vertical columns by inserting additional nonsupporting columns between the true supporting columns. Burnham and Root, on the other hand, stressed the horizontal elements of their Reliance Building [B] by using what came to be called the Chicago window—a large, undivided center pane with a narrow double sash window on each side. The bays increased light and drew attention from the vertical structural columns.

4A

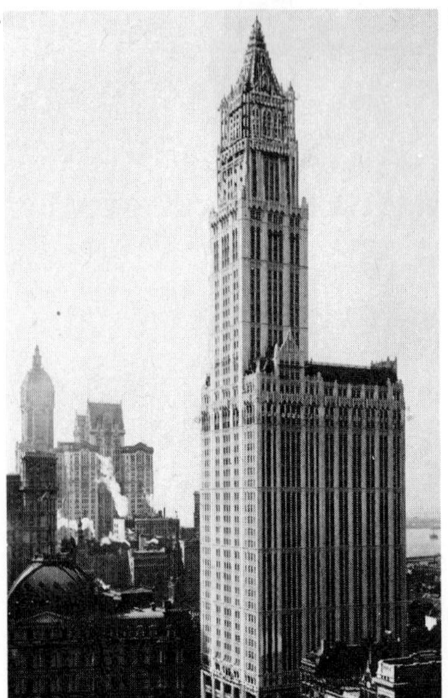

B

C

4 The Gothic skyscraper was, if nothing else, distinctive and solidly three-dimensional. The Woolworth Building [A] (New York City, 1911–13) by Cass Gilbert (1859–1934) was the first and most famous Gothic skyscraper. It was quickly dubbed (to the owners' delight) the Cathedral of Commerce. The 40-ft (12.2-m) flying buttresses atop the Chicago Tribune Building [B] (1923–25) by Raymond M. Hood (1881–1934) and John Mead Howells (1868–1959) are merely decorative. This design won out in a competition over "modernist" designs. The 42-story University of Pittsburgh tower [C] (1924–25) is the tallest academic structure in the world.

Post-World War II developments

With peacetime prosperity many firms commissioned new headquarters, and architects were eager to apply new concepts learned from European colleagues who had fled Europe and to use new or improved materials developed originally for wartime needs. Frank Lloyd Wright (1869–1959) received two skyscraper commissions—the Johnson Company research tower (Racine, Wis., 1944–50) and the Price Tower (Bartlesville, Okla., 1955–56) [7]. Both made imaginative use of the cantilever and of reinforced concrete. Park Avenue, New York City, became the trendsetter for glass curtain-wall skyscrapers, first with Lever House (1952) and then with the Seagram Building (1956–58). Alcoa utilized its own product when it sheathed its new Pittsburgh headquarters (1951) in aluminum [8].

Recent trends

Skyscraper design has demonstrated renewed vitality since the mid-1960s. The height rivalry that had culminated in 1931 in the 1250ft (381.2m) Empire State Building in New York City was resumed. New York hoped to remain on top with the 1353ft (412.7m) twin World Trade Center towers dedicated in 1973, but the Sears Tower (Chicago, 1973) was purposely designed to be 101ft (30.8m) taller.

The tapered, diagonally braced John Hancock Center (Chicago, 1965–70) [9] is among the handsomest of the newer skyscrapers. It is one of many recent nonrectilinear skyscrapers, including the circular Marina Towers (Chicago, 1964), the pyramidal Transamerica building (San Francisco, 1973), and the trapezoidal Pennzoil Place (Houston, 1976) [Key].

Attention is being paid to creating exciting interior spaces, as in the Ford Foundation Building (New York City, 1967), which has a 10-story enclosed garden, and in the extravagant multistory lobbies John Portman has designed for his skyscraper hotels for the Hyatt chain. Some recent skyscrapers, including Boston's long-delayed John Hancock building (1976), are sheathed in mirror glass, which reflects rather than defies the surroundings.

KEY

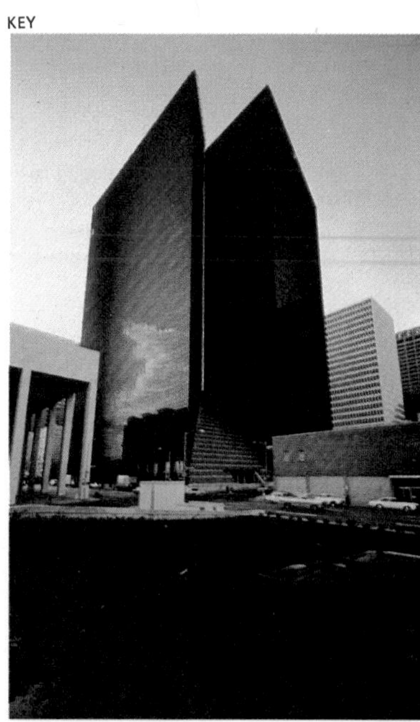

Pennzoil Place (1976) rises in twin 36-story trapezoidal towers in downtown Houston like a giant piece of sculpture. The architects, Philip Johnson and John Burgee, defied Houston's boxy skyline by slicing off the rooflines of their towers at a 45-degree angle. The slanted roofs of the twin towers are echoed in the twin glass-roofed lobbies that rise to a height of eight stories. At their closest, the towers stand only 10 ft (3.05m) apart. The towers are sheathed in a mirror glass that is tinted almost black. Although skyscraper architecture is about 100 years old, this exciting, unconventional project attests to its continuing vitality.

5

6

7

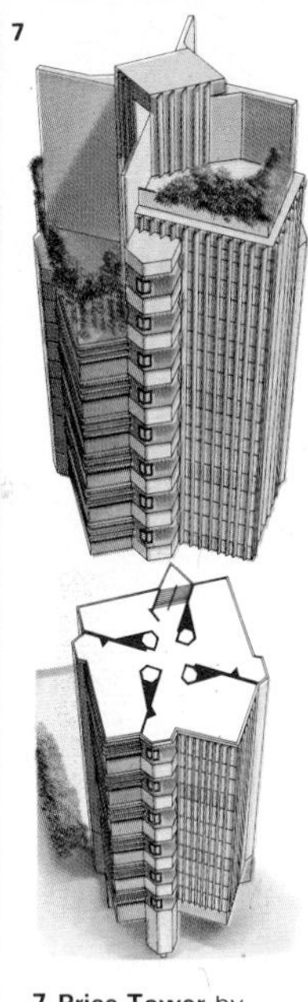

5 The Philadelphia Savings Fund Society Building by George Howe (1886–1955) and William Lescaze introduced the use of the cantilever and curtain-wall strip windows to US skyscraper architecture. It was devoid of decorative embellishments.

8

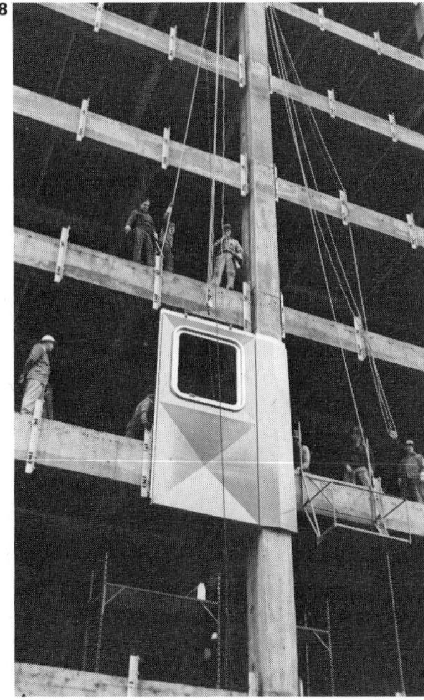

8 Once the steel framework for the 31-story Alcoa Building was in place, prefabricated 6ft by 12ft (1.8m by 3.7m) aluminum panels, complete with built-in windows, were hoisted into place. The x-indent in the siding increases rigidity and provides shadow and scale for the building. Other materials used to sheathe modern skyscrapers include steel, special glass, and an elegant old material, marble.

6 Rockefeller Center (New York City, initial buildings 1930–40), designed by the firms of Reinhard & Hofmeister; Hoat, Godley & Fouilhouz; and Corbett, Harrison & MacMurray, combines office space with entertainment, recreation, and shopping facilities. Originally, the 66-story RCA Building was surrounded by 13 smaller buildings, all formally spaced but turned on different axes to avoid a canyonlike effect and to bathe each building with light from all sides. In the original plan, vehicular traffic was restricted primarily to the perimeter, creating quiet, restful pedestrian malls. Rockefeller Center has been expanded to include newer skyscrapers.

9

7 Price Tower by Frank Lloyd Wright has four hollow concrete cores, containing elevators and service facilities, from which floors cantilever out. Duplex apartments are located in the areas with vertical louvers. Offices are in the areas with horizontal louvers.

9 The John Hancock Tower, Chicago, echoes the Eiffel Tower, completed in 1889, in its cross bracing and upward tapering. It contains both commercial and residential space. Many of its residents commute to work by elevator. Its simple but striking and different design made it a Chicago landmark even before completion.

The American experience: painting

American painting has been marked by boldness, by preoccupation with American space, and by rapid stylistic changes.

Portraying the emerging nation

Early colonial portraitists were often house or sign painters who made rough likenesses on request. By the late colonial era, however, portraiture had, in the hands of professional artists such as John Singleton Copley (1735–1815), become refined [Key].

Capturing the likenesses of the leaders of the American Revolution winning their niche in history was a natural expansion of the portrait painter's art. Fortunately for the emerging nation, there were such excellent artists as Charles Willson Peale (1741–1827), Gilbert Stuart (1755–1828), and John Trumbull (1756–1843).

Primitives, romantics, and naturalists

Artists of the young nation sought to catch the many facets of American life. The untutored primitives, although ignorant of artistic convention, presented a world of native American charm [1].

The romantic impulse found congenial soil in America with its breathtaking landscapes, exotic native Indians, and beckoning frontier. Thomas Cole (1801–48) was the leader of the Hudson River School [3], whose landscapes were a robust tribute to "the virgin charms of our native land." George Catlin (1796–1872), Albert Bierstadt (1830–1902), and others traveled West to capture on canvas in their unspoiled state natural wonders and the Indians [2].

Other, more sentimental artists, including William Sidney Mount (1807–1868), George Caleb Bingham (1811–79), and Eastman Johnson (1824–1906), portrayed picturesque aspects of American life [4]. In the bird paintings of John James Audubon [5] science and art were fused. In the latter half of the nineteenth century, artists such as Winslow Homer (1836–1910) and Frederic Remington (1861–1909) were popular as magazine illustrators, a tradition that has continued into the mid-twentieth century, as with the sentimental-realism of the illustrations by Norman Rockwell (1894–) for *The Saturday Evening Post*.

Impressionism and realism

From late colonial times, American artists had journeyed to Europe to study the masters and to associate with the pathbreakers. James McNeill Whistler (1834–1903) and John Singer Sargent (1856–1925), two of the most sophisticated American artists of the nineteenth century, were more at home in London and Paris than in America. Mary Cassatt (1845–1926) moved to Paris, becoming one of America's leading impressionist painters [6].

Thomas Eakins (1844–1916) had also studied abroad, but only, as he said, to be able to paint Americans "as I see them." His uncompromising realism, based in part on the study of photographs, broke the ground for a group of artists—Robert Henri (1865–1929), John Sloan (1871–1951), George Luks (1867–1933), William Glackens (1870–1938), and Everett Shinn (1876–1953)—dubbed the Ashcan School for their unwillingness to put up with an upper-class aesthetic. They combined an impressionistic palette with an intense vision of urban, polyglot America [7].

CONNECTIONS

See also
1192 British and American art 1530–1790
1252 Realist painting in the 19th century
1294 Fauvism and Expressionism
1318 Dada, Surrealism, and their legacy
1320 Abstract art
1372 Recent trends in the visual arts

1 Edward Hicks (1790–1849), a Pennsylvania Quaker preacher and itinerant carriage and sign painter, produced at least 100 versions of "The Peaceable Kingdom," which illustrates Isaiah's prophecy that "the wolf . . . shall dwell with the lamb, and the leopard shall lie down with the kid." In the background of this version he incorporated a variation of Benjamin West's "Penn's Treaty with the Indians." Hicks gave his paintings to friends.

2 George Catlin traveled among the Plains and Western Indians for eight years beginning in 1829, producing nearly 600 paintings and sketches. His studies of the Mandan are especially important because the tribe was devastated by a smallpox epidemic five years after Catlin's visit. The tall poles within the village in the "Bird's Eye View of the Mandan Village" were supposed to ward off evil spirits. The palisade was set up against enemies. On the plain mummified corpses lay on platforms.

3 "Kindred Spirits" (1849) by the Hudson River School artist Asher B. Durand (1796–1886) was painted as a memorial to Thomas Cole. It shows Cole and his friend the poet William Cullen Bryant standing on a precipice overlooking a picturesque gorge in the Catskill Mountains. It was Bryant who had urged Cole and all artists to "Go forth, under the open sky, and list to Nature's teachings." Other members of the Hudson River School included Thomas Doughty (1793–1856), John F. Kensett (1816–72), Jaspar F. Cropsey (1823–1900), Martin Johnson Heade (1819–1904), and Frederick Church (1826–1900).

4 Eastman Johnson was one of the most popular American painters in the 19th century. Engravings and chromolithographs of his sentimental genre paintings, including "Old Stage Coach" (1871) shown here, "Old Kentucky Home" (1859), and "Corn Husking at Nantucket" (n.d.), hung in countless homes. Like Johnson, William Sidney Mount painted scenes of rural Eastern America. John Caleb Bingham, raised on the Missouri frontier, chronicled the new West. "Fur Traders Descending the Missouri" (*c.*1844) and "Daniel Boone Escorting a Band of Pioneers into the Western Country" (1851) depicted the westward movement of the frontiersmen. After Bingham entered Missouri politics, he recorded American frontier democracy in a number of paintings.

5 "Passenger Pigeon," one of 435 watercolors in John James Audubon's *Birds of America*, is especially valuable because the breed is now extinct, killed off primarily for sport. Unable to obtain a publisher in the United States, Audubon went to England in 1826. *Birds of America* was printed in four volumes in England between 1827–38. A five-volume US edition appeared in 1840–44.

Modern art comes of age in America

The 1913 Armory Show in New York City alerted US artists to the artistic revolution occurring in Europe. Such US painters as Max Weber (1881–1961), Arthur Dove (1880–1946), Marsden Hartley (1877–1943), Joseph Stella (1880–1946), and Stuart Davis (1894–1964) journeyed to Europe to immerse themselves in the radically new techniques—fauvism, cubism, futurism—but returned to adapt them to their own American ends. In the 1920s a Precisionist style, which reduced objects into sharply defined geometric shapes and volumes, evolved in the works of Charles Sheeler (1883–1965), Charles Demuth (1883–1935), and Georgia O'Keeffe [8]. Precursors of the abstract expressionists were the synchromists Stanton Macdonald-Wright (1890–) and Morgan Russell (1896–1953) who used vivid colors and subtle gradation to define nonobjective spaces. The 1930s were dominated by social realism, as in the works of Philip Evergood (1901–73), Reginald Marsh (1898–1954), and Ben Shahn (1898–1969), and by regionalism, as in the works of Thomas Hart Benton (1889–1975), John Steuart Curry (1897–1946), and Grant Wood (1892–1942).

Abstract expressionism versus realism

After World War II, abstract expressionism dominated US art [9]. Willem de Kooning (1904–), Hans Hofmann (1880–1966), Franz Kline (1910–62), and Jackson Pollock (1912–56), among others, made New York City the art capital of the western world. They blazed dazzling new paths into the oldest of artistic concerns—space, color, form, composition, and emotion. The earlier action-painting phase was superseded in the 1960s by the more studied, precise hard-edge works of Mark Rothko (1903–70), Josef Albers (1888–), Kenneth Noland (1924–), and Frank Stella (1936–).

But realism has also remained vital. The "realism" of Edward Hopper (1882–1967), Andy Warhol (1930–), and Andrew Wyeth [10] is as startlingly varied as the multifaceted reality of modern America.

KEY

John Singleton Copley's portrait of Paul Revere (*c.*1768–70) reveals both a sophistication in craft and style remarkable for a self-taught artist and a respect for America's democratic society. Revere is in his shirtsleeves; he holds a teapot he has crafted; before him are his silversmith's tools. But Copley yearned to be more than the finest provincial painter. In 1774, at the urging of the British painter Sir Joshua Reynolds, he sailed for England to improve his skills and expand his reputation. As with Benjamin West (1738–1820), who had left for Europe in 1760, he never returned to his native country.

6

6 Mary Cassatt, despite her banker father's opposition, left Philadelphia for Europe in 1866 to study painting. In Paris she became closely identified with Edgar Degas. "The Boating Party" (1893–94) shows the influence of Edouard Manet and of Japanese wood block prints. French critics praised her works as distinctly American.

7 George Bellows (1882–1925) was Robert Henri's favorite student. His New York City street scenes, such as "Cliff Dwellers" (1913), had the same rough vigor as his famous sporting scenes. His lithographs were as important as his paintings. Bellows lived his whole adult life in New York City; he never visited Europe or traveled widely in his own country. He began teaching at the Art Students League in 1910.

7

8 Georgia O'Keeffe (1887–) is a true native genius. Her works were influenced by the American Precisionists, by American photography (she was married to Alfred Stieglitz), and, most importantly, by the American cityscape and landscape. "Cow Skull: Red, White, and Blue" (1931) is one of her early New Mexico paintings.

9 "Bolton Landing" (1957) was painted by Willem de Kooning after a visit to the studio of sculptor David Smith in that upstate New York village. It is a prime example of action painting. The viewer's eye follows de Kooning's slashing, exuberant brushstrokes almost as if it were observing the actual process of painting.

10 Andrew Wyeth (1917–) regards himself as heir to the realistic tradition of Thomas Eakins and Winslow Homer. His detractors compare his works to those of less esteemed but once more popular sentimental genre painters of the 19th century. In 1976, the Metropolitan Museum of Art in New York City honored Wyeth with a one-man show. But it is still too early to tell what his lasting reputation will be.

8

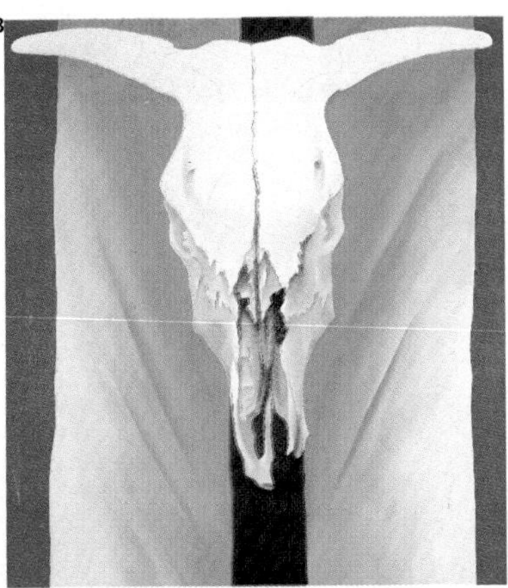

9

10

The American experience: sculpture

American sculpture can be viewed in four historical phases. The oldest applies to native Americans. The second, dealing with the handiwork of artisan-craftsmen, dates from colonial stonecutters and woodcarvers through the folk sculptors of the nineteenth century. The third phase is the European-based tradition of figurative sculpture in marble and bronze that flourished in the nineteenth through the early twentieth century. The fourth phase is one in which American sculptors have pursued individual visions and have dealt with new materials and technology.

Indian sculpture

The most outstanding work of Indian sculpture is the totem pole of the Pacific Northwest Indians [1]. Other distinguished work includes the masks of the Iroquois, the Kachina dolls of the Pueblos, and the masks and carvings of the Eskimos.

Artisan-craftsmen

The earliest colonial sculptures were the wooden altarpieces and stone statues carved for missions in the Southwest and the gravestones of New England stonecutters. The Southwest pieces—executed by Spanish and Indian craftsmen—were the only three-dimensional sculptures of the seventeenth century. In the next century, woodcarvers came to prominence in eastern America. Samuel McIntire (1757–1811) of Salem, Mass., carved elaborate mantel and furniture decorations. William Rush (1756–1833) of Philadelphia raised woodcarving to an art with his portrait busts and free-standing statues, but his works were being carved at the very time that marble was replacing wood in the United States as the preferred medium for sculpture. Woodcarving was soon relegated to the "folk" tradition of ships' heads, cigar-store Indians, and carousel figures [2]. Not until well into the twentieth century would these sculptures be appreciated for their artistry.

The nineteenth century

The new nation was so lacking in trained sculptors that the commissions to commemorate the Revolutionary leaders and to embellish the new capital were given to European sculptors. Horatio Greenough, who had trained in Italy, was, in 1832, the first American to receive a major government commission [3]. Contrasting with his stern, monumental Roman-inspired works were the gentler, more sentimental Greek-inspired statues of Hiram Powers. His "Greek Slave" earned him an international reputation. Other European-trained sculptors who worked in a neoclassical vein included Thomas Crawford (1813?–57), William H. Rinehart (1825–74), and Harriet Hosmer (1830–1908).

Although idealized sculptures on classical and biblical themes were popular throughout the nineteenth century, Americans were never comfortable having their national heroes represented in Roman togas. A naturalistic portrait sculpture, usually in bronze rather than in classical marble, emerged after midcentury. Leading sculptors included Henry Kirke Brown (1814–86), Thomas Ball (1819–1911), John Quincy Adams Ward (1830–1910), and Daniel Chester French [4]. Augustus

CONNECTIONS

See also
1198 Neoclassicism
1318 Dada, Surrealism, and their legacy
1372 Recent trends in the visual arts

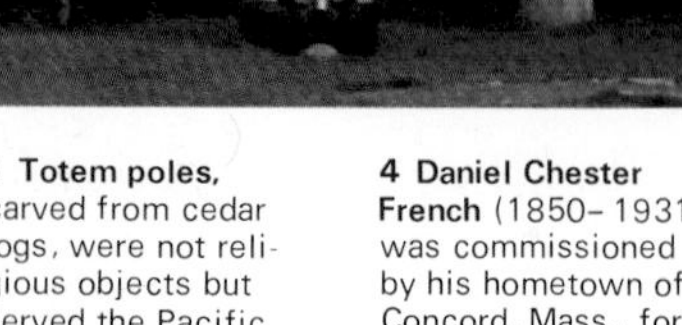

2 This anonymous wooden folk sculpture, carved around 1858 to adorn the top of Fireman's Hall, New York City, represents Henry Howard, Chief Engineer of the New York Volunteer Fire Department.

3 Horatio Greenough (1808–52) carved this colossal statue of George Washington to stand beneath the dome of the Capitol rotunda. Because it proved to be too heavy for the floor, it was moved outdoors and, later, to the Smithsonian Institution. Reaction to the sandaled, semi-nude figure modeled after Phidias' 5th-century BC statue of Zeus was generally negative.

1 Totem poles, carved from cedar logs, were not religious objects but served the Pacific Northwest Indians as family crests by depicting the lineage of the head of the clan. The height of the log and the elaborateness of its carving testified to the importance and affluence of the family. The figures were conventional but arranged uniquely for each family. The earliest totem poles were carved roof supports; only in the 19th century did they become freestanding.

4 Daniel Chester French (1850–1931) was commissioned by his hometown of Concord, Mass., for a statue commemorating the centennial of the stand of the Concord Minute Men against the British. His life-size bronze statue was a realistic portrait of a young farmer standing confidently in his plain, wrinkled work clothes, rifle in one hand, the other hand on his plow. The unveiling was attended by President Grant, Longfellow, and Emerson.

5 For the World's Columbia Exposition, Chicago, 1893, the nation's leading Beaux-Arts sculptors were called upon to design works to embellish and compliment the Beaux-Arts exhibition halls. Frederick William MacMonnies (1863–1937) received the coveted commission for the central sculpture for the head of the grand lagoon. He entitled his imposing piece "The Barge of State" (or "Triumph of Columbia").

Saint-Gaudens (1848–1907), influenced by contemporary trends in France, produced more impressionistic works. Frederic Remington and Charles M. Russell (1864–1926) popularized the West in their bronze sculptures, while the brothers Gutzon (1867–1941) and Solon (1868–1922) Borglum worked the same genre in stone.

By far the most popular sculptor of the nineteenth century was John Rogers. His sentimental, narrative statuettes [6], reproduced in plaster, were sold by the tens of thousands. William Rimmer [Key], a self-taught individualist, created striking, emotively expressive sculptures.

The twentieth century

As in architecture, new trends in sculpture emerged alongside the last, splendid works of the Beaux-Arts school [5]. A few sculptors, such as Jo Davidson [8], retained the realism of portrait sculpture while emphasizing simple lines and materials. Paul Manship (1885–1966) developed a sleek, elegant, realistic style that influenced decorative art of the 1920s and 1930s.

A revolution in sculpture began in 1913 when Robert Laurent, influenced by primitive rather than classical sculpture, began carving in wood [9]. In the 1920s he was joined by William Zorach (1887–1965) and others in creating simple, often abstract, forms directly out of natural materials. In the 1920s and 1930s several major European sculptors moved to the United States—among them Alexander Archipenko (1887–1964), Elie Nadelman (1882–1946), and Jacques Lipchitz (1891–1973).

John Storrs was the first American to produce nonobjective cubist sculpture and one of the first to work in aluminum. Alexander Calder introduced motion with his mobiles [11]. David Smith employed metal welding to create abstract sculptures [7]. Joseph Cornell (1903–72) combined unrelated found (ordinary household or industrial) objects in box sculptures; Louise Nevelson developed a similar technique in her large wall sculptures [10]. Other developments include the use of plastics, neon light, and papier maché and the creation of total sculptural environments.

KEY

"Despair," carved by William Rimmer (1816–79) out of gypsum when he was only 15, is probably the earliest American male nude sculpture. The emotionally charged little figure—it is only 11in (28cm) high—contrasted with the cool, detached neoclassicism then in vogue and preceded the expressive, romantic sculpture of Auguste Rodin (1840–1917), which it resembles, by almost four decades. Although this early sculpture showed great promise, Rimmer completed few other works. A practicing physician, he sculpted and painted visionary fantasies in his spare time. Late in life he became a noted instructor in life drawing.

6

6 John Rogers (1829–1904) sold 8,000 plaster copies of "Coming to the Parson" at $15 each. His works were the sculptural counterpart of Currier and Ives' prints, presenting easily recognizable scenes that appealed to unsophisticated middle-class taste. Rogers employed as many as 60 assistants at one time in his studio-factory, turning out 80,000 reproductions of his statuettes between 1860 and 1893.

7

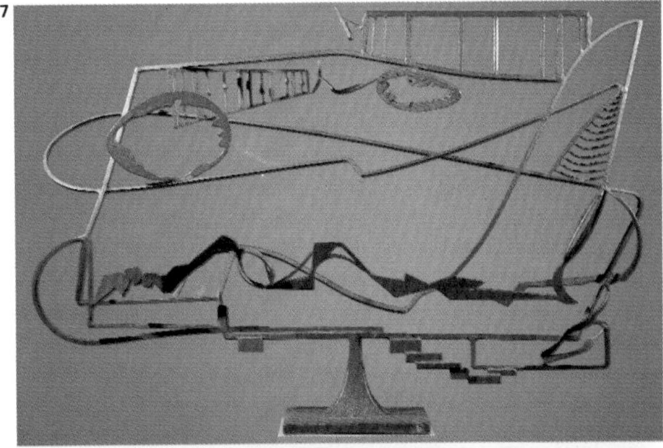

7 David Smith (1906–65) learned to work with metal while employed as a welder and riveter in automobile factories. In Paris he was inspired by Picasso's welded sculptures. After World War II he was influenced by the New York hard-edge school of abstract painting. Works such as "Hudson River Landscape" (1951) have been described as "drawings in air" because of their two-dimensional, brush-like quality.

8

8 Jo Davidson (1883–1952) was the most prolific portrait sculptor of the early 20th century. His simple, direct portraits of leading figures, such as Gertrude Stein shown here in a 1920 work, earned him the title historian in stone.

9

9 Robert Laurent (1890–1970) was influenced by African carving and by American primitives. His first New York exhibit (1915) featured wood reliefs. He then turned to full-round work in wood, such as "The Flame," circa 1917, shown here.

10

10 Louise Nevelson (1900–) creates wall reliefs with found objects as in "Royal Tide II" (1961–63).

11

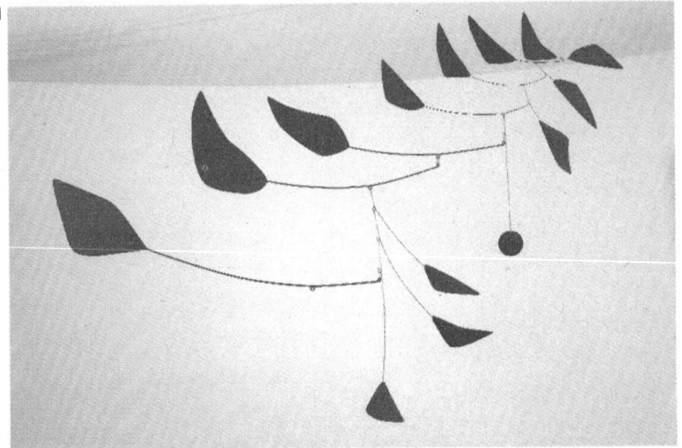

11 Alexander Calder (1898–1976) created his first mobile in 1931. "Big Red" (1959), with outside dimensions of 74in × 114in (188cm × 289.5cm), is painted in Calder's favorite color, red.

The American experience: poetry

The first book published in English America, *The Bay Psalm Book* (1640), was in verse. But in spite of high purpose, early American poetry was not generally of great literary quality. Of the popular *Day of Doom* (1662) by Michael Wigglesworth (1631–1705), Cotton Mather could only write that it was "plain truth dressed up in plain meters." The Revolutionary era poets—Francis Hopkinson (1737–91), Philip Freneau [2], and the Connecticut Wits—were more distinguished by patriotic fervor than by poetic talent.

Since earliest times, some of America's finest poetry was written in obscurity. Edward Taylor's (*c.* 1644–1724) metaphysical poetry remained undiscovered until 1937. Emily Dickinson (1830–86) hid her spare, abstract, and intensely personal lyrics away in boxes and drawers. In this century several major poets went into self-exile, first attaining recognition abroad. T. S. Eliot (1888–1965) became a British citizen. Ezra Pound (1885–1972) left for Europe in 1907, and Robert Frost [6] was first published and praised while living in England.

The nineteenth century

New England dominated American poetry in the nineteenth century as it did other literary forms and philosophy. This New England Renaissance dates from the 1817 publication of *Thanatopsis* by William Cullen Bryant [3]. Bryant's simple, contemplative poem in blank verse fired the American imagination.

The arbiters of nineteenth-century poetry were three poets affiliated with Harvard University: Henry Wadsworth Longfellow [4], Oliver Wendell Holmes (1809–94), and James Russell Lowell (1819–91). For a time Concord, Mass., vied with Harvard's Cambridge as the center of the New England Renaissance. But except for Ralph Waldo Emerson (1803–82), the Concord Transcendentalists wrote little noteworthy poetry. Emily Dickinson wrote outside these intellectual circles as did John Greenleaf Whittier (1807–92), who produced simple poems of country life as well as abolitionist pleas.

Other than Walt Whitman [Key], the great American poet, the most important poet outside New England was Edgar Allan Poe [5]. Regional poets of note were the southerner Sidney Lanier (1842–81) and James Whitcomb Riley (1849–1916) of Indiana.

The twentieth century

Although one region would no longer dominate American poetry, New England continued to make major contributions. Edwin Arlington Robinson (1869–1935) detailed New England life without romanticism or sentimentality. Robert Frost [6] created a uniquely American pastoral, revealing complex and often tragic aspects of life. And a third New Englander, Wallace Stevens (1879–1955) wrote precise, intense, imaginatively rich poems.

In 1912 Harriet Monroe (1860–1936) founded *Poetry: A Magazine of Verse* in Chicago. The most influential US magazine of its kind, it especially stimulated Chicago poets, including Vachel Lindsay (1879–1931), Carl Sandburg [7], and Edgar Lee Masters (1869–1950). *Poetry* also promoted imagism, a movement that advocated the

CONNECTIONS

See also
1374 American writing: into the 20th century

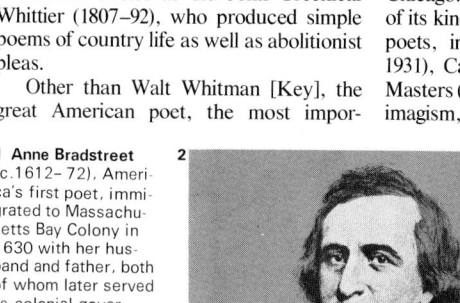

1

THE
TENTH MUSE
Lately sprung up in AMERICA.
OR
Severall Poems, compiled
with great variety of VVit
and Learning, full of delight.
Wherein especially is contained a compleat discourse and description of
The Four Elements, Constitutions, Ages of Man, Seasons of the Year.
Together with an Exact Epitomie of the Four Monarchies, viz.
The Assyrian, Persian, Grecian, Roman.
Also a Dialogue between Old England and New, concerning the late troubles.
With divers other pleasant and serious Poems.
By a Gentlewoman in those parts.
Printed at London for Stephen Bowtell at the signe of the Bible in Popes Head-Alley. 1650.

1 Anne Bradstreet (c.1612–72), America's first poet, immigrated to Massachusetts Bay Colony in 1630 with her husband and father, both of whom later served as colonial governors. Despite the rigors of colonial life and her having eight children, she found time to write poetry. The first edition of her poems, entitled *The Tenth Muse Lately Sprung Up in America*, was published in London in 1650 without her knowledge. An edition of her poems prepared by her appeared in Boston in 1678. She is better appreciated today for her short lyrics of domestic emotion than for her long historical and philosophical verses.

2

2 Philip Freneau (1751–1832), a New Yorker of Huguenot descent, wrote satiric anti-British poems during the American Revolution. In 1780, while returning from the West Indies, he was captured by the British and spent several months on a prison ship. Out of this experience he wrote *The British Prison Ship* (1781). In 1790 he turned to journalism, becoming a leading spokesman for the Jeffersonians.

3 William Cullen Bryant (1794–1878) turned from poetry—he published few poems after 1832—to a distinguished career in journalism as editor (1829–78) of the influential New York *Evening Post*. Yet his influence on American poetry was profound. His call for a return to nature had a direct impact on the Transcendentalists and inspired Thomas Cole, leader of the Hudson River painters.

4 Henry Wadsworth Longfellow (1807–82), more than any other poet, created or popularized American myths. His poem made Paul Revere's ride famous. *The Courtship of Miles Standish* gave life to the Pilgrims. And people think of Hiawatha and Evangeline as if they were historical, not fictional, figures.

5 Edgar Allan Poe (1809–49), both a poet and short-story writer, was more appreciated and influential in France than in the United States. Ralph Waldo Emerson dismissed him as "the jingle man." James Russell Lowell tempered praise with criticism, claiming he was "three fifths pure genius and two fifths sheer fudge." But the French poets Charles Baudelaire and Stephane Mallarmé hailed him as the precursor of the French symbolist movement.

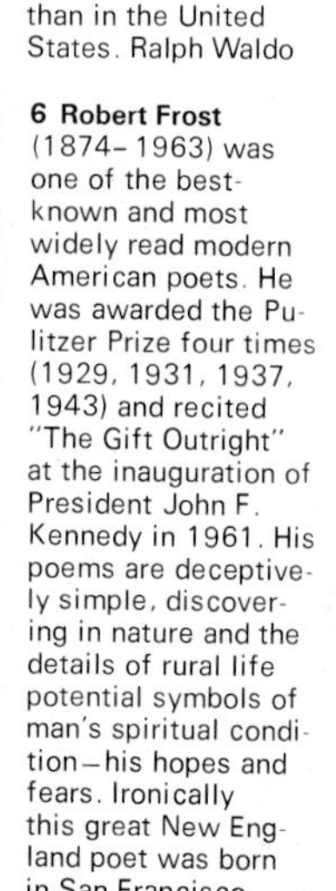

6 Robert Frost (1874–1963) was one of the best-known and most widely read modern American poets. He was awarded the Pulitzer Prize four times (1929, 1931, 1937, 1943) and recited "The Gift Outright" at the inauguration of President John F. Kennedy in 1961. His poems are deceptively simple, discovering in nature and the details of rural life potential symbols of man's spiritual condition—his hopes and fears. Ironically this great New England poet was born in San Francisco.

use of precise image and language. Its practitioners included Ezra Pound (who soon lost interest), H. D. (Hilda Doolittle, 1886–1961), John Gould Fletcher (1886–1950), and Amy Lowell [8].

Fletcher later became a leader of the Agrarians—writers, including John Crowe Ransom (1888–1974), Robert Penn Warren (1905–), and Allen Tate (1899–), who promoted an independent Southern culture. An innovative school of poetry came out of North Carolina's Black Mountain College in the early 1950s. Advocating projective poetry—in which the poet's creative energy surged through the verse—these poets, including Charles Olson (1910–70) and Robert Creeley (1926–), were inspired by the vigorous poetry of William Carlos Williams.

New York City's Greenwich Village has attracted literary figures since the early nineteenth century. Here Edna St Vincent Millay (1892–1962) wrote "My candle burns at both ends" and e. e. cummings (1894–1962) experimented with syntax and typography. In the 1950s, Greenwich Village was co-capital with San Francisco of the Beat poets. In the 1920s, another area of New York, Harlem, saw a renaissance of black poetry [10]. Other poets, such as Marianne Moore [11] and Hart Crane (1899–1932), found inspiration in the whole of New York. In the 1960s a "New York School" of poetry arose around Frank O'Hara (1926–66), Kenneth Koch (1925–), and John Ashbery (1927–).

Although the rewards of poetry—either financial or in fame—are few, American poetry has flourished in the twentieth century. Other outstanding modern poets include Robinson Jeffers (1887–1962), Conrad Aiken (1899–1973), Theodore Roethke (1908–73), Anne Sexton (1928–74), Sylvia Plath (1932–63), Archibald MacLeish (1892–), Kenneth Rexroth (1905–), Muriel Rukeyser (1913–), Karl Shapiro (1913–), Gwendolyn Brooks (1917–), Richard Wilbur (1921–), James Dickey (1923–) [9], W. D. Snodgrass (1926–), Robert Bly (1926–), W. S. Merwin (1927–), Adrienne Rich (1929–), and Gary Snyder (1930–).

KEY

Walt Whitman (1819–92) published the slim first edition of *Leaves of Grass* privately in 1855. Containing only a preface and 12 poems, it appeared anonymously, but with this portrait of Whitman as the frontispiece. This portrait was selected to present Whitman's desired image as a rugged member of the working class—a vigorous, democratic image. Ralph Waldo Emerson praised the work, writing to Whitman, "I greet you at the beginning of a great career." Not until the third, expanded edition (1860) did Whitman obtain a publisher. In all, *Leaves of Grass* appeared in nine editions prepared by Whitman from 1855 to 1892.

7

7 Carl Sandburg (1879–1967) listened to the voices and sounds of America and set them to poetry. In *The American Songbag* (1927) he compiled a valuable collection of ballads and folksongs. *The People, Yes* (1936) is a panoramic verse depiction of the United States and its people. Sandburg was also a biographer of Abraham Lincoln. This portrait is by Sandburg's brother-in-law, Edward Steichen.

8

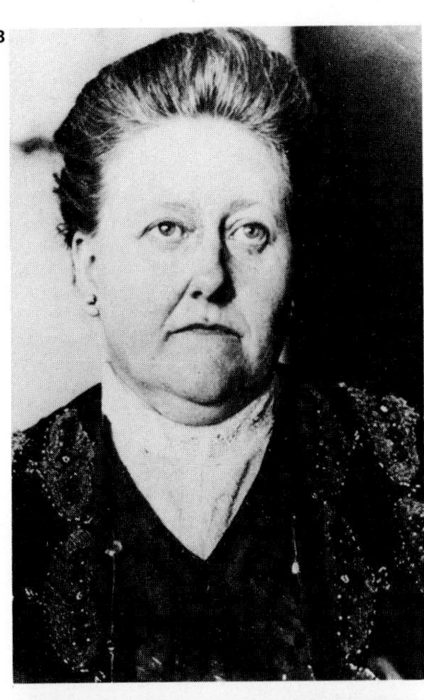

8 The Lowell family of Massachusetts has produced important poets for well over a century. James Russell Lowell began in the *Bigelow Papers* (1848) as a regionalist, employing Yankee humor and dialect. He later turned to more serious verse. Amy Lowell (1874–1925) became the principal promoter of imagism. Robert Lowell (1917–) has written many volumes of serious, well-wrought poetry.

10

OPPORTUNITY

Journal of Negro Life

JULY 1925

15 CENTS the copy

9 Author James Dickey, a native of Atlanta, Ga., remained close to his southern heritage. Collections of his poetry include *Buckdancer's Choice* (1965), while other works include the popular novel *Deliverance* (1969) and the nonfiction *Self-Interviews* (1970) and *Jericho: The South Beheld* (1974).

10 The Harlem Renaissance of the 1920s was inspired by *Autobiography of an Ex-Colored Man* (1912) by James Weldon Johnson (1871–1938). Leading poets were Claude McKay (1890–1948), who explored the politics of race; Countee Cullen (1903–46), who adapted traditional European forms; and Langston Hughes (1902–67), who drew on the musical forms of the ballad and the blues. Countee Cullen is shown here in a drawing by Winold Reiss on a 1925 cover of *Opportunity*, a leading black periodical of the period in which the works of many poets of the Harlem Renaissance appeared.

9

11

11 Marianne Moore (1887–1972) wrote in "Poetry," which appeared in her first collection—*Observations* (1924)—that poets should present "imaginary gardens with real toads in them." The line reveals her quick wit and her insistence upon accurate, close-up detail. Nothing was too topical—"Carnegie Hall; Rescued"—or too commonplace—"To a Steam Roller"—for her discerning poetic eye. In 1951 her *Collected Poems* received the Pulitzer Prize.

The American experience: journalism

Isolation from Europe and from other colonial settlements increased curiosity for news. The colonies were ripe for the advent of newspapers and magazines.

Colonial beginnings

The first American newspaper, Boston's *Publick Occurrences Both Forreign and Domestick,* was suppressed after one issue in 1690 because it lacked a royal license. The first licensed newspaper, the Boston *News-Letter* [1], appeared in 1704. In 1735 the American precedent for freedom of the press was established when New York publisher John Peter Zenger [Key] was cleared of charges of criminal libel for criticizing the provincial governor. The idea for America's first magazine was Benjamin Franklin's, but a rival, *American Magazine,* came out in 1741, three days before Franklin's *General Magazine.*

The Revolutionary and Federal periods

Newspapers and magazines played an important role in the formative years of the United States. Isaiah Thomas' *Royal American Magazine* (1774–75) carried political cartoons by Paul Revere. Thomas Paine [2] edited *Pennsylvania Magazine* (1775–76). Loyalist newspapers vied with patriot counterparts. The virulent political struggles of the early republic were fought out in the press. Attacks against President John Adams' administration became so vicious that the Sedition Act of 1798 was passed to impose press censorship. Before the act expired in 1801, 10 newspaper publishers had been fined and/or imprisoned. Except for this brief lapse, the First Amendment guarantee of freedom of the press has been upheld.

Growth in the nineteenth century

American newspaper and magazine publishers foresaw the potential of an expanding mass audience. The first successful "penny daily" newspaper, the New York *Sun,* appeared in 1833. Hawked in the streets, it contained sensational stories alongside conventional news. It was soon rivaled by the New York *Herald,* founded in 1835, which perfected a direct, precise, and simple prose style that came to typify American journalism. In 1841, Horace Greeley [4] founded the reformist New York *Tribune*. *The New York Times* was founded in 1851 to counter both the sensationalism of the *Sun* and *Herald* and the advocacy of the *Tribune*. By midcentury there were nearly 400 daily newspapers.

One of the earliest popular magazines was *Saturday Evening Post,* founded in 1821. *Knickerbocker Magazine* (1833–65) included works by Irving, Longfellow, Parkman, Hawthorne, Whittier, and Bryant. The most successful magazine of the nineteenth century—*Harper's New Monthly*—appeared in 1850. It serialized works by major English authors. *Atlantic Monthly* (1857) was soon competing with *Harper's*. *Scribner's Magazine* was started in 1870 to promote American rather than English authors; *Overland Monthly,* founded in 1868 in San Francisco and first edited by Bret Harte (1836–1902), promoted Western writers.

Competing with these literary magazines were the illustrateds [3], notably

CONNECTIONS

See also
1776 Newspapers and magazines

1

1 The Boston News-Letter evolved from a handwritten account postmaster John Campbell (1655–1728) sent to New England governors. Between 1704–19, it was the only newspaper in the British colonies. It remained a voice of the loyalists until it ended publication when its last publisher, Margaret Green Draper, left Boston in 1776 with the evacuating British troops.

2

2 Thomas Paine (1737–1809) was probably the most influential political journalist in history. He arrived in America from his native England in 1774 with a letter of introduction from Benjamin Franklin. While editing *Pennsylvania Magazine,* he wrote *Common Sense* (1776), a persuasive argument for independence that laid the groundwork for the Declaration of Independence.

3

3 Frank Leslie (1821–80) has been called the father of the illustrated periodical. He brought out his *Lady's Magazine* in 1854 to compete with *Godey's Lady's Book,* which since 1830 had strongly influenced fashions and manners. The vivid colors and fine quality of Leslie's engravings created an immediate success. In 1855 he started his illustrated newspaper, *Leslie's Weekly,* which—especially during the Civil War—vigorously competed with *Harper's Weekly.*

4

4 The New York Tribune was the one success in Horace Greeley's (1811–72) otherwise often disappointing life. Nominated for the presidency in 1872 by the Liberal Republicans, who opposed the corrupt administration of Ulysses S. Grant, and by the Democrats, he was, nevertheless, overwhelmingly defeated by Grant.

5

HARPER'S WEEKLY.
JOURNAL OF CIVILIZATION

5 Winslow Homer (1836–1910) did not begin painting seriously until 1862. His first paintings were refinements of his war illustrations, such as the one shown here. Engravings made from artists' sketches were the only means newspapers and periodicals had of visually documenting war events. Photographers, notably Mathew Brady (*c.*1823–96), were working at the front, but no method had as yet been perfected for reproducing photographs in print.

Leslie's Weekly (1855–1922) and *Harper's Weekly* (1857–1916). Winslow Homer was an artist-correspondent for *Harper's Weekly* during the Civil War [5]. Thomas Nast's cartoons in *Harper's Weekly* exposed New York's corrupt Tweed Ring.

Yellow journalism and muckraking

In 1895, William Randolph Hearst (1863–1951) purchased the New York *Journal* and determined to outsell Joseph Pulitzer's [6] New York *World*. The two papers vied for audience appeal through sensational headlines and "news" exclusives, and the introduction of color comic strips.

The end of the nineteenth century also saw the advent of the muckraking magazines, most notably *McClure's* (1893–1929). Among important series of articles that ran in *McClure's* were Lincoln Steffens' "Shame of the Cities" and Ida M. Tarbell's [7] "History of Standard Oil."

The twentieth century

The decade of the 1920s was a fruitful time for launching new magazines. In 1922, DeWitt and Lila Wallace began *Reader's Digest*. In 1923, Briton Hadden and Henry Luce founded *Time*, the first, and still most successful, news magazine. The third great success of the 1920s, the *New Yorker*, was founded by Harold Ross in 1925.

In 1936, Time, Inc. launched *Life*, the most influential magazine of photojournalism in history [8]. It was forced to cease publication in 1972 because of soaring production and distribution costs. Not only *Life* but many other, much older popular magazines, such as *Collier's*, *Woman's Home Companion*, and *Saturday Evening Post*, were also forced to cease publication because of high costs. Newspapers, if they survived at all, often did so by merging with others [9].

But the importance of a free, independent press functioning as the Fourth Estate in US political life has not been diminished. It was not Congress, nor television—the rival of the press for advertising revenue—but the Washington *Post*, through its investigative reporters [10], that exposed the Watergate coverup.

KEY

At the trial of John Peter Zenger (1697–1746), his attorney, the distinguished Philadelphia lawyer Andrew Hamilton (c. 1676–1741) successfully urged the jury to uphold "the liberty of both exposing and opposing arbitrary power . . . by speaking and writing truth." Zenger was acquitted of charges of criminal libel and returned to publishing his newspaper.

6

6 Joseph Pulitzer (1847–1911), an emigrant from Hungary, purchased the St. Louis *Post-Dispatch* in 1878 and made it the most influential newspaper in the Midwest. He bought the New York *World* in 1883. His will bequeathed some $2,500,000 to establish the Columbia University School of Journalism and to fund the Pulitzer Prizes in journalism, literature, history, and music.

7 Ida M. Tarbell (1857–1944), as the daughter of an oil producer, knew whom to speak to when she made her incisive investigation of John D. Rockefeller's Standard Oil Company. Her revelations were instrumental in fostering legal constraints on the giant monopoly.

8 Margaret Bourke-White (1906–71) joined Time, Inc. in 1929. Selected as one of the four original staff photographers for *Life*, her photograph of Fort Peck Dam, Montana, was on the cover of the first issue of *Life*. She continued with *Life* as a photojournalist until 1969.

8

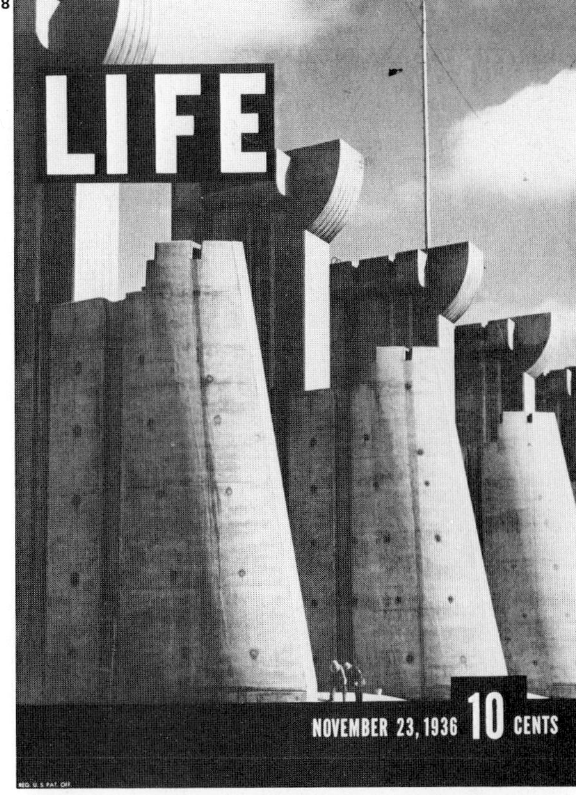
LIFE
NOVEMBER 23, 1936 10 CENTS

7

PRESIDENT TEAPS STANDARD OIL

9

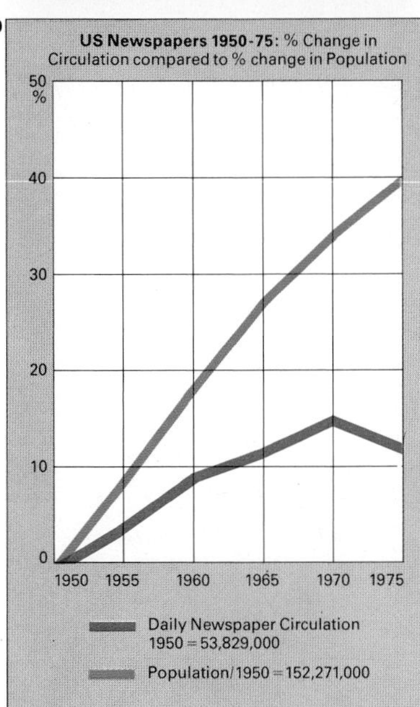
US Newspapers 1950-75: % Change in Circulation compared to % change in Population
50 %
40
30
20
10
0
1950 1955 1960 1965 1970 1975
Daily Newspaper Circulation 1950 = 53,829,000
Population/1950 = 152,271,000

9 Daily newspaper circulation in the United States has failed to keep up with the increasing population. From 1970 to 1975 circulation dropped 2.7%. Since 1950 the number of US daily newspapers has slowly, but steadily, declined.

10

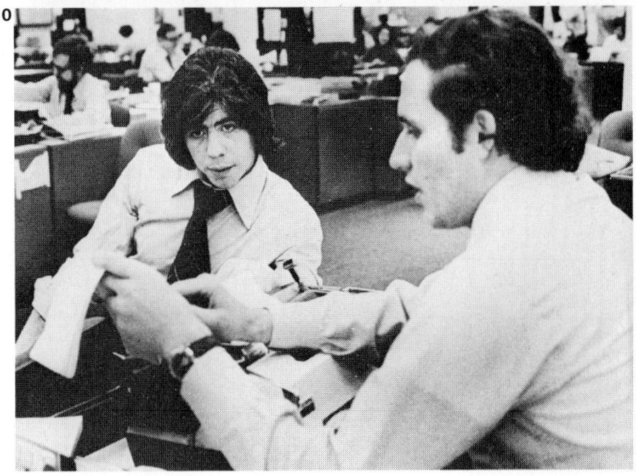

10 The investigation by Washington *Post* reporters Carl Bernstein and Robert Woodward of the June 1972 break-in at the Democrats' Watergate headquarters led to the revelation of Pres. Richard Nixon's role in the coverup.

The American experience: radio and television

In the twentieth century only the automobile has altered US life more than radio and television. Entertainers on radio and television—from Amos 'n' Andy to Lucille Ball—became popular heroes. Politicians who mastered the media, beginning with Franklin D. Roosevelt [Key], found it a significant advantage. Public issues, through prompt and graphic reporting, achieved an immediacy that they had never reached in newspapers and magazines. Finally, radio and television, by creating an enormous demand for products, have had an important influence on the economy.

Beginnings of radio

The potential of radio in communications was seen early in the twentieth century [1] and confirmed by the uses to which radio was put in World War I. Less quick to develop was the awareness of radio as a medium of entertainment and journalism. But in 1920 the Westinghouse Electric Company created station KDKA in Pittsburgh, assembled the transmitting equipment, and went on the air. The first broadcast, on November 2, of the returns for the Harding-Cox presidential election, created considerable public notice. The number of stations increased quickly; by the end of 1922 there were over 500 stations.

The first stations were sponsored by manufacturers of radio equipment in order to develop a market for their products. The advertising of other products soon followed. In August 1922, station WEAF in New York City carried a flowery, 10-minute plug for apartments in Jackson Heights. In January 1923, the actress Marion Davies went on the air to talk about a cosmetic called Mineralava. She offered a free photograph of herself to her listeners; hundreds of requests poured into the station. Advertising agencies and their clients quickly realized the ramifications; radio advertising was soon firmly entrenched.

The Radio Corporation of America founded the National Broadcasting Corporation in 1926 and established two networks (the blue and the red) in 1927. A rival network, the Columbia Broadcasting System, was founded in 1927. The blue network became the American Broadcasting Company in 1943 after being sold by RCA. The Federal Radio (later Communications) Commission was established in 1927 to regulate the new industry. In 1922, 60,000 US families owned radio sets. By 1930, the figure had risen to more than 12,000,000.

The heyday of radio

Commercial network radio blossomed into a major entertainment medium [3]. Stars of vaudeville, the theater, and the concert stage were heard on radio. Al Jolson began broadcasting in 1928, followed by Ed Wynn, Rudy Vallee, and Eddie Cantor. Radio also developed its own stars: Bing Crosby, Kate Smith, and Amos 'n' Andy [2]. The soap opera [8], a daytime serial drama form, became a radio staple, including such shows as *Ma Perkins* and *Just Plain Bill*. Quiz shows were popular, with *Information Please* offering leading intellectuals as panelists.

In 1937, NBC founded the NBC Symphony Orchestra especially for the celebrated Italian conductor Arturo Toscanini

CONNECTIONS

See also
1794 Communications: radio
1796 Communications: television

1

1 David Sarnoff (1891–1971) was a 21-year-old wireless operator with the Marconi Company in New York City when, on April 14, 1912, the British ocean liner *Titanic* struck an iceberg and sank. It was one of the worst disasters of the century—1,513 persons died. Sarnoff, operating his radio from atop the John Wanamaker store, relayed the news of the tragedy to the news services for 72 straight hours. When the Marconi Company was absorbed in 1921 by the Radio Corporation of America, Sarnoff was made its general manager. He became a leading innovator in the radio, television, and recording industries.

2

2 Amos 'n' Andy was the greatest success of early radio. The characters of Amos and Andy were done in traditional minstrel-show black dialect. They were created and performed by two white comedians, Freeman Fisher Gosden (1899–) (Amos, left) and Charles J. Correll (1890–1972) (Andy, right). NBC first broadcast *Amos 'n' Andy* on a national hookup in 1929. It quickly became the rage of the nation. So popular was the program that motion picture theaters, in order not to lose patronage, stopped the movie when the program came on the air and broadcast it over their loudspeakers for the movie audience. The success of the series on radio led to an early television series based on the radio characters. The television series did not win a wide audience and soon went off the air. In recent years, *Amos 'n' Andy* has been faulted for being insulting in its attitude toward blacks.

3

3 Orson Welles (1915–) began his radio career in 1934 as narrator of the *March of Time* news series. He also played Lamont Cranston in the popular mystery series *The Shadow*. In 1938 actors from his Mercury Theater began performing on CBS radio dramas adapted from famous novels. On October 30, 1938 (the night before Halloween), Welles himself broadcast a dramatization of H.G. Wells' science-fiction thriller *The War of the Worlds*. Done in the style of an emergency radio news broadcast, it described an armed invasion of New Jersey by Martians. The play was done with such realism that it caused a degree of panic throughout the country.

4

4 The Texaco Star Theater, with Milton Berle (1908–) as host, began broadcasting in September 1948. It quickly became the most popular show on television and is credited with establishing TV as a major entertainment medium. Shown here (on the 1949 season premiere) are, left to right, comedian Phil Silvers, Buffalo Bob Smith (of the Howdy Doody show), Berle, June Havoc, and Clarabell (a clown from the Howdy Doody show).

5

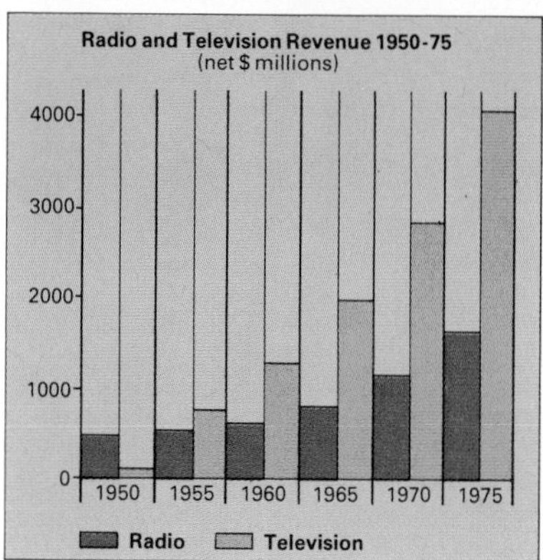
Radio and Television Revenue 1950-75
(net $ millions)
4000
3000
2000
1000
0
1950
1955
1960
1965
1970
1975
Radio
Television

(1867–1957). Saturday afternoon broadcasts of the Metropolitan Opera became a radio institution. Nashville's Grand Ole Opry, broadcasting Saturday nights, created a new country-music audience.

Public affairs and news were not ignored. As World War II approached, network correspondents around the world—including Edward R. Murrow [7], Howard K. Smith, and William L. Shirer—brought foreign affairs closer to the American public than they had ever been before.

The emergence of television

The basic techniques of television broadcasting had been mastered in the 1920s and 1930s. The manufacture of TV sets for public sale and limited TV broadcasting had begun in 1939, but World War II halted all progress in television except specifically for the war effort. In 1946 manufacture of TV sets resumed, and TV broadcasting on a national basis began. Limited color broadcasting began in 1951. By the mid-1950s TV had surpassed radio in revenues and share of the advertising market [5].

The first big star of TV was Milton Berle [4], who began his weekly show in 1948. The early 1950s, now called the Golden Age of TV, saw the regular presentation of plays—by such authors as Paddy Chayefsky and Gore Vidal—written especially for television.

Television was originally produced live, with most programs originating from New York. The success of two early filmed series, *I Love Lucy* and *Dragnet*, brought about a shift to filmed (later, in many cases, taped) shows, most of which originated in Hollywood. The mainstay of commercial television programming in the 1960s and 1970s remained the weekly series: situation comedies, game shows, and police and hospital dramas. Sports consistently drew huge audiences.

Public (noncommercial) television, with emphasis on educational and cultural subject matter, continues to increase its audience [9]. The widespread use of cable and closed-circuit television opened the prospect of pay TV and other forms of limited-interest broadcasting.

KEY

Franklin D. Roosevelt (1882–1945) was the first US president to realize the potential of radio as a political force. He broadcast his famous "fireside chats" to the US public in order to build up confidence in the country and in its economy. In the first fireside chat—broadcast on March 12, 1933—President Roosevelt dealt with the banking crisis.

6

7

8

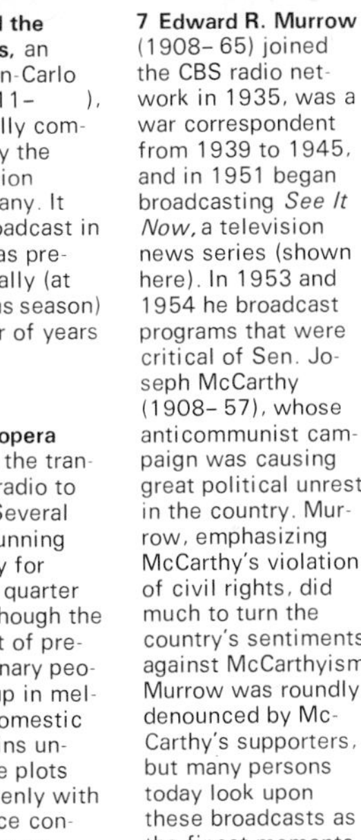

6 Amahl and the Night Visitors, an opera by Gian-Carlo Menotti (1911–), was especially commissioned by the NBC Television Opera Company. It was first broadcast in 1951 and was presented annually (at the Christmas season) for a number of years after that.

8 The soap opera easily made the transition from radio to television. Several have been running continuously for more than a quarter century. Although the basic format of presenting ordinary people caught up in melodramatic domestic crises remains unchanged, the plots now deal openly with subjects once considered taboo on television.

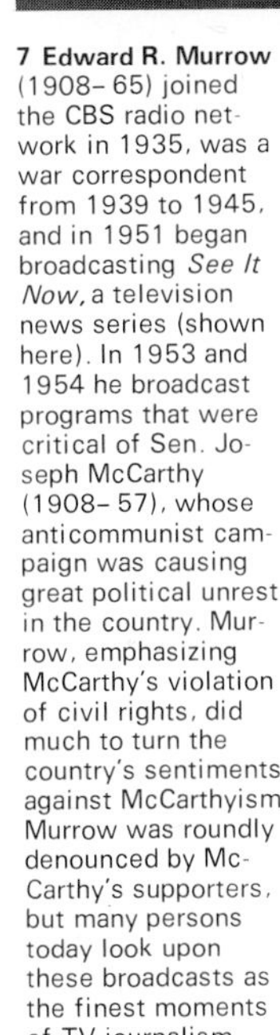

7 Edward R. Murrow (1908–65) joined the CBS radio network in 1935, was a war correspondent from 1939 to 1945, and in 1951 began broadcasting *See It Now*, a television news series (shown here). In 1953 and 1954 he broadcast programs that were critical of Sen. Joseph McCarthy (1908–57), whose anticommunist campaign was causing great political unrest in the country. Murrow, emphasizing McCarthy's violation of civil rights, did much to turn the country's sentiments against McCarthyism. Murrow was roundly denounced by McCarthy's supporters, but many persons today look upon these broadcasts as the finest moments of TV journalism.

9 Sesame Street was an immediate popular success when it went on the air in 1969. Created by the Children's Television Workshop and sponsored by public television, it is aimed at a preschool audience, particularly those in underprivileged households. Its purpose is to increase its viewers' basic learning skills, such as counting, associating sounds with letters of the alphabet, and recognizing shapes. Its techniques are borrowed from those of TV commercials and emphasize a fast pace, tricky camera angles, jingles, and much repetition. Testing has shown that children who watch *Sesame Street* regularly perform better in their early school years.

9A

SESAME STREET
123

B

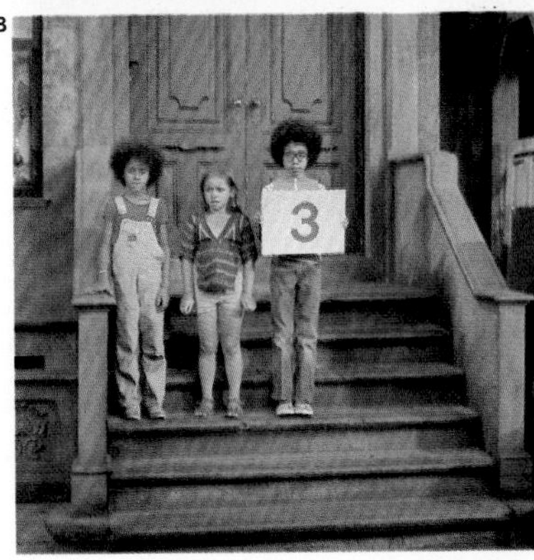
3

The American experience: drama

The 1936 Nobel Prize for literature was awarded to Eugene O'Neill [Key]. (He was only the second American to be so honored; Sinclair Lewis had been the first in 1930.) It is only with O'Neill that American drama comes of age, that it achieves high artistic merit. The history of American drama before this time is a history of Puritan disapproval, of prejudice in favor of European plays, and of sentimental adaptations of works such as Harriet Beecher Stowe's *Uncle Tom's Cabin*.

Drama before the twentieth century

Drama was popular in the colonial and Revolutionary periods, especially as a vehicle for political views. It was only in the nineteenth century that a sense of native cultural inferiority became pronounced. Americans themselves were the strongest critics of native dramatists. Of *Fashion* (1845), a popular comedy by Anna Cora Mowatt (1819–70), Edgar Allan Poe wrote, "Compared with the generality of modern dramas, it is a good play—compared with most American drama it is a *very* good one—estimated by the natural principles of dramatic art, it is altogether unworthy of notice." In 1847, Walt Whitman wrote of New York's finest theater, the Park [1], "It is but a third-rate imitation of the best London theatres. It gives us the cast-off dramas . . . of Great Britain."

Light comedies, sensational melodramas—such as *The Drunkard* (1844) by W. H. Smith (1806–72)—and histrionic performances of Shakespeare dominated the stage [2]. Early attempts at realism, such as *Margaret Fleming* (1890) by James A. Herne (1839–1901), were judged too frank for the commercial theater. Clyde Fitch (1865–1909) wrote well-crafted plays, and William Vaughn Moody (1869–1910) showed promise.

The twentieth century

Eugene O'Neill revolutionized American drama. Although he turned to Europe for many of his themes and forms, he made them his own in the process. He drew on Strindberg and expressionism in *The Emperor Jones* (1921) [3] and *The Hairy Ape* (1922); he used Nietzschean and classical Greek motifs in *The Great God Brown* (1925) and the trilogy *Mourning Becomes Electra* (1931); he employed Freudian and novelistic stream of consciousness in *Strange Interlude* (1928). His radical experimentation and passionate intensity inspired his contemporaries and successors.

The 1920s saw the emergence of other important American playwrights in Elmer Rice (1892–1967), Maxwell Anderson (1888–1959), Laurence Stallings (1894–1968), and Sidney Howard (1891–1939). The best plays of the period were dramas of social criticism. Rice's *The Adding Machine* (1923) [4] dramatized the fate of "Mr. Zero" in a mechanized society. Anderson and Stallings's *What Price Glory?* (1924) ironically questioned America's role in World War I.

Social criticism increased in the 1930s with the Depression. In *Waiting for Lefty* (1935), Clifford Odets (1906–63) attempted to arouse support for a New York taximen's strike. His more sentimental *Golden Boy* (1937) chronicled the corruption of a young

CONNECTIONS

See also
1374 American writing: into the 20th century

1 The Park Theatre, opened in 1821, was the most elegant theater in New York City in the first half of the 19th century. This 1822 watercolor by John Searle shows many prominent New Yorkers at a performance of a farce called *Monsieur Tonson*. Audiences at the Park were apt to be as interested in each other as they were in the play.

2 The three sons of British-born and trained actor Junius Brutus Booth I (1796–1852) appeared together on stage just once, in a performance of Julius Caesar. Edwin (1833–93) remained immensely popular, in spite of the assassination of President Lincoln by his brother John Wilkes (1838–65). Junius Brutus II (1821–83), also kept acting.

3 Charles Gilpin (1878–1930) received the Drama League award in 1921 for his starring performance in Eugene O'Neill's *Emperor Jones*. He was the first black actor so honored.

4 Elmer Rice wrote *The Adding Machine* for the Theatre Guild. The odd-angled, stark sets shared the expressionistic style of the play, touching on reality but emphasizing strain and discord. The Theatre Guild had been founded in 1919 by the Washington Square Players "to produce plays of artistic merit not ordinarily produced by commercial managers." The Guild was so successful that it was able to build its own theater in 1925.

5 The Group Theater's 1935 premier production of Clifford Odets' *Awake and Sing* starred (left to right) John Garfield, Phoebe Brand, Art Smith, Morris Carnovsky, and (not shown) Stella Adler.

prize fighter. The Group Theater [5] was formed in 1931 by directors Harold Clurman, Lee Strasberg, and Cheryl Crawford to produce plays of "social significance." Through it they introduced the acting methods and stagecraft of the great Russian director Constantin Stanislavski. From 1935 to 1939 the Federal Theater Project [6], part of the Works Progress Administration, made modern theater available to tens of millions of Americans. The lyrical social drama *Our Town* (1938) by Thornton Wilder (1897–1975) and Lillian Hellman's [7] *The Little Foxes* (1939) closed the decade.

In the 1940s, Hellman's *Watch on the Rhine* (1941) exposed American isolationism in the face of the Nazi threat. Wilder's *The Skin of Our Teeth* (1942) examined the struggle for survival through the ages. The career of Tennessee Williams (1911–) blossomed in this decade with *The Glass Menagerie* (1945) and the more sensational exploration of Southern genteel decadence in *A Streetcar Named Desire* (1947). Arthur Miller (1915–) began his important contributions to the American theater with *The Death of a Salesman* in 1949. O'Neill's *The Iceman Cometh* (1946) and *Long Day's Journey Into Night* (first produced 1956) enhanced his reputation.

William Inge (1913–73) never fulfilled the promise his four plays [8] of the 1950s seemed to hold. Arthur Miller's *The Crucible* (1953) was both a dramatization of the Salem witch trials and a comment on the contemporary "witch hunts" for Communists. Tennessee Williams wrote several major plays in the 1950s, including *Cat on a Hot Tin Roof* (1955) [10] and *Sweet Bird of Youth* (1959). The provocative plays of Edward Albee [9], such as *Zoo Story* (1959) and *The Sandbox* (1960), were first performed off-Broadway. His *Who's Afraid of Virginia Woolf?* (1962) was widely hailed.

In the 1960s and 1970s American drama reached in new directions. Regional and repertory theater saw new life. Off-off-Broadway theater deliberately violated any number of theatrical conventions. Injustice was attacked with ferocity by such playwrights as Imamu Baraka (Leroi Jones), Megan Terry, and David Rabe.

KEY

Eugene O'Neill (1888–1953) had worked for his father's touring company as an actor and stage manager, but he did not decide to become a playwright until after spending six months in 1912–13 in a tuberculosis sanitorium where he read Ibsen and Strindberg and began writing one-act plays. He then (1914–15) studied playwriting with George Pierce Baker (1896–1949) in Harvard's 47 Workshop. His early plays, beginning in 1916, were produced by the Provincetown Players in Provincetown, Mass., and New York City. *Beyond the Horizon* (1920) was his first Broadway production.

6

6 The Living Newspaper series of plays, including *One Third of a Nation* (1938) shown here, was one of the most innovative and successful activities of the Federal Theater Project. The plays dramatized current social and political problems by quoting newspapers and public addresses. Funds were discontinued in 1939 when Congress objected to the controversial subject matter presented in the Living Newspaper.

7

7 Lillian Hellman (1905–) has written well-crafted, incisive plays exposing personal or political evil, including *The Children's Hour* (1934), *The Little Foxes* (1939), *Watch on the Rhine* (1941), *Autumn Garden* (1951), and *Toys in the Attic* (1960). Her memoirs—*An Unfinished Woman* (1964), *Pentimento* (1973), and *Scoundrel Time* (1976)—have created considerable interest and, in the last case, controversy.

9

9 Edward Albee (1928–) writes plays that are savage commentaries on contemporary America. His characters mercilessly attack each other, physically and verbally. Some of his plays seem to belong to the theater of the absurd—in *The Sandbox* (1960) an old lady lives up to her neck in sand; in *Seascape* (1975) two main characters are reptiles—yet these "absurd" characters reveal sharp truths.

8

8 Come Back, Little Sheba (1950) established William Inge as one of the 1950s' most promising playwrights and made Shirley Booth, shown here with Sidney Blackmer, a star. *Picnic* (1953) received a Pulitzer Prize. *Bus Stop* (1955) and *Dark at the Top of the Stairs* (1957) were also critical successes. Born and educated in Kansas, Inge was the first American playwright to make effective use of the Midwest as the setting for serious dramatic works.

10

10 Tennessee Williams (1911–), by far the most prolific major US playwright to emerge since World War II, has written at least 14 full-length plays since *The Glass Menagerie* (1945). His plays are especially noted for their strong characterizations and for their poetic, often morbidly symbolic, language. *Cat on a Hot Tin Roof (right)* has been revived successfully several times and made into a popular movie.

The American experience: music

Early serious music in America sprang from the religious roots of Puritans and German pietists. American classical music waged a long struggle to shake off European influences. Many forms of popular music were distinctively shaped by black music rooted in Africa.

Colonial beginnings to the nineteenth century

The earliest European music heard in America was the chanting of the Latin Mass by Spaniards in the Southwest. The first blacks may have brought African music with them to Virginia in 1619. The Pilgrims sang psalms from English psalters while landing at Plymouth in 1620. The Boston Puritans published the *Bay Psalm Book* in 1640, although it did not include musical notation until the 1698 edition. In the eighteenth century, singing schools, such as the Boston Society for Promoting Regular Singing (1722), were set up in New England [Key] to teach both religious and secular music. German religious settlements in Pennsylvania developed their own music. The *Ephrata Hymn Collection* of Conrad Beissel (1690–1768), America's first trained composer, was published by Benjamin Franklin in 1730.

Musical activity in America was disrupted by the Revolution. Even patriotic songs, such as "Yankee Doodle" were set to British tunes, as were the later "Star Spangled Banner" (1814) and "America" (1831). Francis Hopkinson [1] was America's first significant native-born composer. Immigrant professional musicians, especially from England and France, dominated American music after the Revolution.

Foreign and native traditions

Early in the nineteenth century, several American composers wrote music on native themes. One of the first such works was the opera *The Indian Princess* (1808) by John Bray, based on James N. Barker's play. Anthony P. Heinrich (1781–1861) produced descriptive orchestral works, including *Pushmataha, A Venerable Chief* (1831). German Romantic music was introduced to America by immigrant musicians in the 1890s. New Orleans-born Louis Gottschalk [4], who was America's first concert pianist of international stature, composed instrumental and orchestral works incorporating black, Creole, and Latin-American tunes. George Bristow (1825–98) pursued the American tradition with the opera *Rip Van Winkle* (1855) and the symphony *The Pioneer* (1874). Edward MacDowell (1861–1908) was the first American to achieve international recognition as a composer. His post-romantic music employing chromatic harmony did not rely on folk tunes, nor was it especially imitative of European models.

Popular music

The minstrel show, which combined elements of black music and white folk tunes, was the most popular musical entertainment of the nineteenth century. Stephen Foster [2] wrote many of his songs for minstrel shows. The minstrel jig influenced the development of ragtime, which swept the country in the 1890s.

The distinctive American musical comedy evolved from three sources: minstrel

CONNECTIONS

See also

1246 Music: the Romantic period
1364 20th-century music—tradition and experimentation
1366 Jazz and pop

1 Francis Hopkinson (1737–1791), besides being a distinguished composer, was a signer of the Declaration of Independence from New Jersey, a poet, an essayist, a political satirist (best known for *The Battle of the Kegs*, 1778), a painter, a harpsichordist, and a US district court judge (1789–91). It has also been claimed that he designed the American flag while chairman of the Continental navy (1776–78). He composed many songs, including "My Days Have Been So Wondrous Free" (1759), and published a *Collection of Psalm Tunes* in 1763. His son Joseph (1770–1842) wrote "Hail Columbia" (1798).

2 Stephen Collins Foster (1826–64) was an untrained amateur who had a natural talent for composing melodies. Among his 188 songs were many popular ones, including "Oh! Susanna" (1848), "Old Folks at Home" (1851), and "My Old Kentucky Home" (1853), for minstrel shows. "Jeanie with the Light Brown Hair" (1854) was written for his wife. Often in debt, he died an alcoholic.

3 Scott Joplin (1868–1917) played the piano in brothels and saloons in St. Louis before entering George Smith College, a black school in Sedalia, Mo., in 1896 to study music. There he learned to write down the syncopated rhythms of his "ragged music." His first published work, "Maple Leaf Rag" (1899), swept the country, making him famous. Other successful rags included "The Entertainer" (1902), "Rose Leaf Rag" (1907), "Fig Leaf Rag" (1908), and "Magnetic Rag" (1914). Joplin saw ragtime as a serious musical form and composed two operas (including *Treemonisha*). *Treemonisha* was performed at Joplin's own expense in 1915.

4 Louis Moreau Gottschalk (1829–69), one of the most popular American piano virtuosos of the mid-19th century, had studied music in Paris. Many of his 103 published piano pieces were unabashedly sentimental *(Dying Poet*, 1864; *The Last Hope*, 1854); others, such as *Banjo* (1855) and *Souvenir de Porto Rico* (1858), drew on American themes and rhythms.

5 John Philip Sousa (1854–1932) wrote about 100 marches. The most noted are "Semper Fidelis" (1888), "The Washington Post March" (1889), and "The Stars and Stripes Forever" (1897).

shows; European-influenced operettas—America's leading operetta composers, Victor Herbert (1859–1924), Sigmund Romberg (1887–1951), and Rudolf Friml (1879–1972), were all born in Europe; and vaudeville, especially in the musicals of George M. Cohan (1878–1942). *Show Boat* (1927) by Jerome Kern (1885–1945) was one of the earliest musicals in which songs were not just set pieces but an integral part of the plot. *Oklahoma!* (1943) by Richard Rodgers (1902–) and Oscar Hammerstein II (1895–1960) integrated dance into the plot of the musical comedy.

Serious music in the twentieth century

Charles Ives [6], the most significant American composer of the early twentieth century, produced highly individualistic works drawing on American themes. Charles Griffes (1884–1920) was influenced by the music of Debussy and Stravinsky. Aaron Copland [7] experimented in many different musical forms. Edgard Varèse (1883–1965) and Henry Cowell (1897–1965) followed European avant-garde models, while Virgil Thomson (1896–), Roy Harris (1898–), and William Schuman (1910–) pursued American themes. Neoclassical composers included Walter Piston (1894–1976), Roger Sessions (1896–), Samuel Barber (1910–), and Gian-Carlo Menotti (1911–). Experimental composers, including Elliott Carter (1908–), Milton Babbitt (1910–), Henry Partch (1901–74), and John Cage (1912–), became prominent.

Some composers move comfortably in both popular and classical music. Thus, Scott Joplin [3] wrote immensely popular rags as well as the opera *Treemonisha* (1915). George Gershwin (1898–1937) wrote Tin Pan Alley songs, Broadway shows, and jazz-influenced classical music—as in *Rhapsody in Blue* (1923) and the opera *Porgy and Bess* [10]. Conductor-composer Leonard Bernstein (1918–) wrote symphonies, such as *Mass* (1971), and the popular musical *West Side Story* (1957). Jazz composer Duke Ellington (1899–1974) also wrote classical music, notably his *Second Sacred Concert* (1967).

KEY

P. Revere sculp
A Canon of 6 in One with a Ground. the Words by ye Rev. Dr. Byles: Set to Music by W. Billings.

William Billings (1746–1800) was the most successful Boston singing teacher-composer. This frontispiece from the first (1770) edition of his *New-England Psalm Singer*, showing a singing group, was engraved by Paul Revere.

6

7

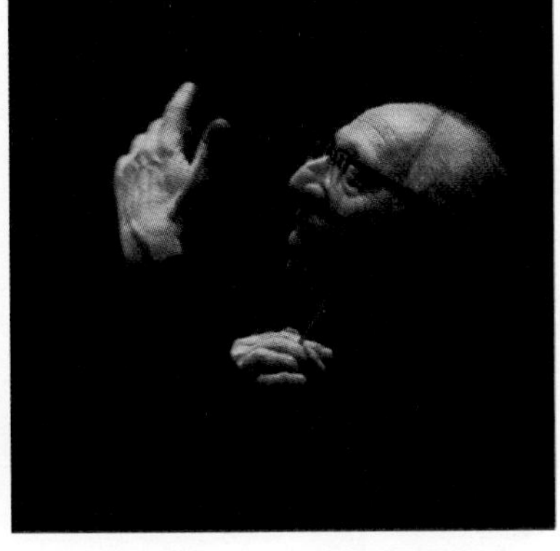

8

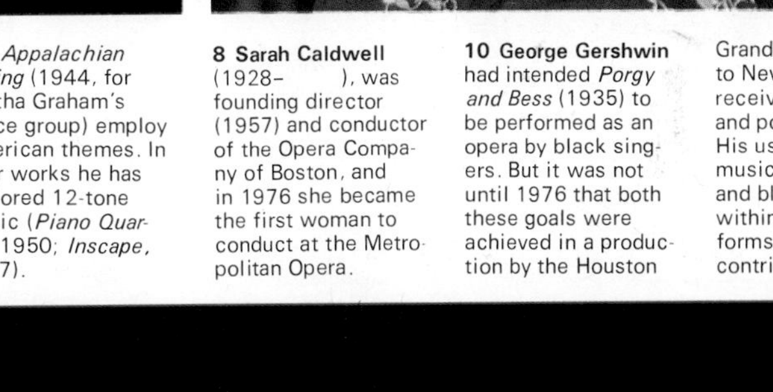

7 Aaron Copland's (1900–) first works were in the French post-romantic manner, but he soon turned to the progressive influences of atonality in *Dance Symphony* (1929). *Billy the Kid* (1938) and *Appalachian Spring* (1944, for Martha Graham's dance group) employ American themes. In later works he has explored 12-tone music (*Piano Quartet*, 1950; *Inscape*, 1967).

8 Sarah Caldwell (1928–), was founding director (1957) and conductor of the Opera Company of Boston, and in 1976 she became the first woman to conduct at the Metropolitan Opera.

10 George Gershwin had intended *Porgy and Bess* (1935) to be performed as an opera by black singers. But it was not until 1976 that both these goals were achieved in a production by the Houston Grand Opera. Brought to New York City, it received both critical and popular acclaim. His use of popular music, including jazz and blues rhythms, within classical forms was his chief contribution.

6 The boldly iconoclastic music of Charles Ives (1874–1954) remained virtually unheard until after he retired from business in 1930. He received a Pulitzer Prize in 1947.

9 Outdoor music complexes have become an important and popular part of American classical music. Tanglewood, at Lenox, Mass., originated in 1934; the Aspen Music School and Festival (1949) at Aspen, Col., features a 9-week summer school and concerts; and, shown here, the Wolf Trap Farm Park for the Performing Arts (1966), Vienna, Va., offers a wide variety of music.

9

10

The American experience: dance

Contrary to popular belief, our colonial forebears did not prohibit dancing. When Francis Stepney offended Boston in 1685, it was not because he gave dancing lessons, but because he held "mixt" dances on Sundays. Dancing was defended as "a natural expression of joy, so that there is no more Sin in it than in laughter." In New Amsterdam (New York City) and New Orleans, holidays featured street dancing.

Early black contributions

Slaves brought a rich dance tradition with them from Africa [2], but not all black dances in America were of African origin. Blacks, who observed whites dancing clogs, hornpipes, and Irish jigs, added expressive hand and body movements to these stiff dances. Thus evolved the buck-and-wing and, eventually, tap dancing. Minstrel shows became the domain of whites mimicking blacks, although the earliest minstrels were blacks. The African Company performed black songs and dances in the North in 1820–21. One of the greatest black minstrels was Juba [3], born William Henry Lane in 1826. He made a triumphant tour of Great Britain in 1848.

Ballet in the nineteenth century

When the Austrian ballerina Fanny Elssler (1810–84) toured the United States in 1840–42 she invited American dancers to perform with her, including George Washington Smith (1820–99), America's first premier danseur, who, before Elssler's arrival, had to content himself primarily with performing hornpipes and clog dances.

The American appearance of the European ballet extravaganza *The Black Crook* (1866) dealt, paradoxically, the death blow to interest in serious ballet. What most pleased the American audience was the corps of 50 beautiful, briefly attired young ladies. *The Black Crook* led not to the development of American ballet companies but to burlesque and revues.

Popular dance

George Washington Smith's son Joseph was also a vaudeville dancer, who, after observing black dancers, developed the turkey trot and the bunny hug for performance on the vaudeville circuit. His audiences quickly adapted them to ballroom dancing. In 1910 he introduced the Argentine tango to America; it caused a sensation. It was adapted and perfected by Irene (1893–1969) and Vernon (1887–1918) Castle, the most celebrated team of US ballroom dancers. Dance crazes have continued as a particularly American phenomenon—among them the Charleston, 1920s; the rumba, 1930s; the jitterbug, 1930s; the mambo, 1950s; the twist, 1960s; the hustle, 1970s—with blacks and Latins first introducing the dances.

Modern dance and ballet

When, in the words of Agnes De Mille (1905–   ), Isadora Duncan [Key] "threw off her corsets and her shoes and danced barefoot across Europe," a true revolution in dance began. While Duncan charmed or scandalized the world's capitals, back home in America Ruth St. Denis (1877–1968) evolved her own style based on Oriental themes. With her husband Ted Shawn

CONNECTIONS

See also
1366 Jazz and pop
1368 Classical and modern ballet

1 John Durang (1768–1822), the new nation's most popular dancer-entertainer, depicted himself dancing a sailor's hornpipe in this self-portrait.

2 This anonymous painting from the antebellum South evidences the African origins of American black dances and music. The pelvic gyrations of the dancers are typical of the dance movements of West Africa, from where most of America's foreign-born slaves came. The gourd drum and gourd banjo shown in the painting are quite similar to West African musical instruments.

3 Charles Dickens, while touring the United States in 1845, saw Juba perform and encouraged him to come to England. Juba made a triumphant dance tour of Great Britain in 1848.

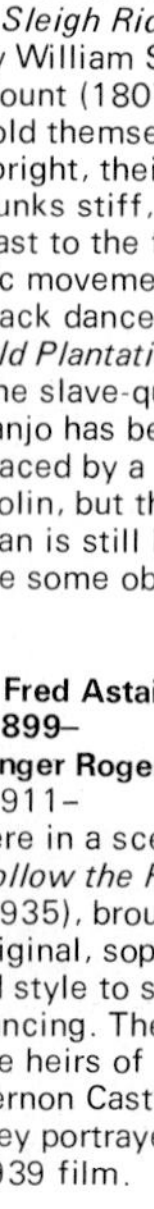

4 The white dancers in *Rustic Dance after a Sleigh Ride* (1830) by William Sidney Mount (1807–68) hold themselves upright, their mid-trunks stiff, in contrast to the fluid pelvic movement of the black dancers in *The Old Plantation* [2]. The slave-quarter banjo has been replaced by a European violin, but the musician is still black, as are some observers.

5 Fred Astaire (1899–   ) and Ginger Rogers (1911–   ), shown here in a scene from *Follow the Fleet* (1935), brought an original, sophisticated style to screen dancing. They were the heirs of Irene and Vernon Castle, whom they portrayed in a 1939 film.

[6] she founded the Denishawn company and school in Los Angeles (1915). Among their students were Doris Humphrey [7], Charles Weidman (1902–), and Martha Graham (1893–).

Isadora Duncan was the inspiration for modern dance; Martha Graham has been its driving force. Seeking to make "visible the interior landscape," she choreographed complex, intellectual dances with themes from Greek mythology, the Old Testament, and American literature and pioneer tradition. Out of Graham's company came many leaders of the third generation of modern dance: Anna Sokolow, Pearl Lang, Erick Hawkins, Paul Taylor. Companies led by Merce Cunningham, Alvin Ailey [8], Alwin Nikolais, Twyla Tharp, and others have kept modern dance in America alive and innovative.

Ballet was almost exclusively an art imported from Europe until Lincoln Kirstein (1907–) established the School of American Ballet in 1934 under the direction of George Balanchine (1904–). In 1948 the school formed the New York City Ballet; in 1949 Jerome Robbins [9] was appointed codirector.

American ballet companies have developed particularly American themes. Ballet Caravan, an offshoot of the School of American Ballet, premiered *Billy the Kid* (1938) by Eugene Loring with music by Aaron Copland. In 1944, Ballet Theatre presented Jerome Robbins' *Fancy Free* with a jazz score by Leonard Bernstein. Ballet choreographers have not shied away from Broadway. George Balanchine choreographed *On Your Toes* (1936), a musical with a ballet story and a memorable ballet sequence, "Slaughter on Tenth Avenue." In *Oklahoma!* (1943), choreographed by Agnes De Mille, a dance sequence in a musical comedy for the first time developed characters and furthered the plot.

In the 1960s and 70s ballet and modern dance began exchanging ideas. Martha Graham choreographed for ballet companies, and ballet dancers came to her for training in modern dance. Such combining of diverse elements helped to attract a wider audience to ballet.

KEY

For Isadora Duncan (1878–1927), dance was, in her own words, "the divine expression of the human spirit through the medium of the body's movement." Her interpretive dancing was based on the natural rhythms and movements of the body rather than on the formal steps of classical ballet. Yet she had a profound impact on the ballet impresario Sergei Diaghilev when he saw her dance in Russia in 1905. She raised interpretive dancing to an accepted art form, since called "modern dance," and inspired renewed vigor and fluidity in ballet. She died of strangulation when her long scarf caught in a car wheel.

6

6 Ted Shawn (1891–1972), after leaving Denishawn, formed a troupe of male dancers that performed original compositions from 1933 to 1940. The vigorous, masculine style enhanced the prestige of male dancers. He also established Jacob's Pillow at Lenox, Mass., in 1933 as an important summer dance theater and school.

7

7 Doris Humphrey (1895–1958) left Denishawn in 1928 to develop a style that explored her own individuality and utilized themes more relevant to America than Denishawn's Orient-inspired works. *The Shakers* (1931) is one of her best known works. Effectively employing group choreography, it told the story of the unique American religious group, the Shakers, who danced away their sins. Arthritis forced her to retire from performing in 1945.

8

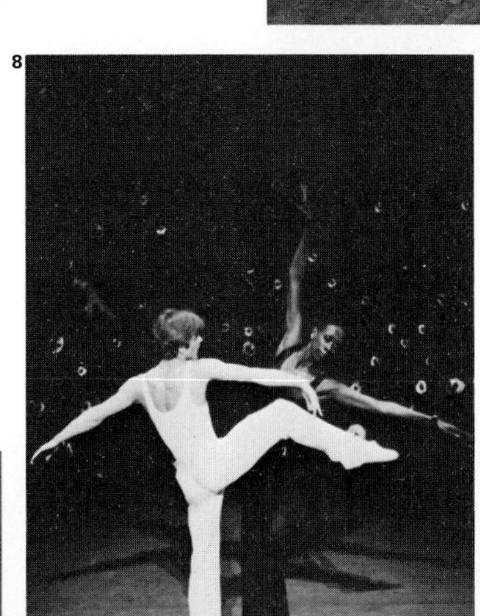

8 Alvin Ailey (1931–) formed his own modern dance company (then called American Dance Theater) in 1958. It is America's most fully integrated dance company, not only in the obvious sense of freely combining dancers of different races (Ailey is himself black), but, even more importantly, in integrating elements of modern dance, classical ballet, jazz, and American musical comedy into its works. Shown here are Judith Jamison of the Ailey Company and Soviet emigrè ballet star Mikhail Baryshnikov in *Pas de Duke*, a work choreographed for them by Ailey in 1976 to music by Duke Ellington. The company has toured worldwide and is a favorite in New York.

9

9 The Goldberg Variations by Jerome Robbins (1918–) is choreographed to the piano music of the same title by Johann Sebastian Bach. Robbins, who began his career as a dancer, choreographed the work for the New York City Ballet, shown here, of which he was long the ballet master.

10

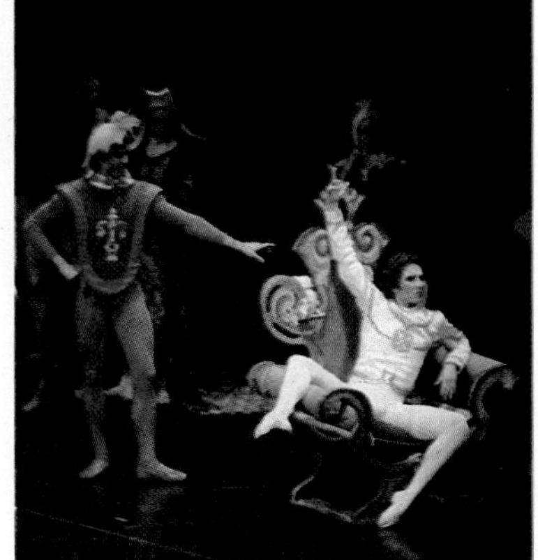

10 Ballet West is one of the most highly acclaimed regional ballet companies in America. Since 1968 it has been the official company of the Federation of Rocky Mountain States. In addition to its regular season in Salt Lake City, Utah, Ballet West tours throughout the Rocky Mountain states, with a special winter season in Tempe, Ariz., and a summer school in Aspen, Col. It sponsors a lecture-demonstration program that visits high schools throughout Utah. This 1976 production of *Cinderella* was choreographed by Ballet West's founder, William Christensen.

MAN AND SCIENCE

MAN AND SCIENCE

by Professor I. Bernard Cohen

Science, in the fourth quarter of the 20th century, stands for notable conquests and achievements: the landing of a man on the Moon, the search for life on Mars, the harnessing of atomic energy and its dreadful counterpart in the atom bomb, quarks and quasars, antimatter, nylon, transistors, jet transport and the SST, polio vaccine, the almost complete disappearance of smallpox from the Earth, chemotherapy, "the pill," hybrid corn, and DNA. Prominent in any such list are those scientific discoveries that affect the life of man—the ways in which people earn their livings, clothe themselves, maintain public health, provide for national defense or conduct warfare, communicate with one another, and transport themselves and their goods. The average man or woman is most aware of science wherever science, or the fruits of science in technology or medicine, impinge upon everyday life, but we are also aware of science as a great adventure into the unknown. So far as anyone can presently foresee, there appears to be no practical benefit to mankind in the explorations of Mars or the study of possible continental drift. And so one is led to the great paradox in modern science: it is, on the one hand, an adventurous assault on the mysteries of matter, living processes, and the universe around us and, on the other hand, the font of both wonderful and frightful innovations in technology, agriculture, and biomedicine that offer a much better world for mankind at the possible price of a perpetual nightmare of violent or total destruction and an erosion of the environment. Because science was not always so closely linked to the human condition and the control of the external environment, an understanding of the place of science in the world today requires an inquiry into where and how science came into being and the ways in which it developed.

The origins of science are difficult to trace, especially because the choice of origin may depend upon one's definition.

Professor of the History of Science, Harvard University; Fellow of the American Academy of Arts and Sciences; Past President of the International Union of the History and Philosophy of Science; Past President of the US National Committee for the History and Philosophy of Science; Past President of the History of Science Society; Recipient of the George Sarton Medal; author of *Benjamin Franklin's Experiments; Isaac Newton's Papers on Natural Philosophy; The Birth of a New Physics; Introduction to Newton's "Principia"; The Scientific Revolution,* etc.

A basic component of modern science is experiment: a reliance on experience, on the direct interrogation of nature. Could this have been a feature of the thinking of distant early ancestors? Probably not—at least in the sense in which experiment and critical observation are basic to science as we know it today. There was lacking in early thought a logically coherent rational system of causes and effects, conceived in a theory that predicts (or retrodicts) the observed or known facts of science. Such theories also predict as-yet-unobserved or unverified new facts—the observation (or nonobservation) of which may serve to confirm, disprove, or modify the theory in question.

A coherent rational system of thought about nature apparently first took form in ancient Greek times, although it, too, was not quite what is considered to be modern science. The missing feature was systematic experiment and controlled observation. Plato, for example, even commended those astronomers who did not pay much attention to the movement of the starry heavens. He conceived the astronomer's job to be the abstract geometrical construction of complex motions by various combinations of uniform circular motions. Since the heavenly bodies were held to partake of a special "perfection," their true motions had to be equally perfect—and the only perfect curve is a circle, constantly folding back on itself and everywhere the same. This doctrine led such astronomers as Eudoxus to the construction of ingenious planetary orbits, and, in the 2nd century of our era, it eventually produced the Ptolemaic system, one of the really high points of ancient science.

Ptolemy reveals a major ambiguity of ancient science. On the one hand, he produced the *Almagest,* in which the apparent motions of the Sun, Moon, and planets were explained nonphysically by a purely geometrical system that served as a means of computing positions, accounting for the changing positions of the heavenly bodies as revealed by observations. On the other hand, he wrote *Planetary Hypotheses,* in which he conceived of a physical system in which the Sun, Moon, and five planets are carried around the Earth by the combined motions of a series of interlocking physical shells. As a mathematical astronomer, he had a computing system whose reality was not in question; as a philosopher, he had a physical system that was not necessarily useful for computations. Even Isaac Newton, many centuries later, continued to make a distinction between his mathematical treatment of models that resemble but do not necessarily truly represent reality and what he considered to be the physics of the true "System of the World."

It is only by being aware of the Greek separation of the abstract discussions of theoretical science from the realities of observation that one can understand how Aristotle could have formulated principles of motion that in application led to demonstrably false conclusions concerning weight and speed. Aristotle was notably more successful in the biological sciences than in physics. In particular, his defense of the study of living things is one of the golden pages of ancient science. Galen, a contemporary of Ptolemy, was heir to a long tradition of direct observation in anatomy and physiology and of animal experimentation. It is easy to forget this aspect of Galen's science because he was so committed to system that the empirical or experimental part of his work was later minimized.

When science shifted from Alexandria to Asia Minor and Arabia, there was greater interest in the Galenic and Ptolemaic systems than in the observations and experiments on which they had, in part, been based. Thus, instead of creating wholly new principles and systems of their own, the scientists of the Islamic world were content to make improvements. Their strength lay in the wealth of new observations and collections of empirical data, but there was no significant relationship between theory and observation—even in astronomy, where there were many observers and well-equipped observatories. In medicine and in plant sciences, however, progress was greater than in the physical sciences. It is not surprising that astronomy and medicine should have been two of the sciences most strongly supported by the Islamic rulers—astronomy, through the associated subject of astrology, foretold man's future on Earth, while medicine guarded his present life and health. But other sciences were encouraged too, chiefly chemistry, optics and vision, and mathematics.

The extensive translation of the corpus of Greek science into the Arabic language is one of the miracles of history. And it was from these Arabic versions, improved by the scholars and sages of the Islamic world, that, beginning about the 12th century, the scholars of Western Europe came into contact with Greek science, hitherto largely unknown to them. This new science was largely Greek and Arabic, plus some of the innovations made by the Hindus and Persians—for example, the system of "Arabic numerals" (0,1,2,3 . . .), invented by the Hindus and introduced into the West through Arabic texts.

The science thus introduced into Europe was not yet the science of modern times. What was lacking was an intimate synergistic interaction between pure thought and experience, a lack most clearly seen in the treatment of motion during the 14th century. The medieval schoolmen, far from being the slavish followers of Aristotle they have commonly been labeled, criticized and improved the Aristotelian principles and invented a new science of motion. Formulating clear and unambiguous concepts of uniform and accelerated motion, these medieval scientists distinguished—just as one still does today—between uniformly accelerated motion (in which there is unchanging acceleration) and nonuniformly accelerated motion (in which the acceleration itself changes from moment to moment). They then stated and proved the Mean Speed Theorem: that the distance traversed during any time interval at constant speed is exactly the same as the distance traversed during the same time interval at a uniformly accelerated speed, provided that the mean or average speed in the accelerated case is the same as the actual speed in the constant case. In other words, if the speed is proportional to the time, the distance will be proportional to the square of the time. This theorem later enabled Galileo, at the opening of the 17th century, to formulate the laws of falling bodies and to devise a test as to whether the motion of a freely falling body is in fact uniformly accelerated—one of the major events in the Scientific Revolution. For the medieval schoolmen, however, the Mean Speed Theorem remained a philosophico-scientific abstraction; having found the law as an exercise in applied logic and mathematics, it never occurred to any of them to see whether it might characterize real events in the external physical world of experience, such as free fall.

If one looks for a convenient date for the beginning of modern science, 1543 will do better than most. In that single year, two very remarkable books were published—one a new conception of the universe, the other a new view of man's body as revealed by actual dissections. These were Copernicus' *De Revolutionibus Orbium Coelestium* (On the Revolution of the Celestial Spheres) and Vesalius' *De Humani Corporis Fabrica* (On the Construction of the Human Body). Copernicus offered an alternative system to Ptolemy's, one that was a conceptual change, not merely a restructure based on new observations; Vesalius presented a wealth of new observations revealed by his own firsthand anatomical dissections, but he had no new system to replace Galen's. Ultimately, the full revolution in the sciences begun by Copernicus and Vesalius came—early in the 17th century—more from Kepler (who refined and altered the Copernican System) and Galileo (who found observational evidence more in support of Copernicus than of Ptolemy) and from William Harvey (who discovered the circulation of the blood and thus sounded the death knell of Galenic physiology). Galileo had made his astronomical discoveries with the newly invented telescope and thus showed scientists how their observational powers might be augmented with new instruments. Particularly in Galileo one can see principles of modern science consciously in use: experiment and critical observation to see if a theory applies to the world of nature, and the use of experiment and critical observation to refine (or to find the limits of) natural laws.

Between the time of Galileo and Kepler and the time of Newton (in the 17th century), modern science began to take its present form. As the number of those engaged in scientific activity grew, there was a desire among similarly minded men to band together to further their cause. They met to perform experiments, to test experiments made by others, and to hear accounts of new advances in science. By the 1660s, national scientific societies had been organized in England and France, and there were regularly published journals in which the new science was disseminated from land to land. One of the signs of the revolution in science was the emergence of a "scientific community" dedicated to the increase and diffusion of the new scientific knowledge. Whereas science in previous centuries had been subservient in its goals to religious ideals or to a higher philosophy, the new science set its own goals. For example, it was agreed that at the meetings of the Royal Society of England there would be no discussions of politics, theology, or metaphysics—these being divisive subjects which were directly relevant neither to science in its new conception nor to practical applications of that science. In particular, as two earlier spokesmen for the new science—Bacon and Descartes—had stated, the society agreed that the developing science would be of practical help to the needs of man in dealing with his environment and the material aspects of his life.

It was method, along with a shared goal of understanding and controlling nature, that held the new scientific community together. Both Bacon and Descartes wrote discourses on method. Bacon saw the method of science as a new tool of inquiry, based on the inductive analysis of many empirically observed examples; his *Novum Organum* was intended to replace the traditional *organum* or logic of Aristotle. Descartes went so far as to say that his own great discoveries (analytical geometry and the laws of optics) had resulted not so much from superior insight or intelligence as from his use of an effective method of scientific discovery, a combination of mathematics and the inductions based upon experiments or controlled observations.

The first major modern triumph, setting the seal on the new science, was embodied in Newton's *Principia* (1687). Here Newton codified the laws of dynamics (force and motion) and set forth the principle and quantitative law of universal gravitation. In this treatise, which came to represent the ideal of all science for a long time to come, Newton showed how a single principle could explain an enormous variety of different phenomena: the falling of bodies on the Earth, the motion of the Moon, the motion of comets and their periodic return, the tides, the action of the Sun in keeping the Solar System together. Newton applied mathematics to the real world, using a set of reasonable postulates and definitions, and his resulting new "System of the World" corrected the principles of Copernicus and Galileo and the laws of Kepler and then embraced the revised statements within itself.

For the next centuries, however, there was no possibility that the life or health sciences might be reduced to an austere mathematical system like Newton's. Indeed, the first great comparable breakthrough in the life sciences—occurring in Darwin's *Origin of Species*—was very different in kind from Newton's *Principia*, although equally profound in its effects and possibly even more far-reaching in its scope. As a sample of the difference, it has only to be pointed out that, although the Darwinian theory of evolution is in its way as exact a science as its counterparts in physical science, it is not a predictive theory.

Throughout the 18th century and the early part of the 19th, scientists continued to bespeak the practical potentialities of their disinterested inquiries into nature—what is now called "pure science" or "basic research"—the quest for knowledge independent of any specific practical goals. Many scientists, feeling a need to justify their pursuit of knowledge apparently for its own sake, invoked Bacon's precepts that the paths to knowledge of nature (that is, science) and power are the same and that true science can alter the material conditions of life, improve man's health, and render him master of his environment. The first such Baconian event of any significance occurred in the 18th century: the invention of the lightning rod by Benjamin Franklin. When Franklin began to study electricity in the 1740s, there were no envisaged practical aspects of this new science; but when Franklin first guessed and then proved that the lightning discharge is an electrical phenomenon, he then—as a good Baconian—turned his knowledge to practical use in the invention of the lightning rod. Benjamin Franklin typifies the scientist of the 18th century: a devoted amateur who had gained his livelihood in some field other than science or who may have possessed inherited wealth, and who was largely self-trained in the experimental art.

In the 19th century, science became professionalized. Schools were established for higher education in the sciences, the first of which were the École Polytechnique and the École Normale, created in Paris in the Revolutionary-Napoleonic era. These were followed by scientific schools in all developed countries; some pioneering institutions in the United States were Lawrence Scientific School at Harvard and Sheffield Scientific School at Yale (in the mid-1840s) and the Massachusetts Institute of Technology (1861). The professionalization of science led to the organization of such large national specialized professional groups as the American Mathematical Society and the (British) Chemical Society. Associations were also formed in which scientists, science teachers, and amateur scientists would be brought together in annual conclaves "for the Advancement of Science." Despite the professionalization of science, much important work continued to be done by amateurs: variable-star observers, microscopists, recorders of meteorological data, and naturalists.

Although the establishment of modern science in the 17th century is generally known today as *the* Scientific Revolution, toward the end of the 19th century there occurred a second scientific revolution: the revelation that science is capable of transforming the economy of nations. The area in which this new revolution occurred most dramatically was chemistry, particularly organic chemistry, a field in which Germany had advanced rapidly to a position of world leadership. The revolution was triggered by a small event, the attempt in 1856 of a young student, William Henry Perkin, to synthesize quinine, using aniline, a residue of coal tar (a by-product of the manufacture of illuminating gas). Perkin failed to make quinine, but he was left with a purplish mass that stained everything it touched—it was the dyestuff mauve. Up to Perkin's time, dyes had been derived from plant and animal material, but before long many dyes were being made commercially by chemical synthesis from coal, water, and air. Because synthetic dyes were much cheaper, had greater stability, and allowed more variety of hue, the traditional economy of whole regions became obsolete within a few years while Germany expanded its dyestuff industry largely at the expense of Britain and of France. One particular synthetic sought by German chemists, indigo, was synthesized and commercially manufactured only after ten years of research and the expenditure of more than five million dollars (a sum never before allocated to a scientific project). Capture of the world dye markets by Germany was the result of a mutually cooperative system of support that involved government, industry, and academic science. Out of this effort came the concepts of the research team, the industrial laboratory, and the large-scale application of scientific research toward a specific practical goal. Germany thus set a model, followed later by other nations, for simultaneously advancing scientific knowledge and putting science to work for the national benefit.

In the 20th century, the most exciting breakthroughs occurred at first in the physical sciences, as a mere listing suffices to show: radioactivity, X-rays, relativity, quantum theory, atomic structure, cosmic rays, nuclear and particle physics. The cyclotron, developed first in America, was a harbinger of larger and more complex machines that were to alter the nature of scientific research because advanced experiments have often required large teams of scientists and technicians as well as very costly equipment. Here was the beginning of "big science," so costly that only national governments of the largest countries or consortiums of smaller nations can foot the bills. In astronomy, too, research often depends upon the limited availability of new large optical and radio telescopes and other large-scale and complex equipment. Astronomy, too, has been a spectacular subject in the 20th century: studies of the internal constitution of stars, the nature of galaxies, the expanding universe, the origin of meteors, the source of the Sun's energy, radio stars, quasars, possible "black holes," and the physical exploration of the Moon and the planets in our Solar System.

The first half of the 20th century was also notable for applied chemistry, as is apparent in the vast range of plastics and other new synthetic materials. One of the most famous of these is, no doubt, nylon—produced by the Du Pont Company on the basis of fundamental research in polymer chemistry by Wallace Carrothers. Within chemical science, a new specialty that came into its own in the 20th century is biochemistry, in which findings have contributed notably to a better understanding of the functioning of the human body and to the cure and control of diseases and malfunctions.

Biology, too, has seen notable advances, beginning in the first part of the century with genetics (especially the mathematical laws of heredity and the theory of the gene), which has led to spectacular increases in the food-producing capabilities of the world, as exemplified by "hybrid corn." The application of new techniques, such as electron microscopy and X-ray diffraction, have made for remarkable advances and have even created a wholly new subject: molecular biology. Who is not familiar with DNA and the "double helix" and the possibilities—both dangerous and beneficent—in "recombinant DNA"? A major new aspect of plant physiology has been the discovery of plant hormones, produced in the tips of sprouts and seedlings, that are the agents promoting growth; they have found a variety of practical applications in increasing crop yields, storing plant foods, controlling weeds, and as an agent in warfare (in the defoliation of trees). A crowning success in the biological realm has been the "modern synthesis" of evolution, bringing together at last what often seemed to be disparate (if not downright contradictory) elements of paleontology, genetics, and systematics.

Throughout most of the 17th, 18th, and 19th centuries, scientists believed firmly in a simple codifiable method, based largely on induction. In the late 19th century, and in the 20th, that belief was to a large degree abandoned, especially as a result of the critical attack by philosophers of science, chief among them Karl Popper. Indeed, it is fair to say that the 20th century has witnessed as active and revolutionary a development of the philosophy of science as of science itself. Some notable figures in this area have been Ernst Mach, Pierre Duhem, Henri Poincaré, Rudolf Carnap, Hans Reichenbach, P. W. Bridgman, and W. V. Quine. The rise of probabilistic or statistical explanations, the recognition that there cannot be a completely causal science, and the impact of relativity and the uncertainty principle have radically changed the concept of scientific explanation. Physical scientists especially have found themselves again and again having to take philosophical positions in the course of their inquiries.

The all but incredible growth of science as an institution has already been mentioned—its vast increase in manpower and its cost, currently having reached as much as 3 percent of the gross national product in the United States and the Soviet Union. In the United States there has been a very great shift in the sources of scientific funding. Prior to World War II, 68 percent of the total expenditure for scientific research and development came from industrial sources and a mere 20 percent from the federal government; today those figures are just about reversed. In 1938 the total expenditure for scientific research in America came to 264 million dollars; in 1974 the federal government spent more than 17 billion dollars on scientific research and development. With the burden of financial support now located in the public sector, the advancement of science, as well as the evaluation and control of the applications or effects, has become the responsibility of every citizen.

One consequence of the increase in the size and success of the scientific enterprise has been the tremendous growth of science-based capabilities for good or harm to man. Atomic energy, for example, can cause the desert to bloom or, in the form of a bomb, wipe out cities and destroy nations. Auxin, which causes growth in plants, can be used to help increase harvests or it can be used in biological warfare to denude trees of all their foliage for years to come. The direct applications of science for good or evil are not the only kind that present major problems to man and society, for we have learned that today's science-based technology may give man benefits only at cost to the very air he breathes, the landscape and the oceans, the whole of the natural environment. Science produces knowledge and it leads to the control and utilization of nature, but it does not of and in itself lead to wisdom. Herein lies perhaps the most significant challenge to the survival of human life in the next century.

Prehistoric and ancient science

Nearly two million years ago the ancestors of man used stones as weapons and tools. The need to master the environment and develop tools for the purpose involved a primitive knowledge of science [Key]. Ever since that time the development of science, technology, and human civilization have all been closely interrelated.

Science of prehistoric man

After perhaps 500,000 years, the descendants of the first tool users had become more selective, concentrating on flint, with its useful cutting edges [1,2]. They discovered how to make fires.

Cave paintings of 15,000 years ago indicate a primitive knowledge of animal anatomy. Some, which show prehistoric elephants with the position of the animal's heart indicated by arrows, may be a record of hunting prowess, or a form of sympathetic magic attempting to influence the outcome of a hunt.

About 10,000 years ago, men began to adopt a more settled way of life. They invented a repetitive system of food production that involved the domestication of animals and the cultivation of plants. Life in such settled communities stimulated invention of various building materials, used to provide better shelter and protection. Fires were kept burning continuously for warmth and cooking and frightening off marauders, and it is possible that the women who tended the fires were the first to notice that when clay is left near a fire it hardens into pottery. When certain stones and earths were roasted, heavy liquids sometimes ran out which hardened into useful metals.

Egypt and Mesopotamia

The people who settled in the Nile valley found an area that was exceptionally safe and fertile. They noticed that the silt brought down by the yearly floods renewed the fertility of the soil, so they dug channels and built embankments to divert the fertile silt-laden flood waters onto their fields. These flood-control operations marked the invention of large-scale engineering. The Nile valley dwellers later applied engineering to construct the pyramids [5].

It is probable that the science of geometry arose from the need to fix positions where landmarks had been washed out by annual flooding. Arithmetic was developed to calculate quantities of crops so that they could be shared among the people. Egyptian arithmetic depended on a method of doubling, much as in the operations of a modern computer. They also needed to determine the seasons and the times of the Nile floods and for this reason devised a calendar of 365 days by observing the positions of the stars and the planets.

The people of Mesopotamia, in the double valley of the Tigris and the Euphrates rivers, were developing in a similar way but under rather different conditions. There was little stone in their land, so they recorded information by making marks on soft clay tablets, which were then baked. The Mesopotamians introduced the idea that the value of a digit depends on its position in a number and they even solved algebraic equations. The Egyptians were primarily concerned with simple, practical calculations, whereas the Babylonians were

CONNECTIONS

See also
1444 Mathematics and civilization
1440 Asian and medieval science
1586 The Stone Age
1588 Fire and bronze
1590 Bark, hide, and horn
1006 Greek science

1

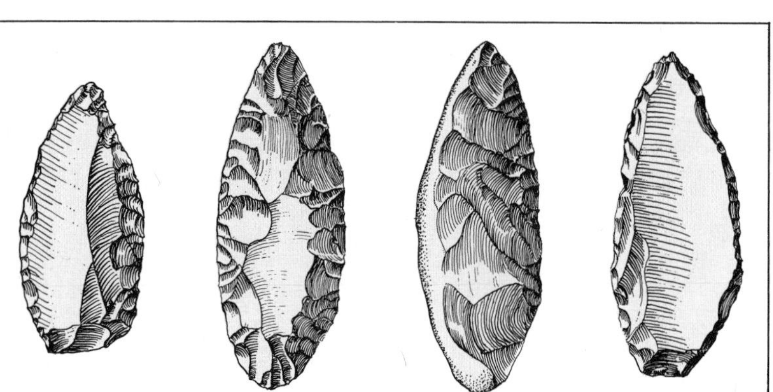

1 Tools of the middle Paleolithic, or Mousterian stage, in France date from 70,000 to 32,000 years ago. There were various human groups living in Europe in this period. They left many traces of their culture in shelters and entrances to caves. Tools are found dating from the beginning of the last period of glaciation and the scrapers and knives shown here illustrate fine stone tool technology.

2

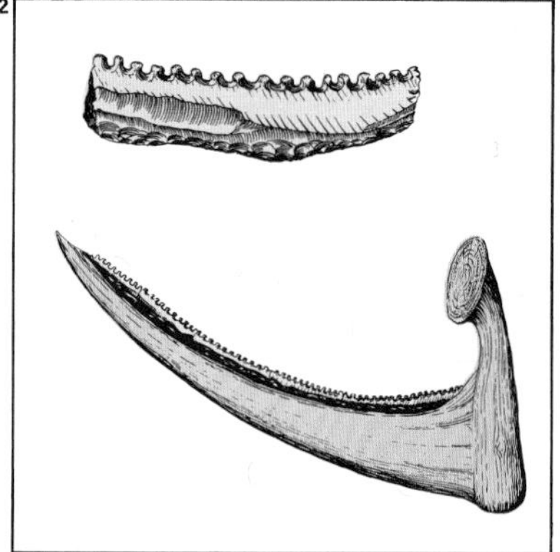

2 Bones, antlers, and wood were used by early men as raw materials for tools and weapons. A wooden tool could be given an efficient cutting edge by adding a row of suitably shaped flint slivers, as in this early Egyptian wooden sickle from about 3000–2500 BC. Pointed wooden implements could also be hardened by charring the point. Antlers were shaped by carving or heating.

3 A

B

3 The Neolithic people who occupied the region of Stoney Littleton, England in about 3000 BC, constructed large barrows for the burial of their dead [A]. A barrow was a long structure with an entrance passage crossed by transept chambers; this barrow had three pairs. The passage [B] contains a vault with corbels, or projections from the walls to carry "capstones," in a manner similar to those in vaults found on islands lying off the coast of Scotland.

much more sophisticated, especially in the field of astronomy.

One of the first Greeks to visit and study other civilizations was Thales of Miletus, who was born in about 630 BC. He returned from Egypt well versed in the techniques of Egyptian geometry. From experience in building, the Egyptians had learned that if a triangle has two sides of equal length, then the angles at its base are also equal. Thales looked for a way of proving this fact. He made two identical triangles, each with two equal sides, and found that when one was picked up and turned over, it could be laid on top of the other and fitted exactly. In this way, a mathematical proof was developed.

Famous Greek scientists

To Pythagoras, born about 50 years after Thales, is attributed a proof of the famous theorem that the square on the longest side of a right angled triangle is equal to the sum of the squares of the other two sides. Pythagoras sought to explain the properties of matter in terms of numbers. He discovered, for instance, that the musical note produced by a vibrating string is arithmetically related to the length of the string.

Another Greek, Euclid (born 330 BC), provided the basic principles for the teaching of classical geometry. Less than half a century later, in 287 BC, Archimedes was born in Sicily. He applied the new mathematics with extraordinary power and logic and made many inventions. He established the principle that when a body is weighed in a liquid, its apparent loss in weight is equal to the weight of the liquid displaced; he is credited with inventing a screw for raising water [7].

Astronomy was first placed on an adequate scientific basis by Eudoxos, who was born about 408 BC. He showed that the motions of the Sun, Moon, and planets could be explained on the assumption that they moved with uniform motion in perfect circles, the centers of which are near, but not exactly at, the center of the Earth. Later Greek astronomers arranged far more complex systems of circular motions, equaling in accuracy the work of Nicolas Copernicus (1473–1543), nearly 2,000 years later.

KEY

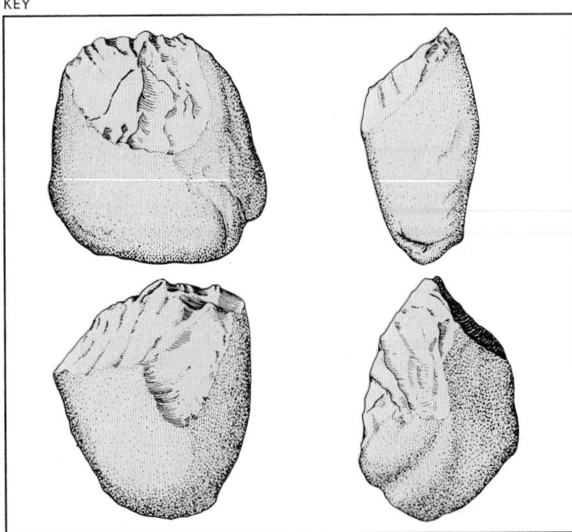

These Oldowan tools were first discovered by Louis Leakey (1903–72) in 1931 in the Olduvai Gorge in northern Tanzania, East Africa. They range from simple broken pebbles to chopping tools, and are 1.8 million to 12 million years old.

4

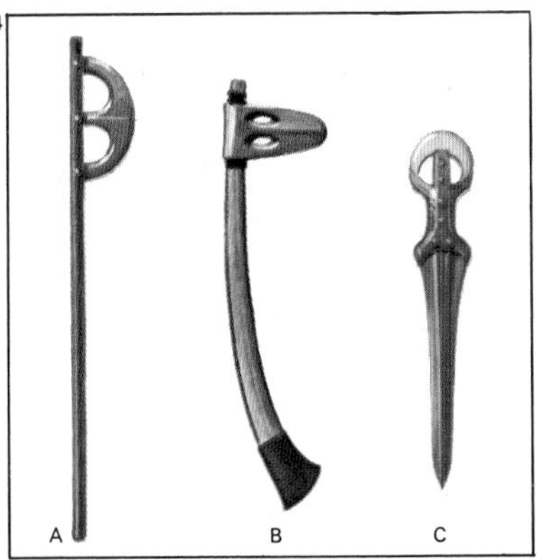
A
B
C

4 The introduction of metals gave early toolmakers much more manageable raw materials—first soft metals such as gold and copper, later bronze, and finally iron. Shown here are an Egyptian eye axe [A] from Megiddo (*c.* 1900 BC), an Egyptian duck-bill axe [B] from Ugarit (*c.* 1800 BC), and an Egyptian bronze dagger [C] of the Hyksos period (*c.* 1650 BC). But iron made the best edge.

5

5 The Great Pyramid in Egypt was erected by the Pharoah Khufu (in Greek, Cheops) of the 4th dynasty, about 2500 BC. It contains 6.5 million tons of limestone. A primary purpose of the pyramids was to provide tombs. They may also have had other purposes. The whole group of the major Egyptian pyramids was built within little more than a century. They involved an enormous concentration of labor and it has been suggested that their construction may have provided a convenient means of organizing the whole population of Egypt and creating a centralized state—hence the short building period.

6

6 The Mesopotamians, lacking the Egyptians' papyrus for writing, made records on clay tablets. Characters were formed by pressing the wedge-shaped end of a stylus into the soft clay and a permanent record could be obtained by baking the clay in a fire until it was hard. From its wedge shape, the writing is known as cuneiform. The associate number system used strokes that, to our eyes, faintly resemble the Roman numerals of 30 centuries later.

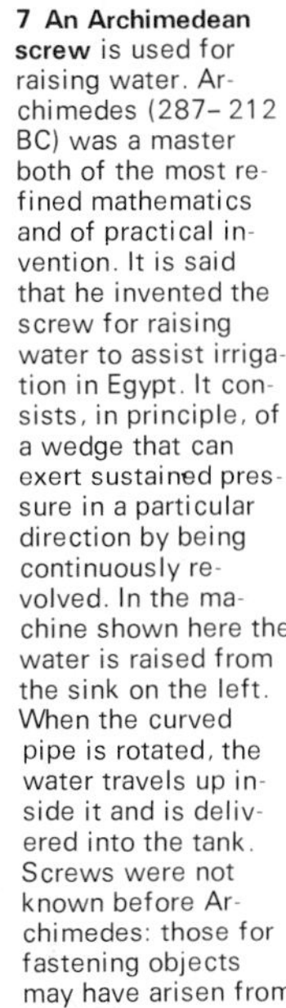

7 An Archimedean screw is used for raising water. Archimedes (287–212 BC) was a master both of the most refined mathematics and of practical invention. It is said that he invented the screw for raising water to assist irrigation in Egypt. It consists, in principle, of a wedge that can exert sustained pressure in a particular direction by being continuously revolved. In the machine shown here the water is raised from the sink on the left. When the curved pipe is rotated, the water travels up inside it and is delivered into the tank. Screws were not known before Archimedes: those for fastening objects may have arisen from his device.

7

F
E
C
D
B
G
D
E
D
C
A

Asian and medieval science

By the fifth century AD the long-ailing Roman Empire lost control of Western Europe. It was overcome by its excessive size, by the "softness" of its citizens, and by a population explosion in Asia that propelled vigorous new peoples against Rome's extended frontiers. At the same time, the Eastern Roman Empire, whose capital was at Byzantium (later Constantinople and now Istanbul) flourished until a new attack from the east in the seventh century.

International influences

The Arabs emerged from Arabia as the followers of the new prophet Mohammed (*c.*570–632), a trader from Mecca. Within about 100 years they captured much of the Middle East and North Africa and invaded Spain and even France [2]. These new conquerors had little learning of their own, but they borrowed from Syriac, Greek, Indian, and other people whom they encountered through their conquests and travels. They became the founders of the internationalism that is one of the most striking features of science. They aimed at all-embracing knowledge; perhaps Avicenna (980–1037) came nearest to attaining it.

The Muslims had a strong trading tradition. Like other peoples, they were interested in the exact calculation of shares in goods and the allocation of family inheritances. They assessed the declining value of female slaves in much the same way as cars are depreciated today. When they invaded India, they discovered and adopted Indian mathematics.

The Indians introduced the number system now universally in use, together with the zero symbol and decimals. Their work became known to Al-Khwarizmi (780–*c.*850), the greatest of the Arab mathematicians. He was librarian to the caliph Al-Mamum (786–833) in Baghdad and published in 830 his treatise on *Al-jabr wa'l muqabala*, from which the word *algebra* is derived. He studied various classes of quadratic (second order) equations and called the unknown quantity to be calculated "the root." Knowledge of mathematics in medieval Europe was based mainly on Latin translations of his works. One of his most famous successors was the Persian poet Omar Khayyám (*c.*1048–1122), who dealt with special classes of cubic (third order) equations.

The Arabs devoted much attention to pharmacy [5] and to astronomy. They calculated elaborate trigonometric tables, which were used to determine the exact times of prayers and to navigate the Indian Ocean. Córdoba in Spain became the most advanced intellectual center in Europe. The dependence of medieval Europe on Arab knowledge is illustrated by the example of Adelard of Bath, who went to Córdoba disguised as a Muslim student in 1120. He returned to England with a copy of Euclid, which served as a mathematical textbook for feudal Europe for four centuries.

Chinese science and technology

The Arabs also brought knowledge of Chinese inventions and discoveries to Europe, including gunpowder, the magnetic compass, and printing.

The Chinese invented an escapement mechanism for a water clock [1], generally

CONNECTIONS

See also
1444 Mathematics and civilization
1452 Finding unknown quantities: algebra
1534 Magnets and magnetism
1032 Early Oriental and Western science
1042 China 618–1368

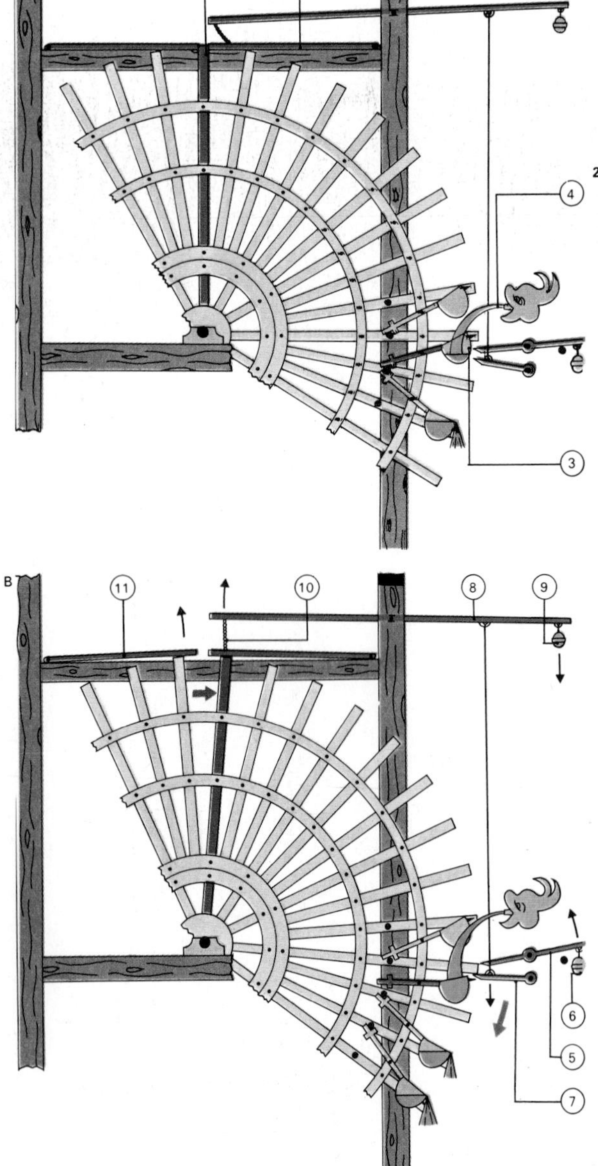

1
A
1
2
4
3
B
11
10
8
9
6
5
7

1 This clock escapement mechanism was invented in China in the 8th century. [A] A spoke [1] is arrested by a lock [2] while a scoop [3] fills with water [4] from a tank at a constant rate. The lock is released [B] when the filling scoop trips a checking fork [5], overcomes its counterweight [6], and trips a coupling tongue [7], which pulls down an upper lever [8] with its own counterweight [9]. This jerks a chain [10], freeing the lock and allowing the wheel to swing clockwise until the lock drops again, arresting the following spoke, which is also held steady by a ratchet lock [11].

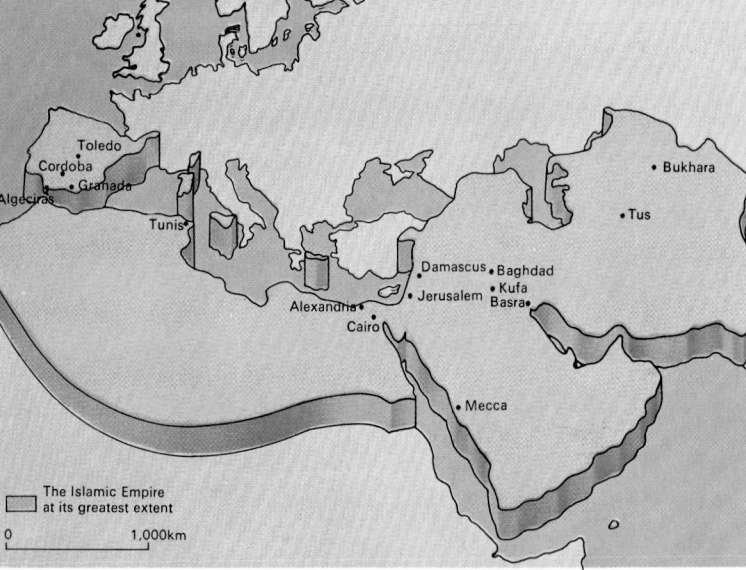

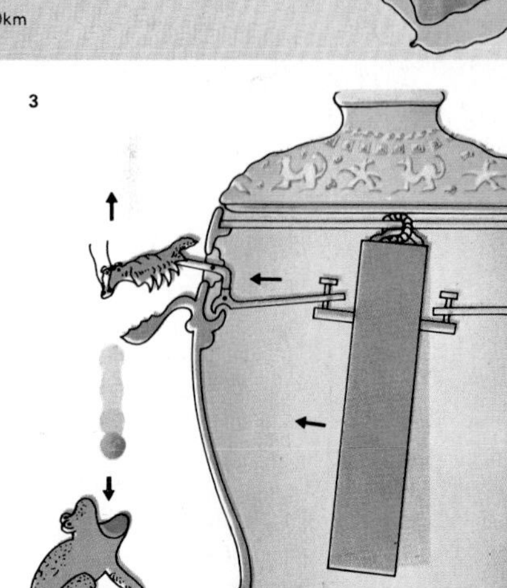

2
Toledo
Cordoba
Granada
Algeciras
Tunis
Bukhara
Tus
Damascus
Baghdad
Jerusalem
Kufa
Basra
Alexandria
Cairo
Mecca
The Islamic Empire at its greatest extent
0
1,000km

2 The Arab Empire, by the 8th century, stretched from India to the Pyrenees, making major contributions to mathematics and chemistry and laying the basis for the international spread of learning.

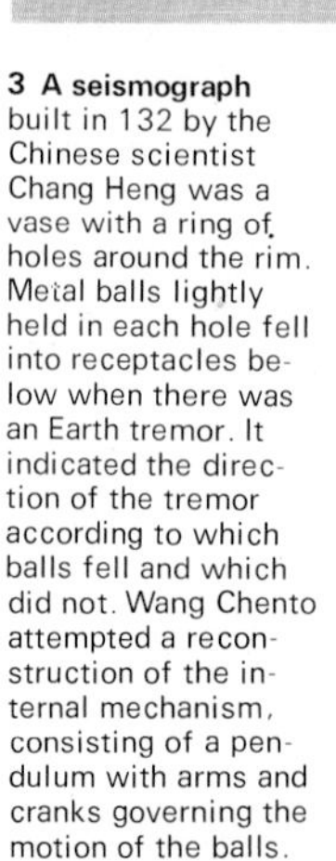

3 A seismograph built in 132 by the Chinese scientist Chang Heng was a vase with a ring of holes around the rim. Metal balls lightly held in each hole fell into receptacles below when there was an Earth tremor. It indicated the direction of the tremor according to which balls fell and which did not. Wang Chento attempted a reconstruction of the internal mechanism, consisting of a pendulum with arms and cranks governing the motion of the balls.

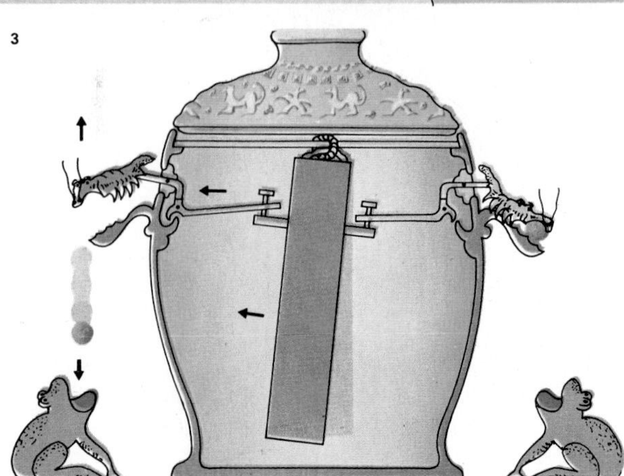

3

credited to Yi Hoing, in 725. It enabled them to build the first accurate mechanical clocks. Chinese science also produced the first seismograph, for detecting earthquakes [3], built by Chang Heng in 132. In 1054 they observed the great new star—a nova, the parent of the Crab Nebula—later to become one of the most important objects in the development of radio astronomy.

The Arabs performed a unique service as world informants on ancient and contemporary science. They introduced the ideas of India and China to the Western world. But they were not the founders of modern science, for this arose in Europe.

Medieval science

The Roman Empire in Europe disintegrated into a multitude of individual strongholds of local military chieftains. So the feudal period began. People who settled around the strong points came to be known as the bourgeoisie, because they lived outside the castle or burg. Many of them were craftsmen. They were dependent on what they could learn from the Arab encyclopedists but they looked at the old knowledge in a more individual way. One such man who played a significant role in the advance of medieval science was Leonardo Fibonaci of Pisa (*c.* 1180–1250). His father was employed on the Barbary coast and there Leonardo learned the Arabic language and arithmetic. On his return to Pisa he introduced Arabic numerals into Europe.

The most eminent of English medieval scientists was Roger Bacon (1214–94). He proposed combinations of lenses for telescopes and microscopes and may have been the first to suggest spectacles [4]. Bacon said that the only man he knew who was to be praised for his experimental science was Petrus Peregrinus of Maricourt, who published a treatise on magnetism in 1269. Peregrinus explicitly pointed out the importance of manual skill in science. He was one of the forerunners of modern science, in which experiment and theory are equally balanced. This became possible only through the emancipation of the craftsman in medieval Europe, a change that was to lead to the Renaissance.

KEY

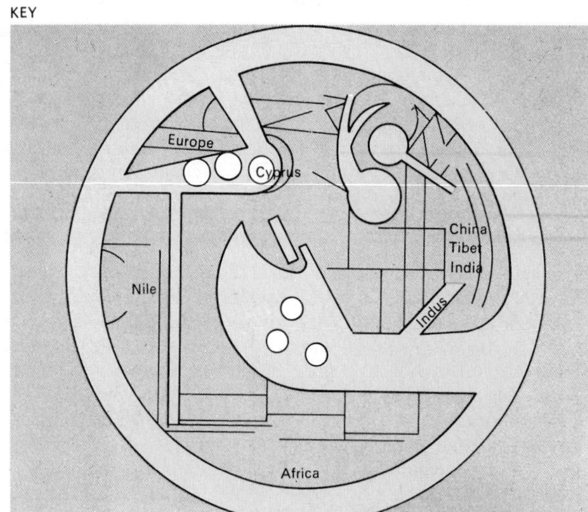
Europe
Cyprus
China
Tibet
India
Nile
Indus
Africa

An Arab map in remarkably modern graphic style shows the seas and land masses known to medieval Arab geographers. The concept of a round world with an encircling ocean and the territorial extent of the map indicates the importance of the Arab contribution to man's knowledge.

4 A

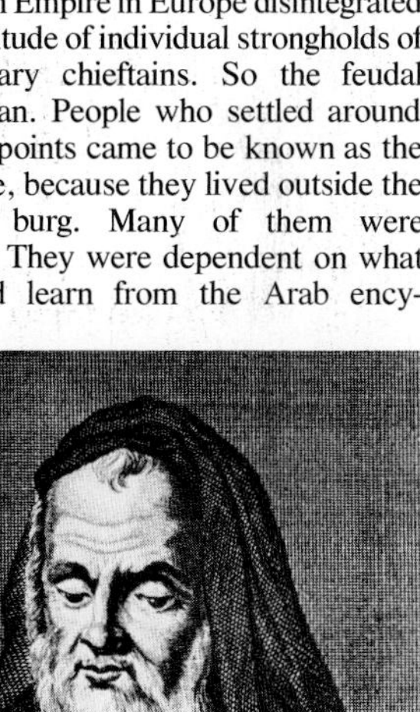

4 Roger Bacon [A] was not personally an experimenter or mathematician but he realized the importance of experiment and mathematics for the advancement of science. His imagination enabled him to make a remarkable collection of scientific suggestions, culled from many sources and ranging from vague hints to clear diagrams. He gave substantially correct optical explanations of [B] why a spherical flask of water [2] acts as a burning glass [3] to concentrate the rays of the Sun [1], and [C] how a convex lens [4] produces a magnified image [5] of an object [6] beneath it.

B

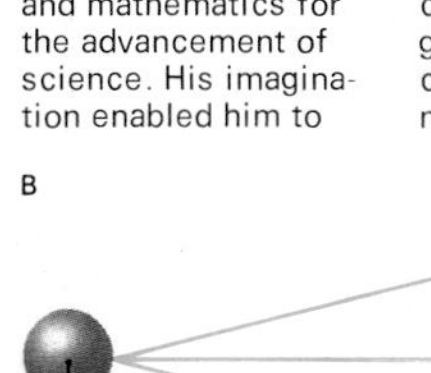
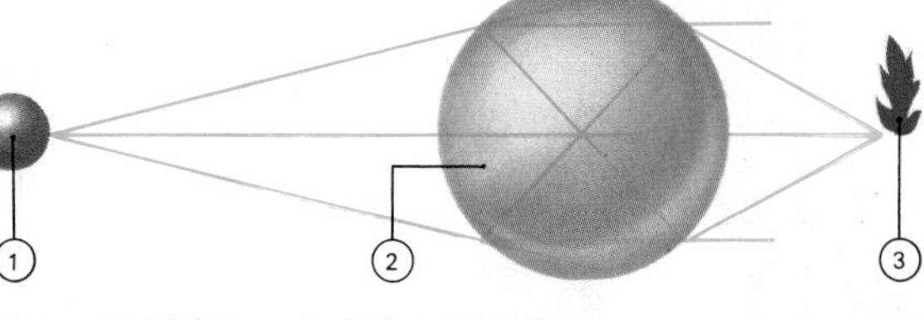
1
2
3

C

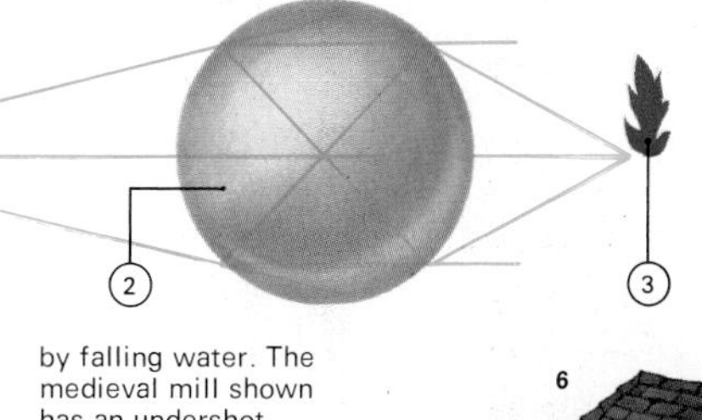
4
5
6

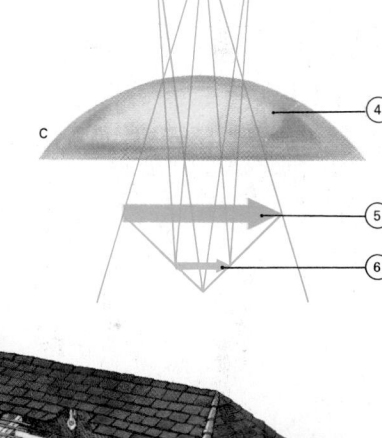

5 A typical pharmacy of the Middle Ages was based on Arab traditions. The Arabs brought knowledge of Persian and Indian drugs and spices. Their influence on European pharmacy was exerted chiefly through Benedictine monks. In the 14th century pharmacy, medicine, chemistry, and the grocery business were combined, and apothecaries and grocers organized themselves into trade guilds.

6 Corn mills originated with the Romans, who spread techniques that helped them to exploit their empire. They built undershot and overshot water mills, one driven by flowing water and the other by falling water. The medieval mill shown has an undershot drive [6] with a hopper [1] for the corn and a chute [2] conveying it to grindstones [3]. The flour fell into a chute [4] and into a bag [5].

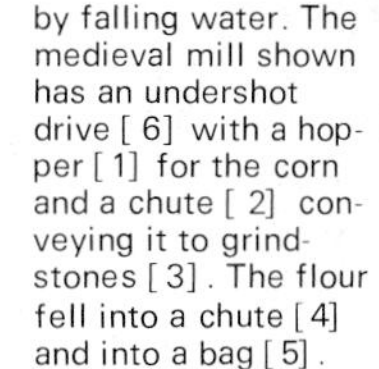

5

Mitro datio

6

1
2
3
4
5
6

Alchemy and the age of reason

Men gained some practical knowledge of the working of materials in early times but work in the crafts (what is now called technology) was regarded as a lowly pursuit. One reason for this attitude was the disagreeable working conditions associated with it. An Egyptian of 1500 BC noted that the metalworker "stinks like fish-spawn."

Alchemy and the Renaissance

In the second century AD, Diocletian (245–313) ordered that all books on the working of gold, silver, and copper should be destroyed to prevent counterfeiting and inflation. The effect was to reduce rational research on practical problems and to increase interest in magic as a method of transmuting base metals into gold. The center of the development was Alexandria and the Arabs called the new science "alchemy" after Khem, or "black," the name given to Egypt because of its black earth.

The Alexandrians invented apparatus for heating, melting, filtering, and distilling substances. The Arabs [1] adopted, extended, and transmitted these advances. Their greatest chemist was Jabir ibn Haijan, or Gebir (*c.* AD 721–817), who worked on the transmutation of metals and propounded a theory of their constitution that was not completely superseded until the eighteenth century. Besides being familiar with chemical operations such as crystallization, solution, and reduction, he attempted to explain them. His most useful discovery was nitric acid.

Modern science was founded during the Renaissance in the urban society of the Italian cities where artisans became emancipated and even famous. The supreme example was Leonardo da Vinci (1452–1519), who knew little Latin and no Greek but analyzed processes scientifically.

Copernicus and Galileo

Nicolas Copernicus (1473–1543) was a Polish scholar who studied at Cracow and Bologna in the 1490s. He noted from astronomical references in Latin and Greek literature that Heraclides (388–315 BC) had assigned a motion to the Earth "after the manner of a wheel being carried on its own axis." Copernicus found "by much and long observation" that a consistent account of the movements of the planets could be given on the basis that the Earth revolves around the Sun. The account of this in his treatise *Concerning the Revolutions of the Heavenly Spheres* was published in 1543 when he was on his deathbed. The Copernican theory [Key] is perhaps the most important scientific theory in history, for it changed man's conception of his place in the universe. Formerly man had believed that the universe revolved around the Earth and himself; now he realized that man was but a minute incidental speck in a universe of almost inconceivable vastness.

The Renaissance effort in science climaxed in Galileo Galilei [2], who cleared the way for modern science. Copernicus defined the workings of the Solar System but Galileo gained the first precise knowledge of how things on the Earth move. He was born in Pisa in 1564, the same year as Shakespeare, and died in 1642, the year in which Isaac Newton was born. He went to the local university. Ac-

CONNECTIONS

See also
1440 Asian and medieval science
1464 Lines and angles: trigonometry
1484 Beyond the atom
1552 Classification of elements
1088 European learning in the 13th century

1

1 Alchemical processes are represented by the figures on this Arab manuscript reflecting cross-cultural influences. The Arabs gained their main introduction to alchemy through Alexandria and spread it to Western Europe in about the eleventh century. Although they improved on the experimental techniques of the Alexandrians, they did not escape the influence of their mystical theorizing, which was based on animistic beliefs in objects possessing souls.

2 A

B

RECENS HABITAE 29

Ori. Occ.

percipi possent; a Ioue, & inter se non magis distabant minuto vno: incertus eram, nunquid ex occidente duæ an tres adessent Stellulæ. Circa horam sextam hoc pacto erant dispositæ. Orien-

Ori. Occ.

talis enim a Ioue duplo magis aberat quam antea, nempe min. 2. media occidentalis a Ioue distabat min. o. sec. 40 ab occidentaliori vero min. o. sec. 20. Tandem hora septima tres ex occidente visæ fuerunt Stellulæ. Ioui proxima aberat ab eo min.

Ori. Occ.

o. sec. 20. inter hanc & occidentaliorem interuallum erat minutorum secundorum 40. inter has vero alia spectabatur paululum ad meridiem deflectens; ab occidentaliori non pluribus decem secundis remota.

Die 21. hora o. m. 30. aderant ex oriente Stellulæ tres, æqualiter inter se, & a Ioue distantes; in-

Ori. Occ.

terstitia vero secundũ existimationem 50. secundorum minutorum fuere, aderat quoque Stella ex occidente a Ioue distans min. pr. 4. Orientalis Ioui proxima erat omniũ minima, reliquæ vero aliquãto maiores, atq; inter se proxime æquales.

Die 22. hora 2. consimilis fuit Stellarum dispositio. A Stella orientali ad Iouem minu-

Ori. Occ.

torum primorum 5. fuit interuallum a Ioue

2 Galileo [A] was 18 when he discovered the constancy of the swing of a pendulum, which he later adapted into a pendulum clock [C]. His development of the telescope led to original observations on the planets, including the discovery of the satellites of Jupiter, first described in a pamphlet of 1610, a page of which [B] is shown here. His conversion to Copernican theory alienated the Church.

C

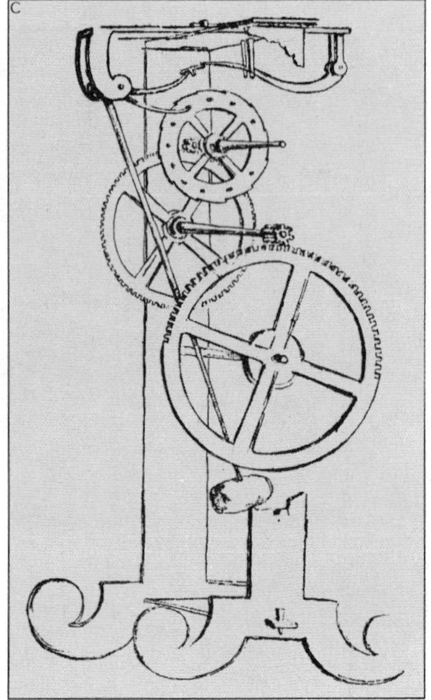

3

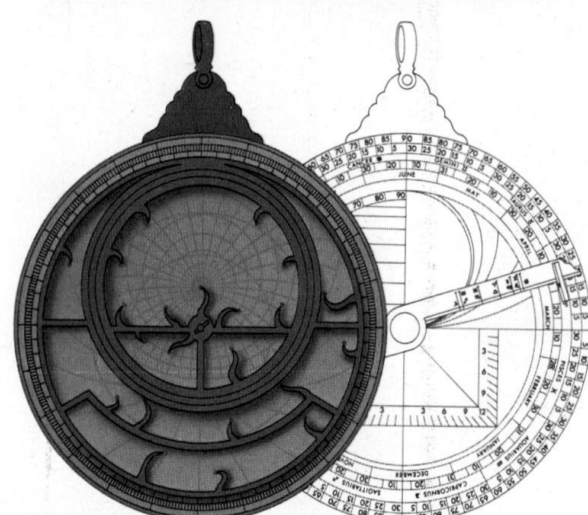

3 The astrolabe enabled an observer to find, at any instant, the position of a known point or object in the sky. It was much used for astrological predictions by the Greeks and Arabs and was introduced to Europe in about the tenth century. Two metal disks bore projections of the celestial and terrestrial spheres. A rotating arm on the back enabled the user to set the inclination of an object from the horizon and to calculate various angles.

cording to legend, a swinging lamp in the cathedral attracted his attention. He noticed that the time of the swing was independent of the size of the swing (its amplitude). When he arrived home he checked the fact with a bullet and a piece of string. He later used this fundamental property of a pendulum in designing a pendulum clock.

When Galileo was appointed professor he was obliged to teach Aristotelian science. This caused him to make a careful study of Aristotle's ideas, especially those on the motion of objects. Aristotle (384–322 BC) based his theory on the assumption that objects fall with a speed proportional to their weight. Galileo devised experiments to measure exactly how fast objects do fall and found that all that fall freely do so at the same speed. He made many other discoveries. The results of his application of the telescope to astronomical observation were particularly spectacular evidence that Aristotle's picture of the Universe was incomplete and mistaken.

Galileo's demonstration that the movement of objects could be exactly determined by a combination of experiment and mathematical reasoning was extended by Isaac Newton (1642–1727). Newton [5] showed that all the then known physical aspects of the universe and nature could be completely described by mathematical theory utilizing laws consistent with experience. Newton's account, in his *Philosophiae Naturalis Principia Mathematica* (1687), was possibly the greatest single intellectual effort yet made.

The Age of Reason

Newton's achievements increased confidence in the power of human reasoning. They had a particularly striking effect in France where Pierre Laplace (1749–1827) and Joseph Lagrange (1736–1813) extended the Newtonian theory and its supporting mathematics. The new confidence in experiment and calculation developed also in other sciences. Antoine Lavoisier (1743–94) revolutionized chemistry, dispatching the magical and mystical remnants from it and laying the foundations of modern chemistry [6].

KEY

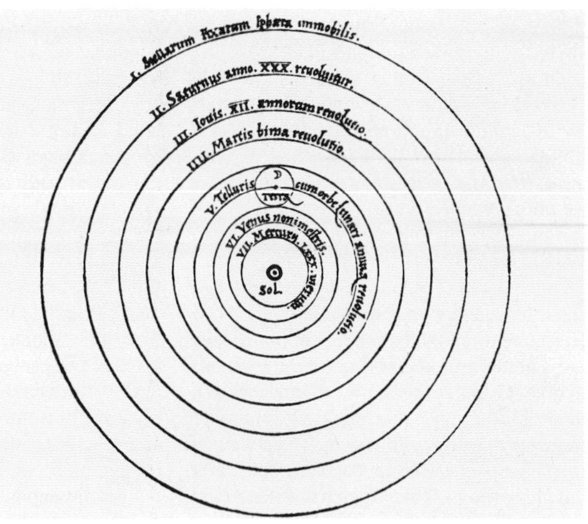
Sol.

Copernicus pictured the planets as revolving around the Sun in a simple pattern of circular motions, the basis of which is shown here. His theory did not give more accurate planetary predictions than Ptolemy's of AD 140, but it was a triumph of ideas that showed man in his true place in nature. Proof that the planets revolve in ellipses came in 1609 with the work of the German astronomer Johann Kepler (1571–1630).

4

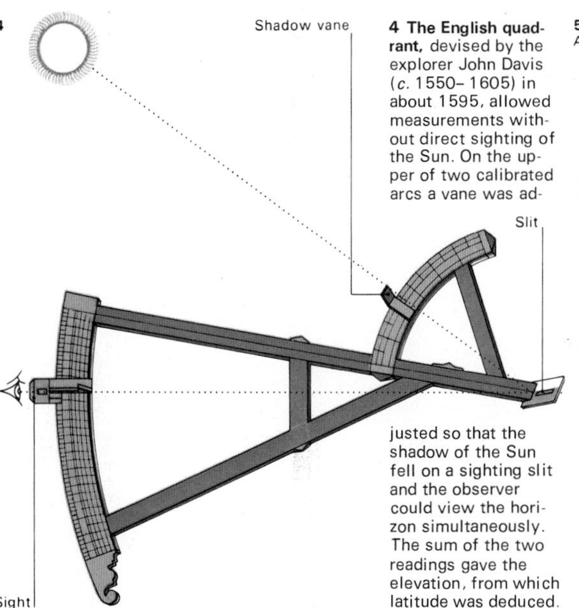
Shadow vane
Slit
Sight

4 The English quadrant, devised by the explorer John Davis (*c.* 1550–1605) in about 1595, allowed measurements without direct sighting of the Sun. On the upper of two calibrated arcs a vane was adjusted so that the shadow of the Sun fell on a sighting slit and the observer could view the horizon simultaneously. The sum of the two readings gave the elevation, from which latitude was deduced.

5 A

5 B

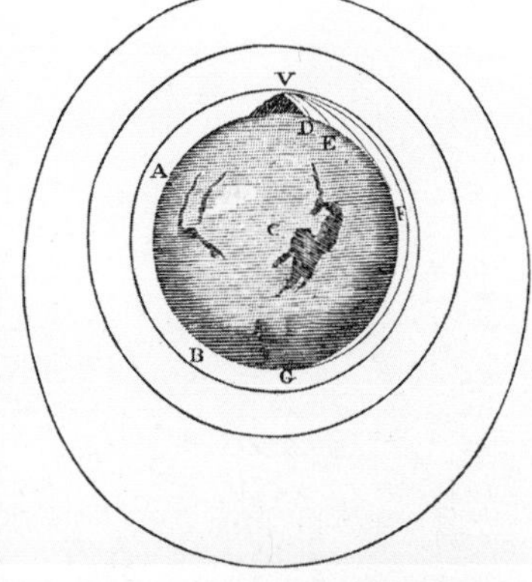
V
D
E
A
F
C
B
G

5 Isaac Newton [A] calculated the speed at which a body projected horizontally from the top of a mountain would leave the Earth and begin revolving around it. His diagram of the path of an artificial satellite [B] was published in 1728, the year after his death. Within a few years after he left Cambridge he had laid the basis of differential and integral calculus, elucidated the nature of light and color, and had begun to explore the usefulness of mathematical analysis to physical theories. His main achievements in physical science were expressed in his *Principia* (1687) and *Optiks* (1704).

6 A

6 B

6 Antoine Lavoisier [B] founded modern chemistry by means of experiments leading to his theory about the nature of combustion. This had previously been ascribed to the transfer of a substance called phlogiston, the main agent of chemical change sometimes released as fire. Lavoisier heated mercury and air in a flask with a curved neck, which enabled him to measure exactly the decrease in volume of gas and gain in weight of mercury during 12 days' heating. By means of this apparatus (illustrated here from Lavoisier's own diagram [A]) he showed that the changes could be explained completely in terms of the active constituent of the air discovered by Joseph Priestley (1733–1804), to which Lavoisier gave the name oxygen. The idea of phlogiston was superfluous and chemistry could develop as a rational science based entirely on quantitative measurements. Experiments gave rise to theories that were then tested by other experiments.

Mathematics and civilization

Mathematics is a continuously expanding system of organized thought. It is employed in almost every aspect of human activity—and has influenced, and often determined, the direction of philosophical thought concerned with man and his universe. Throughout history mathematics has not only reflected developments in civilization but also made a major contribution to those developments.

Algebra, geometry, and calculus

There are three major aspects of mathematics. The assembling and combining of sets of objects led to concepts of number [1], computation, and the algebra of number theory. Concern with the measurement of time and space led to geometry, astronomy, and chronology. The struggle to understand ideas of continuity and limit led to mathematical analysis and the invention of calculus in the seventeenth century. These three aspects of mathematics overlap considerably. There are now algebras of sets, logic, vector and transformation geometry, probability theory, and a host of specialities that employ the concepts, techniques, and language of other fields of study.

Everything natural or man-made has a structure made up of elements that are related in some special way [Key]. A rock crystal, a plant [6], a spaceship, and a political system each has a structure, the study of which is mathematical. Mathematics is the result of the thought process known as abstraction, in which activities related to a physical structure can be organized in such a way that the physical structure is replaced by a mental one, an abstract mathematical model. The power of mathematics is further demonstrated when abstract concepts, such as those of number and space, can be represented by concrete symbols, which may be algebraic, geometric, or graphical [3].

Mathematics can be described as a form of inquiry made according to defined rules for drawing conclusions from accepted mathematical truths. History shows, however, that mathematics is also a field of creative activity inspiring great flights of intuition and imagination [7]. The driving force for creativity is usually the need man has to solve the problems of his society. But the motivation may also simply be the challenge of intellectual activity for its own sake. The Greeks, for example, had a good understanding of conic sections, although they made no practical application of it.

The first mathematicians

All primitive civilizations developed concepts of number and measure as soon as trade progressed beyond the process of barter. Almost 6,000 years ago the Sumerians were using a numeration system based on 10 (denary system) as well as one based on 60 (sexagesimal system). The sexagesimal system still survives in the measure of time and rotation, reflecting the Babylonian preoccupation with the motions of the Sun, Moon, and planets and their influence.

The knowledge acquired became not only a religious force but also solved basic problems of agriculture and social organization. The flooding in Babylon and Egypt demanded seasonal surveys of land, the techniques of which led to geometry. Political, commercial, and religious pressures to

CONNECTIONS

See also
1446 The grammar of numbers
1448 The language of numbers
1452 Finding unknown quantities: algebra
1464 Lines and angles: trigonometry
1468 Shape and symmetry
1440 Asian and medieval science
1438 Prehistoric and ancient science
38 The restless sky
1006 Greek science
1160 Science and technology 1500–1700

1

1 The concept of number is fundamental to mathematics. It probably developed originally out of the need for farmers to count their animals and produce. Numbers also led to money systems, making buying and selling possible.

2

2 Stonehenge was built in the Bronze age as a sort of calendar, which probably also had a religious significance. The positions of the stone blocks can be used to measure the movements of the Sun and Moon and to "predict" eclipses.

3

(A) $131,137

(B) $4 \times \sqrt{27} = 20{\cdot}7846$

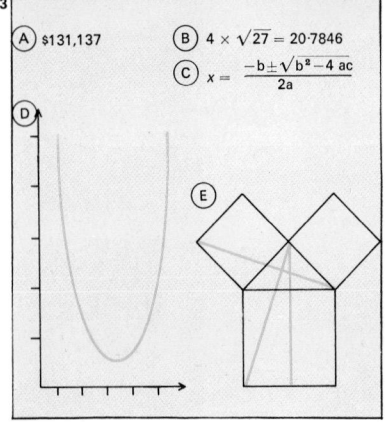

(C) $x = \frac{-b \pm \sqrt{b^2 - 4ac}}{2a}$

(D)

(E)

3 Mathematics has generated its own "language." Numbers are themselves shorthand forms of words and, linked with units, define precise amounts [A]. Other symbols stand for operations, such as multiplication and square roots [B]. In algebra letters often stand for unknown quantities, as in this formula [C] for finding the solutions to a quadratic equation. A graph [D] can "draw" algebraic functions. Pythagoras created his own geometric conventions [E].

4

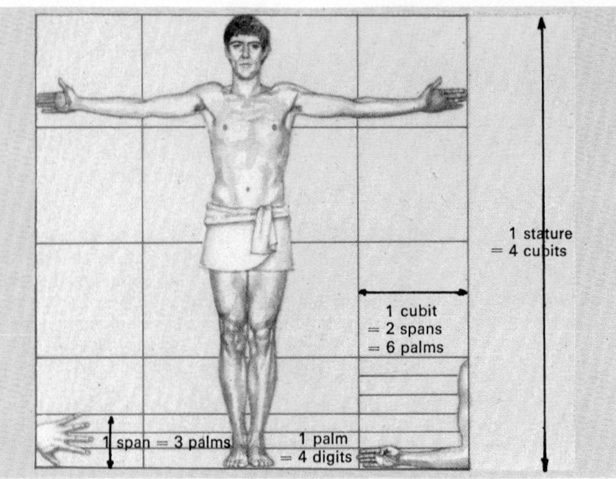

1 stature
= 4 cubits
1 cubit
= 2 spans
= 6 palms
1 span = 3 palms
1 palm
= 4 digits

4 Man probably first counted on his fingers and sized objects in terms of his own body. This diagram shows some of the ancient units of length. "Body units" are still used in some countries today. A hand, equal to 4in (about 10cm), is a standard unit for measuring the height of horses; in North America and England a foot–12in (30.5cm)–is still used in measurement as a unit of length. The metric system is now the most widely accepted system.

build palaces, ships, temples, and tombs stimulated the further development of geometry. At the same time, astronomy regulated social and religious events [2].

The Greeks established mathematics as a rigid study, placing mathematical argument on a logical basis so that propositions, previously not self-evident, could be deduced from basic assumptions. Euclid's *Elements,* produced in about 300 BC, was a prime example of this approach and dominated geometric thinking for 2,000 years. The Greeks saw beauty in number and shape and their excitement with the Golden Ratio [5] manifested itself in their art and architecture and has been echoed by later civilizations in such places as Notre Dame in Paris, in the architecture of Le Corbusier, and in the UN building in New York.

Every civilization has demanded techniques for measuring and each new system has borrowed ideas from previous ones. As civilizations expanded their influence, the need for standardized units increased. The earlier systems were based on convenience, so that parts of the body were used for measuring length [4], the working capacity of oxen for area, stones for weight, skins for volume. Each society learned to standardize; in 1791 the French devised the metric system based on the meter, one ten millionth of the Earth's quadrant (a quarter of the circumference), a distance calculated from an actual survey. International trade has now forced most of the world to accept the metric system.

The heritage of numbers

Mathematics resembles a living organism in that its growth is affected by the environment in which it lives. The golden age of Greece produced mathematical beauty that afterward lay dormant for centuries. The Romans used earlier mathematics but solved no new problems. Not until the sixteenth century was there another great advance. Today the whole world is experiencing change at a pace unequalled in the past. This is mirrored in the development of new mathematics and its applications in solving the problems of science, technology, industry, and commerce [8].

KEY

Everything on Earth, from the atoms in this crystal to the leaves on a tree, consists of individual components. Mathematics seeks to establish their relationships.

5

5 Greek mathematicians extended their logical thinking into the arts, establishing mathematical relationships in music and art. The Golden Ratio (approximately 1.618) was to the Greeks a pleasing proportion, incorporated here in the Parthenon.

6

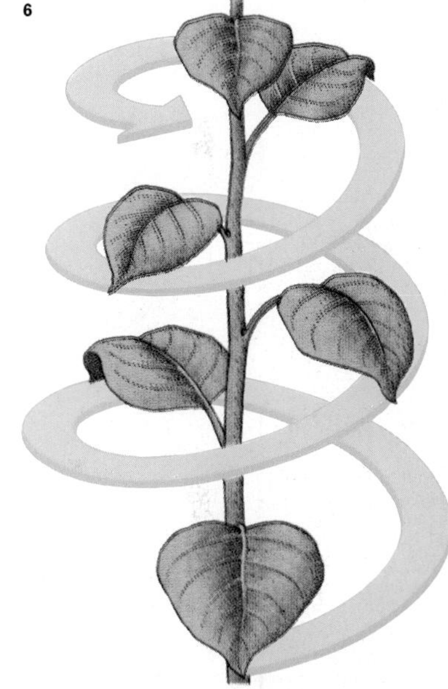

6 Fibonacci ratios are functions in the series 1/1, 2/1, 3/2, 5/3, 8/5, 13/8, and so on. These values approach the Greek Golden Ratio. Both the numerators and the denominators in the series are formed by adding consecutive members of the series. These ratios occur in nature; a spiral following leaves on this stalk has gaps and turns in the ratio of 5/3.

7

7 The Grand Canal at Venice was a favorite subject of the Venetian painter Canaletto, whose real name was Giovanni Canal (1697–1768). Renaissance painters studied perspective and so laid the foundations of projective geometry in mathematics, map making, and the draftsmanship used in architecture and engineering, enabling a three-dimensional object to be represented in two.

8 An electronic calculator is a modern machine for "doing sums." It and the much more complex digital computer have replaced earlier calculating devices such as the mechanical adding machine, the slide rule, and the abacus.

8

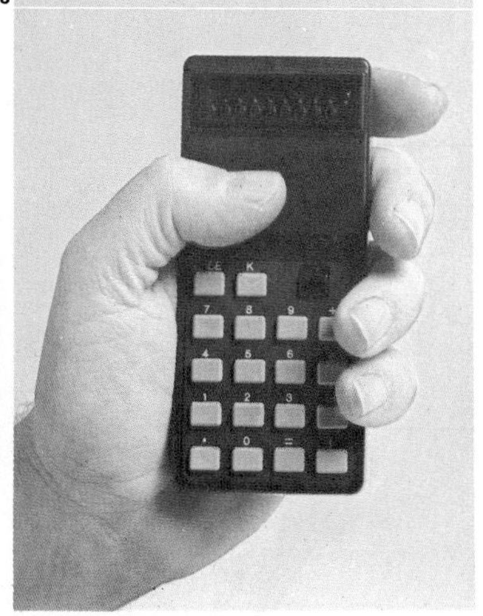

The grammar of numbers

People use arithmetic so frequently in everyday life that they hardly ever think about it. Yet every time someone buys something and counts his change [Key] he uses the basic concepts of addition and equality. These ideas have been used ever since counting and trading began.

Basic rules of arithmetic

The four main types of calculations are addition, subtraction, multiplication, and division. They are carried out following basic laws—most of which are merely statements of common sense. The commutative law holds for both addition and multiplication. It simply states that the sum of seven and two $(7 + 2)$, for example, is the same as the sum of two and seven $(2 + 7)$. In other words, the order in which numbers are added does not matter. The same is true of multiplication: $4 \times 3 = 3 \times 4$ or, in general terms, $a \times b = b \times a$.

The associative law states that, in adding or multiplying a series of numbers, the order of addition or multiplication does not matter [1]. Using symbols to stand for any numbers, $(a + b) + c = a + (b + c)$, or $(a \times b) \times c = a \times (b \times c)$.

The distributive law states that if two numbers are to be added together and the sum multiplied by a third number, the same result is obtained if each of the first two is first multiplied by the third and the two products added. This law is easier to state using symbols: $(a + b) \times c = (a \times c) + (b \times c)$, and is made clear by an example: $(5 + 7) \times 3 = (5 \times 3) + (7 \times 3) = 36$.

Multiplication is equivalent to repeated addition. 7×5, for instance, is a shorthand way of writing $7 + 7 + 7 + 7 + 7$. People learn multiplication tables because it is quicker to apply them than to add columns of figures. Electronic calculators, renowned for their speed, cannot multiply; they work by successive addition, but do so extremely quickly.

Just as subtraction is the reverse of addition, so division can be regarded as the reverse of multiplication—a repeated subtraction [3]. This is the method employed in doing long division. Often it is not possible to subtract successively one number from another an exact number of times—there is generally something "left over," called the remainder: 38 divided by 7, for example, is 5, with a remainder of 3.

Squares and square roots

When a number is squared, it is multiplied by itself (the area of a square is the length of one side multiplied by itself). Three squared (written 3^2) equals 9. The reverse operation is called taking the square root: what number multiplied by itself equals a given number? Squaring a whole number (integer) gives an integer result, but taking the square root of a whole number often does not. And as the Greek mathematician Pythagoras and his coworkers discovered, there is not always a rational number (expressible as the ratio of two integers) that when squared will equal a particular integer. The square root of 4 is 2 (both integers), but the square root of 2 is somewhere between 1.4142 and 1.4143. However fine the intervals are divided, the square root of 2 cannot be defined as an exact number and it is called an irrational number.

CONNECTIONS

See also

1444 Mathematics and civilization

1448 The language of numbers

1452 Finding unknown quantities: algebra

1456 Logarithms and slide rule

1468 Shape and symmetry

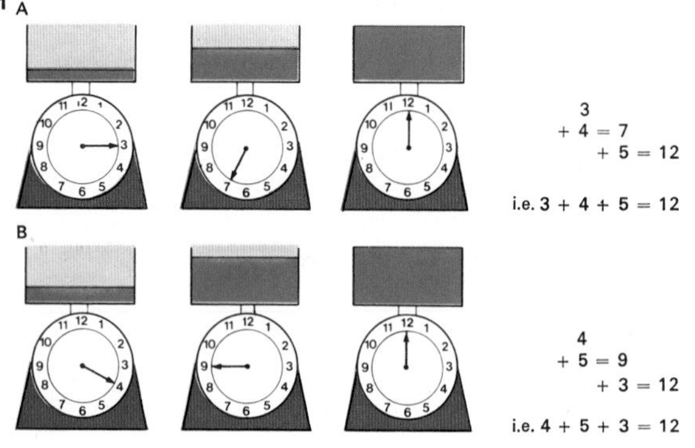

1 A
B

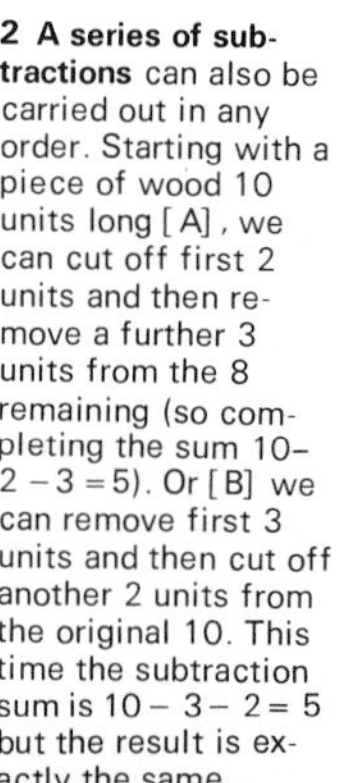

3
+ 4 = 7
+ 5 = 12
i.e. 3 + 4 + 5 = 12
4
+ 5 = 9
+ 3 = 12
i.e. 4 + 5 + 3 = 12

1 Addition is associative—that is, a series of additions can be carried out in any order without affecting the result. This diagram shows the effects of successively weighing [A] 3, 4, and then 5 units of a substance on a spring balance and [B] weighing 4, 5, and then 3 units. In both cases the total weight—the sum of the additions—is 12 units. As in many other mathematical laws, this is applied common sense.

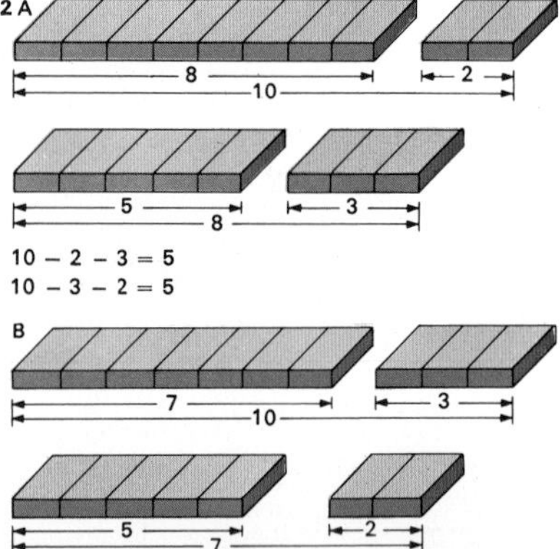

2 A
8
10
2
5
8
3
10 – 2 – 3 = 5
10 – 3 – 2 = 5
B
7
10
3
5
7
2

2 A series of subtractions can also be carried out in any order. Starting with a piece of wood 10 units long [A], we can cut off first 2 units and then remove a further 3 units from the 8 remaining (so completing the sum 10–2 – 3 = 5). Or [B] we can remove first 3 units and then cut off another 2 units from the original 10. This time the subtraction sum is 10 – 3 – 2 = 5 but the result is exactly the same.

3 Multiplication and division are needed to solve many everyday problems. A man wants to tile the two plain walls of a room [A], which is 5.5m long by 3m wide and 4m tall, using tiles 0.5m square. The walls can be drawn [B] as two areas of 22m² and 12m², giving a total area of 34m². A single tile 0.5m by 0.5m has an area of 0.25m². The number of tiles required [C] can be found by dividing the area of one tile (0.25m²) into the total area to be covered (34m²) giving the result 136 tiles. The same problem can be tackled another way [D]. If the whole area to be tiled is considered, it measures 8.5m by 4m. The long side will accommodate 17 half-meter tiles and the short side only 8 tiles. The total number of tiles required is therefore 17 × 8 = 136, the same result as before.

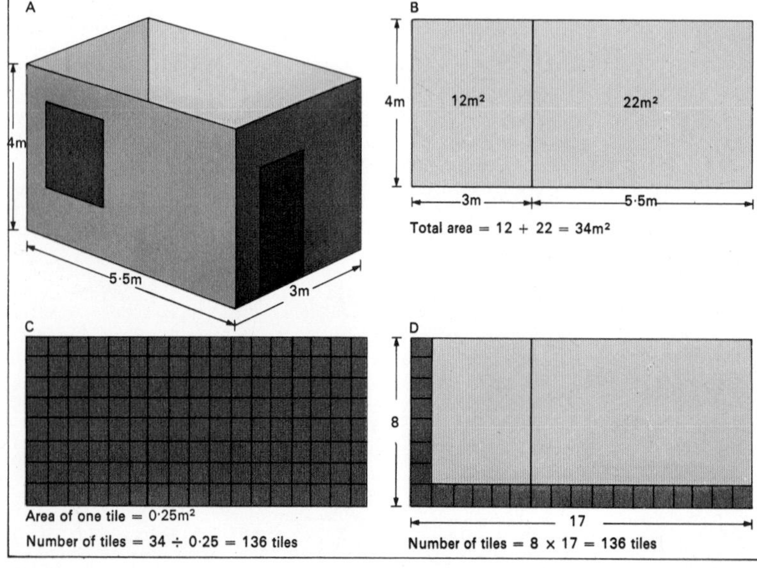

3
A
4m
5·5m
3m
B
4m
12m²
22m²
3m
5·5m
Total area = 12 + 22 = 34m²
C
Area of one tile = 0·25m²
Number of tiles = 34 ÷ 0·25 = 136 tiles
D
8
17
Number of tiles = 8 × 17 = 136 tiles

4
CATA-POLE

4 Dividing quantities into equal parts is a method of forming them into fractions. An athlete such as a pole vaulter intuitively judges his run by dividing it into an equal number of paces so that the pole is in exactly the right place for the jump—he cannot make half a pace. The same is true when we speak of a bottle being half full or say that we have read a third of a book. In a fraction such as three-quarters, written 3/4, 3 is called the numerator and 4 is the denominator. If the numerator is smaller than the denominator, the fraction is termed "proper"; in an improper fraction the numerator is larger than the denominator, although it can be simplified to a whole number and a fraction.

Fractions, proportions, and ratios
Three-sevenths is written as 3/7, meaning 3 divided by 7; it is a fraction. In books, a fraction may be printed as $^{1}/_{3}$ or 1/3. The number below or to the right of the line is called the denominator and is the number of parts that a unit quantity has been "broken" into. The number above or to the left of the line is the numerator and represents the number of such parts being considered. Two pieces of wood 3ft and 7ft long have lengths in the proportion of 3 to 7, or in the ratio 3 to 7 (often written 3:7). The shorter piece is $^{3}/_{7}$ the length of the longer.

There are two types of fractions: proper and improper. In a proper fraction, the numerator is less than the denominator: $^{3}/_{7}$, $^{7}/_{8}$ and $^{29}/_{54}$ are examples. An improper fraction has a larger numerator than denominator, as in $^{5}/_{4}$ and $^{22}/_{7}$. Generally these are simplified by dividing and expressing the remainder as a fraction, as in $1^{1}/_{4}$ and $3^{1}/_{7}$.

The laws of arithmetic also apply to fractions, but special techniques are sometimes needed in manipulating them. Multiplication is simple—the numerators are multiplied together and the denominators multiplied together, and the result expressed as a new fraction. Thus $^{2}/_{3} \times {}^{7}/_{11} = {}^{14}/_{33}$. To divide, invert the second fraction (the divisor) and multiply: $^{2}/_{3} \div {}^{7}/_{11} = {}^{2}/_{3} \times {}^{11}/_{7} = {}^{22}/_{21}$. Here the result is an improper fraction that can be simplified to $1^{1}/_{21}$. Addition and subtraction of fractions is more complicated. They must first be written in terms of the same denominator and for simplicity the smallest possible one is chosen (called the lowest common denominator or LCD). Then the numerators can be added or subtracted as necessary, the result expressed in terms of the LCD and simplified if possible [5, 6].

Decimals are a way of writing fractions whose denominators are powers of ten. $1^{9}/_{10}$, for example, is the fraction $^{19}/_{10}$ and is written in decimals as 1.9. The decimal point separates the whole number part (the argument) from the fractional part. Every fraction can be expressed as the sum of a series of such fractions (tenths, hundredths, thousandths, and so on) and can be represented in decimal form.

KEY

A cash register at a supermarket adds together the cost of each item purchased. Some machines will also calculate and even issue the correct change and print a receipt.

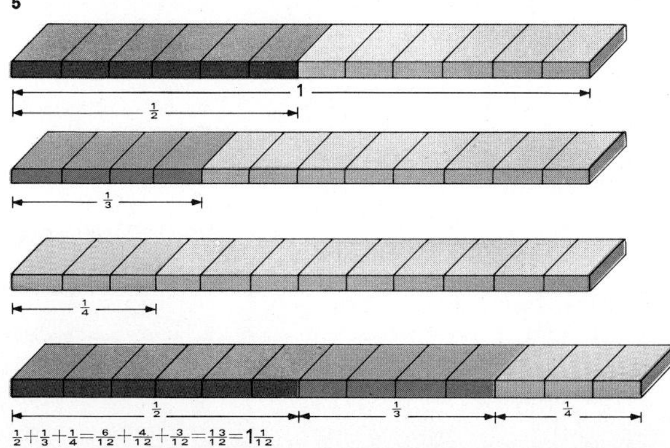
5
1
1/2
1/3
1/4
1/2
1/3
1/4
1/2+1/3+1/4=6/12+4/12+3/12=13/12=1 1/12

5 Before fractions can be added they must all be expressed in terms of the same denominator. To add 1/2, 1/3, and 1/4 they must all be stated in twelfths (in this example, 12 is the lowest common denominator) as 6/12, 4/12, and 3/12. They can then be added to give 13/12. This sum explains why it is impossible to divide anything into "shares" of 1/2, 1/3 and 1/4—their sum is larger than 1.

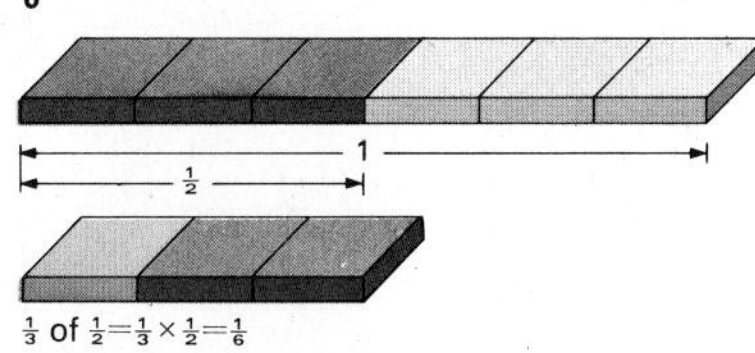
6
1
1/2
1/3 of 1/2=1/3×1/2=1/6

6 To multiply fractions merely multiply the numerators and then multiply the denominators. A third of a half is 1/3 × 1/2 = 1/6 (the same as a half of a third—order does not matter).

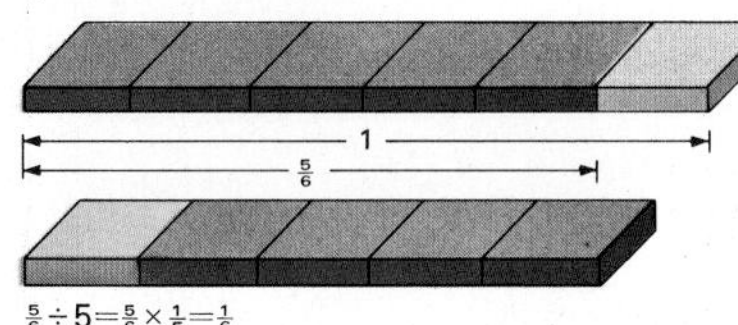
7
1
5/6
5/6÷5=5/6×1/5=1/6

7 To divide fractions invert the divisor and multiply. For example, 5/6 divided by 5 is 5/6 x 1/5= 1/6, which is exactly the same as the quantity described as a third of a half, as shown in illustration 6.

8

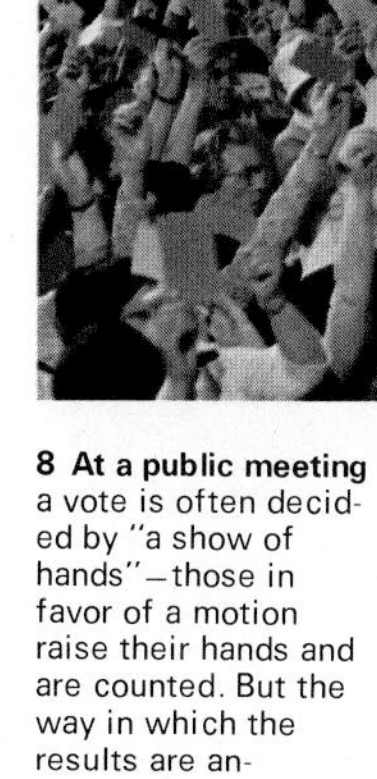

8 At a public meeting a vote is often decided by "a show of hands"—those in favor of a motion raise their hands and are counted. But the way in which the results are announced or reported—as fractions or percentages—can convey different shades of meaning. At such a meeting, with 580 people present, 348 voted for the motion and 232 voted against. This basic fact can be expressed in various ways: "Three out of five people voted in favor"; 40 percent of the voters were against the motion" and "The motion was carried with a 20 percent majority" are all true statements based on these figures. Fractions, proportions, and ratios (often expressed as percentages) are merely different ways of presenting the same information. But if 200 of the people present abstained, a figure of "60 percent voting in favor" means that of the 580 present only 228 people were in favor of the motion—less than half those present.

9

1:9
Low gear
for ½ mile
alexon

9 Proportions are also used to define slopes—for example, gradients on roads. "A slope of one in nine" means, mathematically, that a slope rises one unit of length for every nine horizontal units. In practice distances are measured along the road's surface and a one-in-nine hill climbs one yard for every nine yards traveled along the road. Mathematically this hill has a slope of 1 in 8.944—close enough for a road sign. But proportions can best be compared as percentages. Thus the ratios 7 to 13 and 28 to 53 (corresponding to fractions 7/13 and 28/53) are difficult to compare. But as the percentages 53.85% and 52.83%, the former is obviously larger than the latter.

The language of numbers

The idea of number is a basic concept. The distinction between one and many is probably the easiest for a child to understand. A boy on a beach can pick up one pebble although he can see many more. If he picks up a handful, he obviously has more than one pebble but far less than the total number he can see. To obtain a precise idea of how many he has, he can count the number of pebbles in his hand and find, for example, that there are 12. "Twelve" is the name given to that number of pebbles. It is a property possessed by all collections of 12 objects: 12 cows, 12 seagulls, and 12 buses.

Positive and negative integers

Whole numbers such as 1, 5 and 212 are called positive integers and have been used ever since men began to count. In the Middle Ages the Hindus developed the concept of negative integers to deal with amounts owing in a trading transaction. A man might own five (+5) sheep and owe three (−3), so that he really owned only $5 + (-3) = 2$.

As long as mathematical operations are limited to counting, integers are sufficient as numbers. But as soon as men started to measure they found that nature is not organized into integer lengths and areas. A farmer could make a measuring stick (a ruler) by marking off a piece of wood into similar lengths equal to, say, the length of his foot. He might find that one of his animals was 5 "feet" long, whereas its offspring was only 2 "feet" long. Then he might find an animal that was $3^1/_3$ "feet" and another of $2^2/_3$ "feet." He would thus discover a whole new family of numbers, called rational numbers. Any number that can be written in such a form as $^8/_3$—as a fraction (the ratio of two integers)—is a rational number. Such numbers can be positive or negative and all integers are rational [1A].

In the sixth century BC Greek mathematicians discovered that a square with sides one unit long has a diagonal whose length cannot be measured exactly. No matter what scale of length is used, such a length cannot be measured with precision nor can it be written as a fraction. The system had to be extended again to include this new class of numbers, which are now called irrational numbers [3A].

Today we use zero (0) to denote the absence of a number, but this has not always been so. The Roman numeral system, for instance, had no zero. It was introduced for its present role in about 600 BC by mathematicians in India who formulated rules for calculating with it: multiplying by zero always gives a zero result and addition or subtraction of zero leaves a number unaltered. Indian mathematicians also recognized that dividing by zero does not produce a result that can be defined by the number system. They also deduced that a fraction in the form $^0/_0$ is meaningless.

Infinite and imaginary numbers

The concept that there are infinitely large numbers was first discussed by the Greek mathematician Archimedes (*c.* 287–212 BC). Starting with the largest number in the Greek number system, "a myriad myriads" (a hundred million), he constructed even larger numbers. He then estimated the number of grains of sand in the universe and

CONNECTIONS

See also
1444 Mathematics and civilization
1446 The grammar of numbers
1452 Finding unknown quantities: algebra
1456 Logarithms and slide rule
870 Communication through writing:1

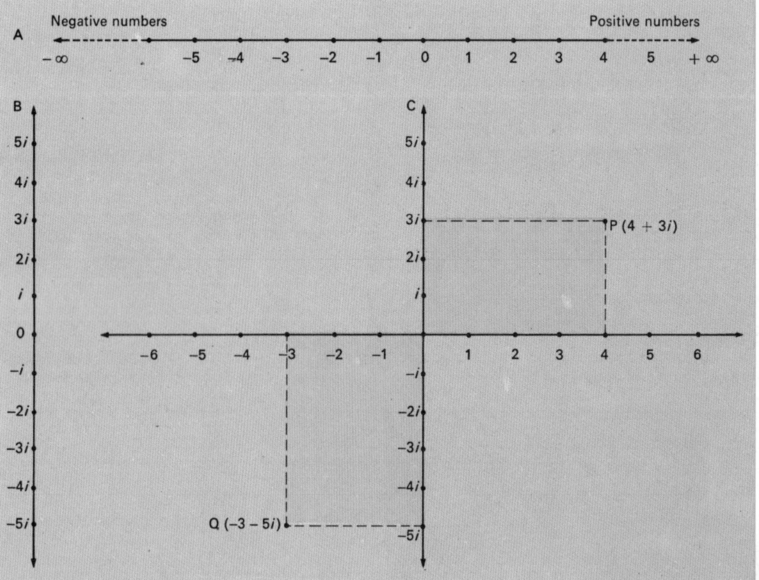
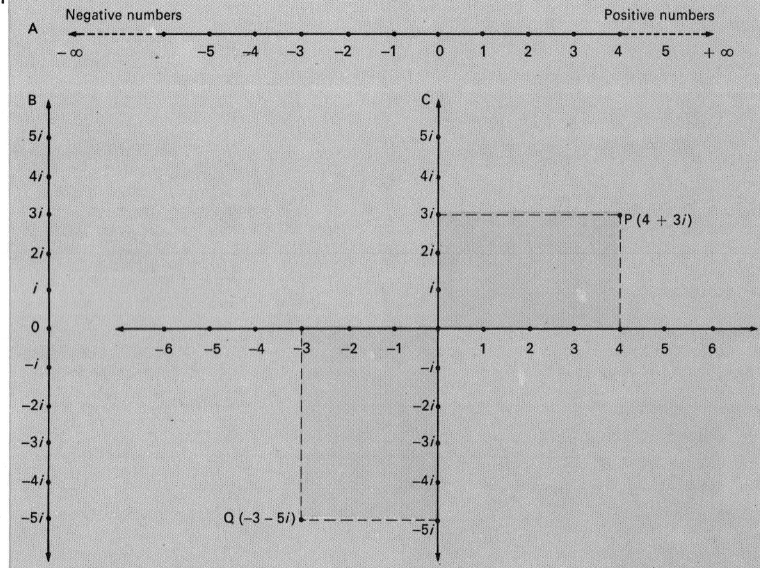

A
Negative numbers
Positive numbers
−∞ −5 −4 −3 −2 −1 0 1 2 3 4 5 +∞
B
C
5*i* 4*i* 3*i* 2*i* *i* 0 −*i* −2*i* −3*i* −4*i* −5*i*
P (4 + 3*i*)
Q (−3 − 5*i*)
−6 −5 −4 −3 −2 −1 1 2 3 4 5 6

1 Three types of numbers are the real, imaginary, and complex numbers. Real numbers [A] can be represented as points along a line extending from minus infinity to plus infinity. They include all negative and positive numbers. Imaginary numbers [B] are based on *i*, the square root of −1, and can also be positive or negative. Complex numbers [C] each have a real and an imaginary part. They can be pictured as points defined by a distance along the real number axis and a distance along the imaginary number axis. Complex number P, for example, is 4 + 3*i*, and Q is −3 − 5*i*.

2 Five oranges, five hens' eggs, and five bottles all have the same property of "fiveness." The number 5, fifth along the positive real number scale shown in illustration 1A, can be applied to any such group of five objects. The bottles do not all have the same shape, but this obviously does not affect their number. Only adding or removing some bottles would alter their "fiveness."

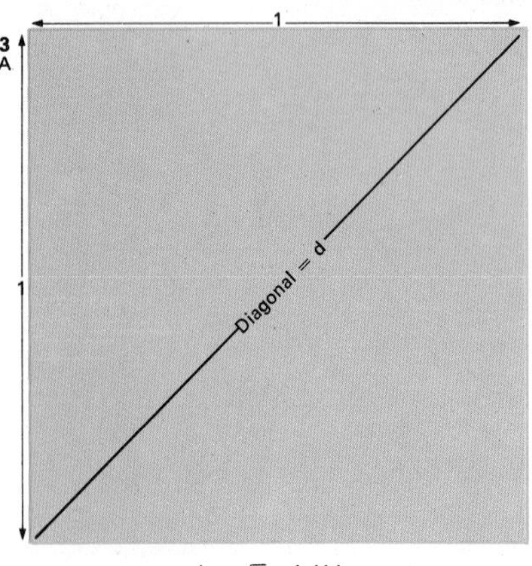

3
A
1
1
Diagonal = d
d = √2 = 1·414...
B
Circumference = C
Diameter = D
C/D = π = 3·1415...

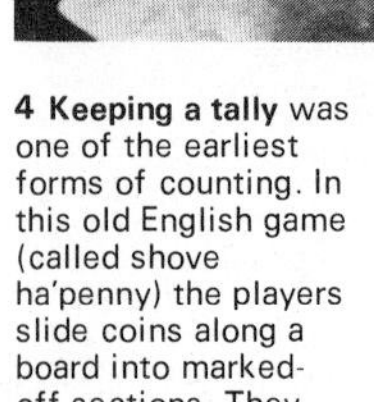

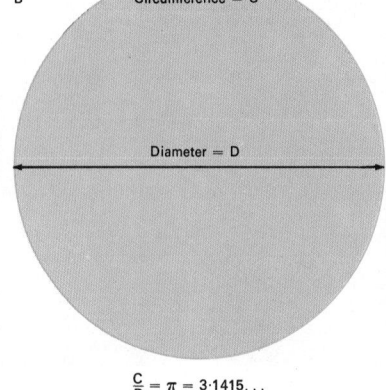

3 An irrational number cannot be expressed as a fraction using integers (whole numbers). A square with sides each one unit long [A] has a diagonal equal in length to the square root of 2. This is approximately equal to 1.414 ..., with a never-ending series of numbers after the decimal point. Another irrational number is the ratio of the circumference of a circle to its diameter [B], represented by the Greek letter π. It is equal to 3.1415 . . . , again with a never-ending series of numbers after the decimal point. A rough approximation to π is given by the fraction (rational number) 22/7, which is equal to 3.1428 . . . . Irrational numbers were discovered by the Greek mathematician Pythagoras (*c.* 582– *c.* 507 BC).

4 Keeping a tally was one of the earliest forms of counting. In this old English game (called shove ha'penny) the players slide coins along a board into marked-off sections. They keep their scores with chalk tally marks at the edges of the board. Ancient farmers probably counted their animals using a tally stick, a piece of wood carved with a series of notches. In some European beer halls today, the waiter gives a customer a new beer mat with each drink and keeps the old mats as a tally of the total drunk by the customer.

showed that this was less than the largest number he could construct. Archimedes showed that there is no upper limit to a number system. Infinity, unlike zero, is not a number. No matter how large a number is, there is still an indefinite number larger than it.

With the concepts of zero and infinity, men had a complete number system that could be pictured as every real number along a line stretching from minus infinity to plus infinity. But with the development of squares and square roots, mathematicians encountered such problems as: what is the square root of -5? At first, such problems were thought to be impossible to solve because there is no real number which, when squared, gives a negative result. Then in the sixteenth century Italian mathematicians introduced the "imaginary" quantity i which, when squared, gives the result -1. Numbers involving i are now called imaginary numbers [1B].

Complex numbers consist of a real part and an imaginary part, such as $5 + 3i$. They can be manipulated in the same way as real numbers. Many branches of modern engineering depend on their use [1C].

The system of numbers commonly used today was adapted from the Arabic numbering system [5], which, in turn, was based on Indian ideas. In this system the position of a digit (numeral) in a number is significant. Using the basic digits 0 and 1 to 9 it is possible to construct any number. This base-10, or decimal, system was introduced into Europe by Adelard of Bath (flourished in 12th century) in about 1100 and by 1600 was in almost universal use.

What is the base?

The base, or radix, is the number of digits in a number system. Position is important because in a number such as 333, the first 3 stands for 300 (three hundreds), the second for 30 (three tens) and the third for 3 units. But any convenient base can be used. Modern digital computers, for example, "count" using the base of 2—the binary system of numbers—because its only digits, 1 and 0, can easily be represented by "on" or "off" pulses of electricity [9B].

KEY

An abacus is an ancient type of calculating machine still used in China and Japan. It has a number of beads on wires, generally divided into two sections with two beads (each standing for 5) and five beads (each of which stands for 1). Numbers are added or subtracted by moving the beads.

5

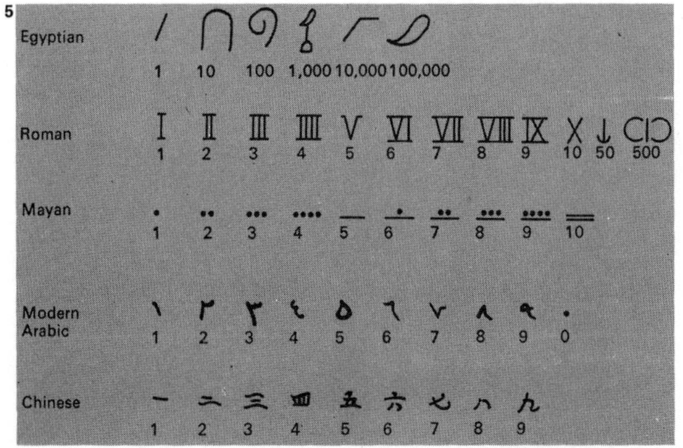

Egyptian
1 10 100 1,000 10,000 100,000
Roman
I II III IIII V VI VII VIII IX X ↓ CIↃ
1 2 3 4 5 6 7 8 9 10 50 500
Mayan
1 2 3 4 5 6 7 8 9 10
Modern Arabic
١ ٢ ٣ ٤ ٥ ٦ ٧ ٨ ٩ ٠
1 2 3 4 5 6 7 8 9 0
Chinese
一 二 三 四 五 六 七 八 九
1 2 3 4 5 6 7 8 9

5 Various numeral systems have been used through the ages. The earliest, such as the Egyptian, used a simple pen stroke or a mark in clay to represent 1; other numbers up to 9 were formed by repeating the 1 symbol. The Romans and Mayans had an additional symbol for 5. Modern Arabic and Chinese have different symbols for each number, although 1 to 3 are formed by adding successive strokes.

6 A B C

6 Clockfaces may have Arabic numerals [A], Roman numerals [B], or no numerals at all [C], because in a clock the numbers have come to stand merely for positions.

7

	English	French	Italian	German	Dutch	Spanish
1	One	Un	Uno	Ein	Een	Uno
2	Two	Deux	Due	Zwei	Twee	Dos
3	Three	Trois	Tre	Drei	Drie	Tres
4	Four	Quatre	Quattro	Vier	Vier	Cuatro
5	Five	Cinq	Cinque	Funf	Vijf	Cinco
6	Six	Six	Sei	Sechs	Zes	Seis
7	Seven	Sept	Sette	Sieben	Zeven	Siete
8	Eight	Huit	Otte	Acht	Acht	Ocho
9	Nine	Neuf	Nove	Neun	Negen	Nueve
10	Ten	Dix	Dieci	Zehn	Tien	Diez

7 The names of numbers in various European languages reveal common word origins. But all these countries use the same number symbols, originally based on early Arabic numerals.

8 Large numbers are awkward to write and have different names even among English-speaking countries. American and British names are different. The scientific use of powers of 10 is unambiguous.

8

Number	American name	British name	Powers of ten
100	Hundred	Hundred	10^2
1,000	Thousand	Thousand	10^3
1,000,000	Million	Million	10^6
1,000,000,000	Billion	(Milliard)	10^9
1,000,000,000,000	Trillion	Billion	10^{12}
1,000,000,000,000,000	Quadrillion		10^{15}
1,000,000,000,000,000,000	Quintillion	Trillion	10^{18}

9 A

DAILY DOUBLE 3 &
1 97,005 5 106.20
2 100,306 6 111.00
3 93,507 7 113.90
4 106,608 8 109.80

B

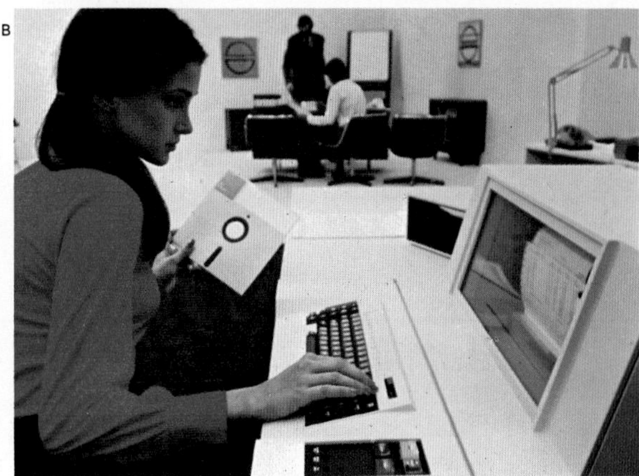

9 High-speed calculations are needed to deal with a changing situation in which numerical quantities vary continually, as at the tote board at a race track [A], which computes winning odds for individual horses in accordance with the amount of money bet on them. For more complicated varying situations, a computer [B] is needed in order to complete the calculation in "real time"—that is, in time for the information to be of use.

Measurement and dimensions

Four students—a chemist, a physicist, a mathematician, and a humanities graduate—were each given a barometer and told to measure the height of a church tower. The chemist knew all about gases. He measured the air pressures at the top and bottom of the tower with his barometer and from the barely perceptible difference produced an answer of "anywhere between 0 and 200ft" (0–60m). The physicist was used to handling expensive equipment casually. He dropped his barometer off the tower and timed its fall, calculating the height as 90–110ft (27–33m). The mathematician compared the length of the tower's shadow with that of the barometer, arriving at a height of 99–101ft (30–30.5m). The humanities graduate sold the barometer, bought the building custodian a few drinks with the money, and found out that the tower was exactly 100ft (30.4m) tall.

Putting numbers on things

This apocryphal story illustrates the variety of ways of arriving at dimensions and the different results that can be obtained. Life in the modern world depends greatly on man's ability to make accurate measurements, and laboratories throughout the world maintain standards of length, time, mass, and voltage to ensure uniformity. Every large factory has a set of reference gauges that have been calibrated against a standard that, in turn, has been checked against a national copy of the standard.

Behind the practice of measurement lies theory. There is the physical theory of the process and also mathematical principles such as dimensional analysis. This derives the "dimensions" of measured quantities in terms of the fundamentals length (L), mass (M), and time (T). Area, for example (square feet, square meters, acres, or hectares), has dimensions (L^2); volume (cubic feet, cubic meters, and so on) has dimensions (L^3). If the volume of a paraboloid were stated to be $\pi H^2/8D$, with H as its height and D its base diameter, then without making any calculations at all a student can be sure that the formula is wrong. It involves the product of two lengths divided by a length and so has dimensions (L^2/fi) = (L). It must therefore represent a length; it cannot possibly represent a volume. (The correct formula is $\pi H^2 D/8$.)

Similarly, given that the time-of-swing *(t)* of a pendulum might depend on its length *l*, the mass of its bob *m* and the acceleration imparted by gravity g, any formula for *t* based on a relationship between *l*, *m*, and g must yield a number with the dimensions of time. Acceleration is measured in feet per second per second, and has dimensions (L/T^2). Thus

$$t \equiv T = \sqrt{T^2} = \sqrt{L \Big/ \frac{L}{T^2}} \equiv \sqrt{l/g}$$

($\equiv$ is the mathematical sign for "is equivalent to".)

In fact the formula is $t = 2\pi\sqrt{l/g}$ (dimensional analysis can never deduce numerical factors such as 2π). There is no room for any number with the dimensions of mass in the expression, so it has been demonstrated here by pure mathematics that the swing of a pendulum does not depend on the mass of its bob.

CONNECTIONS

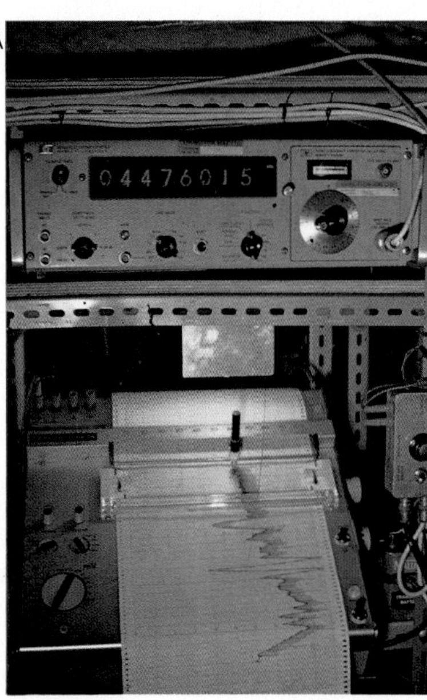

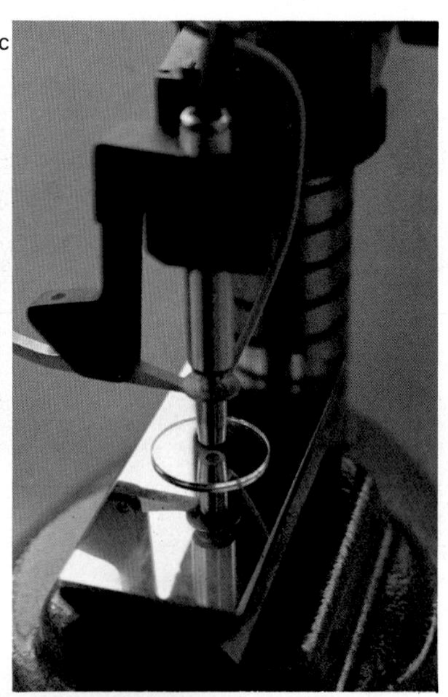

1 Different techniques of measurement have different degrees of precision. The chart-recorder [A, bottom] is precise to about 1 in 100; it is hard to read a chart more accurately than that. The chemical balance [B] can reach 1 in 10^6 and the frequency counter [A, top] 1 in 10^8. Both of these have a numerical display; no meter could be calibrated so finely. An air gauge [C] measures extremely small dimensions by sensing the flow of air through a small gap. Its precision of up to 1 in 10^9 is near the limits of current technology (at about 1 in 10^{11} for a laser gauge). The micrometer is 10 million times less accurate.

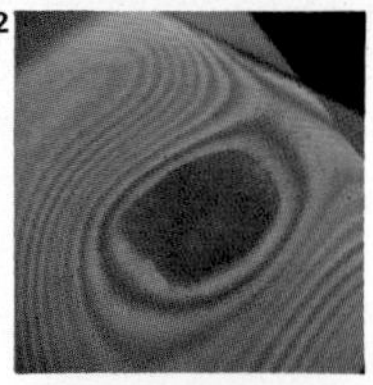

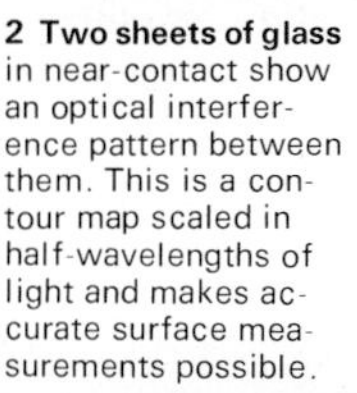

2 Two sheets of glass in near-contact show an optical interference pattern between them. This is a contour map scaled in half-wavelengths of light and makes accurate surface measurements possible.

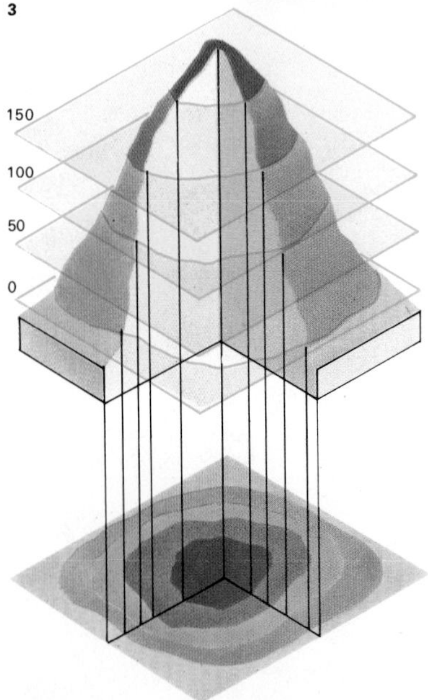

150
100
50
0

3 Recording a three-dimensional shape on a flat surface is a problem that can be solved by the convention of contour scaling. This is shown when the cross-sections of a hill at 50-, 100-, and 150-foot heights are projected on to a map of the hill. The hill can be perceived fairly well from such a map, although the "coarseness" of the contour intervals loses some finer detail. The steepness of the sides can be judged by the contour lines on the map. The interference pattern seen in the contact area of two different lenses is a fine contour map. Special techniques make it possible to reveal tiny deformations of stressed surfaces, or loudspeaker movements as contours.

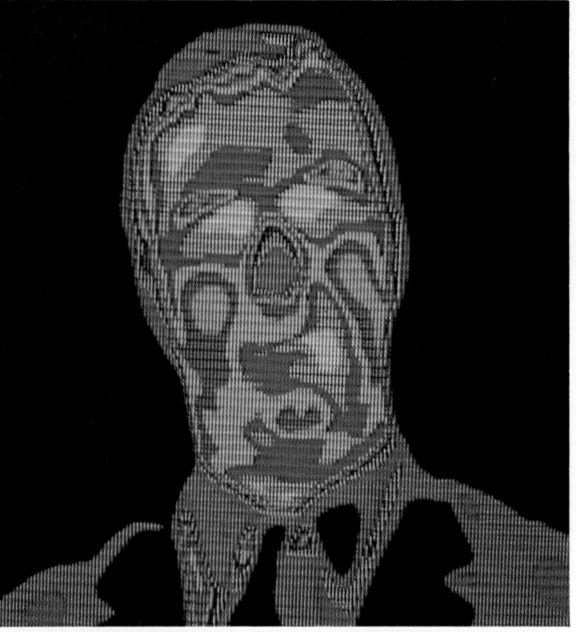

4 A false-color thermogram, also known as a thermoscan, records the temperatures on the skin of a man's face. The technique allows a doctor to study the extent of skin damage caused by burns and has been adapted to aid in the diagnosis of diseases such as cancer of the breast. An infrared camera has a rotating prism scanner that detects the heat levels in a strip of the picture, and the resulting signal is amplified and displayed on a color television screen. Blue colors represent low temperatures; the redder the color, the warmer it is. Thermograms can also help architects design houses for minimum heat loss and aid homeowners to insulate them in the most effective way.

The length in feet and acceleration in feet per second per second must give an answer in seconds. "Coherent" systems of units such as SI units (the international unit system used throughout science) guarantee an answer in correct units. The speed of a piston multiplied by its area and the pressure it exerts gives its power, for example. With units of feet per second, square inches, and atmospheres, the answer would have the dimensions of power (ML^2/T^3) but be in no recognized power-units. Using SI units (meters per second, square meters, and newtons per square meter) guarantees an answer in watts. Other common units are the cgs (centimeter-gram-second) and mks (meter-kilogram-second) systems.

Scaling the heights

If a 20-foot (6-m) scale model of a blade of grass were actually made from grass, it would promptly collapse. Similarly a flea the size of an elephant would not be able even to stand, let alone jump. This is because the weight of an object, like its volume, increases as the cube of its height, whereas its strength increases only as its square. Many related properties scale differently, so it is quite difficult, for example, to calculate what thrust will propel an aircraft from the force needed to sustain a scale model in a wind-tunnel. One way out of this difficulty is to think in terms of "dimensionless groups" like Reynold's Number, valuable in many problems of gas and fluid flow. This is LVd/η, where L is a length (perhaps of a wing-section), V is a gas velocity, d is its density, and η (eta) its viscosity. This particular combination turns out to be a dimensionless ratio—a pure number—and so has the same value in any units and is unchanged by scaling.

Engineers know, for example, that streamline fluid flow becomes turbulent at Reynold's Number around 3,000, no matter what the scale of the experiment. And by working a wind-tunnel at high pressure, thus increasing density d, they can achieve high Reynold's Numbers without the problems of maintaining high gas velocity V. Many other dimensionless groups are known and used in scaling models.

KEY

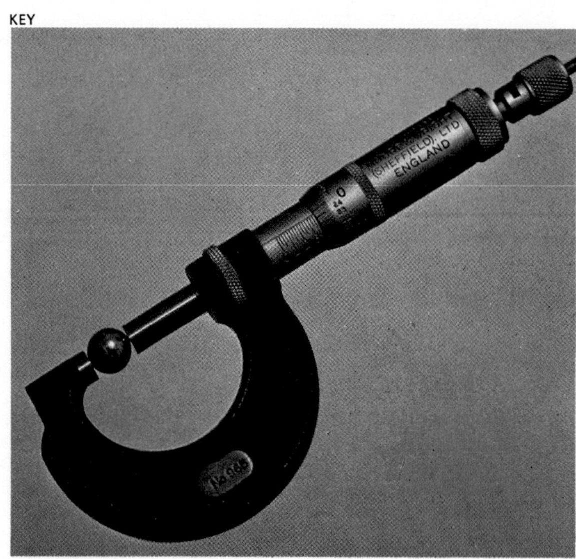
ENGLAND

A micrometer can measure a small object with a precision of up to 1 in 10,000. This is adequate for most high-grade engineering, but far higher precision is possible using other tools.

5

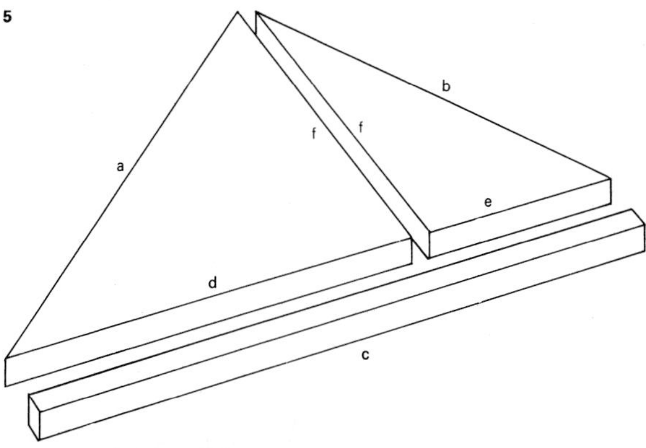
a
b
f
f
e
d
c

5 With c accurately known, *d* is found by measuring *e* and subtracting; error in *e* is diluted in the longer *d*. But obtaining *e* as *c* − *d* is inaccurate; it is a small difference between two larger numbers. Obtaining *f* by the Pythagorean theorem as $\sqrt{a^2 - d^2}$ is worse; squaring the two similar and large values increases their uncertainty. But *e*, *f*, and *b* are all similar lengths, so that *b* could be obtained more accurately as $\sqrt{e^2 + f^2}$.

6

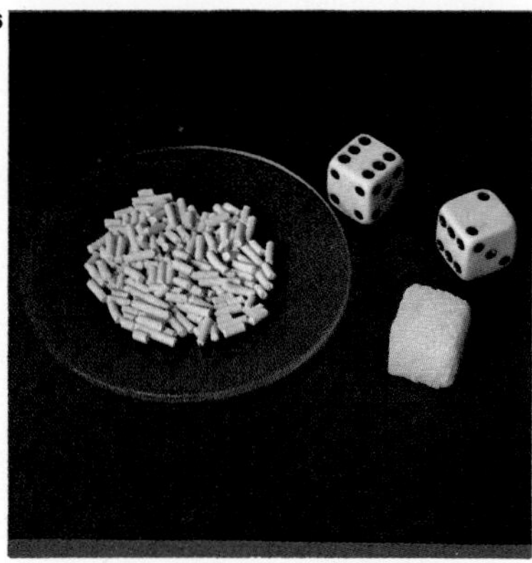

6 By the surface volume scaling law, fine structures have relatively more surface to their volume. Each die weighs .07 oz (2g) and has 1.4in² (9cm²) of surface. The sugar lump is made of .02in (.5 mm) grains and has about 31in² (200 cm²) of total surface. The .07oz (2g) of "molecular sieve" on the watch crystal is porous to the molecular level and has a remarkable 16,150 sq ft (1500m²) of total surface area.

7 A

B

7 If the size of a balloon is doubled, its surface (and therefore weight) goes up four times, but its volume (and therefore lift) goes up eight times. This surface/volume scaling law shows that balloons grow more efficient with size (A). Conversely, doubling an aircraft's size increases its weight by eight times, but the wing area by only four times [B]. Small aircraft pose fewer design problems.

8

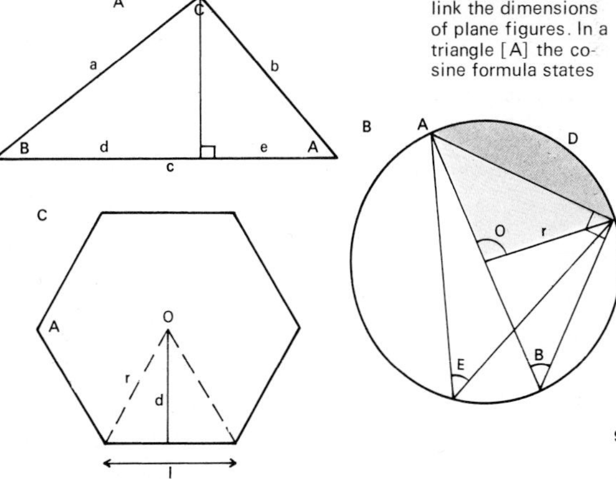
A
a
b
B
d
e
A
c
C
B
A
D
O
r
C
E
B
C
A
O
r
d
l

8 Various formulas link the dimensions of plane figures. In a triangle [A] the cosine formula states $a^2 = b^2 + c^2 - 2bc \cos A$; and the sine formula that $a/\sin A = b/\sin B = c/\sin C$. If $s = \frac{1}{2}(a + b + c)$, the area of the triangle $= \sqrt{s(s-a)(s-b)(s-c)}$. In a circle [B] angle $O = 2B = 2E$ and the circumference of arc *ADC* is $\pi rO/180$. In a regular *n*-sided polygon [C] angle $A = 180\,(1 - 2/n)$; angle $O = 360/n$; the area of the polygon $= \frac{1}{2}nld$ and the radius $r = d \sec(360/n)$.

9 A B

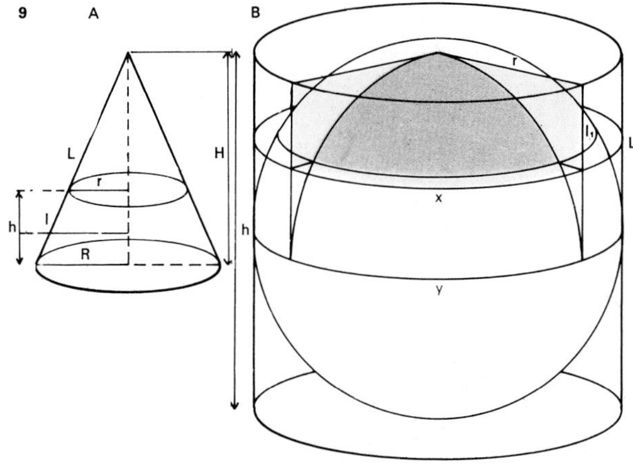
L
H
r
l
h
R
r
L₁
L
x
h
y

9C

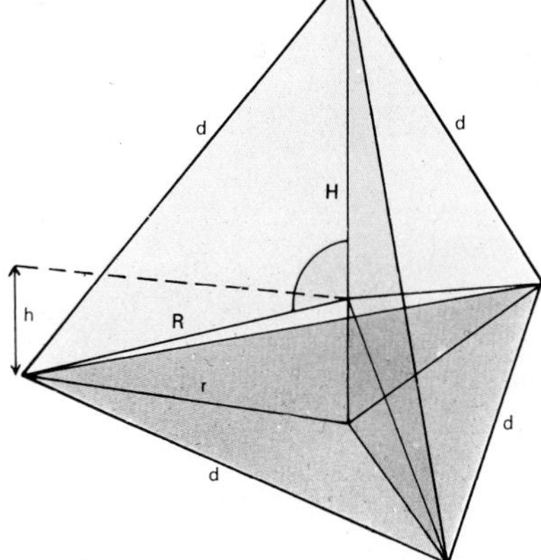
d
d
H
h
R
r
d
d

9 The volumes and areas of solid figures can be linked by formulas. In a cone [A] the volume of the full cone $= \frac{1}{3}R^2H$; and the area of the curved surface is given as πLR. In the frustrum of the cone (the lower section) the area of the curved surface $= \pi l(R + r)$ and the volume $= \frac{1}{3}\pi h(R^2 + Rr + r^2)$. In a sphere and cylinder [B] the surface area of the sphere $= 4\pi r^2$. The curved surface of the cylinder $= 2\pi rh$. The volume of the sphere $= 4\pi r^3/3$; and of a cylinder is given as $\pi r^2 h$. The volume of the section of sphere between planes *x* and *y* $= V\ \pi[L^2(r - L/3) - L_1^2(r - L_1/3)]$. In a regular tetrahedron [C] the formula of distance $r = d/\sqrt{3}$; $H = d(\sqrt{2}/\sqrt{3})$; and $R = \frac{1}{2}d(\sqrt{3}/\sqrt{2})$. The height of the center of gravity is $h = H/4$.

Finding unknown quantities: algebra

In arithmetic various quantities such as lengths, areas, and sums of money are represented as numbers. But some mathematical problems are concerned with *finding* a number—an unknown quantity. If two numbers add up to 10 and one of them is 6, what is the other? The answer to this simple problem in arithmetic is, of course, 4 and yet the method of formalizing it is a basic technique of algebra.

To solve this problem in algebra, let the unknown number be x. Then $6 + x = 10$ (this is an algebraic equation). By subtracting 6 from each side of this equation, it simplifies to $x = 10 - 6 = 4$. By making a letter, x, stand for the unknown quantity, the problem can be solved.

Greek and Arab mathematicians

Greek mathematicians such as Diophantus (*c.* 3rd century AD) used letters in their equations. But the word algebra is derived from the Arabic words *al-jabr*, meaning restoration and reduction, which formed part of the title of a book by the Arab mathematician Al-Khwarizmi. By the sixteenth century, mathematical problems were fully formulated in algebraic terms, initially in France by Franciscus Vieta (1540–1603). The normal convention of using the last few letters of the alphabet *(x, y,* and *z)* to denote unknown quantities and the first few letters to stand for known, prescribed numbers was introduced by the French mathematician René Descartes (1596–1650).

Algebraic equations and formulas

Common practical applications of algebraic equations are the various formulas used in science, particularly in mathematics and physics. The volume of a cylinder, for example, is given by the formula $V = \pi r^2 h$, where V is the volume, r is the radius of one end, and h is the cylinder's height [1]. The formula provides a shorthand way of saying "the volume of a cylinder equals the area of one end multiplied by the height of the cylinder."

Algebraic equations [2] and formulas can be manipulated according to established rules. The cylinder equation can be changed to find the radius or height of a cylinder of known volume. For example, $h = V/\pi r^2$. Such formulas are general—they apply to all cylinders, whether they are tall and thin or short and squat. There are similar formulas for the areas and volumes of all common geometric figures.

Many problems in algebra involve more than one unknown quantity. Consider the problem of finding two positive numbers whose product is 15 and whose difference is 2. Let the two numbers be represented by the letters x and y. Then the "product" information can be stated as the equation $xy = 15$. There are several possible solutions to this equation: 1 and 15, 3 and 5, 7.5 and 2, and so on. To proceed we must use the "difference" information, which generates the equation $x - y = 2$, rearranging to give $y = x - 2$. Substituting this expression for y in the first equation yields $x(x - 2) = 15$, or $x^2 - 2x - 15 = 0$.

Now this third equation contains only one "unknown" quantity: x. The only positive number that satisfies it is 5 (when the equation becomes $(25 - 10 - 15 = 0)$. Finally, to find y we substitute this value of x

CONNECTIONS

See also
1444 Mathematics and civilization
1446 The grammar of numbers
1448 The language of numbers
1456 Logarithms and slide rule
1458 Sets and groups
1454 Mathematical curves
1442 Alchemy and the Age of Reason
1474 Facts and statistics
1476 Odds and probability

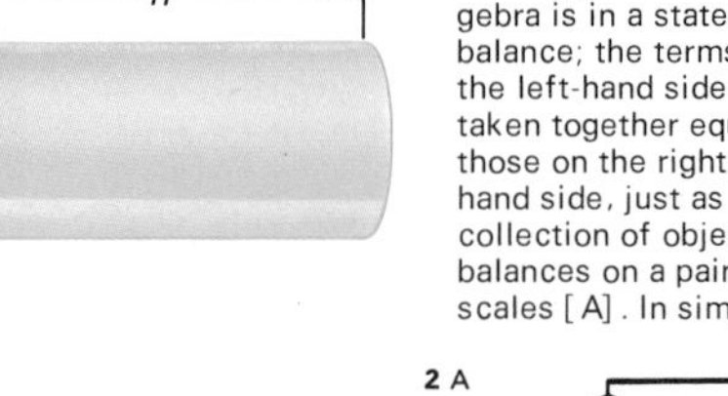

1 A
R
h

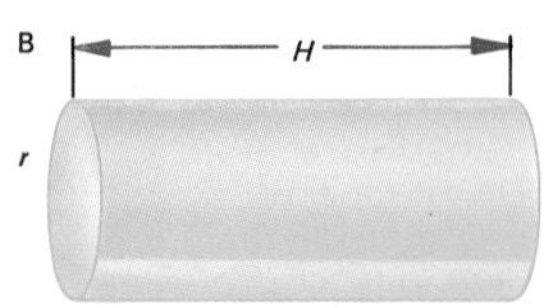

B
H
r

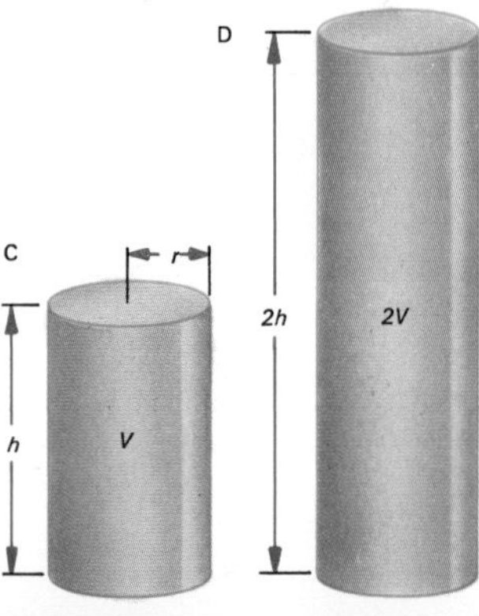

C
r
h
V
D
2h
2V

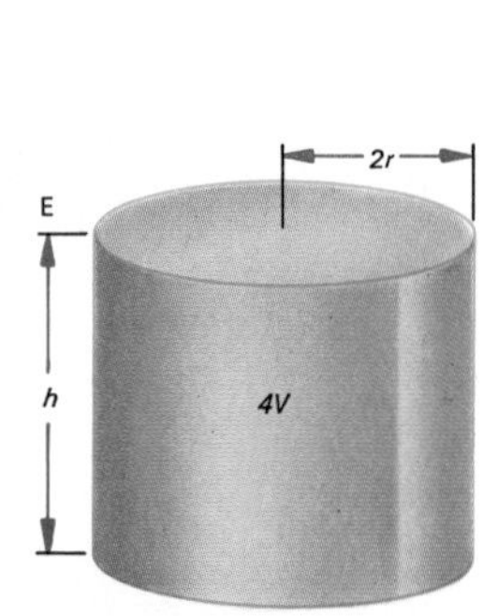

E
2r
h
4V

1 The formula for finding the volume of a cylinder is $V = \pi r^2 h$, where r is the radius of one end and h is the height. The two cylinders [A and B] have the same volume, but very different radii and heights. In fact, the diameter of one is almost equal to the height of the other, that is h is almost equal to r and R is almost the same as H. Another cylinder [C] has volume V. Doubling its height doubles its volume [D] (for C volume $= \pi r^2 h$, for D volume $= \pi r^2 h$). But doubling the radius of the cylinder increases its volume four-fold [E] (for E volume is equal to $\pi(2r)^2 h = 4\pi r^2 h$. Algebra predicts these changes

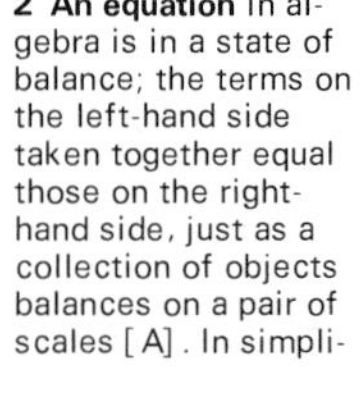

2 A
3x
5y
4x
2y
3x + 5y = 4x + 2y

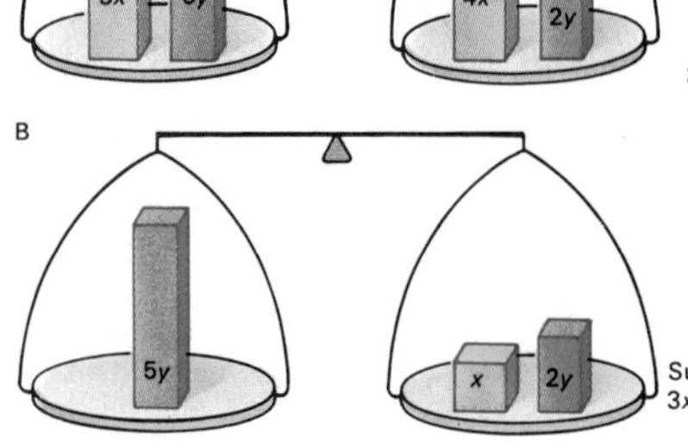

B
5y
x
2y
Subtract 3x from each side:
3x − 3x + 5y = 4x − 3x + 2y
5y = x + 2y

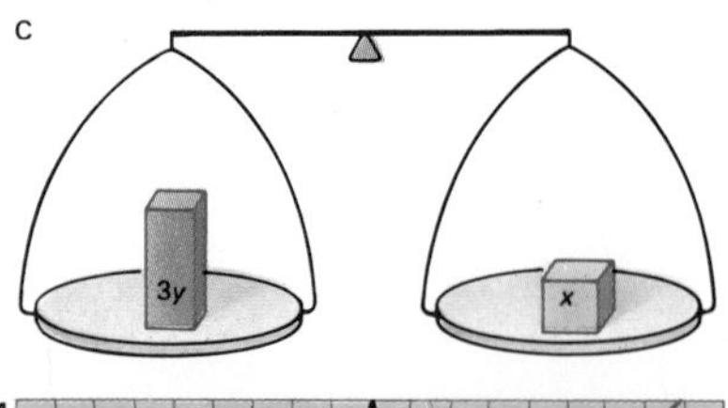

C
3y
x
Subtract 2y from each side:
5y − 2y = x + 2y − 2y
3y = x

2 An equation in algebra is in a state of balance; the terms on the left-hand side taken together equal those on the right-hand side, just as a collection of objects balances on a pair of scales [A]. In simplifying an equation it is essential that the same operation be carried out on each side. For example, $3x$ is subtracted from each pan of the balance [B] (and from each side of the equation). A further simplification is made [C] by subtracting $2y$ from each side. As a result the original equation $3x + 5y = 4x + 2y$ reduces to $3y = x$. It is also possible to multiply or divide each side by a factor.

3 Houses in this street are numbered consecutively. A man notices that four times his number is 10 more than three times his next-door neighbor's. What is his number? Let the house number be x, then the neighbor's is $x + 1$. So $4x = 3(x + 1) + 10 = 3x + 3 + 10$. Subtracting $3x$ from each side of this equation gives $x = 13$. The house number is 13 (and his neighbor's is number 14).

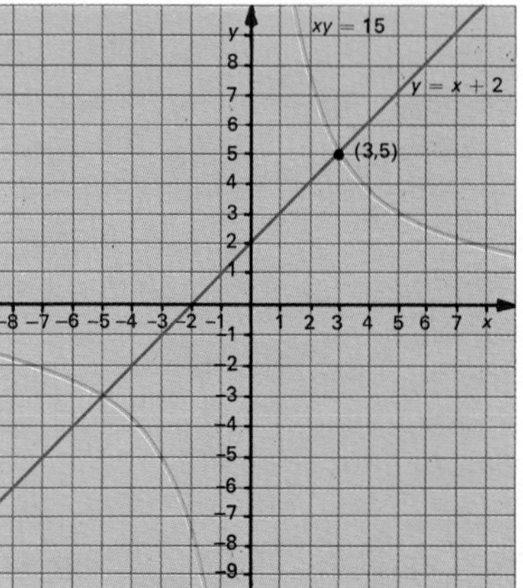

4
y
xy = 15
y = x + 2
(3,5)
x

4 Algebraic equations can be plotted as lines on a graph, a technique that is the function of analytic geometry. This graph shows plots of the equations $xy = 15$ and $y = x + 2$. Treated as simultaneous equations, they are both true at the points where the lines cross. When the equation to a straight line is expressed in the form $y = mx + c$, where m and c are numbers, the letter m is a measure of the slope of the line, here equal to 1.

in either of the two original equations. According to the first, $y = 15/x = 15/5 = 3$ and from the second $y = x - 2 = 5 - 2 = 3$. The answer to the problem is therefore 5 and 3. In algebraic terms, we have solved two equations that are both true at the same time—called simultaneous equations.

By considering points in space defined by referring to their distances from a line (the x-axis) and another line (the y-axis), the equations of algebra take on a new meaning. The equation $xy = 15$, for example, represents a line on which all points have the product of their x-distance and y-distance equal to 15. The equation $y = x + 2$ represents a straight line and all points along it satisfy this equation.

If these two curves are drawn [4] (to a mathematician, even a straight line is a "curve"), they intersect at the point whose x-distance is 3 and whose y-distance is 5—the point defined as (3,5). The graphic approach to the problem gives exactly the same solution as the purely algebraic approach. It also reveals another point at which the curves intersect, corresponding to $x = -3$ and $y = -5$. These solutions are, however, disallowed by the original problem, which called for two *positive* numbers.

The whole procedure of plotting algebraic equations as curves is the function of analytic geometry. It is the branch of mathematics in which algebra and geometry come together.

Algebra also supplies an insight into other puzzles and paradoxes. Any three-digit number whose middle digit is the sum of the other two is divisible by 11. Why? The answer can be supplied by using algebra [5].

Maintaining the balance

The examples already described serve to show the power of algebra in solving problems, particularly by manipulating equations. But there are rules about such manipulation. If there are two unknowns, such as x and y, an equation is simplified by having all the terms in x on one side and all the terms in y on the other. This can be achieved by adding or subtracting equal quantities from each side [2].

KEY

Arithmetic deals with numerical quantities—for example, the number of people in this crowd. But algebra can tackle problems involving unknown quanities, generally by assigning to them a letter which might stand for the number of men.

5

110	220	341	473	671
121	231	352	484	682
132	242	363	495	693
143	253	374	550	770
154	264	385	561	781
165	275	396	572	792
176	286	440	583	880
187	297	451	594	891
198	330	462	660	990

5 The three-digit numbers in this table have two properties in common: the middle digit is the sum of the other two and all of them are divisible by 11. If the first digit is x and the third y, the middle one is $(x + y)$. The whole number has the value $100x + 10(x + y) + y$. This expression can be simplified to $11(10x + y)$; it is a general formula for all the numbers in the table and each has 11 as a factor.

6

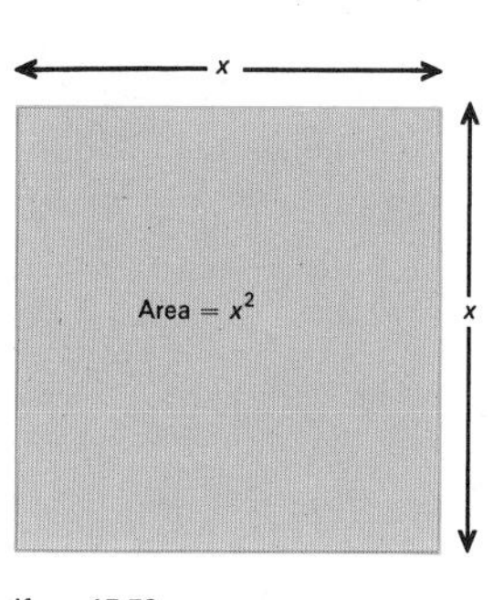

x
Area = x^2
x
If x = 17·72
Area = 314·2

r
Area = πr^2
If r = 10
Area = 314·2

6 Squaring the circle—drawing a square with exactly the same area as a given circle—defies mathematicians. But it can be approximated by using algebra. The area of a circle of radius r is πr^2 and of a square of side x is x^2. For equal areas $\pi r^2 = r^2$, or $x = \sqrt{\pi r^2}$. If $r = 10$ for example, $x = \sqrt{314.2}$, which is about 17.72. The area of a square of side 17.72cm approximately equals a circle of radius 10cm.

7 A

B

Minutes (x)	1·0	2·5	4·0	6·5	7·5	9·0	11·0
Litres (y)	0·6	1·7	2·3	4·0	4·5	5·5	6·6

C

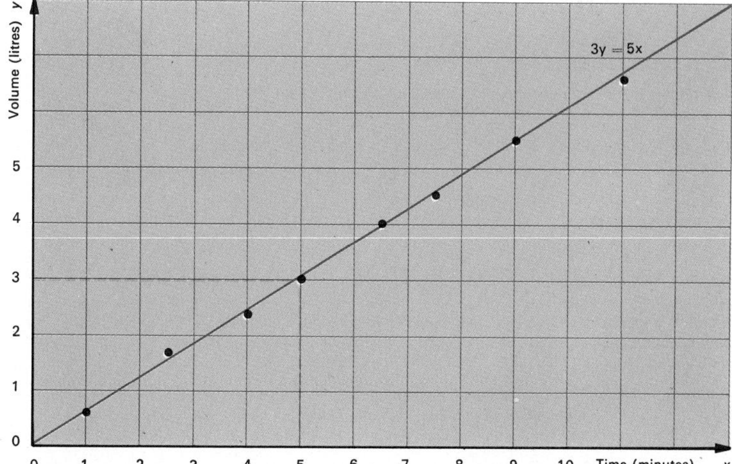

Volume (litres) y
3y = 5x
0
1
2
3
4
5
0 1 2 3 4 5 6 7 8 9 10
Time (minutes) x

7 A woman uses a photographer's clock to time the rate at which a bucket is filling with liquid [A] (the volume of the bucket is calibrated in liters on a scale inside it). The results of the measurements are shown in the table [B]. How much liquid flowed into the bucket after five minutes? To solve this problem she can draw a graph showing the rate of flow [C], which plots volume (liters) against time (minutes). The volume discharge in five minutes can be read off the graph as 3 liters. The graph is a straight line, which best approximates the actual data. It shows that during the time in which she made the measurements the rate of flow was almost constant. The line passes through the origin, at which both axes are zero. It therefore has an equation of the general form $y = mx$, where m is the slope of the line. In this example, the slope is 3/5, so the equation of the line is $y = 3x/5$ or $5y = 3$, from which volume or time can be calculated.

Mathematical curves

Anyone who can catch a ball has an intuitive grasp of mathematical curves and their transformations in space. A thrown ball travels in a mathematical curve that is (very nearly) a parabola: and many athletes can, with the ball still rising far away, begin to run at once to where it will fall. This is not just a simple matter of "seeing where it will go" by elementary estimation. A ball on a long piece of elastic, as is used in some tennis-trainers, is almost impossible to catch even if it is close and moving slowly. It travels in some curve other than a parabola, baffling parabolically-attuned reflexes.

Curves, equations and laws

Gunnery fire-control and ballistic-tracking systems have to predict curves as does the athlete. Lacking his intuitive reflexes, they need high-speed computers to represent the trajectories mathematically. This is done by developing a precise and complete "specification" of the trajectory in the form of an equation. Mathematics is the art of making precise statements, and a mathematical curve is merely one that has such a specification. It does not have to be put in equation form and indeed an informal statement is sometimes clearer. Thus the statement that a circle is a curve on a plane in which every point is the same distance from a given point is easier to understand than the curve of equation $x^2 + y^2 = R^3$ [2].

A mathematician can always translate the specification into an appropriate equation that is true for every point on the curve or surface but false for all other points. He can work out all the properties of the curve by manipulating algebraic symbols, which is much easier than pictorial geometry. When Thomas Telford (1757–1834) built the suspension bridge over the Menai Strait, Wales, in 1826, he had to determine the curve of the hanging chains by setting up a large model across a dry valley and measuring it—a sad consequence of mathematical ignorance. Today an engineer can derive the equation of a suspension bridge cable and find out all he needs to know about it without even drawing a diagram.

Because the world is governed by simple mathematical laws, mathematical curves are all around us. A stone falls in a straight line if dropped or a parabola if thrown; the Moon and artificial satellites move in (very nearly) ellipses; the Sun and Earth are nearly spherical; and a static liquid surface is (very nearly) flat—all because of the mathematical form of the law of gravity. A rainbow is a circular arc and the bright cusp sometimes seen in a sun-lit cup or pan is an epicycloid [9B] because of the laws of optics. Much of the process of scientific discovery consists of observing such things, or conducting experiments to reveal them and then deducing "laws" that must hold to give rise to them. But most often the scientist finds mathematical curves in his results only when he draws them (plots them as a graph). Then the equation of the graph tells him the "law" revealed.

Spheres occur in nature in objects that adopt this shape as the "line of least resistance" to forces affecting them. Small droplets of water and soap bubbles are spherical to minimize their areas under the effect of surface tension. Lead shot was once made by pouring molten lead down

CONNECTIONS

See also
1452 Finding unknown quantities: algebra
1462 Lines and shapes: geometry
1464 Lines and angles: trigonometry

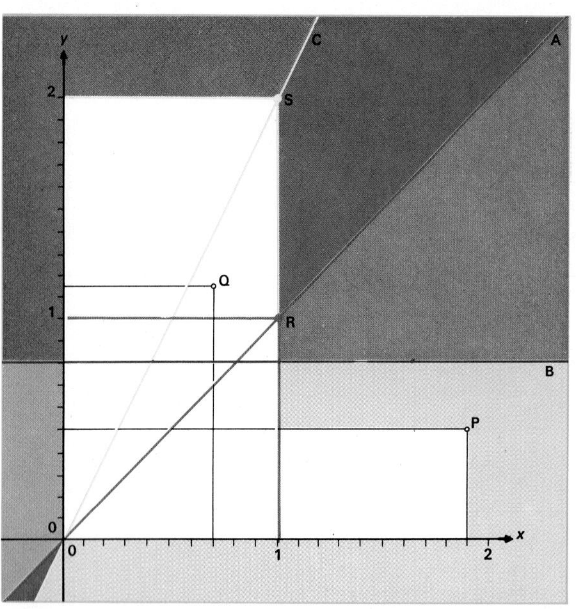
y
C
A
2
S
Q
1
R
B
P
0
x
0
1
2

1 To give a mathematical curve an equation first draw two lines at right H angles: the x axis ([Ox] on the diagram) and the y axis [Oy]. Then every point on the paper can be defined by its "x distance" and "y distance" along these axes. Thus point O has $x = 0.7$ and $y = 1.15$; point P has $x = 1.9$ and $y = 0.5$. On the straight line A it is obvious that for every point on it (eg R, with $x = 1$ $y = 1$) the x distance equals the y distance or $x = y$. This then is the equation of line A as a mathematical curve, true for all points on it and false for all others. Line C has equation $y = 2x$ (as point S shows); line B, equation $y = 0.8$.

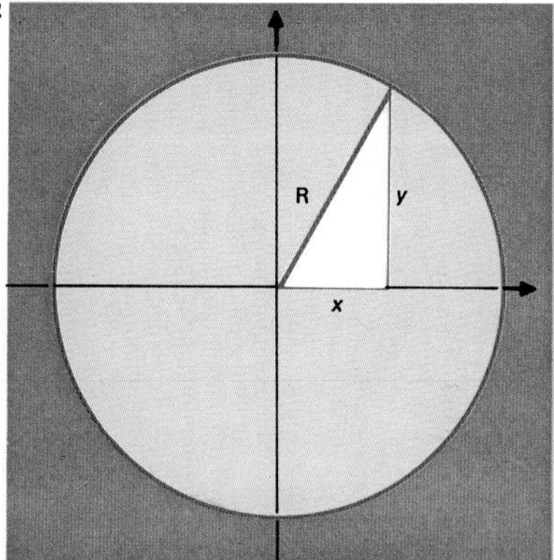
R
y
x

2 To find the equation of a circle, observe that each point on it forms a right-angled triangle whose sides are the x distance and y distance and whose hypotenuse is R. Pythagoras's theorem tells us that $x^2 + y^2 = R^2$. For points outside the circle $x^2 + y^2$ exceeds R^2; inside it $x^2 + y^2$ is less than R^2. Along the intersection the equation balances. All mathematical curves divide space in this way.

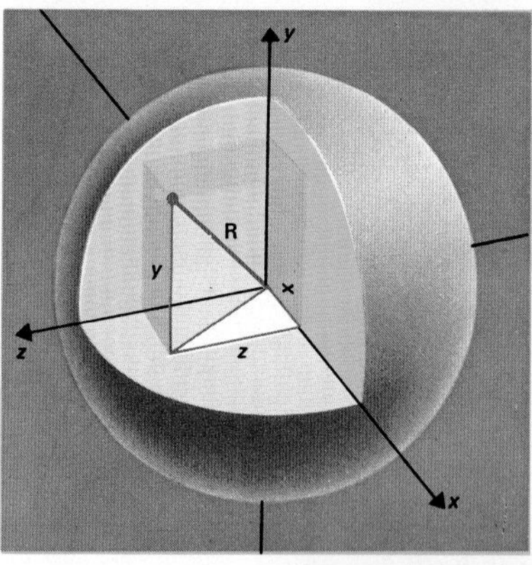
y
R
y
x
z
z
x

4 A mathematical surface can be defined using three perpendicular axes in space, x, y, z. The equation of the sphere is $x^2 + y^2 + z^2 = R^2$. All points outside it have $x^2 + y^2 + z^2$ greater than R^2; those inside have $x^2 + y^2 + z^2$ less than R^2; the equation balances on the boundary. An equation such as $x^2 + y^2 + z^2 - 2x - 8z + 17 = R^2$ also defines a sphere but its center is not on the axes.

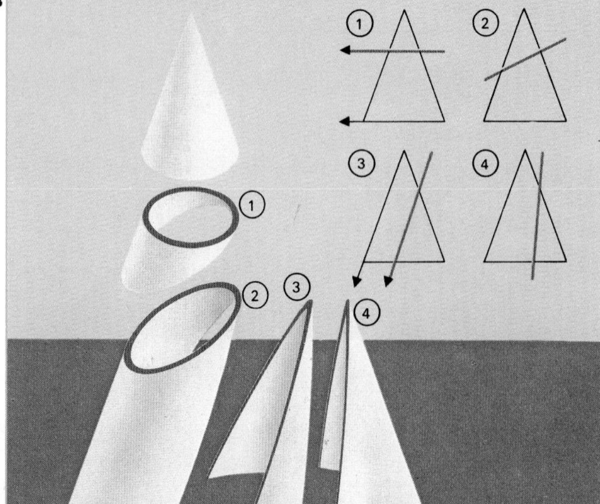
1
2
3
4
1
2
3
4

3 A family of curves results from sectioning a cone. A horizontal section [1] gives a circle; an inclined one [2] an ellipse. A section parallel to one side of the cone [3] gives a parabola and still greater inclination [4] a hyperbola. All these have the same general equation: $ax^2 + by^2 + 2hxy + 2gx + 2fy = c$. With h^2 greater than ab, it is a hyperbola; with $h^2 = ab$, a parabola; h^2 less than ab gives an ellipse, of which the circle ($h = 0$, $a = b$) is a special case. The terms a, b, c, h, g and f are chosen constants; with $b = c = h = g = 0$, $a = 1$ and $2f = 1$, the equation becomes $y = -x^2$. As $h^2 = ab$ (both $= 0$) this is the equation of a parabola.

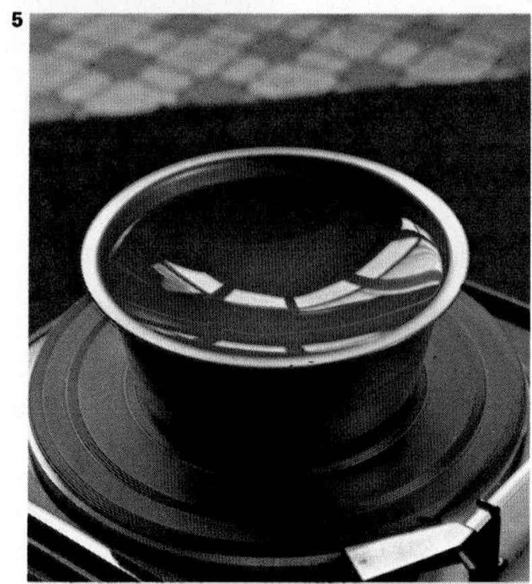

5 A parabola rotated about its axis of symmetry gives a mathematical surface, the paraboloid. A uniformly rotating liquid acquires a paraboloidal surface from the interaction of gravity and centrifugal force, as can be seen by spinning a pan of liquid on a turntable. This surface is perfect for radio- and optical-telescope mirrors; a mirror surface can be made by spinning plastic resin in a dish while it sets and coating it with metal.

inside a tall building into a tank of cold water. During their fall down the tower the droplets of lead formed spheres and cooled sufficiently to retain their shape when they hit the water.

From theory into practice

Mathematical curves and surfaces are involved in all sorts of human activities. Lenses, for example, have spherical surfaces not only because this is a good optical shape but also because it is so easy to make. A spherical surface is the only one that presents the same form and curvature no matter how it is turned. Therefore a hard surface and a soft one, rubbed together with back-and-forth and mutual twisting movements, will wear together into mating spherical surfaces since these are the only ones that enable the two surfaces to fit exactly together every time. As a result, simple grinding processes are sufficient to produce spherical surfaces; where other surfaces are needed manufacture is much more difficult.

Similarly, cylindrical objects (tubes, rods, bolts) and holes are common because this type of surface is readily created by rotating machinery. Boilers and pressure vessels are cylindrical because this shape resists pressure better than others. Cooling towers are hyperboloidal because the two-way "saddle" curvature resists weight and wind loadings well. A trumpet has an exponentially flared horn because this is the mathematically ideal way of launching the intense sound vibrations from its throat into the open atmosphere.

Beauty and the mathematician

The cooling tower, trumpet, bridge arch, and radio-telescope dish all derive their forms from pure mathematical physics. Yet they and other engineering creations have an aesthetic appeal that is sometimes missing in those architectural and automobile creations whose "styling" lacks any mathematical necessity. An interesting consideration is whether the same intuition that enables a person to recognize and respond to the unity and inevitability of mathematical curves at work, also enables him to catch a ball in flight.

KEY

These three bridges over the River Tyne, England, are curves at work. The arches are close to parabolas of different forms. The parabola is ideal for an arch whose weight is negligible compared to the even weight of the roadway. For an actual bridge the arch's own weight must be allowed for.

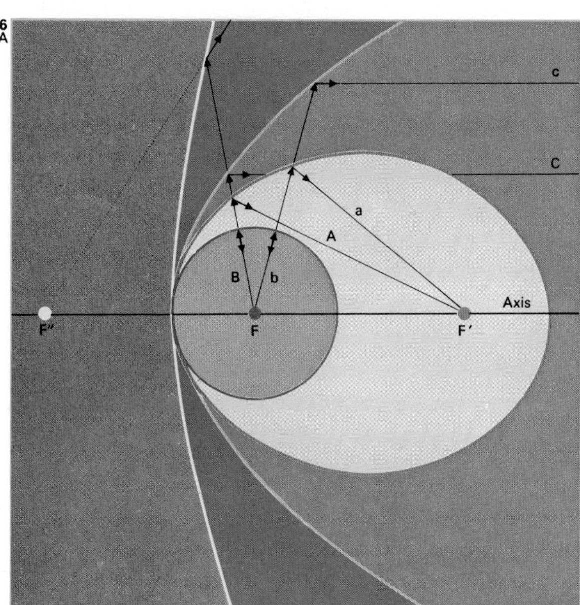
6
A
c
C
a
A
B
b
Axis
F''
F
F'

6 The conic sections [A] all have characteristic "reflecting" properties. An ellipse has two foci [F, F'] such that rays emitted from one converge [A, a] on the other. A circle is an ellipse with its foci coincident and an emitted ray is reflected straight back [B, b]. A parabola is like an ellipse with the other focus infinitely far away. Rays emitted from the true focus are reflected parallel to its true axis [C, c]. The hyperbola reflects rays from F as if they came from another focus F'' behind it. Paris subway tunnels are almost elliptical and whispering on one platform can be heard on the other by the focusing effect [B].

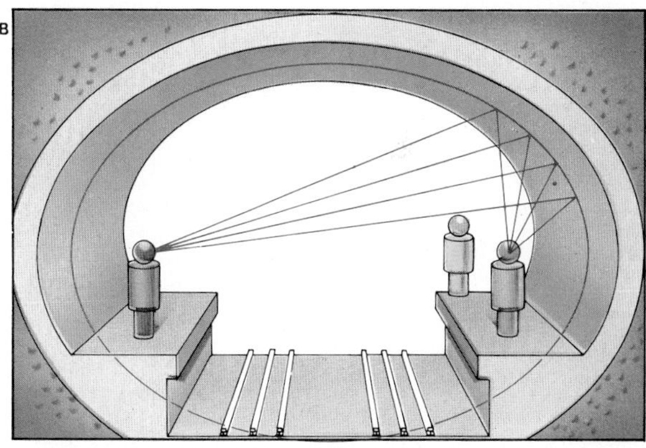
B

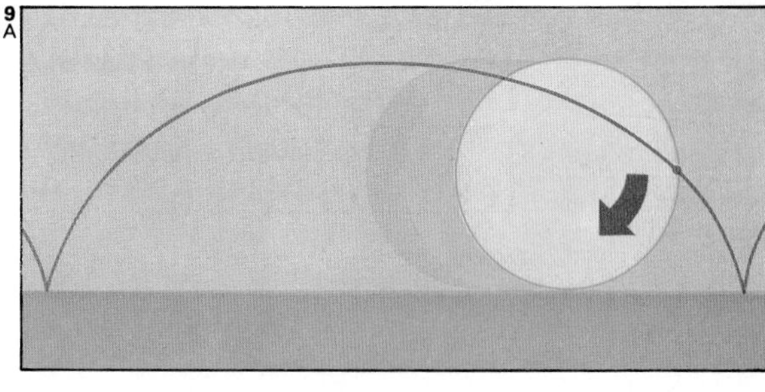
9
A

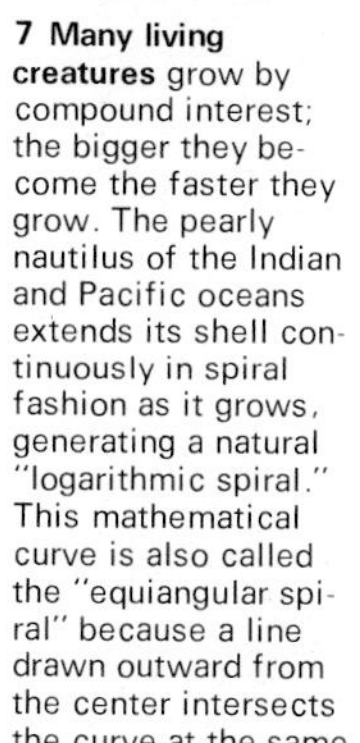

7 Many living creatures grow by compound interest; the bigger they become the faster they grow. The pearly nautilus of the Indian and Pacific oceans extends its shell continuously in spiral fashion as it grows, generating a natural "logarithmic spiral." This mathematical curve is also called the "equiangular spiral" because a line drawn outward from the center intersects the curve at the same angle.

7

8

8 An "Archimedean spiral" is traced by a point that travels around a center varying in distance from it in proportion to the angle it moves through. Similarly a helix is the curve of a point that moves around a cylinder, traveling along it in proportion to its total angular rotation. Both are created automatically by a lathe whose cutting tool traverses a rotating workpiece. Many cylindrical objects show their machine finishing as a fine helical pattern on the surface.

9 A point on the rim of a rolling wheel traces out a cycloid [A]. This famous mathematical curve received attention from Galileo, who suggested it as an archform for stone bridges, and Newton, who proved that inverted, it was that surface down which a particle slid in the minimum time. A wheel rolling on another wheel generates an epicycloid [B]. To mesh smoothly without "stepping" from tooth to tooth gear wheels need teeth of defined curves. The rise of an epicycloid from the inner wheel is one ideal curve. The point on the rim of a wheel rolling inside another wheel generates a curve called a hypocycloid.

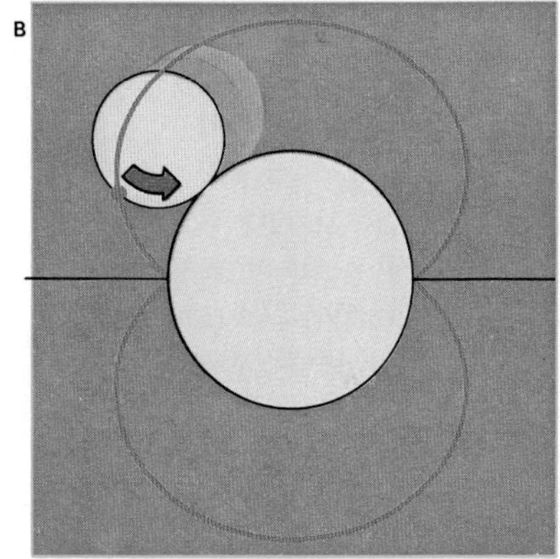
B

Logarithms and slide rule

As the science of mathematics and its applications progressed, men found themselves having to carry out more and more complicated calculations—especially ones involving multiplication and division. Even a modern computer or electronic calculator takes longer to multiply two numbers than to add them, and this is certainly true of human mathematicians.

Both multiplication and division were simplified during the sixteenth century by the introduction of decimal notation. Then a Scottish mathematician, John Napier (1550–1617), published his book *Mirifici Logarithmorum Canonis Descriptio* (1614), which announced the discovery of logarithms. At the time of his death Napier was still working on preparing a set of logarithm tables and the task was completed by the English mathematician Henry Briggs (1561–1631).

Arithmetic and geometric progressions

A practical form of Napier's ideas about logarithms was a set of numbered rods, or "bones," that could be used for carrying out multiplication by merely using the mathematical operation of addition [1]. As with logarithms (and the slide rule) they made use of two types of progressions, called arithmetic and geometric.

An arithmetic progression is a series of numbers in which each is obtained by adding a "common difference" to the one before it in the series. The ordinary ordinal sequence of numbers for example—1, 2, 3, 4, and so on—is an arithmetic series with a common difference of 1. In a geometric progression, each term is obtained from the previous one by multiplying it by a "common ratio." In the series 2, 4, 8, 16, and so on, the common ratio is 2.

In the three following series:

1	2	3	4	5	. . .
10	100	1,000	10,000	100,000	. . .
10^1	10^2	10^3	10^4	10^5	. . .

the first is an arithmetic progression and the second a geometric one (with a common ratio of 10). The third row, equivalent to the second, shows how the succeeding powers of ten in the second series are in an arithmetic progression.

The powers (exponents) in the bottom row are called the logarithms of the corresponding terms in the middle row "to the base 10." The logarithm of a number is the power to which the base must be raised in order to equal the number. Thus the logarithm of 100 to the base 10 is 2 (because $10^2 = 100$).

Logarithms, pianos, and guitars

Ten is not the only base for logarithms; Napier's original tables were to the base "e" (an irrational number) and are still much used in science, where they are called natural, or Naperian, logarithms. The pitch of the notes on a piano is in a logarithmic ratio to the base 2, whereas the keys are in a linear sequence of octaves [2].

The sound wavelength of any note is twice that of the one an octave above it. The pieces of metal called frets across the fingerboard of a guitar also form a logarithmic series (in terms of spacing).

Numbers expressed in terms of powers or exponents are multiplied by adding the exponents. Thus $10^2 \times 10^4 = 10^{2+4} = 10^6$.

CONNECTIONS

See also
1448 The language of numbers
1446 The grammar of numbers
1452 Finding unknown quantities: algebra

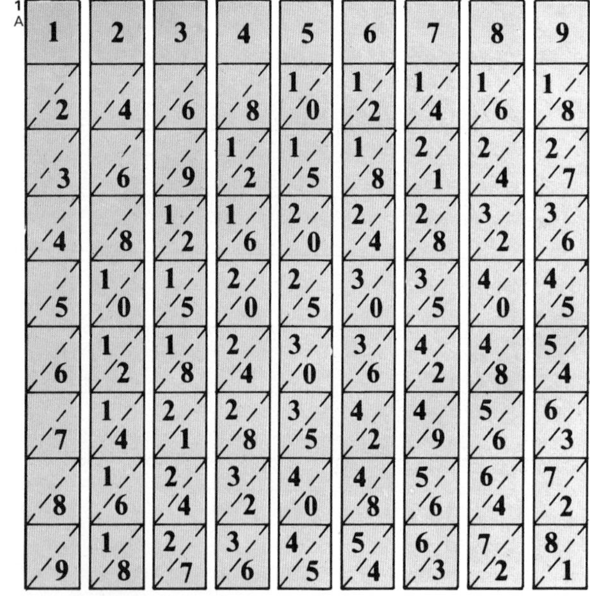
1
A

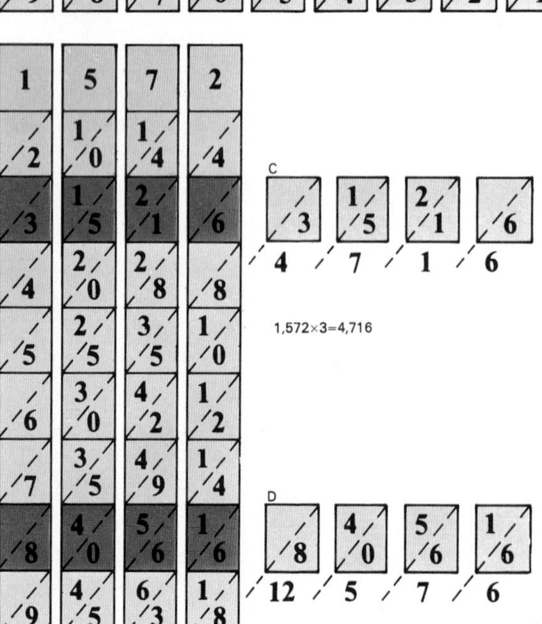
B
C
4 7 1 6
1,572×3=4,716
D
12 5 7 6
1,572×8=12,576

1 Napier's bones consisted of a set of nine square-section rods [A] housed in a tray. They were numbered 1 to 9 in the first segment and the lower segments on each rod were divided diagonally. These segments were numbered down the rods in arithmetic series, the "one" rod numbers increasing by 1 (to give 1, 2, 3, 4, and so on), the "two" rod by 2 (2, 4, 6, etc), the "three" rod by 3 (3, 6, 9, etc), and so on for the whole set, ending with the "nine" rod, which was calibrated in nines (9, 18, 27, 36, etc). The other faces of each square rod were similarly calibrated, so that each number (1 to 9) was represented four times somewhere in the set. To find the multiples of a number—for example 1,572—the rods numbered 1, 5, 7, and 2 are removed from the tray and laid side by side [B]. To find 3 × 1,572 the third row of rod segment is used, as at [C]. The numbers displayed can be added diagonally as shown, to yield 4,716, which is the required product. To find 8 × 1,572, the segments in the eighth row are used, as at [D]. When added diagonally, the numbers displayed this time add to 12,576—again the required product. To multiply by a larger number, say 38, the appropriate products are added together (47,160—a zero is added because we are now multiplying by 30—and 12,576) to give 59,736.

2 The frequency of a note in music is twice that of the one an octave below it. On a keyboard instrument the frequencies of a note and its successive octaves are in the proportions 1: 2: 4: 8: 16, etc. This is a logarithmic scale to the base 2. The spacing of the metal frets across the fingerboard of a guitar are also in a logarithmic sequence, and by pressing his fingers against each in turn the guitarist is able to play the notes up a chromatic scale. An unfretted instrument such as a violin works on the same principle but the divisions are not marked on the fingerboard and must be judged by ear.

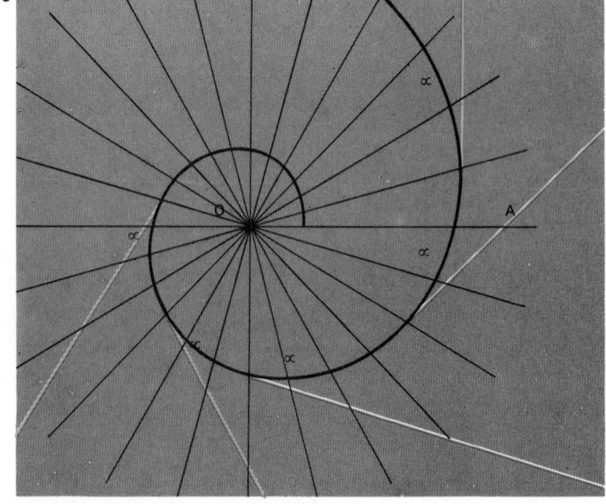
O
A

3 In this curve the angle between a tangent at any point and the radius drawn from the center is constant. For this reason it is called an equiangular spiral. The lengths of the radii to the curve are proportional to the logarithms of the angles between the radii and the initial horizontal direction OA, so it is also known as a logarithmic spiral.

And since logarithms are also exponents, to multiply two numbers their logarithms are merely added and tables can supply the number whose logarithm is the result. In this way multiplication is reduced to the much easier task of addition. Similarly, logarithms can be used to perform division by actually carrying out a subtraction.

To calculate in decimal numbers, logarithm tables need be compiled only for the numbers between 0 and 9.999 (in four-figure tables; five-figure tables include 9.9999, and so on to as many figures as required). Large numbers are expressed by adding a whole number (integer) called the characteristic, which represents in base-10 logs the corresponding power. The four-figure logarithm to the base 10 (written $\log_{10}$) of 2, for example, is 0.3010 [4]. The log of 200 is 2.3010 and of 2,000 is 3.3010 (200 is $10^2 \times 10^{0.3010} = 10^{2.3010}$.

The slide rule

A slide rule [5] is a mechanical device for multiplying and dividing numbers. Logarithmic scales are engraved on rods that can be slid in relation to each other, and numbers on them added or subtracted as needed—added for multiplication and subtracted for division. Because of the log scale, the numbers become closer together along the slide. Unlike an ordinary ruler the scale is geometric rather than arithmetic [6].

In its simplest form a slide rule has only two scales (called the *X* or *D* scales on a complicated slide rule). To multiply two numbers, the 1 on the upper scale is set opposite one of these numbers on the lower scale and the required product read off it opposite the second number on the upper scale [6A]. For division the two numbers are lined up and the quotient read off against the 1 [6B].

The accuracy of a slide rule is limited mainly by its length. A cylindrical slide rule [7] has scales up to a yard long wound around it like a screw thread. Most ordinary slide rules have additional scales to aid various types of calculations: reciprocal (a scale of all the numbers divided into 1), square (numbers multiplied by themselves), square root, and even trigonometric functions.

KEY

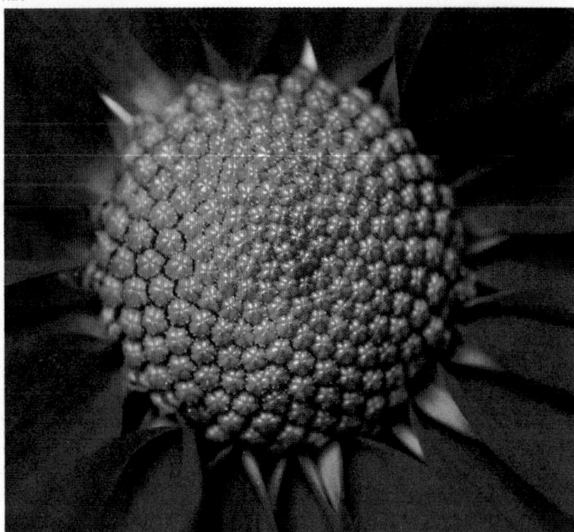

The curve shown in illustration 3 is a logarithmic spiral. Such curves occur in nature, generally revealing the effects of accelerating growth, as in the spiral shells of snails and various other mollusks and in the centers of flowers like this one.

4

	0	1	2	3	4	5	6	7	8	9	1	2	3	4	5	6	7	8	9
10	0000	0043	0086	0128	0170	0212	0253	0294	0334	0374	4	8	12	17	21	25	29	33	37
11	0414	0453	0492	0531	0569	0607	0645	0682	0719	0755	4	8	11	15	19	23	26	30	34
12	0792	0828	0864	0899	0934	0969	1004	1038	1072	1106	3	7	10	14	17	21	24	28	31
13	1139	1173	1206	1239	1271	1303	1335	1367	1399	1430	3	6	10	13	16	19	23	26	29
14	1461	1492	1523	1553	1584	1614	1644	1673	1703	1732	3	6	9	12	15	18	21	24	27
15	1761	1790	1818	1847	1875	1903	1931	1959	1987	2014	3	6	8	11	14	17	20	22	25
16	2041	2068	2095	2122	2148	2175	2201	2227	2253	2279	3	5	8	11	13	16	18	21	24
17	2304	2330	2355	2380	2405	2430	2455	2480	2504	2529	2	5	7	10	12	15	17	20	22
18	2553	2577	2601	2625	2648	2672	2695	2718	2742	2765	2	5	7	9	12	14	16	19	21
19	2788	2810	2833	2856	2878	2900	2923	2945	2967	2989	2	4	7	9	11	13	16	18	20
20	3010	3032	3054	3075	3096	3118	3139	3160	3181	3201	2	4	6	8	11	13	15	17	19

To calculate 1·113×1·456

Logarithm of 1·113=

0·0453 + 0·0011 = 0·0464

Logarithm of 1·456=

0·1614 + 0·0018 = 0·1632

To multiply, add the logarithms:

0·0464
+ 0·1632
= 0·2096 log

i.e. 1·113×1·456= 1·620

4 Log tables can be used to multiply or divide numbers. In this example 1.113 is found by adding the log under 1.11 to that for 0.003, to give 0.0464. Similarly the log of 1.456 is 0.1632. The two logs are then added to give 0.2096 and the required product is the number that has this logarithm—the number 1.620 in the table. In practice, results are found by consulting tables of antilogarithms.

5

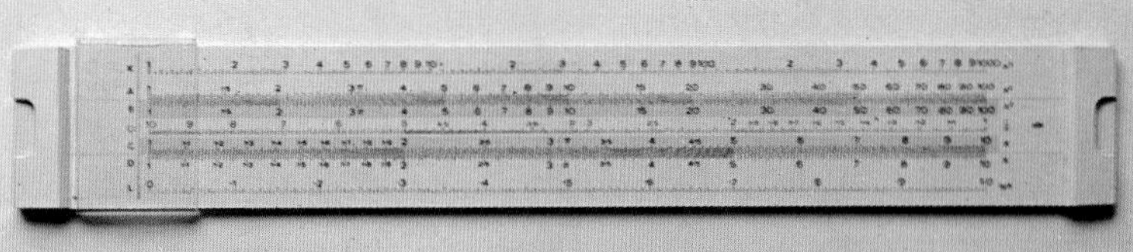

5 A modern slide rule has various scales such as *x*, x^2 $1/x$, square root of *x*, and so on. Some also have trigonometric and other functions for calculations by navigators, engineers, and others.

6

A

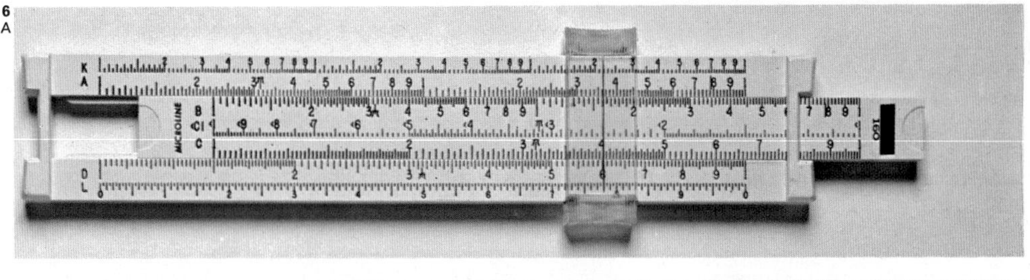

B

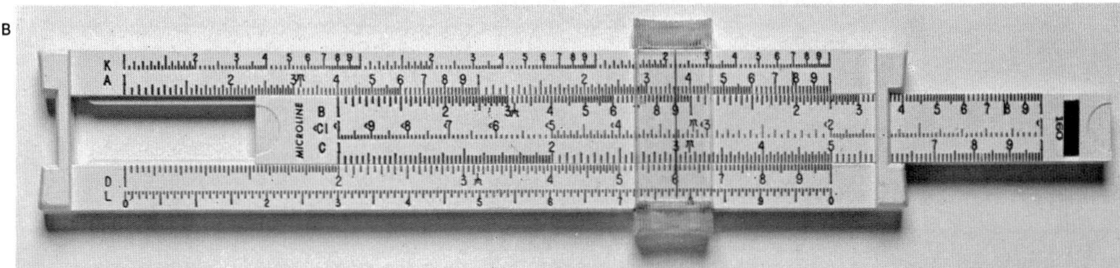

6 To multiply using a slide rule [A], for example to find the product of 1.5 and 4, the 1 on the upper (C) scale is lined up with 1.5 on the lower (D) scale. The product is read off on the lower scale opposite the 4 on the upper—in this example to give 6. The example of division [B] is 6 ÷ 3. The 3 on the C scale is lined up with the 6 on the D scale and the answer read off opposite the 1 on the C scale. In this example the required answer is seen to be the number 2 on the D scale.

7

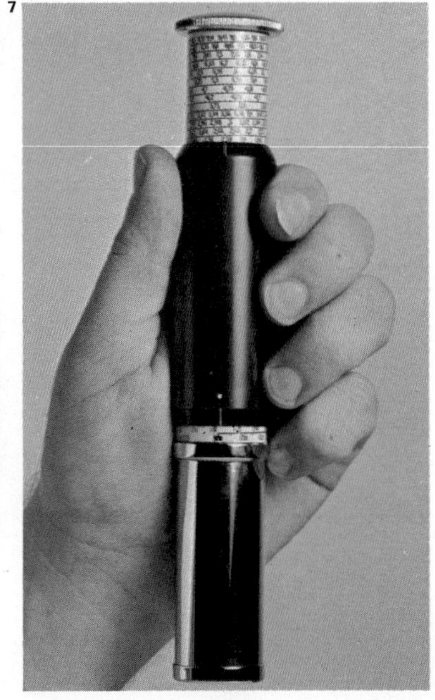

7 A cylindrical slide rule can be pictured as a set of long scales wound around the cylinder like a screw thread.

Sets and groups

The mathematical theory of sets was first investigated by Georg Cantor (1845–1918) and later systematized by Ernst Zermelo (1871–1956), but the basic concepts were known earlier. Some adults who are new to these ideas find them difficult, but children have an intuitive grasp of them. The concepts of number and operations on numbers are abstractions from the concrete experience of sorting and combining sets of physical objects.

Collecting objects together

The idea of a set is the most fundamental concept in mathematics. A set is a collection of objects with a common description or definition, listed in any order or according to a formal law. The set of oceans, for example, is defined as: oceans = {Pacific, Atlantic, Indian, Arctic, Antarctic} or O = $\{x \mid x$ is an ocean$\}$. The letter O labels the set; x is called a variable; {and} are called braces; and the symbol | means "where" or "such that." This kind of set is a finite set because its cardinality (number of elements) is finite—it has a known value, in this case five. The set of counting numbers is an infinite set because we cannot say even in theory exactly how many elements it has: counting numbers = {1, 2, 3, . . . }, or C = $\{x \mid x$ is a counting number$\}$.

The set of natural numbers is J^+ = {1,2, 3, . . . }, with the same elements as the set of counting numbers. We say that C and J^+ are equal sets. Sets with the same cardinality are called equivalent sets. For example, the set {blue, green, yellow, orange, red} is equivalent to the set of oceans—they each have five elements.

The language of sets can be understood by studying a particular example. A universal set [1], the set of all elements under consideration, can be divided into what are called disjoint subsets—that is, non-overlapping sets. If there are only two such sets, one is the complement of the other [2]. The set of elephants living at the North Pole is an example of the empty, or null, set, since it has no elements. The null set is written as ϕ. In illustration 2, for example, there is no intersection of sets A and B, or P and C, so the intersection equals ϕ. The concepts of subsets, complement, intersection [3], and union [4] are fundamental to the processes of classification of information.

Networks [5] give rise to the Cartesian product of two sets. This is obtained by finding all possible ordered pairs of elements, taking one from each set. The word Cartesian is derived from René Descartes (1596–1650), who propounded the concept of coordinates. If set X is associated with the infinite set of points making one line in a plane, and set Y is associated with the infinite set of points making another intersecting line in the same plane, the Cartesian product of X and Y is associated with the infinite set of points making the plane containing the two lines [6].

Boolean and propositional algebra

The algebra of sets is known as Boolean algebra. It is isomorphic—that is, it has a one-to-one correspondence—with the algebra of propositions or logic. It is named after George Boole (1815–64), who founded the modern study of logic. The two types of algebra use different symbols, with *union*

CONNECTIONS

See also
1452 Finding unknown quantities: algebra
1472 Mathematics and mapping
1448 The language of numbers
854 Logic and the tools of philosophy

1 A

B

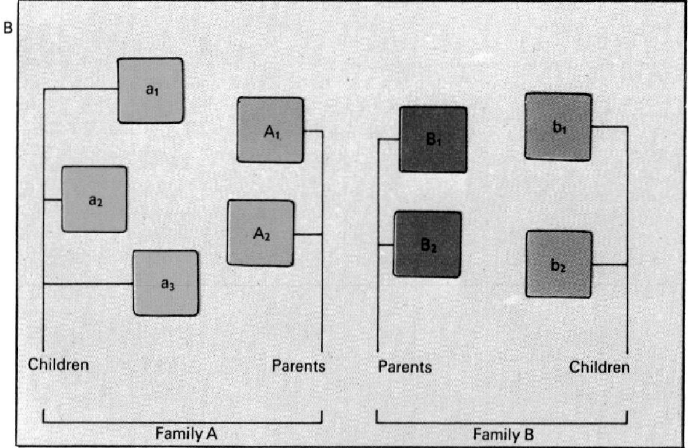

a₁
A₁
B₁
b₁
a₂
A₂
B₂
b₂
a₃
Children
Parents
Parents
Children
Family A
Family B

1 Two families – one with three children and one with two—together make up a universal set [A]. It can be represented diagrammatically [B] and letters given to each of the elements in the set. The letters are then sufficient for the mathematical manipulation of the set in what are called Venn diagrams, first introduced by the mathematician John Venn in 1880. In such diagrams, areas represent sets of things.

2 A

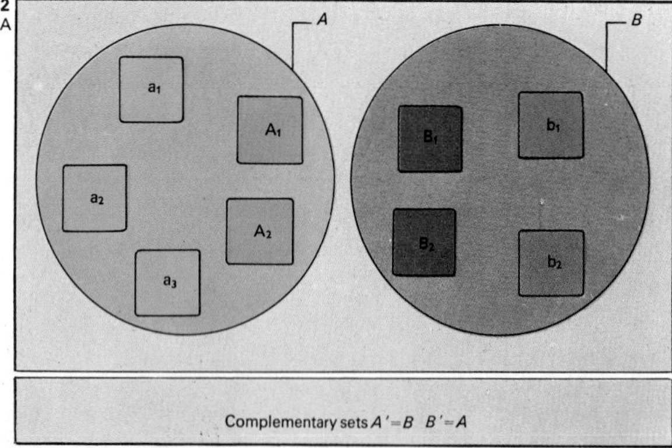

A
B
a₁
A₁
B₁
b₁
a₂
A₂
B₂
b₂
a₃
Complementary sets A′=B B′=A

B

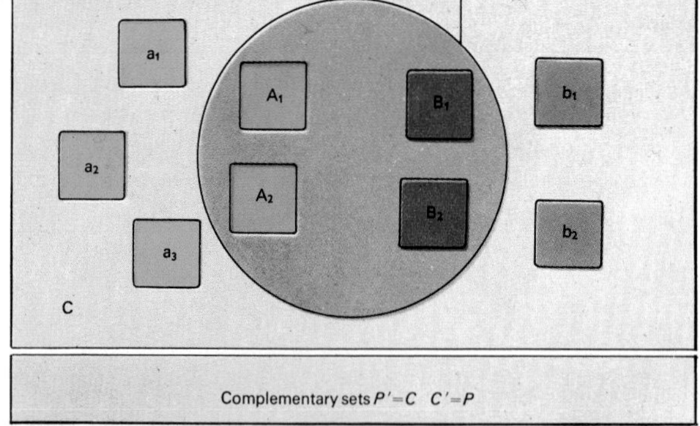

P
a₁
A₁
B₁
b₁
a₂
A₂
B₂
b₂
a₃
C
Complementary sets P′=C C′=P

2 These Venn diagrams show how the universal set of illustration [1B] can be split into two non-overlapping subsets. Each family can make up a subset [A] or the parents and children can each form subsets [B]. In each case the subsets are complementary because they include among them all the elements of the original universal set. The complementary relationships in [A] are written as $A' = B$ and $B' = A$.

3

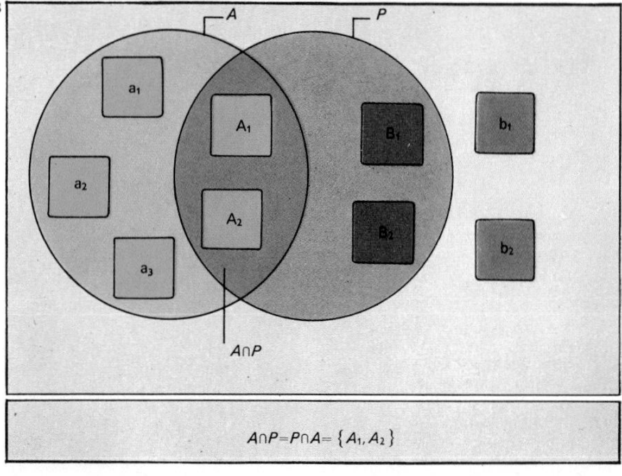

A
P
a₁
A₁
B₁
b₁
a₂
A₂
B₂
b₂
a₃
A∩P
A∩P=P∩A={A₁, A₂}

3 Intersection of sets generates another subset that contains all the elements common to both. Here the intersection of A and P (written as $A \cap P$) gives a subset containing only A_1 and A_2.

4

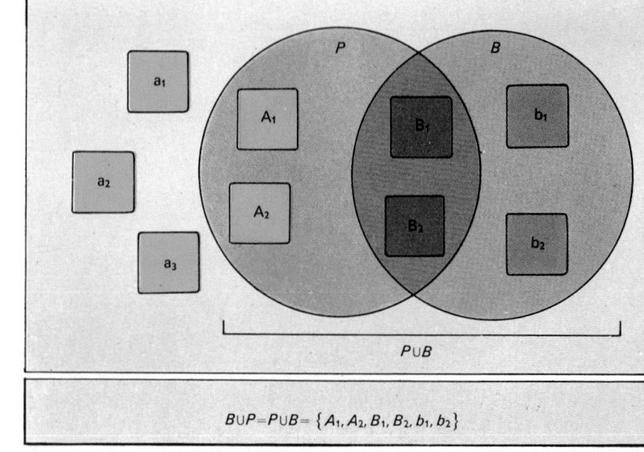

P
B
a₁
A₁
B₁
b₁
a₂
A₂
B₂
b₂
a₃
P∪B
B∪P=P∪B={A₁, A₂, B₁, B₂, b₁, b₂}

4 Union of sets generates yet another subset that contains all the elements in two original sets, in this example B and P. It is written $B \cup P$ and contains the elements A_1, A_2, B_1, B_2, b_1 and b_2. $B \cup P = P \cup B$ shows the commutative law.

(∪) and *intersection* (∩) corresponding to *or* (∨) and *and* (∧). Propositional algebra analyzes the sets of logical possibilities in which various statements and combinations of them are either true or false.

A mathematical system is created when one or more binary operations are applied to a set of elements. A binary operation combines two elements into a third of the same set. One of the most valuable systems is the "group," as it occurs in many diverse situations and helps to unify the study of mathematics. The concept of a group can be illustrated by studying a simple case of formation dancing [8] in which four dancers change their positions or remain still according to various movements. The movements form the set and the operation is a combination of movements called "follows," indicated mathematically by the symbol ⊗. Combining any two movements results in one of the four. The identity element is I and each element is its own inverse in this particular example. We have the relationships $(J \otimes K) \otimes L = L \otimes L = I$ and $J \otimes (K \otimes L) = J \otimes J = I$, so that the associative law $(J \otimes K) \otimes L = J \otimes (K \otimes L)$ is valid. In the particular example of dancing there is another law, the commutative law: $A \otimes B = B \otimes A$.

From the four possible choices available in moving a rectangle [9], a set of four transformations arises. These can be paired by the operation "follows" to produce a combination of movements that is in a one-to-one correspondence to those in the dancing example. The two systems are said to be isomorphic. The search for isomorphisms is essentially the core of mathematical study since they are the basis of abstraction.

The usefulness of group theory

Group theory is useful in the study of number systems. The set of integers (whole numbers) with 0 included, $\{\ldots -3, -2, -1, 0, +1, +2, +3, \ldots\}$, is a group under addition with 0 as the identity element. The set of rational numbers is a group under addition if 0 is included. It is a group under multiplication if 0 is excluded. The use of group theory in the study of arithmetic not only enriches it but leads to higher mathematical concepts.

KEY

Any collection of objects constitutes a mathematical set—a collection of cans of soup, bottles of vinegar, shopping carts, or customers in a store are all definable sets.

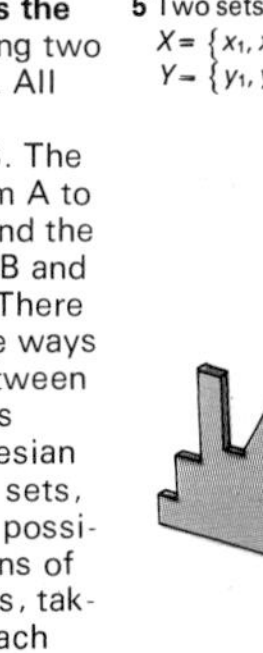

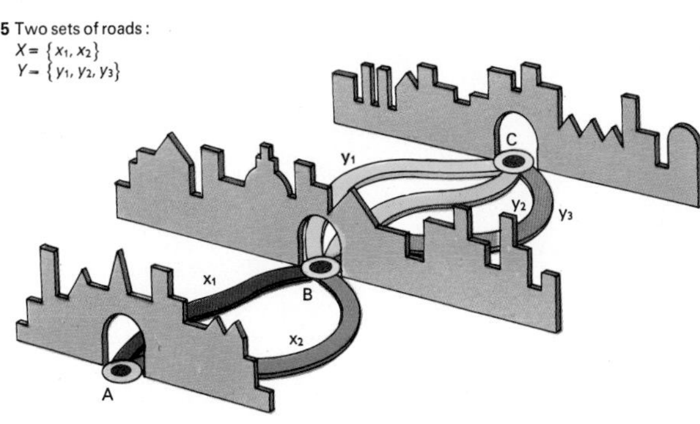

5 Two sets of roads:
$X = \{x_1, x_2\}$
$Y = \{y_1, y_2, y_3\}$
A
B
C
x_1
x_2
y_1
y_2
y_3
Six possible routes: $X \times Y = \{(x_1, y_1), (x_1, y_2), (x_1, y_3), (x_2, y_1), (x_2, y_2), (x_2, y_3)\}$

5 A map shows the roads connecting two towns A and C. All the roads pass through town B. The two routes from A to B are one set and the three between B and C another set. There are six possible ways of traveling between A and C. This is called the Cartesian product of two sets, in this case all possible combinations of paired elements, taking one from each set. The study of networks is one aspect of topology.

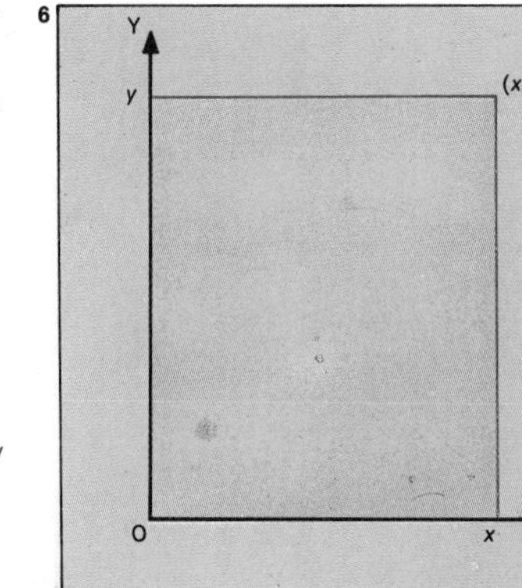

6
Y
y
(x, y)
O
x
X

6 A plane defined by two lines is related to the Cartesian product of two sets that represent an infinite number of points along the lines. The point of intersection of the two red lines is defined by the coordinates x and y, written (x,y). These are called Cartesian coordinates and are used in coordinate, or analytic, geometry in which all lines, whether straight or curved, can be expressed in algebraic equations.

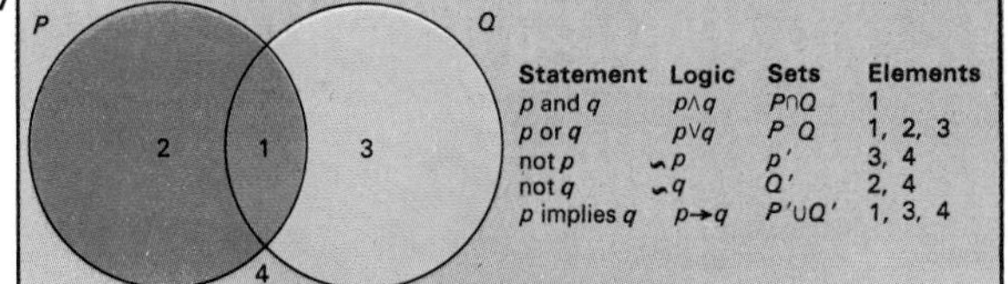

7
P
Q
2
1
3
4

Statement	Logic	Sets	Elements
p and q	p∧q	P∩Q	1
p or q	p∨q	P Q	1, 2, 3
not p	~p	P'	3, 4
not q	~q	Q'	2, 4
p implies q	p→q	P'∪Q'	1, 3, 4

7 Union and intersection in set theory correspond to "or" and "and" in logic. This relationship enables particular elements and combinations of elements from sets to be defined by logical statements.

8
A

8 Four dancers [A], starting at the corners of a square, can have various positions [B], represented by the symbols I, J, K, and L. Carrying out pairs of movements results in new positions [C] described as J follows I, for example. Sequences of three movements can be analyzed as two and the final position predicted. L follows K follows J reduces to L follows L, equals I.

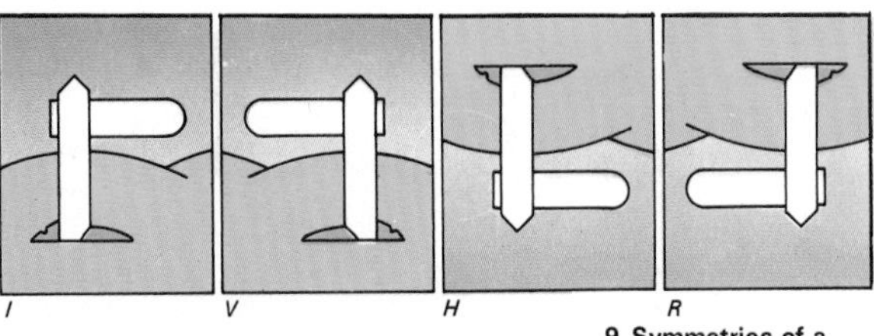

9
I
V
H
R

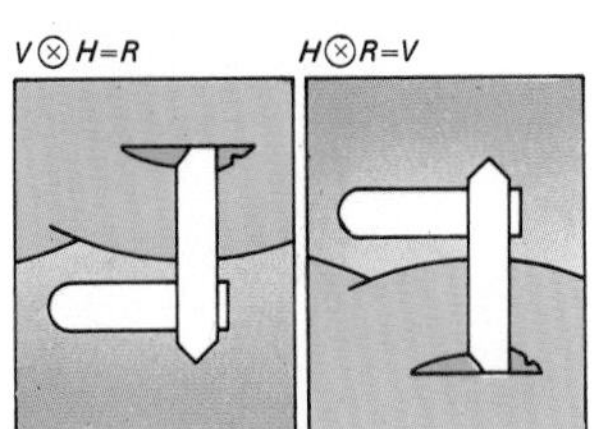

V⊗H=R
H⊗R=V

9 Symmetries of a rectangle involve rotating it in various ways—vertically V, horizontally H, or in the plane of the picture R. The letter I represents its original position. Again successive pairs of movements result in one of the four.

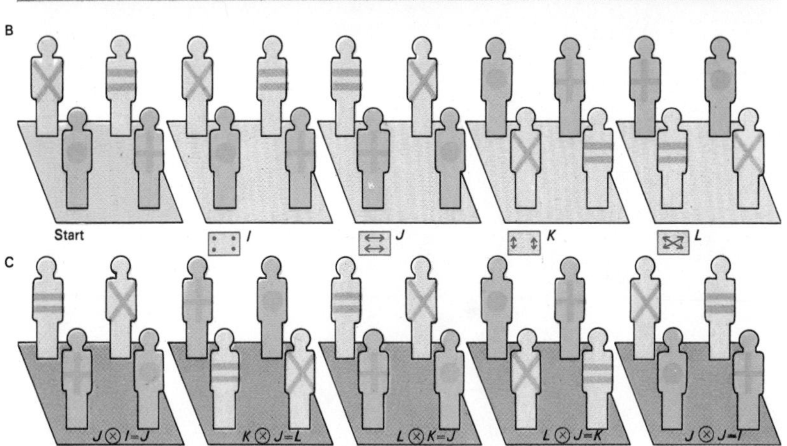

B
Start
I
J
K
L
C
J⊗I=J
K⊗J=L
L⊗K=J
L⊗J=K
J⊗J=I

Finding changing quantities: calculus

In a "political vocabulary" compiled for a newspaper, the noun "decrease" was cynically defined as: "reduction in rate of increase—as in unemployment, crime, inflation, taxation, etc." This not only exposes official double-talk [2] but also highlights the universality of a central concept of calculus—rate of change.

Rates of change became important in physics in 1638 when Galileo (1564–1642) concluded that a falling or thrown body had a downward velocity that increases steadily—that is, its rate of increase of downward velocity is constant [1]. What then is its trajectory? It took the genius of Isaac Newton (1642–1727) and Gottfried Leibniz (1646–1716) to solve this problem; the tool they created was calculus.

Velocity, said Newton, is rate of change of position with time—60mph, for instance. Similarly, acceleration is rate of change of velocity with time. A car that takes 10 seconds to reach a speed of 60mph from a standing start has an average acceleration of 6mph per second. Galileo's law is that the downward acceleration of a falling body is constant. Calculus provides the methods for obtaining velocity from acceleration and position from velocity, and the whole problem is neatly solved. The calculus operation of deriving velocity from position, for example, is called differentiation. Its inverse—finding position from velocity—is called integration.

The simplicity in symbolism

All mathematics is a kind of symbolic machinery for making subtle conceptual deductions without having to think them out—all the thought has been built into symbolism. Calculus is perhaps the supreme example of a symbolism whose economical elegance reduces intractably complex and elusive problems to simplicity. With it, any student can solve problems of motion, growth, and form vastly more complex than the one that resisted the genius of Galileo for half a lifetime.

In mechanics, the branch of physics for which calculus was invented, it is omnipresent in Newton's second law of motion: force equals mass multiplied by acceleration. Given any two of these quantities, the equation defines the third. Consider an internal combustion engine. What is the instantaneous acceleration of the piston as it passes the top of its compression stroke? Calculus provides the answer, so that knowing the piston's mass, it is possible to find the force on it that must be withstood by the connecting-rod. For what speed will this force become excessive? Again, the pressure on the piston during the power stroke is changing every instant with the burning of the charge and the changing volume of the gases in the cylinder as the piston descends. What then is the total energy imparted to the piston by the whole stroke and for what moment of ignition is it a maximum? This and a myriad other mechanical problems could hardly be formulated, let alone solved, without calculus.

Electronic applications

Analogous applications occur in electrical engineering [Key]. Take, for example, a resistor, across which the voltage is propor-

CONNECTIONS

See also
1446 The grammar of numbers
1448 The language of numbers
1452 Finding unknown quantities: algebra
1454 Mathematical curves
1492 Speed and acceleration
1548 Basic electronic principles

1
A

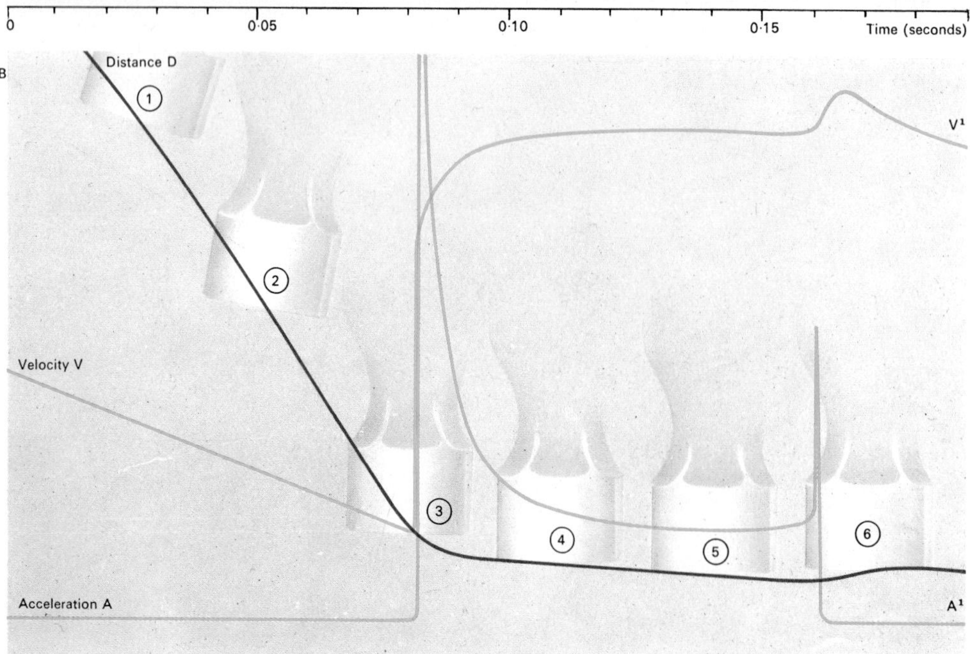

0
0·05
0·10
0·15
Time (seconds)
B
Distance D
V¹
Velocity V
Acceleration A
A¹
1
2
3
4
5
6

1 A falling hammer is shown [A] in six exposures 0.03sec apart and the hammer position curve [D in diagram B] follows them [1–6] exactly. Its changing slope is important and diagram C explains how this is measured, like a road gradient, by tangent triangles with so many units vertically for each one horizontally. The slopes at points 7–11 of line 12 are 0:2, 1:2, 2:2, 3:2, and 4:2, respectively—or 0, 1/2, 1, 1 1/2, and 2. Line 13 plots the increasing slope of line 12. (Obtaining a slope curve from a curve is called differentiation; the reverse is integration.) In [B], the slope of the distance curve for the first exposure is given by a vertical drop of 2.8 cm for a time-interval, measured horizontally, of 0.02 sec. So the velocity here is 2.8cm in 0.02sec = 140 cm/sec. Similar slope measurements give the velocity at other points and yield velocity curve V, which initially increases downward, like the distance. The acceleration (the rate of change of velocity with time) is the slope of the velocity curve—constant while the hammer is falling freely (curve A). At exposure 3, the hammer hits the nail at 200 cm/sec and things start to happen. In a millisecond (thousandth of a second) the velocity is reduced to about 40 cm/sec (curve V); this rapid deceleration drives A off-scale upward to perhaps 100 times its free-fall value. Newton's law then gives a correspondingly large force on the nail, 100 times the weight of the hammer, and this is how the hammer works—driven by the force generated by rapid deceleration of the head. As the wood seizes the nail the shock kicks the hammer upward; then in free fall again the hammer resumes steadily increasing downward velocity V¹ and constant acceleration A¹.

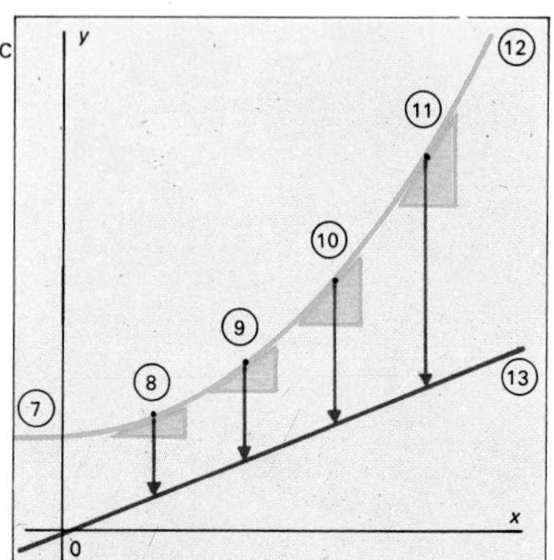

C
y
x
0
7
8
9
10
11
12
13

tional to the current; a capacitor, in which the current is proportional to the rate of change of voltage with time; and an inductor, where the voltage is proportional to the rate of change of current with time. Connect them together and apply an alternating voltage. What happens? Calculus swiftly expresses this seemingly mind-boggling tangle as a differential equation and solves it to show, among other things, that at a certain frequency the whole system "resonates" and very large currents can flow for very little applied voltage. Resonance is of fundamental value throughout electronics. The tuning control of a radio selects one station out of many be setting a circuit to resonate at the station's transmission frequency.

One powerful application of calculus is in seeking maximums, minimums, and optimums generally. A vertically thrown ball is momentarily stationary at the top of its flight; when the height is a maximum, the rate of change of height with time is zero. It can be formed by differentiating the expression relating height and time and setting this equal to zero. This is a general rule of great value—for all technology is governed by the search for optima.

What is the optimum speed for a journey, for example? Too slow wastes time, too fast wastes fuel; both of these have an assignable cost. Calculus enables the rate of change of overall cost with speed to be found and the speed for which it is zero. This must then be the speed for minimum cost. Such calculations are essential in making the best use of ships and aircraft, and the same principles apply in all searches for the best design or flow-rate or working temperature of almost every industrial system [6].

Universal principle

Many physical laws embody the same principle [3, 4, 5]. Thus light traverses an optical system by a path that takes less time than any other possible path—a principle from which the whole of classical optics can be derived. Indeed Leibniz proposed that the whole universe had been designed in some such mighty self-optimization process and that this world was the best of all possible worlds.

KEY

Faraday's "anchor ring" was the first transformer. It revealed the law that the voltage on the output coil depends on the rate of change of voltage on the input coil.

2

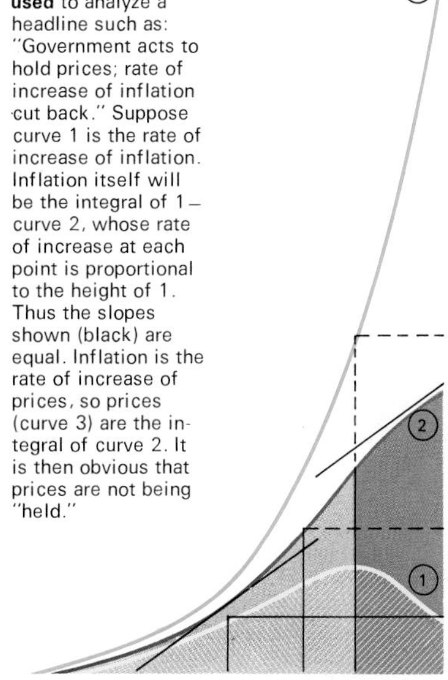
3
2
1

2 Calculus can be used to analyze a headline such as: "Government acts to hold prices; rate of increase of inflation cut back." Suppose curve 1 is the rate of increase of inflation. Inflation itself will be the integral of 1—curve 2, whose rate of increase at each point is proportional to the height of 1. Thus the slopes shown (black) are equal. Inflation is the rate of increase of prices, so prices (curve 3) are the integral of curve 2. It is then obvious that prices are not being "held."

3 The stability of ships, buoys, and other floating objects depends on whether a small tilt raises a greater weight than it allows to fall. In calculus terms, stability requires a positive rate of change of height energy with tilt. The picture shows that with more than a critical volume of ballast liquid, a cylindrical tube floats vertically [1]. Tubes 2 and 3 have too little of the ballast liquid.

4 A

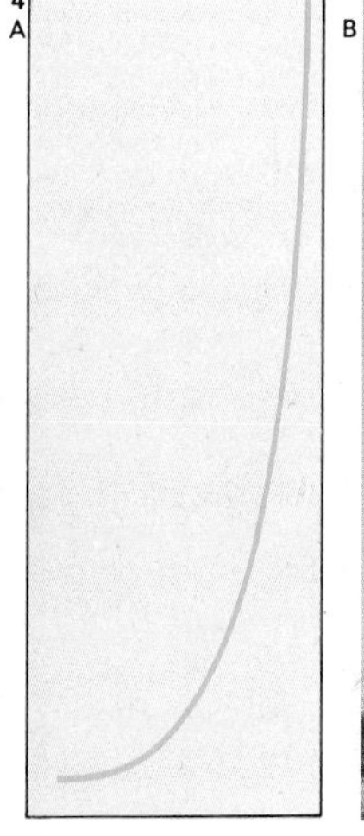

B

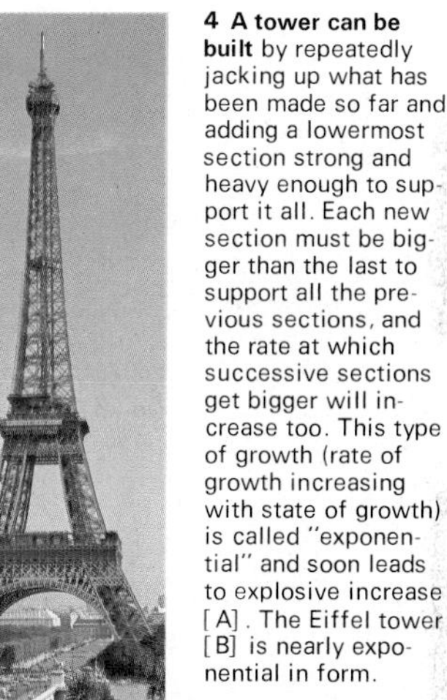

4 A tower can be built by repeatedly jacking up what has been made so far and adding a lowermost section strong and heavy enough to support it all. Each new section must be bigger than the last to support all the previous sections, and the rate at which successive sections get bigger will increase too. This type of growth (rate of growth increasing with state of growth) is called "exponential" and soon leads to explosive increase [A]. The Eiffel tower [B] is nearly exponential in form.

5

5 The curvature of a beam at any point depends on its load. A projecting strip is bent at each point by the weight of the length beyond it and calculus-based beam-theory adds all these changing curvatures to arrive at the final shape of self-loaded beams. These plastic strips have different thicknesses and their degrees of deflection vary roughly as the inverse square of their thickness. Engineering beams do not sag as much but the same design principles apply.

6A

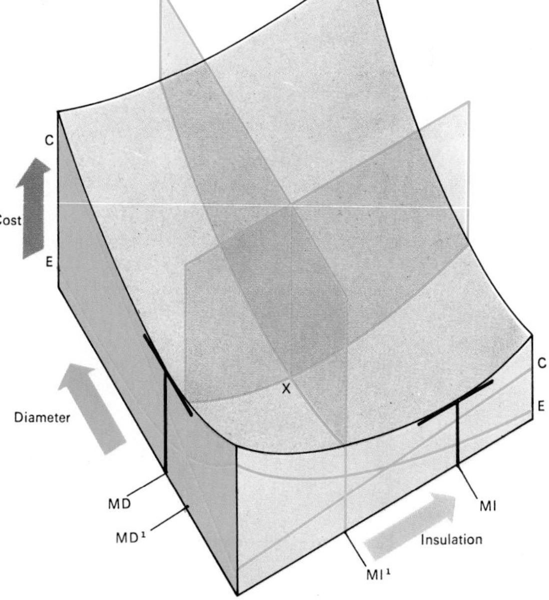
C
Cost
E
Diameter
X
C
E
MD
MD¹
MI
Insulation
MI¹

B

6 The cost benefit of increased insulation on a pipe [A] depends on reduction of heat loss (E on the pale blue) offsetting higher capital costs C. Their sum is least at MI. Increasing diameter reduces pumping costs (E on the dark blue), while raising capital cost (least at MD). The overall minimum cost is (MI¹, MD¹) at X. A chemical plant [B] must minimize cost over hundreds of variables.

Lines and shapes: geometry

Imagine that the United Nations decided to encircle the world at the Equator with a steel band symbolizing international unity. If the contractor made it too long by one part in ten million—13ft in 24,900 miles (4m in 40,075km)—how high would it stand above the surface all around the globe? The answer is 25in (63.5cm).

Lines and shapes at work

The foregoing is an example of simple geometry, the mathematics of size and shape. Since all solid objects have size and shape, geometry is one of the most practical mathematical studies. If someone wants to know how thick to make a rotating shaft to transmit a certain amount of power, or what contour to give a ship's propeller, or even how much paint is needed to cover a room or concrete to lay a path, he uses geometry to provide the solution [5]. Indeed, geometry arose from the surveying needs of the early Egyptians, who had to divide fairly the featureless acres of fertile mud left by the annual flooding of the River Nile. The ancient Greeks adopted geometry [3] and built an amazing intellectual edifice out of it. Euclid's *Elements of Geometry*, written in about 300 BC, developed a complete "axiomatic system"—a web of interlocking proofs all derived from a few basic axioms. "If you can't prove it, you don't know it!" challenged the Elements, and ever since the business of mathematicians has been clarifying basic axioms and proving or disproving statements derived from them.

A practical engineer seldom bothers with proofs; he generally accepts the mathematician's formulas and uses them. And almost instinctively, because geometry makes it simple, he designs objects from rigid parts joined at pivot joints. Many mechanisms around us embody the truths of plane geometry. The motions of a typewriter, the pantograph of an electric locomotive, the suspension of a car, the linkages in a sewing machine or the record changer of a phonograph are all working "models" of a set of geometric theorems.

Some machines—printing presses and knitting machines, for example—appear almost magical in the motions they generate by ingenious geometric linkages. And most rigid structures use the geometric fact that a triangle is the only rigid figure. A triangle of rods joined at pivots cannot deform, whereas a square can distort to a diamond shape. As a result, girderwork is generally made up of triangles (a big girder bridge is a good example, as is a geodesic dome [Key]).

Pi in the sky, and elsewhere

The circle is a simple geometric shape but one that is mathematically rich. The Greeks succeeded in proving its circumference to be $2\pi r$ and its area πr^2, where r is its radius and π is some number between $3^1/_7$ and $3^{10}/_{71}$. In fact π cannot be expressed as any whole-number fraction. In decimals it begins 3.1415926535 . . . and goes on forever, with a never-ending series of numbers after the decimal point with no block of numbers repeating in the series. It is a fundamental constant in trigonometry, a numerical branch of geometry invented for mapping the stars and now fundamental to naviga-

CONNECTIONS

See also
1464 Lines and angles: trigonometry
1466 Surfaces and volumes: solid geometry
1468 Shape and symmetry
1438 Prehistoric and ancient science
1450 Measurement and dimensions
1470 The language of space: topology

1

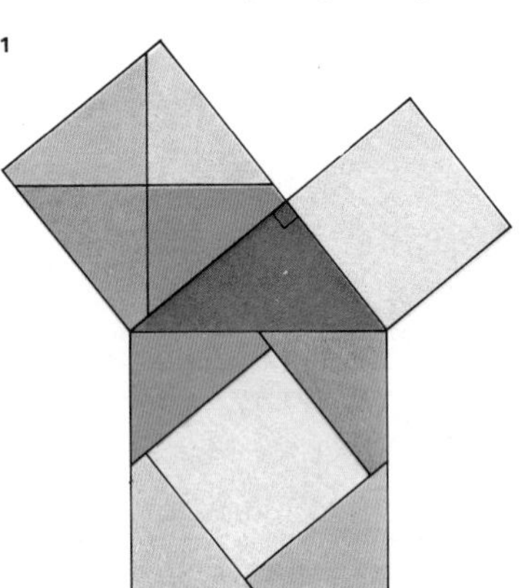

1 Pythagoras' theorem is the famous one children learn at school. The square of the hypotenuse (the longest side of a right-angled triangle) is the sum of the other two sides. The big bottom square (the hypotenuse square) divides into four corner sections, which can be reassembled into the top left square, and the one in the center, which is the size of the top right square.

2

2 An electric locomotive must always maintain contact with the overhead wire which itself is not perfectly level. The geometry of the pantograph achieves this. A spring system pulls points P and Q together, pivoting arms A and B to shorten distance ST. This distortion of triangle STC keeps C against the overhead wire. As arm A pivots, linkage RQ makes B pivot, preserving symmetry.

3

3 The ancient Greek Eratosthenes measured the Earth's circumference by geometry. He found that when the Sun was overhead at Syene it was 7° from the vertical at Alexandria. He knew the distance between them, about 500 miles (800km), and he reasoned that it represented 7° at the Earth's center. The full 360° representing Earth's circumference must be 360 ÷ 7 × 500 = about 25,700 miles.

5A

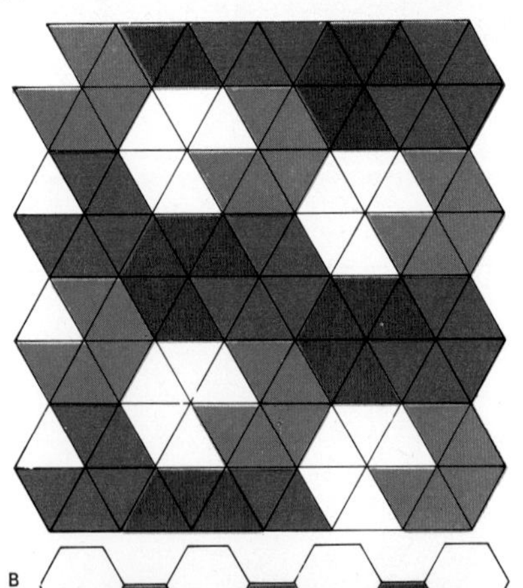

B

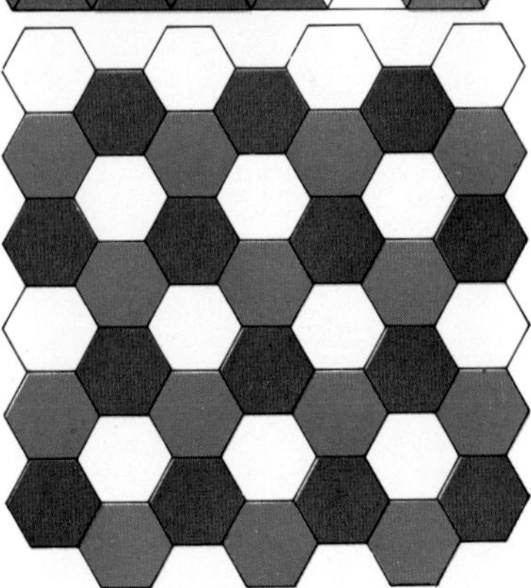

C

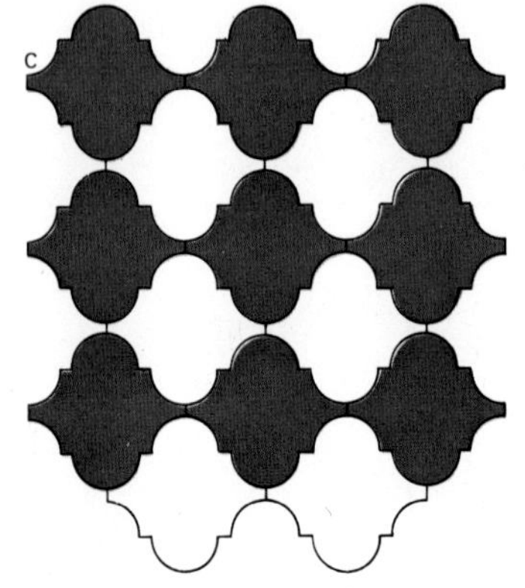

5 Tiling a floor with identical tiles can be done in various ways. Obviously it can be done with equilateral triangles [A], hexagons [B], squares, or with tiles made by fusing shapes together [C]. But it cannot be done with pentagons or any tiles with pentagonal symmetry. Geometry proves that there are just 17 basically different tiling patterns—including the most ornate—using identical tiles.

4 A

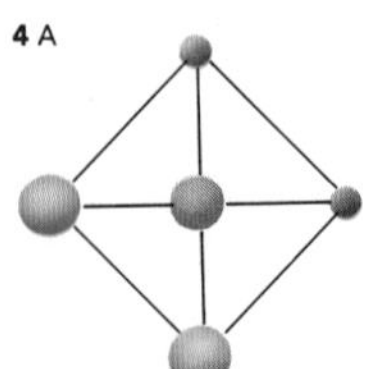

B

C

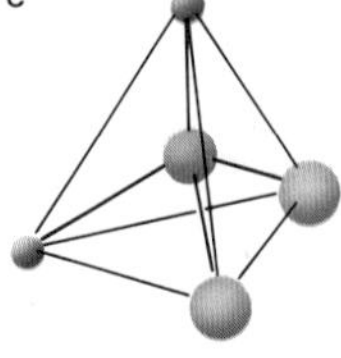

4 Molecules are too small to be visible, so chemists use geometry to deduce molecular structures. Dichloromethane, a solvent used in paint remover, has one carbon atom, two hydrogen atoms, and two chlorine atoms in its molecule. If they were arranged as a square with the carbon in the middle, two forms of dichloromethane should exist, one with the chlorines adjacent [A] and one with them opposite [B]. But if the atoms are arranged tetrahedrally only one form is possible [C]. Only one form has ever been obtained so the square structure is wrong. By such reasoning chemists deduced the spatial arrangements of thousands of molecules long before methods such as crystallography.

tion, surveying, and all kinds of practical measurement. In fact π has "escaped" from geometry and now pervades all numerical measurements.

Some of the most elaborate geometry based on the circle is used in lens design. Almost all lenses—for cameras, eyeglasses, telescopes, and so on—have circular cross sections. Tracing the light path through a multi-component lens system is a complex geometric task now carried out by computers. The computer programs calculate the characteristics of possible lens designs and select the one with the fewest aberrations (for no lens system can be absolutely perfect). The result is a compromise, but the best that can be reached bearing in mind the practical difficulty of actually grinding the lenses.

Geometries beyond intuition

Euclidean geometry takes a number of intuitive notions for granted—the idea of a straight line, for example. Euclid thought of it as a line of zero curvature, the shortest line that could be drawn between two points. In practical matters, such as surveying, we assume that light travels in straight lines. But the physicist feels free to question these suppositions. He considers it possible that light flashed from the Earth might go all around the universe and return to its starting point, just as a person would who traveled in what he regarded as a "straight line" on the spherical Earth. Indeed cosmology, the study of the universe as a whole, currently favors a "closed curved" universe with a finite volume but no boundaries, just as the Earth's surface has a finite area but no edges.

Mathematicians see Euclidean geometry as just one of many imaginable geometries, each true of space of a particular curvature [10]. Their theorems may be strange, but if they can be derived from the stated axioms (assumed facts), mathematical protocol is satisfied. And which of them is true of real space is a matter of scientific experiment, not of axiomatic assertion. Fortunately, any curvature must be very small, so that Euclidean geometry works in the small volumes we can deal with.

KEY

A geodesic dome is a rigid structure made from many triangles and designed for both lightness and strength.

6

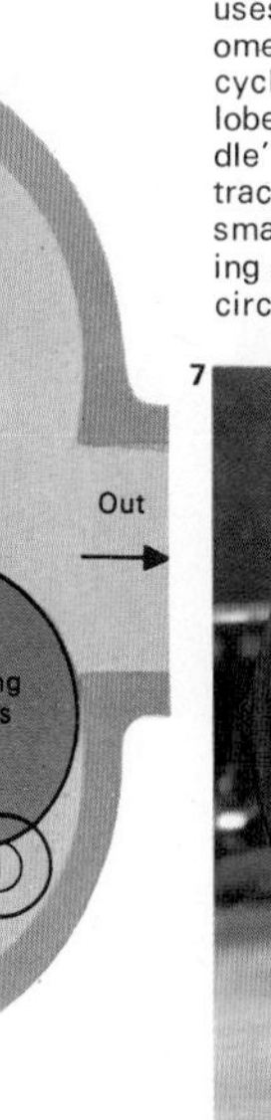
In
Out
Pitch circle
Rolling circles
Hypocycloid
Epicycloid
1
2

6 An air compressor uses the subtle geometry of interlinked cycloids. The end lobes of each "paddle" have the curve traced by a point on a small circle [1] rolling outside the pitch circle. Its waist has the curves from a similar circle [2] rolling on the inside of the pitch circle. As the paddles mesh, they always touch each other, trapping successive volumes of air and compressing them.

7

7 This model of Felton and Murray's early steam engine is a geometric theorem in action. The inner cogwheel rolls around a fixed outer gear of twice its diameter. Geometrically, this implies that one point on it reciprocates in an exact straight line. A piston rod attached at this point is driven from a cylinder; a crank takes the drive from the center of the rolling wheel, to drive other machines.

8

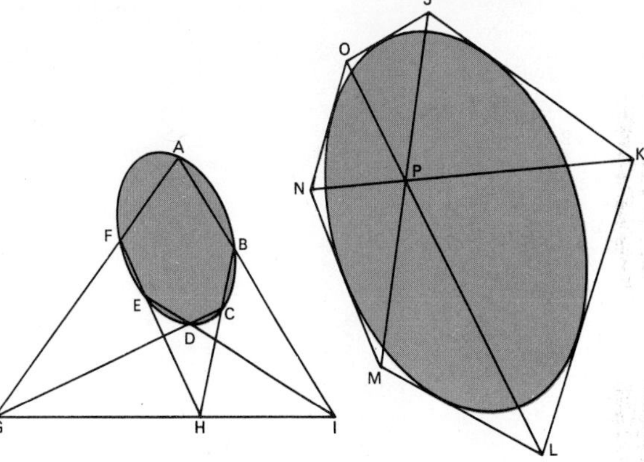
A
B
C
D
E
F
G
H
I
J
K
L
M
N
O
P

8 The principle of duality in geometry states that any two lines define a point (their intersection) and any two points define a line (the one joining them). If six points [A–F] touch an ellipse, then the lines joining them form three opposite pairs whose points of intersection meet at a single line [GHI]. The dual of the theorem is that if six lines touch an ellipse then the points at which they intersect [J–O] form three opposite pairs whose lines of connection meet at a single point [P]. So points and lines are "duals" of each other and if these words are interchanged a new theorem results.

9

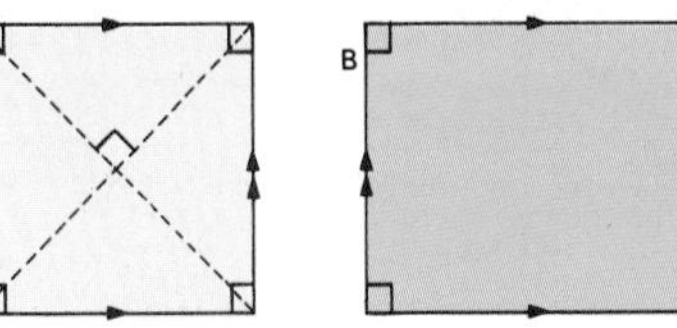
A
B

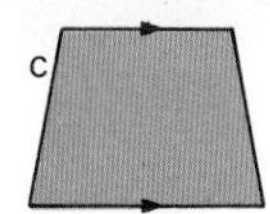
C

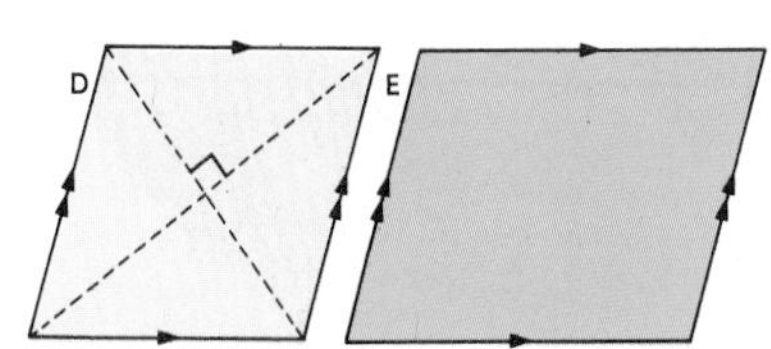
D
E

9 Quadrilaterals include a square [A], with 4 right angles and all its sides equal and parallel; a rectangle [B] with only opposite sides equal; a trapezium [C] with only two opposite sides parallel; a rhombus [D] and a parallelogram [E], both with opposite sides parallel and no right angles.

10 A B

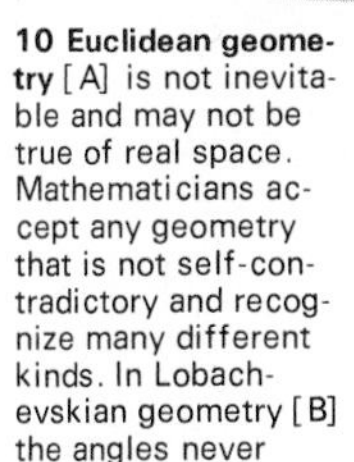

C

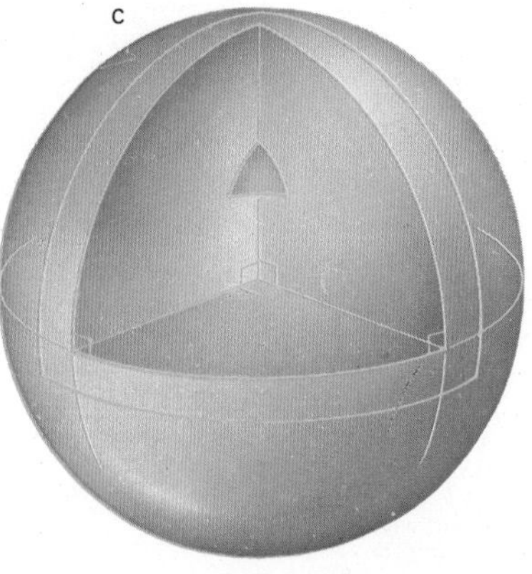

10 Euclidean geometry [A] is not inevitable and may not be true of real space. Mathematicians accept any geometry that is not self-contradictory and recognize many different kinds. In Lobachevskian geometry [B] the angles never reach 180°, like geometry on a trumpet surface. In Riemann geometry [C] angles of a triangle always exceed the Euclidean 180°, like geometry on the surface of a sphere. In three dimensions, this is geometry of "curved space."

Lines and angles: trigonometry

The Simplon tunnel, between Italy and Switzerland, is about 12 miles (20km) long and was bored from both ends through the Alps. When the headings met in the middle, in 1906, they were in exact horizontal alignment and only 4in (10cm) out vertically. The engineers managed to smooth out the discontinuity. Using trigonometry they had set up their machines to cut along the 6 mile (10km) sides of two huge triangles.

Sines, cosines, and tangents

Trigonometry is the art of calculating the dimensions of triangles. The basic idea [1] is that the ratios between the sides of a right angled triangle depend on its base angle [A]. The ratios have been named the sine of A (sin A), the cosine of A (cos A), the tangent of A (tan A) and others. They have been tabulated for many values of the angle A. Sin A is the length of the triangle side opposite the angle A divided by the longest side; cos A is the length of the side adjacent to the angle A divided by the longest side; and tan A is the ratio of the length of the opposite and adjacent sides of the triangle.

Armed with trigonometric tables anyone can determine the dimensions of any triangle with great accuracy. Since nearly any shape can be broken into a series of triangles this is a powerful method of solving even complex spatial problems. To use it in tunneling, engineers set up a station from which both the ends are visible or (as this may be difficult with mountains all around) a station from which other stations are visible, from which in turn the ends can be seen. They measure the angles between all the stations by optical sighting and thus relate the two ends. Trigonometry then tells them the tunneling angles that will align the two headings. The required accuracy of a thousandth of a degree implies a certain professionalism; but the principle is extremely simple.

Trigonometry in everyday life

Trigonometric ratios have, however, "escaped" from their simple geometric interpretation and uses in surveying and measuring, and now crop up in all sorts of mathematical problems that do not seem to be at all "angular." Some of their most fruitful applications are in circuit theory, radiation physics, and information handling, in which the angles are not real but introduced merely for convenience.

The sine of 0° is 0 and it increases with increasing angles up to 90°, whose sine is 1. Between 90° and 180° the sine reduces again to 0. From 180° to 270° the sine is negative, decreasing to −1. And from 270° to 360° the sine increases again from −1 to 0. Thus if a trigonometric angle is regarded as winding up continuously [5], its sine swings between +1 and −1 and back at each revolution of 360°. This periodic behavior gives mathematicians a framework for handling waves, vibrations, oscillating radiation such as light and radio waves, and alternating current (ac) electricity. In the United States a power generator spins at 60 revolutions a second. As a result its output voltage (which depends on the sine of the angle of rotation) swings back and forth between positive and negative at 60 cycles per second (60Hz) to generate main-frequency ac. Any other source of oscillation, even light with a fre-

CONNECTIONS

See also
1462 Lines and shapes: geometry
1454 Mathematical curves
1444 Mathematics and civilization
1440 Ancient and medieval science
1494 Circular and vibrating motion
40 Measuring the restless sky

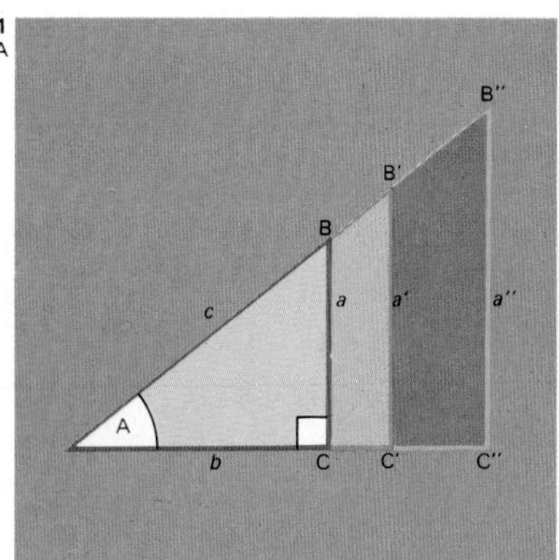

1
A
B''
B'
B
c
a
a'
a''
A
b
C
C'
C''

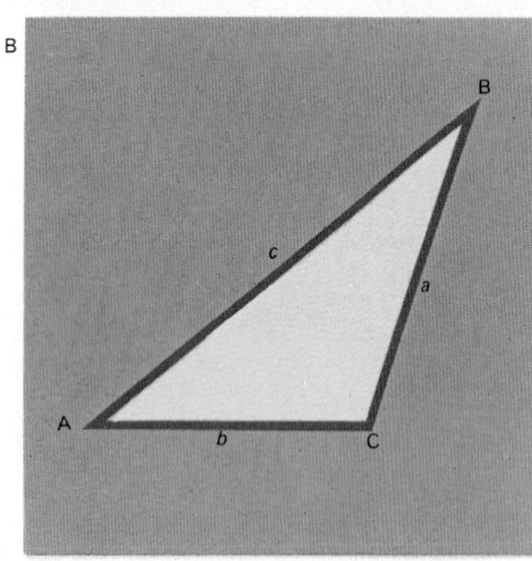

B
B
c
a
A
b
C

1 Trigonometry (literally, "triangle measuring") is based on six named ratios in a right-angled triangle. Triangles ABC, AB'C', and AB''C'' [A] all have base angle A. Clearly they have the same relative proportions so $a/b = a'/b' = a''/b''$. In fact any right-angled triangle of base angle A will have this fixed ratio between those sides. It is called the tangent of A or tan A. Thus when A = 45°, $a = b$, so tan 45° = 1. The other ratios are: b/a, cotangent (cot A); a/c, sine (sin A); b/c, cosine (cos A); c/b, secant (sec A); c/a, cosecant (cosec A). These are tabulated for all angles; today some pocket calculators can work them out. They will give the dimensions of any triangle, not just right-angled ones, via the formulas [B]: $a/\sin A = b/\sin B = c/\sin C$ and $a^2 = b^2 + c^2 - 2bc \cos A$. (Side a is always opposite angle A, side b opposite angle B, etc.)

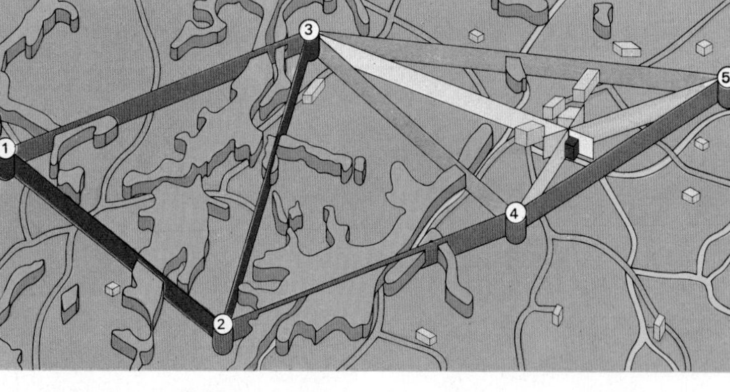

2
1
2
3
4
5

2 Surveying by "triangulation" uses the formulas that fix any triangle if one side and two angles are known. Distance [1–2] is carefully measured as the fundamental base line. Reference point [3] is selected and the angles of triangle 123 determined by optical sighting. This fixes point 3 and enables distance 2–3 to be calculated. Sighting from these reference points will then locate any others [4, 5].

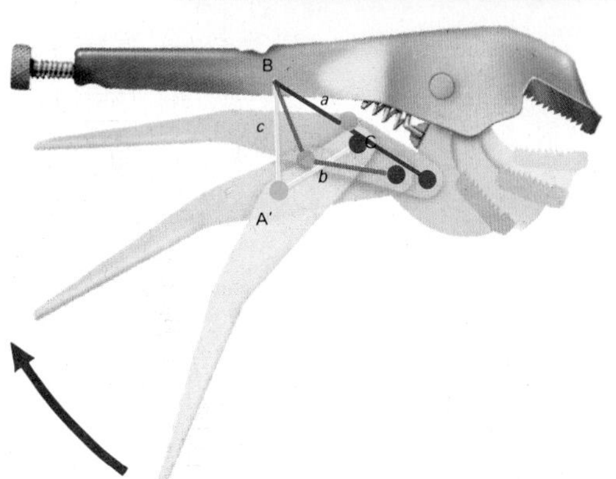
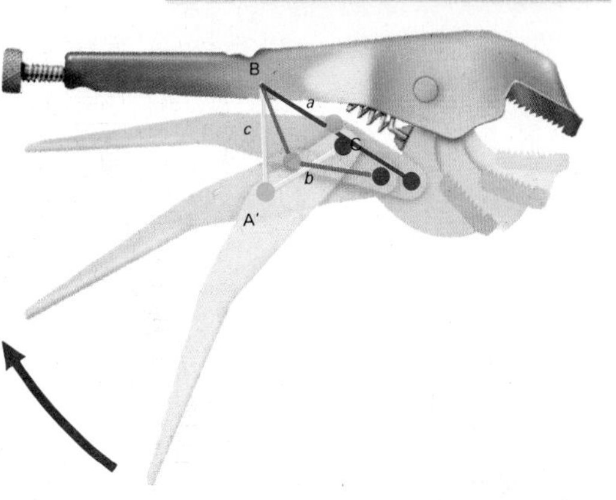

4
B
a
c
b
A'

4 In triangle A'BC of the self-grip wrench, $a^2 = b^2 + c^2 - 2bc \cos A'$. As b and c are constant lengths a^2, and hence a, change only with the cos A' term. Increasing angle A' increases cos A' and hence a, closing the jaws. When A' is near 90°, a small increase increases cos A' substantially. But as A' approaches 180°, cos A' is near its limit of −1 and changes little. The final closure moves the jaws slightly, giving a big leverage ratio.

3 On a sphere such as the Earth any distance can be represented by the angle it makes at the center. Thus distance PB may be represented by angle POB. Accordingly positions are defined by angles of latitude (with the Equator) and of longitude (north/south line). Point A has latitude x° west, longitude y° south; B has x'° east, y'° north. The "spherical trigonometry" of "spherical triangles" such as PAB tells a navigator the distance AB and the compass bearing (angle A) of the journey. Similarly in mapping the heavens astronomers locate stars on spherical celestial triangles like $\pi\alpha\beta$.

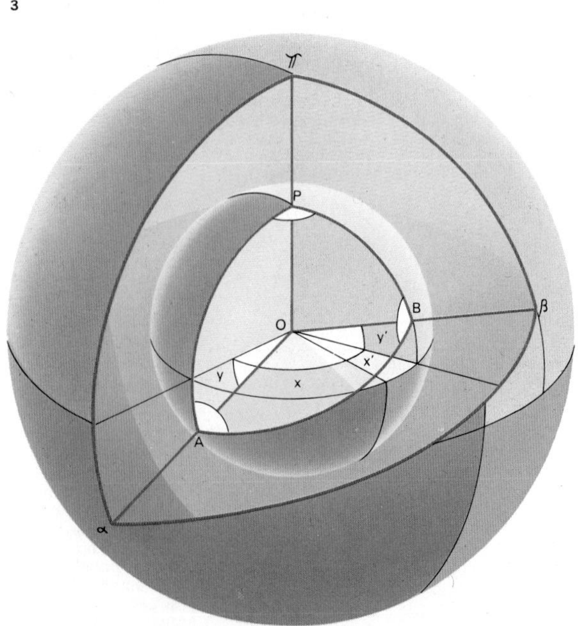

3
P
O
B
β
y
y'
x
x'
A
α

quency of 600 trillion Hz, can be similarly assigned an imaginary "phase angle" winding up at the appropriate rate of time.

Any vibration, however complicated, can be made up of a set of sine-wave components (or cosine-wave ones that are similar), each with its own frequency. Each frequency is independent of the rest. (Two stones thrown into water together generate two sets of spreading ripples that intersect and pass through each other, emerging unaffected.) Similarly, the human ear can pick out the notes in a chord although they make a single vibrational pattern in the air or a single groove on a phonograph record.

Angles in a radio beam

Many electronic techniques process these frequency components of vibrations in ways governed by trigonometry. An AM (amplitude modulated) radio transmitter, for example, has to take a sine-wave audio frequency A (say the musical note A, 440Hz) and attach it somehow to a radio sine-wave "carrier" C, being broadcast at perhaps one million Hz (1MHz, in the medium-wave band). It does this in effect by multiplying the audio voltage at each instant by the carrier voltage at that instant and transmitting the result. Now one of the many trigonometrical formulas for simple angles asserts that $\sin A \times \sin C = \frac{1}{2}\cos(A - C) - \frac{1}{2}\cos(A + C)$. Since A and C are phase angles of audio and carrier frequencies the result of the multiplication is two cosine waves (just like sine waves), one at (1,000,000 − 440) Hz and the other at (1,000,000 + 440) Hz, each of half the intensity of the original carrier.

The splitting of the carrier into two closely spaced "sidebands" is called amplitude modulation, or AM. A transmission generally has many such pairs of sidebands continuously changing in their spacing and intensity with the changing frequency components of the audio signal. At the receiver the audio signal is recovered by the reverse process of demodulation. Thus, a mathematical formula first proved for static triangles on paper can be applied to the imaginary rotating angles of an electronic signal.

KEY

The quadrant was an early instrument used by astronomers to find the altitude of the heavenly bodies. The surveyor's quadrant developed as a portable version for surveying and artillery ranging. This example was made by Jacob Lusuerg of Rome in 1674. It features a Vernier scale – invented by Pierre Vernier (*c.* 1580–1637) in 1631 – for measuring to 1/60°. This is the lower arc-scale joining the legs of the pivoting V-shaped unit that slides over the static quadrant base plate. Another scale shows the tangent of the angle.

5

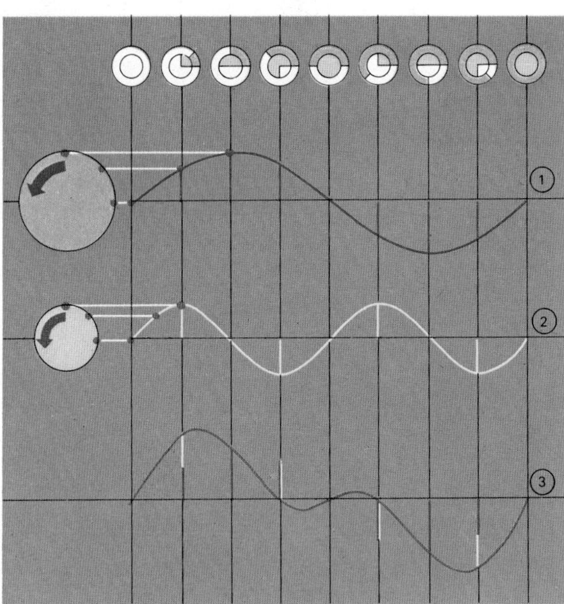

1
2
3

5 As a rotating radius sweeps out an ever increasing angle, the angle's sine varies cyclically, repeating itself for every additional 360° of rotation. For a circle of unit radius the sine is the height of the end of the radius above the horizontal. Such sinusoidal wave forms occur in vibrations. The frequency is the number of radius rotations per second. Two simultaneous sine waves of different frequency will add together to a complex wave form: thus sine waves [1] and [2] add to give the wave form [3], which might represent the variation in sound pressure of two notes sounding together.

6

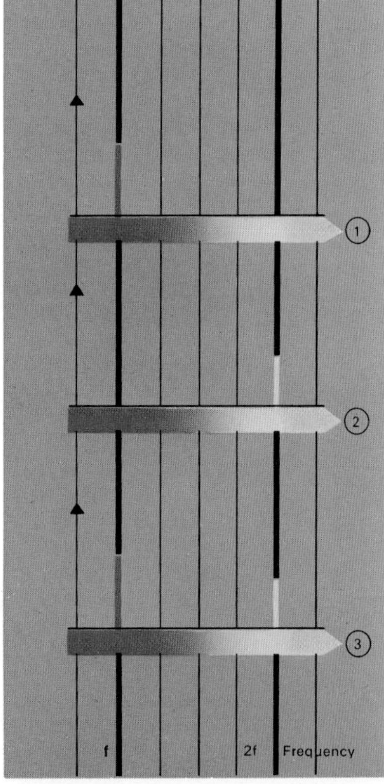

1
2
3
f
2f
Frequency

6 A wave form can be made up of component sine waves; it can also be broken down into them. This diagram shows the amplitude (intensity) spectra of the wave forms of illustration 5. Wave form 1 has only one component in its spectrum, at the frequency f. Wave form 2 has a single component of frequency 2f but of lower intensity. Their combination [3] has both these lines in its spectrum.

7

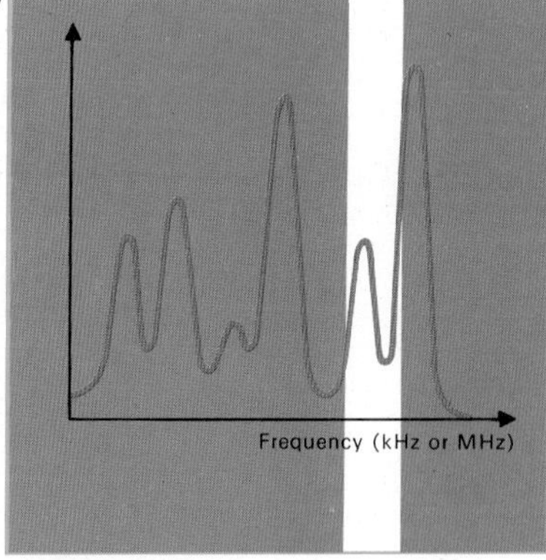

Frequency (kHz or MHz)

7 The complex wave form of all the signals entering the radio receiver's antenna will have many components in its frequency spectrum. Each peak is a broadcast on a specific frequency. Some stations are weak, some strong; tuning the radio moves a narrow frequency-acceptance band along the frequency scale to select just one. The small modulation is then decoded to give sound.

8 A

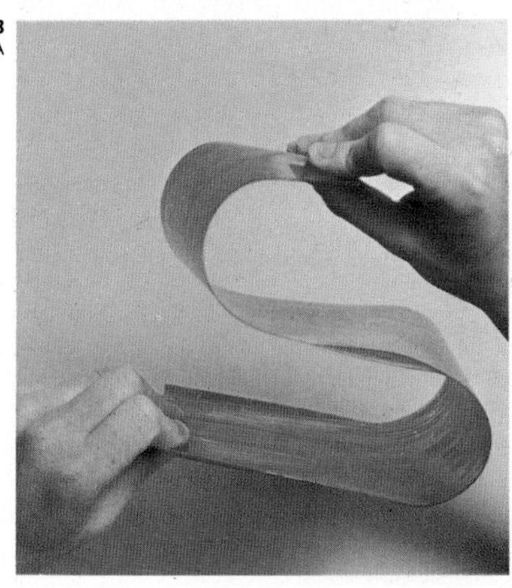

B

8 A bent steel strip [A] does not adopt a sine-wave form but a related "sine-generated" curve. The direction of the strip from point to point varies sinusoidally with distance along the strip. This minimizes the energy of bending stored in the steel. This curve is created on a grand scale [B] when a slow-moving river meanders to the sea. The water has little energy and so seeks the line of least resistance.

Surface and volumes: solid geometry

In 1826 the German astronomer Heinrich Olbers (1758–1840) asked what may seem to be a silly question: Why is it dark at night? Silly questions are sometimes the most profound and Olbers tackled this one using straightforward solid geometry. He imagined the universe divided into a series of concentric shells around the Earth, like the layers of an onion spreading out to infinity. He supposed that the stars were more or less uniformly distributed. Then, through solid geometry, Olbers calculated that a shell twice as far away is bigger and contains four times as many stars. But, in theory, only a quarter as much of their light should reach the Earth. Each shell therefore contributes the same radiance to the night sky no matter how far away it is. Because there are an infinite number of shells the night sky should be infinitely bright—or at least as bright as the face of the Sun.

So why is the night dark? Even today, astronomers do not agree on the structure of the heavens. The universe might be finite in space, with only a limited number of shells; or finite in time, so that light from the most distant shells has yet to reach here; or it may be expanding, weakening the light from distant shells. And distortions and obstructions no doubt play a part. Olbers's paradox remains an outstanding example of how simple mathematics can provoke the most surprising conclusions from uncontroversial assumptions.

Sizing things up

Mathematicians and engineers alike have to be able to calculate the areas and volumes of various solid objects. For an object with flat faces the surface area equals the sum of the areas of the faces. Thus for a cube, the surface area is six times the area of one face. For a sphere the area is four times π times the square of the radius. The volume of a cube is the length of one side multiplied by itself three times (the length cubed), and the volume of a sphere is 4/3 times π times the cube of the radius.

Pyramids, prisms, cylinders, cones, and ellipsoids present more complex problems, but all can be calculated using solid geometry, the geometry of shapes in three dimensions. Mathematicians use solid geometry to find the surface areas of such shapes and whether they can be made by forming a flat paper shape (a cylinder, prism, pyramid, and cone can be made this way, but not a sphere or ellipsoid). The path that a grinding wheel of known dimensions must traverse to cut a given shape from a metal blank, or how much earth must be shifted to make a railroad embankment of a given height, or what size cylinders can be bored in an engine block for a given safe spacing between them—to determine all these quantities, engineers use solid geometry.

Networks of force

The subject matter of solid geometry includes not just the shapes of objects and assemblies, but the invisible strains and forces that traverse them. The center of gravity of a cylinder is halfway up it; stood on end and tilted it will not fall over provided that any part of the top surface is still vertically above any part of the bottom surface. But the center of gravity of a cone is a

CONNECTIONS

See also
1462 Lines and shapes: geometry
1454 Mathematical curves
1450 Measurement and dimensions
1468 Shape and symmetry
1470 The language of space: topology

1 A

B
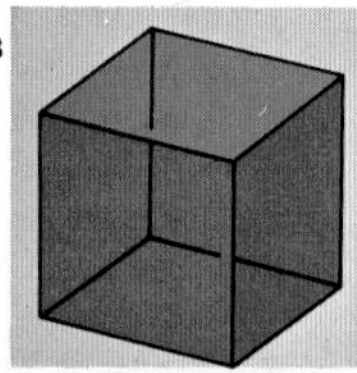
C
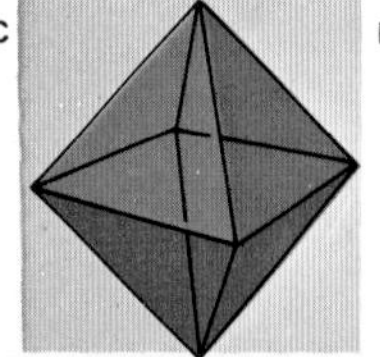
D
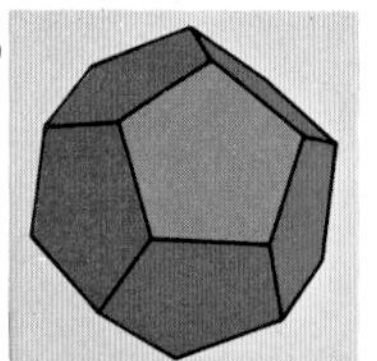
E
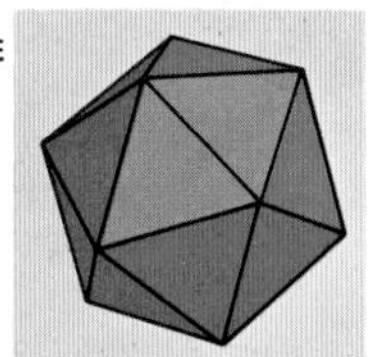

1 A regular polygon has all its sides and angles equal, as in the equilateral triangle, square, and pentagon. Euclid proved that there can be only five regular solids whose faces are all identical regular polygons: the tetrahedron [A], the cube [B], the octahedron [C], the dodecahedron [D] (with 12 faces), and the icosahedron [E] (with 20 faces). Only cubes pack together to fill space completely.

2
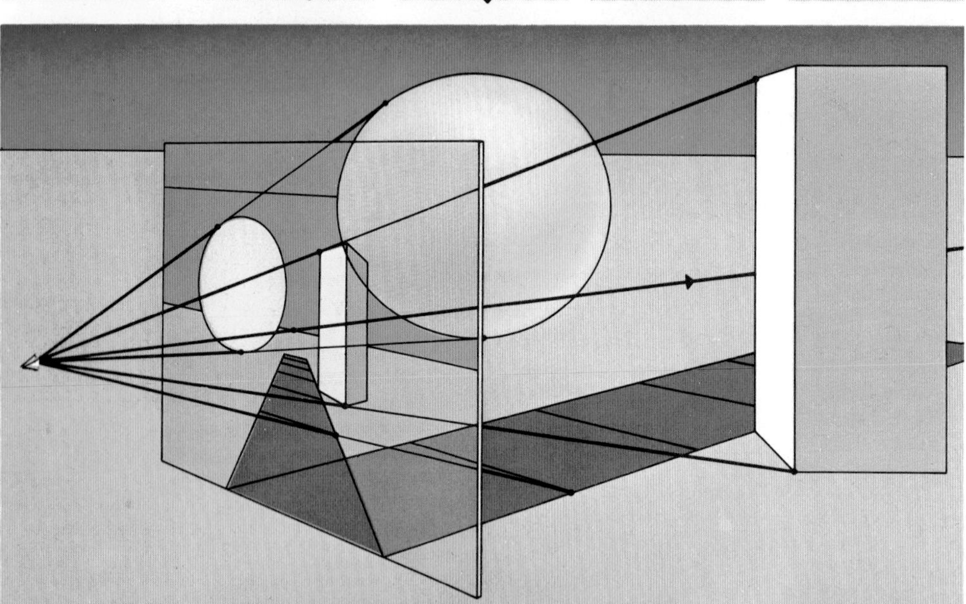

2 Solid geometry controls the perspective appearance of the world because light travels in straight lines. The laws of perspective envision a picture-plane between the eye and the scene to be represented. Connect each point in the scene to the eye by a straight line: the place where this penetrates the picture-plane is its position in the perspective representation of the scene. Viewed from the eye a perspective picture appears perfect.

3
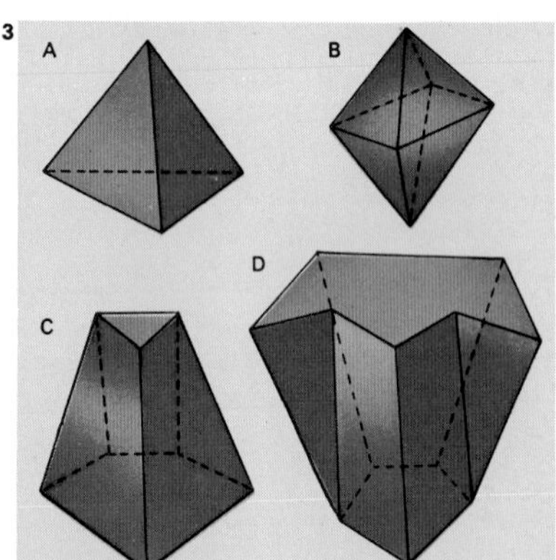

A
B
C
D

3 All solids that do not have holes through them obey Euler's theorem: $V+F=E+2$ where V is the number of vertices (corners), F the number of faces and E the number of edges. For the tetrahedron [A] $4+4=6+2$; for the octahedron [B] $6+8=12+2$. The shapes [C, D] also obey the rules. The theorem is intriguing because the shape and size of the solid does not matter at all.

4
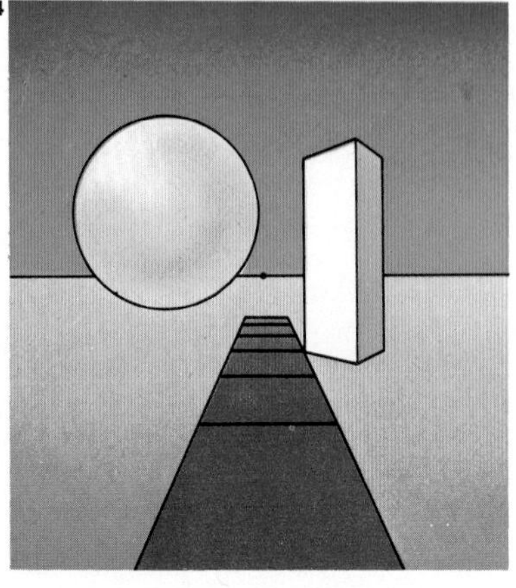

4 A perspective picture has a central "vanishing point" to which parallel lines perpendicular to the picture-plane all converge. Other horizontal lines (such as edges of the cuboid box) converge to other points on the picture's horizon. A circular disk is distorted by perspective representation unless it is directly in front of the eye; the effect is small for most deviations from this position. This picture is the perspective view shown in illustration 2.

5
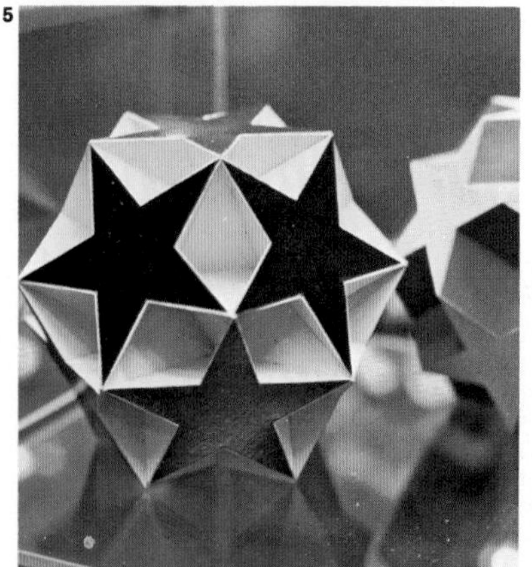

5 Uniform polyhedra can have several different regular polygons contributing to their faces. There are 13 "Archimedean solids" (not counting the infinity of simple prisms allowed by this definition) each of which has a regular polygon top and bottom, joined by square faces around the middle. If faces are allowed to intersect, 53 additional uniform polyhedra result. This one is composed of star-shaped dodecagons and equilateral triangles.

quarter of the way up it. It can be tilted until its tip is one-and-a-half times as far to one side as the base area extends on the other.

Such simple results, elaborated for far more complex shapes, determine for example what form a dam must have in order that the water pressure should not push it over; how high in the water a boat of given shape will float, and how far over it will heel if loaded lopsided; and what overloading of a tower crane will topple it.

For forces more complex than gravity still more intricate questions arise. What pressure can a gas cylinder withstand, and where will it fail if overpressurized? What structure must an aircraft wing be given in order that, when loaded by lift and thrust and weight and drag, it will deflect into the desired shape without overstressing any of its parts? Problems such as these can be solved by modeling, or by computing and translating the solid geometry of the model into its numerical equivalents.

There are systems whose geometry reveals the active forces directly. A magnetic-liquid labyrinth [Key] reveals the opposing magnetic forces that mold it. And in nature, a bone or a tree that grows against the forces on it reveals those forces by the shape into which it grows—the ideal shape for the loads it has to bear.

Molecular architecture

The solid geometry of molecules is important in chemistry. It determines not only how they pack into crystals, but how they react. It is particularly significant for understanding enzymes, the powerful biological catalysts that bring about reactions that the chemist is often helpless to imitate. An enzyme is a huge molecule with a complicated active surface on which only the right reacting molecules can fit. And having fitted they are then held in the right positions to react. In doing so the reactants' geometry alters and they spring from the surface, leaving it ready to accept more reagents. The double helix of the DNA molecule consists of two interlinked twisting strands. The whole marvelous mechanism of the human body depends on the submicroscopic solid geometry of the fundamental catalysts of life.

KEY

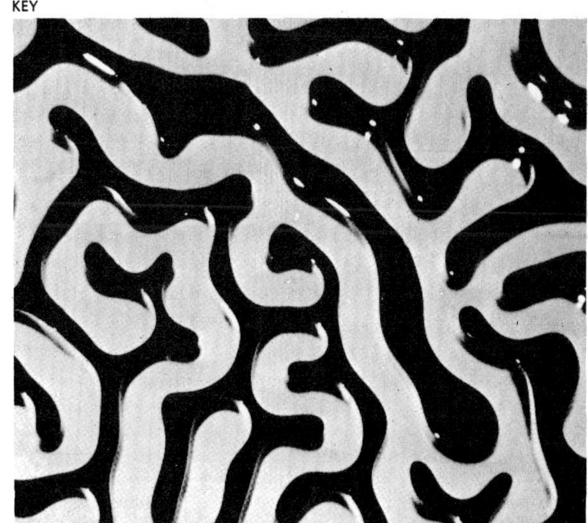

This mixture of a magnetizable liquid and an immiscible transparent one is in a magnetic field. Every part of the magnetic liquid then repels every other part, so it seeks to divide into many small sections. But every division uses energy, so the liquid adopts the compromise shape shown.

6

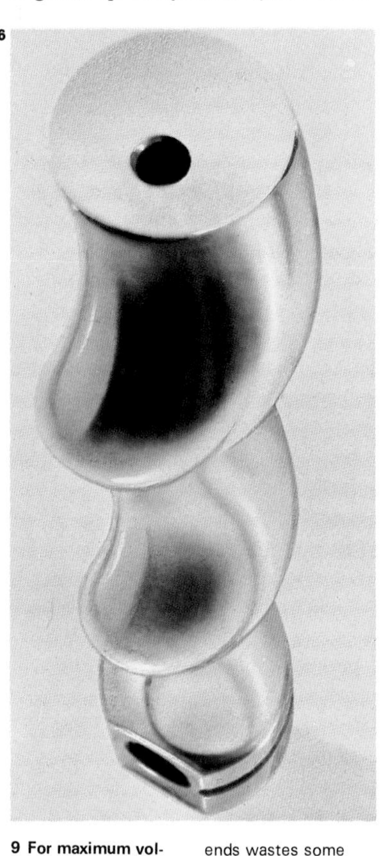

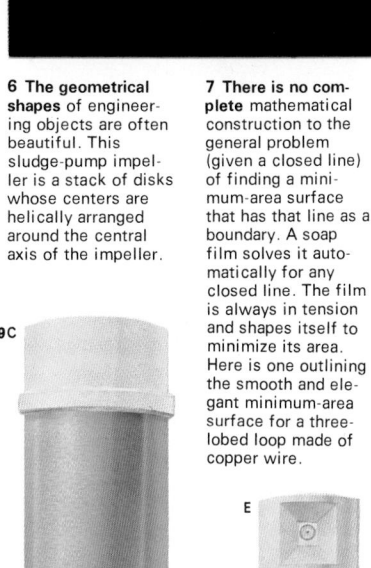

6 The geometrical shapes of engineering objects are often beautiful. This sludge-pump impeller is a stack of disks whose centers are helically arranged around the central axis of the impeller.

7

7 There is no complete mathematical construction to the general problem (given a closed line) of finding a minimum-area surface that has that line as a boundary. A soap film solves it automatically for any closed line. The film is always in tension and shapes itself to minimize its area. Here is one outlining the smooth and elegant minimum-area surface for a three-lobed loop made of copper wire.

8

GRUBB - PARSONS
THERMOCOUPLE
TRANSFORMER

8 Optical components have surfaces governed by the laws of optics and the solid geometry of ray paths. The big rectangular outline mirror of this infrared spectrometer has an ellipsoidal surface. It intercepts a diverging beam of infrared radiation coming from the left and reflects it so that it all converges on the radiation detector, that is, the stalk mounted in front of the mirror. The mirror [bottom left] has a spherical surface and processes the invisible beam at an earlier stage of its journey through the instrument. The complete instrument has about 20 reflecting surfaces.

9C

E
D
9A
B

9 For maximum volume from a given area of sheet steel, the height should equal the diameter. A standard 15 oz can [D] has a height 1.4 times the diameter because stamping out and forming the ends wastes some steel. This is thus the practical optimum. The polish cans [A, B] are wider than ideal for easy access to the contents; the aerosols [C, E] are narrower to resist pressure.

10

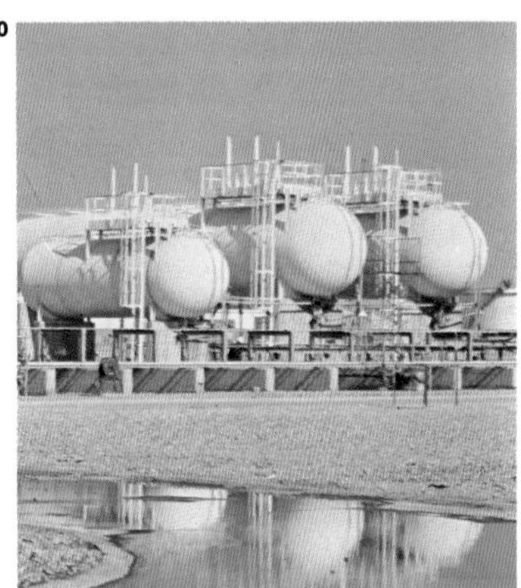

10 The absolute minimum surface area for a given volume container is a sphere. (A soap bubble proves this by minimizing its surface area around an enclosed volume of gas.) This also gives the greatest resistance to internal pressure. Spherical tanks are used to store liquids under pressure. Such tanks are also used for liquids held at low temperatures where the absolute minimum wall area minimizes leakage of heat from outside.

Shape and symmetry

If in the same boarding houses there are two rooms of equal size and furnishings, then their rents will be equal. Suppose the rents are different: then one tenant will be paying less than he might, which is absurd. This amusing theorem formulated by the Canadian humorist Stephen Leacock (1869–1944) illustrates the mathematical idea of symmetry.

Symmetry is a powerful concept and its workings can be seen in many aspects of the world. The two halves of a bridge span, the wings of a bird or of an aircraft, the blades of a propeller, all have symmetry. Mathematicians recognize many different types of symmetry all described by the group of real or imaginable "symmetry operations" that leave the symmetrical entity apparently unchanged. A square, a cube, or a four-bladed propeller can all be rotated 90 degrees without apparent change; they are said to have a "four-fold axis of symmetry." An irregular object has the lowest symmetry because any twist or turn is detectable. A sphere has the highest possible symmetry; no twist or turn is detectable. This made it the "perfect" figure to the ancient Greeks and makes it highly useful today. Thus a ball bearing is so simple because the balls need no aligning; no matter how they roll they cannot jam the bearing. A roller bearing of lower symmetry needs guides to keep rollers parallel to the bearing axis; a tapered roller-bearing of lower symmetry has even more geometrical constraints.

Symmetry of nature

The snowflake [Key] shows how the laws of nature give symmetry to their products. It has 120-degree angles between many faces because in the water molecules of which it is comprised two hydrogen atoms form a 120-degree angle with an oxygen atom. The crystal lattice in ice is formed by the regular interpacking of the molecules and reflects this symmetry.

But this does not explain why the whole elaborate structure has a six-fold axis of symmetry. How does one branch of the flake know how its fellows are growing, so as to imitate them exactly? The physicist Samuel Tolansky (1907–73) made the suggestion that the snowflake, as it falls and takes up water vapor from the cold air, is vibrating with the symmetry of its crystal structure. All the branches move and twist together in a complex and changing pattern; the fastest points on each branch intercept the most water vapor and so grow together. Such symmetries of process are common. The radial shatter pattern of a broken window betrays the symmetrical stresses that radiated from the impact point.

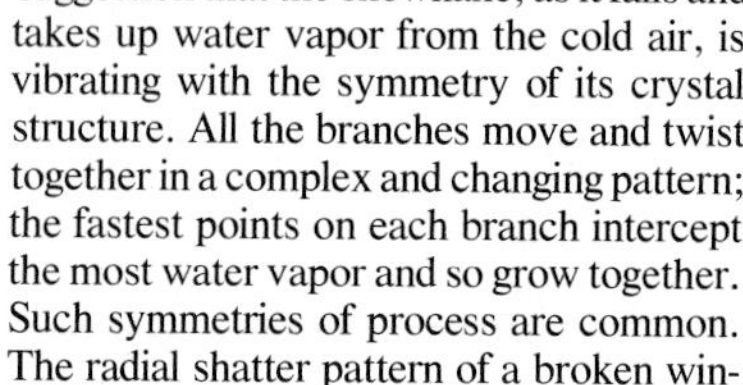

Symmetry in the abstract

Mathematics manages symmetry by "group theory," a fascinating topic, which, from a few apparently trivial axioms, develops rapidly into a structure of subtlety and elegance. The oddest thing about it is that, unlike number theory, it allows $a \times b$ not to equal $b \times a$. This lack of symmetry in the mathematics of symmetry may seem like complete nonsense, but in practice the order of events can also be important. Sanding a door, then painting it, for example, gives a different result from painting it and then sanding it down.

CONNECTIONS

See also
1444 Mathematics and civilization
1466 Surface and volumes: solid geometry
1446 The grammar of numbers
1470 The language of space: topology
1556 Joining atoms
504 Starfish and sea urchins

1

A

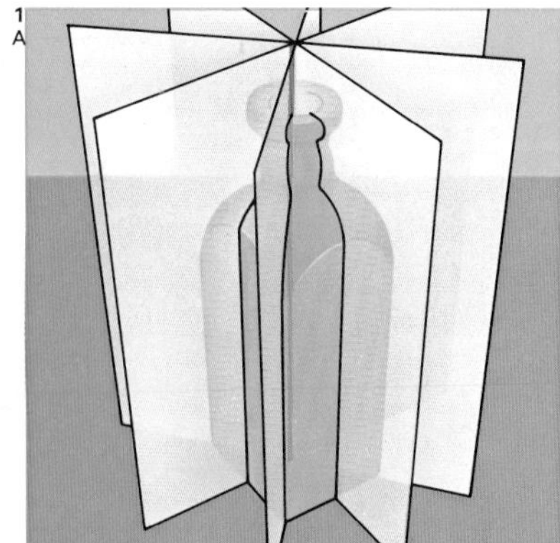

B

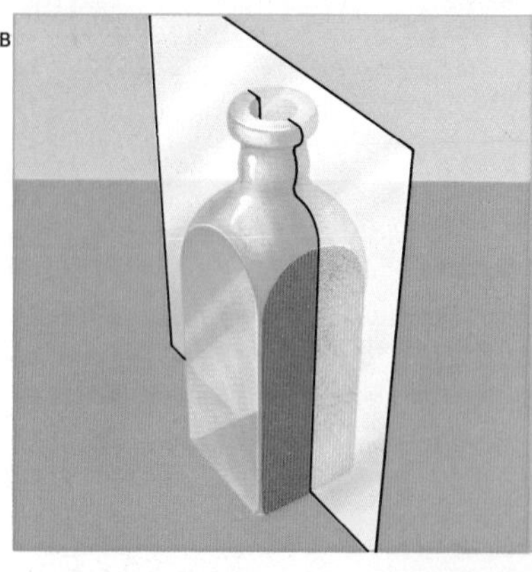

C

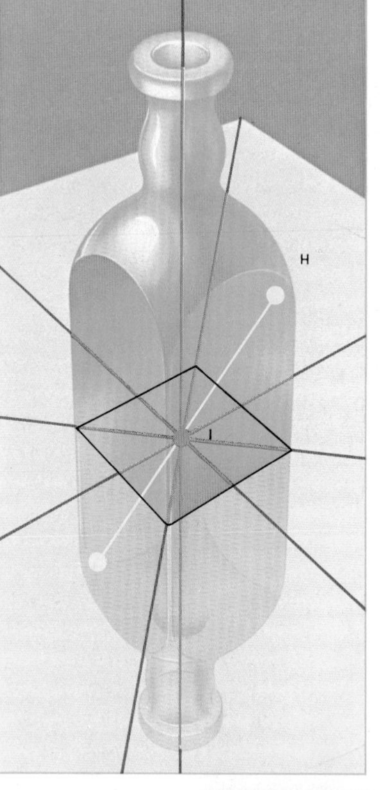
H
I

1 An object or mathematical entity has symmetry if some defined "symmetry operation" on it leaves it unchanged. If the bottle [A] is rotated through 90° about its vertical axis it presents its original appearance again. Because this symmetry operation would recur four times in a complete revolution the axis is a "four-fold axis of rotational symmetry." The bottle's other "symmetry elements" are four mirror planes. Reflecting every point on the bottle through such a plane to the corresponding position on the other side is a symmetry operation. A bottle with a blank label [B] has no rotation axis and only one mirror plane as symmetry element. The pseudo-bottle [C] has new symmetry elements: a horizontal mirror-plane H and four two-fold axes in it, as well as a center of inversion [I], about which the bottle can be rotated and remain unchanged.

2

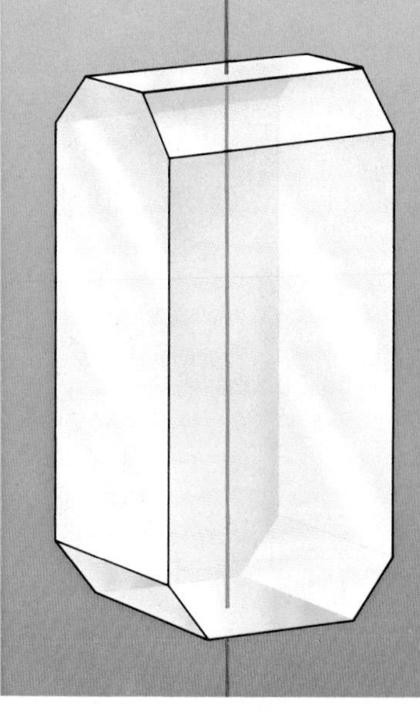

2 Crystals of chemical substances show symmetry that derives from the lattice of molecules composing them. The urea crystal has a vertical "improper axis of symmetry" for a symmetry element. This means that rotating the crystal through 90° and then reflecting it in a bisecting horizontal plane leaves it apparently unchanged. It also has two mirror planes and two 2-fold axes.

3

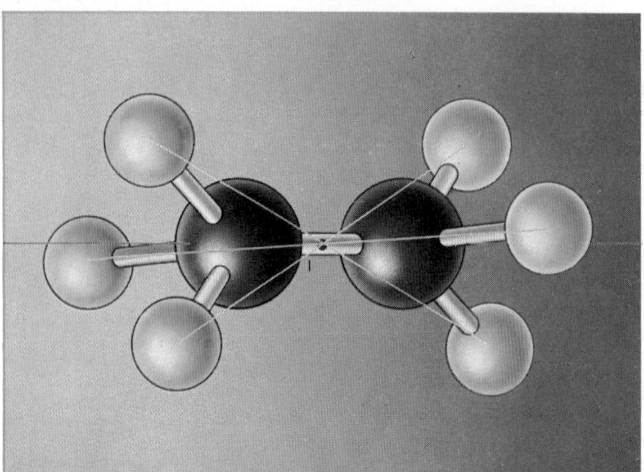

3 Ethane is a gas each molecule of which has two carbon atoms [blue spheres] and six hydrogen atoms [green spheres]. It has the center of inversion [I] but the two CH_3 groups are not related by a mirror plane between them. These groups can mutually rotate into alignment, giving the molecule such a mirror-plane but destroying the center of inversion. Molecular symmetry and its alteration with internal motion dominates much of chemistry.

4

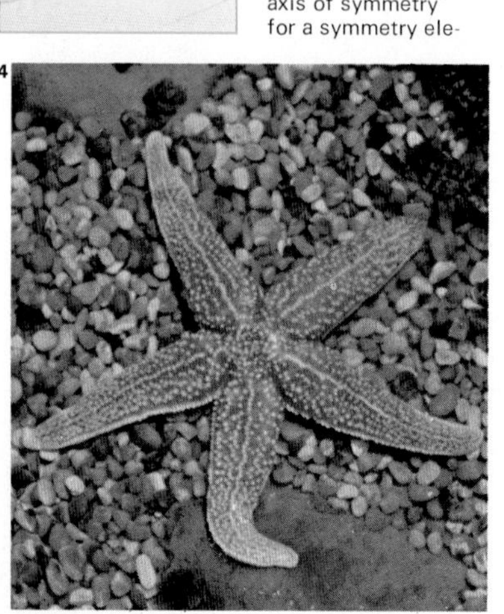

4 The common starfish *(Asterias rubens)* has five appropriate planes of symmetry and a 5-fold rotation axis. Among animals only a few specialized sea creatures (radiata) have such high symmetry. They probably evolved from ancestors of lower symmetry, as inferred from their larvae, which have the approximate mirror-symmetry of most creatures, including man. The starfish has no horizontal mirror plane; it has a true "top" and a true "bottom."

For an object with symmetry its group consists of the "operations" that can be carried out on it: turning it through 90 degrees, reflecting it in a plane, and so on. Take a squat square-shouldered pill bottle without its label, hold it upright and pivot it through a right angle about its top-left and bottom-right corners. It will then be horizontal with the neck on the left. Rotate it clockwise 90 degrees and it will be upright again. That is a symmetry operation. But if the latter is performed first and then the former the bottle will finish upside down: $a \times b$ does not equal $b \times a$ and there is a lack of symmetry.

The uses of group theory

Group theory is one of the many inventions of nineteenth-century mathematics that later found scientific use. Indeed, the rapid spread of its strange but potent "arithmetic" in twentieth-century physics earned it the title, among an older generation of physicists, of *die Gruppenpest* ("group nuisance"). But its incorporation into modern physics and chemistry, with their need to understand the subtle symmetries of molecules and crystals and their energy states, has made possible the theories that resulted in such modern marvels as semiconductor electronics.

So much symmetry exists in scientific theories and mathematical topics that researchers acquire a feeling for it and "lopsided" features of a theory or experiment make them uneasy. In electromagnetism, for example, the fact that electric charges (positive and negative) can be isolated, whereas magnetic poles (north and south) cannot, seems somehow to be "wrong." Many physicists have sought magnetic monopoles to complete the symmetry of the situation but, so far, attempts to discover such particles have been unsuccessful. But the most daring of all such insights was that of Albert Einstein (1879–1955); he reasoned that the speed of light (and indeed every phenomenon of physics) must be the same for all observers, no matter how fast they themselves were traveling. Implicit in that mighty assertion of symmetry was nuclear power and the atomic bomb.

KEY

The symmetry of a snowflake echoes the symmetry of its molecules but owes its perfection to the process of crystal growth by vapor-deposition on a vibrating surface.

5

5 Just as an object can have symmetry, so can an infinite repeating lattice. The symmetry operations for objects also apply to lattices. But there are other operations that, applied to an infinite lattice of appropriate symmetry, will leave it apparently unchanged. One is "translation," that is, shifting the lattice sideways. Every lattice can be divided into repeating "unit-cells" and displacement by one unit-cell spacing is a symmetry operation. Another is "gliding," reflection in a line followed by translation along it. This painting, "Angels and Devils" by M. C. Escher (1898–1970), has symmetry elements decreasing in size.

6 A

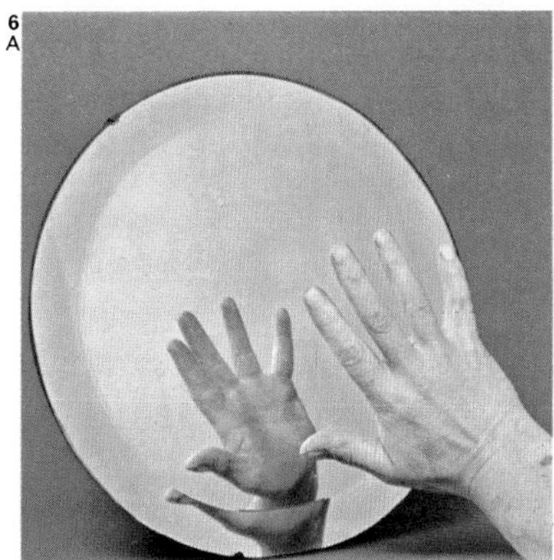

B

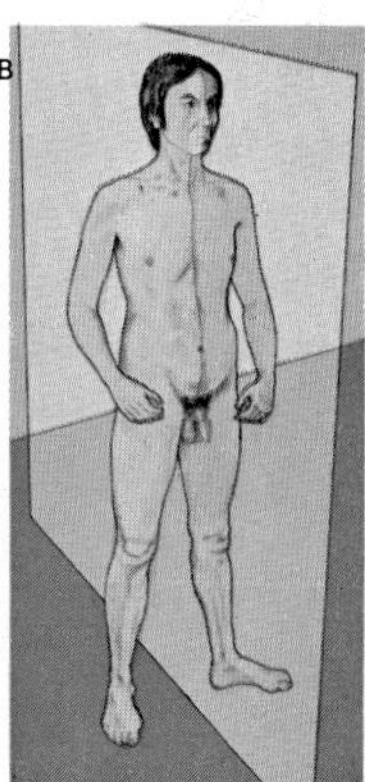

6 Why does a mirror turn an image right-to-left and not upside down? The answer to this confusing question is that the mirror's transformation is neither right-to-left nor up-to-down, but back-to-front. The left side stays on the left and the top stays on top, but the back becomes the front. Because hands [A], like other pairs of body parts related by mirror symmetry, are called "right" and "left," a right hand becomes a left one, starting the confusion. Some lack of symmetry is not obvious; in man [B] the heart and other organs are on the right if he considers his mirror image.

7

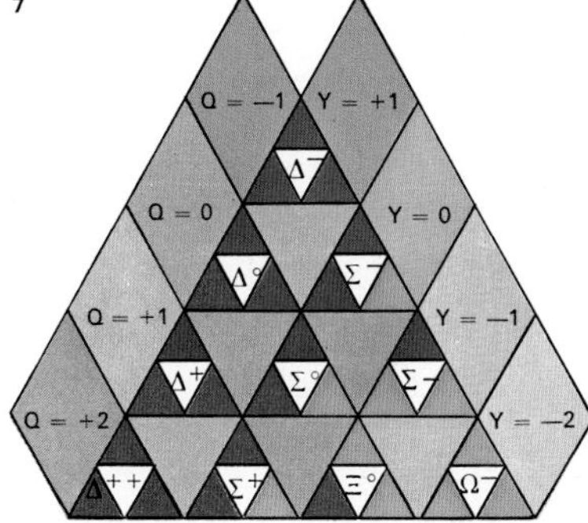

Q = −1
Y = +1
Δ^-
Q = 0
Y = 0
Δ°
Σ^-
Q = +1
Y = −1
Δ^+
Σ°
Σ^-
Q = +2
Y = −2
Δ^{++}
Σ^+
Ξ°
Ω^-

7 Symmetry considerations are basic to nuclear-particle physics. Many fundamental particles are now known, but the laws governing their occurrence and properties are poorly understood. One attractive theory has them composed of "quarks." The diagram shows how the d-quark [blue], the u-quark [red], and the s-quark [green] might combine in threes to form each of 10 particles called hyperons (−, 0, or +). The charge [Q] and "hypercharge" [Y] of each hyperon is correctly predicted by this type of symmetry classification, which also predicted the $\Omega-$ particle before its discovery.

8 A

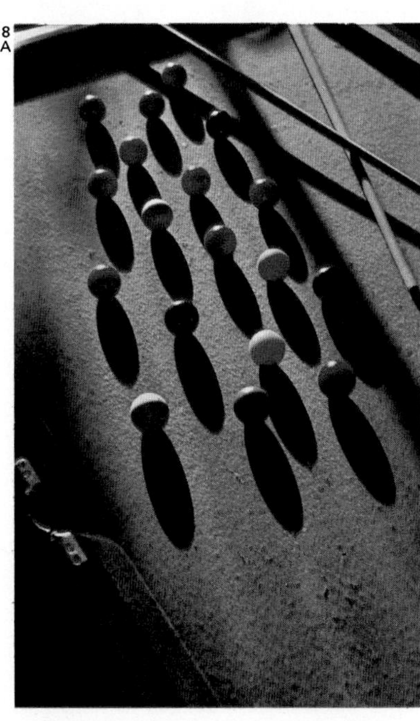

B

8 One of the most paradoxical of physical laws is that of time symmetry: any process can go backward. This may seem absurd but in a film of two or more billiard balls colliding [A], it might not be possible to tell if it was run backward. The reversed film would still show a possible physical event. But it might not be a probable one and most processes (eg, throwing a stone into a pond) are unlikely to reverse. Nonetheless, dispersed molecular motions could converge on a stone and eject it spontaneously through a calm surface. Similarly, light rays can always retrace their paths exactly, so a camera could be used backward [B] as a projector, exchanging object and image, and remain in focus.

The language of space: topology

When a cartoon character follows along a tangled hose from a tap and finds it leads back to the tap again, why does the audience laugh? And what is so odd about a household hint in a newspaper that reads: "Mending a hole in a tablecloth: lay the cloth on a table with the hole uppermost . . . "? Both items offend our instincts about topology—a branch of mathematics that deals not with shape or size but with much more fundamental properties of objects and of space.

Spheres, nets, and knots

It is a topological truth that, regardless of its length or curvature, a hose has two ends. Similarly, we feel sure that no matter what the size of a tablecloth, or the outline of a hole in it, it would be hard to spread the cloth out with the hole underneath. Topology takes such intuitive matters and formalizes them into mathematical logic. It is concerned with all those properties of objects that are unaffected by any change of form, however extreme. For instance, any simple solid object without holes is a "ball" to a topologist, for if made of soft clay it could be rounded into a ball without being torn.

A button with four holes in it is not a topological ball. It is a "quadruply-connected solid" because you would have to make four cuts in it, opening out the holes to the edge of the button, to make a shape that is a topological sphere. Small creatures living on the button would find it a different kind of space from the surface of a sphere. Any closed curve on a sphere [1], for example, must fence off and enclose a definite area. On a button this is not so. A closed curve around one of the holes does no such thing. The pure topologist's main concern is to decide whether particular abstract entities (objects or spaces of many forms and dimensions) are or are not topologically equivalent. Human intuition in comprehending the basic topology of even simple figures is relatively limited and sometimes leads to wrong conclusions.

This strange branch of mathematics has links with the real world [7]. An electrical circuit is a topological entity, for example; its exact layout does not matter because only the pattern of interconnections is electrically significant. Graph theory [3, 4], the branch of topology that handles networks, is fundamental in advanced circuit design. And the age-old crafts of knitting and weaving are really exercises in applied topology. A loop with a knot in it retains that knot however it is deformed and cannot be "undone;" it is topologically different from an unknotted loop. Textile manufactures practice topology in their efforts to produce garments with specific topological properties; ones that can be knotted in one piece or that will not unravel if a fiber breaks [Key].

A mathematical playground

Most serious topology has, as yet, little to do with the practical world. No branch of it is as closely tied to human affairs as, say, arithmetic is to banking. It is therefore a subject full of potential—for time and again in the history of mathematics such theorists' playgrounds have become the workshops of a new science or discipline. At present, however, theorems in topology are less di-

CONNECTIONS

See also
1462 Lines and shapes: geometry
1468 Shape and symmetry
1466 Surfaces and volumes: solid geometry
1472 Mathematics and mapping

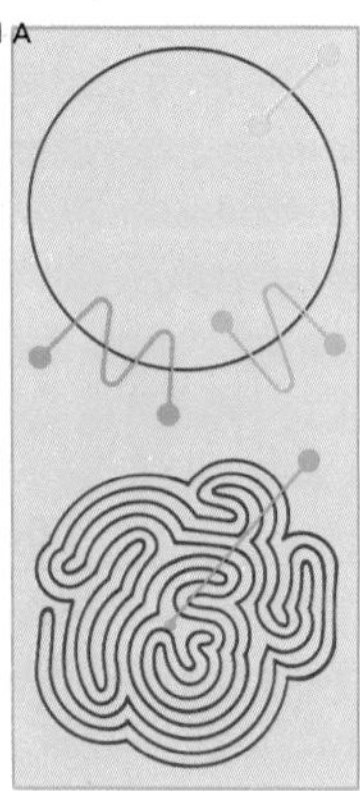

1 A

B

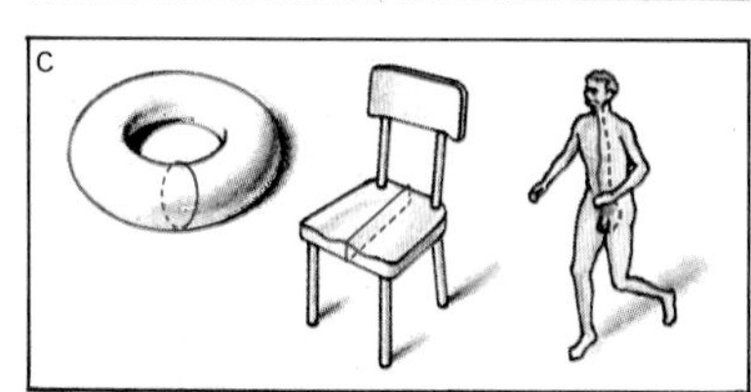

C

1 "Any closed curve divides a surface into an inside and an outside, and a line connecting these crosses the boundary an odd number of times." This theorem [A] is not true of all surfaces. A table and a statue [B] are topological balls, for which the theorem holds. But a chair and man (because of his alimentary canal) have holes through them, like a doughnut [C], which need not obey the theorem.

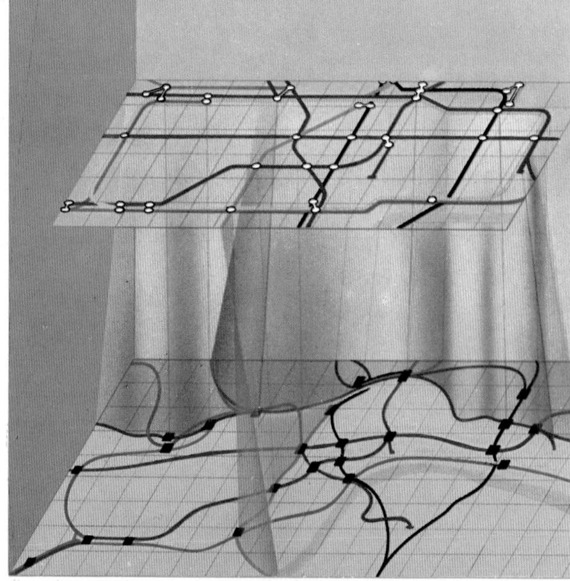

2

2 A subway map is a very distorted plan of the lines. But they correspond point-by-point, and two points joined on the map are connected in reality. This fundamental test makes them topologically identical.

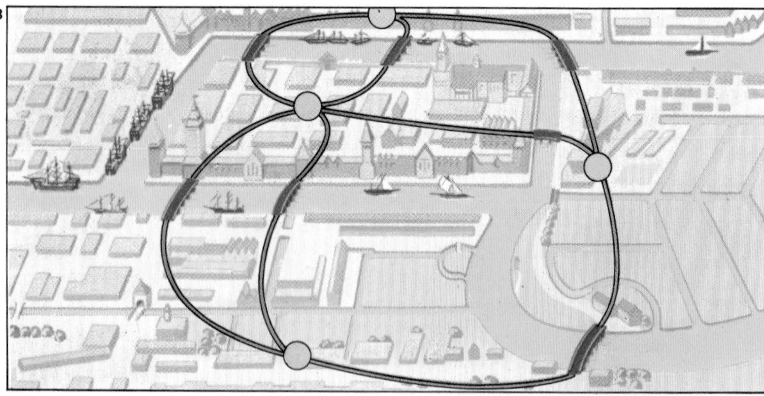

3

3 Königsberg, a Prussian town, posed a teaser that led to topological "graph theory." Could you take a walk crossing each of its seven bridges only once? In 1734 the Swiss mathematician Leonhard Euler analyzed the problem to form a theory of the traversability of a network or "graph" (shown superimposed on the city). One bridge has to be crossed twice. The problem depends on connections.

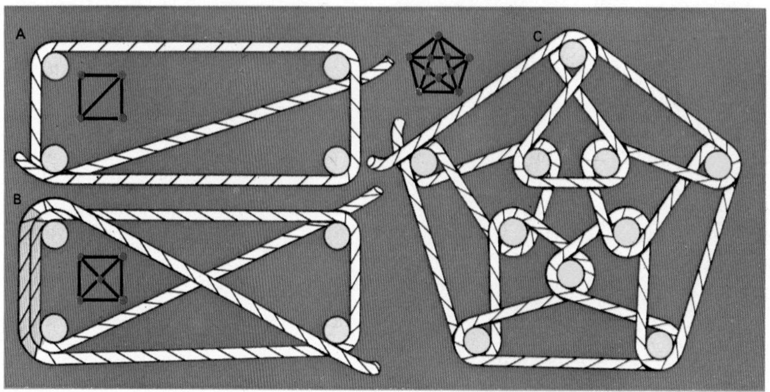

4
A
B
C

4 A graph traversable in one pass must have an even number of lines meeting at each junction. The pentagram [C] is traversable but the rope makes a double pass on rectangle [B] and begins and ends at different points on rectangle [A].

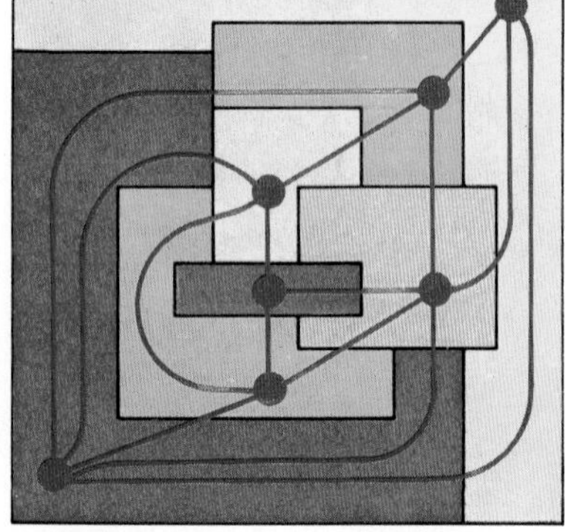

5

5 A flat map needs no more than four colors to prevent adjacent areas sharing the same color. This proved theorem is part of graph theory, for every map can be drawn as a graph with areas as junctions and boundaries as lines.

rectly useful than those of a subject like geometry.

A typical topological theorem says that in coloring a flat map no more than four colors are ever needed to ensure that adjacent areas need not share the same color [5]. The theorem does not state how this can be accomplished for any given case but merely asserts that it can always be done. The theorem was proved in 1976 after an enormous number of computer calculations. Similarly, it is topologically certain that however briskly a cup of coffee is stirred, at any instant at least one point in the liquid is not moving. The topologist is not concerned about identifying this point; he just proves that it must exist. In different types of space different theorems hold good. There need be no fixed points in a stirred inner tube full of water; on a doughnut, up to seven colors may be needed for a map without adjacent colors [6]; and on a Möbius strip, up to six colors may be needed.

A Möbius strip is a contradiction of the strong human intuition that a piece of paper must have two sides. It is named after the German astronomer and mathematician August Möbius (1790–1868). His strip can be made simply by cutting out a ribbon of paper, making a half turn in the middle of it, and sticking the ends together to form a twisted loop. This loop now has only one side, as you can prove by drawing along it with a pen, never going over the edge until you meet your starting point again. Cutting along the line creates another surprise.

Twisted space

Topologists study such "twisted spaces" in more dimensions than two, hard though they are to imagine. Indeed it is topologically entirely possible that the universe itself has a Möbius twist in it. One result of this might be that a traveler who went far enough out into space would return reversed in mirror-image fashion with his heart in the right side of his chest. Glove manufacturers might then be able to make only left-handed gloves and ship half their output around the universe from where the left-handed gloves would return as matching right-handed ones.

KEY

The significance of topology in textile manufacture is shown in the structure of a pair of stockings photographed through a microscope. The complex system of knots is designed to avoid a "run" if a fiber is broken.

6 On a doughnut, or torus, a map can need up to seven colors to prevent adjacent areas sharing the same color. The map shown (with its mirrored reflection for completeness) needs all seven because each area touches the other six. The sections form a continuous helix winding around twice before closing.

7 Any structure has many "modes of failure." Engineering disasters such as the collapse of the Yarra River bridge in Melbourne, Australia, can occur because of modes the designers have not recognized. As a novel design such as the box girder bridge is refined and made lighter and cheaper, unsuspected modes of failure may be discovered the hard way. Classification of abstract entities by their "spatial" properties can help. Topological "catastrophe theory" is concerned with the ways shapes can change; its principal application is to morphogenesis, the biological study of the ways in which organs and tissues develop.

7

6

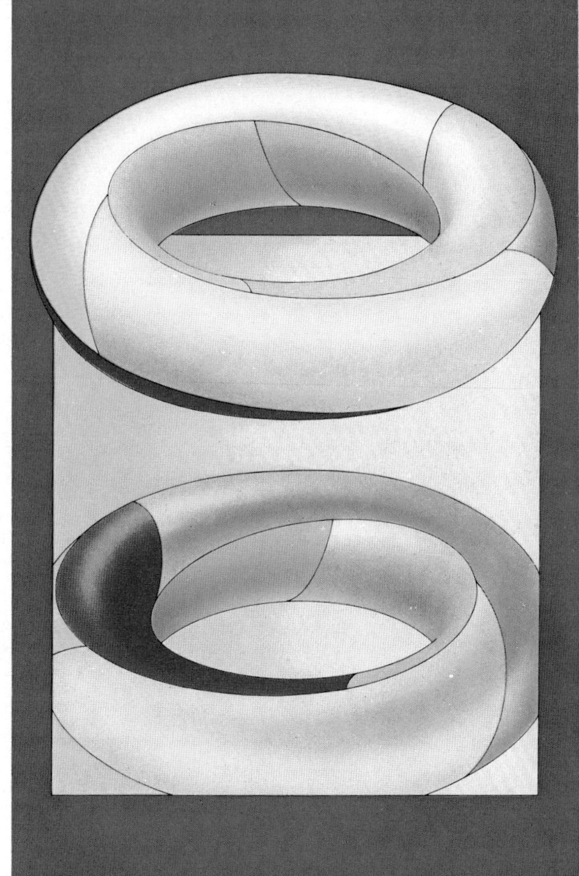

8

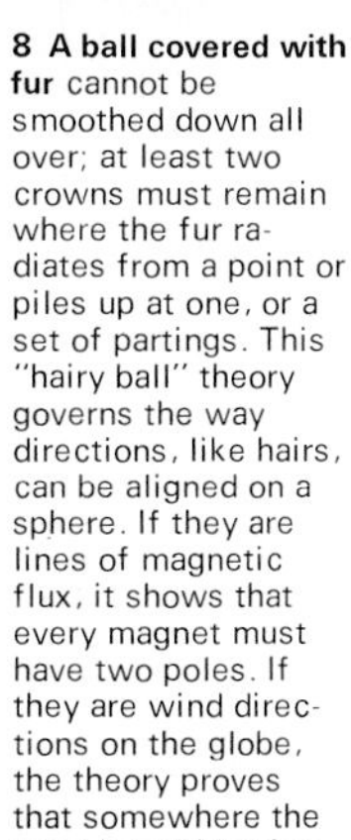

8 A ball covered with fur cannot be smoothed down all over; at least two crowns must remain where the fur radiates from a point or piles up at one, or a set of partings. This "hairy ball" theory governs the way directions, like hairs, can be aligned on a sphere. If they are lines of magnetic flux, it shows that every magnet must have two poles. If they are wind directions on the globe, the theory proves that somewhere the wind is not blowing.

9

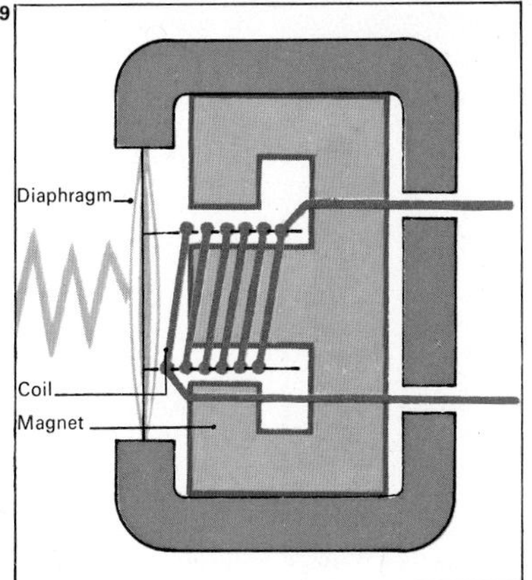
Diaphragm
Coil
Magnet

9 In electromagnetic machines such as motors, loudspeakers, or meters, motion occurs and electric and magnetic fields intersect. Each field is a closed loop; topologically, two loops must intersect at an even number of points. In a moving-coil microphone the reverse effect takes place, again involving two intersecting fields. Sound waves vibrate a diaphragm, which moves a coil in a magnetic field. The relative movement generates a current in the coil.

Mathematics and mapping

Can you read a map? A blueprint? A circuit diagram? Morse code? Then you are a mathematician because these are all examples of mathematical mappings. The idea is simple; a map is any way of relating one set of objects to another set [1]. In a geographical map [3], every one of the infinite number of points on the Earth's surface corresponds to just one of the infinite number on the map. Similarly, blueprints and circuit diagrams map certain features of a physical object onto a pattern on paper.

Maps and their meaning

One interesting thing about such maps is what they can and cannot do. It is impossible, for example, to map the whole globe onto flat paper without sacrificing some features to preserve others. True directions on a map are impossible to achieve without some distortions. But even distorted mapping is still mathematically acceptable—like the hidden painting of a skull in the Key illustration. The apparently meaningless set of circular smears at the bottom is an anamorphic painting (one that appears in proportion when viewed from a particular angle, generally using a lens or mirror), designed to appear as a recognizable image when reflected in a viewing cylinder.

Mathematical maps embrace much more than these simple correspondences of points in space. They deal with anything: points, numbers, sets, and abstract entities with no meaning beyond themselves. They even handle the mapping of a set of objects onto itself. This seeming paradox is commonplace, for example, in secret coding. A code is a rule for replacing each letter of a message by another from the same alphabet; it is a complex mapping of the alphabet onto itself. Similarly, the two-times table relates a number to its double and (if fractions are included) is a mapping of the set of all real numbers onto itself.

One-to-one maps are not the only kind. The "zero-times table" that takes all numbers to zero is a good mathematical map. But the mapping must specify a definite image or images for every element in its "domain" of operation. Therefore there is the old puzzle of the village whose barber shaves everyone who does not shave himself. This purports to describe a mapping that sends all the "shavers" to themselves and the "non-shavers" to the barber. It is not a well formed mapping because it leaves the barber himself in a paradoxical position. Does he map to himself? (That is, does he shave himself?) If so, he shouldn't, and if not, he should.

By contrast the marriage map between n men and n women (where n is any whole number) is a proper map and defines a possible set of marriages. Assuming that each individual has some order of preferences for his or her n possible partners, then it is a wry outcome of mapping theory that of all possible such maps—ways of pairing off the men and women—one and one only is stable. In all others, cases will occur in which a man and a woman not married to each other will prefer the other to their own spouse.

Maps between one thing and another

The above mappings are examples of "discrete" instead of "continuous" maps. Unlike those of points on a surface or a set of all

CONNECTIONS

See also
1470 The language of space: topology
1458 Sets and groups
180 Mapping the Earth

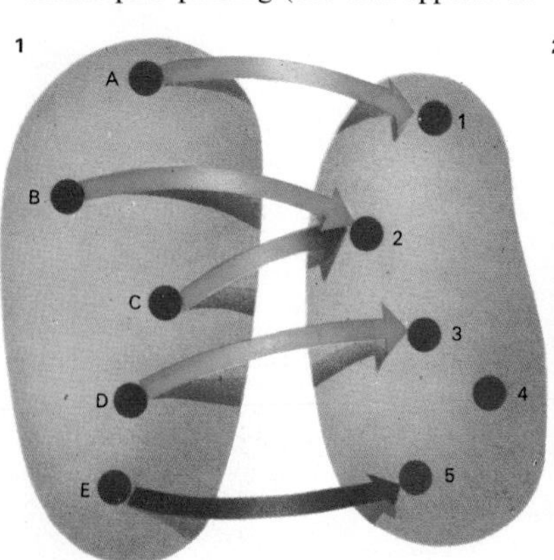

A
B
C
D
E
1
2
3
4
5

1 A mathematical map relates one set of objects (eg, A, B, C, D) to an "image" set (eg, 1, 2, 3, 4), symbolized by the arrows. One-to-one correspondence is not necessary; both B and C are sent to 2, D is sent to 3, and nothing is sent to 4. But the map must act on every object in its domain. Without the purple colored arrow E would be unimaged and the mapping therefore would be improper.

2 Light is transmitted by a fiber from one point to another; the bundle maps an object onto its image [A]; it may be deformed by reduction [B] or by scrambling the fibers [C]. This is fiber-optic mapping

3 Each point on the globe is sent to one on the map in this diagram. The "zenithal projection" is mapping the Southern Hemisphere; each point is projected along a line from the North Pole onto a plane touching the South Pole. The Equator becomes a circle, as do other lines of latitude. Lines of longitude become radii. The scale is not constant; it increases dramatically toward the edge of the map.

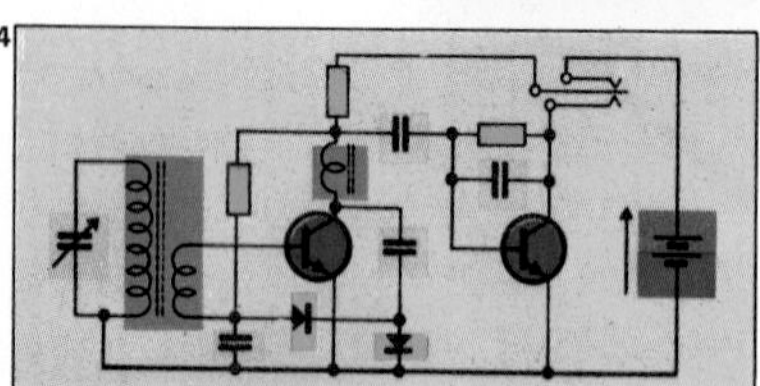

4 An electronic circuit diagram is a map unconcerned with scale or shape. It shows the connections between components using stylistic conventions—wires become straight line segments.

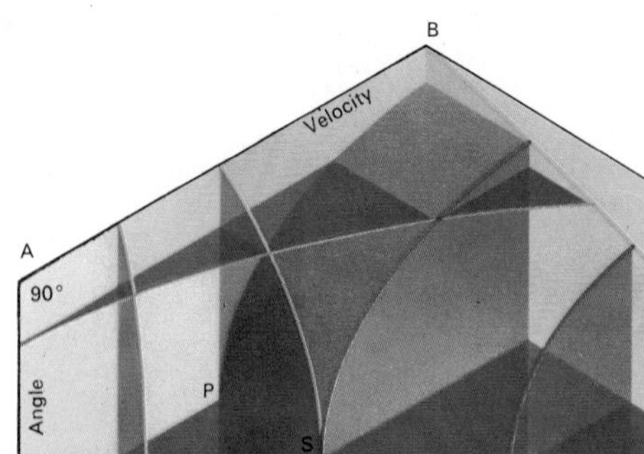

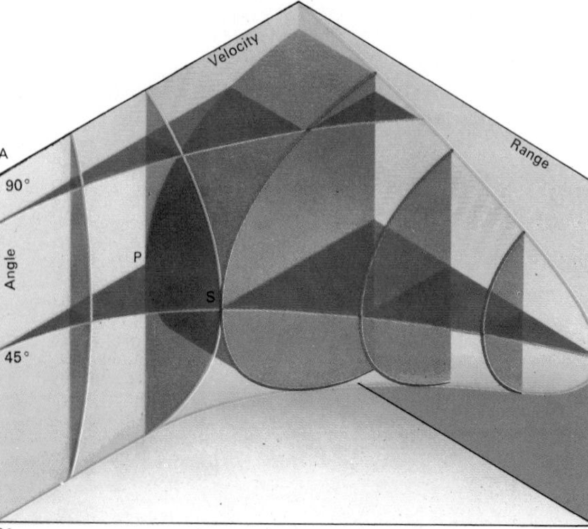

A
B
O
P
S
Velocity
Range
Angle
90°
45°
0°

5 The muzzle-velocity and elevation angle of a gun are mapped onto the range of the shell. The plane OAB is a "map" of angle and velocity; the height of a point [P] represents elevation angle, and its horizontal distance from OA represents muzzle velocity. The perpendicular distance of the surfaces from P represents the range for those settings. The surface contour shows that range increases with velocity and is greatest at 45° elevation.

6 A reflex AM radio-receiver circuit has the circuit diagram shown in illustration 4. They do not look alike but are related by a mapping that ensures that the connections are the same in both the physical and schematic layouts. The manufacturer is unconstrained by circuit-diagram conventions and routes the wiring for tight packing of components for example. But adjacent components may interact, by their electric or magnetic fields.

real numbers, they handle a finite set of elements only. The mapping of telephone subscribers onto their telephone numbers is like this, too. Each subscriber has his own number, but not all numbers are represented. For example, there is no number 000 0000. A reservoir of possible but unused numbers is held by the telephone companies. This map illustrates a new point. Previous examples sent points to points, numbers to numbers, people to people; this one sends people to numbers.

The mapping of one set of entities onto another apparently quite different set is a powerful mathematical technique. For instance, analytical geometry maps geometry onto algebra [11]. Each geometric curve or line is sent to its corresponding equation; for each geometric theorem there is a corresponding algebraic identity. The mapping preserves the relational features of geometry so that geometric problems of great difficulty (for example, those in many dimensions) can be mapped by easier-to-handle algebra, solved, and then mapped back to give the required geometric truth.

Morse code is another example of such mapping. Letters and numbers are mapped onto combinations of dots and dashes. These in turn can be transmitted as short and long flashes of light or pulses of current. At the receiving end the dots and dashes are mapped back to letters and numbers.

A vast range of scientific and technical enterprise depends on mapping from the real world into symbolic systems that preserve the important features. An astronomer maps the positions of the heavenly bodies into terms of a set of equations. From the ensuing calculations, he can recover terms that map back into future positions of the bodies.

Mapping: theory into practice

It is the business of mathematical science to make sure that mappings work. All scientific theories are maps in this sense and so are the calculations and designs of an engineer who decides on paper that an aircraft as yet unbuilt can fly. Like geographic maps of the globe, these maps sacrifice some features to preserve others.

KEY

Anamorphic art is a technique in which an artist draws or paints a familiar shape in a grossly distorted form. It is an example of mapping, just as maps of the curved Earth's surface can be drawn on a flat sheet of paper by a suitable choice of projection. In this detail of "The Ambassadors" by Hans Holbein (1533), the stretched shape at the bottom is a "map" of a skull; it can be seen [below] by viewing from the lower left.

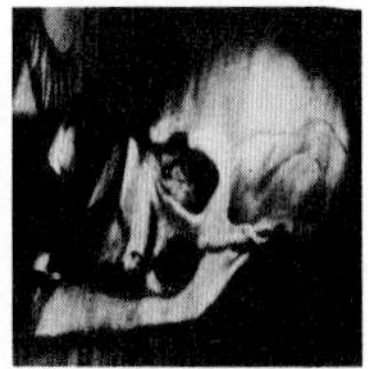

7

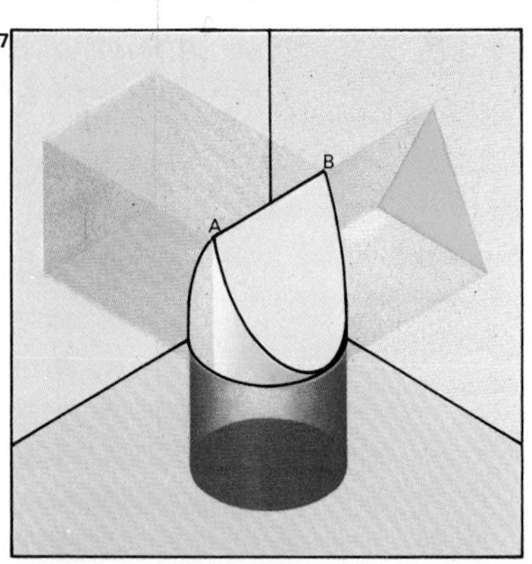

A
B

7 A draftsman's projection is a mathematical map in which many points on the object go to the same point on the image. In the blue triangular projection all the points on the line AB are sent to the top vertex of the triangle. They retain their identity in the yellow square projection. All projections "compress" information in this way, so drafting practice makes use of several different projections for clarity.

8

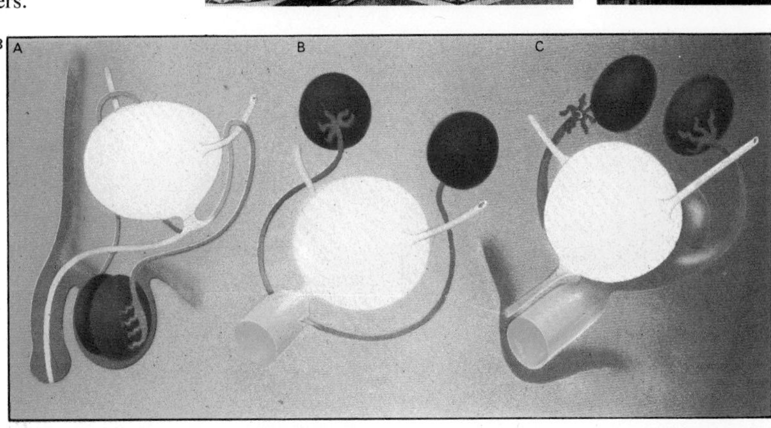

A
B
C

8 The male and female sex organs are both distortions of a primitive system and are mappings of each other in the mathematical sense. The testicles [A] map into the ovaries and the penis and bladder map into the elaboration of uterus and urogenital tract [C] This suggests that both systems may have evolved from a common one [B] and that, in nature, different structures can have the same form.

9

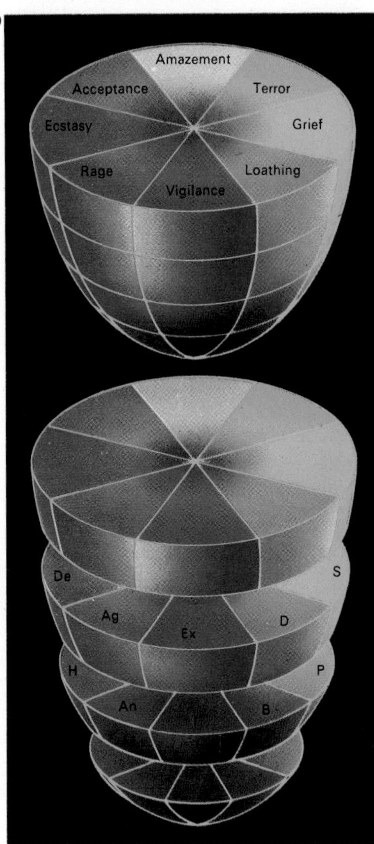

Amazement
Acceptance
Terror
Ecstasy
Grief
Rage
Loathing
Vigilance
De
S
Ag
D
Ex
H
P
An
B

9 The psychologist Plutchik mapped the emotions onto this "emotional solid." The most intense ones map to the top. The next layer shows diluted versions of these (by their initial letters): delight, anger, expectancy, disgust, sadness, etc, and the next layer happiness, annoyance, interest, boredom, pensiveness, etc. The lower marks neutrality. Any sequence of emotions is a "worm-track" through this solid.

10

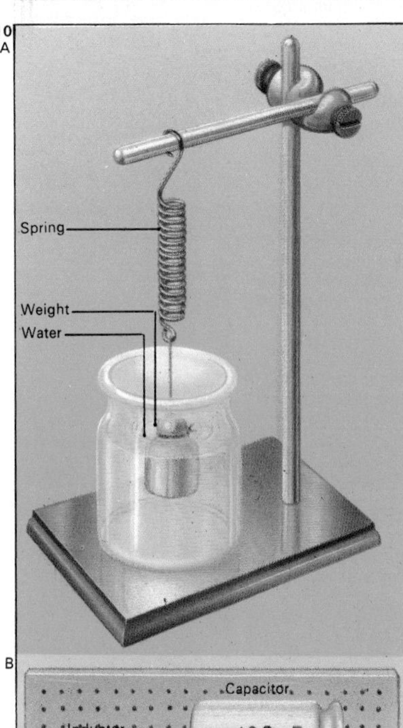

A
Spring
Weight
Water
B
Capacitor
Inductor
100 μF
16 V
Resistor

10 A weight suspended by a spring in water [A] and an electrical circuit [B] are mathematical maps of each other. If disturbed, the weight will vibrate with decreasing vigor and an electrical pulse will cause oscillations in the circuit to fade away gradually. Both examples have an energy-storing element (the spring or capacitor), an inertial element (the weight or inductor), and an energy-dissipating element (the water or resistor).

11

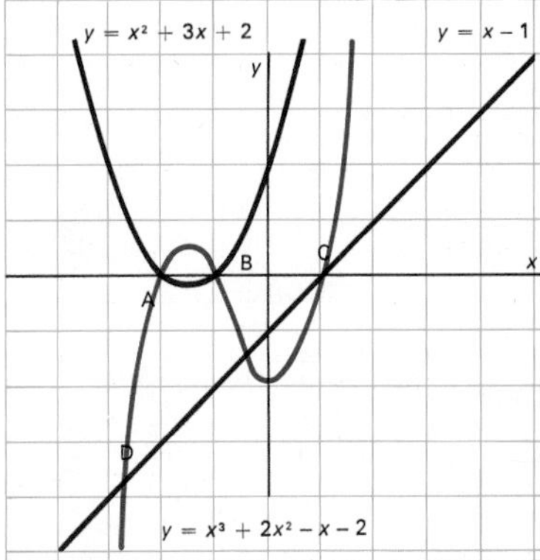

$y = x^2 + 3x + 2$
$y = x - 1$
y
x
A
B
C
D
$y = x^3 + 2x^2 - x - 2$

11 "Mathematics is the art of saying the same thing in different words" (Bertrand Russell). The curves are geometry, their equations algebra. The mapping between these is analytical geometry. The two curves intersect at A and B; their equations will yield two solutions whose values give the coordinates of A and B. Similarly, the straight line intersects one of the curves at C and D whose coordinates are found by solving the equations simultaneously.

Facts and statistics

In the next minute at least 60 and not more than 310 babies will be born. This statistical claim requires no knowledge of any individual women. It just assumes the average world birth rate of three per second—and it has only one chance in 1,000 of being wrong.

Making reliable statements about chance events is the business of statistics. Think of a tossed penny—the classic uncertainty. An unbiased penny tossed a million times gives, with 99 percent certainty, between 498,700 and 501,300 heads. Conversely, if bias is suspected, one toss will not confirm it. But a million tosses giving 500,000 heads indicates, again with 99 percent certainty, that the bias is between 0.4987 and 0.5013 (a perfect coin has a bias of 0.5000).

Chance and certainty

Phrases such as "99 percent certainty" are common to all reliable statistical statements. Certainty is never 100 percent and for this reason a reputable statistician always states his error and confidence limits. Ninety-nine times out of 100 he would be right in predicting the penny's bias between the given limits. Only once in 100 times would a coin of greater bias give, by chance, equal numbers of heads and tails. If it is really necessary to predict the penny's bias with greater confidence than this, or to define it more accurately, it would have to be tossed more times. In statistics there is always this trade off between the information necessary and the reliability of the knowledge it yields, with complete certainty forever unattainable. The art of practical statistics lies in knowing the probability sufficient for the task at hand and knowing how much data to collect in order to derive it.

Making good and bad guesses

Insurance companies depend on statistics. Will a client aged 20 die in 40 years time? Nobody knows. But an insurance company, with its records of thousands of men and women, estimates how many clients are likely to die and be the subject of claims and therefore how much it must charge in premiums to remain in business. From its widely amassed survival statistics it can deduce how dangerous overweight, smoking, and so on, are to health. This is achieved by seeking "bias" in the death records of various groups, just as one might seek it in the tossing records of various pennies.

Medical science gains from this, too. It was statistical analysis that correlated the taking of the drug thalidomide during pregnancy with deformed babies, and cigarette smoking with lung cancer. But such correlations need careful interpretation. Statistics cannot say why smokers are more likely to contract cancer than nonsmokers. Perhaps people predisposed to lung cancer also tend to have a taste for smoking—an odd hypothesis, perhaps, but one that is statiscally feasible. Similarly, cancer of the cervix in women shows a slight but definite correlation with the number of children they have borne. Does this mean that childbirth causes cancer? Further studies show that the correlation fails for Jewish women. This clue leads to the conclusion that the correlation is with sexual activity rather than with its natural outcome. In fact the correlation

CONNECTIONS

See also
1476 Odds and probability
1452 Finding unknown quantities: algebra
1460 Finding changing quantities: calculus

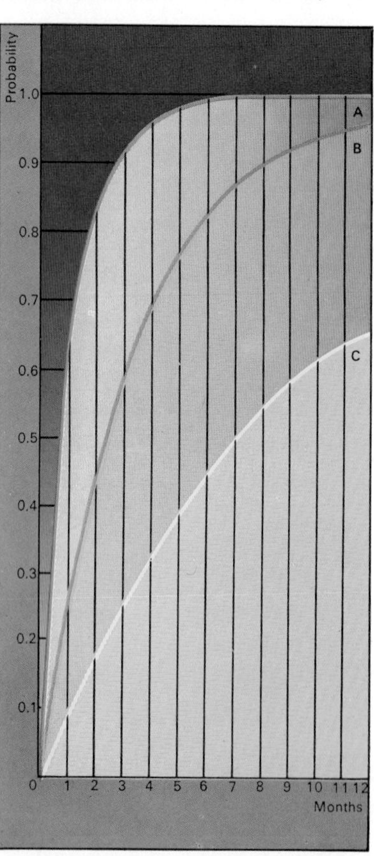

1
Probability
1.0
0.9
0.8
0.7
0.6
0.5
0.4
0.3
0.2
0.1
0
A
B
C
1 2 3 4 5 6 7 8 9 10 11 12
Months

1 Conception depends on many small chances. Even when a couple is very fertile, the chance of conceiving might be a curve [A], reaching 0.9 (90%) in 3 months. An average couple [B] might have a 60% chance of conceiving in this time and a couple with a low fertility [C] of only 25%, chance of conceiving in a year.

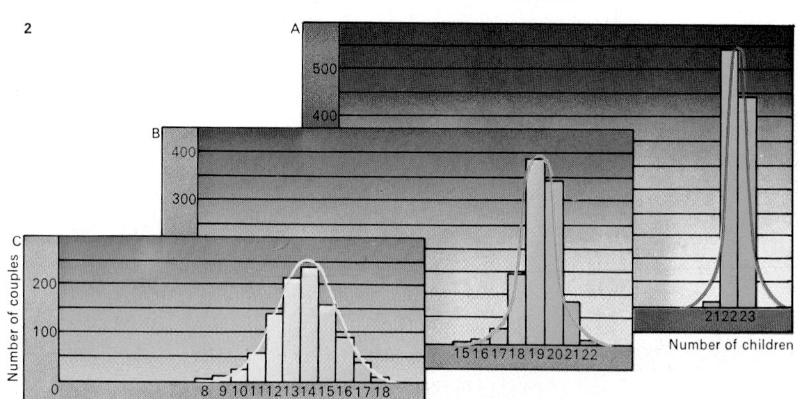

2
A
500
400
B
400
300
C
200
100
0
Number of couples
8 9 10 11 12 13 14 15 16 17 18
15 16 17 18 19 20 21 22
21 22 23
Number of children

2 Computer calculations show the range of family size that 1,000 couples of each type might expect after 25 years. [A] will probably have 21–23 children, [B] 15–21, and [C], probably 10–17.

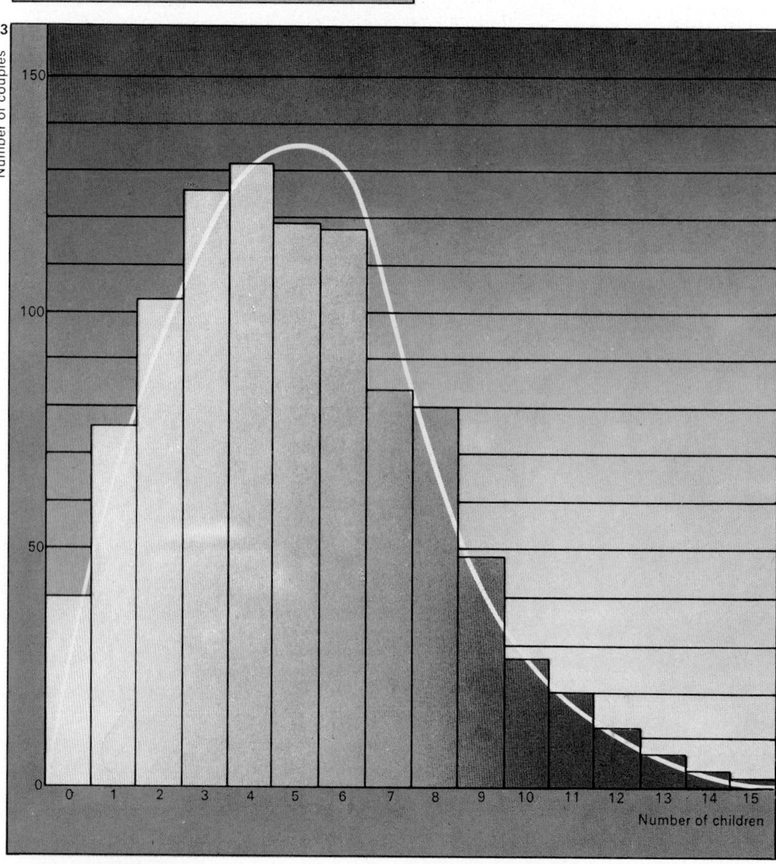

3
Number of couples
150
100
50
0
0 1 2 3 4 5 6 7 8 9 10 11 12 13 14 15
Number of children

3 Even in a primitive community very large families are rare. Limiting factors include the death of the mother or her becoming infertile. If, for such reasons, the chances of a family being complete after the birth of the first child is assessed as 4%, at 8% after the birth of the second child, and so on, then families of high, average, and low fertility each have an average of five or six children and produce the same curve.

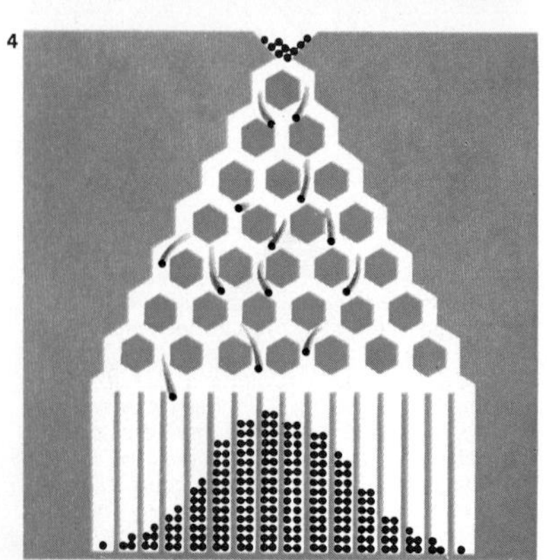

4

4 A rain of balls through this Galton board is distributed in the bell-shaped "normal" curve. This and similar curves are commonplace in statistics. It shows the outcome of events under many individual chances—most stay near the average; a few stray farther away.

arises because of the irritant substances that can form under the foreskin of an uncircumcised man if he is careless about personal hygiene. Jewish men, being circumcised, do not expose their wives to this slight hazard. So mathematicians must not jump to hasty conclusions. Correlations are not causes and statistical data are dangerously easy to misuse.

Molecules and magnetic tape

In a sense the world is ruled by statistics, for its individual atoms and molecules are, by the uncertainty principle, not completely predictable. Only when considered in countless millions is their behavior reliable. It is unlikely, for example, although theoretically possible, that all the air molecules around someone should rush away spontaneously and leave him to suffocate. On a smaller scale chance molecular fluctuations are inevitable and modern technology, in its quest for sensitivity, occasionally encounters them. A good audio amplifier with the volume turned up, for example, produces a slight hissing which is the amplified random motion of the electrons in the input circuit. It is as if the amplifier handles information by "tossing electrons," and residual uncertainties cannot be avoided.

In a similar way magnetic recording maps an audio signal onto millions of metal-oxide particles on the tape [Key]. Each can have one of just two magnetic states, equivalent to heads and tails. The faster the tape runs, and the wider the track processed by the recording head, the more particles are used to record a given sound by the changes in their distribution and magnetic states. For this reason the best quality machines use high speeds (15in [38cm] per second) and wide tracks (up to 0.5in [1.26cm]) to reduce tape hiss. Domestic recorders use lower speeds down to only 1.5in (3.75cm) per second and track widths down to .02in (0.05cm). They suffer accordingly from the smaller sample of magnetic particles from which they must reconstruct the signal. The same statistical principles underlie extraction of information from the tossing of pennies, the fate of smokers, and the reading of magnetic tape.

KEY

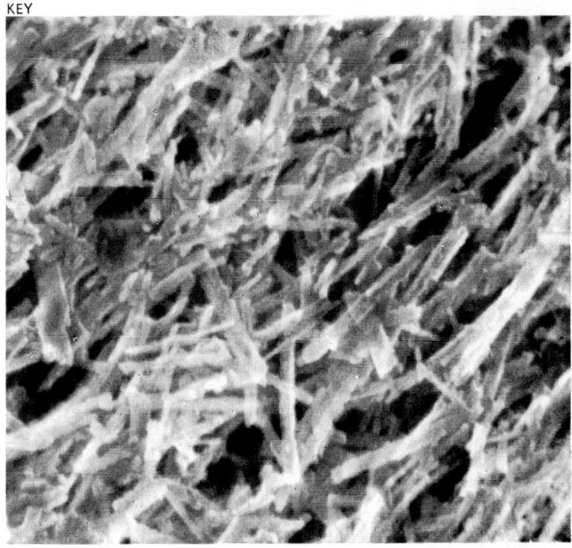

Metallic particles on recording tape, here highly magnified, have their magnetic state changed by the recording process. The quality of recording depends on how many are affected.

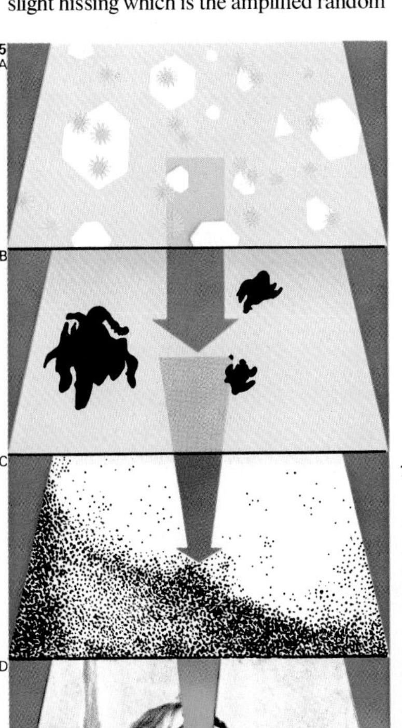

5
A
B
C
D

5 In photographic film sensitive grains are distributed in gelatine. Two photons (light particles) must hit a grain [A] to render it developable [B]. In a random hail of photons this is pure chance for any one grain. But there are so many [C] that statistically the number of developed grains follows the illumination closely [D]. There is a remote chance that the picture might look like something completely different.

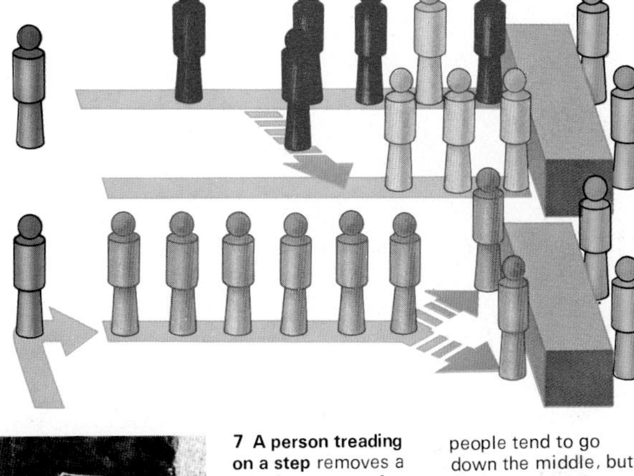

6

6 People arrive at a counter quite unpredictably. How many clerks are needed for efficient service? This is a question for queuing theory, which predicts that one line served by two clerks is more efficient than two lines served by one each. It also decides how much switchgear a telephone exchange needs to handle randomly arriving calls, how many machinists a machine shop needs to cope with irregular repairs, and so on. It proves that if some lines are not to grow infinitely long there should be one line that splits at the head, although a few machinists, clerks, or telephone operators may be idle for a fraction of the time.

7

7 A person treading on a step removes a certain amount of stone from his path. Over the years the stone wears away according to the average distribution of paths down the steps. Since most people tend to go down the middle, but deviate randomly to either side, the steps tend to wear into the bell-shaped "normal" curve. This is a statistical curve that has literally "drawn" itself.

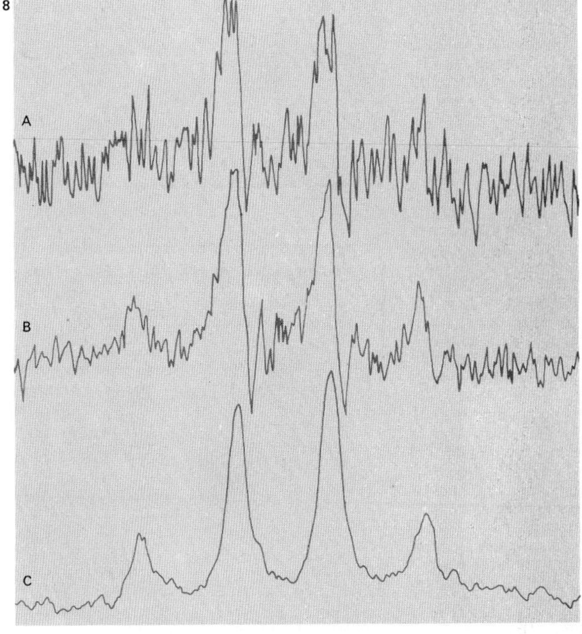

8
A
B
C

8 Many scientific instruments must register a weak signal against a background of random interference. One strategy is to keep repeating the measurement. The signal is always there, the interference is positive or negative and statistically tends to cancel out. The top trace [A], from a nuclear magnetic resonance spectrometer, shows a spectrum heavily degraded by random interference. In [B] 16 scans have been added and in [C] 256 scans.

9
2
3
4

9 A liquid of one color is poured into another and left. Soon the boundary becomes fuzzy and in due course the mixture is uniform. Any one molecule wanders at random, but the statistical effect of all their travels is a perfect mix, the most disordered arrangement possible. The gradual but inevitable increase of disorder is a basic law of physics.

Odds and probability

A racing-car driver worried by the possibility of a blowout consulted a mathematician. "Don't worry," he was told, "there is only one chance in a thousand of any one car blowing a tire." "But I do such a lot of racing," said the driver. "Then always carry a flat tire yourself," came the reply, "because there's only one chance in a million of a car having two flat tires."

How to find the probabilities

This is an elementary but popular fallacy about probability theory. If two independent events each have a known probability such as one-thousandth, the chance of their both occurring together is indeed obtained by multiplying the two probabilities, giving in this example one-millionth. But they must be independent: the chance of one cannot be altered by tampering with that of the other—such as ensuring its certainty.

This multiplication rule is one of the two great pillars of probability theory. The other, the addition rule, says that given two mutually exclusive events (such as rolling a one or a two with a die—both cannot be rolled), then the chance of either occurring is the sum of their probabilities. In this case each has a 1/6 probability; so if either one or two wins, the chance of success is 1/6 + 1/6 = 1/3.

These two rules, carefully used, can solve most problems of probability. They rest on a subtle sort of probabilistic "atomic theory" that treats any chance event as being compounded from a set of basic "equiprobable events." By calculating what combination of these will result in the desired chance coming up, its probability is obtained. But the idea requires subtle handling. Many misleading arguments depend on a deceptive choice of basic equiprobabilities. What is the chance of there being monkeys on Jupiter, for example? Either there are or there are not—and it could be argued that, since nobody has yet been to Jupiter, these mutually exclusive situations are equally probable. Then each has half a chance of truth and there is a 50 percent chance monkeys live on Jupiter.

More subtly, what is the chance of getting one head and one tail on two tosses of a coin? It might be reasoned that there are only three basic possibilities: two heads (HH), head and tail (HT), and two tails (TT). Only one of these is favorable, so the chance is 1/3. But this is not so. There are actually four "atomic" equiprobabilities: HH, HT, TH, and TT, of which two are favorable. The chance is 2/4 or one half.

Calculating the chances of success

In mathematical notation, chances vary from 0 (impossible) to 1 (certain). If there are 7 equiprobable possibilities, and 2 of them will result in success, the chance of success is 2 in 7, or 2/7, or 0.2857. This can also be expressed as 28.57 percent, or in betting parlance 2 to 5 for, or 5 to 2 against. Such figures make most intuitive sense when applied to situations that can occur many times. In a run of 7,000 trials, each with a 2/7 chance of success, about 2,000 successes would be expected. A gambler would break even in the long run by accepting odds of 7 to 2 (that is $7 return for a $2 stake). Where the basic equiprobable events are clear and knowable (as in the fall

CONNECTIONS

See also
1474 Facts and statistics
824 Parapsychology

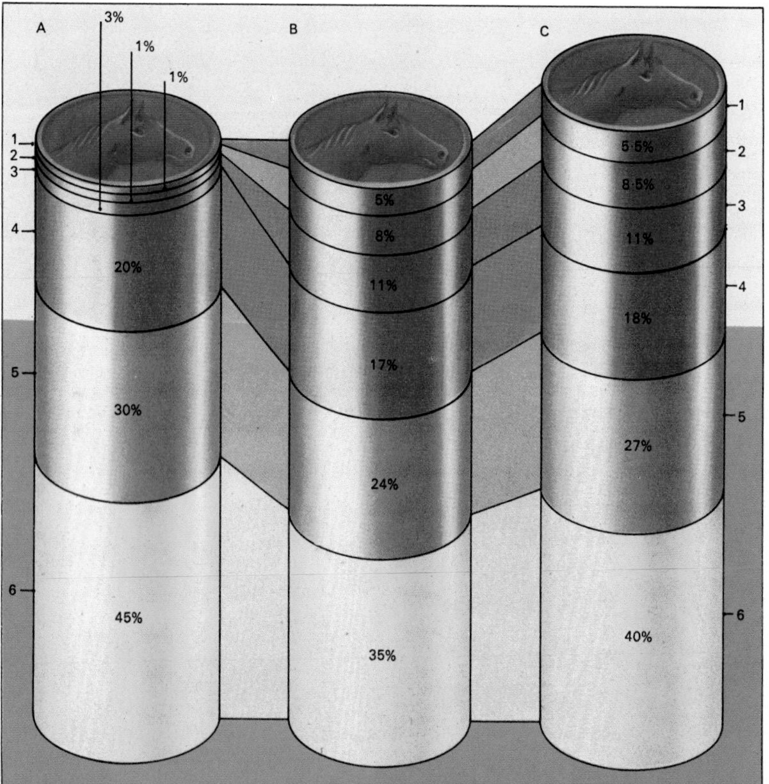

1
A
B
C
3%
1%
1%
20%
30%
45%
5%
8%
11%
17%
24%
35%
5·5%
8·5%
11%
18%
27%
40%
1
2
3
4
5
6

1 The bookmaker aims to offer odds that give him the same predictable profit whichever horse wins. Thus if he received $3 on one horse and $5 on another, he might offer odds of 7:3 on the first (4 to 3 for) and 7:5 (2 to 5 for) on the second. Whichever wins, he pays out $7 and makes $1 profit. So his odds reflect the money bet. "Long shots" attract little money, so he offers long odds on them. The chances of six horses are shown in A; 1, 2, 3 are long shots with very long odds against them. But amateur bettors find them reasonably seductive, so the money placed distributes itself as in B. The bookmaker changes the total odds upward in his own favor, as in C. He is sure of a profit in the ratio of C to B: But even so, some winning odds – on the favorite [6] – are undervalued in C compared with the "reality" of A: 40% (ie, offering a return of 100 to 40) compared with its actual chance of winning, 45%. Thus 6 favors the bookmaker and a series of such bets should clear an average of 10% profit to him. But the gullible backers of long shots, in the long run, also lose. The same mathematical calculation of odds – probabilities – occurs throughout science. In atomic theory, for example, the location of an electron within an atom is defined in terms of probabilities.

2 A tossed coin can land either "heads" or "tails." On each toss the probability of a head (or tail) is 1/2 (0.5) – the chances are even. If a coin lands heads (or tails) eight times in succession, a gambler might be tempted to expect that a tail (or head) is more likely to occur on the ninth toss. But the mathematical probability of either outcome is still exactly 1/2 – an even chance.

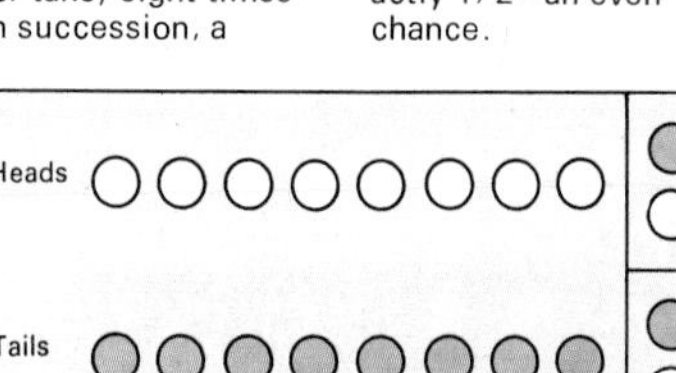

2
Heads
Tails

3 Crown and anchor uses three dice inscribed with the six symbols of the matrix below, which shows all outcomes for the first die "diamond" (five other matrices are similar). Players bet on their symbols against a banker, who returns twice the stake for one symbol displayed, three times for double, and four times for triple. Assume each symbol is backed, giving six stakes "input" per throw. 20 out of 36 times (by the matrix), three different symbols come up and the banker makes no gain, returning three 2-fold stakes to the winners. On doubles (15 in 36) he pays out two on the singlet and three on the doublet and keeps one. On the only triple, he pays four and keeps two. So in 37 rounds he has gained (with one unit staked on each symbol) 15 + 2 = 17 of the 216 stakes: 7.9% return.

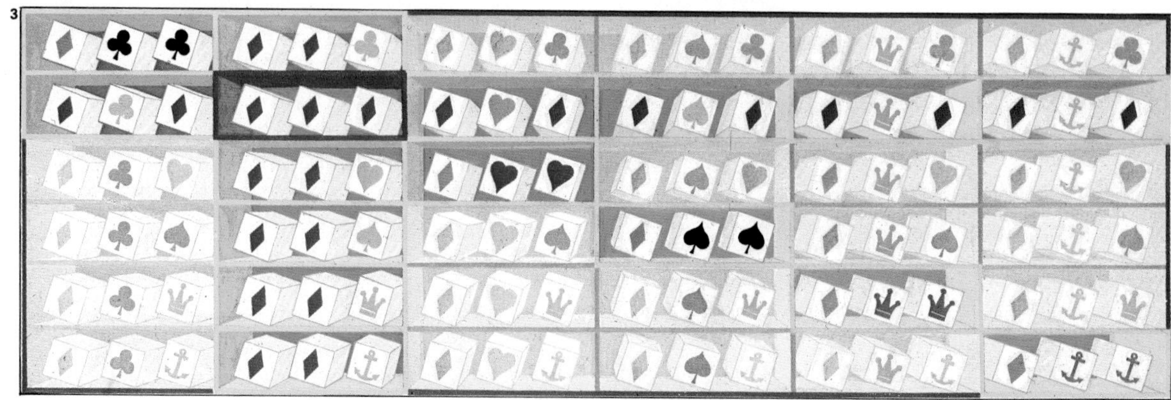

3

of coins or dice), probability theory can give unambiguous chances of success for any outcome. All gambling houses use this principle to set fixed odds that guarantee them a steady average income.

In sports and business assessments, odds are subjective and different people guess them differently. By betting on the favorite in a horse race with a number of unproven "long shots," however, the gambler's chances of winning are demonstrably better [1]. If one of the horses is known to be doped, or a rival's business strategy is known, it is possible to place investments with better than average insight. This is the province of "game theory"—the theory of competing for gains against opponents with assumed aims and knowledge.

In the child's game of button-button, a button is hidden in one hand and the opponent has to guess which. He wins a penny if he is correct and loses one if he is wrong. If the same hand is always played, or hands are switched regularly, the opponent will soon outguess the holder. Game theory proves that the best strategy is to decide the switch at random—for example, by tossing a coin before each round. This is entirely foolproof; even if the opponent discovers the strategy he cannot win more than he loses in the long run. But if two pennies are lost for a right-hand disclosure and only one penny for a left-hand one, the opponent could then win steadily by always choosing the right hand, and making on the average bigger gains than losses. For this modification, game theory prescribes for the holder a "weighted random switch" of 2:1 toward the left—say by tossing a die and playing to the right on 1 and 2, and left on 3,4,5, and 6.

Uses in real-life conflicts

In real-life conflicts, such as war and business, game theory is often used for clarifying options, but seldom slavishly followed. If two people make an agreement, for example, game theory recommends to each that he double-cross the other, for he will gain more if the other is honest. And in a world of unique events that either happen or do not, the whole concept of probability needs careful handling.

KEY

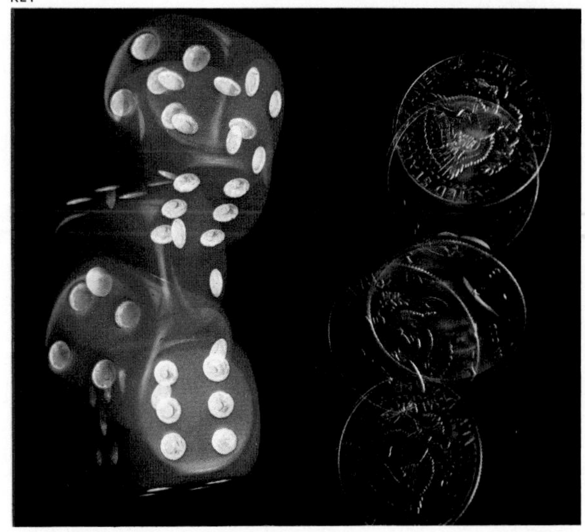

Probability theory cannot predict the outcome of a chance event such as the rolling of a die or the tossing of a coin. But in the long run (thousands of rolls) any one number on a die will occur with a probability of 1/6 (0.16666).

4 A

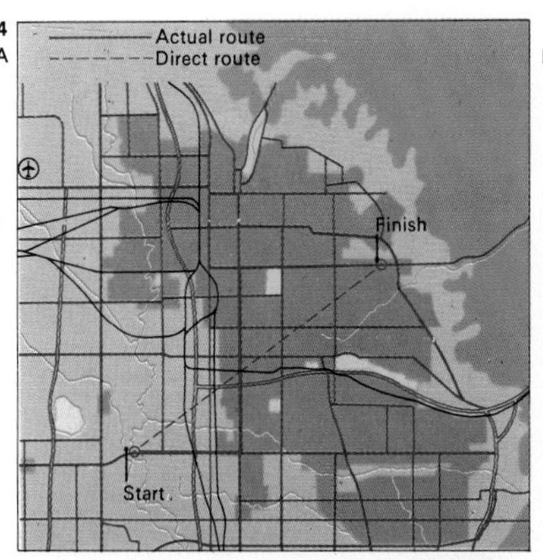

Actual route
Direct route
Finish
Start

B

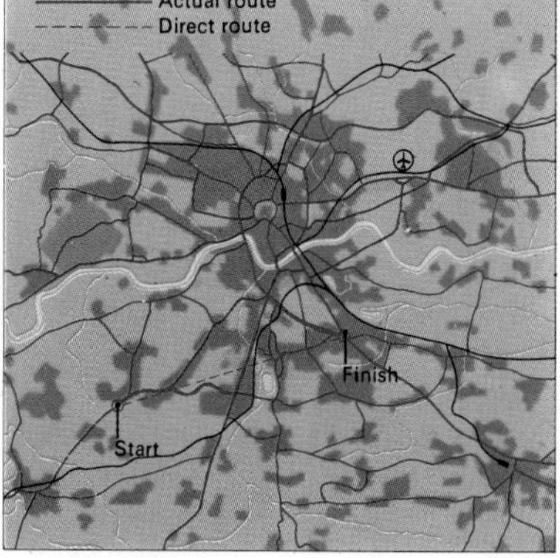

Actual route
Direct route
Finish
Start

C

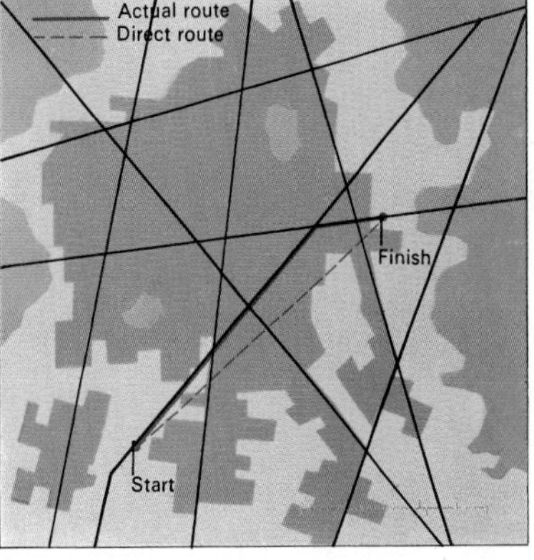

Actual route
Direct route
Finish
Start

4 Is the rational grid layout of Salt Lake City [A] more efficient than the rambling European city of Krakow [B]? A diagonal journey on a grid forces you to traverse the equivalent of two sides of a triangle, even if you zigzag. Probability theory shows that to facilitate many unpredictable point-to-point journeys, a random distribution of straight lines is best [C], a style close to Krakow's.

5

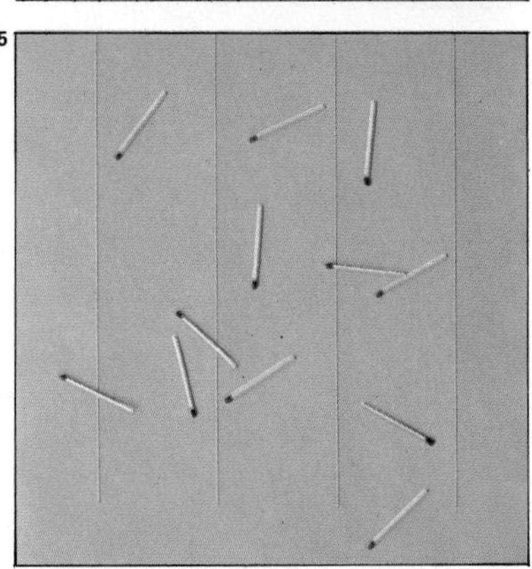

5 In the "buffon match problem," a match is thrown at random on a striped cloth. If the stripes are n match-lengths wide, the chance of it coming to rest across a line is $2/n\pi$. It is surprising to find π in this answer: it enters because the match can lie at any angle; like a spoke in a wheel thrown onto the stripes. Mathematicians have evaluated π experimentally by repeated throwing of matches in this way.

6

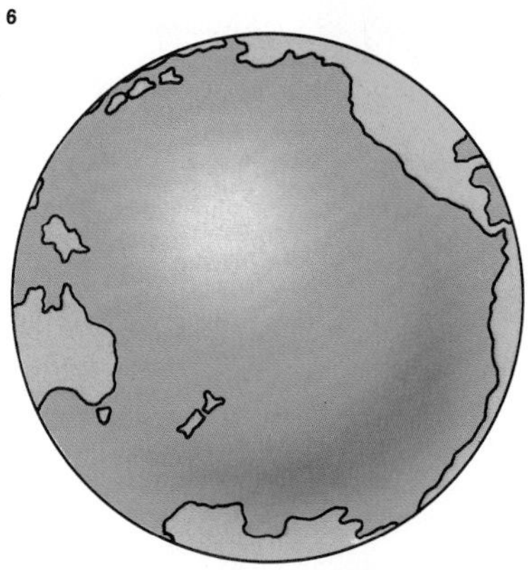

6 Are the shape and distribution of the continents random? The fact that they are crowded into half the globe, leaving the Pacific Basin occupying a whole hemisphere, suggests they are not. But modern plate tectonics proves otherwise. The continents are "floating" on the crustal surface and for most of past geological time converging subcrustal rock currents held them all in one small area, although they are generally now spreading out.

7

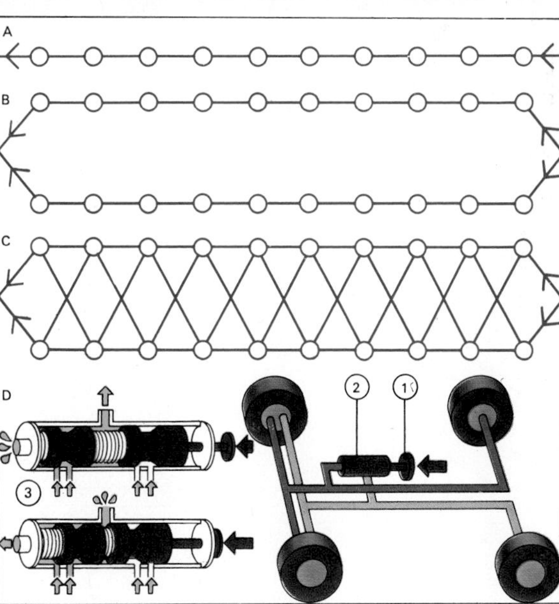
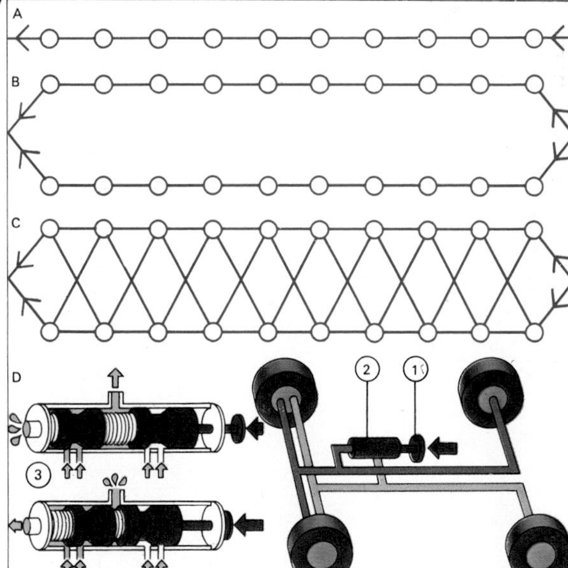

A
B
C
D
1
2
3

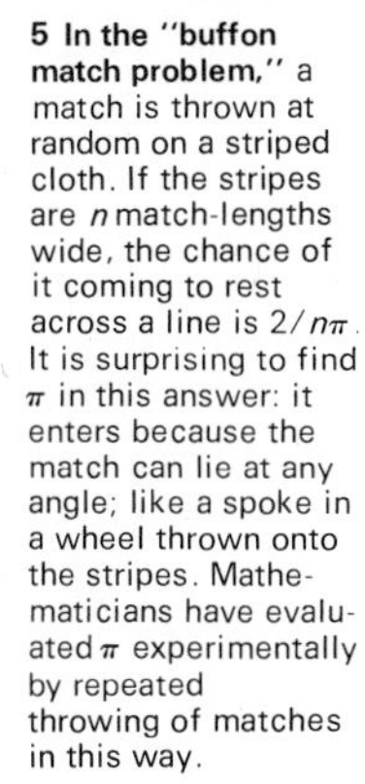

7 A chain of components, all of which must work if the system is to function, is less reliable than its members. With 10 elements each of 99% reliability [A], the whole thing has about 90% reliability. One improvement is duplication [B]; with two such chains in parallel, the chance of at least one of them working is 95%. But it is better to parallel each element separately, so that a paralleled pair will still function if either of its members is working [C]. Then each pair has a reliability of 99.99% and the whole chain of them has 99.9%. This principle is built into a car's dual braking system [D]. Pressing the pedal [1] moves pistons in the master cylinder [2]. Three brakes work even with a leak [3].

8

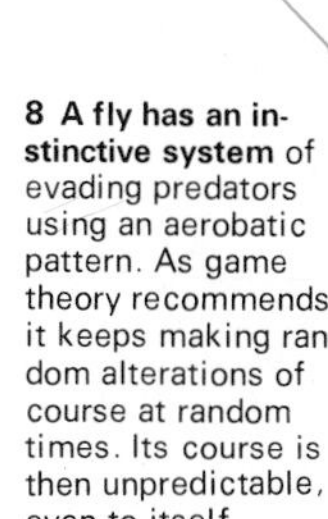

8 A fly has an instinctive system of evading predators using an aerobatic pattern. As game theory recommends, it keeps making random alterations of course at random times. Its course is then unpredictable, even to itself.

The scale of the universe

Every object around us—indeed, all matter—is made up of countless tiny fragments called atoms. And the Earth is but a tiny speck in the vastness of the universe [Key]. But how large are these fragments? How big is an atom? And how large is the universe?

According to current thinking, the universe is about a billion billion billion billion (10^{36}) times as large as a single atom. But this statement gives no clue to the absolute size of either of them. To define the sizes of atoms, galaxies, and the universe—as for a table or a garden—scientists use a series of units. An understanding of these is essential to understanding modern science—and to help the imagination to grasp the range [1] between the immensity of the universe and the smallness of an atom.

Units of scale

Small objects can be measured in millimeters (about 0.04 inch) and longer distances are quoted in kilometers (about 0.62 mile). It is difficult to imagine the number of millimeters in a kilometer. But 10mm=1cm; 100cm=1m; 1,000m=1km. Or, writing the numbers as powers of ten, 10^1mm=1cm; 10^2cm=1m; and 10^3m=1km. Therefore one million or 10^6mm=1km. To denote something smaller a negative index is used: 10^{-1}cm (a tenth of a centimeter)=1mm.

Today an atom is visualized as being almost all empty space with a few tiny subatomic particles. Very roughly, a subatomic particle [2] may be thought of as having a diameter of 10^{-13}cm. Ten trillion (10^{13}) laid in a row might extend a centimeter. The nucleus of an atom is made up of such particles—protons and neutrons—and may be about 10^{-12}cm in diameter. An atom is the next jump in size; measured by pioneers of X-ray crystallography in ångstrom units, Å$=10^{-8}$cm, an atom is about 100 thousand times as large as the proton. Atoms can be bound together to form molecules that can be grouped to make a volume of any size: molecules of gas, a crystal, a droplet of liquid, or all the water in the oceans. The paper of this page is a few million atoms thick.

The wavelength of visible light is 4×10^{-5}cm to 7.2×10^{-5}cm. As a result, particles with a larger diameter than this can be seen using an ordinary microscope. To make smaller objects visible scientists use electron microscopes, because fast electrons have much shorter wavelengths. The smallest living organisms, such as bacteria, are microscopic. Smaller bodies such as viruses [3], which are submicroscopic, cannot live and develop alone but are parasitic on cells of living organisms. All visible living things are made up of millions of atoms.

Distances—from men to the stars

The tallest men are about 2m (6.5ft) in height and the Earth is more than 12,000km in diameter. The diameter of the Sun is more than a million kilometers. The nearest heavenly body to Earth is the Moon, about 384,000km away. Since man landed on the Moon and looked back to the Earth [7] this distance has acquired a more tangible reality.

The Sun is about 1.5×10^8 (150 million)km away from the Earth and the planet Pluto nearly 6×10^9km. These numbers are already becoming difficult to visualize and

CONNECTIONS

See also
1480 What is an atom?
1484 Beyond the atom
126 The expanding universe

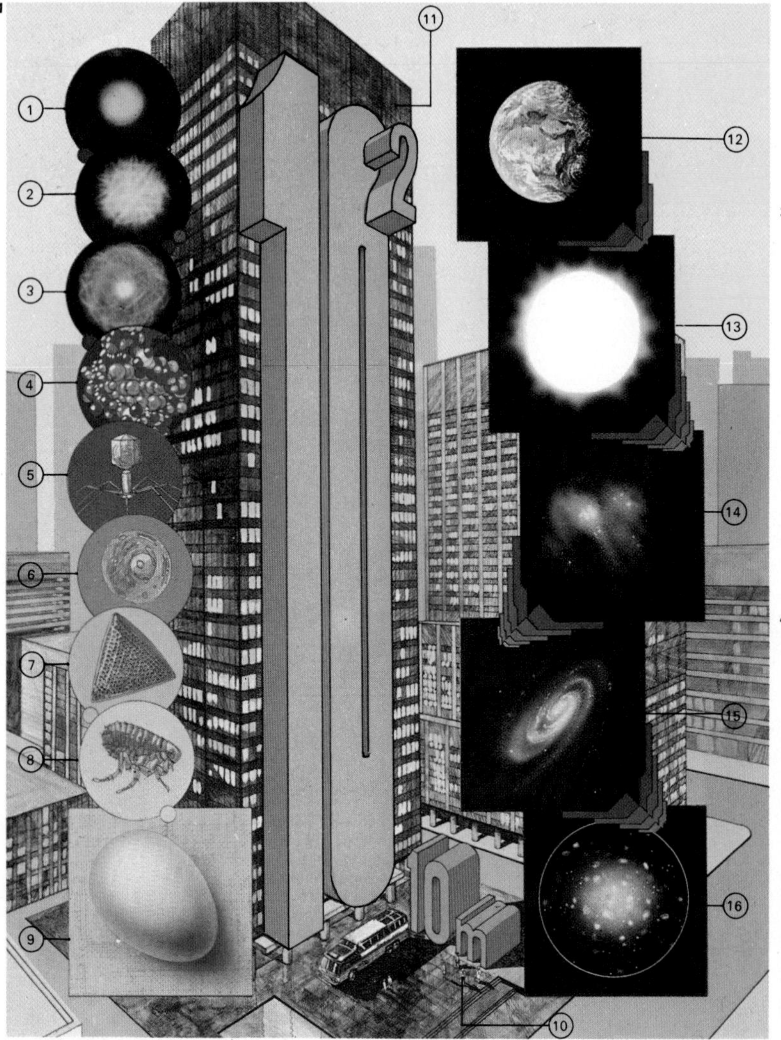

1
2
3
4
5
6
7
8
9
10
11
12
13
14
15
16

1 Within the known universe the dimensions of tiny, subatomic particles and the distance attainable by astronomers' telescopes stand in a ratio of about 10^{40}. The objects shown spanning this staggering range are a proton [1]; an atomic nucleus [2]; an atom [3]; a giant molecule [4]; a virus [5]; a small cell, an ameba [6]; a large cell, a diatom [7]; a flea [8]; a hen's egg [9]; a man [10] 2m (6.5ft) high and one of his buildings [11]; the Earth [12]; a giant star [13]; an interstellar gas cloud or nebula [14]; our Galaxy [15] and the limits of the theoretically observable universe [16]. The 10m symbol is 10m (32.5ft) tall—five times as tall as a man—and the skyscraper [11] is more than 10^2 = 100m (325ft) tall.

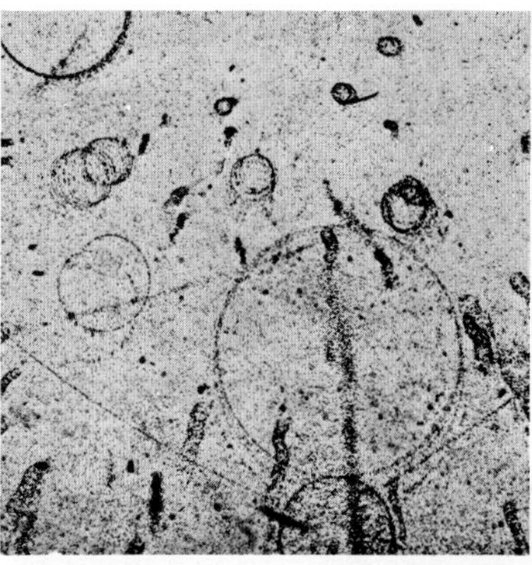

2 Particles are so remote from our experience that indirect methods must be used to make them visible, such as the cloud chamber invented by Charles Wilson (1869–1959) in the 1920s and developed by Patrick Blackett (1897–). It uses water vapor condensing on particles to track and identify them. Particles can also be tracked in bubble or spark chambers, or by using stacks of photographic plates.

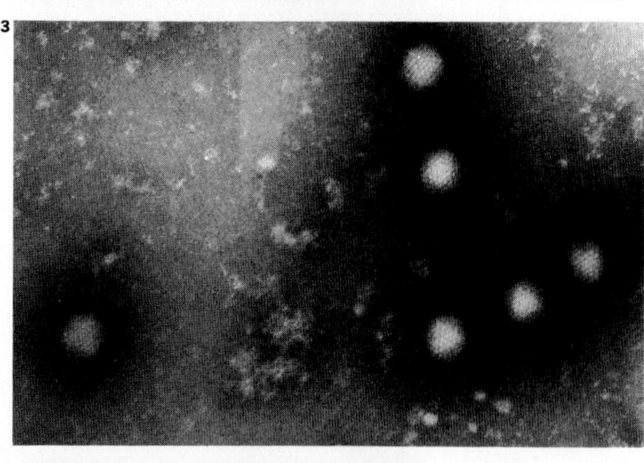

3 Viruses are too small to be visible under an ordinary microscope but can be seen with an electron microscope. They are nonliving matter but affect the properties of living cells.

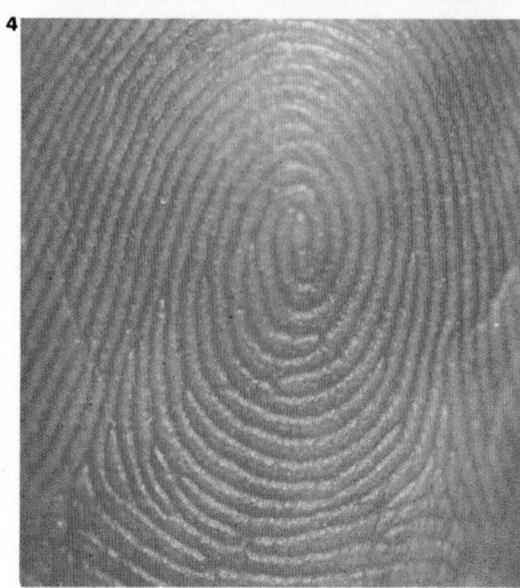

4 The unique pattern of a fingertip exemplifies the enormous number of individual cells that make up even the smallest piece of living matter visible to the naked eye. There are about 10 million cells in each square centimeter of human skin.

the whole Solar System, the Sun with its attendant planets [8], is the merest speck in space. Therefore to describe the geometry of the stars a different unit of distance is used: the light-year, or the distance light travels in a year. In just one second light travels 3×10^5 (300,000) km. In a year light travels about 10^{13}km and the nearest star is more than four light-years from the Sun.

It is only in relation to these kinds of figures that the granulation of the universe can be sensed. The atomic nucleus is formed of densely packed particles, but the atom is almost all empty space. Similarly, in the universe the atoms on the planets and stars are closely packed to form solids, liquids, or gases. But the stars are separated by huge distances compared with their diameters, and so the universe around us, like the atom, is nearly all empty space.

Toward infinity

The stars themselves, at their immense distances, are grouped into great clusters called galaxies or nebulae. So huge are their numbers that through telescopes they look like great white clouds. In our Galaxy alone, the Milky Way, there are more than 10^{11} stars. The Galaxy is about 10^4 light-years thick in the middle and 10^5 light-years across.

Galaxies have greatly differing appearances according to the wavelengths of the light used to observe them. One of the most rapidly developing branches of astronomy is radio astronomy, in which observation is made by radio waves. The largest known object in the universe is a galaxy designated 3C236, observed by radio telescope. A curious object in which the principal radio sources are two bulges at each end, it measures about 2×10^7 (20 million) light-years from end to end. The nearest large galaxy to our own is 2×10^6 light-years away. The farthest objects probably lie at a distance of about 10^{10} light-years, although it is difficult to be confident about such estimates.

The scale of the known universe from the atomic nucleus to the farthest star is about 10^{40}. But what is beyond the limits of present-day astronomy? Does the universe stretch to infinity? Or could it be curved in a way so that its mass and size are finite?

KEY

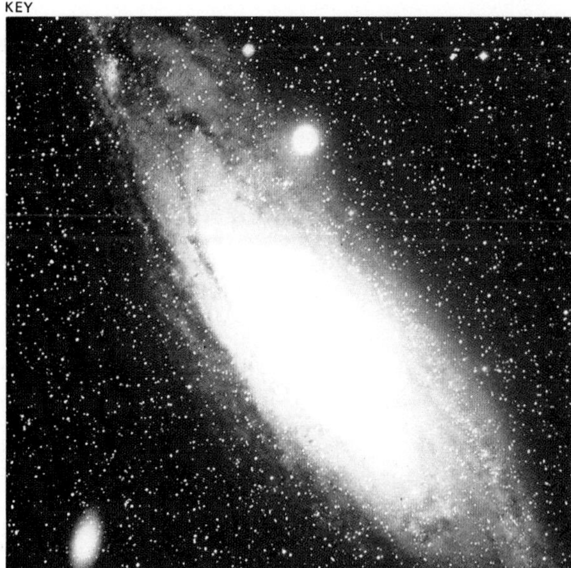

The spiral nebula in Andromeda has a measurable size, but it is difficult to grasp: 120,000 light-years across.

5

6

5 "Man is the measure of all things" said Protagoras in the 5th century BC—a humanist view that established man at the center of the universe and related objects to a human scale. The personification of nature was a theme of such Renaissance painters as Botticelli (1444–1510), who painted "The Birth of Venus." In modern science man is no longer the standard of length.

6 Man's most visible artifact, the Great Wall of China, runs for more than 2,400 km (1,500 miles), about 5% of the circumference of the Earth. It can be seen from well out in space.

7 The Earth, as a body floating in space, has acquired a new reality since man left his own planet and looked back at his terrestrial home. For the first time, it has been seen as merely one minute body in immeasurable space. The idea of other planets having other life forms is no longer regarded as improbable. The number of possibly inhabited planets could be in the millions.

8 The Solar System has been brought within man's reach during the past 20 years. White paths represent the orbits of the nine planets. The blue and red ellipses are typical cometary orbits.

7

8

What is an atom?

The first recorded suggestion that matter might consist of separate particles was made in the fifth century BC, probably by Leucippus of Miletus [1], and the idea was developed by his pupil Democritus, who adopted the word *atomos* (from the Greek word meaning indivisible). John Dalton (1766–1844) revived the word at the beginning of the nineteenth century when he provided a scientific basis for the simple Greek idea. To Dalton an atom was like a tiny indivisible particle that acted as the basic unit of matter that takes part in chemical reactions.

The atom and electricity

The simple Daltonian view of the atom was overturned in 1897 when J. J. Thomson (1856–1940) discovered that atoms could emit even smaller particles of negative electricity (later called electrons) [5]. Clearly the atom itself must have some form of internal structure. Thomson's discovery also implied, as the whole atom was electrically neutral, that it must also contain positive electricity. He suggested that the electrons were like currants dispersed throughout a positively charged bun. This model failed to explain a number of the properties of atoms, but a better one had to await the discovery of radioactivity by Antoine Becquerel (1852–1908). He found that certain heavy atoms spontaneously emit radiation. Three forms of this are now known: beta rays (streams of electrons), alpha particles (helium nuclei consisting of two protons and two neutrons), and gamma rays.

The Rutherford and Bohr models

In 1911 Ernest Rutherford (1871–1937) produced an entirely new model of the atom based on the results of his own experiments and those of Hans Geiger (1882–1945) and his co-workers, who measured the scatter of alpha particles when shot at gold foil. Rutherford's suggestion was that the positive charge and most of the mass of the atom were concentrated in a central nucleus and that the electrons rotate around this nucleus. We now know that the atom is mostly empty space with a minute central nucleus some tens of thousands of times smaller than the atom. The atoms themselves are extremely small—ten million of them side by side would measure only 1 mm (0.039in).

Rutherford later discovered that the positive charge of the nucleus is carried by particles 1,846 times heavier than electrons; he christened them protons. The charge of the proton is equal, but opposite, to that of the electron. A hydrogen atom, in this model, consists of a single positively charged proton (the nucleus) with one electron traveling in an orbit around it [Key].

Heavier atoms have increasing numbers of protons in their nuclei, but the number of protons in the nucleus (called the atomic number) is always balanced by an equal number of orbiting electrons. It was later discovered that all atoms except hydrogen have another type of particle in their nuclei. These are uncharged particles called neutrons and they have almost the same mass as the proton.

Quantum theory and spectroscopy

Two other fields of investigation helped the Danish physicist Niels Bohr (1885–1962) to

CONNECTIONS

See also
1482 Nuclear physics
1484 Beyond the atom
1530 What is electricity?
1536 Electromagnetism
1552 Classification of elements
1556 Joining atoms
1566 Electrochemistry

1 The city of Miletus was the first known home of natural philosophy. Thales (*c.* 630 BC) was born there. He was a member of the Ionian School, the earliest known in Greek philosophy. He discovered the electrical properties of amber. Anaximander also dwelt there, as did Leucippus (*c.* 400 BC), credited by Aristotle with developing atomic theory, a central element in scientific thought.

2 Modern science pictures matter as having a dual existence as waves and particles. Waves are created by the vibrations of water molecules (particles) disturbed by passing ducks, just as particles that are sufficiently small and energetic may behave as waves. Light waves consist of photons, particles without mass but with precisely measurable energies.

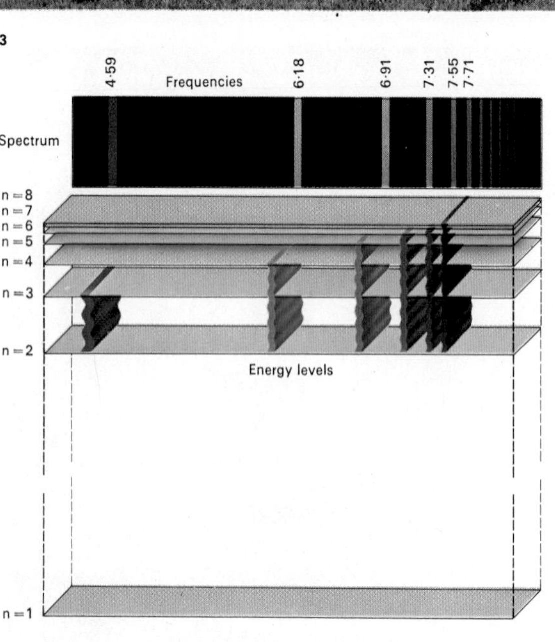
Frequencies
4·59
6·18
6·91
7·31
7·55
7·71
Spectrum
n=8
n=7
n=6
n=5
n=4
n=3
n=2
Energy levels
n=1

3 Lines in the spectrum were observed by Fraunhofer in light from the Sun. These emission lines result from emission of light by atoms. A test of Bohr's theory was its ability to explain the wavelengths of the lines in the spectrum of hydrogen in terms of electron energy level changes.

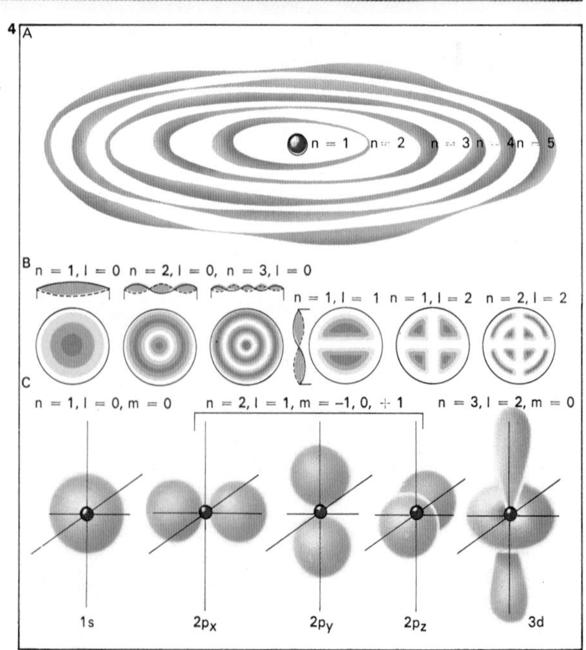
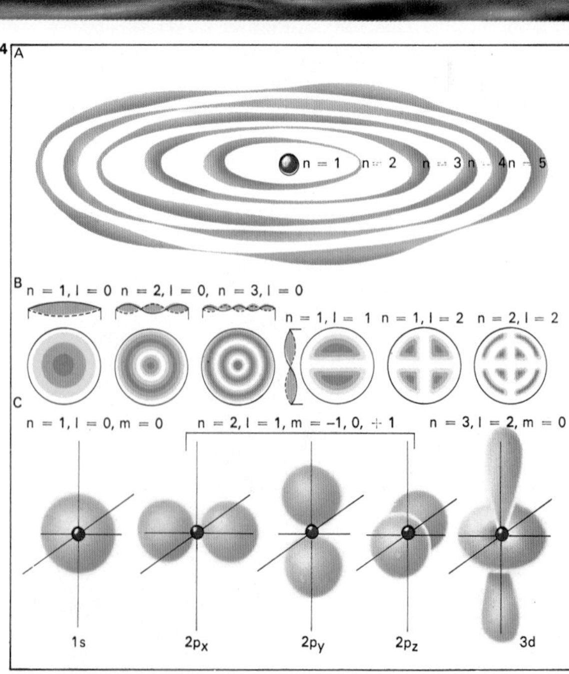
A
n = 1
n = 2
n = 3
n = 4
n = 5
B
n = 1, l = 0
n = 2, l = 0,
n = 3, l = 0
n = 1, l = 1
n = 1, l = 2
n = 2, l = 2
C
n = 1, l = 0, m = 0
n = 2, l = 1, m = −1, 0, +1
n = 3, l = 2, m = 0
1s
2px
2py
2pz
3d

4 Possible orbits of an electron around an atomic nucleus can be pictured [A] as circles that exactly accommodate a whole number of wavelengths, denoted by the principal quantum number n. A two-dimensional analogy (a vibrating drum skin) is described by two quantum numbers, n and l [B], and the shape of an atom [C] in terms of three (n, l and m).

construct the next atomic model [Key]. The first was the quantum theory, the other was the science of spectroscopy. Quantum theory was proposed by Max Planck (1898–1947) [7] in 1900 as a way of explaining the emission of heat (and light) by a hot body. He speculated that energy can be emitted and absorbed only in discontinuous amounts, called quanta.

Spectroscopy began when Issac Newton (1642–1727) passed a ray of sunlight through a glass prism, breaking the ray into all the colors of the visible spectrum. In 1814 Joseph von Fraunhofer (1787–1826) had discovered that the spectrum of sunlight contains a number of black lines, which were later found to coincide with the position of colored lines in the spectrum formed by electric discharge in hydrogen gas [3]. Bohr postulated that the circulating electron in an atom of hydrogen can exist only in fixed orbits [4A], and that the spectral lines correspond to the absorption (black lines) or emission (colored lines) of a quantum of energy when this electron jumps from one fixed orbit to another. This theory, later modified by Arnold Sommerfeld (1868–1951), has been very successful in explaining the hydrogen spectrum.

Modern developments of the quantum theory suggest that the fixed orbits of Bohr should be visualized less precisely and that the position of an atomic electron should be treated as a probability that it will be in a certain place at a certain time. This treatment, known as quantum mechanics [2], was largely the work of Werner Heisenberg (1901–76) and Erwin Schrödinger (1887–1961).

The substitution of a probability for a fixed orbit is a reflection of Heisenberg's uncertainty principle. This says that if the momentum of a particle is known precisely there must be an uncertainty as to its position. In the wave mechanics developed by Louis de Broglie (1892–), matter in the form of atomic particles is like light in that some of its properties are best explained in terms of particles, others in terms of waves. A stream of electrons, for example, behaves like particles in cathode rays and like waves in an electron microscope.

KEY

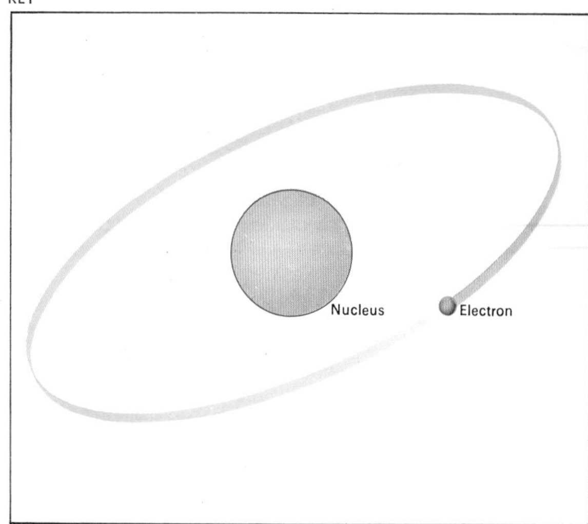
Nucleus
Electron

The pictorial representation of the model of the atom proposed by Niels Bohr is an established part of the iconography of modern physics, even though Bohr's ideas have largely been superseded by quantum mechanics. This example is a hydrogen atom.

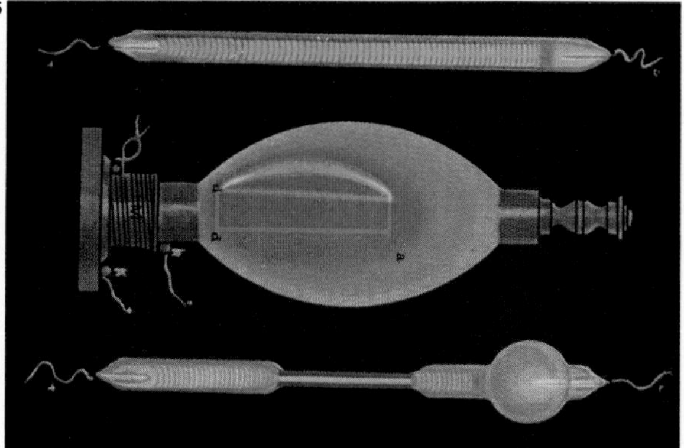

5 Geissler tubes, Victorian toys for adults, depended on electronic rays in a near-vacuum long before the principles of cathode rays were understood. The study of the rays, principally by J. J. Thomson, the British physicist, was the crucial one in the elucidation of the structure of the atom, by establishing the mass and charge of the electron, in conjunction with other experiments.

6 The new ideas about atomic physics were brought together at a series of conferences, such as this Solvay meeting at Brussels in 1911, attended by Bohr, Rutherford, Planck, Curie, and others.

7 Max Planck suggested in 1900 that light was absorbed and emitted in packets or "quanta," with energies proportional to the frequency of light. This was known as the quantum theory.

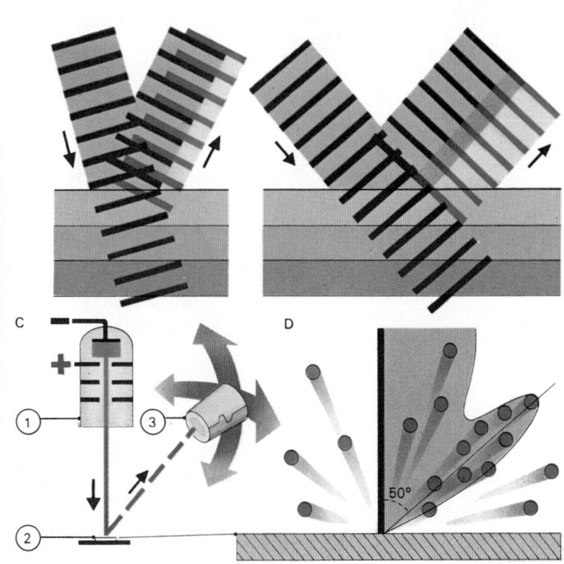
8 A
B
C
D
1
2
3
50°

8 When waves are reflected from parallel surfaces they are out of step [A] or in step [B]. An electron beam [C] from a gun [1] can be reflected from an element [2] to a detector [3] and angles plotted [D].

9 Erwin Schrödinger played a principal part in the mathematical development of the modern model of the atom. He developed wave mechanics from de Broglie's picture of wave-particle duality.

Nuclear physics

Nuclear energy plays a decisive part in shaping the modern world: nuclear weapons not only haunt the statesman but cast a threatening shadow on every living person [Key]. And while the image of limitless nuclear power attracts a civilization hungry for energy, the disposal of radioactive waste threatens lasting pollution of the world. In fact, life has always depended on nuclear energy: nuclear fusion heats the sun [1], and is also the process by which the same elements that form the Earth are created in the interior of stars. Nuclear energy depends on the immense forces holding positively-charged protons together in the nucleus of the atom. These forces may be released in several ways: radioactive decay, the spontaneous release of a particle from the nucleus; fission, the splitting of a heavy nucleus into two or more lighter nuclei; and fusion, the joining of two or more light nuclei into a heavier nucleus.

Radioactivity: its discovery and source

Radioactivity was discovered by Henri Becquerel (1852–1908). With the isolation of radium by the Curies in 1898 [3], it became clear that enormous amounts of energy were involved. Radium decays over many decades and contains 2×10^5 times as much energy as an equal mass of coal. Most elements consist of isotopes, whose nuclei differ in their number of neutrons. The total number of constituents (protons and neutrons) in a particular isotope is indicated by a superscript, for example He^4. It is on the properties of individual isotopes that nuclear power depends.

Deliberate transformation of one nucleus into another was achieved by Ernest Rutherford (1871–1937) [4] in 1919: $He^4 + N^{14} \rightarrow O^{17} + H^1$. In words, an alpha particle (the nucleus of helium) and a nitrogen nucleus momentarily combine and then split into the oxygen isotope O^{17} and a proton.

As mass spectrometers [7]—instruments that measure the individual masses of ions and thus of the nuclei—became more accurate, it was found that the masses of the nuclei of the various isotopes were not equal to the sum of the masses of the constituent protons and neutrons. This discrepancy, according to Einstein's relativity formula, $E = mc^2$, is the source of nuclear energy. Modern theory views the nucleus to be rather like a "liquid" droplet of neutrons and protons. Any such system tends to decay—that is to say transfers itself—into a state of lower energy. If it does so by breaking into two nearly equal parts, that is called fission; if a nuclei gives off one or more particles, that is radioactivity; if two nuclei join together to form a heavier nucleus, that is fusion. Two nuclei are both positively charged so one of them must be accelerated to high speed to achieve fusion, or both must be moving fast due to high temperature.

Generating nuclear energy

The generation of nuclear energy in large quantities by fission requires a chain reaction [6]: when a neutron is absorbed by the isotope uranium-235 it induces fission into two major fragments and two or three neutrons. If on the average two of these neutrons are absorbed by other U-235 nuclei the

CONNECTIONS

See also
1480 What is an atom?
1484 Beyond the atom
1530 What is electricity?
1638 Nuclear power
1746 Nuclear, chemical, and biological warfare

1

1 The sun is powered by nuclear fusion, which needs temperatures of the order of hundreds of millions of degrees centigrade. On earth the necessary conditions and temperatures for fusion reactions have so far been achieved only in nuclear bombs and, for short times, in experimental devices.

2 Volcanic energy is provided by radiation—a source of energy so powerful that a scattering of radioactive atoms with slow decay rate is presumably sufficient to heat the center of the earth. The liquid core that results underlies the continents and powers volcanic eruptions.

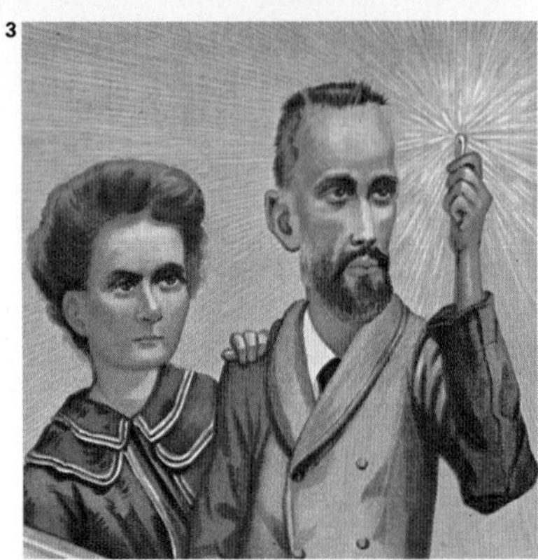

3 Marie Curie (1867–1934) and husband Pierre Curie (1859–1906) formed one of the most famous husband and wife teams in the history of science. During investigations of the radiations given off by uranium, they found an inexplicably high level of radiation. Through painstaking chemical detective work they tracked down and isolated its source in the radioactive elements radium and polonium.

4 Ernest Rutherford [A], a New Zealand-born physicist who first worked at Cambridge University in 1903, established the nuclear theory of the atom in 1911 and later achieved the first splitting of the atom when he produced protons from the nuclei of nitrogen atoms. He and his team used remarkably simple "string and sealing wax" apparatus at the Cavendish Laboratory [B] and were able to change our picture of the structure of atoms.

process will spread explosively through the fissionable material.

In order to generate electricity the process must be slowed down and controlled, and means must be provided for removing the heat. There is a higher probability of fission occurring in U-235 if the neutron absorbed is moving relatively slowly, about 1.2mi (2km) per second. For this reason special materials such as graphite or deuterium, called moderators, are incorporated into the atomic pile in order to slow down the neutrons.

The amount of fissionable material brought together is crucial for a sustained chain reaction. If more neutrons are lost by absorption or escape than are produced, the reaction will not be self-sustaining. If more neutrons are produced than are lost on the average, a self-sustaining and expanding reaction occurs. The smallest amount in which fission is self-sustaining is called the critical mass. In an atomic pile it is necessary to keep the flux of neutrons nearly in balance and constant. To control the reaction rate in a pile, rods of neutron-absorbing material can be moved in and out as required [8].

Fast reactors and their make-up

Structural supports in atomic piles are made of materials that absorb as few neutrons as possible. Fast reactors have a small core of fissile material and no moderator to slow the neutrons. There is little absorbent material and few neutrons are wasted. Natural uranium is 99.3 percent U-238 and 0.7 percent U-235. While U-235 is fissionable, U-238 is not, but after absorbing a neutron can decay radioactively to plutonium Pu-239, which is. Atomic bombs and fast reactors require fairly pure fissionable material, so U-235 must be separated out—for example in a giant diffusion plant—or U-238 turned into Pu-239 in a reactor and separated chemically. In a fast reactor, the fissile core is surrounded by a blanket of natural uranium so that neutrons escaping from the core can turn U-238 into Pu-239. If more fissionable material is made than consumed the reactor, or pile, is called a breeder reactor.

KEY

The mushroom cloud of an atomic explosion haunts civilization. Although the spread of nuclear weapons has been banned by treaties, and some nations have accepted technical limitations on testing, the number of countries with access to nuclear weaponry continues to grow.

5

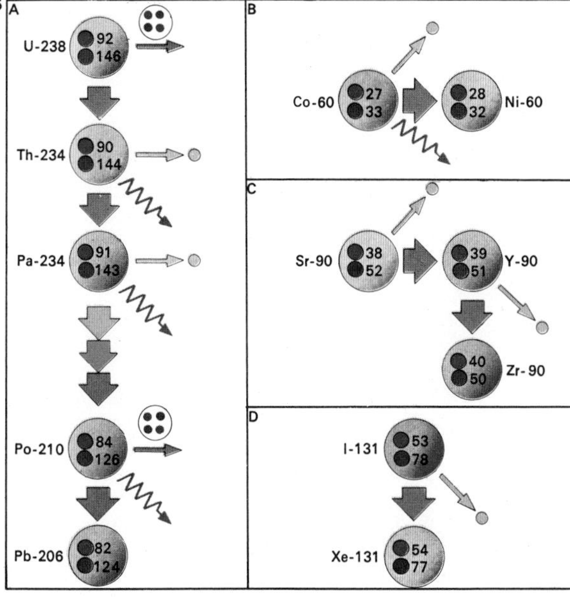
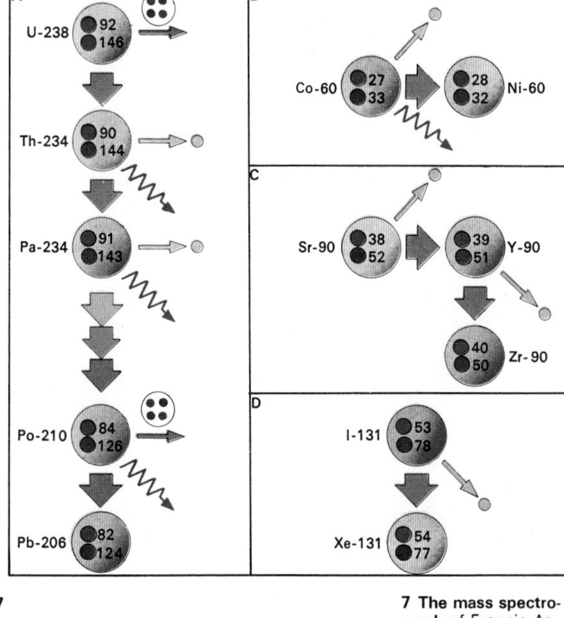
A
U-238
92
146
Th-234
90
144
Pa-234
91
143
Po-210
84
126
Pb-206
82
124
B
Co-60
27
33
28
32
Ni-60
C
Sr-90
38
52
39
51
Y-90
40
50
Zr-90
D
I-131
53
78
54
77
Xe-131

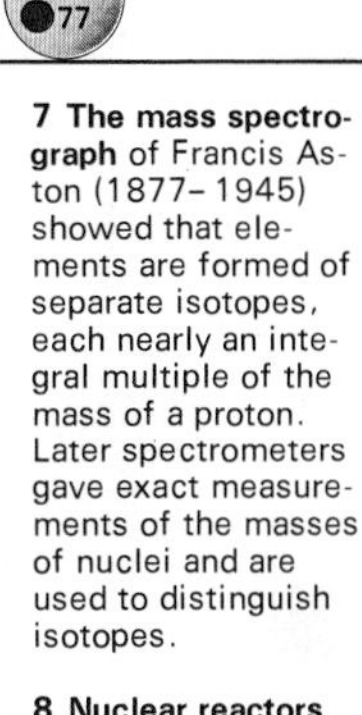

5 The nucleus of an atom, containing protons (red) and neutrons (brown), may change to produce radioactivity: gamma rays (electromagnetic radiation, violet), beta rays (electrons or positrons, grey), and alpha particles (helium ions, orange). Naturally radioactive uranium-238 [A] decays as shown to form lead. [B] shows the decay of cobalt-60, [C] strontium-90, and [D] iodine-131.

6

92
143
U-235
1
92
144
U-236
Ba-141
56
85
Kr-92
36
56
2
52
83
Te-135
54
81
Xe-135
4
3
92
146
5
U-238
92
143
U-235

6 When uranium-235 is hit by a slow neutron [1] it may split and release energy and neutrons [2]. One of these may strike more uranium-235 [3] and lead to a chain reaction, or be absorbed by other atoms [4] or U-238 [5].

7

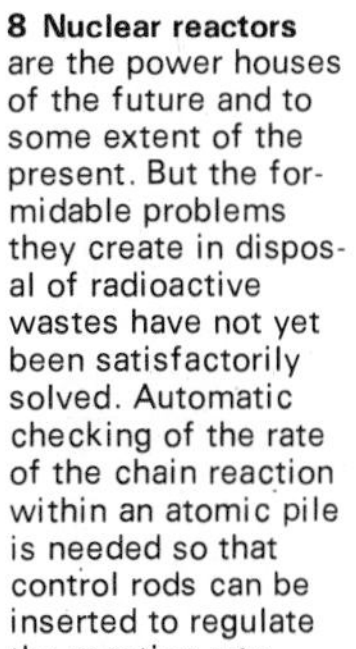

7 The mass spectrograph of Francis Aston (1877–1945) showed that elements are formed of separate isotopes, each nearly an integral multiple of the mass of a proton. Later spectrometers gave exact measurements of the masses of nuclei and are used to distinguish isotopes.

8

8 Nuclear reactors are the power houses of the future and to some extent of the present. But the formidable problems they create in disposal of radioactive wastes have not yet been satisfactorily solved. Automatic checking of the rate of the chain reaction within an atomic pile is needed so that control rods can be inserted to regulate the reaction rate.

Beyond the atom

One of the characteristic features of science is the way in which it attempts to explain a collection of different phenomena in terms of a few basic concepts. A striking example is the atomic theory of John Dalton (1766–1844) in which many different substances are considered to be made up of a few different types of atoms. According to this view atoms are the fundamental "building blocks" of all matter.

In the late nineteenth and early twentieth centuries evidence accumulated to show that atoms themselves have an internal structure. By 1932 it had been realized that atoms are combinations of subatomic particles: protons and neutrons (together forming a small positively charged nucleus) with orbiting negatively charged electrons.

Interactions between particles

To give a full description of matter it is necessary to describe not only the particles but also the way in which they are held together—that is, the way in which they interact. Four types of interaction are recognized; two of these are fairly well known because they are observed in matter in bulk as well as on the atomic scale. The gravitational interaction [1] produces an attraction between objects that depends on their masses. It is an extremely weak effect and plays no part in the binding within atoms, but it is responsible for the forces between heavenly bodies. The electromagnetic interaction [2] occurs between particles that have an electric charge. This force is many millions of times stronger than the gravitational effect and is responsible for the force of attraction between the nuclei of atoms and the orbiting electrons.

Within the nucleus itself a quite different effect must occur. Here neutrons and protons are held together strongly in spite of the electromagnetic repulsion between them. This strong interaction [3] is independent of charge, for it acts between neutrons as well as protons, and is about 7,000 times stronger than the electromagnetic interaction. Moreover, it falls off sharply with distance—its influence extends only over distances comparable with the dimensions of the atomic nucleus, less than 10^{-13}cm.

The fourth type, known as the weak interaction, is about one thousandth of the strength of the electromagnetic interaction. It is observed in certain processes in which tranformations of particles occur, as in beta decay [4], where a neutron changes into three new particles, a proton, an electron, and an antineutrino.

Fields of force

The four types of interaction take place through free space. One way of explaining this action-at-a-distance uses the idea of a field of force. A charged particle, for instance, is thought of as affecting the surrounding space in such a way that another charged particle placed in this region experiences a force. The region of influence is called an electromagnetic field. Similarly a mass has an associated gravitational field.

A different model, based on quantum mechanics, uses the idea of an exchange of virtual particles. Two charged particles interact by emitting and adsorbing photons (particles of light). Gravitational interaction is similarly explained by exchange of

CONNECTIONS

See also
1480 What is an atom?
1482 Nuclear physics
1494 Circular and vibrating motion
1524 The idea of relativity
1536 Electromagnetism
1548 Basic electronic principles

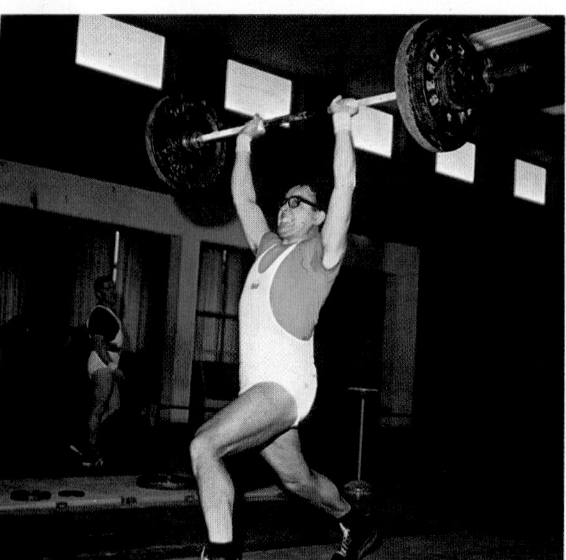

1 The force of gravity is encountered in all its power and immediacy by a weightlifter. The gravitational force was the first to be studied quantitatively and the first to receive, in Isaac Newton's *Principia* (1687), detailed discussion of its theoretical principles. It is experienced by all matter.

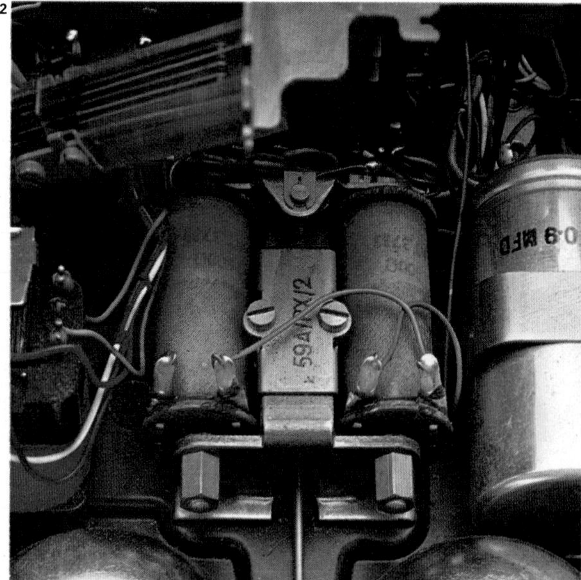

0·9 MFD
59AMX12

2 Electromagnetism (used in an electric bell) was the second interaction of which man became aware. Magnetism and static electricity were known earlier, but the combination of electricity and magnetism in a single theory was achieved only in the nineteenth century by the work of James Clerk Maxwell.

3 Hideki Yukawa (1907–) predicted a particle, later identified as the pi meson, as the quantum of nuclear force. It was found in cosmic ray photographs by C. F. Powell (1903–69) at Bristol University.

4 Enrico Fermi (1901–54) developed the theory of weak interactions, illustrated by the process of beta decay. He was largely responsible for the development of the first atomic pile.

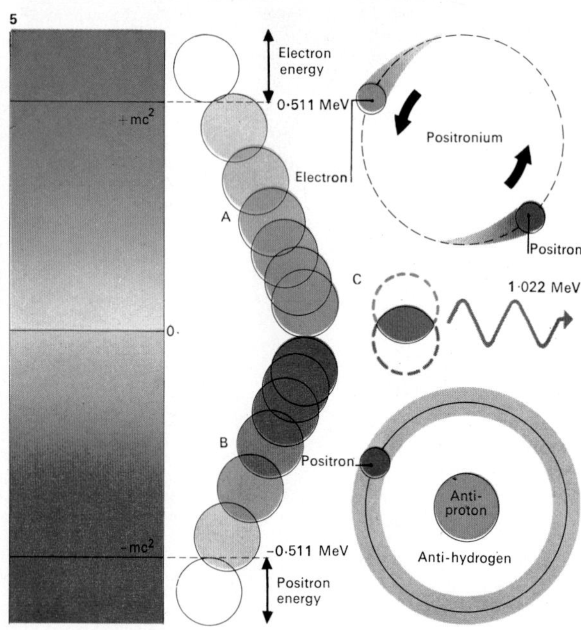

Electron energy
0·511 MeV
+mc²
Electron
A
0
B
Positron
−mc²
−0·511 MeV
Positron energy
Positronium
Positron
C
1·022 MeV
Anti-proton
Anti-hydrogen

5 The existence of a particle equal in mass to an electron [A] but having negative energy was predicted by Paul Dirac (1902–). The discovery of the positron [B] confirmed this. If the two meet, they annihilate each other, releasing their combined mass-energy [C]. Positronium—an electron and positron in orbit—is known to exist briefly and recently anti-hydrogen has been produced for very short periods.

hypothetical particles called gravitons. In 1935 Hideki Yukawa [3] suggested that the strong interaction holding the nucleus together was caused by the exchange of a particle with a mass between that of the electron and the proton. This particle is now known as the pi meson (or pion). Another particle, the intermediate vector boson, has been suggested as being responsible for weak interactions, but so far scientists have been unable to prove the existence of such a particle.

Other fundamental particles

In 1932 only three particles were necessary to explain atomic structure. Since then the situation has been complicated by the discovery of many more particles through work on cosmic rays and experiments using particle accelerators [6, 8]. It is found that high-energy collisions between particles lead to the production of new ones. Now more than 200 are known, most of them very unstable [7]. They are characterized by their mass and charge. They also have other characteristic properties, such as average lifetime, that describe the ways in which they interact.

The numerous subatomic particles are classified into groups: particles that partake in strong interactions are called hadrons (including nucleons, hyperons, and mesons). Particles that do not take part in strong interactions are called leptons (including electrons and neutrinos).

The problem of high-energy physics is to produce a single theory explaining the existence and behavior of this multitude of particles. One suggestion is that the particles themselves are made up of even more basic particles. It is possible, for instance, to describe all hadrons as combinations of three particles called quarks. These have charges that are one-third or two-thirds the size of the electron charge.

Another goal is the creation of a single theory to account for all the types of interaction. So far some success has been achieved in unifying the electromagnetic and weak interactions, but a single mathematical theory encompassing all four types of interactions is still far off.

KEY

The essence of matter summed up in the Chinese symbol of yin and yang was a symmetry of complementary principles – aptly representing the modern theory of particle-wave duality.

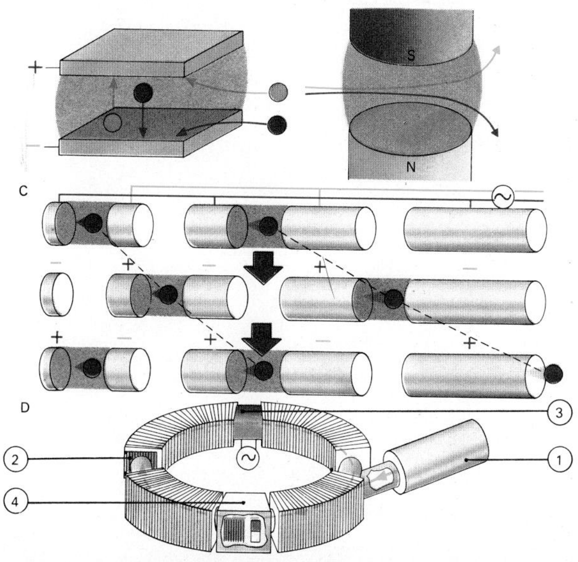

6 Particle accelerators use the principle that an electric field [A] accelerates positive [red] or negative [blue] particles parallel with the direction of the field, whereas a magnetic field [B] makes them curve at right angles to the field. In a "drift-tube" accelerator [C, E] oscillating electric fields speed up at the same rate as the particles. A synchrotron [D] is used for particles brought close to the speed of light by a linear accelerator [1]. A magnetic field [2], increasing to balance the growth of centrifugal force, causes particles to circulate through an accelerating field [3], seen through a viewer [4].

E

7

Type of particle	Symbol	Mass in units of electron mass	Electric charge
Photon	γ	0	0
Leptons			
Neutrino (electronic)	υ	0	0
Antineutrino (electronic)	$\bar{\upsilon}$	0	0
Neutrino (mesonic)	υ_{μ}	0	0
Antineutrino (mesonic)	$\bar{\upsilon}_{\mu}$	0	0
Electron	e^-	1	−1
Positron	e^+	1	1
Mu (muon) plus	μ^+	207	+1
Mu (muon)	μ^-	207	−1
Mesons			
Pi plus	π^+	273	+1
Pi minus	π^-	273	−1
Pi zero	π^0	264	0
K plus	κ^+	967	+1
K minus	κ^-	967	−1
K zero	κ^0	974	0
Anti-K zero	$\bar{\kappa}^0$	974	0
Nucleons			
Proton	p^+	1,836	+1
Antiproton	p^-	1,836	−1
Neutron	n	1,839	0
Antineutron	$\bar{n}$	1,839	0
Hyperons			
Lambda zero	Λ^0	2,183	0
Antilambda zero	$\bar{\Lambda}^0$	2,183	0
Sigma zero	Σ^0	2,332	0
Antisigma zero	$\bar{\Sigma}^0$	2,332	0
Sigma minus	Σ^-	2,328	−1
Antisigma minus	$\bar{\Sigma}^-$	2,341	+1
Sigma plus	Σ^+	2,328	+1
Antisigma plus	$\bar{\Sigma}+$	2,328	−1
Xi plus	Ξ^+	2,566	0
Antixi zero	$\bar{\Xi}^0$	2,580	0
Xi minus	Ξ^-	2,580	−1
Antixi minus	$\bar{\Xi}^-$	2,582	+1

7 Fundamental particles are now so numerous that the term fundamental seems inappropriate, but there is insufficient information for a unified theory and some vital clues may be missing. One day order will be brought to the apparent chaos of information, just as physicist Niels Bohr clarified atomic theory.

8 The ring cyclotron was invented by Ernest Lawrence (1901–58) at the University of California in 1930. Its vacuum chamber, in which charged particles were accelerated by being circulated past two D-shaped electrodes with a high-frequency voltage, measured only 4in (10cm) across. The giant machine now at CERN in Geneva has a diameter of 3mi (4.8km). Accelerated to high speeds in cyclotrons, particles can be used to bombard nuclei – with creation of other particles.

8

The nature of energy

Energy is required for work to be done—work being the operation of a force over a distance. Thus energy is expended when a golf ball is struck, when a dumbbell is lifted, when a spring is compressed or stretched, when a bomb explodes, and when electrons flow in a wire as an electric current.

Additionally, living organisms need energy for movement and growth. Green plants get their energy as light from the Sun [Key], which they utilize by photosynthesis. Animals use the chemical energy of food—the energy of plants or other animals that they eat. From these examples it can be seen that energy exists in many forms.

Potential energy

Potential energy can be considered as stored energy. The potential energy of food and fuels such as coal and oil, for example, is the chemical energy stored in these materials. The potential energy in the water of a high dam or river is stored gravitational energy [1]. The nucleus of an atom consists of a number of subatomic particles held together by an immensely strong force that is the potential energy of the nucleus. In a coiled spring, the potential energy is proportional to the amount of compression or extension. A copper sphere insulated from electrical leakage can be charged with static electricity and the electrical potential energy of the sphere is determined by the amount of static electric charge and the voltage.

Kinetic energy

When matter is in motion it is said to possess kinetic energy. For this reason, molecules of a gas always have kinetic energy because they are always moving. The temperature of a gas is a measure of the average kinetic energy of its moving molecules—the faster they move the higher the temperature. The pressure of a gas is also a measure of its kinetic energy, because the pressure is a measure of the number and energy of the collisions made by gas molecules on the walls of the container. Gas pressure is often used, as in pneumatic drills and lifts, to do useful work. Finally, the kinetic energy of the gas molecules, or of any other moving object, can be expressed in mathematical terms as $\frac{1}{2}mv^2$, where m is the mass of the object and v is its velocity.

Internal energy

That part of the energy of any system apart from the system's kinetic energy is called its internal energy. This quantity is not usually measurable and not all of it can be used to do work. A hot object does work in cooling, for example, but even if it is cooled to near absolute zero, namely −273°C (−459°F), its molecules still possess most of their internal energy. The potential energy of a system is, therefore, measured not as the total internal energy but as that part of it that is available to do work.

Conservation of energy

Heat energy can be regarded as energy of movement. To take the example already used, a gas has kinetic energy proportional to its absolute temperature (its temperature above absolute zero). If the same gas heats an object, the molecules of the object gain kinetic energy. This transfer of kinetic

CONNECTIONS

See also
1498 What is sound?
1508 Heat and temperature
1516 Light and color
1530 What is electricity?
1534 Magnets and magnetism
1490 Attraction and repulsion

1 A dam holds water at a height and when the water is released its potential energy changes to kinetic energy that can be converted into useful electrical energy by water turbines. Other hydroelectric processes rely on the kinetic energy of water moving in the form of waves and tides being turned into useful energy.

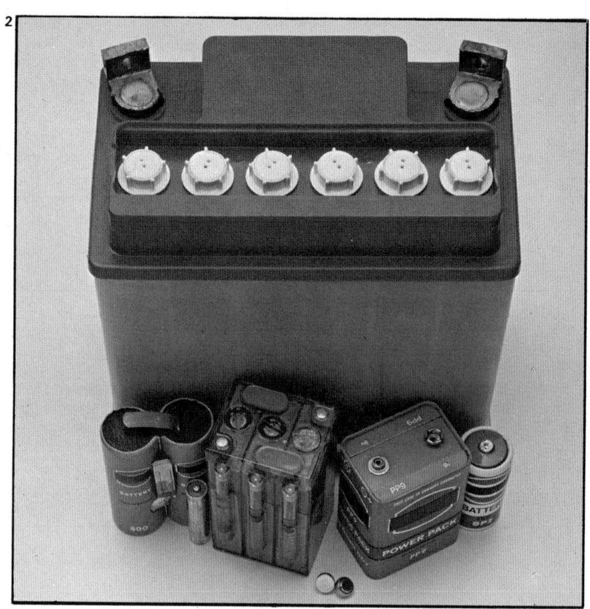

2 In batteries the energy of chemical reactions is converted into electrical energy, which is used for many purposes. Batteries run down as their chemical activity declines. Storage batteries are recharged by electricity, which is converted back to stored chemical energy to be used again.

3 A nuclear power station uses the great energy released when the nucleus of an atom disintegrates. Under controlled conditions the nuclear energy of uranium or plutonium is carefully released, mostly as heat, which is used to raise the temperature of water in boilers. This heat energy is converted in steam turbines into mechanical energy, which is then converted to electricity.

4 In a microphone-loudspeaker system a double energy conversion takes place. Sound is converted into electrical energy by the microphone, and the loudspeaker reverses the conversion process.

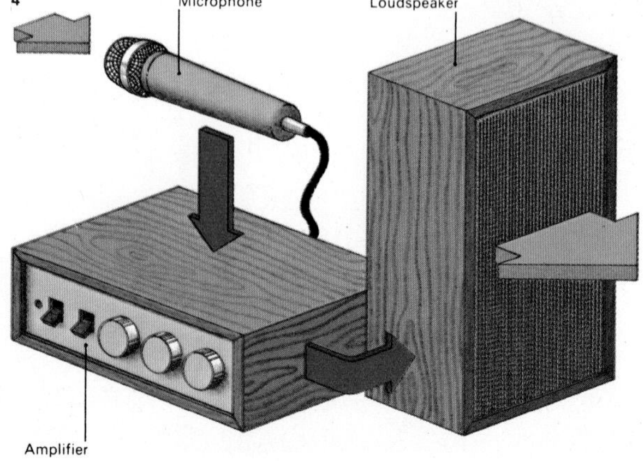
Microphone
Loudspeaker
Amplifier

energy takes the form of a flow of heat from the hot gas to the cooler body.

Useful energy is usually thought of in such terms as the heat of burning coal, the electricity flowing in electric wires and the mechanical energy produced by burning gasoline vapor in a car engine. But in each of these familiar examples, energy must be converted from one form to another to be of practical use. The chemical potential energy of coal is released by burning the coal and is thereby converted into hot gases and useful radiant energy; in a power station these are further converted into useful electrical energy by a system of water boilers, steam turbines, and electrical generators. The chemical potential energy of motor fuel is released by rapid burning as kinetic energy of a hot gas, which is translated into the useful mechanical energy that propels the car.

Energy conversions always involve a loss; no conversion is 100 percent efficient. A coal fire, for example, releases only about 20 percent of the chemical energy of the coal as useful heat. By contrast, an electric motor converts about 80 percent of the electrical energy supplied to it into useful mechanical energy [7].

The principle of conservation of energy is usually stated as "energy can neither be created nor destroyed." In energy conversions the amount of useful energy output is always less than the input energy. The total energy of the system, however, always remains the same, the "missing" energy being wasted energy. Not all the electricity flowing through a lamp filament, for instance, is converted into light, most being wastefully converted to heat. The heat and light together are equivalent to the input electricity, and so energy is conserved. But after the conversion, less energy is available to do work; useful energy has been lost.

What happens in this particular instance is true for the sum of all energy reactions in the universe at any one time; the overall result of these reactions being a degradation in energy level. At some remote time in the future, all energy will have degraded to a level where no work can be done: the universe will then have "run down."

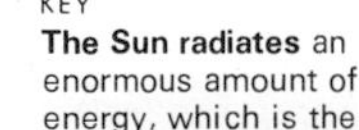

KEY
The Sun radiates an enormous amount of energy, which is the ultimate source for all life in the Solar System. In this photograph the Sun is seen after a total eclipse.

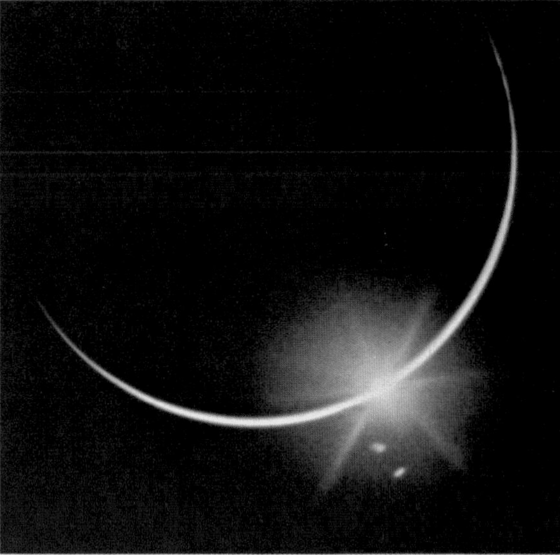

5

5 Solar cells, as fitted on this satellite, convert radiant energy from the Sun directly into electrical energy. A solar cell contains a wafer of semiconductor material, usually silicon. This is made so that when light falls upon it, electrons move in one direction within it and "holes" (positively charged regions) in the other direction. In a circuit, each solar cell produces about half a volt and must be used in large arrays.

6

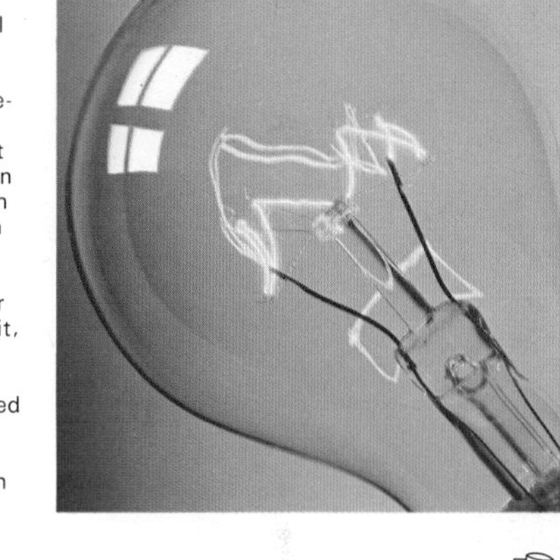

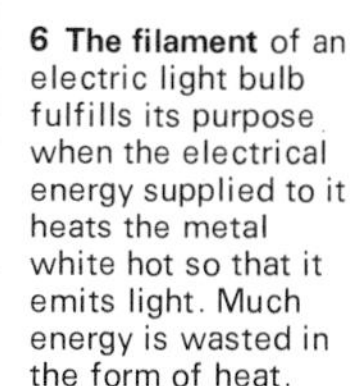

6 The filament of an electric light bulb fulfills its purpose when the electrical energy supplied to it heats the metal white hot so that it emits light. Much energy is wasted in the form of heat.

7 An electric motor converts electrical energy into mechanical, or kinetic, energy. Most familiar is this rotary type in which a rotor revolves within a fixed stator.

7

8 The hydraulic ram raises water, converting its kinetic energy into gravitational potential energy. A lake or reservoir [A] supplies water [1] through a pipe [2] to the ram chamber [3], which is at a lower level, ensuring that the water has adequate kinetic energy on reaching the chamber. This fills with water [B] which briefly escapes through a spring valve [4] before closing it. The water passes on around a one-way valve [5] into a second chamber [6] where air is first compressed by the water [C] then reexpands to force water up the delivery pipe [7]. A backsurge allows the valve to reopen and the process to be repeated.

8

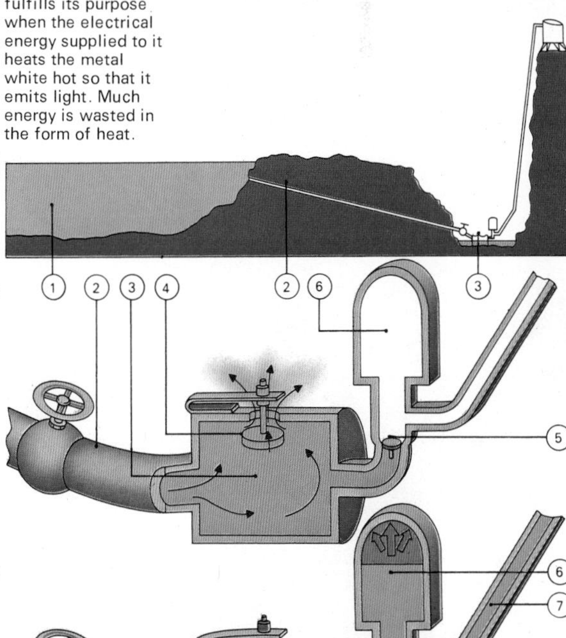
A
B
C
1
2
3
4
2
6
3
5
6
7
5

Statics and forces

The sudden movement of an object with seemingly no cause—for example, the unexpected movement of a table in the middle of a room—would obviously cause consternation. Most people would probably think a trick was responsible for such a happening because they expect a cause for this effect of motion. The scientific name for the cause is "force"—it is anything that causes an object to start to move when it has been at rest, or vice versa. A force is also required to change a condition of motion that already exists—to change the direction of an already existing motion or to alter the velocity of the motion. Once made to move, an object continues to move without stopping or changing direction until it is acted on by another force. This idea has now become almost self-evident following its original expression and generalization by Isaac Newton, and is generally known in physics as Newton's first law of motion.

In many cases the cause that stops, or modifies, already existing motion is provided by the force of friction. This acts in the direction opposite to the movement of an object. It is produced by the rubbing together of the surface of the moving object and the surface it is moving on or, in a gas or a liquid, the medium it is moving through.

States of equilibrium

When several forces act at the same time on the same object, each tries to move the object along a line pointing in its own direction at a rate that depends on the size of the applied force. If it happens that the object does not move as a result of all these forces, then it is said to be in equilibrium [5]. The magnitude and direction of any one of the forces is balanced by the total effect of the other forces and there is no resultant movement. The study of forces applied to objects in a state of equilibrium is called statics (as opposed to dynamics, the study of forces acting on moving objects).

Someone sitting still on a chair is an example of an object in equilibrium—the upward force of the chair on the person balances the downward force of the earth's gravitational attraction that is trying to pull the person through the chair to the floor. A tree standing upright in the ground is a similar example—its downward gravitational force, commonly known as its weight, is balanced by the upward force of the ground in which it is rooted. As a consequence of this equilibrium, neither the person nor the tree is in motion up or down. This state of affairs can be modified only if another external force is brought into the arrangement—for example, by the person moving about on the chair and possibly making it topple or by chopping down the tree [7]. Thousands of everyday objects stay where they are and do not move unaided because of the existence of this equilibrium of forces both in magnitude and direction.

Moments and levers

So far, only those forces that try to move objects along straight-line paths have been considered. There are many other forces, however, that can act on objects and try to rotate them around a central point. These forces have an effectiveness that depends on how far from the central point they are acting. Everyone knows that a much great-

CONNECTIONS

See also
1490 Attraction and repulsion
1502 States of matter: gases
1510 Order and disorder: thermodynamics
1652 Levers and wedges

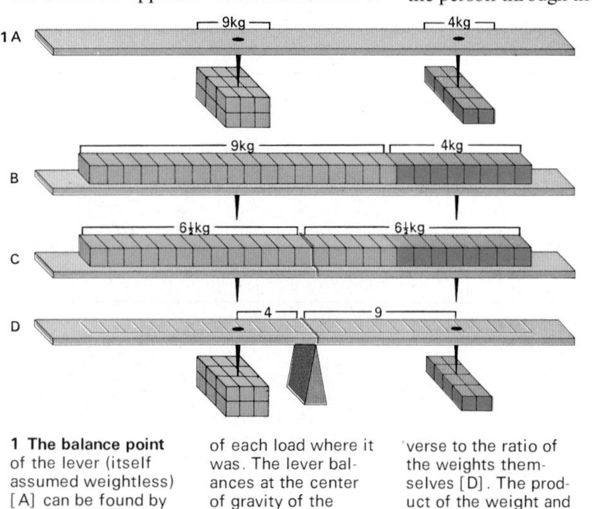

1 A
9kg
4kg
B
9kg
4kg
C
6½kg
6½kg
D
4
9

1 The balance point of the lever (itself assumed weightless) [A] can be found by dividing each load into equal small weights and distributing them along the lever [B], keeping the center of gravity of each load where it was. The lever balances at the center of gravity of the whole line. This point is halfway along the line [C] of equal weights at the distance from the weights that is inverse to the ratio of the weights themselves [D]. The product of the weight and its distance from the fulcrum (pivot) is the same on each side—the moments are equal and opposite each other.

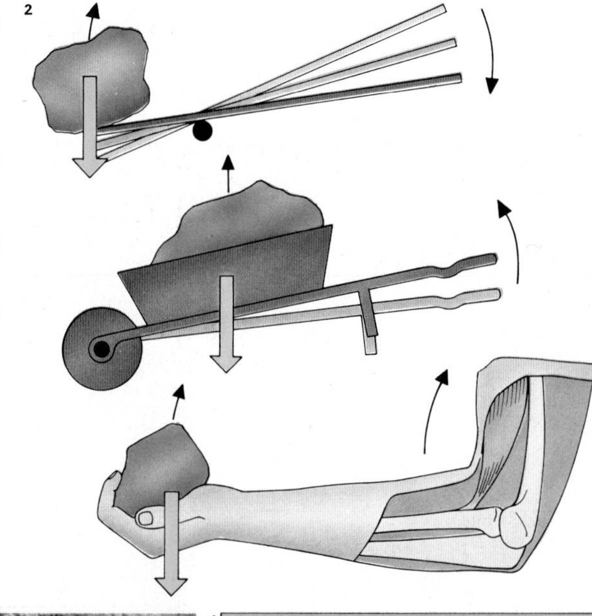

2

2 The see-saw principle is used in the first class of levers and has the fulcrum, or balance-point, between the load and the applied effort. The wheelbarrow is a familiar example of the second class of levers, with the load between the fulcrum and the effort. The third class of levers, with the effort between the fulcrum and the load, is used when lifting a weight with the forearm—the elbow is the fulcrum. If both lever and load remain the same in all three cases, the principle of moments shows the required force is the greatest for the third order and least for the second order.

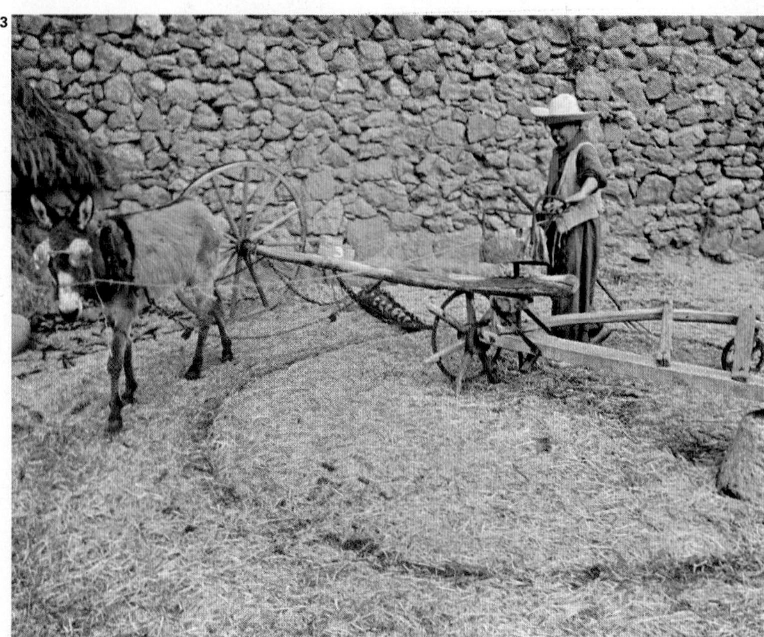

3 Force applied by an animal tethered to the arm of a grinding mill produces a moment or turning effect about the central axis. This turns the mill and grinds the corn poured between heavy stones at the center of the mill.

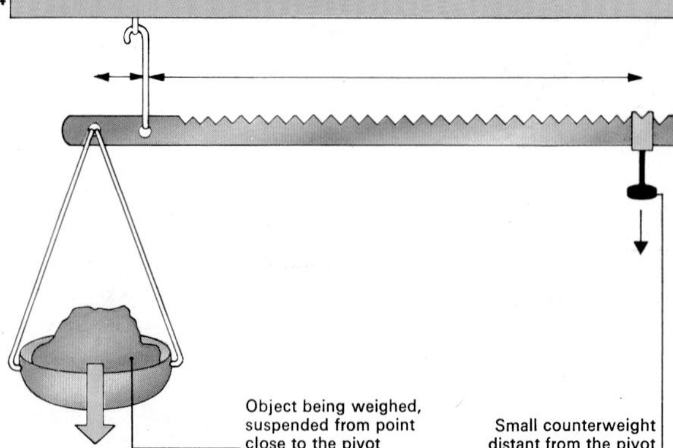

4
Object being weighed, suspended from point close to the pivot
Small counterweight distant from the pivot

4 A steelyard is a balance often used by butchers for weighing carcasses that are too heavy for ordinary scales. The small sliding jockey weight is moved along the long arm of the steelyard until the whole beam is horizontal. The sliding weight, at a greater distance from the fulcrum than the heavy load, can be much lighter. The principle involved is the same as the first order of levers—like the see-saw. The first recorded use of such a scale was in 315 BC.

er turning effect is achieved by pulling on a wrench that has a long, rather than a short, handle. The combined effect of the magnitude of the force multiplied by the perpendicular distance from the turning point (called the axis of rotation) is called the moment of the force. The greater the applied force or the distance of action, the greater is the resulting moment or turning effect. Simple machines that employ the phenomenon of moment of a force are levers [2].

Of course several forces may simultaneously act on an object through more than one point within its boundary. In this case, each has its own moment about a particular axis, through which the object can still be in equilibrium if these moments produce no collective rotational effect. That is, if the total magnitude of the clockwise moments about the axis exactly balances that of the counterclockwise moments, there is no movement. This result is called the principle of moments and it may apply to an object at the same time as the equilibrium that arises from forces acting through a particular point trying to move the object in a straight line.

For the example of a person sitting still on a chair and being in equilibrium for vertical motion, it is clear that if someone tries to tilt the chair backward, the seated person will topple over unless the chair is pulled in the opposite direction with an equivalent force. The vertical equilibrium through the point of contact of the chair with the floor acts at the same time as the equilibrium for the moments of the forces trying to twist the chair around at the same point of contact.

How couples operate

One further type of force that a study of statics includes is called a couple [6]. Actually this is the application of two equal forces arranged so that they both tend to rotate the object in the same direction. The couple produces only rotation with an *equal* moment about any point between the forces, and does not produce any straight-line motion. Consequently, it can be balanced only by another equal or opposite couple if equilibrium is to be achieved.

KEY

The principle of moments is used in most of the activities in the children's playground. The see-saw obviously demonstrates the lever, as shown here; in addition, the umbrella and swings in the background each use the moment of a force about their axis or fulcrum to achieve movement.

5

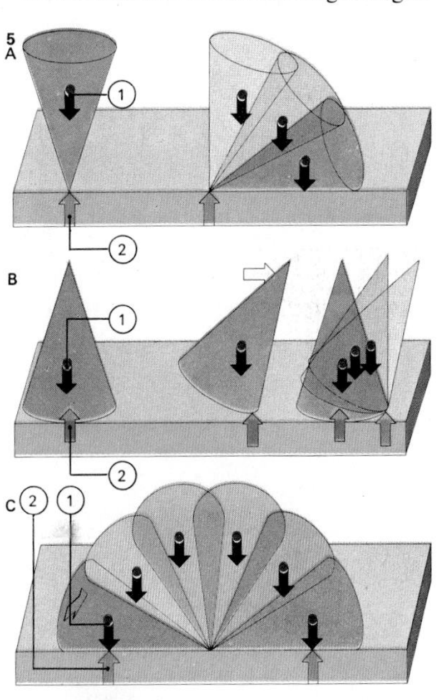
A
1
2
B
1
2
C
2
1

D

5 If a cone standing on its point [A] is slightly displaced, its weight produces a moment that continues to topple the cone about the point of contact. This is an unstable equilibrium position. With the cone on its base [B], displacement produces a moment that restores the original position—a stable equilibrium. If the cone lies on its side [C], displacement produces no moment since the weight and its reaction [1, 2] still act along the same line—the cone remains in its new position and is in neutral equilibrium. The very low center of gravity of the bus [D] keeps it in stable equilibrium even for large displacements.

6

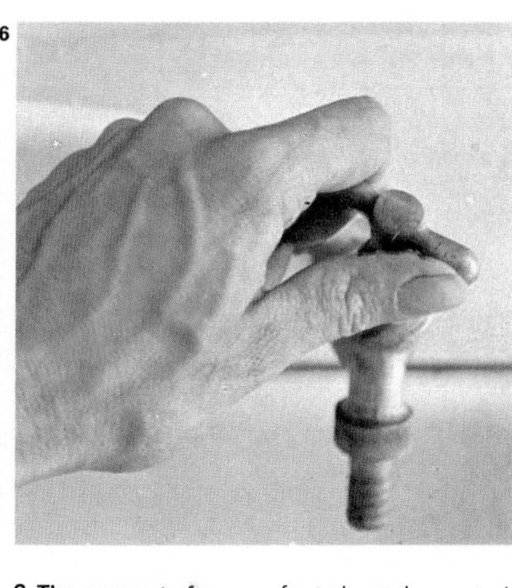

6 The moment of a couple is equal to the product of one of the forces and the distance between the two. This hand is applying an equal force to each end of the top of a tap, producing a rotating effect about the central axis to turn it on and off. Both these forces are trying to turn the tap in the same direction, and together form a couple. The larger the top, the more effective is the force.

7

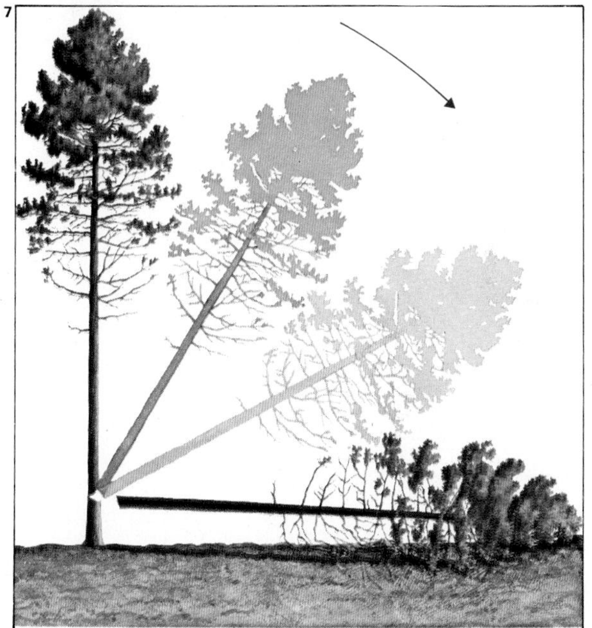

7 A tree stands in equilibrium (its center of gravity acts downward in a straight line through its base) until a wedge is cut into its trunk. This starts to destroy the equilibrium by allowing the tree's weight to develop a toppling moment that is not balanced by an equal and opposite reaction.

8

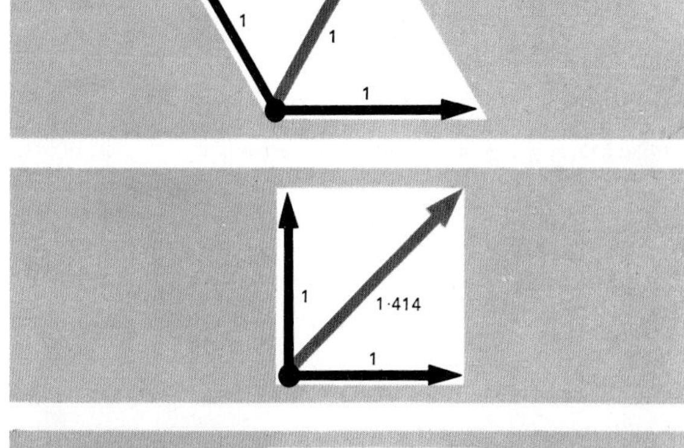
1
1
1
1
1·414
1

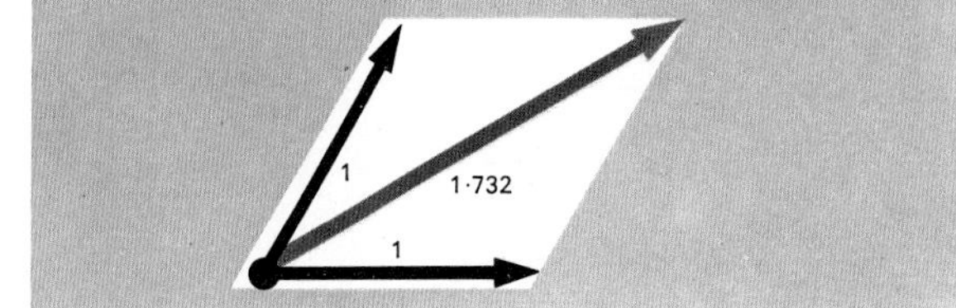
1
1·732
1

8 Two forces act simultaneously on an object in different directions. The resultant force, and the direction of any subsequent movement, is defined by the diagonal of a parallelogram whose sides are drawn parallel to the applied forces with lengths proportional to their magnitudes. This is an application of vector diagrams.

Attraction and repulsion

To many people, the most mysterious natural forces are those that produce an effect on objects at great distances, reaching across even empty space without any material contact between the body producing the force and that being affected by it. This phenomenon is often called "action at a distance," and two fundamental forces of nature act in this way. They are gravitational and electromagnetic. Other fundamental forces act within the limits of the atomic nucleus, over short ranges only.

The inverse-square law

The two forces acting at a distance obey a common law that describes how the magnitude of the force depends on the object producing it, the object affected by it, and the distance separating the two. It is called the inverse-square law [Key]. If the distance between two bodies is doubled, then the force between them falls by one quarter (the inverse square), and so on.

Isaac Newton (1642–1727) first speculated that gravitation obeyed this relation. He proved his theory by calculating the moon's orbital velocity from a knowledge of its distance. His law of gravity [1] states that "the attractive force between two bodies is proportional to the product of their masses divided by the square of the distance between them," and it should be noted that this force is a mutual one—there are equal and opposite forces on the two objects.

About 100 years later, in 1798, Henry Cavendish (1731–1810) used this theory of gravitation to produce the first estimate of the mass of the earth [2]. He was also responsible for one of the best experimental verifications (in 1785) of the use of the inverse square law to describe the force between electrostatic charges (that is, electric charges at rest). Its use was further verified in 1870 by James Clerk Maxwell (1831–79), who showed that the inverse-square law was true to one part in 20,000. More modern methods have taken this limit to one in 1,000,000,000.

The volume of space within which the force exerted by a body produces a detectable effect (usually by causing movement of a second body) is normally called the field of force. The directions along which movement can occur are known as the lines of force. These are merely imaginary "lines" in space that are used to help describe the possible directions of any motion within the field—they spread out from the force-producing object, filling the complete field.

Gravitational and electromagnetic force

Any object with mass, however small, can produce a gravitational force field. The force is always attractive. (A repulsive force could be produced by objects with negative masses, but no such objects have been shown to exist.)

It is gravitational attraction that gives all objects their weight, trying to pull them towards the center of the earth [3], and which keeps the planets in orbit around the sun. A weightless condition may be achieved by falling—as in a satellite, which is constantly falling toward the earth—or by being located far from any gravitational source—as in interstellar space.

The electromagnetic force has two common manifestations: magnetic and elec-

CONNECTIONS

See also
1488 Statics and forces
1534 Magnets and magnetism
1536 Electromagnetism
1532 What is an electric current?
1538 Using magnets
1504 States of matter: liquids
178 Gravity and the shape of the Earth

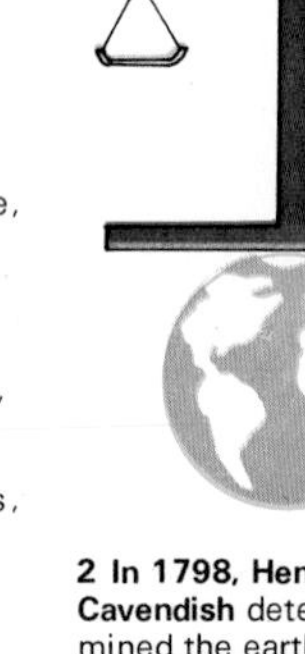
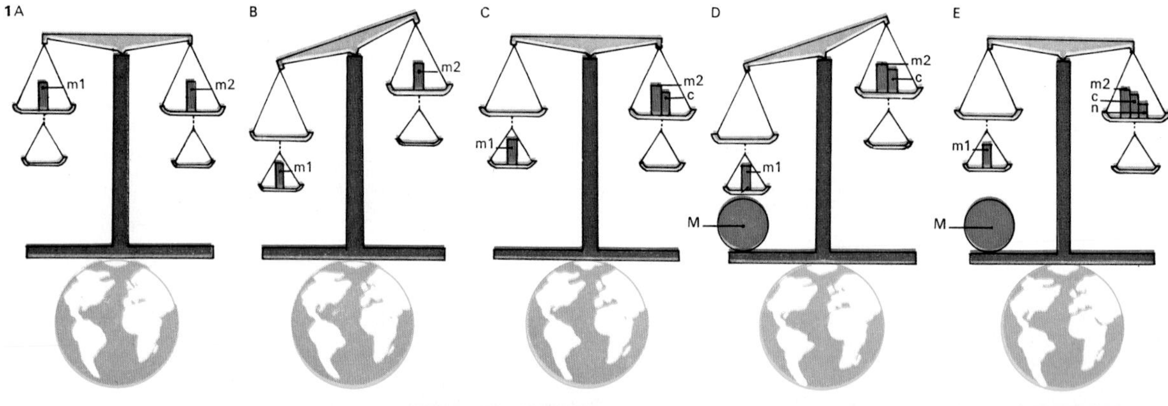

1A
B
C
D
E
m1
m2
c
n
M

1 The earth's mass could be measured with a tall balance. Initially, m1 balances m2 [A] but when m1 is moved to the lower pan it weighs more, being closer to the earth [B]. Mass c restores the balance [C]. Next, the large mass M is used to make m1 weigh more, by gravitational attraction [D]. Balance is restored [E] with weight n. If R is earth's radius, d is the distance between m1 and M, and E is earth's mass, then Newton's law states:

$$\frac{m1 \times M}{d^2} \quad \frac{n = E}{R^2}$$

The distance between the pans must be enough to prevent M from exercising significant gravitational pull on masses on the other side.

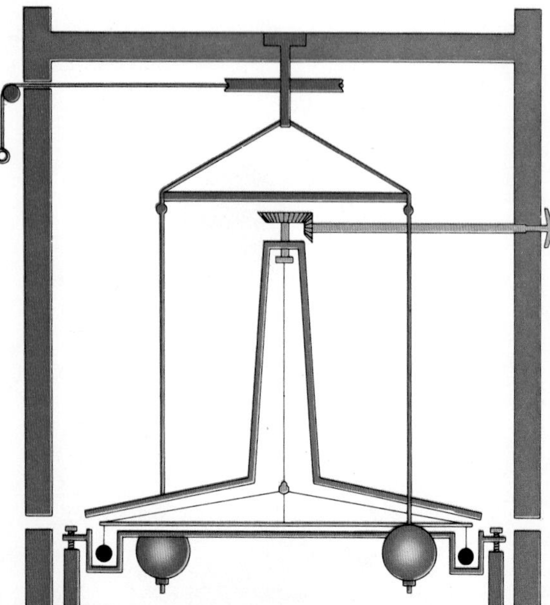

2 In 1798, Henry Cavendish determined the earth's mass using a quartz fiber torsion balance. Two small lead spheres were attracted by two larger lead spheres and from the size of the deflection, the force of attraction between the spheres was calculated. To work out the earth's mass he compared this force with the gravitational pull of the earth on the spheres (that is, their weight).

3 On a roller-coaster, power is needed to pull the car to the top of the highest incline against the gravitational force exerted by the earth. The resulting potential energy of the car is then transformed into kinetic energy of motion as it is allowed to free-wheel down the track. According to the principle of energy conservation, the total kinetic energy at the bottom of an incline should equal the potential energy at the top; the car would be able to travel to the top of another equally high incline with no further application of external power. Some of the potential energy, however, is lost as a result of its conversion to heat energy by friction between the speeding car and the track. Therefore the remaining kinetic energy will allow the car to climb only a smaller vertical height each time it travels downward. To raise the height of the car again, it is necessary to apply additional power against the force of gravity.

tric force. Magnetic force [4] is familiar in connection with the working of a normal compass. This force also acts over large distances, although in this case both attractive and repulsive forces may occur, a fact that is easily tested with two simple bar magnets. The ends, or "poles," of the magnets are distinguished by being called north and south and it is always found that two north or two south poles will not remain in contact, whereas a north and south combination will. This fundamental effect is summarized by the rule: "like poles repel, unlike poles attract."

The different poles are given the descriptive labels north and south for historical reasons—the north pole of a magnet is the one that is always attracted to the North Pole of the earth, though in fact a magnetic south pole must be sited there to achieve this magnetic effect [5]. The inverse-square law determines the magnitude of the magnetic force, although this is now proportional to the product of two magnetic pole strengths that can be positive or negative (instead of two masses that can only be positive, as in the case of the gravitational force).

Electric force [6] can also be either attractive or repulsive since its source, an electric charge, can be either positive or negative. According to the type of charge either a positive (attractive) or a negative (repulsive) force is obtained.

What is an electric charge?

Every electric charge is in fact a multiple of a unit charge that is equal in magnitude to the irreducible charge associated with a single electron, a fact first noted and evaluated in 1909 by the American physicist Robert Millikan (1868–1953). The dual nature of the electric charge had been known from Greek times, however, and is best demonstrated, as then, by electrostatic effects. If a glass rod is rubbed with silk the two objects attract each other, while two glass rods rubbed with silk repel each other. Each rod acquires a net positive electric charge, whereas the silk collects excess electrons by the action of friction and becomes negatively charged.

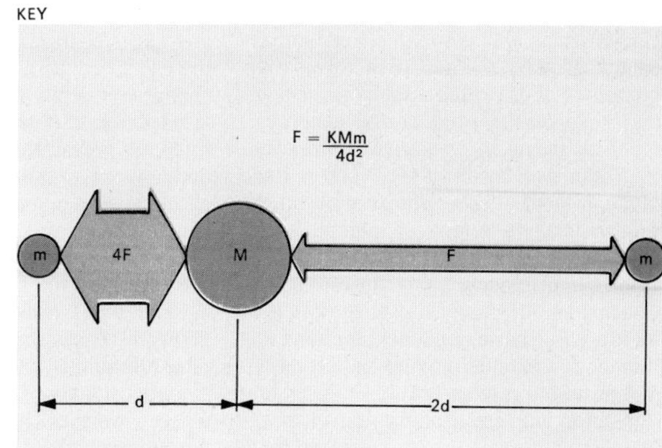
KEY
$F = \frac{KMm}{4d^2}$
m
4F
M
F
m
d
2d

The inverse-square law governs gravitational, electric, and magnetic forces. M and m represent the masses of two bodies (for the gravitational force), their charge values for the electric force, and their pole strengths for the magnetic force. In all cases, d represents the distance between the two bodies. K is a constant quantity that has a different value for each of the three forces. Gravitational force is much the weakest, the gravitational attraction for two electrons being 10^{39} times less than the electric force of repulsion. (Consequently one is aware of gravity only when great masses are involved.) The inverse-square law equation thus varies for the three forces with the value of K.

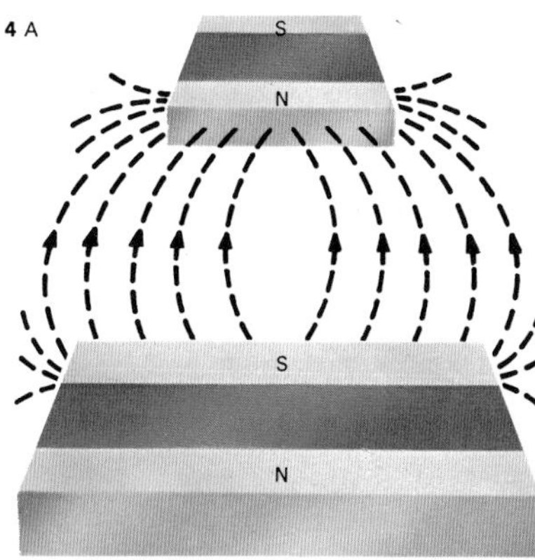
4 A
S
N
S
N

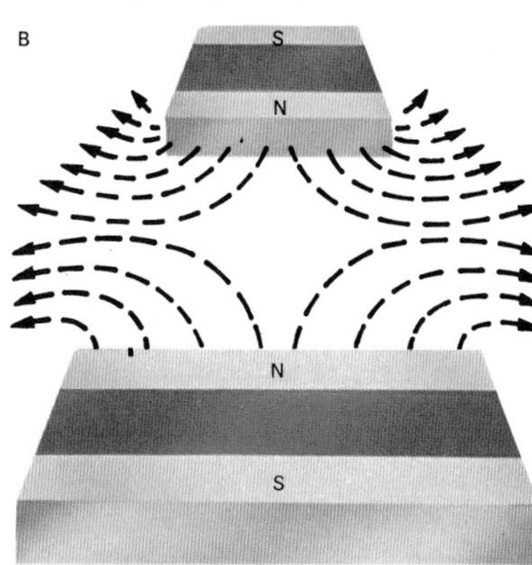
B
S
N
N
S

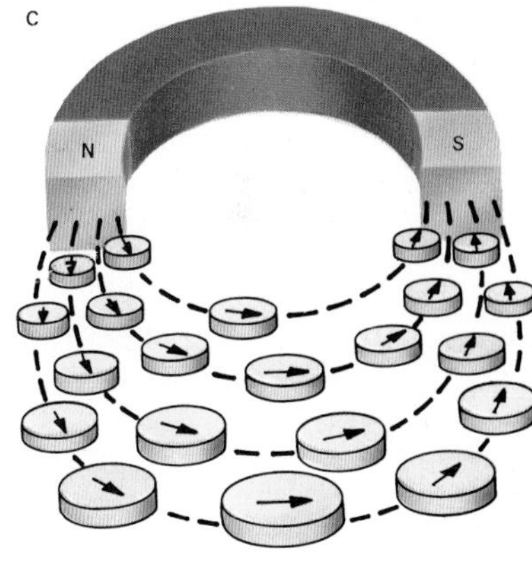
C
N
S

4 A field of force exists all around a magnetic material and the associated lines of force indicate paths along which a unit magnetic north pole would move. Iron filings sprinkled on paper laid over a pair of magnets will display negative [A] or positive [B] lines of force. In a similar way, a small compass needle will line up along lines of force with its north pole pointing out the field direction [C].

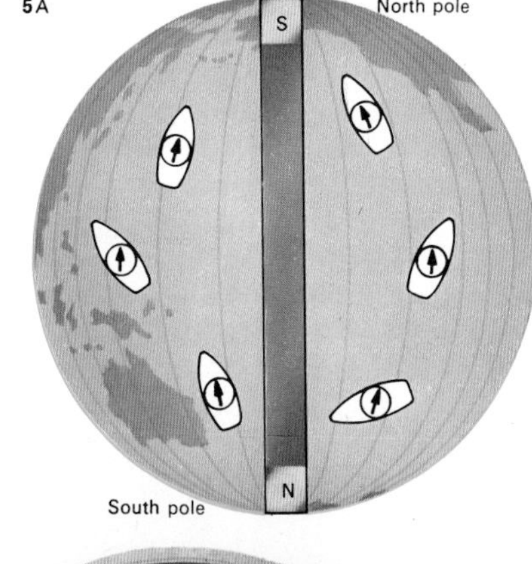
5A
North pole
S
N
South pole

5 The earth's magnetic field is created by phenomena below the crust as if it had been formed by an immense bar magnet with its south pole approximately aligned with the north geographic pole sited at one end of the earth's rotational axis [A]. The needle of a ship's magnetic compass [B] swings to a position where its ends point to north and south, along a line of force of the earth's magnetic field.

B

6

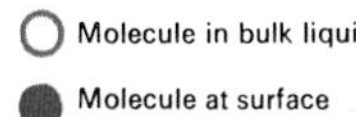
Molecule in bulk liquid
Molecule at surface

6 Electric forces that exist on a molecular and atomic scale within a substance are responsible for the cohesive forces that hold it together and give it shape and strength. Both attractive and repulsive forces exist in a state of equilibrium, the attractive holding the substance together and the repulsive effectively preventing the atoms collapsing in on each other. A striking result of these cohesive forces between atoms is seen in liquids. Within the body of the liquid, any one atom has equal and opposite forces on either side of it in any direction; there is therefore no resultant force. But at the surface there is a net force pulling atoms into the body of the liquid and as a result the surface appears to behave like an invisible elastic "skin" pulled across the liquid. This surface tension effect is used by insects such as water boatmen and mosquito larvae to keep themselves floating on a pond's surface.

Speed and acceleration

Cars, rockets, falling weights, and footballs all move under the action of forces. The branch of physics that studies movement, and the forces that produce and influence it, is called dynamics. It was given a firm scientific basis as a result of the work of Isaac Newton (1642–1727), who formulated the fundamental three laws of motion.

Principles of motion

The first law [1] summarizes the principle of inertia—the basic tendency for anything moving to continue moving and for an object at rest to remain at rest. It states that "an object will remain at rest or in motion at constant velocity unless acted on by a force." Once a car is in motion, both it and its passengers continue to move unless acted on by a force—such as a braking force. A head-on collision may stop the car, but the inertia of the passengers will cause them to fly forward from their seats. They may be thrown against the windshield unless held in place by safety belts.

As a result of this law, it is apparent that the greater the applied force on an object the greater its change of velocity. Velocity is merely speed in a certain direction, and change of velocity in a given time is called acceleration. So the greater the applied force, the greater the acceleration. The second law of motion states that, in addition, acceleration is inversely proportional to the mass of the object being moved. For example, a bus is given a smaller acceleration than a car by the same force.

The third law considers the way forces act against each other. If an object rests on a table, the table exerts an upward force equal and opposite to the downward force of the object's weight. The third law generalizes this by saying that "for every applied force there is an equal and opposite reaction." Two spring balances hooked together and pulled in opposite directions register the same force. Another much more spectacular application of this law is the rocket. The force of the expanding gases in a rocket's combustion chamber acts equally in all directions. The forward thrust is produced not by the gases escaping at the rear but by the reaction to the force of expansion on the closed front end of the combustion chamber [1].

Newton's laws of motion also connect with several other concepts. Thus the second law describes how acceleration (a) is dependent on mass (m) and applied force (F) in the equation $F = ma$. This can be used to calculate the weight of an object, because weight is the force with which a body is attracted toward the center of the Earth. This force equals the product of the mass and the acceleration with which a falling object drops to the ground (called the acceleration caused by gravity). Consequently mass and weight are completely different quantities, having different units to describe their magnitudes. Mass is a property of an object derived from the quantity of matter it contains; weight, a force that acts on it because of gravity.

Definition of momentum

The equation of the second law also shows that, because acceleration is the rate of change of velocity, force can be expressed as the rate of change of the product of mass

CONNECTIONS

See also
1488 Statics and forces
1490 Attraction and repulsion
1494 Circular and vibrating motion
1524 The idea of relativity
1460 Finding changing quantities: calculus

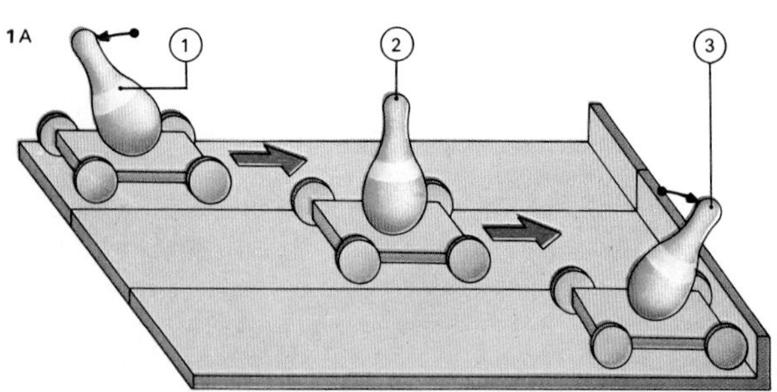
1A
1
2
3

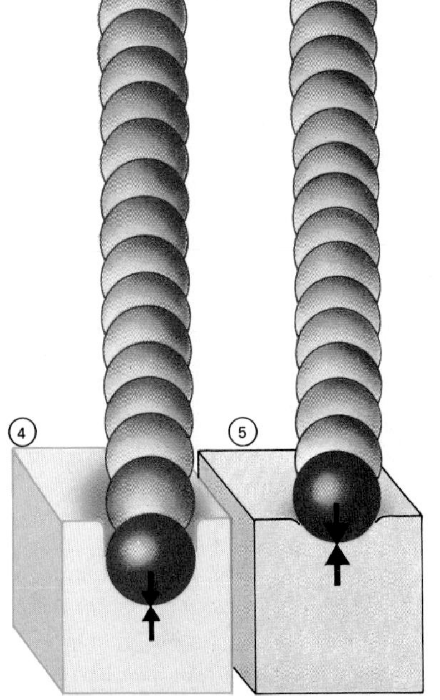
B
4
5

C

1 Newton's first law describes inertial effects. [A] An object resists being moved from rest by toppling backward [1], although moving steadily it is undisturbed, as if at rest [2]. When stopped it tends to continue moving [3]. The second law explains that acceleration or deceleration is proportional to the force producing it. [B] A ball falling onto a soft material [4] sinks deeper than into a harder one [5] because the deceleration force is smaller. The third law states there is an equal and opposite reaction to every force. [C] A rifle recoils when fired [6], although the bullet's velocity is much greater. Successive firings cause successive recoils [7]. A rocket ejects gas and moves forward [8] because of reaction to this ejection.

2 A heavy gun recoils when firing and an equal and opposite reaction propels the shell forward. The principle of conservation of momentum states that the total momentum before and after is zero but the shell is given its forward velocity because it is lighter than the gun. The chemical energy stored in the propellant is transformed to the kinetic energies of gun and shell.

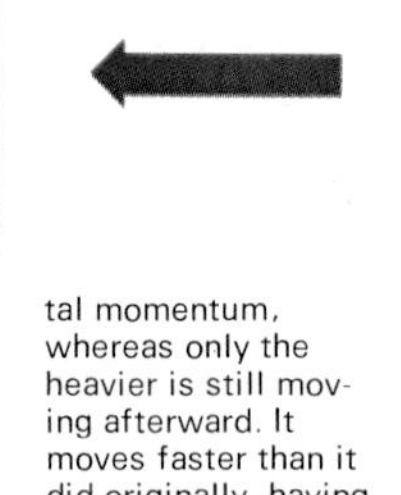

3 The collision of two balls of different mass traveling in the same direction occurs as the smaller ball is moving faster [A]. The total momentum before and after impact [B] is unchanged. Before contact both balls contribute to the total momentum, whereas only the heavier is still moving afterward. It moves faster than it did originally, having experienced the impulse of the lighter ball, but slower than the original velocity of the small ball [C].

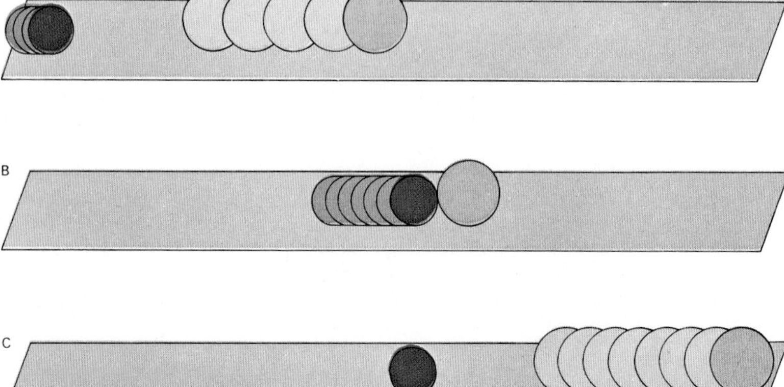
3A
B
C

and velocity. This product is called momentum and can be thought of as a quantity of motion that, for a definite velocity, increases with the object's mass. In effect the momentum indicates the effort needed to move an object or to stop or change the direction of its motion. For instance, a brick carefully placed on someone's foot does not hurt. But the pain caused when the brick is dropped from a height of a foot or so testifies to the effect of momentum.

Probably the most important reason for calculating momentum is that it is conserved throughout events involving changes of motion—for example, sudden collisions or explosions. This means that the total momentum before and after such an event stays absolutely constant [3]. Following the event, momentum may be lost through the action of friction reducing the velocities, but during its occurrence this law of conservation of momentum holds exactly.

Energy and the study of dynamics

Another phenomenon occurring during this kind of event is the transfer of energy. It can exist in many forms, such as heat, light, sound, chemical, and electrical energy. All of these can be transformed into one another—gasoline's stored chemical energy is transformed in the combustion engine to mechanical energy for moving a car. If the energy transfers occurring in any process are considered collectively, very careful measurements have shown that energy is never created or destroyed. This is the law of conservation of energy and it implies that no machine can produce a net gain of energy.

For the study of dynamics two forms of energy are fundamental—kinetic energy, possessed by objects that are in motion, and potential energy, possessed by objects normally at rest and able to do work by virtue of their position [5]. The pile driver has work done on it to lift it against the Earth's gravitational force and then can expend the stored energy when again allowed to fall. In fact, the potential energy is transformed to kinetic energy as the hammer falls and it is the kinetic energy that finally does the work.

KEY

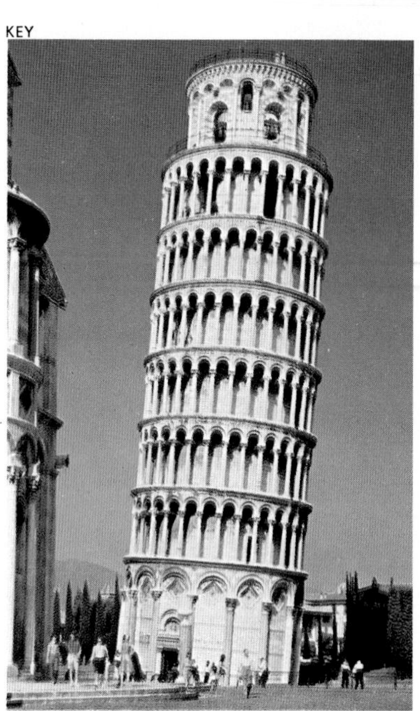

Galileo's legendary experiment, dropping a cannon ball and a pebble from the tower at Pisa, showed that objects of different masses fall to the ground together, proving that the acceleration caused by gravity is the same for all objects. With objects of different cross-sectional area, air resistance to downward motion may also be different and prevent the objects hitting the ground together. If resistance equals the gravitational attraction a limiting velocity is reached. Also there will not be a total transformation of potential to kinetic energy as the objects fall because some heat energy is lost by friction with the air.

4

4 A highway pile-up can occur after one or two cars stop. Other cars that are unable to stop in time collide with the stationary vehicles and transfer their forward momentum to them, creating a ripple effect that moves along an ever-extending chain. Conservation of energy controls the transformation of a car's mechanical kinetic energy to wasted heat and the energy imparted to the stationary cars.

5 Total energy remains constant even though it may be converted from one form to another. Any object in a gravitational field [G] has potential energy [P] proportional to its height. If a ball is allowed to roll down a slope, its potential energy diminishes as an equal amount of kinetic energy is gained. Some energy is wasted by friction, so that if it rolls horizontally it eventually comes to rest. If the ball swings at the end of a string, kinetic energy is reconverted to potential energy during the upward motion. The pendulum's energy can, in this situation, oscillate between kinetic [red] and potential [white].

5

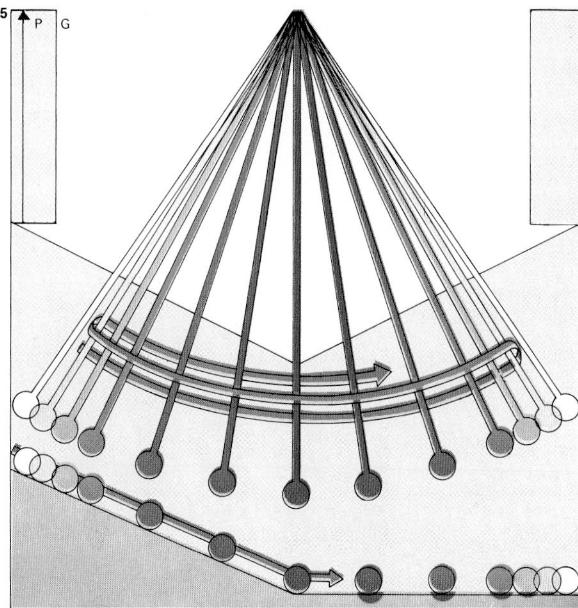

P
G

6 A steam catapult, driven by the pressure of gas built up in the rams, effectively stores a great quantity of potential energy that, when released, can be transformed to the kinetic energy of movement. Thus even the large mass of an aircraft can be accelerated to a speed that will allow it to take off from rest in the relatively very short distance available on an aircraft carrier's deck.

6

7

7 In 1789 Count Rumford (1753–1814) noticed that, in boring cannon barrels, the barrels, borer, and metal chips became hot despite there being no apparent heat source, except for friction. He realized that the mechanical energy needed to turn the barrel against this friction was converted to heat energy. Subsequently other experimenters, notably J. P. Joule (1819–89), demonstrated the transformations between other energy forms.

Circular and vibrating motion

If a driver presses the gas pedal of his car, the car speeds up—in scientific terms its velocity changes. But even when he goes around a bend at constant speed, the car's velocity also changes. This is because velocity is speed in a certain direction; if either its magnitude or its direction alter, velocity changes.

Motion in a circle

The rate of change in velocity is called acceleration. Thus an object that changes direction while traveling at constant speed experiences an acceleration. When a stone is tied to the end of a string and whirled around in a circle at constant speed, the velocity's magnitude is unchanged but the direction alters continuously. If the string were cut at any instant, the stone would fly off along a tangent to the circle.

A force must be acting on the rotating stone to produce its acceleration. Here the force is caused by the tension in the string and one can feel this force on the hand as the stone is whirled around. It is called the "centripetal force" because it acts toward the center of the circle. The acceleration it produces is therefore similarly directed toward the center. For a car moving around a circular track, frictional forces at the ground acting on the wheels provide the centripetal force.

Also, by Newton's third law of motion, there must be an equal and opposite reaction force to the centripetal force that acts on a rotating object—it is called the "centrifugal force" because it acts outward from the orbit center. The effect of centrifugal force is used in the centrifuge machines that subject pilots and astronauts to the high acceleration forces they will encounter in their flights and, on a smaller scale, in domestic spin driers.

Periodic motion

Both centripetal and centrifugal forces depend on the mass *(m)* of the object and its velocity *(v)* in the circular motion (circle of radius *r*). A heavy object needs a greater centripetal force to hold it in orbit and a greater force is also required for high speeds of rotation. Experiment shows that, in addition, the required force *(F)* is inversely proportional to the radius of motion, and $F = mv^2/r$ where v^2r gives the magnitude of the centripetal acceleration.

Uniform circular motion is periodic—that is, the events occur over and over again. The time taken for a complete revolution of the object remains constant. This periodic character is further demonstrated by considering how the object's distance from any fixed diameter of the circle varies with time. If a graph of these distances is plotted, the resulting curve is one of a uniformly oscillating amplitude of motion [1].

For a swinging pendulum, the force that pulls the bob back through the central vertical position is its weight. It undergoes oscillatory motion with an acceleration that is proportional to its distance from the point of suspension and it is also directed toward that point. Movement of this type is called "simple harmonic motion" and for the pendulum the time taken for a complete cycle of forward and backward swing (the oscillation "period" *t*) is proportional to the square root of its length *(l)*. The number of

CONNECTIONS

See also
1492 Speed and acceleration
1498 What is sound?
1516 Light and color
1542 Basic DC circuits
1794 Communications: radio

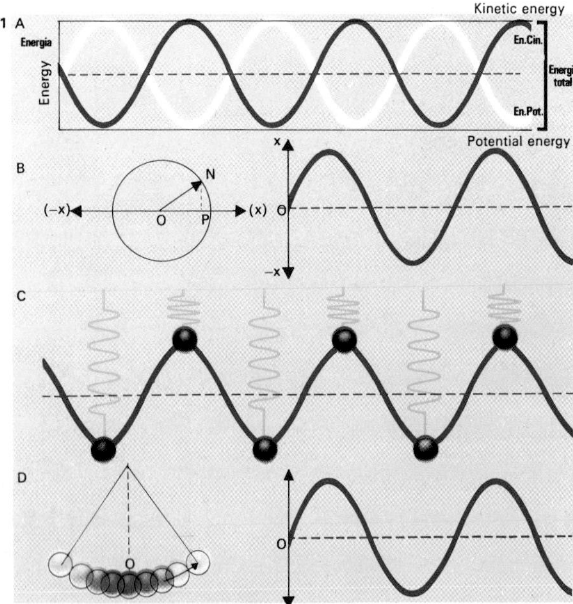
1 A
Kinetic energy
Energia
Energy
En.Cin.
Energia total
En.Pot.
Potential energy
B
N
(-x)
O
P
(x)
x
-x
C
D
O

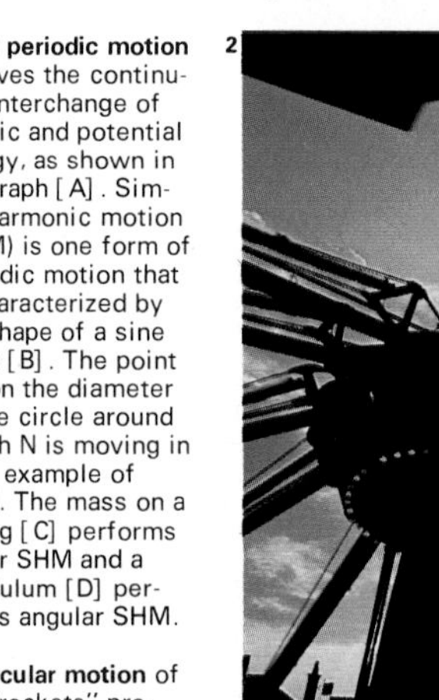

1 All periodic motion involves the continuous interchange of kinetic and potential energy, as shown in the graph [A]. Simple harmonic motion (SHM) is one form of periodic motion that is characterized by the shape of a sine wave [B]. The point [P] on the diameter of the circle around which N is moving in is an example of SHM. The mass on a spring [C] performs linear SHM and a pendulum [D] performs angular SHM.

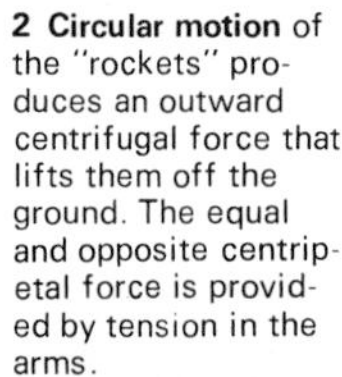

2 Circular motion of the "rockets" produces an outward centrifugal force that lifts them off the ground. The equal and opposite centripetal force is provided by tension in the arms.

3 The constant periodic time of oscillation of a pendulum is used to control clocks, especially case clocks [A]. The periodic time needed to drive the escapement correctly can be exactly matched by choosing a pendulum [B] of correct length. It can be calculated from the equation $t = 2\sqrt{l/g}$ where *t* is the oscillation period, *l* is the length, and g is the acceleration due to gravity.

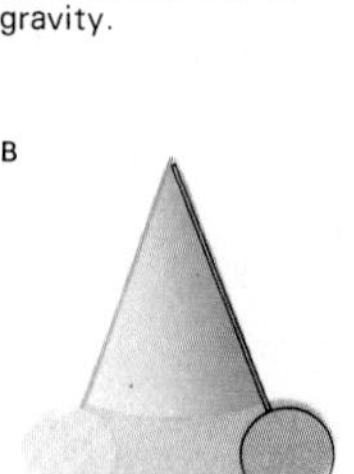

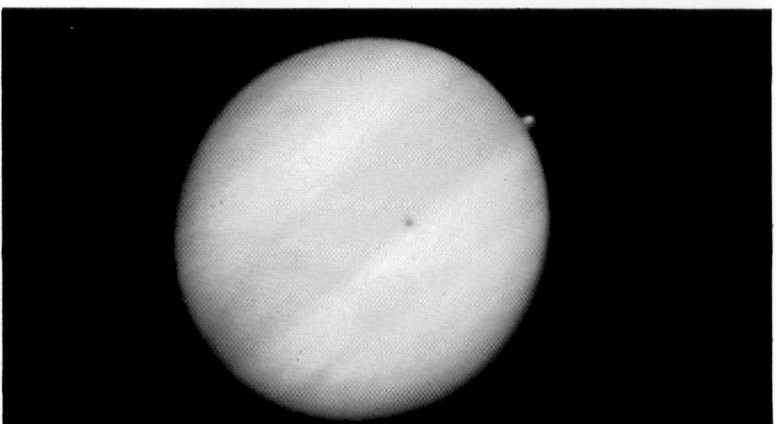

4 The moons of Jupiter, as well as all other natural and artificial satellites, move in orbits around their mother planet at great speeds. The force of gravity between them provides the centripetal force toward the center of motion that keeps a moon in orbit and produces its centripetal acceleration. As the speed of rotation remains almost constant, it is the continuously changing direction of the moon that implies acceleration. If the inward gravitational force were removed, the equal centrifugal force would cause the moon to hurtle out into space. The orbits are not exactly circular, so that the speed of rotation does not remain constant; the associated forces are analogous to those of a system performing circular motion.

cycles completed per second is called the "frequency" of oscillation.

The amplitude in all types of simple harmonic motion rises and falls like a sine wave. This also characterizes many other wave motions. If a long rope is clamped at one end and its free end is whipped, a wavelike disturbance travels along the rope and the amplitude of the rope's displacement at any point from the fixed end is described by the waveform shown in [6].

Moving and standing waves

The characteristics of this wave picture describe amplitude changes for the plane waves that move through the sea, the spherical waves (ripples) that spread from the point at which a stone is dropped in a pond, the air pressure waves of sound, and the electromagnetic waves of radio and light (which are distinguished by their wavelengths). For all these waveforms, energy is transmitted in the direction of the wave motion. Actual vibrations of the medium in which they travel may occur in the same direction, producing "longitudinal waves" such as those of sound, or in a direction at right angles to the motion, producing the transverse waves of all the other examples. In water, a floating object merely bobs up and down as the waves pass, and it does not move in the direction of the wave motion.

If a string is clamped at both ends and then plucked, it still vibrates but in this case the wave appears to stay in the same place—a stationary, or "standing," wave has been produced. The string vibrates at its natural frequency, which is inversely proportional to its length and directly proportional to $\sqrt{T/m}$ where T is its tension and m is its mass per unit length. This state of vibration is called "resonance" because it occurs with the natural frequency of the string. Blowing into the end of an organ pipe makes the air in it resonate at a natural frequency that depends on the pipe's length. Similarly, when struck, a tuning fork vibrates with one particular frequency. There are many useful applications of resonance, as in tuning circuits on radio receivers [8], and in musical instruments.

KEY

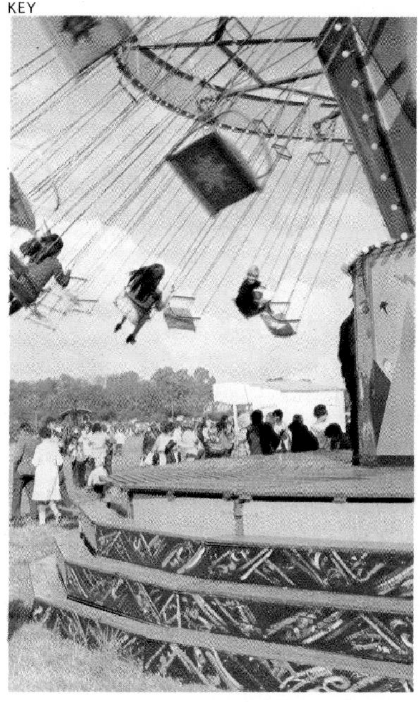

Many fairground rides depend on circular motion and the resulting centrifugal forces for the excitement they can provide. They all use different variations of this type of motion, ranging from the slow revolutions of the merry-go-round to the much faster and more complex movements of the flying chairs. The magnitude of the centrifugal force depends on the mass of the circling object. When this fairground ride gets up to speed, the heavier children will "fly" higher than the lighter ones. The same force squeezes water out of wet laundry in a spin drier and causes precipitation in a centrifuge.

5

5 Sea waves move with a transverse wave motion that transmits energy in their direction of motion, while floating objects only move vertically up and down as the waves pass them.

6

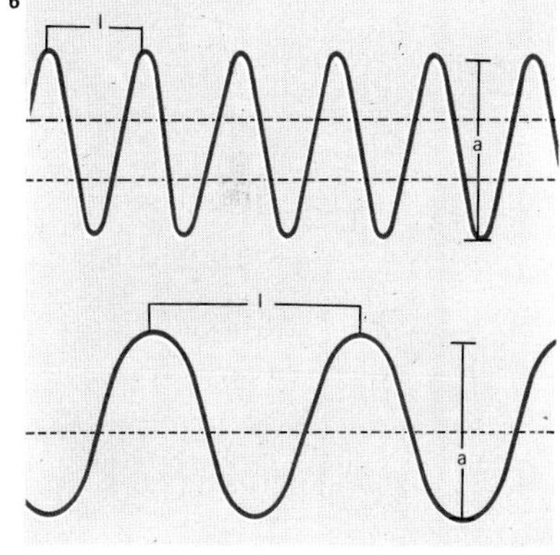

l
a

6 The forward velocity (v) of a wave of frequency (f) and wavelength (l) is given by v= fl. The amplitude (a) of these waves follows a sine wave, even though the wavelengths differ.

7

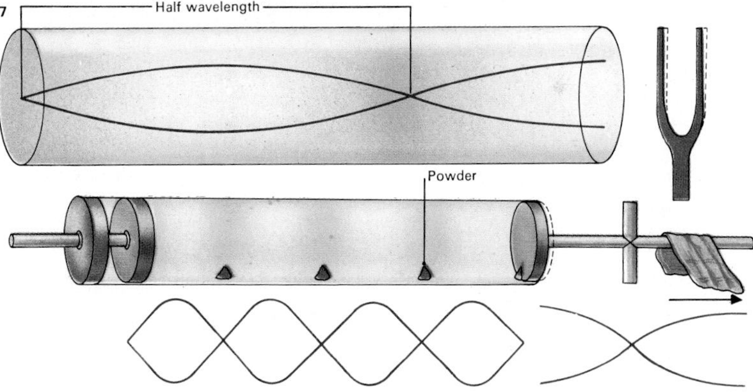

Half wavelength
Powder

7 The air inside a pipe will vibrate at a natural frequency that depends on the pipe's length. If the external impulse has this frequency, resonance occurs. Powder in the lower tube shows the wave.

8

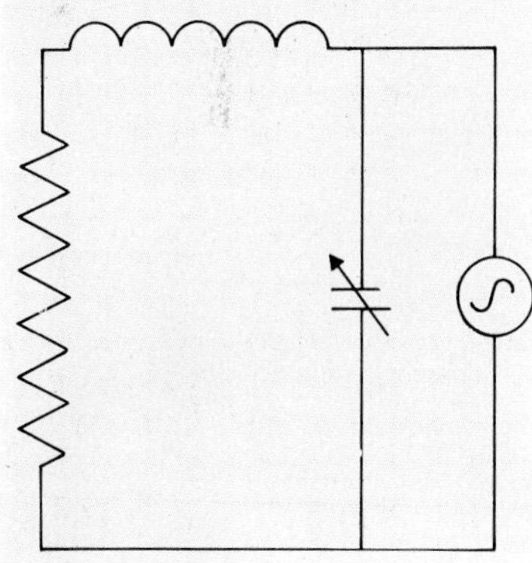

8 This circuit, with the AC source from a radio's antenna, can be "tuned" so that its natural frequency is matched to that of the incoming radio signals. Resonance excites it to oscillate and work the radio.

9

9 Winds can produce oscillations in very large and heavy structures. If they continue, the oscillations may gradually increase in amplitude and if their frequency equals the natural vibration frequency of the structure resonance may occur, leading to catastrophic break-up of the structure. This has happened with bridges, the most renowned being the Tacoma Narrows Suspension Bridge ("Galloping Gertie") in Washington (1940).

Pressure and flow

The branch of physics that deals with the forces, pressures, and flow of liquids and gases is called fluid mechanics. It also deals with the forces experienced by stationary or moving objects within the fluid. It includes, for example, problems ranging from deep-sea diving to airplane altimeters and from floating and sinking to the design of hydraulic car jacks.

Archimedes' principle

Hydrostatics is the study of stationary fluids. Both liquids and gases are fluids and each is able to exert or transmit a force. If a cork is pushed below a liquid surface and then released, it immediately bobs to the surface. The cork has experienced an upward force, or buoyancy, caused by the liquid, and it is this that keeps the cork floating on the surface. In exactly the same way, buoyancy acts on a floating balloon, although here it is produced by a gas rather than a liquid.

It was the Greek scientist Archimedes (287–212 BC) who first quantified this fact by stating that "when an object is totally or partially immersed in a fluid the buoyant force on it is equal to the weight of fluid displaced." Using Archimedes' principle [1] the magnitude of the buoyant force can always be found and it makes itself apparent as a loss of weight of the object.

A floating object has its weight exactly balanced by the buoyant force. But if the object is too dense, the buoyant force may not be sufficient to counterbalance its weight, and the object sinks. This principle of flotation is used directly by a hydrometer, an instrument for measuring liquid densities. A hydrometer floats at a level that depends on the weight of a liquid it displaces and, since the submerged volume is known, the density can be calculated.

Internal forces in fluids

As well as being able to exert a buoyant force, a fluid can produce an internal force at any depth because of the weight of the fluid above it. It is normal to measure this effect as the force per unit area, or pressure, developed by the fluid's weight; this increases with depth (in both liquids and gases). Thus the greater water pressure at the bottom of a dam requires a form of construction in which strength also increases with depth—a triangular cross-section getting thicker with depth is generally used. For a similar reason, the suit of a deep-sea diver must contain a jacket of compressed air whose pressure counteracts the external water pressure, so that he can breathe without his muscles having to expand his chest against this pressure. Another example of a fluid is the earth's atmosphere. The weight of air produces a pressure at the surface, commonly called atmospheric pressure, which is about 14.7 pounds per square inch at sea level. In other unit systems it is equal to 760mm of mercury, 101,325 newtons/m², or 1,013 millibars. Variations in this pressure affect the weather and are caused by atmospheric disturbances. They are measured by the common barometer. The simplest form of barometer measures the height of a column of liquid, often mercury, supported by the atmospheric pressure. An aneroid barometer transforms the effect of pressure on a

CONNECTIONS

See also

1502 States of matter: gases

1504 States of matter: liquids

1634 Wind and water power

1718 How an airplane works

1682 Hydrofoils and hovercraft

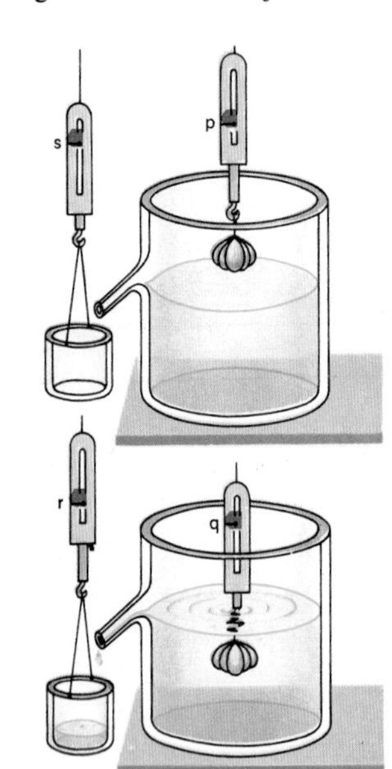

1A
s
p
r
q

B

1 Archimedes' principle states that for an object immersed in a fluid the buoyant force equals the weight of fluid that it displaces [A] The round object suspended on the balance has weight p in air and lesser weight q when immersed in a liquid. The difference in its weight (p-q) is equal to the buoyant force on it, that is, to the weight of displaced water in the beaker (r-s). An application of Archimedes' principle is the hydrometer [B], which is used to test the condition of a car battery by checking the acid density. The tube is immersed in the battery acid and the bulb is squeezed to expel air; it is then released to suck acid into the main stem. The hydrometer then floats in the acid, at a depth that depends on the liquid's density. The hydrometer is calibrated to give accurate readings of the specific gravity of the battery acid.

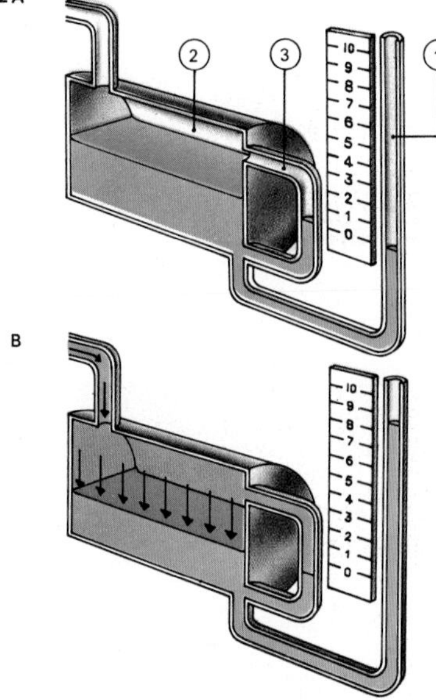

2A
B

2 The manometer is a U-shaped liquid column gauge used to measure differences in fluid pressure. The "well-type" has one column [1] of relatively small diameter; the other acts as a reservoir [2]. The difference in columns ensures that the level in the reservoir does not change much with pressure, but that the level in the small diameter column does, allowing precision in reading these variations. Small adjustments of the scale with the help of the level indicator [3] compensate for the small reservoir changes. At first [A] both columns are equal. With the reservoir pressurized [B] the new level shows the pressure.

3 In the lift pump the piston [1] is moved upward by the downward stroke of the handle, producing a vacuum in the cylinder [2]. The piston valve [4] is kept closed by the water already filling the pump chamber. Water is then forced into the cylinder by atmospheric pressure acting on the surface of the reservoir. This water passes through the open valve [3] filling the upper chamber. On the upward stroke the piston moves down, valve 3 closes and valve 4 is forced open by the pressure of the water below the piston. With the next stroke this water is lifted out of the pump and the cycle begins again. In theory, atmospheric pressure "lifts" up to 34 ft (10m).

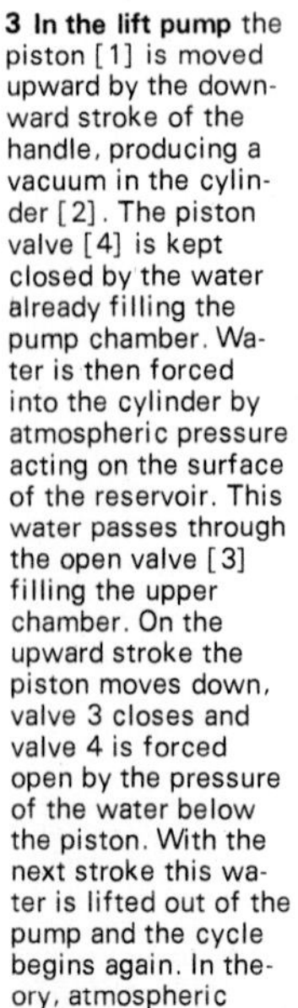

3
10m

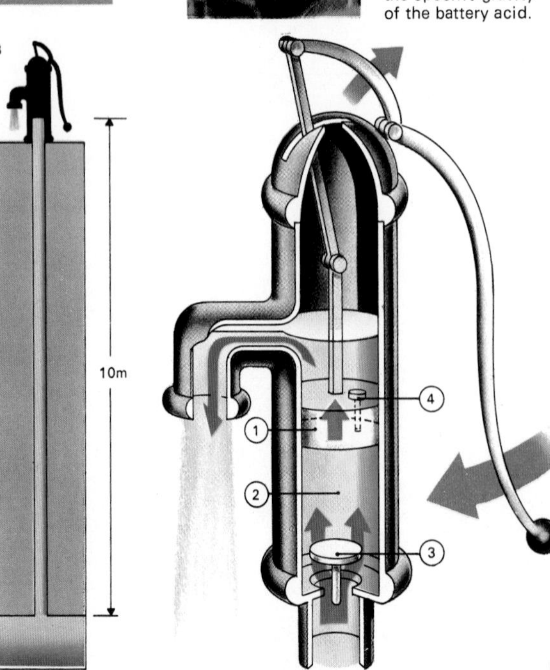

4 A water cannon has water pumped into it under great pressure and forced through an exit nozzle of relatively small diameter. As a result a great force propels the water forward (pressure is the force per unit area) and accelerates it to a high velocity. The water acquires considerable momentum and kinetic energy which can be used to cut relatively soft china clay from a quarry wall. The great power of the water cannon is also often used to clean the outside walls of buildings. In this case, an abrasive in the form of a powder can be put into the water to increase the corrosive effect of the water jet as it strikes the surface to be cleaned, scouring accumulated dirt.

thin-walled metal cylinder into the mechanical movement of a needle moving across a calibrated dial. This form is used as an altimeter in many aircraft.

The possibility of supporting a column of liquid by gas pressure is also used in a manometer [2]. This generally consists of a u-shaped glass tube containing a liquid that moves around the u-bend by an amount depending on the difference between the pressures applied at each end. The same principle is employed in the common pump that lifts water from a well. It "taps" a column of water supported by atmospheric pressure acting on the surface of the water source. The height of this column can theoretically be 34ft (10.36m), although in practice the so-called lift-pump [3] can raise water from only about 28ft (8.5m).

External pressure can be used to move a fluid, but its own internal pressure can also be most effectively employed. A liquid is virtually incompressible, so that pressure developed at one point is transmitted equally in all directions. This fact can be utilized in a hydraulic press or jack to exert very large forces. A force acting on a very small area produces an enormous pressure that can be transformed into a much greater force acting over the large area of the hydraulic jack ram [5], since the pressure remains constant throughout the liquid.

The study of hydrodynamics

All these effects use the static properties of fluids. But by definition a fluid is something that flows and the properties resulting from this are described by hydrodynamics.

Motion changes the pressure within a fluid and this can be difficult to predict accurately. The flow can be either smooth (streamlined) or turbulent, when the fluid is broken up into eddies; it is then harder to calculate the pressure at different points within the fluid. The Swiss scientist Daniel Bernoulli (1700–82) first noticed that pressure decreases as fluid velocity increases and this principle creates the necessary lift on an aircraft's wing [Key]. The wing shape is arranged to produce a greater flow velocity above the wing than below it and so there is a net upward pressure, or lift.

KEY

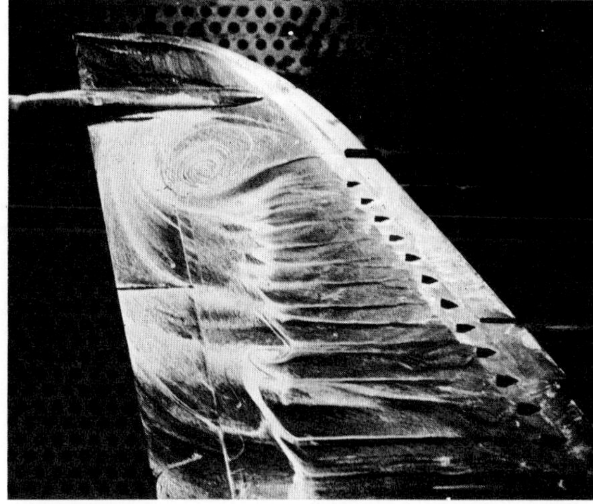

The way air flows around objects can be studied using a wind tunnel. Thus the aerodynamic properties of aircraft wing shapes, or of complete planes and cars, for example, can be investigated. Tiny plastic spheres are injected into the airstream so that flow patterns can be examined visually and photographed and streamlined designs created.

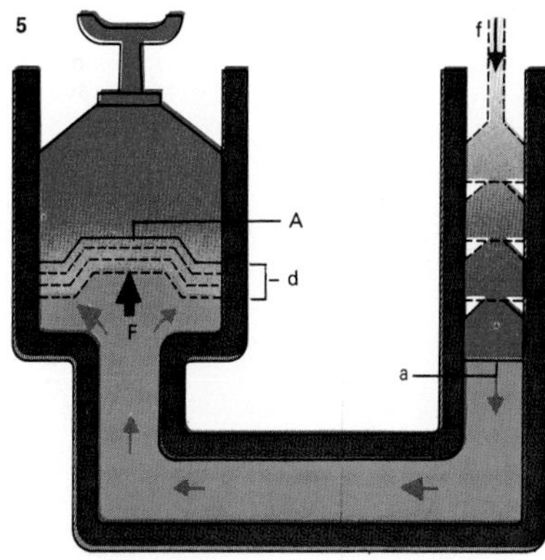

5
f
A
d
F
a

5 An hydraulic lift works on the principle that an incompressible liquid transmits pressure equally in all directions. The small force f acting on area a produces pressure f/a, which is transmitted unchanged to the much larger area A, resulting in larger force F so that $F/A = f/a$. This can be used to move great weights. But the weight moves through only the small distance d.

6
SEEBOARD

6 The principle of hydraulic lift has many applications, the most familiar of which is probably the car lift used by mechanics in garages. Other types of hydraulic machinery have many other applications in agriculture and industry, as in this hydraulic hoist used by engineers to rig or maintain overhead telephone and electric power lines. If such machines worked exactly as described in illustration 5, the pressure-developing force would have to move several yards to produce only a small movement of the actuating piston. The hydraulic fluid is therefore pressurized by a pump, which transfers the necessary pressure.

7 A shock absorber is used to reduce or dampen oscillating motions. Several damping systems can be employed—oil damping is shown in A, air damping in B, and friction damping in C. The most common type is the oil damper [D], which is used especially in road vehicles. It consists of a plunger that on its downward stroke allows oil to pass through a small valve in the piston. The viscosity of the oil and the size of the valve determine the damping characteristics; that is, the manner and speed with which the oscillation is reduced. For rapid loading conditions, a second valve channels oil into a reserve.

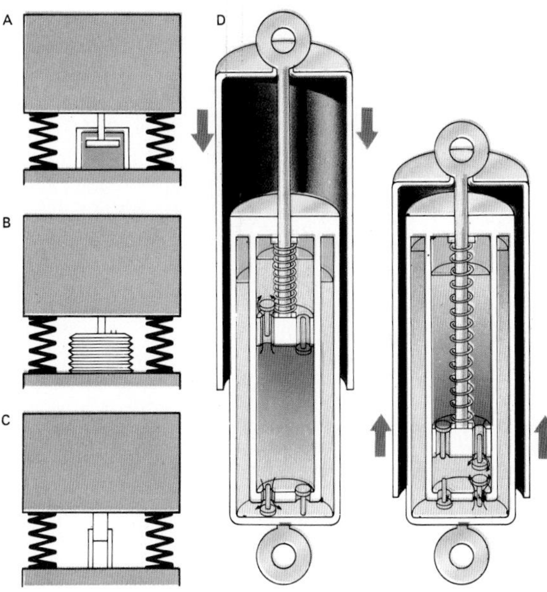

7
A
B
C
D

8 A stream of gas tends to adhere to any adjacent solid surface, a phenomenon called the Coanda wall-attachment effect. A gas stream that is free to enter two identical channels [A] chooses one by adhering to its walls. A side-stream [B] can then deflect it to other output channels [C] where it remains even when the disturbance ceases. This is the fluid analogue of an electric switch.

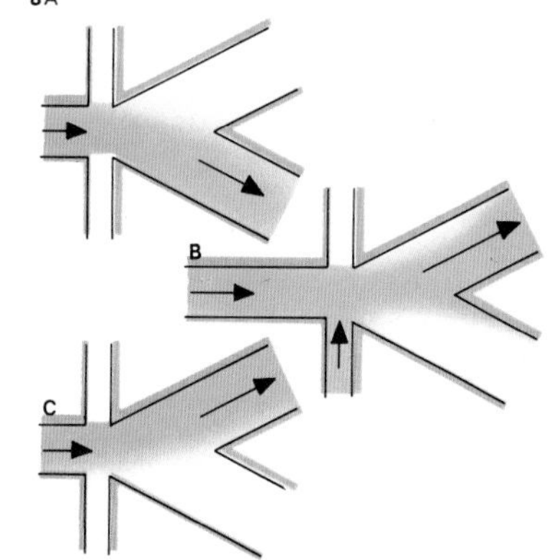

8A
B
C

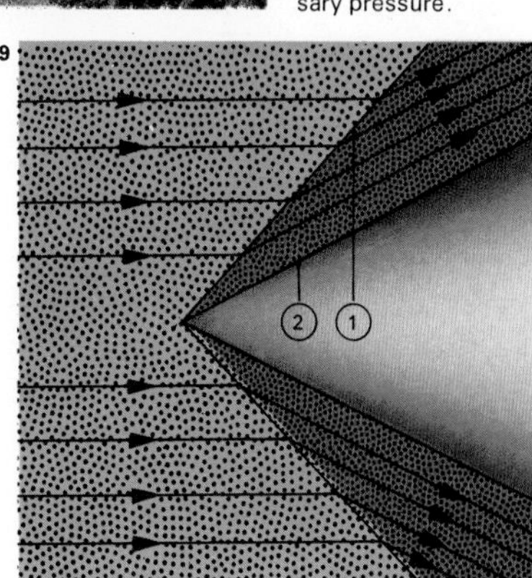

9
2
1

9 When the velocity of a gas is low compared with that of sound its flow can be described without considering the compressibility. Above 0.3 of the speed of sound (Mach 1) a gas is compressed when it meets a solid and there is a consequent temperature change. Above Mach 1, compression occurs abruptly and a shock wave forms. The diagram shows a shock wave [1] at an aircraft nose-cone [2]. At the shock front direction of relative flow changes and air becomes more dense.

What is sound?

Sound is energy and, like other forms of energy, can be useful to man. The vast range of possible frequencies and timbres that characterizes both speech and music makes sound an effective medium of communication. Even ultrasound—sound above the hearing range of man—has many practical uses. Most sounds do not carry a great deal of energy. The noise of a symphony orchestra playing as loudly as possible involves, for example, sound energy equivalent to the light and heat energy from only a low-powered electric lamp. Our hearing sense is more easily saturated (in energy terms) than our visual sense.

How sound is produced

Sound is a particular form of kinetic energy (energy of motion) produced when an object vibrates and a medium, such as air, vibrates in response. The sound of a car crash booms out as the surfaces of the two colliding vehicles vibrate with the force of the collision; music comes from a radio as a loudspeaker vibrates; and talking and singing result from vibrations of the vocal cords.

As an object vibrates it sets the air molecules around it vibrating. Where the air molecules gather together a region of higher pressure (compression) forms. Where they move apart a region of lower pressure (rarefaction) occurs. As compressions and rarefactions move through the air they form a sound wave. At the ear they set the eardrum vibrating and we hear sound.

If a surface vibrates more strongly, the pressure difference between the compressions and rarefactions is greater and the sound is loud [1]. The frequency of vibrations affects the pitch, or note, of the sound. Fast vibrations produce compressions and rarefactions that are close together and the pitch is high. A slower speed of vibration causes the compressions and rarefactions to be farther apart and the sound is lower in pitch.

A sound wave moves out from its source in all directions, traveling at a speed of 1,087ft (331m) per second or 741mph (1,194kph) in air at 0°C at sea level. The speed is slower at high altitudes as air is less dense there, and faster in water and metal because these substances are more elastic than air and transmit vibrations more rapidly. The speed also correlates with the temperature of the medium. Sound cannot move through a vacuum because there are no gas molecules to vibrate and transmit the sound.

Like other waves of energy, sound normally travels in straight lines, but sound can turn corners. It is reflected whenever it strikes a surface such as a wall [2] or floor and is diffracted or spreads out as it passes through an opening such as a window [3].

Dynamics, pitch and frequency

The loudness of a sound can be measured with a decibel meter and the result given as a number of decibels (dB). The scale is logarithmic—a sound that is twice as loud as one at the threshold of hearing is 10dB greater, not twice as great. Strictly, the meter measures the intensity of the sound, which is related to the pressure differences in the sound wave. (Loudness is the strength of the sensation received in the eardrum and transmitted to the brain.) The

CONNECTIONS

See also
1500 Musical sounds
1494 Circular and vibrating motion
1486 The nature of energy
1752 Airports and air traffic
676 Hearing and balance

1 A

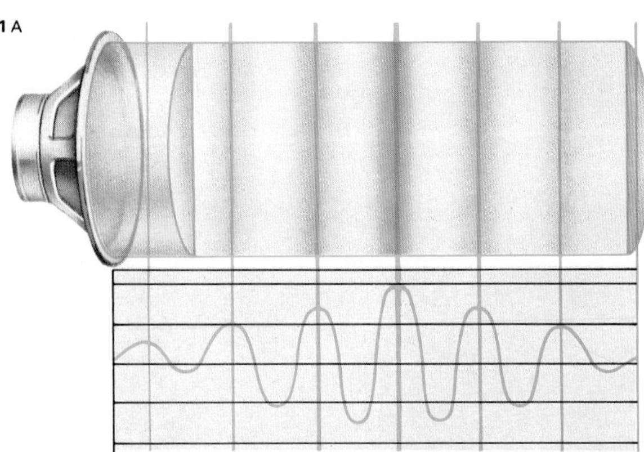

B

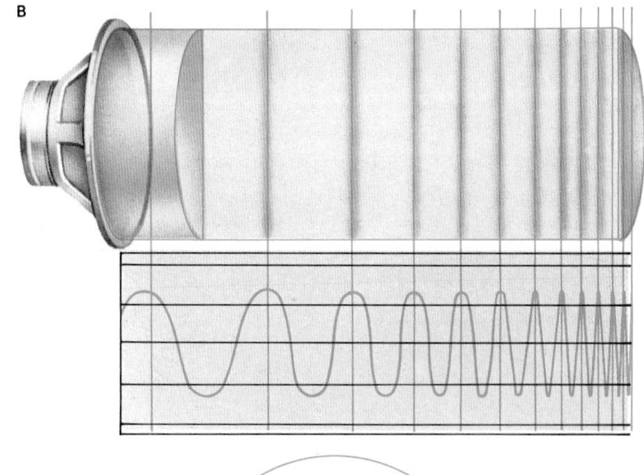

1 A sound wave consists of pressure differences, shown as dark and light bands [A]. The curve shows how pressure changes with time. This wave has a constant frequency (a single note) but decreases and increases in intensity. It would have a "wah" sound. A falling note [B] would be heard as this sound wave passes. The frequency decreases as the note becomes lower, but intensity is the same.

2

2 The Whispering Gallery in the dome of St Paul's Cathedral in London is renowned for its acoustics. A sound whispered against the wall near one side of the gallery can be heard clearly near the other side. Being elliptical in shape, the walls reflect the sound of the whisper made at one focus of the ellipse through the other focus, about 100 ft (30m) away. Normally, a whisper would be inaudible at such a distance.

3

Source of sound

Window

3 Both reflection and diffraction enable a sound to be heard even though the person or object producing the sound is hidden from view. Sound is reflected from surfaces such as walls, floors, and ceilings and, further, undergoes diffraction at an opening such as a door or window. As they pass the edges of the opening the sound waves spread out and the opening appears to be the source of the sound.

human ear does not hear all frequencies of sound in the same way, and a low sound is perceived as being less loud than a high sound of the same intensity.

The number of compressions occurring every second is called the frequency of the sound wave and is measured in hertz (Hz), equal to cycles per second. The higher the frequency the higher the pitch. A note of 440Hz (the A above middle C in music) is said to be an octave above one of 220Hz (the A below middle C).

Noise and acoustics

Noise does not have any particular pitch and covers a wide frequency range [4]. Very loud noise is dangerous as well as a nuisance, because continuous exposure to sound of more than 100dB—the levels produced by jet aircraft [5] and machines in many factories—soon results in a permanent reduction in hearing ability. Low-frequency noises are particularly hazardous because they do not seem to be as loud as higher pitches, and tests have shown that very high levels of low-frequency sound and infrasound (sound below the hearing range of the ear) quickly result in vertigo, nausea, and other physical effects; military scientists have even experimented with using infrasound as a potential weapon.

Acoustic engineers work to reduce noise and improve sound in many ways. A consideration of acoustics in the design of a machine such as a jet engine can reduce the amount of noise it makes. Buildings can also be designed to prevent the transmission of sound through them. A steel framework tends to distribute sound throughout a building, but the use of soft sound-absorbing materials in and on floors, walls, and ceilings prevents sound from getting into and out of rooms. In concert halls the reflection of sound inside the hall is rigorously controlled to provide an exact amount of echo and give the best quality sound [6]. This may be assisted by electronic amplification, although very loud music loses clarity in a concert hall. Some recording studios have completely absorbent walls to remove all echo and ensure total clarity whatever the type of music being performed.

KEY

10 100 1,000 10,000 100,000 Hz

The range of hearing varies widely in man and other animals. Birds and man have fairly similar hearing ranges and both use sound to communicate. Bats and dolphins are sensitive to ultrasound (beyond human hearing), which they use to avoid obstacles and to find their prey by echolocation. There is good evidence that dolphins and other whales communicate by means of ultrasound. Nightmoths make use of ultrasound to avoid predators. Mosquitoes hear a narrow range of sound, corresponding to their own buzzing. The range of sound heard by fish and snakes is also extremely small.

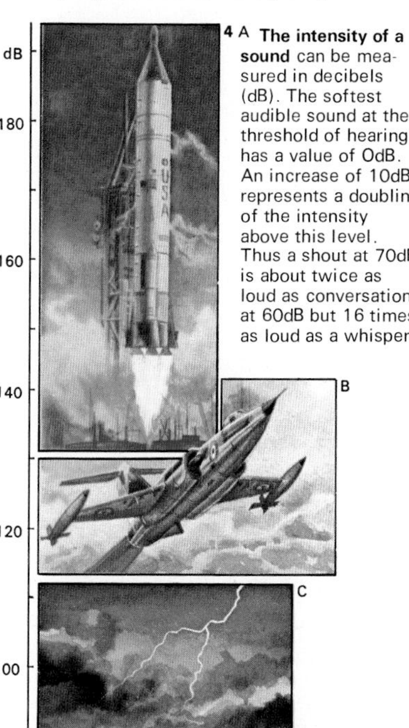

dB
180
160
140
120
100
80
60
40
20
0
A
B
C
D
E
F
G

4 A The intensity of a sound can be measured in decibels (dB). The softest audible sound at the threshold of hearing has a value of 0dB. An increase of 10dB represents a doubling of the intensity above this level. Thus a shout at 70dB is about twice as loud as conversation at 60dB but 16 times as loud as a whisper at 30dB. The chart shows the loudness of some sounds near their sources. At 140dB sound causes pain. These fairly common sounds illustrate the range that can be heard by human beings: [A] space rocket at lift-off, 140–190dB; [B] a jet aircraft on take-off, 110–140dB; [C] thunder, 90–110dB; [D] a train, 65–90dB; [E] loud conversation, 50–65dB; [F] quiet conversation, 20–50 dB; and [G] a rustling of dry autumn leaves, 0–10dB.

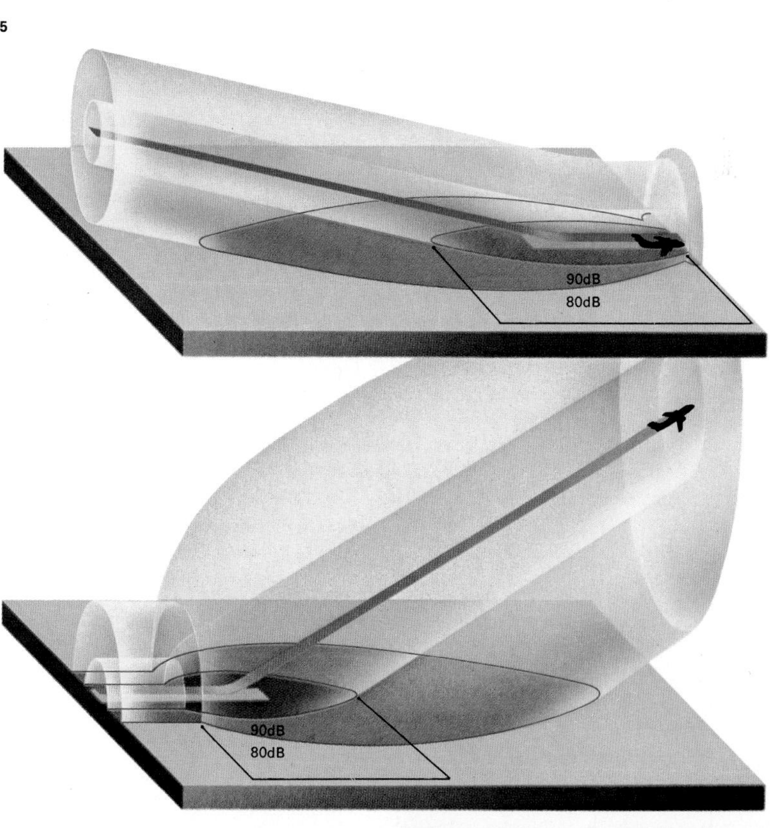

5
90dB
80dB
90dB
80dB

5 Noise is a hazard, particularly near aircraft and airport personnel, who may wear earmuffs for protection. Farther away, noise is a severe nuisance but not physically dangerous. Near an airport noise levels are about 90dB—sufficient to drown all conversation—and for miles around noise levels may be 80dB—roughly that of heavy traffic. The problem is usually worse when aircraft are landing than at take-off. A landing aircraft flies nearer the ground for a longer time and its noise consists of disturbing high-pitched whines. After takeoff an aircraft climbs rapidly and leaves a smaller area affected; also its sound is more of a rumble. Newer jet aircraft—supersonic airliners excepted—have quieter engines and may affect an area only a tenth the size of that disturbed by older jet aircraft.

6 The acoustics of a London concert hall were altered when it was discovered that the reverberation time—the time taken for the sounds made on the stage to die away in the hall—was too short for the lower frequencies. Electronically amplified resonators were placed in the ceiling to add echo to the hall. The graph shows the reverberation time before [1] and after [2]. The result was a more balanced and pleasing sound throughout the hall.

6

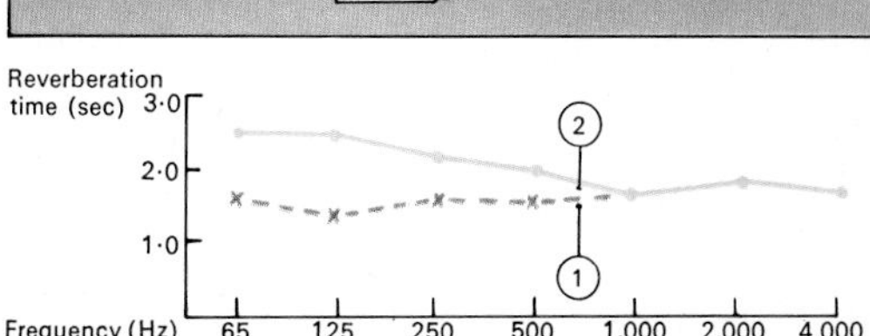

Reverberation time (sec)
3·0
2·0
1·0
2
1
Frequency (Hz)
65
125
250
500
1,000
2,000
4,000

Musical sounds

Why should one musical instrument sound so different from another? Instruments are played in various ways; some are struck, some are blown, while others are bowed or plucked to produce many kinds of sounds. But what is different about the sound itself?

Frequency and pitch

Every instrument produces a sound by making something vibrate, and the frequency of the vibration determines the pitch of the note produced. If the vibration is more rapid, the number of vibrations in the sound wave that reaches the ear in a given time interval is greater and the pitch is higher or more to the treble. If the frequency is less, the pitch will be lower or more to the bass.

The frequency of a sound wave (number of vibrations per second) is measured in hertz (Hz). The audible range of frequencies for human beings usually lies between 20 and 20,000Hz. But some animals have a far wider range of hearing.

Every instrument produces notes within a particular range of frequencies. But each note is in fact a combination of many more notes. The pitch of the main note heard by the ear is called the fundamental, and above it every instrument also produces a group of higher-pitched notes called harmonics. The harmonics are produced because the object making the sound vibrates at several frequencies at once. The extra frequencies are multiples of the fundamental frequency.

These higher notes can sometimes be produced deliberately on certain instruments—on brass instruments by tightening the lips to make them vibrate faster and on string instruments by shortening the part of the string free to vibrate—but normally they are not heard individually. If they were, each note on an instrument would sound like a vast chord. Instead, all the harmonics combine with the fundamental note to produce a complex waveform. Each instrument produces its own particular waveform because the relative intensity of the harmonics is different. The modern music synthesizer works by producing several waveforms of basic shapes—a sine wave, a saw-toothed wave and a square wave—and then combining them to make all kinds of sounds.

Not all instruments produce a note of definite pitch. Several, such as drums and cymbals, produce noise, which consists of a wide range of frequencies without any particular dominant frequency.

The effect of volume

Volume, or the degree of loudness, is another quality of musical sound. Music employs contrasts of volume on a large time scale for dramatic effect, but on a small time scale the change of volume at the beginning of a note is essential to the quality of a sound. The starting characteristics [3], called transients, determine whether a note begins quickly or takes some time to build up; transients are complex and involve changes in the waveform as well as in volume as the instrument begins to sound. Transients are vital to recognition; if the transients are removed from a recording of an oboe, for example, the character of its sound changes until it sounds more like a harmonica.

CONNECTIONS

See also
1498 What is sound?
1244 Development of the orchestra
1366 Jazz and Pop

1 Sound waves combine and the waveforms show that the first tuning fork [A] has twice the frequency of the second one [B]. The combination [C] produces a sound equal to the sum of the frequencies and the altered shape of the waveform [green curve] shows that it has changed in tone. Two waves that are only slightly different in frequency combine to give a slow beating (pulsing) sound.

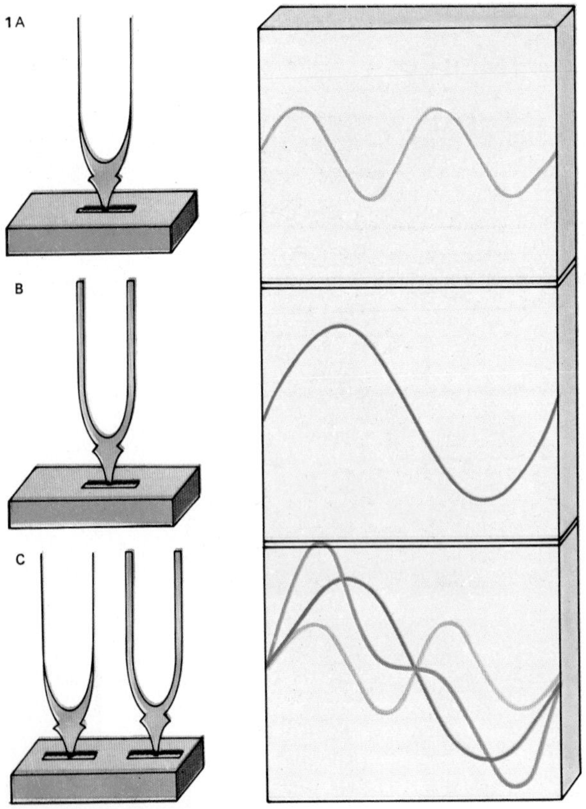

2 The waveforms of a flute [A], oboe [B], and clarinet [C] show the differences in tone among them. The flute's rounded waveform displays the instrument's gentle, fluid sound. The clarinet wave has a similar shape with "jinks" indicating a reedier sound. The oboe's jagged waveform shows that its sound is very reedy. The lowest note of the violin [D] has a fundamental frequency of 196Hz (G below middle C), but it also vibrates at frequencies that are simple multiples of this, giving a range of harmonics above the fundamental note. The second harmonic has a frequency twice that of the fundamental (the first harmonic). These harmonics collectively color the basic note by combining with it to give a complex waveform. The relative intensity of the harmonics [E] shows that the fundamental [red] is less intense than some of the harmonics. But it is reinforced because the harmonics interact with each other.

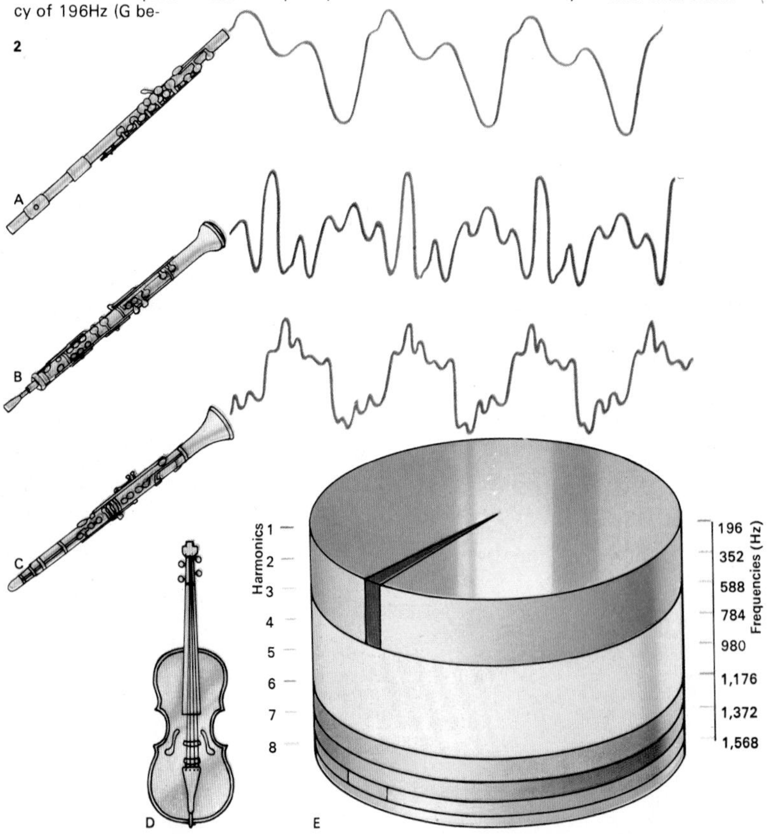

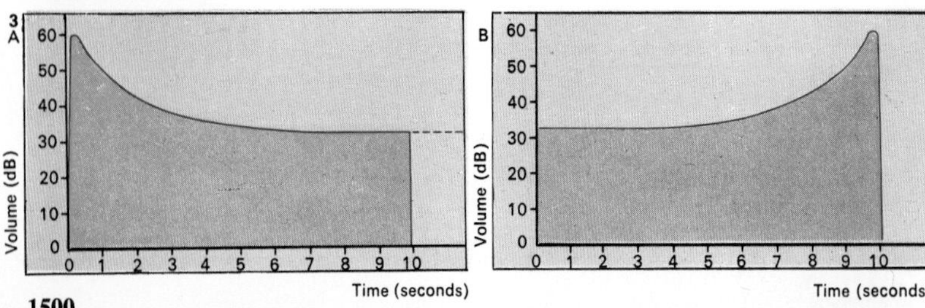
3
A
B
Volume (dB)
60
50
40
30
20
10
0
0 1 2 3 4 5 6 7 8 9 10
Time (seconds)

3 The start of a sound must be heard if it is to be recognized. The graph shows that a piano note, for example, reaches its peak volume very soon after it is struck [A]. It then begins to fall away with great rapidity at first, before trailing away slowly for several seconds. This is what gives the instrument its "attack." The same note produced on a gong takes a comparatively long time to build up and, although of the same pitch, sounds completely different. The same piano note played backward on a tape recording [B] slowly increases in volume and then suddenly stops. Shorn of its start, the sound is totally unlike a piano and more like an organ.

Two other qualities often present in a musical sound are echo and vibrato. Echo is often believed to improve music, giving it a more rounded sound, and it is produced by the reflections of sound from the walls of a concert hall or added artificially to recordings. Vibrato is a slight wobble in pitch that many musicians use; a violinist moves his left wrist to and fro to produce vibrato.

Types of musical instruments

The nature of the vibrating object is the basis of family grouping of instruments. In string instruments—the violin [2D], viola, cello, double bass, guitar, piano, harpsichord, and harp—a taut string is set in motion by stroking it with a bow, plucking it with the fingers or a plectrum, or striking it with a soft hammer. A longer string produces a lower note, and the pitch is altered either by pressing the string against a fingerboard to change its length, or by playing a string of a different length. The tension and thickness of the string also affect the note, a tauter or thinner string giving a higher note.

Wind instruments work by making a column of air vibrate. In brass instruments—the trumpet [5], trombone, and horn—the player's lips vibrate in the mouthpiece. In some woodwind instruments, such as the bassoon, oboe [2B], and clarinet [2C], the mouthpiece contains one or two vibrating reeds, and in the flute [2A] the player blows across a hole to set the air column in the instrument vibrating. When a player presses down keys or valves, he alters the length of the air column and produces notes of different pitch [6].

Some percussion instruments are played by striking a taut skin, as in a drum, or a solid object of some kind—a cymbal, for example. Tuned percussion instruments give definite pitches. They include the vibraphone [7] and xylophone, in which metal or wooden bars of different lengths are struck to sound various notes.

Electric instruments pick up the vibration of a string, as in an electric guitar and convert the vibration into an electric signal that passes to an amplifier and loudspeaker to produce the sound.

KEY

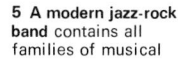

Musical instruments, from the deepest to the highest members of each family, cover almost the entire range of human hearing. The woodwind family has a particularly wide compass, the lowest note of the contrabassoon and the harmonics [dotted line] of the piccolo nearing the limits of audibility.

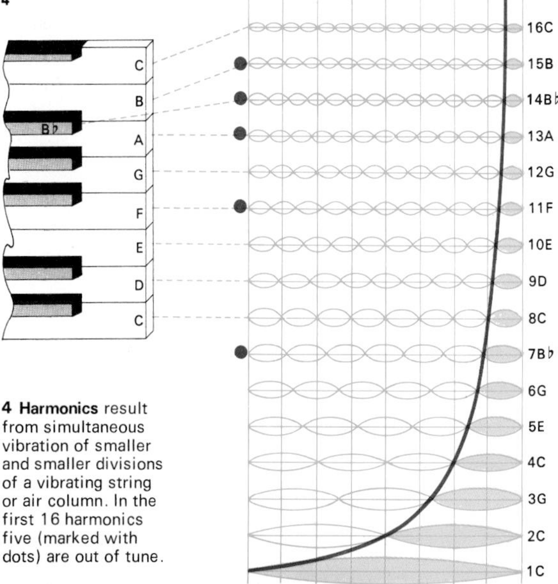

C
B
B♭
A
G
F
E
D
C
16C
15B
14B♭
13A
12G
11F
10E
9D
8C
7B♭
6G
5E
4C
3G
2C
1C

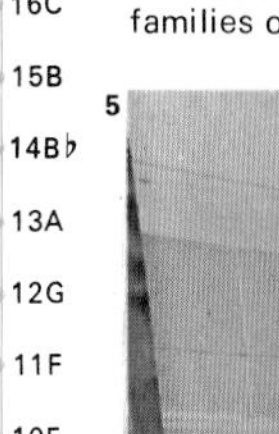

4 **Harmonics** result from simultaneous vibration of smaller and smaller divisions of a vibrating string or air column. In the first 16 harmonics five (marked with dots) are out of tune.

5 **A modern jazz-rock band** contains all families of musical instruments, mingling the acoustic sounds of trumpet, saxophone, and drums with the electric sounds of synthesizer, electric piano, bass guitar, and electric guitar.

6 **Resonance** is an important part of musical sounds. It can be demonstrated with a milk bottle and a tuning fork. The fork is struck and held over the neck of the bottle. The bottle can also sound, but its frequency depends on the length of the air column inside. It is possible to "tune" the bottle by adding a liquid until the remaining air space resonates at the same frequency as the tuning fork. The sound of the fork is then much louder. Many musical instruments make use of resonance. The low-volume sound produced by the vibrating string of a violin or guitar, for example, is made much louder by the air resonating inside the instrument's body.

7 **Sound production** in musical instruments often involves resonance. Amplification of sound is achieved in the vibraphone in the same way as in the tuning fork and milk bottle. Beneath each bar is a tube of sufficient length to resonate at the frequency produced by the bar when it is struck. Small motor-driven fans over the top of each tube blow air into it and at slow speeds produce a "wavy" vibrato quality in the notes produced.

States of matter: gases

Most things on Earth exist in one of three basic states: gases, liquids, and solids. Most substances can exist in all three states, depending on the temperature. Water, for example, is a liquid at ordinary temperatures. But above 100°C (212°F) it changes to a gas (steam) and below 0°C (32°F) it becomes a solid (ice).

Ordinary matter is composed of atoms or molecules and these are held together in liquids and solids by what are called intermolecular forces. The molecules are in continuous motion with their velocities increasing with temperature. This "thermal motion" is restrained by the intermolecular forces of attraction, which hold the molecules together. Scientists call this view of matter the kinetic theory ("kinetic" means relating to movement or motion).

Kinetic theory of gases

In gases, thermal motion predominates and the molecules move rapidly, colliding with each other and with the walls of their containing vessel. Collisions with the walls account for the pressure exerted by a gas [1].

Scientists have made measurements that confirm the kinetic theory of gases. A liter (1.75 pints) of oxygen, for instance, is known to contain about 3×10^{22} (30,000 million million million) molecules. At 0°C (32°F) and a pressure of 760mm (29.9in) of mercury, known as standard temperature and pressure (STP), the molecules move with a speed of about 430m/sec (1,411ft/sec). Molecules are extremely small, measured in ångström units (1 Å = 10^{-10}m). Each oxygen molecule is 3.5 Å across. The molecules are, on an average, 70 Å apart, and they travel about 905 Å between collisions; this distance is the mean free path.

Boyle's law and Avogadro's principle

The quantity known as "temperature" is actually a measure of the kinetic energy of the molecules (their energy of motion). An increase in energy produces a proportional increase in absolute temperature.

When a gas is compressed—that is, if its volume is made to change at a constant temperature—the volume is inversely proportional to the pressure. This relationship is known as Boyle's law [3] after its discoverer, the British scientist Robert Boyle (1627–91). It persists because, when the volume is reduced, collisions with the container walls become more frequent and the pressure rises. If the temperature of a gas rises but it is not allowed to expand, the pressure again increases because molecular collisions with the walls become more forceful as well as more frequent.

Another basic gas law is called Avogadro's principle after the Italian physicist Amadeo Avogadro (1776–1856). It states that, at the same temperature and pressure, equal volumes of all gases contain the same number of molecules. A liter of a dense gas such as carbon dioxide contains the same number of molecules as a liter of a light gas such as hydrogen.

Gases slowly diffuse through the walls of a porous vessel because their molecules are smaller than the minute holes in the walls of the container. The rate at which they do so is inversely proportional to the square root of their density. Discovered by the British physicist Thomas Graham

CONNECTIONS

See also
1490 Attraction and repulsion
1496 Pressure and flow
1504 States of matter: liquids
1510 Order and disorder: thermodynamics
1512 Toward absolute zero

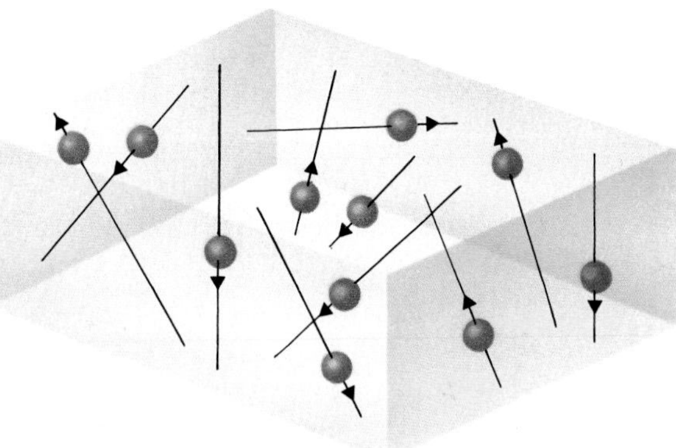

1 The molecules of gas move continuously at various speeds and in various directions. Collisions with the walls of the container cause pressure and there are so many molecules in even the smallest volume that the pressure is the same everywhere in it. The actual pressure is proportional to the number of molecules in a unit volume and to the average kinetic energy (energy of motion) of the molecules.

2 A compressed gas is a store of potential energy and it can be made to do useful work when it expands to atmospheric pressure, as in pneumatic drills, jackhammers, and spray cans.

3

P

2V

2P

V

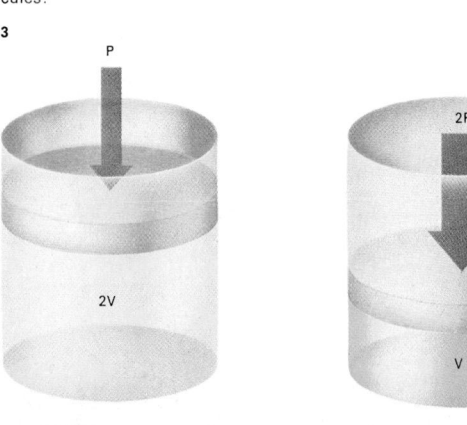

3 When the pressure exerted by the piston is doubled, the gas volume is halved (provided temperature does not change). This is an example of Boyle's law: pressure is inversely proportional to volume:

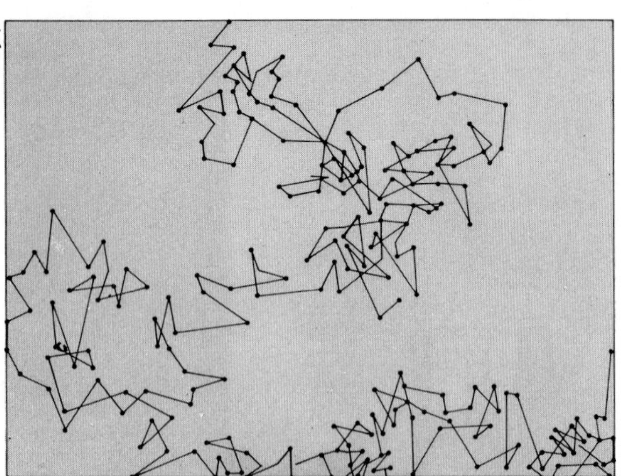

4 In this diagram of Brownian movement [A]—which is evidence for kinetic theory—the dots represent the position of a particle recorded after equal small intervals of time and the lines joining them indicate the paths taken by the random motion of the particle. A beam of sunlight passing through smoke [B] is made visible by reflection from the smoke particles. The same priniciple is used to view Brownian movement with a microscope.

(1805–69), this relationship is called Graham's law [7]. It is explained by the kinetic theory: in any gas left to itself for a sufficient time, the molecules will exchange energy by collisions until all have the same energy. If different gas molecules have the same kinetic energy, the lighter ones must move more quickly. Thus light gases diffuse more quickly than dense ones.

Brownian movement

More direct evidence for the kinetic theory is provided by the phenomenon known as Brownian movement [4]. Smoke can be seen in a sunbeam crossing a room. This effect can be produced in the laboratory by looking through a microscope at smoke particles in a box. Specks of light can be seen moving in a haphazard manner, first a short distance in one direction, then in another, and so on. The cause is unequal bombardment of the smoke particles, from different sides, by air molecules. The movement is less with larger smoke particles because air molecules have the same kinetic energy, so the larger particles move more slowly.

When a gas expands it has to do work against the external pressure. As a result it becomes cooler because the necessary energy must come from the kinetic energy of the gas. This phenomenon, known as the Joule-Thomson effect [6], accounts for the coldness of the air escaping from a car tire, for example. When such a change occurs without heat exchange it is called an adiabatic change. The pressure changes in air as a sound wave passes are adiabatic.

The amount of heat needed to raise the temperature of unit mass of a substance through 1°C is called its specific heat capacity. A gas has two principal heat capacities: that measured at constant pressure (c_p), and that at constant volume (c_v).

Subjected to sufficient pressure, most gases turn into a liquid. But above a certain "critical temperature" it is impossible to liquefy a gas using pressure alone [5]. This is because, above this temperature, the kinetic energy of the molecules overcomes the intermolecular attractions of their neighbors. Scientists apply the cooling effects of adiabatic expansion to liquefy gases [6].

KEY

Huge storage tanks for natural gas enable the pressure of the supply to consumers to be kept almost constant, even with fluctuating demand. A gasometer consists basically of a large movable cylinder with a water seal at the base.

5 A

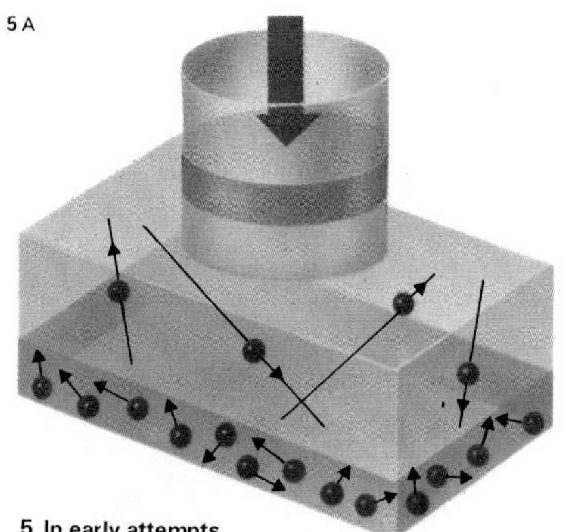

B

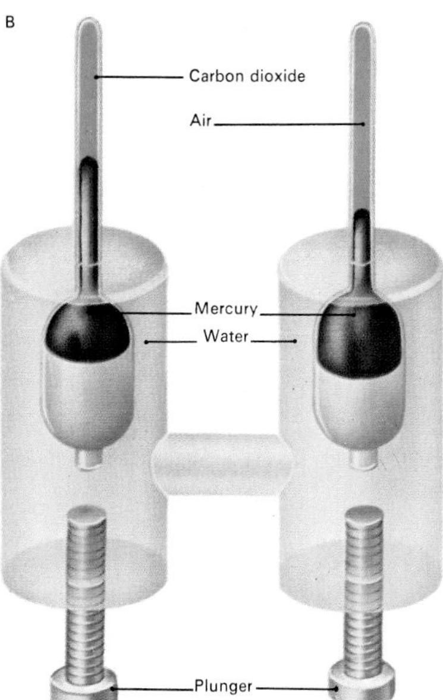

Carbon dioxide
Air
Mercury
Water
Plunger

C

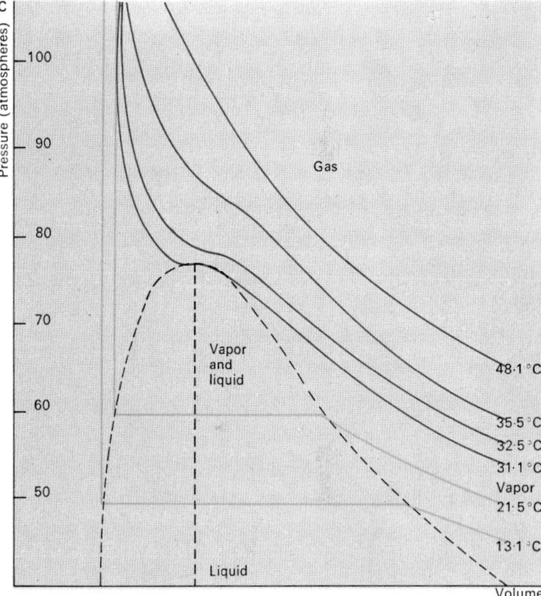

Pressure (atmospheres)
100
90
80
70
60
50
Gas
Vapor
and
liquid
Liquid
48·1°C
35·5°C
32·5°C
31·1°C
Vapor
21·5°C
13·1°C
Volume

5 In early attempts to liquefy gases [A] they were subjected to high pressure. Some gases liquefied under these conditions when a dynamic equilibrium was established between the liquid and vapor states – molecules left and entered the surface at the same rate. The experiments of Thomas Andrews (1813–85) [B] resulted in techniques that allowed other gases to be liquefied. Pressure is increased by screwing in the plungers and transmitted through the water to the gas and air in the upper tubes. The air is assumed to obey Boyle's law so that its change in volume is a measure of the pressure. Graphs of volume against pressure, called isothermals [C], reflect the various states of the gas. The horizontal blue line shows liquefaction and does not appear until temperature falls below 31.1°C (86°F), the critical temperature of carbon dioxide.

6 In an air liquefier, air free from water vapor and carbon dioxide is compressed and then cooled by a refrigerator to −25°C (−13°F). It moves the piston of an adiabatic engine and is further cooled to −160°C (−256°F). This air cools the other part of the high-pressure air flowing down the central pipes. Final cooling occurs by the Joule-Thomson effect as air expands through the valve.

6

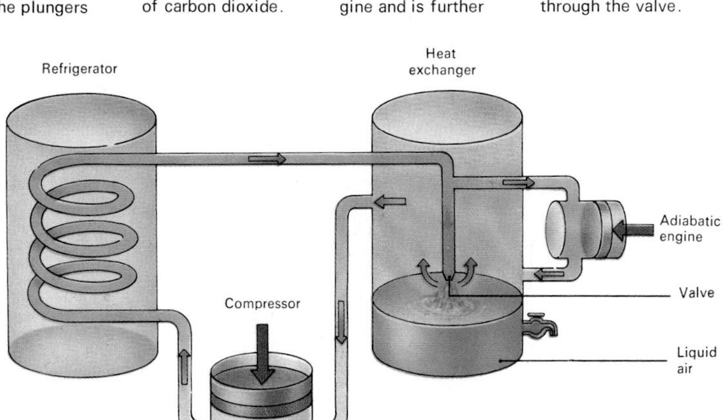

Refrigerator
Heat exchanger
Adiabatic engine
Compressor
Valve
Liquid air

7

7 The rate of diffusion of a gas is inversely proportional to its density. This principle (Graham's law) was used to separate the isotopes of uranium during World War II to make the first atomic bombs and nuclear reactors in this plant at Oak Ridge, Tenn. The uranium had to be converted into its fluoride, which is a volatile solid.

States of matter: liquids

A liquid occupies a definite volume and yet it can flow. The first property is evidence that a liquid's molecules are attracted to each other, whereas the second shows that they have greater freedom than those locked in the lattice of a solid. In a liquid, the molecules vibrate continually (at a rate of a million million times a second) and they change places with each other at nearly the same rate.

A stationary liquid cannot support any stress trying to shear it (as can a solid), which is why the pressure at any point is the same in all directions. The actual value of the pressure is the product of the depth, the density of the liquid, and the acceleration caused by gravity. For this reason, solid objects can float in a liquid and even a submerged object is acted on by a buoyant force equal to the weight of the liquid displaced (Archimedes' principle).

Structure of liquids

Scientific methods used to study the structure of solids (such as X-ray diffraction) reveal that there are sometimes small volumes in a liquid with molecules in an ordered array. But there is no overall order as in a solid. In a hexagonal solid, for example, each molecule has 12 nearest neighbours. In a liquid the number varies between four and 11 and is continually changing.

The average distance between a liquid's molecules is greater than between those of a solid, which explains why most solids take up more room (expand) when they melt. But in a liquid the molecules cannot be squeezed close together (a liquid is almost incompressible). As a result, a liquid can transmit pressure along a pipe [5].

Evaporation and boiling

When a liquid is heated, its molecules move more and more until, at the boiling point, the liquid turns into a gas or vapor. The heat energy needed to achieve this is called the latent heat of vaporization. Similarly, when a liquid is cooled its molecules move less quickly until they take up fixed positions and the liquid freezes into a solid. The heat needed to melt a solid at its melting point is called the latent heat of fusion.

Even at ordinary temperatures (below boiling point) some molecules "jump" out of the surface of a liquid to form vapor—they evaporate. In a closed vessel there is an equilibrium between a liquid and its saturated vapor; the rate at which molecules leave and enter the liquid is the same.

When a liquid boils, some work has to be done by the escaping vapor to overcome atmospheric pressure. If the pressure on a liquid is reduced it boils at a lower temperature. If the pressure is increased the boiling point rises. But if there are no tiny particles in the liquid on which vapor can form bubbles, boiling is suppressed. This effect is the principle of the liquid hydrogen bubble chamber [6]: particles entering the superheated liquid immediately cause large bubbles to form around them, making their paths visible. Water does not follow many of the general rules that apply to liquids [3]. Most substances expand by between five and 15 per cent on melting, for instance, but ice contracts by about ten per cent. These properties arise from the highly directional nature of intermolecular forces in water (the

CONNECTIONS

See also
1502 States of matter: gases
1506 States of matter: solids
1490 Attraction and repulsion
1496 Pressure and flow
1508 Heat and temperature
1510 Order and disorder: thermodynamics
1512 Toward absolute zero

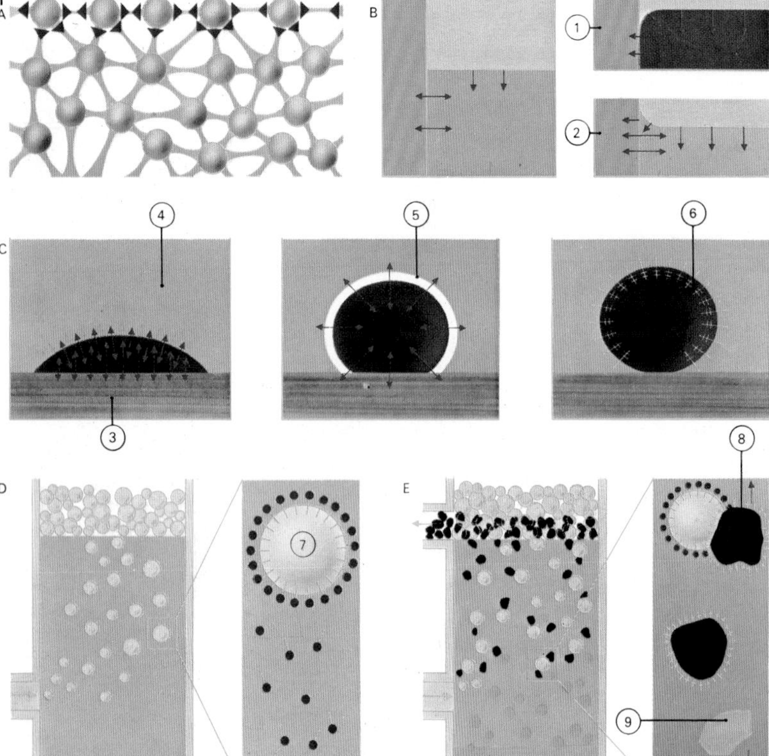

1
A
B
C
D
E
1
2
3
4
5
6
7
8
9

1 At the surface [A], the force between a liquid's molecules causes the surface to behave like a stretched membrane. The surface in a glass container [B] curves depending on whether the glass attracts the liquid weakly (mercury) [1] or strongly (water) [2]. An oily liquid [C] adhering to cloth [3] is weakly attracted by water [4]; a detergent forms a new surface layer [5] attracted to both (detergent [6] is partly oil-like and partly salt-like). Some detergents [D] prevent gas bubbles [7] collapsing, making it possible [E] to separate a powdered ore [8] from sand [9].

2
MARISA

2 Oil is a prime source of energy and chemicals, and huge quantities of crude oil are carried in tankers from the producing countries to highly industrialized ones, such as the US, Japan, and western Europe. By Archimedes' principle a tanker displaces its own weight of seawater in order to float and the cargo (oil) is less dense than water. The tanker sinks slightly deeper in warmer water and on the return journey water ballast is carried in the tanks to keep the vessel stable. If a mishap occurs, escaping oil floats on the water: oil slicks are hazardous to aquatic life.

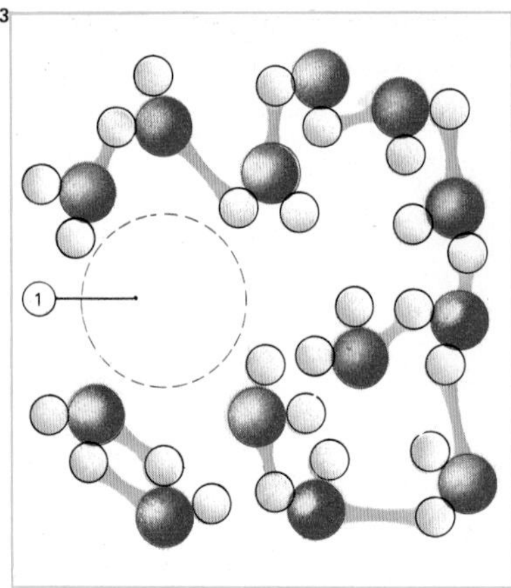

3
1

3 In all materials the atoms or molecules are in continuous motion. The energy of this motion determines the temperature. In a liquid, the motion prevents any permanent intermolecular structure from forming, but forces of attraction govern the overall volume. In water there are many temporary linkages (shown blue) between the molecules; very small cavities [1] form and vanish, giving water an ever changing structure.

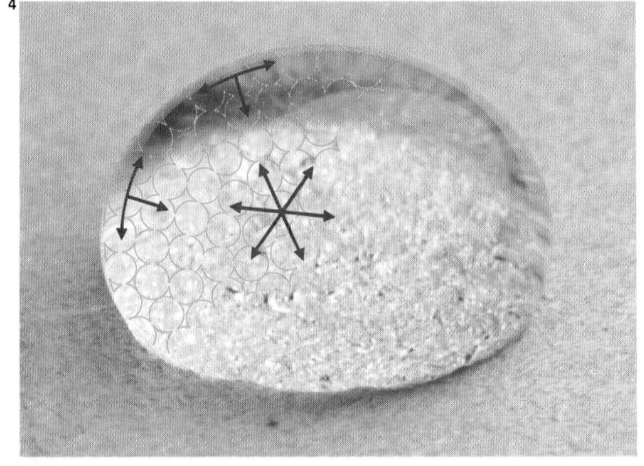

4

4 All the molecules in a liquid exert attractive forces on their immediate neighbors. Within the main body of the liquid the effects of these attractions cancel each other out. But on the surface the attraction can take place only inward (there are no molecules outside the surface to counteract it). As a result the surface is in tension. This surface tension behaves like a "skin," which pulls a droplet of water into a spherical shape.

result of hydrogen bonding). In the solid state (ice) these produce a very open structure, which disappears on melting. Water has its maximum density at about 4°C (39°F), probably due to a crystal-like ordering of small groups of molecules which disappears on warming.

Surface tension and viscosity

In the center of a liquid each molecule is attracted by all those surrounding it and the net effect is zero. But at the surface there can be no upward forces to balance the attractive downward forces. As a result, a surface molecule tends to be pulled into the body of the liquid [4]. The number of molecules at the surface becomes the smallest possible, and the surface behaves as if it were in tension and had a "skin" on it. The membranous effect of surface tension allows small, dense objects, such as needles or insects, to "float" on the surface of water. If the cohesive forces of attraction between a liquid's molecules are large, it has a high surface tension and a large viscosity (stickiness).

Water wets glass because the cohesive force between a water molecule and a glass molecule is greater than that between two water molecules. The opposite is true of glass and a liquid such as mercury. A liquid such as water rises in a fine capillary tube dipped into it and the meniscus (shape of the surface) curves inwards, or is concave. Mercury, on the other hand, is depressed in a capillary tube and displays a convex (outward curving) meniscus.

Water pours more easily from a jar than molasses; the latter is said to be more viscous than water. A simple model of this assumes one layer of liquid molecules under a shearing stress sliding over another layer. For this to happen any molecule in the faster-moving layer must overcome the attraction of the nearest one in the adjoining layer. And having moved one place along the line it must repeat the process. To do this it must use some energy and this slows it down. The relative velocity between the layers is reduced and the result is viscosity. Heating a liquid provides it with more energy and, as expected, viscosity falls.

KEY

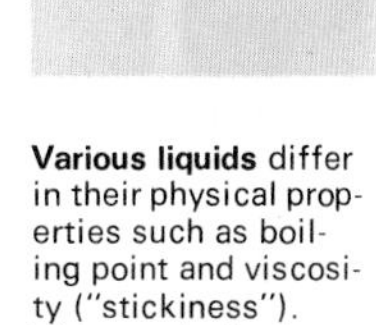

Various liquids differ in their physical properties such as boiling point and viscosity ("stickiness"). Water and wine have roughly the same boiling point and low viscosity. Oil is more viscous and boils at a higher temperature, whereas exceptionally viscous liquids such as honey, molasses, and tomato ketchup have extremely high boiling temperatures.

5

5 Liquids are almost incompressible and as a result can transmit pressure. This important principle finds many applications in the branch of engineering called hydraulics. Many trucks have an hydraulic jack in which pressure transmitted by means of oil is used to tilt the load. A pump is used to provide the pressure and provision has to be made for the oil to run back when the pressure is released.

6

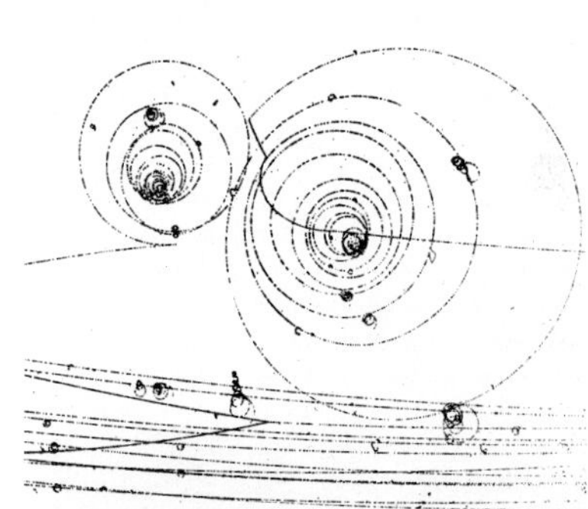

6 In a bubble chamber, a dust-free liquid in a perfectly clean vessel is heated to a temperature above its boiling point and extra pressure is applied to stabilize it. If charged particles are then directed into the chamber, bubbles form on the charged "nuclei" left by the particle along its track, making it visible. Liquid hydrogen is generally used, as it is a good source of protons on which bubbles can form.

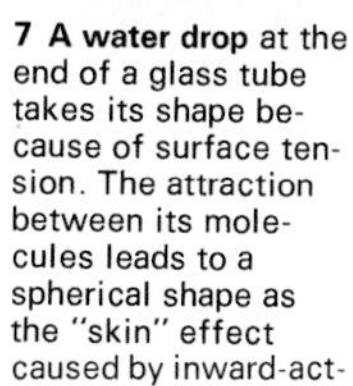

7 A water drop at the end of a glass tube takes its shape because of surface tension. The attraction between its molecules leads to a spherical shape as the "skin" effect caused by inward-acting forces in the surface holds the bulk of the liquid back. But a water droplet becomes a distorted sphere because gravitational as well as surface tension forces are acting on it.

7

8

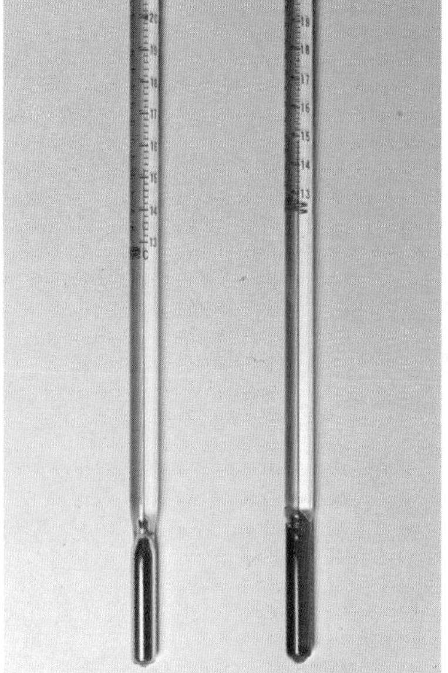

8 The most common method of measuring temperature makes use of the expansion of a liquid on heating. Mercury thermometers have a wide range (−39°C to +360°C), but need a large bulb (reservoir) and a narrow stem if small temperature changes are to be detected. Alcohol can be used in thermometers for measuring lower temperatures; it expands more, but boils at 78°C. The great advantage of liquid-in-glass thermometers is that they can be read directly.

9

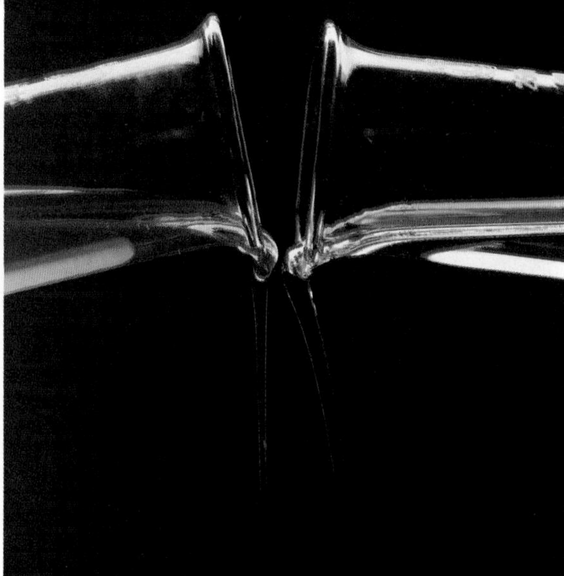

9 Motor oil is more viscous than water, as can be seen when each is poured; the water flows much more easily than oil because layers of water molecules slide over each other more easily than do layers of oil molecules. Normally, the viscosity of a liquid decreases with rise in temperature. Different lubricating oils must be used for different operating temperatures. Much research has been done to produce the correct oils for car engines and gearboxes, including oils whose viscosities change only a little when they get hot. When a liquid flows in a pipe in streamlined motion, the layer in contact with the pipe is still and that near the axis has the greatest velocity, because of friction between the layers.

States of matter: solids

The crystalline shapes of many solids indicate that the atoms in them take up some kind of regular arrangement. In the amorphous or noncrystalline substance, there is no regular order. There are seven main crystalline structures, of which the cubic system is the simplest. Sodium chloride (common salt) is composed of sodium ions and chloride ions. In the solid salt these ions take up what is called a face-centered cubic structure. This and other arrangements can be confirmed by making the crystals diffract an X-ray beam and such X-ray photographs can be used to work out the structures of complex crystals.

Sodium chloride is an example of an ionic crystalline substance [1]. Other crystalline substances, such as diamond, consist of a regular array of atoms linked to each other by covalent chemical bonds, in which one or more electrons are shared between neighboring atoms. In waxes and similar substances, molecules are held together only weakly by what are called Van der Waals' forces. And a metal has a lattice of positive ions in which free electrons occupy the spaces. Applying a voltage across the metal makes electrons drift between the ions, which explains why metals are good conductors of heat and electricity.

All intermolecular forces can be thought of as electrical in origin, causing attraction between molecules at relatively large distances and causing repulsion at close quarters. The elastic properties of solids can be explained in terms of such forces. When a material is stretched, the distances between its atoms increase slightly and the resulting strain is found to be proportional to the stress producing it (the relationship known as Hooke's law). Compression moves the atoms closer together, while shearing makes layers of atoms slide over each other.

Vibrating and slipping atoms

The atoms in a solid—even a crystalline one—vibrate about their average position in the lattice. Heating a pure solid makes its atoms vibrate more vigorously. Sufficient heat energy overcomes the forces holding the atoms together, the crystalline structure 'falls apart," and the solid melts.

A single crystal of a pure metal is much weaker than might be expected. This may be the result of imperfections in the lattice that cause dislocations [7]. Under stress, the layers of atoms move in such a way that the dislocation shifts toward the edge. An ordinary metal is polycrystalline, consisting of an irregular arrangement of many small crystals. Stress makes layers of atoms in individual crystals slip over each other. But atoms of an impurity within a crystal can "anchor" dislocations and prevent slipping. Consequently, an alloy is usually harder than the two or more metals of which it is composed.

Metal fatigue: cause and cure

Strain deforms some solids over a period of time—a phenomenon called creep. This can be caused by the movement of dislocations in crystalline grains, slip between grain boundaries, or slip along well-defined glide planes. "Fatigue" is the name given to a change in metallic properties that may result in sudden breakage. It resembles work-hardening (caused by hammering) in that

CONNECTIONS

See also
1504 States of matter: liquids
1508 Heat and temperature
1534 Magnets and magnetism
1512 Toward absolute zero
240 Shapes and structures of crystals

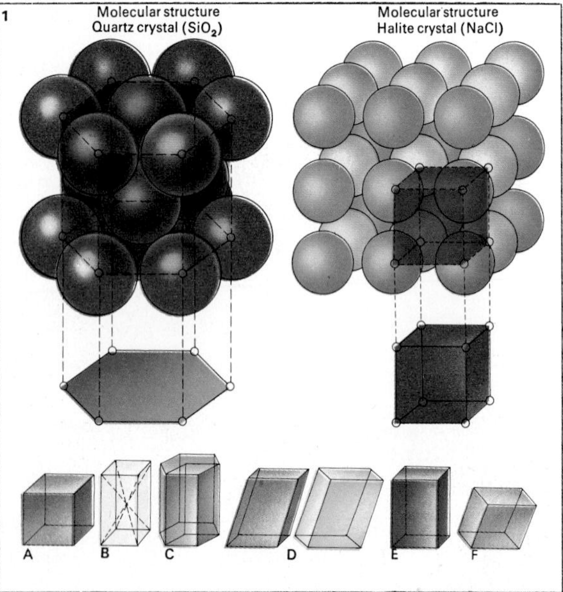

1
Molecular structure
Quartz crystal (SiO_2)
Molecular structure
Halite crystal (NaCl)
A
B
C
D
E
F

1 The main systems of crystal structure are cubic [A], tetragonal [B], hexagonal [C], monoclinic [D], triclinic [E], orthorhombic [F], and trigonal. Scientists who studied crystals examined their shapes and optical properties. Their research established the seven basic systems. The molecular structure of a quartz crystal is hexagonal and relates to the three-dimensional arrangement of its atoms. This crystal has three equal axes [C] inclined at 120° to each other with a fourth unequal and perpendicular to the other three. The crystal of halite (sodium chloride) has three axes equal and mutually perpendicular to each other [A].

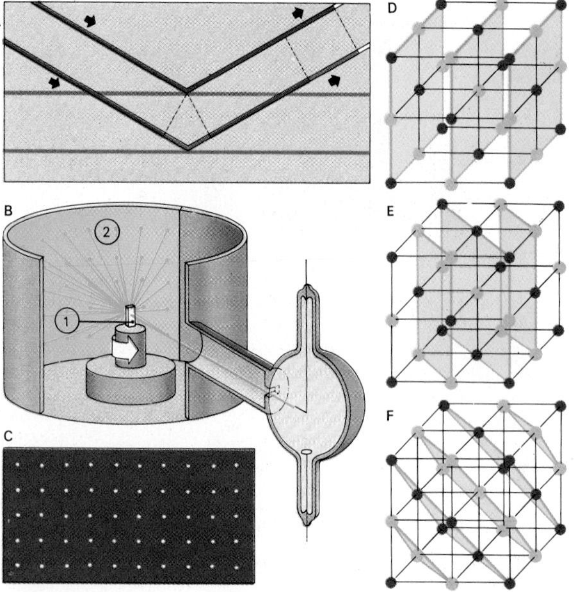

2
A
B
2
1
C
D
E
F

2 Regular layers of atoms in a crystal [A] diffract (bend) a beam of X rays passing through it. A goniometer [B] uses this effect to reveal crystal structures. The crystal [1] rotates on a pillar and scatters X rays onto a photographic plate [2] to produce an X-ray diffraction photograph [C]. From the pattern of spots, a scientist can work out the structure. If halite is used, the X rays reveal sheets of atoms arranged in planes [D], [E], and [F]. It is these planes that reflect the X rays when the crystal rotates around an axis that coincides with one of its main axes, revealing the cubic crystal structure.

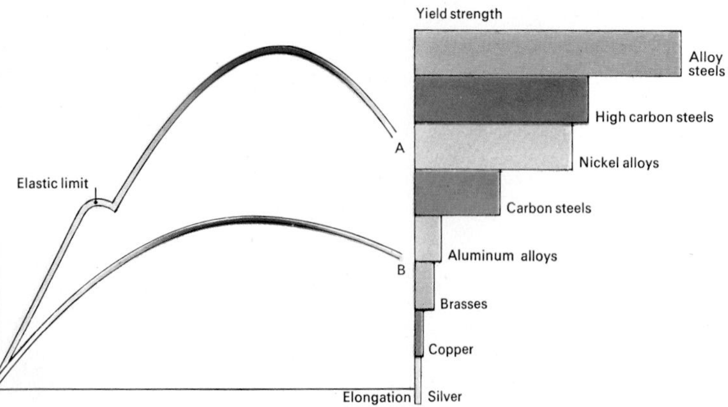

3
Load
Elastic limit
A
B
Elongation
Yield strength
Alloy steels
High carbon steels
Nickel alloys
Carbon steels
Aluminum alloys
Brasses
Copper
Silver

3 Tensile strength is tested by stretching a metal. As it is tested, it extends overall at first, but later expansion concentrates around the point of fracture. Curves [A] and [B] show typical extensions. Curve [A], for mild steel, remains linear to its elastic limit. If the load is released early, the metal returns to its original length. Curve [B] is typical of softer metals. A range of relative strengths of metals, including silver and various ferrous and nonferrous alloys, is also shown (right).

4 Engineers use high-grade steel girders in their work because good steel is highly resistant to cracking. If a crack appears in a good steel, the metal is generally ductile enough for the edges of the crack to flow together, which will diminish the danger of the crack extending far. In poor steels cracks may develop rapidly until they cause fractures. This is a particular danger in bridges, where the steel must resist the expansion and contraction due to temperature changes.

dislocations in crystallites interlock, causing brittleness.

Structural effects in solids

Molecules in natural and man-made polymers have a complex arrangement. X-ray photographs reveal that, when rubber is stretched, its coiled long-chain molecules line up. When tension is released, the molecules snap back into their former shapes, thus giving rubber its elasticity. Similarly, a stretching process during the manufacture of nylon lines up long chains of molecules.

Semiconductors—the keys to modern solid-state devices such as transistors—make use of subtle variations in an otherwise normal crystal lattice. The basic element, usually silicon or germanium, has incorporated in it minute traces of a deliberately introduced impurity element. The impurity has either one more or one fewer electron in its atoms than the basic semiconductor element. As a result, there is a slight excess of electrons or a slight deficiency (an absence of an electron is in this context called a "hole"), and it is the movement of these electrons or holes that gives the materials their special electrical properties. When extra electrons are present the semiconductor has negatively charged current carriers and is called an *n*-type semiconductor. The holes in the second type are considered to be positive carriers and it is called *p*-type.

X-ray diffraction enables scientists to study the microstructure of solids. Other methods reveal the macrostructure. The grain structure of a metal, for example, can be revealed by etching the surface and viewing it by reflected light through an optical microscope.

Higher magnifications are possible using an electron microscope. Scientists make a copy of the etched surface by depositing on it a layer of carbon or plastic and stripping it off as a thin film to be viewed with the microscope. They may use a very thin foil of the metal to be studied. The fine structure of the surface is revealed in three-dimensional detail by a scanning electron microscope.

KEY

Seen under a microscope sugar crystals reveal their regular shapes. Perfect–that is, unbroken–crystals have precise shapes, such as the cubic shape of common salt. There are six other basic crystal shapes, or systems.

5

5 Metalworkers hammer sheet metals to harden them without making them brittle. The hammering moves dislocations along intersecting slip planes until they meet and stop. These meeting places act as barriers to the movement of any other dislocations, making the metal stronger.

6

6 Foundryworkers separate metals from ores by smelting them. Metals are heated to break down the lattice of atoms so that the metal flows. They are poured into molds or cooled and rolled into sheets. Melting points of metals range from mercury, at −38.8°C (−38°F) to tungsten, at 3,410°C (6,170°F).

7 A

B

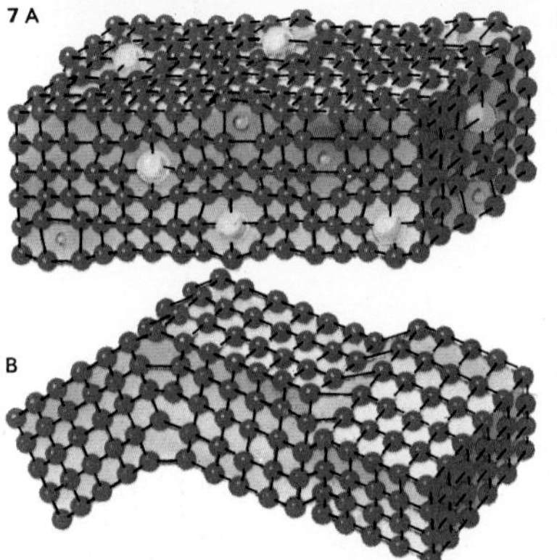

C

D

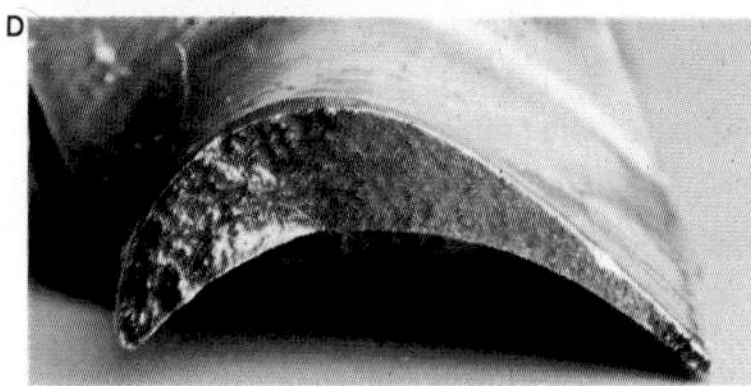

7 Strong metals restrict the free movement of dislocations. A metallurgist may achieve a strong metal by making an alloy, or he may make the metal's crystals as small as possible. In [A], large atoms are at the crystal corners and small ones in the lattice center, distorting the whole crystal and preventing any free dislocation movement. In [B] the crystal boundaries are mismatched and they too have the effect of creating barriers against dislocation movement. Where dislocation of the atomic lattice occurs, or where there is slipping between grain boundaries and along glide planes, the metal will fail. Frequently repeated strains and fluctuating loads may eventually cause metal fatigue [C]. The edges of the fractures may show signs of metallurgical recrystallization. Strain over a long period produces a similar effect, called creep failure [D]. The examples of failures occurred in a nickel alloy turbine blade.

8

det
ökar
mest

8 Increased pressure lowers the melting point in substances, such as water, which expand when they solidify. Ice melting under the pressure of a skate acts as a lubricant that makes the skater's motion across the ice smooth and easy.

Heat and temperature

A bicycle pump becomes warm when pumping up a tire, an effect that can be explained by the kinetic theory of heat, first put forward by Isaac Newton (1642–1727) and Henry Cavendish (1731–1810) in the eighteenth century. The theory explains what heat is—the kinetic energy (energy of motion) of the vibrating atoms or molecules that make up every substance. In the bicycle pump, air molecules are speeded up by collisions with the pump's piston. The increase in their molecular kinetic energy is perceived as heat.

Thermal agitation and molecular motion

Molecules perform a continuous motion known as "thermal agitation," which increases in vigor as heat is transferred to an object. Indirect evidence of this incessant motion was first obtained by the botanist Robert Brown (1773–1858) in 1827. He discovered that tiny pollen grains suspended in water were continually making jerky movements. It is the continual unequal bombardment of each tiny speck by the molecules of the liquid that produces this "Brownian Motion." The smaller the particle, the more violent is the motion.

The kinetic theory also explains why, when a hot gas is mixed with a cooler one, a common temperature is eventually reached. Molecular kinetic energy of the hot gas molecules is transferred by collisions to the cold gas molecules, until the average kinetic energies of both types of molecules are the same. The molecules travel with different velocities, changing after each collision. The temperature of a gas (or other substance) is a measure of the average molecular kinetic energy. Heat is a form of energy and is proportional to the total change of kinetic energy of all the molecules of the substance.

The changes of state that may occur when a substance is heated can be described by the kinetic theory [1]. In a solid, the atoms or molecules are tightly bound together and vibrate closely about an average position. As the solid is heated its internal kinetic energy increases and the particles vibrate more vigorously. They move farther and farther apart until the attraction between them is insufficient to keep them in a fixed position. They can then slide about and exchange partners—the solid melts and a liquid is formed. The heat needed to achieve this change of state from tightly bound solid to loosely bound liquid at the same temperature is called the latent heat of fusion. If more heat is applied, the atoms or molecules gain more kinetic energy, move with greater velocity within the liquid, and the proportion of those escaping from the surface increases (vapor pressure increases). Eventually, at the boiling point, so many atoms have enough energy to escape from the liquid that the vapor pressure equals atmospheric pressure. In the gaseous state the atoms or molecules move almost independently; the conversion of a liquid at its boiling point into a gas requires supplying an amount of energy equal to its latent heat of vaporization.

Changes of temperature

Instead of changing the state of a substance, applied heat energy may merely raise its temperature. The temperature change de-

CONNECTIONS

See also
1502 States of matter: gases
1504 States of matter: liquids
1506 States of matter: solids
1512 Toward absolute zero
1510 Order and disorder: thermodynamics
100 Star types

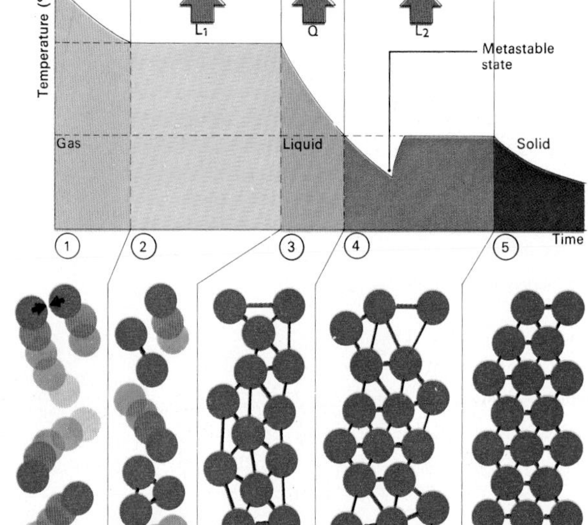
1
Temperature (°K)
L1
Q
L2
Metastable state
Gas
Liquid
Solid
Time
1
2
3
4
5

1 Vibration of atoms and molecules in a substance governs its temperature. In a gas [1] atoms move independently and their average velocity and mass determine the internal energy and temperature. After cooling, loss of latent heat of condensation [L_1] converts the gas at boiling point to a liquid state [2] when its atoms become locked in a weakly bonded arrangement. Further cooling [3] to freezing point loses a quantity of heat [Q] and a solid then forms through [4] release of latent heat of fusion [L_2]; the atoms then become rigidly bonded together [5]. A colder, marginally stable phase can precede actual freezing.

2 The three ways in which heat moves all take place when a pan [A] is heated—conduction through the metal walls of the pan [1], convection by fluid motion [2], and radiation from the heat source to the pan [3]. In theory an insulated good conductor with ice at one end and boiling water at the other varies in temperature linearly with distance along the bar [B], as in the straight-line graph. Without insulation the dotted line results. A vacuum flask [C] has a vacuum [4] to prevent conduction, and silvered walls [5], like mirrors, to minimize heat loss by radiation.

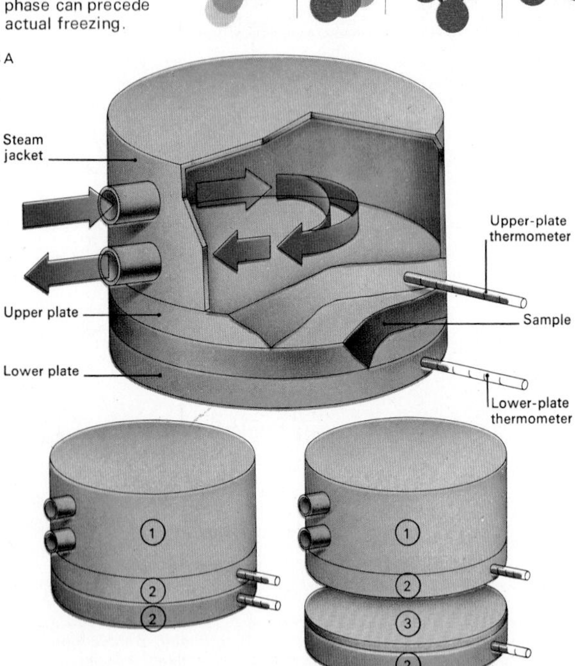
3 A
Steam jacket
Upper plate
Lower plate
Upper-plate thermometer
Sample
Lower-plate thermometer
1
2
2
1
2
3
2

3 Conductivity is the amount of heat passing in unit time across unit cross-section per degree of temperature difference between the substances in contact. It can be measured [A] by noting the time taken for a known quantity of heat to pass through a sample. Two plates of equal area [2] are put against the material [3]. Thermometers measure the temperatures as the upper plate is heated by a steam jacket [1]. Materials of high conductivity [B] are tested in a cylinder [8] heated at one end by steam [4] to 100°C [5]. Other thermometers [6] measure the temperature of the sample and the rise in water temperature in a jacket attached to the other end [7].

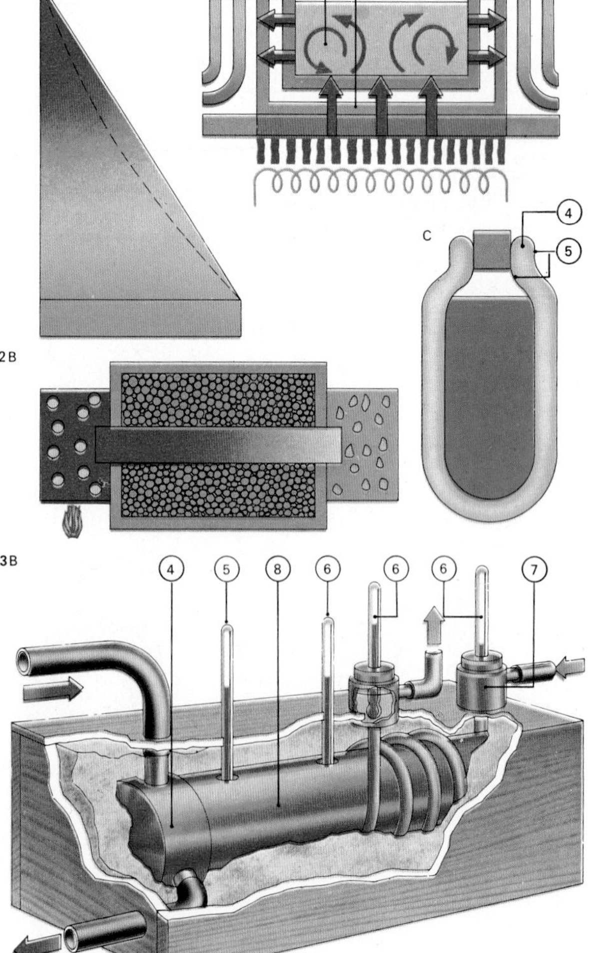
2
A
2
1
3
C
4
5
2 B
3 B
4
5
8
6
6
6
7

pends directly on the quantity of heat transferred and this is measured in units called calories or joules (4.2 joules = 1 calorie). The calorie is defined as the quantity of heat that raises the temperature of 1 gram of water by 1°C. The quantity of heat needed to raise the temperature of 1 gram of any substance by 1°C is called its specific heat. The quantity of heat that raises the whole bulk of a substance by 1°C is called its thermal capacity.

It is possible for heat to be transferred from place to place. There are three ways in which this can occur: by conduction, convection, and radiation [2]. The first two rely on the fact that atoms that have received kinetic energy from a heat source can transmit this to their neighbors by collisions with them. In a tightly bound solid only nearest-neighbor collisions occur—this type of heat transfer is called conduction. In a fluid (liquid or gas), the medium itself can move and transport atoms of high kinetic energy to the cooler parts of the fluid where they then transfer their heat—this is convection. Even when no physical contact exists between atoms, heat can still be transferred. For instance, heat from the Sun reaches the Earth through the vacuum of space. This method is radiation.

Different substances conduct heat at different rates. Their ability to transmit heat is known as their thermal conductivity. Metals have high thermal conductivity. Nonmetals such as glass and wood are poor conductors and are called thermal insulators [3].

Measuring temperature

All methods of measuring temperature changes are based on the ways in which materials change physically when heated. The most commonly used characteristic is the expansion of solids or liquids when heated. In making any thermometer [5, 6, 7], two constant temperatures or "fixed points" are marked. The range between them is then subdivided as finely as desired. The numbers assigned to the fixed points and the numbers of degrees between them define the temperature scale. Most common are the Celsius (centigrade), Fahrenheit, and Kelvin (absolute) scales [4].

KEY

A furnace converts the chemical energy in coal to heat energy used to produce the steam that drives an engine. The heat of the furnace brings the water to its boiling point and provides latent heat of vaporization to turn it into steam.

4

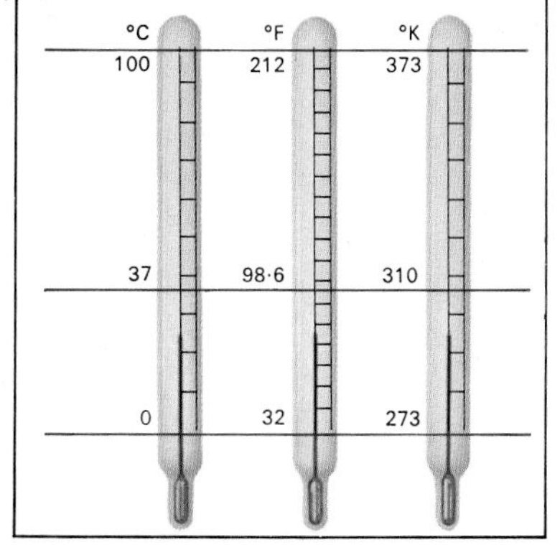

°C
°F
°K
100
212
373
37
98·6
310
0
32
273

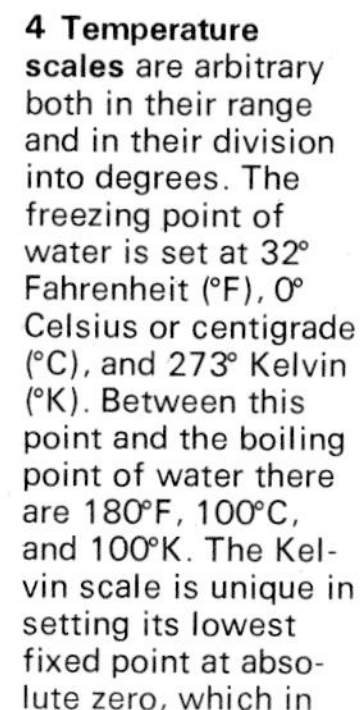

4 Temperature scales are arbitrary both in their range and in their division into degrees. The freezing point of water is set at 32° Fahrenheit (°F), 0° Celsius or centigrade (°C), and 273° Kelvin (°K). Between this point and the boiling point of water there are 180°F, 100°C, and 100°K. The Kelvin scale is unique in setting its lowest fixed point at absolute zero, which in practice is unobtainable.

5 A B C

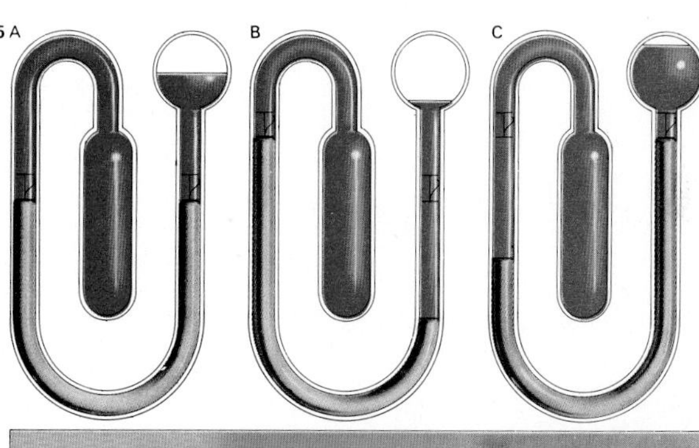

5 The indicators [A] in a maximum and minimum thermometer are pushed along by mercury in a U-tube and stay put at the farthest point of travel. Liquid in a cylindrical reservoir contracts [B] or expands [C] with changing temperature displacing the mercury along scales at each side of the U. The steel indicators inside the U-tube can be reset simply by moving a small magnet along the outside of the tube.

6 A bimetallic strip thermometer uses a helical metal strip that unwinds when heated and rotates a pointer over a calibrated scale. When warmed, the inner metal (usually copper) expands more than the outer one, so causing the bimetallic strip to unwind. The material used for the outer strip is usually Invar, an alloy of iron and nickel, which has a low coefficient of thermal expansion.

6

7 A

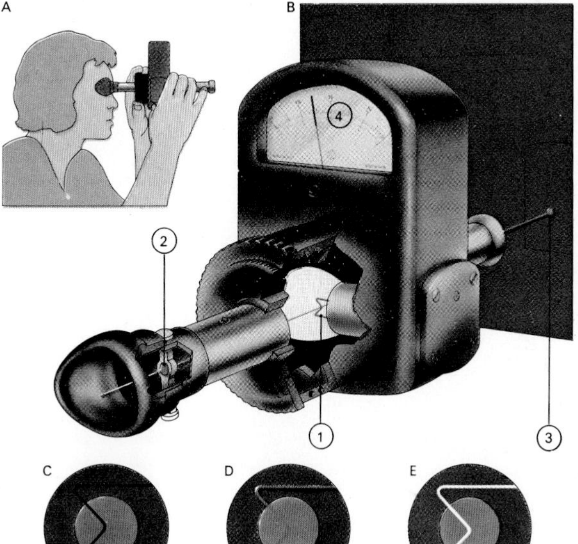

B
4
2
1
3
C
D
E

7 An optical pyrometer allows very high temperatures to be measured at a distance from the temperature source [A]. It exploits the fact that two substances at the same high temperature radiate light with the same color. To measure the heat of a furnace [B], an electrically heated filament [1] fixed in the tube of a telescope with a special lens [2] is heated until it glows with the same color as that emitted by the furnace [3]. Comparison with the background image shows if the furnace is hotter [C], as hot [D], or colder [E] than the wire. A meter [4] indicates the current passing through the heated filament and the meter scale can be calibrated to read directly in temperature degrees.

8

8 Liquid air can be produced by cooling air, which is normally gaseous at room temperature. During the change to a liquid state, latent heat of condensation is released. To cut down heat input the liquid is kept in a Dewar vacuum flask. But if it is poured out of this flask, heat from the surroundings makes the liquid boil rapidly. Large amounts of gas are generated during this process and cause a fog of condensed water vapor to form above the liquid.

Order and disorder: thermodynamics

Thermodynamics (meaning "the movement of heat") deals with the ways in which heat energy travels from one place to another and how heat is converted into other forms of energy. In a heat-transfer process temperature, pressure, and volume may each or all undergo various changes. Much of thermodynamics consists of ways of mathematically manipulating these and other parameters to be able to make predictions about the ways in which they will and do change. This mathematics can be used to formulate the so-called laws of thermodynamics, which are definite relationships between certain of the parameters.

The four laws of thermodynamics

Historically scientists first derived three laws called the first, second, and third laws of thermodynamics. Then a fourth law was recognized. It has been labeled the "zeroth law of thermodynamics."

If a hot and a cold object are brought into contact, they finally reach the same temperature [1]. The hot object emits more heat energy than it receives and the cold object has a net absorption of heat. Both objects absorb and emit energy continually, although in unequal quantities, and the exchange process continues until the temperatures equalize. Each object is then absorbing and emitting equal amounts of heat, and the objects are said to be in "thermal equilibrium." The zeroth law states that, if two objects are each in thermal equilibrium with a third object, then they are in thermal equilibrium with each other.

The first law really has two parts—the first is the law of conservation of energy and the second effectively defines "heat energy" and how types of energy can be converted into one another [2]. If heat energy is supplied to a system, then the first law states that this equals the change of internal energy of the system together with the mechanical energy that allows the system to do external work. Thus in a gasoline engine an air-gasoline vapor mixture is ignited after being compressed. The burning of the mixture releases heat energy by a chemical reaction, thereby causing the gases to expand and do work against the piston by moving it. The burned gases are finally hotter than the system was before the explosion, so there is a change in the internal energy of the engine system. The sum of this energy change and the external work done equals the released heat energy.

The second law of thermodynamics governs the direction of flow of heat energy between objects at different temperatures. It says that heat flows of its own accord only from a hot to a cold object.

Cooling substances

The third law states that it is impossible to cool any substance to absolute zero. This zero of temperature would occur for example in a gas whose pressure was zero. All its molecules would have stopped moving and possess zero energy, so that extracting further energy and achieving corresponding cooling would be impossible. As the temperature of a substance approaches absolute zero, it becomes progressively harder to cool further—the temperature reductions become smaller for given energy inputs and prevent the attainment of absolute zero.

CONNECTIONS

See also
1508 Heat and temperature
1502 States of matter: gases
1504 States of matter: liquids
1506 States of matter: solids
1512 Toward absolute zero

1 The thermic lance produces incredibly high temperatures. If it is directed onto a substance the temperature of the substance near the lance is raised to its melting point, allowing it to be carved at will. Here US scientists are seen using a thermic lance to cut deep into the Arctic ice cap.

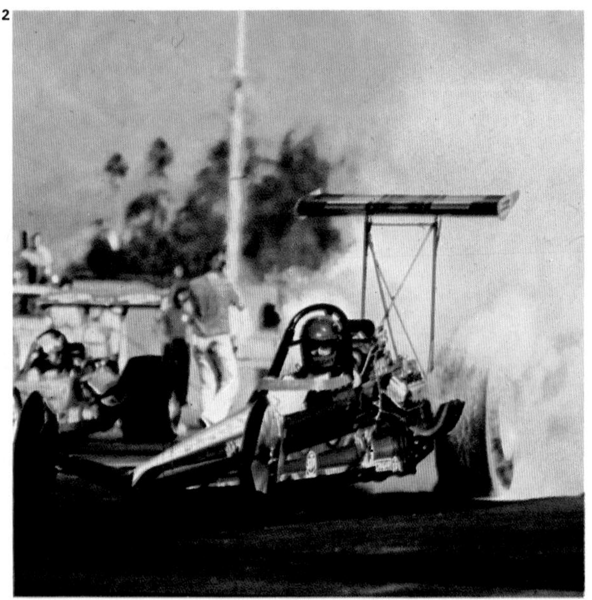

2 Friction occurs whenever two surfaces rub together and this in turn generates heat. The sudden surge of power at the beginning of a "drag" race spins a car's rear wheels and the heat generated burns the rubber of the tires. Similar heating occurs in a car's brakes when they are used to slow or stop the car.

3 Carbon dioxide, released as a solid from a fire extinguisher, turns into a gaseous form and prevents oxygen reaching the fire.

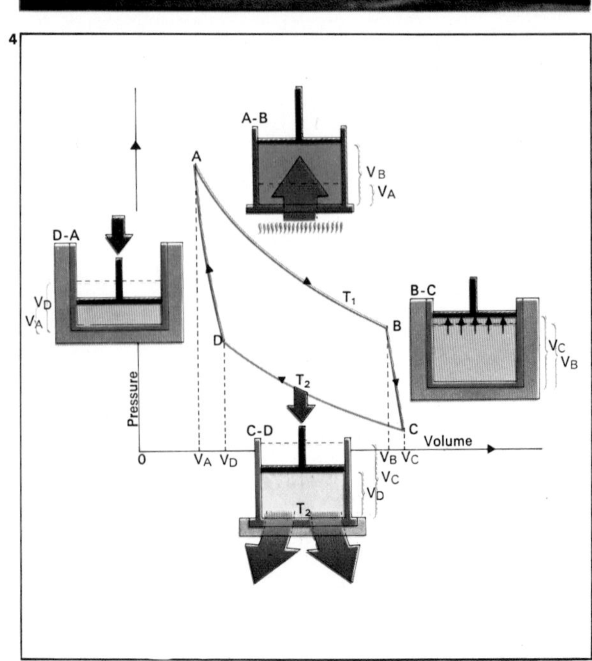

A-B
VB
VA
A
D-A
VD
VA
T1
B-C
B
VC
VB
D
T2
Pressure
C-D
C
Volume
0
VA VD
VB VC
VC
VD
T2

4 Heat can be converted to mechanical work by allowing a heated gas to expand. Maximum efficiency comes from the "Carnot cycle" of alternate adiabatic [BC, DA] and isothermal [AB, CD] processes. The former take place without gaining or losing heat, the latter without changing temperature. From A to C the gas raises the piston and performs work equal to the area below the curve; ie, V_aABCV_c. From C to A it has work done on it equal to area V_aADCV_c. The net work obtained equals area ABCD.

From the statement of the second law, a heat transfer process naturally proceeds "downhill"—from a hotter to a cooler object. The parameter of the system that is a measure of its internal state (its order or disorder), and which has different values at the start and the end of a possible process is termed the "entropy" of the system. The second law maintains that entropy cannot be destroyed but only created.

Careful observation of all types of machines shows that they consume more energy than they convert to useful work. Some energy is wasted in wear and friction or lost by necessity, as in a shock absorber or a radiator. In all these ways the energy is degraded. The entropy of the system is a reflection of its inaccessible energy, and the second law says that it is always increasing. Heat is a random motion of atoms and when the energy is degraded toward the inaccessible energy pool, these atoms assume a more disorderly state; entropy is a measure of this disorder.

Under the constraints imposed by the laws of thermodynamics it is possible for a system to undergo a series of changes of its state (in terms of its pressure, volume, and temperature). In some cases the series ends with a return to the initial state, useful work having been done by the system during the series. The process can then be repeated continually if necessary.

Heat cycles and efficiency

The sequence of changes of the system is called a heat cycle and the theoretical maximum efficiency for such a "heat engine" would be obtained from following the so-called Carnot cycle [4], which is named after the Frenchman Nicolas Carnot (1796–1832). If it were possible to construct a machine operating in cycles that, in any number of complete cycles, would generate more energy in the form of work than was supplied to it in the form of heat, then the perpetual motion machine would be possible [5]. The first law states the impossibility of achieving this result, and the second law denies the possibility of even merely converting all the heat to an exactly equivalent amount of mechanical work.

KEY

A flame applied to one end of a metal bar transfers heat energy to the atoms of the metal. This raises their kinetic energy so that the atoms begin to vibrate much more vigorously about their fixed mean positions within the lattice network of the metal. As the extent of vibration increases, collisions with neighboring atoms transfer energy to these atoms causing them to increase their vibrations. Heat energy is eventually transmitted to the other end of the bar and if the flame is kept in position for some time the temperature at each end of the bar may become nearly equal.

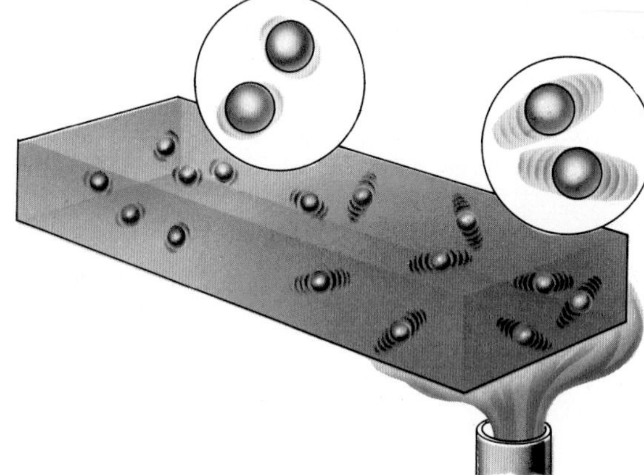

5

5 Perpetual motion machines have been the aim of many inventors. Usually these have been mechanical arrangements designed to continue moving for all time once set in motion. The failure of all such attempts provides one of the best verifications of the laws of thermodynamics. Machine A contains a quantity of liquid that it is assumed will drop back into the large vessel from the bent spout and so maintain circular movement of the liquid. But once the height of liquid in the spout equals that in the vessel, the pressures within the liquid on either side equalize and the fluid motion cannot continue. Machine B has a set of equal weights attached to a rotating wheel. Although there are few weights on the downward side, their longer distance from the axis provides the extra moment of force needed to raise the greater number of weights on the upward side. Unfortunately energy is wasted in overcoming the friction opposing the turning motion of the wheel; this upsets the energy balance and the rotation stops. Friction prevents most of the machines from working; machines C, G, and H all employ almost the same thinking as B and therefore do not function as perpetual motion machines. Machine D does not work because energy is lost against friction as the screw-like construction is turned and as heat is generated and lost when the water cascades down against the paddle wheels and lower reservoir levels. Machine E tries to keep the balls moving around by having the resultant buoyant force acting in one direction through the liquid. But the water levels in each tube would equalize under the force of gravity so that the balls would not get buoyed up one tube further than the other. In machine F the sponges raising and lowering water on the conveyor belt would not retain all the water they first absorb so that the lighter sponges on the downward belt would not raise the heavier ones just leaving the water. Energy loss by friction in the idler pulleys would occur and prevent perpetual motion of even ideal sponges.

Toward absolute zero

Every substance contains a certain amount of heat, even a relatively cold substance such as ice. The heat is the result of the continual motion of the substance's molecules, which, by that motion, possess kinetic energy. Temperature is a measurement of the average kinetic energy of the molecules. The cooler a substance becomes the less its molecules move. Thus it should be possible to continue cooling to the point at which molecular movement ceases completely. This point, "absolute zero," is of great interest to scientists but in practice is unattainable. At temperatures close to absolute zero some materials exhibit remarkable properties, such as superconductivity [6] and superfluidity [Key].

Calculation of absolute zero

On the Celsius, or centigrade, temperature scale, absolute zero is 273.15 degrees below the freezing point of water. Its value can be predicted as a result of the behavior of gases when they are heated or cooled. When heated, a "perfect" gas expands in volume *(V)* proportionally to its absolute temperature *(T)* if its pressure *(P)* is kept constant. Its pressure increases in the same proportion if its volume is kept constant. These relationships are described by the equation $PV = RT$, where R is known as the universal gas constant. The pressure actually falls by a factor of 1/273.15 for every 1°C temperature decrease. Thus at −273.15°C zero pressure would be reached and thus must be the absolute zero of temperature. No gases exactly follow the ideal law.

Absolute zero is denoted as 0° on the Kelvin scale of temperature, named after the British scientist William Thomson, Baron Kelvin of Largs (1824–1907). Its temperature increments equal those on the centigrade or Celsius scale [1].

Aiming at absolute zero

Since the concept of absolute zero was first established toward the end of the nineteenth century, many experiments have been performed with the aim of approaching it in practical terms.

Gas temperatures can be lowered by first compressing the gas and then removing the resultant heat with, for example, a surrounding water jacket. If the gas is allowed to escape into a larger volume it becomes even cooler because its molecules lose kinetic energy during the expansion. This cycle is used in a refrigerator and can liquefy and even freeze many gases.

The gas most useful in experiments at very low temperatures has been helium, the gas with the lowest boiling point, 4.2°K (−269°C). The temperature of liquid helium can be further reduced to 1°K by vacuum pumping the gas immediately above the liquid to reduce its pressure and thereby force down the boiling point. Liquid helium is generally produced in an air liquefaction plant [2].

Below 1°K it is much more difficult to achieve further cooling and a low-temperature effect that occurs in some solids is used [3]. Some salts act as magnets when close to a strong magnetic field but stop being magnetic when the field is removed, a phenomenon known as paramagnetism [4]. If a paramagnetic solid is cooled to 1°K by liquid helium that is allowed to

CONNECTIONS

See also
1504 States of matter: liquids
1506 States of matter: solids
1510 Order and disorder: thermodynamics
1530 What is electricity?
1508 Heat and temperature

1

°C	°K	
0	273	Water freezes
−7	266	Bromine freezes
−33	240	Ammonia boils
−39	234	Mercury freezes
−107	166	Xenon boils
−112	161	Xenon freezes
−152	121	Krypton boils
−183	90	Oxygen boils
−186	87	Argon boils
−196	77	Nitrogen boils
−210	63	Nitrogen freezes
−218	55	Oxygen freezes
−240	33	Critical point of hydrogen
−246	27	Neon boils
−253	20	Hydrogen boils
−269	4	Helium boils
−272	1	Helium freezes under pressure
−273	0	Absolute zero

1 The temperatures on this diagram are stated in both the Kelvin (absolute) and Celsius (centigrade) scales, below a temperature equivalent to the melting point of ice in equilibrium with water.

2 In a helium liquefier, which can be carried by road [A], a mixture of helium gas and air is first compressed and the heat generated removed. Air contains, in addition to oxygen and nitrogen, other "inert" gases, such as argon, neon, krypton, and xenon. At about 20°K all the gases of air except helium can be liquefied in the separator [B]. The helium can be expanded and liquefied.

2 A

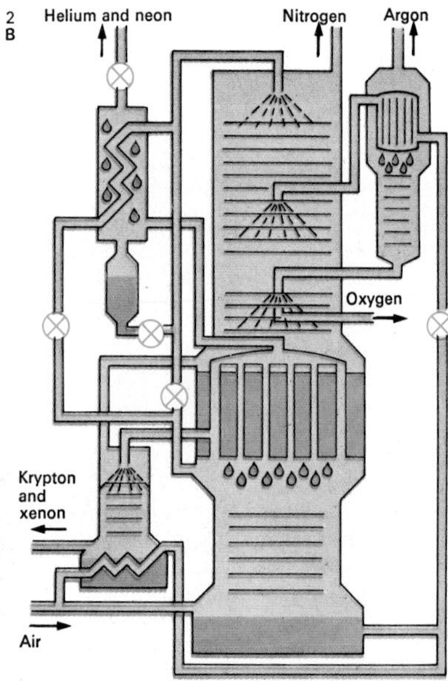

2 B
Helium and neon
Nitrogen
Argon
Oxygen
Krypton and xenon
Air

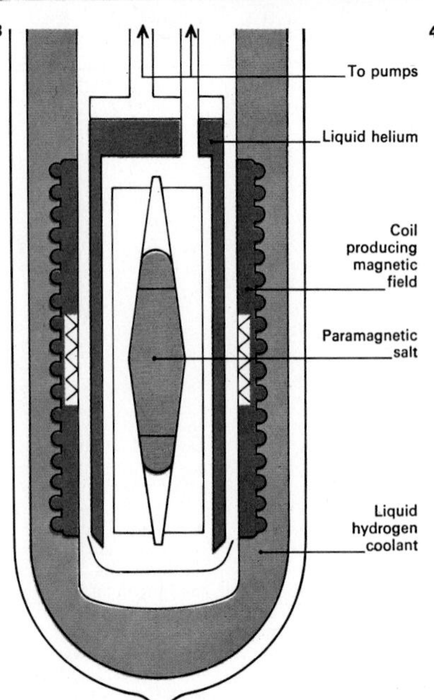

3
To pumps
Liquid helium
Coil producing magnetic field
Paramagnetic salt
Liquid hydrogen coolant

3 To approach absolute zero below 1°K (−272°C) a phenomenon called adiabatic demagnetization of paramagnetic salts is used. A paramagnetic salt is one that acts as a magnet only when near a strong magnetic field. The field forces the molecules into an orderly array. But when they are ordered the molecules have less energy and the balance is given up to the circulating coolant. Now the magnetic field is shut off, and the molecules of the salt extract energy from the surrounding helium, reducing its temperature below 1°K.

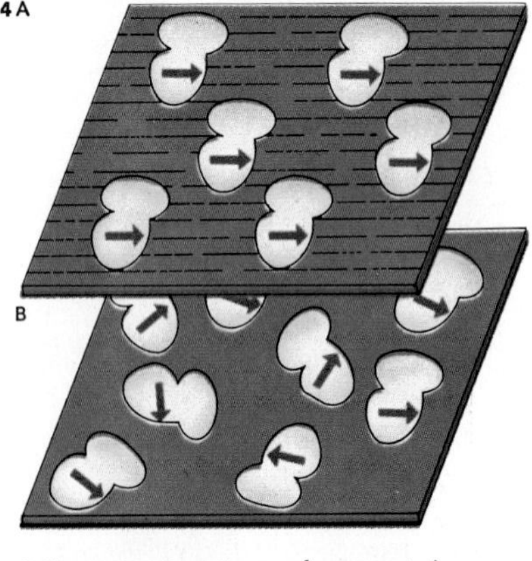

4 A
B

4 The molecules of a paramagnetic salt are normally in continual disordered motion, even if the temperature is as low as 1°K (−272°C). As long as the molecules behave in this way there is no part of the salt that appears to be like either pole of a magnet. As soon as the salt is placed in a magnetic field [A], however, the molecular magnets line up along the field and endow the bulk substance with north and south magnetic poles. Disorder returns when the field is removed [B].

evaporate, heat energy is removed. When a strong magnetic field is switched on, the molecules align themselves and create heat by their motion. This is removed by the surrounding helium gas, which is pumped away. When the field is switched off, the molecules become disordered and cause a further lowering of the solid's internal energy. The cold salt can then absorb heat from a second helium container. A cycle of magnetization and demagnetization can produce temperatures of a few thousandths of a degree Kelvin.

Liquid helium at very low temperatures is not only difficult to produce but behaves in a most unusual way. Boiling occurs as the vapor pressure falls, but at 2.18°K the internal bubbling of helium gas suddenly ceases, although boiling continues. Below this so-called "lambda point" liquid helium exhibits "superfluidic" properties [Key]. The liquid flows through gaps in material as small as one-thousandth of a millimeter. The internal friction or viscosity that normally inhibits the flow of fluids is apparently completely absent in this strange liquid.

Superconductivity and its uses

Near absolute zero, certain substances show remarkable properties; for example, a kind of perpetual motion in electric current becomes possible—that is, some metals and alloys exhibit superconductivity [6]. As their temperature is lowered (for example, to 7.2°K for lead) the electrical resistance of the material disappears completely. If an electric current can be made to flow in a ring of such metal it continues to flow.

The phenomenon of superconductivity was discovered by the Dutch physicist Heike Onnes (1853–1926). It can theoretically be used as the basis for some computer memories, for once stored in a superconductor, information remains unaltered. A magnetic field of sufficient strength can destroy the superconducting state and this effect can be used to achieve a high-speed current-switching facility. As a superconducting material has zero electrical resistance, very high currents can pass through it. Thus superconducting windings for electromagnets can be used to generate extremely powerful magnetic fields. [6].

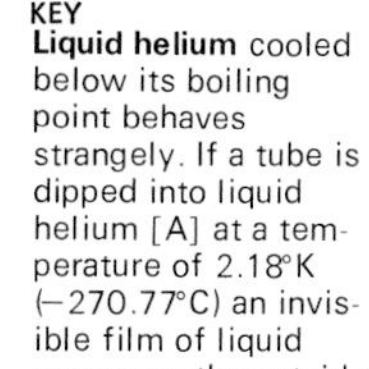

KEY
Liquid helium cooled below its boiling point behaves strangely. If a tube is dipped into liquid helium [A] at a temperature of 2.18°K (−270.77°C) an invisible film of liquid creeps up the outside of the beaker and then down the inside. The helium fills the tube until the liquid levels are the same inside and out. If the tube is raised a little [B] the "superfluid" helium flows the other way to equalize the levels. Drops of the liquid drip off the bottom of the tube. The thickness of the liquid film can be measured (by light polarization) as about 3 millionths of a centimeter at a height of 1 cm above the liquid.

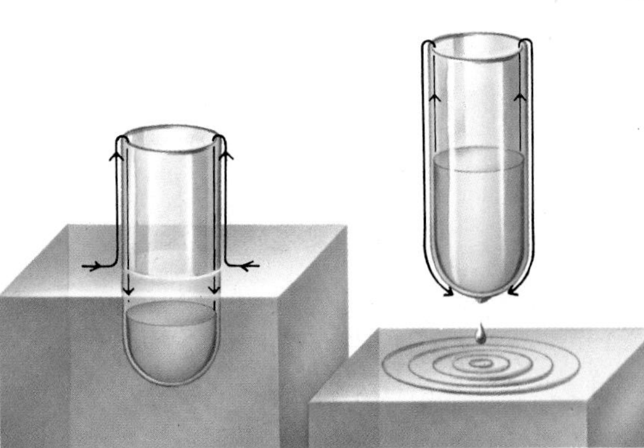

A
B

5 Liquid air has a temperature of only 83°K (−190°C) and thus a flower dipped in it will solidify completely as all the fluid in its cells freezes [A]. When this happens the flower becomes so brittle that it can be broken into small pieces with a blow from a hammer [B]. Liquid air is used industrially for freezing other substances and for the commercial production of oxygen and nitrogen.

6 The superconducting magnets [A] of a particle accelerator, such as those used in the giant proton synchrotron at CERN in Geneva, Switzerland [B], are products of low-temperature physics. Normally superconductivity is destroyed by a high magnetic field. But materials such as niobium-zirconium alloy, with distorted crystal structures, remain superconductive in very strong magnetic fields.

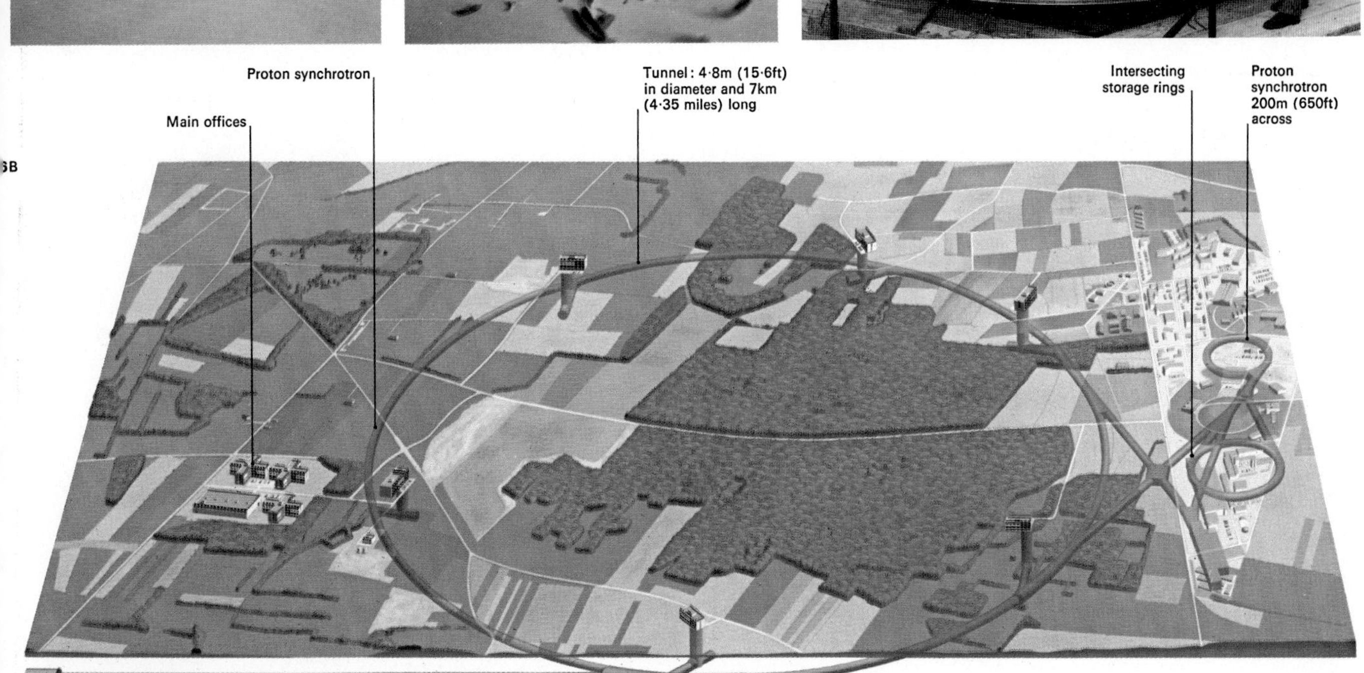

Proton synchrotron
Main offices
Tunnel: 4·8m (15·6ft) in diameter and 7km (4·35 miles) long
Intersecting storage rings
Proton synchrotron 200m (650ft) across

Extremes of pressure

The extremes of pressure—both vacuum (low pressure) and very high pressure—have varied and sometimes remarkable effects on different materials. Matter exists as either solid, liquid, or gas, and all are compressible to various degrees. Perfect gases are compressible to almost any extent, following at low pressures Boyle's law, which states that the volume of a gas varies inversely with its pressure. But liquids are much less compressible, and the changes in their volume brought about by pressure follow no simple law.

Solids are the least compressible. Their rigid structure, in which atoms have their mean separation distance fixed by very strong forces, is the most resistant to externally applied pressure. Their structure can be distorted or destroyed by sufficiently high pressures, but the way in which they actually behave is governed by their internal atomic or molecular arrangement.

The compressibility of a gas can be calculated by its equation of state, but that of a liquid or a solid has to be determined experimentally. For the liquid metal mercury at 0°C (32°F), for example, it has been shown that the volume changes by less than one-millionth part over a pressure range of 0–7.340 kg/cm² (0–7000 atmospheres).

Effects of pressure

Pressure applied to any substance can, under certain conditions, cause a change of state. Thus below a certain critical temperature pressure can turn a gas to liquid.

Extremely high pressures have many industrial applications. Hydraulically generated and transmitted pressures are employed for lifting extremely heavy loads. In the auto industry they are used to press completely shaped car body panels [3] from flat sheet metal. The behavior of metals under compression is also the basis for processes involving rolling and forging. Again, if sufficiently high pressures are brought to bear, metal enters its "plastic" range. That means that the metal continues to yield (ie, to extend its dimensions), even though the load applied remains constant. In the normal elastic range, the dimensions change in direct proportion to the applied load and return to normal when the load is removed. The plastic property is used in processes such as extrusion [2], but enormous pressures must be applied to achieve it.

At the other end of the pressure range is the vacuum, which can be of varying degree. To obtain a vacuum, gas atoms or molecules are removed from an enclosed vessel. The number of intermolecular collisions is correspondingly reduced and thus there is a reduction in the internal energy and pressure of the gas.

The creation of a vacuum is not, however, limited to vessels that previously contained nothing but gas. A partial vacuum can also be achieved above the surface of a liquid—but the space is filled by the vapor of the liquid. As the gas pressure above the liquid is reduced by pumping, the liquid boils at a lower temperature than it does at atmospheric pressure.

As with high pressures, high-vacuum states also have many industrial uses. The process of vacuum deposition by evaporation allows solid objects to be thinly coated with metal [4]. The object to be coated is

CONNECTIONS

See also
1496 Pressure and flow
1556 Joining atoms
1666 Moving heavy loads
106 Nebulae and pulsars

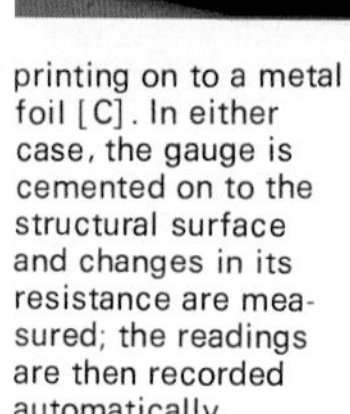

1 The pressures operating on large structures, like the bridge spanning the River Severn [A], are measured by an electrical strain gauge [B]. This device depends on the phenomenon (first noted by Lord Kelvin in 1856) that if a wire is strained, its electrical resistance is changed. The principle was first employed practically in the United States in 1938 and now the strain gauge is the most common instrument used for analysis of stress. Gauges can consist of a grid of fine metal wire that is then bonded to a thin backing, but more commonly, a grid of wire filaments is obtained by printing on to a metal foil [C]. In either case, the gauge is cemented on to the structural surface and changes in its resistance are measured; the readings are then recorded automatically.

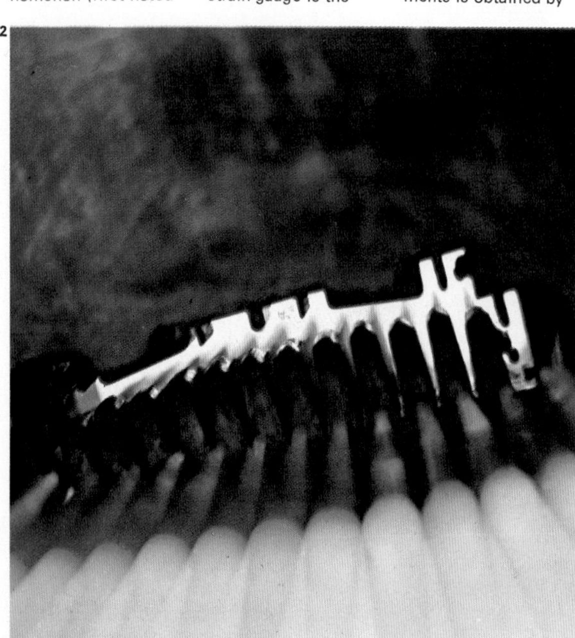

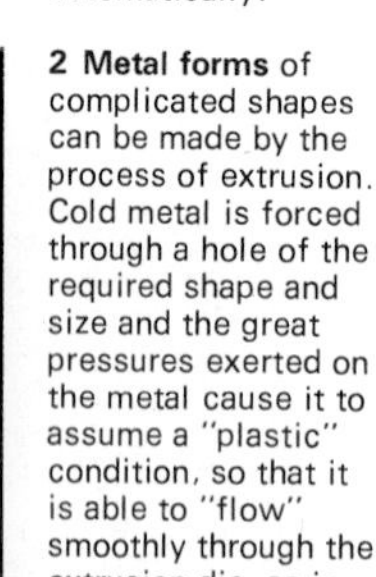

2 Metal forms of complicated shapes can be made by the process of extrusion. Cold metal is forced through a hole of the required shape and size and the great pressures exerted on the metal cause it to assume a "plastic" condition, so that it is able to "flow" smoothly through the extrusion die, as in this machine.

3 Hydraulic presses can make shaped body panels in one step from single flat sheets of metal. A piston carries a die of the shape required and then a hydraulic ram presses this against the metal sheet with tremendous force. The high pressures generally needed call for costly presses, but their speed justifies the expense.

placed in an enclosed vessel that can maintain a high vacuum. When the coating metal is vaporized within that vessel, it forms a thin mirrorlike film over the object.

Vacuums and electronics

There are other manufacturing processes in which the controlled deposition of impurities on substances is performed by means of a high vacuum. Sophisticated electronic circuitry is based upon this use of an ultra-high vacuum [5].

But technological processes are not the only applications of extremes of pressure. Given that all substances are compressible to some degree, consideration of the effects of increasing pressure on materials to be used in construction work is obviously important. Compression and tension tests of various building materials provide the knowledge of the extremes of stresses and strains sustainable by different substances.

The behavior of materials under the two extremes of pressure is well demonstrated in the varying conditions of space. Extremely high-vacuum conditions exist in interstellar space, with probably only a few atoms per cubic centimeter. Separate chemical radicals have also been observed in interplanetary space.

When atoms are smashed

In the denser clouds of gas and dust (nebulae) that are found in galaxies, the pressures become greater because of gravitational attraction, generating higher temperatures, so that eventually the electrons are forced to change orbit within the atom. As they jump back to their original orbit, energy is given up as light [7].

Within the stars, the radiation temperature and pressures are extremely high. At the center of the Sun the temperature is probably about 10 million °C (18 million °F) and the density fifty times that of water; the pressure amounts to about 400,000 million kg/cm² (6 million million lb per sq in). In other stars, the pressures can be so great that the normal arrangement of an atom is completely broken. Protons and electrons are squashed together, creating densities of up to several tons per cm³.

KEY

Artificial diamonds are produced when graphite is subjected to very high pressures and temperatures. Most of the stones are inferior to those that have been produced by nature.

4 A

4 Vacuum deposition is widely used to form metal coatings on plastic objects. The object to be treated is enclosed in a chamber [A] along with a wire filament carrying beads of the metal that is to be deposited. Then the chamber is pumped down to a very low pressure and an electric current is passed through the wire. The beads vaporize and are then deposited as a metal film on the object[B].

B

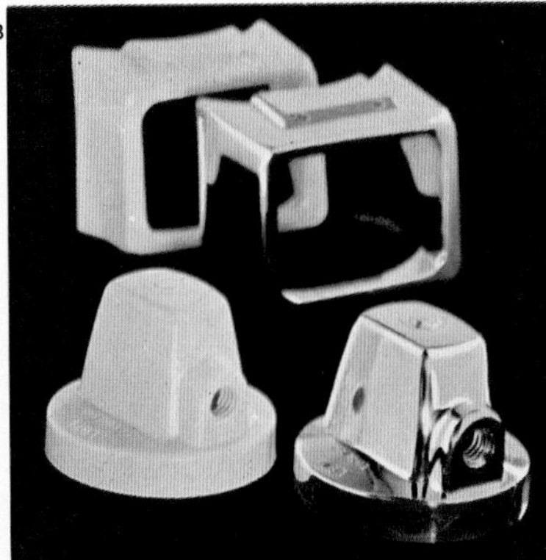

5

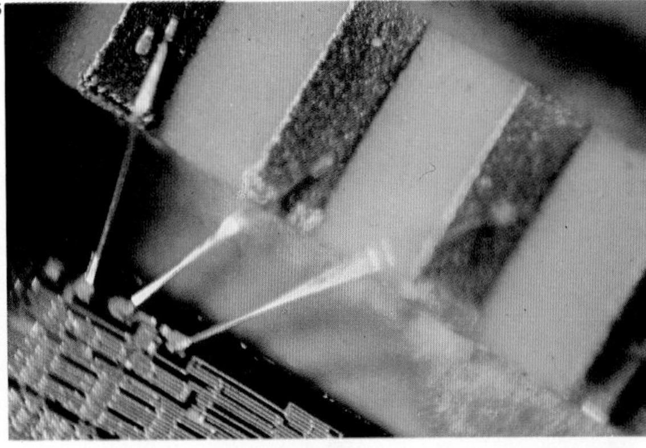

5 Silicon "chips" can be modified by the use of high-vacuum methods so that whole electronic circuits can be integrated into a single piece. To achieve this, certain "impurities" are diffused into or layered onto the base material, these impurities affect the conductivity of the base and perform equivalent functions to electronic components such as transistors, diodes, capacitors, and resistors. The pure silicon base is held in a vacuum during the implantation or layering process. Connections to the circuit are made by fine wires welded at gold-plated electrical contacts.

6

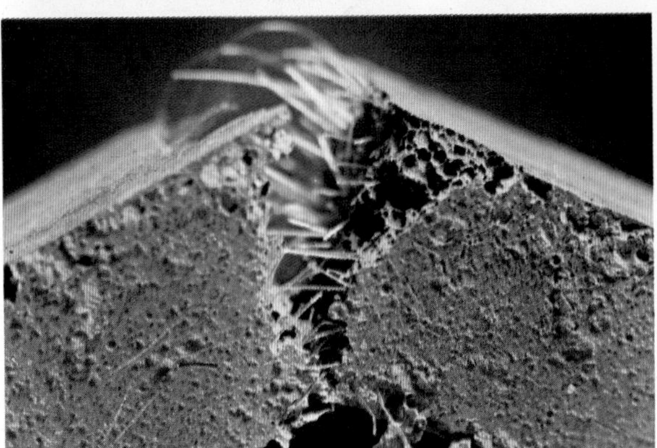

6 Testing materials to destruction is often necessary to discover their real strengths and weaknesses. These tests are carried out in a machine capable of exerting compressive and tensile (stretching) forces, and it records automatically the applied pressure on the material at the instant of its failure. Such tests are not confined to ductile metals (those that can be drawn out as wire), but are also applied to brittle materials such as this fiberglass.

7

7 The evolution of stars illustrates the dramatic effects of extremes of pressure on matter. A cloud of gas at very low pressure condenses, becomes hotter, and forms a star. The star may evolve into the densest known object —a neutron star.

Light and color

We are surrounded by various forms of energy, namely light, heat, chemical, and mechanical energy. Of these, light is as necessary as heat energy and chemical energy—and all are essential to life. By virtue of its basic nature light enables people to sense the world around them in great detail. This is because light consists of a wave motion of extremely high frequency. If human beings were sensitive instead to radio waves, which have a much lower frequency than light, they would detect no more detail in their surroundings than the blurred outlines seen on a radar screen.

How light travels

Light travels in waves, as sound does. In light the vibrations of the wave consist of vibrating electric and magnetic fields, whereas in sound they are vibrations of a medium such as air or water. Both kinds of waves may vary in intensity, producing stronger vibrations. In sound an increase in intensity causes an increase in loudness, and in light it produces an increase in brightness.

Light waves also possess a range of frequencies—the number of vibrations passing every second. In sound people hear different frequencies as sounds of different pitch; in light they see different colors. Blue light, for example, has a higher frequency than red light. Light may also be considered in terms of wavelength—the distance between successive vibrations in a wave; blue light has a shorter wavelength than red light. Light frequencies are very high and the wavelengths are very short (about 55 millionths of a centimeter).

Paint manufacturers include white and black among their ranges of colors, but these are not strictly colors at all. Black is simply an absence of light, and therefore of color, and white light is made up of a mixture of basic colors. This can be shown by passing sunlight through a prism. The white light of the sun is split up into a band of colors called a spectrum. The spectrum looks exactly like a rainbow [5], which is no coincidence because raindrops act as prisms and split up sunlight to produce a rainbow. The beam of colors from a prism can be made to recombine and produce white light once more. This is a proof that white light is a mixture of all the colors.

The science of spectroscopy

Splitting up light to form a spectrum is important in science [Key]. Different elements glow with different colors when they are heated sufficiently or subjected to an electric discharge; examples are gases in sodium street lights or neon advertising signs. By passing the light from a glowing substance through a prism and examining the resulting spectrum, which has a different pattern for different elements, the glowing substance can be identified. This is useful in all kinds of analysis, but particularly in finding out which elements are present in the Sun and the stars. This branch of science is called spectroscopy.

Most of the color we see is reflected light from objects that are naturally colored, painted, or dyed. When white light strikes the surface of a red object, red light is reflected from it, but all the other colors in the white light are absorbed by the surface.

CONNECTIONS

See also
1486 The nature of energy
1518 Mirrors and lenses
1520 Light waves
1522 The speed of light
1524 The idea of relativity
1526 Light energy
46 Invisible astronomy
94 The Sun and the sola spectrum
100 Star types
674 Sight and perception

1

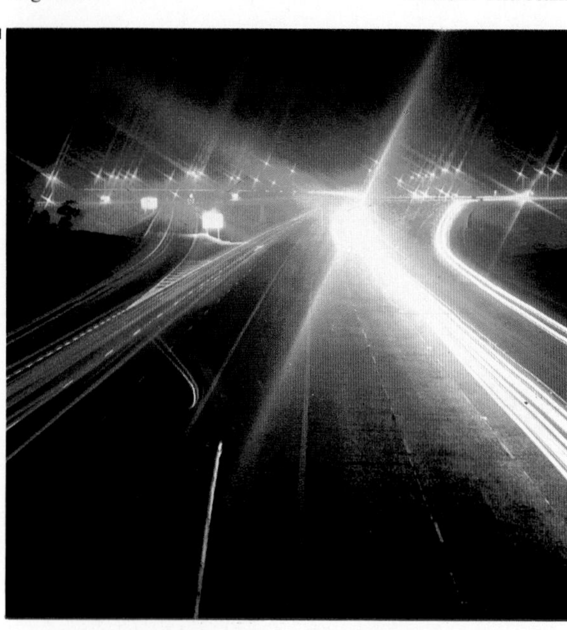

1 Color is used as a means of imparting simple information quickly and unambiguously. On the road, for example, red taillights on cars indicate "stop" or "danger".

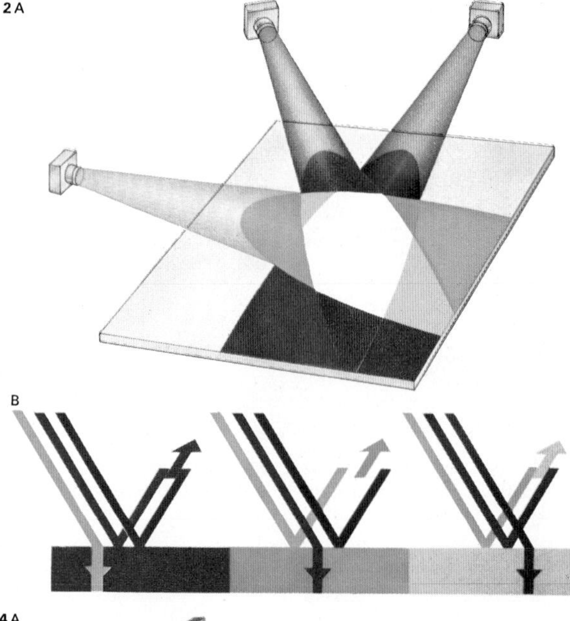

2 A
B

2 Mixing colors depends on whether colored lights or pigments are being used. Lights combine by additive mixing [A] in which three basic, or primary, colors, red, green and blue, combine to give white. Yellow, cyan, and magenta are secondary colors formed by equally mixing two primaries. Pigment colors combine by subtractive mixing [B] in which some color is absorbed before mixing of the remaining colors occurs.

3

3 The Munsell color tree is a system of grading any color. The hue (basic color), chroma (amount of color), and value (degree of lightness or darkness) are measured and the color's position found in the tree. Hue is denoted by its place on the circumference of the tree; chroma by its distance from the trunk; value by its place up the trunk.

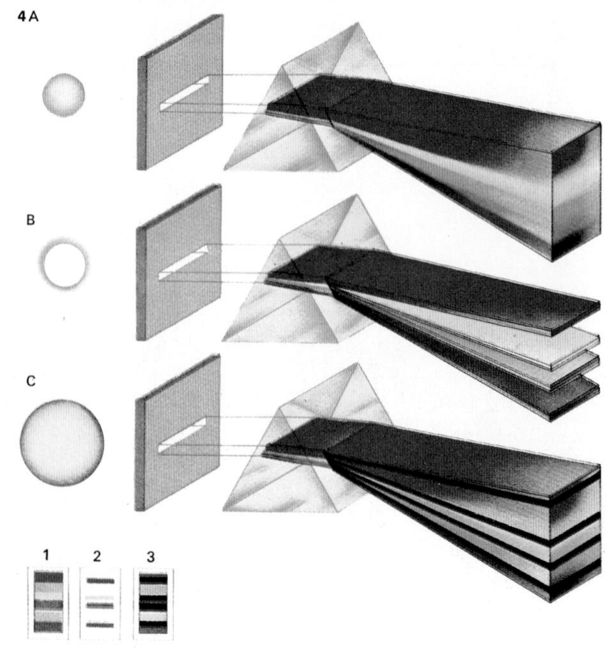

4 A
B
C
1
2
3

4 A solid or plasma under pressure heated to incandescence emits a continuous spectrum [A]. At low pressure a gas produces an emission spectrum [B]. In the Sun [C], light from the inside [1] is partly absorbed as it passes through the outer regions [2] to form an absorption spectrum [3].

Color is also produced in other ways. A substance can be heated so much that it glows with color, and luminous compounds such as the phosphors in a color television screen light up with color when they are struck by invisible cathode rays or ultraviolet rays.

Human beings (and many animals) can perceive color because the retina in the eye contains three kinds of light sensors. These detect different ranges of light frequencies, roughly corresponding to red, green, and blue. All other colors can be produced by combining light of these three basic colors in various amounts. Red and green combine to produce yellow; green and blue to give cyan; and blue and red to make magenta. All three basic colors combine to give white light.

Additive and subtractive mixing

It may seem strange, to anyone used to mixing red and green on a paint brush and obtaining brown, to read that red and green make yellow. This is because colored lights and colored paints combine in different ways. A color television set produces colored light and close examination of a lighted screen reveals that it contains patterns of red, green, and blue dots or stripes. At a distance the dots or stripes merge into a color picture. But close up, the yellow light can be seen to be made up of red light and green light. This kind of color mixing, in which light combines directly, is called additive mixing [2]. Any three colored lights, such as red, green, and blue, that combine to form any other desired color or in the right proportions to form white light are known as the primary colors.

In producing colors by mixing paints, dyes, and inks, subtractive mixing occurs [2]. The mixture selectively absorbs some wavelengths from the light striking it and reflects others. Thus yellow paint absorbs blue from the illuminating white light but reflects red and green, which combine to reach the eye as yellow. Cyan paint absorbs red light, leaving blue and green to mix and make cyan. Mixing yellow and cyan subtracts red and blue from the white light, but leaves green to be reflected: so cyan and yellow paints mix to give green.

KEY

D

Dispersion of light by a prism produces a spectrum of colors. In 1800 the British astronomer William Herschel placed thermometers just beyond the red end of the spectrum and observed a rise in temperature. He deduced that the prism was dispersing invisible heat rays (now called infrared rays).

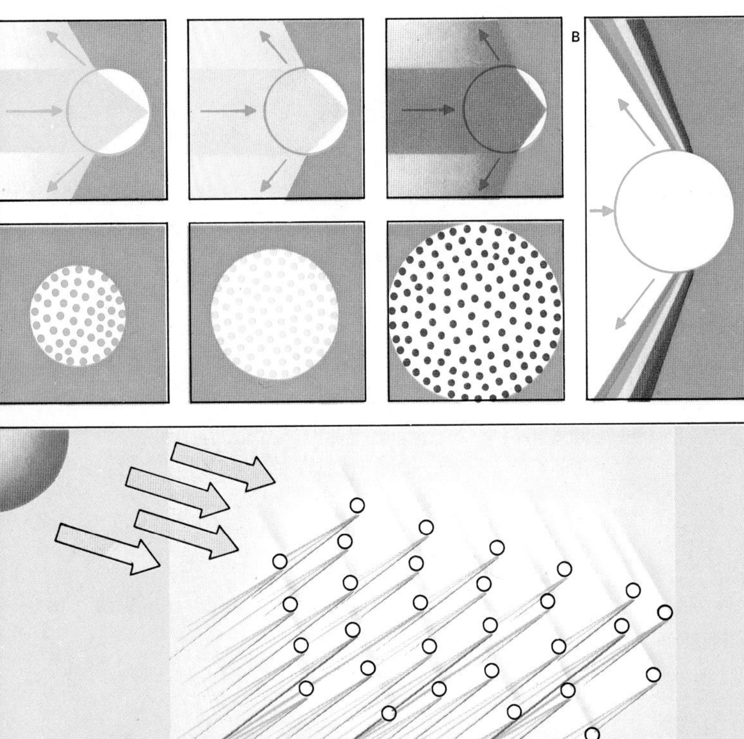
B

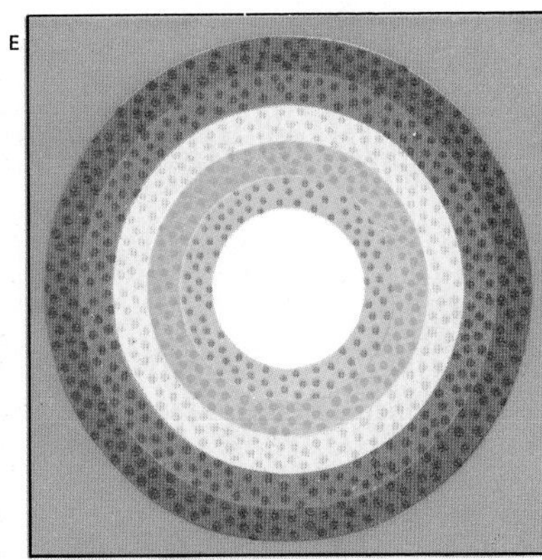
E

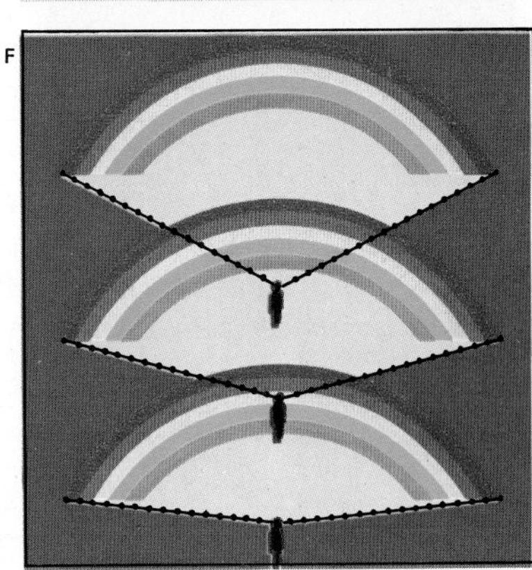
F

5 A rainbow occurs when raindrops reflect sunlight back toward the observer, dispersing the light into its component colors [A]. The colors are reflected back at various angles from each drop, blue being bent more than red [B]. Each raindrop lit up by the sun produces a circle of color [C], but only the lower part of each circle is directed toward the ground [D]. The observer sees the colors coming from many raindrops as a rainbow. Of the reflected rays that reach him the red are at a greater angle than the blue [E] so that, to the observer, the red side appears higher than the blue. To other observers the rainbow may look nearer or farther away, but it is always in the same direction and has the same apparent size [F]. Outside the first bow a secondary rainbow in which the colors appear in reverse order may also be seen.

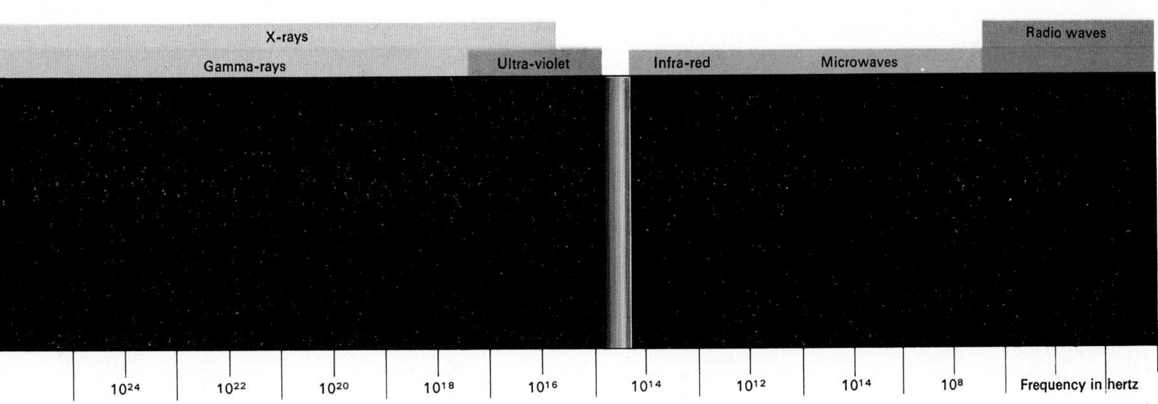
X-rays
Gamma-rays
Ultra-violet
Infra-red
Microwaves
Radio waves
10^{24}
10^{22}
10^{20}
10^{18}
10^{16}
10^{14}
10^{12}
10^{14}
10^{8}
Frequency in hertz

6 The spectrum of visible light is only a small part of the much greater spectrum of all electromagnetic radiation. Beyond the blue end lie the invisible ultraviolet rays, X rays, and gamma rays, while infrared rays (heat rays), microwaves, and radio waves lie beyond the red end. All electromagnetic radiation has the power to penetrate matter to a certain extent. High frequency radiation—that is, X rays and gamma rays—penetrates most.

Mirrors and lenses

Nearly everyone looks in a mirrror at least once a day and people with poor vision spend most of their lives looking through eyeglasses or contact lenses. Telescopes, binoculars, microscopes, cameras, and projectors help us to examine the world about us in far more detail than can be perceived by the unaided human eye. All these visual aids and optical instruments are mirrors or lenses. They work using the simple laws of optics, but before these laws can be understood it is necessary to appreciate how an image is formed.

Light rays and images

Any illuminated or luminous object sends out light rays that spread in all directions in straight lines. An image forms if any of the light rays coming from the same point on the object happen to meet. Normally images do not form because there is nothing to bend the light rays to make them meet, but a lens will do this. The image produced can be seen on a screen placed at the point where the rays meet. If the rays meet exactly, a sharp image is formed and the image is said to be in focus. It is known as a real image and is the kind produced in a camera or by a projector. If the incoming light rays are parallel, the image is produced at a distance called the focal length of the lens.

Plane (flat) mirrors, on the other hand, produce images that cannot be shown on a screen. In this case the light rays are bent but they continue to become farther apart (diverge) rather than closer together (converge). But the human brain always assumes that light rays reach the eyes in a straight line, and we therefore see an image at the point that the object would be occupying if the rays were not bent [6]. This kind of image is called a virtual image and it is always sharp.

Except when illuminating the deepest black objects light is reflected from every surface it strikes. A dull or matte surface scatters the rays at all angles. But a very smooth surface acts as mirror and reflects all rays so that the angle of incidence equals the angles of reflection. A plane mirror, being flat, bends all the rays that strike it by the same angle and so a virtual image, unchanged in size and shape, is seen in it. Left and right are interchanged because a light ray leaving one side of the object is reflected by the mirror to the opposite side of the eye from the one it would otherwise strike [1].

Curved mirrors [2] produce images changed in size and shape. A convex mirror, one that bends outward toward the observer, gives a smaller virtual image. It makes the rays diverge more than if they came directly from the object. This produces the same effect as if the object were farther away and it therefore appears smaller, as in a car's rearview mirror. A concave (inward-bending) mirror has the opposite effect. It makes the rays converge more than they otherwise would, making a close object appear nearer and therefore larger.

Bending of light

If light rays meet a transparent object, most of the rays enter the object and emerge from the other side. The rays are bent as they pass through the surface, being deflected away from the surface if they are entering a denser medium and toward the surface if

CONNECTIONS

See also
1516 Light and color
1522 The speed of light
1520 Light waves
1784 Photography
1786 Taking pictures
1788 Motion-picture photography
42 Telescopes

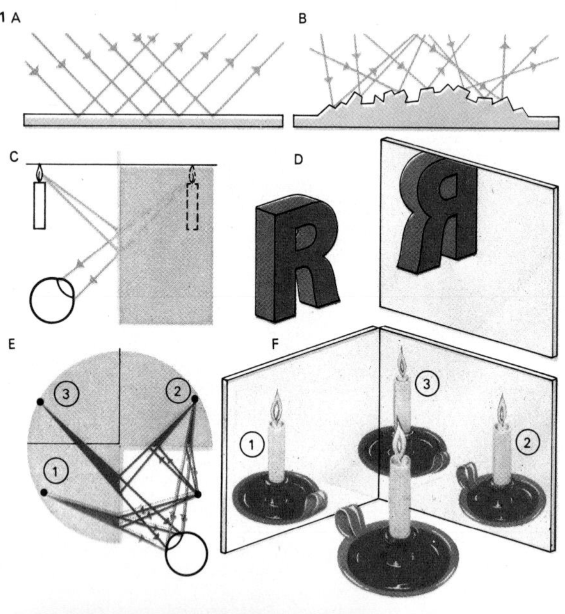

1 A
B
C
D
E
F

1 A plane mirror reflects all light rays at the same angle [A], whereas a matte surface [B] scatters light. The brain imagines that light rays reaching the eye from a mirror come to it in straight lines. An image is seen at that point where the rays would seem to originate if their paths had not been bent by the mirror [C]. The image is laterally inverted [D], because the reflected rays reach opposite sides of the eye. An image can be seen the right way around in two plane mirrors at right angles [E]. Although an image reflected once appears laterally inverted [1,2], one reflected twice [3] is seen correctly [F], left to right.

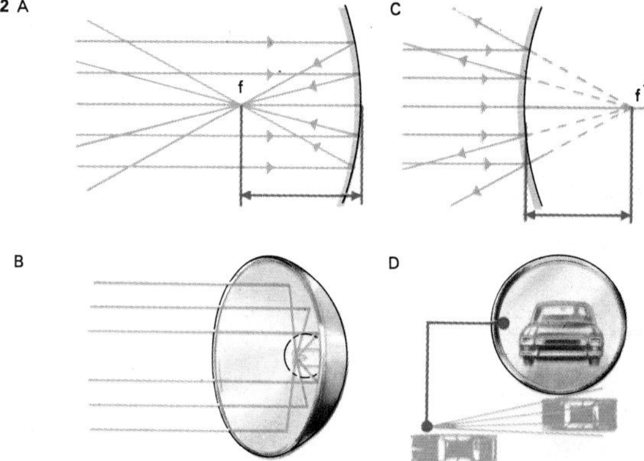

2 A
C
f
f[1]
B
D

2 Curved mirrors form real and virtual images. A concave mirror [A] reflects the rays of a parallel beam of light so that they converge and meet at the focus of the mirror [f]. A real image of a distant object will be formed on a screen placed at the focus. If the eye is placed closer to the mirror than the focus, a magnified virtual image will be seen behind the mirror. In a lamp reflector, the light reverses its path [B]. A convex mirror [C] makes the rays of a parallel beam diverge as if they were coming from the focus[f'], which produces a diminished virtual image, as in a driving mirror [D].

3 Lenses form images because light rays are bent by refraction as they pass through a lens. The rays are made to converge on passing through a convex lens [1] or diverge through a concave lens [2], regardless of the direction in which the rays are moving. Thus convex lenses can make light rays meet and produce real images; concave lenses give only virtual images.

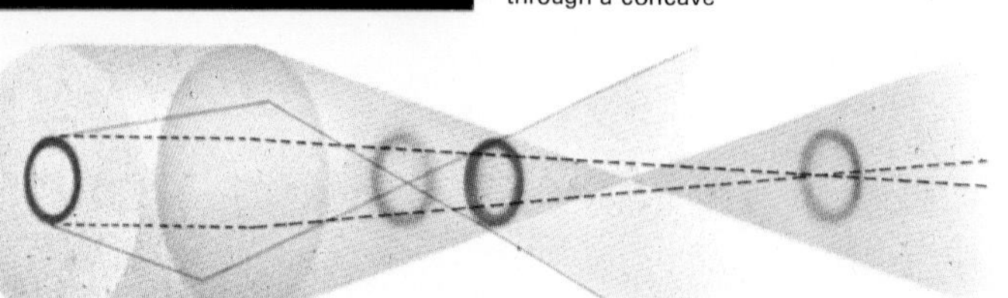

4 Spherical aberration produces a blurred image. Rays passing through the center of the lens are brought to a focus at a different point from rays passing through the edge of the lens and there is no place at which all the rays come to a single focus and give a sharp image. Spherical aberration may be reduced by narrowing the lens so that rays do not pass through the edges and by combining lenses in such a way that the defects in each kind of lens cancel each other.

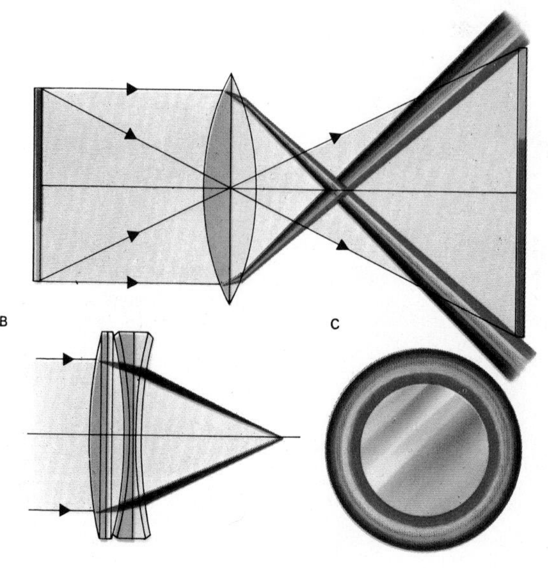

5 A
B
C

5 Chromatic aberration produces colored fringes around the lens edges, and parts of the image may not be sharp [C]. This aberration occurs with single lenses because they behave like prisms and bend blue light more than red [A]. Combining the lens with a weaker concave lens [B] made of a different glass cancels this dispersion effect, and both red and blue rays are brought to the same focus to produce a sharper, more distinct image.

Where two peaks or two troughs of vibrations meet, an increase in energy (brightness) occurs, but where a peak meets a trough they cancel each other out so that no energy is present and there is no light. As a result, a series of light and dark fringes is produced instead of a single image of the opening [2]. This effect, in which waves reinforce each other or cancel each other out, is called interference [4].

If a ray of light is divided into two rays that later recombine, then interference effects are seen if one of the divided rays travels a longer path than the other before the recombination. The peaks and troughs may be out of phase and the light is affected. This happens between two surfaces that are very close together, as in a thin film or two pieces of glass pressed together, and it produces colorful fringed patterns [5]. The iridescent colors seen in the plumage of some birds and some butterflies' wings are produced by interference.

Because interference can be produced by a path difference of only a wavelength or so, interference effects can be used to detect very small changes in length. Interferometers are used for this purpose. They produce interference by dividing a light ray into two or more beams and then recombining them.

Polarization of light waves

Another effect to be seen with light waves is polarization [7]. In an ordinary light wave the electric and magnetic fields vibrate in many randomly oriented planes about the direction of wave motion; in polarized light they vibrate in only one plane. Light is polarized by passing it through a filter that cuts out all vibrations except those in one particular plane. The polarized beam will then pass through a second filter only if it is set at the correct angle to allow the vibrations through. Otherwise the beam is stopped. Light reflected from surfaces at certain angles is polarized and polarizing sunglasses [8] cut out glare by stopping reflected beams in this way. Solutions of some chemical substances, such as various sugars, rotate the plane of polarization of light passing through them. The effect is used in chemistry for analyzing such solutions.

KEY

Shadows form with sharp edges when they are cast on a nearby object, but the outlines become less distinct the farther away they are cast. This can easily be explained because light travels in straight rays and every light source has a certain size. The ray paths show that a region exists at the edge of the shadow that is partially illuminated; this region, the penumbra, makes the outlines of the shadow fuzzy. The dark part of the shadow, the umbra, is completely shielded from the light source. The penumbra is less broad the closer the shadow is to the object casting it, and so nearby shadows look sharper to the observer.

5

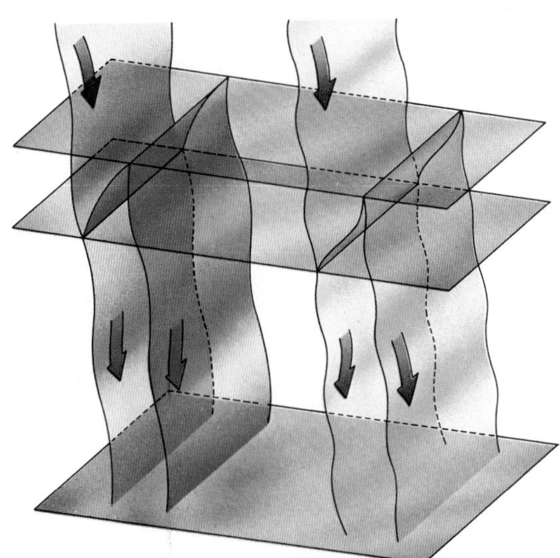

5 A thin film, such as a soap bubble or oil film, glistens with color. Part of the light passing through the film is reflected between the inner surfaces of the film and emerges to interfere with the rest of the light that passed straight through. Traveling paths of different lengths, some of the waves are in phase and reinforce each other [red], while others [blue] cancel each other and are not seen.

6

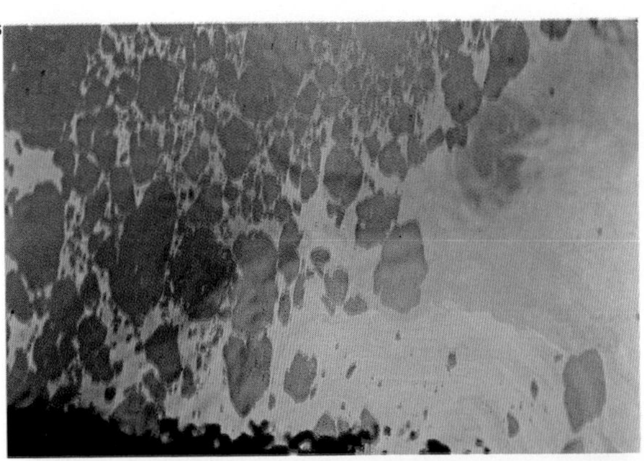

6 Interference is responsible for the colored reflections from bubbles and oil films on water. The light reflected from the top of the film interferes with light reflected from the lower surface.

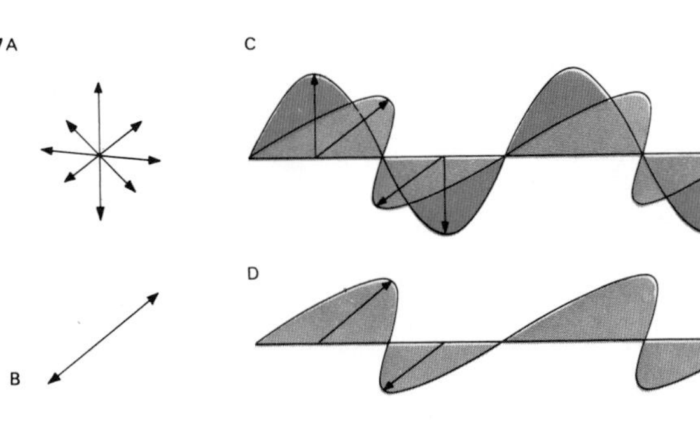
7A
C
D
B

7 Unpolarized light consists of vibrations in all planes at right-angles to the direction of the light wave; the arrows show the wave approaching head on [A]. Polarized light consists of vibrations in one plane only [B]. Light rays consist of vibrating electric and magnetic fields at right angles [C]; only the electric vibration denotes the plane of polarization [D].

8A

TOKY
TOKYO
京

8B

8 Light reflected from glass or water is partly polarized. Here [B] a reflection makes it difficult to see through a shop window. A similar photograph taken with a polarizing filter over the camera lens gives a reflection-free view [A]. Polarizing sunglasses reduce glare this way.

9

9 Stresses and strains in transparent materials such as glass and plastic become visible when viewed with polarized light. Here the regions of strain in a heat-treated car windshield become visible as spectral colors.

The speed of light

Every time we press a light switch, light floods the room instantaneously—or almost instantaneously. It takes a fraction of a second for the light to pass from the light bulb to our eyes, but the time taken is too brief for us to be aware of it. Many early scientists claimed its velocity was infinite.

Determining the velocity of light

Others, notably Galileo (1564–1642), the Italian astronomer, challenged this view. He attempted to measure the velocity of light by trying to find out how long light took to travel between two hills a known distance apart. His experiment was inconclusive but it did show that if light has a particular velocity then it is very great. The first close estimate came with observations of the moons of Jupiter by the Danish astronomer Olaus Roemer (1644–1710) in 1676 [1]. The moons, which had been discovered by Galileo in 1610, are often eclipsed by Jupiter but Roemer found that predictions of the eclipse times were as much as 16 minutes off. Roemer reasoned that the variations occurred because the distance between Earth and Jupiter varies depending on their positions in their orbits around the Sun and light therefore takes different times to reach the Earth from Jupiter. Knowing the distances involved, Roemer made a good estimate of the velocity of light, obtaining a value of 141,000 miles (227,000km) a second. The true velocity is almost 186,000 miles or 300,000km a second.

Another astronomical determination of the velocity was made by the English astronomer James Bradley (1693–1762) in 1728. He observed that the stars are seen in slightly different directions depending on the position of the Earth in its orbit. This phenomenon, called stellar aberration, is caused by the Earth's motion and the differences in direction are simply related to the difference between this motion and the velocity of light. Bradley was therefore able to obtain a value for the velocity of light.

Later determinations of the velocity were completely terrestrial; sensitive instruments were used to measure very precisely the time light took to travel a known distance. The instruments contain mirrors to reflect a ray of light along a particular path and time its passage by a variety of shutter mechanisms. Modern methods use an electronic shutter capable of very rapid action.

The accepted value for the velocity of light is now 186,281.7 miles (299,792.58km) a second. This is the velocity in a vacuum, for light slows when it enters a medium such as air, water, or glass. The change in velocity causes the light to bend and refraction occurs. The refractive index of a medium is the ratio of the velocity of light in a vacuum to its velocity in the medium. For example, the refractive index of water is 1.333 or $^4/_3$, and thus the velocity of light in water is only $^3/_4$ of that in a vacuum.

Scientists next began to wonder how light waves could travel through space. Other wave motions need a medium in which to travel. Sound, for example, moves through air or water, but not through a vacuum, and light had to have a medium, too.

The mystery of the ether

As the medium through which light traveled could not be seen to exist, one was in-

CONNECTIONS

See also
1518 Mirrors and lenses
1520 Light waves
1524 The idea of relativity
120 The local group of galaxies

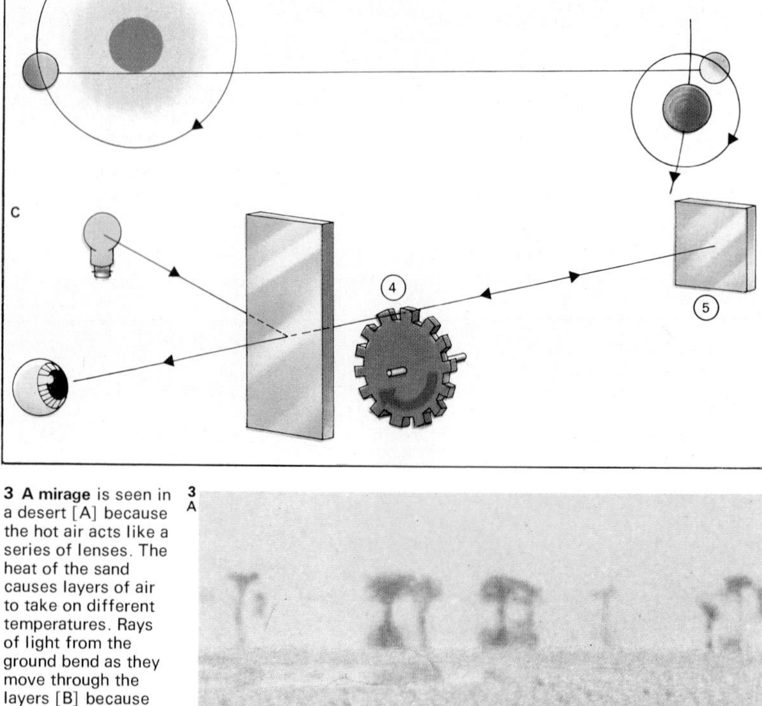

1
A
B
C
1
2
3
4
5

1 The velocity of light was first determined by Olaus Roemer in 1676 [A]. He saw the eclipses of Jupiter's moons [1] by Jupiter [2]. Light from the moons takes less time to reach the Earth [3] when its orbit nears Jupiter than when it is far away toward the other side of the Sun [B]. Knowing the distances and times involved he could work out a good estimate of the velocity of light. Another determination was made by Armand Fizeau (1819–96) in 1849 [C]. Light was reflected through the teeth of a rotating wheel [4] to a mirror [5] and back through the teeth to the observer. The light was seen only when the wheel rotated at a speed such that no teeth blocked its return journey. From the spacing of the teeth the speed of rotation of the wheel and the distance of the mirror (5 miles) the velocity of light could be accurately calculated.

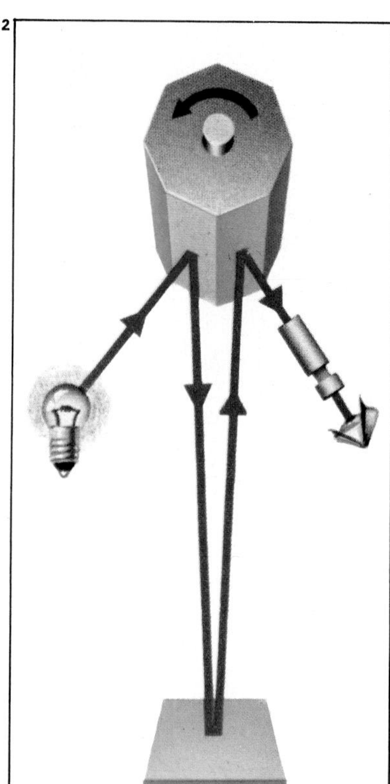

2

2 A rotating mirror was used by Michelson to measure the velocity of light in 1927. Light travelled from one face of the mirror to a plane mirror 22 miles (35km) away and then back to another face and an eyepiece. An image of the light source was obtained with the mirror first stationary and then rotated at sufficient speed for the image to be seen in the same position. At such a speed the mirror turned so that the next face moved into position as the light made its 44 mile (70km) journey to and from the plane mirror. Velocity of light was calculated from the speed of rotation.

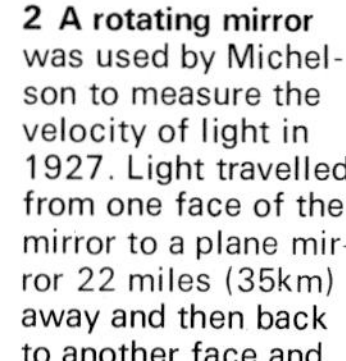

3
A

3 A mirage is seen in a desert [A] because the hot air acts like a series of lenses. The heat of the sand causes layers of air to take on different temperatures. Rays of light from the ground bend as they move through the layers [B] because each layer has a different refractive index. In extreme conditions, the light rays bend so much that an image of the sky may appear to be a lake on the desert.

3
B
Direct ray
Bent ray
Apparent position of image

vented. It was called the ether and it was supposed to pervade the whole universe. Thorny problems surrounded the ether. Known wave motions move more rapidly in denser, more elastic substances and a wave motion as fast as light should theoretically need a medium denser than steel. Yet the planets continue to sail through space, unimpeded by the ether. There were many other contradictions; to resolve the matter, an experiment was made to detect the motion of the Earth through the ether.

In the 1880s two American physicists, Albert Michelson (1852–1931) and Edward Morley (1838–1923) [5], made a simple instrument to detect the ether. In it a beam of light was split into two beams at right angles, and the two beams were reflected from mirrors before recombining. Combined beams show interference effects if one travels a slightly longer path than the other. Michelson and Morley observed the combined beams in one direction and then turned the instrument at right angles and observed the beams again. If the light were traveling in an ether it would take longer to travel a given distance in the direction of the Earth's motion ("upstream and downstream") than at right angles to it. Turning the instrument at right angles should show a difference in the interference effects if the ether existed. None was observed and none has been observed in many repeats of this classic experiment.

The basis of relativity

The conclusion of the Michelson-Morley experiment was that ether does not exist and light does not need a medium for its propagation, or that the ether can never be detected. Without a stationary ether there is no basis against which the absolute motion of everything can be measured, except for light. The Michelson-Morley experiment showed that the velocity of light is the same in the direction of the Earth's motion as at right angles to it and is always the same whatever the observer's motion. These conclusions had profound implications but to realize them it took a genius—Albert Einstein (1879–1955)—who used them as a basis for the theory of relativity.

KEY

Light that reaches us from heavenly bodies does not travel instantaneously. It takes 1.25 seconds to get to Earth from the Moon, 8 minutes from the Sun, over an hour from Saturn and the outer planets, and over four years from the nearest star. We see the galaxies as they were millions of years ago.

4 The blue glow coming from the water surrounding this nuclear reactor is called Cerenkov radiation. It is produced because nuclear particles emitted by the reactor are moving faster than light does itself in water, which slows light by about a quarter. The particles cause a shock wave to be produced in the water, just as a supersonic plane produces a shock wave in the air. We hear the sound shock wave as a supersonic boom and see the light shock wave as blue light. The production of Cerenkov radiation is used as a method of detecting fast-moving particles in nuclear physics. The radiation was first observed by the Russian physicist Pavel Cerenkov (or Cherenkov) in 1934.

5

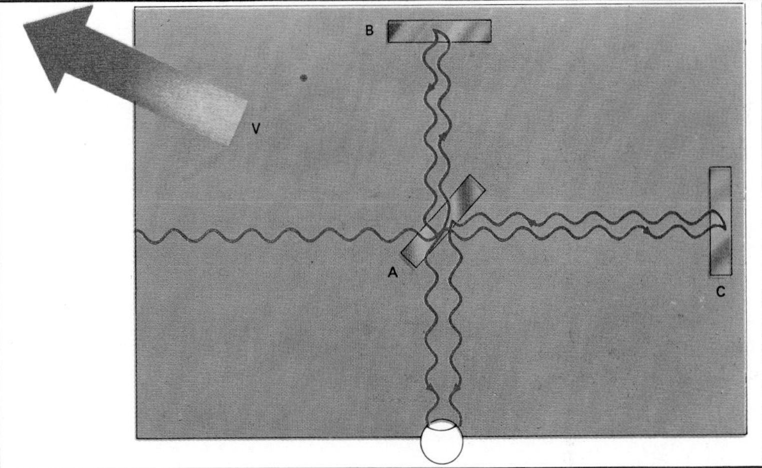

B
V
A
C

5 The Michelson-Morley experiment, first made in 1881, used an interferometer to produce a pattern of interference fringe, from two beams at right angles. The Earth's motion [V] was expected to make the light take longer along one path [AC] than along the other [AB], so that a change in pattern would be seen on turning the interferometer. No change was detected.

6

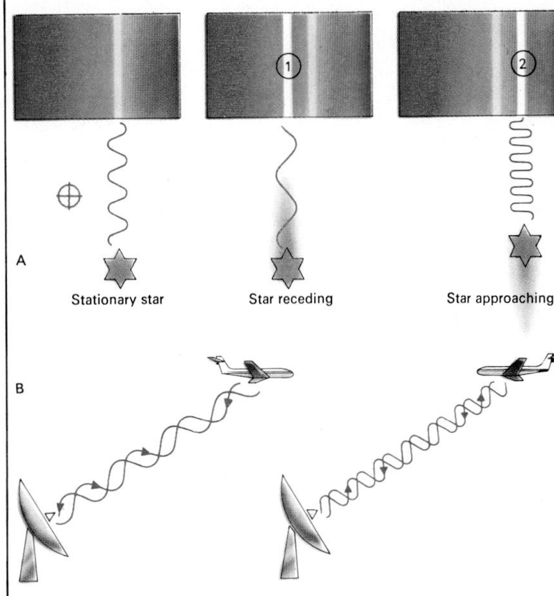

1
2
A
Stationary star
Star receding
Star approaching
B

6 The motion of an observer does not affect the velocity of light but it does change the frequency or color of light because of the Doppler effect. Only stars [A] move fast enough to show the effect. If the star and the observer are moving apart, the frequency decreases because the individual waves are encountered less frequently. The light is redder than if the star were stationary and this red shift shows as a shift in the lines of the spectrum of the star [1]. If a star and observer are approaching, frequency increases and the light appears bluer [2]. A similar frequency shift is used in radar to detect the motion of aircraft or cars [B].

The idea of relativity

Relativity theory eliminated from physics the idea of absolute values for space and time. Such values had been held to be fixed and quite independent of the person measuring them or of the instruments used. To Isaac Newton (1642–1727) they existed as a backdrop against which he could formulate general "laws" about such quantities as acceleration and force. It was the genius of Albert Einstein (1879–1955) that, through the special and general theories of relativity, showed that such absolutes did not exist and that Newton's laws were not universally true.

The special theory of relativity

Einstein's special theory of relativity (1905) was based on the postulate that the speed of light in a vacuum will have the same value measured in any non-accelerating frame of reference. This postulate was suggested by the classic experiment made by Albert Michelson (1852–1931) and Edward Morley (1838–1923), who found the same value for the speed of light no matter which direction the Earth was moving with respect to the fixed stars [2]. From these results Einstein deduced an astonishing set of conclusions. They showed that the mass, length, and time coordinates of an object will appear to change when the object begins to move relative to an observer.

If, say, an astronomer were to observe an extremely fast-moving spaceship, then his instruments would indicate that the mass of the spaceship had increased, that all lengths in the direction of the spaceship's motion had decreased, and time aboard ship was slower. Yet in the spaceship itself nothing would appear to have changed, although if the pilot looked back at the astronomer—who would be in the same motion relative to him—he would observe that mass, length, and time there had changed in exactly the same way.

The light clock [4A] shows why time varies with motion and by how much. Normally the effects of special relativity are undetectable in an object until it is traveling at nearly the speed of light (186,000mi, or 300,000km, per second) [3], although very sensitive atomic clocks have been used to detect clocks "going slow" on aircraft in flight. The effects do become large for subatomic particles moving at close to the speed of light. Thus, because of their high speed, very fast unstable particles in cosmic rays live longer in the Earth's atmosphere than would otherwise be expected [4B]. Subatomic particles can be so speeded artificially that their masses are increased many thousandfold; particle accelerators have to be designed to allow for this effect.

It is Einstein's famous equation "$E = mc^2$," relating the energy E and mass m of a moving particle with the velocity of light c, that shows why in special relativity a particle given ever greater energy will increase its mass. Because c^2 is so large, only a small amount of mass is equivalent to a vast amount of energy. The conversion of mass into energy takes place in nuclear reactors, in nuclear weapons, and in the stars.

As the speed of a particle approaches that of light its energy increases indefinitely. But Einstein's law of velocity addition shows that even an infinite amount of energy applied to a particle cannot make it

CONNECTIONS

See also
1522 The speed of light
1526 Light energy
1492 Speed and acceleration
1638 Nuclear power
48 Evolution of the Solar System
108 Pulsars and black holes

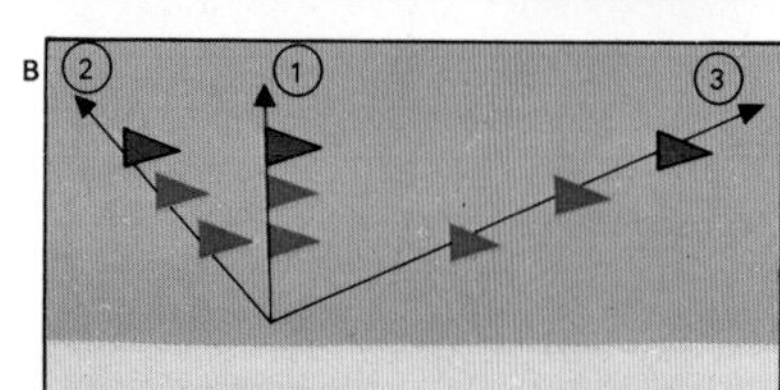

1 Relativity hinges on the simple idea that all motion is relative. A sailor in a yacht hauls a pennant up the mast [A]. To him, it appears to move vertically up [1]. To a man on the shore, the pennant appears to move forward and up [2], because it is being carried past him as it is raised. A passenger in a passing aircraft sees the pennant disappearing rapidly behind him as it is raised [3]. Each observer records the same motion differently [B]; none is any more "correct" than the rest, for the planet on which all this happens is also moving. Their views confirm the relativity of all motion.

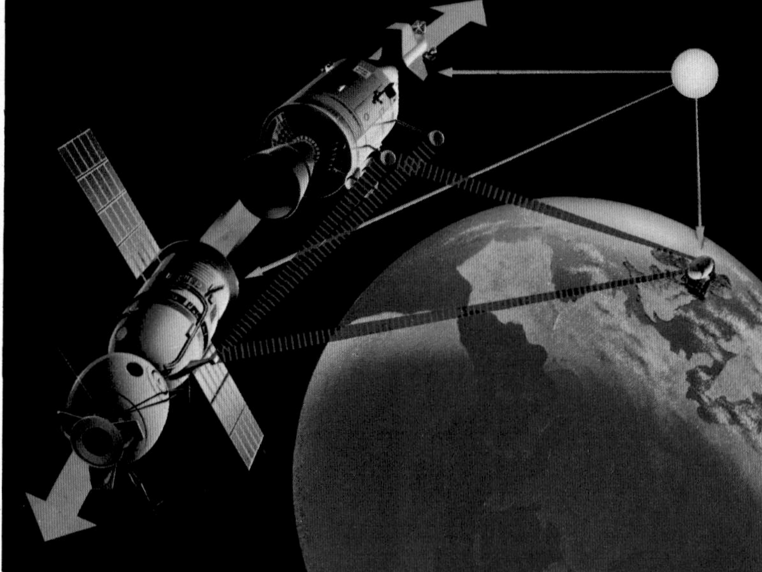

2 The special theory of relativity states that all motion is relative and that the speed of light is always constant. When two spacecraft pass each other in orbit, each traveling at 5 miles (8km) a second as measured by radar at the tracking station below, the pilots detect that they are traveling relative to each other at 10 miles (16 km) a second. If the two spacecraft and the tracking station then measure the speed of light from the Sun, they all get the same result. The craft moving toward the Sun does not obtain a value for the speed of light that reflects its motion relative to the Sun, the speed of light being constant for all observers.

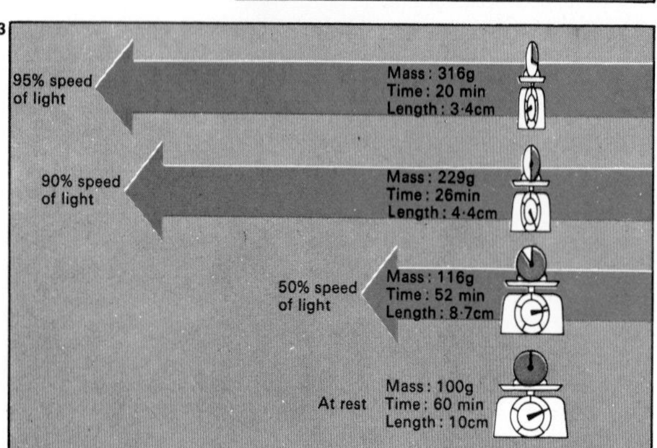
95% speed of light
Mass: 316g
Time: 20 min
Length: 3·4cm
90% speed of light
Mass: 229g
Time: 26min
Length: 4·4cm
50% speed of light
Mass: 116g
Time: 52 min
Length: 8·7cm
At rest
Mass: 100g
Time: 60 min
Length: 10cm

3 Einstein's special theory states that the measurement of mass, length, and time depends totally on the relative motion of the measuring instrument and the object being measured. Compared with measurements made at rest, the mass will appear to be increased, length to be decreased in the direction of motion, and time to be slowed. The effects are apparent only at extremely high speeds. At 90% of the velocity of light, apparent mass more than doubles, length reduces by over a half, and a clock on one object records an hour while a clock on the other shows 26 minutes have elapsed. At the velocity of light, mass would become infinite, length zero, and time would slow to a complete stop.

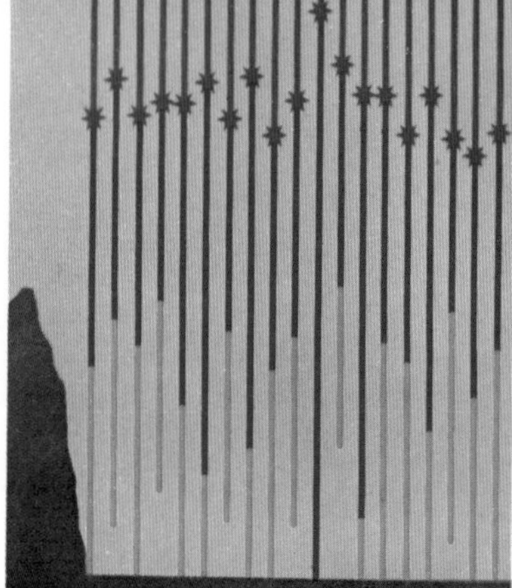

4 A light clock [A], in which light moves to and fro between mirrors, shows in theory how time is slowed by motion. When the clock is in motion, its mirrors travel along and the light travels farther between reflections. It thus takes longer to reach the mirrors, although its own velocity is constant and observed time is slowed down. Time slowing was actually proved when particles from space reached the Earth in greater numbers than predicted [B]. Because of their speed, they had lived longer than expected, as measured by clocks on Earth.

travel faster than light. The special theory showed that neither space nor time had wholly separate existences, but only a combination of the two—space-time—could adequately describe the universe.

The general theory of relativity

Einstein's general theory of relativity (1915) extended the special theory to take account of accelerated frames of reference. Einstein's Equivalence Principle stated that accelerated motion could not be differentiated from motion produced by a gravitational field. Thus both types of motion could be explained by a geometric model of the universe in which massive bodies are replaced by regions of curvature: the greater the distortion, the greater the gravitational force. This "curvature" occurs not in ordinary space but in the four-dimensional space-time continuum.

Experimental observations, such as the small deviations in the motions of planets from those predicted by Newton [7], make the general theory of relativity the most satisfactory of several recently introduced competing theories. Confirmation also comes from the bending of the path of a ray of light near a massive body. Light travels along geodesics—the shortest path available to it—and therefore moves in a curved path in the distorted path around the body [9]. Such bending of light by the Sun was confirmed at a 1919 solar eclipse [10].

Holes in the heavens

All these effects involve weak gravitational fields and cannot put general relativity through the most searching test. When stars have used up their nuclear fuel they may evolve into extremely condensed objects in which strong gravitational fields occur, and so they are good testing grounds for general relativity. It is postulated that very heavy stars collapse in on themselves so completely that the escape velocity on their surface is greater than the speed of light. As a result, nothing can ever escape from them again—not even light—and so they are known as "black holes." Good candidates for black holes in our own Galaxy are the variable X-ray stars such as Cygnus X-1.

KEY

Albert Einstein, working without the aid of a laboratory or university post, thought out the revolutionary concepts of the first theory of relativity from simple and seemingly unconnected ideas. Einstein was 26 and working as a patent officer when he published his special theory of relativity in 1905. Ten years later he announced his general theory of relativity. Einstein's fame was worldwide, but this did not stop the Nazi ruler of Germany from persecuting him for being Jewish. From 1933 he lived in the United States.

5

5 Nuclear weapons are one consequence of Einstein's discovery that mass can be converted into energy. But so too are atomic power stations and our understanding of the Sun's energy.

6 Low velocities accumulate by simple arithmetic. If a tank moving at velocity *V* fires a shell that leaves the gun at velocity *v*, then the shell will be traveling at *V*+ *v* [A]. Addition of velocities near that of light (c) is more complex. If a planet moving relative to Earth at 0.5c had a supergun that fired a shell at 0.5c, the shell would appear from earth to move at only 0.8c [B].

6

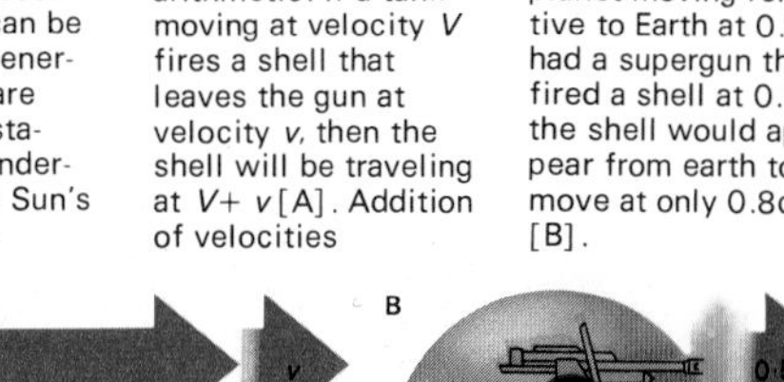

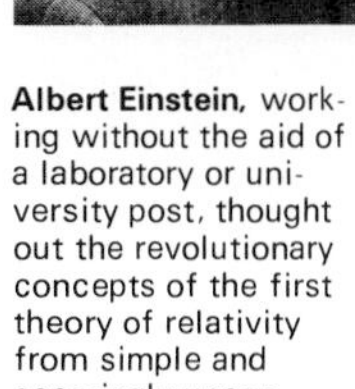

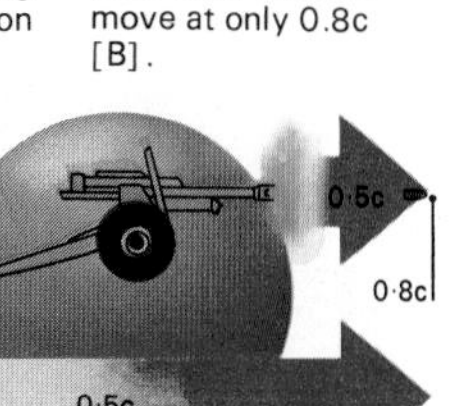
A
B
V
v
V + v
0·5c
0·8c
0·5c

7

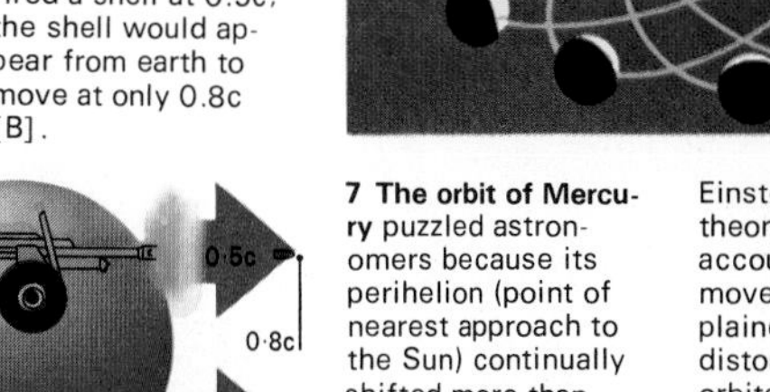

7 The orbit of Mercury puzzled astronomers because its perihelion (point of nearest approach to the Sun) continually shifted more than could be accounted for by the influence of the other planets. Einstein's general theory of relativity accounted for this movement. He explained that gravity distorts space so the orbits of the planets do not follow the simple orbits described by Newton.

8

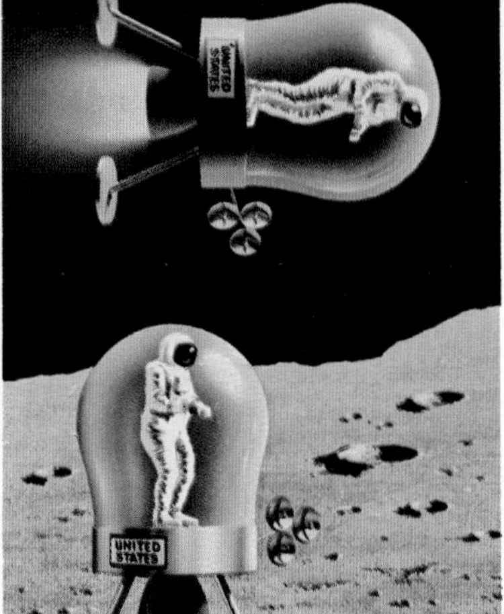
UNITED STATES
UNITED STATES

8 The principle of equivalence on which Einstein based his general theory of relativity states that gravity cannot be distinguished from acceleration. An astronaut is pulled to the floor of his stationary craft by gravity [bottom], in the same way as the floor is pushed toward him when the craft accelerates [top]. The effects are identical; if he let go of an object it would "fall" in either situation.

9 A ray of light passing a rotating wheel bearing a line of people would appear to be straight to an outside nonrotating observer [A]. As it passes, the people are carried away from it by the movement of the wheel. To them the ray appears to bend [B]. This analogy demonstrates the bending of light in an accelerating system and therefore, by equivalence, in a gravitational field.

9

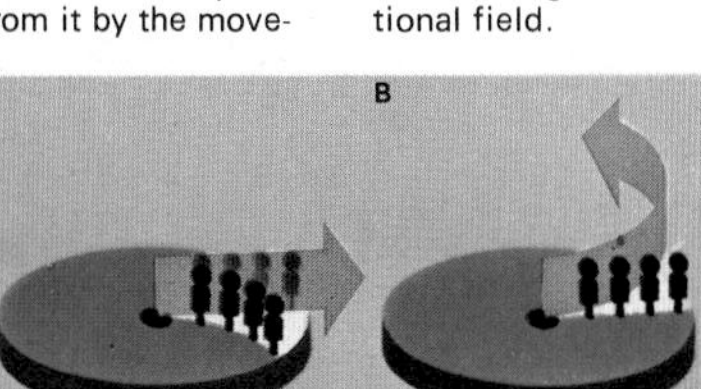
A
B

10

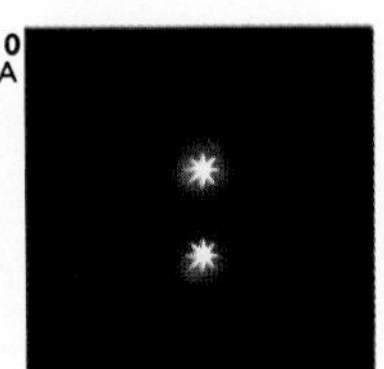
A

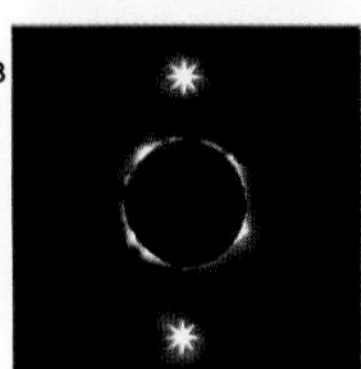
B

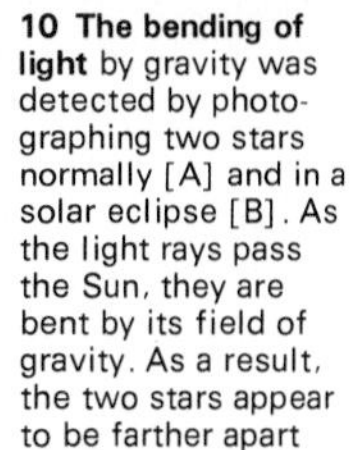

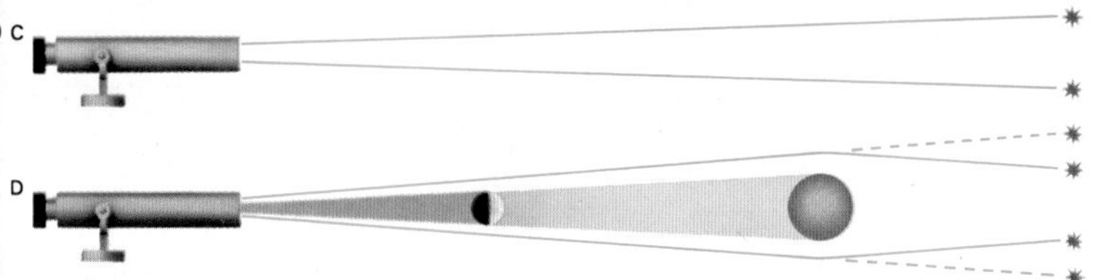
C
D

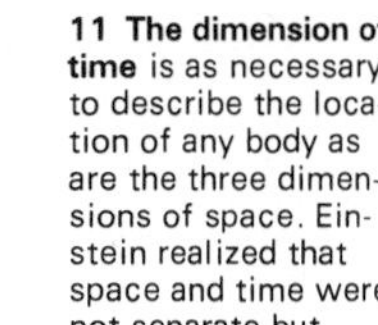

10 The bending of light by gravity was detected by photographing two stars normally [A] and in a solar eclipse [B]. As the light rays pass the Sun, they are bent by its field of gravity. As a result, the two stars appear to be farther apart [D] than usual [C].

11

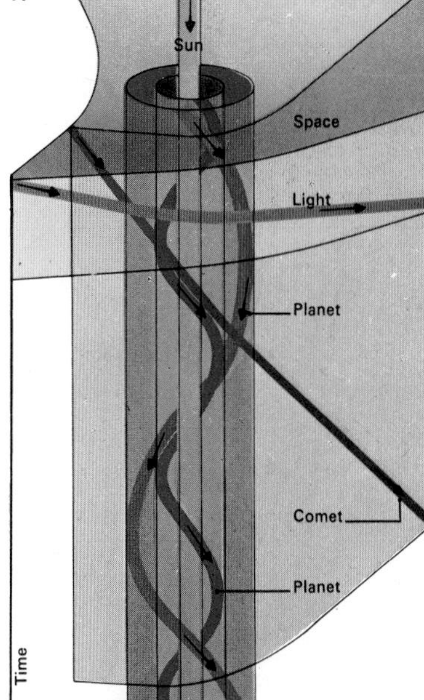
Sun
Space
Light
Planet
Comet
Planet
Time

11 The dimension of time is as necessary to describe the location of any body as are the three dimensions of space. Einstein realized that space and time were not separate but could be transformed one to another, and actually formed an inextricable union, the space-time continuum. This diagram shows the Sun, planets, and a comet moving in time as well as space. The varying velocity and widely changing path of the comet demonstrates the effects of gravitational fields on its motion, as Einstein predicted in his general theory.

Light energy

Light is energy and, in systems of constant mass, energy cannot be created but only changed from one form to another. Light therefore can only be produced from the conversion of some other form of energy. Electrical energy is changed into light in an electric lamp or discharge tube; heat is converted into light in a fire or a red-hot poker; chemical energy is changed into light in luminous animals such as glowworms. The conversion may also go the other way—light produces electrical energy in a photoelectric cell and causes a chemical reaction in photosynthesis which takes place in green plants.

Radiation and quantum theory

The conversion of energy involving light puzzled scientists at the end of the last century. A perfectly black object absorbs all light falling on it and all the invisible radiations such as ultraviolet rays and infrared rays. When it is heated the object gives out radiation over a spectrum of wavelengths, with its maximum energy output occurring at different wavelengths depending on the temperature. Like the poker in the fire, it first gives out infrared rays (which can be felt as heat rays), then it glows red, yellow, and finally white as it gets hotter. The wave theory of light [2], however, predicted that the maximum energy should be given out at the highest frequencies, toward the ultraviolet end of the spectrum. This dilemma became known as the "ultraviolet catastrophe."

In 1900, the German physicist Max Planck (1858–1947) put forward a convincing although revolutionary theory. He suggested that all energy, including light, consists of whole units of energy: an object can have one unit or a million, but not 0.8, 2.5, or 354.67 units, for example. Each energy unit is called a quantum of energy, from the Latin for "how much." The amount of energy in a quantum is minute and we are unable to make out the individual quanta in light rays as they strike the eye. A quantum of light energy is called a photon.

The quantum theory explains why a poker glows in the way it does. As more heat is applied to the poker, the light produced has more energy, and this is shown by a change in color—a blue photon has more energy than a red photon. Planck explained that the energy content of each photon of light depends on its frequency; the higher the frequency (more toward the blue or ultraviolet), the greater its energy.

CONNECTIONS

See also
1486 The nature of ener
1520 Light waves
1522 The speed of light
1524 The idea of relativi
1528 Energy from lasers

Particles and waves

The idea of light existing as indivisible units was a return to the particle theory of light. A light quantum is included in the fundamental particles that make up matter. If light consists of streams of particles, then it will cross empty spaces with no need for the medium of "ether" that scientists had sought in vain. But such effects as diffraction and interference could be explained only if light behaved as waves. Scientists solved this dilemma by assuming that light can behave both as particles and as waves, depending on the situation. This was not just an easy way out of a difficult problem, because the duality can be shown to exist—both experimentally and mathemat-

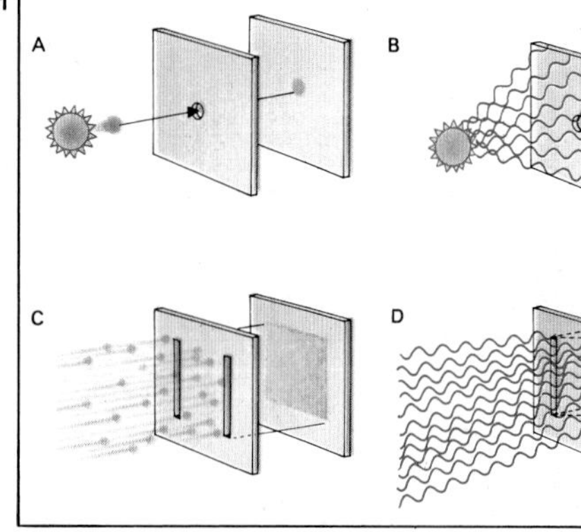

A
B
C
D

1 The wave nature of light is demonstrated by the way light passes through openings. If light consisted of particles, it would produce a pinpoint of light on passing through a pinhole [A]. In fact diffraction gives a larger image [B]. Particles passing through two slits would give a broad band of light [C], but interference fringes are seen [D]. Diffraction and interference are properties of waves.

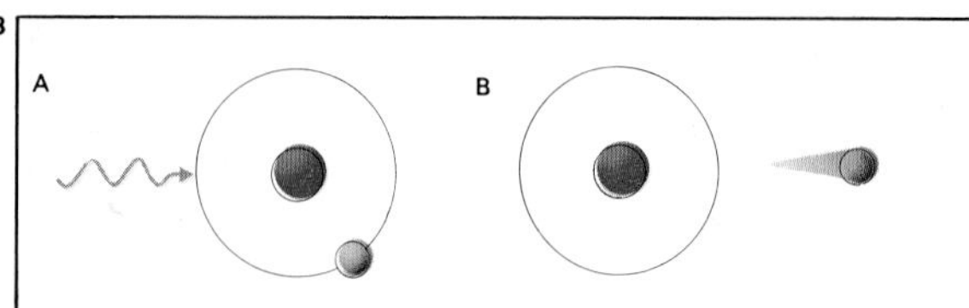

A
B

3 The photoelectric effect was explained by Einstein in 1905 as the absorption of a quantum of energy [A] by an atom and the resulting emission of an electron [B], which can form an electric current.

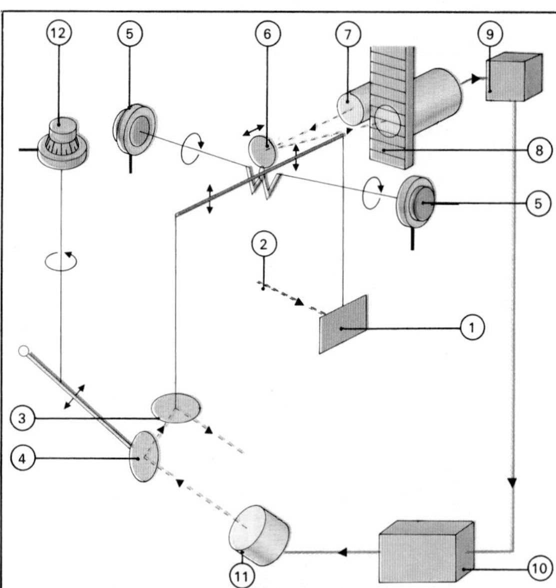

12
5
6
7
9
8
5
2
1
3
4
11
10

2 Light exerts pressure on any object it encounters. A vane [1] struck by light [2] moves under this pressure, and the movement is counterbalanced by a horizontal mirror [3] onto which light is directed by a vertical mirror [4]. The torsion heads [5] first level the balance arm. The mirror [6] reflects light from a lamp [7] on to a scale [8]. A timer [9] detects motion of the light across the scale and adjusts a power source [10] to change the intensity of the lamp [11] illuminating the mirror [4] and thus keeps the arm in balance. Mirror deflection is detected by the torsion head [12].

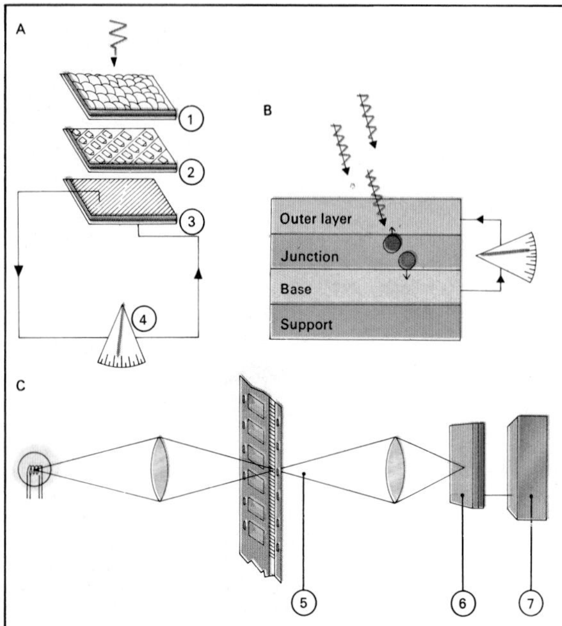

A
1
2
3
4
B
Outer layer
Junction
Base
Support
C
5
6
7

4 A light meter [A] contains a glass honeycomb [1] and a grid [2] through which light passes to a light-sensitive metal element [3]. There it causes electrons to be excited and these pass around the circuit to the meter [4]. The solar cell [B] is another application of photoelectricity. It consists of layers of semiconductor, usually silicon. Light crosses the outer layer and produces electrons at the junction. These are emitted and travel toward the base, producing a current. The optical sound track [C] on a motion-picture film transmits a varying light signal [5] to a photoelectric cell [6], which produces an electric signal that goes to a loudspeaker [7].

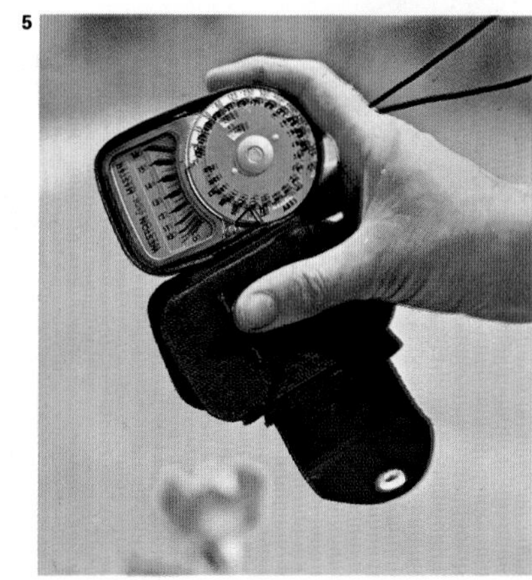

5 A photographic exposure meter measures the light coming from a scene. The light strikes a photoelectric cell, which produces an electric current that varies in strength according to the intensity of the light. The current is low but sufficient to move a needle across a dial and give a value for the light. Many cameras have built-in exposure meters that measure the light entering the lens of the camera.

ically. Also, fast-moving particles were found to have wavelike properties.

The quantum theory—especially its application to light—finally resolved the problem that had polarized scientific thought for centuries. Isaac Newton (1642–1727) had championed the particle theory and Christiaan Huygens (1629–95) had maintained that light travels as waves. With Max Planck's proposal the dilemma ceased to exist—light can be regarded as behaving as particles *or* waves.

Certain metals emit electrons when light falls on them—a phenomenon known as the photoelectric effect [3]. It had been observed that brighter light produces more electrons than dim light but not electrons of greater energy; whereas blue light always gives electrons of greater energy than red light, regardless of the intensity of the light. In 1905, Albert Einstein (1879–1955) explained that each electron is released by one photon of light; a bright light has more photons of the same energy than a dim light, but a blue light has photons of greater energy than red light.

Changing the frequency of light, or converting an invisible frequency into a visible one, has several uses. Fluorescent substances take up light of several frequencies and immediately radiate them at a different frequency, making the resulting color very bright because extra light has been transformed into it [9]. The fluorescent paints and inks used in some advertisements work in this way. Some laundry powders contain optical brighteners that convert invisible ultraviolet rays into blue light and thus cause the wash to appear brighter.

Effects of phosphorescence

Phosphorescence is similar to fluorescence, but the production of light continues for some time after the initial radiation has ceased. Television screens contain phosphors that glow for a short time after being struck with the electron beams inside the cathode ray tube and give a picture on the screen. Many instruments make use of the light produced by phosphors to detect invisible rays such as X rays and fast-moving particles such as cosmic rays.

KEY

The radiometer, invented by William Crookes (1832–1919), measures radiant energy. When sunlight falls on it, the vanes move around. Heat is absorbed by the black side and the few gas molecules left in the bulb's vacuum rebound faster, exerting pressure on that side.

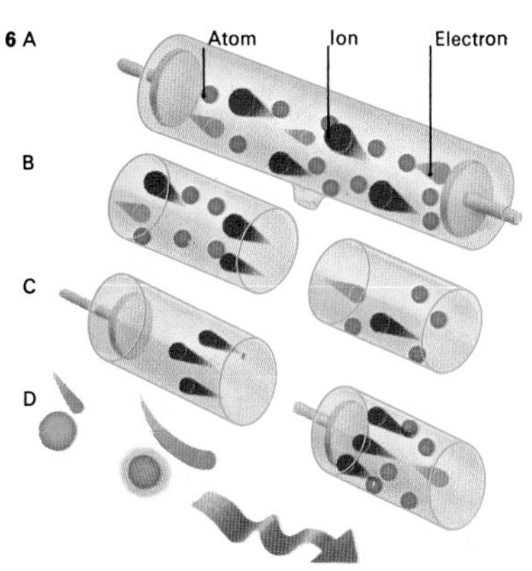
6
A
B
C
D
Atom
Ion
Electron

6 A discharge tube contains a gas at low pressure through which electricity is passed [A]. Electrons (negative) and ions (positive) move toward the electrodes [B]. Ions strike electrodes to produce more electrons [C]. Light is produced as electrons collide with gas atoms [D].

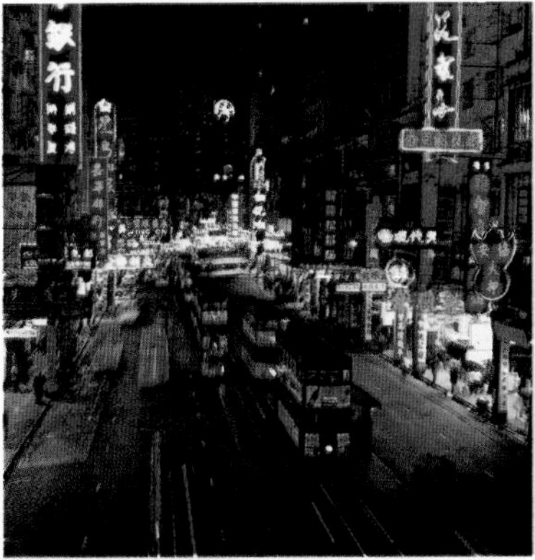
7

7 Advertising signs contain a gas such as neon or are coated with phosphors to give various colors.

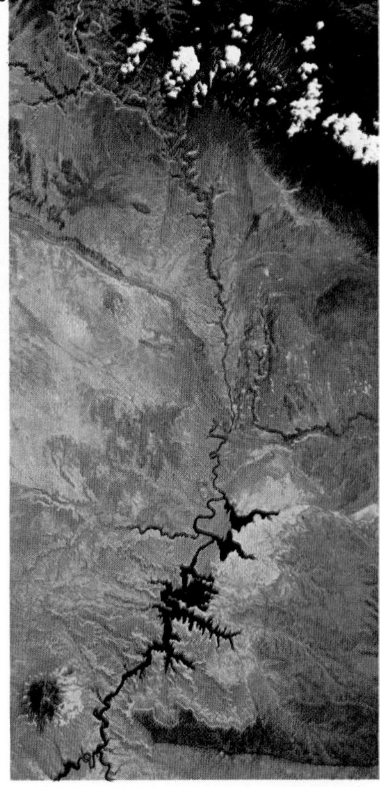
8

8 An infrared view of the Colorado River and Lake Powell taken by a satellite shows vegetation in various shades of red and water as black. Areas of diseased plants can be detected by color.

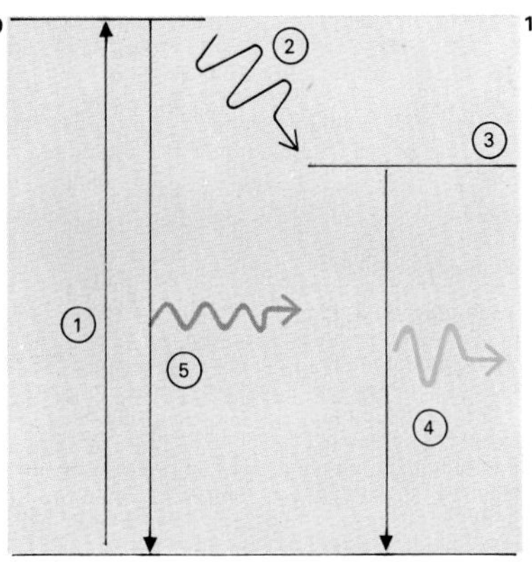
9
1
2
3
4
5

9 Fluorescence occurs when an atom absorbs light energy [1] and emits the energy in two stages: a small energy change producing infrared [2] at an intermediate energy state [3] and a large change giving light at a lower frequency than that received [4]. Normal light production occupies one change [5]. Phosphorescence is similar but stage two takes some time.

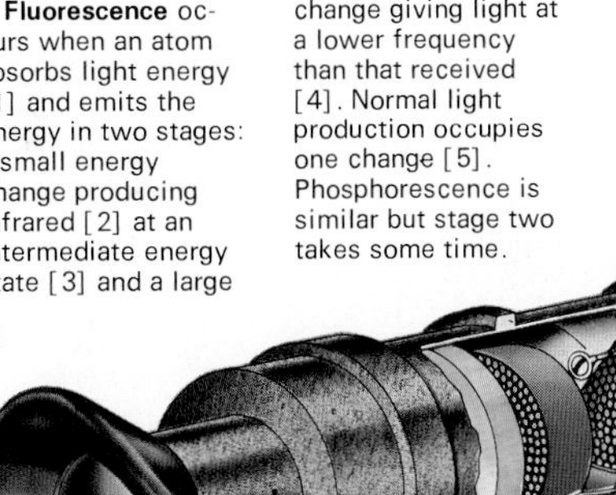
10

10 Automatic letter checking utilizes ultraviolet light. Invisible phosphor codes printed on the stamp glow as the letter passes an ultraviolet scanner, which directs the letter to a mailbag.

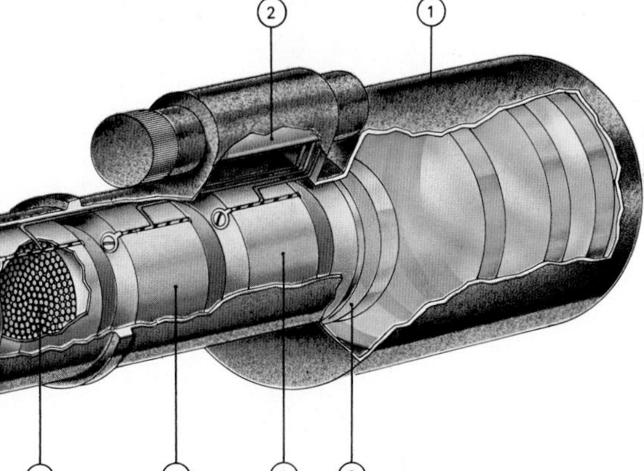
11
1
2
3
4
5
6
7
8
9

1 Night lens system
2 6·75 volt mercury battery
3 Photocathode
4 15kV channel plate
5 30kV channel plate
6 45kV channel plate
7 Fluorescent screen
8 Ocular lens system
9 Eyepiece

11 An image intensifier gives a bright picture of a dimly lit scene. Light from the scene is focused onto the photocathode, which emits electrons. These pass to the electron multipliers that contain tubes lined with electron emitting substances and produce more electrons from each electron entering the tubes. The resulting intensified electron beam is focused on a fluorescent screen that is viewed through an eyepiece.

Energy from lasers

From boring holes through diamonds to performing delicate eye operations, from spanning space between the earth and the moon to detecting the smallest movement, the laser has found an amazing range of uses. Its future looks no less extraordinary with the promise of three-dimensional television and cheap nuclear power. Clearly the laser is no ordinary source of light.

What is a laser?

A pulse laser is basically a device for storing energy and then releasing it all at once to give an intense beam of light. The heart of the laser is a crystal or tube or gas or liquid into which energy is pumped [1]. This is usually done by surrounding it with a device to produce a powerful flash of light or an intense beam of radio waves or electrons. As pumping occurs, more and more of the atoms inside take up energy and are excited to high energy states. Suddenly an atom spontaneously returns to its first energy state and gives out a particle of light (a photon). This photon strikes another excited atom and causes it to produce another photon. Very rapidly, a cascade of photons develops. The crystal or tube is closed at both ends by mirrors and the photons bounce between them, building up the cascade. Finally the light becomes powerful enough to escape through one of the mirrors, which is half-silvered, and an intense flash of light emerges from the laser.

The first pulse laser, invented by Theodore H. Maiman in 1960, contained a ruby crystal and produced a short flash of red light. Continuous wave lasers now produce continuous beams of many colors and some give out infrared or ultraviolet rays.

The activities of photons

The atoms that discharge photons are stimulated to emit them by the arrival of other photons. The light that is pumped into the laser consists of many frequencies but what emerges is a far more intense light at a single frequency. The result—light amplification by the stimulated emission of radiation—gives the laser its name.

Each photon triggers the production of another one and so they all travel together and produce light waves that are exactly in step. This light is said to be in phase, or coherent. (In ordinary light, the waves are all out of phase.) Because the waves are all in step, they reinforce each other and laser light is very bright. The laser produces a narrow beam that hardly spreads at all—even at the distance of the moon, a laser beam directed from the earth is only 2 miles (3km) wide [3]. A narrow beam of intense, coherent light is extremely concentrated in energy, and if a laser beam is focused to a point by a lens, it will heat the air to incandescence (bright and glowing with heat) or burn a hole in a steel plate.

The use of lasers

A straight, narrow beam of laser light can be used for precise alignment in the construction of tunnels and pipelines, for example. The beam is directed along the proposed route and can be seen by the construction engineers only when they are exactly in line with it. Laser beams can also be used to measure distances and speeds. These have included firing a laser beam at the moon to

CONNECTIONS

See also
1526 Light energy

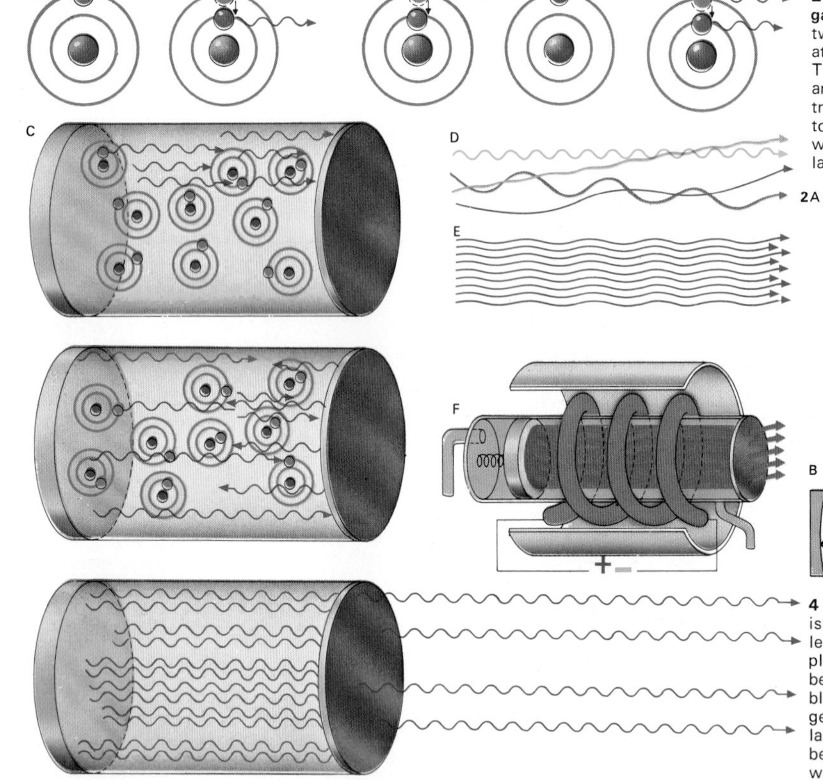
1A
B
C
D
E
F
+

1 Normal emission of light occurs when an electron in a high-energy orbit falls to low orbit [A]. Stimulated emission [B] is triggered by light emitted from an identical atom. In a laser [C], most atoms are brought to a high-energy state by pumping in energy. Some begin to produce light by normal emission, and mirrors at each end reflect the light, producing stimulated emission until all the atoms are in a low-energy state. The light leaves the laser through one of the mirrors. Ordinary light [D] is a mixture of different frequencies moving in various directions, whereas laser light [E] has a single frequency and moves in the same direction with all waves in phase. The first laser [F] contained a synthetic ruby crystal surrounded by a flash tube (to pump in light energy) and a pair of reflecting mirrors.

2A
Energy
20
16
0
He Ne He Ne He Ne He Ne

B
1 2 3 4

2 The helium-neon gas laser contains two gases and operates continuously. The helium atoms are first excited and transfer their energy to the neon atoms, which then produce laser light [A]. The laser [B] consists of a glass tube containing the gases and electrodes [2, 3] connected to a power supply [1] to excite the gas. The beam emerges through the half transparent mirror [4].

4 A detached retina is quickly and painlessly welded into place by a laser beam, curing partial blindness. The surgeon lines up the laser by directing a beam of ordinary white light into the unaffected eye. When the white beam is in place, the laser is fired briefly and the green laser ligh enters the other eye and is focused on the affected retina to seal it back into place.

3A
B

3 Laser communication would be ideal for interplanetary missions because the narrow, powerful beam [B] can reach a small, distant target. A laser carries a television or other signal by modulating the beam at the transmitting end, focusing the beam on a detector at the receiving end, and demodulating the signal produced [A]. Ordinary light is unsuitable for communication because its many frequencies interfere with each other; only lasers can be used.

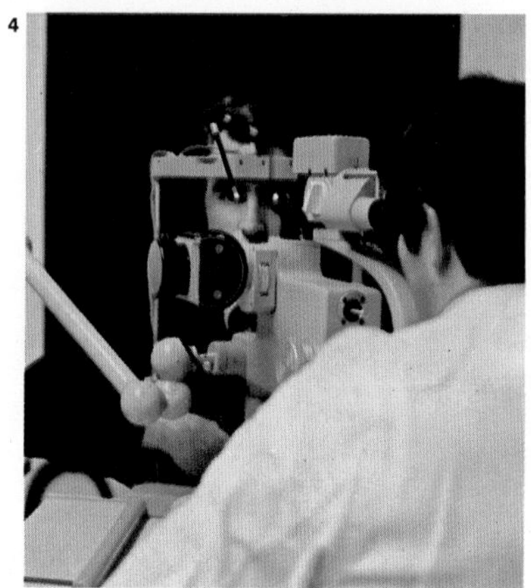
4

reflect it from a special mirror placed there by the Apollo astronauts and thus give an accurate measure of the moon's distance.

In meteorology, laser beams are used to detect invisible air layers and movements as well as clouds, and they are useful in studies of air pollution.

The intense heat of lasers gives them all kinds of uses in medicine and industry. A laser beam directed into the eye at insufficient power to damage the lens is focused by the lens on to the retina, where it can painlessly weld a detached portion back in place and restore failing sight [4]. Laser beams can burn away skin growths without surgery, by being transmitted along fiber-optic tubes inserted into the body, and painlessly drill decayed teeth. In industry, lasers cut out patterns, drill holes in diamonds to make dies for wire manufacture, and shape and weld parts for microelectronic circuits [Key].

Communication by laser beams instead of radio waves is desirable because light beams can carry many more channels of information than can radio. Data, sound, and pictures can be transmitted by a laser beam, which must be routed along an enclosed path of some kind to avoid loss of signal from fog or mist in the air.

One of the most amazing results of producing coherent light in lasers is the development of holography, with which three-dimensional images can be made [5, 6, 7]. Although three-dimensional color television and motion pictures may one day result from it, holography has several uses now. Double-exposure holograms record any movement of the subject between the exposures and so readily picture the vibrations in a surface. Vibration analysis is essential to the design of components such as aircraft and engine parts that must perform faultlessly at high speeds and stresses.

Another field that may be revolutionized by the laser is nuclear energy. Research is being carried out to see if thermonuclear fusion (the reaction that takes place in a hydrogen bomb and in the stars) can be initiated by a laser beam instead of confining a high-temperature plasma in unstable magnetic fields.

KEY

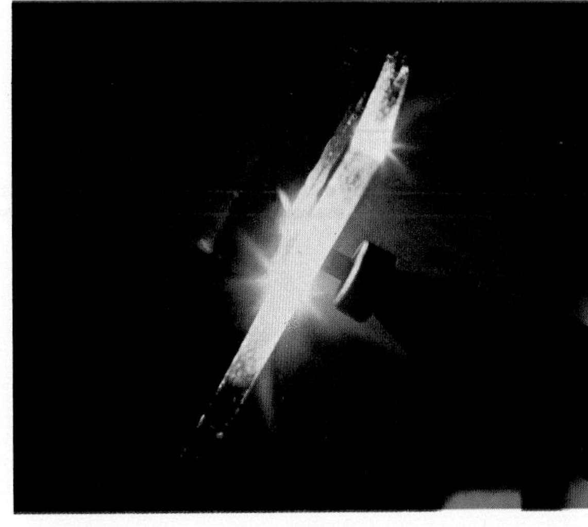

A lasar beam contains sufficient energy to "burn" a hole in hard materials such as steel and diamond. Here a laser beam is drilling a hole in a sheet of toughened glass. Laser-drilled diamonds are used as dies for drawing metal into extremely fine wires for use in electronic devices.

5

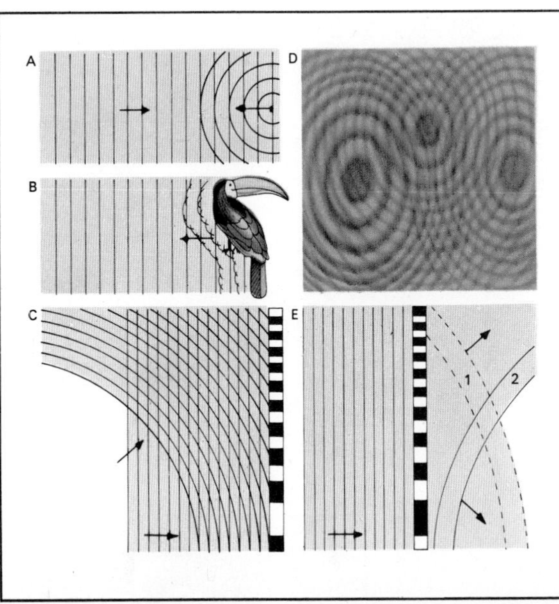
A
B
C
D
E
1
2

5 Holography reconstructs light waves. An illuminated point produces spherical wavefronts [A] and the surface of an object makes a complex wavefront [B]. When a curved wavefront combines with a plane one [C], a pattern [D] is formed on a photographic plate. When laser light is passed through this hologram [E], the original wavefront is reconstructed [1, 2].

6

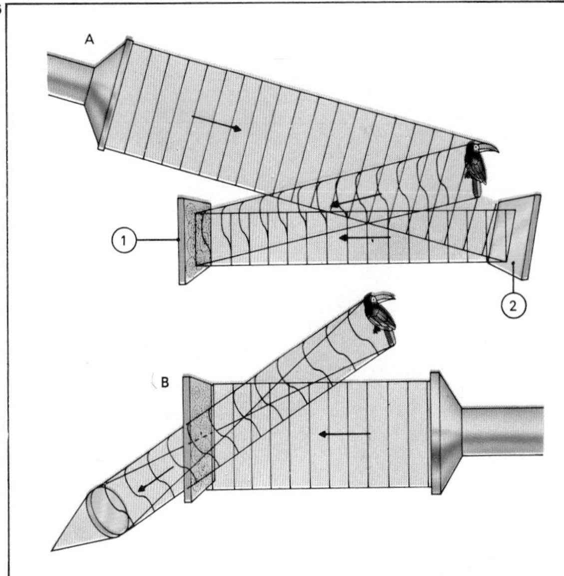
A
1
2
B

6 A hologram is made [A] by placing a photographic plate [1] near an object lit with laser light and reflecting some of the light onto the plate [2]. The image is re-created [B] by illuminating the hologram with a laser.

7 A

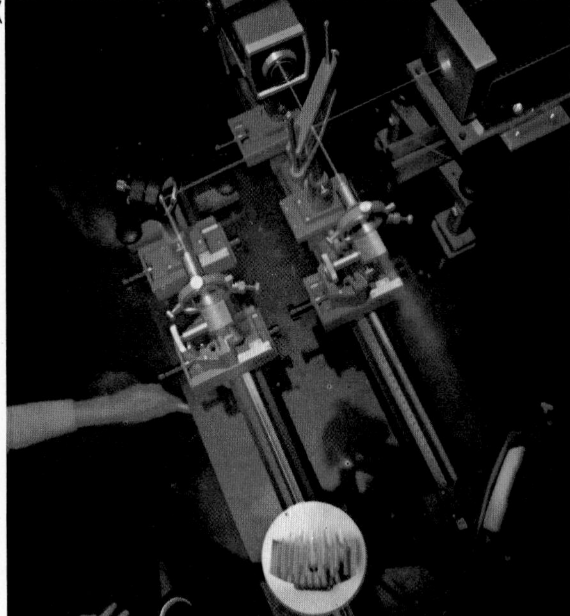

B

C

7 3-D images can be obtained by holography. A hologram of an object is made by the technique described in the caption for illustration 5, using apparatus such as that shown in [A]. It is arranged so that laser light reflected from the object travels about the same distance as the reference laser beam reflected onto the photographic plate by a mirror. When the hologram is illuminated from behind with laser light, an image of the object is seen which is not only 3-dimensional but also demonstrates parallax: as the head is moved, a different view of the object is obtained. This shows in two views of chessmen [B, C]. The image has depth because the hologram completely reconstructs the light rays coming from the object and striking the plate. The color of the object can also be produced by using several lasers of different colors. It is possible that holography may one day give us totally realistic motion pictures or television.

What is electricity?

To the man in the street, electricity is the cause of a lightning flash [1–3] or the form of energy that powers his television set and washing machine. He knows that electric trains use electrical power and he is reminded of his dependence on it by the network of power lines criss-crossing the countryside or by a power cut, when he has to read by candle light. But there are other less well-known everyday processes that involve the use of electricity. A beating heart, a running athlete, a dreaming baby, and a swimming fish all generate electricity just as surely as a power station does.

Electrons and protons

To a scientist, electricity results from the movement of electrons and other charged particles in various materials. A scientific understanding of electricity therefore depends on a knowledge of atoms and the subatomic particles of which they are composed. The key to this understanding is the tiny electron—tiny even when compared with the minute atom in which it may be found.

Atoms of all materials have one or more electrons circling in orbits or various sizes—much as the planets move around the Sun. Normally the number of electrons equals the number of protons in the nucleus. The protons, however, being much heavier than the electrons, are virtually stationary in the atom's center. This extremely simplified model of the atom is sufficient to explain the basis of electricity.

The electrons and protons each have an electric charge (but of opposite polarity) and attract each other. Charges of the same polarity repel each other. To distinguish the proton's charge from that of the electron the former is called positive and the latter negative. An atom that has more, or fewer, electrons than normal is called an ion. If it is deficient in electrons, it is called a positive ion; if it has an excess of electrons, it is called a negative ion. When an electron moves away from an atom the atom is left with a net positive charge. The electron, deprived of its positive counterpart in the atom's center, moves about another atom or returns to the atom it has left.

There are a number of possible causes for the movement of electrons. A common one is simply that if an incoming electron or light pulse hits an atomic electron, the latter can be knocked out of its orbit. Heat makes atoms vibrate faster, causing the electrons to move so energetically that they may shoot away from the parent atoms. Chemical activity will also cause electrons to move out of atoms.

A good example of the relationship between chemical and electrical activity is found in the muscles. Muscle fibers contract when they are electrically stimulated [4]. Normally this is caused by the release of a chemical from an associated nerve, following the receipt of an electrical signal from the nervous system. When part of this system is damaged and muscles become weak or fibers are destroyed, it is possible to apply external electrical signals to stimulate muscle activity and strengthen their fibers.

Conductivity

The electrons of some materials move more freely than others. This characteristic is

CONNECTIONS

See also
1480 What is an atom?
1484 Beyond the atom
1532 What is an electric current?
1542 Basic DC circuits
1544 Basic AC circuits
1536 Electromagnetism
1648 Electricity generati and distribution
1650 Electric power in tl home
1548 Basic electronic pr ciples
1546 Semiconductors
1794 Communications: radio

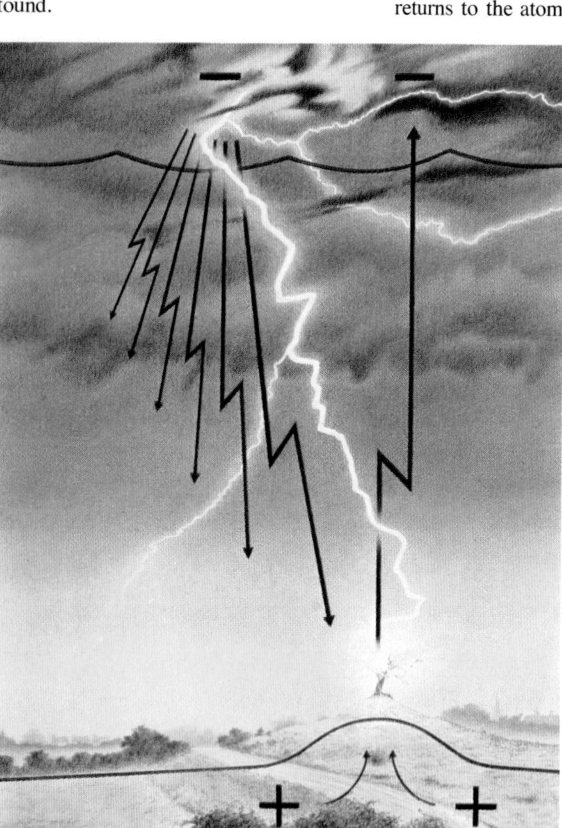

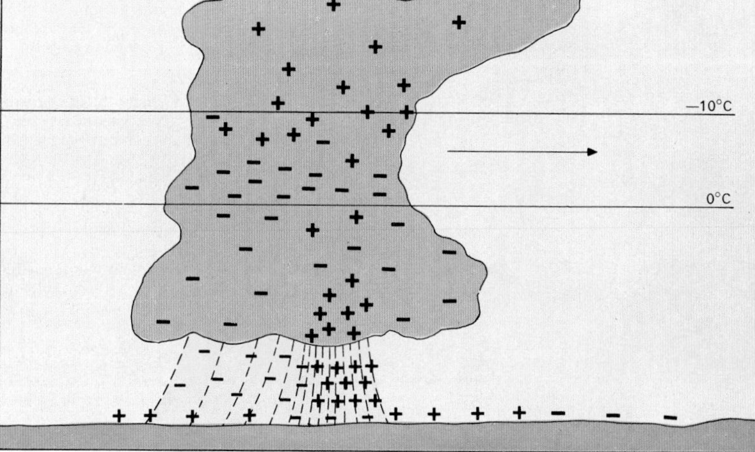
–10°C
0°C

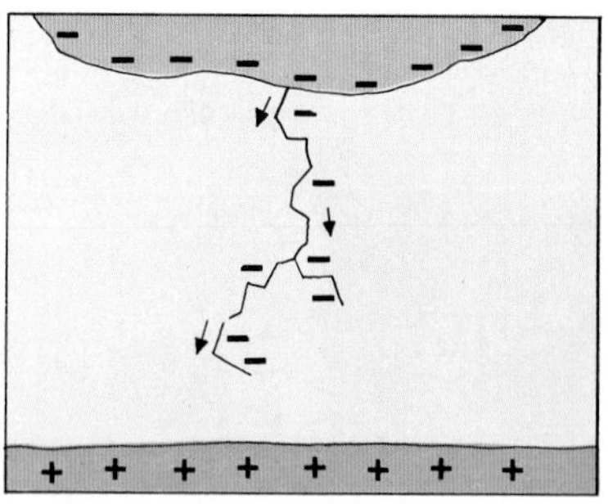

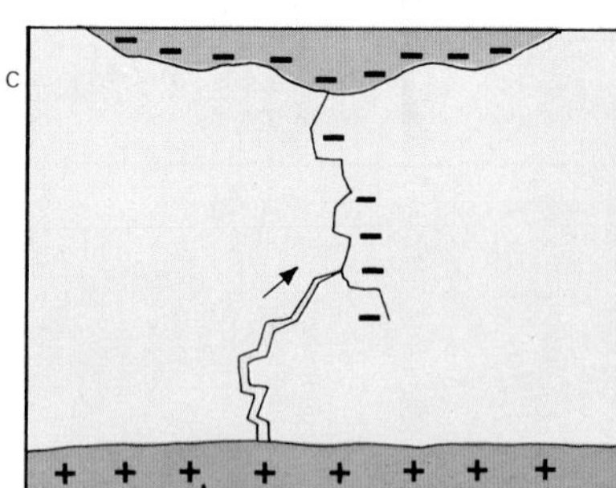

1 Lightning strokes were not properly explained until about 200 years ago. They are caused by an electrical imbalance between clouds or between clouds and earth. The base of the cloud can have an excess of electrons and then draws positive ions to the ground underneath it. The potential difference grows until there is a sudden flow of electrons (the flash), neutralizing charges on both the ground and the cloud or between the clouds.

3 Benjamin Franklin (1706–90) was the first man to recognize the true nature of lightning. During a thunderstorm he induced a flash of lightning to flow along the string of a kite to the earth.

4 Galvanism was the term used to describe the twitching effect produced by an electric current on a pair of frog's legs. Luigi Galvani (1737–98) used this experiment to show the connection between muscle activity and electricity.

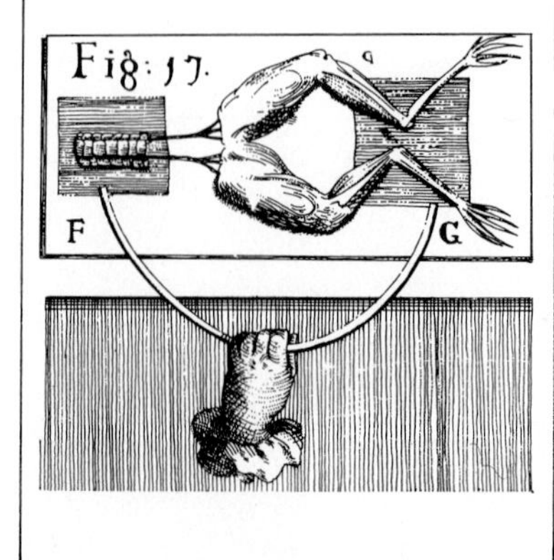
Fig: 17.
F
G

2 Formation of lightning starts with a big storm cloud [A], within which there is a significant temperature difference. Electrons move downward and positive ions move upward within the cloud, causing positive ions to gather on the earth below. When there are sufficient electrons, a sudden breakdown of the electrical resistance of the air occurs and a stream of electrons shoots earthward [B] to be met by an upward stream of ions [C].

known as conductivity. Most metals, hot gases, and some liquids are good conductors. Air, rubber, oil, polyethylene, and glass are poor conductors and can be used to cover good conductors without themselves taking part in electron flow [6]. These poor conductors are called insulators. No insulator is "perfect." Under certain circumstances the electrons of any atom can be forced out of it. But the conditions required are generally so unusual and difficult to arrange with these materials that they can be considered inactive.

There is also a group of materials—the semiconductors—that behave partly as insulators and partly as conductors. Among these are germanium, silicon, and copper oxide. Their properties can be exploited for many purposes. For example, using one of the semiconductors it is possible to make an electric valve that, like the valve on a bicycle tire, allows easy electron movement in one direction only. This device is called a rectifier; it is used in both radio sets and large power stations to change an alternating current to a direct current.

Heat is simply a chaotic form of molecular activity or electronic motion and temperature is a measure of its violence. When the temperature of most metals is reduced, it is easier for electrons to move freely; that is, the electrical resistance (to free electron movement) falls as the temperature drops and the conductivity of the metal increases.

Superconductivity

If in certain materials the temperature drops low enough, the resistance to electron flow ceases completely and electrons, once started on their journey, continue to move indefinitely provided the temperature is kept sufficiently low. The condition of zero resistance is called superconductivity. It occurs in metals such as tin, lead, aluminum, and niobium [7] at a few degrees above absolute zero (−273°C or −460°F).

Electricity, therefore, is simply the movement of electrons or other charged particles. These particles are among the smallest components of matter and yet the way in which they move and interact has a great influence on every aspect of life.

KEY

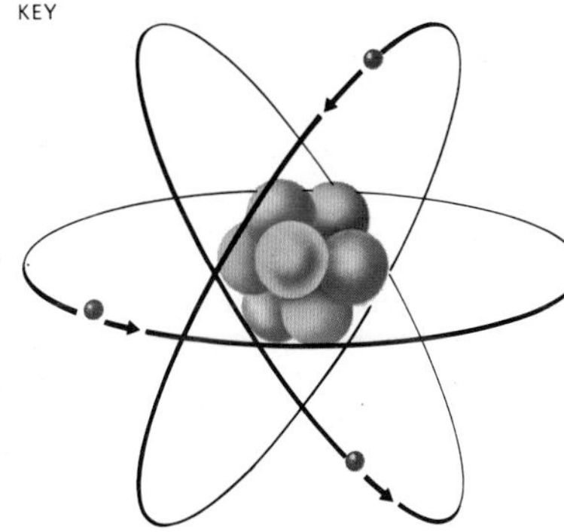

The electron is the basic unit of electricity; it is also a fundamental particle found in all kinds of atoms. In this simple model of an atom of the metallic element lithium, three electrons (red) can be seen circling the central nucleus. Larger particles called protons (blue) and neutrons (grey) make up the nucleus. Each electron carries a negative electric charge and each proton carries a positive one, so that the three electron charges are exactly balanced by the three proton charges, making the whole atom electrically neutral. In a conductor—ie, most metals—an external electromotive force (voltage) causes electrons to "drift" from atom to atom, and it is this flow of electrons that constitutes an electric current. Electron movement occurs because in a conductor the outermost electron is not tightly bound to its nucleus. In a nonconductor, or insulator, the electrons are too tightly bound to leave the nucleus easily and so such substances do not conduct electricity. In some situations atoms can lose or gain one or more electrons and become permanently charged. Such charged atoms, called ions, can also act as current carriers.

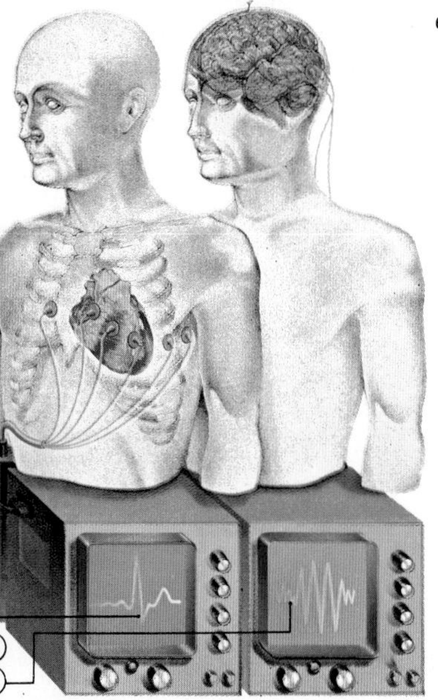

1
2

5 The beating heart generates tiny electrical currents that, after being suitably amplified, can be displayed on a cathode ray tube. These current shapes can be recorded permanently on paper, in which form they are called electrocardiograms for the heart [1] and electroencephalograms [2] for the brain. Existing or potential malfunction of both these vital organs can be diagnosed with their aid.

6

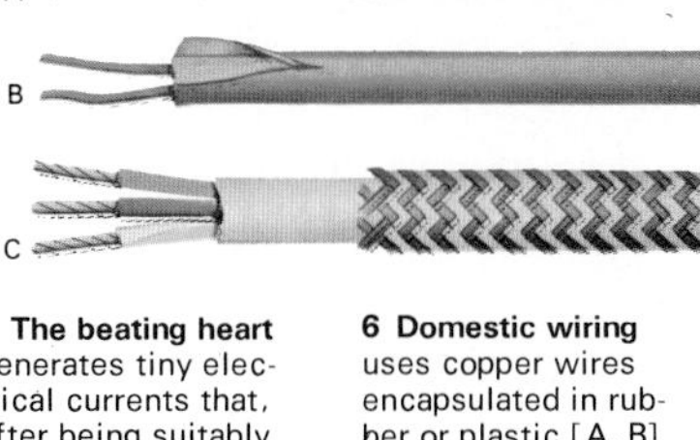

A
B
C

6 Domestic wiring uses copper wires encapsulated in rubber or plastic [A, B]. In fireproof wiring [C], the wires are embedded in a nonflammable powder surrounded by a copper tube.

7

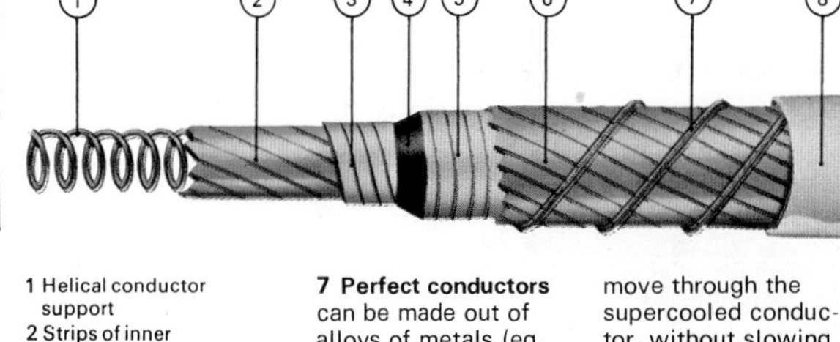

1
2
3
4
5
6
7
8

1 Helical conductor support
2 Strips of inner conductor
3 Inner conductor screen
4 Lapped tape dielectric
5 Outer conductor screen
6 Strips of outer conductor
7 Helical skid wires
8 Helium pipe

7 Perfect conductors can be made out of alloys of metals (eg, tin, lead and niobium) at temperatures close to absolute zero (−273°C). Once electrons become detached from their parent atoms they move through the supercooled conductor, without slowing down or coming to rest, for infinitely long periods. At such low temperatures, the atoms in the metal vibrate only slightly.

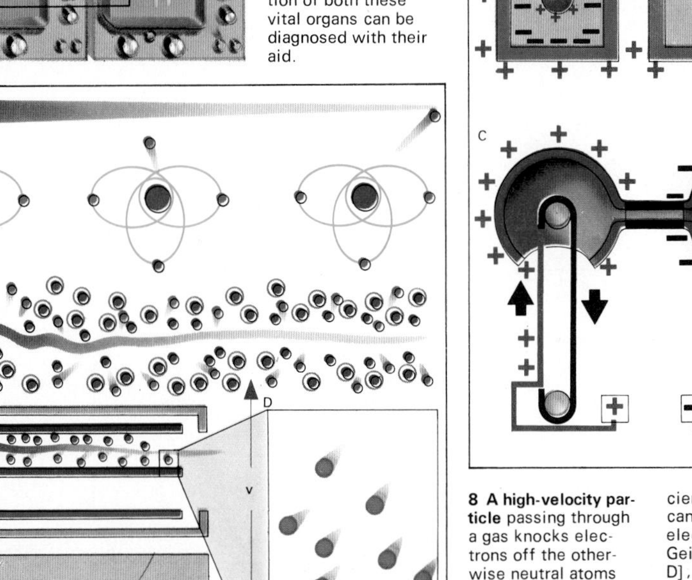

A
B
C
D
E
V
Current per particle
0
400
800
1200
1600
Voltage V

8 A high-velocity particle passing through a gas knocks electrons off the otherwise neutral atoms [A]. As it sweeps through the gas, it leaves behind a stream of free electrons [B], shown here in blue. If these break free with sufficient energy, they can knock other electrons out. In a Geiger counter [C, D], radioactive particles enter the chamber where they are accelerated to produce more free electrons. These are attracted to the positive plate and are led from there to drive a meter or earphones. The current flow depends on the voltage V between the plates [E]. The meter reading or frequency of clicks in the Geiger counter indicates the amount of radioactivity of the source.

9

A

B

C

1

2

3

9 Extremely high voltages can be produced with the Van de Graaff generator [B]. If a body having an excess of positive ions is placed inside a container, the inside acquires electrons [A] and the outside an equal number of positive ions. If the charged body touches the inside all the free electrons flow into it, thus making it neutral. The outside of the container still retains its positive ions. In the Van de Graaff generator, positive ions are sprayed from a suitable source [1] onto an endless conveyor belt, which carries them inside a metal sphere. The belt connects to the inside wall through a conductor in the form of a comb [2], thus permitting an electron flow to the belt. This causes positive ions to form on the sphere's outside wall [3]. The effect may be enhanced by using two generators connected as in [C]. Potentials of millions of volts can be obtained.

What is an electric current?

Electricity flowing along a wire is known as an electric current. The wire is the conductor. When an electric lamp is connected across a battery and switched on, current flows along a wire from one terminal of the battery to the lamp through its filament, making it glow white hot, and back along a second wire to the other battery terminal. If the switch is opened, the circuit is broken and the lamp is extinguished.

Movement of electrons

The current carriers in most circuits are electrons from the metal making up the conductors. In all conductors there is always a random movement of electrons (minute charged particles), even when no current flows. The electrons may be relatively free to move or more tightly bound. Good conductors have freer electrons and hence more electron movement than do bad conductors, or insulators, in which most of the electrons are too tightly bound to their parent atoms to move easily. Sometimes, through natural or contrived processes, there can be a net movement of electrons in a specific direction. This concerted flow is the electric current and it is measured in amperes, generally given by the abbreviation A. Other current carriers include ions (charged atoms or molecular fragments) in gases and solutions, and "holes" (a deficiency in electrons in some types of semiconductors; the holes behave as positively-charged carriers).

A force must be applied to upset the random character of electron motion in a conductor. In nature this can be derived from a number of sources such as sunlight, magnetic action, or chemical activity. Some of these have been exploited to generate electric current. Two common devices designed for this purpose are the generator [9], which utilizes magnetic effects, and the cell (sometimes called a battery) [6], which depends on chemical action. Both force electrons to move in one direction in a circuit by virtue of the electromotive force (emf) they generate. The emf is measured in volts, using a voltmeter.

The voltage of an emf and current flow are related in a way similar to that of water pressure and water flow. In a household, all the pipes are full of water at a certain pressure. But there is no movement until a tap is opened, allowing water to run. An electrical circuit may be connected to a source of emf without causing any specific electron flow (current) until a path is provided through which the electrons can move. This may be a light bulb [Key] or a vacuum cleaner; an electric switch is like a tap that turns on the current.

Relationship between voltage and current

As the voltage in an operating circuit increases, so does the current; however, an electrical circuit is made up of a number of different parts. There is normally a switch, conductors, and the appliance. All these taken together have a resistance to current flow, which is constant (provided the temperature remains the same) for that particular group of components. Therefore, although the same voltage may be applied to a light bulb and an electric iron, the actual current flow is different in each, because each has a different resistance. So it is not only the

CONNECTIONS

See also
1530 What is electricity
1534 Magnets and magnetism
1536 Electromagnetism
1548 Basic electronic p ciples
1546 Semiconductors
1540 Transformers, mot and generators
1566 Electrochemistry

1 When two metals with different numbers of free electrons are joined, the electrons redistribute themselves equally on both sides of the junction [A]. Joining the other ends of the metals stops this action because electrons cannot move two ways at once [B]. A temperature difference between the junctions can upset this [C], and electrons will start moving in one direction. An arrangement of many junctions forms an "electrical" thermometer [D]. This also occurs at junctions between two kinds of semiconductors, known as *n*-type and *p*-type. Current flows from the hot to the cold end of *n*-type [E] and opposite in *p*-type [F].

2 A circuit breaker can be used either in conjunction with, or in place of, a fuse to interrupt dangerously high currents. When too large a current flows through the coil [1], a magnetic field is produced that activates the catch [2], causing the spring-loaded contact [3] to rise. The current is interrupted, protecting the circuit of which the breaker is a part. No further current can flow until the circuit breaker is closed again, which is achieved by pressing the reset button [4]. To test the circuit breaker, or to operate it manually, a push button [5] is pressed to move the contact.

3 A gas discharge lamp gets its light from energy changes in gas atoms. A positive and negative electrode (anode and cathode) at opposite ends of a gas-filled glass tube [A] attract electrons and positive ions. Reducing the pressure [B] speeds this up. As ions hit the cathode [C] they dislodge electrons that speed toward the anode, colliding with gas atoms on the way. The atoms absorb the energy of collision for a moment, then release it in the form of light [D].

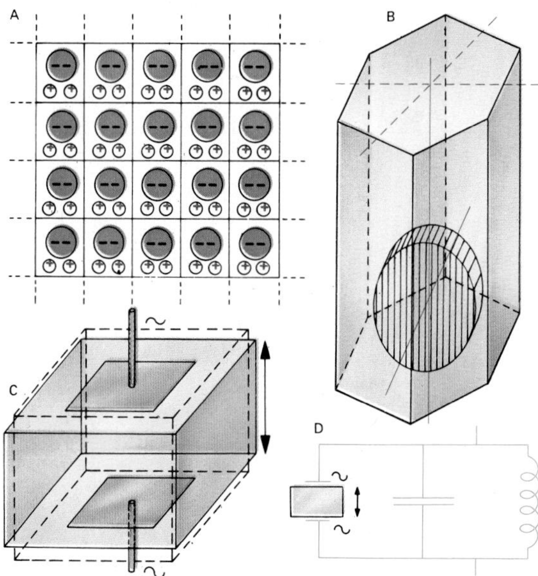
A
B
C
D

4 Quartz and sapphire are among certain crystals formed of cells in a delicate state of electrical equilibrium [A]. Subjecting the crystal to a varying voltage disturbs this balance and causes the crystal to vibrate and emit sound or ultrasonic waves, generally at a specific angle to the direction of applied voltage [B]. Conversely, when it is mechanically vibrated such a crystal generates a voltage. This effect—which is known as piezoelectricity—is the basis of a phonograph pickup [C] and crystal microphones. In the pickup, rapid vibrations of the stylus while it is running in the record's groove vibrate a piezoelectric crystal and generate a tiny electric current. Conversely, in a crystal microphone sound waves vibrate a diaphragm coupled to a crystal, generating current. Most crystals respond strongly to only one frequency, depending on their dimensions. This property is useful because it can "hold" radio transmitter circuits at a certain fixed frequency [D]. Accurately vibrating quartz crystals can keep nearly perfect time. They are used in quartz clocks and watches, which are accurate to within a few seconds over a period of several years.

magnitude of the voltage that determines how much current flows through a particular piece of equipment, it is also the resistance of that equipment and the conductors. This property of electrical resistance is measured in ohms (Ω). For any conductor, or system of conductors and equipment, the relationship between voltage, current, and resistance is given by the formula: voltage ÷ current = resistance. This is the mathematical expression of Ohm's law, named after Georg Ohm (1787–1854), who was the first person to specify the interdependence of these three factors in a precise way.

The resistance of electrical conductors depends on their dimensions and on their composition. As the cross-sectional area increases, the resistance falls; but as the length increases, the resistance rises. A long, thin conductor therefore has more resistance than a short, thick one with the same volume of material. Silver has less resistance than copper, whereas aluminum and iron have more.

According to a convention adopted before the nature of electricity was properly understood, a direct current (that is, current from a battery or generator) is assumed to flow from a positive point to a negative one. As it happens, electrons move from negative to positive, so that electron movement is opposite to that of the assumed current flow.

Effects of current flows

Three phenomena that typically occur when a current flows (and by which it can be detected) are heating, magnetic, and chemical effects. Its heating effect is used to provide warmth in electric heaters, stoves, kitchen appliances, and industrial furnaces. Such heating can also be unwanted. Large cables carrying thousands of amperes have to be cooled to prevent the current-generated heat from melting the insulation or even the wires themselves.

The chemical effect of current is used in electroplating and in energy storage, particularly in cells, the most familiar of which is the lead-acid battery [7]. The magnetic effect is used in motors [8], electromagnets, and many other devices.

KEY

Heat generated by the passage of electric current is the source of light in a so-called "filament" or "incandescent" lamp. Because it is enclosed in a vacuum, or inert gas [1], the filament [2] cannot oxidize when the current passes through, causing it to become hot. It is made of a tungsten alloy, combining mechanical and thermal strength. Though it is extremely thin, it glows white hot when enough current passes through it. It is supported on two glass columns [3] through which the connecting wires pass. The whole assembly is enclosed in a thin glass envelope [4]. Only about two percent of the electrical energy is converted into light.

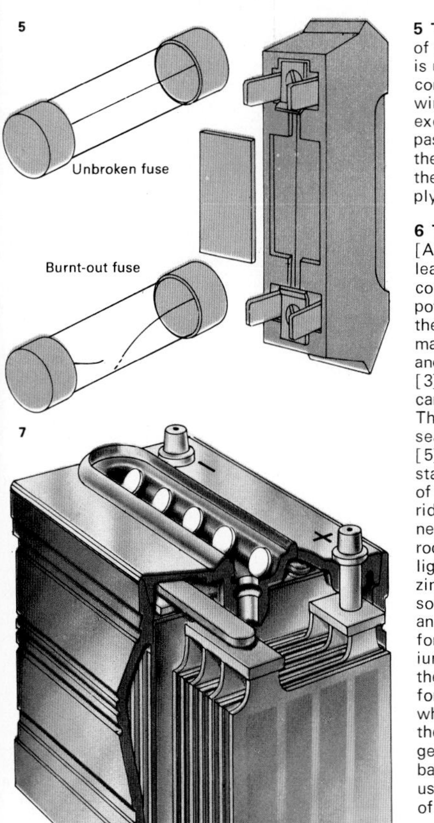
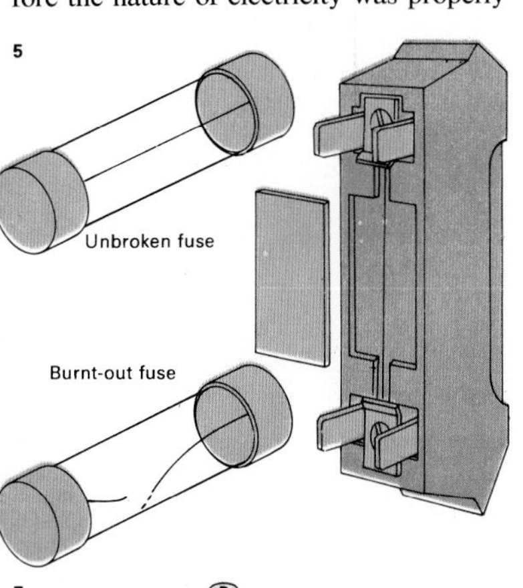
5
Unbroken fuse
Burnt-out fuse
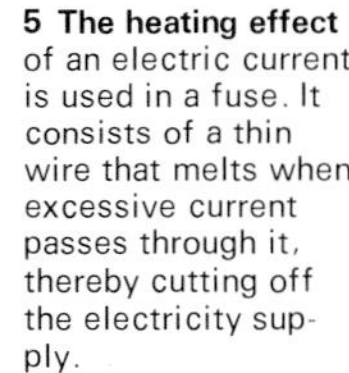

5 The heating effect of an electric current is used in a fuse. It consists of a thin wire that melts when excessive current passes through it, thereby cutting off the electricity supply.

6 The Léclanché cell [A] consists of a leakproof jacket [1] containing a porous pot [2] in which there is a paste of manganese dioxide and carbon granules [3] surrounding a carbon rod [4]. The top can be sealed with pitch [5]. A zinc rod [6] stands in a solution of ammonium chloride [7], and is connected to the carbon rod via a circuit and a light bulb [8]. The zinc dissolves in the solution, setting up an electromotive force. The ammonium ions migrate to the carbon anode and form ammonia, which dissolves in the water, and hydrogen ions. Flashlight batteries [B and C] use wet paste cells of the same type.

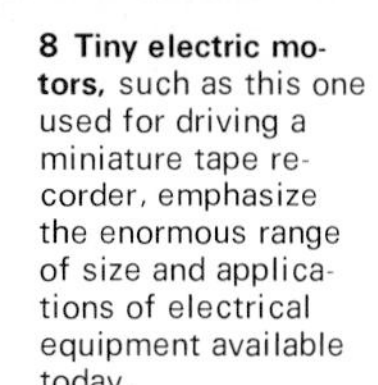

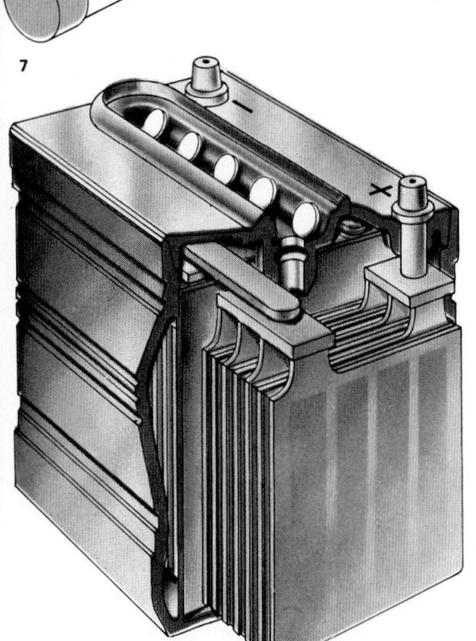

7 A 12-volt battery has six two-volt cells connected in series. The cells have anodes of brown lead oxide and cathodes of porous grey lead immersed in sulfuric acid. An electric current flows if the electrodes are connected through a conductor. When the battery supplies current the acid converts the anode to lead sulfate, thus reducing the strength of the acid. This process is reversed during recharging. Each cell of the battery is made of several anodes and cathodes separated by porous insulators. The six two-volt cells are housed in a hard rubber case and interconnected with lead bars to make it complete.

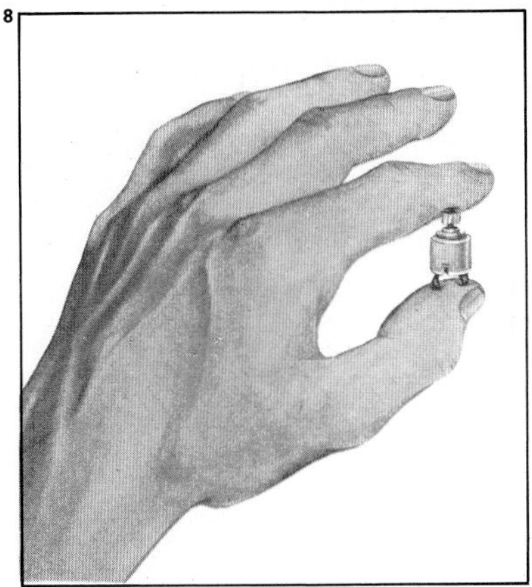

8 Tiny electric motors, such as this one used for driving a miniature tape recorder, emphasize the enormous range of size and applications of electrical equipment available today.

9 The heart of a power station is the generator, which sends electricity over hundreds of miles through a wide network of transmission lines. The generator is the point at which mechanical energy is converted to electrial energy.

Magnets and magnetism

Magnetism and electricity are not two separate phenomena. The error of thinking they are arose from the fact that their interrelation was not appreciated until 1820. In that year the Danish scientist Hans Christian Oersted (1777–1851) showed that an electric current flowing in a wire deflects a compass needle close to it. In fact, whenever an electric current flows, whether in the form of lightning or through a muscle in the body, a magnetic field is created.

Thousands of years before electricity was recognized and used, magnetism was observed and applied—mainly for navigation. Eventually, when science became aware of the atomic nature of matter, it was finally realized that the properties of magnetism and electricity are both bound up in the nature of the physical structure and arrangement of atoms and their electrons.

Whenever magnetism can be detected there must be a current of electricity. Those materials that appear to be magnetic without any external source of electricity depend on electron movements within their atomic structure to provide the electric current; this is the class of magnetism dealt with here.

The property of attracting iron and iron-based materials occurs naturally in a mineral called lodestone [3], itself a chemical compound of iron. It is likely that some form of lodestone was used in the first magnetic compasses that the Chinese are thought to have made [1]. It is relatively easy to transfer magnetic properties between various materials.

Permanent magnets

Iron-attracting materials form a class of so-called permanent magnets, although they may retain their magnetic properties for only a limited time. In the form of a bar, a permanent magnet experiences a force caused by the Earth's magnetism such that, if it were free to move, one end would point roughly in the direction of the Earth's North Pole and the other to the South. The two ends [2] are named the north-seeking (or north) and south-seeking (or south) poles.

Unlike magnetic poles attract each other. A magnet that attracts other material does so by first turning the material into a weak magnet. Like poles repel each other (although this is not as obvious as attraction) because whenever an iron or steel object comes within the influence of a magnet, and itself becomes a magnet, it acquires the opposite polarity. As a result it is automatically attracted. But when two identical magnets of equal strength are positioned with their *like* poles close to each other, each experiences a repulsive force equal to the attractive force that results when the two unlike poles are placed close to each other.

Ferrous (iron-containing) metals are not the only materials that are affected by magnetism. But its effects are easiest to observe in pure metals, such as iron and nickel.

Domain strengths

In general the metals affected by magnetism consist naturally of tiny magnets within the structure of the material, all of them aligned in a random manner. These magnets occupy areas known as domains [6], which can be seen with an electron microscope. In

CONNECTIONS

See also

1536 Electromagnetism
1490 Attraction and repul sion
1538 Using magnets
1540 Transformers, motor and generators
1512 Toward absolute zer
168 The Earth as a magne

NE
E
SE
S
SW
W
NW
N

1 The Chinese were probably the first to realize the directional properties of magnetic materials. They built compasses to help them navigate. By the 12th century magnetic compasses were in the West. This 13th-century one consists of a disk of lodestone (meaning "way stone") engraved with the compass points, mounted on a block of wood and floating in a bowl of water.

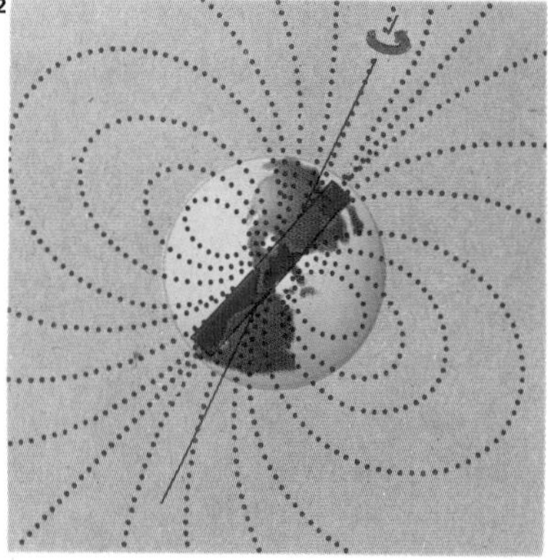

2 A simplified model of the earth's magnetic field may be made by picturing a long bar magnet lying in the center of the Earth. Magnetic materials on the globe's surface tend to align themselves so that their north-seeking poles point to what is called north (actually the south pole of the imaginary magnet) and their south-seeking poles point to the south (north pole of our imaginary magnet).

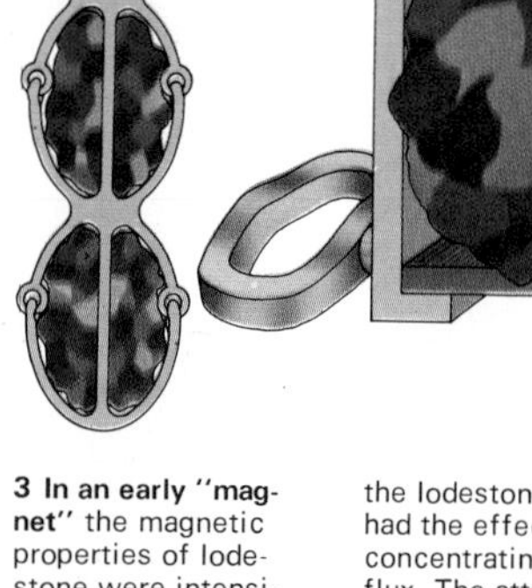

3 In an early "magnet" the magnetic properties of lodestone were intensified by placing lumps of it within a soft iron structure [A]. This provided a path of low resistance to the magnetic flux of the lodestone, and had the effect of concentrating the flux. The attractive force depends on the square of the flux density, so that by directing the flux through a small section the lifting power of the lodestones was increased. Further improvements to lodestones' attractive qualities were gained using iron pole-pieces [B]. The flux lines follow the iron path to produce the two poles.

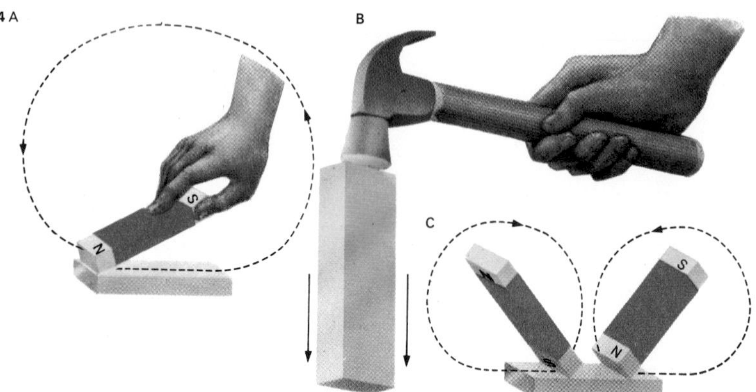

S
N

4 A simple way to magnetize a material such as iron or its alloys is to stroke it with a bar magnet [A], the nearness of which, coupled with its movement, tends to align the magnetic domains within the material. They then reinforce each other rather than keeping their normally random arrangements. The south-seeking ends of the domain try to follow the movement of the original magnet's north pole so that the right-hand side of the new magnet becomes a south pole. The domains lie with south poles to the right, and so their north poles are to the left. Another way to magnetize a bar of suitable material is to hit it [B]. The domains receive a mechanical shock and the earth's field tends to align them with itself. Adapting the technique shown in [A] it is possible to make a bar magnet of suitable material using two magnets [C]. In this case, the right-hand side of the object acquires a south pole and the left-hand side a north pole.

5 William Gilbert (1544–1603), an English physician and philosopher, demonstrated magnetic phenomena to Elizabeth I. His *De Magnete* was the first major work in Europe to describe the characteristics of magnets and magnetism in an organized way. Some of the theory is now known to be incorrect but it was the most important contribution to the subject for many years. He suggested that the Earth itself is a large magnet. The compass was already used as a navigational aid—an important tool for the long commercial and military ventures of the 16th century—but the process by which the compass worked had never been explained. This painting of Gilbert's demonstration is by A. Ackland Hunt.

the unmagnetized material, the result of these millions of tiny magnets, acting in different directions, is to produce a neutral field—one with no magnetic properties whatsoever. It is as if hundreds of children were all tugging at a maypole from different positions; the result of their combined efforts is that the pole does not move.

The process of magnetizing consists of causing all the domains to assist each other by lining them up in the same direction. As they all come into line the total effect is additive and the whole of the material begins to display the properties of a magnet. If all the domains become perfectly aligned then the material has reached the limit of its magnetic capability. As a result, the magnetic strength of a material depends ultimately on its domain strength, and this is determined, in turn, by its atomic structure.

Earth's magnetic field

The magnetic field of the Earth has been accurately measured and charted but it still cannot be adequately explained [2]. In very simple terms, it is as if a single bar magnet lies between the geographic North and South Poles to produce some of the observable effects. But this does not explain the very unusual variations of strength and even the complete and apparently instantaneous reversal of direction of the magnetic poles. Present theory envisions a complicated dynamo interaction between the fluid core of the Earth and the slow cellular currents of molten rock through the mantle.

Both terrestrial magnetism and that exhibited by small pieces of iron can be better understood by considering that lines of magnetic force (often called flux lines) leave the north pole and enter the south. But this is an entirely arbitrary concept, in the same way as lines of latitude and longitude on a map are merely for convenience.

In a bar magnet, lines of flux [Key] are pictured as forming an approximate cylinder stretching in air from one pole to another and enclosing the magnet itself. The flux lines are of the same polarity and thus repel each other. They all start from and end at the same poles, but they each follow unique paths that can never cross.

KEY

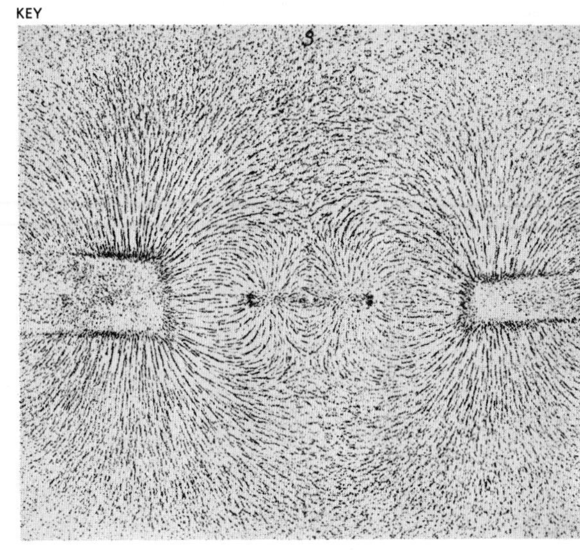

The pattern of iron filings in a magnetic field demonstrates how the lines of magnetic flux are distributed. The lines never cross and they have a mutual repulsive effect.

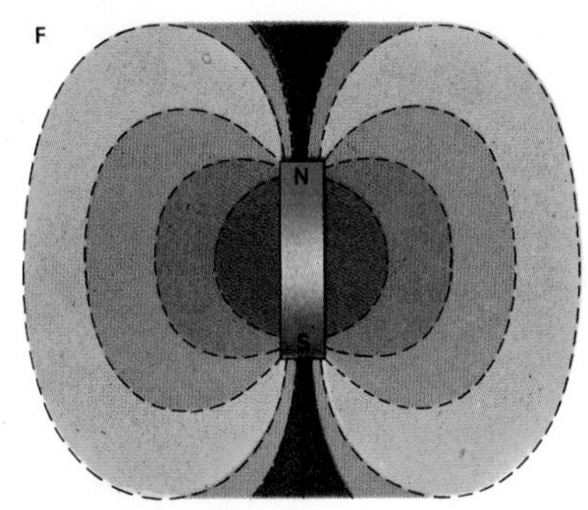
F
N
S

6 The random arrangement of domains in unmagnetized materials [A] becomes highly ordered in a strong external magnetic field [B]. On removing the field the domains do not revert completely but retain a degree of alignment [C]. Domains on each side of any breaks ensure that large bar magnets always split into smaller replicas [D]. Increasing the magnetizing force beyond a certain limit [E] cannot increase alignment, and the material "saturates." Reversing H causes demagnetization. Different materials have similar shaped curves [1 and 2]: Removing H leaves the material partly magnetized [F].

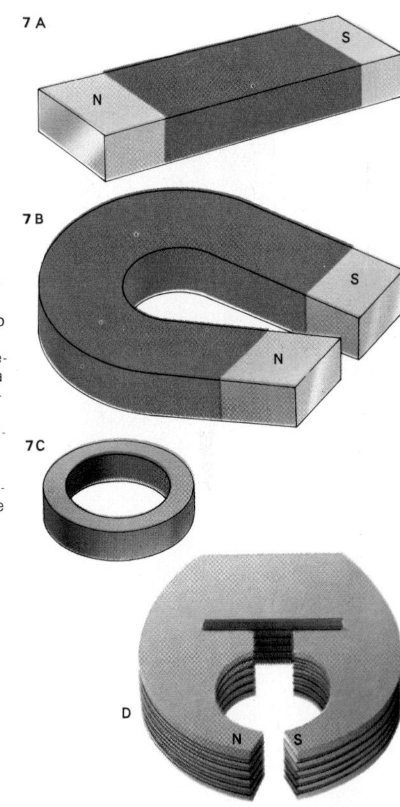
7 A
S
N
7 B
S
N
7C
D
N
S

7 Magnets can be made in almost any form, from the bar [A] to a horseshoe [B], a ring [C], or a shape like that of D, used in an electrical measuring instrument. The polarities are marked N and S.

8 Magnets of complicated shapes for special uses can be made using powdered iron, mixed with a suitable bonding agent and cast into the required form. In granular form the structure is similar to bricks and mortar, the bricks being the particles, the mortar the bonding agent. Each magnet is separated from the next by nonmagnetic material. Thus the whole structure makes a weaker magnet than it would be if made from solid material.

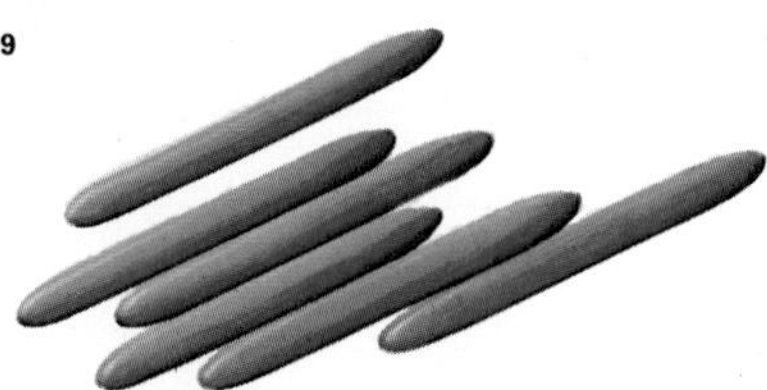

9 Powdered iron can also be bonded as needlelike particles magnetized in such a way that their poles lie at their points. The flux lines tend to run along the axes so that the bonding agent has a limited weakening effect on the magnet.

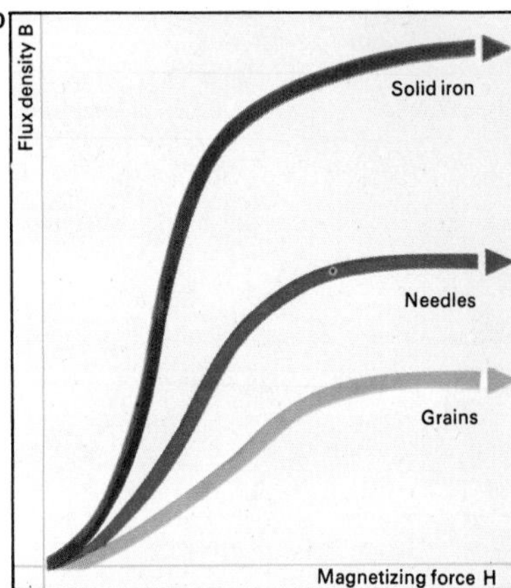
10
Flux density B
Solid iron
Needles
Grains
Magnetizing force H

10 Solid iron is more easily magnetized than any of the forms of powdered iron (such as the grains of iron in illustration 8 or the needles of illustration 9, which are joined with a bonding agent) as the domains form an uninterrupted array.

Electromagnetism

Electromagnetism is the effect by which electrical currents produce magnetic fields. Occasionally the process is unwanted, such as when a current flowing through a piece of equipment or cable on a ship deflects the ship's magnetic compass. Often the effect passes unnoticed because it is very weak. But sometimes electricity is deliberately used to produce magnetic fields of great strength, as in the electromagnets used for lifting scrap iron.

Current flow and magnetic flux

The intensity of a magnetic field is measured in flux lines or webers (Wb). These lines are produced whenever a current flows; and in air there is a simple proportional relationship between electric current flow and magnetic flux. A straight wire carrying a current can be looped to form a single turn. Provided the radius is reasonably small, the effect of forming a loop is to increase the concentration of magnetic flux without having to increase the current.

This concentrating effect can be further intensified by using more turns of wire to form a coil. At the point of maximum flux density—that is, maximum flux lines per unit area—the relationship between electric current A, turns of wire T, and magnetic flux B is such that AT is proportional to B. Additional turns are simply a way of making the same current pass the same way more than once, and 12 amps flowing through three turns has the same magnetic effect as three amps flowing through 12 turns.

Solenoid is the name given to a coil of wire wound to produce a magnetic field. Solenoids may be wound on iron (iron-cored) or on a nonmagnetic support (air-cored). As far as flux is concerned, any nonmagnetic core has the same properties as air, which means that the relationship connecting current, turns, and flux holds good.

The presence of iron influences the magnetic field in two ways. It enhances the magnetic effect of the current, often by a factor of a thousand or more, but it also destroys the simple relationship applying to air-cored coils. Both these effects are a result of the structure of iron.

Microscopic regions called domains in the iron tend to align themselves with the magnetic field produced by the current. The iron provides an easy path for the magnetic flux passing through it. As a result, a given current produces more flux per unit of cross-sectional area—that is, there is a high flux density. When all the domains have been aligned, further increase in current (or in the number of turns of wire in the coil) increases the flux density only negligibly.

Limiting characteristics

An iron-cored solenoid has a vastly stronger magnetic field compared with that of an air-cored one but is limited by the characteristics of iron. Theoretically there is no maximum to the magnetic field produced by an air-cored solenoid. But generally the enormous currents required to make them comparable to iron-cored ones are too expensive and too difficult to produce.

A changing magnetic field can produce a current just as a current can produce a magnetic field. As a magnet moves toward a conductor, the flux lines sweeping past

CONNECTIONS

See also
1534 Magnets and mag netism
1532 What is an electri current?
1540 Transformers, mot and generators
1548 Basic electronic p ciples
1486 The nature of ene
1538 Using magnets

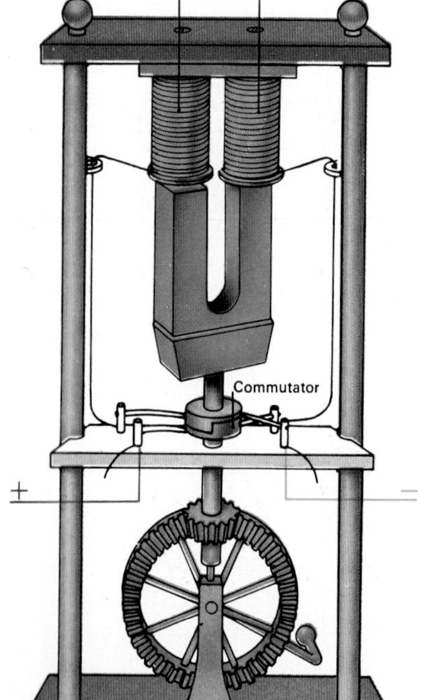

1
Coils
Commutator
+
−

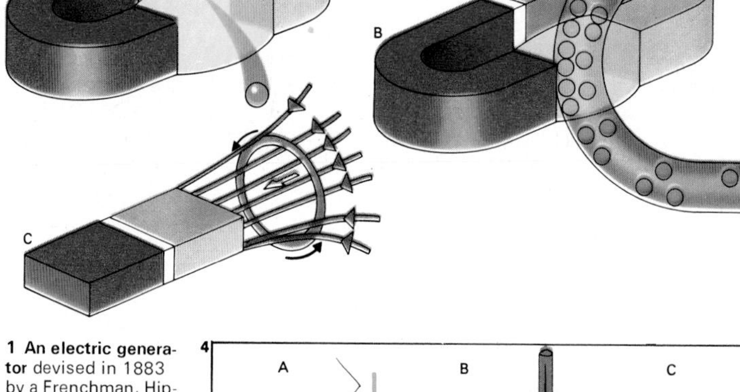

2
A
B
C

2 Pixii's generator is based on the principle that moving electrons [A], having their own magnetic field, are affected by a moving magnet, which attracts or repels them according to the relative polarities: if a path [B] is provided for them, electrons tend to move along it. Electrons will flow in a closed conductor [C] if there is relative movement between it and the magnetic field.

1 An electric generator devised in 1883 by a Frenchman, Hippolyte Pixii, consisted of a horseshoe magnet set on end between two coils. The magnet was rotated through a gear system driven by a hand crank. As the magnet rotated an alternating voltage was induced in the coils. A commutator enabled positive voltage to be picked off one side, and negative off the other, to produce direct current.

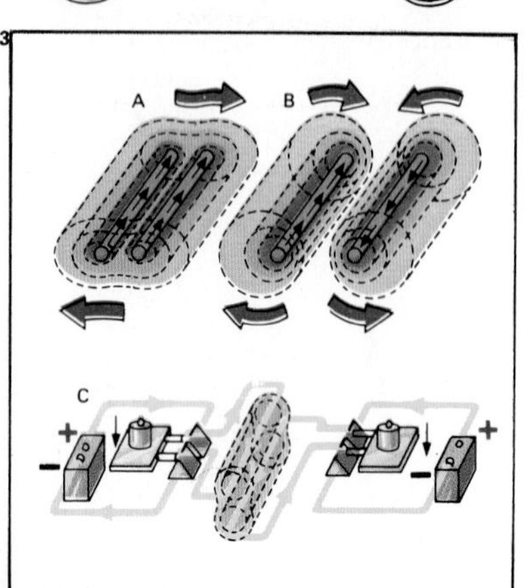

3
A
B
C

3 An electric current carried by a wire sets up a magnetic field around itself. As a result, when parallel wires carry currents in the same direction [A] they attract each other, but when the currents flow in the opposite direction [B] they repel. The ampere balance [C] measures the force of attraction or repulsion between two electric current-bearing conductors. Such forces can be very destructive when the currents are high and the conductors close.

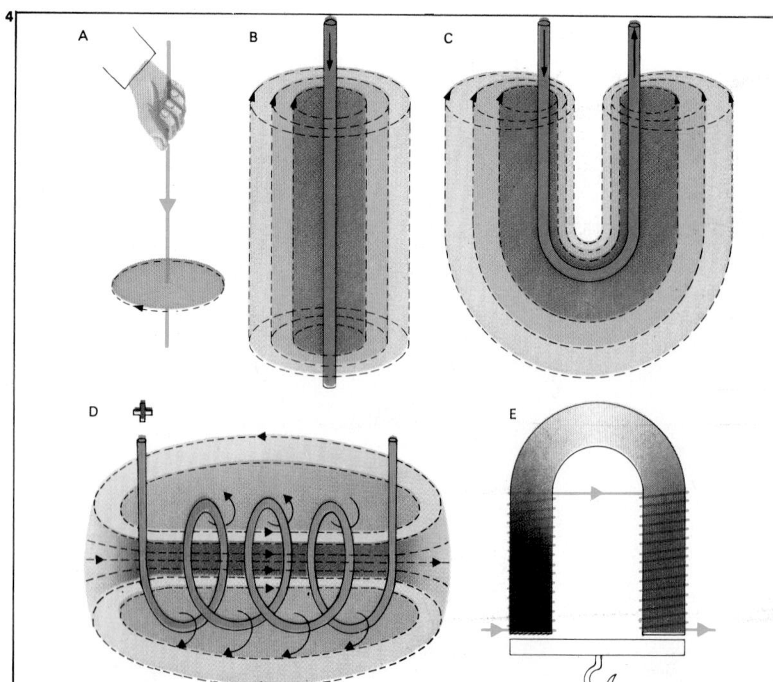

4
A
B
C
D
E

4 An electric current in a conductor produces a magnet field in a plane at right angles to its flow. The direction of the field can be found using the "right-hand rule." Holding the wire in the right hand [A] with the thumb pointing in the direction of the current flow, the curled fingers indicate the field's direction. The field pattern around the wire is symmetrical [B] even if the wire is bent [C]. The magnetic effect is increased by winding the wire into a coil [D]. A powerful electromagnet [E] can be made by winding a coil on an iron core.

cause an electromotive force (voltage) to be induced. The polarity of the induced voltage depends on the polarity and the direction of flux movement. The effect is greater in a coil than in a single wire, and is in proportion to the number of turns of wire in the coil. Similarly, if the coil is iron-cored, the induced voltage is more than in an air-cored coil because the flux changes are larger. In inducing a voltage in this way an essential factor is that there must be relative movement between the flux and the conductor (or coil). If not, flux lines will not move relative to the conductor and no current will flow.

How power is produced

Electric generators produce current using precisely these principles. In their basic form a magnet is rotated between coils. A voltage is induced depending on the strength of the magnet and its speed of rotation (since this determines the rate of flux change). The voltage in a conductor is directly proportional to the rate at which flux sweeps past it. In many generators the magnet is replaced by a solenoid that must be energized or "excited" with current to produce the magnetic field necessary for the generator to function. It is the combination of voltage and current that constitutes the electrical power output from a generator.

Another aspect of the interrelationship between current in a conductor and magnetic flux makes use of the flow of an electric current in a magnetic field to produce physical movement. This is the principle on which motors and some electrical measuring instruments operate, but electrical power must be supplied to cause movement against a mechanical force.

Magnetic fields far stronger than ever before are now created by means of superconductivity, the zero-resistance effect in some metals at temperatures approaching absolute zero. As a result, current can flow without losses or heating, and it is possible to use vast currents in air-cored coils, avoiding the limitations of saturation imposed by iron. These strong magnetic fields open up prospects for electromagnetic levitation and new forms of motors and generators capable of high outputs at reduced costs.

KEY

The "lift" obtainable using magnetism has been applied to make a magnetic levitation train. The train has no wheels, but instead "floats" over a long metallic strip that takes the place of a conventional track, below which a series of electromagnets generate the necessary magnetic field. The electric current can be supplied to these electromagnets in such a way that they behave as a linear motor, so driving the train along the track. Such "maglev" trains are frictionless, pollution-free and virtually silent. This full-scale experimental prototype train, built and successfully tested in West Germany, travels at a speed of 120mph (193kph).

5

5 Electromagnets are often used in scrap-metal yards to lift ferrous metals. This method not only reduces manhandling but also provides a means of separating the iron from other scrap materials.

6

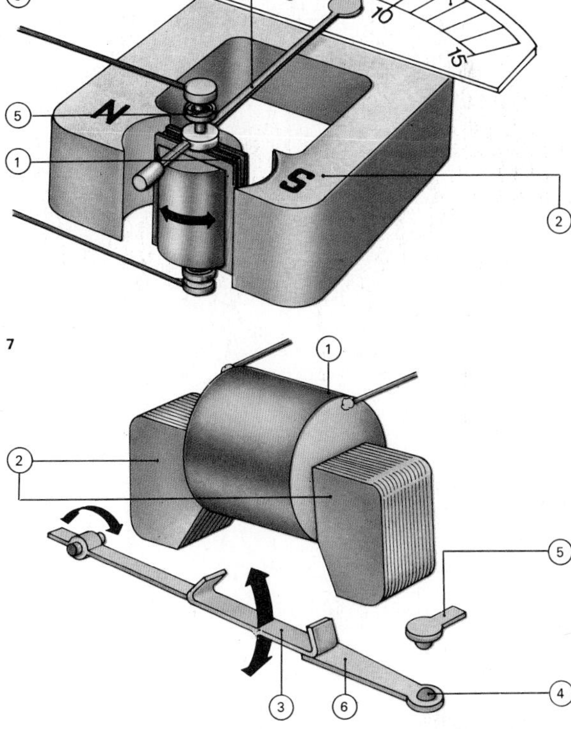
5
10
15
N
S
1
2
3
4
5
7
1
2
3
4
5
6

6 In electrical indicating instruments a coil [1] turns when energized in a magnet's field [2]. The pointer [3] shows the strength of current on the scale [4]. The hairspring [5] returns the pointer.

7 Relays are used to allow a low-power source to switch off a high voltage circuit. When the coil [1] is energized by a small current, magnetic flux appears between the poles of the core [2] attracting the armature [3]. The moving contact [4] then engages the fixed contact [5], closing the high-voltage circuit. When the coil is de-energized, the weight [6] overcomes the weakened field and opens the circuit.

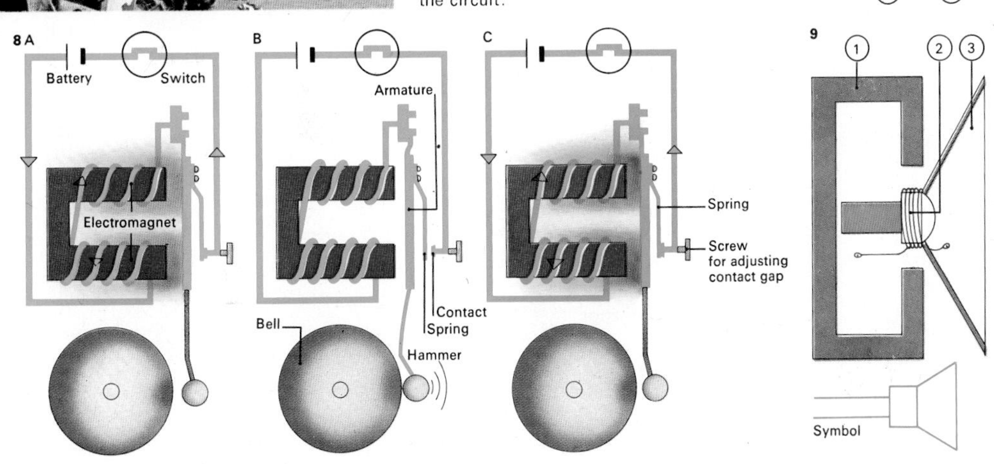
8A
Battery
Switch
Electromagnet
B
Armature
Contact
Spring
Bell
Hammer
C
Spring
Screw
for adjusting
contact gap

8 In an electric bell, the magnetic field of an electromagnet is turned on and off rapidly to make a hammer strike the bell. Pressing the switch [A] allows current from a battery to energize the magnet, pulling over a spring-loaded armature and with it the hammer [B]. This action also breaks the circuit at a point contact and "turns off" the electromagnet. The armature springs back, remakes the circuit [C] and the whole sequence is repeated.

9

1 2 3

Symbol

9 A loudspeaker commonly has a permanent magnet [1] to provide a magnetic field in which a coil [2] attached to a fiber core [3] is held balanced but is free to move backward and forward. A varying electrical current is fed to the coil from the amplifier output, resulting in a varying magnetic flux in the coil. This reacts with the permanent magnet's field, causing the coil and hence the core to move back and forth, producing sound.

Using magnets

The two main types of magnets used in apparatus such as electric bells, motors, generators, speedometers, and the like are permanent magnets and electromagnets. Permanent magnets, chiefly made from iron-based alloys, retain their magnetism all the time. An electromagnet consists of a coil of wire, sometimes wound around a soft iron core, and behaves as a magnet only when an electric current flows in the coil.

The magnetic field

Those processes that generate motion by creating a strong and then a weak magnetic field (as in the electric bell) expend more electrical energy in the electromagnet than is gained from the resulting mechanical motion. But weakening a magnetic field (or alternatively "turning it off") is in fact the basis of many devices with characteristics that would be difficult or expensive to obtain in other ways. In permanent magnets the field cannot be turned off without destroying it. But it can be diverted.

The best example of diversion of the magnetic field is the magnetic chuck [Key]. This is a device for holding ferrous metals tightly on to a work table. The chuck is used almost exclusively in grinding machines because a vise could distort the metal, or not hold it level relative to the grinder.

The chuck comprises a number of small bar magnets embedded on a movable metal plate so that north and south poles are pointing vertically. The metal plate is of a material with low magnetic properties and the poles of the magnets are positioned alternately north-south and slightly separated. A second metal plate is placed above the magnet assembly. This incorporates soft iron pieces that correspond to the position of the magnets fixed in the base plate.

When a workpiece is placed on the upper plate it provides a flux circuit for the embedded magnets through the soft iron pieces of metal and is attracted to them, holding the workpiece in position. The operation of a simple lever allows the lower plate to be moved horizontally in such a way as to bring the magnet poles out of alignment with the pieces of soft iron in the upper plate. This diverts magnetic flux from the workpiece and it goes instead through the metal of the upper plate to link the embedded magnets north to south. The workpiece is then free to move.

Magnets and railroad safety

A system in which permanent and electromagnets complement each other for reasons of safety is commonly used in railroads. A strong permament magnet is attached close to the track at a set distance from the signals. As the train passes over the magnet it causes a pivoted permanent bar magnet in the cab to swing (like a seesaw) through a small angle and rest in this new position. The bar magnet's movement closes a switch to bring an alarm into action. A few seconds later the cab passes over an electromagnet connected to the signals. If they are set at "clear" the electromagnet is energized and the pivoted magnet in the cab is repelled so that it returns to its position, turning off the alarm.

But if the signals are set at "stop" or "caution," the electromagnet is not energized and, after a short preset delay, the

CONNECTIONS

See also

1534 Magnets and magnetism
1490 Attraction and repulsion
1536 Electromagnetism
1798 Sound recording and reproducing
1800 Video recording and reproduction

1 Magnetic mines took a great toll of merchant ships during World War II. Placed in busy shipping lanes, the strong magnets in the devices were attracted to metal-hulled ships and on impact they exploded. Countermeasures, such as electrical cables to reduce the ships' magnetic fields, were devised, and are sometimes used in case there are still mines about in ocean waters.

2 A system of permanent magnets attached to movable metal plates can be suspended above a fixed set of magnets. Provided there is a guide rail to stop sideways motion, it can be used to move heavy loads around a factory or within an area where it is convenient to build a magnetic "track." The advantage over comparable methods such as rail systems is the absence of friction and moving parts.

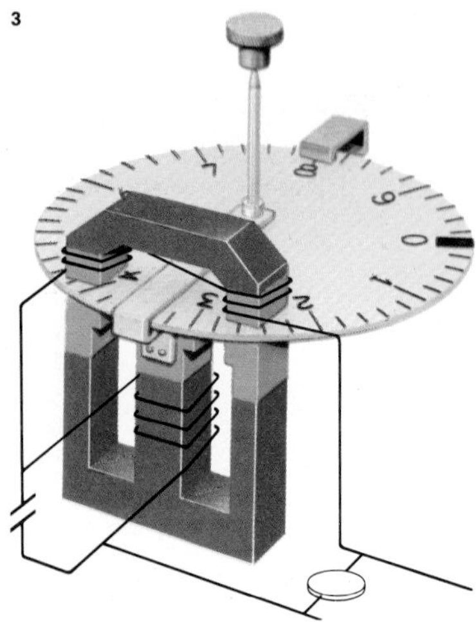

3 A domestic electric meter—a watt-hour meter for recording the amount of electricity consumed—makes use of electromagnets. When current is being used, it flows in coils that energize magnets and make a disk rotate. The disk is coupled to a kilowatt-hour counter.

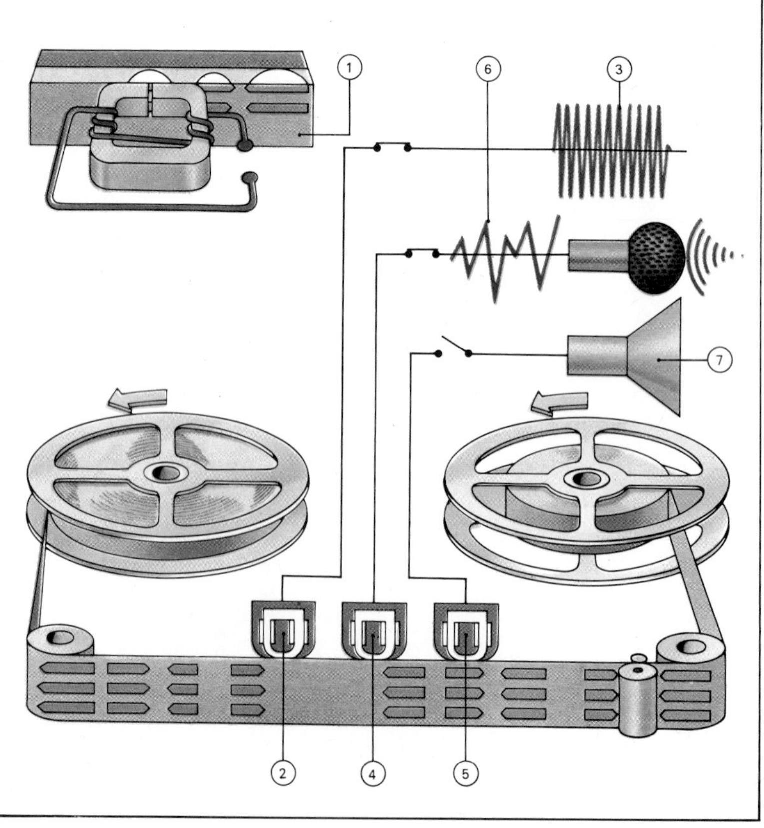

1
6
3
7
2
4
5

4 Magnetic metal oxide development has led to a revolution in the sound-recording industry. Metal oxides in powder form are bonded to flexible plastic tape [1], forming a moving surface on which magnetic patterns can be imposed corresponding to sound, visual, or other signals. These tapes are used in machines that consist of an erase head [2] using high-frequency input [3] to demagnetize the tape as it is driven past, and record [4] and replay [5] heads. These either magnetize the tape according to the signal input [6] or reconvert the previously imposed magnetic patterns into the signals that formed them (ie play back) [7]. Stereo or twin-track recording combines two record/replay heads in one. The erase head is taken out of circuit when playing back and, to prevent accidental erasure, most tape recorders have a built-in fail-safe arrangement.

brakes are automatically applied if the driver fails to apply them. The brake-time circuit (like the audible alarm) is energized from the moment the pivoted magnet moves. If this magnet is returned to its original position (within the preset time) the brakes are not applied.

Meters and medicine

A phenomenon associated with magnetic fields is the eddy current. When there is relative motion between an electrical conductor (not necessarily one with magnetic properties) and a magnetic field, currents called eddy currents are induced. These, in turn, produce another magnetic field of opposite polarity. There is a tendency, because of the attraction between the opposite fields, for the conductor and original magnetic field to move together while the relative motion exists.

This principle is the basis of the car speedometer. A permanent magnet within the instrument housing rotates at a speed related to the crankshaft speed. It turns within a specially shaped aluminum disk which itself can rotate, but only through about 270° because of the restraint of a spring. As the magnet rotates, eddy currents are induced in the disk, which tries to follow the magnet. The strength of these currents is proportional to the speed of rotation and therefore the disk moves according to the speed of the car. A pointer attached to the disk moves over a calibrated scale.

An electric meter [3] works on similar principles. Current used by the consumer passes through an electromagnet, which induces eddy currents in an aluminum disk. In this case the disk can rotate freely through 360° and its movement is coupled to a gear train that drives the indicating dials.

Medical science also benefits from the use of powerful magnets. Experimenters have inserted magnetically guided "pills" within the body. The "pill," which may be swallowed or inserted in a vein, is a minute radio, capable of transmitting information about such factors as temperature and salinity. It may be guided to particular organs by a magnet operating outside the body, thus aiding doctors in diagnosis.

KEY

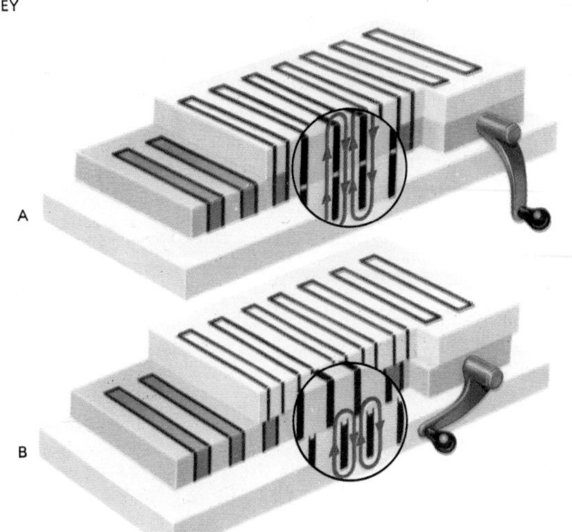
A
B

A permanent magnet cannot be switched off as electric currents can. Instead, its magnetic flux can be diverted. A magnetic chuck holds a workpiece in position on a grinding machine. Flux enters the workpiece and holds it in place [A]. When the flux is cut, the workpiece is released from the chuck.

5

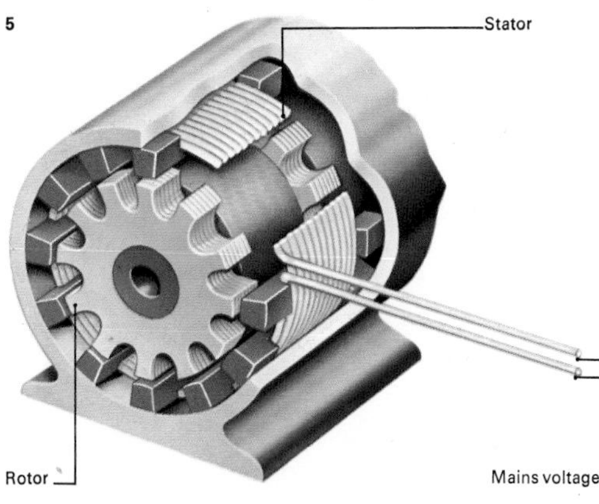
Stator
Rotor
Mains voltage

5 Magnetically polarized rotors are essential elements of modern timing devices and similar equipment. Because the current frequency is fixed precisely at the power station, motors whose rotation is tied to this frequency have a highly accurate speed. Using magnets in the rotor (often permanent for reliability) ensures that once it is "locked" to the stator frequency, the rotor follows the speed exactly. The rotor is made from thin sheets of silicon steel cemented to form a cylinder. The ridges are then magnetized to form poles.

6

6 Electric meters are often difficult to read. The cyclometer type shown here suffers from the disadvantage that the digits representing the high numbers (on the left) rotate slowly and give ambiguous readings. One version has a small magnet attached to every wheel behind the figure 7. A bar magnet is fixed over the wheels as shown. When the wheels move from 9 to 0 magnetic attraction ensures a quick changeover of figures. Only the highest number wheel is excluded from this arrangement because when it changes to 0 all the other figures will change to 0.

7

8

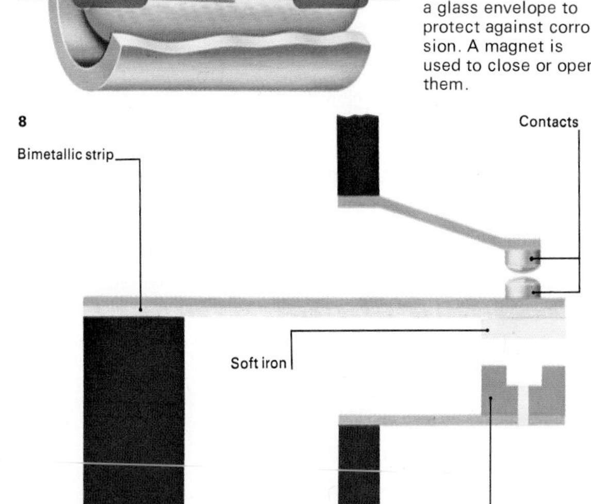
Bimetallic strip
Contacts
Soft iron
Magnet

7 The reed switch, used as a safety switch and in electronic counters, has contacts enclosed in a glass envelope to protect against corrosion. A magnet is used to close or open them.

8 A thermostat often incorporates a bimetallic strip, which moves to open or close a circuit according to the temperature. One way of ensuring a quick "on" or "off" is to use a fixed magnet and a soft iron pellet (armature) attached to the moving contact arm. As the bimetal starts to curve it is either attracted swiftly to the magnet or else is released suddenly giving a fast "snap" action to the thermostat.

9

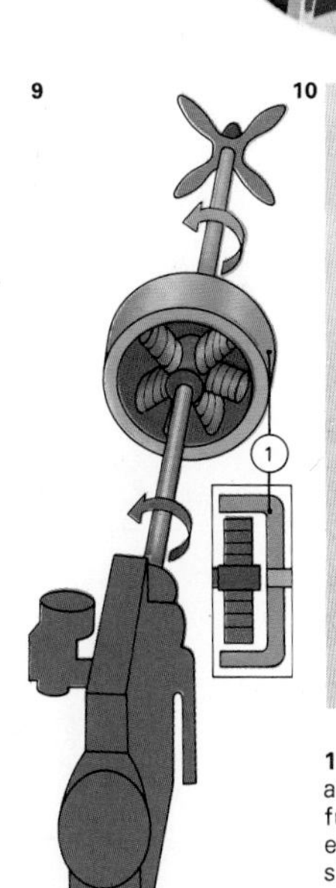
1

9 The electromagnetic clutch, often used on ships, has a soft iron cup [1] attached to the propeller shaft and electromagnets on the engine shaft. Energizing the coils produces a strong field and transmits the drive motion.

10

10 Magnetic catches are used on doors of furniture and refrigerators to hold them shut. A common type on a refrigerator uses "magnetic rubber" (rubber with ferrous particles magnetized to form a convenient pole pattern) on the door edge. As the door touches the frame the rubber pulls the door forcefully into place giving a strong, effective, and flexible seal between the door and frame.

Transformers, motors, and generators

One of the most essential and efficient of electrical machines, the transformer, has wide uses in the supply of electricity. It is used in power stations and at substations—in the former to boost voltages for transmission over power lines and in the latter to reduce voltages to levels suitable for industrial or domestic use. Transformers are also used in many electrical appliances—such as radios, television sets, and battery chargers—wherever alternating voltages different from the supply are required.

Motors and generators

A transformer, with its two main elements, magnetic and electrical, linked by a laminated soft iron core [Key, 1] has no moving parts and is up to 98 per cent efficient. This is not true of electric motors and generators (seldom more than 75 percent efficient), both of which have rotating elements.

Motors and generators are basically the same in construction, although their functions are different. Motors are supplied with electrical power to provide mechanical power; generators are supplied with mechanical power to give electrical power. But it is important to remember that they are so similar that some machines can act as motors or as generators, depending upon whether they are supplied with electricity or mechanical power.

The magnetic field

The two most essential elements of each of these machines are the field and the armature. The field is a magnetic field, which may be derived from permanent magnets or electromagnets. The former are cheaper but the latter are more convenient because, with an electrically energized field it is easy to increase or decrease their strength. It is, however, a convenience gained only at the expense of having to provide the coils for the electromagnets that form the field (field "windings") and to do all the work that goes into insulating and installing them.

How the armature works

The armature is also a winding but is arranged differently from the field. It is essentially a conductor (or conductors) arranged to cut the field's magnetic lines of flux at right angles. The armature conductors may be wound onto a cylinder that rotates in a field. Or they may be fixed to the inner walls of a cylinder, within which the field windings rotate. The static part of the machine is called the stator and the revolving part the rotor. Both the field windings and the armature may be on either the stator or the rotor.

By a basic principle of electromagnetism, a voltage is induced in a conductor that moves in a magnetic field and a conductor in a magnetic field experiences a force and tends to move when a current flows in it.

To make the best use of this basic effect, the magnetic and electrical elements in electrical machines (the field and the armature) have to interact in the most efficient manner possible. The armature is generally wound on a soft iron core so as to be in the path of the maximum number of magnetic flux lines. The field coils are also wound on soft iron cores, to produce the maximum flux for

CONNECTIONS

See also
1536 Electromagnetism
1534 Magnets and magnetism
1532 What is an electric current?
1648 Electricity generation and distribution

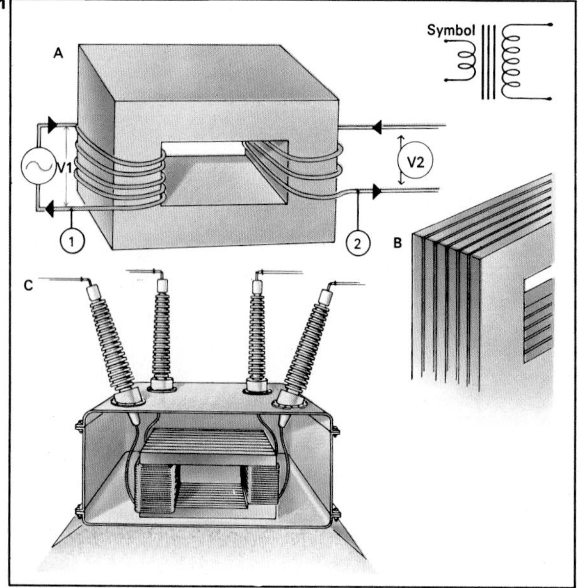

1
A
Symbol
V1
V2
1
2
B
C

1 In the transformer [A], the input, or primary, current [1] causes lines of magnetic flux to form in the iron core, linking it to the output or secondary [2]. As the supply alternates in time the flux lines collapse and reform in the same pattern, but with different polarities. They cut the output coil, inducing a voltage. The ratio of input to output voltage (V1 to V2) is the ratio of turns on the input and output coils. The iron core is laminated [B] to reduce eddy currents. The high-voltage transformer [C] has its terminals insulated to prevent "flashover."

2 Electricity can be generated by a magnet, an electrical conductor, and relative movement. Moving the magnet [1] causes the flux lines surrounding it to cut the conductor of the coil [2] and induce a voltage in it—coinciding with the movement; the faster the movement the higher the voltage induced. Opposite movements produce opposite voltages—any current in a circuit between the coil ends flows first one way then the other as the magnet is moved in and out. These are alternating currents and the generators producing these electrical currents are called alternators.

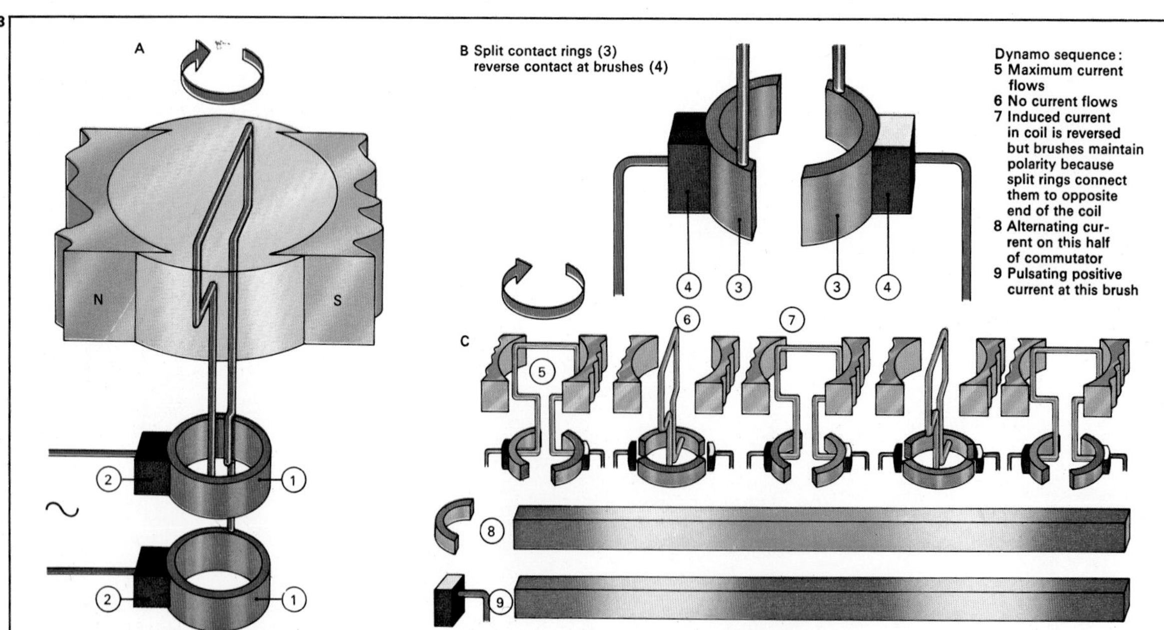

3
A
N
S
B Split contact rings (3) reverse contact at brushes (4)
Dynamo sequence:
5 Maximum current flows
6 No current flows
7 Induced current in coil is reversed but brushes maintain polarity because split rings connect them to opposite end of the coil
8 Alternating current on this half of commutator
9 Pulsating positive current at this brush
C

3 Electricity is generated mechanically when a coil is rotated in a magnetic field [A]. An AC voltage is induced in the coil and is connected to the external circuit by contact rings [1] and carbon brushes [2]. A current flows when a circuit is made between the brushes. To produce direct current the generator is modified [B]; the contact rings are split [3] and the halves insulated from each other. A fixed pair of brushes [4] contacts the ring segments in turn. The arrangements of split segments is called a commutator; the sequence [5-9] describes how it works in a cycle dynamo.

a given current. The soft iron for both the field and the armature is laminated—that is, made up of thin slices [1]. This is to prevent the currents from circulating and "eddying" in the iron itself, and generating wasted heat and opposing magnetic fields as a result of the magnetic flux in the machine.

The armature must be supplied with current (through rotating contacts) if it is the rotor in a motor and there must be a way of taking current from it if it is in a generator. The same applies to the field if it is electrically energized. The rotating contact arrangement can be either a set of slip rings or a commutator [3]. These rotate under fixed contacts, called brushes, made of carbon and held in place by springs. From time to time the brushes have to be replaced when the carbon wears away.

Varying the field

The armature and field of a motor are supplied with current, and, by using a resistor in the field circuit, it is possible to vary the field strength. Weakening it causes the motor to revolve faster—provided the armature current is constant—but with less torque (turning force), and vice versa [4]. In a generator driven at constant speed, strengthening the field increases the voltage output; weakening the field decreases the voltage output.

Induction motors

The motors and generators already described are generally suitable either for AC (alternating current) or for DC (direct current) supplies. There is a group of machines, however, that is suitable only for alternating current supplies. These are induction motors in which the armature is the rotor and can be wound or made in the form of a "squirrel cage" [5]. It obtains its current from the constantly changing flux gained from the field, which is energized by alternating current. No slip rings are necessary and maintenance is easier.

Some induction motors have a wound rotor, and slip rings may be used. The purpose of the rings is not to supply current to the armature but to alter its characteristics with the use of external resistances.

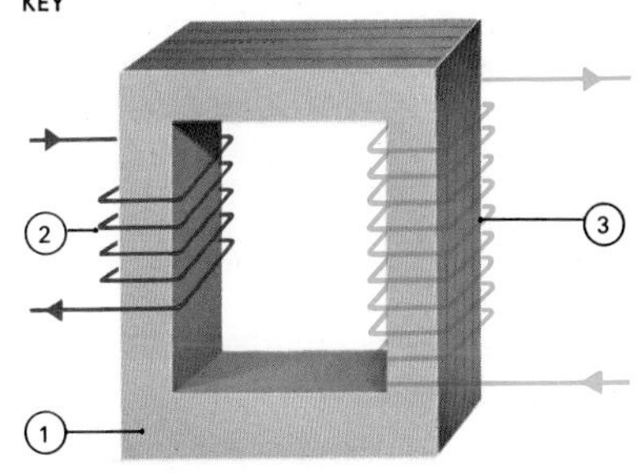
KEY
2
3
1

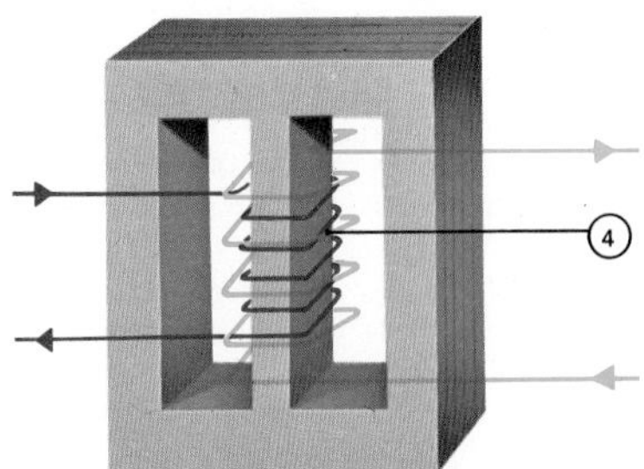
4

The transformer, a simple and efficient means of raising or lowering AC voltage, usually consists of three basic elements: an iron core [1] which provides a magnetic link between the primary, or input [2], coil and the secondary output coil [3]. The turns ratio between the input and the output determines the ratio between AC voltages "transformed;" fewer turns on the output side give a proportional decrease in voltage and vice versa, transforming the flow of current. The core may take various shapes; sometimes more than two coils are used and sometimes the two coils are wound on each other [4].

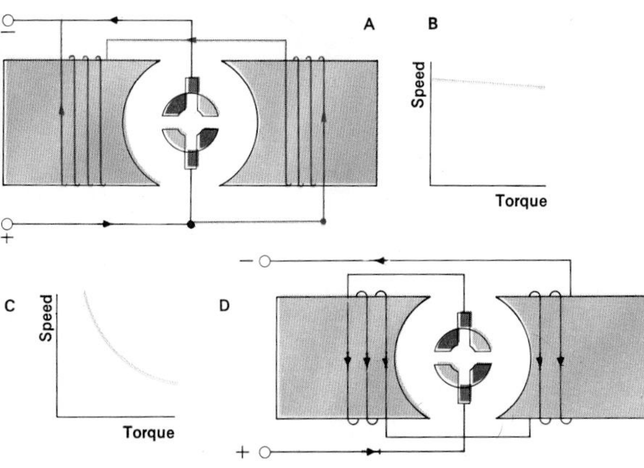
4
A
B
Speed
Torque
+
–
C
Speed
Torque
D
+

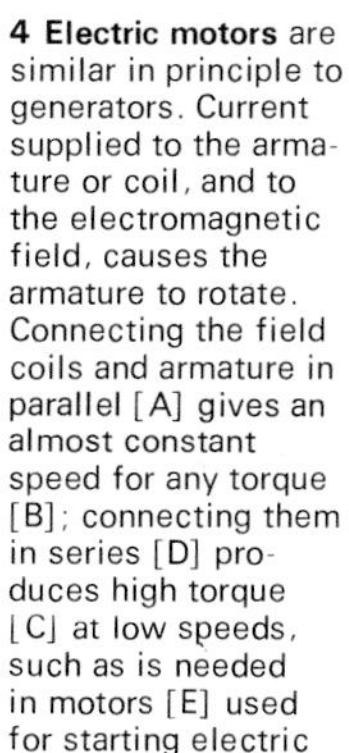
E

4 Electric motors are similar in principle to generators. Current supplied to the armature or coil, and to the electromagnetic field, causes the armature to rotate. Connecting the field coils and armature in parallel [A] gives an almost constant speed for any torque [B]; connecting them in series [D] produces high torque [C] at low speeds, such as is needed in motors [E] used for starting electric trains.

5 The induction motor is the one most widely used; the coil forming the armature of a simple DC machine is replaced by a "squirrel cage." This consists of aluminum or copper bars connecting each end to a ring, the whole embedded in a laminated soft iron rotor. The field, at least two coils inside the motor body, is shaped to allow the rotor to revolve inside with a small clearance. Flux lines caused by an alternating current passing through the field cut the cage bars, inducing a current in them—hence the "induction" motor.

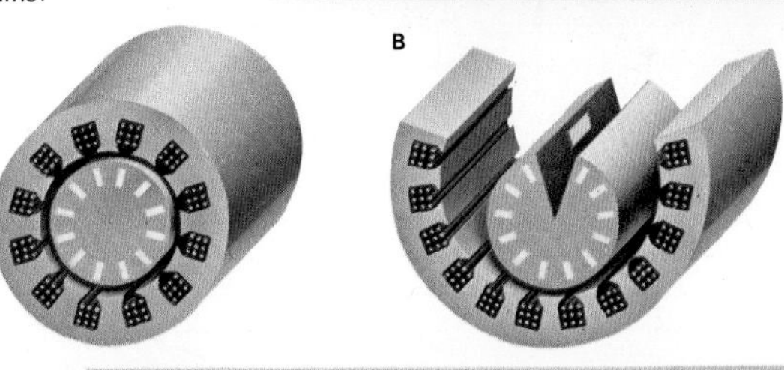
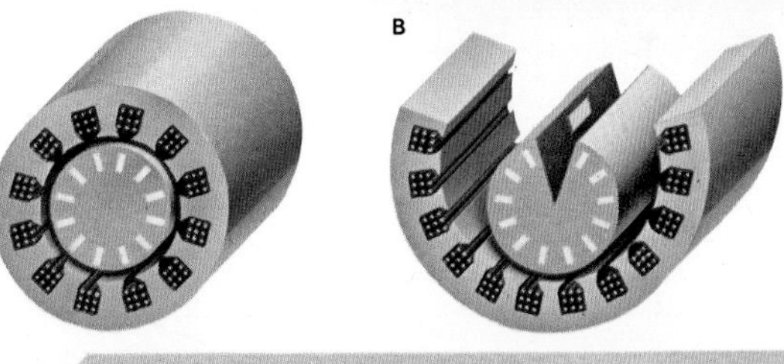
6A
B
C

6 The "rotor" of a linear motor [C] moves lengthwise rather than revolving. It is a flat plate, either sandwiched between two long field windings or resting solely on one. Energizing the fields with AC causes the plate to move, using exactly the same principles as an induction motor [A], from which it can be pictured as being "made" by opening it out [B, C].

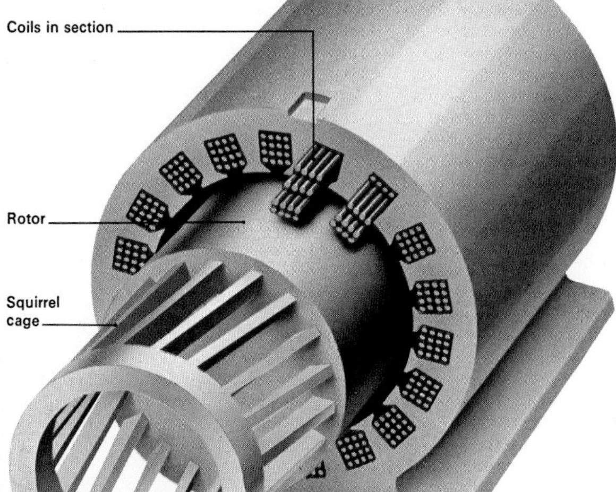
5
Coils in section
Rotor
Squirrel cage

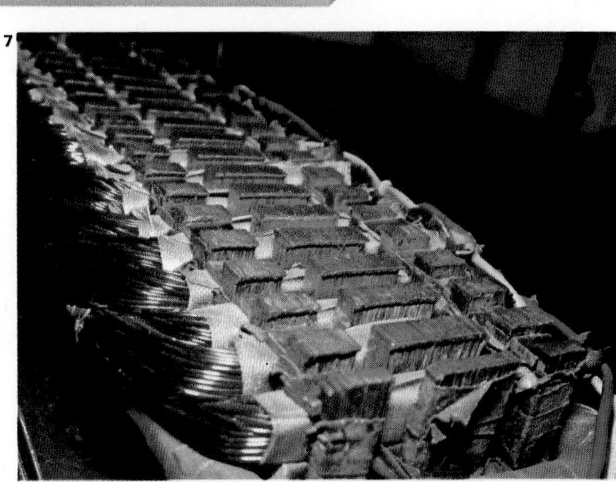
7

7 A large linear motor, the field windings of which are shown here, could be used to drive a silent, non-wheeled train or other vehicle. Smaller motors are already used—for example for opening and closing sliding doors. The armature, or metal plate, usually aluminum, is fixed to the upper part of the door and the windings attached to the door frame. When the field is energized, the plate passes along the field, moving the door.

Basic DC circuits

An electrical circuit is the system by which an electric current is directed, controlled, modified, switched on, or switched off. Circuits can contain from two or three to many hundred different components, according to the way in which the current is to be controlled, but all share certain common characteristics.

Formation of a circuit

The primary requirement of a circuit is that it form a complete path; electrons must be able to flow around the whole system so that as many electrons pass back into the source of the current as leave it. Certain occurrences, such as lightning strikes or electric shocks, seem to deny this first requirement, but are nevertheless examples of electrical circuits. This apparent contradiction can be resolved by considering the Earth and all the structures on it as a vast electron bank. If clouds develop an electron imbalance, the Earth makes it up by generating a flash of lightning, and the net result is that the numbers of electrons leaving the Earth and arriving are equal.

Electric current can also be "carried" by charged atoms, or ions. Ions of dissolved salts and other chemicals conduct current through the electrolyte in an electroplating bath and gas ions conduct electricity in a fluorescent light. But whatever the current carriers, all circuits share three characteristics: a current (I), a voltage (V), and a resistance (R) [6].

Completing the circuit

An illustration of this electron movement (and the use of high-voltage direct current) is the arrangement of the transmission line from the Cabora Bassa dam in Mozambique to the South African town of Apollo some 310mi (500km) away. There are two lines to carry the current, one taking electrons to Apollo, the other returning the same number to Cabora Bassa. If one of the lines breaks, the Earth itself "replaces" the broken line and carries the electrons in the appropriate direction.

In a similar way, the chassis of many vehicles are used as the so-called ground, or return, circuit, although this is a loose and generally inaccurate term. One terminal of the battery is connected to the bodywork and a single wire is brought from the other terminal through a switch to each piece of electrical equipment. These in turn are also connected firmly to the chassis. The circuit so established allows the number of electrons leaving the battery to be matched exactly by the number of those arriving. Using the chassis of a vehicle to complete the circuit in this way makes a second wire unnecessary.

Direct and alternating current

One major practical difference in circuit components (although there are no differences in principle) is determined by whether they are used for direct current or alternating current. Direct current is unidirectional; the electron flow is always in the same direction and although it may stop and start, grow or diminish in quantity, it never reverses direction.

Current flow (as opposed to electron flow, which is always against the conventional direction of current flow) is assumed

CONNECTIONS

See also

1532 What is an electric current?

1540 Transformers, motors and generators

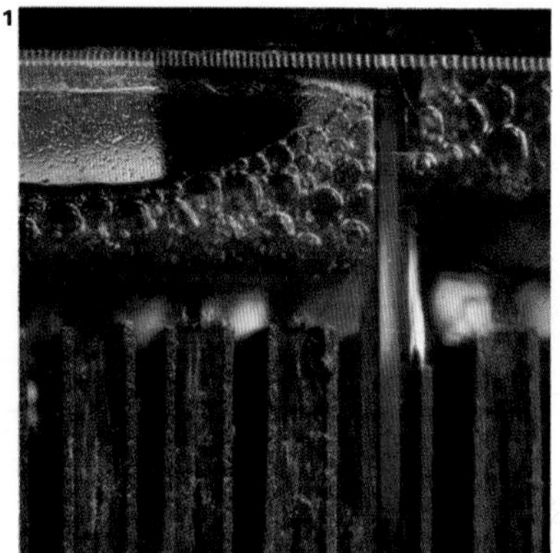

1 A cell or battery sends electrons around an electrical circuit as a result of chemical action. This unidirectional character of the electron flow is called direct current (DC), even if it varies greatly or stops altogether from time to time. In a primary cell current flow stops as soon as one of the chemicals or electrodes is consumed. A secondary cell, or storage battery, can be recharged, often forming gas bubbles.

2 Electrical generators can be AC or DC machines. Generators provide DC current at a fixed level with a small pulsation superimposed as a result of commutator switching action. Batteries give very smooth output but it gradually diminishes in value. AC generators supply alternating current, characterized by a rapid periodic reversal of electron flow. The current falls to zero every time the direction is reversed.

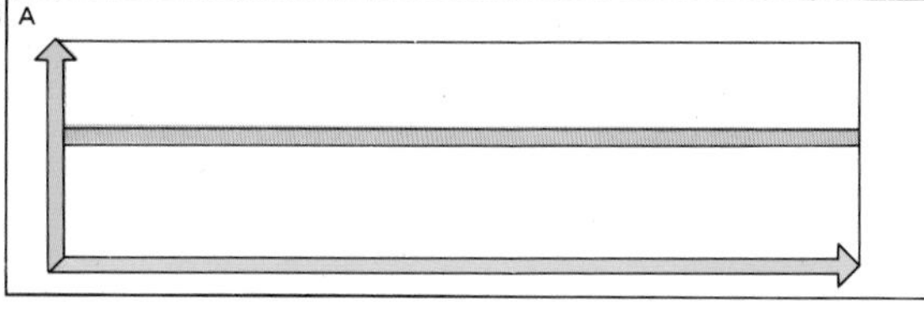

A

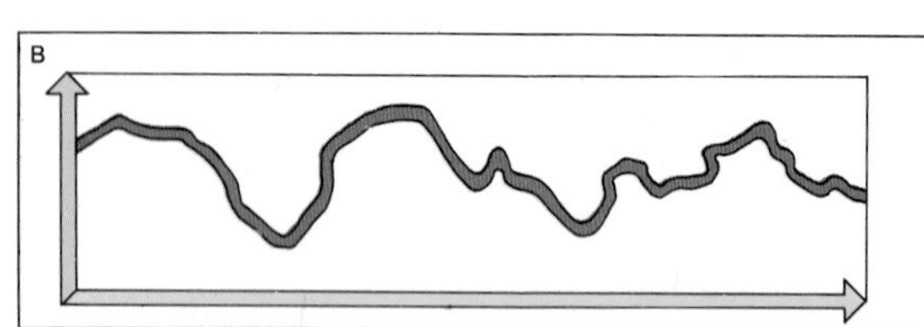

B

3 One method of examining direct current is to measure how it varies over a fixed period. Graph A shows a current, such as that used by a lamp supplied by a battery, which does not alter over the time it is measured (the vertical axis represents current and the horizontal one time). Graph B shows a direct current typical of a welding circuit. It varies with time, although its value is always positive.

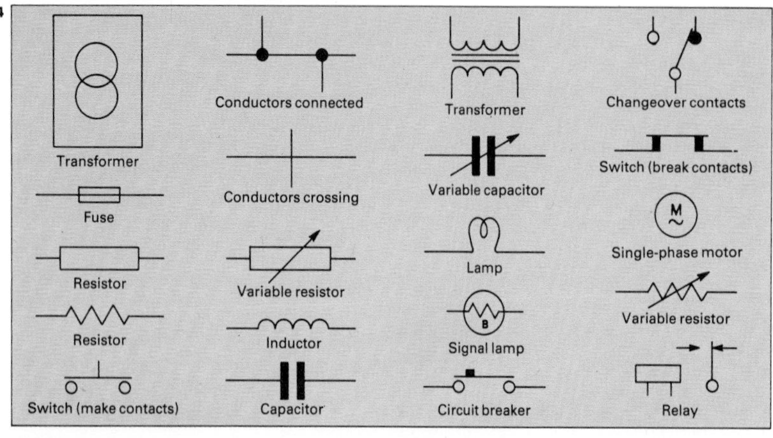

Transformer
Fuse
Resistor
Resistor
Switch (make contacts)
Conductors connected
Conductors crossing
Variable resistor
Inductor
Capacitor
Transformer
Variable capacitor
Lamp
B
Signal lamp
Circuit breaker
Changeover contacts
Switch (break contacts)
M
Single-phase motor
Variable resistor
Relay

4 The drawings used by engineers and other workers in the electrical industry have to be clear to the reader irrespective of his language. These symbols are just a few of the hundreds used.

5 It is often economical to use direct current at high voltage when transmitting large amounts of electrical power. Only in the last few years has reliable equipment been available to switch large DC voltages on and off. This large thyristor "switch" operates on principles similar to transistors used in radios. Because power stations are being sited farther away from population centers, high voltage DC is increasingly used instead of AC.

by convention to be from a positive to a negative terminal. In direct current (DC) generators, batteries, and some other sources, the terminals are determined by the nature of the machine or equipment and are irreversible. The most common example of direct current source is a chemical cell or battery, in which the nature of the chemicals themselves fixes the polarity of the system. Although the output of the cell may vary, the current flow is always in the same direction. The same applies to a DC generator, because the structure of the machine determines the polarity. Another device, known as a rectifier, also has fixed polarity. A rectifier is used to convert alternating current to direct current; irrespective of how the input varies the current direction at the output terminals of the rectifier is always the same.

DC applications

Alternating current (AC) is the more common mode, although in certain instances direct current is particularly appropriate and alternating current cannot be used. In electroplating, for example, direct current is used because it is vital that the current always flow in the same direction. If it did not, plating material would pass back and forth from the coating metal to the surface to be coated and no plating would take place.

The recharging of a battery [1], which is a specialized form of "electroplating," can also be carried out only by direct current and AC-powered battery chargers must contain a rectifier.

In systems for transmitting power over long distances, alternating current is normally used because it provides a more practical way of reducing transmission losses than direct current. The losses are decreased by reducing the current through the transmission conductors by raising the generated voltage to very high values and then lowering it at the distribution points. Transformers, which operate only on alternating current, provide the efficient, safe, and economical means of raising and lowering (transforming) the voltages in power transmission lines.

KEY

Electroplating of metals was one of the earliest uses of direct current. The inherent electrical properties of certain chemicals in solution make it possible to coat metallic surfaces with a thin durable coating of another metal. In this plant car components are given a protective coating of chromium.

6

A

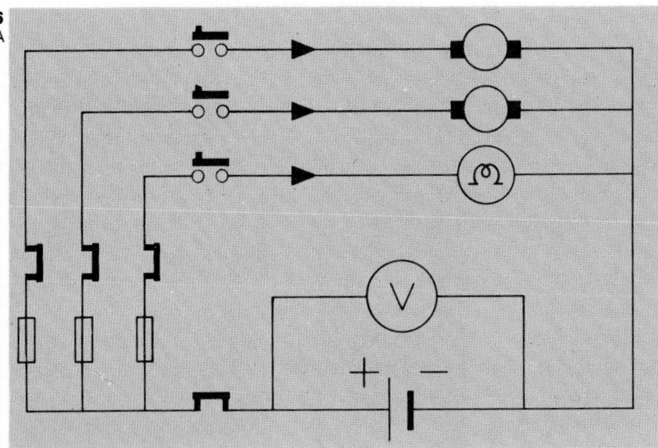

V
+
−

B

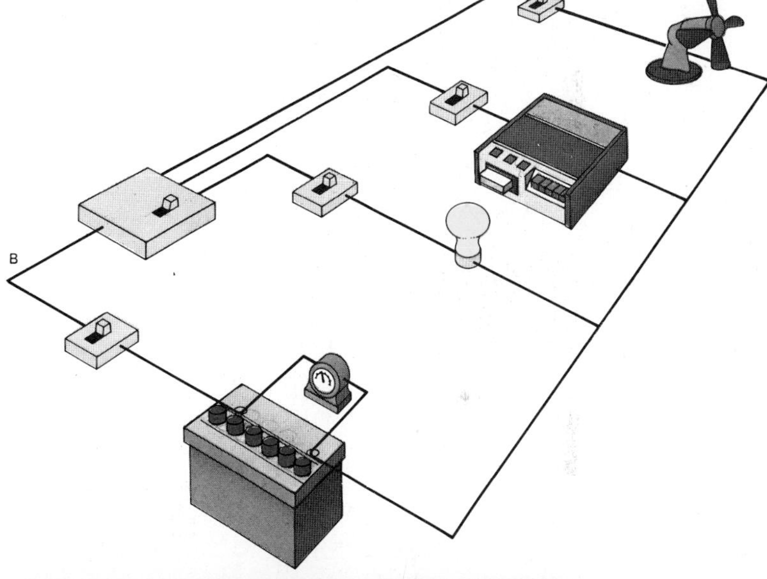

6 This diagram of a circuit [A] shows a typical but simplified electrical system [B] of the kind used for battery-powered equipment. Switches control the current flow into three leads to a lamp and two appliances containing electric motors. The voltmeter records the electromotive force (that is, the voltage) of the battery, which remains virtually constant. The current flowing through the lamp will also remain virtually constant, but those through the appliances may vary, depending on the demands made by their motors. Fuses and circuit breakers protect the circuit from current surges.

7

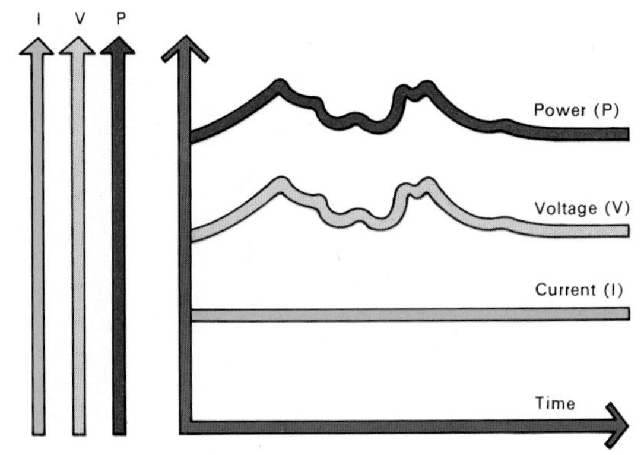

I
V
P
Power (P)
Voltage (V)
Current (I)
Time

7 The circuit shown in illustration 6 has many interdependent electrical variables. Representing them as a graph indicates how they are related. (There are different scales on the vertical axes but the horizontal axis, time, is the same for all the other variables.) Three of the most important variables—voltage, current, and power—are shown. The voltage [V] is fixed by the battery. If the battery is in good condition the voltage will not vary significantly. The current [I] depends on the voltage and the resistance of the appliance it is feeding. This may vary (as it does in the motors) or may be fixed (as it is in the lamp). The power [P] is a product of voltage and current and is measured in watts.

8

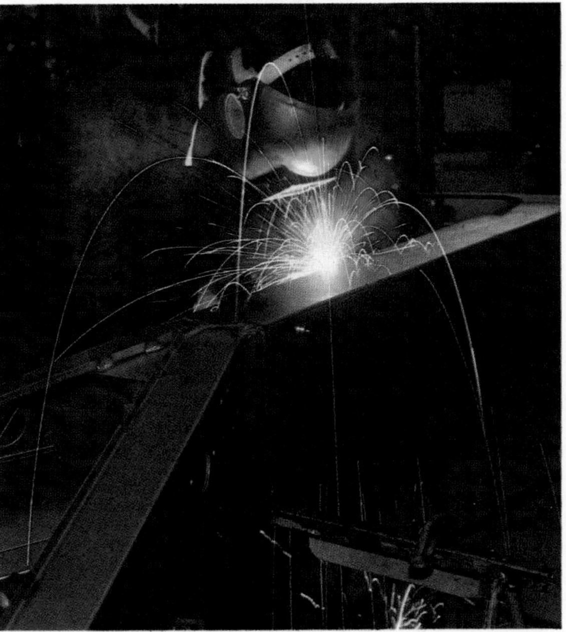

8 Welding is a process of joining metals together with a bond so strong that it is often superior to the parent materials. A large electric current—perhaps 2,000 amps—at low voltage can be used to provide the necessary heat, so that the metal in a particular area is melted. The current passes as an arc from an insulated electrode in the welder's hand and enters the workpiece across a short air gap. The object to be welded is connected to one terminal of the current source and the welding electrode to the other. Electric welding generally uses direct current generated by special equipment because of the large currents needed.

Basic AC circuits

The physical processes that take place in electrical circuits carrying alternating current (AC) differ from those in direct current (DC) circuits, reflecting the differences between the two types of electricity. Alternating current regularly reverses its direction, becoming zero before each reversal (120 times a second in North America and 100 times a second in Europe, corresponding to 60 Hz and 50 Hz supply frequencies). With reference to zero, the current is negative and positive alternately. Direct current always flows in the same direction.

The shape of the "current wave" (the curve representing its change of value with respect to time) can take an infinite variety of forms. For most purposes it is sinusoidal (like a sine wave [Key]).

The number of times the curve repeats the whole alternating cycle in a second is called the frequency and is measured in hertz (Hz)—one cycle per second equals 1Hz. A sinuosoidal voltage (V) applied to a circuit produces a sinusoidal current whose value at any instant in the cycle is equal to V/Z, where Z is called the impedance (which depends on the resistance, capacitance, and inductance of the circuit and the supply frequency); Z is measured in ohms (Ω). The equation is analogous to that used to express Ohm's law, named after George Ohm (1787–1854), who discovered that the direct current flowing through a conductor is directly proportional to the electromotive force (voltage) that produces it and inversely proportional to the resistance.

The three main types of circuit components are inductors, capacitors, and resistors. A resistor behaves in the same way in either an AC or a DC circuit; inductors and capacitors, however, do not. In these devices, currents are out of phase with the applied voltage in parallel circuits (in which there is more than one path for the current) and out of phase with the common current in series circuits (in which the source and output devices are connected by only one path).

Phase lead and lag

A simple analogy to the phase differences in alternating current and voltage is the action of a yo-yo, where the hand from which the spinning mass derives its energy can move in the opposite direction to the mass. The current taken by a capacitor is out of phase with the applied voltage; it is zero when the voltage is maximum and vice versa. Sine waves may be represented by rotating vectors (a vector is a quantity that has both magnitude and direction) [5], and on a vector diagram the capacitor current is 90° out of phase with the voltage and is said to be leading.

For a pure inductance the reverse applies—that is, the current lags the voltage by 90°. This can be explained in another way by saying that for a capacitor, the voltage lags the current by 90° and for an inductor the voltage leads. With a resistance, the current and voltage are in phase [3].

In a circuit that has both capacitance and inductance, one current leads by 90° and is equal in magnitude to another lagging by 90°. The overall effect is subtractive—they cancel each other out. When this happens the circuit is said to experience current resonance. In effect, the capacitor's current

CONNECTIONS

See also
1532 What is an electric current?
1540 Transformers, motors and generators
1548 Basic electronic principles
1536 Electromagnetism
1546 Semiconductors
1794 Communications: radio
1796 Communications: television

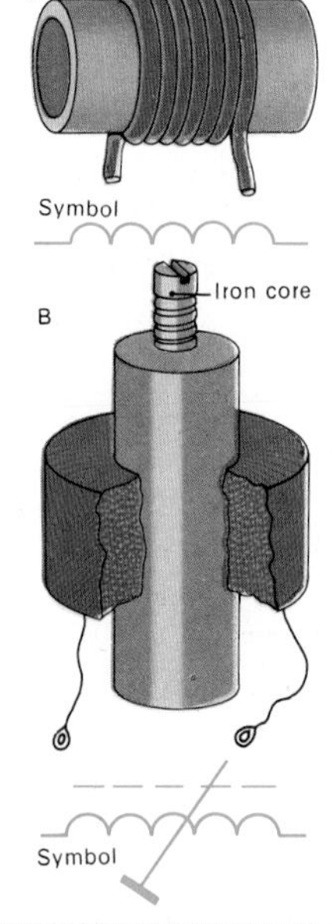

1A
Symbol
Iron core
B
Symbol

1 An inductor [A] is a circuit component consisting of a coil of wire. When current flows through a coil a magnetic field is set up whose lines of magnetic flux thread through the coil. Their number and distribution depend on the design of the coil. As the field changes in strength with the changing current, flux lines increase or decrease, cutting the windings of the coil. This is the principle of a generator, and an emf (electromotive force) is generated in such a way as to oppose current changes. The effectiveness of an inductor can be changed by screwing a threaded iron core in or out of the coil [B].

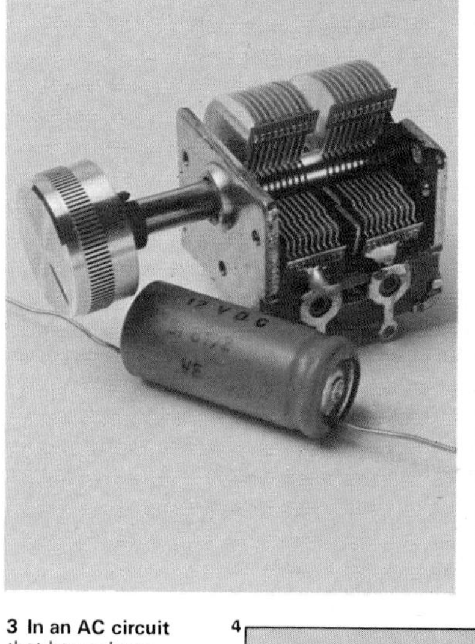

2 A fixed capacitor or condenser (foreground) and a variable capacitor (background) [A] are used in alternating current circuits (particularly in electronic applications). The two parallel surfaces in a capacitor are electronically charged and discharged as the voltage varies. The capacitor holds the electrons in balance and releases them at the same rate as the supply current, but out of phase with it. The capacitance of a capacitor may be intensified by increasing the surface area and reducing the gap between the plates. A large industrial capacitor is shown in use [B]. Variable capacitors are used to tune radios.

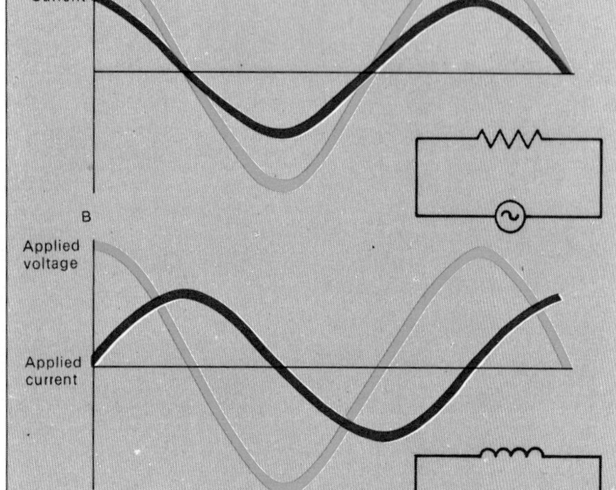

3
A
Voltage
Current
B
Applied voltage
Applied current

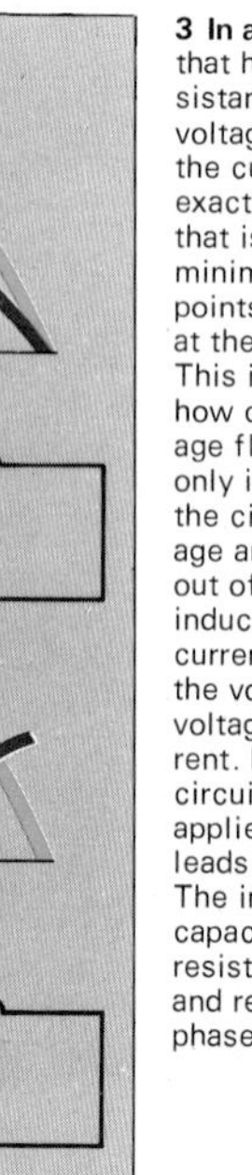

3 In an AC circuit that has only resistance in it, the voltage applied and the current flow are exactly in phase [A], that is, their maxima, minima, and zero points always occur at the same instant. This is true no matter how quickly the voltage fluctuates. With only inductance in the circuit, the voltage and current are out of phase. In an inductive circuit [B], current is said to lag the voltage, or the voltage lead the current. In a capacitive circuit, the reverse applies—the current leads the voltage. The inductor and capacitor (unlike the resistor) store energy and release it out of phase with the input.

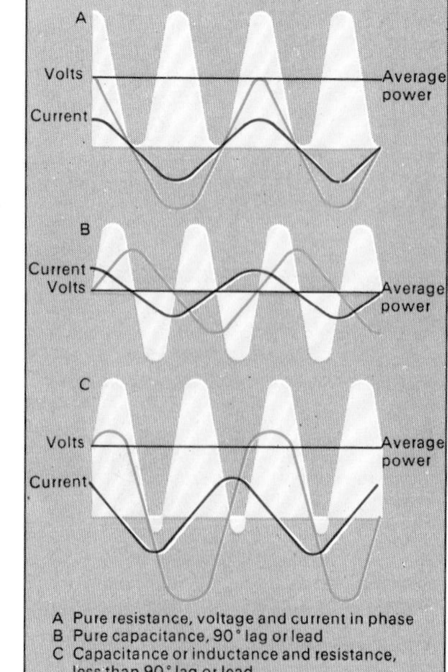

4
A
Volts
Average power
Current
B
Current
Volts
Average power
C
Volts
Average power
Current
A Pure resistance, voltage and current in phase
B Pure capacitance, 90° lag or lead
C Capacitance or inductance and resistance, less than 90° lag or lead

4 Power in an AC circuit is the instantaneous product of voltage and current averaged over a fixed period. In a resistive circuit, the voltage and current are in phase [A] and the power dissipated is given by the formula VI (voltage x current). In a capacitive circuit [B] the current and voltage are 90° out of phase and the circuit returns as much power to the source as it absorbs. This also applies to a purely inductive circuit. Circuits that have a mixture of resistance, capacitance, and inductance [C] take power according to the formula VI cos Ø, where cos Ø (the power factor) varies from 0 to 1 depending on the phase angle O.

feeds the inductor and vice versa, because each needs the current at different times in the cycle. The same applies to a circuit in which a 90° leading voltage is of the same magnitude as a 90° lagging one. The two "cancel out" and the circuit is said to exhibit voltage resonance.

The actual value of the current taken by a capacitor or inductor depends on three factors: the voltage, the frequency, and the value (size) of the capacitor or inductor. The higher the capacitance the higher the current, but for an inductor the current is smaller as the inductance rises. Current or voltage vectors may be added or subtracted to give a resultant vector, combining all the individual ones.

Root mean square values

In an AC circuit the magnitude of the alternating voltage or current is defined as the rms (root mean square, or "effective") value. It is used because the average value is zero, since during any short interval of time the number of half cycles in one direction equals those in the other. The rms value can be derived using simple mathematics and is that quoted in all descriptions of electrical equipment. This figure represents the power that would be consumed if a DC voltage/current of that value could be used. On an electric iron, a plate reading "23OV, 2A" refers to rms values. The voltage and current in this case vary constantly in the form of a sine wave, reaching ±325V and +2.828A—both reaching a peak 60 times every second.

AC applications

All electrical appliances that are essentially resistive in structure—such as incandescent lamps, heaters, and irons—operate perfectly well in either alternating or direct current circuits (provided they are of the same voltage). But equipment that depends on inductive or capacitative properties, such as some motors, transformers, and fluorescent lamps, can operate only with alternating current. Alternating current is preferred for the domestic electricity supply because it can be transmitted efficiently and easily.

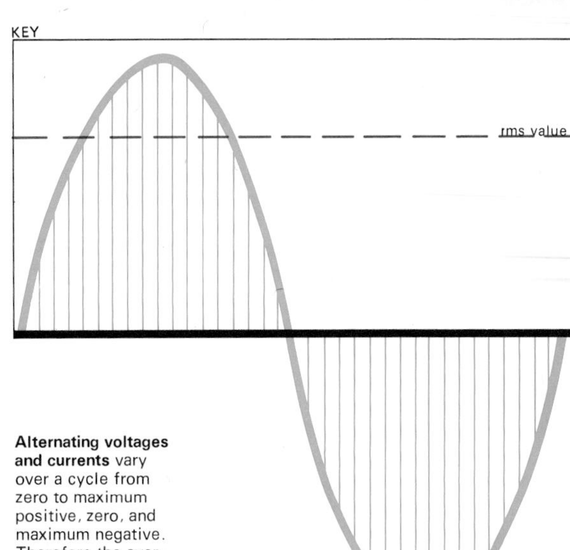
KEY
rms value

Alternating voltages and currents vary over a cycle from zero to maximum positive, zero, and maximum negative. Therefore the average value over the complete cycle is zero, and the rms, or effective, value is used as a measure.

5 A vector diagram shows the relationship among the three branches of current—capacitance, resistance, and inductance. Three currents and their phase relationships with the applied voltage are depicted, by convention, by lines whose lengths represent the various values of current (they are vectors). A is said to lead, B to be in phase, and C to lag behind the voltage.

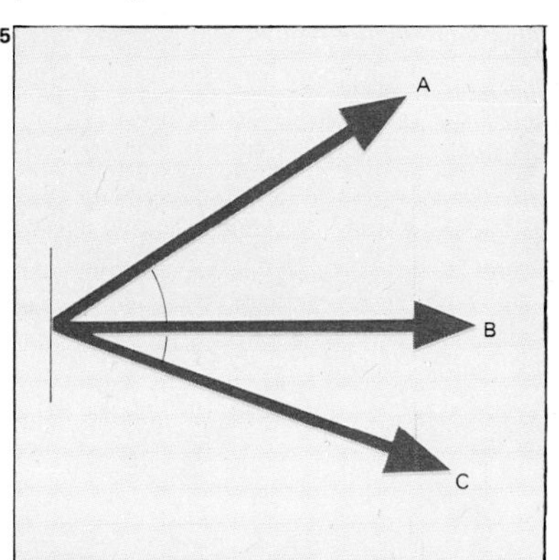
5
A
B
C

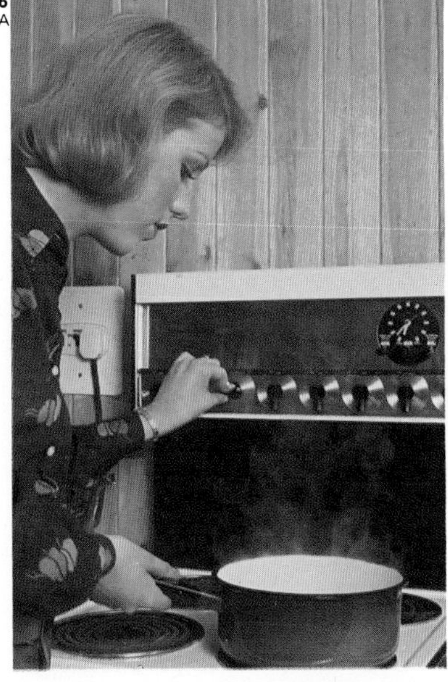
6
A

B

6 Electric clocks connected to the AC network depend on the system frequency for keeping accurate time. This is why the kitchen clock [A] always shows the same time as the master clock in the power station [B]. A reduction in frequency makes the clock read slow and vice versa. Because many essential timing devices depend on the power frequency, it is maintained at a constant value (normally 60Hz, or 60 cycles per second, in the United States). Any fall in frequency can be made up by adjusting the frequency gradually. The frequency rarely varies by more than one percent.

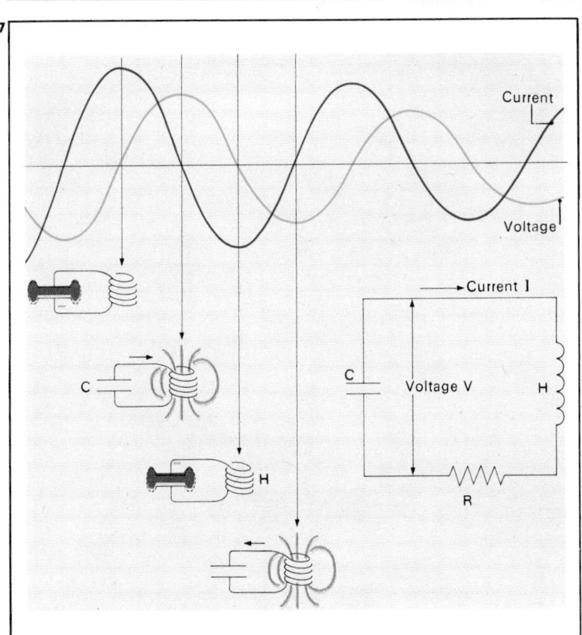
7
Current
Voltage
Current I
C
Voltage V
H
R
C
H

7 A circuit with inductance [L], resistance [R], and capacitance [C] may contain some voltages out of phase with the common current. When those of leading components cancel out those of lagging components, the circuit is said to be resonant.

8

8 The power given by an AC generator depends on its voltage, current output, and frequency. The power-to-weight ratio becomes more favorable as the frequency increases, which is why aircraft generators operate at 400Hz. Here an auxiliary generator is being used to power electrical circuits in an aircraft while its engines are idle and its own generators not working.

Semiconductors

Metals, such as copper and aluminum, are good conductors of electricity. Glass, rubber, and most plastics are nonconductors, or insulators. But there are some materials, such as germanium and silicon, which are neither good nor poor conductors, and they are called semiconductors. They are used for transistors and other solid-state devices.

Current carriers

The atoms in a semiconductor easily lose one of their electrons, allowing another from a nearby atom to replace it. Although this electron exchange process goes on, the overall charge of the material is nil; it is electrically neutral. But by adding some different atoms in the form of a slight impurity, for example with one more electron per atom than the atoms of the material itself, an entirely new material is created. Just one of these new atoms (such as phosphorus, arsenic, or antimony) for every one hundred billion germanium or silicon atoms can make a semiconductor called an *n*-type material, in which a few extra electrons are available for carrying current.

The opposite situation can be produced, making a material deficient in electrons, by adding atoms with one fewer electron per atom than those of the original material. In this case, aluminum, gallium, or indium in the same small proportion is added to the germanium or silicon to produce *p*-type material [Key]. In both *n*-type and *p*-type materials, the electrons involved in the creation of the particular type of semiconductor are known as the valence electrons—the ones in the outer shell of the atom.

In *n*-type materials, the surplus electrons provide the means for current flow, whereas in *p*-type surplus "holes" are created for the electrons to settle into. And as a hole exerts forces of attraction on the surrounding electrons, it can be thought of as if it were a positively charged particle. The most numerous—electrons or holes—are called majority carriers, or current carriers, in contrast to the minority carriers, which are the few residual electrons or holes [1].

The simplest form of semiconductor device, a *p-n* junction diode [3], is made by joining pieces of opposite types of semiconductor material together, attaching a wire to each, and enclosing the combination in a metal or plastic shield, with the leads protruding. By connecting a battery so that the positive terminal is connected to the *n*-type material, a very small current flows consisting of minority carriers only. But if the battery is reversed [4], a large current flows, because it consists of majority carriers.

Forming a transitor

When a layer of one type of semiconductor material is sandwiched between two layers of the opposite type, a conventional two-junction, three-layer semiconductor device is formed, known as the junction transistor [5]. This arrangement can be used to form either a *p-n-p* or an *n-p-n* device. Apart from voltage-polarities, both can be connected in a circuit to provide current amplifying devices. The voltages in each instance are low—for example, a voltage of 6 volts DC between the collector and base of an *n-p-n* transistor.

When the base/emitter voltage is increased from, say, 600 to 620 millivolts, the

CONNECTIONS

See also
1542 Basic DC circuits
1544 Basic AC circuits
1548 Basic electronic principles
1794 Communications: radio
1668 Electronic devices

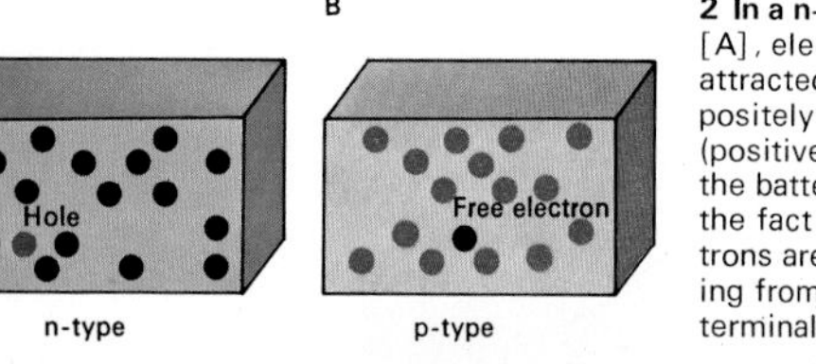

1A
B
Hole
Free electron
n-type
p-type

1 Electrons and holes deliberately introduced into the intrinsic (pure basic) material are seen here to be much more numerous than the carriers (holes [A] or electrons [B]) of thermal activity.

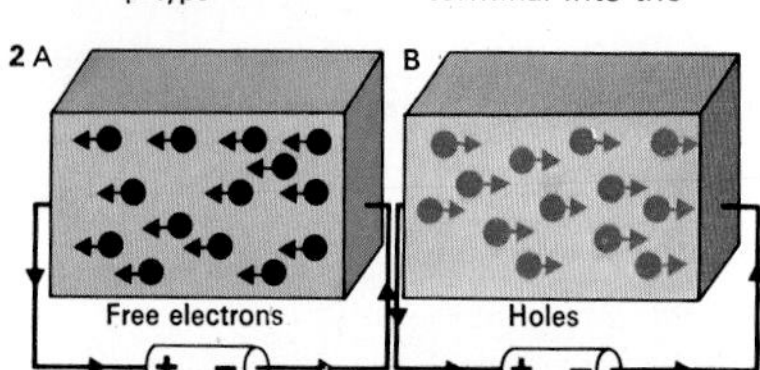

2A
B
Free electrons
Holes

2 In a n-type material [A], electrons are attracted by the oppositely charged (positive) terminal of the battery. But for the fact that electrons are also flowing from the negative terminal into the other end of the material, it would be left with a net positive charge. With *p*-type material [B] a similar action ensues, but initial attraction is between positive holes and the negative terminal. The invention of the transistor in 1948 revolutionized electronics. Before this no one had ever considered how vitally important semiconductors would become to the electronics industry.

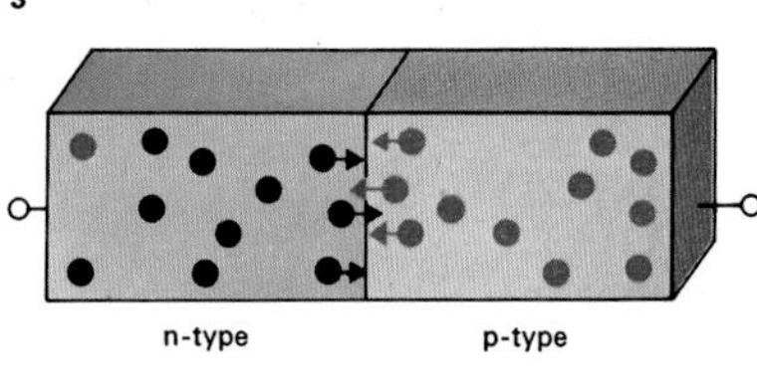

3
n-type
p-type

Diode symbol

3 Joining together two different semiconductor materials (*n*-type and *p*-type) causes carriers to start drifting across the junction area. As soon as a few holes and electrons have crossed the junction, they make a thin section of each material oppositely charged from the rest. A barrier free from carriers is therefore produced. The combination behaves as a semiconductor diode.

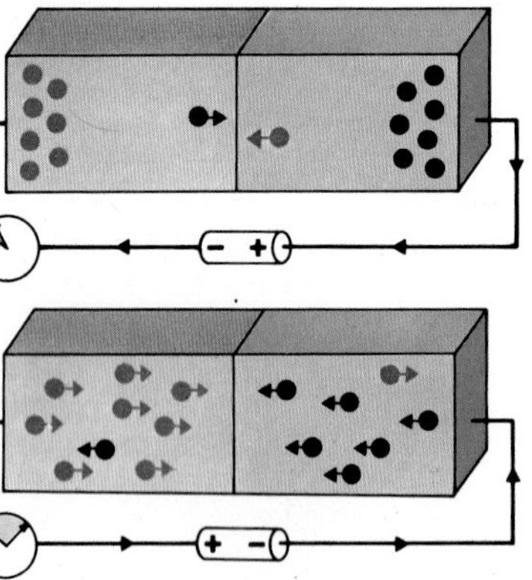

4A
B

4 Wiring the terminals of a battery across a piece of joined *n*-type and *p*-type semiconductor material, in which a barrier free from carriers has been produced, simply widens the barrier if the positive pole of the battery is connected to the *n*-type [A]. Little current flows. But if the battery is reversed, forward bias is created together with the breakdown of the barrier and a large current flows [B].

5A
B
C
D
E
Symbol
F
Input
Output

5 A transistor is a sandwich of particular crystal types, produced by taking two pieces of the same semiconductor material and sandwiching the opposite type between them. The crystal structures behave as if the *p*-type is carrying positive electrical charges and the *n*-type carrying negative charges [A]. If a voltage is applied, the charges drift in the directions shown [B]. Amplification of a signal with a negative bias can be achieved [C], the oscillations of the signal influencing the drift of the charges. Also shown is the actual size of the device [D], its symbol [E] and a transistor amplifier circuit [F].

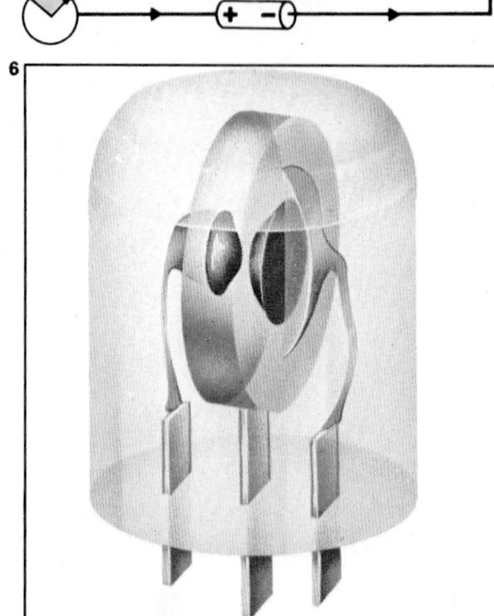

6

6 Most alloy junction semiconductor devices are of the *p n p* type, with germanium as the *n*-type base material in the form of a wafer. *P*-type areas are created by melting and then allowing impurities (such as indium) to crystallize on each side of the base material. Lead wires are connected and the device is encapsulated. Silicon base transistors are created by planar diffusing either *n*- or *p*-type materials into a silicon chip.

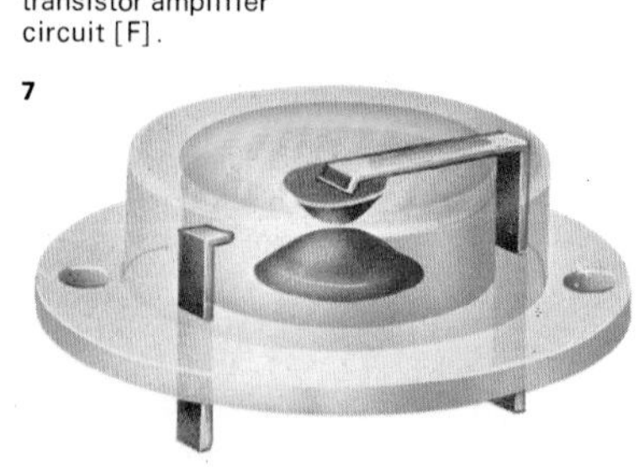

7

7 Where more power is needed than would be possible from an ordinary alloy junction, a different type of construction is used, with larger pieces of material. The collector is cut and bonded to a piece of material called the header. To enable the device to handle high powers continuously, it is attached to a piece of metal known as a heat sink. With the larger junction transistor more heat is produced and it is generally dissipated by means of a metal heat sink.

collector current might increase from 0.995 to 1.990 milliamps (mA), whereas the corresponding base current would probably increase only from 0.005 to 0.010mA. Therefore the gain of 0.005mA in the base current has caused a gain of 0.995mA in the collector current, an amplification of 200.

The earliest transistors were of the point contact type, but this method of manufacture was quickly replaced by the alloy junction [6]. It involves the use of heat to form two regions of *p*-type material in an *n*-type germanium wafer. The resulting device is a *p-n-p* semiconductor, although it can only handle low currents. When more power is needed, larger pieces of each material are used to form an alloy junction power transistor [7]. To ensure cool running, a large heat sink is essential, bolted to the metal plate which is bonded to the collector.

Thyristors and photocells

Thyristors [8] are used to control voltage in light dimmers for the home and in electric trucks for railroad stations, factories, and warehouses. Also known as a silicon controlled rectifier (SCR), a thyristor has four layers, three *p-n* junctions and three electrodes—the cathode, anode, and gate. When reverse biased (cathode positive relative to the anode), an SCR blocks the flow of reverse current, just like an ordinary diode. When forward biased (cathode negative relative to the anode), an SCR also blocks forward current flow until a trigger signal is applied to the gate. The device then switches to a highly conductive state. It remains in this state until the anode current is reduced below a given maintenance level, or the anode voltage is reversed. When this happens the gate must be triggered again to make the thyristor conduct. A photocell-actuated circuit [9] provides automation for street lights.

Integrated circuits [10] are a development from transistors and are finding increasing applications in all types of electronic apparatus. These circuits incorporate hundreds or even thousands of transistors, resistors, and capacitors, and interconnecting circuitry on a single piece of silicon up to 20mm by 20mm, and about 0.2mm thick.

KEY

Electron

Impurity atom

Hole

If a "foreign," or impurity, atom with three electrons in its outer shell enters an array of atoms that have four electrons in their outer shells, a "hole" is created in the lattice. This hole acts as an attraction to the surrounding electrons; it can be considered as a virtual positive charge in its behavior.

8 A

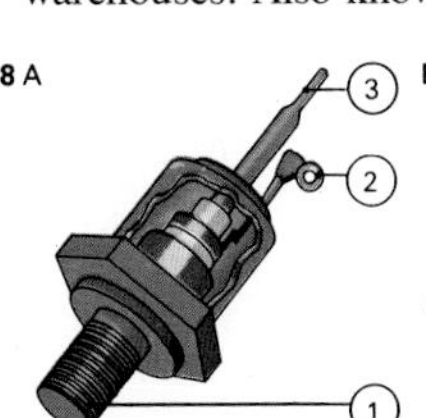
3
2
1

B

C

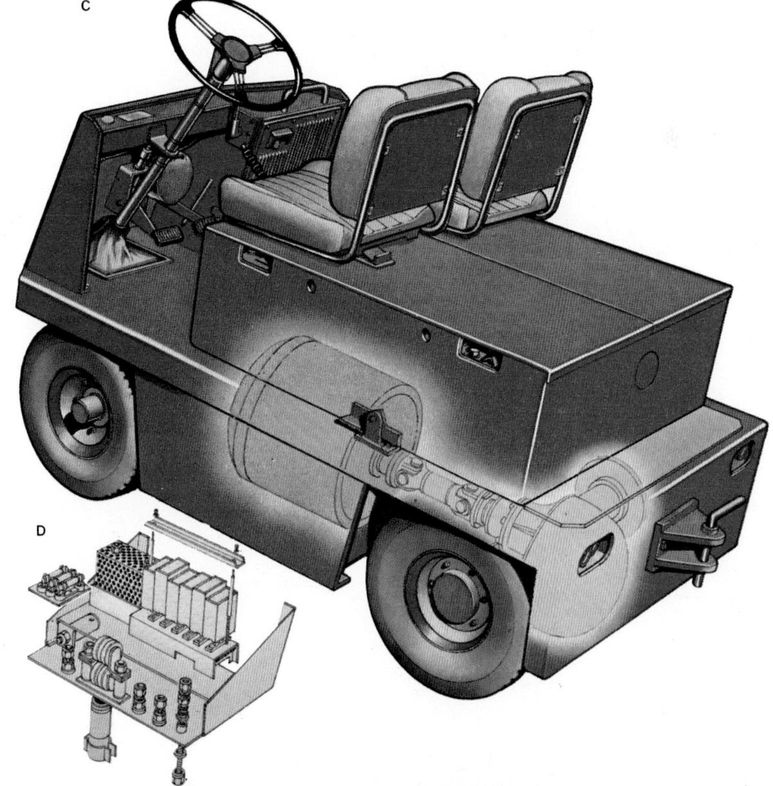

D

8 The thyristor family includes reverse blocking triode thyristors (also known as silicon controlled rectifiers [SCR], or just simply as thyristors), diacs, and triacs. A thyristor [A] has four layers, three *p-n* junctions and three electrodes – the cathode [1], the gate [2], and the anode [3]. Thyristors are used to achieve controlled conduction in apparatus such as temperature controllers, lamp dimmers, power supplies, and inverters. Extremely small thyristors are made to fit within a domestic light dimmer [B], which is based on the action of a thyristor to control the degree of illumination, from zero to full power. Thyristors capable of handling very high powers are used in layers, or banks [D], in electric vehicles such as this small tractor [C] to give precise control of the speed whatever the load it may have to pull.

9 A

B

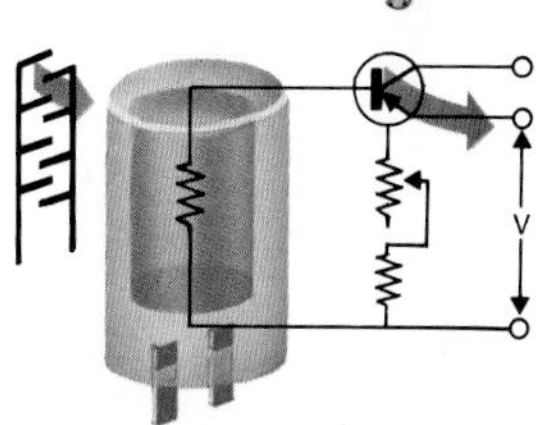
V

9 A photocell-actuated circuit incorporated into a street light [A] turns on the light when natural light falls to a preset level. At that point, the output voltage falls to trigger another circuit and operate the lamp. A photoconductive cell is superior to a time switch because no time-switch can be programmed to anticipate fog or sudden storms. The basic construction of a photoconductive cell is simple [B] and reliable.

10 A

B

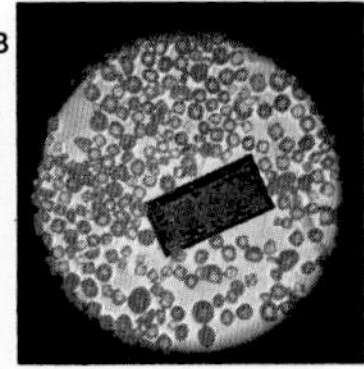

10 Integrated circuits make feasible the miniaturization of all kinds of electronic devices. Such circuits are used in this electronic watch [A]. The tiny size of the circuits can be compared with surrounding crystals of common salt [B].

Basic electronic principles

Everything in electronics begins with the electrons that are part of every atom. Scientists have painstakingly built up the modern picture of the atom, but no one has ever seen one. Even smaller are the minute, negatively-charged electrons, which can be thought of as orbiting at a distance around the atom's central nucleus, where most of its mass is concentrated.

The movement of electrons

Although atoms are normally neutral they can acquire an extra electron and so become negatively charged, or lose an electron and become positively charged. It is this ability of certain atoms easily to "exchange" electrons that enables a stream of them—an electric current—to flow in a conductor [1]. By using a battery or a generator a surplus of electrons can be provided at one terminal and a deficit at the other, to produce an electromotive force (emf). If a conductor is connected between these terminals the emf causes electrons to flow (or rather "drift"—the rate is seldom more than 2cm [0.75in] a minute) from the "surplus" terminal (negative) to the "deficit" terminal (positive). This is opposite to the adopted convention that assumes that electric current flows from positive to negative. Unfortunately this convention was firmly established before anyone knew anything about electrons and has been allowed to remain ever since.

In electronic circuits, conductors (in the form of wires or thin copper strips on an insulating material) act as paths for the free flow of electrons from one part of a circuit to another. But elements are needed to control the flow, to allow precise currents of electrons to pass through various circuit components such as vacuum tubes and transistors. These elements are known as resistors [2], and are available in a wide range of values from a fraction of an ohm (the unit of resistance) up to tens of millions of ohms.

Vacuum tubes

The diode is the simplest form of vacuum tube [3A] and can change an alternating current (such as that at the power line) into a series of pulses—direct current—by a process known as rectification. A diode with a single anode produces half-wave rectification [3B]. The efficiency of the process is improved by full-wave rectification [3F]. To obtain a direct current that has virtually no pulses in it at all the pulsating current can be fed into additional circuit elements, such as capacitors and chokes, which "smooth" it.

Today tube diodes are usually rejected in favor of their solid-state semiconductor equivalents. Virtually all modern domestic circuitry is made up of solid-state components, apart from a few television sets that still employ one or two tubes as well as semiconductors.

Although the solid-state diode [3C] is much smaller than the vacuum tube equivalent it performs exactly the same rectifying function when used in a similar type of circuit [3D]. But it does not have a filament or heater and so a semiconductor diode does not consume a large amount of power. It makes cooling the equipment unnecessary as well as enabling the size and cost of any associated transformer to be reduced.

CONNECTIONS

See also
1532 What is an electric current?
1544 Basic AC circuits
1546 Semiconductors
1668 Electronic devices

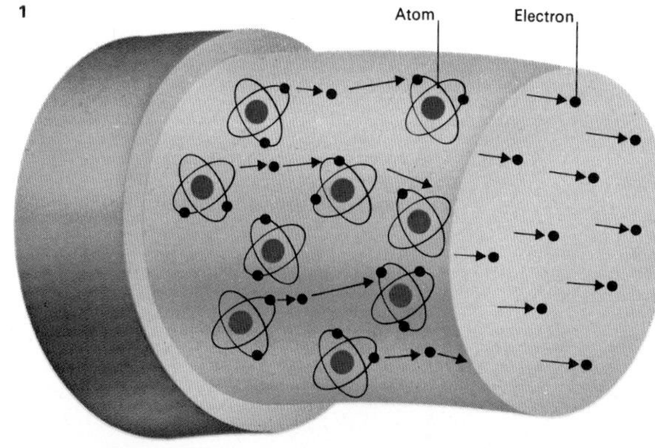
1
Atom
Electron

1 By applying an electromotive force (emf) to the ends of a wire made of a metal such as copper a flow of electrons can be maintained. Such a current is possible because the atoms of good conducting materials allow their electrons to escape easily under the influence of an emf. And just as easily these atoms pick up other electrons that have drifted from neighboring ones.

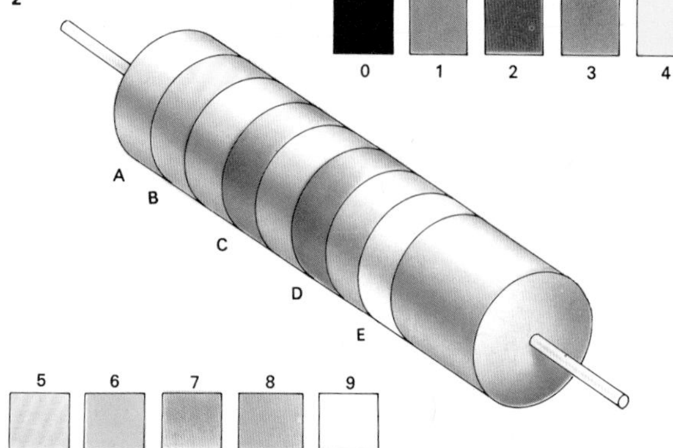
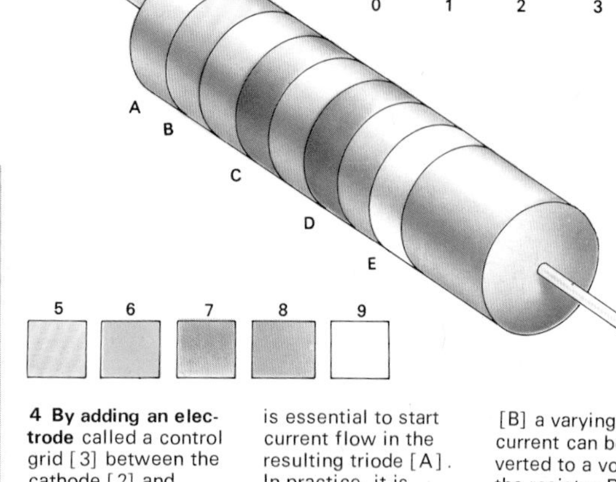
2
0
1
2
3
4
A
B
C
D
E
5
6
7
8
9

2 Carbon resistors usually have their resistance value in ohms (ranging up to millions of ohms) marked on them in an internationally recognized color code. This resistor has a value of 470 ohms with a tolerance (accuracy) of 10%. The key to this simple code is as follows: body color [A] has no significance; ring B gives the first figure, ring C gives the second figure, ring D gives the numbers of zeros to be added to the digits in B and C. If there is a fourth ring E it indicates tolerance: silver 10%, gold 5%. An absence of a fourth ring would indicate a tolerance of 20%.

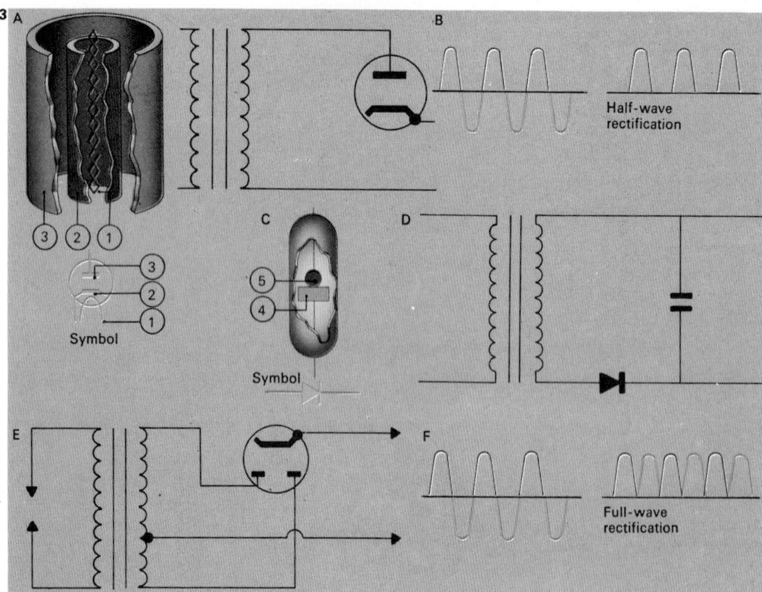
3 A
B
Half-wave rectification
C
D
Symbol
Symbol
E
F
Full-wave rectification

3 When a voltage is applied [A] to the filament [1] of a diode it causes the cathode [2] to emit electrons that are instantly attracted to the anode [3]. As the anode cannot emit electrons, current flow is possible only in one direction. Therefore the diode is ideal as a rectifier of alternating current, either as a half-wave rectifier [B] or a full-wave rectifier [F] using a different circuit with a pair of anodes to produce a "double diode" [E]. The solid-state component, known as a semiconductor diode, is more efficient as it does not need a filament or a heater. This device [C] has a layer of *p*-type semiconductor material [4] and a bead of *n*-type [5]. This combination has a low resistance in one direction and a high resistance in the other, allowing current to flow in only one direction and therefore producing rectification. A half-wave rectification circuit using such a diode is shown in [D].

4 By adding an electrode called a control grid [3] between the cathode [2] and the anode [4] the current in the tube can be controlled by the voltage on the grid. As with the diode, a filament [1] is essential to start current flow in the resulting triode [A]. In practice, it is found that a small change in grid voltage results in a large change in anode current. By using this effect in the circuit [B] a varying anode current can be converted to a voltage in the resistor R. The result is a signal amplified relative to the input at the control grid [C].

By adding an extra electrode to the diode in 1906 the American inventor Lee De Forest (1873–1961) controlled the flow of electrons between the cathode and the anode [4A]. And by adding other basic circuit elements, in this case resistors and capacitors, the triode could be used as a voltage amplifier [4B]. Later, other grids were added to the triode to improve performance, especially in early radio receivers.

The transistor

Following a successful research program directed by William Bradford Shockley (1910–) at the Bell Laboratories in New Jersey, the world of electronics was suddenly presented with the first solid-state three-electrode device, which was destined to end the supremacy of the vacuum tube. Shockley, John Bardeen, and Walter Houser Brattain, were awarded the Nobel prize for physics in 1956 for work on the development of the transistor in 1948.

As a result of this work the world now enjoys the benefits of small, inexpensive portable radios that run on small batteries [5]. Inspecting a circuit shows that transistors are even smaller than many of the other conventional components, despite the fact that these are miniaturized. A transistor consists of a layer of one type of semiconductor material between two layers of a different type. These materials are called *p*-type and *n*-type and either of them can form the inner layer. Taking up even less room, an integrated circuit has one or more transistors and other circuit components formed within a single "chip" of semiconductor material.

An interesting feature of practical tube and transistor circuits is the use of "feedback" to improve the quality of the sound produced by an amplifier. This is a refinement to overcome the distortion of the signal that can take place between the input and the output circuits of a tube or transistor or of several such devices.

In small portable transistor radios, there is seldom any output transformer at all because a "single-ended" push-pull output stage is used. This reduces both cost and weight.

KEY

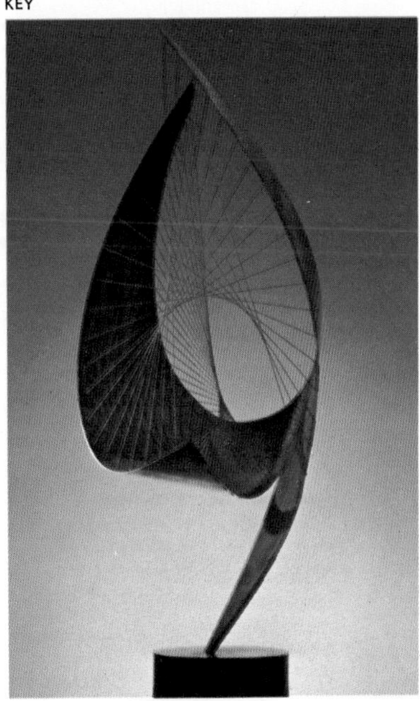

The mysteries of the atom have fascinated many artists. "Theme on Electronics" by the sculptor Barbara Hepworth (1903–75) was executed in 1957 for the Mullard Electronics Centre in London. It symbolizes the world of the electron. Every atom can be pictured with one or more electrons orbiting a central nucleus (with one or more protons and sometimes one or more neutrons as well). The electron always carries a negative charge and the central nucleus a positive one. Normally these charges balance each other exactly, so that neither the negative nor the positive charge predominates – in other words an atom is normally electrically neutral.

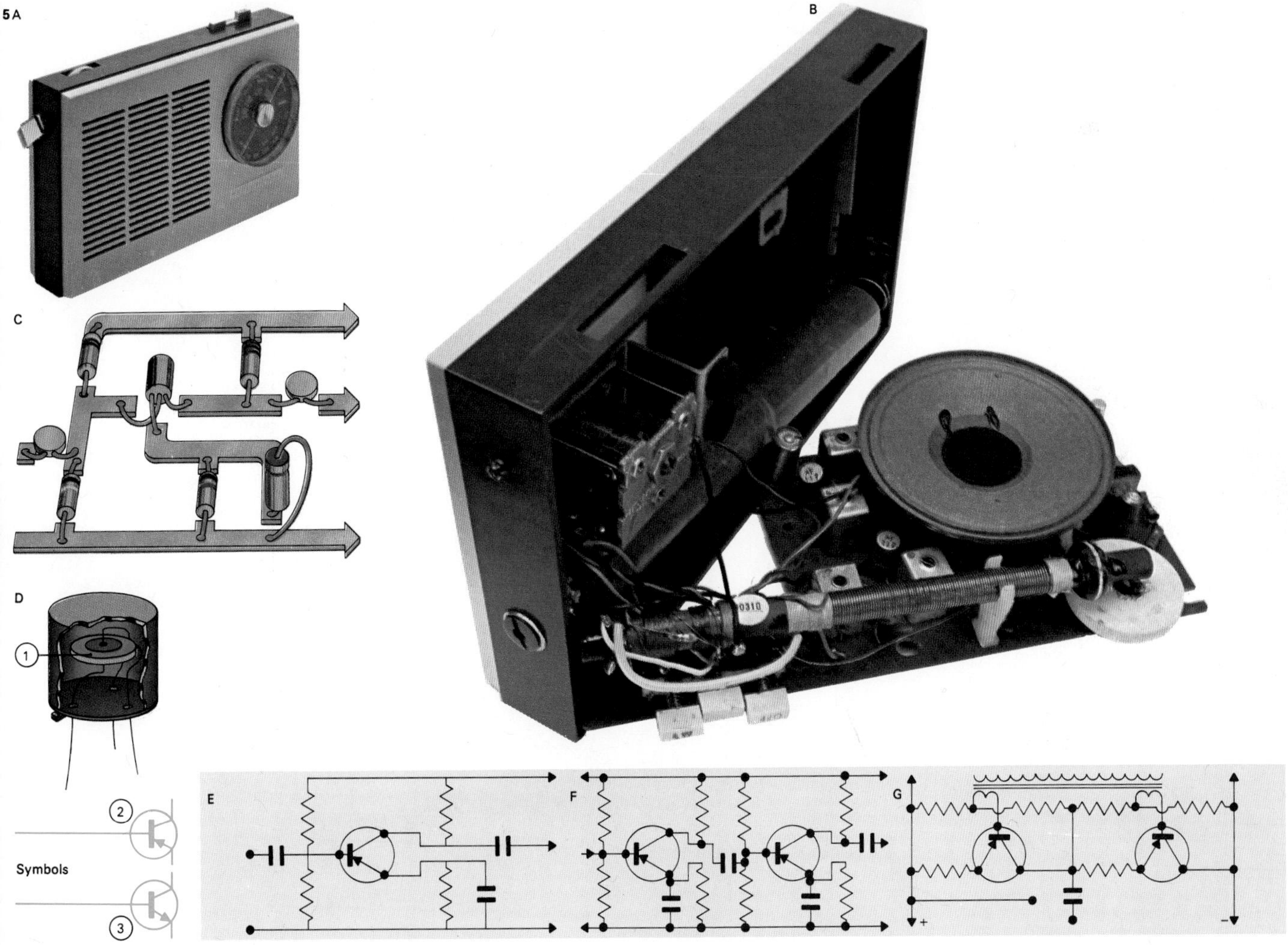

5 A modern portable radio [A] owes its existence to the invention of the transistor in 1948. Without transistors such devices as this one were almost out of the question as far as mass production was concerned because tubes and most other parts were too large. Looking inside the set [B] it is possible to see how many transistors and other components can be packed into such a small space and yet leave room for the batteries and loudspeaker. Within a portable transistor radio there are several types of amplifying circuits. In a typical one-stage transistor amplifier [C], several components are grouped around the transistor, which emphasizes its small size even more. The upper wires of the various capacitors and resistors are folded back and joined onto the printed circuit board. Basically the transistor itself [D] comprises a center layer called the base [1] of one type of semiconductor material sandwiched between two other layers of the opposite type of semiconductor material (the collector and the emitter). The two types are *n*-type and *p*-type and the composition of the sandwich is denoted by the names of the transistor types: *pnp* [2] and *npn* [3]. The essential difference is in the polarities of the three terminals, and the two types of transistors are distinguished by the directions of the emitter arrows in the symbols. The circuit [E] of the transistor amplifier [C] is used in a portable radio with a negative feedback circuit [F] for improving sound quality. Where high output is needed a "single-ended," push-pull circuit [G] is used, each amplifying half of the signal.

What is chemistry?

The basic building block with which chemistry is concerned is the atom. Chemistry deals with the properties of different atoms, the ways in which they join together to form molecules, and the interactions of molecules with one another.

The stuff of atoms

To the chemist, an atom is made up of three kinds of subatomic particles—proton, neutron, and electron. The only difference between a neutron and a proton is that a neutron has no electric charge, whereas a proton has a unit of positive charge. An equal unit of negative charge is carried by the electron, which is much smaller.

In any atom, the protons and neutrons are packed closely together in the central nucleus. Surrounding this, but much less closely packed, are the atom's electrons. The radius of a neutral atom—that is, one in which there are as many electrons as protons—is about 10,000 times larger than the radius of its nucleus. An atom is composed largely of empty space. Because of this, it is much more likely, when two atoms collide, that their electrons will interact with one another than that the two nuclei will ever come into contact.

Different kinds of atoms result from the combination of different numbers of protons, neutrons, and electrons. The number of protons in an atom is its atomic number, and the total mass of all the subatomic particles (protons, neutrons, and electrons) is its atomic weight. The simplest atom, that of hydrogen, consists of a single proton and a single electron. If a neutron is added to the nucleus of hydrogen, a different kind of atom, called deuterium, is formed. In many ways, the behavior of hydrogen and deuterium are the same—as one might expect of two atoms each with only one electron. As a result, the hydrogen atom with no neutron (sometimes called protium) and the deuterium atom are classed by the chemist as being different isotopes of the same element. There is also a third isotope of the element hydrogen. This is tritium, with two neutrons and one proton in its nucleus. But if a second proton is added to a tritium nucleus and, to balance the electric charge, another electron is placed around this nucleus, the situation is quite different. The atom shows no resemblance in its chemical behavior to any of the hydrogen isotopes. It is an atom of a different element—helium.

How elements are built up

The element to which any atom belongs is defined by the number of protons in its nucleus. The number of neutrons can usually vary slightly, to give a range of isotopes. The isotopes of an element have different masses but identical chemical properties. There are many stable isotopes in nature, but among the elements with about 90 or more protons, such as uranium, the isotopes tend to be unstable and the nuclei break down to form atoms of other elements [4]. Nuclear reactors and atomic bombs depend on this instability.

As the elements build up, their nuclei are surrounded by more and more electrons which are arranged according to definite rules. The positive charge of the protons in the nucleus attracts the negatively charged electrons. The electrons, however, do not

CONNECTIONS

See also
1552 Classification of elements
1480 What is an atom?
1484 Beyond the atom
1554 Survey of groups of elements
1558 Simple chemicals an their structures
1562 Chemicals in solutio
1566 Electrochemistry
1570 Toward the chemistr of life

1 This iron rosette, dating from the 7th century BC, once decorated an Etruscan chariot. Techniques of working iron and, earlier, copper and bronze, go back thousands of years. They allowed men to make tools and weapons, implements that advanced both agriculture and warfare. Extraction and purification of metals probably developed accidentally, but led to the founding of present-day chemistry.

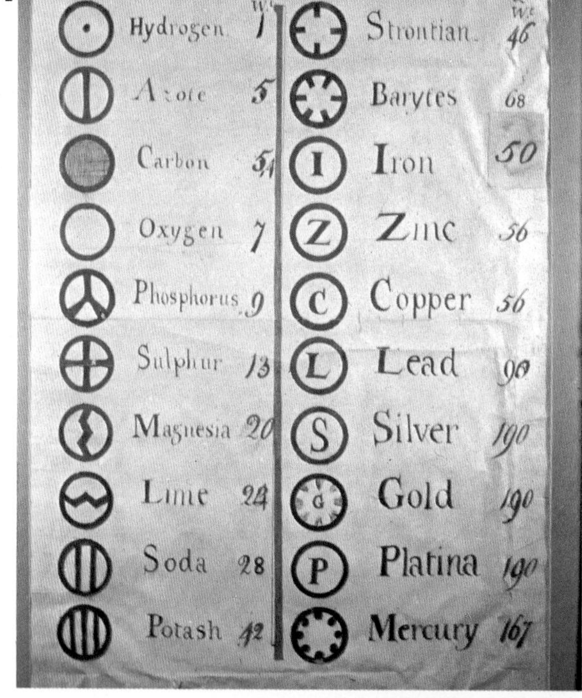
Hydrogen 1
Azote 5
Carbon 5,4
Oxygen 7
Phosphorus 9
Sulphur 13
Magnesia 20
Lime 24
Soda 28
Potash 42
Strontian 46
Barytes 68
Iron 50
Zinc 56
Copper 56
Lead 90
Silver 190
Gold 190
Platina 190
Mercury 167

2 Ancient Greeks, such as Democritus, believed that matter is made from tiny particles, which they called atoms. But "atomism" did not become a useful part of chemistry until John Dalton (1766–1844) proposed that atoms have different weights, and that the weight of any particular atom is constant. By 1808 Dalton had drawn up this list of symbols for the different types of atoms (elements) and their atomic weights.

3 John Dalton, the son of a weaver, is one of chemistry's most distinguished figures as a result of his work on the atomic theory. He was born in Cumberland, England, in 1766, into a Quaker family. At the age of 12 he became a schoolteacher. He moved to Manchester in 1793 and stayed there until his death in 1844, earning his living by teaching mathematics and natural philosophy (physics). Dalton was color-blind and in addition to the atomic theory, which he developed during the first decade of the 1800s, he also investigated color blindness (sometimes called Daltonism) and meteorology, the study of weather.

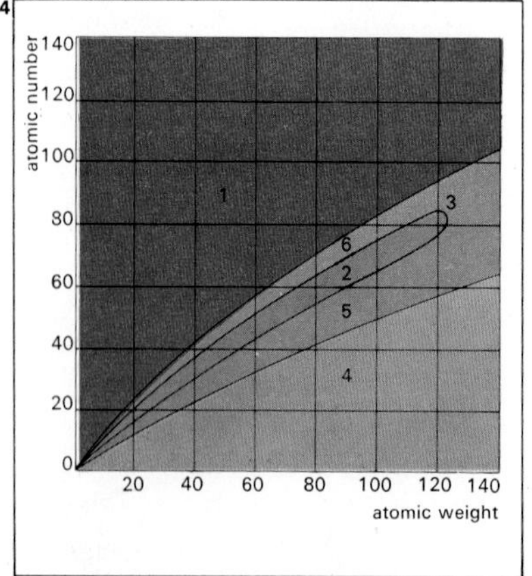
atomic number
140
120
100
80
60
40
20
0
20 40 60 80 100 120 140
atomic weight
1
2
3
4
5
6

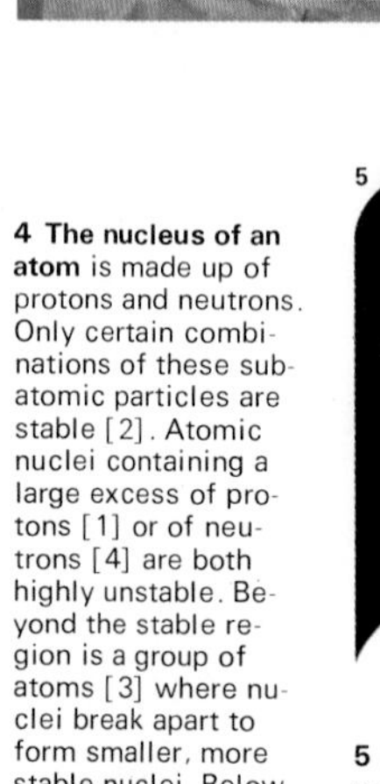

4 The nucleus of an atom is made up of protons and neutrons. Only certain combinations of these subatomic particles are stable [2]. Atomic nuclei containing a large excess of protons [1] or of neutrons [4] are both highly unstable. Beyond the stable region is a group of atoms [3] where nuclei break apart to form smaller, more stable nuclei. Below [5], and above [6], the stable regions are unstable nuclei, which decay into stable elements.

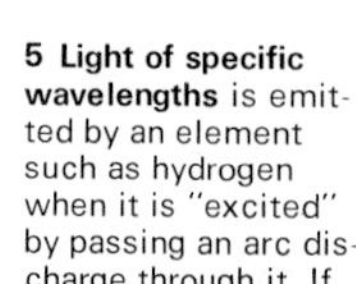

5 Light of specific wavelengths is emitted by an element such as hydrogen when it is "excited" by passing an arc discharge through it. If light of these wavelengths is passed through the vapor of the same element, it is absorbed to form an absorption spectrum. In the 19th century scientists wondered why elements should have such discrete spectra, and why the spectral lines could be divided into four classes—called sharp, principal, diffuse, and fundamental. Only when modern atomic theory was developed was an answer found.

fall into the nucleus—their momentum about it prevents this, just as the earth's momentum in its orbit around the sun prevents gravitational forces from making the earth "fall" into the sun.

Electronic orbitals

The electron in a hydrogen atom spreads out around the nucleus in a spherical shell. It is possible to assign to any point only a probability that the electron is there at an instant in time. The region around a hydrogen nucleus where there is the highest probability of finding the electron is the electron's orbital.

In 1925, the German physicist Wolfgang Pauli formulated rules for electronic orbitals. His major rule was that no two electrons in the same atom can be in exactly the same quantum state. The quantum state of an atom is defined by four different numbers. The first of these, known as the principal quantum number, describes the average distance between the electron and the nucleus. The second and third quantum numbers are related to the shape of the orbital, which is not always spherical. The final quantum number is the spin of the electron, which can only be $+1/2$ or $-1/2$. The possible values for the second and third quantum numbers depend on the value of the principal quantum number in such a way that, when it is 1, there are only two possible quantum states (and orbitals); when it is 2, there are 8; when it is 3, there are 18; and so on, according to the formula $2n^2$, where n is the principal quantum number.

The energy of any electron depends upon the first two quantum numbers and, because its behavior depends largely on its energy, chemists have developed a kind of shorthand for describing an electron's energy level. Each electron in an atom can be described by a number followed by a letter. The number is the same as the principal quantum number, but the values 0, 1, 2, and 3 for the second quantum number are represented (for historical reasons) by the letters s, p, d and f [7]. By knowing the numbers of electrons in different orbitals, a chemist can predict the behavior of any particular atom.

KEY

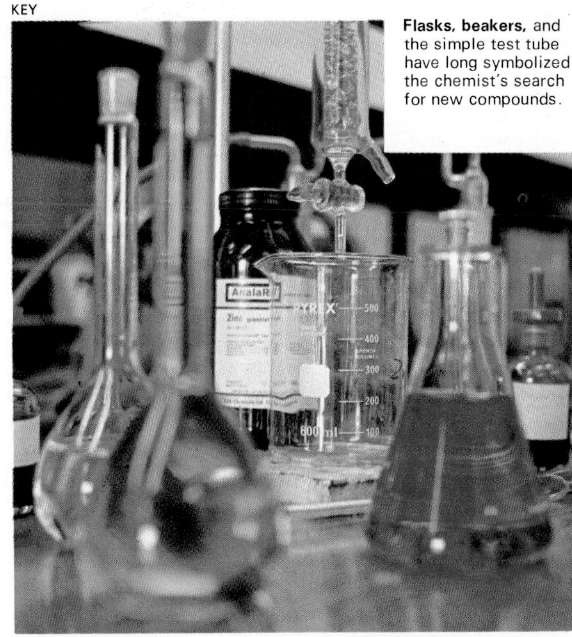
AnalaR
PYREX
500
400
300
200
100
600 ml

Flasks, beakers, and the simple test tube have long symbolized the chemist's search for new compounds.

6 A B C D

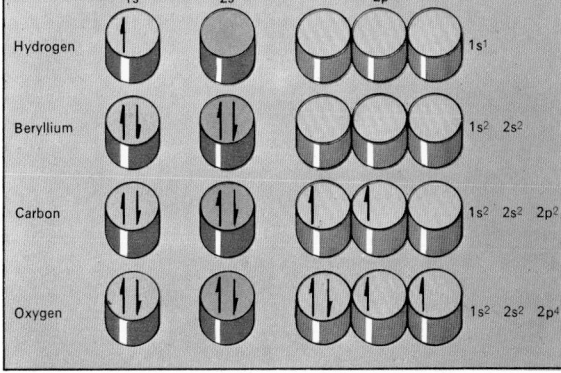

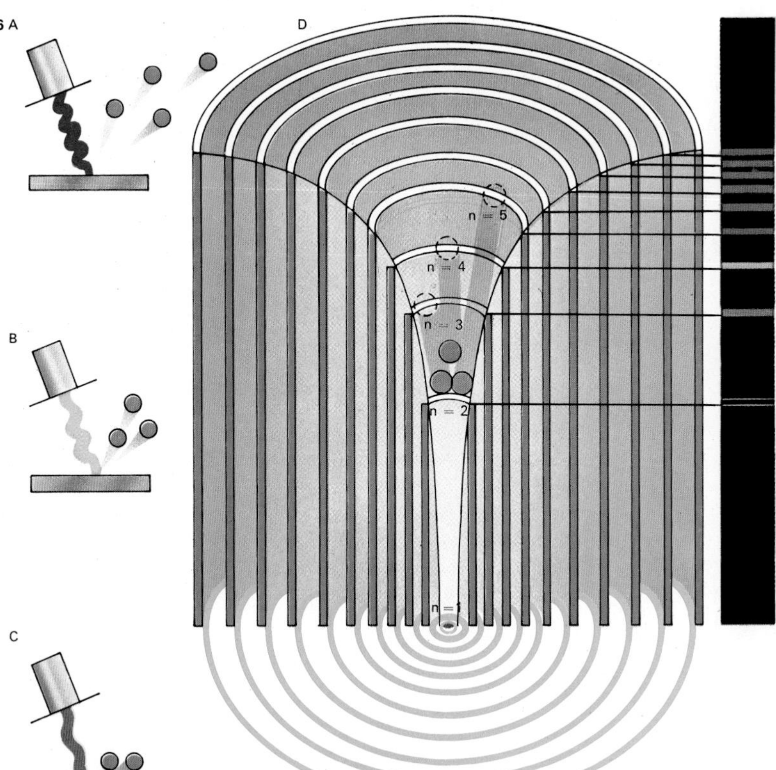
n = 5
n = 4
n = 3
n = 2
n = 1

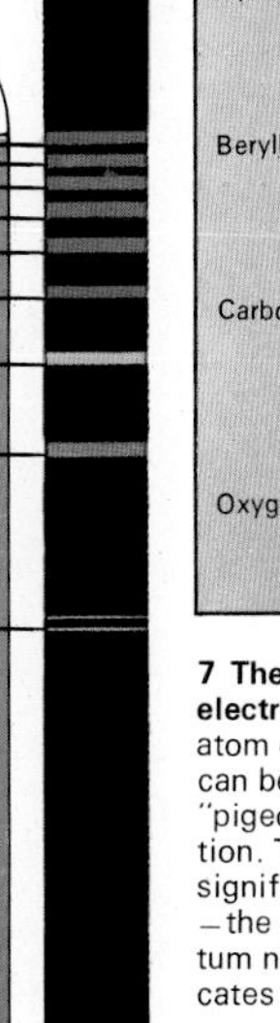

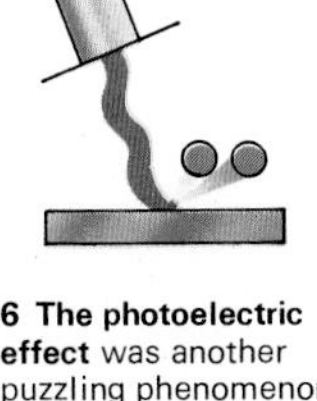

6 The photoelectric effect was another puzzling phenomenon for 19th-century physicists. Some metals give off electrons when light is shined on them, but the number of the electrons depends on the intensity of the light [A-C] and not its wavelength, and demonstrates the quantum nature of light [D]. Electrons occupy orbitals that have specific energies associated with them and they absorb or emit energy when they "jump" between the orbitals.

7

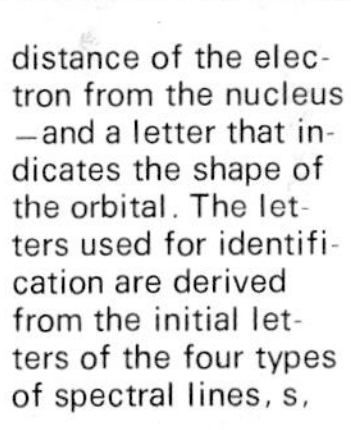
1s
2s
2p
Hydrogen
1s¹
Beryllium
1s² 2s²
Carbon
1s² 2s² 2p²
Oxygen
1s² 2s² 2p⁴

7 The positions of electrons in a neutral atom of any element can be shown in a "pigeonhole" notation. The orbitals are signified by a number—the principal quantum number that indicates the average distance of the electron from the nucleus—and a letter that indicates the shape of the orbital. The letters used for identification are derived from the initial letters of the four types of spectral lines, s, p, d, and f, and then proceed alphabetically. Because electrons—shown by half arrows—are able to spin in completely opposite directions, each pigeonhole is able to hold two electrons.

8

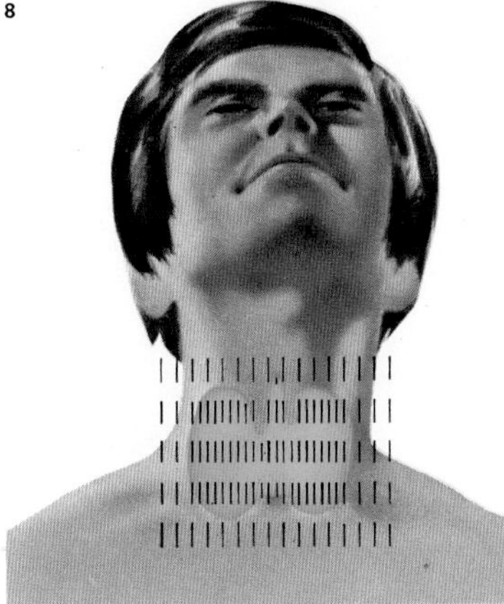

8 The breakdown of unstable isotopes of different elements can be detected and sometimes utilized. Radioactive isotopes (also called radioisotopes) have widespread applications in medicine. For example, a dose of radioactive iodine is taken up preferentially by the thyroid gland in the neck. Its presence can be detected and used to map the gland, to see if it is diseased, cancerous, or (as in the one pictured here) enlarged well beyond normal.

9

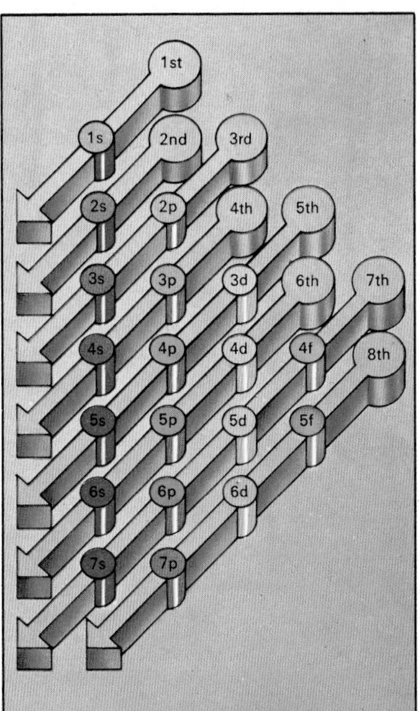
1st
1s
2nd
3rd
2s
2p
4th
5th
3s
3p
3d
6th
7th
4s
4p
4d
4f
8th
5s
5p
5d
5f
6s
6p
6d
7s
7p

9 Atoms have more and more electrons as they build up to form the heavier elements. The order in which they occupy orbitals depends on the particular binding energy. In general, the closer an electron is to the nucleus, the greater is the energy. As electrons get farther away from the nucleus, the energy relationships become more complex. For example, the 4s orbital is more strongly binding than the 3d orbital, and is filled with electrons before 3d. The chart shows the general order for the filling of orbitals as atoms get larger. Even this is an approximation, however, and there are a few exceptions to it. The rules for electronic orbitals were formulated by W. Pauli in 1925.

Classification of elements

Since man first began to purify metals from rocks thousands of years ago, he has been learning how different substances behave and trying to detect a pattern in that behavior. But the major breakthrough in discovering the pattern of chemistry did not come until just over 100 years ago, when the Russian chemist Dmitri Mendeleev [Key] proposed his periodic system of elements.

Earlier, the French chemist Antoine Lavoisier (1743–94) had revived Robert Boyle's use of the word "element" for substances that could not be broken down into anything simpler. During the next 75 years, many new elements were discovered [4] and substances previously thought to have been elements were shown to be compounds—two or more elements combined.

Atomic weights

As more elements were discovered, and more of their properties cataloged, it became clear that some elements were similar to others. Sodium and potassium, for example, first isolated in the early 1800s by Humphry Davy (1778–1829), are both soft metals that react violently with water to produce alkaline solutions. It gradually became obvious that there must be a way of tabulating the elements so that those with similar properties were grouped together.

One property of elements that was being cataloged at that time was atomic weight. An atom is extremely small. Nevertheless each atom does have a definite mass. Most of this comes from the neutrons and protons in its nucleus. For example, a deuterium atom—with one proton and one neutron in its nucleus—is almost twice as heavy as a hydrogen atom, with its one proton. An oxygen atom, with eight neutrons and eight protons, is about 16 times as heavy.

Using various analytical skills, nineteenth-century chemists gradually cataloged the comparative atomic weights of the elements with increasing accuracy. The weight of a hydrogen atom was formerly taken as 1 and the weights of other atoms related to it: atomic weights are now based on a value of 12 for carbon-12 (six neutrons and six protons), giving hydrogen a value of 1.008.

By organizing the elements in tabular form in order of increasing atomic weight, Mendeleev produced a periodic table. Unlike those proposed by other chemists, his had gaps in it. Where the difference in atomic weight between two neighboring elements seemed exceptionally large, he assumed that there was an element of intermediate weight that had yet to be discovered. Because his scheme also arranged elements in families, he was able to predict the properties of some of these undiscovered elements [6]. Before the end of the nineteenth century, his assumptions were vindicated by the discovery of some of these "missing" elements.

Atomic numbers

It is known that the physical basis underlying the periodic classification is not the atomic weights of the elements, but their atomic numbers—that is, the numbers of protons in their nuclei. The regularities observed in different families of elements result from similarities in their electronic arrangement. [5].

CONNECTIONS

See also
1550 What is chemistry?
1554 Survey of groups of elements
1556 Joining atoms

1

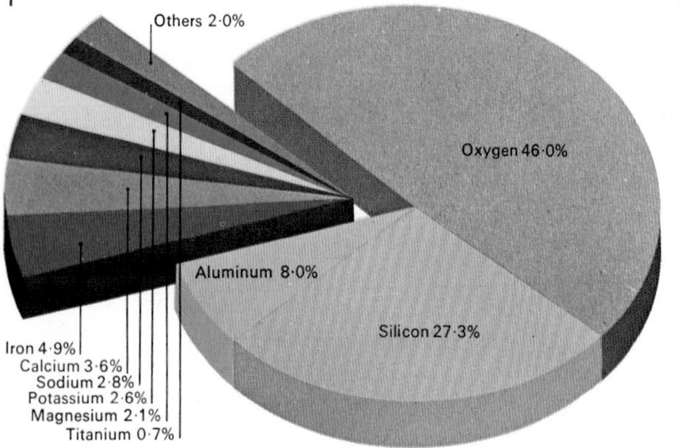

Others 2·0%
Oxygen 46·0%
Aluminum 8·0%
Silicon 27·3%
Iron 4·9%
Calcium 3·6%
Sodium 2·8%
Potassium 2·6%
Magnesium 2·1%
Titanium 0·7%

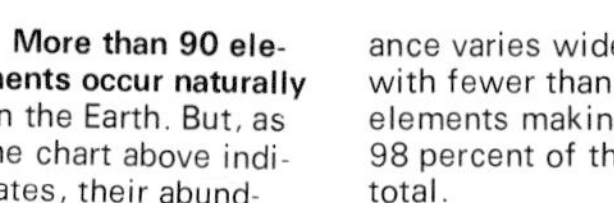

1 More than 90 elements occur naturally on the Earth. But, as the chart above indicates, their abundance varies widely, with fewer than 10 elements making up 98 percent of the total.

2 Energy is needed to remove a single electron from an atom of any element. The amount needed, called the first ionization potential, is different for each element. When all these energies are plotted, with the elements in order of increasing atomic number along the bottom, it can be seen that they vary in a periodic manner—rising gradually and then suddenly falling, before rising again.

3

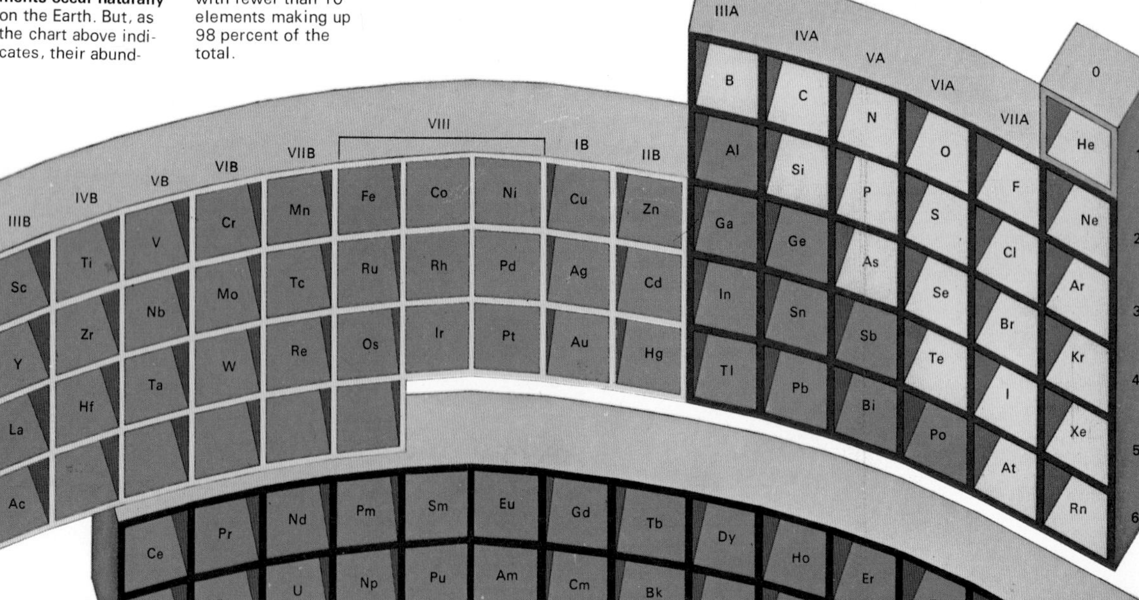

IA
IIA
IIIB
IVB
VB
VIB
VIIB
VIII
IB
IIB
IIIA
IVA
VA
VIA
VIIA
0
H He
Li Be B C N O F Ne
Na Mg Al Si P S Cl Ar
K Ca Sc Ti V Cr Mn Fe Co Ni Cu Zn Ga Ge As Se Br Kr
Rb Sr Y Zr Nb Mo Tc Ru Rh Pd Ag Cd In Sn Sb Te I Xe
Cs Ba La Hf Ta W Re Os Ir Pt Au Hg Tl Pb Bi Po At Rn
Fr Ra Ac
Ce Pr Nd Pm Sm Eu Gd Tb Dy Ho Er Tm Yb Lu
Th Pa U Np Pu Am Cm Bk Cf Es Fm Md No Lr
1
2
3
4
5
6
7

3 The periodic table in its modern version shows the arrangements of 103 elements in increasing atomic number. The vertical columns, or groups, marked by roman numerals, contain elements having similar properties. Metallic elements are in yellow boxes, nonmetallic ones in blue. The seven horizontal rows or periods, indicated by arabic numerals on the left-hand side, relate to the building up of the atomic constituents of each element. The two rows of elements shown separately are the lanthanide and actinide series. These show similarities because the structure of the outermost electronic shell is the same for each.

Lithium (Li) has three electrons and potassium (K) 19. According to the rules for the occupancy of orbitals (the regions in space where electrons are most likely to be found), lithium has as many electrons as are allowed (two) in the orbital with the principal quantum number 1. It also has one electron left over; this occupies the next lowest energy orbital, called 2*s*. Potassium on the other hand, has electrons filling all possible orbitals in the first three levels, and one more. This last electron is in the 3*s* orbital. Thus, in both elements, the outermost occupied orbital has a single electron in it.

If two atoms have the same number of electrons in the outermost orbital layer, or "shell" as it is usually called, it is reasonable to expect that their chemical properties should be similar. All the elements listed beneath lithium in a modern periodic table [3] have one electron in their outer shell.

Man-made elements

For many years, it was believed that element 92 (uranium) had the heaviest atoms occurring naturally on Earth. It was believed that as atomic size increases, the atoms become less stable and any atoms of heavier elements that might once have been present on Earth had broken down. Since 1940 chemists in the United States and the Soviet Union have been making "transuranium" elements artificially [7]. Glenn Seaborg (1912–   ), involved with much of this work, used the periodic table to predict the likely properties of transuranium elements. His predictions go as far as element 168, although, for physical reasons, few of these elements would be stable for long enough to check whether or not their properties did coincide with predictions.

But another of his theories based on the periodic table has been proved. Because of their chemical similarities, members of the same family of elements often occur in the same minerals. Seaborg predicted that, if there were any traces of transuranic elements left on Earth, they would be found in minerals rich in other elements of the same family. In 1971, he discovered naturally occurring plutonium in a sample of uranium ore.

KEY

The Russian chemist Dmitri Mendeleev (1834–1907) was responsible for proposing the periodic table of the elements in 1869. This major theoretical breakthrough provided the necessary classification system for making the similarities in the properties of certain elements understandable. Mendeleev was born in Siberia in 1834 and trained as a teacher in St Petersburg. Subsequently he became professor of chemistry at St Petersburg University, a post he held until 1890. The most convincing justification for Mendeleev's periodic table was his correct prediction of the properties of two then-unknown elements.

4 The elements, their symbols and atomic numbers

Element	Symbol	No.	Element	Symbol	No.	Element	Symbol	No.
Actinium	Ac	89	Hafnium	Hf	72	Promethium	Pm	61
Aluminum	Al	13	Helium	He	2	Protactinium	Pa	91
Americium	Am	95	Holmium	Ho	67	Radium	Ra	88
Antimony	Sb	51	Hydrogen	H	1	Radon	Rn	86
Argon	Ar	18	Indium	In	49	Rhenium	Re	75
Arsenic	As	33	Iodine	I	53	Rhodium	Rh	45
Astatine	At	85	Iridium	Ir	77	Rubidium	Rb	37
Barium	Ba	56	Iron	Fe	26	Ruthenium	Ru	44
Berkelium	Bk	97	Krypton	Kr	36	Samarium	Sm	62
Beryllium	Be	4	Lanthanum	La	57	Scandium	Sc	21
Bismuth	Bi	83	Lawrencium	Lr	103	Selenium	Se	34
Boron	B	5	Lead	Pb	82	Silicon	Si	14
Bromine	Br	35	Lithium	Li	3	Silver	Ag	47
Cadmium	Cd	48	Lutetium	Lu	71	Sodium	Na	11
Caesium	Cs	55	Magnesium	Mg	12	Strontium	Sr	38
Calcium	Ca	20	Manganese	Mn	25	Sulfur	S	16
Californium	Cf	98	Mendelevium	Md	101	Tantalum	Ta	73
Carbon	C	6	Mercury	Hg	80	Technetium	Tc	43
Cerium	Ce	58	Molybdenum	Mo	42	Tellurium	Te	52
Chlorine	Cl	17	Neodymium	Nd	60	Terbium	Tb	65
Chromium	Cr	24	Neon	Ne	10	Thallium	Tl	81
Cobalt	Co	27	Neptunium	Np	93	Thorium	Th	90
Copper	Cu	29	Nickel	Ni	28	Thulium	Tm	69
Curium	Cm	96	Niobium	Nb	41	Tin	Sn	50
Dysprosium	Dy	66	Nitrogen	N	7	Titanium	Ti	22
Einsteinium	Es	99	Nobelium	No	102	Tungsten	W	74
Erbium	Er	68	Osmium	Os	76	Uranium	U	92
Europium	Eu	63	Oxygen	O	8	Vanadium	V	23
Fermium	Fm	100	Palladium	Pd	46	Xenon	Xe	54
Fluorine	F	9	Phosphorus	P	15	Ytterbium	Yb	70
Francium	Fr	87	Platinum	Pt	78	Yttrium	Y	39
Gadolinium	Gd	64	Plutonium	Pu	94	Zinc	Zn	30
Gallium	Ga	31	Polonium	Po	84	Zirconium	Zr	40
Germanium	Ge	32	Potassium	K	19			
Gold	Au	79	Praseodymium	Pr	59			

5 The periodicity of the elements is caused by their electronic structures. The electrons in any atom can be envisaged as occupying "shells," each of which can hold only a certain number of electrons. For the first three shells, the numbers are 2, 8, and 18. If the outermost shell is either completely filled, or holds 8 electrons, the element is chemically unreactive: the gases helium (He), neon (Ne), argon (Ar), and krypton (Kr) all fulfill this condition. Lithium (Li) and potassium (K) are similar because they both have one outer electron, and both differ chemically from magnesium (Mg) and bromine (Br).

5

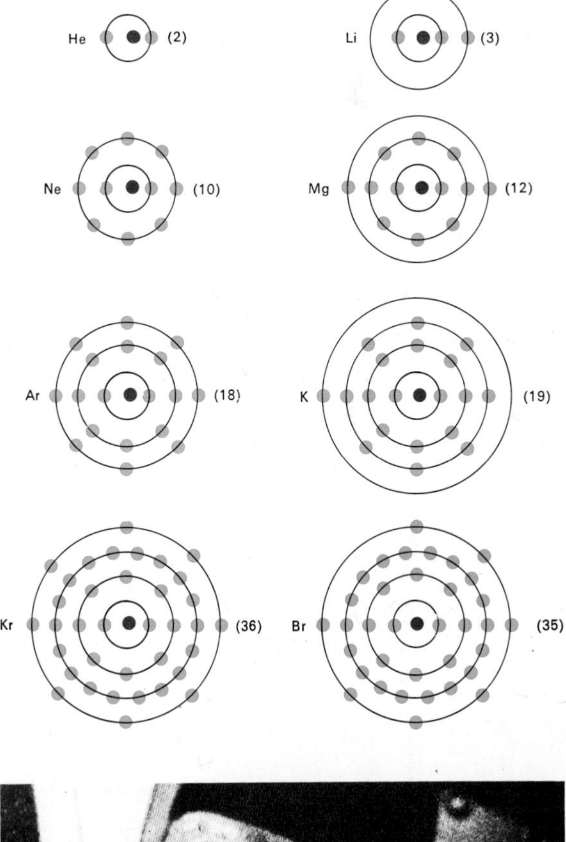
He (2)
Li (3)
Ne (10)
Mg (12)
Ar (18)
K (19)
Kr (36)
Br (35)

6

6 Germanium, a metal "grown" in this form for making transistors, was unknown when Mendeleev proposed his periodic table. In 1871, however, he predicted the existence of an element with the properties of germanium and called it eka silicium, from silicium (the old name for silicon) and the Sanskrit word eka meaning "one." Germanium was discovered 15 years after he had made his prediction.

7

7 The first samples of element 94, plutonium, were produced in 1940 in a US laboratory. One of 11 "transuranium" elements that have now definitely been synthesized, it is used as a fuel in some types of nuclear reactors.

Survey of groups of elements

Atoms of all elements consist of a central nucleus surrounded by a "cloud" containing one or more electrons. The electrons can be thought of as occupying a series of shells. The behavior of a particular element depends largely on the number of electrons in its outermost shells. Other factors, such as the total number of electron shells, also play a part in determining behavior, but it is the dominance of the outer electron configuration that underlies the periodic law and justifies the grouping of the elements into groups or families.

The s-elements and their reactions

Each electron shell is made up of various volumes in space called orbitals, known as *s*-, *p*-, *d*- and *f*-orbitals, and each is at a higher energy than the one below it. Those elements in which the outermost shell can have only one or two electrons can be grouped together as the "*s*-elements" (because it is only the *s*-orbital that is occupied in the outer shell). These are lithium, beryllium, and the elements directly below them in the periodic table [1]. All readily form positive ions by the loss of their outer electrons and they are therefore mostly found as components of ionic compounds, commonly called salts. Many common substances contain these elements—for example, soda (sodium, Na), potash (potassium, K), gypsum (calcium, Ca), and carnallite (magnesium, Mg).

The *s*-elements with only one electron are more reactive than those with two. Thus if dropped in water, sodium reacts so violently that it catches fire; in the case of magnesium the reaction (release of hydrogen) gives off light, but is less violent.

The energy levels of electrons in the heavier elements are slightly complicated and, for this reason, many elements have a filled *s*-level but only a partially filled *d*-level below it. The part of the table ten elements wide beginning with scandium (Sc) includes the "transition" elements in which a *d*-level is successively filled. The outermost electron shell of these elements has an *s*-configuration, but it is the underlying layer of *d*-electrons that determines the element's chemical behavior. The lanthanide and actinide series form further subgroups; in their cases an *f*-group on a lower level begins to fill while the levels beyond contain one *d*-electron and two *s*-electrons.

The *d*-elements: "rare earths" and metals

For the elements scandium, yttrium (Y), and lanthanum (La), as well as the entire 14-element lanthanide series, the chemical behavior is dominated by the presence of the single *d*-electron. All these elements tend to form positive ions by the loss of this electron and the two *s*-electrons—giving ions with a charge of +3. The elements are all fairly reactive and all are rare, but some of these "rare earths" have found commercial uses, for example in transistors.

The other subseries, the actinides, is of greater importance as it contains the nuclear reactor fuel elements uranium and plutonium. But the importance of these is based on their nuclear instability rather than their chemical properties.

The other transition elements [4] are also important. They are all metals and many have large-scale industrial uses. All of these

CONNECTIONS

See also
1552 Classification of elements
1550 What is chemistry?
1556 Joining atoms
1558 Simple chemicals and their structures
1564 Key chemical reactions

1

Li	Be											B	C	N	O	F	Ne
Na	Mg											Al	Si	P	S	Cl	Ar
K	Ca	Sc	Ti	V	Cr	Mn	Fe	Co	Ni	Cu	Zn	Ga	Ge	As	Se	Br	Kr
Rb	Sr	Y	Zr	Nb	Mo	Tc	Ru	Rh	Pd	Ag	Cd	In	Sn	Sb	Te	I	Xe
Cs	Ba	La	Hf	Ta	W	Re	Os	Ir	Pt	Au	Hg	Tl	Pb	Bi	Po	At	Rn

1 Elements are extracted from minerals in different ways, according to their position on the periodic table. In the red group are reactive metals usually extracted by electrolysis. In the orange group, the elements frequently occur in ionic compounds, often combined with oxygen. These are often prepared by electrolysis. The third group (colored green) is commonly found as sulfides and the elements are obtained by roasting these and reducing the resultant oxides. Group four (colored yellow) contains relatively unreactive elements, found free or as compounds that yield the element when they are heated to a certain temperature. The fifth group (light brown) comprises nonmetals that occur free or as negative ions that can be converted to elements by electrolysis.

2 Magnesium is one of the reactive *s*-elements. It burns with an intense white flame, which made it useful in early "flash" photography. It is now used in torches employed underwater.

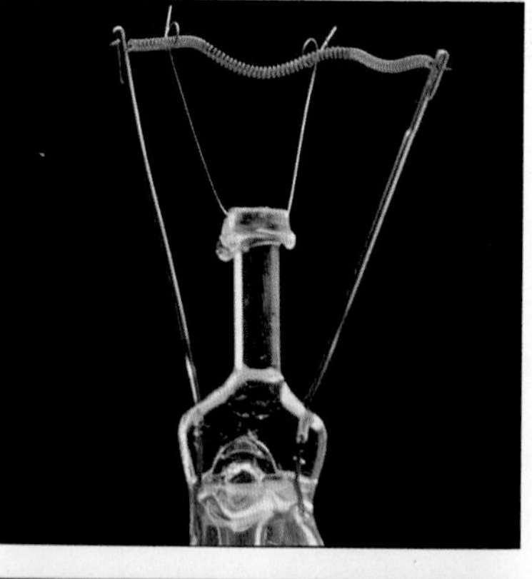

3 Tungsten was discovered in 1783 by the brothers Fausto and Don Juan d'Elhuyar. A fine wire made from tungsten becomes white hot when carrying an electric current, as in an electric light.

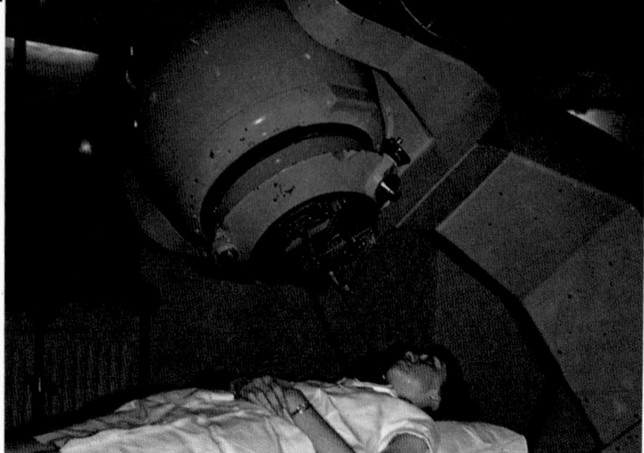

4 Cobalt, one of the transition metals, is the basis of various blue pigments. It is also an important constituent of some biological molecules. A most important use in recent years has been in the medical "cobalt bomb." A radioactive isotope of cobalt (cobalt-60), which gives off high-energy gamma rays, is used to direct this cell-destroying radiation at tumor sites in humans. It is used extensively in hospitals in the treatment of certain cancers to arrest their growth.

5 A compound exhibits a specific color when it absorbs white light—a mixture of all colors—by selectively reflecting a few wavelengths. Many salts of transition metals, such as iron and nickel, are colored. The exact color depends on which other atoms are associated with the metal. Thus chromium compounds have for centuries been used by painters for yellow pigments. Vincent van Gogh's "Sunflowers," shown here, is a good example of their use.

elements—except copper, silver, and gold [6]—have two electrons in an outer *s*-orbital and between two and ten electrons in the underlying, but more energetic *d*-orbital. Silver, copper, and gold could be expected to have two *s*-electrons and nine *d*-electrons. But, because the complete filling of a *d*-shell increases stability, they have only one *s*-electron and a full complement of ten *d*-electrons.

The transition elements are characterized by the ability to form several different ions, because of the complex behavior of electrons in the *d*-orbitals. Thus iron is found in ionic compounds as both Fe^{2+} (ferrous, with two electrons lost) and Fe^{3+} (ferric, with three electrons lost).

The *p*-elements and their grouping

To the right of the transition elements in the periodic table are the *p*-elements. In the groups headed by boron, carbon, nitrogen, oxygen, fluorine, and helium, it is the three *p*-orbitals (capable of holding a maximum of six electrons) that are the most important in determining chemical behavior. From left to right through this group the *p*-orbitals become increasingly filled, until the "completed octet" (two *s*- and six *p*-electrons) of the noble gases—the group headed by helium. These elements are unreactive and only recently have chemists made compounds including them.

The group headed by fluorine—the halogens—all need only one electron to complete the octet and they readily do this to form ions carrying a single negative charge. The oxygen group can form double-negative charged ions, but tend more to link with other atoms through covalent (non-ionic) bonds. The tendency toward covalent bonding is even more marked in the groups headed by nitrogen and carbon. The group headed by boron, where there are two *s*- and one *p*-electrons, like the group headed by scandium, shows more of a tendency to form ions. Aluminum, for example, readily loses its three outer electrons to form Al^{3+}, but aluminum chloride ($AlCl_3$) is not an ionic compound. The bonds joining the chlorine and aluminum atoms are partly ionic, partly covalent.

KEY

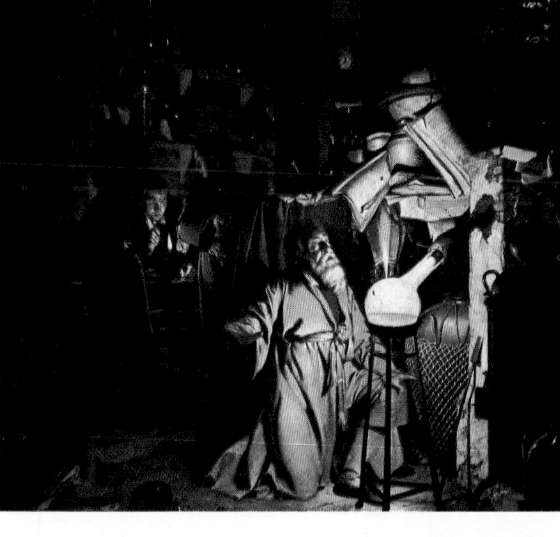

Elements such as iron have long been known. Others were first purified by alchemists such as Hennig Brand (died *c* 1692), shown after discovering phosphorus.

6

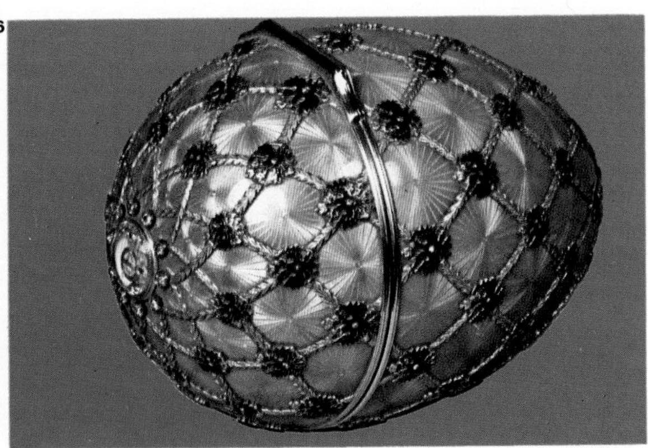

6 Precious metals often occur as free elements in nature. Not only gold and silver, which for centuries have been used in jewelry and ornamentation, such as this Fabergé egg, but others such as platinum and iridium also fall into this category. Silver and mercury are borderline cases. Mercury, for example, occurs as its sulfide, but heating releases the metal, which readily alloys with other metals.

7

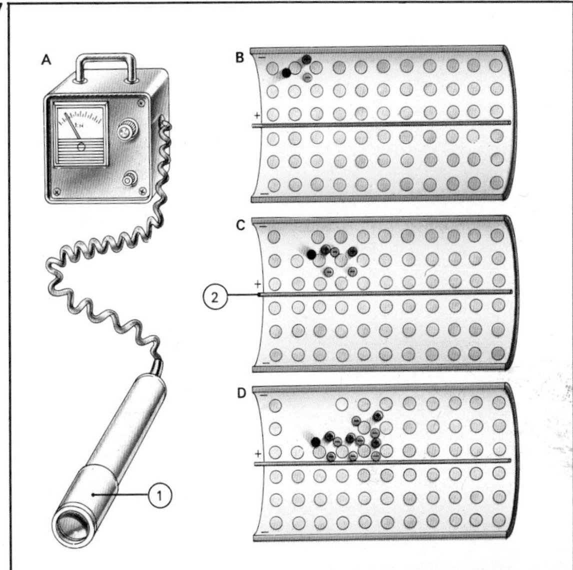
A
B
C
D
1
2

7 A Geiger-Müller counter [A] detects radioactivity in a chamber [1] containing neon atoms at low pressure [B]. The chamber contains neon atoms [grey] that are ionized by beta particles [black] to form positive ions [red] and electrons [blue]. [C] An electric field around an anode [2] accelerates electrons, which collide with other neon atoms [D] and split them to release more electrons.

8

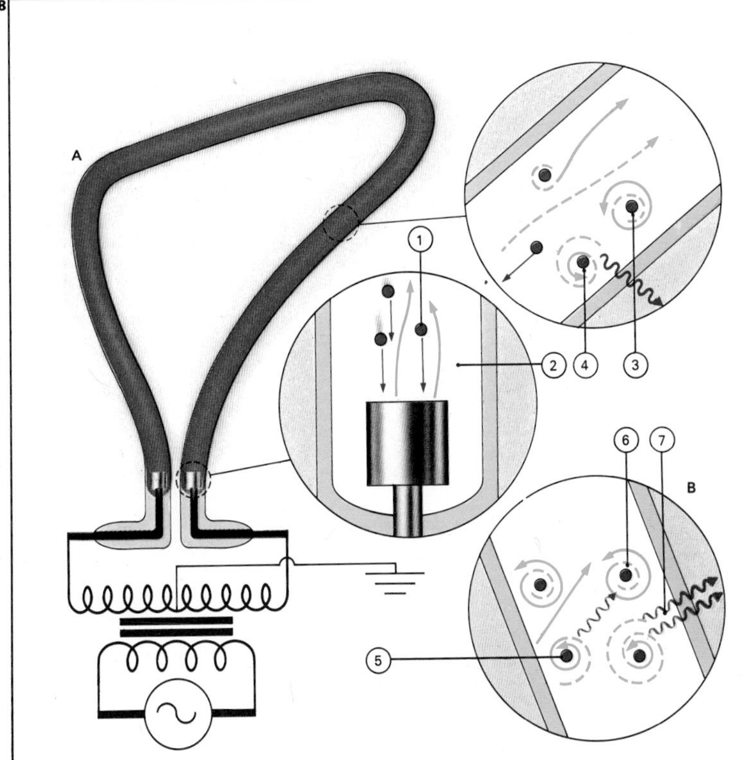
A
B
1
2
3
4
5
6
7

8 Neon is an unreactive element, yet it can be used to produce colored lights [A]. Positively charged ions [1] strike a negative electrode, causing emission of electrons [2], which "energize" electrons in neon atoms [3]. When the energized electrons return to their stable "ground" state [4], red light is emitted. Mercury vapor [B] emits ultraviolet light [5]. This may be absorbed by a fluorescent substance [6], which can release the energy in stages [7].

9

9 Marie Curie (1867–1934) was the first person to win two Nobel prizes; one in physics, the other in chemistry. She discovered polonium and radium and was responsible for much of the early research on radioactive elements.

Joining atoms

CONNECTIONS

See also
1480 What is an atom?
1558 Simple chemicals and their structures
1560 Complex chemicals and their structures
1566 Electrochemistry

Human beings and the world in which they live exist because atoms of elements join together to form compounds or molecules [Key]. Such compounds may have as few as two atoms or they may contain thousands linked together. From the basic building blocks—consisting of less than 100 elements—natural processes have produced hundreds of thousands of different compounds and chemists have synthesized thousands more.

Every atom consists of a small central nucleus surrounded by a "cloud" containing one or more electrons. When two atoms approach closely their clouds of electrons interact. Each electron has a negative electric charge, and for this reason the electron clouds repel one another. But when two atoms are close together the electrons of each, located in space in "orbitals," are attracted by the nucleus to which they "belong" and also by the nearby nucleus.

Forming a bond

The net result of these dual forces of repulsion and attraction can be a rearrangement of the electron orbitals to form new orbitals that encompass and hold together both nuclei. When this happens a chemical bond [1] has been formed and a molecule created. The electrons involved in the chemical bond now occupy molecular, not atomic, orbitals. The rules that apply to electrons occupying atomic orbitals also apply to those in molecular orbitals [4, 5]. Using the normal "pigeon-hole" notation for showing how electrons occupy atomic orbitals it is also possible to show how electrons are distributed in chemical bonds.

In the commonest form of chemical bond, in which a single "pigeon-hole" is involved, the molecular orbital contains two electrons. Such a bond, in which two electrons are shared between two nuclei, is called a single, covalent bond [3]. In some cases an atom may have more than a single electron available for bonding. If this atom meets up with a similar atom, two (or more) covalent bonds may form between the two nuclei.

The number of electrons in an atom available for forming chemical bonds depends on the outer electronic structure of the atom. (All the inner electrons are in completely filled atomic orbitals, which generally cannot accept any more.) For this reason elements such as neon and helium that have completely filled outer shells are highly unreactive and were once thought to be unable to form compounds.

Complete electron shells are very stable structures, and there is a tendency for atoms to borrow or share as many electrons from other atoms as they need to complete a shell. If two oxygen atoms meet, for example, to fill their outer shells, they each take a share of two electrons from the other. As a result, for part of the time at least, each nucleus has eight (instead of six) electrons around it.

Hydrogen needs—and can accept—one electron to complete its outer, and only, shell [4]. This means that if oxygen and hydrogen atoms come together, two hydrogen atoms each form a single bond to oxygen. In the resultant compound, H_2O (water), the oxygen shares two of its own electrons and has a share in two others, so it

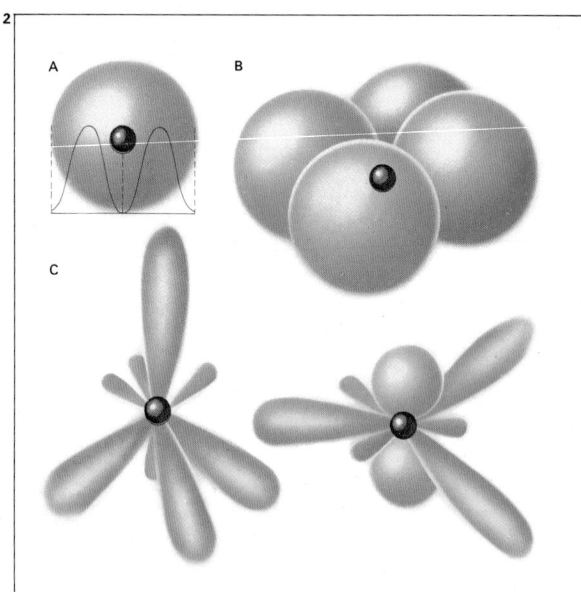

A
B
C

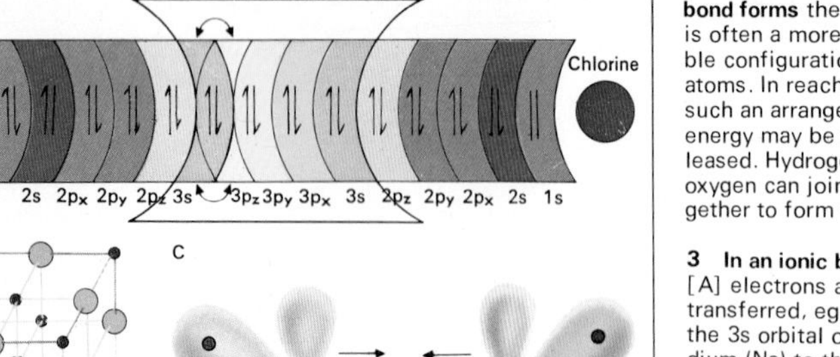

A
Sodium
Chlorine
1s 2s 2px 2py 2pz 3s 3pz 3py 3px 3s 2pz 2py 2px 2s 1s

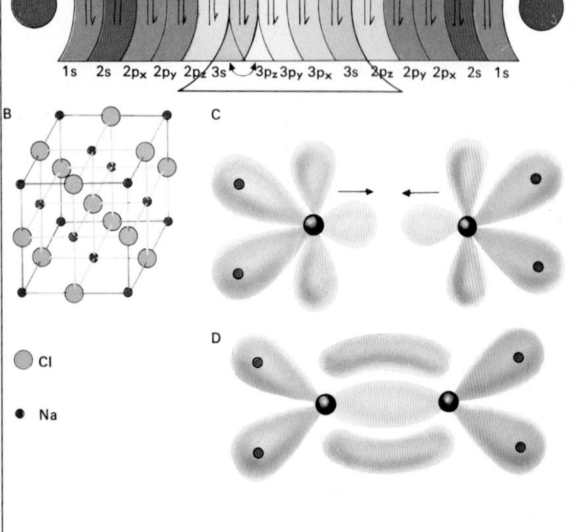

B
C
D
Cl
Na

1 When a chemical bond forms the result is often a more stable configuration of atoms. In reaching such an arrangement, energy may be released. Hydrogen and oxygen can join together to form water

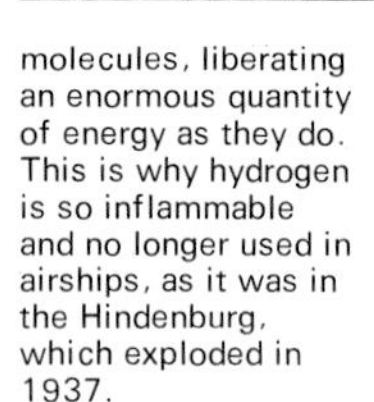

molecules, liberating an enormous quantity of energy as they do. This is why hydrogen is so inflammable and no longer used in airships, as it was in the Hindenburg, which exploded in 1937.

2 The nucleus of any atom has its complement of electrons distributed in orbitals, or volumes of probability. For hydrogen's single electron the orbital is spherical [A], while the two available electrons of oxygen are each distributed in a pair of spherical probability regions [B]. The outer electrons of carbon can adopt a variety of distributions such as the two configurations shown here [C].

3 In an ionic bond [A] electrons are transferred, eg, from the 3s orbital of sodium (Na) to the 3p orbital of chlorine (Cl). Ionic compounds often have geometries in which ionic charges balance [B]. But in a covalent bond two electrons in a molecular orbital are shared by both nuclei. Such orbitals have specific shapes as in the "double bond" linking the carbon atoms in ethylene [C, D]. The other carbon orbitals are bound to hydrogen.

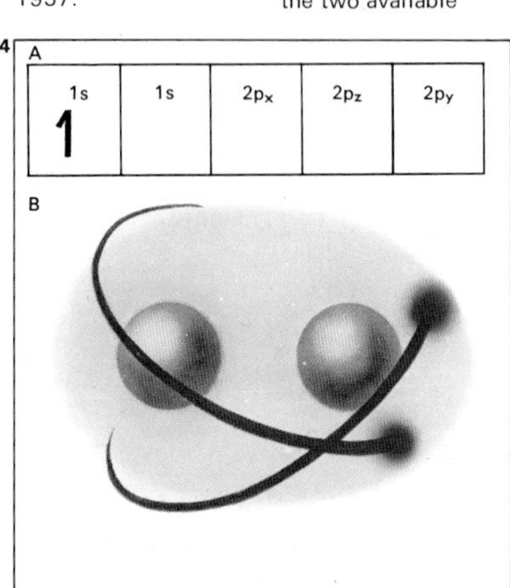

A
1s
1s
2px
2pz
2py
1
B

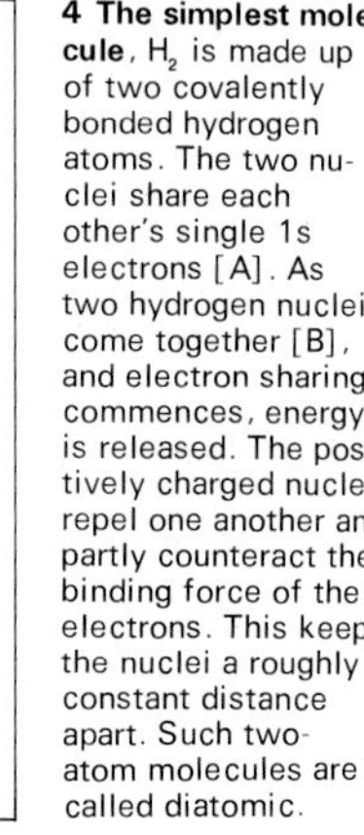

4 The simplest molecule, H_2 is made up of two covalently bonded hydrogen atoms. The two nuclei share each other's single 1s electrons [A]. As two hydrogen nuclei come together [B], and electron sharing commences, energy is released. The positively charged nuclei repel one another and partly counteract the binding force of the electrons. This keeps the nuclei a roughly constant distance apart. Such two-atom molecules are called diatomic.

again completes its outer octet in the molecule.

Exchanging electrons

When two electrons are shared between atoms the bond is said to be covalent [5, 6]. But some atoms have a stronger affinity for electrons than others and gain or lose—rather than share—electrons. This type of combination is called an ionic bond. The resulting atoms are no longer neutral; they carry a positive or negative electric charge (depending on whether they have lost or gained electrons) and are known as ions. Chlorine, for example, with seven electrons in its outer shell, needs only one more to achieve the stability of a completely filled shell. When it gains this electron it becomes a chloride ion and carries a negative charge. Sodium, by contrast, with only one electron in its outer shell, readily loses this to form a positively charged sodium ion. Sodium chloride, or common salt, is a compound with an ionic bond. When it is dissolved in water the chloride ions each carry an electron borrowed from the sodium ions.

The coordinate bond

A third possibility exists for joining atoms in a simple way. This is an extension of the sharing arrangement of covalent bonding. But in this case both electrons in the bond, called a coordinate bond, come from a single atom and use a totally empty orbital in the second atom involved in the bond. Nitrogen, for example, has five electrons in its outermost shell. Three of these may be involved in covalent bonds with three hydrogen atoms, to form the compound ammonia, NH_3. Nitrogen now has shares in eight electrons—a complete outer octet. In a molecule of ammonia, however, there remains a pair of electrons in the nitrogen atom that have not formed covalent bonds with hydrogen atoms. These can be donated to an empty orbital of various metal atoms, such as copper, to form a third type of bond called a coordinate bond. The resulting compounds are known as complexes or coordination compounds.

When more than two atoms are involved in joining together, more complicated arrangements are possible.

KEY

Atoms join together to form molecules. Only since the discovery of the wave nature of matter in the 1920's has it been possible to describe this bonding of atoms clearly. Before this time the way in which atoms held together was a mystery, often shown fancifully, as in this "model" of benzene. Today benzene is pictured as a hexagonal ring of six carbon atoms linked together by equivalent bonds.

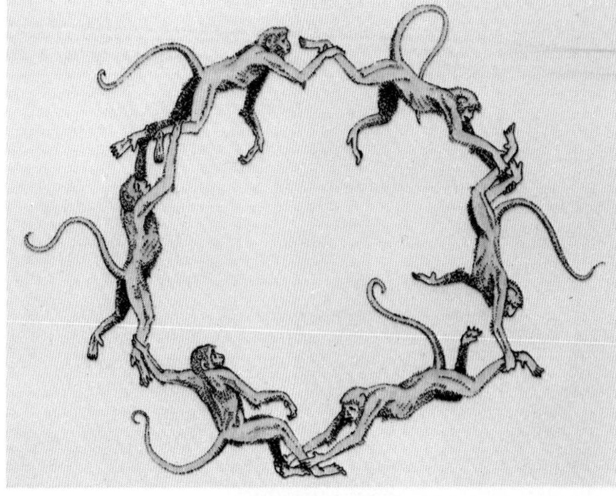

5

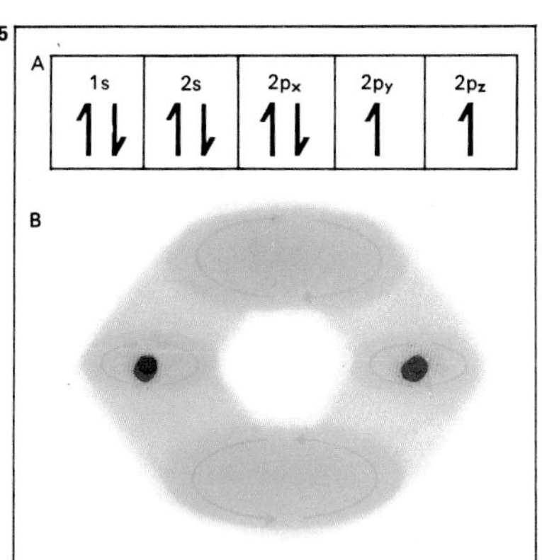
A
1s
2s
2px
2py
2pz
B

5 The "pigeon-hole" notation for the electron structure of an oxygen atom [A] shows that it has two partially filled orbitals ($2p_y$, $2p_z$). To complete its outer octet it therefore needs to take over, or share, two electrons from other atoms. In nature, oxygen is usually found as a diatomic molecule (o_2) in which two oxygen atoms (red) share a total of four electrons, forming two covalent bonds [B].

6

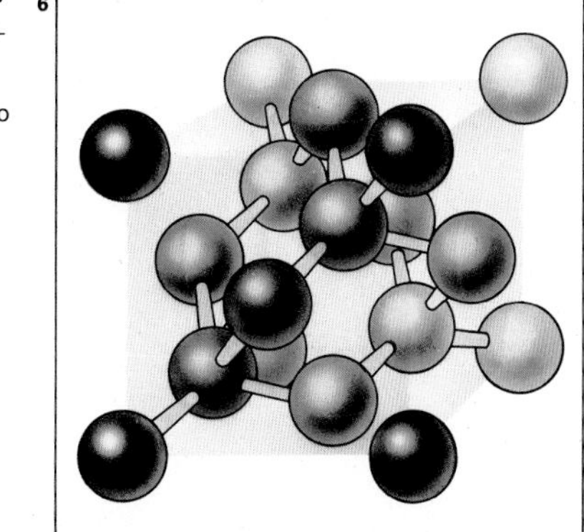

6 In a diamond any one carbon atom is covalently bonded to four others, positioned at the corners of a tetrahedron. This strain-free covalent configuration accounts for diamond's hardness.

7

7 By mimicking the strain-free structure of diamonds chemists have been able to "engineer" even tougher compounds, such as the tungsten carbide on the tips of drills used in oil wells.

8

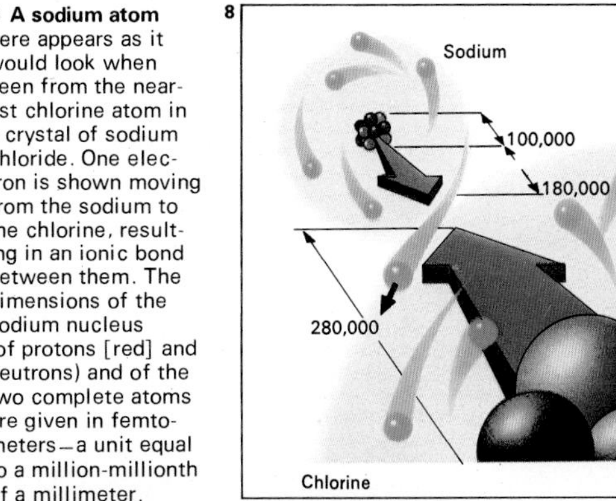
Sodium
100,000
180,000
280,000
Chlorine

8 A sodium atom here appears as it would look when seen from the nearest chlorine atom in a crystal of sodium chloride. One electron is shown moving from the sodium to the chlorine, resulting in an ionic bond between them. The dimensions of the sodium nucleus (of protons [red] and neutrons) and of the two complete atoms are given in femtometers—a unit equal to a million-millionth of a millimeter.

9 A

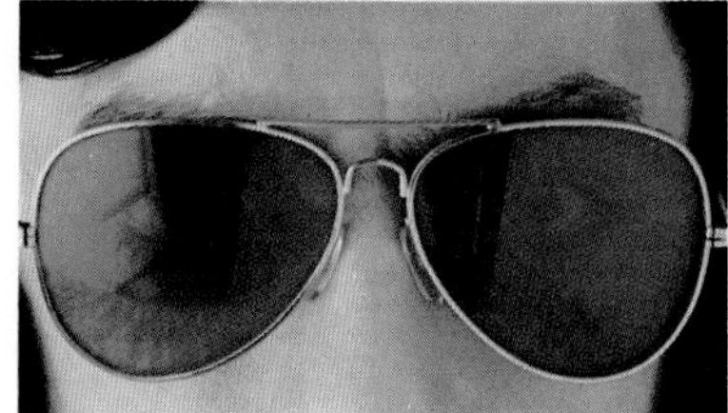

B

9 When two atoms spontaneously form a bond, the release of energy stabilizes the compound. The process may be reversed by supplying energy. Colorless silver salts used in automatically dimming sunglasses [A] and an astronaut's helmet [B] take the form of silver ions in a glass matrix. In sunlight the glass darkens because light energy breaks the ionic bonds and reconverts the silver into metallic atoms. Colorless ions re-form when the light is removed.

10 A B C D

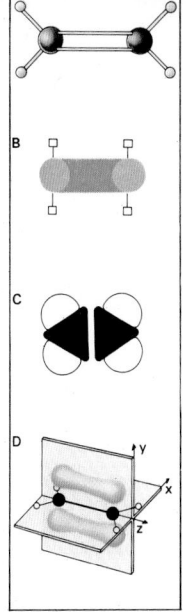

10 Chemical bonding can be illustrated in many ways. The four diagrams shown here depict the simple molecule ethylene, made up of two carbon atoms and four hydrogen atoms. As in the diamond structure, each carbon atom can form four bonds; two of these link the two carbons together, and each carbon also has two hydrogens attached to it by single covalent bonds. The simple ball-and-stick model [A] shows the atoms and the number of bonds linking them. Model [B] gives similar information but is designed especially for biological molecules, while models [C] and [D] reveal more about the actual molecular shape, and the distribution of orbitals, respectively.

Simple chemicals and their structures

Mankind's interest in chemistry derives from the useful information that the subject can provide about the properties of different substances. By understanding the structure of molecules and the way they interact with one another it is possible to invent new compounds that are useful, for example, as drugs or building materials or fibers for clothing. It is also possible to acquire a better understanding of how the Earth on which we live came to its present form and how it is still developing. Geochemistry (as this branch of the subject is called) can lead to the discovery of new supplies of fuels and metal-bearing ores and new ways of processing these ores.

Structures of molecules

All substances are made up of molecules that, in turn, are composed of individual atoms. One of the basic aspects of chemical knowledge is an understanding of the structure of molecules. An atom is a relatively insubstantial entity: a small, hard nucleus surrounded by electrons occupying a volume of probability. Molecules composed of such atoms are similarly made up, in terms of volume, largely of electron orbitals (the areas in space occupied by the electrons). Nevertheless, despite the fact that an orbital can contain a maximum of only two electrons, they often have definite directions in space, so that molecules have particular shapes. In complex molecules such shapes may be crucial to the behavior of the substance. This is particularly true of biological molecules, which contain thousands of individual atoms linked together, but even simple molecules have shapes that can determine their properties.

The structures of ionic compounds [1] depend on the electric charge of the ion and on its ionic volume. An ion of sodium, for example, can be regarded as a small sphere having a particular diameter. In general, provided ions of different elements have the same electric charge and similar radii, they can substitute for one another in different materials. As the Earth settled down after its formation rocks gradually solidified from molten material. Many of these original rocks contain crystalline compounds, nearly always impure. For example, the common mineral potassium feldspar, an ionic compound containing potassium, silicon, and oxygen, is always contaminated with rubidium because rubidium forms a singly-charged ion of approximately the same radius as potassium.

Exchange of ions in crystals is peculiar to ionic compounds. In covalent (non-ionic) compounds the bonds between the different atoms are separate. Covalent compounds can still form crystals, but this is because the molecules as a whole can arrange themselves in geometric arrays, whereas with ionic compounds it is the geometric arrangement of ions that leads to crystallinity. With a crystal of a covalently bonded compound each molecule has its own characteristic shape.

Shapes of covalent compounds

The shape of a covalently bonded molecule [3] depends on the shapes of the orbitals occupied by the electrons—both those involved in chemical bonding and any others in the outermost shells of the individual

CONNECTIONS

See also
1556 Joining atoms
1554 Survey of groups of elements
1550 What is chemistry?
1564 Key chemical reactions

1

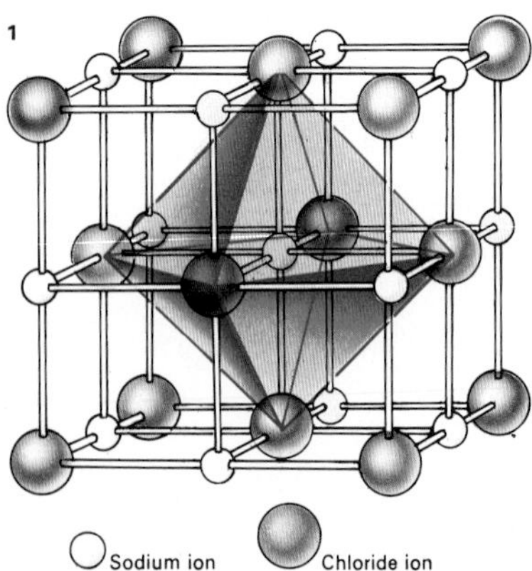

Sodium ion
Chloride ion

1 Sodium chloride, common salt, has a simple cubic crystal structure in which each sodium ion (Na) is surrounded by six chloride ions (Cl) and vice versa. Around each ion, the six ions of opposite electrical charge are situated at the corners of an imaginary octahedron. The main force responsible for holding the ions in position is the balanced electrical attraction of the neighboring ions.

2

2 The shape of any crystalline, ionic solid depends on the size and the number of ions that make it up. Different chemical substances may look alike, even though they have different compositions, molecular structures, and chemical properties. Iron sulfide, shown here, is called "fools' gold" because of its resemblance to the much more valuable element, gold.

3

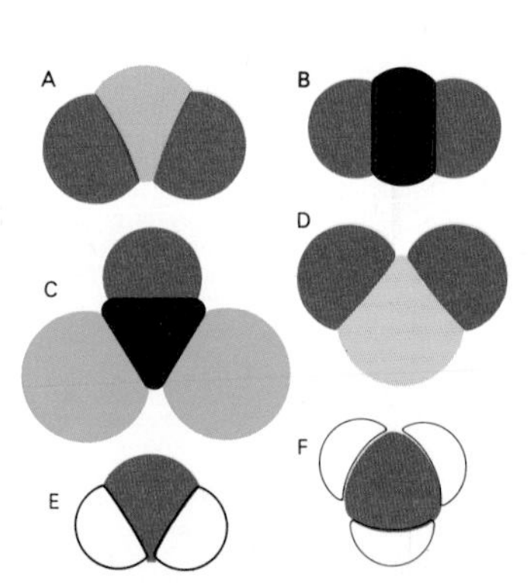

A
B
C
D
E
F

A Nitrogen dioxide NO_2
B Carbon dioxide CO_2
C Phosgene $COCl_2$
D Sulphur dioxide SO_2
E Water H_2O
F Ammonia NH_3

3 Covalently bonded molecules have individual molecular orbitals holding different atoms together, unlike the balanced geometric cluster of an ionic compound. Because of the forces of repulsion between the electron clouds surrounding adjacent nuclei, even small molecules have distinct shapes, which may differ markedly from one another, as in the half-dozen common molecules here.

4

4 In hydrogen peroxide two hydrogen atoms and two oxygen atoms are joined in a single molecule. It readily releases an OH group whose oxygen can, for example, bleach hair (as here) or kill germs and act as a mild disinfectant.

5

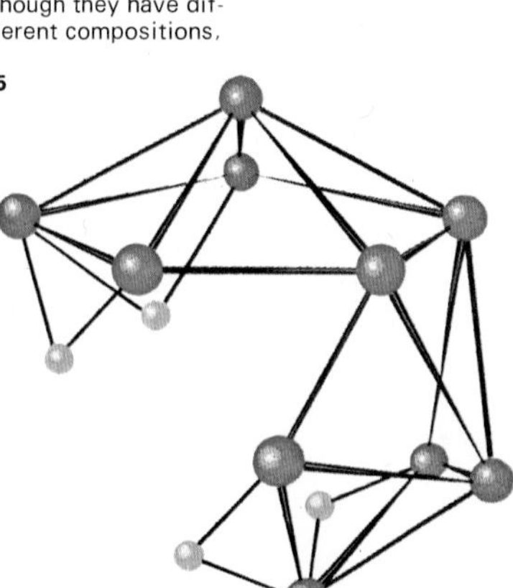
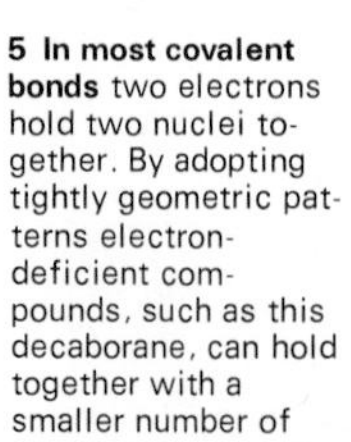

5 In most covalent bonds two electrons hold two nuclei together. By adopting tightly geometric patterns electron-deficient compounds, such as this decaborane, can hold together with a smaller number of electrons.

6

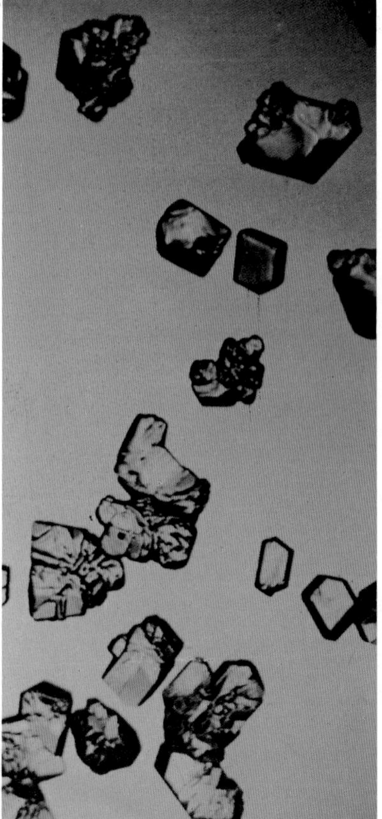

6 In addition to electron-deficient compounds, there are also compounds that seem to have too many electrons. For many years it was believed that the noble gases—helium, neon, xenon, krypton, and radon—would not form any compounds because their outer electron shells had eight electrons in them already. In 1963 Neil Bartlett discovered that xenon would react to form colorful crystalline compounds. An extension of chemical bonding theory has shown how the formation of such compounds does not violate any chemical law, and since 1963 a large number of compounds of xenon (shown here) and krypton have been made in laboratories throughout the world.

atoms. A water molecule, for example, in which two hydrogen atoms are each singly bonded to a central oxygen atom, might be visualized as the three atoms joined in a straight line. Electrons, all being negatively charged, repel each other, so this in-line arrangement might seem best. It would mean that the regions of electron probability around the two hydrogen atoms are as far apart from each other as they possibly could be, thus reducing repulsion to a minimum. But, in addition to the two electrons from the oxygen's outer shell, which are involved in bonding, there are four other electrons in this shell, situated as two "lone pairs" in filled orbitals. Their effect on neighboring electron clouds has to be taken into account. When this is done it is found that a shape almost like that of one segment of a diamond [3E] is adopted. It is a tetrahedral structure in which the hydrogen atoms and the two pairs of oxygen electrons (not involved in bonding) all lie as far away from each other as possible.

Methane [8], in which one carbon atom is surrounded by four hydrogen atoms and all the outermost carbon electrons are involved in bonding, adopts a regular tetrahedral configuration. Intermediate in structure between methane and water is ammonia (NH_3), in which there are three nitrogen-hydrogen bonds and one filled orbital, which contains a single pair of electrons [3F].

Coordination compounds

The lone-pair electrons in water and ammonia molecules sometimes form bonds to metal atoms that have empty orbitals. Anhydrous copper sulfate, for example, is white. When water is present the molecule turns blue as a number of water molecules "coordinate" to empty copper orbitals through the unbonded oxygen lone pairs. Because the empty orbitals in such metals have definite shapes "coordination compounds" generally have highly geometric structures [7].

Some atoms can form several bonds with other atoms, so it is often possible for a number of different molecules to be made up from the same mixture of atoms [10].

KEY

Washing soda (Na_2CO_3)
Baking soda ($NaHCO_3$)
Vinegar (containing CH_3COOH)
Common salt ($NaCl$)
Epsom salt ($MgSO_4$)

Everything around us is made up of chemicals, most of them as complex mixtures. But these familiar substances from the home are comparitively simple chemical compounds.

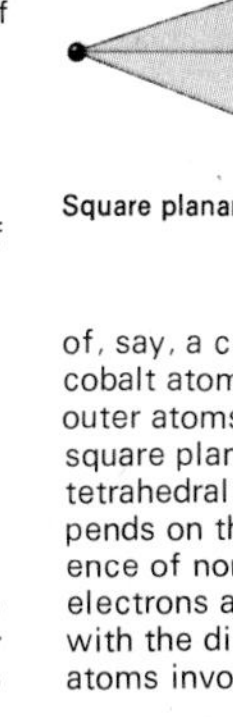

7
Square planar
Octahedral
Tetrahedral
Trigonal bipyramidal
Tetragonal pyramidal

7 Where a central atom in a molecule can bond a number of other atoms, or groups of atoms, a variety of different molecular geometries is possible. In the particular case of coordination compounds, in which the central atom is sharing electrons from other atoms and not contributing any of its own electrons to the bonding, the commonly found geometries are those shown here. Whether a compound made up of, say, a central cobalt atom and four outer atoms adopts a square planar or a tetrahedral form depends on the influence of nonbonding electrons associated with the different atoms involved.

8

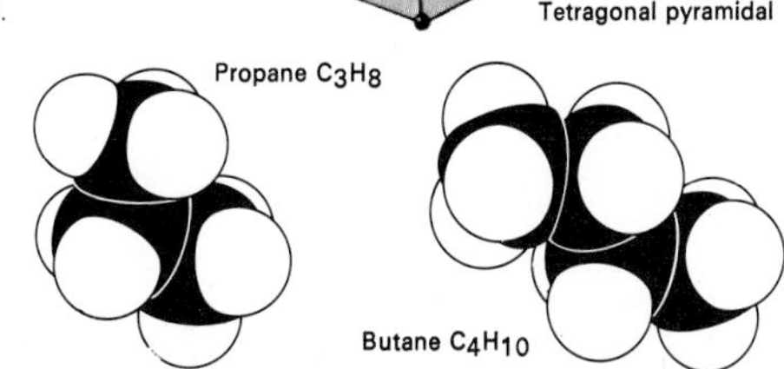

Methane CH_4
Ethane C_2H_6
Propane C_3H_8
Butane C_4H_{10}

8 Carbon atoms can combine covalently to form long chains. Consequently carbon compounds occur in series such as the alkanes (paraffins); the first four (beginning with methane) are shown.

9

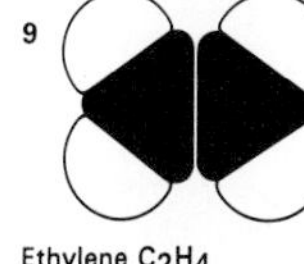

Ethylene C_2H_4

Acetylene C_2H_2

9 In addition to forming chains joined by single bonds, carbon atoms can be joined by two or three molecular orbitals. Ethylene and acetylene are, respectively, the double-and triple-bonded analogues of ethane, all of which contain two carbon atoms.

10

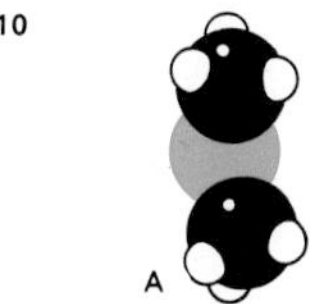

A

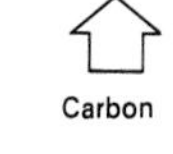
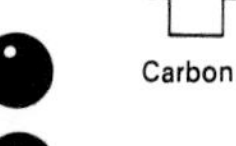

Carbon

Carbon

Oxygen
Six hydrogens

B

10 Where the same numbers of the same kinds of atoms are joined to one another in different ways the resultant compounds behave differently. Because the gross structures of the molecules are different they are called structural isomers; examples are dimethyl ether [A] and ethyl alcohol [B].

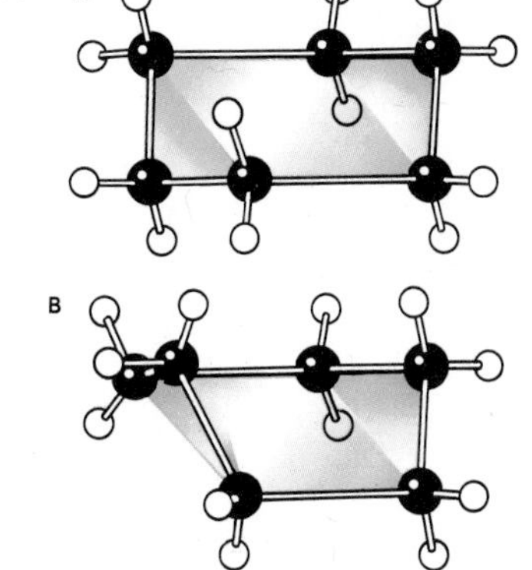

11
A
B

11 Some compounds, such as cyclohexane, can exist in two forms, differing only in the way their chemical bonds are arranged in space. This illustration shows the "chair" [A] and "boat" [B] forms of cyclohexane. Such compounds are known as conformations: they may "flip" from one form to the other, and the compound may contain both.

12 During the 20th century hundreds of thousands of carbon compounds unknown in nature have been synthesized in chemical laboratories. Some of the simplest such molecules of commercial significance are insecticides. The active ingredients in many insecticides are chlorinated hydrocarbons, with molecules containing only one or two dozen atoms. Most are long-lasting and toxic to animals other than insects and should therefore be used with extreme precaution.

Complex chemicals and their structures

Carbon atoms have the ability to link together in large numbers to give an infinite variety of different substances [2]. Most complex chemicals are carbon-based, although there are some important complex materials, such as glass, that contain no carbon.

At one time it was believed that most carbon compounds could be made only by living processes. For instance, urea was discovered in the urine of mammals. Consequently, this and similar compounds were called organic chemicals, a name that has stuck. Then organic chemicals were synthesized in the laboratory—for example, urea (organic) was made from ammonium cyanate (an inorganic compound). Today organic chemicals account for about half the output of the chemical industry.

The basis of an organic chemicals industry

The discoveries that led to the development of an organic chemicals industry came toward the end of the nineteenth century [3]. It was found that a wealth of useful substances could be obtained from coal tar, a by-product of the manufacture of domestic gas from coal. At that time many of the substances extracted from coal tar were too complex in structure to be made in the laboratory. Once purified, however, it was possible to use them as starting materials from which to produce a range of commercial substances. Dyes, aspirin, saccharin, and explosives such as TNT were all made before the end of the nineteenth century from coal-tar chemicals.

A basic constituent of many of the coal-tar products, and of many other complex organic chemicals, is the group formed of a ring of six carbon atoms joined together. As in many other molecules, the chemical bonds between the carbon atoms take the form of electron-carrying orbitals. These orbitals are not located strictly between adjacent carbon nuclei but spread over all six, so that each carbon atom is effectively joined to the next by one-and-a-half bonds.

The simplest of such compounds, in which each carbon atom is also linked to a hydrogen atom (giving a formula C_6H_6), is benzene—originally a coal-tar product but now made mainly from petroleum [1]. In some compounds several benzene rings are fused to give what are called polycyclic structures such as naphthalene (used in mothballs) and benzpyrene (a cancer-inducing chemical).

Many complex organic chemicals found in nature do not contain benzene-type rings. Instead, they are made up of long chains of carbon atoms, with other atoms attached. The other atoms nearly always include hydrogen and often oxygen and nitrogen as well. These compounds include natural products such as fats, waxes, sugars, and proteins.

Synthetic polymers and their products

Organic molecules have been the basis of one of the major industrial developments of the twentieth century—the widespread manufacture and use of synthetic polymers as plastics, rubbers, and fibers. Polymer is a general term for any large molecule that is made by repeatedly linking together the same small molecular unit, which is called the monomer.

CONNECTIONS

See also
1556 Joining atoms
1558 Simple chemicals and their structures
1570 Toward the chemistry of life
1572 The chemistry of life: biochemistry

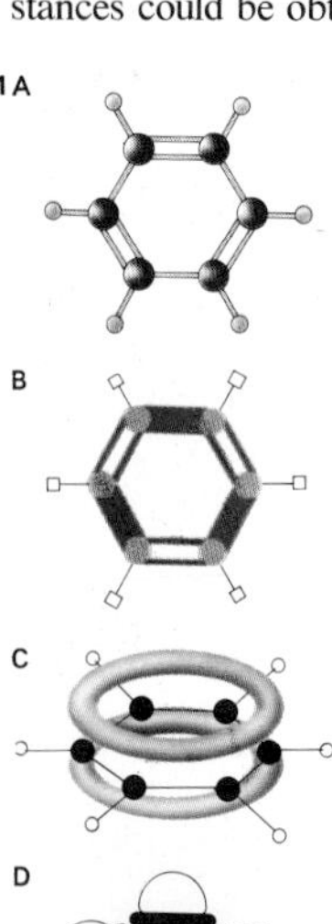

1 The six-carbon benzene ring is one of the most important molecules in organic chemistry. Each carbon atom is attached to a single hydrogen atom, so it can form three other bonds with its two neighboring carbon atoms. It was once thought that single and double bonds alternated around the benzene ring [A, B], although if this were so not all the carbon atoms would have the same chemical reactivity. It is now known that all the carbon-carbon bonds in the ring are equal, because the molecular orbitals (blue [C]) spread out over the whole ring. Below [D] is a more convenient representation of the actual shape of the molecule.

2 In benzene other atomic groups can replace hydrogen atoms. In aniline [A] one hydrogen is replaced by an amino ($-NH_2$) group, while phenol [B] has a hydroxyl ($-OH$) group in place of one hydrogen. Styrene [C], from which polystyrene is made, has a small carbon chain attached to the benzene ring. More than one hydrogen can be replaced: catechol [D], for example, has two $-OH$ groups, while aspirin [E] has two different groups attached to the ring. The shared orbital structure of benzene is sometimes retained even when carbon atoms are replaced, as in pyridine [F].

3 The English chemist William Perkin (1838–1907) tried to make quinine from aniline. Instead, his experiments of 1856 accidentally produced the dye aniline purple. This was the first synthetic dye. Until that time all dyes were natural compounds from plants or animals.

4 Modern pigments brighten this train with contrasting colors, and paint makers are no longer dependent on natural substances.

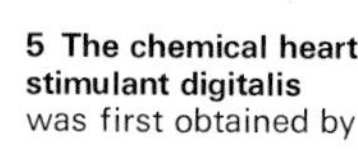

5 The chemical heart stimulant digitalis was first obtained by herbalists from foxglove *(Digitalis purpurea)*.

Most organic polymers are formed either by addition reactions or by elimination reactions. In the first type the monomer molecule has a double bond and links with others by using electrons from the double bond. In the second type atoms at the ends of two monomer molecules are "eliminated" and a bond forms between the remaining parts of the monomer molecules.

Natural rubber is an addition polymer, as are many of the man-made rubbers developed in the past few decades. Many synthetic fibers, on the other hand, are elimination polymers or condensation polymers (in which water is eliminated), as are their natural counterparts such as wool and cotton. A synthetic polymer can have characteristics built into it by the careful choice of starting materials. As a result, different synthetic fibers have different properties.

Plastics [6] can be fibrous, rubbery, clear, hard, opaque, or flexible. The possibilities are almost endless, as the widespread use of synthetic polymers in everyday life confirms.

Linking silicon atoms

Silicon falls directly below carbon in the periodic table of the elements and so logically should have similar chemical properties. But because of their larger size, silicon atoms cannot link to form long chains by themselves. Nevertheless, the important polymers called silicones are based on long chains of alternating atoms of silicon and oxygen. The commercially available silicones are often partly organic, and their forms range from plastics to lubricants.

In silicones, carbon groups are linked to the silicon atoms and stick out on each side of the polymer chain. Like carbon, silicon can form four bonds, whereas oxygen forms only two. This means that, in a repeating —Si—O— chain, there must be other atoms joined to the silicon atoms. These do not have to be organic; each silicon atom can be bonded to four oxygen atoms. If each of these oxygens has two silicons attached, the result is a three-dimensional polymer matrix with the overall formula SiO_2. Sand and glass are composed largely of this inorganic polymer [7], often known as silica.

KEY

A modern pharmacist deals in hundreds of drugs. The old apothecary displayed in his shop rows of glass jars filled with tinctures and essences extracted from botanical plants. Many balms and medicines made from the contents of such jars are still manufactured today, not from natural extracts but from substances that are produced in chemical plants. Increasing knowledge of the complex molecules found in nature has enabled man to copy and in some cases, improve nature's own efforts. Synthetic drugs, rubber, and pigments are only a few of the products that man's ingenuity has created to replace natural materials.

6

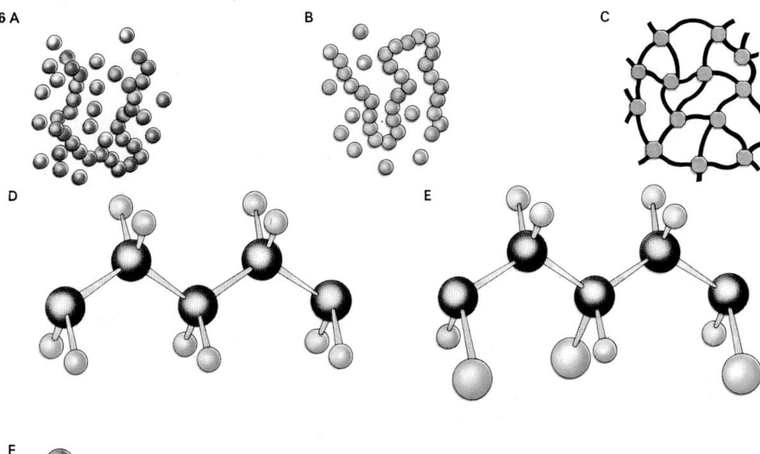
A
B
C
D
E

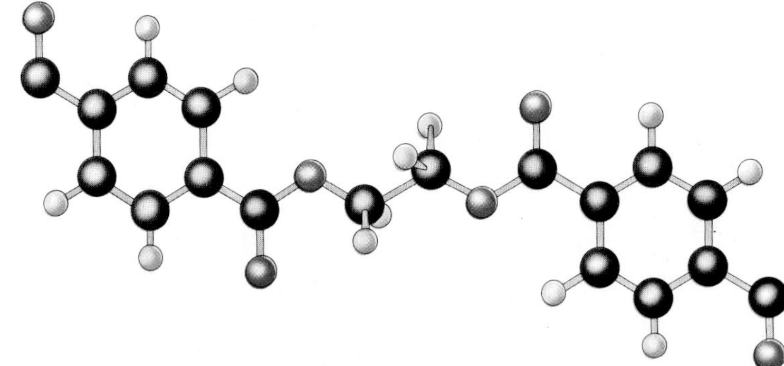
F

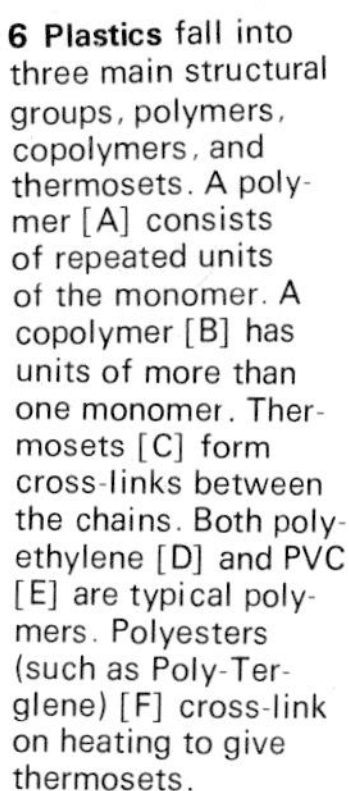

6 Plastics fall into three main structural groups, polymers, copolymers, and thermosets. A polymer [A] consists of repeated units of the monomer. A copolymer [B] has units of more than one monomer. Thermosets [C] form cross-links between the chains. Both polyethylene [D] and PVC [E] are typical polymers. Polyesters (such as Poly-Terglene) [F] cross-link on heating to give thermosets.

7 Colors in glass, such as those in the windows of Coventry Cathedral, come from added metallic compounds. Cross-linked polymers are not all based on organic molecules and glass is probably the oldest synthetic polymer.

7

8

8 Modern plastics are replacing metals in many applications, such as the bodywork of motor vehicles.

9

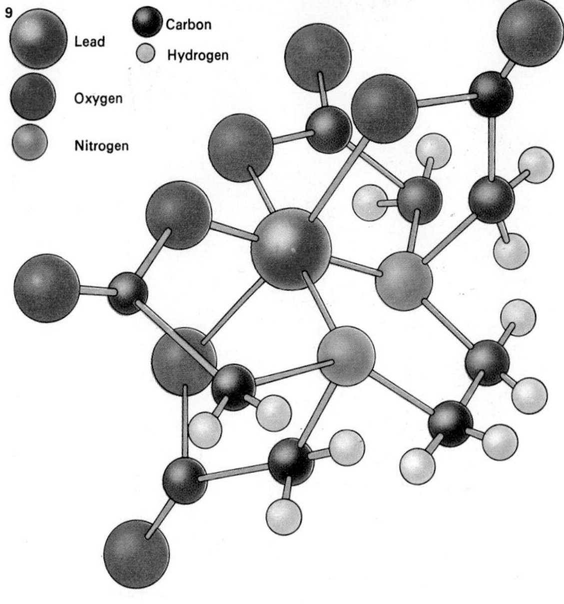
Lead
Carbon
Hydrogen
Oxygen
Nitrogen

9 Metal-organic chemistry bridges the gap between organic and inorganic chemistry. It can lead to important new products, for example, poison antidotes. A chelate, such as EDTA (containing carbon, hydrogen, oxygen and nitrogen atoms) can surround ions of metals and remove them from unwanted places.

Chemicals in solution

Every day millions of people make solutions. Many start at breakfast, when they dissolve sugar in tea or coffee. So common is this action that it is taken for granted. But where does the sugar go when it dissolves? Why, if a spoonful of sand is stirred into hot liquid, does it not dissolve?

In chemical terms, a solution is a homogeneous mixture of different sorts of chemical compounds. The criterion of homogeneity is that the two or more types of molecule involved are thoroughly mixed —as water and sand clearly are not.

Solutes and solvents

Solutions are usually thought of as solids dissolved in liquids—coffee in water, sugar in the coffee, salt in water in the sea, detergent in washing water, iodine in alcohol in tincture of iodine, and many more. But there are other kinds of solutions. Gases can dissolve in liquids, as in carbonated water. Many solutions are made by dissolving liquids in other liquids. Gases can also dissolve in some solids, and solutions of solids in solids are found in metal alloys.

For a solution to form, there must be an interaction between the substance that dissolves (solute) and the material it dissolves in (solvent). Sugar, for example, usually occurs as crystalline arrays of sucrose molecules. To dissolve it, energy is needed to break apart the crystal lattice so that sucrose molecules can disperse evenly through the solvent. Where water is the solvent, the attraction for solute molecules comes from the "polar" character of the water molecule. The central oxygen atom in H_2O is electrically slightly negative, while the hydrogen atoms are slightly positive. Molecules of water tend to attract one another—which is why water is a liquid at room temperature whereas most such small molecules are gases. Water molecules also tend to attract (ie, dissolve) other "polar" compounds, such as sugar, with many OH groups in their molecules.

Molecules and compounds

For similar reasons, but via weaker attractive forces, nonpolar molecules such as hydrocarbons will dissolve other nonpolar compounds, such as fats. Modern detergents work by a compromise between both types of attraction. Part of the molecule dissolves in grease, the other part dissolves in water, so the detergent molecule acts as a bridge and disperses grease in water.

Some compounds, such as ethyl alcohol, dissolve completely in either water or hydrocarbons—substances that will not dissolve in one another. Other compounds show a preference for polar or nonpolar solvents, according to their chemical structures. The attraction between individual molecules of different types can be seen easily where it results in a reduction of the overall volume of material. If, for example, equal parts of water and ethyl alcohol are mixed, the total volume of solution is about 97 percent of the sum of the components.

When a substance will not dissolve, it is because the solvent does not overcome the intermolecular forces that hold the molecules together. With any substance, there are limits to solubility, which may vary according to the temperature of the solution [1]. A solution containing the

CONNECTIONS

See also
1554 The element groups
1564 Key chemical reactions
1566 Electrochemistry
1558 Simple chemicals and their structures
412 The cell in action

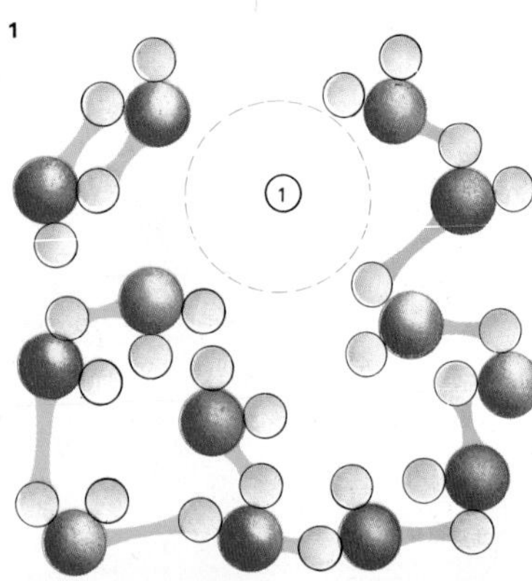

1

1 The atoms and molecules of all materials are in motion, the energy of this motion depending upon the temperature. In liquid, the motion prevents any permanent intermolecular structure from forming, but forces of attraction govern the overall volume. In water, there are many temporary linkages (shown blue) between the H_2O molecules; very small enclosed cavities [1] form and disappear.

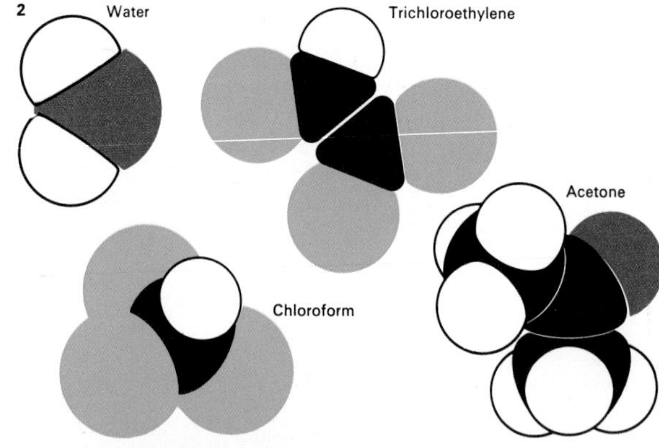

Water
Trichloroethylene
Acetone
Chloroform

2 The slight positive charge on the hydrogen atoms and slight negative charge on the oxygen atoms of water make it particularly suitable for dissolving inorganic salts. Trichloroethylene, widely used in dry cleaning, and chloroform both dissolve many organic compounds. Acetone, with behavior intermediate between water and trichloroethylene, is able to dissolve both organic and inorganic compounds.

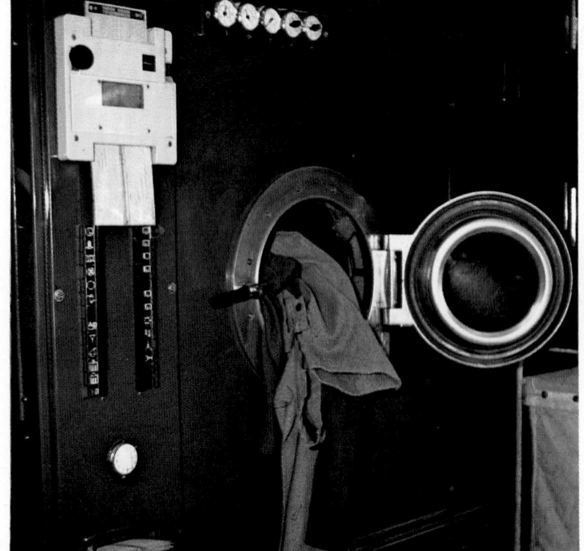

3 Ordinary washing removes water-soluble dirt and also non-soluble dirt that can be emulsified in water by the addition of detergents. (Milk is a typical example of an emulsion where one liquid mixed and joined with another does not separate.) In dry cleaning, an organic solvent is employed; most of those used commercially are small, halogen-containing molecules, such as trichoroethylene. These solvents dissolve grease; however, because their fumes are unpleasant they have to be used in special machines, as shown here. Similar compounds are also used in industrial degreasing operations, such as cleaning metal prior to machining, or in the manufacture of various electronics components.

4 The solubility of a substance is different in different solvents. When immiscible solvents are shaken together, any compounds present are divided between the two liquid phases. If a solution of iodine and salt in water is shaken with benzene, iodine dissolves in the benzene layer, but salt does not; thus it is possible to separate the two. Many different compounds can be purified in this way.

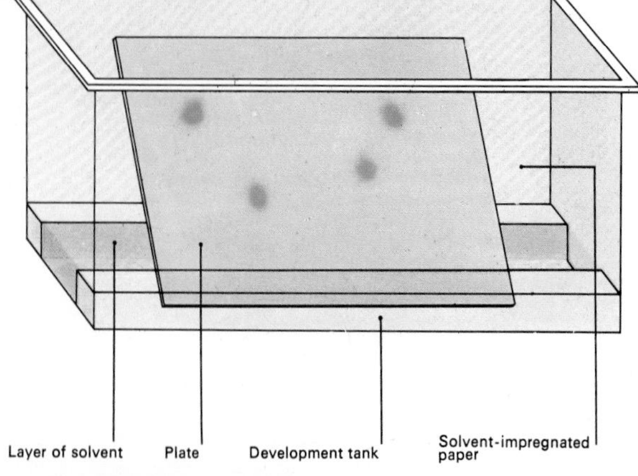

Layer of solvent
Plate
Development tank
Solvent-impregnated paper

5 Different compounds can also be separated by partitioning them between a solid and a liquid. In thin-layer chromatography, a spot of a mixture is placed on a plate coated with absorbent powder, which is put into a development tank containing a solvent (ensuring the tank is saturated with its vapor). As the solvent ascends the plate, the mixture separates into its component chemicals, which may then be separately identified by specific tests.

maximum possible amount of solute (dissolved substance) is called saturated. A hot liquid generally has a greater capacity for holding solid in solution than a cold one (with gases in liquids, the reverse is true). Consequently, if as much solid as possible is dissolved in boiling water, some of it may crystallize out when the water cools. If it does not, the solution is said to be supersaturated. This is the basis of many experiments for growing giant crystals in school laboratories.

Dissolving a solid in a liquid affects the liquid in a variety of ways. For example, pure water freezes at 0°C (32°F) and boils at 100°C (212°F). The freezing point of a solution of common salt, however, is less than 0°C; thus, salt sprinkled on roads in winter prevents ice from forming.

Osmotic pressures

One of the more important properties of solutions is their ability to exert osmotic pressure. If a solution encased in certain types of membrane is brought into contact with pure solvent, the solvent molecules pass through the membrane into the solution, making it more dilute. The molecules of solute, on the other hand, are unable to pass through the membrane, which is called "semipermeable" in consequence.

Osmosis is crucial to all living organisms. For example, the absorption of water by the root hairs of plants depends on it. If the concentration of dissolved matter in the plant cells is greater than in the water surrounding them, water is drawn in. On the other hand, if the reverse is true—in very salty soils, for example—water may be drawn out of the plants, and they may die.

Plants and animals are also responsible for producing complex substances that form so-called colloidal solutions. These are part-way between a solution and a suspension. Gelatin desserts are one type of colloidal solution, and non-drip paint is another. Gelatin sets on cooling and "melts" again on heating, but a non-drip paint becomes more liquid as it is stirred and more solid when it is left standing. These differences are accounted for by the "solutions'" different types of colloidal substances.

KEY

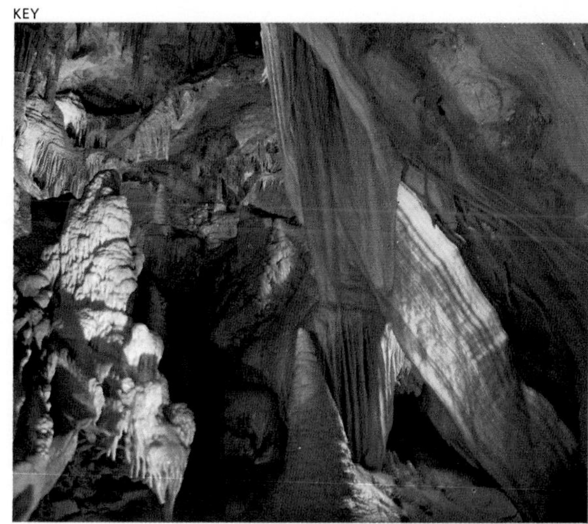

Rivers and streams dissolve small quantities of minerals. Under certain conditions, these minerals can be precipitated from solution sometimes in impressive forms, such as these stalactites and stalagmites formed over thousands of years in limestone caves in various parts of the world.

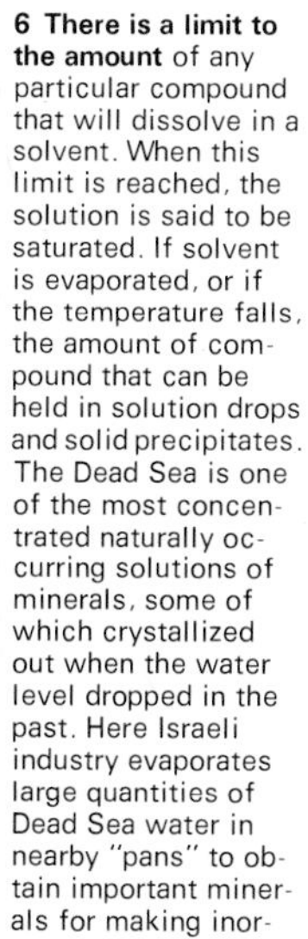

6 There is a limit to the amount of any particular compound that will dissolve in a solvent. When this limit is reached, the solution is said to be saturated. If solvent is evaporated, or if the temperature falls, the amount of compound that can be held in solution drops and solid precipitates. The Dead Sea is one of the most concentrated naturally occurring solutions of minerals, some of which crystallized out when the water level dropped in the past. Here Israeli industry evaporates large quantities of Dead Sea water in nearby "pans" to obtain important minerals for making inorganic chemicals.

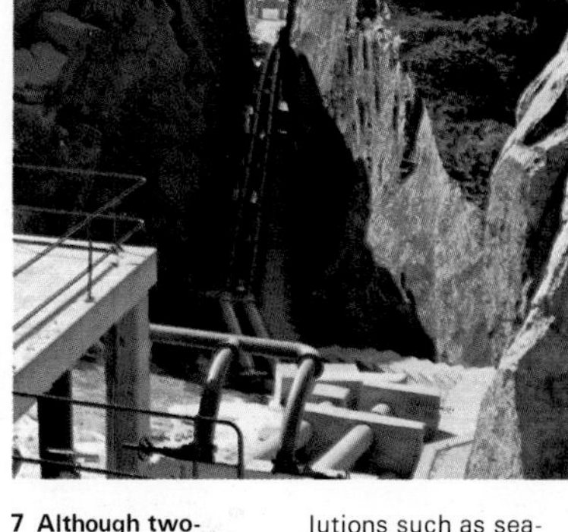

7 Although two-thirds of the earth's surface is covered with water, in many countries there is a lack of pure water for drinking. In this modern desalination plant, pure water is evaporated from solutions such as seawater and then condensed in large tanks. The concentrated brine left over from the process is usually returned to the sea, where it is diluted by tidal mixing.

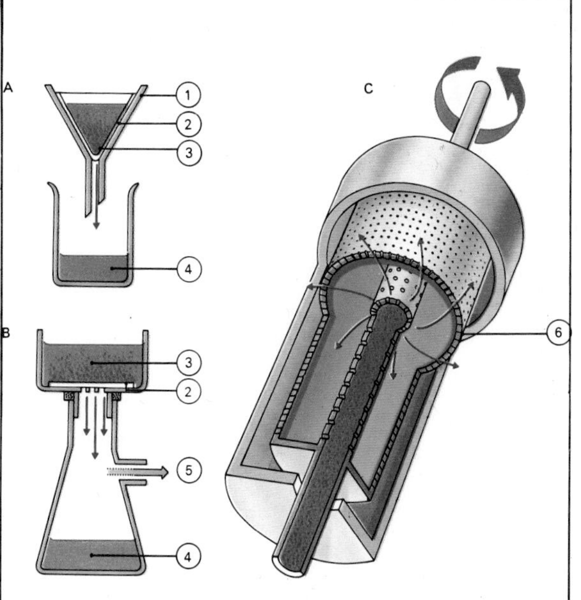
8
A
B
C
1
2
3
4
5
6

8 Filtration removes solid particles from solution. A mixture placed [A] in a filter funnel [1] drains through the filter paper [2] by gravity, leaving sediment [3] trapped while the filtrate [4] flows through. In the Buchner funnel [B], the same principle is enhanced by suction [5]. In the industrial rotary filter [C] the spinning action of the drum drives the mixture onto the fine mesh filter [6].

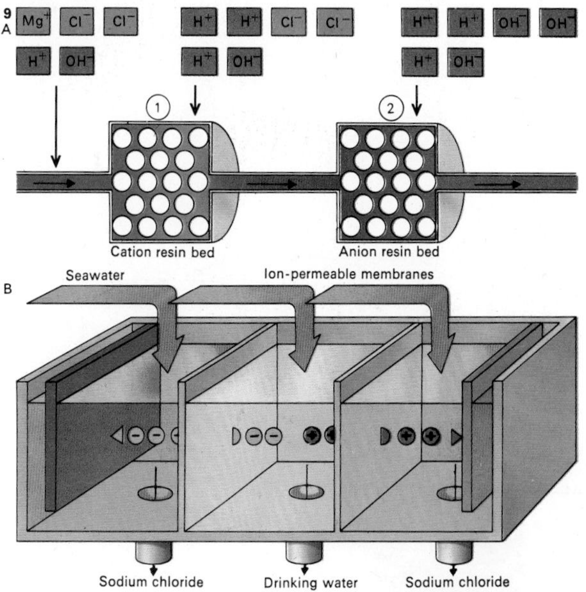
9
A
B
1
2
Cation resin bed
Anion resin bed
Seawater
Ion-permeable membranes
Sodium chloride
Drinking water
Sodium chloride

9 Ion exchange removes ionic compounds from solution [A]. A cationic resin [1] exchanges cations in solution for H^+, while an anionic resin [2] exchanges anions for OH^-. An extension of the exchange process is electrodialysis [B].

Key chemical reactions

In an enclosed space, air and an organic vapor composed mainly of hydrocarbons are pressed together. The hydrocarbons consist of molecules in which several carbon atoms are chemically bonded to each other and to a number of hydrogen atoms. A spark is generated. In an instant, many of the bonds between carbon and hydrogen and between carbon and carbon are broken and replaced by chemical bonds that combine these atoms with oxygen from the air. An explosion results, and a chemical reaction has taken place. This particular reaction takes place millions of times each day as people use internal combustion engines.

Molecular energy

Chemists are interested in how individual compounds react: how quickly they will react, what the products are, and how much "persuasion" is needed to cause a reaction.

Why, for example, is a spark needed before the hydrocarbons that compose gasoline will react with oxygen? Why, no matter how many sparks are provided, will exhaust gases such as carbon dioxide and steam not burn? Why does the spark cause an explosive reaction in a gas/air mixture, whereas a spark landing on this page would probably only char a small portion of the paper; and, if the paper did catch fire, why would it burn steadily rather than explode?

The answers to all these questions are related to the energies of different molecules. The world is full of molecules, rather than unlinked atoms, because the formation of chemical bonds releases energy and makes the resultant product more stable. The same is true of molecular reactions. If a reaction occurs spontaneously, energy is usually released, and more stable molecules are produced.

It is theoretically possible to get water and carbon dioxide to react to form gasoline and oxygen. But, because gasoline and oxygen are less stable molecules, large quantities of energy would have to be put into the reactants (starting materials) to succeed. A better example is, perhaps, metallic corrosion. Many metals are more stable as compounds, such as the oxide or sulfide, than as pure metal. Using processes that supply energy to metallic compounds, scientists can refine their ores to make metals for steel girders or silver teaspoons. But if unprotected, the metals gradually corrode—that is, spontaneously form compounds such as iron oxide (rust) or silver sulfide (tarnish) that are more stable.

Kinds of reactions

While certain reactions may occur spontaneously, they do not necessarily do so. A gas/air mixture needs the spark to set it off because, in between the reactants and the products, there is a transition state which is of higher energy. It is necessary to give many reactants an energy "lift" to help them over the activation barrier. The larger the amount of energy arising from a reaction, the more molecules can be lifted over the barrier. And if the reaction happens fast enough, the result is an explosion.

The energy to initiate a reaction can come from a variety of sources. Heat is commonly used by chemists to help reactions along. But other forms of energy, such as light, can sometimes initiate reactions.

CONNECTIONS

See also
1562 Chemicals in solutio
1556 Joining atoms
1558 Simple chemicals an their structures
1566 Electrochemistry
1642 Oil and natural gas
1808 Soaps and detergent
1810 Explosives and fireworks
1812 Color chemistry
1804 Chemical engineerir
1806 Materials for industr

1 The application of heat [A] alone to aluminum sulfate [1] and potassium sulfate [2] produces no reaction, but they react when dissolved in water [3]. If heating is continued to evaporation, alum [4] forms. Dry copper sulfate crystals [B] do not conduct current; but dissolve them in water [C] and electrolysis can proceed. Metals may react with a liquid [D]; a grain of sodium [5] dropped into water melts, generating hydrogen. Solutions and other liquids react readily [E]. Phenolphthalein [6] added to a solution of alkali [7] produces a red solution [8]. When this is added to an acid solution [9], the red disappears.

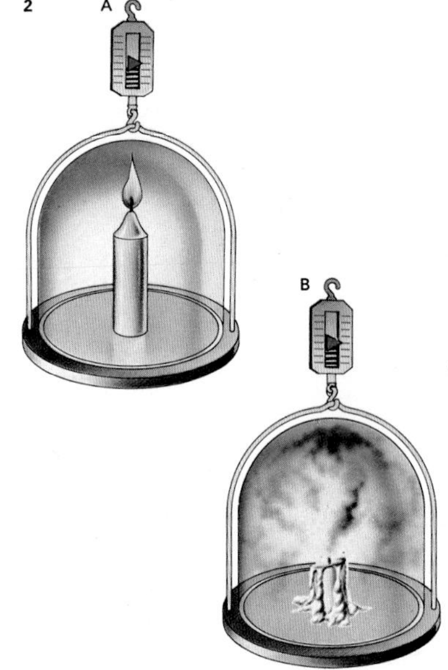

2
A
B

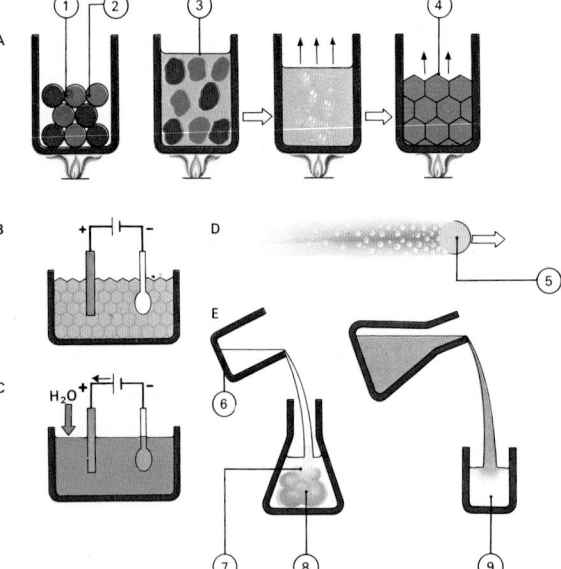

2 In a chemical reaction, matter is neither created nor destroyed. This conservation of mass can be shown by a classic experiment in which a candle is burned inside a weighed bell jar [A]. At the end of the experiment, the weight of the jar and its contents [B] are the same as at the beginning, although a part of the candle—made up largely of carbon and hydrogen—has "disappeared" as volatile reaction products (water and carbon dioxide). It was only after scientists accepted the principle of conservation of mass in the late 1700s that a quantitative approach to chemistry became possible.

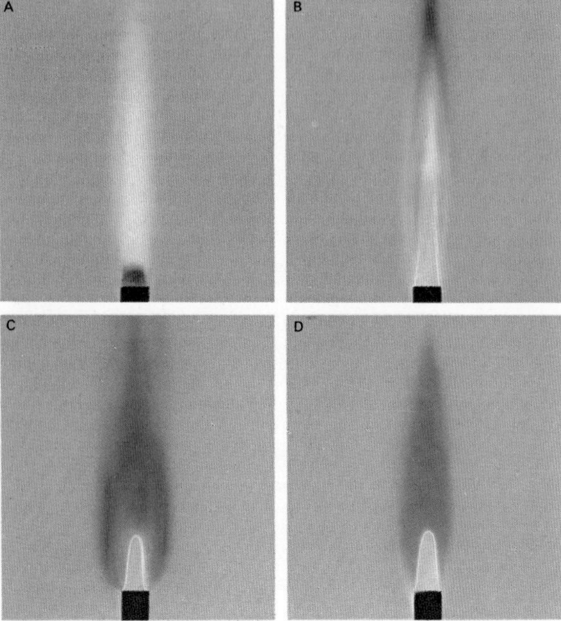

3 A
B
C
D

3 Unmixed ethylene burns with a luminous diffusion flame [A], reacting with oxygen drawn in from around the flame. If mixed with a little air, the ethylene gives a flame with three distinct layers—an inner cone of unburned gas, a blue-green layer of reacting premixed gas, and an outer cone where partially oxidized products of the premixed layer are burned by diffusion flame [B]. Addition of nitric oxide to the mixture cuts down the amount of oxygen available for immediate combustion and the resultant flame [C] shows a complex series of reactions, as in B. But if more air is added to the gas mixture, the diffusion layer disappears [D] from the flame.

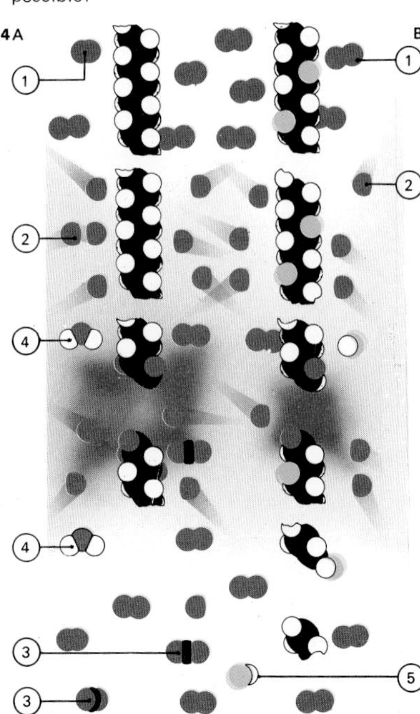

4A
B
1
2
4
3
5

4 A hydrocarbon fuel [A] will burn more readily than similar molecules in which some of the hydrogen atoms have been replaced by chlorine [B]. When mixed with oxygen [1] and subjected to a spark, both types of molecules burn, but the chlorinated one burns more slowly. The spark breaks oxygen molecules into reactive oxygen atoms [2]. These combine with carbon and hydrogen in the hydrocarbon to give carbon dioxide [3] and water [4]. Sufficient heat is produced to keep the reaction going rapidly. With the chlorinated material, more complex reactions take place more slowly. These produce, in addition, hydrogen chloride [5] but generate less heat.

There are a great many types of reactions, but they can all be broken down into simple categories. There are reactions in which a single substance rearranges its chemical bonds to produce a different substance (rearrangement); alternatively, it may break into two or more different parts (decomposition, fragmentation). Conversely, two, or occasionally more, compounds can combine to form a single compound (addition). More often, there are two reactants and a number of products.

Reaction requirements

When there is only one starting material, the activated state is achieved by molecules absorbing sufficient energy to initiate a change. For example, when the visual pigment rhodopsin in the retina of the eye absorbs light, one of its electrons is energized and the molecule is catapulted into a more energetic state. As a result, the molecule changes shape to form a different geometric isomer (substance whose molecules are made of the same numbers of the same atoms, but differently arranged).

When different starting materials are involved, not only must they have enough energy to form the activated intermediate state, but they must also collide physically before the rearrangement of bonds can be completed. This is why some reactions take place under high pressure, as in a car engine, because packing molecules more tightly together makes collisions more likely.

Another way to improve the chances of a successful collision is to provide a surface that has an appropriate geometry for bringing molecules together. Substances that provide such surfaces are among the various types of catalysts. They speed up reactions by lowering the activation barrier. Other, negative, catalysts slow or even prevent reactions.

To follow reactions as they occur and identify the various products, modern chemists use a large range of different techniques [6, 7]. Some of them, such as nuclear spin resonance and Mossbauer spectroscopy, are based on physical phenomena discovered during the past 30 or 40 years.

KEY

A reaction takes place as drops of alkali fall into a dilute solution of a copper salt. This is a precipitation reaction – one of many different kinds that can take place in chemistry. One of the chemist's major tasks lies in discovering how various materials react with each other.

5

A C_6H_6 B C D E $C_6H_5NO_2$

Hydrogen
Carbon
Nitrogen
Oxygen

5 The nitration of benzene produces a reaction that goes through several stages. Initially [A], the entering group approaches and associates weakly with the benzene ring [B]. Then, rearrangement produces an unstable high energy intermediate [C] that breaks down to a complex [D] in which the leaving group is weakly associated with the ring. It ends with the departure of the leaving group [E].

6 In a mass spectrometer [A], outer electrons of a compound are removed in an ionization chamber [1]. Positively charged ions pass into an adjacent chamber under vacuum [2] and are focused by electric [3] and magnetic [4] fields. The way they are deflected by these fields is characteristic for each ion, which can be identified by its position on a photographic plate [5]. A molecule such as n-dodecane breaks down into a number of fragments that produce various "peaks" on a graph [B]. From their position, the parent molecules can be precisely identified.

6

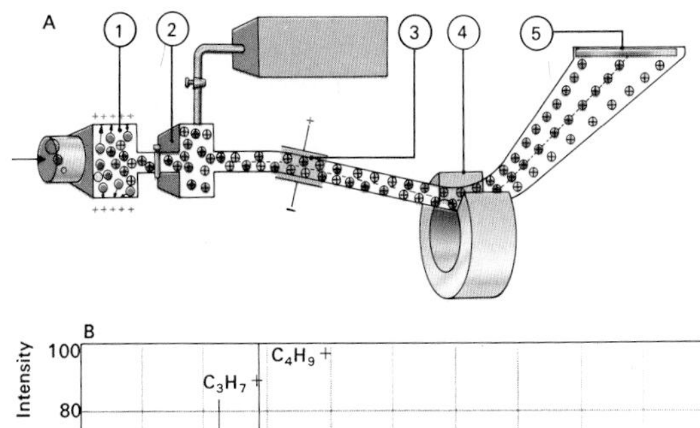
A
1
2
3
4
5

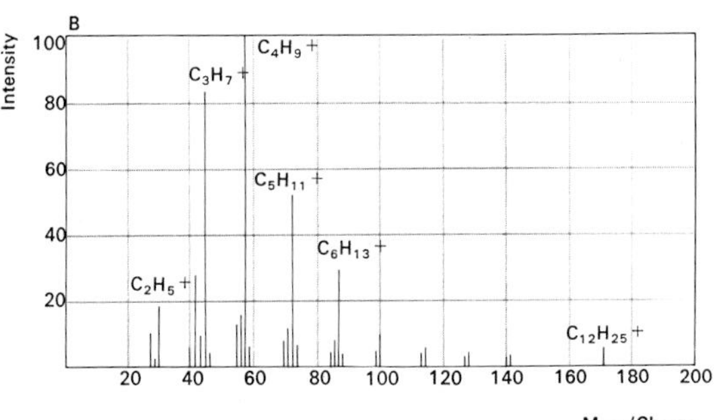
B
Intensity
100
80
60
40
20
C_4H_9 +
C_3H_7 +
C_5H_{11} +
C_6H_{13} +
C_2H_5 +
$C_{12}H_{25}$ +
20 40 60 80 100 120 140 160 180 200
Mass/Charge

7 Mixtures of compounds can be separated by gas chromatography. Gaseous molecules travel down columns of liquid-impregnated solids at different rates. Special detectors reproduce on a graph the peaks produced by the molecules as they leave the column. Each can frequently be identified by the time it takes to go through the column – the "retention time." The chromatogram shows the separation of hydrocarbons: isobutane [A], n-butane [B], n-butene [C], isobutene [D] trans-but-2-ene [E], cis-but-2-ene [F], cis-1-3-butadiene [G].

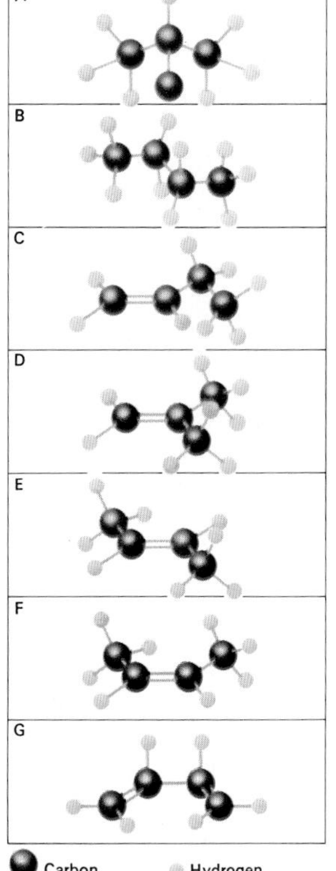
7
A
B
C
D
E
F
G
Carbon
Hydrogen

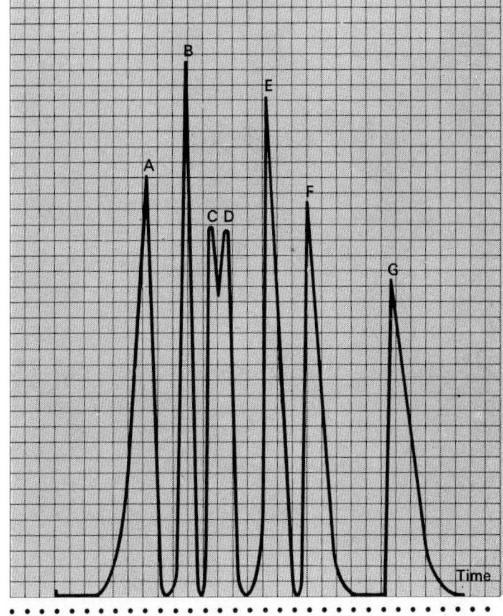
A
B
C D
E
F
G
Time

Electrochemistry

Electrons are negatively charged particles that form a part of every atom and it is with the interactions of electrons from different atoms that chemistry is mainly concerned. An electric current is no more than a flow of electrons. It is not surprising, then, that electricity and chemistry are connected.

Early research

Studies of electricity and chemistry went hand in hand long before anyone knew of the existence of electrons. During the eighteenth century, there was much interest in static electricity, leading to the development of the Leyden jar (for storing "electric fluid" generated by friction) and the lightning conductor, but it was not until the Italian physiologist Luigi Galvani (1737–98) found, toward the end of the century, that frogs' legs would contract if different metals were applied to nerve and muscle that current electricity was discovered. In 1795 another Italian, the physicist Alessandro Volta (1745–1827) [1], showed that this "animal electricity" could be produced without living tissue. He separated two pieces of metal by a cloth moistened with salt solution and thus made the first electrical battery. Within five years, it was discovered that current from such a battery could decompose water into hydrogen and oxygen gases. Thus, the foundations of electrochemistry were laid. By a chemical reaction involving two metals, a flow of electrons can be produced; such flow can bring about other reactions.

Batteries soon became important equipment in every laboratory and led to many new discoveries, such as the isolation of the elements sodium and potassium in the first decade of the nineteenth century by Humphry Davy (1778–1829).

Chemical reactions

When a metal such as zinc forms compounds, it does so in many instances by losing two electrons to form a doubly positive zinc ion (Zn^{2+}). Metals differ in the ease with which they lose electrons, so that if a piece of zinc metal is placed in a solution of copper sulfate (which contains Cu^{2+} ions), the zinc gives up electrons to the copper. The net result is that zinc is converted to zinc sulfate while the copper ions become metallic copper.

When an element gains electrons to form a negatively charged ion, it is said to be reduced; if it loses electrons to form a positively charged ion, it is said to be oxidized. A reaction in which reduction and oxidation cancel each other out, as in the zinc/copper sulfate case, is called a redox reaction. Redox reactions can be tapped to supply electric currents by preventing the reduction and oxidation from occurring at the same place. A battery can be made by suspending zinc in zinc sulfate and copper in copper sulfate and linking the two solutions by a porous partition and the two pieces of metal by a wire.

Each of the reactions in such an arrangement is called a "half cell." When two "half cells" are added together, a cell is completed and the voltage it produces depends on its particular half cells.

That different batteries produce different, but specific, voltages depending on their chemical composition is not surprising, in view of the differences in reactivity

CONNECTIONS

See also

1532 What is an electric current?
1562 Chemicals in solution
1556 Joining atoms

1 Alessandro Volta, professor of natural philosophy at the University of Pavia, Italy, constructed in 1800 an "artificial electrical organ," an apparatus he described as like the electric organ of the electric eel. Made by piling alternate disks of copper and zinc, each pair separated by a piece of brine-soaked cloth, his electrical organ was one of the first scientific batteries.

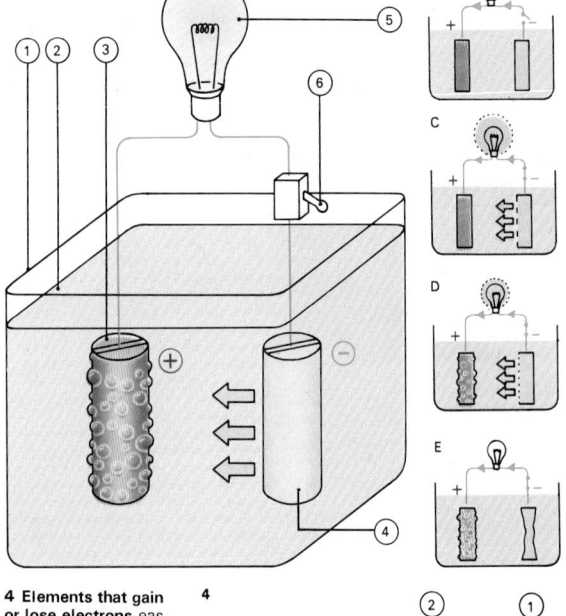

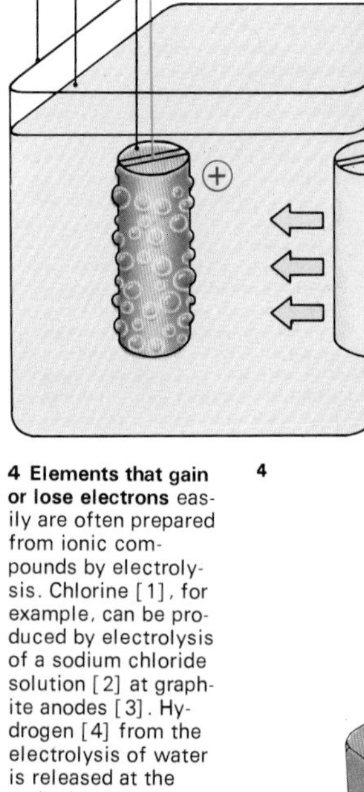

2 A
1
2
3
5
6
4
B
C
D
E

2 The voltaic cell [A] named after Volta, consists of a jar [1] containing sulfuric acid [2] in which are suspended a copper anode [3] and a zinc cathode [4]. These are connected by a circuit containing a light bulb [5] and a switch [6]. When the switch is open [B] no reaction occurs. When it is closed [C] an electromotive force (emf) is set up in the circuit and the light bulb glows weakly, but the light gradually decreases [D] while the cathode is steadily eroded. Hydrogen bubbles are seen on the anode. The hydrogen bubbles then polarize the anode [E] setting up a "back emf," breaking the circuit.

3 Heart pacemakers like the one shown, and miniature hearing aids, can be powered by batteries. These are examples of primary cells. Secondary cells, or storage batteries, can be recharged. Early batteries all had metallic plates separated by solutions of salt-like chemicals. The dry, or Leclanché, cell replaced the liquid with a paste. Such batteries, which use zinc and carbon (with a manganese dioxide depolarizer) as electrodes, are the type used in transistor radios, flashlights, and many other everyday appliances. In recent years, battery technology has led to the production of very small but highly reliable, long-lived batteries, which also use zinc and a metal oxide, in this case mercury.

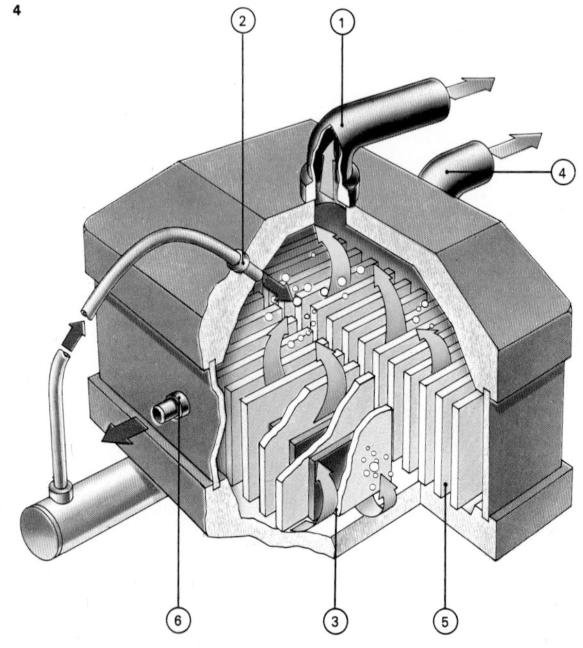

4
1
2
3
4
5
6

4 Elements that gain or lose electrons easily are often prepared from ionic compounds by electrolysis. Chlorine [1], for example, can be produced by electrolysis of a sodium chloride solution [2] at graphite anodes [3]. Hydrogen [4] from the electrolysis of water is released at the cathodes [5]. Left behind in solution are sodium and hydroxyl ions, giving a solution of sodium hydroxide [6]. If the hydroxyl ions are not kept away from the chlorine – for example, by means of a diaphragm – they react with it to produce sodium hypochlorite, used as a bleaching agent. Under slightly different conditions, the weed-killer sodium chlorate is formed in the reaction.

between different elements. The reverse also seems logical: that a particular quantity of electrons should produce a particular amount of change in a substance. The quantitative relationships between electricity and chemical reactions were stated during the nineteenth century by Michael Faraday [Key]. The extraction and electroplating of metals, and the production of reactive electronegative elements such as chlorine [4] and fluorine, are often done electrolytically.

Electrolysis

The products from electrolysis reactions [2] sometime depend on the conditions used, as well as the amount of electricity. If fused (molten) sodium chloride is electrolyzed, sodium metal forms at one electrode and chlorine gas at the other. When a solution of sodium chloride is electrolyzed, however, using a graphite anode (positive electrode) and an iron cathode (negative electrode), chlorine and hydrogen gases are produced, leaving behind sodium hydroxide.

The ions of different elements may be positive (cations) or negative (anions). In a solution that is being electrolyzed, cations are attracted to the cathode and anions to the anode. If aluminum is made into an anode in an acid solution, a very thin layer of aluminum oxide forms on it. This anodization protects the aluminum from corrosion and is used on a wide range of articles.

Many oxidation reactions are used in everyday life: for example, the burning of gasoline in a car is such a reaction. Instead of releasing the energy from such a reaction as heat, it can be converted into a flow of electrons in a "fuel cell." These cells are theoretically much more efficient energy converters than heat engines. Difficulties in designing suitable fuel cells for everyday purposes have meant that their use has been limited largely to applications where cost is not an important factor.

The chief commercial application of electrochemistry is electroplating. For example, decorative metals such as gold and silver are electroplated onto articles of jewelry; chromium electroplated onto steel (preferably on copper and nickel base layers) provides corrosion resistance.

KEY

As a youth, Michael Faraday (1791–1867) attended Humphry Davy's lectures at the Royal Institution in London. He copied these and sent them to Davy with a request for employment. From Davy's assistant, he rose to become professor of chemistry at the Royal Institution, a post he held for more than 30 years. Most of Faraday's work was in physics—particularly in the field of electromagnetic induction. He also founded the science of electrochemistry through his discovery of the quantitative relationships between the amount of electricity passed through a solution and the amount of substances deposited as a result.

5 Electrolysis can easily be shown. A current is passed between platinum electrodes [1] through a dilute hydrochloric acid electrolyte [2]. Positively charged cations [3] move toward the negative electrode (cathode), and anions [4] move to the positive electrode (anode). The hydrogen ions combine with water to form hydronium ions H_3O^+; when two hydronium ions [B] reach the cathode, they each receive an electron, the atoms of hydrogen, which combine to form a molecule of gas. In copper plating [C], copper from the copper sulfate electrolyte is deposited onto the object to be plated [5], while copper from the anode [6] is drawn into solution. A modern barrel electroplating machine [D] can plate a large number of small objects [7] simultaneously.

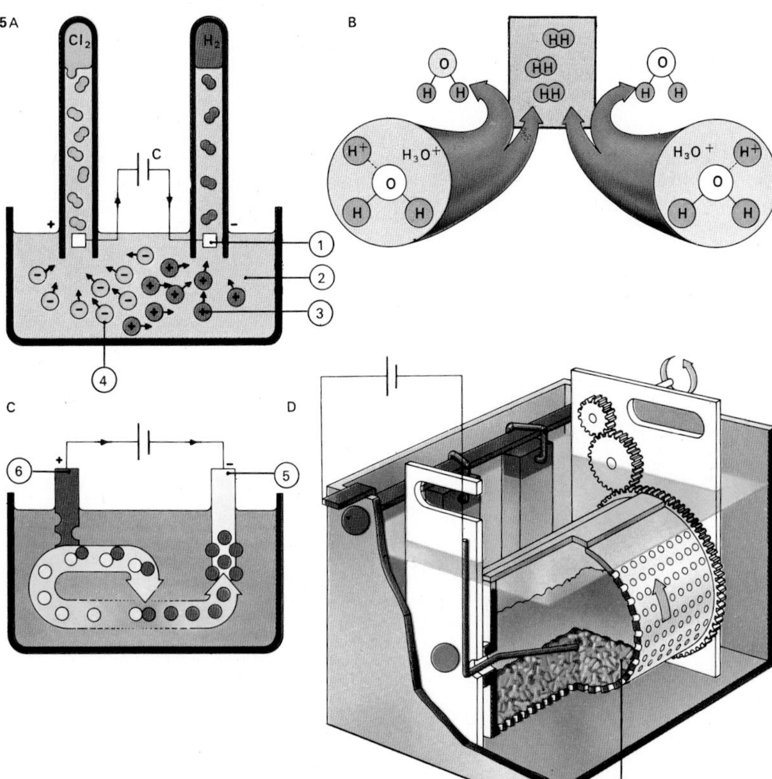

5A
B
C
D
Cl_2
H_2
H_3O^+
H^+
O
H
1
2
3
4
5
6
7

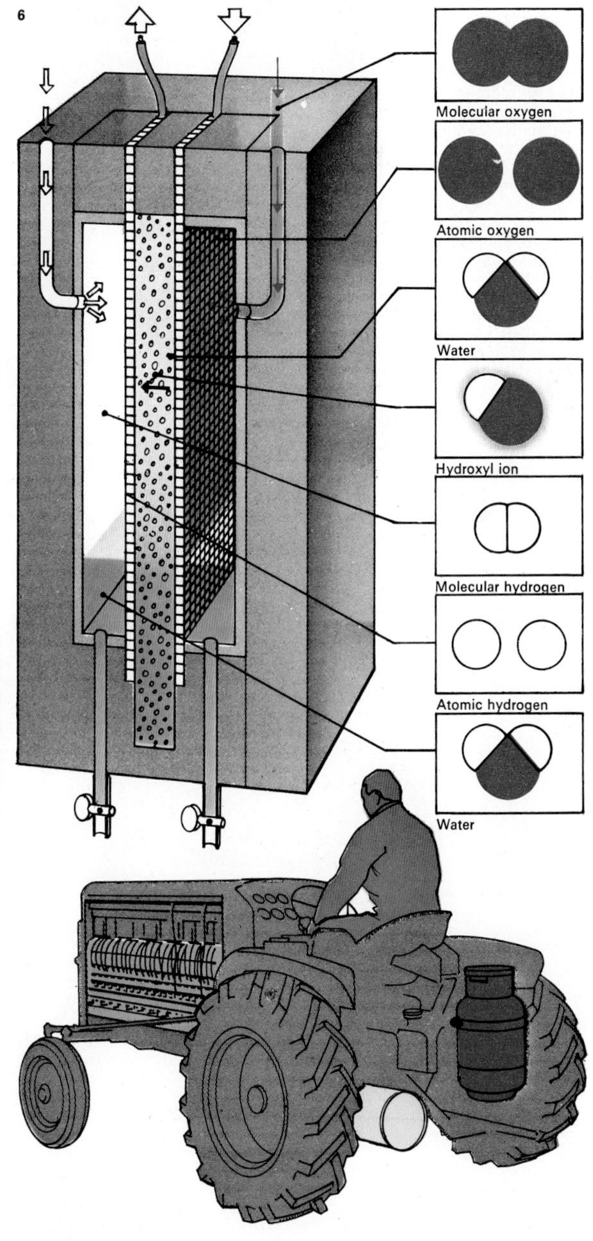

6
Molecular oxygen
Atomic oxygen
Water
Hydroxyl ion
Molecular hydrogen
Atomic hydrogen
Water

6 The fuel cell, like a battery, uses the energy generated during a chemical reaction to produce electrical power. One simple cell uses oxygen and hydrogen as "fuels" to produce electricity, the water formed being a byproduct. The electrolyte in this case is located in a very thin, water-saturated membrane. This allows ions to pass through it, but does not allow the passage of atoms or molecules. The electrodes are of wire mesh, coated with platinum. Molecular hydrogen and oxygen are fed to them from gas chambers. The cathodic platinum converts oxygen to hydroxyl ions, which move across the membrane and react with hydrogen at the anode to form water. Electrons released by the hydrogen traverse the external circuit—as an electric current—to help form hydroxyl at the anode. A battery of such cells can power a tractor, with fuel tanks holding liquid oxygen and hydrogen either in the form of a liquid or as solid hydride.

Chemical analysis

One of the main branches of chemistry—chemical analysis—is concerned with determining the composition of a substance or a mixture of substances. Identifying the ingredients is termed qualitative analysis, whereas determining their precise proportions is called quantitative analysis. Organic chemicals (the large class of compounds containing the element carbon) and inorganic chemicals (all other compounds) require different analytical techniques in the laboratory.

Methods of inorganic analysis

Qualitative inorganic analysis is generally carried out on a semi-micro scale [1] using small quantities—less than a gram. Chemists make preliminary tests on a dry sample of a substance and these give general information about its composition. The effect of heat, for example, may cause a color change, sublimation, or the evolution of a gas. A reagent is added to a solution of the sample and the resulting mixture examined for the release of a gas, a precipitate, or a change in color.

Metal ions are identified by a systematic separation into "groups." A variety of techniques exists, but metals are usually split into groups by adding a series of reagents and collecting any precipitate produced.

Quantitative inorganic analysis may be carried out using either volumetric or gravimetric methods. Volumetric analysis involves reacting a solution of known concentration, referred to as a "standard" solution, with a solution of the substance to be determined. After preparing the standard solution the chemist carries out a titration [Key] in which one solution is slowly added to the other. From the concentration and volume of the standard solution, the "unknown's" concentration is established.

Gravimetric analysis involves preparing a solution with a known mass of the sample. This solution is then reacted with a chosen reagent so that the desired component is completely separated, generally as a precipitate. The product, which must be pure, is isolated and weighed and the amount of the component calculated.

Methods of organic analysis

Merely identifying the elements present is insufficient to make a definite description of an organic compound. The ability of carbon compounds to exhibit isomerism (in which two different substances can contain the same chemical elements, in the same proportions, but combined in a different way) means that the arrangements of the elements present must also be determined.

Identification of the elements in an organic component involves systematic elimination of all possible elements one by one. Carbon and hydrogen are nearly always present and tests for them are rarely carried out. But tests are made to identify other elements. An example is the Lassaigne sodium fusion, which reveals the presence of nitrogen, the halogens (chlorine, bromine, and iodine), and sulfur. A knowledge of the elements allows a chemist to allocate the compound to a main group. This is followed by the application, within the group, of classification tests for functional groups, which determines the types of organic compound present.

CONNECTIONS

See also
1552 Classification of elements
1554 The element groups
1562 Chemicals in solution
1564 Key chemical reactions

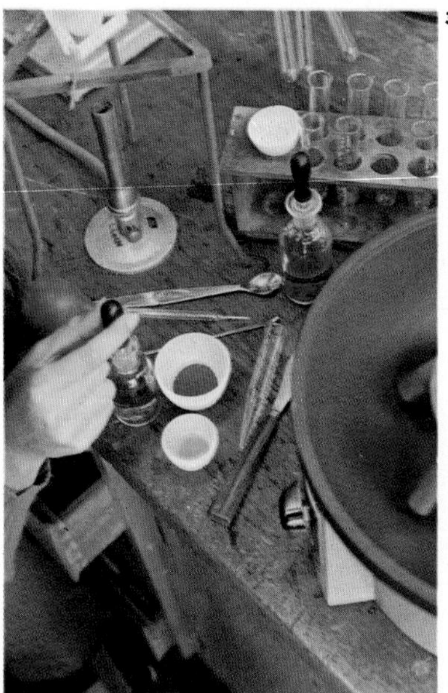

1 Analysis on a semi-micro scale saves time and money. Small test tubes are used for reactions and tapered tubes are used for the centrifuge. Solutions do not mix well in these small tubes, so a stirring rod is used. Solutions are handled in a pipette and each reagent bottle is fitted with its own dropper. Solids require the use of a semi-micro spatula. To avoid "bumping" during heating, solutions are heated indirectly in a metal block, although evaporation to dryness requires the use of a small crucible. Identification of gases is usually carried out with a bubble-cap fitted to a test tube.

Mettler FP 61

2 The melting-point is a characteristic of an organic compound and can be measured, using this automatic apparatus. A sample is first heated quickly to get an approximate value and then slowly melted to obtain a more accurate reading.

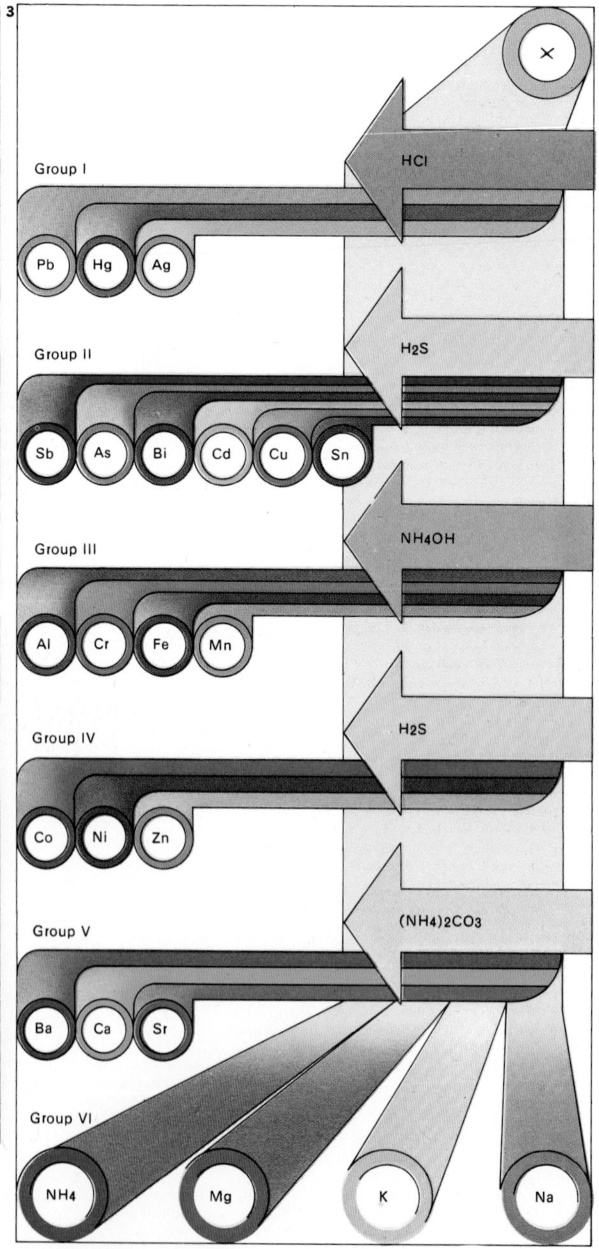

X
Group I
HCl
Pb
Hg
Ag
Group II
H2S
Sb
As
Bi
Cd
Cu
Sn
Group III
NH4OH
Al
Cr
Fe
Mn
Group IV
H2S
Co
Ni
Zn
Group V
(NH4)2CO3
Ba
Ca
Sr
Group VI
NH4
Mg
K
Na

3 Metal ions can be detected in qualitative chemical analysis by a systematic separation into groups by means of a series of characteristic precipitation reactions. The chemist tries to dissolve a sample of the substance to be analyzed in dilute hydrochloric acid. Metals with insoluble chlorides—lead, mercury, and silver—constitute Group I. Next, hydrogen sulfide is bubbled through the acid solution; a sulfide precipitate indicates one of the Group II metals—antimony, arsenic, bismuth, cadmium, copper, or tin. The addition of ammonia solution precipitates the hydroxides of the Group III metals—aluminum, chromium, iron, or manganese. The Group IV metals have sulfides that are precipitated from alkaline solution by bubbling in hydrogen sulfide gas; they are cobalt, nickel, and zinc. The addition of ammonium carbonate to the remaining solution at this stage of the analysis precipitates the carbonates of barium, calcium, or strontium, the Group V metals. Group VI of the analysis table contains the metals magnesium, sodium, and potassium as well as the "metallic" ion ammonium, left after eliminating all other possible metal ions. This analysis program can be carried out on the semi-micro scale and it can be enlarged to include some of the less common metals. It reveals only the presence of a metal.

Quantitative organic analysis also involves estimation of the elements present, followed by purification and a determination of molecular weight to give the empirical and molecular formulas. The amounts of carbon and hydrogen are found by completely oxidizing a known mass of the organic compound and weighing the carbon dioxide and water formed. Various methods are used to estimate other elements.

These results allow the chemist to calculate the percentage composition of the substance (the proportions of each element present) and to determine its empirical formula. The molecular formula is found by comparing the empirical formula with the molecular weight. Dissolving a sample of the substance in a solvent affects the physical properties of the solvent. The lowering of vapor pressure, the elevation of boiling point, and the depression of freezing point are all proportional to the mole fraction (concentration in terms of molecular weight) of the dissolved substance present in the solution. The concentration also affects the osmotic pressure, viscosity, and light-scattering properties of solutions. Careful measurement of one of these effects is followed by a calculation of the molecular weight before the analysis is complete.

Modern instrumental analysis

Various forms of chromatography are based on the fact that different substances diffuse or are absorbed at different rates. Spectroscopy [7] makes use of the fact that each species of atom has a unique characteristic spectrum. A spectrum is produced when atoms, ions, or molecules are excited by absorbing energy and may be observed by using a prism or, preferably, a diffraction grating.

In mass spectroscopy [5] a substance is bombarded with low-energy electrons and fragmentation produces a number of positive ions. Ions of the same mass/charge ratio are focused by magnetic or electrostatic fields and detected photographically or electronically. The highest mass/charge ratio can give the molecular weight. Investigation of the fragmentation pattern determines the molecular structure.

KEY

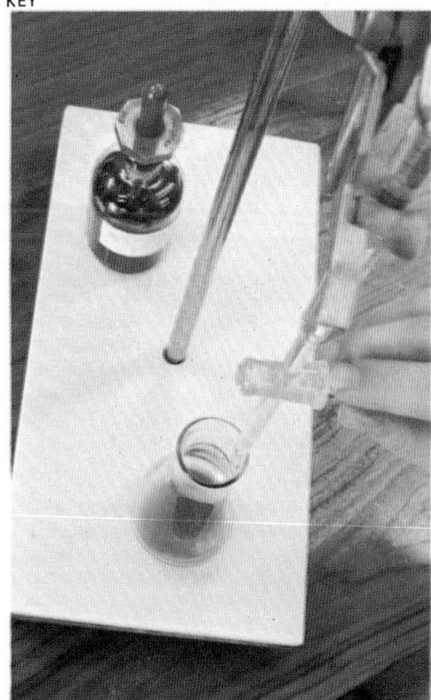

A titration is performed to estimate the unknown concentration of a solution by reacting it with a "standard" solution of known concentration. This is usually added from a burette to a fixed volume of the "unknown." The end point of the reaction is shown either by a visible change in the reactants or by the addition of a chemical indicator. Acid/base indicators have different colors according to the hydrogen-ion concentration (pH) of the solution and change as the pH of the solution changes. The pH at which color changes occur varies so an indicator can be selected that shows a color change at a pH close to the end point.

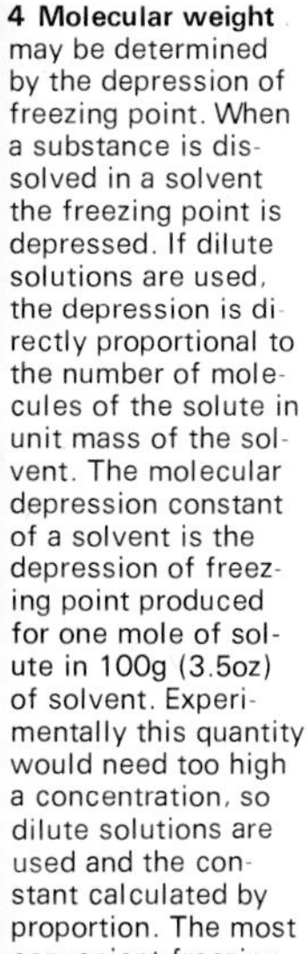

4 Molecular weight may be determined by the depression of freezing point. When a substance is dissolved in a solvent the freezing point is depressed. If dilute solutions are used, the depression is directly proportional to the number of molecules of the solute in unit mass of the solvent. The molecular depression constant of a solvent is the depression of freezing point produced for one mole of solute in 100g (3.5oz) of solvent. Experimentally this quantity would need too high a concentration, so dilute solutions are used and the constant calculated by proportion. The most convenient freezing agent is ice and water.

4

5 The masses of atoms can be compared with great accuracy using a mass spectrometer. A vaporized sample is ionized by electron bombardment and the beam of positive ions produced is accelerated to a constant speed. Application of a strong magnetic field deflects the beam—the lightest ions being deflected most and the heaviest least. The field is adjusted so that ions of a particular mass fall onto a detector, either a moving photographic plate or an electrometer. From an electrometer the signal is amplified and recorded on a graph. Further adjustment of the magnetic field allows ions of different mass to be recorded.

5

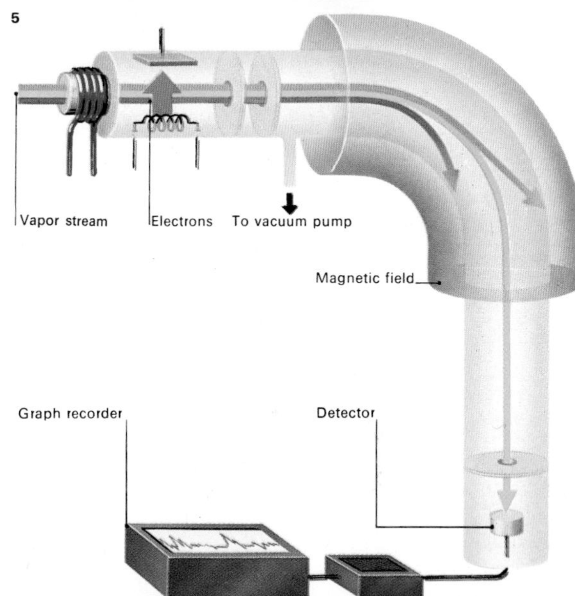
Vapor stream
Electrons
To vacuum pump
Magnetic field
Graph recorder
Detector

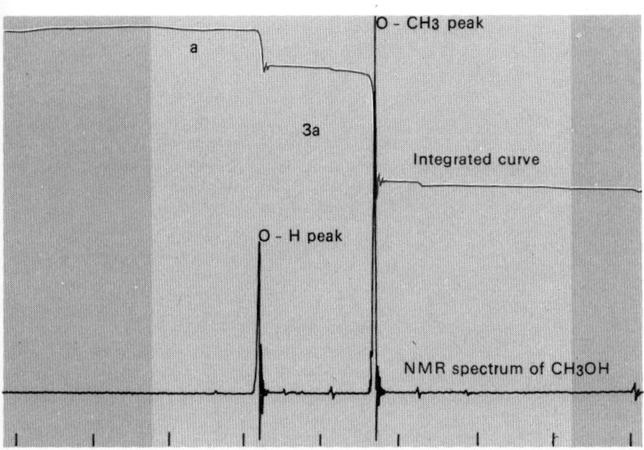
O - CH3 peak
a
3a
Integrated curve
O - H peak
NMR spectrum of CH3OH

7

Infra-red spectrum of CCl4

Transmittance (%)

C-Cl peak

Frequency (cm−1)

6 Nuclear magnetic resonance (NMR) spectroscopy of a substance with a molecular formula of CH_4O shows two peaks. The areas under the peaks are integrated automatically and indicated by the upper curve. This shows a ratio of one to three. The inference is that the hydrogen atoms in the molecule are arranged so that three of the four are in the same environment, and the other is different. The larger peak is produced by those in the O-CH_3 group and the smaller by that in the O-H group—indicating the structure CH_3OH: methanol. Normally a "standard" is added and all lines are measured relative to it. Tetramethylsilane or a sodium salt of 4, 4-dimethyl, 4 silapentanesulfonic acid is a suitable standard.

7 Infrared radiation is absorbed by the chemical bonds in an organic compound and can cause vibrational effects in them. The frequency of the absorbed radiation is characteristic of the bond concerned, so that measuring these frequencies provides a means of determining the bonds present and of analyzing the compound. This is the basis of infrared spectroscopy. The absorption frequencies are measured electronically and plotted as a series of peaks on a graph. In this example the main absorption peak at a frequency of 750cm^{-1} is caused by the stretching of a carbon-chlorine bond, indicating that the substance producing it is probably tetrachloromethane (carbon tetrachloride, CCl_4). The minor peak at 1,550 cm^{-1} is probably a harmonic of the main one. The bending and rocking of chemical bonds after infrared absorption also produce characteristic peaks on the spectrograph and aid the analysis.

Toward the chemistry of life

Only half a dozen of the 93 or more chemical elements that occur naturally on Earth make up the bulk of living matter, and life's diversity is largely the result of the combining properties of just one element: carbon. Carbon atoms can form chemical bonds with each other to produce an extensive range of basic structures. These can be modified by the addition of the atoms of other common elements of life—hydrogen, oxygen, nitrogen, phosphorus, and sulfur—to produce the living world's enormous diversity of chemical substances.

Isomers and polymers

Many naturally occurring carbon compounds have another distinctive property. A single atom of carbon can form chemical bonds to four different atomic groupings. The bonds can be arranged in space in two distinct ways to produce two different molecules that are as similar to and as different from each other as a pair of gloves [1]. They are called optical isomers and where two of these are possible, usually only one form occurs naturally.

Many key substances in living organisms are polymers—giant molecules containing thousands or even millions of individual atoms linked together. Carbohydrates, proteins, and nucleic acids are all polymers. But they are all made by joining together small molecular building blocks rather than individual atoms. Carbohydrates, for example, are made from small molecules called sugars, or saccharides. Common table sugar is not one of the simplest; it is made by linking two smaller saccharides. Chemists call it a disaccharide. It is an ingredient of many processed foods, such as pickles and ketchup [3].

Like all carbohydrates, saccharides are composed of carbon, hydrogen, and oxygen. These elements are generally linked together in such a way that a loop is formed between the ends of the molecule by an oxygen atom bridging two carbon atoms.

Sugars and fats

Sugars [2] not only supply living organisms with energy, but also make up a broad range of polymeric substances, such as starch and cellulose. Starch, for example, is the chief carbohydrate in potatoes, rice, and bread [3]. Human beings cannot digest cellulose, but the polymer can be broken down chemically to form molecules of glucose, which is a simple sugar (monosaccharide).

Virtually all food has sugars or polysaccharides in it. Almost as common in food are the lipids, composed solely of carbon, hydrogen, and oxygen. Lipid is a general term that includes oils, fats, and waxes, all of which have similar chemical structures. In a simple lipid, a carbon-oxygen-carbon bond similar to that which holds a disaccharide together joins three fatty acids to a small molecule called glycerol (also known as glycerine) [B]. The resultant triglyceride may be a liquid (oil) or solid (fat) at room temperature, depending on the structures of the fatty acids, which can all be the same (as in olive oil) or all different. All meats contain some fat [3].

The so-called unsaturated fatty acids contain carbon-carbon double bonds. In recent years, margarines containing them have been available in many countries be-

CONNECTIONS

See also

1560 Complex chemicals and their structures
1572 The chemistry of lif biochemistry
406 Life and its origins
414 The genetic code

1

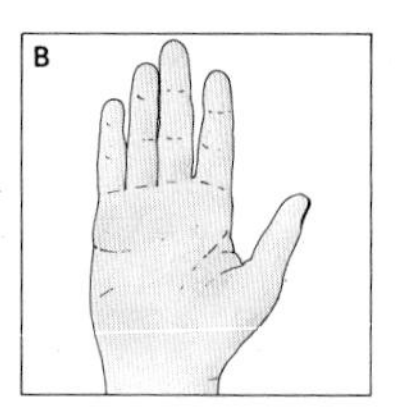

A
B

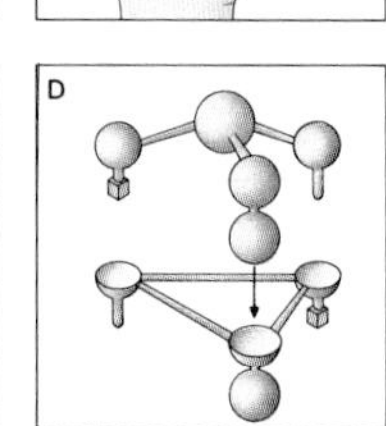

C
D

1 Most biologically active molecules depend on a particular shape for their function because they interact with other molecules and must fit them like a key in a lock [C]. Because of the ways in which molecules are constructed, it is possible for many of them to exist in more than one form. This variation in form is called isomerism. The most important type of isomerism in biological chemistry is optical isomerism in which molecules differ only in so far as they are mirror images of one another (just as a left and right hand [A, B] are mirror images). The upper molecule in C fits the lower one. But the upper molecule in D, the mirror image of that in C, does not fit. When they are made as a result of biological processes the result is nearly always 100 percent of one particular isomer.

2

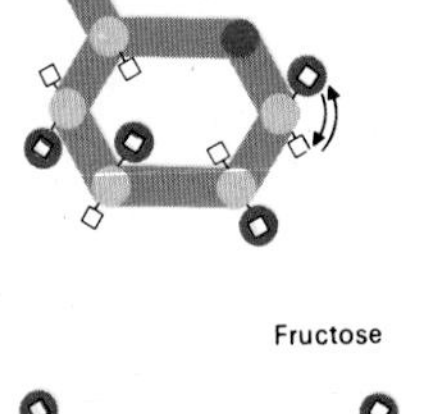

Glucose
Maltose

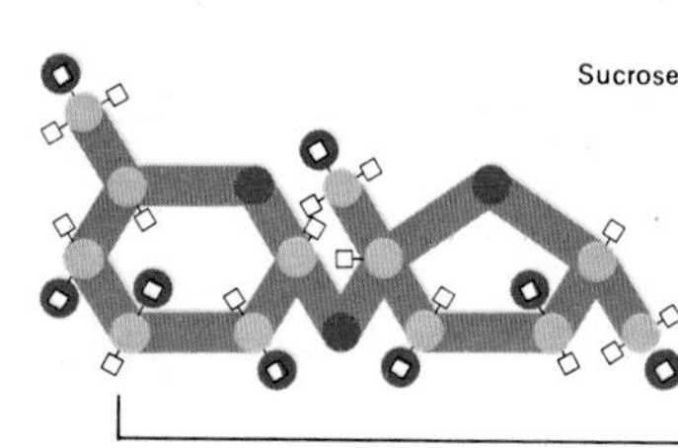

Fructose
Sucrose

2 Among the simplest of life's molecules are the saccharides, or sugars. They are made only of carbon, hydrogen, and oxygen atoms, the hydrogens and oxygens almost always in a 2:1 ratio, as in water. They therefore are known as carbohydrates (hydrates of carbon). The simplest sugars, or monosaccharides, are the pentoses and hextoses, with 5 or 6 carbon atoms. Often the carbon atoms form into a ring, as in glucose and fructose. Glucose molecules can link together to form medium-sized molecules, such as maltose, an important sugar in bread and beer making, or very large molecules such as starch. When monosaccharides link together, they need not all be of the same type. Common table sugar, or sucrose, is made by linking one molecule of glucose with one of fructose.

3

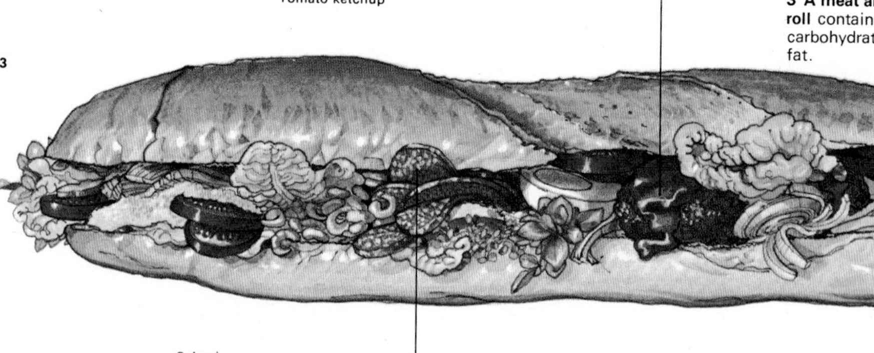

Tomato ketchup
Salami

3 A meat and salad roll contains protein, carbohydrate, and fat.

4

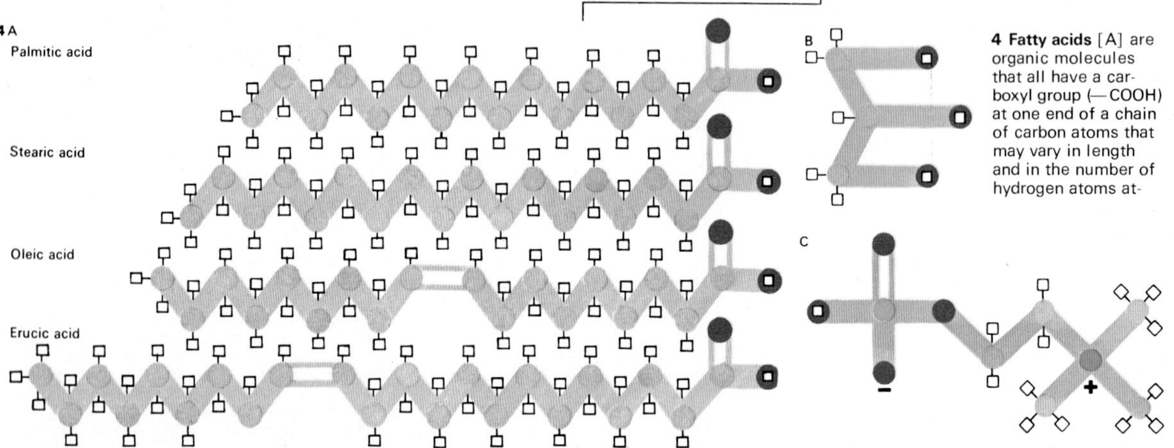

A
Palmitic acid
Stearic acid
Oleic acid
Erucic acid
B
C

4 Fatty acids [A] are organic molecules that all have a carboxyl group (—COOH) at one end of a chain of carbon atoms that may vary in length and in the number of hydrogen atoms attached to each carbon. They are a fundamental component of lipids, compounds found in materials as diverse as bacon fat and olive oil. In the most common lipids, 3 fatty acid molecules are linked to a single molecule of glycerol [B]. In some important biological molecules, one of the fatty acids may be replaced by a phosphorus-containing molecule, such as choline phosphate [C] to form a compound known as a phospholipid.

cause a link has been suggested between high consumption of saturated fats and the incidence of heart disease. Lipids are also important in providing energy for animal cells, but, in more complex forms, they play such roles as "insulators" for nerve fibers.

Triglycerides are the simplest lipids. An important and more complicated example is cholesterol, widely found in dairy foods such as cream and cheese [3]. It is a major constituent of gallstones and also implicated in heart disease. Cholesterol, with a complex chemical structure related to that of human sex hormones, is a type of molecule called a steroid. Steroids may be synthesized in living systems from a molecule called squalene, a kind of terpene. Some terpenes are made from only carbon and hydrogen, but others also contain oxygen and nitrogen. They include not only substances such as turpentine, vitamin A, and cholesterol, but flavors and fragrances.

Amino acids

From small groupings of carbon, oxygen, hydrogen, and occasionally sulfur, all joined in a particular pattern, come the amino acids [5], the building blocks for proteins. Proteins are major constituents of meat, fish, and eggs [3]. They are usually made from only 20 different amino acids and yet they have a wide range of valuable properties. In addition a number of other, less common amino acids are known. These can combine to form compounds such as the antibiotic valinomycin, which is made by linking together a small number of amino acids, and the extremely poisonous seven and eight amino-acid rings occurring naturally in fungi of the genus *Amanita*.

More complex than the amino acids are the nucleotides, the basic building blocks of the nucleic acids, which carry genetic information. Each nucleotide is made from one of the five types of base [7], which is joined to a sugar and this, in turn, is joined to a phosphate grouping. Some foods are very rich in nucleic acids and eating too much of them can cause illness, such as gout, in which the mechanism that usually deals with the bases falters or fails from overwork.

Carbon, the basic element of organic chemistry, undergoes a natural cycle in the environment. It exists in the form of carbon dioxide in the atmosphere. From there it is absorbed by plants [1] to build carbohydrates in green leaves. When plants burn [2], and animals breathe out [3], carbon dioxide passes back into the air. Also in decaying plant and animal remains [4], carbohydrates are broken down to release carbon dioxide into the atmosphere.

5

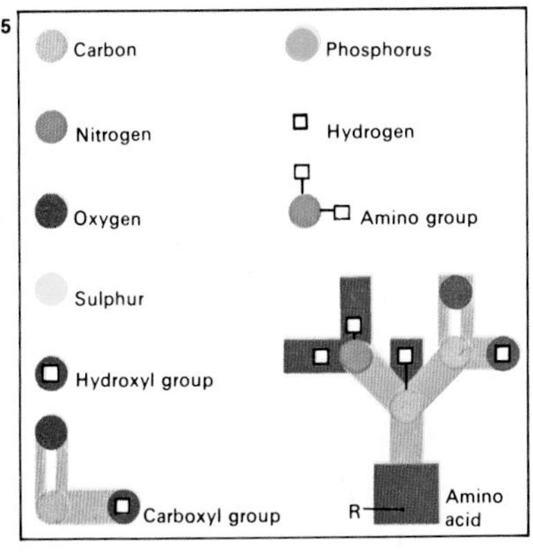

Carbon
Phosphorus
Nitrogen
Hydrogen
Oxygen
Amino group
Sulphur
Hydroxyl group
Carboxyl group
R
Amino acid

5 About 20 amino acids play essential roles in the structure and function of living organisms. All contain carbon, hydrogen, nitrogen, and oxygen atoms. All except proline have a free unsubstituted amino group and a free carboxyl group. Each amino acid has a characteristic "R" (radical or some organic entity) group attached to this carbon atom. This key applies to both of these pages.

6

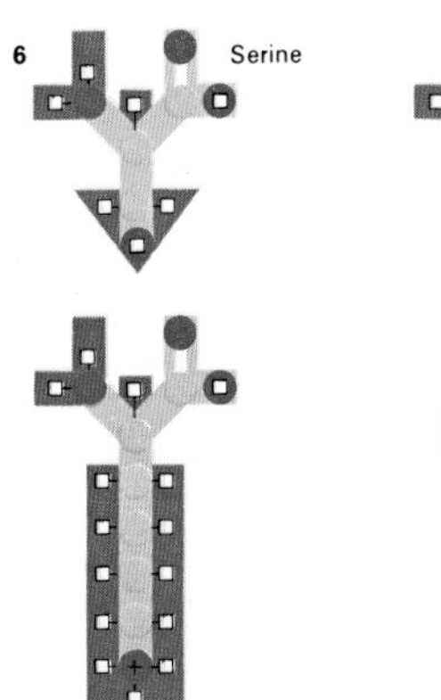

Serine
Lysine

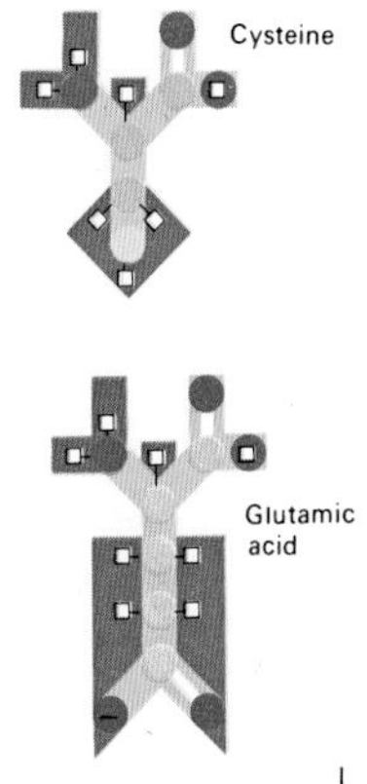

Cysteine
Glutamic acid

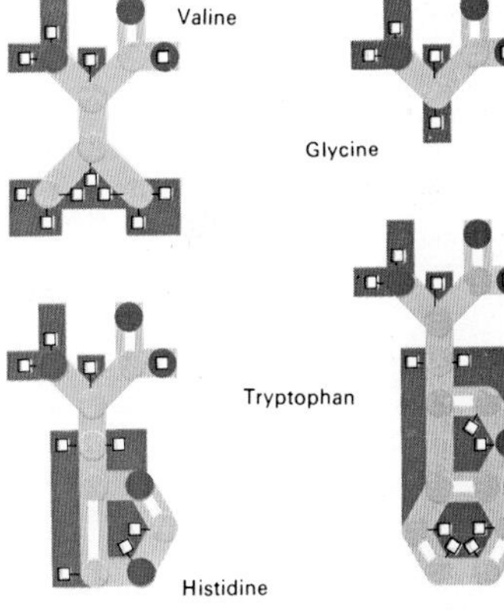

Valine
Glycine
Tryptophan
Histidine

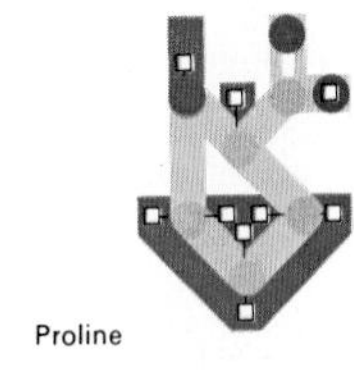

Proline

6 Amino acids usually occur in living organisms linked together in hundreds to form complex molecules. Monosodium glutamate, however, a simple derivative of glutamic acid, has been used as a food additive to enhance the flavor of meat. The "R" group attached to the central carbon atom in an amino acid can vary widely—from the simple hydrogen atom in glycine to the complex groups found in the other amino acids illustrated here. In proline, the end of the "R" group is linked to the nitrogen atom of the amino group, looping around to form a ring structure.

7

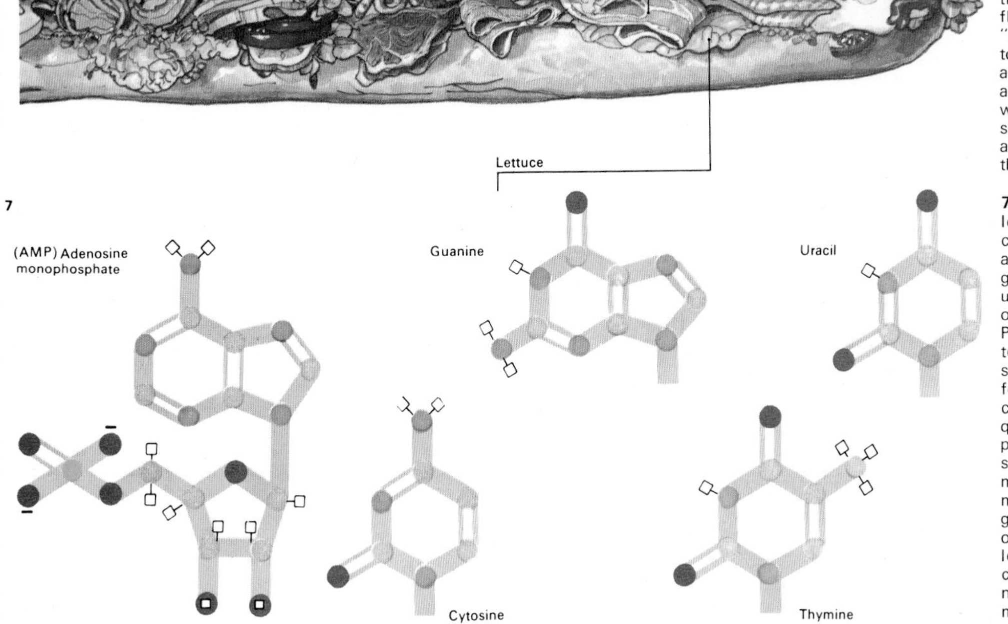

Meat
Lettuce
(AMP) Adenosine monophosphate
Guanine
Uracil
Cytosine
Thymine

7 Any living matter—lettuce or liver—contains nucleic acids. These are the giant molecules that ultimately control all our living processes. Protein made by bacteria, a possible source of synthetic food, is rich in nucleic acids. Large quantities of these produce unpleasant side-effects in human beings. They are made by linking together large numbers of a few simple molecules called nucleotides. A single nucleotide is, in turn, made by linking together three even simpler chemical groupings: a phosphate, which is joined to a 5-carbon monosaccharide (either ribose or deoxyribose), to which a nitrogen containing base is attached. Only five of these bases are common: adenine (here shown linked into the nucleotide adenosine monophosphate), cytosine, guanine, thymine, and uracil. DNA and RNA contain chains of four bases linked through a sugar and phosphate.

The chemistry of life: biochemistry

All living things—plants and animals—build up and break down different chemicals. These chemical processes ensure that an organism has an adequate supply of both the basic materials and the energy it needs for survival. A person eating hamburger derives energy from it, which he may use up by running several miles; but there is no obvious, direct link between the hamburger and the exercise. Biochemistry, through interlocking reactions, provides that link.

Fundamentals of biochemistry

The complexities of biochemistry can be reduced to two fundamental processes. The first is the way in which living cells develop an energy "currency." This can be used to exchange one vital commodity for another. The second is the use of substances called enzymes [2] as go-betweens to reduce the amount of energy needed to make many chemical reactions take place fast enough.

The "currency" used by living cells is a chemical called adenosine triphosphate, ATP [1]. Closely related to one of the units from which nucleic acids are built, ATP can break down to form adenosine diphosphate (ADP) and phosphate. In doing so, it can supply energy for a biochemical reaction—either one in which simple molecules are built up into more complex ones, or one that controls an activity such as muscle contraction [Key]. On the other hand, where a biochemical reaction gives off energy, as in the breakdown of sugars, that energy can be used to reform ATP. Consequently, an organism can balance energy inputs and outputs by recycling ATP.

Although some biochemical reactions ultimately give off energy and others use it, all need an energy push to get them started. The strength of this push can be decreased if the reacting molecules are close together and are lined up in the correct relationship to each other. Substances called catalysts introduce reacting molecules to one another more efficiently and so reduce the amount of energy needed to get the reaction moving. The overall effect is to make chemical reactions proceed much more quickly.

Life relies heavily on a special class of catalysts, the enzymes [4]. These are made mainly from protein, but they may also include metal atoms or small nonprotein organic molecules called coenzymes. Many of the vitamins included in a balanced and nutritional diet are used by a person's body as coenzymes.

The shape and activity of enzymes

Enzymes [3] are very large molecules whose activity is governed by their shape. By changing their shapes it is possible to inactivate them, and thus stop certain reactions from occurring at a noticeable rate. For example, the important protein-digesting enzyme chymotrypsin occurs in an inactive form called chymotrypsinogen. Only when a few of the amino acids that make up this protein are removed does it adopt the catalytic shape of chymotrypsin. This change is triggered by the presence of food in the digestive tract. If the chymotrypsin were active all the time it would rapidly digest the intestine wall while waiting for food to arrive.

In many biochemical processes a molecule is passed from enzyme to enzyme

CONNECTIONS

See also
1570 Toward the chemistry of life
1560 Complex chemicals and their structures
406 Life and its origins
414 The genetic code
690 Glands and their hormones

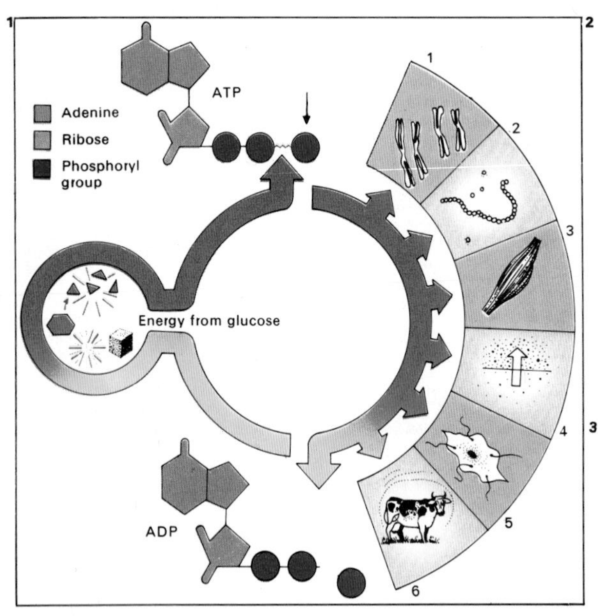

1
ATP
Adenine
Ribose
Phosphoryl group
Energy from glucose
ADP
1
2
3
4
5
6

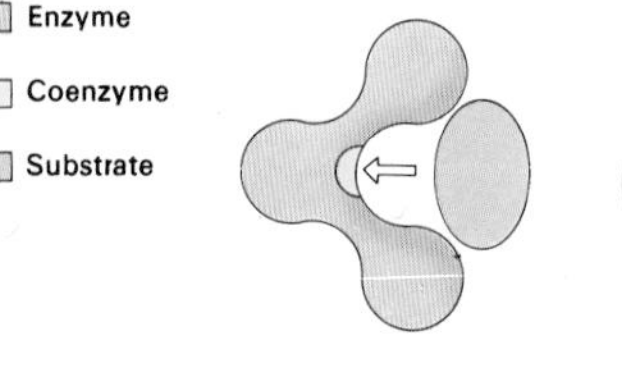
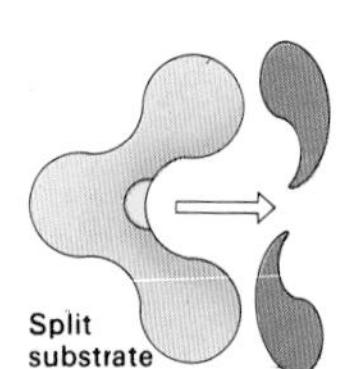

2
Enzyme
Coenzyme
Substrate
Split substrate

1 Adenosine triphosphate (ATP) plays a unique role in the cell, acting as carrier between reactions that supply energy and those that use it, such as [1] cell regulation and division; [2] synthesis of important biochemicals (proteins); [3] muscle contraction; [4] transport of materials into cells; [5] conduction of nerve signals throughout the body; and [6] regulation of the body temperature.

2 Enzymes cause molecules to divide or join together much faster than they would otherwise. To work effectively, a good physical fit is needed between the enzyme and the other molecule(s)—the substrate(s). Only a part of the enzyme, the active site often containing a coenzyme, comes into contact with other molecules. The rest of the enzyme is needed to give the active site its shape.

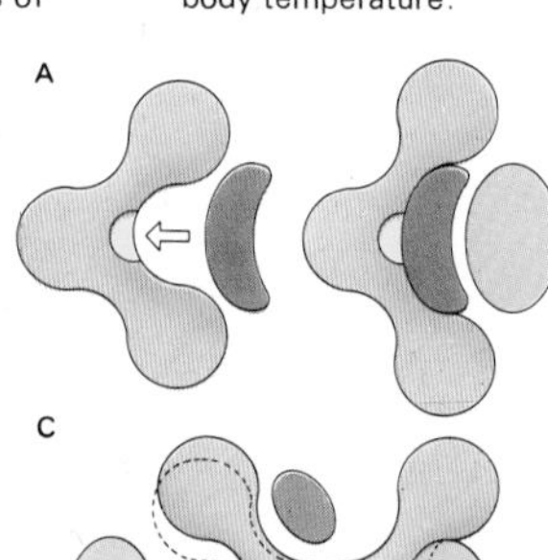

3
Enzyme
Coenzyme
Substrate
Activator
Inhibitor
A
B
C
D

3 The shapes of enzymes can be changed by small nonsubstrate molecules. A molecule of similar shape to a true substrate may compete for the active site [A], thereby slowing down the desired reaction. A substance at a different site [B] changes the shape of the active site, affecting the fit of the substrate. Some enzymes possess more than one active site. The occupation of one or an activator may change the shape of the second site so that it can also accept the substrate [C]. An inhibitor molecule may prevent either of the sites from being used [D].

4

4 Enzymes can lower the "energy hump" that must be overcome in a biochemical reaction. They act as catalysts and are found in many common reactions, such as the rotting of fruit.

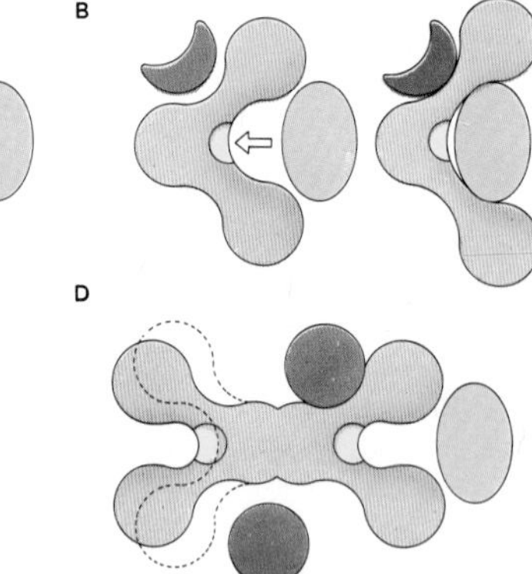

5
Glucose
ATP
Lactate
Pyruvic acid
Alanine
Other amino acids
Proteins for organic structure
CO_2
ATP
Alcohol
CO_2
Acetyl-CoA
O_2
Fatty acids
Fats for storing O_2
CO_2
+H_2O
Energy like ATP

5 Pyruvic acid, a key biochemical, is formed during the breakdown of glucose and some amino acids. Further breakdown varies, depending on the biochemical system. In yeast, for example, the end product can be gas to raise dough.

before it becomes an end product. At each stage, an intermediate compound is formed. Sometimes the final product, or one of the intermediates, can combine with an enzyme farther back along the chain and switch it off. Other small molecules may combine with an enzyme to increase its activity.

Energy from combustion

The many-step processes involving enzymes are a necessary adaptation to circumstances. Most organic chemicals are combustible. Common sugar, for example, can be burned completely to produce carbon dioxide, water, and heat. But heat energy from total combustion is of no use to living cells. To use such energy a large temperature difference is needed, as in a car engine. Living organisms have roughly the same temperature throughout—the temperature of a healthy human being rarely deviates far from 37°C (98.6°F). Consequently, chemical energy is extracted from the "combustion" process by breaking it down into a large number of small steps, each of which produces energy measurable (and removable) in one or two units of the cell's energy currency.

A molecule of glucose, which contains six carbon atoms, can be broken down into two three-carbon pyruvic acid molecules [5]. The process takes ten different steps, uses up two molecules of ATP, and produces four new molecules of ATP. The net result of the process is therefore the production of two units of energy currency.

Pyruvic acid becomes involved in one of the key cycles of biochemistry, the citric acid cycle or Krebs cycle. It is converted into carbon dioxide and other chemicals [8]. At the same time, energy is transferred to another type of "currency" molecule, but this is soon exchanged for more ATP. Another example of energy-generation is photosynthesis, the primary process taking place in the leaves of green plants. Sunlight is absorbed by complex molecules, particularly chlorophyll, to produce "excited" molecules. These power chemical cycles that, after a number of steps, produce the ATP necessary to pay the biochemical cost of living.

KEY

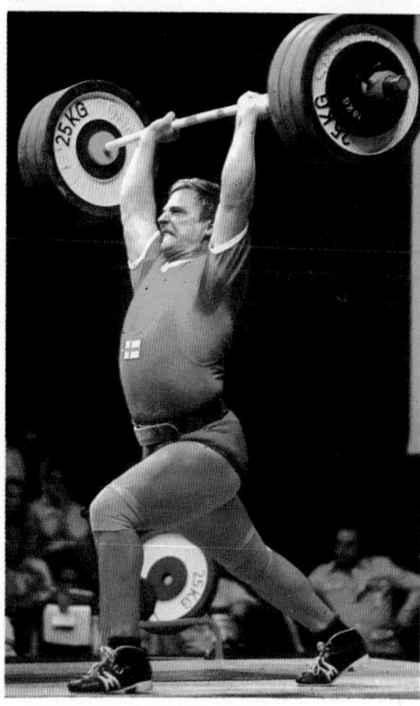

The energy that a strong man uses to lift weights comes ultimately from the sun. Plants use light to make energy-rich chemicals. Animals eat these and make even more complex substances, which eventually supply both the weight lifter's muscles and the energy necessary to flex them. The detailed study of these interactions is included in the science of biochemistry

6

Hexose
Derived monophosphate
Reduced coenzymes
Electron transport
O_2
H_2O
ADP
ATP
Glycolysis
Acetyl CoA
Fatty acids
Fats
Cycle of tricarboxylic acid
CO_2
Cycle of urea
Urea
Pyruvic acid
Ammonia
Glucose
Amino acids
Glycogen
Nucleic acids
Nucleotides
Proteins

6 Every cell is the site of a complex series of chemical reactions that includes both synthesis (anabolism) and breakdown (catabolism). These processes are known collectively as metabolism. Pathways that are basically catabolic are shown in blue, those basically anabolic in green. Paths directly concerned with energy production and use are in brown. Many thousands of separate chemical reactions are involved, each controlled by a different enzyme. Overall balance and control is ultimately maintained by the genetic material of the cell, which governs the production of enzymes.

7

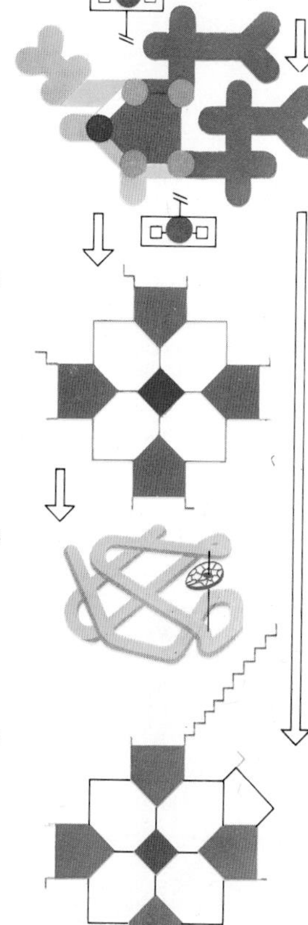

1
2
A
3
A
4
5
6
7

Oxygen
Carbon
Nitrogen
Hydrogen
A Coenzyme
Iron
Magnesium

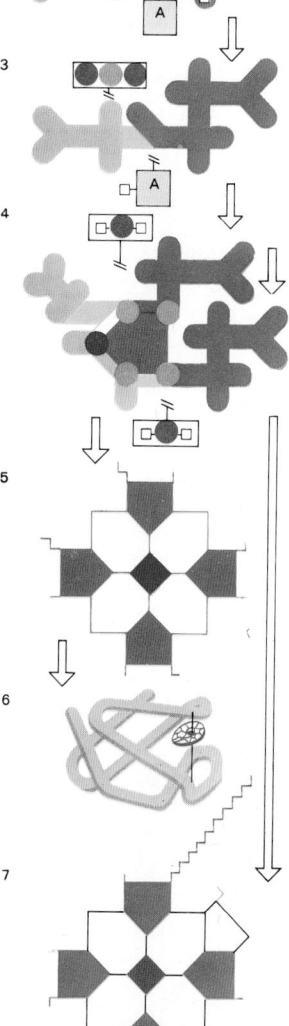

7 Nature's wide diversity is achieved with a remarkable degree of chemical economy. Large molecules are built from a small range of simple ones such as glycine [1] and succinyl coenzyme A [2]. Also certain key structures can have widely different functions. Both hemoglobin [6], which transports oxygen in the bloodstream, and chlorophyll [7], with which plants trap the energy of sunlight, need metal atoms in order to function. In hemoglobin iron is used; in chlorophyll, magnesium. In both cases the metals are attached to an organic molecule called a porphyrin [4], made from a compound such as d-aminolevulinic acid [3]. Thus the red pigment heme [5] and the green pigment chlorophyll are synthesized from the same smaller molecules, although one of them occurs in animals and the other in plants. Similar compounds play key roles in other biochemical processes. Vitamin B^{12}, a prophyrin-like compound with a cobalt atom at its center, is needed in the diet to prevent pernicious anemia.

8

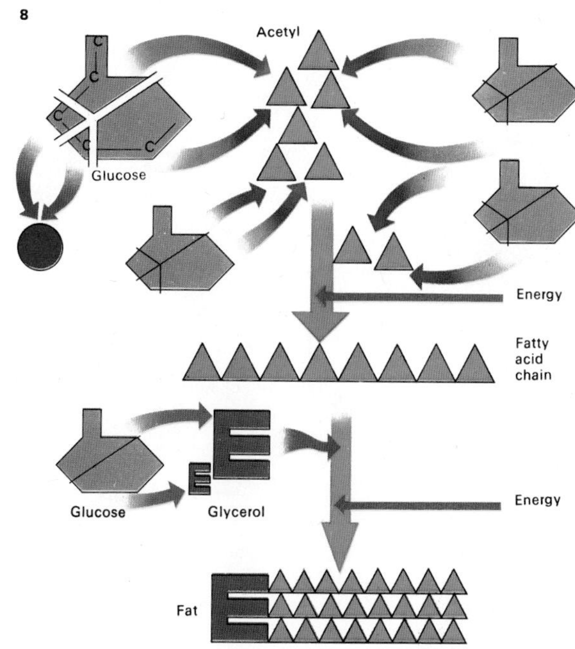

Acetyl
C
C
C
C
C
Glucose
Energy
Fatty acid chain
Glucose
Glycerol
Energy
Fat

8 All cycles interlink so that the energy from breaking down one type of chemical can be used to make another. If a man overeats, he will put on excess weight—in other words he becomes fat. Yet as the dieter is frequently warned, it is carbohydrates such as sugar, more than fats, that increase weight. Pyruvic acid is the key to this apparent paradox. When it is broken down, in addition to carbon dioxide, a substance called acetyl coenzyme A can be formed. The acetyl part (the triangles) is the basic building block for the fatty acids, which, together with glycerol (E-shape), make up oils and fats such as the one pictured at the bottom.

Polymers: giant molecules

The metals that make up a car's body and engine are chemically quite different from the oil products that power and lubricate them. Nature is more economical; the same few elements used to build living organisms are also those that trap and transport the energy, all of which is derived from the sun's light.

Proteins: polymers of amino acids

The important structural molecules of plants and animals are polymers, very large molecules known as macromolecules, made by joining together a succession of simple chemical building blocks. Proteins, for example, are polymers of amino acids that are small molecules, each containing an amino group and a carboxylic acid group. These two groups can react with one another to form a chemical bond. As a result, different amino acids can be linked through these groups in large numbers. A small protein, such as insulin [1], may be made up of only 50 or so amino acids, but many proteins contain hundreds of individual amino-acid units.

Animals employ proteins [2] both to build tissues and in the biochemical processes that take place in them. Collagen, for example, is a common structural protein. One of its jobs is to provide materials for tendons. A tendon "rope" of intertwined collagen molecules can have the strength of light steel wire. Another structural protein, keratin [8], occurs in hoof, hair, horn, and feathers, and actin and myosin are important constituents of muscle. Proteins also supply the major (in some cases the sole) component of enzymes, the cell's catalysts that speed up biochemical reactions, and antibodies, which fight infection.

Essential to these differing roles are the various physical structures of proteins. When amino acids link together, they do not just form long chains. According to the shapes and the chemical properties of the side chains of the individual amino acids used in a protein's make-up, it can be long and thin, or compact and globular. The structures contain electrically charged groups and, in addition, sulfur atoms can form bridges between amino acids. In insulin, sulfur atoms bridge adjacent chains of amino acids. In cytochrome C, a sulfur atom attaches a nonprotein organic molecule (in this case heme) to a protein.

Polysaccharides: polymers of sugars

The essential structural components of plants are polysaccharides, polymers of the small sugar molecules that provide most of the energy for cells. Not surprisingly, some polysaccharides are also used a convenient means of storing energy.

It has been estimated that up to 50 percent of the carbon atoms incorporated in plant tissues are in molecules of cellulose, a structural glucose polymer. In some forms cellulose has commercial value; cotton, for example, is 98 percent cellulose.

The main energy reserve polymer of plants is starch, which is composed of two polymers—amylose and amylopectin. Like cellulose, amylose is a straight-chain polymer of glucose. The only difference between the two molecules is in the shape of the chemical bond that links the units together. This single difference is enough to

CONNECTIONS

See also
1572 The Chemistry of life: biochemistry
1618 Rubber and plastics
412 The cell in action
430 The way plants work
414 The genetic code
686 Skin and hair

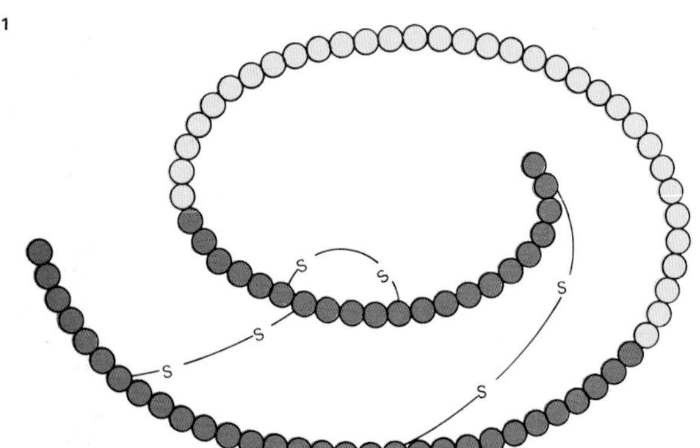

1
S
S
S
S
S
S

1 The small protein insulin is formed in the body from a simpler substance called proinsulin, a single chain with 84 amino acid molecules linked together. In addition to the chemical bonds linking each amino acid chain, there are bridges between sulfur atoms [S] from the amino acid cysteine. When insulin is formed by removal of the 33 amino acid units [yellow], 2 chains are formed.

2 Proteins are not simply amino acid molecules strung together like beads. Superimposed on the primary structure is a secondary structure, either an alpha-helix [A] or a pleated sheet [B]. Both of these secondary structures arise from the formation of weak hydrogen bonds between similar parts of amino acid units. Although weak, hydrogen bonding is important in many biological macromolecules.

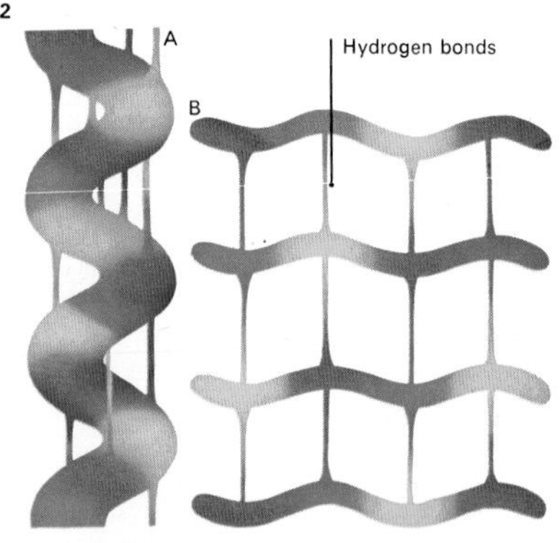

2
A
B
Hydrogen bonds

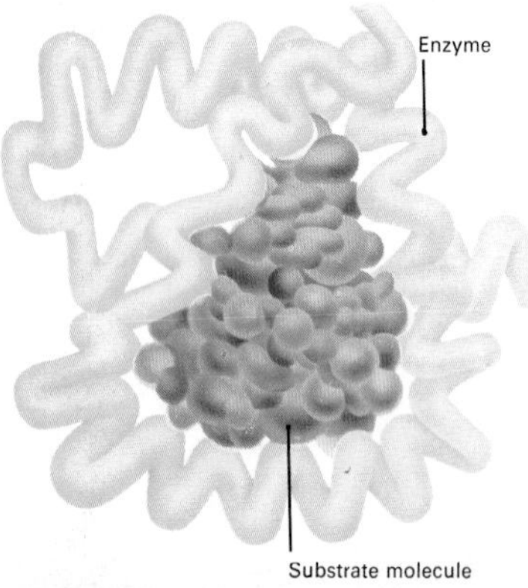

3
Enzyme
Substrate molecule

3 In addition to hydrogen bonds, interactions, such as those between the side chains of similar amino acids, make the shape of some proteins even more complex. This may cause some disruption of the secondary structure, to produce the "tangled spaghetti" shape exemplified by this model of an enzyme, which has a substrate molecule fitted into its active site.

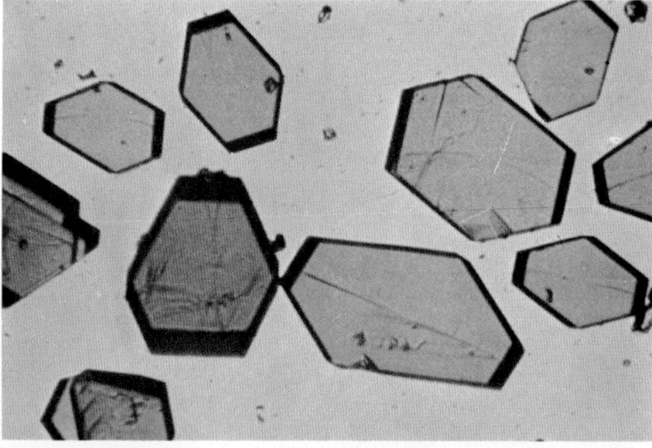

4
A

4 Some proteins can be purified sufficiently to form crystals. Myoglobin, a protein involved in carrying oxygen in muscles, occurs in many species, including sperm whales from which the crystals [A] are obtained (seen here enlarged 40 times). If a beam of X rays is directed at a single crystal, it is possible to obtain a diffraction photograph [C]. Analysis of such photographs, often with the aid of computers, provides information from which electron density maps can be drawn. Made from sheets of Lucite stacked on top of one another, these maps show where particular atoms in the protein molecule are located [B]. It is then possible to construct an accurate 3-dimensional model of a protein. Much of the early work in determining protein structures by this method was done in Cambridge, England, by John Kendrew and Max Perutz.

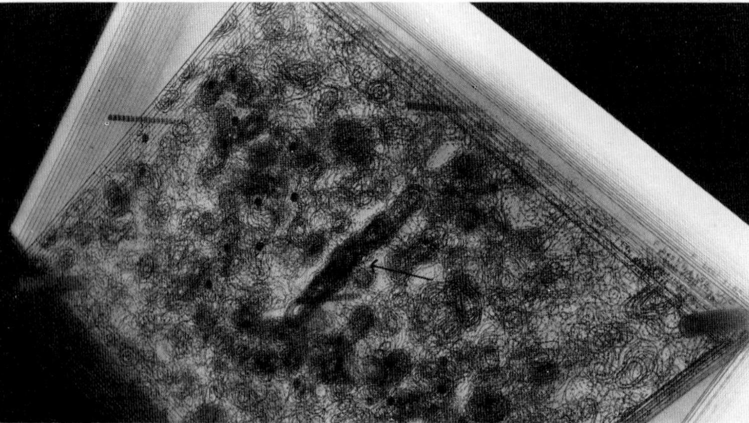

B

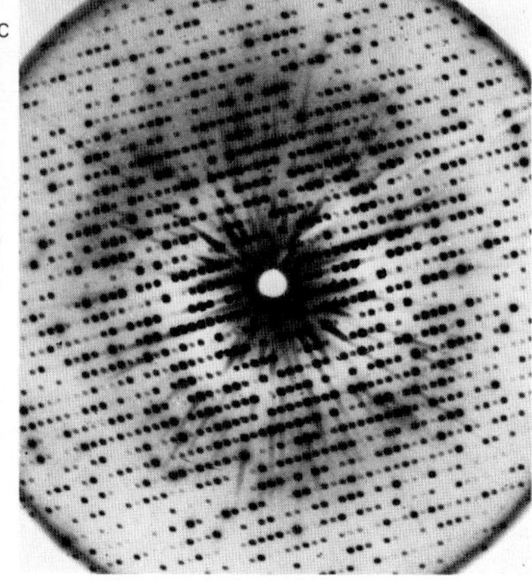

C

make starch a readily digestible dietary ingredient and cellulose completely indigestible to human beings. In amylopectin, there are chemical links at more than one point on some of the glucose units, so that a branched-chain polymer is produced. The same sort of structure occurs in glycogen, the glucose polymer used by animals for energy storage.

Many other sugars, apart from glucose, can form polysaccharides. Chitin, the hard shell material of insects, crabs, and lobsters, is a polymeric amino sugar. Alginates, important food additives that keep the head on beer and give dehydrated soups their thickness, are polysaccharides from seaweed, while the pectins, which are widely used in jam-making, occur notably in apples. Natural adhesives, such as gum arabic, are polysaccharides, as in heparin, an important substance that prevents blood clots and is often used in the treatment of thrombosis.

Nucleic acids

Although not present in such large quantities in most cells as proteins and polysaccharides, the most important macromolecules are the nucleic acids [7]. These make up the genetic material that controls each cell, making it not only a man cell or a mouse cell, but a man liver cell or a mouse tail cell. Nucleic acid polymers are able to reproduce themselves accurately, allowing any species to produce more of its own kind. They also control the chemical building of proteins. As the latter effect includes production of various enzymes, nucleic acids control all other chemical building up and breaking down in living tissues.

Complex polymers [7] can be thousands of units long. The basic repeating unit is made up from a nitrogen-containing base and a phosphate group. Both of these are attached to one of two types of sugar: ribose (RNA) or deoxyribose (in DNA). Because of the chemical properties of the bases, particularly those in DNA, it is possible for two strands of nucleic acids to fit together readily to form the "double helix." Synthetic rubber and plastics are also polymers—often man-made copies of the molecules found in nature.

KEY

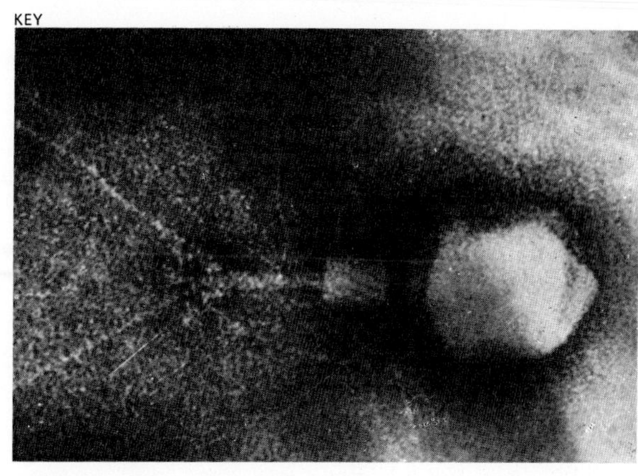

On the margin of life lie the viruses, each made up of a few macromolecules, all of which can be defined in purely chemical terms. Yet, when placed in a living cell, a virus is able to take over that cell's biochemical machinery and make it reproduce virus components. This electron micrograph of a bacteriophage—a virus that attacks bacteria—shows the shape of its protein molecules: inside the diamond-shaped head is the bacteriophage's nucleic acid, which directs the build-up of further examples of both itself and protein components after it has infected a cell.

5 Carbohydrates, proteins, and polynucleotides are the basic polymers of life. They are not, however, the only ones. Natural rubber, for example, is a polymer made up mainly of repeating units of the unsaturated hydrocarbon isoprene. From 1,000 to 5,000 such units join together in a single molecule of rubber. The cell walls of some bacteria are made from a combination of sugar and amino acid molecules, to form a mixed polymer. This photograph, taken at a magnification of 280,000 times with the aid of an electron microscope, shows part of the outer cell wall of the bacterium *Clostridium thermohydrosulfuricum*. At this magnification it is possible to see the individual subunits, arranged in regular rows, that make up the surface of the bacterium's cellular wall.

6

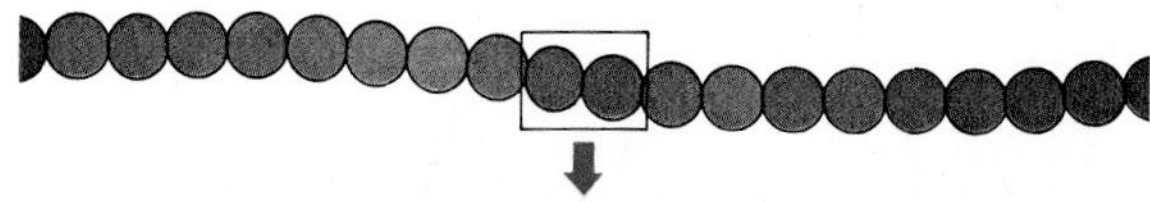

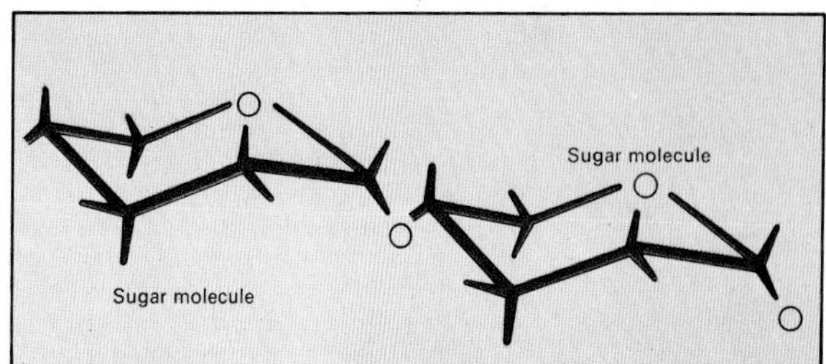

Sugar molecule
Sugar molecule

6 Monosaccharides, the simplest of the sugar molecules, can join together to form very large molecules such as starch. According to where the links form, the macromolecule may be a single chain (as shown), or branched.

7

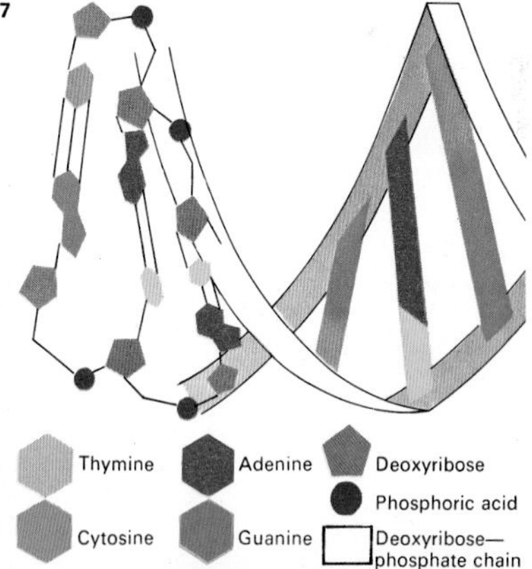

Thymine
Adenine
Deoxyribose
Phosphoric acid
Cytosine
Guanine
Deoxyribose—phosphate chain

7 Deoxyribonucleic acid (DNA) is the master molecule of life. It occurs as a double helix in which two complementary strands of polymer are held together by hydrogen bonding. This bonding occurs between the nitrogen-containing bases that form part of the nucleic acid unit.

8

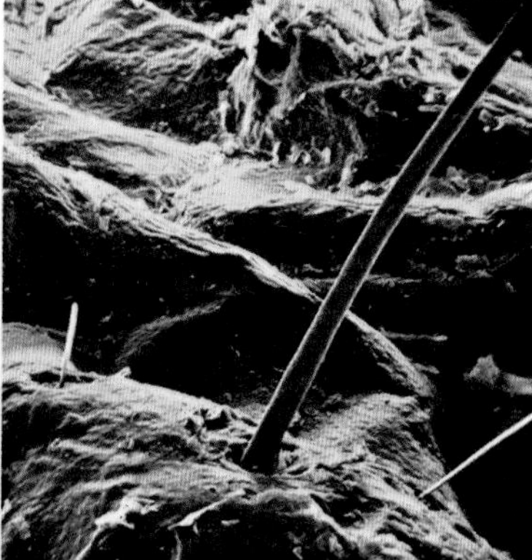

8 Hair is composed mainly of the protein keratin, which also occurs in feathers and skin. Although these hairs are magnified many times, it is still not enough to make individual keratin molecules visible. Whether a person's hair is straight or curly depends on the tertiary structure of the keratin molecules.

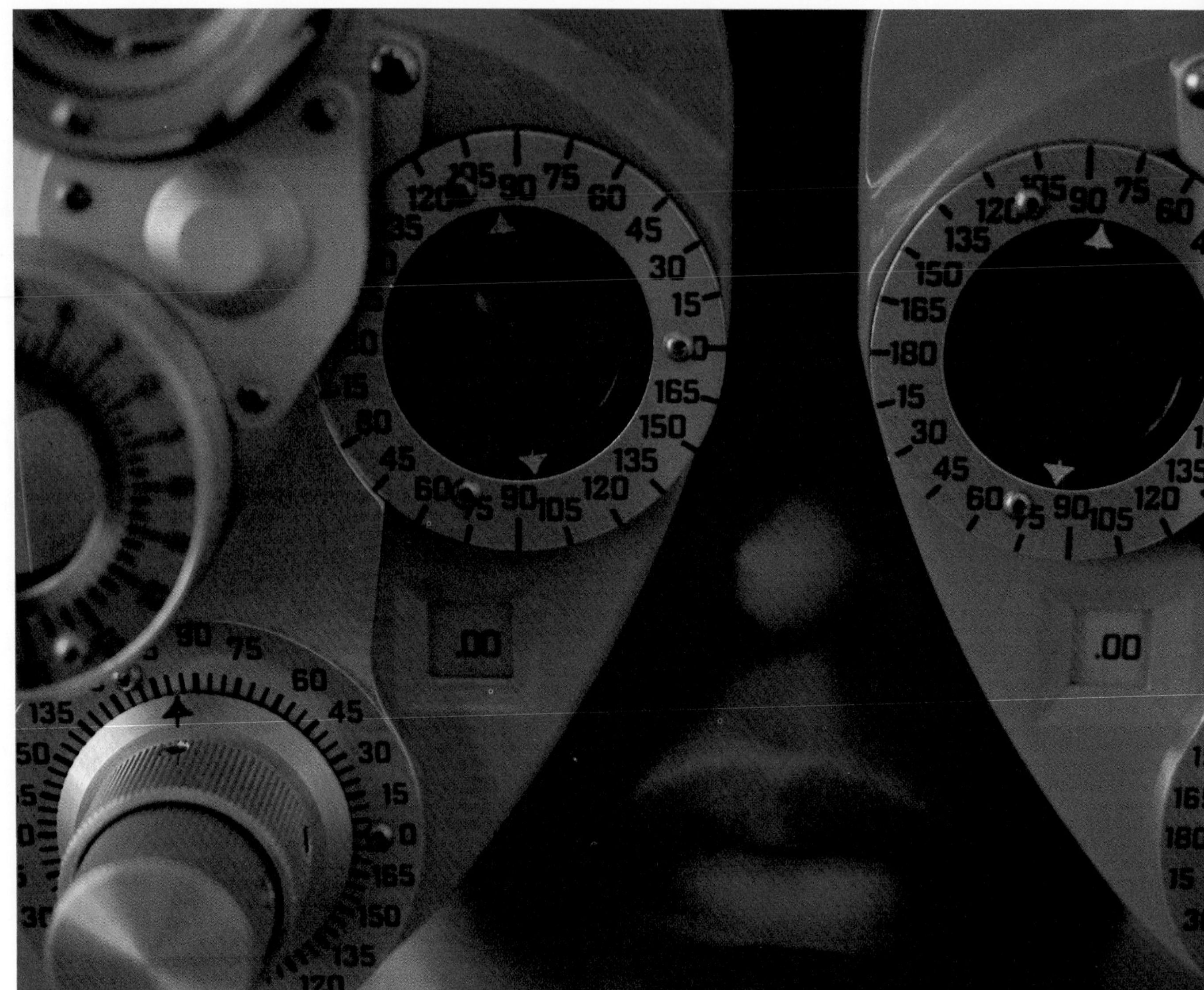
.00
.00

MAN AND MACHINES

MAN AND MACHINES

by Dr. William O. Baker

Technology means ways of making things and doing things —growing food, weaving clothes, building houses, curing disease, communicating with others, and traveling about the world and into space. Thus, technology is a civilizing and inspiring part of human life. It is civilizing because it helps humans to live with less exhausting work and with less damage to other creatures on the planet and because it frees more time for recreation and the arts, for health and growth of body and spirit. It is inspiring because it is a creative expression of the mind and hands working together to meet people's needs. Technology is often a response to compassionate feelings, such as the desire to help feed others, to alleviate pain, to prolong life, to rear the young well, and to live peacefully.

The story of technology covers the entire saga of human prehistory and history, from Stone Age tools to Bronze Age weapons to Steel Age ships and autos and spacecraft. The record of technology is a record of inventions—intuitions about how matter can be shaped and used to make new things: flint and steel for starting fires, the wheel, the lever, the pulley, the gear, the roller bearing, the airplane wing, the herb derivative that eases pain. All these are inventions, inspired by needs and achieved by creative combinations of thought and action.

One characteristic of inventions is that many were made by essentially practical men and women—mechanics, artisans, farmers, technicians—who were trying to meet an immediate need and were not too much concerned with the theory behind their devices and machines. Success often came from hard work in a shop rather than from application of a broad theory. In fact, a brilliant theory does not always get immediate practical application. For example, Hero of Alexandria, a 1st-century mathematician and engineer, conceived the idea of a steam engine, but he did not put this inspiration to practical use. It was not until the 18th century that workable steam engines were developed to meet specific needs such as pumping water from coal mines.

The practical work of craftsmen in developing machines and other products is often contrasted with the more speculative realm of science. Sometimes the term "pure science" is used for theoretical study and "applied science" for the translation of theories into new technologies. Pure science grew out of philosophy. Aristotle, Plato, and other great philosophers of the ancient world were curious to know the nature of human beings and the structure of the universe; they pursued knowledge just so that they could understand, not so that they could produce inventions. It was the same intellectual curiosity that inspired Albert Einstein and other thinkers of the 20th century.

Although some scientists may not be particularly interested in technological applications, science and technology have become interrelated in modern times. For example, the craftsmen-inventors (like James Watt) who built the 18th-century steam engines used scientific knowledge about atmospheric pressure. Because the technicians wanted to improve the efficiency of the engines, they conducted research that helped to develop the science of thermodynamics. In turn, these theoretical principles of thermodynamics helped engineers to build still better steam machinery. The curiosity, the intellectual speculations about gravity and electricity and light by such scholars as Isaac Newton, Michael Faraday, and James Clerk Maxwell led to the growth of new areas of scientific knowledge—knowledge that has been used by applied scientists and engineers to create new technologies. Thus, in our world today, the inspired insights of Einstein are basic to nuclear physics as well as to many of the applied uses of nuclear energy.

The rapid spread and application of scientific knowledge in recent times have been made possible particularly by one vital field of science and technology—information science and engineering, which began with the inventions that enabled us to preserve and disseminate ideas by written symbols. Major

---

President of Bell Laboratories; Vice Chairman of the President's Committee on Science and Technology; Member of the National Cancer Advisory Board; Member of the National Academy of Sciences, the National Academy of Engineering, and the Institute of Medicine; Fellow of the American Philosophical Society; Fellow of the American Academy of Arts and Sciences; Recipient of Perkin Medal (world chemical societies), Priestley Medal and Parsons Award (American Chemical Society), Frederik Philips Award (Institute of Electrical and Electronics Engineers), Gold Medal (American Institute of Chemists), Proctor Prize (Sigma Xi), IRI Medal (Industrial Research Institute); contributor to *The Technological Catch and Society; Annual Review of Materials Science; Science: The Achievement and the Promise; Technology and Social Change*, etc.

modern developments in information technology include the cathode-ray tube used in television, typing machines to which computers are connected, micrographics, and optical character-setting and recognition. The progress of technology depends greatly upon such means of recording and communicating ideas and experience.

The remarkable growth and scope of 20th-century technology can be illustrated by a few facts about information and communications concepts and machines. According to information theory (as developed by such experts as Claude Shannon), all information can be encoded by use of binary digits, called "bits." These are commonly zero and one. They fit admirably the electrical encoding that is their principal medium in computers, communications systems, etc. Any twofold state—such as north and south magnetic poles used in computer memories, plus and minus charges as obtained from electronic diodes, or on and off positions of a switch—can be represented by binary digital states. Thus, bits can be used to store and process encoded words, pictures, formulas, and designs.

It is extremely interesting to compare the work of information-processing machines—designed, of course, by human brains—with the speed of the brain itself. Experiments have determined the approximate rate at which some persons can receive information by hearing, seeing, or feeling and can put out information by talking, writing, or motioning. The average rate is about 40 bits per second. Even the early computers could remember about 1,000 words and make about 2,000 calculations per second. Present-day computer systems have memory capacities of more than 1,000,000 words and can perform about 100,000,000 operations per second. Technology has thus taken us more than a million times beyond the natural capability of humans.

Other technologies have also enormously multiplied what unaided humans can do. For example, while people can walk at about four miles an hour, airplanes have reached speeds beyond 2,000 mph (3,200 kph)—about 500 times the walking pace. Hydraulic lifts can manage 50 tons—about a thousand times the weight an average human can handle. But the increase in the speed of storing, retrieving, analyzing, and communicating information is far and away the greatest leap beyond unaided human capacities. Of course, the volume of information handled by computer systems is important only in terms of the beneficial ways that men and women use it to change ways of life on Earth.

There are many other examples of the exciting modern interactions between science and technology. The needs of long-range radio, for instance, led to the development of more sensitive antennas and receivers. These were also used in radio telescopes, thus giving rise to modern radio astronomy. Radio telescopes have revealed a host of chemical molecules in what had previously been thought to be empty outer space and have detected unanticipated energy conditions in the cosmos. Some of these areas may be vast natural laser systems. These findings, which have great interest for pure science and philosophy, may well point ways to new technologies for energy conversion on Earth.

The roles and the problems of technology and science in the 20th century can be further illustrated in the fields of biology and medicine. The need for more knowledge and better techniques—for instance, in human health—is intense, but research is difficult and the experts are just beginning to find their way in some areas. Yet there has been rapid and heartening progress—so much so that, in the last few decades, some people have come to expect doctors to show almost miraculous powers to stop infection and cure disease. The "miracle drugs" have indeed saved many lives, but the experts still prefer to be cautious in applying new drug technologies. They are now building a science of immunology, of how the body fights infections, foreign disturbances, and even modifications of its own cells (as in cancer). The technology of immunization, introduced by Edward Jenner and others in the technique of vaccination, has proved heroic in the virtual eradication in the United States of smallpox, typhoid, and poliomyelitis. There is now hope that influenza epidemics can be prevented or halted. Yet the scientists' knowledge of immune reactions is still so primitive that they really are not sure whether the use of serums is fully compatible with the build-up of existing resistance in the body. So this case of the linking of science and technology calls for more research, which may lead to new applications, more effective techniques, and new systems of technology.

In the 20th century, technology is a matter not so much of individual pieces of equipment or operations but of whole technical systems. The new science and technology of systems research and engineering have largely developed from telecommunication and automation. Telephone systems involve an enormous and complex variety of wires, cables, radio links, switches, terminals, and other devices that have to function simultaneously and compatibly in response to vast numbers of signals scattered over thousands of miles. One major telephone system, for example, now involves the interaction of ten million billion possible connections among telephones that together have billions of parts! Many automated systems developed rapidly during and after World War II. Military aircraft used to be flown and managed in combat very much by the eyesight and reactions of their crews. Now the airframe, motors, navigation devices, guns, bombs, missiles, and fire control are all parts of a precisely balanced weapons system, controlled to a large extent by automated devices such as radars and computers. Similarly, naval guns are now parts of weapons systems; radars and computers aim the guns and automated systems feed the ammunition.

Going far beyond military applications, systems engineering and systems technology should have increasing uses. They represent a rational way of dealing with the complexity of modern economic, scientific, and social knowledge. For example, there is the very great problem of how to collect, organize, study, disseminate, and apply the information and ideas that already exist. The volume of scientific theory, research reports, field studies, proposals for new techniques and new machines, etc., is so vast—and growing so rapidly—that it is difficult for even a great expert to know more than a corner of a field of study. On top of that, furthermore, is the need to interrelate the thought and work of scientists and technicians with the ideas and experience of economists, psychologists, anthropologists, political scientists, and other scholars and leaders.

Systems engineering and technology can be of great help in the coordination of diverse knowledge. The capacity of computers to store and handle massive amounts of information has already been noted. The value of computer systems in analyzing problems of our civilization can be shown by reference to one of our critical oncoming needs, energy resources and conservation. It is necessary to balance such factors as supply, cost, rate of use, and ecological impact. As of the mid-1970s, the United States has no comprehensive engineering plan for energy. The country currently uses the energy equivalent of about 41,000,000 barrels of oil a day, and, if the present rate of increase of use continues, the country will

CASTINGS
Norwalk Ste
With Wheeler's Paten

need the energy equivalent of about 95,000,000 barrels of oil a day by the year 2000. Through appropriate systematic conservation, that figure might be modified to 84,000,000 barrels. But systems analysis predicts that we will be able at best to scrape up from all sources—coal, oil, water power, solar energy, nuclear power—the equivalent of 60,000,000 barrels of oil a day. Thus, we will be 24,000,000 million barrels short of our needs, if we are to keep up our existing levels of energy consumption. The magnitude of the shortage is clear: one expert estimate indicates that, to catch up with our needs as of 2000, we would have to build nuclear-power plants at the rate of one every ten days from now on.

In the above case, systems analysis and computer modeling show us energy needs—and related economic and ecological problems—of dimensions that are almost inconceivable from actual experience. One challenge to the new technology comes from a well-known machine, the steam engine. Present steam plants for generating electricity convert only about a third of the heat into electric power. New engines—using potassium vapor, which can operate at a temperature of 815°C, in contrast to 538°C for steam—may be able to convert at least 50 percent of their heat into electricity. In this and other areas the demands on science and technology, research and invention, are as great as, or greater than, at any time since the world entered the industrial age.

The challenge to technology—as well as to the social sciences—is dramatically illustrated by the fundamental agricultural technologies that provide fiber and food. On an average, many people are getting by with a diet (not often nutritionally balanced) of about 2,400 calories a day, although 2,600 calories per day are judged to be necessary for a sustaining diet. Some technological remedies that have been suggested are not realistically feasible; for example, providing enough nitrogen to make large areas of land arable would require the building of fertilizer factories on an impossibly vast scale—not to mention the staggering ecological burdens involved. Yet there is hope in the research of agricultural scientists and technicians. It has been found that *Rhizobium* bacteria fix nitrogen in legume plants. This suggests that it may be possible to transplant other bacteria, such as those living in the tropical grass *Digitaria*, to increase greatly the crop yield on a given amount of land. Such studies are of the highest importance because they point the way to techniques for increasing crop production in all nations of the world. Even with new methods, however, crops are always subject to droughts, cold spells, variations in climate. One of the pressing missions for science and technology is, therefore, to learn how to predict weather accurately and for long-range periods, and possibly to modify the weather.

There have been encouraging advances in plant genetics and agricultural technology. Researchers at Purdue University have produced corn hybrids that contain nearly all the constituents necessary for human sustenance. This work has recently been extended to sorghum, producing a strain with a particularly high content of the essential amino acid, glycine. And the "green revolution" in rice production has already helped many countries in Asia. Although such new technologies have not yet solved the world's hunger problem, they have accomplished major benefits in a short time and they can be expected to increase food production significantly in the future. For example, more meat may be produced by using embryo transplants to increase the number of offspring (20 to 30 per year) of a given mother host.

To sum up, technology has become a pervasive factor in 20th-century life. It is viewed in conflicting ways. On the one hand, technology is supposed to solve our problems—if we need more energy, more food, or a new vaccine, the laboratories and the engineers are expected to produce what we want. On the other hand, technology is blamed for overloading us with gadgets, making us slaves of machines, polluting our environment, and leading us to nuclear destruction. Some thoughtful critics of society urge that we stop, or at least slow down, the pace of modern technology. Against this view stands the long-held principle that in a free society there should be no limits on inquiry, that research should progress freely wherever the mind takes it.

The answers are not easy. We cannot, for example, be sure what will come from greatly improved modes of separation of isotopes. Will it be nuclear bombs so easy to make that a laboratory mistake or the act of a terrorist or an irresponsible government will spread radiation over half the Earth? What about intensified research on aging? Should we focus on prolonging life? Scientists and humanists are debating the studies of polynucleotides, which have led to the synthesis of genes and the possibility of genetic control and design. Genetic research might alter the balance of races, cultures, and capabilities with which the world has slowly learned to live. Hence, some argue that "meddling with heredity" should be stopped now. This attitude blends with the contention that there should be a tight rein on all physical and biological science and technology until the "humane sciences" are able to catch up.

Perhaps this would be the most dangerous policy of all—fettering the human mind, chaining it back from its free flights into the unknown. It is the essence of science and technology to discover, to explore, to create—often though not always—what people want and need. Scientists and technicians have helped improve the human condition over the centuries. Can we not seek next to increase wisdom and kindness and prudence? If we can, then it need not be necessary to hold back technical discovery but only to hold on to the best and noblest ways of using it.

Early technology

Perhaps the first event in the history of technology was the making of a crude stone tool more than two million years ago. Another achievement of prehistoric technology was the control of fire for hardening the points of wooden tools and weapons. By the end of the Old Stone Age, some tens of thousands of years ago, man-made objects of stone, horn, bone, and wood often reached a high level of craftsmanship.

Advances in Neolithic technology

It was not until the New Stone Age, or Neolithic, however, when people first settled down in one place, that there arose a need for a technology extending beyond the manufacture of a few kinds of tools, weapons, and garments. From about 7000 BC, technological development began to increase rapidly. In the three thousand years that followed an urban civilization arose in Mesopotamia. Plows, first with blades of stone and later of bronze, sledges for transport, and buildings of baked mud brick were among the earliest major technological developments.

By 3500 BC a number of city states were established between the Tigris and Euphrates rivers. The potter's wheel and the solid cartwheel were introduced not long after. The Sumerians also made inventories of their property in the first written records—cuneiform carvings on clay.

Mesopotamian architecture reached its peak in the ziggurats, great stepped buildings made from clay bricks. The Egyptians, however, had earlier built monuments that were even larger, but in stone. The Great Pyramid of Cheops still stands, 485ft (148m) high and covering 13 acres (5 hectares), yet accurate in design and construction to a tiny fraction of an inch. One of the greatest feats of engineering, it was built without the use of the wheel.

Far from the Middle East, other civilizations began to emerge with their own special technological achievements. In ancient China, silk is reputed to have been made as early as 2000 BC, although it did not reach the West until the sixth century AD. The Indus civilization, *c.*2300 to 1750 BC, built the northern Indian cities of Harappa and Mohenjodaro, which had vast complexes of houses, granaries, and wells, complete with the earliest known planned drainage and sewage system.

Europe, Africa (excluding Egypt), and great tracts of Asia, however, experienced only patchy technological developments at that time. Central and South America generated several elaborate civilizations, but not until the beginnings of the Christian era. The Mayan people (of Middle America) remained essentially in a Stone Age, although they worked gold and copper and built great stone temples. They also developed the most accurate of calendars and perfected an arithmetic that contained a symbol for zero for the first time in human history.

The mastery of materials

Ancient technology, therefore, developed in fits and starts in limited areas of the world. Surprisingly, the Hellenic Greeks did not make great advances in technology. Although they enjoyed scientific speculation, they held inventions and manufacturing in low esteem. One thousand years before the

CONNECTIONS

See also
1586 The stone age
1588 Fire and bronze
1590 Bark, hide, and horr
1592 The iron age
1726 Early weapons and d fense
1748 Road building
1756 History of bridges
1438 Prehistoric and ancient science
1440 Asian and medieval science
304 History of agricultur
650 The first men
876 Origins of human society
1160 Science and technology 1500–1700
1584 Modern technology

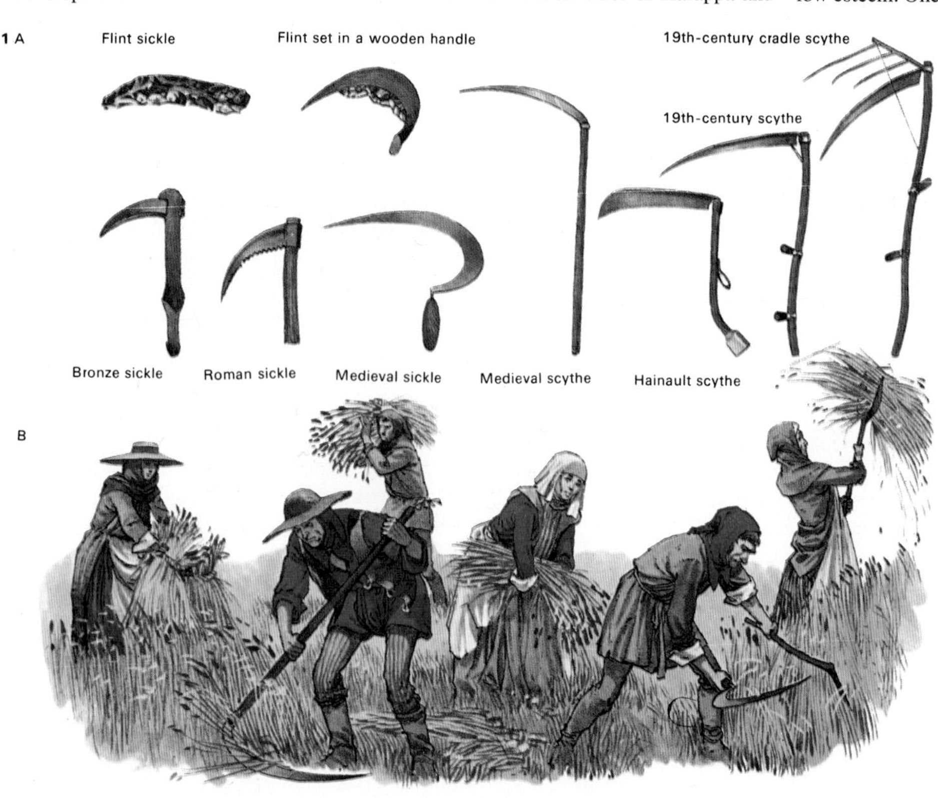

1 A
Flint sickle
Flint set in a wooden handle
19th-century cradle scythe
19th-century scythe
Bronze sickle
Roman sickle
Medieval sickle
Medieval scythe
Hainault scythe
B

1 Farming tools [A] for cutting and reaping form an unbroken sequence down the ages. The Egyptians used flint-edged wooden sickles at first and later bronze ones. By the Middle Ages the sickle had developed a curve and was set in a wooden handle. Medieval harvesters [B] used either short-handled sickles or scythes. Later developments include the Hainault scythe still in use today.

3 A

B

3 Greek metalsmiths [A] fashioned delicate ornaments from silver as early as 700 BC. This silver, later part of the vast wealth of democratic Athens, was mined using slave labor exclusively. In Roman times, mining extended throughout the empire and Roman smiths [B] formed themselves into powerful guilds, the fabri. Much of the smith's equipment, except for the open forge, would be familiar to a smith of today.

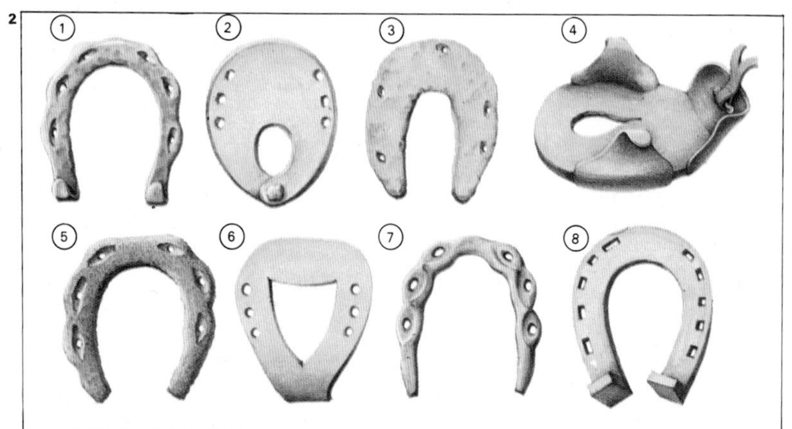

2
1
2
3
4
5
6
7
8

2 Prehistoric Celts were the first to fit horses with shoes, but heavy iron horseshoes were not common in Europe in medieval times. Horseshoes of various designs are associated with certain cultures and they achieved their final form only in the late 19th century.

1 Frankish
2 Syrian
3 Saxon
4 Roman hipposandal
5 Celtic
6 Moorish from Algeria 12th-century
7 Roman
8 16th-century French

Greeks, Hittite smiths in Mesopotamia had worked in iron, a technology that they handed on to many later civilizations [Key].

Egyptian tombs were rich in objects made from pottery, wood, glass, ivory, copper, and bronze and, later, iron. During Roman times mining activities extended throughout Europe and beyond, and bronze and iron were used in large quantities for armor and engines of war. After the rise of Islam in AD 622, the Arabs became the custodians of scientific ideas but, like the Greeks, they made few technological innovations.

Apart from cathedral architecture, clocks, and stained-glass windows, Europe had contributed little new technology for hundreds of years. But the fourteenth century saw the start of the Renaissance, which released scientific thought from religious shackles.

Renaissance and later technology

By 1450 Johannes Gutenberg's printing press was active in Germany, European canals were busy with trade, and early blast furnaces were making iron. In the sixteenth century mining was improved by mechanized drainage and ventilation systems [6]. This was also the age of Galileo's telescope, and many other scientific instruments followed [7, 8].

Windmills had been in use for a thousand years and waterwheels for half that time, but neither of these inventions advanced industry generally. Then three developments stimulated the Industrial Revolution; these were steam power, coal mining, and iron smelting. The application of steam power required the engines of Thomas Newcomen (1663–1729) and the availability of coal to heat their boilers. Coal was also employed in the early 1700s by Abraham Darby (*c.*1678–1717) to make coke, and this new fuel was used by him in blast furnaces to produce a plentiful supply of iron. Later the steam engine, developed by James Watt (1736–1819), introduced powered transport, and sulfuric acid manufacture by the lead chamber process established the beginnings of the modern chemical industry.

KEY

The control of fire is fundamental to technology. As early as 3000 BC, copper and tin ores were smelted in charcoal fires, refined and alloyed into bronze. Two thousand years later, iron objects were being made in Egypt and elsewhere as the result of a technique handed down by Hittite smiths. Iron could not be melted over a fire, even with the aid of bellows such as these, but it could be made red hot and then hammered into ornaments and implements.

4

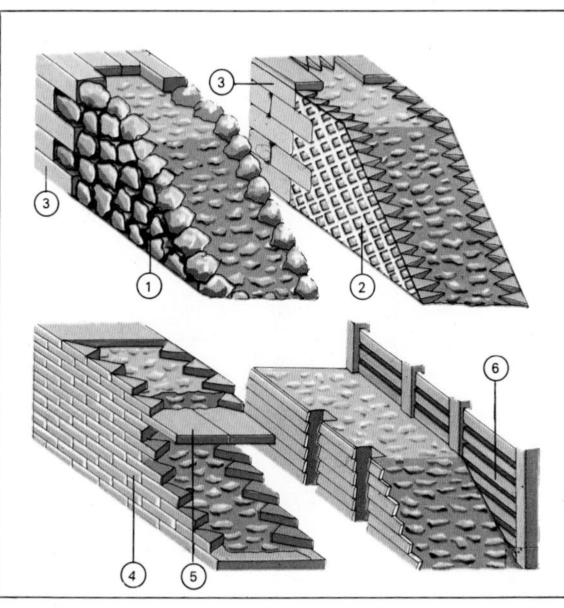

5

4 Roman wallbuilding included small stones laid in mortar–opus incertum [1]. Opus reticulatum [2] was a later diagonal pattern. These walls had outer vertical angles finished with stone quoins [3]. Opus testaceum had a brick facing [4] often strengthened by bonded tiles [5]. Walls of foundations were cast in a timber framework [6], removed when the mortar had hardened.

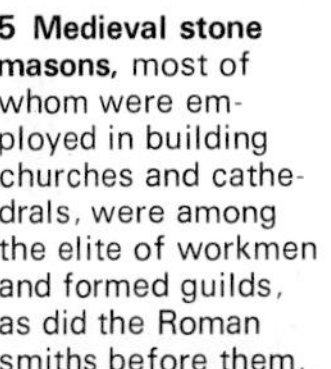

5 Medieval stone masons, most of whom were employed in building churches and cathedrals, were among the elite of workmen and formed guilds, as did the Roman smiths before them.

1 Carving decorated stonework with hammer and punch
2 Measuring out a design on stone with compass and rule
3 Cutting stone with a frame saw
4 Shaping a molding with pitching tool

6

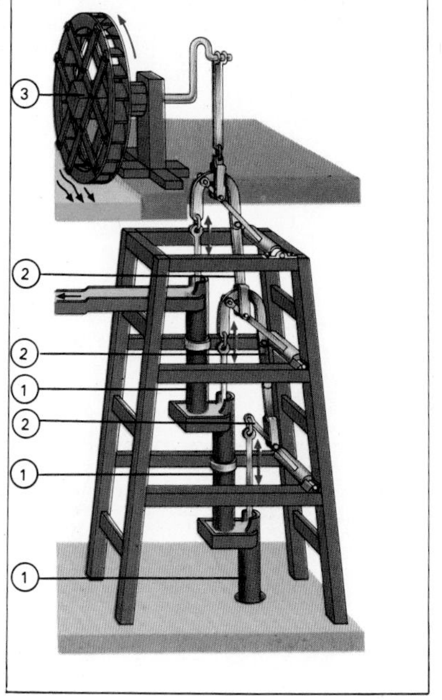

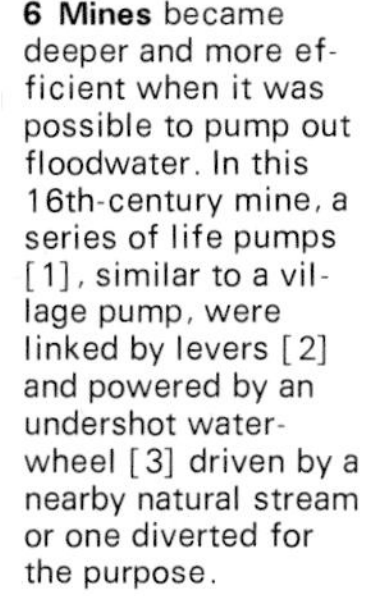

6 Mines became deeper and more efficient when it was possible to pump out floodwater. In this 16th-century mine, a series of life pumps [1], similar to a village pump, were linked by levers [2] and powered by an undershot waterwheel [3] driven by a nearby natural stream or one diverted for the purpose.

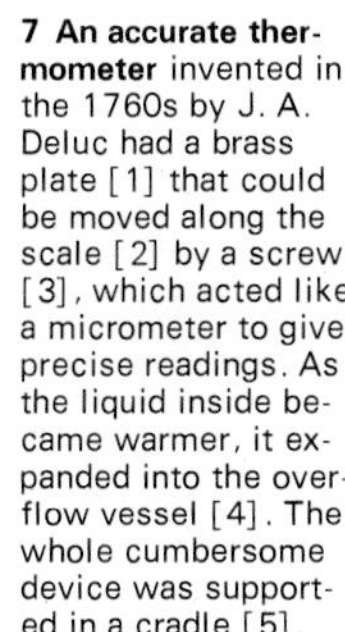

7 An accurate thermometer invented in the 1760s by J. A. Deluc had a brass plate [1] that could be moved along the scale [2] by a screw [3], which acted like a micrometer to give precise readings. As the liquid inside became warmer, it expanded into the overflow vessel [4]. The whole cumbersome device was supported in a cradle [5].

7

8

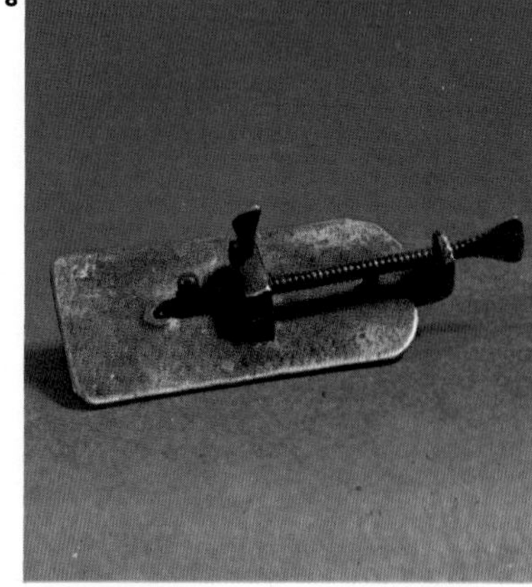

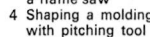

8 A microscope made by the Dutch scientist Anton van Leeuwenhoek (1632–1723) is an example of 17th-century precision engineering. It had a single lens mounted between two plates and ground so accurately that it gave a clearer magnification than other compound microscopes made at that time. The specimen was mounted on the point of the longer of the two focusing screws.

Modern technology

The great events that directed science and technology to the paths they pursue today were the profound social changes that occurred in the eighteenth century. One of these events was the French Revolution; another the Industrial Revolution.

The age of revolution

The French Revolution stressed the need for the rational conduct of human affairs. One effect was to give a strong impetus to calculation and mathematics. This French development inspired the English mathematician Charles Babbage (1791–1871) to build the first "computer-type" calculating machine.

The Industrial Revolution [4] posed new problems. Its central features were the extensive use of coal and iron and the development of the steam engine by Thomas Newcomen (1633–1729) and James Watt (1736–1819) [2]. Industry was thus presented with the prospect of unlimited power, and the problem of the nature of power and energy was brought to the forefront of science. The Industrial Revolution created a new demand for a knowledge of the properties of materials and a fresh motive for the development of chemistry. It made mankind aware of the possibility of fundamental change.

The Industrial Revolution stimulated a search into the principles of motion associated with other phenomena, such as electricity. Michael Faraday (1791–1867) conceived the idea of the electromagnetic field to explain electrical motions. He also demonstrated the principles of the dynamo and the electric motor. With the coming of power-generating stations, electricity could be produced and distributed almost anywhere to factories and individual homes.

A few pioneering scientists concentrated on working out the laws of thermodynamics—the branch of physics concerned with processes involving heat changes. Sadi Carnot (1796–1832) gave a mathematical theory to the cycles of heat changes in the steam engine as determined experimentally by James Watt. James Joule (1818–89) measured the mechanical equivalent of heat (how much heat is generated by a given amount of mechanical energy, and vice versa) and how various other forms of energy are interrelated. From this the concept of the conservation of energy was developed—the basic idea of physics that energy can be neither created nor destroyed, but only converted from one form into another.

James Clerk-Maxwell (1831–79) gave expression to Faraday's ideas of lines of force acting in space in his equations of the electromagnetic field. He showed that light waves are a form of electromagnetic waves and deduced that other forms, different from light waves, might exist. One such form, now used in radio, was discovered by Heinrich Hertz (1857–94) about 1887.

The new chemistry, which Antoine Lavoisier (1743–94) had taken the chief part in founding, was developed especially in Germany by Justus von Liebig (1803–73). He was followed by August Hofmann (1818–92), who worked for a long period in England. Hofmann had a student in his London laboratory, William Perkin (1838–1907), who at the age of 18 discovered the

CONNECTIONS

See also

1594 The steel age
1626 Basic types of engines
1646 Saving fuel and energy
1660 The factory and assembly line
1670 Automatic control
1280 The impact of steam
1220 The early Industrial Revolution
1236 The Industrial Revolution
1284 European industrialization 1870–1914
1582 Early technology

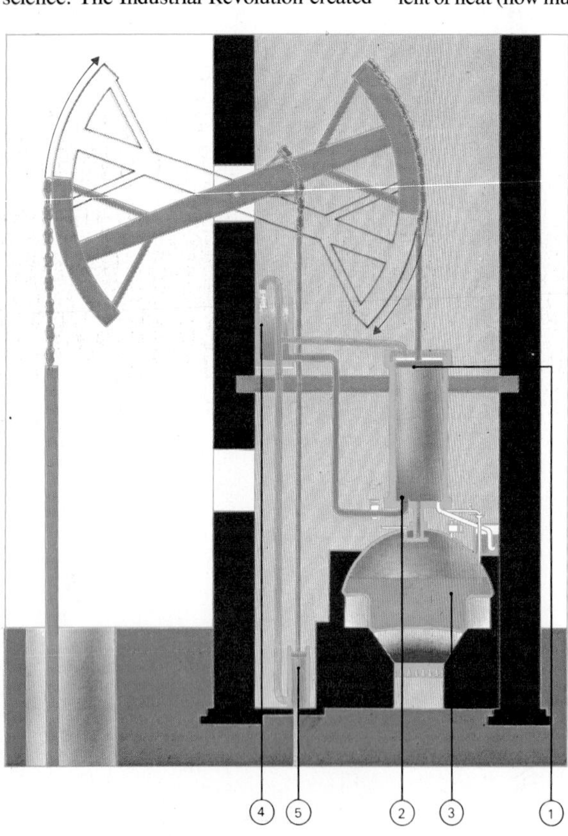

1
4
5
2
3
1

1 Thomas Newcomen's steam engine of 1712 was a great advance on Thomas Savery's earlier machine, although it was also only a pumping engine. The piston [1] was forced up by steam pressure and the weight of the pump mechanism. A cold-water spray [2] condensed the steam creating a vacuum, which "sucked" the piston down. A boiler [3] provided steam and a tank [4], fed by a secondary pump [5], the cold water.

2 James Watt's engine of the 1770s condensed steam with water, but in a separate condenser [1]. This technique, and that of admitting steam to both sides of the piston [2], greatly increased the efficiency of the steam engine. Pushing the piston in both directions made it double-acting. Watt soon adapted it to produce rotary motion, used for machines other than pumps.

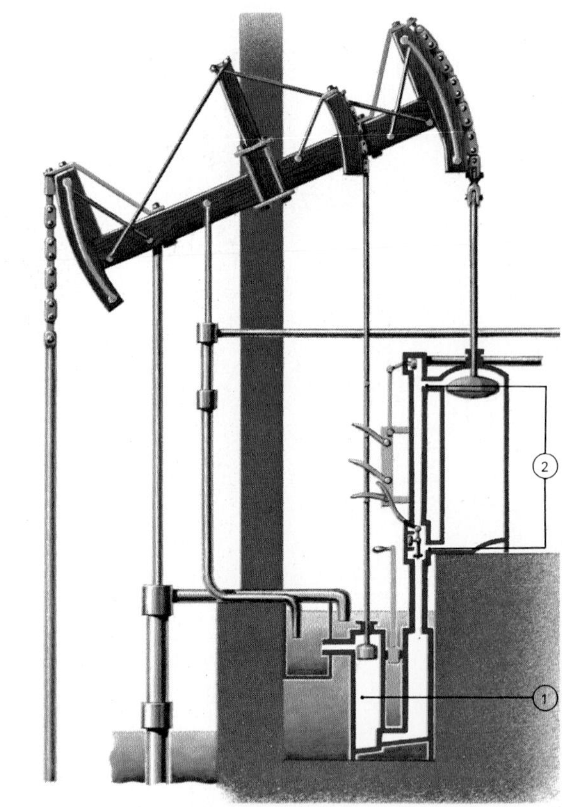

2
2
1

3

3 Agriculture was also revolutionized by new machines. A reaper invented by Patrick Bell in 1828 was pushed by two horses and could cut an acre of grain in an hour. A large bevel gear on the main axle drove a high-speed shaft that worked crank rods and an oscillating cutter bar A belt on the same shaft turned the blades of a collector to push the grain into the blades. A sideways moving belt moved the cut grain to the side of the reaping machine.

first synthetic chemical dye, mauve, which led to the foundation of aniline dye manufacture. This was the start of the modern chemical industry.

Modern science

Following Hertz's discovery of long electromagnetic waves, Wilhelm Roentgen (1845–1923) discovered short electromagnetic waves in 1895 and called them X rays. They came as a surprise to physicists. Searches were immediately made for other new rays, and in 1896 Antoine Becquerel (1852–1908) discovered that uranium emitted a new kind of radiation. Pursuing this discovery Marie Curie (1867–1934) and her husband Pierre (1859–1906) showed in 1898 that far more powerful sources of this kind of radiation existed in certain new elements that they named polonium and radium. While these researches were progressing, other scientists were investigating how electricity is conducted in gases. This culminated in the discovery of the electron by Joseph Thomson (1856–1940) in 1897, which led to the development of the cathode ray tube, vacuum tubes, and the whole science of electronics.

Developments in atomic theory provided scientists with new instruments of investigation. Ernest Rutherford (1871–1937) utilized radioactivity to discover the structure of the atom, and how atoms could be transmuted, opening the way to the release of atomic energy.

Molecules of life

Lawrence Bragg (1890–1971), working with his father William (1862–1942), explained how the structure of molecules can be determined by means of X rays. Working in Bragg's laboratory, James Watson (1928–) and Francis Crick (1916–) discovered in 1953 the double-helix structure of the molecule of DNA (deoxyribonucleic acid), upon which one of the fundamental processes of life, the transmission of hereditary qualities, depends. Such knowledge has made "genetic engineering" possible and has led, for example, to new strains of crop plants to help feed the world's growing population.

KEY

The first cast iron bridge, built over the River Severn at Coalbrookdale, England, in 1779, represented the beginnings of iron as a construction material. The key to cheap iron was the development of blast furnaces and a smelting process using coke instead of coal. This was introduced in 1709, also at Coalbrookdale, by the Englishman Abraham Darby (1678–1717).

4 The Industrial Revolution began in Georgian and Victorian Britain. Based on coal and iron and powered by steam, the world's first industrial society could by the mid-nineteenth century claim to be "the workshop of the world" and stage a Great Exhibition of Trade and Industry at the Crystal Palace in London's Hyde Park in 1851. One of the products of this industrialization, and the one that probably most affected the way of life of the people, was the factory town. By 1851 in Britain, more people lived in towns and cities than in country areas. Often the dominant factories were mills. The steam-powered machinery demanded that men, women, and even children work for 72 hours a week, often in dangerous and unhealthy conditions. Textile mills produced cotton and woolen cloth and yarn to be exported throughout the world. Shown here [left] are carding machines and spinning jennies. Iron foundries made everything from pots and pans to great iron beams and girders and, of course, the machines themselves. But neither machines nor products would have been any use without efficient transportation. Improvement of natural waterways and then the digging of hundreds of miles of canals [right] provided a transportation network linking all the major industrial centers. Itinerant laborers dug the canals, at first largely by hand using picks, shovels, and wheelbarrows. With the coming of the railroads in the nineteenth century the laborers took on the job of making excavations and building huge earth embankments. The railroads completed the transportation system.

The stone age

According to the most recent discoveries our first ancestors, the Australopithecines, lived from three to one-half million years ago. These creatures, only 4ft (1.2m) tall, were distinguished from apes mainly by features of the skull and because they walked upright. Crude stone implements have been found in association with the Australopithecines, but it is not certain that they were the makers [Key]. Many Australopithecine remains have been found in southern and eastern Africa [3].

We do not know how or when people discovered the use of fire. We are sure, however, that by the time of the lower Paleolithic (early Old Stone Age) about 500,000 years ago, they not only made fire safely but also hardened wood in it to make tools and weapons.

The Stone Age in Europe

Human fossils from the first half of the Paleolithic are rare, but it seems likely that the type of person called *Homo erectus* gradually gave way to, or evolved into, a number of later types of which only one, *Homo sapiens* or modern man, has survived. Human artifacts of this long period of the middle Paleolithic include improved types of stone flake tools. These are associated with the Levalloisian culture first discovered in France.

About 30,000 years ago the last human type recognizably different from *Homo sapiens* (although sometimes classified within this species) became extinct. This was the Neanderthal, who was stocky in build and had heavy brow ridges and a sloping forehead, but whose brain was as large as ours. Neanderthals are associated with the Mousterian culture of the middle Paleolithic, first found in the region of the Vézère River in southwest France. They made fire and elegant hand axes [Key B] and buried their dead with funeral rites.

The rest of the Paleolithic is the story of prehistoric cultures of *Homo sapiens:* the Aurignacian of the upper Paleolithic, named after a site at Haute Garonne, France; Gravettian of the upper Paleolithic, after a site on the Dordogne, France; Solutrean of the upper Paleolithic, originally found at Saône-et-Loire, France; and Magdalenian cave dwellers of the upper Paleolithic, after a site on the Vézère, France.

Sophisticated artifacts

Weapons of these cultures were often finely made [Key C, D]. The Solutreans were particularly sophisticated toolmakers. But men were also becoming creative in a totally new way: they began to make carvings representing the human figure and cave paintings of animals.

The carvings were dumpy "Venuses" that possibly had a magical significance [1]. The cave paintings of Laseaux in France and Altamira in Spain [4], both of the Magdalenian culture, probably served magical purposes connected with hunting.

People of these cultures also made simple stone vessels, including lamps [2A]. They used flint, bones, and antlers as materials for tools and they probably worked in wood and leather as well, although these materials have not survived. In a later culture the Azilian people (located at Ariège, southwest France) of the Mesolithic—the

CONNECTIONS

See also
1582 Early technology
1590 Bark, hide, and horn
1438 Prehistoric and ancient science
304 History of agriculture
650 The first men
876 Origins of human society
950 The art of prehistory

1 This "Venus," carved from a mammoth bone, is from the Gravettian culture of the Old Stone Age. It was one of 43 figures found at Kostienki in southern Russia. It is probably a fertility symbol and refers to woman and the earth.

2 From the late Old Stone Age to the time of his settling down the Neolithic or New Stone Age man worked in a number of materials and made many kinds of objects. The cave painters made small household objects such as the stone lamps [A], which date from 15,000 BC. The painted pebbles [B] of the Mesolithic Azilian culture date from 10,000 BC and may be toys or magical objects. Also Mesolithic, but from the Maglemosian culture of 8000–5000 BC, are decorative animals carved in amber [C]. Neolithic tools were often elaborately manufactured, as in this flint-bladed one-handled sickle of about 5000 BC [D]. Antlers were used as picks and ox shoulder blades as shovels [F]. Stone tools were used until later times in Britain. A good example is the stone-headed axe [E].

3 Man probably first evolved in Africa. Fossils resembling men rather than apes were dug up in the Olduvai Gorge of Tanzania by Louis Leakey in 1959. Some date from 2 million years ago.

4 Man was an artist 20,000 years ago–but his paintings also carried a magical significance. This example is from the cave paintings at Altamira, Spain. The Altamira paintings were the first to be recognized as Paleolithic.

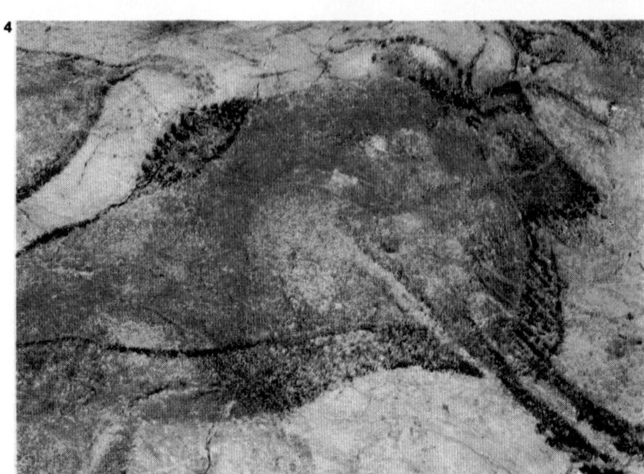

Middle Stone Age—made objects such as painted pebbles [2B].

The Mesolithic, lasting from 10,000 to 7000 BC in the Near East and later in Europe, was a time of great changes. The end of the Ice Age freed men to wander; indeed, it forced them to, because game animals were able to spread out from local areas and became more difficult to hunt. In the milder European climate forests sprang up. The Maglemosian culture (named after Maglemose, Denmark) associated with these forests produced some carvings that were purely decorative [2C].

Man—settled and nomadic

From 7000 to 5000 BC, in the equable climates of Turkey and Mesopotamia, tribes that had been nomadic began to settle down in the first villages and raise animals and grow crops for food. This was the beginning of the Neolithic, or New Stone Age. In the fertile plain between the Tigris and Euphrates rivers this village life eventually gave rise to the first great city civilization, Sumeria.

In the Near East the Stone Age lasted only until 3500 BC after which, as men learned how to smelt metals, it gave way to the Bronze Age. In more backward northern Europe the Neolithic persisted until about 2000 BC. Intermediates were such village cultures as that at Habasesti in Romania [5].

The Neolithic was also a time of great migrations of peoples, particularly those moving east and west from southwest Russia. These people spoke the language from which many Eastern and nearly all European languages have been derived.

In the West the Neolithic wanderers left behind many weapons and tools of stone and bone [2D, E, F], as well as clay vessels and toys. More impressively, they left behind, from the Mediterranean to northern Europe, massive stone blocks arranged in lines and circles erected for astronomical or perhaps religious purposes. These stones (megaliths) are the last great relics of the Stone Age and were probably used to calculate the times of sunrise and sunset at various seasons of the year.

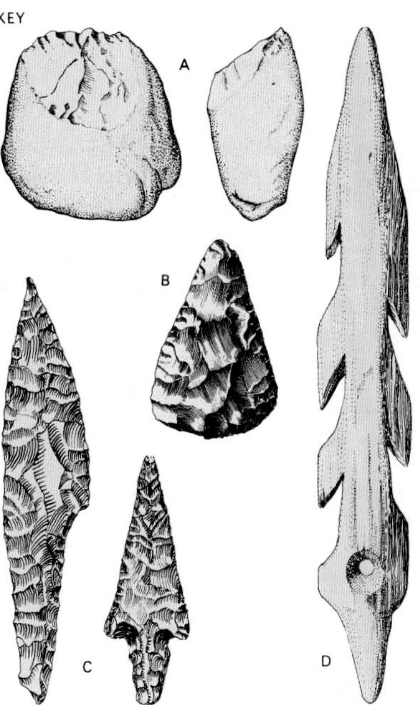
KEY
A
B
C
D

The earliest tools of ancient man were crude stone hand axes, some of which (from East Africa) [A] are more than 2 million years old. Much later, about 50,000 years ago, Neanderthal man made stone hand axes of a more sculptured kind [B]. These were shaped by being hammered carefully with another stone. Late in the Old Stone Age, about 18,000 BC, Solutrean hunters were making very elegant scrapers and arrowheads [C]. By about 15,000 BC, *Homo sapiens* was also an expert fisherman who carved bone harpoons [D]. This was the time of Cro-Magnon man, who was physically indistinguishable from modern man.

5

5 At Habasesti, a site in Romania dating from 3000 BC, edged tools such as axes and hoes were made of stone and sickles were edged with flint. Thus the site (illustrated here) belongs to the New Stone Age. But ornaments and tools of copper are also found. Perhaps these are copies of items imported from Anatolia to the east, which was already in the Bronze Age. Habasesti shell ornaments, with holes for stringing, are probably also copies but this time from the ornaments of visiting Mediterranean peoples. Neolithic villages of the European forest-steppe zones were often larger than villages 4,000 years later. Habasesti contains remains of 44 longhouses, each of which could house 500 people. But these were probably built and occupied over a long period by a smaller number of people. The long houses had walls of clay on a framework of tree branches. Roofs were reed and thatch. House furnishings in these villages were often surprisingly sophisticated. The pottery vessels of Habasesti bear a distinctive S-shaped design. They were painted on red and white bases and outlined by channeled grooves and white, black, and red paint. They were fired, together with many small animal and human clay figures, in top-draft kilns. The Habasesti settlers were farmers who raised wheat and other grains, and kept cattle, goats, pigs, and dogs. The remains of roe deer and wild pigs show, however, that the settlers also hunted for food. Their lives were busy and prosperous because the settled life allowed them to collect a surplus of food, weapons and ornaments. Life at Habasesti also had its dark side: defensive ditches dug around the settlement show that attack was likely.

Fire and bronze

Metal was first used about 8,000 years ago in an era from which the beginning of Western civilization can be dated. Earlier the stones people had picked up, perhaps first to throw at an attacker, had been refined into the sharp tools and weapons of the Neolithic (New Stone Age). But now a new material was at hand—the malleable copper first, perhaps, picked up as the native (pure) metal and beaten into the required shape. When the pure metal became scarce, copper was smelted from the ores containing it. Soon it was found that the rather soft copper could be alloyed. It was mixed with tin, to produce the harder, more useful bronze.

Increasing use of metals

The longest Copper Age, that of ancient Egypt, extended before the first dynasty from about 5000 BC until about 3700 BC, after which bronze was used. But bronze objects had been made earlier still, in the city states of the Fertile Crescent of Mesopotamia where the earliest of known city dwellers, the Sumerians, were the first to use copper. They probably obtained it by trading with miners in Asia Minor.

Europe in general saw the introduction of the Bronze Age about 1,000 years later than did Asia Minor [Key 1, 5], although some copper finds from eastern Europe date from times as ancient as those of Sumeria [4]. Beyond the deserts and mountains of central Asia, the great civilization of China was pursuing its own course, producing ceramics and intricate jade and bronze vessels from 1500 BC onward. But some ancient societies, such as those in Central America, had no metals at this time, not using copper until about AD 100.

The first civilizations were controlled by the priests in theocratic Sumeria and the civil servants and administrators of bureaucratic Egypt. They also created the first slaves, war captives more profitably put to work than killed. Thus a labor force existed that released artisans to do skilled work in shaping tools and ornaments.

The largest class, however, remained the peasant farmers. They also needed metals, in the form of plows, hoes, axes, and other edged tools, which in Neolithic times had been made of wood and stone. In times of war, many peasants were recruited as soldiers and, as at other times in history, peaceful metalworking was adapted to the production of bronze helmets, battleaxes, spearheads, daggers, and later swords.

Bronze Age achievements

Huge sacred buildings were constructed by slaves both in Mesopotamia and Egypt. In Mesopotamia, ziggurats were used for astrological observations and as temples. In Egypt, the pyramids were the greatest and grandest tombs ever built. Interred with each Egyptian luminary were all kinds of domestic and luxury objects to be taken into the next world. The tomb of the pharaoh Tutankhamen, the most undisturbed yet discovered, contained a wealth of luxury articles made of bronze, gold, silver, ivory, and glass. If a relatively unimportant 18-year-old pharaoh deserved all this, then it is probable that even richer tombs once existed, containing still greater funeral hoards.

CONNECTIONS

See also
- **1582** Early technology
- **1604** Working metals by hand
- **1596** Metals and their uses
- **1726** Early weapons and defense
- **1732** History of artillery
- **1438** Prehistoric and ancient science
- **304** History of agriculture
- **650** The first men
- **876** Origins of human society

1

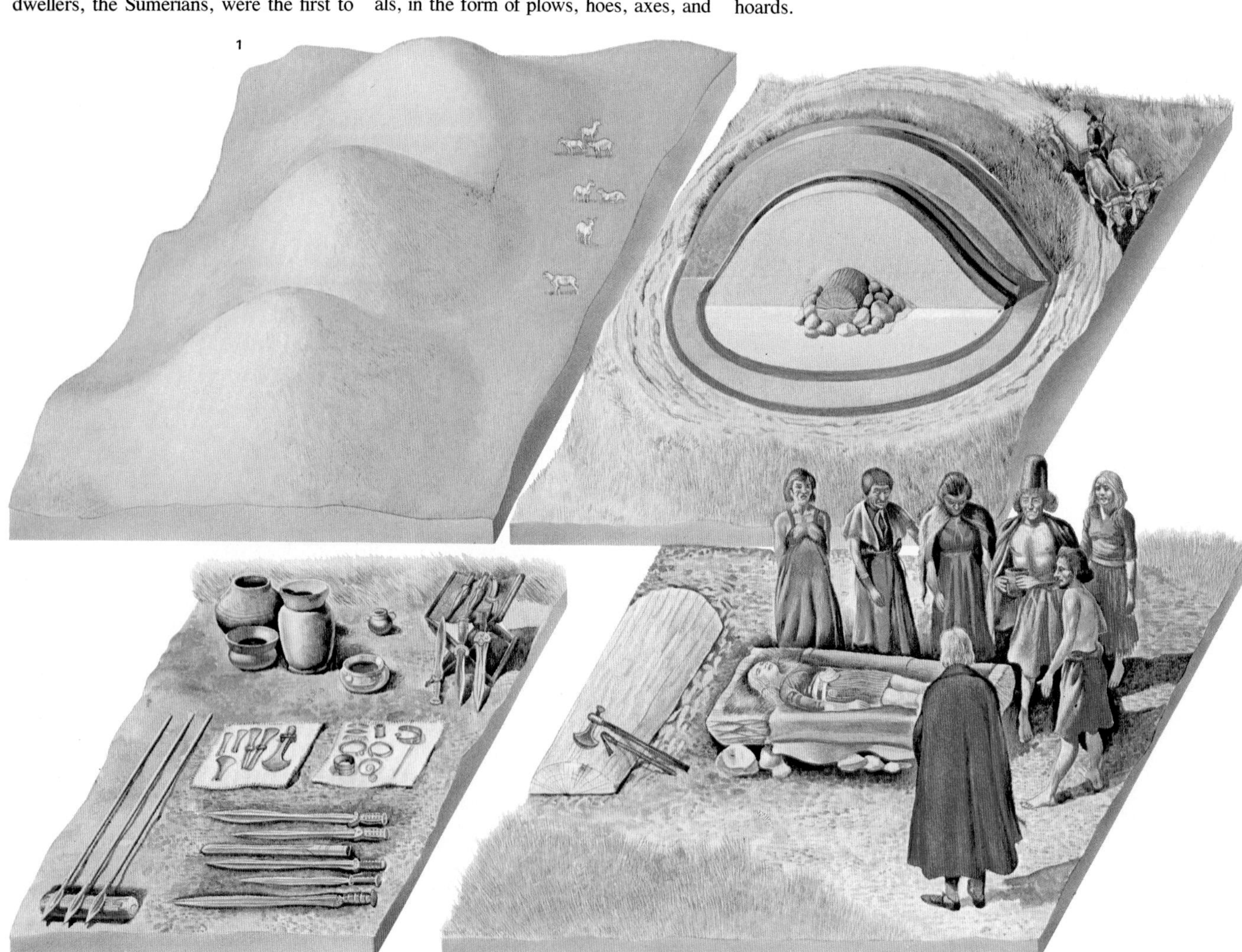

1 The ancients left their messages for posterity in the graves of their dead, whether great pyramids or simple turf burial mounds. This reconstruction depicts a burial ceremony at Egtved, in east Jutland, a few centuries after the Bronze Age culture had reached northwestern Europe, about 1500 BC. The corpse was interred in a round barrow, or tumulus grave mound. Such Bronze Age barrows and long barrows from the Neolithic (New Stone Age) are widespread in Europe. The corpse, that of a rich young woman, was discovered in a barrow, in a coffin made from a split and hollowed tree trunk. The coffin was enclosed in a heap of stones and then surrounded by an enormous quantity of turf, enough to strip several fields. The dead woman wore a belt ornamented by a large bronze disk, bronze arm rings, and an earring of bronze. The grave objects laid out for the ceremony are varied and plentiful, since they are those of a rich woman. They include weapons, jewelry, and pottery. The weapons are typical of the period and culture, and include palstaves—narrow bladed axes with high flanges on either side—and small thrusting swords with hilts only large enough for a three-fingered grip. Decorations on the weapons echo those of Mycenaean Greece of about 1500 BC. Shown with the dissected mound is an aspect of Bronze Age agriculture, a cart drawn by cattle. Seed would have been scattered in front of the animals to be trodden in by their hooves. The harvest, if it was of grain, would have been reaped with bronze bladed sickles.

Egyptian civilization, with only a few major upsets, endured for more than three thousand years. In contrast, the civilizations in Mesopotamia came and went over the centuries. The Sumerians, who had invented writing and the wheel, disappeared and were replaced by the Akkadians by 2350 BC. The Akkadians left behind one of the great Bronze Age sculptures, that of their warrior-king Sargon I, which still survives. In their turn, the Akkadians were swept away by the Amorites, who gave way to a Hittite invasion around 1600 BC. The Hittites had founded a powerful kingdom in Anatolia about 2000 BC and were the greatest ironworkers and steelmakers. They started the Iron Age that replaced the Bronze Age in the Near East.

Technology of metals

Why copper and bronze should have been employed for so long to make axes, hammers, and heavy weapons is at first glance odd, since iron ore was plentiful, and iron is harder and tougher than bronze. The answer lies in available technology. The Bronze Age persisted for more than 3,000 years because copper melts at 1,981°F (1,083°C). Iron melts at 2,802°F (1,539°C), and cannot be melted for molding without the use of some kind of forced draft or blast furnace. Even the skilled Hittites lacked such a furnace: they beat the metal out of roasted, but not melted, ore.

Bronze could be strengthened by the addition of small amounts of zinc, antimony, and other elements that improved its hardness and toughness. These elements were at first present in ancient bronze as impurities, but later were probably added deliberately. At first, the mixtures of copper and tin or their ores [6] were made haphazardly. But later, as skills improved, they were mixed in definite proportions for different bronzes.

The Sumerians also hardened bronze by hammering, and made nails from it. They made wire, sheet, and castings (in gold and silver, also) in clay molds by the *cire perdue*, or lost wax, process, afterwards used for thousands of years (as in the Benin sculptures of West Africa).

KEY

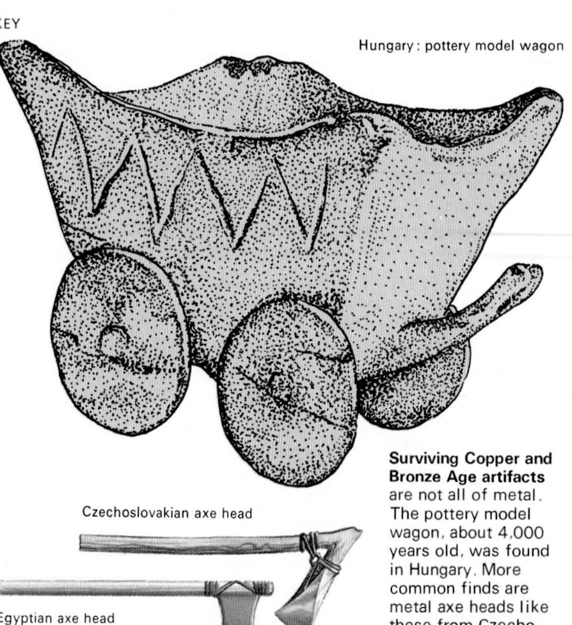
Hungary: pottery model wagon
Czechoslovakian axe head
Egyptian axe head

Surviving Copper and Bronze Age artifacts are not all of metal. The pottery model wagon, about 4,000 years old, was found in Hungary. More common finds are metal axe heads like these from Czechoslovakia and Egypt.

2

2 Unable to multiply or divide, the ancient Egyptians achieved a wonder of practical mathematics when they built the Great Pyramid. Its base covers an area of 13 acres (5 hectares) yet differs from a perfect square by only 0.6in (1.5cm). The stone blocks of which the pyramids were built weighed up to 1,000 tons and were moved into position without the use of wheels.

3

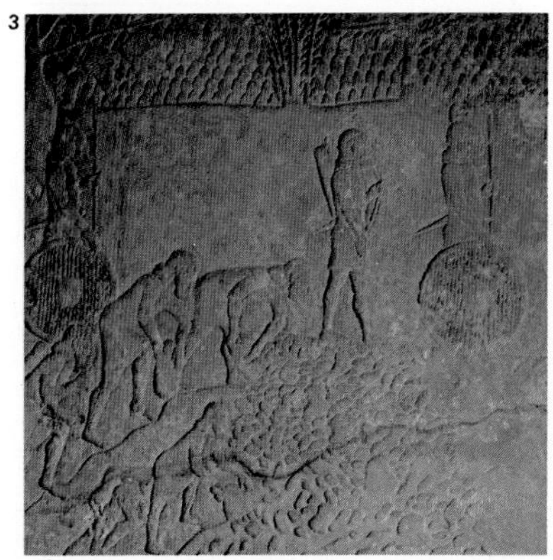

3 Some Egyptian tombs contain pictures carved in relief in rock. Others have paintings executed in water-based paints, to which were often added honey, gum, or egg white to give substance to the color. The pictures themselves provide a record of the ways of life in various classes of Egyptian society. Officialdom thrived; here a dignitary is attended by many servants.

4

5A B

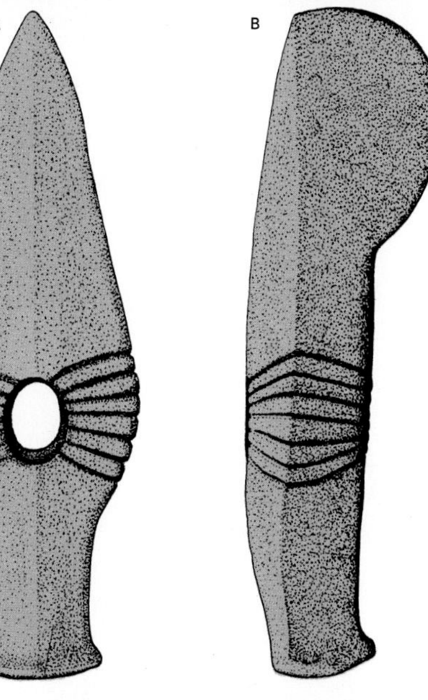

4 A terracotta figurine from the Copper Age of Romania dates from before 3500 BC and gives some idea of the spread of culture along the Danube during the time of the early metal ages of Sumeria and Egypt.

5 Across the Black Sea, north of the Fertile Crescent, traces of the Copper and Bronze ages have been found in the Soviet Union. This axe (top [A], side [B]) was found at Fatyanovo and dates from the early Bronze Age, about 1000 BC.

6A

B

6 Bronze alloys are made primarily from two metals, tin and copper. In the metallurgy of the Bronze Age bronzes could have been made—and probably were—in a number of ways. Tin occurs mainly in nature as an oxide called cassiterite [A], which is often found in rivers or lakes as an alluvial deposit. Copper occurs as many kinds of ores, as well as the "ready-to-use" native metal [B]. In some regions, a Copper Age preceded the Bronze Age.

Bark, hide, and horn

Early cultures made use of available materials to satisfy their needs. Archeologists have found a profusion of the stone tools they used, but because skin, bone, and wood are far more likely to disintegrate than to turn into fossils and to be preserved, there is less evidence of how early cultures used those materials. There is no reason to doubt, however, that they did use them.

The skins of animals

Animal fur makes ideal clothing. When hunters learned to trap and kill larger animals the skins of the great cats—lions [9], tigers, and leopards—made magnificent and prized garments, which were a mark of courage and power as well as being effective clothing. Small skins were sewn together using bone needles. Bones were also used to make buttons.

The hide of almost any animal—pig, goat, cattle, sheep, camel, horse, snake, crocodile, and many others—can be tanned into leather. The skin was scraped [3] with flint tools and preserved by smoking or rubbing salt into it. Hunters tanned hides into lasting leather by soaking them in a wide variety of solutions made from roots or the bark of trees and which sometimes included urine. They then softened the leather by rubbing in animal fats. The Eskimos used fish oils or seal oil to make skins soft and durable.

As technology evolved, peoples became more skilled in working and decorating leather. It is such a versatile material, pliable and strong, that its range of uses is almost a catalog of the activities of early cultures: pouches and bags [6A] of all sorts; casks for liquids; sheaths for knives; covers for tents, wagons, and boats; saddles; skins for drums; slings, shields, and armor; ornaments; and later, parchment for writing.

Animal hair into cloth

The skin of all mammals carries some hair, even if sparse. Hair can be used as thread or made into rope, and employed as stuffing for saddles and cushions. The hair of some animals, including goats and camels, is longer and can be spun or woven into textiles [5]. But by far the most important is the wool of the sheep. The fleece of domestic sheep is derived from the undercoat of the wild sheep, the long guard hairs having disappeared with selective breeding.

Unlike most hair, domestic sheep's wool grows continuously throughout the life of the animal. It will trail to the ground if not shorn or torn away on bushes. The origins of the use of wool are unknown. Woven woolen cloth was used during the Scandinavian Bronze Age and wool was widely used in antiquity by the Greeks and Romans. The Roman author Pliny (AD 23–79) classified wool into three types: soft wool, long-fiber wool and rustic wool. It was also classified according to color, the most valuable being white. Sheep were selectively bred to improve standards. In the Middle Ages the quality of English wool was famous. It was exported to many other European countries and used to weave the finest cloth in Flanders and Florence. The wool was classified according to its place of origin, even down to the individual market town. It was only in the eighteenth century that scientific breeding began to estab-

CONNECTIONS

See also
1582 Early technology
1610 Materials for buildir
1438 Prehistoric and ancient science
1624 Making paper
304 History of agricultu

1 Early people used the natural materials available. Plants provided ample sources of raw materials and some idea of early uses can be seen among modern tribes. The Ainu women of Japan weave cloth from the bark of elm and linden trees. The bark is soaked, dried, and teased out into threads [A]. The cloth is then woven on a loom [B] into material with traditional geometric patterns [C].

2 Some natural objects make convenient containers. The fashioning of gourds into vessels is widely practiced among members of the African Nuer tribe. A gourd of suitable shape is chosen, an opening cut in it, and the inside cleared of seeds. The gourd is then dried in tne sun.

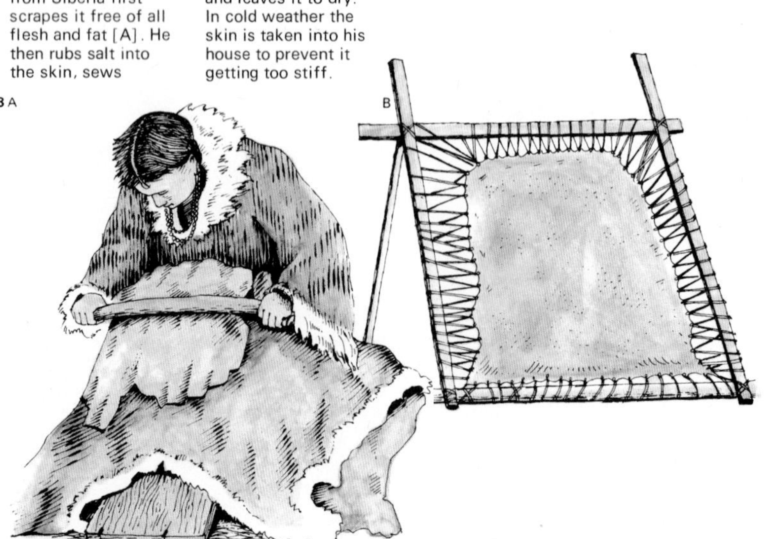

3 To prepare an animal skin this Chukchi tribesman from Siberia first scrapes it free of all flesh and fat [A]. He then rubs salt into the skin, sews thongs around its edges, stretches it taut on a frame [B], and leaves it to dry. In cold weather the skin is taken into his house to prevent it getting too stiff.

4 A fish-skin robe is one of the traditional garments made by the Nanays of Siberia. In common with tribes in many parts of the world the Nanays have evolved styles of cut and patterns of decoration all their own. Their tribe consists of clans, members of which may not intermarry. Hence identification is important to the peaceful life of the tribe. This quick recognition is effected by certain conventions in dress and ornamentation. Many of the styles are of great age and may have had their origins in various cult beliefs that clans observed in the past.

lish the various breeds of sheep that are now recognized.

Rhinoceros "horn" is a compact fibrous material with the same composition as hair. It owes its value to a misconception: it is thought by many people in the East to be an aphrodisiac and powdered rhinoceros horn still fetches a high price in eastern Asia.

Strong and shapely horn

The horns of oxen, buffalo, and sheep, and the antlers of stags, are two different kinds of tough material that can be worked fairly easily. Horn can be carved, drilled, and molded [7C] and, after heating in hot water, welded together. Among the earliest known decorative works are Paleolithic carvings on reindeer antler and mammoth ivory. In their natural form horns and antlers look attractive [6B] and are conveniently shaped [7A] for various purposes. Antlers were used as picks and horn as handles for tools and weapons, and hollow horns as drinking vessels.

Horn is a material with particularly tough, springy properties. In Siberia, in later times, powerful compound bows were made by laminating strips of antler and horn to strips of wood. Such bows, if short, were convenient and effective weapons for horsemen. Apparently responsible for much of the military success of the Turks in the later Middle Ages, they are said to have had twice the range of the English longbow, which had an effective range of about 650ft (200m). In more recent times people made horns into containers for gunpowder.

Ivory is the finest of the bonelike materials. Usually obtained from the tusks of elephants, ivory is a beautiful but difficult material to carve [8]. Inferior ivories come from hippopotamus and walrus tusks. To the Eskimos, who had neither wood nor metal, ivory and bone were especially important and were used to make clubs, snow knives, harpoons, fish hooks, combs, and many other implements. A tradition of fine carving in ivory developed in many places [8]. The ancient Minoans used ivory seals to stamp oil and wine jars with their individual marks and made lifelike ivory carvings of people.

KEY

The stripes of the zebra evolved as a form of camouflage. When the skin of the zebra is used, for example, as a cover for a shield, the stripes form a bold pattern. The cured hide is remarkably tough and is strong enough to deflect spears and arrows and ward off blows from a club.

5

5 The yak of Tibet serves the Sherpas of the high mountain region well. They take from it leather for shoes and harness, coarse wool for blankets, and clothing. The yak gives milk to drink and the herdsmen churn it into butter or make it into strongly flavored cheese. The herdsmen open one of a yak's veins to take some of its blood, which they dry into a cake. Added to soups and stews this gives them a protein-rich source of food that is easily carried. Yak dung, when dried, provides one of the few sources of fuel in a high mountain region almost devoid of trees. The animal is also a durable, if fractious, pack animal.

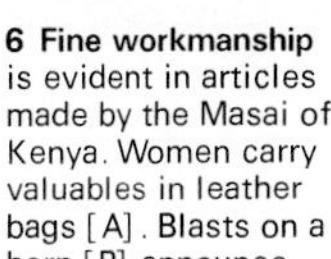

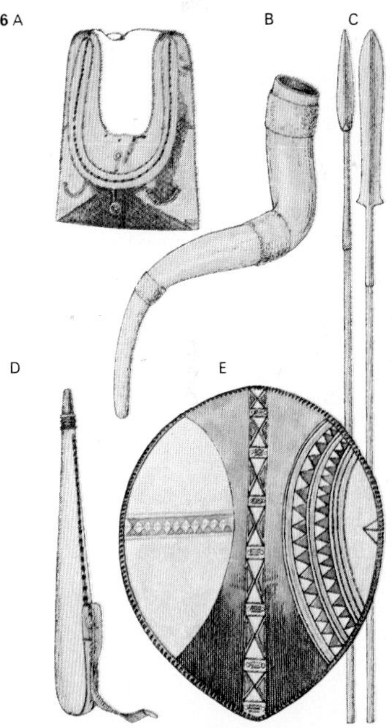

6 A
B
C
D
E

6 Fine workmanship is evident in articles made by the Masai of Kenya. Women carry valuables in leather bags [A]. Blasts on a horn [B] announce ceremonies. Warriors arm themselves with spears [C], carry blood and milk in gourds [D], and bear shields [E] for defense.

7 A B

C

7 Antler, flint, and horn are the basis of these objects. The Stone Age antler harpoon [A] has a detachable head that stays in the prey. The 5,000-year-old flint knife [B] has an ivory handle. The Haida Indians' ladles were carved out of horn [C].

8

8 Exquisitely worked ivory chessmen were highpoints in the workmanship exhibited by Chinese craftsmen in many materials. Each piece in their chess sets was imbued with individual character, reflecting the carver's experience of the feudal society in which he lived. The expendable pawns were commonly portrayed as peasants and were carved with sympathy.

9

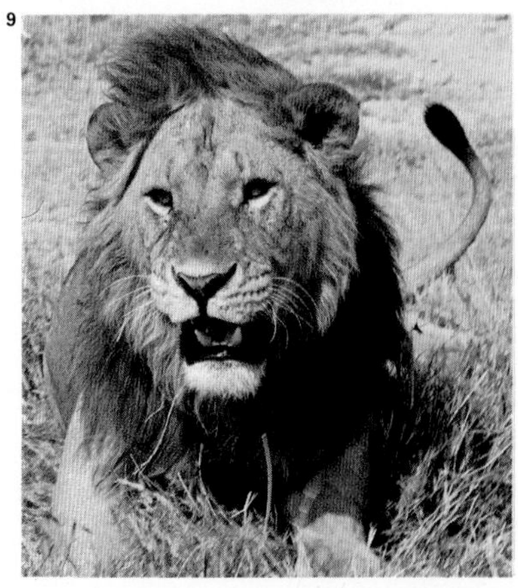

9 To kill a lion with a spear in individual combat was considered one of the noblest achievements among the Masai of Kenya and other African tribes. The lion's skin was worn by the hunter as a coat of courage, admired by others of his tribe as well as by strangers.

The iron age

Iron may have been first encountered as a gift from the heavens: iron meteorites might have supplied the metal for weapons and ornaments made in about 3000 BC or even earlier. The manufacture of iron tools had to wait another thousand years until the introduction of iron smelting—the extraction of the often impure metal from iron ores. Iron's high melting temperature means that it cannot be melted directly over a wood or coal fire. Some kind of forced-draft, or blast, furnace must be employed to attain the required temperature of 2,802°F (1,539°C).

Primitive smelting ovens did produce a malleable iron of fair quality and were used for several centuries in different countries. Iron was of fundamental importance to a number of civilizations. The first significant steel production was started in India using a process already familiar to ancient Egyptians.

The methods of the Hittite smiths

Iron in the form of bog ore is quite plentiful, widespread, and easy to obtain. To make iron objects the ore is first smelted to make a "bloom" of iron. It must then be heated and hammered to remove the slag, then quenched in water. This process, repeated several times, makes iron of adequate strength. The technique was used widely by Hittite ironsmiths, the first true technologists of the Iron Age, in the latter half of the second millennium BC [2].

These Hittites closely guarded their smelting method, but after the destruction of the Hittite empire in 1200 BC the smiths were scattered, so that other tribes and nations benefited from their skill in making tough metal tools. At this time a kind of steel—iron containing 1.5 percent or less of carbon—had also been made and was used for tools and weapons needing a sharp cutting edge. An early Iron Age spearhead or sickle [3] was limited by lack of a socket, which could be made only by casting the metal in a mold. A few socketed iron weapons have been found dating from as early as the second millennium BC, but their sockets are made from gold or copper (copper melts at 1,981°F (1,083°C) and gold at 1,947°F (1,064°C). so these metals could be melted over a fire for casting). Iron swords of this period were stronger and less brittle than the bronze swords they supplanted. The Assyrians used Hittite iron swords. More peaceful early Iron Age objects include the tongs, hammers, and anvils used by the ironsmiths, and iron nails.

The first iron plows, from Palestine, date from about 1100 BC but the Greeks of the sixth century BC do not seem to have used iron for this purpose and iron-shod plows became common only in Roman times. By 600 BC the Catalans of northeastern Spain were able to soften, but not melt, iron in a type of furnace having a forced draft provided by two sets of bellows.

The Romans and their use of iron

If the Hittites were the first ironsmiths, then the Romans were the first mining engineers. Sites of Roman metal mines range from southern Scotland to southern Spain in the west to Romania in the east.

As would be expected, Roman iron and steel were put to many military uses. The famous short sword, the nine-foot spear,

CONNECTIONS

See also
1602 Hand tools
1582 Early technology
1438 Prehistoric and ancient science
304 History of agriculture
656 Spread of man: 2
976 The Hittites 1700–1200 BC
1008 The Celts 500 BC–AD 450

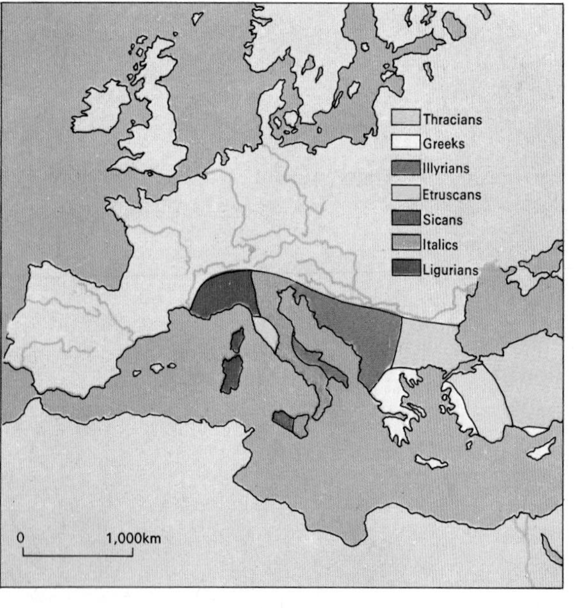

1
Thracians
Greeks
Illyrians
Etruscans
Sicans
Italics
Ligurians
0
1,000km

1 Iron ores are common and widespread, second only to those of aluminum. But early Iron Age man would not have used the richer ores such as hematite and magnetite, which can contain as much as 60% iron. These ores must be mined. He would more probably have first exploited bog iron ore, which occurs freely in marshy ground. It is formed by the decomposition of other iron minerals and is finally precipitated in the water by the action of bacteria. It needs only to be sieved out to be used. However, by 850 BC several other iron ores were being worked in Europe, and regions occupied by various peoples who worked iron ore.

2 A
B
C

2 Earliest of man-made iron objects were ornaments and small weapons, dating from about 3000 BC. The Hittite dagger-sword [A] was made somewhat later. Its blade would have been beaten out from heated iron ore. This produces a relatively crude form of iron, but the Hittite smiths eventually became the masters of iron technology. They influenced European ironwork, such as this collar [B]. By 500 BC, in central Europe, ironsmiths were making a kind of steel by hammering charcoal into heated iron. The iron-headed mace [C] is a late example of primitive iron technology from Chieti, Italy. It dates from about 600 BC.

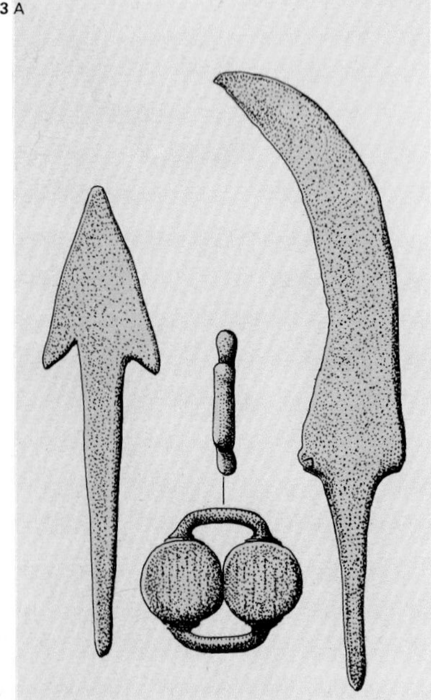

3 A

B

1 2 3 4 5 6

Turf
Chalk
Chalk parapets
Clay
Earth

Unexcavated

3 Maiden Castle is a large Iron Age fort in Britain. The site, a saddleback hill [B], was occupied from Neolithic times (3rd millennium BC) and by 100 BC had grown to a town-sized fortress with six phases of ramparts [1–6], the earliest dating to about 500 BC. The iron arrowhead and small sickle and the bronze belt buckle [A] are objects that were made by a Wessex Iron Age people who inhabited Maiden Castle from about 100 BC until 70 BC; they were known at the time as the Durotriges. These Celts also left behind them many artifacts made of iron, including rings, axes, and "currency bars" (shaped like swords) that were used for trading. The castle was attacked by the Romans under Vespasian in AD 43 and a cemetery of the defenders has been found. The castle continued to be occupied until about AD 70, when it was replaced by the nearby Roman town of Dorchester.

and the breastplate inherited from the Greeks were all made largely of iron. Later Roman soldiers also used iron long-swords and throwing spears and shot iron darts from their catapults. Iron-headed battering rams had been used since the Assyrians.

In architecture the Greeks had made the most imaginative use of iron, in wrought-iron beams. In the construction of the Parthenon, such beams acted as cantilevers to hold up the heaviest statues on the pediment. The Romans later made use of T-shaped iron girders, as in the Baths of Caracalla, where they help to support a dome 118ft (36m) across.

Little is known about mining and metallurgy in the early Middle Ages except that Saxon miners were at work in the Harz mountains before AD 1000. Knowledge of later medieval mining technology is much greater, largely because of a single man, the Saxon physician known as Agricola. His great book *De re metallica* (1556) details methods and machinery and demonstrates that by this time mining had become a profitable industry.

Iron and the manufacture of armaments

Centuries before Agricola's time, the iron industry was essentially an armaments industry. From the time of Charlemagne (AD 742–814) onward, iron armor was invented afresh, very little being copied from the Romans. Later there evolved a totally new iron technology—firearms [5].

The final great discovery of the Iron Age was that iron could be melted and cast in molds. The first blast furnaces were developed as enlarged versions of medieval ovens. They used first charcoal, then coal, both as fuel and as a necessary ingredient (carbon) for the smelting process. By 1711 Abraham Darby (1677–1717) in England began to use coke to smelt large quantities of ores to make good quality cast iron suitable for forging as well as for casting in sand molds. Previously, cast utensils, such as pots, could be made only from expensive metals such as brass. Soon every home in the land had cast-iron cooking pots and pans. Iron was used for making bridges and the iron tracks of railroads. The Industrial Revolution and the age of steel had begun.

KEY

Iron Age peoples occupied hill-forts in many parts of Europe often fortifying them with a series of concentric earth ramparts, as pictured here at Maiden Castle, England.

4

4 After the fall of the Roman Empire metalworking in Europe declined, surviving mainly in the elegant iron swords made by the Burgundian and Frankish smiths. These had patterns formed by strips of welded iron. The horsemen of Charlemagne, king of the Franks in the 8th century AD, were clothed in heavy iron armor of a design that owed little to the Romans: the Germanic conquerors of the Roman Empire had apparently despised the thought of copying the armor of a defeated foe. Chainmail came later still as an import from the East. This feudal knight wears up to 110lb (50kg) of mail and plate. Mail was made from rings of iron wire riveted or welded together and shaped to cover the arms, feet, and head. By the 14th century, plate armor, originally a reinforcement for chainmail, was beginning to take its place. Ironsmiths were by this time adept at shaping accurately the joints necessary for properly functioning plate armor and were also skilled at producing decorative metal inlays.

5

5 The first iron cannon and mortars were brittle and likely to blow up in the user's face. From the 15th century they were cast in a more reliable iron.

6

6 Charcoal, and to a lesser extent coal, was employed in furnaces for ironmaking during the Middle Ages. The charcoal came from native timber and many of Europe's forests disappeared for this use, among them those of the Sussex Weald (shown here) in southern England.

The steel age

From human beginnings to about ten thousand years ago the technology of our ancestors was based upon the use of stone, five thousand years ago upon bronze, and three thousand years ago upon iron. Thus we refer to the Stone Age, the Bronze Age, and the Iron Age. There is no corresponding period that archeologists can specify as an age based upon steel. Steel has been made in large quantities only for about 120 years, during which time it has become vital to our civilization. But the origins of steel lie in the remote past.

The first steelmakers

Plain, or mild, steel, as it is used in a host of applications, is an alloy of iron with a little carbon. Mild steel contains between 0.15 and 0.25 percent carbon, partly in the form of iron carbide or cementite. Steel is much harder than pure iron and less brittle than cast iron (which contains more carbon than steel does); its strength, toughness, and springiness account for its great usefulness.

The first makers of iron tools and weapons on a large scale were the Hittites, and it was men of a subject tribe of the Hittites, the Chalybes, who first made steel in about 1400 BC. Chalybean steelsmiths in Asia Minor employed a cementation process; that is, they hammered hot but still unmolten iron together with charcoal until the iron became steel. During the hammering, carbon from the charcoal diffused into the iron, forming cementite—hence the name for the process.

Molding and hardening

Variations on the cementation process continued in use for more than a thousand years, spreading from the Middle East into Europe and India. But it was in southern India that iron was melted for the first time and steel cast into molds. The Romans imported this steel in the shape of small, rounded cakes. They thought that it originated in China and called it "Seric" (meaning Chinese) iron.

In Europe steel was sometimes made directly from an ore with the correct carbon content, but this was rare. More often steel resulted from the cementation process and, from the eighth century AD onward, cementation steel began to be exported from the iron-rich parts of central Europe known as Styria and Carinthia. This steel had been further hardened by quenching it from red heat in water.

By the fifteenth century early printers were using steel punches in the manufacture of their type molds and, midway through the seventeenth century, tempered steel coach springs added a little comfort to travel on Europe's rutted and pothole-strewn roads. Such examples show a thorough appreciation of the possibilities of steel, but these were not to be fully realized until cheap steel became available with the coming of the Bessemer furnace in the 1850s.

The Bessemer process

A great problem with early steel was the presence in it of slag waste from the ore, which made it difficult to manufacture large steel objects without structural weaknesses. This problem was solved by the mid-eighteenth century as the result of the work of Torbern Bergmann (1735–84), a Swedish

CONNECTIONS

See also
1592 The iron age
1604 Working metals by hand
1606 Metalworking machines
1584 Modern technology
1612 Making large buildings
1734 Modern artillery
1736 Armored fighting vehicles
1740 Modern fighting ships
1758 Modern bridges
1236 The Industrial Revolution

1 A complex modern steelmaking plant uses coal as the initial fuel. Iron and limestone [1] are brought in by train or ship and are conveyed [2] from storage to a blast furnace. But some ore and limestone are first heated with coke [3]. Coal from a coal store [4] is converted into coke in a coking plant [5]. All these materials are then fed to the blast furnace [6] in which the iron takes up carbon from the coke and the other materials to form a layer of molten slag. A pump [7] supplies the furnace with air, which is preheated in heat exchangers [8] by hot gases [9] from the blast furnace. Too much carbon is absorbed by the iron in the blast furnace and this excess is removed in a second basic oxygen furnace [10] containing an oxygen lance [11] fed from large spherical tanks [12]. Coke and limestone are also used in the refining process. Gas from the oxygen furnace is taken off [13] for cleaning before being discharged into the atmosphere. The refined steel, containing between 0.15 and 0.25 percent carbon, is poured from the oyxgen furnace [14] and cast into ingots [15].

1

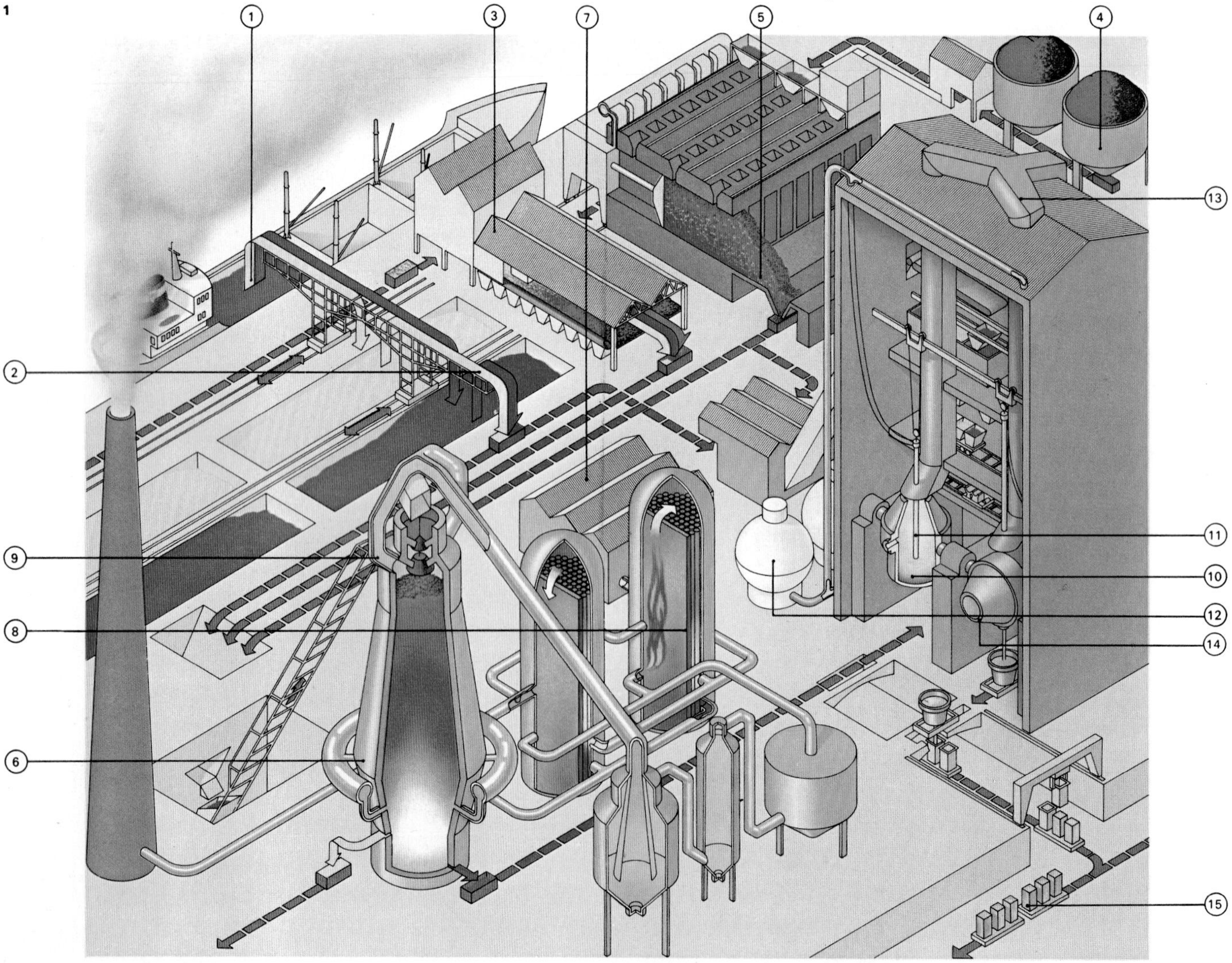

1 3 7 5 4 13 2 11 9 10 12 8 14 6 15

metallurgist, and Benjamin Huntsman (1704–76), a British steelmaker. "Swedish" steel had a controlled carbon content and was free from slag. But it was still quite expensive. In 1850 the entire output of steel in Britain was only about 60,000 tons. Twenty years later, Bessemer furnaces, or "converters," made steel at an average rate of one ton per minute, and steel could be made as cheaply as cast iron.

The secret of the Bessemer process—developed in 1856 by Henry Bessemer (1813–98) and based on the experiments of a bankrupt Kentucky steelmaker, William Kelley—was that excess carbon could be oxidized (combined with oxygen) by forcing bubbles of air through a mass of molten iron. Moreover, the carbon burned to carbon dioxide in the blast of air, thus acting as a fuel. Once started, the process continued without the addition of more fuel coal and was thus extremely economical.

Within five years the Bessemer process [3] had a rival in the open-hearth method of steelmaking [2] in which iron, iron ore, and scrap steel are melted in such proportions as to drive off most of the carbon and oxygen as carbon monoxide. This inflammable gas is then burned "regeneratively" to preheat the blast. This efficient operation was, by 1900, producing more steel than even the Bessemer process.

The twentieth century saw further revolutions in steelmaking, notably the development of continuous casting of steel [4] and special steels such as those for making machine tools and turbine blades. The newer steels include stainless steels, which contain chromium, nickel, and sometimes molybdenum, and are made in an electric furnace [5]. They are used mainly for cutlery, kitchen utensils, and in chemical plants. Since 1970 the Bessemer process has been partly replaced by the basic oxygen process [3B].

By the end of the nineteenth century, world production of steel was already about 30 million tons. In the years since, it has received further boosts from the two world wars, which demanded steel for armaments, and from the development of the automobile.

KEY

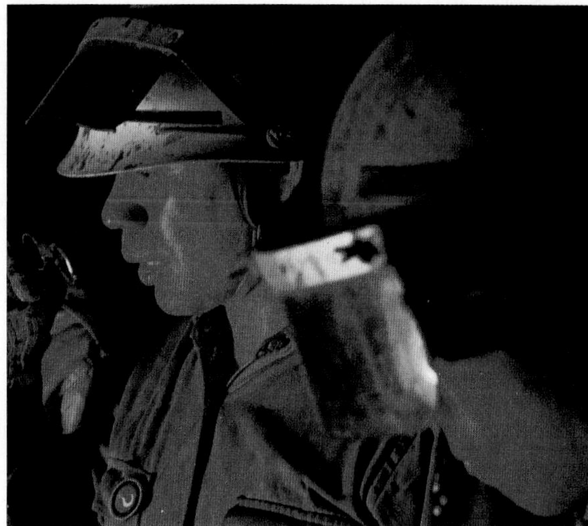

Steelmaking is often hot, tough work, as the faces of these Japanese steelworkers show. In the 19th century men whose job it was to tap or release the molten steel from the furnaces wore no protective clothing, and the intense heat could kill them. Today automatic controls protect workers.

2

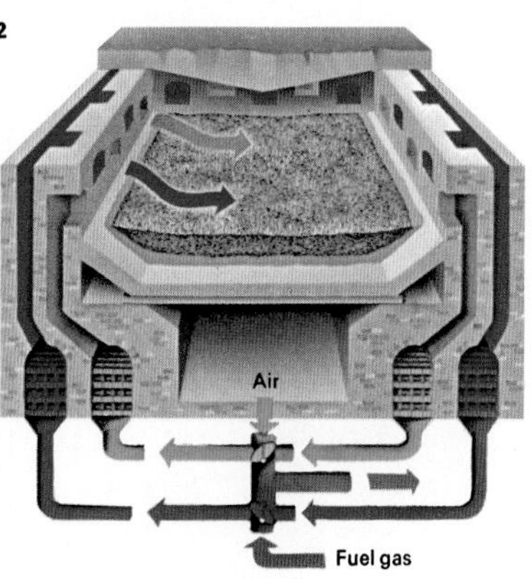
Air
Fuel gas

2 The Siemens-Martin open-hearth process has made most of the steel in this century but it is being superseded by electric and basic oxygen methods. It uses the gases from the molten charge to preheat the air blast and so economizes on fuel. As the air cools, valves switch the flow to other channels that have been heated; after a while, it is switched back. Alkaline linings are used when the ore is acidic.

3

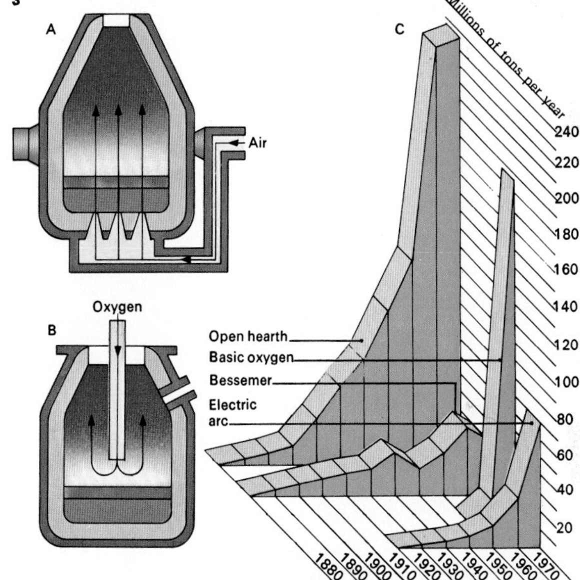
A
Air
B
Oxygen
C
Millions of tons per year
240
220
200
180
160
140
120
100
80
60
40
20
Open hearth
Basic oxygen
Bessemer
Electric arc
1880
1890
1900
1910
1920
1930
1940
1950
1960
1970

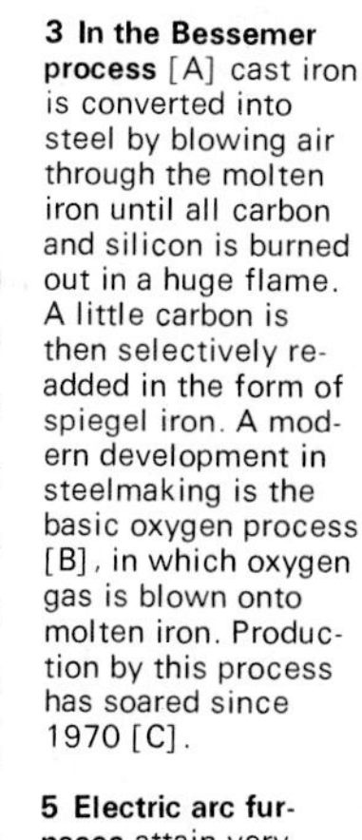

3 In the Bessemer process [A] cast iron is converted into steel by blowing air through the molten iron until all carbon and silicon is burned out in a huge flame. A little carbon is then selectively re-added in the form of spiegel iron. A modern development in steelmaking is the basic oxygen process [B], in which oxygen gas is blown onto molten iron. Production by this process has soared since 1970 [C].

5 Electric arc furnaces attain very high temperatures, without any oxygen being used. For this reason, they are employed to make steels containing oxidizable metals such as chromium.

4

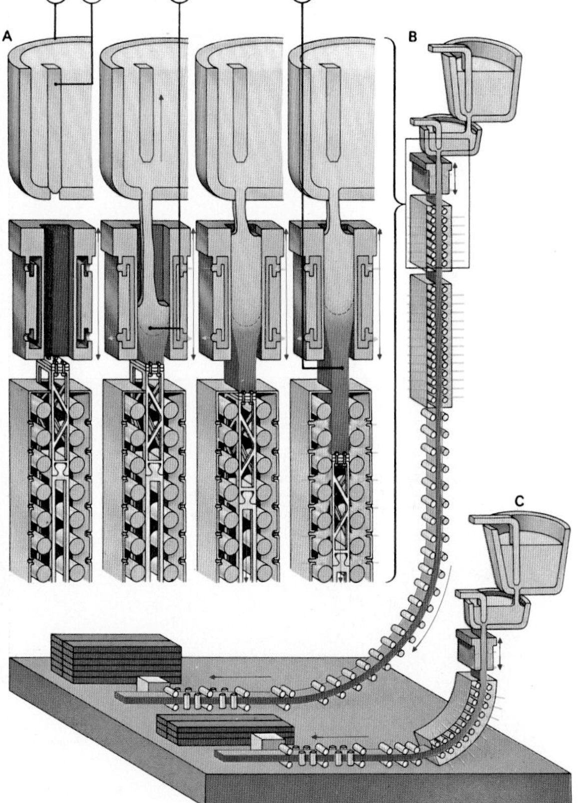
1
2
3
4
A
B
C

4 Continuous casting is a modern method of making steel cheaply and quickly in the form of bars and rods. A casting run [A] starts with molten steel being poured into a copper mold [1] which is closed by a plug [2] at its lower end. The steel is cooled by water in the mold and when it is nearly solid the plug is withdrawn. The molded steel moves down [3] and is then further cooled by means of water sprays before being cut into the required lengths. While the plug is withdrawn molten steel is poured continuously [4]. The original casting process [B] had a straight, vertical cooling section, but a newer type [C] has a curved section requiring less space.

5

Metals and their uses

Iron and its alloys are dominant metals today and so it is customary to group all other metals into the category "non-ferrous." But non-ferrous metals have little in common apart from the negative attribute implied by the name. There are more than 20 non-ferrous metals of industrial importance, and some of the chief ones—copper, silver, lead, tin, and mercury—have been known since antiquity. Others such as aluminum and titanium have found wide application only recently.

Gold, copper, and silver

The legendary metal gold [1] occurs in nature almost exclusively in a native (free or uncombined) state. First found by chance, it was being mined by 3000 BC and was being chemically extracted from crushed quartz (by amalgamation with mercury) by 1000 BC. Gold is yellow and lustrous, outstandingly workable for drawing or hammering into shapes, and is resistant to corrosion and to chemical attack.

The conventional test for gold is to drop hydrochloric or nitric acid separately onto the metal; pure gold resists either acid alone but dissolves in a mixture of the two, known as aqua regia. Other solvents for gold are chlorine water, alkaline cyanides, and mercury. Gold is extremely soft and generally used only in alloys, usually with silver or copper. The number of "carats" indicates the number of parts of pure gold in 24 parts of the alloy (9 carat gold is $^{9}/_{24}$ pure gold and $^{15}/_{24}$ copper).

Copper was being smelted by about 4000 BC, although it was probably found earlier than this in its native state. The campfire was probably the original smelting furnace—copper ore among the stones being reduced accidentally by wood charcoal in the fire to yield metallic copper. Today copper is a major commercial metal, produced at the rate of many thousands of millions of tons a year.

Copper is easily worked and readily alloyed [5]. Only silver is a better conductor of heat and electricity. Copper is also readily joined by brazing, soldering, or welding and is relatively resistant to corrosion. This combination of properties gives it widespread uses in electrical work or where heat is to be transferred quickly—as in radiators, heaters, coolers, or heat exchangers. Sometimes it is used in its pure state, at other times in one of its many alloys such as in brasses (with zinc), bronzes (with tin), and nickel silver (with zinc and nickel).

Silver is another legendary metal, and ornaments of silver have been dated to 4000 BC. It is thought to have been discovered first as the free metal, then in chlorides and later from its occurrence with lead in galena ores. Silver's main uses are industrial and are based on its resistance to corrosion. It is also used widely in the form of salts, for photographic emulsions, as well as for medals, decorative plate, and other commemorative products. Silver's excellent electrical properties determine many of its applications.

Lead, tin, and their alloys

Described by Shakespeare as "base" (compared with the "nobler" metals), lead [7] has a long history. Yet it is not found free in nature. It is thought to have been discov-

CONNECTIONS

See also
1594 The steel age
1598 Aluminum and its uses
1604 Working metals by hand
1606 Metalworking machines
1588 Fire and bronze
1592 The iron age

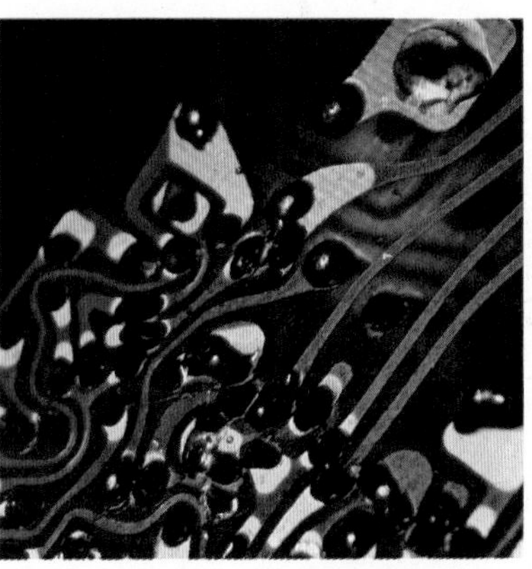

1 Gold has always been a symbol of material wealth and, because of its unique qualities, has been used to create art treasures of dazzling beauty, such as this medieval goblet [A]. Complete freedom from corrosion also makes gold technically valuable. To minimize contact resistance, the terminals of electrical sub-assemblies, such as a printed circuit board [B], may be thinly electroplated with gold.

2 Bronze is thought to have been the first metal alloy ever made, although it was probably produced originally by the accidental smelting of mixed ores of copper and tin. People in the Middle and Far East used it both for practical objects, such as mirrors, and for ornaments, such as this Egyptian cat, which is thought to have been sculpted and cast in bronze at least 4,000 years ago.

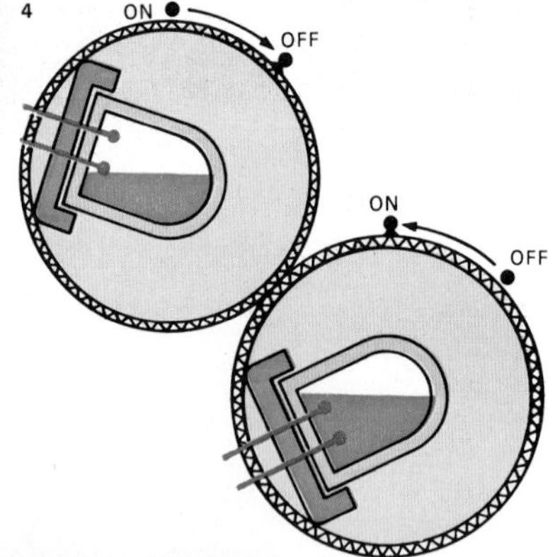

ON
OFF
ON
OFF

4 In a mercury switch a pool of mercury completes an electrical circuit. Terminals are fused into a glass bulb, which can be tilted. In the "on" position the mercury flows around the terminals: in the "off" position it flows away, breaking the connection.

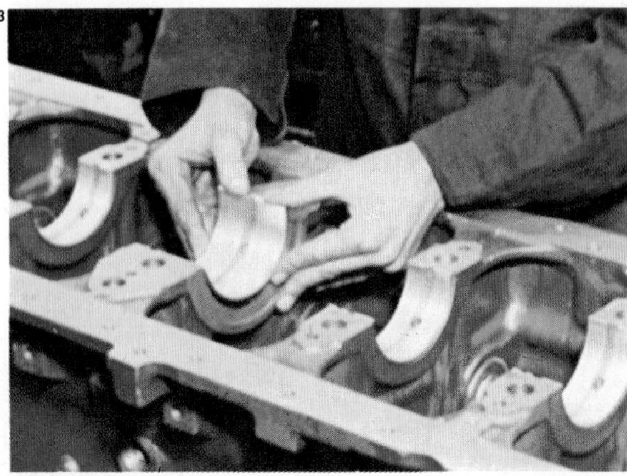

3 A new alloy of aluminum containing 20% tin was developed by tin researchers to improve the strength of white metal bearings and meet modern requirements for higher bearing loads. Here, an aluminum bearing is being fitted to a large diesel engine.

5 Alloys of copper find many uses in marine engineering. High-tensile brass, as used in ship propellers, is based on Muntz metal containing about 40% zinc. Other elements are often added to promote particular properties for various uses. To produce the range of high-tensile brasses employed today tin, aluminum, iron, and manganese are used; some of these are known as manganese bronzes, although technically they are classified as brasses.

ered by accidental smelting, much in the same way as copper. In this case, however, the ore was galena (lead sulfide). Tumblers of lead have been found in remains dating from 3500 BC. The Romans used lead extensively for water pipes, known in English as "plumbing"—*plumbum* being the Latin name for lead—and it was later used as a roofing material. Lead has a low melting point (620°F [327°C]), is easily cast, and makes a number of valuable alloys—with tin for solders, with antimony for electric storage batteries, and with several other metals for alloys for bearings and as sheathing for electric cables. An organic compound of lead is used in gasoline as an anti-knock additive. In recent years there have been increased efforts to prevent its discharge into the air.

In antiquity, tin was used with copper in the alloy bronze, but compositions were variable. Again, it is thought that the first discovery was caused by accidental smelting of mixed ores of copper and tin. Later the alloy was made deliberately from the component metals. Today its main use is as a coating on steel to make what is called tin plate. Tin protects steel from corrosion, allows soldering to be carried out quickly and easily, and is non-toxic.

The second largest use for tin is in solders and there are also extensive uses in modern bronzes, metals for bearings [3], and as a minor alloying additive to control the structure of cast iron. Organic compounds of tin have wide applications as chemical stabilizers and pesticides.

Mercury—the liquid metal

Mercury, the only metal that is liquid at ordinary temperatures, has long fascinated poets, who referred to it variously as "fluid silver" or later "quicksilver." It was probably known by about 500 BC and was prepared by treating cinnabar, its sulfide (also used directly as a red cosmetic), with vinegar, or simply by roasting it. The Romans used mercury to extract gold from ores. Today it is extensively used in scientific instruments—barometers, thermometers, micro-switches [4], and others—and as a compound for detonating explosives.

KEY

Coins are now used mainly for the lower values of money, but were once the only form of currency in international use. They need to be made of metal that is fairly strong, such as a copper-nickel alloy, resistant to corrosion and abrasion, and at the same time readily malleable for ease in stamping.

6 Nickel is a non-corrodable metal used with small amounts of alloying metals in vacuum tubes, such as this electronic tube, and in cathode ray tubes for television. But in most of its metallurgical uses it is alloyed—for example, to form a constituent of steels for high strength and low corrosion, notably with chromium in stainless steel. Nickel also has many chemical applications.

7 A lead tank made in the 1880s shows no sign of corrosion, demonstrating how well this metal resists attack by ordinary water. Roman architects made extensive use of lead in their elaborate systems of water distribution and public baths. Very soft water attacks lead and, since an accumulation of the metal in the body is poisonous, lead pipes are now rarely used to carry drinking water.

8 Chromium plating, here applied to car bumpers, improves durability as well as appearance. Chromium is a major alloying element in the making of stainless steels or other steels that need extra hardness and resistance to corrosion. Alloyed with nickel it is used for resistance wires for electrical heating elements in space heaters and industrial plants. But the most important use of chromium is as a hard layer plated onto the surface of steel or plastic components.

9 Uranium, which is chemical element number 92, has the highest atomic weight of any naturally occurring metal. Uranium or its compounds are used in atomic reactors or bombs because they are fissionable, with an atomic nucleus that breaks down when bombarded with neutrons, yielding further neutrons that can establish a chain reaction. Transuranic elements are also formed in reactor piles such as these and in bombs; they include the metal plutonium.

Aluminum and its uses

Before about 1890, few people outside the scientific community had heard of aluminum. Yet today this metal and its alloys are among the most versatile of those commonly used [Key]. They are particularly valued by the aerospace industry, which makes good use of their three principal properties: lightness, strength, and noncorrodibility. Aluminum's excellent electrical conductivity [8] also makes it important in high-voltage electrical conductors.

Location and extraction

Aluminum is the most abundant metallic element in the earth's crust. It is chemically reactive and so is never found naturally as a free element, but always in combination with other elements. It is a constituent of nearly all kinds of rock and its average concentration in the upper 10 miles (16km) of the Earth's crust is eight percent. Commercially it is extracted from a mineral called bauxite, a weathered aluminum oxide.

Aluminum was first isolated in 1825 by the Danish scientist Hans Christian Oersted (1777–1851). At the beginning of the century the British chemist Humphry Davy (1778–1829) had postulated the metal's existence but had been unable to isolate it. It was not until 15 years after Oersted's discovery that enough aluminum was produced to establish some of its properties—notably its low density. Napoleon III (1808–73) believed that such a lightweight metal could have an important future in military applications and provided money for the French chemist Henri Sainte-Claire Deville (1818–81) to develop a process for the large-scale production of aluminum.

Deville devised a process based on the chemical reduction of aluminum chloride using sodium metal, and aluminum was first displayed publicly at the Paris Exhibition of 1855. At this time it cost about $250 per kilogram, but by 1886 the price had dropped by $15 per kilogram and a total of 50 tons had been produced.

The production of aluminum

The future of aluminum was assured in 1886 when, at almost the same time, Charles Martin Hall (1863–1914) in the United States and Paul Héroult (1863–1914) in France devised the process for extracting aluminum by electrolysis that is still used today. They discovered that when pure alumina (aluminum oxide) is dissolved in a molten aluminum mineral called cryolite and an electric current passed through it, aluminum metal is liberated at one electrode (the cathode) and oxygen at the other (the anode). Within six years of this discovery, the price of aluminum had fallen to $1.30 per kilogram.

Large quantities of electricity are needed to produce aluminum (about 13–18 kwh/kg). For this reason the industry grew up in such places as Niagara Falls and Norway, where cheap supplies of hydroelectricity are available. But aluminum has become so important that most industrial countries have now established their own aluminum smelting industries.

Bauxite, generally obtained by strip mining, must be purified before it can be used for aluminum manufacture. To be acceptable, the bauxite must contain more than 32 per cent aluminum oxide, although

CONNECTIONS

See also
1716 Modern aircraft
1744 Modern military ai craft
1596 Metals and their us
1722 Space vehicles

1

1 Bauxite mine
2 Transport of bauxite to extraction process
3 Bauxite store
4 Grinding mill
5 Addition of lime and water to form a slurry
6 Addition of soda ash
7 Heating to dissolve alumina (but not impurities)
8 Settlement tank
9 "Red mud" of impurities
10 Filter
11 First settlement tank
12 Second settlement tank
13 Kiln in which hydrated alumina loses water
14 Cooler
15 Carbon-lined electrolysis cell
16 99·8% pure aluminum
17 Refining cell
18 99·99% pure aluminum

1 The main extraction process for aluminum makes use of electrolysis. Alumina (aluminum oxide), obtained from bauxite, is dissolved in molten cryolite and direct-current electricity is passed between carbon electrodes. Aluminum, 99.8 per cent pure, sinks to the bottom and can be further purified if need be.

2

2 The engine of the Wright brothers' *Flyer* was made largely from aluminum. It weighed only 180lb(82kg) but powered the first flight at Kitty Hawk, North Carolina, in December 1903.

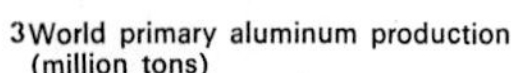
3World primary aluminum production (million tons)

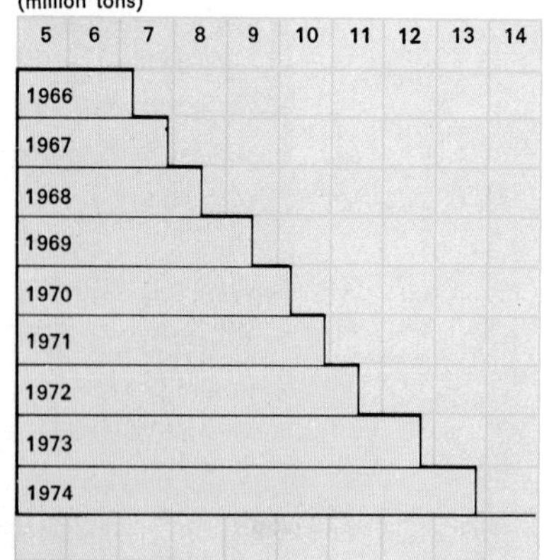
5
6
7
8
9
10
11
12
13
14
1966
1967
1968
1969
1970
1971
1972
1973
1974

3 Primary aluminum, extracted from ore and excluding that reclaimed from scrap, has been produced in steadily increasing quantities over the last few years. Production doubled between 1966 and 1974, although the price (at an all-time low of 31¢ per kg in the 1940s) slowly continues to rise as more and more uses are found for this versatile metal and its alloys. Recently, more effort has been made to reuse scrap aluminum.

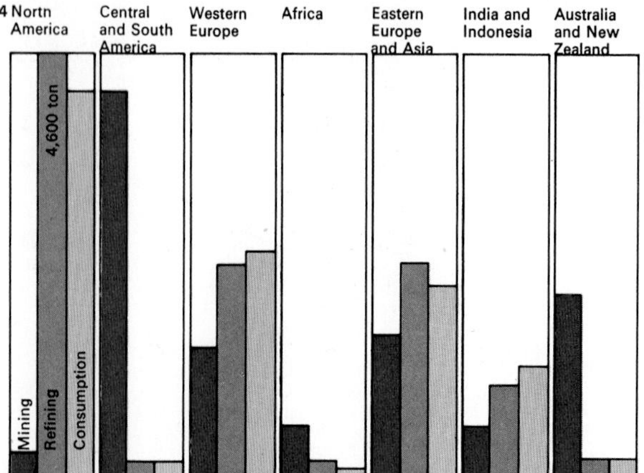
4 Nortn America
Central and South America
Western Europe
Africa
Eastern Europe and Asia
India and Indonesia
Australia and New Zealand
4,600 ton
Mining
Refining
Consumption

4 The world's largest user of aluminum, the United States, is not the greatest producer of the ore, bauxite, although more aluminum (66 percent of the total output) is refined in the US than anywhere in the world. The chief ore producers are Jamaica and Australia. This diagram shows where bauxite is mined and aluminum refined and used. It takes 4kg of bauxite to produce 1kg of aluminum. Current world production is 26,000 tons a day.

the level is usually as high as 45 to 55 per cent in bauxite used today. The Bayer process [1] is the most common purification method, during which the impurities form a "red mud," although this caused pollution problems for some countries. The red mud still contains some alumina, mixed with silica. Alcoa developed a process that can be used to extract this aluminum, or to obtain it from ores containing high proportions of silica.

There have been various attempts to develop alternative processes. In 1973 Alcoa announced a method based on the electrolysis of aluminum chloride, which uses 30 percent less power than the Hall-Héroult process. There has also been research into "carbothermic" processes, in which the oxide is reduced by heating it with carbon.

The multi-purpose metal

The first major application of aluminum was in the manufacture of cast cooking utensils in the 1890s. In the first decade of this century, usage included electrical conductors (first used for telephone lines in the Chicago stockyards in 1897), marine and aeronautical components, engineering and scientific instruments, paint pigments, and bottle caps.

During World War I, the German Alfred Wilm invented duralumin, an alloy of aluminum with small amounts of copper, magnesium, and manganese, which has physical properties similar to those of structural steel. This was the first of a large range of alloys that have greatly extended the use of the metal. In the United States in 1975 the major estimated uses were building and construction, transportation, electrical, and containers.

Modern uses of aluminum are many: metal window frames, coinage, saucepans and cooking foil, aircraft, bus and train components, catalysts for the petrochemicals industry, constituents of deodorants, giant storage tanks for liquid natural gas [11], soft drink and beer cans, aluminothermic smelting of high-melting metals such as chromium, and corrosion-resistant metal paints.

KEY

NASA

Aluminum and its alloys have myriad uses, from spacecraft to cooking foil. Many different elements may be added to aluminum to produce alloys with a remarkable range of properties and those properties may be further modified by heat treatment, aging, solution treatment with various chemicals, and mechanical working. Copper, magnesium, and zinc are alloyed with aluminum to produce strong metals. Silicon, manganese, chromium, and nickel are used in various combinations to make alloys for special components or to make the alloys suitable for casting, chemical treatment, and certain machining operations.

5 Time Strength A B C

5 The hardness of aluminum is increased by alloying and by heat treatment. When cooled rapidly from high temperatures [A], alloying element atoms are evenly dispersed. The alloy is strengthened by short-term heating, called aging. At lower aging temperatures [B] the alloying atoms cluster, making it hard. At higher temperatures the formation of intermetallic compounds [C] makes soft alloys.

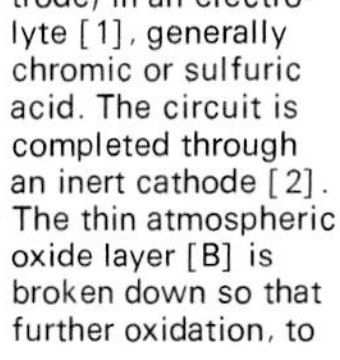

6 A thin film of oxide rapidly forms on aluminum on its exposure to air. Unlike rust on iron the oxide film is hard and non-porous, making aluminium corrosion resistant but difficult to weld.

7 Anodizing [A] is the name of the electrolytic process for deliberately forming a relatively thick film of oxide on aluminum and its alloys. The article to be anodized [3] is made the anode (positive electrode) in an electrolyte [1], generally chromic or sulfuric acid. The circuit is completed through an inert cathode [2]. The thin atmospheric oxide layer [B] is broken down so that further oxidation, to form a thicker layer [C], can take place. Anodized aluminum can be dyed various colors, including metallic ones to make it resemble, say, brass or copper. The oxide layer is then sealed [D]. Letters and symbols can be made photographically. The anodizing process does more than merely provide a decorative finish. It creates a tough surface that is considerably harder than the original base metal.

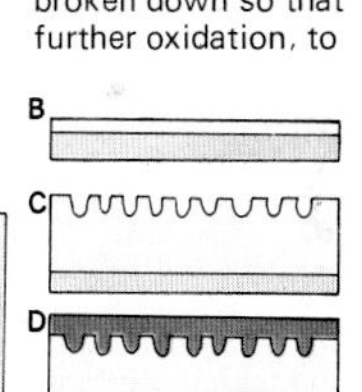
7A
B
C
D
1
2
3

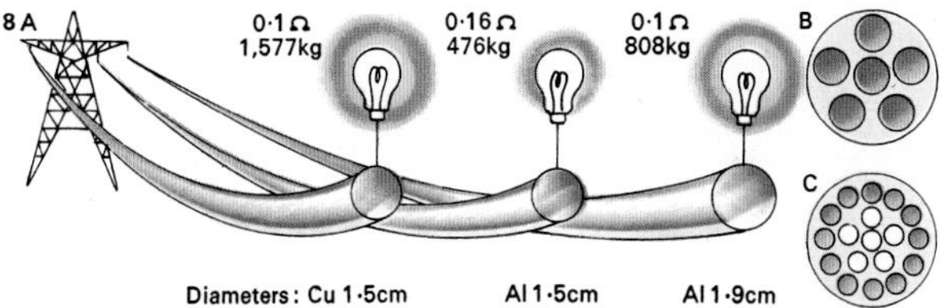
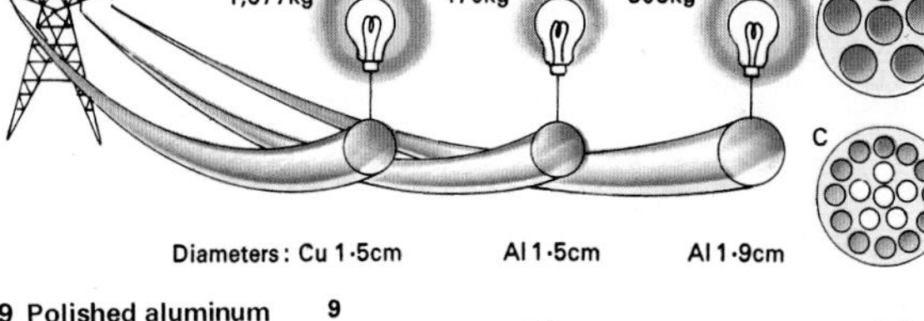
8A
0·1Ω
1,577kg
0·16Ω
476kg
0·1Ω
808kg
B
C
Diameters: Cu 1·5cm
Al 1·5cm
Al 1·9cm

8 The electrical conductivity of aluminum is only about 60% of that of copper but is lighter and cheaper. Here [A] weights and resistances are compared for cable—copper [B] and aluminum [C].

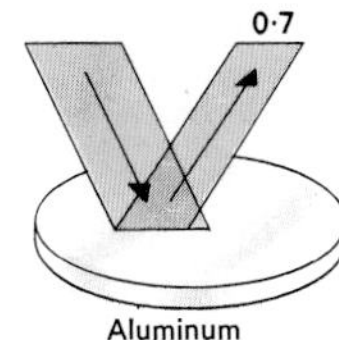
9
0·9
0·7
0·4
Silver
Aluminum
Iron

9 Polished aluminum reflects much more light than iron and nearly as much as silver, making it an ideal material for mirrors for telescopes and other optical instruments. The metal can also be used for making heat shields.

10

10 Alloying aluminum can rob it of some of its corrosion resistance. To overcome this drawback, thin sheets of pure aluminum can be pressure-welded to the surfaces of alloy sheets.

11 A large, spherical "tank" at a nuclear power station makes good use of many of aluminum's properties: the tank is light, can be polished to reflect heat, and is strong enough to withstand pressure.

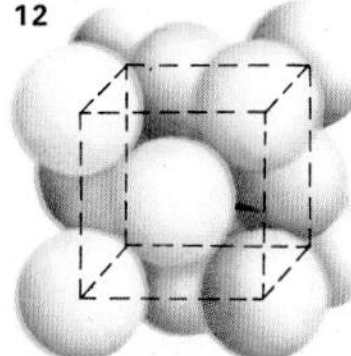

12 Aluminum is soft because its atoms form a close-packed, cubic structure. This has many glide planes to let the atoms easily slide over each other. It is malleable and easily drawn out into wires.

Tailor-made materials

The development of modern civilization has been closely connected with the increasing ability to master the environment and adapt parts of it for use. For centuries primitive peoples relied on the natural materials around them, such as stone and wood, to provide shelter and protection. Later they learned to modify these materials, producing such improvements as pottery, bricks and metals. But it has been only during the past century that the science of materials has enabled technologists to tailor materials to withstand extreme conditions.

The importance of alloys

Alloys (combinations of a metal with one or more other elements) have played an important role in human development for thousands of years—a role recognized by terms such as the Bronze Age.

Bronze is generally a mixture of copper and tin, with the two components varying widely in proportion. By contrast, many of today's alloys are made by precise mixtures of several main elements or of a single element, the properties of which are modified by the addition of carefully determined minute quantities of "impurities." From the now common stainless steels, made from iron mixed with small percentages of such elements as carbon, chromium, and nickel, the technology of materials has advanced through the nickel superalloys, which retain their strength even when white-hot, to titanium alloys [2], which are essential components of many jet engines as well as airframes.

Improvements since the 1950s

The molecular principles used in producing diamond substitutes (and improvements) such as boron nitride have spread throughout many industries since the 1950s. For instance, with attempts to achieve more speed or efficiency, the conditions under which machinery operates become more extreme and it has been necessary to develop not only new structural materials but also new lubricants. In many applications, conventional mineral oils have been replaced by especially tailored chemical lubricants. Some of these do more than merely operate effectively at high temperatures and pressures. Some sulfur-containing lubricants, for example, are good for "breaking in" new machinery. Even with modern machining techniques, surfaces are likely to be irregular and to produce "hot spots" during running, which explains why some new cars have to be "broken in" cautiously. The sulfur-containing lubricants react with hot spots, removing them as soft metal sulfide particles.

Another field in which "tailor-making" plays a crucial role is replacement-part surgery [7]. The silicone polymers have made an outstanding contribution in this area because there is no interaction between them and body fluids and tissues. A replacement part for a heart valve, for example, has to be resistant to the corrosive effects of the gallons of blood in which it will be bathed during its lifetime and the blood must not react abnormally or at all to the presence of material foreign to the body. In biomedical technology, the trend is now toward the development of materials similar to those evolved by nature. Thus scientists

CONNECTIONS

See also
1608 Working with ceramics
1618 Rubber and plastics
1620 Fibers for fabrics
1808 Soaps and detergents
1812 Color chemistry

1A

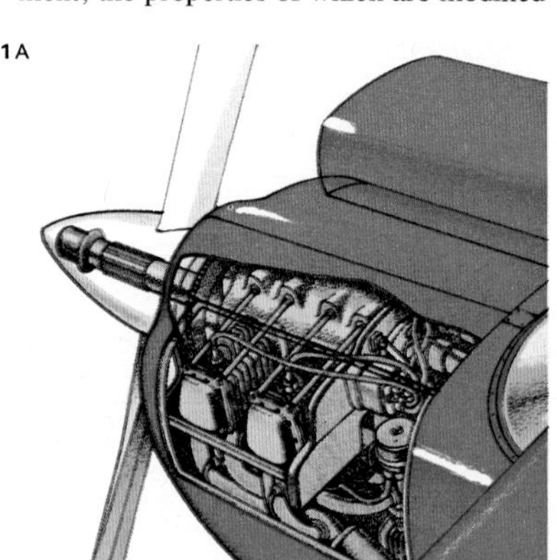

B

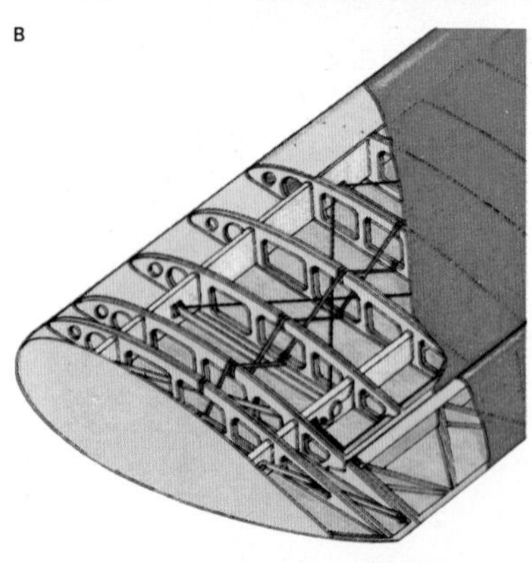

C

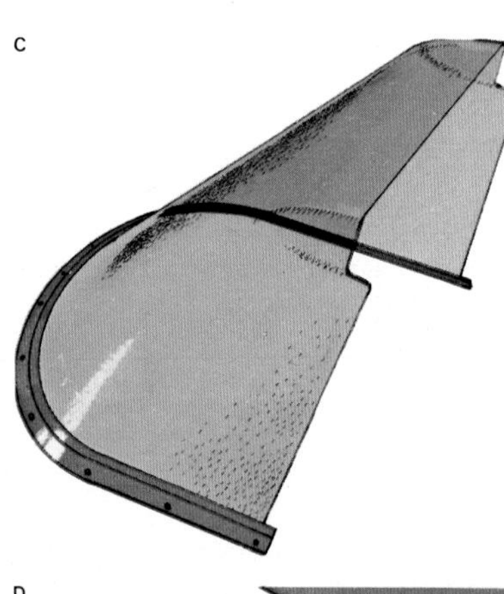

D

1 A light airplane such as this Bellanca Champion Scout would be impossible to make without a wide ranges of modern tailor-made materials. The propeller [A] is made from aluminum alloy and the wings [B] from aluminum ribs covered with the synthetic polymer Dacron, with glass-reinforced polyester wing tips. The Scout has a fuselage of molybdenum steel tubing, also covered with Dacron. The transparent material in the windows is Perspex, and synthetic rubber is used for the tires [D], which are supported on landing gear made from high-tensile strength steel.

2

2 The Lockheed YF 12A broke four major world records on May 1, 1965, and still holds the official air speed record of just over 2000 mph (3200 km/h). This airplane is built largely of titanium, a metal that was not available in commercial quantities until after World War II. Commercial titanium has the strength of steel but only half the weight, hence its advantage for use in aircraft. It is the ninth most plentiful element in the Earth's crust.

3

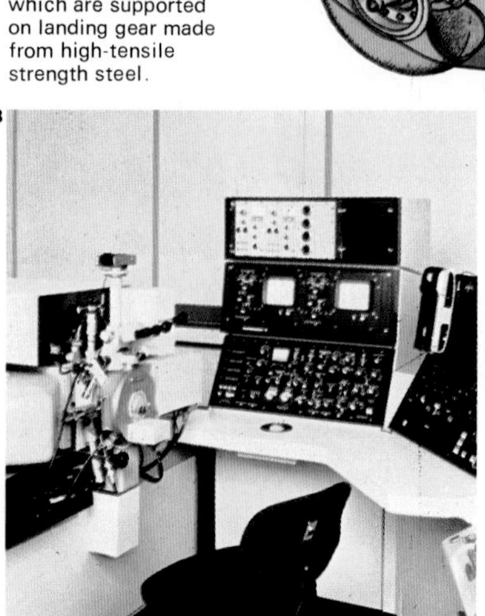

3 Development of new materials has been made possible by the increased range of scientific techniques available for studying the properties of different substances. This electron probe microanalyzer sends a carefully focused beam of electrons onto a selected portion of the materials being studied. From the X-rays being emitted as a result, it is possible to identify elements present in the sample and analyze for impurities on surfaces.

in different parts of the world are currently working on the development of bone substitutes that are chemically and physically similar to real bone.

In dealing with materials for biomedical use, high standards of purity are clearly necessary. The ability to produce ultra-pure materials has also been a major factor in the development of several other modern technologies—particularly solid-state electronics. Just as the properties of a metal can be altered by alloying it with some other element, so its properties may by altered by refining it from, say, 99 to 99.99 percent purity. Without techniques such as zone refining (in which impurities are concentrated at one end of a rod by melting it progressively along its length) it would have been nearly impossible in the 1950s to prepare materials pure enough to make workable semiconductors and transistors.

The formation of composites

Another important aspect of materials science is the way in which several materials can be combined together to form composites. Often two or three different materials may be blended together in a precisely controlled manner to produce a new material with properties different from any of the individual components. Thus plastics reinforced with glass fiber are now used widely in automobile bodies and boat hulls.

Not all attempts to "compose" new materials have been so successful. A few years ago it was predicted that composites would soon replace leather for making shoes. Synthetic shoe materials are now available, but some companies lost large sums of money on research that failed to produce materials as good as natural leather. Another case in which technology overreached itself occurred with the fan-blades for the Rolls-Royce RB2-11 turbine engine. In the original specification these were to be manufactured from a carbon-fiber reinforced composite [5]. Unfortunately this was not satisfactory in practice and more expensive, heavier titanium blades had to be used. Despite failures it seems likely that technologists will continue to tailor new materials.

KEY

P&H

Coins were once made from pure, rare metals such as gold and silver. For years now they have been made from a variety of common metal alloys, as shown in this stamping mill at a mint. Sophisticated alloys and nonmetallic, tailor-made materials play an ever increasing role in modern technology.

4

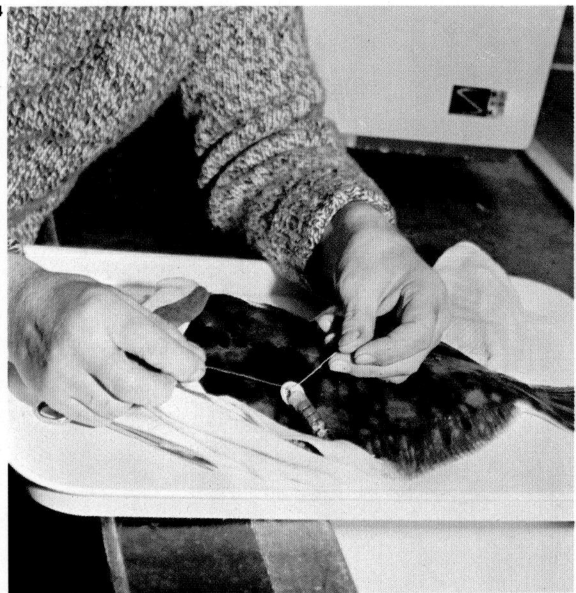

4 The miniaturization of electronic circuitry that followed the development of semiconductor materials has produced unexpected "spin-offs." For example, animals such as this flounder can now be fitted with small radio transmitters so that their migration patterns can be studied.

5

5 Carbon fibers, long whiskers of pure carbon produced under carefully controlled conditions, were heralded as the miracle material of the 1960s. It was believed that they could be used to reinforce plastics to make them as strong as metals, but they require more development for certain applications.

6

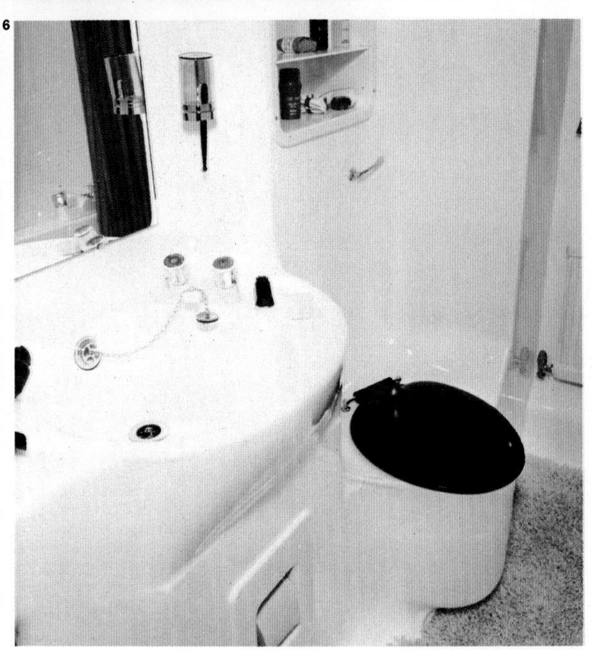

6 New materials enter into all areas of daily life, from the transistor radio to the instant bathroom. With the increasing cost of traditional building materials, and, in many countries, a shortage of skilled labor, the building or renovating of houses is becoming more difficult and more expensive. With modern technology it is possible to mold an entire bathroom in plastics. It can then be lowered into place in a house where the walls are constructed of traditional materials that will provide the basic structural strength. After a few plumbing connections have been made the bathroom is ready to be used. Such molded bathrooms are easy to maintain.

7

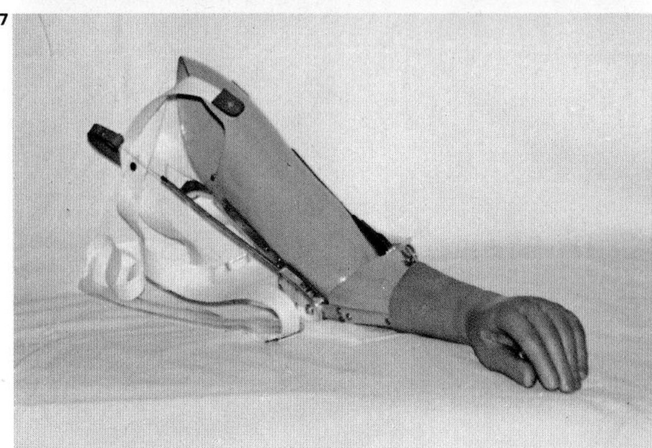

7 The most complex materials on earth are possibly those present in living tissue such as skin, bone, muscle, and cartilage. To devise new synthetic materials to replace worn out or damaged parts of the human body is one of the greatest challenges facing materials scientists and technologists today. For internal use, rugged materials are required that will withstand the corrosive environment and yet produce no undesirable side effects, such as inflammation. For external use, as in this prosthetic hand, the ideal is a combination of materials that not only will give the right appearance in terms of color and texture, but also will provide the power and diversity of action of the natural limb.

Hand tools

Hand tools are "powered" by the muscles of the user. Craftsmen in almost every trade use a profusion of many kinds of tools. Modern materials and manufacturing methods have led to the development of new hand tools such as a tool that combines some of the functions of a plane and a file. But traditional forms can usually be recognized immediately in the modern version. In addition, today's consumer society has led to the development of special tools for the amateur—gardening tools are a good example [2]. Almost all craftsmen's tools have evolved from a limited number of standard types and may be grouped according to their principal functions; hammering; cutting; splitting and shaping; piercing and boring; measuring and marking; grasping and holding; sharpening; and screw-based.

Hammering, cutting, and piercing

The most familiar kind of hammer is the carpenter's claw-hammer, whose primary function is to drive nails into wood and, when necessary, pull them out. But there are many other kinds of hammering tools [1, 9] including mallets, sledgehammers, and pestles. Blacksmiths, boilermakers, bricklayers, prospectors, woodcarvers [4], stonemasons, jewelers, and sculptors use a great variety of hammers. They vary in weight from a sledgehammer, almost too heavy to lift, to the jeweler's delicate instrument for embossing precious metals. Each type has its own special form for a particular function. The head of the tool may be hard enough to forge iron or soft enough to avoid damaging the wooden handle of another tool. One of the most important parts of the hammer is the handle, which must be carefully balanced for convenience and maximum efficiency in use.

Cutting, splitting, and shaping tools may be classified according to the number of cutting edges they possess. Single-edged tools are probably the most numerous, and include razors, chisels, gouges, edging-tools, and axes. Even an ax, which is generally regarded as an instrument for cutting down trees, and its smaller relation the hatchet, are available in many special forms. Knives and swords are made in endless variety from the saber to the surgeon's scalpel. The carpenter's plane is an example of a specialized form of knife that is used for smoothing. Another is the bricklayer's trowel, used for applying mortar.

Knives may have two edges, although each can function independently. The action of scissors and shears depends on two edges working in opposition. A file or saw has many cutting edges; it may have small teeth for cutting hard materials or coarser teeth for relatively soft ones. Saws also vary in the "set" of the teeth—that is, by the amount each is slightly bent to the left or right away from the saw blade. In the carver's rasp the cutting edges are reduced almost to points and scattered at random on the surface. And there are a vast number of cutting points on sandpaper.

Cutting tools can be sharpened on artificial materials such as carborundum, but often natural stone is used. A rotary stone can be used for sharpening flat chisels, but hand finishing is generally necessary. For curved-edge tools the stones must be chosen to match the required shape.

CONNECTIONS

See also
1604 Working metals by hand
1582 Early technology
1652 Levers and wedges
1654 Pulleys and gears
1704 Technology and transportation in developing nations

1

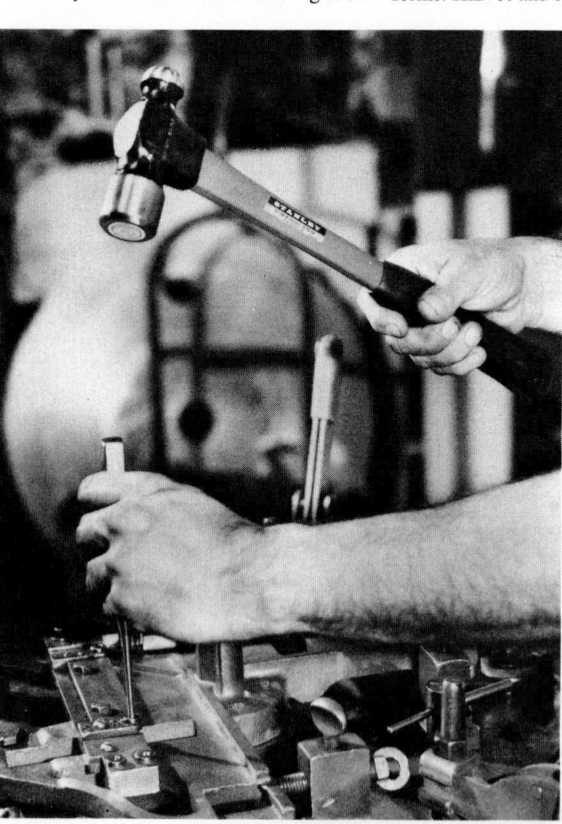

1 Hammers are probably the oldest tools of man. At the end of the Paleolithic Era hammers had acquired handles. Today there are three basic types of hammers. Woodworking hammers have a claw for pulling nails and prying boards apart. Metalworking hammers, such as the ball-peen shown here, have one regular face and one special face for particular tasks. Mallets have big-faced heads.

2

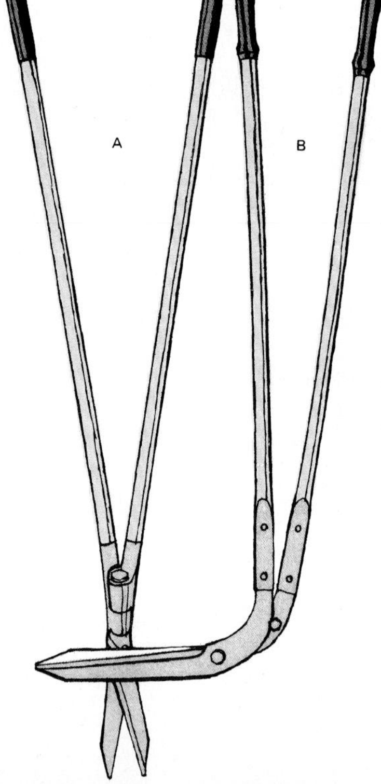
A
B

2 Cutting tools are a valuable aid to the gardener as well as to the carpenter. Garden shears operate on the scissors principle of two cutting edges working in opposition to each other. Lawn shears [A] are employed to cut the grass in awkward corners that would be inaccessible to a lawnmower. Edging shears [B] are shaped differently for neatly trimming the grass on the edges of lawns on raised beds.

4

4 Grinling Gibbons (1648–1721) was a complete master with woodcarving tools. His delicate designs ranged over a diversity of subjects including fruits, flowers, and shellfish. They can be seen today in a number of historic English homes and in churches and cathedrals, including Petworth House in West Sussex, Canterbury Cathedral, and the chapel at Windsor Castle. This ornamentation is from the interior of Trinity College, Oxford.

3

3 Woodworking tools have changed little over the centuries. This detail from the painting "Christ in the Carpenter's Shop" by the English Pre-Raphaelite artist John Millais (1829–96) shows a plane, pliers, and a bow saw in which the blade is held under tension by a twisted cord across the top of the "bow." Other tools can be seen in the rack on the wall, including chisels, drills, and a gimlet for boring; there is a bench vise in the foreground.

Making holes in hard materials calls for special tools such as drills [8]. Drills are generally made of hardened steel that is carefully shaped to deal with the material to be cut and the cutting speed. A drill can be held in a three-jaw chuck turned by a brace. A drill for boring timber is called a bit and is held in the two-jaw chuck of a carpenter's brace. Electrically powered drills are also in common use today.

Measuring and marking instruments

Science has devised instruments of remarkable precision for a wide variety of measurements, but many of those in everyday use are straightforward derivatives of prototypes used hundreds of years ago. A vertical is defined by a plumbline—a thin cord with a weight at one end. The horizontal is usually established with a spirit level, a transparent tube containing alcohol or other liquid with a bubble of air sealed into it. Compasses and dividers are used to draw circles and arcs; calipers are used to mark or measure distances and the micrometer is used to measure small diameters accurately. For making larger measurements a flexible steel rule is more convenient. A try square is used for marking and checking right angles.

Grippers and screw-based tools

Pliers, tongs, and tweezers are grasping instruments that handle objects more conveniently and more securely than the hand that manipulates them. They range from blacksmith's tongs for holding glowing hot iron bars to surgical forceps [7]. Workbenches and vises are commonly used by carpenters and metalworkers. The material that forms the face of a vise varies from hard steel to felt, according to the delicacy of the piece being worked on and the force applied. There are also other forms of clamps, including G-clamps.

Wood-screws and nuts and bolts are made in various shapes and sizes and of various materials, including plastics. Screwdrivers and wrenches [6] must fit their particular job. A tool that is too heavy may cause damage; too fine a tool will be ineffective and may itself be damaged.

KEY

Hand tools have been developed for a wide range of specialized jobs. The human hand is a versatile instrument, but unaided it has its limitations where power or precision are required. The tool used so skilfully by the engraver, is, for all practical purposes, merely an extension of his hand.

5

5 Cobblers' awls, seen in the bench rack, are typical piercing tools.

6

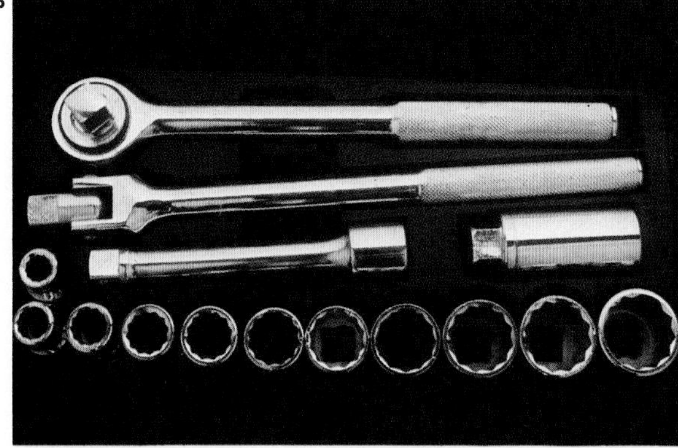

6 A set of socket wrenches provides a range of sizes with a single handle, so making the set very compact. By means of a torque wrench they can be used to tighten nuts to a precise tension.

7

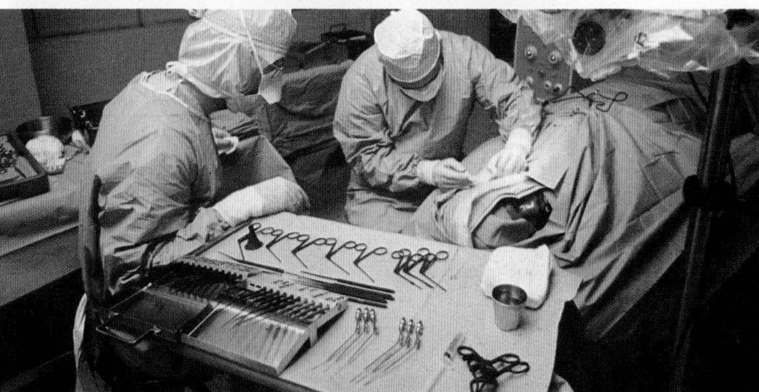

7 A modern operating room is equipped with a wide range of precision instruments made from durable, stainless materials. The surgeon's forceps are a kind of specialized gripping tool.

8

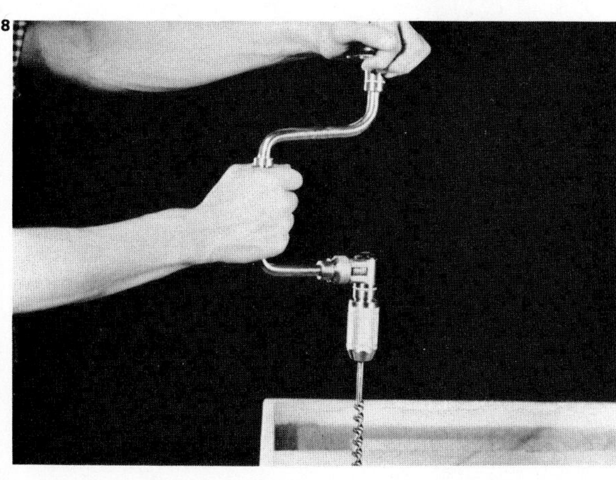

8 Drilling with a bit and brace dates from the Middle Ages. It was the first drill to provide a continuous unidirectional rotation. It is made of metal and usually has an adjustable chuck, which holds the bit.

9

9 A woodcarver uses a set of chisels and curved gouges with a wooden mallet to cut intricate designs or make sculptures in wood. The tools need to be extremely sharp; even big cuts are made using a series of carefully controlled small blows.

Working metals by hand

Most metals conduct heat and electricity well and many common metals can be mixed together to form alloys—substances with properties different from those of the parent metals but more useful in particular applications. Primitive people were not aware of many properties of metals, yet they appreciated their toughness and durability, their hardness and their ability to be worked into almost any desired shape. They also found that some metals retain an untarnishable luster. Because of this, and because of their attractive appearance and rarity, these metals were used for money and personal adornment and became known as "precious."

Early steps in metallurgy

Civilized people of 6,000 years ago had learned to work with gold, copper, silver, and probably tin. The earliest metallurgy stemmed from the discovery of native metals (which occured naturally in their metallic state) but gradually people learned how to extract metals from minerals—metallic compounds—by heating them in a furnace, usually in the presence of charcoal. By about AD 1400 water-driven bellows could make a furnace so hot that even iron could be smelted.

Once metal could be melted it could be cast by pouring it as a white-hot liquid into a mold and leaving it to cool. Gradually metal workers learned how to make more complicated molds, designed to open so that the cast object could be extracted. But long before smelting, the most important early method of shaping metals was forging. The metal is not melted, but merely softened by being heated to a bright orange; then it is shaped by blows from a hammer. The smith [1] developed the anvil and an increasing range of shaped tools for hammering against hot metal [Key]. He learned to know the quality of metal by eye, to judge its exact temperature and to shape it accurately before it cooled.

Over the centuries a host of familiar objects gradually matured, differing from one region or country to another but each serving its purpose. Knives, ploughshares, horseshoes, door hinges, clasps, roasting spits, fire-irons, and spurs were typical everyday objects made with no prior drawing or measurement but simply by skill and experience. The art of the jeweler also relied wholly on the craftsman's experience [5] and on the manual dexterity needed to fashion objects that were both valuable and delicate.

It was in the making of jewelry that workers first used the technique of soldering [7], in which a special alloy with a low melting point is used to join other metal parts. It was also in jewelry that metals were first beaten out into thin wires, although during the Renaissance a way was found to "draw" wire by pulling it through a small opening.

Drawing and welding

The ability to be drawn is a characteristic of metals, stemming from their tensile strength and ductility (ability to change shape without breaking). Because the earliest metals were all farily soft, unless especially treated such as sword edges, they could be cut and pierced readily. This had to be done

CONNECTIONS

See also

1602 Hand tools
1606 Metalworking machines
1704 Technology and trar portation in develop ing nations

1
2
3
4
5
9
8
10
6
7
14
13
11
12

1 The smithy is centered around the open-hearth forge, where the temperature is kept high with bellows [1]. Anvils are pierced with a tool hole (hardie hole) [2] and punch hole [3], the heavy body [4] resting on an elm block [5]. The anvil face [6] terminates in the beak [7]. A rake [8] lies near a tool rail [9]; a water trough [10] is used for quenching hot work. The smith [11] carefully positions work for the striker [12]. A floor mandrel [13] holds additional tools near the hearth [14]. Blacksmiths not only shod horses but made every kind of locally needed metal artifact for agriculture, engineering, and for the home.

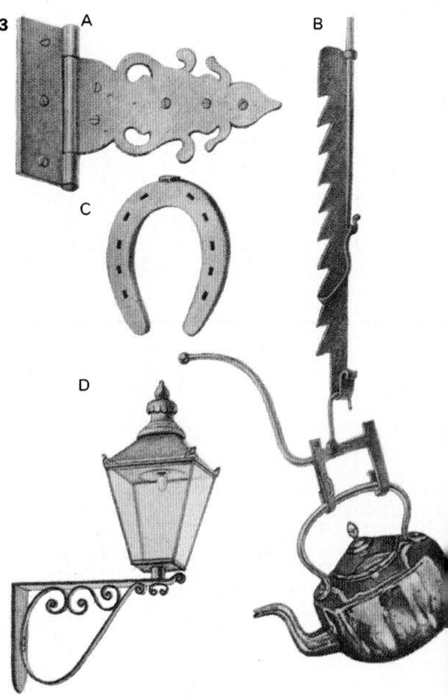

A
B
C
D

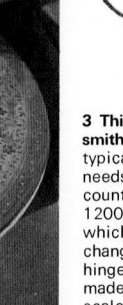

2 In India, delicate metalworking for decorative purposes reached a standard 1,000 years ago that has never been surpassed. Methods were devised for chasing and engraving soft metals, filling in the cavities with enamel, and even for inlaying one metal into a base of another metal of contrasting color. Two of the best metals for decorative work are gold and brass, because they are highly malleable and can be deformed cold without splitting. This brass engraver in Jaipur (Rajasthan) is making a tray that will probably be sold in the West for hanging on a wall. In many countries such handwork would not be economically feasible.

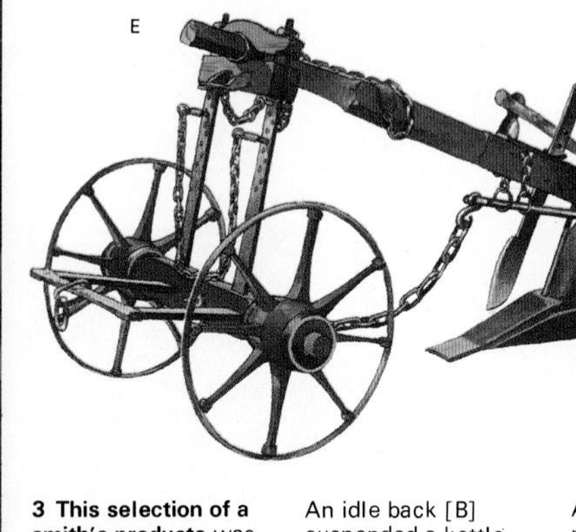

E

3 This selection of a smith's products was typical of customer needs in Western countries in 1200–1850, during which period designs changed slowly. Door hinges [A] could be made on a small scale in brass for a decorative casket. An idle back [B] suspended a kettle over the hearth and could be tipped to pour the boiling water safely. A horseshoe [C] was an item made by the millions in distinct family designs that often reveal the place and time of manufacture. A lamp [D] could be pinned or screwed to a house wall and was an item on which the smith could demonstrate his skill with fine wrought ironwork. The 17th-century Kentish plough [E] is wooden but incorporates iron components.

with large items while they were hot, but small objects could be shaped cold. The most delicate work of all was the beautiful technique of inlaying patterns of one metal into recesses in another metal of contrasting color. Sometimes the inlaid pieces were secured by hammering the edges of the recesses. But in other cases soldering or brazing was employed, the latter using a brass (an alloy of copper and zinc), which was melted and run into the joints.

By 1800 the technique of welding metals using a hot gas flame was being developed and by the end of the century it had reached a high degree of perfection and had been supplemented by welding with an electric arc. Welding, in which some of the metal is melted, exerts a profound effect on the metal's properties and much patient research was needed to find the best methods while simultaneously avoiding distortion caused by the severe heating.

The value of hand tools

In many places and communities men and women work with metals to make or repair objects that are useful or beautiful, or both. Using hand tools with the manual skill and judgment born of experience, craftsmen often provide the most efficient solution to many metal-working problems, especially where the objects are made to order.

The same is true in countless jobs in which metalworking plays a part, such as building construction, plumbing, farming, automobile bodybuilding and repair, and in do-it-yourself handyman tasks about the home. A special part is played by artists who work with metal, either in creating jewelry or in the larger forms grouped under the heading of sculpture [4].

Most of these tasks involve some form of joining, such as welding or soldering, and a few require a forge. All use hand tools such as shears, hacksaws, and files to cut, shape, and trim metal while cold. In nearly every case the exact dimensions are unimportant, provided that mating parts fit precisely. In modern manufacturing, however, the aims are entirely different. Mass production calls for metalworking machines instead of craftsmen.

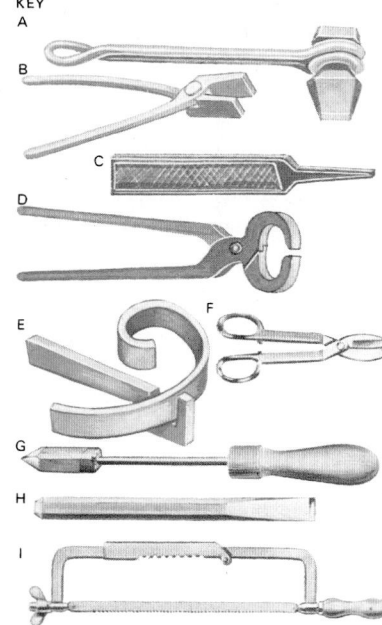

KEY
A
B
C
D
E
F
G
H
I

Tools for metal handwork have changed little over the centuries. Cutting tools have either a single chopping blade (like a chisel), two shearing blades (like scissors), or many blades (as in a saw or file). Other tools were devised for gripping the hot metal while a workman bent or cut it. Blacksmith's tools shown here include a hot set [A] for cutting iron softened to red heat, plain tongs [B], horse rasp [C], hoof clippers [D], and a scrolling dog [E] for bending wrought iron. Also shown are tin snips [F] for cutting thin sheets, soldering iron [G], a cold chisel [H] which is used on cold metals as opposed to hot metals, and a hacksaw [I].

4

5 Jewelers fashion delicate designs in gold and silver by brazing previously shaped pieces together. A propane torch provides a fine needle flame; the delicate parts must be held with tweezers. Because precious metals are used, the jeweler must be careful to collect even the smallest pieces of waste material. Larger ornamental pieces, such as silver cups and bowls, are fashioned from a flat sheet that is beaten with a roundheaded mallet on a leather cushion until the required shape gradually emerges. Final shaping may be done on a series of anvils especially designed for this purpose.

5

4 Modern sculptors use oxy-acetylene welding gear to cut, join, and shape metals. If it is made hot enough, the molten metal flows and the artist can control the effect to create new textures not obtainable in any other way. Such techniques also allow a sculptor to employ a wide range of materials. At one time, most metal sculptures were made by casting, using metals such as bronze. Today a sculptor can work with such high melting point metals as stainless steel. Like all welders he must wear dark goggles to protect his eyes from the glare and flying sparks.

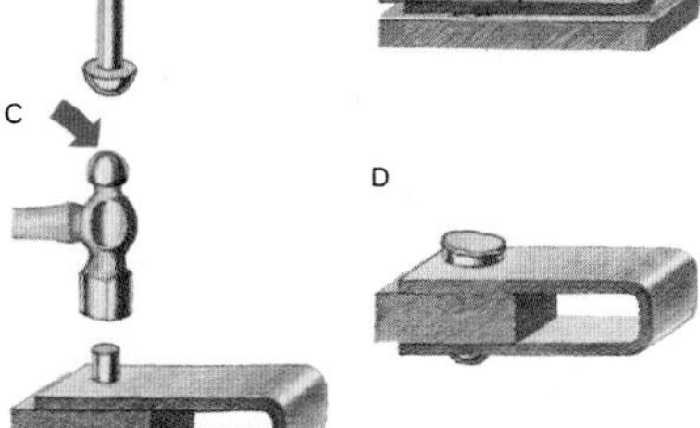

6 A
B
C
D

6 Riveting is a method of joining metals without melting them. A hole is drilled through the parts to be joined [A] and a hot rivet passed through it [B]. The end of the rivet is beaten with a ball-peen hammer [C] until it flattens over, making a tight joint [D]. Large structures such as girders and plating on ships' hulls can also be joined using rivets and mechanical hammers.

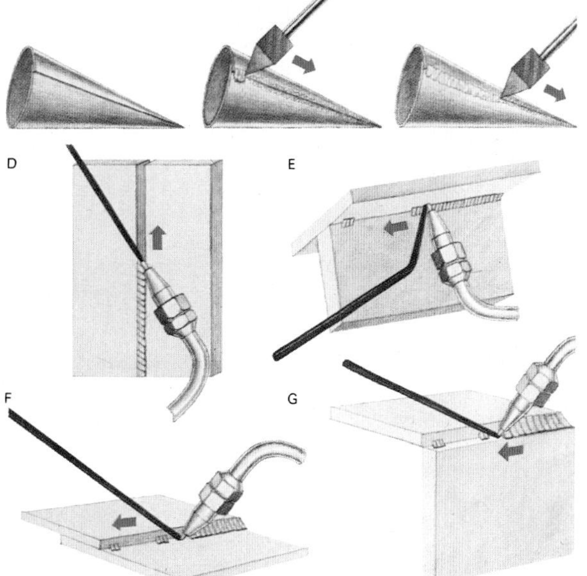

7 A
B
C
D
E
F
G

7 Soldering can be used for joining sheet metal, particularly copper and brass. In making this seam, the metal is first bent into shape [A]. The metal is treated with a flux (to clean the edges to be joined) and the two edges "tinned" with a thin film of solder [B]. Finally a hot soldering iron is passed along the joint to fuse the two tinned edges together [C]. There are various ways of joining sheet metal by welding. Butt welds can be used to join two plates in line [D] or at right-angles to each other [E]. A lap joint [F] is welded on each side and a corner joint [G] has a fillet of weld run along each seam.

Metalworking machines

Ever since Hiram of Tyre made the pillars of Solomon's temple in metal, men have continued to work metals into a required shape mainly by casting and forging. In casting, molten metal is poured into a mold; in forging, the metal—hot or cold—is beaten into shape with a hammer. These are still the two basic processes for working with metals.

Casting and forging can be used to produce articles in which accuracy is not of prime importance. But when accuracy in a product is essential, then foundries supply metal in stock forms such as ingots, castings, sheet, bar, and tube for subsequent machining to the required shapes.

Casting and forging

Traditional sand casting [1], such as a sculptor might use, has to be employed for bulky or irregular shapes, especially in iron and steel. Huge solid masses, such as a propeller for a giant tanker, could hardly be made in any other way. Even so, the finished casting needs to be machined or ground to the exact profile and smoothness.

Some small metal parts can be made by the repetitive process of die casting [2]. There are also special items, such as turbine blades for jet engines, which have to be made of metals that stay very strong even when extremely hot and casting is often the only economic way of making them.

For many other items of all sizes, forging can be the answer. The modern equivalent of the blacksmith's hammer is the giant hydraulic press [Key]. Used for large masses of metal, it squeezes white-hot billets under a force of perhaps 50,000 tons. For small products die forging is used. The soft, hot "blank" is banged into shape between two precisely shaped dies that come together in perfect register.

A variation of forging is hot rolling. An ingot or "bloom" is passed, glowing with heat, between pairs of shaped rollers like a giant mangle. It may make dozens of passes, sometimes being reheated, as it grows longer and thinner. Eventually it will become an exact strip, an angle-section bar, a structural girder, a railroad rail or, in a modern plant, a seamless length of tube.

Using machine tools

Machine tools work with much greater power than a craftsman can exert with his hands. They therefore fashion metal parts faster and at a lower cost. But far more important is the fact that they exert rigid control over the workpiece and are cutting or shaping it all the time. They can go on making the desired number of parts, each identical to the last, so that the machine-made parts are interchangeable. Each conforms exactly to an original drawing showing precise shapes, dimensions, and tolerances. The tolerances indicate by how much a dimension can be slightly larger or smaller than the desired value, and are measured in micrometers or thousandths of an inch. A craftsman would be hard-pressed to maintain such accuracy and output would be very low.

Machining a metal involves cutting it with a machine tool such as a milling machine (miller), planer, router, or lathe. Millers [4] hold the work still while rotating cutters pass over it. Planers draw large items past a fixed cutter, whereas a router

CONNECTIONS

See also
1584 Modern technology
1594 The steel age
1596 Metals and their uses
1598 Aluminum and its uses
1604 Working metals by hand

1 Sand casting is the most widely used casting method. A wooden pattern is made up from the original design, then packed with sand up to its largest cross sectional area in a steel box [A]. The top part of the mold is assembled. It is clamped on to the bottom box and more sand is rammed into it. A wooden runner and riser are fixed in position [B]. The sand core for a hollow in the casting is made. The sand is mixed with sodium silicate, which forms "silica gel" when carbon dioxide is pumped through it. This "gel" has a syrupy consistency and binds the sand together. The mold is split and the pattern removed. The core is placed in position and the mold assembled [C]. Runner and riser are removed. Molten metal is poured into the dried mold through the conical-shaped runner. Displaced air escapes through the riser [D]. After cooling, the mold is split open and the casting removed [E]. The runner and riser are cut off and the sand core is knocked out. The finished casting [F] shows the hollow produced by the core.

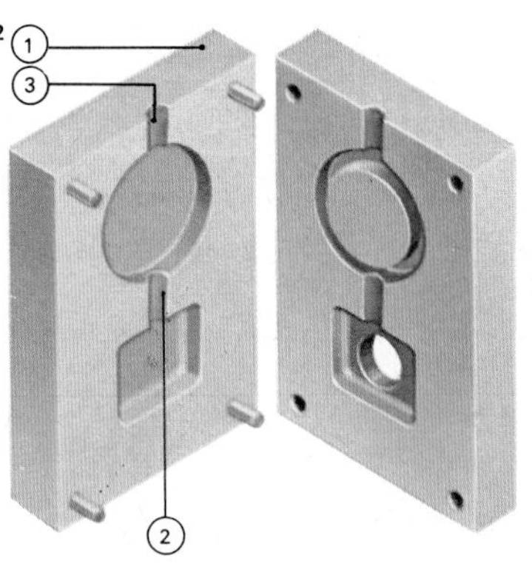

2
1
3
4
2

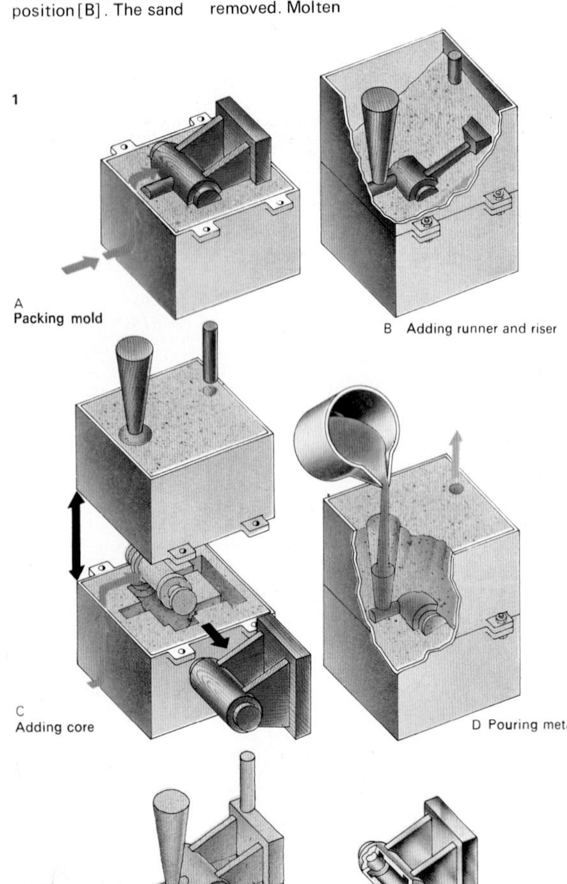

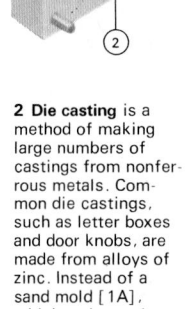

1
A
Packing mold
B Adding runner and riser
C
Adding core
D Pouring metal
E
Rough casting
F Finished casting

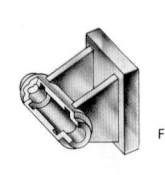

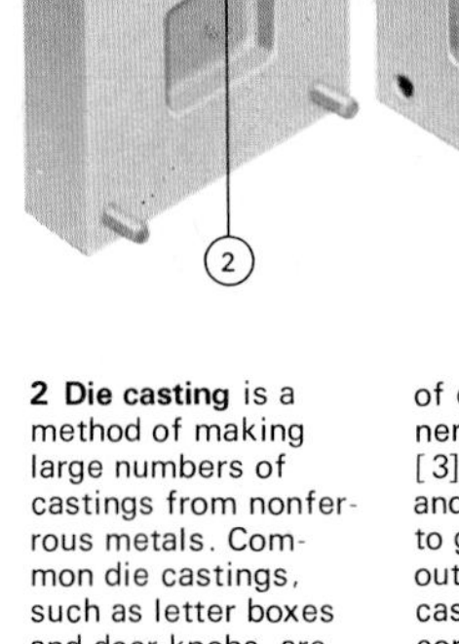

2 Die casting is a method of making large numbers of castings from nonferrous metals. Common die castings, such as letter boxes and door knobs, are made from alloys of zinc. Instead of a sand mold [1A], which makes only one casting, a die or permanent mold [1] is used. This is made of cast iron with runners [2] and risers [3] like a sand mold, and it can be opened to get the casting out. For a hollow casting, the metal cores are either part of the die or retractable to release the casting. The metal may be cast by either of two methods, gravity or pressure from a plunger [4].

3 Press tools, which consist of a die [1] and a counter [2] are made of hard steel [A]. A piece of sheet metal [3] is put between the two and the press closes on it [B]. This method is used for forming sheet metal into various shapes, including simple bends and complex curves. The various sections of body panels of an automobile [C], for example, are generally pressings. Sharp curves may require several successive pressings, each with a tighter curve than the one before, on different machines. The different press operations such as blanking (cutting a piece to the right shape in the flat) or piercing (making holes in it) may be done on different presses or some may be combined, depending on the size and thickness of the material.

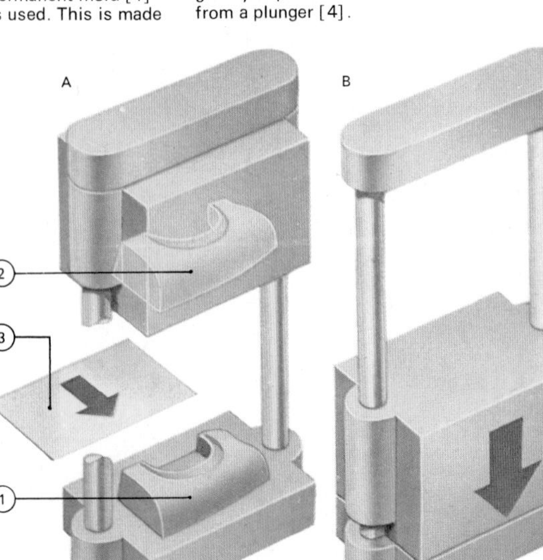

3
A
B
2
3
1

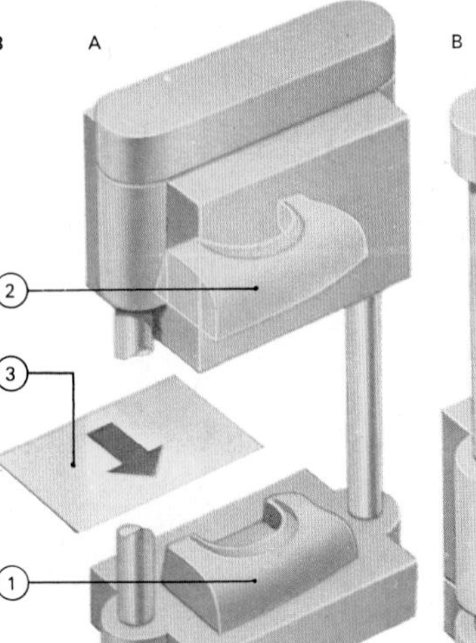

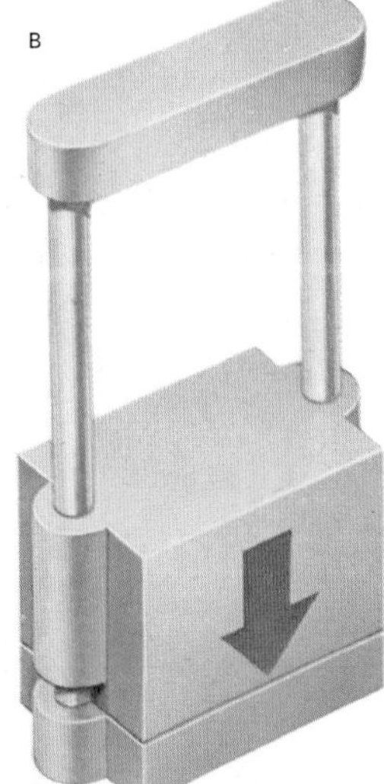

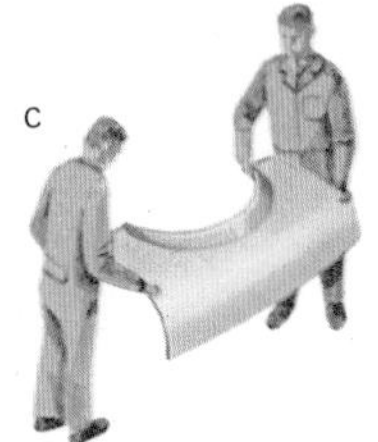

C

resembles a drill that mills the surface instead of boring holes. Grinders [5] use another method of machining, but instead of having cutting tools of very hard metal (or sometimes even diamond) they use wheels with surfaces made up of millions of hard fragments, each of which takes a small cut. Turret lathes [6] rotate the workpiece while tools are arranged in various positions to cut it.

Advances in metalworking

Since 1950 many completely new ways of working with metal have been brought from the research laboratory to the production plant. The aircraft industry pioneered chemical milling, in which sheets of any size are etched away in baths of acid or other corrosive chemicals. Portions of sheet can be protected by a surface mask that prevents them from being attacked. The rest can be eaten away in a controlled way, with no scratches or machining marks on the surface. This is important because even the smallest scratch or imperfection can induce metal fatigue.

Electrochemical machining (ECM) [8] is a variation in which the liquid bath is not corrosive but an electrolyte (carrier of electric current). The workpiece is connected in an electric circuit and then eaten away by a shaped electrode, rather like electroplating in reverse. Another electrical method is spark erosion [8], in which even the hardest parts are gradually shaped by millions of sparks. Yet another, and totally different, electrical method is electromagnetic forming, when massive currents are suddenly switched through magnetic coils that slam the workpiece against shaped dies.

In contrast there are other new methods of extreme delicacy used for shaping on a microscopic scale. Ultrasonic machining [8] is a form of grinding, useful for extremely hard material or non-metals that must be finely shaped. Electron-beam machining uses a concentrated beam of electrons to melt away parts not wanted. Laser machining [8] does the same with an intense beam of light. Such methods can be used to shape electronic circuits that would easily fit on a pin's head.

KEY

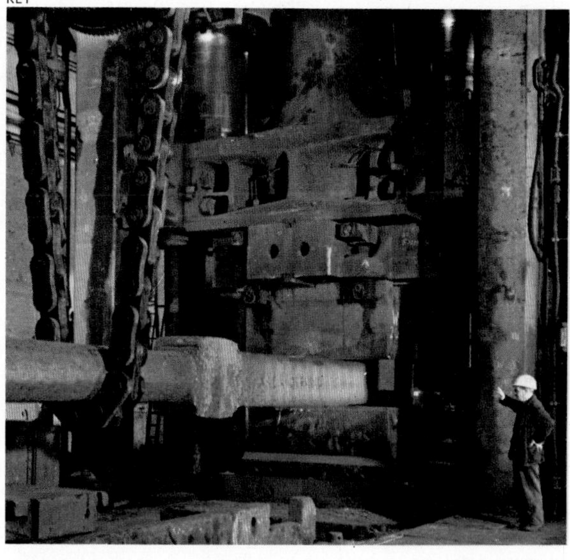

In forging, ingots or billets of metal are heated red hot and stamped roughly to shape in powerful hydraulic presses.

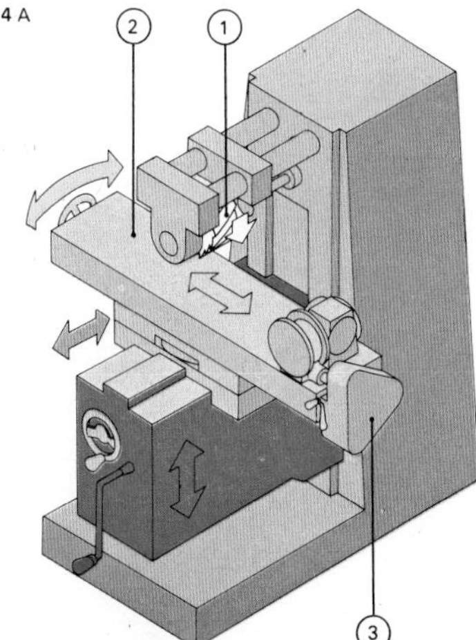

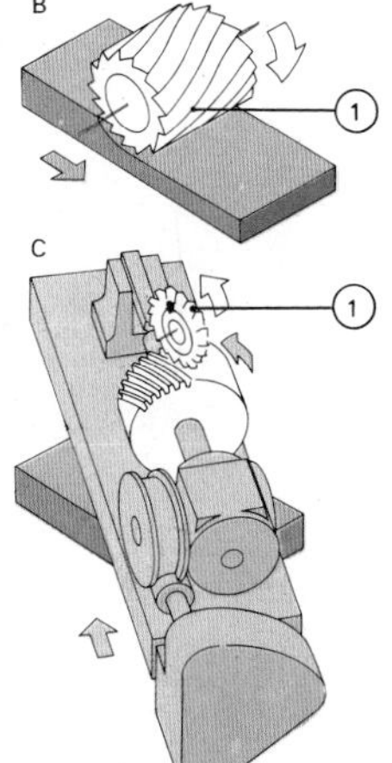

4 Milling machines cut metal with a rotary cutter [1]. The universal mill [A] has a table that can be moved in all 3 planes [2]. A workpiece is clamped to the table or to the dividing head. Gears [3] allow the workpiece to be rotated during or between strokes. As well as milling surfaces and grooves, the machine can plane a flat workpiece [B]. A cutter can be angled to mill threads. [C] shows the dividing head being used to make a helical cut on a workpiece.

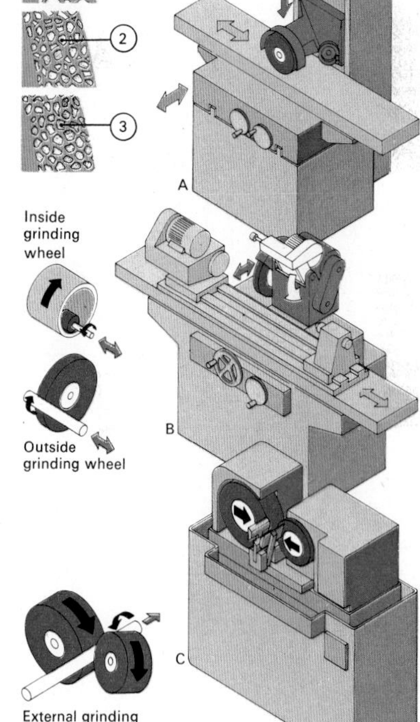

Inside grinding wheel
Outside grinding wheel
External grinding

5 Grinding is used mainly as a finishing operation giving a smooth surface. The grinding wheel consists of hard particles, usually alumina or silicon carbide bonded together with a resin. Three types of grinding machine are shown: the surface [A], universal [B], and centerless grinders [C]. [A] smoothes plane surfaces, [B] is restricted to internal and external cylinders, and [C] to external cylinders or long bars. 1, 2, 3 are soft, medium, and hard grinding wheels.

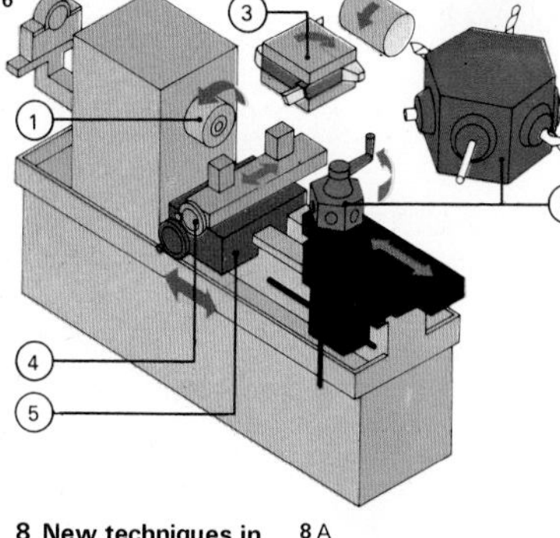

6 Turret lathes are for repetitive work where large numbers of the same component have to be made from bar or tube-fed through the chuck [1]. Six tools can be used on the turret [2], and a front tool post [3] on the cross slide [4] of the saddle [5] can carry four more. A rear tool post can also carry tools.

7 Drilling machines of many different kinds are used in workshops. The multi-spindle model shown is a time saver in mass production. It can be installed as part of a machining line for a particular component and tooled to drill all the holes in that component in one simple and time-saving operation.

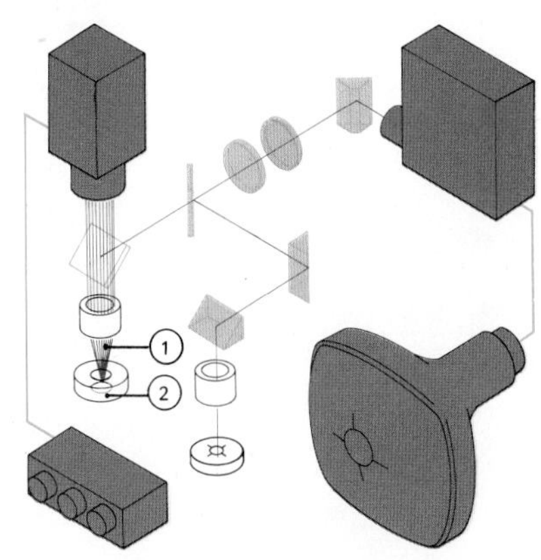

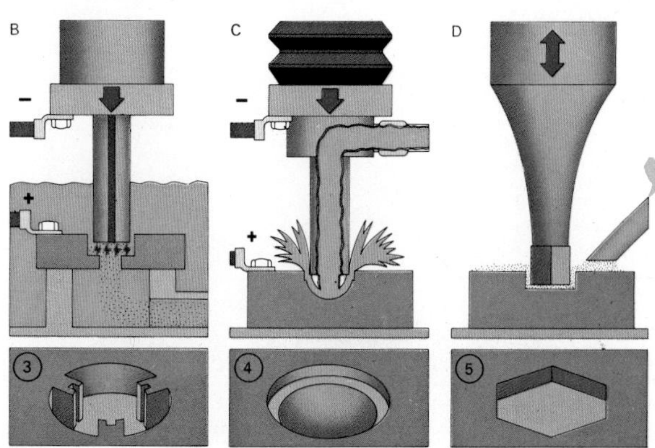

8 New techniques in metalworking include laser machining [A], in which an intense beam of light [1] cuts hard material [2] such as diamond and tool steel. The image of the work and that of the pattern are combined on a closed-circuit TV display. In spark erosion [B], a high-voltage spark etches away small pieces of a hard material. In electrochemical machining [C], corrosion of metal in salt solution (brine) is speeded up using a high voltage. The hole is cut the same shape as the electrode. Ultrasonic machining [D] uses high-frequency sounds beyond the range of human hearing to vibrate a cutting tool. An abrasive powder then cuts through the workpiece, which could therefore be a non-metal. A cavity is produced that is a mirror image of the tool. Typical shapes produced by these various methods are shown in [3]; [4], and [5].

Ceramics and glass

Ceramics and glass are among the oldest products of human ingenuity. Yet so great is their versatility that, even today, new uses are being found for these materials [Key], from high-voltage insulators to radar and computer components and nuclear fuels.

Early technology

During the last Ice Age, hunters made clay images of animals and hardened them near fires. Clay is basically a mixture of aluminum and silicon oxides, together with various impurities. When heated moderately it loses its chemically-bound water and forms a porous, hard material suitable for making hearths, images, and, if pre-shaped, pots. To make a nonporous product, higher temperatures are necessary so that a portion of the material melts, or fuses, thus filling up the tiny holes in it.

If silica is fused and then allowed to cool slowly the result is glass rather than pottery. Glazing—the production of a glassy surface on a solid object—dates back to 4000 BC, but the first all-glass vessels did not appear until 1500 BC, and it was nearly another 1,500 years before the technique of blowing glass vessels was developed.

The production of ceramics and glassware was a highly mechanized industry, even in the nineteenth century. But in the second part of that century developments in technology put the craft on a more scientific footing. The chemical structures of ceramics contain no free electrons, so they are nonconductors of electricity. This property became important when large-scale electricity generation began. The development of satisfactory insulators, for example, required much more knowledge of materials than did the manufacture of teacups. Consequently, scientific studies of raw material composition and firing methods had to be undertaken.

Chemical composition

Chemically, ceramics and glass are composed largely of compounds of oxygen with other elements. Glass, which is composed largely of silica (SiO_2), is a special case—most oxides do not form glasses but many ceramics contain a glassy component. Porcelain, for example, is made from a mixture of clay, sand, and an alkaline flux. Such fluxes, often common minerals such as feldspars, lower the temperature at which silica fuses. A fragment of porcelain viewed through a microscope can be seen to have several different kinds of particles bound together by a glass matrix.

Many of the particles in a ceramic are tiny crystals in which the atoms are arranged in simple geometric patterns. In a glass there are no such geometric regularities and the atoms are oriented at random. Physically, glass is a gel with a structure more like that of a liquid than of a solid.

If glass is not cooled properly (annealed) from the molten state [5], tiny crystals do appear and the result is a brittle, semiopaque material. Some crystal formation can occur with slow decomposition and some very old glass, as in Roman bottles, is partly opaque [3] because of the chemical action that has taken place over the hundreds of years that the glass has been buried. Recently, techniques have been devised to encourage controlled crystal forma-

CONNECTIONS

See also
1610 Materials for building
1616 Small technology in the home
1600 Tailor-made materials

1 Glass was made in antiquity by [A] fusing raw material held by a glass thread on a sand core to form a bottle, or [B] by shaping it in a mold. A wine glass was made [C] by blowing a gather of molten glass in a mold, adding a stem, shaping the foot, and trimming. Press molding [D] is a more modern technique. A decorative paperweight [E] was made by fusing colored glass rods and surrounding them with molten glass. Glass-working tools [F] include a blowpipe, rod, tongs, shears, and rolling plate. Glass was originally melted in a crucible [G]; later bell [H] and cone [I] furnaces were used.

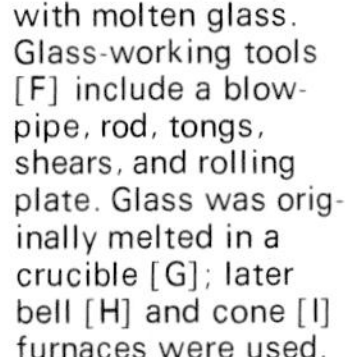

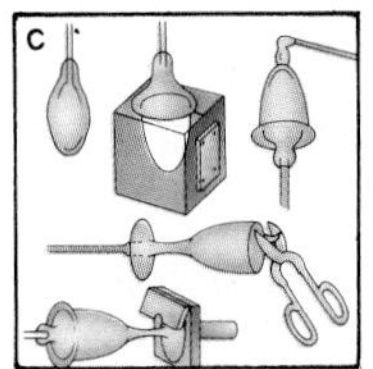

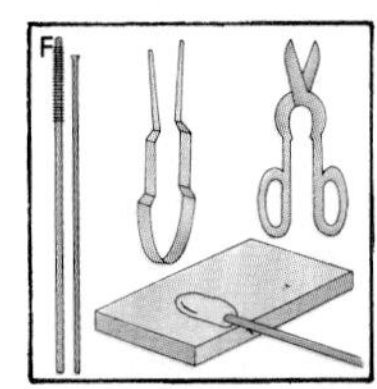

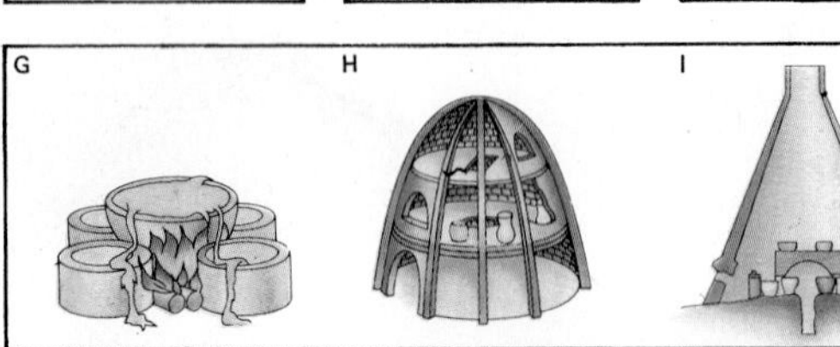

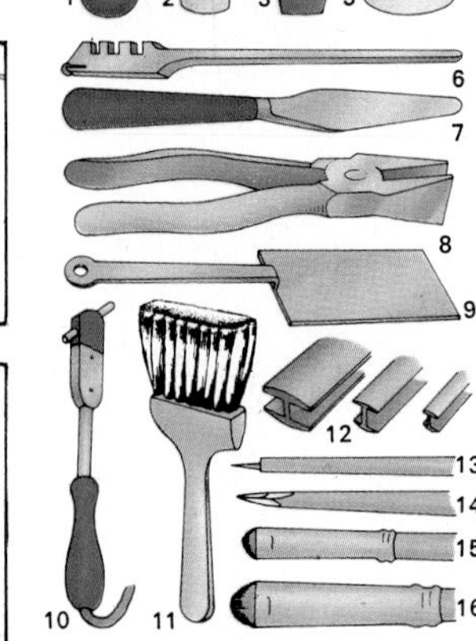

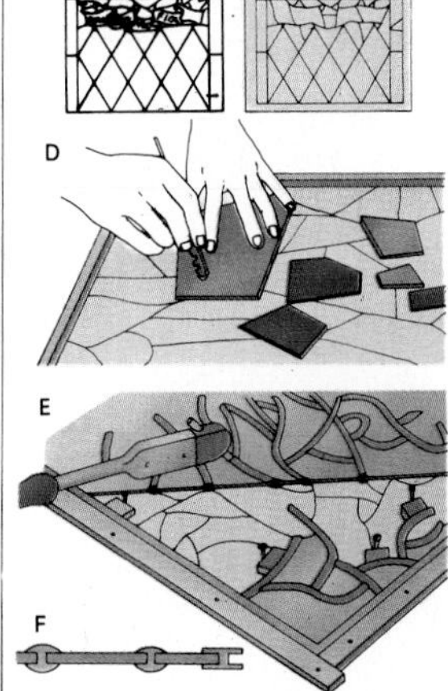

2 Stained-glass windows are made from many small pieces of colored glass joined by lead strips. An artist first makes a full-scale drawing of the design. From this sketch [B], a cutline [C] is traced onto linen. Glass is cut to the exact shape of the cutline [D] and the pieces are leaded up and soldered [E, F]. Tools [A] used are: [1] cutting knife; [2] stopping knife; [3] lathekin; [4] nails; [5] muller for mixing paint; [6] glass cutter; [7] palette knife; [8] grozing pliers; [9] tray lifter; [10] soldering iron; [11] badgerhair brush; [12] leads; [13] needle point; [14] sharpened wood; [15] and [16] hogshair brushes.

3 Long ago, glass was colored by the addition of small amounts of metal to the melt. Gold, for example, can be used to make glass red or blue. The color depends on the size of the individual particles dispersed in the melt. A remarkable example of Roman glass colored with gold and silver is the Lycurgus cup in the British Museum. If seen by reflected light it appears an opaque green; by transmitted light, translucent purple-red.

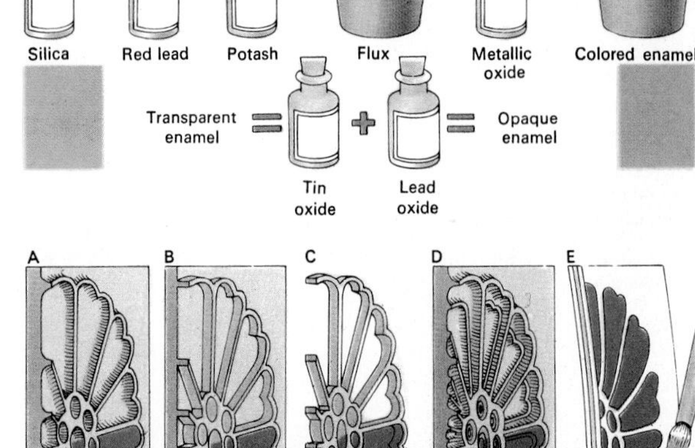

Silica
Red lead
Potash
Flux
Metallic oxide
Colored enamel
Transparent enamel
Opaque enamel
Tin oxide
Lead oxide
A
B
C
D
E

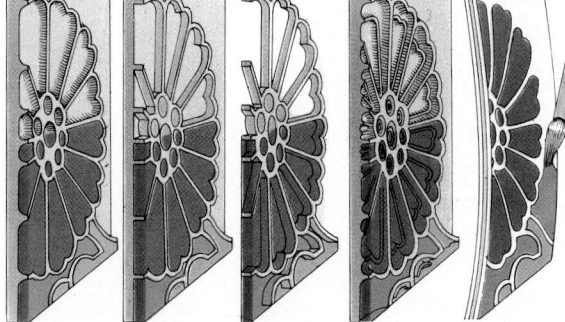

4 In enameling, a coat of glass is fused to a metal surface. Silica, red lead, and potash are melted to make a flux, which can then be colored by the addition of a broad range of metal oxides; addition of tin and lead oxides gives an opaque enamel. In *champlevé* enameling [A], pieces of metal are cut away, leaving a pattern of raised metal lines between them to form the outline of a design. Pulverized enamel is laid in the troughs and then fused. Afterward, the enamel is filed and polished. The other techniques of enameling shown here—*cloisonné* [B], *plique à jour* [C], *basse-taille* [D], and enamel painting [E]—are all variants of *champlevé* enameling.

tion in glass by reheating it under specific conditions [8]. The result is a tough heat-proof and flame-proof glass ceramic, now widely used in kitchen ovenware.

In firing some ceramics it is not necessary to form much glassy material in order to hold it together. Where the solid has formed solely as a result of sintering (aggregating as a result of applied heat) with no fusing, however, it is usually porous like brick. This is because the particles of material come together more closely but, in most cases, do not drive out all the air holes.

It is because of their very high melting points that the raw components of many ceramics have to be sintered rather than fused. Such high melting points mean that ceramics act as good refractories—lining materials for crucibles and furnaces.

Modern uses of ceramics

High-density ceramics can now be prepared as "whiskers," which may be used to strengthen other materials or even to strengthen more conventional ceramics. Thus ceramics can play an important part in modern engineering, in some cases replacing metals, as in engine parts that must operate at ultra-high temperatures.

Not all ceramics are oxides, and some of the newer ones are compounds of different elements with carbon or nitrogen [7]. Carbide-tipped drill bits exemplify the everyday uses of new ceramics.

Electricity and magnetism are usually associated with metals, but in the developed countries the electrical and magnetic properties of ceramics are widely used. Solar batteries, which convert sunlight directly into electricity, rely on modern ceramics.

If some iron-containing ceramics are cooled in a particular way the materials that result are capable of converting mechanical into electrical energy (and vice versa) because of the alignment of electrical dipoles in the material. Much of today's sound transmission and recording is based on such "ferroelectrics." Similarly, "ferrites" are ceramics in which the magnetic rather than the electrical dipoles have been aligned, and they form an essential part of computers, radar equipment, and small electric motors.

KEY

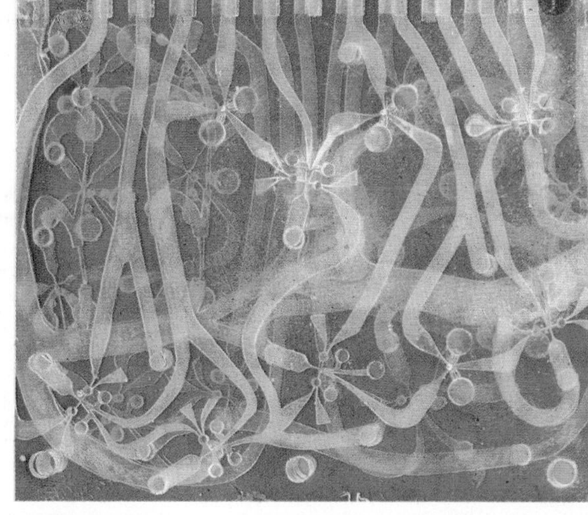

Glass, one of the oldest materials known to man, can be used for some of the most up-to-date technology. These fluid circuits have been etched in photosensitive glass. A special formula assures that on treatment with radiation the glass crystallizes, making it easy to etch with acid.

5

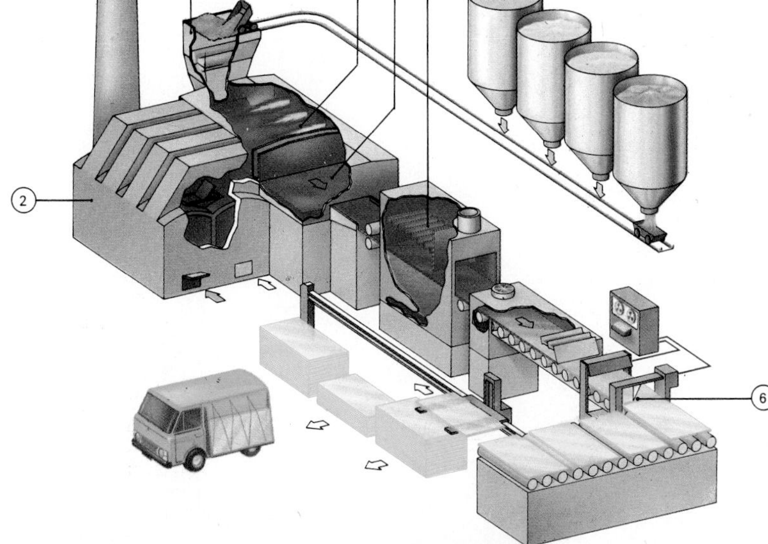

1
3
4
5
2
6

5 The float glass process was developed by Pilkingtons Ltd in 1959 in the United Kingdom and is now used throughout the world for the production of flat glass of the type used, for example, in windows. The ingredients are mixed in a hopper [1] and then melted in an oil fired furnace [2]; the molten glass [3] then passes on to a float bath of molten tin [4] in a special non-oxidizing atmosphere. The glass spreads out over the molten metal surface to form a uniform, flat sheet. As the glass passes through the bath it is gradually cooled so that it emerges with a firm surface that is not deformed by the rollers that take it into an annealing lehr [5], where it undergoes further cooling before it passes over more rollers to a computer-controlled cutting and stacking operation [6].

6

6 Pottery is generally defined as a porous ceramic material made from clay by firing until it is hard. The firing temperature is comparatively low, so that the individual particles in the clay do not melt and fuse together, as can be seen in this microscopic section of a piece of pottery. To make it waterproof a glasslike glaze has to be fired onto the surface. Nonporous ceramics such as porcelain, which do not necessarily have to be glazed, are fired at higher temperatures, so that some particles melt and fuse together. Often silica is added to give a glassy texture.

7

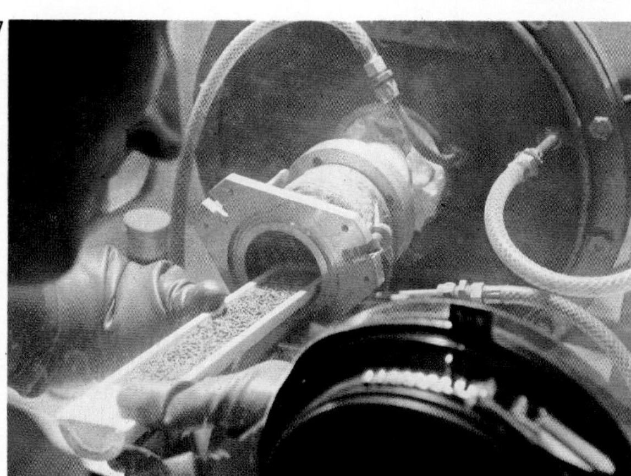

7 Oxides or carbides of fissionable elements such as uranium are sintered to form ceramic pellets that are packed into metal containers and used as fuel elements in nuclear reactors.

8

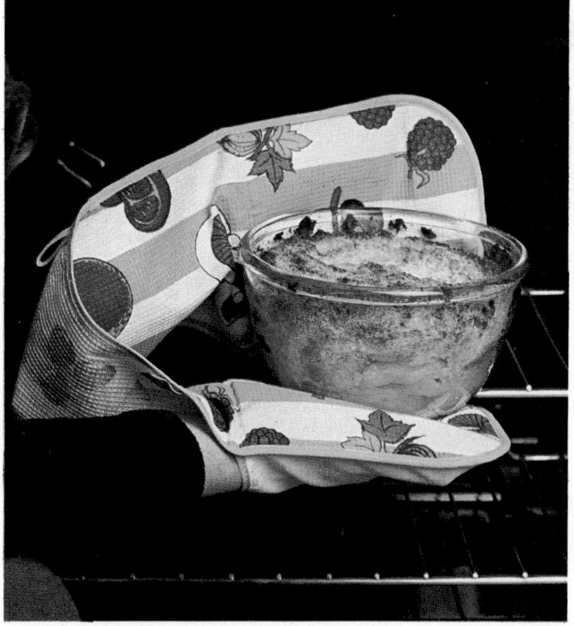

8 Glass ceramic is made by heat-treating preformed glass so that it devitrifies. By carefully controlling the crystal formation, glass ceramics that combine mechanical strength with good heat-proof properties are produced.

Materials for building

Shelter from the natural elements is a basic need. Early people met this need by dwelling in caves and then their descendants began to construct buildings. Key factors in the design of these shelters were the climate and the materials available. For example, in hot, dry countries houses with tiny windows and thick walls of mud were built to keep out the heat and sunlight; in rainy climates people normally built sloping roofs of grass and rushes, so that the rain ran off the house without penetrating the interior; in earthquake areas, houses were built of light materials—in Japan, for example, some internal walls are still made of paper.

Building with timber

Originally an ancient building material, timber [2] is now being applied to major structures, although its widest use is still in house building. Improved design techniques and treatments now overcome many weaknesses. The strength of timber is different along and across the grain, so it is made more uniform by using adhesives to bond multiple layers with the grain running in various directions. Durability is improved by better methods of preservation and the timber is treated so that it does not burn readily. Devices for joining timber structures have also been improved, notably metal plate connectors with multiple projecting teeth. These spread the applied load over a wide area.

Timber is now used to make fully prefabricated houses [6], which are factory finished and ready for erection on a firm base. More extensively it is used for joists, rafters, window frames, doors, floors, and studding [3] for internal non-load-bearing walls which are to be faced with plasterboard. Timber also has appeal for conservationists because it is renewable—we can plant more trees—and its manufacture into a usable form involves no pollution of the environment.

Building with stone and brick

Natural stone is still used for building, although it has taken on a comparatively minor role in industrialized countries, being confined mainly to facings and other decorative finishes. Stone is obtained from quarries by blasting or splitting with wedges. If, like limestone, it is layered, it must be used in such a position that its layers lie at right angles to the pressure.

Fired bricks are used extensively for houses in developed countries. Their size and type are governed by national standards and there is a move to set up international standards. The size and proportions are broadly chosen so that a bricklayer can hold a brick using only one hand and the brick can bond with others lying both parallel and at right angles to the wall face.

Most bricks are made from clay or shale and are "burned" in a kiln. Some, however, are made of silica sand and lime and these are known as calcium silicate bricks. Building blocks are a little larger than bricks and are generally made of concrete.

Building with concrete

Most people think of concrete as a modern material, but its history begins with the Romans, who used it to build their aqueducts and amphitheaters. Another common mis-

CONNECTIONS

See also
1612 Making large buildings
1614 Building with local resources
1750 Traffic engineering

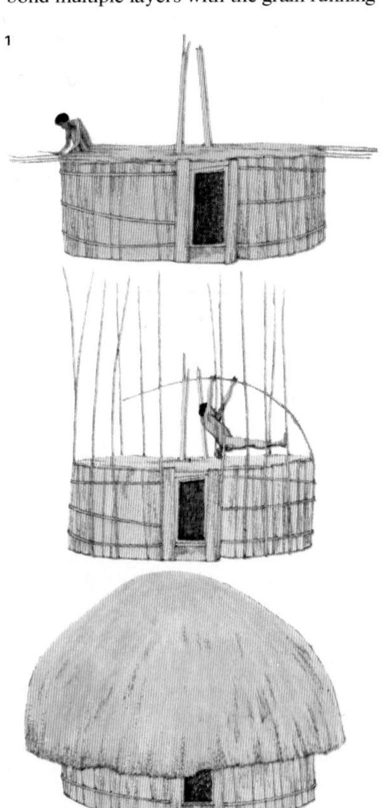
1

1 A complex house belonging to a woman of the Dani tribe, who live in the forests of New Guinea, illustrates the use of traditional materials. It is made with tools of stone, wood, bamboo, and bone. It has a lower room and a sleeping loft; the lower room has wooden walls and a tall doorway. The dome is made with saplings, which form the frame of the whole house, bent over and attached to the center posts. Then the house is covered with long grass thatch made by the men. The sleeping area in the roof has a reed floor, but it is provided with a hearth on a mud base to keep people warm at night. Grass is trimmed and prepared for use with a stone adze, a tool rather like an axe with an arched blade mounted at right angles to the handle. Vines are used to lash the building together.

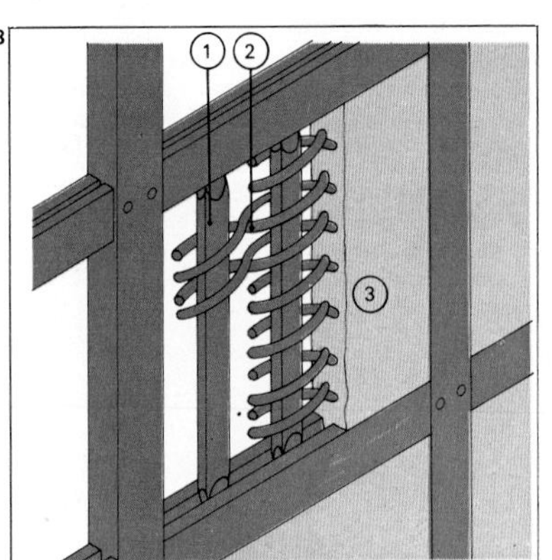
3
1
2
3

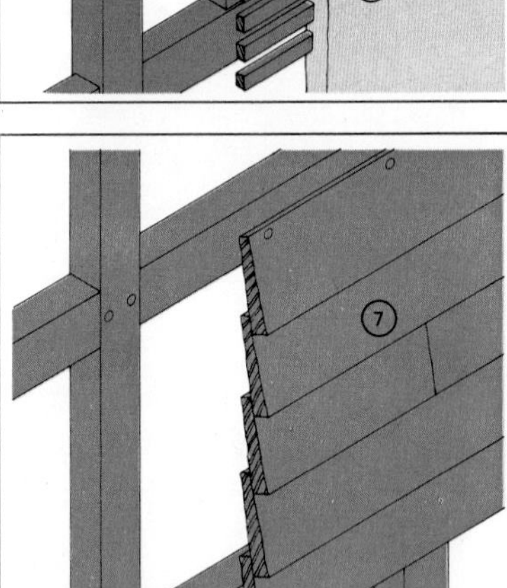
4
5
7

6

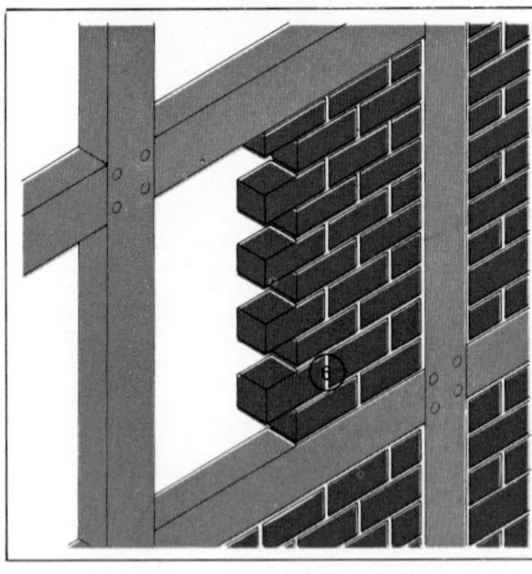

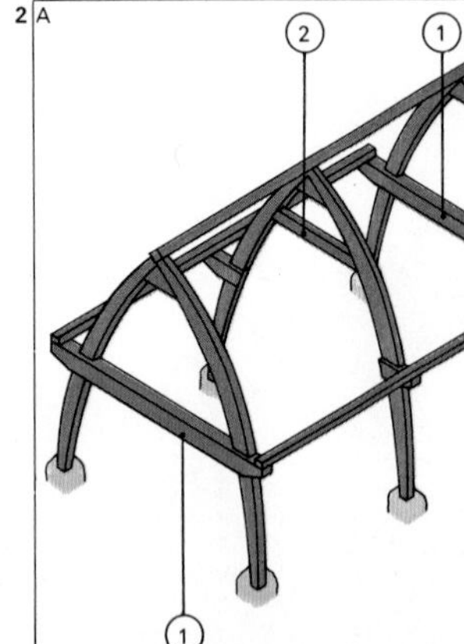
2 A
2
1
1

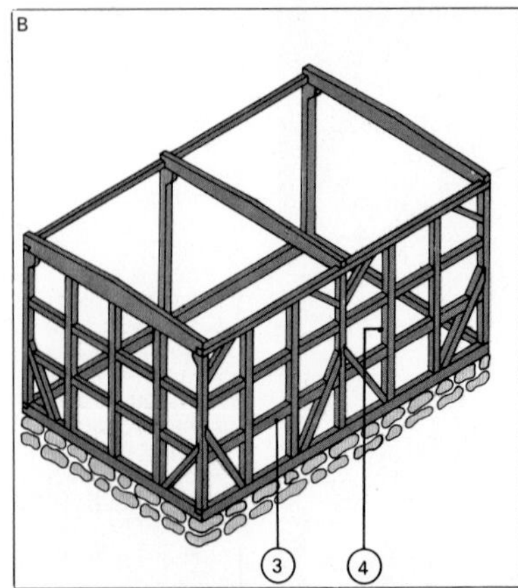
B
3
4

2 Timber was the main structural material used to build small houses in the forested areas of Europe from the Stone Age to the 1700s. Cruck constructions [A] were formed by arched timbers that supported the roof and walls. Horizontal beams [1, 2] formed trusses to take the weight. The box frame [B] had added rails [3] and studs (vertical timbers) [4]. These help to stiffen the structure and provide attachment points for cladding (siding).

3 In frame walls the space between the timber frames can be filled by timber staves [1] surrounded by wattle [2] and covered by daub and plaster [3]; or timber laths [4] covered by plaster [5]; or with brick filling [6]. The frame can also be covered with weatherboard or clapboard [7]. In Europe, timber was soon eclipsed as the principal material for frame structures. In the early 19th century, the development of rolled iron and steel girders enabled builders to construct larger buildings. At about the same time glass was being made into large sheets, and by the close of the century reinforced concrete was in use. Recent innovation and improvements in timber technology—notably better methods of connecting beams by using metal plates and improved methods of lamination—have reopened the possibilities of its use for making frames.

conception is that concrete is used only in the construction of large buildings (apart from foundations). Concrete is a mixture of water, stone, and sand with a binder (usually Portland cement). Today an industry has grown up that precasts concrete into forms suitable for house walls and roofs, as well as for applications in bigger buildings. When a set of molds is made for this purpose, the process is called "battery casting." A recent extension of this idea is a system of battery casting concrete panels for rapid building of dwellings in developing countries. They can be set up on site without the need for factories to process them. A "package" is supplied consisting of a vertical battery unit for casting, a transporter vehicle, a tower crane, and accessories that enable a sub-contractor to construct medium-sized blocks of apartments at a rate of one per day. The basic design is standard, but even so the system gives great architectural and planning flexibility using only a few units. These units can be assembled in various ways, according to the needs and styles of a community or country.

Other composite materials are gaining importance in building homes. In essence they are well established; for example, the old wattle (interlaced rods and twigs) and daub of mud or clay. A modern form used in house building is glass-reinforced polyester resin. Panels of this material are themselves composites; they are applied to timber framing and act with the frame to give so-called "racking resistance," which prevents distortion of the frame. Similarly, internal walls may be composites of timber frames or metal frames fitted with honeycombs of metal strips, faced with plasterboard.

So far, few plastics have been used as structural materials, although they are widely used for a variety of accessory roles in buildings. These include panels, gutters and their supports, drainpipes, and decorative ceilings. Water can be stored in plastic tanks and led through plastic pipes. Foamed plastics can be injected into cavity walls to improve thermal insulation. Some designers have built all-plastic houses, but these have not been commercially successful because they are too expensive.

KEY

Standardization in building makes use of basic units that can be assembled in various ways in order to provide flexibility in design. The idea was pioneered by Walter Gropius (1883–1969), the German architect who founded the Bauhaus school of architecture in 1919. His own house was one of four residences for the teaching staff, built among the trees of the Bauhaus school in Dessau, Germany. These buildings illustrate Gropius's theory of standardization. The houses are built of similar slag concrete blocks, with the walls as the main supporting elements. His own two-story house is basically L-shaped with terraces at different levels. The external appearance of the building was as important to Gropius as the functional planning of the interior. Today unit construction, using prefabricated sections, permits the rapid building of substantial homes by relatively unskilled workers in developing countries.

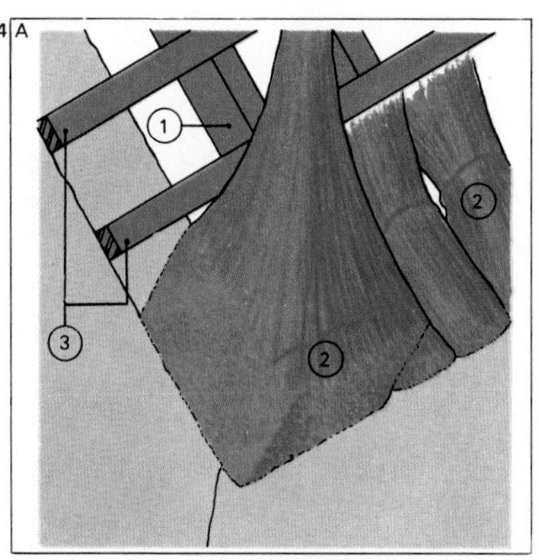
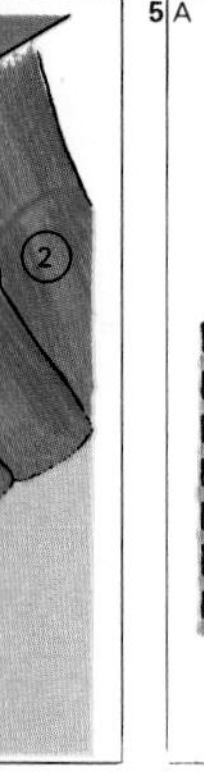
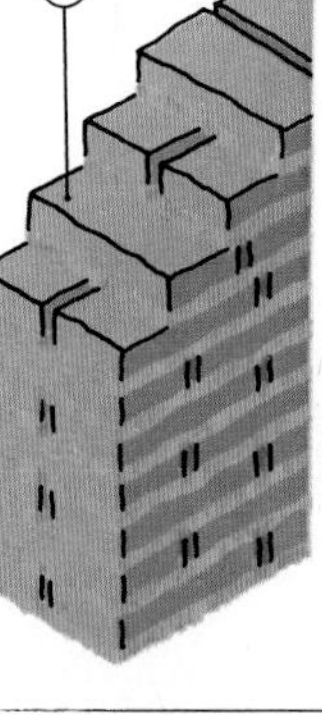
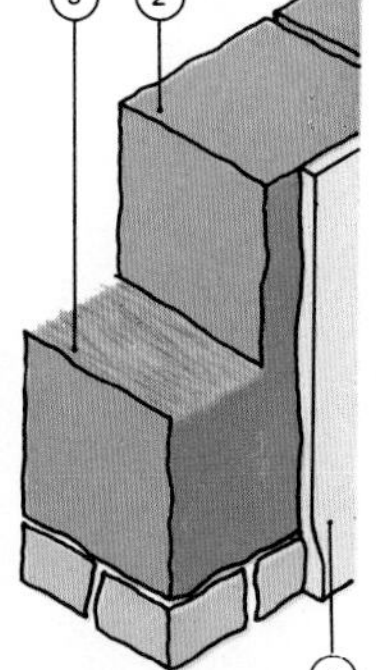

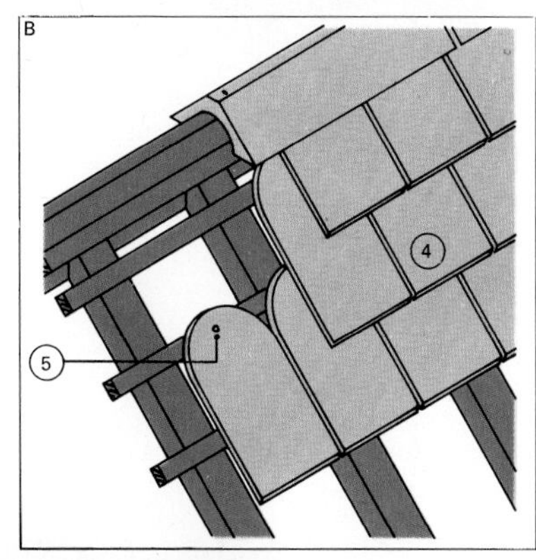

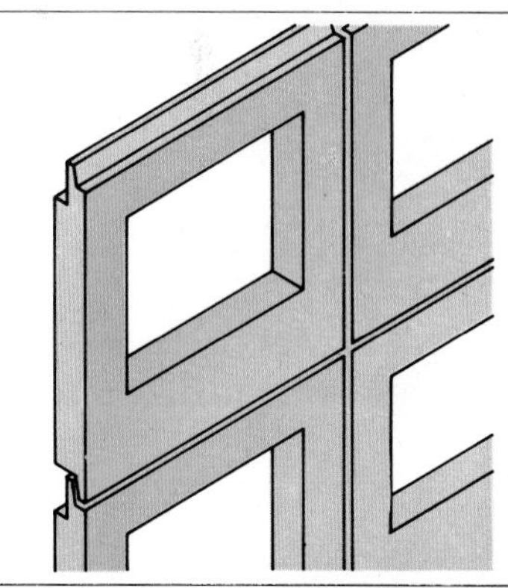

4 Thatching is an old roofing technique [A] that involves covering rafters [1] with straw layers [2] vertically fixed to horizontal battens [3]. There is no crossing or weaving, though rods may be used to secure the thatch on a straw roof. Chief materials used are straw and reeds. Stone tiles [4] were also used, with round tops and a peg-hole [5] for securing them to battens [B]. Regional and economic conditions have influenced building, particularly since earlier times when transport was difficult, slow, and expensive. As it became more efficient, manufactured goods were applied over a wider area. Where slate was available it was used; if not, then clay tiles were made. With the new rail systems, slate came into use in the countryside and other materials, usually reserved for one area, were used everywhere.

5 Walls may be built of a wide variety of materials [A] including a mixture of sods of turf [1] and thick clay mixed with pebbles [2] linked together with straw [3] and then faced with a plaster coating [4]. Alternatively, there may be thin clay layers [5] linked with straw [6] and faced with a plaster coating [7] or a wall built of clay "lumps" [8] like bricks but unburned. They are generally sun dried, like adobe. True burned brick walls [B] may resemble the early irregular brick [9] or be like the standardized brick laid in what is known as English bond [10]. Walls may also be made of precast concrete sections [C]. Other materials used for walls include stone in a wide variety of presentations using regular or unusually shaped stones, sometimes backed by brick and faced with plaster.

6 Complete home unit systems are now made of timber (with steel corner columns) in factories and delivered to the building site fully finished and ready for assembly. [A] A concrete base is prepared in advance with points for connections to mains services. The house is ready for occupation within days. [B] Where road regulations limit the width of the load, the home unit may be transported on its side, then turned upright for assembly.

Making large buildings

The highest building constructed by 1975 was Sears Roebuck Tower in Chicago. It is 1,454ft (443m) tall with 110 floors. It houses 16,500 people and has 103 elevators and 18 escalators. Structural engineers have calculated that buildings up to 1.75 miles (3km) tall are technically feasible.

Why have large buildings?

The chief reason for constructing large buildings has been to make the best use of the limited (and expensive) land area available in the world's major cities. New York City, largely confined to an island, could not spread outward so it spread upward. A secondary justification for large buildings for commercial purposes is that the whole of a large company's staff can be housed together, with obvious gains in efficiency.

Large buildings for homes, such as tower blocks of apartments, also make the best use of land and simplify the installation of services such as electricity and heating. But they can also create social problems—living many feet above street level can lead to lack of contact with the surrounding community. In terms of people, a large tower block is the size of a village; many skyscraper hotels are complete with shops, restaurants, and recreation facilities.

Whatever its size, a building must shelter people from the elements and have some system for controlling the climate. It must provide spaces for specific uses and such services as escalators, elevators, and stairways for its users. As structures, buildings must be able to carry not only their own loads, which vary according to the heights and materials used, but also the weights of the people and objects within them.

Building materials

Most larger buildings are structures of steel, reinforced concrete, and prestressed concrete. But a timber home-unit system can be built up to ten stories high and masonry (blocks or bricks) can take up to 18 floors built in cellular form—flat slabs arranged in boxlike fashion giving mutual support.

Aluminum alloys are seldom used on large buildings except for roofing over wide spaces without supporting columns. High tensile cables may be used in low-rise structures of a novel skeletal design, particularly where a large open space is needed, as in the Olympic tent at Munich, in airplane hangars, or in sports halls. Timber tends to be used for skeletal structures such as post and beam constructions and common trusses (the supports for roofs and bridges). It is likely to be found in single-story buildings —although timber structures can be built up to greater heights and spans for schools, hangars, exhibition halls, and for lightly-loaded floors, footbridges, and roofs. Joints are made by mechanical means such as multiple nails, staples, and bolts, or with adhesives. Treatments for preserving wood against biological attack and for retarding fire, as well as guidance on timber designs, have all improved considerably in recent years.

Masonry is brittle, strong in compression but weak in tension. Its use is therefore largely limited to columns, walls, and arches. Designs have to ensure that lateral forces are resisted and that structures cannot buckle or fail by horizontal sliding.

CONNECTIONS

See also
1610 Materials for buildir
1662 Machines for lifting
1760 Harbors and docks
1614 Building with local resources
1320 Modern architecture after 1930
1414 The American expe ience: the skyscrap

1
4
1
2
3
5

1 Staging can be eliminated by carrying out work close to the ground and then lifting the work up to its final position. One method of doing this is the "lift slab" system. This technique is applied to the type of structure based on columns and flat slabs. Here the upright columns [1] are first cast at only a part of their height or sometimes at their full height. Using moveable molds, the roof and floor slabs are then cast in sequence as a pile or stack into their plan positions around the upright columns at ground level, one on top of the other. The slabs are separated by special linkages that are later used for connecting them to the columns. The stacks of slabs are lifted, one at a time, by means of hydraulic jacks [4] until each reaches its allotted level. Each floor [2] is then secured into its final position, using special kinds of anchors [3]. The slabs are lifted by jacks at the very tops of the columns, and for this reason great care is needed to ensure that the columns themselves are upright and stable. Sometimes the method is modified and whole units of slabs with cast-in beams, or shell roofs, are jacked up from below. The system still demands formwork for casting the units, but it means that all this type of work can be completely carried out at ground level. This results in more economical formwork, virtually eliminating the need for raised supports. When each pair of floors has been secured, the outside walls [5] are built between them using brickwork or precast concrete slabs, leaving openings for window frames and doors to be fitted at a later stage.

Steel [3] is used in skeletal structures, which have a self-supporting framework clad with other materials. Or it may be used in "surface-active structures," where the frame, the beams supporting the covering sheets, and the sheets themselves—particularly when they are of steel—are regarded as acting as a single unit. Ultra-high-rise buildings [Key], with heights of more than 328ft (100m) are rare outside the United States and demand more sophisticated frame techniques.

Reinforced concrete [6] is now widely used for building frames. The concrete may be cast on the site or precast, depending on the ease of using formwork (the wooden mold into which concrete is poured) on location and the number of times the process has to be repeated [5]. Other factors are the nearness of the concrete plant to the site, the availability of cranes, and the construction schedule.

Concrete may also be compressed by tensioning its reinforcements and it is then known as "prestressed." This treatment enables embedded rods or high-tensile wires to carry an amount of direct or bending tension without the concrete itself going into tension, making it much stronger.

Reinforced concrete can be used for skeletal structures, often based on precast units and used mainly for industrial and shed-type buildings. Concrete may also be used in a shell form of construction, where the surface is an intrinsic part of the structure. Exciting and original shapes of shell have been designed, notably in South America and Spain. Probably the most famous such structure, however, is the group of concrete shells of the Sydney Opera House in Australia.

Pneumatic buildings

Large "tents," kept up by inflating them with air under slight pressure, are called pneumatic structures. They are made of strong fabrics and, depending on the degree of curvature and span, may be reinforced with membrane ribs and cables. So far these structures have been used mainly for temporary buildings, sometimes for protecting permanent ones while they are being built.

KEY

The Empire State Building in New York City was the tallest building in the world until 1972 and remained the third tallest after completion of the Sears Roebuck Tower in Chicago and the World Trade Center in New York City. The latter is 1,350ft (412m) tall, excluding the 223-ft (68-m) television mast that surmounts it; it has 102 stories. The main Empire State Building was opened in 1931. It has a steel structure and has been reported to have swayed a total of 2.97in(75.4mm) during a gale of 100 miles(164km) per hour in 1936. Four power beacons shine from the top of the building. The television mast was added in 1950–51.

2 The lift slab system in section.

1 Reinforced concrete floors assembled at ground level
2 Reinforced concrete column
3 Steel rods
4 Hydraulic jack
5 Floors fitted at appropriate levels

3A

B

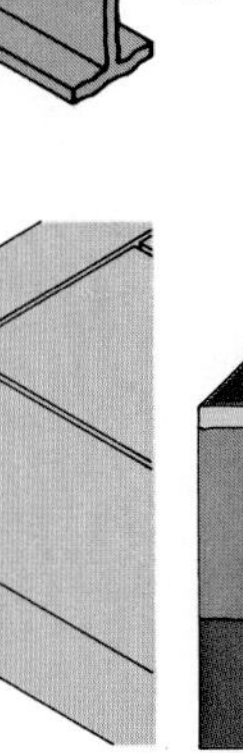

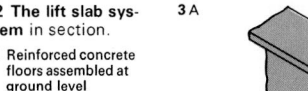

3 Steel beams are riveted together [A] to form a rigid framework. The horizontal beams are fixed to vertical columns. The frame construction using reinforced concrete [B] shows the vertical column [1] with its reinforcing rods, the main beam [2], again showing reinforcing rods, and the precast slab floor [3], which is partly cut away here to show how it is attached to the main beams.

4 Three modern pile-driving methods are: driven piles [A], where a prefabricated pile is driven into hard rock, providing a firm base; driven and cast piles [B], where the vibrator drives a steel tube into the ground; it is reinforced by a steel grid and withdrawn after concrete is cast into it; and bored and cast piles [C], where a hole is drilled and a concrete mixture is cast directly into the hole.

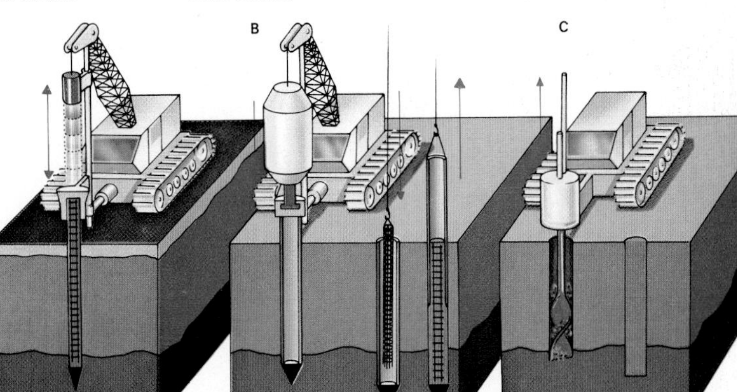

4A
B
C

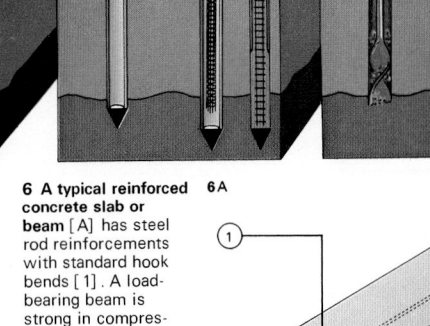

5 Slip forming is the application of continuous casting of concrete to the construction of tall buildings. Formwork in the form of a steel shuttered mold [1] about 4.5ft(1.3m) deep is erected on the foundations. It contains a network of heavy steel wires or rods, which act as reinforcement [4]. Concrete [6] is continuously cast into the mold; and the forms are slowly raised by a screw or hydraulic jack [3]. They then effectively "climb" steel pipes or rods [2] previously cast into the foundations. The upward movement of the formwork is transmitted by means of the yokes [5].

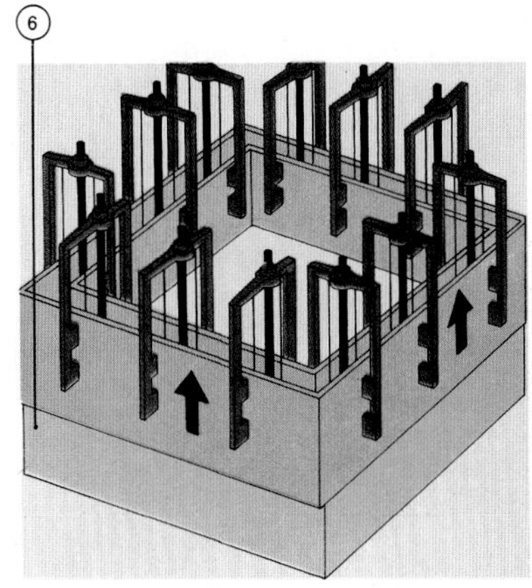

6 A typical reinforced concrete slab or beam [A] has steel rod reinforcements with standard hook bends [1]. A load-bearing beam is strong in compression but weak in tension. Without reinforcement, concrete will crack under strain, whereas a reinforced beam will not. A concrete block [B] with metal sheathing [2] encloses the tendons [3], which are tensioned [blue arrows]. One end is anchored and the other released so that the tendon compresses the concrete to form a prestressed block. Ordinary cast concrete [C] has a variety of uses in road and foundation construction using wooden forms [4] with anchoring pegs [6] on a stone base [5].

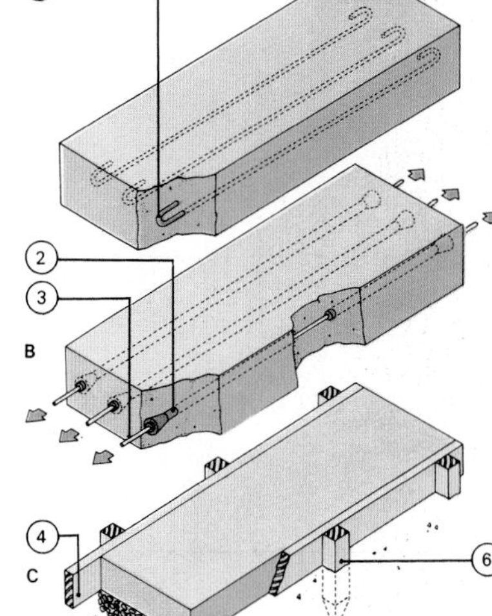

6A
B
C

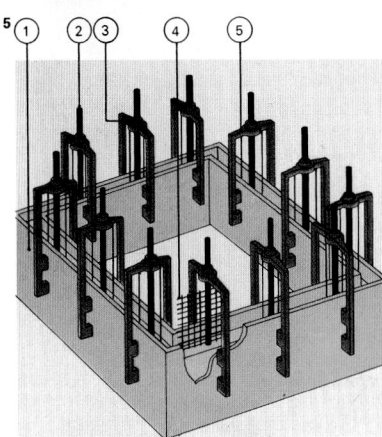

Building with local resources

Over the centuries industrious people with both the will and opportunity to create wealth found ways to make their lives comfortable. The ancient Romans knew nothing of modern technology yet they had a water supply system that provided Rome with nearly 220 million gallons (1,000 million liters) of water each day, homes warmed with hot air flowing in channels under the floor, an efficient sewage system and thousands of miles of excellent roads with fine bridges. These achievements were accomplished by making the maximum use of local resources within their limited technical knowledge.

Overcoming cost barriers

Today the world has developed an enormous fund of sophisticated technology and with its aid men have walked on the moon. Such advanced technology costs a great deal, however, and not all nations have the means of payment. One of the major problems of these nations is their inability to produce enough to create the wealth needed to buy the technology for increasing production.

The financial problem can be solved with outside aid or through self help. Each can contribute independently, but a combination is often even more fruitful. In Indonesia, Latin America, and some African countries, food production is being significantly increased by huge irrigation projects. The engineering know-how is Western, financed by the World Bank and similar organizations, but the works themselves are the product largely of the art of using local resources.

Water, energy and labor

Since the dawn of history, there has been water in the world's rivers running to waste. In some countries canals and reservoirs are being dug by hand, with animals being used to move the soil. The banks are waterproofed with hand-puddled clay. And even deserts often have vast reserves of water under them. The sun shines daily on millions of square miles of the Earth's surface, providing immeasurable quantities of free energy that is never used. Some of the underdeveloped countries have enormous reserves of labor. The problem is to harness this water, energy, and labor—along with the numerous other unexploited resources such as fertile soil, timber, and minerals—and to make them productive without having to make investments in contemporary technologies beyond the financial resources of those concerned.

There are several methods of developing local domestic water supplies cheaply [2, 3, 4]. If the water has to be raised to a higher level, a simple pump such as the Humphrey pump [5] can be used. And when there is a plentiful supply, as in a fast-flowing stream, a hydraulic ram can be used. This makes use of the energy of flowing water to pump small volumes to a higher level. Where bamboo is plentiful and water pipes hard to get, the bamboo can be drilled out and used to carry water, as is done in Ethiopia and Indonesia.

The sun's energy can be used to heat water in a solar heat collector consisting of a folded length of piping in a frame under glass. By connecting a storage tank at a higher level the water heated by the sun will

CONNECTIONS

See also
- 1610 Materials for building
- 1616 Small technology in the home
- 1704 Technology and transportation in developing nations
- 1602 Hand tools
- 752 Development of surgery

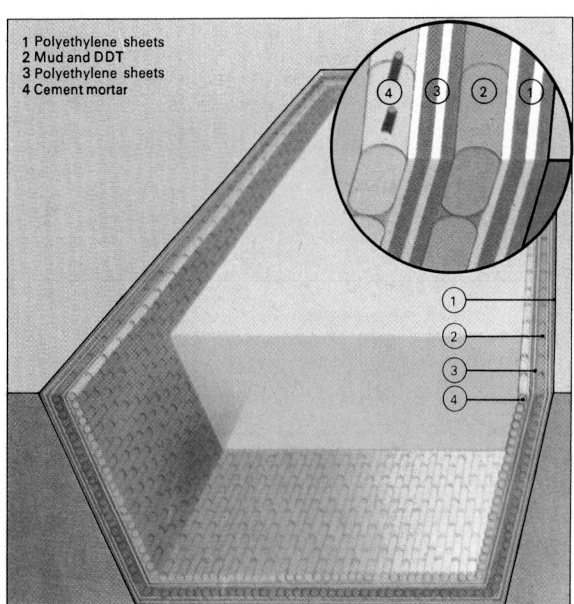

1 Polyethylene sheets
2 Mud and DDT
3 Polyethylene sheets
4 Cement mortar

1 Water storage in the Western world is achieved by the construction of huge reservoirs. To convey the water to where it is wanted canals and pipelines are built. A new approach, suited to countries that cannot afford to pay for major civil works, is the provision of a large number of rainwater tanks sited where the water is needed. These "tanks" are dug in the ground and lined with three or more layers of polyethylene sheet, separated by a mud and DDT mixture to kill termites that bore through the outer skin. The tank shown in the diagram has a wearing surface of cement mortar "sausages" made with polyethylene tubes.

2 In stored water, before it is filtered, sediment that would quickly block a sand filter must be removed if the water is for human use. The large sedimentation tanks used in water treatment plants in the West are costly. The process can be carried out in a small community supply scheme by means of a simple concrete-lined tank with a sloping bottom. Important features are the inlet baffle [1] (which stops incoming water from "stirring" the tank), the scum board [2] (to stop floating matter from passing out), and the sludge drain, which is located at the lowest point of the tank [3].

3 The filtration of drinking water for a small community supply scheme can be carried out efficiently by means of a relatively cheap "slow" sand filter in a concrete-lined tank. The sand particles should be between 0.2 and 0.5mm in size and the bed [1] about 4ft(1.2m) deep, supported on a layer of graded gravel [2] surrounding a porous pipe drain [3]. At least 20in(50cm) of clean water must be maintained over the sand and there should be an underwater upward flow inlet [4] that will not disturb the sand. Flow must not exceed 18.4gal/yd². In such a slow filter a layer of living organisms forms at the top of the sand bed adding biological purification to the mechanical filtration.

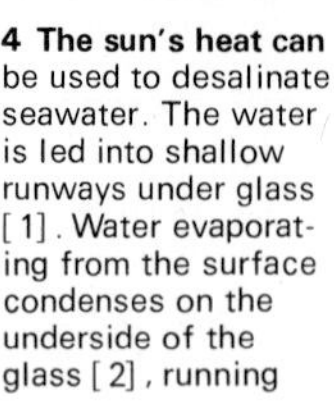

4 The sun's heat can be used to desalinate seawater. The water is led into shallow runways under glass [1]. Water evaporating from the surface condenses on the underside of the glass [2], running down the slope to the edge where it drips into a freshwater channel [3]. Additional freshwater can be collected from rain falling on the glass [4] and draining into other runways [5].

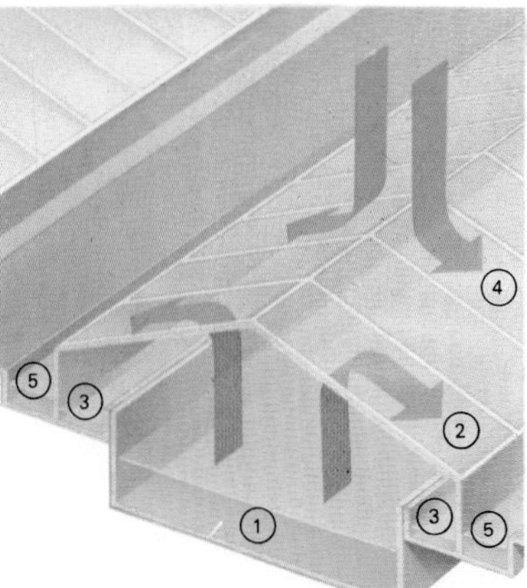

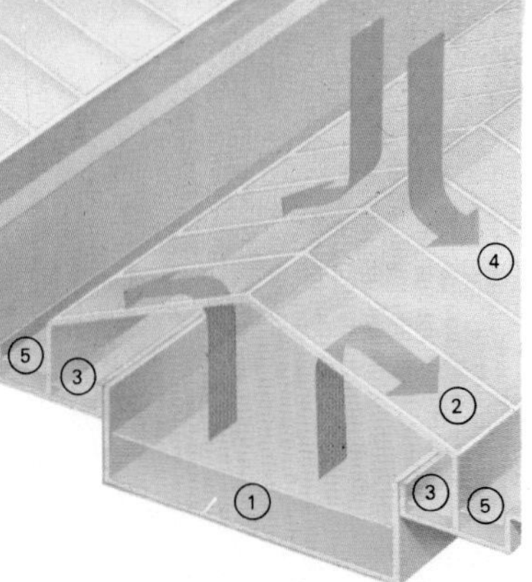

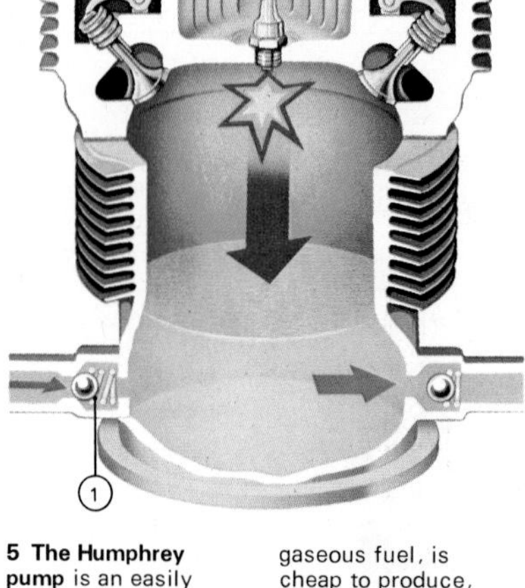

5 The Humphrey pump is an easily made internal combustion unit in which the water being pumped replaces both the piston and flywheel of the conventional power unit and needs no separate pump. It will operate on almost any gaseous fuel, is cheap to produce, and easily maintained. The water inlet valve [1] is automatic. Operating on a four-stroke cycle the "bounce" of the water produces the compression, suction, and exhaust strokes.

rise to the tank and be replaced by cooler water. A solar heater of this kind, fitted with a sufficiently large heat collector, will heat water for washing and cooking.

Draft animals walking in a circle can drive simple crop processing machines using a device that works like a ship's capstan coupled by a crown wheel and pinion to a horizontal shaft. Water power can be harnessed to operate small machinery using a simple hardwood turbine of the kind used in Nepal to drive village flour mills.

For small-scale irrigation there are a number of ways of leveling land using ox-drawn graders and scrapers, which can be made by a blacksmith. A metal barrel, cut in half and fitted with a steel cutting edge on one side, can be used to scrape and carry soil, pulled by a team of oxen. Numerous other improved and new farm implements have been found invaluable [8, 9].

Industrial applications

A wide range of village industries can be introduced to create nonagricultural employment. Good soap, for example, can be made from caustic soda and locally available fats. A pottery can be established with a small brick firing kiln to make domestic vessels. A foundry to cast aluminum or iron can be set up fairly inexpensively.

An excellent example of the application of appropriate, as opposed to advanced technology can be seen in the increased efficiency and productivity being achieved in the coastal fishing industry of Ghana. Most Ghanaian fishermen use 33-ft (10-m) canoes made from tree trunks. Small trawlers would undoubtedly be more efficient, but a less expensive improvement has been made by fitting outboard motors to the canoes. Between 1961 and 1971 the number of motors used increased from 19 percent of the canoes to 86 percent.

Another example is found in India where the manufacture of cement is insufficient to meet city needs. In rural districts lime is widely used as an alternative material where the superior strength of cement concrete is not essential. Small-scale lime manufacture is carried on in villages throughout the country.

KEY

The march of technology has made us creatures of habit. Someone entering a room at night takes the existence of electricity for granted, forgetting that people lived for many centuries with only oil lamps and candles. The technology of reinforced concrete depends on steel rods or wires to withstand tension while the concrete itself stands immense compression. Yet costly steel is not the only material strong in tension. A concrete structure requiring some reinforcement against surface cracking can sometimes be adequately strengthened with natural bamboo, a material that is plentiful and cheap in some of the poorer countries.

6

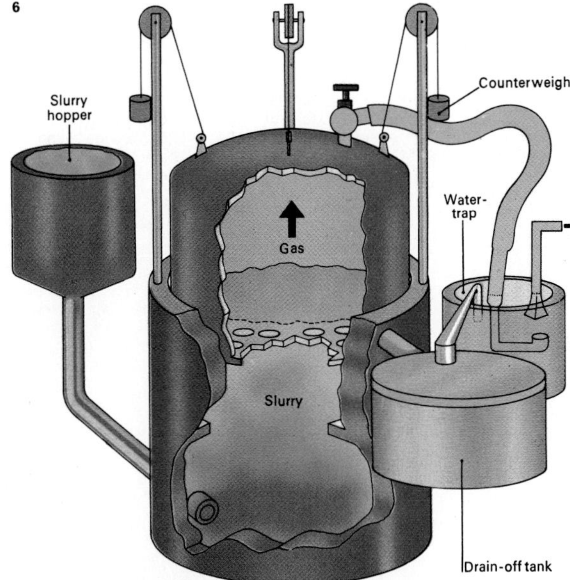
Slurry hopper
Counterweight
Water-trap
Gas
Slurry
Drain-off tank

6 In the developing countries the lack of a reliable, cheap and convenient supply of energy is a considerable problem. Dried cattle dung is a widely used fuel but its value as a fertilizer is lost when it is burnt. By subjecting dung to anaerobic fermentation (without oxygen), methane is produced and the waste slurry has a high nitrogen content which is more readily available as a fertilizer than the natural nitrogen in unprocessed dung. The diagram shows how a cheap methane generator can be built with provision for continuous recharging with dung slurry, steady production, and gas storage.

7

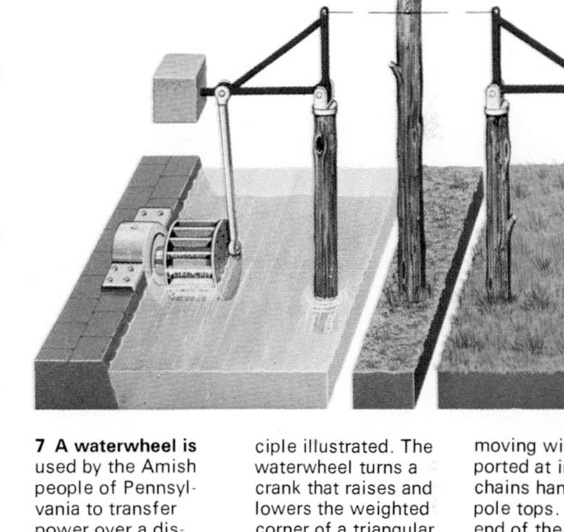

7 A waterwheel is used by the Amish people of Pennsylvania to transfer power over a distance of up to nearly 0.6 mile by a reciprocating wire power transmission system operating on the principle illustrated. The waterwheel turns a crank that raises and lowers the weighted corner of a triangular frame [left], which pivots on another corner to transfer the motion to the horizontal wire. The moving wire is supported at intervals by chains hanging from pole tops. At the far end of the wire a second frame transfers the motion to a vertical reciprocating pump for raising water.

8

8 Rice cultivation is widespread in poorer countries where it provides the staple diet for the bulk of the population. Because there is usually a surplus of cheap labor in these countries cultivation is traditionally carried out by hand, often by women. In particular the "puddling" of rice fields so that they will retain water as long as possible is normally a tedious hand job. The multi-action puddling tool shown here is pulled by oxen and does the job quickly and economically. Rotating chopper blades first cut the soil transversely. Then disks cut it longitudinally. Finally a row of 6.3in (16cm) long knives cut through the chopped soil like tiny plows. This implement was developed in Japan.

9

9 The peanut lifter, drawn by a pair of oxen, is a simple tool developed in Nigeria. The oxen walk each side of a row of peanuts, which is also straddled by the two "depth" wheels whose height can be easily adjusted. The sharp lifting blade cuts its way horizontally through the soil under the peanuts, leaving them in loose soil on the surface ready for quick gathering by hand. The tool, assembled with bolts, can be made by any blacksmith. It has proved itself after extensive trials in the six northern states of Nigeria and is now in common use there. It has also been successfully field tested in southern regions of Zambia.

Small technology in the home

People have three basic needs—food, clothing, and shelter—and it is the last of these that represents a family's most valuable and most durable possession. It is as necessary to an African tribesman as to a European or American office worker. In the Western world the design and equipping of the home has been developed with the aid of an advanced technology, many of the products of which are beyond the means of people living in less developed countries.

Simple technologies and community needs

To enable people in rural communities to build houses that are more comfortable and will last longer, the designs and construction techniques must be simple. The materials used should come from the kind of technology that can be applied locally. As a result the people can have better protection from the elements, better cooking [4] and washing facilities, and better sanitation [6].

Some personal needs are also community needs—a reliable and pure water supply, a cheap and effective source of energy (such as methane gas), and access to inexpensive building materials. Rural industries, which provide the community with such essential products as soap, agricultural implements, and cooking pots, are another need—and, incidentally, help to create wealth where it is most needed.

Before high-quality, low-cost housing can be built, there must be research and experiment focused on specific local needs. Designs must be appropriate to local style [Key] and to the climate, as well as being flexible, so that small houses can when necessary be enlarged. They must fully exploit local materials and the ability of local labor. Finally, cooperative organizations must be set up to mobilize local resources and to encourage a desire for improvement.

Sanitation and food storage

Sanitation is as much a community as a family responsibility. But it begins in the home, where the introduction of the inexpensive water-seal toilet [7] can be the greatest single method of reducing the incidence of disease.

Methods of storing food are also important for family and community health. In many developing countries the climate is such that a refrigerator would be considered essential by contemporary western standards. In places where ice is available, an insulated ice-box may provide a partial solution. The box itself is cheap and easy to make, but the ice may well be too costly for most rural families.

In regions where the humidity is not too high an evaporative food cooler may provide a practical alternative. The cooler, which is designed as a cabinet with wire mesh walls and shelves to allow air to circulate, is placed in a shallow pan of water and has a second pan as its top. Jute burlap or sacking "curtains" hang from top to bottom, with their ends in the water. The burlap absorbs water like a wick thus keeping damp. When the cabinet is placed in a breeze, away from direct sunlight, heat absorbed from the interior is used by the water in evaporating. As a result the inside of the cabinet is significantly cooler than the surrounding air.

CONNECTIONS

See also
1614 Building with local re-sources
1602 Hand tools
1636 Power direct from the Sun and Earth
306 The small farm
732 Diseases of the Third World
734 World health

1

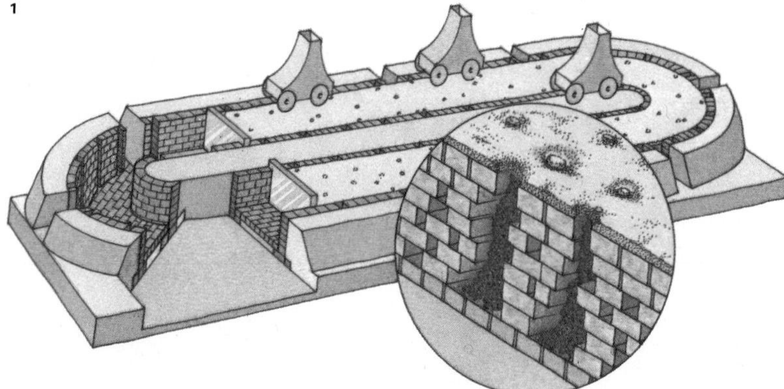

1 In rural areas bricks are made by ancient manual processes. In India, where a rural brick industry provides about half a million jobs, efforts have been made to improve the output of these brickworks by the introduction of an inexpensive kiln designed for simplicity of installation and use. An Indian trench kiln is illustrated here. A typical kiln with a capacity of up to 28,000 bricks each day would be 213ft (65m) long and 82ft (25m) wide overall, the depth of the "trench" being 7ft (2.25m). There is no roof. The top courses of "green" bricks are laid close and covered with ash, leaving only coal feed holes. The kiln is fired section by section, one each day, the 55ft (17m) tall steel chimneys, mounted on wheels, being moved to the next section to be fired.

2 This traditional mud house, which can rarely survive more than five years of tropical rains, could be made to last three to four times as long if its weak point – the base of its outer walls – was protected. This has been successfully achieved in Zaïre The method shown in [3A] is to dig a shallow foundation 14in (35cm) deep by 14 in (35cm) wide round the house close to the existing walls. The trench is filled with stones and clay mortar on which is built a low stone wall 39in(1m) high against the house wall. The top and upper mud wall are protected with cement.

2

3 A B C

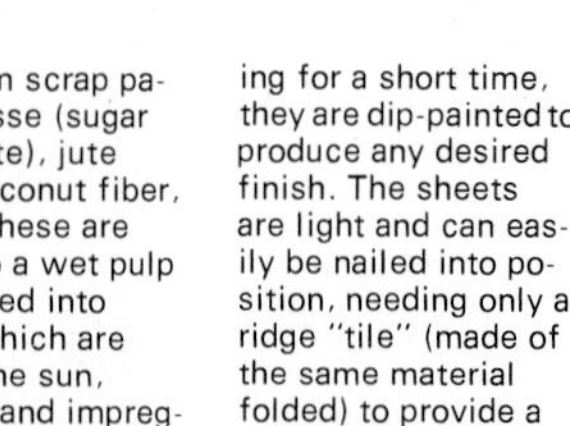

3 Thatch is one of the traditional roofing materials [A], even in regions with a heavy rainfall. Thatch needs support and timber is generally used for this purpose. But sawn timber is expensive and its cost tends to offset the only advantage of thatch – its cheapness. Thatch can also present other problems: it is susceptible to attack by fungi and vermin, and it burns easily, constituting a fire hazard. Commonly used alternatives include sheets of galvanized steel, corrugated asbestos cement sheets [A], and, in some developing countries, clay tiles [B]. None of these is cheap, and corrugated sheets made from asphalt and paper felt [C] provide a good substitute at less cost. The material is made from scrap paper, bagasse (sugar cane waste), jute waste, coconut fiber, or rags. These are made into a wet pulp and pressed into sheets, which are dried in the sun, trimmed, and impregnated in a bath of paving asphalt. After curing for a short time, they are dip-painted to produce any desired finish. The sheets are light and can easily be nailed into position, needing only a ridge "tile" (made of the same material folded) to provide a completely watertight roof. This is an excellent example of how local materials and labor can be used. Timber also has a cheap available alternative in bamboo, which is long-lasting and strong. Until now it has been little used as a building material because local people have not known how to joint it effectively. But they now use the results of research that has shown that the application of modern engineering practice can produce relatively large bamboo structures with a good strength-to-weight ratio.

Heating and laundry

A heating system that has proved successful in Zambia uses an airtight brick enclosure, about 39in (1m) high and 27in (70cm) wide, built 14in (35cm) from an outside wall. Two holes in the wall lead to the enclosure. The hole at ground level is just large enough to take a lighted coal pot; the second, 31in (80cm) above it, is made large enough for a single air brick. A thick clay outer wall reduces heat loss to a minimum.

After a coal pot is put in, the bricks of the enclosure heat up in about an hour. They hold the heat (in much the same way as does a Western storage heater) long after the fuel has burnt away. In Zambia the charcoal cooking pot is put into the enclosure as soon as the evening meal has been prepared and no more fuel is needed.

Even the electric washing machine has a low-cost equivalent, which has been successfully introduced in Afghanistan. A washing machine works by continually agitating hot water and the laundry immersed in it. Washing by hand has three drawbacks: the skin of the hands becomes sore and unsightly, the temperature of the washing water is limited to that which the hands can bear, and a considerable amount of human effort is wasted in the task of bending over the tub and agitating the wash.

The "rural" washing machine is basically a tub in which a vertical plunger, about half the diameter of the tub, is used to agitate the laundry. The plunger has a long wooden handle and is centered in the tub by passing it through a hole in the lid. A long tub can have two plungers—one at each end—operated by a lever pivoted between the two and having a handle at one end. All three disadvantages of hand-washing are avoided: the operator's hands are kept dry, the water can be heated almost to boiling, and the plunger makes the best use of muscle power.

These few examples demonstrate that the potential for the applications of low-cost technology are enormous. Many people could benefit from them today, instead of waiting for their individual society to attain the levels of sophisticated Western technology.

KEY

In many developing areas of the world houses are small and have no separate kitchens. The wife may squat on a stool by a charcoal stove in the corner of a partly roofed courtyard, pots and basins around her. A replacement "modern" kitchen, as shown here, must reflect her local life style.

4

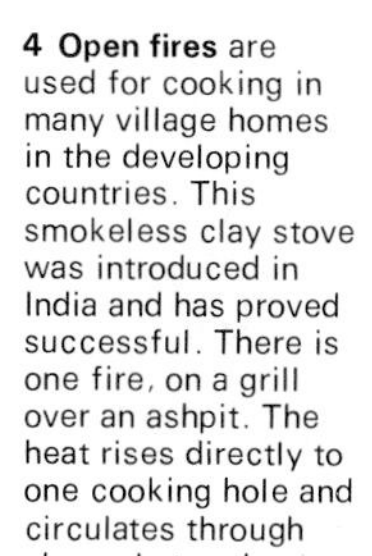

4 Open fires are used for cooking in many village homes in the developing countries. This smokeless clay stove was introduced in India and has proved successful. There is one fire, on a grill over an ashpit. The heat rises directly to one cooking hole and circulates through channels to others.

5

2
1

5 This simple solar water heater gives a steady supply of hot water when used in countries that have plenty of warm sunshine. Basically it consists of a flat heater tank [1] angled toward the midday sun and a storage tank [2] at a higher level. The tanks are connected by large-bore pipes. Circulation is by gravity.

6 Open pits are still used as outdoor toilets in many villages in the Third World. A water-seal bowl improves such a toilet by keeping odors in and flies out of the pit. The Western porcelain water closet has been successfully copied in concrete in the Philippines at a fraction of the cost. A wooden mold is packed with two parts sand to one cement with enough water to make the mix workable. After 20 minutes the bowl and outlet are dug out with a spoon. Next, dry cement is sprinkled over the wet interior surface to make it smooth. The mold is removed after 48 hours.

6

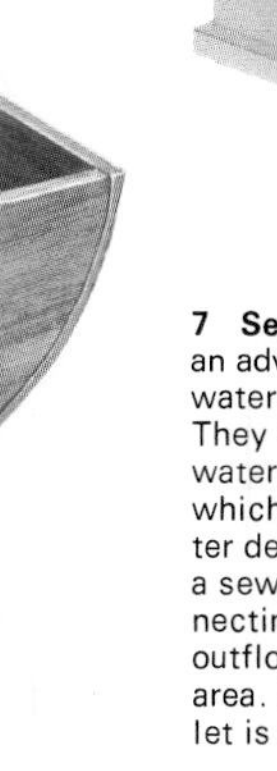

7

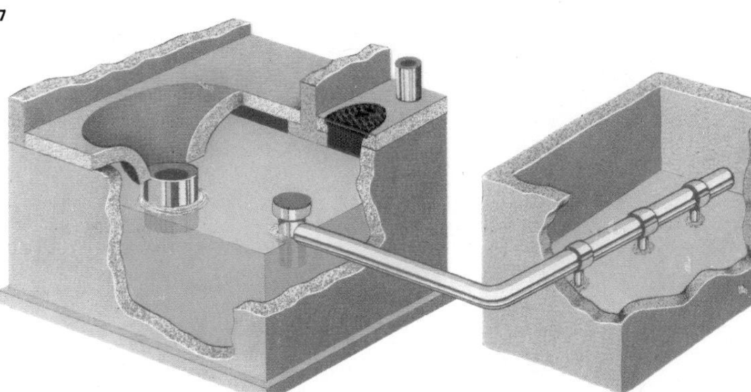

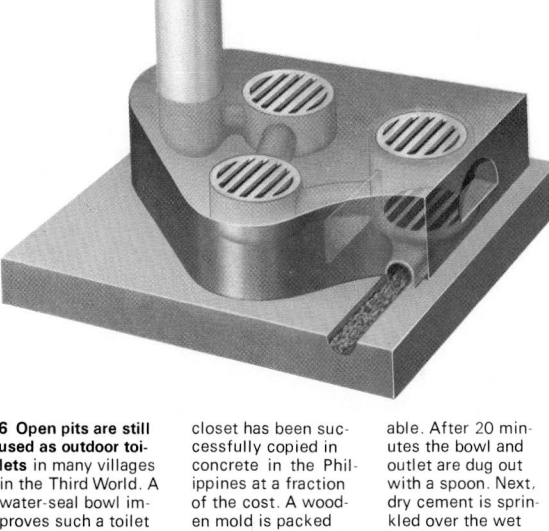

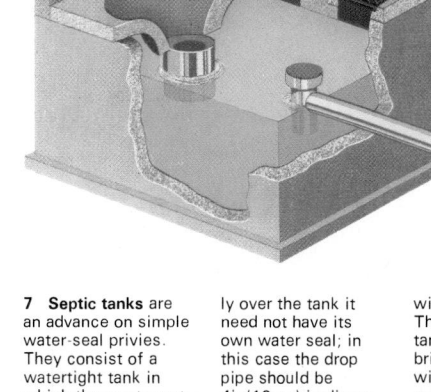

7 Septic tanks are an advance on simple water-seal privies. They consist of a watertight tank in which the waste matter decomposes and a sewer pipe connecting the tank's outflow to a drain area. If the water toilet is situated directly over the tank it need not have its own water seal; in this case the drop pipe should be 4in(10cm) in diameter and dip 10 cm below the natural water level of the tank. The pipe is connected directly to the squatting plate with an airtight seal. The decomposition tank can be made of brick or stone faced with rich cement mortar. Alternatively it can be made of concrete or from a 36-in(90-cm) or 47.2-in(120-cm) sewer pipe set vertically, its bottom sealed with concrete. For use by one family it should have a capacity of not less than 36cuft(1m³). Natural decomposition forms a sludge that settles, an effluent that passes into a seepage pit, and gas that must be given an outlet through a soil stack.

Rubber and plastics

Rubber and plastics are two commonly used modern materials that both consist of complex molecules known as polymers. These polymers have long molecules built up from simpler units attached to each other repeatedly, like links in a chain. The type of chemical reaction by which they are formed is called polymerization. Most rubbers are elastic—that is, they return to their original shape after being stretched or bent. This property and the fact that rubber was originally a natural product are generally supposed to distinguish rubbers from man-made plastics.

Natural rubber: extraction and treatment

Nearly all natural rubber comes from a South American rubber tree *(Hevea brasiliensis)* although several other plants, including some nettles, contain a rubbery liquid sap, or latex. The rubber tree originally grew in Brazil. But in the late 1800s seedlings were raised, first in London's Kew Gardens and then in Malaya, and today most of the world's natural rubber comes from Malaysia.

Natural rubber is a polymer of isoprene. The latex is obtained from the tree by "tapping"—it seeps out through spiral cuts made in the bark. The liquid latex is coagulated (made solid), dried, and exported as sheets of raw rubber [1, 3]. This is a weak, sticky, and not very elastic material. Its strength and elasticity are improved by the addition of sulfur in a process known as vulcanization, or curing, of rubber. Vulcanized rubber is harder and springier than raw rubber because atoms of sulfur form cross-links between the long polymer molecules so that these can no longer slide over one another so easily. Rubber containing a great deal of sulfur has many cross-links and so is rigid; this hard material is called ebonite.

The strength and wear resistance of rubber are also improved by the addition of fillers, which are powdery or fibrous substances mixed into the rubber and include carbon black, silica, and cotton flock.

Natural rubber, vulcanized and filled, is a useful elastic material and is widely employed although it is rather expensive to produce. Since the mid-1960s its production has been greatly outstripped by that of synthetic rubbers [2].

Man-made rubbers and plastics

The first useful synthetic or artificially made rubbers were produced during World War II. Since that time many kinds have been developed. Perhaps the most important, in terms of the quantity produced, is styrene butadiene rubber (SBR). Most of the raw materials for this rubber come from petroleum. SBR is a copolymer made from two chemicals, styrene and butadiene [5].

Other synthetic rubbers include Neoprene and Hypalon [Key], both employed in industry because of their resistance to chemicals. Silicone rubbers are a fairly recent development. They are remarkable polymers because, unlike most others, their long chainlike molecules have "backbones" not of carbon atoms but of silicon atoms. This makes them resistant to extremes of heat and cold and they are widely used as seals for jet engines and aircraft windows.

Plastics are now taken so much for granted that it is difficult to imagine what life

CONNECTIONS

See also
1620 Fibers for fabrics
1600 Tailor-made materials
1804 Chemical engineeri
1560 Complex chemicals and their structures
1574 Polymers: giant molecules

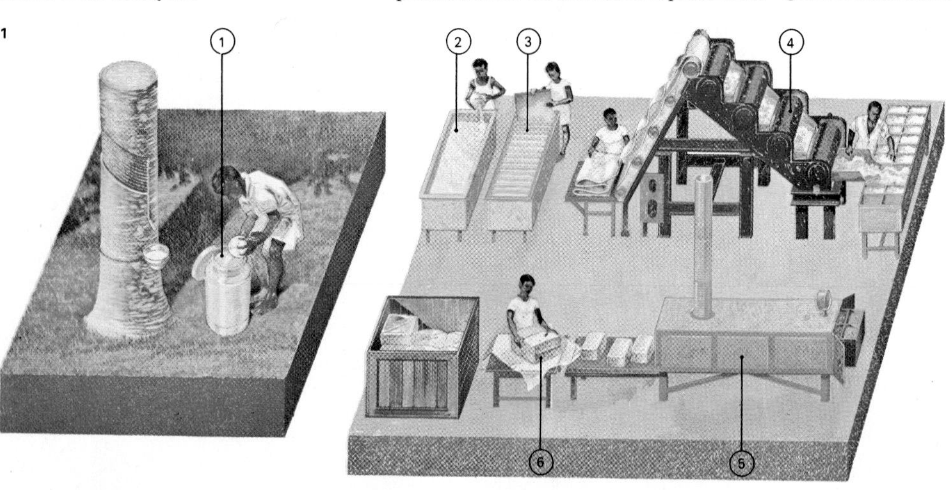

1 Plantation rubber begins life as a watery latex tapped from a spiral cut on a rubber tree *(Hevea brasiliensis)*. Foreign matter is filtered out and the latex coagulated into solid rubber with an acid [2]. In coagulation tanks the rubber is separated into slabs by partitions [3]. The slabs are dried first by rollers [4] then by passing them through a drying tunnel [5]. The raw rubber is then packed for export [6]. Malaysia is the world's largest producer of natural rubber.

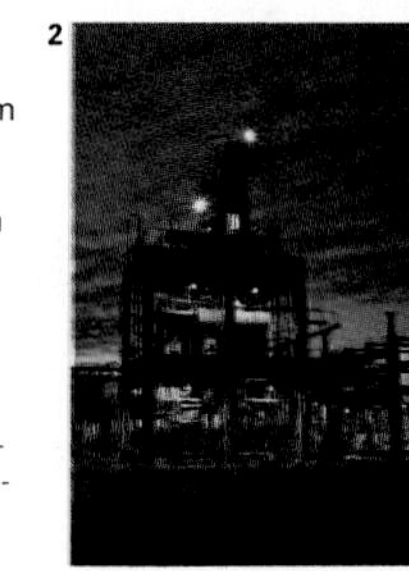

2 Since the mid-1960s the production of petroleum-based synthetic rubbers has far outstripped the production of natural rubber.

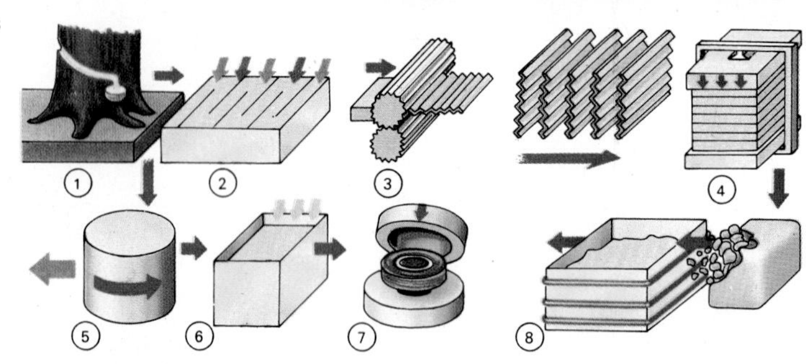

3 At the factory, latex from a rubber tree can be acid-coagulated and squeeze-dried [1–4] or concentrated by centrifuge [5]. Rubber is melted [8] or vulcanized [6] (hardened) with sulfur after which it can be shaped in molds [7].

4 An inflatable boat makes use of rubber's unique properties. Not all rubbers resist stresses equally. Special compounding methods produce rubbers with particular, required properties. The rubber itself is often a mixture of natural and synthetic products. The degree of vulcanization and the presence of reinforcing and filling materials also determine the final properties of the rubber.

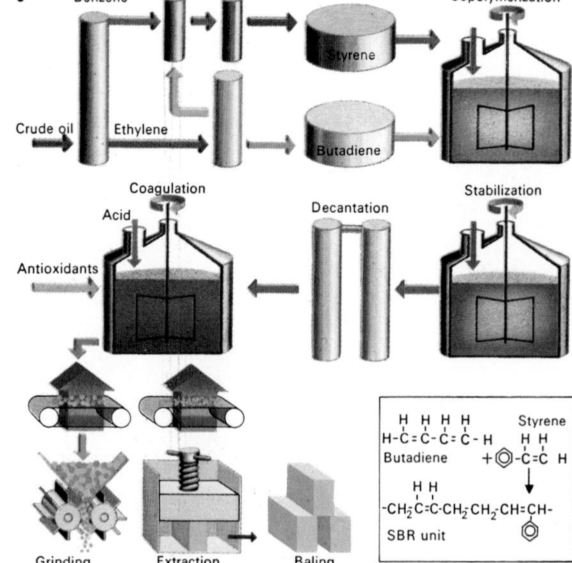

Benzene
Copolymerization
Styrene
Crude oil
Ethylene
Butadiene
Coagulation
Acid
Decantation
Stabilization
Antioxidants
Grinding
Extraction
Baling
Styrene
Butadiene
SBR unit

5 Styrene butadiene rubber (SBR) is the major synthetic rubber used widely for tires, conveyor belts, and other commercial and industrial products. It is a copolymer made by polymerizing two chemicals together. These are styrene and butadiene, which originate in crude oil. A catalyst is required, as in most polymerization reactions, to speed up the reaction. In later parts of the process stabilizers and antioxidants are added to prevent the rubber breaking down and to protect it from oxidation by air. It is then dried and baled.

was like without them [8]. The first man-made polymers to be called plastics were compounds made from a naturally occurring polymer, cellulose. Celluloid (cellulose nitrate) was one such early plastic. It was most famous, or infamous, as the material of highly inflammable films and dolls.

Bakelite, another early plastic, is still used in large quantities for making electrical plugs and connectors. Bakelite was the first of the thermosetting plastics—that is, plastics that set hard on heating and cannot be remelted without decomposing. More recent thermosetting plastics include urea and melamine plastics, used for plastic dinnerware and decorative laminates and the epoxy resins, most familiar as tubes of household glue. When mixed with a chemical called a catalyst (provided in a separate tube), an epoxy cement polymerizes to become very strong, hard, and resistant to chemicals. For these reasons many protective paints and coatings also contain epoxy compounds.

The other large group of plastics consists of the thermoplastics, so called because they soften on heating. Familiar articles made from them include polyethylene bowls and buckets; polyester and nylon fabrics; Teflon (PTFE) non-stick pan liners and polyvinyl chlotide (PVC) clothing.

Like rubbers, plastics become stiffer when their long polymer molecules are cross-linked. Thermosetting plastics that are hard and stiff contain many cross-links, those that are more pliable contain fewer cross-members.

Techniques of molding

Plastics are generally molded into the shapes required. Thermosetting plastics are often molded in pellet form. The pellets are compressed, heated until they flow and allowed to harden to take on the shape of the mold. Thermoplastics are frequently pressure-molded [7]. Pipes, rods, and sheets of plastics and rubbers are generally formed by extrusion in which the material is forced through a hole like toothpaste being squeezed from a tube. The extrude often is equipped with a screw for forcing the materials through a shaped hole or die [6].

KEY
A
Polyethylene
1
2
3
B
Hypalon
Hydrogen
Carbon
Oxygen
Sulfur
Chlorine

Plastics and rubbers are chemically similar—they are all polymers. They can even be made from the same starting material, called a monomer. This diagram shows [A] the polymerization of ethylene [1] to form the plastic polyethylene. The same monomer [B] will react with sulfur dioxide [2] and chlorine [3] to produce the synthetic rubber called Hypalon. Natural rubber is composed of similar long-chain polymer molecules. They extend when the rubber is stretched and contract rapidly back to their original length when the tension is released, giving both kinds of rubber their elasticity.

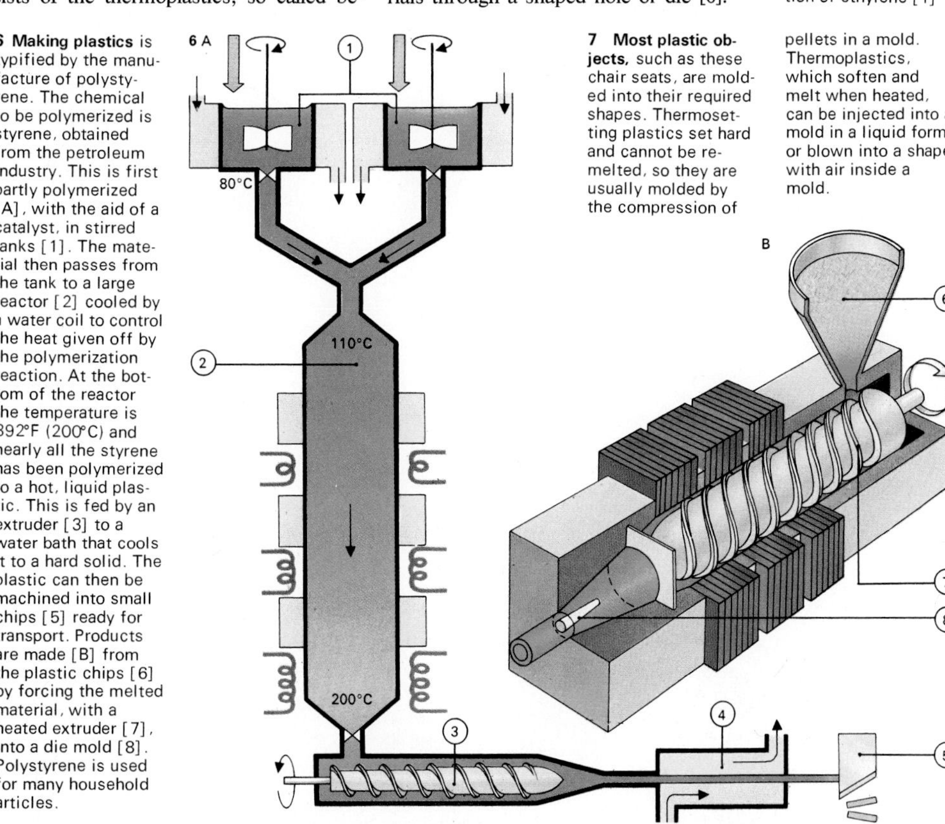
6 A
1
80°C
2
110°C
200°C
3
4
5
B
6
7
8

6 Making plastics is typified by the manufacture of polystyrene. The chemical to be polymerized is styrene, obtained from the petroleum industry. This is first partly polymerized [A], with the aid of a catalyst, in stirred tanks [1]. The material then passes from the tank to a large reactor [2] cooled by a water coil to control the heat given off by the polymerization reaction. At the bottom of the reactor the temperature is 392°F (200°C) and nearly all the styrene has been polymerized to a hot, liquid plastic. This is fed by an extruder [3] to a water bath that cools it to a hard solid. The plastic can then be machined into small chips [5] ready for transport. Products are made [B] from the plastic chips [6] by forcing the melted material, with a heated extruder [7], into a die mold [8]. Polystyrene is used for many household articles.

7 Most plastic objects, such as these chair seats, are molded into their required shapes. Thermosetting plastics set hard and cannot be remelted, so they are usually molded by the compression of pellets in a mold. Thermoplastics, which soften and melt when heated, can be injected into a mold in a liquid form or blown into a shape with air inside a mold.

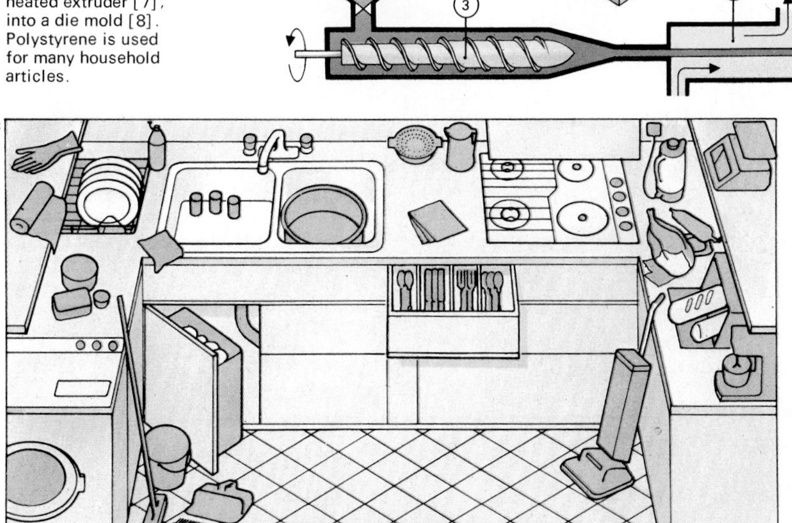

8 The domestic uses of plastic are many. Utensils range from food containers to dishpans. Even wine is sometimes bottled in plastic. Deprived of plastics, modern kitchens appear unfurnished.

9 Transparent plastics, such as polyesters and the acrylics, can be used to preserve biological specimens and also find use as materials for ornaments. Clear plastic is now widely used as a glass substitute for the tops of tables.

Fibers for fabrics

The word fabric once described any material made from wool, silk, cotton, or other animal or vegetable fiber. But today the choice of fabrics has been greatly increased by the introduction of man-made fibers. Synthetic fabrics made from them are relatively cheap and have special properties such as high strength and resistance to creasing and rotting. In many modern fabrics a natural fiber such as wool is interwoven with a synthetic fiber such as Dacron thus combining the advantages of the two.

Animal and vegetable fibers

Cotton is the most widely used of the vegetable fibers. Cotton fiber comes from the seed pod of the cotton plant *(Gossypium)* and, like other vegetable fibers, is composed mostly of cellulose. The shorter fibers of the cotton plant supply most of the world's pure cellulose and only the longer fibers are used for textiles.

Next in importance is linen, which is made from long fibers in the stalk of the flax plant *(Linum)*. Jute *(Corchorus)*, hemp *(Cannabis)*, and ramie *(Boehmeria nivea)* are other stalk, or bast, fibers. Sisal is a fiber taken from the leaf of the agave plant *(Agave sisalana)*. Cotton and linen are the only vegetable fibers widely used for textiles. The others are generally too coarse and are used mainly for sacking, carpet backing, and ropes.

Wool is the best known animal fiber. Wool fabrics have low strength but are uniquely comfortable and warm because the soft, springy fibers trap air, which insulates the wearer against cold. The main source of wool is the sheep, but some of the best wools come from goats. Cashmere is a fine fabric made from the fleece of the Kashmir goat living in northern India and Tibet. Mohair is a high quality cloth made from the wool of the Angora goat, also a native of Asia. Fine, soft wools also come from members of the camel family—the llama, alpaca, guanaco, and vicuña [2], all of which live in South America.

Wool is one of the few fibers that can be matted into felt. This process adds to its softness. All wools, however, have the disadvantage of vulnerability to attack by pests.

Silk, the only other animal fiber of importance, has long been used to make fabrics of delicate luster and smoothness. Because of its cost, however, it has largely been superseded by synthetic fibers. The home of silk production is the Far East where silkworms [3], fed on mulberry leaves, eventually spin a continuous silk thread up to 0.5 mile (800m) long to make a cocoon.

The methods used in spinning, weaving, and knitting natural fibers into fabrics are all very similar to one another [1].

Synthetic fiber production

There are two kinds of synthetic fibers. The first is derived from plant cellulose, and so can be considered as "semi-synthetic" because cellulose ia a natural polymer with molecules made up of thousands of glucose sub-units linked together in a chain.

Rayon is a fabric made of fibers of pure cellulose. Plant cellulose is dissolved by various chemical processes into a thick liquid and then regenerated in the form of spun fibers. A chemical solution of cellulose is

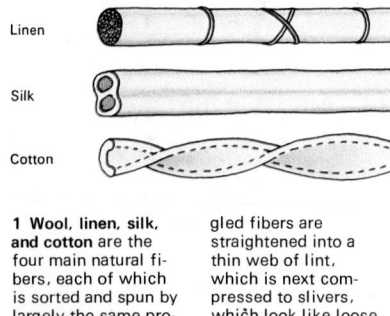

CONNECTIONS

See also

1618 Rubber and plastics
1622 Making cloth
1590 Bark, hide, and horn
1812 Color chemistry
362 Fiber and oil crops

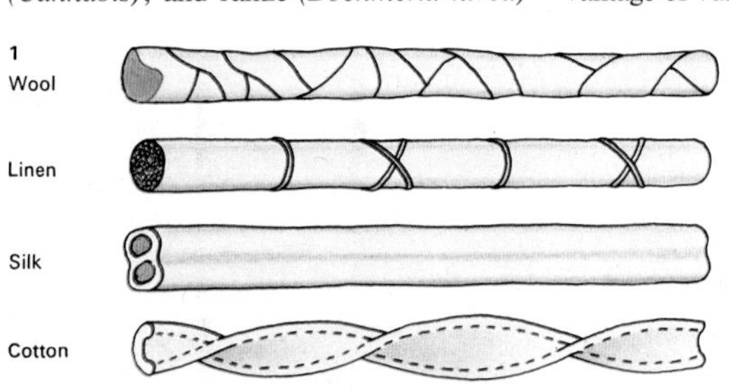

1
Wool
Linen
Silk
Cotton

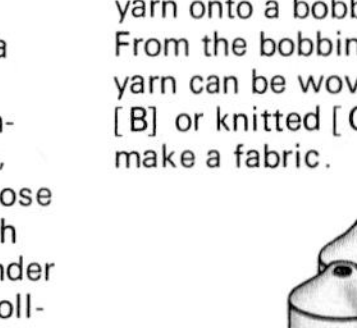

Beater cylinders
A
Carding

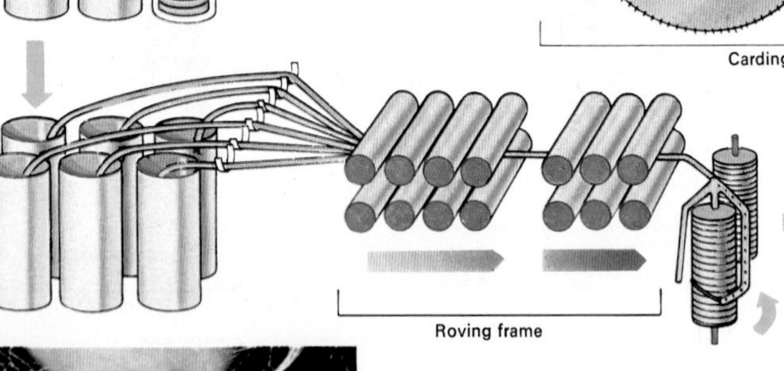

Roving frame

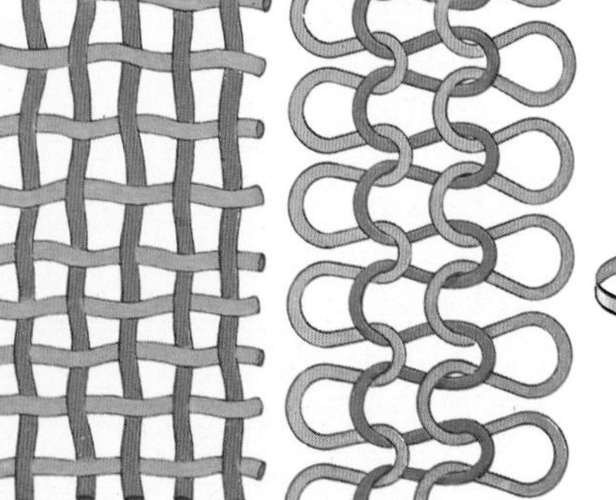

B
C

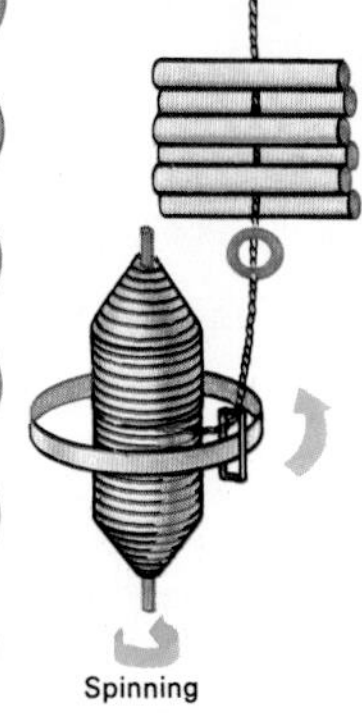

Spinning

1 Wool, linen, silk, and cotton are the four main natural fibers, each of which is sorted and spun by largely the same processes [A]. After the raw material has been cleaned it is "opened" or arranged into a thick mat by passing it through a beater cylinder. It is then "carded" or combed by huge rollers covered with wire teeth. The tangled fibers are straightened into a thin web of lint, which is next compressed to slivers, which look like loose ropes of yarn. Each sliver is drawn, under tension, through rollers and coiled onto a roving frame. The "roving" is twisted and retwisted, becoming continually finer and stronger, before it is finally wound as finished yarn onto a bobbin. From the bobbin the yarn can be woven [B] or knitted [C] to make a fabric.

2 The dense coat of the vicuña *(Lama vicugna)* protects it from the cold of the high Andes, where it lives at altitudes of 14,000ft (4,270m). A vicuña is a South American member of the camel family and its wool is valued for its high quality.

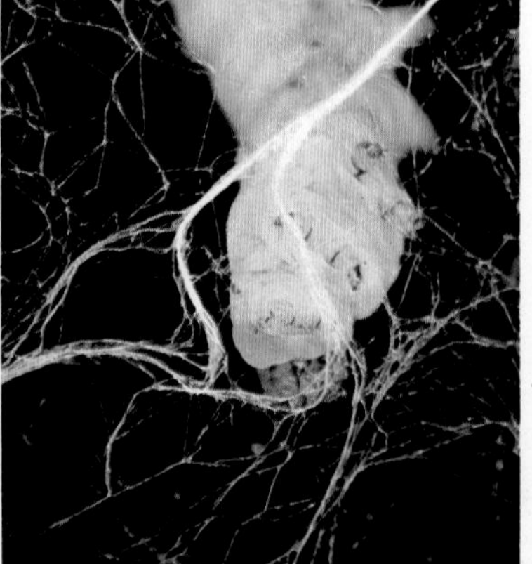

3 Silkworms, such as the Chinese silkworm *(Bombyx mori)*, differ from other caterpillars not by producing silk but by making much more of it. Silk is forced out through a small spinneret between the jaws and hardens on contact with air.

pumped through a spinneret (named after the silkworm's spinning gland) into a chemical solution, in which it coagulates into fine threads (filaments) [Key]. These filaments are then twisted together to make the rayon yarn. Another cellulose fabric is rayon acetate, the fibers of which are made by treating cellulose with acetic and sulfuric acids. The fibers of cellulose acetate are also made through a spinneret. Rayons dye easily and they also lose their strength when wet, only to regain it again when dry.

The second and much larger group contains the purely synthetic fibers—nylon and polyester—known by such trademarks as Antron and Dacron. The materials for these are made entirely from chemicals (often by-products of petroleum).

Spinning plastics into fibers often involves melting and extrusion through a spinneret [4]. For plastics that are sensitive to heating, including the acrylics used to make such fabrics as Acrilan, it may be necessary to dissolve the plastic before spinning the fiber. Acrylic fibers have a soft, woollike feel and are often used for making blankets and winter clothing. Synthetic fibers are often superior to natural fibers. They can be stronger, more flexible, and are usually resistant to heat, rot, or abrasion.

Dyeing and finishing

Natural fibers, with the exception of silk, are easy to dye, but special chemical processes are sometimes necessary to make dyes adhere to synthetics. Unwanted natural color is removed by bleaching. Natural fibers and rayon can be treated with resins to render them crease-resistant or with an elastic plastic to make them waterproof and stainproof.

There are two fibers used in fabrics that are entirely mineral in composition. Asbestos fibers, from the mineral chrysotile, are woven into fire-resistant matting and clothing [5]. Glass fibers are made by melting glass in a tank perforated with tiny holes through which the glass drips as filaments, which are chilled and snapped into short fibers by air or steam. Fiberglass fabric, hardened with a synthetic resin, is very strong.[7].

KEY

Spinnerets are finely perforated plates or tubes that extrude threads from chemical solutions of polymers during the course of manufacturing all man-made fibers.

4

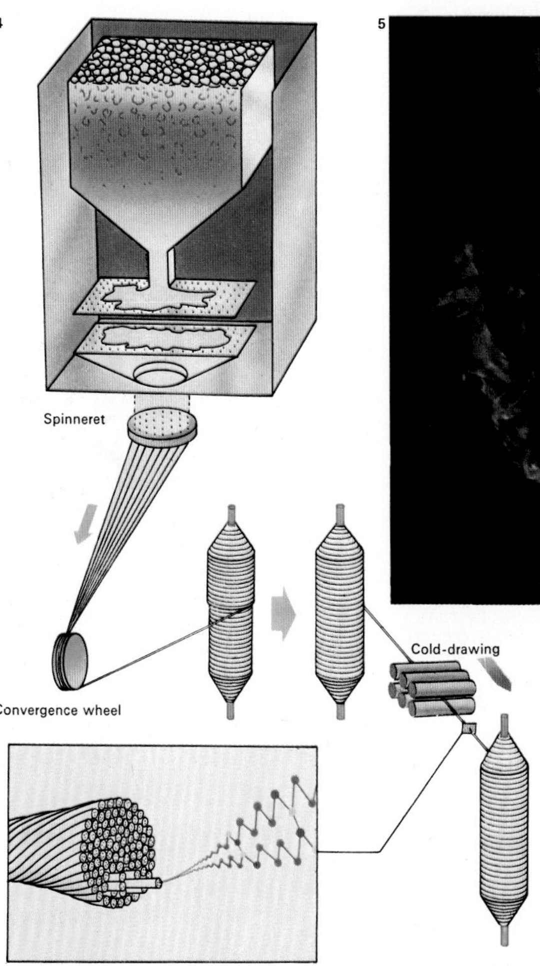

Spinneret
Convergence wheel
Cold-drawing

4 In making nylon two chemical compounds, such as hexamethylenediamine and adipic acid, are melted and combined under pressure in a hopper. The liquid nylon thus formed is filtered through metal gauze or sand and extruded as very fine filaments, or strands, through a spinneret. The filaments are twisted and united into yarn by a convergence wheel, which feeds the yarn onto bobbins. It is then cold-drawn or stretched, to alter the molecular structure of the yarn filaments and thus to give them greater strength and elasticity. This process is carried out by unwinding the yarn from the bobbin, passing it through rollers to stretch it, and then winding it onto another bobbin. Nylon is one of the strongest and most elastic of all plastics and is used for domestic and industrial purposes.

5

5 Asbestos fibers are mineral, and so do not burn or char. For this reason clothing woven from asbestos is invaluable for fire-fighting and is often aluminized or "silvered" to reflect heat and keep the wearer cool. Asbestos clothing is also resistant to chemicals and, because asbestos is a poor conductor of electricity, it protects against electric shocks. Asbestos is also used in soundproofing.

6

6 Synthetic fibers are used for many purposes calling for great strength, as in parachute making. Nylon cords and ropes vie with steel in strength and are much stronger than natural fibers.

7

7 Automobile bodies and many other products are now made of materials woven from fiberglass. The flexible glass fibers are stronger than steel and resistant to heat, corrosion, and rust.

Making cloth

Nearly all textiles for clothes, sacks, carpets, and other coverings are made by looping or interlacing fiber strands together. The strands can be of natural origin—for example wool and cotton—or they can be synthetics such as nylon and Dacron. Additionally, natural and man-made fibers are often woven together, as in the Dacron/cotton mixtures used for shirts and blouses.

Fibers into fabrics

Each fiber strand, or yarn, is composed of many short fibers twisted together by an operation called spinning [1, 2]. When two or more yarns are interlaced in the process of weaving, carried out on a machine called a loom [Key, 3], a length of cloth is made. But when a single continuous length of yarn is looped into a fabric the operation is called knitting. Industrially, knitting is also carried out on machines [4, 5].

Lace fabrics are made by interlacing and twisting yarns together. Felt fabrics are exceptional in that they are not knitted or woven. They are made by pounding hot, wet wool and other fibers together. The soft feel of "cut velvet" is given by many tufts of severed yarn endings [7], although "figured" velvet, also a woven fabric, is not cut. Its softness is derived from the raised loops of fibers of wool, cotton, or synthetics.

The preparation of fibers involves a number of processes. For cotton these include brushing fibers from the seed bolls in a cotton gin; beating the fibers to loosen them; rolling or lapping them flat and scutching (beating) them into fleecy masses. All of these processes are now carried out completely by machines.

Cotton fibers are straightened in a carding machine, which also forms them into a loose rope or sliver. Only the longest fibers are used for high-quality yarns and are obtained by combing them out on a machine in which the fibers are held by rows of pins. The slivers are then drawn through a series of rubber rollers, each pair of which moves faster than the previous pair so that the fibers elongate to form rovings. These rovings are then ready for spinning.

Wool needs to be washed in detergent to remove dirt and grease. Fine worsted wool yarns use only the longer fibers, selected by a combing operation. Retting is the name of a treatment for flax fibers (for linen) in which they are rotted in water to soften them. Silk comes from the cocoon of the silkworm and requires a special treatment with soap or detergent to remove the gum that bound the filaments in the cocoon.

Spinning and weaving

The textile industry grew up only in the eighteenth and nineteenth centuries, although spinning and weaving are age-old traditional occupations. The industry progressed as the result of a series of British inventions. The inventors included Richard Arkwright (1732–92), whose spinning frame of 1768 first provided a cotton yarn strong enough to be used as the warp, or lengthwise thread, for machine-operated looms. Two years later, in 1770, James Hargreaves (died 1778) patented the spinning jenny, which spun many threads at once. Other early inventions included the spinning mule of Samuel Crompton (1753–1827) and the power loom of Edmund Cart-

CONNECTIONS
See also
1620 Fibers for fabrics
1590 Bark, hide, and horn
1220 The early Industrial Revolution
1812 Color chemistry
1808 Soaps and detergents

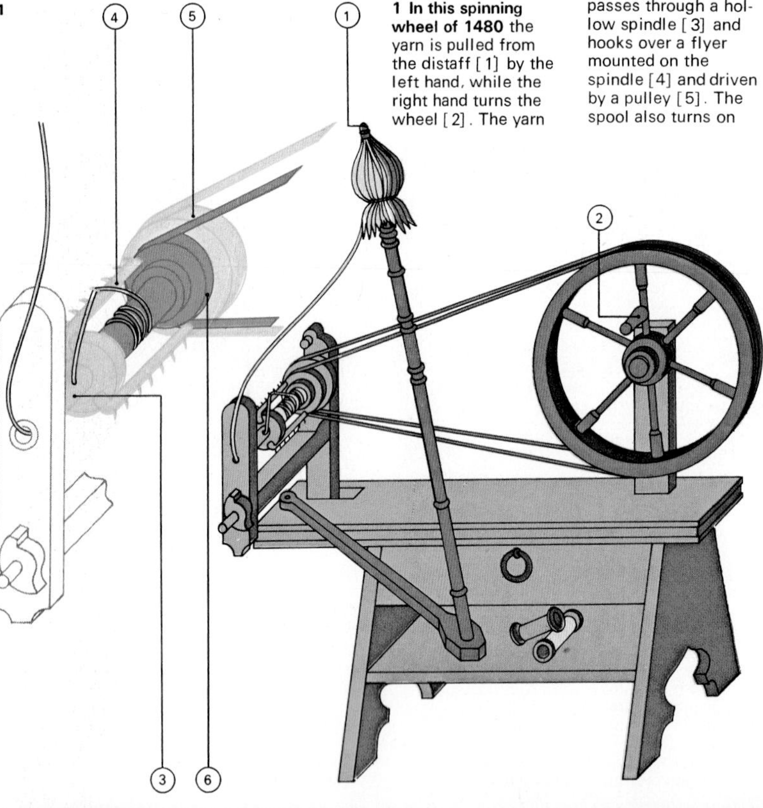
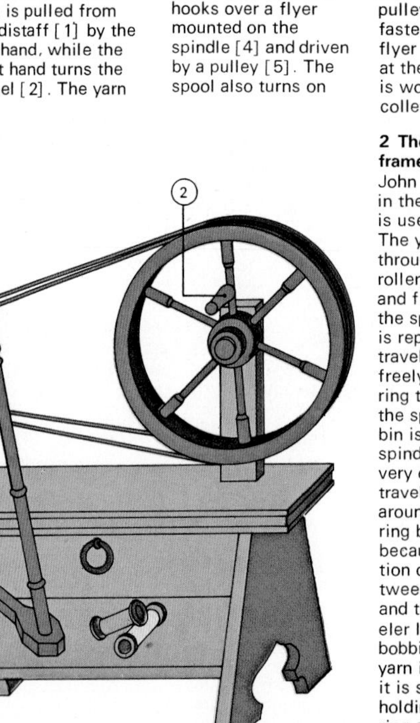
1
4
5
1
2
3
6

1 In this spinning wheel of 1480 the yarn is pulled from the distaff [1] by the left hand, while the right hand turns the wheel [2]. The yarn passes through a hollow spindle [3] and hooks over a flyer mounted on the spindle [4] and driven by a pulley [5]. The spool also turns on the spindle but is attached to a smaller pulley [6] that turns faster, so that the flyer twists the yarn at the same time as it is wound onto the collecting spool.

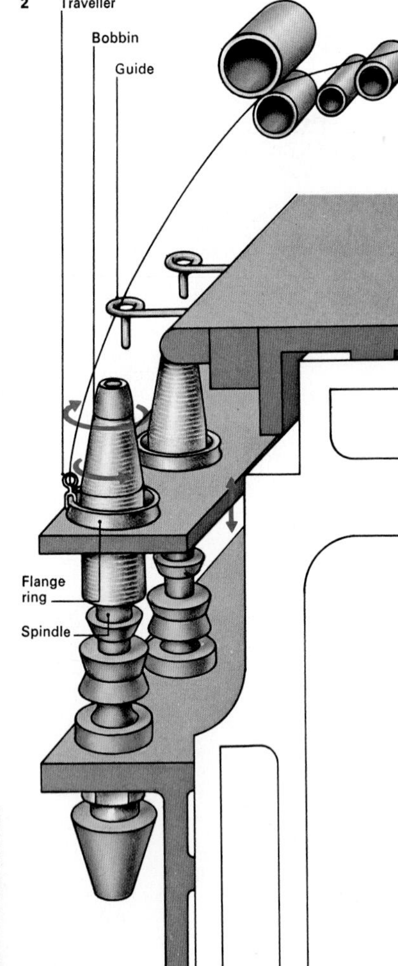
2
Traveller
Bobbin
Guide
Flange ring
Spindle

2 The ring spinning frame, invented by John Thorpe in 1828 in the United States, is used for cotton. The yarn passes through a series of rollers and a guide, and finally down to the spindle. The flyer is replaced by a small traveler that runs freely on a flange ring that surrounds the spindle. The bobbin is carried on the spindle and rotates very quickly. The traveler is pulled around the flange ring by the yarn and, because of the friction occurring between the traveler and the ring, the traveler lags behind the bobbin so that the yarn is wound on as it is spun. The plate holding the flange ring and traveler rises and falls, distributing the yarn evenly on the bobbin.

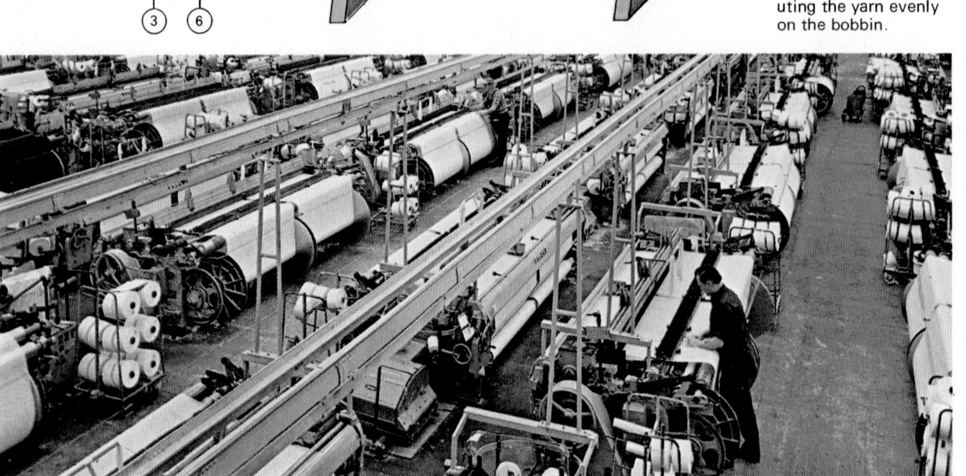

3 A modern textile factory generally has a number of looms all working at the same time. An attendant watches one or more machines, joining any broken yarn and supplying the loom with full bobbins. The strength and elasticity of yarn varies with temperature and amount of moisture in the air, and so the whole room is air-conditioned to keep breakages to a minimum and to stabilize the settings of the fine controls of the high-speed machines.

wright (1743–1823). One of the greatest contributions to textile production was the invention of the cotton gin by the American Eli Whitney (1765–1825) in 1793.

In spinning, the rovings are passed to rotating spindles carrying bobbins, all mounted on a moving frame of the kind originally invented by Samuel Crompton and called the spinning mule. The frame first moves outward, pulling out the roving to form a yarn and twisting it. Then it moves back and the yarn is wound evenly onto the bobbins, guided by wires. Worsted and cotton are now usually spun on a ring spinning frame invented in 1828 by John Thorpe in the United States [2].

In weaving, two yarns are employed: the warp, a set of lengthwise strands held firmly on a loom and alternately pulled apart, and the weft, which is carried crosswise through the parted warp strands by a shuttle to which it is attached. The warp strands are then closed together and the new weft strand is pushed back against the previous one by a device called a reed. Factory looms weave quickly because the weft threads are shot through the warp by an extremely fast shuttle. The edges of a cloth are strengthened by doubling the thread or using a stronger warp yarn. This edge is known as a selvage.

Finishing the fabrics

Fabrics are finished in a number of operations that include bleaching, dyeing, and printing. Bleaches such as hydrogen peroxide hypochlorites may be used to whiten a cloth before dyeing. Printing on cloth resembles that on paper: flat or cylindrical printing blocks or silk screen processes can be used.

The luster of a fabric, particularly cotton, can be improved in a number of ways, including singeing and mercerizing, a process using caustic soda. Wool fabrics are treated against shrinking by chemical treatment of the fibers. Creaseproofing is another finishing process, although it is not necessary for many synthetic fabrics that resist creasing well anyway. Fireproofing, waterproofing, and mothproofing are other finishing treatments carried out on a large scale.

KEY

In the first looms, weaving proceeded like darning, the weft being passed over and under the warp. In other early looms every other warp thread was attached to a stick, the heddle, which could be lifted to part the warp, allowing passage of the weft thread. The heddle eventually gave way to a device called the shaft, which parts the warp threads in various combinations to allow the weaving of patterns.

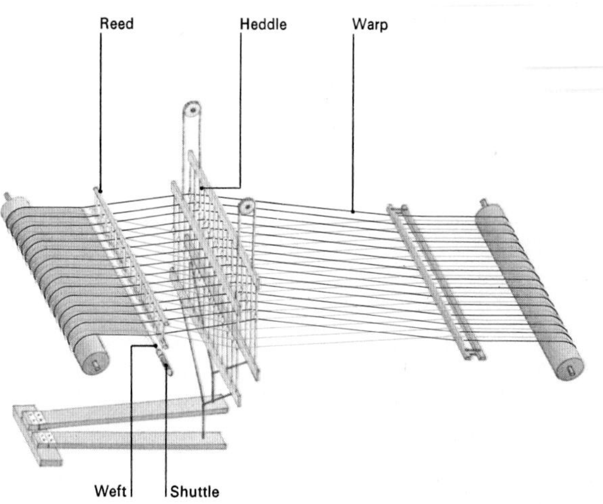
Reed
Heddle
Warp
Weft
Shuttle

4 Treadle and pulley operated the first really successful knitting machine, which was invented by William Lee in 1589. It could knit at the surprisingly fast rate of 600 stitches every minute.

1 Hooked needles
2 Presser bar
3 Shank of needle
4 Sinkers
5 Handle
6 Hinged arms
7 Bent bar
8 Bent pulley
9 Locker bar
10 Slur
11 Wheel

5 Modern knitting machines resulted in mass-produced hosiery. The power-driven circular knitting frame came into operation in the 1840s and the machine for closing seams 20 years later.

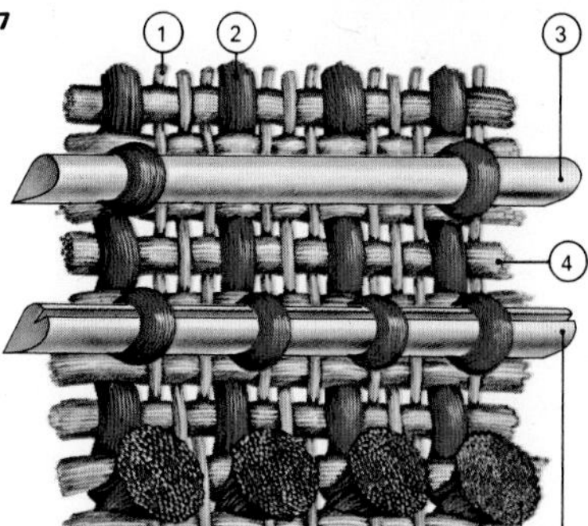

7 Velvet weaving originated in China. The pile warps are lifted for the insertion of the wire, which forms a loop in the pile. This wire has a blade at its end to sever the loops and leave the tufts as the wire is withdrawn.

1 Foundation warp
2 Pile warp
3 Wire for uncut pile, or terry
4 Foundation weft
5 Grooved wire for cut pile
6 Cut pile tufts

6 Designs are printed on cloth after it has been woven. Flat printing blocks with the design raised in relief or etched below the surface (intaglio) may be used or, as here, the cloth can be printed by means of inked rollers.

8 The seed heads of the teasel plant form a "brush" of hooked bristles. They are traditionally used for raising a nap on coarse tweed cloth such as Harris tweed and this method has not yet been bettered by a machine tool.

Making paper

Paper is one of the most common everyday materials of industrialized societies and one that man has been using for nearly two thousand years. He does not rely on paper merely to record his noblest conceptions but also uses it to fulfill his most basic needs. Apart from newspapers and books, paper is used for clothing, as containers for food and drink, and for decorating houses. As yet, a comparably cheap, light, and durable substitute for paper has eluded technology.

Most modern paper consists of interlaced fibers derived from wood, although some papers may also contain fibers from rags, other vegetable sources, and even synthetic materials. The production principle is as simple as the material itself. Timber is chopped up and, to some extent, purified. The fibers are next treated with chemicals and dispersed into water. They dry out as a thin film, so producing paper.

Industrial papermaking

The industrial manufacture of paper is a far more complex and far-reaching operation. Millions of trees are harvested every year solely to make paper [3]. There has been public concern about the depredations of the paper industry on natural forest areas, but responsible paper companies now arrange careful ecologically based programs to ensure that forests yield regular crops. Screens of standing trees are left around cleared areas to promote natural reseeding. In many places seedlings are planted to reestablish the forest.

In the forests of North America and Scandinavia the trees are cut and transported to rivers, which are often frozen over in winter. In spring they are then floated downstream by the thousands. In some places the logs are made into huge rafts and then towed to the factory, or trucks are used to carry the logs to the mill.

After arriving at the pulp mill the logs are stripped of bark and then treated in one of two ways. They may be disintegrated by grinding with huge grindstones and so reduced to what is known as mechanical pulp, or the logs may be "cooked" in large digesters, a process that breaks down the wood chemically. Wood has two principal constituents: cellulose and a complex substance called lignin that holds the cellulose fibers together, thus making the wood rigid. During the "cooking" the lignin is removed.

The product of this second process is known as chemical pulp [5]. The method is more gentle on the wood fiber than the mechanical process and the fibers, because they are less damaged, make stronger paper. Usually, however, the two types of pulp are mixed in proportions that vary with intended use.

Processing the pulp

If the pulp mill and paper mill are located close together liquid pulp may be pumped straight from one to the other. If they are distant then the pulp is partly dried and pressed before being dispatched. The dried pulp has to be broken up again at the paper mill in a machine called a Hydrapulper. It is then thoroughly dispersed in a process known as beating or refining. Next come the additives—such as china clay, coated whiting, rosin (usually mixed with alum)—plus other chemicals used as retention aids to

CONNECTIONS

See also
1770 History of printing
1772 Modern printing
1774 Copying and duplicating
1776 Newspapers and magazines
1778 Books and book publishing
1780 Reference books
872 Communication through writing: 2

1

1 Papyrus, the writing material of the ancient world, predated paper by at least 3,500 years. It was made from the papyrus reed *(Cyperus papyrus)*, an aquatic plant of the sedge family that still grows in the Nile Delta. It was prepared by laying strips of the reed side by side and then crossing them with other strips. It was then soaked in the water of the Nile, which created an adhesive and stuck the strips together. Finally, the sheet was hammered and left out to dry in the sun. Any surface roughness was removed by polishing the papyrus with ivory or a smooth shell.

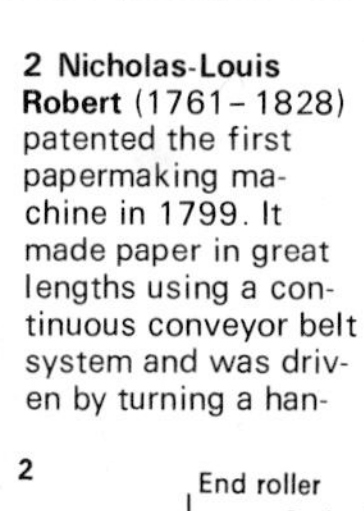

2 Nicholas-Louis Robert (1761–1828) patented the first papermaking machine in 1799. It made paper in great lengths using a continuous conveyor belt system and was driven by turning a handle. The prepared mixture of water and pulp was poured into an oval chest, then picked up by rotating copper bars and discharged onto the upper surface of an endless wire mesh running on two end rollers. The pulp passed between felt-covered squeezing rollers, removing most of the water, so that the web lifted off the wire and could be coiled on a roller. The tension of the wire was adjusted by a screw. The wire was shaken by a cross-bar driven by a wheel. This cross-bar could also be raised or lowered to alter the slope of the wire and thus the rate of water loss.

2

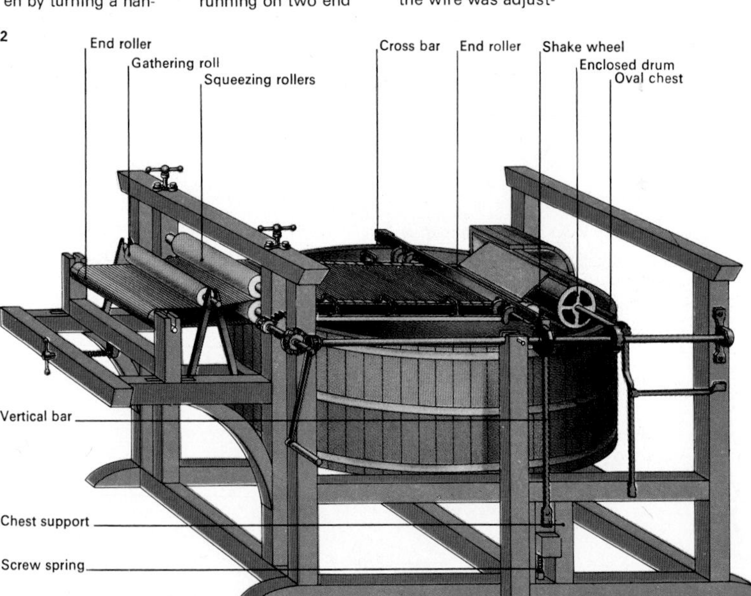

End roller
Gathering roll
Squeezing rollers
Cross bar
End roller
Shake wheel
Enclosed drum
Oval chest
Vertical bar
Chest support
Screw spring

3

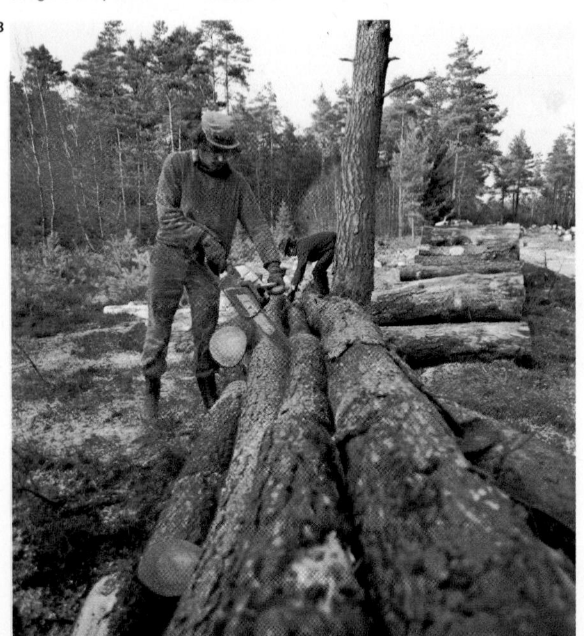

3 The growing demand for paper and board is depleting the world's forests of adult trees. One tree is needed for every 400 copies of a 40-page tabloid newspaper. But as forests are being cleared to meet the rising demand, the stock of trees is not being replenished. Even if sufficient land were available to plant new trees, it would still take 20–40 years for them to reach maturity. The need to recycle more waste paper therefore is becoming increasingly urgent. World consumption of paper and paperboard in 1973 was nearly 147 million tons, of which about 20% had been recycled. Clearly this proportion will have to increase significantly if there is not to be a world shortfall of pulp and paper, already predicted by the United Nations for 1980. Possible substitutes for wood pulp, such as certain grasses, are also being explored.

4

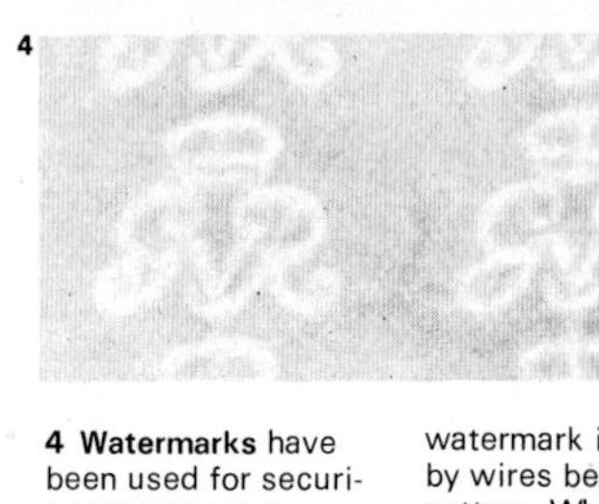

4 Watermarks have been used for security reasons or as marks of distinction since the latter part of the 13th century, when they were first used in Italy. They are still employed on documents and banknotes as a guarantee of authenticity. The watermark is made by wires bent into a pattern. When this comes into contact with a layer of wet pulp a translucent impression is made, which can be seen when the finished paper is held up to a light.

keep the additives on the fibers when the water is removed. Pigments to color the paper or to improve its whiteness—titanium dioxide is used—may be added.

The papermaking machine most often used—known as a Fourdrinier machine—has three main sections. At the wet end the slushed pulp of beaten fibers flows onto a moving band of finely woven wire or plastic mesh. There, aided by suction, much of the water drains away, leaving the fibers and most of the additives on the mesh. The wet "web" of paper runs onto the press section where it is carried on felt and passes between rollers that remove more water. The web is finally transferred to another felt surface in the drying sections and passes over as many as 60 drying cylinders.

Papermaking machines, some of which are more than 75ft (25m) wide, operate at a rate of more than 3,000ft (900m) per minute. Pulp, which enters the machine with more than 99 percent moisture, is transformed in a matter of seconds into finished paper with no more than five to ten percent moisture. This paper is then wound onto a reel and is sometimes processed even further. It may be remoistened and passed through a stack of rollers, to impart a polished effect known as calendering, or it may be coated with china clay and latex to produce high-quality art papers.

Paper in the modern age

There has been much discussion in the past concerning the way in which cellulose fibers in paper hold together. Today, this adhesion is largely attributed to so-called "hydrogen bonding." This is a weak link between a hydrogen atom already chemically bonded and a neighboring hydrogen atom.

Paper is more than just a subject of research in modern science. It is among the components of some of the world's most sophisticated machinery and has some special technical applications—such as forming part of the dielectric in electric capacitors that are not seen by the general public. It seems that although science produces more and more new synthetic materials every year, it still finds new applications for paper.

KEY

Ways of making paper have changed little in 2,000 years. A suspension of cellulose fibers is made by beating the fibers in water, then separating and soaking them. The wet sheet is pressed to remove water and then refined further.

5

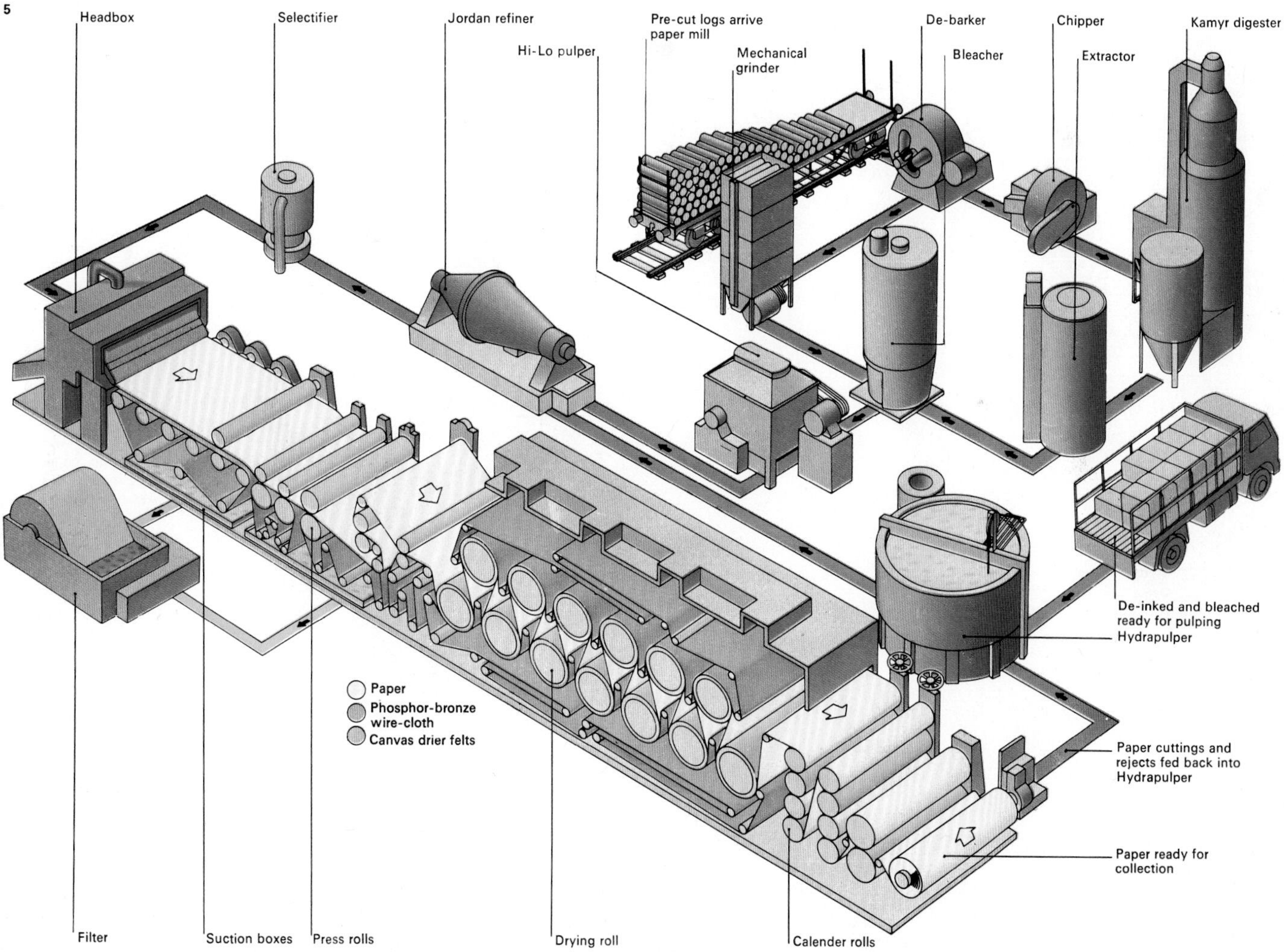

Headbox
Selectifier
Jordan refiner
Hi-Lo pulper
Pre-cut logs arrive paper mill
Mechanical grinder
De-barker
Bleacher
Chipper
Extractor
Kamyr digester
De-inked and bleached ready for pulping Hydrapulper
Paper cuttings and rejects fed back into Hydrapulper
Paper ready for collection
Paper
Phosphor-bronze wire-cloth
Canvas drier felts
Filter
Suction boxes
Press rolls
Drying roll
Calender rolls

5 The modern papermaking process is shown here in a diagrammatic and simplified flow chart. Pre-cut logs arrive at the paper mill. They then pass to the debarker, which has cutters that penetrate the bark and force it off without damaging the timber. The wood may then go to the chipper. This machine has rotating knives that cut wood into pieces about 0.125in(3mm) thick. From there it goes to the Kamyr digester. There treatment with boiling chemicals yields a "chemical pulp" from which chemicals are removed at the extractor. Alternatively, debarked logs may then pass to the mechanical grinder. The two streams meet in the bleacher, pass to the Hi-Lo pulper, and from there to further treatment in the Jordan refiner. De-inked and bleached waste paper is pulped in the Hydrapulper by means of a spinning multivane motor and joins the other pulp at the refiner. All the pulp moves on to the Selectifier which is a pressurized sieve, and into the headbox. There the pulp is adjusted for consistency and fed at a controlled rate through a sluice gate onto a fine phosphor-bronze wire-cloth that is traveling at high speed. At this point suction boxes extract most of the water and the paper then forms a web. The drained water is filtered out; both it and the recovered pulp may be recycled. The web is pressed to the required thickness in the press rolls and then dried over drying rolls. It is given its finish in the calender rolls. The paper cuttings are not wasted but are fed back into the Hydrapulper. Finally the completed paper roll is ready for collection and use.

Basic types of engines

Engines are machines that convert other types of energy into mechanical energy, capable of doing work. The energy is generally heat from the burning of a fuel oil, gasoline, gas, or coal—and the work done by the engine can be used in many different ways: to drive other machines, to generate electricity, to pump water, or to power vehicles such as automobiles, locomotives, ships, and aircraft.

The rules governing the way in which heat can be converted into work were discovered through experience by early engineers. In the early nineteenth century these rules were formalized as the science of thermodynamics. By using them it is possible to calculate how much power an engine will produce, what fraction of the heat will be turned into work, and what might be done to improve its performance.

The first engines, invented during the eighteenth century, burned coal to produce steam in a boiler [1]. The steam was then used to drive the engine. An engine of this sort, in which the source of heat is outside the engine, is known as an external combustion engine. An example of this type is the steam turbine. [2].

By far the most successful form of engine, however, is the internal combustion engine. In an engine of this sort fuel is burned inside the engine and the expansion of gases produced by the explosion of fuel is employed to drive a piston backward and forward inside a cylinder.

Early gas engines

The internal combustion engine was invented in the second half of the nineteenth century. The first successful design was produced by a German engineer, Nikolaus August Otto (1832–91), who used coal gas as his fuel. Otto's gas engine used the four-stroke cycle first proposed in 1862 by Alphonse Beau de Rochas—and so called because only one stroke in four produces power. The other three are taken up in drawing in the fuel, compressing it, and finally, after it is burned, exhausting it.

Since only one stroke in four produces power the output of a single-cylinder four-stroke engine is very uneven and requires a heavy flywheel to smooth it out. Most practical four-stroke engines have more than one cylinder—usually four or six, but often as many as sixteen. Increasing the number of cylinders produces smoother power.

The internal combustion engine using the four-stroke cycle is the engine found in almost all cars and trucks and many motor cycles. Such engines will run on gas but are normally fueled with a liquid fuel, usually gasoline. The fuel is turned into a vapor, mixed with air in the carburetor, and ignited inside the cylinders of the engine by the plugs, which are timed to produce a spark at the right moment in the four-stroke cycle.

The diesel engine

Many internal combustion engines, including most of those used in modern commercial vehicles, employ a heavier petroleum fuel called diesel oil. This type of engine is named after the German inventor Rudolf Diesel (1858–1913). Instead of a carburetor to mix the fuel with air, a diesel engine has a fuel injector that pumps a measured quantity of fuel into the cylinder at precisely the

CONNECTIONS

See also
1628 Steam engines
1632 Oil and gas engines
1634 Wind and water power
1638 Nuclear power
1696 How an automobile works
1706 Locomotives
1718 Principles of flight
1722 Space vehicles
1540 Transformers, motors, and generators

1

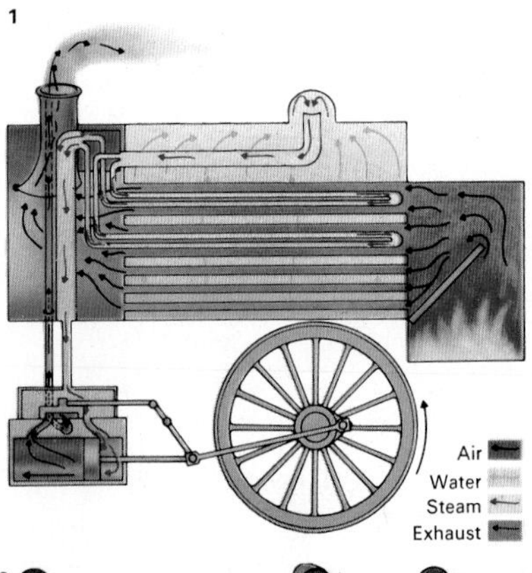

Air
Water
Steam
Exhaust

1 In a steam engine, as used in steam locomotives, heat from burning fuel (coal or oil) boils water in a boiler. The pressure of the steam produced then forces a piston backward and forward.

2

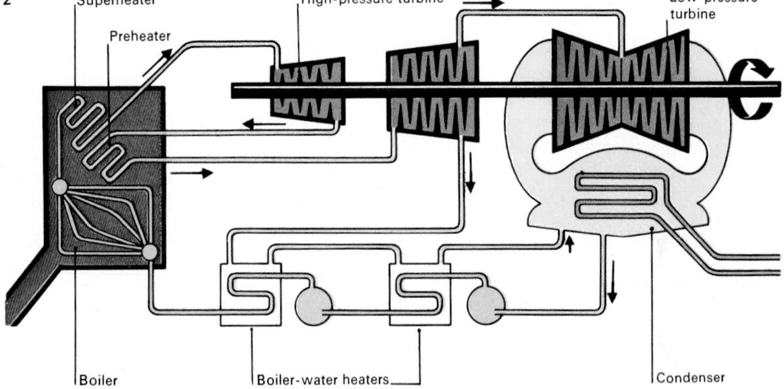

Superheater
Preheater
High-pressure turbine
Low-pressure turbine
Boiler
Boiler-water heaters
Condenser

2 A steam turbine uses steam from a boiler to drive the rotary blades of a series of turbines, each at a lower pressure than the one before it. Exhaust steam is condensed to water and reused.

3

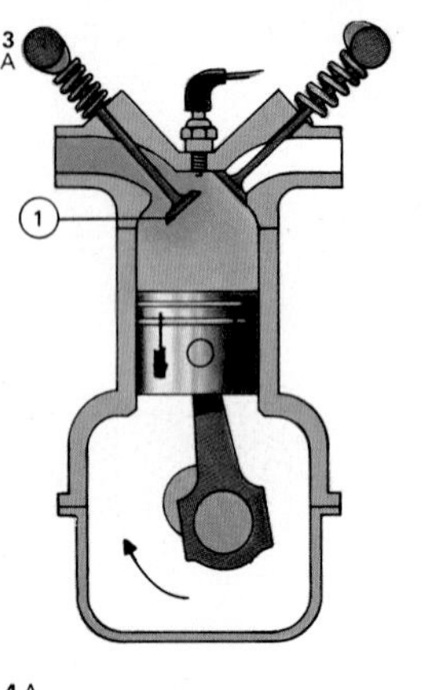

A
1

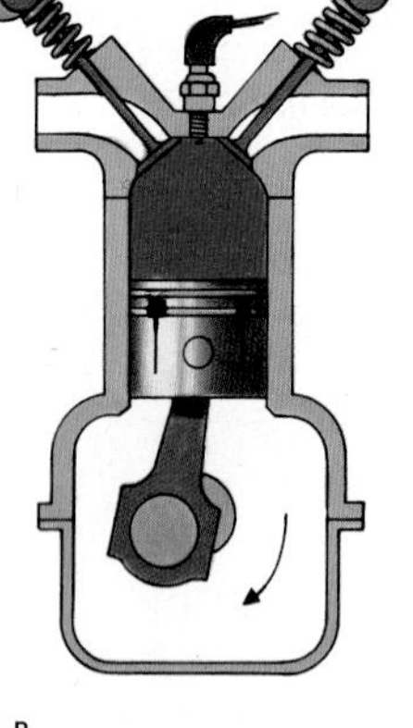

B

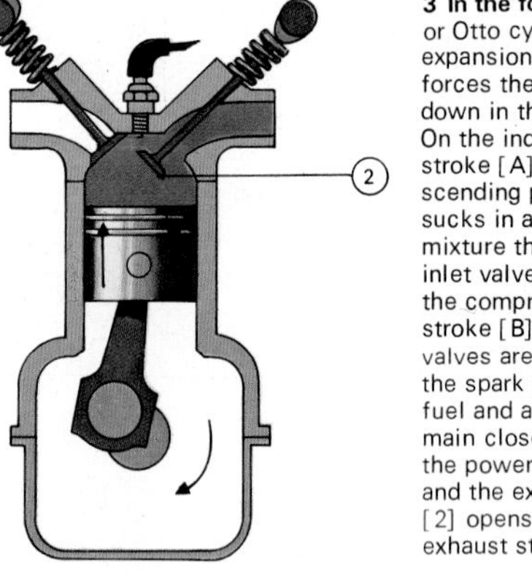

C
D
2

3 In the four-stroke, or Otto cycle, engine, expansion of gases forces the piston down in the cylinder. On the induction stroke [A] the descending piston sucks in a fuel-air mixture through the inlet valve [1]. On the compression stroke [B] both valves are shut and the spark plug ignites fuel and air. They remain closed during the power stroke [C] and the exhaust valve [2] opens during the exhaust stroke [D].

4

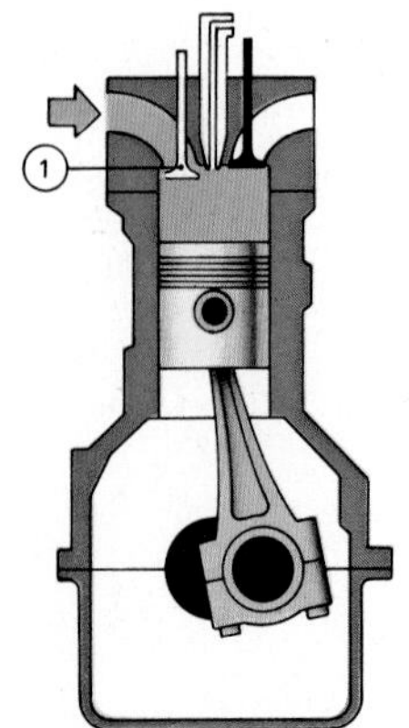

A
1

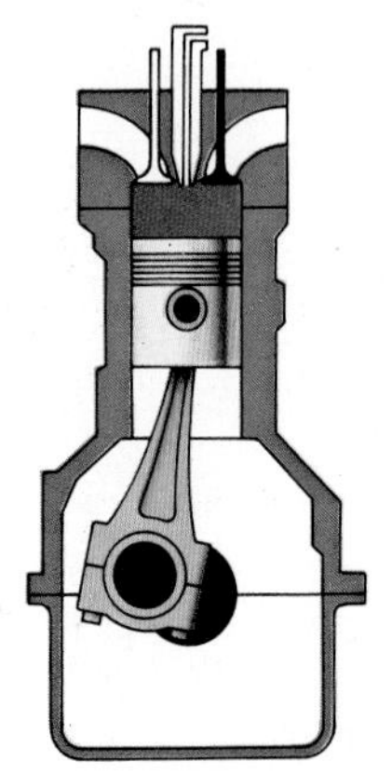

B

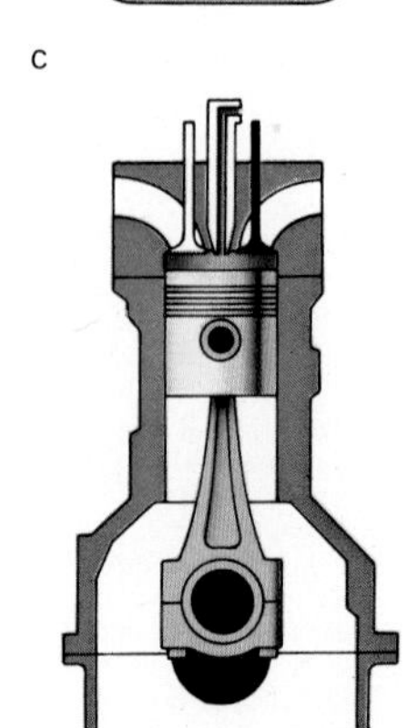

C

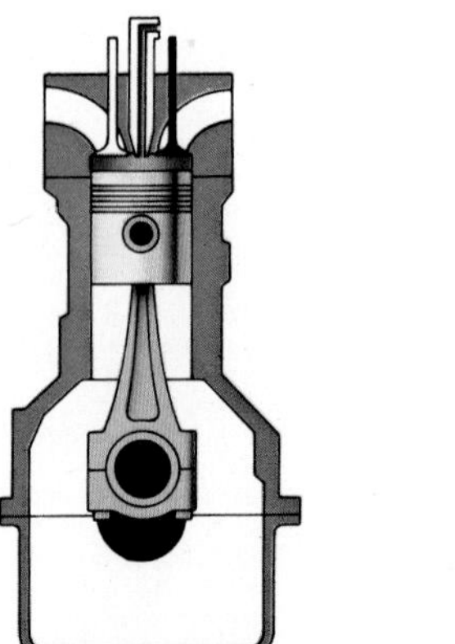

D

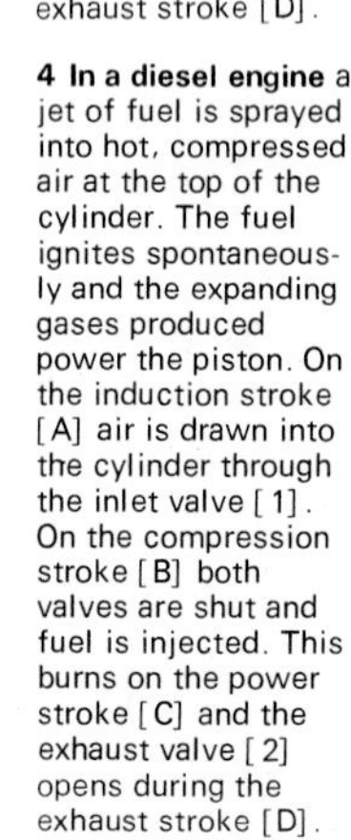

2

4 In a diesel engine a jet of fuel is sprayed into hot, compressed air at the top of the cylinder. The fuel ignites spontaneously and the expanding gases produced power the piston. On the induction stroke [A] air is drawn into the cylinder through the inlet valve [1]. On the compression stroke [B] both valves are shut and fuel is injected. This burns on the power stroke [C] and the exhaust valve [2] opens during the exhaust stroke [D].

right moment. And, instead of spark plugs, diesel engines depend on the compression of the gas in the cylinder to achieve ignition. As the pressure of a gas increases so does its temperature. In a diesel engine the fuel ignites spontaneously at the end of the compression stroke. For this reason a diesel engine is more correctly called a compression-ignition engine.

Converting heat into work

Internal combustion engines do not convert heat into work efficiently. A typical car engine converts no more than a quarter of the energy contained in the fuel into useful work, and even a highly developed engine is little better than 35 percent efficient. The explanation of this disappointing performance lies with the laws of thermodynamics.

The first law states that the energy generated by an engine as work cannot exceed the energy put into it as heat. The second law goes further. It shows that the amount of work produced by an engine is always less than the amount of heat supplied. In other words the efficiency of any type of engine is always less than 100 percent.

The efficiency of a heat engine depends on the difference in temperature between the heat used to drive it and the heat rejected as waste. The higher the temperature of the engine's working fuel and the lower the temperature of the waste heat the more efficient the engine. Complete 100 percent efficiency can be achieved only if the waste heat is at absolute zero (−273°C [−459.4F]). In practice, of course, this cannot be and thus the efficiency of a heat engine cannot be 100 percent. Under ideal circumstances a heat engine operating at 1,000°C (1,832°F)—possible for an internal combustion engine—and rejecting waste heat at normal exhaust temperatures (say 150°C [302°F]), has a theoretical efficiency of 67 percent.

The difficulties of designing a perfect engine mean that all actual engines fall far short of the theoretical efficiency. Friction, vibration, the energy consumed by the engine itself in driving camshafts, fans, etc., and losses in the transmission reduce the efficiency to even lower levels.

KEY

PK 6730

Air-cooled, small, light engines were developed in the first quarter of this century, chiefly for powering motorcycles. The British Morgan company used a motorcycle engine as the power unit in this 1927 three-wheeler car. Known as a V-twin, the engine had two cylinders inclined at an angle to each other. It drove a propeller shaft along the floor of the car to a gearbox, with a final chain drive to the single rear wheel. The car had controls mounted on the steering column.

5 A

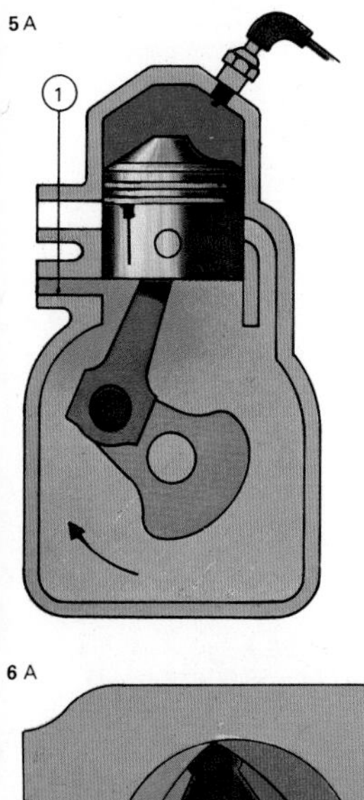

B

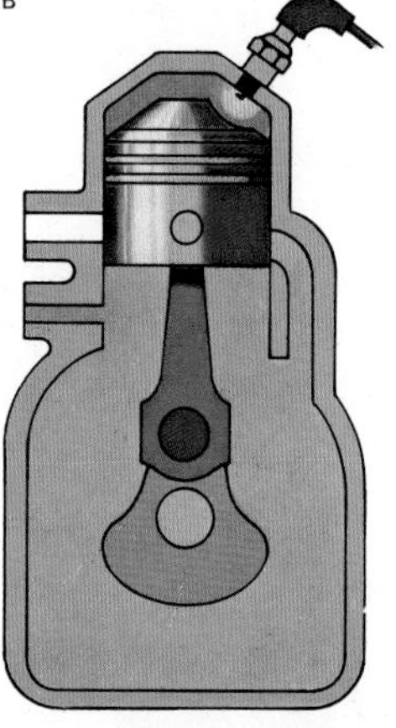

C

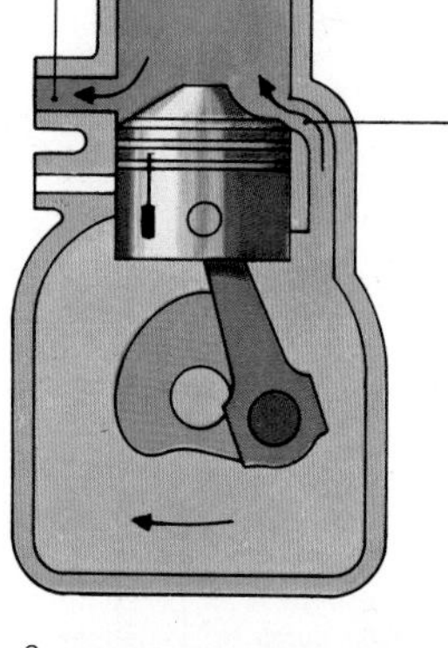

5 In a two-stroke engine the upstroke [A] opens the inlet port [1] and compresses the mixture already in the cylinder. A spark plug ignites the fuel [B] and after combustion the descending piston [C] first opens the exhaust port [2] and then the transfer port [3], letting fresh fuel-air mixture enter the combustion chamber. Thus the piston also acts as the engine's valves and oil is added to the fuel to lubricate it. In many two-stroke engines, the cylinder is air-cooled.

6 The Wankel engine has a rotor in the form of a curved triangle within a chamber. The "points" of the rotor have gas-tight carbon-fiber seals. The four stages of the cycle are the same in principle as the Otto cycle: induction [A], compression [B], power [C], and exhaust [D]. All three spaces in the chamber are used at once. There are two spark plugs and the rotary motion produced can be used as direct drive, without the need for a crankshaft.

6 A

B

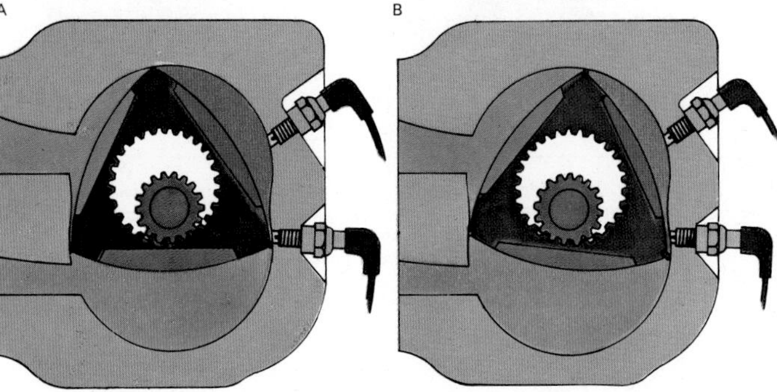

C

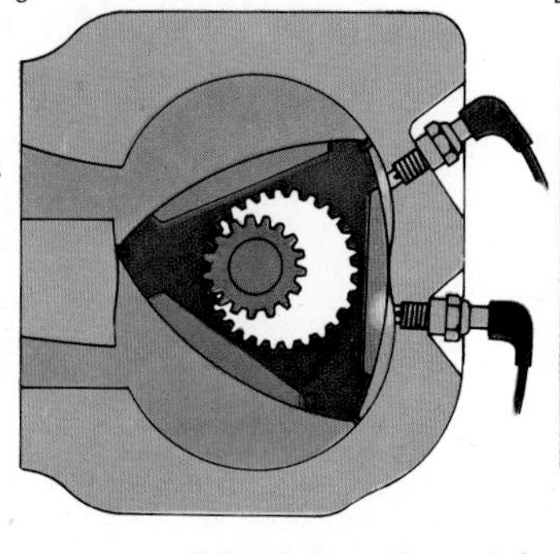

D

7

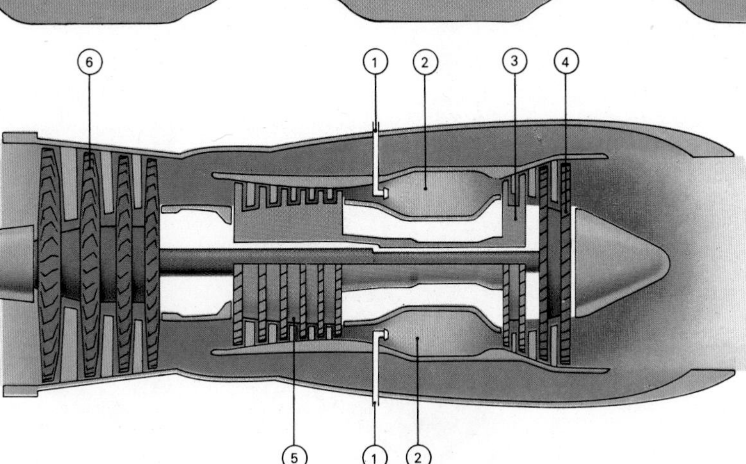

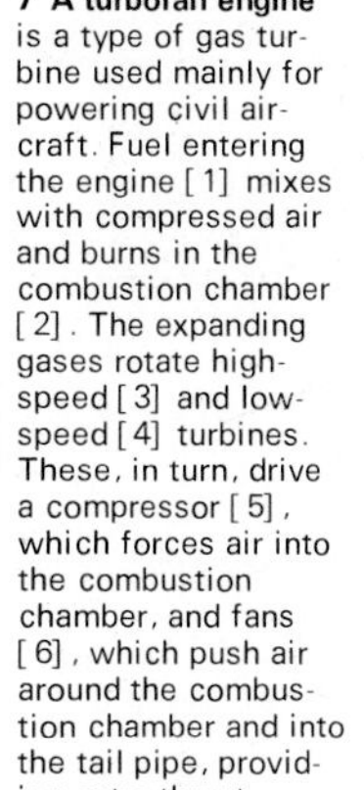

7 A turbofan engine is a type of gas turbine used mainly for powering civil aircraft. Fuel entering the engine [1] mixes with compressed air and burns in the combustion chamber [2]. The expanding gases rotate high-speed [3] and low-speed [4] turbines. These, in turn, drive a compressor [5], which forces air into the combustion chamber, and fans [6], which push air around the combustion chamber and into the tail pipe, providing extra thrust.

8

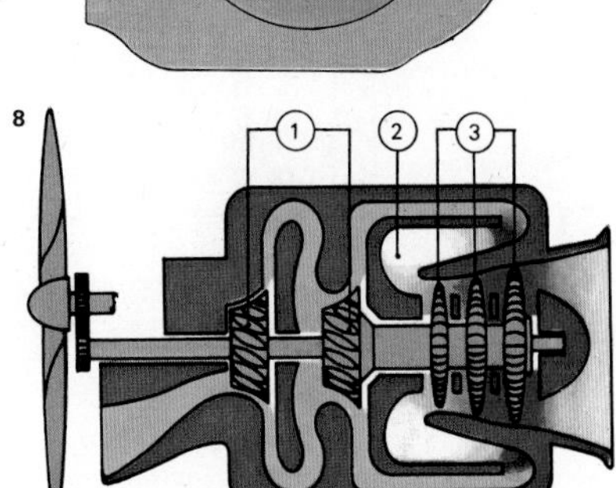

8 A turboprop engine is basically a gas turbine in which most of the power in the rotating shaft drives a propeller through reduction gears. Incoming air is compressed [1], mixed with fuel [2], and burned to rotate the turbine [3]. A typical turboprop output is 2,000hp.

Steam engines

The steam engine is generally acknowledged as one of technology's greatest contributions to human progress. In the two centuries following its introduction, commerce and industry developed at a greater rate than ever before. And the steam engine is one of the few inventions that have been almost wholly beneficial.

The influence of steam power

The steam engine's first impact was on the development of coal mining. Before 1712, deep coal seams were impossible to work because they were flooded with water. Then Thomas Newcomen (1663–1729) developed a steam engine [2] that could be used to pump out water. The engine was extremely simple and, except for a few parts, could be made by local craftsmen. But it wasted fuel because the cylinder had to be cooled after every stroke, and so the engine was used only at mines where fuel was plentiful.

The engine invented by James Watt (1736–1819) in 1769 [5] separated the heated and cooled parts of the work cycle and so avoided the energy losse´ caused by combining them in the cylinder, reducing fuel consumption by two-thirds. As a result, Watt's engine could be used even where fuel was scarce and costly.

The Watt engine also enabled the development of ironworks, making cast iron readily available and leading to a period of great industrial expansion in Britain. By the mid-nineteenth century, horizontal and vertical types of steam engines had evolved and were developed into powerful mill engines.

The other great impact of steam power was in transport. Steam locomotives, pioneered by Richard Trevithick (1771–1833) [4], led to railroad networks offering faster and cheaper carriage of freight than by canal barge. Steamships cut many days off the time needed for an intercontinental sea passage.

The next great breakthrough in steam power was the invention in 1884 by Charles Parsons (1854–1931) of the steam turbine. One of its advantages was that its "output" was a rotating shaft instead of the backward and forward motion of earlier steam engines. There was no longer any need for the complicated mechanical linkages of connecting rods, cranks, and eccentrics. Within 20 years, 70,000 horsepower Parsons turbines were driving liners across the Atlantic Ocean at up to 28mph (about 24knots).

Principles of the steam engine

Any steam engine converts the heat energy stored in steam into usable power. Steam is the vapor produced by heating water until it changes from a liquid to a gaseous state. If this process takes place in a closed vessel (a boiler), adding more heat raises the temperature and pressure of the steam. Heat from any source—fuel, the sun, or a nuclear reactor—can be used. In a conventional steam engine, the pressure of the steam imposes a thrust on a piston connected by a linkage in such a way that its movement is made to rotate a shaft. In a turbine, the steam passes through jets and strikes the blades of a turbine wheel, making it turn.

The process is reversible, and if steam is cooled in a condenser it turns back into water. If this takes place in a closed vessel,

CONNECTIONS

See also
1706 Locomotives
1630 Power from steam
1680 Modern ships
1584 Modern technology
1280 The impact of steam
1282 The foundations of 20th-century science

1

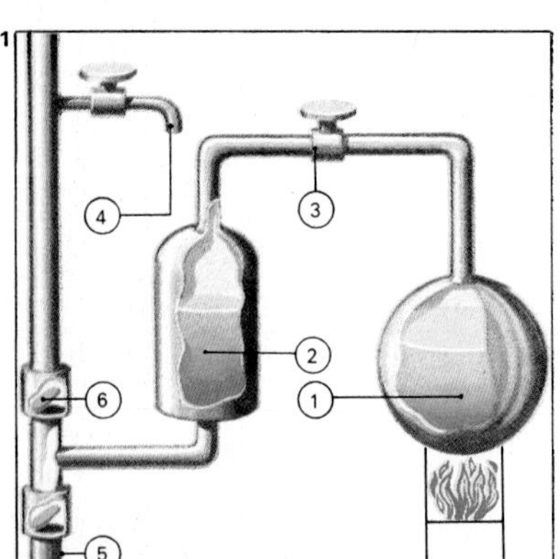

4
3
2
1
6
5

1 Savery's steam engine of 1696 was the first to combine steam pressure, vacuum, and condensing for continuous operation. Steam from the boiler [1] passed to the working chamber [2] and the cock [3] was closed. Cold water from a spray [4] condensed the steam, creating a vacuum in [2] and lifting water into it from [5]. Steam was again let in [2], forcing the water out through the valve [6] and upward.

2

5
3
2
4
1

2 Newcomen's steam engine of 1712 was the first to use a piston and linkage to transfer the movement to pumps. Steam from the boiler [1] passed to the cylinder [2], and the weight of the pump rods pulled the piston [3] to the top. The steam was shut off and cold water [4] sprayed in to condense the steam. The vacuum created caused pressure to force the piston down again, and a link to the crossbeam made it rock and work the main pump. A pipe led air and condensed water out of the cylinder, and a small pump lifted water up to the header tank [5].

3

3 Small, powerful steam engines were a logical development of Trevithick's locomotive of 1804. Coupled to existing and, later, especially designed machines, they reduced human drudgery, increased production, and reduced costs in many industries. Richard Hoe's steam-powered newspaper press of 1847, shown here, was a rotary machine with the type of cylinders that turned at high speed in contact with a moving band of paper. Steam power also influenced agriculture, where traction engines—the first successful self-propelled road vehicles—could haul and work heavy trailers and threshing machines. Two engines at opposite ends of a field could draw a large multiple-bladed plow back and forth.

4 Richard Trevithick pioneered the use of high-pressure steam and obtained great power from relatively small engines by raising the pressure to 50lb/sq in. He also did away with the condenser, thus reducing the weight, and achieved further economies by enclosing the furnace within the boiler shell, and using the exhaust steam to preheat the boiler feed water. From this, it was but a short step to mount the whole engine on wheels to run on iron rails, and the locomotive shown here proved the feasibility of railroads in 1804. The single horizontal cylinder was enclosed within the boiler, and the flywheel drove both axles through a set of gear wheels.

4

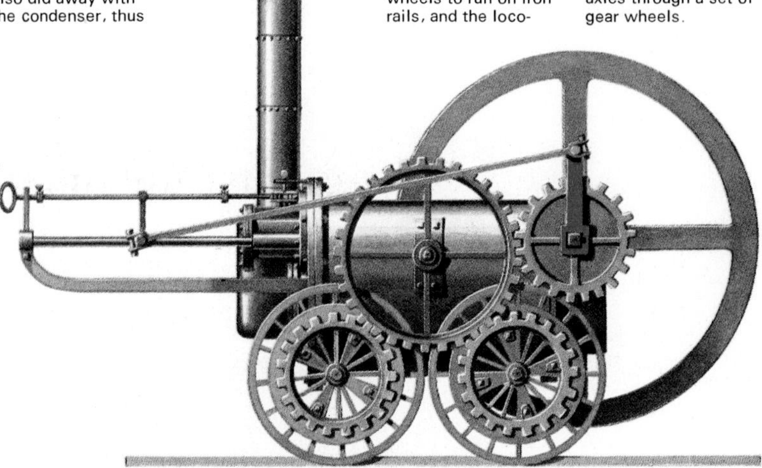

the reduction in volume creates a vacuum that can be used to recover further energy. These two principles were known for nearly a century before Thomas Savery (1650–1715) combined them in a machine for pumping water in 1696 [1].

Condensation of steam during use in the work cycle represents a loss of energy. Steam engines were designed to raise steam to the highest possible temperature, to minimize condensation during the cycle, and to expand the steam until it was exhausted at the lowest possible temperature. The idea was to extract the maximum heat energy from the steam. It was achieved by leading the steam on its way to the engine through pipes exposed to hot flue gases from the boiler—a so-called superheater. In a modern power station, superheated steam reaches temperatures up to about 1,100°F (600°C). Even better efficiency can be obtained by taking the steam after use in part of the cycle and again leading it in pipes through hot boiler gases, in a reheater. In this way, the heat from fuel burned in the boiler is used three times to inject energy into the steam. Exhaust steam tends to cool the walls of the cylinder, and so it is enclosed by an outer container full of hot steam, called a steam jacket.

Fuel economy

There are other ways of saving fuel. Water fed to the boiler has to be raised to boiling point before evaporation to steam takes place. Any way of heating the water before it reaches the boiler must save fuel. There are two ways of doing this. An economizer consists of a set of pipes exposed to hot gases leaving the boiler, and boiler fed water can be passed through these, heating the water to about 200°F (93°C). But a modern power station, with an evaporation temperature of 700°F (370°C), requires much more preheating. The boiler feed water is heated by steam, drawn from various points along the turbine system, which has already given out power in the main turbines. Called interstage feed-water heating, this system is less costly in energy terms than, for example, using the hottest steam straight from the boiler to preheat the water.

KEY

Many early designs for making use of steam engines applied them to road vehicles, generally conceived as steerable mechanical carriages. All designs had to solve the problem of converting the steam engine's reciprocal (side-to-side) motion into a rotary one for driving the wheels.

5 James Watt's engine of 1769 reduced fuel consumption by separating the condenser and the cylinder, but it was still only a pumping engine. The growing industries needed power to drive machines, provided by Watt's double-acting engine of 1784. It included the basic features of modern engines, and was a great advance on the Newcomen engine. A furnace [1] heated the base and sides of a boiler [2]. Steam at a pressure of 7lb/sq in passed into a cylinder [6] that was closed at the top to allow the steam to drive the piston [7] both down and upward. The effort was transmitted via a parallel motion linkage [22] to the beam [23], which rocked about its center. Its movement was transmitted to the factory via the connecting rod [24], which had a non-rotating planet wheel [25] fixed rigidly at the end, driving the sun wheel [26] on the flywheel shaft. The sun and planet wheels were kept in mesh by a link behind them. Teeth on the flywheel [27] meshed with those of the pinion [28] at the end of the mill drive shaft. The engine framing was made of timber, and the engine speed was controlled by the governor [11]. Steam was let in and out of the cylinder by two pairs of valves, and the exhaust was condensed in [14] by the cold-water jet [15]. Air and water were removed by a pump [16], and water pumped to the boiler [18] via the float control [4].

1 Furnace and firedoor
2 Boiler
3 Water
4 Float control
5 Steam pipe
6 Engine cylinder
7 Piston
8 Steam throttle valve
9 Top valve chest
10 Bottom valve chest
11 Governor
12 Governor drive
13 Condensing water tank
14 Condenser
15 Cold-water jet
16 Air pump
17 Feed water tank
18 Feed water pump
19 Feed water pipe
20 Condenser water supply
21 Piston rod
22 Parallel motion
23 Engine beam
24 Connecting rod
25 Planet wheel
26 Sun wheel
27 Toothed flywheel
28 Toothed driving wheel

5

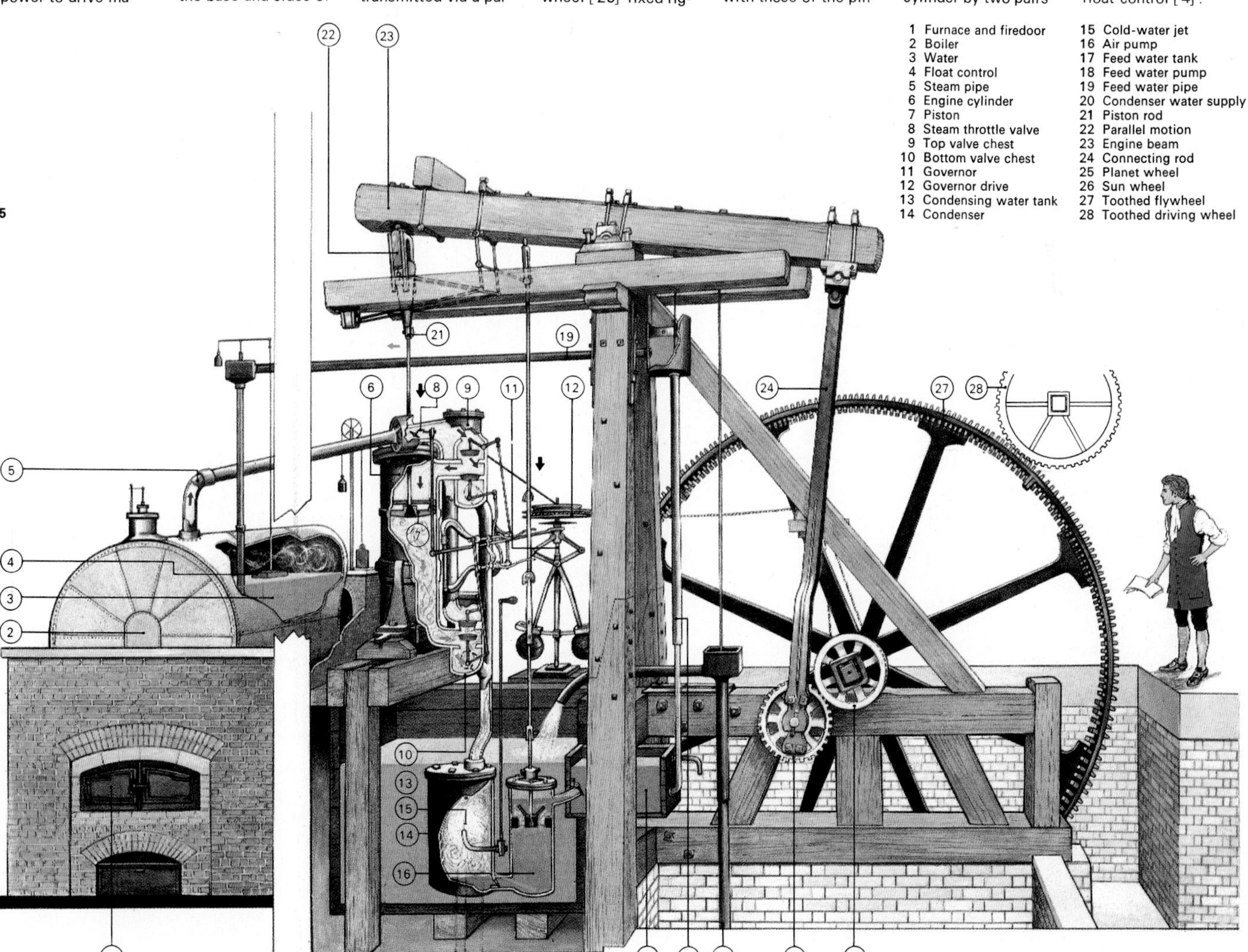
22
23
21
19
6
8
9
11
12
24
27
28
5
4
3
2
10
13
15
14
16
1
17
18
20
25
26

Power from steam

The power of steam created the Industrial Revolution, yet today hardly any steam engines remain. For generating electricity, however, steam—driving a turbine—is still the chief motive force employed.

Modern power stations [key]
A modern thermal power station uses the heat from burning coal or oil, or from a nuclear reactor, to boil water circulating in boiler tubes to produce high-pressure steam [1]. The steam travels along pipes to a steam turbine that consists of a series of propeller-like vanes mounted on a single shaft. Nozzles direct jets of steam toward the vanes, driving the turbine around. A generator coupled to the end of the turbine shaft converts the rotary motion of the shaft into electric power.

Each of the three elements of a power station—the boiler, turbine, and generator—has undergone intensive development to produce the most efficient machines possible. As a result, the efficiency of electricity generation (the amount of electrical energy output compared with the heat energy input) increased from about five percent in 1900 to nearly 40 percent in 1975. In other words, without this increase in efficiency a power station would burn eight times as much fuel to produce the same amount of electricity.

The boiler of a large conventional power station burns powdered coal at a rate of up to 200 tons per hour. Rail wagons carry the coal to the plant and dump it in huge coal stores from which it is taken by conveyor to the boiler. It is weighed and pulverized to a powder as fine as flour, then mixed with air and carried by fans to the furnace.

Producing the steam
The boiler consists of a tall chimneylike structure lined with vertical pipes carrying water. The heat produced by burning the coal-air mixture boils the water, producing steam. This is first collected in a steam drum, then recirculated through the hottest part of the boiler in another set of tubes that superheat it to even higher temperatures.

From the superheater steam goes directly to the turbines [2]. The steam is taken first to the high-pressure turbine, where it passes through a ring of stationary blades. These act as nozzles and direct the blast of steam onto the rotating blades. As it passes through, the steam makes the turbine turn, just as a windmill turns in the breeze. Immediately after passing through the high-pressure turbine the steam is led back to the boiler and reheated. It then passes through the intermediate and low-pressure turbines [3], gradually giving up its energy and generating more rotational power.

Finally, the steam, with most of its energy spent, changes back into water in a condenser. This is a large vessel containing cooling pipes carrying cold water from a nearby river or estuary. The cooling water takes the last remaining heat from the steam, producing hot water that passes back to the boiler to be reheated. Condensation creates a vacuum in the condenser, allowing more energy to be extracted from the steam.

The turbine shaft rotates at a speed set by the frequency of the electricity supply. In Great Britain and many other European countries the speed is 3,000 revolutions per

CONNECTIONS

See also
1628 Steam engines
1648 Electricity generation and distribution
1638 Nuclear power
1646 Saving fuel and energy

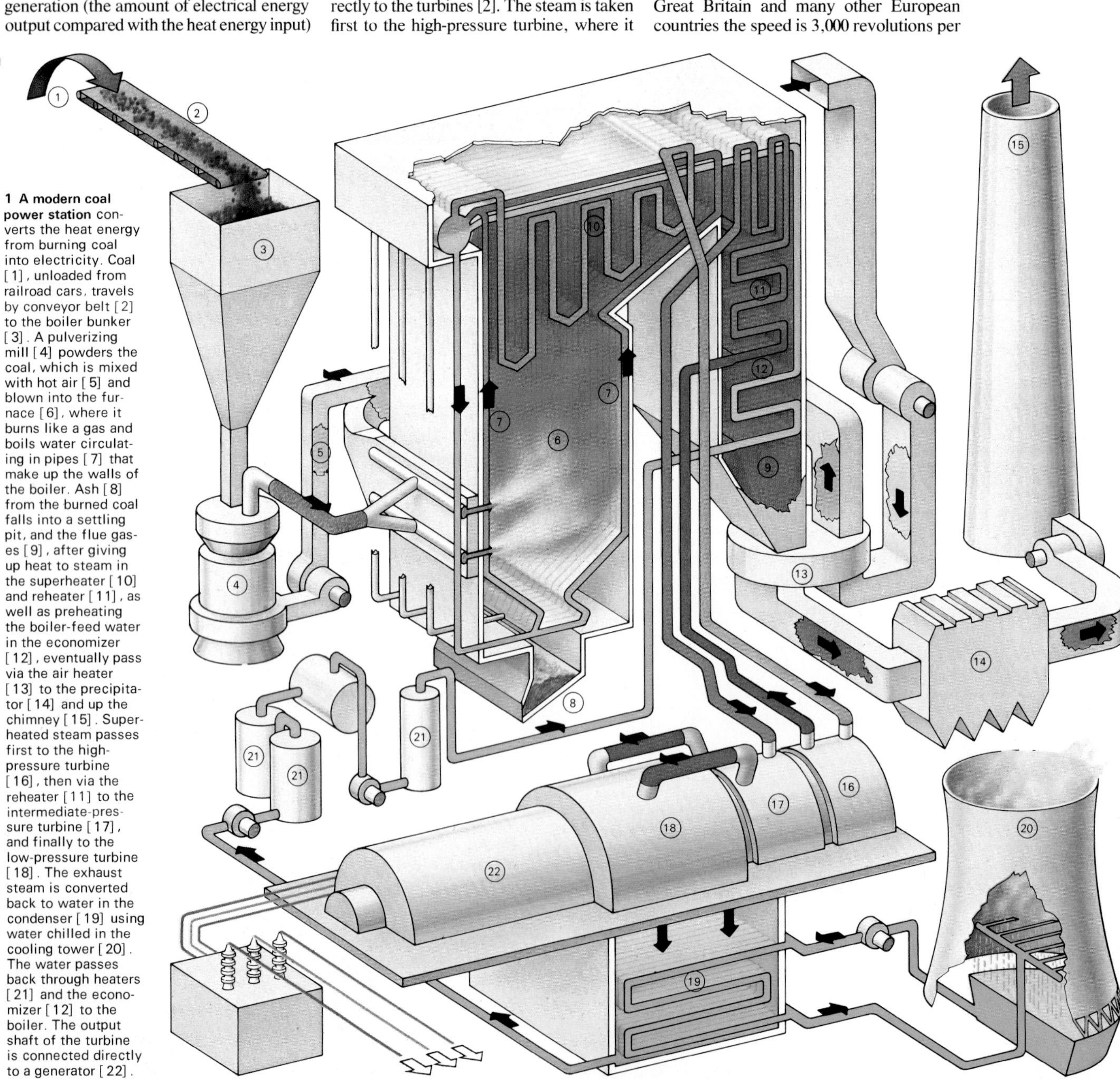
1
2
3
4
5
6
7
8
9
10
11
12
13
14
15
16
17
18
19
20
21
22

1 A modern coal power station converts the heat energy from burning coal into electricity. Coal [1], unloaded from railroad cars, travels by conveyor belt [2] to the boiler bunker [3]. A pulverizing mill [4] powders the coal, which is mixed with hot air [5] and blown into the furnace [6], where it burns like a gas and boils water circulating in pipes [7] that make up the walls of the boiler. Ash [8] from the burned coal falls into a settling pit, and the flue gases [9], after giving up heat to steam in the superheater [10] and reheater [11], as well as preheating the boiler-feed water in the economizer [12], eventually pass via the air heater [13] to the precipitator [14] and up the chimney [15]. Superheated steam passes first to the high-pressure turbine [16], then via the reheater [11] to the intermediate-pressure turbine [17], and finally to the low-pressure turbine [18]. The exhaust steam is converted back to water in the condenser [19] using water chilled in the cooling tower [20]. The water passes back through heaters [21] and the economizer [12] to the boiler. The output shaft of the turbine is connected directly to a generator [22].

minute (50 revolutions per second), corresponding to an alternating supply at 50 hertz (cycles per second). In the United States the turbine speed is normally 3,600rpm, corresponding to a 60Hz supply.

The electricity generator consists of two electrical windings [2]. One, called the rotor, is mounted on the turbine shaft, and rotates with it. The other, the stator, is arranged as a shroud around the rotor and is fixed to the floor. The relative motion of rotor and stator generates electricity by induction.

Generators and efficiency

To get the best performance out of the generator it must be continuously cooled. At one time natural cooling or forced cooling by air fans was used, but since the early 1950s hydrogen gas has been employed because it is much more efficient. The rotor and stator operate in an atmosphere of hydrogen, which removes the heat. Rotor windings are now made of hollow copper tubes with hydrogen circulating through them, and the stator windings are cooled individually by tubes carrying hydrogen. With "direct" or "inner" cooling, as this technique is called, generator output can be doubled.

The generator produces electricity at about 25,000 volts. Most domestic supplies operate at only 250 volts but it is much more economical to transmit electricity over long distances at very high voltages. The first step in distribution, therefore, is to step up the voltage to several hundred times the original value by using a transformer. It is then fed to a large grid that links country- or state-wide generating plants.

Linking power plants helps to operate the entire network in the most economical way. The efficiency of a large generator becomes less when it operates at only part-load. So, rather than reduce output to match demand, it may be best to turn the generator off altogether and switch in power from another station that is kept going at full power. Electricity authorities turn off the least economical stations first as demand for power drops. This enables them to keep the cheapest stations in operation all the time on so-called base-load.

KEY

2

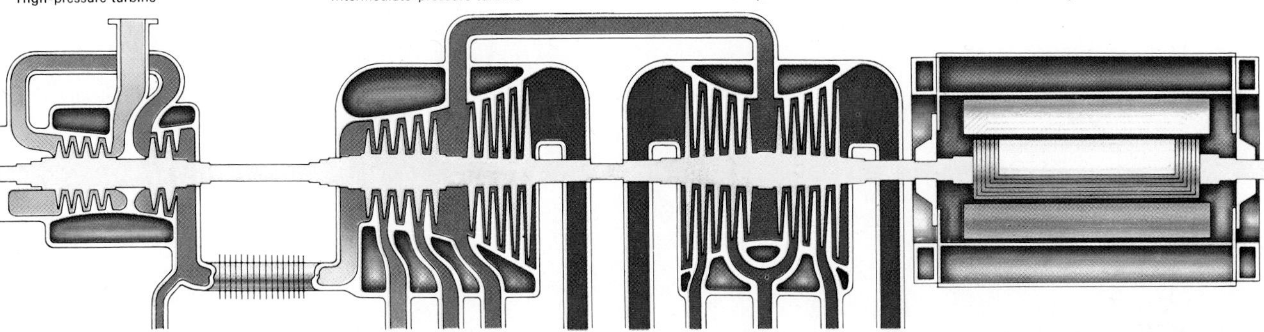
High-pressure turbine
Intermediate-pressure turbine
Low-pressure turbine
Electrical generator

2 Turbines and generators are the components that convert the rotary motion produced by steam power into electricity. To obtain the maximum energy from the hot steam, there are several stages of turbines – up to five in a large power station – each using steam at a slightly lower pressure than the previous one. Superheated steam at up to 1,112°F (600°C) gives up much of its energy in a high-pressure turbine. The exhaust steam from this stage is reheated and passed to an intermediate-pressure turbine and then to the low-pressure turbine. The output shaft drives an electrical generator connected to it.

3 A low-pressure turbine, shown here diagrammatically, illustrates how steam pressure is made to turn the blades. There are two similar sets, mounted back to back on the same shaft for efficiency. The central blades, where steam pressure is highest, are smaller than those at the ends, where pressure is lowest.

4 The turbine hall of a modern power station contains a mass of heavy machinery and insulated pipes carrying steam between the various turbines. Galleries and catwalks halfway up the machines enable engineers to inspect and maintain them. The steam-generating boilers may be placed beneath the floor.

3

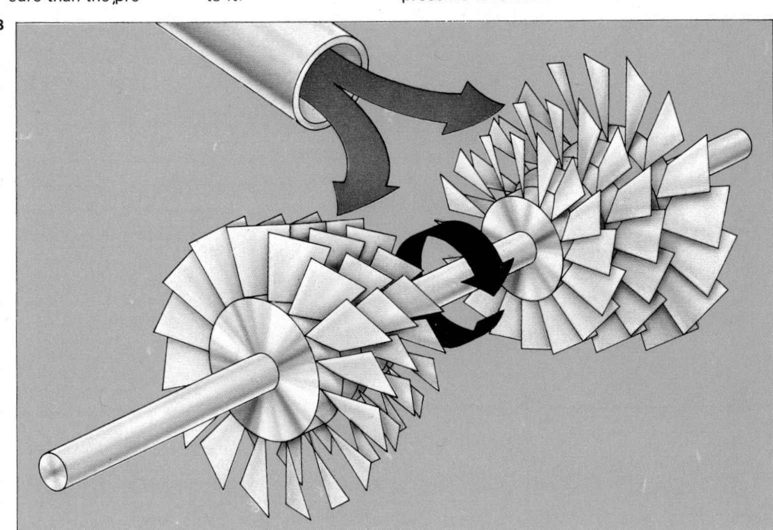

4

Oil and gas engines

In the traditional steam engine, and even in a modern steam turbine, fuel is burned outside the engine to heat water and raise steam to drive the engine. But it is more efficient to burn fuel inside an engine and let the expanding gases drive a piston or turbine.

The first such internal combustion engine, running on gas [Key], was built by the German engineer Nikolaus August Otto (1832–91). His engine, demonstrated in Paris in 1867, was large, noisy, and not very efficient. But it became the forerunner of 99 percent of all today's engines.

The four-stroke cycle

Nine years after the first gas engine Otto devised another, based on the four-stroke cycle. The crucial advance in this engine was that the gas was compressed before it was ignited, yielding a considerable improvement in efficiency.

Every four strokes of the engine include one of power, so this system is known as the four-stroke cycle. It is by far the most common type of engine in use today. The four main stages are an induction stroke in which a downward movement of the piston sucks in the fuel-air mixture; a compression stroke in which upward movement of the piston compresses the gas; a power stroke—a second downward piston movement caused by the explosion of the fuel; and an exhaust stroke in which the upward-moving piston forces exhaust gases out of the cylinder.

Many motorcycles and a few small cars use the two-stroke cycle first devised by Dugald Clerk in 1880. In this type of engine the movement of the piston admits the fuel and exhausts the burned gases by uncovering "ports" in the side of the cylinder.

Fuel and exhaust pass in and out of a four-stroke engine using a more sophisticated system of valves, controlled automatically by a camshaft driven by a timing chain from the engine's crankshaft. As the engine operates, the valves are successively opened and closed by camshaft rocker arms.

The moment of ignition of the fuel must also be accurately controlled. This is done by a distributor, again mechanically connected to the crankshaft, which sends a current of electricity to each of the cylinders. The electric current "fires" a spark in the spark plugs and the fuel is ignited.

Otto's engines ran on coal gas, a perfectly satisfactory fuel but one that is difficult to store. The gas engine was greatly improved by the use of liquid fuels such as gasoline, made by refining crude oil. To turn gasoline into a combustible vapor it is mixed with air to form a fine mist of droplets that can be drawn into the cylinders. The mixing is carried out in a carburetor.

Unlike steam engines, most internal combustion engines do not produce great power at slow speeds. The cylinders are small and each individual ignition stroke produces comparatively little power. To obtain a useful amount of work from such an engine it must be run fast, to put the maximum number of ignition strokes into each second. Automobile engines commonly produce their maximum power at speeds of 5,000 revolutions per minute or more. The upper limit on speed is set by the wear and tear on the engine caused by the oscillating pistons and valve gear. Espe-

CONNECTIONS

See also
1626 Basic types of engine
1642 Oil and natural gas
1680 Modern ships
1690 History of motorcycle
1692 History of automobiles
1696 How an automobile works
1718 Principles of flight

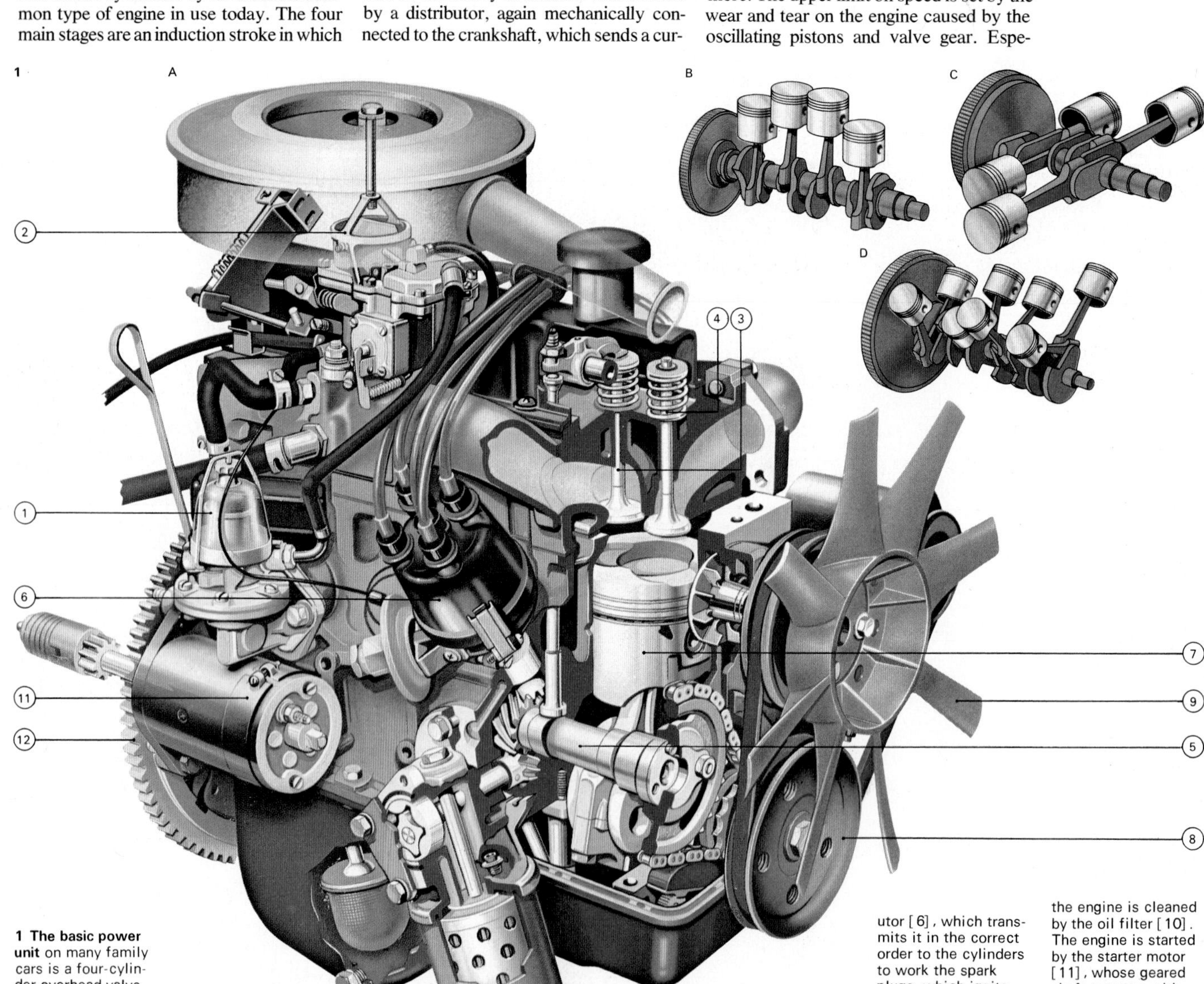

1
A
B
C
D
1
2
3
4
5
6
7
8
9
10
11
12

1 The basic power unit on many family cars is a four-cylinder overhead valve gasoline engine [A]. The gasoline pump [1] draws fuel from the gas tank; in the carburetor [2] it is vaporized and mixed with air. The gasoline-air mixture passes into the cylinders through inlet valves [3]. The valves are closed by springs [4] and opened by tappets controlled by push rods via the camshaft [5]. High-tension electric current from the coil passes to the distributor [6], which transmits it in the correct order to the cylinders to work the spark plugs, which ignite the fuel. Expanding burned gases depress pistons [7], whose movement rotates the crankshaft. A pulley [8] drives a cooling fan [9] by means of the fan belt. Lubricating oil circulating around the engine is cleaned by the oil filter [10]. The engine is started by the starter motor [11], whose geared shaft engages with the toothed flywheel [12]. Common engine configurations include the in-line four [B], a horizontally-opposed or flat four [C], and a V-8 [D], with two sets of four cylinders inclined at an angle.

cially prepared engines can obtain more power by running up to 12,000 rpm or more.

The economical diesel engine

The compression-ignition engine, designed by the German Rudolf Diesel (1858–1913) in 1896, dispenses with the carburetor and spark plugs of the gasoline engine. The gas inside the cylinder on the compression stroke is pure air, which is compressed to $^1/_{14}$ to $^1/_{20}$ of its initial volume—a much higher compression ratio than is used in gasoline engines. At the top of the compression stroke a fine spray of oil fuel is injected into the cylinder. As a gas is compressed its temperature increases, so that the oil spray meets the air charge at a temperature sufficiently high to ignite it spontaneously.

Because of its high compression ratio the compression-ignition or diesel engine is more efficient than a gasoline engine. But for the same reason it must be more heavily built, thus offsetting the advantage. Diesel engines offer economies in fuel use and type at the expense of a loss in performance; they are particularly well suited to frequent stop and start duties, and are widely used in taxis, buses, and trucks.

The powerful gas turbine

The gas turbine, a completely different kind of engine, was first devised at the beginning of the twentieth century and was perfected in the 1930s. It usually has a single shaft carrying a series of propellerlike fans divided into two groups, those of the compressor and of the turbine.

In an operating gas turbine air is drawn in by the compressor fans and its pressure increased. The compressed air is mixed with fuel and ignition takes place, further increasing temperatures and pressures. The burned mixture leaves the engine through the turbine, driving the blades around. Much of the power produced is taken up by the compressor, which is often driven directly by the turbine, but enough is left over to make the gas turbine an exceedingly powerful form of engine. Efficiencies are not high, but the power-to-weight ratio of a gas turbine is good, making it suitable for aircraft propulsion.

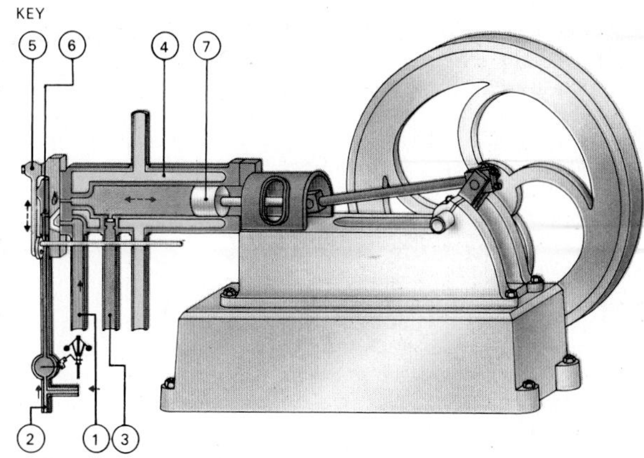
KEY

Otto's engine of 1876 was the first successful internal combustion engine. A four-stroke horizontal engine, it used a mixture of gas and air as fuel. The charging stroke drew in air [1] and gas [2] through a slide valve [5] into the cylinder, pulled in by movement of the piston [7]. On the return stroke, the fuel mixture was ignited by a flame carried through a narrow opening in the slide valve from a continuously burning gas jet [6] outside the engine. The expanding products of combustion produced the working stroke. On the fourth and last stroke the exhaust gases were forced out of the engine [3]. A jacket of cold water [4] cooled the engine.

A

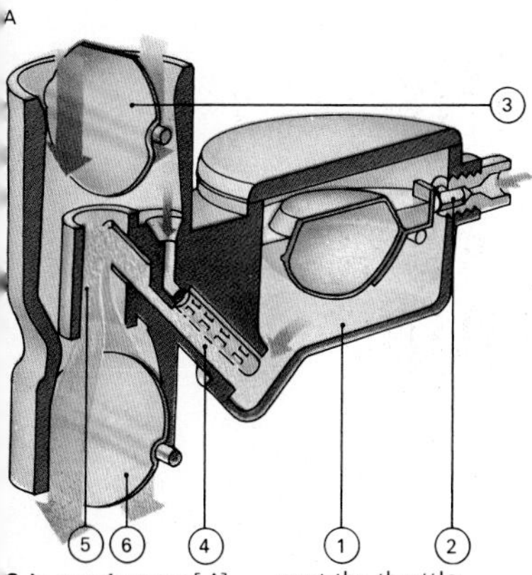

2 In a carburetor [A], gasoline enters the float chamber [1] controlled by a needle valve [2]. Part of the air passing the choke valve [3] mixes with the fuel [4]. The mixture passes into the main airstream [5] and past the throttle valve [6]. In an overhead valve engine [B] the valves [1] are worked by push rods [2] moved by cams on the camshaft [3], which is rotated by a chain [4] from the crankshaft [5].

B

3

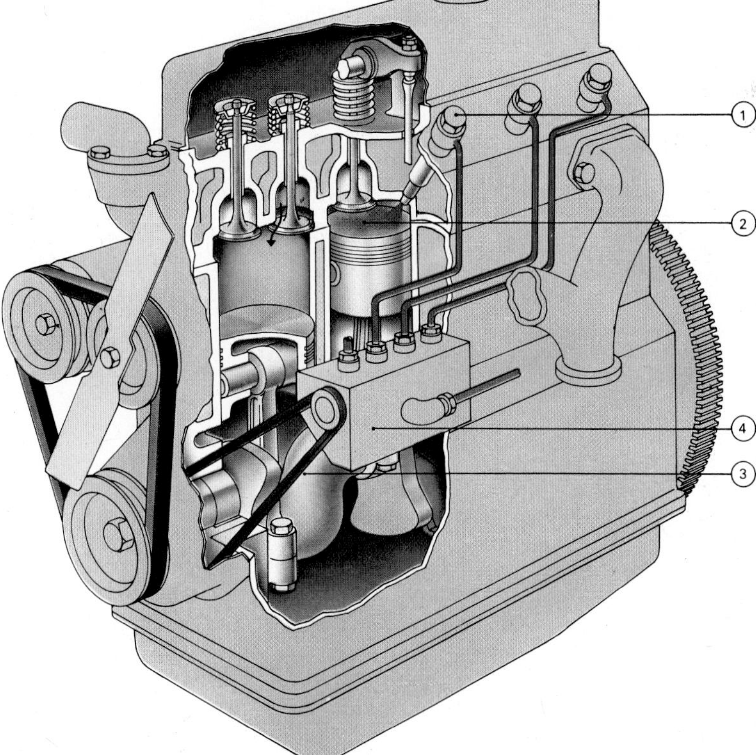

3 A diesel engine has no spark plugs and works on the principle of compression-ignition. An injector [1] squirts fuel into the cylinder [2], where the upward stroke of the piston compresses the air. Under these conditions the fuel ignites spontaneously and the expansion of the combustion products forces the piston downward. A drive-belt from the crankshaft [3] works the fuel pump [4]. As in a gasoline engine there is a pair of valves on each cylinder, but in a diesel one controls the admission of air only and the other lets exhaust gases out of the cylinder. The power of the engine depends on the amount of fuel delivered by the pump, and this, in turn, is controlled by the vehicle's accelerator pedal. A fan belt around a pulley at the end of the crankshaft drives a cooling fan and a generator or alternator to work the electrical accessories.

4

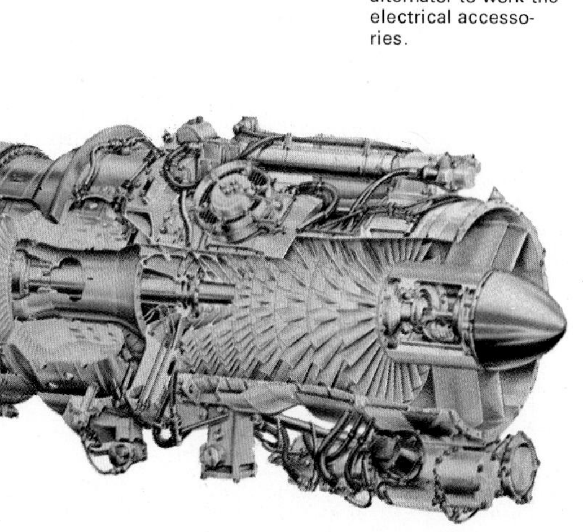

4 A gas turbine, such as this turbojet, uses the hot gases from the burning of fuel to turn sets of turbine blades at the rear of the engine. Other blades, mounted on the same shaft but at the front of the engine, compress the incoming air. Generating up to 4,000lb thrust, the engine is used in trainer, light attack, and business jet aircraft.

Wind and water power

The windmill [Key] and the waterwheel [1] are two of the oldest forms of power. Waterwheels were in use in Rome in 70 BC to grind corn and the windmill made its first appearance in Persia in AD 644. The modern waterwheel, in the form of the hydroelectric turbine, is more important, but the use of wind for power shows signs of reviving.

From waterwheels to turbines

A waterwheel or turbine converts the energy of flowing water into a rotary motion [3]. Early waterwheels used the undershot principle, in which the lower half of the wheel was simply immersed in a flowing stream [1]. They had an efficiency of only 30 percent. Overshot wheels, in which the flow of water is directed over the top of the wheel, produce efficiencies of 70 to 90 percent, similar to modern turbines.

Turbines replaced waterwheels in the second half of the nineteenth century. There are three categories: impulse turbines, reaction turbines, and axial-flow turbines [4]. An impulse turbine needs a high head of water pressure. The falling water is directed through a nozzle and the rapidly moving jet produced hits "buckets" on the edge of a wheel. A reaction turbine operates on the same jet principle as a rotating lawn-sprinkler: an axial-flow turbine has a variable-pitch propeller in a large tube.

Hydroelectric schemes and tidal power

Most water turbines are used to exploit the runoff of water from mountain areas, which is stored behind a dam. These turbines drive electrical generators. In countries with many mountains such systems provide cheap, pollution-free power. Hydroelectricity is the fourth largest source of energy in the United States.

A considerable capacity of such conventional turbo-power remains untapped: the Fraser River in Canada, for instance, could generate 8,700 megawatts (Mw) of electrical power, the Brahmaputra in India 20,000 Mw. The Yenisei-Angara river system in the USSR, with 11,000 Mw installed, has the capacity for a further 53,000 Mw.

Water turbines can also be used to generate power from the small heads of water produced by the tides [2]. The only full-scale power station of this kind is in the Rance river estuary in the Gulf of St Malo in northern France. The range of rise and fall produced by the tides varies widely from place to place—from as little as 0.75in (2cm) in Tahiti to as much as 50ft (15m) in the Bay of Fundy in eastern Canada. But only places at the upper end of this range make suitable sites for tidal power stations, and even then the economics of such a scheme may not be easy to justify.

Unfortunately the times of the tides do not always coincide with peak demand for electricity. A tidal power station might reach its full power in the middle of the night, when electricity demand is lowest. One way of reducing this problem is to divide the tidal basin into two: a high basin that fills between mid-tide and high tide and a low basin that empties between mid-tide and low tide. The setting up of such a system allows a continuous difference in level to be maintained at all times.

An alternative is to use the high basin as a pumped storage system [4]. In pumped

CONNECTIONS

See also

1678 Sailing ships
1682 Hydrofoils and hov craft
1764 Building dams
1646 Saving fuel and energy

1
A
B

1 The two basic types of waterwheels are called overshot [A] and undershot [B]. In the overshot wheel, a stream of fast flowing water is directed on top of the wheel, which turns forward. The paddles of the undershot wheel dip into the mill stream and the water current turns the wheel backward. In both types of waterwheels the energy of flowing water is converted into rotary power. It can be used to drive various machines, such as pumps or mills for grinding wheat. Water can even be harnessed to drive a dynamo or alternator for generating electricity. Waterwheels are virtually silent and pollution-free.

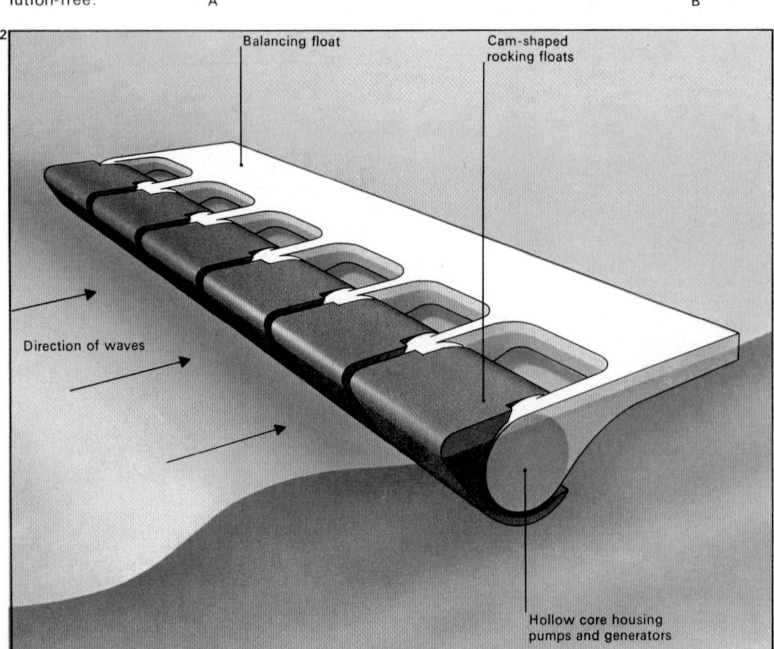

2
Balancing float
Cam-shaped rocking floats
Direction of waves
Hollow core housing pumps and generators

2 Water waves in the continuous swell of the open sea are a vast and as yet largely untapped source of energy. When a wave passes a certain point no water moves sideways. Instead, large masses of water move up and down. This can be confirmed by watching a cork or other light object floating on a pond. When ripples pass it, it does not move along but merely bobs up and down. The assembly of rocking floats shown here is designed to harness wave power and generate electricity. The structure would be about 1,000ft(300m) long – the size of a supertanker. The movement of the floats works pumps that power turbines that drive electrical generators.

3 A simple turbine of the 16th century used running water to work a pump for irrigation. Rotation of the turbine [1] turned a wheel [2] with teeth on half its circumference. The cog wheels [3] turned alternately in opposite directions making the pump wheel [4] oscillate. Self-acting valves allowed the pistons [5] to draw water into one cylinder while pushing it out the other.

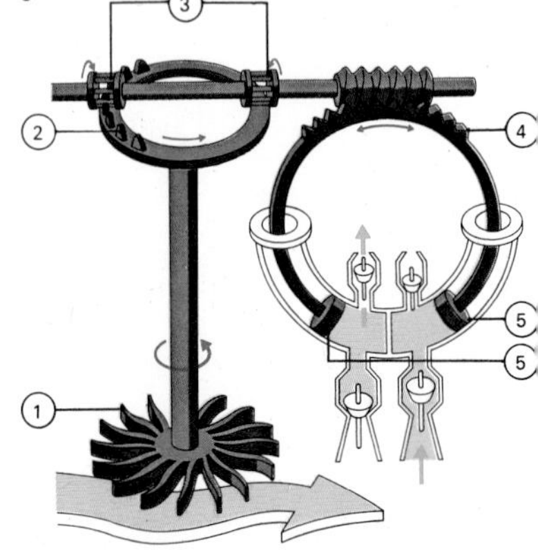

3
1
2
3
4
5
5

storage electricity generated by conventional plants and not needed by consumers is used to pump water from a low-lying basin into a high-lying one. When demand picks up, the water is allowed to flow down again, generating electricity like an ordinary hydroelectric plant. Such a method is not a net generator of electricity but it provides a means of storing large amounts of power efficiently.

Harnessing wind power

The use of wind to generate electricity has been less successful. Despite the immense amounts of power theoretically available (America could meet most of its electrical energy needs by harnessing just a fraction of its available wind energy) the problem of harnessing it economically has yet to be solved.

The power available to a windmill [Key] is proportional to the cube of the wind velocity and the area swept out by the blades. The ultimate efficiency possible is 59 percent, but practical machines would be unlikely to do better than 45 percent. Estimates suggest that the generation of electricity by wind could compete with nuclear power in a limited number of sites where average wind speeds exceed 20mph (32kph). But there are not many such sites and wind power is thus unlikely to be able to generate more than about one percent of electricity needs.

For this reason more interest is being shown in exploiting the stored power of the wind in sea waves [2]. Winds blowing over a long stretch of ocean generate powerful waves, and could be used as a source of power. The most promising design, produced by S. H. Salter at Edinburgh University in Scotland, uses a float that rocks to and fro as the waves pass, operating pumps to compress a fluid which would then be allowed to expand through turbines to generate electricity.

The amounts of wave power available are large. The amounts of power available are also greater in winter, when demand is at its highest, but the problems of building and maintaining such floats at a distance from the coastline are formidable.

KEY

Windmills have been used for many centuries for harnessing the power of the wind. Originally the power was used for grinding wheat – hence the name mill – but later windmills were used to drive pumps, particularly for draining low-lying regions of the Netherlands and eastern England in the Fens and East Anglia. Some early windmills had canvas sails, developed from those used on ships. Then slatted wooden sails were developed, as in this bonnet mill. The sails turned with the bonnet or cap on the top of the mill so that they always faced into the wind. In a post mill the structure pivoted on a central post to face the wind.

4A

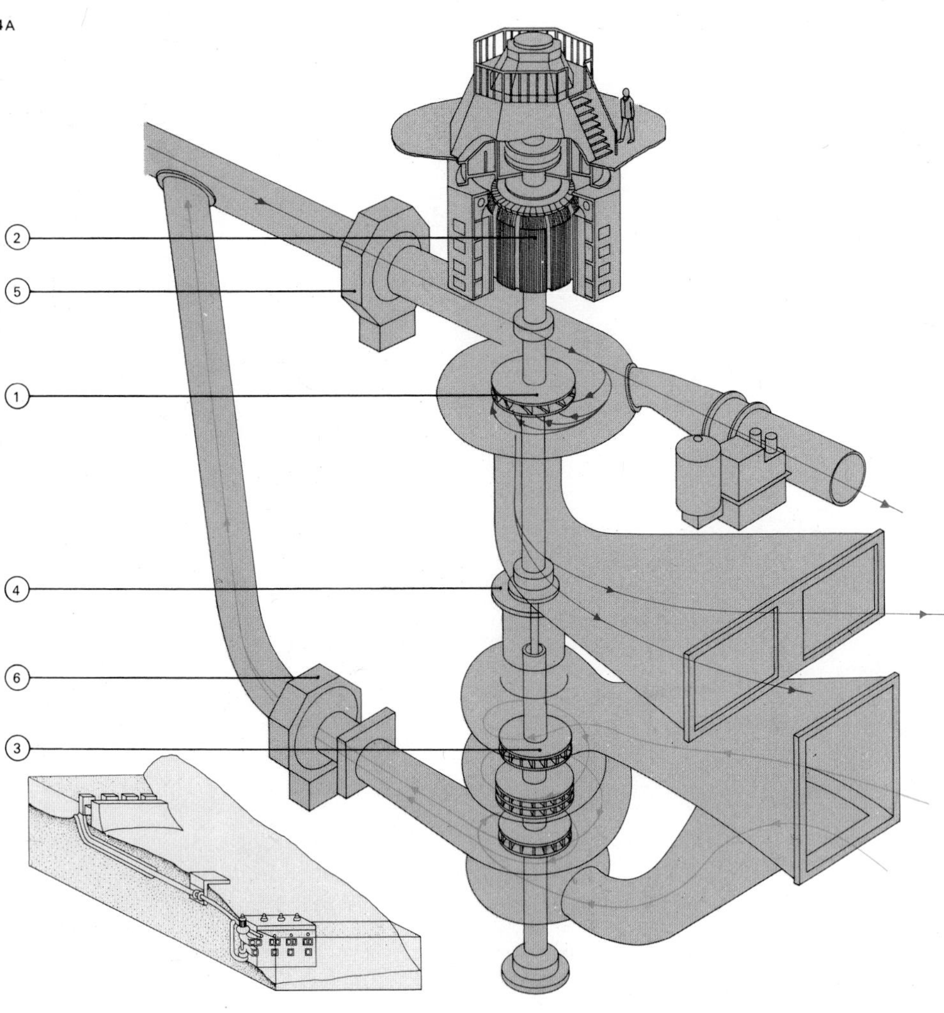
2
5
1
4
6
3

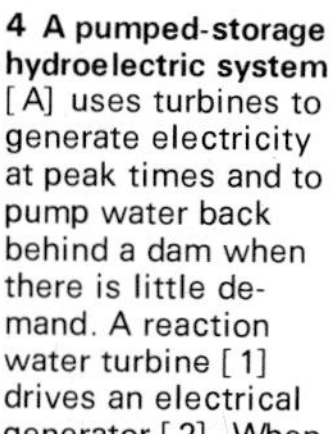

B

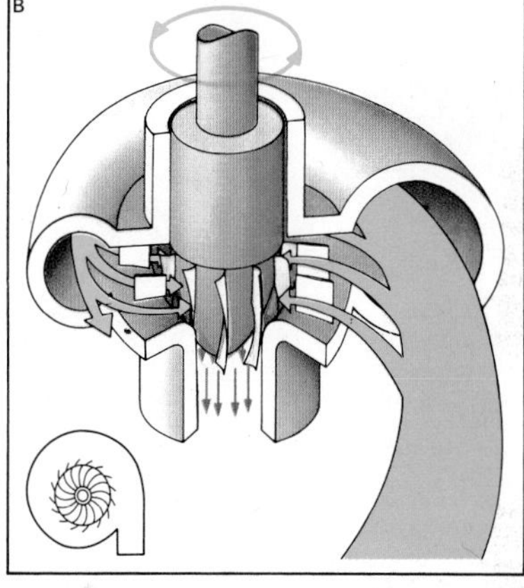

C

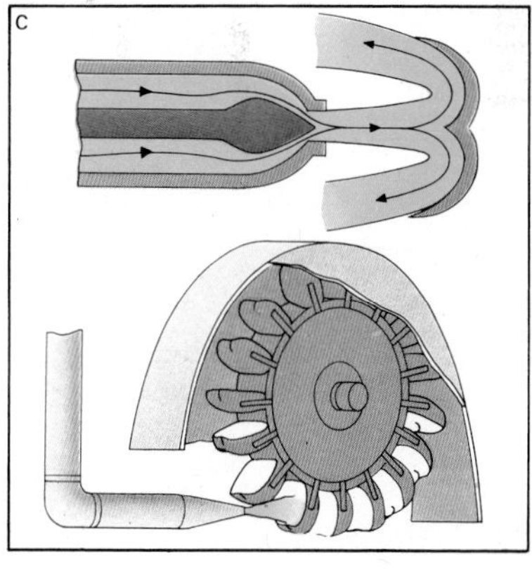

D

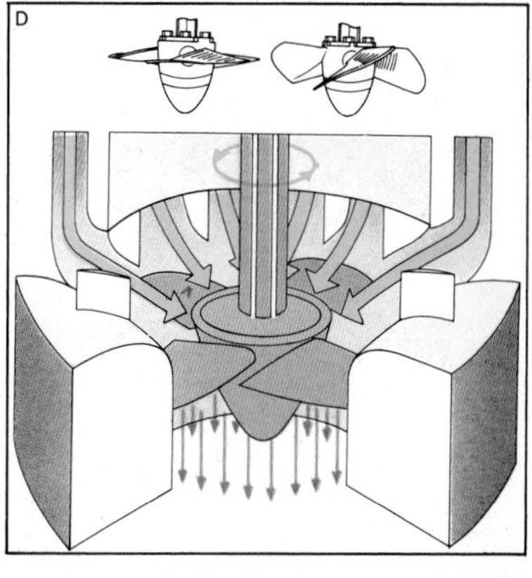

4 A pumped-storage hydroelectric system [A] uses turbines to generate electricity at peak times and to pump water back behind a dam when there is little demand. A reaction water turbine [1] drives an electrical generator [2]. When the centrifugal pumps [3] are uncoupled the machine acts as a normal hydroelectric generator. But when the geared coupling [4] is engaged the water turbine drives the pump up to operating speed. Then the generator is connected to the electricity supply for which it acts as a motor. The turbine valve [5] is closed, the pump valve [6] is opened, and water is pumped back behind the dam, adding to the volume of stored water available for later hydroelectric generation. Three types of water turbines are in common use. The Francis reaction turbine [B] has adjustable fixed blades that divert the water stream in such a way that it strikes the rotating turbine blades at a tangent. Water flows out of the turbine downward. In the Pelton wheel or impulse turbine [C] the water passes through a jet and strikes paddles on the wheel. The direction of the water flow is reversed. The blades on the Kaplan axial-flow turbine [D] resemble a ship's propeller.

Power direct from the Sun and Earth

Much of the energy man consumes comes indirectly from the Sun. Coal, oil, and hydroelectricity can all be thought of as forms of solar energy, stored as long-dead plant and animal remains or as water, evaporated from the sea by the Sun, which falls as rain and provides water power. Today, however, the search is on for a way to use solar energy directly; coal and oil take millions of years to produce and many of the best hydroelectric sites are already in use.

Collecting solar energy

There are many possible ways of tapping solar energy. It may be intercepted in space by a satellite and beamed to earth as an intense beam. More simply, it can be collected as it reaches the earth's surface by collectors that are basically hot water radiators working in reverse. Such collectors can provide space heating in houses or can be used as the basis for air-conditioning systems. Solar energy can also be converted directly into electricity, at low efficiency, by solar cells similar to those used in satellites. Alternatively, it can be collected by using it to grow plants that are then used directly as fuel, or converted into a liquid fuel by chemical conversion, or by the use of micro-organisms. Finally, the heat stored in the sea can be used to provide energy by employing the temperature difference between surface water and cold deep water.

The systems compared

Of these possibilities, only the humble solar collectors are so far used. They consist of panels, usually mounted on the roof of a building and angled so as to obtain the maximum amount of sunlight. Water is pumped through the panels, picking up heat from the Sun as it goes. The pump is controlled by a sensor so that it operates only when the collector is several degrees hotter than the water in the storage tank. Unfortunately, the Sun does not shine all the time, particularly in northern areas such as Great Britain and parts of the United States, but despite this it is estimated that a well-designed solar collector system could halve hot water and space heating costs.

Systems for converting solar energy directly into electricity are less attractive. The solar cells used by spacecraft are expensive and typically have conversion efficiencies of only ten percent or less. In principle electricity could be generated by covering rooftops with solar cells [2] but this would depend on producing cheap cells on the order of a dollar per square foot; they now cost over $100 per square foot.

An alternative would be to collect solar energy by using transparent pipes carrying a molten mixture of sodium and potassium. The mixture would be heated to well above the boiling point of water by concentrating the Sun's rays onto the pipes with reflectors. The hot metal would then be used in a heat exchanger to raise steam, which could be used to generate electricity. Such a scheme, based in a desert area, would need a lot of land—19.3 to 77 square miles (50 to 200 square kilometers) for every 1,000 megawatts of electricity—and might be feasible to introduce in the 1980s.

The other possibility is to make use of the difference in temperature between deep ocean water and surface water. The circula-

CONNECTIONS

See also
1634 Wind and water powe
1638 Nuclear power
1640 Coal: production ar uses
1642 Oil and natural gas
1646 Saving fuel and energy

1 A solar furnace harnesses the Sun's energy by focusing its heat and light, using large lenses or mirrors. This furnace at Mont-Louis in France gets hot enough—up to 5,430°F (3,000°C)—to melt metals. The heat, which is completely clean and uncontaminated by fuel gases, could be concentrated on a boiler to raise steam for domestic heating or for driving a turbine for generating electricity. Generally a set of flat mirrors is arranged to follow automatically the path of the Sun and reflect its rays onto the stationary furnace mirror. The tracking mirror is called a heliostat and be driven by an electric motor so that it moves through exactly 15 minutes of arc every hour. Alternatively the angle of the heliostat may be controlled by a photocell or thermocouple that detects the absence of light or heat rays.

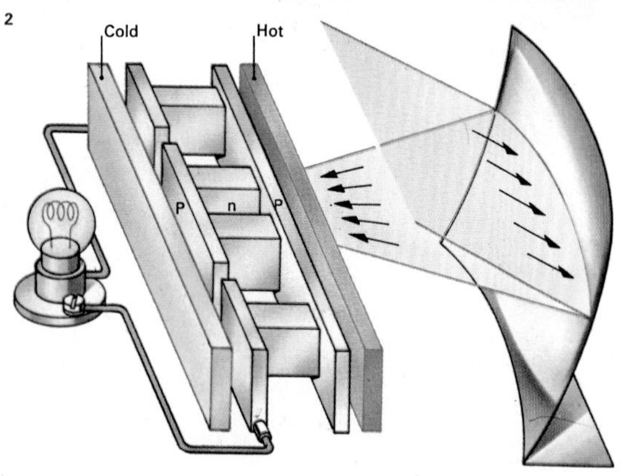

Cold
Hot
p
n
p

2 In one type of solar cell, heat from the Sun is focused onto a surface backed by a semiconductor thermocouple (a series of p-n junctions) that converts the solar heat into electricity.

3 Solar collectors, seen here on the roof of a house, provide energy for domestic space and water heating. Flat-plate collectors are sheets of metal painted black and they transfer heat to air or water circulating behind them.

tion of ocean water is limited, which means that there is often a difference of as much as 27°F(15°C) between deep and surface water. By making use of this difference the vast quantities of solar heat stored in the sea could be used. But the efficiency of operation would be only about five percent.

Energy from the earth

The eruption of volcanoes is graphic evidence of the energy stored inside the Earth. Geothermal heat is believed to be produced continuously by the slow decay of radioactive elements deep inside the Earth's core.

In some places on the Earth's surface this heat escapes, either as a volcano or as hot springs and geysers [Key]. The first attempt to make use of geothermal heat [5] was at Larderello in Italy, where natural steam is now used to generate 390 megawatts of electricity. Other geothermal plants are in operation in Iceland, Japan, New Zealand, the USSR, and the United States. In the United States, geysers 90 miles (145km) northeast of San Francisco generate 302 megawatts.

The number of places where steam or hot brines occur naturally is limited and depends on a supply of water. If a hole is drilled anywhere on the Earth's surface it becomes hotter the deeper the drill goes, but the rate at which the temperature increases—the temperature gradient—varies widely. In places with a steep temperature gradient it may be possible to extract heat by drilling holes, fracturing the rocks at the bottom, then passing down water from the surface to be turned into steam and used to generate electricity. Experiments to test the feasibility of this scheme are in progress at Los Alamos Scientific Laboratory in New Mexico [6]. If it works, the potential energy reserve will be enormous. A volume of about 125 cubic miles (520 cubic kilometers) of underground rock a few hundred degrees hotter than the surface rocks contains as much energy as the entire world uses in a whole year. If only a small fraction of this energy can be extracted, geothermal power plants could supply huge amounts of pollution-free power.

KEY

Geysers spout steam and superheated water. They occur in regions that have active or recently active volcanoes, such as Iceland, Wyoming, and, as shown here, New Zealand. It is possible to "tap" the hot water for energy.

4

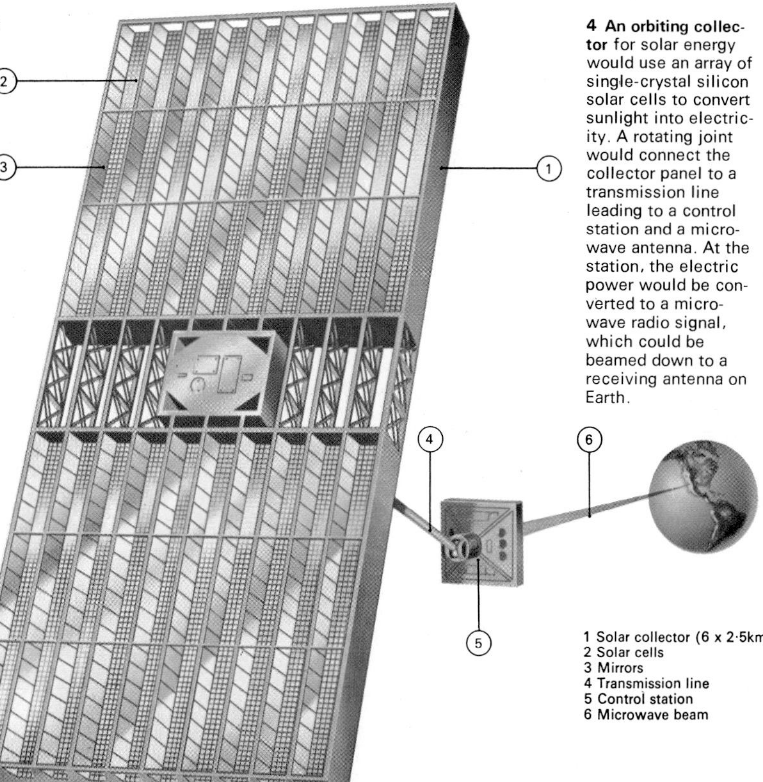

1
2
3
4
5
6

4 An orbiting collector for solar energy would use an array of single-crystal silicon solar cells to convert sunlight into electricity. A rotating joint would connect the collector panel to a transmission line leading to a control station and a microwave antenna. At the station, the electric power would be converted to a microwave radio signal, which could be beamed down to a receiving antenna on Earth.

1 Solar collector (6 x 2·5km)
2 Solar cells
3 Mirrors
4 Transmission line
5 Control station
6 Microwave beam

5

5 Geothermal energy (the heat of the earth in deep rocks) can give rise to hot springs when water naturally accumulates underground. A bore-hole drilled down into the water can be used to get a supply of hot water for industrial or domestic heating. A whole town sited over a geothermal field could obtain most of its heating by this means, and experimental systems have been tried in Scandinavia, the USSR, and the United States.

6

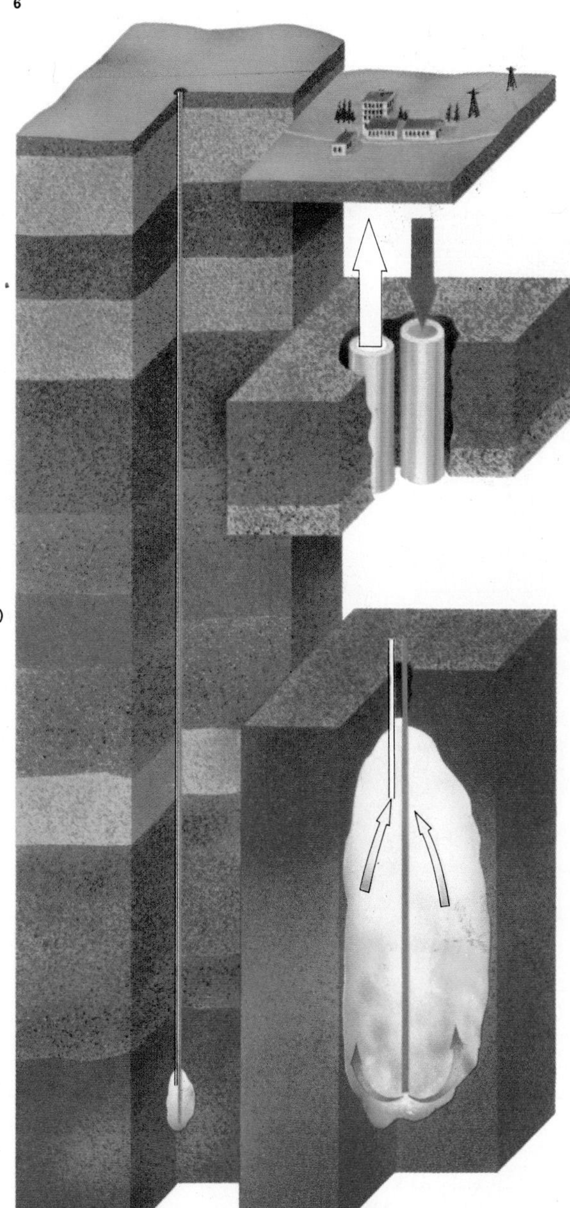

6 A man-made hot spring can be used, as in this experiment at Los Alamos, New Mexico, as a source of heat energy. A bore-hole is drilled several thousand feet into a natural cavity in the earth in which the temperature may be as high as 572°F (300° C). Water pumped down the bore is heated and led up a second bore-hole. At the surface the hot water passes through a heat exchanger, which transfers its heat to air blown over it.

Nuclear power

Nuclear power is the controlled release of the most concentrated source of energy man has yet discovered—the energy of the atomic nucleus. When the nucleus of a heavy atom divides into two, in a process called fission, it releases prodigious amounts of energy—suddenly in an atomic bomb, slowly and controllably in a nuclear reactor that is generating electricity.

The only naturally occurring element that will spontaneously undergo fission is uranium. As it is found in nature, uranium ore is a mixture of mainly two isotopes; uranium-235 and uranium-238, and only the first of these will undergo rapid spontaneous fission. (Isotopes are two forms of an element with different masses and other physical properties but identical chemical properties.) In the ore, U-235 makes up no more than 0.7 percent of the uranium present. The proportion of this isotope is increased, through ore enrichment, to produce an isotope mixture about 90 percent U-235.

The fuel is sealed into thin, pencil-shaped containers [5] so that it and the poisonous products of the fission process cannot escape. The fuel elements are supported, usually vertically, so that water or gas can flow between them to take away the heat produced by fission. After flowing past the hot fuel elements and picking up their heat, the coolant is taken away and used to raise steam to produce electricity in turbine generators.

Controlled chain reactions

Most reactors, however, need more than just fuel and a coolant. The fissioning of a U-235 nucleus is triggered off by a neutron, which strikes the nucleus and disturbs it just sufficiently to make it divide into two. In the process of dividing, the nucleus produces two or three fresh neutrons, which fly off and strike other U-235 nuclei, creating a chain reaction.

A nuclear reactor [1] must be so contrived that of the neutrons produced by each fission one, and only one, must cause a second fission. Only then will the reactor work steadily and at a constant speed. If on average more than one neutron from each fission causes a second fission, the reactor will accelerate and become a bomb; if less than one, the reactor will gradually lose power until it stops altogether.

The neutrons produced by each fission travel extremely fast—about 10,000 miles (16,000km) per second—and tend to escape from the reactor altogether before they can cause an additional fission. To make the reactor work they must be slowed down, using a material called a moderator, to increase the chances that they will collide productively with another U-235 nucleus and cause another fission. Moderators are light atoms that slow the neutrons down by a series of collisions.

Safety and refueling

The reactor is controlled by neutron-absorbing rods that can be moved in and out of the core at will. As the control rods are moved, the number of neutrons absorbed declines, so that more are available for fission and the reaction speeds up [2]. To stop the reactor in a hurry—a procedure known as scramming—the control rods are pushed into the core as quickly as possible. The

CONNECTIONS

See also
1482 Nuclear physics
1746 Nuclear, chemical, and biological warfa
1646 Saving fuel and energy
1734 Modern artillery

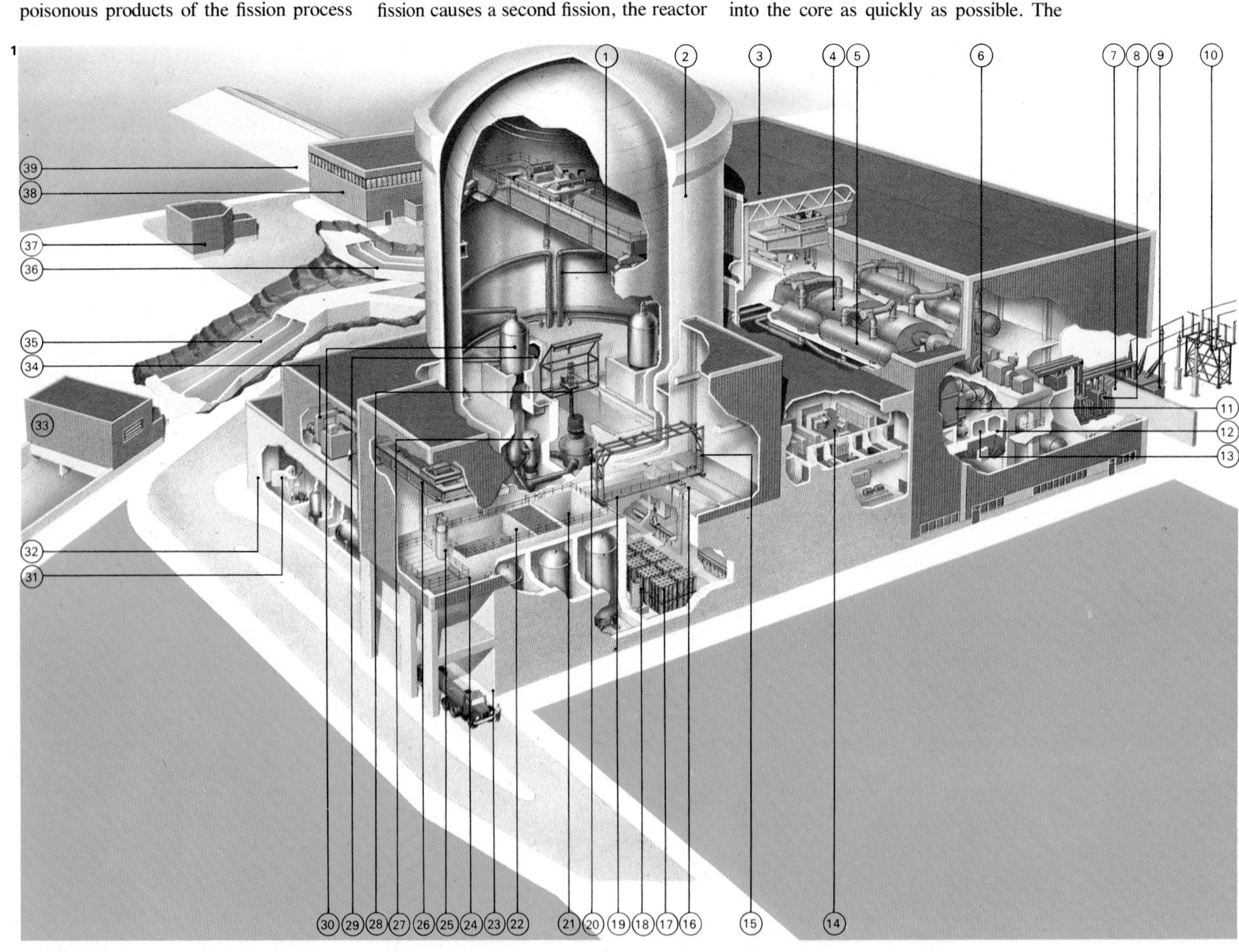

1 Nuclear reactors generate electricity using the heat produced by controlled fission of atoms of uranium or other similar elements. The heat is used in much the same way as in power stations that burn coal or oil to produce high-pressure steam to work turbine generators—only the source of the heat differs. Large volumes of cooling water are needed. Various liquids can be used to "carry" heat from the reactor to the heat exchanger. These include liquid sodium metal or, as here at the Ko-Ri power station near Pusan in South Korea, water under high pressure. Pressurized water reactors are today the most common type worldwide. The various parts of this highly complex installation are: [1] pressurized water pipes; [2] reactor building; [3] turbine building; [4] high-pressure turbine; [5] low-pressure turbine; [6] generator; [7] fire wall; [8] transformers; [9] main transformer; [10] switch-gear; [11] cooling water outlet; [12] condenser; [13] cooling water inlet; [14] control room; [15] spent fuel bridge; [16] new fuel lift; [17] spent fuel storage rack; [18] spent fuel drum. [19] drum loading; [20] reactor vessel; [21] decontamination pit; [22] new fuel store; [23] fuel loading bay; [24] fuel handling hatch; [25] spent fuel drum; [26] fuel crane; [27] reactor coolant pump; [28] refueling gantry; [29] pressurizer; [30] steam generator; [31] drum store; [32] waste drum loading area; [33] cooling water discharge; [34] auxiliary ventilation; [35] cooling water from turbines; [36] seawater (coolant) pump house; [37] cooling water to turbines; [38] cooling water pump house; and [39] seawater inlet.

rods "soak up" neutrons, leaving fewer available for taking part in fission, and the reactor slows down.

Surrounding the reactor are concrete and steel walls thick enough to absorb any accidental radiation escape. And, to make sure that the whole system is safe, the reactor must have emergency systems designed to cope with any unexpected failure of the fuel elements or the cooling system.

When the fuel elements are exhausted they are taken out of the reactor and replaced by new ones. The old ones, which still contain some unused U-235, are taken to a reprocessing plant to extract what is left [3]. At this point the nuclear reactor produces a useful bonus. Among the products inside the old fuel elements is a new man-made atom, plutonium-239, created by the neutron bombardment of U-238.

Plutonium-239 (Pu-239), just like U-235, is spontaneously fissionable, so that it can be used to make atomic bombs or to find new nuclear reactors. The first reactors were designed and built as plutonium factories for the production of atomic bombs. Plutonium is, however, extremely poisonous and in recent years people have become concerned about the world increase in the amount of this element.

The fast breeder reactor

The latest type of reactor, the fast breeder [6], is also designed to make use of the accidental production of Pu-239. It is fueled by uranium and around the outside of the core, to catch the escaping neutrons, is a "breeding blanket" in which U-238 is converted into Pu-239. So effective is this arrangement that a fast breeder should produce PU-239 more quickly than it uses up its own fuel. The fast breeder therefore creates more nuclear fuel than it actually consumes.

To date, all existing reactors use the fission reaction in which heavy atoms split to produce energy. It has so far proved much more difficult to tame the other powerful nuclear reaction—fusion—that gives the hydrogen bomb its awesome power [7]. In this reaction light atoms heated to two million degrees fuse together to build heavier atoms, producing energy.

KEY

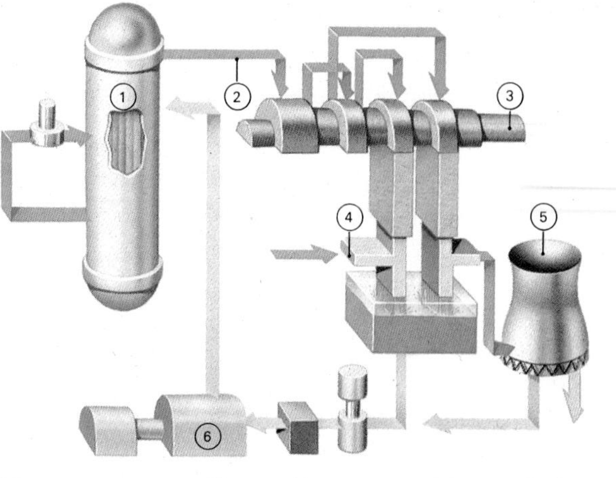
1
2
3
4
5
6

All nuclear power stations have basically the same layout. A reactor [1] heats water and converts it (either directly or indirectly) into steam [2], which then drives a turbine generator [3] to produce electricity. Exhaust steam is converted back to water in a condenser [4], using cold water from a cooling tower [5], and the water is circulated by a pump [6] back through the hot part of the reactor. The cooling tower needs a supply of cold water from a river or the sea.

2

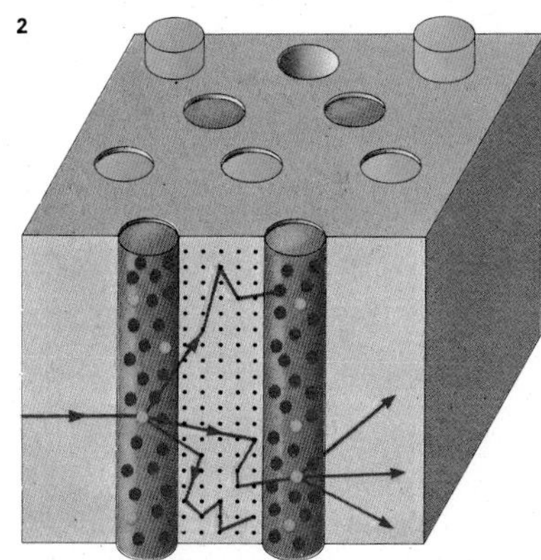

2 A graphite-moderated reactor also raises steam to power turbine generators. Neutrons, slowed down in a surrounding block of graphite, split atoms of uranium-235. Each of these produces more neutrons, which are again slowed and produce further fissions. Rods of cadmium (blue) are lowered into the "pile" to mop up some of the new neutrons to control the rate of heat production

3

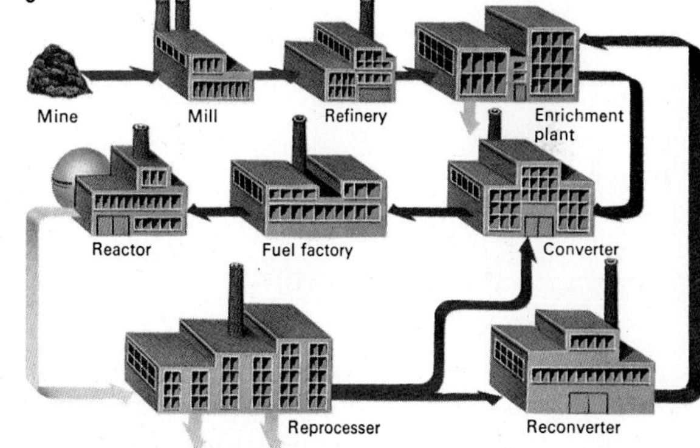
Mine
Mill
Refinery
Enrichment plant
Reactor
Fuel factory
Converter
Reprocesser
Reconverter

3 Nuclear fuel is used cyclically. From the mine, uranium ore passes to a mill to be converted to uranium oxide. This is refined and, as the fluoride, goes to an enrichment plant before being converted back to the oxide and made into fuel. The enriched fuel is then used in the reactor, from which spent fuel is reprocessed and the recovered uranium reconverted into fluoride and fed back to the enrichment plant.

4

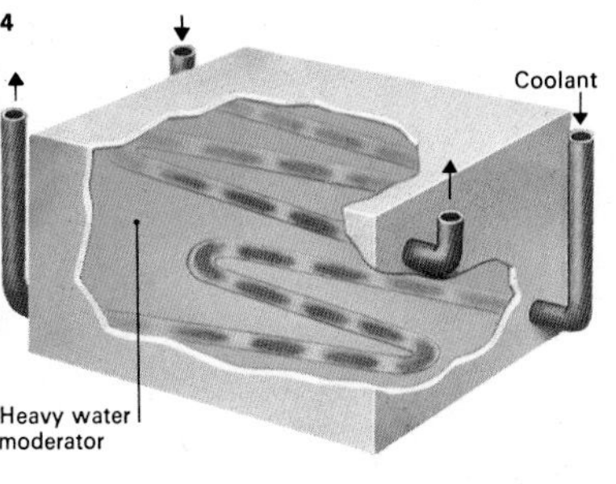
Coolant
Heavy water moderator

4 In a pressure-tube reactor the pressurized coolant (water, heavy water, or an organic liquid) passes through the reactor vessel, surrounded by a neutron-absorbing heavy water moderator.

5

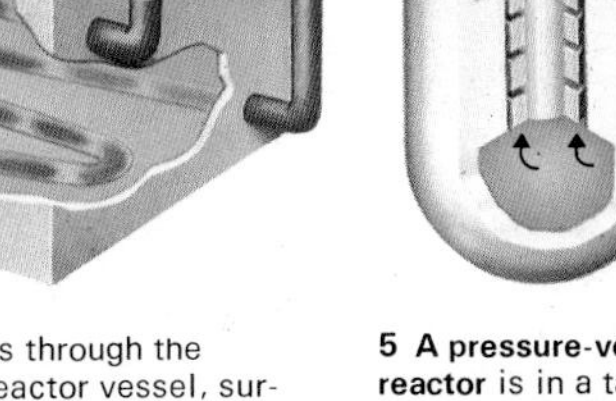

5 A pressure-vessel reactor is in a tank of steel 8–12in thick and clad with stainless steel.

6

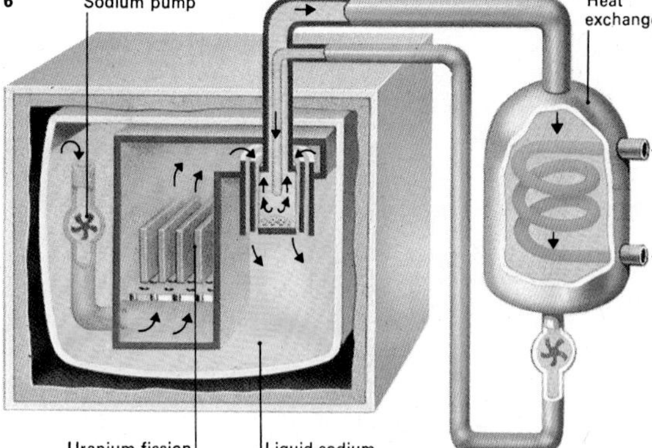
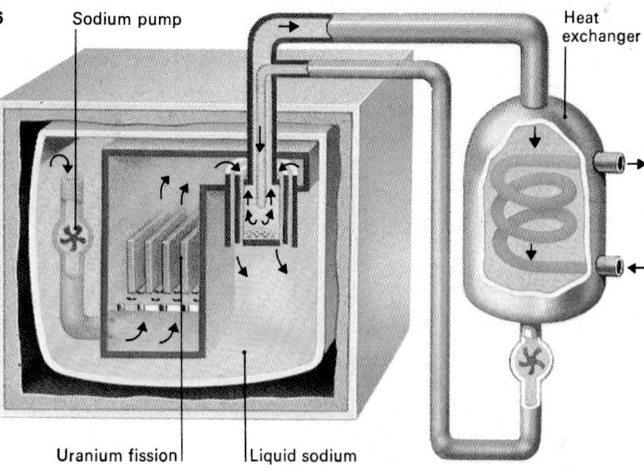
Sodium pump
Heat exchanger
Uranium fission
Liquid sodium

6 In a fast breeder reactor, uranium fuel is used and at the same time converted into the fissile element plutonium. Liquid sodium metal carries heat from the reactor to a heat exchanger, converting water to steam to drive turbine generators. A condenser turns the exhaust steam back to water for recirculation. The plutonium produced is used to enrich the uranium fuel or is used in other reactors.

7 Scientists are trying to harness the fusion reaction that powers a hydrogen bomb. At extremely high temperatures the reacting gases, now called a plasma, are confined by magnetic fields.

8

8 Nuclear reactors for power stations, such as this one at Dounray, Scotland, need a plentiful supply of water for cooling. This water, drawn from the sea or an estuary, is used in condensers to convert exhaust steam to water.

Coal: production and uses

Coal is a hydrocarbon deposit that can be burned to provide heat energy. It is found in layers known as seams, usually below the ground [2], but in some places it appears near the surface immediately under a layer of soil [4]. It is generally hard, opaque, and black. It was little used before the sixteenth century, but thereafter it became the basis of a great fuel industry—first in Great Britain, then elsewhere in Europe and throughout the world.

Origins of coal

Coal is the product of low-lying forest growths from several tens of millions to some 300 million years ago [1]. The residues of the plant debris were submerged in swamps, then buried beneath great thicknesses of sandstones and shales. This process was repeated many times. The plant deposits were subjected to pressure, heat, and breakdown by micro-organisms; as a result they were transformed into a range of combustible solids.

This process of transformation is often called "coalification" and the degree to which it has taken place determines the "rank" of the coal. Anthracite is the highest rank coal. Rank may vary across a single seam and when this occurs all seams above and below vary in a predictable way. In undisturbed vertical sections the deeper seams are of higher rank than those nearer the surface.

To simply quality control, coal is often specified in terms of its "proximate analysis"; this gives its percentage composition of moisture, volatile matter, fixed carbon, and ash as determined by standard methods. The "ultimate analysis" determines the amount of carbon, hydrogen, oxygen, nitrogen, and sulfur in coal. In addition, users may wish to know the "heating power" or calorific value of the fuel in units of heat generated per unit of weight burned.

Coals may also be described in terms of their petrographic constituents—that is, considered as rock types. The four physical structures recognized are clarain (smooth, shining constituent), durain (dull, hard, granular), vitrain (shining, black, glassy luster), and fusain (black, friable, fibrous).

History of the coal industry

The growth of the coal industry was one of the main spurs to general industrial growth from the seventeenth to the twentieth centuries. Today, coal is not used merely as fuel but is the basis of the manufacture of such diverse commodities as perfumes, nylon stockings, pain-killing drugs, and cloth dyes.

Until World War II the coal industry was of key economic importance in the industrialized countries. Even in 1950 coal provided 56 percent of world energy supply; by 1974 this had declined to 29 percent because of marked increases in both oil and natural gas production. After the sharp rises in oil prices in 1973, and the estimates of limited reserves of oil and gas, coal production was being increased in many countries that had conducted a policy of decreasing production since the mid-1950s [Key].

Coal was first scratched from the surface of the earth where it was found by chance. It was later extracted from "drifts" (gently sloping tunnels that followed the seam into the ground) and later still by

CONNECTIONS

See also
1648 Electricity generatic and distribution
1754 Tunnel engineering
1810 Explosives and fireworks
1646 Saving fuel and energy
282 Energy resources: coal
562 Plants of the past

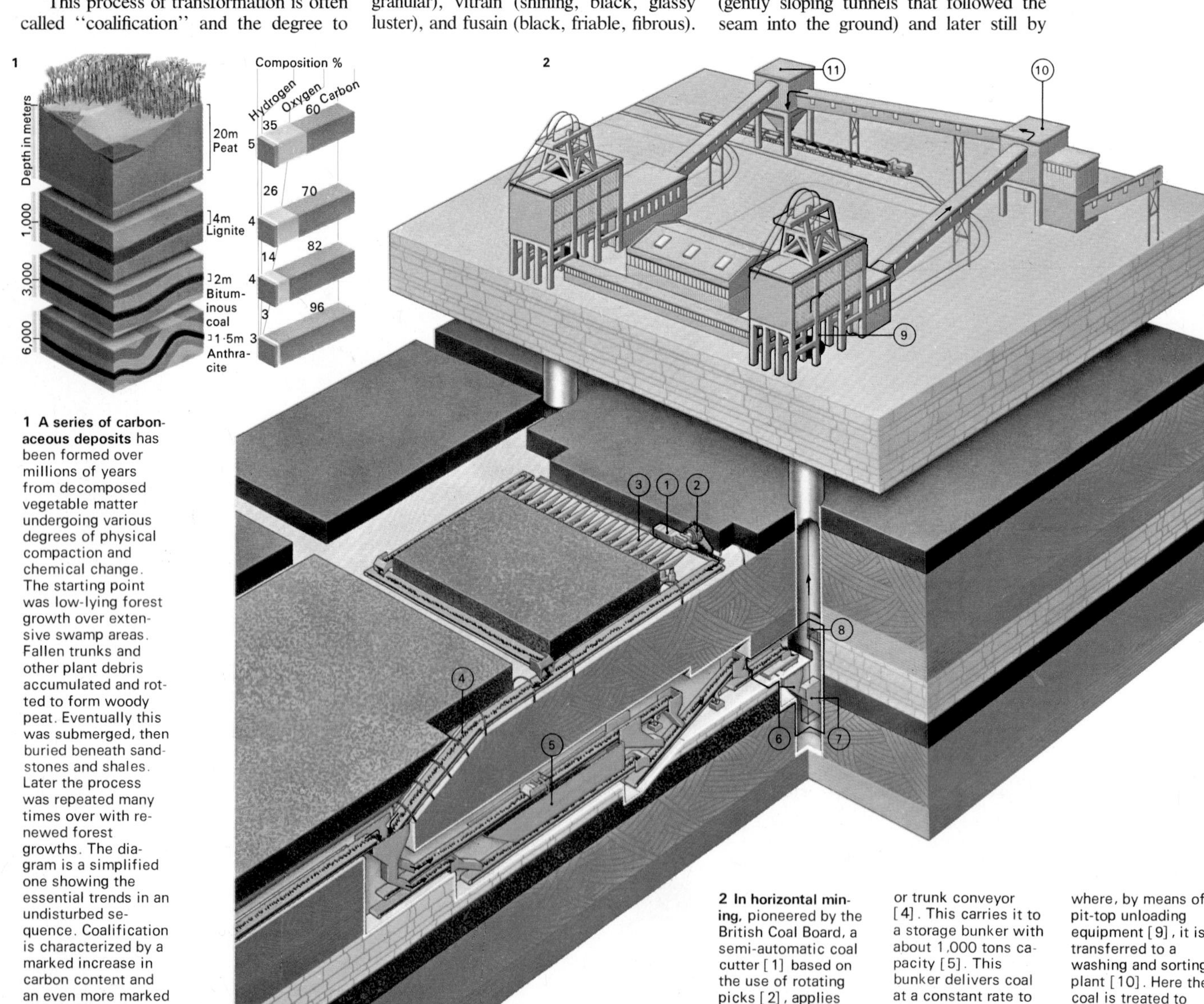

1
Depth in meters
1,000
3,000
6,000
Composition %
Hydrogen
Oxygen
Carbon
20m Peat 5
35
60
26
70
]4m Lignite 4
14
82
]2m Bitum-inous coal 4
3
96
]1·5m Anthra-cite 3
2
1
2
3
4
5
6
7
8
9
10
11

1 A series of carbonaceous deposits has been formed over millions of years from decomposed vegetable matter undergoing various degrees of physical compaction and chemical change. The starting point was low-lying forest growth over extensive swamp areas. Fallen trunks and other plant debris accumulated and rotted to form woody peat. Eventually this was submerged, then buried beneath sandstones and shales. Later the process was repeated many times over with renewed forest growths. The diagram is a simplified one showing the essential trends in an undisturbed sequence. Coalification is characterized by a marked increase in carbon content and an even more marked decrease in oxygen and hydrogen. The effect of these changes is that higher rank fuels are more chemically condensed and give off less volatile matter when tested.

2 In horizontal mining, pioneered by the British Coal Board, a semi-automatic coal cutter [1] based on the use of rotating picks [2], applies self-advanced hydraulic roof supports [3] on the coalface. The coal is discharged onto an armored conveyor that carries the coal to a transfer point where it is put onto a main or trunk conveyor [4]. This carries it to a storage bunker with about 1,000 tons capacity [5]. This bunker delivers coal at a constant rate to the measuring hopper [6], which in turn loads the coal skip [7] in the area devoted to pit-bottom loading equipment [8]. In the skip the coal is raised in the shaft to the pithead where, by means of pit-top unloading equipment [9], it is transferred to a washing and sorting plant [10]. Here the coal is treated to reduce the ash content and also graded into size groups. The cleaned and graded coal is then loaded at the train loading tower [11] for delivery.

sinking shafts. Today, coal prospecting is a major scientific undertaking employing geophysicists and advanced instruments for investigation before trial borings are made. Sinking a pit is now a major project that takes between five and ten years and the investment of many millions of dollars.

Coal was originally dug out by pick and shovel and removed to the surface in baskets. Today, in all industrialized countries, coal mining is wholly mechanized and pit outputs may range up to more than a million tons a year [2]. The miners operate mechanical cutters and the coal is transferred by conveyor or underground trains. The tendency is toward remotely operated equipment so that men are increasingly withdrawn from the dangerous areas where the coal is actually being mined. In one development a coalcutting machine is automatically steered along the face using a radioactive probe to measure the thickness of the skin of coal left in the roof as it cuts its way along. Although coal miners continue to be subject to specific dangers and medical problems, the death and accident rates have been steadily reduced in industrialized countries. The inflammable gas methane may be released from the coal during working and for this reason all equipment used must meet strict safety requirements.

Products from coal

Coal was at one time an important source of gas and chemicals obtained by heating the coal, out of contact with air, in the process called "carbonization." This process has sharply declined in importance since the mid-1950s. Nevertheless, widespread research is in progress to make coal once again an important source of chemicals using new processes, such as hydrogenation, that can make it into both gas and liquid fuels. Of all the primary fossil fuels coal has by far the greatest reserves, amounting to probably hundreds of years of use at expected rates; thus it will far outlast gas and oil. The coke produced by degassing coal is an essential ingredient in the smelting of iron for making steel. The coal gas produced from coking ovens can be used for heating at the coke-making plant.

KEY

World Coal Production
(Millions of metric tons)

700, 600, 500, 400, 300, 200, 100

USSR, US, China, East Germany, West Germany, Poland, United Kingdom

1969 1970 1971 1972 1973 1974 1975

The five-fold increase in oil prices during 1972–74 caused many countries to reconsider their policy regarding coal production. Some coal producers had seriously reduced coal output, but the US had generally maintained the level of production while the USSR and other Eastern European producers had continued to develop their coal industries. In Eastern Europe the relationship between prices of oil and coal is the result of political decisions. In the free market economies the state of the coal industry in the postwar period has been determined by the ratio of prices of oil and coal. Today scientists in Western Europe are finding new uses for coal.

3

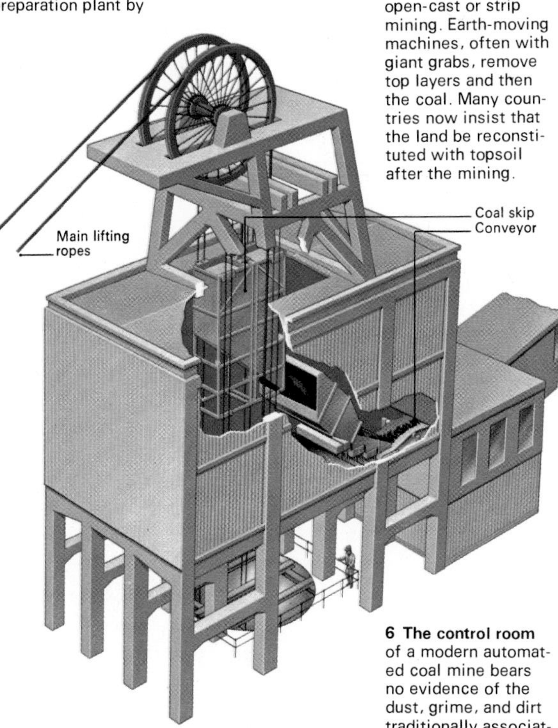
Coal skip
Conveyor
Main lifting ropes

3 In modern plants the pithead equipment, which transfers the coal to the preparation plant by conveyor, is housed within a building designed not to conflict with its surroundings.

4

4 When seams are close to the surface the cheapest way to obtain coal is by open-cast or strip mining. Earth-moving machines, often with giant grabs, remove top layers and then the coal. Many countries now insist that the land be reconstituted with topsoil after the mining.

5

5 Coke, shown here leaving a coking oven, is a typical smokeless fuel for industrial use. Coal is heated in ovens, out of contact with the air, until it is white hot. This process removes most of the tarry substances and the fuel thus produced burns leaving very little ash.

6

6 The control room of a modern automated coal mine bears no evidence of the dust, grime, and dirt traditionally associated with mining. In this control room a single engineer monitors the workings of machines both underground and on the surface.

7

1
2
3

7 The Anderton Shearer [1] is a rotary drum cutter coupled with a diverting plow [2] that loads the coal onto an armored coal conveyor [3].

Oil and natural gas

The world's first oil well was drilled at Titusville, western Pennsylvania, in August 1859 by Colonel Edwin L. Drake. He found crude oil 69.5ft (21m) below the surface and started an industry that is now the world's biggest. By 1975 there were more than 600,000 oil wells throughout the world, producing a total of more than 55 million barrels of oil a day (a barrel equals 35 imperial gallons, 42 US gallons, or 159 liters).

Composition, origins, and location

Oil is a complex mixture of hydrocarbons—chemical compounds consisting of carbon and hydrogen. They range in density from light gases such as methane to heavy solids such as asphalt. And the color ranges from yellow, through green, red, and brown, to black. A typical crude oil contains about 85 percent carbon and 15 percent hydrogen. Natural gas consists of the least dense fraction of crude oil [7], but it can often occur in the absence of oil.

Oil (including most natural gas) is thought to be the product of the decay, under special conditions, of single-celled plants and animals that lived hundreds of millions of years ago and settled to form sediments when they died. Some natural gas has a simpler origin; methane can be formed by the bacterial decomposition of vegetable matter in marshy areas.

After their formation, oil deposits frequently moved until they became trapped in porous rocks at depths ranging from as little as 100ft (30m) to more than 25,000ft (7,600m). For this reason oil deposits are not vast caverns filled with a sea of liquid oil and gas but are more widely dispersed.

The first prospectors drilled for oil in places where it seeped naturally to the surface. Today prospecting has to be more scientific [2], although surface methods can still sometimes be helpful. The appearance of the ground and the presence of the appropriate kinds of sedimentary rocks can suggest likely places to drill. Seismic surveys (measurements of the effects of shock waves in rocks) are widely used. Engineers detonate explosives in a shallow hole and use microphones to detect the depths of the echoes from underground structures. Gravity surveys may also be used; sensitive instruments, sometimes carried by aircraft, detect variations in the gravitational field and these may suggest the presence of oil-bearing geological structures.

Methods of drilling

The first drills operated with a pounding action in a dry hole. If oil was found there was nothing to stop it shooting out of the hole as a "gusher." Modern techniques prevent this by using rotary drills [1] immersed in drilling "mud"—especially formulated compounds that fill the hole as it is drilled to prevent gushers.

The drilling bit is driven downward on the end of a hollow steel tube through which mud is pumped. As the bit drives through the rock the pieces of debris are carried away by the mud and brought to the surface. There, the mud is examined by geologists, who check the nature of the stratum through which the drill bit has passed. This should agree with their survey. The mud is screened to remove rubble and then recirculated down the hole.

CONNECTIONS

See also
1644 Oil refining
1626 Basic types of engines
1646 Saving fuel and energy
284 Energy resources: oil and gas

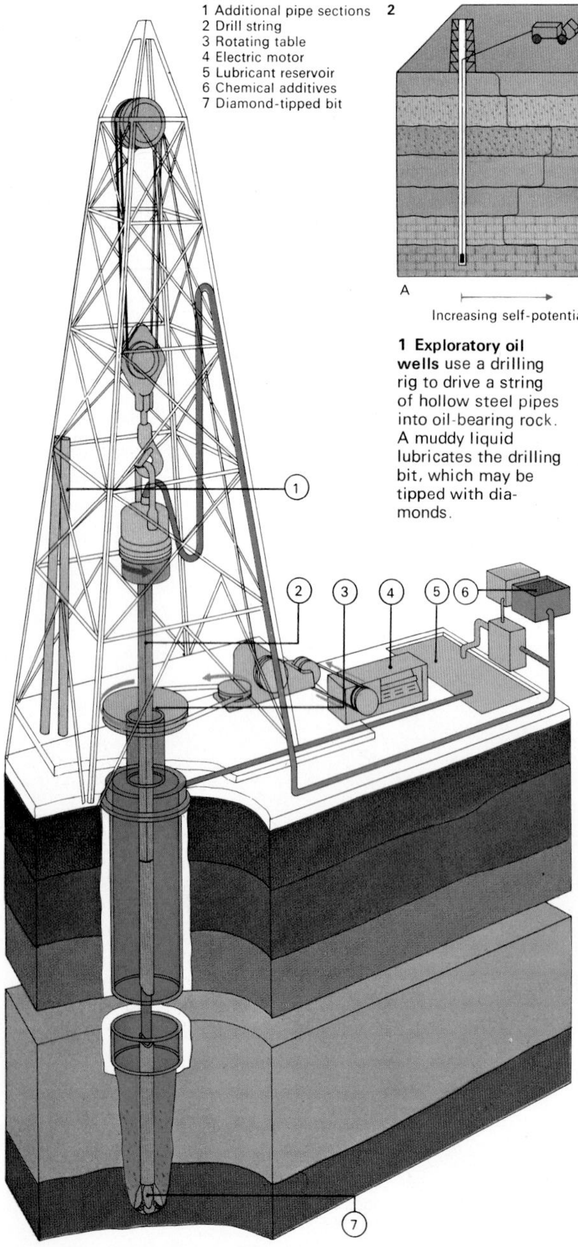

1
1 Additional pipe sections
2 Drill string
3 Rotating table
4 Electric motor
5 Lubricant reservoir
6 Chemical additives
7 Diamond-tipped bit

2
A Increasing self-potential
B Increasing resistivity
C Increasing gamma-ray intensity
D Increasing gamma-ray intensity
Shale
Oil/gas sand
Water sand
Black shale
Limestone
Porous limestone

1 Exploratory oil wells use a drilling rig to drive a string of hollow steel pipes into oil-bearing rock. A muddy liquid lubricates the drilling bit, which may be tipped with diamonds.

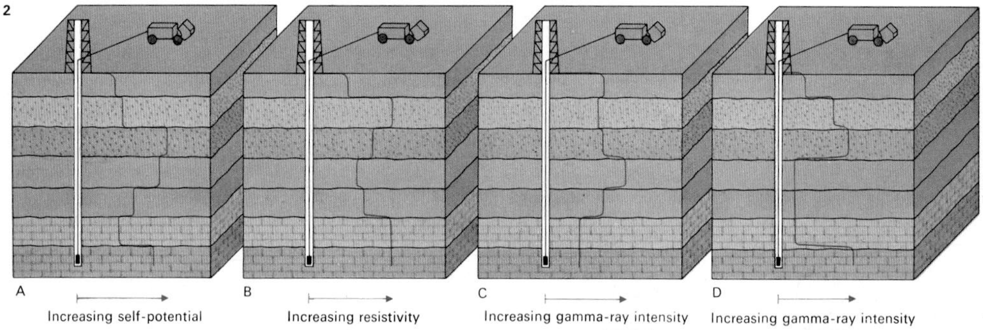

2 Test drilling rock is called well logging. Scientists measure electrical and radioactive properties of potential oil-bearing rocks. They drill a test bore and measure [A] electrical voltages generated by the rock (self-potential logging); [B] the resistance of the rock to current passed through it (resistive logging); [C] the intensity of gamma rays emitted by the rock (gamma-ray logging); or [D] the gamma rays emitted after a radioactive source is lowered down the bore with a detector. The fluid content and porosity of the rock give additional clues.

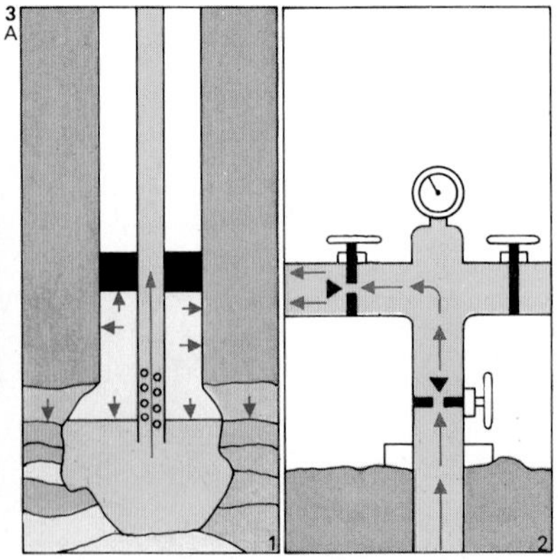

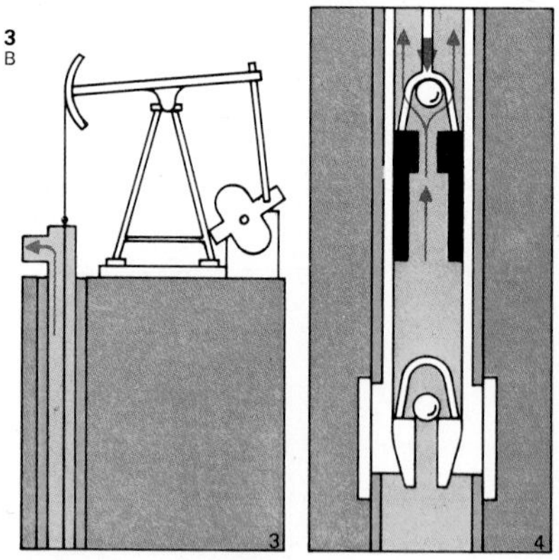

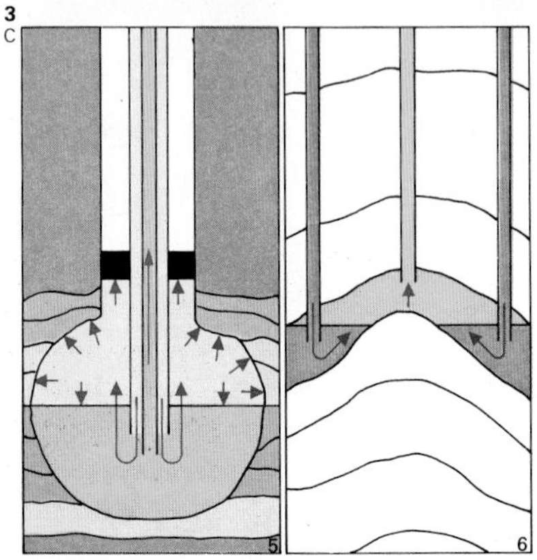

3 A
3 B
3 C
1
2
3
4
5
6

3 There are various ways of extracting oil from the bore of a well. Natural gas pressure [A] above the oil will force it up the bore [1] to a system of pressure-reducing valves [2] called a Christmas tree. Or [B] the oil can be lifted [3] by a pump at the bottom of the shaft [4], driven by a beam engine at the surface. And when an oil well is nearly dry [C] the remaining oil can be forced up the bore by applied gas pressure [5] or by pumping in water [6] to displace the oil.

Two hazards of drilling are blowouts of oil or gas and stuck drill pipes. Blowouts are infrequent, but to prevent them drilling rigs are fitted with safety equipment that can seal off the hole rapidly. Stuck drill bits can sometimes be freed with special equipment. Failing this they are abandoned in the hole, as much as possible of the drill string is recovered, and a new hole is drilled close by.

Once drilled, a well is completed by inserting a 9-in (22.9-cm) pipe in the bore and pumping concrete around it to seal the sides of the hole. A production string of 3-in (7.6-cm) tubing is inserted to the right depth. An explosive charge called a "down-hole perforator" is then lowered into the bore and detonated to puncture holes through the casing and concrete to let oil in.

Transportation and storage

Pipelines [6] are generally the most economical way of transporting oil and gas from wells to the processors. Pipes are made of welded steel up to 48in (1.22m) in diameter, covered with asphalted felt for protection and often buried underground. Pumping stations along the pipeline maintain the flow and pressure.

Sea transport is more expensive. The huge tankers used to transport oil from the Middle East are the largest ships afloat, carrying a million barrels of oil or more. Liquefied natural gas can also be carried by sea in even more expensive vessels called liquefied natural gas (LNG) carriers [5].

Oil is usually stored in tanks up to 100ft (30m) across and 30ft (9m) tall. Natural gas can be stored as a liquid either in refrigerated tanks or in ground storage caverns, which are made gas-tight by first freezing the surrounding ground. Then pits up to 130ft (40m) in diameter are dug and the liquefied gas pumped in. Once filled the contents keep the reservoir frozen.

An ideal way of storing gas uses depleted oil and gas reservoirs underground and near consumers. This is a technique widely used in the United States. Disused coal mines can also be used for natural gas storage. The one at Fontaine L'Evêque, Belgium, can hold 17,650 million cubic feet (500 million cubic meters) of gas.

KEY

Natural gas is often found under the sea floor. It is used directly as a fuel, being burned for domestic heating and cooking or for industrial heating and electricity generation. The gas can also be treated as a raw material for the petrochemical industry and be made into a range of other chemicals.

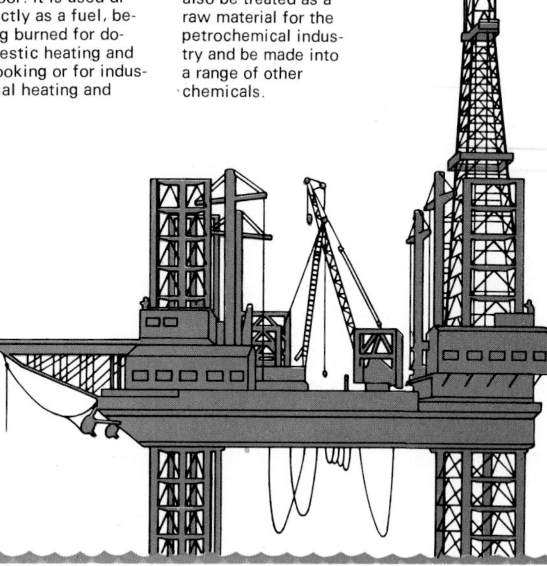

4 A gas drilling rig [1] leaves a string of pipes [2] in the natural gas pocket [3]. These are connected to the mainland by a pipeline [4].

5 Gas is transported by pipelines or in special ships [1]. Before being used it must be treated to remove various chemicals. Water and liquid hydrocarbons are removed in an expansion chamber [2]. Alkali remove any sulfur compounds [3], which are purified and stored [4] as a useful by-product. Any remaining liquids are removed [5] and excess gas is liquefied under pressure and stored underground [6]. When gas is required the liquid is evaporated [7], metered, and pumped [8] into the national gas grid [9]. Smaller pipes lead to the consumers [10]. Some European countries import gas liquefied for storage.

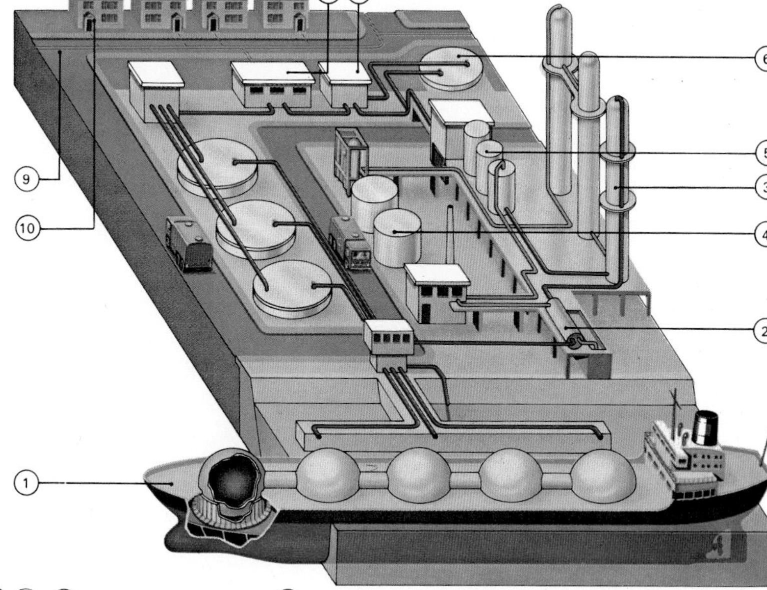

6 Pipelines for oil or gas may be laid underwater [A] or underground [B]. Lengths of pipe from a supply boat [1] are welded together [2], X-rayed for flaws [3], and cased in concrete [4] before being laid. On land a machine [5] cuts a trench and the cast-iron pipes are again welded and X-rayed [6], given a chemical corrosion protection, and laid in the trench.

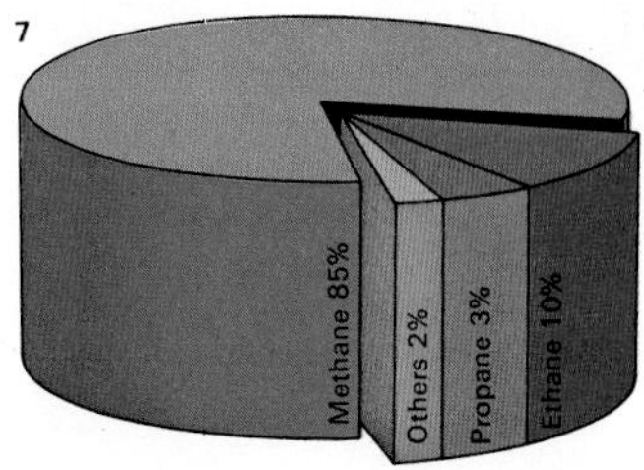
Methane 85%
Others 2%
Propane 3%
Ethane 10%

7 Natural gas is largely composed of methane and higher hydrocarbon gases, with some nitrogen, carbon dioxide, and sometimes helium. It varies from locality to locality, but the methane generally makes up between 85 and 95 percent of the gas. It is often economical to extract the helium, which is a light non-flammable gas. Sulfur compound impurities must be removed.

Oil refining

Crude oil—often called petroleum, meaning "rock oil"—is the source of a wide variety of chemicals, such as plastics, pharmaceuticals, cosmetics, adhesives, polishes, paints, explosives, and pesticides. It is a complex mixture that contains hundreds of different kinds of chemicals called hydrocarbons, because they are composed primarily of hydrogen and carbon. Physically, crude oil is a sticky, inflammable liquid varying in color from yellow, green, red, or brown to black. It may also be fluorescent. Its composition varies considerably from source to source.

The hydrocarbons may be paraffins (straight-chain compounds), naphthenes (compounds with ring structures), or aromatics (compounds related to benzene with one or more six-carbon rings).

How petroleum is refined

Crude oil is processed in a refinery [1]. First the mixture of hydrocarbons is separated into various components (called fractions). Various hydrocarbons boil at different temperatures, and so the mixture can be separated by fractional distillation—heating so that the fractions boil off, condense, and separate at different levels in a long vertical fractionating column [2]. These may then be further refined or chemically changed and sometimes blended back into the straight distilled fractions to improve their qualities.

The eight main fractions, in order of boiling point, are petroleum gases (which pass off from the top of the column), gasoline, kerosene, diesel fuel, lubricating oil, fuel oil, and wax (which all distill off) and a bituminous residue discharged from the bottom of the column. To achieve the degree of separation needed to yield the great range of petroleum products, the oil is passed through a series of columns. The relative quantities—and properties—of the products are adjusted as required in accordance with the needs of the market. As the number of cars grows, so the demand for gasoline increases; the market for kerosene has grown with its use as a jet fuel.

Added flexibility in refinery operation is provided by "cracking"—breaking down larger molecules into smaller ones. In this way, heavy fractions such as those used in diesel fuel can be made into gasoline. For upgrading the quality of the gasoline fraction, it may be "reformed"; this is a process in which it is mixed with hydrogen and heated over catalysts. Straight-chain hydrocarbon molecules are rearranged into ring structures, which perform better in automobile engines. The resulting mixture is again fractionated. Products include—as well as the improved gasoline—toluene and xylenes, which are used for making various chemicals.

Conversion processes

Small molecules may be treated so as to build up larger molecules as a further source of gasoline. More processes are designed to remove impurities [3]; these are of growing importance in view of rising concern about atmospheric pollution. Sulfur, for example, is removed by treating the raw material with hydrogen to form hydrogen sulfide, which is then separated; the sulfur forms a valuable by-product.

CONNECTIONS

See also
1642 Oil and natural gas
1804 Chemical engineerir
1806 Materials for indust
284 Energy resources: o and gas

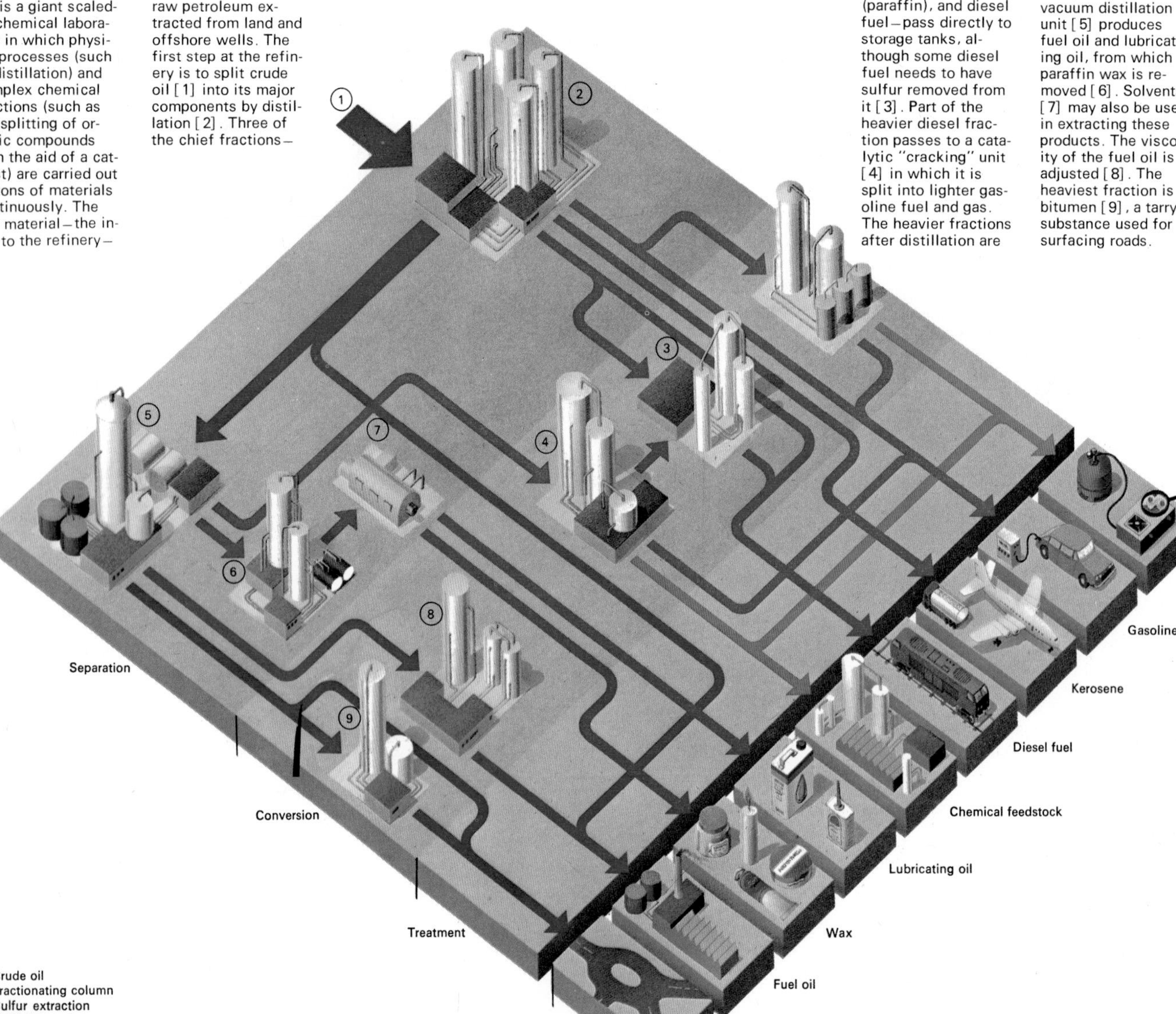

1
1
2
3
4
5
6
7
8
9
Separation
Conversion
Treatment
Gas
Gasoline
Kerosene
Diesel fuel
Chemical feedstock
Lubricating oil
Wax
Fuel oil
Bitumen

1 A modern oil refinery is a giant scaled-up chemical laboratory in which physical processes (such as distillation) and complex chemical reactions (such as the splitting of organic compounds with the aid of a catalyst) are carried out on tons of materials continuously. The raw material—the input to the refinery—is crude oil, the raw petroleum extracted from land and offshore wells. The first step at the refinery is to split crude oil [1] into its major components by distillation [2]. Three of the chief fractions—gasoline, kerosene (paraffin), and diesel fuel—pass directly to storage tanks, although some diesel fuel needs to have sulfur removed from it [3]. Part of the heavier diesel fraction passes to a catalytic "cracking" unit [4] in which it is split into lighter gasoline fuel and gas. The heavier fractions after distillation are also processed. A vacuum distillation unit [5] produces fuel oil and lubricating oil, from which paraffin wax is removed [6]. Solvents [7] may also be used in extracting these products. The viscosity of the fuel oil is adjusted [8]. The heaviest fraction is bitumen [9], a tarry substance used for surfacing roads.

1 Crude oil
2 Fractionating column
3 Sulfur extraction
4 Catalytic cracker
5 Vacuum distillation unit
6 De-waxing unit
7 Solvent extraction unit
8 Viscosity breaker
9 Bitumen blower

Petroleum derivatives

Many organic chemicals used in industry and medicine were originally made from surplus refinery gas, but today they can be derived during the refinery process. One example is butylene, which may be converted to butadiene, the basis of many synthetic rubbers.

By far the most important base chemicals are ethylene [6] and propylene. These "building blocks" polymerize directly to form the plastics polyethylene and polypropylene. Ethylene is also converted to such materials as PVC, polystyrene, antifreeze, polyesters, and ethyl alcohol and some is used to form synthetic rubbers. Derivatives from polypropylene include solvents, acrylic fibers, polyurethane, foam plastics, nylon, and materials called "plasticizers," which are used to give flexibility to paint films and resins.

Next in importance are the aromatics—benzene, toluene, and the xylenes. Their main source is catalytic reforming but some arise during the special cracking of naphthas after hydrogen treatment of the gasoline fraction. This produces more toluene than is needed and the excess is converted to benzene. From this, nylon, polystyrene, synthetic rubbers, resins, and detergents are made. Toluene is also a base for making solvents and polyurethane resins. Higher up the series, xylenes are used for conversion to polyester fibers and plasticizers. Acetylene, itself a base for syntheses, is now often made from petroleum sources. Another important inorganic base chemical, after sulfur, is ammonia.

Kerosene is a petroleum derivative that is used for domestic heating, lamps, and as a fuel or fuel component for jet engines.

Petroleum provides substantially more than 90 percent of the world's plastics and resins, synthetic rubbers, fibers (excluding those made from cellulose), and chemical solvents, and about 50 percent of the world's synthetic detergents. Only a little more than a generation ago, these came largely from vegetable sources, wood, and coal. But oil supplies are known to be limited and it seems possible that this picture will be greatly altered in the future.

KEY

An oil refinery takes delivery of crude oil, often directly from ocean-going tankers, and converts it into gasoline and other fuels and raw materials for the production of chemicals.

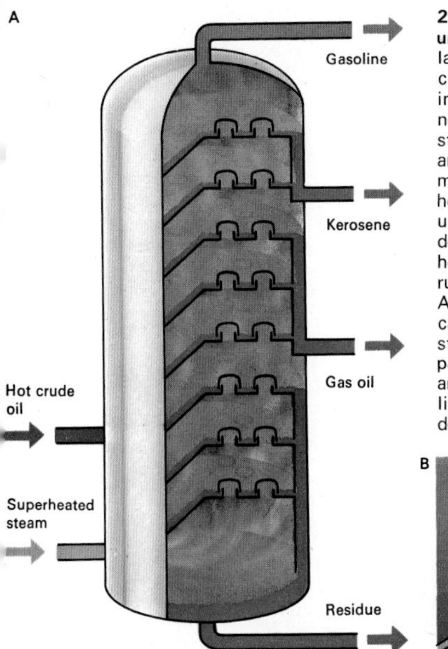
A
Gasoline
Kerosene
Gas oil
Hot crude oil
Superheated steam
Residue

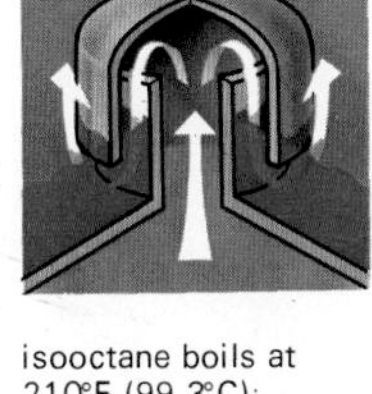
B

2 A fractionating column [A] is the distillation unit in which crude oil is separated into its chief components. Superheated steam boils the oil and the vapor accumulates at various heights up the column. The vapor condenses to a liquid in horizontal trays and runs off to the side. A series of bubble caps [B] allows steam and vapor to pass up but prevents any of the condensed liquids from running down. The most volatile component of all is gas, similar in composition to natural gas. The next fractions include liquid fuels and solvents such as gasoline, kerosene, benzene, and domestic fuel oil. Lower boiling heavy oils are used as fuels for marine diesel engines and as lubricating oils. The solid components include paraffin wax (a hydrocarbon known also as paraffin) and the tarry substance bitumen.

3

Heavy gas oil 300°C
Light gas oil 200°C
Kerosene 175°C
Naphtha 120°C
Benzine 90°C
Gasoline 30°C

3 Crude oil has a variable composition, depending on its source. This diagram shows the make-up and boiling points of a typical sample. All the substances named are hydrocarbons – compounds of hydrogen and carbon – although other elements such as sulfur are generally also present as impurities. These have to be removed to limit pollution caused when the fuels are burned, but they are valuable by-products.

4

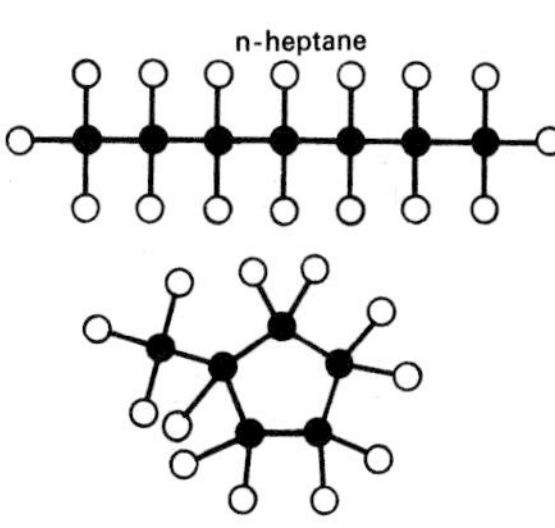
n-heptane
Methyl cyclopentane

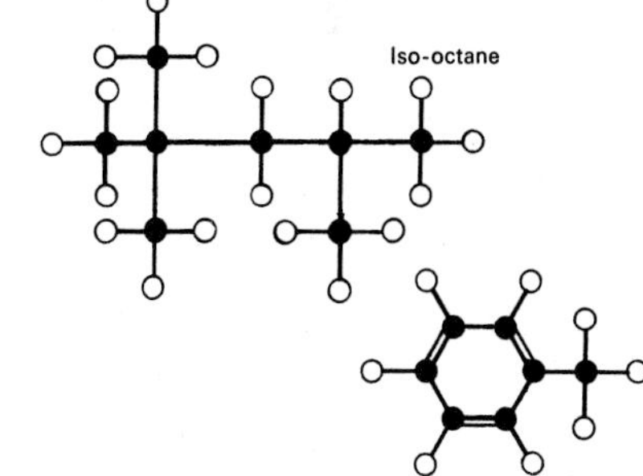
Iso-octane
Toluene

4 Hydrocarbons from petroleum take the form of molecules that may be linear or long-chain (with a long "backbone" of carbon atoms, with or without a branch) or basically cyclic (with most of the carbon atoms in a ring). The sizes and shapes of the molecules determine such properties as boiling point and octane number (fuel rating). Normal heptane boils at 209°F (98.4°C), whereas isooctane boils at 210°F (99.3°C); isooctane is a good fuel, but n-heptane has a low rating. Methyl cyclopentane has a five-membered carbon ring and toluene has a six-membered ring.

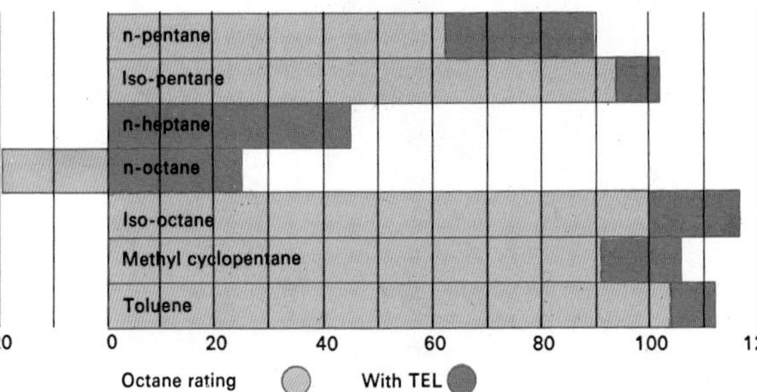
n-pentane
Iso-pentane
n-heptane
n-octane
Iso-octane
Methyl cyclopentane
Toluene
20
0
20
40
60
80
100
120
Octane rating
With TEL

5 The octane rating of an engine fuel, such as gasoline, is a measure of its efficiency for modern engines. Hydrocarbons with branched chains or cyclic structures (see illustration 4) are better than straight-chain compounds. All are improved by the addition of the organometallic compound tetraethyl lead (TEL), although this can cause pollution.

6

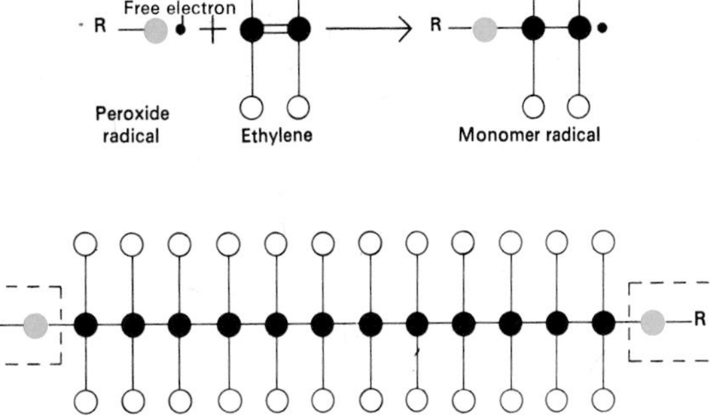
A
B
Free electron
R
R
Peroxide radical
Ethylene
Monomer radical
C
R
R
Polyethylene

6 Simple hydrocarbons such as ethylene can be made from petroleum products. They are valuable for making plastics such as polyethylene and detergents. The double bond in ethylene [A] can be "sprung" and made to react with a radical R to give an active compound [B] that can spring other double bonds repeatedly and give a long-chain polymer—a plastic [C]. Such long-chain radicals can be treated with acids to form more complex molecules.

Saving fuel and energy

Historically, the efficiency with which man has used his energy resources has been very low. The steam engine, one of the foundations of the Industrial Revolution, turned only a few percent of the energy supplied to it into power and the first steam turbine power stations wasted the energy of 95 percent of the coal they burned.

While fuel—that is, energy—was cheap, this inefficiency was less important. But as resources dwindle and the prices of coal and oil have increased significantly many nations have made greater efforts to conserve energy—particularly fossil fuels such as oil [2] and the fuels derived from it. But the inertia of the complex system devoted to energy and the need to spend large amounts of money to make even small savings have resulted, as yet, in little significant achievement.

The uses of energy

In a modern economy basic fuel expenditure is dominated by four major uses: domestic space and water heating, industrial and commercial uses, transportation, and electricity generation [1]. The total amount of primary energy used in the United States in 1974 was the equivalent of 12 billion barrels of oil, or approximately 56 barrels of oil for every man, woman, and child in the country. The corresponding figure for Great Britain is 27 oil-barrel equivalents; for West Germany, 20; and for France, 15.

Improvement of efficiency

The most convenient form of energy, electricity, is also one of the most inefficient. Steam turbine efficiencies have risen from five percent early in this century to about 35 percent in the mid 1970s for the biggest power stations, but this still means that 65 percent (nearly two thirds) of the coal or oil burned in power stations is wasted. The generating efficiency of an electricity network, including losses in transmission, is about 25 percent. A further small loss takes place when electricity is converted into heat, producing an overall efficiency for electric heating of about 22 percent. This compares with a heating efficiency for natural gas or oil of more than 60 percent. Electricity, however, can do things that gas and oil cannot; it can drive a whole variety of household machines, power record players and television sets, and provide instant, clean, and effective lighting. In industry electricity is essential to many processes, such as ore refining and metals fabrication.

Various attempts have been made to improve the overall efficiency of electricity generation. One possibility is district heating in which the "waste" heat from power stations is used directly to heat houses or factories. In ideal circumstances overall efficiencies of up to 75 percent can then be achieved, but this theoretical calculation demands that heat and electricity needs keep in step. More practical efficiency figures for district heating are around 45 percent. Sweden has pioneered the use of combined electricity and heat production. The town of Vasteras, which has a population of about 100,000, is supplied with 600 megawatts of heat and 300 megawatts of electricity from a single power station.

CONNECTIONS

See also
1636 Power direct from Sun and Earth
1650 Electric power in t home
1638 Nuclear power
1640 Coal: production a uses
1642 Oil and natural gas
286 Energy supplies
288 Energy for the futu

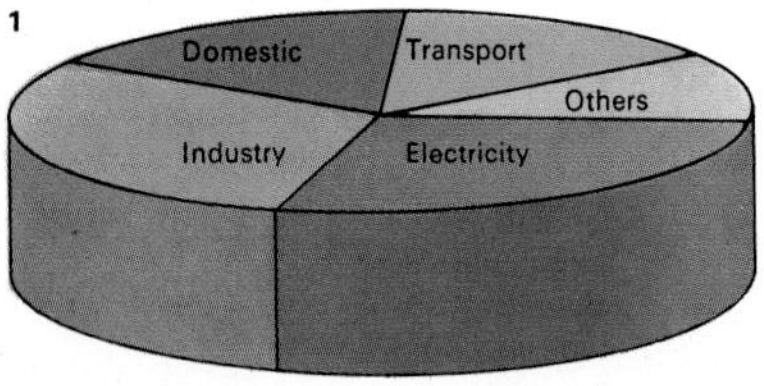

1 In the United States most energy is used by industry. Of 12 billion barrel equivalents of oil used, 30% is used by industry, 22% is used to produce electricity, 23% is used in homes and business, and 24% in transportation. Great Britain uses 40% more for electricity and 40% less on transportation.

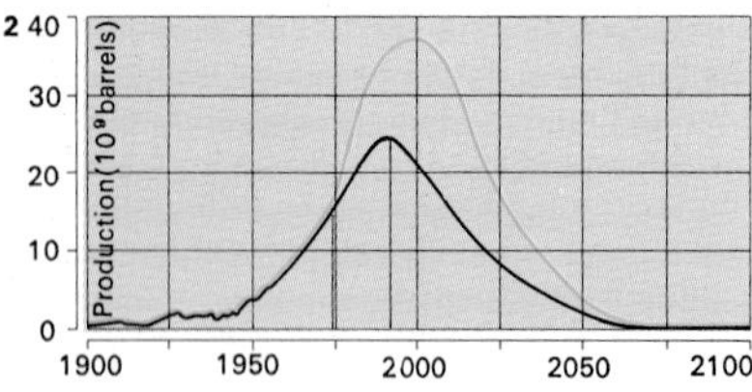

Production (10⁹ barrels)
0
10
20
30
40
1900
1950
2000
2050
2100

2 Oil reserves will not last forever. The curves predict the use of oil based on two estimates of total reserves – 2.1 trillion barrels and 1.35 trillion barrels. Both show an increase in production until the end of the century with total exhaustion of reserves by the year 2100. The areas beneath the curves equal the reserve volume and the barrel quoted is equal to the standard one of 35 gal (159liters).

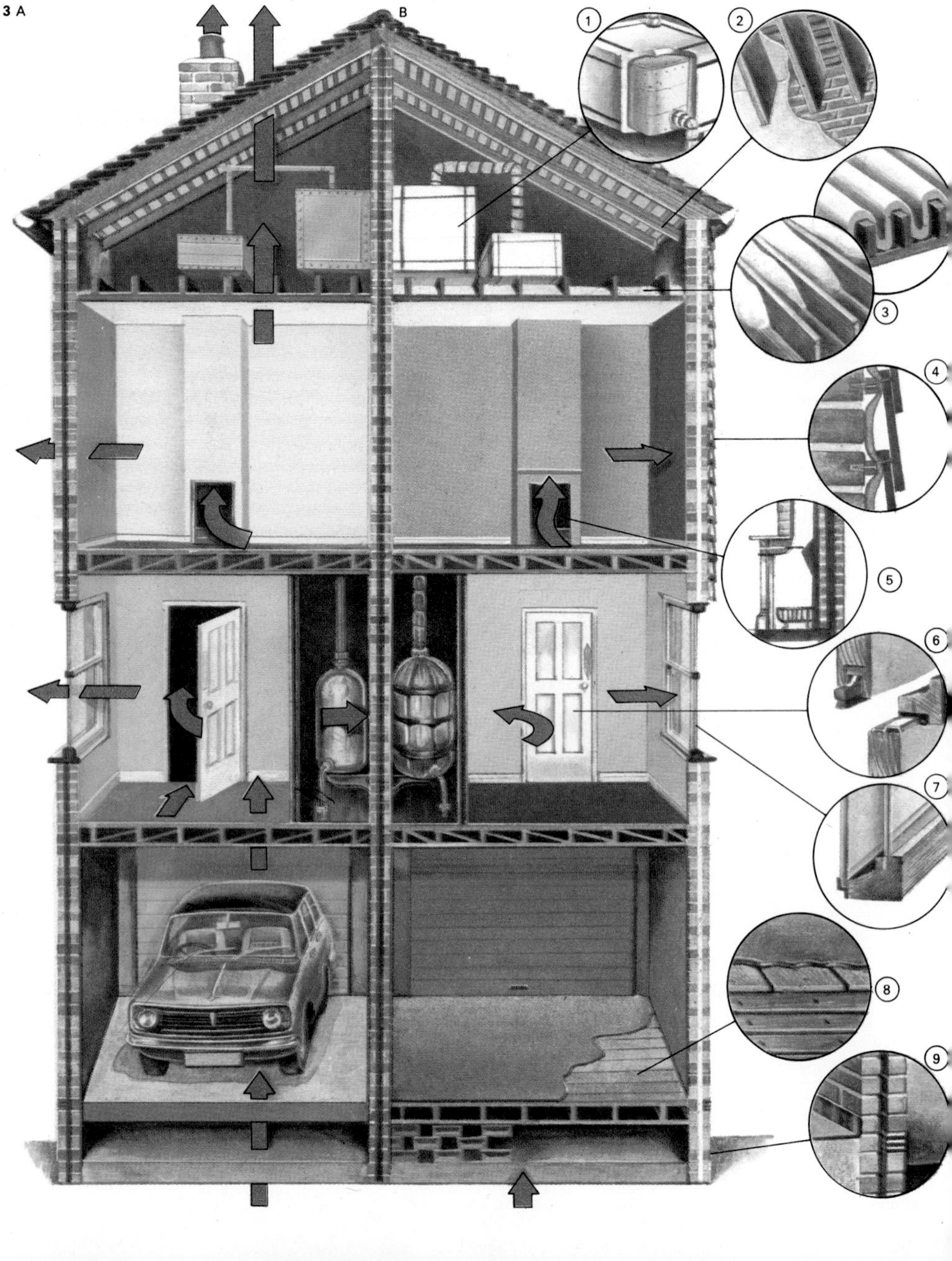

3 In ordinary homes much energy can be wasted by allowing heat to escape through walls, windows, and roof spaces. The secret of conserving heat is insulation and efficient (preferably central) heating. House A has no insulation and is heated by an inefficient open fire burning ordinary coal. House B has thermally-insulated cold-water tanks [1] and pipes in its attic, the roofing is insulated with felt or paper [2], and the ceiling joists with glass wool [3]. Additional siding on the exterior wall [4] provides extra insulation for the bedrooms. The fireplace [5] is blocked and the room heated electrically or by central heating radiators. Heat loss from a room is reduced by draft-excluding strips around the door [6] and by double glazing [7]. A wooden floor [8] to the garage insulates it from the foundations and heat flow through the hollow walls is minimized by plastic foam [9].

The electricity and transportation industries are well aware of the cost of energy and generally make all the economies they can. But a large amount of primary energy —about 17 percent—is used by consumers in the home.

Conservation and pollution

Conservation of energy can be achieved in a variety of ways. In the home, thorough insulation and the use of storm windows and doors can reduce energy consumption by half [3]. A widespread shift from inefficient private cars to public transportation —with one engine transporting up to 40 people instead of only three or four—would also achieve savings. Technical improvements in all energy uses, but particularly in industry through the expansion of waste recycling programs, could help further. But all of these solutions suffer from the need for major outlays of money to bring these changes about either in the short or long term.

Energy consumption and electricity generation can also create pollution and in some cases the need to reduce consumption may conflict directly with the need to reduce pollution. This is certainly true of the automobile. For reasons of health it would be desirable to reduce the amount of lead compounds added to gasoline [6], and by doing so the lead pollution of the environment would be lowered. But leaded gas is more efficient in modern high-performance engines and leaving out the lead has resulted in greater fuel consumption.

In the same way urban pollution has been reduced by the growth of electricity consumption—but at the cost of using more fuel. The fuel used in power stations to raise steam for turbine generators could instead be burned in houses to heat them. The fuel would be more efficiently used, but at a considerable price in pollution and convenience. And new power stations are generally built far enough away from densely populated areas so that the polluting gases they produce can be dispersed from high chimneys, thus avoiding the build-up of dangerous concentrations in the lower atmosphere.

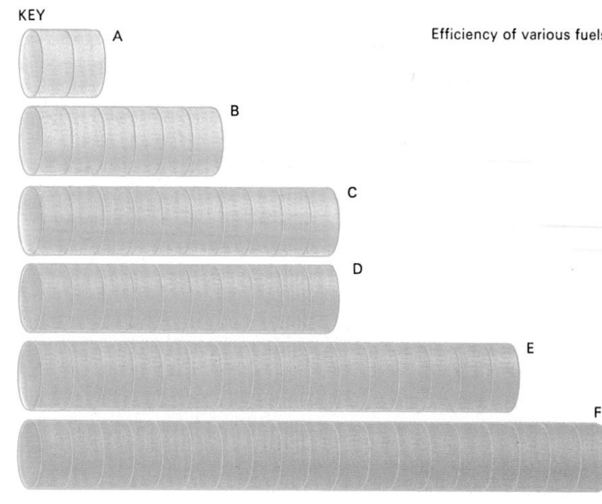
KEY
A
B
C
D
E
F
Efficiency of various fuels

Natural gas is the most efficient fuel for heating. The diagram compares the amount of energy produced by burning 1lb of coal [A], wood [B], coal gas [C], anthracite coal [D], petroleum [E], and natural gas [F]. Each bar represents the number of pints of water that can be boiled using heat from each fuel. Anthracite is as efficient as coal gas. The production of electricity by each one follows the same order of efficiency.

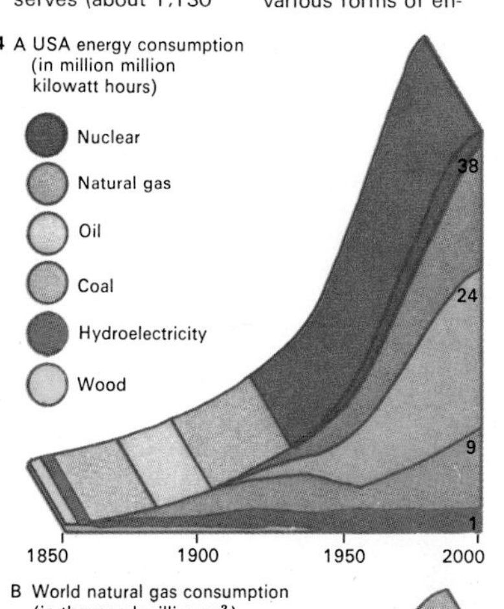
4 A USA energy consumption (in million million kilowatt hours)
Nuclear
Natural gas
Oil
Coal
Hydroelectricity
Wood
38
24
9
1
1850
1900
1950
2000

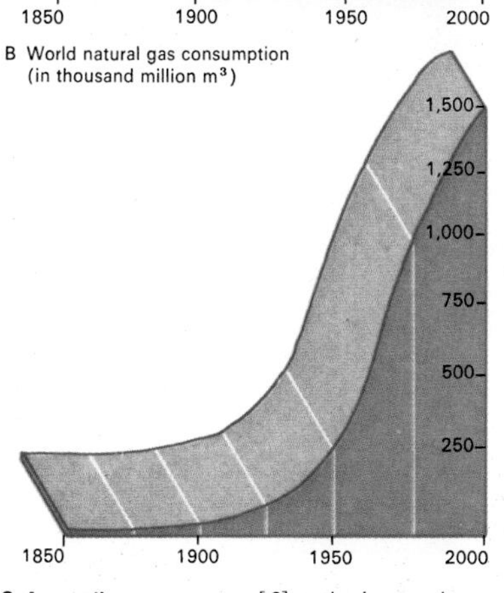
B World natural gas consumption (in thousand million m³)
1,500
1,250
1,000
750
500
250
1850
1900
1950
2000

4 The consumption of natural gas, at present supplying about 20% of the world's energy, increased by 3.5 times between 1965 and 1975. The known world reserves (about 1,130 trillion cu ft) will last about 20 years at this rate. Even if new reserves are discovered natural gas will run out as a fuel supply in about 50 years. The curves compare the consumption of various forms of energy in the United States [A] with total world usage of natural gas [B]. A significant factor, in the United States and elsewhere in the world, is the growing return to coal as a fuel.

5
Rover Jewellery
club danshoku
Florsheim shoes
RED LIPS BAR
TURKISH STEAM BATH MASSAGE
JOHAN'S LTD

5 The impending energy crisis is barely in evidence in a large city, such as Hong Kong, when lit for the night. Thousands of kilowatts of electrical power are consumed by advertising signs and shop window displays. During the night this electricity could be "saved" in an energy-storage system. It could then be made available to help meet the peak demand that always occurs in the morning.

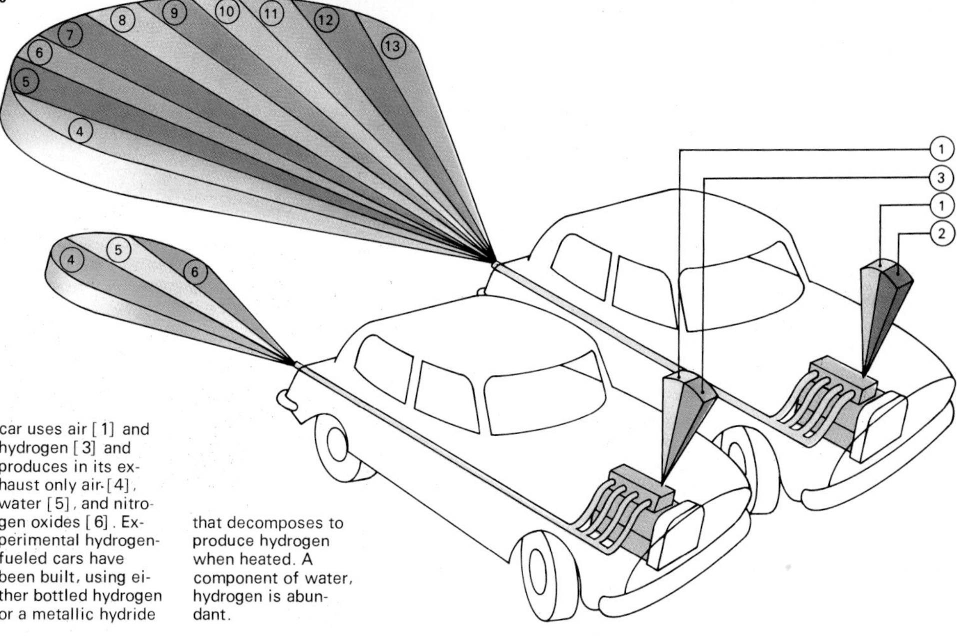
6
1
2
3
4
5
6
7
8
9
10
11
12
13

6 A gasoline-powered car is inefficient and produces a wide range of pollutants. Running a car on the more efficient hydrogen as a fuel would almost totally eliminate pollution. A gas-powered car uses air [1] and gas [2] and releases, in its exhaust, air [4], water [5], nitrogen oxides [6], carbon [7], carbon dioxide [8], carbon monoxide [9], lead compounds [10], sulfur dioxide [11], hydrocarbons [12], and aldehydes [13]. The hydrogen car uses air [1] and hydrogen [3] and produces in its exhaust only air [4], water [5], and nitrogen oxides [6]. Experimental hydrogen-fueled cars have been built, using either bottled hydrogen or a metallic hydride that decomposes to produce hydrogen when heated. A component of water, hydrogen is abundant.

Electricity generation and distribution

CONNECTIONS

See also
1630 Power from steam
1638 Nuclear power
1650 Electric power in the home
1530 What is electricity?

Much of the electricity that supplies the enormous variety of needs in homes, offices, and factories originates in fuel-consuming power stations. These vast buildings contain generators, machines to drive them, transformers [Key], and switching systems. They convert the chemical energy of coal, oil, or natural gas or nuclear energy into thermal energy and then into electricity on a large scale.

The generation of electrical power is often an inefficient process, although it compares well with other forms of energy use. In power stations burning fossil fuels (coal or oil) nearly two-thirds of the thermal energy released is lost as heat to the atmosphere or surrounding area, and only a little more than a third is actually used to produce electricity. There are additional losses as the current is transmitted over the distribution network [3]. When a consumer uses this electrical power he probably turns it back into heat, either intentionally or incidentally during some other process. Imperfect as the system is, electricity is still the best power source available for the thousands of different uses in homes and factories. At the point of consumption it is clean, convenient, and safer than almost any other form of energy.

Alternative forms of generation

There are some important exceptions to the inefficient consumption of fuel in the generation of electricity. When power is derived from behind a dam [5], or from tidal motion [6], for instance, there are no "fuel" losses. Less common are a few systems that use solar energy [2] or wind power [4]. The capital costs of manufacturing cells that convert sunlight into electricity are very high. But the rapid depletion of fossil fuel resources and the increasing pollution from thermal power stations are factors that may in time override purely economic considerations. Where political pressures make access to fossil fuel reserves difficult, the economic case for developing systems that exploit other forms of energy may become even stronger.

For this reason nuclear power stations are being used to generate an increasingly large proportion of power in the industrialized nations. Their overall efficiency is no greater than that of thermal stations [1], but their long-term fuel costs are so small that nuclear stations may prove economical to operate.

Whether the source of power is oil, coal, nuclear, wind, or moving water, electricity is produced by the same kind of machines—turbines and generators. In themselves, generators are highly efficient, converting mechanical to electrical energy with losses no greater than about two percent.

The supply system

Most power stations have more than one generator to allow for some degree of reliability in case one machine breaks down. Many stations have four, and at periods of peak demand all of them may be working at maximum output. As demand slackens each may be brought out of circuit in turn and shut down, although some may be left partly loaded.

From the generators big, solid conductors in the form of metal bars (called bus-

1 A thermal station uses steam to drive its generators. Until about the mid-1950s the steam was obtained by burning oil, coal, or lignite. More recently, nuclear reactors have been used as heat sources. Steam is passed at high pressure through turbines, which are on the same shaft as the generators. These large machines generate electricity as they rotate. Because electricity consumption varies from hour to hour, steam supply to the generators must follow the load consumption. Rapid steam-generating capacity is needed to meet peak demands and forecasts of supply needs must be made on the basis of previous experience.

1
2
3
4
5

2 A solar panel in semi-stationary orbit is one system proposed for deriving energy from the sun. Clear of the Earth's atmosphere, the solar cells would be in the direct rays of the Sun, unhindered by dust, water vapor, and atmosphere. The electricity (in the form of direct current) generated in the panel would be transmitted along a short conductor [1] to a device for converting the current into microwaves [2]. After a small loss of energy in the atmosphere [3] the microwaves would reach large collecting panels [4] and be passed to a station [5] for conversion from direct to alternating current for use by consumers.

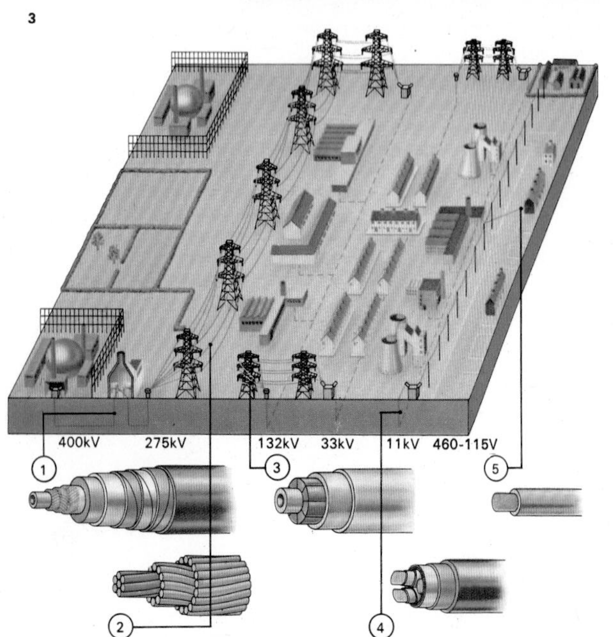
400kV
275kV
132kV
33kV
11kV
460-115V
1
2
3
4
5

3 Transmission of electricity from power station to consumer is by a network of overhead lines or underground cables of varying voltages. Because more energy is lost at low voltages the voltage must be kept as high as possible while still ensuring safety. In a typical network underground cables [1 and 3] use oil, plastic, and similar materials for insulation, whereas overhead conductors [2] are uncovered, as the air acts as the insulator. A fabric tape cable [4] takes power to a local substation. Then it goes to consumers via sheathed cable [5].

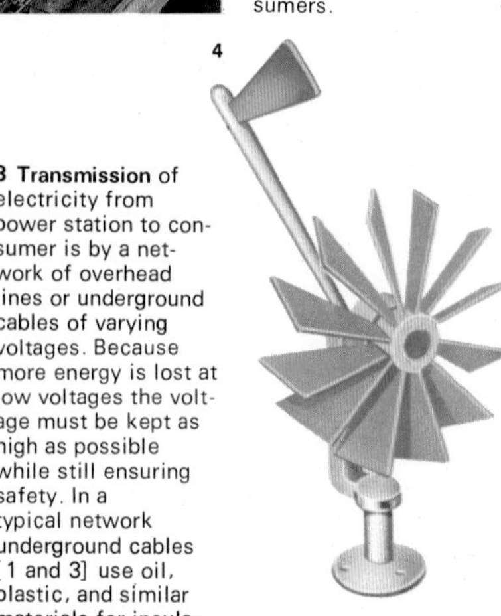

4 Wind power was widely used in Europe until the advent of cheap fuels. Windmills need large blades and steady winds, but linked to storage batteries they can often provide cheap power.

bars) connect to transformers, where the voltage is increased for transmission. Conductors slung between pylons spread out from the station in all directions. Where necessary or desirable the voltage is lowered by other transformers to a level safe for distribution to consumers. Some of this distribution may take place underground and may eventually terminate at a sub-station where the supply cable is split into a number of feeders, again after appropriate voltage reduction. From there it is taken overhead or underground into industrial or residential areas where further voltage reduction takes place before it is fed into homes and factories. Overhead lines may themselves terminate in sub-stations, thus avoiding an underground section, but many consumers are supplied by underground cables.

Typical voltages at the three chief stages are 33,000 volts (33kV), 11kV, and 460 volts and 208 volts (or 115 volts single phase). The high-voltage alternating current (AC) in the distribution system is normally three-phase, generally transmitted along four wires—three phase conductors and a neutral, or common, conductor. For domestic use at low voltage, the power is supplied as single-phase AC with two wires (''live'' and neutral) or three wires (two ''live'' and one neutral).

At various points along the line between the power station and the user there are switches, circuit breakers, and similar devices to protect lines and equipment in case of overload or disruption by lightning.

Network links, national and international
The output from each station is linked to that from others by conductors called ''interties,'' running between convenient points, generally on pylons. All the stations in one country are thus electrically connected. This enables some stations to be shut down for maintenance or repair and allows the most efficient stations to run continuously, supplying what is termed ''base load.'' The networks of many countries are also linked together; the United States and Canada, for example, and England and France. This enables some countries to sell or lend power to others.

KEY

A transformer (shown here is the core) is used to connect generators to an electricity grid. The transformer's function is to raise the voltage from perhaps 23kV to about 400kV.

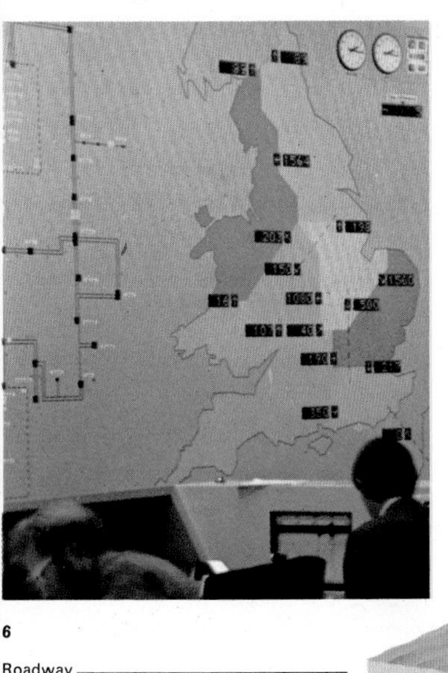
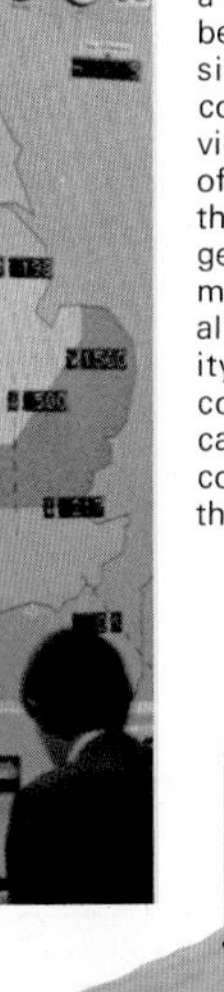

5 Control of electricity distribution in a small country may be controlled from a single room. The country may be divided into a number of regions, each with the responsibility for generating and transmitting power and all under the authority of the national control center. Because the regions are connected through the network, it becomes convenient to send power from one region to another, particularly if there are breakdowns of some generators. Regions with more costly fuel supplies are able to import some power. At the central control room engineers must assess the most economic way of using regional resources, bearing in mind such factors as weather, fuel costs, plant efficiency, and cable capacity. They are in constant touch with regional headquarters and can use computer information. A computer-controlled display on the engineer's desk shows in detail the position of all the transmission lines, the state of the equipment, and the current carrying capacity of the network.

6 Power from ocean tides is being harnessed by an experimental station at La Rance in France. The experience gained here may be used throughout the world. Special turbines have been developed that can be driven by water flowing in either of two directions. This enables them to function when the tide is either ebbing or flowing. When the tide comes in, water is directed through large tunnels housing the turbines, causing them to rotate. When the tide starts to ebb, the water is held behind a dam until the tide is on the turn and is then released again, driving the turbines. These machines also act as pumps so that when the demand for electricity is low they can increase the amount of stored water over and above that gained naturally, allowing extra power to be generated by the station when the demand increases. The Rance station has 24 generating bulbs lying in horizontal tunnels.

6

Sea at high tide
Roadway
Sea at low tide
Basin
Tunnel
Access to alternator
Turbine generator bulb
Service chamber
At high tide, water flows from the sea to the basin
At low tide, water flows from the basin to the sea

Electric power in the home

Electricity is man's servant, providing power for heat, light, and labor-saving appliances. But its advantages are accompanied by some serious risks, if it is carelessly used, in the forms of fire or shock, which can injure or kill.

How electricity reaches the home

Electricity is generally brought to a house through a three-wire cable and connected via a meter (for indicating power consumption) and a circuit breaker or fuse box into the household distribution box. This may contain the branch circuit breakers or fuses [6]. The third wire, or neutral, is brought out to a household grounding bar or attached to a metal cold water pipe.

The neutral wire is brought to all the power outlets in a house and almost every appliance that is plugged into such an outlet has a ground connection. This is usually connected to a piece of metal on the case of the equipment. One or both of the other wires is also brought to every power outlet, as well as to utility boxes for lighting. Each of the two live wires is at a voltage of 115 volts relative to ground and 230 volts relative to the other wire. If these two should inadvertently come into contact with each other or the ground, an enormous current begins to flow, so large that it may melt the wires with a loud explosion. But in a properly wired house, such a short circuit causes a protective fuse to melt or a breaker to open and thus break the circuit.

Distribution within the house

The two live wires are divided at the distribution box into a number of branch circuits [1] in order to distribute them around the house. The live conductors are connected to fuses (or circuit breakers) before being taken to the various parts of the house, but the neutral (ground) conductor is taken there directly.

Fuses and circuit breakers are rated at various amperages—usually, 15, 20, or 30 amps—depending on the power consumed by the equipment in the particular branch circuit. Power consumed (watts) is equal to the voltage (volts) multiplied by the current (amperes). To find the current consumption of an appliance, its wattage should be divided by the voltage. A 1,500-watt toaster-oven on a 120-volt line, for example, draws a current of 12.5 amps; a 3-kilowatt (3,000-watt) electric heater on a 230-volt line draws 13 amps. Screw-in and plug-in fuses contain a metal-alloy strip that melts when overloaded before the overload can damage the entire circuit. Circuit breakers are essentially heat- or current-activated switches that open when overloaded. Time-delay fuses are used to protect circuits in which there are fairly large, capacitor-start motors, such as in refrigerators or washing machines. The fuses "ignore" the surge of current necessary to start up such motors.

At the different power and lighting outlets no current flows until a lamp or piece of equipment has been plugged in and switched on. But there is always a voltage at that point whether current flows or not. It is like a water tap; the pressure of water is always there, although there is no flow until it is turned on.

There is always a danger when using a metal-cased electric appliance that the live

CONNECTIONS

See also
1648 Electricity generati and distribution
1530 What is electricity?
1532 What is an electric current?
1818 Everyday machines and mechanisms:
1820 Everyday machines and mechanisms:
1668 Electronic devices

1

Light switch
Power switch
Light switch
Power switch
Power switch
Fuse box and switch

1 A simplified circuit diagram of the way in which electricity is distributed around the home shows how the fuse box is used to protect the house and its wiring from the effects of short circuits. In the branching system shown here some circuits supply equipment that takes heavy current—such as an iron, color TV, and heater. Other circuits are for lights; for greater safety in the event of a fault, no more than three or four lamps are on one circuit. Additionally, ground wires are routed to the power switches and outlets. Some of the appliances shown, such as the electric iron and the electric heater, should always be grounded. Some European domestic wiring installations use a ring system, which can be simpler and more economical.

2

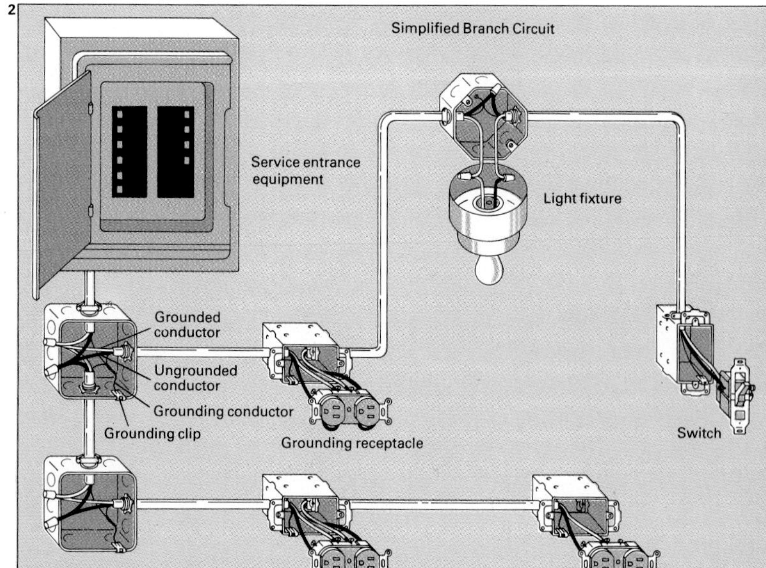

Simplified Branch Circuit
Service entrance equipment
Light fixture
Grounded conductor
Ungrounded conductor
Grounding conductor
Grounding clip
Grounding receptacle
Switch

2 A branch circuit is used in modern homes for the distribution of current. In a branch circuit all electrical fixtures are connected to separate fused circuits, which in turn are connected to the main distribution box by cable. Thus if one branch is faulty only that branch's circuit is affected. The cable may contain two insulated conductors and one bare grounding conductor. These three wires are appropriately joined by solderless connectors. In a grounding receptacle the wires are connected to colored screws: black wire to gold, white to silver, ground to green. Alternating current (AC) is the most economical and simplest to generate. The standard frequency in the United States is 60 Herz (cycles per second).

3

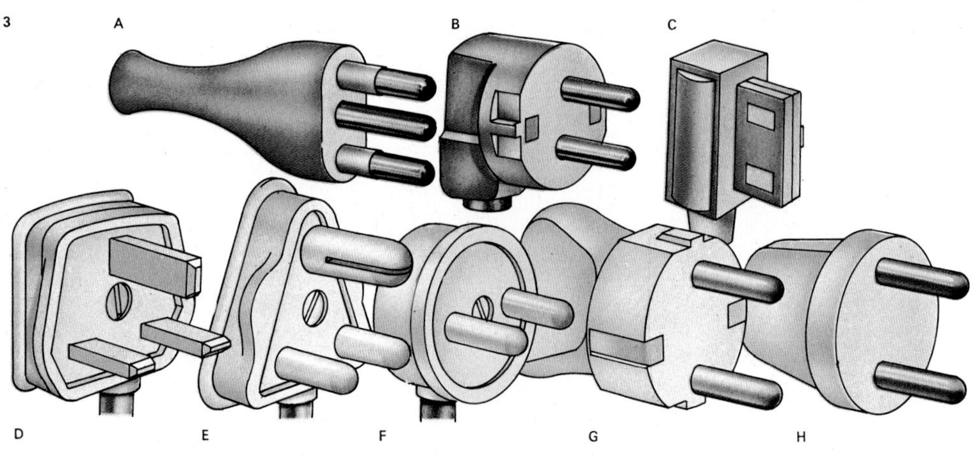

A
B
C
D
E
F
G
H

3 The design of electric plugs varies from country to country. The wide variety shown here comes from only three European countries. The plugs are not interchangeable. Plugs A-C are from Italy, although only A and B have ground pins. Of the three British plugs [D-F], D is the standard fused, square-pin plug for use with ring circuits, E is an older 15-amp three-pin plug, and F is used for low currents. G (grounded) and H are Dutch plugs.

4

4 In a flexible cable colors of the conductor insulation show the way in which connections should be made to an outlet box. In this wire the neutral (ground) conductor is striped green and yellow, one live wire is red and the other is blue.

conductor may become loose or that a fault will develop in its insulation, causing it to touch the case. If the ground wire has been properly installed, a current flows along the ground connections and back to the distribution box. This current will be large, and the fuse (or circuit breaker) of that particular circuit will operate, disconnecting the faulty equipment. If there is no ground connection, anyone touching the live case will almost certainly provide the grounding path for the current and will get an electric shock. The amount of current passing depends on the body's electrical resistance and the remaining ground circuit path. Moisture lowers the resistance and for this reason it is extremely hazardous to handle electric appliances in wet areas or with wet hands.

Certain kinds of electrical fittings, such as lamps and some specially built equipment labeled "double insulated," do not require ground conductors because they have cases that are heavily insulated.

In modern house wiring systems, a branching circuit is used for the distribution of a current [2]. This can be compared to a tree in which the trunk is the distribution box and each branch is a separately fused circuit. Each branch may have three or four lamps on it, so that if one of them is faulty, and the branch fuse "blows," then all the lamps on that circuit are cut off.

Some European systems of house wiring use "ring" circuits in which all the power outlets are connected to a loop circuit, so that they are like stations on a circular railroad. The system makes the most economical use of conductor wires and each outlet box has its own fuse, so that if a fault develops in the appliance connected to it, that particular fuse will blow, leaving the rest of the ring operating.

Safety in the home

Good workmanship, thoughtful design, and new materials selected for their safety value have reduced the potential dangers of electricity in the home to almost negligible proportions. These safety factors, however, can be negated by careless practice, such as using the wrong size fuse or failing to maintain proper ground connections.

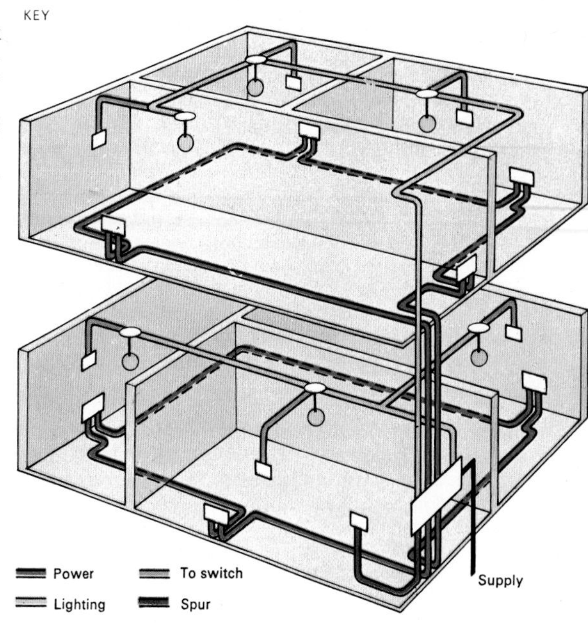

KEY
Power
Lighting
To switch
Spur
Supply

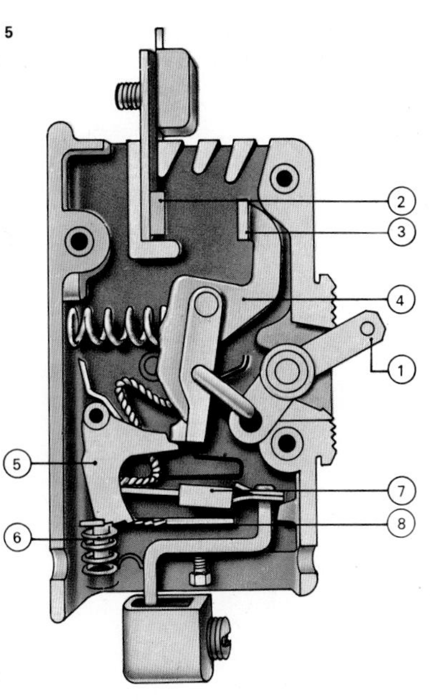

5
1
2
3
4
5
6
7
8

5 The miniature circuit breaker is often installed as an alternative to a fuse in the distribution box. It is more convenient to use because it "trips" (switches) the circuit off. It is then simply reset after the fault is repaired, whereas a "blown" fuse must be replaced. Pushing the lever [1] closes the circuit between terminals [2, 3]. The moving contact [4] is held in place by a linkage [5] against spring [6] pressure. A sudden rise in current (above the safe level) causes a magnetic device [7] to disturb the linkage, tripping the breaker. A gradual rise causes the thermal overload [8] to do the same.

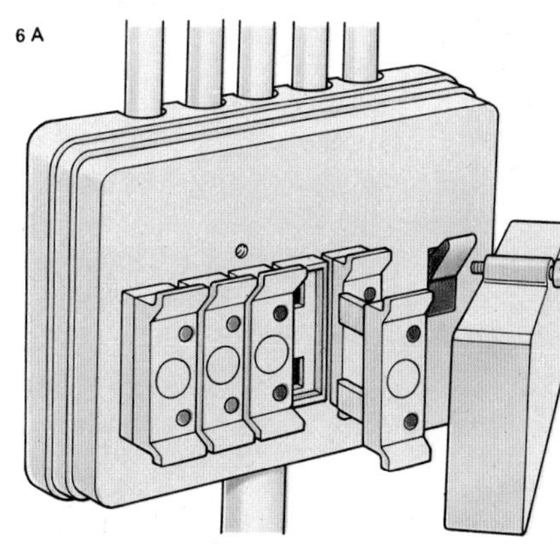

6 A

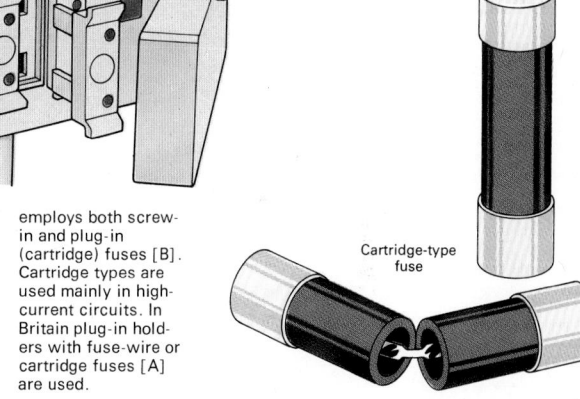

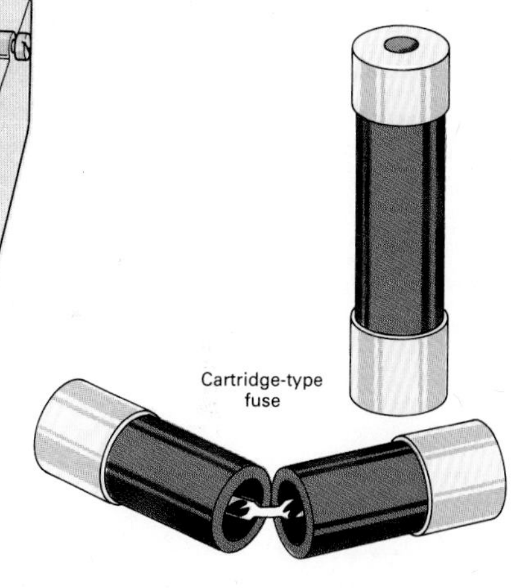

B
Screw-type (plug) fuse
Cartridge-type fuse

6 Fuses are used to protect electric circuits. In the event of a short circuit, current surge heats and melts the fuse instead of slowly heating the wiring and possibly causing a fire. US practice employs both screw-in and plug-in (cartridge) fuses [B]. Cartridge types are used mainly in high-current circuits. In Britain plug-in holders with fuse-wire or cartridge fuses [A] are used.

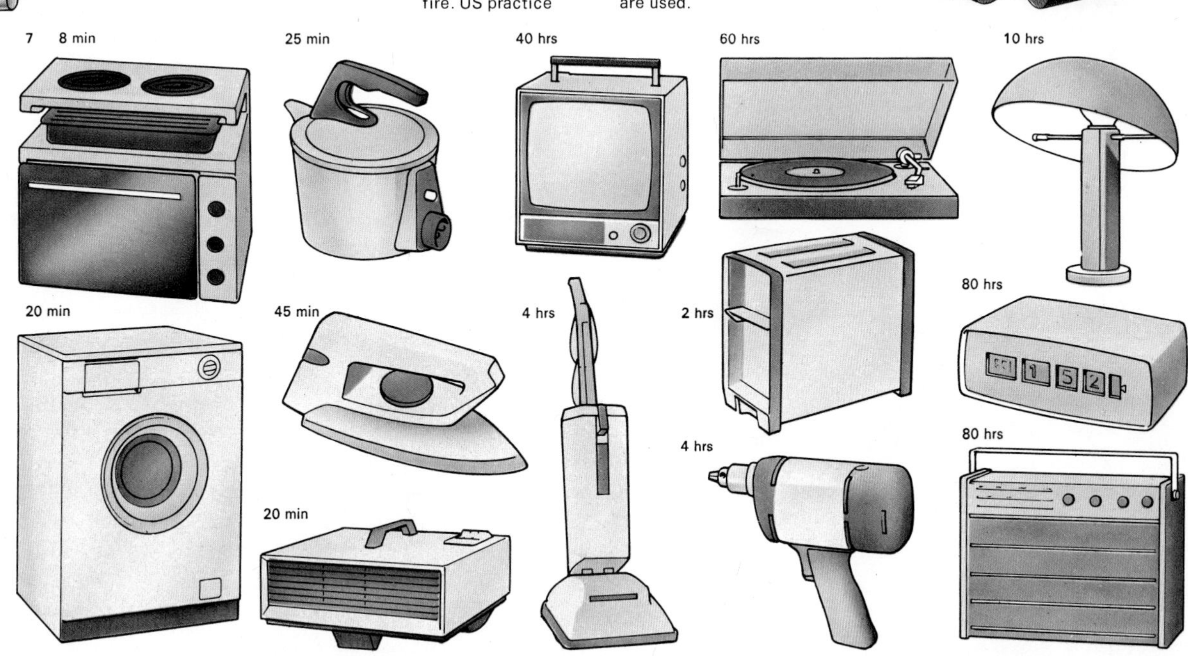

7
8 min
25 min
40 hrs
60 hrs
10 hrs
20 min
45 min
4 hrs
2 hrs
80 hrs
80 hrs
4 hrs
20 min

7 The unit of electrical energy is the kilowatt-hour (kWh), which is the consumption of 1,000W for one hour continuously. A 100W lamp bulb will consume 1 unit in 10 hours, although an 80W fluorescent lamp will also consume the same amount in the same time, because it includes some equipment that accounts for about 20W. Its light output, however, is about four times greater than a conventional 100W bulb. A refrigerator consumes about 1 to 2 units in 24 hours; a black-and white TV can run for 40 hours, whereas a color set will run for only 9 hours on the same amount, that is, one unit. This illustration shows various running times on one unit of power.

Levers and wedges

Today we are surrounded by a vast range of machines, from clocks, washing machines, and other domestic appliances to computers, hovercraft, and rockets. All machines are in some sense labor-saving devices—and for once the popular definition matches the scientific one. To a scientist a machine is any device that provides a mechanical advantage—that is, allows a limited amount of effort to do useful work in lifting or moving a load. The mechanical advantage of a machine is the load divided by the effort. In this sense, the simplest machines are levers, wedges, and screws.

Magnifying an effort

Levers have hundreds of uses—a crowbar, an oar, a screwdriver, scissors, a seesaw, and a wheelbarrow all make use of the various classes of levers [1]. Their effect is to "magnify" an effort to make it easier to move a load. Each makes use of a pivot, called a fulcrum, and the sizes of the load and effort and their distances from the fulcrum determine the lever's mechanical advantage.

How can a four-year-old child lift a man weighting 165lb (75kg)? One simple way is to sit them both on a seesaw. If the man sits fairly close to the pivot, the weight of the child at the far end of the other side will be enough to lift him. The child will move down farther than the man moves up, and this additional movement is the price that has to be paid for the advantage in lifting a large load. The load must move, however, and the Greek mathematician Archimedes (c.287–212BC) is reputed to have said "give me a firm place on which to stand and I will move the Earth."

A stationary seesaw—and any lever in which the load and effort balance each other—is said to be in equilibrium. In such cases, the load multiplied by its horizontal distance to the fulcrum equals the effort times its horizontal distance to the fulcrum. If the child on the seesaw in the above example weighs 30lb (13.6kg) and sits 9ft (2.7m) from the pivot, he would exactly balance the 180lb (81.5kg) man sitting 1.5ft (0.46m) from the pivot on the other arm of the seesaw ($30 \times 9 = 180 \times 1.5$). The mechanical advantage (the load divided by the effort) is 180 divided by 30, equal to 6 in this example. It can also be calculated by dividing the effort's distance to the fulcrum by the load's distance; in this case, 9 divided by 1.5, again equal to 6.

The load multiplied by the distance is called the moment of the load (which is a force). At equilibrium, the moment on the load side equals that on the effort side. If one moment is larger than the other, there is a turning force and that side of the seesaw will move downward.

Using ramps and wedges

When the ancient Egyptians were making the pyramids or Bronze Age men were building Stonehenge, they were faced with the task of raising huge blocks of stone. They knew that it is easier to push a heavy object up a slope than to lift it directly, so they probably constructed long ramps (called inclined planes by physicists) of earth up which they dragged the stones.

To lift a 10-ton block vertically requires an effort of 10 tons. But, neglecting friction,

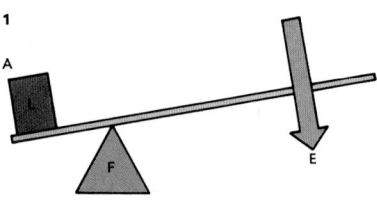

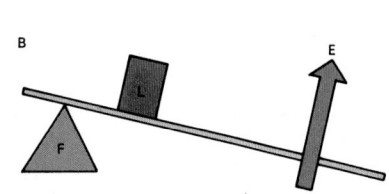

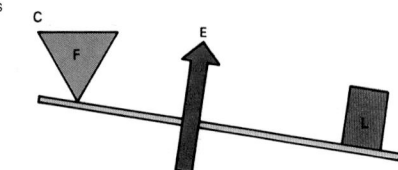

CONNECTIONS

See also
1488 Statics and forces
1654 Pulleys and gears
1662 Machines for lifting
1656 Machines for weighing and measuring
1664 Earth-moving machines
682 Skull, skeleton, and joints

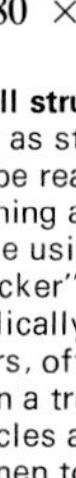

1
A
L
F
E
B
C

1 All levers belong to one of three classes, depending on the relationship between the effort E, load L, and fulcrum F (the pivot). In the seesaw arrangement of the first class [A], the fulcrum is between the load and the effort. In the second class of levers [B], an upward effort raises a load placed between effort and fulcrum. A wheelbarrow uses this principle. In the third class [C], the effort acts between the fulcrum and the load. Many hydraulically operated machines employ leverage of this class and some complex machines—such as printing presses—have examples of all the classes of levers somewhere in their mechanism.

2 Tall structures such as street lamps can be reached for cleaning and maintenance using a "cherry picker" with hydraulically operated levers, often mounted on a truck. Similar vehicles are used by firemen to provide a high point for hoses or for rescuing people trapped in tall buildings. Hydraulic linkages can work such hinged joints in much the same way as muscles bend a man's arm at the elbow; both are examples of the third class of levers. Because the effort is applied so close to the fulcrum (pivot), a large effort is required to move the load at the end of its long arm. This is why engine-powered hydraulics are used.

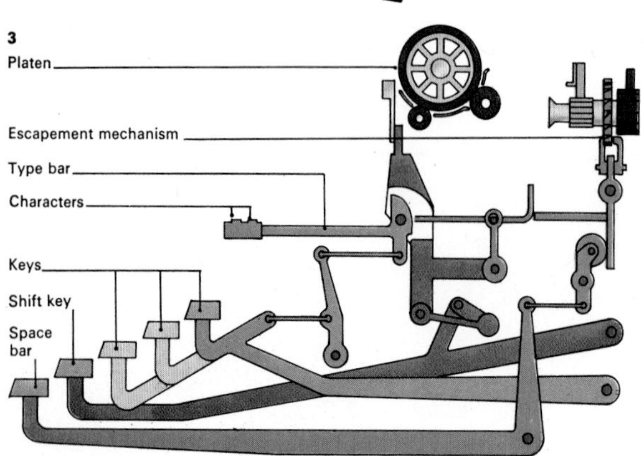

3
Platen
Escapement mechanism
Type bar
Characters
Keys
Shift key
Space bar

3 The keys of a typewriter are operated through a series of linkages acting as levers. As a key is tapped, the levers move a type bar and make a character print on paper wrapped around the platen. Pressing the space bar releases an escapement mechanism to advance the carriage without a character being typed. The levers controlled by the shift key raise the whole lever system so that, on tapping a type key, the lower character on the type bar makes contact with the typewriter ribbon and prints on the paper. Other levers are used to move the carriage and tabulator.

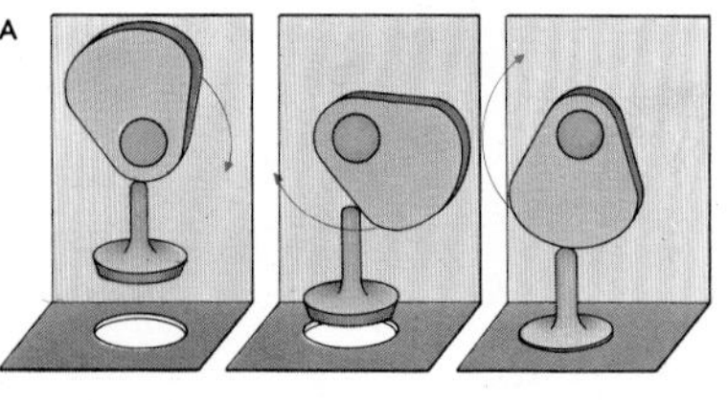

4 A

4 A disk cam [A] can be regarded as a lever of variable length that changes rotary motion into an up-and-down or side-to-side reciprocating motion. Disk cams are commonly used to operate the valves in a car engine. The rotary motion of a slot cam [B] drives a vertical arm up or down—or a horizontal one sideways. Using such a cam, a twist can produce linear motion to work the bolt on a lock.

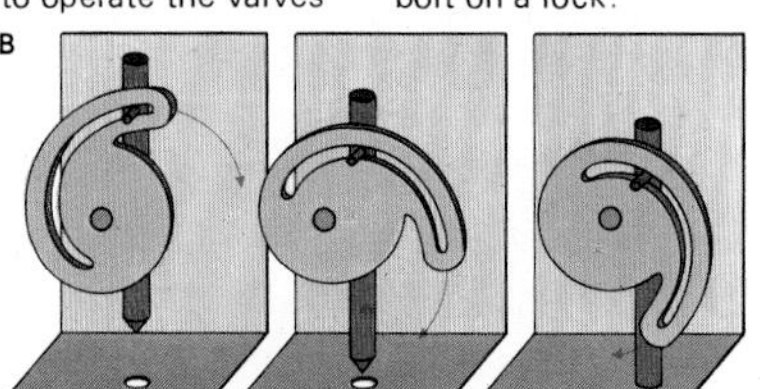

B

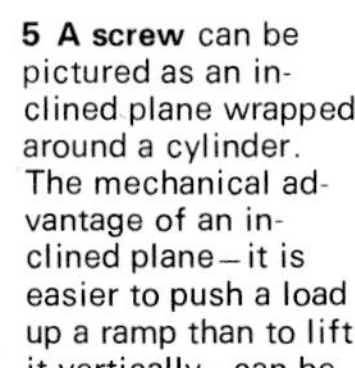

5

5 A screw can be pictured as an inclined plane wrapped around a cylinder. The mechanical advantage of an inclined plane—it is easier to push a load up a ramp than to lift it vertically—can be realized by rotating the screw, often to exert considerable force. The distance between the threads is called the pitch of the screw and is the distance the screw advances after one revolution.

the effort needed to push or drag it up a slope of 1 in 20 is only about half a ton. To raise it 1ft the load must be moved about 20ft so that, as with levers, a large movement of the effort is needed for a small load movement to gain significant mechanical advantage. The ratio of the ramp's height to the length of the slope determines how much effort must be used. Modern technology can achieve some space-saving with long ramps by coiling them [8].

Lifting a heavy block slightly (perhaps to pass a rope around it) can be achieved by driving a wedge underneath it. A wedge is like two inclined planes back to back. But instead of moving a load up the plane, the plane is pushed past the load to move it. Driving a wedge into a crack, for example, exerts a tremendous force [Key]. An ax uses this principle, as do chisels, plows, and pneumatic drills.

Screws—wound-up wedges

A screw thread can be pictured as an inclined plane wrapped around a cylinder [5]. This shape is called a helix and its geometry was studied in the 3rd century BC by the Greek mathematician Apollonius of Perga. Archimedes invented screw-cutting machinery and used the screw as the key principle in his famous "screw" pump for raising water.

Just as a wedge can be driven into an object by hammering, the helical wedge of a screw can be driven in by turning. The turning movement requires leverage—a screwdriver or wrench—and the simple screw is, in use, a "machine" that combines the lever and the wedge.

The distance between the threads of a screw is called the pitch and is a measure of the slope of the corresponding inclined plane. In one complete turn a screw moves through a distance equal to its pitch. The length of the lever turning the screw, divided by the pitch, gives its mechanical advantage.

Other applications of screw threads are found in a vise, a corkscrew, a screw jack, propellers for ships and aircraft, and in various taps and valves [7]. The most common is in nuts and bolts [6].

KEY

A wedge driven into a crack in a log or a block of stone can split it apart. In this quarry in Malta, sandstone is partially sawed into blocks, then wedges are used to split them.

6 A B C D E

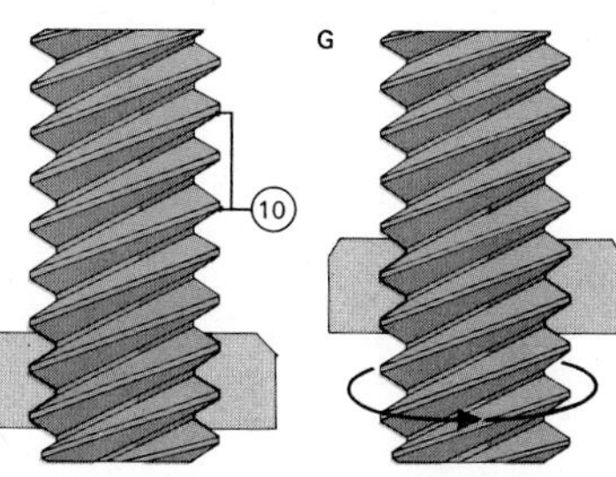
F
G
10

6 Screw threads on bolts generally conform to a few major types and there is a set of specialized terms to describe them. Engineers use this "thread terminology" to define kinds and parts of screws [A], including the two major diameters, the root diameter [1] and the pitch diameter [2], the thickness of the thread [3], the crest [4], and root [5]. The pitch [6] is the spacing between threads, but the properties of the screw depend also on the thread angle [7] and the helix angle [8]. The two main kinds of screw are round-sectioned [B] and square-sectioned [C]. In a single-start thread [D] the lead [9] and the pitch are the same. After one revolution [E] a nut moves along a distance equal to the pitch. In a double-start thread [F] the lead [10] is twice the pitch, and a nut moves through a distance twice the pitch [G].

7

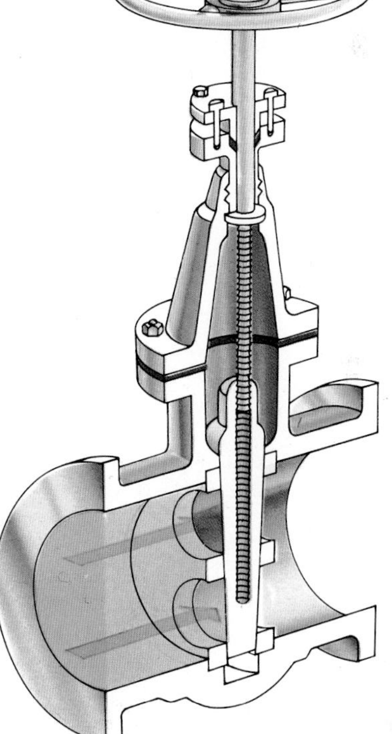

7 A screw with a fine thread can control precise movements—the distance it moves is equal to the fineness of the pitch. A micrometer, for example, makes use of a fine screw thread to measure small dimensions with a high degree of accuracy. But in other applications a coarse pitch ensures a positive action. In this gate valve, turning the wheeled handle opens it quickly. It normally operates fully open or closed.

9 Levers of the first class can be paired, as in scissors or pliers. The same idea can be extended to form a "set of scissors," as in lazy tongs. The principle can, with modern hydraulics, make a powerful machine for raising or lowering loads, such as cargo and luggage at an airport. The same scissors principle is used for some car jacks, which have a screw thread for pushing the lower arms together.

8

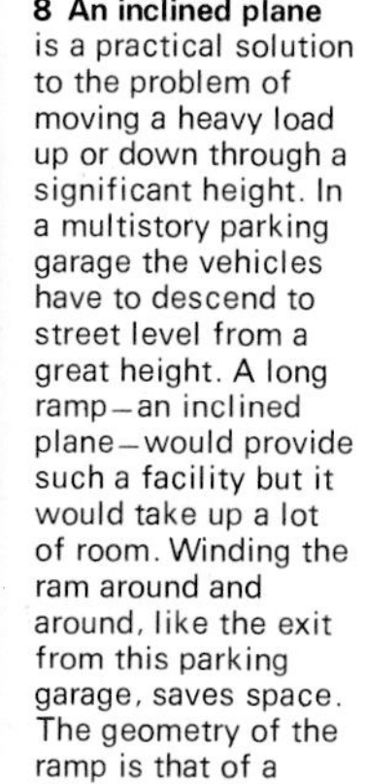

8 An inclined plane is a practical solution to the problem of moving a heavy load up or down through a significant height. In a multistory parking garage the vehicles have to descend to street level from a great height. A long ramp—an inclined plane—would provide such a facility but it would take up a lot of room. Winding the ram around and around, like the exit from this parking garage, saves space. The geometry of the ramp is that of a screw thread.

9

Pulleys and gears

Pulleys and gears are wheels arranged to transmit motion and are among the earliest machines invented by man. A gearing system of wooden pins was used to drive the mechanisms in medieval flour mills, windmills, and mines. Pulleys were probably known by the ninth century BC and Archimedes demonstrated the efficiency of a compound pulley [Key].

Pulley action and design

In a pulley the wheel is used in conjunction with either a rope, chain, or belt. On a gear the rim of the wheel is cut with teeth or a worm thread to mesh with similar projections from another gear. Both pulleys and gears can be used to transmit rotary motion between two or more shafts. If the shafts are close together, as in a clock or a car engine, then gears are generally employed. If the shafts are farther apart, pulleys are more often used. Gear-wheels can also be used to change the direction of rotation by as much as 90 degrees. Wheels of various diameters (both pulleys and gears) produce a change in the speed of rotation.

Belt-driven pulleys are common driving arrangements for factory and agricultural machines. A circular (endless) belt transmits motion between one pully on the shaft of a motor and another on a machine shaft, for example that of a lathe. By giving the pulley on the motor or driving shaft a different diameter from the pulley on the machine or driven shaft, the speed of rotation of the driven shaft can be varied. Several pulleys of different sizes are often fitted together on the driving shaft to provide a range of speeds for the driven shaft. This is known as a stepped pulley system. The rim of a pulley may be broad and flat to take a wide belt. Alternatively, the rim face may be grooved to accommodate narrower belts that are V-shaped or circular in cross-section, which prevents them from slipping from the pulley.

Cranes and hoists are the other common applications of pulleys. Here the motion is usually transmitted to provide a mechanical advantage. The force or effort employed by the person hoisting is magnified by an arrangement of two or more pulleys so that heavier weights can be lifted than would otherwise be possible. Hoists with two or more pulleys are widely used in industry for lifting components or packages and transferring them from one place to another [4].

How gear-wheels work

Most gear-wheels have teeth with slightly curved surfaces. These are the surfaces that come into contact with those of another gear. The action of one gear tooth on another generally results in a combined rolling and slipping motion of the curved faces, so that friction and the risk of jamming are very much lower than they would be if the contact faces were flat. Even so, a gear-wheel must be made so that its teeth fit more or less loosely into the spaces between the teeth of its mating gear. The looseness is called backlash.

Pairs of gear-wheels are generally chosen to change the speed, and often also the direction, of rotational movement [5]. If one gear is much larger than the other they are known as the gear (large) and pinion (small). When the gear drives the pinion an increase of rotational speed is obtained and vice

CONNECTIONS

See also
1662 Machines for lifting
1666 Moving heavy loads
1658 Machines for measuring time

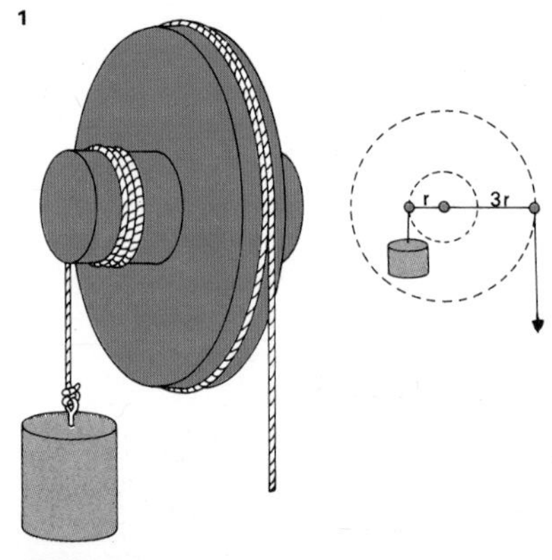
1
r
3r

1 Mechanical advantage is the ratio of force exerted by a machine to the force exerted on it. In this wheel-and-axle pulley the radius of the wheel is three times that of the axle. Theoretically, then, the mechanical advantage is three; that is, a downward force on the rope should result in an upward force on the weight three times greater. In practice, however, friction always lowers mechanical advantage.

2 A simple arrangement of two pulleys has one fixed pulley [1]; the other [2], to which a weight [3] is attached, is free to move. If someone hauls on the free end of the rope, the movable pulley and weight are pulled upward by twice the hauling force (less the frictional resistance) because they are held by two lengths of the rope. But the weight is raised through only half the distance hauled on the rope.

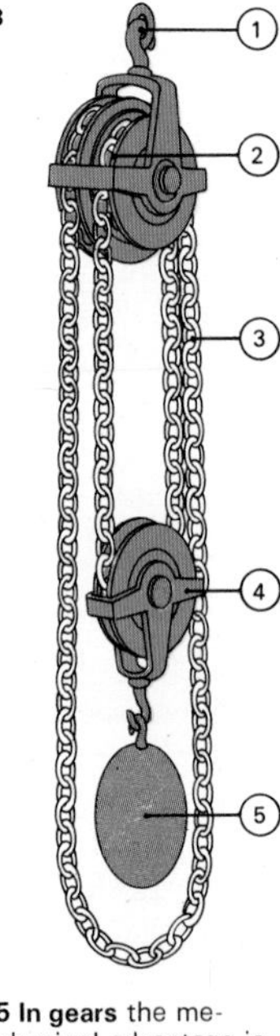
3
1
2
3
4
5

3 This factory hoist is hooked to a support [1] and has two fixed pulleys of different sizes [2] together with a movable pulley [4] to which a load [5] is attached. An endless chain [3] passes around the whole system of pulleys. A pull on one side of the chain loop extending over the larger fixed pulley exerts a much greater force to lift the load. A pull on the other side of the endless chain loop lowers the load.

4 Pulley hoists are often used in the automobile industry to lift bulky or heavy components. Hoists are usually suspended from mobile overhead cranes or gantries, allowing the transfer of parts from one place to another on the factory floor.

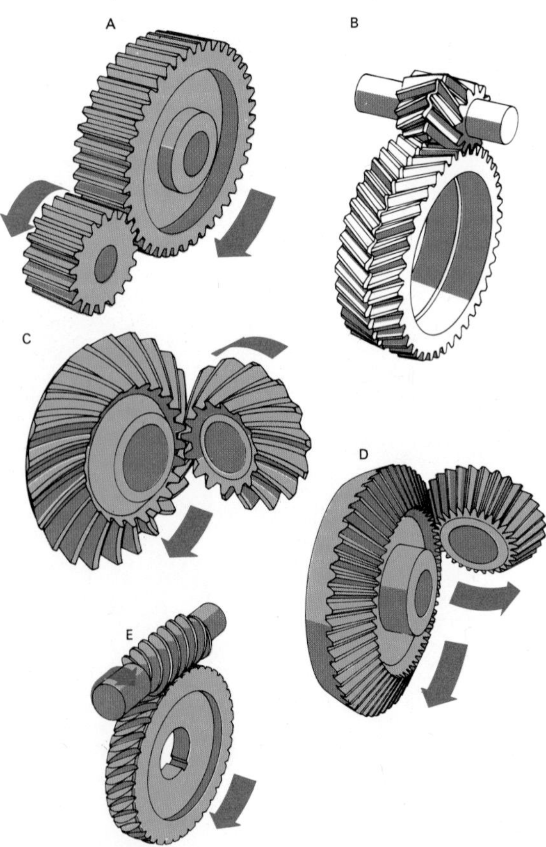
5
A
B
C
D
E

5 In gears the mechanical advantage is related to the number of teeth. Gear teeth are cut to shapes that vary with the use of the gear. The teeth of spur gears [A] are cut parallel to the axis of rotation, while those of helical gears [B] are "twisted" to form part of a helix and often cut double to avoid thrusts that result in wear. The teeth of bevel gears [D] are longer than those of spur gears, giving a greater area of contact that permits the transmission of much greater thrusts. This advantage applies more particularly to bevel gears with spiral teeth [C]. In a worm gear [E] the worm has a single spiral thread and turns a spirally toothed gear at right angles to its own axis.

versa. The amount of change of speed is directly proportional to the numbers of teeth on the gear-wheels. A gear of 100 teeth driving a pinion of 20 teeth, for example, increases the speed of rotation five times.

Motion from a smaller driving gear to a larger driven gear, apart from reducing speed, obviously confers a mechanical advantage. Such an advantage was obtained in the old-fashioned clothes mangle: a small effort in turning the handle was sufficient to turn the rollers against considerable resistance from the squeezed clothing.

When shafts to be rotated by gear-wheels are not immediately adjacent, one or more idler gears may be placed between the driving and driven gears to couple them together.

Changing the direction of motion

Rack and pinion gears convert rotary motion into linear motion. The pinion is an ordinary circular gear-wheel that meshes with the rack, which is a "gear" with its teeth set in a row. This kind of gear system is used, for example, in the focusing mechanism of a microscope or old camera, in which the focusing adjustment turns pinions that move the lens. In cars with rack-and-pinion steering the rotary movement of the steering wheel is converted into sideways movement of a linkage to steer the wheels.

The teeth of gear-wheels may be set parallel to the gear axis, as already described, or spirally, as in helical and worm gears [5]. A worm gear is used to drive a shaft at right angles to its own. Bevel gears [5, 7] also transmit motion through an angle and can have parallel or spiral teeth. A gear system with a central "sun" gear meshing with several "planetary" gears is often fitted to bicycle hubs [8]. This is one example of a gearbox, which consists of a number of intermeshing gears together with a device for selecting gear combinations, or ratios. Another example is the gearbox of an automobile. Early models had gear systems almost as simple as those of bicycles [9]. Those of today, however, are more complicated and often have automatic gear selection.

KEY

A

B

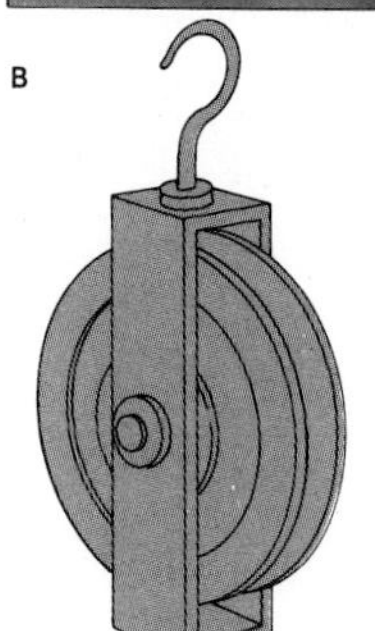

The block in a simple pulley [B] comprises a wheel or sheave that runs inside a housing, the whole block being hung from a hook. The wheel is grooved to accommodate a rope, belt, or chain. A single fixed pulley of this kind confers no mechanical advantage for lifting a load, although a person raising a load is able to add his own weight to the pulling force exerted by his arms. However, systems of two or more pulleys, in which some of the pulleys are free to move, can give a considerable mechanical advantage, as shown by the compound pulley [A] said to have been used by Archimedes to move a large sailing vessel single-handed.

6

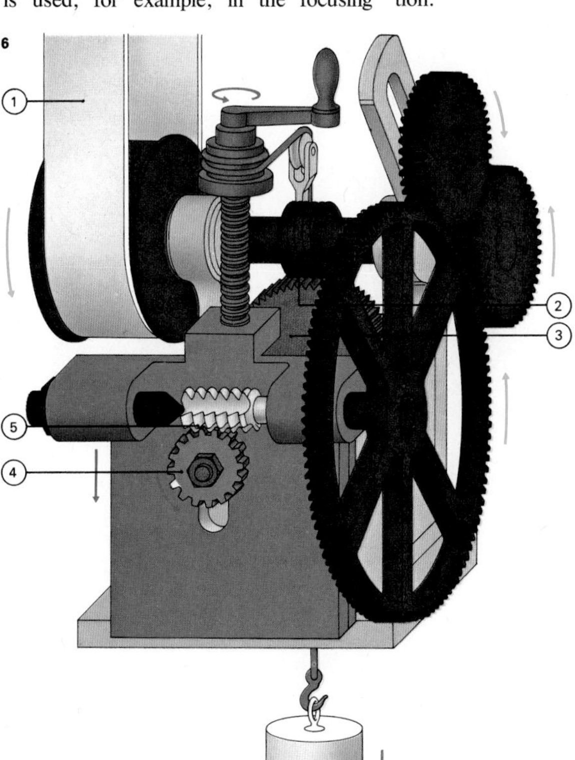

1
2
3
5
4

6 Joseph Whitworth's gear-cutting machine of 1835 contains a belt and pulley [1] driving a worm gear [2] that by engaging a cogwheel [3] turns the gear that is being machined [4]. The same drive shaft turns a cogwheel meshed with a second cog and a large wheel that turns the milling cutter [5]. The cutter is mounted in a block that is lowered by means of the screw and counter-weight until the gear is fully cut.

7

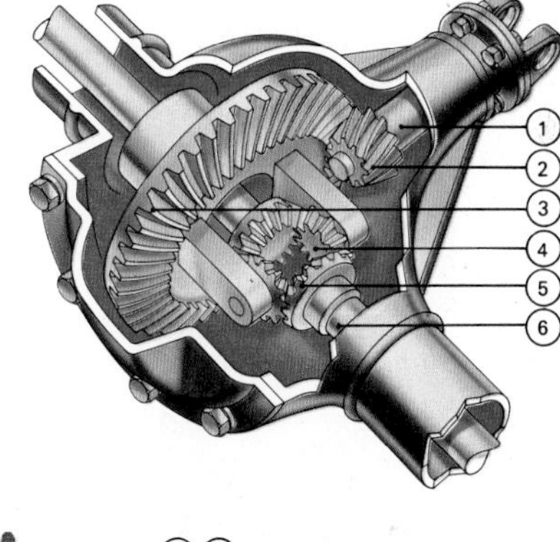

1
2
3
4
5
6

7 The differential of an automobile transmits rotary movement produced by the engine through right angles to the half-shafts [6] driving the wheels. The pinion [2] of the propeller shaft [1] rotates the crown wheel [3], turning the pinion [4] of the bevel gears [5]. The differential gears let the wheels turn at different speeds when the car turns a corner and the outer wheel rotates faster than the one on the inside.

8

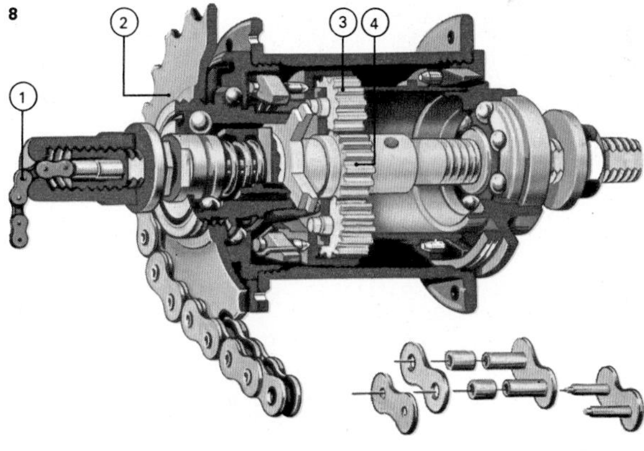

2
3
4
1

8 This bicycle hub gearbox has a central sun gear [4] surrounded by planet gears [3], a typical arrangement that is known as epicyclic gearing. The thrust given by the rider is transmitted to the hub through a chain and sprocket [2] connected to the hub by a cable-operated clutch [1]. The illustration shows the medium (direct drive) gear selected. The components of the chain drive are also shown.

9 A gearbox permits a vehicle to move at different speeds while the engine revolutions remain more or less steady. This is done by altering the ratio of input to output gears. More power is provided by a high ratio (low gears), allowing the vehicle to climb hills easily. All gear-wheels except those needed for reverse are always in mesh. When a gear-wheel is engaged it is locked (manually, in this gear box) onto the output shaft, thus transmitting power.

9

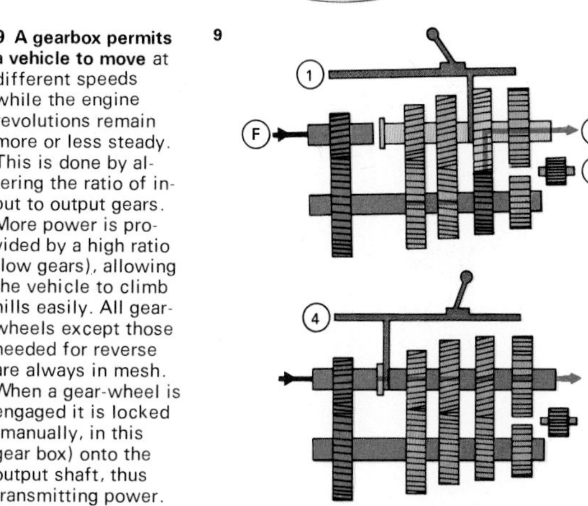

1
F
L
I
4

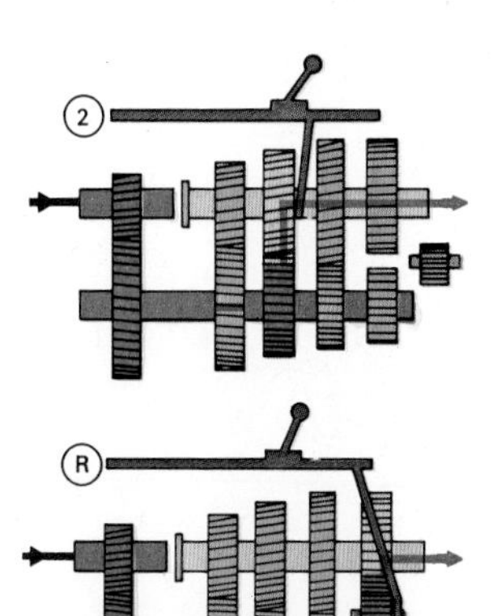

2
R

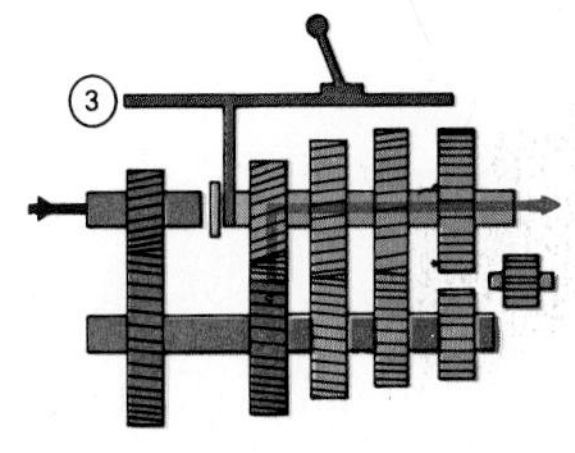

3

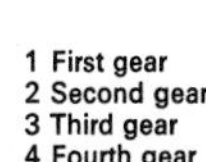

1 First gear
2 Second gear
3 Third gear
4 Fourth gear

R Reverse gear
F Input shaft
L Output shaft
I Idler wheel

Machines for weighing and measuring

Methods of measuring mass, time, and distance are among the oldest skills of man. Modern life requires ever more complex measurements and depends on the accuracy and consistency of a whole range of machines for the functioning of industry, transportation, medical care, and meteorology. At one end of the scale are everyday instruments such as the micrometer [Key], which in engineering can measure diameters and thickness to an accuracy of 0.000254mm (0.0001in). At the other extreme are specialized machines that set absolute standards—atomic clocks, for example, are synchronized to keep time with the vibrations of caesium atoms pulsing exactly 9,192,631,770 times a second.

Weight, time, and temperature

The chemical balance [5] is based on one of the oldest principles of all—the idea that the unknown weight of a given mass can be found by balancing it against a known weight. By suspending two pans from a beam the Egyptians used balances to weigh grain and gold against stone weights at least 7,000 years ago. By 1350 BC they were able to achieve an accuracy of 99 percent. The Romans added an important refinement when they fixed a triangular fulcrum to the underside of the beam, thus making balances more sensitive to lighter weights.

Measurement of time with sundials, hourglasses, and clocks is also ancient. The Chinese developed a water clock in 1000 BC. By the fourteenth century there were mechanical clocks moved by weights with a system of gears connecting these to an escapement wheel—a device to release the energy to the hour hand in small, regular amounts. But it was Galileo (1564–1642) who is credited with introducing a pendulum [2] to control the escapement, achieving a regularity that led to the accurate timepieces of today.

In 1593 Galileo also played an important part in the development of the thermometer with his gas thermometer (air trapped below water). A more accurate alcohol thermometer was invented in 1641, and in 1714 Gabriel Fahrenheit (1686–1736) developed the mercury thermometer and the temperature scale named after him. Thirty years later the Swedish scientist Anders Celsius (1701–44) constructed the centigrade thermometer, so called because on its scale the boiling point of water is 100°, its freezing point 0°. The Celsius scale is used in nearly all scientific temperature measurement. The clinical thermometer [8] is designed to measure human body temperature from 95° to 113°F (35°–45°C).

Many industrial processes require measurements of temperatures that are much higher or lower than body heat. A variety of different instruments is used, each designed for a particular temperature range [9]. For measuring high temperatures, an optical pyrometer is used to compare the color of a hot object with an electrically heated wire filament. The effect of temperature on the electrical resistance of a wire is employed in a platinum resistance thermometer.

Establishing position

Successful navigation, at sea or in the air, depends on the ability to fix a position in relation to some known point. Instruments

CONNECTIONS

See also
1658 Machines for measuring time
1652 Levers and wedges
100 Star types

1 The sextant is still the basic tool of navigation and is simple to operate. It is held so that the horizon is visible through the telescope [1]. A movable arm [2] carries a mirror [3], and the arm is moved so that an image of the sun reflected from this mirror, and from another half-silvered mirror [5], is aligned with the horizon. On a vernier scale [6]—a scale that measures subdivisions of the main scale—the angular distance between the sun and the horizon is then read. A piece of dark glass [4] reduces the intensity of the sun's image. The sextant is also used to measure angles in astronomy.

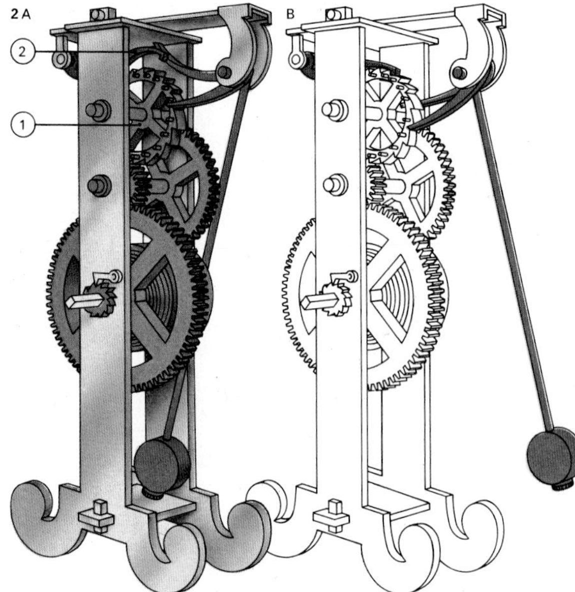

2 A
B
2
1

2 As a device to regulate speed a pendulum operates on the simple principle that the longer the pendulum the longer its period—the time taken for one complete swing. Galileo applied this principle to regulate the escapement wheel of a clock. His wheel [1] had 12 projecting pins lined up with notches around the circumference. As the pendulum swung inward [A] it lifted a restraining pallet [2] and pushed the pins, allowing the wheel to rotate but only until, with the reversal of the pendulum swing [B], it was once again restrained by the pallet.

Gimbal rings
Revolving wheel

3 Stability is the vital contribution made to the science of measurement by the gyroscope. The instrument depends on a rapidly spinning wheel with a heavy rim suspended with a minimum of friction in a system of gimbal rings that allow it to rotate on its axis in any plane. If momentum is maintained at a given speed (by an electric motor for instance), the axis of the wheel maintains the position it took up when first spun. As the earth revolves, the axis continues to point to a particular position in space although the gimbals change their angle relative to it. Early applications were gun-sighting at sea and torpedo steering.

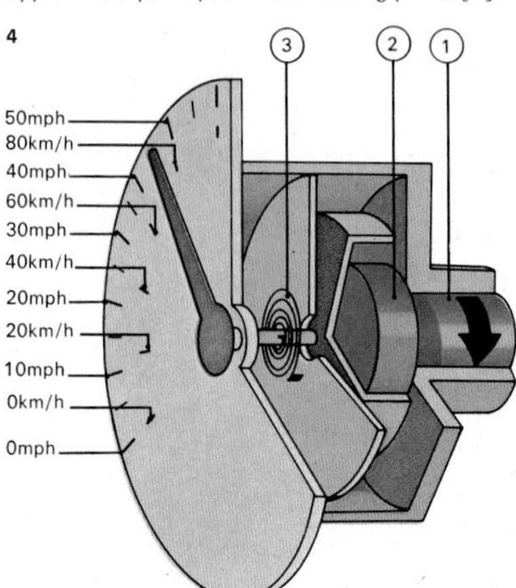

50mph
80km/h
40mph
60km/h
30mph
40km/h
20mph
20km/h
10mph
0km/h
0mph
3
2
1

4 The speed of a vehicle is read on a speedometer connected by a flexible cable to gears in the transmission system. According to the speed, the core of the cable rotates a magnet [1], which pulls a drum [2] mounted around it. A pointer on the speedometer dial moves with this drum but is stabilized, if the speed is constant, by a hairspring [3] that balances the force of the magnet and holds the pointer.

to measure the angle of the sun, moon, and stars above the horizon have been gradually refined since the invention of the astrolabe, perhaps as early as the third century BC. This permitted measurement of the positions of celestial bodies, but it was difficult to use accurately on the heaving deck of a ship. In 1730 John Hadley (1682–1744) invented a reflecting quadrant that brought the horizon and the observed object in line by mirrors. It soon developed into the sextant [1]. The sextant, so called because it usually has a scale of 60° (one-sixth of a circle), enabled mariners to measure angles at any inclination and to fix their positions much more accurately.

Measurement of absolute movement relative to the stars was significantly improved after a French physicist, Jean Foucault (1819–68), built a gyroscope [3] to show that the earth revolved on its axis. The principle of the gyro is that the axis of a spinning wheel suspended in gimbal rings holds its original position in space regardless of gravity or magnetic force. Gyroscopes have been made for automatic steering of machines from submarines and space vehicles to oil drills.

Pressure, speed, and radiation

In 1643 Evangelista Torricelli (1608–47), an Italian mathematician and physicist, found that the pressure of air at the surface of the earth was equal to that of a 76cm (30in) column of mercury. At higher altitudes the pressure falls. Working on this principle, Torricelli devised a practical form of barometer. Measurement of changes in atmospheric pressure were soon being used to gauge the height of mountains as well as climatic conditions. In addition to the barometer and various adaptations of it, a wide range of instruments is available to measure the pressure of liquids and gases. A common one is the Bourdon gauge [7].

Accurate measurement of vehicle speed was achieved only in the 1920s with the development of the magnetic speedometer [4]. Today this instrument is usually linked with an odometer that records distance traveled. The nuclear age has brought still newer devices, such as the film badge [6].

KEY

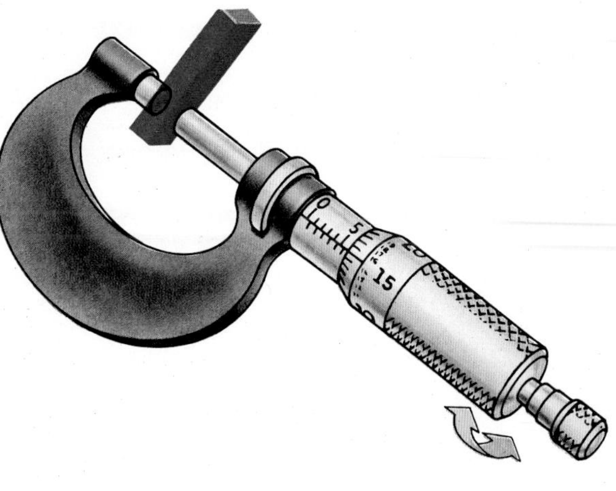

The micrometer is a standard measuring instrument for dealing with precise dimensions in the engineering industry. It consists basically of a bolt that can be turned through a fixed nut. As the end of the bolt is turned in a clockwise direction it closes toward the workpiece being measured. The required dimension, which is related to the number of turns made by the bolt, is read off a graduated scale.

5

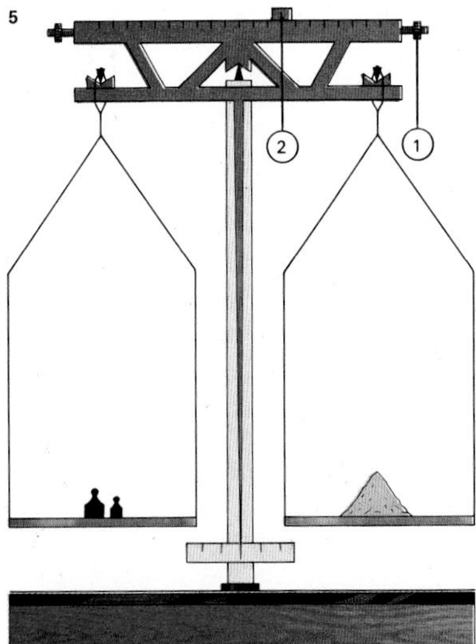

5 Measurement of mass is most accurately carried out by balancing. A high-sensitivity balance used by chemists has screw weights [1] for fine adjustment. When correctly adjusted, a long, vertical needle in the center of the unit rests exactly over a central zero on a scale at the base of the balance column. To achieve finer measurements than are possible by placing known weights in one pan, a "rider weight" is sometimes used. This small weight [2] slides along a direct-reading scale.

6 A film badge worn by those likely to be exposed to radiation consists of a film [7] in a plastic holder of known absorption properties [1]. A window [2] lets through all types of radiation. As neutrons [3] do not themselves affect film they are slowed by a lead filter [5] and absorbed by a cadmium filter [6], which emits a gamma ray for each neutron, blackening the film. Gamma rays [4] themselves penetrate all filters. X rays [9] penetrate the plastic filter, whereas beta particles and other types of radiation [10] blacken the film through the window. Developed film [8] shows blackening.

6

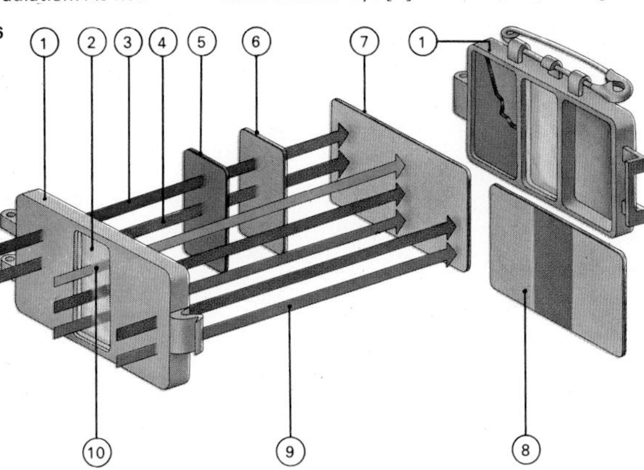

7

7 Pressure is measured in a Bourdon gauge by allowing a liquid or gas to flow into a curved flattened tube sealed at one end. Higher pressures produce a tendency for the tube to straighten out. The resulting small movement at the sealed end of the tube is amplified by a system of levers fixed to an indicator that moves over a scale to show the pressure applied. It was developed in 1850.

8

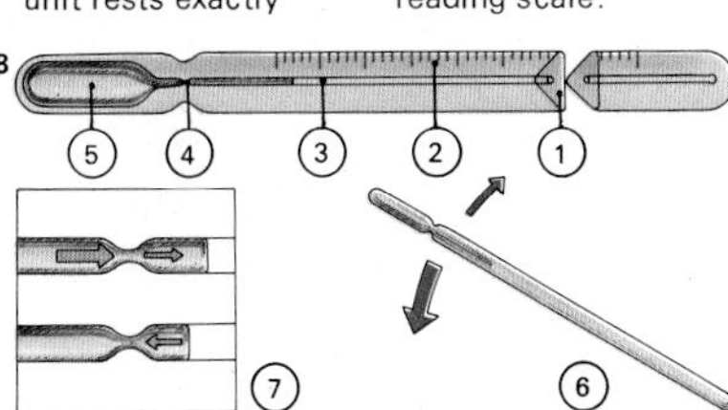

8 A clinical thermometer is an ordinary mercury-glass thermometer with a particularly fine capillary [3]. A constriction [4] allows mercury to flow easily from the bulb [5] but, by surface tension, prevents flow back [7]. A temperature reading can thus be maintained on the scale [2] until the mercury is forced back by shaking [6]. For easy reading the stem is lens-shaped as in cross-section [1], to magnify the mercury visually.

9

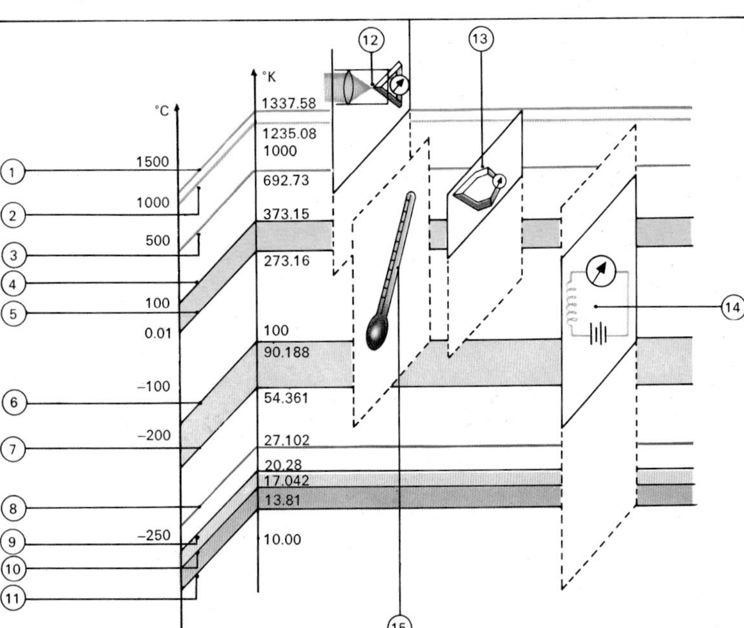
°C
1500
1000
500
100
0.01
–100
–200
–250
°K
1337.58
1235.08
1000
692.73
373.15
273.16
100
90.188
54.361
27.102
20.28
17.042
13.81
10.00

9 Temperatures are defined in the International Practical Temperature Scale in degrees absolute (above 0°K or –273°C). The "fixed points" are melting points of gold [1], silver, [2] and zinc [3]; the boiling point of water [4] and its "triple point" [5] at which steam, water, and ice are in equilibrium; boiling [6] and triple [7] points of oxygen; boiling point of neon [8]; triple [11] and boiling points of hydrogen at atmospheric [9] and at 25mm of mercury [10] pressures. Instruments for measuring temperatures in certain ranges are the pyrometer [12], platinum-rhodium thermocouple [13], electrical resistance of platinum wire [14], and thermometer [15].

Machines for measuring time

CONNECTIONS

See also
1652 Levers and wedges
1654 Pulleys and gears

The earliest mechanical clocks containing movable parts were built about 700 years ago. But the first means of measuring daily time was devised more than 3,000 years ago. This was probably the Egyptian shadow stick, dating from about 1450 BC. Like a sundial, it measured daily time by the movement of a shadow thrown across markers.

The first kinds of clocks

The shadow clock was soon followed by the water clock or clepsydra [1] and the sandglass or hourglass, in which time is measured by the change in level of flowing water or sand. These remained the only methods for measuring daily time until the Anglo-Saxons began to use candles marked at regular intervals [2]. In medieval times, instruments were made with dials marked in hours. These included the sundial and star dials such as the nocturnal [3].

All familiar clocks and watches work by the regular recurrence of some mechanical movement. The first mechanical clocks, of the thirteenth and fourteenth centuries [5], were driven by falling weights that moved gears. For the clock to run for more than a few seconds, the power from the falling weights must be released slowly. To do this, one of the gears (the escape wheel) is regularly held and released by an escapement mechanism.

Early clocks used the verge escapement. Two projections or pallets, formed on the balance axis, engaged with and disengaged from the teeth of the escape wheel, causing the balance to oscillate regularly. The motion of the escape wheel was transmitted through a series of gears to a single hand on the clock face.

As early as the mid-fifteenth century, compact and portable clocks driven by springs were developed. Early spring-driven clocks were inaccurate. A minute hand had appeared on the faces of some of these clocks, but a hand telling the seconds remained almost unknown until the arrival of the pendulum.

In 1657 the Dutch scientist Christian Huygens (1629–95), influenced by a suggestion from the Italian scientist Galileo (1564–1642), specified the conditions for a perfectly swinging pendulum and applied it to a clock. From the mid-seventeenth century, more accurate clocks were made with pendulums.

Problems with pendulums and escapements

Problems of accuracy remained. Pendulums are affected by changes in temperature, which cause them to expand or contract and so change length. In about 1715 George Graham invented the first of many pendulums compensated for temperature changes. The principal shortcoming of clock mechanisms, however, was the verge escapement, which interfered with pendulum action. In 1673 the anchor escapement [4] was invented. It allowed a heavy pendulum to swing in a small arc with such a gain in accuracy that it is still used in some modern clocks.

Another oscillator is the balance and balance spring, or hairspring [6], introduced by Huygens in 1675. One end of the spiral balance spring is fixed and the other is attached to the axis of the balance. The bal-

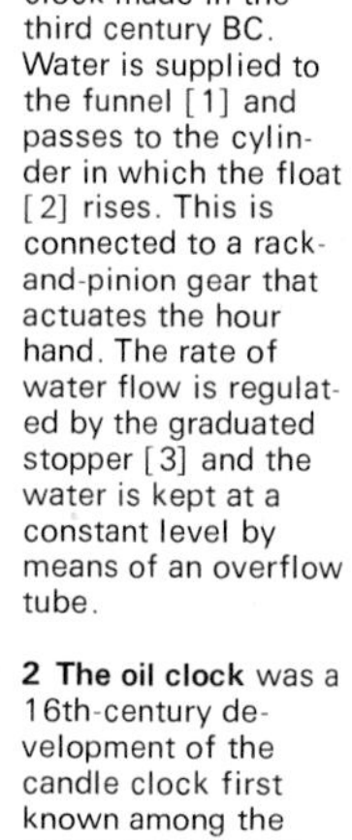

1 This water clock, or clepsydra, is based on an Egyptian clock made in the third century BC. Water is supplied to the funnel [1] and passes to the cylinder in which the float [2] rises. This is connected to a rack-and-pinion gear that actuates the hour hand. The rate of water flow is regulated by the graduated stopper [3] and the water is kept at a constant level by means of an overflow tube.

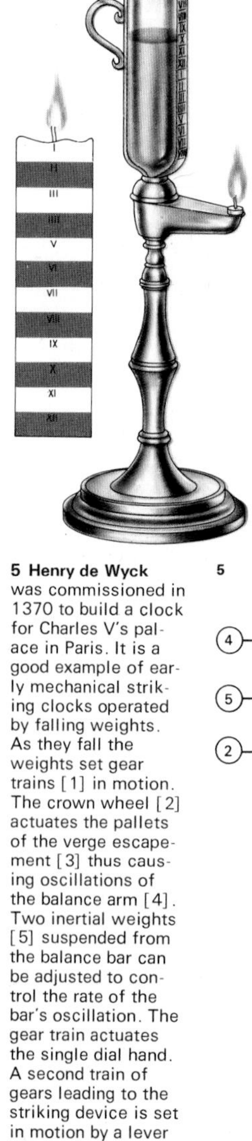

2 The oil clock was a 16th-century development of the candle clock first known among the Anglo-Saxons. Both have a scale recording the dropping level in hours as the oil or wax burns away.

3 To measure time at night, a nocturnal or night dial was used. The North Star was sighted through a central hole and the pointer was rotated toward the two "pointer" stars of the Dipper.

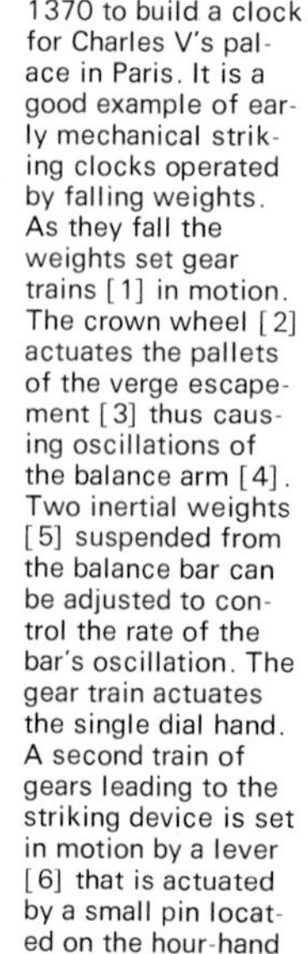

4 The accuracy of a mechanical clock depends above all on the escapement mechanism that releases the energy of a spring or weight regularly in small "bursts" to the timekeeping part of the clock. The anchor escapement of a pendulum clock [A] has an anchor that swings about its center and is connected to the pendulum. A main spring (not shown) moves the escape wheel clockwise. A tooth of the wheel pushes one pallet of the anchor [B] until the other pallet checks another tooth [C], the curve of the pallet forcing the wheel slightly backward. After this recoil the pallet receives a push until the first pallet checks the wheel. In this way, the to-and-fro movement maintains the oscillations.

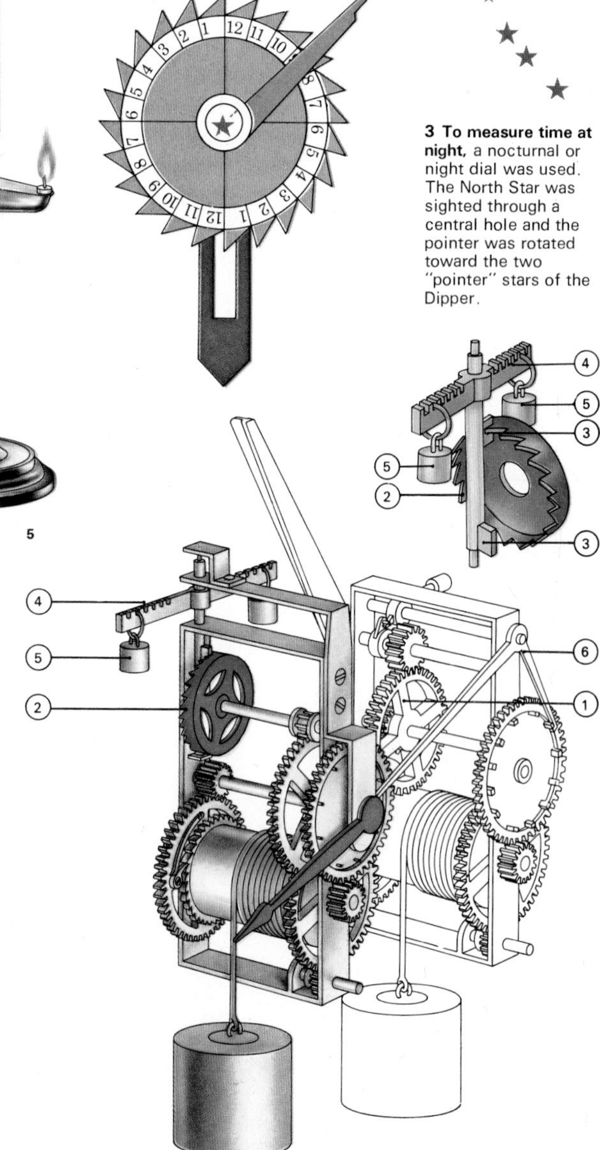

5 Henry de Wyck was commissioned in 1370 to build a clock for Charles V's palace in Paris. It is a good example of early mechanical striking clocks operated by falling weights. As they fall the weights set gear trains [1] in motion. The crown wheel [2] actuates the pallets of the verge escapement [3] thus causing oscillations of the balance arm [4]. Two inertial weights [5] suspended from the balance bar can be adjusted to control the rate of the bar's oscillation. The gear train actuates the single dial hand. A second train of gears leading to the striking device is set in motion by a lever [6] that is actuated by a small pin located on the hour-hand wheel.

ance spring alternately winds and unwinds as the balance swings. He later incorporated it in a watch intended for determining longitude at sea. But balance springs, like pendulums, were adversely affected by temperature variations. In 1753 an effective compensation was made for a watch by John Harrison (1693–1776), whose chronometer of 1759, made in response to a government competition, erred by only five seconds in a sea voyage lasting six weeks. Accuracy had also been improved by the introduction of jewels used as bearings. Sapphires and rubies were the most generally used jewels for bearings, and they are still used in watches.

Watches were developed and refined with various escapements until the mid-nineteenth century, when the lever escapement was almost universally adopted. In this mechanism, invented by Thomas Mudge in about 1755 but neglected for half a century, the pallets are attached to a lever that is detached from the balance for most of its swing. This arrangement, together with the lever's robustness, promotes highly accurate timekeeping. In the nineteenth century standardized parts were introduced.

Modern and electric clocks

Other kinds of clocks, including those employing an electric motor to wind a spring or weight, now rival purely mechanical clocks. An electric clock has a "synchronous" motor that keeps in step with the frequency of the alternating current supply. Electric pendulum clocks use electromagnets to keep a pendulum swinging accurately.

Oscillators include piezoelectric crystals such as quartz. The crystal vibrates and continues vibrating when the correct alternating voltage is applied across it. Compact electronic circuits reduce such high-frequency oscillations to only a few per second; these then operate gears driving hands. Such clocks can be accurate to a tenth of a second per year. Even more accurate are atomic clocks, which employ oscillating energy changes within atoms. Clocks of this kind are now used as international standards of time [9].

KEY

T C
1872

Shadow clocks such as sundials were used for centuries for telling the time. They have to be accurately set up with the 12 noon position pointing due north on a horizontal dial or, on a wall clock, downward, with seasonal adjustments.

6A

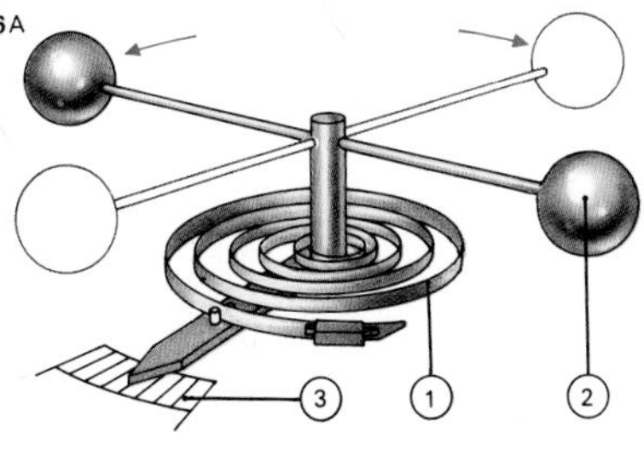

3
1
2

B

3

6 This 17th-century watch [B] has its balance spring [1] attached to the staff of a balance [2], which swings first one way, then the other, under the tension of the spring. The regulator [3] shortens or lengthens the spring to alter its tension, which in turn controls the swings and thus the accuracy of the watch.

7

MARINE CHRONOMETER
OMEGA
3437185

7 Quartz clocks and watches use the piezoelectric properties of a quartz crystal. Such crystals vibrate at a specific frequency when placed in an alternating electric current circuit, and the circuit frequency becomes that of the crystal. In a quartz timekeeper this "crystal current" is amplified and used to drive an electric motor, which in turn actuates the hands of the time-display on the face of the clock.

8A

Regulator

2

8B

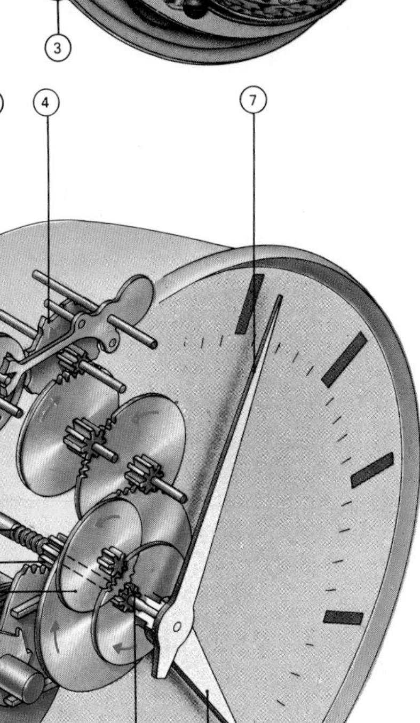

2
3
4
7
9
8
11
5
1
6
10

8 A typical mechanical clock of today [B] is operated by energy stored in a mainspring [1]. This energy is released in small controlled "bursts" in an escapement mechanism [A] comprising a spring [2] and balance [3] together with an escape wheel [4]. The mainspring drives a great wheel [5] which in turn rotates the center arbor [6] and minute hand [7] via the center pinion [8] and friction spring [9]. The hour hand [10] is turned at one-twelfth the speed of the minute hand by gears [11] that are driven by a cannon pinion in small controlled increments.

9A 9B

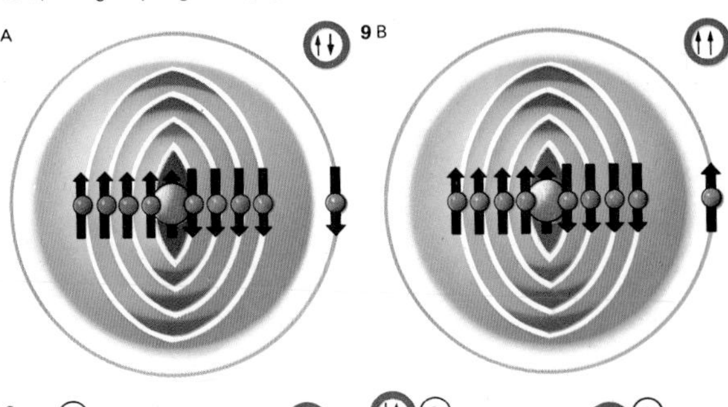

C

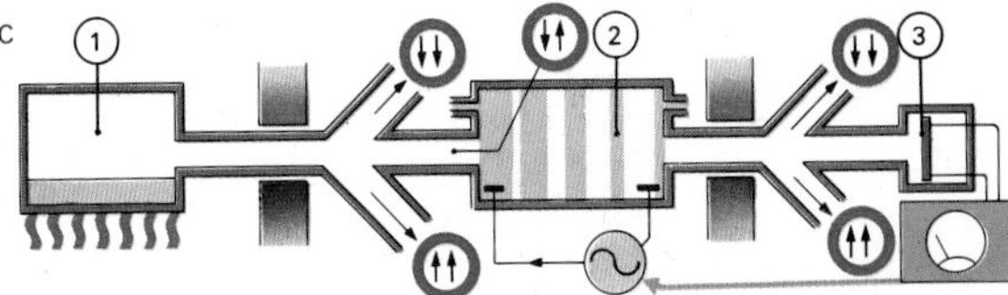

1
2
3

9 Atomic clocks use the frequency of vibration of atoms (about 10,000 million per sec) to regulate a quartz crystal clock. Caesium atoms [A] are normally unmagnetized but radiation can magnetize them [B]. A caesium clock [C] has a boiler [1] yielding a supply of atoms whose magnetic axes are lined up by a magnetic field. In the chamber [2] they encounter an oscillating field and the axes flip over so that they are deflected by a second field toward a detector [3]. Signals from here control a quartz crystal clock.

The factory and assembly line

In modern industrial society nearly all consumer goods are made in factories that are complex organizations of machines, processes, materials, people, and products. Underlying the organization of a factory is the principle of the division of labor, formulated by Adam Smith (1723–90) in his book *The Wealth of Nations* (1776), in which he described methods used to make pins. The manufacture of pins was divided into several different tasks, each carried out by a different person. It has been found that this type of organization, in which the work is divided up into a series of separate operations, is essential for efficiency in large-scale production.

The factory system

A craftsman generally carries out all the stages of manufacture of an article himself. But even he relies on apprentices or other help; few woodcarvers make their own tools, for example. Some processes are now being envisaged in which a modern master-craftsman, using computerized systems, will design and control the manufacture of goods by mass production, and in so doing restore the unity of craft techniques.

In Europe the factory system became firmly established for the making of cloth in the seventeenth century. The process was subdivided into carding, spinning, and weaving, sometimes with many machines in one factory. Even so, factory production accounted for only a small proportion of the total output of cloth.

A decisive step came with the design and manufacture of machinery with standardized interchangeable parts. In 1803 Marc Isambard Brunel designed machinery with interchangeable parts for making pulley blocks for the Portsmouth (England) naval dockyard [1]. The machinery was manufactured by Henry Maudsley and there were 45 machines of 22 different kinds. By 1807 the machinery was capable of supplying the entire pulley block requirements of the Royal Navy and by 1808 there was a yearly production rate of 130,000 blocks.

The first automatic assembly line [4] was begun when the Olds Motor Works in Detroit was destroyed by fire in 1901. The factory was rebuilt so that a car could be wheeled from worker to worker. This idea was later employed by Henry Ford, who started up the first moving assembly line using interchangeable parts and a moving conveyor belt to transport the vehicle around the factory floor. (This meant that cars of the same model could be repaired or assembled from stock parts.) By 1914 Ford was turning out the Model T at a rate of one every hour and a half. This time-saving cut production costs, and the price of a Model T fell from $850 in 1914 to $400 in 1916.

Modern assembly lines

On modern assembly lines complex products are assembled at great speed. Goods are produced in greater quantities and at a lower cost. Production lines even manufacture complex machined parts, such as cylinder blocks for automobile engines, as well as large finished items [5].

The assembly line is undoubtedly efficient, but the work is not only extremely boring for the workers but has to be per-

CONNECTIONS

See also
1670 Automatic control
1606 Metalworking machines
1608 Working with ceramics
1804 Chemical engineering
1644 Oil refining
1584 Modern technology
928 Work: management and organization
938 Industry and economics

1 The machinery that was set up in the Royal Dockyard at Portsmouth was the first instance of the use of mass production of interchangeable parts with machine tools. The machines were so well built that several were still in use in the 1950s. The total saving in the first year was £24,000, of which the inventor, Marc Isambard Brunel (1769–1849), received £17,000.

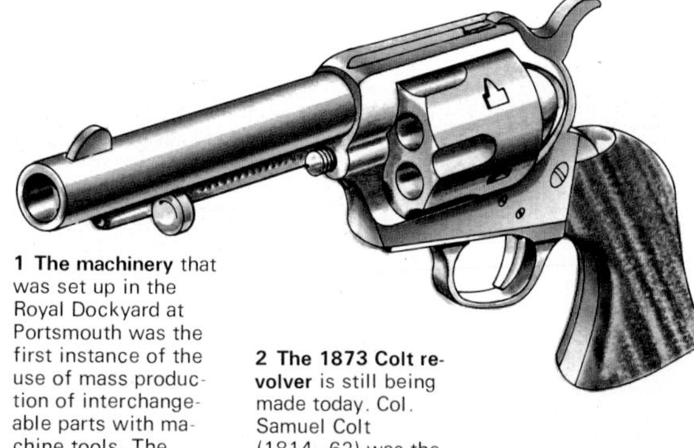

2 The 1873 Colt revolver is still being made today. Col. Samuel Colt (1814–62) was the first mass-producer of firearms. His revolvers had single-action mechanisms and therefore had to be cocked before firing. They were first supplied in .44 calibre to the US Army after the Mexican War (1846–8).

4 Assembly line techniques are still used in the automobile industry, although they are now being superseded by modified systems that are both easier on the worker and less regimented.

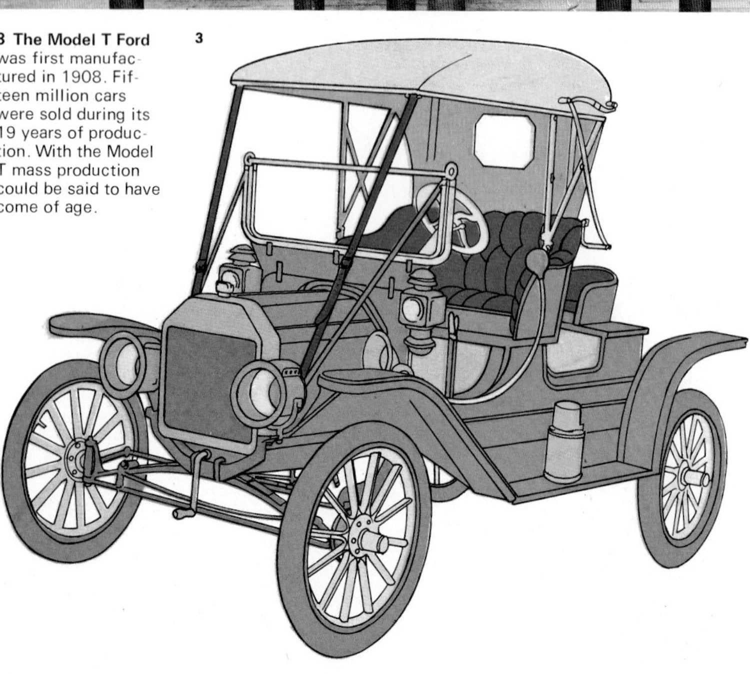

3 The Model T Ford was first manufactured in 1908. Fifteen million cars were sold during its 19 years of production. With the Model T mass production could be said to have come of age.

formed under tremendous pressure. The whole process of mass production is, however, beginning to change. Work is being reorganized to make each person's job more interesting and factories under almost total computer control are planned.

The attempt to improve job satisfaction was pioneered in Sweden. Instead of a "one man, one machine" line, departments are divided into a series of teams. Each team receives the same pay, with each person in it performing a variety of tasks. Instead of working to orders, each team devises its own methods. The new system has succeeded. Using it, the Saab-Scania automobile division at Sodertalje opened a new factory for engine assembly in 1972 and Volvo opened a plant for the assembly of complete cars in 1974.

Other new methods

New methods of organization and manufacture are being developed in most industries, with mass production reserved for the production of identical parts in large quantities. One-of-a-kind parts and prototypes remain expensive. Between these two extremes there are batch-produced items made at moderate expense. This is a surprisingly important area of production and it has been estimated that more than 50 percent by value of the goods manufactured in the United States are made in batches of 50 or less.

The manufacture of computer-controlled parts [6–8] depends on numerically controlled machine-tool stations that can be instructed to carry out a range of machining tasks. There are also versatile handling systems that transfer manufactured parts from one station to another and position them according to instructions. The type of design must be made to suit the computerized control system. Japan is the most advanced country in computer-controlled parts manufacture, but the most ambitious system is at Karl-Marx-Stadt in the German Democratic Republic. The system is housed in an air-conditioned building the size of two football fields. Work is transferred around the factory floor on pallets supported on air cushions and propelled by linear induction motors.

KEY

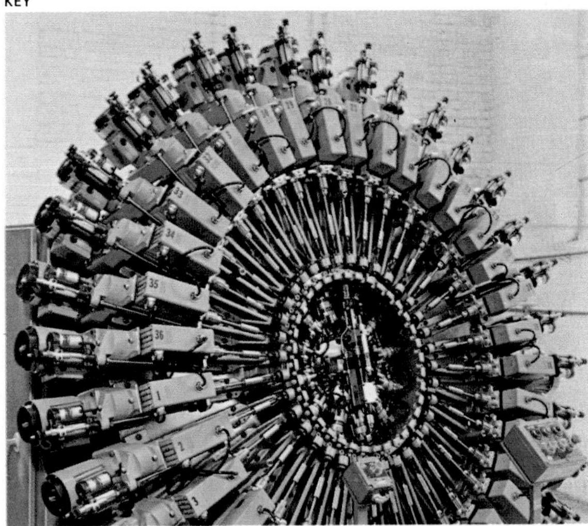

The automatic tool-changing carousel provides a versatile machine tool suited to numerical control. A computer selects the tool and it is automatically brought into position in a few seconds. This system is expensive compared with standard tools and its use has not always proved justified.

5 A

B

C

5 Products made on assembly lines, such as these automobile engines, pass from one group of workers to another. Each worker repeats a specific job on a part-built engine as it reaches him [A, B]. The completed product passes to inspectors, who carry out a series of examinations [C] to test its quality. The advantages can, however, be counterproductive because of the boring, repetitive nature of the work.

6

6 Computer-controlled parts manufacture uses a versatile handling system. Depending on the complexity of the part, it can be directed to just two or three machines, bypassing the others. The computer is also able to direct the machining of at least 16 different kinds of parts. The engineering drawings of a part to be made resemble a map, and the dimensions can be coded as instructions to the computer's memory and then to the machine that makes the part.

7

7 A computer is the heart of any fully automatic manufacturing process. It can collect and sort production data, control the ordering of raw materials and stock and, most important of all, instruct automatic machine tools to fabricate various components.

8 Computer-managed parts manufacturing uses computer technology to lower the cost of machining a small number of parts. Because the computer stores all the information about the part it is able to organize the manufacture of that unit in a "batch" that can consist, if necessary, of only one unit.

8

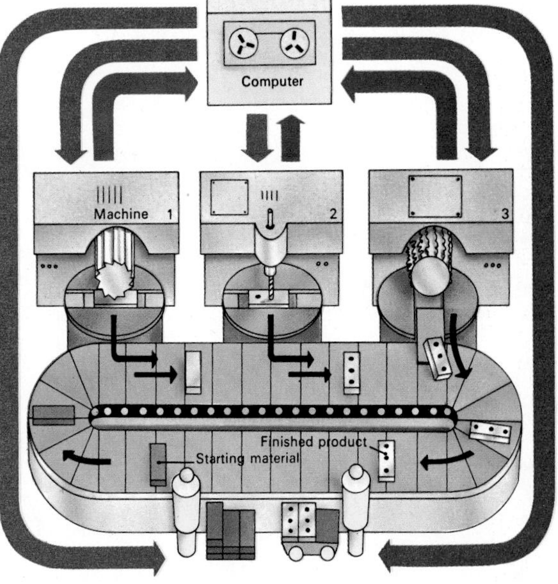
Computer
Machine 1
2
3
Finished product
Starting material

Machines for lifting

The strongest athletes can lift close to 1,000lb (455kg) just off the ground, but few ordinary people can lift more than about 150lb (68kg). Early man soon developed machines for lifting large stones and tree trunks. A simple device is a single pulley wheel arranged as a hoist. But a rope around one pulley merely changes the direction of the pull and friction in the pulley's bearing in fact makes this simple machine less efficient than a straight pull. If the rope is wound around a wheel or cylinder to form a windlass [Key], a mechanical advantage is gained, by means of which a man can easily lift more than his own weight. A small windlass can be driven by a hand crank—first used in the ninth century—and many early cranes and hoists used this principle.

Screws and pulleys

Many basic inventions, such as the screw and the pulley, cannot be credited to any one man. The Greeks were probably using screws by about 400 BC and by the time of Archimedes (who died in 212 BC) the screw certainly had various applications. Archimedes himself invented a type of pump consisting of a long helix in an upward-sloping tube; by turning a handle at the upper end the operator could "screw" water from the lower end of a spiral to its upper end until it flowed out of the top. This kind of pump was used for irrigating the Nile Valley. In Roman and medieval times, screw presses were used for crushing olives and grapes.

In the thirteenth century the French monk Villard de Honnecourt made a machine that used a screw for lifting instead of pressing downward. Today known as the screw jack [2], the device has many applications from lifting a car to change a wheel to jacking up whole buildings while a story is slipped underneath.

Pulleys were also known to the ancient Greeks who used them to lower a statue of a god onto the stage as the climax of a religious drama. By the time of Christ, Roman engineers were designing and making multiple pulley blocks for lifting heavy loads. A 200-ton Egyptian granite obelisk, similar to the so-called Cleopatra's needles now standing in New York and London, was erected in ancient Rome using many pulley blocks and teams of slaves to provide the muscle power. Today's compact hoists [3] use exactly the same principles.

Hoists and cranes

Machines for lifting can also be made using gears to obtain mechanical advantage. With only horse power, sixteenth-century miners hauled loads of ore and other minerals [1]. Later hoists using steam engines—and even modern ones with electric motors—use similar principles.

Early cranes were merely rope-and-pulley hoists rigged between two or three wooden "legs" straddling the object to be lifted. Power was provided through a windlass or, for heavy loads, by a treadmill. The building projects and dock installations of the Middle Ages depended on such machines for lifting huge blocks of stone.

Modern cranes are of two main types—bridge cranes and jib cranes. Both use a windlass with steel wire rope wrapped around a powered drum. A bridge crane has

CONNECTIONS

See also
1654 Pulleys and gears
1666 Moving heavy loads
1664 Earth-moving machines
1720 Helicopters and autogiros
1722 Space vehicles
1612 Making large buildings
1712 Balloons, blimps, and dirigibles

1 In the earliest days of mining tubs full of ore were dragged along horizontal or gently sloping tunnels driven into a hillside. The development of hoists by the 16th century allowed miners to sink vertical shafts. The horse-powered capstan [1] turns a cogged wheel [2] to winch up a leather bucket [3] containing the ore. To lower a load the miners reversed the horses' harnesses and made them walk in the other direction. The brakeman [4] working below stopped the hoist by pulling down the beam [5] to make the timber baulk [6] press against the outer edge of the brake drum [7].

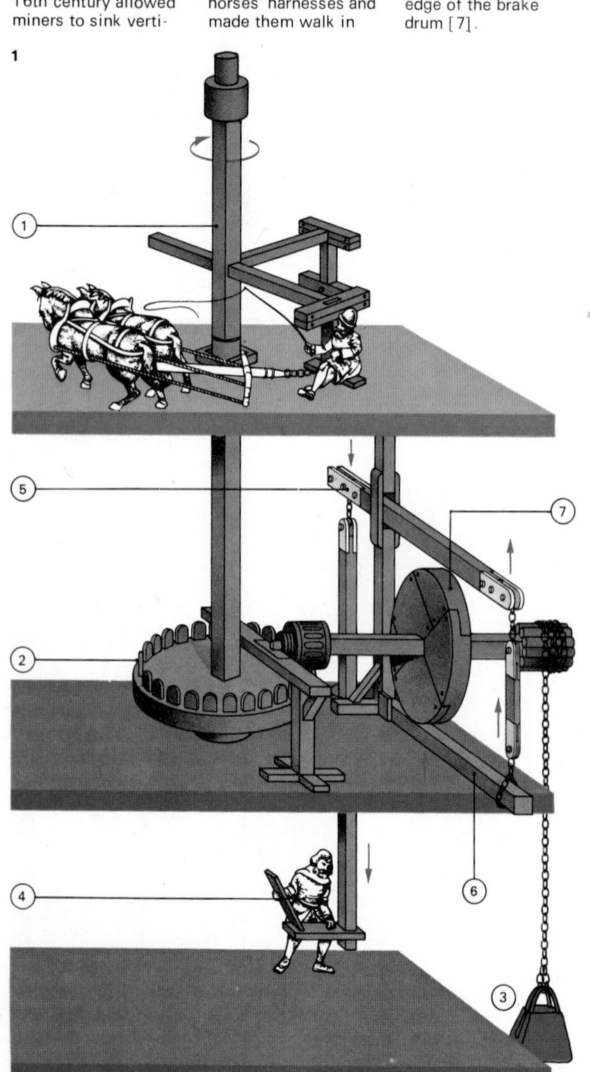

1
1
5
7
2
4
6
3

2 The winding lever[1] of a screw jack is turned once to raise the jack through a distance equal to the pitch of the screw's thread. With a fine pitch a small effort can lift a very heavy load.

3 A compact hoist can be made using two pulley blocks. This one has a mechanical advantage of eight, although 24ft (7.3m) of rope have to be pulled through to raise the load only 3ft (0.9m).

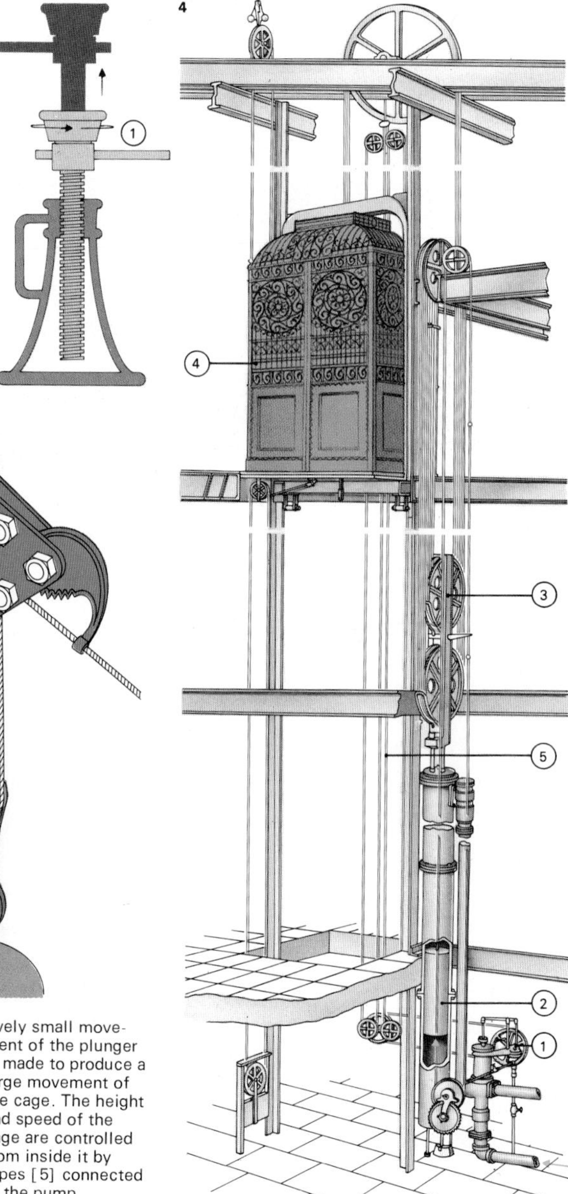

2
1
3
4
4
3
5
2
1

4 A hydraulic elevator of the 19th century also uses pulleys. A pump [1] pressurizes water to move the plunger [2]. This movement is transmitted to the lower pair of pulleys [3] to raise or lower the elevator cage [4]. In this way, the relatively small movement of the plunger is made to produce a large movement of the cage. The height and speed of the cage are controlled from inside it by ropes [5] connected to the pump.

a box-girder beam (called a gantry) running on long elevated tracks at each of its ends. The gantry can move backward and forward along the tracks. The hoisting system is carried in a trolley, which moves along the gantry beam. Bridge cranes are commonly set up above a working area to handle such loads as tree trunks and steel beams.

A jib crane has a long boom that can swing horizontally to move the load sideways. Many such cranes can also "luff" to control the reach of the crane by angling the boom more or less to the horizontal. A cantilever crane [5] is a typical example.

Lifting people

Skyscrapers and high-rise apartments would have been impossible without elevators interconnecting the floors and giving access to the ground. In 1857 the American inventor Elisha Otis (1811–61) installed a steam-powered elevator in a New York department store.

Early elevators used the screw-jack principle, soon to be replaced in the 1870s by elevators using hydraulic pressure. Water, oil, or other fluid is pumped to provide pressure against a piston, which in turn raises the load. Many buildings use a combination of hydraulics and pulleys [4] which allows the elevator to go up higher. In the twentieth century buildings were made even taller, especially in the United States. The ultra-high-rise buildings need passenger elevators using electric motors that travel at more than 1,200ft (365m) per minute, or about two floors each second.

In subway stations and large stores, there is a more or less continuous flow of people between various levels. Here the people-lifting problem is solved by using escalators, which are continuously moving staircases based on the conveyor belt principle with an endless belt of steps. The original patents of 1891 were obtained and improved by the Otis Elevator Company that, together with Westinghouse Electric Elevators, developed the modern escalator in the 1930s. An escalator 4ft (1.25m) wide moving at 90ft (27m) per minute can carry about 8,000 people an hour.

KEY

The effort of lifting a man is reduced by the mechanical advantages (ma) of the windlass on a mine's winding gear. If the shaft has a radius of 12in(30cm) and the windlass 96in (240cm) the ma is 8 – by exerting 22lb(10kg) of effort a 176-lb (80kg) man can be lifted, ignoring friction.

5

5 A cantilever or tower crane is used in constructing high-rise buildings. Anchored to the ground or to the building itself, the crane is extended upward as the work proceeds. Standard sections form the tower, which supports a horizontal boom whose weight, and that of the load, is counterbalanced by a block of concrete. The hoist is in a trolley that can travel along the boom.

6 Each step on the endless belt forming an escalator has two pairs of wheels. The upper pair [1] run on an outer rail and the lower ones [2] run on an inner rail. On the sloping part of the "staircase," the rails are in line. But at the top and the bottom they separate to make the steps line up to create flat sections for people to step on and off. Even when stopped, an escalator can be used.

6

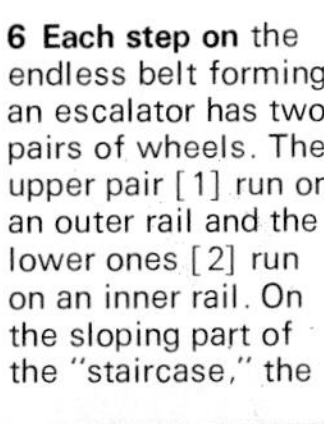
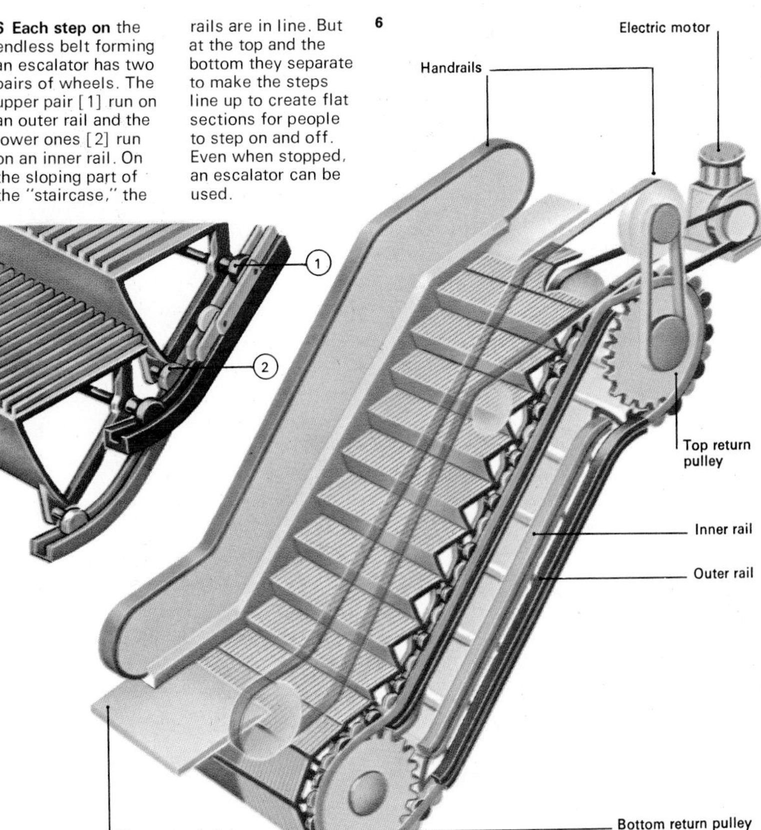
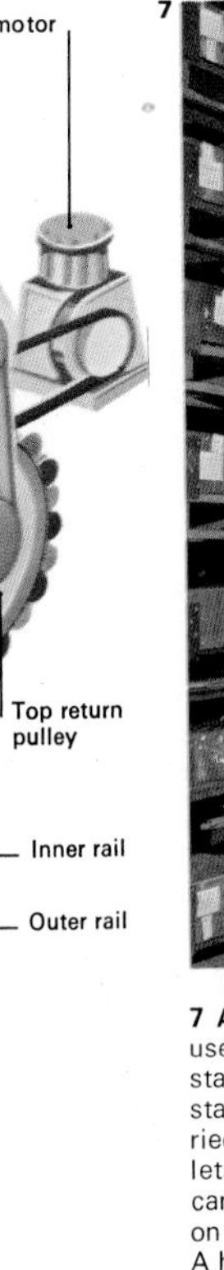

Electric motor
Handrails
1
2
Top return pulley
Inner rail
Outer rail
Bottom combplate
Bottom return pulley

7

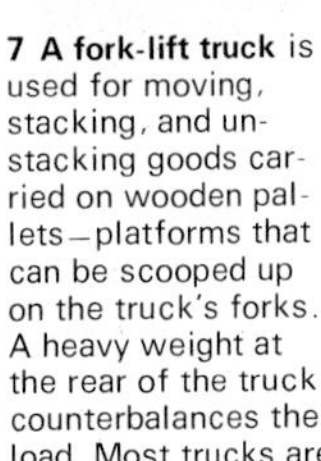

7 A fork-lift truck is used for moving, stacking, and unstacking goods carried on wooden pallets – platforms that can be scooped up on the truck's forks. A heavy weight at the rear of the truck counterbalances the load. Most trucks are driven by electric motors, although some have diesel or low-pressure gas engines. The same power unit drives the hydraulic mechanism or chains that raise and lower the forks, which may tilt backward to make the load safer when being moved. Some trucks have telescopic masts that extend upward to allow the forks to stack loads up to 16ft (5m) above the ground. Carrying capacities vary from five tons with small machines to 50 tons or more for larger ones.

Earth-moving machines

Building Iron Age forts, digging canals, making railroads, and constructing modern highways have all required the shifting of hundreds of tons of soil. As a result, from the Iron Age to the present men have devised various machines for moving earth.

One of the earliest earth-moving machines was the wheelbarrow, developed in China before AD 118. The Chinese version had a large wheel 39in (1m) or more across, with the load carried above and at the sides of the wheel. The early European wheelbarrow, similar in style to that used today, had a fairly small wheel and the load was carried between it and the handles. Using only wheelbarrows, picks, and shovels, the navvies (short for "navigators") built the whole system of European canals and many early railroads [Key].

Modern earth-moving machines

Wheelbarrows are still used on small-scale building projects, but today's civil engineers can choose from many specialized earth-moving machines. The digger, or excavator, was one of the first of these and a mechanical digger was an early nineteenth-century application of the steam engine.

Today there is a wide range of excavator designs, each suited to a particular task. The dragline excavator, for example, has caterpillar tracks for moving over uneven or soft ground [3]. The digging bucket is suspended from a boom and after scooping up its load is winched back to be dumped. The size of the "bite" taken by the bucket has to suit the material being excavated. For soft earth and for moving existing stockpiles of earthy minerals, such as crushed ore, a light bucket is used. A medium-weight bucket is employed for general digging duties, but for deep digging, or in rocky terrain, heavy buckets are essential to give enough penetration and prevent undue wear. In all these operations, the digging action occurs as the bucket is dragged back along the ground after being dropped from the boom.

For size and capacity the bucket-wheel excavators [2] are among the greatest engineering achievements. They are among the largest of self-propelled land machines and can be used for rapid excavating or for shifting vast quantities of loose material such as crushed ores or coal. They can move up to 354,000 cubic feet (10,000 cubic meters) of material in an hour.

Dredges are floating excavators used for keeping docks, harbors, and river channels free from mud and silt. They can also be used for "mining" underwater, to scoop up sand and gravel and other minerals. They have boatlike hulls, which may be passive and thus have to be towed to the site of operation, or may be fully powered and equipped with the necessary machinery to travel in the open sea. They have diesel engines that drive the machinery directly or power a generator for electric motors.

There are three main types of dredges: bucket dredges [6], grab and dipper dredges, and suction dredges [7]. Bucket dredges have an endless chain of buckets, on the conveyor belt system, that scoop up material from the bottom. A grab and dipper dredge has either a mechanical shovel (the dipper) pivoted at the end of a boom or a "clamshell" (the grab) for excavating materials in bulk. Most grab and dipper dredges

CONNECTIONS

See also

1748 Road building
1762 Canal construction
1754 Tunnel engineering
1760 Harbors and docks
1704 Technology and transportation in developing nations

1

CATERPILLAR

1 A bulldozer has rams hinged at the base of the bucket. By skillfully controling these rams the driver is able to excavate material without having to move the machine forward. For speed of operation most have crawler (or caterpillar) tracks so that they can swing around to dump into a truck parked behind in less than 15 seconds.

2

2 A digging-wheel excavator, with a scoop-tipped wheel up to 65ft(20m) across, can shift many cubic yards of soft material onto its internal conveyor belt. It is particularly useful for shifting dumps of powdered minerals such as china clay or coal-dust.

3

3 A dragline excavator, which is a kind of revolving shovel with a long boom, is ideal for stripping the topsoil, called overburden, from near-surface deposits of coal and other minerals. With very long booms, the bucket must be light or the machine must have a counterweight.

4

4 A front loader, designed for digging and loading, can also be used for moving "spoil" over short distances. The crawler-mounted type can have a bucket holding up to 140cu ft (4 cu m) of soil. Special attachments allow the machine to lift and remove rocks and tree stumps.

have a pair of metal legs, called "spuds," which are lowered to the bottom to stabilize the craft. Suction dredges work like giant vacuum cleaners and use powerful pumps to suck sludge from the bottom.

Shovels and dozers

The workhorse of land-based earth-moving equipment is the hydraulic loader, also known as a bulldozer [1]. It may have crawler (or caterpillar) tracks or wheels (with two-wheel or four-wheel drive). The crawler version can turn in very confined spaces—even in its own length—but the wheeled loaders travel much more quickly. In both, the usual cycle of operation consists of loading the excavator bucket, traveling to a heap of "spoil" or to a dump truck, dumping, and returning.

The dump trucks, also essential machines in a modern operation, have a capacity of 20 tons or more. Even so, several may have to be used to keep pace with a giant excavator.

If the soil or other material does not have to be moved too far it can be pushed to its new site by a bulldozer or carried there by the hybrid machine known as a shovel dozer. An angledozer merely pushes the material to one side. A shovel dozer, or front loader [4], can be mounted on tracks or wheels, depending on the requirements of the site. It can dig, load, and transport material.

Scrapers and graders

For building level, modern roads the specialized earth movers employed are scrapers and graders. A scraper may be self-propelled or pulled by a tractor [5]. It has a knifelike cutter that planes off a layer of soil into an internal reservoir that can hold up to 1,400 cubic feet (40 cubic meters) of soil. The depth of cut is controlled by hydraulic rams and the machine can transport its load to a nearby site, where it is dumped.

For precise finishing of the road foundation before concreting, a grader is used. It has an angled blade 7–13ft (2–4m) wide, hydraulically controlled and slung between its wheels. Most graders are self-propelled.

KEY

In the early days of railroads, excavations were largely made by hand; picks and shovels were used to dig out the soil and wheelbarrows to cart it away. The 2-mi(3-km) Tring Cutting between London and Birmingham was dug in 1838. Horses pulled the loaded barrows up planks laid on the sloping sides of the excavation but "navvies" had the dangerous job of guiding the barrows. Accidents were frequent.

5

5 A scraper is one of the key machines in modern road-building projects. Self-powered or hauled by a tractor, large ones can carry 3,500cu ft (100cu m) of soil. For extra power, a second diesel engine may be mounted at the rear. It is this massive power that enables the scraper blade under the machine to skim off layers of earth and force them back into the body of the machine. The heights of the scraper and of the tailgate, which is lifted or slid aside to release the load, are controlled by hydraulic rams, also powered by the main engines. All scrapers have huge tired wheels to cross uneven ground.

6

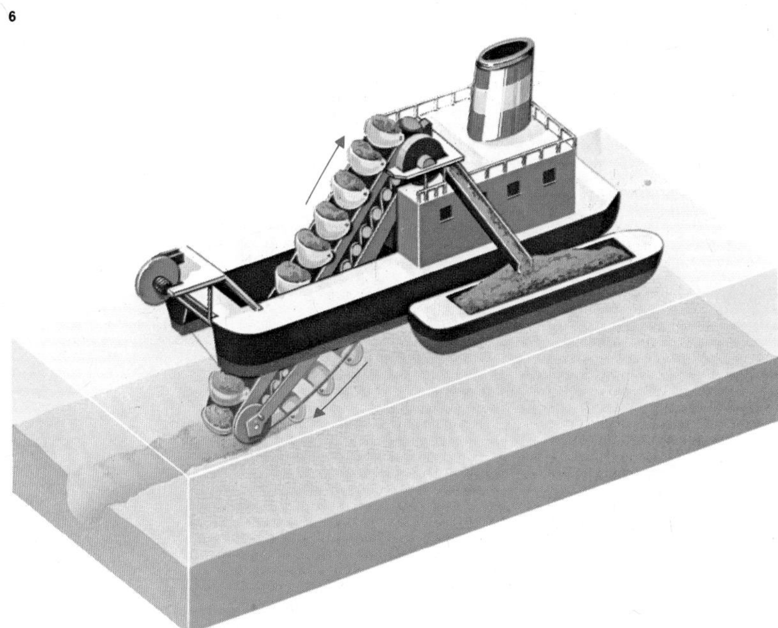

7

6 A bucket dredge has an endless chain of buckets that scoop up sludgy material from the bottom of the sea or a river. The "spoil" is automatically tipped into a discharge chute and into a barge moored alongside or, when working in a dock, directly into a dump truck. Most bucket dredges have no engines and therefore have to be towed into position by tugs, although self-propelled ones are sometimes used for excavating canal banks or other confined areas.

7 A suction dredge has powerful pumps that suck up the "spoil" in the form of a watery mud called slurry. Any hard material is broken up by high-pressure water jets or cutters. Most suction dredges are self-propelled.

Moving heavy loads

Ordinary cranes, used in the construction industry or for loading ships, can lift weights of up to 200 tons. But consider the following problems: a prefabricated 1,500-ton section of a ship (such as the whole superstructure or the front part of the bow) has to be placed in its final position [2]; a 6,000-ton rocket has to be moved 3mi (5km) to its launching site [3]; a 7,000-ton section of a stadium has to be placed in a new position [4]. Each problem involves moving a heavy load, and each has been solved.

What are heavy loads?

The ability to move heavy loads is increasingly important to the engineering industries because the cost-saving of building assemblies on a specific site before moving them to their final places is now accepted. But prefabricated structures are becoming larger and heavier. As new load-moving techniques have been developed, other industries have adopted them.

The word "heavy" is arbitrary, but for these purposes it includes loads ranging from hundreds of tons to tens of thousands of tons. Moving heavy loads has presented engineers with problems for thousands of years. Many suggestions have been put forward as to how stone was moved in the building of the pyramids and Stonehenge. Certainly a method using tree trunks as rollers would have been known then, and animal or human power could have provided the moving force.

Man started with the lever and soon discovered the arrangements of the moving force, the load, and the fulcrum (pivot) that would be most useful in particular applications. Archimedes [Key] is reputed to have claimed, "give me a firm place on which to stand and I will move the earth." He knew that given a lever long enough to gain the necessary mechanical advantage a small movement of the heaviest load could be obtained with a sufficiently large movement of even a small applied force.

The problems involved

Moving heavy loads involves reducing the friction underneath the load and providing sufficient force to overcome the friction remaining once the load is moving. To reduce friction, rolling logs were used and later wheels of various types. Grease was also applied to ease the movement of the load, particularly in the shipbuilding industry. More recently various "slippery" plastic coatings, such as polytetrafluorethylene (PTFE), have been used, as well as air and water cushions that operate like hovercraft.

There are two kinds of friction involved in moving anything. Static, or stationary, friction has to be overcome to start something moving, and dynamic, or moving, friction opposes its continued movement. The coefficient of friction between two materials is defined as the ratio of the force required to move the load to the weight of the load. Static and dynamic coefficients have wide ranges. These maximum values drop between the traditional slippery slopes of steel on greased steel (used for ship launching) from 0.25 and 0.17, down to 0.10 and 0.05 for steel on PTFE plastic. The values fall to 0.01 for air-bearing systems.

The use of friction-reducing systems can introduce further difficulties. Loads of

CONNECTIONS

See also
1652 Levers and wedges
1664 Earth-moving machines
1764 Building dams
1612 Making large buildings
1680 Modern ships

1 A

B

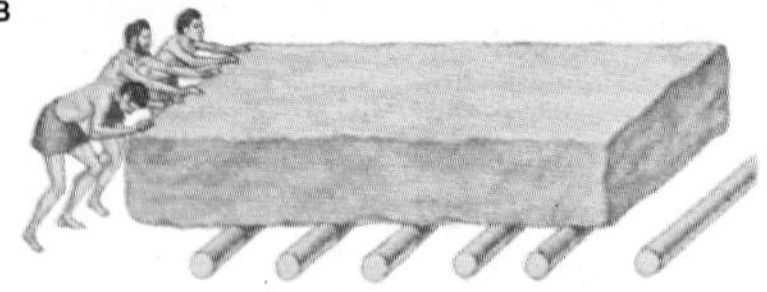

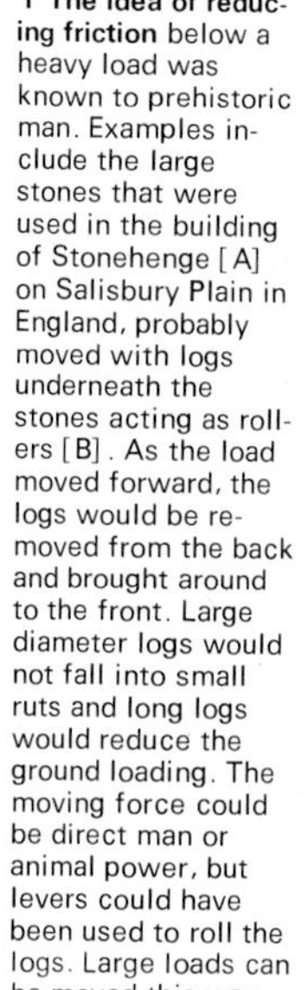

1 The idea of reducing friction below a heavy load was known to prehistoric man. Examples include the large stones that were used in the building of Stonehenge [A] on Salisbury Plain in England, probably moved with logs underneath the stones acting as rollers [B]. As the load moved forward, the logs would be removed from the back and brought around to the front. Large diameter logs would not fall into small ruts and long logs would reduce the ground loading. The moving force could be direct man or animal power, but levers could have been used to roll the logs. Large loads can be moved this way.

2 A

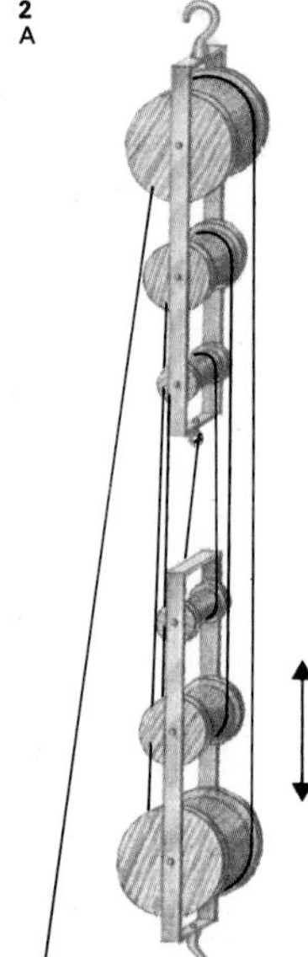

2 B

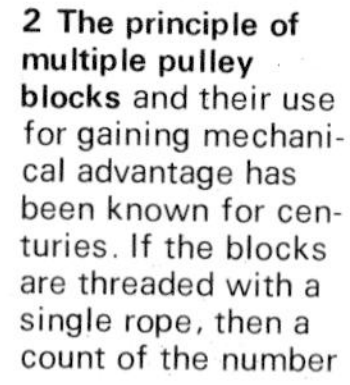

2 The principle of multiple pulley blocks and their use for gaining mechanical advantage has been known for centuries. If the blocks are threaded with a single rope, then a count of the number of lines effectively supporting the load gives the gain. In [A] a mechanical advantage of six is shown. Nearly every crane system uses this technique. A disadvantage of the technique is that a great length of hauling rope must be winched in to achieve only a small movement of the load. Large portal cranes [B] can lift 15,000 tons and are now used in shipyards throughout the world.

3 A

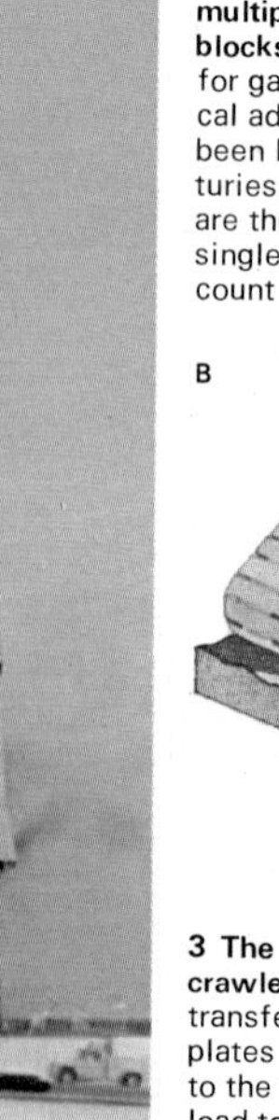

USA
USA

B

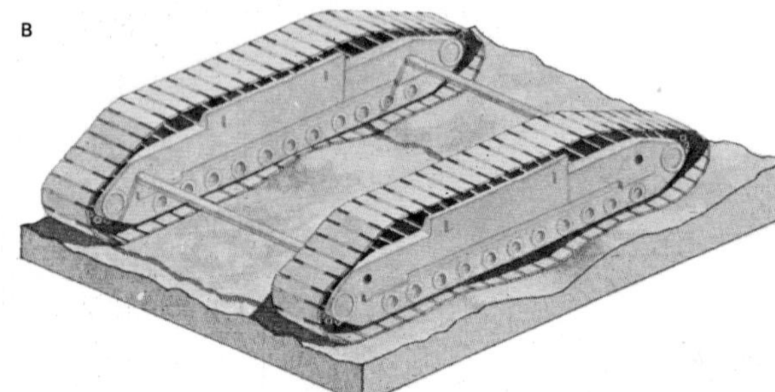

3 The caterpillar crawler mechanically transfers linked plates from the back to the front for the load to roll over them [B]. By increasing link width, ground loading is reduced. The motive force is also supplied through the wheels and track. This technique was chosen to transport the 6,000-ton US Saturn moon rockets [A].

thousands of tons, once started moving, also have to be stopped. For this reason, when coefficients of friction are low, suitable braking systems must be incorporated. After a ship is launched, strong chains and cables are needed to stop it.

Any conventional system can be used for moving power, providing that it can overcome the frictional forces that remain. When large cranes, such as portal cranes [2], are used to move a load from one point to another, they are merely lifting the load to reduce the coefficient of friction between it and the ground. This means that stresses are then put into the ground at chosen points, which have previously been strengthened to bear the loads.

Strengthening the surface

A third difficulty concerns the amount of preparation required for the surface on which the load is to be moved. This involves a calculation of the maximum permissible ground loading. For many materials this quantity is known—for example, compacted gravel will withstand a ground loading of 3.3 tons per square foot and wet sand 0.55 tons per square foot. At greater loadings the gravel or sand "collapses" and the load sinks. The loading is a pressure—a weight on a given area—and for a given load increasing the area of contact obviously lowers the pressure. This is why snowshoes support a man on loose snow whereas in ordinary boots he would sink.

In most heavy load-moving techniques there must be a way of spreading point loads. But even this is not a complete answer to ground-loading limitations. A hovercraft or air-cushion system that can carry loads over water has been known slowly to bury itself in dry sand as the sand is blown out from under the load.

It rapidly becomes clear that there is no universal way of moving a variety of loads over various surfaces for different applications. The answers to the problems illustrated here are merely a few modern solutions—a portal crane to lift a ship structure, caterpillar crawlers to move the Saturn rocket, and air-cushion units to move the stadium stands.

KEY

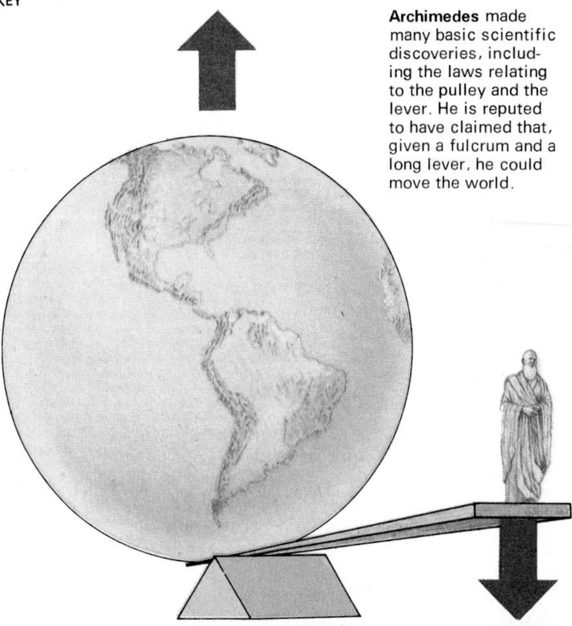

Archimedes made many basic scientific discoveries, including the laws relating to the pulley and the lever. He is reputed to have claimed that, given a fulcrum and a long lever, he could move the world.

4 A

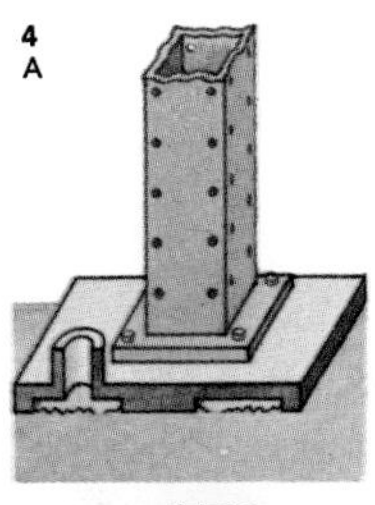

B

C

HAWAII

4 The air-cushion technique uses high air pressure underneath a load to lift the load slightly so that air can escape [A]. This continually escaping air acts as a bearing for the load and very low coefficients of friction can be obtained. The loading is spread over the area of the cushion. The Oahu Stadium in Hawaii was designed so that the stands could be moved from a rectangular shape [B] for football to a diamond shape [C] for baseball. The air-cushion system was chosen because it reduces friction. Problems on the smooth surface have arisen because of wind loadings and slopes that could cause the loads to run away. Movable friction grippers are used for braking the stands.

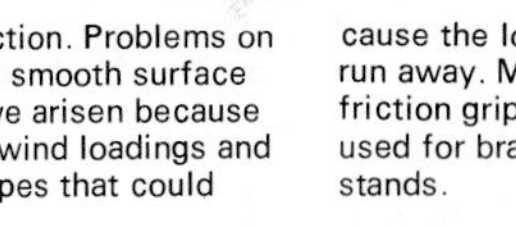

5 A

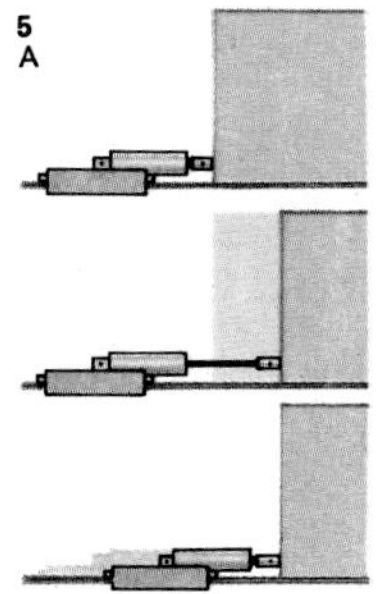

B

5 Hydraulic jacks can move extremely large loads, such as this 4,000-ton ship section [B], if they have reaction points. Hydranautic gripper jacks provide these by using hydraulic forces to give grip as well as push [A]. The sequence shows the grippers being pulled up behind the load and repeatedly locked into position.

6 A

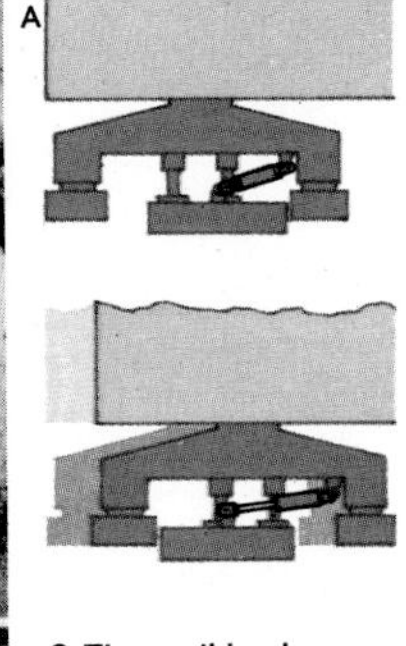

B

6 The walking beam uses two "footprints," that take the load alternately [A]. The area of the footprint can be designed to suit any ground loading. By choosing appropriate geometry, the walking beam can be made to move in any direction and also to rotate. Four walking beams carry and rotate this oil platform module [B].

Electronic devices

Electronics is the science that deals with electric currents moving in components such as tubes, transistors, diodes, cathode ray tubes, and many others. When various components are assembled to make circuits to perform specific tasks the resulting apparatus is an electronic device.

Our world is increasingly dependent upon electronic devices of all kinds—in industry, commerce, and the home. The devices themselves are legion, yet the types of components from which they are constructed are relatively few. Today, electronic circuit designers prefer to use solid-state components such as transistors and integrated circuits because they are smaller, cheaper, and more reliable than vacuum tubes. High-power applications, for which there are no solid-state equivalents, are exceptions. A transistor is a discrete electronic component that, with other transistors, capacitors, and resistors, can be wired to form a circuit. In an integrated circuit all such components are formed in a single "chip" of semiconductor material only a few millimeters across.

From the countless applications of electronics the eight devices described here demonstrate the possibilities of electronic devices, which are continually being invented throughout the industrialized world.

Electronics and light

Optoelectronics is the name given to the combination of optical and electronic techniques and hardware. A typical application is a method of counting on mass-production lines. In this, a beam of light is repeatedly interrupted by the products moving along a conveyor belt. The light pulses so produced are focused onto a photoelectric cell, to be counted electronically.

Another labor-saving application of optoelectronics is the remote control of a television set [1]. Basically the system is a torch-like hand-held device. Merely by switching on, directing the light beam at specially fitted "light-control" positions on the TV set, and turning the rotary control, it is possible to adjust the volume, contrast, and channel received. With such a device a viewer can control his television set without moving from his chair.

About 20 percent of modern cameras now feature optoelectronic circuits, mostly to control shutter speed [3]. These techniques enable even the most inexperienced photographer to be sure of getting the exposure time right, whatever the light conditions. Some cameras now incorporate automatic systems that prevent the photographer from making an exposure if there is not enough light. Usually, the light sensor is a cadmium sulfide (CdS) photoconductive cell. Its spectral response (the range of light to which it is sensitive) matches that of modern photographic emulsions, and so this cell is ideal for automatic exposure.

Electronic digital clocks

Unlike mechanical digital clocks, the all-electronic variety is silent. It is designed around several integrated circuits and uses the alternating electricity supply to get the necessary pulses of current. For greater accuracy a crystal-controlled oscillator can be used. The pulses are eventually used to

CONNECTIONS

See also
1548 Basic electronic principles
1546 Semiconductors
1670 Automatic control
1672 How computers work
1674 What computers can do
920 Crime detection

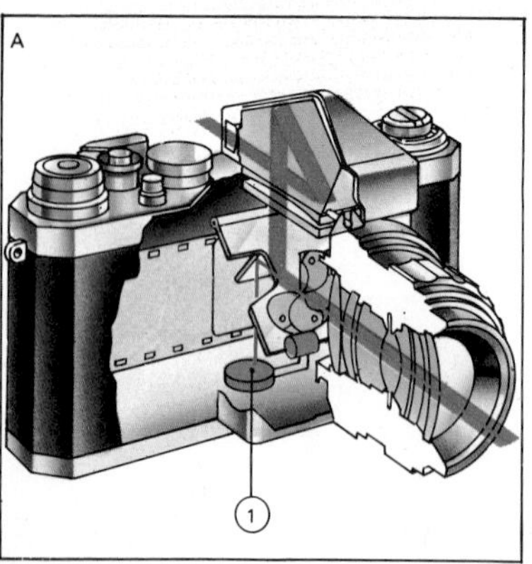
1
3
6
1
4
2
5
7
8

1 In an optical remote controller, a multivibrator [1] produces pulses [2] using a rotary control [3]. The pulses are amplified [4] and modulate light to produce a set of saw-tooth pulses [5]. These are received by a photo-transistor [6] in the TV, amplified [7], and used to work a trigger to re-form the pulse shapes [8]. This signal can then be used to control the channel selection or volume of the receiver.

2 A metal locater works by subtracting two supersonic frequencies to produce an audio frequency in headphones. One frequency is produced by an oscillator including the search coil and a capacitor. The other is produced by internal circuitry. When the search coil is not near a metal object a note is heard. As soon as metal is located, the note changes because the coil's inductance has changed.

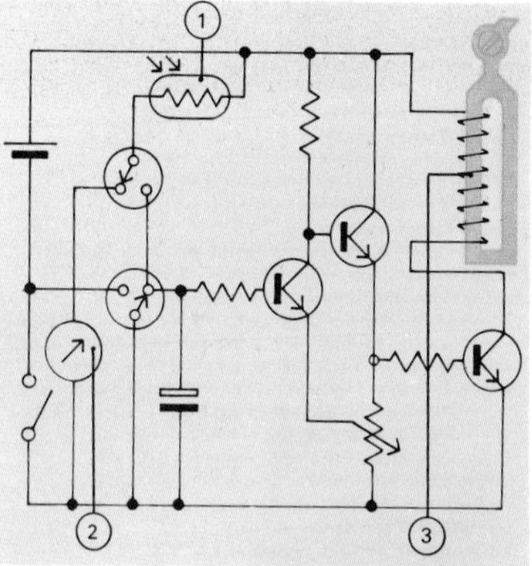
3
A
1

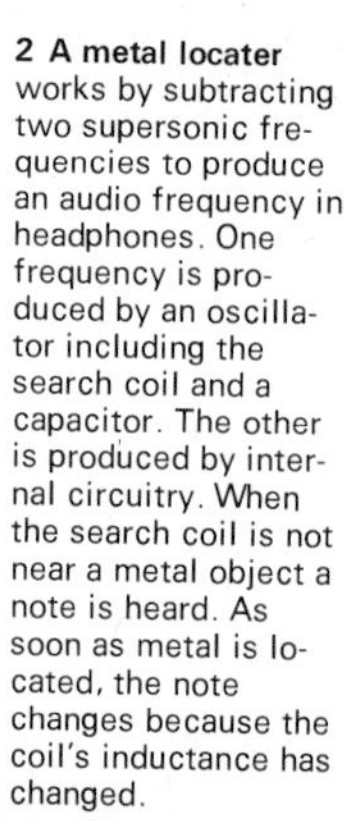
B
1
2
3

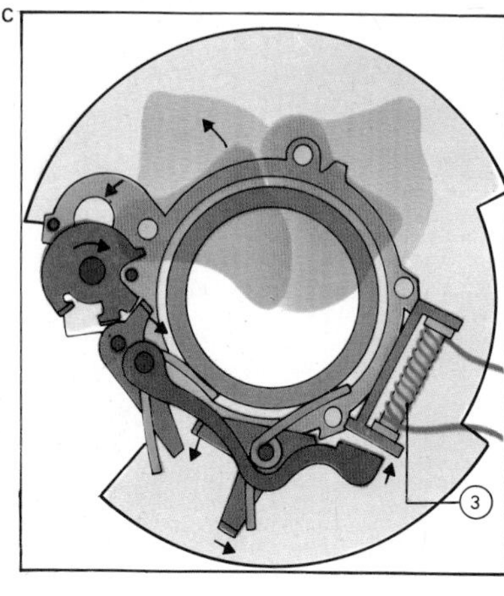
C
3

3 An automatic camera shutter makes the correct exposure for a perfect photograph. The light path diagram [A] shows how some of the incident light is reflected onto a photosensitive cell [1]. This is part of the electronic shutter-control circuit [B]. Initially, the cell output powers an exposure meter [2], but is switched into the timing circuit immediately before the exposure. The shutter [C] has an electromagnetic release mechanism [3].

4
A
0 1 4

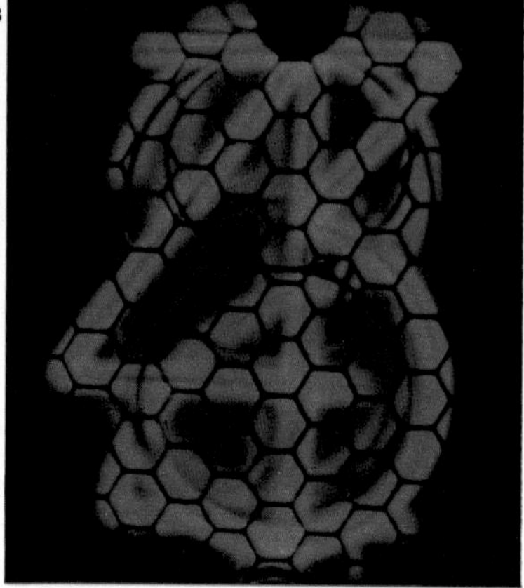
B

4 A modern digital counting device [A] indicates numerals with groups of light-emitting diodes shaped to form the numbers 0 to 9 and activated under the control of the counter circuitry. Older digital displays employed "Nixie" glow tubes [B] having ten wire cathodes shaped as numerals. Activation of a voltage between the common tube anode and one of the cathodes would electrically ionize the gas within the tube in the shape of the selected numeral.

energize a series of light-emitting diodes (LEDs). These LEDs are grouped to form the numbers 0 to 9. Circuitry within the clock causes the appropriate numbers to glow, displaying the time in digital form on a 12- or 24-hour basis. The division between hours and minutes (and between minutes and seconds, if seconds are included) can be either another LED or simply shown by appropriate spacing of the LEDs in groups. Similar types of displays are used on electronic counters, such as those used in Geiger counters and electrostatic photocopying machines [4A]. An older method of digital display utilized "Nixie" vacuum tubes [4B] with internal cathodes shaped as numbers. The latest method of time indication uses liquid crystal displays. In these, a liquid crystal film is sandwiched between two parallel glass plates and there is a light source in front of or behind the display. When an electric field is applied to the plates the liquid becomes milky and different numbers can be formed. This type of display is used in some electronic pocket calculators and digital watches.

Detecting metals and thieves

There are two ways of finding old coins, or something more valuable, buried in the ground. The traditional method is to dig. But the modern way is to use a metal locater [2]. It gives a clear audible signal when a metal object is below the surface.

Robbery is an increasing menace to modern industry and commerce, so the sophistication of anti-theft devices must keep pace. Electronics play a dominant role in this field, with experts continuously devising new ways of preventing or detecting criminal acts. A jeweler's shop [5], for example, may have one or more electronic devices to thwart thieves. In addition to round-the-clock visual observation using closed-circuit television cameras, other anti-theft devices detect changes in air pressure, capacitance, or vibration. An output from any one of these can sound an alarm at a nearby police station or at a private security organization. The radio signals to police cars—even transmitted images of fingerprints and suspects—all make use of modern electronic devices.

KEY

Audio units are a fast-growing part of the domestic electronics industry. This stereo music player incorporates a radio tuner, a cassette recorder, and a record turntable. To make it into a complete stereo system it is necessary to connect only a pair of loudspeaker enclosures. When dealing with a quadraphonic system, four speakers would be needed at equal distance from the listener. When an audio system is capable of reproducing sound very close to the original program material, then the term high fidelity, (or "hi-fi") is used to describe it, rather than "audio."

5

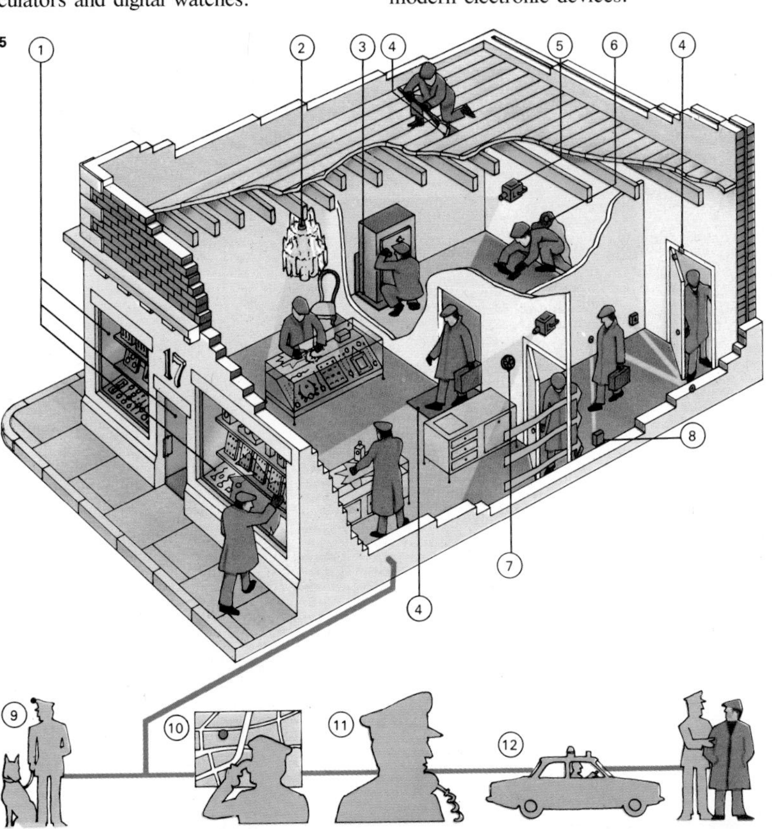
1
2
3
4
5
6
4
17
8
7
4
9
10
11
12

5 Electronic anti-theft devices operate by electrodes [1] attached to glass, detecting capacitance changes as the glass shatters. Changes in surrounding light are detected by a phototransistor [2]. A safe and a wire beneath it form a capacitor [3], which is altered by intruders, activating the alarm. Contact devices [4] make or break circuits. A TV camera [5] is linked to a security display. An electromagnetic detector [6] senses vibrations. A fan maintains low pressure; as a door opens a pressure-sensitive diaphragm [7] detects pressure increase. An ultraviolet or infrared beam is reflected by mirrors onto a photoelectric cell [8]; the current generated changes when the beam is interrupted. The alarm is relayed to security guards [9]. An autodialer [10] alerts a police station. The message relayed by radio [11] is received by a patrol car [12].

6 A

ZOOM
22.5-90mm

B

6 A modern closed-circuit TV camera makes use of miniaturized electronic components and circuits. Its zoom lens [A] is worked electrically by small motors. It uses integrated circuits and other components mounted on printed circuit boards, which are located along the sides of the camera case for easy access and maintenance. As a result, the whole camera [B] is light and compact.

7

CLASSIC
CLASSIC

7 An intercom system has an interesting feature—the use of a single unit as both loudspeaker and microphone. A loudspeaker in shape and construction is designed to serve as a microphone as well. In the home, intercoms are often used as baby alarms while parents, or babysitter, watch television. In large houses, or even small ones where there are several levels, an intercom system can solve a number of communication problems.

Automatic control

In 1788 James Watt (1736–1819) applied his fly-ball governor to maintain the speed of a steam engine—it was probably the first mechanism specifically designed to act as a controller [Key]. Eighty years later James Clerk-Maxwell (1831–79) supplied the mathematical theory of the governor and laid the foundation for the modern science of automatic control. Today machines from household appliances to supersonic airliners are controlled automatically. The ultimate development would be a humanoid robot—an electronic and mechanical copy of a human being. But the human brain is so complex that even a primitive mechanical man is still only a dream.

Open and closed loops

There are the two basic categories of automatic control systems, the open and closed loops. An open-loop system [1] is one that does not involve any feedback. Feedback is the routing of information from the output end of a device back to the chief operating part to control its workings. There are dozens of domestic appliances with open-loop controls. These include automatic dishwashers, record changers, and washing machines. They follow a preset "program" and perform a series of operations in an ordered sequence.

In closed-loop automatic control systems there is negative feedback to bring conditions back to a stable state. An electric thermostat, for example, can detect the temperature produced by an electric heating appliance; when a preset upper value is reached, the thermostat cuts off the current. Conversely, positive feedback leads to instability or oscillation, as when a rock group's microphones pick up the output from the loudspeakers and produce a screaming sound.

The human body has some remarkable examples of biological feedback systems. To maintain conditions for the various life processes under the most favorable conditions the body follows the principle known as homeostasis. This principle ensures that the status quo is maintained in the organism—for example, the temperature of the human body [5] is maintained within limits, despite variations in the local environment.

It was not until the twentieth century that feedback systems could be applied over the whole of industry. With the invention of the triode and other vacuum tubes it became possible to amplify the tiny electronic signals provided by various types of transducers, which convert a physical property, such as temperature, into electricity.

Transducers and servomechanisms

Engineers are now able to design electronic circuits capable of detecting extremely small changes in the signals from transducers in domestic, industrial, and medical equipment. These include changes in light intensity (automatic cameras), temperature (refrigerators) [2], liquid flow (kidney machines), gas pressure (heart-lung machines), thickness (steel and paper mills), and color (paint production). By amplifying and processing the error signals provided by transducers, and feeding back an amplified signal to earlier stages in the process, automatic control is achieved.

CONNECTIONS

See also
1660 The factory and assembly line
1674 What computers can do
1718 How an airplane works
1722 Space vehicles

1 With open-loop control [A] there is no feedback from the system. If, in this hotwater system, the valve is set to provide a flow of water at a particular temperature, but incoming water temperature or gas pressure varies later, then output temperature will vary. In a closed-loop system [B] a link between the output temperature and the cold supply is established, providing feedback control and steady temperature.

2 A refrigerant gas is compressed [1] and changed to liquid [2]. The valve [3] maintains pressure behind it but as soon as the gas passes the valve, pressure drops. The refrigerant is well above its boiling point at the new pressure and so some vaporizes, cooling the interior to below freezing and eventually causing the thermostat [4] to switch off the compressor. Rising warm air later causes the thermostat to switch the compressor on again, cooling the refrigerator.

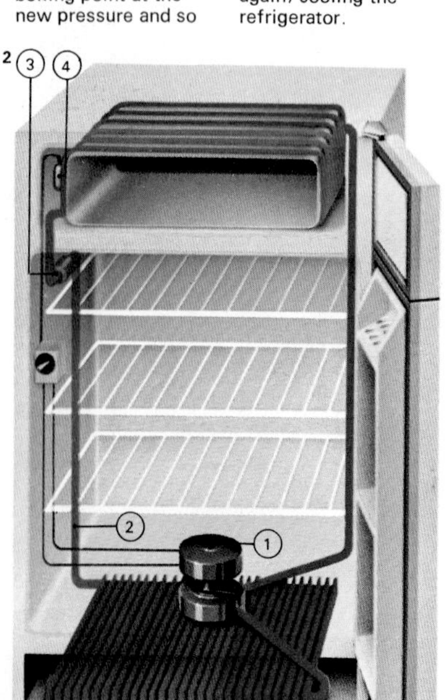

3 A servo [2] coupled to a ship's gyro [1], can produce error signals when the vessel deviates from a preset bearing. These signals are passed to a servo amplifier [3], which activates a servomotor [4] driving a rotary/linear converter [5]. This turns the rudder [6] to correct the deviation. As it turns, feedback [7] returns the gyro and its servo to its original position, thereby reducing the signal to zero.

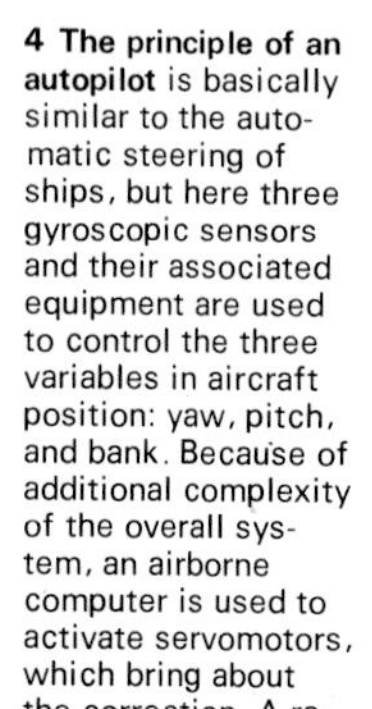

4 The principle of an autopilot is basically similar to the automatic steering of ships, but here three gyroscopic sensors and their associated equipment are used to control the three variables in aircraft position: yaw, pitch, and bank. Because of additional complexity of the overall system, an airborne computer is used to activate servomotors, which bring about the correction. A radio or radar link to the computer allows for ground-controlled landings.

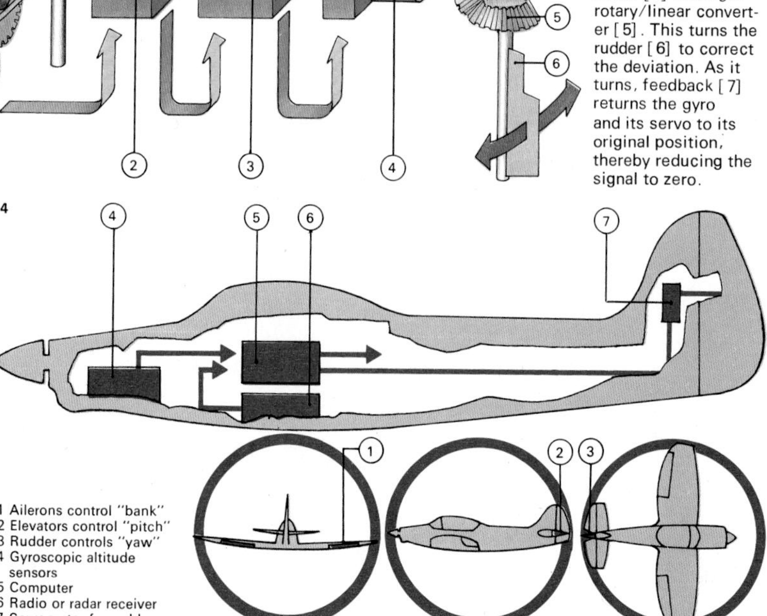

1 Ailerons control "bank"
2 Elevators control "pitch"
3 Rudder controls "yaw"
4 Gyroscopic altitude sensors
5 Computer
6 Radio or radar receiver
7 Servomotor for rudder

A servomechanism, like all feedback systems, is concerned with automatic control. But the term is usually reserved to describe equipment in which control is maintained over the relative alignment of two remote shafts. Typical examples are radar-controlled guns or missile launchers, automatic steering of ships [3], autopilots [4], and controlled machine tools.

By using servos it is possible to detect small changes in the rotation of shafts. Like other types of electrical transducers servos provide error signals and these signals can be amplified and fed back to a servomotor to control shaft alignment. Much power amplification is needed to convert a tiny error signal into a voltage sufficient to drive a correcting device. The radar signal reflected back from a target might be measured in microwatts, whereas the power needed to move a gun turret can be measured in kilowatts.

Cybernetics and robots

The science of cybernetics has no well defined area of activity—it is concerned with control and communication generally. Cybernetics includes in its scope both engineering and biological feedback systems and is derived from various aspects of mathematics, physiology, electrical and computer engineering, and psychology.

One practical application of cybernetics enables disabled people to control their own movements. One of the best-known workers in this new and socially useful area of activity is the British scientist Meredith Thring (1915–), who has designed and built many prototype machines. These include a machine to carry a seated adult up stairs and a chair for paralytics [6].

Robots have fascinated people since the dawn of engineering. But the full possibilities of robot design have had to wait for the comparatively recent introduction of tiny integrated circuits—like other machines, notably the computers, the efficiency of the robot is only as good as its human designer or programmer. Now many more machines and domestic appliances can be made to behave more like robots and yet retain their familiar shapes [7].

KEY

Designed by James Watt in 1788, this original fly-ball governor controlled the speed of a steam engine. The shaft [1] is driven by the steam engine, causing the revolving weights [2] to move outward under the action of centrifugal force. As they move, the control linkage [3] gradually closes the steam valve [4] between the boiler and the engine until a point of equilibrium is reached. If the engine speeds up for any reason the weights move farther out, throttling back the steam and slowing down the engine [5]. As the weights move downward and inward [6] the control linkage [7] gradually opens the valve again [8]. Overall, the result is a working engine whose speed is largely independent of its load.

5

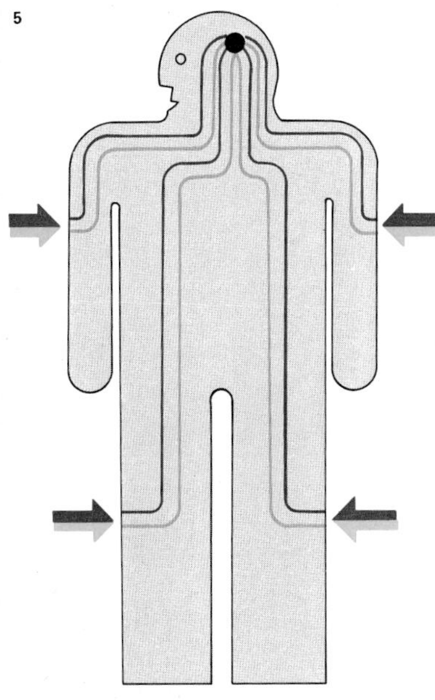

5 Heat changes in the local environment arrive at the body's hypothalamus, an area in the brain. Biological feedback signals trigger the appropriate response to maintain steady body temperature. If it becomes too hot, sweating begins, more blood is brought to the skin surface, and muscle activity is reduced. If the body becomes too cold, less blood flows to the skin surface, sweating is suppressed, and shivering starts.

6

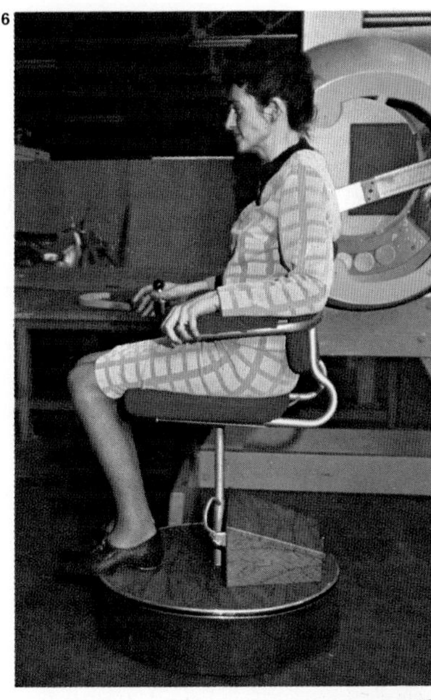

6 By using this mobile chair, developed by Meredith Thring, paralytics can move around. The controls are devised to enable them to operate the chair despite their physical condition.

7 A robot lawn mower is driven by a battery-powered motor [1]. The unit has a sensing coil [2] that locates a cable below the surface of the lawn, in a way similar to that of a metal detector. A steering motor [3] is controlled by electronic circuitry so that the lawn mower is always directly above the cable. By placing the cable correctly the whole lawn can be cut and the mower returned.

7

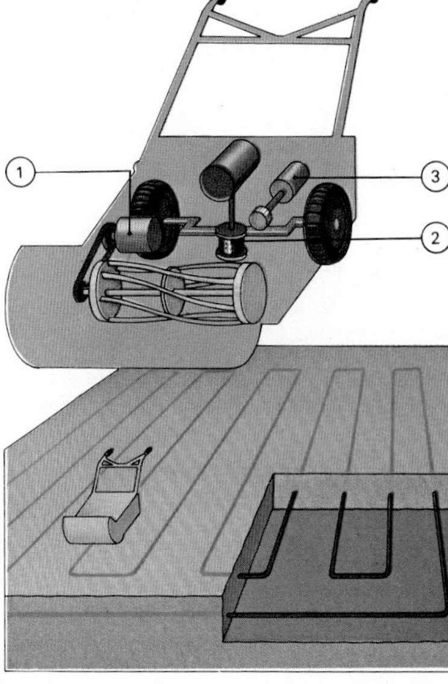

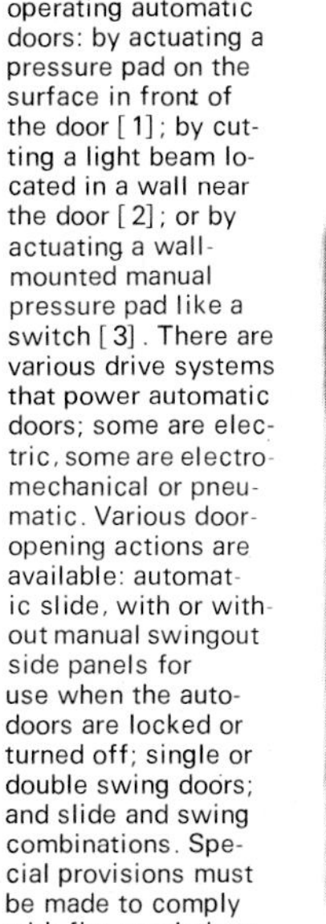

8 There are three common ways of operating automatic doors: by actuating a pressure pad on the surface in front of the door [1]; by cutting a light beam located in a wall near the door [2]; or by actuating a wall-mounted manual pressure pad like a switch [3]. There are various drive systems that power automatic doors; some are electric, some are electromechanical or pneumatic. Various door-opening actions are available: automatic slide, with or without manual swingout side panels for use when the auto-doors are locked or turned off; single or double swing doors; and slide and swing combinations. Special provisions must be made to comply with fire regulations.

8

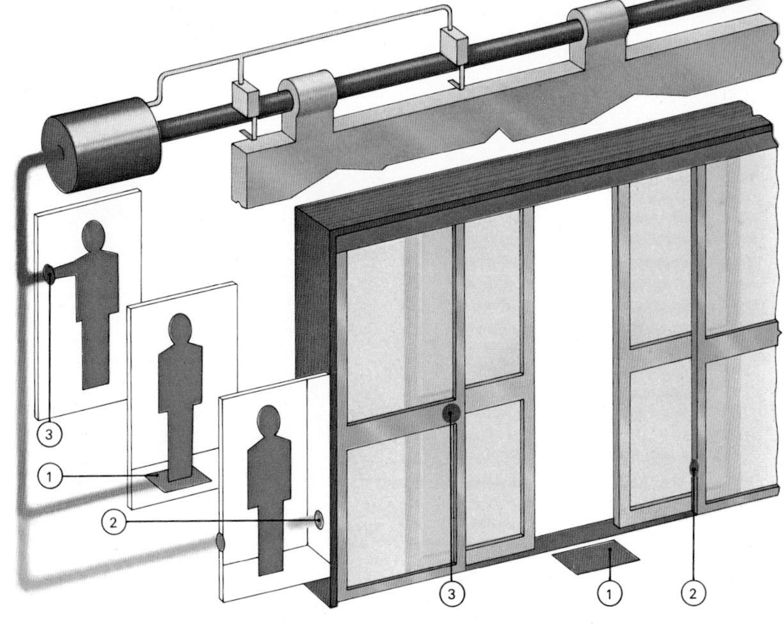

9 An electronic tortoise can even "feed" itself, when its batteries run down, by plugging itself into the socket of a battery charger and replenishing its cells. Features of this electronic animal include a sensor for locating the charger [1]; pins to connect with the charger socket [2]; obstacle detector [3]; driving wheels [4]; steering wheels [5]; and steering sensors (photocells).

9

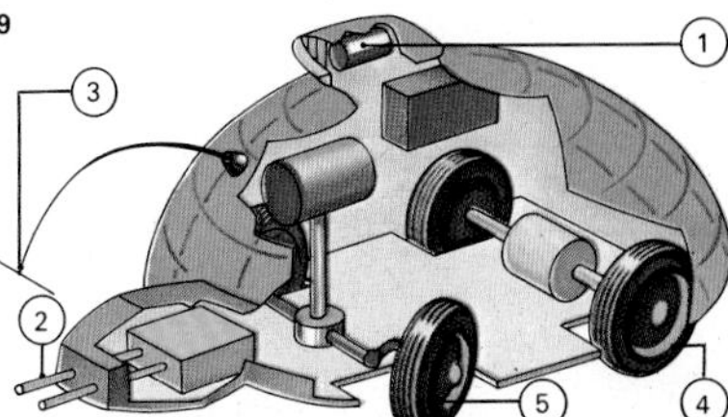

How computers work

Most people regard the computer as an electronic marvel, yet the principle on which it works is relatively simple. The heart of the computer is an arithmetic and logical unit (which adds, subtracts, multiplies, divides, and compares numbers at high speed by electronic means) and a memory unit, in which many thousands of numbers can be electronically stored and recalled on command.

Programming the computer

The use of the computer is based on the technique known as programming—the conversion of the problem the computer is to solve, or the tasks it is to perform, into the simple steps the computer can carry out. A programmer defines precisely what has to be done in each succeeding step. The value of the computer over the human being lies in its ability to work without error and at immense speed; it can carry out hundreds of thousands of calculations every second, storing intermediate results in its memory, and recalling them instantly when required. The various instructions for the stages in the program are stored in the computer memory in numerical form for instant access.

To program, for example, the multiplication of 683 by 67 (an unwieldy sum for an amateur human mathematician, although much too simple to be worth feeding into a computer), the computer would first reduce the number 67 to simpler components, probably as powers of ten, thus: $67 = (6 \times 10^1) + (7 \times 10^0)$. So 683×67 becomes $(6 \times 10^2)\,[(6 \times 10^1) + (7 \times 10^0)] + (8 \times 10^1)\,[(6 \times 10^1) + (7 \times 10^0)] + (3 \times 10^0)\,[(6 \times 10^1) + (7 \times 10^0)]$. Doing a multiplication problem in this way means remembering the method and answers to each step. This is why the computer needs a memory. Also future operations can be made to depend on the result of the calculation so far—that is, the computer makes decisions.

The binary system

Ordinary calculations are carried out using the decimal system, with the numbers 1 to 9 and 0. A computer can be designed to do the same, but electronic engineers found that computers could be designed more simply using the binary system, which employs only two numbers—0 and 1. This system is simple because an electric current can be switched on and off, using "off" for 0 and "on" for 1. Because the binary system uses only these two numbers it contains many more digits than its decimal equivalent [3]. This makes calculations in binary extremely unwieldy for a human being, but a computer calculates so fast that the length of numbers is of no importance.

The binary system also makes the memory much simpler to design. Most modern computers have a magnetic core memory [4]. Each core is a tiny magnetizable ferrite ring, usually about a millimeter (0.04in) in diameter, which can be magnetized by passing an electric current through wires inside it. The polarity of magnetism depends on the direction of the current, one direction standing for 0, the other for 1. A computer memory has thousands of these tiny cores and, provided groups of them have a specific "address," numbers can be stored as collections of individual digits and recalled when required.

CONNECTIONS

See also

1674 What computers can do
1668 Electronic devices
1548 Basic electronic principles
1822 Everyday machines and mechanisms: 4
666 How the brain work

1 Charles Babbage (1791–1871), an English mathematician, was the first to realize that if a machine could be built to remember numbers and recognize simple arithmetic situations, it could then be programmed to carry out complex calculations automatically. His ingenious "Difference Engine," part of which is shown here, was able to compute complicated tables, although it lacked a memory. A later invention of his, resoundingly named the "Analytic Engine," would have been a true computer but was never completed because mechanical engineers of the time were unable to meet the specifications of his design.

2 The electronic desk calculator is built on the lines of the modern computer. The numerical and function keys comprise its input device, the display and printout facility giving its output. Like the computer it contains an arithmetic unit and an electronic memory but the latter is fairly small, thus limiting the scope of the instrument to simple calculations. Calculator memories vary widely.

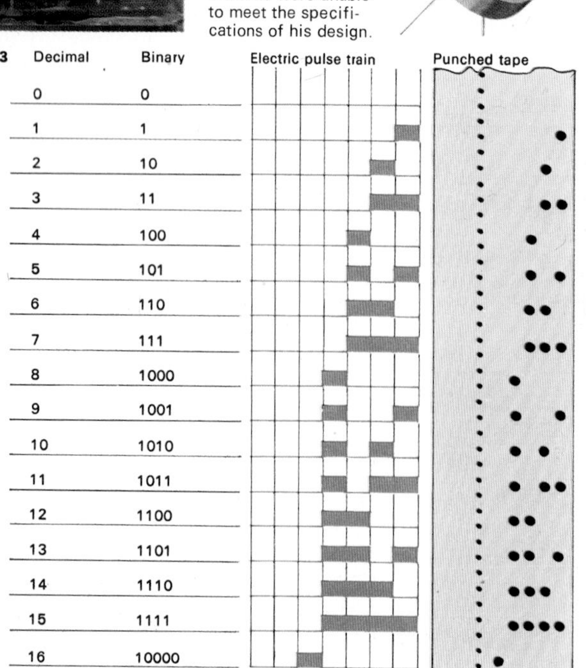

Electric pulse train
Punched tape

Decimal	Binary
0	0
1	1
2	10
3	11
4	100
5	101
6	110
7	111
8	1000
9	1001
10	1010
11	1011
12	1100
13	1101
14	1110
15	1111
16	10000

3 The binary system is the simple secret behind the computer. The paper tape [right] shows one method of recording binary numbers. Binary works on the same principle as the decimal system, but in ascending orders of 2 rather than 10. Decimal units are counted up to 9 and then carried to the "tens" column where they are recorded as 1, but binary units are counted only up to 1. To add another 1 (total, 2) the 1 is carried to the "twos" column, indicating a 2. Thus 10 in binary means one "2" plus no "1s"—total, 2. The third column in binary (signifying "hundreds" in decimal calculation) is the "fours" column, thus 101=4+0+1=5.

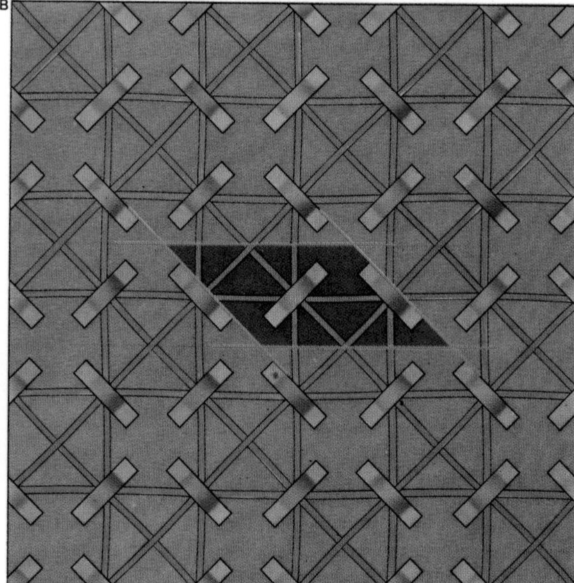

4A
Write
Read
Write
B

4 A computer memory consists of ferrite cores threaded on so-called address and read-out wires. Each core can be "written on" by passing simultaneous currents along the vertical and horizontal wires that intersect it [A]. This magnetizes the core in one direction indicating a "1." Changing current direction reverses the polarity, thus indicating a "0." The third wire is the "read" wire [B]. In fact the unit cell of such a memory contains two cores (one such pair is in the dark area) which differ only as do mirror-images. A typical array of cores might number 10,000, all identical, and all threaded on a 100 × 100 matrix, each core being defined by its coordinates. A computer memory may contain many arrays.

The magnetic core memory is widely used because it is extremely fast and reliable, but it is only one of several kinds. A solid-state memory is even faster. The computer's own memory is often augmented by a slower back-up store, of which magnetic tape and magnetic disk systems are the most widely used. These make possible the storage of a virtually unlimited quantity of information.

The processing unit

Because a computer cannot read more than one number at a time the basis of computer operation is an electronic "clock" producing an endless series of identical pulses—up to millions every second. In one type of computer, these pulses are switched on or off, one after another, to indicate the successive components of a binary number. So the binary number 100110 (which in decimal is expressed as 38) is read as "no pulse, pulse, pulse, no pulse, no pulse, pulse," the unit digit being read first, as in all arithmetic calculations. Each number in a computer circuit is thus a set of pulses, and to avoid confusion each set must have the same total number. If the full set, in this case, were 16 pulses, the six-digit example would be completed by ten more "no pulses." As each number is defined, it is stored in the memory core where it stays until the next number (or series of numbers) is also stored and ready for use [Key].

Once these numbers have been read in (automatically, controlled by the program), the computer can then be made to juggle them in accordance with a program already stored in its memory. If two numbers in store are to be added, a code number in the calculation program (previously stored in another part of the memory) switches the computer circuits so that the two numbers in store are fed together, pulse by pulse, into an adder circuit. The adder combines the incoming pulses, carrying where necessary, and produces an output train of pulses that defines the added number.

Despite their great flexibility of operation and application, all computers depend for their efficiency on the ability of the programmer to simplify problems.

KEY

Input device

Central processor

Output device

Memory

The heart of any computer installation is a processing unit (essentially a high-speed calculator), which operates in conjunction with a memory unit. Data are fed into the computer by means of an input device that converts information and instructions into trains of electronic pulses representing numbers. These data are often fed in by means of punched cards or paper tape on which the position of the holes forms a code that the computer can "read." Operators prepare the cards on key punch machines, paper tape usually being punched on a special form of typewriter. When more information is to be stored than can be accommodated in the computer's own memory, this can be transferred to magnetic tape or disk. An output device converts the electronic pulses back into information that may be printed on paper, displayed on a screen, or communicated via other media.

5 A modern computer installation consists of a number of interconnected machines. Data can be fed into the system by various input devices such as a keyboard (resembling a typewriter), a punched-card reader, a punched-tape reader, and a magnetic-tape input. An operator can even use a light pen to "draw" designs on the face of a cathode-ray tube. All input passes to the central processor and is stored in its memory or, if necessary, recorded in various back-up stores such as magnetic tape stores or ones using magnetic disks or magnetic drums. The operation of the computer is controlled by a program, which also has to be fed in and stored. The central processor consults the program as necessary to carry out its various tasks. Information produced by the computer is presented on an output device, such as a card punch, paper tape punch, or a visual display. Some displays have a cathode-ray-tube screen and some, called alpha-numeric displays, present information electronically as letters or numbers "written" on the screen. Printed information, known as "hard copy," is provided by some form of printout device. The most common is a line printer, which generates a whole line of typed copy at a time. Output information can also be provided on magnetic tape, possibly for feeding into another computer or for controlling a typesetting machine.

5

Magnetic tape stores
Tape control unit
Central processor
Control console
Disk control unit
Magnetic disk stores
Card punch
Card reader
Visual display unit
Line printer

What computers can do

The essence of a computer is an arithmetic unit that performs calculations and an electronic "memory" that stores numbers. The computer solves every problem as a series of extremely simple steps, using the memory to store both the details of the program to be followed and the results of each intermediate step while the program is being carried out. In practical terms there are two kinds of problems: those in which the power of the computer to carry out complex calculations at high speed is paramount, and those in which its capacity to store immense quantities of information is more important. To solve either kind there must be a means of communication between man and machine.

Information is commonly fed into a computer using a device that resembles a typewriter, which produces a typed record of the fed-in data as a check. Its main purpose is to produce electronic signals—a binary number for each letter and numeral—that the computer can "read." Alternatively it produces either a punched paper tape or a series of punched cards. These are subsequently fed into a "reader" that generates the required electronic binary numbers. By means of the teletypewriter the operator can feed data and instructions into the computer using a "code" that the computer is programmed to understand.

There are other means of communicating with a computer. One is the use of magnetic printed characters [5]. Another uses an optical "reader" that scans ordinary printed type, passing the information to the computer, which is programmed to "recognize" characters and numerals and convert them into its own language of binary numbers. A third employs a "light pen," with which the operator can trace over a diagram on the screen of a cathode ray tube, with the computer programmed to process the diagram as required [1].

Output devices in common use

There are three principal output devices in common use. The line printer is a high-speed typewriter operated directly by the computer. It prints a whole line simultaneously and can print 10 to 15 lines a second, each with 100 or more characters.

The plotter is an automatic computer-controlled drawing instrument. A pen moves across the paper under the control of an appropriate computer program, to record in graphical form the output of the calculations [6].

The visual display is a form of cathode ray tube (similar to that in a television set) on whose screen the computer may produce either "written" messages or drawings. This type of output is used where the operator needs continuously updated information but where a permanent record is not required. The display has numerous special applications such as in airport control, engineering design [1], and in teaching machines [7].

The computer's ability to calculate at high speed and store enormous quantities of information is being applied to everwidening fields of activity. In weather forecasting the main problem is to relate continually changing readings of temperature, humidity, and barometric pressure from numerous observation points and to build up a chart. If carried out manually, the work

CONNECTIONS

See also
1672 How computers work
1670 Automatic control
1660 The factory and assembly line
1722 Space vehicles
1782 Information retrieval
218 Forecasting

1 A computer can be programmed to simulate perspective. The designer traces the outline of an object with a light pen. The computer retains the spatial relationships of the object's shape in its memory.

2 Various forms of accounting are among the most common uses for computers. Banking, stock market transactions, wages control, and tax deductions can all be done rapidly by computer.

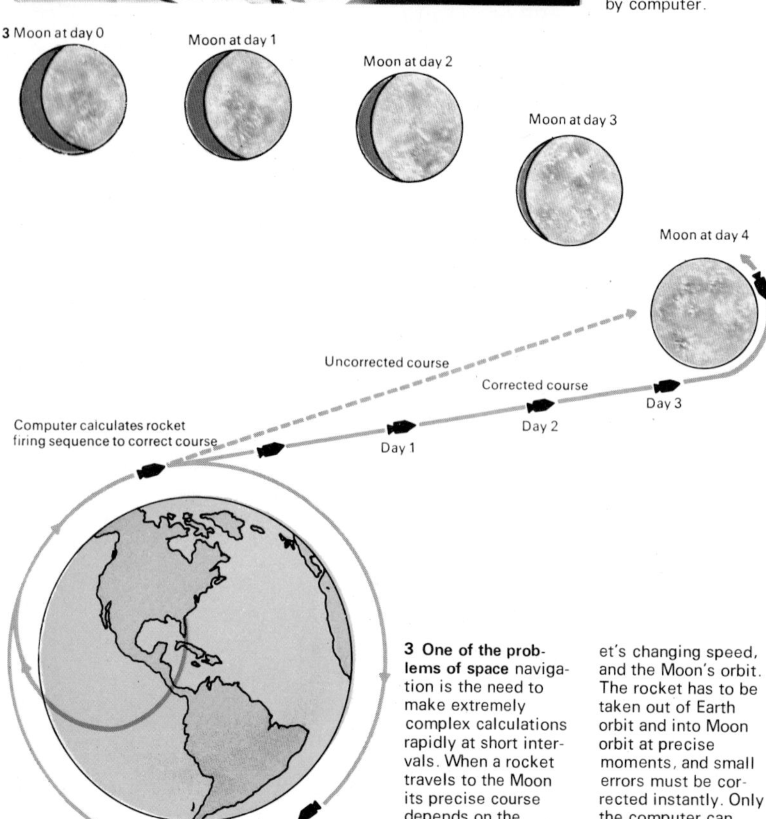
Moon at day 0
Moon at day 1
Moon at day 2
Moon at day 3
Moon at day 4
Uncorrected course
Corrected course
Computer calculates rocket firing sequence to correct course
Day 1
Day 2
Day 3

3 One of the problems of space navigation is the need to make extremely complex calculations rapidly at short intervals. When a rocket travels to the Moon its precise course depends on the Earth's spin and orbit at launch, the rocket's changing speed, and the Moon's orbit. The rocket has to be taken out of Earth orbit and into Moon orbit at precise moments, and small errors must be corrected instantly. Only the computer can calculate fast enough.

4 When an airline booking is made from a computer terminal it is not only the seat availability that is checked for each section of a long-distance flight. The computer can also be programmed to offer alternative flights that have seat vacancies. It first makes a provisional booking, then calculates the cost, asks for payment, makes the appropriate entry in the airline's accounts and prints the ticket for the flight with all relevant details. As the flow chart shows, there are a number of alternative paths in the program depending on the fulfillment of certain conditions.

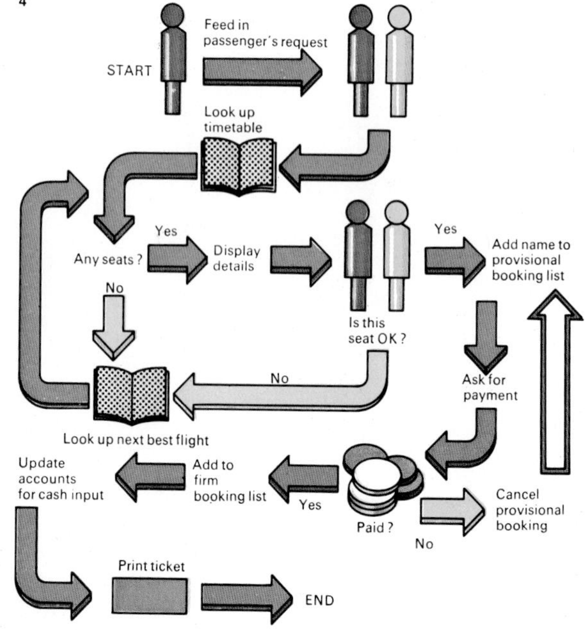
START
Feed in passenger's request
Look up timetable
Any seats ?
Yes
No
Display details
Is this seat OK ?
Yes
No
Add name to provisional booking list
Ask for payment
Look up next best flight
Paid ?
Yes
No
Add to firm booking list
Cancel provisional booking
Update accounts for cash input
Print ticket
END

can hardly be completed before new factors develop to affect the forecast. A computer can accept new data as fast as they are received and can produce an up-to-date weather forecast chart in minutes.

Computers used in engineering

The mathematics involved in the design of a modern long-span steel bridge is so complicated that it takes a team of engineers working with slide rules and tables several months to calculate the stresses and quantities necessary in the evaluation of a design. Today a computer, fed with data by two or three engineers, can complete the calculations in minutes—not only saving time but releasing experienced men for other work. A consulting engineer's computer can carry out the mathematics of reinforced and pre-stressed concrete design; it can also be programmed to specify the steel required for reinforcement and to print out the details for immediate use.

In antimissile defense, radar detects a missile a few minutes before its arrival. To destroy it a rocket must be fired, before the missile is visible, so that the rocket will intercept the missile. To calculate the trajectory of the missile from continuous radar data, and fire the antimissile rocket with the correct direction and elevation within a few seconds, is possible only by using the computer. The computer's ability to carry out complicated mathematics at high speed is used in space navigation [3].

Applications of "memory" computers

"Memory" computers also have numerous applications. These include the maintenance of details of licensed vehicles and drivers; world-wide airline bookings [4]; recording of personal bank accounts on magnetic tape, including automatic print-out of monthly statements and provision of cash-drawing facilities [Key]; accounts of gas and electricity users and telephone subscribers, including automatic preparation of invoices; and in-factory inventory accounting, where the smooth running of a production line depends upon the availability of raw materials and components in the quantities required at the moment needed.

KEY

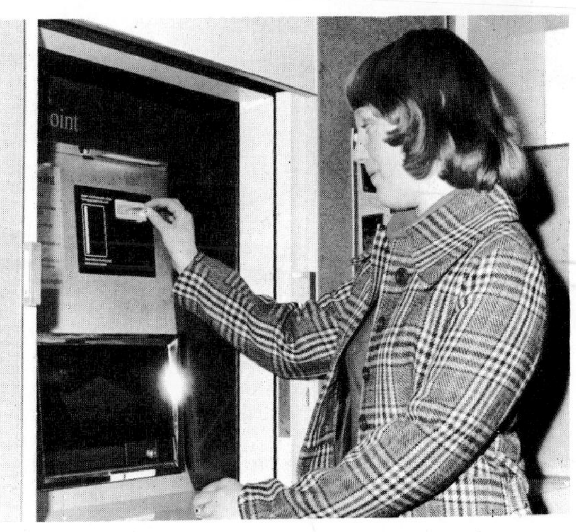

An automatic "teller," widely used to save customers' and bank clerks' time, typifies the use of computers in everyday life. The customer inserts his personal card in the machine, then presses buttons to "read in" his account number and the sum of money he wishes to withdraw. A central computer checks his balance before cash is dispensed.

5 The oddly shaped numerals used on checks are printed in magnetic ink and can be read by a computer reader as well as by humans. The numerals seen here are designed seven units wide and nine units high. The figures in line A below each magnetic numeral show the number of squares filled with magnetic ink in each vertical column. The electronic reader produces a pulse where four or more squares are filled and no pulse where three or less are occupied. Each magnetic numeral thus generates the binary numbers shown in line B. This is the computer's own language.

5

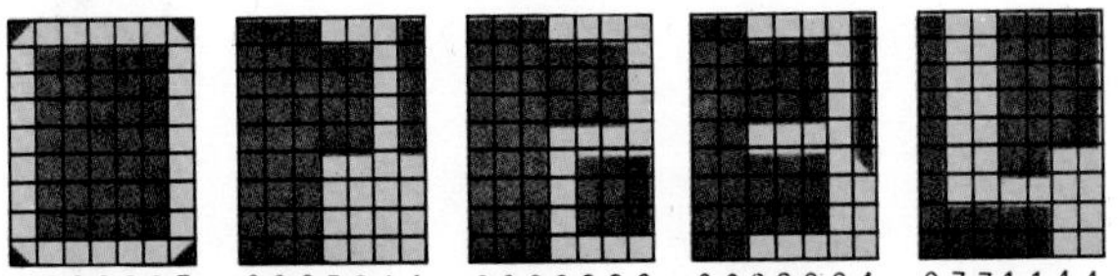

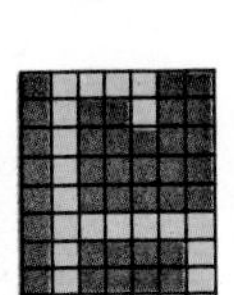

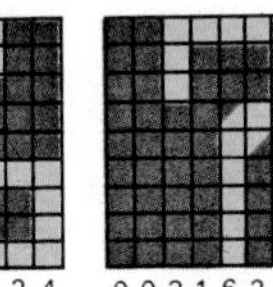

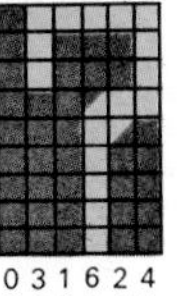

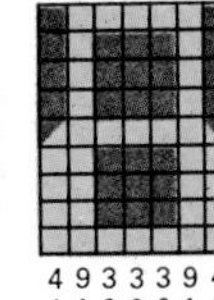

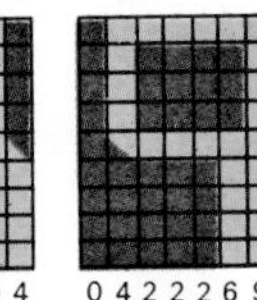

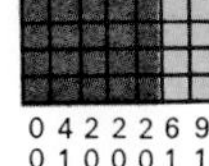

A	7222227	0005944	0006336	0033994	0771144
B	1000001	0001111	0001001	0000011	0110011

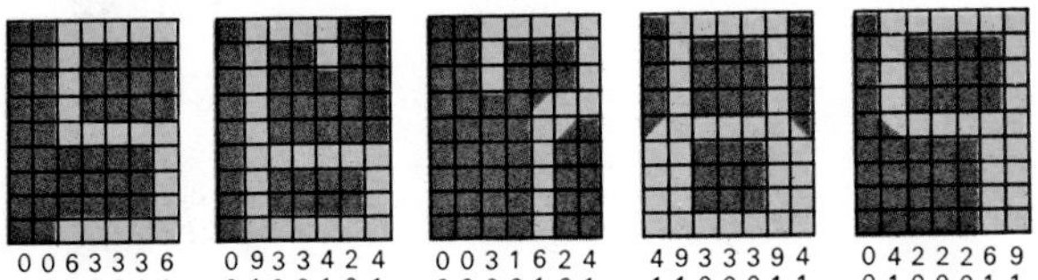

0063336	0933424	0031624	4933394	0422269
0010001	0100101	0000101	1100011	0100011

6 The "contours" of equal light intensity in a lecture hall are seen here. They were drawn by an automatic plotter controlled by a computer that was programmed to calculate these contours from data defining the position and power of the lights that the architect proposed to install. The "map" shows clearly where more light is needed and enables the engineer to correct the lighting plan.

6

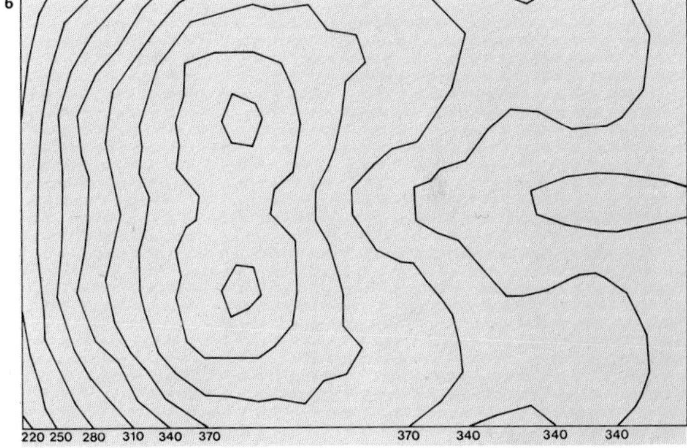
220 250 280 310 340 370
370 340 340 340

7 Teaching machines are designed to involve the student, who must respond to each step in the lesson before it proceeds. In early days machines told the student only whether his answer to a question was right or wrong. Later machines worked on programs that gave the student an explanation when a wrong answer was given, before proceeding with the lesson. The most recent machines go further. They assess the student's performance and adapt the lesson to his potential, relying on a mass of information and an ability to follow a complex branching program.

7

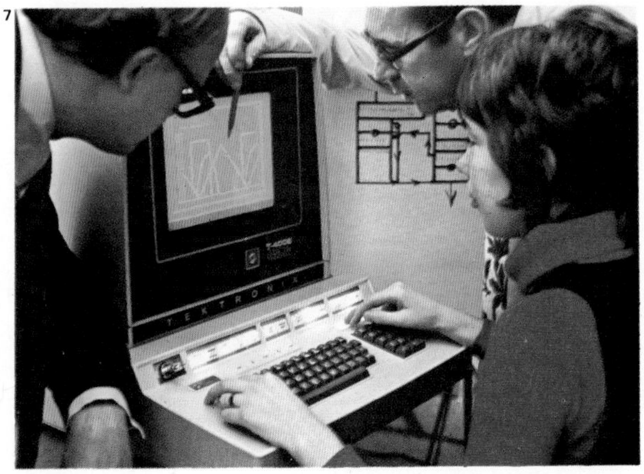

8

A

```
PAGE   1     AIMBR2/TXT

  1.  99999   021        2880       20  15   0
  2.  99999    11  315:57:13           44123                76  AIMBR2  1AIMBR2
  3.             152
  4.       00    121
  5.       11    131 The essence of a computer is an arithmetic
  6.       12    211 unit that performs calculations and an electronic
  7.       13    221 "memory" that stores numbers. The
  8.       21    231 computer solves every problem as a series of
  9.       22    311 extremely simple steps, using the memory to
 10.       23    321 store both the details of the program to be
 11.       31    331 followed and the results of each intermediate
 12.       32    411 step while the program is being carried out.
 13.       33    421 In practical terms there are two kinds of
 14.       41    431 problems: those in which the power of the
 15.       42    511 computer to carry out complex calculations
 16.       43    521 at high speed is paramount and those in
 17.       51    531 which its capacity to store immense quantities
 18.       52    611 of information is more important. To
 19.       53    621 solve either kind there must be a means of
 20.       61    631 communication between man and machine.
 21.       62    711   Information is commonly fed into a computer
 22.       63    721 using a device that resembles a typewriter.
 23.       71    731 which produces a typed record of the
 24.       72    811 fed-in data as a check. Its main purpose is to
 25.       73    821 produce electronic signals - a binary number
 26.       81    831 for each letter and numeral - that the computer
 27.       82    911 can "read". Alternatively it produces
 28.       83    921 either a punched paper tape or a series of
 29.       91    931 punched cards. These are subsequently fed
 30.       92   1011 into a "reader" that generates the required
 31.       93   1021 electronic binary numbers. By means of the
 32.      101   1031 teletypewriter the operator can feed data and
 33.      102   1111 instructions into the computer using a
 34.      103   1121 predetermined "code" that the computer is
 35.      111   1131 programmed to understand.
 36.      112   1211   There are other means of communicating
 37.      113   1221 with a computer. These inlude the use of
 38.      121   1231 magnetic printed characters [5]; an optical
 39.      122   1311 "reader" that scans ordinary printed type.
 40.      123   1321 passing the information to the computer
 41.      131   1331 which is programmed to "recognize" characters
 42.      132   1411 and numerals and convert them into its
 43.      133   1421 own language of binary numbers; and a "light
 44.      141   1431 pen", with which the operator can trace over
 45.      142   1511 a diagram on the screen of a cathode ray tube,
 46.      143   1521 with the computer programmed to process
 47.      151   1531 the diagram as required [1].
 48.      15299999] ****************************************************************
```

B

The essence of a computer is an arithmetic unit that performs calculations and an electronic "memory" that stores numbers. The computer solves every problem as a series of extremely simple steps, using the memory to store both the details of the program to be followed and the results of each intermediate step while the program is being carried out. In practical terms there are two kinds of problems: those in which the power of the computer to carry out complex calculations at high speed is paramount and those in which its capacity to store immense quantities of information is more important. To solve either kind there must be a means of communication between man and machine.

Information is commonly fed into a computer using a device that resembles a typewriter, which produces a typed record of the fed-in data as a check. Its main purpose is to produce electronic signals – a binary number for each letter and numeral – that the computer can "read". Alternatively it produces either a punched paper tape or a series of punched cards. These are subsequently fed into a "reader" that generates the required electronic binary numbers. By means of the teletypewriter the operator can feed data and instructions into the computer using a predetermined "code" that the computer is programmed to understand.

There are other means of communicating with a computer. These include the use of magnetic printed characters [5]; an optical "reader" that scans ordinary printed type, passing the information to the computer which is programmed to "recognize" characters and numerals and convert them into its own language of binary numbers; and a "light pen", with which the operator can trace over a diagram on the screen of a cathode ray tube, with the computer programmed to process the diagram as required [1].

8 When a book is to be printed the type is first set in a predetermined format that defines the width and length of each column. While the modern typesetting machine aids the operator in maintaining column width and inserts space automatically between words, it is the operator who must ensure that the rules of style are maintained. These rules lay down the system of paragraphing, punctuation, capitalization, the use of italic and bold typefaces, and hyphenation. Computer typesetting eliminates most of the intellectual effort required. The operator has only to type the copy accurately, the machine organizing the setting according to its program. It produces a coded proof, which is used by the proof-reader for checking errors in the usual way, corrections being fed into the computer before the type is set. The example shows the coded proof [A] and the finished print [B].

History of transportation

Transportation is probably our oldest technology, predating both house building and agriculture. There is no reason to doubt that prehistoric men and women carried burdens on their backs and heads and used especially constructed litters, and rollers for transportation.

Water and rail transportation

The oldest artifacts that could be described as transport vehicles were crude boats of prehistoric times; people had progressed to the dugout canoe about 20,000 years ago. At the same time ancient people must have developed ways of building rafts.

Rafts are still made in more or less the same way, using bundles of reeds, logs, grasses, and other material, sometimes with added flotation from skin bags or sea-kelp bladders. From the raft, many peoples progressed to making boats with built-up hulls, sometimes using a framework covered by skins or bark (eucalyptus bark was the favorite in the countries of Australasia.)

About 5,000 years ago canals were being constructed, at first to link close river channels and eventually to carry people and supplies over considerable distances. In more recent times canals were dug throughout Britian and much of western Europe as primary transportation routes, largely because of the inadequacy of roads. From 1770 to 1840 canals were almost unchallenged in these areas as means for slow but cheap transport of a rapidly growing volume of manufactured goods.

One great advantage of the canal was its ability to move very heavy loads for a minimal expenditure of energy. Compared with the canal barge, no land vehicle could move such loads until the coming of railroads.

The first crude railroads were used for commercial rather than private or passenger transportation. Metal rails had been used in local industries such as mines [9] since medieval times, but by about 1800 their use began to spread. By 1830 it had been realized that a uniform kind of track should be adopted, and the two-rail system was introduced with smooth steel rails at standardized spacings and with flanges on the inner edges of the wheels.

Like a canal, a railroad could carry heavy loads with minimal resistance to motion. Competition between the two forms of transportation in many regions was intense, railroads usually enjoying an advantage because of the ease of extension (branches and spurs could be built to serve almost every town) and because they were unrivaled in hilly areas. At the same time progress was made in the design and construction of roads, which in Europe until 1800 had been inferior to the roads built by the Romans many centuries earlier.

Road transportation

In theory roads have always had an advantage over railroads because of their greater flexibility. They cost less to build, which means that a national road network can serve almost every factory and house. They can carry a wide range of vehicles up and down steep grades. On the other hand, the resistance to motion is much greater than on a railroad because the friction of the relatively small area of the train wheels against the smooth rails is less. On a road surface

CONNECTIONS

See also
1582 Early technology
1584 Modern technology
1688 History of bicycles
1690 History of motorcycles
1692 History of automobiles
1706 Locomotives
1712 Balloons, blimps, and dirigibles
1714 History of aircraft
1738 Fighting ships: the age of sail
1678 Sailing ships

1

1 Tree trunks were probably the earliest vehicles. More than 20,000 years ago wood and other materials were used to make rafts and the precursors of the later kayaks, coracles, and canoes.

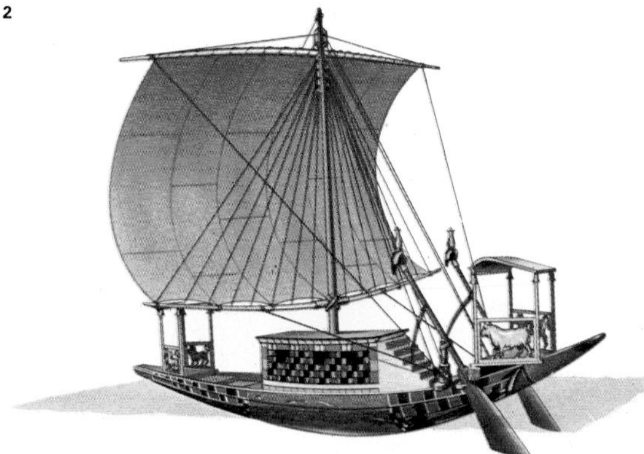

2 Egyptian ships date from about 2500 BC. The broad spoon-shaped hull was made from acacia, a tree yielding only short, irregular timbers. The ship was steered by two stern-mounted oars.

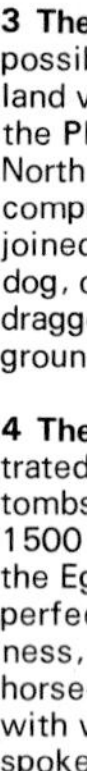
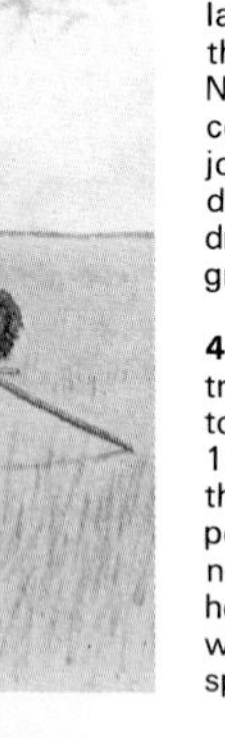

3 The travois was possibly the earliest land vehicle. Used by the Plains Indians of North America, it comprised two poles joined to a man, a dog, or a horse and dragged along the ground.

4

4 The chariot is illustrated on one of the tombs at Thebes (*c.* 1500 BC). Although the Egyptians never perfected the harness, they used many horse-drawn vehicles with wheels of spoked construction.

5 The first hydrogen balloon carried Jacques Charles and M. N. Robert from Paris to a field 25mi (40km) away in December 1783 in under two hours. It looked like a balloon with a "boat" below.

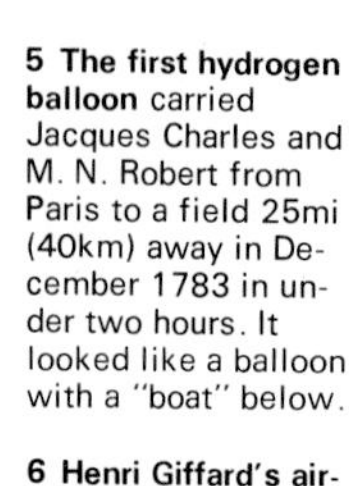
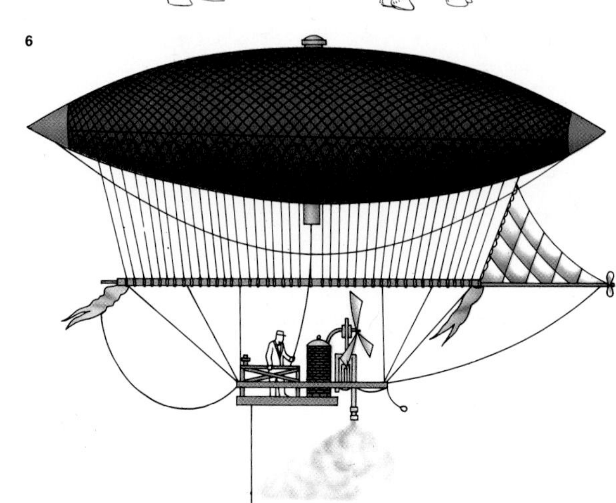

6 Henri Giffard's airship could sustain an airspeed of 5mph (8kph) on its steam-driven propeller. In 1852 Giffard navigated it from Paris to Trappes, making the first powered cross-country flight. Progress was delayed by lack of good engines.

the friction factor is much higher, and until quite recently the surface was irregular. Until late in the nineteenth century roads were marred by ruts, bumps, and potholes, which not only slowed vehicles but often caused damage and even serious accidents. In many places it was accepted procedure to disassemble coaches or wagons and use teams of men to carry them over the worst sections of road surface.

Mechanically powered vehicles

All the earliest forms of propulsion had relied on natural forces such as wind and river currents or muscle power. By the early years of the nineteenth century mechanical power was being applied to move vehicles—at first steam engines in railroad locomotives and ships. Then mechanically propelled road vehicles gained importance with the advent of the internal combustion engine after 1885. Automobiles multiplied in an amazing way, as did those convenient muscle-driven vehicles, bicycles. A key innovation with both of them was the introduction of pneumatic tires. The replacement of the horse and horse-drawn carriage by the rubber tired car forced governments to build smooth, all-weather roads.

Today's rail and road networks are more complex, and many have automatic traffic-control systems involving computers, electronic communication and display systems, as well as methods for dealing instantly with emergencies.

There have also been several revolutions in marine transportation. At one time merchant ships had to be equipped to fight off pirates. By 1800 many kinds of true cargo vessels were built and for 100 years they monopolized all transportation between continents.

The newest form of transportation, the airplane [11], swiftly supplanted the ship as the vehicle for long passenger journeys, while economies of scale led to a startling growth in the size of oil tankers, bulk carriers, and other cargo ships. The pressure on shipping lines to reduce travel time has also been relieved because over short distances hydrofoils [8] and hover-craft travel four times faster.

KEY

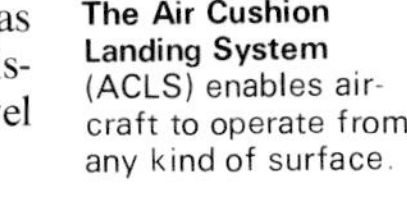

The Air Cushion Landing System (ACLS) enables aircraft to operate from any kind of surface. This is a converted Buffalo short-field transport plane that helped to prove the concept. The result is a vehicle able to land on any level part of the Earth, including water.

7

7 This river boat typifies hundreds that served US southern states in the 19th century. Paddle-driven, often with a stern wheel, they had shallow-draft but could carry heavy loads.

8

8 The hydrofoil of V. Grunberg ran in 1934. Driven by tandem air propellers, it had two forward floats and a central submerged foil, which was adjusted automatically. It predated the modern foil by 30 years.

9

9 This wooden hopper car ran on wooden track in a German mine (*c.* 1510) and is probably typical of an early form of railroad vehicle. By 1670 wagons had flanged iron wheels for strength and durability.

10

10 This Daimler car (1897) was built by the English Daimler Co. formed initially in 1893 to import cars from the factory in Germany. It had a two-cylinder engine with four forward speeds and a reverse.

11

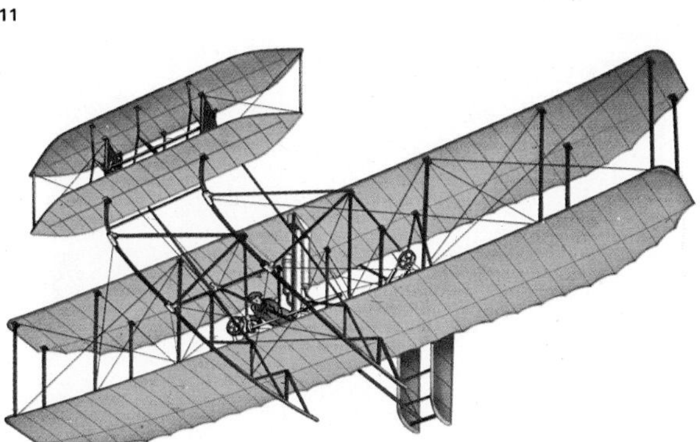

11 The Wright Flyer III was an improved version of the first airplane to make a successful flight. The Wright brothers learned how to control a glider, and then added a light-weight gasoline engine.

12

12 Paul Cornu, the French inventor, made the first heavier-than-air machine to take off vertically in free flight. Tethered to the ground by a rope, his primitive helicopter rose 5ft (1.5m) on November 13, 1907, but lacked stability.

Sailing ships

No one knows when or where the first sail was invented, but it was probably one of the earliest attempts at harnessing a natural force and putting it to work. The first evidence of sailing craft comes from Egypt and dates back to the third millennium BC. Ancient Egyptian ships [5] had single square sails spread by two wooden spars, a yard at the top and a boom at the foot; they could sail only downwind, but since the wind in the Nile valley is nearly always from the north, this allowed them to sail upstream. Going downstream did not require a sail.

Sailing against the wind

It was some time before it was realized that sails could be made that would propel a ship against a wind—not directly into it, but at an angle of less than 90°—and it is only recently that the aerodynamics of such sails has been understood [1]. Another early breakthrough was the keel, a long plank running from stem to stern, from which the rest of the hull could be built up.

The square-rigged ships of the Middle Ages could not sail much closer to the wind than 90° and even the latest square-riggers cannot sail closer than about 70°. The "fore-and-aft" sail (in which the forward edge is secured to, and pivots around, a mast or stay), such as the Mediterranean lateen and the triangular Bermudan sail of modern yachts, can hold a course as close as 45° to the wind [4].

The fore-and-aft idea appears to have evolved in the Indian Ocean from the Egyptian square sail in the third century AD—leading to the lateen sail of the Arab dhows and to the lug-sail of the Chinese junk. The square sail did, however, survive until the end of commercial sailing ships because it was more efficient than the fore-and-aft sail on long voyages with following winds.

The Romans improved on the Egyptian rig by adding the *artemon* (spritsail) and a triangular topsail [6], but as in the Egyptian ships before and in the Viking ships later, steering was done with an oar lashed near the stern. The Chinese, however, had known the axial rudder and the compass since about the first century AD. The former allowed better steering and was more robust than the steering oar; the latter allowed navigation out of sight of land without fear of overcast skies hiding the stars. These discoveries reached Europe only in the later years of the eleventh century and had great consequences on seafaring.

Development of ship and sail

The multi-masted ship originated in China, and the idea was brought to the West at the time of Marco Polo in the thirteenth century. Before this time, vessels such as the single-masted double-ended cog had been used extensively for trade around Europe and the Mediterranean. By the end of the fifteenth century three-masted ships had become a common feature of European waters. The deep, broad carrack [7] was one such common trading vessel, and the caravel was also developed at this time. Used mainly by the Portuguese, the caravel was a simpler and lighter vessel. It carried lateen sails (fore-and-aft) but sometimes the foremast was square-rigged.

The galleon [9], which appeared in the mid-sixteenth century, was a cross between

CONNECTONS

See also
1676 History of transportation
1738 Fighting ships: the age of sail
1680 Modern ships
1740 Modern fighting ship
1760 Harbors and docks

1

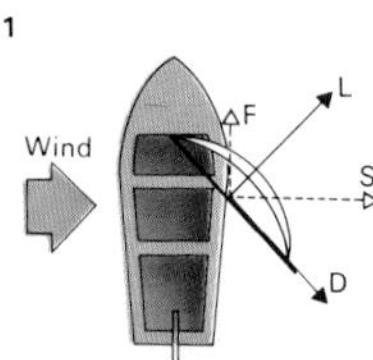

Wind
F
L
S
D

2 3

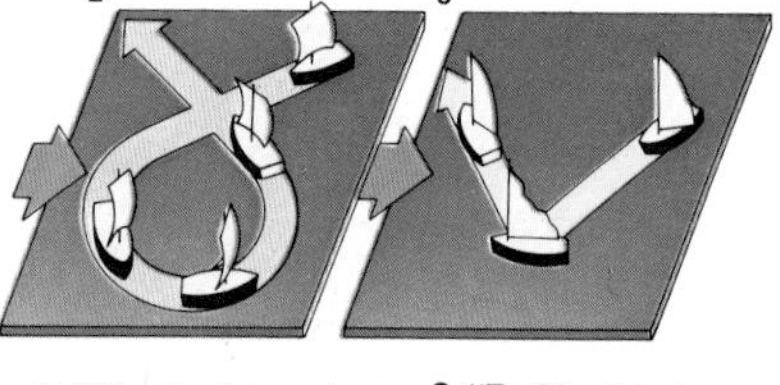

4

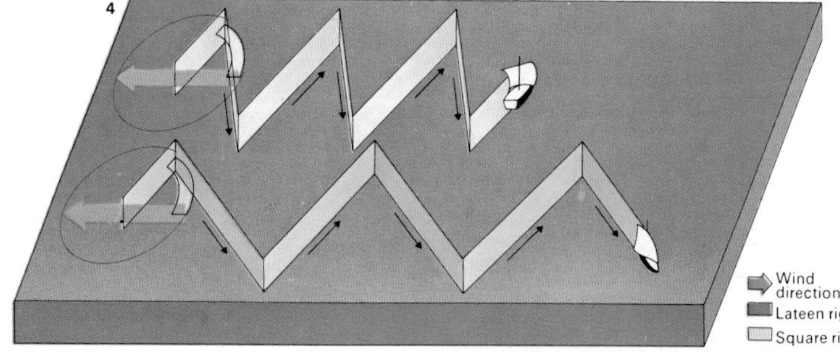

Wind direction
Lateen rig
Square rig

1 Sailing against the wind is possible because the wind acting on a sail creates a lift [L] and a drag [D]. These are equivalent to a driving force [F] and force driving to leeward [S].

2 "Wearing" is making a downwind turn, a method often used by square-rigged ships such as carracks and galleons, when sailing into wind. This method loses some ground to windward.

3 "Tacking" is turning into and across the wind. This is a maneuver more easily done by fore-and-aft vessels than by square-riggers and loses less ground to windward than wearing.

4 Fore-and-aft rigs are able to point much closer to the wind than square-rigs when tacking in a zigzagging course to windward. After sailing the same number of miles the fore-and-aft (lateen-rigged) vessel is thus much farther ahead.

5

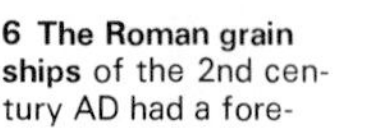

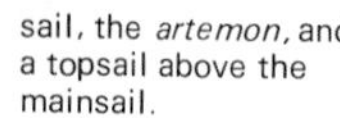

5 Egyptian ships of *c.* 1300 BC had a square sail and were steered by oars. The hull shape derived from reed boats.

6

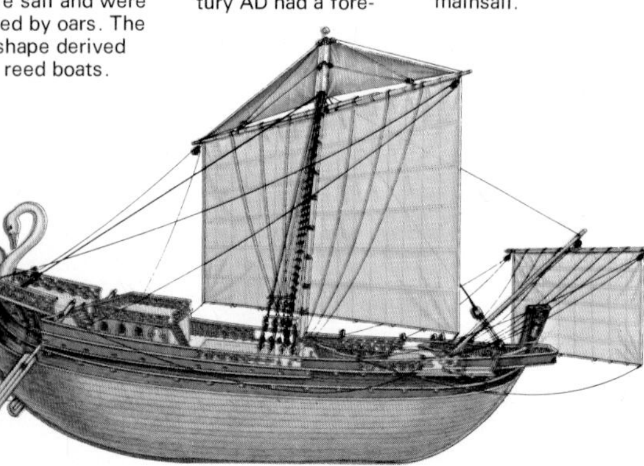

6 The Roman grain ships of the 2nd century AD had a foresail, the *artemon*, and a topsail above the mainsail.

7

A B C D E F

7 The shape of ships' hulls changed considerably between 1400 and 1600. The nef of 1400 [A] was double-ended, with a "pointed" stern, and had "castles" added at both ends. Multi-masted ships (inspired by Chinese junks) appeared with the carrack [B] (1450) and [C] (1465). The flat or *transom* stern appeared with the 1520 great ship [D], whose hull was also pierced for guns. Bringing the forecastle inboard produced the galleon [E] (1545) and [F] (1587).

8

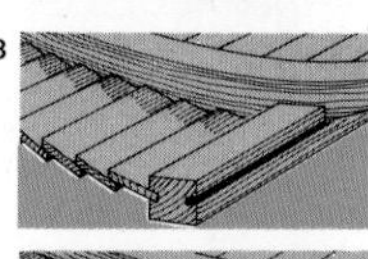

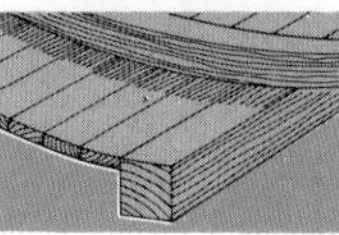

8 Clinker [A] and caravel [B] built hulls were characteristic of North European and Mediterranean ships respectively. From 1520 onward all large ships adopted the caravel build with the butting of bottom planks edge to edge.

the heavy carrack and the slim Venetian galley. Galleons had slimmer hull lines [7] than the carracks, a square stern where the carracks were "double-ended" and a forecastle well inboard instead of hanging over the bow.

The transition from the carrack to the galleon was the last big technological "jump" for sailing ships. The difference between a sixteenth-century galleon and a nineteenth-century packet ship, such as the Blackwall frigate, was one of detail, although the performance of the latter was far superior. The gradual evolution since the early galleons involved an increase in the size and number of sails, and the introduction of fore-and-aft staysails.

From the mid-eighteenth century onward, the Western sailing ship branched out in a variety of rigs, from two masts to as many as six.

The last of the sailing ships

The fastest, the most beautiful, and the most short-lived of the great sailing ships was the clipper [11]. She was developed in the 1820s in the United States, reached the height of her fame in the 1850s and 1860s, and by the end of the century was obsolete.

The clipper was built primarily for speed. She was slim and light, with a limited cargo space, and carried an enormous area of canvas. She fulfilled a variety of needs. The Californian and Australian gold rushes (1849 and 1851), the China tea trade and, from the 1870s, the trade in wool and grain from Australia were all served by clippers. The competition between ships' companies in the race to make fast passages and high profits produced crews of the highest quality.

Such factors as steamships, the opening of the Suez Canal, and the transcontinental railroads made the clippers obsolete. They were replaced by larger windjammers that were built of steel, and cargo-carrying capacity and labor-saving devices were given precedence over speed. Despite their much greater tonnage (up to 5,800 tons) they did not require larger crews than the clippers. Even these ships were eventually made obsolete by steamship competition.

KEY

The sails of the 3-masted, fully square-rigged ship are fore skysail [1], fore royal [2], fore top-gallant sail [3], fore topsail [4], foresail [5], main skysail [6], main royal [7], main top-gallant sail [8], main topsail [9], mainsail [10], mizzen skysail [11], mizzen royal [12], mizzen topgallant sail [13], mizzen topsail [14], spanker [15], studding sails [16], outer jib [17], inner jib [18], fore staysail [19], and staysails [20].

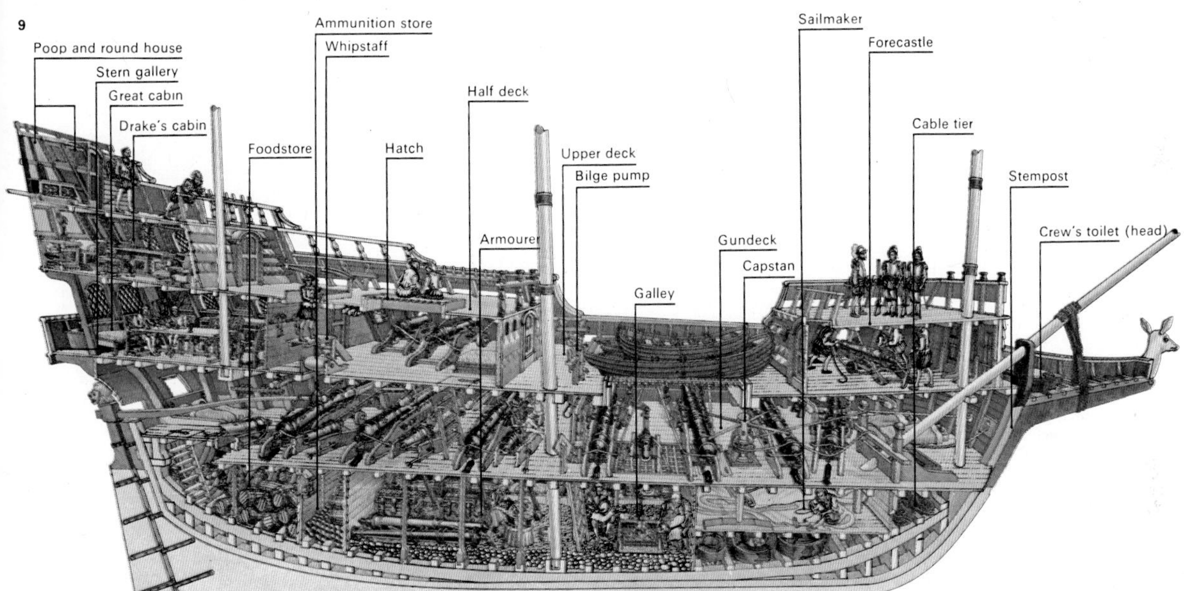
9
Poop and round house
Stern gallery
Great cabin
Drake's cabin
Foodstore
Ammunition store
Whipstaff
Hatch
Half deck
Armourer
Upper deck
Bilge pump
Galley
Gundeck
Capstan
Sailmaker
Forecastle
Cable tier
Stempost
Crew's toilet (head)

9 Drake's Golden Hind was a medium-sized Elizabethan galleon. Her deck was about 90ft (28m) long. The rig consisted of the square bowsprit sail, 2 square sails on the foremast and on the mainmast and a lateen on the mizzen. The hull was characterized by a slim underbody, a projecting head (derived from the galley's ram), a forecastle forming an integral part of the hull, and a transom stern with a stern gallery. Steering was done with a whipstaff (the wheel only appeared during the 18th century). There were 2 full-length decks. Such ships were used both for war and commerce.

10

11

12

13

13 The barkentine (19th-20th century) has three masts with a square rig only on the foremast, thus reducing crew size and running costs.

10 The Dutch East Indiaman (1720) was larger than the *Golden Hind*, but of the same basic pattern. Two new sails appeared: the spritsail topsail and the mizzen topsail. These heavily armed and extremely rugged merchant ships could be used as men-of-war.

14

14 The brig (18th-20th century), a common coastal craft, has two masts, both of them square-rigged, and fore-and-aft staysails.

11 The clipper of the mid-19th century was a particularly efficient sailing ship. Its phenomenal speed made trading between Australia, China, the United States, and Britain more economical. The name clipper came from the way the ships could "clip off" the miles.

15

15 The brigantine (18th-20th century) has two masts, with a square rig on the foremast and mainsails and staysails on the mainmast.

12 The four-masted steel barks of the late 19th century were built of steel, and they carried manufactured goods, grain, and nitrates around the world. Their aftermasts had no yards. The bark rig appeared in he late 18th century and steel hulls in the 1870s.

16

16 The topsail schooner (18th-20th century) is a fore-and-aft rigged vessel with one or more square topsails set on the foremast.

Modern ships

Ships have changed vastly since the first iron-hulled steamer powered by a screw propeller, the *Great Britain* [1], crossed the Atlantic in 1843. Toward the end of the nineteenth century, iron gave way to steel as the standard material for hulls and sail-power declined in usefulness. At first indispensable as an auxiliary to the early crude steam engines, sail was ousted as steam machinery became more reliable. By 1918 there were very few sailing ships trading on main ocean routes.

Types of shipping

Since the introduction of steam there have always been three main divisions of non-military shipping: passenger carriers, cargo carriers (merchant ships), and service craft. The largest passenger carriers are ocean liners, particularly the North Atlantic record-breakers of the twentieth century. Competition from cheap and speedy air travel has driven big passenger liners out of business. But they survive as cruise ships, carrying vacationers to exotic ports instead of travelers on scheduled routes. Many famous liners have ended their careers by becoming cruise ships, and now especially designed ships [11] cater to the packaged vacation market. "Short haul" passenger ships and ferries have proved far more resilient in meeting the competition from air travel. Improvements in ship design have enabled road vehicles to drive on and off a ferry [10], allowing faster turnaround.

The passenger liner was once the largest type of non-military ship, but since the 1950s it has been surpassed by the oil tanker [6]. As world consumption of petroleum products has risen, so has demand for tankers. Individual ships have increased in size from an average of about 50,000 tons deadweight in 1955 to 500,000 tons in 1976 (deadweight is the carrying capacity of a ship, including cargo, ballast, fuel, water, crew, and passengers). The "supertanker" is relatively slow but can be operated by a small crew and it is the most economical way of shipping crude oil. The growth in size is likely to be limited only by safety factors and the risk of pollution from accidental spillage.

The cargo carrying ship is still the mainstay of world trade, but here too there has been a striking expansion in size. In order to save on operating costs, bulk carriers handling dry cargos of iron ore, grain, or coal have grown to deadweights of more than 100,000 tons. Some are equipped to unload their own cargo, but many still need dockside facilities.

The most important development in cargo handling is the container ship [5], which loads cargo in prepacked, weather-tight containers by means of special dockside cranes. The main advantage is that time in port is reduced and containers are easily handled by an integrated road or rail system. Loading and unloading of diverse cargos, with its risk of damage and theft, is eliminated. The disadvantage is that container ships can operate only on fixed routes with terminals especially equipped to load and unload them.

Smaller vessels

A few general purpose cargo vessels still "tramp" from port to port seeking any

CONNECTIONS

See also
1740 Modern fighting ships
1678 Sailing ships
1738 Fighting ships: the age of sail
1682 Hydrofoils and hovercraft
1684 Submarines and submersibles
1760 Harbors and docks
1762 Canal construction
1676 History of transportation
236 Oceanographic exploration
298 Pollution of the sea
386 Commercial fishing

1 The first iron screw steamship, the SS *Great Britain* (1843), was not an immediate commercial success but showed that iron ships could carry more cargo than wooden ones.

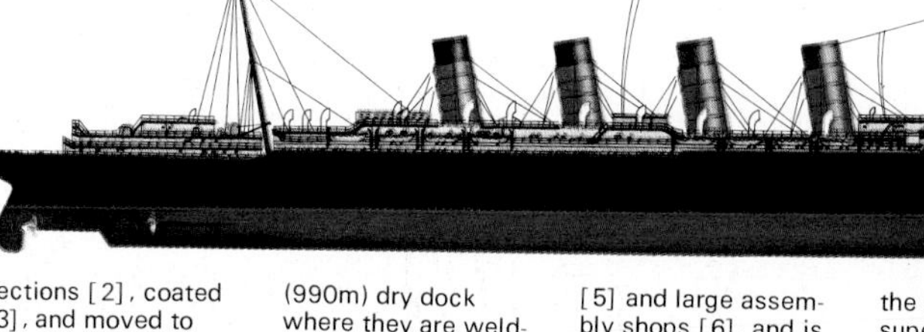

2 The Lusitania was torpedoed in 1915 by a German U-boat with the loss of 1,198 lives. Introduced in 1907, she helped to establish the Parsons steam turbine as a means of propulsion for liners.

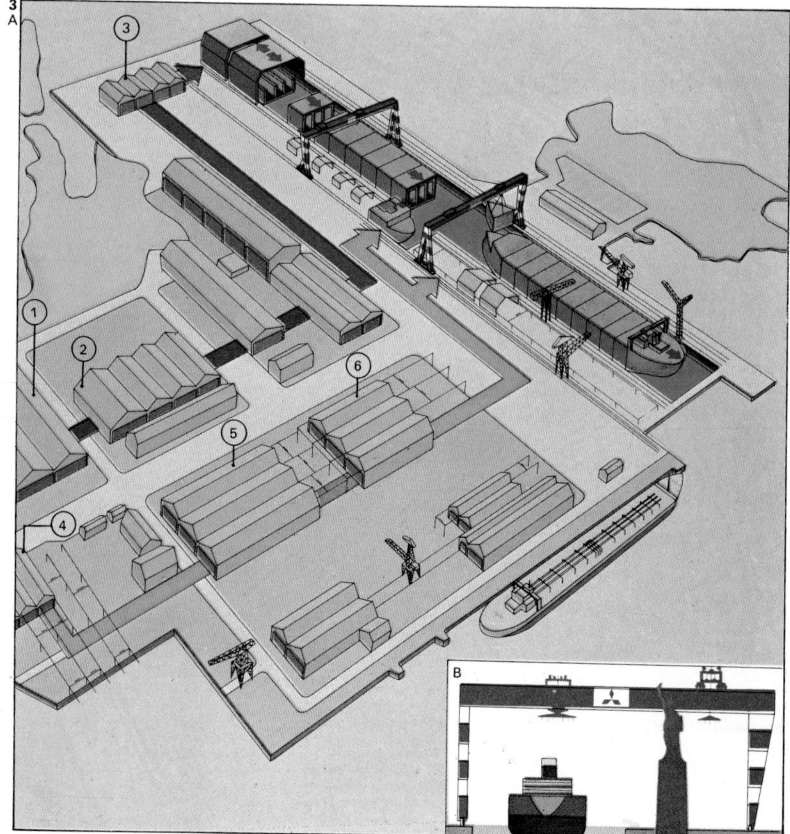

3
A
B
1
2
3
4
5
6

3 Production line assembly of giant oil tankers is carried out in drydock shipyards like the extensive Mitsubishi yards at Koyagi in Japan [A]. Treated steel plate is cut to size [1], assembled in small sections [2], coated [3], and moved to the dockside to be assembled into sections that can weigh up to 600 tons. Powerful gantry cranes [B] are used to lift each section into a 3,246ft (990m) dry dock where they are welded together. Steel plate for the stern and bow is handled on another assembly line. The steel for these sections leaves a treatment shop [4], goes to subassembly [5] and large assembly shops [6], and is built up in a pocket dock to be added as the ship is slid to the seaward end of the main dock. Final fitting out is done afloat. Yards like the one at Koyagi build the 500,000-ton supertankers needed to meet world demands for oil. The Japanese have the world's biggest tanker building industry.

4 The Lanka Devi is a conventional cargo ship of a type still widely used. She can load or unload cargo with her own derricks if cranes are not available on the dockside. Though the *Lanka Devi* has her machinery placed amidships, a more recent trend in cargo vessels is for the bridge superstructure and the propulsion unit to be positioned either at or near the stern.

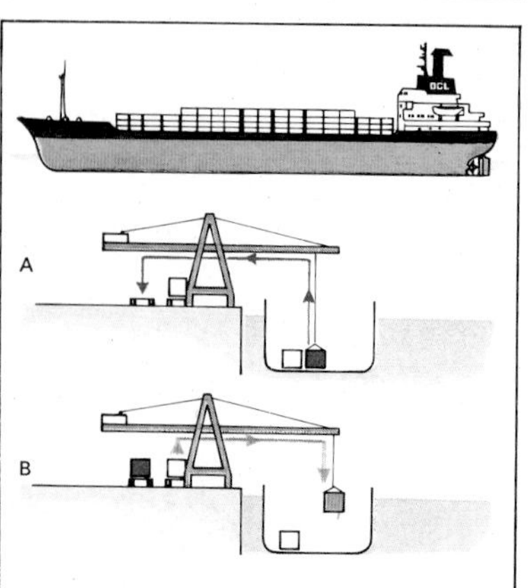

A
B

5 A container ship like the *Encounter Bay* must use special terminals to handle her 1,500 containers, each measuring 1,280cu ft (36cu m). Unloading [A] and loading [B] can be carried out simultaneously. Like most container ships, the *Encounter Bay* has a high freeboard and an unobstructed deck, allowing containers to be stacked there. Bigger ships can carry up to 3,000 containers.

cargo they can find. Or their owners allow the whole vessel to be chartered for a single cargo, like a conventional cargo vessel [4]. Such vessels operate on routes where container ships would be too costly, or they act as a "feeder" to container routes. The "reefer," or refrigerated cargo liner, also remains important because it handles perishable cargos such as fruit and meat. Smaller coasters and coastal oil tankers, which transship cargo between ports, act as vital links both as distributors of cargo to lesser ports and as feeders to the major ports and container terminals. Roll-on roll-off ships are used to carry truck trailers from point to point. Another variant is the LASH, or Lighter Aboard Ship concept, with barges or lighters hoisted aboard a large ship. After being dropped at the mouth of a river, the barges are towed upriver without any transshipment of cargo, as with containers.

Shipping could not function without a host of service craft. Foremost among these is the tug [9], which exists primarily to maneuver larger ships in confined waters. Tugs are also used to salvage damaged ships on the high seas and to fight fires, and special "pusher" tugs handle barges on rivers and canals. Dredgers keep the channels in harbors and estuaries open to deep-sea shipping, and a variety of small craft are employed for piloting and maintenance of buoys and other navigational aids.

Marine engines

The main propulsion systems of ships are either diesel or steam engines, driving screw propellers. Diesel engines are favored for their simplicity and economy, and they have steadily driven out the one-time workhorse, the vertical triple-expansion steam engine. Larger ships requiring high speeds rely on steam turbines. The new container ships and bulk carriers designed for fast running have drawn for the first time on naval experience with high-speed steam propulsion. Gas turbines have been used experimentally, although they have not yet proved sufficiently cheap and reliable. Similarly, nuclear power for ships still remains uneconomical.

KEY
Astern
Ahead
Topsides
Freeboard
Boot-topping
Draft
Length between perpendiculars (BP)
Overall length (OA)
Port quarter
Port side
Port bow
Aft
Forward
Amidships
Starboard quarter
Starboard side
Starboard bow

Terms used on ships include the following: *Ahead:* In advance of the bows. *Amidships:* Near the middle of the ship's length. *Astern:* Behind the ship. *Athwartships:* From one side of the ship to the other. *Beam:* Greatest breadth of the ship. *Boot-topping:* Paint on hull between load line and waterline when ship is empty. *Bows:* Foremost part. *Draft:* Depth to which ship sinks in the water. *Forward:* Toward the bows. *Freeboard:* Distance from main deck to waterline. *Lee side:* Sheltered from the wind. *Port:* Left side looking forward. *Quarter:* Direction between stern and beam. *Rake:* Slope of funnel, masts, or stem. *Sheer:* Fore-and-aft curve of a hull rising toward bow and stern. *Starboard:* Right hand side looking forward. *Topsides:* Outer surface of vessel above waterline. *Trim:* The way a vessel sits in the water. *Windward:* Direction from which wind is blowing.

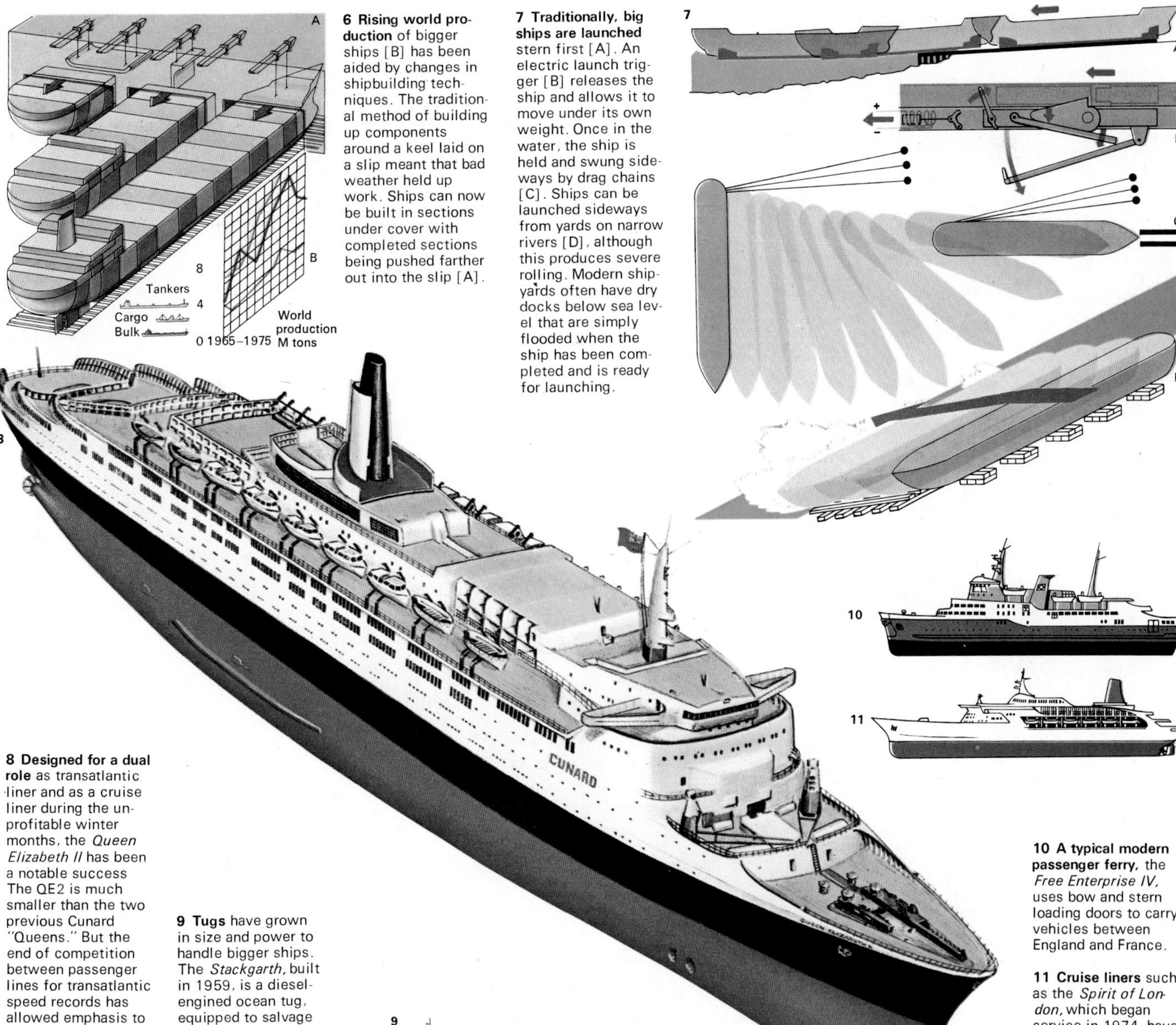

6
A
B
8
4
Tankers
Cargo
Bulk
0 1965–1975
World production M tons
7
A
B
C
D
8
CUNARD
9
10
11

6 Rising world production of bigger ships [B] has been aided by changes in shipbuilding techniques. The traditional method of building up components around a keel laid on a slip meant that bad weather held up work. Ships can now be built in sections under cover with completed sections being pushed farther out into the slip [A].

7 Traditionally, big ships are launched stern first [A]. An electric launch trigger [B] releases the ship and allows it to move under its own weight. Once in the water, the ship is held and swung sideways by drag chains [C]. Ships can be launched sideways from yards on narrow rivers [D], although this produces severe rolling. Modern shipyards often have dry docks below sea level that are simply flooded when the ship has been completed and is ready for launching.

8 Designed for a dual role as transatlantic liner and as a cruise liner during the unprofitable winter months, the *Queen Elizabeth II* has been a notable success. The QE2 is much smaller than the two previous Cunard "Queens." But the end of competition between passenger lines for transatlantic speed records has allowed emphasis to be placed on better facilities especially for lowerfare passengers.

9 Tugs have grown in size and power to handle bigger ships. The *Stackgarth*, built in 1959, is a diesel-engined ocean tug, equipped to salvage disabled vessels and for firefighting in addition to normal towage work.

10 A typical modern passenger ferry, the *Free Enterprise IV*, uses bow and stern loading doors to carry vehicles between England and France.

11 Cruise liners such as the *Spirit of London*, which began service in 1974, have special sports and entertainment facilities for vacationers.

Hydrofoils and hovercraft

Hydrofoils and hovercraft [Key] are machines that reflect today's demand for greater speed and flexibility in transportation. In common with airplanes and helicopters these craft use energy for both upward and forward motion. A hydrofoil's hull is raised out of the water to reduce drag (friction) and thus enable it to travel faster than a conventional ship. A hovercraft lifts itself in order to become independent of the surface over which it travels, which can be water, snow, marsh, or sand.

Hydrofoils and their uses

The first hydrofoils were built at the beginning of the twentieth century. Designers calculated that a sea wing (a lifting plane designed for running through water) [2] could be made much smaller than an air wing capable of generating the same lift force. Early experiments used foils stacked [1A] so that, as the craft accelerated and lifted, fewer foils were in the water.

By 1940 the more efficient surface piercing foil [1C] had become preferred. In this type of hydrofoil a large foil slopes up on each side of the center line, looking from the front like a V with the tips emerging from the water. These foils provide built-in stability in banked turns or through waves.

Most modern hydrofoils are of this type, although two other designs are also current. Many Soviet hydrofoils have depth-effect foils [1B], which stabilize automatically an inch or so below the surface of the water. They are ideal for use on shallow draft vessels for inland waterways but are useless in a rough sea. For this application, submerged foils [1D] are the best solution and these are the type used on most high-speed military hydrofoils. Small foils run deep in the water, supporting the vessel on streamlined struts. The angle of the foil can be varied by an autopilot, enabling the craft to run true even in heavy seas.

Most hydrofoils are fairly small, few civil types reaching 150 tons and the largest military version being 320 tons. As inshore ferries they can travel at high speeds without damaging river banks or disturbing smaller craft with their wash, and they give a smooth ride across choppy water. Naval hydrofoils provide maneuverable platforms for guns, missiles, and antisubmarine search and attack systems. At slow speeds, a hydrofoil behaves like a conventional ship and floats with its hull in the water. Control is precise, and it can ride out storms.

The story of the hovercraft

A hydrofoil is restricted to water and at low speeds needs deep water to float in. By contrast, a hovercraft—more properly called an air-cushion vehicle (ACV)—is able to go practically anywhere.

In the nineteenth century engineers such as John Thornycroft (1843–1928) tried to reduce drag by pumping bubbles out of holes in a ship's hull. Later ACV developments sprang from the experimental work in the 1950s of Christopher Cockerell (1910–), who realized that some sort of "curtain" to contain the air cushion under the vehicle was essential to provide sufficient lift within the practical limits imposed by engine size.

Modern ACVs ride on a single bubble or cushion of air blown by fans through slots or

CONNECTIONS

See also

1702 Special purpose vehicles
1666 Moving heavy loads
1710 Railroads of the future
1676 History of transportation

A

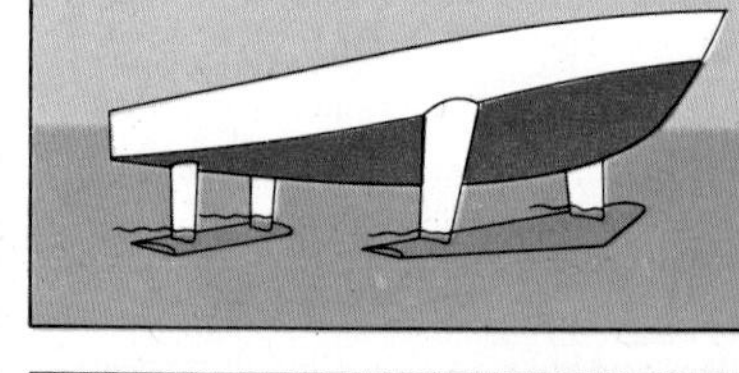

B

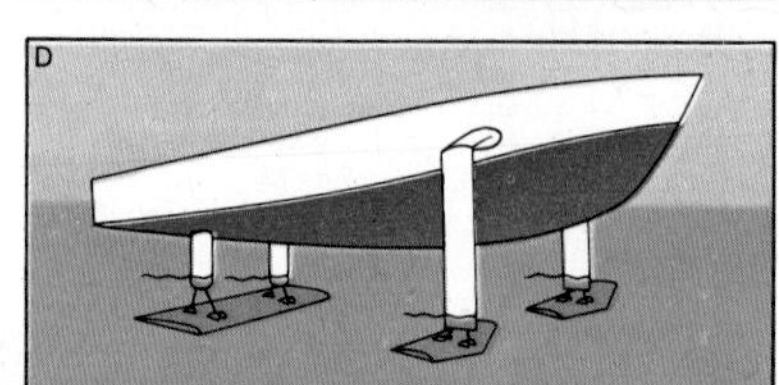

D

1 Almost all hydrofoils belong to one of four classes. Ladder foils [A] emerge progressively from the water as speed is increased. Depth-effect foils [B] are suited to shallow water without waves. Surface-piercing foils [C] are the most common form for passenger hydrofoils, while submerged foils [D] are preferred for rough seas. The foils are adjustable and their angle is controlled by an autopilot.

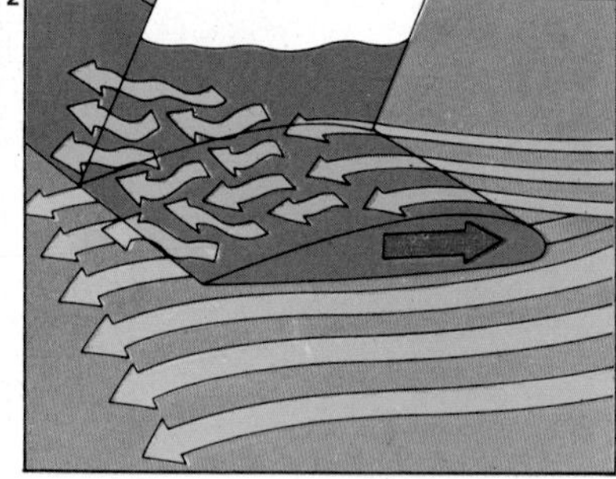

2 Foils are sea wings. At speed they generate enough lift to raise the vessel out of the water, thus reducing drag.

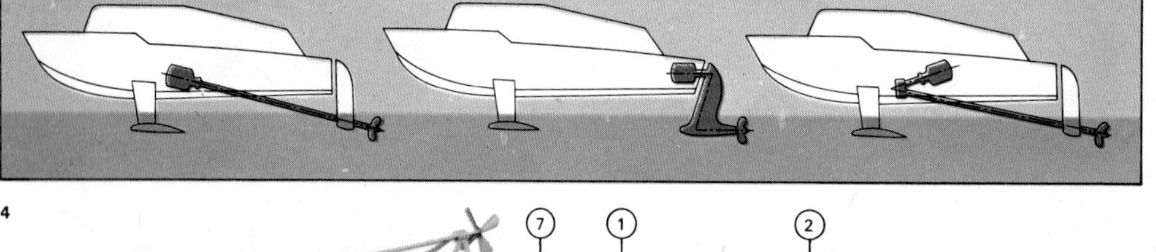

A
B
C

3 Propulsion poses problems because a hydrofoil's screw is lower than the engine. The sloping drive [A] is simplest, but the thrust acts at a sharp angle. The Z drive [B] is best for deeply submerged foils, but requires two sets of bevel gears. The V form [C] is common on surface-piercing foil boats. An alternative is to use the engine to drive a pump, which squirts a water jet to provide thrust.

4 The first fullscale hydrofoil was built in 1906 by Enrico Forlanini (1848–1930). Lifted on three sets of ladder foils and propelled by front and rear air screws, it successfully ran at 44mph (71kph). In 1918 a foil boat built by Alexander Graham Bell (1847–1922) reached 71mph (114kph). Commercial development of the hydrofoil began in the 1930s.

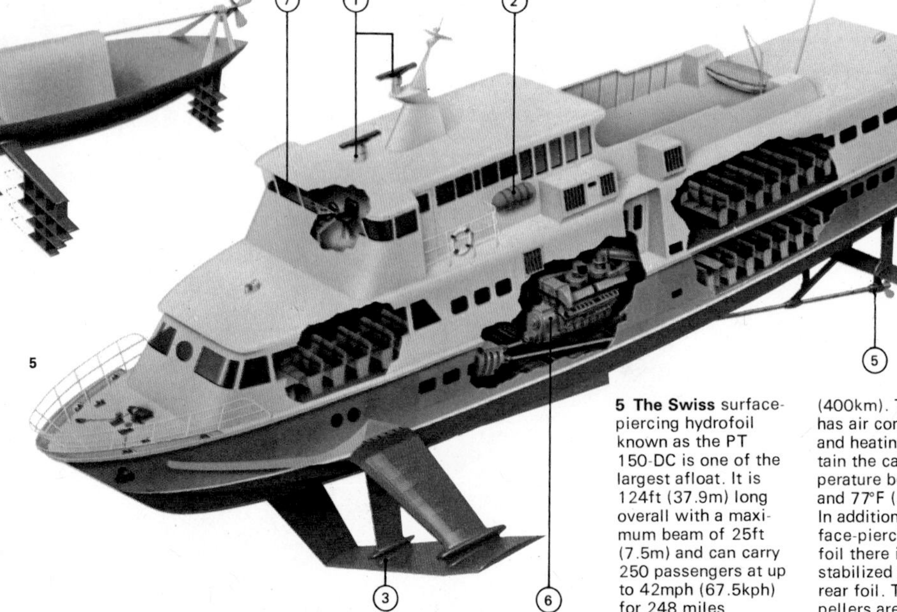

7
1
2
5
4
3
6

1 Radars
2 Liferaft
3 Front foil
4 Rear foil
5 Propeller
6 Two 3,400hp diesel engines
7 Bridge

5 The Swiss surface-piercing hydrofoil known as the PT 150-DC is one of the largest afloat. It is 124ft (37.9m) long overall with a maximum beam of 25ft (7.5m) and can carry 250 passengers at up to 42mph (67.5kph) for 248 miles (400km). The vessel has air conditioning and heating to maintain the cabin temperature between 68 and 77°F (20-25°C). In addition to the surface-piercing front foil there is an air-stabilized submerged rear foil. Twin propellers are located below the rear foil. There are four passenger cabins, two on the main deck and two on the lower, and passengers can be served with drinks and refreshments in their seats. The Malmo-Copenhagen ferry uses a PT 150-DC hydrofoil.

jets round the underside of the hull [6]. The main part of the hull serves as a buoyancy tank, enabling a water-borne ACV to float when the lifting power is switched off. Air pumped by the lift fans raises the ACV on a cushion of slightly pressurized air, which leaks away around the edges at the same rate as it is fed in. The propulsion and lift systems may be driven either by one power plant or by separate units.

Early ACVs had flat undersides and daylight was visible beneath them when they were operating, although clearance was often only a few inches. To improve their performance over waves and other obstacles, later ACVs were fitted with flexible skirts [7]. These skirts contain the cushion of air but pass easily over obstructions. This facility makes them truly amphibious, and they can operate equally well in or out of water. Unlike hydrofoils they are not limited in size, and large passenger-carrying craft and car ferries are being used. Various types of propulsion and steering systems have been tried [8], some combining both functions.

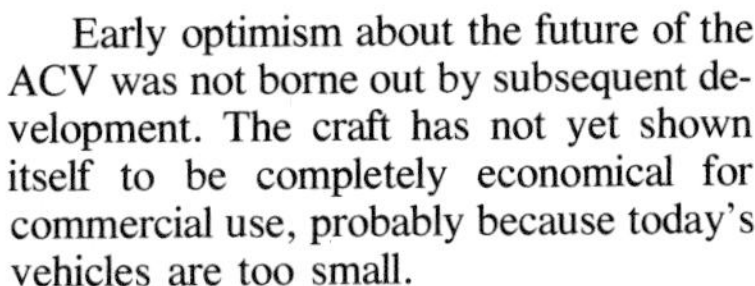
Early optimism about the future of the ACV was not borne out by subsequent development. The craft has not yet shown itself to be completely economical for commercial use, probably because today's vehicles are too small.

Other uses of ACVs

Apart from conventional passenger transportation ACVs have proved their value in the military sphere and the principle of the air cushion has been applied successfully to other modes of transportation. The ACV system can be used on a train running over a smooth track, the air cushion reducing friction while propulsion is obtained from ducted fans or linear induction motors. As heavy load carriers ACVs are able to transport machinery weighing 500 tons over surfaces that could not possibly be traversed by wheeled or tracked vehicles. Air-cushion pallets for industrial use are easy to move and reduce strain on floor surfaces. The ACV principle has also been used in the design of hospital beds to lessen the discomfort of patients suffering from burns.

KEY

A
B

The hydrofoil and hovercraft are lifted and supported by the expenditure of energy—unlike water-borne ships or land vehicles resting on wheels. A hydrofoil [A] lifts itself to reduce drag, so as to run at high speed and travel smoothly across rough water. A hovercraft [B] does the same, but has the ability to traverse almost any kind of surface, including swamps, mud, river rapids, and ice. The skirt fitted to amphibious hovercraft helps retain the supporting air cushion and lifts the rigid structure higher above the surface.

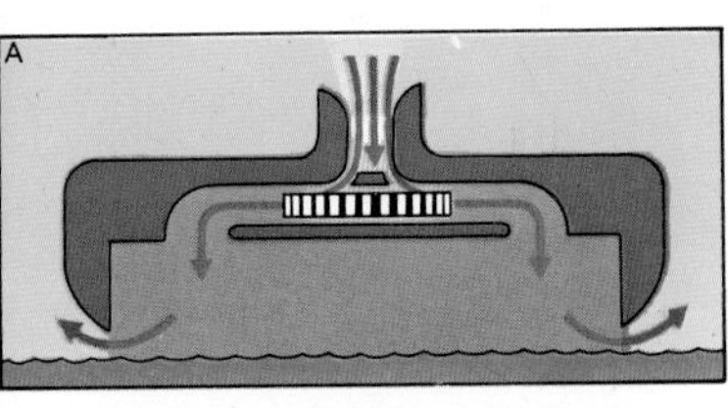
A

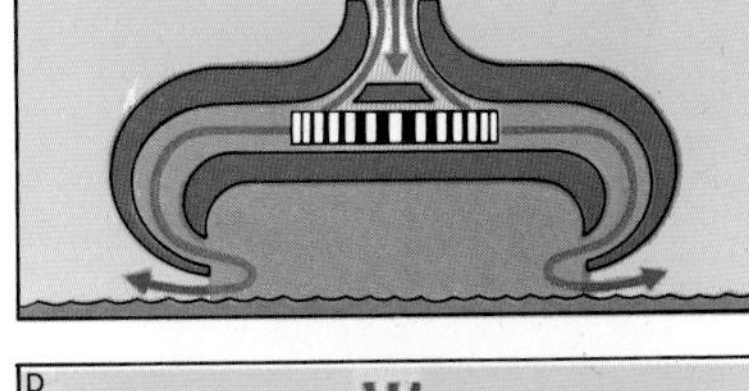
B

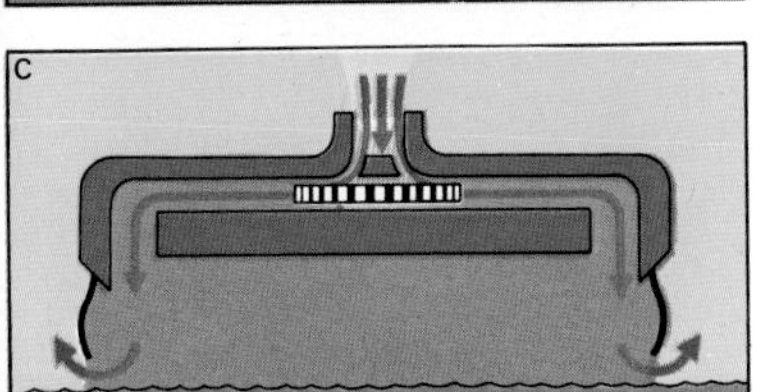
C

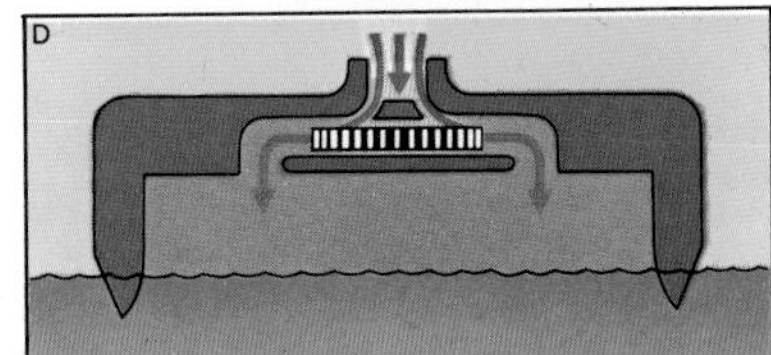
D

6 There are four types of hovercraft, each with a central lift fan. The simple "plenum chamber" [A] blows in air that escapes beneath the downturned edges. The peripheral jet [B] blows air inward from a surrounding slit. With a skirt [C] the rigid body is raised above waves and solid obstructions. ACVs designed solely for use over water have side walls [D], saving lift power but adding extra water drag.

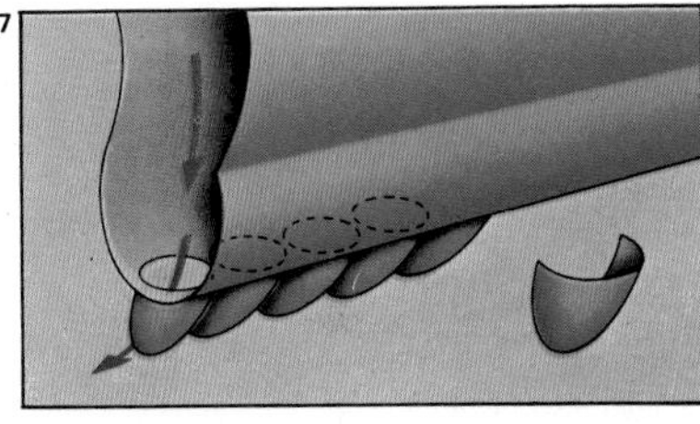
7

7 The skirt of an amphibious ACV is made of tough, rubberized fabric to withstand heavy wear. Air inflates the inner and outer walls, escaping through inward facing ducts or "fingers." These inflate the main cushion. They are designed for quick and easy replacement, since they are most likely to be damaged.

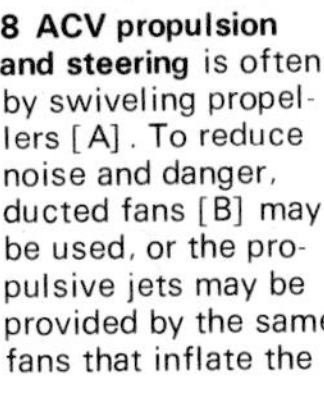
8 ACV propulsion and steering is often by swiveling propellers [A]. To reduce noise and danger, ducted fans [B] may be used, or the propulsive jets may be provided by the same fans that inflate the cushion [C]. Like the fast hydrofoil, the seagoing ACV may be propelled by water jets [D]. Unless the propulsion system swivels, deflectors or rudders are needed to control the craft at speed.

8 A
B
C
D

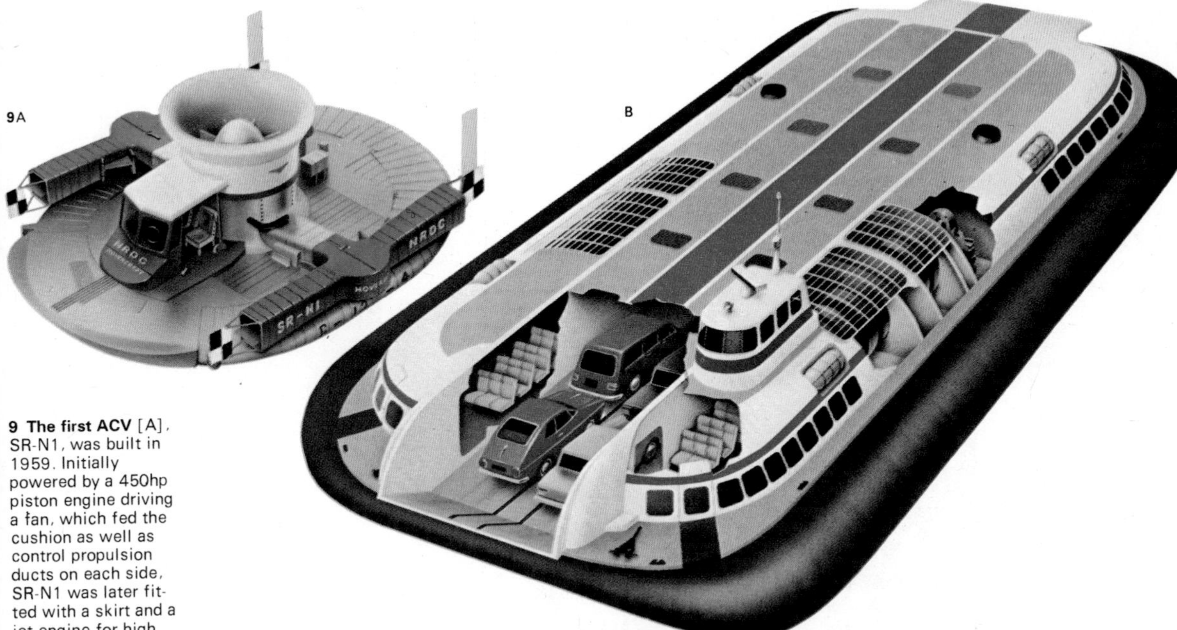
9A
B
NRDC
NRDC
SR-N1

9 The first ACV [A], SR-N1, was built in 1959. Initially powered by a 450hp piston engine driving a fan, which fed the cushion as well as control propulsion ducts on each side, SR-N1 was later fitted with a skirt and a jet engine for high speeds. The VT1 [B] was a large commercial ACV built in 1969 by Vosper Thornycroft. Designed to carry 10 cars and 146 passengers, it was propelled by water screws, yet had a skirt and could run out of the water up a slipway for loading. This design combined advantages of high speed with economy and low noise levels. The subsequent civil and military versions of the VT1 were fitted with a new propulsion system—large ducted air propellers.

Submarines and submersibles

The invention of the submarine is usually credited to an Englishman, William Bourne. In 1578 he described a vessel that could take on and expel water to vary its buoyancy and that used a snorkellike tube for its air supply. There is no evidence that Bourne's craft ever sailed, and the first submarine was probably a leather-covered rowing boat built by a Dutch engineer, Cornelius van Drebbel (1572–1634), in about 1620. According to the British chemist Robert Boyle, such a boat took King James I (1566–1625) for a ride beneath the River Thames and even had some kind of "liquor" for renewing the air inside. Unfortunately no drawings of this craft have survived.

Submarines in wartime

The *Turtle* [Key], a one-man submarine invented in 1776 by an American, David Bushnell (*c*.1742–1824), was the first underwater vessel to be used in war. It pioneered two essential features of the modern submarine—a closed hull and screw propulsion, although the latter was worked by hand. But two further developments were necessary before the submarine could become an effective fighting machine: a good undersea weapon and a source of power.

The Confederate navy used submarines during the American Civil War. Small craft known as Davids—named after the biblical David who vanquished the giant Goliath —were each armed with an explosive charge at the end of a long spar and powered by hand or steam. In 1864, a David, the *Hunley,* rammed the Union ship *Housatonic* off Charleston harbor; both vessels sank, and the crew of the *Hunley* were killed. A self-propelled torpedo was also invented at about that time.

By the turn of the century the American inventor John P. Holland (1840–1914) was designing submarines powered by gasoline engines. Holland's vessels were the first modern submarines and contained all the basic features of those that fought in both world wars. German submarines (U-boats) during World War I were highly effective as raiders of unarmed merchant ships, thereby threatening to cut Britain's vital supply lines. In World War II submarines took a toll of warships as well [6].

The effectiveness of the submarine remained limited by the slowness and short duration of undersea travel when vessels depended on electric motors powered by batteries. The batteries soon became exhausted and submarines had to surface frequently to obtain air for the diesel engines to recharge the batteries (through a generator driven by the engines). The diesel engines were also used for surface propulsion. In World War II a snorkel tube was developed to supply air to the diesel engines, which could be run just below the surface. This helped the submarine to escape detection.

How submarines work

Part of a submarine's hull is double-skinned. Water admitted into ballast tanks in the hull lowers the buoyancy of the vessel; diving planes on the sides of the hull control the angle at which the vessel sinks and level it out. Buoyancy is restored by expelling the water from the ballast

CONNECTIONS

See also
1740 Modern fighting shi
1734 Modern artillery
1746 Nuclear, chemical, and biological warfa
1802 Radar and sonar
238 Man under the sea

1

580

1 Hunter-killer submarines—this is the USS *Barbel*—were designed to destroy other submarines. They represented the ultimate development of undersea warfare until the advent of the nuclear submarine. A modern nuclear submarine is a deadly weapon on an unprecedented scale. Each of its 16 guided missiles can carry up to 10 separate nuclear warheads, each sufficient to destroy a city. It need not surface and can fire its missiles from beneath the sea, thus remaining invulnerable. The United States and the USSR each possess more than 100 nuclear submarines.

2

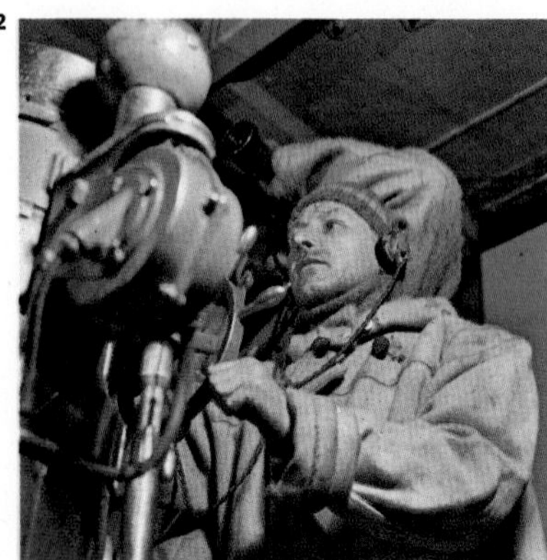

2 Locating submerged submarines from a ship, or locating surface vessels from a submarine, is achieved by listening for echoes of supersonic sound pulses transmitted through water. The system, originally called "Asdic" by the British Royal Navy, is now called sonar. Submarines can be located using sonar buoys, which transmit signals back to a nearby mother ship, or by using a "dunking" sonar suspended from a helicopter and dipped just below the surface of the water.

3 The torpedo, invented by an Austrian engineer, G. Luppis, in 1864 and developed by an English engineer, Robert Whitehead (1823–1905), made the submarine into an effective fighting force. It is fired from a tube inside the submarine. Torpedo attacks on merchant shipping, as shown here, were successful in both world wars, but the torpedo is now primarily an antisubmarine weapon. Accurate positioning is no longer necessary, as modern torpedoes home in on their targets acoustically or are guided by wire. Short-range missiles have been developed for firing from torpedo tubes.

3

4

4 Rising from the sea on a test flight, the *Polaris* missile has a range of nearly 2,875mi (4,630km) and carries three nuclear warheads. The *Poseidon* missile has ten warheads. The missiles are ejected from their launching tubes by compressed gas, and the two-stage solid-fueled rocket motor fires at the surface. They are computer guided and the warheads separate on reentry.

tanks with compressed air. The central structure—the conning tower or sail—contains a periscope, radio and radar antennas, and a snorkel tube. Tracking of an enemy vessel is accomplished by sonar (underwater) and radar (when surfaced), and communications are by radio. A submarine can receive messages underwater but has to have at least its radio antenna clear of the water in order to transmit signals. Navigation is by means of an inertial guidance system (a computerized information system) assisted by sonar and radar in coastal waters or beneath ice floes. The periscope is used for photographing targets or coastal installations and for checking navigation.

The nuclear submarine is a true undersea craft. It needs no air for its motors and can make long undersea voyages without refueling. The first of these vessels, the USS *Nautilus*, was also the world's first nuclear-powered warship of any kind. Launched in 1954, its capabilities drastically changed the military strategy of the Great Powers. Instead of raiding surface vessels, nuclear submarines carry long-range intercontinental missiles armed with nuclear warheads that can be launched underwater. The submarines constitute a strike force that is practically invulnerable because they cannot easily be located when submerged. They are intended to respond to the first attack and thus deter aggression.

In addition to intercontinental missiles [4] the submarine can carry torpedoes [3] that "home in" acoustically or are guided by a wire trailed behind the torpedo. Weapons that are part torpedo and part missile can also be carried.

The role of submersibles

The term submersible may be used to describe any underwater vessel, but today it usually indicates a non-military vessel. Small electrically powered submersibles [7] are used to inspect and carry out maintenance of underwater structures, especially oil and gas drilling heads and pipelines; to check undersea cables and bury them in the mud on the sea floor; to search for minerals on the sea bottom; and to carry out oceanographic research.

KEY

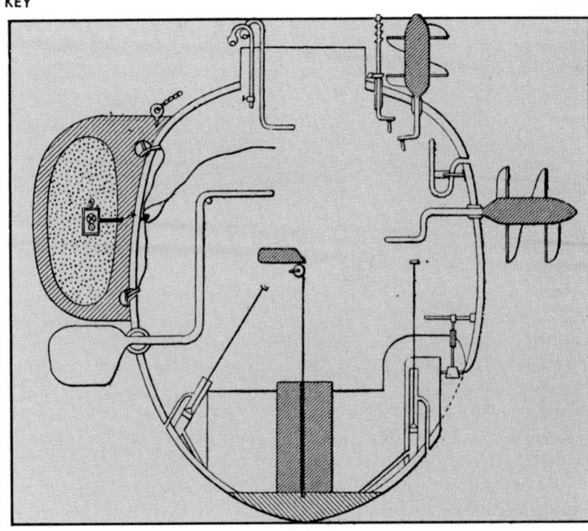

The Turtle, an American submarine, was in 1776 the first to operate in war. The single crew member worked all the controls—lateral and vertical propellers, rudder and pumps—by hand. The packet of explosives (left) was detachable and designed to be fixed to the hull of an enemy vessel.

5

6

5 The largest submarine of World War I was the K-class of the British Royal Navy. It was 338ft (103m) long and had a crew of 55. The war proved that submarines were not greatly effective against warships but could be used to sink merchant ships and disrupt supply lines. Germany had no ocean supply lines, but the Allies lost 32 ships for every German submarine they sank.

6 The German U-boat *(Unterseeboot)* was responsible for sinking millions of tons of Allied shipping during the early stages of World War II. Working in packs and armed with fore and aft torpedo tubes, the U-boats stalked convoys by day and attacked by night. The Allied development of radio direction-finding and radar made surfaced submarines vulnerable to aircraft attack.

8

DEEP DIVER

7 Star III is a submersible capable of operating to a depth of 2,000ft (610m). Powered by batteries it is 25ft (7.7m) long and carries a crew of two sealed inside the spherical steel pressure hull amidships. *Star III* is highly maneuverable as it has horizontal and vertical motors. It operates from a support ship and has been used to investigate the deep scattering layer of plankton that is so important to ocean ecology. Submersibles have also been used to locate deep-swimming schools of fish to help improve catches. They are capable of delicate undersea work on cables and oil rigs.

7

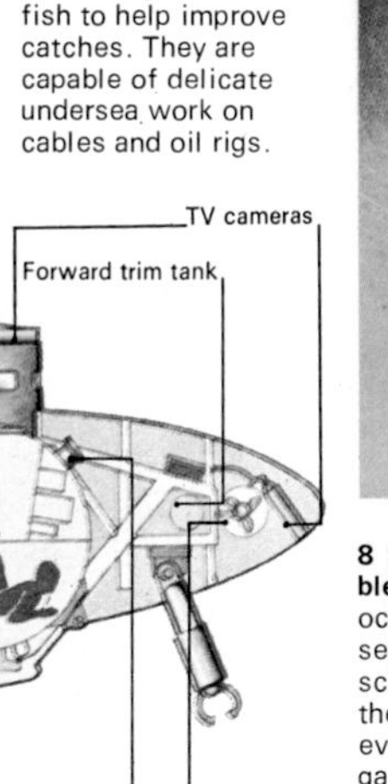

Aft trim tank
Vertical propulsion motor
TV cameras
Main ballast tank
Forward trim tank
Batteries
Pressure hull
Main propulsion motor
HP air flasks
Viewing ports
Bow thruster

8 Modern submersibles are important in oceanographic research. Using them scientists can search the ocean floors for evidence of oil, manganese nodules, and other minerals. Similar vessels are used to inspect and maintain underwater structures such as offshore drilling rigs (for natural gas and oil) and submarine telephone cables. Mechanical "hands," controlled from inside the submersible, are used to collect samples or to hold tools. The vessel can also be equipped with powerful lights, television cameras, and underwater cutting torches. At shallower depths, a submersible can act as a base and even living quarters for divers, who leave and enter the craft through an airlock. Communication to the surface may be by telephone along a cable, or a sonar (supersonic sound) beam may be used to transmit suitably coded voice messages or even slow-scan television pictures. All equipment is worked by electricity from storage batteries.

Carts, coaches, and carriages

When early people were hunters they found that they could transport their kill more easily if they dragged it on a crude sled [1] rather than carrying it on their backs. Soon they found that lengths of tree trunks used as rollers could move even heavier loads.

A solid wheel fixed to a platform by a simple axle was a logical development of the roller system [2]. The first reported use of a wheel was in Mesopotamia, the land between the rivers Tigris and Euphrates, some 5,000 years ago. Oxen-hauled wheeled transportation then developed, and its use spread slowly to the Mediterranean, Europe, and China. When the Romans turned their attention to the building of wheeled vehicles their fine roads permitted fast travel in chariots—an important factor in the empire's administration.

In the period between the fall of the Roman Empire and the fifteenth century, progress in the development of vehicular transportation lapsed. Most travellers were soldiers, pilgrims, or pedlars who relied largely on horses or pack animals. Farm carts used for local haulage were drawn by heavy horses especially bred for the work and in later times used as battle chargers. The few wheeled vehicles of the Middle Ages had no springs [4], and a long journey through Europe could take several uncomfortable months.

Transportation on wheels develops

As communication between peoples increased, the use of carriages began to develop. The first vehicles used rigid axles until suspensions in the form of flexible wood laths, then leather straps, were introduced. Early sixteenth century carriages, often extravagantly decorated, were much resented. The public envied those rich enough to afford them, the Church considered private conveyances sinful, and the authorities kept a close watch, thinking them ripe for taxing—attitudes very similar to the ones of those who opposed the introduction of the automobile some 400 years later.

By the seventeenth century, the period of mechanical and scientific awakening in Western Europe, some coaches and carriages had metal spring suspensions. Large rear wheels allowed the vehicles to travel at higher speeds over the poor roads and also provided a more comfortable ride.

During the seventeenth century, Great Britain changed, mainly because of trade, from a farming community to a commercial nation with the need to convey goods and people over long distances. Smaller, lighter vehicles were developed for rapid short trips. But for longer journeys the early stage coaches could travel little more than 30mi (48km) a day, stopping periodically at staging posts. A journey from London to Edinburgh—a distance of 420mi (675km)—took 12 days even by fast coach.

From mail coach to rail travel

The first coaches to carry both mail and passengers traveled from Bath to London in 1783. Mail coaches were so reliable that clocks could be set by their 10mph (16kph) schedule. Coaching inns, some of them able to cater to a hundred coaches a day, provided passengers with meals and accommodations along the main routes.

CONNECTIONS

See also
1676 History of transportation
1700 Buses and streetcars
1748 Road building
1692 History of automobiles

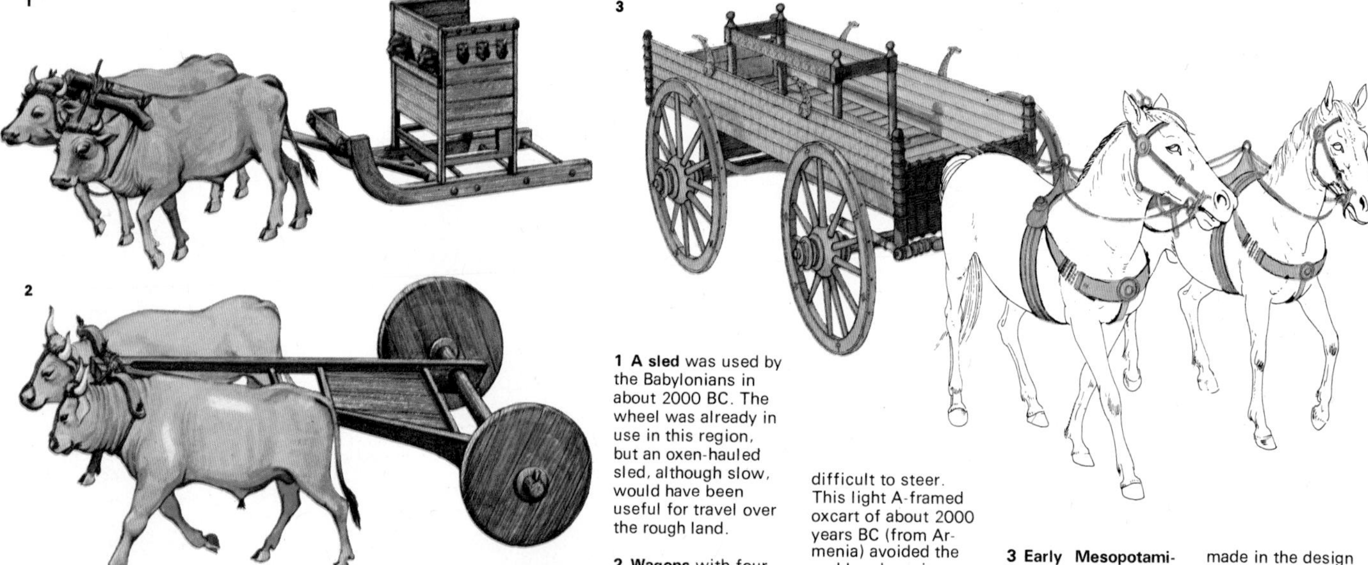

1 A sled was used by the Babylonians in about 2000 BC. The wheel was already in use in this region, but an oxen-hauled sled, although slow, would have been useful for travel over the rough land.

2 Wagons with four fixed wheels were difficult to steer. This light A-framed oxcart of about 2000 years BC (from Armenia) avoided the problem by using only two wheels.

3 Early Mesopotamian civilizations had cattle, sheep, goats—but no horses. Horses were first tamed on the plains of central Asia. Early Celts had very little knowledge of either wagons or horses but by the first century BC a considerable advancement had been made in the design and use of horse-drawn vehicles, as shown by this illustration of a two-horse ceremonial Celtic or Teutonic wagon used on feast days. The picture was reconstructed from fragments found on the western coast of Jutland, Denmark.

4 Horses, mules, and pack animals were the main forms of transportation in the Middle Ages, but this type of "longwagon" was used to carry women of rank and wealth in relative comfort.

5 French elegance can be seen in the design of this heavy seventeenth century funeral coach. Leather strap suspension and the large rear wheels (the front wheels were smaller to allow them to turn on a central steering pivot without fouling the body) gave passengers in this type of coach a reasonably comfortable ride on roads that had improved little for about a thousand years. In Britain, Charles II issued a royal charter to all coachmakers demanding that attention be paid to the problems of transportation.

The nineteenth century saw great changes, including the brief introduction of steam coaches. Traveling became more comfortable with the development of elliptical leaf springs made of several thin, flat springs bound together; these are still used for many purposes today. The design of carriages and coaches became more elegant and lighter following the improvement of roads by the engineer John McAdam (1756–1836), whose type of road surfacing, designed to compact by the weight of passing traffic, greatly facilitated travel.

The Victorians used numerous types of horse-drawn vehicles for short journeys, ranging from the light gig to the family brake. Wealthy families kept staff to drive or maintain a private coach or drag, a dog cart for sportsmen and gun dogs, a governess cart for the children, a phaeton for rapid journeys, a victoria for park and town use, a brougham for privacy, and perhaps a stately landau for formal occasions.

In the United States the stagecoach enjoyed a longer span of life and helped to open up the West through a vast network of scheduled services operated by coaching companies such as Wells Fargo. The lightweight highwheeled buggy [1] and canopied phaeton or surrey were extensively used for private travel. Both were North American vehicles. A buggy seated two people, whereas a surrey was essentially a family vehicle with two rows of seats.

Cabs, trams and buses

In Europe the hire-cab designed by Joseph Hansom (1803–82) in 1834 (and bearing his name) plied the streets of almost every city, and horse-drawn trams and omnibuses provided reasonably inexpensive travel for the masses. The boxlike omnibus, French in origin, was first introduced to London in 1829 by George Shillibeer at the time of the demise of the coach. By the 1840s the single-decker bus had developed into the double-decker with seating along the length of the top deck [8]. With further development improvements were added, and the double-decker became the design adopted by bus companies as motor-driven vehicles replaced horse-drawn carriages.

KEY

The brougham, a type of small, closed carriage for town and winter use, was first made in 1839 for Lord Brougham (1778–1868). It was unique in Britain and led to a revolution in carriage design, although similar vehicles were already in use in Paris. Eventually the brougham became one of the most common town carriages. The original version, known as the single brougham, was drawn by one horse and carried two people. Later models, known as double broughams, were drawn by two horses and carried up to four people.

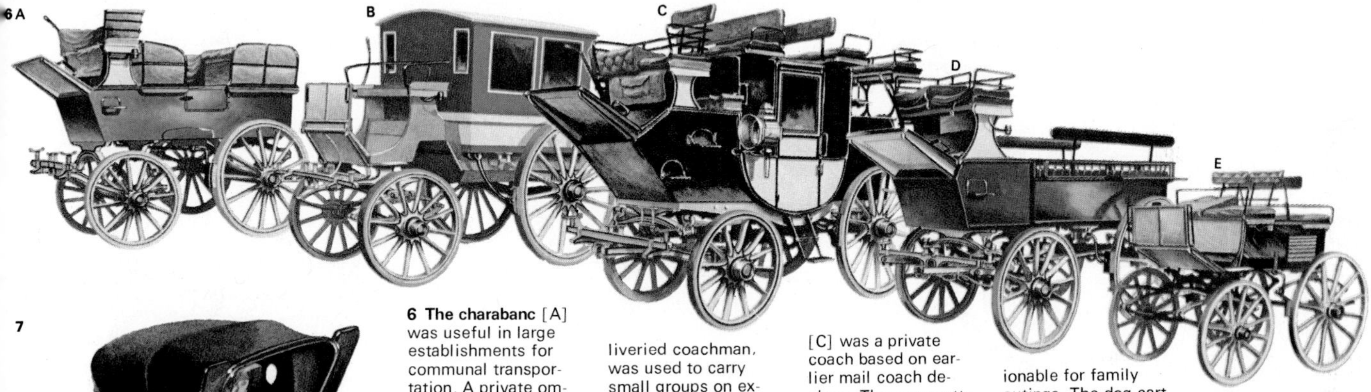

6 The charabanc [A] was useful in large establishments for communal transportation. A private omnibus [B], driven by a liveried coachman, was used to carry small groups on excursions. The drag [C] was a private coach based on earlier mail coach designs. The wagonette [D], with seats down each side and a rear entrance, was fashionable for family outings. The dog cart [E], originally designed to carry sportsmen and their dogs, became widely used for everyday travel.

7 European carriage design influenced many early American models. But the buggy had a very definite North American character, although the word "buggy" was originally an English word meaning a hooded gig. The distinctive American buggy, which made its appearance in about 1850, was a light, fast carriage with two or four high wheels and a thin frame supporting the carriage and canopy. It was drawn by one horse and seated two passengers.

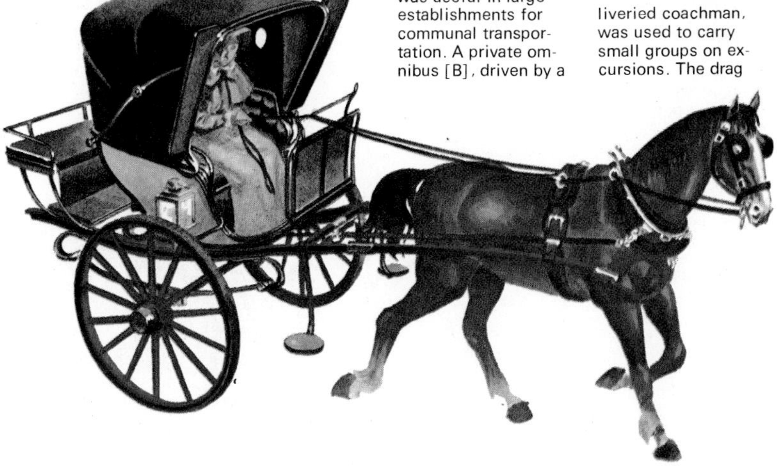

8 The word "omnibus" (meaning "for every one") originated in France in about 1825 for a transportation service operating in Nantes. Introduced to London in 1829 by the Englishman George Shillibeer (1797–1866), the omnibus was an immediate success. The initial service, which ran between Paddington and the Bank for a fare of one shilling, was provided by a horse-drawn vehicle carrying 18 to 22 passengers. A liveried conductor stood guard by the rear entrance door. Soon people adopted the practice of perching on the roof of these single-deckers, leading to the development of the double-decker "knifeboard" bus with no weather protection on the upper deck (fares on top were half price). By the 1880s it had developed into the two-horse "garden seat" bus pictured here, in which forward-facing seats replaced the long bench. Horse-bus service operated in London until 1914.

History of bicycles

Bicycles driven by cranked pedals date from the 1860s, and since then the machines have become popular throughout the world, particularly in Great Britain, France, Italy, the Netherlands, and other European countries. Troops riding bicycles were employed by the major powers in World War I and, more recently, by the Vietcong in Vietnam.

The first bicycle

The history of the bicycle begins with non-powered machines developed in France in the late 1700s. In 1791 the Comte de Sivrac built his *célérifère*. It was a wooden machine consisting of two wheels in line joined by a bar that carried a seat. The rider straddled the bar and "walked" the machine along. Similar machines were made by Nicéphore Niepce (1765–1833; also the inventor of an early photographic process) in 1816 and by the German Baron Karl von Drais a year later. Drais' *Laufmaschine* soon became popular in Britain and Germany as the hobbyhorse.

In 1839 the Scotsman Kirkpatrick Macmillan produced a "powered" hobbyhorse propelled by pedals at the front that worked backward and forward driving connecting rods to turn the rear wheel. Rotating pedal cranks, driving the front wheel directly, were introduced by the French brothers Pierre and Ernest Michaux in about 1861. They called their machines *Vélocipèdes* and within four years were manufacturing 400 bicycles a year. By 1869 bicycle racing was established in France.

The "ordinary," or "penny-farthing," bicycle [Key] had a large front wheel driven directly by pedals and a small rear wheel. Invented in 1871 by the Englishman James Starley (1831–81), it rapidly became the most popular type of bicycle. The size of the large wheel was chosen to suit the length of the rider's legs and varied from 39in (1m) to 59in (1.5m) across.

Chain-driven bicycles

The first chain-driven machine was built in 1874 by H. J. Lawson. Pedals mounted on the frame turned a large sprocket wheel that drove an endless chain around a smaller sprocket on the rear wheel. Bicycles again had wheels of roughly equal sizes. The Rover safety bicycle of 1885 was mass produced and within a few years completely replaced the penny-farthing. All these early bicycles had solid rubber tires mounted on steel-rimmed wheels.

The modern machine

A milestone in the history of the bicycle came in 1888 when John Dunlop (1840–1921) invented the air-filled or pneumatic tire. The diamond-shaped frame became standard, and there were no major changes in bicycle design for the next 70 years. In the 1960s various manufacturers produced small-wheeled bicycles—some of which could be folded to fit into the trunk of a car—for urban use. Earlier unusual designs included the tandem, a long-framed bicycle for two riders, and the three-wheeled bicycle, which became important as the type of machine into which Karl Benz (1844–1929) and Gottlieb Daimler (1834–1904) fitted gasoline engines to make the first automobiles in 1885.

A modern bicycle has fenders, electric

CONNECTIONS

See also
1690 History of motorcycl
1704 Technology and transportation in developing nations

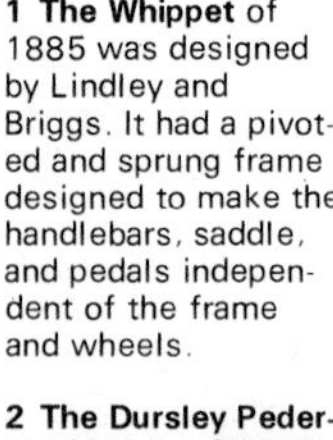

1 The Whippet of 1885 was designed by Lindley and Briggs. It had a pivoted and sprung frame designed to make the handlebars, saddle, and pedals independent of the frame and wheels.

2 The Dursley Pederson bicycle of 1893 was designed by M. Pederson and built at Dursley in England. The frame members were of twin narrow-section tubes, side by side for rigidity, giving a lighter frame.

3 The Raleigh Safety bicycle of 1901 had an all-steel frame joined by a new brazing process using pressed steel sockets brazed to the frame tubes by dipping the joints in molten brass.

4 The Swift ladies' bicycle of 1926 had no crossbar on the frame, making it easier for a woman wearing a skirt to get on and off. The lightweight frame was an advance over early heavy designs.

5 The Velocino bicycle, made in Italy in the mid-1930s, was an attempt at a compact design that was easy to store and carry. Its inventors also claimed it to be easier to dismount in an emergency.

6 The Moulton bicycle, produced in the UK in 1962, had small wheels, rubber suspension, and a low center of gravity. The frame could be adjusted to "fit" the build of almost any rider and was strong enough to carry heavy loads.

lamps powered by batteries or a generator, and lever or caliper brakes acting on the rims of both wheels [7]. It may have variable gear ratios and a guard to enclose the chain and transmission. Accessories include extra carrying capacity in the form of a rear-mounted rack, a basket in front of the handlebars, and a saddlebag or a pair of baskets mounted on each side of the rear wheel. The frame is generally made of seamless steel tubing brazed or welded together. In the brazing process pre-cut lengths of tubing are fitted over angled sockets and secured in place with molten brass. In welding there are no sockets, and the tubes are joined with molten steel.

Between 24 and 40 wire spokes join the wheel hub to the rim. The rim end of each spoke is threaded, and a nut or nipple is screwed onto it to keep the spoke taut. The rim may be made of aluminum alloy, stainless steel, or chromium plated stainless steel. Hard rubber brake blocks, worked by levers (called stirrups) or calipers (which act like pincers to nip each side of the wheel), press on the rim for braking. An alternative type of brake acts by pressing inside the hub of the rear wheel and is brought into action by back-pedaling.

The rear wheel of a bicycle rotates faster than the large sprocket wheel turned by the pedals. There are generally about 48 teeth on the large sprocket wheel and about 18 on the smaller rear sprocket. This provides a gear ratio of about 2.66 to 1. Variable gears allow different speeds for a constant pedaling effort. There are two main types. In a *dérailleur* gear there are up to six rear sprockets of different sizes plus up to three on the pedal wheel to provide a variety of gear ratios.

An epicyclic gear, developed by Sturmey and Archer, is more complicated. A small cog called the sun gear inside the rear hub is rotated by the rear sprocket. A ring of teeth line the inside of the hub and the drive is transmitted from the sun gear by a set of planetary gears. Three different gear ratios are available. Sturmey-Archer and *dérailleur* types can be combined on the same hub to provide the rider with an eight-gear combination.

KEY

The penny-farthing or ordinary bicycle first appeared in the early 1870s, invented by Englishman James Starley (1831–81). The rider pedaled cranks mounted at the center of the large front wheel, which he also turned to steer the machine.

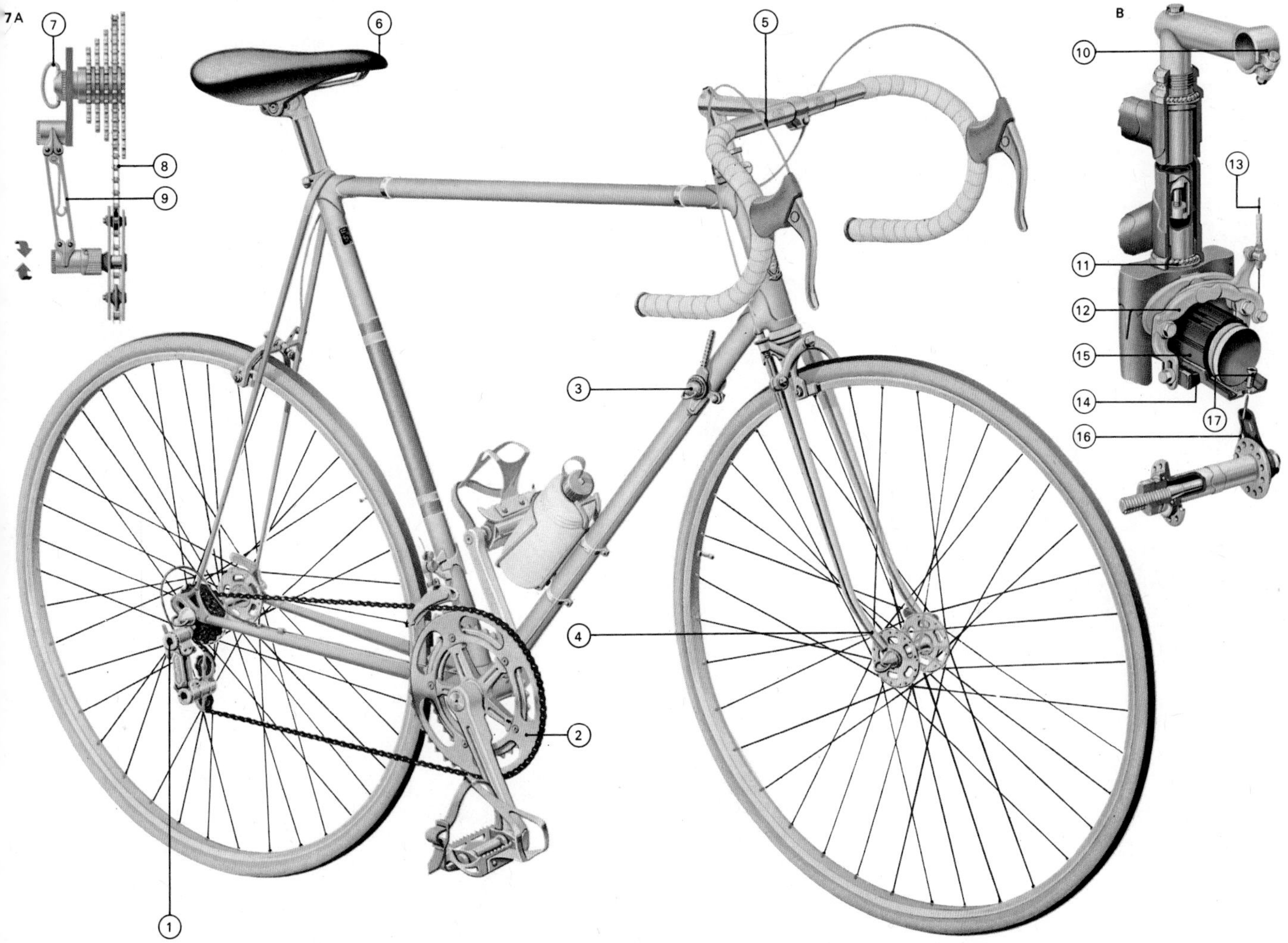

7 A modern touring bicycle has a short wheelbase for maneuverability and is made of lightweight alloys to reduce the weight of the machine. It has two sets of *dérailleur* gears, one [1] on the rear hub and the other [2] on the main sprocket, giving it up to 28 different gear ratios. The gears are changed by means of two levers [3] on the frame. The front forks [4] are nearly straight, to reduce the wheelbase, but have enough curvature to act as springs. The handlebars [5] and saddle [6] are both adjustable, and the saddle is fixed so that the distance from it to the handlebars is about the same as the length between the rider's elbow and fingertips. The height of the saddle above the lowest point of the pedal is ideally 9% longer than the rider's inside leg length. The *dérailleur* gear [A] on the rear hub has up to six sprockets, or increasing sizes, mounted on a quick-release hub [7]. Small sprockets give high gears and larger ones low gears. The drive chain [8] can be shifted from one sprocket to another by a parallelogram arrangement [9] held in sideways tension by a spring. The stem and fork assembly [B] of a modern bicycle has to bear much of the weight and still pivot freely for steering the machine. Handlebars are fitted to an angled sprocket [10] at the top of the stem. A ballrace [11] provides a friction-free bearing. Most modern machines have brakes consisting of a caliper [12] operated by a bowden cable [13]. When the cable is pulled the caliper nips brake blocks [14] against the wheel rim. The tire [15] has a canvas carcass covered by synthetic rubber tread. Each spoke [16] is tensioned by a nipple [17].

History of motorcycles

The motorcycle is an older invention than the automobile. Two Frenchmen, Pierre and Ernest Michaux, built the first motorcycle—a steam powered "boneshaker" in Paris in 1869, sixteen years before Karl Benz (1844–1929) and Gottlieb Daimler (1834–1900) made the first cars. But the advantage of Daimler's gasoline engine was soon put to use.

Early developments

Other technical innovations soon improved these early machines. The pneumatic tire of J. B. Dunlop (1840–1921), invented in 1888, helped to absorb some of the bone-jarring shocks from the road surface. The final drive was generally a leather belt, which tended to break or slip in wet weather. The engine was started by pedaling, to turn over the motor, or by "bump starting" in which the rider pushed the machine, running alongside and jumping onto the seat when the engine fired. The Butler spray carburetor of 1889, modified and refined by Wilhelm Maybach (1847–1929) in 1893, was the forerunner of those still used today.

Motor tricycles also date from about 1880. Some were little better than motorized wheelchairs. But the De Dion Bouton of 1898 had a rear-mounted engine, a differential, and was capable of the then staggering speed of 25mph (40kph).

In Britain the Road Acts of 1861 and 1865 had required that all motor vehicles be preceded by a man carrying a red flag. The repeal of these laws in 1869 removed the restrictions that had cramped British designs for so long. In the same year Colonel Capel Holden patented a motorcycle with a four-cylinder opposed engine. This had a commutator-type distributor powered by a coil and a battery, as on a modern car. External connecting rods drove the rear wheel directly by means of overhung cranks.

Wider applications of motorcycles

The motorcycle movement was also growing in the United States, where by 1905 the main manufacturers were Harley Davidson and Indian. Both companies pioneered the use of twistgrips [1] on the handlebars to control the throttle and advance and retard the ignition timing. The 1.75hp Indian of 1905 had a single cylinder engine with a steel cylinder machined from a solid casting. Harley Davidson produced its first V-twin cylinder engine in 1909 and has used the same layout in most of its engines ever since. By 1914 the motorcycle speed record had risen to 93.5mph (150.5kph). In the same year, the first of World War I, the British Army began to use motorcycles for dispatch riders and used machines fitted with sidecars that could also carry a machine gun.

By the 1920s nearly all large engined machines had a chain or shaft as final drive. Overhead valve engines began to appear and some, such as the 1,000cc units in Harley Davidsons and Indians, had four valves to each cylinder. In Germany BMW produced its first motorcycles with a horizontally opposed twin cylinder engine, an arrangement that has survived.

As the volume of traffic increased, particularly in the United States, police forces began to use motorcycles for patrol duties.

CONNECTIONS

See also
1688 History of bicycles
1626 Basic types of engines
1692 History of automobiles

1

Indian

1 Indian (1911) became popular by taking 1st, 2nd, and 3rd in the Isle of Man TT races. This rarer single cylinder machine also had twist grip controls.

2

2 Brough Superior (1924) was the first production machine generally available with a top speed of more than 100mph (160kph). This 1930 version, the Black Alpine, had a JAP 680cc V-twin engine, a heavy-duty four-speed Sturmey-Archer gearbox, and a bottom link front fork developed by Harley Davidson.

3

Norton
2

3 Norton International (1932) was so successful it became known as the "Unapproachable Norton." This 490cc version had hairpin valve springs and others had rubber-mounted handlebars. Optional extras included plunger-type rear springs, straight through exhaust pipes, and a Norton TT-type gearbox.

4

4 Velocette KTT (1949) resulted from the firm's considerable racing success in the 1930s. The machine had a 348cc overhead camshaft engine, air-filled "hydraulic" rear shock absorbers, and "girder" front forks (later superseded by "teledraulic" forks).

5

USA 619028

5 Harley Davidson WLA and WLC (1945, produced for the Canadian Government) were adapted from earlier civilian machines. They had strengthened frames, bearings, gearboxes and clutches. The 750cc twin side-valve engine was rugged and reliable. It was one of the machines for Allied dispatch riders and military police at the end of World War II.

Large four cylinder machines produced by companies such as Henderson and Indian were particularly suited for driving on the long, straight American roads.

Two-stroke engines

A two-stroke gasoline engine has fewer moving parts than a four-stroke and is easier to maintain. By 1930 Villiers and other companies were producing a wide range of single cylinder two-stroke engines. During the late 1920s and the 1930s the motorcycle underwent a social change. It ceased to be a luxury machine and evolved into a relatively cheap and utilitarian form of transportation. A second passenger could be carried behind the driver, and a sidecar gave the "combination" a carrying capacity of up to four (two adults and two children).

By 1937 a Brough Superior fitted with a 1,000cc JAP engine had pushed the world speed record up to nearly 170mph (275kph). Once again the motorcycle industry was preparing for war. In 1938 BMW produced the R75 model, with a sidecar, for the German army.

Postwar development was characterized by smaller, higher-revving engines, and in Europe thousands of motor scooters were produced. Between 1950 and 1965 manufacturers of expensive "luxury" machines such as the Vincent and Sunbeam (which used rubber mounted engines) were forced to close down in the face of competition from mass produced machines from Triumph, BSA, Norton and AMC. A wide range of special purpose machines became available, for scrambles, trials, and road racing.

During the early 1960s the Japanese Honda company began to enter Western markets with its small, 50cc four-stroke machines. Followed by Suzuki and Yamaha producing two-strokes, the Japanese soon dominated the market with models ranging from 50cc "monkey bikes" to 750cc four cylinder machines capable of 130mph (210kph). Most motorcycles sold today are economical and comfortable machines. Electric starters and hydraulic disc brakes are becoming standard, and rotary engines have been introduced.

KEY

The first recorded motorcycle was built in France in 1869, based on an existing Michaux velocipede—a type of "boneshaker" pedal bicycle. It was fitted with a small single-cylinder steam engine. A flexible leather belt linked a pulley on the engine with a larger one on the rear wheel, thus gearing down the speed of the engine. Within 20 years other inventors constructed steam bicycles and tricycles, and in 1886 the German engineer Gottlieb Daimler fitted his air-cooled gasoline engine into a wooden bicycle. At about the same time the English inventor Edward Butler patented his "Petro-cycle," a three-wheeler with two-cylinder water-cooled engine. The first commercially successful gasoline engined motorcycle was produced in 1893 by Henry and Wilhelm Wildebrand in Munich.

6
7
8

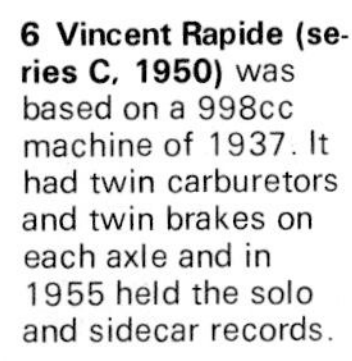

6 Vincent Rapide (series C, 1950) was based on a 998cc machine of 1937. It had twin carburetors and twin brakes on each axle and in 1955 held the solo and sidecar records.

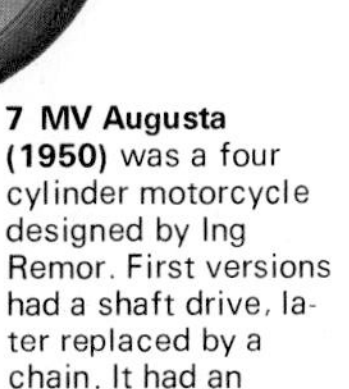

7 MV Augusta (1950) was a four cylinder motorcycle designed by Ing Remor. First versions had a shaft drive, later replaced by a chain. It had an electric starter.

8 Honda's highly successful 250cc four-cylinder racing machine was produced in 1961. There were four valves to each cylinder, and the engine had a double overhead camshaft. With this model Honda reintroduced the multi-valve configuration originally evolved in Europe 25 years earlier, but discarded. The configuration is now considered the norm for successful racing. A train of gears from the center of the five-bearing crankshaft drives the transmission, camshafts, and ignition generator. The design of the engine permits very high peak revolutions.

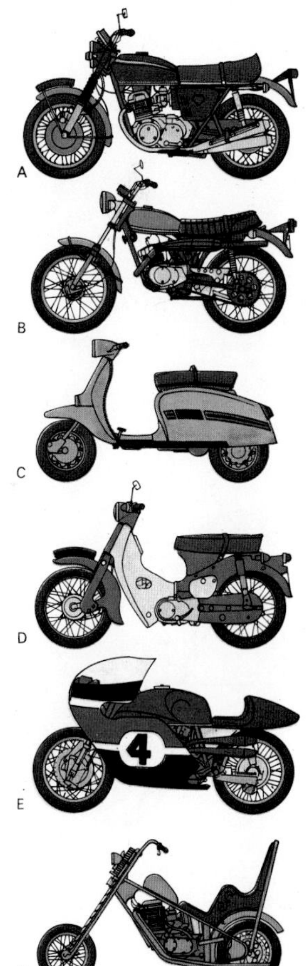
9
A
B
C
D
E
F

9 Types of modern motorcycles include [A] standard 750cc road-going sports, capable of carrying two people at high speed; [B] trail bike with high-mounted engine, wide handlebars, and knobby tires for cross-country riding; [C] Italian pioneered motor scooter with good weather protection; [D] "step-through" motorcycle with small engine and automatic clutch for use in towns; [E] fully modified road racer with a highly tuned engine in a special frame giving a 175mph (280kph) machine suitable for only the most experienced riders; and [F] the "chopper" using a standard engine in a highly modified frame with upswept handlebars and a sit-back saddle.

History of automobiles

The automobile was not invented overnight. It took shape from an accumulation of technical advances that resulted in a light and efficient engine. The accepted "fathers of the modern automobile" are two Germans, Karl Benz (1844–1929) and Gottlieb Daimler (1834–1900), who built their first gasoline-fueled motor vehicles within a few months of each other (1885–86).

More than a hundred years earlier, the first self-propelled road vehicle had rumbled through the streets of Paris at nearly 3mph (5kph) when Nicolas Cugnot (1725–1804) demonstrated his steam-driven wagon [1].

The first automobile

The German Nikolaus Otto (1832–91) made the first four-stroke internal combustion engine in 1876, and in 1885 Daimler had installed a small four-stroke engine in a cycle frame. He drove his first four-wheeled gasoline-driven vehicle around Cannstatt in 1886. In neighboring Mannheim, Benz tested his three-wheeled car.

Daimler licensed the French firm of Panhard and Levassor to build his engine. Levassor placed it at the front of his crude car [2], and it drove the rear wheels through a clutch and a gearbox. Thus in 1891 the first car to use modern engineering layout was seen. Within three years of the appearance of the first Panhard, France was staging auto races on public roads.

At the turn of the century, gasoline, steam, and electric power shared almost equal popularity for powering automobiles. Steam was reliable and electric vehicles held the land speed record. France had several established automobile manufacturers —Panhard, Peugeot, Renault, Daracq, Delehaye, and others. In Germany Benz had made the world's first standard production car, the Velo (1894), and the Daimler company was just about to present the Mercedes to the public (1901) [3].

In the United States the automobile would develop along different lines. There the car was seen not as a rich man's toy, but as a new method of transportation in a continent in which travel had been restricted by a lack of roads and great distances that had to be covered.

American cars

One of the first cars to capture the imagination of America was the Stanley Steamer, built in 1896 by the Stanley brothers of Massachusetts. It set a land speed record of 127.66mi (205.4km) per hour in 1906. Most authorities credit Charles E. and J. Frank Duryea with the invention of the first American gasoline-powered automobile. Driven for the first time in 1893, it had a one-cylinder gasoline engine.

Ransom Eli Olds (1864–1950) developed the first commercially successful American-made automobile in 1901. He employed many companies, each producing a different part for his three-horsepower car, thus utilizing a mass-production system. In 1904, 5,000 of these unique cars were sold.

In 1908, Henry Ford introduced the Model T [5]. This automobile had been built by a new type of manufacturing system—the assembly line. This lowered the price of the Model T, enabling more people to buy the "Tin Lizzie." Soon automobile companies, such as Fiat, Citröen, and Austin,

CONNECTIONS

See also
1694 Classic cars
1696 How an automobile works
1626 Basic types of engine
1748 Road building
1750 Traffic engineering
1698 Cars and society
1700 Buses and streetcars
1676 History of transportation

1 The first self-propelled road vehicle, built by Cugnot in 1769, was a tiller-steered, two-cylinder, steam-powered tractor. Its "engine" was on the single front wheel and was designed to pull guns. It involved its inventor in the world's first motor accident when it hit a wall.

2 Panhard and Levassor (1894) was developed from the 1891 design. It had a Daimler engine mounted at the front of the car, with the drive passing through a clutch and gearbox to the rear wheels. This French design was to be adopted as the standard modern layout.

3 The Mercedes, built by Daimler, appeared in 1901. Technically advanced for its day it had a 35bhp/5.9-liter engine.

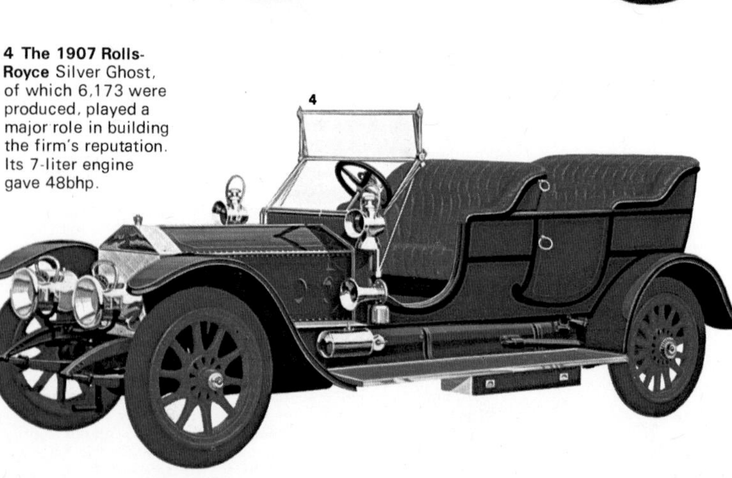

4 The 1907 Rolls-Royce Silver Ghost, of which 6,173 were produced, played a major role in building the firm's reputation. Its 7-liter engine gave 48bhp.

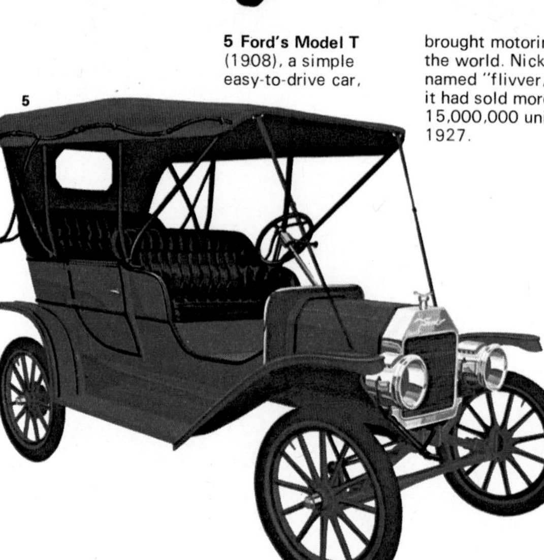

5 Ford's Model T (1908), a simple easy-to-drive car, brought motoring to the world. Nicknamed "flivver," it had sold more than 15,000,000 units by 1927.

were emerging in Europe and following Ford's techniques.

By 1910 automobile design had become fairly settled, with a side-valve, four- (or six-) cylinder, front-mounted engine. Weather protection had been developed, and the electric starter introduced by Cadillac in 1912 had encouraged women to take to the wheel by removing the physical hardship of the starting handle. Interchangeable parts made to fine tolerances opened the gates to mass production. Heavy, unstable coach-built sedan bodies encouraged the trend to wood and fabric and later to the rigid, welded pressed-steel body. In the 1930s power brakes and independent front wheel suspension appeared. Cars in the 1940s and 1950s were being equipped with automatic transmission, sealed-beam headlights, and power steering. Pressure from the public and the government brought safety changes in cars during the 1960s.

Cheaper cars

From the 1930s to the 1960s American cars were getting larger and more luxurious, while in Europe the emphasis was on basic medium-sized cars. In 1934 Citröen produced the Traction Avant [7], the first medium-sized car to have front-wheel drive and independent suspension. In 1955 the hydro-pneumatic suspension system of the Citröen DS 19 astonished the automobile world. The end of 1959 saw the introduction of the Morris Mini-Minor, now known as the Mini. It had a transversely mounted engine, front-wheel drive, and rubber suspension. In the United States only American Motors produced a compact car, the Rambler, at this time.

During the 1960s and 1970s foreign car imports to the United States rose. The success in the United States of the Volkswagen [8] from Germany and of the Toyota and Datsun from Japan led US producers to manufacture compact cars such as the Dodge Aspen [10] and Ford Maverick.

The energy crisis of the 1970s put even a greater emphasis on small energy-saving cars and a trend started toward the manufacture of subcompacts such as the Chevrolet Chevette.

KEY

Gottlieb Daimler (1834–1900) in 1883 made one of the first relatively fast-running, lightweight engines using gasoline. Developed in the experimental laboratory he had set up in 1882 in Cannstatt, Germany, with Wilhelm Maybach, he had built it into a wooden motorcycle by 1885 and within a year produced his first car. At almost the same time, but independently, Carl Benz built his first car. This three-wheeler had a 1.5hp single-cylinder, water-cooled gasoline engine mounted horizontally at the back of the car. Final drive was by means of a chain to a gear on the back axle.

6

6 A classic of the vintage era, the Vauxhall 30/98 was famous for its successes in sprints and hill-climbing competitions.

7

7 The revolutionary front-wheel drive Citröen of 1934 was the model for this 1939 15CV and subsequent models.

8

8 The Volkswagen, "car for people," was designed by Ferdinand Porsche (1875–1951). First planned in 1934, the design of the air-cooled rear-engined "Beetle" changed very little after that.

9

9 The Fiat 128 is typical of the European car of the 1970s. It follows the world trend forced by the shortage of fuel and has a small high-revving engine for economy and front-wheel drive.

10

10 The Dodge Aspen is an example of recent trends in styling and engineering in American compact cars. While reducing the overall length, the emphasis is on adequate interior space. Economy of operation is stressed. Today's compacts may some day be thought of as standard-size cars.

Classic cars

The history of the automobile spans less than 100 years from the spluttering experiments of pioneers such as Benz, Daimler, and Panhard to the mass-produced, energy-conserving designs of the 1970s.

Between the two world wars, the fundamental principles of the machine had become well established. Henry Ford (1863–1947) in the United States had proved the economic common sense of mass production, and motoring became available to an ever larger section of the population.

Yet during this time there emerged a few really great cars. They were carefully, almost lovingly, built—generally one at a time, to individual customer's orders. Some incorporated radical innovations, although most merely represented the best available combination of design and engineering skills. Their names became synonymous with quality and status. Some, such as Alfa Romeo, Rolls-Royce, Cadillac, and Mercedes, survive as names. A whole list of others has gone. But these classic cars were the ancestors of the modern workhorses that are a major world industry.

1 Mercedes (Germany, 1914) was designed by Paul Daimler for that year's Grand Prix. Its 4.5-liter engine gave it a maximum speed of 112mph (180kph). It had two coils and three spark plugs per cylinder. Front-wheel brakes were a post-World War I addition to the car.

CONNECTIONS

See also
1692 Historyof automobiles

1

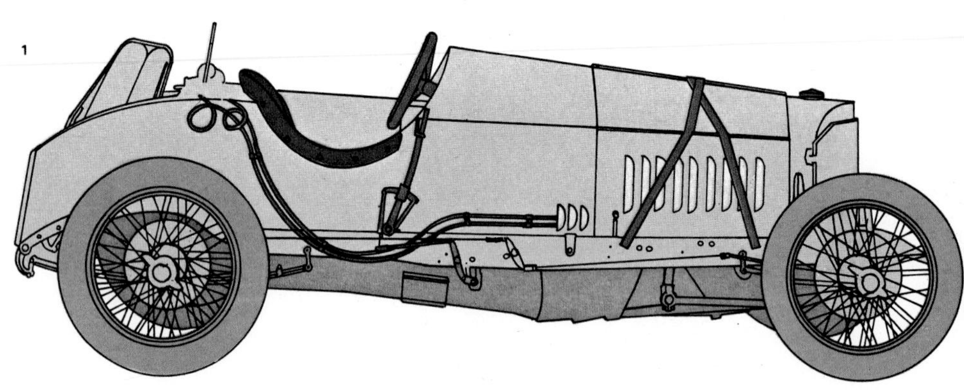

2

2 Hispano-Suiza (France, 1922) had a steel and aluminum engine, based on earlier airplane engines by the Swiss designer Marc Birkigt, of 6.6-liter capacity. It was the first car to have power brakes on all four wheels, and had a maximum speed of 85mph (137kph).

3 Isotta-Fraschini A (Italy, 1929) had twin carburetors to feed gasoline into its 7.4-liter eight cylinder engine, giving an output of 120bhp. Its Italian manufacturer pioneered the use of four-wheel brakes.

3

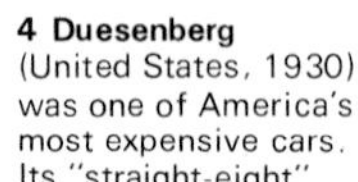

4 Duesenberg (United States, 1930) was one of America's most expensive cars. Its "straight-eight" 6.9-liter engine had more than 260bhp to give the car a top speed of more than 110mph (175kph).

4

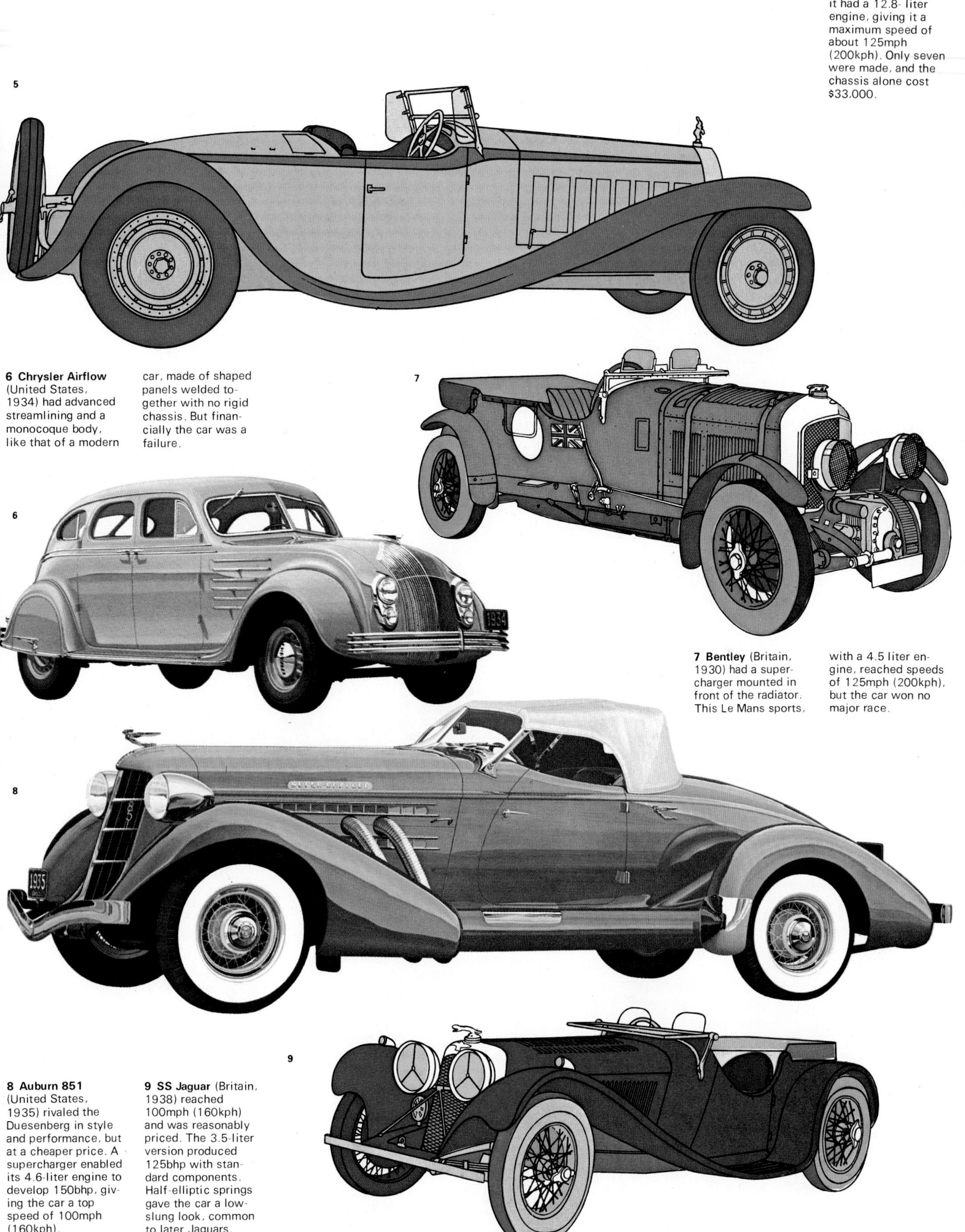
1934
1935

5

5 Bugatti Royale (France, 1927) was one of the largest cars ever built. More than 20ft (6m) long and 6.5ft (2m) wide, it had a 12.8- liter engine, giving it a maximum speed of about 125mph (200kph). Only seven were made, and the chassis alone cost $33,000.

6

6 Chrysler Airflow (United States, 1934) had advanced streamlining and a monocoque body, like that of a modern car, made of shaped panels welded together with no rigid chassis. But financially the car was a failure.

7

7 Bentley (Britain, 1930) had a supercharger mounted in front of the radiator. This Le Mans sports, with a 4.5 liter engine, reached speeds of 125mph (200kph), but the car won no major race.

8

8 Auburn 851 (United States, 1935) rivaled the Duesenberg in style and performance, but at a cheaper price. A supercharger enabled its 4.6-liter engine to develop 150bhp, giving the car a top speed of 100mph (160kph).

9

9 SS Jaguar (Britain, 1938) reached 100mph (160kph) and was reasonably priced. The 3.5-liter version produced 125bhp with standard components. Half-elliptic springs gave the car a low-slung look, common to later Jaguars.

How an automobile works

A typical modern car can be divided into four main component systems: the engine, producer of the power; the transmission, which feeds the power to the road wheels; the electrical system; and the body/chassis, including steering, brakes, and suspension [Key]. Wherever the engine is placed—at the rear, driving the rear wheels, in front, driving the front wheels, or even in the middle—the working principle is basically the same. In the conventional front-engined rear-drive car, the engine feeds rotary power via the clutch, gearbox, propeller shaft, and differential to the rear axle and back wheels.

Transmission

By using the clutch [6] in a standard transmission, the driver is able to connect or disconnect the engine's power to the road wheels, to engage gears to start smoothly, and to stop the car without stopping the engine. When the driver depresses the clutch pedal while the car is in gear, the drive (power) is disconnected from the gearbox and the rest of the transmission; releasing the pedal reconnects the drive.

Generally located just behind the clutch, the gearbox (either manual or automatic) is designed to vary the ratio of speed between engine and road wheels. The normal gasoline engine works best at between 2,000 and 5,000 revolutions per minute (the rate at which the crankshaft turns). To permit this while the car is moving at anything from 10 to 90mph (16–150kph), the standard manual gearbox has a selection of from three to four different forward gear ratios, through three or four pairs of gears [5] respectively. Selecting low (first) gear allows the engine to turn at its working speed while driving the road wheels slowly, resulting in a greater torque or turning effort needed to overcome inertia, heavy loads or a grade. When the car is moving more quickly and less effort is needed to power it, successively higher gears are engaged.

The propeller shaft, running under the floor along the length of the car, is attached at its forward end to the gearbox and at the rear to the differential. The differential has two functions [7], to "bend" the driving power at right angles and feed it to the rear axle and wheels and, when the car is steered around corners, to allow the outer wheel to travel faster than the inner one.

Electrical system and brakes

In pre-1907 motoring days, the sole function of the battery was to produce the spark for plugs (which ignite the fuel-air mixture in the cylinders), but today the car depends on several electric devices for its operation [4]. These are all powered by the battery, which is recharged by a generator (or alternator), driven by the crankshaft through a belt that also turns the cooling fan. The 6- or 12-volt battery supplies the coil (an induction coil), which produces the necessary voltage for the plugs via a distributor. The battery also provides current for the horn, lights, heaters, windshield wipers, radio, and, the heaviest drain of all, the starter motor.

Almost all modern cars, benefiting from racing practice, have disc brakes on the front wheels and drum brakes on the rear. Some cars have discs all around. Metal discs that rotate with the wheels are gripped by stationary pads when the brake pedal

CONNECTIONS

See also
1626 Basic types of engine
1698 Cars and society
1750 Traffic engineering
1692 History of automobiles
1694 Classic cars
1702 Special purpose vehicles
1700 Buses and streetcars

1
- Engine and exhaust
- Fuel system
- Electrical system
- Cooling system
- Transmission
- Steering and suspension
- Brakes

1 Terms used in cars: *Alternator:* charges the battery, often instead of a generator. *Anti-roll bar:* tough steel bar attached to the suspension to minimize roll when cornering *BHP:* brake horse power, measure of engine power. *Brake shoes and pads:* shoes are curved steel segments covered with lining that press on the brake drums. Pads grip exposed discs. *Shock absorbers:* pistons fitted to cushion bounce from springs. *Half-shafts:* the two parts of the rear axle, taking drive from the differential.

2 Cross-ply tires have their cords crossing one another trellis fashion, giving equal stiffness to wall and tread. Radial-ply and cross-ply tires should not be used together.

3 Radial-ply tires, with the cords of the inner case braced and running directly from one side of the tire to the other without criss-crossing, hold the road better and last longer than cross-ply but can be more sensitive to uneven road surfaces.

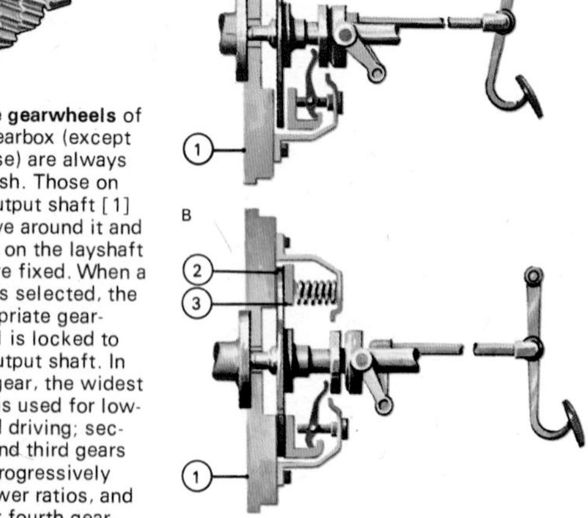

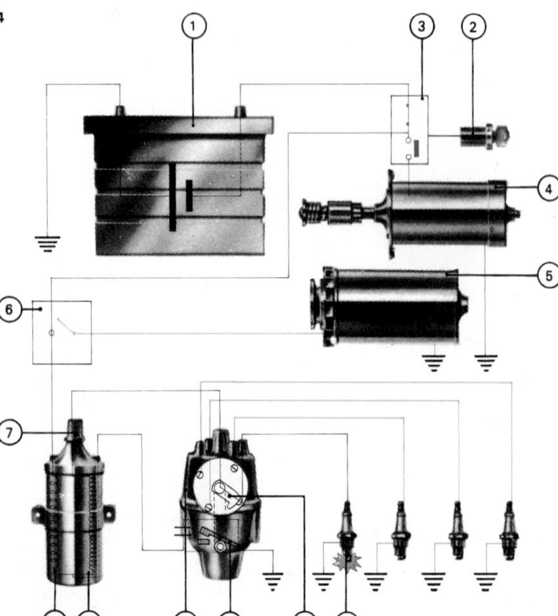

4 The 6- or 12-volt car battery must, through the coil, deliver 10,000 volts at up to 300 times a second to the plugs, and must also provide current for starting, heating, lighting, and electrical accessories. The diagram shows only the starting, ignition, and recharging electrical systems.

1 Battery
2 Ignition key
3 Electromagnetic relay, activated by the key when starting, connecting the battery to the starter motor
4 Starter motor
5 Generator or alternator, driven by the engine to recharge the battery.
6 Control box
7 Ignition coil
8 Primary coil
9 Secondary coil
10 Distributor
11 Contact breaker
12 Rotor arm
13 Spark plug

5 The gearwheels of the gearbox (except reverse) are always in mesh. Those on the output shaft [1] revolve around it and those on the layshaft [2] are fixed. When a gear is selected, the appropriate gearwheel is locked to the output shaft. In first gear, the widest ratio is used for low-speed driving; second and third gears use progressively narrower ratios, and top or fourth gear, when it exists, is obtained by coupling the input shaft directly to the output shaft. Overdrive is a separate and higher top gear fitted to some cars to reduce wear and tear and fuel consumption. It may be engaged automatically or by the driver.

6 The clutch is basically made up of three plates: the flywheel [1], which is fixed to the engine shaft and rotates with it; the clutch plate [2], which is connected to the gearbox shaft; and the pressure plate [3], which clamps the clutch plate to the flywheel when the clutch is engaged by releasing the clutch pedal [B]. Disengaging the clutch by depressing the pedal [A] separates the plates so that the flywheel and clutch plates rotate independently.

is applied [8]. Because the discs are open to the cooling air, heat is quickly dissipated, avoiding brake-fade. All four brakes are operated by the brake pedal via hydraulic lines. The parking (hand) brake operates on the rear wheels only.

Suspension and construction

Suspension is designed to give the passengers a comfortable, smooth ride, and to protect the body and parts of the car by reducing the shocks from the uneven surface of the road [10]. Springs alone would give a bouncing ride, hence shock absorbers are fitted to "damp" down the oscillation that the springs themselves produce. Traditional elliptical or semielliptical springs have in many cars been replaced by helical or coil springs, torsion bar springs (in which a twisting action is used as springing), gas-and-fluid (combined springs and shock absorbers) or rubber springs, or several combined types.

The front wheels of a car are each mounted on separate short axles, so that when the steering wheel is turned and the movement passed to them, each wheel turns on its own axis (the inner one describing a slightly tighter arc than the other). Rack-and-pinion steering [9], the most popular of several systems, has a pinion on the end of the steering column that engages a transverse toothed rack. The rack, connected at its ends to track-rods attached to each road wheel, is moved right or left by the action of the steering wheel, steering the wheels in the required direction.

Until the 1930s, the traditional way of building a car was by making a rigid chassis (the wheels, machinery, and frame). Everything else was bolted onto the chassis. Now many manufacturers use the body itself as the frame. When welded together, the pressed-steel body panels form a rigid "box," each unit contributing to the strength of the structure. Using unit-construction (monocoque) methods, cars can be made more cheaply, and are considerably lighter than earlier models built on a separate chassis. A number of small manufacturers produce cars using light alloy or fiber glass bodies.

KEY

A typical modern car has the engine mounted at the front driving the rear wheels through a gearbox and propeller shaft. The engine, suspension, and steering system are all fixed into the main body of the car, which is constructed as a welded rigid "box" from separate curved body panels. Many manufacturers design cars that can be adapted for right- or left-hand steering, for sales around the world.

7 The differential allows one of the half-shafts and its road wheel to rotate more slowly than the other when the car is turning although both are still being driven, thus improving the cornering and reducing tire wear. The two half-shafts transfer the drive from the differential to the road wheels. The diagram shows that when the driver is turning the steering wheel the rear inner road wheel describes a tighter, shorter arc than the rear outer wheel. Turning a corner would result in tire scrub and loss of handling qualities without the differential. A pinion on the end of the propeller shaft turns the crown wheel in the differential, which rotates four bevel gears, allowing the half-shafts to be driven at different speeds.

8 When the brake pedal is depressed, a piston in the master cylinder forces fluid through hydraulic pipes to slave cylinders on each wheel, pushing shoes or pads into contact with drums or discs. (Brake-shoe pads are curved steel platforms covered with tough fibrous shoes that act on the inside of the brake drums. Pads act on exposed discs holding them in a vise-like grip).

1 Brake pedal
2 Master cylinder
3 Hydraulic pipe
4 Brake shoe and lining
5 Brake drum
6 Slave cylinder
7 Drum brakes on
8 Drum brakes off
9 Disc brakes on
10 Disc brakes off
11 Brake pad
12 Disc

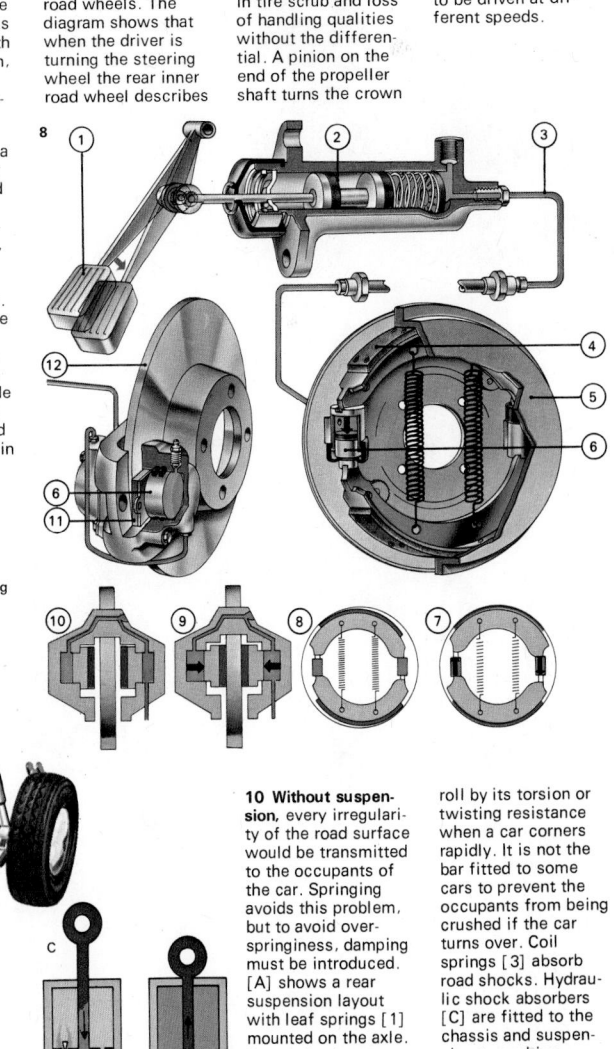

9 Two main types of steering systems are commonly used. Rack-and-pinion steering has a toothed pinion [1] at the end of the steering column [2], which engages with a transverse rack [3] moving it right or left as necessary. Tie rods [4] at each end transmit the movement to the wheels. The steering box system (not shown) has a box that houses a worm reduction gear. The gear drives a drop arm, and, via a transverse link, a slave arm. The power assisted system is a modern refinement of steering, which facilitates driving larger cars by using power steering worked by hydraulic pressure.

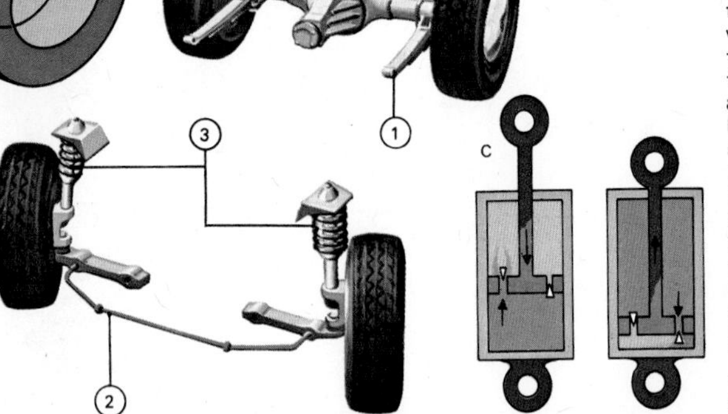
10 A
1
B
3
2
C

10 Without suspension, every irregularity of the road surface would be transmitted to the occupants of the car. Springing avoids this problem, but to avoid over-springiness, damping must be introduced. [A] shows a rear suspension layout with leaf springs [1] mounted on the axle. Front-wheel suspension [B] incorporates an anti-roll bar [2]. This is a steel bar attached to the suspension to minimize roll by its torsion or twisting resistance when a car corners rapidly. It is not the bar fitted to some cars to prevent the occupants from being crushed if the car turns over. Coil springs [3] absorb road shocks. Hydraulic shock absorbers [C] are fitted to the chassis and suspension to cushion bounce from springs. Oil is forced through the constricting valves and slows down the recoil.

Cars and society

CONNECTIONS

See also
1750 Traffic engineering
1700 Buses and streetca
1710 Railroads of the futu

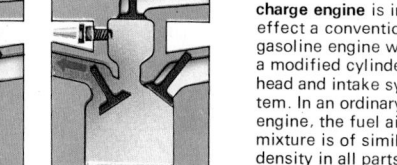

The automobile powered by the internal combustion engine has been in common use for less than 70 years. At first a toy, then a mode of transportation for the rich, and later part of the pattern of living, it was designed as man's mechanical servant. Together with the truck, it revolutionized the world's trade and social life.

The introduction of cheap, mass-produced cars, pioneered by Henry Ford's Model T of 1908, brought personal transportation to ordinary people. They could go almost anywhere, and the new-found freedom created the beginnings of domestic tourist industries. More expensive cars became status symbols.

The threat to society

Now it is a question of the car's survival or demise. Today, with 220 million vehicles on the world's highways, many people think that the answer to the rapidly increasing problem of pollution and fuel shortages can at last clearly be seen. They consider that sometime in the future society must forget the automobile as we know it—a five-passenger four-wheeled vehicle up to 16ft (5m) long and 8ft (2.5m) wide using the extremely inefficient internal combustion engine, pouring toxic wastes into the air, damaging people's ears and minds with its noise, congesting cities, creating fuel shortages, and beginning to take away the very freedom of movement for which it was developed. There may have to be a radical change in size, engines, and people's approach to personal travel.

What type of engine?

All combustion, from that in a bonfire to a car engine, produces undesirable by-products—carbon monoxide, various unburned hydrocarbons, and, from cars, nitric oxide, lead salts, iron oxide, and soot in exhaust smoke. New regulations governing the toxic content of exhaust fumes have done much to reduce air pollution. But they cannot (even with the most stringent emission curbs, such as those laid down in the United States in 1975), hope to eliminate automobile-related pollutants entirely. Similarly, the most vigilant noise-abatement organizations cannot hope to damp effectively the roar of heavy, under-powered vehicles working under stress. And even the most ambitious planning of city centers can at best clear only a fraction of shopping space—at the cost of adding to the numbers of vehicles elsewhere.

In the short term, current and planned regulations will help in certain respects. But automobile designers have long been investigating the future particularly with regard to engines, fuels, and overall size reduction, in addition to various public transportation systems.

Modern steam road vehicles have been tested for more than 25 years; their basic problems are weight and water supply. Research continues on low-emission systems such as the stratified-charge engine, gas turbine, Stirling (hot-air) engine, and hybrid-electric (in which such an engine powers a generator to charge batteries that can be used for cruising). Other possible power units are pure electric (one of the great goals, because electricity supplies can be made almost unlimited, but still handi-

1

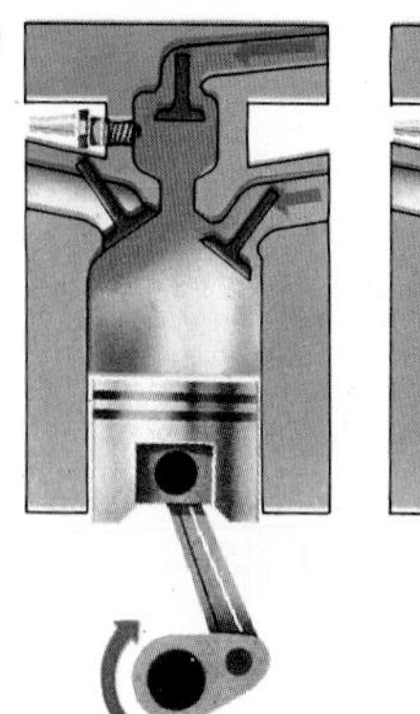

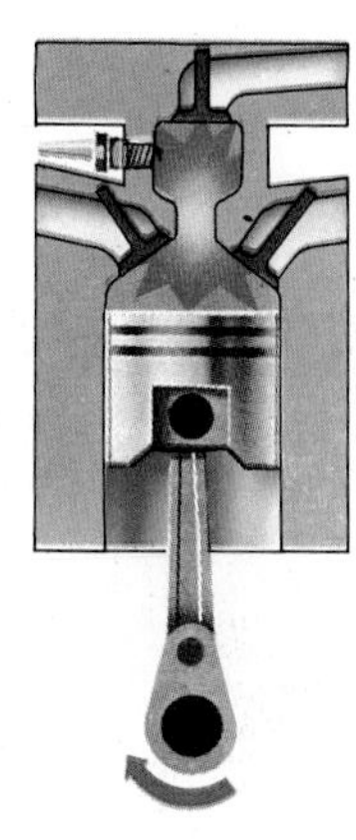

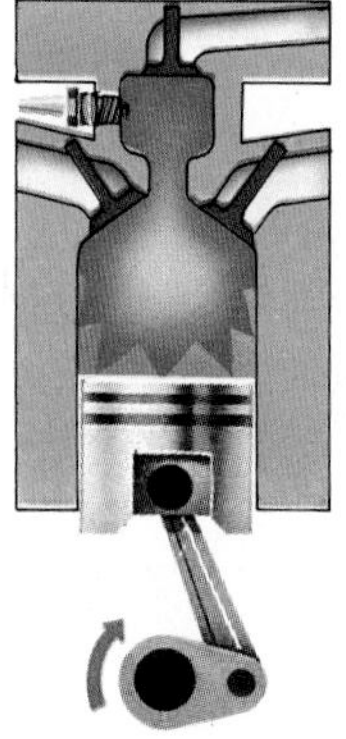

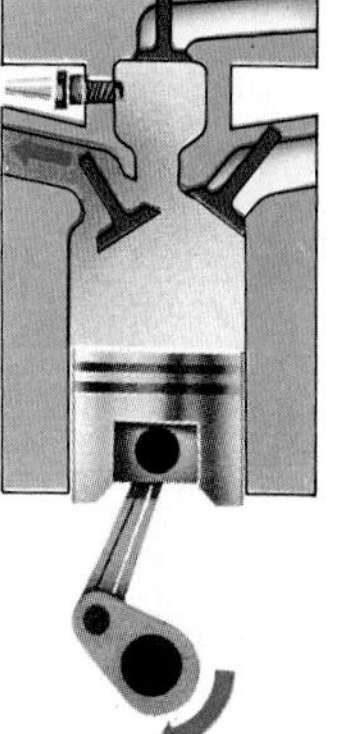

1 The stratified-charge engine is in effect a conventional gasoline engine with a modified cylinder head and intake system. In an ordinary engine, the fuel air mixture is of similar density in all parts of the combustion chamber. In the stratified-charge unit, it is richer near the plug and weaker elsewhere. The rich mixture near the plug ignites readily and the weaker mixture burns more completely.

2A

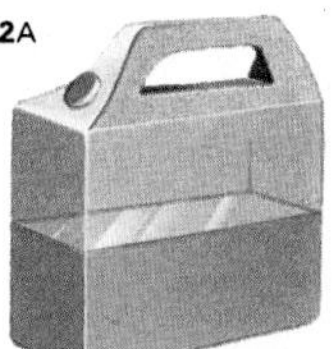

B

2 Diesel-fuel exhaust emission from a correctly adjusted engine pollutes the air much less than does a gasoline-fueled unit. Of all the toxic fumes discharged by any type of internal combustion engine, invisible and odorless carbon monoxide is the most damaging. A gasoline engine produces thirty times as much as a diesel engine. Car A represents gasoline engine emission, B diesel.

3

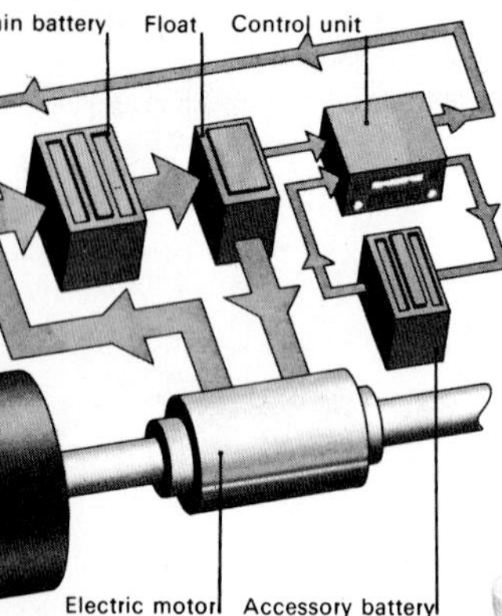

Main battery
Float
Control unit
Electric motor
Accessory battery

3 In an experimental urban car electric-drive system, power for accessories is taken from either an accessory battery or from the main source.

4

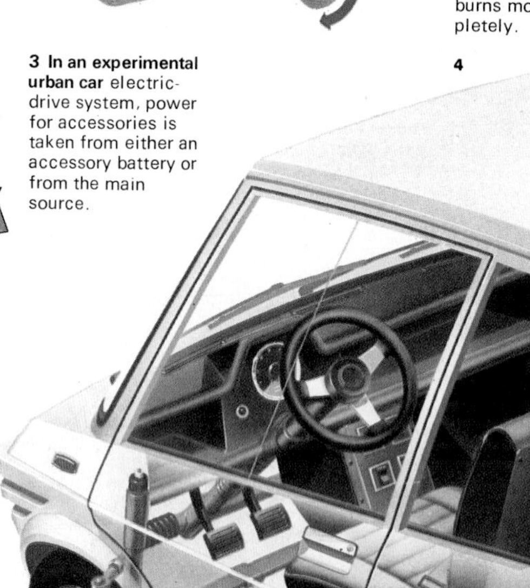

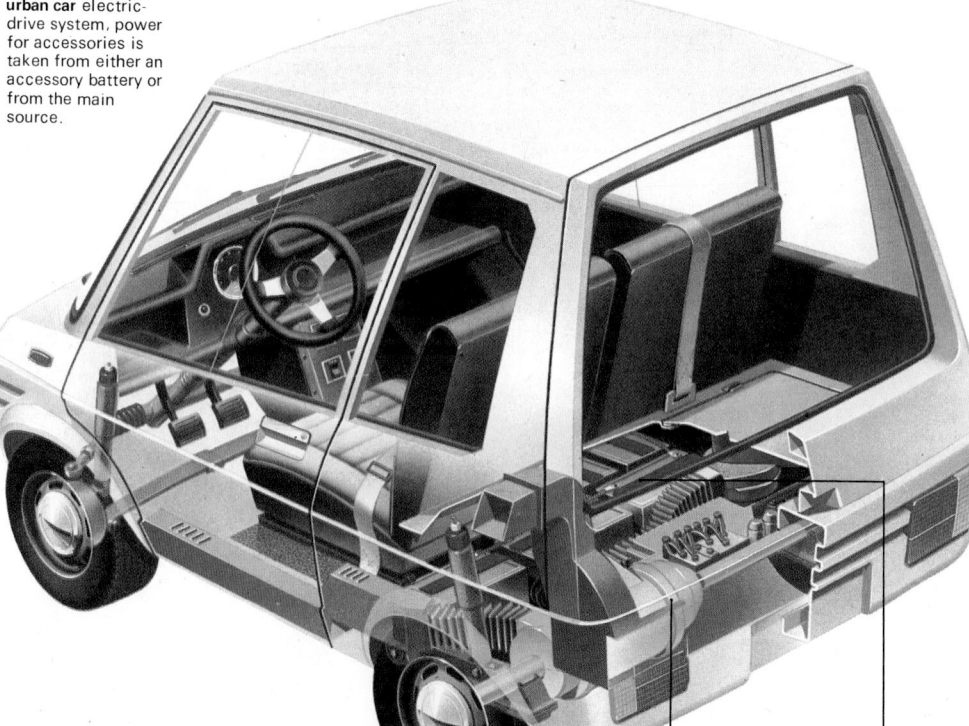

Electric motor
Batteries

4 Short-range personal transportation is provided by this experimental urban electric car. A direct current electric motor mounted on the rear axle is driven by a special 84-volt lead-acid battery, which gives the car a greater range than conventional batteries. A built-in charger can be plugged into a household socket and recharges the battery in 7 hrs. This car built by General Motors has a range of 60mi (97km) at 25mph (40kph).

capped by heavy batteries and the need for frequent recharging), and fuel cell power, which would convert conventional fuel energy directly into electric power without burning it. This would be one of the most significant developments of our time, but is not likely to be practical for some years. More than 250 designs of small electrically powered "city" or urban cars have been produced; if the cars were made commercially they could help congested cities and relieve parking problems (three can be parked in one normal bay), although light and heavy vehicles would probably have to be segregated.

The future of the car engine

Current research has already produced technical advances aimed at improved economy and ecology, although most of them would, at best, provide only partial relief. The car industry has produced the catalytic converter [6], a type of de-polluting muffler for use with low-lead gasoline. Fuel economy has been improved by electronic ignition, by steel-ply radial tires, which have less rolling resistance, by lower rear-axle ratios, scaled down engine capacities, and, mainly in the United States, the reintroduction of overdrive.

There are three immediate goals. First, future engine design (internal combustion engines will probably remain for the next 15 years) must aim at conserving fuel and reducing exhaust pollutants. Second, a way of controlling traffic density in cities, and its flow elsewhere, must be found. Third, and most urgently, greater safety must be built into structural design and additional equipment provided (such as collapsible steering wheels, rigid "boxes," and deflecting properties), not only to combat the injuries likely to be received in a collision but also to prevent road accidents in the first place (improved tires, brakes, lights, and visibility).

Long-term aims must be to find an alternative power system now that oil supplies —even offshore supplies—are unpredictable. And a fundamental reappraisal in society's attitude toward highway transportation, its appearance, and its function, must be made.

KEY

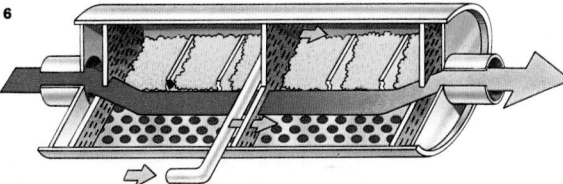

Batteries

Electric motor

Gasoline engine

The hybrid city car was developed as a possible answer to pollution in towns. For city and urban use the car runs on its electric motor, but on out-of-town trips the small internal combustion engine is started. The electric unit is used on its own only where there must be no pollution, and the gasoline engine charges the batteries at other times.

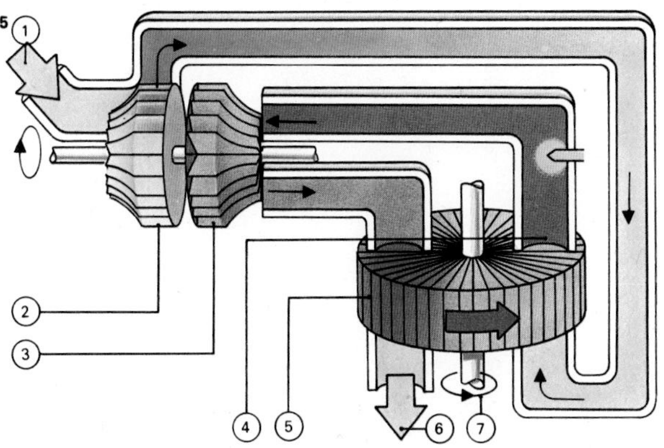

5 The gas-turbine car engine was developed originally by the British Rover Company, which tested the first gas-turbine car in 1950. It is quiet, powerful, has low maintenance costs, and runs on low-grade, lead-free fuel. But it is expensive to manufacture.

1 Air in
2 Radial compressor
3 Compressor turbine
4 Fuel in
5 Power turbine
6 Exhaust
7 Power out

6 Catalytic converters, built into mufflers have been used as a partial solution to prevent exhaust pollution. Nitrogen oxides are reduced to ammonia at the first catalyst bed, and hydrocarbons and carbon monoxide are converted to carbon dioxide and water at the second. The most suitable catalyst is platinum, but this is extremely expensive. The system has proved to be efficient enough for some manufacturers to recalibrate their engines for higher peak performance, using catalytic converters to "clean up" the extra pollution in the exhaust gases.

Moment of impact
1
2

Full impact
1
2

7 The ideal safety car [1] has a rigid compartment protecting passengers restrained by seat belts and head rests. The car body is designed to absorb impact and, in a collision, the engine deflects downward, and the steering column collapses. The injuries sustained by unrestrained passengers [2] depend on the speed of the collision (here 60mph [97kph]).

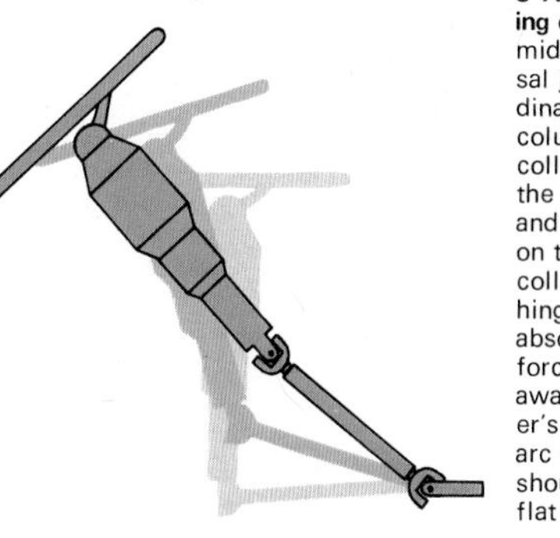

8 A collapsible steering column is hinged mid-way at a universal joint. With an ordinary rigid steering column, a head-on collision can make the wheel break off and impale the driver on the column. The collapsible column hinges on impact, absorbs some of the force and swings away from the driver's chest. The lower arc of the wheel should be padded or flat to lessen injury.

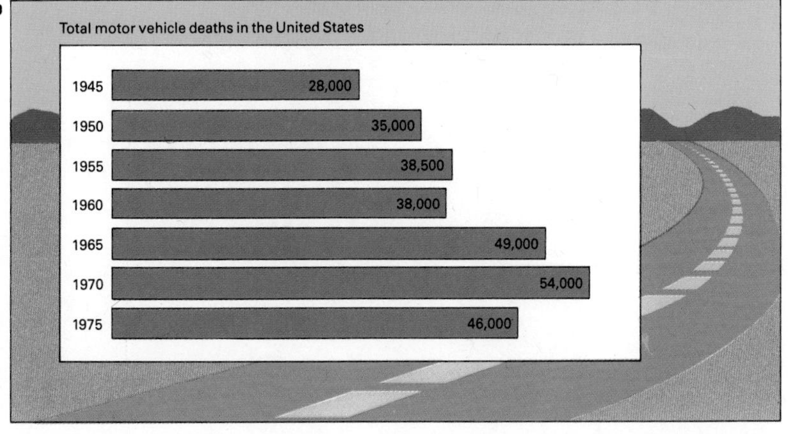

Total motor vehicle deaths in the United States
1945 28,000
1950 35,000
1955 38,500
1960 38,000
1965 49,000
1970 54,000
1975 46,000

9 Deaths due to motor vehicle accidents in the United States are shown on the graph at 5-year intervals, 1945–75. The highest death count occurred in 1970, when 54,000 people died.

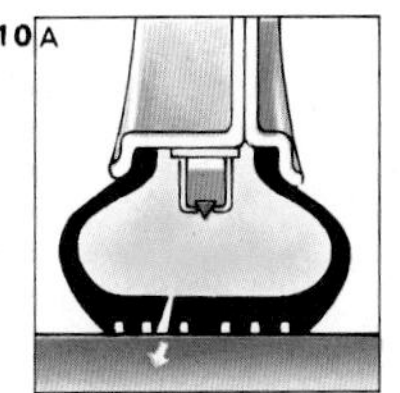

A

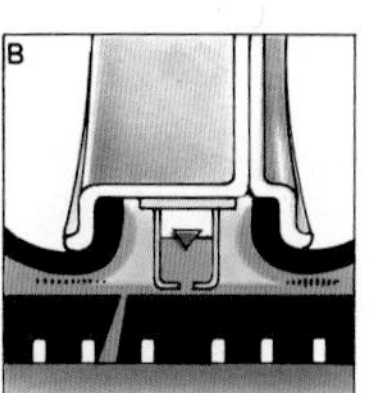

B

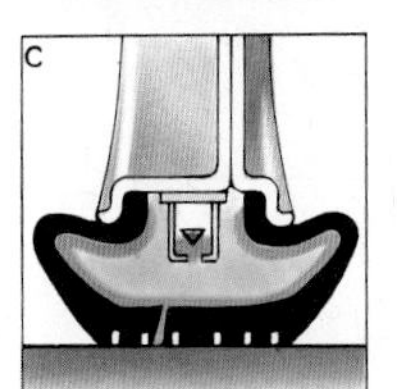

C

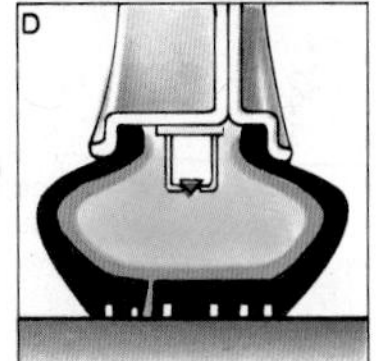

D

10 A puncture at high speed is extremely dangerous—the tire collapses. A recent development uses a ring of containers [A] that burst when the tire deflates releasing fluid that seals the hole [C] and vaporizes to reinflate the tire [D].

Buses and streetcars

Industrialization—the transformation of scattered cottage industries into centralized factories and offices—creates a need for good public transportation. In the early stages of industrialization people moved in from rural areas to live within walking distance of their places of work. But as the developing cities sprawled outward, an efficient system of commutation became necessary to feed industry its manpower.

The automobile is inefficient for such a purpose because it takes up far too much road space for the average number of passengers it carries, and it produces congestion. Moreover, it was invented too late to form the basis of a good system. Bicycles are a solution, but few people will ride them in all weather or over long distances.

Early passenger transportation systems

Cities in Europe and America began to grow large enough to need public transportation systems in the early 1800s, when the only feasible source of motive power was the horse. The horse-drawn bus might have seemed the obvious choice of vehicle, being a logical development of the stagecoach, but roads were in such poor condition in cities that coachlike vehicles provided a very uncomfortable ride. The first extensive transportation systems used horse-drawn streetcars rather than buses because vehicles on rails not only carried people smoothly but also allowed a horse to pull twice as many passengers, because of easier rolling. Medieval miners transported minerals by pushing wheeled tubs along primitive rails made of wooden beams. The word "tram" reflects this origin—being derived from the Low German *traam,* meaning "the shaft of a wheelbarrow"—although in the United States the more descriptive word "streetcar" is used.

From streetcar to trolley bus

Streetcars and railroads developed together. The first city streetcar network spread through New York in the 1830s, at the same time that steam railroads began to appear in Britain. The first steam engine to pull a streetcar chugged its way around New York in 1837. Europe lagged behind—the first horse-drawn streetcar network did not open in Britain until 1860, and steam-powered streetcars did not appear until 1872. Europe pioneered the next important development, however, with trolleys [1] in Berlin in 1881. In 1873 the cable car, invented by Andrew Hallidie, made its appearance on the steep hills of San Francisco. The car, which gripped a cable moving just below the street surface, became briefly popular in other US and European cities. They could not compete, however, with the electric cars that soon followed. The first US electric trolley line opened in Cleveland in 1884.

Coincident with the development of the electric trolley came the trolley bus. By the first years of the twentieth century, commercial systems were in operation. Trolley buses had twin poles and overhead wires because the rubber wheels insulated the vehicles from the ground. (Streetcars needed only a single wire for current pickup, the circuit being completed through the metal wheels and rails.) The first trolley buses collected current through a trolley

CONNECTIONS

See also
1702 Special purpose vehicles
1698 Cars and society
1708 Railroad transportation

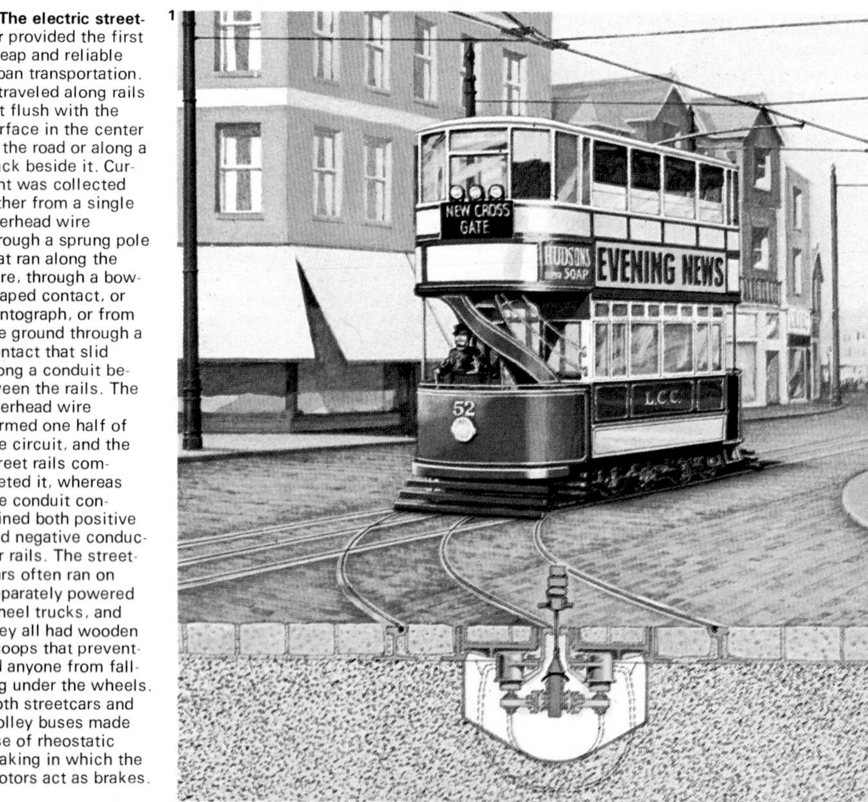

NEW CROSS GATE
HUDSONS SOAP
EVENING NEWS
52
L.C.C.

1 The electric streetcar provided the first cheap and reliable urban transportation. It traveled along rails set flush with the surface in the center of the road or along a track beside it. Current was collected either from a single overhead wire through a sprung pole that ran along the wire, through a bow-shaped contact, or pantograph, or from the ground through a contact that slid along a conduit between the rails. The overhead wire formed one half of the circuit, and the street rails completed it, whereas the conduit contained both positive and negative conductor rails. The streetcars often ran on separately powered wheel trucks, and they all had wooden scoops that prevented anyone from falling under the wheels. Both streetcars and trolley buses made use of rheostatic braking in which the motors act as brakes.

2 San Francisco has the oldest cable car system; it opened in 1873. Other hilly cities soon introduced cable-hauled streetcars. In 1884 the first cable cars in Europe appeared on Highgate Hill in London. Other cities noted for cable systems were Kansas City, Melbourne, Australia, and Wellington, N.Z. Cable cars are no longer in use except in San Francisco and Wellington.

3 Buses, the major mode of city public transportation, are continually being improved and modernized. Shown here is a sleek new 47-seat transit bus from General Motors.

METROPOLITAN ELECTRIC TRAMWAYS LTD

4 The first trolley buses were introduced by the streetcar companies soon after the turn of the century. At first current-collecting trolleys ran on top of a pair of overhead wires, but later ones contacted the conductors below them.

slung on the wires, hence their names, but the sprung poles used on streetcars were soon found to be more efficient.

The trolley bus was a silent and fume-free form of travel capable of fast acceleration and greater maneuverability than the streetcars. Trolley bus networks were built in cities that did not want to pay the cost of laying rails for streetcars; they were also used in suburbs.

Buses versus streetcars

Both streetcars and trolley buses had to contend with buses and found the competition more and more intense. Buses have a long history, the first horse-drawn vehicle being run in Paris by Blaise Pascal in 1662.

The name *bus*—from the Latin *omnibus,* meaning "for all"—appeared shortly before the introduction of the first horse-drawn bus in London in 1829 and in New York City in 1830. Steam buses soon followed, but the first motorbus—an elegant gasoline-driven coach built in Germany by Benz—did not begin service until 1895, when streetcars were established.

Compared with streetcars, the early buses were small, noisy, and smelly, and the solid tires gave the passengers a bone-shaking ride. But buses soon improved, and streetcar lines began to decline.

As motor traffic increased, streetcars often impeded cars, and severe congestion occurred, exacerbated by wire and power failures. Buses became more economic and were more flexible in routing than either streetcars or trolley buses. After World War II streetcars and trolley buses began to disappear. Today they are common only in some European cities.

Modern streetcar designs include articulated vehicles of several interconnected coaches, but flexibility of design has always been a feature more typical of motorbuses. The descendants of the elegant many-doored, open-air motor coaches of the 1920s are the luxurious air-conditioned, reclining-seated, long-distance coaches of today [7]. Today buses are the only means of public transportation in most cities, and minibuses and dial-a-bus services now carry passengers on less productive routes.

KEY

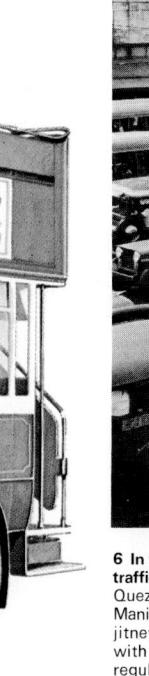

The first streetcars were pulled by steam "locomotives," generally with vertical boilers and side panels that totally enclosed the moving parts and wheels. This streetcar ran in East London in 1887. Its engine used a steam pressure of 100lb per sq in and it burned about 20lb (9kg) of coal for an hour's operation. Passengers rode in a trailer, with no weather protection for those on the upper deck. Other streetcars were propelled by compressed-air engines.

5 Motorbuses were introduced to the streets of Paris and London at the end of the nineteenth century. Their gasoline engines were noisy and smelly, but the new buses soon demonstrated their advantage over the streetcar—the ability to go anywhere served by a road. This type of English bus was "drafted" at the beginning of World War I, and many saw service with the British army in France.

5

W. CROYDON Stn
PURLEY
COULSDON
MERSTHAM
REDHILL
REIGATE
DORKING
CAPEL
414
KNIGHTS of REIGATE
DRAPERS AND OUTFITTERS
EAST SURREY
129
PD1537

6

6 In the rush-hour traffic on crowded Quezon Boulevard in Manila, Philippines, jitney buses compete with the full-sized regular city buses. The "Jeepnees," as they are called, are actually jeeps that have been converted for public transportation use. They are colorfully decorated vehicles and can accomodate 12 passengers. Their availability offers city dwellers additional transportation.

SPECIAL
GREYHOUND

7 An intercity bus network covers the whole of North America. Large coaches provide a cheap, reliable means of intercity travel. Passengers may spend several days aboard.

8 A tourist coach makes its way through the resort of Sitges in Spain. Such vehicles are often extravagantly decorated to attract tourists and designed to provide a view of the town rather than a means of rapid urban transport.

8

Special-purpose vehicles

Conventional vehicles such as cars and trucks are designed to run on firm roads, normally with only slight grades, and carry average loads. A special purpose vehicle has some extra features. It may be able to travel over unusual terrain or to carry a load that is beyond the capacity of ordinary vehicles.

For economy, speedy development and, sometimes, reliability, specialty vehicles are designed to make the best use of components already available. A standard truck chassis can be fitted with a special body or be used to tow various trailers [7]. Existing components can be built onto a new chassis or into a single-unit hull welded from flat sheets of metal.

Basic design considerations

The first consideration must be the type of load to be carried. This may be two oil explorers and their instruments, 30 tons of timber, or a 120mm gun, ammunition, and crew. In general, large vehicles are best for bulk loads. Off the road their size makes obstacles relatively easy to surmount—what would be an obstacle to a conventional vehicle becomes less significant. But on the road, many special purpose vehicles are difficult to maneuver because of their excessive width and weight.

The terrain over which loads are to be taken is another important consideration in the design of a special purpose vehicle. Soft ground calls for knives or tracks that spread the load over a large area to lessen the chance that the vehicle will sink into the ground. There must be enough traction to overcome the resistance of loose soil and to cope with slippery grades. The two main choices are four-wheel drive or caterpillar tracks.

A wheeled vehicle tends to be less expensive and quieter than a tracked vehicle. Extremely large wheels can be fitted to small vehicles, making them as good as tracked vehicles on soft ground and giving the added advantage that, with low-pressure tires, they can float. In some so-called all-terrain vehicles (ATVs) the tires are so broad that the wheels cannot be pivoted for normal steering. Instead they employ "skid" steering by braking the wheels on one side of the vehicle.

For a given size and weight, caterpillar tracks grip better than wheels and distribute the vehicle's weight more evenly, making them a good choice for cross-country use. Tracked vehicles also have a lower fuel consumption under severe conditions. They are steered by braking the track on one side.

Suspension for cross-country travel

The type of suspension is determined by the speed at which the vehicle has to travel over the roughest ground it is likely to encounter. Trucks and cars designed for smooth roads have only slight suspension resilience. If driven fast across country their suspension is liable to break. For this reason, vehicles adapted with only minimum modification for off-road use have a "hard" suspension giving the driver such an uncomfortable ride that he will not go too fast. Agricultural tractors and their derivatives normally operate so slowly they manage without any suspension at all, although wheeled tractors

CONNECTIONS

See also
1700 Buses and streetcar
1664 Earth-moving machines
1666 Moving heavy loads
1682 Hydrofoils and hove craft
1736 Armored fighting vehicles
1710 Railroads of the futu
310 Farm machinery anc buildings

1 Concrete carriers transport large quantities of concrete that has been mixed away from the site to where it is needed. The drum revolves slowly during the journey to keep the concrete properly mixed. The convenience of off-site mixing justifies the cost of transporting concrete by road.

2 Tracked commercial vehicles are used in snow and on marshy ground. In the Arctic areas of Alaska, Canada, and the Soviet Union they are used by the lumber industry and by oil and ore prospecting companies. They range from small tractors for hauling sleds, and slightly larger personnel carriers with heated cabins, to huge 40-ton load platforms.

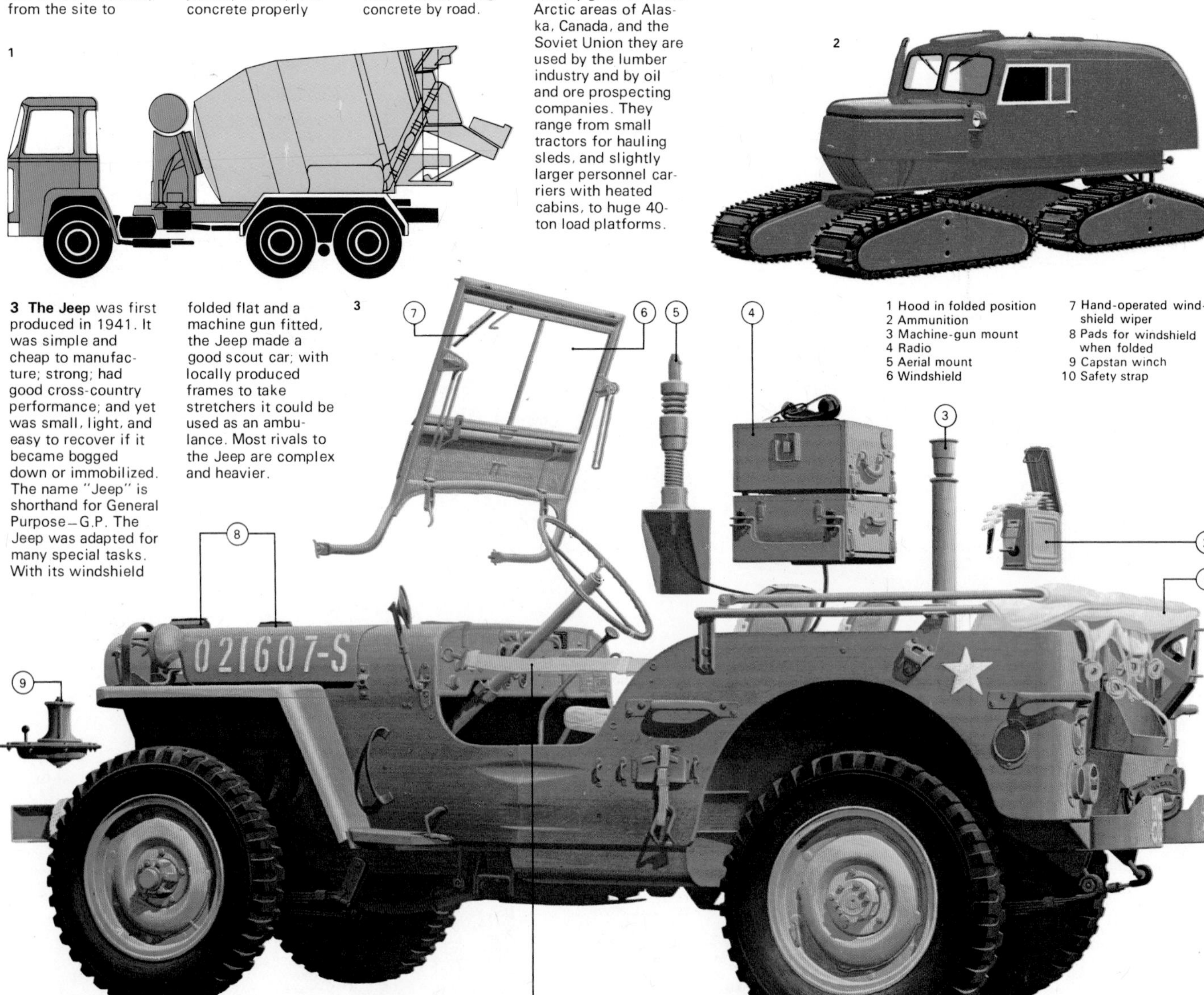

1
2
3
021607-S
1 Hood in folded position
2 Ammunition
3 Machine-gun mount
4 Radio
5 Aerial mount
6 Windshield
7 Hand-operated windshield wiper
8 Pads for windshield when folded
9 Capstan winch
10 Safety strap

3 The Jeep was first produced in 1941. It was simple and cheap to manufacture; strong; had good cross-country performance; and yet was small, light, and easy to recover if it became bogged down or immobilized. The name "Jeep" is shorthand for General Purpose—G.P. The Jeep was adapted for many special tasks. With its windshield folded flat and a machine gun fitted, the Jeep made a good scout car; with locally produced frames to take stretchers it could be used as an ambulance. Most rivals to the Jeep are complex and heavier.

have resilient tires, producing bounce. Tracked "crawler" tractors have no suspension; they are slow and are used only for heavy work where tracks are essential. The prime examples of fast cross-country machines are armored fighting vehicles (AFVs), such as tanks, self-propelled artillery, and various armored personnel carriers, with tracks and suspensions of high resilience.

Engine power and transmission

A small family car carrying the driver alone has power in relation to the vehicle weight of about 60bhp (brake horsepower) per ton, whereas an expensive sports sedan might have 180bhp per ton. For economy of operation, a diesel engine is best in heavy comemericial vehicles. Such engines are generally used unless high power output is needed for minimum weight, when a gasoline engine is a better choice.

Generally the transmission must suit both road journeys at relatively high speeds and slow, heavy work across country. It must also provide the power for winches and other equipment. Except in simple vehicles, the transmission is usually as heavy as the engine.

Steering a special purpose vehicle

Short tracked vehicles can be steered by using the transmission to drive the tracks at different speeds. A long, narrow vehicle is built in two parts, with a powered and articulated joint in the middle, and the vehicle steered by "bending" it sideways at the joint. Such vehicles have a good performance on soft soil such as clay or on snow. In the same conditions, a wheeled vehicle should have wheels of large diameter rather than of broad section, but there is seldom enough room to fit them. A deep tread on the tires is necessary when the surface is soft. In dry sand fat tires are used.

Reliability is difficult to achieve in special purpose vehicles. Often their use cannot be simulated accurately in trials, and "over-design"—making all parts stronger than absolutely necessary—must be avoided or the vehicle will be excessively heavy.

KEY

A dump truck justifies a special design, because its body is so short. The loads it carries are massive yet consist of small particles, such as sand. The dumping mechanism allows rapid unloading by the driver alone.

MAGIRUS DEUTZ

4
6
5
COLES

4 The Coles Colossus is a 14-wheeled truck designed as a crane carrier. It has hydro-pneumatic suspension, and the engine is a Rolls-Royce 300hp turbo-charged diesel. Sections can be added to the jib-strut crane in order to convert it into a tall tower crane.

5 The racing car's wedge shape helps to keep it on the track. Its low wind resistance and its wide tires give it stability on corners.

6 Swamp buggies use large, low-pressure tires to carry men and materials over inland waters, shifting sand, and deep, soft swamp.

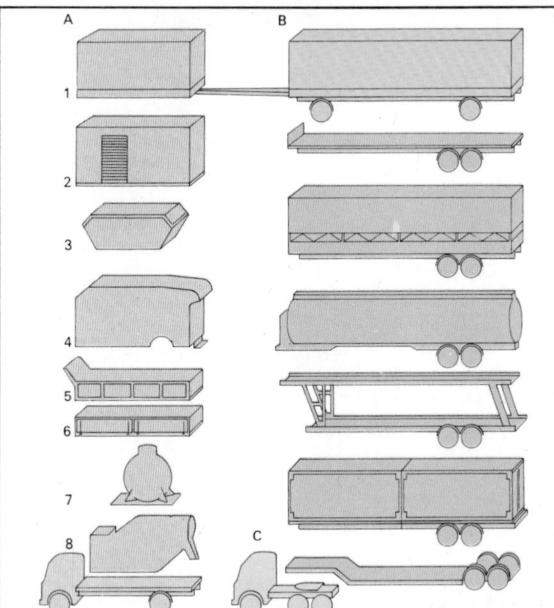
7
A
B
1
2
3
4
5
6
7
8
C

7 A basic truck [A] can have various vehicle bodies, such as a plain van [1], side entry van [2], rubble carrier [3], garbage truck [4], dumper [5], open truck [6], liquid gas carrier [7], or cement carrier [8]. It can also be adapted to tow a trailer [B]. One tractor [C] can be used to haul various kinds of articulated semi-trailers, giving good maneuverability and giving full and economic use of the vehicle.

8 This European riot vehicle weighs 20 tons, has bullet-proof steel and glass for protection, and carries a 15-man squad. It is armed with a water cannon, special sprays, and a high intensity siren. It can assist authorities in controlling crowds and rioters in situations where minimum force is desired.

8

9 A hovercraft is also a special purpose vehicle, although the craft shown is limited to water travel. It uses two gas turbine engines to drive the fans that supply high pressure air on which it "floats" over water.

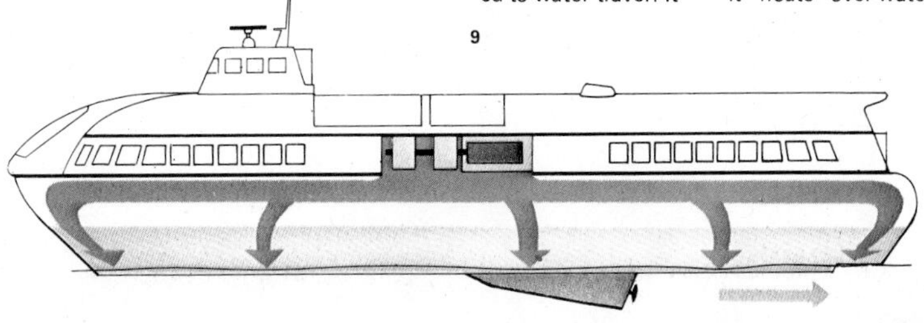
9

Technology and transportation in developing nations

Physical communications—basically roads and railroads to transport people from place to place—are an essential ingredient of progress. When irrigation canals were built in Indonesia more than half a century ago, the building of roads parallel to the canals did not seem worthwhile. But the lack of such roads led to a decline in standards of inspection and maintenance and as a result the canals steadily deteriorated. Today, to transport additional food for growing populations, the canals are being rebuilt—with service roads, and costing much more than they would have originally.

An adequate transportation system is equally necessary for the distribution of food and for the more general trade without which there can be little continuing improvement in the quality of life in any community.

The basic ingredients of physical communication are products of technology. The richer the community, the more sophisticated the technology that develops. Progress is the result of man's mastery of the world he lives in and of his ability to use the resources within his reach. In regions in which modern mechanized road building and modern transportation is too costly for the local communities, and where progress is limited by the lack of adequate physical communication, there are two ways in which the problem can be solved. The first is by foreign aid—the system in which the richer nations provide the poorer ones with money, materials, or trained personnel. The second is by the use of simpler, less costly technologies. Even where outside aid is available, it may be productive to use it for a wide range of schemes based on low cost local technology than on a few highly sophisticated and correspondingly more expensive projects.

Building low cost roads

The principles of road design are simple, and road building can also be a relatively simple process [1, 2]. Earth, and sometimes rock, must be moved and stones must be quarried, crushed, collected, and spread according to a plan. The checking of levels is important because the drainage of the finished road depends on it. But even leveling does not require expensive instruments and techniques. A cheap but accurate method uses a length of transparent plastic tubing with its ends tied along a pair of wooden rods. The rods are placed upright on the ground and the tubing filled with water. If the roads are graduated from the bottom up, the difference in ground levels where each is placed can be quickly found by reading off the height of the water level in each tube, and subtracting one from the other. The tube can be as long as 100ft (30m).

The building of bridges

Some roads have to cross a watercourse. It may be possible to construct a shallow ford, but the roadway under the water will be quickly worn away unless it is made of well cured concrete. In most cases, therefore, a bridge is needed.

In the Western world a modern road bridge is generally a structure made of reinforced concrete or, for longer spans, steel. Both materials have advantages where the loads to be carried are frequent and heavy.

CONNECTIONS

See also
1748 Road building
1756 History of bridges
1602 Hand tools
1604 Working metals by hand

1
2
3
4
5
6
7
8

1 Low cost methods of road construction vary according to the climate and availability of materials and labor. The basic principles are universal and the following alternatives to more generally accepted methods can often be adapted to suit varying situations. To build an earth road, the first step is to clear trees, shrubs, and roots [1]. Trees are cleared to keep the road in sunshine and therefore dry. The topsoil is removed [2] and dumped not closer than 26ft (8m) from the center of the road. Wide side ditches [3] are dug, and soil from them spread to raise the road level between them. The road surface is compacted by rolling [4], ensuring a cross slope (for drainage) of not less than 1 in 20. The ditches must be graded along their length so that excess water can run away [5]. The original topsoil should be put back on the ditch slopes to encourage the growth of grass [6]. A waterproof surface can be given to a compacted earth road [7] by spreading a layer of 2in (5cm) stones, then brushing and watering in finer grades of crushed stones to fill the spaces. A final rolling produces a dense surface [8]. Bridges can be built using a number of standard prefabricated timber sections supported on an iron beam and fixed together with interlocking metal plates (shown in insert).

But this does not mean that they are necessarily the best for a bridge carrying light traffic in undeveloped areas where cement and steel have to be brought at considerable expense from distant sources of supply, and yet where suitable timber, quarried stone, and bricks may be available locally. Before the general use of iron (from about 1830) and concrete (from about 1890), most bridges were built of masonry or timber.

The design of bridges is not usually considered a field for standardization. But a recent scheme by the forestry department in Kenya has shown that enormous savings in cost can be achieved by standardization. A civil engineer working for the department designed a standard 100ft (30m) timber truss panel made from Kenya cyprus. The panels are prefabricated at a central workshop, carried to each site and joined together there to form a bridge with a roadway running over the top layer. Two panels, set parallel to each other, can safely carry a 20-ton truck. If a route has to be upgraded for heavier vehicles, more panels can quickly be added.

For longer bridges, intermediate timber piers can be built up from the river bed to support two or more spans. A pilot project has been set up that produces an average of one bridge span every three days. Some steel is used for panel couplings and ties, but most of the bridge is built from local materials, using local labor, which helps to reduce expenses.

Low cost transportation

Modern motor vehicles may be necessary for carrying heavy loads in rural areas, but medium sized loads can be transported by traditional means provided friction and grades are kept to a minumum. The systematic construction of roads provides an opportunity for avoiding steep grades. It also ensures a smooth, hard road surface on which rubber tires roll with a minimum of friction. Modern wheel bearings eliminate the other main source of resistance. By such means [3] an ox team can be used to carry heavier loads more efficiently. Other means of providing low cost rural transportation depend on the local environment.

KEY

A

B

A well designed road does not collect water [A] but allows it to drain off [B]. John McAdam (1756–1836) first applied the basic principles of a serviceable road—it is the subsoil that supports the traffic, and any soil sufficiently compacted and kept dry can support any reasonable weight.

2 Land and water routes can be built without costly modern machinery. The 8-ft (2.4m) drag-grader [A] has metal edges and is drawn by two oxen. This form of grader was used on the construction of many early US roads. One man can shift a load of soil with a team of oxen and a fresno scraper [B]. It is made from a strong oil drum. The steel nosed V-drag [C] is used for cutting ditches.

2A B C

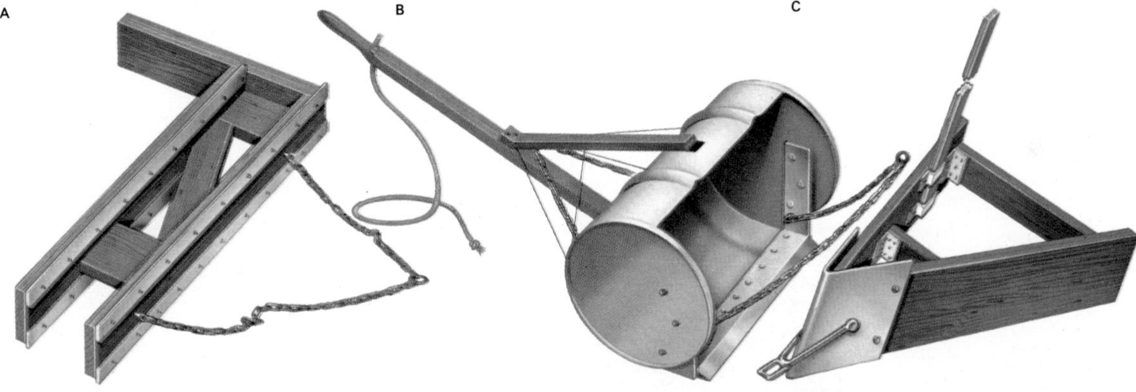

3

3 The ox cart is still the most widely used load-carrying vehicle in the rural areas of most of the world's developing countries. Among its advantages is the fact that, unlike a motor vehicle, it is simple to maintain, easy to repair, and uses the energy of fodder and not of oil. The ox causes no air pollution and provides manure as a valuable by-product. The main disadvantage of the traditional ox cart is the wasted energy due to primitive wheel bearings and the friction between solid wheels and the road. By fitting the back axle, leaf springs, and wheel and tire assembly of scrapped automobiles, the disadvantages of the ox cart can be overcome at low cost to produce a more efficient vehicle.

4

4 Where there are water routes the barge provides an economical method of transporting heavy loads. In coastal China an experiment in the mass production of reinforced concrete sampans has resulted in a cheaper product with a longer life. The six- and ten-ton sampans are hand built upside down over a pit, using prefabricated bulkheads over which mesh is laid before cement plastering.

5

5 The cycle rickshaw is a cheap and convenient form of transport in several Southeast Asian cities where there are marked differences in income and much unemployment. It often competes directly with the more sophisticated buses and taxis. Opinions may differ about the moral desirability of public transportation propelled by human energy, but cyclists such as the one seen here resting are able to work, supporting their families as well as filling a need.

Locomotives

The spread of railroads, which transformed life in the nineteenth century, is linked inextricably with the steam locomotive. To its devotees the steam locomotive was one of the most romantic and beautiful machines ever built. It first appeared in 1804 in a simple version [1] invented by an Englishman, Richard Trevithick (1771–1883).

Early rail systems

The first steam locomotives to do useful work were ordered and used by coal mines in northeast England in 1813–20. In 1825 a public railroad was opened between the English towns of Stockton and Darlington. It had been planned for horse traction, but George Stephenson (1781–1848), a leading builder of colliery locomotives, persuaded the directors to operate a steam locomotive hauling trains heavier than horses could manage. The success of this line led to the much bigger and more important railroad between Liverpool and Manchester. It was opened in 1830 after bitter opposition from landlords, coachmen, canal bargemen, and the large sector of the population that abhorred any change and considered smoke-spouting locomotives to be engines of Satan. Against spirited competition, Stephenson's *Rocket* [2] was chosen to provide the motive power. It was small and light enough to run on only four wheels without breaking the flimsy iron track. Steady improvements in manufacturing made it possible to make boilers stronger, cylinders and pistons more accurate and better fitting, and the whole locomotive capable of developing more power at higher speeds.

For a century steam locomotives provided nearly all the traction of the world's railroads. There were no dramatic technical advances but size, power, and speed grew constantly. In Europe many rail systems used excellent track, capable of bearing 100-ton locomotives running at up to 100mph (160kph). But in the United States in early days, and in most other young, developing countries, track was lighter, and often badly laid by men racing to complete more miles each day. This called for more wheels to spread the load. Engines came to be identified by their wheels, so that 4–6–2 designated the number of leading, driving, and trailing wheels. Speeds were limited and seldom exceeded 50mph (80kph).

The steam locomotive had reached its zenith by the 1930s. European "steamers" were clean, splendidly painted in the colors of their operating companies, and, when designed for express passenger haulage, often capable of reaching 100mph. American locomotives tended to be more utilitarian. Demands for greater power led to increase in size until they became the biggest land vehicles in history [7].

Electric locomotives

The first rival to steam came in the form of the direct current electric motor, adopted in cities (especially in underground railroads), to avoid smoke pollution. The first electric train ran at an exhibition in Berlin in 1879. Soon countries such as Switzerland and Norway found that it was cheaper, with the development of hydroelectric power, to generate electricity than to burn fuel, and their networks became all electric.

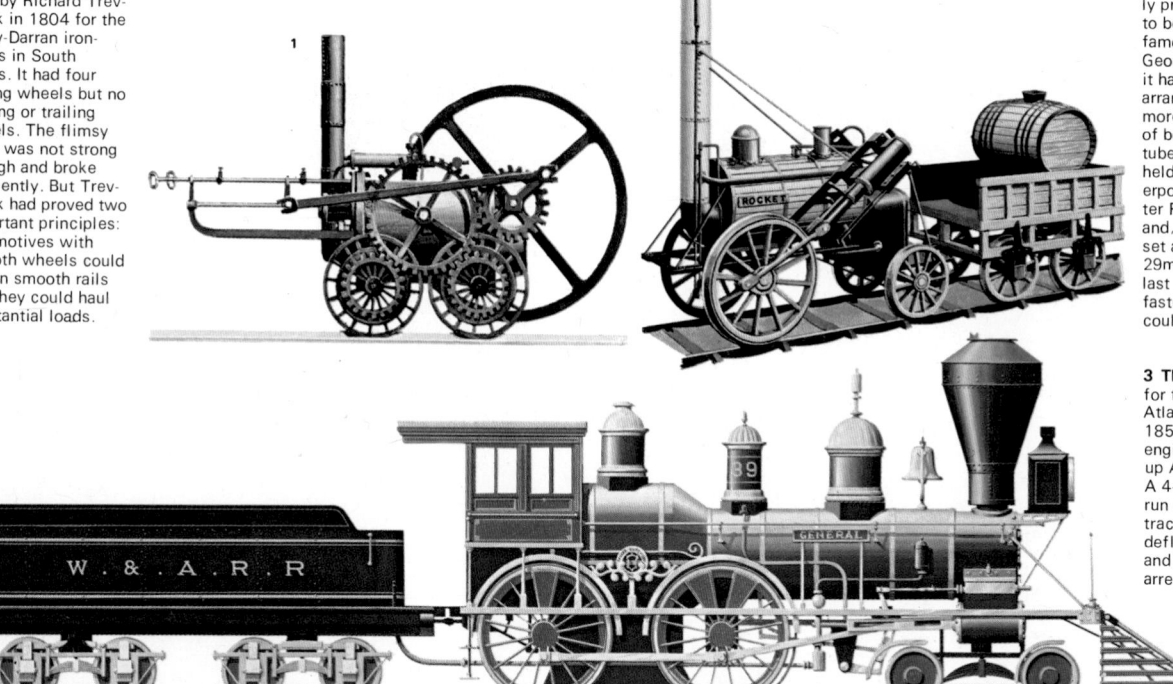

CONNECTIONS

See also
1628 Steam engines
1708 Railroad transportation
1710 Railroads of the futur[e]
1700 Buses and streetcar[s]
1676 History of transporta[tion]
1584 Modern technology
1280 The impact of stea[m]
1236 The Industrial Revol[u]tion
1284 European Industrialization 1870–1914

1 The first commercial locomotive was built by Richard Trevithick in 1804 for the Pen-y-Darran ironworks in South Wales. It had four driving wheels but no leading or trailing wheels. The flimsy track was not strong enough and broke frequently. But Trevithick had proved two important principles: locomotives with smooth wheels could run on smooth rails and they could haul substantial loads.

2 The Rocket was the first mechanically propelled vehicle to become world famous. Designed by George Stephenson, it had an 0-2-2 wheel arrangement and a more advanced type of boiler with heating tubes. It won trials held by the new Liverpool and Manchester Railway in 1829 and, without a train, set a record speed of 29mph (47kph); at last man could travel faster than horses could carry him.

3 The General, built for the Western and Atlantic Railroad in 1855, typifies the engines that opened up America's West. A 4-4-0, it could run on poor, unfenced track. A cowcatcher deflected animals and a huge funnel arrested sparks.

L N E R
4468
MALLARD

4 Electric traction was introduced in 1890 on the City & South London underground railroad in the heart of London.

5 Class 53/6 of the Bavarian State Railway, dating from 1908 and used to pull prestige passenger trains, had a four-cylinder compound engine with a 4-6-2 "Pacific" wheel arrangement.

6 Britain's Mallard set the world steam speed record at 126mph (203kph) in 1938, pulling a seven-coach train.

Today the electric motor, with its linear form still under development, is regarded as the best form of traction for railroads, but the huge capital costs impede its introduction except on the busiest routes. As long ago as 1955, French Railways demonstrated that electric trains of conventional type [9] could run at more than 200mph (320kph), but average speeds of public trains have risen only slowly. The Japanese New Tokaido line [10] achieved a sudden jump in speed because the line was laid for high speed. Even so, track and trains need constant maintenance.

Diesel power

About 1920, the first diesel locomotives and railcars came into general use, powered by compression-ignition oil engines developed by the German Rudolf Diesel (1858–1913). Though often noisy, diesel engines pick up speed faster and convert 25 to 45 percent of their fuel energy into useful haulage, whereas the fuel efficiency of steam traction seldom exceeded eight percent. Despite greater capital cost, diesel locomotives gradually ousted steam from 1935 onward, until today steam engines are confined to a shrinking number of railroads in Africa and Asia and a few local lines elsewhere. Diesels can be started and stopped easily, burn no fuel when not working, and can run at close to maximum power for hours at a time with no strain on either machines or crew (in contrast to the grimy slavery of the former stoker, or fireman, on the steam footplate). Many diesel locomotives regularly run more than 100,000mi (160,000km) a year, and modern examples are highly reliable.

Only in the smallest sizes does the diesel engine drive the wheels through a mechanical gearbox, as on a truck. Generally the two are linked hydraulically or electrically. Hydraulic transmissions are arrangements of turbines linked by oil under high pressure, and they can smoothly transmit 2,000 horsepower with any ratio between input and output speeds. In the diesel-electric locomotive the engine drives a generator or alternator. This is used to supply current to traction motors.

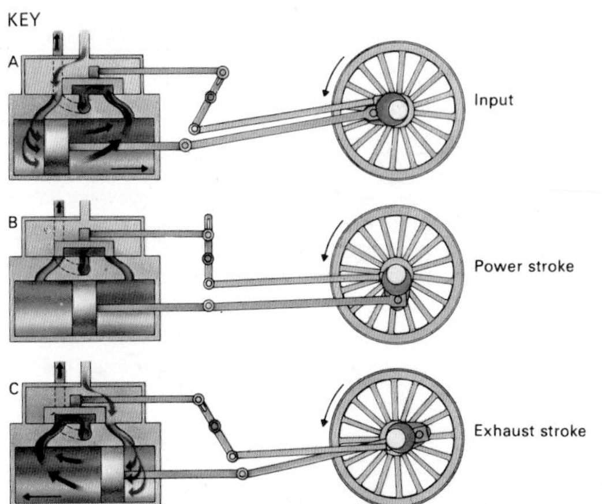
KEY
A
Input
B
Power stroke
C
Exhaust stroke

The double-action engine used to drive a steam locomotive uses superheated steam generated in a heating tube boiler. Steam entering the cylinder [A] drives the piston back and exhausts steam from the other side of the piston. [B] shows the midposition, with both inlet valves closed. In [C], steam is led to the other side of the piston and the cycle is repeated. The exhaust steam passes directly into the atmosphere, and this wasted energy, coupled with the design of the boiler, gives this type of steam engine the remarkably low efficiency of only eight per cent.

7

4021
UNION PACIFIC

7 The "Big Boys" of the Union Pacific were the heaviest locomotives built (540 tons). With a 4–8–8–4 layout, they hauled heavy freight trains in the Rocky Mountains at up to 75mph.

8

9

SNCF
CC7107

8 The Beyer-Garratt (4–6–4– + 4–6–4) of Rhodesia Railways shows how articulated design can fit powerful locomotives to light track. The boiler supplies a pair of engines pivoted at their ends.

9 Class CC 7100 of the SNCF (French Railways), pulling a light train, ran at 205mph (331kph) in 1955. It was a regular electric locomotive modified with a high gear ratio for high speed.

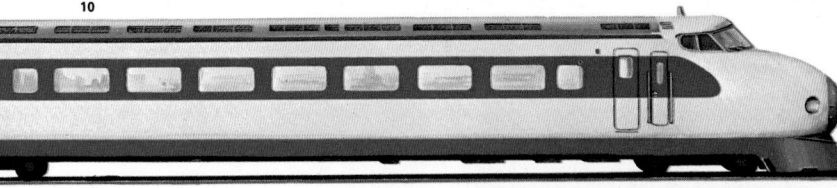

10

10 New Tokaido trains began running between Tokyo and Osaka in 1964. With 12,000hp per train, the new electric route 320mi (515km) is covered in three hours, but costs are high.

11 Typical of the locomotives of today is a diesel-electric built in Montreal in 1972 for East Africa. Devoid of frills, it spreads its weight on eight axles in two pivoted trucks and can haul big loads.

11

E A R

12

41 001

12 The High Speed Train, introduced by British Rail in 1973, set a world record for diesel trains when it reached a speed of 143mph (230kph). Planned for general service from 1976, it has a light but powerful diesel at each end and with 4,500hp can carry passengers at 125mph (200kph). To increase normal service speed to 150mph without major alterations to track and signals, British Rail is developing an electrically propelled Advanced Passenger Train. A prototype is planned to run in 1978.

Railroad transportation

Man built railroads long before he built steam engines and before he had even mastered the basic technology of engineering with iron and other metals. The earliest trains were constructed of timber and were in operation not later than the fourteenth century. They were built to overcome the severe limitations of other forms of land transportation. The provision of a special purpose track avoided pot holes and ruts and deterioration caused by the weather, and simultaneously reduced the friction so that heavier loads could be transported by the same amount of power.

The first railroads

Most trains built before 1825 [1] were what might today be called tramways. They ran over distances of 2mi (3km) or less and carried a single commodity such as coal or stone (for example between a mine or quarry and a loading wharf for ships). Wagons were pulled by horses or by human beings. Rolling stock was solidly made of wood, reinforced and joined by metal. Wheels were crude, but the smoothness of the track meant that they could be much smaller than those for carts and coaches running on roads. The track, either of wood or iron, was built with inner, outer, or double flanges to hold the trucks.

At first trucks were pushed individually. Then growing traffic led to two or more being coupled together, by simple iron links or even by ropes, to operate as a train. Usually the horses or human beings had to push only over short sections or on the return journey, since the slope from a pithead to a wharf was mainly downhill. Often a horse would ride down in an empty truck, ready to pull the unladen train back to the mine again. There was no signaling or traffic control, and the absence of brakes meant that coal laden trains ran downhill completely out of control.

Improvements and standardization

Not until after 1820 were crude friction brakes fitted to any rolling stock, but the really big step forward was the invention of powerful air, steam, and vacuum brakes. The air brake, introduced by George Westinghouse (1846–1914) in 1869 [6], cut the stopping distance needed on level track by as much as 90 percent.

By 1820 several of the variable features had been firmly decided upon. Track was no longer of wood but of iron, with high-strength steel in standard sections following at the end of the 1860s. The flange was no longer on the track but on the inner edges of the wheels, which were fixed in pairs to the axles. This feature enabled trains to run faster and more smoothly.

Rolling stock had to be designed to fit the loading gauge of the line so that no part projected far enough outward or upward to strike a tunnel, bridge, or signal. The restriction of the loading gauge meant there were capacity advantages in making vehicles longer, but they had to run around corners without forcing the flanges off the rails. Most early stock had only two axles. By 1845 three-axle freight and passenger equipment was common, all axles being held in axle-boxes fixed to the vehicle frame. By 1875 the biggest coaches were fitted with pivoted two-axle trucks, which

CONNECTIONS

See also
1706 Locomotives
1710 Railroads of the futur
1756 History of bridges
1758 Modern bridges
1676 History of transportation
1754 Tunnel engineering

1

2

1 Early railroad cars ran on wooden rails. The plain wooden wheels were kept on the track by flanges, grooves, or other guideways built into the track. This car hauled iron ore in the 1500s.

2 Railroad gauges throughout the world range in width from 5ft 6in (1.68m) to less than 2ft (60cm). Most European countries, and North America, use the standard gauge of 4ft 8.5in (1.43m).

3 A B

C

3 Early passenger cars established the idea that there should be three different classes of accommodation for rail travelers, priced at different levels. Third class [A] was simply an open car, second class [B] had bench seats, and first-class travelers were housed in something resembling three opulent horse carriages on a single chassis [C]. All these had to be designed to function together.

4 Underground trains have been carrying the residents of the world's major cities since London's Metropolitan line opened in January 1863. In its first year the line carried 9.5 million passengers. Today the entire London network carries more than two million passengers each day. Subways of some cities are shown.

4 New York Berlin Montreal London

F
2431
2431
3006

allowed increased length and reduced the minimum radius of curve that could be traversed. By this time trains often comprised 12-pivoted axle passenger cars, or had standard couplers.

In the twentieth century it became necessary to try to standardize rail gauges [2] and to fit all rolling stock with standard braking and control systems, vehicle heating and lighting supplies, and, above all, with standardized couplers. Early couplers were merely heavy hooks and links, connected by hand, but by 1925 automatic couplers were beginning to come into use. These resembled strong claws that could snap shut by pushing vehicles together and prevented an individual vehicle from overturning if its wheels accidentally left the track [5].

Railway passenger transport

The early years of the twentieth century saw the growing construction of urban underground or rapid-transit railroad systems. This led to a fresh class of rolling stock [4], designed for passenger transport only, often with a small loading gauge for subway lines and propelled by electricity (picked up from one or two extra current carrying rails). Unlike most earlier trains these were powered by electric motors placed along the train, instead of having a separate locomotive.

Such "multiple unit" (m.u.) trains are completely flexible in that they can be made up of any number of small groups of cars and can run equally well in either direction. They are also capable of rapid acceleration and braking because they have a very high ratio of power to weight and powerful brakes. Some have been fitted with rubber tires (to reduce noise) and almost all have power-driven sliding doors. The latest type is fitted with automatic control so that if a driver rides with the train he does so only as a passive overseer. Similar technology operates on long-distance passenger trains for surface use. Propulsion is being applied to most or all axles right along the train, and water-turbine brakes are fitted to slow trains down from very high speeds. The latest trains have bodies that can tilt smoothly on curves [Key].

KEY

The most advanced rail rolling stock of the late 1970s is that of the British Rail Advanced Passenger Train (APT). It has a dramatically lightened body and a new form of swiveling axle designed to exceed 150mph (240kph) even around the curves of existing track.

5

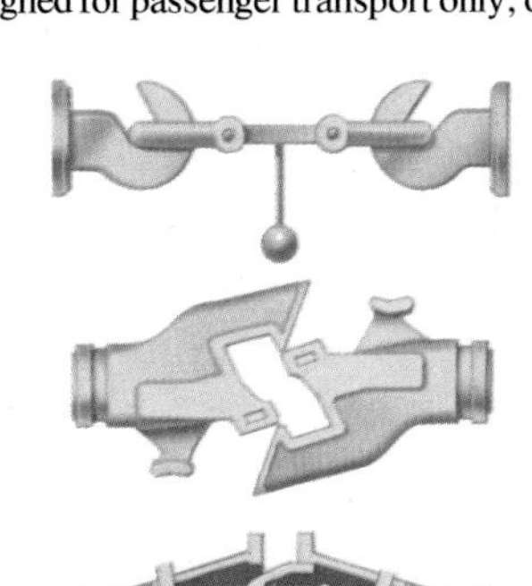
A
B
C

5 Couplings between railroad cars began as simple hooks and chains [A] with buffers to absorb the shock. Automatic couplers and uncouplers [B] were introduced in the US in 1882 and led to today's buck-eye coupler [C]. Some include connections for the brakes, electrical controls, and heating. American train cars have "draft" gear that uses springs, friction, or hydraulics to absorb operating shocks.

6

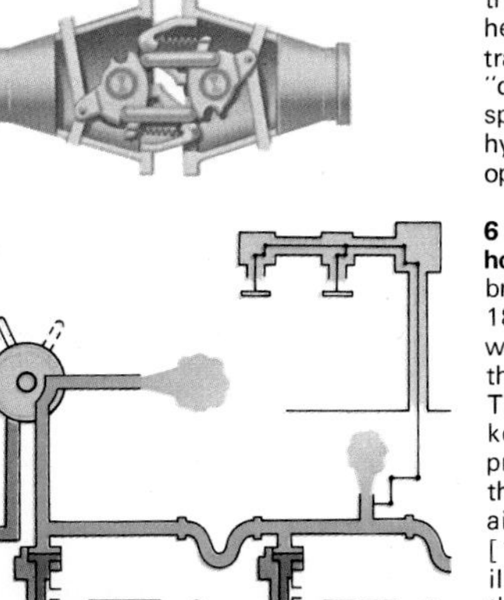

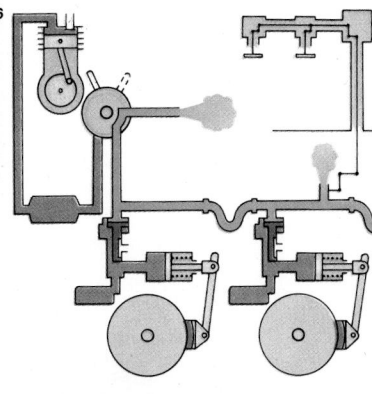

6 George Westinghouse's pneumatic brake, patented in 1869, is used more widely by railroads than any other type. The brake pipes are kept full of compressed air. When the brake is applied air in the main pipe [1] escapes. Auxiliary reservoirs [2] that still contain compressed air are then automatically connected to the brake cylinders, in which the pistons [3] move outward and force the brake shoes onto the wheels.

7

A
B
C
D
E
F
G
H
I
J
K
L
CP Rail
WESTERN PACIFIC
DISTRIBUTION "DIVIDEND"
NZR COAL

7 Modern freight cars are designed to carry particular kinds of commodities. Vehicles have now probably reached the maximum size that can be accepted with today's track, but recent research has opened the way for freight trains of the future to run with greater safety at speeds of at least 145mph (235kph).

A CIE (Ireland) containers on flat car
B SNCF (France) car transporter
C Austrian Federal liquid-gas tank car
D Canadian Pacific box car
E Western Pacific (USA) box car
F New Zealand Railways coal hopper
G Penn Central (USA) open gondola
H South Australian bulk grain hopper
I Finnish State flat car (timber)
J Italian State refrigerated van
K British Rail bulk cement
L Indian Railways hopper

Stockholm
Paris
301
2794

Railroads of the future

The railroads of the future will probably not involve any spectacularly new principle but will be developments of those we use today. Most rail administrations have built their entire system to a stereotyped model, with two steel rails of a particular type separated by a "gauge" of about 4ft. 8.5in (1.43m), 3ft. 6in (1.07m), 3.28ft (1m), or 5ft 6in (1.68m). Sums of money equivalent to hundreds of millions of dollars were invested in this track and, in today's economic environment of inflation and rapidly rising material and labor costs, it is not easy to see how any major change can ever occur. Only in places with no existing railroad at all can new railroad principles be adopted without the financial loss of scrapping an existing system. Yet already much is being done to improve efficiency of "traditional" two-rail systems.

Rewarding trends in railroads

One of the most rewarding efforts is the elimination of traffic bottlenecks, level crossings, sharp bends, and trackway restrictions of all kinds. Another improvement is to construct the track in a different way. Instead of laying rails and ties (sleepers) on a bed of ballast, which constantly needs attention, track could be made up into prefabricated concrete-based sections laid directly onto firm ground [2]. The maintenance cost of such track could be cut to less than one-tenth of that of a traditional track.

Another vital area for improvement is automatic train control. Today railroads are introducing electronically based control and communication systems [1]. These involve fixed beacons or cables laid along the track for communications between trains and a control center with a computer [3]. Trains can be started automatically, accelerated at an exact rate, held to precisely the best speed at all times and automatically guided onto the right track or made to comply with any special limitations. Any emergency can be instantly known throughout the system, the computer changing its program to re-instruct all traffic. Using early forms of such control, city transit systems such as San Francisco's BART and London's Victoria Line operate automatically.

Use of such automatic control, coupled with arrangements for stopping trains in a safe distance, has been allied with advances in the design of rolling stock to allow dramatic increases in speed. One alternative to the traditional railroad is the monorail [Key], which has been in use for most of this century in various forms. Its main advantage is not extra speed but the fact that it is easy to erect on stilts across a city.

With changes to the track, speeds greatly in excess of 155mph (250kph), a speed that approaches the limit for conventional track, will be possible.

Wheels obsolete

The most radical new developments in the final quarter of this century involve the elimination of wheels. High-speed vehicles can run along smooth tracks by air-cushion lift or magnetic levitation [Key]. Although both methods demand the consumption of energy—doing what the wheel does for nothing—the wheel-less train can run much faster than a wheeled one and needs less costly track. By getting rid of any contact

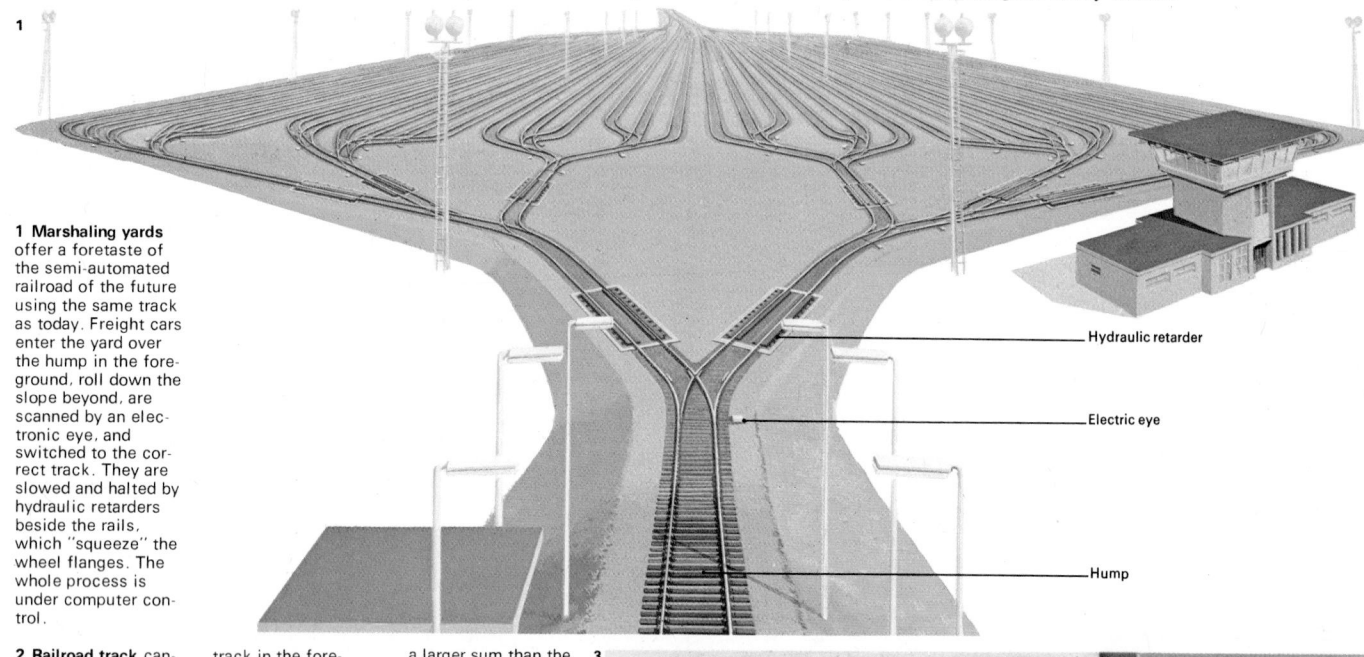

CONNECTIONS

See also
1708 Railroad transportation
1706 Locomotives
1754 Tunnel engineering

1

Hydraulic retarder

Electric eye

Hump

1 Marshaling yards offer a foretaste of the semi-automated railroad of the future using the same track as today. Freight cars enter the yard over the hump in the foreground, roll down the slope beyond, are scanned by an electronic eye, and switched to the correct track. They are slowed and halted by hydraulic retarders beside the rails, which "squeeze" the wheel flanges. The whole process is under computer control.

2 Railroad track cannot break away from the established form and spacing of rails, but it is continuously being developed to reduce costs, especially the cost of maintenance. The track in the foreground, laid on prefabricated concrete base sections, needs no ballast and in theory little attention for years. In a large rail system this type of advance would save a larger sum than the total annual bill for the cost of the energy to drive the trains. The possibility of eventually changing to a totally different form of track is extremely remote.

2

3

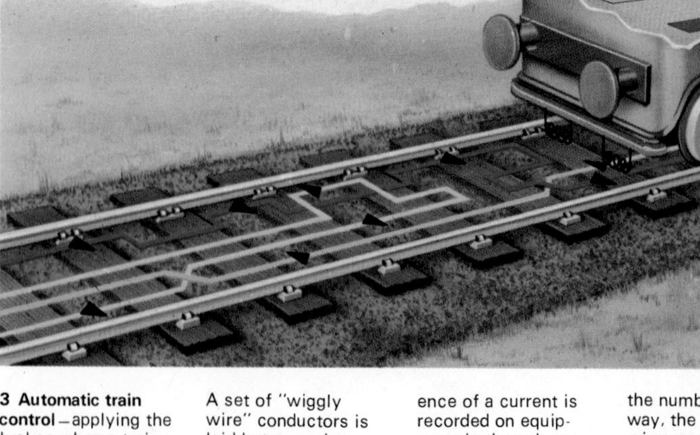

3 Automatic train control—applying the brakes when a train is approaching an obstruction—has been employed on a number of railroads for many years. But this fully automatic system is still in the experimental stage. A set of "wiggly wire" conductors is laid between the running rails of the track and the electric currents in them detected (using induction) by coils suspended from the underside of the locomotive. The presence of a current is recorded on equipment in the cab as a digit, say a number 1. Where a second wire runs in the opposite direction to the first, its current effectively cancels that of the first wire and the equipment records the number 0. In this way, the pattern of wires can relay a series of coded instructions as consecutive digits, standing for "reduce speed to 30mph" or "stop train in 2 miles" and so on, controlling the train automatically.

between train and track the need for maintenance would also virtually be eliminated, or so it is hoped. There would be no noise save for the aerodynamic rush of air past the vehicle and the only power needed to maintain cruising speed would be to overcome air drag. The track, basically made of concrete box sections, would have to be rather straight in comparison with today's rails because at, say 500mph it would be impossible to climb grades comfortably, to breast summits, or to negotiate curves. The TACV (tracked air cushion vehicle) [4] is a well developed technology, but no extensive system has been built.

From present to future

The magnetic-levitation method (maglev) dates from as recently as 1968 and many systems are operating over short test stretches. The fundamental feature of maglev is the use of the same magnetic field both to lift and to propel the train (probably a single vehicle). Superconducting magnets are used to effect dramatic savings in consumption of current.

For the more distant future there is a wealth of fantastic possibilities. Undoubtedly the most rewarding, somewhat frightening, and least likely in the foreseeable future is the gravity tunnel train [6A]. If a tunnel were to be bored from, New York to London, it would seem at each end to dive quite steeply down into the earth. A vehicle placed in the tunnel would fall toward its destination. If the tunnel were empty of air the vehicle would reach a speed of many thousands of miles per hour at the midpoint, when it would appear to be traveling on level ground. It would then increasingly seem to climb, coming to rest at its destination (with no expenditure of energy, save that of pumping out the air). Man does not yet possess the technology to build such a "railroad," but he could build shorter gravity vacuum systems that would dive down in curving tunnels between stations only a few miles apart, with atmospheric pressure behind the car and a near vacuum in front. Another "train" of the future might zoom along an air-filled tube by sucking in air in front and discharging it behind [6C].

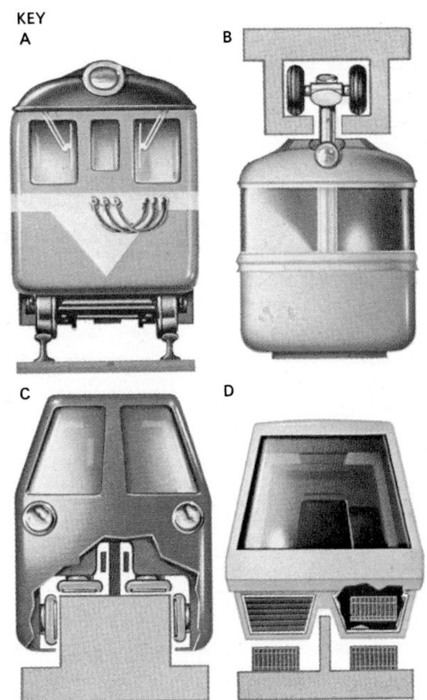
KEY
A
B
C
D

There are many kinds of railroads already in use. Almost all the world's public rail track is of the two-rail variety [A], with steel rails spaced side by side. In urban areas the monorail is sometimes found, with the cars either riding above the track or hanging from it [B]. Advocates of air cushion trains [C] claim that the track, made from reinforced concrete box sections, is cheaper. One of the latest systems uses magnetic levitation [D] to support the train. Examples of all these have been tested. Various futuristic designs exist only on paper and nobody can foretell with certainty what trains will look like even 25 years ahead.

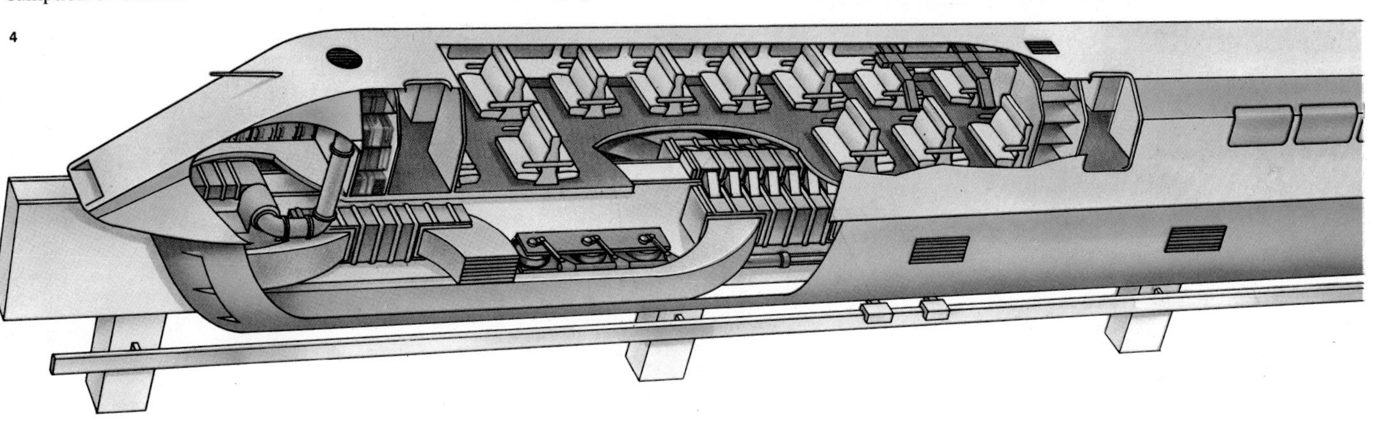
4

4 The hovertrain, a tracked air-cushion vehicle (TACV), illustrates the kind of system that one day may supersede the steel two rail. The track is assembled from cheap concrete boxes carried on short stilts. The only physical contact between vehicle and track is the sliding electric current pick-up that serves the linear motor. Electrically powered blowers form an air-cushion to lift and guide the vehicle.

5

5 A city could be linked to a distant airport using three kinds of rail links. A conventional surface railroad (diesel or electric) could serve the city and be a junction to other rail routes. An underground railroad could serve outlying suburbs and the center, and a high speed monorail could form a non-stop rapid link directly to the city. But only a subway can be built with little disruption to existing buildings.

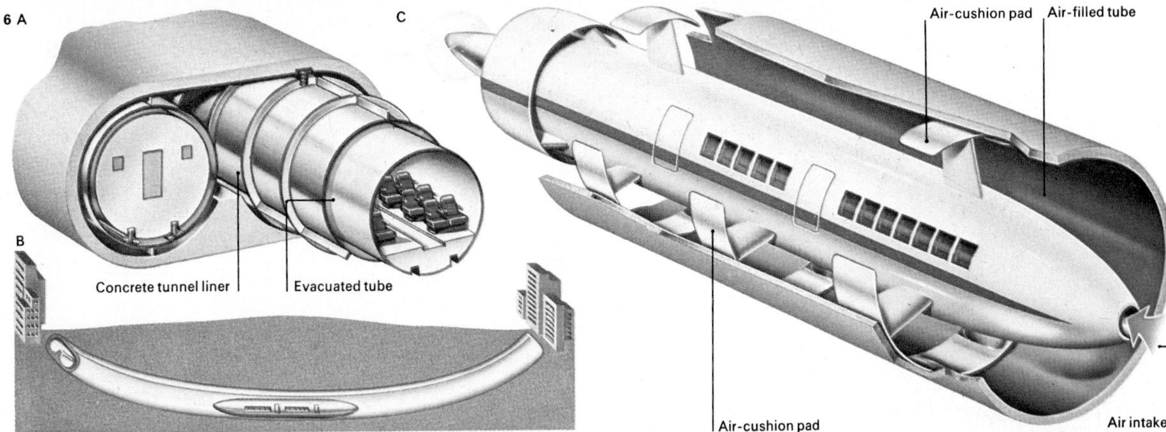
6 A
B
C
Concrete tunnel liner
Evacuated tube
Air-cushion pad
Air-filled tube
Air-cushion pad
Air intake

6 Futuristic ideas for railroads, not yet even in the experimental stage, include a vacuum train and an airtube system. The vacuum train [A] is "sucked" along by low pressure in front of it; gravity aids acceleration and deceleration because the tunnel slopes down steeply from one station and slopes upward to the next [B]. The tunnel for the airtube train [C] is filled with air and air cushion pads center the train. Airflow through the train propels it.

Balloons, blimps, and dirigibles

When people first dreamed of flying they usually imagined "flying machines" that resembled artificial birds. It so happened that, more than a century before the technology existed to make flying possible in this way, a totally different method of flying was developed in France. This method involved the use of balloons and is called lighter-than-air flight. The technical term for such aircraft is an aerostat. Aerostats are buoyant in the atmosphere and float at a particular level that depends on their mass, on the surrounding atmosphere, and also on the volume of air that they displace.

Balloon construction

The concept of making a balloon from some light material and filling it with a gas having a density less than that of air dates from medieval times. In 1670 Francesco de Lana proposed an aerial ship to be lifted by four large copper spheres from which the air had been pumped out (he did not know that spheres strong enough not to collapse would weigh many times more than the mass of air they displaced). In the next century the balloon came much closer with the discovery of the gas we now call hydrogen, the least dense of all the elements. The British chemist Joseph Black (1728–99), who studied hydrogen, thought of making a hydrogen-filled balloon.

A few years later, in France in 1782, the papermakers Joseph and Etienne Montgolfier (1740–1810 and 1745–99 respectively) had been watching charred fragments spiraling upward above a bonfire. Why, they wondered, did the fragments rise? Thanks to their skill with paper the Montgolfier brothers were able to build small balloons that, when filled with hot air from a fire, took off and sailed upward. On June 4, 1783, they publicly flew a 36-ft (11-m) balloon of linen and paper that climbed to about 6,000ft (1,830m).

The balloon caused a sensation. Jacques Charles (1746–1823) had meanwhile set to work to build a hydrogen balloon, while the Montgolfiers constructed a hot-air balloon large enough to lift a man, carrying a fire beneath it. On October 15, 1783, Pilâtre de Rozier was carried aloft in a tethered balloon, while five weeks later [Key] he and the Marquis d'Arlandes flew the first aerial journey in history, covering 5mi (8km) in a gentle breeze in 25 minutes. Charles's hydrogen balloon made a manned flight the following week, on December 1, 1783. For the next 100 years lighter-than-air flight dominated man's attempts to fly, with balloons reaching heights of 3.7mi (6km) and traveling hundreds of miles. For example, in 1859 John Wise flew 804mi (1,300km) from St Louis to Henderson, NY. In 1870, during the Franco-Prussian War, balloons were the only link that existed between Paris and the outside world.

Uses of balloons and airships

It was natural for early aeronauts to wish to devise some means of locomotion to free themselves from the mercy of the wind. Some attempted to use oars and others tried propellers cranked by hand, but it was not until the invention, in 1852, of the steam driven dirigible (meaning "steerable") by Henri Giffard (1823–1921) that the airship emerged as a vehicle. The earliest airships

CONNECTIONS

See also
1714 History of aircraft
1720 Helicopters and autogiros
1676 History of transportation
218 Forecasting

1

1 Ferdinand von Zeppelin (1838–1917) pioneered the rigid airship, which was to take his name. His first vessel, LZ1, flew in 1900 and was followed by a whole series, including this LZ13 of 1912. It was 460ft (141.5m) long and 45ft (13.8m) in diameter and could carry more than six tons of passengers and cargo. This airship, named *Hansa*, made nearly 400 flights carrying a total of more than 8,000 passengers 30,000mi (45,000km). LZ14 (renumbered L1) was ordered by the German navy; some commercial airships were taken over by the army.

2

U.S. NAVY • C-7

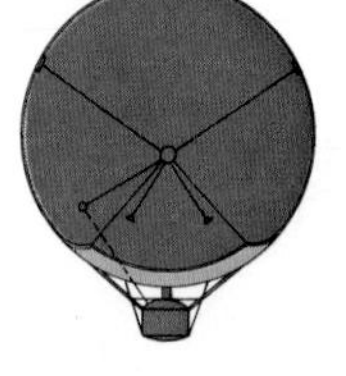

2 Nonrigid airships all have flexible envelopes that are stabilized by being inflated to a pressure slightly higher than that of the surrounding atmosphere. The load is suspended by a system of ropes or wires that distributes the weight around the fabric envelope. The sea patrol blimp illustrated dates from 1913 but closely resembles many used in World War II. Similar ships filled with noninflammable helium are still flying. Some are used for advertising and carry huge arrays of lights that can be made to display slogans or pictures. Others are being developed as freight carriers.

3

3 Semirigid airships are uncommon, but the *Norge* was one of a series of Italian airships of the 1920s and achieved fame by making a voyage to the North Pole in May 1926. There was no rigid structure inside the gas envelope, but a rigid keel ran from bow to stern and served as a structure to which everything could be attached. Cords and cables extended upward from the keel to secure the envelope, preserve its shape, and enable it to lift the whole ship. Below the keel were braced frames carrying the control car and engine nacelles.

4

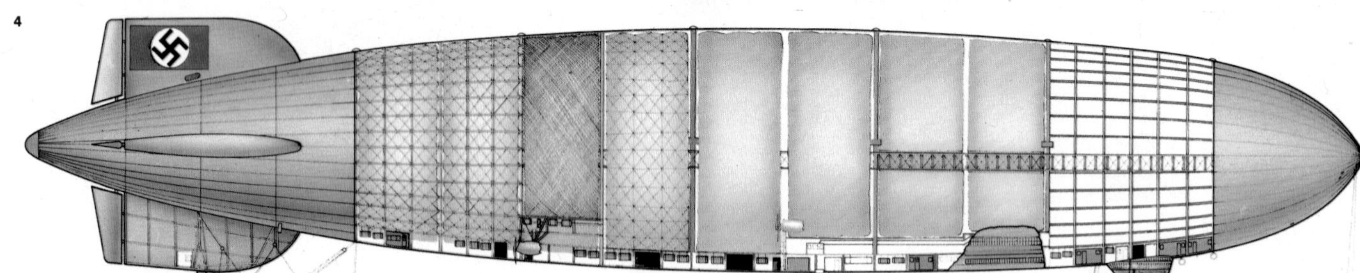

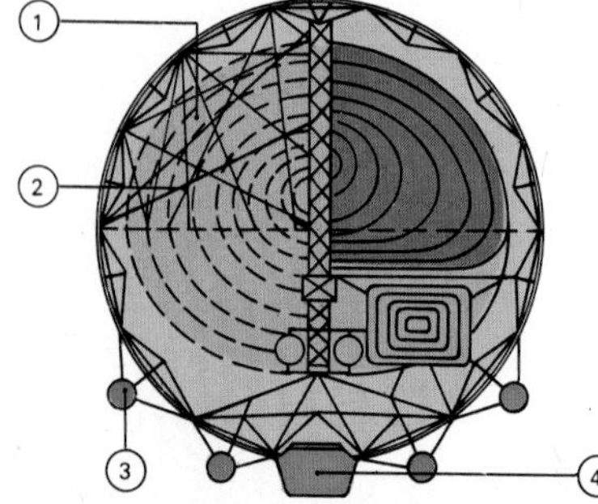

1
2
3
4

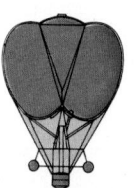

4 Rigid airships have a skeleton framework that contains the lifting gas in a series of bags. The largest ever built were the German LZ 129 *Hindenburg* (1936) and LZ 130 *Graf Zeppelin* (1938), named after the earlier LZ 127 of 1928. Each had 7 million cu ft of hydrogen, giving a lift of about 232 tons, contained in gas bags [1]. These were housed inside the aluminum framework [2] from which were hung the four 1,050hp diesel engines [3] and the payload [4] comprising 50 passengers and their baggage and 12 tons of freight and mail. The *Hindenburg* exploded in flames at Lakehurst, N.J., in May 1937 with 36 deaths resulting.

5

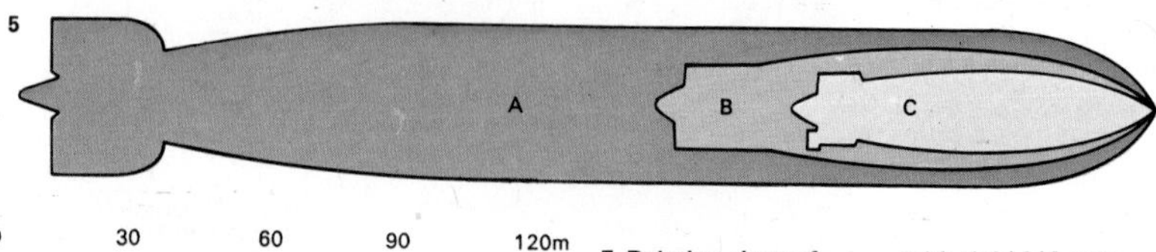

A
B
C
0 30 60 90 120m
0 100 200 300 400ft

5 Relative sizes of the three types of airship show the greater size possible with rigid [A] compared with semirigid [B] and nonrigid [C] ships.

were what are today called nonrigids [2]: each had an envelope of flexible fabric from which the load was suspended by cords. In the semirigid airship [3] there is a rigid keel, and in the rigid type [4] the entire envelope is built around a rigid framework. All were fully developed by the start of World War I in which airships, tethered "kite balloons," and nonrigid "blimps" played roles.

The operation of all aerostats depends on balancing their mass against the volume of displaced atmosphere. With gas balloons and airships the normal technique is to vent gas from the envelope to descend and to release sand or water ballast to rise. Airships in cruising flight can also change their direction or height by using aerodynamic tail controls, but these are not effective at low speeds. With hot-air balloons the lift depends on the difference in temperature between the air inside and that outside the envelope.

The future of the airship

By the beginning of World War II the large airship was dead—killed by a series of major disasters. Among the last of these was the destruction by fire in 1937 of the German airship *Hindenburg* [4], with 36 deaths. Barrage balloons and blimps had their uses but after 1945 there remained very few devotees of the sporting hydrogen balloon. Then, in about 1965, the scene was transformed. The modern hot-air balloon gradually came into worldwide use and today many hundreds are sold each year. They use immediately controllable propane burners with which climb and descent can be governed for a whole day if necessary.

The airship is also being recognized once more as a potential cargo carrier. All over the world designers and freight carriers are studying plans of completely new kinds of airships that would make use of modern technology to carry loads of hundreds or thousands of tons in safety and at low cost. Such giant cargo airships—the *Skyship* [8] is an example—could become a reality before the end of the century. They may be especially useful in opening up undeveloped regions and in carrying large freight containers and possibly even bulk cargo.

KEY

Man's first balloon flight took place on November 21, 1783, when two men travelled about 5mi (8km) across Paris. They rose aloft standing on a gallery of wickerwork suspended beneath the gaily painted envelope of the Montgolfier brothers' largest hot-air balloon. Made of paper-lined linen and coated with alum to reduce the fire risk (although not with complete success) the envelope was 49ft (15m) high and the whole balloon weighed about 1,730lb (785kg). The air inside, a volume of about 77,700cu ft (2,200cu m) was heated by a large mass of burning straw resting on a wire grid in the center of the gallery.

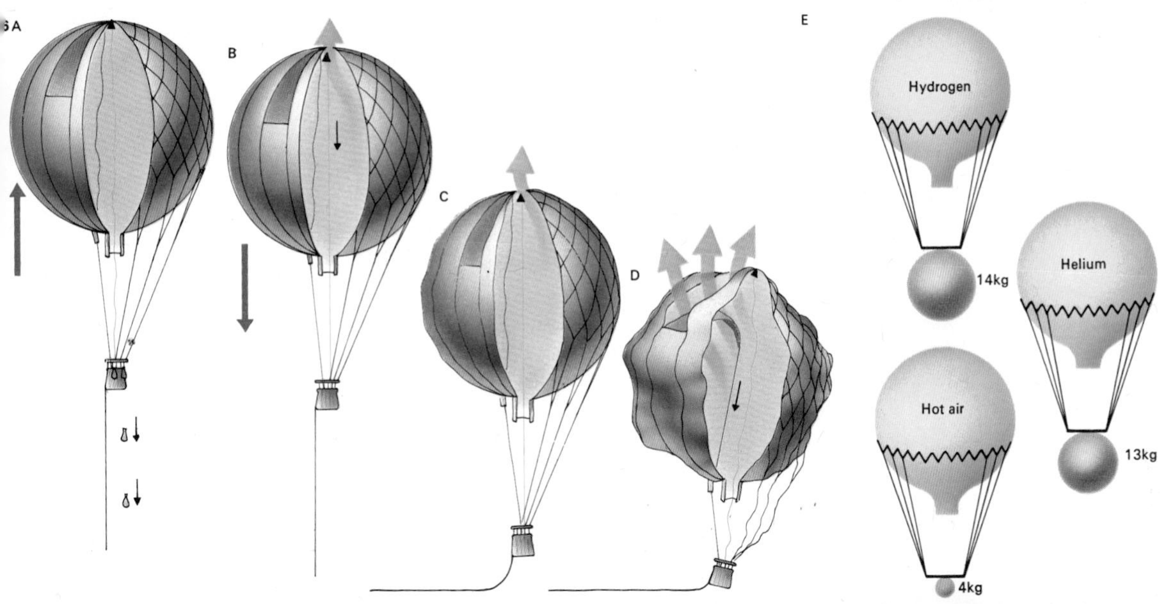

6 A
B
C
D
E
Hydrogen
14kg
Helium
13kg
Hot air
4kg

6 Balloons rise because the gas they contain is less dense than air. Control is limited to upward movement by releasing ballast [A] and downward by letting gas out of the top [B]. A drag rope [C] gives stability and slows the balloon on landing, when the rip panel is opened [D] to let the gas out. The lifting power of about 1,000 cu ft of gas is shown in [E].

8 Skyship is a proposal for a modern cargo airship. This 32ft (10m) model was demonstrated in 1975. A full-scale *Skyship*, 700ft (215m) across, would cruise at about 100mph (160kph) and have a crew of 24 with a payload of 400 tons.

7

8

7 The British R101 airship crashed on a hill at Beauvais, France, in 1930. Burning hydrogen created a fireball hot enough to melt the metal of which it was built. This and the fatal disaster to the *Hindenburg* seven years later sealed the fate of the hydrogen airship. The R101 was on a voyage from England to India when it crashed, killing all but six of the 48 passengers and crewmen on board.

History of aircraft

Contrary to popular belief, Orville (1871–1948) and Wilbur Wright (1867–1912) were not the first men to build an aircraft that could fly. Otto Lilienthal (1848–96) in Germany, for example, had already made hundreds of flights in his gliders. The Wright brothers' place in history is assured because their airplane was the first powered, controllable heavier-than-air craft to fly.

Louis Blériot's pioneering flight

After the Wright brothers, one of the important contributors to airplane design was Louis Blériot (1872–1836). He introduced a number of new features in his design, including a tractor (pulling) propeller, single wing (monoplane), and rudder and elevator at the rear. His Type XI achieved world acclaim on July 25, 1909, by flying from France to England. As with almost all other flying machines of its day it was of mixed construction; the main spars of the stubby wing and the four longerons of the lengthy fuselage were made of ash and the whole structure braced by numerous wires. Like the Wrights, Blériot covered both the top and bottom surfaces of his wings, although many other designer-aviators used only a single surface of fabric, on the wing's top.

By 1912 a manufacturer, helped by research in Scandinavia, had built a racer of monocoque (single-shell) construction, which made for strength, lightness, and a completely new streamlined form. The fuselage was built from multiple thin veneers of tulip wood, wrapped to shape and finally glued and covered with doped (lacquered) fabric. Most of the 100,000 aircraft built in World War I used the traditional wire-braced wood structure, but then the monocoque design developed gradually and found new expression in metal. Some early military aircraft, such as the Voisin L series, had all-metal structures. Some were made of steel tubing assembled by welding or riveting, or with bolted joints, and others used the new aluminum alloy Duralumin. Whatever the material, the basic method remained constant: to make a strong skeleton and cover it with fabric.

A few wartime machines designed by Hugo Junkers (1859–1935) were not only all-metal in skeleton but were also skinned with metal. In 1919 Junkers flew his F13, the first all-metal monoplane in commercial service. The low-mounted wing was completely unbraced by struts or wires and, like the fuselage, was skinned with Duralumin sheets having fore-and-aft corrugations for rigidity. From this stemmed a family of transports used all over the world, the best known being the Ju 52/3m—the leading European airliner in the 1930s and an aircraft built in large numbers for Hitler's *Luftwaffe*.

The only other family of transports able to rival the Junkers all-metal monoplanes were those from the Dutch Fokker company. These were also monoplanes, but they had deep wooden wings mounted above a fuselage of welded steel tube with a fabric covering. Together these two companies dominated European air transport until the mid-1930s.

The Schneider Trophy

Throughout the 1920s, much attention and money was lavished on the Schneider

CONNECTIONS

See also
1676 History of transport-tion
1718 How an airplane works
1716 Modern aircraft
1720 Helicopters and au-togiros
1742 Early military aircra
1744 Modern military air-craft

1 Blériot Type XI

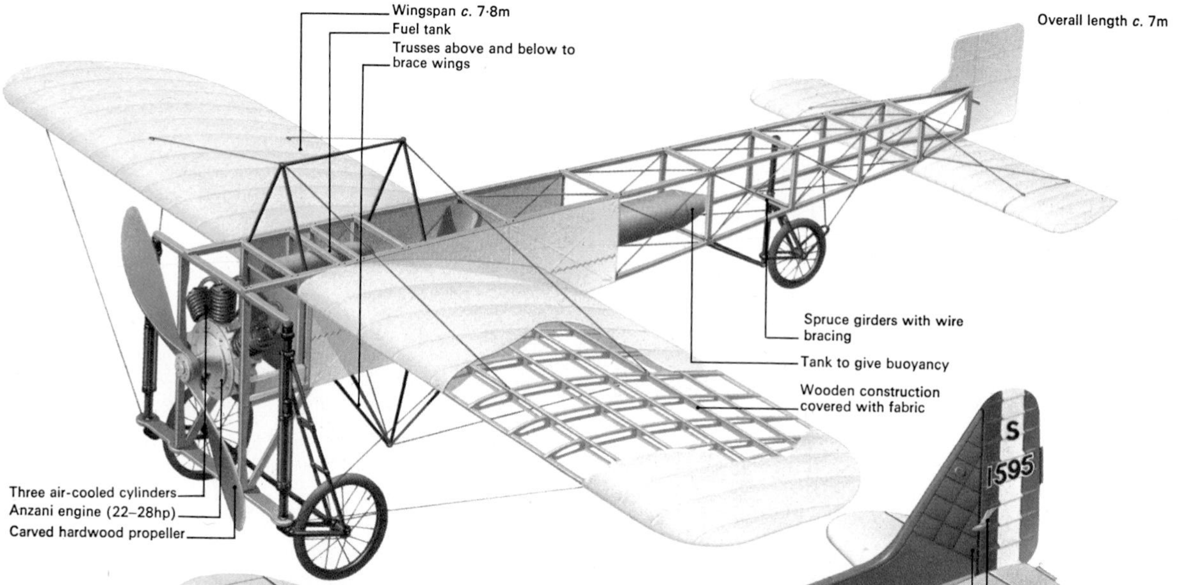

Wingspan *c.* 7·8m
Fuel tank
Trusses above and below to brace wings
Overall length *c.* 7m
Spruce girders with wire bracing
Tank to give buoyancy
Wooden construction covered with fabric
Three air-cooled cylinders
Anzani engine (22–28hp)
Carved hardwood propeller

1 Louis blériot flew his first aircraft in 1907, but it was with the Type XI that he achieved his greatest success. Aided by a shower of rain that saved his engine from overheating, he flew from Les Barraques in France to Dover, England. His flight was the first sea crossing and the first international air journey. Within two days of this feat, Blériot had orders for more than 100 Type XIs.

2 Supermarine S-6B

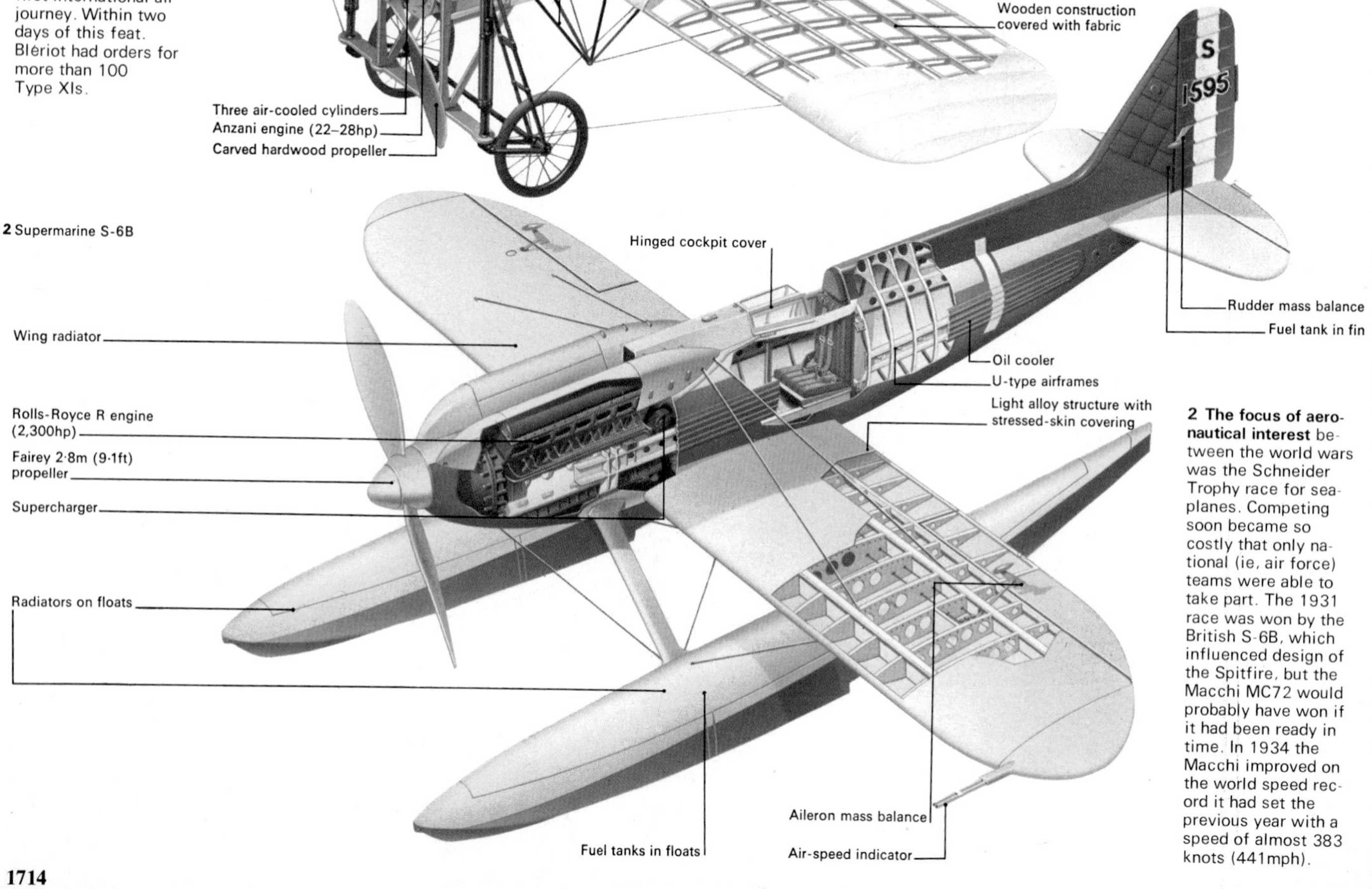

S
1595
Hinged cockpit cover
Wing radiator
Rudder mass balance
Fuel tank in fin
Oil cooler
U-type airframes
Light alloy structure with stressed-skin covering
Rolls-Royce R engine (2,300hp)
Fairey 2·8m (9·1ft) propeller
Supercharger
Radiators on floats
Aileron mass balance
Fuel tanks in floats
Air-speed indicator

2 The focus of aeronautical interest between the world wars was the Schneider Trophy race for seaplanes. Competing soon became so costly that only national (ie, air force) teams were able to take part. The 1931 race was won by the British S-6B, which influenced design of the Spitfire, but the Macchi MC72 would probably have won if it had been ready in time. In 1934 the Macchi improved on the world speed record it had set the previous year with a speed of almost 383 knots (441mph).

Trophy—an international competition for racing seaplanes. Seaplanes rather than conventional aircraft took part because Jacques Schneider thought future international air travel would require the use of such aircraft.

In addition to the public interest it stimulated, the competition had great influence on the mainstream of aircraft design. Also significant was the steady improvement in aviation technology, especially in the United States. The most important factor was the perfection of all-metal stressed-skin construction, in which the light-alloy skin was not just a covering but a crucial load-bearing part of the structure (so permitting a lighter skeleton underneath). Engines were improved and installed in better ways, with cowlings giving reliable cooling and reduced drag. Propellers were no longer fixed blades of wood or metal, but consisted of hub mechanisms carrying blades whose pitch (setting to the airflow) could be varied to suit the different demands of takeoff and high-speed flight. Wings were fitted with flaps to give more lift at takeoff and both lift and drag for landing. Landing gear was made retractable to reduce drag. Inevitably, aircraft acquired "systems" worked by electricity, hydraulics, compressed air, and other methods, which grew in complexity year by year.

The Douglas aircraft

One of the first modern airliners was the Boeing 247 of 1933. In the same year Douglas flew the DC-1, only one of which was built, and took orders for the slightly improved DC-2. In 1934 Britain held an air race to Melbourne, Australia; the outright winner for speed was a special racer, carrying no load, but the second and third places were taken by a DC-2 and a Boeing 247. On December 17, 1935, the thirty-second anniversary of the Wrights' first flight, Douglas flew the DC-3. Over the next ten years this was to become the world standard airliner and the standard Allied transport in World War II, with some 11,000 being built in the United States and the Soviet Union. Large numbers are still in use and individual DC-3s have flown as many as 80,000 hours.

KEY

Boeing 747 "Jumbo"

Douglas DC-3

Junkers Ju 52/3m

Supermarine S-6B

Blériot Type XI

The frailty and small size of early aircraft is emphasized by the comparison of their silhouettes with that of a modern Jumbo jet. This growth has, to some extent, been forced and made possible by huge improvements in propulsion and in airfields. Even the Ju 52/3m and the DC-3 had to operate from small, rough grass fields. These planes represented the most efficient compromise between conflicting demands that was possible in the 1930s, just like the Jumbo Jet today.

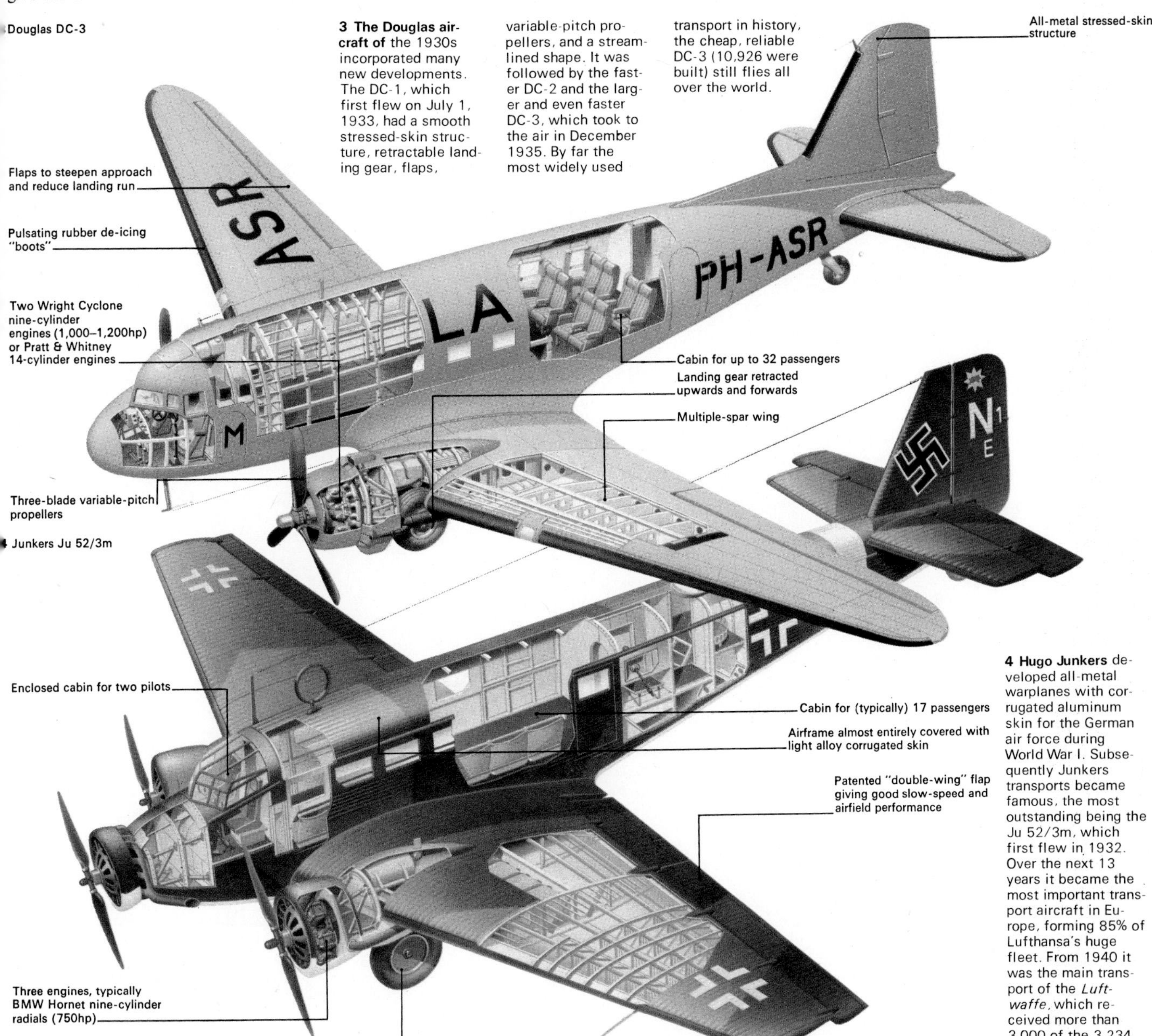

Douglas DC-3
All-metal stressed-skin structure
Flaps to steepen approach and reduce landing run
Pulsating rubber de-icing "boots"
Two Wright Cyclone nine-cylinder engines (1,000–1,200hp) or Pratt & Whitney 14-cylinder engines
Cabin for up to 32 passengers
Landing gear retracted upwards and forwards
Multiple-spar wing
Three-blade variable-pitch propellers
PH-ASR
Junkers Ju 52/3m
Enclosed cabin for two pilots
Cabin for (typically) 17 passengers
Airframe almost entirely covered with light alloy corrugated skin
Patented "double-wing" flap giving good slow-speed and airfield performance
Three engines, typically BMW Hornet nine-cylinder radials (750hp)
Fixed landing gear

3 The Douglas aircraft of the 1930s incorporated many new developments. The DC-1, which first flew on July 1, 1933, had a smooth stressed-skin structure, retractable landing gear, flaps, variable-pitch propellers, and a streamlined shape. It was followed by the faster DC-2 and the larger and even faster DC-3, which took to the air in December 1935. By far the most widely used transport in history, the cheap, reliable DC-3 (10,926 were built) still flies all over the world.

4 Hugo Junkers developed all-metal warplanes with corrugated aluminum skin for the German air force during World War I. Subsequently Junkers transports became famous, the most outstanding being the Ju 52/3m, which first flew in 1932. Over the next 13 years it became the most important transport aircraft in Europe, forming 85% of Lufthansa's huge fleet. From 1940 it was the main transport of the *Luftwaffe*, which received more than 3,000 of the 3,234 aircraft built.

Modern aircraft

The advent of the gas turbine engine late in World War II revolutionized aircraft design. The light plane—although still a recognizable descendant of earlier models—has been dramatically improved by fitting turbine engines. More advanced machines—airliners, heavy freighters, and virtually all military aircraft and helicopters—have been completely transformed. The basic principles of aerodynamics, mechanisms of control, and structural design necessarily remain unchanged, but development of ever more complex and sophisticated control, navigation, and guidance systems has continued to the point where the systems today often account for more than half the cost of an aircraft.

The early pace setters

This equation is true even for the class of aircraft bought by private owners and companies. In the 1930s the Percival Gull and Percival Vega Gull set several world records for long flights, establishing these planes as reliable private and light business aircraft for many years. Built entirely of wood, they were neat low-wing monoplanes powered by air-cooled piston engines of 130–200 hp and seated three or four in a comfortable enclosed cabin. Such aircraft were among the first to be capable of undertaking long flights to distant parts of the world. They cannot, however, be compared with similar planes today, which are equipped with pilot-aids of all kinds. Intense competition means that modern aircraft, such as the Beechcraft Super King Air 200, must be improved and updated constantly, resulting in a superior and more reliable product.

Instead of being made of wood, this Beechcraft model has a light alloy stressed-skin structure designed for fatigue-free use over perhaps 30 years (a factor never even considered 40 years ago). It is as large as some airliners of 1935, with seating for up to eight passengers. Maximum takeoff load is 12,500lb (5,670kg), four times that of the Percival Gull. The two 850hp turboprop engines are almost nine times as powerful. Instead of flying for 700mi (1,130km) at 120 knots (140mph) at a height of 16,000ft (4,880m), the pressurized King Air 200 cruises at 32,300ft (9,850m), far above most bad weather, for up to 2,050mi (3,300km) at over 280 knots (320mph). Yet perhaps the biggest contrast is in complexity of manufacture and operation. The number of items of equipment built into the aircraft that contribute directly to its flight—such as pumps, valves, radios, instruments, and different types of controls—amounted to 33 in the Gull. The total number of flight-related items in a modern machine is over 4,400.

The arrival of jet aircraft

When the British Comet I came into service in 1952, most airlines thought it premature and continued buying piston-engined machines for a while. But new jet aircraft offered the passenger flight that was not only faster but also significantly smoother and more comfortable. The early jets were, however, not so impressive to the man on the ground, although they stimulated unprecedented and sustained growth and profitability for the airlines. They were ex-

CONNECTIONS

See also
1744 Modern military aircraft
1714 History of aircraft
1742 Early military aircraft
1718 How an airplane works
1720 Helicopters and autogiros
1752 Airports and air traffic
1722 Space vehicles
1802 Radar and sonar

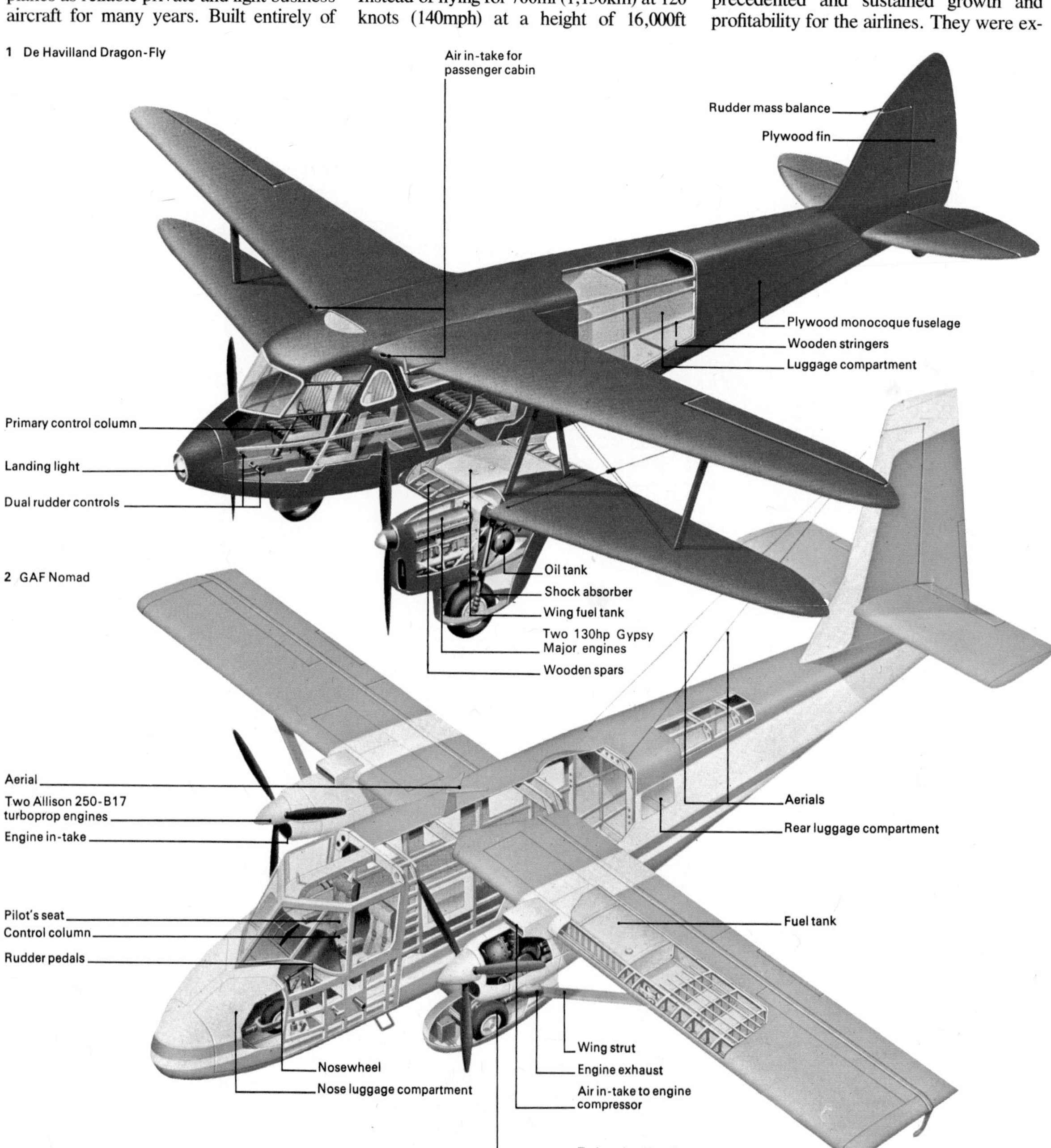

1 De Havilland Dragon-Fly
Air in-take for passenger cabin
Rudder mass balance
Plywood fin
Plywood monocoque fuselage
Wooden stringers
Luggage compartment
Primary control column
Landing light
Dual rudder controls
Oil tank
Shock absorber
Wing fuel tank
Two 130hp Gypsy Major engines
Wooden spars
2 GAF Nomad
Aerial
Two Allison 250-B17 turboprop engines
Engine in-take
Pilot's seat
Control column
Rudder pedals
Aerials
Rear luggage compartment
Fuel tank
Wing strut
Engine exhaust
Air in-take to engine compressor
Nosewheel
Nose luggage compartment
Twin-wheel landing gear

1 Low capital cost has always been of paramount consideration in the manufacture of light aircraft, discouraging new technology; the wooden De Havilland Dragon-Fly, first sold in 1936, carried five passengers at 109 knots (125mph) for up to 600mi (966km). The aircraft cost less than a modern car. Today's light aircraft differ only in details—for example, the layout of the engine cylinders. By 1990, even small ones may be equipped with turbine engines.

2 The latest technology has transformed the larger of the light aircraft types. These are too costly for most private owners and are generally used by companies employing a professional pilot. The Australian GAF Nomad 22 is powered by two turboprop engines and can carry up to 13 passengers in great luxury. It can fly at a cruising speed of 175 knots (202mph) with a range at maximum payload of up to 580mi (930km).

Trophy—an international competition for racing seaplanes. Seaplanes rather than conventional aircraft took part because Jacques Schneider thought future international air travel would require the use of such aircraft.

In addition to the public interest it stimulated, the competition had great influence on the mainstream of aircraft design. Also significant was the steady improvement in aviation technology, especially in the United States. The most important factor was the perfection of all-metal stressed-skin construction, in which the light-alloy skin was not just a covering but a crucial load-bearing part of the structure (so permitting a lighter skeleton underneath). Engines were improved and installed in better ways, with cowlings giving reliable cooling and reduced drag. Propellers were no longer fixed blades of wood or metal, but consisted of hub mechanisms carrying blades whose pitch (setting to the airflow) could be varied to suit the different demands of takeoff and high-speed flight. Wings were fitted with flaps to give more lift at takeoff and both lift and drag for landing. Landing gear was made retractable to reduce drag. Inevitably, aircraft acquired "systems" worked by electricity, hydraulics, compressed air, and other methods, which grew in complexity year by year.

The Douglas aircraft

One of the first modern airliners was the Boeing 247 of 1933. In the same year Douglas flew the DC-1, only one of which was built, and took orders for the slightly improved DC-2. In 1934 Britain held an air race to Melbourne, Australia; the outright winner for speed was a special racer, carrying no load, but the second and third places were taken by a DC-2 and a Boeing 247. On December 17, 1935, the thirty-second anniversary of the Wrights' first flight, Douglas flew the DC-3. Over the next ten years this was to become the world standard airliner and the standard Allied transport in World War II, with some 11,000 being built in the United States and the Soviet Union. Large numbers are still in use and individual DC-3s have flown as many as 80,000 hours.

KEY

Boeing 747 "Jumbo"

JAPAN AIR LINES

Douglas DC-3

Junkers Ju 52/3m

Supermarine S-6B

Blériot Type XI

The frailty and small size of early aircraft is emphasized by the comparison of their silhouettes with that of a modern Jumbo jet. This growth has, to some extent, been forced and made possible by huge improvements in propulsion and in airfields. Even the Ju 52/3m and the DC-3 had to operate from small, rough grass fields. These planes represented the most efficient compromise between conflicting demands that was possible in the 1930s, just like the Jumbo Jet today.

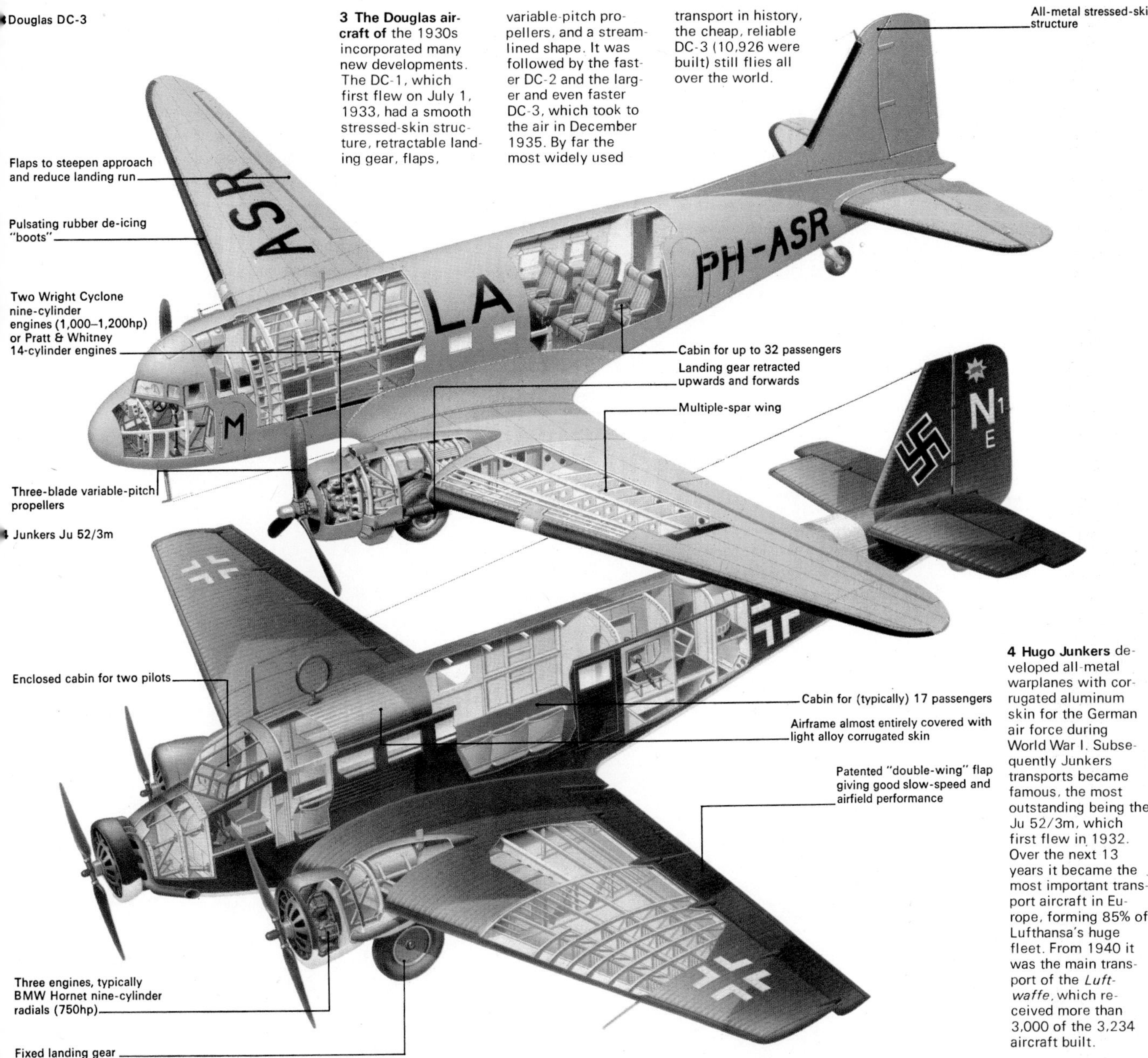
Douglas DC-3
All-metal stressed-skin structure
Flaps to steepen approach and reduce landing run
Pulsating rubber de-icing "boots"
Two Wright Cyclone nine-cylinder engines (1,000–1,200hp) or Pratt & Whitney 14-cylinder engines
Cabin for up to 32 passengers
Landing gear retracted upwards and forwards
Multiple-spar wing
Three-blade variable-pitch propellers
ASR
LA
PH-ASR
M
N1
E
Junkers Ju 52/3m
Enclosed cabin for two pilots
Cabin for (typically) 17 passengers
Airframe almost entirely covered with light alloy corrugated skin
Patented "double-wing" flap giving good slow-speed and airfield performance
Three engines, typically BMW Hornet nine-cylinder radials (750hp)
Fixed landing gear

3 The Douglas aircraft of the 1930s incorporated many new developments. The DC-1, which first flew on July 1, 1933, had a smooth stressed-skin structure, retractable landing gear, flaps, variable-pitch propellers, and a streamlined shape. It was followed by the faster DC-2 and the larger and even faster DC-3, which took to the air in December 1935. By far the most widely used transport in history, the cheap, reliable DC-3 (10,926 were built) still flies all over the world.

4 Hugo Junkers developed all-metal warplanes with corrugated aluminum skin for the German air force during World War I. Subsequently Junkers transports became famous, the most outstanding being the Ju 52/3m, which first flew in 1932. Over the next 13 years it became the most important transport aircraft in Europe, forming 85% of Lufthansa's huge fleet. From 1940 it was the main transport of the *Luftwaffe*, which received more than 3,000 of the 3,234 aircraft built.

Modern aircraft

The advent of the gas turbine engine late in World War II revolutionized aircraft design. The light plane—although still a recognizable descendant of earlier models—has been dramatically improved by fitting turbine engines. More advanced machines—airliners, heavy freighters, and virtually all military aircraft and helicopters—have been completely transformed. The basic principles of aerodynamics, mechanisms of control, and structural design necessarily remain unchanged, but development of ever more complex and sophisticated control, navigation, and guidance systems has continued to the point where the systems today often account for more than half the cost of an aircraft.

The early pace setters

This equation is true even for the class of aircraft bought by private owners and companies. In the 1930s the Percival Gull and Percival Vega Gull set several world records for long flights, establishing these planes as reliable private and light business aircraft for many years. Built entirely of wood, they were neat low-wing monoplanes powered by air-cooled piston engines of 130–200 hp and seated three or four in a comfortable enclosed cabin. Such aircraft were among the first to be capable of undertaking long flights to distant parts of the world. They cannot, however, be compared with similar planes today, which are equipped with pilot-aids of all kinds. Intense competition means that modern aircraft, such as the Beechcraft Super King Air 200, must be improved and updated constantly, resulting in a superior and more reliable product.

Instead of being made of wood, this Beechcraft model has a light alloy stressed-skin structure designed for fatigue-free use over perhaps 30 years (a factor never even considered 40 years ago). It is as large as some airliners of 1935, with seating for up to eight passengers. Maximum takeoff load is 12,500lb (5,670kg), four times that of the Percival Gull. The two 850hp turboprop engines are almost nine times as powerful. Instead of flying for 700mi (1,130km) at 120 knots (140mph) at a height of 16,000ft (4,880m), the pressurized King Air 200 cruises at 32,300ft (9,850m), far above most bad weather, for up to 2,050mi (3,300km) at over 280 knots (320mph). Yet perhaps the biggest contrast is in complexity of manufacture and operation. The number of items of equipment built into the aircraft that contribute directly to its flight—such as pumps, valves, radios, instruments, and different types of controls—amounted to 33 in the Gull. The total number of flight-related items in a modern machine is over 4,400.

The arrival of jet aircraft

When the British Comet I came into service in 1952, most airlines thought it premature and continued buying piston-engined machines for a while. But new jet aircraft offered the passenger flight that was not only faster but also significantly smoother and more comfortable. The early jets were, however, not so impressive to the man on the ground, although they stimulated unprecedented and sustained growth and profitability for the airlines. They were ex-

CONNECTIONS

See also
1744 Modern military aircraft
1714 History of aircraft
1742 Early military aircraft
1718 How an airplane works
1720 Helicopters and autogiros
1752 Airports and air traffic
1722 Space vehicles
1802 Radar and sonar

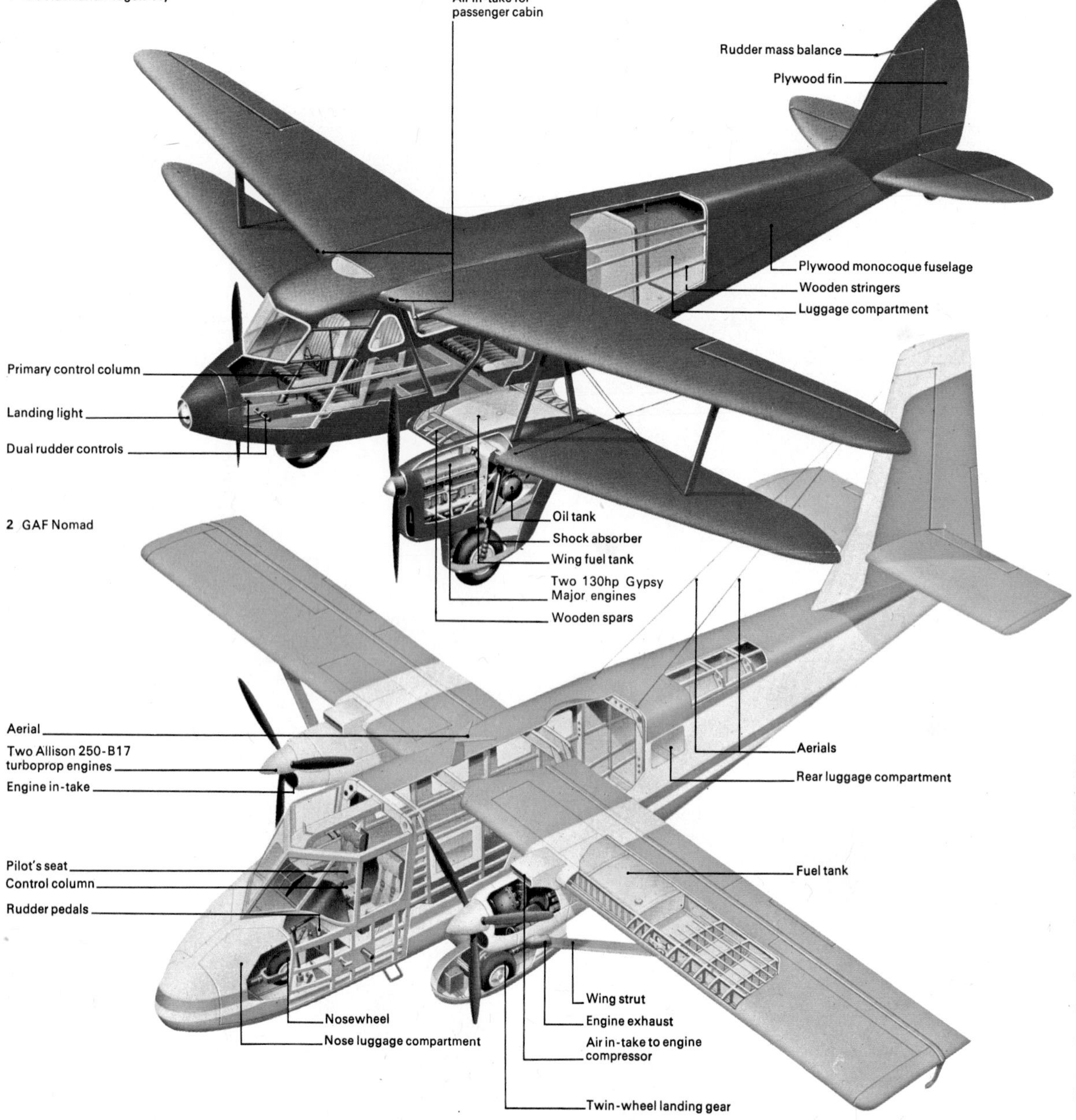

1 De Havilland Dragon-Fly
Air in-take for passenger cabin
Rudder mass balance
Plywood fin
Plywood monocoque fuselage
Wooden stringers
Luggage compartment
Primary control column
Landing light
Dual rudder controls
Oil tank
Shock absorber
Wing fuel tank
Two 130hp Gypsy Major engines
Wooden spars
2 GAF Nomad
Aerial
Two Allison 250-B17 turboprop engines
Engine in-take
Aerials
Rear luggage compartment
Pilot's seat
Control column
Rudder pedals
Fuel tank
Wing strut
Nosewheel
Engine exhaust
Nose luggage compartment
Air in-take to engine compressor
Twin-wheel landing gear

1 Low capital cost has always been of paramount consideration in the manufacture of light aircraft, discouraging new technology; the wooden De Havilland Dragon-Fly, first sold in 1936, carried five passengers at 109 knots (125mph) for up to 600mi (966km). The aircraft cost less than a modern car. Today's light aircraft differ only in details—for example, the layout of the engine cylinders. By 1990, even small ones may be equipped with turbine engines.

2 The latest technology has transformed the larger of the light aircraft types. These are too costly for most private owners and are generally used by companies employing a professional pilot. The Australian GAF Nomad 22 is powered by two turboprop engines and can carry up to 13 passengers in great luxury. It can fly at a cruising speed of 175 knots (202mph) with a range at maximum payload of up to 580mi (930km).

tremely noisy and burned fuel rapidly, often leaving unsightly sooty trails in the sky.

An answer to these antisocial qualities had been lying unheeded since the early days of the jet engine. The turbofan engine, a cross between a turbojet and a turboprop, could move airliners just as fast as a turbojet engine, with much less noise and a considerably lower fuel consumption. The large-diameter turbofan was rediscovered during the development of a US Air Force freighter in the mid-1960s. The losing bidder for that contract, Boeing, took four of the giant yet quiet engines and used them to propel the Boeing 747, the first of the huge, wide-body transports, popularly known as the "Jumbo."

Competition has resulted in a progressive increase in the size of transport aircraft. The DC-3 cabin is 5.5ft (1.7m) wide, and a Constellation of the immediate postwar years had a cabin 10ft (3m) wide at its widest point. The first of the big jets, the Boeing 707 of 1958, had a much longer cabin, which was 11.5ft (3.5m) wide throughout. In 1969 the first Boeing 747 was delivered, with a cabin nearly twice as long and 20ft (6.1m) wide. The capability of such aircraft is much greater than mere size suggests, because they travel faster and fly far more hours a day than older machines. Several airlines have just one Boeing 747F freighter, but a single 747F can carry more cargo each year than all the world's airliners of 1939. And the wide-bodied jets are relatively clean and quiet.

Supersonic transport

These "selling points" are not present in either the Anglo-French Concorde or the Soviet Tu-144, the first supersonic transports to enter commercial service. It is extremely difficult to make supersonic propulsion systems quiet, although the rapid and steep climb of these aircraft creates a local noise problem only around the airport itself. The move toward wider cabins is reversed in the SST (supersonic transport), because at Mach 2 (twice the speed of sound) aircraft must be relatively slim. On the other hand, travel time is cut by half by the supersonic transports.

KEY

Boeing 747 "Jumbo"

AIR FRANCE

BAC-Aérospatiale Concorde

GAF Nomad 22

De Havilland DH90 Dragon-Fly

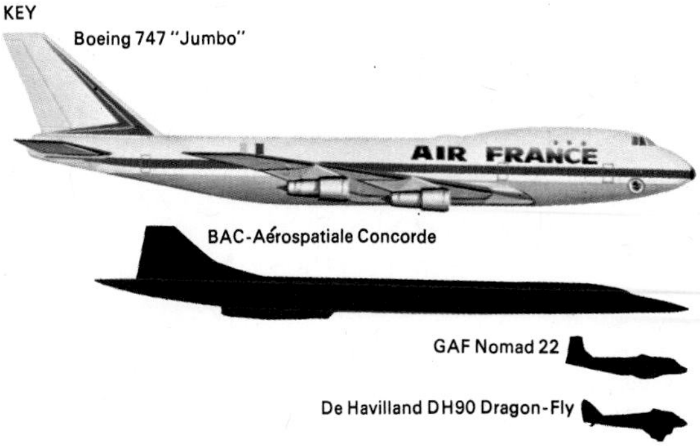

These aircraft silhouettes, reproduced to a common scale, emphasize the size of the Boeing 747 and the slenderness of Concorde. Supersonic aircraft must be relatively slender if they are not to be uneconomical, whereas the subsonic 747 can have a much wider cabin. The next generation of long-haul subsonic airliners may be smaller. The differences between the two light aircraft are less apparent externally and involve mainly the structural materials.

3 The Boeing 747, first flown in 1969, was the largest civil airliner and, in some respects, the largest aircraft in use (the military C-5A Galaxy freighter has slightly greater dimensions but is lighter and less powerful). The 747, with its turbofan engines, heralded a new era of quiet flight. The fuel economy of the turbofan engines has helped to hold down travel costs despite severe increases in the price of fuel. The 747 was developed because of the need to move more traffic without congestion.

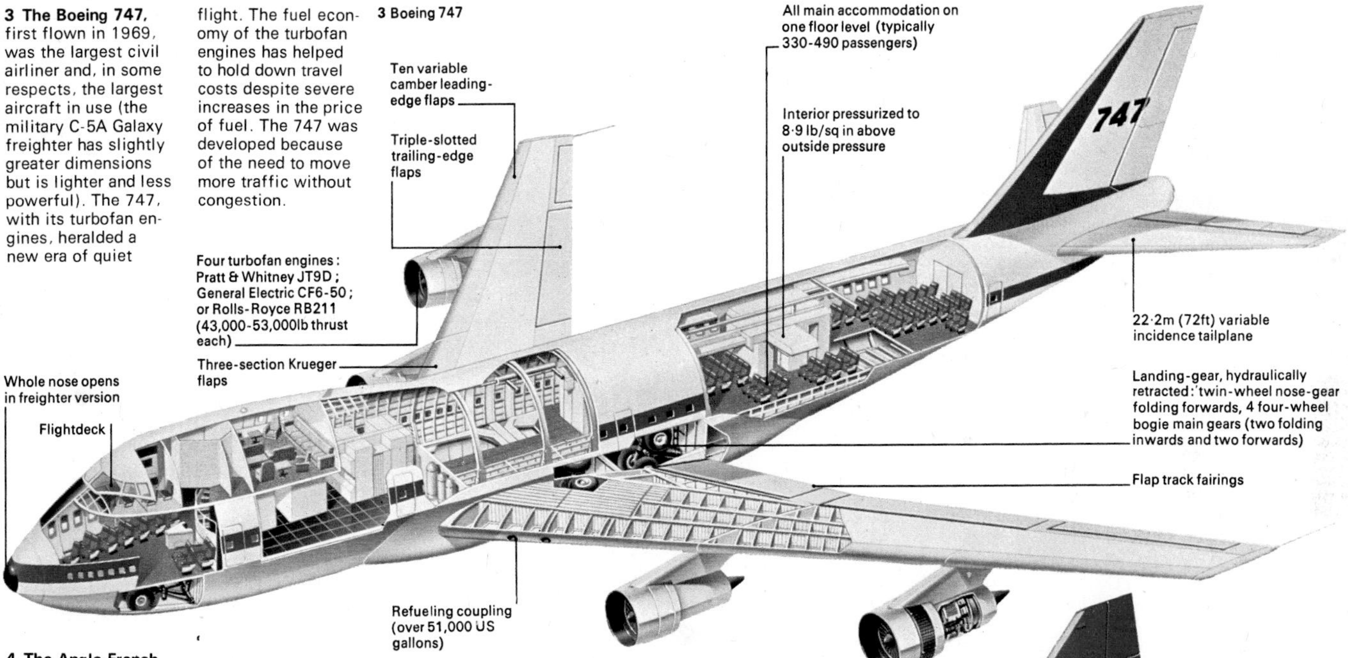

3 Boeing 747

Ten variable camber leading-edge flaps

Triple-slotted trailing-edge flaps

All main accommodation on one floor level (typically 330-490 passengers)

Interior pressurized to 8·9 lb/sq in above outside pressure

747

Four turbofan engines: Pratt & Whitney JT9D; General Electric CF6-50; or Rolls-Royce RB211 (43,000-53,000lb thrust each)

Three-section Krueger flaps

22·2m (72ft) variable incidence tailplane

Whole nose opens in freighter version

Flightdeck

Landing-gear, hydraulically retracted: twin-wheel nose-gear folding forwards, 4 four-wheel bogie main gears (two folding inwards and two forwards)

Flap track fairings

Refueling coupling (over 51,000 US gallons)

4 The Anglo-French Concorde, and its direct rival the Soviet Tu-144, probably represent the next step in fast passenger transport. These aircraft can halve the time previously taken to fly between any two distant places, just as the Comet did in 1952. The Comet, criticized in much the same way as the Concorde is now, paved the way for the jets of today. Political factors, the huge costs involved, and more far-reaching environmental problems of supersonic travel may prevent history from repeating itself.

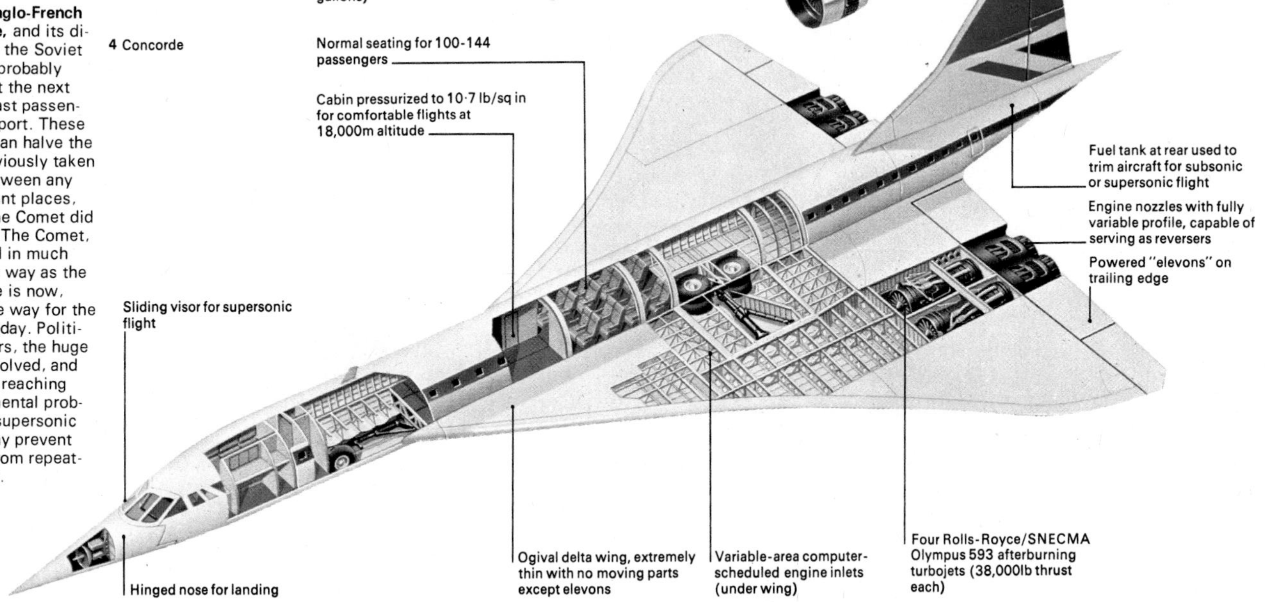

4 Concorde

Normal seating for 100-144 passengers

Cabin pressurized to 10·7 lb/sq in for comfortable flights at 18,000m altitude

Fuel tank at rear used to trim aircraft for subsonic or supersonic flight

Engine nozzles with fully variable profile, capable of serving as reversers

Powered "elevons" on trailing edge

Sliding visor for supersonic flight

Hinged nose for landing

Ogival delta wing, extremely thin with no moving parts except elevons

Variable-area computer-scheduled engine inlets (under wing)

Four Rolls-Royce/SNECMA Olympus 593 afterburning turbojets (38,000lb thrust each)

Principles of flight

If someone holds a sheet of paper in both hands and raises it in front of his face, tilting the near edge slightly downward, most of the sheet (beyond the hands) arches down toward the floor. What happens if he blows across the top of the sheet? Oddly enough, it rises until it is stretched out horizontally. One might have expected this by blowing on the underside, but why is the sheet lifted by blowing over the top?

The answer lies in the effect that speed of flow has on the pressure of air. In the case of the paper, and the arched shape of an airplane wing, air flowing over the top has to flow farther than that passing underneath. The upper air therefore speeds up and, as a result, its pressure falls. The higher pressure of the slower air below creates "lift." This effect is responsible for about 80 percent of the lift on a normal airplane wing moving at less than the speed of sound [Key].

Wings and air flow

Modern airplane wings are not like sheets but are more-or-less fixed in cross section. A conventional subsonic section always has a strongly arching top. The underside may be fairly flat in slow airplanes, with the thickest part of the wing well forward (toward the leading edge). In fast aircraft the wing looks almost symmetrical, so that it would work either side up, and the thickest part is about halfway between the leading edge and trailing edge. In every case most of the lift is generated by reduced pressure as air curves at increased speed over the top.

Factors affecting lift

For any given wing the lift depends on the angle of attack (the angle at which the wing meets the oncoming air). The greater the angle, the greater the lift—up to a point. Some modern aircraft with short but wide wing shapes, such as Concorde, can go on generating lift to seemingly impossible angles; but ordinary wings soon run into trouble. At an angle of about 16° there is little more lift to be had. By 18° the lift is erratic, the flow finds it hard to remain attached across the top of the wing and, suddenly, it breaks away. Instead of smooth, streamlined flow, the air billows away in great eddies. Lift is largely destroyed and any aircraft flown at such an angle of attack stalls [2] and begins to fall.

Wing lift also depends on the square of the airspeed; lift at a given angle of attack may be 1000lb at 100 knots, 4,000lb at 200 knots, and 9,000lb at 300 knots. How does an airplane take off? The pilot knows its gross weight, the airfield's height above sea level, and the air temperature (hot or high places have thinner air and give less lift). For each set of conditions he knows how fast the wing must move through the air in order that maximum lift (with a safe margin left to avoid stalling) will exceed the weight. In all but the most simple aircraft the lift at low speeds can be greatly increased by extending flaps behind and below the trailing edge and, often, by using "Krevaer flaps" along the leading edge that serve to increase the curvature of the wing section. These devices change the apparent cross section of the wing, making it act far more effectively on the airflow and greatly intensifying the difference in pressure between the underside and upper surface. At the correct

CONNECTIONS

See also
1720 Helicopters and autogiros
1716 Modern aircraft
1744 Modern military aircraft
1722 Space vehicles
1752 Airports and air traffi
528 The anatomy of bird

1 A
B
C

1 Control surfaces behave like miniature wings. These surfaces are: ailerons for roll [A] about the longitudinal axis, giving lateral control; elevators for pitch [B] about the lateral axis for longitudinal control; and a rudder for yaw [C] about the vertical axis for directional control. Each surface is hinged and is controlled from the cockpit. When deflected, the surface's main effect is not to push the whole aircraft but to cause it to rotate about one of its axes. Sideways movement of the control column moves the left and right ailerons in opposite directions because, as one wing comes up the other must go down. Fore-and-aft movement of the stick deflects left and right elevators together because both act together in raising or lowering the tail for a dive or climb. The rudder is moved by foot pedals and one of the things a student pilot must learn is how to "harmonize" the various controls, working the stick and pedals together to just the right degree. In very large or fast aircraft, some or all the control surfaces are hydraulically powered and an artificial "feel" is fed back to the pilot's controls in the cockpit.

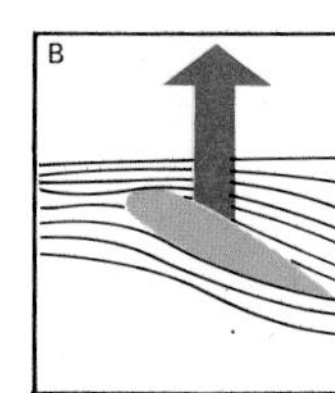

2 A

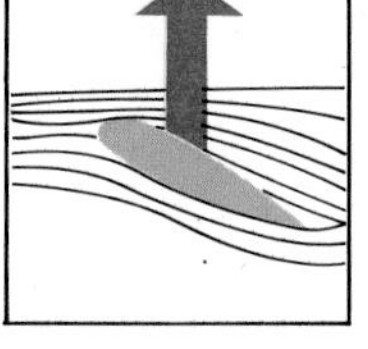

B

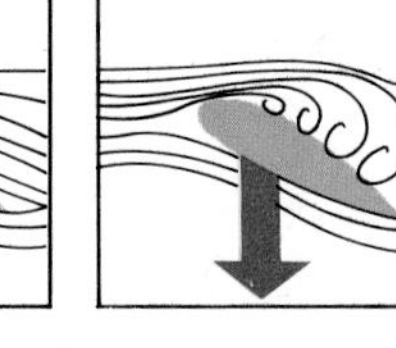

C

2 Stalling occurs when the angle at which the airflow meets the wing exceeds a critical value. At high speed [A] the angle is small. At lower speeds the nose must be pulled up more and more to maintain height [B]. Suddenly the aircraft stalls and a spin [C] may result.

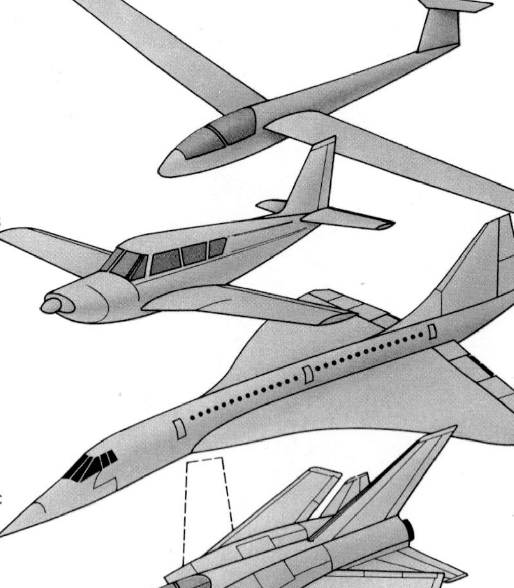

3 A
B
C
D

3 Wing shapes vary depending on their purpose. Sailplanes [A] have long, narrow wings to give maximum lift and minimum drag at low speeds (43–78 knots for a high-performance glider). Light planes [B] have simple, thick wings that provide good lift at low speeds. A supersonic airliner [C] has a wing that is optimised for cruising at twice the speed of sound (Mach 2: 1,350mph). It is less efficient at takeoff and landing. Supersonic combat aircraft [D] often need variable-sweep "swing wings" that can be folded back for operational flying or spread out sideways for cruising.

speed the pilot pulls back on the control column [1]. This deflects the horizontal tail (elevators or, often, the whole tailplane) so that it is tilted sharply, with the leading edge pointing downward. Immediately the airflow pushes the tail down, the whole aircraft "rotates," the wing reaches the angle at which lift exceeds weight, and the aircraft climbs away.

Airborne control

As speed and height are gained the pilot "cleans up" the aircraft by retracting the various flaps. The wing can lift the aircraft without them and, as speed continues to increase, the angle of the wing becomes less and less and the aircraft levels out. At full speed the wing skims virtually edge-on to the airflow. But in any sudden maneuver, such as a tight turn, the wing has to generate vastly increased lift. In the most violent maneuvers it is possible to reach stalling angle even at high speed. Normally a stall-warning system alerts the pilot of any approach to stall and this is especially important in thin air at great heights where wing angles are greater under all conditions. The "absolute ceiling" that the aircraft can reach is, in fact, the altitude at which level flight demands the stalling angle even at maximum speed.

In straight and level cruising flight the control surfaces on the wings form an integral part of the lifting surface. Any movement of the cockpit controls deflects these surfaces or the tail rudder to make the aircraft rotate about one or more of its axes [1]. Roll and pitch commands are often needed; the rudder is used mainly to prevent or induce lateral motion in the turn, with the nose of the aircraft moving left or right along the horizon, the wings tilted to give a lift force acting toward the center of the turn, and the rudder and elevators acting together. When landing the pilot places the aircraft in exactly the right position, aiming along the runway centerline, at such a speed that the wing (with all high-lift devices extended) reaches stalling angle just as the wheels make grazing contact with the runway. Many aircraft extend "spoilers" as they touch down to kill remaining lift.

KEY

Streamlines (paths of particles of air) show airflow over a wing [1] giving lift [2]. The airflow rises across the leading edge [3], arches across the top of the wing, and leaves traveling sharply downward. When high-lift devices, such as leading edge slats and trailing edge flaps, are extended, the effect is accentuated and the air flow over the wing almost resembles an upside-down U. Designers try to achieve the highest possible ratio of lift to drag (aerodynamic resistance) by choosing the correct form of wing.

4 Propulsion must be tailored to the job. The piston engine [A] is cheap and efficient for slow aircraft. The turboprop [B] also handles a huge airflow and is best suited to large aircraft. The turbofan [C-E] is best for aircraft flying at high subsonic speeds, such as airliners. In [C] the fan at the front of the engine displaces air around the main engine. In [D] several fans force air along bypasses and into the tailpipe. Turbofan [E] has an afterburner. Extra fuel is injected to burn in the tailpipe and thus provide more power. But it is noisy and generally used only for highly supersonic aircraft.

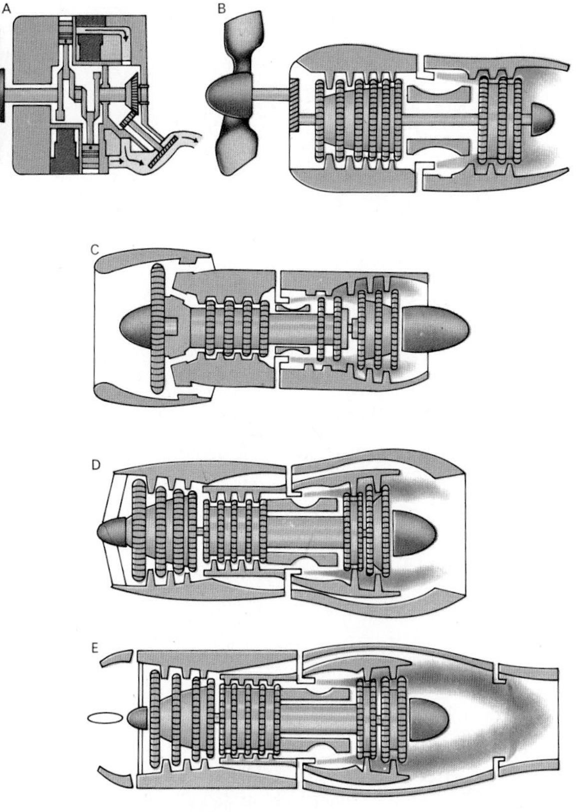
4 A
B
C
D
E

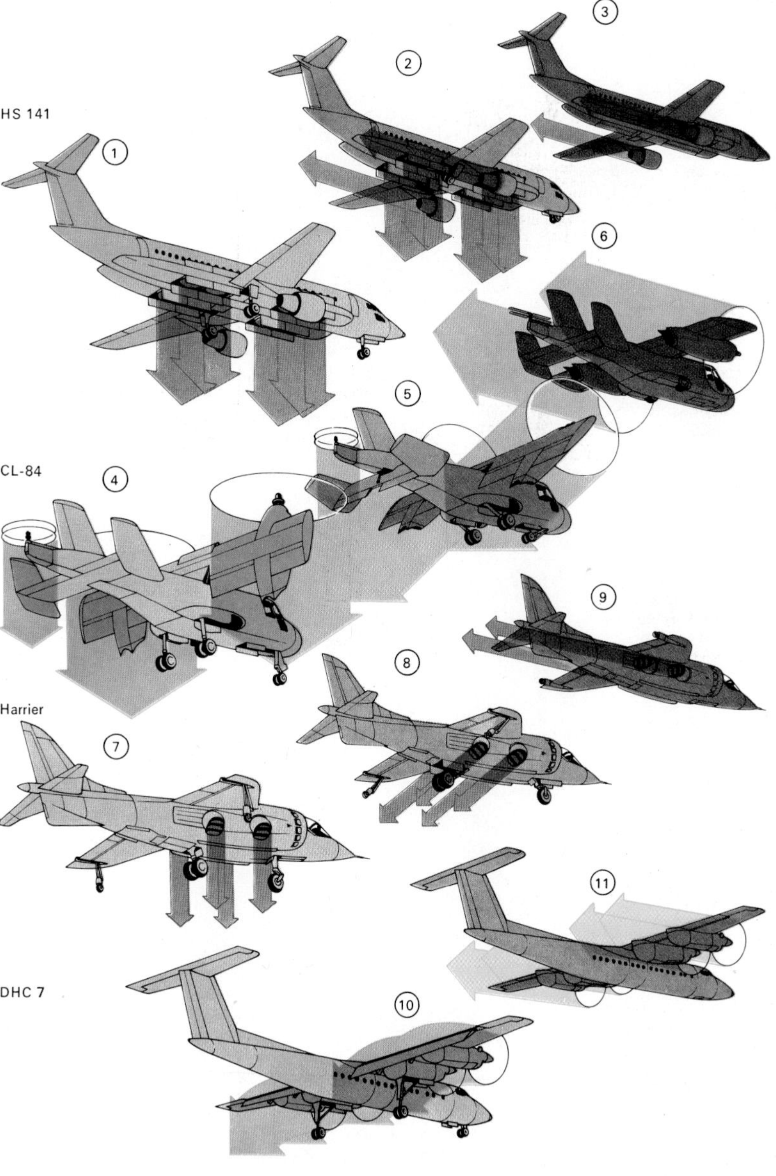
5
HS 141
CL-84
Harrier
DHC 7
1
2
3
4
5
6
7
8
9
10
11

5 Vertical takeoff and landing (VTOL) designs included the HS 141, with lift jets for vertical takeoff [1]; the propulsion turbofans started [2] and the lift engines shut off [3]. It was never built. The CL-84 had two turboprops on a tilt wing set at 90° for takeoff [4]; the wing slowly rotated [5] and then completely straightened [6]. The Harrier has a directional thrust engine blasting downward for takeoff [7]; the nozzles then rotate for acceleration into wing-lifted flight [8,9]. The DHC 7, a short takeoff and landing (STOL) machine, has four turboprops blowing across flapped wings, which deflect the slipstream down for takeoff [10] before the aircraft levels out [11] for normal cruising flight.

Helicopters and autogiros

The conventional airplane copes efficiently with its main task, the moving of people and cargo from one point to another. But it is limited because it cannot hover above the ground to lift or set down an object in one precise position and it cannot land on ground too uneven for the building of an airstrip. For difficult terrain and difficult jobs, a helicopter is needed.

Helicopters in history

All heavier-than-air flying machines stay in the air using the principle known as lift. As an ordinary fixed-wing airplane moves quickly through the air the shape of the wings makes the air pressure above them less than that below. The difference in pressure "lifts" the aircraft and enables it to fly. If the wings can be made to rotate instead of being fixed, lift can be obtained without the machine itself moving forward. This is the principle on which a hovering machine works.

The principle has been known for a long time. Leonardo da Vinci (1452–1519) sketched a design for a rotating-wing machine [Key] and dubbed it *helix pteron,* which is Greek for "spiral wing." The name is in use today in slightly changed form in the word "helicopter."

No helicopter could fly until an engine could be made sufficiently light and powerful. With the development of the gasoline engine about 1900, the power problem was solved and full-scale helicopters just managed to become airborne. These first rotating-wing machines ran into stability problems and test pilots were reluctant to try them out unless the machines were tethered. The problem of keeping a hovering machine aloft without tilting proved very difficult to solve, and yet deliberate tilting proved to be necessary to enable the machine to fly in a particular direction.

Tilting a windmill

In 1923 the Spanish inventor Juan de La Cierva (1896–1936) successfully flew a machine that was a strange hybrid between a helicopter and a fixed-wing aircraft [4]. It had wings and a propeller but it also had a freewheeling rotor on top. As the machine flew, the motion of the air past the rotor whirled the blades like a windmill and provided extra lift, enabling it to fly slowly and to take off with a short run. Cierva called it the "Autogiro," from the way the blades automatically gyrated as it flew. This effect is called auto-rotation and it can enable a helicopter to land safely if it loses power.

A most versatile machine

By World War II the helicopter had been perfected, principally because of the work of Igor Sikorsky (1889–1972) [5], an American of Russian origin. One of the main difficulties was torque—as the engine turned the rotor in one direction, it also turned the body of the helicopter in the opposite direction. Torque is a consequence of action and reaction and has been overcome in two main ways. Either a small vertical rotor, fitted to the tail of the helicopter, acts as a propeller to oppose the torque or the helicopter has two horizontal main rotors that spin in opposite directions, thus canceling the torque. By adjusting the tilt of the rotors the helicopter can be held steady

CONNECTIONS

See also
1718 How an airplane works
1714 History of aircraft
1716 Modern aircraft
1744 Modern military aircraft

1

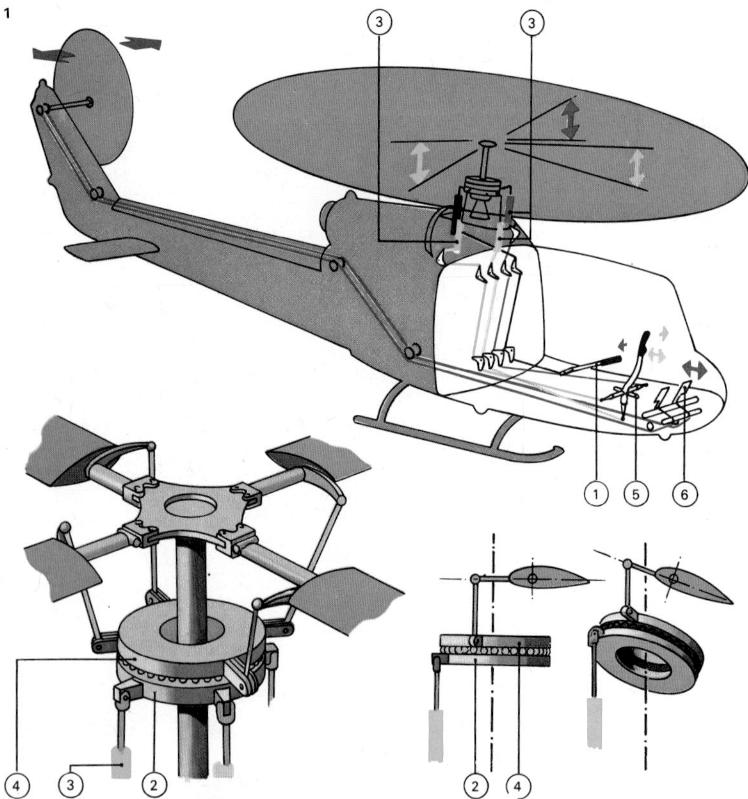

3
3
1
5
6
4
3
2
2
4

1 A tail-rotor helicopter has a cyclic pitch stick [1] that operates jacks [3]; these tilt the lower swashplate [2]. The upper plate [4] also tilts, tilting the main rotor to propel the helicopter. The collective pitch stick [5] raises or lowers the swashplates, thus changing the pitch of the rotor blades and altering the lift of the main rotor. The foot pedals [6] change the pitch of the tail rotor blades, swinging the helicopter around.

2

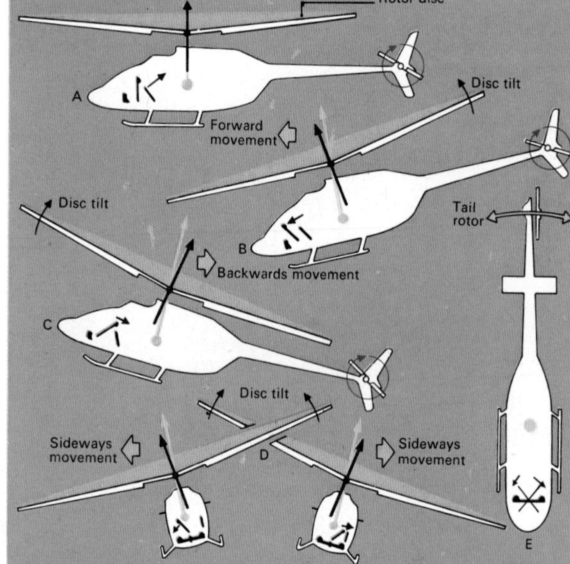

Upward movement
Rotor disc
A
Disc tilt
Forward movement
Disc tilt
Tail rotor
B
Backwards movement
C
Disc tilt
Sideways movement
D
Sideways movement
E

2 Vertical and hovering flight occurs when the axis of rotation of the rotor is in line with the center of gravity [A]. Moving the collective pitch stick increases or decreases lift. Pushing the cyclic pitch stick forward tilts the rotor disk (the space swept out by the blades) forward and moves the helicopter forward [B]. Pulling the stick back [C] makes the helicopter move backward and pushing it to the right or left enables it to "crab" sideways [D]. The tail rotor is controlled by the rudder pedals [E]. This swings the helicopter around in order to allow the pilot to change direction.

3

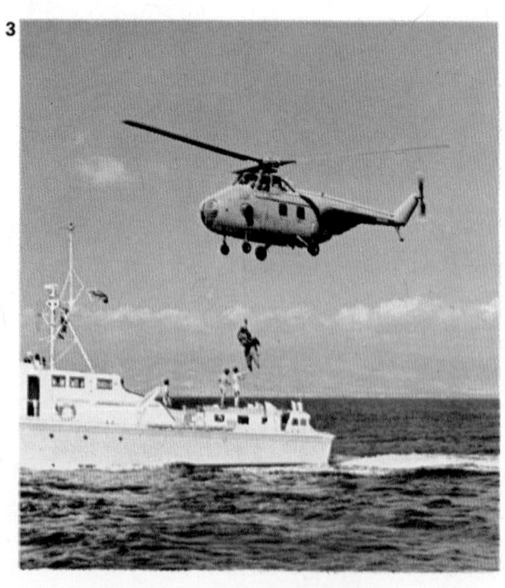

3 Rescue is a task at which the helicopter excels. Injured mountaineers, shipwrecked sailors, stranded tourists, and flood and earthquake victims often owe their lives to helicopters.

4

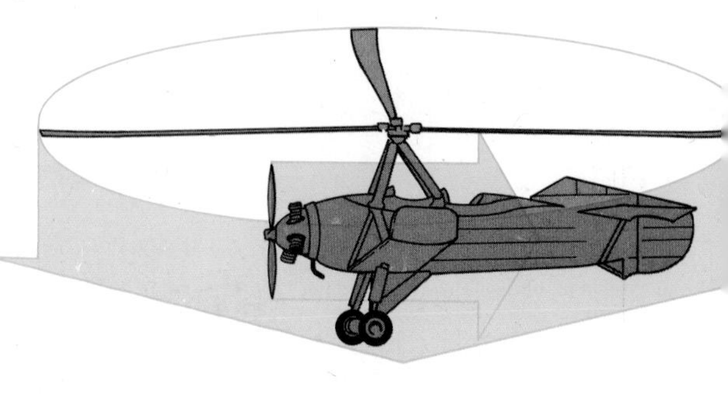

4 The autogiro was designed by Juan de la Cierva in order to make flying safer. The free-wheeling rotor (as well as the wings) provided lift. The propeller produced forward motion. Ironically, Cierva himself was killed in an airplane crash.

or made to turn. Another solution to the problem of torque is to power the rotor by having a jet engine at the tip of each blade; the blade's motion is the reaction to the jet's thrust and no torque occurs. A small ram jet may be used or exhaust air ducts may be connected to a gas turbine in the body of the helicopter.

Once stable in the air, a helicopter can fly easily in any direction. The rotor produces a downwash of air and the reaction to this downwash forces the machine upward. If the lifting force equals the weight of the helicopter, then the craft remains stationary in the air. If the lifting force is lessened by slowing the rotor or if the angle at which the blades sweep through the air is changed, the machine descends. If the rotor is tilted slightly as it whirls, part of the downwash of air is directed to one side, and the helicopter moves in the opposite direction.

Forward speed, however, is not very great and manufacturers are experimenting with aircraft that have the maneuverability of the helicopter and the speed of the fixed-wing machine. Winged aircraft with tilting rotors that can face upward or forward have been tried, although the use of jet engines with swiveling exhausts has been more successful.

Helicopters are used for passenger transport—for example, as a rapid service between airports and city centers and to link islands without airstrips. But helicopters are expensive to buy and to run and thus have generally failed to compete economically with other forms of passenger transport. They are used mainly in special applications for which no other machine would be suitable. Only helicopters can be used for many kinds of rescue work [3]—to lift people trapped in burning buildings, to rescue sailors from shipwrecks or vacationers swept out to sea, and to remove people from areas devastated by earthquakes or floods. Helicopters are invaluable for transferring both workers and materials to remote places and are also used as cranes to hoist heavy objects into position on top of buildings. The flexibility of the helicopter also makes it a versatile war machine for carrying men and equipment.

KEY

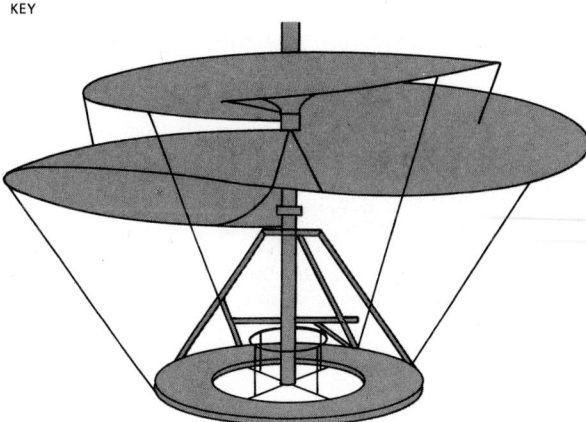

Leonardo da Vinci made this design in 1483 for a rotating-wing aircraft. The spiral wing, which Leonardo suggested should be made of starched linen, would have lifted the machine in much the same way as the rotor of a helicopter. But it is certain that Leonardo's machine never flew. No engine existed that was capable of powering the device and even if there had been it would have spun wildly out of control, for Leonardo did not realize that the engine would also rotate the body in the opposite direction to the wing. This turning effect is known as torque and must be counteracted.

5

5 The VS-300, built by Igor Sikorsky, was the first practical helicopter. It first flew in 1939, but went through many modifications before being perfected. At one stage it could fly in every direction except forward. These problems were overcome by 1941 and production models were tested in World War II. Its single main rotor and small tail rotor became the predominant helicopter design.

6

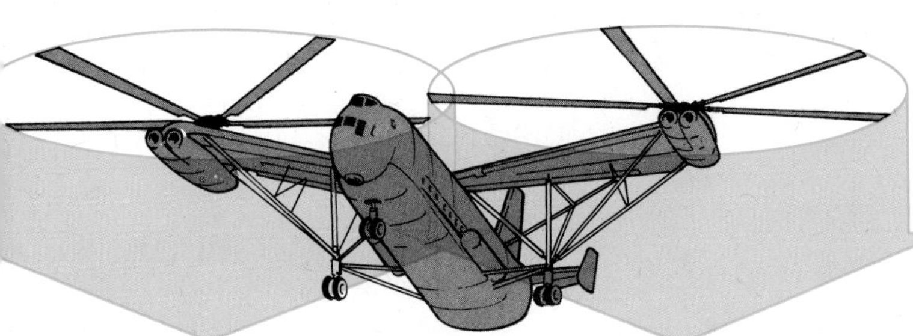

6 A twin-rotor helicopter achieves twice as much lift as a single-rotor machine with a similar rotor. The Soviet Mi-12 is the world's largest helicopter. Built by Mikhail Mil, it set a world record in 1969 by lifting 40 tons to a height of more than 6,560ft (2,000m). It has a span of 220ft (67m) across its rotors, which spin in opposite directions. The Mi-12 is a transport aircraft.

7 A tandem helicopter has twin rotors mounted one behind the other. The first tandem helicopter, the "Flying Banana" was built by US engineer Frank Piasecki in 1945. Such helicopters can be made large enough to serve as passenger vehicles or troop transports. Other twin-rotor machines have side-by-side rotors intermeshing like an eggbeater or coaxial rotors one above the other.

7

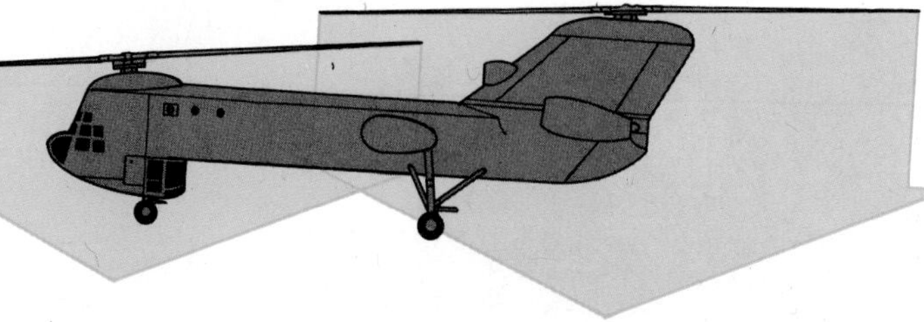

8

8 A "flying crane" lifts a heavy field gun during army maneuvers. Such operations are quick and dispense with the need for towing vehicles. Standard helicopters are useful for carrying freight and some interesting tasks have been proposed for the most powerful machines. They could rapidly unload containers from ships offshore and do away with the need for deep harbors. Another idea envisages the carrying of a Sky-lounge—a bus-like vehicle that would gather passengers in a city and then be lifted by helicopter straight to the door of an airplane at the airport. Flying cranes are particularly useful in wartime for retrieving aircraft that have crashed but are not beyond repair.

Space vehicles

Since the Soviet Sputnik 1 was launched on October 4, 1957, several nations have between them launched hundreds of artificial satellites into orbit around the Earth. The United States and the Soviet Union have sent exploratory "probes" to orbit or soft-land on the Moon, Mars, and Venus. Other planets have been studied at close quarters using unmanned space vehicles. The greatest achievement was probably the landing of men on the Moon during the US Apollo program, and there is good reason to suppose that by the end of the twentieth century the whole Solar System will have been explored—but by unmanned probes.

Getting into space

The use of vehicles to explore space dates from the development of rockets powerful enough to launch the vehicles and enable them to "escape" from the Earth's gravity [Key]. This requires a velocity of about 25,000mph (40,000kph), which is known as the Earth's escape velocity.

To reach such speeds, multi-stage rockets are employed. These make use of the piggy-back principle [1]—the rocket entering orbit is fired at the edge of the atmosphere, having been carried there on top of another rocket that, in turn, may also have been lifted on an even more powerful first-stage rocket. This technique of overcoming gravity was first proposed by the Russian pioneer of rocketry Konstantin Tsiolkovskii (1857–1935). In 1949 a US multistage rocket sent a vehicle to a height of more than 242mi (390km) above the surface of the Earth.

Rockets and satellites

All rockets are reaction motors. They work using the principle of Newton's third law of motion, which states that action and reaction are equal and opposite.

In a rocket the "action" is the escape of hot gases roaring out of the tail; the "reaction" to this action forces the body of the rocket in the other direction. The principle can be demonstrated by blowing up a balloon and releasing it. The action of the jet of air escaping from the neck of the balloon is balanced by an equal and opposite reaction that pushes the balloon through the air. For this reason a rocket will work in the airless near-vacuum of outer space; it does not work, like a jet engine, by pushing against the air behind it. The presence of air is actually a handicap because it sets up a resistance to the rocket's motion.

The fuel in a firework rocket is a solid propellant explosive such as gunpowder. But solid fuels are too weak and uncontrollable to be used alone in space rockets. Instead, two liquids are used—a fuel and an oxidant. When mixed in a combustion chamber they react together to produce hot gases that are expelled from the exhaust and create thrust. The first successful liquid-fueled rockets were made in the United States in 1926 by Robert Goddard (1882–1945). By the time of Goddard's death German scientists, led by Werner von Braun (1912–), had developed the V2. This was a liquid-fueled rocket that carried a one-ton explosive warhead and was the direct ancestor of modern space rockets. After World War II von Braun and his colleagues went to the United States to continue their work.

CONNECTIONS

See also
1724 Man in space
1794 Communications: radio
1796 Communications: television
1802 Radar and sonar
54 Moon missions
70 Mars missions
142 A history of space achievements

1

3rd stage
2nd stage
1st stage
2,542m
127,868m
922
118,420kg
4,489m/sec
481,441kg
71,526m
2,972m/sec
2,283,034kg

1 Multi-stage rockets consist of a number of smaller rockets combined to make one big one. At the start of the flight the large, lower stage is used; here it accounts for 83.3 percent of the propellant but accelerates the rocket to only 33 percent of its final velocity. When it has used up its fuel, it drops away and the second stage takes over. Only the third stage goes into orbit around the Earth.

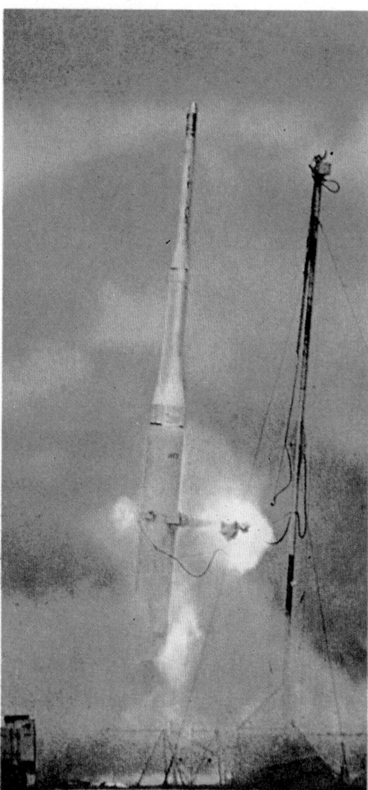

2 The US Vanguard rocket was launched in 1958 in the early days of space research. Rockets were not reliable then, but this craft was a major US success, although with only a minute payload.

3 The Soviet "Moon crawler" Lunokhod 1 [A] was taken to the Moon by a Luna rocket probe; after landing it was sent down a ramp [B] onto the surface. Lunokhod 1 landed upon the grey plain of the Mare Imbrium and crawled along for months, controlled from the USSR, sending back invaluable data. A second Lunokhod operated in the Mare Serenitatis near the landing site of the Apollo 17 module.

4 Since 1957 hundreds of space probes have been launched. The Soviet Cosmos vehicles [A] are artificial satellites, brought back to Earth after limited flight times. The US Mariner 9 [B], went into Mars orbit in late 1971. Continuing well into 1972 it sent back detailed photographs of the Martian landscape. The first probe launched by the Soviet Union to Venus [C] was unsuccessful.

Sputnik 1 was the size of a football and carried little apart from a radio transmitter. Some of today's satellites are the size of a large truck. They have been used in many ways: for mapping [7], communications, and scientific research into phenomena impossible to study properly from the ground because of the Earth's atmosphere. Communications satellites have evolved from the early passive type, which consisted of a "silvered" balloon that acted like a mirror to reflect radio signals beamed up to it back down to Earth, to the modern active satellites that amplify received radio and television signals before re-transmitting them.

Manned satellites have now become relatively common, and in 1973 the US Skylab was placed into orbit as the first true space station. Docking procedures have also been carried out between two spacecraft; in 1975 a US vehicle docked with a Soviet one, the first such meeting between traditional rivals in space. All such maneuvers require precise information about orbits and velocities. This is provided by radar sets on the craft and on Earth, and the necessary complex calculations are carried out using computers.

Probes to the Moon and planets

The first target for unmanned space probes was the Moon. In 1959 the Soviet Luna 3 made a circumlunar voyage and subsequently the whole of the Moon's surface was mapped by automatic probes. Soft landings on the surface were made [3], and mechanical fingers collected dust and rock.

The lunar probes were followed by the first attempts to explore the planets. In 1962 the US Mariner 2 made a fly-by pass of Venus, and vehicles have since been sent to Mars, Mercury, and Jupiter. By 1975 a Soviet probe had soft-landed on Venus and in the same year a vehicle was on its way to Saturn. In 1976 two US Vikings made soft landings on Mars.

Vast amounts of unique information have been collected. Telescopes and spectrometers in space vehicles aid Earth-bound astronomers. And infrared photographs of Earth taken from space can reveal new resources.

KEY

This rocket launched the US Mars probe Mariner 9 in 1971. It was the first probe to be put into a close path around Mars and transmitted back to Earth thousands of high-quality pictures. Similar rockets have launched space vehicles to other planets, either to pass close to them and take photographs or to soft-land and relay valuable information to Earth.

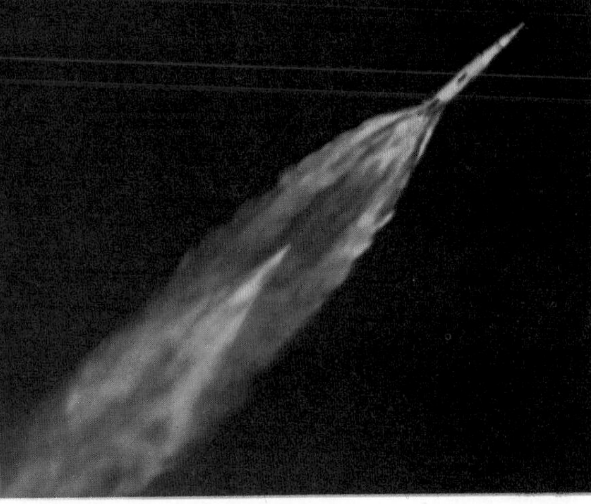

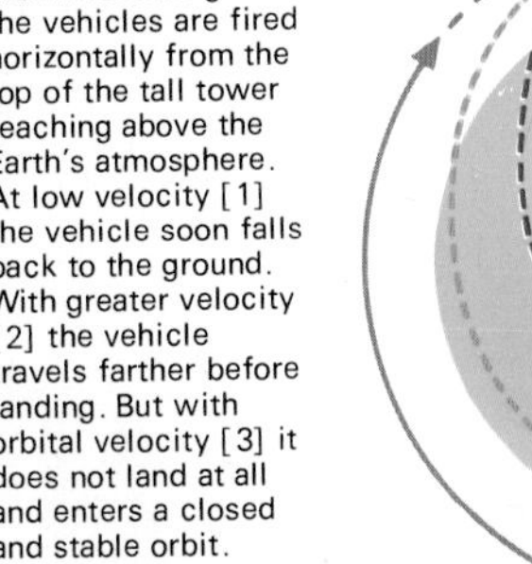

5 Various paths for space probes can be drawn assuming that the vehicles are fired horizontally from the top of the tall tower reaching above the Earth's atmosphere. At low velocity [1] the vehicle soon falls back to the ground. With greater velocity [2] the vehicle travels farther before landing. But with orbital velocity [3] it does not land at all and enters a closed and stable orbit.

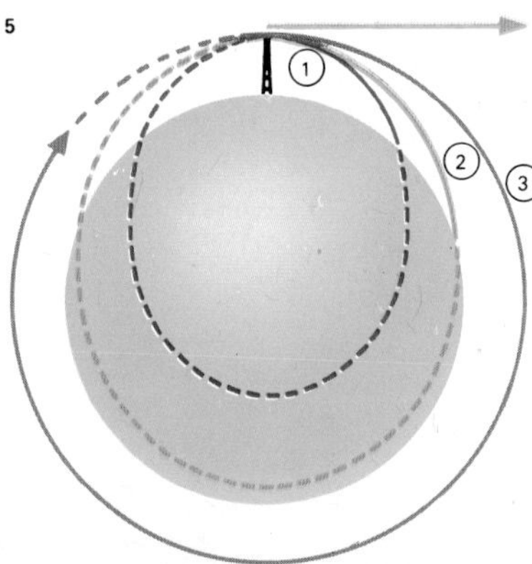
5
1
2
3

6 Satellites may travel in orbits of various kinds [A]. Some move in the plane of the Equator [1], others have inclined orbits [2], and some use polar orbits [3]. For a "stationary" satellite of the Syncom communications type [B] the period is exactly one day. Its distance from Earth is 22,300mi (35,900km); it appears stationary and is ideal for use in television relays.

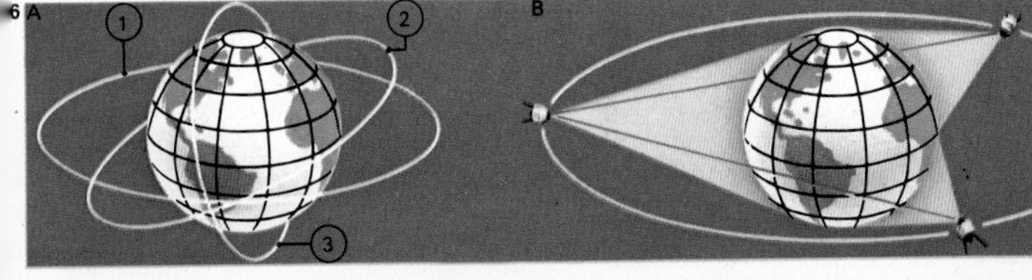
6 A
1
2
3
B

7 An orbiting satellite is better for photographing the Earth than an aircraft. One exposure from a space vehicle can cover an area that would need hundreds of photographs from an aircraft. The whole area can be shown with greater accuracy and detail. Also, a vertical space photograph does not have the distortion inherent in aerial mosaics of a wide area. Aerial photographs require lengthy and specialized processing to make them into a mosaic map, whereas this task is greatly reduced using space photographs. Any necessary revisions can be made more easily.

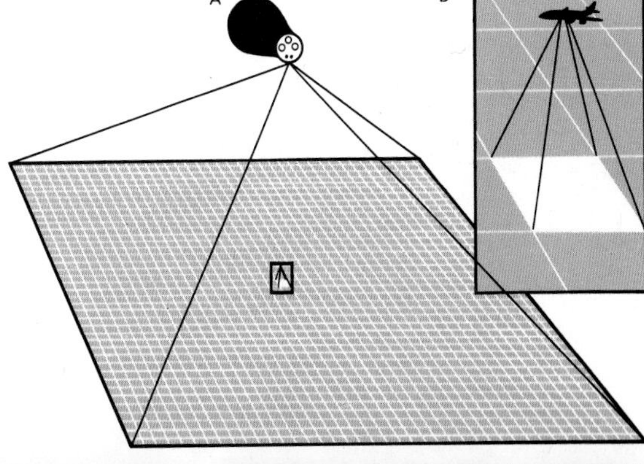
7
A
B

8
A

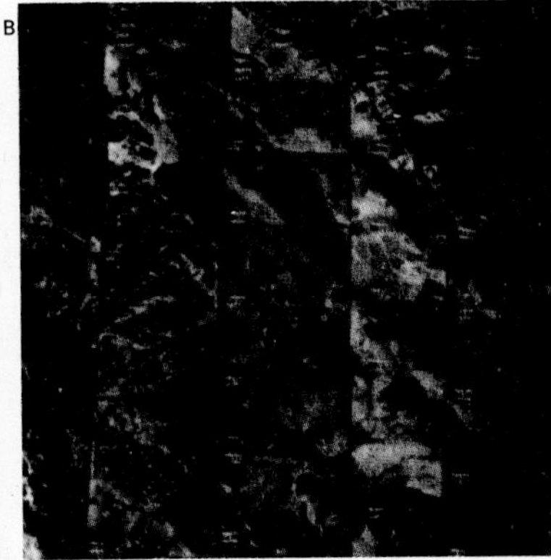
B

8 A comparison of aerial and space photography clearly shows the superior structural definition obtained from the latter. The Richat craters in Mauritania, West Africa [A], probably of volcanic origin, are well defined in the photograph from the orbiting Apollo 9 vehicle. A mosaic of aerial photographs of the same area is shown in [B]. The Apollo photograph clearly reveals previously unrecorded features including depressions up to a mile across.

Man in space

Yuri Gagarin (1934–68) of the Soviet air force was the first man in space. In April 1961—less than four years after the ascent of the first artificial satellite, Sputnik 1—he made a complete circuit of the Earth in Vostok I, above the bulk of the atmosphere, before landing safely in a prearranged area.

Gagarin and zero gravity

Gagarin's flight was a truly pioneering venture. Nobody at that time had any real idea of how the human body would react to a prolonged period of weightlessness. Yet during his flight Gagarin experienced conditions of zero gravity—something that can only be simulated briefly on Earth.

Zero gravity [1] does not mean that the orbiting astronaut has completely escaped the pull of the Earth's gravity. The best way to picture it is to think of a book placed on a piece of card: the book presses on the card and with reference to it the book is "heavy." If both are then dropped the pressure of book on card ceases; the two objects move in the same direction at the same rate during the fall.

The same situation occurs when an astronaut is inside his vehicle; the two move at the same rate so that the passenger does not press down upon his craft, and "weight" vanishes. (His mass—the quantity of matter in his body—does not change.)

Gagarin found that zero gravity was neither inconvenient nor unpleasant. This was confirmed by all later space travelers although "walking" in space [4, 5] is extremely exhausting. The first man to venture outside an orbiting vehicle was the Russian cosmonaut Aleksei Leonov, and this has since been repeated many times by both Americans and Soviets.

Americans in space

The first American in space was Alan B. Shepard, Jr., who made a sub-orbital flight lasting for about 15 minutes in May 1961. In the 1960s manned satellites (Mercury and Gemini programs) carrying two or three astronauts were sent up and there were docking operations in which two independent spacecraft were brought together and joined.

One initial difficulty facing international docking was that US and Soviet designs differed because their space programs had been developed independently. But following the success of the US Skylab, space station plans were made for a joint exercise and this was accomplished with the Apollo-Soyuz mission in 1975. Both vehicles had been suitably modified—the Soviet cosmonauts generally breathe ordinary air at normal pressure, for example, whereas the Americans prefer pure oxygen at reduced pressure. For the joint mission a special "adaptation chamber" was set up between the two control cabins.

During manned flight many experiments are carried out. The Earth can be closely studied and there have been vast improvements in man's knowledge of the circulation of the atmosphere, which should bring better weather forecasting; plant and mineral resources can be assessed; and nearly all other sciences can benefit.

Predicted space-flight dangers from meteoroids (solid particles moving in space), cosmic radiation, and weightless-

CONNECTIONS

See also
1722 Space vehicles
144 Stations in space
142 A history of space achievements

1 Free fall is the condition of weightlessness, or zero gravity. [A] shows an astronaut training in a flying aircraft. In [1] he is experiencing normal gravity; in [2] the plane is put into a curving dive that simulates the free-fall state for a very brief period; in [3] he takes to a pressure couch to counter the extra g force as the aircraft levels off. [B] shows how, in an orbiting capsule, gravitational pull (mg) is balanced by centrifugal force (mv^2/r) to produce zero gravity (m-mass; r-radius of orbit; v-velocity and g-acceleration caused by gravity).

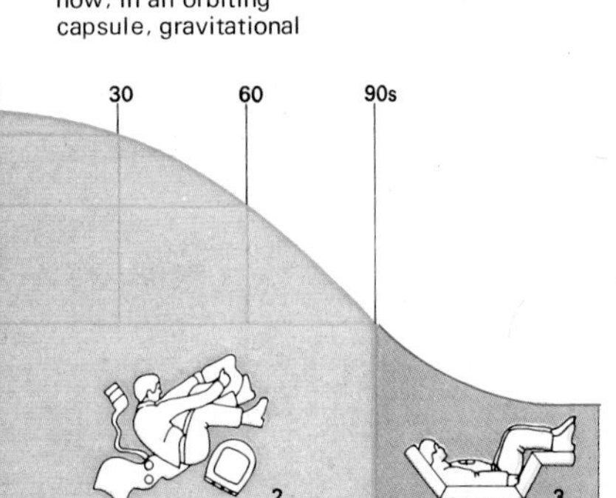

1
0
30
60
90s
30
60
90s
1
2
3

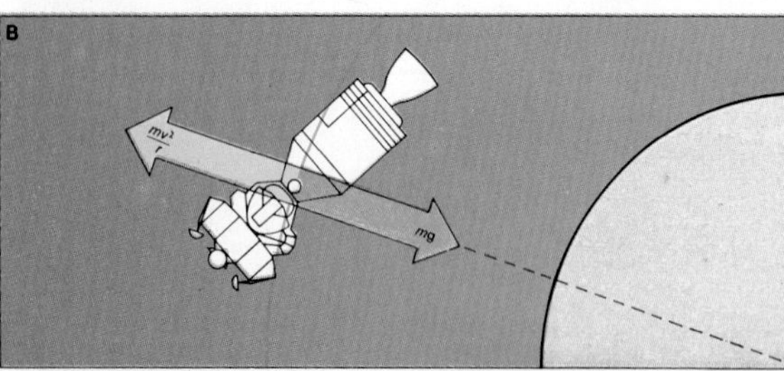

B
mv²/r
mg

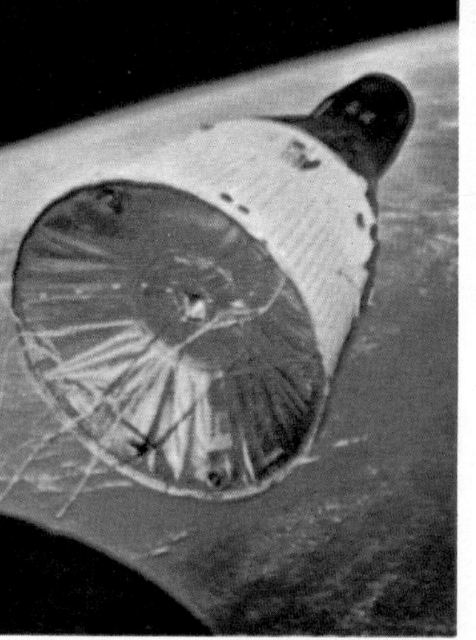

2 The Gemini program followed the first US manned program (Mercury). Gemini 7, shown here, was able to carry two men, could conduct docking procedures, and allowed for "spacewalking."

3 Apollo 15's command and service modules were photographed by lunar module pilot David Scott. At this time the probe was orbiting the Moon above the Sea of Fertility (Mare Fecundatis).

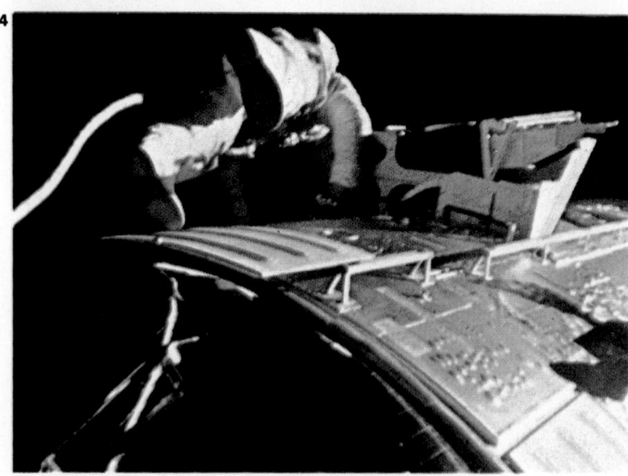

4 Astronaut Alfred M. Worden spacewalked outside Apollo 15 on the return trip; he recovered film equipment that had been used earlier. At the Moon he did not go to the surface with Jim Irwin and David Scott but remained in orbit in the Apollo command module.

5 Astronaut Edward H. White carried out the first US spacewalk in 1965 during the Gemini program. (The first spacewalk ever was made by the Russian Aleksei Leonov earlier in 1965.) Astronauts outside a craft do not drift away but remain in the same orbit. White was later killed in the fire at Cape Kennedy that destroyed a capsule under test.

ness have failed to materialize. On the other hand, mechanical mishap both on earth and in space is a danger and there have been tragic deaths of both Americans and Soviets. Manned flights to the Moon have so far been the preserve of Americans; the USSR has concentrated on automatic exploration.

The Apollo program [6–9], initiated in the early 1960s, reached its climax with the Apollo vehicles of 1968 and 1969. During the Christmas period of 1968 Frank Borman, James Lovell, and William Anders orbited the Moon in Apollo 8. In the following year the lunar module was tested close to the Moon's surface. Finally, in July 1969 Neil Armstrong and Edwin Aldrin landed on the waterless Sea of Tranquility. The gap between Earth and Moon had finally been bridged by man.

Inherent problems of Moon missions

The fuel problem is such that it is not yet possible to send a single-stage vehicle to the Moon and back. The initial launching is by step-vehicle; the command and service modules combined then travel to the neighborhood of the Moon and enter closed orbit. Next, two of the astronauts make the final descent in the lunar module, the only function of which is to shuttle its crew from the main spacecraft to the Moon's surface and back. Nevertheless, the procedure has its dangers. The explorers depend entirely on the ascent engine of their lunar module; if this fails there can be no chance of rescue for the men on the surface.

All the landings made so far have been successful. The only in-flight failure came when an explosion aboard Apollo 13 on the outward journey put the main propulsion unit out of action. The astronauts were forced to use the motors of the lunar module to pass around the Moon and return safely to Earth.

Apollos 11 and 12, and 14 to 17 made great progress in lunar study. ALSEPs (Apollo Lunar Surface Experimental Packages) were set up and are still operating. During the last three journeys the astronauts were able to drive across the surface in lunar rovers or Moon cars.

KEY

An astronaut's view of Earth taken by an Apollo crewman *en route* for the Moon shows both North Africa and Arabia. There is considerable cloud cover, but a great part of the Earth's surface was still visible to the astronauts.

6

6 Command and service modules of Apollo 16 orbited the Moon in 1972. Below lay the inhospitable lunar surface with several well-defined craters. The photograph was taken from the lunar module that carried astronauts Charles M. Duke and John W. Young to the Moon surface.

7

7 Lunar rover vehicles (LRVs) considerably extend the area of exploration for astronauts on the moon. Charles M. Duke is seen here with the LRV of Apollo 16, near the peak that was soon unofficially named Stone Mountain. In the background the bright rays are from South Ray Crater.

8

8 The first Moon landing was made from Apollo 11 in July 1969. Edwin E. Aldrin, Jr., stands on the lunar surface filmed by Neil A. Armstrong who was first to descend the ladder from the lunar module. The mission was shown on TV.

9

9 Hadley Delta, one of the peaks of the lunar Apennines, forms the background for David R. Scott and the Apollo 15 LRV. It is farther from Scott than it looks—the distance is more than 19mi (30km). On the Moon there is no atmospheric scattering, so distances can be deceptive and the sky is always black. The US flag does not flutter on its pole since the Moon has no wind—the fabric was wired to make it stand out.

10

10 The ascent motor of the lunar module worked perfectly when Apollo craft left the Moon—this is the view from Apollo 15. Yet this was one of the weakest links in the entire program. If for any reason the ascent engine failed there could be no hope of rescue; it is not likely that men will return to the Moon until rescue provision is made. The experimental packages (ALSEPs) left on the lunar surface are powered by solar cells.

Early weapons and defense

To provide themselves with food and protection, people have always needed weapons. Primitive people probably armed themselves with sticks and stones that they found lying around [1]. These hand-held weapons were adequate at close range but were obviously useless for beating off a large predatory beast or for bringing down an animal such as a fleet-footed antelope. With an increase in manual dexterity and intelligence, people began to adapt the materials at hand to make tools and weapons.

The first weapons

A curved stick, carved to the correct cross-section, can be thrown with great accuracy and will return if it misses its target. This weapon—the boomerang—is still used today by Australian Aborigines.

Stones with a groove carved around them and tied together by a length of leather or cord produce a bola, a throwing implement still used in South America. This weapon also has a long history and similarly shaped stones have been found in Stone Age sites in Europe. Such weapons are good enough for hunting game, but people needed better weapons and the techniques for using them in order to overcome other humans.

The spear [5, 6] has been used for thousands of years as both an offensive and a defensive weapon. Originally it was merely a straight stick with a fire-hardened point. With the gradual improvement of weapon making techniques it was successively tipped with stone, bone, bronze, and iron.

Once a spear had been thrown or an opponent had managed to get through the defense, a more convenient weapon was needed for hand-to-hand fighting. Zulu warriors solved this problem with a short-handled, long-bladed stabbing spear called an assegai. Long before, other peoples had arrived at a slightly different solution with the sword [9], although there is little evidence of when or where it originated.

At first, swords were made of bronze and subsequently of iron. The Greek armies needed special swords for cutting as well as short weapons for stabbing. The Romans [Key] fought with a short iron sword—the *gladius*. Wielded from behind a barrier of large shields the *gladius* enabled the Roman legions to rule most of the known world for about 400 years. The slow-moving phalanxes of Rome were eventually overcome by the lightly armed cavalry of the barbarian hordes. With the collapse of the Roman Empire the use of tightly packed foot soldiery almost disappeared.

From their bases in Scandinavia came the "sea-wolves" in their longships. Vikings dealt death and destruction with their long-bladed swords and battleaxes. Organized armies arose whose soldiers were armed not only with a long-sword and battleaxe but also with the bow, and their discipline inevitably beat the loosely organized Viking warriors.

Bows and arrows

The European bow [8] was a much heavier weapon than the light recurved bow of the eastern steppes (made of laminated horn and wood and small enough to be fired from horseback). The western bow was primarily a hunting weapon designed for use on the ground and from cover. Its ultimate form

CONNECTIONS

See also

1582 Early technology
1586 The Stone Age
1588 Fire and bronze
1592 The Iron Age
1728 Development of firearms
1732 History of artillery
1738 Fighting ships: the age of sail
1032 Early Oriental and Western science

1 Neanderthals lived in Europe some 80,000 to 35,000 years ago and represented Paleolithic (Old Stone Age) culture. The weapons of these people were stones, clubs, and spears. The spears were merely shafts sharpened to a point and hardened by fire. The technical development of weapons did not occur evenly throughout the world, but eventually the Neanderthal culture was supplanted by more sophisticated cultures using stone-tipped weapons—the Neolithic or New Stone Age peoples. The Australian Aborigines remained at the Paleolithic stage. Stone weapons were superseded by bronze and eventually iron.

2 The use of worked stone for arrow and spear heads increased the penetrating power of such weapons. This dates from the Old Stone Age (about 16,000 BC) and was found in Europe.

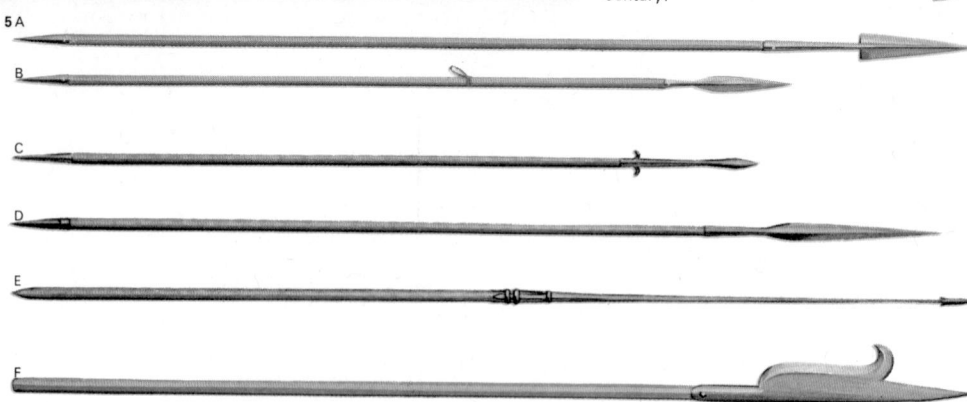

3 Early axes were quite small. Neolithic [B] and Bronze Age [C] axes measured about 3in (7cm) across the blade, compared with 11in (28cm) for the Viking ax [A] of the 7th century.

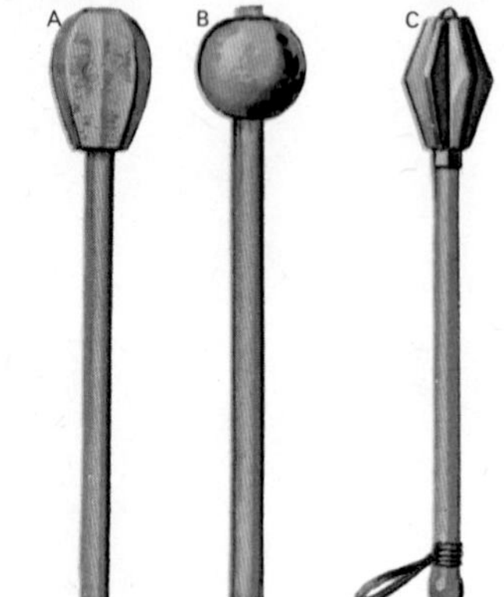

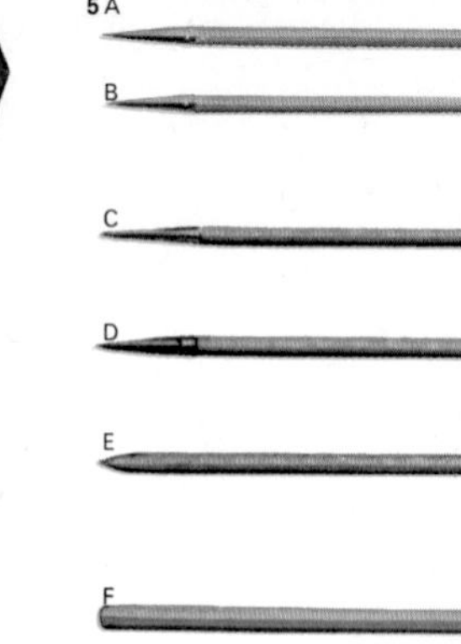

4 The war club or mace grew gradually more formidable. The 2,000-year-old iron mace [B] resembles a 4,000-year-old Egyptian wooden mace [A] but was less likely to break. The fluted head of a 14th-century mace [C] had more power.

5 The early spear [A] and javelin [B] used in 650-500 BC were little different from the Frankish-Gothic spears [C, D] and Roman javelin [E] of the 5th-7th centuries AD. The bill [F] was a medieval development of the spear.

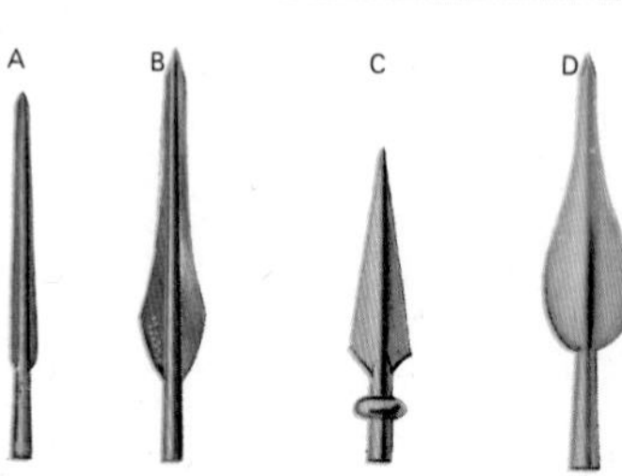

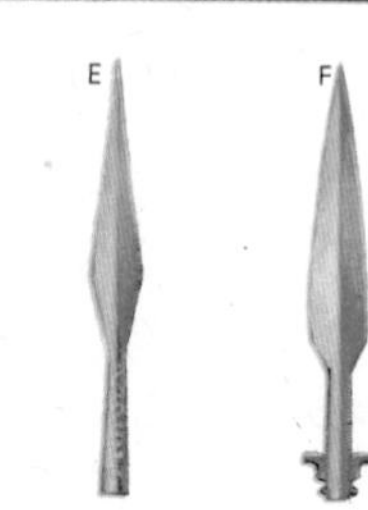

6 Spear heads changed little in their design, despite the different materials—stone, bronze, and iron—from which they were made. Bronze spear heads from Greece [A, B] made in about 700 BC resemble the later iron ones of the Celts [D], Vikings [E], and Saxons [F]. Broad-headed stabbing spears, such as the Macedonian example [C], often had a collar or flange to prevent the spear from being pushed right through the victim's body.

was the English longbow—5ft (1.4m) of yew with a horsehair bowstring capable of loosing an arrow 39 in (1m) long. The Norman troops of William the Conqueror, who in 1066 invaded England, carried bows and were also armed with a shield and sword and they wore long corselets of mail.

Later arms and armor

Mail became standard equipment, at least for those who could afford it, and gave some protection from arrows. But it did not prevent the wearer from being bruised by blows aimed at him. As armor developed, small plates were introduced into the mail at vulnerable points until eventually a knight was completely encased in steel. The mounts, which resembled great lumbering cart horses, also had their own armor.

On their mighty chargers the knights thundered into battle—although somewhat slowly with the weight they were carrying—equipped with a variety of death-dealing weapons. A 12ft (3.7m) lance of ash, tipped with iron, a shield, and a long-sword were standard equipment. Other weapons included a short dagger and often a mace and battle-axe.

Swords of this period were generally long, double-edged, and straight, with a reach of about 6ft (2m). They could be used with one or both hands. The age of chivalry came to an end with the success of the English longbow at the battles of Crécy (1346) and Agincourt (1415). The bow's rapid delivery, accuracy, and range defeated the knights and demoralized foot soldiers. Opposing the longbows were Genoese crossbows that could be operated by untrained troops and did not require the practice needed to use the longbow. Their arrows could also penetrate armor. But although useful, the crossbow had a short range and a low rate of fire.

Swords became narrow and light, with large guards to envelop and protect the hand. By the eighteenth century they had become very light and fairly short, often with decorated hilts. Horsemen favored curved swords, which were used until the present century. In modern times foot soldiers carry bayonets instead of swords.

KEY

A large shield and short-sword were standard equipment for the Roman legionary. The shield provided a defensive wall behind which the soldier was safe from almost all enemy weapons. In phalanx formation shields could be used to form a roof and walls known as the *testudo*, or tortoise. In this way soldiers could attack the walls and gates of fortifications virtually with impunity. A short-sword lacked the reach of a longer weapon and was probably used with a stabbing action. But it was also less cumbersome and less fatiguing to use than a long-sword. A helmet and breastplate helped to protect the body from blows that passed the shield.

7 The medieval knight [A] was a product of the arms race between more effective armor and improved arrows. More vulnerable than a man, the horse also had its own armor, but if the knight was unseated, as often happened, he found it hard to remount and use his weapons, and was at the mercy of any nearby foot soldier less heavily encumbered. The reintroduction of disciplined foot formations armed with pikes and bows spelled the eventual doom of heavily armored cavalry. The lance was the knight's primary weapon, but if this broke he still had a variety of other weapons [B] to use. Most knights carried a war sword [3] with a decorated scabbard and belt [4]. But other popular weapons included a mace [2] and a battle-axe. The war hammer [1] was a direct development of the earlier battle-axe.

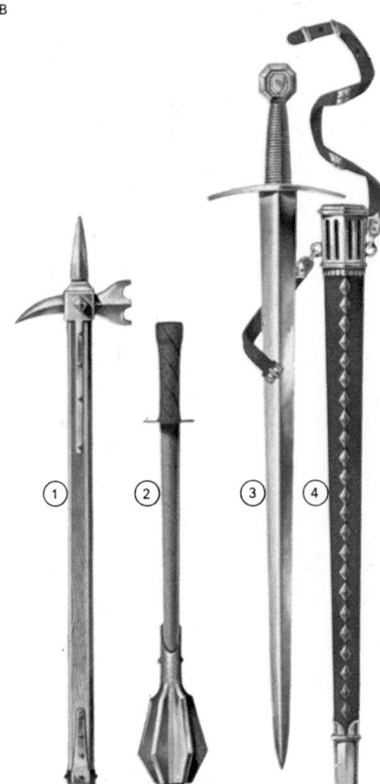
B
1
2
3
4

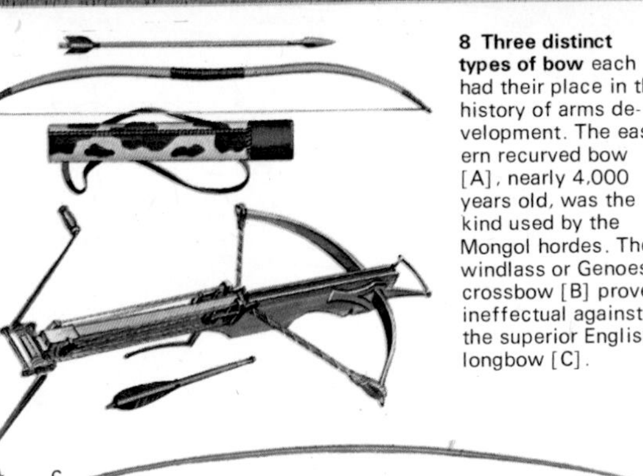
8 A
B
C

8 Three distinct types of bow each had their place in the history of arms development. The eastern recurved bow [A], nearly 4,000 years old, was the kind used by the Mongol hordes. The windlass or Genoese crossbow [B] proved ineffectual against the superior English longbow [C].

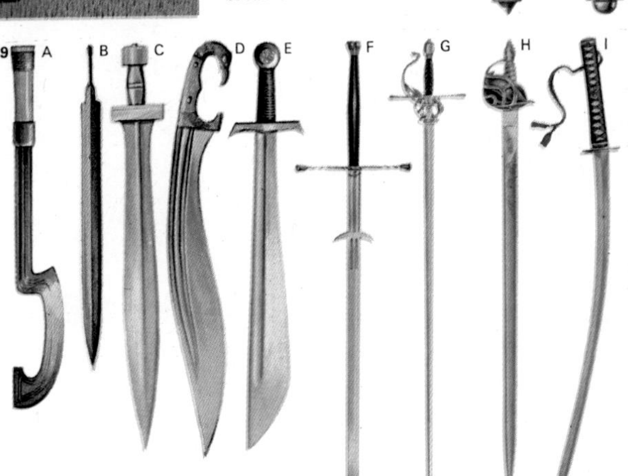
9 A
B
C
D
E
F
G
H
I

9 Primitive swords include the Egyptian sickle sword [A] of 2000 BC and a Swiss sword in bronze [B], 1,000 years later. The Greeks used a double-edged stabbing sword [C] and a single-edged cutting sword [D]. The single-edged falchion [E] dates from medieval times. The straight double-edged sword [F] was a cutting weapon. The later rapier [G] was used with only the point. The cavalry sword [H] and Samurai [I] were slashing swords.

Development of firearms

Firearms, whatever their age, are similar in principle. They consist of a tube or barrel along which a projectile is propelled by an explosion, a means of ignition, and a way of controlling the ignition. The development of firearms is marked by improvements to the firing mechanism or "lock," so called because firearm mechanisms or actions were originally made by locksmiths.

Development of ignition systems

The first firearm was the infantry hand cannon. It was merely a tube with a spike at one end on which it could be supported when fired. It was ignited by a glowing match thrust into a hole (called a vent) in the breech (the closed end of the barrel).

The first spring-powered mechanical ignition system was the matchlock [1] developed in the late fifteenth century. The arquebus was the earliest matchlock musket. Matchlocks remained in use for over two hundred years, establishing many of the accepted characteristics of the long-barreled gun. The first matchlock weapon to be fired from the shoulder was a sixteenth century arquebus, but the early weapons were massive, often needing a support for aiming [2]. Moreover, loading was slow and dangerous. Powder and a ball were rammed down the barrel from the muzzle, with a wad to hold them in place, then priming powder (fine gunpowder) was placed in the priming pan—all while the mechanism held the glowing slow-burning match. These difficulties made the weapon unsuitable for mounted men. Almost all matchlocks were smoothbore (with unrifled barrels), and breechloaders were rare.

The wheellock [3] was an enormous advance over the matchlock because it could be loaded and held ready for long periods for immediate use. It was invented in the early sixteenth century (many of the finest surviving examples are German [4]) but was complex, fragile, and expensive. Because rich men rode on horseback the wheellock, in carbine and pistol [5] form became the weapon of the horseman. Wheellocks were favored by German mercenaries (sixteenth century) and English cavalry (seventeenth century).

The chief need was for a weapon lighter and less cumbersome than the matchlock, yet cheaper and more reliable than the wheellock. Both the snaphance and flintlock relied on a flint for ignition. They differed in that the battery or steel (the piece of metal struck by the flint) and pan cover were one piece on a flintlock [8], two on a snaphance.

The flintlock soon replaced all other firearms. Muskets such as the Brown Bess and the Charleville, and later rifles such as the Ferguson breech-loader, Jaeger rifle, and the Kentucky rifle [7] contributed much to the development of firearms.

Many inventors had tried to increase firepower by using multi-barreled arms, superimposed charges, and other means, but none was really practical.

Percussion and the repeating firearm

The Reverend Alexander John Forsyth (1769–1843) began the percussion era in 1805 with his lock that used a highly sensitive explosive called fulminating powder as priming. Like other later devices the lock

CONNECTIONS

See also
1732 History of artillery
1730 Automatic weapons
1736 Armored fighting vehicles
1734 Modern artillery
1738 Fighting ships: the age of sail
1740 Modern fighting shi
1742 Early military aircra
1744 Modern military aircraft
1684 Submarines and submersibles

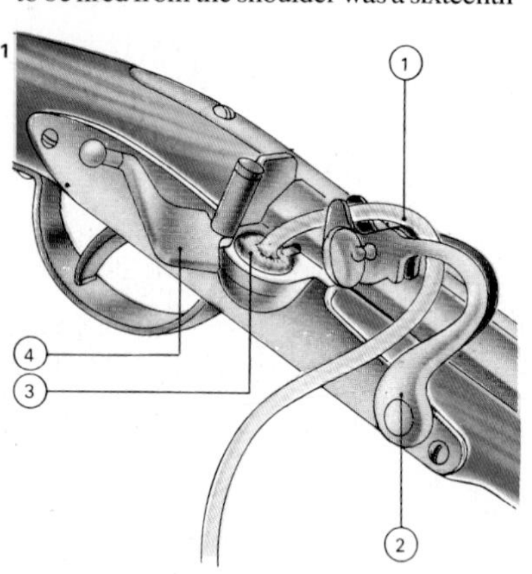

1 **The matchlock mechanism** was introduced in the late 15th century. A slow-burning match [1] was secured in a serpentine cock [2], which, when the trigger was pressed, brought the match down onto the powder in the pan [3]. A pan-cover [4] kept the powder dry and retained it in the pan when the arm was not in use. The lock shown here is typical of those used from the early seventeenth century and became common on infantry firearms. The mechanism was too cumbersome for a pistol, but it was used on the petronel, a carbine with a short, curved butt, intended for use by horsemen.

2

Matchlock musket (England, 1630)

Muzzle support

2 **Matchlocks** of this type were in use in Europe as the common infantry firearm throughout the seventeenth century. Musketeers, protected from the enemy by pikemen, performed the intricate, lengthy drill of loading and firing the massive weapons. Weighing as much as 25lb (11kg), these muskets required a forked support to enable soldiers to aim and fire them accurately.

3 **The wheellock** is shown here externally [A] and internally [B]. Most had to be pre-wound with a key. To ignite the charge the dog [1] holding iron pyrites [2] was lowered into contact with the serrated edge of a steel wheel [3] projecting through the bottom of the pan [4]. Pressure on the trigger released the wheel, causing a shower of sparks that ignited the priming, which fired the charge.

3 A

B

4

Wheel-lock carbine (Germany, *c.* 1540)

4 **Made in southern Germany** about 1540, this carbine probably belonged to a rich man. At that time wheellocks were extremely expensive and usually beautifully decorated. Repairs were also costly.

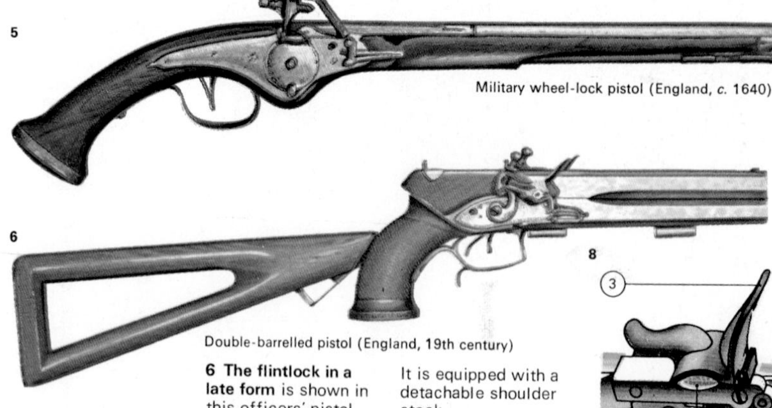

5
Military wheel-lock pistol (England, c. 1640)
6
Double-barrelled pistol (England, 19th century)

5 **This military pistol** of the mid-17th century is similar to the weapons used by the Cromwellian cavalry and other European armies. A trooper with two such pistols had great fire power.

6 **The flintlock in a late form** is shown in this officers' pistol. It is equipped with a detachable shoulder stock.

7

Kentucky rifle (USA, *c.* 1812)

7 **The Kentucky rifle** was a notably accurate flintlock firearm. Believed to have evolved from the Jaeger rifle introduced to America by German colonists, it was developed in Pennsylvania. The hinged box cut into the butt carried patches to wrap around the bullet before it was rammed down the muzzle.

8

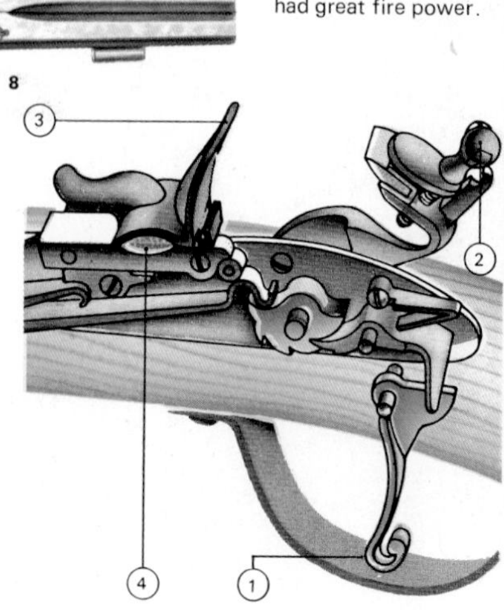

8 **The flintlock was** developed in the early seventeenth century. Pulling the trigger [1] released the cock [2] that held a flint. This struck against the battery or steel [3] forcing it back to expose the flashpan [4], and creating a shower of sparks that fell into the priming.

used the explosive properties of fulminates when struck by a hammer blow as the means of ignition. Of the various percussion ignition systems that followed, the caplock [9], was the most successful.

At first the general design of weapons did not alter, and many flintlocks were converted to cap ignition. Then in 1835–36 Samuel Colt (1814–62) patented his revolving pistol and the repeating firearm had arrived. Even so, Colt's business was not an unqualified success and in 1842 his first venture failed from lack of orders. Then, in 1847, Colt was asked by Captain Walker of the US Dragoons to produce a new weapon of 0.44in caliber for military use. This large, six-shot saddle-holster pistol was the "Walker" Colt.

The Walker Colt was followed by other dragoon pistols, the 0.31in caliber pocket models, the 0.36in Navy [11] and Police models, the 0.44in Army, as well as revolving shotguns, muskets, and rifles. Muzzle-loading revolvers can, if badly loaded, occasionally "chainfire," when more than one chamber discharges in succession. Revolving longarms were hazardous because, as they were held in both hands, a right-handed shooter could shoot off his left hand.

All percussion Colts were "single-action" pistols—that is, the shooter had first to cock the hammer with his thumb. Most were open-frame revolvers and lacked the solid-frame pistols' rigidity [12].

Cartridges and the modern firearm

Cartridges had been used for centuries, but *without* combining the bullet, the charge, and primer. The first successful combined cartridge was made in 1812 and later perfected by the German gunsmith Johann Dreyse (1787–1867) for use with his needle-fire rifle in 1837. In America Daniel Wesson (1825–1906) developed an improved rimfire cartridge in 1856 and a similar cartridge was used in the Henry rifle [13B]. In rimfire the primer is sealed in the rim of the cartridge case. Centerfire cartridges (with a central primer) followed, and were used in the 1873 Colt [14] and Winchester. Centerfire is still used for most modern firearms.

KEY

A

B

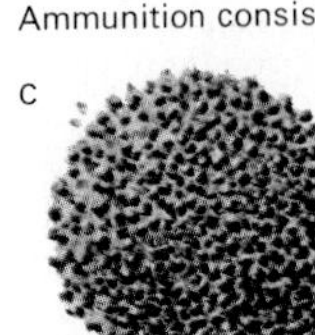

C

D

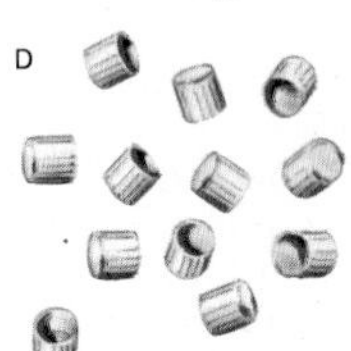

E

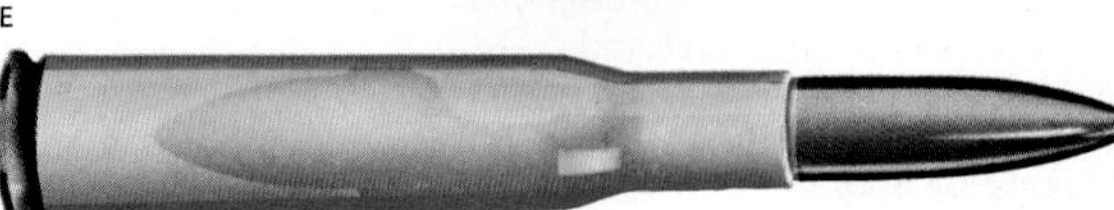

The flight of a bullet is stabilized by spin, caused by spiral grooves (rifling) in the sides of the barrel. Here eight grooves are shown [A]. The distance between opposing grooves is about the diameter of the bullet. The raised "lands" cut into the sides of the bullet, causing it to rotate. Ammunition consists of bullet, charge, and primer, today combined in a metal or plastic case [E]. Earlier firearms used separate bullet [B], powder [C], and percussion cap [D]. The cap consists of a small charge of sensitive explosive sealed in a cap of metal foil. Struck by the gun's firing pin or hammer, it ignites the main charge.

9 Hammer Cap Nipple Charge Vent

9 Percussion-cap priming introduced a new reliability to firearms. It was probably invented by Joshua Shaw in the United States in about 1815. The hammer struck the cap on the nipple, the flash traveling through the vent (a fire hole drilled through the nipple) and firing the main charge. Other methods of percussion ignition included devices using loose fulminate powders and fulminates in pills and tapes, but the cap was the most advanced external ignition system. It made possible the future work on repeating firearms, cartridge weapons, and, finally, machine guns.

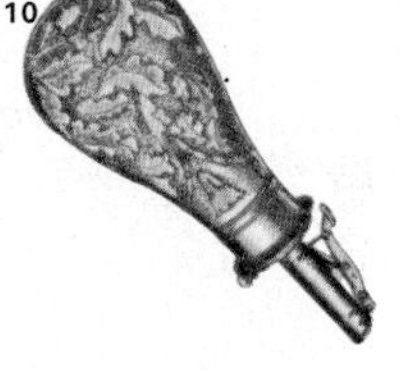

10

10 Powder flasks were used until the introduction of cartridge weapons. A pistol flask such as this was designed to measure the charge as well as pour it; such flasks were safe to use.

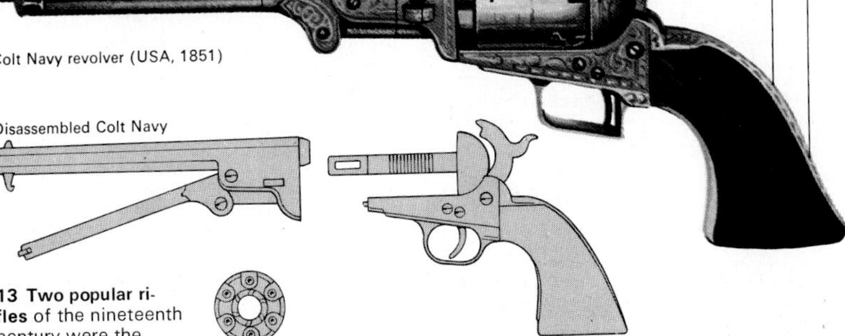

Loading lever
Rammer
Cylinder
Nipple
Hammer
Backstrap
Wedge
Recoil shield
Butt
11

Colt Navy revolver (USA, 1851)

Disassembled Colt Navy

11 The Colt Navy was not the first of Colt's revolvers, but is probably the most famous percussion revolving pistol. In general appearance it is similar to the larger Dragoon and small Pocket models. The Navy was a "belt" pistol, as distinct from the saddle-holster and pocket pistols, and was open framed, having no strap over the top of the frame. It had a six-chambered cylinder and was of 0.36in caliber. Each chamber was normally loaded from the muzzle with powder and ball (or conical bullet) rammed home and the nipples primed with percussion caps in readiness for firing.

12

12 An early double-action revolver was this Beaumont Adams, developed in England in 1886 from the Adams self-cocking revolver. Trigger pressure cocked and fired it, or alternatively it could be cocked with the thumb.

Beaumont-Adams revolver (England, 1856)

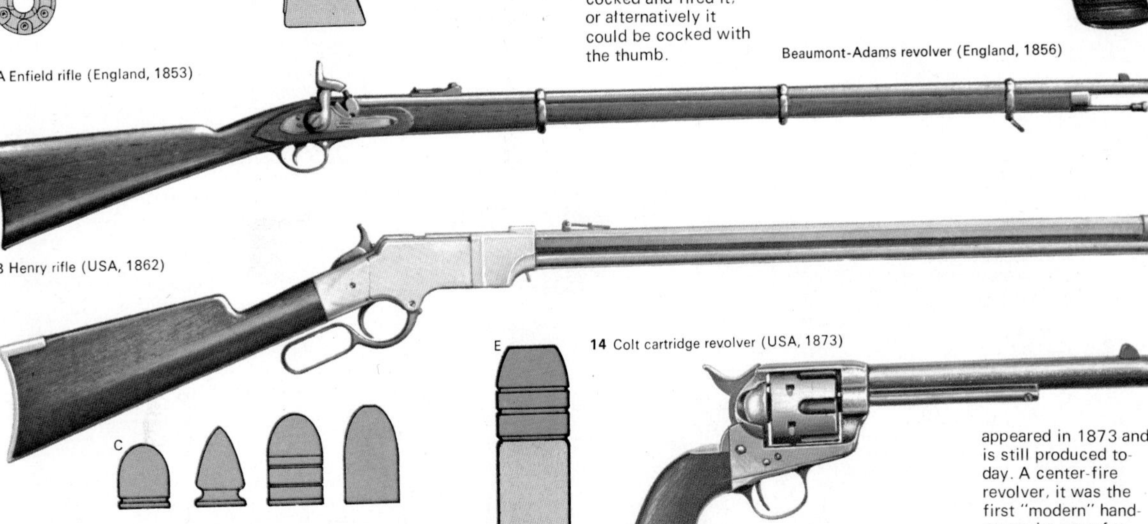

13A Enfield rifle (England, 1853)
B Henry rifle (USA, 1862)
C
D
E
14 Colt cartridge revolver (USA, 1873)

13 Two popular rifles of the nineteenth century were the 0.577in caliber Enfield rifle [A] and the 0.44in Henry [B]. The Enfield was made in England from 1853; it was a single shot muzzle-loader using a paper cartridge [D] that had to be torn open on loading to expose the powder. It was primed with a percussion cap. Several types of bullet for muzzle-loaders are shown in [C]. The US-made Henry carbine, developed by Tyler Henry, was produced from 1862–66. It was an early magazine cartridge rifle and the forerunner of the Winchester. It had a tubular magazine holding fifteen rimfire cartridges [E], with a sixteenth in the chamber.

14 The most famous revolver is the Colt "45," which first appeared in 1873 and is still produced today. A center-fire revolver, it was the first "modern" handgun to be manufactured in quantity for both civil and military use.

Automatic weapons

An automatic weapon is a gun, rifle, or pistol that fires continuously without any external aid such as hand cranking (or even electric power) for as long as the trigger is pressed. Early designs were hand cranked in one way or another, but they laid the framework for the first true automatic weapons.

Early American designs

The best known early mechanical weapon was the Gatling gun [1], developed by the American inventor Richard Gatling (1818–1903) and first demonstrated in 1863. This used six barrels rotated by a hand crank; for 50 years the design was sold and copied throughout the world using a wide variety of calibers (barrel sizes). Later, true automatic weapons used electric motors or gas pressure taken from the barrel. In the blowback action, part of the explosive force propelling the bullet ejects the spent cartridge and re-cocks the firing mechanism. In a gas-operated weapon hot gases, led from the barrel, force back a piston that works the ejection and re-cocking mechanisms.

Another American design was the Lowell gun, produced in 1875. This was also a hand-cranked weapon, but one that overcame the heating problem affecting all machine guns after 300 or 400 rounds (bullets) have been fired, when the barrel becomes too hot for further use. It had four barrels, one of which was used at a time. When this became too hot a new barrel was rotated into position.

The next development came from another American, Hiram Maxim (1840–1916). He designed an automatic weapon [2] in London, by first modifying a Winchester rifle. He used a hook fixed to the barrel to lock the bolt in place for firing. The recoil drove both hook and bolt back until the hook was lifted by passing under a bridge. The bolt continued back, driving around a crank to extract and reload the cartridge, and was then forced back by a spring. Ammunition was fed into the gun by means of a belt, which could be joined to successive belts to provide long continuous firing.

Satisfied with the success of this design, Maxim simplified it and set up a company to produce the gun with Vickers, the shipbuilding firm. Demonstrations in Europe impressed everybody who saw the gun in action. Vickers eventually took over the company and developed an improved version of the Maxim, which became the standard machine gun for many years.

As designs proliferated, three main mechanisms came into use: blowback, recoil (as in the Maxim), and gas operation. With the recoil method, the breech is locked to the barrel and they move back as one to start the cycle of extraction, ejection, cocking, chambering, locking, and firing.

World War II

By the start of World War II machine guns were grouped into three main types: the light machine gun such as the Bren [5], which can quickly be set up and fired; the medium machine gun such as the Vickers, capable of sustained fire but of necessity heavier and more robust; and the heavy machine gun used against aircraft and similar targets. The differences between the types are, however, more tactical than

CONNECTIONS

See also
1728 Development of firearms
1736 Armored fighting ve hicles
1732 History of artillery
1734 Modern artillery
1740 Modern fighting ships
1744 Modern military aircraft
1306 World War I
1338 World War II

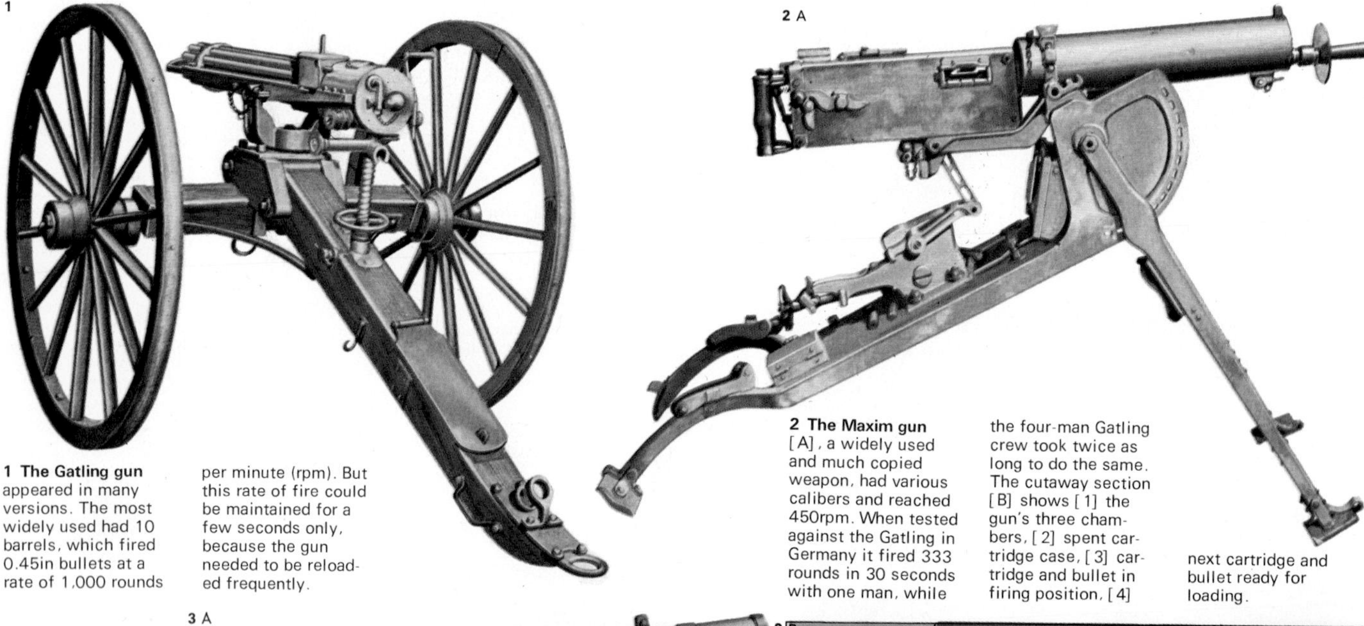
1
2 A
3 A
2 B
2
3
4
1

1 The Gatling gun appeared in many versions. The most widely used had 10 barrels, which fired 0.45in bullets at a rate of 1,000 rounds per minute (rpm). But this rate of fire could be maintained for a few seconds only, because the gun needed to be reloaded frequently.

2 The Maxim gun [A], a widely used and much copied weapon, had various calibers and reached 450rpm. When tested against the Gatling in Germany it fired 333 rounds in 30 seconds with one man, while the four-man Gatling crew took twice as long to do the same. The cutaway section [B] shows [1] the gun's three chambers, [2] spent cartridge case, [3] cartridge and bullet in firing position, [4] next cartridge and bullet ready for loading.

B

3 The Lewis gun [A] was the most successful light machine gun of World War I; more than 100,000 were produced for the Allied armies. Unloaded it weighed 26lb (11.8kg); it was 50.5in (12.8cm) long and held a 47- or 97-round pan magazine firing 550 rounds per minute. It could be made more quickly and cheaply than any similar gun, could be carried and operated by one man, and used the same .303in ammunition as infantry rifles. Isaac Newton (1858–1931), a US Army colonel, had developed the gun in 1911, but it was first used by the Belgians in 1914 and soon after by the British. It was also widely used on aircraft, being first installed on pusher biplanes. When used in single-seat tractor aircraft the Lewis was mounted on a quadrant on the top wing [B] so that the pilot could pull it down to change the drum. Although aerial gun-aiming was imprecise the Lewis, relatively inaccurate, directed an effective "spray" of bullets at the enemy.

technical. The light or submachine gun was not popular until it proved its worth in the war in the shape of the many excellent German weapons such as the Erma (designed by Schmeisser), numerous cheap and simple Russian weapons, and the Sten and Thompson [4].

The Americans relied on massed firepower from the Garand or M1 automatic rifle, described by Gen. George Patton (1885–1945) as "the best battle implement ever designed." This was a gas-operated rifle of great simplicity and reliability. It was augmented later by a shorter carbine for use by troops who found a full-size rifle a hindrance. This was the concept behind the Belgian FN automatic rifle [6] after the war.

Automatic pistols and later developments

"Automatic pistols" (strictly speaking, semi-automatic weapons) started to come into their own at the turn of the century [Key]. One of the best known—the 9mm Luger—went into service in 1908. It was officially replaced by the Walther P38 in 1938, but remained in general use, although, being a particularly well-made gun, it was dependent on the quality of the ammunition. The advantage of the automatic over the revolver was its more rapid rate of fire and larger magazine. But it was more likely than the simpler revolver to jam in dirty conditions. This is one of the crucial points in the designs of all weapons, particularly automatics.

With the coming of fighter planes, then bombers that needed to defend themselves, the machine gun took to the air. The Lewis gun, Spandau, and Hotchkiss were used in World War I fighters, with eight 12.7mm (0.5in) guns being mounted in fighters in the later stages of World War II, and up to 13 in the Flying Fortress bomber. Brownings were the Allies' most popular.

With the coming of fast fighters the target was often in range for only a split second and was generally heavier and stronger. Cannon (with explosive bullets) began to replace machine guns long before the war ended, but the ultimate weapon for this purpose came with the development of the rotating-barrel Vulcan [7].

KEY

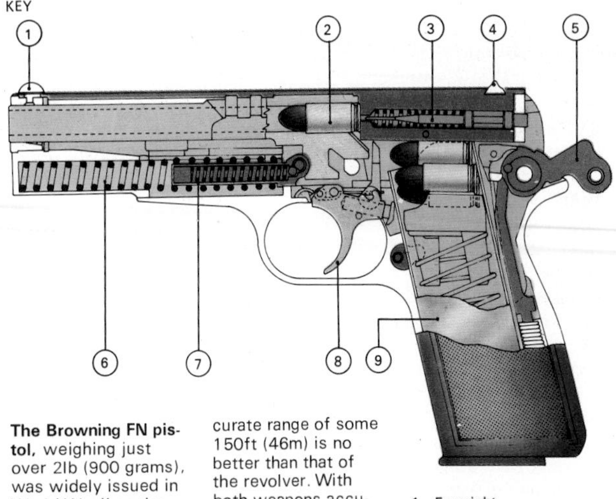
1
2
3
4
5
6
7
8
9

The Browning FN pistol, weighing just over 2lb (900 grams), was widely issued in World War II as the standard British automatic pistol. It carried 13 9mm rounds in a magazine in the butt, an advantage over the usual 6-shot revolver. But its accurate range of some 150ft (46m) is no better than that of the revolver. With both weapons accuracy depends principally on the man behind the gun. Strictly speaking, this and similar firearms are semi-automatic weapons.

1 Foresight
2 9mm cartridge in breech
3 Firing pin
4 Rear sight
5 Hammer
6 Return spring
7 Return spring guide
8 Trigger
9 Magazine

A

B

C

4 Submachine guns proved their worth in World War II. The Thompson [A], built by Colt, was a good weapon but expensive. It was replaced by the Sten [B]. More than 2 million of these were produced. The German Erma MP 40 [C], like the Sten, was made largely from stamped parts; only the barrel and breech were precision made. Many regarded it as the best machine gun of the war.

5 A

5 The Bren was highly regarded and is still in service today [A]. Built by the Enfield factory from a Czech design, the Bren was a good light machine gun and standard equipment in the British and some other allied armies. The mechanism [B] is gas operated. Gas from the barrel [1] drives back the piston [2] and the breech block, which ejects the empty case and then, as it is driven forward again by the return spring [6] picks up new round. The hammer [4] then hits the end of the firing pin [5] and fires the round. The volume of gas in the chamber [7] is controlled by a gas regulator [8].

5 B

8 7 2 1 3 5 4 6

6

6 The Belgian FN was adopted as the standard NATO rifle in the 1950s. It can be used as a single-shot weapon or as an automatic and fires the standard 7.62mm round. The operation of the gun is simplified because the left hand works the cocking, feed and safety while the right hand is free to hold and fire the gun. Like the Bren, the FN is gas operated, but its 20-round magazine is mounted underneath the gun. The gun is self-loading and fully waterproof and is one of the best infantry weapons in the world. It has a maximum rate of fire of 600rpm.

7

7 The GEC Vulcan was designed for use in fighters in its 20mm form. Later the 7.62mm MiniGun was developed for helicopter use in Vietnam against ground targets, where the 6,000rpm rate can have devastating results. The Vulcan is here mounted on a tracked chassis for anti-aircraft work with a power-operated traverse to track low-flying supersonic aircraft. Although wasteful of ammunition, it represents the optimum in current machine guns.

History of artillery

The term "artillery" strictly includes any weapon that projects a missile farther than a man can throw it by hand. But with large missiles, the mechanism used is too heavy to carry, and the definition of artillery is now generally limited to weapons of this type.

Early artillery "engines"

All artillery makes use of stored energy that can be released and expended quickly to propel the missile. Before the invention of gunpowder there were three ways of doing this: the compression and tension of fibers, as in a bow; the torsion (twisting) of sinew or fiber as in the catapult; and the use of a counterweight, as in the trebuchet.

Artillery using the bow principle was known in Syracuse by 399 BC, when a repeating bow firing bolts was developed by Dionysus of Alexandria. Similar weapons were still being used by the Chinese in the 1890s. By about 350 BC similar engines were made using bands of sinew, hair, or fiber into which the bow arms were inserted. Both types fired arrows or bolts and could be modified to fire stones.

A development of the bow, known to the Romans as the ballista, used a single arm inserted into a band of fiber that was tightened by a winch [2]. It could be used to throw a variety of missiles, including stones, Greek fire (a mixture of pitch, sulfur, and naphtha), live or dead prisoners, and filth. A ballista had a range of about 1,640ft (500m) and fired a missile weighing up to 330lb (150kg). The only siege engine to be invented in the Middle Ages was the trebuchet [4], which used a heavy counterweight that imparted velocity to the missile.

Development of firearms

Gunpowder became known in the West about the end of the thirteenth century. Guns first appeared in Europe in the first quarter of the fourteenth century and there seems to have been an industry making and exporting guns in Ghent at that time. Reports of their use include the Siege of Metz (1324), the Battle of Halidan Hill (Scotland) in 1333, and the Battle of Crécy (1346). The first guns fired arrows [5] and later ones shot stones or balls of iron.

Early light guns were breechloaders, each with a separate barrel or chamber, mounted on a wooden frame or sledge. These guns were individual pieces with little standardization. Some, such as Mons Meg [Key], were huge and became legends. Mons Meg was 13ft (4m) long, its caliber 19.5in (49.5cm) and its weight 5 tons. It fired 330lb (150kg) granite balls. A weapon known as the Dardanelles gun, of cast bronze beautifully made in two pieces that screwed together, is at the Tower of London. Its length is 16ft (5m), its caliber 25in (63.5cm), its weight 17 tons, and the weight of the stone shot 670lb (304kg). Tzar Pouchka, in Moscow, cast in 1586 was 18ft (5.4m) long, its caliber 36in (91.4cm), its weight 38 tons, and the weight of the stone ball 2,200lb (998kg). The weight of powder used to fire this monster was 220–300lb (90–136kg).

The barrels of the first true guns were made from a bundle of wrought iron rods arranged in a cylinder and welded together. Molten lead was generally poured into the grooves and the whole barrel wrapped in

CONNECTIONS

See also
1734 Modern artillery
1728 Development of firearms
1730 Automatic weapons
1736 Armored fighting vehicles
1738 Fighting ships: the age of sail
1084 The Crusades

1 The bow introduced into weaponry the principle of storing energy for sudden release. It was used in warfare by the ancient Greeks. Bows and arrows continued to be used in warfare even after the invention of gunpowder because they were cheap, effective, and accurate. The crossbow, developed in the Middle Ages, took less skill to fire accurately but reloading was time consuming.

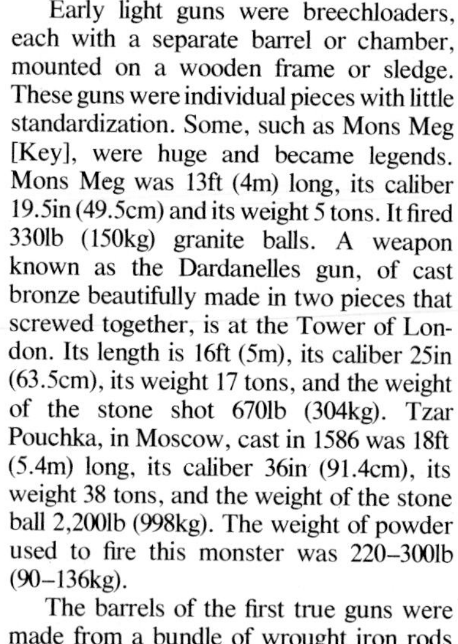

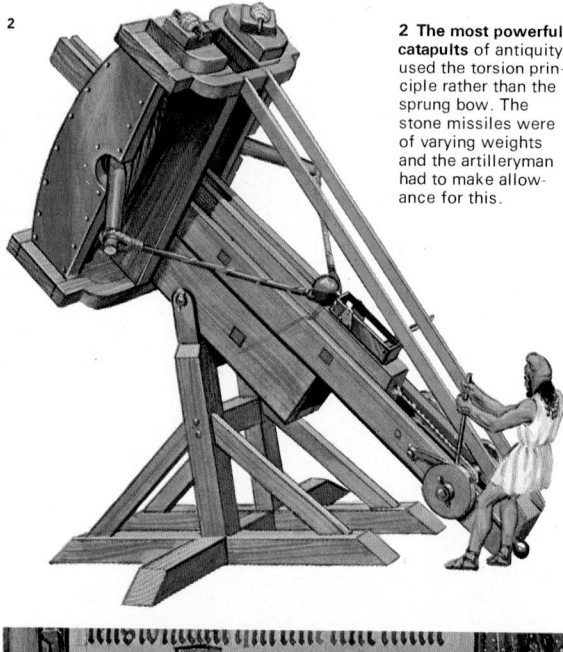

2 The most powerful catapults of antiquity used the torsion principle rather than the sprung bow. The stone missiles were of varying weights and the artilleryman had to make allowance for this.

3 This Graeco-Roman ballista of the first century AD used the principle of the bow. The long wooden arm was pulled down (like half a bow) and suddenly released to hurl the missile.

4 The trebuchet, a medieval siege weapon, was designed to hurl stones and similar missiles for great distances. Also called a mangonel, it worked with a heavy stone counterweight that fell to provide the necessary power.

5 The pot-de-fer, the earliest type of gun used in the West, was first employed in the 14th century. It fired a bolt or heavy arrow. Similar Chinese guns probably fired arrows from bamboo tubes.

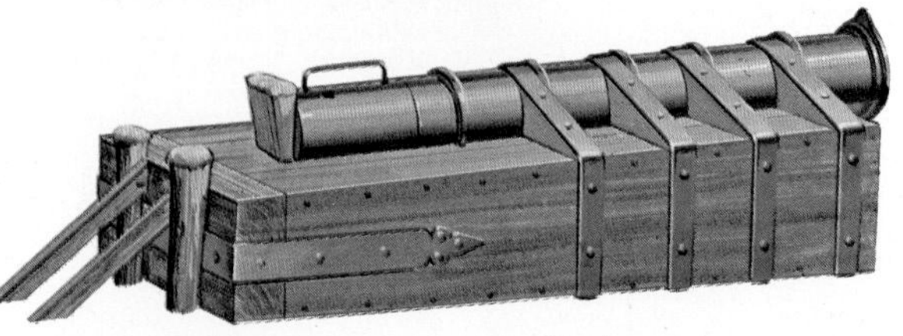

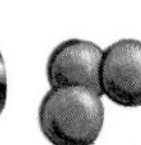

6 This breech-loading cannon of the late 14th century is from Castle Rising, Norfolk, England. The illustration shows a spare breech and balls. The problem of recoil was a major one at this time.

iron hoops. The trunnion, a short stub-axle fitted to the barrel to enable the muzzle to be raised or lowered, was not invented until the mid-fifteenth century. Artillerymen filled cases with small stones or scrap metal, or loaded them loose in the barrel.

Tactics developed slowly. Initially artillery was used to batter down walls or to fire from walls at an approaching army. Turkish siege guns were largely responsible for the fall of Constantinople in 1453. Between 1537 and 1551 the Italian mathematician Niccol Tartaglia (*c.* 1500–77) put forward the first theory about trajectories. He showed that a flying shot follows a curved path—previously gunners had thought that it went straight and then fell vertically.

In 1626 Gustavus Adolphus of Sweden (1594–1642) tried to devise light field pieces to support his troops. He had his armaments industry make copper barrels bound with iron rings and covered with leather. But these barrels rapidly overheated and therefore could not quickly be reloaded. He also organized his artillery into three roles: field, regimental, and siege. This became a fairly standard form of division until 1776 when the French Inspector of Artillery, Jean-Baptiste de Gribeauval (1715–89), grouped them into field, siege, and coastal defence. By that time guns were carried on light horse-drawn carriages.

Artillery at sea

Heavy naval guns were usually employed in unison ("broadsides") at close quarters, although longer range light guns could be used for harassment. Ships were rarely destroyed by ship-based guns but heavy damage could be inflicted. Pebbles or almost any pieces of iron could be used on land or sea as anti-personnel missiles; grapeshot consisted of bags of round-lead shot. Chain-shot, two hemispheres of iron keyed together and joined by a chain, was particularly effective against masts and rigging. Shore artillery could be far heavier and more accurate. Iron shot was sometimes heated before firing in order to start fires on ships. After loading the main powder charge, the gunners added a small damp charge followed by a red-hot cannon ball.

KEY

Mons Meg, a welded wrought-iron cannon made in about 1460, can still be seen at Edinburgh Castle in Scotland.

7 A

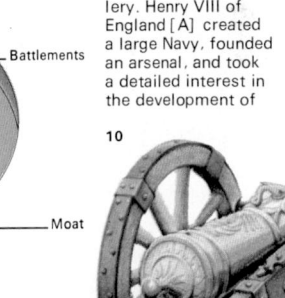

HENRICVS VIII REX
ANGLIE

B

Drawbridge
Outer bastion
Battlements
Living quarters
Moat
Basement stores

7 Commanders played a crucial part in developing the technology of artillery. Henry VIII of England [A] created a large Navy, founded an arsenal, and took a detailed interest in the development of fortifications [B]. He introduced some of his own ideas in fortifications along the Scottish frontier and in Boulogne against the French, and encouraged the science of military engineering.

10

10 A field piece of this type was used by all armies during the War of Spanish Succession (1701–14). It had a chased and elaborately decorated gun barrel of brass or iron [1] and its gun carriage was reinforced with iron binding [2].

9

8

8 This muzzle-loading Parrott rifle – a 10 pounder with a 3in bore – was used by both sides in the American Civil War (1861–65).

9 Used in sieges with devastating effect, this 13in mortar was deployed by Union forces during the American Civil War.

11 This British 18-pounder field gun [B] with its ammunition wagon [A] saw service during the Crimean War (1854–56). Much of the allied artillery, however, was of a lighter caliber. Many of the field pieces in use were 9-pounders and some were as much as 40 years old.

11A

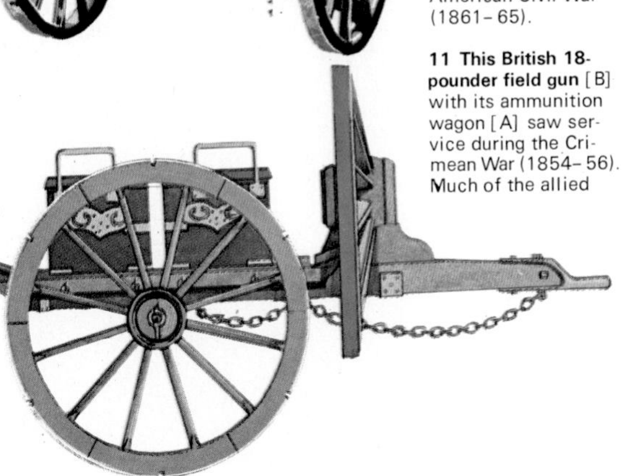

B

12

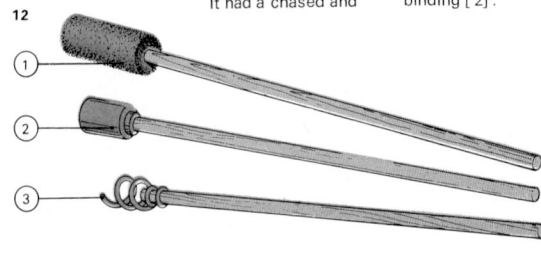

12 Gun tools for breech-loading cannon included a damp sponge [1] – used to get rid of glowing residues in the bore –, a rammer [2], which drove the projectile into position, and a worm [3] for removing any obstruction.

Modern artillery

CONNECTIONS

See also
1732 History of artillery
1730 Automatic weapons
1736 Armored fighting vehicles
1740 Modern fighting ship
1802 Radar and sonar
1306 World War I
1338 World War II

There was little change in heavy guns for the 500 years from the time of their introduction in the 1300s to the early 1800s. Their barrels were cast in bronze or iron and they were loaded from the muzzle using black powder (gunpowder). Then the nineteenth century advances in metallurgy and chemistry were applied to artillery.

In 1855 William Armstrong (1810–1900) of England designed a three-pounder gun with a barrel made of wrought iron wrapped around an inner tube. The barrel was rifled to give spin and therefore greater accuracy to the shell, which was loaded from the breech. Many such guns were made in various calibers [1], but the design was not completely successful. Better was the sliding breech-block, designed by Krupp of Germany, and the interrupted screw system.

In 1888 black powder was replaced by a new propellant explosive—guncotton, or nitrocellulose. It burned more slowly, generating more hot gas and therefore more force. Gun sights were also improved.

In an explosive shell fired from a muzzle-loaded gun the fuse was ignited by the hot gases from the propellant, By 1880 steel projectiles were in general use. A soft metal collar on a steel shell, called a driving band, sealed it from the gases; thus another type of fuse had to be used. Some detonated when they hit a target and others used clockwork or timed powder trains.

A new explosive for the shell, based on picric acid, was introduced in 1886. The shrapnel shell—a case filled with small steel balls—was invented in 1784 and continued in use until 1916. Breech loading and the new explosives gave rise to "fixed ammunition" with a cap detonator, main propellant charge, and the projectile all in one metal case. For calibers of more than about 6in (15cm) separate charge and shell continued.

Developments to World War I

A French field gun of 1897 had a device to absorb much of the recoil. As the barrel was forced back by the explosion in it, the movement was arrested by compressing oil in a reservoir; air in a second reservoir was also compressed and its pressure forced the barrel forward again. A spade at the end of the gun carriage helped to keep it steady. This gun, the famous "75" (it had a 75mm caliber), was still in service in World War II. Its flat trajectory, however, limited its use against well-protected installations, which required high-trajectory howitzers.

Britain had a variety of guns: a 13-pounder (3in caliber, about 75mm), 4.7in and 6in guns, and 4.5in, 5in, 6in, and 9.2in howitzers. Germany used a 77mm field gun firing about 15lb (7kg) shell and howitzers of 42, 105, and 155mm calibers. Nearly all gun carriages were pulled by horses, although there were a few trials using trucks. Some large guns were mounted on railroad wagons. The most famous of these was the 8.3in (21cm) "Paris Gun" with a range of 82mi (132km), successful only for propaganda.

Developments in ammunition included poison gas shells (1915) and white phosphorus smoke shells (1916). The high explosive TNT replaced shrapnel. Trench warfare led to the development of the midget howitzer, or mortar. Mortar calibers increased from 3in (75mm) to 6in (150mm) and even 9.4in (230mm) and large mortars

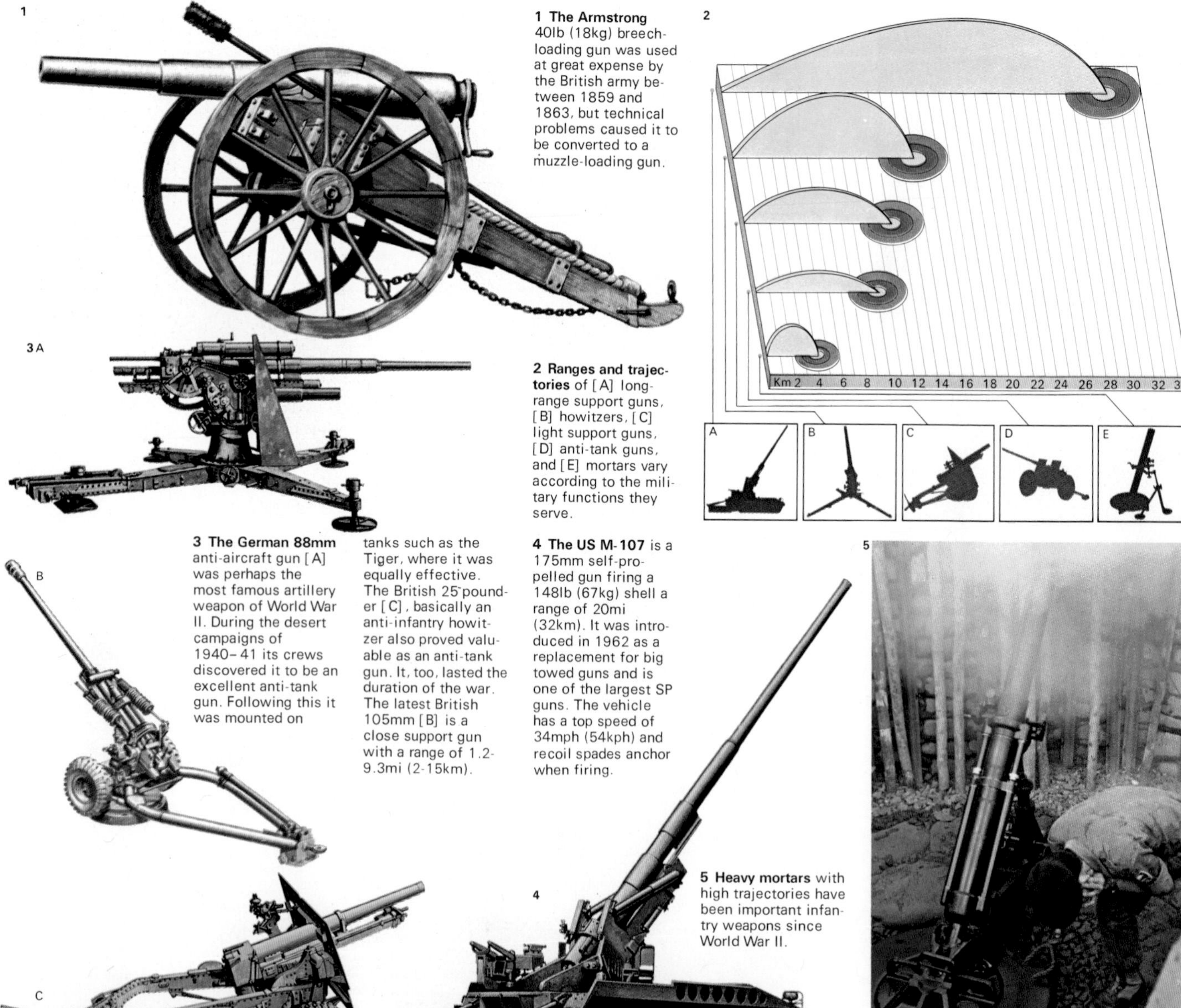
1
2
Km 2 4 6 8 10 12 14 16 18 20 22 24 26 28 30 32 34
A
B
C
D
E
3A
B
C
4
5

1 The Armstrong 40lb (18kg) breech-loading gun was used at great expense by the British army between 1859 and 1863, but technical problems caused it to be converted to a muzzle-loading gun.

2 Ranges and trajectories of [A] long-range support guns, [B] howitzers, [C] light support guns, [D] anti-tank guns, and [E] mortars vary according to the military functions they serve.

3 The German 88mm anti-aircraft gun [A] was perhaps the most famous artillery weapon of World War II. During the desert campaigns of 1940–41 its crews discovered it to be an excellent anti-tank gun. Following this it was mounted on tanks such as the Tiger, where it was equally effective. The British 25-pounder [C], basically an anti-infantry howitzer also proved valuable as an anti-tank gun. It, too, lasted the duration of the war. The latest British 105mm [B] is a close support gun with a range of 1.2-9.3mi (2-15km).

4 The US M-107 is a 175mm self-propelled gun firing a 148lb (67kg) shell a range of 20mi (32km). It was introduced in 1962 as a replacement for big towed guns and is one of the largest SP guns. The vehicle has a top speed of 34mph (54kph) and recoil spades anchor when firing.

5 Heavy mortars with high trajectories have been important infantry weapons since World War II.

evolved into artillery weapons with recoil systems and accurate sights [5].

Developments to World War II

Light close-support guns had been the only addition to artillery since 1918 when war broke out again in Europe in 1939 and trucks began to replace horses. The British used the 25-pounder gun-howitzer, with a range of 13,400yds (12,370m) [3]. The United States and Germany had 105mm howitzers firing 10lb (4.5kg) shells over a range of 6.3 to 7.5mi (10–12km).

Improvements in design allowed heavier shells to be fired over greater ranges—and calibers varied from 0.79in (20mm) to 31.5in (800mm). New fuses exploded shells at a pre-set height above the target. Mountings included wheels, half-tracks, and full caterpillar tracks. Special defensive guns were developed for anti-tank use and for antiaircraft [3].

Then new weapons appeared—rockets that had been tried and abandoned in the mid-1800s. Germans and Americans used Panzerfaust and bazooka anti-tank rockets. Britain and the United States developed a 3in anti-aircraft rocket and a 5in multiple assembly that could lay 1,000lb (455kg) of high explosive per second on a target for nearly a minute. The Soviet equivalent was a 130mm (5.1in) truck-mounted multiple rocket system called Katyusha.

After World War II

In the closing stages of the war Germany introduced two "vengeance weapons," the V1 flying bomb and the V2 rocket. The V1 was a small pilotless aircraft using a pulsejet engine with rocket-assisted takeoff. It was used to bomb London and nearby targets from launch sites in France and the Netherlands. TheV2 [6] was a supersonic liquid-fueled rocket carrying a warhead of nearly a ton of high explosive. It served as a model for later American and Soviet experiments with rockets—soon to be called missiles [9]. For speed of preparation and firing, modern missiles have solid-fuel propellants and, armed with nuclear warheads, they can be fired from underground silos or submarines.

KEY

Soviet missiles, on display in Moscow's Red Square, maintain a balance of power with US weapons.

6 The German V2 rocket was one of the most destructive and sophisticated weapons of World War II. Launched mainly from sites in the Netherlands (at the close of the war in Europe), these rockets killed 2,855 people in England. Built like finned shells, 46ft (14m) high and guided by automatic pilots, each carried nearly a ton of explosives 200mi (320km) at a speed of 3,621 mph (5,794kph).

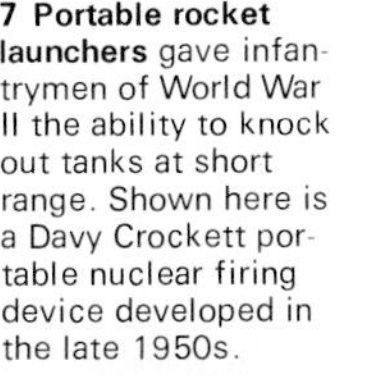

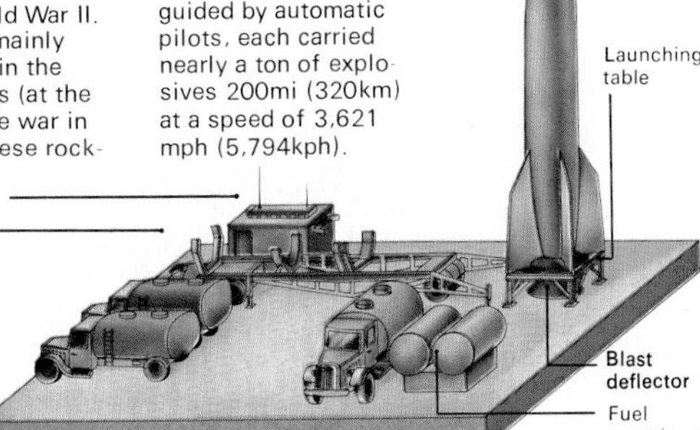
Control room
Trailer and uplift jack
Launching table
Blast deflector
Fuel containers
6

7 Portable rocket launchers gave infantrymen of World War II the ability to knock out tanks at short range. Shown here is a Davy Crockett portable nuclear firing device developed in the late 1950s.

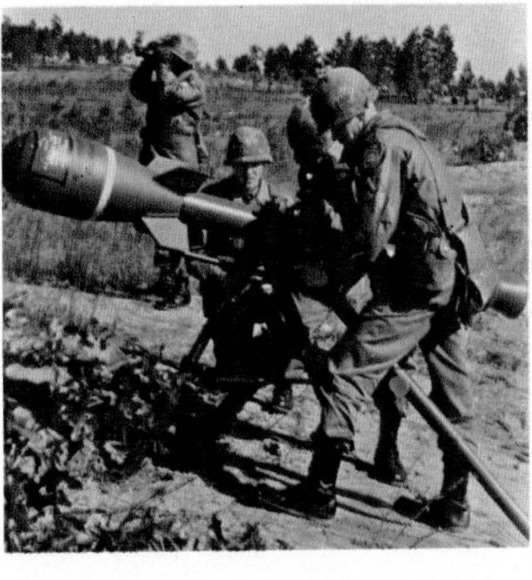

8 Minuteman was the first in a series of US intercontinental ballistic missiles. These three-stage solid-fueled rockets are often fired from below ground and carry nuclear warheads.

9 The command system of a surface-to-air guided missile sometimes has a long-range radar [1] system that detects the target and sends flight-path information to a control computer [2], which activates a tracking radar [3] to lock on the target. In tactical systems the tracking radar both detects and tracks the target. Once the target has been established as an enemy, the control computer launches a missile [4] and activates the missile radar [5]. Information from the target and missile radar is then fed back to the control computer which guides the missile through a command radio [6].

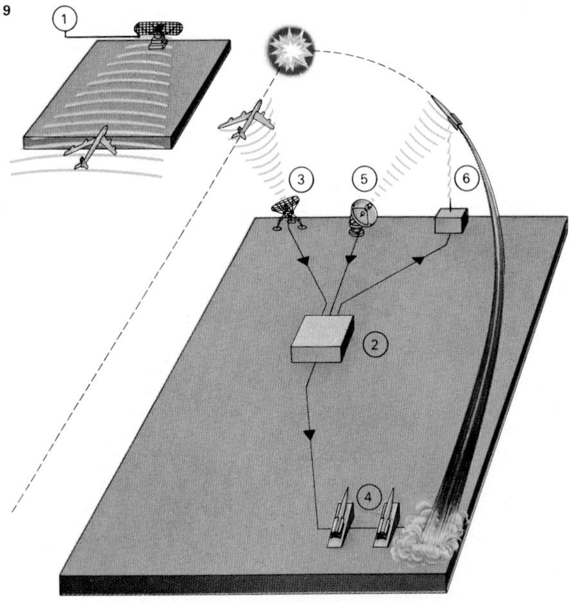
9
1
2
3
4
5
6

10 Rockets with considerable range and firepower, such as *Swingfire*, can be launched from the backs of tanks as well as from fixed sites. They can locate and destroy enemy vehicles before they get within gun range. Another means of achieving speed and mobility in placing rockets for attack or for defense is to launch guided rockets from high-speed naval patrol boats.

Armored fighting vehicles

Of the many types of armored fighting vehicles (AFVs), the tank is the most significant. The idea of such a vehicle can be traced back hundreds of years. But it was not until the internal combustion engine and caterpillar tracks were developed at the beginning of this century that it became practical to devise a war machine that could carry men and weapons protected by armor plate.

Britain took an initial lead in tank development, the early World War I machines being designed by the Admiralty as landships. Then an American, Walter Christie, designed a heavy tank with a more advanced suspension (the T3), which influenced the new Soviet tanks. By 1941 the USSR had T34s [3]—then the best tanks in the world and not matched until 1943.

Between the wars

Between 1939 and 1945 typical gun calibers grew from 37 to 75mm and armor thickness from 25 to 100mm (1 to 4in). Average tank weights rose from 15 to 40 tons. The heaviest tank ever to go into production was the limited traverse *Jagdtiger* of 1944, with a 128mm gun, 250mm (9.8in) armor, and a weight of 72 tons. Such tanks were too expensive, and their size and weight hindered mobility.

In recent years tank design has been aimed at flexibility in use, with the emphasis on relatively light machines and away from the giants of World War II. Advances in gunnery have improved the shooting on the move and at moving targets. Infrared gunsights permit night firing.

In the 1970s, conventional tanks weigh about 50 tons. They carry long-barreled guns of 105–120mm caliber, which can fire high-velocity armor-piercing shot against tanks, high-explosive shells against other targets, and also cannister shot (containing large scatter-gun pellets) against massed infantry. The main gun is generally mounted, together with a machine gun for use against infantry, in a turret that provides all-around traverse. The combination of hitting power, mobility, armor, and good radio communications allows tanks to make flexible, swift responses and give them the shock-action needed to break through enemy defenses.

Most tanks have four man crews. The commander, gunner, and loader/radio operator are in the turret, and the driver is down in front, in the hull. The engine is mounted behind the turret and at the back is the combined gearbox and steering unit. Tanks runs on tracks, with five or six large wheels on each side and large springs and shock absorbers to permit them to travel at high speed over rough ground. Modern tanks have steeply-sloped armor up to 120mm (4.7in) thick.

Among the most prominent tanks of the 1970s are the Soviet T62, a 47-ton tank with a 115mm smooth-bore gun firing spin-stabilized ammunition, and the German *Leopard 1*, a fast 43-ton tank with a 105mm gun. The British *Chieftain*, heavily armored and with a 120mm rifled gun, is one of the heaviest tanks currently in use. The US M60 A2 is a 52-ton tank armed with a main gun firing 152mm conventional ammunition or Shillelagh guided missiles. Tanks rarely operate effectively alone, needing mobile infantry, artillery, engineers, and aircraft for support.

CONNECTIONS

See also
1734 Modern artillery
1730 Automatic weapons
1810 Explosives and fireworks
1306 World War I
1338 World War II

1

2

3

4

1 The Daimler armored car first served in 1941 and was still used in the 1960s. It was a reliable reconnaissance vehicle. Despite four-wheel drive, it had only limited cross-country ability. Its 95hp engine could achieve 50mph (80kph) and had five forward and reverse gears. If the vehicle had to reverse along a road, the commander could steer it by a wheel mounted in the turret. It carried a crew of 3 and a 2-pounder gun.

2 PzKpfw III was Germany's main tank at the beginning of World War II and an important weapon in the *Blitzkrieg* attacks on Poland in 1939, France in 1940, and the USSR in 1941. Early models had a 37mm gun, but this later version had a 50mm gun. It was outclassed by the Soviet T34. A limited traverse version, *Sturmgeschutz III*, with the 75mm gun of the PzKpfw IV, gave excellent service until the very end of World War II.

3 The Soviet T34 with a 76mm gun and 45mm (1.8in) of sloped armor was, in 1941, the best tank in the world, and came as a shock to the Germans. Its 500hp diesel engine was a model of reliability with a speed of 32mph (51.5kph). The Germans were able to advance deep into the USSR despite the T34 because, initially, Soviet tactics, compared with those of the German armored forces, were poor.

4 The US M4 Sherman Tank was the main allied tank of World War II after 1942. It had a five-man crew, 3.1in (80mm) armor, and was equipped with a short 75mm gun. The later version shown here had a longer, 76mm gun.

KEY

Light armored fighting vehicles

Some AFVs, such as the Daimler armored car [1], lack the strong hull armor of main battle tanks and are protected only against shell splinters and machine-gun bullets. This keeps their weight down and enables them to travel at high speed.

Armored reconnaissance vehicles seek out the enemy, patrol open flanks, and act as an early warning screen against surprise attack. Some have wheels and some tracks. A tracked AFV has better cross-country performance, but is noisier and requires more maintenance than its wheeled alternative.

Armored personnel carriers (APCs), such as the US M-113 [7], take infantry into combat. Most have light guns to provide cover for their infantry or to engage other similar vehicles.

Armored self-propelled artillery guns, such as the Abbot [8], provide mobile fire support. Army engineers have armored bridge launch vehicles that carry a folding bridge span on a battle-tank hull. Armored bulldozers dig fire positions or clear debris

Armored recovery vehicles rescue tanks, clear routes, or assist tanks to cross water.

Many of the lighter vehicles are now made of aluminum. They float, or can easily be made to do so with a screen, and they can be carried by aircraft.

The future of tanks

Anti-tank guided missiles can be launched from the air, the ground, or from light vehicles. But control by the firer is difficult and automatic guidance is expensive. Unless they are mounted in an armored vehicle, they are vulnerable and too expensive to use against targets other than tanks. Thus as a weapons system they have not yet supplanted tanks, although they do complement them.

The advent of small, portable anti-tank missiles has not reduced the value of tanks. Just as an infantryman is vulnerable to every weapon, yet plays a vital role in a battle, so tanks have always been vulnerable to some weapons, especially mines, but like infantry and artillery they will probably remain an integral part of most armies.

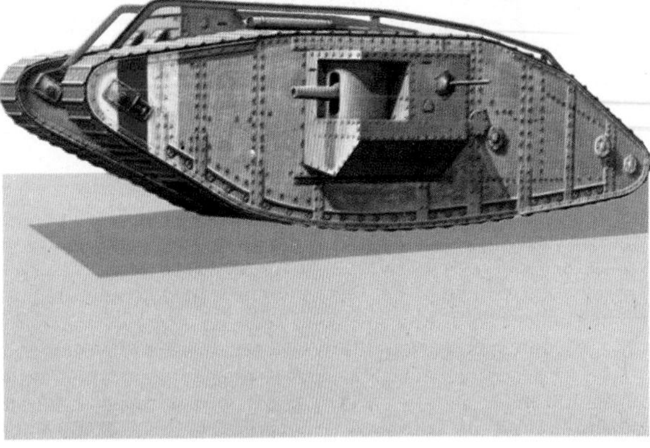

Allied Mark IV tank used in World War I. Its shape was largely dictated by the conflicting requirements of crossing wide trenches after being carried by narrow railroad wagons. Mark IV tanks had rails on top to support bundles of brushwood which were dropped ahead into deep ditches.

5

5 A minesweeping flail was one of the many special AFV devices developed in World War II, here seen mounted as the "Crab" on a Sherman tank. The flail consisted of chains on a rotating drum, which beat the ground in front of the tank and exploded any mines in its path. Now tanks push plows or rollers, or launch sausages of explosives by rockets over a minefield to clear their paths of mines.

6

6 The Swedish S tank is a novel concept with no turret. This allows a low profile and slight weight yet excellent armor. The gun is aimed by moving the whole tank on its suspension and steering. Although it has a crew of three, one man can operate the tank in an emergency. Ammunition is loaded automatically; the magazine is at the rear, limiting the fire risk if hit. The gun breach at the back of the chassis reduces the overhang of the barrel, allowing traverse in confined spaces. But the engine must be running to traverse, and the tank cannot fire while it is moving.

7

7 Armored personnel carriers (APCs) are a valued component of modern armored forces. The M-113 used by US troops is extremely mobile—able to move rapidly over rough terrain, to "swim" across deep water, and small enough to be transported by air. An APC can carry about a squad of soldiers and has machine guns for weaponry. APCs can serve as scouts for armored and infantry units and were used in the Vietnam War.

8

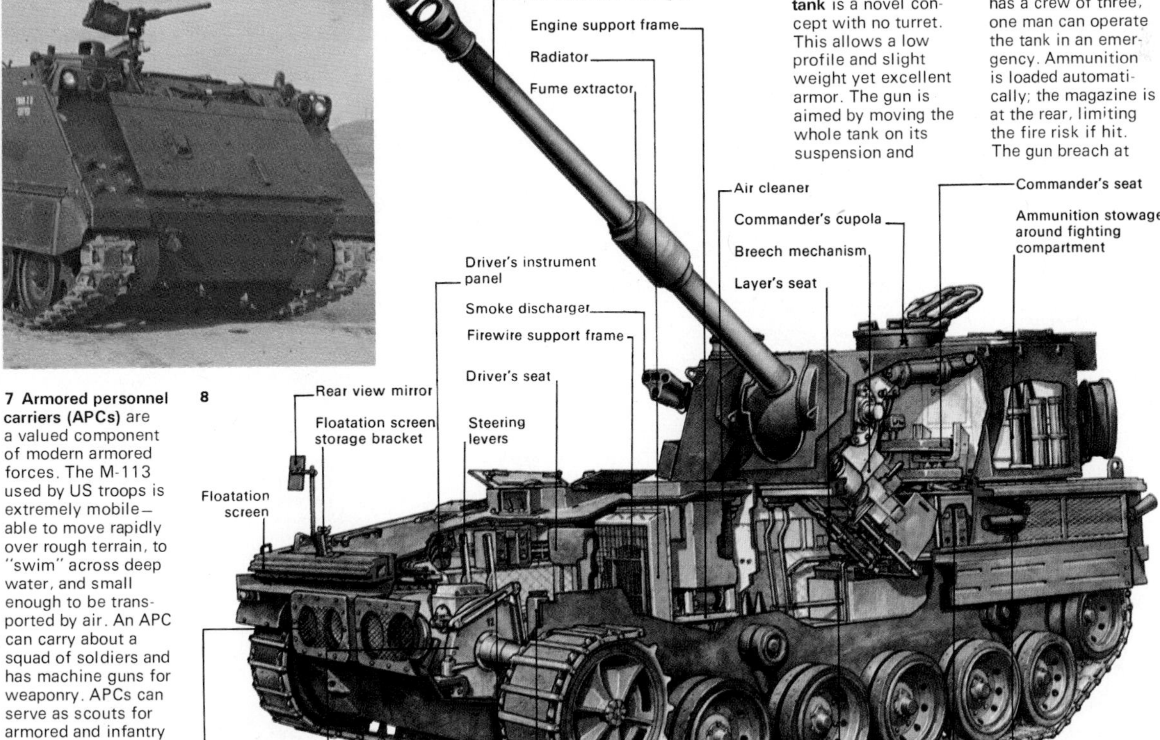
QF 105mm L13A1 gun
Engine support frame
Radiator
Fume extractor
Air cleaner
Commander's cupola
Breech mechanism
Layer's seat
Commander's seat
Ammunition stowage around fighting compartment
Driver's instrument panel
Smoke discharger
Firewire support frame
Driver's seat
Rear view mirror
Floatation screen storage bracket
Steering levers
Floatation screen
Final drive steering unit
Brake operating levers
Headlights (1 pair infra-red)
Steering unit oil tank
Turret batteries
Machine gun ammunition
Exhaust

8 The British Abbot is a self-propelled artillery gun able to keep pace with tank formations. Armor protects it against counter-battery fire and against attacks from enemy who infiltrate the forward battle areas. While some self-propelled guns are little more than heavily armored turretless tanks, most are specialized to support tank advances with scattered artillery fire against distant targets. The Abbot uses the same automotive components as the tracked APC, FV432, and can "Swim" using an extended screen while being propelled and steered by its tracks.

Fighting ships: the age of sail

Nations dependent on sea trade have always needed fighting ships to protect their sea lanes. Peaceful maritime commerce has usually been the result of an acknowledged naval supremacy on the part of one nation or another. By building up sufficient naval strength, interlopers have been able to achieve dramatic reversals of commercial power, as when the Arabs supplanted the Byzantines in the fifteenth century or when the Spanish were pushed aside by the Dutch and English in the sixteenth and seventeenth centuries. Some nations used ships for attacking other countries, as when the Vikings in their longships terrorized eastern Britain in the ninth century. And great territorial conflicts have often led to the build-up of great fighting fleets.

Galley warfare

An early reference to naval warfare in Egyptian temple reliefs of the second millennium BC shows a battle between the Egyptians and the "Sea People," with the former using oared sailing boats and the latter pure sailing boats. The Sea People lost, perhaps because of the superiority of the primitive Egyptian galley.

The ancient Greeks, Phoenicians, and Romans had galleys with up to three (and perhaps more) staggered layers or banks of oars [1]. These boats carried an auxiliary square sail on a single mast. Bows, arrows, and catapults were not decisive weapons and an engagement usually had to be decided by boarding the enemy. Because of the sweeps (oars) this could be done only by head-on attack and the ram was a useful means of holding or capsizing an adversary.

Galleys survived until the early nineteenth century in some areas with remarkably little alteration, the major changes being the replacement of staggered sweeps by a single bank of longer sweeps powered by more men, and the replacement of the inefficient single square sail by triangular lateen sails on one or more masts [2].

The demise of the galley followed the development in northern waters (unsuitable for galleys) of maneuverable sailing men-of-war that could fire devastating broadsides. The galleys could carry at most only five guns placed in the bows and were no match for the men-of-war after the sixteenth century. The last great galley battle was fought off Greece at Lepanto in 1571, when Europeans defeated the Turks.

During the Middle Ages, there was no difference between the design of merchant and fighting ships; the former could be converted readily into the latter if soldiers were carried instead of cargo and wooden battlements were nailed on the bows and stern (the origin of the forecastle and quarterdeck). In fact, the distinction between the type of vessel used for trade, war, and piracy was hazy even up to the nineteenth century.

Importance of artillery

Light anti-personnel artillery was fitted on the rails of vessels during the fourteenth century, and the great ships of the early Tudor period had gun ports pierced in the hull. Larger ships of this period were built primarily for naval purposes but would often engage in trade. The same was true of the Elizabethan galleon, and in the Anglo-

CONNECTIONS

See also
1732 History of artillery
1740 Modern fighting shi
1018 From the civil wars
Caesar's empire

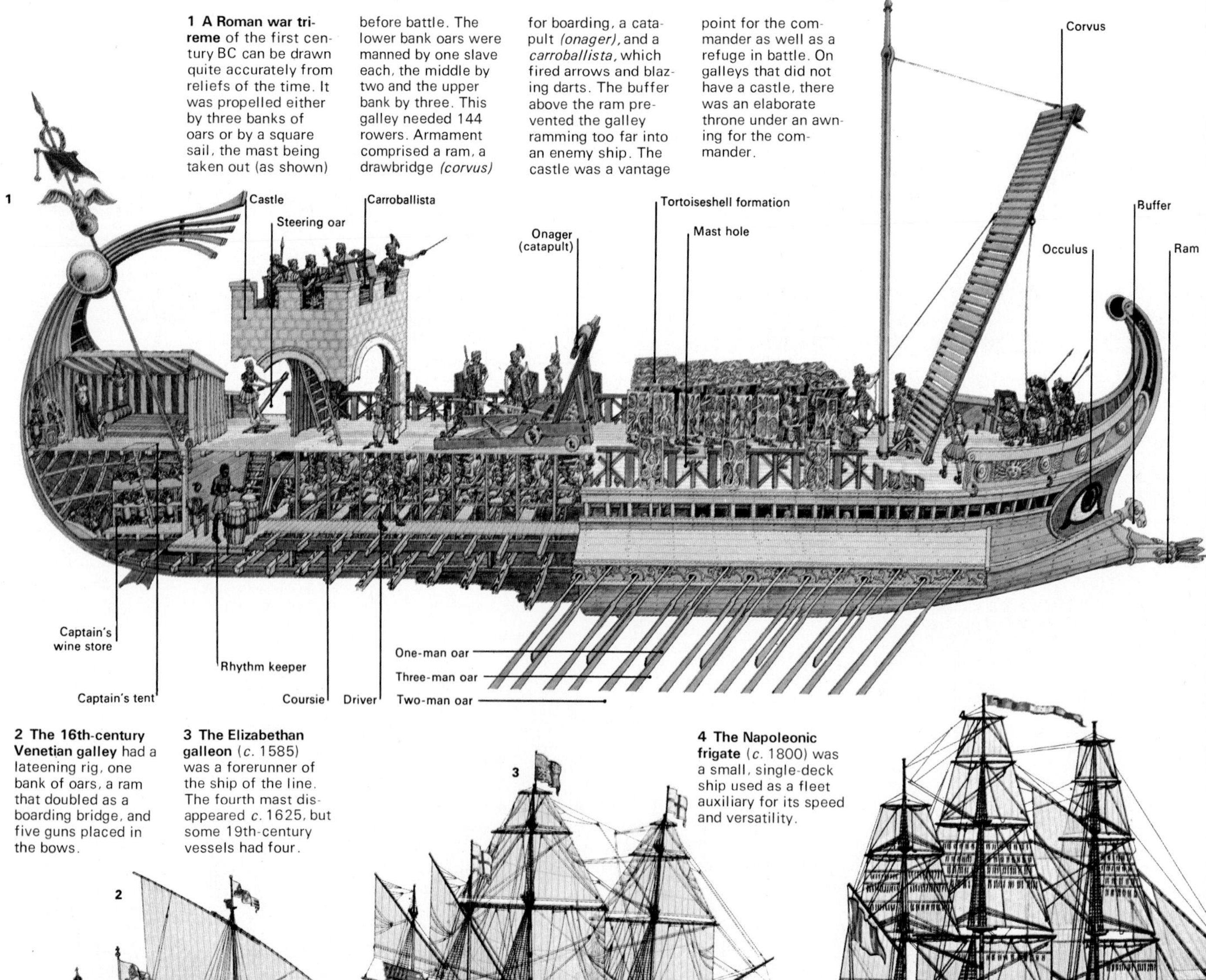

1
Castle
Steering oar
Carroballista
Onager
(catapult)
Tortoiseshell formation
Mast hole
Corvus
Occulus
Buffer
Ram
Captain's wine store
Rhythm keeper
Captain's tent
Coursie
Driver
One-man oar
Three-man oar
Two-man oar
2
3

1 A Roman war trireme of the first century BC can be drawn quite accurately from reliefs of the time. It was propelled either by three banks of oars or by a square sail, the mast being taken out (as shown) before battle. The lower bank oars were manned by one slave each, the middle by two and the upper bank by three. This galley needed 144 rowers. Armament comprised a ram, a drawbridge *(corvus)* for boarding, a catapult *(onager)*, and a *carroballista*, which fired arrows and blazing darts. The buffer above the ram prevented the galley ramming too far into an enemy ship. The castle was a vantage point for the commander as well as a refuge in battle. On galleys that did not have a castle, there was an elaborate throne under an awning for the commander.

2 The 16th-century Venetian galley had a lateening rig, one bank of oars, a ram that doubled as a boarding bridge, and five guns placed in the bows.

3 The Elizabethan galleon (*c.* 1585) was a forerunner of the ship of the line. The fourth mast disappeared *c.* 1625, but some 19th-century vessels had four.

4 The Napoleonic frigate (*c.* 1800) was a small, single-deck ship used as a fleet auxiliary for its speed and versatility.

Dutch wars of the seventeenth century the Dutch fleets were essentially composed of the large two-decker trading vessels (known as "East Indiamen") of the Dutch East India Company. By that time, however, the fleet on the English side was purely naval and included some ships with three gun decks running the whole length of the ship. The upper decks such as forecastle and quarter-deck often carried guns as well.

Up to the time of the Anglo-Dutch wars, naval tactics remained fairly similar to those used by the galley; ships formed a line abreast and "charged" the enemy. But the increasing importance of artillery and its broadside placement led to the line-of-battle tactic [5] in which ships forming the line presented a formidable wall of guns. Only three- and two-decker ships were included in such lines and were known as "ships of the line." Two opposing lines would sail parallel to one another, firing broadsides in an attempt to create confusion in the enemy line so that it could be divided.

Crossing an enemy's bow or stern not only ensured safety from his fire (which could be aimed only sideways) but also provided the opportunity to rake him. The bow and stern were the weak spots of a ship and shot plowing through the whole length of a gun deck was particularly lethal. The side that achieved the windward line had the advantage of being able to disengage more easily in case of trouble. In addition, an enemy could be holed below the waterline.

Close-range fighting

Attack at close quarters remained an important tactic and in the Napoleonic wars the British fleets made effective use of a large-bore, short-range gun called the carronade [10]. The British traditionally aimed at smashing the enemy's hull, while the French, firing on the uproll, concentrated on rigging and upperworks.

Beginning with small, paddle-wheel warships, navies experimented with steam engines early in the nineteenth century. Engines were fitted in ships of the line in the 1850s and in the next decade the appearance of the rifled shell gun rendered the "wooden walls" obsolete and ushered in the ironclad.

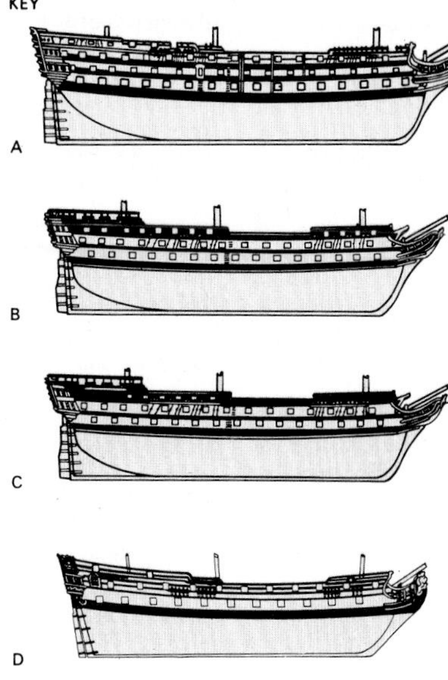

KEY
A
B
C
D

Men-of-war were classed into rates from the 1650s until the end of the era of sailing navies. Rates were based on numbers of guns carried (excluding the carronades) and were altered several times during the era of the line-of-battle ship. In Nelson's day first-raters [A] had 100 or more guns on three decks, second-raters [B] had 90 to 98 guns on three decks, third-raters [C] had 64,74, or 84 guns on two or three decks, and fourth-raters [D] had 50 on a single deck. Only the first three rates were classed as ships of the line. Fourth- and fifth-raters (32-44 guns) were frigates. Sixth-raters (20–28 guns) were sloops and brigs or war.

5

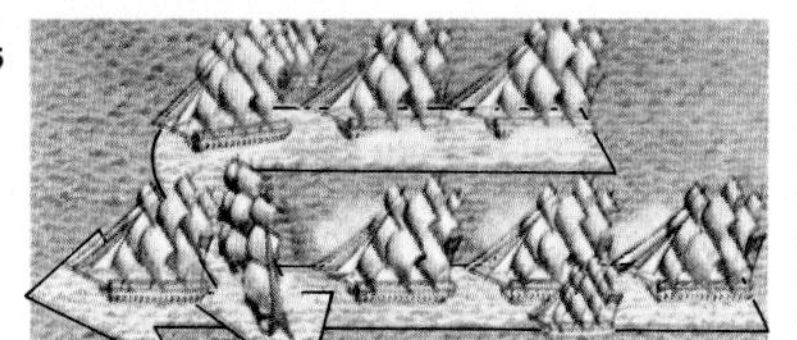

5 Naval fleet tactics of the 17th to 19th centuries were based on a line of battle with two- and three-decker ships forming a line ahead and frigates stationed outside to relay flag signals.

7

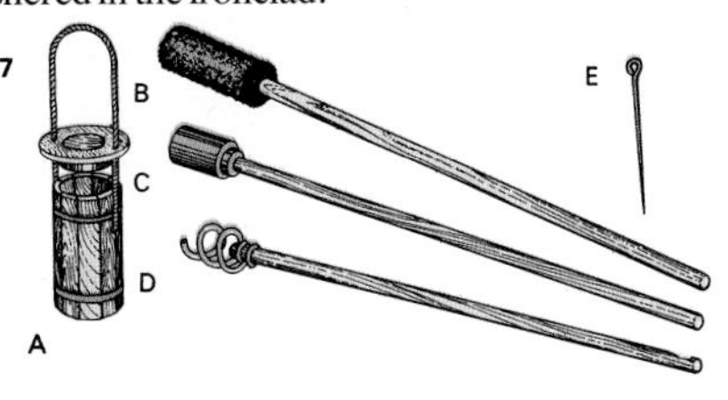

A
B
C
D
E

7 Gunnery procedure changed little between 1560 and 1860. The powder cartridge was carried from the magazine in a box [A] to protect it from sparks. It was pushed down the gun's barrel with a rammer [C] and pricked through the touch hole with a priming wire [E]. The barrel was swabbed, after firing, with a sponge [B] to extinguish embers. The worm [D] extracted unfired charges.

6

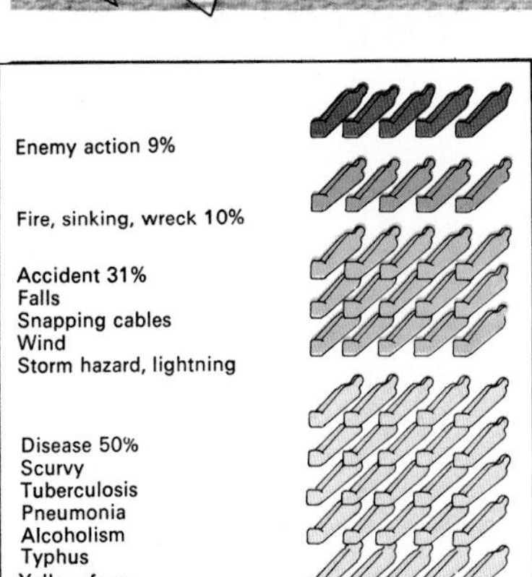

Enemy action 9%
Fire, sinking, wreck 10%
Accident 31%
Falls
Snapping cables
Wind
Storm hazard, lightning
Disease 50%
Scurvy
Tuberculosis
Pneumonia
Alcoholism
Typhus
Yellow fever
Malaria

6 Death at sea during the age of fighting sail were common. Statistics for the British Navy during the late 18th century show that accidents and diseases took many more lives than enemy action. Respiratory diseases like pneumonia and tuberculosis were rife, as were illnesses from bad food and drink. In the tropics, malaria and yellow fever (the "black vomit") were added hazards.

8

8 Naval cannon had a touch hole [1], cartridge [2], wads [3], shot [4], muzzle [5], breech [6].

9

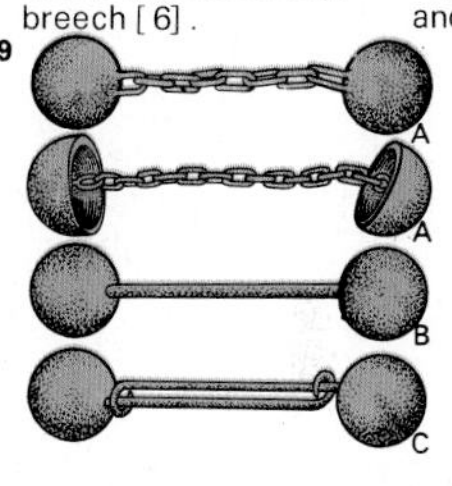

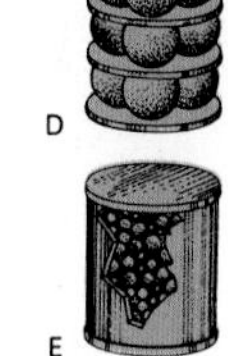

9 Types of disabling shot included chain [A], bar [B], elongating [C], grape [D], and canister [E].

10

10 The carronade or "smasher," first fitted in 1779, was a short, stubby gun that fired a heavy shot and was deadly at close range. Light in weight and more maneuverable than other guns, it was mounted on the upper decks.

11

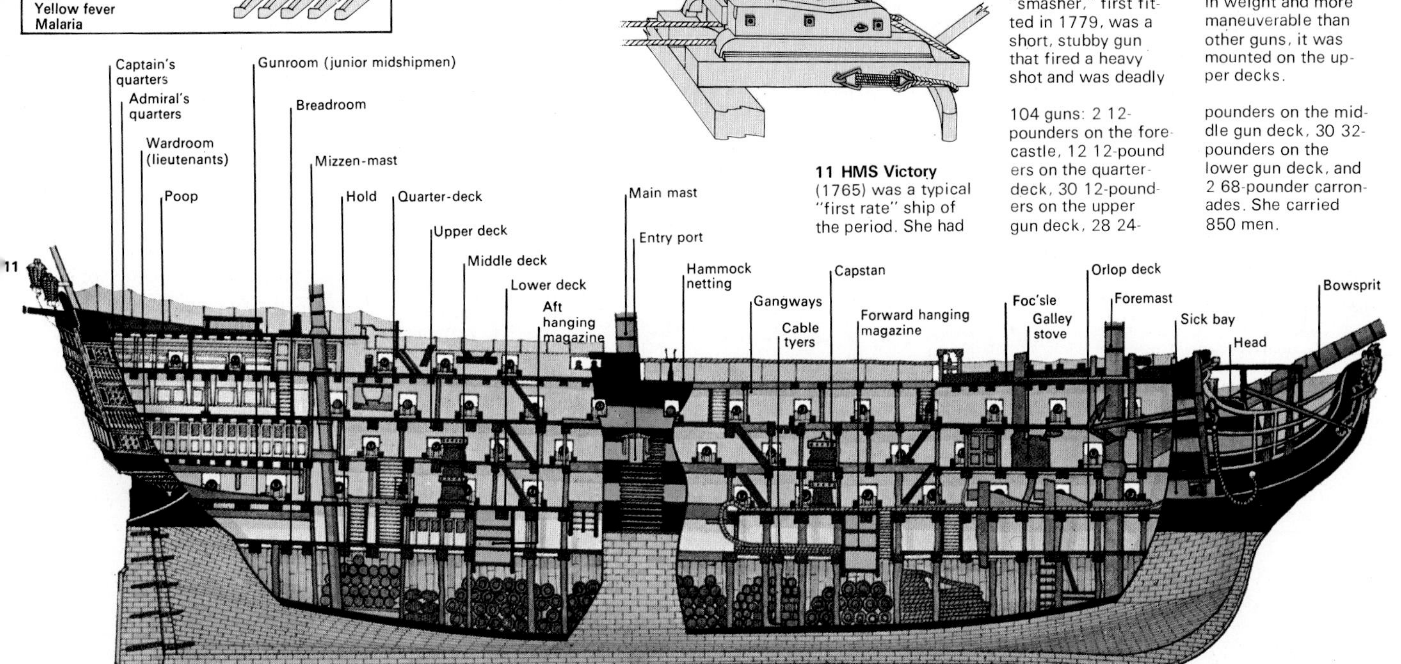

Captain's quarters
Admiral's quarters
Wardroom (lieutenants)
Poop
Gunroom (junior midshipmen)
Breadroom
Mizzen-mast
Hold
Quarter-deck
Upper deck
Middle deck
Lower deck
Aft hanging magazine
Main mast
Entry port
Hammock netting
Gangways
Cable tyers
Capstan
Forward hanging magazine
Foc'sle
Galley stove
Orlop deck
Foremast
Sick bay
Head
Bowsprit

11 HMS Victory (1765) was a typical "first rate" ship of the period. She had 104 guns: 2 12-pounders on the forecastle, 12 12-pounders on the quarter-deck, 30 12-pounders on the upper gun deck, 28 24-pounders on the middle gun deck, 30 32-pounders on the lower gun deck, and 2 68-pounder carronades. She carried 850 men.

Modern fighting ships

Navies are still used to protect shipping lanes, deter invasions, or support military operations on land. But the nature of modern warships has changed radically in the past 30 years. Until World War II, battleships were the most important units of any fleet, armed with large guns and protected by thick armor plate. In essence, they had altered little from HMS *Dreadnought* [1] of 1906, just as most other types of warship, particularly cruisers, destroyers, and submarines, were fundamentally similar to their predecessors of 30 years earlier.

Rise of the carrier

World War II changed the pattern of naval power. Aircraft carriers with dive bombers and torpedo bombers could strike enemy targets at 300mi (500km) range, compared with the 20mi (32km) range of a battleship's guns. Carriers had been under development since 1912, but were perfected as weapon systems only between 1939 and 1945, when it became clear that their mobility and striking power made them supreme. Today large attack carriers [5] are still the most powerful surface warships, carrying about 80 aircraft, all similar in performance to land-based counterparts.

Modern naval aircraft are too heavy to take off from a short deck, so they are launched by powerful steam-driven catapults. An incoming aircraft is arrested on landing by means of a wire across the flight deck that engages a hook under its tail. These special techniques enable carrier aircraft to use a shorter runway than that needed for normal takeoff and landing. Naval aircraft carry the entire range of weapons and equipment used by land aircraft, including guided missiles, bombs, and electronic countermeasures.

The development of Vertical Short Takeoff and Landing (V/STOL) and Short Takeoff and Landing (STOL) aircraft has led to a new type of hybrid carrier, whose main function is to provide air cover for a group of ships and helicopters for antisubmarine defense. Helicopters are now effective weapons against submarines because they carry both detection gear and appropriate weapons.

Air attack is one of the greatest dangers faced by surface warships and modern navies are equipped with a range of defensive guided weapons. Surface-to-air and surface-to-surface missiles are large, and so destroyers armed with them are now as big as the light cruisers of World War II; many of the larger classes are rated as cruisers. American surface warships were the first to be armed with long-range surface-to-surface missiles, but these weapons are now carried by Soviet ships as well.

Development of the submarine

Submarines have changed radically since the introduction of nuclear propulsion. By eliminating the need to use oxygen from the atmosphere for burning fuel in diesel engines, nuclear propulsion has given submarines not only great power for high underwater speeds but also unlimited endurance. When the tactical advantages of nuclear propulsion were combined with the awesome destructive power of nuclear ballistic missiles, submarines suddenly became the most deadly weapons in history [6, 7].

CONNECTIONS

See also

- **1738** Fighting ships: the age of sail
- **1684** Submarines and submersibles
- **1802** Radar and sonar
- **1734** Modern artillery
- **1682** Hydrofoils and hovercraft
- **1746** Nuclear, chemical, and biological warfare
- **1306** World War I
- **1338** World War II

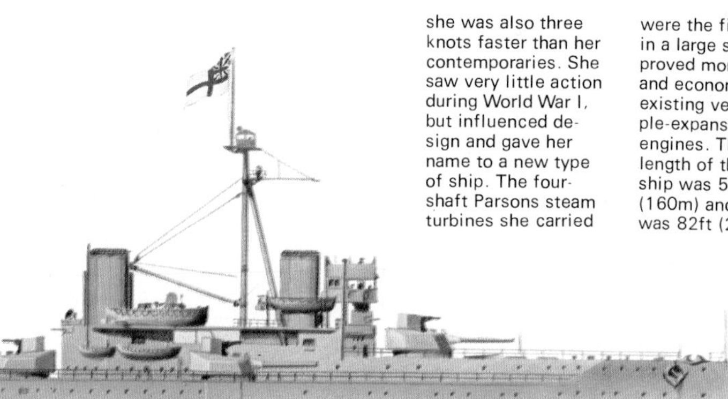

1 HMS Dreadnought the world's most influential battleship, was completed in 1906. She had ten 12-inch guns and was driven at 21 knots by Parsons steam turbines. She made all previous warships obsolete and started a naval arms race that contributed to the outbreak of war in 1914. She was the first warship whose main guns were of equal caliber, essential for correcting fall of shot and firing salvoes at long range; she was also three knots faster than her contemporaries. She saw very little action during World War I, but influenced design and gave her name to a new type of ship. The four-shaft Parsons steam turbines she carried were the first fitted in a large ship. They proved more reliable and economical than existing vertical triple-expansion steam engines. The overall length of the battleship was 526ft (160m) and her beam was 82ft (25m).

2

2 The Motor Torpedo Boat (MTB) was first used in World War I by the British but developed into a more potent weapon in World War II. The German equivalent was the Schnellboot, and the Americans called it the PT. Armed with torpedo tubes and light guns, torpedo boats could reach 40 knots. In World War II these small boats sank hundreds of enemy ships.

3

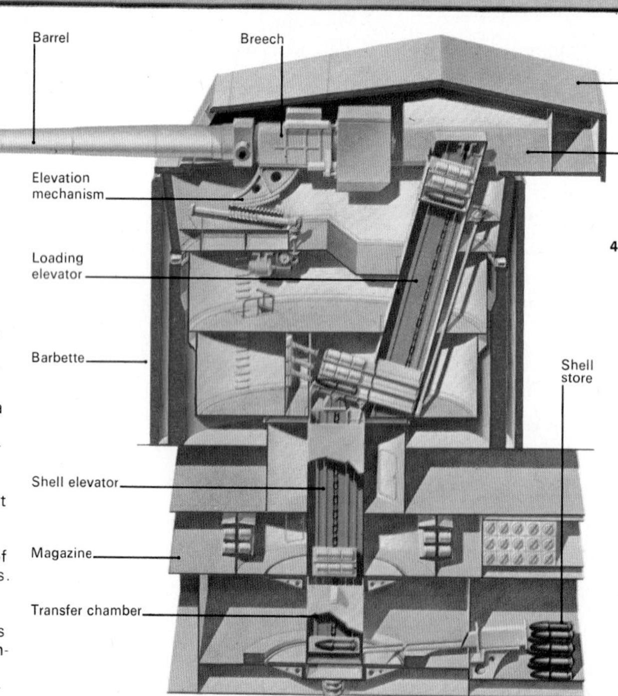

Barrel
Breech
Armored turret
Firing chamber
Elevation mechanism
Loading elevator
Barbette
Shell store
Shell elevator
Magazine
Transfer chamber

3 A large naval gun is still a formidable weapon, used today mainly for bombarding beaches and shore targets before an amphibious landing of troops. Heavy explosive shells are fired by detonating a "bag" of propellant explosive loaded behind them in the breech of the gun. Shells and propellant are carried from magazines below decks on a system of conveyors and hoists. A transfer arrangement at the top of the first elevator lets the turret rotate within its barbette. The gun is laid on its target automatically by a computer that uses data from the ship's radar. Both radar and guns are stabilized gyroscopically to compensate for the ship's pitching and rolling.

4

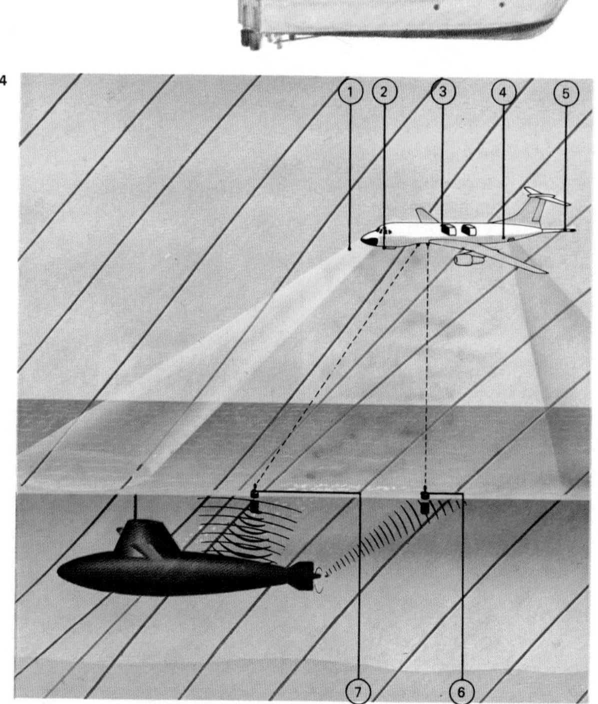

1
2
3
4
5
7
6

4 An aircraft hunting a submarine uses a variety of devices. Radar [1] detects anything above surface. Different types of sensors pick up fumes [2], temperature changes in the ocean [4], or magnetic fields [5] caused by the submarine. Underwater sonar buoys either record sound [6] or send out intense sound and broadcast any reflections [7]. An airborne computer or "tactical display" [3] gives an overall picture of the search being made.

The Polaris missile, and its successors the Poseidon and Trident, are fired from under water and use the surface of the sea as a launch pad. Ballistic missile submarines do not reveal their position until the moment of firing and so there is no countermeasure short of finding and destroying all hostile submarines simultaneously. Even the possible interception of incoming missiles by antimissile weapons is made more difficult in the Trident missile, which has 14 independently targeted warheads. For the foreseeable future, ballistic missile submarines remain almost invulnerable as a nuclear deterrent.

The submarine, together with the aircraft carrier, forms an important part of a fleet; however, to gain full advantage of the submarine, particularly the nuclear-powered submarine, it is never strategically committed to surface ships. The submarine acts independently.

Since 1965 the fast patrol boat (FPB) has become more powerful with the introduction of light but destructive subsonic surface-to-surface missiles. These missile-armed FPBS are small and make fast, difficult targets. They are relatively cheap to build and are highly effective in coastal waters. The success of a Soviet-built missile FPB used by Egypt against an Israeli destroyer in 1967 speeded up the introduction of similar weapons in larger ships, although light rapid-firing guns remain an effective defense against subsonic missiles.

Surface propulsion

Nuclear propulson has been used in a few surface warships, but its extremely high cost and bulk offset many of its advantages. Only the US Navy has shown any inclination to change from conventional forms of propulsion. Other navies, notably the British, have chosen gas turbine engines for their lightness and power, but they are frequently combined with diesel engines or steam turbines for greater economy.

Despite the threat from submarines and aircraft, surface warships have proved adaptable and remain the main vessels of navies. The ideal naval force combines aircraft and surface ships.

KEY

(1) (2) (3) (4) (5) (6)

Warship profiles reflect varying design needs. The aircraft carrier [1] is identified by its size and long, clear deck with superstructure confined to the starboard side. The guided missile destroyer [2], built for versatility and speed, has an air missile launcher. The World War I battleship [3] was heavily armored and equipped with antitorpedo nets. The light frigate [4] is scaled down for escort duties, and the construction of the minesweeper [5] makes its magnetic field negligible. The nuclear submarine [6] is streamlined.

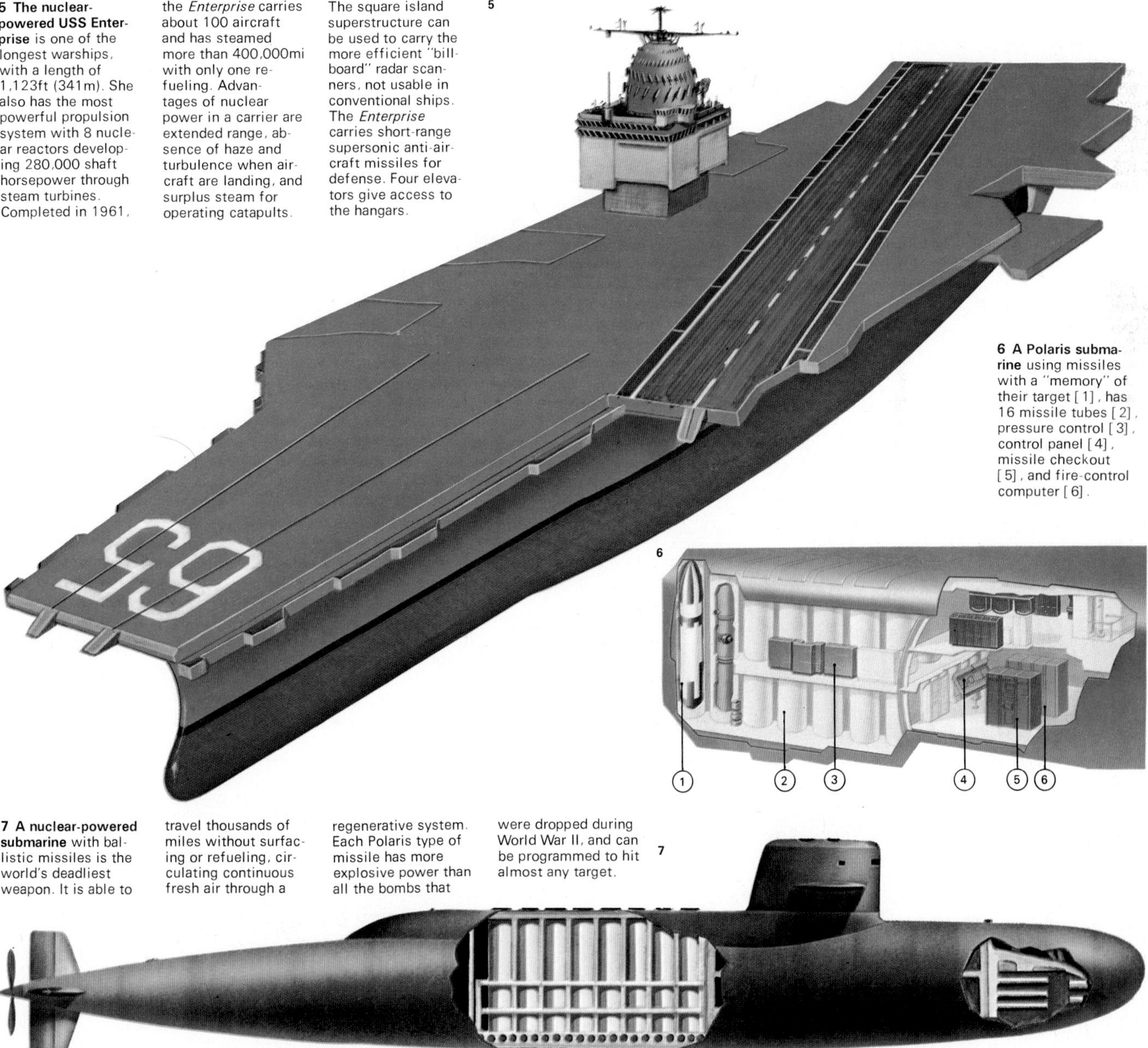

5
6
1
2
3
4
5
6
7

5 The nuclear-powered USS Enterprise is one of the longest warships, with a length of 1,123ft (341m). She also has the most powerful propulsion system with 8 nuclear reactors developing 280,000 shaft horsepower through steam turbines. Completed in 1961, the *Enterprise* carries about 100 aircraft and has steamed more than 400,000mi with only one refueling. Advantages of nuclear power in a carrier are extended range, absence of haze and turbulence when aircraft are landing, and surplus steam for operating catapults. The square island superstructure can be used to carry the more efficient "billboard" radar scanners, not usable in conventional ships. The *Enterprise* carries short-range supersonic anti-aircraft missiles for defense. Four elevators give access to the hangars.

6 A Polaris submarine using missiles with a "memory" of their target [1], has 16 missile tubes [2], pressure control [3], control panel [4], missile checkout [5], and fire-control computer [6].

7 A nuclear-powered submarine with ballistic missiles is the world's deadliest weapon. It is able to travel thousands of miles without surfacing or refueling, circulating continuous fresh air through a regenerative system. Each Polaris type of missile has more explosive power than all the bombs that were dropped during World War II, and can be programmed to hit almost any target.

Early military aircraft

An Italian, Lieutenant Gavotti, is credited with dropping the first aerial bomb (on Turks, in Tripolitania, on November 1, 1911) and two Frenchmen, Sergeant Joseph Frantz and Corporal Quenault, with the first victory in aerial combat. On October 5, 1914, just 11 years after the first successful flight by the Wright brothers, they shot down a German two-seater with a machine gun mounted on the nose of their Voisin III biplane. The Voisin, with its "pusher" propeller at the rear, offered a clear field of fire forward.

At the outbreak of World War I the Germans with 285 aircraft, and the French and British, with a total of 219, were fairly evenly matched. The aircraft were intended mainly for reconnaissance. Though some pilots and observers, like Frantz and Quenault, carried weapons, it was not until the first months of 1915 that the air war became serious. In April of that year Roland Garros of the French Air Force fitted steel plates to the propeller of his Morane-Saulnier monoplane. The plates deflected bullets fired through the propeller disk and for two weeks Garros was unbeatable. Then he was forced to land behind German lines. By this time, however, German engineers of the Fokker works had gone a step further and had developed an interrupter gear that synchronized the firing of the gun with the rotation of the propeller. Single-gunned Fokker Eindeckers fitted with the gear created a reign of terror on the Western Front for almost a year. By the summer of 1917 fighters like the Sopwith Camel [1] had twin synchronized guns.

Specialization

Gradually, as aircraft were made more powerful and reliable, it became possible to design them for specific tasks. Fighters became maneuverable flying guns for attacking other fighters, bombers, and ground targets. Reconnaissance machines carried not only an observer but also cameras and radio sets. Bombers grew in size until by the end of the war the newly formed Royal Air Force had bombs that weighed 3,300lb (1,500kg) as well as aircraft—the Handley Page V/1500, successor to the 0/400 [3]—capable of bombing Berlin from airfields in England. Special torpedo carriers were in service, their crews rigorously trained to drop the 1,760-lb (800-kg) "tin fish" at exactly the correct height and speed.

Between the wars

There was little change in aircraft armament between 1918 and 1935. The fighter still carried two machine guns firing ahead through the propeller disk and the bomber was defended by the same two or three men who aimed their machine guns by hand. But there were dramatic changes in aircraft engineering. Engines had to be improved so that they could run not for the 20 or 30 hours that had sufficed in 1918 but for hundreds of hours, without failure. Airframes became both lighter and stronger, the fabric-covered skeleton of spruce or steel tubing gradually giving way to a monocoque (single shell) structure of light metal alloy.

After 1930 the increasing power of engines and ceaseless competition to outfly potential rivals led to the gradual abandonment of the trusty wire-braced biplane,

CONNECTIONS

See also

1744 Modern military aircraft
1714 History of aircraft
1718 How an airplane works
1730 Automatic weapons
1306 World War I
1338 World War II

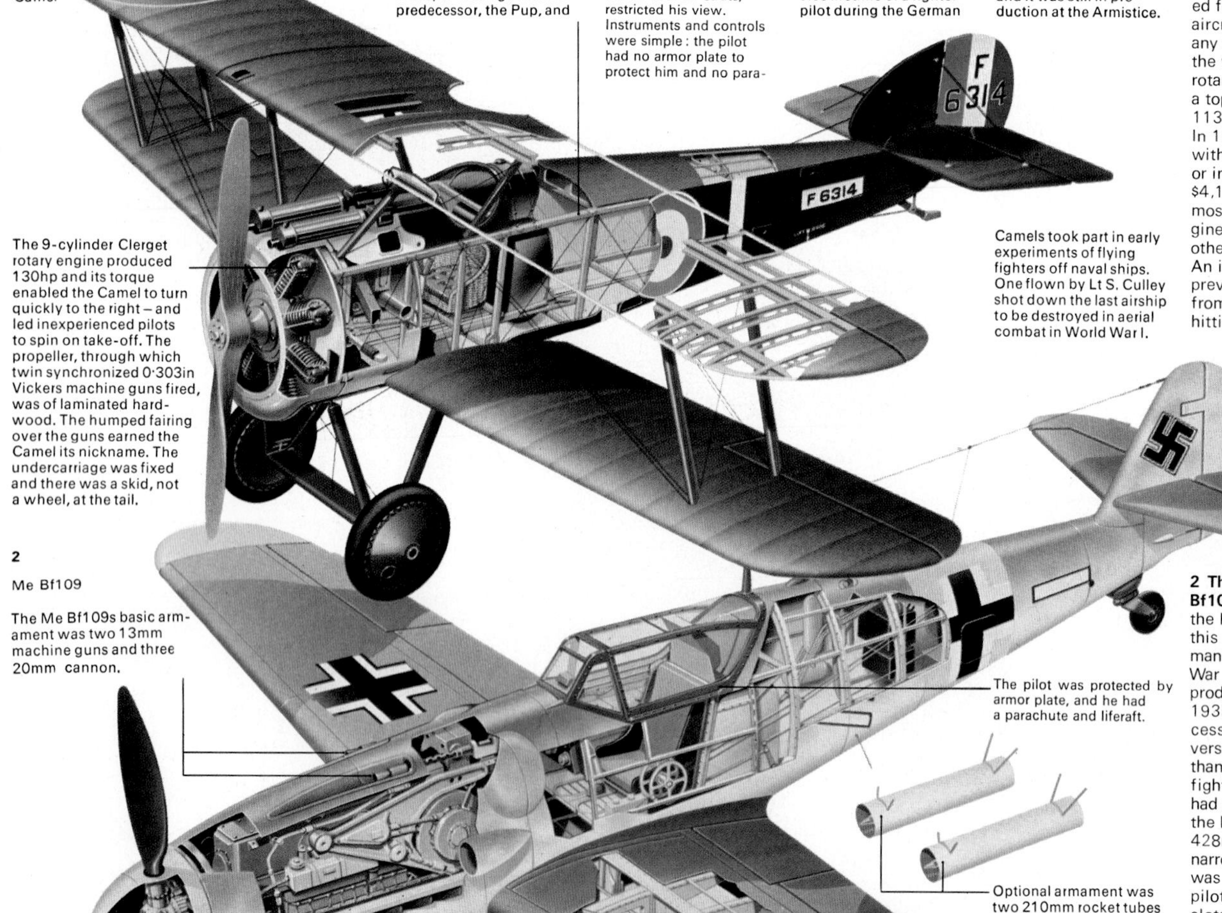

1
Camel
F 6314
F 6314
2
Me Bf109

The Camel, which was made of wooden box girders covered with fabric, had a deeper fuselage than its predecessor, the Pup, and the pilot sat well forward. The position of the open cockpit, between the rear center-section struts, restricted his view. Instruments and controls were simple: the pilot had no armor plate to protect him and no parachute, and the dope-covered fabric could burn fiercely. The average service lifetime of a fighter pilot during the German offensive in March 1918 was one day. More than 5,000 Camels were built and it was still in production at the Armistice.

The 9-cylinder Clerget rotary engine produced 130hp and its torque enabled the Camel to turn quickly to the right – and led inexperienced pilots to spin on take-off. The propeller, through which twin synchronized 0·303in Vickers machine guns fired, was of laminated hardwood. The humped fairing over the guns earned the Camel its nickname. The undercarriage was fixed and there was a skid, not a wheel, at the tail.

Camels took part in early experiments of flying fighters off naval ships. One flown by Lt S. Culley shot down the last airship to be destroyed in aerial combat in World War I.

The Me Bf109s basic armament was two 13mm machine guns and three 20mm cannon.

The pilot was protected by armor plate, and he had a parachute and liferaft.

Optional armament was two 210mm rocket tubes and a 250kg (550lb) or a 500kg (1,100lb) bomb.

Heavy armament reduced top speed of the 109-G6 to 576km/h (359mph) using a 1,475hp Daimler Benz 605 ASM 12-cylinder in-line inverted V engine. A powerful 30mm cannon fired along the hollow propeller shaft.

The Bf109 had an all-metal monocoque construction and a retractable undercarriage.

1 The Sopwith Camel, a British fighter of World War I, accounted for 1,294 enemy aircraft – a record for any type of aircraft in the war. Its stubby rotary engine gave it a top speed of 113mph (182 kph). In 1918, a Camel, without guns, engine or instruments, cost \$4,165(£875). The most expensive engine fitted added another \$4,317(£907). An interrupter gear prevented the bullets from the two guns hitting the propeller.

2 The Messerschmitt Bf109G was one of the last versions of this renowned German fighter of World War II, which was in production from 1935 in many successively improved versions. Smaller than most Allied fighters, the 109G had a top speed (in the Mk 10 version) of 428mph(689kph). Its narrow landing gear was unpopular with pilots of and the slots to increase wing lift sometimes opened in combat, spoiling the pilot's aim. The cockpit was cramped and at high speed the ailerons, needed to roll the aircraft, were hard to use. But the guns of the Luftwaffe fighters were hard hitting and some Me109s were also equipped with rockets.

which seldom reached 200mph (322kph). Instead, aircraft became monoplanes. The retractable undercarriage made its appearance—the first military aircraft to have one was the American Grumman FF-1 of 1933—and guns (up to eight in aircraft like the Spitfire) were located in the wings outside the propeller arc.

The spur of World War II

Engines grew in power from 500hp in 1935 to 1,000hp by 1939, and by 1944 a 2,500hp engine was not uncommon. This meant that aircraft could be heavier and faster. Both the United States and Britain used bombers as strategic weapons. The aircraft were four-engined, carrying up to seven tons of bombs each and defended by power-driven gun turrets. The United States equipped them with turbo-charged engines that enabled aircraft like the B-29 Superfortress [4] to fly as high as 35,000ft (10,700m). German bombers, part of the *Blitzkrieg* (lightning war), were really close-support tactical machines. Shot out of the British daylight sky in 1940, they took to raiding by night.

Ocean patrol aircraft flew for 24 hours at a time, packed with new systems for detecting surface vessels and even submerged submarines. Reconnaissance aircraft brought back clear photographs taken from heights that ranged from 40,000ft (12,200m) to treetop level. Especially built transports and gliders carried airborne forces and supplies, and naval combat aircraft were developed to operate from aircraft carriers.

By 1945, only one or two outstanding machines, such as the Spitfire and Bf109 [2], designed before 1939 still survived in improved form. But the way to the future was being shown by dramatically new developments. In 1944 Messerschmitt introduced the batlike Me163 rocket interceptor and followed this with the formidable Me262 twin jet, which could carry four automatic cannons as well as bombs. Entering service in the same week as the Me262, the British Meteor jet was a more refined aircraft that began its career by destroying V-1 flying bombs—a radical innovation that heralded guided missiles.

KEY

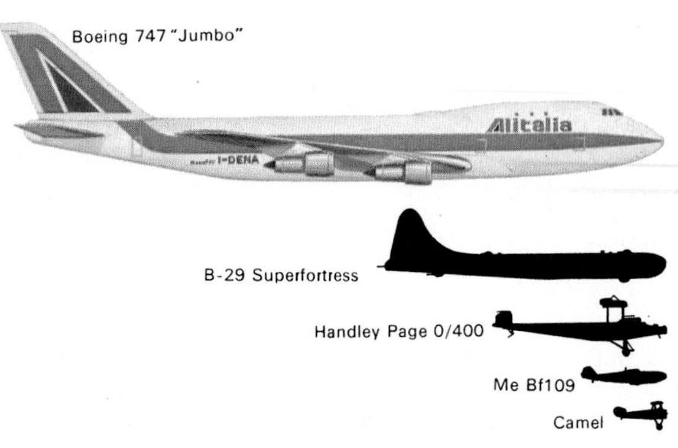
Boeing 747 "Jumbo"
Alitalia
I-DENA
B-29 Superfortress
Handley Page 0/400
Me Bf109
Camel

Even the large B-29 Superfortress, the most highly developed of World War II bombers, is dwarfed by a modern Boeing 747 "Jumbo" jet airliner. Yet compared with the Handley Page 0/400 of World War I, the B-29 was nearly four times as fast and could carry 12 times the bomb load. Fighter development was equally dramatic, 1945 aircraft flying up to six times as fast as their World War I predecessors.

3 Handley Page 0/400

Made of wood and fabric, like the Camel, the Handley Page 0/400 was introduced in 1918. It could carry sixteen 50kg (110lb) bombs or one 750 kg (1,650lb) bomb – the heaviest dropped in World War 1. The aircraft was powered by two 350hp Rolls-Royce Eagle VIII 12-cylinder engines, its maximum speed was 156km/h (97 mph) and its service ceiling 2,590m (8,500ft). It weighed 6 tons.

The crew was three to five men. Two bombs could be carried under the fuselage and there was provision for five Lewis machine guns on board.

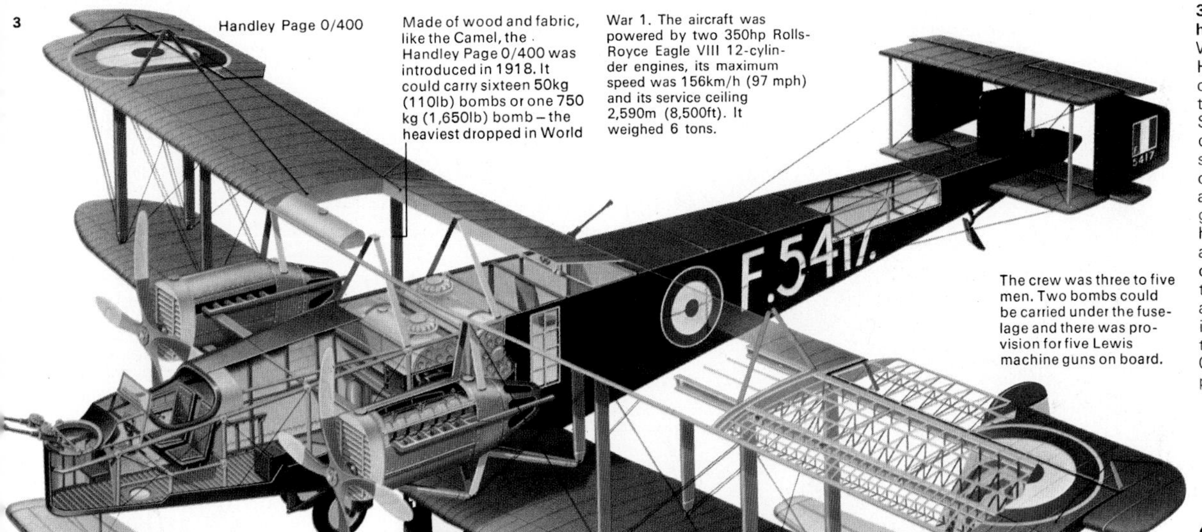

3 The best British heavy bomber of World War I was the Handley Page 0/400, originally ordered by the Royal Naval Air Service. Its wings could fold to fit the small canvas hangars of 1918 and it operated from rough grass fields a few hundred yards across. With an endurance of 8 hours, the 0/400 was used against German cities in late 1918. After the war, some 0/400 were used as passenger aircraft.

4 B-29 Superfortress

The B.29 Superfortress had four 2,200hp Wright Cyclone engines that enabled the 60-ton aircraft to fly at 573km/h (356mph).

Armament consisted of ten 0·50in machine guns.

The 11 crew members of a B-29 flew in pressurized compartments. There were bunks so that they could rest on flights of up to 8,000km (5,000 miles), a galley and a toilet. The aircraft was the first to have remotely controlled guns. B-29s ended World War II by dropping atomic bombs in August 1945.

Little Boy and Fat Man were atomic bombs dropped on Japan.

All-metal construction

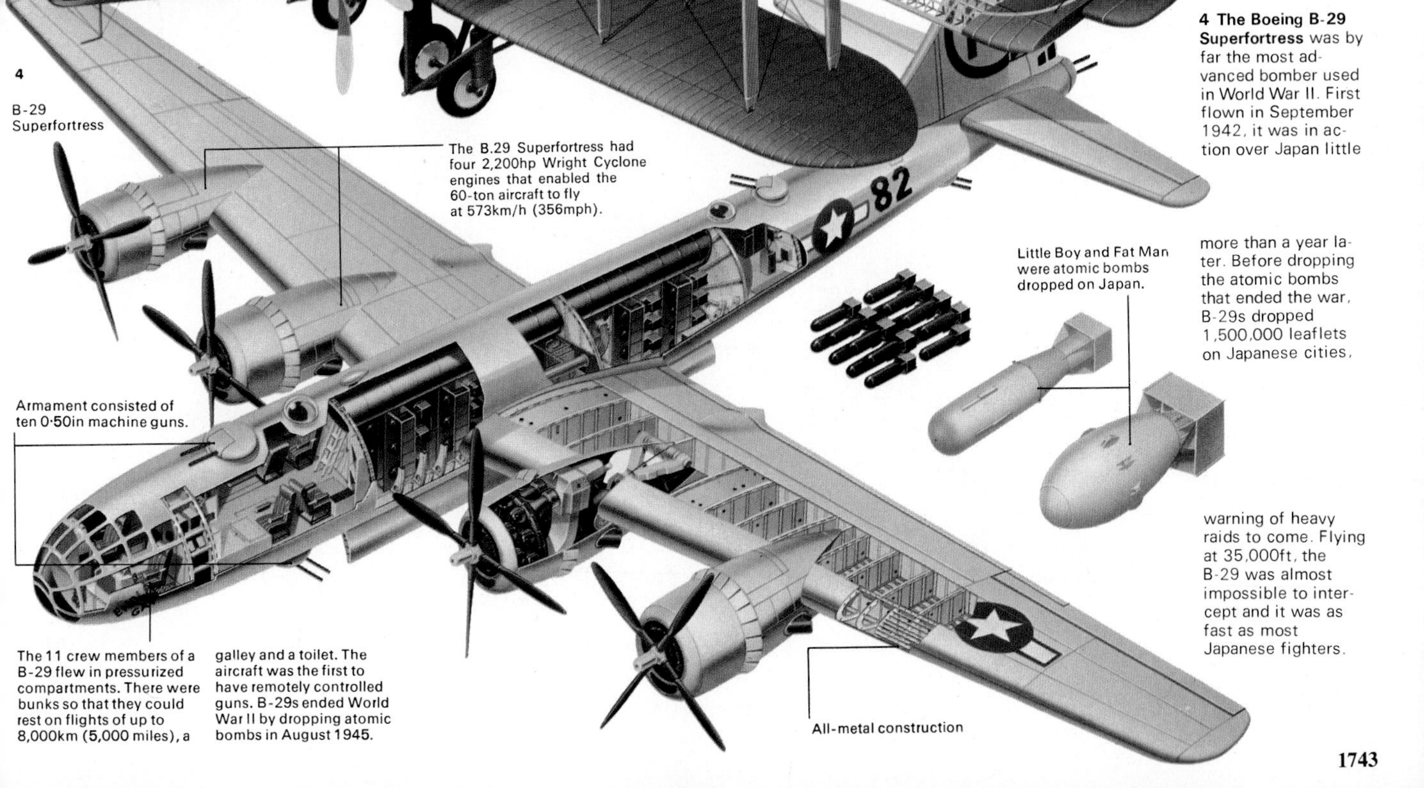

4 The Boeing B-29 Superfortress was by far the most advanced bomber used in World War II. First flown in September 1942, it was in action over Japan little more than a year later. Before dropping the atomic bombs that ended the war, B-29s dropped 1,500,000 leaflets on Japanese cities, warning of heavy raids to come. Flying at 35,000ft, the B-29 was almost impossible to intercept and it was as fast as most Japanese fighters.

Modern military aircraft

The largest single advance in aircraft propulsion was the invention of the jet engine. After World War II two main groups of aircraft design emerged: those with jets in traditional airframes and those with new types of airframes that took better advantage of jet engines. By the outbreak of the Korean War in June 1950 the United States still had only obsolescent piston-engine fighters and a few F-80 jets, which were not as advanced as the MiG-15 [1].

The MiG incorporated the results of wartime German research and had wings and tail swept back to delay the onset of shock waves at regions of local supersonic airflow. The plane could fly 100mph (160kph) faster than "straight-winged" jets. The US F-86 Sabre, although not as fast as the MiG, mastered the North Korean-piloted MiGs mainly because its pilots were better trained.

Unpredictable development

Radical design advances were being made at an accelerating rate, calling for expert judgment in ordering new military aircraft. Unexpectedly, bombers of dramatic new design failed to enter service, whereas the very conventional British Canberra [3] was made in large numbers in Britain and the United States. Used Canberras were still in keen demand more than 25 years after this aircraft's first flight in May 1949. The Canberra had broad upswept wings for good performance and maneuverability at great heights, yet it was used mainly in low-level tactical roles, for which its simplicity, flexibility, low costs and short runway requirements made it suitable all over the world.

By the early 1950s the first supersonic military aircraft were being designed. This meant further major changes in aircraft design—smaller wingspan, broader wings with thicker skins, greater body length, completely rearranged packing of equipment, ejector seats, greater fuel capacity and weight, and considerably more powerful engines with afterburners to boost thrust for supersonic flight. Some designers chose swept wings, some a triangular delta shape (with or without a horizontal tail), some a stubby unswept wing, and a few the canard (tail-first) layout. In each the wing had to be extremely thin and so most or all the fuel had to be in tanks inside the ever-bigger fuselage. Increasingly bombs were carried externally, even in the large B-58 Hustler of the US Air Force, which in 1957 flew at twice the speed of sound (Mach 2). Overloading with equipment could cause problems: the Starfighter crashed frequently when it went into service in West Germany.

Tactical requirements

Until the mid-1950s it had seemed sensible to strive for greater speed and altitude. But it was gradually realized that improvements in surface-to-air missiles would make high-altitude flights risky and attack aircraft had to be redesigned or modified to fly as low as possible to try to escape radar detection and give defenders less warning. A new generation of bombers was planned, some of them notable for variable-sweep wings that could be spread out for takeoff, cruising flight, and landing, yet folded sharply backward for a low-level dash at high speed. The first such

CONNECTIONS

See also
1742 Early military aircra
1720 Helicopters and au
togiros
1730 Automatic weapons
1734 Modern artillery
1746 Nuclear, chemical, and biological warfa
1740 Modern fighting sh
1802 Radar and sonar
1306 World War I
1338 World War II

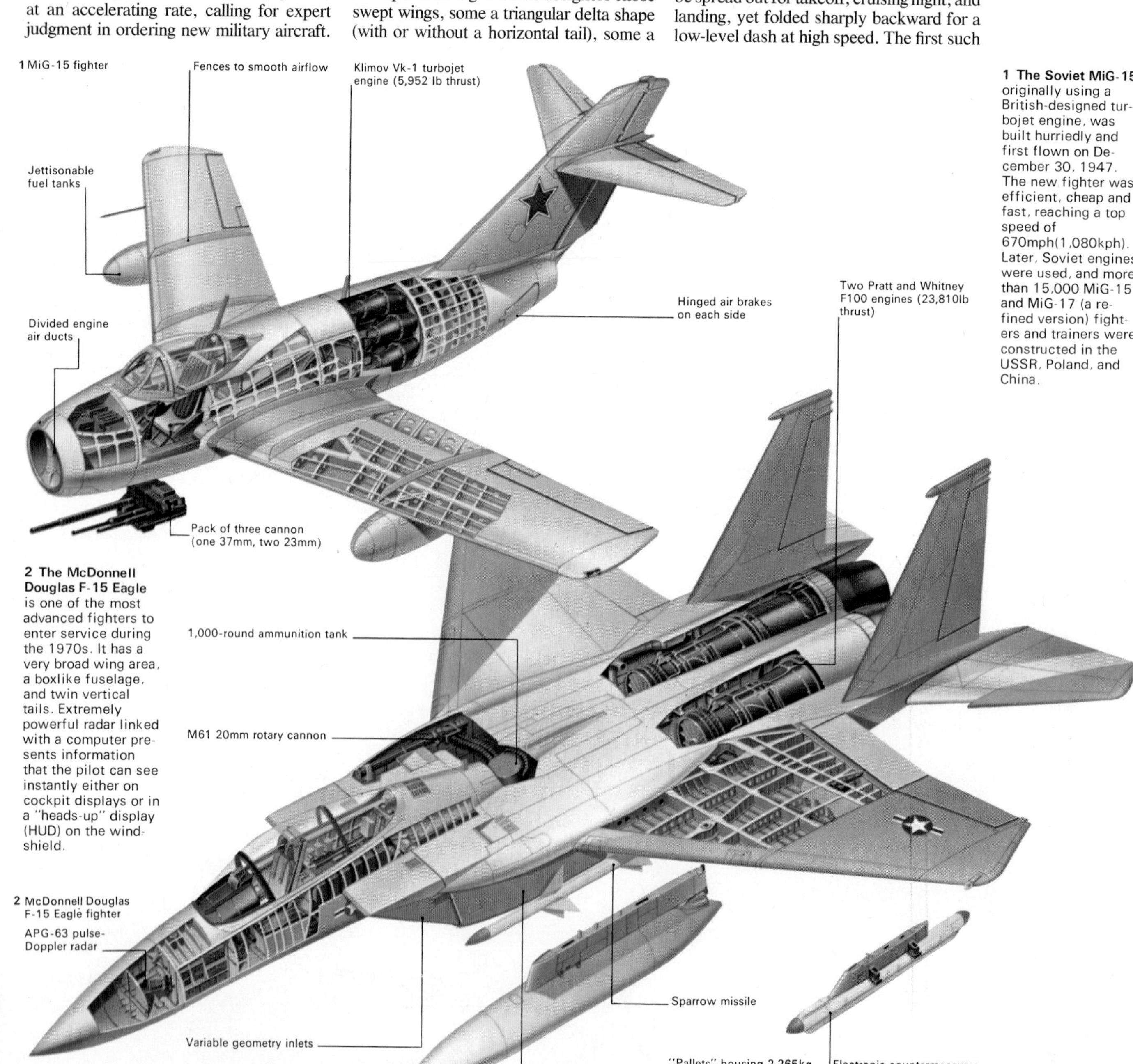

1 MiG-15 fighter
Fences to smooth airflow
Klimov Vk-1 turbojet engine (5,952 lb thrust)
Jettisonable fuel tanks
Divided engine air ducts
Hinged air brakes on each side
Pack of three cannon (one 37mm, two 23mm)
Two Pratt and Whitney F100 engines (23,810lb thrust)
1,000-round ammunition tank
M61 20mm rotary cannon
2 McDonnell Douglas F-15 Eagle fighter
APG-63 pulse-Doppler radar
Sparrow missile
Variable geometry inlets
Extra tank, missile or bomb
"Pallets" housing 2,265kg (5,000lb) of fuel
Electronic countermeasures (ECM) pod

1 The Soviet MiG-15 originally using a British-designed turbojet engine, was built hurriedly and first flown on December 30, 1947. The new fighter was efficient, cheap and fast, reaching a top speed of 670mph(1,080kph). Later, Soviet engines were used, and more than 15,000 MiG-15 and MiG-17 (a refined version) fighters and trainers were constructed in the USSR, Poland, and China.

2 The McDonnell Douglas F-15 Eagle is one of the most advanced fighters to enter service during the 1970s. It has a very broad wing area, a boxlike fuselage, and twin vertical tails. Extremely powerful radar linked with a computer presents information that the pilot can see instantly either on cockpit displays or in a "heads-up" display (HUD) on the windshield.

variable-geometry or "swing wing" aircraft was the US F-111 bomber (originally in production as a fighter). Later examples include the US Navy F-14 Tomcat, the European MRCA (Multi Role Combat Aircraft), and the B-1 strategic bomber [4].

In contrast some pure interceptors of the 1970s have seemingly old-fashioned fixed wings, as typified by the Soviet MiG-25 and its Western rival the F-15 [2]. Here the prime needs are tremendous engine power and a large wing area, for outstanding maneuverability. In 1955 fixed guns were considered obsolete and fighters became equipped with air-to-air guided missiles. But all new fighters now have guns for close-range dog-fighting (feasible only at much less than the speed of sound) as well as special close-range missiles.

Aircraft radar systems

Dramatic advances have been made in radars and infrared and other systems for gaining a detailed picture of the whole battle scene. But several recent tactical aircraft, such as the US Air Force A-10, have no target-seeking radar and rely mainly on the pilot's eyesight to attack targets. In a class of its own, the British-developed Harrier V/STOL (vertical or short takeoff and landing) has a unique tactical role as it can carry weapons or reconnaissance gear out of a forest clearing or from a small ship.

In antisubmarine warfare the task is to pack inside one aircraft a versatile array of sensing systems for detecting a submerged submarine and weapons for destroying it. The aircraft may be a large land-based jet, a carrier-based airplane with folding wings, or a large helicopter. Modern antisubmarine aircraft, bombers, and military transports are increasingly being designed for the ability to use short unpaved airstrips. Helicopters include heavy-load carriers and attack helicopters that are heavily armed.

A major factor in modern military aircraft is their astronomic cost. The Soviet Union and United States build large numbers so that the price can be kept down. Other nations have increasingly chosen to collaborate on joint projects or buy from one of the two superpowers.

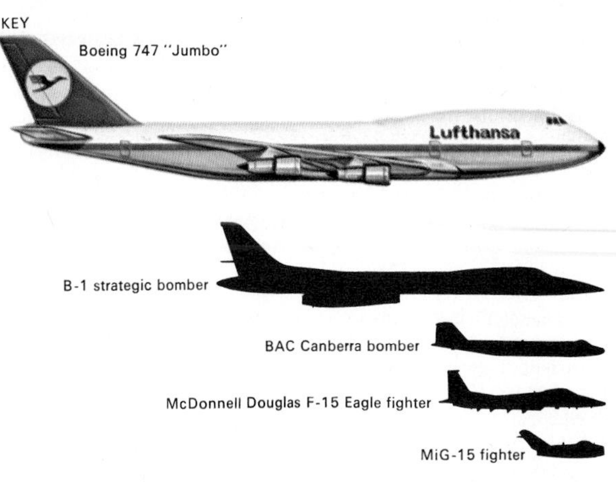
KEY
Boeing 747 "Jumbo"
Lufthansa
B-1 strategic bomber
BAC Canberra bomber
McDonnell Douglas F-15 Eagle fighter
MiG-15 fighter

Military aircraft tend to be smaller than civil transports, partly because the density of weapons and other military equipment is much higher than that of passengers and commercial cargo. Here the B-1 and Canberra bombers and the F-15 Eagle and MiG-15 fighters are compared with a Boeing 747 "Jumbo." Four-engined heavy bombers of World War II were about the same length as the Canberra and F-15, but it seems likely that future combat aircraft will be smaller.

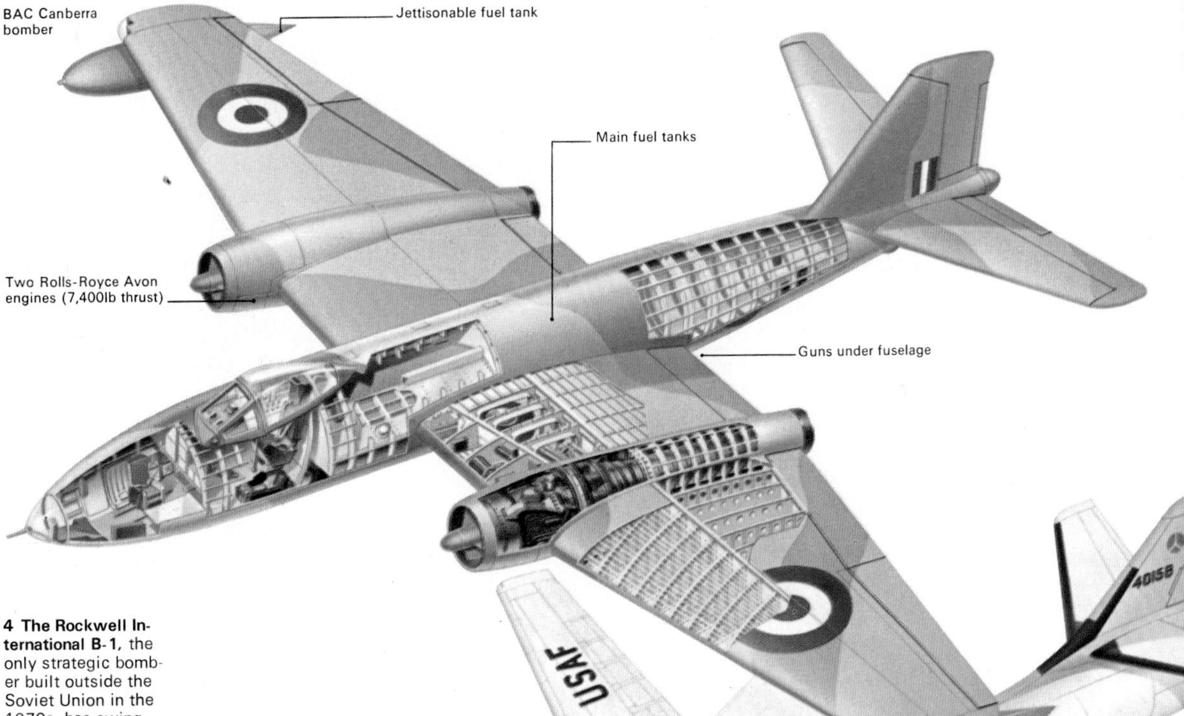

3 BAC Canberra bomber

Jettisonable fuel tank

Main fuel tanks

Two Rolls-Royce Avon engines (7,400lb thrust)

Guns under fuselage

3 The BAC Canberra was one of the first jet bombers and is still used by many air forces. This version has a pilot offset to the left under a fighter-type canopy with a navigator in the nose and a battery of cannon under the belly. Other versions have a broad canopy, often with dual pilot controls, and the navigator in a third seat behind. Designed originally to bomb from 50,000ft (15,000m), Canberras now operate mainly at tree-top levels.

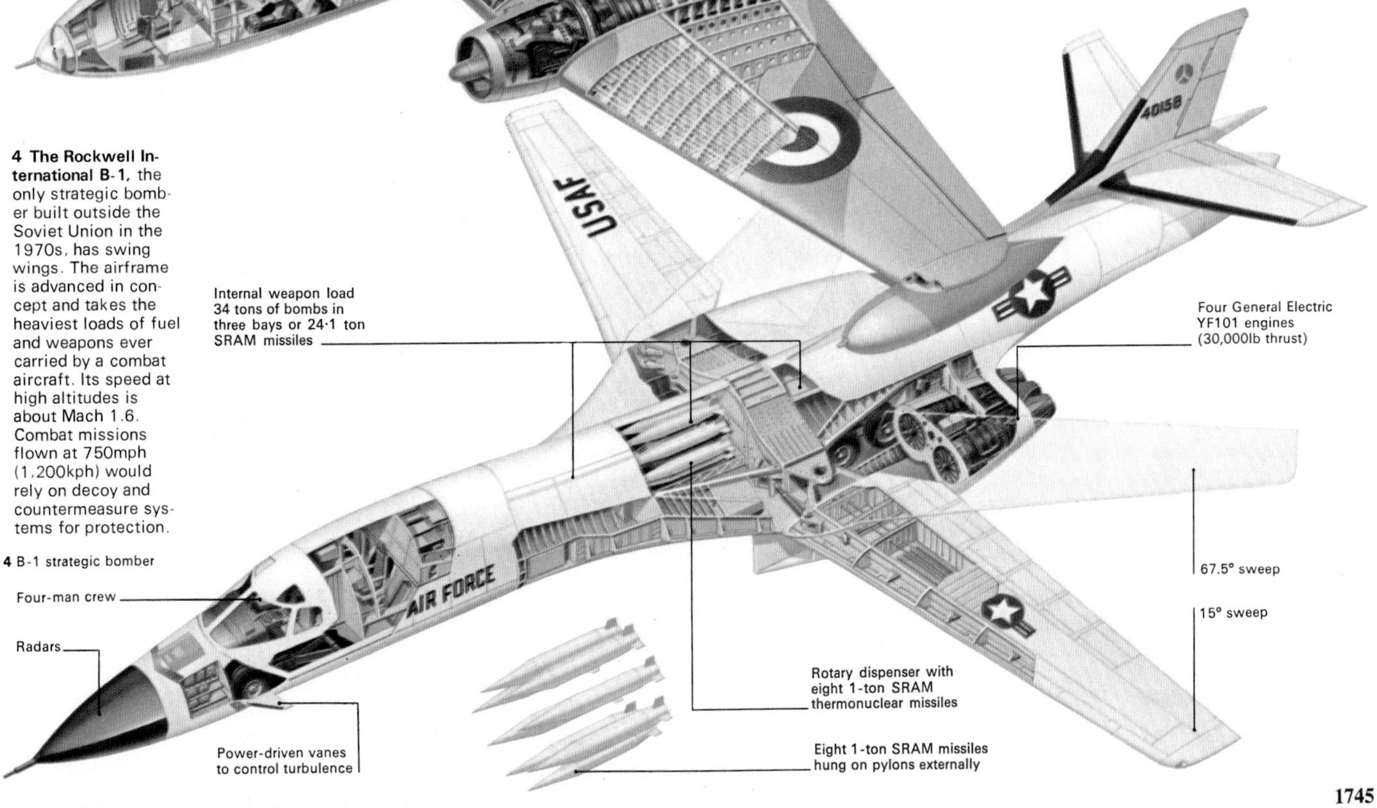

4 The Rockwell International B-1, the only strategic bomber built outside the Soviet Union in the 1970s, has swing wings. The airframe is advanced in concept and takes the heaviest loads of fuel and weapons ever carried by a combat aircraft. Its speed at high altitudes is about Mach 1.6. Combat missions flown at 750mph (1,200kph) would rely on decoy and countermeasure systems for protection.

4 B-1 strategic bomber

Four-man crew

Radars

Power-driven vanes to control turbulence

Internal weapon load 34 tons of bombs in three bays or 24·1 ton SRAM missiles

Rotary dispenser with eight 1-ton SRAM thermonuclear missiles

Eight 1-ton SRAM missiles hung on pylons externally

Four General Electric YF101 engines (30,000lb thrust)

67.5° sweep

15° sweep

Nuclear, chemical, and biological warfare

The nuclear bomb was born at the end of the most destructive war the world has known. The very first nuclear bomb, exploded in 1945, illustrated the awesome power of the new weapon; it was 2,000 times more powerful than any bomb used during the entire war in Europe. Since then, the power of the bomb [5, 6] has increased by another 3,000 times; the largest ever detonated, by the USSR in 1961, was equivalent to almost 60 million tons of TNT.

The first nuclear bomb dropped in a war, on August 6, 1945, killed 75,000 people in Hiroshima, Japan [1, 2], destroyed 62,000 out of 90,000 buildings, created a firestorm that lasted for six hours, and burned out an area of 4sq mi (10.5sq km). It was equivalent to 20,000 tons of TNT. Today the United States and the Soviet Union each has an armory able to destroy more than 100,000 Hiroshimas [3, 4].

Atomic and hydrogen bombs

The first nuclear bombs derived their energy from fission—the splitting of the nuclei of certain uranium atoms (plutonium can also be used). When the atoms split the mass of the fragments produced is slightly less than the mass of the original heavy atoms and the difference in mass appears directly as energy according to Einstein's famous equation $E = mc^2$. The trigger that sparks off nuclear fission is a collision between the nucleus and a subatomic particle called a neutron. And for each uranium atom that splits, three more neutrons are produced. As long as the lump of uranium is big enough (larger than the "critical mass"), these neutrons go on to split more atoms, producing a chain reaction. In a piece of uranium of less than the critical mass the neutrons escape and fission stops.

The Italian physicist Enrico Fermi (1901–54) had recognized the possibility of a chain reaction in the late 1930s. In 1939 Albert Einstein (1879–1955) described the military application to President Franklin D. Roosevelt (1882–1945) and within a year money was made available for atomic research. In December 1942 Fermi and his co-workers produced the first chain reaction in a primitive nuclear reactor at the University of Chicago. The first atomic explosion took place at Alamogordo, N.M., in July 1945 and three weeks later Hiroshima was bombed.

The discovery of atomic energy was yet another example, common in the history of science, of a discovery that could be turned into a weapon of war. But so terrible was this weapon that even the man who was largely responsible for its development—J. Robert Oppenheimer (1904–67)—spoke publicly against its use, and was replaced as a government advisor.

Only two isotopes of uranium and plutonium are suitable for making bombs: uranium-235 and plutonium-239. Neither occurs naturally in a form from which it can readily be made into a bomb. Uranium-235 does occur in ores but it makes up only a small part of the total (0.7 percent of the uranium). Expensive and complicated enrichment plants are needed to make a bomb from it.

The fission bomb was succeeded in the 1950s by the fusion, or hydrogen, bomb. This uses a fission explosion to trigger a

CONNECTIONS

See also
1482 Nuclear physics
1638 Nuclear power
1740 Modern fighting ship
1744 Modern military aircraft
1684 Submarines and submersibles
808 Questions of life and death
1338 World War II

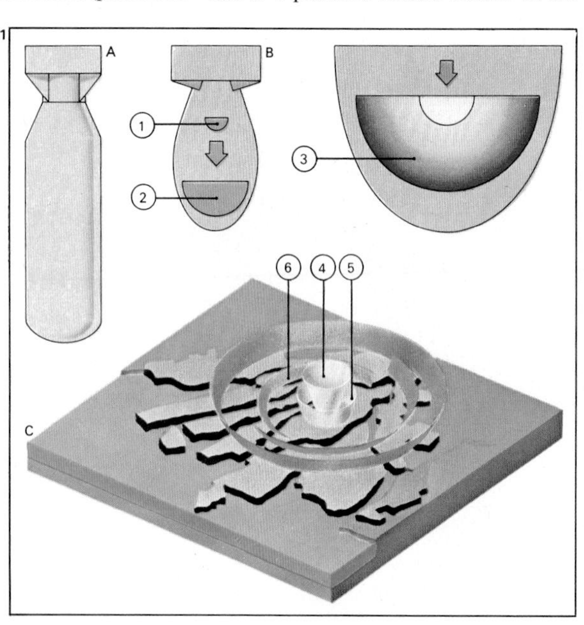

A
B
C
1
2
3
4
5
6

1 Atomic bombs, nicknamed Little Boy [A] and Fat Man [B], were dropped by the United States on Hiroshima and Nagasaki, Japan, in 1945. For a nuclear chain reaction to lead to an explosion the "critical mass" of the fissile material must always be exceeded. An explosion forces a small piece of material [1] into a large, slightly subcritical mass [2] to give a fissile lump [3]. The map of Hiroshima [C] shows the extent of the damage. At "ground zero" [4], directly beneath the explosion, everything was vaporized. All buildings were destroyed in [5] and the severe blast in [6] damaged everything. The bombings horrified mankind.

2 The ruins of Hiroshima, photographed after the atomic bomb blast, show the complete devastation. Hardly any buildings remain standing, for those that survived the initial blast were destroyed in the firestorm that followed. People who survived the blast and the fire were exposed to intense radiation and many subsequently died of radiation sickness or other longer-term effects. Unlike a fusion (hydrogen) bomb an atomic bomb produces no significant fallout of airborne, radioactive material downwind of the site of the explosion. An atomic bomb is limited in size.

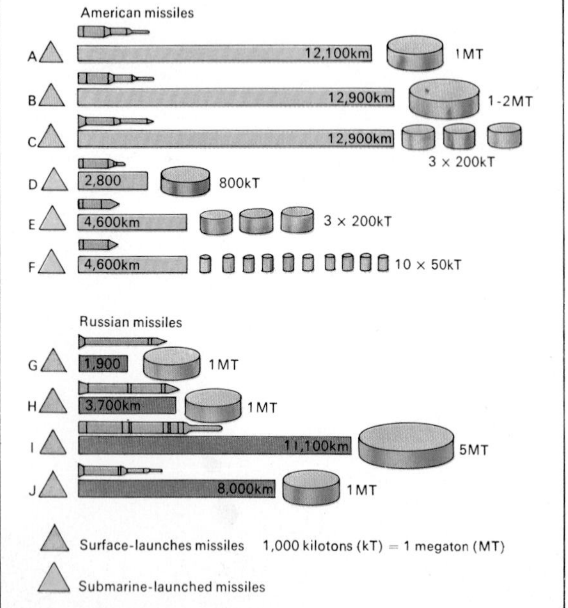

American missiles
A 12,100km 1MT
B 12,900km 1-2MT
C 12,900km 3 x 200kT
D 2,800 800kT
E 4,600km 3 x 200kT
F 4,600km 10 x 50kT
Russian missiles
G 1,900 1MT
H 3,700km 1MT
I 11,100km 5MT
J 8,000km 1MT
Surface-launches missiles
1,000 kilotons (kT) = 1 megaton (MT)
Submarine-launched missiles

3 Ballistic missiles equipped with atomic warheads are the foremost weapons of the US and USSR. America's Minutemen 1 [A] and 2 [B] have been superseded by Minuteman 3 [C]; Poseidon [F] is replacing submarine missiles Polaris A-2 [D] and A-3 [E]. The USSR has Sandal [G] Skean [H] Sasin [I], and Savage [J].

4 Global nuclear balance is controlled by five nations: US, USSR, Britain, France, and China. Both the US and USSR have enough nuclear force to survive an attack and still deliver an unacceptable counter-blow. Each symbol shows approximately 40 missiles or 30 bombers deployed in 1974.

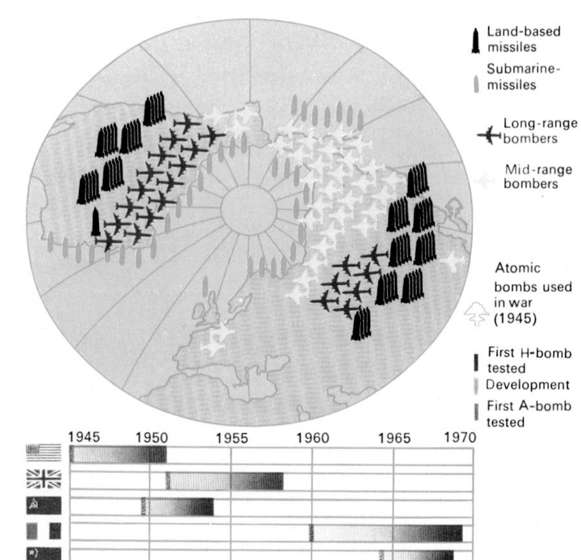

Land-based missiles
Submarine-missiles
Long-range bombers
Mid-range bombers
Atomic bombs used in war (1945)
First H-bomb tested
Development
First A-bomb tested
1945
1950
1955
1960
1965
1970

fusion reaction in which isotopes of the light element hydrogen fuse to form heavier elements. In the process mass is "lost" and converted into energy. A fusion bomb is much more destructive than a fission bomb.

Chemical weapons and their effects

Chemical warfare has been used in a major war only once—during World War I, when gas was used by both sides to poison enemy troops in the trenches [Key]. Since 1925 chemical warfare has been banned.

The most potent antipersonnel weapons in the chemical arsenal are nerve gases, first developed in Germany during World War II. Three such gases were developed, all derivatives of phosphine oxide. If deposited as small drops on the skin they penetrate without blistering or irritation and act by inhibiting the action of an enzyme, cholinesterase, essential for muscle control. Death follows in as little as a minute or, in some cases, as much as an hour. The lethal dose for an adult is about 0.7 milligrams.

In addition to nerve gases there are incendiaries such as napalm and white phosphorus [7], "conventional" poison gases such as hydrogen cyanide, choking gases such as phosgene, and defoliant chemicals that can be used against crops to create famine or against trees to destroy ground cover [8]. Another possibility is the use of incapacitating agents.

Biological warfare: the ultimate weapon?

Biological, or germ, warfare has never been used in human conflict. Like chemical warfare it has been the subject of intense development. During World War II, for instance, the United States perfected a means of isolating botulinus toxin, the natural product of a bacterium so toxic that 500gm (about 1lb) could extinguish all life.

There are growing doubts that the theoretical efficiencies of biological warfare could be achieved in practice and in 1972 it was agreed by convention to ban the production of use of biological weapons. Research, purportedly for people's defense, continues. Meanwhile people's consciences continue to be stirred by the moral issues raised by these weapons.

KEY

Gas was introduced as a weapon during World War I and used by both the Allies and Germany. Gases employed included the poisonous choking chlorine (which revealed its presence as a yellow-green cloud), the poisonous phosgene, and the blinding mustard gas. An unreliable weapon, gas could rebound on the attacker if the wind changed. The only defense was to equip every soldier with a gas mask that absorbed the gas and allowed the wearer to breathe nonpoisonous air. Lingering effects of gas poisoning are among the worst of all the disorders that are inflicted by man.

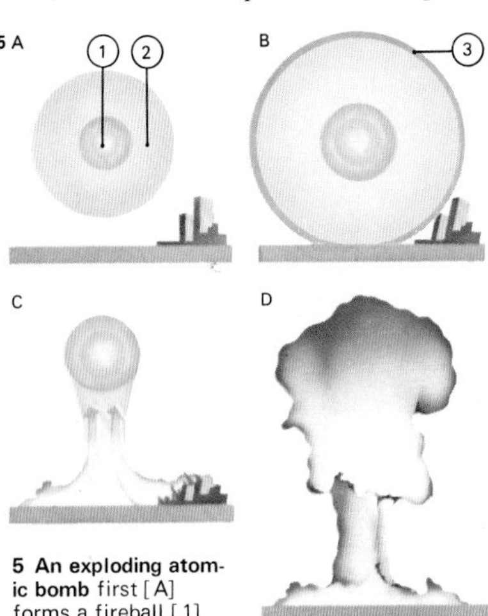

5 A
1
2
B
3
C
D

5 An exploding atomic bomb first [A] forms a fireball [1] at millions of degrees and gives out radiation [2]. Within a few seconds [B] it expands and creates a high-pressure shock wave [3]. The fireball rises [C], sucking up dust and rubble to form the familiar shape of a mushroom cloud [D].

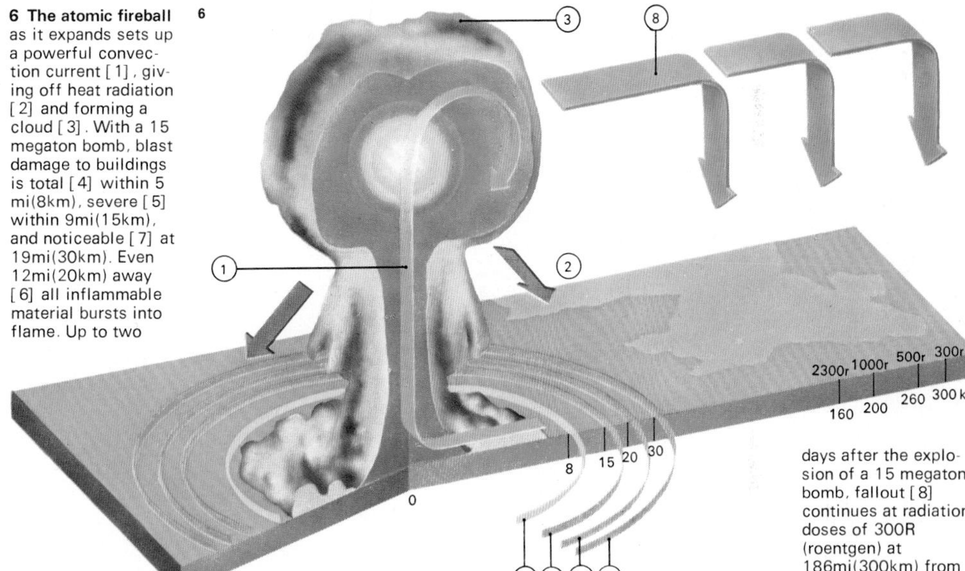

6
3
8
1
2
2300r
1000r
500r
300r
160
200
260
300 km
0
8
15
20
30
4
5
6
7

6 The atomic fireball as it expands sets up a powerful convection current [1], giving off heat radiation [2] and forming a cloud [3]. With a 15 megaton bomb, blast damage to buildings is total [4] within 5 mi(8km), severe [5] within 9mi(15km), and noticeable [7] at 19mi(30km). Even 12mi(20km) away [6] all inflammable material bursts into flame. Up to two days after the explosion of a 15 megaton bomb, fallout [8] continues at radiation doses of 300R (roentgen) at 186mi(300km) from the blast.

7 White phosphorus, once used in warfare to create smokescreens, was used as an antipersonnel weapon in Vietnam. It ignites spontaneously and adheres to the flesh, where it causes appalling burns.

8 In Vietnam the Vietcong sought shelter under the forest canopy for their men, machines, and supply lines. Their American opponents removed this natural cover by stripping the leaves off the trees with defoliants. Similar chemicals can be sprayed on an enemy's crops, destroying his food supply and reducing the civilian population and the armed forces to likely famine. Most defoliants affect trees for one season.

Road building

The first roads used by people were probably beaten out by the hoofs of animals as they made their way between feeding and watering places. Routes that began as mere cattle tracks or hunting and supply trails developed after the invention of the wheel into harder-wearing roads crisscrossing the ancient world and linking great trade markets. The Romans built a more permanent and extensive road network [Key] so that the empire could back up remote administrators by rapid deployment of troops.

Stone paving

Few authenticated records exist of pre-Roman road paving. But given the known skill of the ancient stonemason, we may assume that heavily used roads of the earliest civilizations were surfaced with slabs of cut stone. A drained earthen track becomes compacted by foot and hoof but cannot stand up to the wheel, which gradually cuts and breaks the surface.

The engineering of Roman roads [3] is well documented. Descriptions are detailed and some roads lasted so well that the original formation has been discovered, almost intact in places, by archeologists. The Appian Way, started in 312 BC, which linked Rome with Brindisi, was typical. About 14.75ft (4.5m) wide across its two-way central lane, it was built in five layers and had three features to ensure drainage; it was constructed above ground level with a cambered surface and flanking ditches. The wearing surface was of crushed lava (plentiful in south Italy) on a gravel core. The larger stones of the base layer of many Roman roads were mixed with lime mortar as a binder or with *pozzuloana* (natural volcanic cement), forming what was virtually a concrete footing. The surface of Roman roads varied with local materials.

The Romans employed cheap, expendable slave labor under military supervision for road building. After them, no administration could afford to repair their highways, let alone build new roads, until the introduction of tolls in the late Middle Ages.

Modern road technology evolved in eighteenth-century France. The Corps des Ingénieurs des Ponts et Chaussées was set up in 1720 within the French army. Twenty-seven years later the Ecole des Ponts et Chaussées was established as a state college at which civilians could study. It was Pierre Tresaguet (1716–96) who designed and built the first roads that combined good engineering practice with sound economics. He taught that there were two essentials for a lasting road—a firm foundation protected by a water-resistant surface [6].

Influence of McAdam

The French lead was soon followed elsewhere in Europe and the names of two British engineers became closely associated with improved road design. Thomas Telford (1757–1834), originally a stonemason, built roads similar in section to those of Tresaguet. But Telford's pavement was costly and it was a Scotsman, John McAdam (1756–1836), who found a way to cut costs without impairing efficiency. McAdam eliminated the deep foundation, recognizing that it is the soil that ultimately supports the weight of traffic, and that com-

CONNECTIONS

See also
1750 Traffic engineering
1754 Tunnel engineering
1758 Modern bridges
1698 Cars and society
1704 Technology and transportation in de veloping nations
1686 Carts, coaches, and carriages
1020 Rome: the expansio of the empire

1 A

B

C

D

1 Road construction methods grew from simple compaction of early routes by foot and horsedrawn traffic. The Romans [A] made their routes more permanent by removing obstacles, laying foundations of gravel, surfacing with crushed stones or paving slabs, and leaving drainage ditches at both sides. In the eighteenth century [B], major roads were built of tamped gravel on top of a foundation of large blocks. Roads in the nineteenth century [C] were similar but were sometimes raised and had an upper surface of rolled gravel. With the vast increase of traffic in the twentieth century and the introduction of heavy vehicles [D], roads had to be made more durable. Most modern roads have a concrete base over crushed rock topped with either reinforced concrete or asphalt that has been rolled.

2

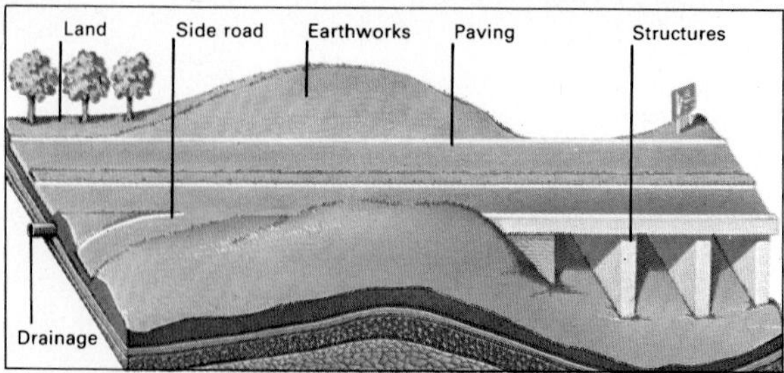
Land
Side road
Earthworks
Paving
Structures
Drainage

2 A cost breakdown for a modern highway shows that earthworks are the most expensive item.

Earthworks	25%
Paving	18%
Structures	18%
Drainage	7%
Land	4%
Side roads	4%
Engineers' fees and miscellaneous	24%

pacted soil, kept dry, will support any load. McAdam's road [4] was cambered for drainage and was surfaced with stone chips that were crushed and rolled by the iron-rimmed wheels into a smooth surface.

The McAdam pavement served its purpose well until the invention of the rubber tire. Tires no longer compacted the crushed stone, but sucked the finer material from between the larger stones until the surface broke up. A binder was needed and the answer was found in natural tar. The new surface was called tarmacadam, tarmac, or macadam.

Concrete paving

The final stage in the development of the modern road followed the steady increase in the weight of heavy road vehicles. Lean concrete (which has a lower cement content) began to be used for the footing and fine concrete for the surface of the "rigid" pavement, which spreads heavy-axle loads over a greater area. The modern "flexible" or "blacktop" pavement usually has a tar surface up to 4in (10cm) thick over a 10in (25cm) base layer, such as lean concrete, laid on a subbase of any locally available granular materials such as stone or clinker. In the modern reinforced concrete road, a granular base layer is topped by a concrete slab up to 12in (30cm) thick, with a mat of steel reinforcement 2in (5cm) below the surface.

The rapidly expanding need for more and more roads has led to the development of sophisticated road-making machinery. Giant scrapers, graders, and other heavy earthmoving machines are used to prepare the roadbed and lay the footing. Machines for automatic laying of an asphalt surface to a predetermined thickness are commonplace.

The modern automatic concrete paver [7] spreads and tamps a continuous slab of concrete up to 12in (30cm) thick and 16ft (5m) wide, handling about 300 tons of material an hour, its hopper fed by dump trucks. Reinforcement, in the form of mats of welded steel rods, is either sandwiched between two layers of wet concrete or pushed down into the body of a single slab.

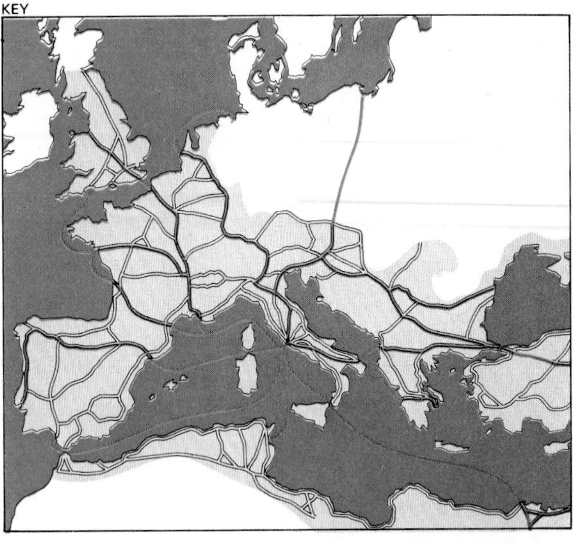
KEY

The Romans built 53,000mi (85,000km) of roads to link Rome to its overseas centers of supply. Major land and water routes are marked on this map in orange; other routes shown are the secondary land routes.

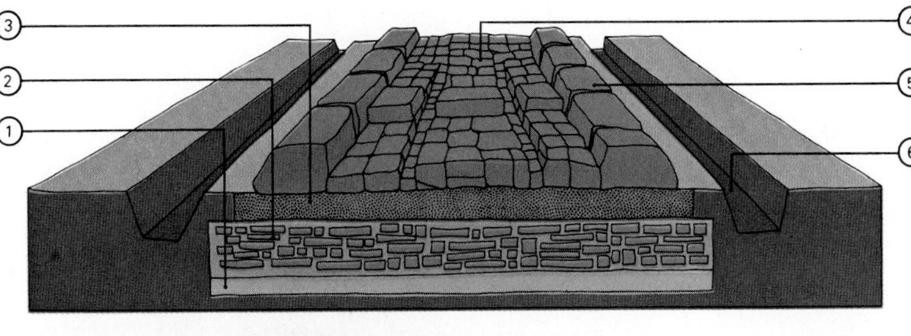

3 The Roman road pavement was based on a compacted earth footing [1] with a layer of small stones in mortar [2], and above this hard filling [3] and a slab surface [4]. At the sides were retaining stones [5] and ditches for drainage [6].

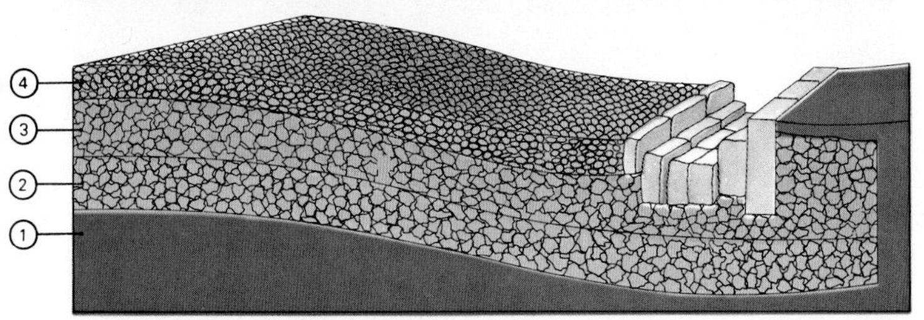

4 McAdam's pavement had a compacted cambered earth footing [1], 4in (10cm) base layer of stones [2], 4in middle layer of stones [3], and a wearing surface of small stones [4], which the iron wheels of the time crushed and rolled to a smooth surface.

5 One kind of modern pavement has a granular subbase [1], a 10in (25cm) base layer of concrete [2], a 2.5in (6.5cm) layer of tar or rolled asphalt [3], a 1.5in (3.5cm) surface of rolled asphalt [4], a concrete haunch [5], and a hard shoulder [6].

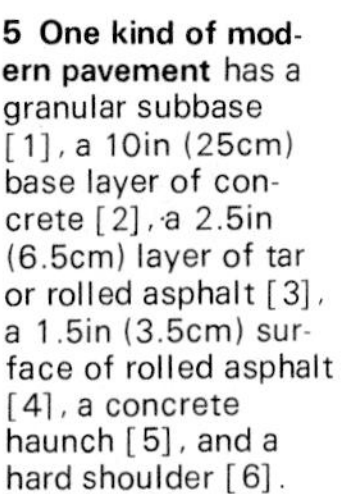

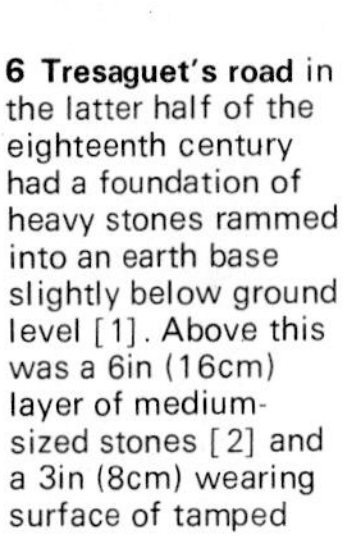

6 Tresaguet's road in the latter half of the eighteenth century had a foundation of heavy stones rammed into an earth base slightly below ground level [1]. Above this was a 6in (16cm) layer of medium-sized stones [2] and a 3in (8cm) wearing surface of tamped small stones about the size of walnuts [3]. Retaining stones [4] were placed at the sides. The construction ensured good drainage. Different surfaces included herringbone [5], *opus testaceum* (brick and tile) [6], and natural cobblestones [7].

7 Road making is automated in the modern concrete "train." Ready-mixed concrete is fed into a paver, which extrudes an even layer as it creeps along. This layer is compacted with vibrators. After a mat of steel reinforcing has been laid over the wet concrete a second paver places another layer of concrete over the steel. A vibrating beam is used to compact this thin layer without disturbing the steel. Surface irregularities are then eliminated with an automatic screeding machine carrying two transverse vibrating metal strips that spread a small amount of excess mix over the surface. After final leveling by means of straight edges manipulated by hand from a traveling bridge, mechanical brushing produces a nonskid surface. The concrete is protected with waterproof tenting while it dries.

Traffic engineering

CONNECTIONS

See also
1748 Road building
1758 Modern bridges
1698 Cars and society
1700 Buses and streetca

Modern road systems evolved over many hundreds of years out of the network of routes that linked villages and townships across the length and breadth of every country. In early times, the farmer's cart threaded its way between fields, skirting woods, avoiding water, and seeking the most convenient routes across hilly ground. In mountainous country, the principle of developing roads in the general direction of contours was developed.

The Romans attempted to reduce the wastefulness of meandering roads by driving theirs, wherever possible, in simple, straight lines, using civil engineering techniques to carry the roadway over soft ground, natural depressions, and rivers.

Development of road construction

By 1826, the British engineer Thomas Telford (1757–1834) had reconstructed the road from Shrewsbury to Holyhead to specifications that minimized curvature and gradient and provided perfect drainage. Now a part of Britain's A5 highway, his road was a model of its time.

Special highways for fast motor traffic appeared in America and Europe in the 1920s, notably around Milan, Italy, where a system of two-lane *autostradas* was developed by private enterprise. In Germany, Adolf Hitler was impressed by the military potential of these roads and a vigorous program of highway building began with the Frankfurt-Darmstadt *autobahn* in 1933–35. With subsequent design improvements, the modern high-speed freeway or turnpike emerged. High speeds do not necessarily imply danger. Research has shown that a grade-separated freeway can handle much more traffic at faster speeds and much more safely than a typical arterial road with at-grade intersections, curbside parking, and other hazards.

The essentials of freeway design are relatively simple—no frontage development, divided opposing lanes, no turns across the path of oncoming traffic, no sharp curves, and marked lanes of 12ft (3.7m) standard width. Simple though these principles are, old roads can rarely be upgraded to freeway specifications. Freeways are therefore built as new roads. A typical modern freeway with a design speed of 70mph (110km/h) meets the following specifications: 3 lanes in each direction totaling 36ft (11m); central median of 16.4ft (5m); transverse grade for drainage 1 in 40; minimum curve radius 2,950ft (900m); super-elevation for 2,950ft curve 1 in 22; uninterrupted visibility at 3.6ft (1.1m) above road surface 820ft (250m).

Urban freeways are designed for lower speeds with more frequent access for local traffic. Because it is impractical to drive urban freeways through existing cities at ground level, they are often built as elevated structures or in tunnels.

Traffic controls

Some of the earliest attempts to control traffic were made in Rome with the banning of daytime cart traffic in the city during the first century AD.

With the expansion of trade and commerce during the Renaissance, several cities introduced rudimentary traffic regulations, including the use of one-way streets and parking restrictions. Leonardo da Vinci

1
A

B
C
D
E

1 Freeway interchanges are designed to minimize traffic conflict. Different needs are met by a number of designs. [A] The Almondsbury interchange between Britain's M5 and M6 highways allows traffic to flow safely toward any destination without much loss of speed. [B] The trumpet interchange provides a freeway T-junction with three-way access and minimum conflict. [C] Where a freeway is crossed by a major road, the major road is divided to form a "jughandle" either over or under the freeway itself. [D] Special purpose junctions are designed to connect a country road network with a freeway. [E] The classic "cloverleaf" freeway interchange achieves safe access to and from all directions with little traffic conflict. Traffic that is changing direction must reduce speed in compact interchanges of this type.

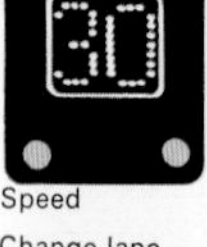

2
Speed
Lane closed
Road clear
Change lane
Leave motorway at next exit
Stop and wait until signal changes

2 Electronic signs on British highways are operated by police at central control stations. These signs are normally blank but can be activated to show a variety of illuminated symbols. Colored lights, above and below, flash to draw motorists' attention.

3
Information
Instructions
30
Warnings
Prohibitions

3 Language problems have been overcome in recent years by the introduction of a standardized system of road signs that can be recognized by motorists everywhere.

even envisaged separation of traffic on two levels.

The arrival of the motor age at the turn of the century saw the tentative beginning of scientific traffic engineering with the adoption of a traffic code for New York in 1903. Customary rules such as keeping to the left in Britain and to the right in Europe and the United States began to be enforced by law. The introduction of traffic signs, automatic traffic lights at busy urban intersections, and traffic circles followed [Key]. Traffic engineering is a distinctively twentieth-century science, born out of the hazards brought to human societies by a torrent of motor vehicles. Its object is to provide safe, convenient, and economic movement of vehicles and pedestrians.

More recently, traffic engineering has been defined as the science of fitting roads to traffic by regulation and control, in order to achieve maximum capacity with safety. This depends on detailed analyses of traffic flows, congestion, and accidents. On highways increased capacity at high speeds with safety is sought by minimizing the chance of traffic conflict. The modern road designer must try to achieve these aims while causing the least possible harm to the environment.

City traffic

The complexity of traffic engineering increases off the freeway as vehicles seek facilities to stop or park throughout the city. Expedients to reduce congestion include parking restrictions, designation of streets where no stopping is permitted, bans on U-turns, extensive one-way systems, and staggered systems of traffic lights to allow an unimpeded path along busy routes. In many cities, the policy is to reduce private traffic by both the improvement of public transport and the control and restriction of car parking. Already in some cities, traffic surveillance by remote-controlled TV cameras enables experienced traffic officers to operate electronic signs to reroute or restrict traffic.

Semi-automatic road systems now under study could conceivably lead to an electronically controlled flow of cars on major roads.

KEY

五反田 大森 横浜

Today's road user is served – or perhaps confused – by a proliferation of warnings, prohibitions, and instructions applied in his own interests by the modern science of traffic engineering.

4

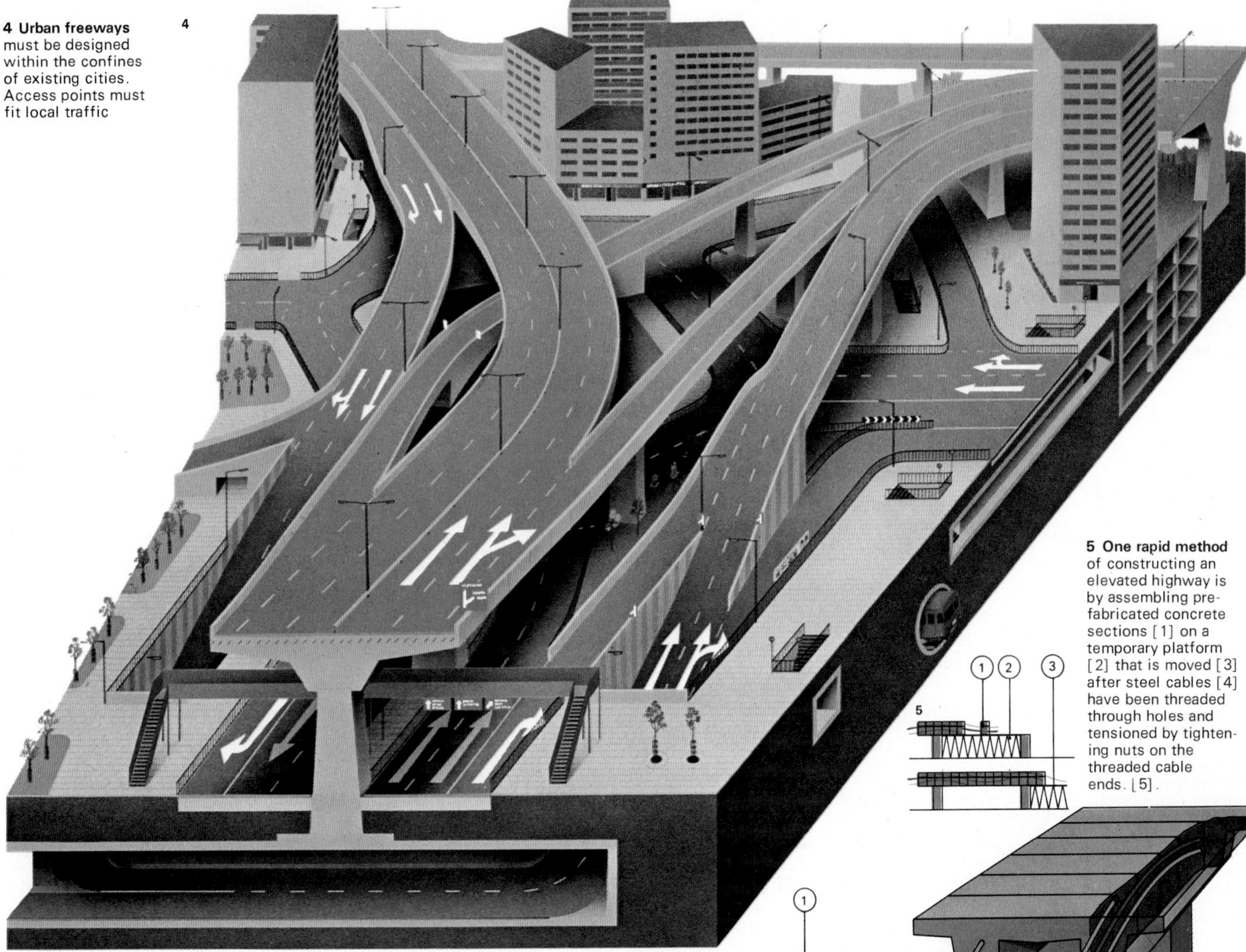

4 Urban freeways must be designed within the confines of existing cities. Access points must fit local traffic needs, both in their location and their capacity. As freeways cannot be accommodated in existing cities at ground level (except where an old rail track, for example, is given over to a roadway), they are often built either in a tunnel or overhead. One of the disadvantages of surface routes and elevated city freeways is pollution of the atmosphere by the high concentration of exhaust fumes in the surrounding area and by the noise of high-density, fast traffic. Overhead roads may also look unattractive or spoil views from existing apartment buildings. Architectural values can be radically affected by the construction of an urban interchange. Complex structures are needed to ensure that traffic leaving a freeway can disperse quickly enough to avoid a buildup of slow traffic on the through roadway.

5

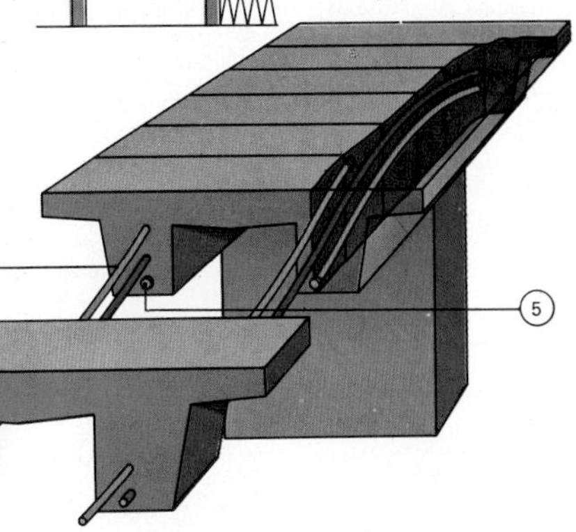

5 One rapid method of constructing an elevated highway is by assembling prefabricated concrete sections [1] on a temporary platform [2] that is moved [3] after steel cables [4] have been threaded through holes and tensioned by tightening nuts on the threaded cable ends. [5].

Airports and air traffic

When Orville Wright (1871–1948) and his brother Wilbur (1867–1912) made man's first powered flight on December 17, 1903, at Kitty Hawk, North Carolina, they revolutionized transportation. In theory the new aircraft made possible the movement of men and goods from any point on earth to any other without the need for massive engineering projects on roads, bridges, tunnels, and seaports. Landing facilities were necessary, but before the 1920s any large, dry, level space served the purpose.

Runway size and strength

From the early 1920s the establishment of public air passenger services, and the increase in size, weight, and speed of aircraft, resulted in the need for complex installations including suitable runways and facilities for passengers and cargo. The rapid growth in the size of aircraft since their invention is illustrated by the fact that during the 1930s an aircraft carried an average of 20 passengers, weighed about 26,000lb (11,800kg) and needed 2,000ft (610m) of runway, while in the 1970s Jumbo jets weighing 820,000lb (373,000kg) were carrying up to 500 passengers and needed more than 11,500ft (3,500m) of runway to take off. These lengths are for sea level airports; at higher altitudes runways must be even longer. Typical commercial air speeds also increased from approximately 170mph (274 kph) to more than 620mph (1,000kph).

Runway width varies today between 150 ft and 230ft (46–70m) with taxiways 80ft (25m) wide connecting the runways with the loading and unloading areas. The heavier airliners have a cluster of landing wheels to spread their weight; thus modern design practice specifies a runway strength sufficient to bear 100 tons per single wheel or 125 tons for a pair of dual wheels.

Most busy airports have at least two runways lined up in different directions [Key]. This enables the aircraft to take off and land into the prevailing wind. A good layout (neglecting noise considerations) is a six-pointed star providing a pair of runways in each of three directions separated by 120 degrees. But such a layout requires a clear area of 4 square miles (10sq km), so it is usual to economize on space by building all airport facilities and control, passenger, cargo, and car parking areas in the center and serving them by approach tunnels. An example of this design is London's Heathrow airport.

Airport location

Airports must be located as near as possible to major population centers if air transport is to retain its advantage of speed, especially on short-haul routes. London Heathrow to Amsterdam Schiphol [2], for example, takes about 45 minutes flying time. But the road journeys from the West London Air Terminal to Heathrow (14mi [24km]) and from Schiphol to Amsterdam city center (7mi [12km]) can take up to 90 minutes and passengers can spend much time at the airports waiting for customs clearance and their flights to be called. Buenos Aires international airport is 30mi (50km) from the city center while Hong Kong airport is only 4mi (7km) from the main shopping center.

Airports must be serviced by good road and rail facilities to enable the efficient

CONNECTIONS

See also
1716 Modern aircraft
1664 Earth-moving machines
1710 Railroads of the future

1

1975 Concorde
1965 DC-8/63
1955 Comet 4
1945 Constellation
1935 DC-3
1925 Fokker
3000
2000
1000
500
0 km/h

1 Flight technology has advanced much more rapidly than that of most other means of transport. Fifty years have seen aircraft speeds increase to as much as 1,450 mph(2,335 kph) in the case of Concorde. When the total area available limits runway length the only solution consistent with safety is to construct a new airport at a new location. It is doubtful, however, that aircraft speeds will increase in the near future because of the controversy over noise levels. Typical passenger transport aircraft and their maximum speeds are shown on the chart.

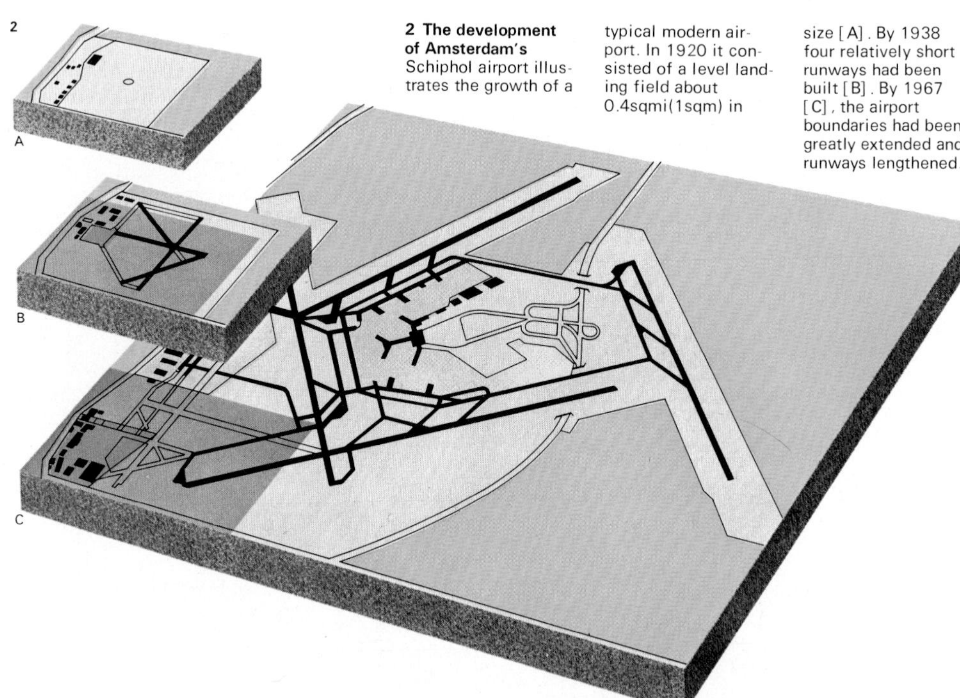

2
A
B
C

2 The development of Amsterdam's Schiphol airport illustrates the growth of a typical modern airport. In 1920 it consisted of a level landing field about 0.4sqmi(1sqm) in size [A]. By 1938 four relatively short runways had been built [B]. By 1967 [C], the airport boundaries had been greatly extended and runways lengthened.

3 The problem of aircraft noise near airports must be faced by all airport management authorities. In the enforcement of noise abatement programs a balance must be struck between the demands of efficiency and the minimization of disturbance. Heathrow airport, London, is the busiest airport in Europe; because of its situation close to a number of suburban localities strict rules have been made to control noise. In 1958 noise limits were set at 110 PNdB (a measure of perceived noise) during the day and 102 PNdB at night, and there has been no relaxation since the advent of the larger, more powerful, and potentially noisier jet-engined aircraft of today. Noise abatement procedures include keeping within a defined flight path, making the approach for landing at a fixed angle of 3° from a height of 1,000ft (300m), and reducing power and the rate of climb as soon as the aircraft has reached 1,000ft after takeoff. The environmental battle over Concorde has been based as much on the question of exceeding accepted maximum takeoff and landing noise as on the question of sonic boom in level flight.

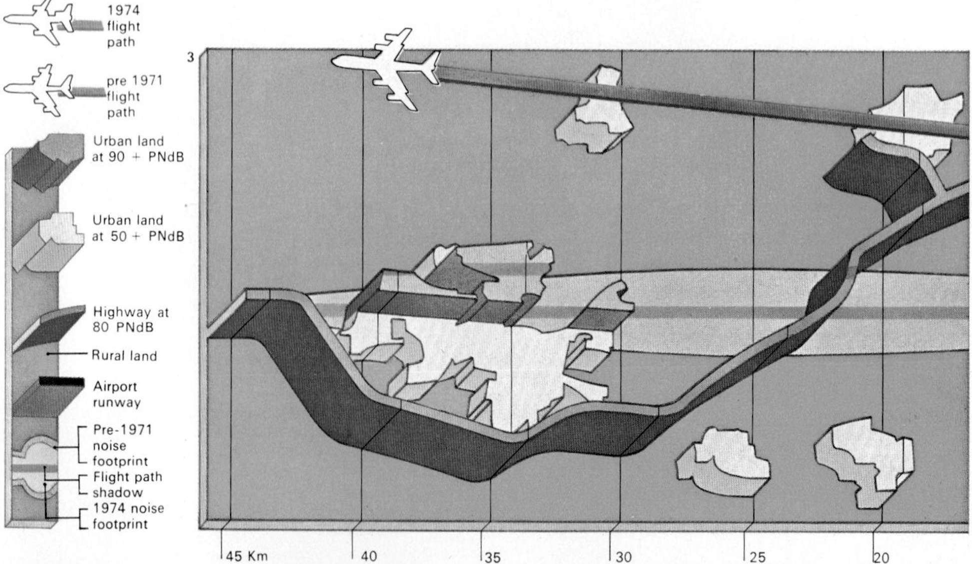

1974 flight path
pre 1971 flight path
Urban land at 90 + PNdB
Urban land at 50 + PNdB
Highway at 80 PNdB
Rural land
Airport runway
Pre-1971 noise footprint
Flight path shadow
1974 noise footprint
3
45 Km
40
35
30
25
20

inflow and outflow of passenger and freight traffic at densities equivalent to the airport's capacity. Some airports such as Kennedy airport, New York, can be reached by means of helicopter shuttle services. Modern jet aircraft are noisy and airports must therefore be located so that the takeoff air lanes avoid populated areas as far as possible. Legislation in most countries limits takeoff noise [3] to between 110 and 120 PNdB (perceived noise decibels) at ground level in the flight path.

Passenger and cargo handling

Passenger facilities [6] at a modern airport have to be designed to deal with a wide variety of services: airline booking and checking in, baggage handling, open and duty-free shopping, departure and transit waiting and restaurant service, passport control, customs and short- and long-term car parking. These must be adequate to service the full loads that arrive with each giant airliner every few minutes. Cargo facilities include vehicle access, booking offices, warehousing, handling gear, and customs. There must also be provision for airport police, and fire and ambulance services.

The air traffic control facilities required at a modern airport are considerable. The control tower must be located so that control staff can see all runways, and airport lighting must allow for comparable visibility during the night as well as providing pilots with adequate airport recognition and runway lighting for landing and takeoff. There must be equipment to provide VHF radio contact between the control tower and pilots of all aircraft on the ground and of those in the air.

Landing aids [4], essential in low-visibility conditions, include radio beacons to provide control signals for blind landing. Full radar scanning is also necessary to enable controllers to "see" all aircraft at night or in fog.

Airports must also be safe places. One of the new safety measures on the ground is the extensive search necessary to thwart potential hijackers. Airport personnel, aided by electronic devices, carry out these searches.

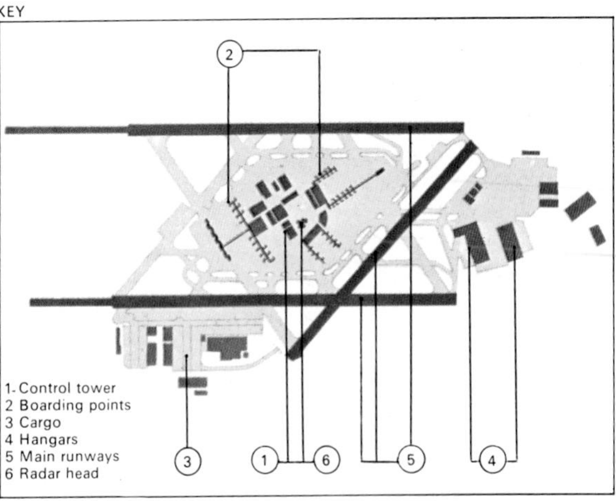
KEY
1 Control tower
2 Boarding points
3 Cargo
4 Hangars
5 Main runways
6 Radar head

The ideal airport provides landing and takeoff directions into, or nearly into, the prevailing wind. This layout is the basis of London's Heathrow airport. As the heavy aircraft of today are less affected by cross winds, the full star is no longer necessary and runway extension has been confined to where it is most needed. The runways have been lengthened from time to time to accommodate these new aircraft. The longest runway today is 12,800ft(3,900m).

4 Aircraft navigational aids include VOR beacons (very high frequency navigational facility) [1] at flight path intersections to give bearings. At airports traffic plotted by a primary radar [2] is called up by surveillance radar [3], individually identified and guided to a holding pattern [4] in which inbound aircraft fly in oval circuits at successively lower levels controlled by a radio beacon [5]. Pattern control is essential at modern takeoff and landing rates; those waiting their turn must remain in the stack. When the aircraft reaches the bottom the pilot locates the radio-defined glide path to the runway, enabling a safe landing even in the worst visibility. Airport surveillance radar [6] "sees" all ground vehicles even in dense fog and the staff at the control center [7] coordinates all movements by means of two-way radio. Near large airports there are additional stacks to hold extra aircraft if landings at the airport are temporarily suspended.

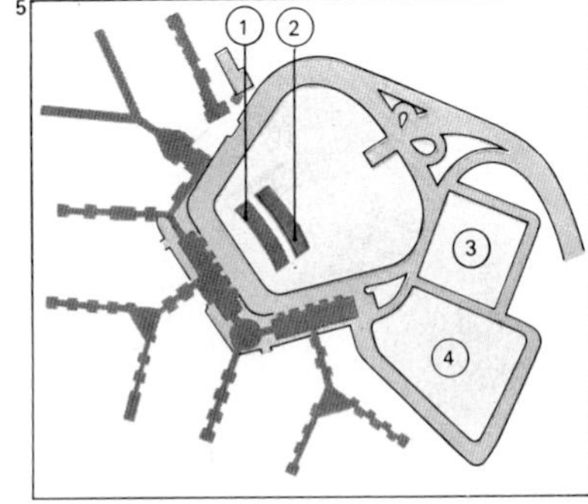

5 O'Hare International airport, Chicago, is one of the busiest in the world. It has two domestic multi-berth terminals [1] in addition to an international one [2], and its other facilities include a hotel [3], parking garages [4,5], and restaurants, as well as the usual passport controls and customs agencies and the means of handling air freight.

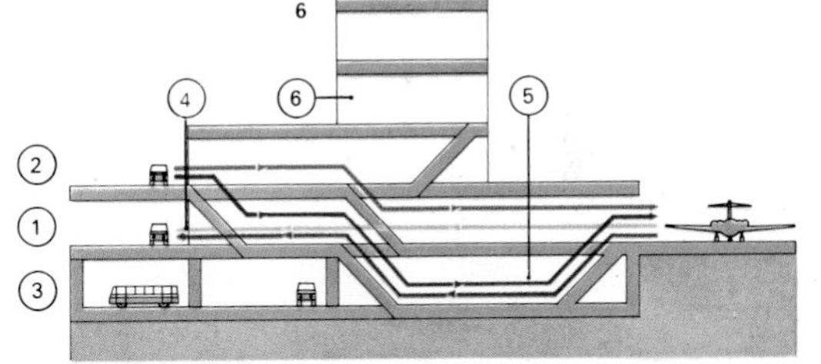

6 Modern airport terminals are designed to handle large numbers of passengers and luggage. The diagram shows traffic flow to [2] and from [1] an aircraft, parking areas [3], customs [4], baggage [5], and service areas [6].

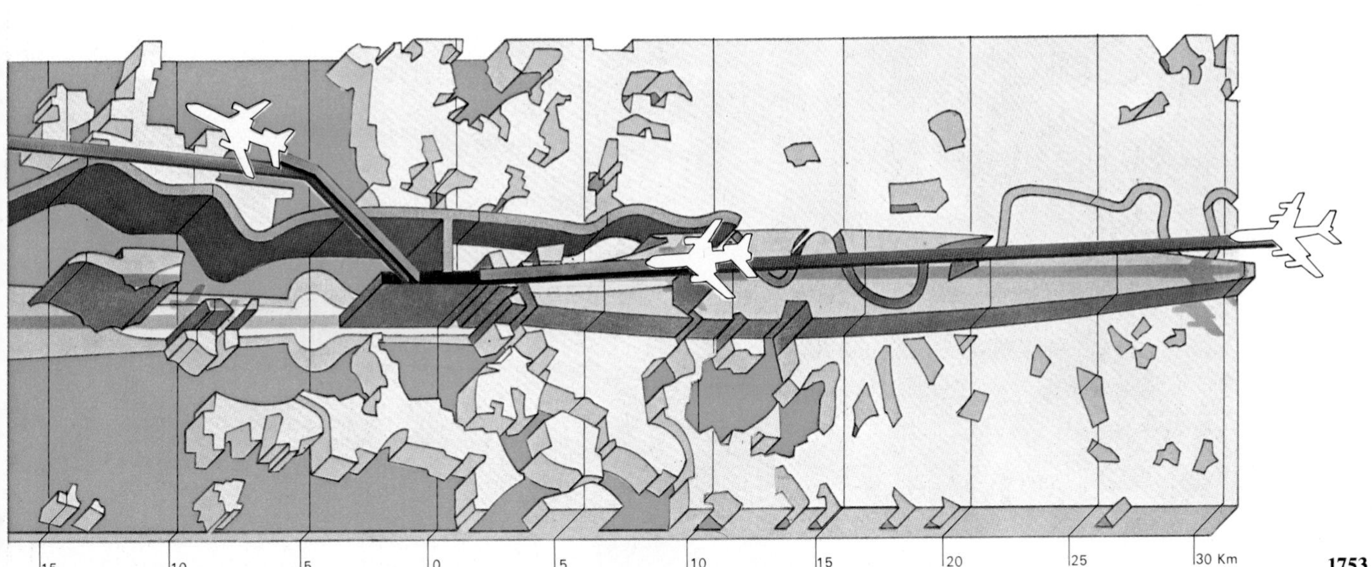
15
10
5
0
5
10
15
20
25
30 Km

Tunnel engineering

Tunneling was probably one of man's earliest exercises in the field of civil engineering. The ancient Egyptians are known to have built tunnels for transporting water and for use as tombs. The Egyptians also undertook mining operations, cutting deep tunnels to excavate copper ores. Today tunnels are used for road, rail, and pedestrian transport, for carrying water and in mining.

Some early tunnels

The first underwater tunnel was probably built in about 2160 BC by the engineers of Queen Semiramis of Babylon. The Euphrates had been diverted and the engineers dug a channel in the river bed. In this they built a brick-lined tunnel some 3,000ft (900m) long, waterproofed with bitumen plaster about 6.5ft (2m) thick. It connected the palace with a temple across the water.

Tunnels have often been used in warfare to penetrate enemy defenses. Historians suggest that the walls of Jericho were almost certainly brought down by driving a tunnel beneath them and then lighting a fire to burn away the wooden props.

Tunnels, some cut through hard rock, were used extensively by the Romans in building their famous system of aqueducts. The Appian aqueduct, built in about 312 BC, ran as a tunnel for almost 16mi (25km).

After the time of the Romans no large tunnels were built for more than a thousand years. It was the coming of the canal age in the seventeenth century that produced a new generation of tunnel builders.

Man's first great tunnel built for transportation was part of the Canal du Midi. It was completed in 1681 and ran across France from the Bay of Biscay to the Mediterranean. At Malpus, near Beziers, a 515-ft (158-m) tunnel was cut to carry the canal through a rocky ridge. It was the first tunnel built with the aid of explosives—gunpowder in hand-drilled holes.

Rail and underwater tunnels

Throughout the eighteenth century canal tunnels were built both in Europe and America, but with the onset of the railroad age in the early nineteenth century canals fell into disuse as a means of transport. The construction of railroads, however, itself produced a huge increase in tunneling. One of the most remarkable and difficult tunnels was the Simplon tunnel under the Alps, completed in 1906. It runs for 12mi (20km) and connects Switzerland and Italy.

Between 1825 and 1841, French engineer Marc Brunel (1769–1849), a British resident, built the first major underwater tunnel—still in constant use by the London Underground (subway)—beneath the Thames. Brunel constructed his tunnel by means of a tunneling shield [1]—a device consisting basically of a vertical face of stout horizontal timber beams that could be removed one at a time to enable clay to be dug out, each beam then being replaced farther forward. Brunel's shield preceded the modern circular tunneling shield.

Soon after Brunel's triumph plans were prepared to build a tunnel under the English Channel. In 1882 an army engineer, Colonel Frederick Beaumont, designed and built a tunneling machine suitable for cutting a hole 7.5ft(2.3m) in diameter through chalk. Driven by compressed air, the machine ad-

CONNECTIONS

See also
1664 Earth-moving machines
1662 Machines for lifting
1764 Building dams

1

1 Brunel's tunneling shield consisted of 12 vertical cast iron sections. The men were protected by horizontal timbers held against the tunnel face. These could be removed for digging, one at a time. When the face had been excavated about 12in (30cm) the jacks holding the timbers were released and the shield moved forward by means of large jacks that acted against the tunnel's shield.

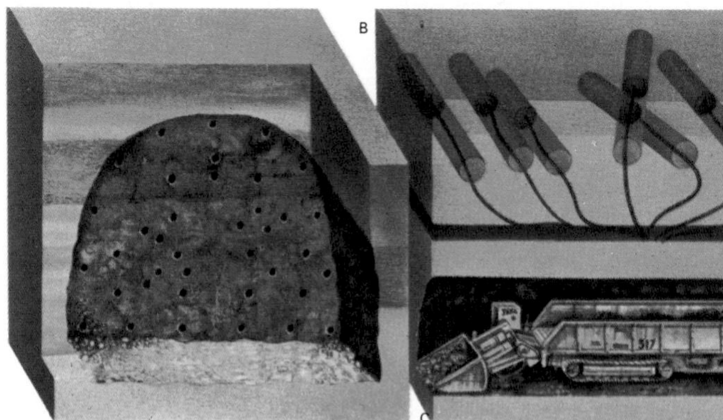
2
A
B
C

2 A typical drilling pattern for blasting through rock involves a center group of holes that are packed with a high explosive such as dynamite. [A] shows the holes in a vertical cross section. [B] is a horizontal section showing the explosive placed in the rock face. After the explosive charges have been detonated, a heap of rock lumps and rubble block the tunnel face. Engineers drill the hole pattern in such a way that the rock is smashed into manageable lumps. The machine for the removal of blasted rock [C] includes a rock shovel near the face, which loads material into a long shuttle car with a steel-slat conveyor for moving the rock rubble back to trucks. The whole machine is gradually moved toward the face.

3
Ingoing passengers to all lines
Ticket offices
Exit

3 London's reconstructed Oxford Circus subway junction provides interchange facilities for three systems: the Central (orange), Bakerloo (brown), and Victoria (blue) lines. The new ticket offices were built under a steel "umbrella" above street level. The Victoria line was excavated mainly by automatic "drum-digger," which advanced up to 59ft (18m) a day. This machine consists of two steel drums, with the edge of the outer drum beveled to cut through the London clay. At one Victoria line station water-bearing ground was frozen by pumping liquid nitrogen into tubes driven 5.5ft (1.6m) apart. Station tunnels in the Victoria line are 21.5ft (6.5m) in diameter.

vanced 39ft (12m) every 24 hours and had cut a hole 1mi (1.6km) long eastward from Dover when work was stopped for political reasons. A second tunnel, begun in 1973, was abandoned in 1975 because of the escalating construction costs.

Modern tuneling methods

Tunnels through hard rock are usually built by drilling and blasting [2]. A pattern of holes is drilled into the rock face by using compressed air drills operated by men on a moving carriage or "jumbo" running on temporary rails. A drill tipped with a tungsten-carbide bit can penetrate 6 to 10ft (2 to 3m) in four to five minutes. When a round of holes is ready a high explosive such as dynamite is packed in and detonated. A mobile rock shovel lifts the shattered rock into dump cars, which are hauled away by a locomotive.

Soft material such as sandstone, clay, and chalk is cut through by automatic machines [Key]. One of the largest of these machines to be used cut five 29-ft (9-m) tunnels through 1,600ft (480m) of sandstone and limestone during the building of Pakistan's Mangla Dam in 1963. Machines of this kind have a hydraulic cutting head that turns slowly and scrapes out the material at the face of the tunnel. This is lifted by a mechanical shovel on to a conveyor that carries it back to dump cars behind the machine. Mechanical arms lift and place in position huge prefabricated sections of concrete tunnel lining.

Shallow tunnels are sometimes built by the "cut and cover" method. A deep trench is excavated, the completely roofed tunnel lining is built at the bottom, and this is then covered with excavated material.

In underwater tunneling the working area may have to be pressurized so that the internal air pressure exceeds the pressure of water. After placing the tunnel lining, engineers pump cement grout, a sealing mixture, around it to make it watertight. Another method sometimes used in water-bearing gravel is to sink tubes on each side of the path of the tunnel and pump in liquid nitrogen. The water in the gravel is frozen solid and the tunnel can then be cut.

KEY

The Mersey Mole, a new soft tunneling machine, was used in 1967 to cut a 34-ft (10.3-m) hole through the soft rock under the River Mersey at Liverpool, England. The machine can cut away the tunnel face and convey the material back to skips running on rails. It also contains handling gear to position prefabricated concrete lining sections.

4

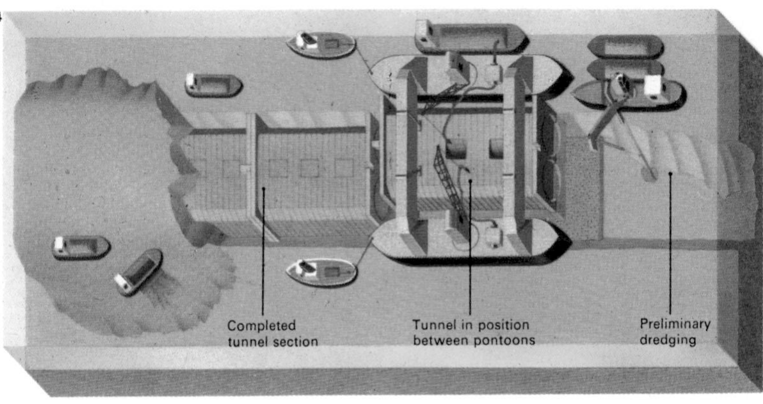
Completed tunnel section
Tunnel in position between pontoons
Preliminary dredging

4 Underwater tunnels are increasingly being built by the immersed tube method. Prefabricated steel or concrete sections of tunnel are sealed at the ends and floated into position. There they are sunk into a trench dredged into the bed of the lake or river. The sections are then joined together end to end with watertight joints and covered with previously dredged material. It is economical to make all the tunnel sections close to the tunnel site and factories for this purpose may be built on the shore; the tunnel sections are floated to the site on barges. Alternatively, prefabricated concrete or steel tunnel sections can be made in a floating dry dock that is moored alongside the site at which they are to be sunk into the dredged trench.

5

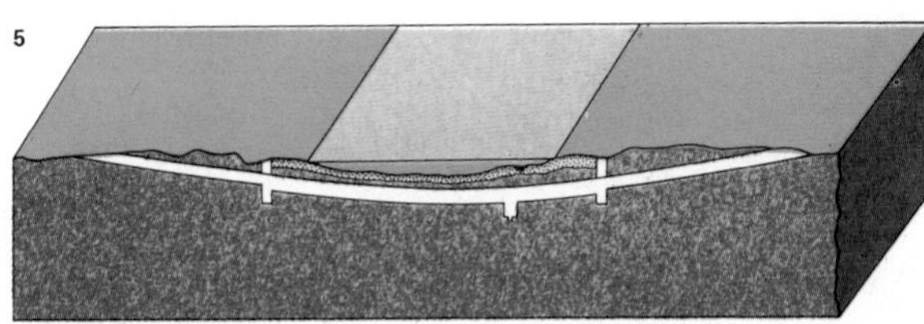

5 The first Mersey road tunnel at Liverpool is shown here in section. The tunnel falls steadily from its portals to a central point where pumps operate to remove any water that may seep in. This tunnel has a diameter of 44ft (13.5m), carries four traffic lanes (with space, never used, for two double-decker trolley lines below), and runs for 2mi (3.2km), half of it under water. The tunnel was hand excavated in four stages. First two pilot tunnels were cut, one above the other, then the entire tunnel was opened out, the top portions first. The Mersey road tunnel was completed in 1934.

6

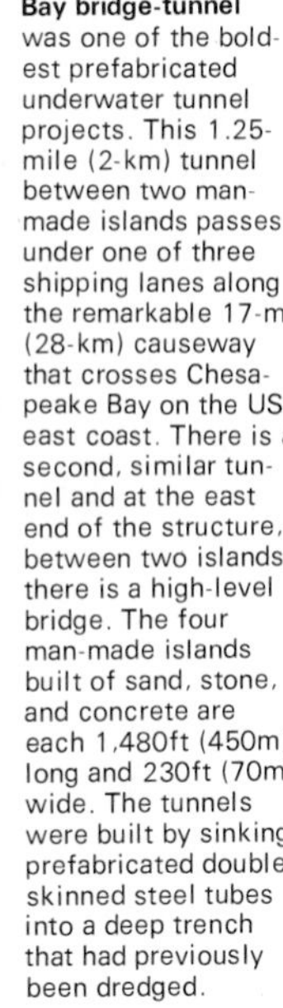

6 The Chesapeake Bay bridge-tunnel was one of the boldest prefabricated underwater tunnel projects. This 1.25-mile (2-km) tunnel between two man-made islands passes under one of three shipping lanes along the remarkable 17-mi (28-km) causeway that crosses Chesapeake Bay on the US east coast. There is a second, similar tunnel and at the east end of the structure, between two islands, there is a high-level bridge. The four man-made islands built of sand, stone, and concrete are each 1,480ft (450m) long and 230ft (70m) wide. The tunnels were built by sinking prefabricated double-skinned steel tubes into a deep trench that had previously been dredged.

7

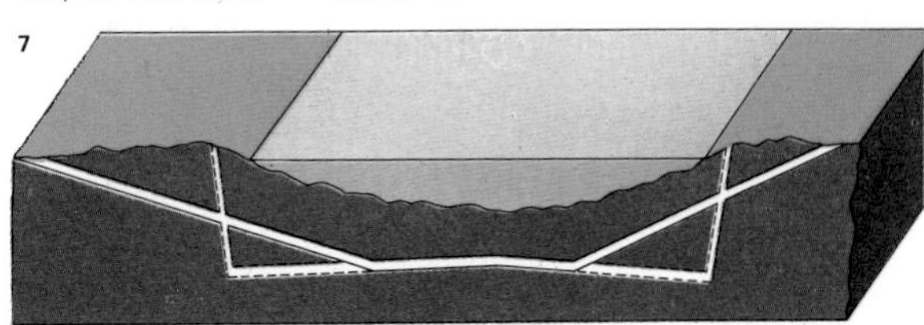

7 The Seikan tunnel, links Japan's main island of Honshu with the north island, Hokkaido. At 22mi (36km) it is the world's longest tunnel. Although 328ft (100m) of rock cover the tunnel under the deepest water, the danger of a leak at high pressure prompted the designers to extend the low section to a lower level at each end, providing a major drain-off facility to the high-power pumping plant. The tunnel runs for 14mi (22km) through volcanic rock. The drilling and blasting method and rock tunneling machines were both employed to excavate the Seikan tunnel.

8

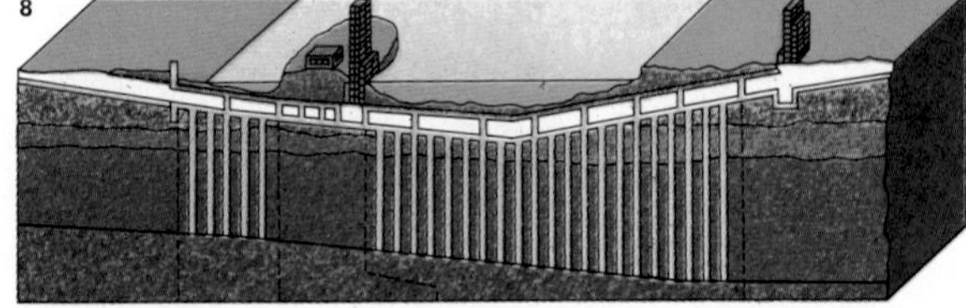

8 The four-lane road tunnel under the IJ river in Amsterdam, completed in 1967, was built mainly by the immersed tube method, although one section, where the ventilation facilities are located, was constructed on site. The prefabricated reinforced concrete tunnel elements were from 220-300ft (70-90m) long and weighed up to 17,000 tons. They were designed as a flat box with two 23-ft (7-m) roadways side by side with service ducts between them and a fresh air duct below each. As the river bed was very soft the tunnel sections were laid on sliding plastic bearings on a concrete raft supported by long piles. The tunnel sections were, waterproofed with a bituminous membrane and steel skin.

History of bridges

The earliest bridges were probably logs thrown across streams or the stone slab "clapper" bridges such as those still surviving in Devon, England. Another type of water crossing was provided by bridges formed by boats fixed together. The Greek historian Herodotus (*c.* 485–425 BC) provided the earliest documentary evidence of a more permanent structure. This crossed the Euphrates River at Babylon about the eighth century BC.

Less durable perhaps, but certainly as remarkable technically, was the bridge of boats built for King Darius (548–486 BC) in 512 BC. It enabled the advancing Persian army to cross the Bosporus and invade southeastern Europe. Darius's successor Xerxes (*c.* 519–465 BC) instructed his engineers to repeat the Bosporus exercise on the Hellespont (now the Dardanelles) [2]. On this occasion two bridges using 674 boats were built side by side spanning 0.87mi (1.4km).

Rivers in mountainous country pose different but equally difficult problems and provoke some equally impressive solutions. Fâ-Hsien, a Buddist monk, writing in AD 412, came across a 300ft (92m) bridge of ropes traversing a deep ravine while he was traveling in India. This form of primitive suspension bridge is known to have been widely used in South America, Central Africa, Southeast Asia, and China as well as in India. Jungle vines served as ropes for many of these bridges, woven split bamboo being used in the construction of others. The Incas of Peru were still building such bridges in the sixteenth century [3].

Roman bridge building

The Romans developed the art of bridge building, like most things they tackled, systematically. The Pons Sublicius built over the Tiber River in Rome in 621 BC was 492ft (150m) long and famous for being defended by Horatius in 508 BC. Built entirely of timber, it was founded on timber piles driven deep into the river bed. The most remarkable Roman timber bridge was the 1,378-ft (420m) structure built across the Rhine River in 50 BC. The last plank was placed just ten days after Julius Caesar had ordered its construction.

The Romans' legacy to bridge building was the heavy masonry arch bridge, hundreds of which were built throughout Europe [5]. In this, large stone blocks were wedged against each other to form an arch. The central stone at the top of the arch was known as the keystone. The finest surviving example of such a bridge is the Pons Fabricius in Rome. Completed in 62 BC, the bridge (now called the Ponte Quattro Capi) has two fine semicircular arches each spanning 78ft (24m). A small "relief" arch in the central springing of the two main arches releases excess water in times of flood.

Priests and professionals take over

So prolific and efficient was Roman building that it was hundreds of years before Europeans took to bridge building anew. Then, surprisingly, it was the Christian Church that, recognizing the advantages of good road communications in a developing society, took the lead. In France a group of interested priests formed a new order, the Frères du Pont, to design and build lasting bridges. Most famous of this order's works

CONNECTIONS

See also
1758 Modern bridges
1750 Traffic engineering
1766 Water supply
1662 Machines for lifting
1704 Technology and transportation in developing nations

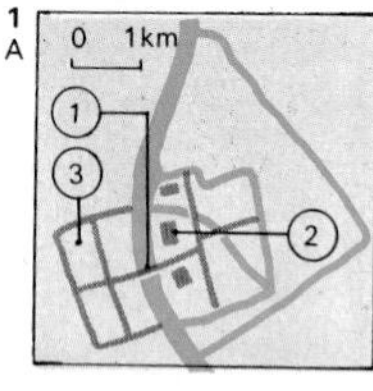

1
A
0 1km
1
3
2

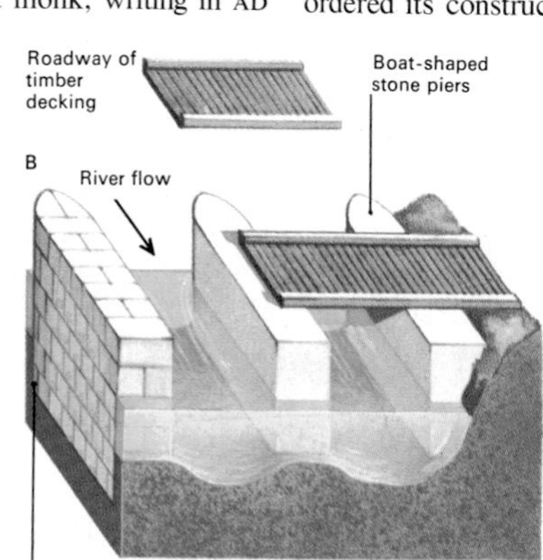
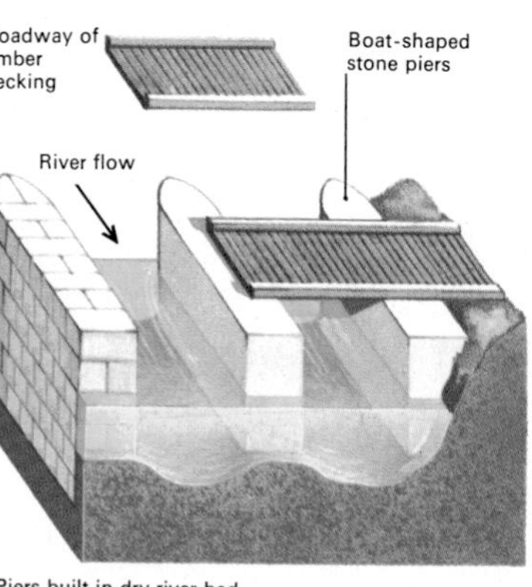

Roadway of timber decking
Boat-shaped stone piers
B
River flow
Piers built in dry river bed

1 This drawing of the Euphrates bridge [B] at Babylon has been projected from ancient records [A]. The bridge [1] connected the old city [2] with a newer residential suburb on the west bank [3].

2 A unit of King Xerxes' army of 480 BC crosses the Hellespont by a bridge of boats in this artist's impression. Alexander the Great crossed the Indus in India on a pontoon bridge.

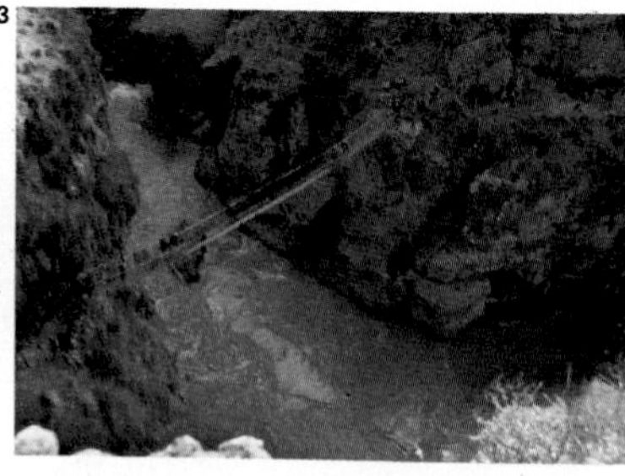

3 Suspension bridges built from jungle vines and stakes have been used for centuries by primitive societies in hilly regions. This Indian bridge in Peru is a typical modern example.

4
Heads of martyrs, traitors and criminals displayed over Great Stone Gate; collapsed and rebuilt 1437–40
Houses joined by gallery (hauptas) spanning street
Nonesuch House (1577) built on site of Newstone Gate
House and shop built over chapel remains
Remains of Peter of Colechurch's chapel

4 Old London Bridge was designed by a priest. Finished in 1209 after 30 years of toil, it had piers built on heaps of rubble dumped in the river and held in place by encircling rows of closely spaced wooden piles driven deep into the river bed. Over one of the piers stood a chapel dedicated to Thomas à Becket. The sixth span from the south was a timber draw span, which could be opened for tall ships to pass. Multi-storied houses and shops were built along the bridge with a wide enclosed corridor forming the roadway below. These buildings were destroyed by fire on several occasions and rebuilt each time in the current architectural style. The bridge's 20 pointed arches varied in span from 15ft (4.5m) to 34ft (10.5m), the pier occupying half the total river width. London's only dry crossing, old London Bridge stood for more than six centuries before being replaced in 1831.

was the Pont d' Avignon, built in 1177 over the Rhône River. It had 21 arches in all, the longest being 115ft (35m) in span. Similarly in England it was Peter de Colechurch who designed and built the first stone bridge over the Thames—the famous London Bridge [4].

Until the late seventeenth century bridges continued to be designed and built largely by priests or architects with a flair for engineering. In Florence the local chamber of commerce commissioned the architect Taddeo Gaddi (*c.*1300–66) to replace the Ponte Vecchio, which had been destroyed by flood. Gaddi's chief design innovation, incorporated in his bridge over the Arno River, was arches that were only part of a semicircle. Gaddi's idea was adopted by the architect-priest Giovanni Giocondo (*c.* 1433–1515). He used the segmental arch in Paris' first masonry bridge, built in 1507.

Such complex and essential work could not rest in the hands of gifted amateurs forever. In 1716, following the work of French army engineers, France took the lead on the rest of the world by forming the Corps des Ingénieurs des Ponts et Chaussées (Corps of Bridge and Road Engineers). Jean Rodolph Perronet, chief engineer of the corps, replaced the segmental arch with the even more daring and flatter elliptical shape [7].

Iron and steel bridges

In 1779 the first bridge to be made of iron was built across the River Severn, England, at Coalbrookdale. The iron ribs and plates were cast at the local works of the ironmaster Abraham Darby.

Wrought iron was the next major material for bridges, and Thomas Telford (1757–1834) used it for the chains of his 580-ft (178-m) bridge of 1826, which spanned the Menai Strait to link Wales and Anglesey. Robert Stephenson's (1803–59) nearby tubular railway bridge (1850) also used wrought iron. For long-span railroad bridges carrying heavy loads, an arch or cantilever is the best design. The steel arch over the Mississippi River at St Louis (1874), built by James Eads (1820–87), was an early type.

KEY
A
B
C

Bridges as a means of transporting people or goods have evolved to meet the needs of society. In medieval times [A] road bridges were used in conjunction with ferries. In the 19th century [B] these were supplemented by rail bridges and in modern times [C] by multi-purpose bridges.

5 A most impressive Roman bridge was built over the Tagus River at Alcantara, Spain. Finished in AD 109, it was 670ft (204m) long with six stone arches and stood 170ft (52m) above the water. The Romans built aqueducts in a similar way, to carry the water supply to Rome. Some of these also had a roadway. All Roman arches were semicircular, giving the name Romanesque to this type.

6 This timber cantilever bridge is of a type that has stood for centuries in Srinagar, capital of Kashmir. Built on stone foundations, these bridges have log piers bridged by Indian cedar.

7 The Pont de la Concorde, Paris, was completed in 1791 by Jean Perronet. He was the engineer who replaced the circular arch with the more graceful ellipse, later to be widely copied by others. The arch under construction is shown supported by timber falsework; a coffer dam enclosing the pier keeps it dry.

8 The stayed suspension bridge at Niagara Falls, completed in 1855 by John Roebling (1806–69), had a rail track above and road below. Spanning 820ft (250m), the main supports for the rail and roadway were cables of wrought iron wire. The stays anchored the structure and reduced vibration in it in winds or when trains passed over it. The decks were hung on wires from the cables.

9 Eads' bridge over the Mississippi at St Louis was opened in 1874. It was the world's first major steel bridge and carried a roadway above a train track. The center arch is 512ft (156m) in span; the others 20ft (6m) less. Eads sank the foundations down to rock using pressurized caissons to exclude water from the working area on the river bed. The main arch had to allow sufficient room above the water level for boats to pass.

Modern bridges

Two nineteenth-century inventions led to a revolution in bridge building. These were Portland cement and mass-produced steel. Cement is the vital ingredient of concrete, and mass concrete can be used to build piers, abutments (bank supports), and arches of "artificial" stone to any required shape. Well-made concrete is extremely strong in compression (when squeezed), but it has very little strength in tension (when stretched). On the other hand, steel can withstand great tension as well as compression, and can be used for building girders of far greater strength than the wooden trusses of early days. High-tensile steel wire cables will support immense suspension bridges.

Reinforced concrete bridges

These materials, concrete and steel, can also be used in combination with each other. For example, a concrete structure does not have to be designed so that the material is entirely in compression, because steel rods can be used to carry the tension.

The French engineer Eugene Freyssinet (1879–1962) overcame the remaining weakness of reinforced concrete (the fact that steel in tension stretches, allowing the concrete immediately around the steel to stretch and frequently to crack) by using high-strength tensioned steel wires as the reinforcement. This technique permitted Freyssinet to "prestress" concrete (preload it in compression), so that it would never be subjected to tension at all. The result was a material so versatile that it could be used to make stronger, lighter, and more architecturally satisfactory bridges.

Type of bridges

There are four basic types of bridge: beam, arch, suspension, and cantilever [1]. The beam bridge is, in effect, a pair of girders supporting a deck spanning the gap between two piers. Such a beam has to withstand both compression in its upper parts and tension in its lower parts. Where it passes over supports, other forces come into play. A beam may be a hollow box girder or an open frame or truss.

An arch bridge can be designed so that no part of it has to withstand tension. Concrete is well suited to arched bridge design. When reinforced concrete is used, a more elegant and sometimes less costly arch can be designed and most concrete arch bridges are reinforced.

A suspension bridge consists, basically, of a deck suspended from cables slung between high towers. The cables of high-tensile steel wire can support an immense weight. The towers are in compression and the deck, often consisting of a long slender truss (used as a hollow beam), is supported at frequent intervals along its length.

A cantilever bridge is generally carried by two beams, each supported at one end. Unlike a simple beam supported at both ends, the cantilever must resist tension in its upper half and compression in its lower.

There are also many composite forms of bridges. The bridle-chord bridge is a combination of a long beam (usually a trussed girder) partially supported by steel wires from a tower at one end, or from towers at each end. Most cantilever bridges are designed so that a gap remains between two cantilevered arms that reach out from their

CONNECTIONS

See also

1756 History of bridges
1750 Traffic engineering
1662 Machines for lifting
1736 Armored fighting vehicles

1

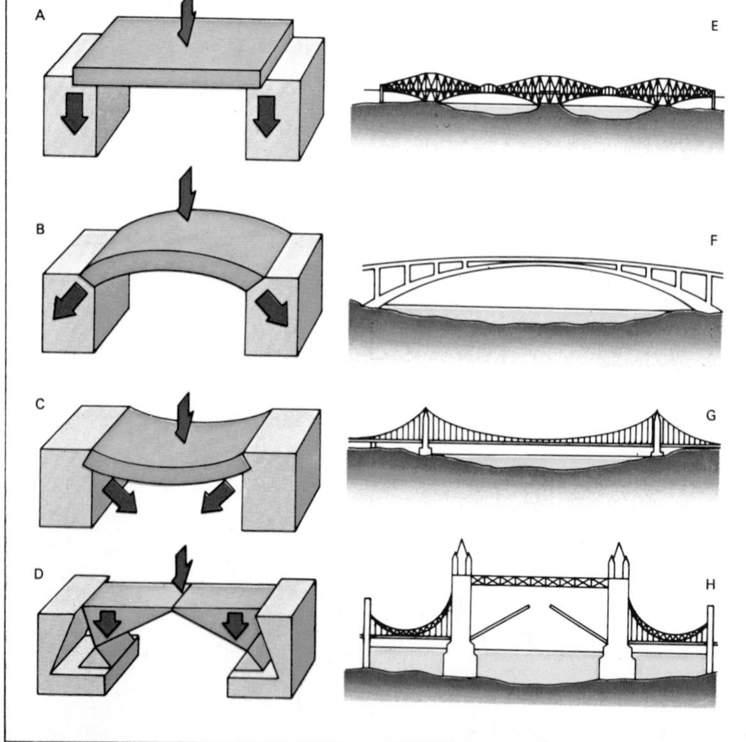

A
B
C
D
E
F
G
H

1 Bridges are of four main types: the beam bridge [A], the arch bridge [B], the suspension bridge [C], and the cantilever bridge [D]. The three main structures of the railway bridge [E] are cantilevers and the two steel trusses that connect them are end-supported beams. In [F] it is the lower member that forms the arch. The suspension bridge [G] has its roadway hanging from enormous steel cables passing over tall towers. The two rising arms of Tower Bridge in London [D, H] are cantilevers, whereas the slender truss that connects the top of the towers is a long beam.

2

2 The Howrah Bridge at Calcutta is the world's fifth longest cantilever, spanning 1,500ft (457m). The two main piers of this bridge were built hollow with twenty-one vertical shafts. By digging out the sand at the bottom of these shafts, the piers were made to sink steadily down until they reached impervious clay. The bridge was opened in 1943.

3

3 The Gladesville Bridge over the Parramatta River at Sydney, Australia, is the world's longest concrete arch. Completed in 1964, it spans 1,000ft (305m) and carries an 8-lane road.

4

4 The Medway Bridge in southeast England is the longest pre-stressed concrete cantilever bridge. Its 490ft (149m) main span is made up of two 196ft (60m) cantilever arms linked by a 98ft (30m) suspended beam.

abutments; the gap is bridged by a simple beam. "Movable" bridges, like London's famous Tower Bridge, have cantilevered arms or "bascules" that can be raised about pivots like a drawbridge.

Most modern bridges have reinforced concrete foundations, often keyed into bedrock. They may have to be designed to withstand the scouring action of tides, buffeting from pack ice, and even mild earthquake tremors. If solid bedrock is too deep to be reached by excavating, foundations can be built on piles driven into the subsoil.

Theoretical limits of bridge spans

A bridge carries two loads. The useful load is the live load of crossing traffic. In addition, it must carry its own weight, the dead load. The longer the span of a bridge, the greater its dead load. Consequently there is a theoretical span limit for any given material and method of construction. Theoretical limits can be compared with current achievements using modern materials. The longest steel arches in existence are the 1,627ft (496m) Bayonne Bridge in New York City and the 1,650ft (503m) Sydney Harbor in Australia. The theoretical span limit for steel bridges of this type is about 3,280ft (1,000m). In theory engineers have considerable scope here. But the limiting factor is cost, and a long steel arch is not usually the most economical method of bridging a wide gap.

The longest steel cantilever is the 1,800ft (549m) Quebec Bridge in Canada. This was a great achievement considering it was completed in 1918. The theoretical cantilever span limit is about 2,460ft (750m).

The longest reinforced concrete arch yet built is the 1000ft (305m) Gladesville Bridge at Sydney, Australia [3].

The modern suspension bridge has the greatest span potential. The longest yet built is the 4,260ft (1.298m) Verrazano-Narrows Bridge at the mouth of New York harbor. The new Humber Bridge, under construction in Britain, will extend this record span to 4,610ft (1,405m). Experienced designers consider a span of 10,000ft (3,050m) to be possible with currently available high-tensile steel.

KEY

The Bosporus Bridge at Istanbul, opened in 1973, has a main span of 3,520ft (1,074m). An example of the modern trend in suspension bridge design, this bridge is far lighter and therefore more economical than many earlier suspension bridges. A similar bridge, across the Humber at Hull, England, will break the world's long span record.

6

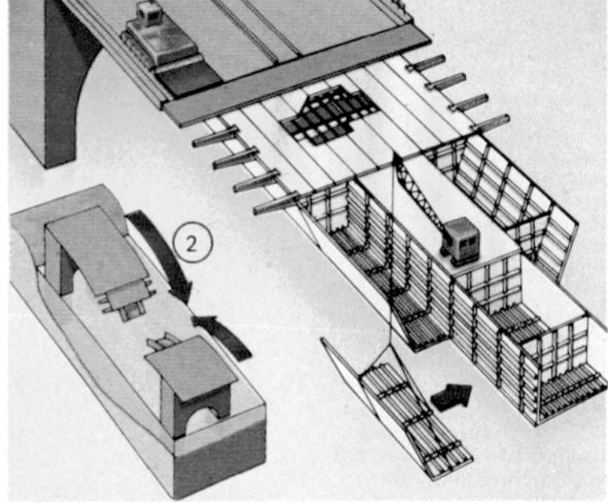
1
2

5 This section of highway interchanges, seen here under construction, is a complex of box girders with simple beams that carry the various links of the interchange over each other. A large number of concrete columns support the many spans. The complete network of highways and box girder bridges is a fine example of the combining of skills of the civil engineer and the traffic engineer.

6 Box girder bridges are increasingly used today because of their high strength-to-weight ratio. Building a bridge of this type often involves construction outward from a support [1] in the form of long cantilevers. The method imposes stresses [2] on the structure that will not occur when it is complete, and it is vital for these to be allowed for. Once complete, the bridge assumes its designed strength.

7 Bascule bridges, which can be either single or double leaf, are shown over the Chicago River. This type of bridge pivots on a horizontal axis and opens upward to allow a clear opening for ships to pass.

8 A vertical lift bridge has two towers spanned by a bridge. Very little power is needed to move the bridge up and down on the towers. Shown is the Arthur Kill Bridge in Elizabeth, N.J., which has a span of 558ft (170.1m).

8

Harbors and docks

A harbor is any place that provides seagoing ships or boats of any kind with a measure of protection from the wind and waves. To fulfil this role, a harbor must be deep enough to accommodate the largest ships that may use it, and have a bottom that will hold them at anchor. A port is a harbor with facilities for transferring passengers and cargo from shore to ship and vice versa.

Natural harbors

A harbor is often a natural product of geography [Key], whereas a port is a manmade communications facility and usually has piers, wharves, quays, and docks. There may be cranes and other cargo-handling equipment, warehouses, customs and excise houses, and passenger facilities, including immigration control. Large ports have repair facilities for ships—perhaps including a dry dock [4]—and means of supplying water, food, oil, and sometimes coal.

The Phoenicians used the natural eastern Mediterranean harbors of Tyre and Sidon from the thirteenth century BC until the Romans ended their power with the sack of Carthage (145 BC). The harbor of Alexandria (founded 332 BC) was an early example of a well-developed port. The natural harbor had land on all sides but the east, where the deep water pier was built within the protection of a line of reefs.

To guide ships safely into the harbor, Ptolemy II of Egypt built the 443-ft (135-m) Pharos lighthouse, one of the Seven Wonders of the ancient world, in about 280 BC.

The growing prosperity of Europe in the Middle Ages led to the establishment of extensive trade through the ports of Venice and Genoa, where docking and repair facilities were provided. Genoa was the terminal for sea communication with western Europe via the Straits of Gibraltar, whereas Venice was the link with Constantinople, which had direct overland trading contact with the countries of the Far East.

Among early British harbors known to have been developed by primitive civil engineering techniques were those built at Hartlepool (1250 AD) and Arbroath (1394), where the works consisted basically of protective breakwaters. Dover, formerly an exposed seaside town, was provided with an artificial harbor in the reign of Henry VIII by the construction of an enclosing breakwater of stone and timber.

Until the eighteenth century most harbors were natural. It was the Industrial Revolution in England that saw the founding of the science of harbor engineering by John Smeaton (1724–92), Thomas Telford (1757–1834) and John Rennie (1761–1821).

One of the most famous harbor constructions in recent times was Mulberry Harbor, built by the Allies and used during World War II for the invasion of Normandy (1944). It was constructed of prefabricated concrete sections and floated to the French coast. There it provided an instant harbor for the landing of troops and supplies.

Harbor types

There are four main types of natural harbors. There are harbors in a coastal bay [1], river estuary harbors [3], inland harbors, and open roadstead harbors where a stretch of coast is relatively sheltered from storms (moorings may be protected by break-

CONNECTIONS

See also
1762 Canal construction
1680 Modern ships
1642 Oil and natural gas

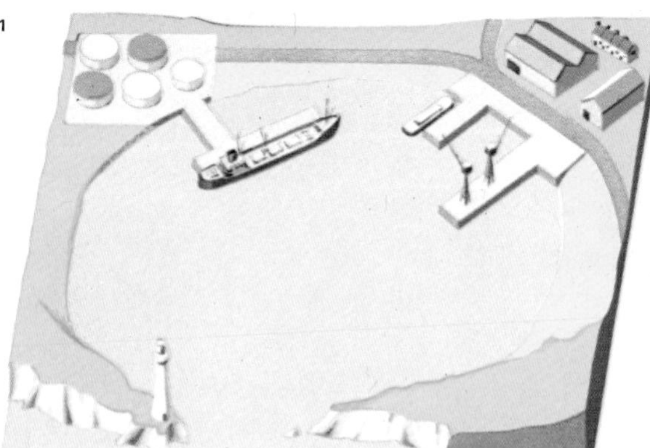

1 **Natural harbors** can be used without necessarily introducing improvements by engineering. They are usually located in sheltered areas, such as enclosed bays or river estuaries. Those at Kingston (Jamaica), Southampton (England), and San Francisco are examples. New York Harbor is one of the finest natural havens in the world with deep water, shelter, accessibility, small tidal variation, and moderate current.

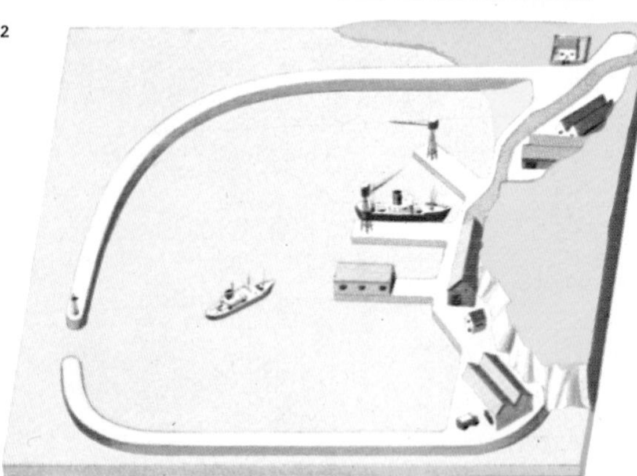

2 **An artificial harbor**, or shelter, can be formed in an exposed bay by the construction of a breakwater projecting from each shore. A single entrance is left open where the deepest water is found. The harbor at Colombo, situated in an exposed location, in an embayment on the coast of Sri Lanka, is typical. Others are the ferry port at Dover in the English Channel and the port of Monaco on the Mediterranean.

3 **Estuaries** often have wide entrances and then the river gradually narrows. Tides, therefore, are accentuated. The great tidal variation necessitates various devices to keep a relatively constant level between vessels and the shoreside facilities. At ports such as London, Liverpool, Le Havre, and Antwerp large artificial basins are provided, separated from the tidal estuary by locks (wet docks) through which sea-going ships can enter.

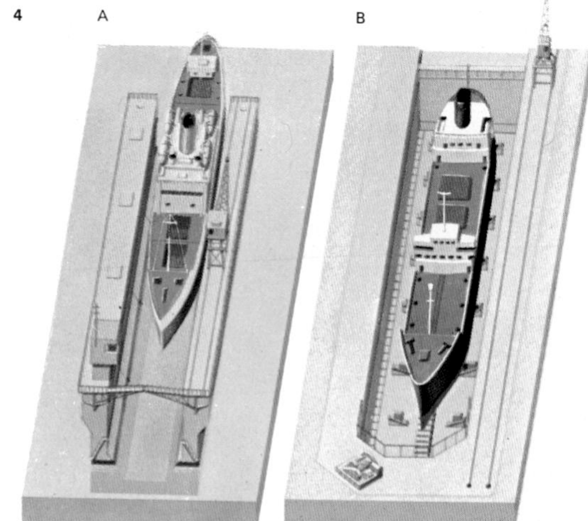

A
B

4 **In a floating dock,** or a dry dock, underwater ship repairs are carried out. A floating dock [A] is partly submerged and the ship is brought in. A dry dock [B] is a solid permanent structure.

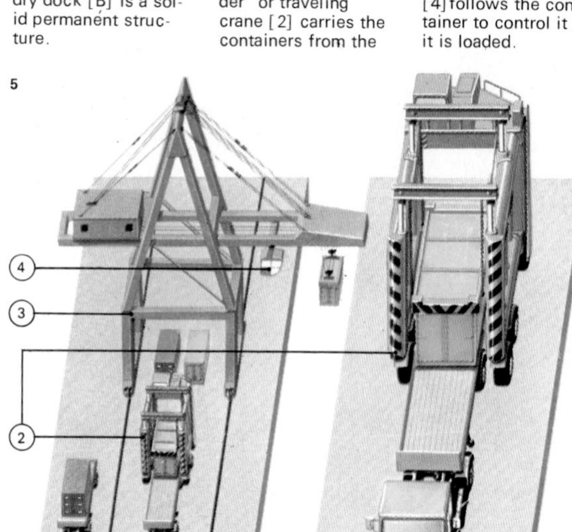
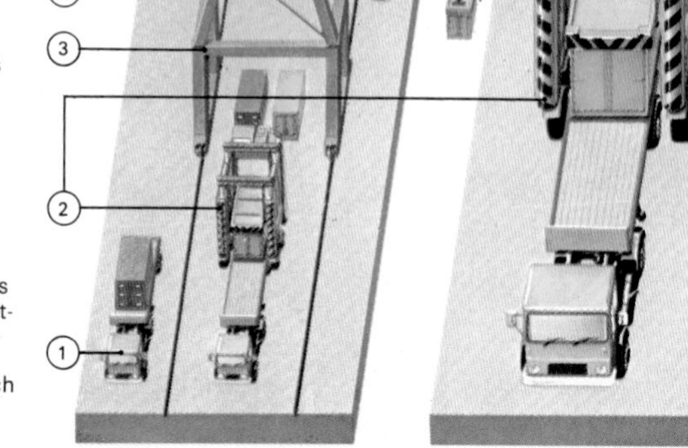

4
3
2
1

5 **The container dock** is equipped with special devices for handling prepacked cargo. A truck [1] brings containers to the dock. The "Spider" or traveling crane [2] carries the containers from the truck and places them in a suitable position for the crane [3], which loads the containers onto the ship. The crane's central cabin [4] follows the container to control it as it is loaded.

waters). Ports, too, are of four main types: commercial ports, naval ports, fishing ports, and (a modern development) leisure ports, often called marinas, for yachts and power craft.

Commercial ports are vital to today's economy based on industry and trade, and they play a variety of specialized roles. There are highly mechanized cargo ports, including container ports [6]; passenger ports for ocean liners; short-haul passenger and drive-on ferry ports; and the new hoverports.

There are many natural harbors in the world, and among the finest in constant use are New York, San Francisco, Liverpool, Buenos Aires, Montevideo, Le Havre, Brisbane, and Sydney. Of these New York has the advantage of enormous capacity providing about 450mi (720km) of potential natural berthing along with 150mi (240km) of man-made piers. The inner harbor is a perfect landlocked haven with adequate depth, a tidal range of less than 5.6ft (1.7m), and moderate tidal currents. The outer harbor, beyond the Verrazano Narrows, is protected by extensive sandbanks.

Inland ports are typified by Chicago, situated on Lake Michigan. It is 1,900 miles (3,000km) from the Gulf of St Lawrence, but connected to it. The channel runs via Lake Huron, Lake Erie, and the 30ft (9m) deep Welland Ship Canal, which carries ocean-going ships 27mi (44km) from Lake Erie to Lake Ontario (bypassing the Niagara Falls). From there it runs along the St Lawrence Seaway, via Montreal and Quebec, to the Atlantic Ocean.

Port maintenance

Most important of the maintenance operations of most river ports (and the majority of the world's ports are river ports) is dredging out the silt that accumulates in estuaries. Most modern ocean-going ships have a draft (depth below the waterline) of between 33 and 49ft (10 and 15m) and trailing suction dredges are kept constantly at work maintaining the depths of the channels. Modern supertankers need up to 82ft (25m) of water, so modern oil ports require unusually deep channels.

KEY

Falmouth's natural harbor on the south coast of Cornwall, England, has had a place in history for hundreds of years as a haven for ships seeking shelter from Atlantic storms, as a coastal port, and as a postal station. Today it is used as the headquarters of the Royal Cornwall Yacht Club.

6

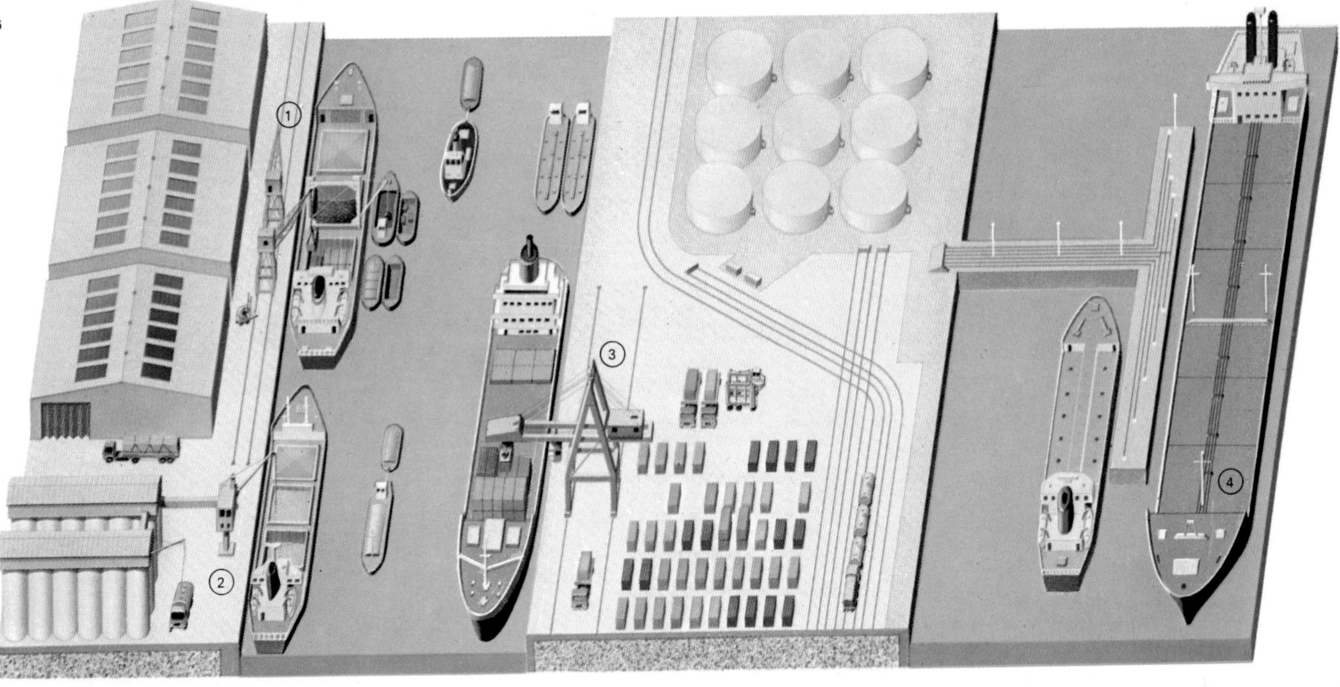
1
2
3
4

6 A multi-purpose port handles various types of cargo from different types of ships. When a regular cargo ship unloads at a typical dockside [1], the cargo is removed from the open hold by cranes and stored in warehouses. The cranes are generally mounted on rails so that they can be moved anywhere along the quayside. Some cargo may be unloaded by means of pumps connected with dockside silos. A container ship [3] provides a maximum speed and efficiency for mixed cargo, as described in [5]. Today's large oil tankers [4] and supertankers have too great a draft to be able to dock normally in a port. They may moor offshore, unloading their crude oil by hose to land or into smaller tankers.

by the ship's own derricks into barges or lighters moored alongside. A bulk grain ship [2] is loaded or unloaded

7

Million tons

250
225
200
175
150
125
100
75
50
25

Rotterdam
New York
Marseille
Antwerp
London
Tokyo

7 The cargo-handling capacity of a modern port is in proportion to the capital invested in cranes and other heavy mechanical handling devices. Apart from the traditional luffing crane running on dockside rails, special grab cranes are used at industrial ports for the handling of coal and ore. Floating cranes, operating from pontoons, are used for unusually bulky and heavy lifts. Rotterdam currently handles more goods each year than any other port. Next in size are New York and Marseille. Each crate on this diagram represents 25 million tons of cargo in and out of the ports each year. The port of Rotterdam handles 268 million tons a year, New York 132 million, Marseille 83 million, Antwerp 67 million, London 66 million, and the port of Tokyo 46 million. In the 20 years up to the mid-1970s the tonnages handled by some of these ports increased by seven times.

8A

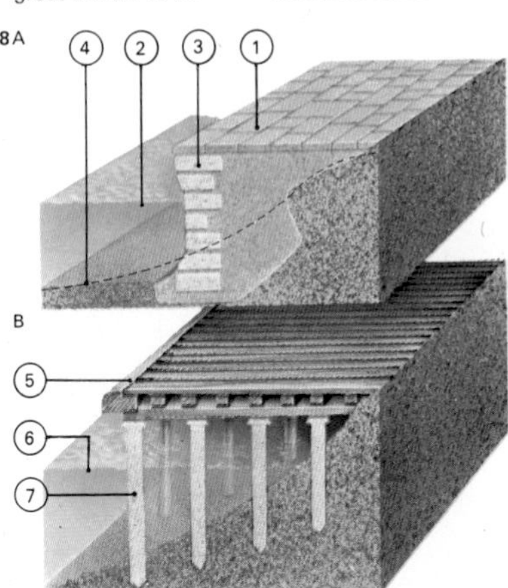
4
2
3
1
B
5
6
7

8 Harbor construction presents many problems. These necessitate building firm foundations and protecting against salt water corrosion. Quay construction varies. The solid type [A] has a paved apron [1] above the water level [2], supported by concrete blocks [3]. The bottom is dredged [4]. In one pile type [B] the timber apron [5] above the water level [6] rests on concrete piles [7]; it can be backed by sheet piling.

Canal construction

Modern canals provide important transport highways throughout Europe and, to a lesser extent, North America. The rivers Rhine and Moselle feed an extensive canal system in Germany that has connections to the Dutch, Belgian, and French networks. A new major waterway is under construction to connect the Rhine with the Black sea, via the rivers Main and Danube, and a great network has already been developed around the rivers Volga, Ob, Yenisei, and Lena across the Soviet Union.

Canals ancient and modern

The four greatest achievements by canal engineers were undoubtedly the Suez Canal, opened in 1868 [8], the Panama Canal, completed in 1914 [6], the canals of the St Lawrence Seaway, opened in 1959 [2], and the 200 miles (320km) of canal linking the White Sea to the Baltic, opened in 1975.

One of the earliest reports of a man-made canal tells of one completed by Ptolemy II (d. 247 BC) of Egypt to link the Nile River with the Red Sea. Natural inland waterways such as major rivers had been used as transport routes since earliest times and primitive single-gate locks are known to have been used in China from about 500 BC. These were openings in dams through which water poured. Boats were carried downstream by the rushing waters or pulled upstream by means of winches. A two-gate lock, built at Vreswijk, Holland, in 1373, is believed to have been the first true pound-lock—a lock in which the flow of water is controlled by alternately lifting up or lowering the gates. The first to have swinging miter gates of the kind used today was designed and built by Leonardo da Vinci (1452–1519). Miter lock gates, when closed, form an angle pointing upstream so that water pressure holds them shut.

In 1681 French engineers made history when they completed the 155-mile (250-km) long Canal du Midi linking the Atlantic Ocean with the Mediterranean Sea by a man-made waterway. It had many locks connecting the Garonne River near Toulouse, with the Etang de Thau River near Séte and included three aqueducts and a tunnel.

The greatest single obstacle to the industrial development of Europe and the United States in the eighteenth century was poor internal transportation. The needs of industry brought about the dawn of the canal age on both sides of the Atlantic.

In the United States canals were built to link the Ohio and Mississippi basins [1] with east coast ports to provide routes from inland areas to the navigable rivers. The most spectacular early American achievement was the completion, in 1825, of the 363-mile (580-km) Erie Canal linking New York City with Lake Erie. The lake was subsequently connected by canal to the Ohio River and so to the Mississippi and the port of New Orleans.

By 1850 England was traversed by more than 5,000 miles (8,000km) of navigable rivers and canals. Canals were also constructed throughout Europe, especially along the North Sea coasts of the Netherlands, Belgium, and France.

During the nineteenth century British civil engineers constructed a perennial irrigation system in northwestern India [5] in

CONNECTIONS

See also
1760 Harbors and docks
1766 Water supply
314 Water and irrigatio
1220 The early Industria Revolution

1

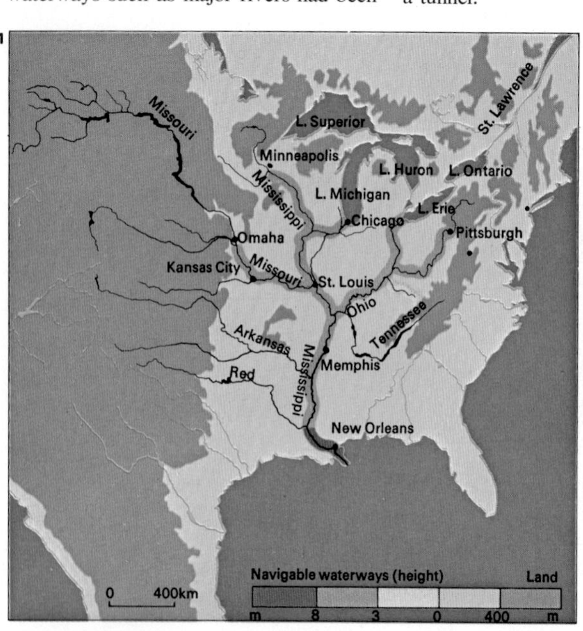

Missouri
L. Superior
St. Lawrence
Minneapolis
Mississippi
L. Huron
L. Ontario
L. Michigan
Chicago
L. Erie
Pittsburgh
Omaha
Kansas City
Missouri
St. Louis
Ohio
Tennessee
Arkansas
Mississippi
Memphis
Red
New Orleans
0 400km
Navigable waterways (height)
Land
m 8 3 0 400 m

1 The river systems of the Mississippi and Ohio form one of the largest in the world. Their basins cross two-thirds of the United States. Many of the rivers are navigable and canals have been constructed to connect other waterways, thus extending the system to provide a continuous water route from New Orleans in the south to Chicago and the St Lawrence Seaway, and, via the Ohio River, to New York City. Pittsburgh and Philadelphia were also in the 19th-century canal network, which connected with Chesapeake Bay. There is also a link from New York City to the St. Lawrence.

2

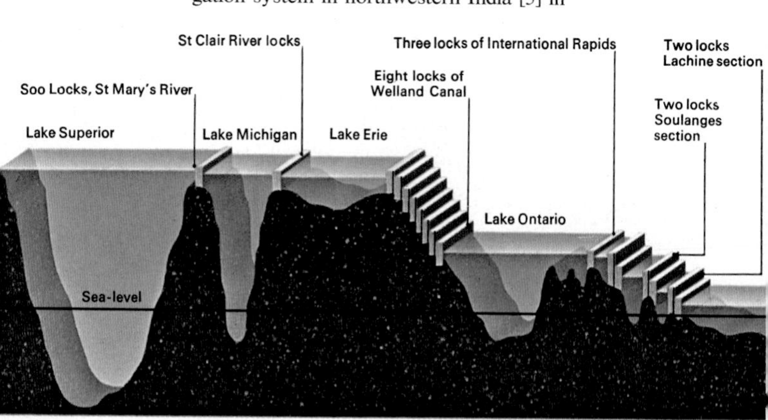

St Clair River locks
Three locks of International Rapids
Two locks Lachine section
Eight locks of Welland Canal
Soo Locks, St Mary's River
Two locks Soulanges section
Lake Superior
Lake Michigan
Lake Erie
Lake Ontario
Sea-level

2 The St Lawrence Seaway provides a 2,380 mile (3,830km) inland route for oceangoing ships from the Atlantic to the heart of Canada and the United States. From Montreal it rises 169ft (51.5m) to Lake Ontario via two small lakes, three canals, and seven locks. Between Lake Ontario and Lake Erie the waterway bypasses Niagara Falls, rising 322ft (98m) in 28 miles (45km) through the eight locks of the Welland Ship Canal. From Lake Erie the route passes via Detroit and the St Clair River and Lake into Lake Huron. This lake connects directly with Lake Michigan, via the Mackinac Strait, thus linking the port of Chicago with the sea. The St Mary's Falls, between the northern point of Lake Huron and Lake Superior, are passed by a canal with five locks.

3

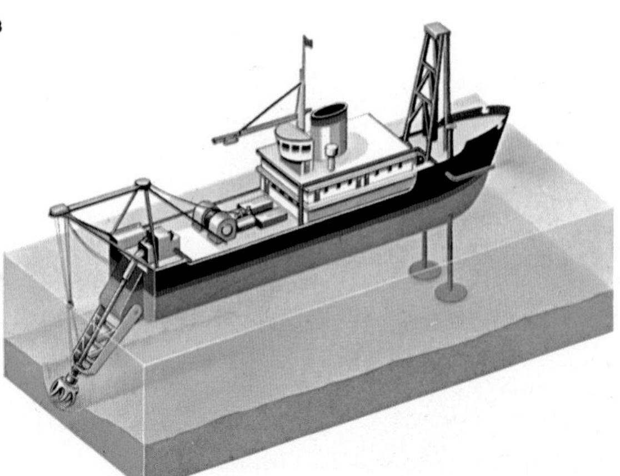

4 A

C

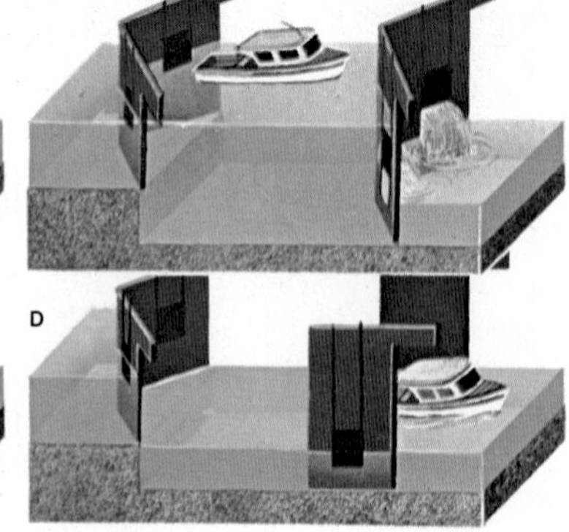

B
D

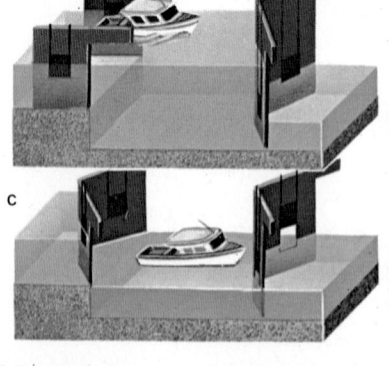

3 The depth of a shipping canal must be rigorously maintained to ensure that ships do not ground, causing delay not only to themselves but to all shipping along the length of the water channel. Dredgers of many types are used. The cutter dredge shown here has a twin-leg bracing system to resist the action of the rotary cutter. A suction pipe close to the cutter draws off the debris and discharges it away from the vessel or into a barge moored alongside.

4 Passing down a lock, a vessel first enters it from the higher level [A], and the gates are shut behind it. Sluices in or around the lower gates are then opened [B], allowing water from the lock to pass to the lower level, lowering the water level and with it the floating vessel. When the lock level equals the lower canal level [C], the lower gates are opened [D]. Sluices in or around the upper gates are used to raise the lock level whenever a vessel passes up the canal.

which huge masonry barriers were built across the rivers to divert part of the water into a great network of canals. By the time India and Pakistan became politically independent in 1947 the subcontinent had more than 50 million acres (20 million hectares) of land under irrigation.

Techniques of canal engineering

A canal, unlike a road, must be built in level sections and the canal engineer's first problem is the selection of a route along which a level can be maintained with the minimum of engineering work. This problem is approached by planning the canal to run as far as possible along natural land contours. Where high ground must be crossed, the cut can be correspondingly deeper or the canal can be built in a tunnel. Where there is an unavoidable depression in the ground, the best solution is to construct the canal along a low embankment. There comes a point where the rise or fall of the land to be traversed requires so deep a cut, so long a tunnel, or so high an embankment or aqueduct that it is more economic to build a lock or series of locks and continue the canal at a new level.

Wherever canals are built there are obstacles, such as roads, streams, and rivers, to be crossed. If there are roads or railroads, bridges must be built; if there are waterways, then either the canal or the waterway must be carried on an aqueduct [9]. Where locks are introduced there must be a sufficient supply of water at the highest level to replace the water that flows each time any lock is used [4].

A canal must not lose excessive water by seepage into the ground. Where the ground is porous, the engineer must waterproof its bottom and sides. In early canals this was achieved by lining the canal with puddled clay. Today there are alternative materials, including bituminous materials, sheet polyethylene, and concrete. Machines have been developed to lay a continuous concrete lining at minimum cost, as in the Jordan Canal in Israel [7]. This type of lining is increasingly used for long-distance irrigation canals in the Middle East and other arid areas.

KEY

A massive excavation 3.5 miles (5.6km) long was made in 1893 across the isthmus at Corinth to link the Ionian and Aegean seas. The Corinth ship canal has no locks, the whole waterway being at sea level to allow direct passage.

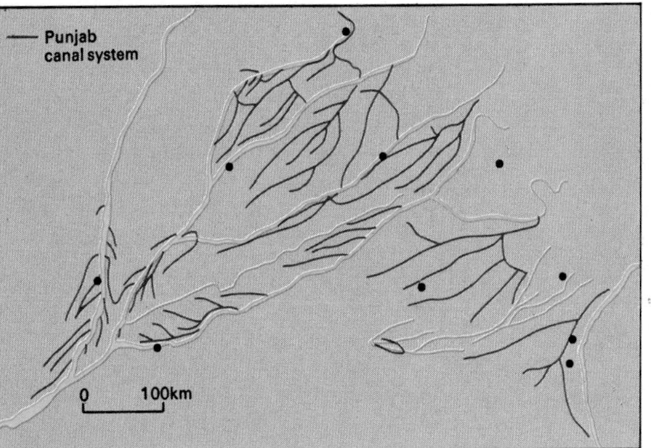
Punjab canal system
0 100km

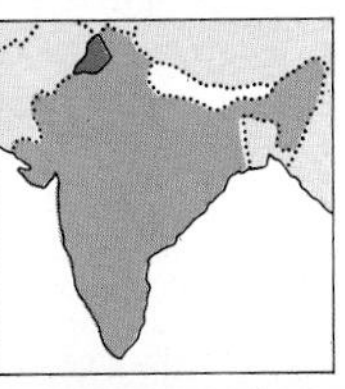

5 A system of irrigation canals in the western Punjab [A] constructed by British engineers was one of the major engineering achievements of the 19th century. These were running water canals fed from the River Indus and its tributaries by building great masonry dams. They turned an arid area half the size of England into northern India's most fertile food producing region [B].

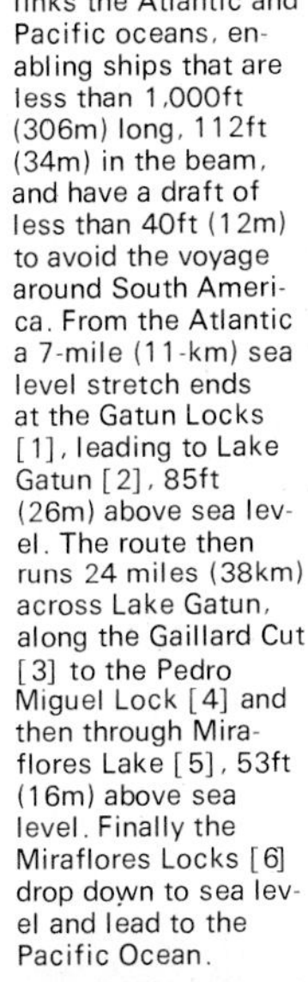

6 The Panama Canal links the Atlantic and Pacific oceans, enabling ships that are less than 1,000ft (306m) long, 112ft (34m) in the beam, and have a draft of less than 40ft (12m) to avoid the voyage around South America. From the Atlantic a 7-mile (11-km) sea level stretch ends at the Gatun Locks [1], leading to Lake Gatun [2], 85ft (26m) above sea level. The route then runs 24 miles (38km) across Lake Gatun, along the Gaillard Cut [3] to the Pedro Miguel Lock [4] and then through Miraflores Lake [5], 53ft (16m) above sea level. Finally the Miraflores Locks [6] drop down to sea level and lead to the Pacific Ocean.

6

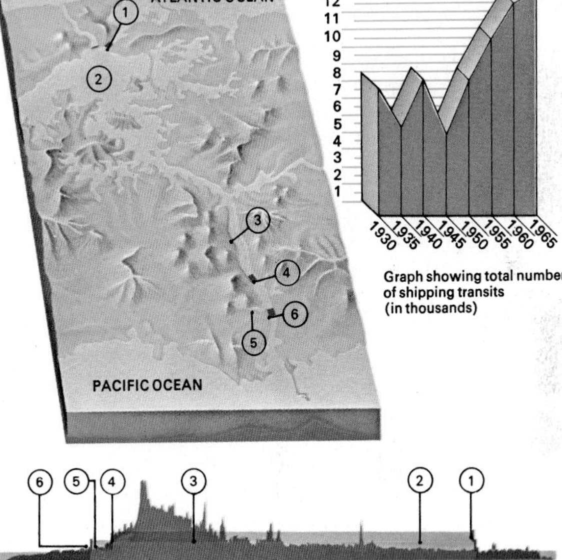
ATLANTIC OCEAN
PACIFIC OCEAN
1
2
3
4
5
6
13
12
11
10
9
8
7
6
5
4
3
2
1
1930
1935
1940
1945
1950
1955
1960
1965
Graph showing total number of shipping transits (in thousands)

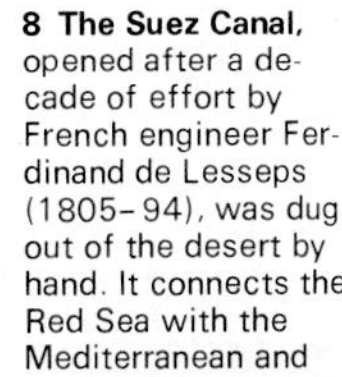

7 Construction techniques in canal engineering include the use of special lining machines, as in the Jordan Canal section of Israel's National Water Carrier. Wet concrete is fed onto a conveyor belt and, as the machine moves forward on caterpillar tracks, an even layer 4in (10cm) thick is laid as a continuous strip. The Israeli system carries water 17 miles (28km) from Lake Tiberius southward in an open canal to feed a pipeline extending much farther to the south.

8

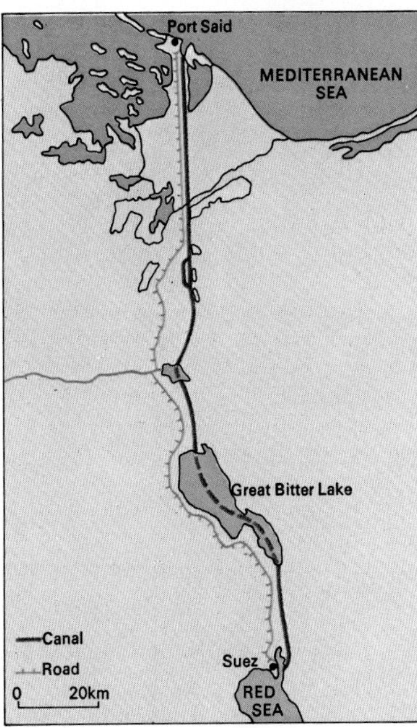
Port Said
MEDITERRANEAN SEA
Great Bitter Lake
Canal
Road
0 20km
Suez
RED SEA

8 The Suez Canal, opened after a decade of effort by French engineer Ferdinand de Lesseps (1805–94), was dug out of the desert by hand. It connects the Red Sea with the Mediterranean and covers a distance of 105 miles (169km). It has a minimum width of 500ft (150m) and a minimum depth of 33ft (10m). Great Britain bought a controlling share in the canal from the Khedive of Egypt in 1873 and retained control until Egypt's President Nasser nationalized it in 1956. The canal was blocked with sunken ships during the 1967 Arab-Israeli war and was reopened only in 1975.

9

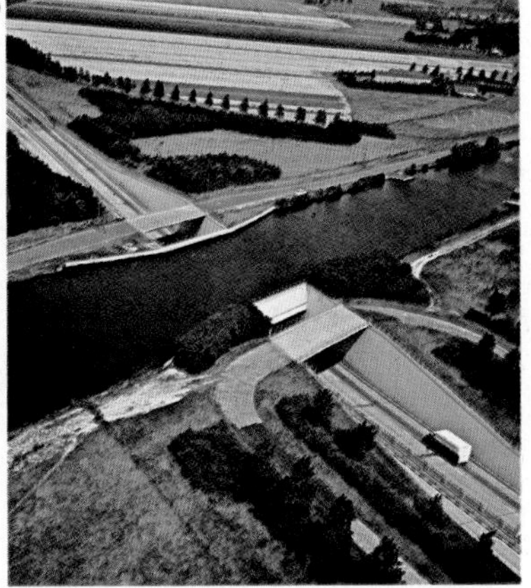

9 An aqueduct built over a road is often necessary in canal engineering for economic reasons, as in this case in the Netherlands. Because the canal is filled with water it has to be built to one level throughout, or in level reaches connected by locks. This is achieved by judicious choice of route, by cutting deeper into high ground, and by building on a raised embankment over low-lying areas. Most roads cross canals by bridges.

Building dams

Control of his life-sustaining water supply has always been one of man's primary concerns. For 5,000 years, dams have been instrumental in this control, being used to avert floods, divert rivers, store water, and irrigate land. Many of today's constructions fulfill these same age-old functions; dams are still used for agricultural irrigation and domestic water storage and supply, as well as for the more sophisticated purposes of hydroelectric power generation, land reclamation, control of erosion by floods, and the prevention of build-up of silt.

The first recorded construction is the earth dam built on the Nile River in about 3000 BC by Menes, first pharaoh of Egypt. Enclosing clay banks were used to retain river water on land when the annual flood receded. This system has been continued into the present day in India and the Far East.

The use of barriers to divert part of a river's flow into irrigation canals was developed by British engineers during the nineteenth century and used widely in the Punjab of northern India. French engineers built a similar barrier across the Nile, which allowed the summer flood to pass over it but formed a reservoir from which the water was led, during the spring and early summer, into irrigation canals.

The development of modern engineering materials and techniques have since made it possible not only to divert part of a river's water, but also to hold and store water by the creation of huge lakes behind a solid dam wall. A typical early example is the Hoover Dam, built across the Colorado River in the United States. Completed in 1936, this great dam has a reservoir capacity of 49 billion cubic yards (38 billion cubic meters) and a power output of 1,340 megawatts.

Dam design

There are two main types of modern dams: embankment dams, built from earth and rock fill, and concrete dams (which may or may not be reinforced). Embankment dams came first and today are generally the cheapest to build because they need fewer workers. They include the world's tallest dams, such as the 1,071ft (310m) Nurek Dam in the Soviet Union, and the 770ft (234m) Oroville Dam in California. They are built from the natural earth and rock found near the site, consisting essentially of a central earth core to hold back the water, faced and supported on each side with more earth or rock. "Filter curtains" between the various layers prevent fine grains from one being washed into the voids of the next.

Embankment dams are suitable for nearly all sites because they can withstand some settlement of the foundation and do not need strong valley sides. A deep trench filled with compacted clay or concrete forms a curtain to prevent water from seeping under the dam. A line of wells under the foot of the dam collects any seepage water and leads it back to the river.

The greater strength of rock fill allows it to be used with steeper slopes. One of the cheapest types of dam has rock fill with a waterproof skin of bitumen concrete.

There are a number of designs for concrete dams. The simplest, the gravity dam, works rather like a bookend, its own weight

CONNECTIONS

See also
1766 Water supply
1610 Materials for build
1648 Electricity generati and distribution

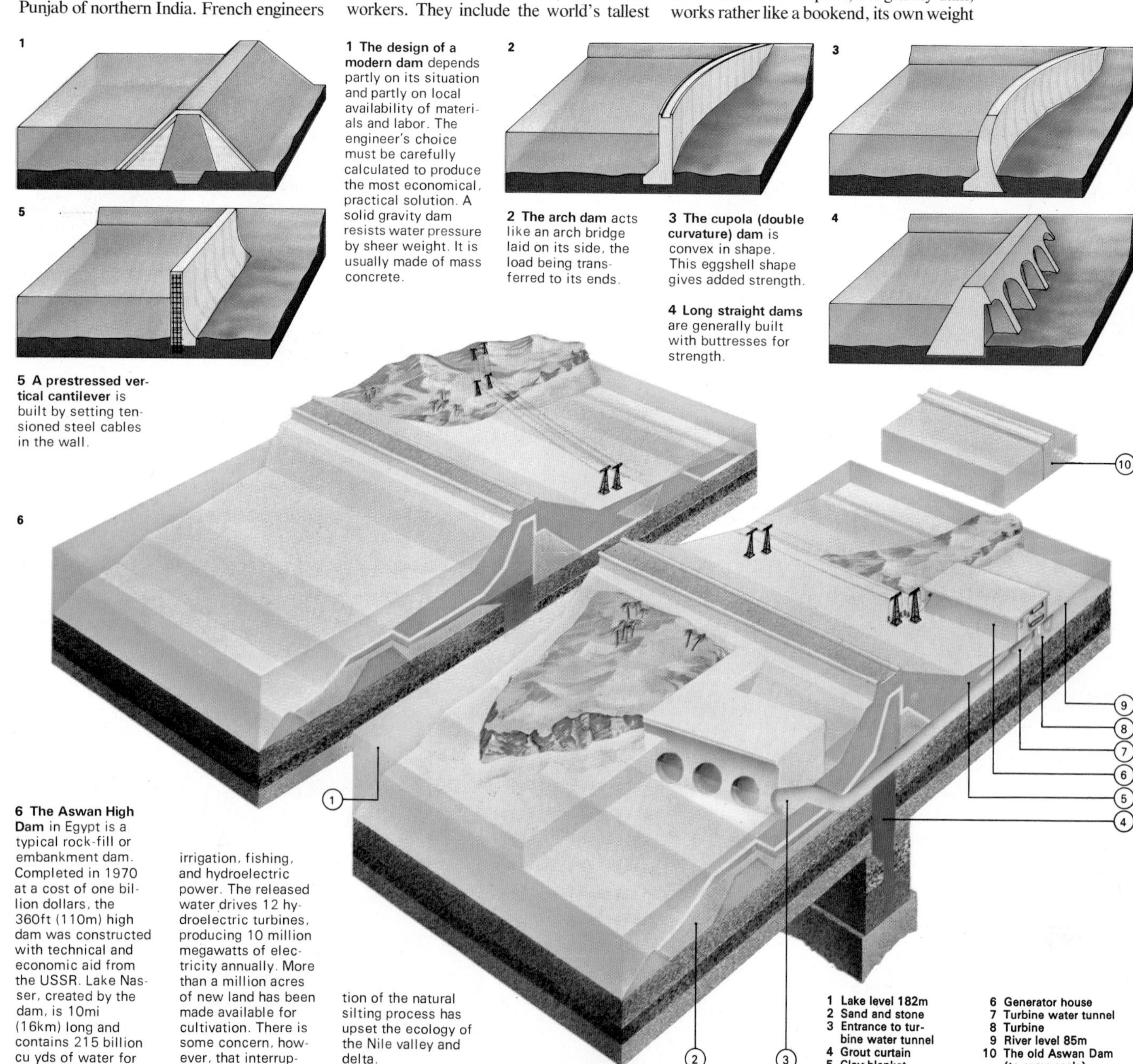

1
2
3
5
4
6
10
9
8
7
6
5
4
1
2
3

1 The design of a modern dam depends partly on its situation and partly on local availability of materials and labor. The engineer's choice must be carefully calculated to produce the most economical, practical solution. A solid gravity dam resists water pressure by sheer weight. It is usually made of mass concrete.

2 The arch dam acts like an arch bridge laid on its side, the load being transferred to its ends.

3 The cupola (double curvature) dam is convex in shape. This eggshell shape gives added strength.

4 Long straight dams are generally built with buttresses for strength.

5 A prestressed vertical cantilever is built by setting tensioned steel cables in the wall.

6 The Aswan High Dam in Egypt is a typical rock-fill or embankment dam. Completed in 1970 at a cost of one billion dollars, the 360ft (110m) high dam was constructed with technical and economic aid from the USSR. Lake Nasser, created by the dam, is 10mi (16km) long and contains 215 billion cu yds of water for irrigation, fishing, and hydroelectric power. The released water drives 12 hydroelectric turbines, producing 10 million megawatts of electricity annually. More than a million acres of new land has been made available for cultivation. There is some concern, however, that interruption of the natural silting process has upset the ecology of the Nile valley and delta.

1 Lake level 182m
2 Sand and stone
3 Entrance to turbine water tunnel
4 Grout curtain
5 Clay blanket
6 Generator house
7 Turbine water tunnel
8 Turbine
9 River level 85m
10 The old Aswan Dam (to same scale)

preventing it from being turned over by the water's force. Volume of material is reduced by a buttress construction.

An arch dam, a more sophisticated construction, is like an arch bridge lying on its side. The curve of the arch is designed so that the concrete (weak in tension) is held permanently in compression. For success, this type of dam has to be firmly keyed into the rock of the valley sides at its ends.

The thinnest type of dam, also with its concrete kept in compression, is the double-curved cupola dam. It is shaped rather like half an egg, with the bulge facing into the pressure of the reservoir water.

Dam foundations

Engineers generally fill fissures in the rock foundation of a concrete dam with a curtain of grout. A drainage system leads away any seepage water, to prevent a build-up of pressure under the dam.

To construct the foundation of a dam while water is flowing, engineers generally drive a diversion tunnel through the rock of the valley wall around the dam site, before construction starts on the dam itself [7]. A temporary dam is then constructed to divert the water into the tunnel.

Every dam construction must allow excess water to flow away in times of flood, without causing erosion in the process. The excess is usually dispersed in one of three ways: by a concrete-lined spillway at a level lower than the top of the dam; by an overflow shaft leading vertically down from a point well within the reservoir; or by an overflow channel or tunnel leading from a point at the side of the reservoir.

Great modern dams

The world's greatest dams (in terms of reservoir capacity) are: Owen Falls, Uganda, built across the Victoria Nile in 1954 and holding a reservoir of about 268 billion cubic yards behind a gravity dam; Bratsk Dam, USSR, built across the Angara River in 1964 (about 220 billion cubic yards), a concrete gravity dam; and Aswan High Dam [6], Egypt, built across the Nile River in 1970 (about 215 billion cubic yards), a rock-fill embankment.

KEY

The Cubuk Dam, 6 miles (10km) north of modern Ankara, straddles the River Cubuk to form a reservoir with a capacity of 13 million cubic yards. This huge man-made lake provides Ankara with most of its water supply and there is a hydroelectric station to exploit the energy of the water flowing out. Set in an attractive wooded valley, this important engineering achievement has played a significant role in the industrial development of eastern Turkey. It has also been promoted as a recreation area and tourist center and has a fine casino and other forms of entertainment.

7

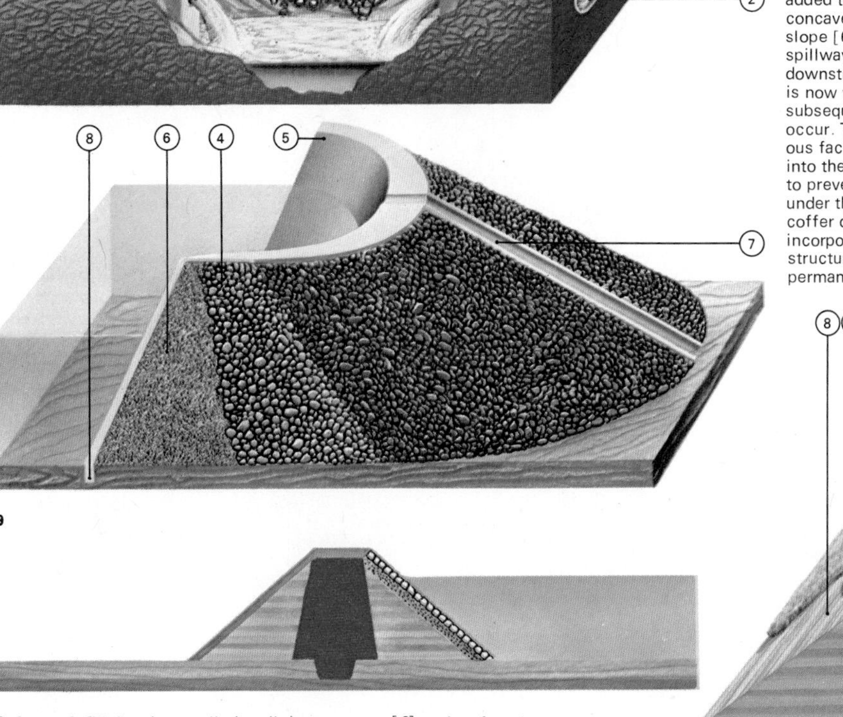

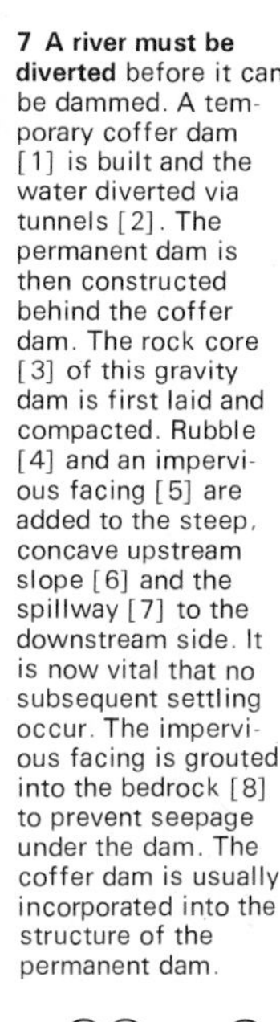

7 A river must be diverted before it can be dammed. A temporary coffer dam [1] is built and the water diverted via tunnels [2]. The permanent dam is then constructed behind the coffer dam. The rock core [3] of this gravity dam is first laid and compacted. Rubble [4] and an impervious facing [5] are added to the steep, concave upstream slope [6] and the spillway [7] to the downstream side. It is now vital that no subsequent settling occur. The impervious facing is grouted into the bedrock [8] to prevent seepage under the dam. The coffer dam is usually incorporated into the structure of the permanent dam.

8

8 Laboratory testing of hydraulic models often precedes the start of work on the actual dam. These models give advance data on patterns of erosion that the water flow may cause. By this means the engineer who designs a river barrier or the outflow channels of a hydroelectric system can avoid the problems of water scour; he includes preventive measures in the design.

9

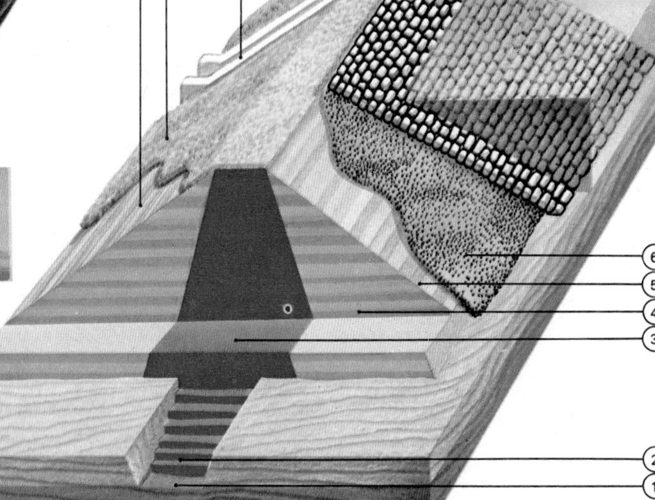

9 An earth-fill dam is begun by digging a trench until impervious rock is reached. This is excavated and the first layer of impervious core material (probably clay) is grouted into this trench [1]. Successive layers [2] of clay are added and rolled until they are completely compact. Once this foundation is ready only the core is formed from impervious material [3]. The rest of the dam is constructed with layers of any soil [4]. The upstream slope [5] is covered with gravel [6] and surfaced with rocks called "rip-rap" [7] to prevent water erosion. The downstream slope [8] is sown with vegetation [9] for stability. A spillway [10] is usually built to allow water to flow over the dam in times of flooding.

Water supply

The more prosperous man becomes, the more water he uses. In developing countries (the Third World), some communities manage with an average of 2.5 gallons (12 liters) of water per person per day. In most European cities the daily domestic consumption per capita of the population is nearer 33 gallons (150 liters). In the most prosperous urban areas of the United States the figure can be as high as 55 gallons (250 liters).

Demands and resources

Domestic water consumption is far outweighed by the demands of modern industry. The production of 2.2lb (1kg) of steel uses 660lb (300kg) of water, although some of this is returned to its source. The total average daily water consumption—domestic, commercial, and industrial—in a large Western city may be as high as 440 gallons (2,000 liters) per capita.

Agriculture's demands are even greater than those of urban consumers. To produce 2lb (0.9kg) of wheat, for example, a farmer may use up to 3,300 pounds (1,500kg) of water from rain, irrigation, or both.

Water is the world's most plentiful natural substance and is in constant circulation [Key]. But man's demand for water often exceeds the local natural supply. It is the engineer's job to transport water to where it is needed and to purify it.

Collection and storage

Water is generally collected from underground sources by drilling and pumping. The old farmhouse well with its bucket—still in common use in many areas—provides an example of the extraction of flowing ground water. A well is made simply by digging a hole until the depth of the natural water table is reached. Trapped "fossil" water, sometimes found under deserts, is not replaced by natural flow and removing it is a form of mining—the extraction of a limited resource. Deep-lying water under pressure can be brought to the surface without pumps by sinking an artesian well, a simple borehole from the surface to the water-bearing strata.

Surface water can be brought into use by pumping it from rivers [2] or lakes, by building a barrier across a river to divert its flow through canals or pipelines, or by constructing a dam across a valley at the lower end of a natural catchment area. Apart from short-term local storage in water towers or tanks, water is normally stored by pumping it into large, open reservoirs or by letting it form huge lakes behind the walls of artificial valley dams.

Water purification

Natural water, other than rain, is rarely pure. Rivers in swampy areas pick up organic acids. Ground water takes up mineral salts including common salt (up to 0.1 percent is tolerable in drinking water), calcium bicarbonate (more than 0.02 percent makes water unacceptably hard), and fluorides (amounts above 0.0001 percent but not exceeding 0.00015 percent are said to help prevent tooth decay).

The Industrial Revolution produced a new problem. The discharge of effluents—factory waste products—into rivers resulted in chemical pollution and the development of waterborne sewage systems

CONNECTIONS

See also
- 1764 Building dams
- 1768 Sewage treatment
- 1614 Building with local resources
- 254 Earth's water supply
- 296 Pollution of rivers and lakes
- 314 Water and irrigation
- 736 Community medicine

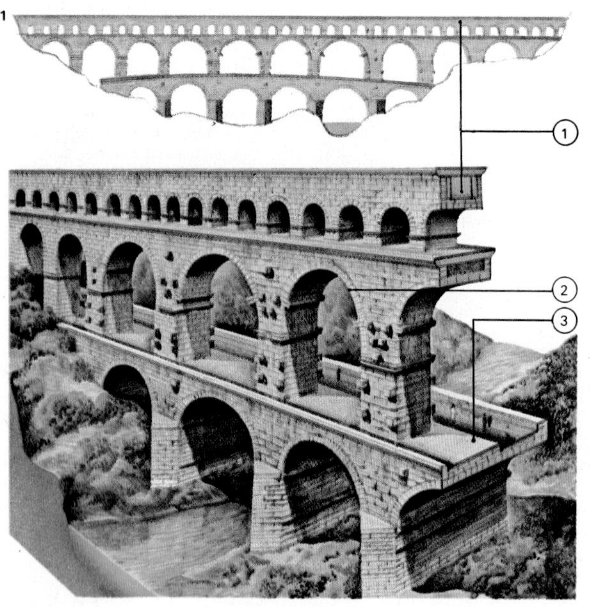

1 One of the first major water supply systems was built by the Romans. Their first eleven aqueducts, constructed between 313 BC and AD 226, conveyed water by gravity feed from various sources to Rome. The longest, the Acqua Marcia, extended 57mi (92km) and bridged low-lying land by a water channel of cut stone slabs raised on a succession of stone arches. Shown here is the Roman aqueduct of Pont du Gard in France. It is 900ft (274m) long. The top tier carries the water channel [1], the lower tier a footbridge [3]. So accurate were the Roman masons that the stones of the two lower tiers of arches, including the keystone [2], were laid dry.

2 As a city grows, so does it demand for water. The London Bridge Waterworks on the Thames River was opened in 1581 to serve the city. The huge waterwheel and pumps could supply 4 million gallons (18 million liters) of Thames water daily. As this substantially lowered the river level, making the passages under the nearby bridge unnavigable at times, the waterworks was later removed. The current turned the great wheel, which rotated the crankshafts [3]. These operated the pumps [4] via levers [1], water being discharged through pipes [5]. The supply of water was controlled by turning the cranks [2], which raised and lowered the pumps.

Lime slurry
Chlorine
Chlorinated ferrous sulphate
Sulphur dioxide
Intake
Sedimentation tank
Activated carbon
Pump
Pump
Sludge lagoon
Rapid gravity filter
Contact tank

3 The modern water treatment plant can be very complex, as this diagram shows. Here raw river water is screened at the intake and drawn by pumps to an upward flow sedimentation tank. A flocculant (chlorinated ferrous sulfate) and softener (lime slurry) are added as the water enters, the lime also regulating the acidity. The sludge formed in the sedimentation tank is pumped to a sludge lagoon from which the clear water is recycled. Activated carbon is then added to absorb impurities of the kind that give an unacceptable taste, smell, or color to water. The water then flows into a rapid gravity filter in which any organic matter is decomposed by nonpathogenic bacteria to form unobjectionable inorganic products. One of two chlorinators supplies chlorine gas as a sterilizer and additional lime is added as the water enters the contact tank. (The second chlorinator feeds the flocculant supply.) A sulfonator feeds the contact tank with sulfur dioxide, which dechlorinates the sterilized water. Finally, the treated water is pumped to the main supply system, where it is stored in water towers or reservoirs before distribution to domestic consumers and industry.

caused bacterial pollution. Today many countries have laws to control chemical pollution and the bacteria of disease are eliminated by treatment.

The principal processes of water treatment [3] are sedimentation, filtration, aeration, and sterilization. The sedimentation process allows solid particles in the water to settle slowly to the bottom of large, shallow basins. Its efficiency is increased by adding a flocculant, such as alum, which causes the smallest particles to clump together. Filtration is carried out by passing water through a bed of sand—328ft by 131ft (100m by 40m) is a typical size. Harmless bacteria—in a layer 12in (30cm) deep—decompose organic matter in the water passing through, forming unobjectionable inorganic substances, but the filtered water is not entirely bacteria-free.

Aeration (generally carried out by passing water over a cascade) increases the amount of dissolved oxygen in the water, reduces the carbon dioxide content by as much as 60 percent, and aids natural purification by aerobic bacteria. Where bacterial pollution has been high, sterilization (killing harmful microorganisms) is achieved by adding small quantities of chlorine or ozone. A dose of 0.0001 percent chlorine destroys all bacteria and viruses within ten minutes.

Water can be demineralized (softened) if it has to be exceptionally pure. In this process the "salt" parts of soluble mineral salts are exchanged for insoluble ones. Sea water can be made fit to drink (and fit for irrigating crops) by removing its salts, a process called desalination. The main processes are distillation, electrodialysis, reverse osmosis, and freezing. Multi-stage flash-distillation [5] is used in most modern desalination plants, using steam as the source of heat.

Today most water is distributed by pumping it to a local storage facility (generally a water tower), which provides sufficient static "head" or pressure to force the water through a network of pipes. Large pipes or mains lead into smaller ones and these in turn are used to supply individual business and domestic consumers.

KEY

The hydrologic cycle, powered by the Sun's heat, keeps the world's stock of water in constant circulation. Enormous quantities are moved by evaporation from seas, lakes, and rivers and by transpiration from trees and other vegetation. Water vapor moves through the atmosphere, condensing as clouds, then falls on the land as rain or snow, forming streams and rivers leading back to lakes and seas. It sinks into the soil forming aquifers, reappearing as springs.

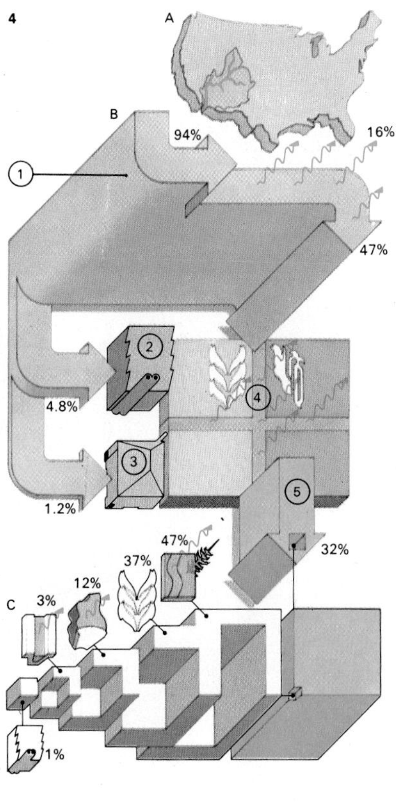
4
A
B
94%
16%
1
47%
2
4
4.8%
3
5
1.2%
47%
32%
37%
12%
C
3%
1%

4 Growing salinity can pollute natural water. Man's "control" of the Colorado River in the United States has caused an excessively high salinity. The map [A] shows the location of the Colorado River. [B] shows how the water obtained from the river is used. The total capacity of the Colorado River [1] is about 27,000 billion gallons (60,000 billion liters) per day; 94 percent is supplied to agriculture, although 16 percent of this is lost in evaporation before it reaches the farms. Of total capacity 4.8 percent is supplied to industry and 1.2 percent [3] for domestic use. Runoff from all uses is 32 percent [5]. Forty-seven percent of total capacity [4] is actually used by agriculture. The runoff is highly saline when it returns to the river. Salinity [C] in the water is caused by evaporation from the river (47%), evaporation from land and transpiration of plants (37%), evaporation from reservoirs (12%), evaporation from canals (3%), and from industry (1%). In highly developed industrial countries industry has been responsible for some other forms of river pollution. Industrial effluents can cause serious chemical pollution and the disposal of waterborne sewage can be responsible for serious biological pollution. Legislation has been passed in many countries to help keep river water clean.

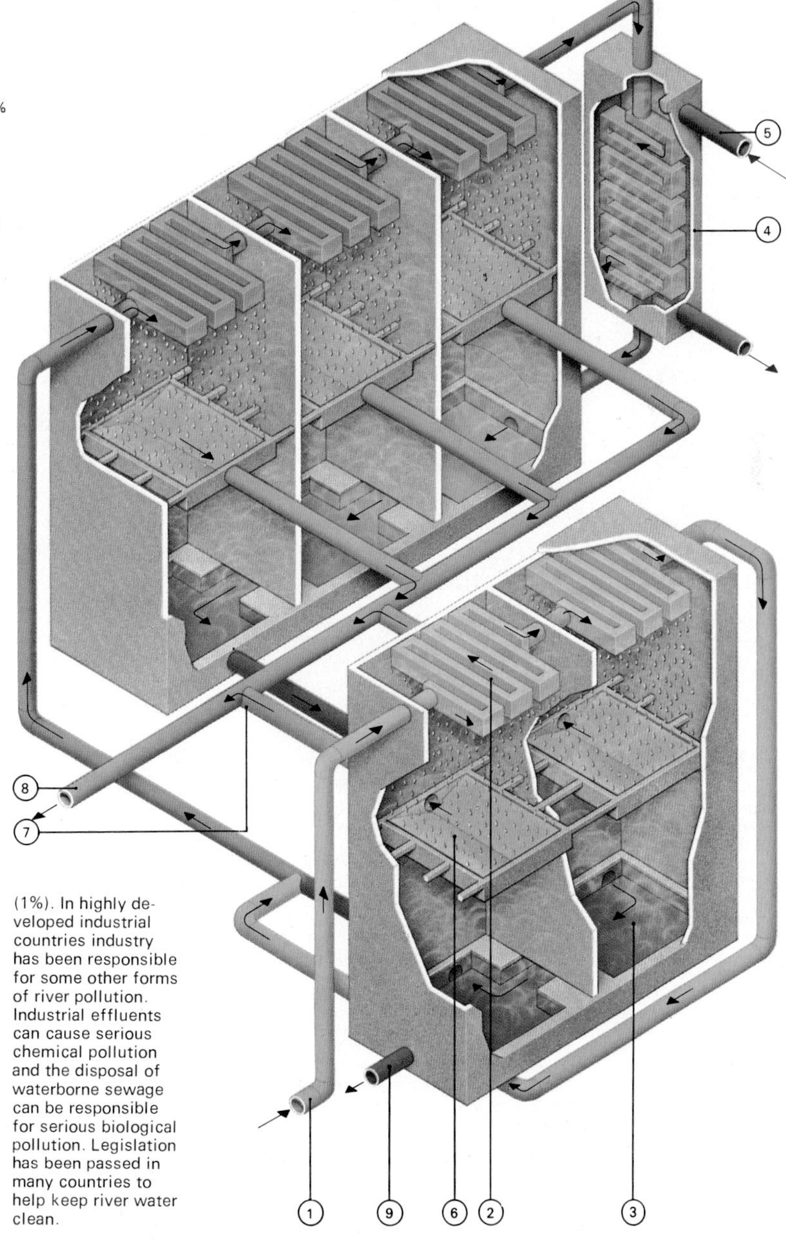
5
5
4
8
7
1
9
6
2
3

5 Desalination by flash-distillation is a widely used process. Raw sea water [1] is fed through the condensing coils [2] of the first two flash chambers. It is then mixed with strong brine from the brine pans [3] of these two chambers before passing on through the condensing coils of the third, fourth, and fifth flash chambers. From there it passes through the heat exchanger [4], where it is heated by steam [5]. The sea water, then at 80°C (176°F), next flows through the brine pans of the five chambers in reverse order. Water vapor rises from the hot brine, condensing on the much cooler coils above. The condensate drips on to the freshwater catchment troughs [6] from which it is piped [7] into the main freshwater outlet [8]. Meanwhile, the hot brine, on its way through the five chambers, grows progressively more concentrated and cooler. When it reaches the first chamber, part of it is recycled by mixing with the sea water passing between the coils of the second and third chambers, the rest being discarded as waste [9]. Modern practice achieves economy in the desalination process by locating the plant, wherever possible, near a nuclear power station. The exhaust steam from the power plant can then be used as the main energy source for the distillation process.

Sewage treatment

As soon as early peoples established settlement they had the problem of getting rid of sewage—their organic wastes and, sometimes, those of domestic animals. Nature disposes of surplus organic material in four principal ways—by dilution, oxidation, putrefaction, and filtration. Early peoples relied on these natural processes and generally dumped sewage in the fields. There its moisture seeped into the land, becoming filtered and purified.

The Roman system of channels, built from 312 BC to AD 226, provided a waterborne sewage system that drained into the Tiber River. Today the large volumes of sewage from towns and cities need the resources of modern technology for efficient treatment and disposal. Industrial wastes present additional treatment problems.

Treatment by dilution

Sewage treatment by dilution works because water contains dissolved oxygen. When sewage contaminates a small volume of water, as in a lake or stream, aerobic bacteria (which oxidize the organic material) absorb the dissolved oxygen at a rate greater than it is naturally replaced from the air. As a result fish cannot live and the water is no longer self-purifying. But if the surface area of the water is large enough to absorb oxygen faster than it is absorbed by the bacteria the water remains pure.

The Thames River in London provides an illuminating case history [Key]. In 1750 the city's population was 750,000 and the river was teeming with fish. It had long been used as a sewer but this had not seriously polluted the water. By 1840 the population was over two million and sewage, swollen in volume by industrial effluents, then exceeded the river's capacity for self-purification.

London's first sewage treatment works were commissioned in 1889. By 1900, with the population at over six million, six of the less sensitive species of fish had returned to its waters. Between the wars London's population grew to eight million people and industry increased. The sewage works could not handle the greater volumes of domestic and industrial effluent and by 1945 there were no fish in the river, which had become more polluted than ever. In the 1950s there was a drive to clean the river. New sewage works were built and by 1970 fish of many kinds had returned.

The dangers of pollution

Health authorities today agree that the disposal of diluted sewage into lakes or rivers is satisfactory—if it contains not more than 30 parts per million of suspended solids and does not absorb more than 20 parts per million of dissolved oxygen in five days. The latter figure, called the "biochemical oxygen demand" (BOD), provides a means of measuring the degree of pollution.

Where there is sufficient water for effective sewage treatment by dilution, as on coasts, on the shores of major lakes, or near large rivers, sewage is sometimes discharged without prior treatment [4]. The growth of industry and high population densities usually require sewage treatment by processes designed to reduce its BOD to a very low figure before discharge and sometimes to eliminate all bacteria.

CONNECTIONS

See also
1766 Water supply
296 Pollution of rivers and lakes
736 Community medicine

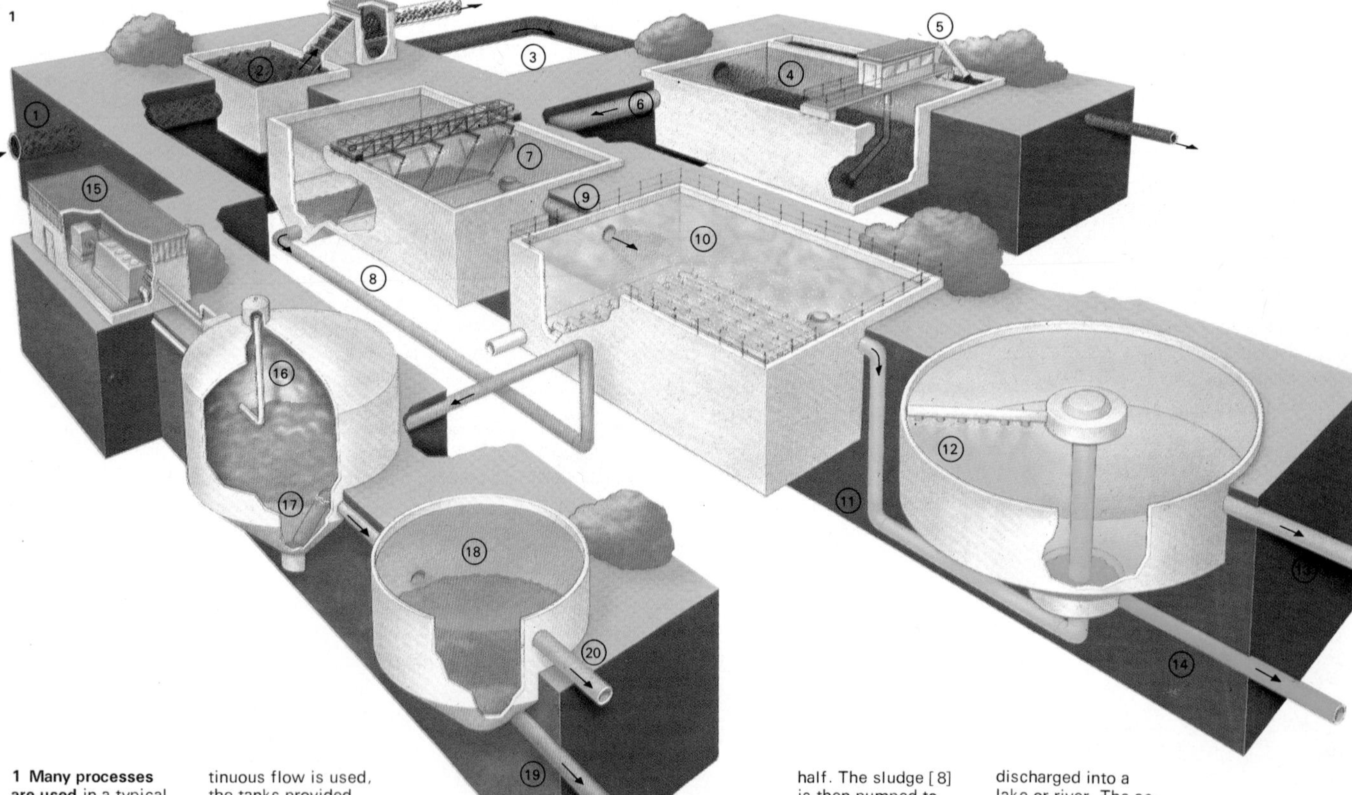
1
1
2
3
4
5
6
7
8
9
10
11
12
13
14
15
16
17
18
19
20

1 Many processes are used in a typical modern sewage plant. The first stage consists of screening to remove solid material including heavy grit. Screenings are burned to destroy microorganisms and render them inoffensive. Fine grit is next removed by gravity settlement. Screened, de-gritted sewage is then led to sedimentation tanks. The remaining suspended solids are eliminated. This reduces the liquid sewage strength by up to one half. As gravity precipitation is a slow process, whether still or continuous flow is used, the tanks provided for this purpose are usually duplicated and made large. The sludge and clear sewage are then treated separately. Clear sewage passes to aeration tanks where the organic content is destroyed by aerobic bacteria. The effluent from the aeration tanks is once again settled, the clear liquid chlorinated and discharged into a river or the sea. Sedimented sludge is fed to digestion tanks where it is warmed and allowed to putrefy in the absence of air. This produces gas, to power the plant itself and to heat the sludge tanks, and a nitrogen-rich "clean" sludge that may be dried for use as fertilizer. A typical process operates in the following way. Raw sewage [1] enters the plant, where coarse screens [2] remove solid trash (wood, rags, and so on) from the sewage so that the machinery is not damaged or pipelines blocked. The screened sewage [3] is then pumped to grit-settling tanks [4], where grit and sand settle out. In some areas these are washed, and used as filling material, such as aggregates for roadbed construction. The settled grit and sand [5] are removed to allow the grit-free sewage [6] to be pumped to the primary sedimentation tanks [7]. During this process a third of the suspended solids settles out to form sludge and the BOD of the settled sewage is reduced by half. The sludge [8] is then pumped to digestion tanks and settled sewage [9] pumped to the aerator [10], in which the sewage is mixed with bacteria-rich activated sludge. As the sewage is aerated the bacteria transform organic matter into harmless by-products. The aerated sewage [11] is pumped to a final settling tank or secondary sedimentation tank [12]. At this stage of the process activated sludge settles out, leaving a clear effluent. The upper liquid part [13] is filtered, chlorine-treated, and then discharged into a lake or river. The activated sludge [14] is removed and reused in the aerator with incoming settled sewage. In the power house [15], gas from the collector [16] – containing about 70% methane – is burned to generate power for pumps and air compressors; some gas is used to heat the digestion tanks. The sludge that settles out is then pumped to the primary digestion tanks [17], which are kept at a temperature of 86°F (30°C). The temperature speeds the action of microorganisms, which, in the absence of oxygen, digest the sludge rapidly, producing gas and a relatively inoffensive sludge. The secondary digestion tanks [18] are where the digestion is completed (unheated), producing concentrated, nitrogen-rich sludge and relatively pure but bacteria-rich water. The sludge [19] is then removed. After going through a drying process it may be used as a fertilizer. Finally, water [20] is drawn off and discharged into a lake, river, or the sea.

Sewage treatment by putrefaction is a natural process in which anaerobic bacteria destroy organic matter by breaking it down into simpler substances. The products are nitrogen-rich humus and a mixture of gases in which methane predominates. The primitive pit latrine and the more sophisticated septic tank [2] are well-known examples that make use putrefaction.

Modern treatment processes

A modern sewage treatment plant [1] uses both the natural oxidation and putrefaction processes in treating sewage. It also uses several other processes that may include screening, sedimentation, flocculation, digestion, aeration, filtration, and chlorination. Industrial effluents often require other special treatments.

Screening is simply the removal of large, solid particles by passing the sewage through a wire screen or other form of mesh. Quiescent sedimentation is natural settlement of sediment by gravity in undisturbed tanks. Continuous-flow sedimentation achieves the same result by passing the fluid slowly, without turbulence, through long, relatively shallow tanks and out over a weir. Flocculation, mechanical or chemical, makes nonsettling material coagulate into particles of sufficient size to settle by gravity. Alum is an efficient flocculent but is too expensive for general use. Mechanical flocculation is achieved by slow stirring.

Digestion uses natural aerobic putrefaction, producing gas and a sludge which, when dried, may be used as fertilizer. Some sewage plants use the gas to produce power and light, and often warm digestion tanks by passing gas-heated water through coils fixed inside them. Heating speeds the digestion process but it is generally too expensive because it consumes too much energy.

Aeration employs natural oxidation to reduce the BOD of clear sewage, following sedimentation. It is commonly achieved by pumping air bubbles through the lower part of the tank and redistributing the clear sewage over the surface in the form of a rotating spray. Filtration and chlorination remove the final effluent from the water, leaving it totally free from bacteria.

KEY

In 1858 the Thames was so polluted that *Punch*, England's weekly humor magazine, printed this savage caricature of Death rowing through its flotsam and jetsam. The flow of sewage, a product of the Industrial Revolution, into the Thames created an enormous health hazard. *Punch* called its cartoon "The 'Silent Highway' Man" and gave it the subtitle "Your MONEY or your LIFE!" In 1889, 31 years later, London commissioned its first sewage plant to be built.

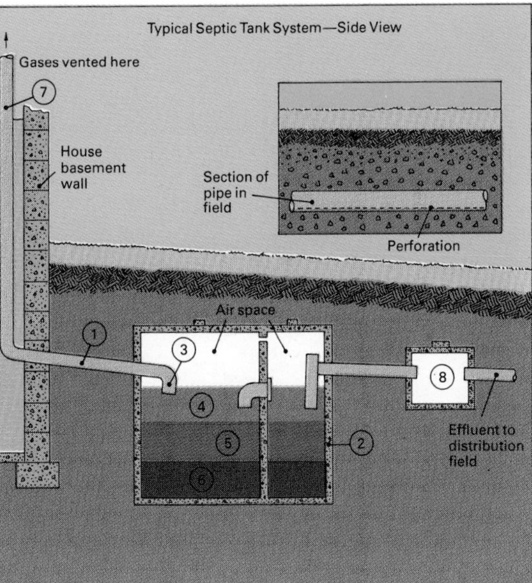
Typical Septic Tank System—Side View
Gases vented here
7
House basement wall
Section of pipe in field
Perforation
Air space
1
3
4
5
6
2
8
Effluent to distribution field

3

9t's a BOYD
Septic Tank Service Unit

3 The sludge from a home septic tank must be pumped out every one to five years. A custom-built tanker is used for this purpose. A sludge removal vehicle must have a tank large enough to empty the largest septic tanks in its area in one pass, for partial emptying results in the scum being left behind. The vehicles pump out liquid sludge through a long flexible hose.

2 A septic tank can process sewage from buildings not connected to city sewage systems. It is a watertight underground tank of concrete, steel, or fiberglass that serves the triple purpose of sedimentation, digestion, and sludge storage. Digestion is automatic, being effected by anaerobic bacteria. Effluent is led to a leaching area and sludge pumped out every one to five years, depending on use and efficiency of the system. The tank's walls are waterproof [2]. Sewage enters through the inlet pipe [1] and is delivered low in the tank [3] without stirring the contents. Relatively pure water [4] separates above the sludge, anaerobic bacteria digest the sewage [5], and the sludge sinks [6]. Gas escapes up the vent pipe [7] and the effluent moves into the absorption field via a distribution box [8].

B

4 Untreated sewage used to be discharged into rivers, estuaries, or the sea [A], leading to pollution and the possible spread of disease. Today most industrialized countries process sewage in treatment plants [B]. One of the problems of modern sewage treatment is the presence in urban waste of ever-increasing quantities of detergents. Domestic detergents must by law be biodegradable, so that they are digested by bacteria, but most sewage treatment plants are unable to remove the phosphates usually found in detergents. These act as nutrients to green algae, which grow too quickly and upset the natural biochemical processes that ordinarily maintains the purity of water in lakes and rivers.

5

Redland Purle Sludge Gulper

5 The digestion of sedimented sewage sludge in modern sewage plants results in the production of a relatively inoffensive nitrogen-rich sludge. After drying, the sewage sludge is sometimes used as a general fertilizer.

History of printing

Movable metal type was probably first produced in the Royal Type Foundry of Korea in 1403 and a book was printed from this type six years later. But not until 1439 is there evidence of printing, as we know it today, in Europe. It was a German, Johannes Gutenberg (1400–68), working in Strasbourg, who developed printing that used movable type.

Early printing methods

In the year 1456 the first substantial printed book appeared. This was a Latin Bible printed in Mainz, almost certainly by Johannes Gutenberg and his associates [2]. How Gutenberg manufactured his type is not known and it was not until 1540, in Vanoccio Biringuccio's book *De La Pyrotechnica*, printed in Venice, that there was a description of type founding. Type was made by pouring molten metal into a copper matrix or mold formed by punching an engraved steel character into a piece of copper.

From the days of Gutenberg there were, for many centuries, no significant changes in the basic methods used for printing. Metal type was set by hand into pages known as forms and these were inked and printed onto single sheets of paper in a hand press [Key]. The first change came around 1790 when Firmin Didot (1764–1836) tested ways of making duplicate printing plates (stereotypes) from set type.

Lithography was invented in 1796 by Aloys Senefelder (1771–1834) of Munich. While seeking a practical method of printing musical scores he tried drawing the music in reverse on a flat slab of stone, using an ink made of wax, soap, and lampblack. His original idea was to etch the stone with acid but his experiments led to an entirely new printing process based on the mutual repulsion of oil-based ink and water.

From plates to printing machines

Didot's stereotype process was perfected in 1800 by Charles Stanhope (1753–1816), who used plaster of Paris to make the molds of the set type. Molten metal was then poured into the plaster molds to produce solid printing plates, a whole page at a time. In 1806 Anthony Berte of London invented a mechanical device for typecasting, using a pump to force molten metal into the matrix.

In 1811 Friedrich König (1774–1833), a German printer who had moved to England, built the first successful printing machine in which a series of leather-covered rollers, fed with ink from a container, automatically inked the type as it traveled to and from the printing platen. Except for the laying on and removing of the paper from the platen, this steam-powered press was automatic. In the following year König designed a cylinder printing machine in which the type form was fixed to a bed that moved first under leather-covered inking rollers and then under a cylinder around which the paper was held.

Nineteenth-century progress

In 1816 an Englishman, Edward Cowper (1790–1852), secured a patent for a method of bending stereotype plates for rotary printing, the plate first being cast flat in a plaster mold of a type form. In the same year Friedrich König and Andreas Bauer (1783–1860)

CONNECTIONS

See also
1772 Modern printing
1776 Newspapers and magazines
1778 Books and publishi
1780 Reference books
1624 Making paper
1160 Science and technc ogy 1500–1700

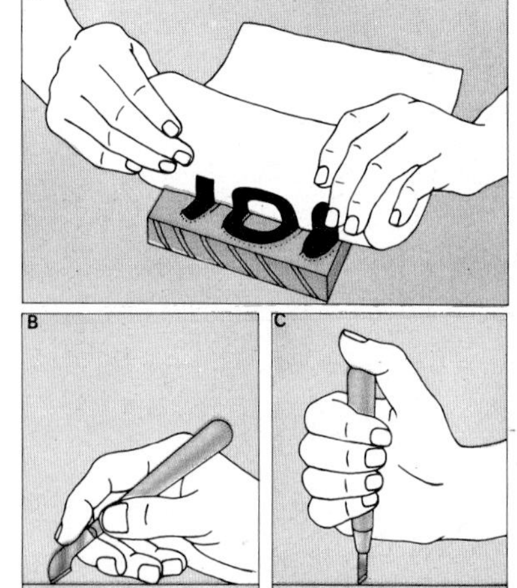

A
B
C

1 The woodcut was developed from the early 15th century onward to produce devotional prints and playing cards. The artist cuts away the part of the design that is to appear white, so that only the parts to be inked appear in relief [A]. The block, made of well-seasoned wood from apple, pear, cherry, sycamore, or oak trees, is cut along the grain. Some early woodcuts were hand-colored but prints can be produced by using a series of blocks. A variety of cutting tools were used, such as the English knife [B] and The Japanese knife [C].

2 The first substantial book printed from movable type was the Latin Bible published in Mainz, Germany, in 1456. This remarkable book had 643 leaves, each page printed in two columns of 42 lines. Known by the name of its celebrated printer, Johannes Gutenberg, the Gutenberg Bible is not only the first major product of modern typography, but is still among the finest examples of the printer's art. This illustration shows the typeface used by Gutenberg. This face was known as Textura and it was cut to resemble the manuscript hand used in the 15th century in Germany to prepare handwritten Bibles. The decorated ("illuminated") initial was painted in by hand. The Gutenberg Bible was printed in ten sections on six presses at once, the edition running to 150 copies on heavy paper and 30 on fine vellum.

3 The first self-inking treadle platen press was designed and built by an American, Stephen Ruggles, in 1839. This improved design built by him 12 years later became the model for the popular jobbing press. In this machine the form of type is clamped in a near-vertical position. Above the form is a rotating disk that serves to distribute the ink. Three composition rollers roll down over the disk picking up ink and then down over the type form. When the rollers have returned, the platen (on which the paper has been laid by hand) moves up against the type form.

4 Type founding is the process of making individual pieces of type by casting molten type metal into molds. Type metal is an alloy of tin and lead, with antimony added for hardness. Lines of type were assembled letter by letter in a hand-held "stick," then moved to a galley for assembly into paragraphs and columns. Single casting of individual type was superseded by the Linotype machine, which casts a whole line at once and is still in use.

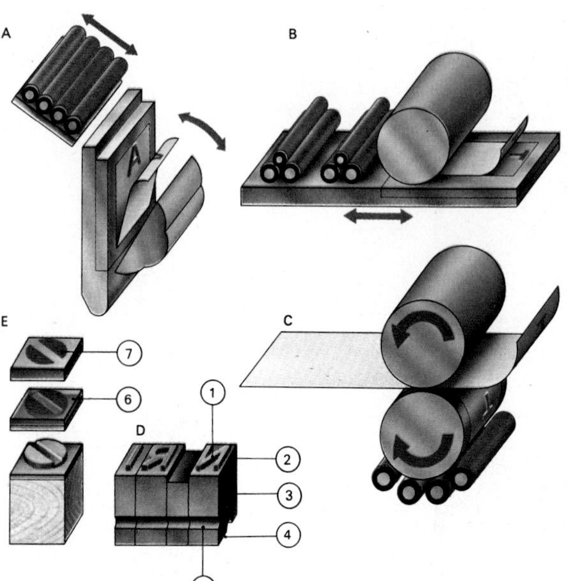

A
B
C
D
E
1
2
3
4
5
6
7

5 Letterpress printing includes the platen press [A] in which paper is pressed up against the inked image. The paper in the flatbed press [B] is laid on the image and pressed down by roller. The rotary press [C] has a curved image on one roller, the paper passing between this and a pressure roller. Metal type [D] has a face [1], a shoulder [2], a body [3], a foot [4], and a nick [5]. Zinc blocks [E] have unwanted metal etched away from the design [7].

built the first perfecting machine—a machine that was able to print on both sides of the paper.

A traditional printing press uses mirror image type. In 1817 the Englishman Augustus Applegath (1788–1871) designed a machine to print bank notes with the same design on each side of the paper and with each color in perfect register with the others. In this machine a curved stereotype first printed onto a leather pad fitted around the printing cylinder. When one revolution was complete the paper was fed between the stereo and the leather pad so that the metal printed on one side of the paper and the inked leather pad on the other. The idea was to produce bank notes that could be forged only with difficulty, and Applegath's machine in fact printed the lower side of the notes by what is now called the offset method. The leather pad was printed with a mirror image of the original type matter which it then transferred to the paper. As a result the printed image on the lower side of the paper was identical to the original stereo. This principle was later made use of in offset printing, in which the type matter is identical to the finished print.

The next 70 years saw numerous advances in the art of printing. Stereotype preparation from papier mâché molds [9] was originated by Claud Genoux of Lyons. These molds or "flongs" were strengthened with clay and glue. In 1845 the French printing firm of Worms and Phillipe patented the idea of casting curved stereos direct from a curved flong. This is the method still used in most newspaper printing today.

In 1838 the American David Bruce, Jr (1802–92) built and patented the first commercially successful mechanical typecasting machine, which produced 100 type characters an hour.

In 1852 the first printing by photolithography was carried out experimentally by Alfred Lemercier, a Frenchman. Lemercier coated his printing stone with a light-sensitive substance that was exposed through a paper negative. After washing with turpentine the design on the stone could then be inked for normal lithographic printing.

KEY

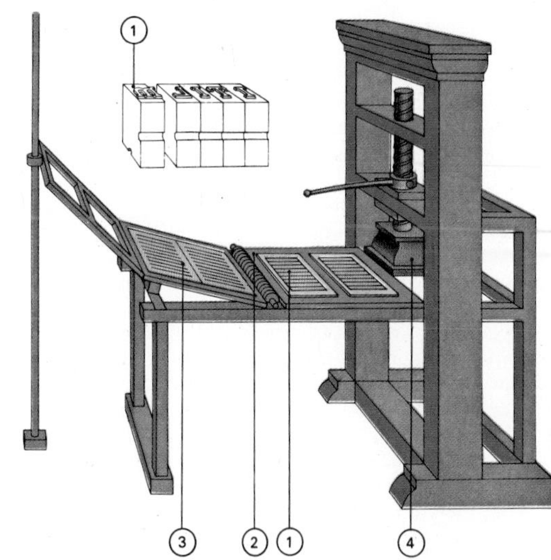
1
3
2
1
4

Early printing presses resembled 15th-century linen presses. The type matter [1] was wedged in a sliding tray [2] and then inked by hand. The paper was placed on a parchment covered "tympan" [3], which was hinged over the type tray. This slid under the screw-down press [4].

A

6 Lithography is based on the mutual repulsion of greasy ink and water. The image to be printed is drawn, in reverse, on stone using a greasy pencil or ink. The stone is then soaked in water and inked. The ink adheres to the image but not to the wet stone. The machine [A] presses paper from the holder onto the stone, thus making the print. The process was used originally for printing music scores [B].

B

A Lass that was loaden with care, set
hear, And thus she be-gan for to mourn
we twa have been, O my Heart it is like to d

7 A

8 When an etched plate has been inked and wiped, ink remains only in the grooves made by the acid and can thus be printed. This is the principle of intaglio, in which the image is below the surface of the printing plate and so retains the ink when the polished surface is wiped clean. James Whistler (1834–1903), who used etching as an art form, made this etching of Black Lion Wharf, Wapping, London.

8

7 In an etched printing plate the ink fills the grooves made by acid in a polished metal plate (copper, zinc, aluminum, or steel). The plate is coated with acid-resisting wax. The image is drawn in the wax with an etching needle [A] exposing the metal. The inscribed plate is then put in acid [B] which eats into the metal where the wax has been removed. After cleaning off the wax the plate is inked, then wiped.

B

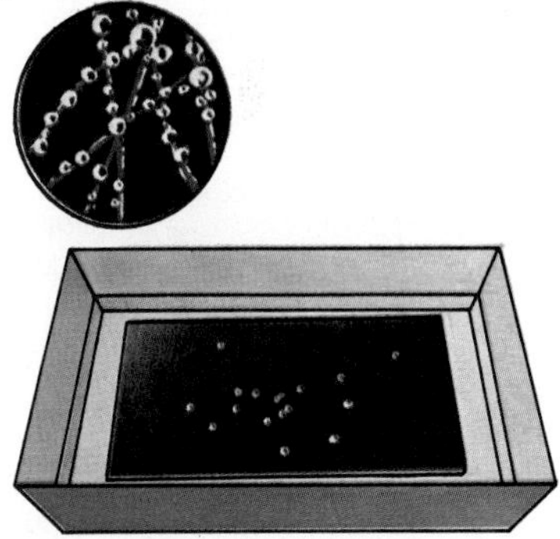

9 The principle of printing on paper fed from a roll with the sheets being cut after printing was invented by Rowland Hill (1795–1879), who later introduced the penny post in England. Rotary machines were developed for newspaper printing from 1846, using curved stereotypes cast from curved papier mâché molds (flongs) of the original flat type forms. This early Victory press printed at high speed and folded the cut sheets.

10

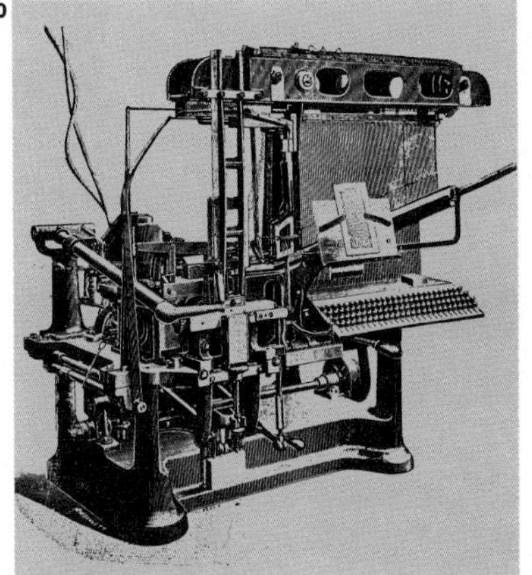

10 The Linotype composing machine, invented by Ottmar Mergenthaler (1854–99), an American of German parentage, was probably the greatest single printing innovation of all time. The machine was first used to typeset *The New York Tribune* in 1886. The operator "types" the copy on a keyboard and the machine sets letter molds (matrices) in the correct order. At the end of each line a complete line of type (slug) is cast in one piece.

Modern printing

There are three main kinds of modern printing processes; relief, intaglio, and planographic.

In relief printing the ink-bearing surface of the type or engravings (for illustrations) stands out above the surrounding non-printing area. Letterpress printing is an example of relief printing and includes printing from one-piece plates made up of both type matter and illustrations, metal line blocks and halftone engravings (which have tonal shades formed from minute dots), stereotype plates, woodcuts, and linocuts. In letterpress printing the platen (flat plate) press and various kinds of cylinder presses are widely used. Paper is fed into the machine by hand or automatically. The mechanism picks up single sheets from a stack (usually by means of suction pads) and feeds them into the machine.

Intaglio printing is relief printing "in reverse." In this case the ink is trapped in cavities in the printing plate surface, the polished non-printing area being "wiped" clean of ink before printing. Photogravure is the principal intaglio process of today; formerly it was used for printing artists' engravings made on steel and copper and for aquatints and etchings (in which lines were etched in the metal by acid).

In planographic printing the printing and non-printing surfaces are completely flat. The printing plates are treated in such a way that the mutual repulsion of oil and water keeps the ink from the non-printing area. Lithography, or offset, is the principal planographic process of printing.

High-speed printing

Modern high-speed printing is carried out on a rotary press [1] using continuous paper from a roll. The printing forms are prepared flat, using type (text) and blocks (illustrations). A papier-mâché "flong" mold is made, again flat. The mold is placed in a casting box that has been bent to a half circle, so that when molten metal is pumped between the flong and the circular backing of the mold a semicircular stereotype plate (stereo for short) is produced. The edges are cleaned up, the white (non-print) areas routed out, the inner side shaved to form a perfect semicircle, and two stereos are fitted around each printing cylinder in the press. This forms a circular printing surface.

Modern photogravure, developed from hand etching, uses photographic techniques to produce copper printing cylinders or plates. Positive prints of the type matter and illustrations are printed photographically onto a gelatin-coated carbon tissue. When developed and laid on a copper sheet this forms an etch-resistant pattern (called a resist), which allows acid or other etching material through the image area, leaving the copper surface untouched in the non-image areas. The etched copper cylinders are then fitted to a high-speed rotary gravure press, which operates in much the same way as a letterpress rotary [1]. Rotary photogravure is widely used for the production of high-quality, large-circulation magazines.

Lithography, originally carried out by forming the image to be printed on a porous stone slab, was soon developed so that the printing surface could be prepared photographically on a sheet of metal such as zinc or aluminum. The methods used for offset

CONNECTIONS

See also
1770 History of printing
1624 Making paper
1774 Copying and duplicating
1776 Newspapers and magazines
1778 Books and book publishing
1780 Reference books
1812 Color chemistry

1

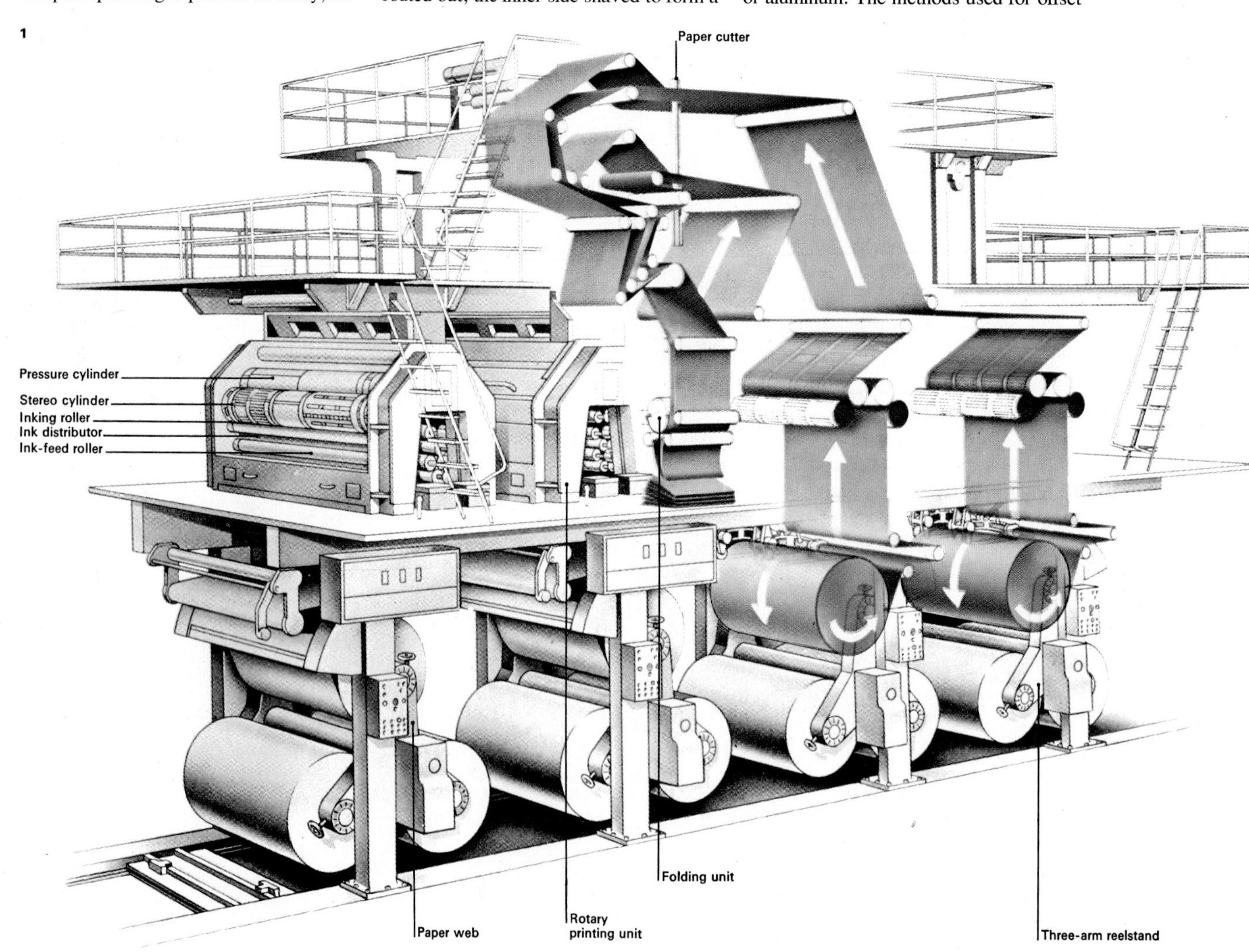

Paper cutter
Pressure cylinder
Stereo cylinder
Inking roller
Ink distributor
Ink-feed roller
Folding unit
Paper web
Rotary printing unit
Three-arm reelstand

1 The newspaper industry has improved and developed its methods of printing over the last 100 years. A modern machine prints both sides of a paper web four pages wide, cutting and folding to make up a finished eight-page newspaper section. Shown here is a typical installation with four presses that can produce a complete 32 page newspaper at once. The three-arm reel stands allow the machine to run without interruption by pasting the paper from the following reel onto the tail of an exhausted web. Color printing can be achieved by rerouting the paper web so that it runs through two machines in sequence, one using black, the other a colored ink, or by adding multi-color press units in the paper path following one of the single-color presses. They then print color in the white space left by the normal press. Presses of this type are designed to deliver at least 50,000 copies per hour. Presses working at such high speeds are fitted with automatic devices to maintain correct paper tension and flow through the mechanism and to apply brakes if there is some failure such as a break in the paper web. Newspapers and magazines are printed increasingly frequently by photo-offset, but many large-circulation magazines, printed in black and one other color, are produced on automatic high-speed letterpress machines similar to newspaper presses. Often, telephone directories and similar publications are printed on rotary letterpress machines at a rate of 15,000 copies per hour. Rotary presses sacrifice quality for speed; in eight hours several presses can print 2.5 million copies of a paper.

platemaking vary widely, but the result is the same—a flexible metal plate that can be fitted around the printing cylinder of a high-speed rotary press [2]. Web-offset presses, printing on a continuous paper roll (the web), have been developed in recent years. As a result many small-circulation newspapers and magazines use this system.

Modern printing methods

In letterpress printing and lithography, the reproduction of continuous-tone illustrations such as photographs is achieved by photographing the picture through a "halftone screen," which is a fine grid of crossed parallel lines. This breaks the picture into tiny elements, which are printed separately as dots of varying size [3].

Linotype machines (which cast a whole line of type at a time) continue to be used widely for newspaper production, and the Monotype machine [4] (which casts one letter at a time), with its facility for rapid change from one type style or size to another, is still used extensively for book production. But phototypesetting, introduced in a practical form in 1955, is superseding the metal type processes in many fields of printing.

Phototypesetting is an entirely new process in which the alphabet and other characters of each type style are stored on film or as tape-recorded instructions. The phototypesetting machine [5] produces positive or negative copy suitable for photographic platemaking processes and has the advantage that the size of any typeface can easily be reduced or enlarged photographically.

A modern phototypesetting machine, with appropriate lens systems, also produces condensed and expanded faces, and italics, from the same master negatives. It operates at high speed— computers control spacing and produce proofs as fast as the operator can use his keyboard. In gravure printing and lithography printing plates are made directly from the positive image produced by the phototypesetter. In letterpress work a negative image is made photographically into a metal printing plate in a manner similar to that used in the production of halftone blocks.

KEY

The essence of modern printing is speed. Millions of copies of daily newspapers appear every morning filled with news stories, many of which were written the previous night.

2

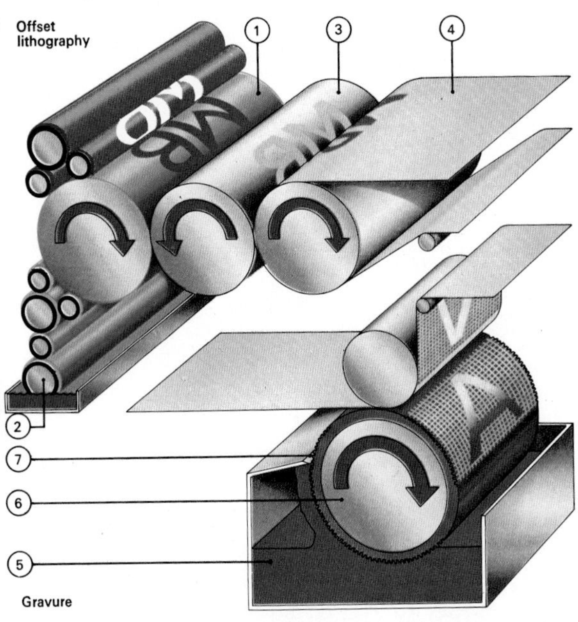
Offset lithography
1
3
4
2
7
6
5
Gravure

2 Image areas of offset lithographic printing plates [1] accept a grease-based ink and non-image areas, damped by rollers [2], reject the ink. The inked image is offset onto a rubber roller [3] and then onto the paper [4]. The copper gravure printing cylinder [6] has the image etched as "cells" (small depressions beneath the surface), the volume of cell determining the quantity of ink and hence the tonal value. The cylinder is covered with ink [5] and the surface is then cleaned by a "doctor" blade [7], leaving ink only in the etched depressions. When the cylinder contacts the paper the ink in the cells is transferred to it. The gravure process is used principally for the production of high-quality pictorial work

3 A

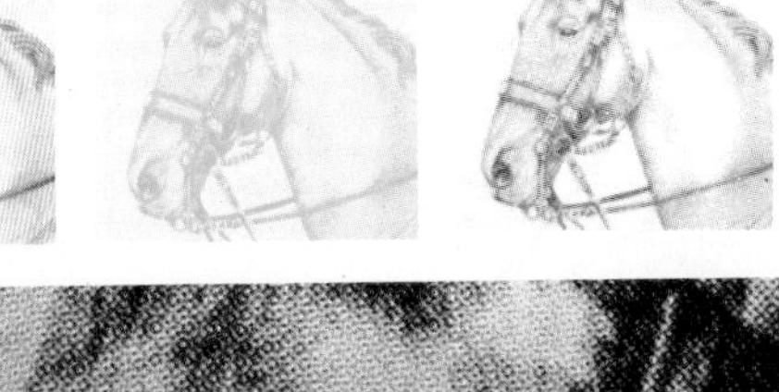
B
C
D

E

3 Yellow, red, and blue are used in various combinations to print a wide variety of shades. Where all three overlap the result is almost black. A greatly improved result is achieved by a fourth black printing. More accurate colors are obtained by using magenta and cyan in place of red and blue. An image is printed in each color [A–D] to give the combined effect, seen here magnified [E].

4

4 The Monotype machine, invented in 1887 by Tolbert Lanston (1844–1913), produces three characters of set type each second, using matrices (molds) and molten metal. It is widely used for books. The operator types the copy on a keyboard, producing a punched paper tape. The tape is later fed into a second machine, which casts individual letters, setting the type in lines of equal length.

5

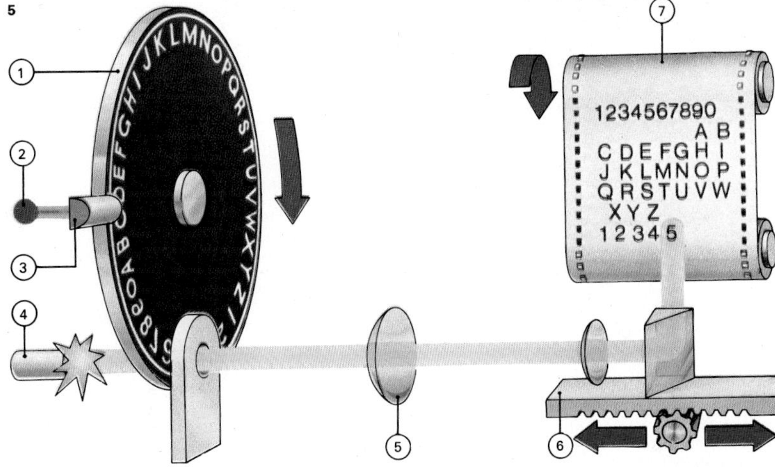
1
2
3
4
5
6
7
1234567890
AB
CDEFGHI
JKLMNOP
QRSTUVW
XYZ
12345

5 A typical photocomposing machine has a continually rotating disk [1] that bears negative images of all the letters, numerals, and punctuation marks in a given type face. An exciter lamp [2] and photoelectric cell [3] sense the exact orientation of the rotating disk. When the chosen character is in line (instructions come from a computer tape by "typing" copy on a keyboard) a microflash unit [4] fires. The lens system [5] focuses an image on film or paper [7]. The transport system [6], also computer controlled, sets the images in lines with justification and hyphenation where necessary to make equal lines.

Copying and duplicating

Reproduction of the written word and of drawings and photographs is not exclusively the art of the printer. An increasingly large volume and variety of reproduced material are prepared quickly and relatively cheaply in offices all over the world by duplicating and copying processes developed for this purpose [1].

The hectograph and rotary duplicator

The oldest of office copying processes is the once familiar hectograph or spirit duplicator [2]. The original material—the master—was drawn by hand using synthetic, aniline inks (purple, red and green were the most usual colors, although black, blue, yellow, and brown inks are also available today) or by typing with special aniline dye ribbons. The master was then rolled face down onto a gelatin bed, which absorbed a proportion of the ink, to form a mirror image on its surface. Plain paper moistened with spirit was then pressed onto the gelatin and peeled off to leave a positive image on each sheet. This convenient process, which can print up to 50 or even 100 copies from a good master, has been modernized and is the basis of the rotary duplicator. A "transfer" sheet surfaced with a wax film containing aniline dye is placed behind the master sheet and material is drawn or typed onto both sheets. In this way a mirror image in aniline ink is formed on the back of the paper, just as though a sheet of carbon paper had been placed below it, black side up. The master so made is fitted on to a cylindrical drum that presses against sheets of paper, moistened with spirit, to provide copies quickly and cleanly. A master can be made using a number of different colored transfer sheets, the process printing the different colors simultaneously.

Modern copying processes

The ink duplicating machine, or mimeograph, has the advantage of being able to produce a thousand or more good copies from the master. This master, once made of wax on porous paper, is now generally made of a pressure-sensitive plastic composition. The image is either hand-drawn with a sharp stylus or typed on any machine with a fine typeface. The lines or letters cut into the surface and break the skin so that ink can penetrate. The master so formed is a negative stencil. The modern mimeograph is a high-speed electrically powered machine and produces good quality copies.

Offset lithography is another process widely used in modern offices. The office offset machine uses the principle employed in commercial lithography—the fact that water and an oil-based ink will not mix. The offset-litho masters can be prepared in several ways: photographically, as in commercial printing; by the use of a suitable toning powder in an electrostatic copier; or simply by typing or drawing with a special ribbon or ink directly onto plastic or thin metal plates.

The blueprint [Key] is no more than a negative prepared photographically by contact with a translucent original. The modern process, which has superseded the blueprint, uses special paper sensitized with diazo compounds. This is placed in contact with the original and exposed to what is known as actinic radiation (mainly blue and violet light, together with ultraviolet rays).

CONNECTIONS*

See also
1772 Modern printing
1782 Information retrieval
1784 Photography

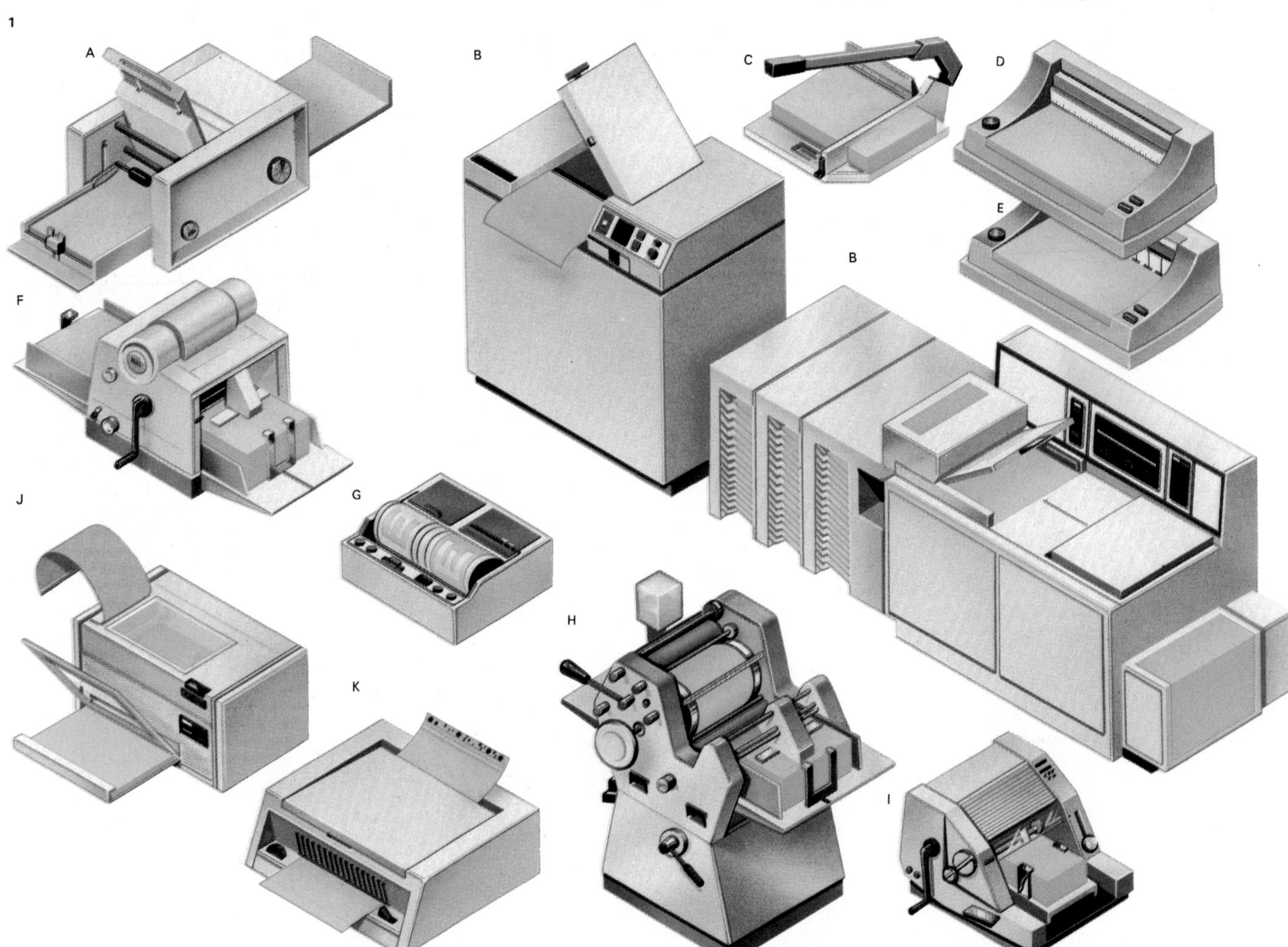
1
A
B
C
D
E
B
F
G
J
H
K
I

1 The in-house print shop of a modern commercial office, research establishment, or other organization where reproduction of printed matter and illustrations is required quickly and often, contains a variety of machines, each serving a specific purpose. Among typical machines shown here there is a spirit duplicator [A] for short runs, a mimeograph [I] for medium runs of non-illustrated material, and an offset-litho press [H] for high-quality printing that may include color work as well as drawings and photographs. For rapid copying and high quality, a type of electrostatic copier [B] is generally used. Large drawings can be quickly reproduced on a diazo copier; "semi-wet" and dry working types are available. Stencils for a mimeograph can be typed by hand on an ordinary typewriter or produced on a thermal stencil maker [K]. A high-speed stencil duplicator [F] can reproduce these much faster than can a mimeograph. Litho plates can also be made on a typewriter, and an electrostatic litho-plate maker [J] can produce them from drawings and photographs. Also shown here are an electronic machine for making mimeograph masters [G], a paper cutter [C], paper punch [D] and binder [E]. A well-equipped print shop can copy any documents, drawings, pages from books, or any other originals, and it can print circulars, memoranda, publicity material, invitations, house journals, technical reports, and even good quality letterheads. Among other methods of graphic reproduction (not shown) are microfilm systems. There are also titling systems such as adhesive transfer lettering and machines for printing serial numbers.

'he radiation passes through the clear aper of the original and chemically alters he diazo compound. But where it is nasked by the lines of the image, the diazo ompound remains unchanged. "Dry" de- elopment by ammonia gas can produce a lack or blue image; wet development can roduce prints in red, sepia, and some other olors. Variations of this process are used in he many dry, "semi-wet," and heat de- elopment diazo copiers available today. 'he process has the advantage of producing opies of large drawings cheaply.

The introduction of electrostatic copying nachines in the mid-1940s [4] has resulted in minor revolution in the copying field. The erm xerography has come into general use or processes marketed by many com- anies. Electrostatic copying depends on he phenomenon of photo-conductivity [5].

reparation of copy

'he first step in the traditional printing pro- ess is the setting of movable type—a com- licated procedure not suitable to the office rint shop. It was the possibility of preparing printing masters on standard typewriters that made the hectograph and the mimeograph, and later the offset-litho press, practical alternatives to commercial printing.

The standard typewriter, however, has three drawbacks. The quality of the typed copy is variable in intensity and clarity, the typeface cannot be altered, and the letter spacing is constant, unlike that of movable type, where "m"s and "w"s, for example occupy much more space on a line than do "i"s or "l"s.

All three weaknesses have been overcome with the invention of more sophisticated typewriters. The modern electric machine, with a carbon or plasticized ribbon used only once, produces uniformly clean and clear jet-black letters. Machines with interchangeable typefaces have also been introduced. Finally, machines with "proportional" spacing were invented, so that narrow, medium, and wide letters do not have to occupy the same space. The most advanced machines also have special spacing facilities for the typing of fixed-width columns.

KEY

The original blueprint used by architects and engineers for the reproduction of plans and drawings is a photographic negative, white on blue, made on paper that has been sensitized with a ferric (iron) salt and potassium ferrocyanide.

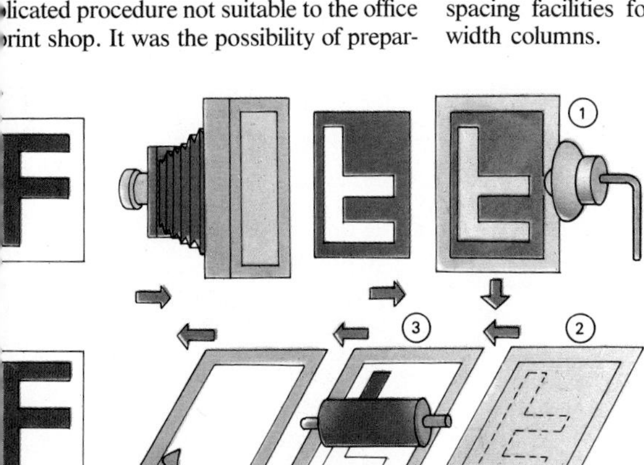

1
3
2

2 **The original spirit duplicator,** or hecto- graph, used a gelatin or clay bed that ab- sorbed some of the aniline ink with which the master copy [1] had been prepared. Some of the ink mirror image in the surface of the "jelly" bed [2] was then transferred back to sheets of paper that had been moistened with spirit and pressed onto it by means of a rubber roller [3]. As aniline inks of various colors could be used on the master, the flat bed hectograph could reproduce several colors simultaneously. Its disadvantage lay in that only short runs – fewer than 100 copies – could be printed.

3 Adhesive transfer lettering, which is available in a wide range of typefaces and sizes, has made possible the preparation of titles quickly and cheaply, complementing the modern electric typewriter's function of producing near-perfect printed material. Line borders, human figures in various attitudes and sizes for use in simple artwork, electronic symbols, mathematical signs, and a wide variety of other symbols and colors are produced in the form of adhesive transfers. Transfer lettering is produced on a transparent sheet. Letters are placed in the position required and rubbed onto the paper below, where they remain fixed after the sheet above is removed. "Instant" lettering is ideal for small-scale print operations at a relatively low cost.

3

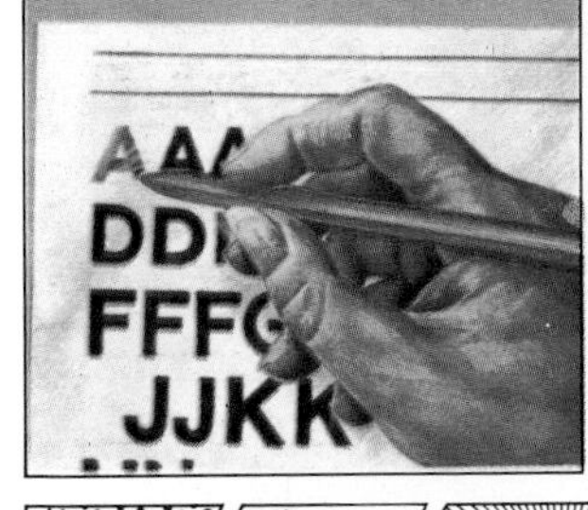

4 Modern electro- static copying ma- chines are produced n a wide range of sizes and types. Table-top machines, designed specifically or use in offices where noise must be kept to a minimum, equire no expertise on the part of the operator. A dial is set to specify the number of copies and the original is then fed in through the slot. The sheet trips a microswitch, which sets the process in motion. The copies emerge singly, followed by the original. Floor-standing copiers usually have a flat bed for the original, making reproduction from open books possible without the removal of separate sheets. Enlargement or reduction of the image is possible on the most comprehensive copiers.

5

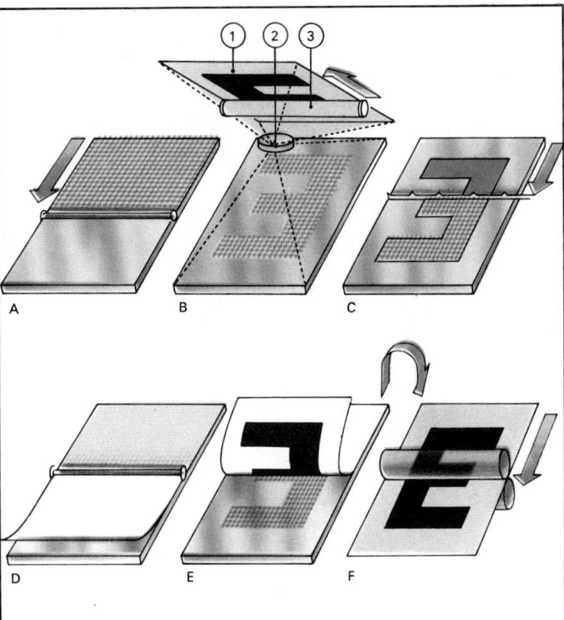

1
2
3
A
B
C
D
E
F

5 The electrostatic copying process uses a metal plate (which is often wrapped around a cylinder) coated with a material that conducts electricity only when exposed to light. In this process the plate is first given an overall charge [A]. Then an image of [B] the original [1] is focused on to the plate using a lens system [2] and a light source [3]. Where the light falls the charge is conducted away. [C] A plastic toning powder (toner) is now dusted over the plate. This adheres to the charged image area but not elsewhere. [D] Resin-coated paper is pressed in contact with the plate. [E] The powder adheres to the paper. [F] The image is fixed by heat.

Newspapers and magazines

Newspapers—a combination of topical information and regular appearance—are probably as old as cities. Early "proto-newspapers" include ancient Rome's *Acte Diurna,* a daily government gazette that was hung in public places from about 59 BC, and China's *pao*, or court circular, which appeared from 618 to 1911.

The advent of the printing press made possible the distribution of public news without government control. Early printed newspapers such as *Mercurius Gallobelgicus* (1594–1634) summarized the news. The first modern newspaper was probably the *Nieuwe Tijdinghen* (Antwerp, 1605); the first daily was the *Frankfurter Zeitung* (1615). The first regular English paper was *The Weekly News* (1622–41).

The first newspaper in the American colonies was *Publick Occurences both Foreign and Domestick,* which appeared as a monthly in 1690 and was immediately suppressed by the British; the first regular American paper was the *Boston Newsletter* (1704). By the Revolution, there was a strong, independent colonial press.

Large paper circulations were made possible by technological advances of the 19th century. *The Times* (London) introduced the steam printing press in 1814, the modern rotary press in 1866, and the electric press in 1884. Armed with this technology, mass journalism became a reality when Joseph Pulitzer (1847–1911) merged three US papers in 1883 to produce a previously unheard of circulation of 250,000. Under the influence of Pulitzer, newspapers mixed sensationalism, aggressive reporting, and social responsibility to sell papers—a pattern persisting to this day.

By 1900 there were 1,950 US papers. The first American tabloid, *The Illustrated Daily News,* appeared in 1919; it later became the (New York) *Daily News*, the largest American daily. Such popular, mass-appeal papers cater to the interests of a mass audience by emphasizing photos and "quick reading." Meanwhile, influential papers, often called the quality press, concentrate on comprehensive reporting. Among these are *The New York Times, The Times,* and *Le Monde* (France).

Developments in 20th-century technology have increased newspaper circulation and multiplied newspaper industry problems. Although most papers are still produced by traditional methods [2, 3], automation of printing processes, including the increased use of offset and computer techniques [6], has lessened the role of manpower.

Editorial content

The editorial content of newspapers can be divided into two major sections: news and features. Predictable news comes from events that are known about in advance, such as sessions of Congress. Unpredictable news includes robberies, disasters, sports events, or political assassination. Editorial page pieces are generally based on a principal news item. Features include articles giving the background of the news, gossip columns, and articles on such special subjects as cooking.

In producing this editorial content [1], the task of the newspaper's managing editor is to direct his journalists in assembling

CONNECTIONS

See also
1772 Modern printing
1778 Books and book publishing
1780 Reference books
1794 Communications: radio
1796 Communications: television
1786 Taking pictures
1422 The American experience: journalism

1

12
11
13
7
3
7
10
1
2
9
4
6
5
8

1 Birth of a story in a newspaper. 7pm: News of a fire at an important politician's home may come over the teletype [1] from a press association or may be phoned in by a "beat" reporter. The story is assessed by the city editor [2], who informs the news editor [3]. They send a reporter [4] to the scene, along with a photographer [6] dispatched by a picture editor [5]. 7:15: The reporter telephones that the man has died. Additional reporters and photographers are sometimes sent to assist in covering events. The news editor [7] decides that the story is the main front-page news – the lead story. A staff writer [8] is briefed to compile the man's obituary, using reference books, interviewing his colleagues and friends, and studying earlier newspaper clippings. Pictures of the man are obtained from the newspaper's files and an artist may draw a map of the house and grounds. 8:00: While one reporter returns to write his story, others phone in details from the scene to the rewrite man. The photographers rush to the darkroom where their film is developed. 8:15: The make-up editor [10] chooses a picture and "lays out" the page, showing the sizes of illustrations and headlines and the lengths of stories. 8:40: The reporters' copy is checked by a copy reader at the copy desk [11]; facts are checked, a headline is added, and the copy is marked for the compositor. Copy and layout go to the news editor [12], who reviews it and sends it to the composing room. The managing editor and chief editors [13] assess the news of the day and decide which stories will be covered for the next edition of the daily newspaper.

stories and pictures that together strike a suitable balance between information and entertainment for his particular readers. Helping the managing editor to assemble this news are the chief editors—city, national, foreign, and specials (finance, sports, arts)—and their staffs of reporters.

The space available for editorial content in each issue is determined in part by the amount of advertising. Each day the managing editor studies a mock-up of the paper that indicates the pages and positions of the advertisements [4]. Knowing the space available, he then holds a conference to deal with stories that are expected to develop during the day.

The magazine world

The first monthly magazine—a periodical of miscellaneous material by several authors—was probably the *Gentleman's Magazine* (1731–1907), which appeared in London. Other early English examples include *Edinburgh Review* (1802–1929).

In the American colonies, Ben Franklin published the short-lived *The General Magazine and Historical Chronicle* in 1741; other early periodicals included the *Royal American Magazine* (1774–75) and Thomas Paine's *Pennsylvania Magazine* (1775–76). By the mid-19th century, weekly magazines, such as the *Saturday Evening Post* (founded 1821) became popular along with nationally circulated monthlies. They had illustrations, fiction, and essays.

In the twentieth century, the large-circulation, general-interest magazines [Key], often featuring photo-journalism, appeared; among them *Look* and *Life*. One of the largest, *Readers Digest*, with a US circulation of about 18,000,000, began publication in 1922. Weekly news magazines, such as *Time* (1923), *Newsweek* (1933), and *U.S. News and World Report* (1933), have enjoyed great success. A drop in advertising revenues, coupled with higher costs, spelled the end for many large-circulation magazines, most notably *Life* in 1972 and *Look* in 1971. Most magazines published today are special interest magazines for professionals, hobbyists, and specific age groups.

KEY

Sales of newspapers and magazines through newsstands are an important revenue source; the balance comes from home deliveries. A news dealer's profit is a percentage of the selling or "cover" price. Most newspapers deliver directly to news dealers, but some papers go first to area wholesalers, who take a percentage of the cover price. News dealers operating on "sale-or-return" send back unsold copies to the wholesaler. To lessen this possible loss, some newspapers ask dealers to place firm orders and bear any loss themselves—but this may encourage under-ordering, resulting in a shortage of papers and in sales for rivals.

2

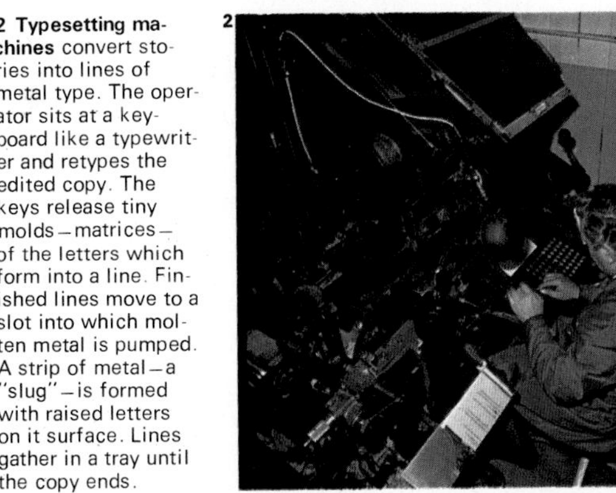

2 Typesetting machines convert stories into lines of metal type. The operator sits at a keyboard like a typewriter and retypes the edited copy. The keys release tiny molds—matrices—of the letters which form into a line. Finished lines move to a slot into which molten metal is pumped. A strip of metal—a "slug"—is formed with raised letters on it surface. Lines gather in a tray until the copy ends.

3

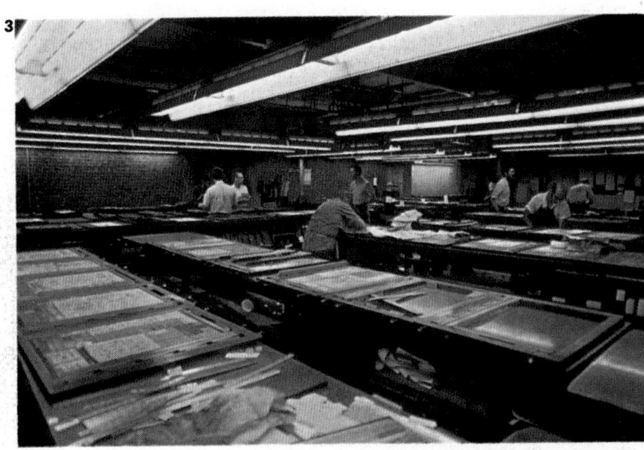

3 Pages are assembled by a compositor. Following the directions of the make-up editor, he assembles slugs of type and metal blocks etched with pictures into a flat metal frame called a page form. A proofreader reads and corrects proofs of each story. An impression of the page form is made, and a curved metal plate is cast from this mold. It is then locked to a cylinder of the rotary drum press.

4

--- Fold of spread

Advertisements

Pictures

Headlines

Text

4 A typical tabloid newspaper contains about 60% advertising and 40% news, commentary, etc. More than half the editorial matter may be text and the rest pictures. Headlines are often strongly attention-getting. Most pages carry advertisements, except for the front page and editorial pages; without them pages look dull. Pictures and headlines are placed to counterbalance advertisements.

5

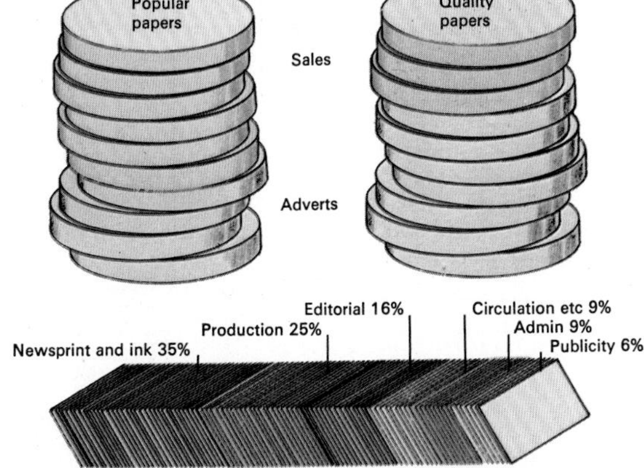
A
Popular papers
B
Quality papers
Sales
Adverts
C
Editorial 16%
Circulation etc 9%
Production 25%
Admin 9%
Newsprint and ink 35%
Publicity 6%

5 A newspaper's income (A, B] is derived from advertisements and from sales of the paper. This chart assumes no profit. It shows [C] paper (called newsprint) and ink as the main costs and demonstrates how popular papers selling millions of copies depend more on sales, whereas quality papers selling perhaps 400,000 copies a day rely on advertisements. In local free newspapers, profit is derived solely from advertising content.

6

6 Future newspaper production will be by computer, with typesetting machines phased out. Writers sit at visual display units, which are keyboards with cathode-ray tubes linked to a computer. When a key is tapped, a letter shows on the screen. The finished stories are kept in the computer until an editor calls one onto his own screen for amendments. The computer then instantly produces a tape that works an automatic typesetting machine.

Books and book publishing

The word "book" can apply to many different ways—some very old—of storing ideas and information in words and pictures. The Egyptian Book of the Dead, the Hebrew and Greek books of the Bible, and the medieval books of hours existed long before modern printing and binding gave us the present-day "book." Reading an ancient book, for example, often required unrolling a scroll. Today, people may read a book by looking at a microfilm of it through a viewer. Still, "book" now most often means a bound volume of text or of text and pictures, intended to be more permanent than a magazine.

The business of publishing

Book production started in ancient times as the process of writing and binding one copy at a time by hand and continued in this way until Gutenberg's invention of printing from movable type in the 15th century. With subsequently improved means of production, publishing has now developed into a major industry. By the mid-1970's, annual US sales had passed $3,500,000,000.

Books and book sales can be classified under eight headings. *Trade books* include fiction [1] (novels, short stories, and mysteries, for example) and popular nonfiction (biography, history, art, politics, travel, cooking, and others) sold to the general public. Other categories are *juvenile* fiction and nonfiction; *religious* books; *professional* works—law, medicine, business, science, and technology; *book clubs,* which select books to sell by mail; *paperbacks,* including all kinds of original and reprinted fiction and nonfiction titles that appeal to large numbers of readers; *textbooks* for schools and colleges; and *reference books* such as encyclopedias and dictionaries.

Sales of individual books vary considerably, and a successful book can be highly profitable to author and publisher. For example, a best-selling textbook writer such as economist Paul Samuelson (1915–) may have millions of copies of his book sold. Some popular fiction writers do even better. The Belgian mystery-novel writer Georges Simenon (1903–) counts 300,000,000 copies sold, and Ross MacDonald [2] has been very popular. In the juvenile category, books for children get large markets, about 8% of all titles sold. Other major areas are fiction (25%), natural sciences (8%), history (8%), the arts (8%), and politics (7%). But the Bible holds the record as a best-seller—since 1800 about 1,500,000,000 copies have been printed in various languages.

Total sales in many categories include much more than bound volumes. One book may be issued in print, in braille for the blind, and on records, tapes, and microfilm. Educational sales may include workbooks, tests, filmstrips, and other aids. Many readers first encounter books when they are serialized in periodicals.

Producing a book

First, an author has to write a manuscript or a prospectus of a manuscript. Many unsolicited manuscripts are sent to publishers but very few are accepted. Numerous manuscripts reach publishing houses through literary agents. Growing numbers of manuscripts, for example in the textbook field,

CONNECTIONS

See also
1780 Reference books
1776 Newspapers and magazines
1800 Video recording and reproduction
1624 Making paper
1772 Modern printing
1130 The Renaissance: humanism

LE PARRAIN
Der Pate
DE PEET-VADER
Der Pate
IL PADRINO
Der Pate

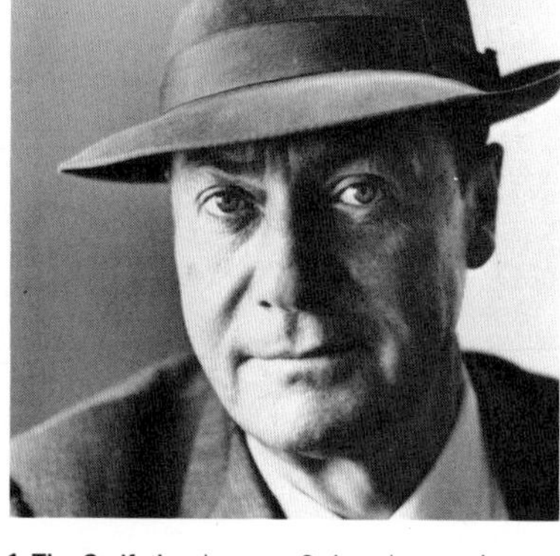

1 The Godfather by Mario Puzo was written originally in English and was translated into most major languages. It became one of the most successful fiction books of recent years and also a popular film.

2 American author Ross MacDonald (1915–), like the Belgian Simenon, has written best-selling mysteries that are also praised for literary merit, such as *The Underground Man* (1971).

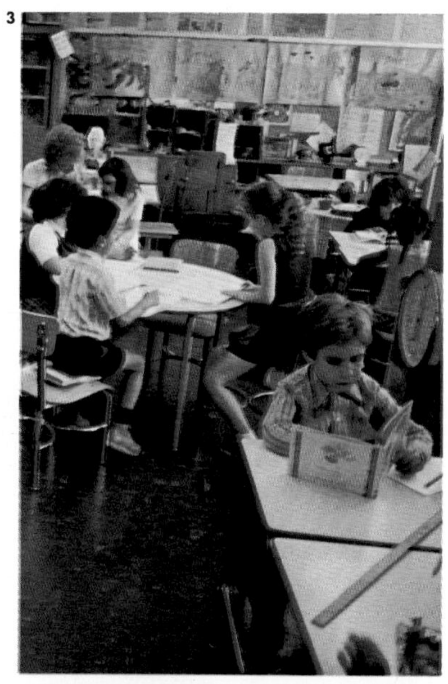

3 Among the most successful books in terms of numbers printed and sold are textbooks and other books for schools and colleges. An elementary mathematics book, for example, may have numerous editions and sell in large numbers for years. In the past, schoolbooks were hardback, with a stiff cloth-covered binding. Many classes used one standard textbook. Today the rising cost of books has encouraged publishers to produce paperbacks for schools and colleges. There is a trend in schools to use several paperback books rather than relying on the more limited resources of a single textbook.

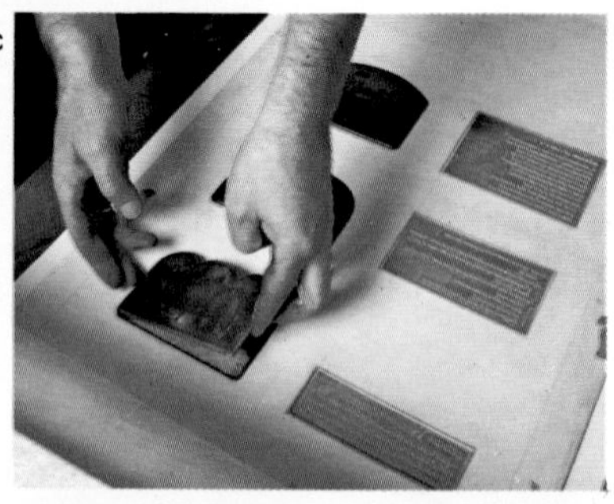

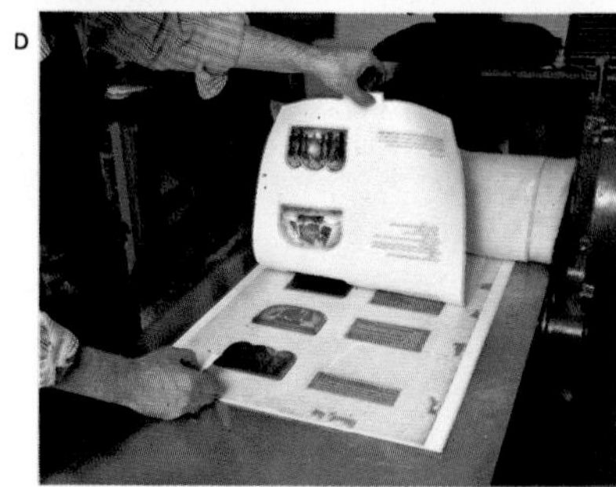

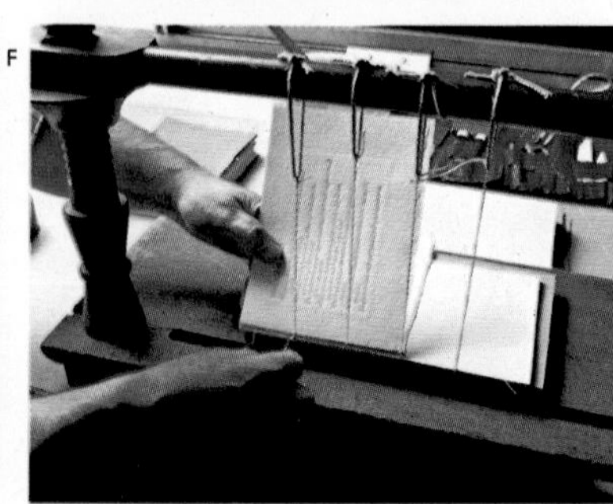

4 Hand production of fine books is still done as it was in the past. Most books are now mass-produced, but the process requires essentially the same steps as hand work. Here a craftsman is inking an etched plate [A] for an illustration, then [B] inking the type with a roller before [C] arranging the plate and type on a form for printing. Sheets of paper for the book's pages are printed [D] on a flatbed press, then any hand-lettering is carefully drawn [E]. Finally the book is bound. The pages are stitched together [F], then boards forming the covers are added and the cover bound in cloth or leather. Few people have all these skills, and their products command high prices.

are commissioned—the publisher finds an author or authors.

The author's manuscript is frequently read and changes are suggested by one or more editors. They may ask: Is the work too long, or too short? Are facts and figures correct? Is the book logically organized? Will the language be clear to those who will use the book? Problems in such areas sometimes require extensive revision. The final copy, marked to show size and style of type, then goes to be set in type.

Most publishing firms do not do their own typesetting, printing, and binding. The great majority of publishers send out their production work to specialized firms using high-speed machinery. A few craftsmen-artists still do all their own work [4], usually in very small quantities.

The compositor returns long sheets, called galley proofs, to the editor and author for correction. Once the proofs have been corrected, the next step is to divide the type up into pages. In an all-text book, proofs need simply be marked to show where pages start and end. If the book is to be illustrated, however, photographs and artwork have to be chosen, and the text, pictures, and captions must be fitted together into pages.

Editors review page proofs, and after type and illustrations for all pages are ready, the job goes to the printer. He arranges the printing plates so that pages will appear in the right sequence on large sheets ("signatures"). When these sheets are folded, the pages fall into their numbered order through the book. The bindery gathers signatures at the back, and binds them [5]. Paperback books are generally not sewn but are "perfect bound" (the backs of the signatures are held together and in the cover with glue).

The next task for the publisher is to promote and sell the finished book [6]. Salesmen for publishers show their new titles to bookstores [Key], schools, and libraries. Large numbers of copies are often sold by mail order, as by book clubs. New titles are advertised mainly in print media, but sometimes radio and TV is used. The number of US books published continues to increase every year.

KEY

YOGA

A large general bookstore may occupy several floors and have several hundred thousand volumes on display. Smaller shops may specialize in one field or in second-hand books.

1

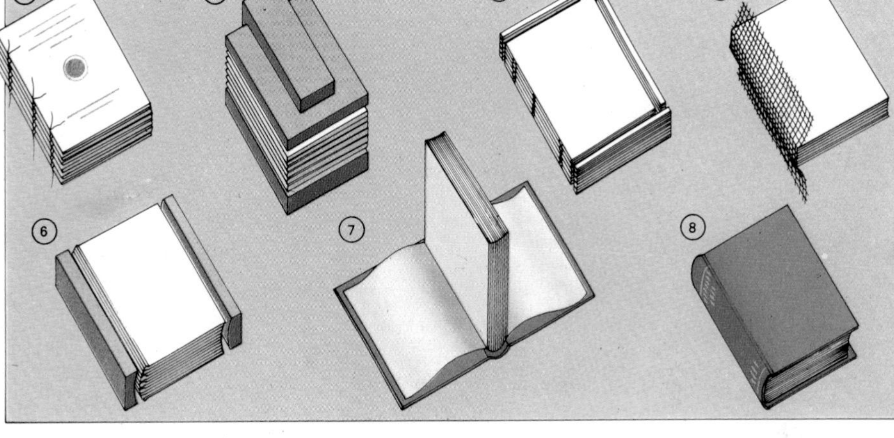
2
3
4
5
6
7
8

5 Modern bookbinding is carried out almost entirely by machines. The pages of a book are printed on sheets of paper, generally 8 to 32, 48, or 64 pages at a time on each side of the sheet. Each sheet is folded [1] into a signature (in this example, of 16 pages). All the signatures for a complete book are collated (put in page order) and sewn [2]. A heavy clamp [3] expels air from the sewn book, which is then trimmed to the finished size [4]. Net fabric, called mull, is glued to the spine [5], and the back of the book is rounded [6]. Endpapers are attached and the book fixed into its covers or "case" [7]. All of these operations may be done by automatic machinery in a modern bindery. The title may be blocked—impressed into the cover [8] and often a printed dust jacket is added. Books are packed into boxes for distribution.

6 The Frankfurt (Germany) Book Fair is held annually in the autumn. It is the foremost marketplace at which publishers display existing and planned works to the international book trade. The fair is a highlight of the process by which publishers promote their books and start the sales effort. International cooperation between publishers is another feature of the fair. They can plan for one book to be produced in several coeditions that differ only in the language in which the text is printed. And a book that is made as a single volume for one country may be produced in several volumes for another. A hardback book in one country may be a paperback in another.

6

7

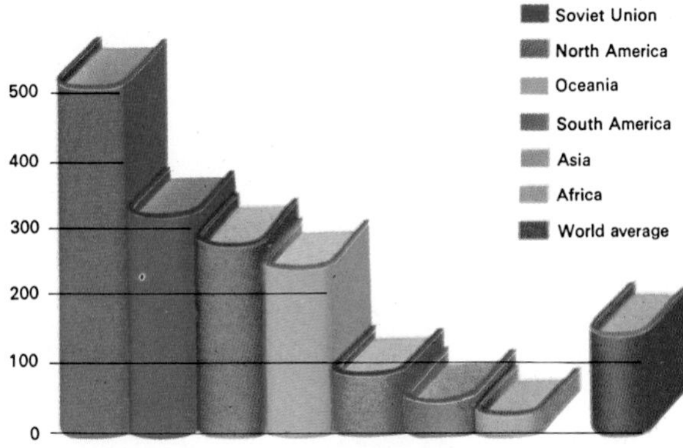
500
400
300
200
100
0
Europe
Soviet Union
North America
Oceania
South America
Asia
Africa
World average

7 The world market for books can be stated in terms of the number of new titles published annually. This diagram shows the number of titles per million inhabitants in each of the major continents and the USSR in the early 1970s. More books were produced in Europe, with the Soviet Union and North America the second and third largest producers. The Soviet total (325 per million), however, has changed little over a period of ten years; those of Europe and North America have increased steadily. The figure for Asia, about 48 new titles published annually per million inhabitants, has remained virtually unchanged for about 20 years.

Reference books

One effect of the expansion of human knowledge during the twentieth century has been to make a good reference library an important adjunct of civilized life. The essential job of encyclopedias, dictionaries, and other reference books is to summarize knowledge in an easily accessible and suitable form. Encyclopedias are about subjects and facts; dictionaries are about words and definitions.

Encyclopedias

The desire to summarize all human knowledge has a long history; the earliest surviving encyclopedia in the West was compiled in Rome by Varro in the first century BC, and in China encyclopedias were in existence a thousand years before that. Varro's work was followed a century later by the *Historia Naturalis* of Pliny the Elder (AD 23–79). Like all early encyclopedias, Pliny's work was arranged by subject, as was the much larger *Etymologiae* [1] of Isidore of Seville (560–636).

Pierre Bayle's *Dictionnaire Historique et Critique* (1696–97) attempted to give a comprehensive summary of human knowledge and appeared in many editions and translations. In 1704–10 John Harris (*c.*1667–1719) brought out his *Lexicon Technicum*. The first true encyclopedia in English, it was compiled at the request of England's Royal Society and had a distinct scientific bias. It was followed in 1728 by the *Cyclopaedia* of Ephraim Chambers (died 1740), a fully cross-referenced work that was a model for subsequent alphabetical encyclopedias, including the largest European encyclopedia ever published—the *Great Complete Universal Lexicon* [2] of Johann Heinrich Zedler (1706–70).

The most famous successor to Chambers' work was the *Encyclopédie* [3] (1751–72) of Denis Diderot (1713–84) and Jean le Rond d'Alembert (1717–83). Their approach was unashamedly radical and their enthusiastic humanism contributed to the undermining of the *ancien régime* in France. The original three-volume *Encyclopaedia Britannica,* published in Edinburgh, Scotland, in 1768–71, was conceived in part as a more objective answer to the *Encyclopédie*. Always a monumental work, *Britannica* has grown through 15 editions.

Alphabetical order of subjects did not become standard practice until the late Middle Ages. Even today some valuable encyclopedias, such as the *Encyclopédie Francaise* (1937–) and the *Oxford Junior Encyclopedia* (1948–), arrange their material in a logical sequence from subject to subject, rather than alphabetically. *The Random House Encyclopedia* uses both systems, presenting subjects thematically in the *Colorpedia* and alphabetically in the *Alphapedia*.

Advent of dictionaries

Without alphabetical order, dictionaries would be impossible to use. They are comparatively recent innovations. John Florio's *World of Words* (1598) was the first Italian-English dictionary, and Robert Cawdrey's little *Table Alphabeticall of Hard Words* (1604) explained in simple English the meaning of some of the obscure, affectedly learned words that had come into English from Latin.

CONNECTIONS

See also
1778 Books and book pu-lishing
1772 Modern printing
1800 Video recording an reproduction
1782 Information retrieva
1184 The Enlightenment
1188 European literature the 18th century

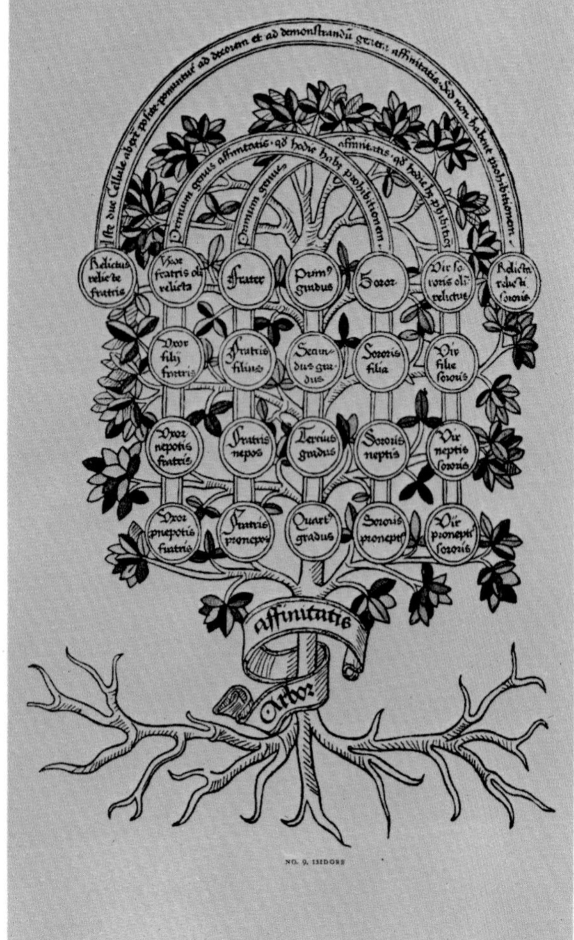
affinitatis
arbor

1 Isidore's Etymologiae was a compilation of seventh century knowledge. This "Tree of Knowledge" is taken from an illustrated manuscript copy. The book was arranged thematically and included liberal arts, medicine, law, a time chart, the Bible, the Church, people, language, statecraft, a Latin dictionary, man, zoology, heaven, air, seas and oceans, geography, cities and towns, building, geology, weights and measures, agriculture, ships, houses, dress and costume, food and drink, tools, and furniture. Isidore remained a standard work of reference for 1,000 years. Today it serves as an important source for information about early medieval life and seventh-century thinking.

Grosses vollständiges
UNIVERSAL
LEXICON
Aller Wissenschafften und Künste,
Welche bißhero durch menschlichen Verstand und Witz
erfunden und verbessert worden,

2 Zedler's Lexicon or *Great Complete Universal Dictionary of all the Sciences and Arts* (1732–50) was particularly strong on biography, genealogy and topography. Zedler, a German publisher and bookseller, claimed that his work was more comprehensive and complete than any previous encyclopedia. His work prompted rival ones that later put him out of business.

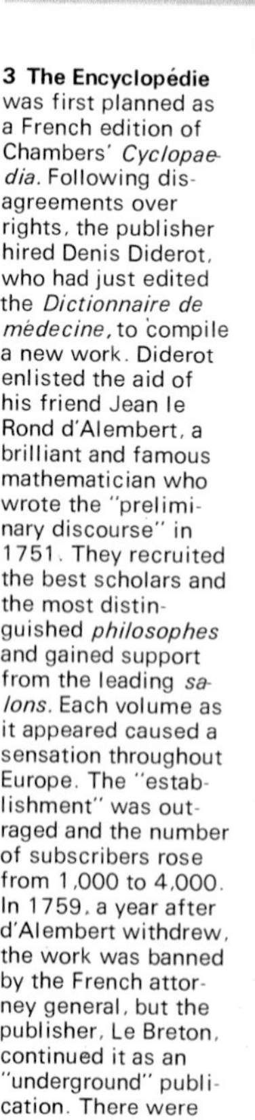

3 The Encyclopédie was first planned as a French edition of Chambers' *Cyclopaedia.* Following disagreements over rights, the publisher hired Denis Diderot, who had just edited the *Dictionnaire de médecine,* to compile a new work. Diderot enlisted the aid of his friend Jean le Rond d'Alembert, a brilliant and famous mathematician who wrote the "preliminary discourse" in 1751. They recruited the best scholars and the most distinguished *philosophes* and gained support from the leading *salons.* Each volume as it appeared caused a sensation throughout Europe. The "establishment" was outraged and the number of subscribers rose from 1,000 to 4,000. In 1759, a year after d'Alembert withdrew, the work was banned by the French attorney general, but the publisher, Le Breton, continued it as an "underground" publication. There were numerous pirated editions.

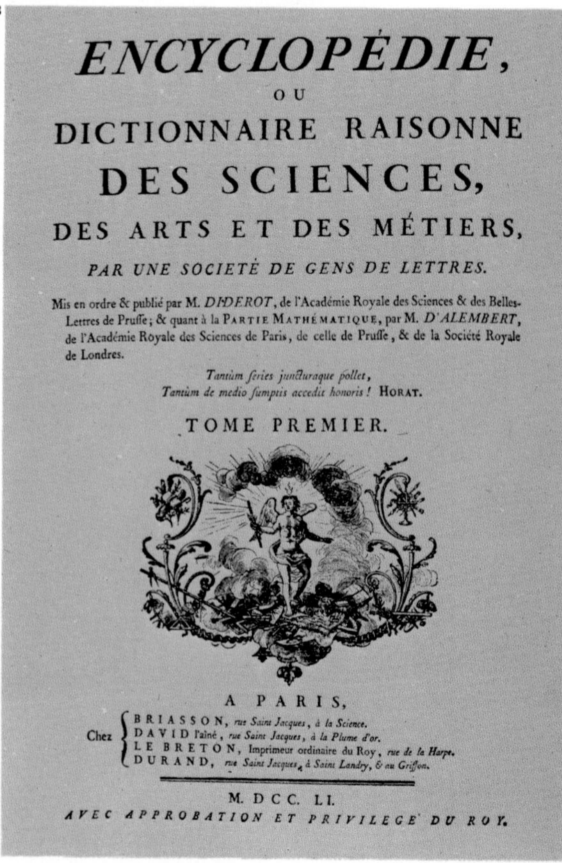

ENCYCLOPÉDIE,
OU
DICTIONNAIRE RAISONNÉ
DES SCIENCES,
DES ARTS ET DES MÉTIERS,
PAR UNE SOCIETÉ DE GENS DE LETTRES.

Mis en ordre & publié par M. *DIDEROT*, de l'Académie Royale des Sciences & des Belles-Lettres de Prusse; & quant à la PARTIE MATHÉMATIQUE, par M. *D'ALEMBERT*, de l'Académie Royale des Sciences de Paris, de celle de Prusse, & de la Société Royale de Londres.

Tantùm series juncturaque pollet,
Tantùm de medio sumptis accedit honoris! HORAT.

TOME PREMIER.

A PARIS,
Chez BRIASSON, *rue Saint Jacques, à la Science.*
DAVID l'aîné, *rue Saint Jacques, à la Plume d'or.*
LE BRETON, Imprimeur ordinaire du Roy, *rue de la Harpe.*
DURAND, *rue Saint Jacques, à Saint Landry, & au Griffon.*

M. DCC. LI.
AVEC APPROBATION ET PRIVILEGE DU ROY.

In the eighteenth century the first modern dictionaries were produced. In 1721, Nathan Bailey (died 1742) issued his *Universal Etymological English Dictionary*, which remained a bestseller for more than a century. It was the first attempt to collect and define *all* English words, as opposed to just "difficult" words, and it was the foundation on which Samuel Johnson (1709–84) based his more famous English dictionary. Johnson's chief innovations were the introduction of illustrative quotations to demonstrate meaning and usage, a willingness to make judgments about usage.

Among Johnson's successors was the American schoolmaster and patriot Noah Webster (1758–1843), who in 1828 issued his *American Dictionary of the English Language*, which first listed most of the spelling differences between British and American English.

Major dictionaries now adopt one of two approaches to language. The first, exemplified by the great *Oxford English Dictionary* (1884–1933; supplements 1933, 1972–), is the historical approach: through a systematic reading of representative writings in the English language, the history of each word is given with numerous dated examples of use. In the other approach—the "synchronic" method—the lexicographers set out to observe and record the language mainly in its contemporary form, as in *The Random House Dictionary* (1966). The most controversial example of the latter method—*Webster's Third New International Dictionary* (1961)—upset many people by its policy of not always indicating the status of words or meanings disapproved by many users of English. The best modern reference-book staffs expend great efforts to keep abreast of developments in all fields of knowledge.

New works of reference

In the future, printed reference books will undoubtedly be supplemented by more technologically advanced ways of storing and retrieving information. Computer data banks can hold an enormous amount of information in a way that enables it to be available instantly and readily updated.

KEY

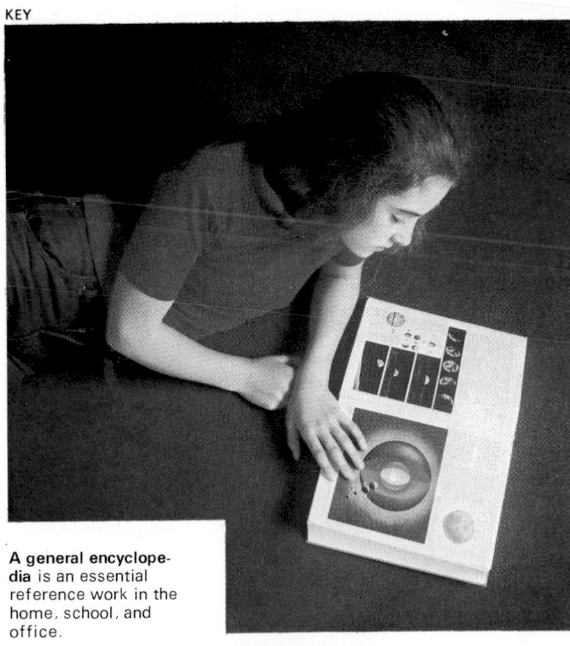

A general encyclopedia is an essential reference work in the home, school, and office.

4 A

B

C

D

E

F

G

H

I

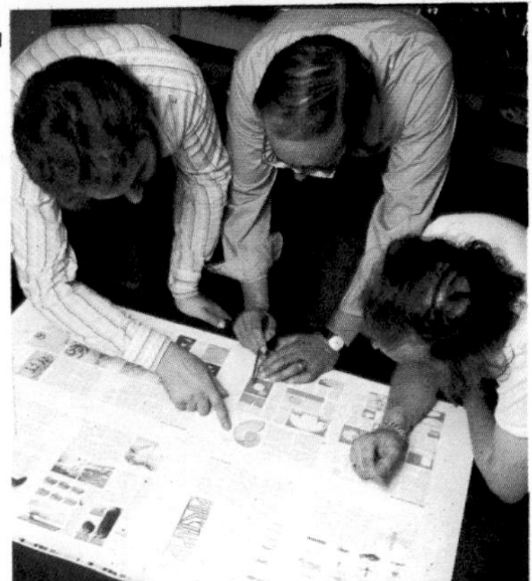

4 Producing a modern encyclopedia is a complex process, with text and illustrations assembled in various stages. First, the editors select and define subjects for articles. An author is commissioned to write about a subject and may attend briefings [A] at the publisher's office with members of the editorial staff. Rough layouts are drawn, indicating the size, position, and content of all pictures. Authors then research and write the text [B] while artists prepare precise page layouts [C]. A picture researcher obtains photographs [D] from picture agencies and photographers, or photographs are taken especially for the book. Artwork—paintings and drawings—is produced by a team of artists [E]. Each author's manuscript—often reviewed by advisors and consultants—is then edited for style and content by the publisher's staff [F], and cross references are developed. After a compositor has set type, proofs are checked for accuracy [G] and assembled into a "paste-up" of the pages [H]. The text is "married" with the color pictures, and a final full-color proof is checked for accuracy and quality [1]. This process is repeated until the entire encyclopedia is finished.

Information retrieval

In the Middle Ages, man's knowledge was mainly in the areas of philosophy, history, medicine, astronomy, and, to a very limited extent, geography. The boundaries of scientific and technical information were limited. All known knowledge could have been recorded in a few hundred books.

The early recording systems

The volume of recorded knowledge grew slowly at first, but, after the second half of the eighteenth century, men began to conduct systematic scientific research in many fields. Soon no one person could hope to read, understand, and remember all recorded knowledge and instead people began to specialize in particular fields of study. The expansion of scientific and technical knowledge into new areas, each producing its own "literature," led to a rapid explosion of scientific information. Even modest libraries found it impossible to cope with the flood of new information.

The new problem led to the evolution of a new expertise called information science—the science of storing, organizing, retrieving, and disseminating information in such a way that anyone who knows the system is able to identify and retrieve all available information on any specific subject as and when it is needed. There are now many aspects of information retrieval, including market research, mail-order selling, and population censuses. Its principles can best be illustrated by considering the problems facing a large library of books.

The first successful system of information classification was the decimal system invented by an American, Melvil Dewey (1851–1931), and first published in 1876.

The Dewey classification system

Dewey divided "knowledge" into ten main numbered classes: 100 Philosophy; 200 Religion; 300 Social Sciences (including Economics); 400 Language; 500 Natural Science; 600 Useful Arts (now Technology); 700 Fine Arts; 800 Literature; 900 History (including Travel and Biography); and 000 General Works (covering subjects not fitting into the other nine categories). Each main class was subdivided into ten subclasses (indicated by the second digit of classification number), and each of these into ten further subclasses (third digit). Dewey made provision for even greater flexibility by adding a decimal point after the first three figures. The virtue of the system lies in the ease with which books can be numbered and grouped together on library shelves.

The Dewey system was widely accepted, but had one major drawback. Many books can be classified in more than one way and the Dewey system made little provision for this. To make it possible for a book or document to be given a classification number that indicates its subject matter more precisely, the Universal Decimal System (UDC) was developed. This used the Dewey system as its basis and was first published by the International Institute of Bibliography, in French, in 1905. The Institute (which later became the International Federation of Documentation) has developed and widened the scope of the UDC progressively ever since.

When the US Library of Congress moved to new premises in 1897 it was al-

CONNECTIONS

See also

1674 What computers can do

1780 Reference books and encyclopedias

1798 Sound recording and reproducing

1800 Video recording and reproduction

670 Memory and recall

1 This carpet loom is controlled by punched cards. It is based on a silk loom invented in 1801 by the French engineer Joseph Jacquard (1752–1834). Compressed air passes through the holes in the cards, joined to form an endless loop, as they pass over a perforated roller. Depending on the positions of the holes, the air operates mechanisms that lift the lengthwise warp threads of different colors. In the modern machine, push rods are used instead of compressed air to "read" the positions of the holes. Single punched cards, "read" by a photocell arrangement, are part of modern data processing.

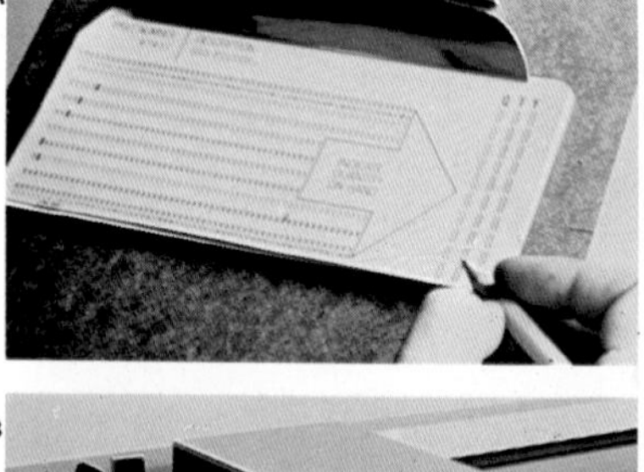

2 The punched card is the basis of most electromechanical data processing systems. Information is stored on the card by punching holes in specific locations according to a predetermined code [A]. In a population census, for example, there would be one card punched for each completed census form. The card sorter [B] uses electrical contacts to sense the holes and thereby sort cards into predetermined groups at high speed. For example, the sorter could sort cards into ten different age groups by sensing the "age" hole on each card, this being carried out in a fraction of the time possible by hand.

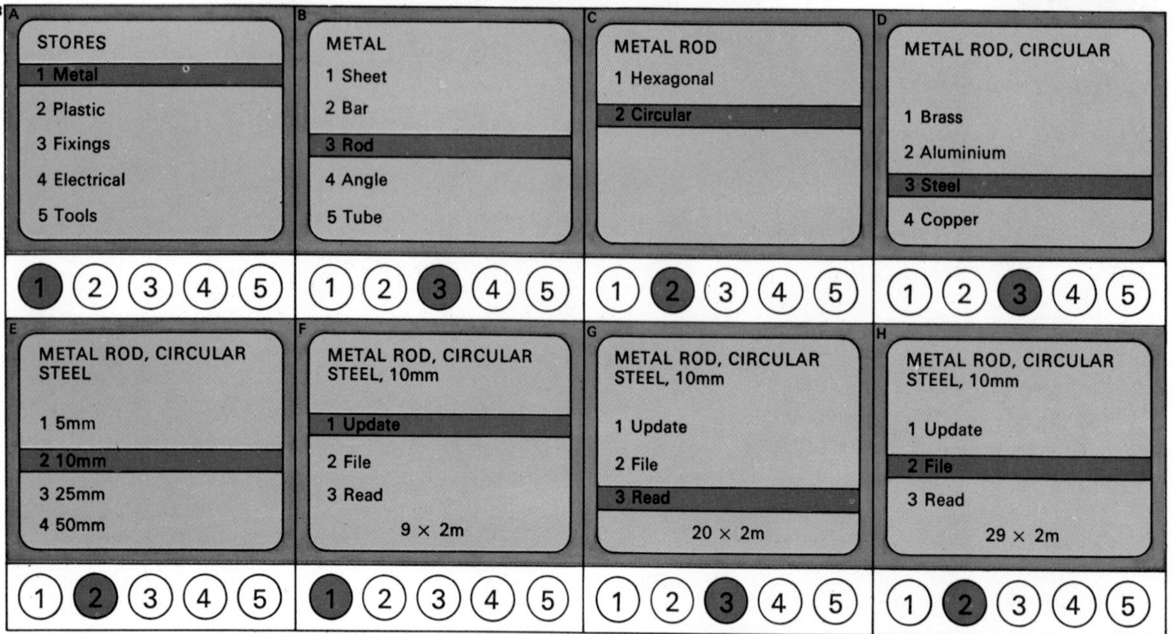

A
STORES
1 Metal
2 Plastic
3 Fixings
4 Electrical
5 Tools
1 2 3 4 5
B
METAL
1 Sheet
2 Bar
3 Rod
4 Angle
5 Tube
1 2 3 4 5
C
METAL ROD
1 Hexagonal
2 Circular
1 2 3 4 5
D
METAL ROD, CIRCULAR
1 Brass
2 Aluminium
3 Steel
4 Copper
1 2 3 4 5
E
METAL ROD, CIRCULAR
STEEL
1 5mm
2 10mm
3 25mm
4 50mm
1 2 3 4 5
F
METAL ROD, CIRCULAR
STEEL, 10mm
1 Update
2 File
3 Read
9 × 2m
1 2 3 4 5
G
METAL ROD, CIRCULAR
STEEL, 10mm
1 Update
2 File
3 Read
20 × 2m
1 2 3 4 5
H
METAL ROD, CIRCULAR
STEEL, 10mm
1 Update
2 File
3 Read
29 × 2m
1 2 3 4 5

3 A computer display screen can be used to provide information about the stock on hand in an engineering factory. Suppose the inventory keeper takes delivery of twenty 2m lengths of steel rod and wants to correct the records. The computer gives the "stock" display [A], from which he selects "Metal" by pushing button number 1. On the "Metal" display [B] he selects "Rod"; from "Metal rod" [C] he chooses "Circular;" and from the available types of circular metal rod [D] selects "Steel." From the next display [E] he selects the 10mm size, and [F] informs him that the present stock is nine 2m lengths. He feeds in the new stock [G] and checks total [H].

ready 97 years old and held about 1.5 million volumes and documents. The directors considered using the Dewey system but finally developed its own. In this, the LC system, subject-matter is first divided into 21 classes bearing the letters of the alphabet from A-Z, excluding I, O, W, X, and Y. Each main class is then subdivided, each subclass again bearing a letter. In this way the classification of every book or document begins with two letters and these give a fairly clear indication of the nature of the contents. The two letters are followed by figures, usually three or four, which are so devised to give the maximum detailed information on the contents of the book. Numerical subclasses, where appropriate, are further subdivided by topics. Many advantages are claimed for the LC system, especially its ease of use.

Other classification systems

Other forms of information classification have particular advantages and are used in modern retrieval systems. Faceted classification recognizes that most subjects are compounds of several elements and seeks to enumerate the principal elements in every classification label. This system has not only been shown to be flexible but also to provide, if well conceived, a precise indication of, say, the contents of every book or document. Faceted classification is also easily adapted to use in punched card information retrieval systems [2]. By defining all the "facets" of a subject on which information is required, a punched card sorting machine can quickly identify all information cards bearing those facets in its classification label.

Information retrieval is an area in which computers are increasingly being used. As long as the "information" can be coded in a form that can be stored in a computer's memory banks, it can quickly be retrieved merely by calling it up using an appropriate code addressed to the computer. In addition, computer information can be continually updated, canceling outdated material and replacing it with fresh data. The updating process in books and most other publications has to await complete new editions.

KEY

A record storage corridor in a US Patent Office gives a vivid impression of the steadily growing problem of information storage and retrieval. When an application for a patent is made, the authority must be sure that the idea is genuinely new. A century ago the descriptions of all existing patents could easily be filed in a single room and classified in such a way that the validity of new applications for patents could be quickly established. Today the number of current patents is so large that the problem of validating these applications in the old way has now become excessively time consuming.

4 A

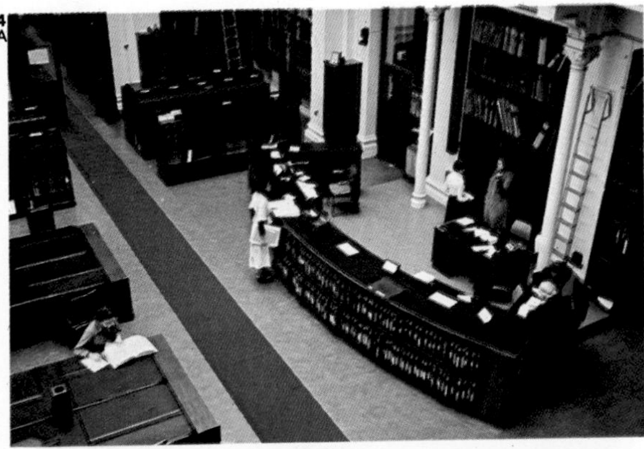

B

4 Libraries of rare books must guard against losses and theft. The Victoria and Albert Museum Library in London [A] uses a system under which all books are guarded [B]. A user enters his request (author and title) on a form in duplicate, and hands this to an attendant. The latter files one copy, takes the book from the shelf (where the other copy is lodged in its place, and gives the book to the reader.

5

5 Large airlines operate 50 or more airliners flying daily on routes all over the world, and passengers may join or leave flights at 20 or 30 different major cities. The airline's information problem is to know instantly, at all ticket offices, how many seats are available on each plane along each section of the route. This is accomplished by having a computer at the head office with terminals at every ticket office. The computer memory has a separate sub-store for every section of every flight and keeps a running total of the number of passengers booked for each section. If a proposed booking will exceed seat capacity on any section, the computer informs the ticket clerk instantly.

6

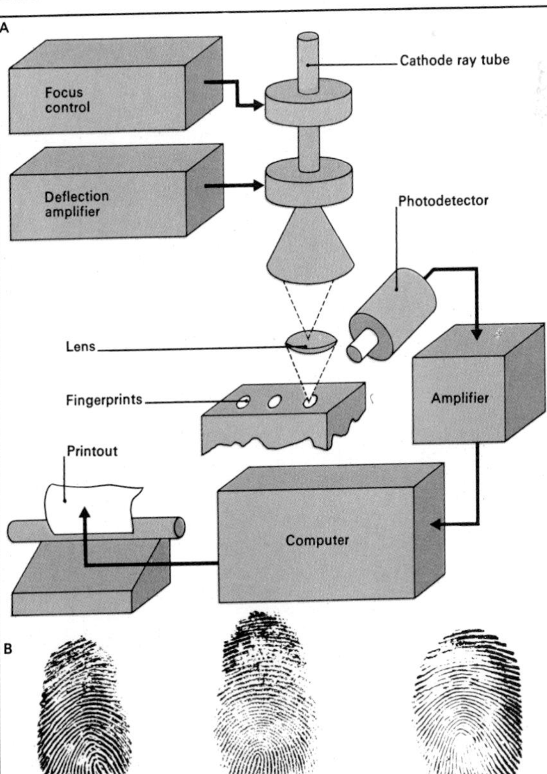
A
Cathode ray tube
Focus control
Deflection amplifier
Photodetector
Lens
Fingerprints
Amplifier
Printout
Computer
B

6 In the early days of police science the criminal investigation departments of even the largest countries held only a few thousand sets of fingerprints. Today the number filed at the Federal Bureau of Investigation is counted in millions. When a crime has been committed and fingerprints found at the scene, it may take days of searching to establish whether the prints belong to a known criminal. To solve the problem, scanning devices [A] are being developed that will provide information that can be read by a computer. When this new technique has been perfected, fingerprint sets will be filed in a single computer store and it will be possible for the computer, if "shown" a print found at the scene of a crime [B], to compare it with every print in its store within a minute or two and come up with references to any matching finger prints.

Photography

In just 150 years photographs, and allied processes such as photocopying, have become almost indispensable. Where words struggled to convey reality and paintings could not capture the fleeting moment, the photograph came to achieve both, presenting in one dramatic image instant history, technical detail, or profoundly moving emotion. "Photography" comes from Greek words meaning "writing with light."

Development of photographic processes

The first photograph was taken by Nicéphore Niepce (1765–1833) in 1826 in a "camera obscura." This was a small dark room with a lens into one wall; the scene outside was projected onto the opposite wall. It took about eight hours to expose a pewter plate covered with chemicals that reacted to light.

In 1837, a Frenchman, Louis Jacques Mandé Daguerre (1787–1851), invented the daguerreotype process in which silver-plated copper sheets treated with iodine vapor replaced Niepce's pewter plate. Development of the latent image (the picture held invisibly in the chemicals) required treatment with mercury vapor. The visible image produced was reversed, with the black parts white and the white parts black. The process became popular, but produced only one picture at a time.

The multiple prints of today were impossible until William Fox Talbot (1800–77) developed the negative in 1839. But his calotype (later talbotype) was not as clear as the daguerreotype. Talbot's paper negatives could be made transparent by wax or oil. They were replaced by glass negatives; in 1861 the first color process was shown.

The modern camera

In 1888 George Eastman (1854–1932) introduced roll film and the simple box camera and thus brought photography to the man in the street. The year 1924 saw the introduction of the Leica, a miniature camera originally designed for testing 35mm motion picture film, and in 1925 the invention of the flash bulb released photography from dependence on sunlight or special artificial lighting.

The modern camera [Key] is a light-tight box with a mechanism that holds a piece of film flat and opposite a lens. The lens focuses onto the film a sharp upside-down image of the scene before the camera. A shutter, located between the film and the lens, prevents light reaching the film until it is opened, usually for only a fraction of a second. The correct exposure is obtained by regulating the relationship between the shutter speed and the diameter of the lens.

The diaphragm controls the amount of light passing through the lens and the shutter determines how long the film is exposed to the light. A fast shutter speed and a wide diaphragm opening will give the equivalent exposure of a slow shutter speed and a small opening. All cameras have a viewfinder—from a simple wire frame to a complex optical system—that enables the user to see what the camera "sees."

These features are common to all cameras, but there is great variation in their complexity and operation. The simplest cameras [3] have a single shutter speed and fixed diaphragm, both so chosen that on an

CONNECTIONS

See also
1786 Taking pictures
1788 Motion picture photography
1796 Communications: television
1800 Video recording and reproduction
1772 Modern printing

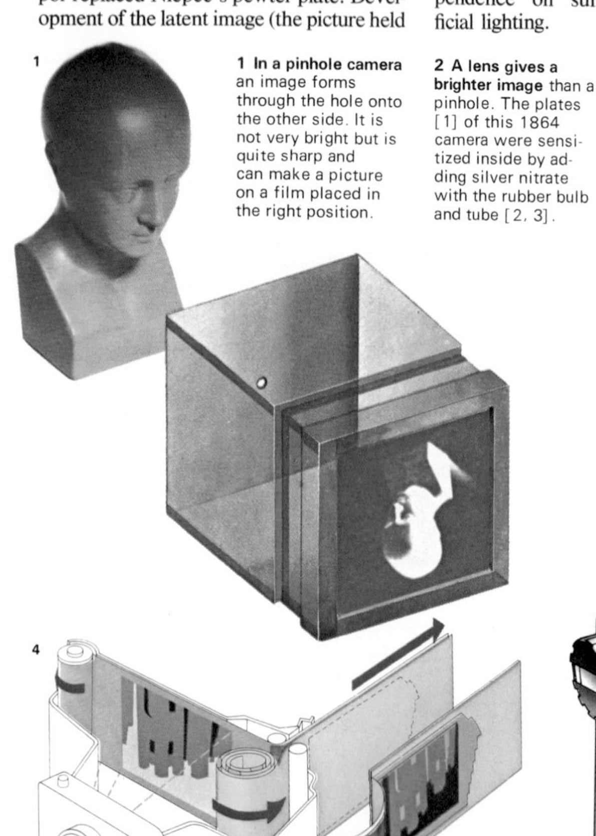

1 In a pinhole camera an image forms through the hole onto the other side. It is not very bright but is quite sharp and can make a picture on a film placed in the right position.

4 Polaroid cameras take composite "film and paper" packs that include processing chemicals. The picture is ready in seconds.

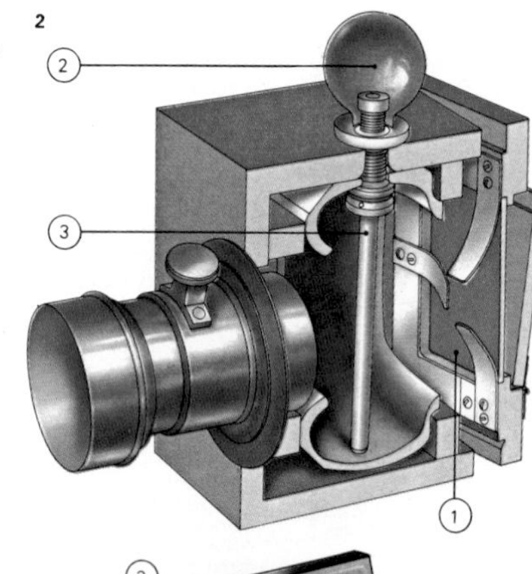

2 A lens gives a brighter image than a pinhole. The plates [1] of this 1864 camera were sensitized inside by adding silver nitrate with the rubber bulb and tube [2, 3].

3 Modern cameras work on the same principle and are much simpler to operate. This pocket model uses film in easy loading cartridges [1]. It has a single-speed shutter [2]. Alongside the main lens [3] is a viewfinder [4] to show what will be in the picture. In bright weather—or with a flash—it takes pictures in color or in black and white.

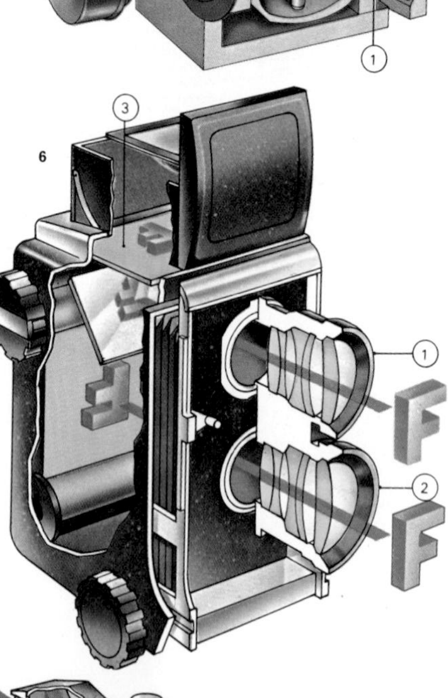

5 The single-lens reflex is a versatile camera design. The viewfinder [1] reveals an image formed via a mirror [2] by light from the main lens [3], showing exactly what is being focused upon.

6 The twin-lens reflex camera is really two cameras, one for focusing and viewfinding [1] and one for photography [2]. The lenses focus on a focusing screen [3].

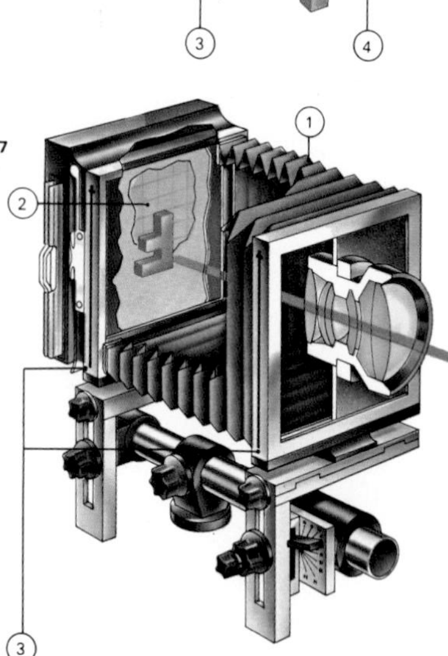

7 The studio camera does not have a viewfinder. The image is focused by means of bellows [1] on a ground glass sheet [2] at the back. Just before exposure this is replaced by a piece of film held in a film holder. The front and back panels can both be tilted, shifted, or swiveled independently [3]. This allows the professional photographer to manipulate subject angles and planes of sharp focus. It is ideal for static subjects and for various forms of copying.

average sunny day the correct amount of light is admitted. Complex cameras, designed to take perfect photographs in all kinds of lighting conditions, have shutters with a wide variety of speeds, from hours to perhaps 1/2000th of a second; lenses that can admit a much greater amount of light (and still focus precisely and clearly); and built-in accessories.

Generally the principal built-in accessory is an electronic exposure meter, which can automatically adjust shutter and diaphragm to the correct relationship. In many miniature (and some other) cameras the shutter is not built into the lens, or set just behind it, but lies almost against the film. These shutters are known as focal-plane shutters.

Film developing and printing

Film may be cut into sheets, loaded in a strip into a light-tight cartridge or cassette, or wound (backed with paper) onto a spool. It is thin transparent plastic coated with a photographic emulsion made of grains of silver salts suspended in gelatine. The grains are relatively large in highly sensitive (fast) film and small in slow film.

The latent image formed on the film [14] is made visible and permanent by chemical processing in four main stages—developing, stopping development, fixing, and washing. With negative film, developers darken the film in proportion to the light that reached it, so that the brighter parts of the scene that was photographed appear dark. In color negative film [13] the colors of the original subject are also reversed, each color being represented by its complement. Thus yellow appears as blue and red as cyan.

Fixing simply removes from the emulsion all the chemicals not affected by light, leaving areas of clear film. These portions print black in the final photograph. A "stop bath" between developer and fixer stops development at the correct point. Washing removes unwanted fixer, which would otherwise eventually spoil the negative. The printing process [10] is identical, except that light-sensitive paper is used (film may be used if the photo is to be projected).

KEY

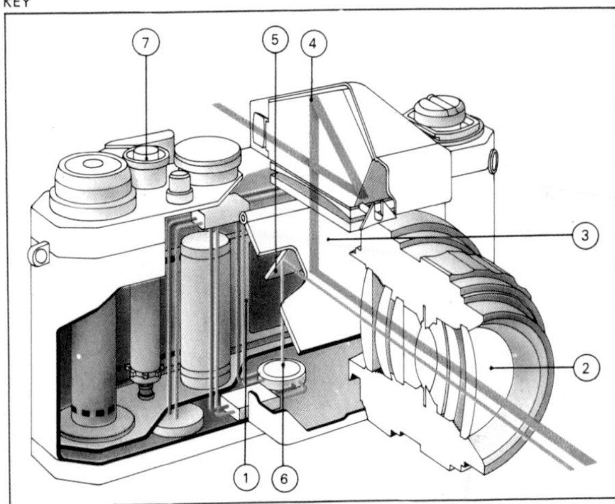

When the shutter [1] is released light reflected from a scene is focused onto film. Before the photo is taken, light entering the lens [2] is split along two paths. Most is reflected upward from a mirror [3] into a viewfinder [4]. A little is either reflected downward from a smaller mirror [5] into the photoelectric cell of an exposure meter [6], or directed to a cell in the viewfinder. The release [7] opens the shutter.

8

8 A black-and-white film is processed by immersion in a proper developer [1]. The action is then stopped [2] and made permanent by "fixing" [3]. The negative is washed [4] and dried [5].

9 After drying, the negative is seen as a picture with reversed tones; the blacks are recorded as clear, the whites as black, with the intermediate tones recorded as their complementary tones.

9

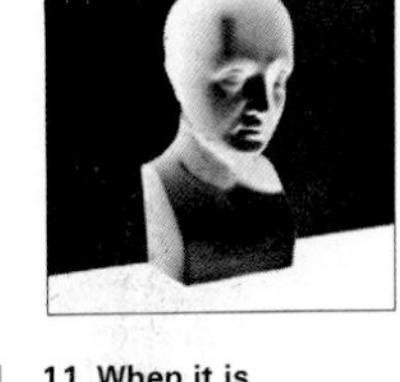

10

10 To make a print, light-sensitive paper is exposed to a same-size or enlarged image of the negative [1], then processed as is a film [2–6]. The paper is not as sensitive as film.

11

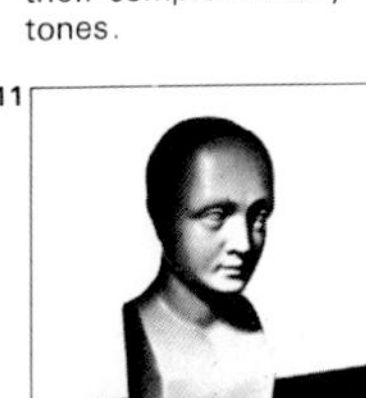

11 When it is washed and dried the paper has a permanent black-and-white image of the subject. The exact range from black to white depends on the paper's contrast and the surface.

12 The processing chemicals are spread onto Polaroid film as it is pulled from the camera [1]. After 15 seconds [2] the paper print is removed [3] from its negative. Fixer may be brushed on [4].

12

13

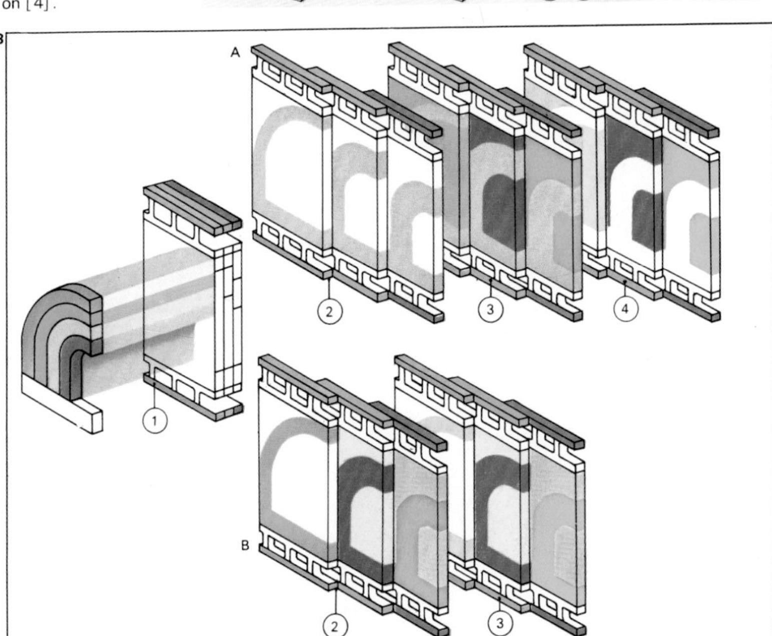

14

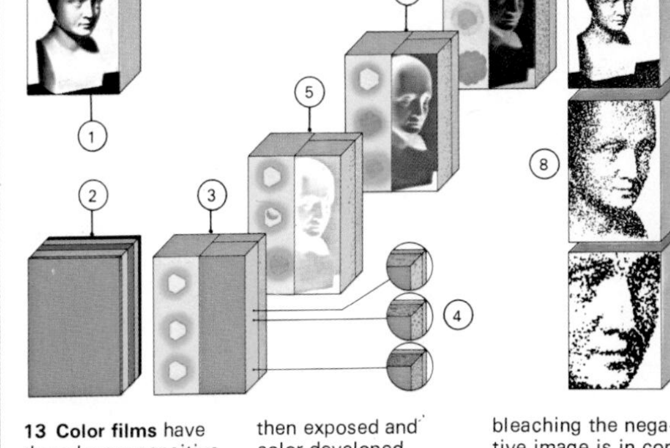

14 When light falls [1] on the light-sensitive emulsion of a film [2] it forms a latent image [3]. Grains of silver halide are slightly altered; the more light reaching the film, the more grains are affected [4]. In developer the grains are converted back to black metallic silver. At first a few are changed [5]; later a denser image forms [6, 7] consisting of clumps of silver grains [8].

13 Color films have three layers sensitive to blue, green, and red light respectively; each forms a latent image on exposure [1]. [A] Most transparency film is first developed to a black-and-white negative [2]. All remaining silver halide is then exposed and color developed. Now the film is opaque, as all silver has been blackened [3]. The silver is bleached out leaving a naturally colored dye image [4]. [B] Dyes form in the first development of color negatives [2]. After bleaching the negative image is in complementary colors [3{, and it also has residual yellow and orange dyes. This ensures the correct colors in the subsequent printing process.

Taking pictures

In the modern world, photography has replaced painting and drawing as the chief means of making pictures. It lets people capture images without the need for graphic skills.

Using a camera

Even with the simplest camera there are rules to be followed. For example, a suitable film must be used, and the camera must be properly positioned so that the subject is not too close and out of focus, nor too far away and too small in the finished picture. A live subject must keep reasonably still, the camera must be held level and steady, and the shutter release pressed gently.

With a more complicated camera the right exposure must be selected. On some cameras the photographer simply sets a pointer to the appropriate weather symbol. With others, the camera automatically sets its own aperture or shutter speed, or both. In the most sophisticated equipment the exposure is set manually, or by overriding the automatic system, to give the photographer creative control.

Lens apertures, or "stops," are normally expressed as *f*-numbers [2]. These are so calculated that the light-passing ability of any lens is the same at the same *f*-number, within the limits set by manufacturing tolerances and lens efficiency. The smaller the number, the more light reaches the film. Most cameras have apertures indicated by numbers from the scale: 1, 1.4, 2, 2.8, 4, 5.6, 8, 11, 16, 22, 32. Each number symbolizes half the light-passing ability of the one before it on the scale. Some cameras have apertures that fall between the scale figures.

Shutter speeds [1] may also be set on a scale that halves the light reaching the film with each step. The commonly used speeds are all fractions of a second, usually on the scale: 1, 1/2, 1/4, 1/8, 1/15, 1/30, 1/60, 1/125, 1/250, 1/500, 1/1000. Any one of a number of combinations of aperture and shutter speed can give the same exposure. For example, many color films need an exposure of 1/125 at *f*11 in bright sun. They receive the same amount of light with 1/30 at *f*22, and 1/500 at *f*5.6.

Filters and focusing

The way in which a black-and-white film records colors as monochrome tone values can be modified by using filters. These are disks of colored glass: when placed in front of the camera lens they transmit light of their own color and absorb light of other colors. A yellow filter can be used in landscape photography to prevent overexposure of the blue sky and to highlight detail in cloud formation.

The chosen combination of aperture and shutter speed is decided by the amount of light available. The aperture determines how much of the picture is in sharp focus. The distance between the nearest and farthest parts of the subject that come out sharp is called the depth of field. It is partly affected by the *f*-number. It is smaller with longer-focus lenses, often called telephoto lenses, and greater with shorter-focus (generally wide-angle) lenses. The depth of field also decreases or increases as the distance between camera and subject changes [7].

Shutter speed determines how sharply moving subjects come out. Slow speeds

CONNECTIONS

See also
1784 Photography
1788 Motion picture photography
1252 Realist painting in the 19th century

1 A

B

2 A

B

C

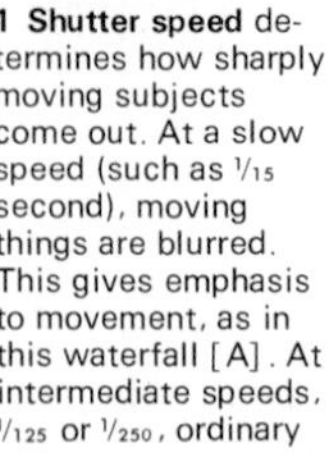

1 Shutter speed determines how sharply moving subjects come out. At a slow speed (such as 1/15 second), moving things are blurred. This gives emphasis to movement, as in this waterfall [A]. At intermediate speeds, 1/125 or 1/250, ordinary movements do not affect the picture, but really fast objects still blur. Fast speeds, such as 1/500 or 1/1000 second can freeze most movement and reveal details that are normally unseen, as shown in this photo of river rapids [B].

2 When the lens is set to a large aperture (such as *f*4) it has little depth of field. Only part of the subject is in sharp focus. The actual plane of the sharp image depends on how close [A] or distant [B] the lens is focused. At small apertures (large *f*-numbers such as *f*16) the depth of field is much larger and most of the subject comes out sharp [C]. Choosing the aperture can thus concentrate the viewer's attention on selected parts of the subject.

carry the risk that the picture will be spoiled by camera shake. Few people can hand-hold a camera steadily enough to use times longer than $^{1}/_{60}$ second.

Simple cameras are pre-set to give about $^{1}/_{60}$ second at f11. They have enough depth of field to take sharp pictures of anything more than about 5ft (1.5m) from the camera.

The professionals

Professional photographers work in a wide range of fields. Some record life as it is for newspapers, magazines, and similar publications. Others set up the situation they want in a studio or on a carefully chosen location. Their pictures are usually used as decorative illustrations for the publication or in advertising to show a product to its best advantage.

Photojournalists and other reporting photographers have to take scenes as they find them. They create their pictures by choosing a suitable viewpoint and manipulating the shutter speed and aperture. They may have some simple portable lighting, such as an electronic flash unit. But this is normally used merely to illuminate a subject that is not well enough lit.

On the other hand, advertising, portrait, and industrial photographers manipulate their lighting to make the most of the subject. A studio set may be lit by several electronic flashes [6], or by a series of theatrical spotlights and floodlights [3]. The first consideration is the angle of the main, or key, light, followed by the amount of fill-in light used to keep the shadows from being too dark. There may also be background lighting, or special effects, such as a backlight to make a model's hair glow.

Professional photographers understand how to get sharp, grain-free, perfectly lit, and accurately colored pictures. But much of the impact of good, exciting photography depends occasionally on breaking the rules to create something more than a mere record of what is in front of the camera. Whether he breaks rules, or follows them, has sophisticated or simple equipment, a photographer creates the picture in the viewfinder the instant that he presses the shutter release.

KEY

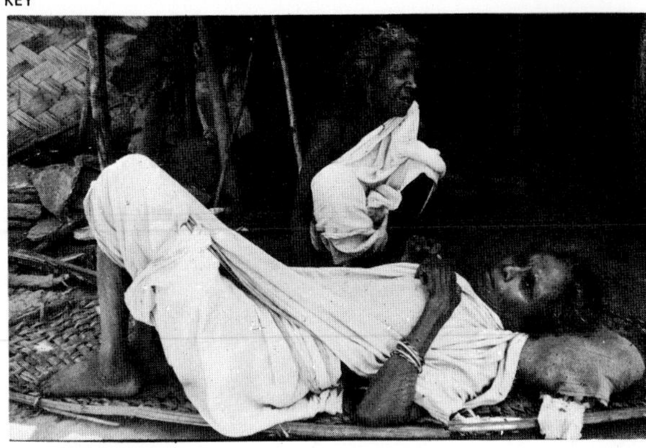

One good picture is worth 1,000 words. This maxim is known and understood by every newspaper editor. For example, this photograph, taken by Chris Steele-Perkins, shows all the agony and despair of the terrible conflict in Bangladesh. It says far more about human suffering than the most eloquent of reports could achieve with descriptive prose. The recent history of war and revolution in Asia, Africa, the Middle East, Southeast Asia, and Northern Ireland has brought to the fore photojournalists able to capture the violence and compassion of the modern age, often risking their own safety in order to take good pictures with the desired impact.

3 A

B

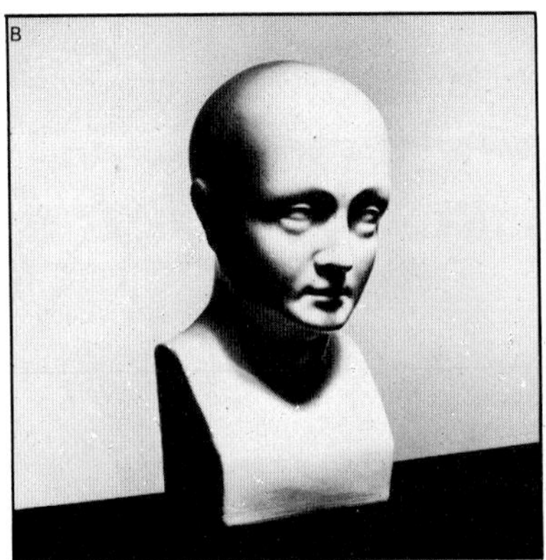

C

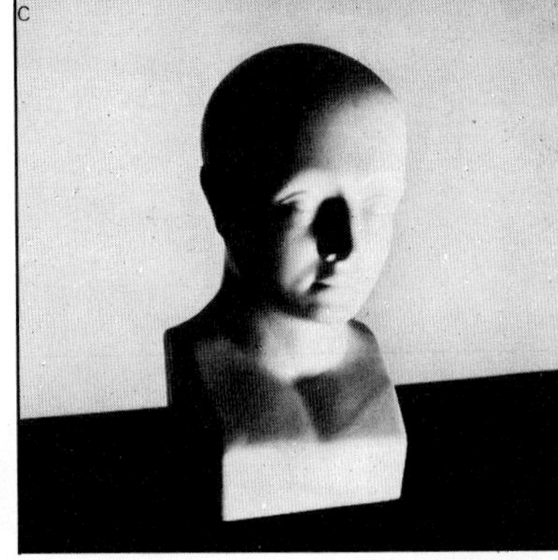

3 The angle at which light falls on the subject changes its appearance in the photograph. Direct lighting from the front gives a flat look. If the key light is moved to the side [A], above [B], or below [C] it creates a more interesting picture. The effect can be harsh with a "hard" light source. To soften it, a fill light is used. It is placed in a more-or-less frontal position.

4

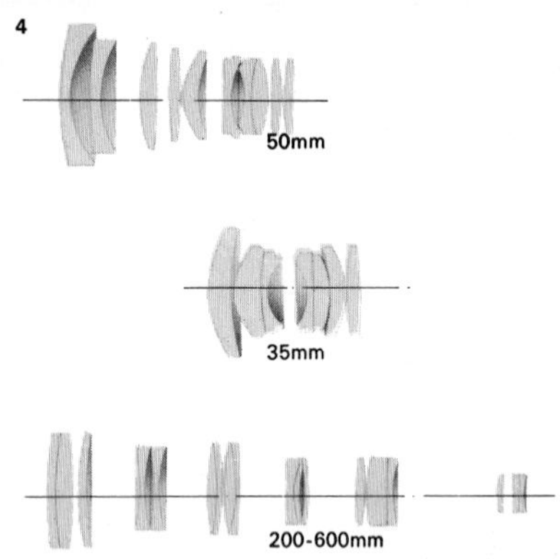
50mm
35mm
200-600mm

4 Camera lenses consist of glass or plastic elements in a tube. Number, shape, and position of the elements determine the focal length and maximum aperture. On a 35mm camera, a 35mm lens covers a wide field of view; a 50mm lens covers a standard field. Some lenses can zoom through a range of focal lengths between two fixed points, as in an extremely long focus or telephoto lens of 200–600mm.

5

5 Simple cameras often take battery-fired flash cubes, with disposable flash bulbs mounted in reflectors, which rotate between flashes.

6

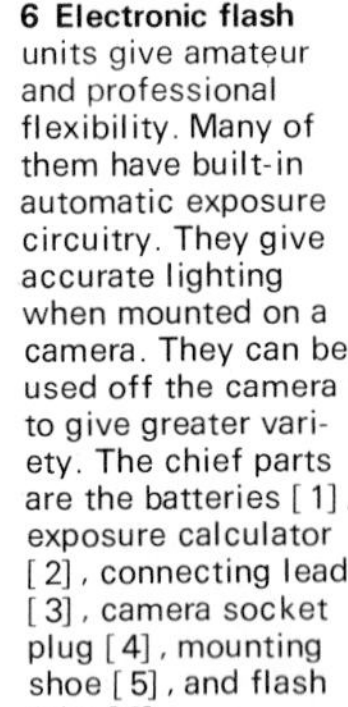

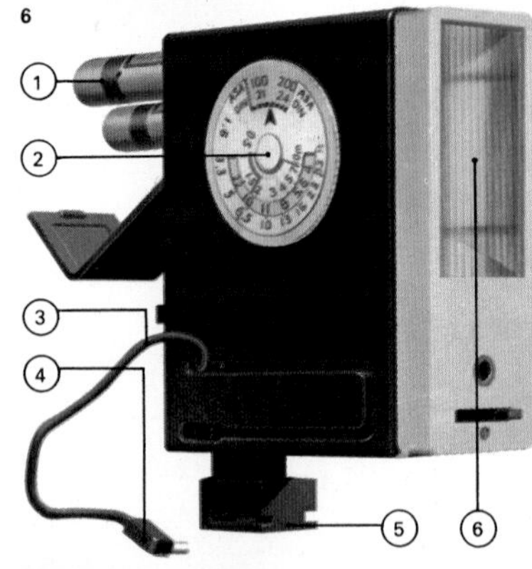
1
2
3
4
5
6

6 Electronic flash units give amateur and professional flexibility. Many of them have built-in automatic exposure circuitry. They give accurate lighting when mounted on a camera. They can be used off the camera to give greater variety. The chief parts are the batteries [1], exposure calculator [2], connecting lead [3], camera socket plug [4], mounting shoe [5], and flash tube [6].

7 A

B

C

7 Altering the focal length alters the subject's size, pictured from a fixed camera position. If the camera is moved so that the subject stays the same size, it comes out a different shape with different angles of view. A wide-angle lens [A] enlarges the nose and chin, while a narrow angle, long focus, lens [C] tends to flatten them, but is preferred for portraits. A standard lens is in between [B], and intended to give a normal view.

Motion picture photography

A motion picture camera [Key] works just like a still camera, with one major exception: instead of taking just one picture of a scene, it rapidly takes a series of pictures or frames [7]. The usual rate for taking and projecting amateur movies is 18 pictures a second and for professional movies 24. Older silent movies were shot at 16 pictures a second. Each exposure produces a static view of the scene; but anything that moves is in a slightly different place in each succeeding frame. When the pictures are projected in sequence the movement is recreated. If pictures are taken at a faster rate, such as 48 or 72 a second, they produce slow motion when projected at normal speed; pictures taken at longer intervals, such as 16 or 8 a second, produce a speed-up motion at normal projection speed.

The camera

All movie cameras have a motor—usually electric, occasionally clockwork—to drive the film from one spool to another; and they all have a lens, shutter, and gate mechanism. Apart from these features, they vary enormously. The simplest cameras have a fixed-focus lens and simple automatic exposure systems—ensuring acceptable results in most outdoor conditions. More versatile cameras are fitted with zoom lenses that allow a range of image sizes. These lenses generally have a focus control and often a built-in rangefinder system. Only in the most sophisticated cameras can the lens be removed and replaced with another. Super 8 cameras range in sophistication from the movie equivalents of box cameras to complex machines hardly distinguishable from 16mm professional equipment.

Motion picture camera film

Motion picture camera film is used in five widths—70mm, 35mm, 16mm, 9.5mm, and 8mm. The 70mm and 35mm sizes are used by major film companies in cameras that are highly complex and expensive. Such cameras are often used with special image-squeezing "anamorphic" lenses to produce wide-screen pictures. 16mm film is used for smaller-budget commercial pictures, documentary films, much television filming, and by serious amateurs. A special format with a larger picture area, Super 16, is made for wide-screen filming to be printed onto 35mm film stock. Although apparently superseded for a quarter of a century, 9.5mm still has its adherents in Europe. The 8mm size is the popular amateur film width and is also used for low-budget television work. There are two picture sizes—Standard 8 and Super 8. With Standard 8 the camera is loaded with special 16mm film either on simple spools or in reloadable magazines. After half the width (that is, an 8mm-wide strip down one side) has been exposed, the film is turned over to expose the other half. It is cut along the middle after processing. Super 8 film in plastic cartridges has virtually superseded Standard 8.

Because the same piece of film is normally used both for filming and projection, almost all amateur movies are shot in color reversal film—usually rated at 40 ASA (17 DIN) in artificial light or 25 ASA (15DIN) in daylight. ASA and DIN ratings are a measure of the "speed" of the film—that is, its sensitivity to light. Super 8 cameras have a

CONNECTIONS

See also
1784 Photography
1786 Taking pictures
1314 Origins of film
1362 Hollywood
1370 Cinema as art

1 Moving subjects were first pictured as a series of still photographs by Eadweard Muybridge (1830–1904) in 1877. He set up 12 and later 25 cameras fitted with high-speed shutters. As a horse galloped or trotted by, it set off each camera in turn by breaking a string or through electrical contacts. Later Muybridge extended his technique to a wide range of subjects, using the principles of moving picture toys (such as the Zoetrope) to produce moving images.

2 The gun camera was produced by Etienne-Jules Marey (1830–1903) in 1882. It was the first single camera to take a series of photographs. It was sighted like a gun and, when the trigger was pulled, took 12 small pictures in one second on a revolving circular photographic plate. Marey was not limited to subjects that could trip the camera shutter, and made numerous series of photographs of birds.

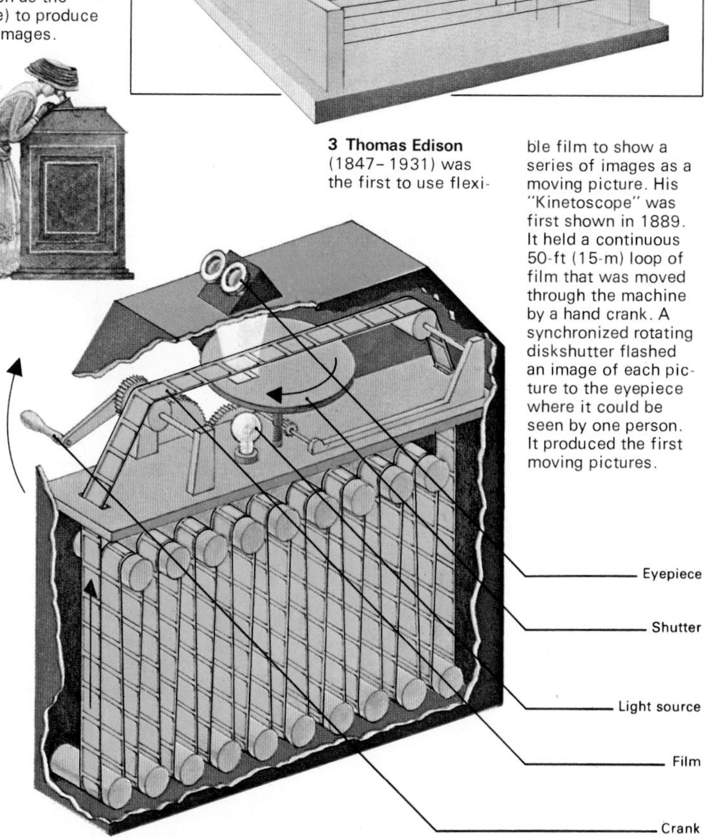

Eyepiece
Shutter
Light source
Film
Crank

3 Thomas Edison (1847–1931) was the first to use flexible film to show a series of images as a moving picture. His "Kinetoscope" was first shown in 1889. It held a continuous 50-ft (15-m) loop of film that was moved through the machine by a hand crank. A synchronized rotating diskshutter flashed an image of each picture to the eyepiece where it could be seen by one person. It produced the first moving pictures.

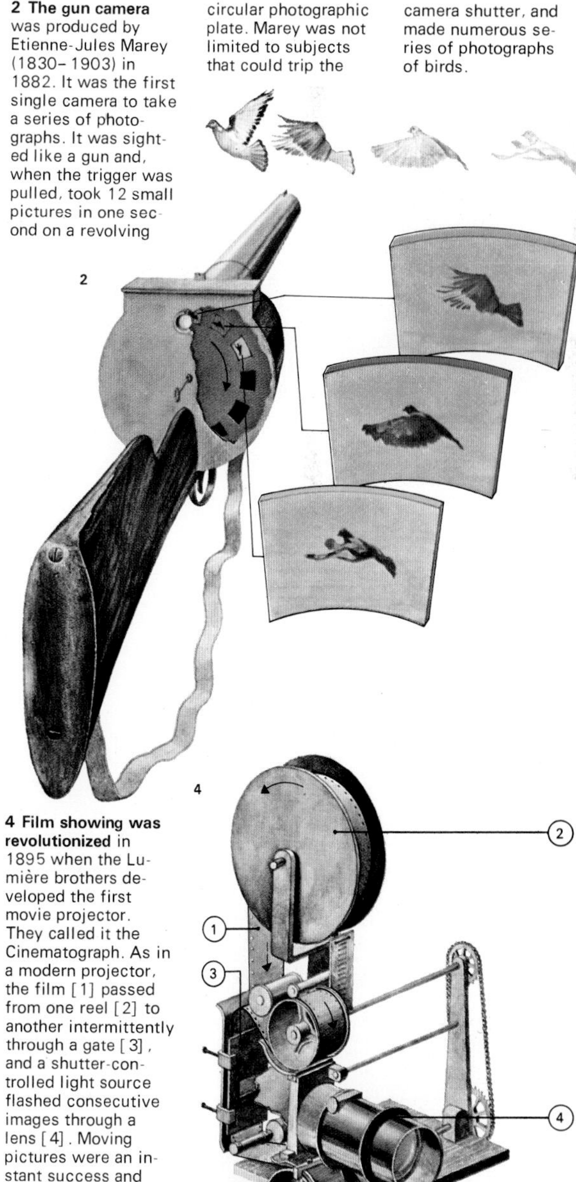

1
2
3
4

4 Film showing was revolutionized in 1895 when the Lumière brothers developed the first movie projector. They called it the Cinematograph. As in a modern projector, the film [1] passed from one reel [2] to another intermittently through a gate [3], and a shutter-controlled light source flashed consecutive images through a lens [4]. Moving pictures were an instant success and within a decade the motion picture industry was a reality.

built-in filter and normally use the 40 ASA (17 DIN) artificial light film with this filter in daylight. The 160 ASA (23 DIN) films are available for poor lighting conditions and, with specially designed lowlight XL type cameras, can make films in ordinary home lighting.

Most professional moviemakers use negative film—either color or black-and-white. The colors or tones of the final copies are determined in the processing laboratory. The films for projection are always positive—like color transparencies, but negatives are used for some television transmission and they are reversed electronically.

Projection and editing

The film is projected as a series of static images. If the images follow one another fast enough, the effect is a moving picture. To reduce flicker, the projector shutter closes and opens during each frame, so we see 48 pictures a second, each of which is repeated with a moment of blackness intervening.

For home movies, the original camera film is projected. In professional work prints are made from the camera negatives and are edited and spliced to make a complete film. The camera negatives are then cut and joined together to match. Any optical effects are added at this stage. Such effects include "fades" to black or white, "dissolves" from one scene to the next, and "wipes" in which a new scene progressively displaces the old one. A master negative is then made from the complete film and used to produce all the prints for distribution. The prints need not be on the same size of film as the camera original. For the largest theaters, 70mm film is used; 35mm is more usual, 16mm copies are made for small theaters and schools.

Soundtracks on movies may be either magnetic or optical. Magnetic tracks are recorded on magnetic strips coated on the film, just like a normal tape recording. Optical tracks record the sound as brightness variations in a dark stripe down the edge of the film. They are replayed by shining a light through them on to a photoelectric cell [7].

KEY

In a movie camera, fresh film [1] is fed from a spool to the gate [2]. A revolving shutter [3] controls exposure to light focused through a lens [4]. This produces an upside down image like that in a still camera. While the shutter is closed, a claw mechanism [5] moves the film through the gate in measured steps. Between steps the film remains stationary and the shutter opens and closes again. The scene is recorded as a series of pictures taken one after the other. The reflex viewfinder uses a mirror shutter [6]. When the shutter is closed, the image through the camera lens is reflected from its mirror surface to the viewfinder. As a result, the image directed through the prism and lens system is exactly the same as that passing through the lens. In the viewfinder, the cameraman sees exactly what the lens "sees."

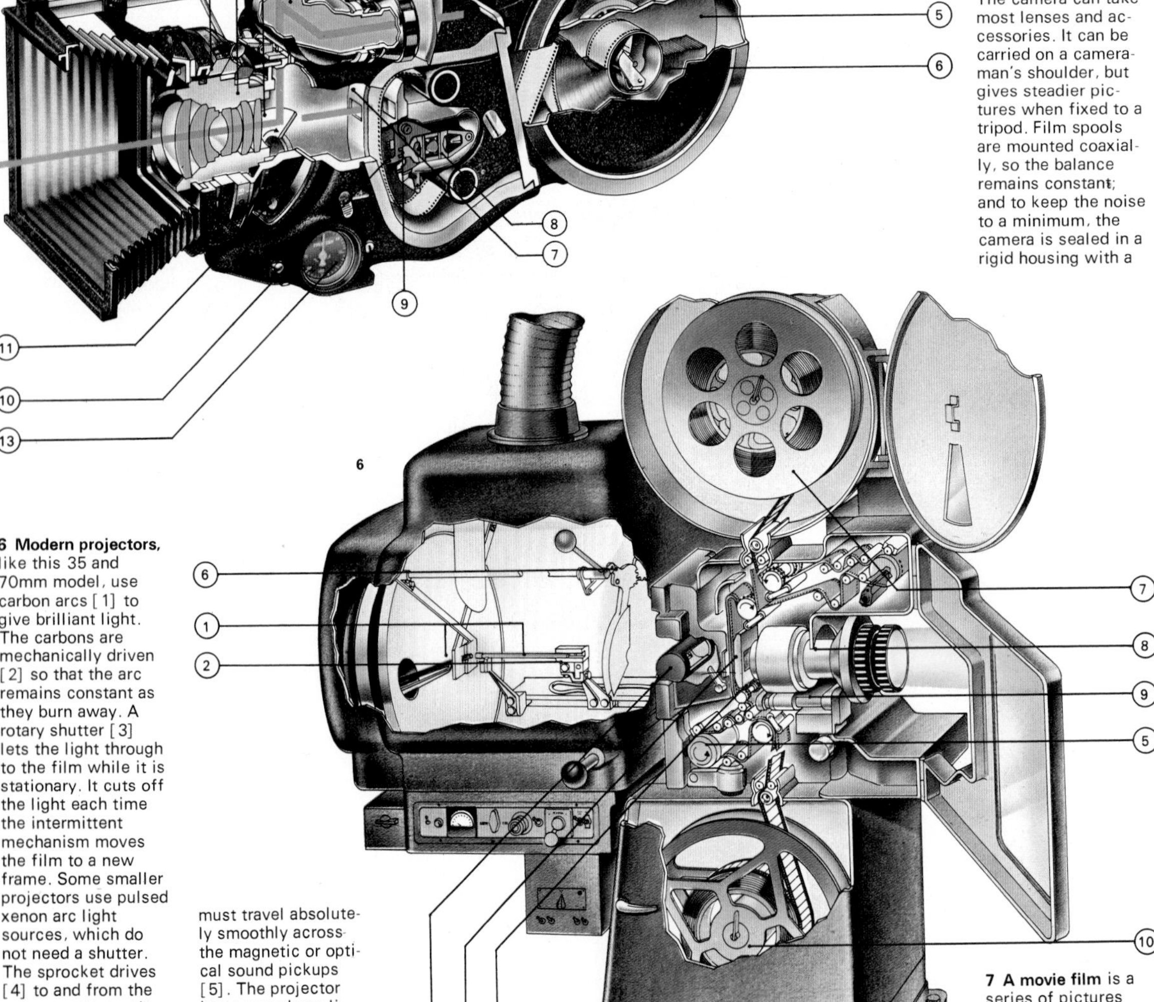

5 Floor-mounted movie cameras are used in studios; lighter cameras such as this 35mm model are used outdoors. The camera can take most lenses and accessories. It can be carried on a cameraman's shoulder, but gives steadier pictures when fixed to a tripod. Film spools are mounted coaxially, so the balance remains constant; and to keep the noise to a minimum, the camera is sealed in a rigid housing with a window in front of the lens. The gate is fitted with register pins to ensure that each frame is accurately located on the film.

Key
- **[1] Focus control**
- **[2] Aperture control**
- **[3] Mirror shutter**
- **[4] Viewfinder eyepiece**
- **[5] Take-up spool**
- **[6] Feed spool**
- **[7] Gate**
- **[8] Sprocket drive**
- **[9] Pull-down claw**
- **[10] Register pins**
- **[11] Indicator**
- **[12] Viewfinder**
- **[13] Footage indicator**
- **[14] Lens**

6 Modern projectors, like this 35 and 70mm model, use carbon arcs [1] to give brilliant light. The carbons are mechanically driven [2] so that the arc remains constant as they burn away. A rotary shutter [3] lets the light through to the film while it is stationary. It cuts off the light each time the intermittent mechanism moves the film to a new frame. Some smaller projectors use pulsed xenon arc light sources, which do not need a shutter. The sprocket drives [4] to and from the gate operate continuously. Small loops above and below the gate allow for intermittent movement. To give good sound reproduction the film must travel absolutely smoothly across the magnetic or optical sound pickups [5]. The projector has a sound amplifier. The shield [6], feed spool [7], lens [8], focus drive [9], take-up spool [10], and film guide [11] are other main parts.

7 A movie film is a series of pictures ready for projection. In each succeeding one, moving objects are slightly displaced. Sprocket holes along the edge ensure that each frame is held in the right place in the projector. A variable area stripe along one edge carries the soundtrack. As this passes a light-sensitive cell, it modulates the light from a lamp and produces sound signals.

Communications: telegraph

Long distance communications, which for thousands of years had depended on the slow and unreliable travel of messengers by foot, horseback, or ship were transformed by telegraphy. Simple forms of semaphore had long been used, but the transmission of messages beyond the range of sight had to wait until the discovery of electricity. The idea was foreshadowed as early as 1753 by a Scottish doctor, Charles Morrison, in a letter to the *Scots Magazine*. In 1764 George Louis Lesages built and operated an experimental electric telegraph in Geneva using static electricity and an electroscope. The mutual repulsion of a pair of pith balls indicated the presence of an electric charge in a wire connected to them and a separate wire was used for each letter.

Single-wire telegraphy

At the end of the eighteenth century, Napoleon Bonaparte, who was the first to make use of a systematic telegraph, still had to rely on a visual system invented by a French merchant, Claude Chappe (1763–1805), to receive intelligence reports and send orders to his army [1]. It was not until 1816 that a single-wire telegraph was invented by an Englishman, Francis Ronalds (1788–1873). He set up disks turned by clockwork at each end of the wire. Each disk was initialed with the alphabet around its rim and, as the desired letter aligned with a pointer, the sender's wire was connected to an electroscope. With the disks synchronized, a man at the other end of the wire could note the letter indicated each time the wire received a charge.

Ten years later an American, Harrison Gray Dyer, built the first practical electrical telegraph by using the recently invented voltaic cell (battery) and a chemical solution that indicated the presence of an electric current by the formation of bubbles at two electrodes. Dyer sent messages along 8mi (12.5km) of wire in Long Island, New York, using the Earth to complete the circuit.

The further step in the evolution of the electric telegraph came in 1831 when another American, Joseph Henry (1797–1878), replaced Dyer's electrolytic indicator with an electric sounder, using the principle of electromagnetism discovered in 1819 by the Danish physicist Hans Christian Oersted (1787–1851). Henry used a code to indicate the different letters of the alphabet.

Two Englishmen, William Cooke (1806–79) and Charles Wheatstone (1802–75), designed and installed the world's first commercial telegraph [2]. This was a six-wire, five-needle system, first tested in 1837 on the London-Birmingham railroad and installed permanently two years later for the Great Western Railway.

Morse code and later developments

Up to this time each inventor had devised his own means of coding messages. It was an American inventor and painter, Samuel Morse (1791–1872), who first recognized the practical and commercial importance of devising a standard code. He demonstrated his own code in 1837 and it was the revised Morse code that eventually made possible the worldwide development of electric telegraphs. Consisting of a single wire, the telegraph circuit was completed by a battery

CONNECTIONS

See also
1792 Communications: telephone
1794 Communications: radio
1796 Communications: television
868 Codes, ciphers, and secret messages

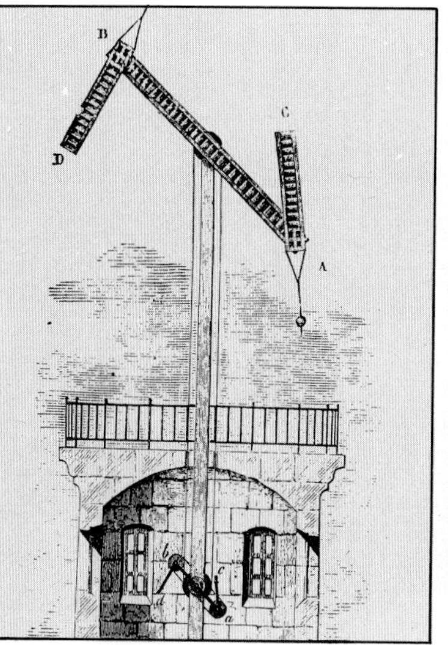

1 The earliest form of long-distance communication, apart from jungle drums, smoke signals, and similar devices, was the visual semaphore invented by Claude Chappe and used by the French army from 1794. The Chappe telegraph consisted of pairs of hand-operated semaphore arms located on a chain of towers built on the tops of hills within sight of each other and used to transmit orders.

2 The first commercial telegraph was a six-wire, five-needle system set up in England in 1839. Shown is a later, two-needle model. Switch pairs made each needle deflect in either direction.

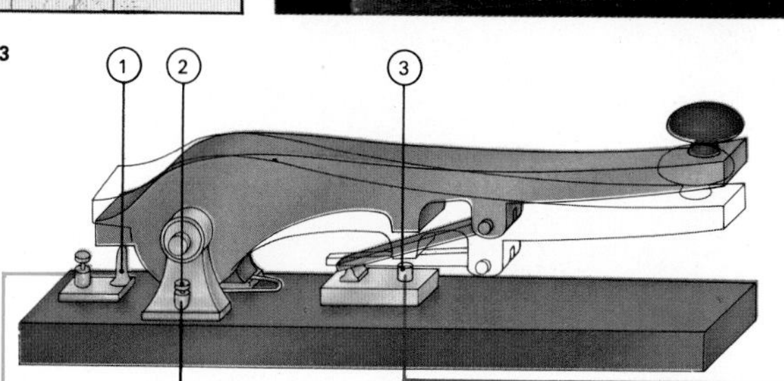
1
2
3

3 A Morse key is basically a switch. This early two-pole key has a closed circuit between points [1] and [2] when at rest. When the key is depressed contact [1] is broken and the circuit made instead through [3]. Current entering via the black wire is switched from blue to red.

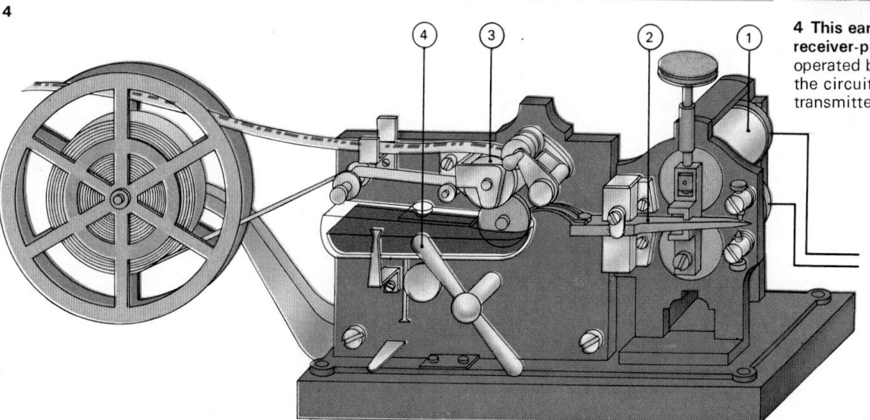
4
3
2
1

4 This early Morse receiver-printer is operated by closing the circuit of the transmitter (a simple key). The current energizes the coils [1]. The lever [2] is moved by magnetic attraction, bringing the printing disk [3] into contact with the paper tape for the duration of the current. The disk is linked by contact with a roller immersed in printer's ink. The movement of the paper tape is effected by clockwork wound by the handle [4]. It was found that a skilled operator could "read" a buzzer faster than an inked tape.

5 Emile Baudot's multiplex system enabled several telegraph operators to send messages over the same line simultaneously. Each operator's set was connected in turn to the line by a distributor for just enough time to allow transmission of a single letter in the form of a five-unit code. By exact phase synchronization outgoing signals could be correctly separated and "read" on receivers at the other end of the transmission line.

and tappable key between the wire and the Earth at the sending end [3], and an electromagnetic sounder between the wire and the Earth at the receiving end.

The laying of submarine cables [6, 8] was a natural development of the electric telegraph. A connection across the English Channel in 1850 encouraged engineers to attempt the more difficult task of laying a cable across the Atlantic. Success came in 1858 when a cable was laid from Ireland to Newfoundland, although a reliable link was not established until 1866 [Key].

Because wire is expensive inventors soon thought of ways of sending a number of messages simultaneously along a single wire. The breakthrough came in 1892 when a Frenchman, Emile Baudot (1845–1903), designed an instrument that, when fully developed, could interlace six messages and decode them separately [5].

Teleprinting systems

Baudot's system, in which every letter consisted of five pulses (or absence of pulses), was replaced by a more sophisticated frequency division multiplex, invented in the 1890s by an American, Elisha Gray (1835–1901).

To reduce the time spent coding and decoding messages much effort was given, over many years, to the invention of an automatic printing telegraph. David Hughes (1831–1900), an Anglo-American professor, built the first practical printing telegraph in 1854 [4], but it, too, was slow. In 1921 a Russian, N. P. Trusevich, invented what is called the "start-stop" system and the modern teleprinter became possible. The new invention solved the problem of keeping the receiving machine perfectly synchronized with the sending machine when the operator's typing speed varied slightly from letter to letter [9]. The modern teleprinter, using the five-unit code, can transmit up to 13 characters a second when working from punched paper tape, which the operator first prepares, typing at his own speed. Telex [7] enables up to 26 teleprinter messages to be on a single telephone cable. Phototelegraphy [10] completes the range of modern telegraphic communications.

KEY

A cable-laying ship is especially designed so that miles of submarine telegraph cable can be fed out over sheaves in the bows. Today cable-laying is a routine task, but it took the American businessman Cyrus W. Field (1819–92) nine years and five attempts before the first successful transatlantic telegraph cable was laid in 1866. For the laying the engineers used the largest ship then afloat, the steam screw and paddle ship *Great Eastern*, built by the British engineer Isambard Kingdom Brunel (1806–59).

1 2 3 4 5

6 A typical early submarine cable was made up of a stranded copper conductor [3], usually of wires or copper tapes woven around a heavy central strand; an insulating layer [2], originally of gutta percha; a layer of jute fiber [4] with galvanized steel wires embedded in it (for strength); another layer [1] of compounded jute; and an outer waterproof layer [5] tough enough to withstand chafing.

7A B

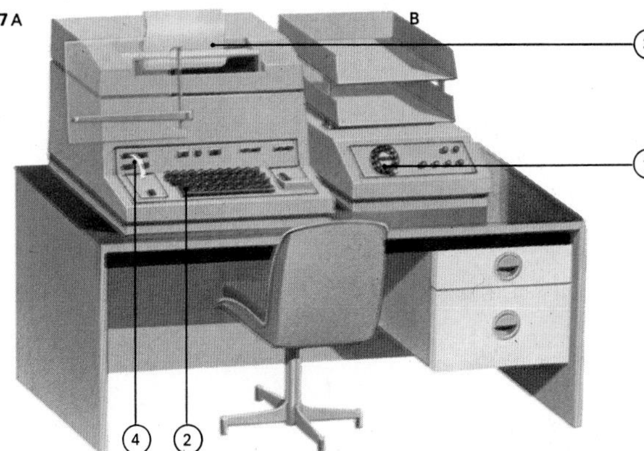

3
1
4
2

7 A modern Telex installation comprises a teletypewriter [A] and a dialing unit [B], both often built into a single console. The operator uses the dial unit [1] to call the receiver's telex number and then types the message using conventional typewriter keys [2]. Alternatively, the message can be pretyped on punched tape [4] and fed in for extra speed in transmission or when a line is free. For checking, the transmitted message is automatically printed out above [3]. When not sending, the equipment is left ready for receiving. A buzzer can alert the receiving operator to an incoming message. If the operator is absent the teletypewriter is automatically activated to reproduce the message on the paper [3]. Incoming messages can thus be "stored" in typed form on the machine until the operator returns.

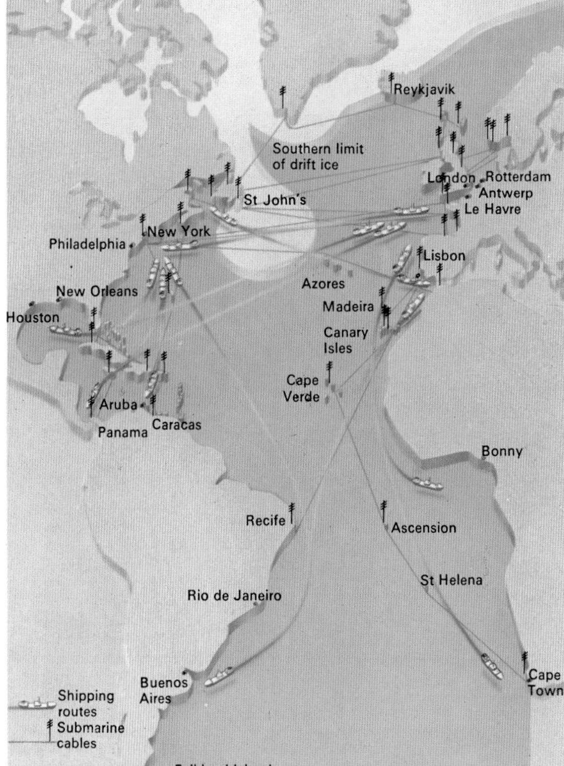

Reykjavik
Southern limit of drift ice
St John's
London
Rotterdam
Antwerp
Le Havre
New York
Philadelphia
Lisbon
Azores
New Orleans
Madeira
Houston
Canary Isles
Cape Verde
Aruba
Caracas
Panama
Bonny
Recife
Ascension
St Helena
Rio de Janeiro
Cape Town
Buenos Aires
Shipping routes
Submarine cables
Falkland Islands

8 Telegraph cabling across the Atlantic first became fully successful in 1866. After this the world's oceans were soon crossed by a network of such cables. The map shows today's transatlantic routes. Cable communications were supplemented by radio in the 1920s and by satellite systems in the 1960s. Cables retain the advantage of privacy because the messages they carry are difficult to intercept.

9

Letter	Morse code	Morse code electrical signals	Five-unit code	Five-unit electrical signals (Start … Stop)
A	•–			
E	•			
O	–––			
Y	–•––			

9 The teleprinter has a seven-unit code consisting of a start signal, a five-unit character signal, and a stop signal. The start and stop signals enable the equipment to keep the five-unit signals in step for each transmitted letter, despite the fact that no two typists operate at the same precise speed or perfectly evenly. Morse signals, being of unequal length, cannot be so used on the teleprinter.

10

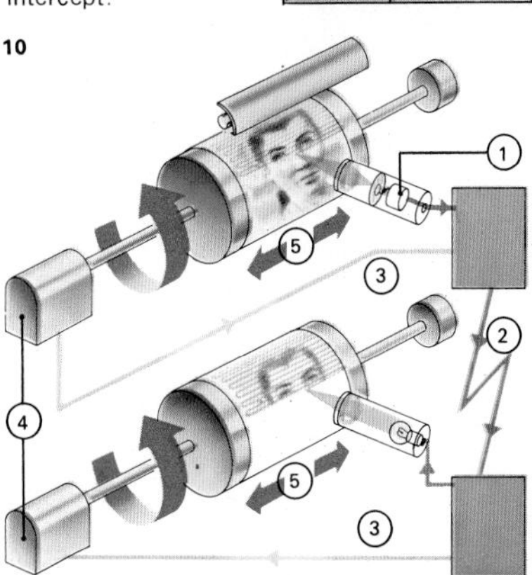

1
5
3
2
4
5
3

10 In photo-telegraphy, used widely by newspapers, the picture is "scanned" by a spot of light that covers its area in a series of parallel lines. The brightness of each element is converted by the cell [1] into an electrical signal that is transmitted [2] by telegraph. A machine at the receiving end converts the signal back into a picture by printing it dot by dot according to the incoming signal. Pulses [3] synchronize the motors [4] and the traverse mechanism [5].

Communications: telephone

Inventors working independently often arrive at very similar solutions to a problem. So it was in 1876 when Alexander Graham Bell (1847–1922), a Scottish professor of vocal physiology living in the United States, applied for a patent for his electric telephone only a few hours before an American from Chicago, Elisha Gray (1835–1901), filed a similar application. Bell was granted the patent and has since generally been credited as the inventor of the telephone.

Bell's instrument [2] was used both as transmitter and receiver and needed no battery. But the current generated when sound vibrated the diaphragm in its "microphone" was small and it was therefore unsuitable for long-distance communication.

The microphone and telephone exchange

In 1877 the American Thomas Edison (1847–1931) invented the carbon microphone. By another coincidence a similar microphone was developed independently a year later by the Anglo-American professor David Hughes (1831–1900), who is now generally credited as the inventor. The carbon microphone [4] modulates an electric current from a DC source, creating a voltage that varies in step with the sound waves. It is used to this day as the transmitter in modern telephones, the receiver being an electromagnetic earphone similar to that patented by Bell. A varying voltage in the earphone's coil causes a metal diaphragm to vibrate and produce sounds at low volume.

For the telphone to become a practical proposition it was necessary to find a means of interconnecting any pair of a number of instruments. The first telephone exchange was opened at New Haven, Connecticut, in 1878 and a similar eight-line exchange was set up in London a year later. An operator used plugs and sockets to connect callers.

In 1889 an American undertaker, Almon Strowger, annoyed by the inefficient service from his local exchange, designed an automatic selector. The first automatic exchange was opened in La Porte, Indiana, in 1892. The Strowger electromechanical selector [5] became standard equipment for telephone exchanges throughout the world during the next half century.

Since 1926 an American invention, the crossbar switch, began to replace the Strowger selector. It is in use today in the United States, Great Britain, and Sweden, although an even more efficient all-electronic exchange was developed in 1960.

Telephone cables

The largest single expense in any long-distance telephone system is the cost of the wires that connect subscribers to each other. Research into the problem of using a single cable for more than one simultaneous telephone call bore fruit in 1936 when the first 12-channel coaxial cable was laid between Bristol and Plymouth in southwest England. The system uses electric carrier waves of different frequencies, which can be transmitted simultaneously along the metal core of the cable and separated at the other end by a series of electronic "filters," each of which accepts signals of one frequency only.

The longer a telephone line, the weaker the electrical signal reaching the end; this is caused by the resistance of the wire. Auto-

CONNECTIONS

See also
1790 Communications: telegraph
1794 Communications: radio
1796 Communications: television

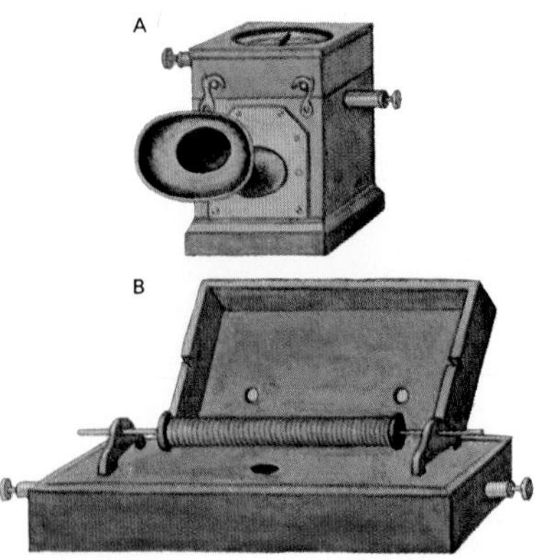

1
A
B

1 An early telephone designed by a German, Philipp Reis, in about 1861 has a transmitter [A] with a metal point in light contact with a metal strip fixed to a membrane. Reis believed that the intermittent circuit caused when the membrane vibrated would produce a varying electric current which could be reconverted into sound. The receiver [B] was based on the change in length of an iron needle in a magnetic field.

2 Bell's first telephone used a parchment drum that vibrated when sound waves reached it. A piece of iron was supported by a short length of clock spring so that it rested lightly on the parchment [A]. An electromagnet [B] was placed so that one pole was close to the iron piece. When the parchment and the iron vibrated a small varying electric current was induced in the coil. When two such instruments were connected the current produced by one energized the magnet of the other, causing the iron piece and the parchment to vibrate in step with the first. By this means a voice or any other sound that vibrated one parchment diaphragm was reproduced by similar vibrations of the other. Alexander Bell obtained the publicity he needed for his invention when it was seen by the Emperor of Brazil.

3 An exchange network allows telephone subscribers to dial any number in a national system. The lines and numbers indicate the direction in which calls can be routed and the dialing code for each route. The squares, always in pairs, are main exchanges, one part for local, the other for long-distance calls. The circles are subexchanges—those top right being directly interconnected exchanges in a city. All city, local, and main exchanges have lines to subscribers. A caller on exchange P can call numbers on exchange N by first dialing the code "9," or numbers on exchange Q by dialing code "987." To call exchange S he must first dial code "991," and to call a number on exchange T the code is "99186." A long-distance call between exchanges P and M is routed by dial code "072188" through trunk exchange N, which has equipment to take care of long-distance billing. A call to city exchange B starts with code "051," which connects the call to "director" exchange A. This automatically routes the call the most convenient way via other city exchanges. Foreign calls are routed by the trunk exchange to the nearest international exchange, where the call is passed to the other country.

tomatic amplifiers (called repeaters) overcame this problem and today these are incorporated in multi-channel cables every 10mi (16km). The first transatlantic multichannel telephone cable, called TAT 1, was laid in 1956. It was a twin coaxial cable—one for speech in each direction—running from Scotland to Newfoundland and included 51 repeaters in each cable. Today, submarine telephone cables with two-way repeaters encircle the world. The repeaters are powered by alternating current from the same cable core that carries the modulated carriers. The power frequency is much lower than the carrier frequencies, so there is no interference.

For many years automatic dialing could be used only for calling a subscriber connected to one's own exchange. The problem of extending the system was largely one of designing a means of automatic billing that would charge according to distance and time.

Today, when a call is dialed the equipment connects the line to an electronic pulse generator. Each pulse records a fixed unit, charged to the subscriber's account. The pulse generator selected depends on the distance of the called exchange.

Modern coaxial cables can carry an increasingly large number of simultaneous conversations—current research is producing multiple cables capable of handling up to 3,000 channels—but microwave radio has been playing a rapidly growing part in telecommunications since the early 1960s.

Microwave telephony

Modern microwave systems use relay towers at 25–30mi (40–50km) intervals. Telephone signals are used to modulate microwave radio carriers instead of the electrical carriers used in coaxial cables [6]. A microwave system [Key] operates with many separate microwave carriers, each able to accommodate 2,700 simultaneous telephone conversations. The channels may also be used to relay television signals. For intercontinental telecommunications microwave carriers are beamed up to satellites where they are amplified and beamed down to ground stations.

KEY

London's Post Office Tower is the hub of the United Kingdom microwave network. This provides thousands of telephone circuits and up to forty television channels connecting all parts of the British Isles, and links them with the international satellite station at Goonhilly Downs in Cornwall and a cross-Channel link station near Dover. The tower is 620ft (189m) to the top of the antennas and has a mass of radio equipment on most of its lower 16 floors. Above is a series of open galleries around which stand an array of parabolic dish and horn antennas for microwave signals. Above are public observation galleries and a restaurant.

4

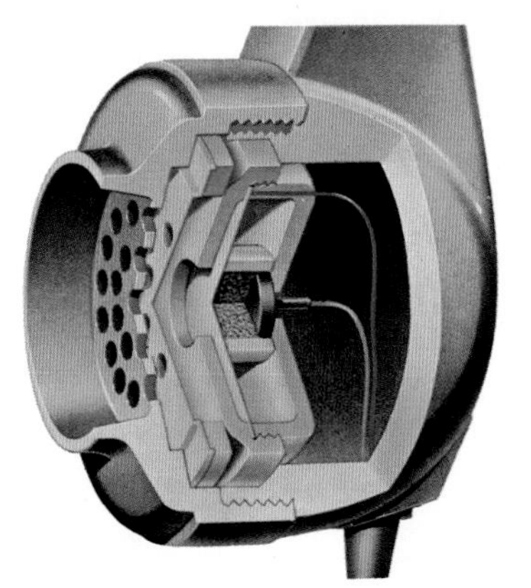

4 The heart of a carbon microphone is a small insulating cylinder packed with carbon granules. The center of a metal diaphragm presses against the open end of the cylinder. When the diaphragm vibrates, the pressure on the granules, and thus the electrical resistance through them, varies. With a DC source connected, a variable current passes. This current will operate a magnetic earpiece.

5

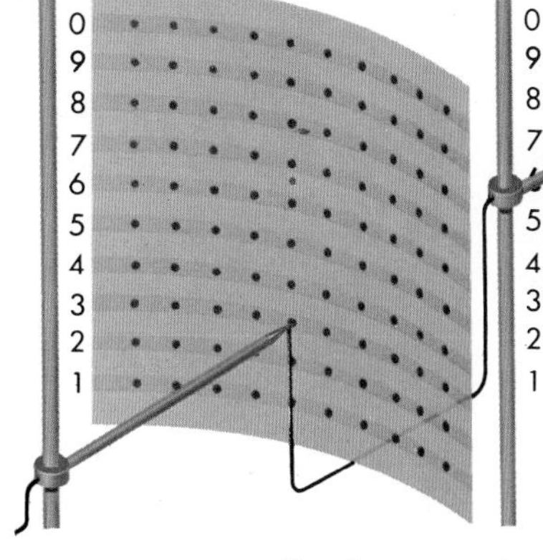
A
B
C
0 9 8 7 6 5 4 3 2 1

5 Imagine a caller's telephone is connected to a wiper [A] of a Strowger selector. He dials 3064. In response to the three electrical impulses produced by dialing the digit 3, the wiper moves up to the third line of contacts and then moves along until a free line is found. (In the illustration the wiper has stopped at the fifth contact because the first four lines are already in use by other callers.) The fifth contact is connected to wiper [B] of another selector. This moves up to the tenth row of lines and then moves around until it reaches a free one—once again the fifth, the first four being busy. This line is connected to wiper [C] of a third Strowger selector. This, unlike the first two, which are "number line" selectors, is a "double-number" selector. The wiper moves up to the sixth row of contacts in response to the dialed third digit 6 and then waits until the final digit 4 is dialed. It then moves to the fourth contact leading to the desired telephone number 3064.

6

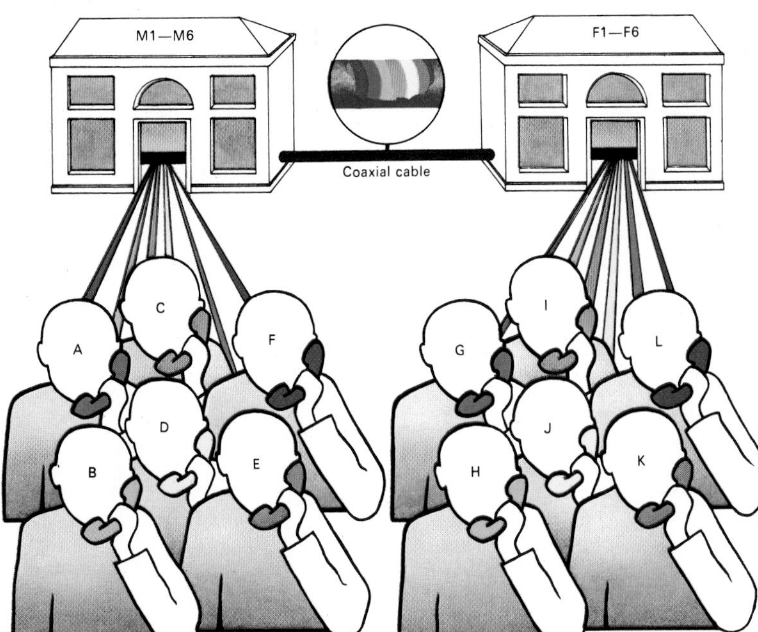
M1—M6
F1—F6
Coaxial cable
A
B
C
D
E
F
G
H
I
J
K
L

6 Coaxial cables enable a number of telephone calls to be made simultaneously over a single circuit. Six calls, on lines A-F, are each passed through one of six modulators M1–M6, which vary six different carrier waves according to the audio signals. The six modulated carriers are then fed into a coaxial cable. At the other end, six filters F1–F6 are each tuned to accept only one of the six carrier frequencies. Only one of the six carriers is thus fed into each of six detectors, which separate the audio signals from the carriers, passing the former to the six subscribers, G–L. All the circuits are duplicated for two-way communication.

7

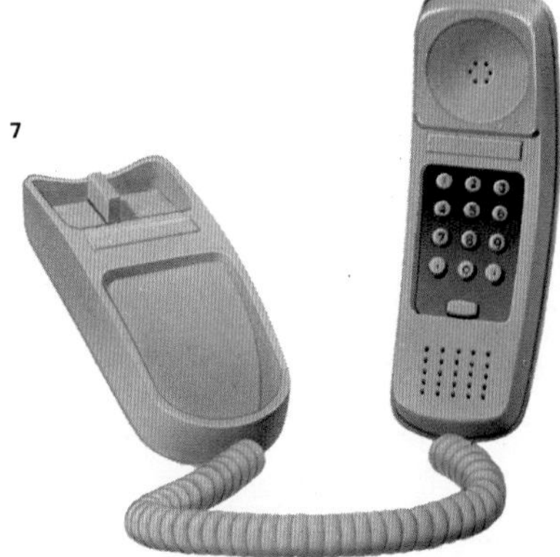

7 Many modern telephones have a set of numbered push buttons in place of the traditional dial. A number can be selected more quickly by push button and cross-bar, and electronic exchanges can work as fast as a user can "dial." If a push-button telephone is used with a Strowger exchange the number has to be stored in a memory and converted into pulses at a speed the selectors can handle. Despite this limitation the push-button system is more convenient.

Communications: radio

Radio waves were predicted before they were discovered. In 1865 James Clerk Maxwell (1831–79), a Scottish theoretical physicist, argued the existence of an unseen form of radiation. But his mathematics was so complex that his theory was at first rejected by some scientists. About 25 years later experiments showed that electromagnetic waves, which include gamma rays, X rays, and visible light and radio waves, all conformed to his formulas.

The first practical demonstration of what we now call radio waves took place in 1879, when the Anglo-American inventor David Edward Hughes (1831–1900) built a crude radio transmitter and receiver and passed signals without wires along Great Portland Street in London. Hughes failed to realize the full significance of his experiment and did not publish his findings for 20 years.

From Hertz to Marconi

In about 1887 the German scientist Heinrich Hertz (1857–94) built a spark generator [Key] that produced radio waves and a receiver that detected their presence at a distance. In a series of experiments he proved conclusively that energy could be transferred over a distance in a way that could not be accounted for by induction and he is generally credited with the discovery of radio.

Oliver Lodge (1851–1940), an Englishman, was the first to build a radio receiver—more sensitive than Hertz's coil and spark gap—that could be used for practical radio communication. It used a coherer [2], a device invented in 1890 by a Parisian, Edouard Branly (1844–1940). In an experiment in 1894, Lodge used his radio to operate an electrical circuit at a distance of 137m (450ft).

The man who was to take wireless out of the purely experimental field was the Italian Guglielmo Marconi (1847–1937). After failing to interest the Italian government in his work he moved to England. In 1898 he set up a radio link between the mainland near Dover and the East Goodwin light vessel moored 12mi (19km) offshore. A year later Marconi fitted the US liner *St Paul* with radio. The first message received was from a transmitter 60mi (97km) away on the Isle of Wight.

In 1901 Marconi astonished the world by transmitting a radio signal across the Atlantic Ocean [1] in Morse code. In 1906 a Canadian, R. A. Fessenden (1866–1932), transmitted from Brant Rock, Massachusetts, a signal in which operators at sea heard a voice and music in their headphones. This was the first audio-modulated transmission.

The nature of radio waves

When electrons oscillate in an electric circuit, some of their energy is converted into electromagnetic radiation. The frequency (the rate of oscillation) has to be very high to produce waves of useful intensity, but once formed they travel through space at the speed of light—186,000mi (300,000km) per second. When such a wave meets a metal antenna some of its energy is transferred to free electrons in the metal, causing them to flow as an alternating electric current having the frequency of the wave. This, in the

Connections

See also
1790 Communications: telegraph
1792 Communications: telephone
1796 Communications: television
1668 Electronic devices
1544 Basic AC circuits
1546 Semiconductors
1802 Radar and sonar
46 Invisible astronomy
212 The atmosphere

1 Three dots—the Morse code for "S"—signaled success for Guglielmo Marconi and for the future of wireless telegraphy in 1901. They were transmitted from Cornwall, England, and received 2,200mi (3,520km) away in Newfoundland by the inventor himself. The transmitter, using electricity generated by a 25hp oil engine, had an antenna supported by four 200ft (61m) masts. Marconi's receiver was connected to a 400ft (122m) antenna supported by a kite. Marconi had proved to doubting science his firm belief that radio waves were capable of traveling around the curvature of the Earth.

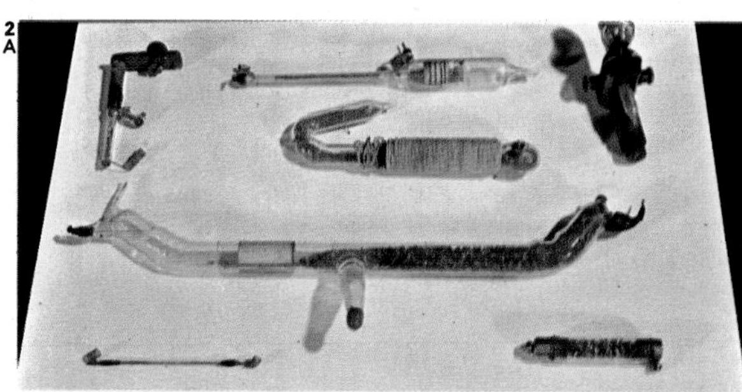

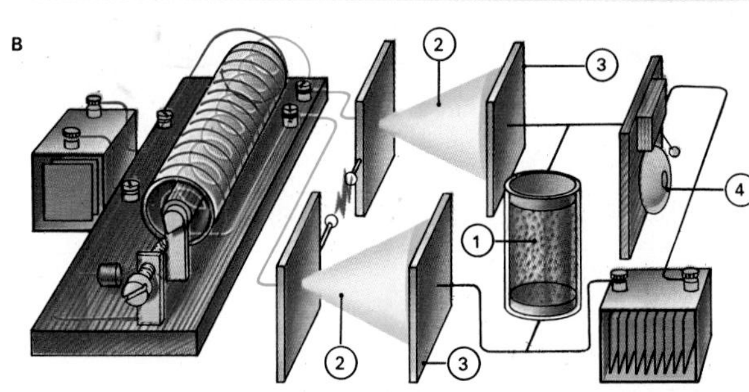

2
3
1
4
2
3

2 The first practical radio detectors were coherers [A], invented by the French scientist Branly in 1890 and developed by Oliver Lodge. They consisted of glass tubes with iron filings packed between two metal plates. In their loose condition the filings did not conduct electricity but when subjected to a vibrating electric wave they cohered (adhered to each other), making a conducting path between the plates. In the circuit shown [B], the coherer [1] acts as a switch in an electric bell circuit. As soon as streams of radio waves [2] reach the antenna plates [3], the coherer filings adhere, ringing the bell [4].

3 A 1920s crystal set, forerunner of the modern transistor, used a crystal of carborundum or lead sulfide, a semiconductor that rectified a radio carrier wave. This crystal produced an alternating current of the same frequency as the sound "carried" on the wave. The low frequency electric current had sufficient power to produce sound from sensitive earphones.

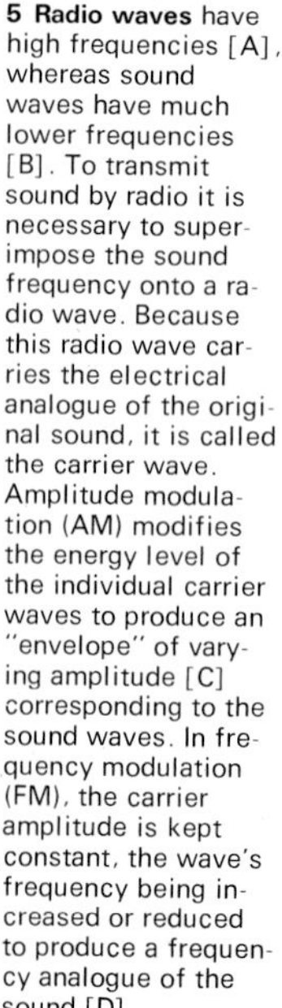

4 The modern transistor radio, like the old crystal set, "detects" (or demodulates) the radio carrier wave, although the process it uses is far more sophisticated. Having created an electrical analogue of the original sound waves, a series of amplifying circuits then produce a signal that had sufficient power to drive a small loudspeaker. Whereas radio wave energy was enough to operate earphones, the transistor set needs a battery.

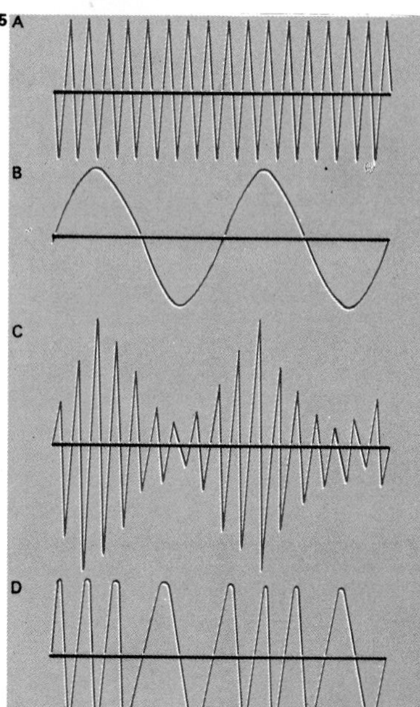

A
B
C
D

5 Radio waves have high frequencies [A], whereas sound waves have much lower frequencies [B]. To transmit sound by radio it is necessary to superimpose the sound frequency onto a radio wave. Because this radio wave carries the electrical analogue of the original sound, it is called the carrier wave. Amplitude modulation (AM) modifies the energy level of the individual carrier waves to produce an "envelope" of varying amplitude [C] corresponding to the sound waves. In frequency modulation (FM), the carrier amplitude is kept constant, the wave's frequency being increased or reduced to produce a frequency analogue of the sound [D].

simplest terms, is the principle of radio communication. A radio transmitter produces concentrated electromagnetic radiation of a chosen frequency. The waves so generated are picked up by an antenna. From all the waves that come into contact with its antenna, the radio receiver amplifies those of a selected frequency to which it is "tuned" and eliminates all others.

To transmit voice and music by radio the waves of a regular "carrier" signal must be modulated (varied) by the audio signal [5]. The waves may vary either in strength (amplitude modulation, AM) or in frequency (frequency modulation, FM). The receiver is then able to eliminate the high-frequency carrier waves, leaving only electrical waves of the same frequencies as those of the original sound. Finally, after amplification, the electrical waves are fed into earphones or a loudspeaker, which are able to convert electrical vibrations back into sound waves.

Frequencies, wavelengths, and channels

Electromagnetic radiation can vary enormously in frequency. It includes gamma-rays, X rays, and ultraviolet, visible, and infrared light rays, all of which have very high frequencies. Electromagnetic radiation of lower frequencies is radio waves. Those waves next in frequency to infrared rays are known as microwaves and are used mainly for telecommunications between towers within visible range, but also for communication with satellites. These waves are followed in order of lower frequency (and so of longer wavelength) by ultra high frequency (UHF)—used for television broadcasts; very high frequency (VHF), for some television and radio broadcasting as well as for local communication, such as between aircraft and ground control; short waves that, at high power, are used for worldwide broadcasting; medium waves for regional broadcasting; and the relatively little used long waves. The whole radio spectrum is divided by international agreement into bands reserved for specific uses and each band is generally further subdivided into channels spaced so that one channel does not interfere with the transmissions of adjacent channels.

KEY

A

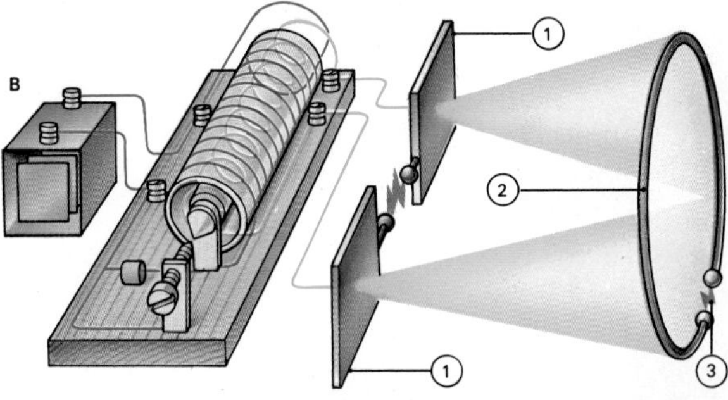
B
1
2
1
3

The first radio transmitters [A], as used by Heinrich Hertz and Oliver Lodge, made use of the radio waves generated when a high-voltage spark jumped between contacts [B]. Hertz beamed the waves from antenna plates [1] and detected them with a loop of wire [2] in which they caused a small spark [3].

6
A

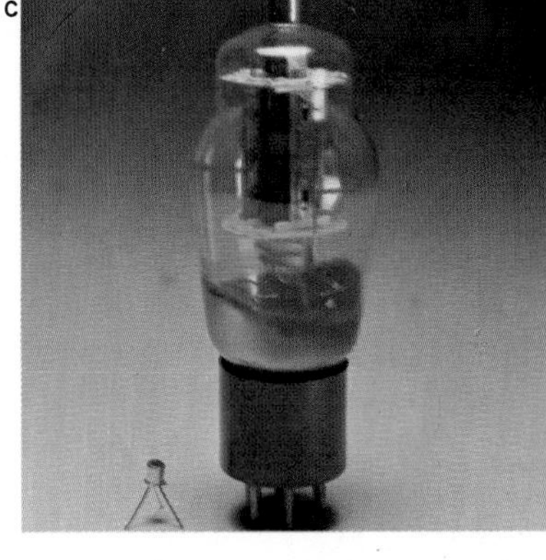
C

6 The nonstop trend towards miniaturization in electronics is shown in this comparison of a typical radio of the 1930s [A] and a transistor radio of today [B]. A loudspeaker must still be large if it is to reproduce the low-frequency components of sound, but now modern technology (much of it a spin-off from space technology) has led to the design of smaller and smaller components of nearly all other kinds. The modern transistor [c, left] has almost entirely superseded the old vacuum tube [right]. Individual electronic components have been growing steadily smaller; moreover new developments have taken the process further, with the introduction of integrated circuits (IC) in which a complete wired set of components is replaced by one minute integrated circuit.

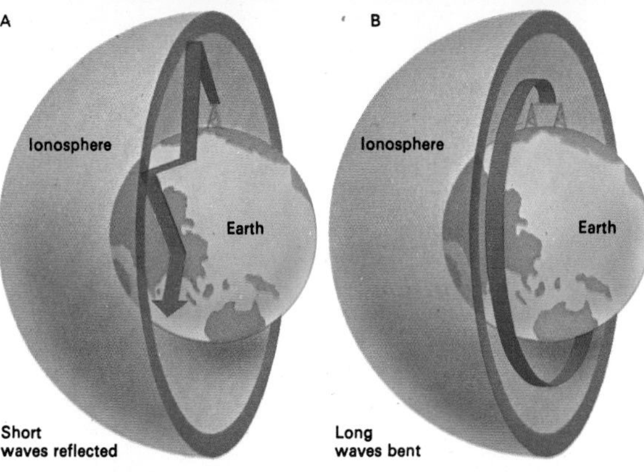
7 A
B
Ionosphere
Earth
Ionosphere
Earth
Short waves reflected
Long waves bent

7 The ionosphere (a layer of ionized gas in the Earth's upper atmosphere) and the curved surface of the Earth below act together as a kind of "waveguide," that bends the path of long radio waves [B] around the Earth. The path of waves of the medium band is not as bent, which is why they cannot normally be received more than a few hundred miles from the transmitter. All radio waves travel in straight lines, but short waves are used for round-the-world communication because they are reflected by the ionosphere and also by the Earth's surface, as though these were mirrors [A]. Even shorter waves pass through the ionosphere and so are used for communications with satellites in space.

8 Communications satellites, owned by an international consortium, provide a major part of the world's global communications. Placed in synchronous orbit [A] 22,375mi (35,800km) above the equator over the Pacific [1], Atlantic [2], and Indian oceans [3], the Intelsat IV satellites remain in fixed positions, each capable of relaying thousands of VHF radio signals to and from about one-third of the Earth's surface. Together they cover most of the Earth with some overlapping [B]. There are more than 70 Earth stations (dots in [C]) capable of communication via the satellites, although submarine cables (red lines) are still used.

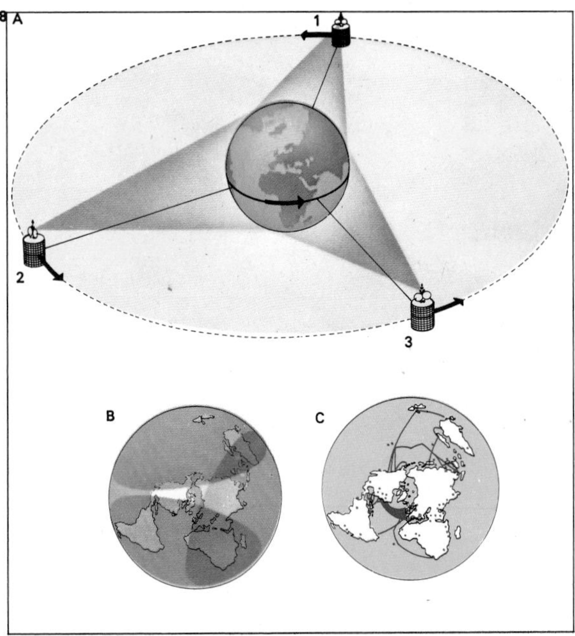
8 A
1
2
3
B
C

Communications: television

Unlike the telegraph, telephone, and radio, television is unique among forms of telecommunications because it was originally developed purely as an entertainment medium. Today, however, it has many other applications, particularly for surveillance.

The dawning image

Paul Nipkow (1860–1940), a German scientist, was the first to develop a scanner disk, in 1884. A perforated, spiral rotating disk, it could break down an image into thousands of individual dots. V. K. Zworykin (1889–   ), a Russian emigrant to the United States, patented the iconoscope in 1923. Forerunner of the modern television camera tube, this was an electronic device in which a lens focused an optical image onto a screen inside a glass container. The image was scanned by an electron beam that covered the area in a continually repeated series of parallel lines. When the beam struck a bright part of the image the electron current flowing back was greater than when it fell on a darker part of the scene. By using this varying electric current to control the intensity of another electron beam in a cathode-ray tube (a beam made to scan the face of the tube in step with the beam in the iconoscope), a replica of the original scene was built up spot by spot and line by line. The scanning covered the entire screen several times a second, the glow caused did not die away instantaneously, and so the human eye could not tell that the image was built up of individual elements.

In 1930 an American, Philo T. Farnsworth (1906–71), developed an electronic scanning system. Another American, Allen B. Du Mont (1901–65), perfected the cathode-ray picture tube, which enabled him to make the first television sets for the public in 1939. On February 1, 1940, the first official network program in the United States was broadcast by the National Broadcasting Company (NBC).

Television standards

The Radio Corporation of America (RCA) began an interlaced scan of 343-line pictures at a rate of 30 frames per second in 1936. Interlacing means that alternate lines are scanned, followed by those between—like reading lines 1, 3, 5 down this column and then going back to read 2, 4, 6. In 1941 the Federal Communications Commission (FCC) raised the broadcast standard to 525 lines, which is still used in North and South America and Japan. Most of Europe uses a standard of 625 lines at a rate of 25 frames per second.

The sideband theory of radio states that, in order that two radio signals do not interfere with each other, the difference between their frequencies must not be less than the highest frequency of the signal being broadcast. Television signals include very high frequencies, so a band width of about 5MHz (5 million cycles/sec) has largely been accepted as the practical minimum. Because this is equal to the radio space occupied by more than 500 voice channels the entire shortwave radio band would accommodate only five television channels. Thus television is broadcast in the VHF and UHF bands (very and ultra high frequency), which can accommodate up to 80 separate channels.

CONNECTIONS

See also
1794 Communications: radio
1800 Video recording and reproduction
1668 Electronic devices
1544 Basic AC circuits
1546 Semiconductors
1674 What computers can do

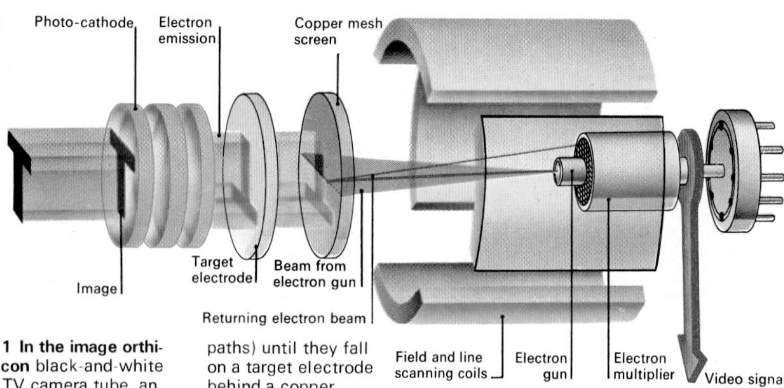

1
Photo-cathode
Electron emission
Copper mesh screen
Target electrode
Beam from electron gun
Image
Returning electron beam
Field and line scanning coils
Electron gun
Electron multiplier
Video signal

1 In the image orthicon black-and-white TV camera tube, an optical image of the studio scene is focused on a photocathode, which emits electrons in proportion to the amount of light falling on it. These electrons pass through magnetic and electrostatic fields (which keep them moving in parallel paths) until they fall on a target electrode behind a copper mesh screen. There a pattern of charges is formed, corresponding to the light and dark areas in the picture. A scanning electron beam from the other side is modulated by the charges, thus forming a varying transmission signal.

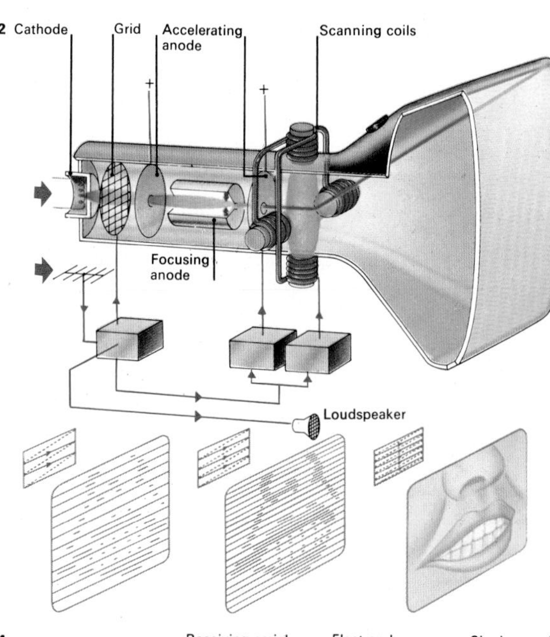

2 Cathode
Grid
Accelerating anode
Scanning coils
Focusing anode
Loudspeaker

2 A cathode-ray tube in a television receiver has a screen coated with a material that fluoresces when struck by an electron beam. The beam is produced by a cathode that emits electrons and is accelerated and focused by anodes. The beam is deflected by two scanning coils fed with signals so that it zigzags across the screen. The velocity of the beam, and therefore the intensity of each picture element, is controlled by a grid that is fed by another signal.

3
Scene to be televised
Final encoder and amplifier
Unmodulated color signal
First encoder
Picture tubes convert colored light into signals
Composite signal to transmitter
Amplifier
Adder combines signals to form monochrome signal
Final encoder and amplifier
Identical picture tubes
Camera separates scene into three primary colors
Mirror
Dichroic mirrors
Lens focuses scene on to tubes
Mirror

3 A color television camera first splits the picture into three primary colors using color-separating mirrors. Each beam of colored light enters one of three picture tubes, which convert the picture into electrical signals. The three signals are combined to form a monochrome signal which is amplified and processed into a color signal. This defines the hue (frequency) and saturation (intensity) of each color.

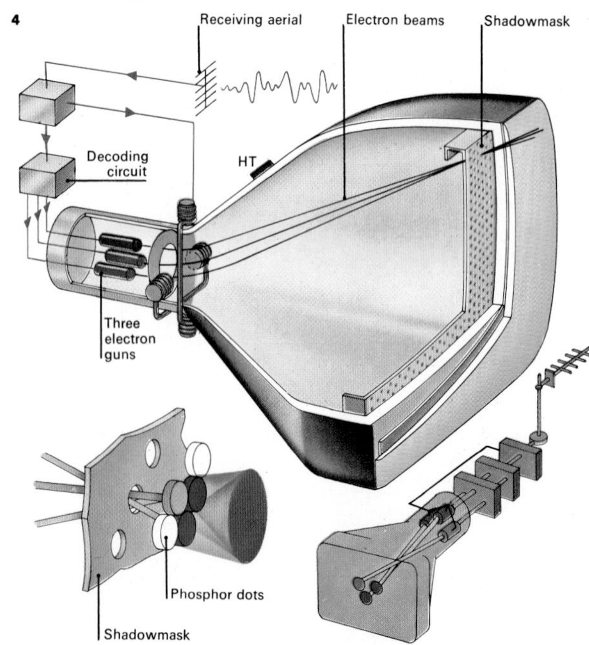

4
Receiving aerial
Electron beams
Shadowmask
Decoding circuit
HT
Three electron guns
Phosphor dots
Shadowmask

4 In a color television receiver a decoding circuit extracts the information of the original color signals. This is used to modulate the beams from three electron guns. The screen has a pattern of tiny phosphor dots, which glow red, green, or blue when struck by electrons. Directly behind the screen is a shadow mask with thousands of holes arranged so that the beam from each gun can strike only dots of the color from which its signal was made.

Color television

In theory the range of pure colors (called "hues") is continuous from violet of the shortest visible wavelength to red of the longest. In practice the sensations perceived by the human eye in response to all these hues can be quite accurately matched by simple mixtures of red, green, and blue light. Color television [3] uses this principle by having three camera tubes to convert the red, green, and blue light present in each televised scene into three simultaneous but separate electrical signals. In theory these three signals could be transmitted separately, received by three separate circuits in the television receiver and then combined to form a color picture, but this method would take up too much signal space on the radio band.

Experiments have shown that, provided the black-and-white detail of a picture is sharply defined, the human eye does not require the color definition to be as high. US engineers devised a clever system to use this information. First the three primary color signals were added to form a detailed monochrome (black-and-white) signal for transmission in the usual way. At the same time the three color signals were converted into a second composite signal that defines the color mixture in terms of hue and saturation (the amount of white used to dilute the pure hue). Because this color signal does not need to be of high definition it is possible to sandwich it between the information giving the detail of each monochrome line without interfering with it. In this way a complete color signal can be transmitted within a 5MHz monochrome signal band width. The television receiver makes a detailed picture from the monochrome signal, extracts the color information interleaved with it, and uses this to deflect the three picture tube electron beams onto the appropriate spots on its screen [4].

In the United States this system has been used since 1953 and is known as the National Television Systems Committee (NTSC) system. It works well but has the disadvantage that the colors produced on the receiver screen can be altered by minor changes in the transmitted signal.

KEY

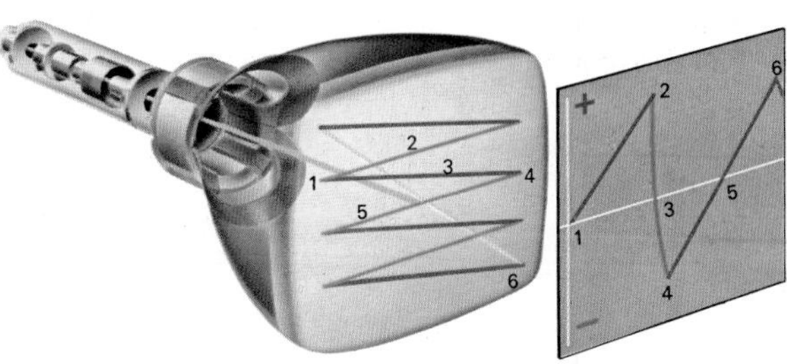
1
2
3
4
5
6
+
–

Electronic scanning is the basis of television. An electron beam scans the screen in a series of horizontal lines, which are kept in step with the lines scanning an optical image in the television camera in the studio from which the broadcast comes. This synchronization of the scanning process is achieved by a set of timing pulses superimposed on the picture information in the transmitted signal. At the end [1] of each horizontal line [2], there is a pulse that triggers the instant return [3] of the electron beam to the opposite side [4], where it scans the next line [5] below the previous one. After the final line of each picture [6] a different pulse triggers the return of the electron beam to the top of the picture. A saw-tooth current, through electromagnetic deflection coils (around the neck of the tube) controls the beam.

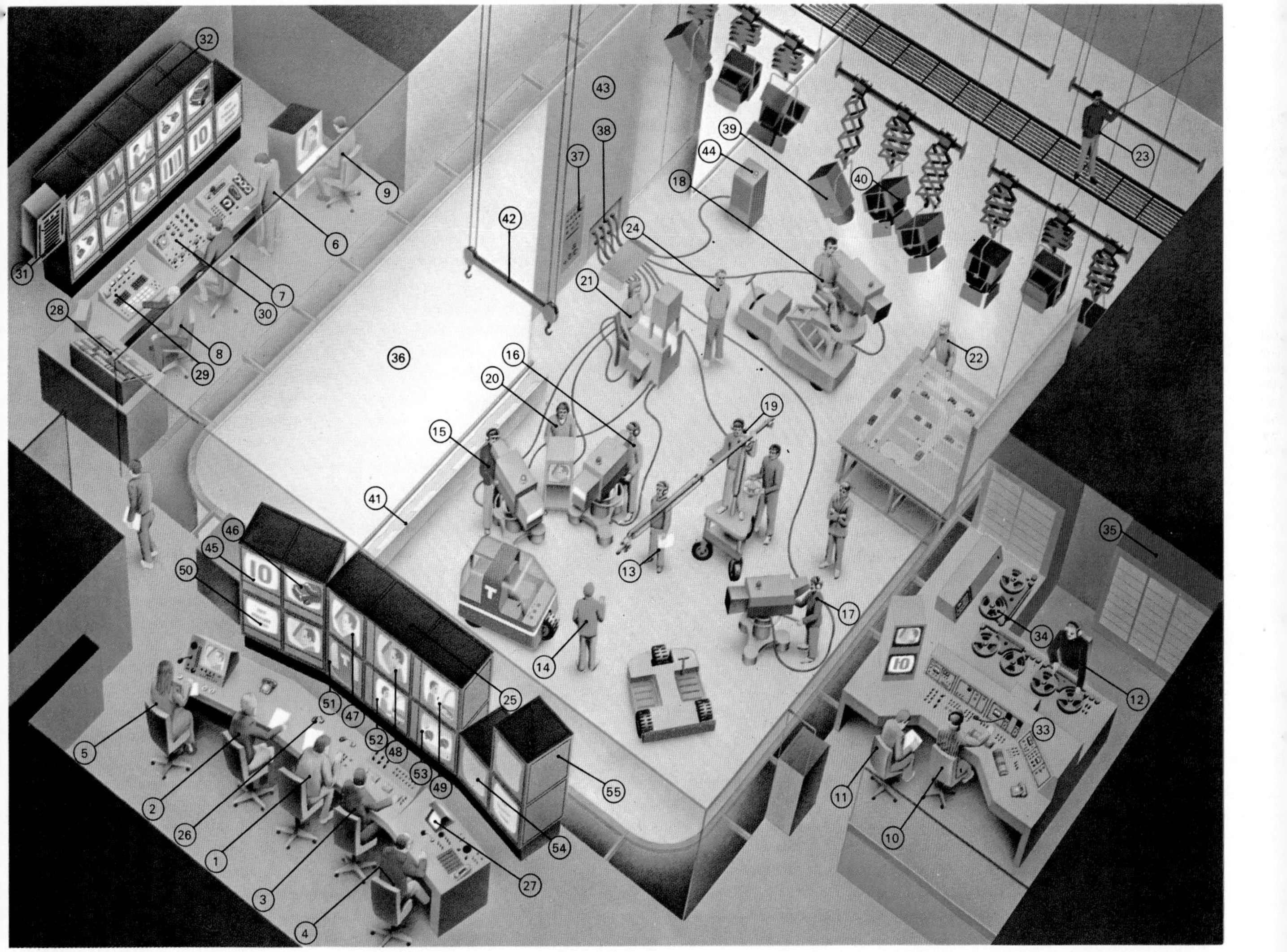

5 The transmission of a live television program requires the combined efforts of a highly skilled team.

1 Director
2 Assistant director
3 Technical director
4 Assistant technical director
5 Timekeeper
6 Lighting director
7 Camera assistant
8 Lighting engineer
9 Color grader
10–12 Audio engineers
13 Floor manager
14 Performer
15–18 Cameraman
19 Microphone-boom operator
20 Monitor pusher
21 Teleprompter
22 Prop man
23–24 Electricians
25 Director's monitor
26 Microphone to studio
27 Test screen
28 Dimmer bank
29 Switchboard
30 Camera iris controls
31 Lighting display
32 Picture quality control
33 Sound console
34 Tape decks
35 Amplifiers
36 Cyclorama
37 Hoist control
38 Output socket
39 Spotlight
40 Floodlight
41 Cyclorama lights
42 Scenery hoist
43 Soundproof wall
44 Studio speaker
45 Slides and stills
46 Videotape picture
47 Monochrome final transmission
48 Color final transmission picture
49 General monitor
50 Credit holder
51–54 Pictures from cameras 1–4
55 Monitor bank for extra cameras and outside broadcasts.

Sound recording and reproduction

It was possible, at about the turn of the century, to reproduce mechanically the sound and "attack" of an actual piano performance on an automatic player piano roll. But the story of sound recording and reproduction as the terms are now understood is the story of the phonograph, the "talking" motion picture, and the tape recorder.

Thomas Edison (1847–1931) invented a hand-cranked phonograph [1] in 1877. The machine converted the air pressure variations of sound waves into a mechanical record consisting of a groove of varying depth in a sheet of tinfoil wrapped round a cylinder. The foil was soon replaced by a hard wax cylinder, and in 1894 Charles Pathé (1863–1957) and his brother Emile (1860–1937) opened a phonograph factory in France.

The development of early sound systems
Meanwhile, Emile Berliner (1851–1929), a German in Washington, DC, patented a "phonograph" in 1887. This used a flat disk instead of a cylinder, the sound groove being cut as a spiral. By 1900 the hill-and-dale recording was replaced by a groove that made a stylus vibrate from side to side. And with the advent of a shellac disk pressed from a "negative" of the original recording, the phonograph, known by the trade name Victrola, became popular [Key].

At first, methods of recording and playback were entirely mechanical and the quality of reproduction was poor. The invention of the triode valve in 1906 opened the way to electrical recording, and by the 1930s music of greatly improved quality could be reproduced electronically from shellac disks running at 78 revolutions per minute (rpm).

In 1948 the American Columbia Company successfully demonstrated an "unbreakable" vinyl plastic record and high-fidelity microgroove records playing for 25–30 minutes a side at 33⅓rpm soon became popular. By 1958 the stereo record had been introduced. It had separate twin soundtracks in a single groove (each corresponding to the sounds received by a listener's left and right ears) and provided a sense of musical presence hitherto unknown in a recording [2].

Soon after the development of silent motion pictures a system of synchronized sound followed in the late 1920s. Early "talkies" used an adaptation of the already popular shellac record. The most successful system had a 16in (40cm) record running at 33⅓rpm, with a motor linked mechanically to the film drive. By 1930, engineers had developed a more foolproof system that recorded the sound optically on one edge of the film in the form of a transparent line varying either in density or in width [3]. A fine beam of light shone through the moving line onto a photoelectric cell, its varying electrical output being amplified and fed to loudspeakers.

Experiments in magnetic recording
The idea of converting the varying pressure waves of sound into a magnetic pattern on a continuous steel wire was developed in the 1920s. In 1929 Fritz Pfleumer patented a recording tape that had a flexible insulated base with a magnetic coating. The German AEG company developed this invention and

CONNECTIONS

See also
1800 Video recording and reproduction
1536 Electromagnetism
1668 Electronic devices

1 Thomas Edison's phonograph consisted of a brass cylinder [1] cut with a spiral groove. Over this was wrapped a sheet of tinfoil [2]. A conical funnel focused sound onto a metal diaphragm [3], which touched a steel stylus held by a flat spring. The sharp tip of the stylus pressed on the foil. The cylinder was mounted on a screw of the same pitch as the groove, so that when the cylinder was turned the stylus pressd always over the groove. A flywheel [4] helped keep the cylinder speed steady. When sound caused the diaphragm to vibrate, the stylus pressed the foil into the groove in step with the vibrations. The cylinder was wound back to its original position, and the sound reproduced by turning the handle. The stylus, and so the diaphragm, were then vibrated by the indentations [5] in the foil.

3 An optical system is used by the film industry for recording sound, the vibrations being reproduced in the form of a transparent line of varying thickness. In the projector, a light beam passes through the line onto a photoelectric cell. The width of the line controls the amount of light reaching the cell, the resulting electrical signal being amplified to produce sound. In home movie equipment the sound is recorded on a magnetic stripe, as on tape.

4 In recording on magnetic tape [A], the tape first passes an erase head, which leaves the magnetic particles on the tape in random disarray. Then the record/replay head, energized by a microphone signal, orients the particles according to the signal's waveform. In playing back [B], the tape again passes the record/replay head. Magnetic variations reproduce in it the currents that formed them [C]. After amplification, the currents drive a speaker.

1 Erase head
2 High-frequency alternating current
3 Record/replay head
4 Microphone
5 Loudspeaker
6 Tape drive capstan
7 Head magnetizes tape coating

2 On a stereo record the groove walls are angled at 90° to each other. When a recording is made [A], sound from one microphone [1] produces a hill-and-dale contour on one groove wall. The second channel sound [2] contours the other groove wall. After being pressed between metal molds [B], the final plastic record is ready to be played back. The cartridge stylus of the playback machine vibrates in two planes perpendicular to each other [C]. The movement in each of these planes actuates separate electromagnets, which are wired to two different amplifiers and separate loudspeakers. The sound is thus reproduced independently.

in 1935 in Berlin exhibited the Magnetophone, the first modern tape recorder. But it was not until the end of World War II that the potential of the reel-to-reel tape recorder using $^{1}/_{4}$in (0.5cm) plastic-based tape with an iron oxide coating [4], was fully realized. The tape can move at various speeds, with higher speeds providing greater fidelity. The most common speeds for domestic recording are $1^{7}/_{8}$in/sec (4.8cm/sec), $3^{3}/_{4}$in/sec (9.5cm/sec), and $7^{1}/_{2}$in/sec (19cm/sec). For stereo recording two separate soundtracks are recorded side by side using two microphones. Stereo reproduction or playback needs two amplifiers and speakers. The system of dividing the tape into four tracks permits stereo recordings to be made on tracks 1 and 3 in one direction and 2 and 4 in the reverse.

The cartridge and cassette revolution

The main drawbacks of a reel-to-reel tape recorder are the vulnerability of the tape to damage during threading and the inconvenience of threading and storing it. To eliminate these, the tape cartridge and cassette were invented. The former contains a single loosely wound reel of continuous tape. The tape is fed out from the center at an angle, guided by rollers to the gate where it touches the playback head of the equipment (it was never designed for home recording) and then back to the outside of the reel.

A cassette recorder [7] has two spools like those of a reel-to-reel recorder, but much smaller, and is suitable for recording, automatic rewind, and playback operations. The tape is only 0.15in (3.8mm) wide and runs at $1^{7}/_{8}$ in/sec (4.8cm/sec). The cassette (plastic case) holds tape for 45, 60, 90, or 120 minutes' playing time and clicks into the cassette player without the need for threading the tape. High-frequency random noise called "tape-hiss" (a consequence of having four tracks recorded on the extremely narrow tape at a slow speed) can lower the quality of the cassette recording. But this defect can often be eliminated by using an electronic noise-reduction circuit, preferably for both recording and playback.

KEY

The marvel of sound reproduction was captured in a narrative painting that became a trademark as "His Master's Voice." In 1899 the British artist Francis Barraud portrayed a fox terrier called Nipper listening for the voice of his dead master. The Gramophone Co., which bought the painting, asked Barraud to paint in a phonograph.

5 The human hearing process, using a pair of ears, can sense the direction of a sound and can thus discriminate between a sound from one direction and background noise from another. This is not so of a microphone, which combines all the sounds it "hears" into one electrical wave. To maintain a high signal-to-noise ratio it is therefore normal to place microphones as near as possible to the desired sound source. To record an orchestra and choir with proper balance between instruments and voices a single microphone would have to be roughly the same distance from each sound source. Except in a perfectly soundproof studio this would result in an unacceptably low signal-to-noise ratio. The engineer solves this problem by providing separate microphones for each section of the choir and orchestra and for the soloists, the combined outputs then being mixed by electronic means. The balance can then also be adjusted.

5

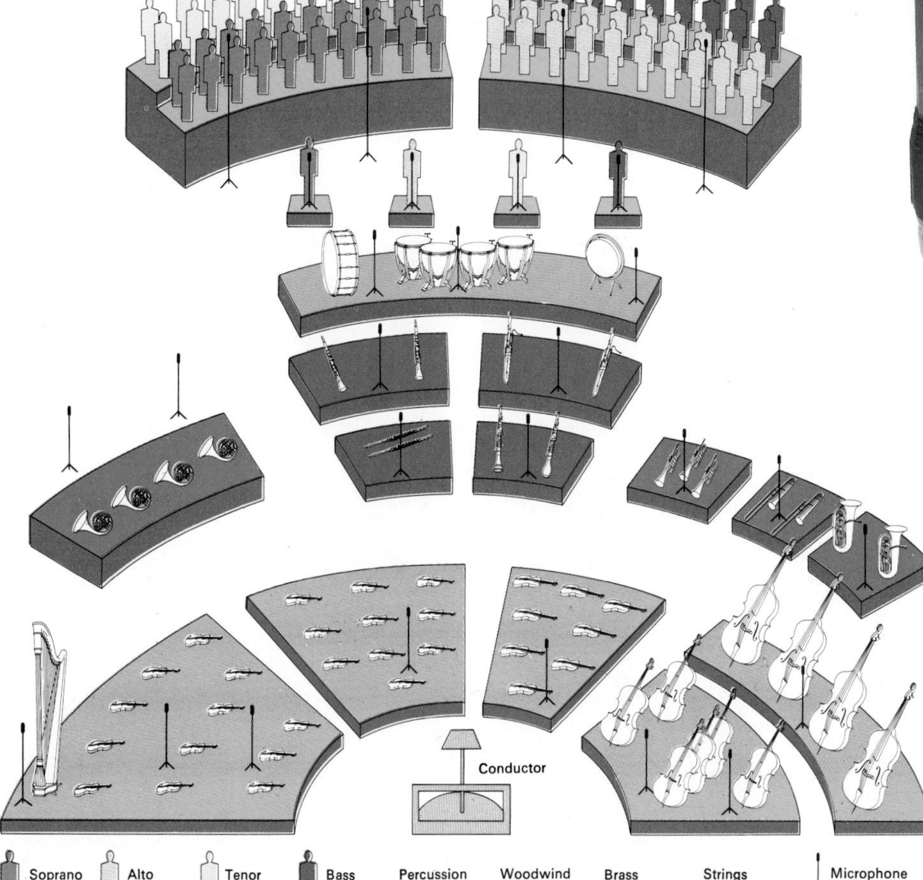
Conductor
Soprano
Alto
Tenor
Bass
Percussion
Woodwind
Brass
Strings
Microphone

6

6 A jukebox, an early example of which is shown here, is a coin-operated phonograph that plays selected music. Some modern jukeboxes hold 200 or more records and provide stereophonic sound.

7

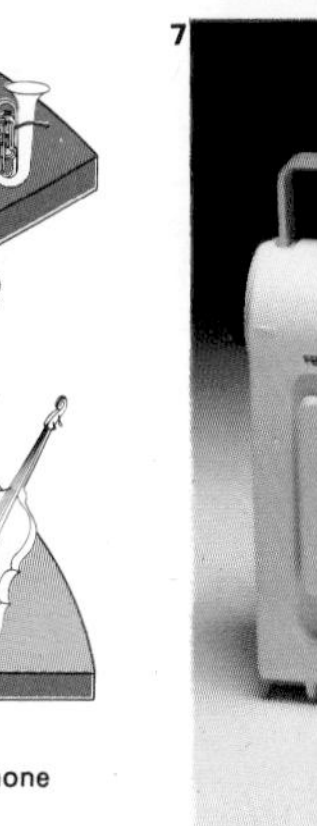

7 A portable cassette player allows tape-recorded music or speech to be heard anywhere. With transistorized circuits it is light and compact and can be used with prerecorded tapes.

Video recording and reproduction

From the earliest days of the television industry, there was a need for a method of recording programs in such a way that they could be played back almost at once. Motion-picture film is often unsuitable because the delay in processing prevents it being shown immediately, and the fact that the film cannot be reused makes it an expensive medium.

A Scotsman, John Logie Baird, (1888–1946), inventor of a mechanical television scanner, was the first man to record a moving picture by other than photographic means. In 1927 he used equipment designed for cutting 10 inch (25.4cm) 78-rpm sound records to record pictures using the output of his 30-line TV scanner.

Magnetic tape recording

The development of magnetic tape recording meant that Baird's aim could be achieved more simply with instant replay. In the meantime, however, television had progressed from the first 30-line format to a picture having 405 to 819 lines. The best of the early shellac records could reproduce audio (sound) signals up to a frequency of about 4,500 hertz (Hz). A hertz is equal to one cycle per second. High-fidelity LP records today reproduce musical overtones up to 15,000Hz or more. But a modern television broadcasting signal includes frequencies that are as high as 5 megahertz (5MHz). A megahertz equals 1,000,000 cycles per second.

The frequency response of a magnetic tape recorder is limited by the size of the head gap and the speed with which the tape passes the head. The finest equipment operating at 7.5in (19cm) per second cannot reproduce frequencies much above 25,000Hz. An increase in frequency response to 5MHz can be achieved only by increasing the tape-to-head speed to at least 500in (1,270cm) per second.

The earliest videotape recorders (which record pictures on magnetic tape just as a tape recorder records sound) were designed to operate at tape speeds of 100in (254cm) per second or more. They required enormous spools of tape and presented speed control problems; also constant head-to-tape contact was difficult to achieve. Research led to the introduction (by Ampex) in 1956 of the first transverse-scan recorder—the system used professionally today. In this system, the tape, normally 2in (5.1cm) wide, moves at either 15in (38cm) or 7.5in (19cm) per second. Four record/replay heads mounted on a drum sweep across the tape producing transverse parallel record tracks for the video signal [2]. Linear tracks at the edges of the tape are used for tape-speed control, picture cueing, and sound. Head-to-tape "writing" speeds as high as 1,500in (3,810cm) per second are commonly achieved.

Helical scanning

The highly sophisticated transverse-scan color videotape recorder is far too expensive for institutional and domestic use. A cheaper method uses what is termed helical scanning. Here the tape passes in a helix around a rotating drum into which one or more record/replay heads are built [2A]. The drum is rotated rapidly in the opposite direction from the tape (it "slips" around

CONNECTIONS

See also
1798 Sound recording and reproducing
1796 Communications: television
1536 Electromagnetism

AMPEX

1 **The earliest video recorder** worked in exactly the same way as an audio tape recorder, using spools of wide magnetic tape. The video track was recorded by a stationary head and the recording of the high frequencies required to produce pictures of acceptable quality was achieved by using very fast tape speeds. In the most highly developed of these machines, 360in (914cm) of tape 2in (5.1cm) wide passed the head each second. Even so, picture quality was poor by modern standards and the machines were suitable only for black-and white pictures.

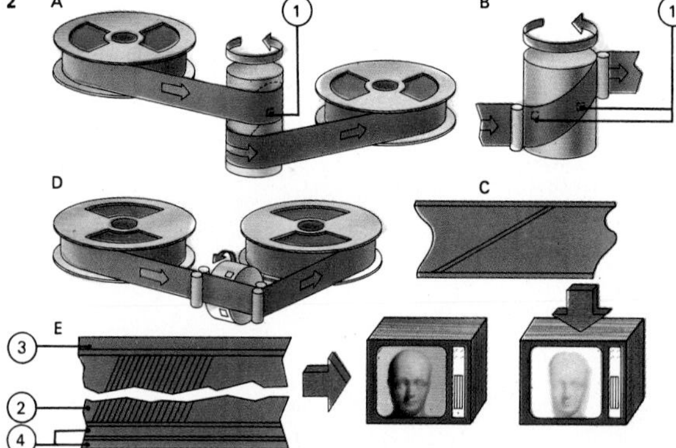

A
B
C
D
E
1
2
3
4

2 **Videotape** may move in a helix around a rotating drum having either one [A] or two [B] record/replay heads [1]. The combined motion of tape and head produces diagonal video tracks [C]. Transverse scanning [D] uses four heads on a horizontally spinning drum to produce tapes recorded as in [E] with video tracks [2], an audio track [3], and picture control tracks [4]. Both have high "writing" speeds.

Scotch
VC-30

3 **The moving head** was invented in 1956 by Ampex (then a little known company in Redwood, California), as a means of achieving the high tape-to-head speed required for video recording without the tape itself having to move at unmanageably high speed. The latest Ampex machine [A] is a self-contained videotape recorder designed for color television. The studio videotape recorder is expensive and heavy and many manufacturers, foreseeing a wide market for a cheaper and smaller machine suitable for home, school, police, and other work, have made cassette videotape recorders that are compact and efficient, yet not too costly. This cassette player [B] is a typical example of such a model.

within a loop of tape). As the tape rises by its own width in its journey around the drum, the heads sweep across the tape at an acute angle. Tape-to-head "writing" speeds of up to 1,000in (2,540cm) per second are achieved with helical-scan portable videotape recorders. In domestic applications, this system has the advantage that a conventional TV set can be used as a combined picture and sound monitor, the signal produced on replay being fed into the antenna socket via a demodulator. Tape 0.5in (1.27cm) wide is commonly used, although some recorders of this kind use 0.75in (1.9cm) or 1in (2.5cm) tape.

Video disks

It is possible for tape to be replaced by disks in video recording, and the system has the advantage of giving rapid access to any part of the recording for immediate replay, in slow motion if necessary. [6]. The production of prerecorded TV tapes is expensive and so some manufacturers have been developing video machines that use disks similar to phonograph records. Such machines are not recorders, but replay programs on relatively cheap disks [4] that are mass produced.

There are three systems of such video disks, which differ in the "pick-up" used to extract the recorded information. In the system developed by Philips in the Netherlands and MCA in the United States, there are small elliptical depressions in the disk [6]. The disk revolves at 1,800rpm. A laser beam scans the lower surface of the disk and then the reflected beam becomes modulated and provides video and sound signals. A disk 12in (30.5cm) in diameter records up to half an hour's television. In the system developed by RCA in the United States, a stylus glides over electronically incised slots on a vinyl-based record [7], which revolves at 450 rpm and reproduces an hour of television. The video disk developed by Telefunken in West Germany and Decca in England is grooved like a long-playing phonograph record, although the grooves are finer and spaced much closer together. Such disks record only about 10 minutes of television.

KEY

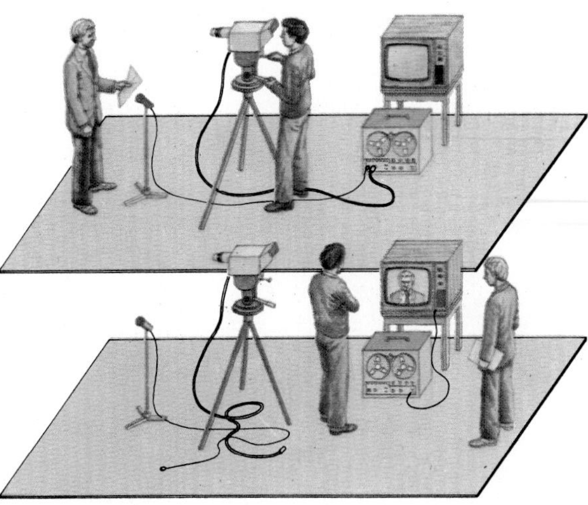

The recording and reproduction of moving pictures on magnetic tape has been developed to such an extent that reproduced television pictures are nearly indistinguishable from originals. Even portable videotape recorders that are suitable for domestic use give remarkably good results.

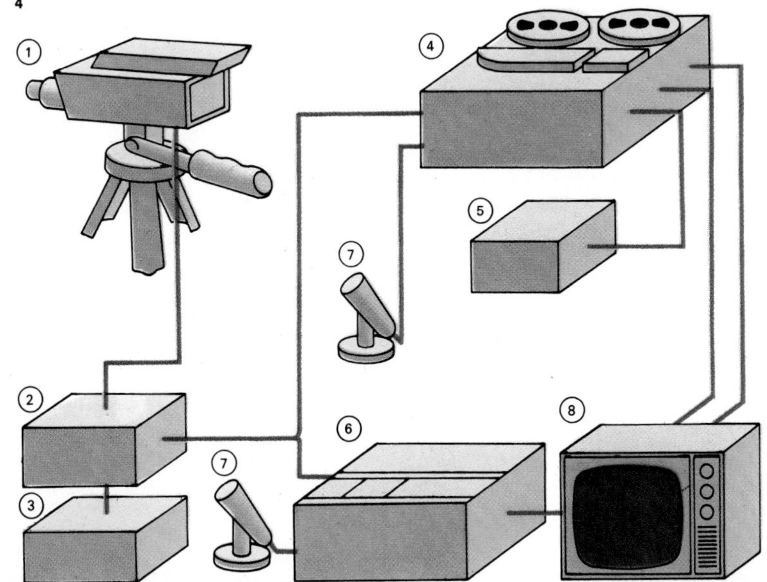
4
1
2
3
4
5
6
7
7
8

4 Live video recordings in black-and-white or color can be made with ease today. The diagram shows a typical set-up using equipment that is readily available. The camera [1] is connected via its control [2] and sync [3] units to the reel-to-reel color video tape recorder [4] (with color pack [5]) or to the video cassette recorder [6]. A microphone is simultaneously connected to record the accompanying sound [7]. The color TV set [8] has special sockets to enable it to be used as a monitor during recording. Recorded tape can be played back through the TV set immediately after the tape is wound back.

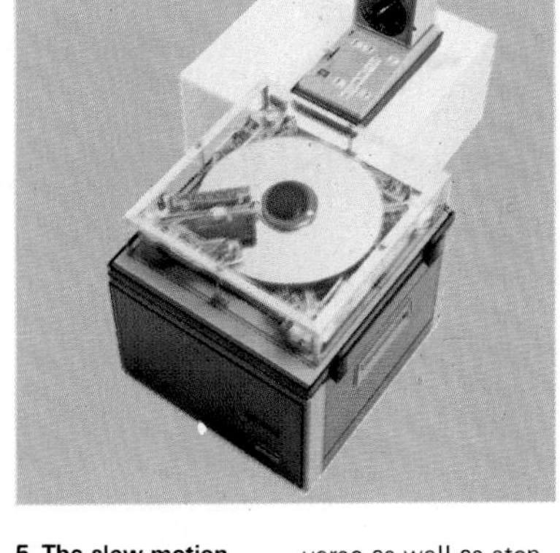

5 The slow motion "action replay" seen frequently on sports programs was made possible by the invention of a magnetic disk recorder that provides continuously variable slow motion forward and reverse as well as stop, "freeze," and natural speed replay. It records about 7.5 to 9 seconds of television program material on a series of concentric magnetic tracks on each side of the disk.

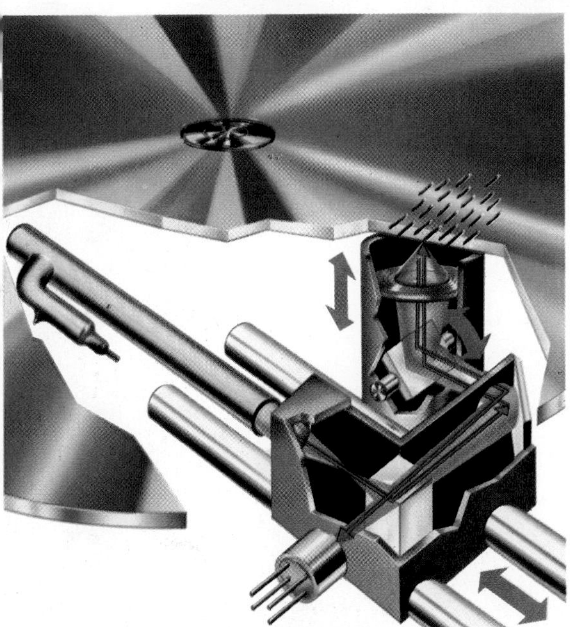

6 The nonmagnetic video disk is used by several firms as an alternative to magnetic tape systems. Philips and other companies have designed systems that use minute elliptical depressions on a 12in (30.5cm) disk to record 30 minutes of color video signals with sound. It is scanned using a laser beam.

7 The RCA SelectaVision VideoDisc player can be connected to the antenna terminals of a regular home television set to produce an excellent picture. The LP disk, which has a special vinyl coating, has a playing time of 30 minutes per side. The VideoDisc has been magnified many times (inset) to show the disk's hairline grooves.

Radar and sonar

Sonar (formerly known as "asdic" in England) is a system of direction finding and rangefinding using sound waves under water. Radar uses essentially the same principles in air, with radio waves instead of sound waves.

The essentials of the two systems are simple. Acoustic (sound) or electromagnetic (radio) waves are transmitted. When they meet a solid object, some are reflected and returned—there is a sound or radio echo. The time that elapses between a wave's transmission and return, multiplied by the speed of the wave, gives the distance traveled. Normally this is twice the distance of the object. Early radar units from World War II [Key] were mounted on trailers for portability.

Development and uses

Sonar (from *SO*und *N*avigation *A*nd *R*anging) was developed principally for the detection of submarines during World War I and to act as a submarine commander's "ear" for detection of other vessels, minefields, wrecks and other underwater hazards. Sonar can be "active" or "passive." In active sonar, an acoustic wave is transmitted and its echo picked up [1]. In passive sonar, other vessels are detected by listening for noise generated by their engines. Today sonar is also used by fishing vessels seeking schools of fish and for surveying the ocean bed.

In 1935 a British team headed by Robert Watson-Watt (1892–1973) started a program of research aimed at developing radio location for military use [5]. By the outbreak of World War II in 1939, Britain had an aircraft detection system along its east coast. Known as RDF (radio direction finding) it was quickly extended to cover the south coast and was a major factor in Britain's ability to win the war in the air over the nation.

The secrets of RDF were passed to the United States, where further research was conducted and a new name, "radar" (*RA*dio *D*etection *A*nd *R*anging), was given to the new technology. German scientists conducted similar research during the early war years and achieved similar results.

A radar installation consists of three separate units: a transmitter that radiates a special form of radio signal; a receiver that picks up and processes any reflected waves; and a presentation unit that gives a visual display from which the operator can immediately read the desired information.

Types of radar aerials

Radar antennas vary in design according to their purpose. Many consist of a metal lattice in the shape of a flat dish or rectangular array, which can be steered at any angle to aim the radar in the required direction. Some can be "locked" onto a target so that they track it automatically. A location radar has a narrow beam, focused by a parabolic reflector, so that the bearing and elevation of reflected waves can be accurately measured. A search radar uses an antenna that radiates waves over a wide arc. The beam is kept relatively flat for a ship's radar, but covers a vertical arc in an aircraft search radar. In both cases, the antenna is sometimes made to revolve horizontally so that the radar sweeps around continuously.

CONNECTIONS

See also
1794 Communications: radio
1734 Modern artillery
1740 Modern fighting shi
1744 Modern military air craft
218 Forecasting
464 Principles of anima behavior
546 Rodents, insect eaters, and bats
552 Whales, porpoises, and dolphins
1304 World War I
1336 World War II

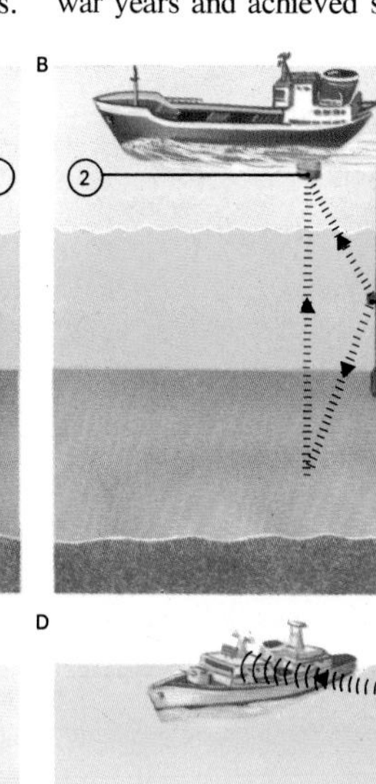

1A
B
1
2

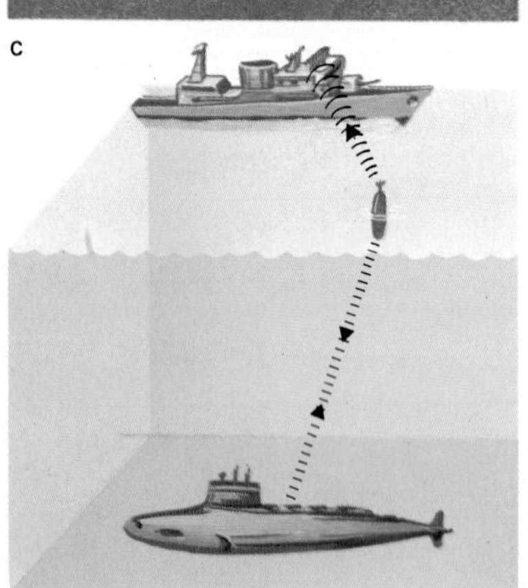

C

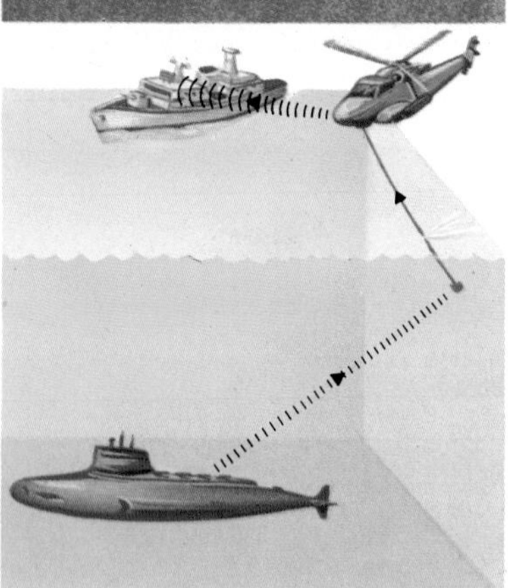

D

1 The time taken for a sound wave, transmitted from a device in the water under a ship, to travel to the sea bottom and echo back to the ships, is measured to calculate the depth of the water. The acoustic generator [1] can be mounted directly under the ship [A] in which case the echo time multiplied by the speed of sound in water gives twice the depth. The signal-to-noise ratio of the echo picked up by the microphone [2] can be improved by lowering the sound generator into the water [B], reducing the total distance that the sound waves must travel. For military purposes, warships, so as not to confuse an echo from a submarine, use a sonar buoy [C]. For maximum mobility a ship makes use of its own helicopter, which suspends a "dunking" sonar in the water [D] and transmits signals back to the mother ship by means of a shortwave radio.

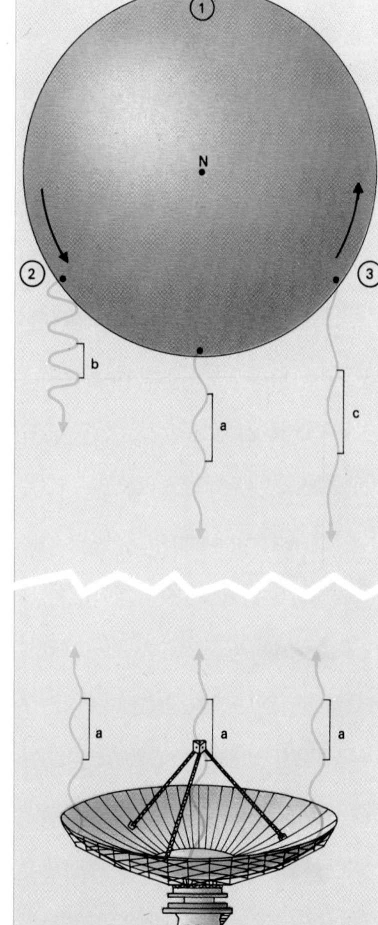

2
1
N
2
3
b
a
c
a
a
a

2 The reflected wave of a radar beam that hits an approaching or receding object has a frequency greater or less than the transmitted wave. If a wave of a given frequency [a] is reflected from a planet [1] spinning about its pole [N], the frequency [b] of the reflected wave from the approaching side [2] will be more than the frequency [c] from the receding side [3]. The difference between b and c can be used to compute the planet's rate of spin and day length.

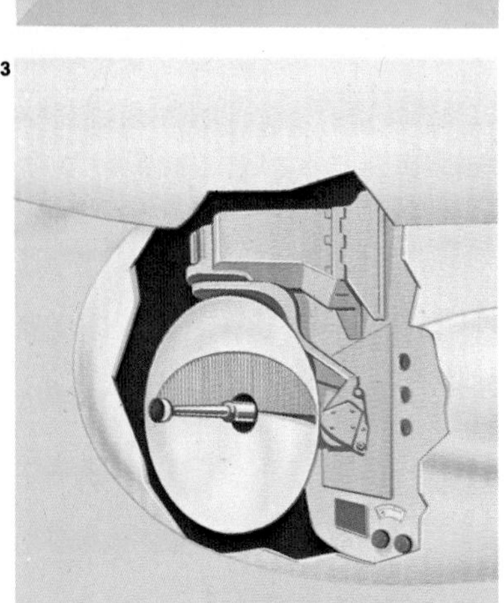

3

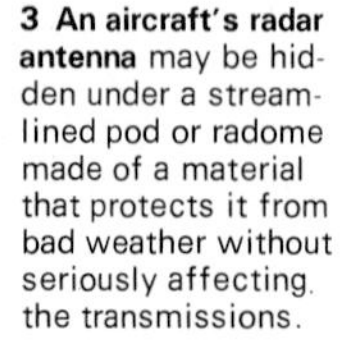

3 An aircraft's radar antenna may be hidden under a streamlined pod or radome made of a material that protects it from bad weather without seriously affecting the transmissions.

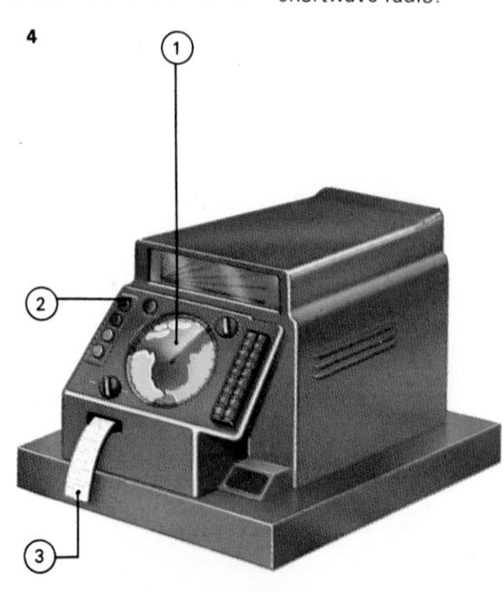
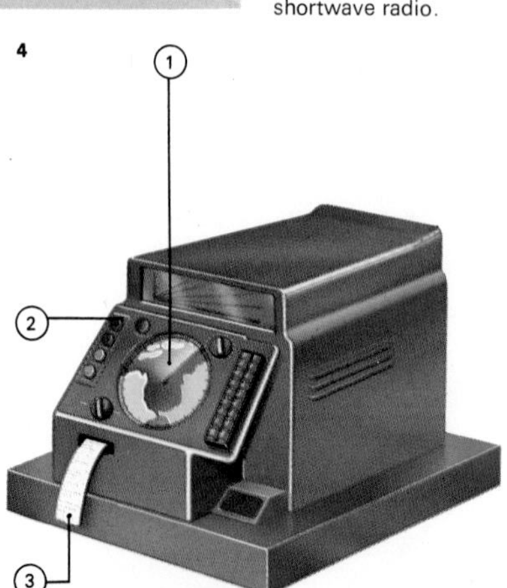

4
1
2
3

4 The presentation unit of a storm-detector radar has a cathode-ray tube [1] that maps signals from a rotating antenna as glowing storm clouds. The function selector [2] controls observed range; paper tape [3] gives a record.

Most radar receivers have large aerial arrays designed to receive as much as possible of a reflected signal, which is usually weak.

Processing and presentation

Radar signals, suitably processed and amplified, are passed to the presentation unit along with the original transmitted signal. The signal presentation system is generally a cathode-ray tube display, based on an oscilloscope, and can give either a simple read-out of range or of elevation, or both. Alternatively it can display a complete electronic "map" of the position of wave-reflecting objects in all directions [4].

In a simple straight-line display, the direction and elevation of the located object (an airplane in the sky, for example) are read from dials indicating the direction and elevation of the radar beam. The range is read off a pulsed straight-line oscilloscope trace in which the time between transmission and reception is twice the range.

The "map" or Plan Position Indicator (PPI) display is produced by a straight-line oscilloscope display arranged with a radial scan that begins at the center of the tube and ends near its circumference. The scan is then made to rotate, with the start of the scan as the center of rotation, in step with the rotation of the antenna. The oscilloscope screen is coated with a material having a long afterglow, so that an echo signal (a bright spot) on the screen remains visible during the time taken for one complete revolution of the antenna. The distance of an echo spot from the tube center represents the range of the object, and its bearing on the screen conforms to its actual bearing.

Most radar installations depend entirely on the weak waves reflected by solid objects, although some systems use a relay receiver-transmitter to receive and retransmit a more powerful return wave. Such a system is known as secondary radar.

When an electromagnetic wave is reflected by an object moving toward or away from the radar installation, the frequency of the reflected wave is altered. This is the Doppler effect, well known in acoustics. The resulting frequency shift can be used to calculate the speed of an object [6].

KEY

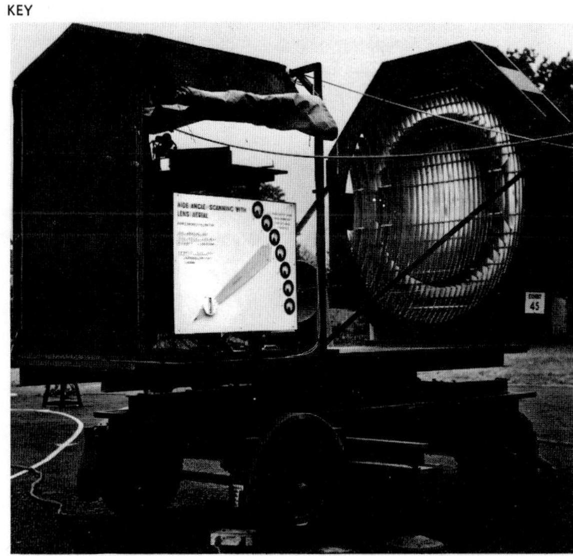

During World War II, the British developed small, transportable radar sets so that their radar defense system was able to monitor any area of potential air attack.

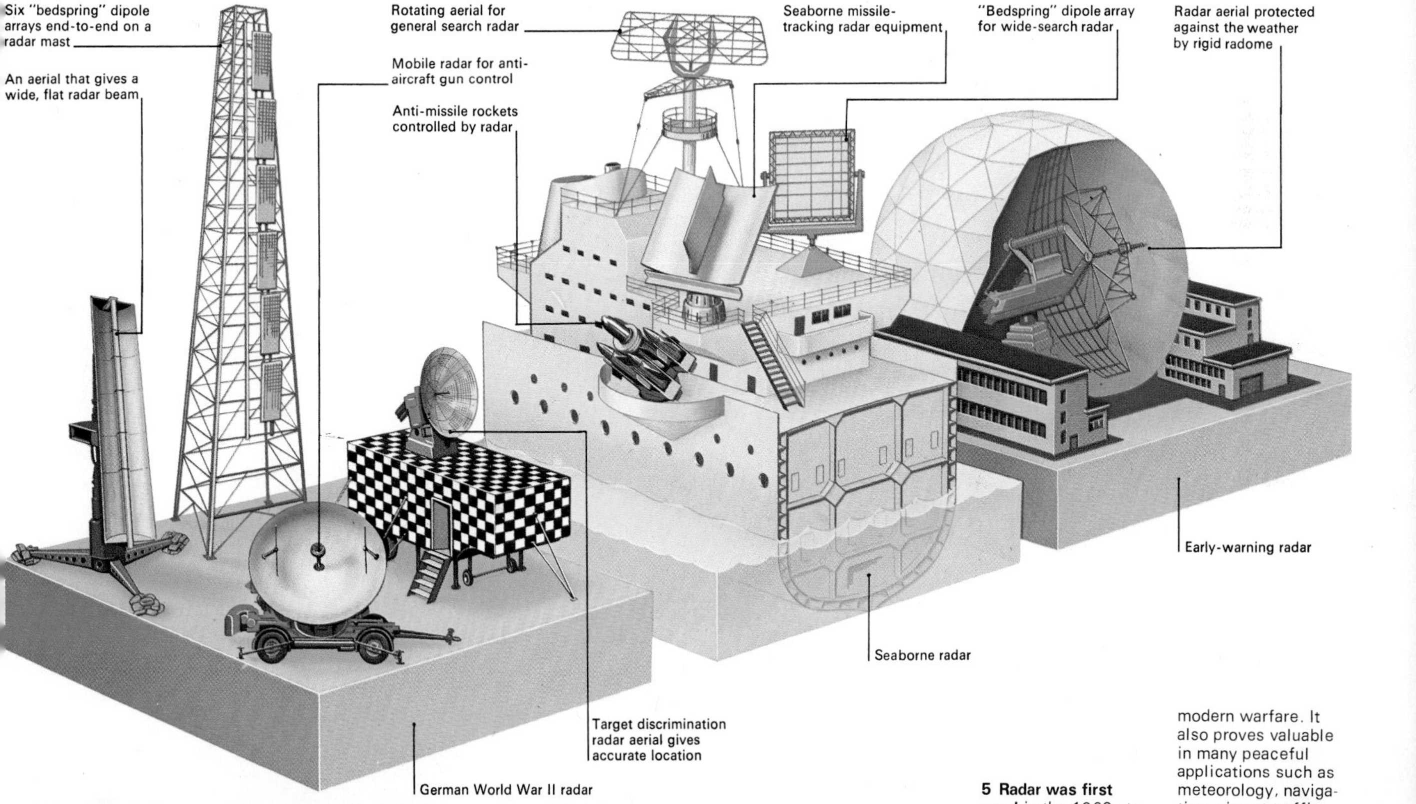

Six "bedspring" dipole arrays end-to-end on a radar mast

An aerial that gives a wide, flat radar beam

Rotating aerial for general search radar

Mobile radar for anti-aircraft gun control

Anti-missile rockets controlled by radar

Seaborne missile-tracking radar equipment

"Bedspring" dipole array for wide-search radar

Radar aerial protected against the weather by rigid radome

Early-warning radar

Seaborne radar

Target discrimination radar aerial gives accurate location

German World War II radar

5 Radar was first used in the 1920s to demonstrate the existence and extent of the ionosphere, which was found to reflect radio waves. Research during the 1930s in Britain, the United States, Germany, and France developed radar for military puposes and it became a vital aid in both defense and attack during World War II when British and German electronic engineers designed and built similar installations. So greatly has its efficiency improved that radar is now an indispensable tool of modern warfare. It also proves valuable in many peaceful applications such as meteorology, navigation, airport traffic control, and surveying. Military uses of radar include long-range aircraft and missile warning systems; location radar for automatic control of anti-aircraft guns; airborne radar for use as a night "eye" to locate enemy bombers in darkness; and naval radar to give information about the presence of enemy shipping in conditions of poor visibility. Radar is also used in sophisticated weaponry as a homing device for steering anti-missile missiles.

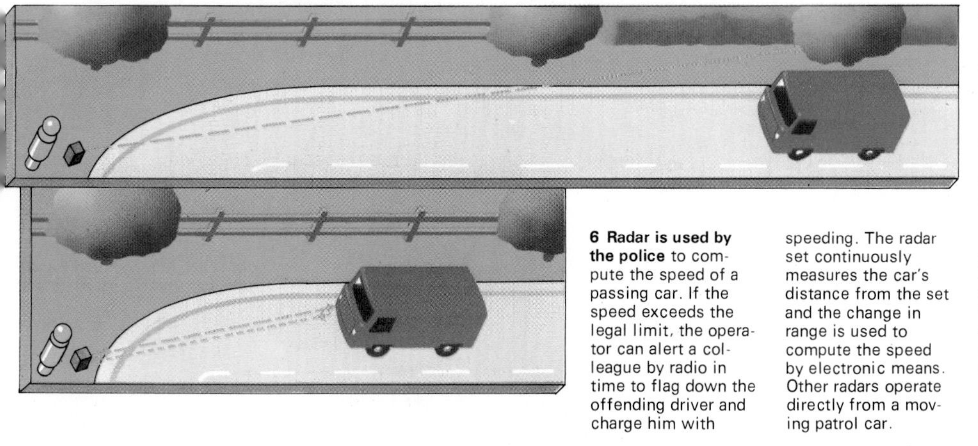

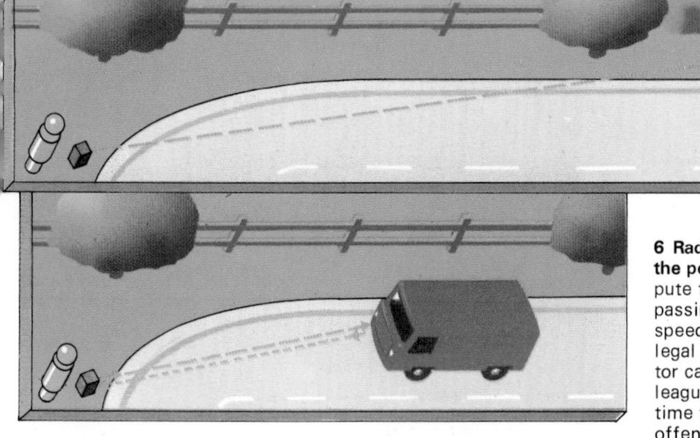

6 Radar is used by the police to compute the speed of a passing car. If the speed exceeds the legal limit, the operator can alert a colleague by radio in time to flag down the offending driver and charge him with speeding. The radar set continuously measures the car's distance from the set and the change in range is used to compute the speed by electronic means. Other radars operate directly from a moving patrol car.

Chemical engineering

Research chemists at their laboratory benches develop new products, generally using only glass apparatus. A new product is made in the laboratory in gram quantities, but if it is to sell in the open market the makers may well have to sell tons—for well-developed commodities such as plastics or fertilizers, up to millions of tons a year. It is this transition from laboratory to production plant that is the basis of chemical engineering.

The chemical plant

The processes in chemical engineering are often basically only refined versions of activities that might take place in the kitchen. But chemical engineering is an exact science devoted to designing, building, and operating equipment on an industrial scale in the special kind of factory known as a chemical plant. Yet the process need not literally be a chemical process. Chemical engineers design plants for physical processes such as evaporation, distillation, liquefaction, and filtration, as well as for changes of chemical composition.

The design of chemical plants and equipment is a separate and distinct discipline, although it overlaps with several others. The task is best done not by a team containing both chemists and mechanical engineers but by individual engineers who have the right combination of skills. They need to know, for instance, how large a vessel should be for "cracking" naphtha from petroleum to change it to ethylene and propylene (which will later be converted to plastics, detergents or dry-cleaning fluids). What should it be made of? How much power is needed for pumping, how much for heating and cooling? Will the immediate products be separated by distilling them? It is practical questions such as these that are applied to changing materials in both composition and form.

The foundation of the discipline of chemical engineering lies in chemistry, physics, and mathematics. Its operation is based on interweaving these with the knowledge gained from older branches of engineering, as well as assessing the economics of processes. Chemical engineers often use computers for assessing design and operational factors [5].

Many chemical engineers are employed in the chemical industries, where their skills have contributed to an exceptionally high growth record. They also work in the petroleum refining, atomic energy, gas, and coal industries.

From theory into practice

The important basic idea of chemical engineering is that processes used for producing quite diverse chemicals—for example, acids, dyes, or drugs—can be considered as a series of "unit operations." These unit operations are the same whatever the detailed nature of the material being processed. Consequently a common body of theory can be applied to a range of process industries.

Unit operations include distilling, filtering, mixing, crushing, and crystallizing. It is even possible to unify the theory further. Many of the operations can be considered as examples of the study of how fluids flow, how heat is transferred, or how material is

CONNECTIONS

See also
1806 Materials for indus
1808 Soaps and deterge
1810 Explosives and fire works
1812 Color chemistry
1814 Cosmetics and per fumes
1550 What is chemistry?

1 A

B

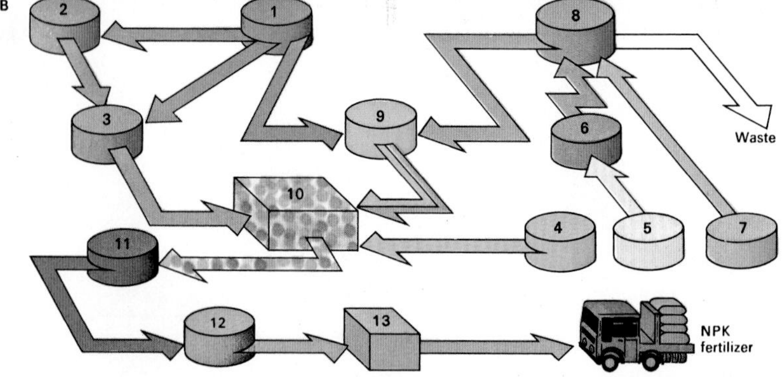
1
2
3
4
5
6
7
8
9
10
11
12
13
Waste
NPK fertilizer

1 The key elements in plant fertilizer are nitrogen, phosphorus, and potassium. The basic processes, therefore, in a factory making fertilizers [A] are extracting nitrogen from the air and phosphorus and potassium from natural minerals, and combining these elements (sometimes individually, sometimes jointly) into soluble chemical compounds that are used to feed plants. A chemical engineer designs and operates processes [B] to obtain the necessary compounds. He extracts nitrogen from the air and hydrogen from natural gas or water. He then combines the two by "fixing" the nitrogen as ammonia [1]. Part of this is converted to nitric acid [2], which reacts with more of the ammonia to form ammonium nitrate [3]. The potassium compound, probably sylvite [4] (potassium chloride), may be used directly. Sulfur [5] is converted into sulfuric acid [6], which is reacted with natural phosphate rock [7] to produce phosphoric acid [8]. With ammonia, this yields diammonium phosphate [9]. The three "NPK" compounds are then mixed and granulated [10], dried [11], coated [12], and packed [13] for sale.

ransferred through surfaces (mass trans-er). Thus what is learned about mass trans-er can be applied to unit operations for ıbsorbing gases, leaching soluble materials ›ut of solids, or crystallization.

The chemical engineer must also con-ider what will happen when he "scales up" he quantities [3]. Sometimes a different eaction takes place in a big tank from that in a small beaker where the reagents have only a short way to travel before meeting. Stirring the contents of the beaker brings hem quickly into contact and heat can read-ly reach all parts or be as rapidly removed. When ammonium diuranate is produced in he laboratory by reacting the nitrate with ammonia, for example, it precipitates al-nost immediately. With tons of solution in a large tank, precipitation may take several ıours, because the practical speed of reac-ion depends on the rate at which pumps can operate and stir the liquid. As another example, nitrobenzene is made in the aboratory in a round glass flask that can be mmersed in water to remove heat. On a arge scale engineers use a different form of vessel to provide enough surface area to remove heat at a reasonable rate, and it is made not of glass but of metal.

Evaporating a liquid in the laboratory may be carried out in a glass vessel over an open flame (if the liquid is not inflammable). But the engineering operation needs large metal vessels with large amounts of surface area to promote efficient transfer of heat between the source and the liquid to be evaporated. Thus the study of materials for making apparatus (and their fabrication) and of the laws governing change of scale are important.

Biochemical engineering

Applied to biological processes or materials the discipline of chemical engineering is called biochemical engineering. An important area of this work has been the growing of food proteins on petroleum products to produce animal feed. Biochemical engineering has also been applied to new forms of fermentation processes for making antibiotics and vitamins, including the extraction and concentration of the delicate products.

KEY

The crowning achievement of a chemical engineer's work is the factory where chemical products such as nylon are made. Chemical engineering serves a modern group of industries rich in challenges because the processes tend to change more quickly than in most other industries. Many of the products help to make life more convenient. Working in close collaboration with chemists and other specialist engineers, chemical engineers choose the process, choose or design the plant, help in its construction and, after starting the process, control its operation to give the most economic results, as technical or general managers.

2 In one type of evaporator heat is transferred from a heating medium [1] (often steam) to a liquid [2]. The two are kept apart by partitions made of metal or sometimes carbon. The liquid circulates through tubes [3] and is heated to give off a vapor [4]. The loss of solvent concentrates the liquid [5], which is discharged at the bottom of the evaporator. The cooled heating medium [6] is removed.

3

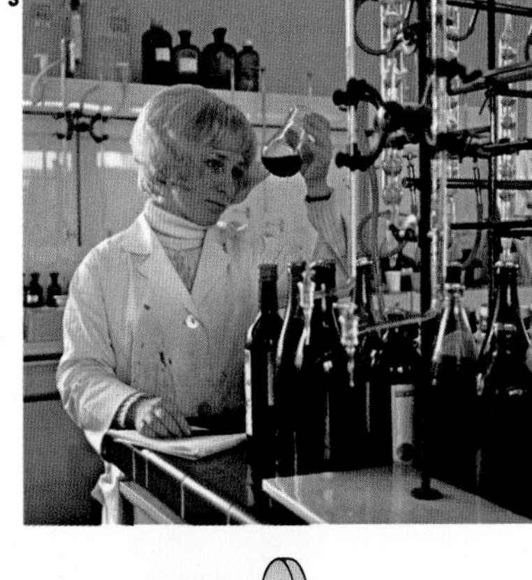

3 The operations of chemical engineering are essentially scaled-up versions of operations in the chemical laboratory, although on a larger scale the equipment and utensils may look different.

4 To make sulfuric acid, liquid sulfur is blown [1] into a burner [3], also fed with air [2], forming sulfur dioxide. This passes through the filter [4] to the cooling tower [5]. In the washing tower [6] it is washed with water then dried in a packed tower [7] of Raschig rings by means of 98% sulfuric acid entering at 8 and leaving at 9. In the converter [10] the dry sulfur dioxide reacts with oxygen [11], is cooled [12] and the resultant sulfur trioxide is absorbed in 98% sulfuric acid [13] to yield oleum [14]. This is diluted [15] with sulfuric acid [16] to produce 98% sulfuric acid [17].

2

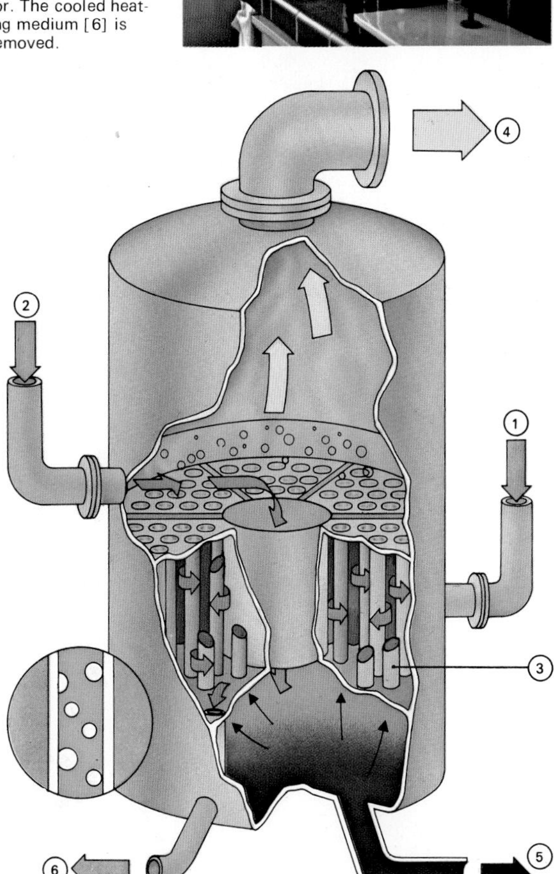

4
2
1
3
6
5

5 Computers are extensively used in chemical engineering for solving design problems and for controlling operations. The basic relationships of a process may be investigated by the computer and corrective action can be applied if some measured quantity in any part of the plant (eg, temperature, pressure, viscosity, or composition) deviates from requirements and would otherwise result in a reduced yield or in poor quality.

5

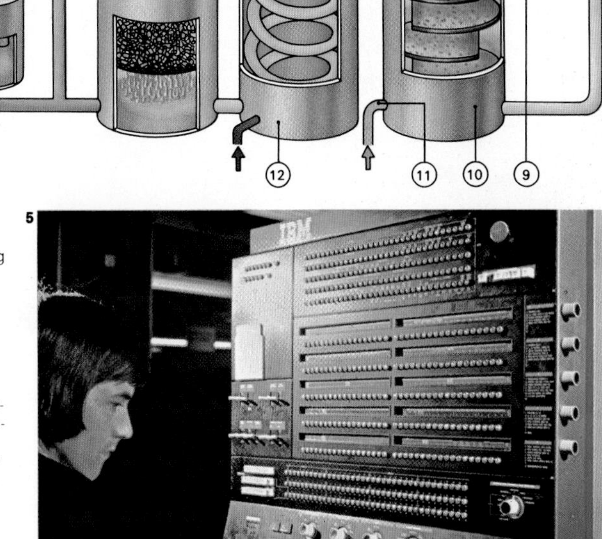

IBM

Materials for industry

Plastics, paints, pills, soap, synthetic rubber, polishes, and pesticides are all products of the chemical industries. They begin as natural materials and are then transformed chemically to make products of value to other industries or to people in their daily lives [Key]. Minerals such as rock phosphate [1] or petroleum are treated so as to yield chemicals in a series of steps known as chemical processes. Before or after each chemical process there may also be other closely allied activities, such as distilling, mixing, crushing, filtering, and blending reactants or products.

Structure of the industry

Chemicals are either organic (mostly compounds of carbon, oxygen, and hydrogen) or inorganic. Most inorganic chemicals are based on rocklike minerals, with some important exceptions: sulfur and ammonia, for example can be extracted from oil and natural gas.

The chemical industries are among the growth industries. World production expanded between 1963 and 1973 at more than nine percent a year by volume, compared with an average growth rate of less than six percent for all industries. Chemical industries need large capital investment—which tends to result in giant companies—but they are efficient, producing a high value of output for each employee. Chemical consumption is particularly high in the United States—about 1.5 times the rate for Western Europe and Japan. But elsewhere (except in Australia and South Africa) consumption is low. The use of such chemicals is one measure of industrialization.

A major development since World War II has been the change from wood, coal, and vegetable matter to petroleum as a source of organic chemicals. About a million tons of petrochemicals were produced in 1945, but output had increased almost 100 times by 1975. The most important group of basic "building blocks" are ethylene, propylene, and butylenes, sometimes known as organic base chemicals. These come largely from oil refinery operations, except in the United States, where they are derived predominantly from natural gas by "cracking" ethane and propane. They are used to make plastics, solvents, fibers, and many other derivatives.

Aromatic chemicals—such as benzene, toluene, and xylene—are another major organic group, largely petroleum-based (but formerly derived from coal tar) with a wide range of uses in resins, plastics, fibers, and solvents [2]. Other important base chemicals used at the rate of many millions of tons a year are acetylene, methanol, ammonia, and sulfur. In most industrial countries development is heavily based on organics resting on an already well developed inorganic chemical industry.

Versatility of chemicals

The chemical industries are of fundamental importance in modern industrial society, often in little-known ways. Their role in providing fertilizers for agriculture and pharmaceuticals for medicine, for example, is widely understood. But the consumption of sulfuric acid is often regarded as an index of the level of commercial prosperity of a country. It is used in making rayon; for

CONNECTIONS

See also
1804 Chemical engineer
1644 Oil refining
1618 Rubber and plasti
1620 Fibers for fabrics

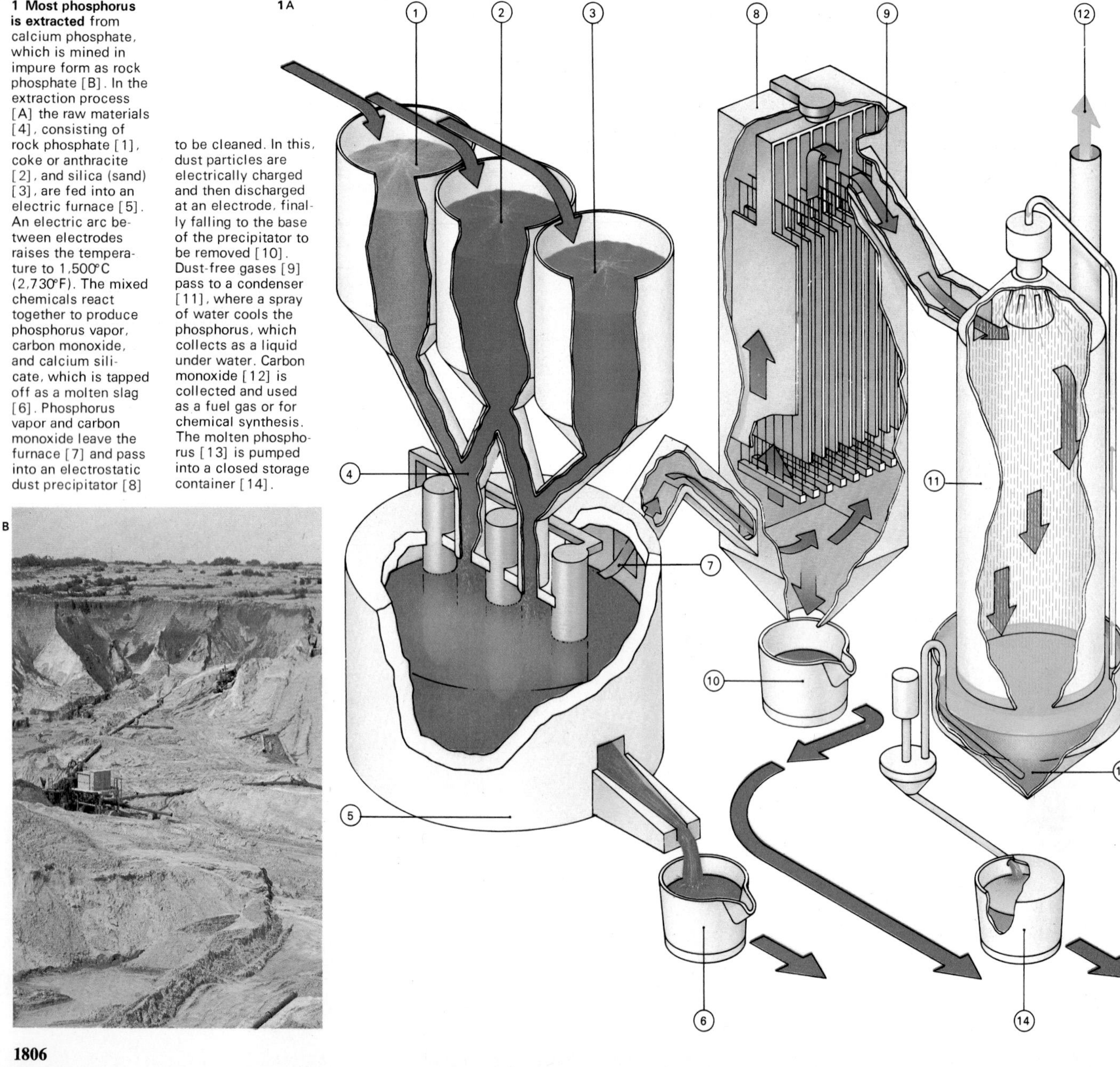

1A
B
1
2
3
4
5
6
7
8
9
10
11
12
13
14

1 Most phosphorus is extracted from calcium phosphate, which is mined in impure form as rock phosphate [B]. In the extraction process [A] the raw materials [4], consisting of rock phosphate [1], coke or anthracite [2], and silica (sand) [3], are fed into an electric furnace [5]. An electric arc between electrodes raises the temperature to 1,500°C (2,730°F). The mixed chemicals react together to produce phosphorus vapor, carbon monoxide, and calcium silicate, which is tapped off as a molten slag [6]. Phosphorus vapor and carbon monoxide leave the furnace [7] and pass into an electrostatic dust precipitator [8] to be cleaned. In this, dust particles are electrically charged and then discharged at an electrode, finally falling to the base of the precipitator to be removed [10]. Dust-free gases [9] pass to a condenser [11], where a spray of water cools the phosphorus, which collects as a liquid under water. Carbon monoxide [12] is collected and used as a fuel gas or for chemical synthesis. The molten phosphorus [13] is pumped into a closed storage container [14].

cleaning metals before plating; for producing pigments, explosives, dyestuffs, and storage batteries; and for making many other chemicals. Acetic acid—commonly thought of simply as a constituent of vinegar—is used to make cellulose acetate for fibers, plastics, and packaging, and vinyl acetate for emulsion paints and adhesives. It is also a starting material for solvents and pharmaceuticals.

Chemical industries invest heavily in research and plants and are highly inventive. Processes change far more frequently than in other industries and they produce a stream of new chemical products—for example improved resins, pesticides, paints, and pharmaceuticals. The main companies are international and need worldwide markets.

Safety regulations

Both the materials and the chemical processes are potentially dangerous. For this reason exceptional attention is paid to safety. There are occasional major disasters at chemical factories, but the overall record of these industries is good. Attempts have recently been made to set up an international marking system for vehicles carrying bulk chemicals, so that firemen, police, and ambulance attendants know what hazards to expect if a vehicle is involved in an accident. These wider attempts have failed, although there are national marking systems.

Regulations to protect workers from potentially dangerous gases and dusts have steadily been tightened in all industrialized countries. A recent American example has been the reduction of the limits for a worker's exposure to vinyl chloride monomer (used in making PVC plastics) to no more than one part per million during an eight-hour working shift.

Current research suggests that in the future coal will once again become an important source of bulk chemicals, but using very different techniques from the former carbonization process of coke making. Development of new techniques was stimulated by the rising price of oil in the 1970s and by supply difficulties that affected US and Japanese petrochemical production.

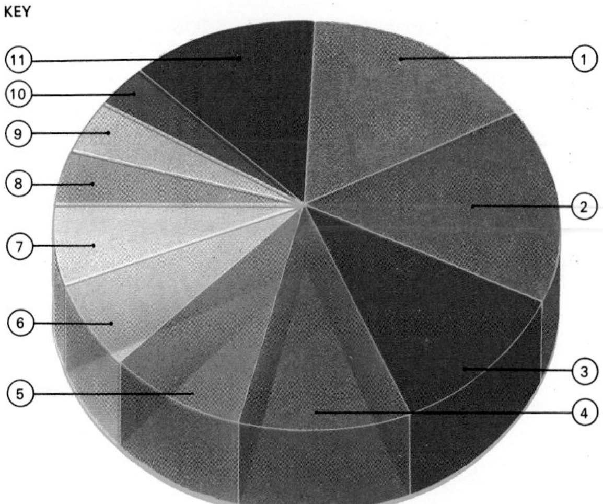
KEY
11
10
9
8
7
6
5
1
2
3
4

Materials produced by the chemical industry can be grouped in ten major categories. In terms of value: [1] organic chemicals 15%; [2] plastics and synthetic rubber 13%; [3] pharmaceuticals 12%; [4] general chemicals 11%; [5] inorganic chemicals 9%; [6] fertilizers 7%; [7] paint 6%; [8] soaps and detergents 5%; [9] dyes and pigments 5%; [10] cosmetics 4%; and [11] others 13%.

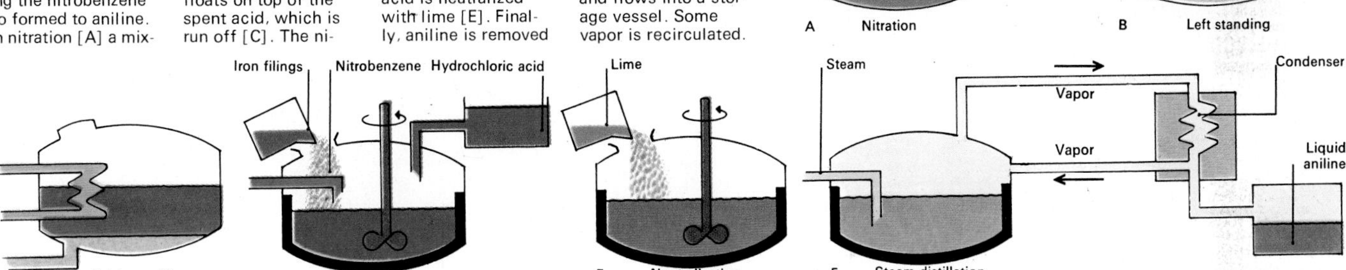
2
Mixed acid
Water
Benzene
A
Nitration
Nitrobenzene
Spent acid
B
Left standing
C
Acid run off
Iron filings
Nitrobenzene
Hydrochloric acid
D
Reduction
Lime
E
Neutralization
Steam
Vapor
Vapor
Condenser
Liquid aniline
F
Steam distillation

2 Aniline is produced in large quantities as the basic aromatic organic chemical used by the synthetic dye industry. It can be made by nitrating benzene and reducing the nitrobenzene so formed to aniline. In nitration [A] a mixture of nitric and sulfuric acids is added to benzene in a cooled, stirred container. The reaction mixture is left to stand [B], when a layer of nitrobenzene floats on top of the spent acid, which is run off [C]. The nitrobenzene is pumped into another reaction vessel in which it is reduced [D] with iron filings and hydrochloric acid. At the end of the reaction excess acid is neutralized with lime [E]. Finally, aniline is removed from the mixture by steam distillation [F]. Steam bubbled through the mixture boils the aniline; its vapor passes through a condenser in which it turns into a liquid and flows into a storage vessel. Some vapor is recirculated.

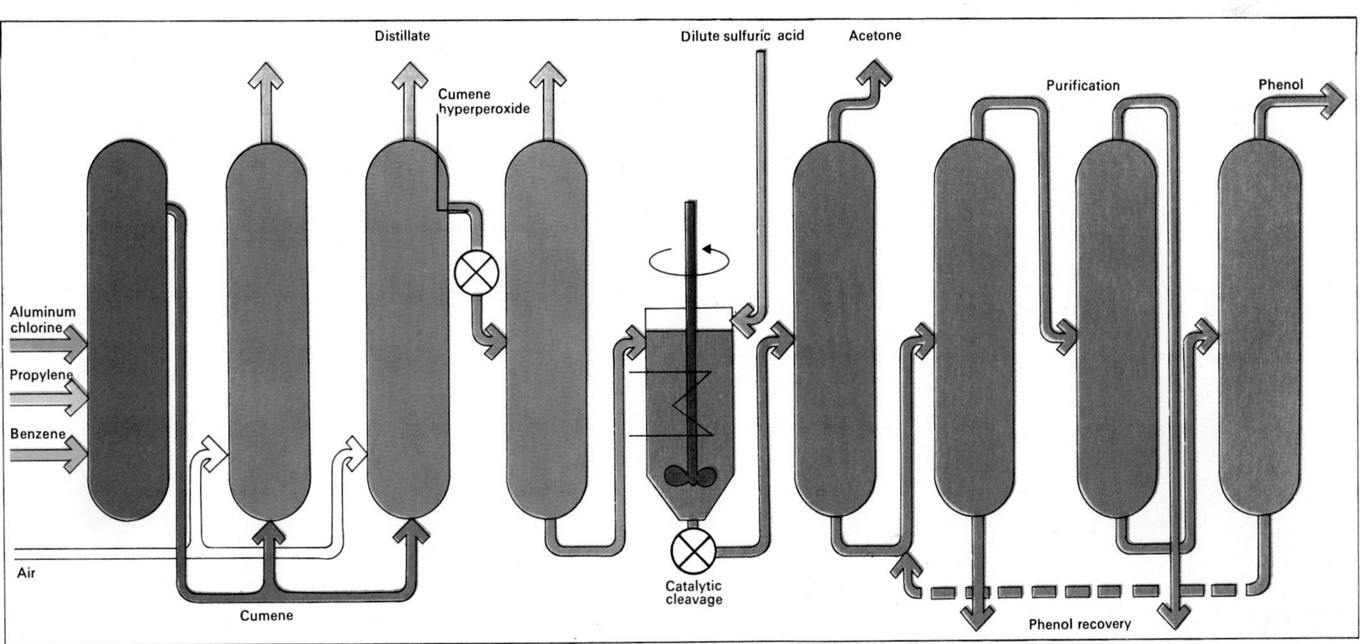
Distillate
Cumene hyperperoxide
Dilute sulfuric acid
Acetone
Purification
Phenol
Aluminum chlorine
Propylene
Benzene
Air
Cumene
Catalytic cleavage
Phenol recovery

3 Phenol (once called carbolic acid) is an organic chemical that, with its derivatives, is used for dyes, plastics and disinfectants. It was once made entirely from coal tar but today the demand for phenol is so great that it is also synthesized. One such process uses cumene, itself made from benzene and propylene by the action of aluminum chloride. The cumene is heated with air in alkaline conditions to form cumene hyperperoxide. This is split catalytically by dilute sulfuric acid into phenol and acetone, an important solvent and useful by-product. Methylstyrene, another by-product of the process, is used for making plastics or can be converted back to cumene and reused. The phenol is purified by distillation and allowed to condense to a solid. Other processes for making phenol make use of toluene or benzene.

Soaps and detergents

People have been using various kinds of cleansing agents for thousands of years, because water itself does not readily get rid of dirt and grease, as our ancestors discovered long ago. Water is not a good "wetter" because of its high surface tension, which causes it to run off a greasy area or stay there without penetrating it. Only when a cleansing agent that lowers surface tension is added, can water penetrate [5].

The Babylonians added alkaline plant ash (potash) to water. Other primitive cleansers were fuller's earth (a type of fine clay that easily absorbs impurities from oil and fat), soapberries (tree fruits containing a soapy substance called saponin), and the sap of the soapwort plant. Soap itself was probably first made in the Nile valley and about 600 BC Phoenician seamen carried the knowledge to the Mediterranean coasts. In the first century AD the best soap was made from goats' fat and beechwood ashes. Animal fat and wood ash remained the raw materials for centuries. Today, manufacture of materials for keeping clean is a major industry [Key].

Soap making was a small domestic industry until the end of the eighteenth century when a number of changes took place [2]. In 1787 it was discovered that the alkali caustic soda could be made from common salt—a plentiful raw material—so manufacturers were no longer dependent on plant ashes. Vegetable oils such as olive oil had been used in soap making by the Spaniards as early as AD 700. In the early nineteenth century other oils became more easily available. Coconut oil, palm oil, sesame oil, and soybean oil were imported from Africa, Southeast Asia, and China and by 1900 were replacing animal fats, which were in short supply. Social changes in the nineteenth century and the discovery of oleic and stearic acids further stimulated soap manufacture.

Modern soap making

The treatment of oil or fat with alkali (saponification) is the first stage in the manufacture of all types of "washing" soap [4]. This reaction produces sodium salts of stearic, palmitic, and oleic acids. After saponification the soap contains about 30 percent water—for making the more dense toilet soaps this has to be reduced to about 12 percent. Then various refinements such as perfumes, preservatives, whiteners, or coloring materials, and, sometimes, germicides (for medicated soaps) are added and thoroughly mixed. The molten soap is then cooled and cut to size; abrasives are added if scouring soap is wanted.

Soap flakes are produced by spreading the molten soap over water-cooled drums and producing ribbons of soap that are rolled progressively thinner and then broken into flakes. Soap powders normally contain silicates and phosphates that are added to the liquid soap—the resultant slush is superheated under pressure and sprayed into the top of a tower. As the droplets fall they solidify to give the familiar soap powder.

Not all soaps are soda based. Some made with caustic potash are used in liquid soaps and shaving cream, and other types are used in textile finishing, as lubricants, in the cosmetics and pharmaceutical industries, in polishes, and in emulsion paints.

CONNECTIONS

See also
1574 Polymers: giant molecules
1504 States of matter: liquids
1806 Materials for indus

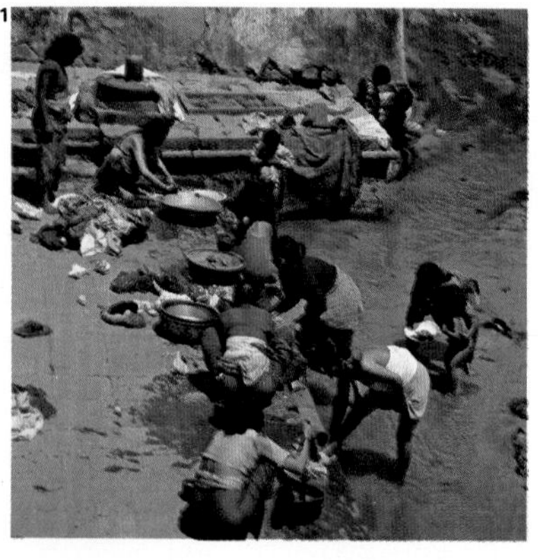

1 Women in some societies still clean their clothes by beating them with rocks in the nearest stream. This method works but shortens the life of the clothes and is hard work for the women.

2 Early soap making was done in open pans, where lye (crude sodium hydroxide) made from plant ash and limestone was heated with animal fats. The soap formed a crust on cooling.

3 Synthetic detergents are mixtures of various ingredients, the chief of which is the cleansing agent, or surfactant. A common surfactant has the chemical name sodium dodecylbenzene-sulfonate. It is made from petroleum products and has the molecular structure shown. Much dirt is held on clothing by greasy substances. The long tail (the dodecyl part) of the surfactant molecule "dissolves" in the grease, while the ionic head (the sulfonate part) dissolves in water. The two types of detergent manufacture shown use common hydrocarbon starting materials.

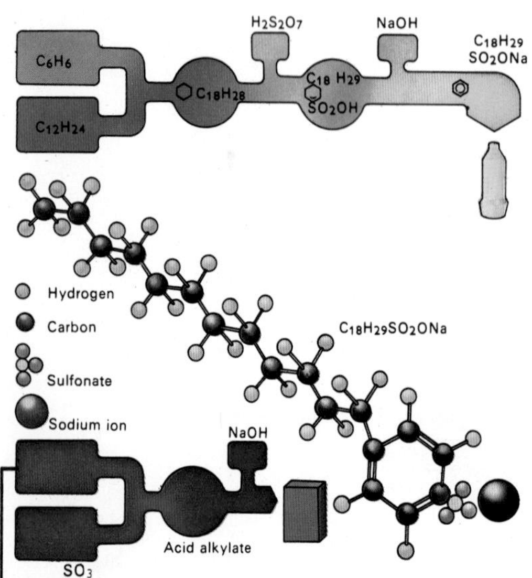

3
$H_2S_2O_7$
NaOH
$C_{18}H_{29}$ SO_2ONa
C_6H_6
$C_{18}H_{28}$
$C_{18}H_{29}$ SO_2OH
$C_{12}H_{24}$
Hydrogen
Carbon
Sulfonate
Sodium ion
$C_{18}H_{29}SO_2ONa$
NaOH
Acid alkylate
SO_3
Alkylbenzene

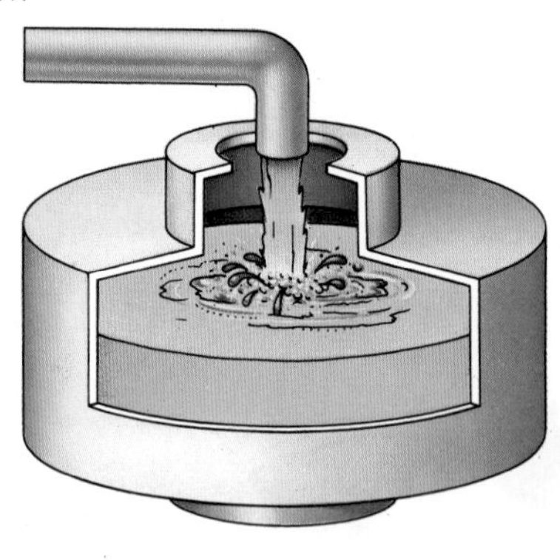

4 A

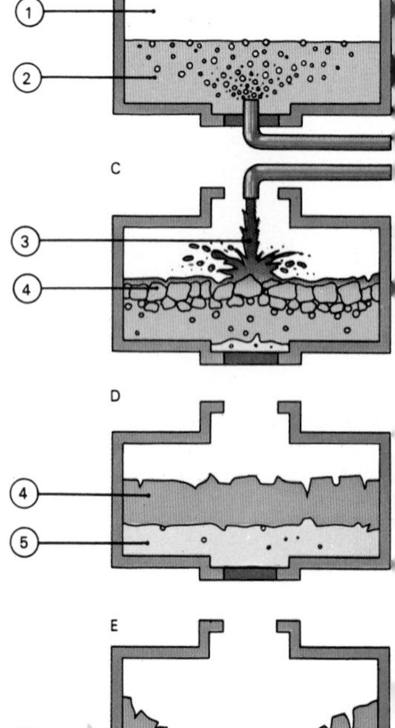

B
1
2
C
3
4
D
4
5
E
4
5

4 Modern soap making methods [A] follow ancient principles. Fat and alkali are saponified, producing soap and glycerol. Today's equipment allows the process to be completed in 15 minutes instead of several days. [B] Fats and oils [2] are reacted with water under high temperature and pressure [1]. [C] Alkali [3] is added to the resulting mixture of fatty acids to produce soap [4]. [D] The soap still contains glycerol [5], which is washed out [E] using brine and the salt solution is separated from the soap in a centrifugal extractor, which works like a spin dryer. Any fatty acid remaining is neutralized with alkali and salt, and again separated in a centrifuge. The molten soap is then poured into mixing machines that blend in other ingredients such as perfumes, softeners, germicides, and color. The blended soap is then ready for shaping into hard soap, toilet soap, flakes, or powder.

Soaps have a number of disadvantages as cleansing agents. They do not work in even slightly acid water, which is why various alkaline substances—carbonates, phosphates, and silicates—are added to household soaps. And, most importantly, they do not work well in hard water. The soap reacts with calcium and magnesium salts to form the familiar insoluble "scum" that leaves rings on bathtubs or a whitish film on glassware. Moreover, the availability of the raw materials (oils and fat) for making soap varies unpredictably. For these reasons manufacturers began looking in the late 1940s for a new type of synthetic detergent.

Synthetic detergents

The first synthetic detergents to be made on a large scale were based on products of the distillation of crude oil—at the time a cheap and readily available raw material. By the 1950s detergents based on the synthetic chemical alkylbenzenesulfonic acid (ABS) had captured more than 50 percent of the fabric washing market.

But early ABS detergents had an important defect. They contained branched chain molecules that made them biologically "hard," or nondegradable, which meant that they were not easily broken down by the bacteria in sewage treatment plants. These were replaced by degradable detergents (linear alkyl sulfonates, LAS).

Threat to the environment

Even the biodegradable detergents are not free from faults. In addition to the LAS, which is the cleansing agent, or surfactant, many other substances are added, such as builders, bleaches, conditioners, optical brighteners, and enzymes. A builder prevents the formation of insoluble compounds in hard water. A typical one is sodium tripolyphosphate, which breaks down into phosphates and can lead to an excess growth of algae and other water plants in rivers and lakes [6]. In the 1970s a search began for a replacement for these phosphates. Several alternatives were developed, but all proved to have worse side effects than the phosphates.

KEY

Cleansing agents such as soaps and powdered or liquid synthetic detergents are widely used in modern homes.

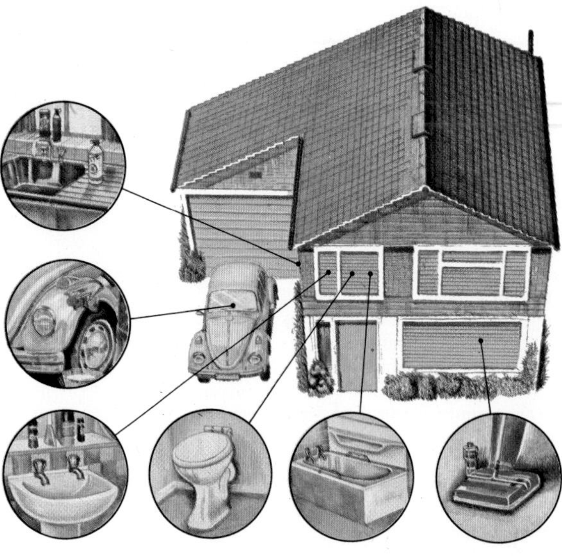

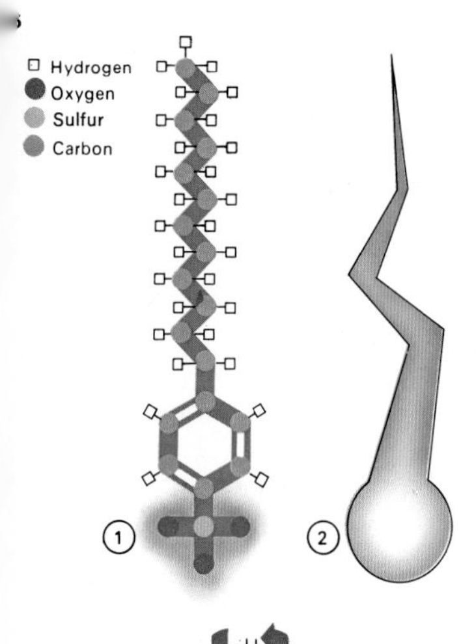
Hydrogen
Oxygen
Sulfur
Carbon
1
2

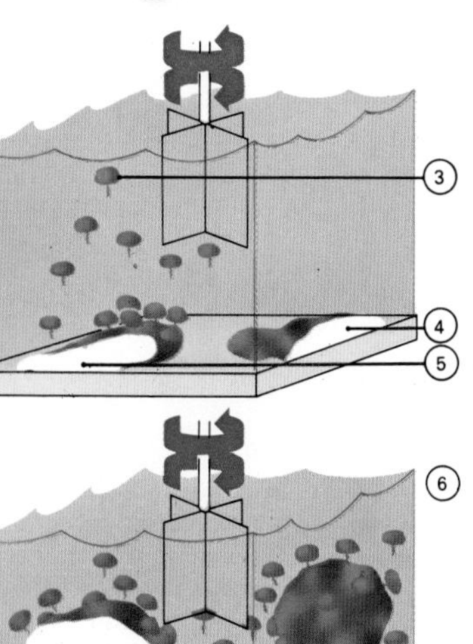
3
4
5
6

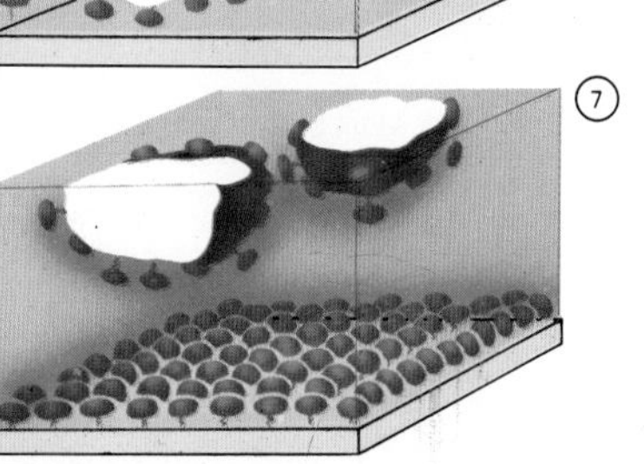
7

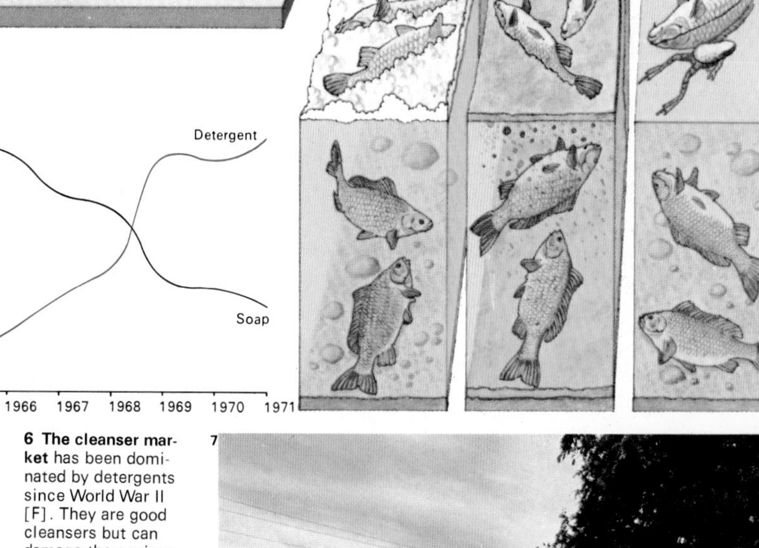
6 A
B
C
D
E
F thousands of tons
360
340
320
300
280
260
240
220
200
Detergent
Soap
1963
1964
1965
1966
1967
1968
1969
1970
1971

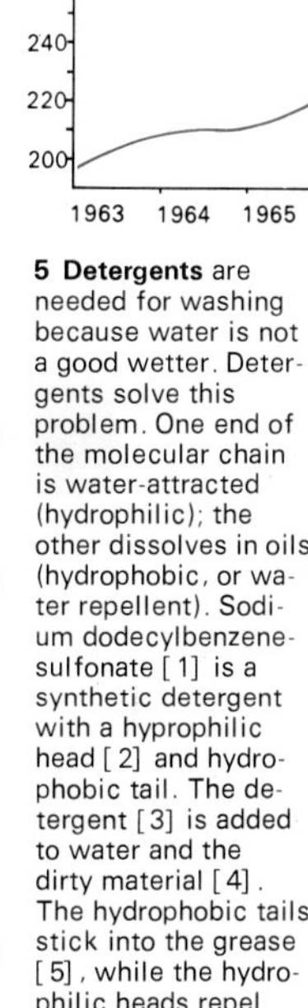

5 Detergents are needed for washing because water is not a good wetter. Detergents solve this problem. One end of the molecular chain is water-attracted (hydrophilic); the other dissolves in oils (hydrophobic, or water repellent). Sodium dodecylbenzenesulfonate [1] is a synthetic detergent with a hyprophilic head [2] and hydrophobic tail. The detergent [3] is added to water and the dirty material [4]. The hydrophobic tails stick into the grease [5], while the hydrophilic heads repel each other, forcing dirt into the water [6]. Dirt particles [7] do not return to the cleaned material because both material and dirt now have the same charge and repel each other.

6 The cleanser market has been dominated by detergents since World War II [F]. They are good cleansers but can damage the environment. Surfactants [yellow], phosphates [pink], and perborates [red] [A] pass unchanged through sewage plants [B] to rivers where the surfactant foam [C] kills birds and fish. Phosphates promote algae, which absorb the water's oxygen [D] and suffocate fish. [E] Perborates poison fish.

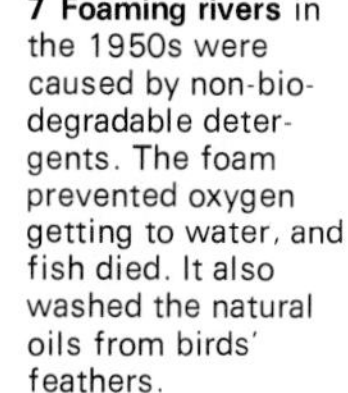

7 Foaming rivers in the 1950s were caused by non-biodegradable detergents. The foam prevented oxygen getting to water, and fish died. It also washed the natural oils from birds' feathers.

Explosives and fireworks

An explosive is a substance that can undergo a rapid chemical reaction to produce a large volume of gas. At the instant the gas is formed, it occupies the same volume as the explosive and is at an extremely high pressure. The pressure is increased by the generation of heat from the reaction and the rapid expansion that follows moves the surrounding matter. This is an explosion.

There are two main types of explosives: comparatively slow-burning propellants and fast-burning types used for their destructive effect in both military and peaceful operations. In quarrying for building stone, a low-power explosive is necessary to avoid shattering the stone, whereas in mining, a high-power explosive is used to break the mineral into suitable pieces [3].

Demolition bombs and mines are designed to exert the maximum blast effect; fragmentation bombs and some types of hand grenades have cases that break into many pieces at or above ground level to cause the maximum number of casualties [4]. Some shells contain an explosive charge that is fused to detonate at a predetermined time after the projectile has left the gun, as in "air bursts." These charges cannot be exploded by the shock of the propellant charge. Peaceful uses of this power include explosive forming, a process in which a shock wave from a small charge of high explosive causes a metal sheet to take the shape of a mold.

The manufacture of explosives is under strict government control. "Homemade" explosives can be particularly sensitive to shock and, apart from being illegal, are extremely dangerous.

The development of gunpowder

The first, and for hundreds of years the most effective, explosive propellant was gunpowder. It was known to the Chinese, who used it for fireworks by 1000 AD, and was introduced to Europe by the Arabs. In the 14th century it was first used as a propellant for the gun, the principle of which the Arabs had helped to develop. The design and development of firearms was to be closely linked with the quality of "black powder," as it was then known. It was not used for peaceful purposes, such as mining, until the 17th century.

Gunpowder is made by mixing potassium nitrate with carbon and sulfur. The mixture is moistened to prevent spontaneous ignition and the paste is milled to reduce the particle size. The "cake" formed after drying is broken into grains of various sizes. Large grains are slow burning and give a relatively long, slow push to a projectile. This was ideal for a cannon ball, but a shell or bullet in a rifled barrel needed the faster burning properties of small grains.

Cordite, a superior smokeless powder, replaced gunpowder as a military propellant in the late 1800s It contains nitroglycerin and nitrocellulose (guncotton) with a small amount of mineral jelly. Manufactured as a paste, it is kneaded into stiff dough and extruded into rods or cords, hence its name. The cords are then cut into suitable lengths.

High explosives are generally based on organic nitro compounds and are detonated by a violent shock, such as the explosion of an adjacent charge—a cap or detonator—or a mechanical blow—for example, the

CONNECTIONS

See also
1722 Space vehicles
1728 Development of firearms
1730 Automatic weapon
1732 History of artillery
1734 Modern artillery
1736 Armored fighting vehicles
1740 Modern fighting sh
1742 Early military aircr
1744 Modern military ai craft
1746 Nuclear, chemical, and biological warfa
174 Earthquakes

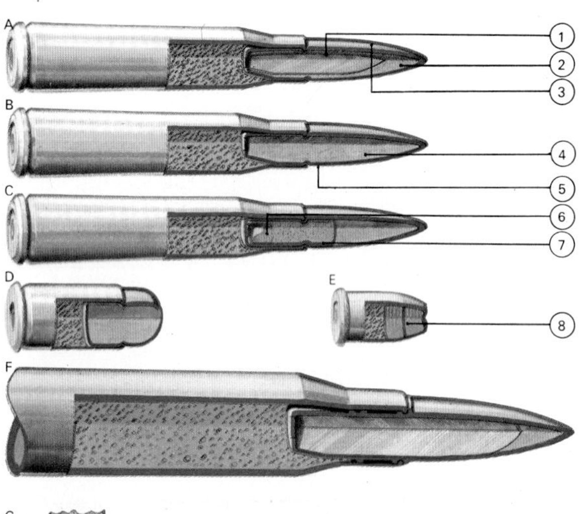

1 Small arms ammunition includes a rifle cartridge [A], with an armor-piercing bullet having a steel core [1], a lead-antimony sleeve [2], and steel envelope [3]; ordinary ball cartridge [B] with lead bullet [4] and steel envelope [5] for antipersonnel use; [C] tracer bullet used to correct machine-gun aiming – the primer [6] ignites the flaring tracer substance [7]; [D] standard pistol cartridge and [E] a pistol blank with felt wadding [8] in place of the bullet; [F] large armor-piercing bullet; and [G] primer assembly. The primer [9] is ignited by the cup [10] hitting the anvil [11], which fires the charge [12].

2 The Grand Slam [A], a 10-ton aircraft bomb, was designed to penetrate up to 100ft (30m) before exploding. The detonator [1] fired the charge [2]. A general purpose bomb [B] has fuses in the nose and tail [3,4] to ensure that the charge [5] detonates. Fragmentation bombs [C, D] have weakened cases [8] that fragment after the detonator [6] ignites the charge [7]. A built-in parachute [9] may be used to slow descent.

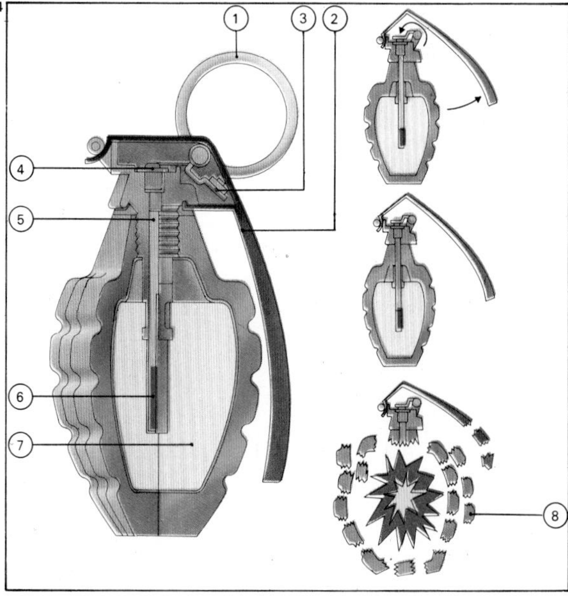

4 The hand grenade, of a type used by the US Army for 50 years, closely resembles the even older British 36 grenade, the "Mills bomb." The thrower hooks his left forefinger through the ring [1], holding the grenade in his right hand. As he pulls the grenade away, the pin is withdrawn and the grenade hurled in an overarm action. The lever [2] flies up, causing the sprung striker [3] to detonate the percussion cap [4], igniting the time fuse [5] made of slow-burning powder. The detonator [6] is fired after a delay of about four seconds, setting off the main charge [7]. Lethal fragments of the cast-iron case [8] are showered in all directions, some of them dangerous for 100ft (30m).

3 In blasting, a hole is drilled for the charge, its depth and size depending on the type of rock, the explosive used, and the purpose. The detonation causes shock waves to be produced radially, in all directions, with the greatest force at the center of the explosion. Low-power explosives are used for quarrying building stone to avoid shattering, but for other stones blasting gelatin or dynamite is used. Varying grades of high explosive are available, depending on the hardness of the rock and the depth of the hole. Charges are fired by detonator exploded by safety or electric fuse. Large-scale blasting is sometimes used for major excavation work and road construction.

firing pin of a rifle. High explosives yield stable decomposition products, such as nitrogen, water, and carbon dioxide.

The development of dynamite

Nitroglycerin, an oily liquid first prepared in 1846, requires only a slight shock to cause detonation. Its use as a high explosive is consequently hazardous. The Swedish chemist and industrialist Alfred Nobel (1833–96) solved the problem in 1866 when he discovered that kieselguhr, a diatomaceous (silica) earth, absorbs up to three times its weight in nitroglycerin, while remaining dry. The granular product, dynamite, retains all the properties of nitroglycerin but is far less sensitive to shock. Nobel later discovered that nitrocellulose (originally called guncotton) can be gelatinized with nitroglycerin to produce a stiff jelly known as blasting gelatin.

Most military high explosives are organic chemicals such as trinitrotoluene (TNT), ammonium picrate, cyclotrimethylenetrinitramine (RDX or cyclonite), and pentaerythritoltetranitrate (PETN), Bombs and explosive shells contain TNT or amatol (a TNT and ammonium nitrate mixture), both of which are sufficiently insensitive to withstand the shock of the propellant. Armor-piercing shells contain ammonium picrate, which is less sensitive than TNT and can withstand the shock of impact before being detonated. Plastic explosives have military and peaceful uses and consist of RDX blended with wax.

Fuses, detonators, and fireworks

A fuse is used to fire an explosive from a distance or after a delay. Safety fuse contains a gunpowderlike substance and is generally used with a detonator. This contains a sensitive primary explosive fired by fuse or electric current.

Pyrotechnics is the use of explosives for signals, display, flares, or fireworks. Various colors are obtained by adding a suitable metal salt, usually a sulfide. Antimony gives a white flame, strontium salts red, barium salts green, sodium salts yellow, and a mixture of copper salt and mercury chloride a blue flame.

KEY

Peaceful uses of explosives include blasting in mines and quarries, the demolition of old buildings, and the removal of tree stumps. Only an expert can decide the type and size of explosive charge to be used. Demolishing a tall structure such as the cooling tower of a power station or the chimney of a factory involves precise placing of small charges that are fired together or in sequence. In this case the space available for falling debris determines the type of explosive and how it is used. A chimney may be made to topple and fall like a tree by demolishing a wedge shape at the base or it can be made to fall vertically by using several charges.

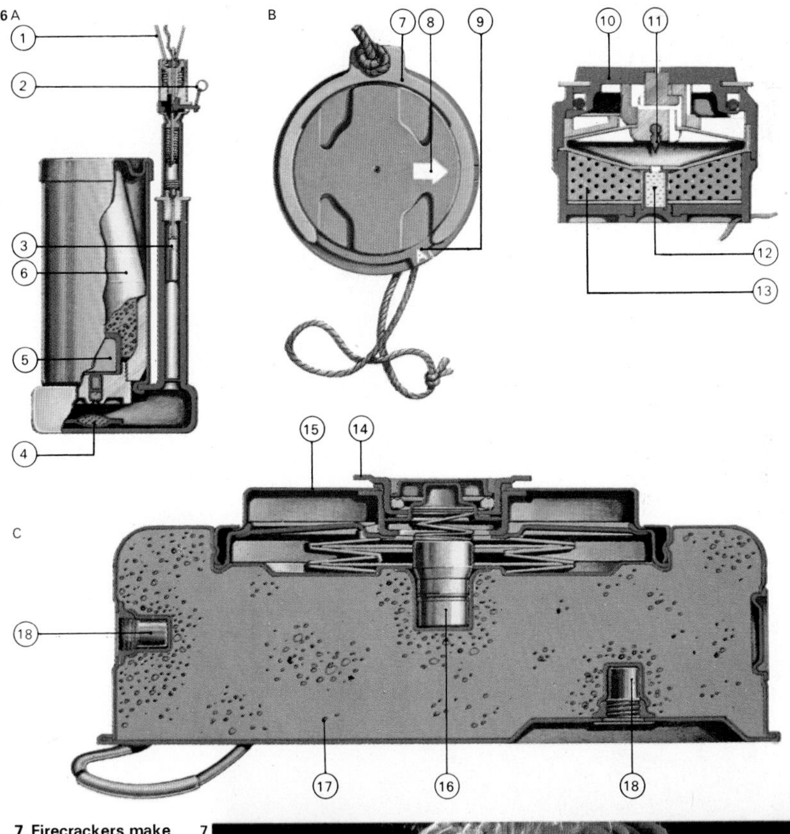
6 A
B
C
1
2
3
4
5
6
7
8
9
10
11
12
13
14
15
16
17
18

6 Mines are hidden hazards. The bounding-type mine [A] is buried with the tips of the prongs [1] showing and the safety pin [2] released. When the prongs are touched the firing pin [3] is released, detonating the igniter [4], which detonates the propellant [5], firing the projectile [6] about 7ft (2mm) above the ground before it explodes. [B] is a conventional antipersonnel mine armed by rotating the safety clip [7] from "safe" [8] to the "armed" [9] position. Stepping on the pressure plate [10] pushes the firing pin [11] into the detonator [12], and the charge [13] is exploded. [C] is a heavy antitank mine that is armed by inserting the fuse and rotating the arming plug [14]. Heavy pressure on the pressure plate [15] activates the fuse, which ignites booster [16] and charge [17]. The activation wells [18] contain fuses to booby-trap it.

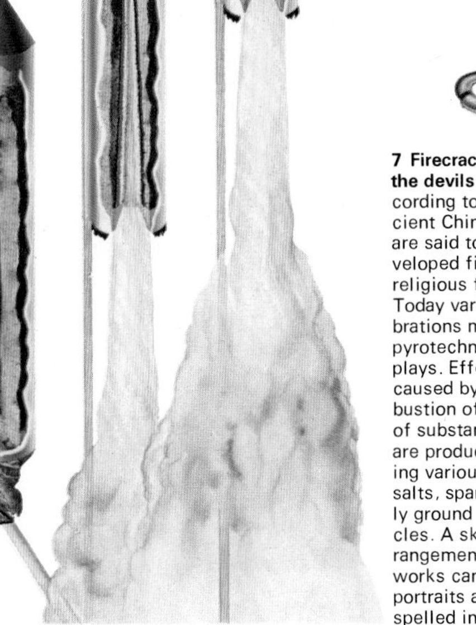

5 The combustion of the propellant in a firework rocket produces its power. The case is wet-rolled and the thrust increased by constricting it near one end (constriction is made with a cord before the case is dry). The propellant is packed into the case so that a conical cavity is formed at the burning end, allowing a large surface area of combustion to give the inital push. The cap of the rocket contains flares, or "stars," which are ejected as the propellant burns out.

7 Firecrackers make the devils jump, according to the ancient Chinese, who are said to have developed fireworks for religious festivals. Today various celebrations make use of pyrotechnical displays. Effects are caused by the combustion of a variety of substances; colors are produced by adding various metal salts, sparks by finely ground metal particles. A skillful arrangement of fireworks can produce portraits and words spelled in fire.

Color chemistry

People have perceived and used color since the earliest times, as the Stone Age cave paintings of Altamira and Lascaux [5], in Italy and the Urals, and in eastern Siberia and Australia all testify. Early artists employed natural materials to produce the color for these paintings and ever since that time have been experimenting with and perfecting methods of extracting dyes and pigments from natural materials and, comparatively recently, producing them artificially.

The composition of dyes and paints

Early people learned how to extract the animal and vegetable dyes with which they daubed their bodies and, later, impregnated their cloth, but it was not until the second half of the nineteenth century that the chemical composition of dyes was understood. It was then discovered that dyes are complex organic substances that are chemically bound to the fibers, as opposed to pigments, which are larger particles that form a film on the surface. The color we see depends on the wavelength of the light absorbed [6].

In paints, finely ground pigments are bound together in an oily medium. When spread as a thin layer the medium dries to form a hard film binding the pigment particles to the surface. Vegetable and animal pigments were used in antiquity—sepia from cuttlefish, ivory black from burnt ivory, and indigo, which was originally a plant extract—although these were less durable than the inorganic pigments derived from minerals. Some inorganic pigments are still used, but most are now derived from synthetic organic chemicals.

Plant and animal extracts have been used as dyes [2, 3] and were often mixed to give other colors: woad [1], when combined with madder, gave dark blue; with logwood and nut gall, black; with weld, green; and with kermes (a dried scale insect), purple-violet.

Classification of dyes

Dyes can be classified in two different ways, either according to how they are used or by their chemical composition [7]. The main dyers' classes are vat dyes, substantive dyes, mordant dyes, sulfur dyes, and ingrain dyes. Vat dyes—such as indigo—are insoluble in water and have to be converted to a soluble derivative, which is absorbed by the fabric. Once in the fabric the dye is reconverted to the original form. Substantive dyes impregnate a fabric directly, whereas mordant dyes have to be fixed in the fibers by substances known as mordants, such as alum, which form insoluble complexes with the dyes on the fabric. Sulfur dyes are direct dyes for cotton. Ingrain dyes are insoluble azo dyes (organic dyes derived from azo-benzene) produced on the fabric itself.

The nineteenth century saw the end of many of the natural dye industries. The first synthetic dye (aniline purple) was discovered by the British chemist William Perkin (1838–1907) in 1856. This was quickly followed by the discovery of magenta in 1858, and Perkin's tutor August Hofmann (1818–1892) then succeeded in showing that magenta could be converted into violet dyes, a group known as the rosanilines.

At about this time an extremely important chemical discovery, the diazo reaction,

CONNECTIONS

See also
1618 Rubber and plastic
1620 Fibers for fabrics
1622 Making cloth
1772 Modern printing
1784 Photography
1788 Motion picture photography
428 Mushrooms and toadstools
434 The lichens
480 Squids and octopus
482 Shells of the world

1

1 The woad plant sustained the manufacture of blue dye for over 1,000 years. Extracting indigotin from woad produced such a stench that Elizabeth I banned woad mills within five miles of her residences, but she also protected the industry from competition from the Indian indigo plant, which was a prohibited import in Britain until the end of the seventeenth century. In France Henri IV sentenced to death anyone using Indian indigo and the home industry was also protected in Germany and Italy. Despite such protectionism, the lower cost and more vivid color of indigo prevailed and the wood trade began to decline.

2

3

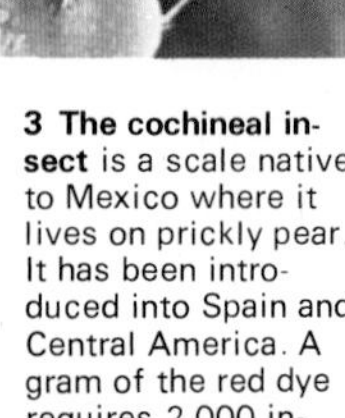

2 Plants, shellfish, and insects have all been used to produce dyes, sometimes at great trouble and cost. 9,000 of these murex snails were needed for one gram of Tyrian purple (imperial purple).

3 The cochineal insect is a scale native to Mexico where it lives on prickly pear. It has been introduced into Spain and Central America. A gram of the red dye requires 2,000 insects.

4

5

4 Ancient Persian carpets dyed with madder, kermes genista, genista (broom), buckthorn, nut gall, indigo, henna, safflower, and tumeric (all vegetable or insect dyes) mellow and improve with age, as in this 400-year-old example.

5 Cave paintings in Altamira and Lascaux of over 12,000 years ago made use of colored earths and clays stained with iron or manganese compounds. Natural ochres and lampblack made from oak charcoal were bound with animal fat, marrow, and blood. Australian aborigines still use the same pigments: black from charcoal; white from pipe clay and gypsum; yellow from limonite, ochre oxide, and some fungi; and red from red ochres and other iron compounds.

was observed by a young German chemist, Peter Griess (1829–88). This enabled azo dyes to be prepared from a wide range of intermediates. The discovery of the ring structure of benzene (by another German, Friederich Kekulé [1829–96]), and other advances in basic chemical understanding meant that the types of molecules responsible for color could be identified and eventually synthesized. A great commercial industry thus grew up producing synthetic dyes from coal tar's organic chemicals.

The modern dyeing industry

Since the nineteenth century the manufacture of both dyes and pigments has been revolutionized by modern techniques. Most are now synthetic compounds derived mainly from organic aromatic chemicals obtained from the distillation of coal tar and crude oil. Using various chemical reactions these compounds are converted into more than a thousand intermediates, which can be made into the desired dye or pigment.

Azo dyes can be made in many colors and are used on all types of materials and as pigments in printing inks and for plastics. Anthraquinone dyes give rise to reddish-blue pigments used in paints, stains, enamels, polishes, soaps, and plastics as well as fabrics. Indigoid colors (blue and red) are used to dye fabrics. The triphenylmethanes create bright green, blue, and purple shades and are used in paper, printing inks, crayons, cosmetics, and in processed food. Copper pthalocyanine is a pigment used in printing inks, lacquers, emulsion paints, rubber, and plastics, and for imparting color to car bodies. Phthalocyanines are also used as dyes; most are bright blue or green.

Dyes or pigments can now be made to suit any purpose. In general, dyes are used to color textile fabrics, whereas pigments are used for paints, printing inks, and plastics. Plastics are colored by mixing the finely divided solid plastic with pigment before molding. Pigments can be made from dyes by precipitating them with a suitable metal salt to form the "lake" colors. Thousands of different color chemicals are now manufactured.

KEY

For centuries the principal way of coloring cloth was by vat dyeing—a method still used today. Bolts of bleached or unbleached cloth are "stewed" in a bath of dye. The invention of synthetic aniline dyes in the 1850s widened the range of color dyes. This illustration of about 1870 shows the equipment used for making synthetic aniline dyes.

6

6 When white light falls upon an object, the chemical composition determines which colors the object absorbs and which it reflects. It is the reflected light that we see and interpret as the different colors. A cloth that absorbs the blue component from white light appears reddish to us.

7

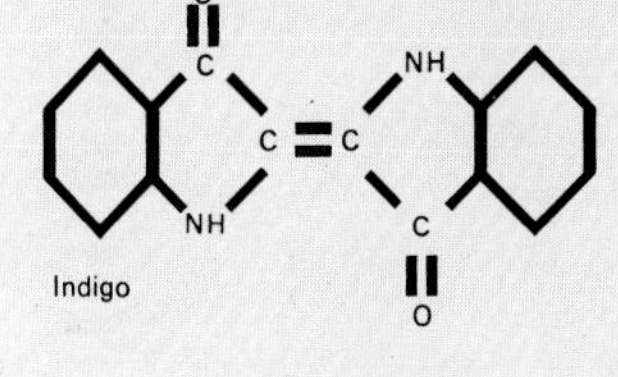

Indigo

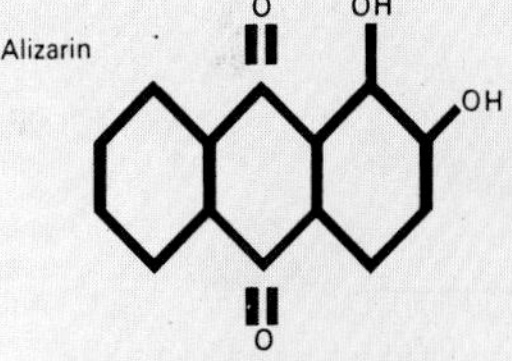

Alizarin

Malachite green

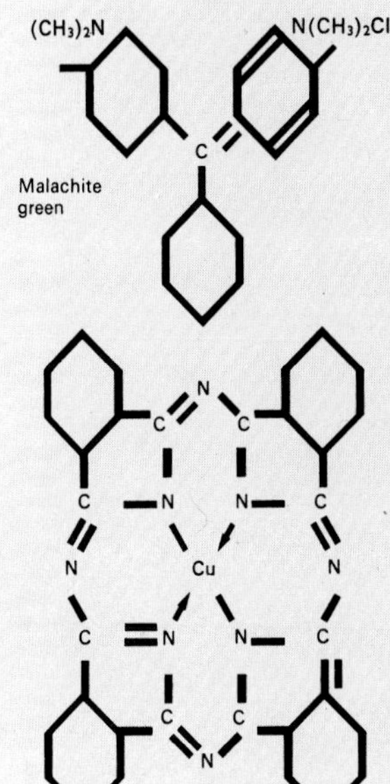

Phthalocyanine

7 There are four main chemical classes of dyes and pigments in addition to the azo colors that provide 50% of all manufactured dyes and pigments. Alizarin, a natural anthraquinone, was first used as a red dye by the Egyptians. Indigo was first synthesized commercially in 1897. Malachite green was one of the first synthetic dyes. The phthalocyanines were discovered in the 1920s.

8 Hematite is one of the iron oxides originally used as pigments for yellow, red, brown, and black shades. Iron oxides are still widely used because of their durability, inertness, and low cost.

9

9 These printing ink samples show the wide range of colors available. Inorganic pigments (Prussian blue and the lead chromes) and the modern synthetic organic dyes and pigments are used.

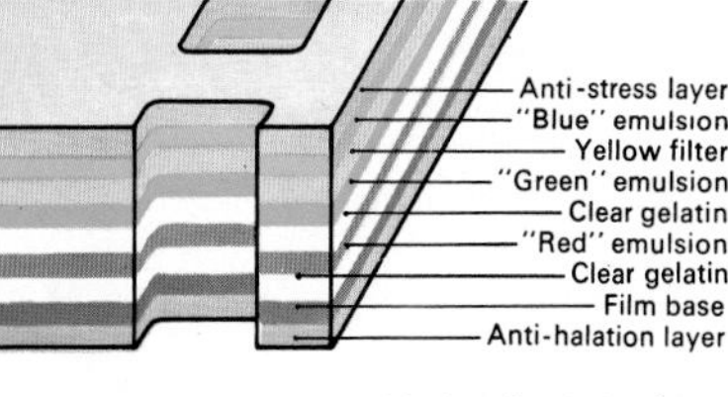

Anti-stress layer
"Blue" emulsion
Yellow filter
"Green" emulsion
Clear gelatin
"Red" emulsion
Clear gelatin
Film base
Anti-halation layer

10 Color film is made up of three silver halide layers that respond to blue, green, and red light. A positive print is obtained from the developed film "negative" by replacing the colors of the "negative" with their complements.

11

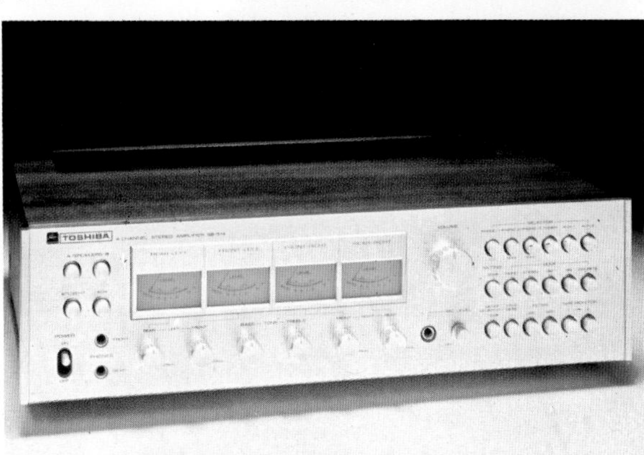

TOSHIBA

11 Anodized aluminum can be colored using dyes that are soluble in organic solvents. Both azo and phthalocyanine solvent dyes can be used. Black dyes can be used to "print" letters on signs or, as here, on electronic equipment.

Cosmetics and perfumes

Cosmetics have been used since the Stone Age, when men painted their bodies as part of a hunting ritual. Excavations in Egypt have provided evidence that decorating the face and body with oils, aromatics, and color had become a sophisticated art by 2000 BC [Key]. As well as being used for decoration, cosmetics are now employed to cleanse, help prevent skin troubles, and to disguise minor imperfections.

Creams and lotions

Many cosmetic preparations are emulsions of water and oils or waxes. On application the emulsion splits up, water is lost, and the oily material remains as a thin film on the skin or hair. Cold cream, often used for removing make-up, is an emulsion consisting of a combination of water, oil, and waxes. It gets its name from the cooling effect produced by the evaporation of the water. It can be prepared by mixing about one part by weight of white beeswax with three parts of liquid paraffin at 158°F (70°C), and adding this to a mixture of two parts water and a sixteenth part of borax. The resulting mixture is stirred as it cools to 95°F (35°C), at which point perfume may be added.

New emulsifiers and better knowledge of emulsion technology have resulted in a large range of different creams. These include foundation creams for use under make-up, cleansing creams that do not degrease the skin, hand creams to maintain the oil and water balance of the skin, and barrier creams.

Cosmetic lotions such as skin tonics or fresheners are mild astringents. They are said to close the "pores" of the skin, but in reality they close the openings of the hair follicles. Such lotions are based on aqueous alcohol and may contain humectants such as glycerol, menthol for its freshening effect, and the astringent witch hazel. Eau-de-Cologne and aftershave lotions may both be regarded as everyday skin fresheners.

Powder, lipstick, and eyeshadow

Face powder gives a smooth, even texture to the skin by masking the shine that results from natural secretions. Basic face powder is a blend of various ingredients including zinc oxide for covering power, precipitated chalk for absorbency and bloom, talc for spreading, and zinc stearate for adhesion. The color comes from organic and inorganic pigments. The perfume is either a flowery fragrance or a synthetic bouquet [3]. Cake make-up is applied to the face with a damp sponge and dries to form a water-repellent film of powder. It contains a perfumed powder base and "fillers" mixed with oily and waxy ingredients. The resultant mixture is compressed into cake form.

Lipstick must have a permanent color, good covering power, and an acceptable taste. The base is a mixture of waxes and nondrying oils, and many variations are possible depending on the proportion of oil to wax and the melting point of the wax. Color is achieved by blending titanium dioxide (for opacity) and inorganic and organic pigments (for intensity and variation of color) with a staining dye (for indelibility). The most widely used staining dyes are eosin derivatives. A simple lipstick can be made by gently melting together about six

CONNECTIONS

See also
1812 Color chemistry
680 Smell and taste
818 Body image and biofeedback

1

A
B

1 The male musk deer secretes a strong smelling substance from a gland situated on the abdomen. A rare perfume base, musk is obtained by killing the deer and extracting the whole gland. This is then dried and sold to the perfume industry whole or as a powdered extract. The perfume base civet occurs in both the male and female African civet cat [B]. It is a yellow glandular secretion and is valued at about one third the price of musk.

2 A

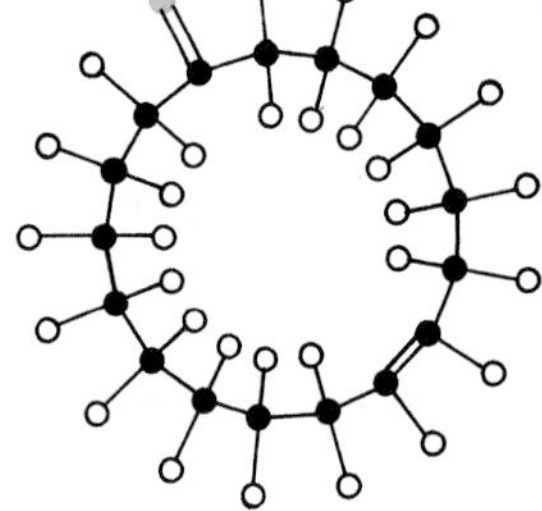

B

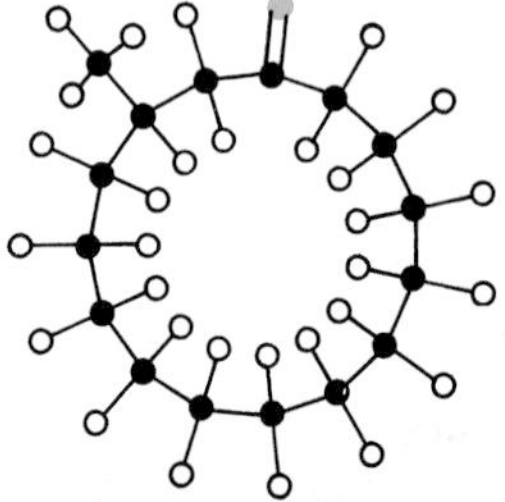

2 These molecular diagrams (black = carbon, white = hydrogen, blue = oxygen) show civetone [A] and muscone [B], active components of civet and musk.

3 A

B

3 The fragrance of flowers such as lavender [A] and roses [B] is caused by minute traces of essential oils. These are not single substances but complex mixtures of odorous compounds. They are generally volatile liquids and may be extracted for use as raw materials in perfumery. Separation of oil from plants is not easy and the method chosen must ensure that the perfume is not decomposed. Steam distillation may be employed, but the high temperature does not suit all oils. The most widely used method is extraction with a low-boiling solvent, which is later removed by distillation. The oils from peels are extracted by crushing and other mechanical means.

parts of ceresin wax, one part olive oil, two parts lanolin, four parts petroleum jelly, and one part liquid paraffin. When these are completely mixed, the pigments are ground in castor oil and eosin paste is added to achieve the desired shade. The melted lipstick is then poured into a mold and allowed to cool. Eye shadow and eyebrow pencils have a suitable coloring material dispersed in a similar wax base. Eyeshadow base contains an increased proportion of petroleum jelly so that it may be applied with a brush or fingertip, whereas eyebrow pencil contains more high-melting wax to increase its firmness.

Nail polish, deodorants, and antiperspirants
Nail polish consists of a nitrocellulose base combined with a plasticizer, a modifying resin, volatile solvents, and colors. The plasticizer ensures that the film is flexible and does not flake. The addition of resins improves adhesion, hardness, gloss, and resistance to detergent solutions. Solvents are chosen to give even drying in five minutes or less. The color comes from blending soluble dyes and insoluble organic pigments with titanium dioxide, which provides opacity. Other materials, such as natural pearl (guanine) or coated micas, may be incorporated to give "metallic" finishes.

Unpleasant odor develops with the bacterial decomposition of perspiration on the skin. This can be prevented simply by frequent washing or by the application of an efficient bactericide in a suitable base. Deodorants have no effect on the flow of perspiration and become less effective after a time. Antiperspirants decrease perspiration by a complicated mechanism. It is thought that sweat passes along the sweat duct by a process known as electro-osmosis and that the application of an electropositive material to the electronegative end of the duct inhibits the delivery of sweat. Antiperspirants generally contain an aluminum salt as the active ingredient. Aluminum chloride and sulfate are effective, but their acidity causes skin irritation and damage to clothes. A buffered form of aluminum chloride in solution has removed many of the undesirable side effects.

KEY

The Egyptians decorated their eyes by painting the undersides green (not shown) and the lids, lashes, and eyebrows black. Green was made from malachite (an ore mineral consisting of copper carbonate) and the black was *kohl*, a fine black powder produced from antimony or lead sulfide.

4

4 A typical manufacturer offers the following selection of cosmetics; mascara in 2 to 3 types, eyeshadow in 4 or more forms, eyeliner (liquid or cake), eyebrow pencils, nail polish and lipstick (both as pearlized or cream), face powder (loose and cake), liquid make-up, and rouge in up to 4 forms. Each product is available in a wide range of shades that is updated to follow or set new fashions.

5 Cosmetics should be applied to clean skin [A]. Foundation cream provides a base for coloring the face, to impart a healthy appearance, and to modify the shape of the face. Powder hides shine or greasiness and gives a matte bloom to the skin. Eye make-up is used to enhance the natural color of the eyes, to alter their shape, or to draw attention to or detract from the line of the eyes [B]. Lipstick modifies the shape of the mouth and enhances the whiteness of the teeth. A layer of lipstick may also be beneficial in preventing cracked lips—possible sites of infection.

5A B

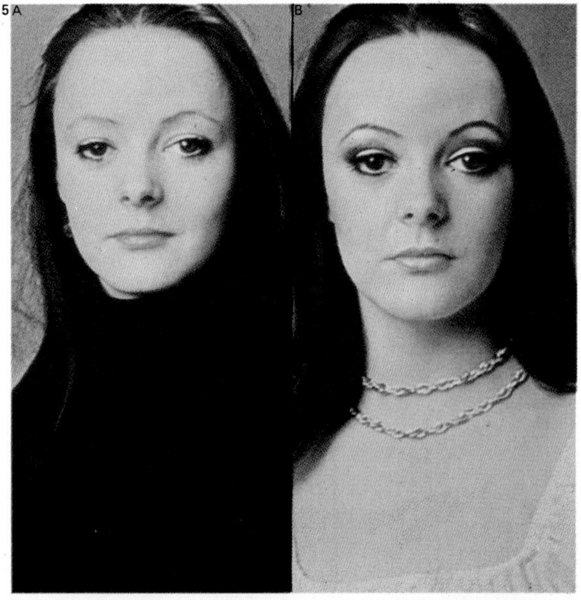

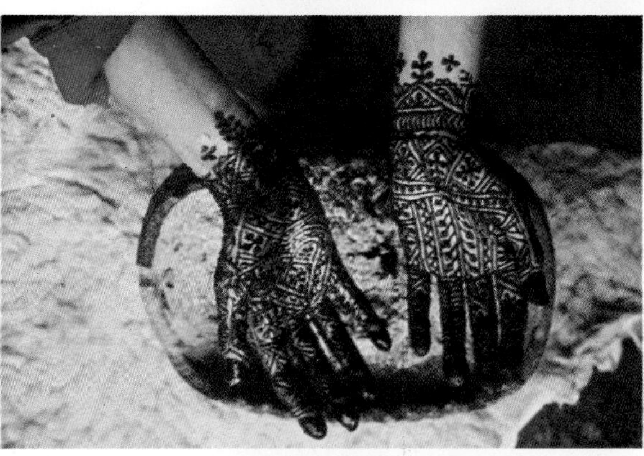

6 Women in North Africa and India use henna *(Lawsonia inermis)*. Before the plant flowers its leaves are collected and powdered. This produces a red dye that has long been used. The powder is made into a paste by mixing it with hot water; this is then spread liberally over the part to be dyed. It is generally left overnight and is used to dye fingernails, hands, hair, and even the manes of horses.

7 Stage make-up can be used to give a face a natural appearance under the whitening effect of strong light [A]. To age the face [B] shading is applied around the eyes, temples, beneath the cheek bones, and at the sides of the nose and mouth. To give an Oriental look [C] white powder and shadow is used to widen and flatten the face and the eyes are elongated with black eyeliner. Grease paint is made in many colors from oil, wax, and spermaceti.

7A

B

C

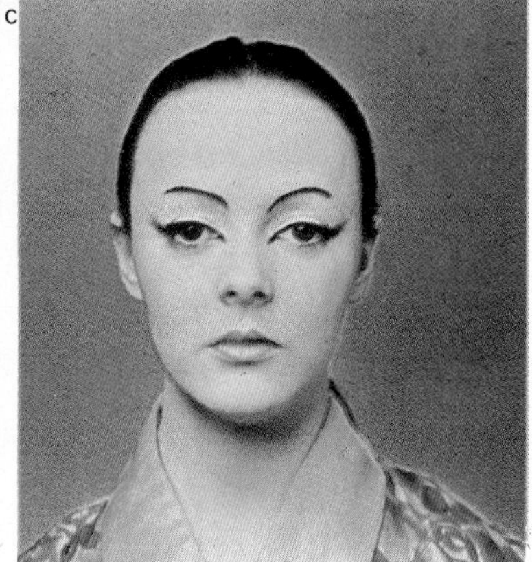

Everyday machines and mechanisms: 1

Most everyday products are used without any thought about the history of their invention or development. But modern life would be inconvenient without practical products such as zippers [1], pens [2], door locks [3, 5], water faucets [4], flush toilets [6], cigarette lighters [7], aerosols [8], and fire extinguishers [9].

Whitcomb Judson invented the zipper in 1891, although the first reliable model was not introduced until 1913 by Gideon Sundback (1880–1954). Before this buttons alone were used, although they did not become common until the thirteenth century. L. E. Waterman (1837–1901) invented the modern fountain pen in 1884. In the years after World War II the ballpoint pen and fiber-tip pen became increasingly popular.

Locks date back more than 4,000 years and were used by the ancient Egyptians. The lock most commonly used today is the Yale, named after its inventor Linus Yale Jr. (1821–68). The modern aerosol has been adopted for many uses. Since the early 1950s it has become a spray applicator for cosmetics, paints, and cleansers.

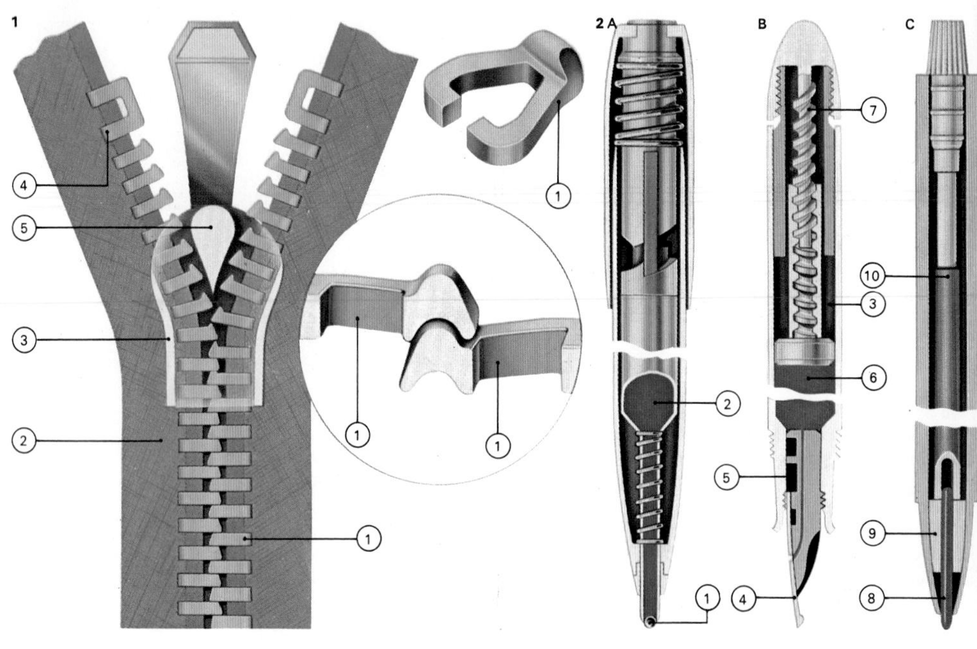

1 The zipper, comprises two chains of teeth [1], each secured to a length of strong fabric [2], a slide [3], a bottom-end piece, and two top-end pieces [4]. By moving the slide upward, the teeth are gradually drawn together within the slide, interlocking as shown in the inset diagram. When the slide moves downward, the divider within it [5] separates the teeth.

2 Pens are of three main types – ball, fountain, and felt-tip. Ballpoint pens [A], developed in 1938, have a ballbearing [1] at the tip of a tube of special ink [2]. Some fountain pens [B] are cartridge-loaded but most have a barrel [3], nib [4], feed [3], an ink reservoir [6], and self-filling mechanism [7]. A felt-tip pen [C] has a fiber tip [8] and "transorb" [9], and an ink reservoir [10].

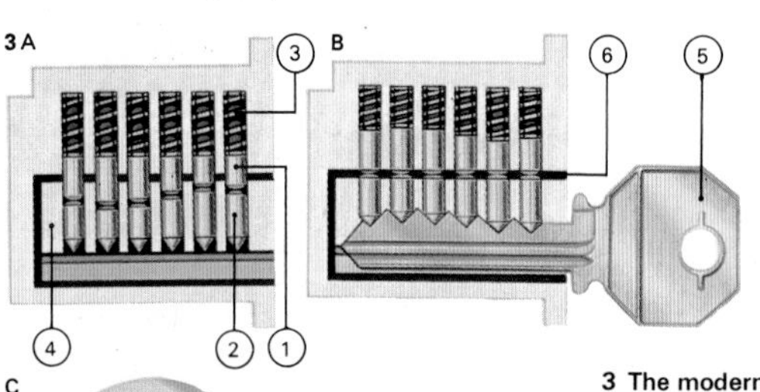

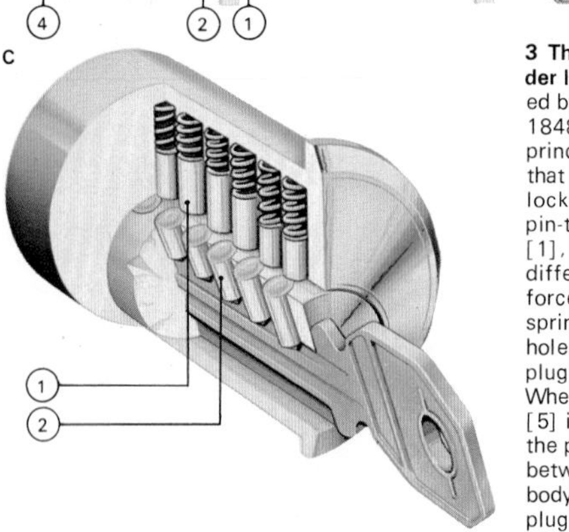

3 The modern cylinder lock [A], invented by Linus Yale in 1848, operates on a principle similar to that used in ancient locks. Two-section pin-tumblers (pins [1], drivers [2]) of different lengths are forced downward by springs [3] into holes in a rotating plug or cylinder [4]. When the correct key [5] is inserted [B], the pins are aligned between the plug and body [6] allowing the plug to turn [C].

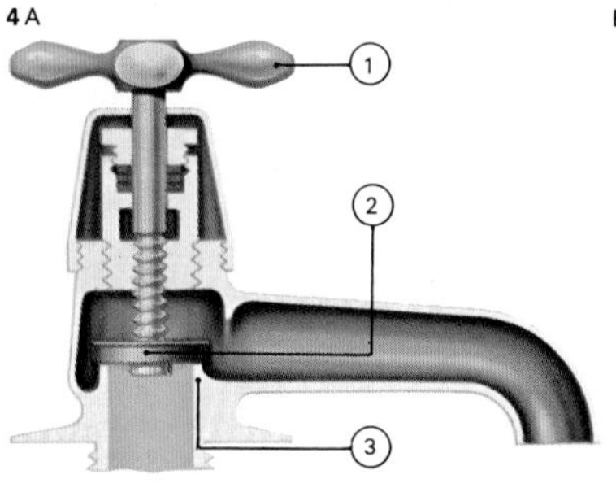

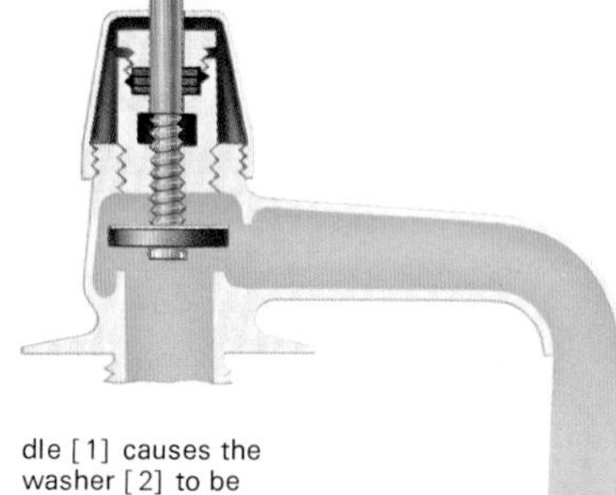

4 Faucets have not changed their basic design for more than 100 years. Most faucets function like the one shown here – closed [A] and open [B]. Turning the handle [1] causes the washer [2] to be screwed downward on the valve seat [3].

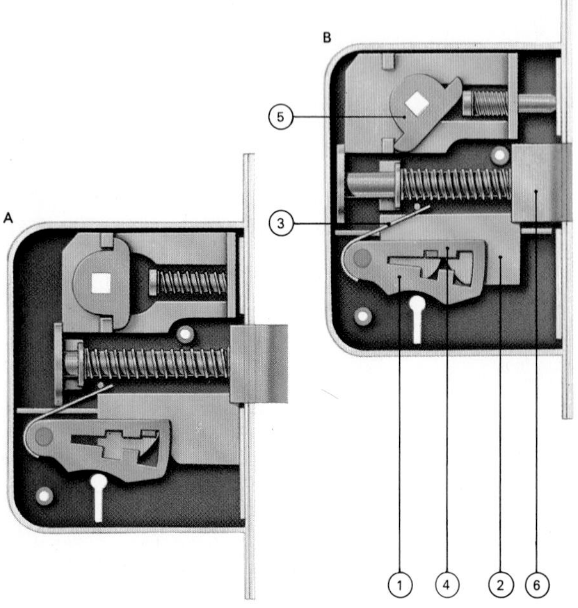

5 Lever tumbler locks dates back to the 18th century. Now used mostly on internal doors [A], their most important component is the tumbler [1] a simple lever that is securely held on the bolt [2] by a spring [3]. A projection on the tumbler, called a stump [4], prevents the bolt from moving back. If a key is inserted, it engages the tumbler and is shaped so that it pushes the tumbler upward [B] by the right amount. The key is then able to turn enough to engage the bolt at a point and move it back into the lock. Turning the door handle then makes the cam [5] move the latch [6] across. For extra security, a series of different tumblers can be used.

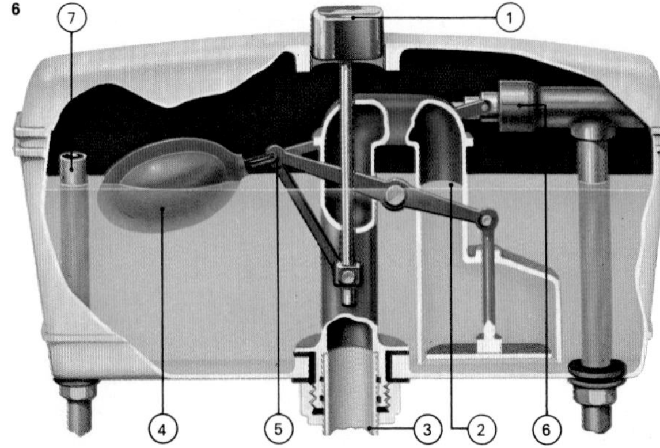

6 The "wash-down" toilet, invented in 1889, worked on exactly the same principle as the one used today. Using plastics and superior design, the slimline reservoir is made for use in modern homes. By depressing the top-press device [1], a siphon is formed [2] and the water is sucked from the reservoir and flushed down into the bowl via a pipe [3]. As the water drains from the reservoir, the ballfloat [4] moves down and a lever system [5] opens the ball valve [6], allowing the reservoir to refill. When it is full, the ball float and lever system closes the ball valve. An overflow [7] allows water to drain off in the event the ball valve does not function properly.

7 Cigarette lighters first appeared in 1909 when flint-wheel lighters with Auermetal flints were used. Auermetal, an alloy of iron and magnesium, was invented by Baron Auer von Welsbach (1858–1929). In a modern flint/fluid lighter [B], a lever [1] turns the flint wheel [2]. Lighter fluid [3], generally in wadding, is drawn up the wick [4], and ignited by a spark from the flint [5]. Flint/gas lighters [C] are similar to flint/fluid models, except that the fluid and wick are replaced by liquid gas [6] and a valve [7]. There are two types of electric cigarette lighters: battery-operated and piezoelectric models. In the battery-operated type [A], a low-voltage battery [8] charges a capacitor [9]. When a switch [10] is pressed, a capacitor is discharged through a step-up transformer [11] that produces a high-voltage spark across a gap [12], igniting the gas released through a valve [13] when the button was pressed. In a piezoelectric cigarette lighter [D] the electric current for a spark is generated when a crystal [14] is squeezed, so igniting the gas.

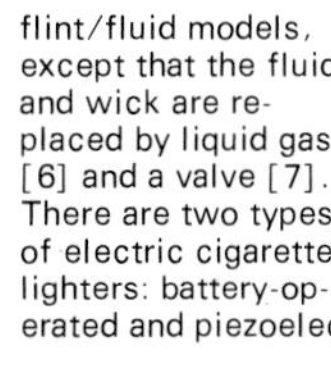

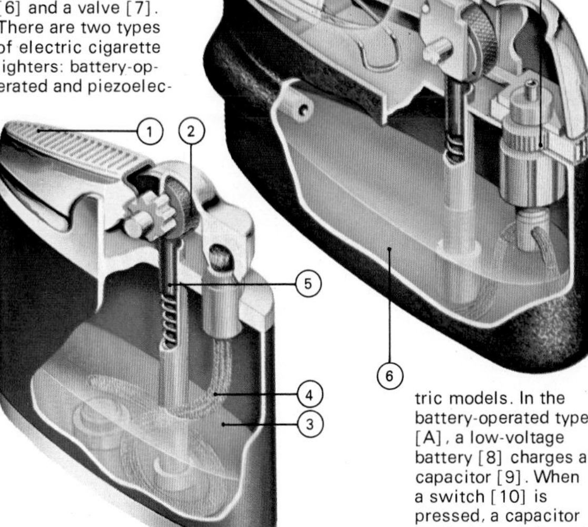

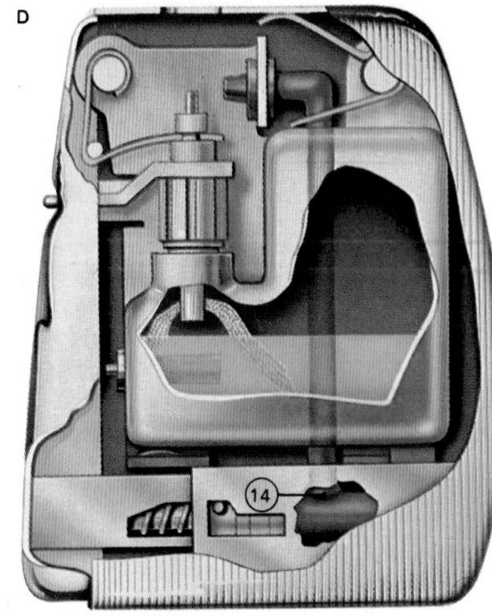

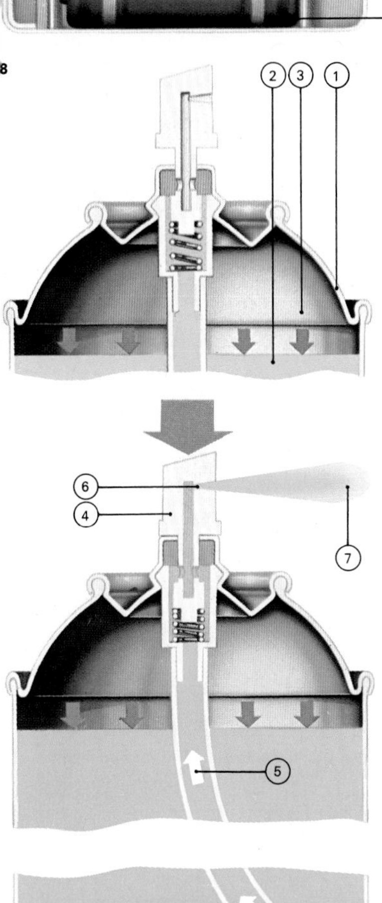

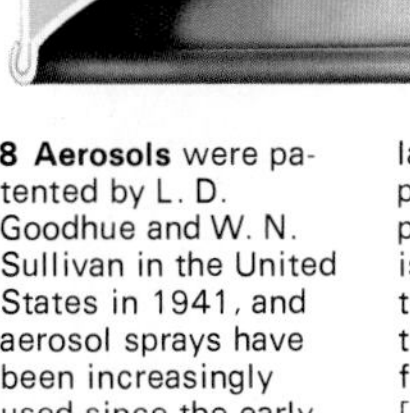

8 Aerosols were patented by L. D. Goodhue and W. N. Sullivan in the United States in 1941, and aerosol sprays have been increasingly used since the early 1950s. The can [1] is filled with the product to be sprayed [2] and the propellant [3]. When the pushbutton [4] is pressed, the product is forced up the dip tube [5] and out of the nozzle [6] in a fine spray of foam [7]. Freon is the most common propellant, although it may be a serious pollutant.

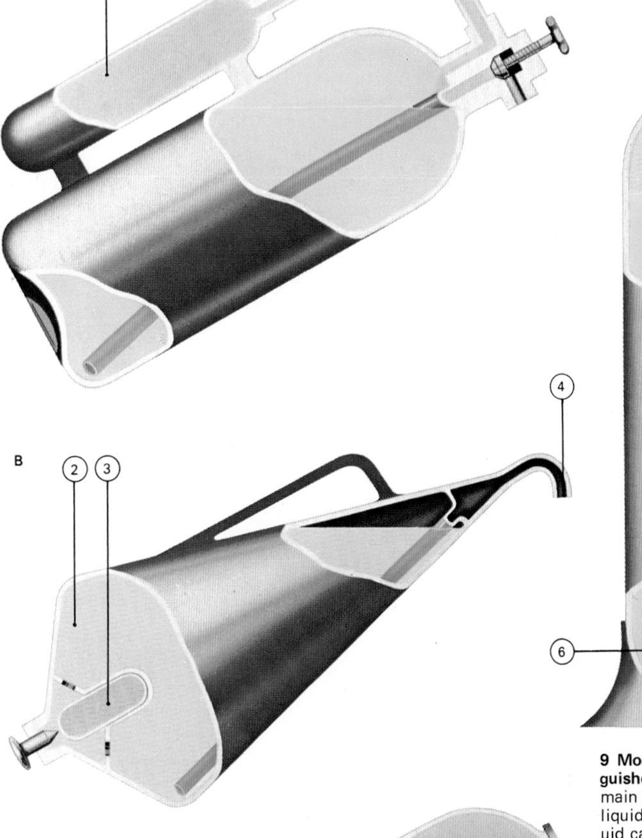

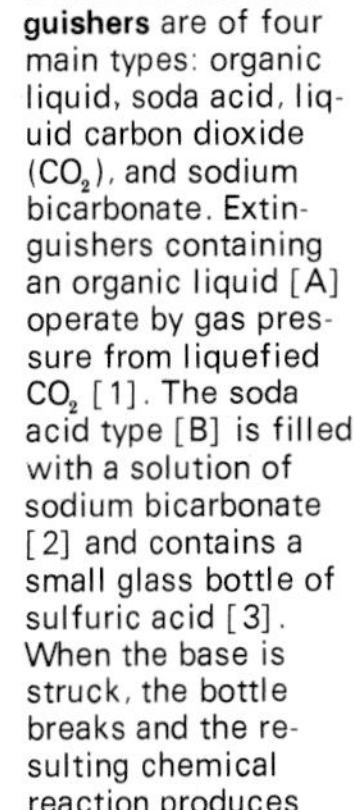

9 Modern fire extinguishers are of four main types: organic liquid, soda acid, liquid carbon dioxide (CO_2), and sodium bicarbonate. Extinguishers containing an organic liquid [A] operate by gas pressure from liquefied CO_2 [1]. The soda acid type [B] is filled with a solution of sodium bicarbonate [2] and contains a small glass bottle of sulfuric acid [3]. When the base is struck, the bottle breaks and the resulting chemical reaction produces CO_2 gas, forcing the solution out of the nozzle [4]. The solid sodium bicarbonate unit [C] is "powered" by liquefied CO_2. In the fire the bicarbonate [5] decomposes into soda (to form an air-excluding crust), water vapor, and CO_2. The carbon dioxide extinguisher [D] contains CO_2 at high pressure [6]. When released, solid CO_2 snow is sprayed onto the fire. In addition to excluding air, it lowers the temperature to below the ignition point.

Everyday machines and mechanisms: 2

Most of the machines described on these pages are commonplace to anyone who lives in an industrialized country. But some of the inventions that they employ are surprisingly old. Few people realize, for example, that the first gas meters (known originally as "wet meters" because they contained a liquid to make them work) were invented in about 1815. This type of meter is no longer used, but it was more than a hundred years before wet meters were superseded by the modern "dry" type—and even these [1B] are based on a design originally developed between 1830 and 1850. Barometers also measure properties of a gas—the pressure of air in the atmosphere. Early barometers, such as the Fortin barometer [2A] used long tubes filled with mercury. Later barometers were superseded by "dry" types, such as the aneroid barometer [2B].

Many modern machines are powered by electricity. Vacuum cleaners [5], electric shavers [6], drills [7], and washing machines [8] all make use of electric motors. A steam iron [3] and blower heaters [4] use the heating effect of an electric current.

1 Most modern homes are supplied with electricity and many also have a gas supply. The amounts consumed are measured by meters. An electricity meter [A] – known technically as an AC watt-hour meter – has a horizontal rotating disk [1] made of aluminum with electromagnetic coils above [2] and below [3]. Eddy currents from the coils turn the disk. The magnetic flux of the upper coil is proportional to the supply voltage and that of the lower one depends on the load current. The speed of rotation is proportional to the power passing through the meter. Gears [4] drive a counting mechanism [5]. The positive displacement gas meter [B] has two diaphragm chambers [6] containing flexible membranes, which are filled and emptied in turn. Their movements are conveyed by levers [7] to slide valves that control the gas flow to and from the membranes. Other levers work an index drive shaft [8], which actuates a counter [9].

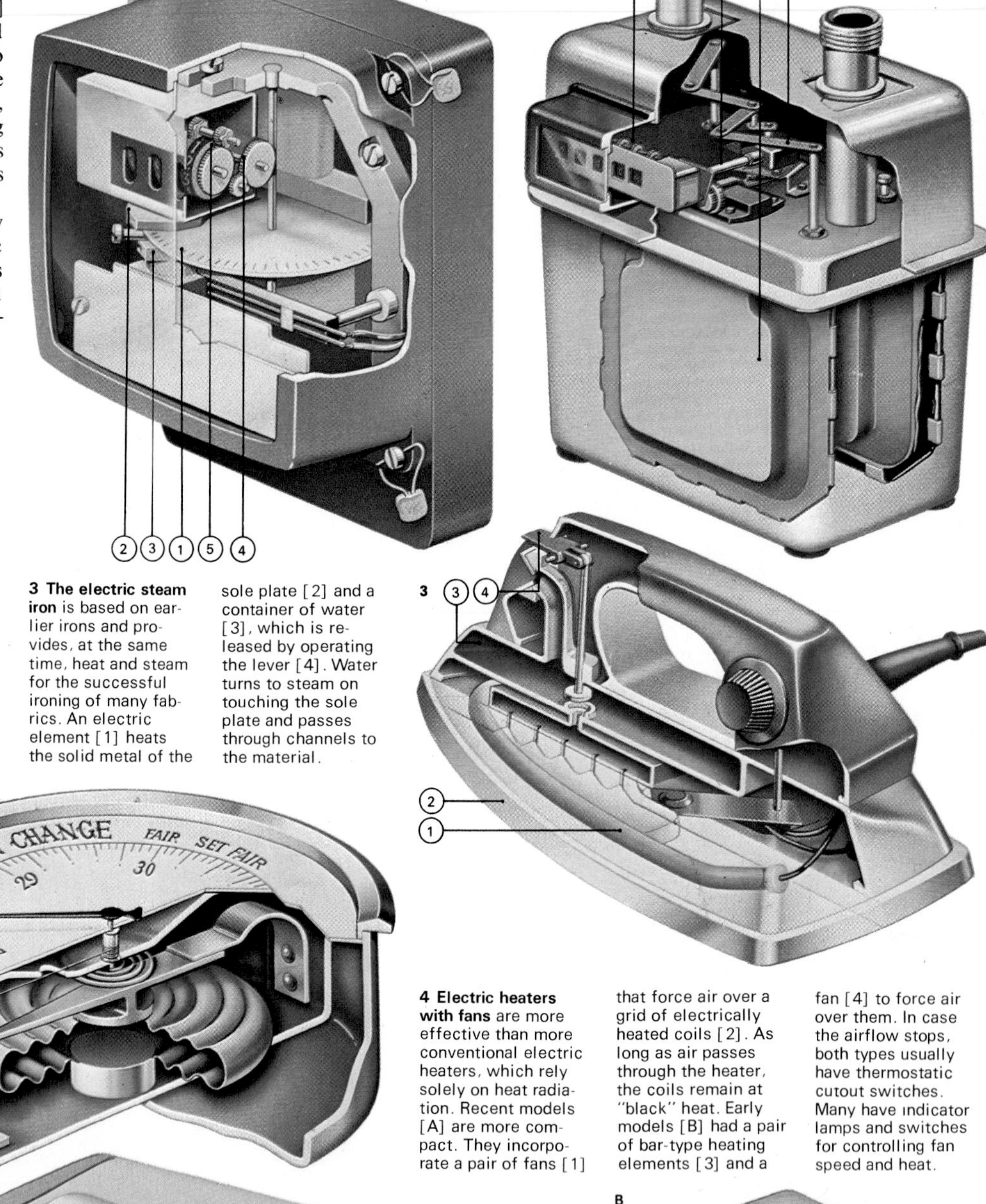
CHANGE
RAIN
FAIR
SET FAIR
STORM
29
30
28

2 The Fortin barometer [A] was designed in the early 1800s. Mercury in a chamois leather bag [1] bears against a screw [2], which is turned until the top of the column touches a pointer [3]. Pressure is read on a scale [4]. The aneroid barometer [B] was invented in 1843. It has an evacuated sealed metal chamber [5] that expands and contracts with changes in pressure and moves a pointer [6].

3 The electric steam iron is based on earlier irons and provides, at the same time, heat and steam for the successful ironing of many fabrics. An electric element [1] heats the solid metal of the sole plate [2] and a container of water [3], which is released by operating the lever [4]. Water turns to steam on touching the sole plate and passes through channels to the material.

4 Electric heaters with fans are more effective than more conventional electric heaters, which rely solely on heat radiation. Recent models [A] are more compact. They incorporate a pair of fans [1] that force air over a grid of electrically heated coils [2]. As long as air passes through the heater, the coils remain at "black" heat. Early models [B] had a pair of bar-type heating elements [3] and a fan [4] to force air over them. In case the airflow stops, both types usually have thermostatic cutout switches. Many have indicator lamps and switches for controlling fan speed and heat.

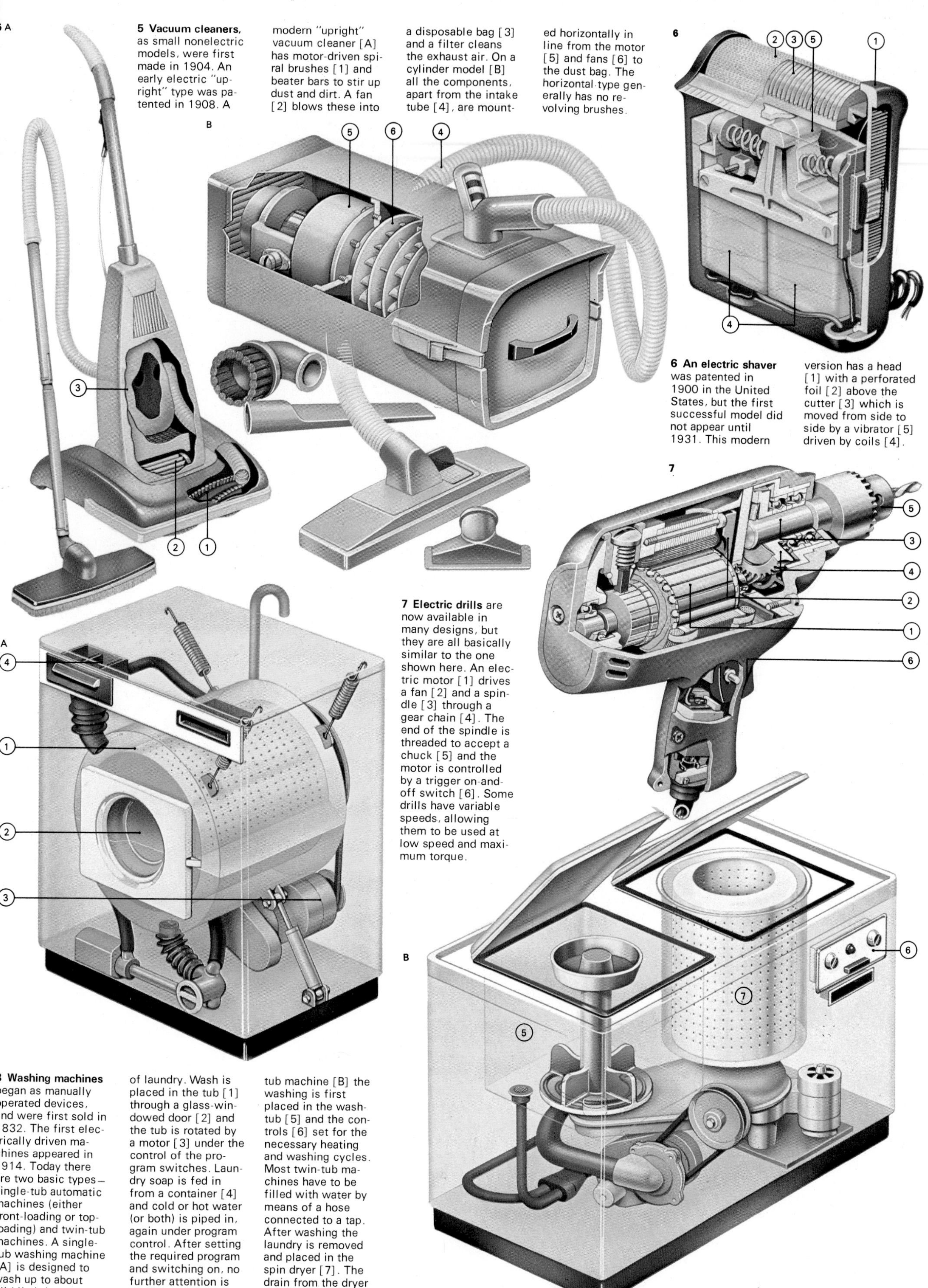

5 Vacuum cleaners, as small nonelectric models, were first made in 1904. An early electric "upright" type was patented in 1908. A modern "upright" vacuum cleaner [A] has motor-driven spiral brushes [1] and beater bars to stir up dust and dirt. A fan [2] blows these into a disposable bag [3] and a filter cleans the exhaust air. On a cylinder model [B] all the components, apart from the intake tube [4], are mounted horizontally in line from the motor [5] and fans [6] to the dust bag. The horizontal-type generally has no revolving brushes.

6 An electric shaver was patented in 1900 in the United States, but the first successful model did not appear until 1931. This modern version has a head [1] with a perforated foil [2] above the cutter [3] which is moved from side to side by a vibrator [5] driven by coils [4].

7 Electric drills are now available in many designs, but they are all basically similar to the one shown here. An electric motor [1] drives a fan [2] and a spindle [3] through a gear chain [4]. The end of the spindle is threaded to accept a chuck [5] and the motor is controlled by a trigger on-and-off switch [6]. Some drills have variable speeds, allowing them to be used at low speed and maximum torque.

Washing machines egan as manually perated devices, nd were first sold in 832. The first elecrically driven mahines appeared in 914. Today there re two basic types – ingle-tub automatic nachines (either ront-loading or topoading) and twin-tub nachines. A singleub washing machine A] is designed to vash up to about lb(4kg) dry-weight of laundry. Wash is placed in the tub [1] through a glass-windowed door [2] and the tub is rotated by a motor [3] under the control of the program switches. Laundry soap is fed in from a container [4] and cold or hot water (or both) is piped in, again under program control. After setting the required program and switching on, no further attention is needed. With a twin-tub machine [B] the washing is first placed in the wash-tub [5] and the controls [6] set for the necessary heating and washing cycles. Most twin-tub machines have to be filled with water by means of a hose connected to a tap. After washing the laundry is removed and placed in the spin dryer [7]. The drain from the dryer must be led to a sink.

Everyday machines and mechanisms: 3

Many modern domestic appliances are not the product of space age technology but owe their existence to nineteenth-century inventors. The first sewing machine was patented in 1830. It was wooden, had a hooked needle, and was made by a French tailor, Barthélemy Thimonnier (1793–1859). In 1841 Thimonnier used 80 such machines to make uniforms for the French army. The sewing machine [2] did not achieve large-scale factory use until the development of the foot treadle in 1851 by Isaac Singer (1811–75).

In 1834 Great Britain issued the first refrigerator patent to the American Jacob Perkins (1766–1849), but a practical machine was not developed until the 1850s. The modern electric refrigerator [4] differs little from the one devised by James Harrison (1816–93) in 1851 for freezing meat on cargo ships. The household carpet sweeper [1], was invented by Thomas Ewbank (1792–1870), and was not made until 1889. The gardener's neat lawn is the result of the work of Edwin Beard Budding (1795–1846), who launched the first practical cylinder lawn mower [3] in 1830.

1

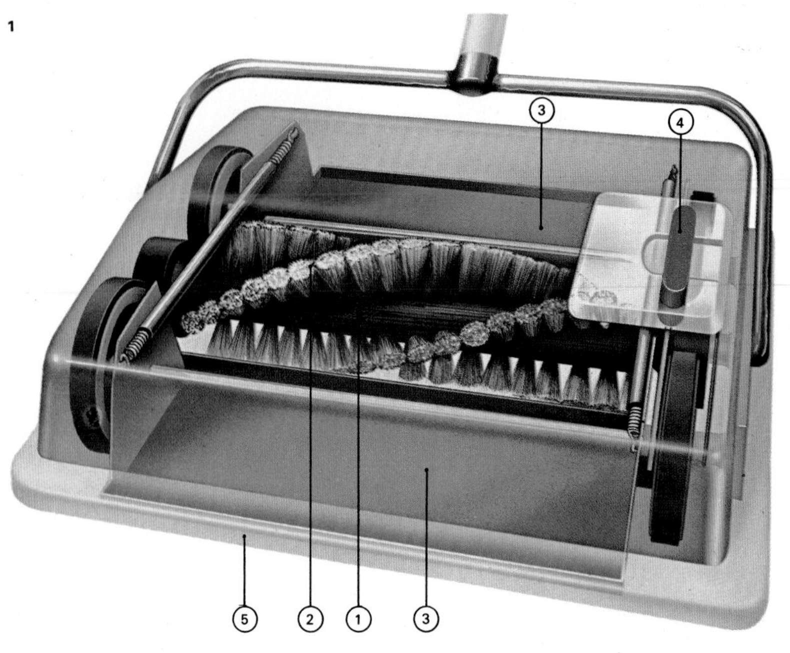
3
4
5
2
1
3

The carpet sweeper cleans both carpets and smooth floor surfaces efficiently. Within the strong, lightweight plastic case is a brush [1] with six helical rows of tufts [2]. Alternate rows are designed to suit flat and carpeted surfaces and the brush height is simply adjusted by means of a plastic slide. As the sweeper is moved manually backward and forward the brush is constantly rotated. Dust is collected in pans [3] that can be emptied by raising the lever [4] on top of the sweeper. The unit is completely surrounded by a flexible guard [5] to protect furniture. This type of sweeper is not only labor-saving but uses no electricity.

2

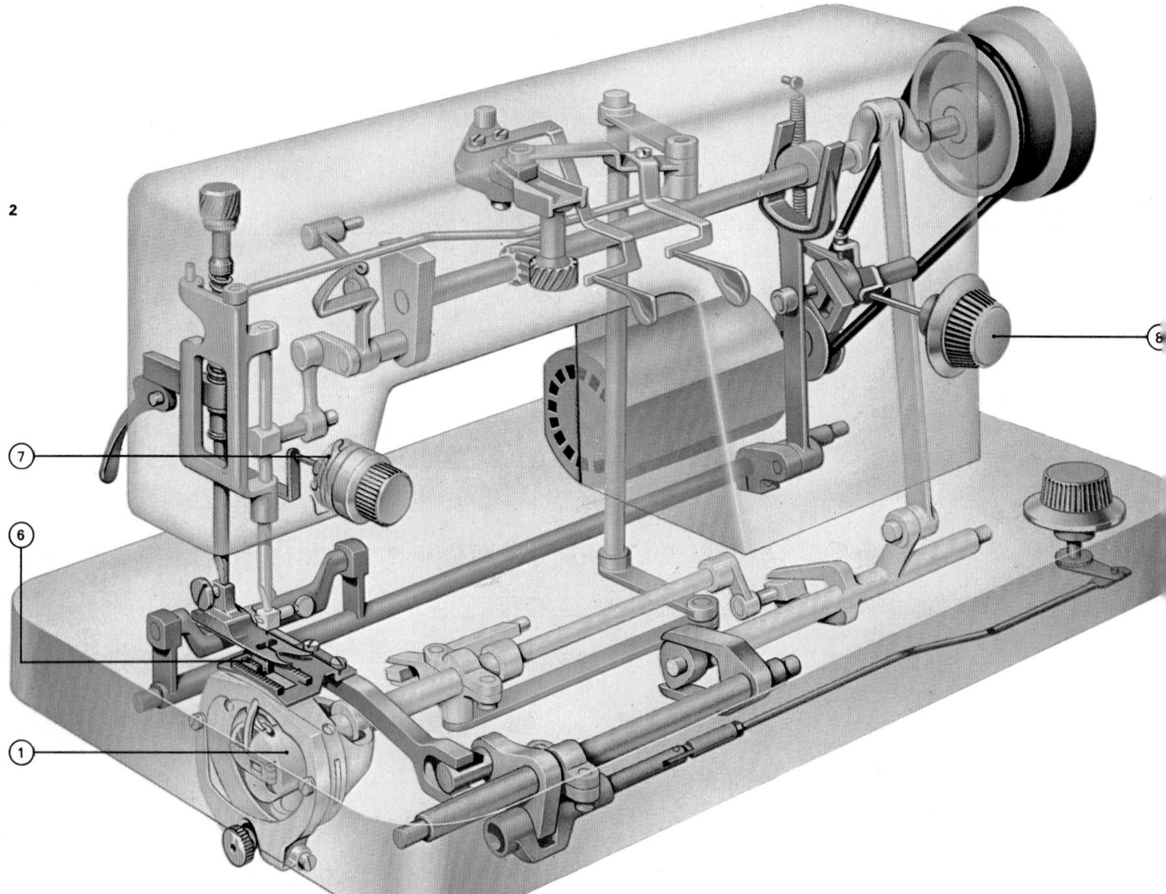

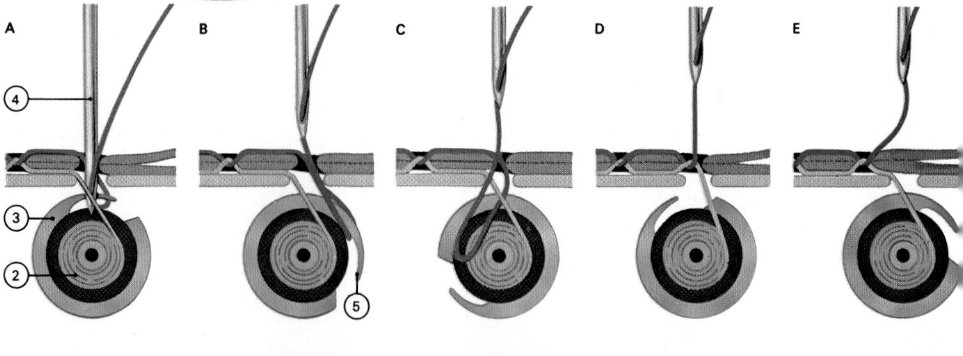

2 A modern electric sewing machine incorporates a rotary or oscillating shuttle [1]. The characteristic machine stitch is created by a pair of threads, one held at the top of the machine on a standard bobbin which holds a cotton reel, the other wound on a special metal or plastic bobbin [2] in the base of the machine – below the fabric. As the motor revolves (at a speed determined by a foot control) the shuttle [3] turns around the bobbin. The series of events in the sewing of a stitch is shown in the sequence A–E. The needle [4], which is threaded near its point, pierces the fabric [A] and the point of the shuttle moves toward the needle. As the needle moves upward [B] the hook [5] on the shuttle enters the loop formed in the needle thread. With further movement of the shuttle around the bobbin [C] the loop is drawn over the bobbin, linking it with the bobbin thread. At this point [D] the needle thread loop slips off the shuttle as the take-up lever moves upward to pull the resulting stitch tight [E]. While the feed-dog [6] moves the material along one stitch length, the shuttle makes one "idle" revolution. The tension of each stitch, the optimum of which varies for different types of fabric, is controlled by tensioning disks [7] and the length is determined by a regulator [8]. The length control mechanism works by varying the amount of rotation of the shuttle at each stroke. Other mechanisms include linkages to move the feed-dog. The most up-to-date "swing needle" electric sewing-machines can produce embroidered stitches and can hem, pleat, smock, tack, and gather.

3 Power mowers have blades that move either by rotary [A] or cylinder [B] action. In the rotary mower the cutting blade [1] is turned by a gasoline engine [2] (or electric motor) at such a high speed that it is not necessary to sharpen the blades. The height of the blades is adjusted using a lever [3] and the engine (and thus the speed of operation) is controlled by a throttle that regulates the flow of gasoline/air mixture into the carburetor of the engine. One special type works on the hovercraft principle and rather than having wheels or rollers floats on an air cushion. A disadvantage of most rotary mowers is the absence of a collector for grass cutting—a standard feature of most cylinder mowers. In cylinder machines a series of cutting blades [4] is mounted on a rotating "cylinder" [5]. In the mower illustrated the unit is powered by an electric motor [6] but most cylinder mowers are driven either by gasoline engines or pushed across the lawn by hand. The largest types of clinder mowers are built with seating arrangements for the operator and when an immaculate finish is required, as on a large expanse of lawn, may also incorporate a heavy roller.

The first domestic lawnmowers, adaptations of agricultural reaping machines, were drawn by horses whose hoofs were covered with sacking to prevent them from damaging the delicate turf.

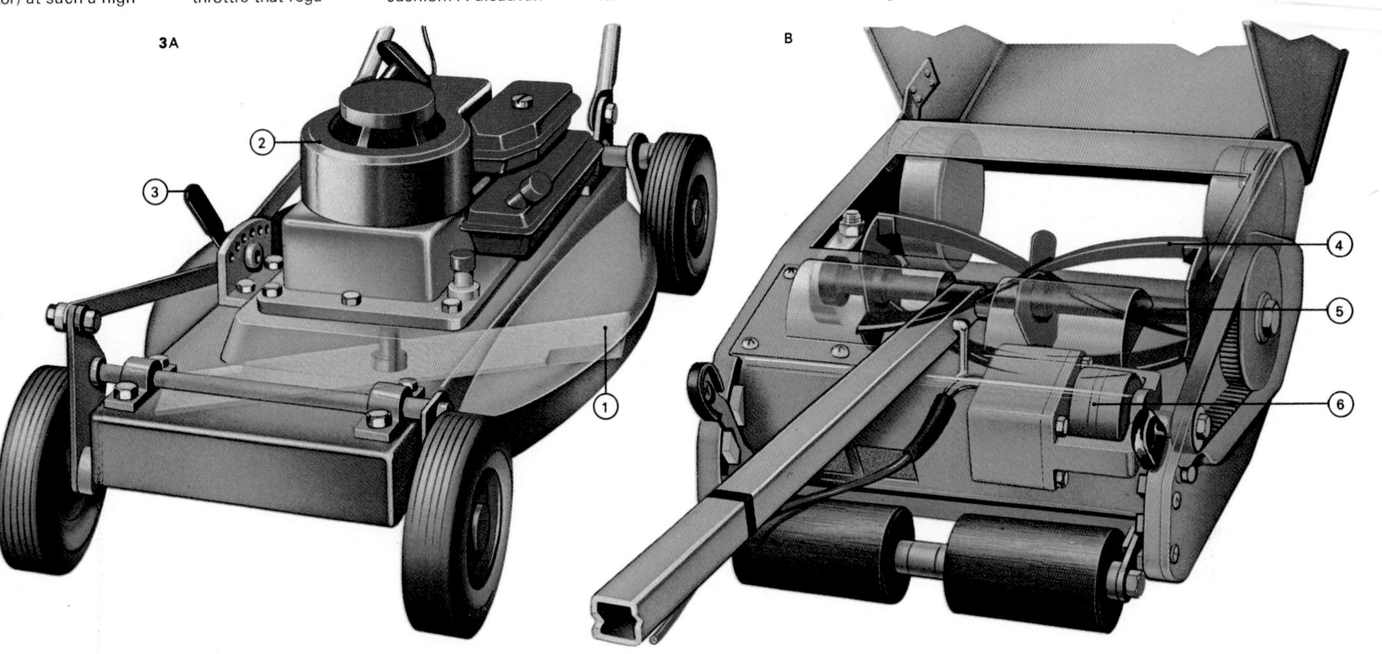
3A
2
3
1
B
4
5
6

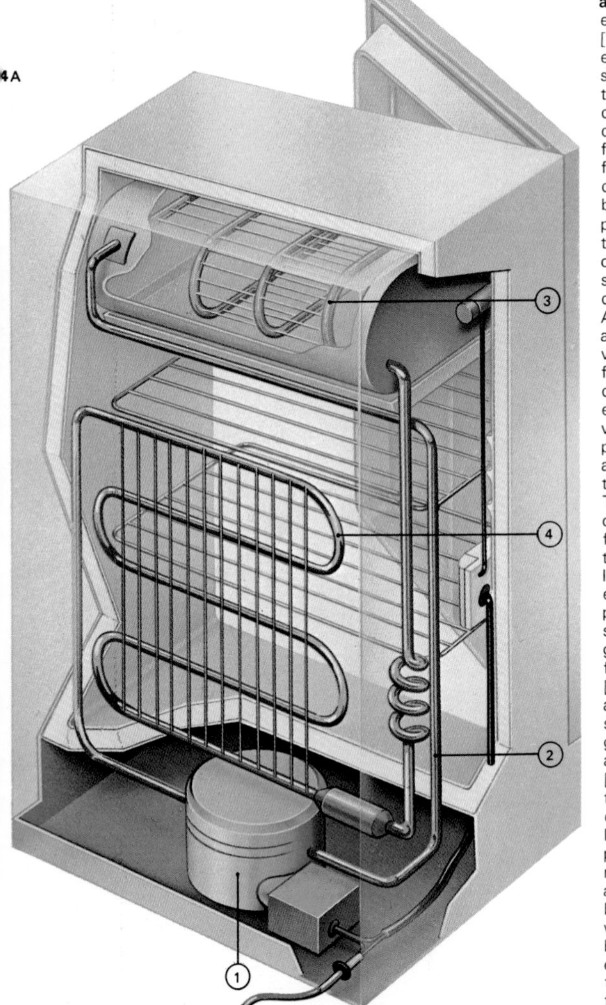
4A
3
4
2
1

4 Household refrigerators are operated either by electricity [A] or gas [B]. In the electric, or compression, model an electric motor drives a compressor [1] to circulate a fluid refrigerant [2]. The refrigerant is a liquid cooling agent; it boils at a low temperature and in electric refrigerators is often freon, a substance containing carbon and fluorine. As the liquid refrigerant changes into a vapor, it absorbs heat from the freezing compartment or evaporator [3]. The vapor is then compressed and passed at high pressure to the condenser [4]. The refrigerant condenses to its liquid form, losing heat to the outside air. The liquid returns to the evaporator after expansion to low pressure at a valve. In the gas or absorption refrigerator a generator [5] is filled with ammonia gas dissolved in water. A gas flame heats this and ammonia vapor [6] is driven off. It is then liquefied in a condenser [7], thus losing heat, and passes into an evaporator [8] where it absorbs heat and becomes a gas, which sinks to the bottom of the evaporator and siphons to the absorber [9]; then to the generator.

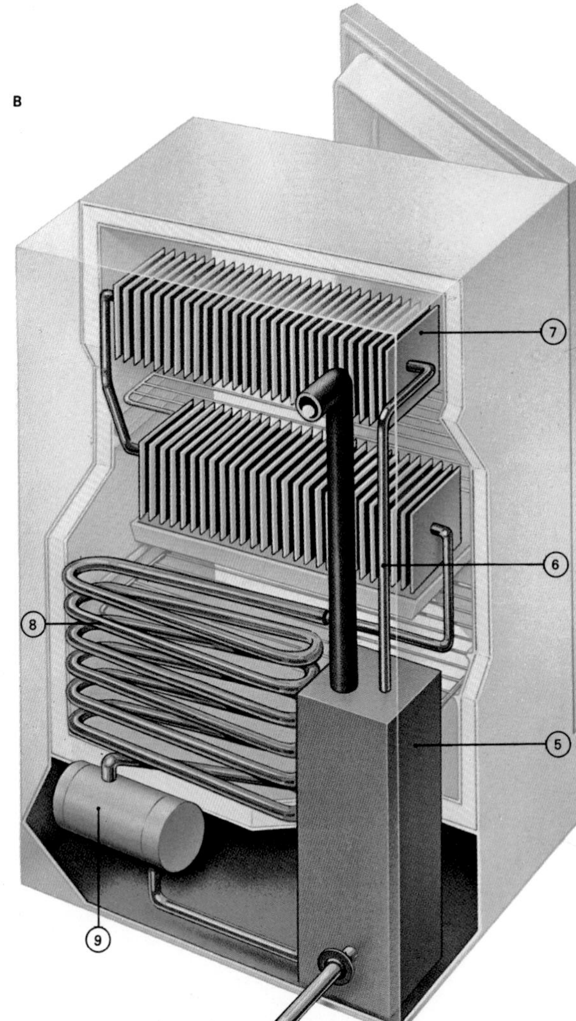
B
7
6
8
5
9

Everyday machines and mechanisms: 4

Two of the most useful devices ever invented are the typewriter and the electronic calculator. Both are based on the work of many past inventors and engineers who designed and built a great variety of such machines.

The origins of the typewriter [1] can be traced back to a patent granted to the Englishman Henry Mill by Queen Anne in 1714. But it was not until 1874 that the first commercially successful machine—a Remington—evolved from one made in the United States by Christopher Sholes (1819–90) in 1867. The first electric typewriter was marketed in the mid-1930s.

Electronic calculators [2]—often small enough to fit in the palm of one's hand—owe their existence to the rapid development of tiny integrated circuit "chips." These incorporate transistors, invented in 1948 by three American scientists, John Bardeen (1908–), Walter Brattain (1902–), and William Shockley (1910–), who were later awarded a Nobel Prize for their work. The same technology permits the present generation of computers to be smaller, more reliable, and more powerful.

CONNECTIONS

See also
1816 Everyday machines and mechanisms: 1
1818 Everyday machines and mechanisms: 2
1820 Everyday machines and mechanisms: 3

1 A

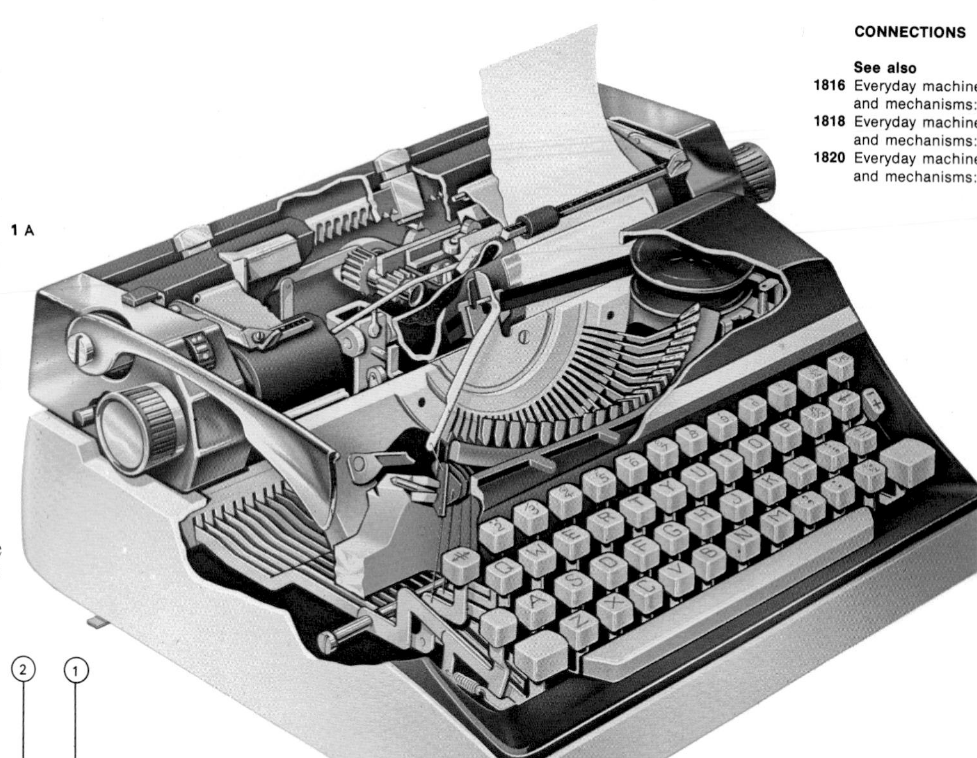

B

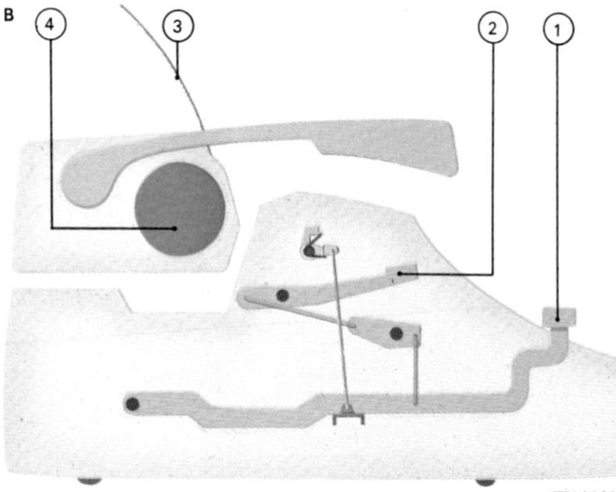

4
3
2
1

1 Modern mechanical typewriters [A] all operate using the same basic principles [B], whether they are portables or desk models. A key [1] labeled with the character to be typed is tapped, and this action moves a series of linked levers that results in the upward movement of the appropriate type bar [2]. The paper [3] is wound around a cylinder or platen [4], which moves along one character at a time during typing. An inked ribbon is forced against the paper by a metal character at the end of the type bar, printing a letter on the paper. As the type bar falls back, the carriage moves one character-space to the left. At the end of a line the typist moves a lever that shifts the carriage to the right and at the same time rotates the paper-carrying cylinder around one line space. The electric typewriter [C] was developed to reduce the manual labor of typewriting. In its mechanism [D] a light depression of a key [5] makes a cam [6] contact a drive roller [7] powered by a constant-speed motor [8]. The cam is drawn upward and the attached cam lever [9] moves back, forcing the type bar [10] upward against the ribbon, marking the paper. The force of the typing strokes is not dependent on the pressure applied by the typist and thus even typing results.

C

electric

D

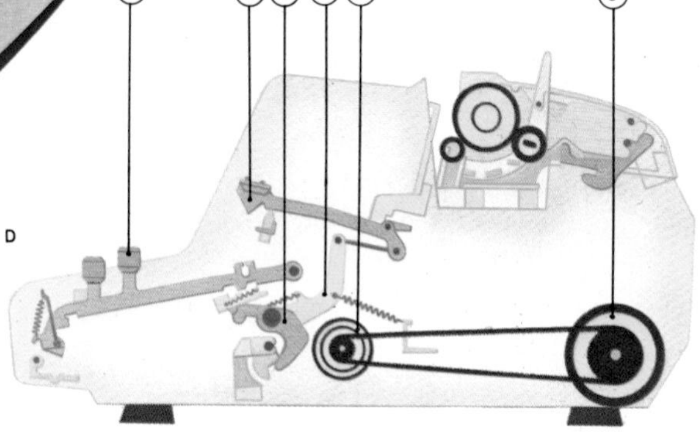

5
10
6
9
7
8

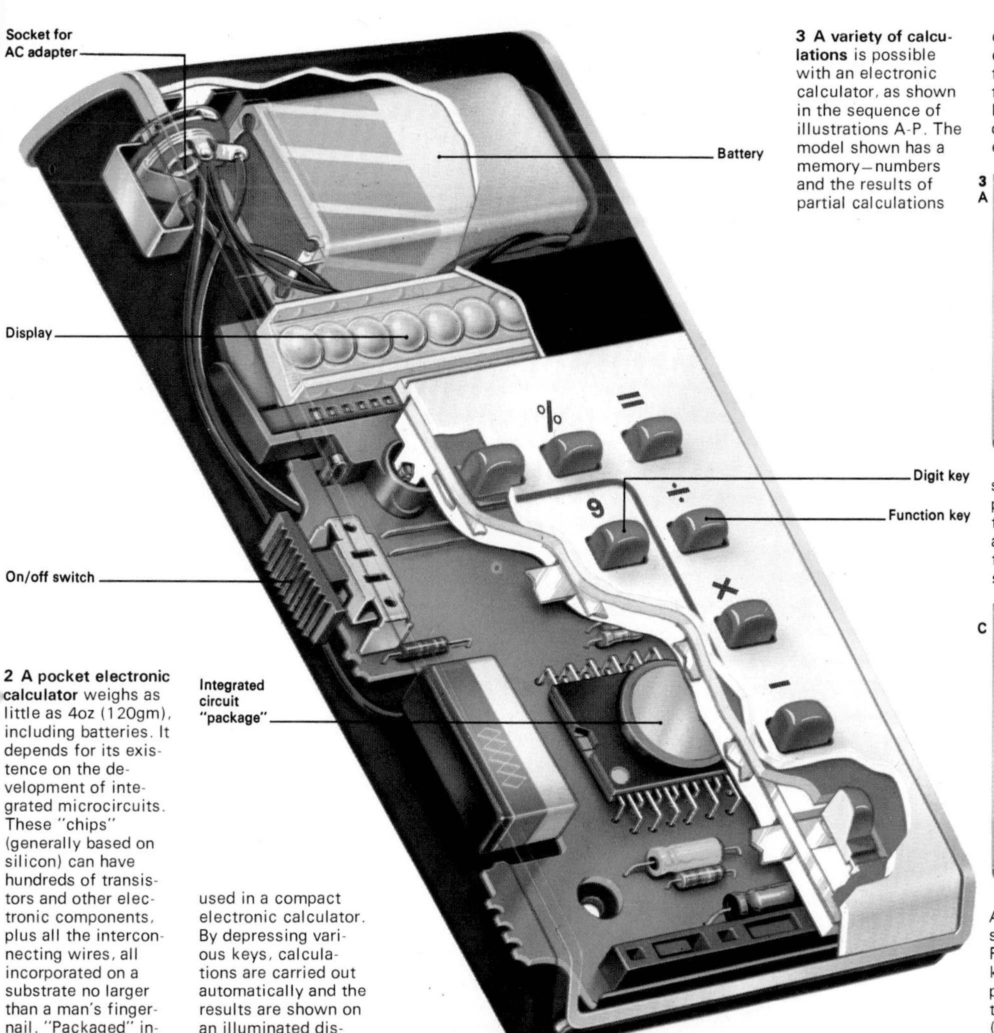
Socket for AC adapter
Battery
Display
Digit key
Function key
On/off switch
Integrated circuit "package"

2 A pocket electronic calculator weighs as little as 4oz (120gm), including batteries. It depends for its existence on the development of integrated microcircuits. These "chips" (generally based on silicon) can have hundreds of transistors and other electronic components, plus all the interconnecting wires, all incorporated on a substrate no larger than a man's fingernail. "Packaged" integrated circuits are used in a compact electronic calculator. By depressing various keys, calculations are carried out automatically and the results are shown on an illuminated display panel.

3 A variety of calculations is possible with an electronic calculator, as shown in the sequence of illustrations A-P. The model shown has a memory—numbers and the results of partial calculations can be stored and called up later as they are required. In this model, the CE/C key, when pressed once, cancels the existing entry; the same key, when pressed twice, clears the display and makes the calculator ready for the next series of operations. A simple addition

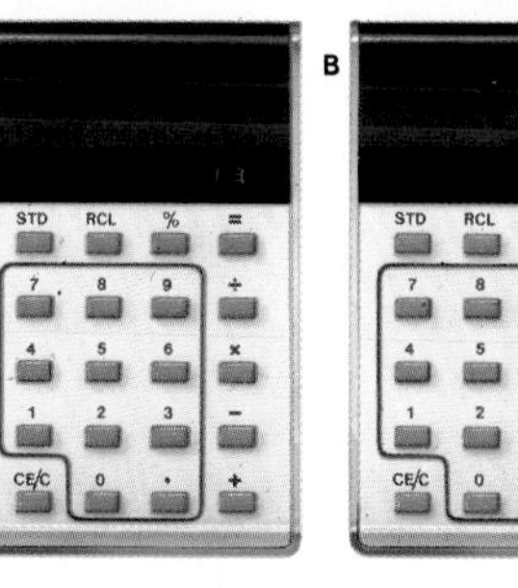

sum is 13+ 92. First press the CE/C key to clear the registers and display. Press 1 then 3 (display shows 13) [A]. Press + (display remains as 13). Press 9 then 2 (display shows 92) then press = (equals) and display shows 105 [B].

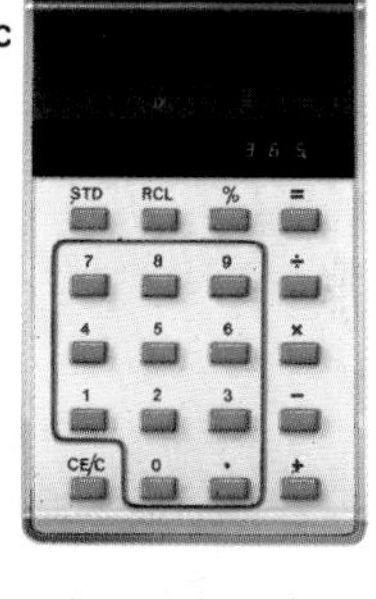

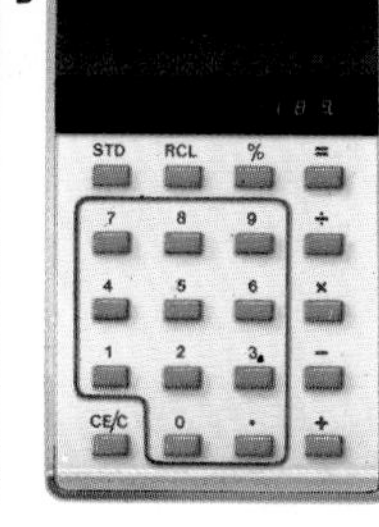

A simple subtraction sum is 365−176. First press the CE/C key to clear the display. Then press 3, then 6, and then 5 (display shows 365) [C]. Press—(minus) key (display remains at 365). Press 1, then 7, then 6 (display shows 176). Finally press = (equals) key (display shows 189 [D], the required answer).

A chain calculation makes use of the calculator's memory. To do the "sum" (25 × 92) + (72 × 5), first press the CE/C key, then 2, then 5. Press × (multiply) key and then key in 9, then 2. Press = (equals) key, and display shows 2300 [E]. Next press STD—the number is stored in the memory. Then press 7 followed by 2; press × then 5; press = (360 displayed)(F). Finally press + then RCL (memory recall) and =. 2660 is displayed [G]. This result could also be stored in the calculator's memory and used as a starting number for additional chain calculations—such as further additions or subtractions. Pressing CE/C twice clears the memory.

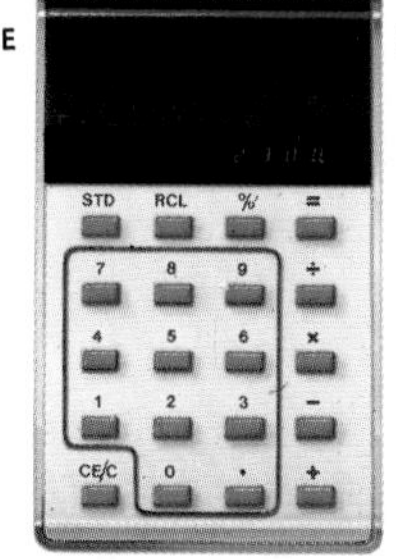

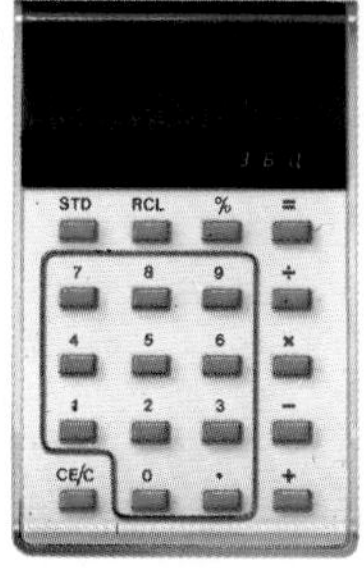

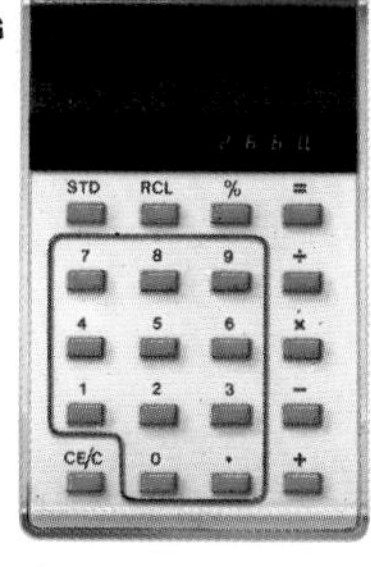

The calculator has a "constant" facility by means of which it can be used for counting. First press CE/C to clear the display. Press 1 and then = (1 is displayed) [H]. The calculator is now set up as a counter; repeatedly pressing the + key makes it count in sequence—1, 2, 3, 4, and so on. For example, after five presses of the key it will have counted up to 5 and displayed the number [I]. The constant can also be used for carrying out a series of multiplications—for example, converting inches into centimeters. The conversion factor 2.54 is made the constant.

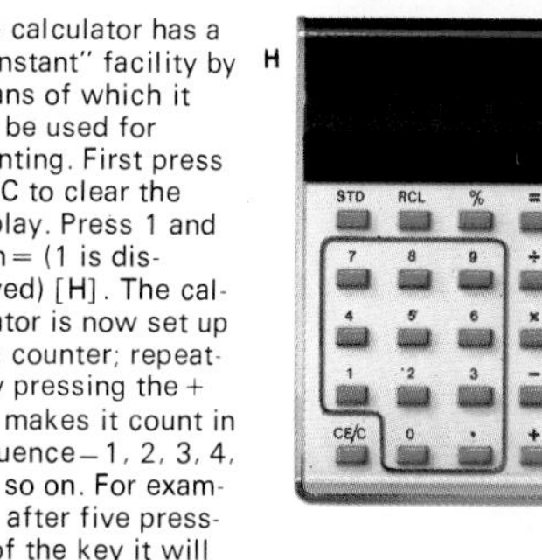

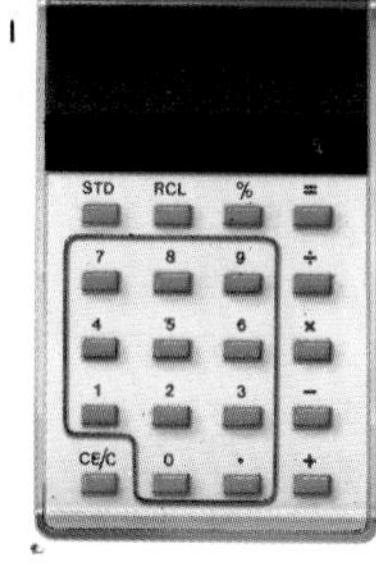

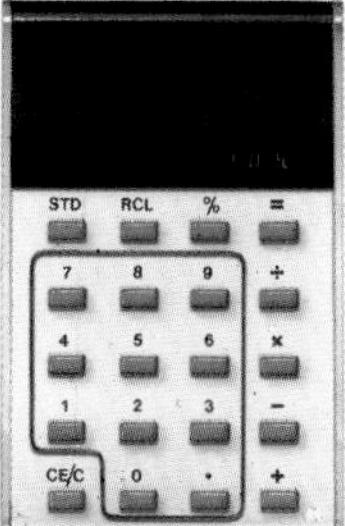

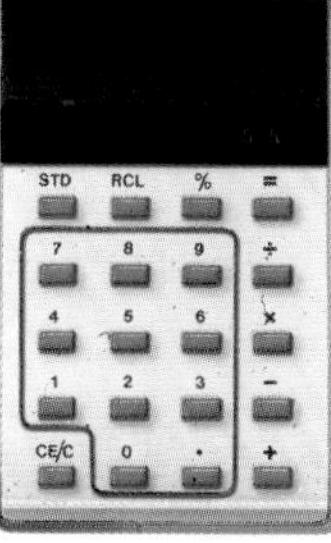

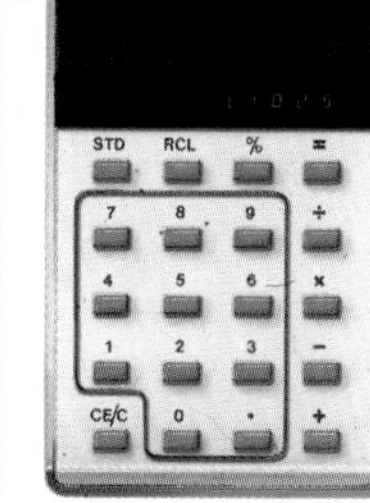

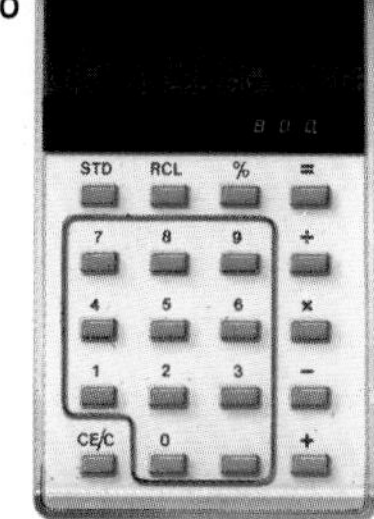

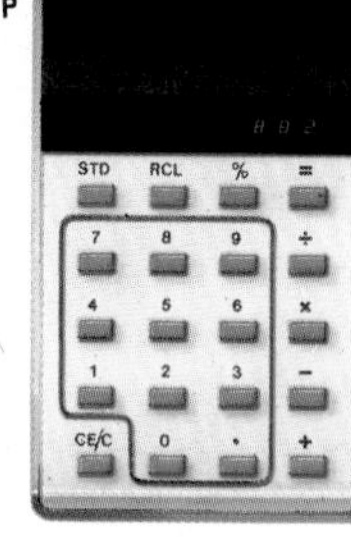

To find 55 percent of 105, first press the CE/C key, then press 1, then 0, then 5 [J]. Press × key, then 5, then 5 again [K]. Press % key, to get 57.75—the result. Percentages can be calculated even without a % key. To find 55 percent of 102, key in 102, press × (multiply) key, then key in 55. Press = key (shows 5610). Press ÷, then 100 and = to give 561 [L]. What is the growth of $800 invested at 5% compound interest for two years? Press CE/C; press 1 then . (decimal point) then 0 followed by 5 to display 1.05 [M]. Press × (to make 1.05 the constant). Press = to give 1.1025 [N], the square of 1.05—the total interest rate at the end of two years. To find the new value of the investment, multiply by 800: press × then 8, then 0, and 0 again [O]. Finally press = to give the result $882 [P]. Simple interest would yield $880.

TIME CHART

The *Time Chart* places most of the significant events in human history in perspective. Each two-page spread moves chronologically, left to right, through the time period under examination. Thus, in the first chart, "The first civilizations," events begin at 4000 BC on the left and conclude at 2000 BC on the right.

By reading across any one of the time charts, the reader can trace general developments in "Principal Events" (set in boldface type) and specific trends in five broad areas: religion and philosophy; music; literature; art and architecture; science and philosophy. Below the "Principal Events" section, there is on each time chart a section that focuses on events in the Americas and the United States.

By reading down the columns of any one of the time charts, the reader can learn what was happening in various areas during a particular period of time and can therefore connect developments in politics, for example, with advances in science and technology.

TIME CHART: CONTENTS

The first civilizations 4000–2000 BC

Principal events

Assisted by the invention of writing and the wheel, the world's first urban civilizations grew up and flourished in Mesopotamia, and later in Egypt, in the fourth millennium BC. Mesopotamian city-states emerged from ancient agricultural and religious settlements, encouraged by the immigration of the Sumerian people into the area, and grew rich from agriculture and long-distance trade. With growth, however, came conflicts between cities, although none achieved permanent supremacy. In Egypt early unification and centralization led to the Pyramid Age with its celebration of the pharaoh's authority. In both areas hereditary monarchies were set up c.3000 BC, with a bureaucracy that placed emphasis on public works, especially canal building. Toward 2000 BC, Sumeria was threatened by barbarian invasions, while Egypt declined from internal stresses, as Minoan civilization emerged.

4000–3800 BC

Farming settlements found in the lower Mesopotamian plain since 5000 BC probably included the sites of the future royal cities of Endu, Uruk, Nippur, and Girsu by 4000 BC.
The need for irrigation led to a more concentrated population and complex social systems.
The site of Babylon was settled by Sumerians c.4000.
The Nile cultures were based on farming villages c.4000.

3800–3600 BC

Jewish tradition dates the creation from 3761 BC.

3600–3400 BC

Uruk (modern Warka), the greatest Sumerian city, already possessed many features of the city-state by 3500 BC. At least twelve autonomous cities, including Ur, Lagash, Umma, and Kish, developed over the next millennium.
The pastoral Sumerians moved into the Mesopotamian plains and encouraged the growth of this civilization, c.3500, building a network of canals for irrigation.

3400–3200 BC

The Nile Valley provinces (nomes) had been merged into two separate kingdoms – Upper and Lower Egypt – by 3300 BC.
City-states began to develop in Syria and Palestine c.3300.
The Proto-literate period, when writing was first used in Sumer c.3500–3000 BC, coincides with the semi-legendary rule of the First Dynasty of Kish.
Mesopotamian influence is thought to have stimulated Egyptian cultural development c.3400 BC.

The Americas

The American continents had been uninhabited until c.40,000 BC, when prehistoric man migrated from Asia across the Bering Strait. Radiocarbon dating of artifacts places man there definitely by 20,000 BC. This early man was a hunter of large animals, using spears with fluted projectile points.

Remains of corn at Bat Cave in central New Mexico indicate that primitive agriculture was developing as a supplement to hunting and gathering.

In Chilca, on the Peruvian Pacific coast, approximately 100 families lived in a cluster of conical grass and cane huts, fishing and cultivating beans and gourds.

In Canada's southwest Yukon, the beaver tooth gouge came into use. It became an important tool for woodworking in the subarctic area.

In Valdivia, Ecuador, pottery has been found dating from c.3200 BC. It is the earliest known in the Western Hemisphere.

Susa ware, c.4000 BC

Sumerian cuneiform

White Temple, Uruk, c.4000 BC

Palette of Narmer

Pyramids of Giza

Religion

The development of religious ideas in early history was closely related to the rise of settled agriculture and the emergence of the first states and empires.

The change from a hunting economy to one based on arable agriculture was reflected first of all in the rise of fertility cults in which the central figure was a mother or earth goddess.

With the growth of urban civilizations in the fertile valleys of the Nile and the Euphrates, a priest-dominated society grew up with a system of gods, each related to a particular city or region. As the authority of the state and the priesthood became more centralized this was reflected in the changing importance of particular gods, and in Egypt in the rise of the doctrine of divine kingship and the construction of increasingly elaborate temples and royal tombs culminating in the Age of the Pyramids.

Fertility cults arose with settled farming. Sacramental concepts and techniques centered on fertility of the soil, its products, and seasons. These cults in the Near East were associated with the cycle of death and rebirth and took as the chief divinity a sexual mother goddess or a nonsexual creator – the earth goddess, known as Ninna in Mesopotamia.

Burial cults had existed since early prehistory. A specific site was often marked by a mound, and sacrifice and ritual eating of the dead were frequently involved. The placing of artifacts in the graves indicated a desire to ensure the continuity of life.
Cave paintings at **Lascaux** and **Trois Frères, France,** indicate that as far back as 20,000 BC Cro-Magnon men had witch doctors. They are pictured along with the animals hunted.

Before the third millennium BC peoples of Mesopotamia worshiped nature gods in human form, each god being associated with a city temple and the temples themselves occupying a central place in city life. The gods were organized as a democratic council, which reflected the political relations among the various city-states.

The religion of Egypt before the foundation of the dynasties was based on totemism, the idea that there is a relation between kinship groups and specific animals and plants. Each independent principality had its own totem. **Horus** the falcon was that of Bedhet in the north, while the god **Seth**, represented by a hegoat, protected Naqadah in the south. Above these local gods was the sun god, Re, the source of all life.

Literature

Writing developed in Mesopotamia as the Sumerians tried to simplify and regularize earlier picture writing and ideograms; a system for depicting sounds rather than ideas was probably invented by temple clerks in response to the need to record tribute payments and wages in the Mesopotamian city temples. With the development of the regular cuneiform style of script, writing became a skill for every aspiring man to acquire.

Literature had its origins in oral chronicles such as the Gilgamesh epic in Sumeria and in written prayers in Egypt, where a hieroglyphic script developed after 3400 BC and poetry emerged during the Pyramid Age. By 2000 BC, China was developing independently an elaborate system of word signs.

The Sumerian language was in use by 5000 BC, and a pictographic script developed by 4000 BC. Although this communicated ideas by the use of pictures, it gradually began to take on a more formal appearance with agreed symbols standing for ideas. This simplified the task of the Sumerian picture writer.

The first use of writing is attributed to the Sumerian city of Uruk. Simplification of the characters in earlier pictographic script led them to the idea of using conventional symbols to represent the sound of a word rather than the idea it conveyed. Motifs on painted pottery indicate that a script incorporating phonetic elements was in use in Uruk by 3700 BC.

Temple clerks recording wages, tribute, and stores had developed after 3500 BC some 2,000 signs, which were engraved on clay tablets. The linking of these signs with sounds made it easier to write names and abstract ideas as well as lists of objects. As Sumerian words were largely of one syllable, the system is called a *syllabary*.

An Egyptian hieroglyphic script developed after 3400 BC, possibly influenced by trading contacts with Sumeria. A hieroglyph could represent either a sound, an idea, or an identifying mark attached to another sign. The syllabic signs did not indicate differences in vowel sounds, as did the Sumerian script.

Art and architecture

In Egypt and Mesopotamia, the development of pottery and small domestic articles, cosmetic implements, and jewelry occurred in the Neolithic period, but with the growth of states and technological advance sophisticated metal crafts and stone sculpture developed. In the absence of stone, builders in Mesopotamia used as their basic medium the baked mud brick, which they later decorated with ceramics and copper reliefs, while the finest sculpture and much beautiful jewelry was produced in metal. In Egypt, stone was used for a series of monuments, culminating in the pyramids, as well as for a highly sophisticated tradition of sculpture with its own rules of proportion that persisted for over 1,000 years.

Throughout this period in China and after c.3000 BC in the Aegean, the manufacture of fine decorated ceramic ware anticipated the artistic achievements of subsequent centuries.

The appearance of painted pottery coincided with the late Neolithic/early Chalcolithic period – a transition period between the late Stone Age and the early uses of copper. Richly decorated pottery dating from c.4000 BC has been found in Anatolia at Hacilar and in Assyria at Arpachiyah.

In Egypt black-topped polished bowls (Badarian ware) and terra cotta figurines were produced. Ivory combs and cosmetic articles also date from this period.

The Sumerians in Susa, capital of Elam (SW Iran), became associated with a variety of remarkably fine pottery vessels, on which sharp geometric devices were brilliantly interwoven with stylized figures of birds, animals, and men.
Egyptian Amratian culture, c.3600 BC, showed technical advances on the Badarian period. Decorated ivory and bone combs were found, and figures of animals such as hippopotamuses appear on pottery.

Undecorated stone vases from Egypt's Gerzean period superseded vessels of the Amratian culture. Spherical and cylindrical jars were light and skillfully hewn out of solid blocks of hard stone by means of flint borers. Votive objects, tomb paintings, and palettes depict battles, ships, animals, and vase bearers.

Music

Music probably originated in man's desire to express himself more richly and formally than he could in speech alone; ritual chants rapidly developed into musical forms with special meanings. Widely separated cultures produced similar kinds of instruments, adapting natural objects: bone flutes and whistles found in Hungary and Russia date from c.25,000 BC.

The harp, in prehistory, probably developed from the archer's bow, played over a covered pit to add resonance. In Mesopotamia musicians played flutes, as well as drums and rattles.

Drum and reed pipe music bloomed in Mesopotamia. Called bull and reed music, it symbolized strength and weakness with the use of drums for a vigorous beat and pipes for the melody.

Religious music was performed by musicians chanting and playing on reed pipes, flutes, drums, and tambourines as part of the liturgy of temple worship in the Sumerian city-states.

Science and technology

The elaborate civilizations of Mesopotamia and Egypt depended for their birth and development on the settled agriculture practiced by Neolithic peoples in these regions since c.8000. Without it they could not have sustained either the increased population or the specialization of urban life. Once secure, these societies spawned a remarkable series of technological advances. The 4th millennium BC saw the invention of the plow, the wheel, the sailing boat, and methods of writing. Stone tools gave way to those of copper and bronze, that came into use c.2500 BC.

Scientific method as we know it – the systematic testing of the theories about the material world – did not develop until much later, but the technical knowledge of these early societies was very sophisticated. The pyramids remain one of the finest engineering feats of all time and in west Asia, as later in China and Mesoamerica, the mathematics used by priests provided the basis for the development of other sciences.

Neolithic or New Stone Age settlements prospered in Egypt, Mesopotamia between the Tigris and Euphrates rivers, and in other parts of the East, between 8000 and 3500 BC. Stone tools included polished stone axes and a type of flint sickle mounted in an animal's lower jawbone. The flints were mined. Buildings were reed and wattle huts or made of hand-molded clay bricks dried in the sun.

Clay seals were used c.4000 in the Middle East, to place the owner's name on pots.
Land transport vehicles in Sumeria included sledges.
The wheel was invented in Mesopotamia during the period of the establishment of city states. It took two forms: a stone potters' wheel, and a cartwheel, made from a single, solid piece of wood.

Copper, fashioned into beads as early as 6000 BC in northern Europe, was smelted from ores or melted as the native metal over wood fires since 4000 BC in Sumeria.
Kilns were introduced c.3400 in Sumeria. Many pots were fired at once, and raised above the fire, thus protecting the painted designs from wood ash. Shadow clocks originated in Sumeria c.3500 BC.

Metal-molding was practiced in Sumeria by 3200 to make copper and bronze axes with molded sockets for holding the shafts. Previous models had weaker sockets of folded metal.
The Egyptian Copper Age began in the Upper and Lower Kingdoms c.3200 and lasted until 2000 BC, after which iron and bronze artifacts were made.

3200–3000 BC

The Delta Kingdom of Lower Egypt was conquered *c.*3100 by Menes (Narmer), who came from the south and unified Egypt into a single monarchy. He is attributed with the founding of the First Dynasty, which he ruled from his new capital at Memphis.
The Phoenicians, a Semitic-speaking people, began to settle the coast of Syria *c.*3000 BC.
Copper was widely used throughout the Near East *c.*3000 BC.

3000–2800 BC

Cretan Neolithic culture gave way to bronze-based culture *c.*3000 BC. **Sumerian cities** came to be ruled by hereditary kings from 2900 onward. The Archaic Tablets of Ur came from this Early Dynastic or Classical Sumerian age. **Public works in Egypt,** especially canal construction, led to the growth of the Egyptian bureaucracy in the Early Dynastic period, when a national government first developed.

2800–2600 BC

Gilgamesh, the legendary king of Uruk, *r.c.*2750 BC.
Records of Sumerian kings began with Mebaragesi of Kish *c.*2700.
The Old Kingdom Of Egypt, a 500-year period of stability and cultural splendor, began *c.*2700 with the reign of Zoser. Egypt also expanded toward Nubia, *c.*2600.
Akkadians came to dominate the northern Mesopotamian plain in the Early Dynastic II period.

2600–2400 BC

Conflict between Sumerian cities such as Ur, Kish, and Lagash reached a climax *c.*2500.
A prosperous culture emerged at Yangshao in China *c.*2500.
Royal power reached its zenith in the Egyptian Old Kingdom *c.*2500 under the pharaohs Khufu and Khaphre.
A sea-going Minoan Civilization developed in Crete *c.*2500.

2400–2200 BC

Sargon the Great built Akkad in northern Mesopotamia, conquered Sumer, and created an empire stretching from the Persian Gulf to the Mediterranean *c.*2350. His soldiers settled at Ashur, the future Assyria.
Urukagina, King of Lagash, introduced reforms but was ousted by Lugalzaggisi of Umma. The Indus Valley civilization around the cities of Harappa and Mohenjo-daro emerged *c.*2300.
The Gutians destroyed the Akkadian Empire *c.*2230.

2200–2000 BC

Gudea of Lagash restored disrupted Sumerian commercial prosperity in southern Mesopotamia.
Ur-Nammu of Ur drove out the Gutians and established a brief Sumerian renaissance. After Egypt had expanded into Nubia and west Asia on a large scale, its Old Kingdom ended in anarchy with the collapse of the central government, 2181.
King Mentuhotep of Thebes reunited Egypt *c.*2060.

Pictograph cave in Montana was first used as shelter, *c.*3000. On its walls are drawings of men and animals in black, white, and red.

People living at Indian Knoll on Kentucky's Green River depended on a shellfish diet. They buried their dead under mounds of discarded shells.

Copper implements and ornaments were fashioned by the "Old Copper" Culture of Wisconsin from ore found in the area around Lake Superior.

The first pottery known to be made in North America was found at Stallings Island, Ga. It was made *c.*2400.

On the shores of Lake Lahonton in northwestern Nevada decoys made of reeds and feathers were used to attract ducks.

In Middle America the earliest pottery was made near Guerrero, Mexico *c.*2000 BC.

Nevada duck decoy

Royal standard of Ur

Bronze bust of Sargon 1

Stonehenge

The religion of Mesopotamia reached its classical form with the rise of more centralized political units in the early dynastic period. There were four main gods: **Anu**, god of heaven; **Enlil,** god of the winds; **Ninhursag,** goddess of birth; and **Enki** (Ea), god of water. Hierarchical relationships between the gods reflected the growing separation between the strata of Mesopotamian society. Divination of dreams and interpretation of entrails were practiced.

The priests at Memphis in Lower Egypt established the Memphite theology after the unification of Upper and Lower Egypt. Their god **Ptah** was believed to have created the world and was known as the patron of craftsmen. The creation myth associated with him is more abstract than those of the pre-dynastic period, and testifies to the sophistication of the Memphite priesthood.

In the Egyptian early dynastic period the king became associated with **Horus,** the falcon deity of Hierakonpolis in Bedhet. **Classical Egyptian religion** described an optimistic vision of an ordered cosmos, itself an expression of the predictability of life in Egypt governed by the regular flooding of the Nile River.
The first pyramid tombs were built in Egypt *c.*2700 BC.

The concept of divine kingship was well established by 2500, as was the existence of a specialized priesthood. Both contributed to the force of royal authority. The king became identified with the god **Horus**, who by this time was associated with the whole land of Egypt.

With the decline of the Old Kingdom, the idea of survival after death was extended to include people other than royalty for the first time. This may have been a reflection of the growing power of the nobility.

Stonehenge, built *c.*2000, to serve as some sort of religious facility, testifies to the astronomical knowledge of Wessex.

A cuneiform script was in use in Sumeria by 3200 BC. It consisted of vertical, horizontal, and oblique strokes made with a sharpened wooden stylus on a wet, hand-sized clay tablet. The name comes from the Latin *cuneus* (wedge) and refers to the wedge-shaped strokes of the stylus.

As cuneiform spread, writing began to serve a wide range of social needs, although there is no indication that it was used for anything but practical purposes. The Babylonians and Assyrians kept lists and inventories for business and legal purposes. There is an Egyptian record of farming procedures.

Literature had yet to emerge, but writing was becoming an important tool of social advancement and literary form was evolving in the oral tradition of the Sumerian-Babylonian epic of *Gilgamesh*, mankind's first great poem.

Another script was evolving on the Indian continent, not yet settled by Aryans—the Indus (or proto-Indian) script, found on seals dating back to *c.*2500 BC in which each sign seems to have had a single phonetic value.
In Sumeria, the Akkadians produced a simplified script of only 550 symbols, seen in the legal code of Urakagina *c.*2400.

The first literature dates from *c.* 2300 BC in the prayers of Egyptian pyramid texts. Also preserved in papyri is the "Pessimistic Literature," which includes the *Prophecy of Neferty* and *Admonitions of an Egyptian Sage*, the *Tale of an Eloquent Peasant*, and *A Dialogue of a Desperate Man with his Soul.*

A Chinese script emerged, although it was not standardized and no examples survive. A "concept script" in which each idea had a corresponding sign, it replaced a system of knotted cords and was used to record commands and perhaps chronicles and poetry.
In Babylon, the first known library, composed of clay tablets, existed by 2000 BC.

Mesopotamian cylinder seals dating from the **Protoliterate period** were used in the business of temple administration and bear the miniature prototypes of the relief friezes that were to become important in Sumerian art. They reached a high degree of craftsmanship by the Akkadian period.
The Palette of Narmer, *c.*3100 BC, a carved slate tablet from Hierakonpolis in Egypt, shows the king wearing the crowns of both kingdoms.

Complex tombs for Egyptian notables were constructed. These *mastaba* consisted of underground funerary chambers with stone or brick structures above.
In Mesopotamia, a typical temple of the Ubaid period, 2900–2800 BC, had a facade decorated with niches dedicated to the cult of the god Enki. Sculpture of the period consisted of terra cotta statuettes of both men and women.

The outstanding advance of Egyptian Old Kingdom architecture was the building, under the direction of royal architect Imhotep, of Zoser's step pyramid at Sakkara *c.*2700. Later the Great Pyramid at Giza and the Great Sphinx of Khafre would be built *c.*2500 BC.
Egyptian royal sculpture concentrated on idealized figures with an emphasis on set proportions.

Early Minoan art was characterized by marble statuettes of goddesses (Cycladic idols). *c.*2500 BC and vases made from Cretan and imported stone.
Mesopotamian decorative arts—in particular the use of gold and copper, lapis lazuli, and other fine inlays—achieved a high degree of craftsmanship. In China the painted ceramics of the late Neolithic Yangshao culture, *c.*2500, have geometric patterns painted in black and red pigments.

Narrative reliefs and stelae proclaimed the achievements of Mesopotamian culture in the Akkadian period, while **King Sargon's bronze bust** is one of the greatest examples of ancient portrait sculpture.
The earliest Indus Valley cities of Harappa and Mohenjo-daro were constructed of fire-baked bricks and utilized such features as corbeled arches. Among the few known vestiges of Indian art are seals with animal motifs and figurines.

A group of diorite statues of Gudea, the famous ruler of Lagash, *c.*2130, represents the finest works of Sumerian artistic revival.
The temple of Ur—a ziggurat dedicated to the moon goddess Nanna—was built by the Sumerian King Ur-Nammu.
Minoan pottery *c.*2200–2000 BC is represented by ceramics with a creamy white glaze over a dark ground.

Egyptian pottery depicts instruments like those used in Mesopotamia, including harps, drums, sistra (metal rattles on a U-shaped frame), and reed pipes of various lengths.

Vertical (end-blown) flutes, sistra, and tambourines were played in processional music, suggesting the possible use of music in courtly ritual in Mesopotamia and Egypt *c.*3000 BC.

A harp from ancient Egypt has been unearthed, dating *c.*2500 BC. It has a lower sound chest to improve its resonance. About the same time, doubled reed flutes were played, probably in unison.

Two kinds of harp, dating from *c.*2400 BC, were uncovered during the excavation of the royal tombs at Ur, in Mesopotamia. One had a lower sound chest and the other an upper sound chest.

Antiphonal forms, in which two choirs or a priest and choir chant responses, appeared in the ritual music of Sumerian temples under the Akkadian ruler Naram-Sin *c.*2200 BC.

Boats, as depicted on Egyptian pottery, had squared sails and many oars. Reed boats navigated the Nile *c.*3000 BC.
Plows take the form of a forked branch in Mesopotamia and Egypt, the forks being held by the plowman and the sharpened end, or share, being drawn through the soil by oxen. Such plows were shown *c.*3000 BC in Egyptian picture writing, although used earlier.
Horse-drawn chariots were recorded in Mesopotamia *c.*3000 BC.

Populations in Mesopotamia and Egypt had increased by 2800 BC owing to improved agricultural methods. Despite its primitive appearance and action the fork-branch plow brought greatly increased crop yields.
Cotton was grown in India *c.*3000 BC.

Mesopotamian metallurgy advanced significantly by 2600, for example in the development of soldering techniques, used to make the ornaments found in the royal tombs at Ur.
The first calendar of 365 days was invented by the Egyptians. The first pyramid, of King Zoser, was built *c.*2700. Its construction involved a practical knowledge of geometry that was not formulated in theory for many centuries.

Bronze alloys were widely made in Mesopotamia by 2500 BC; they were a mixture of copper and tin ores and were fashioned into ornaments, tools, and weapons. Copper ores were plentiful and widespread in Syria; some Sumerian bronzes are very hard as they accidentally contained silicon.
The Great Pyramid of Khufu was finished *c.*2500. It is 481ft (146.6m) high and covers 5 hectares.
Egyptian wooden boats were shown on tomb walls from 2500.

Weaving with looms had been practiced well before 3000 BC in west Asia and Egypt. By 2300, horizontal looms, with the warp thread pegged on the ground, were usual in the Near East.
Weight standards and accurate scales were used in Egypt from 2200 BC. For example, the dried fish eaten by miners in Egypt was measured by their masters using stone weights.
Sewage and drainage systems were built in Harappan cities.

Ziggurats became most refined *c.*2000 BC. These Mesopotamian buildings served both as storehouses for grain and as platforms for astrological and astronomical observations.
The Bronze Age reached the Neolithic settlements and nomadic cultures of western Europe *c.*3000–2000 BC.

Hittites and Assyrians 2000–1200 BC

Principal events

An influx of Aryan tribes, at the beginning of the second millennium BC, disrupted the civilizations of Sumeria, the Indus, and to a lesser extent Egypt, while adapting well to the existing cultures, especially in Babylon. After 1600 the Egyptians, the Hittites in Anatolia, and the Assyrians all developed large-scale military organizations to sustain their growing imperial ambitions. In the Eastern Mediterranean new civilizations began to emerge in this period.

The Cretan Minoans created a sea-based empire and a flourishing, peaceful civilization based on Knossos, and Mycenae began to establish itself as a power in southern Greece, where olive and vine farming formed the basis of future economic development.

After the fall of the Minoan civilization Mycenae took over much of its maritime power and culture, but with further invasions from the north c.1200 BC it too declined.

2000–1920 BC

The brief Sumerian renaissance centered on Ur continued until *c.*1950 BC when Semitic Amorites overran much of Sumeria. This was the beginning of a long period of instability in Mesopotamia.

In Egypt the Middle Kingdom reached its height with the 12th Dynasty, 1991–1785, after Amenemhat I had subdued the nobility and restored prosperity. Building, art, and international commerce flourished.

1920–1840 BC

Senusret III, 1887–1849 BC, further consolidated royal authority in Egypt by suppressing provincial rulers (nomarchs) and assisted the rise of a bureaucratic and trading middle class.

Unrest in Sumeria centered on conflict between the cities of Isin and Larsa, during which the area broke down once more into independent city-states.

The Semitic language of the Amorites gradually superseded Sumerian in Mesopotamia, between 2000 and 1700 BC.

1840–1760 BC

Hammurabi the Great of Babylon, *c.*1792–1750 BC, an Amorite, subdued the other cities of Mesopotamia and built an empire from the north Euphrates to the Persian Gulf, ruling with a code of laws based on principles absorbed from Sumerian culture.

The Middle Kingdom of Egypt ended *c.*1786 BC, weakened by an influx of the "Hyksos," a Semitic people from Syria.

The Indus civilization, already in decline, was destroyed by invading Aryans *c.*1760 BC.

1760–1680 BC

The Hyksos became firmly established in the Delta region of Egypt and adopted Egyptian culture. By 1700 BC a dynasty of Hyksos pharaohs was established.

The Babylonian Empire slowly crumbled under Hammurabi's son *c.*1700 while culture and religion flourished.

A natural disaster on Crete caused the Minoan palaces to be rebuilt *c.*1700 BC.

The Hittites, an Aryan people, grew powerful in Anatolia.

The Americas

The previous period was characterized by the domestication of wild plants in North and South America. In the years 2000–1200 BC this tradition spread, and agricultural villages grew up. Pottery was made in South, Middle, and North America by 2000 and weaving of cloth was developing.

2000–1920 BC

At the site of Boston, fishermen made an elaborate fish weir consisting of 65,000 stakes interwoven with branches to trap their prey in tidal waters.

1920–1840 BC

The Red Paint peoples, who lived on the banks of Maine's Penobscot River, spread red ocher over their dead and their grave offerings.

1840–1760 BC

Cotton textiles decorated with designs of bird, animal, and human figures in contrasting colors, were woven in the Huaca Prieta area of northern Peru.

1760–1680 BC

At La Florida, on the central coast of Peru, a temple of field stones and mud mortar was built around this time. The buildings included a large pyramid.

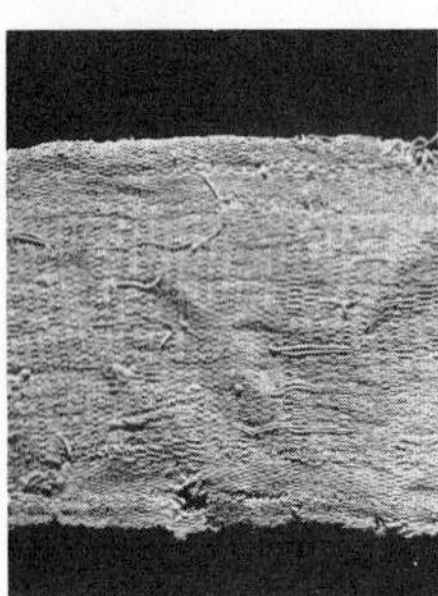

Huaca Prieta textile

Minoan jug, *c.*1800 BC

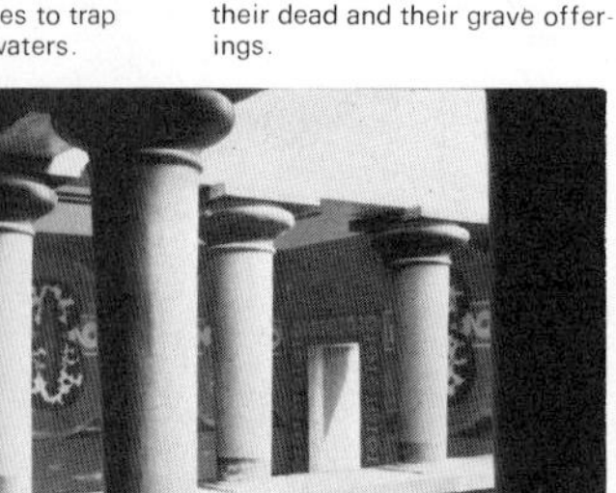

State apartments of the Palace of Knossos

Mask of Tutankhamen

Mycenaean capital, 14th c.

Religion and philosophy

The incursions of Aryans and other invading peoples into the main centers of civilization in the Near East disrupted the established religious traditions, dispersed some of their elements, and introduced new ones. The gods of the newcomers reflected their warlike nature, and the worship of their gods evolved into ecstatic sacrificial cults. Their impact upon Egypt, however, was transitory, and the traditional religious system continued and developed, interrupted by a brief but interesting monotheistic interlude under Pharaoh Akhenaton in the early 1300s BC. Once the more turbulent areas of Mesopotamia had settled to orderly lives of commerce and agriculture in city-centered communities, the first codes of law and concepts of citizenship were devised. In this period the basis of the Judaic tradition, with its emphasis on ethical monotheism, was laid among the Israelite tribes.

2000–1920 BC

Amenemhat I, the founder of the Egyptian 12th Dynasty, claimed descent from **Amun,** a local god of his native Thebes. From this time Amun, a father of the gods, and the Heliopolitan god Re were identified as **Amun-Re,** emphasizing the change in the royal family and confirming the divine right of the king to rule all of Egypt.

1920–1840 BC

The Canaanite religion emerged in Palestine with **El** as supreme god, and **Baal,** god of rain, vegetation, and fertility sharing the central position. The Canaanite religion was an important influence, both negatively and positively, on Israelite culture. It is possible that **Yahweh,** the sole god of Israel, was an Israelite name for the Canaanite El.

1840–1760 BC

The migrations of Aryans and other peoples from the Black Sea area helped to disperse religious ideas and practices. The Hurrians who invaded Upper Mesopotamia at this time transmitted elements of Sumerian beliefs northward to Hittite areas.

1760–1680 BC

The complex law code devised by Hammurabi the Great of Babylon *c.*1792–*c.*1750, was created in response to the needs of increasing trade, usury, and commerce. It sought to end blood feud and personal retribution and replace these with a secular state code based on the idea of citizenship. For example, one of the articles of the code stated that if a man's home fell down and someone was injured, then the owner was to be held responsible.

Literature

Cuneiform became more sophisticated after 2000 BC, but a more important development was the emergence of the first consonantal (BCD) script, far simpler to master than earlier syllabic systems of writing, none of which has remained in use. The Syrian Ugaritic script, however, which developed in the mid-2nd millennium BC, also possessed three vowel signs, although the five-vowel alphabet would not be elaborated until after 1000 BC by the Greeks who would draw on a variety of Semitic scripts.

Literature of the period ranged from narrative and love poetry in Egypt to historical narrative among the Hittites, the religious Vedas in India, and the ethical and divinatory Ching philosophy in China.

2000–1920 BC

The Egyptian Coffin Texts 2040–1786, found on coffins and papyri, include spells, ritual texts, and mythological stories. Their purpose was to give the dead person power in the afterlife, and after 1570 they would evolve into a more unified text, the Egyptian **Book of the Dead.**

1840–1760 BC

The Babylonian ritual poem, the Epic of Creation, first written about 2000 BC, had reached a classic form as part of the ceremonies associated with the new year. It told how the god Marduk slew the sea monster Tiamat, and created men as servants of the gods. Babylonian literature of the period is infused with a sense of metaphysical pessimism.

1760–1680 BC

The ancient Greek script, Linear B, was deciphered only in 1953 by Michael Ventris (1922–56). It flourished at Mycenae in the 12th century BC but dates back earlier than this and may derive from Linear A, an undeciphered script used by the Minoan civilization of Crete. Linear A dates from 1700 BC and is a syllabic script.

Art and architecture

The brilliant civilization that emerged in Crete reached its peak of cultural achievement between 1900 and 1500 BC with palaces of a highly functional design and decorative arts whose grace and vitality reflected a long period of peaceful development. Minoan fresco painting, sculpture, and painted pottery were characterized by a humane outlook and a love of nature and movement. The influence of Minoan art extended to Mycenae.

Temple architecture revived in Egypt with the Middle Kingdom and enjoyed its golden age in the 14th and 13th centuries. The New Kingdom ruler, Akhenaton, who made sun worship the sole cult during his reign, built some of the finest of these and introduced a revolutionary naturalism into royal portrait sculpture.

Chinese bronze workmanship was the most advanced in the world, and calligraphic art was beginning to develop.

2000–1920 BC

In Egypt, the establishment of the Middle Kingdom in 1991 BC was marked by an economic and artistic revival. The Great Temple of Karnak, built during the 12th Dynasty, *c.*1991–1785 showed a high level of craftsmanship in tomb reliefs, gold ornamentation, and paintings. Middle Kingdom sculpture adheres rigidly to rules dictating proportion and posture devised in the Old Kingdom despite a new element of naturalism in royal portraiture.

1920–1840 BC

The Bell-Beaker culture in central and western Europe made good-quality red ceramic beakers decorated with horizontal bands of geometric patterns. **In China,** wheel-turned **Lung-shan** black pottery (named after a site in Shantung) replaced the Yangshao type at the end of the Neolithic period. With thin walls and a metallic, burnished finish, it marked a great technical advance and was commonly used for ritual purposes and funerary ware.

1840–1760 BC

The Minoan palaces at Knossos, Phaestos, and other Cretan sites were rebuilt on a grander scale in the Middle Minoan period, 1900–1600, with more varied architectural features such as light shafts and efficient sanitation. By about 1760 BC, Minoan potters were producing fine Kamares ware pottery in graceful and varied shapes with a profusion of floral and geometric motifs. Craftsmen specialized in small works such as faïence figurines.

1760–1680 BC

A major revival of Mesopotamian art marked the rule of **Hammurabi,** *c.*1792–*c.*1750. Old palaces and buildings were strengthened and new ziggurats constructed. To the north, the city of Mari, partly built under the ruler **Zimrilim,** *c.*1779–*c.*1761 BC, is remarkable for its size. Its 200 rooms cover 10 acres (4 hectares), and the fine painted decorations include narrative pictures such as the investiture of Zimrilim.

Music

The development of a metal-working technology in ancient civilization enabled craftsmen to make metal instruments based on older instruments made from organic materials and stone.

Bells of bronze replaced stone chimes, and bronze, copper, or silver trumpets replaced hollowed horns. A metal tube with a more cylindrical bore than animal horn gave a brilliant tone.

2000–1920 BC

The yellow bell, or huang chung, was the name given to an absolute (fixed) pitch produced by a bamboo pipe of set length. It is attributed to a mythical Chinese emperor of *c.*2000 BC.

Science and technology

Trade and warfare were the main stimuli of technological advance in the 2nd millennium BC. Larger sailing ships were used to bring tin from the Mediterranean countries to Mesopotamia and to carry away bronze objects made using the tin; radical improvements took place in chariot design, but the greatest technological event was the mastery of iron by Hittite smiths. Although they lacked heat enough to melt the metal, the Hittites made iron implements by hammering them out of the heated ore. The resultant metal, albeit flawed by slag, could be tougher and harder than bronze. Weapons, sword blades in particular, benefited while metalwork for decorative purposes in iron, bronze, gold, or silver became highly refined, as the objects found in the tomb of Tutankhamen show. Bronze vessels of superlative craftsmanship were made in China too under the Shang dynasty.

2000–1920 BC

The shaduf, a device for raising water from one level to another with a bucket, appears on Mesopotamian seals *c.*2000. This is an Egyptian invention still used in the Nile region.

Early Chinese technology is suggested by the finding of jade plaques, which could only have been worked effectively with metal tools.

Iron weapons and ornaments, dating from 2000 BC, have been found in the Near and Middle East.

1920–1840 BC

Early iron technology involved repeated hammering of the ore until most of the slag was beaten out. Wood or charcoal fires are not hot enough to melt iron. This can only be accomplished in some kind of blast furnace, which was not developed until the Middle Ages.

1840–1760 BC

Cosmetics in Egypt, already used in the 4th millennium, included perfumery oils extracted from fruits by pressing them through a cylindrical cloth bag, held upright with sticks. Filter pressing methods of this kind are still used in the food and chemical industries.

1760–1680 BC

Bronze-casting in Mesopotamia followed the *cire perdue* method, a one-off process necessarily reserved for valuable items. Objects were modeled or sculptured in wax, covered with clay, and the wax melted out to make a mold for the molten metal. Hollow objects were made by molding the wax around a clay center.

1680–1600 BC

The Minoans established a sea-based empire in the eastern Mediterranean under their semi-legendary King Minos *c.*1650 BC, creating the Minoan golden age centered on Knossos.
The Babylonian Empire was increasingly threatened by the influx of Aryan Kassites from the north *c.*1600 BC.
The Shang dynasty, which introduced writing to China, developed an urban civilization *c.*1600 BC.

1600–1520 BC

The Hittites plundered Babylon in *c.*1550 under King Mursilis I. In their wake the Kassites ruled there for 400 years.
The Hyksos were driven from Egypt in *c.*1570 BC by the Theban kings Kamose and Amosis, who established the New Kingdom, sparking a growth of nationalist feeling.
Mycenaean civilization was growing on mainland Greece and has left rich "shaft graves."
Minoan civilization reached its height *c.*1550 BC.

1520–1440 BC

Mitanni, a kingdom of Aryan Hurrians in northern Mesopotamia, **the Hittites,** and **Assyria** all grew as military powers *c.*1500 BC.
Thutmose I of Egypt established an empire in the Near East between 1520 and 1510 and began the construction of the valley of the tombs of the kings at Thebes.
Minoan civilization was destroyed *c.*1450, probably by an earthquake at Thera.

1440–1360 BC

After the volcanic eruption at Thera, *c.*1450, Cretan civilization revived and continued to spread to mainland Greece.
Mitanni conquered Assyria *c.*1440 BC to become a military power equal to Egypt.
Amenhotep III, 1417–1379 BC, extended the Egyptian Empire and brought peace and prosperity at home, which was threatened by the attempted religious reforms of his successor, Akhenaton, and by internecine murders.

1360–1280 BC

Under Ashur-uballit I, Assyria again became a military power.
Tutankhamen ruled as pharaoh in Egypt, *c.*1348–1340 BC.
Hittites destroyed the empires of Mitanni *c.*1360 BC, conquered north Syria and Aleppo, and built a major empire in the Near East.
Mycenaean civilization reached its height *c.*1320 BC.
Ramesses I reestablished the Egyptian Empire in the Near East *c.*1319 BC. Ramesses II fought the Hittites at the battle of Kadesh in 1299 BC.

1280–1200 BC

A truce was agreed between Egypt and the Hittites *c.*1270 as both came under pressure from migrations of "sea peoples."
The Trojan War reflected stresses in Mycenaean culture from Dorian invasions, *c.*1200.
Shalmaneser I of Assyria, *r.*1274–1245, took Babylon from the Kassites and defeated the Hittites and the Hurrians.
Moses led the Jews from Egypt *c.*1250 BC.

Bitterroot peoples, who had inhabited the Alpha Rockshelter near the Salmon River in Idaho since *c.*6000 BC, lived by hunting, fishing, and gathering.

In Illinois, Wisconsin, Ohio, Indiana, Michigan, and Ontario, the Glacial Kame peoples used the gravel ridges formed by melting glaciers for burial sites.

Ocós, on the coast of Guatemala, developed into one of the first permanent village sites in Mesoamerica.

At a cemetery near Port au Choix, Newfoundland, treasured and useful articles, as well as carved images of animals and birds, were buried with the dead.

The inhabitants of the Pinto Basin of southeastern California used pulverized, hard shell seeds, particularly acorns, to form a large part of their diet.

The Olmec people, who had settled in Mexico by 1500 BC, were developing an agricultural culture that definitely indicated a civilization of high order.

Egyptian ship, *c.*1300 BC

Ramesses II at Luxor

Shang bronze ritual vessel

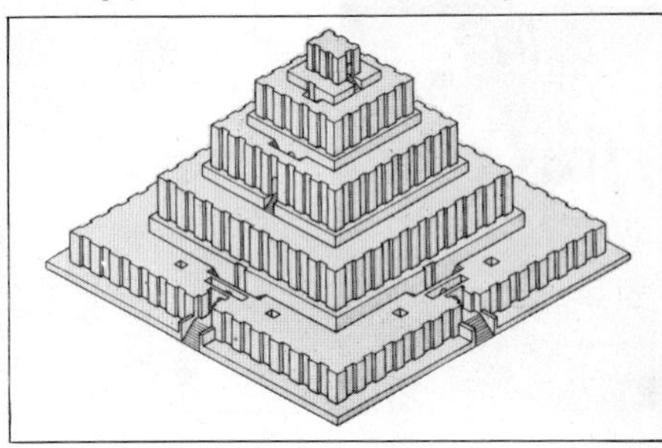

Ziggurat at Elam, 13th c. BC

The royal palace at Knossos was a center for the worship of nature gods with human and animal characteristics. These deities included a fertility goddess associated with snake worship and possibly a bull-god. The surviving palace is decorated with a bull's horn motif and is thought to have provided the model for the Labyrinth in the Greek myth of the Minotaur.

The religion of the Hittites, who overthrew Babylon in the mid-1500s, derived from many sources. Several of their gods were attributed characteristics that varied locally, and they indiscriminately absorbed the gods of other tribes. However, the mother goddess and the weather god were always retained, the dominance of the latter reflecting the importance of rain to fertility.

Egyptian religion went through a short-lived phase in which only one god was worshiped in the reign of **Akhenaton,** *r.c.*1379–1362. He suppressed the older gods including Amun-Re and instituted **Aton,** represented by the solar disk, as the only god. During his reign the only other god acknowledged was King Akhenaton himself, who was thought to be eternally revitalized by Aton's rays. After Akhenaton's death, however, Egypt reverted to its traditional gods.

The Aryan invaders of India brought with them a religion which came to be embodied in the **Vedas,** a set of sacred hymns codified by the end of the 2nd millennium BC. The Vedic pantheon of nature gods included **Indra,** the storm god, **Agni,** the fire god, and **Soma,** the intoxicating ritual juice; these and many other gods were involved in a complex mythology and an elaborate system of ritual.

The Israelites left Egypt *c.*1250 BC under the leadership of Moses, who instituted worship of a single god, **Yahweh,** to whom the tribes were bound by a covenant promising them possession of Canaan (Palestine). The Israelites quickly conquered much of Canaan, and their monotheistic religion became common to the "twelve tribes" of Israel.

The first known Phoenician inscriptions, found at the city of Byblos, date from *c.*1600 BC. From Byblos, a main trading center for papyrus, the Greeks took their word for books, *biblia.* The Phoenicians developed the simplest of all the consonantal scripts, reducing the number of symbols used to represent sounds to 22.

Egyptian love songs had evolved into a sophisticated literary form by 1200 BC. Although the surviving songs date from the New Kingdom (*c.*1570–1085), many are clearly from older sources. They are vigorous, direct, and lyrical in their appeal to the senses. "When the wind comes it desires the sycamore tree; When you come near to me, you will desire me."

Cuneiform had become entirely syllabic with fewer and more simplified characters, each having a phonetic value. This development culminated in the **Syrian Ugaritic script,** one of the first scripts with vowel signs. The earliest examples of writing in this Semitic language date from 1400 BC and describe Canaanite mythology.

Hittite literature flourished between 1600 and 1200 BC. It was written in cuneiform or, for private communication, in an older pictographic script. There are royal decrees, treaties, a law code, religious instructions, and some Sumerian and Babylonian tales. The literary style is distinguished by laconic vigor and lack of verbosity.

The origin of the Greek alphabet is attributed in mythology to the Phoenician Cadmus (son of Agenor, king of Tyre), who is said to have brought 16 letters to Boeotia *c.*1313 BC. Evidence from Mycenae indicates that this legend may have some basis in fact. The Phoenician consonant signs certainly provided a model for the Greeks, who later added vowel signs.

The Vedas, verse hymns dealing with sacrificial and magical formulae, were written in Sanskrit between 1500 and 1200 BC in India. The foremost is the *Rigveda.* The hymns include incantations and spells for good health and long life. Indian literature of this period was primarily religious in inspiration.

Minoan culture was approaching its golden age. Wheel-thrown pottery decorated with figures, a wide range of gold jewelry, and fine quality seals were made, together with miniature sculptures in bronze, terra cotta figurines, and ivory carvings. Carved vases of stone and marble appeared *c.*1600 BC with relief decoration, some in the shape of bulls' heads, reflecting the Minoan passion for bull sports and the religious significance of this animal.

Egyptian art experienced its classical flowering under the New Kingdom, *c.*1570–1085. A standard temple plan, often on a monumental scale, was established, with floral motifs as characteristic decoration on the columns. A spirit of freedom produced lighter and more elegant sculpture, coupled with precise rendering of detail, but formal rules were preserved. Fine quality work in precious materials reflected the influence of new trade links.

Minoan culture was extending its influence to Greece, particularly in Mycenae. The Minoans' love of depicting nature in their art is exemplified in the lively frescoes of the palaces, in works such as the unique painted limestone coffin, *c.*1450, from Hagia Triada, Crete, and in the richly decorated pottery that flourished *c.*1500–1450, depicting marine creatures of many varieties.

A more naturalistic style of Egyptian royal portraiture was encouraged by **Akhenaton,** *r.c.*1379–1362, who constructed a new palace and temple to the sun god at Tell el Amarna. A head of his consort **Nefertiti** is one of the most beautiful works of this short-lived Amarna style. The temple of Amun and Colossi of Memnon were built under **Amenhotep III,** 1417–1379. Examples from **Ras Shamra** (Ugarit) show a high standard of Phoenician decorative art.

The tomb of Tutankhamen with its rich furnishings included a sarcophagus with a gold and lapis lazuli funerary mask.
Under China's Shang dynasty at An-yang, mastery of bronze casting produced distinctive vessels, drums, and bells, some with calligraphic ornamentation.
Tholoi (beehive tombs), including the Treasury of Atreus, with great vaulted ceilings, were built at Mycenae, in the 14th century.

Ramesses II, *c.*1304–1237, completed the colonnaded hypostyle hall at Abydos, with fine funerary reliefs. His rock temple at Abu Simbel was one of the most grandiose achievements of Egypt's New Kingdom. Hewn from a pink sandstone cliff with an entrance 105ft (32m) high, it extended 200ft (61m) into the mountain and was flanked by four massive statues of the king. He also added to the Temple of Luxor and erected a colossus of himself in the forecourt.

A lutelike instrument with fretted fingerboard appears in a wall painting in an ancient Egyptian tomb dating from about 1520 BC. Earlier types are found in Mesopotamian pottery *c.*2000.

The oldest known Chinese instruments are suspended stone chimes and globular bone flutes, dating from about 1500 BC. They were played in the early part of the Shang dynasty.

Bamboo culture in Southeast Asia produced an unusual music, mixing the sounds of blown pipes, such as flutes, and struck pipes in the form of bamboo xylophones.

Copper and silver trumpets found in the tomb of Tutankhamen date from about 1320 BC. The brilliance of their tone contrasted with other instruments in use at the time.

Vedic chant, a sung form of ancient Hindu scriptures, was established by 1200 BC and is the world's oldest continuous musical tradition. It was based on a three-note scale system.

Ships underwent improvement in the second millennium BC. A major impetus for sea trade came from the Mesopotamians, who had probably become cut off from their major sources of tin in Syria and so imported the metal to make bronze. Many vessels sailing the eastern Mediterranean were built from planks and could be made up to 40ft (12m) long. Minoan ship design was particularly influential.
Sea battles took place toward the end of this millennium.

Plows were improved *c.*1600 in Mesopotamia, by the invention of a share and sole that dug deeper furrows.
Glass bottles appeared in Egypt *c.*1500 BC. Glazed beads and glass imitations of precious stones have been found dating from a thousand years earlier, but this is the first evidence of work with molten glass.
Fine metalwork in iron, copper bronze, gold, and silver, with filigree and inlay work reached a new peak in Egypt.

Chinese bronze urns and vases appeared suddenly *c.*1500 BC under the Shang dynasty with no previous evidence of a metal technology (except for jade carving). Shang bronzes were molded in sections to extremely complex designs.
Cementation steel was made by the Chalybes, a subject people of the Hittites. This, the earliest form of steel, is made by repeatedly hammering red-hot iron together with charcoal until carbon enters the iron.

An Egyptian water clock, *c.*1400 BC, had bucket-shaped vessels from which water drained by way of small holes in the bases. Hours were marked inside the vessels. Mathematics may have developed from linear measurement used in the division of land in Egypt and Mesopotamia. Measurements were often made in units based on parts of the body, such as the Egyptian cubit, from the elbow to the fingertip.

Currency, in Egypt, took the form of copper ingots in the shape of a stretched oxhide. These oxhide ingots were often transported by ship, as we know from Egyptian wrecks.
Egyptian chariots were improved by increasing the number of wheel spokes from four to six and the movement of the axle rearward, so that the rider's weight was more evenly distributed. This prevented seesawing movements over rough ground, giving a smoother ride.

Cavalry soon challenged the charioteer in war. Saddles and reins were developed in south Turkey, but stirrups were not used for 1,000 years and did not reach Europe until *c.*700 AD.
Hittite ironsmiths scattered with the destruction of the Hittite Empire, *c.*1200 BC, with far-reaching consequences. The smiths had kept their techniques secret for hundreds of years; but knowledge of them now began to spread, reaching eastern Europe by 1000.

Iron swords and the alphabet 1200–700 BC

Principal events

Barbarian invasions continued to strike the Near East, obliterating the power of the Hittites and Mycenaeans and limiting Egyptian and Assyrian military ambition. In the same period, however, the smaller trading societies, particularly the Jews and Phoenicians, flourished. The Phoenicians built colonies throughout the Mediterranean, and the Jews established their distinctive identity and claim to the region west of the river Jordan. After 900 the military power of Egypt and Assyria recovered, financed by tribute from their subject peoples, but the focus for cultural development moved to Greece, where the adaptation of the Phoenician alphabet marked the end of the Dorian-imposed dark ages.

In India, the Aryans overran the Ganges area and established a caste system based on the Vedic religion. In China the Shang dynasty fell to their former subjects, the Chou, but this had little cultural effect.

1200–1150 BC

The Sea Peoples invaded the eastern Mediterranean from the Caspian Sea area and destroyed the Hittites *c.*1200 BC. Some settled on the Canaanite coast to become the Philistines.
Ramesses III *c.*1198–1166, repelled their invasion of Egyptian soil *c.*1190 BC, after which Egypt withdrew into cultural and political isolation.
The Canaanites, a Semitic race, settled in Syria and developed a flourishing culture based on the production of purple cloth.

1150–1100 BC

Nebuchadrezzar I, *r.*1124–1103, of Babylon restored stability in Mesopotamia, facilitating the recovery of Assyrian trade disturbed by the Hyksos.
The Egyptian monarchy fell under the growing influence of the priesthood of the sun god Re, the Amun, causing political and economic stagnation *c.*1100.
The Shang dynasty in China consisted of 30 kings in fraternal succession but declined through internal unrest *c.*1100 BC.

1100–1050 BC

Tiglath-Pileser I of Assyria conquered Mesopotamia and the eastern Mediterranean, defeating Babylon and exacting tribute from the Phoenician city-states. After his death *c.*1077, **the Aramaeans** took Babylon and destroyed Assyrian power, driving the Canaanites south.
The Philistines, a trading people, conquered **the Jews** who had settled in Palestine after leaving Egypt and were at this time a loose confederation of tribes ruled by the Judges.

1050–1000 BC

Aramaean rule in Assyria produced little military or cultural activity.
In Greece, monarchical city-states including Athens, Thebes, and Sparta developed *c.*1000 based on wealth derived from trade and agriculture.
Saul became the first king of the Jews *c.*1020 BC, with powers limited by religious tradition.
Aryan rule was established in north India by 1000 BC.
The Chou dynasty was set up in China in 1027 BC.

The Americas

Permanent settlements, principally agricultural villages, were being established. The first highly developed civilization—the Olmec—developed in Central America. The Chavin and Paracas cultures of South America produced distinctive art styles. In North America burial mound building began.

An Olmec ceremonial center at San Lorenzo (in Vera Cruz), Mexico, located on a man-made plateau, featured colossal stone human heads.

Woodland hunters in eastern North America depended on the canoe in their search for game. River travel gave them access to new forest areas.

Inhabitation began at Poverty Point, an alluvial fan formed by the Arkansas River in northern Louisiana, 1050 BC.

The peoples of the Paracas peninsula in Peru, beginning *c.*1000, wrapped their dead in richly embroidered textiles, which distinguished the culture.

Phoenician ivory from Nimrud

Bronze axe, *c.*1000 BC

Black obelisk of Shalmaneser III

Olmec head

Hittite relief, *c.*800 BC

Religion and philosophy

Beginning with the period of the Judges, Israelite history shows a continual effort by certain individuals and nomadic groups to defend the purity of the religion of Yahweh against its dilution by the pagan affiliations of the central rulers. This unceasing resistance to the addition of other gods to their faith reinforced the distinctive features of the Judaic tradition.

In China the emergence of a secular philosophy foreshadowed the development of later religious systems, with their characteristic lack of emphasis on the supernatural.

The invasion of Greece by a succession of northern tribes led to a joining of new Olympian gods with older deities. This varied religious atmosphere, contrasting sharply with the rigid, priest-dominated society of Egypt, would play an important part in the emergence of the brilliant culture of 5th-century Greece.

Successive invasions of Greece culminating in that of the Dorians, *c.*1200, brought Aryan gods such as Zeus, Apollo, and Hermes, who largely replaced the more nature-oriented gods of the Minoan-influenced Mycenaeans. These gods, who in Greek mythology became associated with Mount Olympus, bore a far more arbitrary relation to human affairs than the original Mycenaean deities.

The Israelites began to assimilate Canaanite ideas during the period of the Judges, which ended *c.*1050 BC. The Yahweh of Moses and his nomadic followers absorbed features of the Canaanite deities as Israelite society became more settled and structured. Religious purists such as **Rechabites** and **Nazarites** opposed this degeneration of the monotheistic ideal.

Religion in Iran before Zoroaster (6th century BC) bore similarities to the early Vedic religion of India. Many of the Iranian pantheon of gods coincided with Vedic ones, including **Mithras**, the cult of fire, and **Haoma**, the sacred liquor.

Chinese philosophy emerged during the Chou dynasty, 1027–221 BC, as increasing control over nature and the growth of social stability led to a demystification of thought. Irrigation replaced prayers for rain, and heaven *(T'ien)* was seen as rewarding virtue, thus giving man the power to control his own destiny through being virtuous.

Literature

The Greek alphabet, in which letters were used to represent vowels for the first time, had developed from Phoenician forms by the 8th century BC. It provided the most flexible and economical method of writing yet devised. At about the same time the ballads of the Trojan wars, which had emerged in oral form in the 10th century, were compiled and written down by Homer in the Iliad and the Odyssey. It is not entirely clear whether Homer was a single man or the name for a group of poets. But the later Greeks, who drew strongly on Homeric traditions, regarded him as an individual, the father of Greek poetry. Similarly, in Mesopotamia, the Gilgamesh epic neared its final form, and a Chinese poetic tradition grew up.

Ten thousand Hittite cuneiform tablets constituting the state archives at Bögazköy, the capital, survived the destruction of the empire *c.*1200 BC. These represent the main source of information on Hittite history and culture.

The collection of myths and folklore that coalesced into the *Gilgamesh* epic in Mesopotamia was now approaching its final form. It combined religious elements with story themes that were to become widely popular throughout the Middle East, including references to a flood, the quest for immortality, and the friendship of two great warriors.

Traces of the Gilgamesh epic can be found in the Trojan ballads, which culminated in the poetry of Homer, as well as in Hebrew and other classical literature. The adventures of Gilgamesh, king of Uruk, and his friendship with Enkidu, a wild man sent to destroy him, were the center of a pessimistic poetic cycle that combined realism with myth.

The Greek alphabet is thought to have begun evolving after 1050 BC as the Greeks modified symbols they had borrowed from the Phoenicians to suit the sounds of their own language. The name alphabet comes from the first two symbols, *alpha* and *beta*. By using signs for vowels as well as for consonants the Greeks made a crucial advance, enabling any word to be written.

Art and architecture

The trading societies that emerged during this period helped to spread artistic styles and techniques in the eastern Mediterranean. In Greece foreign influences imported especially by the Phoenicians led to the adoption of complex figurative images in pottery, where previously only geometric patterns had been used. The influence of the Phoenicians was similarly felt in the Hebrew kingdom of King Solomon, who employed their craftsmen to build his Great Temple at Jerusalem.

Monumental architecture ceased to be built in Egypt, but in Assyria the political resurgence of the 9th and 8th centuries led to the restoration of Nimrud and the building of Sargon's palace at Khorsabad.

In Central America the isolated Olmec civilization produced colossal sculpture without the aid of metal tools.

With the decline of the Egyptian New Kingdom major architectural programs ended, and the sarcophagus of **Ramesses III**, *d.*1166, is one of the last major works in the classical New Kingdom style.
The earliest form of Greek art was the Proto-Geometric style of pottery decoration painted with zigzags and wavy lines. This pottery probably originated in Athens, the leading city at the end of the Bronze Age.

San Lorenzo, the earliest Olmec site, was established *c.*1150. The chief Olmec art forms were large stone monuments, including colossal heads, some weighing over 40 tons.

In China the artistic traditions of the Shang dynasty were perpetuated by the Chou, *c.*1122–221. Jade and ritual bronze vessels became increasingly elaborate, palace architecture developed, and roof-tiling and bricks were introduced. Wall painting probably began during this period.

Egypt's Late Dynastic period was dominated by the high priests of Amun, and primarily religious artifacts were made. Metal was increasingly used to make figurines, and larger statuary was often made in the harder stones such as schist and basalt.

Music

Noticing that there was a mathematical relationship between the length of a pipe or a string and the pitch it produced, musicians in the ancient civilizations linked this relationship with the underlying order of the universe and phenomena of the natural world. This aspect of musical theory would later be expressed in Pythagoras' concept of the harmony of the spheres.

Secular music was established as an important part of the life of the Assyrian court *c.*1200. Minstrels were highly regarded and music held a recognized place in court entertainment.

Pentatonic scales became prevalent in the East. The five notes of these scales, still characteristic of Eastern music, were often related to north, south, east, west, and center.

The reed mouth organ or shéng developed in China. It has several bamboo pipes rising from a wind chest into which air is blown though a mouthpiece.

Science and technology

The major technological advance of the 2nd millennium BC—a radical improvement in the quality of wrought iron—was a major factor in the expansion of the later Assyrian Empire. Assyrian ironsmiths were able to make a sharp edge using a process of tempering that involved repeated hammering and quenching in water. For the first time, effective iron swords and axes could be made; these weapons, together with siege towers and the use of cavalry, greatly contributed to the image of Assyrian indomitability. Sharpened iron was first used effectively in agriculture with the introduction of iron plowshares in Mesopotamia. Iron blades withstood wear far better than bronze-shared plows and could cut deeper furrows, which led in turn to greater crop yields.

In South America the Chavin produced beautiful objects in hammered gold, and Chinese bronze and ceramic technology was further refined.

Phoenician sea trade, by 1200 BC, supplanted that of Minoan Crete and would later focus on the docks of Tyre and Sidon.
Early food technology included the preservation of fish by drying, smoking, and salting, thus allowing it to be stored. Such methods were used widely in the Bronze Age, but in particular by the Greeks and Phoenicians who were great eaters of fish.

Vitreous enameling was an achievement of the later Mycenaeans. This process involves fusing glass materials onto a metallic base and first appeared in Cyprus in the form of glass decorated gold rings.

Iron plowshares were developed in Mesopotamia *c.*1100 BC. Hard enough to take a sharp cutting edge, they advanced agricultural technology. The Phoenicians are thought to have developed the bireme *c.*1100.

The mass production of iron tools was a major feature of the Assyrian Empire. The Assyrians themselves were not great innovators, but they made use of iron technology practiced by Hittite and other subject artisans.
Early South American farming settlements appeared on the coast of Ecuador and Peru *c.*1000 BC. The simple technology of these Neolithic peoples included building in mud, brick, and stone.

1000–950 BC

David, king of the Jews, 1000–961 BC, defeated the Philistines. His successor, Solomon, 961–922, built the temple at Jerusalem and a trading fleet in the Indian Ocean.
Hiram I, king of Byblos, 969–936, consolidated the Sidonian states and assisted Phoenician trade by building a harbor at Tyre, his new capital.
Damascus and Geshu were founded by the Aramaeans.

950–900 BC

Assurdan II, *r.*935–913, briefly restored Assyrian military authority *c.*935 BC. But by 912 Assyria was at its smallest size.
Egypt re-emerged as a military power, reconquering Palestine in 918, after Shoshenk, *c.*935–914, had reunited Egypt by making his son high priest.
The Jewish kingdom was divided on Solomon's death into the kingdom of the Israelites in the north and Judah in the south, following opposition to his rule in the north.

900–850 BC

The Phoenician city of Byblos grew up *c.*900 BC on the Mediterranean coast and became the center of the cult of Baal.
Egypt and Assyria fought in Syria-Palestine 900–830 BC. At the **battle of Qarqar,** 854, the Aramaeans and Israelites, inspired by Elijah, defeated Shalmaneser III of Assyria.
In Greece there was a gradual shift from monarchies to oligarchies in most of the city-states with the exception of Sparta.
The Chavin culture flourished in Peru *c.*900–*c.*200 BC.

850–800 BC

Shalmaneser III of Assyria, *r.*858–824, defeated the forces of Damascus and Israel and exacted tribute from the Phoenician cities.
Damascus came to dominate the Aramaean states and subdued the Israelites *c.*820 BC.
The Medes, an eastern people noted for their horse raising, were first mentioned in Babylonian records *c.*835 BC.
The Phoenicians colonized the eastern Mediterranean and established Carthage *c.*814 BC.

800–750 BC

Assyrian military power declined under a succession of weak monarchs *c.*800 BC and with it Assyrian wealth.
A Greek renaissance occurred under the stimulus of trading contact with the Phoenicians.
Judah played an important role in a military alliance against the Assyrians *c.*769 BC.
Jereboam, 780–740, brought prosperity to the Israelites.
The caste system was now firmly established in India.
Rome was founded in 753 BC.

750–700 BC

Tiglath-Pileser III, *r.*744–727, Shalmaneser V, *r.*726–722, and Sargon II, *c.*722–705, restored Assyrian military power, founding a standing army and often moving subject peoples. Babylon was conquered and Damascus paid tribute to Assyria.
Greek cities founded colonies in Sicily and southern Italy *c.*750.
The Kushite kingdom in Nubia overran Egypt, 725 BC, establishing a Kushite dynasty, 725–656 BC. A capital, Napata, had been founded *c.*800 BC.

The Woodland tradition of eastern North America began *c.*1000. This tradition was characterized by burial mounds and elaborate earthworks.

The monumental stone sculptures at the ceremonial site at San Lorenzo were mutilated and buried by the Olmecs, marking the end of the civilization there.

Chavin de Huantar, a town and temple site in northern Peru, emerged as the center of the Chavin culture, known for its unique pottery and sculpture.

About 800 BC, at a second Olmec center, La Venta in Tabasco, Mexico, craftsmen produced beautiful jade ornaments and colossal sculpture.

Cultivation of maize was first undertaken in eastern North America *c.*800 in the Ohio River Valley.

The civilization at Poverty Point, La., was at its peak, importing materials from as far away as the Great Lakes and Appalachian Mountains areas.

Gates of Shalmaneser III: Assyrian war machines

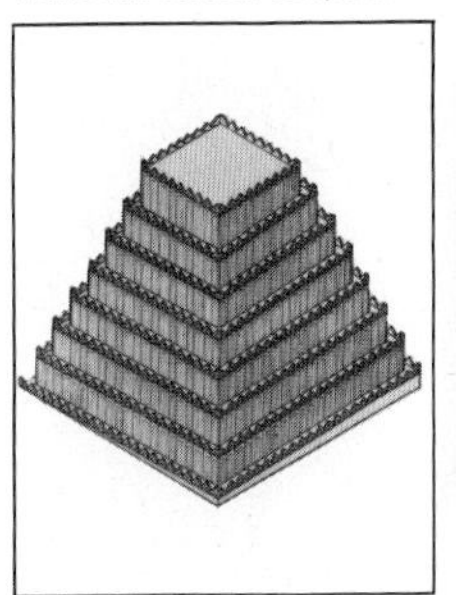

The Ziggurat at Khorsabad

Phoenician musicians, 8th c.

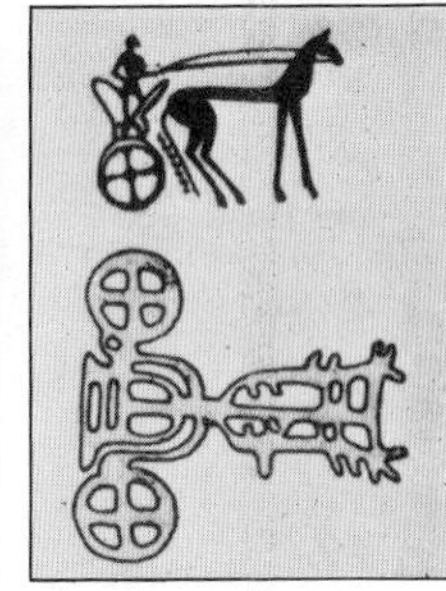

Chariot from a Greek amphora

The foremost Vedic writings were the *Rigveda*, a collection of hymns and sacred formulae of "mantras" that formed the liturgical basis for a priesthood. Cremation of the dead came to replace burial, and there was a differentiation of priestly functions into those relating to actual sacrificial procedures and those relating to the ritual chanting of the sacred hymns.

Primitive Japanese religion, Shinto, was based on a love of nature. The powers of nature, **Kami,** were seen as beneficent rather than awesome, and pollution was "biological" rather than moral. Pollution from contact with death or menstruation had to be removed by ritual cleansing. They practiced the art of divination by burning bones.

Jezebel, wife of the king of Israel Ahab, *r.*874–853 BC, built a temple to the Canaanite god Baal. This aroused opposition among the zealous followers of Yahweh, led by **Elijah,** *fl.c.*875. Elijah's disciple **Elisha** inspired the slaying of Jezebel and the complete overthrow of the royal family.

The orgiastic cult of the nature divinity **Dionysus, or Bacchus,** reached Greece from Thrace and Phrygia. His followers, mostly women known as **Maenads** (mad ones), would take to the hills in ecstasy under the god's inspiration and wander about in *thiasori*, or revel bands. Dionysus was god of fruitfulness and vegetation, and was especially known as the god of wine.

The 8th-century prophets of the Old Testament, **Amos, Hosea, and Isaiah,** castigated the moral turpitude of the Israelite rulers and their syncretist tendencies. The prophets rejected contemporary and foreign standards and urged otherworldly ideals, prophesying that the dilution of the old religion would lead to the fall of the kingdom of Israel. This prediction was fulfilled when the Assyrians conquered Israel in 732 BC.

The concept of caste that had emerged in India was elaborated by the highest priestly caste, or **Brahmins.** There were four main castes, covering occupations of priests, nobles, merchants, and laborers. Brahmins further developed the earlier Vedic traditions in the *Brahmanas*, prose commentaries on the Vedas. The *Aranyakas* (Books of the Forest) foreshadowed later trends toward a mystical ascetic religious life.

Hebrew literature flourished in the tenth century with the composition of the mystical *Song of Songs*, a poetic drama full of lyrical beauty celebrating fantasy and love. It is attributed in the Bible to Solomon, king of Israel, but its origins may be even older.

The Trojan cycle of ballads, which Homer would immortalize in his *Iliad* and *Odyssey*, had probably begun to evolve in the 10th century although they may not have been written down. The cycle told of the 12th-century war between Greece and Troy, the wrath of Achilles, and the wanderings of another Greek hero, Odysseus.

The Moabite Stone, or Mesha Stele, was erected at Dibon *c.*850 BC by King Mesha, who composed the inscription on it to commemorate his successful revolt against Israel in the ancient land of the Moabites. It approximates Hebrew, but the script is the Phoenician one from which the Greeks derived the alphabet.

The Upanishads in India summed up much of the wisdom of earlier Hindu scriptural writing and expressed it in the form of a dialogue between teacher and pupil that would provide the basis for the major philosophical branches of Hinduism. The dialogues bring out the essential unity of Brahman (god) and Atman (soul).

The Iliad and **Odyssey,** Greek poems of 24 books each, belong in style to the 8th century BC, but little is known of their authorship. They combine ancient legends with a vivid evocation of scene and event and masterly delineation of character. Their literary magic is generally attributed to a single poet, Homer, who may have lived in Asia Minor.

The first surviving Greek inscription, the Dipylon vase from Athens, is dated *c.*710: "Who now of all dancers performs most gracefully, he shall receive this."
Hesiod, *c.*750–700 BC, a didactic poet from Boeotia, wrote the *Theogony* and *Works and Days*, providing indispensable information on Greek myths, religion, and agriculture.

The Scandinavian Iron Age developed a high level of metal craftsmanship in grave goods. The most outstanding example is the Sun Chariot from Trundholm, Denmark, *c.*1000. It shows a horse and six-wheeled chariot, with a bronze-gilt solar disk.

The first Temple of Jerusalem was completed *c.*950. Built by Phoenician craftsmen under the direction of King Solomon, it was based on Canaanite and Phoenician models. The main building, decorated with massive carvings in ivory, wood, and gold, was flanked by three-story chambers.
The "Megaron B" temple at **Thermon,** one of the earliest major examples of Greek architecture, has the characteristic form of later Greek temples.

Nimrud in Mesopotamia was restored and enlarged by Ashurnasirpal II, 883–859, who built at least two temples and four palaces, decorated with winged human-headed lions in carved stone and reliefs showing the king himself. Ivories from the northwest palace show the widespread assimilation of Phoenician craftsmanship.

The Black Obelisk, known as "Jehu's stele," describes the campaigns of Shalmaneser III, 859–825. The frieze shows King Jehu of Israel making obeisance to him—the earliest representation of a Semite in traditional costume.

Pottery in Greece flourished between *c.*900 and 750 BC, decorated with a wide range of human and animal figures, which prefigured the classical narrative style. Bronze work, and the small terra cotta figurines made for the new sanctuaries at Delphi and Olympia, herald the emergence of Greek sculpture. New motifs such as floral designs were included in geometric pottery decoration as a result of increased trade with Cyprus and the Near East.

The art of the late Assyrian Empire flowered under **Tiglath-Pileser III,** *r.*744–727, and **Sargon II,** *r.*722–705. Tiglath-Pileser's palace at **Nimrud** was decorated with reliefs in the epic tradition, but freer in style. Sargon's palace at **Khorsabad** was a sophisticated structure covering over 20 acres (9 hectares) with its own drainage system. Man-headed winged bulls guarded the entrance and 7-ft (2-m) reliefs depicted members of the court.

Bronze trumpets or lurs date from about 1000 BC. Found in Danish bogs, lurs were made with conical bores ending in flat disks. They are usually found in pairs.

Psalms were the central feature of the music of the first temple of the Jews. Responses between priests and congregation established the pattern of many later forms of Christian music.

Lyres and harps were used to accompany Jewish temple songs. Trumpets and cymbals were played to signal special moments or interludes in the liturgy.

The lyre was popular in Greece. A large form with from three to twelve strings called the kithara was plucked with a plectrum while the player's other hand dampened the strings' vibrations.

Professional bards in Greece recited or sang epic poems to their own lyre accompaniment, while shepherds played pan-pipes made of reeds of various lengths bound together side by side.

Assyrian military technology, 1000–700 BC, was stimulated by constant warfare. The Assyrian Ashurnasipal II was the first to use cavalry units to any extent in addition to infantry and war chariots. The Assyrians also developed siege weapons for attacking the mud walls of enemy cities. Battering rams that rocked to and fro were not very successful, but iron-shod beams, which were raised and allowed to fall, were extremely effective.

Chinese chariots had wheels with many more spokes than the chariots of the Middle East, but otherwise differed very little from them. The Chinese, however, who had acquired chariot design from nomads who lived to their west, still placed the axle centrally beneath the platform.

Iron mines in Italy were worked from *c.*900 BC, and would later be taken over by the Etruscans.
Peruvian gold ornaments of the Chavín culture date from *c.*900. Goldsmiths used stone hammers to beat gold into stone molds, probably without attempting to melt it.

Leather manufacture originated with the animal skins taken by men of the Old Stone Age. Leather technology, however, developed slowly and few of the dates are certain. The Egyptians treated hides with fat, to increase durability, before 1500 BC. Tanning, or soaking the hides in a solution containing vegetable material to make leather, probably evolved much later, as did a method for hardening leather with alum, but all these techniques were in use *c.*800 BC.

Trade in glassware became widespread, extending as far as the Atlantic coasts. Simple glass technology, such as the manufacture of glass beads, followed this trade and was practiced in Britain *c.*800 BC.
Crops grown in the Middle East included wheat, barley, flax, and later, cotton.

Siege towers were a later development of Assyrian military inventiveness. These wooden towers on wheels, often armorplated and fitted with battering-rams, were used to attack the walls of besieged cities. Although clumsy, they were undoubtedly effective; defenders could retaliate only with spears and arrows, grappling at the battering-rams with iron hooks.
Biremes, ships with double banks of oars, are pictured in Assyrian reliefs of 700 BC.

The birth of philosophy 700–300 BC

Principal events

Middle Eastern civilization entered a phase of turmoil between the 6th and 4th centuries BC with a series of short-lived empires established by the Babylonians, Persians, and Greeks, while the Magadha Empire grew up in India.

The most striking feature of the period, however, was cultural—a massive shift toward the systematization of thought that took place in literature and the sciences and was manifested above all in the founding of many of the Eastern religions and the principal schools of Western philosophy.

Athens, where culture and democracy flourished in the context of a prosperous city-state, stood at the center of the first brilliant flowering of European urban culture, and although her power even in Greece was limited by Spartan and Macedonian militarism, the conquests of Alexander would carry this culture throughout the Middle East.

700–660 BC

Sennacherib II, 704–681, of Assyria made Nineveh his capital after destroying the rebellious Babylon. Esarhaddon, his successor, *c.*681–669, rebuilt Babylon and attacked Egypt, captured Memphis, and drove the pharaohs back to Kush in 671. **Tyrants** (non-hereditary rulers, mostly of the merchant classes) appeared in many Greek cities and in Athens in 683 BC, assuring growth and prosperity. **Twelve Etruscan cities** flourished in central Italy *c.*675.

660–620 BC

Sparta became dominant in the Peloponnese after subduing the Messenians in 630 BC. After the reign of **Ashurbanipal,** 668–*c.*627 BC, a time of military activity in Egypt and artistic splendor, Assyrian fortunes declined suddenly. The **Chaldean Nabopolassar** led a successful revolt in Babylon. **Josiah,** 640–609, inspired a successful political and religious uprising in Judah, and **Phoenicia** won its independence from Assyria in 627 BC.

620–580 BC

Nabopolassar of Babylon destroyed Assyria with Median help in 612 and took Nineveh. **Sparta** introduced barrack life and military education *c.*610. **Nebuchadrezzar II,** *r.*604–562, built a Babylonian empire in Syria-Palestine, taking the Jews to Babylon as prisoners in 586 BC, and ending Pharaoh Neko II's imperial aspirations. **Solon,** who became the archon in Athens in 594, smoothed tensions between aristocrats and merchants.

580–540 BC

Babylonian power waned after Nebuchadrezzar died in 562. **The Peloponnesian League** was founded on Spartan military strength in 560 BC. **Pisistratus,** *c.*600–527, the tyrant, secured Athenian authority in eastern Greece. **Cyrus the Great,** *d.*529, founded the Persian Empire, defeating Media in 549 and Ionia in 547. **The Kushite kingdom** reached southward to Khartoum *c.*550. **The Magadha Empire** was established in Bihar *c.*542.

The Americas

With the sedentary life firmly rooted in most of North and South America, cultural regionalism developed. While Olmec culture flourished in Mexico, another important civilization was forming in the Mayan highlands. Religion played an increasingly prominent role, with more sophisticated beliefs and practices.

Cassava was the major food crop cultivated by the Saladero people, early farmers and potters who lived in the valley of the Orinoco River in Venezuela.

The Olmec culture, at its height *c.*1200–400 BC, was the earliest Mesoamerican civilization to create a primitive state with a political or religious leader.

Archeologists estimate that the Zapotec peoples of Mexico began to level off the top of a mountain where they would build the city of Monte Albán.

Worship of the jaguar god, revered by the Olmecs and the Chavin cultists, had spread to the San Agustín Culture of Colombia.

Monte Albán, sculpture

Greek black-figure vase decoration

Ming portrait of Confucius

The Parthenon on the Acropolis, Athens

Religion and philosophy

Within a remarkably short time, a number of diverse and highly sophisticated religions of world significance arose. Buddhism and Jainism in India marked a break with Brahmanic ritualism. Zoroastrianism in Persia established religious themes that were to spread westward with far-reaching consequences. In China, both Taoism and Confucianism established the doctrine of harmony as their central idea.

The flowering of Greek philosophy is one of the most extraordinary episodes in the history of thought. A questioning of accepted ideas, including the tenets of religion, and an emphasis on rational argument resulted in Greek thinkers from Thales to Aristotle raising most of the issues that have occupied Western philosophy up to the present time. Central concerns were the nature of reality and the basis of virtuous conduct.

Thales of Miletus, *c.*640–*c.*546, believed that the essence of all matter was water. His attempt to find simple material causes was seminal to Greek thought.

Taoism is thought to stem from the work of the Chinese philosopher **Lao Tze,** *c.*604–*c.*531, to whom the *Tao-te Ching* anthology is attributed. The Tao is an imperceptible state of void and was exemplified in the childlike innocence in man. **Zoroastrianism,** proclaimed in Iran by **Zoroaster,** *c.*600 proposed a dualistic cosmology of the spirit of good and evil, between which man is free to choose. The Zoroastrian scriptures were the *Avesta*.

Jainism was developed in India by **Mahavira,** *c.*560–*c.*468, a member of the Kshatriya noble caste. It emphasized self-denial and non-violence, and rejected **Vedic** authority in reaction to the dominance of Brahmin ritual. Within the mainstream of Vedism **the first Upanishads** were written epitomizing the doctrines of samsara (rebirth) and karma (inescapable consequences). Unity with the cosmos through contemplation provided the only escape from suffering.

Literature

From religious mysteries and epic poems, literature began to develop secular forms of many kinds. The most varied and accomplished writing emerged in Athens where theater became a medium into which most poetic energy flowed, whether tragic, epic, comic, or lyrical. Poetry flourished, and prose writing developed in the fields of history and philosophy, although Plato's use of the Socratic dialogue indicated the all-pervading influence of the dramatic form.

Systematization of previous literary developments occurred in all the major cultures of the world. For the first time, the Gilgamesh epic was collected, as were the Indian epics, while in China the teaching of philosophers was written down.

Etruscan inscriptions, mostly liturgical or funerary, dating from *c.*700 BC, have been found at Magliano, Italy, and elsewhere—indicating the existence of a literature that has been lost. The language is incomprehensible and of unknown origin but the alphabet is Greek-based and led to the development of a Latin alphabet.

A library of 20,000 tablets was established at Nineveh by **King Ashurbanipal,** *r.*668–*c.*627, who collected Assyrian, Babylonian, and Sumerian writings, among them the *Gilgamesh* epic and religious and scientific works.

In the Bhagavad Gita, or Song of the Beloved, Hindu sacred literature took the form of poetic dialogues on the soul. In Greece, the period saw the rise of **burlesque plays** with religious themes in which the chorus consisted of satyrs. The **earliest existing Latin inscriptions**—on the Black Stone of the Roman forum and the Manios clasp—date *c.*600.

The poetic style of **Sappho** was echoed in the simpler lyrics of **Anacreon of Teos,** *c.*570–485, but he had no successors in Greece where literature served a public function linked to religion. **Aesop,** a slave from Thrace who died *c.*564, wrote popular animal fables to illustrate moral points, some possibly derived from Oriental sources.

Art and architecture

Although the Assyrians and Babylonians produced much striking monumental art in the 7th and 6th centuries BC the most significant artistic development of the period was the evolution of Classical Greek art in which a new realism superseded the stylization common to the ancient Near Eastern art.

A narrative style grew up in pottery decoration drawn with a fluid hand in black- and red-figure work. In sculpture the traditional kouros figure gradually took on a more relaxed pose, and a representational style developed—the single most vital step in the emergence of European art.

Greek architects, especially in Athens, designed simple but subtle buildings using austerely ornamented lintels and columns as their basic units and counteracting the effects of foreshortening with the help of mathematics.

Assyrian wall reliefs of the 7th century were incised on stone instead of molded, giving finer detail to scenes of savage conquest of the expanding Assyrian Empire. **Saite artists** of the early 7th century attempted to revive the brilliance of the Old Kingdom. Sculpture and bas-relief were elegant, and the new use of hard stone made for a studied and severe style.

Olmec sculptures at La Venta between 800 and 400 BC produced basalt monuments carved in elaborate relief, depicting scenes of historical and contemporary events. **A gold scabbard from Litoi,** *c.*650, showed typical Scythian style of ceremonial weaponry characterized by the designs combining different animals to make a mythical beast.

Babylon was rebuilt by Nebuchadrezzar between 604–562. The decorated glazed bricks of the **Ishtar Gate,** and the famous **Hanging Gardens** were intended to outshine the brilliance of Assyrian palaces. **Etruscan tomb frescoes** began in the mid-6th century. Those at Tarquinii depicted scenes from the life of the dead man in a realistic style.

Attic black-figure pottery achieved technical excellence by the mid-6th century and came to predominate in Greek vase painting. Mythological scenes were depicted in black glaze against a red background. Pottery after 540 was dominated by the red-figure technique.

Music

Music theories developed in the East and the West, and especially in China, as complex scales were devised, but little is known of the style of music produced at this period. The seven-note scale, later to become the basis of most European music, entered Europe from the Near East through Greece c.550 BC. In India, the basis for the raga was evolving.

Terpander, the Greek composer, *fl. c.*675 BC, was a founder of classical Greek music. He is sometimes credited with having completed the octave.

Scale theory was developed in Babylonia in the Chaldean period (626–538 BC). Mathematical division of strings produced a four-note scale, which was associated with the four seasons.

The kettledrum appears as a bowl-shaped drum beaten with sticks in a relief dating from *c.*600 BC found in Persia.

Pythagoras introduced Chaldean scale theory into Greece *c.*550 BC. He based a system of tuning on the fact that a string stopped at two-thirds its length sounds a fifth higher than its full length.

Science and technology

By the 5th century BC the Athenian Greeks had established a rich and complex pattern of manufactures, particularly in pottery and textiles with trading contacts from the Black Sea to the Rhine. They did not introduce many advances in technology, which they preferred to regard as the preserve of slaves. Their theoretical writings, however, have provided the basis for much Western European science even where, as in the case of Aristotle, this consisted of the systematization of earlier thinking or the elaboration of untested hypotheses.

Greek mathematics began in the 6th century with Pythagoras, but by the 4th century the focus of the science had moved to Alexandria where scientific study flourished.

In China, where military technology may have received a spur from constant attacks by nomadic ivaders, the crossbow was invented and a way was found to melt and cast iron.

Greek silver coins, stamped with an owl design, came into usage in 700 BC. Early coins from Lydia, in Asia Minor, were made of electrum, a gold and silver alloy. Coinage was developed because the barter system was inadequate to deal with the growing trade between the countries of the Middle East and the Mediterranean. **Greek silver mines** at Laurion were heavily worked by the Athenians, using prisoner or slave labor.

Central European technology thrived at Halstatt, Austria, with the mining, manufacture, and export of iron and salt.

Thales, *fl.*580 BC, "Father of Greek philosophy," made detailed observations on methods of triangulation navigation. **Anaximander,** *fl.*6th century, who believed the Earth to be cylindrical in shape, is thought to have produced the first map of the known world. The **potter's kick wheel** may have been invented at this time. **Indian mathematical texts** of the 6th-3rd centuries BC deal with simple geometric forms, and calculations involving large numbers.

Pythagoras, *c.*580–500 BC, and his school studied medicine, astronomy, and musical scales and mathematics, particularly the theory of numbers. It is debatable whether Pythagoras invented the theorem that bears his name. **Anacharsis the Scythian** and **Theodorus of Samos,** *fl.*6th century, are thought to have developed the key, a metal anchor with grappling flukes, a lathe, and an improved bellows.

540–500 BC

Cyrus took Babylon in 538 BC, thereby assisting the Jews' return to Jerusalem, and Egypt in 525 BC. Darius I, c.558–486, benevolently ruled a centralized empire from the Indus to the Mediterranean, divided into regions (satrapies) for administrative purposes.
Rome expelled her Etruscan kings in 509 BC and became an independent republic.
Cleisthenes reorganized Athenian local government and laid the basis for democracy in 508.

500–460 BC

Athens checked Darius' invasion of Greece at Marathon, 490. A second Persian invasion by **Xerxes**, c.519–465, in 480 was stopped by the Spartans at Thermopylae and the Athenians at Salamis.
The Delian League was founded in 478 BC, reflecting Athenian ascendancy in eastern Greece.
Celtic culture spread in Europe c.500 BC.
The Greeks defeated Carthage, 480, and the Etruscans, 474, and thus won control of the sea.

460–420 BC

Athenian power and culture was at its height under Pericles, c.490–429, who assisted Egypt in an abortive revolt against the declining Persian Empire, 456–454.
Rome expanded into central Italy and the plebeians won new constitutional rights 445 BC.
Buddhism became popular in India, especially among the merchant classes.
The Peloponnesian War between Athens and Sparta began in 431.

420–380 BC

The Peloponnesian War ended in naval defeat for Athens at Aegospotami in 405 BC.
The Romans captured Veii, an Etruscan city, in 396, but Rome herself was sacked by marauding Celts in 390 BC, who also hastened the Etruscan decline.
Socrates, c.469–399, was put to death in Athens in 399 BC.
The Chou dynasty in China declined in the long "Warring States period," 475–221.

380–340 BC

Athens defeated Sparta in 371 in alliance with Thebes, which became leader of the opposition to Sparta.
Philip of Macedon, r.359–336, built up his military strength in northern Greece. Many of the Persian satrapies had become semi-autonomous.
The Persian Artaxerxes III, r.359–338, restored royal authority and reestablished Persian rule in Egypt in 343 BC, thus ending the last native pharaoh dynasty.

340–300 BC

Alexander the Great, having assured his authority in Greece, defeated Darius of Persia, d.330, at Issus in 333, and crossed the Indus in 327. He died at Babylon in 323 after turning back to consolidate his authority. His empire had fallen apart by 306.
Chandragupta, r.c.321–c.297 created the Mâurya dynasty at Magadha in India.
Rome had effectively destroyed Etruscan power by 300 BC.

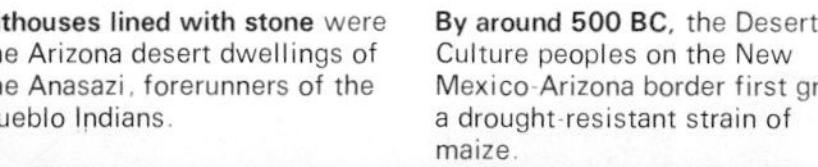

Pithouses lined with stone were the Arizona desert dwellings of the Anasazi, forerunners of the Pueblo Indians.

By around 500 BC, the Desert Culture peoples on the New Mexico-Arizona border first grew a drought-resistant strain of maize.

Mayan civilization was in its formative stages in Central America. Tikal, in Guatemala, later the most important Mayan center, was first inhabited.

Indians in Kentucky were exploring the inner passageways of Mammoth Cave, searching for the gypsum crystals that were plentiful there.

Permanent settlement began at Marksville, on Old River Lake in Louisiana, and continued until the arrival of the white man.

The Marpole peoples of the Fraser Delta area in British Columbia were engaged in heavy wood-working, building plank houses and dugout canoes c.300.

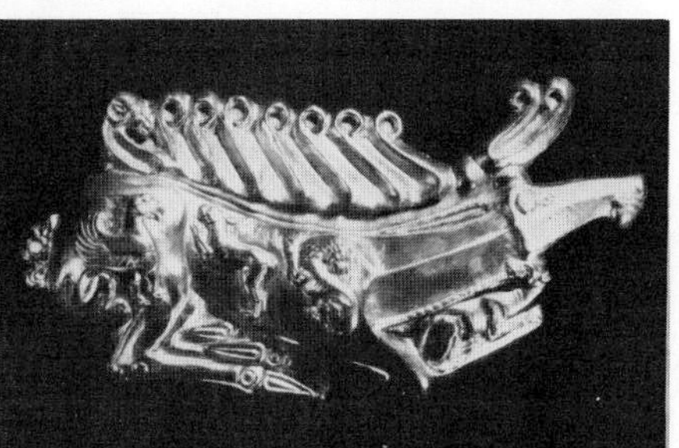

Scythian gold plaque, 5th c.

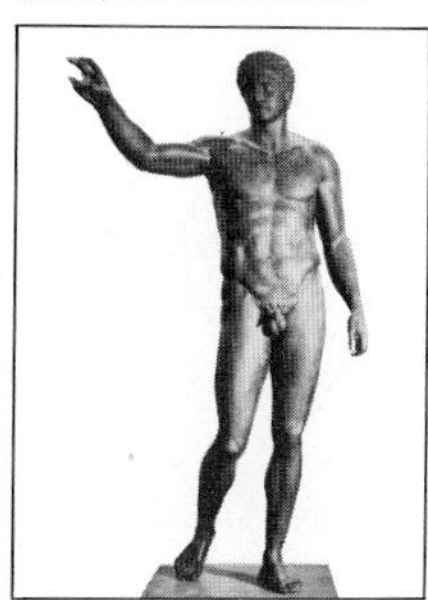

Classical Greek sculpture

18th c. portrait of Aristotle

Alexander the Great in battle

Confucius, or Kung-Fu-tzu, 551–479, taught social ethics in China. His doctrine was taken up by the rulers and governed the Chinese way of life for over 2,000 years. It embraced elements of traditional Chinese religion and emphasized aristocratic social virtues and conduct harmonious with the heavenly order. It stressed awareness of fate and the decrees of heaven. In Greece **Pythagoras' theory of numbers and music** quickly developed into a mystical cult.

Buddhism was founded in India when **Siddhartha Gautama,** c.563–c.483 BC, began propagating the insights he achieved through long periods of contemplation. He taught that suffering can be avoided only by following an eight-fold path of moral conduct, non-violence, and meditation, leading to a state of perfect enlightenment, nirvana. **Zeno of Elea,** c.495–c.430, a Greek philosopher, originated the dialectic and supported his argument with paradoxes.

The Greek Sophists, led by **Protagoras,** c.485–c.410, were agnostic toward the gods. **Socrates,** c.469–399, argued that no one can possibly do that which he knows to be wrong. He followed this principle to the point of political dissent for which he was tried and condemned to death. In China, **Mo Ti,** c.470–391, taught pacifism and universal love; he also established a dialectical method of argument.

Plato, *fl.*4th century BC, founded the Academy in Athens, where philosophy was taught to young members of the Athenian aristocracy, c.387 BC. He advocated subordination of the individual to the all-powerful republic, and also maintained that phenomena perceived by the senses are merely impure copies of the perfect reality of eternal ideas.

The Cynics in Greece, such as **Diogenes,** c.412–323, believed that happiness needed the repudiation of human values and the adoption of a simple animallike existence. **Aristotle,** 384–322, rejected Plato's idealism, urging a more detailed empirical examination of natural and social phenomena and the doctrine that good consists in individuals achieving the state appropriate to their natures.

Zeno, 334–262, of Citium, founded Stoicism, claiming virtue to be the only good and wealth, illness, and death of no human concern.
Epicurus, 342–270, of Samos, believed pleasure to be the essence of a happy life.
Mencius, 372–289 BC, a Confucian philosopher, saw man as inherently good and urged filial piety.

Classical Greek tragedy began with **Aeschylus,** c.525–456. He developed drama from choral cult songs by introducing dialogue between the actors when tragedy became a regular feature of the spring Dionysiac festivals.
The Boeotian Pindar, c.522–c.440, wrote patriotic poems often celebrating athletic prowess.

Sophocles, c.496–406 BC, and Aeschylus continued the tradition of classical tragedy. In his plays like *Oedipus Rex* Sophocles retained a functional chorus but shifted the center of interest to the actors.
During the time of Confucius, 551–479, the five classic *Ching* books reached their final form.

Euripides, c.480–406 BC, last of the great writers of tragedy, dealt with social issues as well as myths, reflecting a growing humanism in Greek drama.
Herodotus, c.485–425, emerged as the first major historian with a lively account of the Persian Wars, while **Thucydides,** 460–400 BC, took a more rigorous approach to the history of the Peloponnesian War.

Aristophanes, c.445–388, was the best comic dramatist and topical satirist at the Athenian drama contests. His *Lysistrata*, 411 BC, deals with a strike by women aiming to end war.
The philosopher Socrates, 469–399, invented the cross-questioning (dialogue) teaching method, but his skeptical approach to religion brought him a death sentence.

Plato, c.427–347, continued the Socratic method in a masterly series of prose dialogues, including the *Republic*, which achieve the quality of a drama of ideas. His pupil **Aristotle,** 384–322 BC, made important contributions to literary criticism, although his books are mainly lecture notes, in *Rhetoric* and *Poetics*, which analyzed classical drama.

The New Comedy flourished in Athens from c.330. This was a comedy of manners, using stock characterization and avoiding touchy subjects. **Menander,** c.342–292 BC, was its best exponent but was less popular than **Philemon,** c.365–265 BC. Greek prose style was meanwhile brought to its zenith by the Athenian orator Demosthenes, c.382–322 BC.

Painted grey ware of the urban Ganges cultures, c.500, was a hard wheel-turned pottery decorated with linear and dotted patterns.
Bronze and ceramic vessels and ornamental and ritual jade carvings were the primary Chinese art forms under the Chou dynasty, 1000–200 BC.
Cyrus' funerary monument at Parsagadae, 529 BC, anticipated Achaemenid success with its artistic traditions of Greece and Mesopotamia.

Early Celtic bronze wine flagons from the Moselle region, c.460 BC, show how classical and eastern elements were assimilated to produce a new and purely Celtic art form. The human mask was a typical motif.
The Palace of Darius, 522–486, records Persia's victory over the Median kings in the bas-relief friezes on the gigantic columns.

Greek art became increasingly independent of foreign influences and more humanistic in style, reaching its High Classical period between 450 and 400. The "Cretan boy," c.450, from the Acropolis showed a relaxation of the 6th-century kouros pose. Doric architecture became less severe in style. The **Parthenon,** 447–432, built entirely of marble, was the least conventional of this style.

The Greek Late Classical period was between 400 and 323. The more complex Ionic capitals superseded the Doric style, with the richly ornate designs of the **Erectheum** begun c.420. A new naturalism dominated sculpture, as seen with the transformation of the archaic kore in the figure of "Victory" from Olympia c.420.

Idealized grace and beauty was characteristic of Late Classical Greek sculpture. The sensual possibilities of carved marble were explored by **Praxiteles** in "Hermes with young Dionysus," 350, at Olympia. The nude female form was introduced, and Praxiteles' "Aphrodite from Cnidus," 350, initiated a feminine ideal of narrow shoulders and broad hips.

Corinthian columns were first used on the exterior of Greek architecture with the monument at Athens, built c.335 to celebrate a victory.
La Tène art from a 4th-century grave at Waldagesheim shows how classical motifs decorating neck torques and bracelets had superseded earlier Celtic styles.
The Appian Way between Rome and Capua was begun c.312.

The ancient Greeks developed modes (patterns of sound in descending order, a basis for tunes) with distinct moods, and named them after Greek tribes, such as the Lydian and Phrygian.

The rise of drama in Greece linked dance, music, and poetry. The chorus performed in an area called the orchestra in front of the stage, after which the modern orchestra is named.

A Chinese text showed how the chromatic scale (of 12 half tones) can be derived from the cycle of fifths, but in practice they used it only to transpose pentatonic scales into "keys."

The Ramayana, a book of Hindu myths, recorded nine basic moods associated with scales in Indian music c.400 BC. Similar to Greek modes, this music anticipated the raga.

Alexander the Great's invasion of India brought with it new instruments and a developed theory. The introduction of the lute c.300 BC and new theories affected Indian music deeply.

Iron welding, by hammering the red-hot metal, is associated with the name of Glaukos of Chios. Before his time iron sections were joined by elaborate lappings and flanges.
Heraclitus, c.540–c.480, held that fire is the fundamental principle of the universe.

Athenian culture, reflected in the volume and variety of their trade and industry, was well advanced, producing large quantities of metals, oil, and cloth. Pottery, too, was of the highest quality in design and manufacture and was in great demand abroad.
Anaxagoras, c.500–c.428, who came to Athens from Ionia in c.480, gave the first scientific explanations of celestial events, especially eclipses. He influenced much of Aristotle's scientific work.

Democritus, c.460–370, held the theory that matter was composed of atoms.
Quarries on Mount Pentelicon provided the Athenians with fine milky-white marble, with which they built the Parthenon.
Hippocrates of Cos, c.460–c.377, called the Father of Medicine, explained mind and body conditions in terms of "humors," glandular secretions whose imbalance caused disease. He emphasized dietary and hygienic factors in the maintenance of good health.

Chinese cast iron appeared c.400 BC. The Chinese, unlike early Western ironsmiths, were able to melt iron to cast it, helped by the high phosphorous content of their iron, which lowered the melting-point; however, it also made the iron brittle. Two centuries passed before the Chinese could produce a satisfactory cast iron.

Aristotle systematized knowledge in the realm of science, logic, politics, and ethics. His scientific thinking, although often merely speculative, was enormously influential. For example, his belief that heavenly bodies move in perfect circles governed Western thinking until the 17th century AD.
Eudoxus, c.408–355 BC, studied mathematical proportions and developed a method of successive addition to determine irregular areas; this theory was the forerunner of calculus.

The elements of Aristotle, **earth, air, water, and fire,** in fact proposed by earlier Greeks, represent an early attempt to systematize nature. These elements could be used to produce each other; for example, smoke (air) and ash (earth) could be made by burning wood (fire).
Epicurus, 342–270, advanced an atomic theory similar to that of Democritus.

Rome conquers the West 300 BC – AD 100

Principal events

Despite the constant political unrest that followed Alexander's fall, a cosmopolitan Hellenistic culture spread throughout the Middle East. This was absorbed by Rome, which now emerged as a great power, creating eight provinces by 146 BC, including Macedonia and Spain. Conquest, however, brought with it chronic social conflict in Italy, which finally helped to destroy the Roman Republic and led to the establishment of the empire in 28–27 BC, a constitutional solution that left the problems of expansion untouched.

By AD 100 the empire stretched from Egypt to Britain, bringing to Rome new manpower, art forms, and the many religious cults it incorporated, among them Christianity.

In the East Buddhism and Confucianism grew influential; the former spread by Ashoka in southern India, the latter becoming an integral part of society in China where it would remain so for 2,000 years.

300–260 BC

Alexander's empire had broken into four parts by 297 BC: the Hellenistic kingdoms of Macedonia and Thrace, the Seleucid dynasty in Syria, and the Ptolemaic in Egypt (whose invasion of Palestine in 301 BC revived old tensions with Syria). **Rome** gained control of southern Italy and with the defeat of Tarentum in 272 BC came into conflict with Carthage in Sicily. **Ashoka,** *c.*274– *c.*236 BC, expanded the Mauryan Empire and promulgated Buddhist principles.

260–220 BC

In the first Punic War, 264–241, Rome built her first fleet, took Sicily and the Lipan Islands, and defeated Carthage, which expanded into Spain. Conflict continued between the flourishing **Hellenistic kingdoms. Ptolemy II,** *r.*285–246, extended Alexandria in Egypt. **Bactria** left the Seleucid kingdom, and developed a combination of Greek and Buddhist social philosophy, *c.*250.

220–180 BC

In the **second Punic War,** 218–210 BC, **Hannibal,** 247–183, invaded Italy across the Alps in 218 but retreated after Roman aggression in Spain *c.*206. His alliance with Macedon, 215, involved Rome in eastern Mediterranean politics. **The Roman nobility** took control of the wealth from the new provinces while smallholders suffered from military service in the new standing army. **Huang-Ti,** *r.*221–210, completed the Great Wall of China in 214.

180–140 BC

Rome invaded and defeated Macedon, and after further unrest annexed Greece in 147. **Carthage** was totally destroyed by a Roman army in the third Punic War, 149–146. **The Arsacid dynasty** ruled in Parthia, stretching from the Euphrates to the Indus *c.*150. Under **Menander,** *r.*155–130, the Indo-Greek kingdoms reached over much of northern India. **The Han dynasty** in China consolidated imperial authority.

The Americas

Increased population brought urbanization and cultural development in both North and South America. Agriculture increased and became more efficient with the introduction of such methodology as fertilization, irrigation, and terracing. Metallurgy, weaving, and pottery-making advanced.

The Zapotecs, who were basically peaceful, probably had an army of some kind at Monte Alban, which was strategically located for defense.

The Chavin culture, which had influenced the architecture, ceramics, and textiles of most of Peru since its beginning *c.*900 BC, was disappearing.

The Nazca People who inhabited Peru's south coast excelled at pottery, weaving, and the making of textiles.

Pok-ta-pok, the Mayan game played by heavily padded contestants, featured a rubber ball. Most Mayan cities had the I-shaped courts.

Roman bust of Hannibal

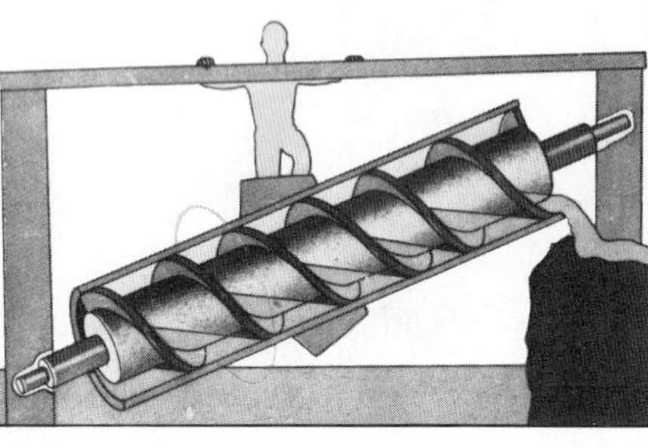
Archimedean screw

Mayan ball court

The Aphrodite of Melos

Religion and philosophy

Christianity grew from being one of several Jewish nationalist sects into a more universally significant religion, as Paul spread it throughout the Roman Empire and introduced Hellenic ideas. The Christian emphasis on the individual conscience and on love brought persecution in Rome where religion was primarily a public or political concern.

In India a proliferation of Hindu sects provided more popular forms of worship than the traditional Brahminical cult, and important additions to the sacred literature expressed further compromises with the everyday needs of worshipers.

New schools of thought grew up in China, while Confucianism became adopted as the official state religion under the Han dynasty c.140 BC.

The Yin-Yang school of Chinese philosophy and cosmology, the leading exponent of which was **Tsou Yen,** 340– *c.*260 BC, considered the universe to comprise five elements: metal, wood, water, fire, and earth. The Yin-Yang school thought the universe was governed by the two complementary forces of yin, female and passive, and yang, male and active.

Ashoka, *r. c.*274– *c.*236 BC, made Buddhism the state religion of the Mauryan Empire. **The developing Shinto religion in Japan** had a hierarchy of deities presided over by the sun goddess **Amaterasu** and her descendants, the imperial family. Past heroes became mythological figures and each clan venerated its own deity. **In China Hsun Tzu,** 313–238 BC, taught that human nature was fundamentally evil. Goodness required training.

Mystery religions and Eastern astrology took hold in Rome in response to the stress of the second Punic War, 218–201 BC. Novel gods, such as the Great Mother of Asia Minor, **Cybele,** and **Dionysus** superseded the traditional deities of Greek origin. **The introduction of the Stoic philosophy** to Rome at this time with its emphasis on Fate, encouraged the development of mystical and astrological thought.

Within the Vedic tradition yogic thought was codified by **Patanjali,** *c.*150 BC, into the four volumes of the *yoga sutras,* rules dealing with transcendental trance states and mystical liberation. **Bhakti** (popular devotional cults) emerged as well as cults centered on the gods Vishnu, Shiva, and Krishna. The *Bhagavad Gita* was added to the earlier epic poem of the *Mahabharata,* and in it a new emphasis on salvation through the performance of duty emerged.

Literature

Although Greek literature itself declined, its influence spread first in the wake of Alexander and then through Rome, which built its culture to a large extent on that of Greece.

A Latin literature arose in the third century BC based on Greek models in poetry, drama, and history although under the late republic a number of writers, among them Caesar, Livy, and Vergil, set out to glorify specifically Roman culture and history. The New Testament was written in Greek, still at the end of the first century the lingua franca of the eastern Mediterranean.

The Chinese classical literature flourished, while in India the epics and Buddhist scripture were finalized.

The last classical writer, Ch'u Yuang, 343–277, is traditionally described as the author of the celebrated *Ch'u Elegies,* the most famous of which is the *Heavenly Questions.* **Bucolic and pastoral poetry** by **Theocritus,** *c.*300–260, was imitated by his fellow Greeks **Moschus,** *fl.*150, and **Bion.**

A Latin literature emerged, based largely on Greek poetry, drama, and history. **Naevius,** *c.* 270– *c.*201, was the first Latin epic poet. A freed Greek slave, **Livius Andronicus,** *c.*284– *c.*204, wrote plays and translated the *Odyssey.* **Ennius,** 239–169, historian and playwright, was important for his efforts to adapt to Latin the methods of writers such as Euripides.

The Chinese Classical period came to a dramatic end with the reign of Ts'in, 221–210. He burned many Confucian texts. **Latin drama** emerged with **Plautus,** *c.*225–184, who used Greek meters and plots from the New Comedy. *Miles Gloriosus, c.* 205, was his best play.

The Indian epic Ramayana, with between 20,000 and 40,000 couplets in its various versions, is attributed to the 2nd century BC. It was the forerunner of court poetry and had much influence on literary developments throughout southern Asia. Latin playwright **Terrence,** *c.*190–159, was less popular than Plautus but more influential with works such as *Adelphi.*

Art and architecture

Throughout the Hellenistic world private patronage helped artistic production, and collectors demands were so great that copying and pastiche developed, although many artists explored new ideas. Styles like that of the Pergamon school, marked by a new and masterful handling of emotion, were still for the most part associated with places rather than individuals. The Roman Empire absorbed the art of both the Hellenistic world and Italy. Etruscan iconography was copied, and the basic design for Roman architecture came from Etruscan models. Roman municipal architecture reflected both a strong civic pride and the varied leisure pursuits of Rome's urban elite. Baths, theaters and basilicas, constructed with careful attention to practical requirements, also served to create a dramatic framework for public life. Monuments were erected to commemorate the victories of the late republic and early empire.

The Colossus of Rhodes, one of the Seven Wonders of the ancient world, was a huge bronze representation of the sun god Helios, which was built astride the harbor at Rhodes between 292 and 280 BC.

The Temple of Horus at Edfu in Egypt, begun by **Ptolemy III** in 237, was planned with one main axis, typical of Egyptian temple architecture. **The Hellenistic period** in Greek art, *c.*323–1st century BC, developed the sensuous possibilities of marble sculpture. The naturalistic poses of the bronze "Eros" from Tunisia and the "Sleeping Hermaphrodite" are typical of three-dimensional realism of 3rd-century Greek sculpture.

Town planning played an important role in Greek architecture. The chaotic market places of Ephesus and Miletus were replaced by public squares.

The "Venus de Milo," *c.*150, was a Pergamene pastiche of preceding sculptural styles. The classical features coldly echoed 5th-century tradition, while the slight twist of the torso accommodated the new taste for multiple view figures. This Hellenistic Aphrodite became the classic source for the Roman models.

Music

Music stagnated in the West under the Roman Empire, but the Jews maintained their vocal tradition from which the Christian Church borrowed heavily later. In the Arab world, music was still a lively art. The progress of music in the East had little influence on Western musicians, but Western incursions affected Eastern music to some degree.

The Indian vina, from which the sitar later developed, was a lute-like plucked instrument thought to have evolved from the instruments carried by Alexander's invading soldiers.

The first keyboard instrument was the hydraulis, a water-powered organ. It was built by Ctesibius, who was working in Alexandria from 246–221 BC.

The Imperial Court of the Han dynasty in China employed more than 800 musicians to impart a rich panoply of sound to the rituals of state occasions.

A Greek hymn to Apollo composed at Delphi survives from this date.

Science and technology

In the Hellenistic world Alexandria became the focus of scientific work particularly in mapping, astronomy, and mathematics. At the same time Greek technology found its greatest mathematician and experimental physicist in Archimedes.

As Rome expanded it developed the use of concrete and the arch in the building of bridges, roads, and aqueducts, creating a series of civil and military engineering projects that surpassed in scale any since those of the Assyrians and Egyptians. Nevertheless, whether because of the widespread use of slave labor or the stifling effects of a powerful bureaucracy, the Romans, like the Athenians, failed to exploit many inventions of their time.

In China, iron metallurgy improved still further, surpassing any in the West. Chinese astronomy was also active, and the preparation of many useful drugs from plants became a specialty of Chinese medicine.

Euclid wrote his *Elements of Geometry* at Alexandria *c.*300. Alexandria became a center of learning in the century that followed Alexander's death, acquiring a great library and museum. Alexandrian inventions were based on the known principles of the siphon, gear wheel, spring, screw, lever, pulley, cam, and valve. The lighthouse of Pharos, a Greek achievement, stood 250ft (76m) high, with a 35-mile(56-km) beam.

Aristarchus, 310–230 BC, was the first to maintain that the Earth moved around the Sun. **Archimedes of Syracuse,** *c.* 287–212 BC, discovered fundamental laws of floating bodies, made advances in mathematics, and was the greatest of Greek inventors; the "Archimedean" screw is still used in Egypt to raise water. **The crossbow** was invented in the 3rd century BC in China. This weapon had a cocking and trigger mechanism similar to that of children's toys today.

A map of the world produced by Eratosthenes, *c.*276– *c.*194, a librarian at Alexandria in the 3rd century BC, was a great improvement on its predecessors. He calculated the diameter of the Earth with great accuracy, and did work in number theory. **Glass-blowing** spread to Alexandria from Syria via the Romans and for two centuries was the most active of the technologies. Larger vessels and dishes were now made, by blowing the molten glass at the end of an iron blowpipe.

A piston bellows with a double action was among Chinese inventions of the 2nd century BC. It provided a regular, steady air draft for the production of higher quality cast iron.

140–100 BC

Han emperor, Wu Ti, r.140–87, established Confucianism as the basis of Chinese civil administration, 136 BC. **The Gracchus brothers** proposed radical land reform to relieve Roman unemployment and poverty 133 BC. Gaius Gracchus, 157–86, introduced state control of grain imports and allowed landless men into the army in 112. **The Senate** feared the destruction of the constitution and the nobility's power and opposed these measures.

100–60 BC

After Marius' death in 86, **Sulla,** 138–78, rescinded his reforms. **Cicero,** 106–43, prosecuted Verres, *d.*43, for corruption while he was governor of Sicily in 70, and denounced Catiline's attempt to gain a consulship by force in 63 BC, defending the constitutional basis of the republic, which depended upon no one man gaining supreme power. **Pompey,** 106–48, and **Julius Caesar,** 100–44, rose to power after Pompey's victories had led to the annexation of Syria.

60–20 BC

The Han dynasty in China, 206 BC–AD 220, expanded into central Asia *c.*60 BC. **Julius Caesar** subdued Gaul 58–51 BC, and after defeating Pompey became "dictator" in 45. Civil war followed his assassination in 44 by a pro-senatorial conspiracy. **Octavian (Augustus),** 63 BC–AD 14, took imperial authority, 27 BC, to centralize power and prevent the unrest from recurring. **Egypt** became a Roman province in 30 BC.

20 BC–AD 20

Augustus strengthened the Roman Empire in the north and east and brought peace to Rome. **Tiberius,** *r.*AD 14–37, did the same, although imperial power became increasingly dependent on the approval of the Praetorian Guard (the emperor's bodyguard). **Judea** became a Roman province in AD 6. **The Kushite kingdom** in Nubia was in decline *c.*AD 10. **Mexican lake houses** were built.

AD 20–60

Tiberius and Claudius, *r.*AD 41–54, expanded the empire, instituted social reforms, and consolidated imperial power, although the danger of palace revolutions increased. **Jesus of Nazareth** was crucified in Jerusalem *c.*AD 30. The **Christian cult** was taken to Asia Minor, Greece, and Rome by Paul, *fl.*1st century AD. **Buddhism** was accepted as the official religion of China by **Emperor Ming,** *r.*AD 58–75.

AD 60–100

Nero, *r.*AD 54–68, rebuilt Rome after a fire in AD 64, which was blamed on the Jews and Christians, who were unpopular because they refused to recognize the emperor's divinity. **Peter and Paul** were executed in the ensuing persecution *c.*64. **Vespasian,** *r.*AD 69–79, became emperor after a civil war that followed Nero's death. **Jewish religious revolt,** 66–70, was defeated by the Romans. **Mongol invaders** brought iron and rice to Japan by AD 100.

The Hopewell culture, which had begun *c.*300 BC in Illinois, was at its height in Ohio. It featured elaborate earthworks and was an extension of the Adena culture.

The origin of the culture at Teotihuacán in Mexico has been dated *c.*100 BC. Teotihuacán grew into the largest ancient city in the Americas.

An Olmec sculpture from Tres Zapotes, Mexico, bears the bar-and-dot date 31 BC, the earliest recorded in the new world, predating Mayan calculations.

A volcano erupted during this period, covering the village of Cuicuilcó, on the southwestern edge of the Valley of Mexico.

The Izapa, a transitional culture in Guatemala between the Olmec and the Mayan, produced a sculpture at El Bául bearing the bar-and-dot date of AD 36.

Pit houses, circular mud-covered dwellings partially sunk in the ground, were built by the Mogollón peoples along the New Mexico-Arizona border.

Julius Caesar

The Great Stupa of Sanchi

Roman civil engineering: the Pont du Gard, Nîmes

Graeco-Roman ballista

Tung Chung Su established Confucianism in China as the state cult *c.*140 BC, combining elements of the Yin-Yang school and Confucianism. He taught that Heaven, Earth, and Man formed a triad that the emperor, ruling by decree of Heaven, must maintain in harmony. This idea was important throughout Chinese imperial history, being associated with the stable order of Chinese society which lasted for 2,000 years.

The Pharisees in Israel opposed the adoption of Hellenistic culture by their conservative Sadducean rulers and were accused of arid formalistic legalism because of their emphasis on the regulation of all aspects of life in accordance with Jewish law. However, they enjoyed the allegiance of much of the population because of their personal austerity and asceticism.

In Rome Marcus Cicero, 106–43 BC, and **Lucius Seneca,** *c.*55 BC–*c.*AD 40, developed an **Eclectic philosophy,** drawing on Platonist, Stoic, Epicurean, and Aristotelian sources. **Titus Lucretius,** *c.*99–55 BC, composed a long poem, *De rerum natura* (On the nature of things), in which he elaborated the Epicurean theory of physical atomism—a doctrine derived from Democritus that the world is composed entirely of microscopic particles.

Jesus Christ was born in Bethlehem in Judea in 4 BC and crucified in Jerusalem *c.*AD 30.

After the Crucifixion, *c.*AD 30, the early Jewish/Christian sect developed a unique emphasis on the resurrection of a Messiah and the imminent transformation of the world at the dawning of a millennium of universal love. **Paul of Tarsus,** *fl.*1st century AD, who saw the death of Jesus as a universal sign reflecting cosmic forces, spread Christian ideals through the Roman Empire. Contact with Hellenic thought turned Christianity into a world religion.

After the death of Paul, AD 64, and the destruction of Jerusalem in AD 70, the **Pauline version of Christianity,** with its more transcendental significance, became completely dominant. A few Christians who still upheld Jewish law became a small sect without links with either synagogue or Gentile Church. The oral tradition of early Christianity was gradually replaced by composed narratives, the earliest of which was probably the Gospel of St Mark.

Fu poetry, influenced by Chu Yuan, was brought to perfection *c.*100 BC. Used mainly for description, it combined elements of prose and poetry in a form that was freer than that of the more personal **sao poetry,** which continued to develop. **Ssu-ma Chien,** *c.*145–86, wrote the first dynastic history of China. His *Historical Record* is notable for its objectivity.

Cicero, 106–43 BC, a politician and philosopher, brought Latin oratory to a peak. His letters are a model of literary style. The Latin poet **Lucretius,** *c.*99–55, gave emotional body to Epicurean philosophy in *De rerum natura.* **Catullus,** 84–54 BC, showed a mastery of technique and lyrical intensity.

Julius Caesar, *c.*100–44 BC, wrote his history *Commentaries on the Gallic War* in a style of exemplary clarity. **Roman history** was idealized in the *Aeneid,* 70–19 BC, by **Vergil** 70–19 BC, second only to Homer as a model for Western poetry. He also wrote fine pastoral poetry, the *Eclogues* and *Georgics.* **Horace,** 65–8 BC, combined elegance with humanity in his *Odes.*

Ovid, 43 BC–AD 17, the supreme Roman poet of love, and one of the most influential of classical writers, developed erotic verse into a major form in his long poem *Metamorphoses.* It was completed in AD 8, the year of Ovid's banishment, partly for his witty but irreverent *Art of Love.* His later poetry is skeptical, often elegaic.

Seneca the Younger, 4 BC–AD 65, made nine melodramatic adaptations of such Greek tragedies as *Oedipus.* They influenced Spanish literature and the revenge tragedies of Jacobean England. A noted orator and philosopher, Seneca exercised power in Rome in AD 54–62 but was finally ordered to commit suicide.

Plutarch, *c.*AD 46–120, the Greek biographer, wrote *Parallel Lives of Illustrious Greeks and Romans,* a work that approached history from the viewpoint of the characters of the men and women who made it. Shakespeare and many other European writers drew from its vivid portraits of life in Rome and Greece.

Roman sculpture at first reproduced and imitated the styles of the past. The "Dying Gaul," *c.*100, was an accurate copy of the Pergamene original. **The steam baths of Stebiae,** *c.*120, were an early example of domed Roman architecture. **The Great Altar of Zeus** at Pergamon was begun *c.*170. The exterior frieze depicts the battle of gods and giants.

Roman arches were used for tenement houses and theaters in the highly populated cities of the 1st century BC. **Silverware** brought to Rome following the sack of Corinth began a new taste for luxury articles in Roman circles. "The Old Republican," a portrait bust *c.*75 BC, captures Roman realism in a grim projection of asceticism and authority.

Wall paintings at the Pompeiian **Villa of Mysteries,** *c.*40 BC, portrayed Dionysiac themes. Roman villas of the 1st century BC increasingly introduced walled gardens and Greek peristyles. The "Augustus" from **Prima Porta,** *c.*20 BC, displays a naturalistic classicism characteristic of Augustan portrait sculpture.

Roman temples derived their typical high podia and deep porches from Etruscan architecture, while the **Maison Carrée** at Nîmes, *c.*16 BC, has colonnades built in imitation of a Greek façade. **Roman bas-reliefs** like that on the **Ara Pacis,** 9 BC, often used a combination of real and mythological figures to evoke contemporary Roman history. **Thermae,** magnificent municipal buildings, were developed at Rome *c.*20 AD.

Roman columns acquired a new function in the support of arches and when used as a free form. The Tuscan and Composite orders developed as more ornate variants of the Doric and Ionic. **Roman villas** of the 1st century AD were often decorated with wall paintings which, like that at the **Villa Albani,** made use of idyllic scenes to evoke the peace of the countryside.

The Arch of Titus, a triumphal arch of the kind developed in the 2nd century BC, portrayed Roman victories in the Judean War, AD 70. **Stupas,** typical Buddhist edifices, derived their dome shape from Vedic tombs. Stupa I at Sanchi, *c.*AD 100, was embellished with a square base, balconies, and ornamental gateways.

Music notation had been devised in China, according to Symaa Chian, 163–85 BC, a chronicler who tells of a music master who wrote down a zither tune.

An Imperial Office of Music was founded in China *c.*100 BC. The office supervised such activities as standardizing pitch and the building and administration of music archives.

Panpipes, rattles, and drums were made by the **Hopewell culture** of American Indians, who developed from the fourth century BC in the Ohio Valley.

Buddhist monks arrived in China *c.*AD 50 from India, bringing with them chants and decorative melodic features that were incorporated into Chinese music of later periods.

Destruction of the Second Temple, AD 70, led to the dispersal of the Jews. To keep their identity, secular music was discouraged and only singing permitted.

Peruvian technology during the last three centuries BC developed the molding of elaborate pottery and metal casting. **Hipparchus,** 190–120 BC, was the greatest Greek astronomer of his time. He estimated the Sun to be millions of miles away, instead of hundreds as previously thought. He also made a catalog of stars.

Only two furnaces, both using charcoal and a draft, could produce iron in a malleable (workable) form in which it could be forged with carbon to produce steel. These were the **Catalan iron furnace** with two bellows and the **two-story shaft furnace.** Neither, however, produced sufficient heat to melt the iron completely. **Lucretius,** *c.* 99–55 BC, a Roman poet, wrote *De rerum natura,* a scientific treatise praising Epicurus and his ideas.

The Julian calendar of 45 BC, introduced under Julius Caesar, took a base year of 365.25 days. It was designed by the astronomer Sosigenes of Alexandria, and was inaccurate by a mere 11 minutes per year. This calendar was not supplanted until the 16th century AD, by which time it was inaccurate by ten days. **Water mills** were a feature of Roman technology as early as the 1st century BC, but were only fully described a century later, by Vitruvius.

Strabo, *b.c.*64 BC, a Greek historian and geographer, wrote on the uses of materials. **A roller bearing** for a cart wheel is another example of sophisticated engineering of the 1st century BC; made entirely from wood, it was found in Denmark but probably made in Germany or France.

Metallurgical developments of the Romans include the manufacture of brass and the amalgamation of mercury with gold in the extraction of gold from its ores. **Roman civil engineering** left an impressive record, including a 3.5-mile(5.6-km) mountain tunnel, many aqueducts, and 53,000m (85,000km) of roads. **The city of imperial Rome** received a million cubic meters of water each day through lead piping, which in turn went to cisterns and centrally heated baths.

Chinese science was very active under the Han dynasty. Astronomers recorded eclipses and observed planetary motions. Mathematicians constructed "magic squares" of numbers that add up to the same answer in any direction and influenced arithmetic and algebra. **Paper** was invented in China *c.*100 AD. Chinese inventions of this time include a camera obscura, and convex and concave mirrors.

Early Christianity AD 100 – 400

Principal events

The Roman Empire reached its greatest extent under Trajan, but further expansion became impossible due largely to pressure from barbarian migrations in the north and east, which brought increased economic and social instability to Rome. Various defensive measures were adopted, such as allying with the barbarians, but Rome remained weak because of the dependence of most emperors on the support of the army. The reign of Theodosius saw the beginning of the close identification of the interests of the Christian Church and the empire in the east.

Cultured and prosperous civilizations arose in India, where the tions arose in India, where the Guptas set up a northern empire and the strong southern Chola kingdom traded with Rome. In Central America the Mayas entered their classic period, while China suffered from instability and lack of central authority.

100–130

Emperor Trajan, *r.*98–117, expanded into Dacia. His heir **Hadrian,** *r.*117–38, pursued an essentially defensive policy, suing for peace in order to limit the eastern boundaries of the empire. He established his personal authority in Rome and traveled widely, consolidating Roman power in Britain while building Hadrian's wall.
The Western Satrap dynasty in Malwa, India, made Ujjain a center of Sanskrit learning.

130–160

Emperor Antonius Pius, *r.*138–61, continued Hadrian's peaceful policies and quelled Senate opposition.
The dispersion of the Jews followed the ruthless suppression of a Zealot revolt in Jerusalem in 135.
Migrating Goths settled on the northern Black Sea coast.
Taoism became popular in China, stimulated by military and social instability during the decline of the **Han dynasty** and the introduction of **Buddhism.**

160–190

Plague brought back by troops returning from the wars with Parthia depopulated the Roman Empire in 166–67.
Marcus Aurelius' reign, 161–80, marked the high point of **Stoicism** as the dominant philosophy, with its emphasis on the empire as a "common weal."
Marcomanni from Bohemia crossed the Danube, 167, and were settled by the Romans in areas depopulated by the plague.
The persecution of Christians in Rome increased *c.*170.

190–220

Praetorian scheming prevented the establishment of a strong emperor, 192–93, until **Severus** *r.*193–211, reformed the army and reinforced provincial administration.
Caracalla, *r.*211–17, expelled the Goths and Alemanni and in 212 bestowed citizenship on most free inhabitants of the empire, a token of Rome's reliance on provincial talent.
The Han dynasty in China fell in 220 and was replaced by three separate kingdoms.

The Americas

By about the time of Christ, peoples throughout the North and South American continents had arrived at a comfortable plateau of living, although it differed from one area to another. Surplus resources were available for the building of ceremonial centers in Mesoamerica and burial mounds in North America.

The 200-ft (60-m) high, 650-ft (195-m) long Pyramid of the Sun, which would dominate the city of Teotihuacán in the Valley of Mexico, was being built.

The Classic Period of Mayan civilization began about this time. Ceremonial centers, which would eventually number in the hundreds, were developing.

Funeral offerings in graves at the Norton Mounds in Michigan were elaborate. Materials imported from great distances indicate vigorous trade.

Although the date of the Great Serpent Mound is unknown, it was probably built before AD 200, when a climate change brought cultural deterioration.

Trajan's column: Romans fighting the Dacians

Late Roman sculpture: "Mithras Slaying the Bull"

Teotihuacán: Pyramid of the Sun

Religion and philosophy

The early Church clarified and developed a sophisticated theology in response to attacks from religions whose origins lay outside the Judeo-Christian tradition, including Gnosticism, Manichaeanism, Montanism, and Mithraism. By 395, Theodosius the Great had finally established Christianity as the religion of the empire but with the barbarian invasions began a long struggle against paganism. Missions were sent out to the Germanic tribes, and those who were converted largely adopted the Arian form of the Christian faith. Under Pope Damasus the Roman see claimed primacy over the five patriarchates of Rome, Constantinople, Antioch, Jerusalem, and Alexandria, basing its claim on the "Petrine" text.

Buddhism began to influence the development of Hinduism in India and similarly affected religion and society in China.

Gnosticism, a diffuse movement based on a variety of religions, some earlier than Christianity, absorbed Christian ideas, giving the Gospels equal weight with Greek and Oriental texts. Many Gnostic sects were proclaimed heretical by the early Church and Gnostic interpretations of the scriptures forced the Church to establish authoritative versions of the Gospels and to consolidate the basis of a universal Church.

The Mahayana school of Buddhism was founded by **Nagarjuna,** *c.*150–*c.*250, in India. This school, often known as "The Great Vehicle," departed from the traditional Hinayana or Theravada, "Little Vehicle," doctrines in holding that laymen as well as monks could achieve nirvana through the intervention of saints. This development resulted from the impact of the Brahmin religion on Buddhism.

Montanus, who appeared in Phrygia *c.*172, preached that prophecy and revelation had not ended with the death of Jesus. This belief and the expectation of the Second Coming of Christ threatened the stability of the Church, and many Montanists were excommunicated *c.*177.
Buddhism reached China in the 1st century AD and began to exert an influence there in the 2nd century, when it received official patronage.

Origen, 185–254, became head of the Christian Catechetical school at Alexandria *c.*212. This was the most famous of the Christian schools and offered a wide curriculum including Greek, philosophy, and science. Origen, a Platonist, furthered the synthesis of the Christian Gospels and Greek philosophy, emphasizing the study of the Bible as essential to a proper understanding of Christianity.

Literature

With the diffusion of Christianity the scriptures began to spread in translation, notably in Latin, although fragments exist of translations into Gothic (mainly from the New Testament) made by Bishop Wulfila. The influence of the Gospels was literary as well as religious, setting the stage for the Christian allegorical treatment of pagan literature that was to dominate European literature until the 17th century. Homer, Vergil, and Ovid were all interpreted in this way. Classical Latin literature petered out after AD 200.

In China, paper (chih) was invented but took nearly a millennium to reach Europe, where papyrus gradually gave way to stitched parchment or vellum.

The Latin satirical tradition had begun with **Lucilius,** *c.*180–102 BC, but culminated with **Juvenal,** *c.*AD 60–127, whose verse *Satires* on folly and Roman corruption profoundly influenced Western satirists. Tacitus, *c.*55–117, like Juvenal, vividly recounted the cruelties of the period up to the death of Domitian in 96, in his *Histories*, 104–09, and *Annals*, 117.

Asvaghosa, *c.*80–150, was the first known poet and dramatist to write in classical Sanskrit. He was a Brahmin convert to Buddhism who wrote two epic poems, *Saundaranada* and *Buddhacarita* (The Life of Buddha), a philosophical work that became the source for later studies of Buddha's life.

The prose romance became a popular literary form in both Latin and Greek. *Satiricon*, a romance of Nero's Rome written by **Petronius** *c.*60, gained popularity during this time.
Elements of science fiction were introduced into a parody of traveler's tales by a Greek writer, **Lucian,** *c.*115–200, living in Syria. His *True History* describes a trip to the moon.

Apuleius, *b. c.*127, wrote the only Latin prose romance that survives in full. His *Metamorphoses*, now known as *The Golden Ass*, relates the hilarious adventures of a man magically transformed into a donkey.

Art and architecture

The Imperial and Hellenistic styles of Rome gradually lost ground, to be replaced in western Europe by the more mysterious and magic art of the Christian period. A recognizable Christian style in art and architecture had developed by the 4th century, by which time the empire was divided into east and west, presaging the lasting division between the Byzantine and Western Christian traditions in art. Into this world of changing imagery the barbarian invaders brought new decorative abilities and tastes, which were also assimilated into the art of Rome.

The Persian culture of the Sassanids and the Indian culture of the Gandhara region were influenced in part by Rome and this influence penetrated China during the late Han period, producing the basis for a recognizable style. Indian art flourished under the Guptas, during whose dynasty the Ajanta cave paintings were done.

The ascending spiral bas-relief narrative on **Trajan's column,** 113, relates and glorifies the emperor's military victories during the Dacian campaign.
The Pantheon, *c.*118, is an architectural realization of the climax of imperial grandeur.
Monumental stone tomb sculpture appeared in China during the Han dynasty, probably due to foreign influence. The tomb of **Ho Ch'u-ping,** *c.*117, includes a figure of a horse trampling a barbarian.

The Temple of Mithras, 2nd century, in London, is a typical architectural design of the period with its small size, basilican plan and central apse. Temples were common throughout the periphery of the empire.

One example of **Roman imperial sculpture** is the bronze equestrian portrait of Emperor Marcus Aurelius, *c.*173, which still dominates the Campidoglio in Rome.
Sculpture from Gandhara in northwest India of the 2nd to 4th centuries exemplifies the meeting point of Greco-Roman and Buddhist canons of beauty. Delicate reliefs depict the life of the Buddha—the first time he is represented figuratively.

Early Christian painting remained stylistically in the tradition of Roman decoration as can be seen in the fresco "The Celestial Refreshment," *c.*200, in the catacomb of St Calixtus in Rome.
The Synagogue of Dura Europus in northern Mesopotamia is decorated with symbolic frescoes on the subject of Ezekiel in the valley of the bones, typical of the art resulting from the development of mystical religions in the Middle East.

Music

Plainsong, a form of religious chant, developed in Europe. St Augustine, 354–430, warned of the "peril of pleasure" in this music, whose austere unaccompanied line would be the basis of later European developments in polyphony (two or more related melodies played together) and harmony (chord progressions). Eastern music, with its sensuous sonorities, reached its peak.

The Chinese zither, adopted by Buddhist monks from *c.*100, brought more instrumental color to their music. Zither players produced sliding runs and delicate harmonic overtones.

Greek modes lived on in the **plainsong chants** of the Christian Church in an adapted form, ascending rather than descending as the Greek modes did.

Buddhism became a vital force in China from *c.*200. Its chants were accompanied by the music of elaborate percussion orchestras of bells, gongs, triangles, drums, and cymbals.

Science and technology

In the Greco-Roman world, there was a decline in science and technology, although a brief revival started in the reign of Constantine the Great. The "occult sciences," astrology and alchemy, were held in great esteem, forming the basis for much technological innovation.

Most Western scientists of the 4th century were engaged in translating, collecting, and commenting on the works of earlier thinkers, rather than making observations or doing experiments of their own.

In China, however, in spite of unsettled times, scientific thought progressed as advances were made in mathematics, astronomy, and medicine, while materials technology remained active and productive.

In Central America Mayan culture began its classic period. This would produce remarkable advances in mathematics and astronomy and massive stone buildings constructed without the aid of metalworking.

Menelaus, a Greek mathematician, *fl.*100, wrote the first work on non-Euclidean geometry.
Hadrian's Wall was begun in Britain *c.*122. It was 73.5 miles (18.3km) long, with many forts.
Surgical instruments were well developed in Rome, as described by Celsus in the 1st century, but no pain-killing drugs were available to sufferers. There is evidence that the **wheelbarrow** was invented in China at the beginning of the 2nd century.

Ptolemy, the Hellenic astronomer and geographer, wrote the *Almagest* *c.*150. This became the "bible" of astronomers for the next 1,400 years, although it contained few new discoveries. Like Hipparchus and other Greek astronomers, Ptolemy accounted for the erratic paths of planets by suggesting that they moved in epicycles (small circles centered on the rim of a planet's orbit). Ptolemy's *Guide to Geography*, which included Africa and Asia, had great subsequent influence.

Galen, *c.*130–*c.*200, a surgeon and philosopher of Alexandria, wrote over 500 works on medical subjects. His experiments on animals led to the science of physiology. Galen's knowledge of the body was influenced by the works of Aristotle and Hippocrates, who believed in vital substances or essences at work in the body. Despite practical knowledge of the circulatory system, he postulated that blood vessels carried the blood to the skin where it was transformed into flesh.

Alchemists of the first two centuries include **Dioscorides of Cilicia,** *fl.c.*60, who described the processes of crystallization, sublimation, and distillation of substances. He also described the use of minerals for medical purposes.
Alchemy, a pseudo-science of obscure origins, sought a philosopher's stone thought capable of changing base metals into gold, and the elixir of life that would preserve youth indefinitely.
The abacus is recorded in use in China *c.*190.

220–250

The murder of **Alexander Severus,** *r.*222–35, instigated a period of military control over the Roman emperor and factional warfare among the troops.
Official persecution of Christians began under **Decius,** *r.*249–51, as the worship of living rulers became proof of loyalty.
The new Sassanid Empire in Persia, founded by **Ardashir I,** *r.*224–41, took Armenia from Rome in 232. **The first written records** in Japan date from *c.*230.

250–280

The Goths took Dacia in 257. A series of capable emperors from Illyria began with **Claudius II "Gothicus,"** *r.*268–70, who defeated the Gothic invasion of the Balkans and settled the Goths in the Danubian provinces. In 271, **Aurelian,** *r.*270–75, drove out the Alemanni who had invaded Italy, but abandoned the Roman province of Dacia. **China** was nominally reunited under the **Western Ch'in dynasty** in 265.

280–310

Diocletian, *r.*284–305, divided the empire into eastern and western spheres in 285 with two equal emperors. In 285 the western capital moved to Milan to defend the northern frontiers more easily.
Rome recaptured Armenia and Mesopotamia in 297.
The Mediterranean economy continued to collapse under heavy Roman taxation, *c.*300.
The Franks, Alemanni, and Burgundians crossed the Rhine.

310–340

Constantine, *c.*285–337, became interested in Christianity and granted religious freedom to all religions in 313. He founded Constantinople as his eastern capital in 330 and gave Christian bishops a major administrative role in the empire.
The Gupta dynasty united much of northern India under **Chandra Gupta,** *c.*320, and introduced a classic period of urban culture in north India.

340–370

Julian, 331–63, tried unsuccessfully to organize a pagan Church and campaigned against the Franks.
The Persians recaptured Mesopotamia in 364.
Samudra Gupta, the Indian emperor, conquered Bengal and Nepal and broke the power of the tribal republics in northwest India. This marked a victory for caste over tribe.
The Pallava dynasty was set up in southern India *c.*350.
Japan conquered Korea *c.*360.

370–400

Roman absorption of the Germanic tribes was reaching its limits.
The Visigoths crossed the Danube in 376 and were settled as military allies by **Theodosius the Great,** *r.*379–95.
Stilicho, *c.*368–408, a Vandal Roman commander, defeated a Visigoth invasion under Alaric.
Christianity received official support from the emperor **Theodosius** ?346–95.
Persian power was at its zenith under **Shapur II,** *r.*309–79.

The Saladero peoples were driven out of coastal Venezuela, migrating to the Caribbean Islands. Their descendants met Columbus.

The Mochica civilization of Peru was a powerful military society with armies ruled by priest warriors. They created a remarkable art form.

A Mayan stone slab, or stela, found at Tikal in Guatemala, had an inscription dated at AD 292. It is one of the earliest long-count dated objects known.

At the Mayan ceremonial center of Uaxactún in El Petéu, Guatemala, a stela dated AD 328 was found. Murals there provide examples of Mayan painting.

Arizona's Canyon de Chelly, with its red sandstone walls, was occupied for about 1,000 years, beginning *c.*350, by Anasazi and later Pueblo Indians.

The building of Old Stone Fort, a series of walls on a bluff overlooking the Little Duck River in Tennessee, was begun about AD 1 and completed by 400.

Roman grain ship

Relief at Naqsh-e-Rustan

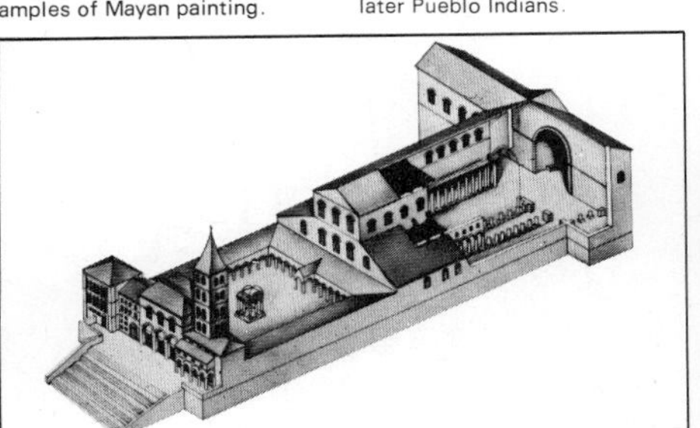
Early Christian churches: St Peter's, Rome

Constantine the Great

Neo-Platonism was founded by **Plotinus,** 205–70, his belief in the superiority of ideas over mundane reality fostered the Christian conception of heaven, widely influencing Christian and Islamic thought. **Mithraism,** a cult based on the recognition of the two powers of good and evil, became popular with Roman legionaries and received official patronage.

Manichaeanism, founded by **Mani,** *c.*216–76, a dualistic religion combining the teachings of Zoroaster, Buddha, Jesus, and Gnosticism became widespread from Europe to China. Mani held that knowledge of oneself and God guaranteed salvation (light) and liberation from one's present fallen condition (darkness). The soul had to be kept pure and in communion with God, both of which could be achieved by an abstemious life.

The Desert Fathers in Egypt formed the earliest Christian monastic orders.
St Anthony, 250–355, organized a group of hermits in 305, and **St Pachomius,** *c.*290–346, founded communal monasteries.
Neo-Taoism was created in China. It was influenced by **Kuo Hsing,** *d.*312, and **Wang Pi,** 226–49, who believed in controlling the emotions and in an ultimate all-uniting principle of non-being.

At the Council of Nicaea, in 325, called by Constantine the Great, a group of bishops from all over the Christian world issued a creed stating that God and Christ are of one identical substance.
The Arianist heresy, stating that only God was divine and that Christ was created as other men, was condemned by the Council. Constantine continued to support Arianism in spite of this.

The Latin Fathers of the Church, **Jerome,** *c.*347–420, and **Ambrose,** 340–97, began their life's work of theological writing and furtherance of monasticism in the West. Jerome was baptized in 366, after he had studied Latin literature. His Latin translation of the Bible, the Vulgate, is still important today.

The spread of Buddhism in China was greatly speeded by **Kumarajiva,** 344–413, who translated Mahayana Buddhist texts from Indian into Chinese.
Theodosius the Great, *r.*379–95, extirpated Arianism and linked the Christian Church with the Roman state.

Early Tamil literature, associated with the kingdoms of southern India, dealt with the themes of courtly love and kingship. Its earliest works are the *Eight Anthologies* and possibly the *Ten Songs*, both written *c.*100–500 by the third of the legendary Sangam literary academies, which are said to have lasted for thousands of years.

Valluvar, *c.*200–*c.*300, was the author of the classic Tamil poem the *Tirukkural* (sacred couplets). The work is a collection of aphorisms dealing with government, society, virtue, and love, and has proved almost impossible to translate. The outlook of the poet is so varied that several religious groups in the Tamil region have claimed him as their own.

A more uninhibited and individualistic writing style evolved in China with Taoist and Buddhist thought. The poet **Lu Chi,** *fl.* *c.*300 was the first to express this movement toward original creativity. Simple language styles and folksongs were used by the poet **Ts'ao Chih,** *c.*300.

Runes were the early Germanic script, used for magical charms and riddles. One of the earliest surviving examples, dating from the 4th century, is the *Mojbro Stone* from Uppland, which says that a man was slain on his horse.

The golden age of classical Sanskrit began with the rule of the Guptas, 320–535. The poet and dramatist **Kalidasa,** 388–455, excelled in the epic genre of the *kavya* school.

The childhood and licentious youth of **Saint Augustine,** 354–430, before the time when he became a Christian convert in 387, is described in his *Confessions*, 397–401.

Realistic portraiture flourished throughout the Roman Empire. Paintings recalled Egyptian mummy portraits in both style and technique. Most exquisite were the delicate miniatures on gold glass medallions, among them the "Family of Vennerius Keramis," *c.*250.
Sassanid Persia reached its cultural zenith during the reign of **Shapur I.** The rock carvings at Naqsh-e-Rustan, 242–73, record the humiliation of the Roman emperor Valerian.

Mochican art flourished on the coast of Peru, *c.*200–500, and was notable for its naturalistic ceramics, particularly of warrior figures.
Mayan culture grew in Central America from about the first century AD and lasted for the next 900 years. The architectural monuments of this civilization and the cities of Palenque, Copan, Uaxactan, and Yaxchilan were built from the 3rd century onward.

Roman architecture was at its most massive in the early 4th century with the Palace of Diocletian at Split and the Baths of Diocletian and Basilica of Maxentius in Rome.
The fixed hieratic expression on the colossal head of Constantine in the Forum marked a break from Hellenistic realism and heralded the formalized style of Byzantine art.

The old church of Saint Peter in Rome was built in 330 but destroyed during the Renaissance. The first religious building designed specifically for the needs of Christian worship, its basilican shape determined the layout of the majority of Western churches. **Sta Costanza,** 323–37, also in Rome, is an early example of the alternative centrally planned style of Christian architecture.

Hsieh Ho's *Six Canons of Painting* is the earliest work on the theory of art, written in the mid-4th century. The Taoist **Ku K'ai Chih,** *c.*344–406, produced masterly landscapes and genre paintings, conforming to Ho's artistic definitions.
Gupta art flowered with some of the greatest paintings at the Ajanta caves in the north Deccan. Massive Buddhist stupas were built, with a marked stylistic influence from central Asia and China.

Roman art became increasingly stiff and formalized, as with the ivory diptych of **Stilicho** (a Vandal leader in the Roman army) and his wife Serena, *c.*396. The Jonah Sarcophagus in the Lateran in Rome shows the merging of late Roman classical style with Christian motifs.

Heroic poems were sung among the German tribes by bards who accompanied themselves on harps. The songs were narrative lays of couplets set to music.

The harp, Europe's main musical instrument, was regarded as a precious possession. Later versions of the instrument became the national emblems of Ireland and Wales.

Psalms used by the Christian Church in its liturgy were among the first Christian chants. They were sung as responses by two choirs, or a priest and congregation sang alternate verses.

Persia under the Sassanid dynasty, 224–642, was rich in musicians and well developed instruments. Azádá's songs were celebrated in poems. Trumpet, lute, and mouth organ flourished.

Chinese music was further enriched by foreign influences. After the conquest of Kutcha in Turkestan, 384, drums, cymbals, and Persian harps with upper sound chests were imported.

In China the use of paper became widespread during the period of the Three Kingdoms, 220–64.
Diophantus of Alexandria, *fl.*250, wrote the *Arithmetica*, of which six volumes survive in Greek manuscripts. He was the first to introduce symbols into Greek algebra. His numerical equations, together with the Hindu system of numbering, influenced the development of Arabian algebra.

In China Huang Fu wrote a treatise on acupuncture, in use since 2500 BC.
Chinese mathematical books describe the Pythagorean theorem; solve problems involving square roots; and give the value of π as 3.1547.
Shafts on chariots and carts first appeared in Europe in the 3rd century although they had been used in China for many hundreds of years.

Hippology—the science of breeding and managing horses—flourished under the Romans.
Clinker-built boats, made from overlapping wooden planks fastened with iron rivets, were developed in northern Europe in the 3rd century.
By order of Diocletian, Roman emperor from 284 to 305, all books on the working of gold, silver, and copper were burned to prevent counterfeiting. The effect was to increase interest in alchemy and magic as a method of turning base metal into gold.

Mathematics developed by the Central American Mayas was the first to make use of a symbol for zero. Mayan arithmetic was based on the number 20 and is notable for calculations involving very large numbers. One reason for this may have been the smallness and cheapness of the Mayan unit of money, the cocoa bean.
Yu Hsi studied the equinoxes *c.*330 and was one of the first astronomers to describe the precession of the equinoxes.

Mayan calandars, superior to those of early Christianity, were developed in order to calculate the year more accurately for religious purposes.
Mayan astronomy was in some ways very advanced, owing to the Mayan concern with time. Thus the Mayas calculated the length of a year on Venus and used it partly to work out the dates of religious festivals.

Chinese astronomers of the 4th century believed, fairly correctly, that the blue of the sky was an illusion and that the Sun, Moon, and stars float freely in space.

The new barbarian kingdoms 400 – 700

Principal events

After the fall of Rome in 476, the Western Roman Empire divided into a galaxy of unstable "barbarian" kingdoms, which adapted Roman institutions, while the Byzantine Empire became cut off from the west despite Justinian's brief expansion *c.***550. The growing independence of the papacy and the new monastic movement made Christianity a powerful political weapon among the barbarian kingdoms, so that national conversion and the suppression of heresy had a more than religious significance.**

The teachings of Mohammed brought a new unity and aggression to the Arabs, who threatened Constantinople and expanded toward India.

The T'ang dynasty completed the development of the Chinese imperial system, on which Japan modeled its own, while India split into smaller kingdoms with the fall of the Guptas, although the classical era they initiated outlasted them.

400–430

The western capital of the Roman Empire retreated to Ravenna in 402.
The Visigoths under **Alaric** sacked Rome, 410, and invaded Spain in 415 under **Ataulf**, displacing the Vandals, who then moved to Africa.
The Franks and Burgundians, who created the first barbarian kingdom inside the empire, occupied Flanders and the Rhineland in 406.

430–460

The Huns' attack on Gaul, led by **Attila**, *c.*406– 53, was defeated by a Roman/Visigothic alliance in 452, and their invasion of Italy stopped on Attila's death.
The Vandals attacked Rome in 455 from North Africa and annexed the Mediterranean islands.
After St Patrick's conversion of Ireland the Irish monasteries developed into centers of Christian learning.

460–490

The Western Roman Empire ended in 476 when **Odoacer**, *d.*493, set up a barbarian kingdom in Italy. But **Theodoric the Ostrogoth**, *r.*471– 526, invaded Italy in his turn in 488.
The Frankish king Clovis I, *r.*481– 511, defeated the Roman governor in Gaul in 486 and set up the Merovingian dynasty. **In China** political fragmentation prevented the development of Chinese culture, while Buddhism won many converts.

490–520

Odoacer surrendered in 493 to Theodoric, who set up an Ostrogothic kingdom that was initially recognized by Byzantium, 497. He built his capital at Ravenna.
Clovis was baptized in 497, becoming the first non-heretical barbarian king and thus winning the support of the papacy and the emperor against the heretical Germanic tribes. In 507 he drove the Visigoths into Spain.

The Americas

Mayan architecture flourished, with many of the great ceremonial sites built. Teotihuacán was destroyed at its height, weakening Kaminaljuyú and the civilizations of the Mayan lowlands. Irrigation facilitated farming in southwest North America, while effigy mounds were built in the woodlands.

Buildings constructed c.400 at Kaminaljuyú in Guatemala were copied from the architecture of Teotihuacán, probably by invaders from that city.

Although there were many sizes and shapes, bows and arrows were definitely in use in southwest North America by *c.*450, increasing hunting potential.

A stela dated 460 was placed at Copán, Honduras, a temple city of the southern Mayan lowlands. Copán was an intellectual center for the Mayans.

The Anasazi, whose descendants were the Pueblos, farmed near Mesa Verde, Colorado. They first built pit houses, but later they moved to cliff dwellings there.

Attila the Hun

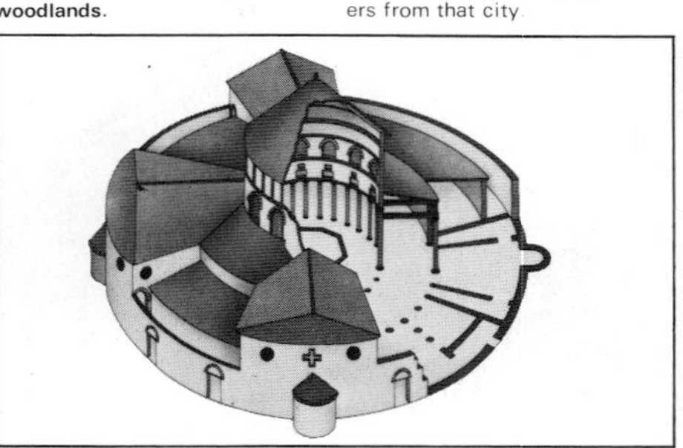

Early Christian churches: San Stefano Rotundo, Rome

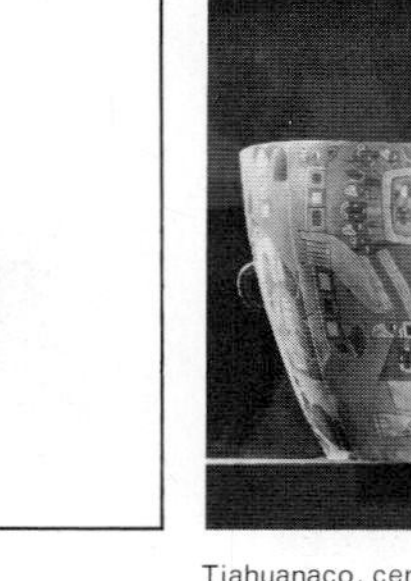

Tiahuanaco, ceremonial urn

Mosaics from San Apollinare, Ravenna, 6th c.– 7th c.

Religion and philosophy

With its consolidation and the removal of the threat of alien ideas, the Christian Church turned in upon itself and became engaged in a series of fierce internal doctrinal disputes centering on the many interpretations of the nature of Christ. At the same time Western monasticism emerged with the founding of the Benedictine rule.

Islam arose as a small sect in the early 7th century and quickly became a powerful cohesive movement with an aggressive evangelical mission. By 700 it had spread throughout the Middle East. After the death of the prophet Mohammed, however, it became subject to internal schismatic tendencies deriving from the conflicts between the temporal and spiritual aspects of the Islamic religion.

Buddhism advanced beyond the borders of the Indian subcontinent; by 700 it had become firmly established in both China and Japan.

Nestorius, consecrated Bishop of Constantinople in 428, maintained that Christ was both divine and human. Three years later **The Council of Ephesus** declared this view heretical.
St Augustine of Hippo, the greatest theologian of Christian antiquity, combined the New Testament with Platonism. In *The City of God c.*410, he described predestination.
The Nestorian Church developed in Asia Minor.

The Council of Chalcedon, 451, in response to the claim of **Pope Leo I** to universal supremacy, declared the Patriarch of Constantinople to be of equal authority. This council also emphasized that Christ had both a human and a divine nature, countering the doctrine of **Monophysitism,** which stated the essential unity of Christ. **St Patrick,** entrusted by Pope Celestine I to convert the Irish people, landed in County Wicklow, Ireland, in 432.

The Shakta and Tantra cults became important in India, emphasizing mystical speculations on divine fertility and energy. These doctrines were regarded as unorthodox by religious teachers. Tantrism was also an important trend in the Buddhist tradition.
Under the Guptas, Vishnaism flourished as a separate cult distinct from **Shivaism.**
The **Yogacara** school of meditative techniques flourished within Buddhism.

Buddhism grew in China at the expense of the more elite cult of **Confucianism.** There were two schools of Buddhism, the **T'ien-T'ai sect,** rationalists who sought to integrate Hinayana and Mahayana Buddhism, and the **Mahayana Amitabha sect,** who believed that salvation required reflection on the **Amitabha Buddha** as well as general meditation.

Literature

The classical tradition of literature largely disappeared with the fall of Rome in 476 but survived in Byzantium and in Christian monasteries where a few late Latin works were influential. Western European literature centered around the heroic myths of the Germanic invaders and the Celts, sung by bardic poets whose verse forms Christian writers later adapted to religious poetry. With the founding of Islam in the Arab world the Koran was collected, but the re-emergence of Arabic poetry would await the prosperous dynasties of the 8th century.

In India and in China under the T'ang dynasty lyric poetry flourished, both religious and secular, while a Japanese writing and literature emerged.

Buddhist sacred literature, in its earliest complete forms, appeared in the 5th century Pali texts that collected together the *Jataka Tales* (birth stories). These 547 tales consisted of prose and verse fables about the former births of the Buddha, often in animal forms. Similar tales are found in Aesop and in non-Buddhist Indian literature.

Japan assimilated Chinese civilization in the first four centuries AD and evolved a writing system of extreme complexity by adapting the script of the monosyllabic Chinese language to convey the phonetics of Japanese. 5th-century songs and myths would not appear in texts until the 8th century histories *Kojiki* and *Nihon Shoki.*

The Jewish Haggadah texts in Palestine and Babylonia used legends, stories, and anecdotes to illustrate ethical and theological matters dealt with in the Talmud. This material, with its lively embellishment of such Old Testament stories as that of Noah, influenced the similar treatment of biblical tales in the miracle plays of medieval Western Europe.

An oral literature of heroic verse known as **Heldenlieder** developed among the tribes of western Germany. From these songs and from pagan hymns and laments emerged later epic narratives, notably the story of Siegfried and Brunhild, which was incorporated into Germanic epics like the 13th-century *Song of the Nibelungs* and into the heroic sagas of Iceland.

Art and architecture

The fall of the Western Empire in 476 enabled new art forms combining Celtic, Scandinavian, German, and Roman styles to develop in northern Europe, reaching their high point in the exquisite illuminated manuscripts produced by the Irish and Northumbrian monasteries.

Byzantine art, a sacred and stylized offspring of late Roman art, spread from Greece to Italy, blossoming in the 6th century with the building of Hagia Sophia in Constantinople and S Vitale at Ravenna—the main cultural center in Italy after the fall of Rome.

Middle Eastern culture, divided until the 7th century between Byzantine and Persian influences, later collapsed before the onslaught of Islam, which absorbed certain elements of church design but forbade the use of representational imagery.

Japanese art during the Asuka period developed a style of its own distinct from that of China and Korea.

The hieratic and stylized form of Roman art can be seen in the ivory carvings "Scenes from the Passion," dating from the early 5th century. Classical ideals of proportion and anatomy were no longer considered important.
Christian architecture was a blend of Roman and indigenous styles, AD 400– 600. In Egypt monasteries with frescoes were built at Bawit and Sakkara, and the basilica of St Mena was constructed near Alexandria.

The Mausoleum of Galla Placidia in Ravenna, *c.*450 shows a Byzantine influence in its plan and its decorations. The mosaics were made over a period of one hundred years and illustrate the shift from the light, decorative qualities of Rome to the somber and awe-inspiring images of a wholly Byzantine style.

The church of St Stefano Rotondo in Rome, 468– 83, is exceptional for its entirely circular plan, although the centrally planned style continued a tradition that reached back to the Pantheon.
Chinese art during the Six Dynasties period, 220– 589, developed the Han tradition of monumental stone sculpture. In 460 a series of rock-cut shrines were begun in the caves of Yunkang which contain a 45-ft (13.7-m) figure of a Buddha.

Manuscript illumination was an important art form of the early Christian period. Only four religious texts survive, including the *Vienna Genesis*, a luxurious work on purple ground, and the *Rossano Gospels*, the earliest illustrated version of the New Testament. Both texts date from the early 6th century.

Music

In India, ragas were well established by the fifth century, having evolved from traditional melodies and scale theory that utilized many seven-note scales and complex rhythms to evoke various moods. In the West, by 600, Christian monks had developed plainsong to a level of accomplishment, codified by Pope Gregory I, that placed it lastingly in the liturgy.

The marimba, played today by the Bantu in Africa, developed from a xylophone introduced to Africa by Indonesian immigrants in the 5th century.

Japan adopted music and dance that were to die in their countries of origin. Supple Indian and Chinese forms were considered female, and Korean and Manchurian forms male in character.

Confucian ceremonies in China closely integrated music, dance, and poetry. Chinese court music and dance expressed the form and calligraphy of poems around which they were created.

Irish song, carried through Europe by minstrels and monks, revitalized musical composition. It was classical verse, which might be sung to a melody repeated as often as required.

Science and technology

Chinese science and technology were by far the most active and inventive of this time. Under the T'ang dynasty the sciences and arts were encouraged and science was no longer hampered in any way by religious dogmas or prohibitions. Chinese attitudes to medicine were particularly enlightened: even before the 5th century medical treatment was regarded as a public service and was administered by the state. In astronomy, practical chemistry, and mathematical calculation China also led the world.

By contrast Western science had dwindled to commentaries, and even these often met with discouragement of an extreme kind. Boethius, one of the last important Western commentators of science and philosophy, was executed in 524 by Theodoric the Ostrogoth for advocating a return to political and intellectual liberty. Although overshadowed by China, Indian mathematical, astronomical, and medical sciences also advanced.

The university of Constantinople was founded in 425 by **Theodosius II**, 401– 50, the Roman emperor of the East, who later (438) produced the **Theodosian Code**, a systematization and simplification of the Roman legal code.

Chinese scientific instruments of the 5th century included water-driven armillary spheres, which revolved in phase with the stars, and a compass, in use since the 2nd century, whose pointer was a metal spoon balanced on its bowl. These spoons would not be replaced by magnetic needles until the 9th century.

Boethius, 480– 524, wrote on the four advanced "arts," geometry, arithmetic, music, and astronomy. Two of these manuscripts survive, *De Institutione Musica*, and *De Institutione Arithmetica.*

Indian astronomical literature shows an upsurge that lasted a century, beginning with the publication in the late 5th century of the work of the astronomer **Aryabhata,** 476– 550. This mentions rotation of the Earth and the epicyclic movements of planets. He also obtained an extremely accurate calculation for π. **Metal stirrups,** invented in 5th-century Korea and used by the Avars on their incursions from Asia, were first seen in southern Europe *c.*500.

520–550

The Byzantine emperor Justinian the Great, *r.*527–65, temporarily reconquered North Africa in 534 and Italy in 554, and codified Roman law. His alliance with the papacy led to the suppression of heresy in the empire. **Khosru I,** *r.*531–79, brought Persia to its greatest strength in a protracted war with Byzantium. **The Gupta dynasty** in north India fell in 550.

550–580

Byzantium had reconquered most of the Mediterranean seaboard by 560, but by 571 the Lombards had taken Italy and settled in the North.
The Frankish kingdom stayed divided because of the Merovingian custom of equal division of inheritance between the king's sons.
Persia took southern Arabia from the Abyssinians in 576.
The introduction of Buddhism to Japan in 552 marked the start of a period of Chinese influence.

580–610

Pope Gregory I, *r.*590–604, assisted papal authority by defending Rome against the Lombards.
Persia and Byzantium were at war in Syria–Palestine, 602–28.
The Sui dynasty reunified China in 589 by conquering the southern Chen dynasty.
In Japan, the Soga clan rose to power in 587, introducing a paternalist, Chinese-style constitution.
Irish missionaries worked in Scotland and Germany *c.*600.

610–640

The Muslim era began with the flight of Mohammed, *c.*579–632, from Mecca to Medina in 622. His ideas brought a new unity, sense of responsibility, and aggression to the diverse Arab traders and tribesmen. After Mohammed's death **Caliph Omar,** 581–644 (the head of Islam), expanded the Islamic realm in the Near East.
The T'ang dynasty was founded in China in 618, ruling with a large and powerful imperial bureaucracy.

640–670

Disputes about the authority and succession of the caliphate under **Othman,** *d.*656, and **Ali,** *d.*661, led to civil war, which destroyed the unity of the Ummah and led to the establishment of the **Umayyad dynasty** at Jerusalem in 638. The Muslims then took Iran and Egypt, 642, Armenia, 653, and Afghanistan, 664, ruling as an autocratic but tolerant minority.
Japan entered a period of reform in 646, imitating Chinese society.

670–700

The Islamic world was divided by disputes, which led to the emergence of the Sunni, Shi'ite, and Khawarij sects, reflecting the problems of succession and the growing discontent at the prosperity of the Meccans, which was increasing at the expense of other Muslims.
A 30-year truce was concluded between the Byzantine and Muslim empires after the failure of the Muslim blockade of Constantinople in 673–78.

Tiahuanaco was the site of a pre-Inca culture near Lake Titicaca on the Peru-Bolivia border, forming in time a widespread cultural "empire."

Merovingian buckle, 6th c.

In the Upper Mississippi and Great Lakes area, Woodland peoples constructed their burial mounds in the shapes of birds or animals.

T'ang pottery figure

A Mayan ball court marker, dated 590, in glyph numbers instead of the bar-and-dot system, is carved with the figure of a ball player.

Teotihuacán, at its zenith *c.*500, with a population greater than that of Rome, was conquered and burned. A general decline would begin about 700.

Early Islamic architecture: the Dome of the Rock

The Mayans' most impressive architectural expression, Palenque in the Chiapas area of Mexico, was being built in a rain forest.

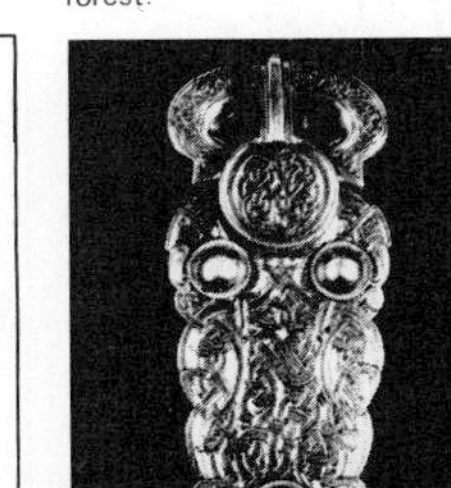

Gold buckle, Sutton Hoo

The sculptured portal, Gateway of the Sun, at Tiahuanaco, Peru, was carved *c.*700 with 48 relief figures and a central gateway god.

Japanese Buddha, 7th c.

St Benedict, *c.*480–547, founded the first Benedictine monastery *c.*529. He laid down a complete set of rules for monastic life, including a period of probation before full membership in the monastic community, prohibition of ownership, and most important of all, rules for obedience, celibacy, and humility. His monastic ideal was of a self-contained and self-sufficient community.

Buddhism, supported by the **Soga clan,** was officially introduced into Japan in 552. **Mazdakism,** founded by **Mazdak,** *fl.* 560, in Iran was an offshoot of **Manichaeanism.** Mazdak held that good (light) acted by free will and evil (darkness) by chance. Light could only be released into the world by asceticism, vegetarianism, and non-violence.
The prophet Mohammed, was born in *c.*570 in Mecca.

Mohammed, founder of Islam, received his first prophetic call in 610. Thereafter he began to proclaim his message publicly. His revelation was of a majestic being, the one God, Allah, whose command was that Mohammed was to be his prophet. This and subsequent revelations form the content of the *Koran,* which emphasizes generosity, the goodness and power of God, and retribution on the Day of Judgment.

In 622 Mohammed and a small following emigrated to Medina after opposition and harassment in their native Mecca. The **Ummah,** or Muslim community, claimed supremacy over tribal or familial loyalties, regarding all Muslims as brothers. In so doing it helped to make Arab society more cohesive. The crucial concept of **jihad** (holy war) was instituted at this time by Mohammed and led to the conquest of Mecca in 630. Mohammed died in 632.

Following the death of Mohammed, 632, there was a period of conflict in the Ummah over the succession. The supporters of his son-in-law **Ali** were the forerunners of the major **Shi'ite** division of Islam. The puritanical **Kharijites** who opposed Ali withdrew from the main body of the Ummah. The Shi'ites stressed leadership, the Kharijites community and permanent religious aggression.

The Monothelites were condemned as heretics at the ecumenical council at Constantinople in 681. The heresy concerned the divinity and humanity of Christ. The Monothelites, following the decision reached at Chalcedon, claimed that although Christ had two natures he had a single will. The Council insisted on Christ's duality by asserting that both a divine and a human will were in Christ's person.

Aristotelean logic was translated into Latin by **Boethius,** *c.* 480–524, the last great Roman writer. A Christian who served as a minister under Theodoric the Ostrogoth, he was condemned to death and in prison wrote *De consolatione philosophiae,* 523, a treatise in verse and prose on free will, good, and evil that helped spread Greek thought in the Germanic world.

Alliterative bardic verse romanticizing the heroism of Celtic warriors had become an established literary form by the middle of the 6th century. Odes and lays in praise of **King Urien,** *fl.*547–59, were attributed to a Welsh bard Taliesen (by Nennius, *c.*800) who may have been a mythical figure. These would later be collected in the 14th century *Book of Taliesen.*

An Irish bard, Dallan Forgaill, *d.*597, is credited with the *Eulogy of St Columba.* Its vigorous alliterative style is also found in Irish sagas about the hero **Cú Chulainn,** possibly 7th century, known as the Ulaid cycle. Ireland had a class of professional poets, the filiad. **A Welsh poet, Aneirin,** *c.*600, celebrated northern British heroes in *Y Gododdin.*

In India, classical Sanskrit literature, which had thrived under the rule of the Guptas, 320–550, reached its late flowering in the poetry of **Bhartrhari,** *c* 570–651, a philosopher who wrote three collections of verses, the *Sataka,* on the sensual pleasures of love, the nature of justice, and the means of liberation from earthly existence.

The Koran reached its final form, 651–52. Written partly in rhymed prose reflecting the mood of Mohammed during his life as a solitary visionary preacher, it was regarded by Muslims as the perfect word of God. Its style and thought permeated the literature of Islam, an expansionist force that took many Persian stories to Europe.

The first named English poet, Caedmon, *fl.*670, used the meter and diction of Old English pagan verse to compose poems on biblical and religious themes at the monastery of Whitby. A nine-line "Hymn on the Creation" is the most generally accepted of several works attributed to him in a 10th-century MS. He was an untutored herdsman, according to the Venerable Bede.

The age of Justinian saw the flowering of Byzantine architecture. The architecture and mosaics of **S. Vitale,** Ravenna, 526–48, were the splendor of Italy. The great cathedral of **Hagia Sophia** in Constantinople, 532–37, was an architectural and engineering triumph.
King Theodoric's mausoleum in Ravenna, *c.* 530, is surmounted by a colossal domed monolith, a fitting tribute to the half-barbarian, half-civilized king.

The distinctive Japanese art style of the Asuka period, 552–645, culminated with the temple complex of Horyu-ji Nara. The courtyard with its Pagoda, Konda (Golden Hall), and Kodo (for meetings) was based on the traditional Chinese and Korean layout.
The solid ivory throne of Maximian, archbishop of Ravenna, was carved in Constantinople and was a gift from Emperor Justinian *c.*550.

The Basilica at Turmanin in Syria is a typical eastern variation of Roman Christian architecture, which was common throughout Syria and Palestine before the rise of Islam.
The art of Sassanid Persia of the 5th and 6th centuries shows a combination of Byzantine and Irano-Buddhist styles. Metalwork was highly developed and decorated with complex motifs and intricate filigree work.

The Great Chalice of Antioch is typical of Christian metalwork from the Roman provinces. It probably dates from the early 7th century, when there was an enormous output of silverware and fine gold jewelry.
The Ashburnham Pentateuch is a masterpiece of vivid narrative illumination dating from the late 6th or early 7th century. It is not known where it was made, nor whether by a Jewish or Christian illuminator.

The Sutton Hoo treasure comes from the grave of an East Anglian king who died in 654. It includes superb examples of Anglo-Saxon decorative metalwork.
Christian scholars and artists who took refuge in Ireland during the period of the Anglo-Saxon invasions produced an abstract and extremely ornate style of illumination, the 7th-century *Book of Durrow* being one of the best surviving examples.

The Dome of the Rock in Jerusalem is the first great Islamic architectural monument. Construction began in 688 in the reign of Abd al-Malik, but the design was a creative adaptation of Christian church buildings.
Book illumination reached great heights in Northumberland. The *Lindisfarne Gospels, c.*700, combine the Roman narrative tradition with the decorative skill of the Celts.

Musical letter notation was introduced by Boethius, *c.*475–525, in *De Institutione musica,* his treatise that was the authoritative work on music until about 1500.

Harps of six to twelve strings were played by European musicians. The instrument became a symbol of their calling.

Pope Gregory I supervised the compiling and codifying of plainsong *c.*600, giving his name to Gregorian chant, an unaccompanied and unharmonized style that is still used today.

Under the T'ang dynasty, 618–907, orchestral suites and programmatic works, some describing battles, were composed in China. Music-dramas incorporating folk-song developed.

Classical Arab music evolved richly under the Umayyad caliphs, 661–750, in Damascus. **Ibn Misjah,** died *c.*715, codified its theory, embracing eight modes for lute music.

Arab modes were nearly identical to Greek modes, but were performed with rich embellishments characteristic of the sinuous ornamentation of much Arab visual art and architecture.

Justinian, Byzantine emperor, *r.*527–65, closed the Athenian university because the teachers were not Christians. **John Philoponus,** *fl.c.*530, speculated that a projectile would gain momentum from the mechanism which fired it, thus arriving at a crude idea of inertia. **Paleontology** was furthered in China in 527 with a book by **Li Tao Yuan** in which he described animal fossils.
Indian decimal notation began in the 6th century; on later inscriptions a dot signified zero.

The Ma'daba mosaic, the oldest known map of the Holy Land, shows the area from ancient Byblos to Thebes and has a street plan of Jerusalem. It was made in Palestine *c.* 550.
Silk production was attempted at Byzantium in the 6th century after silkworm eggs had been smuggled out of China and taken there, reputedly by Nestorian monks.
Abacus calculators are described in a mathematical work thought to have been written by **Chen Luan** *c.*570.

The diagnosis of disease in China in the 7th century was documented by **Chao Yuan Fang,** *c.*610, who wrote a treatise listing 1,720 diseases classified into 67 groups.

Chinese surgical treatment in the 7th century included the removal of cataracts.
Windmills, probably invented in Persia in the 7th century, may have had their origin in wind-driven prayer wheels. Another theory, unproven, is that they were inspired by ships' sails. The axis of a wheel, driven by some 6 to 12 sails, was mounted on the first story of a Persian windmill. Stone wheels used for grinding grain were located on the story above.

Greek fire, used in the defense of the Byzantine Empire in the 7th century, was a highly inflammable substance of uncertain composition. Probably a mixture of pitch, naphtha, and potash, it could be discharged from tubes in the prows of ships.
Fine metalwork including cloisonné, enamel, and lathe-turned jewelry was found at the Sutton Hoo ship burial dating *c.*650, showing that metallurgy in the Dark Ages was not only used to make swords.

Swords were the most advanced product of Burgundian and Frankish metallurgy in the 7th and 8th centuries. Their blades were expertly forged, with strips of decorative metal running along the whole length. Handles and scabbards were inset with jewels and welded decorations. **In northern England** the tides and moon were studied by the **Venerable Bede,** *c.*673–735, who also wrote a treatise on finger reckoning.

Islam reaches India and Spain 700–1000

Principal events

Invasions from the Muslims in Spain, Vikings in the north, and Magyars in the east destroyed much of Europe's culture and economic strength, although Charlemagne's conquests east of the Rhine brought Germany within the European orbit.

The Muslim world reached from Spain to Afghanistan by 736, and the papacy, although relatively isolated by Muslim control of the Mediterranean, used its new states for political ends, reviving the Roman ideal by crowning its main supporters Holy Roman Emperor. Royal authority in Europe at this time was often precarious, based only on the personal allegiance of a provincial nobility whose power was strengthened by the need to defend the kingdom's frontiers.

In China constant warfare weakened the T'ang armies and the Sung dynasty gained control, while in Japan the Heian period marked a moment of transition to a society run on feudal lines.

700–730

Pope Gregory II, *r.*715–31, appointed St Boniface, *c.*672–754, to convert Germany.
The Umayyad Arabs took Spain in 715.
Leo III, *r.*717–41, defeated the second Arab siege of Constantinople, 717–18, and began the iconoclastic controversy in 726, asserting the religious authority of the emperor and limiting the spread of monasticism.
The Nara period in Japan began with the establishment of a capital at Heijō in 710.

730–760

Charles Martel, *c.*688–741, stopped the Muslim invasion of Europe at Poitiers, 732, and assisted Boniface in Germany. His son **Pepin**, *r.*747–68, campaigning in Italy, established papal temporal power by a donation of land to the papacy, 756.
Al Mansur, *r.*754–75, founded the **Abbasid Caliphate**, defeating the Umayyads in North Africa and the Near East, 750.
The Gurjara-Pratihara dynasty defended India against the Muslims after 740.

760–790

Charlemagne, *r.*768–814, united France and conquered Italy in 774, northern Spain in 777, Saxony in 785, and Bavaria in 788.
Baghdad became the Abbasid capital in 762.
An Umayyad dynasty emerged at Córdoba in Spain, 756, tolerating Jews and Christians. **Scandinavian trade** with Byzantium began *c.*770.
Turkish and Tibetan tribesmen threatened western China *c.*763.

790–820

Charlemagne was crowned Holy Roman Emperor, 800, reviving the idea of a Western Roman Empire. Byzantium recognized the title in 812.
The Bulgar kingdom reached its peak under **Krum**, *r.*808–14.
Ghana was an important trading kingdom, bringing gold from southern Africa to the Sahara.
Emperor Kammu, *r.*781–806, instituted the Heian period in Japan, 794–1185, in which indigenous feudalism superseded the Chinese-based social order.

The Americas

The year 900 marked the change from the Classic to the Post-Classic period of Mayan civilization in Mesoamerica. In North America, the Mississippian tradition developed in the eastern woodlands and the Pueblo civilization in the southwest. The Tiahuanaco-Huari culture dominated in South America.

In the transition period the Pueblo Indians of the North American Southwest gave up their pithouses and began building above-ground communal dwellings.

In 756 the Hieroglyphic Stairway at Copán, Honduras, was dedicated. Copán hosted, *c.*765, an assembly to correct the Mayan calendar.

An influential civilization, the Mississippian Culture, flourished in the central and lower Mississippi River valleys, after 700.

The Frescoes at Bonampak in the Mexican jungle were painted *c.*800. A splendid example of Mayan art, they illustrate the Mayan lifestyle.

Islamic architecture: Mosque at Cordoba, 8th c. interior

The stupa of Borobudur, Java, 8th c.–9th c.

Crown of Charlemagne

Carolingian church, *c.*800

Religion and philosophy

The Christian Church continued the struggle to assert its authority over the secular powers of the Holy Roman and Byzantine empires while the assertion of the primacy of the Roman popes over the Eastern Church led to an increasing separation of Eastern and Western forms of Christianity. In the West, papal sanction of Charlemagne's empire brought the Church additional prestige. The practices of the clergy, however, were becoming increasingly lax and would eventually prompt the Cluniac reform movement.

In the Islamic world, the Sufi movement was founded and grew, emphasizing an austere mysticism in response to the rational ideal and the reason of orthodox Islam.

The spread of Buddhism within Japan continued and won official support.

Mayan religion reached its most elaborate hierarchical form at the height of the empire's power in Central America.

Iconoclasm as a movement began, 726, when the Byzantine emperor **Leo II** prohibited the use of icons as idolatrous, claiming the emperor was God's "vice-regent" on earth.
A period of severe repression and conflict between Church and state followed in which sacred images of Christ, the Virgin Mary, and various saints were destroyed.
The Islamic religion reached India in 712 and Spain in 715.

The Classical period in Mayan culture in Central America reached its height. Mayan cosmology saw the earth as a crocodile, and the Mayans placated their gods with sacrifices.
Buddhism in Japan became the state cult in the reign of **Shomu**, who built a magnificent Buddha (**Daibutsu**) and a temple (**Todaiji**) in Nara, in 743–52.

The new Anglo-Saxon humanism was introduced in France by the Northumbrian monk **Alcuin**, *c.*732–804, who met **Emperor Charlemagne,** 781, and became an important figure in the **Carolingian Renaissance.** Alcuin encouraged the study of the liberal arts. His revision of the liturgy of the Frankish Church was carried throughout Charlemagne's empire and he created a new edition of the *Vulgate*.

The Tendai and Shingon sects were founded in Japan *c.*805 by Buddhist monks returning from a visit to China.
Sankara, 780–820, the most important member of the new **Vedanta school of philosophy** in India, affirmed the one true reality (**Brahma**) as the source of all things. He also wrote commentaries on the *Upanishads* and *Brahma Sutra*.

Literature

Chinese literature of the T'ang dynasty reached its finest form in the evocative poetry of Li Po, Tu Fu, and Wang Wei in the 8th century. With the later decline of the dynasty, social criticism and an elegiac mood appeared. Chinese influence on Japanese literature gave way to new vernacular forms of Japanese verse and prose.

The spread of Islam led to more sophisticated themes in Arabic poetry and to an extension of Arabic influence into Persian literature.

The epic saga took shape in Norway and Iceland. In England scholastic Latin developed and the growing power of Anglo-Saxon vernacular literature showed itself in the saga of Beowulf, in religious poetry, and in the Anglo-Saxon Chronicle.

The Venerable Bede 673–735, wrote his *History of the English Church and People*, a major source of information on England between 597 and 731. He drew on wide sources in creating a work of literary and historical value.
In India, the Sanskrit dramatist Bhvabhutti, *fl.*730, wrote three outstanding plays, two of which tell the story of **Rama.**

Nearly 49,000 poems survive from China's golden age of poetry, the **T'ang dynasty. Tu Fu,** 712–70, showed his mastery of imagery in such lines as "Blue is the smoke of war, white the bones of men." Equally famous is **Li Po**, 701–62 who wrote of wine and companionship. **Wang Wei**, 699–759, was a painter and poet of nature. The strict 8-line *shih* form predominated.

Beowulf, the greatest surviving Anglo-Saxon epic poem, dates between 700 and 1000. A vivid narrative of a warrior's struggles against dragons and sea monsters, it is based on north European heroic legend, with elements of moral and religious significance probably added by later Christian writers. Chinese poet **Po Chü-i**, 772–846, wrote didactic verse.

A rebirth of European learning took place under **Charlemagne,** 768–814, who encouraged the copying of old manuscripts. His biography was written by the German monk **Einhard,** 770–840, in personal and political terms. Charlemagne's court at Aachen attracted scholars such as **Alcuin,** *c.*732–804, an Anglo-Latin writer and cleric with a humanistic outlook.

Art and architecture

After the period of confusion that followed the decline of the Roman Empire, European art again flourished. A Germanic decorative style subordinating realistic representation to stylized patterns is found in jewelry, Viking carving, and Celtic manuscripts. In architecture, elements of the Romanesque developed, based on a combination of Roman, Byzantine, and Carolingian art, replacing the utilitarian basilicas of the early northern churches with more complex structures using a system of bays often with vaulted roofs.

Islamic art entered its classical age in the 9th century, the religious ban on figurative art producing a wealth of geometric designs in architectural detail, while Islamic and Christian styles mingled in Spain.

Buddhist art flourished throughout the East, contributing to a mingling of cultural styles as Chinese influence reached Japan, while China itself felt the impact of Indian ideas.

Byzantine icons have survived from Sinai, Constantinople, and Rome. The early beginnings of defined painting schools can be seen in the life-size "Enthroned Virgin and Child," *c.*705, commissioned by Pope John VII.
Chinese Buddhist sculpture combined the traditional linear delicacy with the Indian sense of form, resulting in such superb statues as the seated stone Buddha, 711.

The Iconoclastic age lasted in the Byzantine Empire from 726–843. In order to stop the cult of images and discourage monasticism, all figurative representations, except of the Cross, were either defaced or destroyed.
The earliest Orissan-style temples were built at Bhuvanesvar in east India, 700–800. A hollow terraced pyramid supported a conical beehive-shaped spire.

The Great Mosque at Córdoba was built by Spain's Arab conquerors, 785–990. The naves use elegant star vaulting and the whole was intricately decorated with colored marbles and precious stones.
The Book of Kells was produced in Ireland at the end of the 8th century. It is the finest and most elaborate of early Western illuminated manuscripts.

A Viking earth barrow, *c.*800, contained the Oseberg ship, as well as a cart, several sledges, and numerous small decorated objects. The delicate interwoven wood carvings of figures and abstract motifs are typical of northern art.
Charlemagne's Palace Chapel at Aachen in Germany was consecrated in 805. Local Roman remains and the church of S. Vitale in Ravenna were used as models in an assertion of the continuity of the empire.

Music

The establishment of the Divine Office and Mass by the 9th century encouraged the development of chants more complex than Gregorian chant. At the same time, the Muslim invasion of Western Europe brought schools of singing, lute playing, and musical theory, which would have a lasting influence on European music over the next five hundred years.

The first composition by known European composers took the form of tropes, melodic passages added to the liturgy either as new music or as variations on the preceding plainsong melody.

The Arabs in conquering Spain brought with them **the lute** (the first fretted instrument to arrive in Europe), **the rebec** (an ancestor of the violin), and the violin type of bow.

"Ut Queant Laxis"—written *c.*770—was an early medieval hymn tune in the then unusual form of six separate phrases, each starting a step or half step higher than the previous one.

Arab music entered its golden age under **Harun al-Rashid,** *c.*764–809, whose musical tastes are revealed in *The Arabian Nights*. A style of romantic song flourished in the period.

Science and technology

The rise of Islam transformed the course of European science and philosophy. The Arabs were heirs to the Hellenic Greeks and acknowledged their role as custodians of that culture. Following the Athenian tradition they founded a number of schools for wide-ranging, unprejudiced, and objective study, most important of which was the Academy of Science at Baghdad. A great respect for Greek learning, and particularly for Aristotle, may have held them back from even greater discoveries, but some Arab scientists rejected Aristotle, arguing for a more experimental approach to science. With the spread of the Arab Empire, Arabic became the language of science outside the Far East, absorbing elements of Indian astronomy while benefiting to a lesser extent from achievements in China. Many Arabic texts on astronomy, chemistry, and mathematics retained their influence until modern science began in Europe with the work of Galileo and Newton.

Mayan science, with its detailed astronomical observations and advanced use of mathematics, reached its peak.

Jabir, or Gebir, *c.*721–815, the "father of Arabic chemistry," left evidence of a systematic approach to this science, relatively uncluttered by alchemical superstitions. For example, Jabir described the manufacture of nitric acid and how it may be used in extracting silver and gold from their ores or salts.
Gunpowder, probably invented in China in the 8th century, was used initially to make fireworks and only much later in weaponry.

Printing with blocks from which the letters stand out in relief was invented in Japan in or prior to the 8th century.
Bells and organ pipes, made at this time from bronze, indicate an advance in European metal-working.

Arab paper was made in Baghdad for the first time, 793, following the capture of Chinese paper-makers during the battle for the city of Samarkand in 751.
Viking ships of the 9th century were clinker-built (using overlapping planks) with square sails, a single steering oar aft, and many rowing oars. Their narrow hull shape made them faster than Mediterranean ships.
The Baghdad Academy of Science replaced Jundishapur, Persia, as the center of scientific learning *c.*800.

820–850

The Carolingian Empire was divided into three parts at the Treaty of Verdun in 843. **Scandinavians,** having founded Kiev and Novgorod, absorbed Byzantine culture and religion through trading contacts, *c.*850. **Al-Mamun the Great,** *r.*813–33, set up a House of Knowledge in Baghdad and encouraged the most glorious epoch of the Abbasid dynasty. **The Abbasid capital** moved to Samarra in 836.

The civilizations of Tiahuanaco and Huari merged and began to spread their influence and cultural style over most of Peru.

Nunnery at Uxmal

Ahmad Ibn Hanbal, 780–855, within the **Sunni branch of Islam,** founded the most orthodox of the four schools of Islamic law, which holds that the *Koran* as interpreted by the Islamic community contains the answers to all moral questions. In 833 **Hanbal** was imprisoned for refusing to accept **Mutazili** rationalist doctrines. **The Ch'an school,** the precursor of Japanese **Zen Buddhism,** developed in China.

Arabic literature had a strong tradition of lyrical desert poetry, which re-emerged at the peak of the **Abbasid Empire,** 786–861. The lyrics of **Abu Nuwas,** *c.*762–815, reflected the town life of the caliphates, while Islam influenced the religious poetry of **Abu al-Atahiya,** 748–826. Another poet, **Abu Tamman,** *c.*807–50, edited the fine Hamasu anthology.

The constructional and geometric skills of Islam are seen in the spiral ramped minaret of the **Malwiyya Mosque,** begun at Samarra in 848.

Plainsong notation, which originated in Europe in the 9th century, first consisted of marks like accents over syllables to denote a rise and fall in pitch; they did not indicate by how much.

Spanish metal mines were taken over *c.*850 by the Moors, who also prepared pure copper by reacting its salts with iron—a primitive forerunner of modern electroplating methods. **Al-Farghani,** or Alfraganus, *d.*850, wrote the *Elements,* a summary of Ptolemaic astronomy studied in Europe until 1600. **Algebra,** as a word, first figures as al-jabr, meaning transposition, in a treatise by the Arab mathematician **Al-Khwarizmi,** d. *c.*850. The Arabs based their algebra on both Greek and Indian maths.

850–880

Frequent invasions and the weakness of the monarchy gave new power to the provincial nobility in the Carolingian states and in Italy caused a decline in papal authority. **Roman and Byzantine** Christianity officially split in 867. **Basil I** of Byzantium, *r.*867–86, attacked the Muslims in Mesopotamia and stimulated a revival of Byzantine civilization. **The Bulgarians** were converted to Christianity in 865.

The Mayans completed two waves of migration that took them out of the Mexican lowlands and into the Yucatán Peninsula.

Viking ship

The Fourth Council of Constantinople was called in 867–70 by **Basil I.** It deposed Photius, patriarch of Constantinople, who had challenged the pope's authority in the East, and reinstated Ignatius, *c.*800–877, thus ending the schism with Rome.

Vernacular literature in both prose and verse was created in Germany and Britain, best shown in the plain narrative style of the *Anglo-Saxon Chronicle,* a history begun during the reign of **Alfred the Great** *c.*870–99. The heroic **Edda** lays began to develop in Iceland after 860.

The Middle Byzantine age, 867–1025, saw a second flowering of Byzantine art with the energetic redecoration of pre-Iconoclast churches. The mosaic of the "Madonna and Child" in the church of Hagia Sophia dates from 867. Figurative representation became increasingly stylized with the characteristic Byzantine distortion of a face—a small mouth, a long nose, and huge, wide open eyes. **The early German abbey** of Corvei was begun in 873.

Organum, the practice of singing extra lines of music at intervals of a fourth or a fifth above or below plainsong, appeared in the 9th century. This was primitive polyphony.

Al-Rhazi, a physician and encyclopedist, *c.*920, and **Al-Khindi,** a scientist and philosopher, *c.*873, were exceptional in objecting to alchemical and Aristotelian dogmas. They sought new concepts of the nature of motion and heat and encouraged the use of experiments to solve scientific problems. **Bardas** reorganized the University of Constantinople in 863 for the teaching of science. Soon afterward the teaching was again suppressed by **Basil II,** *r.*963–1025.

880–910

Urban development in northern Europe, stimulated by long-distance overland trade, was disrupted by Norse raiders *c.*900. **The Bulgarians** warred constantly with Byzantium under **Symeon I,** *r.*893–927. **The Chola dynasty** displaced the Pallavas in India in 888. **The T'ang dynasty** in China fell in 907 and was followed by a period of weak imperial authority and constant barbarian invasions.

Monks Mound, or Cahokia, which was under construction *c.*900 and took over two centuries to complete, extends over 18 acres in Illinois.

The Abbey of Cluny in France was founded, 910, marking a revival of the monastic movement. It was here that the **Cluniac reform movement** began, which introduced the notion that the Church hierarchy has a responsibility for clerical discipline and formed the basis of a widespread attack on abuses and corruption in the Church.

Classical Japanese literature emerged in the **Heian period,** 794–1192. The *Kokinshu,* 905, was an anthology of short poems with themes of love and nostalgia, showing the flexibility made possible by the phonetic *kana* script. The Welsh monk **Asser,** *d.*909, wrote a biography of Alfred the Great, 893.

Phnom Bakheng became the new administrative and religious center of Cambodia during the Angkor period, 889–1434. The "mountain temple" design has a single base supporting six tower-like structures.

Pitch notation was required to communicate to singers the relationship of two parts in an organum. A Flemish monk called **Hucbald,** 840–930, first used letters to denote pitch.

Cotton and silk manufacture was introduced into Spain and Sicily by the Moors in the 9th and 10th centuries. **Lateen sails,** triangular fore-and-aft sails, which may have appeared in the eastern Mediterranean in the 2nd century, were brought to the West in the 9th century by the Arabs.

910–940

Rollo, *c.*860–932, founded an independent dukedom of Normandy in 911 and was baptized in 912. **Henry I,** *r.*919–36, became the first Saxon king to rule a unified Germany, whereas the French monarchy was weak. **Umayyad** culture reached its zenith in Spain under **Abd ar-Rahman III,** *r.*912–61. **The rise of a military class** in Japan resulted in civil strife in the provinces, 935–41.

A struggle for control of the Oaxaca Valley of Mexico had begun *c.*900 when the Mixtecs invaded the Zapotec stronghold.

Islamic art: tomb facade, *c.*900

Sufism, a mystical literary and philosophical movement within Islam, stressed divine love through the immediate personal union of the soul with God. It developed as a reaction against more orthodox interpretations of the *Koran,* and **Al Halláj,** who was crucified in 922 for his teachings, became revered as a Sufi martyr.

Lyric and elegiac Anglo-Saxon poetry survives in a manuscript known as the *Exeter Book.* This included individualistic poems such as "The Seafarer" as well as work by an earlier poet, **Cynewulf,** *fl.*850. "The Dream of the Rood" was a notable poem on the Crucifixion.

During the Chola period, 907–1053, in India, improved metal-casting techniques enabled notable achievements in figurative images, especially in portraying the complex and balanced poses of the dancing Shiva.

Organs were installed in abbeys and cathedrals of Europe by the 10th century. They were played to support parts of the organum sung by the choir, and followed the sung lines.

Córdoba, in Spain, reached its height as a center of Islamic science in the 10th century under **Abd-ar-Rahman III,** 912–61. **Optical lenses** of four kinds were described by **Than Chhiao** in China *c.*940.

940–970

Otto I, *r.*936–73, ended the recurrent Magyar invasions at the battle of Lechfeld in 955 and became the first Saxon Holy Roman Emperor in 962. **The Northern Sung dynasty,** founded in 960, brought a more modern humanism to Chinese government, social organization, and thought. A Muslim **Ghaznavid** dynasty grew up in Afghanistan in 962.

The Nunnery at Uxmal in Mexico was the highest achievement of a very late Mayan architectural style called Puuc. It was completed in the 10th century.

Arab manuscript showing preparation of perfumes

Sa'adia ben Joseph, head of the **Jewish academy in Babylon,** is known as the father of Jewish philosophy. He defended orthodox Judaism by reaffirming a belief in one God against gnostic dualism. He also repudiated the earlier **Koraite** rejection of the Talmud (the oral tradition of law) in favor of the Torah (the original scriptures that were given to Moses).

In China, with the continuing decline of the T'ang dynasty and the unrest of the 10th century, nostalgia suffused the **tzu poetry** of **Li Yu,** 937–78. The *tzu* poets adapted the irregular structure and colloquial language of Chinese folk verse, usually sung to a tune.

An Imperial Academy of painting was founded in western China during the Ten Kingdoms period, 907–80. **Ching Hao,** 900–60, wrote an essay on landscape painting that stressed the metaphysical implications of the art.

The tambura, a 4-stringed lute-shaped instrument, developed in India in the 10th century as a drone accompaniment to melodic instruments.

The alembic, an apparatus for distilling chemicals and perfumes, was illustrated in Arabic books of this time. The alembic played an important part in Arab chemistry and strongly influenced its development.

970–1000

Hugh Capet, *r.*987–96, became king of France and reasserted royal authority over the nobility, pope, and emperor. **Venice** was given trading privileges in the Byzantine Empire in 992. **Viking invasions** of Europe reached their peak *c.*1000, threatening southern France and Italy. **Basil II** of Byzantium, *r.*963–1025, took Greece from the Bulgarians in 996.

Quetzalcóatl, priest-ruler of the military aristocracy of the Toltec people in central Mexico, abdicated in 987.

The Vikings, whose incursions into the Christian world reached a peak *c.*1000, worshiped gods similar to those of the Germans. There were two tribes of gods, one of them (**the Aesir**) led by **Odin,** who lived in the castle Valhalla where he was joined by heroes killed in battle and assisted by them in a perpetual fight against wolves.

A revival of Persian poetry using the Arabic alphabet produced the national epic *Shah-Nama* (Book of Kings) by **Firdausi,** 935–1020, who used legend and history in verse that became a model for Arab epics. **An Anglo-Saxon historical poem** with a central theme of feudal loyalty was *The Battle of Maldon,* *c.*995.

Romanesque architecture after 950 possessed a grandiose quality that derived partly from the use of stone vaults below the roofs and partly from a more unified concept of the church, which developed in response to the needs of the clergy, monks, and pilgrims who used them. Two main plans were influential—that of an ambulatory with radiating chapels as at St Martin at Tours, and the chapels on either side of the main apse at Cluny Abbey.

Chinese temple music under the Northern Sung dynasty, 960–1279, involved huge choruses with orchestras of zithers and mouth organs in an organum style of complex sonority.

The windmill reached Muslim Spain from Persia in the 10th century. **Mining in Christian Europe** centered on the Harz Mountains in the 10th century, where the Saxons mined copper and iron. **Gerbert,** a French mathematician, 940–1003, who became Pope Sylvester II, is thought to have introduced the astrolabe and Arabic (Indian) numerals into Europe from Córdoba. He has also been credited with the invention of a mechanical clock *c.*996.

The Crusades 1000–1250

Principal events

Europe now began to take the offensive, expanding geographically and economically, her population rising. A new spirit of confidence, epitomized by the cosmopolitanism of Norman culture, brought a series of attacks on the Muslims in Spain and in Syria, where the Crusades provided an aggressive outlet for the military nobility of the flourishing feudal system. The papacy reached the height of its power during the reign of Innocent III, 1198–1216, in spite of continuing opposition to the gradual concentration of its power both from within the Church and from secular rulers.

In the 13th century Genghis Khan set up a Mongol Empire in China, swept across Asia and threatened Europe and North Africa, creating the largest empire ever known and bringing a new peace and unity to Asia in his wake. He did not, however, conquer India, where the various Muslim rulers built up their authority in the north.

1000–1025

Basil II, 958–1025, briefly restored Byzantine authority in Syria, Crete, and south Italy and destroyed the Bulgarian army.
Canute, 994–1035, built a unified Danish Empire comprising England, Norway, and Denmark.
Mahmud, the brilliant Muslim ruler of the Ghaznavid Empire in Afghanistan, 997–1030, plundered and annexed the Punjab.
The Chola dynasty of Tamil kings unified southern India and took Ceylon and Bengal, 1001–24.

1025–1050

William I, a vassal of the French king, became Duke of Normandy in 1035, organizing Normandy on full feudal and military lines.
The Umayyad dynasty in Spain fell as a result of racial and religious pressures in 1031. The support of **Pope Leo IX,** *r.*1049–54, for monastic reform stimulated the concept of papal supremacy over secular rulers.
Yaroslav, *r.*1019–54, brought Kievan Russia to its peak (promoting education and building).

1050–1075

Ferdinand of Castile, *r.*1035–65, recovered Portugal from the Muslims in 1055.
William of Normandy, introducing a fully feudal society, conquered England in 1066, while another Norman kingdom was established in southern Italy in 1068, finally ousting the Byzantines.
The Berber dynasty of Almoravids built a kingdom in Algeria and Morocco, 1054.
The Ottoman Empire began with the capture of Anatolia in 1071.

1075–1100

Pope Gregory VII, *r.*1073–85, and Emperor Henry IV, *r.*1050–1106, clashed on the investiture issue, over the respective rights of the Holy Roman Emperor and the papacy in appointing bishops. **The Almoravids** annexed Moorish Spain 1086, but **Alfonso VI,** *r.*1072–1109, retook Toledo. The First Crusade, 1096–99, captured Jerusalem and set up Frankish kingdoms in the Near East. **Alexius I,** Byzantine emperor, *r.*1081–1118, recovered some territory.

The Americas

The first white men to explore the Americas came from Scandinavia, but their visit had little impact. The Inca Empire was beginning in the Cuzco Valley in Peru, while in another valley in Mexico the Aztecs appeared. The Pueblo tradition flourished in the southwest United States.

1000–1025: **Leif Ericson** visited North America *c.*1000, calling the area Vinland. A Norse colony was established at L'Anse aux Meadows in Newfoundland.

1025–1050: **The architecture of Chichén Itzá,** in the central Yucatán, Mexico, began to show strong Toltec influences after 1000, particularly the feathered-serpent motif.

1050–1075: **An elaborate underground water system** was begun *c.*1050 to irrigate crops and supply the city of Casas Grandes in northern Chihuahua, Mexico.

1075–1100: **According to Inca legend,** Manco Capac led his followers to the Cuzco Valley in Peru. There the Inca Empire was founded with Cuzco its capital.

Bayeux tapestry: William the Conqueror and companions

Chichén Itzá: Kukulkan

Crusading knights: Hospitaller, Teutonic Knight, Templar

Early Gothic: Laon Cathedral

Religion and philosophy

In the emerging struggle for power between the Church and the rulers of the new European states, the papacy succeeded in asserting its right to judge the morality of secular political actions at the same time as it took the lead in the reform movements within the Church.

In both the Muslim and Christian worlds, there was a revival of philosophy and a return to the Greeks, especially Aristotle. This was essential to the rise of scholasticism, an important philosophical movement within the Catholic tradition, based on the notion that dialectical reasoning as well as faith and revelation could illuminate the mysteries of Christian belief.

The Mahayana form of Buddhism, which allowed lay salvation, spread from China to Japan. There it evolved into a popular devotional cult centered on ritual chanting, in sharp contrast to the elitist monasticism of Zen, which was also emerging within Japanese Buddhism at this time.

1000–1025: **Saint Symeon** (Simon), *c.*949–1022, "The New Theologian," developed the orthodoxy within the Greek Church on meditation and revelation in a mystical direction.
Pope Benedict VIII, *r.*1012–24, promulgated a decree against clerical marriage and concubinage at the Council of Pavia in 1022.

1025–1050: **Avicenna,** 980–1037, also known as Ibn Sina, was an eclectic Muslim thinker and physician. He wrote *The Book of Healing*, a monumental encyclopedia elaborating mainly Aristotelian theories of philosophy and medicine.
Buddhism became firmly established in Tibet in 1038.
Pope Leo IX, *r.*1049–54, issued stern decrees against simony (the purchase of ecclesiastical office), thereby identifying the papacy with Cluniac reform.

1050–1075: **The schism** between the papacy and the Greek Christian Church was fixed in 1054, when **Pope Leo IX** closed Greek churches in southern Italy for unorthodox practices, such as the use of leavened bread in the Mass.
Berengar of Tours, 999–1088, argued that reason could justify the contravention of authority. He denied the doctrine later known as transubstantiation, but was finally forced to recant, 1059.

1075–1100: **The Dictatus Papae** of 1075 by **Pope Gregory VII** (Hildebrand), *r.*1073–85, decreed that popes were able to depose emperors.
Roscellinus, *c.*1050–1120, was an early proponent of the scholastic tenet of nominalism, holding that the qualities we ascribe to objects, like color, do not exist in reality but are just the product of thought or language. He denied the unity of the Trinity, but he was forced to recant by the Synod of Soissons in 1092.

Literature

Of the European literatures, French was the most influential in the development of new literary forms in the 11th and 12th centuries, producing the chanson de geste in written form, the Arthurian romance tradition, and the lyrical vernacular poetry of the troubadours, all of which soon became international. The common heritage of warfare against the Muslims in Spain was the subject of the French Chanson de Roland and also of the great Spanish epic El Cid.

In the Near East the solitary genius of Omar Khayyam flourished, while in Japan the late Heian period saw the emergence of underivative Japanese styles including the literary diary of which The Tale of Genji, written by a lady at court, is the best-known example.

1000–1025: **The greatest of all Japanese novels, The Tale of Genji,** was written by the court lady **Murasaki Shikibu,** 978-*c.* 1031; it is an elaborate, realistic tale of court life. Japanese ladies of the Heian court wrote witty prose, notably the *Pillow Book of Sei Shonagon*, *c.*1000.

1025–1050: **The Sung period,** 960–1279, in China was mostly an age of prose. Its great writers were **Ou-Yang Hsiu,** 1007–72, and **Sung Chi,** 998–1061, who collaborated on a Confucian history. **Su Shih,** 1037–1101, widened the subject matter of tzu (song form) poetry and introduced vernacular words, thus contributing to Yan "drama" which resembled opera.

1050–1075: **In Persia** the scientist, mathematician, and poet **Omar Khayyám,** *c.*1048–1122, wrote *The Rubaiyat* (quatrains), which expresses a rational, pessimistic, and hedonistic philosophy—ideas then unacceptable to orthodox Islam. It is not certain how many of the almost 500 quatrains were written by him.

1075–1100: **The chansons de geste,** epic poems consisting of a series of stanzas using a single rhyme and celebrating the history of the Age of Charlemagne, were sung by traveling musicians. The earliest written example, *The Song of Roland*, dates from *c.*1100.

Art and architecture

The transition from Romanesque to Gothic architecture involved a structural and visual change in the aisled church, beginning in France and England. Separate inventions—stronger pointed arches at Cluny and rib vaults at Lessay—were then combined as in the vaults of Durham, which were supported by buttresses beneath the gallery roofs. External flying buttresses, first used at Notre Dame, allowed Gothic architecture to develop. With these the building became an independent frame in which larger windows were inserted.
Bar tracery produced the lovely patterns of French 13th-century architecture, which spread swiftly across Europe, reaching Cologne in 1248 and England with the additions to Westminster Abbey in 1245.

Castles developed from the primitive motte-and-bailey to the sophisticated designs of the Crusaders' permanent garrisons, such as the Krak des Chevaliers (first fortified 1110) in Syria.

1000–1025: **Ottonian architecture** in Germany took its cue from **St Michael's Hildesheim** (designed apparently by Bishop Bernward) with its unvaulted double choirs and arcades of square piers alternating with round, short columns. **Dravidian architecture** reached a peak of sophistication under the Chola period in India. The great **Temple of Shiva** at Tanjore with its pyramid and dome-shaped finial profoundly influenced Southeast Asian architecture.

1025–1050: **The Muslims** raided west India between 1000 and 1026, defacing many of the temples. This led to the building of the most important **Gujarat temples** with characteristic colonnaded halls and "pyramids" of massed cupolas. **Wulfic's Rotunda of St Augustine's Abbey,** Canterbury, 1049, marked the end of English architectural isolation; both this and the later **Westminster Abbey,** 1055–65, of Edward the Confessor, used Continental models.

1050–1075: **The Byodo-in Temple,** 1053, in Japan has the brilliance and delicacy of ornament typical of the **Fujiwara** culture. The Phoenix Hall houses a wooden Amida Buddha by the contemporary sculptor **Yocho.**

1075–1100: **Durham Cathedral,** unlike all previous church architecture, was vaulted throughout. It used a new and more stable combination of round and pointed arches and had buttressed arches beneath the gallery roof.
The Bayeux tapestry, *c.*1080, whose continuous narrative describes the Norman victory over the English and the events preceding it, was sewn to adorn Bayeux Cathedral, though it was probably made in Canterbury.

Music

Polyphony developed further in both the religious and secular music of Europe in the Middle Ages, having long existed in folk music, particularly in Britain. At the same time set musical forms, like the ballade, virelai, and rondeau, evolved from songs and dances. Both developments reflected the medieval delight in uniting contrasting elements in a consistent whole.

1000–1025: **A cantus firmus** was used as a fixed melody about which a line of embellishment could be worked. In this could be seen the origins of counterpoint.

1025–1050: **Guido d'Arezzo,** *c.*997–*c.*1050, advocated the use of the staff (a grid of horizontal lines) in notation and made simple rules for defining relative pitch of notes, later revived as the tonic solfa.

1075–1100: **Troubadours** appeared in Provence late in the 11th century, singing to their own harp accompaniment. They set stanzas of poems to music, producing complete compositions in new forms.

Science and technology

Arabic science and philosophy reached its height in the 11th century with the work of such major figures as Avicenna, al-Biruni, and Alhazen in the Middle East and Averroes in Spain, but soon afterward it declined. It was at this time, in the early 12th century, that the influence of Arab science began to show in Europe with the introduction of Arabic numerals. These were used in the already powerful business world of Italy which, unlike China and the Arab lands, was to develop an economy based on money. Other signs of the power Europe was to achieve were rapid growth in the silk and glass industries in the south and the use of coal and the beginnings of cast iron manufacture in the north. This technology owed a heavy debt to Chinese expertise, brought to Europe at this stage via the Arab world but later derived directly from China, which would trade extensively with Italy after the visits of Marco Polo.

1000–1025: **Avicenna** (Ibn Sina), 980–1037, and al-Biruni, 943–1048, were two of the greatest Arab encyclopedists of science. **Avicenna** wrote on astronomy, physics, and medicine, which he also practiced, and his theory and methods were taught in Europe for the next 700 years. **Al-Biruni** wrote on mathematics, astronomy and astrology, geography, and history, and was the first botanist to analyze the structure of flowers by methods important to plant classification.

1025–1050: **Illustrated botanical texts** were published in China in the 11th century. These had medical as well as botanical importance since the pharmacology of drugs obtained from plants was a highly advanced science in China. **Alhazen,** or Ibn al-Haitam, *c.*965–1038, wrote *Optical Thesaurus*, the first important work on dioptrics (the optics of the eye), which influenced the work of **Roger Bacon,** the 13th-century English scholar.

1050–1075: **Mold boards,** curved boards on plows which overturn the plowed earth and thereby improve soil structure and aeration, came to be used in Europe from the 11th century onward, although they had been known in China for 1,000 years.
Omar Khayyám, *c.*1048–*c.*1122, a Persian poet and mathematician, solved cubic equations by geometric methods *c.*1075, and worked at the sultan's court in Merv, reforming the Muslim calendar.

1075–1100: **Chinese medical texts** written in the 11th century include one of a qualifying examination for doctors and enlarged editions of medical pharmacopoeias.
Indian commentators on science in the 11th and 12th centuries described the medical uses of yoga meditational techniques.

1100–1125

The Seljuk Empire gradually split into separate regencies.
The Concordat of Worms, 1122, brought a compromise to the investiture controversy.
Louis VI of France, *r.*1108–37, granted urban charters to many French Towns. In **Manchuria** the Jurchen tribes overthrew the Khitai with Chinese assistance, 1116, and destroyed the Chinese Sung dynasty, 1136.
The Khmer Empire in Cambodia reached its peak, *c.*1100.

1125–1150

Alfonso VII, *r.*1126–57, resumed the conquest of Spain while the Muslim dynasties of Spain and North Africa fought each other. After the fall of the **Frankish kingdom of Edessa** to the Seljuk Turks, 1144, the disorganized Second Crusade failed to halt the Turkish advance, 1147–49.
The communal movement of the north European towns claiming independence from royal authority reached Rouen, 1145.
Kiev declined after the death of **Vladimir Monomach,** 1125.

1150–1175

Henry II of England, *r.*1154–89, added Aquitaine and Gascony to the Angevin Empire in France, and heightened the conflict of secular and papal authority by having **Becket,** Archbishop of Canterbury, murdered in 1170.
Saladin, *r.*1169–93, united the disparate Muslim tribes in Egypt and Syria under the Egyptian **Ayyubid dynasty. Civil War in Japan** among the local clans, 1156–81, accelerated the decline of imperial authority over the feudal magnates

1175–1200

The Seljuks took Anatolia, 1176, and Saladin took Jerusalem, 1187. The third Crusade, 1189–91, rewon the city.
Muhammad of Ghur, *r.*1176–1206, took Delhi and Bihar in India. A Muslim kingdom was set up at Delhi on his death.
Yoritomo's defeat of the Taira clan, 1185, in Japan inaugurated the Kamabura period.
Emperor Frederick I (Barbarossa), *r.*1152–90, was defeated by the league of Lombard towns in his invasion of Italy, 1176.

1200–1225

Venice persuaded the **Fourth Crusade,** 1202–04, to take Constantinople, setting up the Latin Empire of the East 1204–61.
King John of England, *r.*1199–1216, was forced to sign the Magna Carta, 1215, subjecting the monarchy to the rule of law.
Alfonso VIII, *r.*1170–1214, defeated the Almohades, 1212.
The Mongols, under **Genghis Khan,** *r.*1206–27, had invaded China, Persia, and southern Russia by 1225.

1225–1250

Assimilation of native ideas by the ruling minority created a fusion of Muslim and Hindu cultures in northern India by 1230.
The Mongols annexed the Chin Empire in China, 1234, overran eastern Europe, and set up the Tatar state of the Golden Horde on the lower Volga in 1242.
Alexander Nevsky, *r.*1236–63, prince of Novgorod, defeated the Teutonic Knights, 1242.
Jerusalem was lost to the Turks in 1244 and the Seventh Crusade, 1248–50, achieved little.

A Mogollon-Anasazi pueblo at Kinishba, Ariz., was inhabited *c.*1100–1350. It is one of the largest ruin sites in the Southwest.

The Chibcha culture of Colombia had a highly organized political organization that involved five states, each with a chief. The major one was near Bogotá.

The Aztec Ruins pueblo in New Mexico was abandoned *c.*1150 soon after it was completed, probably due to climate change. The inhabitants returned *c.*1225.

The Toltec cities of Tula and Chichén Itzá, in Mexico, declined. Tula was burned by Chichimecs, and Chichén Itzá was defeated and then abandoned.

The nomadic Mexica Indians migrated south into the Valley of Mexico, bringing religious practices that included human sacrifice. They became the Aztecs.

The people who lived at Moundsville, Ala., were skilled architects who built remarkable mound enclaves and created a unique art form.

Classical Khmer architecture: temple complex at Angkor Wat

Pope Innocent III

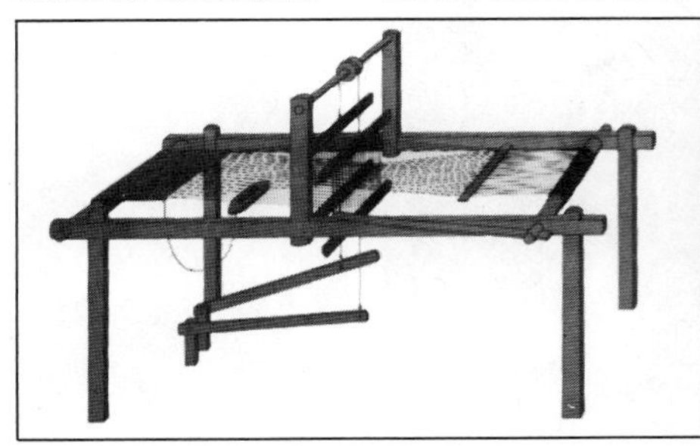

European treadle loom, 13th c.

Genghis Khan

St. Anselm, Archbishop of Canterbury 1093–1109, one of the first scholastic philosophers, sought to establish the existance of God by reason, arguing that God must necessarily exist since He is perfect and it is more perfect to exist than not.
Peter Abelard, 1079–1142, French theologian and philosopher, advocated reason as a source of truth. His nominalist ideas led to his condemnation at the Council of Soissons in 1121 for his views on the Trinity.

St. Bernard, 1090–1153, Cistercian abbot of Clairvaux in France, strongly encouraged mysticism and contemplation in opposition to the scholastic rationalism prevalent in Western Christendom. **Honen,** 1133–1212, founder of the Pure Land Sect in Japan, joined the **Tendai Sect** in 1148.
Gratian, a Benedictine monk, compiled the *Decretum Gratiani*, a collection of canon law *c.*1140.

Averroes, 1126–98, the Islamic scholar, began writing his influential commentaries on Aristotle in 1169. He also argued that reason could serve to establish religious truths.
The Waldenses, founded by **Peter Waldo** in 1173 in southern France, rejected the license of the official Church and adopted a simple way of life, electing their own priests.

Zen Buddhism was introduced into Japan in 1191 by the monk **Eisai,** 1141–1215. Zen stressed personal instruction by a master, rather than the study of scriptures, as the way to enlightenment. His techniques included sudden physical shocks and meditation on paradoxical statements. **Neo-Confucianism** emerged in the 12th century in China. **Chu-Hsi,** 1130–1200, one of its most influential exponents, completed his commentaries, *The Four Books*, in 1189.

Islam became firmly entrenched in India with the establishment of the Delhi kingdom in 1206.
The True Pure Land Sect (Jodo Shin) was founded in Japan in 1224 by **Shinran,** 1173–1262. For him, salvation came only through faith and the Buddha's grace. Because it rejected monasticism and ascetic practices, this became, and still is, the largest Buddhist sect in Japan.

The Franciscan and Dominican orders of friars, devoted to the care of the poor and the sick, spread quickly, 1225–30.
Nicherin, 1222–82, a Japanese Buddhist monk, added a highly nationalist element to Japanese Buddhism. By 1250 he had proclaimed the *Lotus Sutra*, the central writing of the Mahayana tradition, as the supreme Buddhist scripture. He desired to end Buddhist sectarianism in order to regenerate and unify Japan against China.

A miracle play was performed at Dunstable *c.*1100. In such Latin plays, performed in churches and drawing on both the scriptures and the lives of saints, lie the roots of the medieval drama as later practiced.

The first bardic period of Hindi literature began in India. Among the important early epics is the *Prithvi Rah Raso*.

The lyrical poetry of the troubadours grew up in 12th-century France. Written in a Provencal dialect and sung to music, it lauded a concept of love as a knightly duty then fashionable in the southern French courts.
Mystère d'Adam *c.*1175, marks a major development toward popular drama; it is in French, not Latin, uses the vernacular, and was later played outdoors.

The long Middle High German epic Nibelungenlied, which has survived in thirteenth-century manuscripts, was written by an unknown Austrian; its hero is Siegfried, it has connections with Scandinavian legends and has influenced many writers and composers, notably Wagner.
Chretien de Troyes, *fl.*1165–80, developed the prose romance in *Conte del Graal*.

The German minnesinger tradition, parallel to the Provençal courtly poetry, is exemplified in the songs of **Walther von der Vogelweide,** *c.*1170–1230, a wanderer and a beggar. He discarded the older strict form, as did his contemporary. **Wolfram von Eschenbach,** *fl.*1200–20, author of the great German romance, the grail-story *Parzival*, *c.*1210.

The Icelandic Classical period culminated in the work of **Snorri Sturluson,** 1179–1241, who wrote the *Edda*, a handbook that set out the Icelandic myths and the types of poetic diction used in old Norse poetry.
Literature in Japan declined with the Kamakura period, 1192–1333, but war tales, especially the *Heike monogatari*, *c.*1215–50, became an established form.

Chinese landscape painting reached its zenith under the patronage of **Hui Tsung,** *r.*1101–25. Great care was lavished on tiny details in an attempt to reveal the inner life of the objects shown. Li Chieh's treatise on **Sung architecture** is a blend of learning and practical instruction on survey geometry, uses of building materials, and decorations, and includes recipes for colored glazes for floor and roof tiles.

At Autun Cathedral in France Gislebertus sculpted all the nave capitals, *c.*1125–35, the west door tympanum depicting the Apocalypse.
Abbot Suger rebuilt the choir and westwork of **St Denis,** near Paris, *c.*1140–44. The first example of mature Gothic, its slender pillars and pointed arches allowed big lancet windows with stained glass in the apse chapels; statues adorned the porch.

A change in the design of Cistercian monasteries followed the death of **St Bernard of Clairvaux** in 1153. After the harsh simplicity of **Fontenay,** built in 1139, **Clairvaux III,** 1153, and **Pontigny** apse, *c.*1185, are richer and more imposing.
External flying buttresses, first used at Notre Dame, Paris, *c.*1163, enabled clerestory as well as ground floor windows to be treated as a frame, with a thin web of stone and glass between.

In the second Angkor period the Cambodian capital of **Angkor Thom** was rebuilt, 1181–95, followed by temples in **Angkor Wat.** The ashlar façades were deeply carved to resemble gigantic faces.
High Gothic architects used the new construction techniques to varied aesthetic ends and made structure itself ornamental. Most important were **Chartres** and **Bourgues,** 1195, **Canterbury,** 1174, and **Lincoln,** 1192.

The Peruvian Chimú capital of Chanchan had adobe buildings with trapezoidal doors and intricate geometrical surface designs. Pottery played an important part in decoration. **An International style** known as **Rayonnant Gothic** was born in 1220 at Amiens Cathedral.
The massive "Black Pagoda," a Jain temple of the sun, was begun at Kanarak in Orissa *c.*1200. Only the base, carved with erotic reliefs, survives.

The Sainte Chapelle, Paris, was built, 1240–48, as **St Louis'** palace chapel and to house the Crown of Thorns relic. The walls are like continuous sheets of glass and made the design a symbol of prestige.

Three- and four-part polyphony was composed round a *cantus firmus*, but early in the 12th century two parts were more usual. The harmony often used sounds dissonant to modern ears.

Trouvères in northern France developed on similar lines to the troubadours, producing *formes fixes* (set structures of contrasting phrases), among them the ballade, virelai, and rondeau.

The conductus developed as processional music in a chordal style late in the 12th century. Composed for voices or instruments, it was based on original themes rather than plainsong.

The minnesinger created a tradition of German song inspired by the art of the troubadours. Notre Dame choir school in Paris flourished under the great masters Léonin and Pérotin.

Muslim rule in northern India after 1206 strengthened secular music and featured the use of the **sitar.** Southern Indian music remained restrained and classical, favoring the **vina.**

"Sumer is icumen in," an English song of astonishing form, written *c.*1240, was the first recorded canon. It is a four-part round over a two-part repeated pattern in the bass parts.

Silk manufacture began in south Italy in the 12th century as a result of Arab influence and by the 13th century water-powered silk mills were in operation.
Stained-glass windows of the early 12th century demonstrate the high-level glass technology found in Europe. Glass was colored by the addition of particular metal salts; those of copper for green, copper or gold chloride for red, iron or silver for yellow, and cobalt for blue.

Coal was used at Liège for iron-smelting beginning about 1150.
Alcohol was probably first distilled from wine at Salerno in the 12th century. Although fully able to do so, the Arabs had not made alcohol because it was prohibited by the Koran.

Maimonides, 1135–1204, the great Jewish thinker, worked at the court of Saladin and wrote on medicine, theology, and philosophy. He described diseases and cures in a way that we now recognize as that of psychosomatic medicine.
Averroes, or Ibn Rushd, 1126–98, the leader of Arabic science and the major encyclopedist of his day, worked in Córdoba. His scientific writings led to the Averroist school of scientific thought in Europe.

Old London Bridge and the Avignon bridge were built *c.*1175.
Cast iron, made by melting and molding the metal, was first produced in Europe. It was made possible by higher furnace temperatures.
Leonardo Fibonacci, *c.*1170–*c.*1240, the greatest medieval mathematician, wrote the first Western textbook on algebra about 1200.

Stückofen, the precursors of blast furnaces, operated in Styria, central Europe, as early as the 13th century. These furnaces burned charcoal.
Universities founded in Europe in the early 13th century included those of Paris and Oxford.
Roger Bacon, *c.*1214–*c.*94, was one of the few important experimenters in medieval English science. He had an extensive knowledge of astronomy and medicine and employed lenses to correct defective vision.

Frederick II, Holy Roman emperor, *r.*1220–50, a serious student of natural science, wrote a treatise on falconry that is a model of natural history for its combined learning and observation.
Stern-mounted rudders were first fitted to European ships at this time, although the Chinese had invented them centuries earlier.
Navigational charts came to be first used by Western sailors in the 13th century.

The Mongols Unify Asia 1250 – 1400

Principal events

In Europe the crusading mentality gave way to a more flexible, commercial society, epitomized by the rise of the Italian city-states, the Hanseatic League of trading towns in the north, and merchant and trade guilds. Kings came to depend more closely on popular support and called parliaments in which they consulted a wider section of the population, including townsmen. After 1300, the growth of European population and prosperity gave way to famine and plague, which reduced many towns and introduced a period of retrenchment. The population decline, however, increased the bargaining power of the laborers, later enabling the peasantry to escape serfdom.

The Mongols brought prosperity and trade to much of Asia, but their empire was fragmented by religious conflict. Their benevolent rule in China was replaced by the native Ming dynasty in 1368.

1250–1265

Gold currencies were introduced in Florence and Genoa, 1252, and bankers, such as the Bardi in Florence, flourished.
Chinese silk became available in Europe in 1257 along the silk route opened up as a result of Mongol expansion.
Kublai Khan, *r.*1260–94, set up the Yüan dynasty in China.
In England, de Montfort's Parliaments, 1264–65, reflected the improved status of townsmen and lesser knights.

1265–1280

Louis IX of France, *r.*1226–70, the most powerful and respected monarch in Europe, died in Tunis on the ninth and last Crusade.
Mongol peaceful rule in Asia inspired a Venetian trader, **Marco Polo,** 1254–1324, to visit China in 1271–95.
Rudolf of Hapsburg, from an old Swabian family, was elected King of Germany in 1273 and thus became founder of the Hapsburg dynasty.

1280–1295

The defeat of the Mongol invasions of Japan in 1274 and 1281 strengthened the Japanese military clans.
The Danish Magna Carta, 1282, united royal power.
Tripoli and Acre fell to the Mamelukes, 1289–91.
The Yüan dynasty in China restored canals and built roads.
Osman, 1259–1326, founded the Turkish Ottoman principality in Bithynia in 1290.
The western Mongols rejected the khan's authority in 1295.

1295–1310

Venice was governed by a narrow oligarchy of merchants who consolidated their power by crushing the popular and patrician revolts of 1300 and 1310.
A conflict over papal authority led **Philip IV,** *r.*1285–1314, of France to call one of the first Estates-General in 1302 to appeal for national support.
Military anarchy in Italy drove the papacy to Avignon in 1309.
The African Empire of Mali, based in Sudan, flourished.

The Americas

The first known white colony (established *c.*1014) continued in Newfoundland. The prehistoric Pueblo culture reached its peak *c.*1300 and began to decline.

Prehistoric Mayan civilization was in its last centuries, while the Aztec Empire emerged. The Chimú and Inca empires, were expanding by conquest.

The Mayans, who were excellent navigators, were engaged in extensive trading by sea-going canoe. They ranged as far south as Panama and Nicaragua.

A severe drought in the Southwest, which was to persist for 23 years, began in 1276 in the area of Mesa Verde; the culture there was in its classic stage.

Mayapán, the capital of the Itzá, who were the last strong Mayan tribe, *c.*1283 was the last site of prehistoric Mayan civilization, which disappeared by 1450.

Emerald Mound, which extends over eight acres near Natchez, Miss., was built *c.*1300 as a ceremonial center for the Natchez Culture peoples.

The harbor of Venice, late 12th c.

Kublai Khan

Summa Theologica
St Thomas Aquinas

"San Croce Crucifix," 1283

The Black Death: flagellants

Religion and philosophy

The scholastic tradition in European philosophy, which sought to strengthen religious faith with the help of reason, culminated in the work of Thomas Aquinas, Duns Scotus, and William of Ockham, all of whom looked to the work of Plato and Aristotle. Ockham, however, was also an empiricist, disputing the self-evidence of the principles of Aristotelian logic, like the final cause, and of Christian teachings, like the existence of God.

The reign of Pope Boniface VIII marked the summit of papal power. Following the move to Avignon, 1305, the power of the papacy declined.

The vernacular writings of Langland and Wycliffe, both Englishmen, foreshadowed the Reformation in condemning priestly corruption while advocating spiritual as well as social equality.

The Islamic world produced its most original thinker, the scholar Ibn Khaldun.

St Thomas Aquinas, *c.*1225–74, the greatest scholastic philosopher, stated his belief in the power of reason in *Summa Contra Gentiles*, 1264, in which he presented arguments designed to convince the non-believer of the power and truth displayed in Christianity. This work, together with his *Summa Theologica*, 1266–73, was influential in giving a strong Aristotelian basis to Catholic philosophy.

Roger Bacon, *c.*1214–*c.*94, a Franciscan philosopher interested in science, magic, and mathematics, in 1272 wrote *Compendium Studii Philosophiae*, attacking clerical influence. He was unusual in valuing experiment as a worthwhile and useful source of knowledge.
Madhava, 1197–1276, an Indian thinker whose life was remarkably similar to that of Christ, denied the Sankara doctrine of the illusory nature of the world.

Duns Scotus, *c.*1265–1308, an English scholastic philosopher and a Franciscan monk, drew on the work of Plato. He was a realist, denying the nominalist view that the qualities we perceive, such as the color green, are merely products of thought and do not exist in the real world. He rejected the idea of predestination and inclined to the Pelagian view that man can alter his fate by his conduct.

Pope Boniface VIII instituted the Jubilee year of 1300, when plenary indulgence was granted to those visiting Rome.
The papacy moved to Avignon in 1309, under Clement V, where it remained for nearly 70 years. The French influence over the papacy in this period marked the beginning of the decline in its temporal power.

Literature

Italian writers of the early Renaissance, particularly Dante, Petrarch, and Boccaccio, drew on the passionate and poetical faith of St Francis, the philosophical theology of Aquinas, and the new lyricism of the French troubadours to forge a brilliant literature. Honored by the princes of the Italian states, they explored in allegories, love poems, and philosophical writings the contradictions between classical humanism and Christian ideals. Italian vernacular poetry and prose was the latest to emerge among the Romance languages, but the work of writers such as Boccaccio opened the way to the vivid portrayal of contemporary life that marked the work of Chaucer in England and became characteristic of Renaissance literature.

Laudi (praises to God) became a common form of religious song in Italy during the period following the death of **St Francis,** 1226. The Franciscan friar **Jacapone da Todi,** *c.*1230–1306, was the greatest poet of this style. Written in an Umbrian dialect, his ardent mystical laudi counterposed a love of God with a harsh awareness of the secular world.

The ghazal—a 7th-century form of Arabic love poetry celebrating mystical and worldly love in mono-rhymed verses without logical sequence—was developed by Persian Sufi mystics, notably **Rumi,** 1207–73, in "Divan."
Roman de la Rose, a French poem of 22,000 lines in 8-syllable couplets, completed by 1280, included an elaborate allegory on the psychology of love.

One of the major figures in Catalan literature, Raymond Lully, 1232–1315, was a poet, mystic, philosopher, and theologian who produced 243 works. *Blanquerna*, 1289, is notable as a philosophical study of Utopia and the forerunner of the novel.
The exploits of the 13th-century Tannhäuser, a knight and poet of the **Minnesinger** school, were described in legend and ballad.

Marco Polo recorded in a Genoese prison, *c.*1298, the story of his travels in China and Asia. His account was the basis of Western knowledge of China.
Heinrich von Meissen, *c.*1250–1318, was a representative of the school of middle-class poets who succeeded the knightly Minnesingers adapting Minnesinger traditions to poems dealing with theology and philosophy.

Art and architecture

Art and architecture in Europe between 1250 and 1400 show their initial indebtedness to France, a nation that had achieved success both politically and artistically. German patrons sent for architects to build "in the French manner," while Italian masons grafted details from Rayonnant Gothic architecture onto buildings that were essentially the piled masses of Italian Romanesque. Everywhere much time, skill, and money were lavished to make buildings bigger and more ornate and objects more intricate and naturalistic, both in religious and secular spheres. The period saw the "birth" of Italian painting in the works of Cimabue, Giotto, and Duccio and the beginnings of modern sculpture with Nicola Pisano and his son, Giovanni.

Cultures in Southeast Asia became more distinct, yet borrowed freely from each other. Comparatively little survives from India at this time.

The French Rayonnant Gothic style, characterized by circular windows with wheel tracery, was exemplified on the western façade of **Rheims Cathedral,** begun in 1255, and also in Spain at **Leon Cathedral,** 1255–1303. The choir of **Old St Paul's,** London, begun in 1256, also incorporated French features. **Nicola Pisano,** *c.*1225–*c.*84, the greatest sculptor of his generation, completed a pulpit for the baptistery at Pisa, 1260.

The influence of the Four Great Masters on landscape painting of the Mongol **Yüan dynasty** in China, 1264–1368, brought a greater robustness and broader color spectrum to this important art form.
The Benin (Nigeria) bronze-casters' "lost wax" technique was developed in the late 13th century, introduced by tradition from Ife.

Cimabue, *c.*1240–1302, one of the first great Italian painters, worked toward the realistic depiction of physical form and human emotion, as in his "Sta Croce crucifix," 1283.
In England one of the earliest lierne vaults, characterized by small ribs running from one major rib to another, was built at **Pershore Abbey,** 1288. Lierne vaults became a purely decorative, typically English device.

The frescoes by Giotto, 1266–1337, in the Arena (Scrovegni) chapel in Padua, painted *c.*1305, show solidity, naturalistic detail, and perspective, and represent the turning point in Italian painting. By contrast **Duccio di Buoninsegna,** *c.*1260–1315, the first great Sienese painter, summed up the mastery of the Byzantine tradition in his "Maesta" for Siena Cathedral, commissioned in 1308.

Music

Late medieval European music was increasingly complex and brilliant, requiring more exact systems of notation. The beginning of the Renaissance produced an easing of the Church's nearly exclusive hold on serious composition and, as patrons began to sponsor secular music, compositions began to show signs of greater individuality and independence.

The motet, a polyphonic form with different words sung simultaneously in the various parts, in which the *cantus firmus* was reduced to a repeated rhythmic phrase, developed after *c.*1250.

Notation was developed for shorter time values as intricate parts were introduced to overlie lines of long notes. The new notation clarified the time relationship between the parts.

In China, during the Yüan dynasty, 1264–1368, music was encouraged. Opera developed in the theater with recitative (musically declaimed words), arias, and melodies for set moods.

The madrigal emerged in Italy. Usually set for two or more voices, it was in a strict poetic structure corresponding to the *formes fixes* of France.

Science and technology

European trade and industry, although violently arrested in the mid-14th century by the Black Death, expanded rapidly in the first century of this period. Italian galleys carried cargoes of glass, silk, and finished metal goods to northern Europe and elsewhere, returning laden with textiles from the Hanseatic cloth towns and metals from the mines of central Europe.

Intellectual life, including that of the newly founded universities of Oxford and Paris, was also vigorous. Although in science Scholasticism was still the rule, signs of a breakthrough to a more experimental approach began with the works of Oresme and Buridan in Paris and William of Ockham in England, whose ideas conflicted with those of the scholastic's ultimate scientific authority, Aristotle.

By the end of this period Arab science was limited to the teachings of a few wandering scholars, and China, the home of accurate scientific reasoning and technology, had declined due to an unwieldy bureaucracy.

Gold florins were first struck in Florence in 1252.
The first cannons, employed by the Moors perhaps as early as 1250, were simply iron buckets charged with gunpowder and filled with stones. They were ignited by means of a touch hole near the bottom of the bucket.
Vincent of Beauvais, *d.*1264, was a major encyclopedist. His *Speculum Majus*, unequaled in length until the 18th century, summarized the scientific and philosophical views of the major scholastic writers.

Commercial fishing, encouraged by the many meatless fastdays of the Christian calendar, grew rapidly during the Middle Ages in Europe. The Hanseatic League fishery, in the Baltic, reached its peak, 1275–1350, with catches of 13,000 tons of herring a year.
The spinning wheel may have been invented by 1280 but was not commonly introduced into Europe until the 14th century when it would replace the distaff and loose spindle.

Spectacles, with convex lenses, were first recorded by an Englishman, Roger Bacon, 1286. By the early 14th century they were factory-made in Venice.
Albertus Magnus, *c.*1200–80, a German encyclopedist, classified plants by their structures.

Stanches, or navigation weirs, which maintain a depth of water for ships, were built in European rivers and canals and include one built on the Thames in 1306.
Gunpowder for artillery appeared in Europe *c.*1300.
Watermarks were first used in papermaking in Italy in the late 13th century.

1310–1325

Bad harvests in 1315 brought famine to much of Europe, slowing population growth.
In north India, where Muslim dynasties ruled from Delhi since 1206, a Turkish Tughluk dynasty was founded in 1320.
In Mexico the Aztecs founded the capital Tenochtitlán in 1325 and began to colonize Central America.
Uzbeg, *r.*1312–41, converted the Mongol Golden Horde to Islam and brought Mongol prosperity to its height.

The Pueblo Culture's golden age ended, and a regressive period, marked by abandonment of the great cities and migration south and east, began.

Piers Plowman frontispiece

Giovanni Monte Corvino, 1247–1328, established the first Christian missions in China and baptized **Khaistan Kuluk,** *r.*1307–11, the third great Khan of the Chinese Yüan dynasty.
Marsiglio of Padua, *c.*1275–1342, wrote *Defensor Pacis,* 1324, a famous treatise espousing the supremacy of lay power over the Church, and claimed that all power derives from the people, for whom the ruler is a delegate.

The theme of spiritual love developed by such Tuscan poets as **Guido Cavalcanti,** *c.* 1260–1300, was given expression by **Dante Alighieri,** 1265–1321. In his *Divina Commedia,* begun *c.* 1307, he describes his journey through *Inferno, Purgatorio,* and *Paradiso,* giving insight on medieval views and religious beliefs. It made Tuscan Italy's literary medium.

The Paris school of manuscript illumination flowed in the work of **Master Honoré,** *d.*1318.
Second generation "decorated" Gothic architecture in England developed with the building of Ely Cathedral Lady Chapel, 1321–48, whose undulating blind arcading and curvilinear tracery derived from geometrical forms.
Giovanni Pisano, *c.*1245–1314, completed the pulpit in Pisa Cathedral, 1310, synthesizing Gothic and classical elements.

Drainage mills, windmills that operate drainage scoops, were invented in the 14th century. (In the 16th century the Dutch used such mills for recovering land for agriculture.)
Chaulmoogra oil, for the treatment of leprosy, was first seen in 14th-century China. It was the only effective treatment for leprosy until the 20th century.
Linen clothes were widely worn in the 14th century for the first time. This led to an improvement in personal cleanliness and decline in diseases.

1325–1340

The Ottoman Empire expanded into Thrace, 1326–61. **Edward II** of England, *r.*1307–27, was deposed and killed, 1327.
The Hundred Years War of England and France broke out in 1337 as a result of the rival claims to the French throne of **Edward III,** *r.*1327–77, and **Philip of Valois,** *r.*1328–50.
The Hanseatic League grew politically powerful *c.*1340. Alfonso XI of Castile, *r.*1312–50, ended the African threat to Spain in 1340.

The Aztecs settled on an island in Lake Texcoco with their capital, Tenochtitlán, which would flourish until the Spanish conquest.

William of Ockham, *c.*1300–*c.*49, an Englishman, was the last of the great scholastic Franciscan philosophers. He broke with the Aristotelian realism of **Aquinas** and took a nominalist position. His importance lies in his development of a sophisticated logic and epistemology of more than a purely theological significance, which was to have a great effect on later secular philosophy.

Petrarch (Francesco Petrarca), 1304–74, gave passionate form to Italian love poetry in his "Canzoniere," sonnets and madrigals inspired by his unrequited love for Laura. An admirer of Roman and Greek ideals, his humanistic outlook influenced other writers.
The Persian mystic poet Hafiz, 1320–88, used complex lyrical imagery in ghazal form.

In the Muromachi (Ashikaga) period in Japan, 1392–1573, painters followed previous traditions such as continuous narrative scrolls. Renewal of contact with China and Korea introduced new techniques such as the art of painting.
The Perpendicular style of architecture in England first appeared in Gloucester Cathedral cloister, where the ribs of the vault spread out into fan-vaulting.

Ars nova was a term coined by **Phillipe de Vitry,** 1291–1361, to describe new and freer forms of music. The earlier forms became known as *ars antiqua.*

Salt-glazing of pottery was practiced in the Rhineland from the 14th century. The potter threw salt over wares in the final stages of firing in the kiln; this produced a fine glaze that sealed off the wares.
The cross staff, a primitive form of sextant, was popularized for use in navigation by **Levi ben Gerson** of Provence, 1288–1344. **The spinning wheel** was pictured in the Luttrell Psalter of 1338.

1340–1355

Italian economic decline followed the fall of the Bardi bankers after the English monarchy repudiated its debts.
Cola de Rienzo, 1313–54, was murdered after his attempt to set up a Roman republic independent of the papacy.
The Black Death destroyed up to half Europe's population between 1348 and 1350, totally disrupting commerce.
During the Hundred Years War England profited from pillage and the ransom of captives.

The sixth Inca ruler, Inca Roca, expanded the city of Cuzco, as well as building a bridge across the Apurimac River.

Ming vase

The Flagellant movement arose in response to fear of the Black Death, but was condemned by **Pope Clement VI,** 1349. The Flagellants sought to avoid divine wrath by whipping themselves thrice daily. They began in Italy and spread to Germany and the Low Countries, where they toured the countryside proclaiming flagellation as the way to salvation.

The Italian novella was developed by **Giovanni Boccaccio,** 1313–75, in the *Decameron,* 1353, a collection of 100 witty and bawdy tales set in the time of the Black Death. Their humanism and breadth of social and psychological observation had an enormous influence on Renaissance literature everywhere. Boccaccio was influenced by Greco-Roman styles.

Italian painting followed the Sienese tradition in the works of **Simone Martini,** *c.*1284–1344, and of **Pietro and Ambrogio Lorenzetti,** both active in the first half of the 14th century. Papal patronage in the palace of Avignon brought numerous Italian artists to France. Giotto's earlier detailed studies of nature influenced the decoration of the **Tour des Anges,** *c.*1340, by **Matteo Giovanetti.**

Religious music still favored triple time as symbolic of the Trinity, but growing acceptance of **duple** (beats in groups of two) time advocated in *ars nova* showed growth of secular music.

The Black Death of 1348–51 caused a severe decline in European trade and power, badly affecting labor intensive industries such as agriculture, mining, and fishing, which did not recover for over a century.
Double-entry bookkeeping methods are known to have been used by the Massari family of Genoa *c.*1340, although they were probably used before that by the Hanseatic League, the Medicis, and the Fuggers.

1355–1370

The Holy Roman Empire was changed by papal decree, the **Golden Bull,** from a monarchy to an aristocratic federation.
The ransom of John II of France by England provoked the **Jacquerie,** a peasant revolt against war taxes, which was violently suppressed in 1358.
The Ming dynasty in China was created after a popular revolt against the Mongols, 1368.

The Norse colony in Newfoundland was less closely tied to Europe after 1367, when the last royal ship made the voyage to North America.

The English Parliament deposing Richard II

The Sufi branch of Islam spread into India, Malaya, and Africa south of the Sahara. **"Piers Plowman,"** a vernacular poem probably by the English parson **Langland** begun *c.*1362, attacked corruption in the state and Church. The poem is an appeal on behalf of the poor and a plea for spiritual equality.

A great Christian allegorical poem, "Piers Plowman," attributed to **William Langland,** *c.* 1332–1400, brought to Middle English the alliterative tradition of Anglo-Saxon verse in a series of 11 dream visions.
A more mysterious allegory was the anonymous *Sir Gawain and the Green Knight, c.* 1370, an Arthurian romance. *Pearl* was found in the same manuscript.

Potters of the Ming dynasty in China, 1368–1644, discovered underglaze painting using imported Persian cobalt. Their harmonious blue designs on white ground balanced their favorite opulent shapes and sinuous line.
Italian architecture's continuity with Romanesque was shown in the new design for the east end of Florence Cathedral by **Francesco Talenti.** Only external details such as windows are borrowed Gothic.

Guillaume de Machaut, *c.*1300–77, was the chief figure of *ars nova.* The complex forms he used involved modulation, intricate cross-rhythms, and great independence of line.

Oresme, *c.*1325–82, and **Buridan,** 1300–58, in Paris, criticized Aristotle's doctrine of motion. They were influenced by the idea of *impetus,* conceived by **Philoponos,** *c.*530, and later developed into a theory of motion by Galileo.
Iron cannons were used by the Germans from 1350 onward.

1370–1385

The Ottomans took Adrianople.
Rival popes were created in Rome and Avignon, 1378, after the breakdown of negotiations over plans to reform the papacy.
Popular revolts in Florence in 1378 and England in 1381 were suppressed.
Constitutional reform in Florence marked the beginning of Florentine power in 1382.
Moscow emerged as the focus of Russian opposition to the Mongols after the defeat of the Tatars at Kulikovo in 1380.

Ñancen Pinco, ruler of the Chimú Empire *c.*1370, began his conquests along the Peruvian coast. The empire was overcome by the Inca *c.*1465.

John Wycliffe, *c.*1320–84, and his followers the Lollards, a religious group with noble supporters in England, spread ideas that were unacceptable until the Reformation. In *On Civil Dominion,* 1376, Wycliffe proposed a propertyless church and argued for direct access to God for individuals.
In the Netherlands disciples of Gerard Groote, 1340–84, who espoused a nonritualized, humane Christianity, formed the Brothers of the Common Life.

The No play emerged in Japan in a classic form established by **Kanami Motokiyo,** 1333–84, and his son **Zeami Motokiyo,** 1363–1443, who wrote most of the 100 plays that survive from this period. No drama is formal in style, incorporates music and dancing, and is performed without scenery by males who wear masks to portray women, old men, or supernatural beings.

English Perpendicular architecture matured. Canterbury Cathedral nave had smoothly shafted columns rising to the lierne vaults.
The Hindu Vijanagar dynasty of the Deccan, India, 1336–*c.*1614, favored an almost baroque style. Groups of small buildings were characteristic, and columns were often sculptured with groups of figures and animals.

Meistersinger in Germany took over the lyric art of the aristocratic Minnesinger. Meistersinger were traders and craftsmen who founded guilds to set and keep up standards for their art.

Lock gates on Dutch canals date from at least 1373. By 1400, locks were an integral part of navigation and drainage systems of Italy and Germany.
Geoffrey Chaucer, an English writer, *c.*1345–1400, described what may be the first scientific work in English, *The Equatorial Planetarie,* which deals with a device for predicting the paths and positions of planets.

1385–1400

Portugal assured its independence by defeating Castile at Aljubarota in 1385.
Tamerlane, *r.*1369–1405, conquered Central Asia, defeated the Golden Horde, 1391, and destroyed the kingdom of Delhi in 1398, delaying the Ottoman advance westward into Europe.
The Ming dynasty began to develop a naval empire *c.*1400.
In England, Richard II's absolutist reign, 1377–99, was ended by the nobles; Henry IV took the throne, 1399.

The Southern Death cult was part of the Mississippian culture from *c.*1400–1700. Human sacrifice was depicted on artifacts in this period.

Chimú portrait jar

Ibn Khaldun, 1332–1406, the Islamic scholar, was unique in the medieval era. The greatest social thinker until modern times, he based a theory of society on social cohesion and cyclical patterns of growth and decay. In his masterwork the *Muquaddimah,* he outlined a philosophy of history and laid the foundations for what he called "a science of culture."

The first truly native English poetry was created by **Geoffrey Chaucer,** *c.*1345–1400, influenced by French and Italian styles. His best works include *Troilus and Cressida, c.*1387, and *Canterbury Tales, c.*1395.
Confessio Amantis, *c.*1390, by English poet **John Gower,** 1325–1408, told moralistic stories of courtly love.

The rebuilding of Milan Cathedral, 1387, in the northern Late Gothic style showed the influence of and enthusiasm for French ideas. Building continued throughout the Renaissance.
Tamerlane's mausolea at Samarkand were built in the decade after Baghdad's capture, 1393. Their tall domes on high drums and colorful glazed relief-tile decoration would be the inspiration for Timurid architects 1405–1500.

Dissonances and great embellishment in music were part of the general concern with richness and diversity seen in European art of the time. Paris produced the best examples.

Forged iron guns weighing 600lb (272kg) were used by Richard II, *r.*1377–99, to defend the Tower of London.
Mechanically wound steel crossbows were developed.
Weight-driven clocks, often employing elaborate striking mechanisms, appeared in Europe at this time. The earliest surviving clock in England is in Salisbury Cathedral, installed in 1386.
Observatories were among the last achievements of Arab science.

Printing and discovery 1400 – 1500

Principal events

In spite of a generally static economic climate the move toward national sovereignty increased at the expense of papal authority. The process of the consolidation of the European states continued, and the power of the monarchs over the nobility grew gradually with the help of ostentatious artistic patronage and ambitious foreign wars. In Spain, united under Ferdinand and Isabella, the Moors were finally expelled, and Ivan I established the power of Moscow by bargaining with the Tatars.

Byzantium fell to the Ottoman Turks in 1453, closing the eastern Mediterranean to Christian traffic, but European expansion began to the west as the Spanish and Portuguese thrones sponsored the exploration of alternative routes to India around the coast of Africa.

In China, the Ming dynasty made contact by sea with India and Africa and fought to protect its weak northern frontiers.

1400–1410

Tamerlane's victory at Angora in 1402 brought temporary disorder to the Ottoman Empire.
Chinese naval expeditions to India and Africa for commercial and military prestige began in 1403.
Burgundian ambitions led to a French civil war with the Armagnacs in 1404.
Venice seized Vicenza, Padua, and Verona to become the dominant power in northern Italy.
Florence won access to the sea by buying Pisa in 1405.

1410–1420

Mehmet I, *r.*1413–21, reunited the Ottoman power in the Balkans.
Henry V of England, *r.*1413–22, captured Normandy, 1417–19, after his victory at Agincourt in 1415.
The papal schism was ended at the Council of Constance, 1414–17, where **Huss**, 1369–1415, the Bohemian religious reformer, was burned for heresy.
Henry the Navigator, 1394–1460, began his systematic exploration of the African Coast.

1420–1430

The Bohemian Hussites under **John Zizka**, *c.*1370–1424, were defeated in a series of imperial crusades, 1420–33.
Henry V of England was recognized as heir to the French throne, 1420. **Joan of Arc**, *c.*1412–31, then inspired a new French national unity in support of **Charles VII**, *r.*1422–61.
Peking became the Ming capital in 1421.
Murad II, *r.*1421–51, led an Ottoman attack on Constantinople in 1422.

1430–1440

Alfonso V of Aragon, *r.*1416–58, campaigned in Italy and took Naples in 1435.
The banking and wool merchant Medici family controlled Florence, 1434–94.
Hapsburg control of the Holy Roman Empire became virtually hereditary with **Albert II**, *r.*1438–39.
John VIII, *r.*1425–48, of Byzantium, inspired serious opposition by accepting the primacy of the pope in 1439.

The Americas

The century ended with the exploration and discovery of America at Cuba and the Bahamas by Christopher Columbus. It was to be the last period in which the civilizations of North and South America would be untouched by European influence. The empires of the Incas and the Aztecs expanded.

In Kentucky, near a saltwater spring that had been visited by animals and hunters for centuries, peoples of the Fort Ancient culture settled permanently.

A 12-year period of drought began in 1413 in the southwestern part of New Mexico. Salado peoples moved into the valley of the Gila River about this time.

Itzcoatl, *r.*1428–40, led the Aztecs in a series of wars of conquest that would result in the emergence of a large and powerful empire in Mexico and Guatemala.

A very well fortified settlement was under construction at Angel Mound on the Ohio River in Indiana. A clay-and-mud wall surrounded a village with 11 mounds.

"David" by Donatello

Facade, San Maria Novella

The conquest of Constantinople by the Turks

Gutenburg's printing press

Jain manuscript, 14th–15th c.

Religion and philosophy

The relationship of Church and state was a major subject of controversy in 15th-century Europe, while the corrupt practices and moral laxity of the established religious orders came under attack. Reformers and critics of religious authority spelled out many of the themes that would be elaborated in the Protestant Reformation of the next century. Savonarola, an Italian monk, denounced corruption in Florence and the abuse of political power, calling for a regeneration of spiritual values and a steadfast devotion to asceticism.

In Bohemia the Hussites identified religious reforms with Bohemian nationalism while humanist writers in Italy, England, and Holland argued for the separation of religious and secular law and the freedom of conscience of the individual. In another sense the power of the universal Church was challenged in Spain where the crown set up the Spanish inquisition.

The Chinese emperor Ch'eng Tsu, *r.*1403–24, sponsored the publication of an 11,095-volume encyclopedia in 1403.
The Council of Pisa, 1409, attempted to resolve the Great Schism in the papacy. This had arisen in 1378, with Urban VI in Rome and Clement VII in Avignon as rival claimants, backed by the empire and France.
John XXII, the compromise candidate, satisfied no one however and the schism continued until 1417.

Pope Martin V, *r.*1417–31, whose election ended the Great Schism, moved the papacy permanently to Rome in 1420 and consolidated Church unity.
John Huss, *c.*1369–1415, a Bohemian follower of Wycliffe, criticized the papacy for the sale of indulgences (absolutions from sin) and urged a literal interpretation of the Bible. He denied the infallibility of an immoral pope and claimed the supremacy of the state over the Church.

The Hussites were Bohemian followers of John Huss. They believed that the laity should receive both the wine and bread in communion instead of bread alone. **Thomas à Kempis**, *c.*1379–1471, wrote the *Imitation of Christ c.*1425. This simple book, emphasizing the need for a moderate asceticism, was considered at the time to be the most influential Christian work since the Bible.

Nicholas of Cusa, 1401–64, in his *De Concordantia Catholica*, 1433, argued for the General Council's authority over the pope. However, the council's lack of power led him to reverse his position by 1437. Cusa also contributed to the sciences and philosophy. He wrote *Of Learned Ignorance*, in 1440, arguing against the possibility of ever attaining eternal truths.

Literature

Compared with the vitality and initiative of Boccaccio and Chaucer, European writers of the early 15th century produced less distinctive work. Learning rather than literature held sway and the revival of interest in classical studies led by the Humanist scholars in Italy had its main impact only after 1454, when the development of printing by Gutenberg in Germany produced a rapidly increasing flow of books. Two outstanding writers who drew on medieval traditions were Villon, France's first great lyrical poet, and Malory, who dominated English prose with an adaptation of Arthurian legend. Lively vernacular poetry emerged in Scotland with Henryson and Dunbar and also in Florence and Naples late in the century.

The Mabinogian collection of Celtic tales and heroic legends was preserved in the Welsh *Red Book of Hergest*, *c.*1375–1425. These anonymous stories contained a wealth of ancient mythology. They fused narrative with dialogue, conveying the vitality of the oral tradition from which these tales emerged, probably during the 11th century.

Miracle plays based on biblical themes or the lives of saints were enacted in popular style in England and Europe. **John Lydgate**, *c.*1370–1451, English imitator of Chaucer and Boccaccio, produced the *Troy Book* and *Siege of Thames*, *c.*1420. **Perez de Guzman**, *c.*1370–*c*-1460, Spanish historian and poet, examined the theory of history and role of the historian.

Alain Chartier, *c.*1390–1440, wrote the allegorical poem "La Belle Dame Sans Merci" in 1424. An attack on courtly love, it reflected political unrest in France after the defeat at Agincourt. In *Le Quadrilogue invectif*, 1422, a political pamphlet, he called for French solidarity to combat the turmoil of the Hundred Years War, using prose form to convey his plea.

The Italian Leon Battista Alberti, 1404–72, a brilliant Renaissance figure who was an architect, sculptor, and musician, wrote *Della Famiglia*, 1434, containing a theoretical treatise within a discussion of household affairs. Styled on Latin models, it displayed a pessimistic view of contemporary life. He also published works on ethics, jurisprudence, and architecture.

Art and architecture

Fifteenth-century European art was profoundly affected by the artistic Renaissance that emerged in Italy—a stylistic revolution characterized by a revival of interest in Greek and Roman antiquities that brought with it a new interest in the anatomy of the human form, in proportion, and in perspective, combined with a new sense of human dignity and confidence. Beginning in Florence, and fostered by widespread court patronage both ecclesiastical and secular, it spread rapidly to other parts of Italy and culminated at the end of the century in the masterpieces of Mantegna, Botticelli, Bellini, Leonardo, Michelangelo, and Bramante.

The Gothic style in architecture still flourished even in Italy and took new forms with the Perpendicular style in England, while International Gothic brought a new realism to European painting and sculpture.

The International Gothic style introduced a new realism into the painting of landscape, costume, and animals, exemplified in the wings of the altarpiece at Dijon, by **Melchior Broederi** *d.c.*1410.
Gothic and Renaissance styles were linked in the bronze doors of the Florence Baptistery, sculptured by **Lorenzo Ghiberti**, 1378–1455, from 1403–52.
Burgundian sculpture was characterized by the "Well of Moses," 1401, by **Claus Sluter**.

The Duc de Berry commissioned the "Très Riches Heures," *c.*1415, from the Limbourg brothers. His extensive patronage included the less-known "Très Belles Heures," and he built twelve elegant castles.
The design for Innocenti (Foundling) Hospital in Florence, 1419, by **Filippo Brunelleschi**, 1377–1446, began the architectural Renaissance in Italy and established Brunelleschi's reputation as one of the finest Renaissance architects.

Masaccio, *c.*1401–28, the first of the great *quattrocento* painters, used simplicity, naturalism, and light in a new way in his Brancacci Chapel frescoes, Florence, 1425–28.
One of the masterpieces of the International Gothic style in Italy was the "Adoration of the Magi," 1423, by **Gentile de Fabriano**, *c.*1370–1427.

Donatello, 1386–1466, an Italian and one of the greatest figures of 15th-century art, executed his classic bronze masterpiece "David" *c.*1435.
Flemish painting was revolutionized by **Jan van Eyck**, *d.*1441, who not only perfected an oil painting technique using brilliant color and subtle light effects but also brought an everyday realism to such works as "The Adoration of the Lamb," 1432.

Music

European music was dominated by the brilliance of the Franco-Flemish composers, the first great musical school. The Church favored an international style of music and would admit no other styles, but national composers successfully challenged the Franco-Flemish school in the quality of their work, especially in the field of polyphonic songs.

Under the Ming dynasty, 1368–1644, music declined in China. Long pieces, interspersing new material with a refrain, were played on the zither and tunes modulated for special effect.

Composers set parts to imitate each other. Polyphony related melodies to the *cantus firmus*, and **counterpoint** used rhythmically related tunes.

Choral polyphony using four independent parts now grew up. The voices (parts) were finely blended and the harmony euphonious, avoiding the dissonances common in earlier music.

Secular polyphony developed as part-songs were combined with the four-part texture of "learned" music. This is a style that still lives on in barbershop quartet singing in the United States.

Science

Important changes occurred in the economic and industrial organization of Europe. The Hundred Years War ended and with the Renaissance feudal methods of exchange gave way to more dynamic systems of trade. Technological change—in agriculture, mining, textiles, and glassmaking—continued, bringing a steady expansion of industry. The breakthrough of the century was the creation of Gutenberg's book-printing industry at Nuremberg.

Ships and navigational instruments had been undergoing steady improvement and by the end of the century provided explorers with the means to sail to all parts of the globe. Maritime successes stimulated the founding of schools of navigation, which produced men trained in mathematics and curious about science but relatively untrammeled by the religious ideas that had ruled the minds of educated people of earlier medieval times.

Technical treatises on military engineering and ballistics abounded in the early 15th century, especially in Germany and Italy. Among the most famous was the *Bellifortis* of 1405 by **Conrad Kyeser**, a German.
Archimedean screws, used for lifting water in Dutch polder dams, are known from 1408.
Perspective, used first in painting but later in scientific and architectural drawings, was discovered in the early 15th century by **Filippo Brunelleschi**, 1377–1446.

Drift nets up to 360ft (140m) long, towed behind fishing boats, were introduced by the Dutch fishing industry in 1416. These nets greatly improved the size of herring catches. The fish were preserved by a salting process improved by the Dutch.
Navigation was studied by experts from many nations at the court of **Henry the Navigator**, 1394–1460.
Observatories were among the last achievements of Arab science. **Ulugh-Beg**, 1394–1449, made astronomical tables.

Nicholas of Cusa, 1401–64, wrote that the Earth, and not the heavens, revolved daily, a refutation of the accepted Ptolemaic astronomical system. Nicholas's idea was based upon philosophic notions and not on observable scientific data.
Hollow-post mills, invented *c.*1430 in Holland, were an improved form of windmill in which the size of the rotating sail arms was reduced and a shaft was passed from them through a hollow post to drive machinery in a building below.

Textile industries in the 15th century used **alum** to fix vegetable dyes, such as indigo, madder, and saffron, to cloth. Black dyes were made at this time by mixing green vitriol (iron sulfate) with oak galls to make the intensely black iron stannate. In textile finishing, **gig-mills** (as first drawn by Leonardo da Vinci) were being used to raise the nap of cloth into a woolly texture.

440–1450

fter losing Serbia, the Ottoman ırks defeated a Hungarian cru-ade against them in 1444.
harles VII created a French anding army free from feudal bligations.
ars in Italy caused a rise in dip-matic activity, and artistic pa-onage became a major factor in ruler's prestige *c.*1440.
pan, under Ashikaga rule since 336, underwent a period of cul-ral refinement *c.*1440.

1450–1460

The alliance of Florence, Naples, and Milan, 1450, inspired by Medici diplomacy, ensured the balance of power among the Italian states.
The fall of Constantinople in 1453 to the Ottoman ruler **Mehmet II,** *r.*1451–81, ended 1,000 years of Byzantine rule.
George Podiebrad, 1420–71, ended the Bohemian religious wars with conciliatory policies.
The Wars of the Roses between the houses of Lancaster and York began in England, 1455.

1460–1470

Venice fought the Turks for control of the Mediterranean, 1463–79.
Louis XI, *r.*1461–83, aided French unification by ending provincial and urban privileges.
The Onin War, 1467–77, resulted from a succession dispute among the Ashikaga in Japan. This was a prelude to a century of war.
The kingdom of Songhay, based on the Middle Niger region, reached its zenith under **Sonni Ali,** *r.*1464–92.

1470–1480

Ivan the Great, *r.*1462–1505, adopted the title of tsar in 1472 and subjected Novgorod to Muscovite rule in 1478.
Burgundy was reunited with France, 1477. In spite of the Pazzi plot to assassinate him, **Lorenzo de' Medici,** 1449–92, ruled in Florence and exhausted the stagnant economy with his flamboyant foreign policy.
The marriage of Ferdinand and Isabella, 1469, would unite Aragon and Castile in 1479.

1480–1490

Ivàn the Great ended the Tatar threat to Moscow, 1480, and annexed Tver in 1485.
The Spanish Church and the **Inquisition** came under royal control after a concordat with the pope in 1482.
The Portuguese Bartolomeu Diaz, 1450–1500, rounded the Cape of Good Hope, 1487–88.
The Wars of the Roses ended with the dominance of **Henry VII** (Tudor), *r.*1485–1509, who established royal independence from baronial support.

1490–1500

Spain captured Granada, the last Moorish outpost, and expelled 200,000 Jews, 1492.
Christopher Columbus, 1451–1506, discovered the New World, 1492, on his search for a western route to India.
Vasco da Gama reached India around Africa, 1497–98.
Charles VIII of France, *r.*1483–98, invaded Italy, 1495, but was expelled by an alliance including the empire, the papacy, and Venice, formed to protect Italy from foreign domination.

---

e Xius, one of the Mayan bes, revolted in 1441 against e rival tribe, Cocoms. Mayapan sintegrated.

Among the Aztec artisans were the feather workers who mounted feathers on cloth. The feathers were part of tribute paid to **Montezuma I,** *r.*1444–69.

By c. 1466, ruler Pachacuti Inca Yupanqui, *r.*1438–71, had completed his subjugation of the Chimú Empire, extending Inca control over all of Peru.

The year 1476 marked the completion of the Inca Empire's conquest. Topa Inca Yupanqui, *r.*1471–93, took control of parts of Bolivia, Argentina, and Chile.

The magnificently carved 20-ton Aztec Calendar Stone, also known as the Sun Stone for the image of the Sun God it bears, was completed about this time.

For the English, John Cabot, 1450–98, explored North America. **Treaty of Tordesillas,** 1494, divided the colonial world between Spain and Portugal.

ıristopher Columbus

LAVRENTIVS MEDICES PETRI FILIVS

Lorenzo de Medici

"Venus" by Botticelli

The burning of Savanarola in Florence

1440, **Lorenzo Valla,** 07–57, attacked papal politi-l claims by asserting that the *nations of Constantine*, an onymous document that sup-sedly granted universal tempo-power to the papacy, was a gery. As a humanist of the lian Renaissance, Valla ac-sed the medieval philosophers deliberately misunderstanding d poorly interpreting the works Plato and Aristotle.

The Indian mystic Kabir, 1440–1518, attempted to merge some aspects of the Hindu creed with Sufist Muslim ideas. Kabir, originally a weaver from Benares, rejected Hindu beliefs in idols and castes but accepted the institutions of reincarnation and eventual release. His followers were known as **Kabirpanthis.** This movement was a forerunner of the movement of Sikhism.
The first printed Bible was produced in Mainz in 1456.

The Unitas Fratrum (Bohemian Brethren), founded by Peter of Chelchich, *d.*1460, broke with the Utraquists in 1467. They were a militantly democratic sect who, like the Taborites, rejected subordination to Rome.

Sir John Fortescue, *c.*1394–*c.*1479, in *De Laudibus Legum Angliae*, *c.*1470, praised English over Roman law and introduced the principle of "innocent until proven guilty."
Set up in 1478 by Ferdinand and Isabella with the reluctant permission of the pope, who regarded it as a breach of Church privilege, **the Spanish Inquisition** persecuted converted Jews and Muslims as well as Catholic intellectuals, among them Ignatius Loyola.

Rodolphus Agricola, *c.*1443–85, was an early Dutch humanist who influenced Erasmus. In his lectures at Heidelberg, given from 1484, he expounded a philosophy emphasizing the freedom of the individual and the intellectual and physical development of the self.
The existence of witchcraft was admitted by the Church in 1484 and its practices condemned. *Malleus Maleficarum*, 1487, described witchcraft and encouraged its suppression.

The French statesman **Phillippe de Comines,** *c.*1447–*c.*1511, argued that taxes needed sanction of the Estates-General, the representative body of nobles, gentry, and clergy.
With the defeat of the Medicis in Florence, **Savonarola,** 1452–98, established city rule free from corruption and along democratic lines. His sermons criticizing aristocratic and papal corruption led to his death at the stake in 1498.

---

ngali literature, which had sted in India since the 10th ntury, was enriched by the ymed version of *Ramayana*, de *c.*1440 by Kirttivasa, 385, and by the lyrical *Song Krishna* by **Chandidas,** 1417–. **In Spain, the Marquis of ntillana,** 1398–1458, wrote lian-style sonnets that en-hed the poetic tradition.

Medieval French verse forms were infused with vigor and blunt realism in the lyrical poetry **of François Villon,** 1430–*c.*63, in which he recalls his wasted life. He was awaiting execution when he wrote *Ballad of a Hanged Man*.
Diego de San Pedro, *fl.*1450, was best known for his sentimental novels that influenced the Spanish novel.

Scottish poetry flourished with "The Testament of Cresseid" by **Robert Henryson,** *c.*1425–1508, a tragic and powerful sequel to Chaucer's poem. **William Dunbar,** *c.*1460–1520, was less earnest but more versatile. His "Dance of the Seven Deadly Sins" is similar to Villon in its macabre vigor. The Scottish poets combined romance and satire with idiomatic language.

Arthurian legend was unified in the epic prose romance *Morte d'Arthur*, 1469–70, by **Sir Thomas Malory,** *d.*1471. Its admirably plain style and its creative adaptation of medievalism to modern thought deeply influenced later writers. It was published in 1485 by **William Caxton,** a key figure in the development of English printing, which he began in 1476.

Humanist poetry emerged in Italy where **Luigi Pulci,** 1432–84, treated the heroic Charlemagne theme irreverently in *Morgante Maggiore*, *c.*1483. Another Florentine poet, **Angelo Poliziano,** 1454–94, wrote the first secular play "Orfeo," 1480.
Matteo Maria Boiardo, *c.*1441–94, wrote Latin eulogies and lyric love poems including his epic *Orlando Innamorato*.

German satirical writing reached the common man in the popular and influential *Ship of Fools*, 1494, by **Sebastian Brant,** *c.*1458–1521, which mocked vice in rhyming couplets.
In Persia, the death of the poet and mystic Jami, 1414–92, ended the classical period of Persian Sufi poetry. He was notable for such romantic verse as "Salaman u Absal."

Italy Domenico Veneziano, 461, represented the most vanced stage of mid-century rentine painting in his "St cy" altarpiece, 1445.
gier van der Weyden, 00–64, a major mid-15th cen-y Flemish artist, produced a re emotional style than van ck. His great "Deposition" was nted *c.*1435.
Angelico, *c.*1387–1455, and **Filippo Lippi,** c.1406–69, h linked Gothic and Renais-nce styles.

The study of perspective absorbed **Paolo Uccello,** *c.*1397–1475, whose famous "Battles," 1454–57, also possess an eerie, dreamlike atmosphere.
The frescoes of S. Francesco, Arezzo, 1452, by **Piero della Francesca,** *c.*1420–92, were outside the mainstream of Italian painting and closer to the diffused naturalism of Flemish art with their mathematical precision and use of light and shade.

Leon Battista Alberti, 1404–72, writer, musician, painter, and architect, crystallized Renaissance ideas on architectural proportions and harmonious design. His use of classical elements for the church of San Sebastiano, Mantua, 1470, deprived it of an "ecclesiastical" flavor.
Hans Memling, *c.*1440–94, a German who settled in Bruges, became a successful Flemish painter and influenced later Italian art.

The equestrian monument to Bartolomeo Colleone, in Venice, commissioned in 1479 and executed by **Andrea del Verrochio,** *c.*1434–88, showed a masterly rendering of movement and a use of light and shade that anticipated Michelangelo.
In Mantua Andrea Mantegna, 1431–1506, painted his fresco "Camera degli Sposi" at the Gonzaga Palace, 1474, and in Florence **Sandro Botticelli,** 1444–1510, produced his "Primavera" *c.*1478.

English Perpendicular Gothic style with its extremely intricate vaulting is seen in the **Divinity School** at Oxford University, completed 1480.
The rebirth of Venetian painting began with **Giovanni Bellini,** *c.*1430–1516, whose "Madonna and Saints," 1488, has resonant colors and novel lighting.
Medici patronage in Florence produced the first great Renaissance villa, **Poggio a Caiano,** begun *c.*1482 by **Giuliano da Sangallo,** 1445–1516.

The two giants of the Italian **Renaissance** emerged. **Leonardo da Vinci,** 1452–1519, painted his "Last Supper" in the refectory of Sta Maria delle Grazie, Milan, in 1495–98. His rival **Michelangelo,** 1475–1564, sculpted the St Peter's "Pietà" in 1499 when 24 years old.
Donato Bramante, 1444–1514, one of the greatest architects of the High Renaissance, designed the spacious gallery of **Sta Maria delle Grazie,** Milan, dating from 1492.

---

e use of the interval of a third ng established in England) ndardized harmony in poly-ony but the increasing preoc-pation with harmony itself led dull and static rhythms.

National forms evolved in polyphonic song, with the *frottola* in Italy and the *lied* in Germany matching the richness of the established *chanson* in France.

The Franco-Flemish school included Guillaume Dufay, *c.*1400–74, Johannes Ockegham, *c.*1430–95, and Josquin des Prés, *c.*1450–1521, who used popular tunes in his work.

The mass attained a great variety of structure, although the use of the *cantus firmus* throughout, in many ingenious modifications, brought unity to the form.

Keyboard instruments improved in Europe. A Flemish painting of 1484 depicts an organ with a chromatic keyboard. The clavichord had a range of up to four octaves.

Music printing began in Germany but was developed fully in Venice by **Ottaviano dei Petrucci,** who patented his process in 1498. His technique led to the birth of music publishing.

---

ann Gutenberg, *c.*1400–68, Strasbourg, began printing h movable metal type, a pro-s invented in Korea in the h century. Gutenberg's books re the first to be printed in s way in the West, yet no nted work bearing his name sts. Letters were cast in type tal, composed into sentences a type stick, and set up as es of type before being inked the press. It is possible that enberg designed his press ng the lines of wine and linen sses.

Instrument-making in Europe became centered on Nuremberg *c.*1450, and Augsburg *c.*1475.
Calendar reform was undertaken *c.*1450 under the direction of the astronomer **Puerbach,** 1423–61. The Julian calendar, commissioned by Julius Caesar and accurate to 1 day in 128 years, was wrong by 10 days in 1450. However, revision was not finished until 1582.
Quadrants, for determining latitude at sea, were used by European seafarers *c.*1456.

Carracks, the earliest form of modern sailing ships, are illustrated on a French seal of 1466. These ships had three or four masts, raised decks fore and aft, and a stern rudder and tiller for steering; by 1500 they weighed as much as 600 tons. They supplanted the trading galleys for ocean voyages, and a military version followed—the galleon.
Tables for navigation were revised by the German astronomer **Johann Müller,** 1436–76.

Rifles were first made *c.*1475, according to armory records in Turin and Nuremberg. These were muzzle loaders, in which the lead bullet was made slightly larger than the bore so that it had to be forced into the barrel, giving a tight fit.

Leonardo da Vinci, 1452–1519, painter, sculptor, architect, engineer, and scientist, began service as a military engineer with Cesare Borgia, 1476–1507, in 1502. Working mainly in Milan and Florence, he made scientific drawings of animals, human, and plant anatomy, rocks, and optical systems. He also conceived and drew a helicopter, a mobile canal cutter, and several kinds of pumps. However, most of his designs were never built, as mechanics lagged behind his inventiveness.

The voyages of Diaz, Vasco da Gama, Columbus, and Magellan, in the late 15th and 16th centuries, encouraged the founding of navigation schools in Portugal and Spain. These schools produced a new group of expertly trained mathematical and nautical technicians, which greatly influenced the standing of science in Europe.
Dissection of human cadavers had been practiced for a century in Europe but systematic dissections, in medical schools of Padua, began *c.*1500.

The Reformation 1500–1600

Principal events

The Reformation brought a new dimension to Europe's dynastic wars and social conflicts. As the Italian states declined, Spain, invigorated by wealth from the New World, led the Catholic offensive against England, the Netherlands, and the Protestant German princes. Royal authority increased with the decline of papal authority, but the religious and political debates, and the new wealth from confiscation of church lands, enabled an eloquent and powerful middle class to challenge royal power.

European expansion continued. Much of the American coastline and the Far East was reached by all the major powers, although only the American civilizations succumbed to the explorers. Japan experienced vigorous expansion, and the Moguls brought a stable and flourishing culture to India with the establishment of an extensive empire under Babur and Akbar.

1500–1510

The Italian wars provided an opportunity for conflict between the Hapsburgs and the Valois (French kings) until 1559. This caused a decline in the prosperity and autonomy of the Italian cities.
The Portuguese claimed Brazil and established regular trade with India, 1500. The Spanish introduced African slaves to the West Indies, 1501.
Ashikaga prestige in Japan was in decline.

1510–1520

Russia took Smolensk from Poland in 1514.
Charles V, 1500–58, created the Hapsburg Empire, inheriting the Spanish crown, 1516, and being proclaimed Holy Roman emperor in 1519.
Ferdinand Magellan, *c.*1480–1521, sailed through the Pacific Ocean, 1519–21, and **Hernando Cortés**, 1485–1547, conquered the Aztecs in Mexico, 1519–21. **Portugal** controlled the import of spices from the East Indies *c.*1520.

1520–1530

Portuguese traders reached China, 1520–21.
Frederick III of Saxony, *r.*1486–1525, led the princely support for Luther, 1483–1546.
Peasant revolts in Swabia, inspired by Luther's example and by discontent with feudal obligations, were ruthlessly suppressed in 1525.
Babur, 1483–1530, founded the brilliant Mogul Empire in north India in 1526.
The Medici were driven out of Florence in 1527.

1530–1540

Protestantism spread throughou[t] northern Europe. **Henry VIII** of England, *r.*1509–47, dissolved the monasteries, 1536–39.
Francisco Pizarro, *c.*1471–154[1], a Spaniard, conquered Peru for booty, from 1531.
The Afghan Sher Khan, *r.*1539–45, expelled the Mogul empero[r] Humayan and reformed the administration.
Suleiman the Magnificent, *r.*1520–66, brought Ottoman power to its zenith.

The Americas

European settlement in the Americas began on Santo Domingo, 1494. There was exploration and colonization by England, Spain, Portugal, the Netherlands, and France. The civilizations of Mexico and Peru. Explorers sought glory and wealth, the extension of Christianity, and new trade routes.

Amerigo Vespucci, 1454–1512, in 1501 led a Portuguese voyage to explore South America, which he called a "New World." In 1507 it was named America.

Juan Ponce de Léon, 1460–1521, explored Florida, 1513. **Vasco Núñez de Balboa**, 1475–1519, crossed the Isthmus of Panama to the Pacific, 1513.

Spaniard Hernando Cortés, 1485–1547, 1519, subjugated central America. **Montezuma**, *r.*1502–20, was killed, and the Aztec Empire ended, 1521.

Francisco Pizarro, leaving Panama, 1531, captured (and later executed) Inca ruler **Atzhualpa**. Pizarro's men fought over Inca wealth.

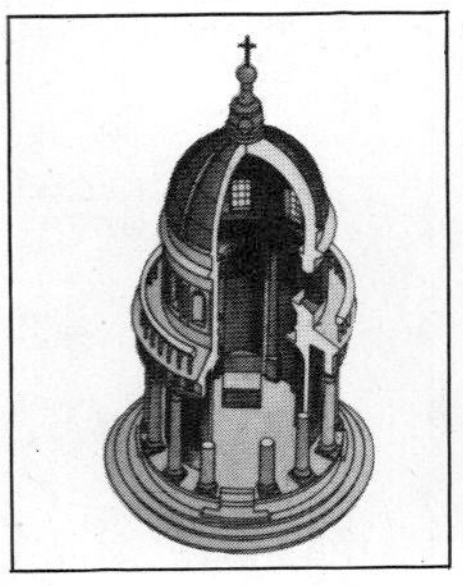

Tempietto of San Pietro

Sistine chapel frescoes: the "Birth of Adam"

Ottoman Emperor Selim 1

MARTINVS
LVTHERVS

Martin Luther

The German Peasants' war

Religion and philosophy

The Protestant Reformation took place in western Europe, arising from objections to many of the doctrines and practices of the medieval Church. Reformers attacked the worldliness of clergy, the stifling of intellectual progress, and the inability of the Church to provide spiritual leadership. Luther stated that faith alone was the basis of salvation, believing that no intermediary between man and God could alter his salvation. Calvin in Geneva also rejected the power of his Church to alter who was saved and who damned by God. The general questioning of religious authority gave a new dimension to the already critical question of the relation of Church and state, leading for example in England to rapid changes in official religion. By 1600 the Reformation had spread to almost all of northwest Europe, and there were also large numbers of Protestants in France, Poland, and Hungary.

Erasmus, *c.*1466–1536, a humanist scholar, wrote *Praise of Folly*, 1509, which satirized church corruption and scholastic philosophy.

The **Utopia**, 1516, of **Thomas More**, *c.*1478–1535, depicted an imaginary island lacking the evils of Europe.
Machiavelli, 1469–1527, wrote *The Prince*, 1513, a ruthlessly pragmatic analysis of politics.
Martin Luther, 1483–1546, affixed his 95 Theses to the door of Wittenberg Castle Church in 1517.
Sikhism, a combination of Hinduism and Islam, was founded *c.*1519 by **Nanak**, 1469–1539.

Luther was excommunicated in 1520. At the Diet of Worms, 1521, he argued for "justification by faith alone," the doctrine that no intermediary priest can aid salvation. Luther's attacks on the Catholic Church led to a rejection of papal authority and marked the start of the Protestant Reformation. This doctrine was adopted by many princes for its political implications. Luther translated the Bible into the vernacular *c.*1525.

The Anabaptists, who prophes[ied] the imminent end of the world gained control of Munster in Germany in 1534.
The Mennonites, a Dutch sect, shared the Anabaptists' belief [in] pacifism and pastoralism.
In 1534, Henry VIII of England assumed full authority over the English Church.
Ignatius de Loyola, 1491–155[6], formed the Catholic Jesuit ord[er] in 1540.

Literature

With the spread of the Renaissance the sixteenth century brought moments of great brilliance to national literatures, particularly those of England, France, Italy, Spain, and Portugal. In England, the work of Wyatt and the Elizabethan poets and dramatists culminated in the genius of Shakespeare, who created a body of lyric poetry and drama of unmatched scope and power. Rabelais and Montaigne dominated French writing, and poets such as Ronsard began the move toward classical themes in French literature. Pastoral idealism found expression in the Iberian Peninsula and Italy, and epic poetry flourished.

In China the novel form emerged, and in both India and Turkey, Islamic influence revitalized literary traditions.

Commedia dell'arte developed from earlier peasant traditions in Italy. Actors improvised farce from a set scenario using stock characters such as Pedrillo, who became the French Pierrot, and the stupid but agile Harlequin. This boisterous form of theater had little literary merit but influenced later drama, especially the comedies of **Molière** in France.

The Portuguese dramatist **Gil Vicente**, 1470–1536, wrote naturalistic plays, full of intrigue and psychological insight. The innovative English poet and humanist **John Skelton**, 1460–1529, wrote scathing attacks on the court and clergy. His German contemporary **Ulrich von Hutten**, 1488–1523, used dialogues to champion the cause of the Reformation.

Italian court life and etiquette were vividly portrayed in the *Libro del Cortegiano*, 1528, by **Baldassare Castiglione**, 1478–1529.
Portuguese poetry reached its peak with the epic *The Lusiads*, 1572, by **Luis Camoes**, *c.*1524–80.

Meistersang, a form of poetic song based on minstrel traditi[on] was popular in Germany. It wa[s] enlivened by the work of the devout Lutheran poet **Hans Sachs**, 1494–1576, a cobbler with a talent for comic verse.
Ludovico Ariosto, 1474–1533 poet, dramatist and satirist, pu[b]lished *Orlando Furioso*, 1532, the greatest Italian epic of romantic chivalry.

Art and architecture

With the work of Michelangelo, Leonardo, Raphael, and Bramante at the beginning of the 16th century, Italian Renaissance art reached a climax in the development of perspective, the analysis of the human form, and the celebration of classical models. By 1520, however, this peak was past. Mannerism followed with its lack of harmony, distorted forms, and search for novelty. Later in the century, the naturalistic experiments of Caravaggio, and Carracci's reassertion of classical canons in new dramatic compositions, pointed toward a new style—Baroque. Italy remained the official arbiter of taste in Europe, but the styles were more readily absorbed by the still solidly Catholic France and Spain. In the Protestant north the Reformation replaced Church patronage with that of merchants, encouraging the growth of secular art forms. Exploration in the New World carried European art abroad.

The Renaissance reached its height in Florence and Rome *c.*1500–20. **Leonardo da Vinci**, 1452–1519, painted the "Mona Lisa," 1503–06, achieving a more naturalistic effect by leaving outlines blurred. **Michelangelo**, 1475–1564, also in Florence at this time, completed the statue of "David," 1504. **Donato Bramante**, 1444–1514, built the Tempietto of S. Pietro, Rome, 1502, and was invited by Pope Julius II to design the new St Peter's, 1506.

Michelangelo in Rome completed the Sistine Chapel frescoes, 1512, and **Raphael**, 1483–1520, the Stanza frescoes in 1514, with their dazzling use of perspective.
Leonardo left for Amboise, France, 1516.
English Gothic art in its final stage was seen in Henry VII's Westminster Chapel, 1503–19. His tomb in the chapel by **Torrigiano**, 1472–1528, was the first use of Italian Renaissance motifs in England.

German painting showed two trends: **Grunewald**, 1480–1528, painted the Isenheim altarpiece, *c.* 1512–16, in the late Gothic style but **Dürer**, 1471–1528, who had visited Italy, made use of Renaissance ideals in his "Four Apostles," 1526.
Venetian painting broke from the Renaissance emphasis on drawing and perfect form. The Pesaro altarpiece, 1519–26, by **Titian**, *c.*1487–1576, used a dramatic juxtaposition of contrasting colors and diagonals.

The Reformation had interrupte[d] patronage in Basel and forced **Hans Holbein**, 1497–1543, to seek work in England, where h[e] arrived in 1526 with a letter o[f] introduction from Erasmus to [Sir] Thomas More. After 1532 he settled there and painted cour[t] portraits. **The Wu school** in China, including **Wen Chengming**, 1470–1559, and **T'ang Yin**, 1470–1523, worked awa[y] from the Imperial Academy, painting ink landscapes with genre scenes.

Music

The growing Protestant Church in Europe redefined the liturgy for its own use, and sacred music began to be performed by lay people in church and in their homes, widening the basis of religious music. City councils and individual patrons established their own groups of musicians, raising instrumental music to the same status as choral music.

The single or solo line drew the interest of composers of the early 1500s, reacting to the increasing complexity of polyphony. Their interest is seen in their airs and lute songs.

The fantasia, toccata and variations, and the ricercar (forerunner of the fugue) were new instrumental forms devised to exploit the individual qualities of musical instruments.

German hymns or chorales were composed in the 1520s and were firmly established by the end of the century. Set in four or five parts, they were often written to existing popular tunes.

Consorts of instruments (viols[,] recorders) were cultural perqu[is]ites found in many wealthy homes. Families of instrumen[ts] were usually played separatel[y] to give euphonious sonorities.

Science

A scientific revolution began in Europe in the 16th century and with it a long-held conception of the nature of the universe died. The century began with the later work of Leonardo da Vinci—a series of brilliant inventions that came to little because the scientific principles needed to realize them were hardly known—and culminated in Kepler's exact scientific calculations, based on Copernicus' idea of a Sun-centered universe and the precise astronomical observations of Tycho Brahe. This work finally destroyed the Aristotelian picture of the universe as a group of perfect crystal spheres centering on, and revolving about, the Earth, and opened the way for Galileo.

Advances were also made in medical science, particularly in anatomy, chemistry, larger-scale iron production, and mining technology. Despite opposition from the Church, by 1600 science was firmly based on the experimental method and had turned its back on theology.

T. B. von Hohenheim Paracelsus *c.*1493–1541, professor of medicine at Basel, made advances in chemistry although his system of iatrochemistry (chemical doctoring) was a mixture of observed fact and superstition.
The coach was invented in Hungary, probably in the early 16th century, but would not appear in England until the 1580s. It differed from covered wagons in having a strap suspension and a pivoted front axle. Queen Elizabeth I owned an early coach.

Coins containing copper mixed with gold or silver came into use in Europe in the early 16th century as a result of the great increase in prices caused in part by large imports of Spanish silver from Peru. **Henry VIII of England**, *r.*1509–47, in particular, debased the currency in this way. Although later recoinage partly improved the real value of money, alloying became the rule.
A mass production technique for casting small brass objects was practiced in Italy at this time.

Blast furnaces, able to produce large quantities of cast iron, gradually evolved from earlier Stückofen. Cast iron so made was mostly used in weaponry, an industry in which England led Europe, selling to any customer who could pay the price, whether friend or enemy.
Coal became a major fuel in mid-16th century industrial Europe as the price of wood soared and forests disappeared. Coal mines opened in Liège and Newcastle.

Telesio, an Italian who lived 1509–88, proposed the first system of physics to rival Aris[to]tle's. His theory argued that h[eat] and cold were the motive powers of the universe, an ide[a] that would later influence the work of the English philosoph[er] **Francis Bacon**, 1561–1626. **A[n]dreas Vesalius**, 1514–64, accepted the chair of anatomy i[n] Padua, 1537, and shocked the Church by dissecting corpses His book *De Humani Corporis Fabrica* (1543) would advance knowledge of internal anatom[y].

540–1550

ohn Calvin, 1509–64, estab shed a puritan theocracy at ieneva in 1541.

he Catholic Counter Reforma on inspired Charles V to con uct the Schmalkaldic War, 546–47, against the Protestant rinces.

rittany was united with France 1547.

he Portuguese were the first uropeans in Japan, 1542, here the Jesuit **Francis Xavier**, 506–52, founded a mission in 549.

rance's Jacques Cartier, 1491–557, attempted to colonize uebec in 1541. **Hernando e Soto**, *c*.1500–42, discov red the Mississippi River, 1541.

Charles V" by Titian

ohn Calvin 1506–64, promoted ne Reformation in Geneva, 541. He espoused the doctrine f predestination—that God had lready elected those to be aved—but it was believed that xemplary conduct signified lection. **Decrees issued by the ouncil of Trent** on Church re orm in 1545–47 initiated the atholic, or Counter, Reforma on.

homas Cranmer, 1489–1556, ssued the Church of England's *ook of Common Prayer*, 1549.

a Pléiade, a group of seven rench poets, of whom the reatest was **Pierre de Ronsard**, 524–85, established the Alex ndrine meter of a 12-syllable ne and emphasized the dignity f the French language while urning to classical themes. **heir manifesto was written by oachim du Bellay**, 1522–60, in *efense et Illustration de la angue Française*, 1549.

rench Renaissance art copied alian models as the painters **osso**, 1494–1540, and **Prima ccio**, 1504–*c*.70, and the archi ects **Vignola**, 1507–73, and **erlio**, 1475–1554, came to rance to work on the Palace of ontainebleau, 1528–60. **Man erist painting** in Italy, like the Madonna with the Long Neck," 534–36, by **Girolamo Parmigi nino**, 1503–40, shows an elon ation of figures, a lack of har ony, and a search for the new nd unusual.

ne lute became popular as an ccompanying instrument. It ould be used to accompany the ew contrapuntal madrigal style at grew up in Italy after 1530. ater the English adopted it.

Sun-centered universe was roposed in the book *On the evolutions of the Celestial Orbs* **Nicolas Copernicus**, 1473–543, published in the year his death. In this revolu onary work, the Earth, Moon, nd planets, and outside them e stars, orbited around the un in circles. This theory is e basis of modern cosmology. **ological and botanical** works ere published in the mid-16th entury by the French biologists **esner**, 1516–65, **Belon**, 1517–4, and **Rondelet**, 1507–66.

1550–1560

The Peace of Augsburg, 1555, permitted each German prince to decide the religion of his subjects. After Charles V's retirement and later abdication **Philip II of Spain** *r*.1556–98, took over the Catholic offensive, while **Elizabeth I**, *r*.1558–1603, confirmed England's Protestantism.

The influx of American silver to Spain accelerated inflation and caused hardship to the poor, but encouraged the rise of a European middle class.

The Indian population of Spanish America, about 7,000,000 in 1550, declined as Indians died of European diseases. By 1600 they numbered about 1,000,000.

Elizabeth I: Armada jewel

Many English Protestant bishops, including Cranmer, were burned at the stake in the reign of Queen Mary. Elizabeth, her successor, reestablished the Protestant Church but continued to burn heretics.

The Holy Roman Empire acknowledged Lutheranism in the Peace of Augsburg, 1555.

Protestantism in Scotland was united by the Calvinist **John Knox**, 1513–72, and became the national faith by Act of Parliament in 1560.

Among the great comic prose works of world literature, *Gargantua* and *Pantagruel* were completed in 1552 by **François Rabelais**, *c*.1494–*c*.1553. This bawdy, satirical tale of two grotesque giants was an erudite allegory vigorously attacking established institutions and conventional wisdom, mocking superstitious fears and defending free will.

The historian and painter **Vasari**, 1511–74, published the *Lives of the most excellent Painters, Sculptors, and Architects* in 1550.

Palladio, 1508–80, designed the Villa Rotunda, Vicenza, *c*.1550, beginning work *c*.1566. With its four porticos and symmetrical plan, it is an example of his search for classical and harmonious proportions. **Benin bronze figures** of West Africa adopted freer poses as a result of contact with Portuguese culture.

Sacred polyphony declined in influence after the Council of Trent, 1545–63, regularized the musical forms suitable for the mass of the Roman Catholic Church.

Georg Bauer (Agricola), 1494–1555, a German doctor, gave a full description of mining, smelting, and chemistry in *De Re Metallica*, published at Basel in 1556. Agricola's book is still the major source on technology in the later Middle Ages.

Discoveries of metals in the 16th century included that of mercury, *c*.1550, in Peru. Mercury was later used to extract silver from its ores by amalgamation. Zinc, bismuth, cobalt, and nickel were other metals used in alloys or mixtures.

1560–70

The French wars of religion began, 1562, between the Catholics and the Protestant Huguenots (mostly nobles and townsmen in west and south France).

The Calvinist and predominantly mercantile Dutch provinces began a long war of independence from Spain, 1568.

Nobunaga, 1534–82, introduced a dynamic period of Japanese centralization and expansion.

Akbar, *r*. 1556–1605, expanded the Mogul Empire and created a tolerant cosmopolitan culture.

Britain's John Hawkins, 1532–95, transported black slaves from West Africa to the Spanish West Indies, 1562–67. **St. Augustine, Fla.**, was founded, 1565.

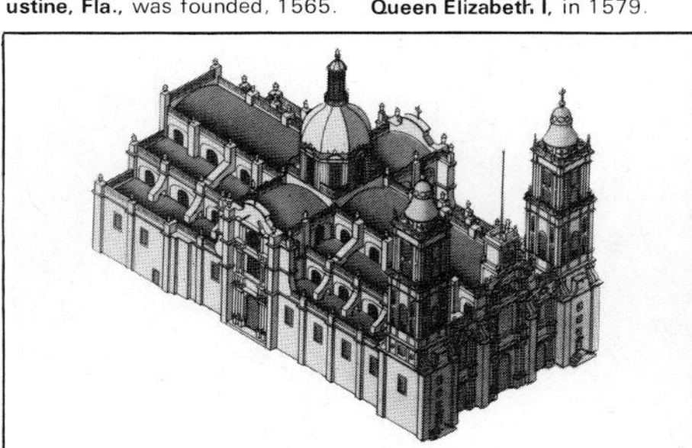

Mexico City: cathedral

The adoption of the 39 Articles in 1563, combining Protestant doctrine with Catholic church organization, finally established the Church of England. There were many dissenting groups, among them the Puritans, who opposed church ritual, the Separatists, who rejected Anglicanism entirely, the Presbyterians, who had synods instead of bishops, and the Brownists, a communistic sect. All but the Brownists and Catholics were tolerated.

The English poets **Thomas Wyatt**, 1503–42, and the **Earl of Surrey**, *c*.1517–47, wrote in sonnets and blank verse—forms perfected by the Elizabethan poets **Shakespeare**, **Walter Raleigh**, 1552–1618, and **Edmund Spenser**, 1552–99.

Flemish painting saw the emergence of the individualist **Pieter Bruegel the Elder**, *c*.1525–69, one of the greatest landscape painters and a remarkable satirist, whose series "The Months" dates from 1565. **Indian Mogul art** assimilated the Persian tradition of miniature painting, which emphasized sumptuous decoration and lively color patterns. This was combined with indigenous styles in the illustrations of Akbar's life in the *Akbarnama*.

Japanese music began to win its individual character with the popularization of national forms of vertical bamboo pipe *(shakuhachi)*, three-stringed guitar *(samisen)*, and zither *(koto)*.

Letter symbols for algebra and trigonometry were pioneered by **Vieta**, a French mathematician, 1540–1603. Words had previously been used for variables; the substitution of letters such as *x* and *y* greatly speeded up calculations and also removed many previous ambiguities.

Gerhard Kremer Mercator, 1512–94, published a map, 1568, using a projection that has since borne his name.

The potato was introduced to Europe from South America by the Spaniards *c*.1570.

1570–80

A European alliance defeated the Ottoman fleet at **Lepanto** in 1571, but Venice failed to use the opportunity to regain control of the eastern Mediterranean.

The Portuguese began their settlement of Angola, 1574.

The Dutch provinces, with increasing involvement in trade outside Europe, united in opposition to Spain, 1579.

England's **Sir Francis Drake**, *c*.1540–96, circumnavigated the world, 1577–80.

British navigator Sir Francis Drake, *c*.1540–96, on a voyage around the world in the *Golden Hind*, claimed California for **Queen Elizabeth I**, in 1579.

Jean Bodin, 1530–96, a major French political theorist, published his *Six Books of the Commonwealth* in 1576, arguing that the basis of any society was the family. His most important contribution was an analysis of sovereignty. He argued that in any state sovereignty was necessary to prevent anarchy and that the exercise of monarchical power in conformity with the natural law was unquestionable, as it had divine authorization.

Michel de Montaigne, 1533–92, began his *Essays* in 1580.

In China the realistic, erotic novel the *The Golden Lotus* was published *c*.1575.

John Lyly, *c*.1554–1606, wrote *Euphues*, 1578–80, an early novel of manners.

Torquato Tasso, 1544–95, published *Jerusalem Liberated* in 1575 and the pastoral romance *Aminta* in 1573.

The brilliant Monoyama period in Japan, 1573–1615, is seen in the castle at Azuchi, built for **Nobunaga**, 1576–79, which contained large rooms decorated with murals. Screens painted with strong colors on gold ground came into fashion.

Spanish colonial architecture in the late 16th century, like Mexico Cathedral, 1563–1667, was based on contemporary Spanish mannerist styles but derived a pre-Columbian flavor from the native Indian labor.

Javanese fleeing the spread of Islam reached Bali and kept early traditions of Indonesian music in the works for the gamelan orchestra (mostly tuned percussion instruments).

Sir Thomas Gresham, 1519–79, established by will the first British institute for teaching science, which later housed the Royal Society.

Decimals were introduced to mathematical calculations in physics by **Simon Stevin**, 1585.

1580–90

Portugal and Spain were united under **Philip II** of Spain, 1580.

England assisted the Dutch revolt in 1585, executed the Catholic **Mary, Queen of Scots** in 1587, and defeated the **Spanish Armada** in 1588. **Pope Sixtus V**, *r*.1585–90, a supporter of the Counter-Reformation, began the internal reform of the papacy.

Hideyoshi, *r*.1584–98, expelled the Portuguese missionaries from Japan in 1587.

The first British child in America, **Virginia Dare**, was born, 1587, on Roanoke Island. The colonists had mysteriously disappeared by 1591.

Benin bronzes, 16th c.

Akbar, the greatest Mogul emperor of India, *r*.1556–1605, attempted to establish **"Din Ilahl"** as a universal religion acceptable to his many Hindu subjects. Vegetarianism and other Hindu practices were supported by Akbar. Although the Din Illahl movement was influential for some time after Akbar's death, it would be discouraged by **Emperor Aurungzebe**, *r*.1658–1707, and would eventually collapse under the 18th-century Muslim revival.

English drama entered its great period. **Christopher Marlowe**, 1564–93, in his *Dr. Faustus*, *c*. 1588, perfected the blank verse of *The Spanish Tragedy* by **Thomas Kyd**, 1558–94. **Sir Philip Sidney**, 1554–86, in his verse-prose *Arcadia*, 1590, drew on a tradition of pastoral romance established in Spain by **Jorge de Montemayor**, *c*.1520–61, in his *Diana*.

English court portraiture and domestic architecture were given impetus by the Reformation. **Longleat**, 1567–80, was a house built in the rectangular style with large expanses of windows by **Smython**, *c*.1536–1614.

The Mannerist style emphasizing the bizarre and the tortuous spread through Europe, to Spain with **El Greco**, 1541–1614, to Germany in the works of artists like **Spranger**, 1546–1611, and to France with the second **Fontainebleau School**.

Equal temperament (based on equal half-tone divisions) was proposed by Prince Tsai-Yu in his *Handbook of Music*. It predated the West's recognition of its importance to harmony.

Tycho Brahe, 1546–1601, and his assistant **Johannes Kepler**, 1571–1630, extended Copernican theory. Brahe made accurate observations of planetary movements. Using these results, Kepler calculated the actual orbits of the planets, which he found to be ellipses and not perfect circles. Kepler's results established astronomy as an observational science, free from any religious considerations.

1590–1600

Henry IV, *r*.1589–1610, ended the French wars of religion and granted equal rights to Catholics and Huguenots in the **Edict of Nantes**, 1598.

The Dutch took over much of Portugal's former trade with the East Indies, 1595.

Japan invaded Korea, 1592–93 and 1597–98, but was expelled by the Chinese.

Spanish power gradually declined owing to the stagnation of her internal economy and the lack of a middle class.

The conquest and colonization of New Mexico by Spanish explorer **Juan de Onate**, ?1549–1624?, began in 1598. The settlement of **San Juan** was established.

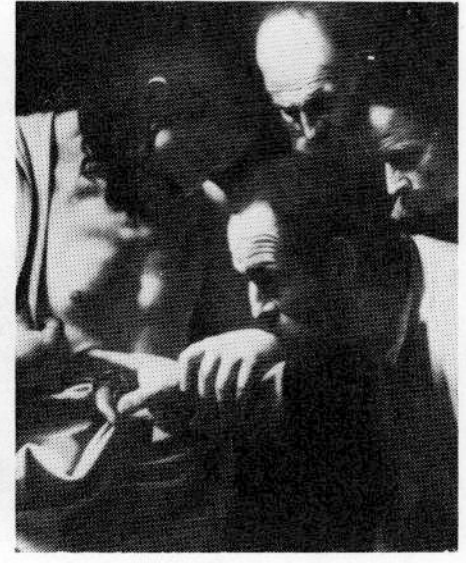

Work by Caravaggio

A Protestant movement, opposed to Calvinism, grew up in the United Provinces, denying the doctrine of predestination and arguing for religious tolerance. The movement came to be called **Arminianism**, after **Jacobus Arminius**, 1560–1609, who defended the Arminians in a controversy with his colleague **Gomarus. The Edict of Nantes**, 1598, granted liberty of worship to the Huguenots, the French Protestant sect.

William Shakespeare, 1564–1616, consummate master of the English language, began *c*.1591 to produce a stream of comedies, tragedies, and historical dramas revealing a remarkable range of human experience and thought. By 1600 he had written some 20 plays, including the comedy *As You Like It* and the romantic tragedy *Romeo and Juliet*.

The precursors of Italian baroque painting were radically opposed to each other. "The Loves of the Gods," 1597, in the Palazzo Farnese by **Annibale Carracci**, 1540–1609, returned to the classical ideals, but with an emotional, anecdotal appeal and complex composition. "Doubting Thomas," *c*.1600, by **Caravaggio**, 1571–1610, introduced a vivid realism and simplicity seen in the portrayal of Christ and the Apostles as ordinary men.

Sonata Pian'e Forte, 1597, by Giovanni Gabriele, 1557–1612, was composed for two consorts, the first ensemble piece in which instrumentation was specified.

Chinese pharmacology was summed up by **Li Shi-Chen** in his *Great Pharmacopoeia*, 1578. Chinese medicine was completely conservative and few new treatments were reported.

Galileo, 1564–1642, wrote in 1597 stating his agreement with the Copernican system. Three years later,

Giordano Bruno was burned by the Inquisition as a heretic for propagating the same idea.

Galileo and the new science 1600–1660

Principal events

The political and religious tensions generated by the Reformation in the previous century were brought to a head in the Thirty Years War, which involved most of the European powers and left the Holy Roman Empire in particular devastated from constant military activity. Although England remained out of the war, the same conflicts over religion and constitutional authority led to the execution of Charles I in 1649, but the establishment of the Commonwealth proved no solution.

Colonial trade expanded throughout the world bringing skirmishes and trade wars in India, America, and Europe as the European powers jostled for supremacy, regarding control of trade as a tangible form of political power.

In China the Manchu dynasty brought strength and prosperity, while Japan withdrew into isolation after experiencing the disruptive impact of Christianity and European trade.

1600–1606

Power struggles in Japan resulted in the Tokugawa (Edo) period, 1603, which advanced education and economic growth.
Charles IX, *r.*1604–11, a Protestant, succeeded to the Swedish throne after the deposition of his Catholic predecessor.
The anarchy in Russia resulting from rivalry among the boyars (nobility) began under **Boris Godunov,** *r.*1598–1605, who was opposed by a pretender, the false **Dmitry.**

1606–1612

In Japan the Tokugawa introduced **Confucianism** as the official religion, 1608, and Dutch traders arrived, 1609, rivaling the Spanish and Portuguese in the Far East.
The settlement of the French Wars of religion was threatened by the murder of **Henry IV,** *r.*1589–1610.

1612–1618

The influence of the English East India Company extended to India, ousting the Portuguese as a rival to the Dutch.
Persecution of Christianity began in Japan, 1612, although trade with Europe increased.
The accession of Mikháil Romanov, *r.*1613–45, in Russia established royal authority by ending local autonomy and strengthening serfdom.
A group of Tungus tribes in Manchuria grew powerful under **Nurhachi,** 1615–16.

1618–1624

The Thirty Years War began in 1618 after a nationalist and Pro estant revolt in Bohemia. By 1619, **Emperor Ferdinand,** *r.*1619–37, had restored Catho icism in Bohemia.
Spanish troops invaded the Prot estant Palatinate to ensure a route to the Netherlands.
The Pilgrim Fathers landed in North America in 1620.
Batavia was established by the Dutch as the center of their Eas ern spice trade, 1619.

National events

The 17th century saw the colonization of the New World. The religious situation in Europe influenced colonial development, as Protestant and Catholic nations competed for wealth and power. Dissidents escaping persecution were among those who sought refuge in the colonies. Others sought opportunity.

The Gulf of St Lawrence and the St Lawrence River were explored for France by **Samuel de Champlain,** *c.*1567–1635, during voyages beginning in 1603.

The first permanent English colony was founded at Jamestown, Va., in 1607. In 1609 Champlain fired on the Iroquois, setting a pattern of Indian relationships.

French Roman Catholic missionaries arrived in Canada, 1615. In Virginia, 1612, **John Rolfe,** 1585–1622, began the cultivation of tobacco.

In 1620, the Mayflower arrived at Cape Cod, Mass., bearing the Pilgrims. In Virginia, 1619, the first black slaves arrived.

Baroque: facade of St Peter's Rome by Maderna

Defenestration of Prague

"Apollo and Daphne"

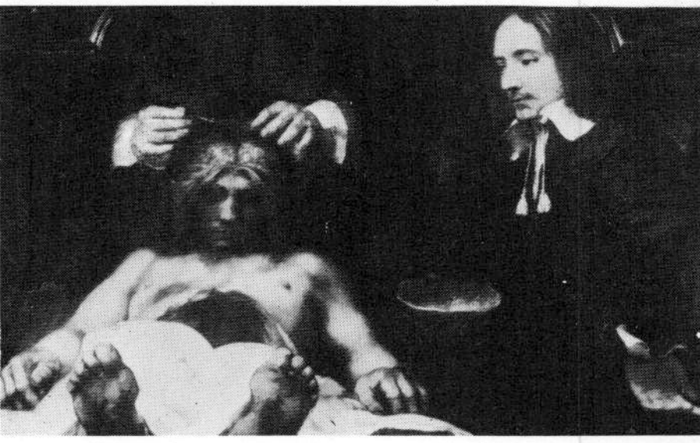

"The Anatomy Lesson" by Rembrandt

Religion and philosophy

As the basic assumptions and methodology of the natural sciences underwent a dramatic change with Galileo's suggestion that the workings of natural phenomena could be described exactly, philosophical and religious thought was also transformed. Theories of society based on the natural condition of man were common and resulted in the concept of the social contract, which could be renounced if the ruler rejected his duties to his subjects. Such ideas were used to justify widespread political revolts.

Descartes and Hobbes laid the foundations of modern philosophy by attempting to return to first principles, using only scientific or mathematical tools, and the same reliance on reason brought the beginnings of Deism, which would become popular in the 18th century.

In England in the Civil War, utopian ideas linking political and religious aims abounded.

Faustus Socinus, 1539–1604, in Poland, argued that Christ, although sinless, was not divine. He inspired the **Polish Unitarian movement,** which denied the existence of the Holy Trinity.
Johannes Althusius, 1557–1638, a Dutch Calvinist, said in 1603 that voluntary agreement should be the basis of political association. He advocated republican government.
The Tung-lin Academy, founded in China, 1604, revived Confucianism and attacked graft.

John Dee, 1527–1608, Elizabeth of England's astrologer, helped to revive interest in mathematics in England. As a magician and scientist he was a leading representative of the Hermetic tradition of alchemical study. This tradition, which sought to establish mystical connection among empirical phenomena with the help of experimentation, influenced the Cambridge Platonists and the development of Newtonian science.

Francisco Suarez, 1548–1617, a Spanish Jesuit, argued in *On Laws*, 1612, that a contract between ruler and subject was the basis of sovereignty. He hoped to refute James I of England's claim to rule by divine right.
The Dutch rejected Arminianism at the Synod of Dort, 1618. But after the publication of Arminius' works in 1629, they would be granted freedom of worship in the United Provinces.

Francis Bacon, 1561–1626, elaborated a sophisticated method of establishing scientif truths, using observation and experiment to test hypotheses, in *Novum Organum*, 1620. He argued for the usefulness of sci entific knowledge in giving mar mastery over nature and later conceived a scientific Utopia in *The New Atlantis*, 1627, which foreshadowed later developments in mid-17th century scientific thought.

Literature

The Elizabethan age in English literature culminated in the later work of William Shakespeare whose plays and sonnets epitomize the innovative power and humanism of the Renaissance, while in Spain Cervantes produced his picaresque Don Quixote. As the century wore on the religious and political conflicts between Royalists and Puritans were reflected in English literature with the poetry of Marvell and Milton.

In France an attempt to systematize the rules of language and literature was made by the newly founded Académie Française, which would stand until the 19th century, and an interest in classical models produced the dramas of Corneille and the verse of Malherbe.

Miguel de Cervantes, 1547–1616, blended and transcended the realistic and idealistic veins of Spanish prose writing in *Don Quixote*, published in two parts in 1605 and 1615. Its satirical theme of an amiable landowner who fancies himself an adventurous knight had a universality and a delicate juxtaposition of humor and sadness that influenced many later novelists.

Ben Jonson, *c.*1572–1637, poet, critic, and playwright, wrote *Volpone*, 1607, *The Alchemist*, 1610, and other comedies notable for their honesty. Other English dramatists were **John Webster,** 1580–1625, with *The White Devil*, 1608, **Thomas Middleton,** 1570–1627, **Thomas Dekker,** 1570–1641, and the prolific **Francis Beaumont** and **John Fletcher,** *fl.*1606–16.

Shakespeare's profound tragedies including *Hamlet*, *Lear*, and *Othello*, dealt with heroes trapped as much by the human condition as by their individual flaws of character. After 1608 he began writing his last, enigmatic plays, in which a spirit of reconciliation appears, among them *The Tempest*, *c.*1612. He retired to Stratford in 1613.

The English metaphysical poets, who included **George Herbert,** 1593–1633, explored the unity of flesh and spirit in a style tha influenced modern poetry. Erud tion, wit, reason, and passion were best combined in the devo tional and love poems of **John Donne,** 1572–1631, *(Anniversaries)*, who as dean of St Paul's from 1621 preached a series of fine sermons.

Art and architecture

Baroque art emerged in Italy in the 1600s and reached its peak in the mid-17th century in the works of Bernini, Pietro da Cortona, and Borromini. Its stylistic emphasis was on unity of composition, so that the parts were subordinate to the whole, an effect most expertly achieved in sculpture and architecture. Throughout the 17th century, Baroque spread from its basically Roman origins to Catholic Europe but had least influence in northern Protestant countries in spite of the achievement of Rubens and Vandyke.

Bourgeois Dutch art flourished during the long war of independence from Spain, while native English painting was relatively unaffected by European developments, although Charles I patronized many continental artists. In France the tradition of rationalism produced the restrained classicism of Poussin and Claude.

Indian art flourished at the height of Mogul power.

Parisian town planning, like the Place Royale, 1605, with its smaller terraced houses, was the result of Henry IV's policy to support the new merchant classes and improve traffic circulation.
Painting in China within the traditional schools was dominated by literati and theorists, like **Tung Ch'i-ch'ang,** 1555–1636, who, in his "Dwelling in the Ch'ing-pien Mountains," emphasized the spiritual message of landscape.

Art and architecture in Mogul India reached its greatest achievement during the reigns of **Jahangir,** *r.*1605–27, and **Shah Jehan,** *r.*1628–58. Painting was characterized by the realism and vigor of Jahangir's picture albums, which were primarily portraits and depictions of the hunt. Later, Shah Jehan would build the **Taj Mahal,** 1632–43, the most renowned structure in India, as a mausoleum for his dead wife.

Italian baroque painting was dominated by the influence of the Carracci and Caravaggio. **Guido Reni,** 1575–1642, painted "Aurora," 1613, in the Carracci style. In Flanders, **Peter Paul Rubens,** 1577–1640, shows the influence of Caravaggio in his work "Descent from the Cross," 1611–14.
Palladian architecture was introduced to England by **Inigo Jones,** 1573–1652, whose Queen's House, Greenwich, 1616, is thoroughtly classical.

The baroque style was epitomized in the magnificent sculptures of **Gianlorenzo Bernini,** 1598–1680, whose "Apollo an Daphne," 1622–25, establishec him as the greatest sculptor since Michelangelo.
Reality, allegory, and myth are combined in one of **Rubens'** masterpieces, the gigantic Med ici cycle painted for the Luxem bourg Palace, Paris, 1622–25.

Music

Many of the forms of music current today had their beginnings in 17th-century Europe. The suite was developing to provide the basis of the later sonata, and opera and ballet were evolving from court entertainments. Italy was the center of the stage, and interest in the solo line pressed forward the development of a new style of madrigal and fine singing styles.

Dances for lutes and consorts became popular, providing musical forms such as the *pavane*, *galliard*, *allemande*, and *gavotte*, which were later gathered into composite pieces called suites.

Orfeo, 1607, by Claudio Monteverdi, 1567–1643, is the earliest European opera extant. The form arose from a search for a new way to express the ideals of classical drama.

The violin made its orchestral appearance in the *Vingt quatre violons du roi*, set up by Louis XIII, *r.*1610–43, as a court band. Later, bands of several consorts had up to 35 players.

Figured bass developed in Italia lute songs. Beneath the melody was written a base line with fig ures and signs to indicate the harmony of the inner parts with out writing chords in full.

Science and technology

Religious dissent marked this period in Europe, and from it rose the beginnings of modern science. The century was only a few weeks old when the Italian Giordano Bruno was burned at the stake for heresy. He had conceived of the universe as infinite in time and space and filled with a multitude of suns each bearing planets, everything being in constant motion. His views were a major threat to orthodox theology at a time when the Catholic Church was threatened by the Reformation. Bruno's death probably persuaded Galileo, another Italian, to retract his belief that the Earth moves, and helped to shift the scene of progress toward the Protestant countries of Northern Europe.

The concept of scientific method was established and practical endeavor stimulated invention and inquiry. For example, the pumps required to clear water from mines prompted the investigation of air pressure and facilitated an understanding of the heart's action.

De Magnete, a study of magnetism and electricity, was published in 1600 by an Englishman, **William Gilbert,** *c.*1540–1603. He suggested that the Earth was a giant magnet with its own magnetic field.
Galileo Galilei, 1564–1642, studied the motions of falling bodies and discovered that they accelerated constantly toward the Earth. Galileo, the father of experimental science, drew conclusions from observation and experiment only, without theological speculations.

The telescope was invented by the Dutchman Hans Lippershey, *c.*1570–1619, in 1608.
Astronomia Nova, published in 1609 by Johannes Kepler, 1571–1630, argued that the planets moved around the Sun in ellipses and at varying speeds.
The moons of Jupiter and phases of Venus were discovered by Galileo in 1610.

The Art of Glass Making, 1612, by the Italian Antonio Neri, was one of many handbooks that helped the spread of technology.
John Napier, 1550–1617, introduced logarithms in 1614. Logarithmic tables prepared by **Henry Briggs,** 1561–1631, greatly facilitated their use.
Sanctorius, 1561–1636, founded the study of metabolism with his *De Medicina Statica*, 1614. He weighed himself over thirty years, recording changes in weight, pulse, and temperature.

Harmonice Mundi, 1619, by Kep ler, returned to the ancient concept of the harmony of the spheres in trying to find a relationship between music and as tronomy. This work neverthele contained a third law of planetary motion.
Francis Bacon published *Novum Organum*, 1620, in which theories are drawn from hypothese and tested by observation and experiment.

1624–1630

England, the United Provinces, Denmark, and France allied against the Hapsburgs, 1625. **In France, Richelieu,** 1585–1642, rebuilt royal power, attacking the Huguenots, 1628. **French settlements in the West Indies** began in 1625, exporting sugar and tobacco, and emigration to Canada was encouraged among traders and fishermen. **The Tungus Manchus** overran Korea, ousting the Ming dynasty from the Liao Basin, 1627.

1630–1636

The Dutch East India Company seized part of Brazil for its sugar and silver, 1630. **Gustavus Adolphus,** *r.*1611–32, of Sweden invaded the Holy Roman Empire, 1630, to protect the Protestant cause against ruthless Catholic suppression. **Magdeburg was sacked** in 1631 by the Catholic general **Tilly,** 1559–1632. **The war in Europe** dislocated previous patterns of trade and industry and the search for colonial wealth increased.

1636–1642

After the Shimabara revolt of the Christian peasantry, 1637, Japan cut her foreign trade and cultural contacts. **France** first entered the Thirty Years War in 1639. **Spain** was weakened by the establishment of Portuguese independence and a Catalan nationalist revolt in 1640. **England** was close to civil war in 1641 after constitutional opposition to royal absolutism.

1642–1648

The New England Confederacy was founded in 1643 for defense against the Indians. **The Manchus** set up the **Ta Ch'ing** dynasty at Mukden, 1644, replacing the Ming dynasty. **The English Civil War,** 1642–46, resulted in military victory for Parliament and the Puritans after the reorganization of their army, in 1645. Attempts to find a constitutional settlement failed. **France** confirmed its new military superiority by defeating Spain at Rocroi, 1647.

1648–1654

The Peace of Westphalia ended the Thirty Years War in 1648 with every participant exhausted. **The Fronde,** a series of noble and peasant uprisings in France, tried to substitute government by law for royal power and voiced economic grievances but was crushed,1648–53. **Charles I,** *r.*1625–49, of England was executed and a Commonwealth set up under **Oliver Cromwell,** 1599–1658. His Navigation Act, 1651, led to war with the Dutch, 1652.

1654–60

The rise of Brandenburg and Russia as military powers brought a new conflict in the Baltic and Poland, 1655–60. **The Venetians** drove the Turks from the Dardanelles, 1656, following a period of anarchy among the Ottomans. **Anarchy after Cromwell's death** led to the restoration of the English monarchy, 1660. **The war between France and Spain** ended, 1659, emphasizing the Spanish decline and the rise of French power.

Virginia became a royal colony, 1624. In 1626, **Peter Minuit,** *c.*1580–1638, governor of New Netherlands, bought Manhattan which became New Amsterdam.

In 1630, the Puritan "Great Migration" brought more than 1,000 settlers to Massachusetts. **Roger Williams,** *c.*1603–83, founded Providence, 1636.

Anne Hutchinson *c.*1591–1643, banished from Massachusetts, joined **Roger Williams.** In the **Pequot War,** 1636–37, in New England over 600 whites died.

Massachusetts, Plymouth, Connecticut, and New Haven formed the New England Confederation, 1643, for defense.

Maryland, 1649, granted rights to all Christians who asserted belief in the Trinity. Parliament, 1651, passed the first **Navigation Act** for colonial administration.

The Navigation Act of 1660 restricted colonial trade. Peter Stuyvesant, 1592–1672, was the New Netherlands' harsh governor, 1646–64.

The trial of Galileo

The Taj Mahal

OCromwell

Oliver Cromwell

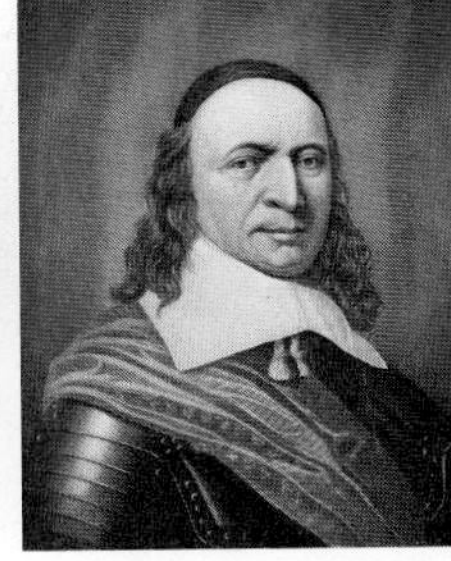

Peter Stuyvesant

Herbert of Cherbury, 1583–1648, attempted to establish a belief in God based on rational inquiry rather than faith in *On Truth*, 1624. His belief that the basic tenets of religion were reasonable and universal was central to the growth of Deism. **Hugo Grotius,** 1583–1645, a Dutchman, developed the theory of international law in *On Law*, 1625. He aimed to make war more humane, arguing that nations, like individuals, are bound by natural law.

Galileo Galilei, 1564–1642, an Italian, began modern science by uniting mathematics with physics. He distinguished real or "primary" qualities such as mass, from subjective "secondary" qualities such as color. The religious opposition to his work highlighted the challenge of experimental science to the Aristotelian world view, both philosophically and politically.

Cornelis Jansen, 1585–1638, a Frenchman, attacked the Jesuits and proclaimed strict predestinarianism, while staying within the Catholic Church, in the *Augustinus*, 1642. **Blaise Pascal,** 1623–62, supported the Jansenist movement in France, where it appealed to the nationalist opposition to papal power. The Jesuits rejected these views because they implied the denial both of free will and the universality of redemption.

René Descartes, 1596–1650, who founded modern philosophy, attempted to establish a philosophical system from first principles alone, relying on mathematical logic and using systematic doubt as his method. He espoused a total dualism between mind and matter, arguing that the physical world was governed by deterministic laws, while the clarity and distinctness of ideas established their truth independently of any experience.

Utopian social and religious ideas flourished in England after the civil war. **George Fox,** 1624–91, founded the pacifist and egalitarian Friends, or **Quakers,** in 1652, while the **Diggers,** an agrarian communistic group, believed that religious ideas had diverted man from asserting his political rights in this world. **The Levelers,** another Puritan group, led by John Liburne, 1614–57, demanded an egalitarian and republican society.

In **De Corpore,** 1655, Thomas Hobbes, 1588–1679, following Descartes' mathematical method, suggested that the universe comprises material particles moving in a void. This atomism had also been stated in his political tract, *Leviathan*, 1651, in which he argued that in a state of nature men would fight because of their natural selfishness; they could only escape by means of a contract whereby they renounced their freedom to a supreme ruler.

Spanish drama was dominated by the popular and prolific **Lope de Vega,** 1562–1635, whose ingeniously plotted verse plays mixed comedy and tragedy. **Pedro Calderón de la Barca,** 1600–81, added deeper characterization in plays that reflected the richly ornate **culteranismo** style of the poet and satirist Luis de Gongora, 1561–1627.

The Passion Play at Oberammergau, Bavaria, the most famous survival of its genre, was inaugurated in 1634. It has been performed every ten years except for three wartime interruptions.

French writers applied strict classical rules under the influence of **François de Malherbe,** 1555–1628. **Pierre Corneille,** 1606–84, successfully adapted these in a series of tragedies in Alexandrine couplets, starting with *Le Cid*, 1637. His artificial but powerful plays based on Spanish and Roman heroes made drama the chief form of French classical literature.

English prose had acquired a new eloquence in *Anatomy of Melancholy* by **Robert Burton** 1577–1640. This tradition was extended by **Sir Thomas Browne,** 1605–82, whose *Religio Medici*, 1643, was a reflective study of a doctor's spiritual life. An equally individualistic writer, **Izaak Walton,** 1593–1683, began to write *The Compleat Angler.*

English poetry reflected the political conflict of Puritans and Royalists. The Cavalier lyricists included **Sir John Suckling,** 1609–42, **Robert Herrick,** 1591–1674, and **Richard Lovelace,** 1618–57, whose best work was collected in *Lucasta*, 1649. On the Puritan side, **Andrew Marvell,** 1621–78, wrote poems on nature during the 1650s.

The greatest Dutch poet, Joost van den Vondel, 1587–1679, turned from satire to write his religious drama *Lucifer*, 1654. **In Germany,** literature revived after the Thirty Years War, 1618–48. Poetry was much influenced by Lutheranism, and the poet and mystic **Paul Gerhardt,** 1607–76, wrote outstanding hymns, including "O sacred head sore wounded."

Classicism in French painting was developed by **Nicolas Poussin,** *c.*1594–1665, whose "Triumph of David," 1626, shows an abstraction and modeling based on antique ideals. **Realism** and the skillful use of color and light began to appear in Spanish painting in such works as the "Scenes from the life of St Bonaventura," 1629–30, by **José Ribera,** 1591–1652, and in the works of **Francisco de Zurbarán,** 1598–1664.

Roman high baroque painting was represented in the works of **Pietro da Cortona,** 1596–1669, whose masterpiece, the ceiling of the Gran Salone, Palazzo Barberini, painted in 1633–39, was a skillful illusion, its center seemingly open to the sky. **Anthony Van Dyke,** 1599–1641, working at the English court, brought sophistication and elegance to English portraiture in the "Equestrian portrait of Charles I," 1633.

Dutch art found its greatest painter in Rembrandt van Rijn, 1606–69, whose psychological insight and technical virtuosity produced "The Night Watch," 1642. **Jan Vermeer,** 1632–75, painted domestic interiors and **Frans Hals,** *c.*1580–1666, lively portraits. **The greatest of the baroque architects, Francesco Borromini,** 1599–1667, produced his masterpiece of spatial ingenuity, **S. Carlo alle Quattro Fontane,** 1634–44.

French landscape painting as developed by **Claude Lorrain,** 1600–82, involved the formal arrangement of trees and a panoramic background as the setting for diminutive foreground figures, as in "Hagar and the Angel," 1646. **Individualist schools in China** broke away from traditional painting. **Kung Hsien,** *c.*1620–89, painted vast landscapes of great originality, such as his "A Thousand Peaks and a Myriad Rivers."

French classical architecture was initially developed by **François Mansart,** 1598–1666, whose Château of Maisons Laffitte, with its elegance, clarity, and cool restraint, epitomized his subtly proportioned style. **Classical compositions** and the use of indirect lighting are combined in the highly personal style of **Georges de la Tour,** 1593–1652, whose "St Sebastian," *c.*1650, suggests the influence of Caravaggio.

Realism and a superlative handling of color distinguish the works of the Spanish court painter **Diego de Velazquez** 1599–1660. His "Las Meninas," 1656, an informal royal group, represents the culmination of his remarkable style. **Bernini's genius as an architect** was affirmed in his Piazza of St Peter's, begun in 1656, which was both simple and original in design and reflected the dignity and grandeur of Mother Church.

Fugue developed, principally in Germany, as a contrapuntal treatment of one main theme. It remained the dominant form for solo organ until the 1700s but also had wider applications.

Bel canto, a lyrical style of singing, developed in Italy. *Castrati*, men who had been castrated before puberty, were renowned for their high, sweet, powerful voices, often used in opera.

Dynamic markings, such as *p* (piano) and *f* (forte), were used for the first time in 1638 by **Domenico Mazzochi,** 1592–1665, in Italy. He was quickly followed by other composers.

Ballet developed at the French court in the reign of Louis XIV, *r.*1643–1715, who first danced it in 1651. Brought from Italy, ballet had been known at the French court since *c.*1581.

The koto became the national instrument of Japan. Its strings and movable bridge produced various five-note scales. Its solo music was often composed in the form of variations.

The violin was perfected in Italy by the Amati, Stradivari, and Guarneri families from 1650 to 1740. The great brilliance of violin tone soon overwhelmed the softer viols, which died out.

Johann Glauber, *c.*1603–68, discovered many chemical compounds, including benzene, acetone, and hydrochloric acid. **William Harvey,** 1578–1657, discovered the circulation of the blood in 1628, but this was not confirmed until later improvements in the microscope took place. By studying valves Harvey realized that blood must flow in one direction only. His mechanistic view of man perfectly complemented Galileo's mechanistic universe.

In **Dialogues Concerning Two World Systems,** published in 1632, Galileo presented the evidence for a heliocentric solar system in which the Earth moves. In 1633, Galileo was forced to retract his views. **Fen drainage** in England since the 1620s had increased farm land. Fertilizer experiments also aided agriculture. English trade and industry prospered, especially coal production, iron mining, and metallurgy. **The slide rule** was invented in 1632 by Oughtred, 1575–1660.

Le Discours de la Méthode, 1637, by René Descartes, 1596–1650, established the deductive method, by which theories are deduced from observations and experimentally tested for validity. He also invented coordinate geometry, in which position can be described mathematically, an advance vital to the growth of engineering and the calculus. **Two New Sciences,** published by Galileo, 1638, dealt with dynamics and helped to establish experimental science.

Blaise Pascal, 1623–62, invented an adding machine in 1642. He also discovered the principles of hydraulics and investigated the theory of probability, showing that chance can be assessed mathematically. **Evangelista Torricelli,** 1608–47, demonstrated in 1643 that air pressure is sufficient to hold up a column of mercury about 76 cm high, thus producing the first barometer. This discovery laid down the fundamental principles of hydromechanics.

The air pump, developed *c.*1650 by Otto von Guericke, 1602–86, was used to show that sound cannot cross a vacuum. In 1654 Guericke conducted a famous experiment in which two teams of horses tried and failed to separate two evacuated hemispheres, thus demonstrating the power of air pressure, later to be harnessed in the first steam engines.

Christiaan Huygens, 1629–95, a Dutchman, invented the pendulum clock from 1656. **Accademia del Cimento,** the first scientific research institute, was founded in Florence, 1657.

The Age of Louis XIV 1660–1720

Principal events

Louis XIV's schemes for the expansion of France brought him into conflict with the major European powers. The spectacle of his rule as an absolute monarch dominated 17th-century European politics, arousing the envy of lesser rulers including James II of England who was expelled in 1688 for trying to emulate him. This second English Revolution finally confirmed the victory of Protestantism and the rule of Parliament, which would serve to inspire the Enlightenment thinkers of the following century, particularly in France itself.

Outside Europe the major powers fought for colonies—valued for their dual role as sources of raw materials and luxury goods like tobacco, sugar, and spices and as markets for the produce of the home country.

The Mogul Empire in India declined after Aurungzebe had made the dynasty unpopular with his policy of intolerance toward Hinduism.

1660–1666

Louis XIV began his personal rule in 1661 marked by a suppression of noble authority and the creation of a bureaucracy for local government.
K'ang Hsi, *r.*1662–1722, introduced a period of Chinese cultural splendor.
The English acquired Bombay in 1661 and took New Amsterdam from the Dutch in 1664.
The Spanish colonies became a prize sought after by the major naval powers in the reign of **Charles II**, 1665–1700.

1666–1672

Louis XIV invaded the Spanish Netherlands but was opposed by the United Provinces, 1667–68.
The English and Dutch fought an indecisive trade war, 1665–67.
Russia defeated Poland for the Ukraine, 1654–67.
The Mogul Emperor Aurungzebe revoked Hindu toleration in 1669, causing unrest in India.
The English founded the Hudson Bay Company for the exploration of North America.

1672–1678

The French again attacked the Dutch in 1672, backed by riches gained through the mercantilist economic policy of **Jean-Baptiste Colbert,** 1619–83. They were opposed by Spain and the empire, who feared French strength in the north.
A two-party system emerged in England in the 1670s.

1678–1683

Brandenburg sent an expedition to West Africa in 1680.
Louis XIV moved his court to Versailles to consolidate his independence from the nobility and the Parisians, 1682.
K'ang Hsi took Formosa, 1683, which had been wrested from the Dutch by a Chinese pirate i 1661.
The Turks besieged Vienna, 1683, but later were defeated **Mohacs**, 1687.
Robert de la Salle explored the Mississippi for France.

National events

A rivalry for dominance in the New World between the French and the English was underway. European conflicts brought war to the colonies. The English colonial population was larger, but the French had alliances with numerous Indian tribes. By 1713, with the Treaty of Utrecht, Britain had gained the advantage.

The British defeated the Dutch in New Amsterdam, 1664, renaming it New York. French crown took control of Canada, 1663, from a private company.

The Massachusetts Bay Colony had taken over the government of Maine by 1669. **Carolina's Fundamental Constitutions,** 1669, drew on **John Locke.**

Jacques Marquette, 1637–75, and **Louis Joliet,** 1648–1700, explored the Mississippi River, 1673. **King Philip's War,** 1675–76, ravaged New England.

In 1682, William Penn, 1644–1718, arrived in Pennsylvania. The colony's **Frame of Government** granted religious toleratic and an elected assembly.

Louis XIV

Chinese Emperor K'ang-hsi

Newton's first telescope

Molière

Versailles: the Hall of Mirrors

Religion and philosophy

European theories of knowledge and politics underwent important changes in the latter half of the 17th century, at a time when Newton's revolutionary ideas on the workings of the universe were transforming Western science. In Britain Newton himself, Locke, and Berkeley took the empiricist position that knowledge was obtained by experience alone, in direct contrast to the rationalist views of thinkers like Spinoza and Leibniz, who argued that knowledge of the world could be obtained by deductions from certain key principles like the nature of substance. Empiricism would dominate British philosophy thereafter and was to have a major influence on the thinkers of the French Enlightenment. Among political theorists, Locke and Pufendorf argued that political authority depended upon consent and took the form of a contract between the people and the king.

Mercantilists, such as **Thomas Mun** 1571–1641, in England and **Jean-Baptiste Colbert,** 1619–83, in France held that governmental regulation of the economy was necessary to increase the power of the state, since a nation's economic power depended on the bullion at its disposal. A key factor was the monopolization of colonial trade by the mother country.
The Royal Society was founded in England in 1662.

The German Pufendorf, 1632–94, based his concept of natural law on "socialitas," the essentially social nature of man. He believed that agreement was the basis of political relationships and that human dignity implied the equality of all men.
The Old Believers broke with the Russian Church in 1667 to counteract the reforms of the patriarch **Nikon,** 1605–81, who introduced Greek practices and reformed the parish clergy.

Spinoza, 1632–77, a Dutch philosopher, attempted to find a rational explanation of the universe and argued that since God cannot be other than He is then the world, His creation, cannot be other than it is. In his *Ethics*, 1675, he held that free will was an illusion, which would be dispelled by man's recognition that the world was completely determined. He supported democracy as the most natural form of government, and rejected Descartes' dualism of mind and body.

Ralph Cudworth, 1617–88, an Englishman, published his *True Intellectual System*, 1678, admitting mental as well as mate al forces to science. He belonged to the **Cambridge Platon ist** group of Christian humanist associated with the religiously tolerant "Latitudinarian" follow ers of Arminius.
Jacques Bossuet, 1627–1704, upheld Louis XIV's absolute monarchy against Protestantism arguing that any legally formed government is sacred.

Literature

Neoclassical drama, based on logic and Greco-Roman stylistic rules, reached a peak in France in the tragedies of Racine and comedies of Molière. After the comic license of early Restoration drama, English writers such as Dryden also turned to classical models, laying the ground for the Age of Reason. English journalism began with Addison and Defoe, and satire developed with Alexander Pope.

The period also saw the publication of the chief work of the two greatest English Puritan writers, Milton and Bunyan, as well as developments in baroque poetry and picaresque prose in Germany and the emergence of new prose and verse forms in France with La Fontaine.

In Japan, Basho emerged as the supreme haiku poet.

German baroque literature was dominated by the influence of **Andreas Gryphius,** 1616–64, whose comedies and religious poems were collected in 1663. Another baroque writer was **Hans Grimmelshausen,** *c.*1621–76, whose *Simplicissimus*, a graphic account of the experiences of the peasantry in the Thirty Years War, is regarded as the start of the German novel.

The Greek "unities" of action, time, and space were given dramatic form in the French classical drama of **Jean Racine,** 1639–99, and **Molière,** 1622–73. Racine's *Andromaque*, 1667, blended poetic style with tragic passion. In comedies such as *Le Misanthrope* and *Tartuffe*, Molière exposed upper- and middle-class hypocrisies, mastering both plot and dialogue.

John Milton, 1608–74, an English poet who was politically prominent on the Puritan side, published in 1674 his final version of *Paradise Lost*, written, 1658–63, in strong blank verse, showing man as obsessed by sin. **In Mexico,** a Spanish nun, **Juana Inez de la Cruz,** published *A Nosegay of Poetic Flowers*. Her works are among Latin America's best.

A forerunner of the English novel, *Pilgrim's Progress*, 1678, was an allegorical journey through life, told in plain prose with a wealth of narrative detai that overrode the narrow purita ism of its author, **John Bunyan,** 1628–88.
Madame de Lafayette, 1634–9 wrote *La Princess de Clèves*, th first French court romance of psychological depth.

Art and architecture

France replaced Italy as the center of the arts in Europe. They were dominated by the royal patronage of Louis XIV, who rebuilt Versailles using the talents of Lebrun, Le Vau, Hardouin-Mansart, and Le Nôtre. Baroque architecture was at its purest in Italy, at its most restrained in England, and at its most extravagant in Spain and Portugal. Painting during the latter half of the 17th century produced few masterpieces although the works of Murillo in Spain, Pozzo in Italy, Claude Lorrain in France, and the landscapists in Holland were exceptional. In the American colonies architecture and painting adapted European styles to their own conditions.

The Rococo style emerged in France in the late 17th century, bringing to interior decoration the use of swirls, scrolls, and conchs in design, and finding a stylistic parallel in the elegant paintings of Watteau, dealing with life at court.

Spanish painting was represented by the works of **Bartolomé Estebán Murillo,** 1617–82, who founded the Seville Academy and became its first president, 1660. Eight of his 11 paintings for the almshouse of St Jorge, 1661–74, are regarded as his masterpieces.
The greatest exponent of Baroque, Gianlorenzo Bernini, 1598–1680, went to Paris to redesign the Louvre, 1665. His plans were rejected, but he made a superb bust of Louix XIV.

Dutch landscape painting was exemplified in "The Avenue of Middleharnis," 1669, by **Meindert Hobbema,** 1638–1709, and in "Windmill at Wijk," *c.*1670, by **Jacob van Ruisdael,** *c.*1628–82, a great Dutch landscapist.
The palace of Versailles in France was first remodeled in 1669 by **Louis Le Vau,** 1612–70, France's leading baroque architect. The park and gardens at Versailles were designed by **André Le Nôtre,** 1613–1700, from 1662.

The classical landscape tradition of Poussin in France continued with **Claude Lorrain,** 1600–82, whose "Evening," 1672, expresses a questioning melancholy. **Jules Hardouin-Mansart,** 1646–1708, officially supervised building at Versailles after 1678. **Christopher Wren,** 1632–1723, the greatest English architect, began work on St Paul's Cathedral, 1675. It is a classical work with baroque overtones.

The Poussinistes/Rubensistes controversy was sparked off by the French Academy's publication of rules for painting, 1680 **André Félibien,** 1619–95, defended the orthodox view, whic valued drawing, idealism, formalized rules, and the work of Poussin. **Roger de Piles,** 1635–1709, led the revolutionaries and argued the importance of color, imagination, and the works of Rubens. The Academy was officially associated with the ideas of Poussinistes.

Music

Baroque music grew up in Europe in the second half of the 17th century in the princely states of northern Italy and Germany. The freewheeling melodic lines and firm harmonic structure in the works of such composers as Diderik Buxtehude, 1637–1707, and Johann Sebastian Bach, 1685–1750, paralleled the ornamented but firm qualities of Baroque architecture.

The Restoration in England brought the first public concerts in the modern sense. But music there would decline for two centuries after the death of **Henry Purcell,** 1659–95.

The trio sonata was developed by Germans and Italians, using a quick first movement adapting *aabb* dance form with sections in contrasting moods and keys, and a slow second movement.

The chorale prelude, a free composition based on a hymn tune, exploited the varied capabilities of the organ. **Buxtehude's** chorale preludes influenced young composers such as **Bach.**

Continuo was played on a keyboard instrument—often a harpsichord—filling in the harmony between treble and bass lines, as in the cantatas of **Alessandr Scarlatti,** 1660–1725.

Science and technology

Isaac Newton's account of the workings of the universe surpassed Galileo's and provided a new framework for scientific thought. His exceptional insight into nature found definitions for concepts such as inertia and gravity that cannot easily be sensed. Newton's view of the universe, as one obeying set laws, accorded with the spirit of Protestant inquiry into the purpose of creation, in complete opposition to the Catholic world of personal salvation and divine intervention. Scientific advance in England and Holland was also stimulated by wealth from their growing trade.

Scientific communities grew up and provided scientists with the means to pool their researches, facilitating the spread of information and ideas internationally, while increasing the scientist's stature by granting him royal patronage. However, the growth of these communities contributed to the new division in men's minds between the impersonal sciences and the humanities.

The Royal Society was founded in London, 1660, and the French **Académie Royale des Sciences,** in 1666.
Marcellio Malpighi, 1628–94, used a microscope to discover capillary blood vessels in 1661, thereby confirming Harvey's theory of blood circulation.
Robert Boyle, 1627–91, a British physicist, found that gas pressure varies inversely with volume (Boyle's law, 1662). His book *The Sceptical Chymist*, 1661, defined the concepts of element, alkali, and acid.

Isaac Newton, 1642–1727, conceived of gravity, 1664–66, correctly concluding that it obeys an inverse square law. He discovered the spectrum, 1666, and invented the reflecting telescope, 1671.
Francesco Redi, *c.*1626–97, disproved previous theories of the spontaneous generation of lower animals by showing in 1668 that flies are needed to produce the eggs of maggots.
A calculating machine that could multiply and divide was made by Leibniz, 1646–1716, in 1671.

Greenwich Observatory, founded in 1675 principally to improve navigation, marks the standard meridian of longitude.
The speed of light was calculated for the first time in 1675 by **Olaus Roemer,** 1644–1720, and shown to be finite.
A single-lens microscope was made by **Anton van Leeuwenhoek,** 1632–1723, a Dutch biologist who discovered protozoa, 1677, and bacteria, 1683.
The calculus was independently developed by Leibniz and Newton.

The pressure cooker was inven ed, 1679, by **Denis Papin,** 1647–1712. Papin also experi mented on steam engines, usir both the vacuum made by condensing cylinders and the powe produced by the expansion of steam as water boils.
John Ray, 1627–1705, laid the groundwork for modern plant classification in his *Historia Generalis plantarum*.

684–90

ıe Edict of Nantes, granting eedom of worship to Huguen- :s in France, was revoked by ɔuis XIV in 1685. Many Hu- ɹenots emigrated. **ıssian eastward expansion** led conflict with China, 1683–89. **ames II of England,** *r.*1685–88, as expelled for trying to re- :ore Catholicism. **The Bill of ghts,** 1689, confirmed a con- :itutional monarchy. **Japan,** the Genroku year peri- d, 1688–1704, saw the rise of merchant culture.

1690–1696

William of Orange, *r.*1688–1702, who reigned jointly with his wife, James II's daughter **Mary,** brought England into the war against France. **Peter the Great,** *r.*1689–1725, began his policy of Russian expansion toward Azov for an outlet to the Black Sea and visited western Europe. **English trade in India** grew and a factory was set up in Calcutta in 1690. **European sugar traders** competed in the West Indies.

1696–1702

Charles II of Spain died in 1700 leaving **Philip, duke of Anjou** and grandson of Louis XIV, as heir to his lands. This led to the **War of the Spanish Succession,** 1702–13. **Hungary** was recaptured from the Turks and by 1699 was restored to Austrian control. **Frederick III,** the elector of Brandenburg, assumed the title King of Prussia with the consent of the emperor and became **Frederick I of Prussia,** *r.*1701–13.

1702–1708

The French won control of the *asiento* contract in 1702, which allowed them to transport black slaves to the Spanish colonies. **Portugal** joined the alliance against France, acting as a base for operations in Spain, 1703. **The duke of Marlborough,** 1650–1722, defeated the French at **Blenheim,** 1704. **After Aurungzebe's death** in 1707, the Mogul Empire disintegrated as local princes asserted their autonomy, seeking assistance from European traders.

1708–1714

The Sikhs became militant and made the Punjab virtually independent of Mogul rule, 1708. **A mass emigration** of Germans to America began in 1709. **War between the native Brazilians** and the Portuguese erupted after France attacked Rio de Janeiro in the course of the Spanish War of Succession. **The Treaty of Utrecht,** 1713, confirmed that France and Spain should not be united and left Britain in control of the *asiento* slave trade.

1714–1720

The English East India Company won trading concessions over rival companies from the Mogul emperor in 1717. **Frederick William of Prussia,** *r.*1713–40, laid the foundations of Prussian military power by setting up a standing army. **Louis XIV** died in 1715, with France's economy exhausted. **Manchu rule in Tibet** was assured by 1720. **The South Sea Company,** set up in 1710 to increase British South American trade, collapsed, 1720.

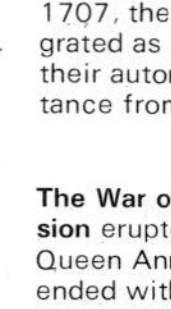

North America the English and :ench vied for control. **King Wilam's War,** 1689–97 was inconusive. **The Dominion of New ıgland** was established, 1686.

The settlement of Salem, Mass., was the site, 1692–93, of a series of witchcraft trials. Nineteen people were convicted and executed.

Biloxi, Miss., was founded, 1699, by **Pierre le Moyne,** 1661–1706. Detroit, Mich., was founded, 1701, by **Antoine de la Mothe Cadillac,** 1658–1730.

The War of the Spanish Succession erupted in the colonies as Queen Anne's War, 1702–13. It ended with France losing territory in Canada to Britain.

The Parliamentary Act of 1709 offered immigrants who swore allegiance and took the Sacrament the privileges of British citizens.

Many Scotch-Irish immigrants arrived in the New World, most of them settling in Pennsylvania. New Orleans was founded in 1718.

: Paul's Cathedral

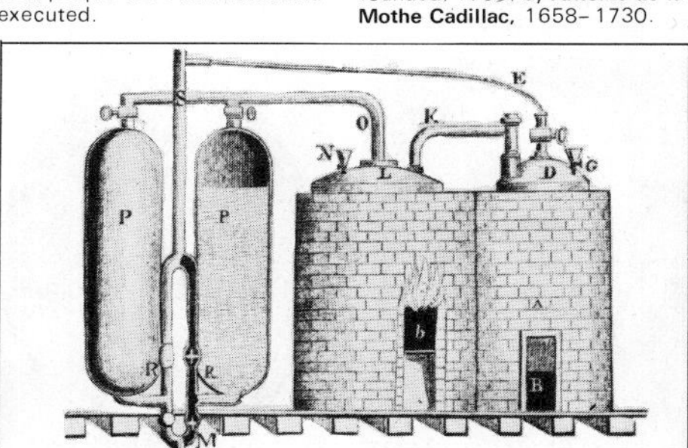

E
O
K
N
L
D
G
P
P
b
A
B
R
R
M

Thomas Savery's steam engine

Johann Sebastian Bach

Salem witchcraft trial

ıac Newton, 1642–1727, pubshed the *Principia* in 1687. He efended the idea of a gravitaɔnal force by arguing that sciıce should merely establish ɔserved regularities, without eculating about underlying echanisms. His view that the me set of laws, comprehensie with the aid of the physical :iences, apply throughout the ıiverse was fundamental to the evelopment of the mechanistic ıd optimistic philosophy of the 3th century.

John Locke, 1632–1704, produced the first thorough empiricist study in *An Essay Concerning Human Understanding,* 1690. He denied the existence of innate knowledge, arguing that the mind was a "tabula rasa" (a blank slate) that was only filled in by sensory experience. His *Two Treatises on Government,* 1690, which justified the English Revolution of 1688, claimed that rulers' legitimacy depended on their protecting the citizens' rights.

Govind Singh, 1666–1708, the tenth guru of the Sikh religion, began a strategy of armed resistance to Mogul persecution and in 1699 gave the common surname Singh (meaning "lion") to the Sikhs. He also introduced the strict practices of the Sikhs, who were pledged to wear a turban, to carry a knife, and never to cut their hair. The Sikhs eventually dominated the Punjab.

In **The Grumbling Hive,** 1705, **Bernard de Mandeville,** 1670–1733, argued that all individual actions are motivated by self-interest, but the net effect of many such actions is the general good. This idea influenced later *laissez-faire* economists. **The Earl of Shaftesbury's** *Letter concerning Enthusiasm,* 1708, helped to popularize **Deism,** or Natural Religion. Deists criticized formal religions, intolerance, and extremism.

In **The Principles of Human Knowledge,** 1710, Bishop Berkeley, 1685–1753, starting from the belief that all knowledge must come from perception, went beyond Locke and argued for an extreme idealism. He claimed that all we perceive is in the mind alone. As a result, to exist is merely to be perceived, and thus the continuing existence of the external world depends on God's external perception of it. Berkeley thus hoped to refute atheism definitively.

The metaphysical views of Gottfried Leibniz, 1646–1716, were summed up in the *Monadologie,* 1714. He saw the universe as comprising an infinity of "monads," dimensionless entities endowed with souls, in pre-established harmony with each other. Leibniz held that God had chosen this as the best of all possible worlds and that the evil in it was necessary. He also worked influentially in symbolic logic.

ıe French poet Jean de la Fonine, 1621–95, read his *Disurs en Vers* to the Academy in 384. His verse *Fables,* begun in 368, conveyed human insights rough the old tradition of anial stories. **Japan,** the succinct three-line ɔetic form called **haiku** reached peak in the poetry of **Matsuo asho,** 1644–94.

Restoration English drama, which had been dominated since 1660 by the influence of the poet, critic, satirist, and playwright **John Dryden,** 1631–1700, culminated in *Love for Love,* 1695, by **William Congreve,** 1670–1729. This was an improvement on the comedies of **William Wycherley,** 1640–1716, including the bawdy play *The Country Wife, c.*1674.

John Dryden ended a fruitful career with *Fables Ancient and Modern,* 1699. He also wrote a significant political satire on Monmouth and Shaftesbury, *Absalom and Achitophel.* His clear, elegant verse and prose had influenced many, including **Samuel Butler,** 1612–80. *All for Love* was Dryden's best play.

English journalism arose to satisfy the new middle class market. **Daniel Defoe,** 1660–1731, journalist, novelist, merchant, and spy, issued the *Review,* 1704, later followed by **Richard Steele's** *Tatler,* 1709, and **Joseph Addison's** *Spectator,* 1711. Addison and Steele were informed and sensible essayists on literary, political, and social issues.

English Classicism found its wittiest poet in **Alexander Pope,** 1688–1744, whose *Rape of The Lock* was published in its full form in 1714. The main defenders of classicism in France were **Nicolas Boileau,** 1636–1711, **Jean de la Bruyère,** 1645–96, and **Jacques Bossuet,** 1627–1704.

The tradition of the picaresque novel (recounting exploits of an adventurer), which derived from Spain, was used by **Alain Le Sage,** 1668–1747, in his *Gil Blas,* 1715–35. **The romantic Japanese dramatist Chikamatsu Monzaemon,** 1652–1725, wrote *Love Suicides,* the last of many successful plays both in **Kabuki** (song-dance) and **jojuri** (puppet) forms.

ıe arts in France under Louis V were dominated by **Charles Brun,** 1619–90, who was ɾector from 1663 of the French cademy and was also responsie for the Versailles Galerie des aces, completed 1684, and e Salons de la Guerre and de la aix, 1686. **ɜnetian architecture** was repreınted by the Sta Maria della alute, *c.*1631–87, by **Baldasre Longhena,** 1598–1682. It as classical in conception but ıd baroque overtones.

Spanish Baroque style in architecture was derived from the works of **José Churriguera,** 1665–1725, whose east end of St Esteban, Salamanca, 1693, shows the extravagant surface decoration and richly gilded ornament called Churriguesque. **The leading exponent of the Baroque style of illusionist decoration** in Italy was **Andrea dal Pozzo,** 1642–1709, whose ceiling of S Ignazio, Rome, 1691–94, was a masterpiece of perspective and trompe l'oeil.

Baroque architecture in England was exemplified in Castle Howard, designed by **John Vanbrugh,** 1664–1726, from 1696. He worked with **Nicholas Hawksmoor,** 1661–1736, on this and other buildings. **The beginnings of the Rococo** style were seen in the "arabesques" and "grotesques" designed by **Jean Bérain,** 1640–1711, and **Claude Audran,** 1658–1734.

The grandeur and formal design of Versailles were emulated throughout Europe in the 18th century with the founding of St Petersburg, Russia, 1703, and in England with Blenheim Palace, 1705, built for the duke of Marlborough by **Vanbrugh.**

European artists, like **Gustavus Hesselius,** 1682–1755, from Sweden, settled in Philadelphia in 1711 and executed realistic portraits and history paintings. **A triumph for Rubensistes** was evident in the vast ceiling of the Chapel at Versailles, 1708, by **Antoine Coypel,** 1661–1722, which is in the manner of Roman baroque illusionism.

The "fête galante," a new genre of painting characterized by exquisite scenes of pleasure and dalliance, was introduced by **Antoine Watteau,** 1684–1721, in the "Departure for the Island of Cythera," 1717. **The first phase of the Rococo in France,** 1700–20, largely in sculpture and interior design, was exemplified in the fountains of **Gilles Marie Oppenordt,** 1672–1742, designed about 1715 and showing twisting figures, shells, and scrolls.

ıroque composers' awareness modulation through a cycle of ths brought more harmonic terest to their music, but tun3 problems grew when harmowandered from the home key.

The concerto was developed by **Arcangelo Corelli,** 1653–1713, and others as a concerto grosso for a group of instruments and orchestra or for a virtuoso solo performer with orchestra.

Fugues in organ music were often paired with a free composition for contrast, giving the prelude and fugue or toccata and fugue found in many works by Buxtehude and Bach.

German suites by Bach and others mixed free forms such as prelude and toccata with dance forms such as *allemande, sarabande, minuet, gavotte,* and *gigue.*

The pianoforte was invented. It is usually attributed to the Italian **Bartolomeo Cristofori,** 1655–1731, who in 1709 substituted hammer action for the harpsichord's plucking action.

Italian became the usual operatic language in Europe although France still kept its own opera. **George Friderie Handel,** 1685–1759, composed Italian opera in England after 1719.

ɜwton's *Principia,* probably the ɔst important book in science, ıs published in 1687. The first ction deals with the behavior moving bodies and enunciates ɜwton's three laws of motion, well as the principles of gravtion. The second deals with ɜ motion of bodies in fluids, d also wave motion. The third lizes the principles expounded the earlier sections to explain ɜ motion of bodies on the rth and in the universe. It was ɾevolutionary conception.

Christiaan Huygens, 1629–95, a Dutch physicist, put forward a wave theory of light, 1690. Newton at this time proposed a particle theory. Later science would prove them both right.

The first practical steam engine was invented, 1696, by **Thomas Savery,** 1650–1715, a British engineer. **Thomas Newcomen,** 1663–1729, another British engineer, invented the atmospheric steam engine, used until 1934 to pump water from mines. Both engines had a great drawback: the cylinder had to be cooled at each stroke, wasting 99% of the heat from the fuel. **Agriculture** was improved by sowing seeds in rows with a drill invented in 1701 by **Jethro Tull,** 1674–1741, in England.

Opticks, published by Newton in 1704, encapsulated his work on light. His particle theory of light held great sway for a century before Huygens' wave theory was revived. **Edmond Halley,** 1656–1742, British astronomer royal, proposed the idea that comets orbit the Sun and, using Newton's principles, correctly predicted in 1705 the return of the comet that now bears his name.

Jesuit missionaries made an accurate map of China, 1708. **High quality iron** was produced in 1711 by **Abraham Darby,** 1677–1717, a British iron worker. The iron was smelted with coke and molded in sand for cheap production, making the cast iron steam engine an economic proposition. **Francis Hawksbee,** an Englishman, made the first accurate observations of capillary action in glass tubes in 1709. **Prussian blue,** a colored dye, was produced from 1710.

The mercury thermometer was invented in 1714 by **Gabriel Fahrenheit,** a German physicist, 1686–1736. **Jethro Tull** brought the horsehoe to England from France. **Thomas Lombe,** 1658–1739, an Englishman, patented a machine to make thrown silk in 1718.

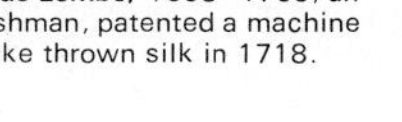

Reason and the Enlightenment 1720–1760

Principal events

A series of dynastic and trade wars overtook Europe, contributing to the growing conflict between centralized monarchical authority, the nobility, and the newly strong mercantile class. In France the supremacy of the monarch over the nobles broke down, producing a political stalemate. In Prussia, Russia, and Portugal, however, the liberal ideas of the Enlightenment were harnessed to the growth of royal absolutism and industrial reform.

The English moved inland in India into the vacuum of the collapsing Mogul Empire, prized both for the value of its produce and the quality of its culture. Here they competed successfully with the French despite the unwillingness of the English government to take on imperial responsibility. At the same time the American colonies, whose economies were beginning to grow, were becoming impatient with Britain's rigid mercantilist policies.

1720–1724

The English South Sea Company and the French Mississippi scheme, which had both aimed to restore royal finances, collapsed in 1720.
The Pragmatic Sanction, 1713, establishing the indivisibility of Austria-Hungary, was accepted in 1720.
In North America, Spain occupied Texas 1720–22, to prevent a French invasion, and the Piedmont region was colonized by Swiss, Germans, and Scots.

1724–1728

Peter the Great of Russia died, 1725, having encouraged industrial growth, centralized the administration, and subdued the nobility.
The ministry of Fleury, 1653–1743, in France began, 1726, introducing a period of peace and economic growth that led to a strengthening of the middle classes.
The Russian border with China was fixed in 1727.

1728–1732

The Anglo-Spanish War, 1727–28, forced Spain to end her siege and confirm England's possession of Gibraltar, 1729.
Anna, *r.*1730–40, empress of Russia, founded the Corps of Cadets to encourage the nobles' participation in administration.
By the Treaty of Vienna, 1731, the Holy Roman Empire dissolved the Ostend East India Company, England's colonial trading rival in cotton, spices, and saltpeter.

1732–1736

England prohibited trade between her American and West Indian colonies by the Molasse Act of 1733.
War over the succession, 1733 35, weakened Poland.
The French Compagnie des Ind was firmly established in India by 1735.
Class distinctions between the merchant and military groups i Japan became blurred during a long period of economic declir

National events

The American colonies continued to develop, each in its own way, but with a common English identity. As English power in America grew, colonists began to chafe under British economic policies. Colonial assemblies were unable to exercise independent action. Settlers began to move westward increasingly.

French forts along the Mississippi River spread northward from New Orleans. The first smallpox inoculations were given, 1721.

The Great Awakening, a spiritual revival in the colonies, began in 1726. Prominent figures were **Jonathan Edwards,** 1703–58, and **George Whitefield,** 1715–70.

North Carolina became a royal colony, 1729, as had South Carolina in 1721. Georgia, planned as a refuge for prisoners, was chartered, 1732.

Independence Hall in Philadelphia was begun in 1732. **Benjamin Franklin,** 1706–90, began publication of *Poor Richard's Almanack.*

Gulliver's Travels

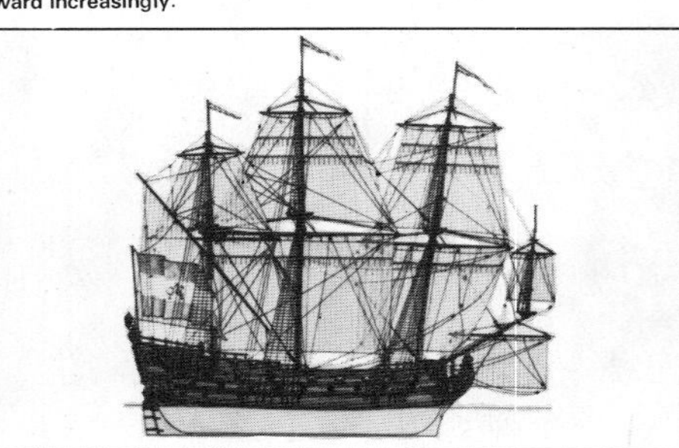

Dutch East Indiaman

Marble bust of Voltaire

Carl Linnaeus

House of Menander, Pompeii

Religion and philosophy

The influence of English empiricist ideas on the philosophical tradition stemming from Descartes led to the great intellectual development known as the French Enlightenment. Montesquieu, Voltaire, Rousseau, and other "philosophes" who contributed to the French Encyclopedia believed in the power of reason and knowledge to liberate man from restrictive political and religious systems.

On religious questions these thinkers tended toward deism or even atheism, and accepted a materialist conception of the universe. In politics they were liberals. Montesquieu sought to classify social systems and analyze their function. The Physiocrats laid the foundation of scientific economics. Others such as Condillac elaborated the basic ideas of materialist philosophy.

In Britain David Hume showed how empiricism could lead to an extreme skepticism.

Christian von Wolff, 1679–1754, a follower of Leibniz, made rationalist antitraditional philosophy popular in Germany. Puritan Pietists engineered his expulsion from the University of Halle in 1723, but he later became its chancellor.
Ba'al Shem Tov, *c.*1700–60, founded **Hasidism** in Poland. This vibrant orthodox movement within Judaism stressed the joy of religious practice and expression, and rejected academic formalism and elitism.

Giovanni Battista Vico, 1668–1744, an important forerunner of the modern social scientists, outlined his ideas in *Universal Law,* 1720–21, and elaborated them later in his masterpiece, *The New Science,* 1725. Vico held that societies pass from a bestial stage through a patrician stage ruled by a hereditary elite, to a stage where men are equal. He warned that man was never wholly rid of his bestial aspect and might always regress into barbarism.

Voltaire, 1694–1778, returned to France in 1729 after over two years in England. His *Lettres philosophiques,* 1734, advocating the empiricism of **Isaac Newton** and **John Locke** and the merits of the English political system, had a great influence on the French Enlightenment. Voltaire was a deist and an active liberal fighting for the exercise of tolerance in both religion and politics.

In his Treatise on Human Natur written from 1734 to 1737, **Da vid Hume,** 1711–76, argued from empiricist presupposition that knowledge was unattainable. He said that since connections were unobservable our belief in them was irration Hume held that the basis of moral judgment was man's sub jective reaction of approval or disapproval of the effects actions have on himself and others.

Literature

European literature was dominated by the critical spirit of the Age of Reason expressed in the work of essayists and satirists such as Pope and Swift in Britain or Voltaire and Montesquieu in France, where polemical writing was in the ascendant. The same desire to grasp social reality found expression in the English novel, whether in the vein of a new realism, with Defoe or Fielding, in the psychological studies of Laurence Sterne, or the picaresque novels of Smollett. In Italy, Goldoni's comedies began a parallel move in the theater away from stock characterization and toward a greater realism.

The basis of modern Russian poetry was established by Lomonosov.

Daniel Defoe, 1660–1731, a prolific writer and one of the founders of modern journalism, turned to fiction (disguised as fact) and revealed a powerful imagination. His novels, including *Robinson Crusoe,* 1719–20, and *Moll Flanders,* 1722, are noted for their highly realistic descriptions.

Jonathan Swift, 1667–1745, poet, polemicist, and churchman, published *Gulliver's Travels,* 1726, a highly imaginative satire on mankind. Swift wrote brilliantly abusive essays.
The Beggar's Opera by John Gay, 1685–1732, was first played in 1728. It uses elements of Italian opera and traditional songs to create a new style of political satire.

German ideas of the Aufklärung (Enlightenment) were summed up in *Critische Dichtkunst,* 1730, a critical work by the playwright **J. C. Gottsched,** 1700–66. He argued that literature must imitate classical models and be didactic.
Romanticism was foreshadowed in France by the **Abbé Prévost,** 1697–1763, the prolific author of *Manon Lescaut,* 1731.

The Italian **Scipione Maffei,** 1675–1755, published his erudite study of the history of Verona, *Verona Illustrata,* in 1732
Montesquieu, 1689–1755, a leading French thinker and sati rist, wrote his *Considerations the Causes of the Grandeur of the Romans and their Decadence,* 1734, an outstanding piece of sociopolitical analysis

Art and architecture

Late manifestations of the more emotional baroque and rococo forms were seen in Austria and Germany as well as in European colonial architecture in the mid-18th century. But as concepts of "good taste" emerged during the Enlightenment, combined with a more exact and careful study of the aesthetics of classical art, the exuberance of the early 18th century became restrained within realist, or neoclassical modes. Interest in fantasy shifted from the Baroque to chinoiserie or rococo "Gothick," in the search for new stylistic forms.

Native Indian art was in decline, and European styles were introduced to India by the advancing colonialists. The impact of European expansion in the cultural sphere was also found in China.

In Japan color printing techniques were developed, and the art reached a new peak in the work of Utamaro.

Easter Island was discovered by the Dutch, 1722. Archeologists have since been baffled by the significance of, and building methods used to erect, the megalithic statues found there.
Austrian art reached its peak in the architecture of palaces, churches, and monasteries, especially those of **Lukas von Hildebrandt,** 1688–1745. Known as "Austrian Baroque," this style with its florid shapes and lavish decoration paved the way for late German Baroque.

Indian art was in decline with the collapse of the Mogul Empire, and European architectural styles began to be introduced in colonial towns, including Bombay where **St Thomas Cathedral** was built.
Catholic Bavaria accepted Italian baroque forms, which in the later work of **Balthasar Neumann,** 1687–1753, took on an almost rococo lightness. His church at Vierzehnheiligen, 1743–72, is richly painted in pink, gold, and white.

Palladianism, a revival of interest in the restrained classicism of Vitruvius, Palladio, and his English follower Inigo Jones, marked an English reaction against Baroque. It was pioneered by **Colin Campbell,** *d.*1729, and taken up by **Lord Burlington** 1694–1753, who encouraged **William Kent,** *d.*1748, and **Isaac Ware,** *d.*1766.
Giuseppe Castiglione 1698–1768, settled in China *c.*1730, and was the first Western painter to be appreciated there.

Venice took the lead in Italian a with the painting of **Giovanni Tiepolo,** 1696–1770, and **Anto nio Canaletto,** 1697–1768.
Servandoni, 1695–1766, bega work on the facade of Ste Sulpice in Paris, 1732. It relied on antique architecture and heralc ed a reaction against Rococo.

Music

Italian influence on European music waned, except in opera and song. The French evolved instruments and musical theory, but the Germans and Austrians, patronized by their princes, made the most use of these developments and ushered in the classical age of music. In the work of Joseph Haydn, 1732–1809, the symphony found a champion to establish its form.

Traité de l'harmonie, 1722, by **Jean Philipe Rameau,** 1683–1764, provided the foundation of harmonic thought for two centuries, with its clear statement of the function of tonality.

Light opera emerged in Germany, where **Reinhard Keiser,** 1674–1739, wrote operas with catchy tunes. He wrote a comic opera in 1726 that used spoken dialogue rather than recitative.

Virtuoso players such as **Antonio Vivaldi,** *c.*1675–1741, advanced the techniques of their instruments and led to a distinction between music for professional and amateur players.

Religious cantata and oratorio were developed on a grand sca by **Bach** and **George Frideric Handel,** 1685–1759, to embra all musical techniques but wit out the use of operatic staging

Science and technology

Great technological innovations were created, and were stimulated by, the Industrial Revolution. In England the textile industry, with its need for large-scale bleaching and dyeing processes, gave a boost to practical chemistry and to machine technology. The flying shuttle produced the large quantities of cloth that demanded bleaching, and modern methods were invented to provide the great amounts of acid employed in the process. Similarly, the need to transport more raw materials and finished products by sea than ever before encouraged navigational innovation. An early form of the sextant and the first accurate chronometer were invented. Meanwhile pure scientific research continued in the form of discoveries, particularly in plant physiology and growth. Early work on electricity was performed at Leyden University and in America, providing the basis of later experiments into the nature of electric currents and their potential.

Smallpox inoculations were first administered in the New World during an epidemic in 1721, when **Zabdiel Boylston,** 1679–1766, inoculated 240 persons, of whom all but six survived.

The chronometer was developed from 1726 by John Harrison, 1693–1776, an Englishman, to aid navigation, as longitude could be determined only by time. He invented the compensating pendulum, so that his chronometers would keep perfect time in any climate.
Plant physiology was founded by the publication of *Vegetable Staticks,* in 1727, by **Stephen Hales,** 1677–1761. Measuring plant growth and sap production, Hales realized that air is necessary for plants to grow.

Stellar aberration, a change in the position of stars caused by the Earth's motion, was detected in 1729 by an Englishman, **James Bradley,** 1693–1762. This was the first absolute confirmation of Copernicus' theory that the Earth moves around the Sun.
Cobalt was discovered in 1730 by George Brandt, 1694–1768, a Swedish chemist.
The reflecting quadrant, a forerunner of the sextant, aided navigation. It was invented in 1730 by John Hadley, 1682–1744.

Systema Naturae was publishe by Carl Linnaeus, 1707–78, a Swedish botanist, in 1735. He defined the differences betwe species and formed the idea of classifying plants and animals into species and genera, classe and orders.
The flying shuttle was invente in England in 1733 by John Ka 1704–64.
Rubber was found in South America by Charles Marie de la Condamine, 1701–74, while o an expedition to measure the curvature of the Earth, 1735.

736–1740

ıssia and Austria clashed with e Turks over their Polish pol-y. The Russians captured Azov ıt by the Treaty of Belgrade, 739, were prevented from eeping a fortified Black Sea ıse there.
ommercial rivalry in America etween England and Spain ought an end to a period of eace for England, with the war Jenkins' Ear, 1739–48. The ar resulted from a dispute over ading rights in the Spanish col-ıies.

1740–1744

Frederick II the Great of Prussia, *r.*1740–86, introduced religious toleration and agricultural reform, consolidated royal authority, and reformed the army. In 1740 he occupied Silesia, thus striking the first blow in the War of the Austrian Succession, 1740–48.
Elizabeth of Russia, *r.*1741–62, gave new authority to the Senate.
The Marathas took Bengal, 1742–44, and disturbed English trade in Bombay.

1744–1748

Frederick II began the Second Silesian War, 1744–45. France and Prussia defeated the Austrians and their allies at the battle of Fontenoy, 1745.
In North America, English forces took Louisbourg, 1745, and made new conquests from the French in the West Indies.
In India, the Frenchman **Joseph Dupleix,** 1696–1763, took Madras, 1746. However, all these conquests were restored by the **Treaty of Aix-la-Chapelle,** 1748.

1748–1752

Louis XV, *r.*1715–74, met united opposition from the nobility and clergy in France when he tried to introduce new taxes on their wealth to pay for his war expenses, 1751.
Robert Clive, 1725–74, seized Arcot, 1751, in search of personal power and booty, and thus established English authority over southern India, ousting the French opposition.
The Chinese invaded Tibet, 1751, following a growth in Chinese population and wealth.

1752–1756

Sébastião Pombal, 1699–1782, introduced Enlightenment ideas to Portugal, 1751–77, ruthlessly attacking clerical and noble privileges and stimulating industrial growth.
Dupleix was recalled to France in 1754, leaving India to the British. Delhi was sacked by Afghan invaders, 1756–57.
Moscow University was founded in 1755 to promote education among the Russian nobility.
Lisbon was destroyed by an earthquake in 1755.

1756–1760

In the Seven Years War, 1756–63, Austria was at first defeated by Frederick II.
Clive won control of Bengal at Plassey, 1757.
The Marathas occupied the Punjab in 1758.
Pombal expelled the Jesuits from Portugal in 1759.
Most of Canada came under British control after the surrender of **Montreal,** 1760. This ended the need for British garrisons to defend the American colonies.

ıhn Peter Zenger, 1697–1746, ppointed public printer for ew Jersey and New York, 737. Zenger had been acquit-d in 1735 of libel.

Alaska was discovered, 1741, by **Vitus Bering,** 1680–1741, sailing from Russia to see if North America and Asia were connected by land.

The Presbyterian College of New Jersey, renamed Princeton University in 1896, was chartered, 1746, to educate clergy.

In 1749, Britain granted 200,000 acres of land on the upper Ohio to a group of Virginians who formed a land company.

George Washington's troops at Fort Duquesne, 1754, opened the French and Indian War.
Franklin proposed Plan of Union at the Albany Congress, 1754.

French General Montcalm, 1712–59, and **British Brig. Gen. James Wolfe,** 1727–59, died on the Plains of Abraham. France ceded Canada to England, 1763.

ederick II of Prussia reviewing troops

Jean-Jacques Rousseau

Sandoe
22 Dec
1788
B
Robert Bakewell's improved sheep

JOIN, or DIE.
JOIN, or DIE.
Albany Congress: flags

ıhn Wesley, 1703–91, an An-ican minister, founded the ethodist movement in England. fter a spiritual experience in 738, Wesley began evangelical pen air preaching and drew up a et of "Rules" for his followers, ho formed "bands"—small oups for mutual encourage-ent and for teaching and pray-. They believed in a personal lationship with God and were oted for their good works. The ethodists finally broke with the hurch of England in 1795.

The puritanical Wahhabi movement within Islam was founded by **Muhammed ibn Abd al-Wahhab,** 1703–92. He advocated a return to the original principles of Islam and condemned as polytheistic the decoration of mosques and the cult of saints, which he saw as intervening in the personal and direct relationship between the faithful and God. In 1744 the powerful Saudi family in central Arabia adopted the principles of the Wahhabi sect.

In **The Spirit of Laws,** published 1748, the French social theorist **Charles Montesquieu,** 1689–1755, examined the relationships between a society's laws and its other characteristics such as religion and economic organization, drawing on an immense range of information about other cultures. He elaborated a study of types of governmental systems and analyzed the prerequisites of their proper functioning.

The first volume of the French Encyclopédie appeared, 1751. Edited by **Denis Diderot,** 1713–84, and completed in 1772, this was a monument to the "philosophes" of the French Enlightenment and aimed to advance reason, knowledge, and liberty. The contributors, who included **Etienne Condillac,** 1715–80, the Lockean philosopher, were deists or atheists who held liberal political views and a materialist conception of the universe.

Jean-Jacques Rousseau, 1712–78, published his *Discourse on Inequality* in 1755. In this work, and in *The Social Contract*, 1762, he argued that in a natural state men were equal and that it was only society that creates inequality and misery. He argued that the injustices of society could be minimized if citizens resigned their rights to a government that acted on the "general will."

The Physiocrats of the 18th century were the first scientific school of economics. They regarded agriculture rather than manufacturing as the source of wealth, and advocated the doctrine of *laissez-faire*, or free trade, against the complex trade regulations then in force. The most important Physiocrat was **François Quesnay,** 1694–1774, whose *Tableau economique*, 1758, was the first work to attempt an analysis of the workings of an entire economy.

oltaire (F. M. Arouet), 1694–778, wit, poet, dramatist, and pitome of the Enlightenment his scorn for prejudice and strust of accepted ideas, wrote e philosophical poems *Le Mondain*, 1736, and *Discours ur l'Homme*, 1738. Stressing e value of experience, he later atirized ideas of human perfect-ility in *Candide*, 1759, a tale innocence abused.

The crowning achievement of Augustan poetry in England, *The Dunciad* of **Alexander Pope,** appeared in its final version, 1743. This was a mock heroic attacking the betrayal of literature by hack writers, using elements of Homer, Vergil, Dante, and Milton and defending a role for the poet as a conserver of the values of society.

Italy's greatest comic dramatist, Carlo Goldoni, 1707–93, wrote *The Servant of Two Masters*, 1745. A skillful and prolific craftsman, he substituted a script and more realistic treatment of character and situation for commedia dell'arte, the traditional Italian comic form in which actors playing stock roles improvised upon an outline scenario.

The English novel, which had been developed by **Samuel Richardson,** 1689–1761, in *Pamela*, 1740–41, flowered in the masterpiece *Tom Jones*, 1749, by **Henry Fielding,** 1707–54. **Laurence Sterne,** 1713–68, mastered a vein of black humor in *Tristram Shandy*, **Tobias** and **Smollett,** 1721–71, the picaresque tradition in *Roderick Random*, 1748.

The father of modern Russian literature, Mikhail Lomonosov, 1711–65, published his *Grammar*, 1755. Poet and linguist, he set up verse rules and three styles of literary diction that opened up new possibilities in Russian literature.
The lyrical poetry of the German F. G. Klopstock, 1724–1803, who took Greek verse as his model, anticipated Romanticism.

Realism in Chinese fiction, exemplified in the satirical novel *Unofficial History of Scholars* by **Wu Ching-tse,** 1701–54, was further developed by **Tsao Chan,** *c.*1719–63, in *The Dream of a Red Chamber*. In this novel, the grandeur and decline of a Chinese family was described with convincing detail and a new sense of humanity.

ench art was divided between e officially accepted art in the ococo vein, like the frivolous, ildly erotic work of **François oucher,** 1703–70, who had dopted much of Tiepolo's tech-que, and the more solid realis-c genre scenes of **Jean Char-n,** 1699–1779, which re-ected a contemporary taste for orthern painting, especially 7th-century Dutch masters.
erculaneum was discovered in 738.

Color printing was developed in Japan, *c.*1742 with outstanding results by **Kitagawa Utamaro,** 1753–1806, who was one of the greatest exponents of the ukiyo-e school of painting. This "floating world" art form was famous for its depiction of sensuous women. In England, **William Hogarth,** 1697–1764, attacked the social abuses of his time. He often followed a narrative of events in a series of paintings as in "Marriage à la Mode."

Chinoiserie, a taste for Chinese art and design, became popular in Europe in the 1740s.
Spanish colonial architecture was executed in a baroque style, especially in Mexico. The collision with existing cultures introduced new motifs like the Puebla tiles on the Church of San Francisco, Acatepec.

The "Gothick rococo" became a fashion in England with the remodeling of Strawberry Hill House, 1749, by **Horace Walpole,** 1717–97. The library fireplace combined motifs from medieval tombs in Westminster and Canterbury Cathedrals.
British and French artists such as **Joshua Reynolds,** 1723–92, and **Jacques-Germain Soufflot,** 1713–80, would revolutionize art and architecture after studying art in Rome *c.*1750.
Pompeii was found in 1748.

A torrent of publications heralded a change in taste in European art, foreshadowing **Neoclassicism,** which would be based on a detailed study of ancient Greek and Roman art. The archeological discoveries engraved by **Piranesi,** 1720–78, in *Antichita Romana*, 1757, and such dissertations on taste as *Dialogue on Taste*, 1754, by **Allan Ramsay,** 1713–84, resulted in an ability to distinguish different phases in antiquity.

Russian architecture was based largely on French developments, the combination of baroque forms with rococo decoration producing the extravagant splendor of the Winter Palace, 1754–62, in St Petersburg by **Bartolomeo Rastrelli,** 1700–71.
A positive reaction against Rococo in France was seen in the fleeting fashion of **"Le Gout Grec"** and also in a more significant dependence on antique precedents in the design of the Pantheon by **Soufflot** in Paris.

ontrapuntal writing reached a asterful zenith under Bach, ith music of great power and tricacy, as in the "Kyrie" from s *Mass in B minor*, 1738.

Equal temperament was worked out in Germany. It made modulation to distant keys possible, as in the *Well-tempered Klavier*, 1722–44, by **J. S. Bach,** 1685–1750.

The symphony orchestra gained the basis of its present form at Mannheim court under **Johann Stamitz,** 1717–57, who trained his players to produce controlled extremes of loud and soft.

American settlers began making a distinctive music with easily carried instruments. Barn dances were held as buildings were completed, and hymn-singing meetings were held in homes.

The symphony in the hands of Haydn developed greatly from 1750 to 1760, advancing its instrumentation and the form of its contrasting movements, usually four in number.

Sonata form was advanced by **C. P. E. Bach,** 1714–88, who made imaginative use of key relationships and conflicts in the development sections of first movements of his symphonies.

aniel Bernoulli, 1700–82, a enchman, related fluid flow to essure in 1738.

Anders Celsius, 1701–44, a Swede, devised the Celsius scale of temperature, *c.*1744, with 0° the freezing point of water and 100° the boiling point.
The crucible method of making steel by heating scrap iron was found in England, 1740, by Benjamin Huntsman, 1704–76.
Mikhail Lomonosov, 1711–65, rejected the phlogiston theory and suggested the law of the conservation of mass.
Traité de Dynamique, 1743, by **Jean d'Alembert,** 1717–83, solved problems in mechanics.

The Leyden jar, developed at the University of Leyden, 1745, was able to store a large charge of static electricity. It was used in the first investigations into the nature of electricity.
John Roebuck, 1718–94, a British inventor, developed a process for manufacturing sulfuric acid, used to bleach textiles, on a large scale in 1746.

Benjamin Franklin, 1706–90, working in America, flew a kite in a thunderstorm, 1752, to prove that lightning is electrical, and from his results developed a lightning conductor.
Selective breeding, pioneered by **Robert Bakewell,** 1725–95, in England, improved livestock.
The experimental farming of Viscount Townshend, 1674–1738, improved crop rotation.
Georges Buffon, 1707–88, published the first volume of his massive *Histoire Naturelle*, 1749–88.

Immanuel Kant, 1724–1804, in Germany, published his views on the formation of the solar system in 1755, anticipating the work of Laplace. He also suggested that galaxies of stars exist and that the tides slow the rotation of the Earth. Both of these ideas were verified much later.
René Réaumur, 1683–1757, proved that digestion is a chemical process and invented an 80 degree thermometer scale.

Carbon dioxide was discovered in 1756 by Joseph Black, 1728–99, a British chemist.
Lomonosov was the first man to observe atmosphere on the planet of Venus, 1761.
The sextant of John Bird (1758) made navigational observations far more accurate.
John Dollond, 1706–61, produced the first achromatic lenses in 1757 in England.

Revolution in America and France 1760–1800

Principal events

The old order in Europe was fundamentally shaken by three major revolutions—in America, France, and England—which dramatically changed the political and economic basis of Western society and would ultimately transform the world. The American Revolution represented the overthrow of the old colonial and trading system and installed the ideas of liberty and democracy as the ideals of the United States. The French Revolution of 1789 swept away the privileges of the outdated ancien régime and established a new idea of popular right, which would be carried by Napoleon's conquests to stir the rest of Europe to revolt.

In England the Industrial Revolution began in earnest in the 1780s, providing the basis for a fundamental transformation of Western and ultimately global society by accelerating urbanization and creating new sources of wealth, new social classes, and democratic demands.

1760–1764

Prussia increased its military power after 1760 and an inconclusive settlement to the Seven Years War followed.
The Treaty of Paris, 1763, confirmed English supremacy in Canada and India.
The War left French government finances in a precarious state despite expanding trade.
Pontiac's Rebellion, an American Indian revolt, was suppressed by the English in Canada, 1763–66.

1764–1768

The Sugar Act and Stamp Act 1764–65, by which Britain aimed to recover revenue from the American colonies, aroused local opposition.
England ruled Bengal and Bihar by 1765, maintaining a puppet Mogul emperor.
Ali Bey *r.*1768–73, declared Egyptian independence from Turkish rule, 1766.
Catherine II of Russia, *r.*1762–96, consulted a convention of all social classes to reform Russian law, 1767.

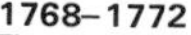

1768–1772

The American colonies began their westward expansion, settling Tennessee in 1769.
French trade with India increased after the French East India Company lost its monopoly, 1769.
Opposition to absolutism in France increased among intellectuals.
James Cook, 1728–79, began the exploration of Australia in the *Endeavour*, 1768–71.

1772–1776

After Pugachev's revolt, a larg peasant and cossack uprising, 1773–75, Catherine II reform Russian provincial administration.
The Regulating Act establishec an English governor general in India, 1773. **Warren Hastings,** 1732–1818, reformed the Ber gal administration. Demands b the American colonists that th be represented in the English Parliament led to the **American Revolution,** 1775–83.

National events

The American colonists had become so "English" in their political beliefs that they could not tolerate the inferior status of colonials. Resentment of British rule, particularly taxation without representation, led to a war to ensure that Englishmen in America would enjoy all the rights of Englishmen in England.

Ottawa chief Pontiac, *c.*1720–69, led an Indian uprising, 1763, but the British defeated the Indians. The Sugar Act was passed, 1764.

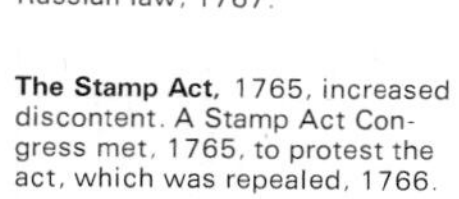

The Stamp Act, 1765, increased discontent. A Stamp Act Congress met, 1765, to protest the act, which was repealed, 1766.

British troops in Boston fired on civilians, and five died in the Boston Massacre, March 5, 1770.

The Boston Tea Party proteste the Tea Act, 1773. The First Continental Congress met, 177 Lexington and Concord, 1775, opened the Revolution.

Thomas Paine

American Revolution

Iron bridge, Coalbrookdale

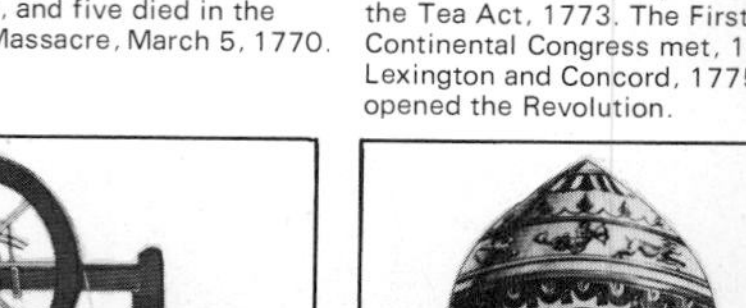

Mechanized spinning: Samuel Crompton's mule

Montgolfier's balloon

Religion and philosophy

The question of the existence of God became subordinate for many European thinkers to questions of social organization.

In America the revolution was associated with ideas of democracy, liberty, and equality, which in turn inspired the French Revolution.

In Britain new economic thinking reflected the emergence of the industrial system. Adam Smith laid the foundation of modern economics, fostering the liberal doctrine of the free market and the absence of state encroachment on individual freedom. Bentham argued that desire and pursuit of pleasure motivated human behavior. The Scottish Enlightenment advanced social thought with Ferguson's and Monboddo's work on social development and man's origins.

Kant, however, laid the basis for German idealism with his opposition to pure empiricism, claiming that such concepts as time were innate.

The Scottish School of Common Sense Philosophy was begun by **Thomas Reid,** 1710–96, who argued in *An Inquiry into the Human Mind on the Principles of Common Sense*, 1764, that Hume's skepticism about attaining true knowledge was against common sense. **Dugald Stewart,** 1753–1828, sought rejection of fruitless metaphysical speculation and the creation of scientific philosophy.

Adam Ferguson, 1723–1816, an early British sociologist, put forward the theory that man's unceasing desire to control nature was the cause of social development in his *Essay on the History of Civil Society*, 1766.
The Judaic religion was interpreted by **Moses Mendelssohn,** 1729–86, in terms of the metaphysics of Leibniz, paving the way for a synthesis of Judaism and modern philosophical and scientific thought, later to develop into **Reform Judaism.**

Johann Herder, 1744–1803, German poet and philosopher, was among the first modern thinkers to question the limits of reason. He emphasized the immediacy and therefore the power of feeling—ideas that were later to become the essence of the Romantic movement.
Paul d'Holbach, 1723–1803, the most ardent materialist of the French Encyclopedists, wrote in his *System of Nature*, 1770, that man's life is determined from birth.

Lord Monboddo, 1714–99, a British anthropologist, believed man's present social state evolved from a previous animal one. This conflicted with the view then current that man was unique. He began publication of his work on language in 1773.
The "Shakers," a group of puritanical nonconformists led by **Ann Lee,** 1736–84, began their first colony in America in 1774. They believed total sexual abstinence was the basis of man's spiritual salvation.

Literature

Forerunners of Romanticism emerged in Germany, France, and Britain. The emphasis on unity and order in literary style and the skeptical and rational attitudes of mind that marked the Enlightenment were beginning to give way to increasing respect for human instincts and emotions, sincerity of feeling, and freedom and naturalism of style. This transition, initiated by Rousseau in France, was carried on in Germany by the Sturn und Drang movement whose greatest voice, Goethe, combined passion with discipline. The work of the British poets Gray, Cowper, Burns, and Blake exemplified the transition from classicism to romanticism in English poetic style. Samuel Johnson's work advanced literary criticism.

Jean-Jacques Rousseau, 1712–78, whose concept of the "noble savage" deeply influenced romanticism, published *La Nouvelle Hèloise*, 1761, a novel advocating simple relationships in a natural setting. *The Encyclopedie*, edited 1751–72, by **Denis Diderot,** 1713–84, and **Jean Le Rond d'Alembert,** 1717–83, expressed the skepticism of the Enlightenment.

Gothic themes involving the supernatural and the crime of passion appeared in the ultra-romantic novel *The Castle of Otranto*, 1764, by **Horace Walpole,** 1717–97.
Thomas Percy, 1729–1811, published *Reliques of Ancient English Poetry*, 1765.
Karl Bellman, 1740–95, a Swedish poet, began his *82 Epistles* in 1765.

Thomas Gray's *Poems by Mr Gray*, 1768, included the "Elegy Written in a Country Churchyard." Gray, 1716–71, treated themes of history and death in a sensitive, meditative manner.
Gotthold Lessing, 1729–81, a German dramatist, wrote *Emilia Galotti*, 1772.

Sturm und Drang (Storm and Stress), a German literary movement expressing subjectivity anc contemporary unease, found a genius in **Johann Wolfgang von Goethe,** 1749–1832. His novel *The Sufferings of Young Werther*, 1774, began a cult of the hero ruled by the heart rather than the head. Romantic pessimism was exemplified in the poems of **Novalis,** 1772–1801.

Art and architecture

The arts in Europe, and particularly in France, reflected the critical spirit of the Enlightenment by returning to an austere style based on moral and aesthetic theories. Antiquarian and archeological investigation had transformed ideas on cultural development so that the various styles of Greek and Roman antiquity, the Middle Ages, and the Renaissance could now be distinguished. Neoclassicism, which developed toward the end of the 18th century, incorporated this knowledge, adopting Greek and Roman ideals of beauty and ethics derived from antique sculpture, architecture, painting, and literature. This historical concern was also to lead to acceptance of eclecticism and the concept of a modern style.

The European colonial presence in Asia tended to paralyze the development of indigenous artistic styles, but native traditions survived in areas remote from foreign influence.

Robert Adam with his brother James introduced a new eclectic style of architecture to town and country houses in Britain, like **Syon House,** 1762–69, in which they combined elements of English Palladianism with details of Roman architecture and Renaissance palaces.
Neoclassical painting was developed in Rome, under the impetus of the German archeologist **Johann Joachim Wickelmann,** 1717–68, by his follower **Anton Raffael Mengs,** 1728–79.

Soufflot's church of Ste Geneviève in Paris progressed. The design combined Greek post and lintel systems and attempted to achieve the lightness of Gothic architecture.
The Royal Academy of Art, London, was founded in 1768 under royal patronage. The first President, **Joshua Reynolds,** 1723–92, in "13 Discourses," promoted the "Grand Manner" in English painting.

An empirical, scientific attitude to art in England was shown by **George Stubbs,** 1724–1806, in the *Anatomy of the Horse*, published 1766, and in *The Experiment with the Air Pump*, 1768, by **Joseph Wright** of Derby, 1734–97.
French Neoclassic architecture was governed by the severe unadorned classicism seen in the works of **Jacques Gondouin** 1737–1818, of which the **Ecole de Médecine,** Paris, 1769, is a fine example.

Reynolds' supremacy in English portraiture was challenged in 1774 when **Thomas Gainsborough,** 1727–88, moved to London. His "William Henry, Duke o Gloucester," *c.*1775, was deliberately glamorous and richly colored. His later paintings introduced a more lyrical note to English portraiture.
Indian artists in the late 18th and early 19th centuries were dominated by European techniques. The Patua paintings of east India were exceptions.

Music

The classical age of European music was dominated by Joseph Haydn, 1732–1809, and Wolfgang Mozart, 1756–91. Composers pursued variety within movements, building bigger structures by manipulating musical themes and utilizing key relationships and contrasts of instrumental sound, appealing equally to the heads and hearts of their educated audiences.

The symphony and sonata grew in complexity under the hand of Haydn from *c.*1760. The first movement had contrasting themes worked over in a development section.

Christoph Gluck, 1714–87, reformed opera in Paris, stressing the balance between the musical and the dramatic elements. He expressed his ideals in a preface to *Alceste*, 1767.

Counterpoint declined in importance and the continuo disappeared. Contrapuntal forms such as fugue continued to be used but usually as part of a movement in a larger work.

String quartets were written in large numbers. They were an ideal vehicle for the development of classical designs and allowed the composer to hear his work immediately.

Science and technology

In Britain the Industrial Revolution began to transform the face of the nation. James Watt produced the first rotary engine, which could be used to power factories anywhere in the country, while the spinning jenny and the water frame furthered mechanization of the textile industry. Agricultural improvements, including more efficient crop rotation and selective breeding, increased the amount of food produced and provided a surplus for the towns. Developments in hygiene and medicine, such as the water closet, vaccination, and the widespread use of soap, would form the basis for substantial improvements in urban living conditions, many of which, however, were not realized until the nineteenth century.

Science was linked with liberty in revolutionary Fance as many academies of science were founded after 1789, while American technology worked against freedom—the success of the cotton gin helping to prolong slavery in the South.

Joseph Black, 1728–99, a Scottish chemist, defined the difference between heat and temperature, and discovered specific and latent heat, 1760–63. His basic work on heat enabled his friend **James Watt** to build a steam engine.
The spinning "jenny" was invented in England, 1764, by **James Hargreaves.** It could spin several threads at once.

The Lunar Society, an informal society of technologists, was founded in England *c.*1765.
Neurology was established with the work of Swiss physiologist **Albrecht von Haller,** 1708–77. Haller located nerves and showed that nerve impulses stimulate muscles.
Henry Cavendish, 1731–1810, a British scientist, discovered hydrogen in 1766. He also made fundamental, unpublished discoveries in electricity. In 1798 he would calculate the Earth's mass.

The water frame was invented in 1768 by **Richard Arkwright,** 1732–92. Powered by water, it spun cotton into a strong thread.
James Watt, 1736–1819, patented his steam engine in 1769. This engine used a separate cylinder for condensing steam and worked quickly and efficiently. Watt's engine was the first to produce rotary motion.
Luigi Galvani, 1737–98, an Italian, found in 1771 that two metals in contact with a frog's leg cause it to twitch. He had produced current electricity.

Oxygen was discovered, 1772, by the Swede **Carl Scheele,** 1742–86. He withheld his findings until after the independent discovery by **Joseph Priestley,** 1733–1804, in 1774. Scheele was also involved in the discovery of chlorine, 1774, tungsten, 1781, and other elements.
Daniel Rutherford, 1749–1819, discovered **nitrogen** in 1772.

776–1780

ne American colonies declared ɪeir independence, 1776, and llied with France, 1778, and pain, 1779. The English over- n the southern states, 1778, ut were weakened by a French ockade of shipping.
ne French government was ɪined by the war in spite of the ontinued financial reforms of acques Necker, 1732–1804.
ombal, 1699–1782, completed ne reorganization of the admin- stration in Portuguese Brazil, 777.

1780–1784

American independence was assured by the British surrender at Yorktown, 1781, and formally recognized at the 1783 **Treaty of Paris.**
A sudden growth in the English cotton industry after 1780 marked the beginning of the English **Industrial Revolution.**
Russia occupied the Crimea in 1783.
Hastings made an effective peace with the Marathas, 1784.

1784–1788

The United States began trading with China, 1784, but suffered postwar depression through loss of contact with the West Indies 1784–87.
The American Constitution was signed in Philadelphia, 1787.
The aristocratic parliaments in France blocked proposals for financial reform, 1787.
The founding of The Times newspaper in England, 1788, accompanied the growth of an informed middle class in Europe.

1788–1792

England established convict settlements in Australia, 1788.
Louis XVI, *r.*1774–92, was forced to summon the estates-general in 1789 because of the financial crisis.
The French Revolution began when a group of middle-class radicals took over the administration with the help of the Paris mob and tried to set up a constitutional monarchy, 1789.
George Washington, 1732–99, became the first president of the United States, 1789.

1792–1796

France was declared a republic, 1792. Louis was executed, 1793, and during the ensuing terror, 1793–94, many of the nobility were also guillotined as a result of the fear of a counter-revolution backed by Austrian forces.
The French overran Holland and established the Batavian Republic in 1795.
Revolutionary ideas led to the freeing of slaves in the French West Indies, arousing hostility among the European powers.

1796–1800

By the **Treaty of Campo Formio,** 1797, Austria ceded Belgium to France.
Napoleon, 1769–1821, defeated Austria, 1796, but his plans to invade England, 1798, failed and he was prevented by **Horatio Nelson,** 1758–1805, from cutting England off from India at the Battle of the Nile, 1798. In 1799 he overthrew the moderate **Directory** and established a dictatorship, 1799–1804.

ɪ **1776,** *Common Sense* by **homas Paine,** 1737–1809, ppeared. The Declaration of ndependence, was signed uly 4, 1776.

Gen. George Washington led the Colonial army against the British, who surrendered at Yorktown, 1781; the Treaty of Paris was signed in 1783.

By the Articles of Confederation, ratified 1781, Congress controlled the western lands. The Northwest Ordinance, 1787, provided a plan of government.

The Constitution of the United States was ratified in 1788. The Bill of Rights, ten amendments to the Constitution, was adopted in 1789.

Federal troops ended the Whiskey Rebellion in Pennsylvania, 1794. **John Jay,** 1745–1829, negotiated Jay's Treaty to settle Anglo-American grievances.

An undeclared naval conflict over French interference with American shipping was precipitated by the XYZ affair, 1797. The Convention of 1800 ended the war.

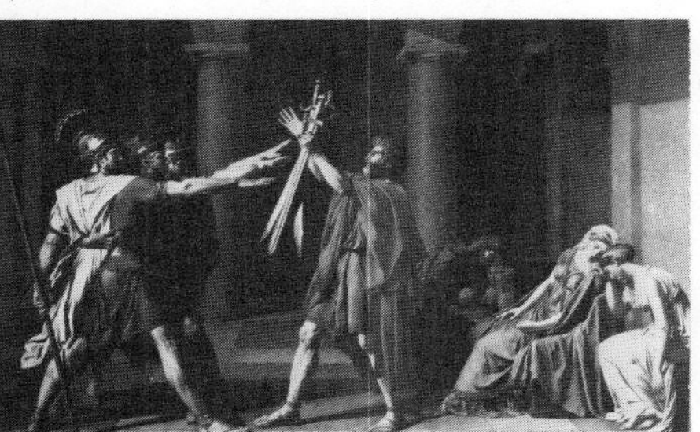

The Oath of the Horatii" by David

James Watt's rotary steam engine

French Revolution: the execution of Louis XVI

---

dam Smith, 1723–90, founder f modern economics, argued nat although manufacturers do ot intend to satisfy the general ood, they are led to do so by ne "invisible hand" of the competitive market. When a producer satisfied his self-interest by elling goods for which there is demand, he also satisfied a eneral social need. Smith's *Vealth of Nations* was published 1776.

Immanuel Kant, 1724–1804, in his *Critique of Pure Reason,* 1781, wrote that although knowledge cannot transcend experience, the concepts that organize perception are innate to the human mind and prior to experience. In *Metaphysics and Morals,* 1785, he argued that man's idea of morality is *a priori* and that people act morally when the maxim on which they act is one that they can desire all men to follow.

Liberalism, the belief that the state should not encroach on individual freedom, was proposed by **Jeremy Bentham,** 1748–1832, in *A Fragment on Government,* 1776. He argued in his *Principles,* 1789, for utilitarianism, the theory that the happiness of the majority of individuals was the greatest good. This was to be achieved by allowing each individual the freedom to maximize his useful achievement by avoiding pain and pursuing pleasure.

In France, 1789–90, Church lands were nationalized and religious orders suppressed.
Edmund Burke, 1729–97, in *Reflections on the French Revolution,* 1790, argued that the replacement of practical politics by utopianism had led to extremism. **Tom Paine,** 1737–1809, in America, wrote *The Rights of Man,* 1791, to oppose Burke's *Reflections.* Paine believed revolution could be avoided only if the causes of the discontent were eradicated.

Equal opportunities for women to develop their talents were demanded by **Mary Wollstonecraft,** 1759–97, in her *Vindication of the Rights of Women,* 1792. Her husband, **William Godwin,** 1756–1836, published *Enquiry Concerning Political Justice,* 1793. A radical, he argued that government powers over citizens inevitably bred corruption.
The Cult of Reason and later the **Cult of the Supreme Being** were substituted for Christianity in France, 1793–94.

The English Evangelical Movement had emerged within the Church of England, influenced by Methodism. Its followers believed in the certainty of salvation, emphasizing evangelism and social welfare.
Reverend Thomas Malthus, 1766–1834, published his *Essay on the Principle of Population,* 1798, rejecting the possibility of infinite improvements in human conditions on the grounds that population expands more rapidly than the available food supply.

---

omedy of manners, revived in ngland by **Oliver Goldsmith,** *c.* 730–74, in *She Stoops to Conɥer,* 1773, reached a peak in *he School for Scandal,* 1777, y the Irish wit **R. B. Sheridan,** 751–1816.
alian patriotism was stirred by **ittorio Alfieri,** 1749–1803, hose 19 verse tragedies in the lassical mode opposed tyranny.

The influential French novel *Les Liaisons Dangereuses,* 1782, by **P. A. F. Choderlos de Laclos,** 1741–1803, had a savage tone in contrast to the vogue for high moral sentiment established by Rousseau. The privileges of the upper class were satirized by **Pierre de Beaumarchais,** 1732–99, in *The Barber of Seville,* 1784, and *The Marriage of Figaro.*

Scottish folk traditions found a passionate and lyrical voice in the poems of **Robert Burns,** 1759–96, whose *Kilmarnock Edition,* 1786, established him as a skilled writer of songs, satires, and narratives. A deep love of nature, a major theme in romanticism, is found in the blank verse of "The Task," 1785, by the English poet **William Cowper,** 1731–1800.

A new tradition of candid biography was begun by **James Boswell,** 1740–95, in his *Life of Johnson,* 1791, bringing to life his friend **Samuel Johnson,** 1709–84. Johnson, a brillant conversationalist, editor, poet, and critic, had dominated English literature after 1750 with his *Dictionary,* 1755, the Gothic novel *Rasselas,* 1759, and *Lives of the Poets,* 1779–81.

William Blake, 1757–1827, one of the most powerful, imaginative artists in English literature, published the lyrical *Songs of Experience,* 1794, complementing *Songs of Innocence,* 1789. Poet, painter, engraver, and above all, visionary, he issued prophetic warnings of the danger of industrialization and materialism in *The Marriage of Heaven and Hell.*

The Romantic movement in England began with *Lyrical Ballads,* 1798, by **William Wordsworth,** 1770–1850, and **Samuel Taylor Coleridge,** 1772–1834.
The novels of Jean Paul, 1763–1825, included *Hesperus,* 1795, and *Siebenkäs,* 1796–97, which contained both idealism and sentimentalism.

---

lassicism in Russia under Catherine the Great was led by foreign artists such as the French culptor **Etienne-Maurice Falconet,** 1716–91, who had executed the equestrian statue of Peter ne Great, 1769, and Scottish rchitect **Charles Cameron,** .1740–1812, who went to Russia in 1779. Cameron decorated everal apartments in the palace f Tsarkoe Selo (now Pushkin) ear Leningrad for Catherine.

Neoclassical painting was firmly established in France with "Oath of the Horatii," 1784, by Jacques Louis David, 1748–1825, in which the subordination of color to drawing enforces the theme of heroic self-sacrifice as exemplified by ancient Rome.
The Nightmare by **Henry Fuseli,** 1741–1825, and the works of **William Blake,** 1757–1827, reveal an emphasis on the bizarre and supernatural in contrast with Academic aims.

The Academy of Fine Arts in Mexico City, founded in 1785, was staffed primarily by Spanish trained artists who were largely instrumental in introducing Neoclassicism to Mexico.
English caricature was developed by **James Gillray,** 1757–1815, in "A New Way to Pay the National Debt," 1786, and by **Thomas Rowlandson,** 1756–1827, who illustrated Smollett, Goldsmith, Sterne, and Swift, and produced "Imitations of Modern Drawings," 1784–88.

The "Style Troubadour" originated in France when anecdotal scenes from the lives of wise kings of early French history were used by antiroyalists to accentuate the incompetence of Louis XVI.
Classicism in English architecture was exemplified in the work of **John Soane,** 1753–1837, whose austere and original manipulation of the antique was seen in his **Bank of England Stock Office,** 1792, with its top-lit vaulted hall.

Painting in Revolutionary France was used as a political weapon. David's "Death of Marat," 1793, combines classicism with an element of realism to deify a revolutionary hero and muster republican support.
John Flaxman, 1755–1826, published his illustrations to Homer's *Iliad* and *Odyssey* in 1793. With their simple outline figures they immediately became a major model for Neoclassical painters and influenced later generations.

The success of Napoleon's Italian campaign, 1796–97, galvanized French art with the public display in the Louvre of looted art treasures. This enhanced the image of Napoleon as a national hero.
The Capitol, Richmond, Va., 1785–98, built by Thomas Jefferson, 1743–1826, was based on the Maison Carrée, Nîmes, and brought Neoclassical architecture to the United States.

---

frican music as described by Vestern observers probably reembled music heard today, in hich groups of instruments, uch as marimbas and drums, reely explore areas of sonority.

Ludwig van Beethoven, 1770–1827, son of a court musician at Bonn, was acknowledged a child prodigy in 1783, the year he published his first composition.

Mozart, 1756–91, was one of the first great composers who tried to live independently without the support of a patron, but he died a pauper.

Domenico Cimarosa, 1749–1801, "the Italian Mozart," composed his most celebrated opera, *Il Matrimonio Segreto,* in Vienna in 1792.

Niccolò Paganini, the Italian virtuoso violinist, 1782–1840, made his debut in Genoa in 1793, playing his own variations on "La Carmagnole."

The violin was taken to India by British rulers. Indian musicians absorbed it into their music, utilizing its subtleties of intonation and tone color.

---

practical water closet was paented in 1778 in England by **oseph Bramah,** 1748–1814. ramah's many inventions introuced practical techniques that ounded the engineering industry.
he spinning mule was invented England in 1779 by **Samuel rompton,** 1753–1827. It was ble to spin high quality thread n many spindles at once.
heap soap resulted from the ork *c.*1780 of **Nicholas Leanc,** 1742–1806, in France. He atented his process of producng soda from salt in 1791.

Uranus was discovered by **William Herschel,** 1738–1822, in 1781. It was the first planet to be discovered that was not known to ancient civilizations.
The first manned flight took place in 1783 in a hot air balloon made and flown by the French **Montgolfier** brothers Joseph, 1740–1810, and Jacques, 1745–99.
James Watt invented the double acting engine in 1784.

Chlorine was first used for bleaching cloth in 1785 by **Claude Berthollet,** 1748–1822.
The threshing machine was patented, 1788, by a Scotsman, **Andrew Meikle,** 1719–1811.
Jacques Charles, 1746–1823, a French physicist, formulated **Charles's law** *c.*1787, that at constant pressure the volume of a gas is related to its absolute temperature.
The power loom, invented in 1785 by **Edmund Cartwright,** 1743–1823, mechanized weaving.

Traité Elèmentaire de Chimie, by **Antoine Lavoisier,** 1743–94, written in 1789, founded modern chemistry with its insistence on measurement and standard nomenclature. Lavoisier stated the law of the conservation of mass; he also defined chemical reaction.
Coal gas was first produced in 1792 by **William Murdock,** 1754–1839, a British inventor. In 1790, **Watt** applied his fly-ball governor to control the speed of a steam engine.

Theory of the Earth, 1795, by **James Hutton,** 1726–97, began modern geology by viewing all geological change as continuous.
The cotton gin, a device used to strip cotton from bolls, was invented, 1793, by **Eli Whitney,** 1765–1825, revitalizing cotton growing in the United States.
The metric system was adopted in France in 1795.
Scientific institutes abounded in revolutionary France, including the Jardin des Plantes and the Ecole Polytechnique.

Vaccination, discovered in 1796 by Edward Jenner, 1749–1823, led to the eradication of smallpox.
The nature of heat, or kinetic energy, was discovered in 1798 by the American **Count Rumford,** who noticed that the boring of cannons produced heat and reasoned that heat is a form of motion and not a fluid.
The battery was invented by **Count Volta,** 1745–1827, in 1800. He developed Galvani's observations into a practical idea for an electricity supply.

The rise of industrial power 1800–1825

Principal events

Inspired by a vision of himself as head of a European empire, Napoleon Bonaparte overran most of Europe but was unable to maintain his conquests. With his final defeat at Waterloo in 1815, the ancien régime was restored to France. His conquests, however, sparked off a multitude of constitutional and nationalist demands throughout Europe, while his occupation of Spain encouraged the Latin American countries to grasp their independence. They remained, however, unable to reorganize themselves economically or to free themselves politically from European influence.

In England, the Industrial Revolution caused the emergence of a new wealthy class and social tensions gave a greater urgency to demands for parliamentary reform, while British naval strength and leadership of the final coalition against Napoleon left Britain the dominant trading power in the world.

1800–1802

Napoleon established the prefecture as the main instrument of local government subject to central control. He improved education and made a compromise with the Church, 1800–01. His agressive nationalist campaigns led to victory over the empire and Austria, conquest in Italy, 1800, and temporary peace with England in 1802. With the murder of Paul I, **Alexander I**, 1801–25, became tsar of Russia.

1802–1805

Nationalist feeling brought a Serbian uprising against the Ottoman rule in 1804.
Napoleon assumed the title of emperor in 1804. **Britain** resumed the war against him in 1803 and was joined by **Russia, Austria,** and **Sweden** in 1805. Russia was defeated at **Austerlitz**, 1805, but Britain's naval victory at **Trafalgar**, 1805, resulted in a crippling blockade of French shipping.
Napoleon proclaimed himself **King of Italy**, 1805.

1805–1807

After defeating Prussia, 1806, Napoleon allied with Russia, 1807, and set up the **Continental System** (which Russia was forced to leave for economic reasons in 1810) to exclude British trade from Europe.
The Holy Roman Empire came to an end when **Francis II**, *r.*1792–1835, who was also emperor of Austria, renounced the title, 1806.
The slave trade was abolished in the British Empire, 1807, although slavery continued in the colonies.

1807–1810

A nationalist revolt broke out in Spain when Joseph Bonaparte, 1768–1844, assumed the throne, 1808. Britain exploited this to attack Napoleon in the Peninsular War, 1808–14.
Austria and Prussia reformed their army and taxation systems to improve military capacity.
Archduke Charles of Austria appealed to the Germans to oppose Napoleon but was defeate at **Wagram,** 1809.
France assumed control of Swedish foreign affairs.

National events

The American nation was developing a spirit of nationalism, of identification not as a colony or state, but with the United States. Land purchases provided room for expansion of a growing population. National authority was expressed in the readiness of Americans to defend US interests.

In 1801 war began with the North African Barbary states. Barbary pirates had interfered with American shipping and demanded tribute. Peace came in 1805.

The territory between the Rocky Mountains and the Mississippi River was bought from France for $15,000,000 and was called the Louisiana Purchase.

Meriwether Lewis, 1774–1809, and **George Rogers Clark,** 1752–1818, returned in 1806 from their expedition to the Pacific Ocean.

In 1808 federal law forbade importation of slaves into the United States. The Embargo Ac 1807, aimed at keeping US shi out of European conflicts.

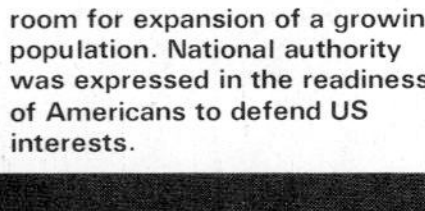

Lewis and Clark

Napoleon at Eylau, 1807

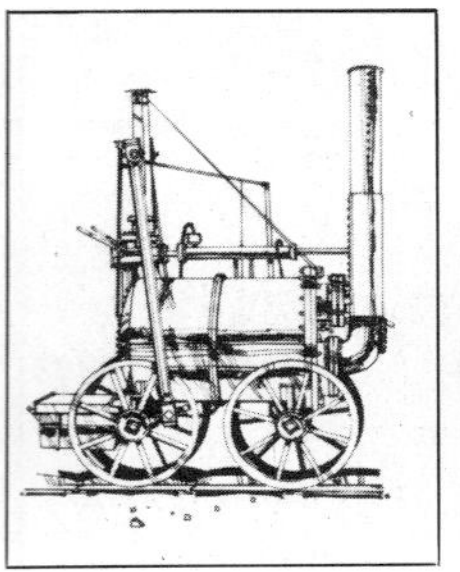

Trevithick's steam engine

"The 3rd of May" by Goya

Religion and philosophy

Classical economic theory was developed and systematized in the work of Say in France and Ricardo in England, the latter influencing both sides of the debate about laissez-faire doctrines, which dominated social thought in the early 19th century. At the same time reaction to the social evils of industrial capitalism ranged from Sismondi's warning of class antagonisms to the social experiments of Robert Owen and the Utopianism of Charles Fourier.

The major philosophical school of the period, German idealism, emerged in a country as yet relatively sheltered from the major social upheavals of the time. In particular, Hegel, who would greatly influence the young Karl Marx, argued that historical progress was identical with the advancement of human consciousness, while Schopenhauer and Schelling emphasized man's darker, irrational impulses and prepared the way for Freud and existentialism.

Friedrich Schelling, 1775–1854, published his *Transcendental Idealism*, 1800, in Germany, grounding his idealism on external nature. His philosophy of man stressed the force of irrationalism, which, as the source of all evil, could dominate the intellect, wherein lay the power for good.
William Paley, 1743–1805, an Anglican, advanced the idea in *Natural Theology*, 1802, that the design evident in the world implied the work of a creator.

Jean Baptiste Say published his Traité d'économie politique in 1803, putting forward his "law of markets," which states that supply creates its own demand with the consequence that depression is the result of overproduction in some markets and underproduction in others, an imbalance that would automatically correct itself.
The Code Napoléon of 1804 nationalized French law and established the principle of equal citizenship.

G. W. F. Hegel, 1770–1831, the German idealist philosopher, published his first great work, *Phenomenology of Mind*, in 1807. In this and later works Hegel expressed the view that reality is essentially a whole (which he called the Absolute) comprising both mind (subject) and matter (object). The physical world would cease to be alien and objective when, with the attainment of total comprehension, object and subject merged into the Absolute.

Charles Fourier, 1772–1837, writing in France *(The Social Destiny of Man*, 1808) and later **Robert Owen** in England (*A New View of Society*, 1813) advocat ed social reconstruction on the basis of workers' cooperatives. Owen organized mills at New Lanark, 1800–29, on principles of welfare and justice, but his American experimental community at New Harmony, 1825, wa short-lived, as were the communes based on the even more Utopian ideas of Fourier.

Literature

English Romanticism reached its peak with the work of the poets Wordsworth and Byron, who explored the individual quest for harmony with nature and stressed the independence of the genius from social convention. The historical novel developed by Scott linked the interest in the past with an implicit concern for national identity—a trend echoed in the German concentration on folk-tales and mythology. In other respects, however, German Romanticism, as displayed by Goethe and Schiller, involved a less violent break with 18th-century humanism.

Chateaubriand and Madame de Staël tried to introduce the ideas of the movement to France, but met little success, as classicism still reigned until the work of the poets in the 1820s.

A more subjective emphasis developed in German literature with the two unfinished novels of **Novalis,** 1772–1801, published in 1798–1800. Both were *Bildungsroman*—novels on the education of the hero and the development of character and temperament, like Goethe's *Wilhelm Meisters Lehrjahre.*

Le Génie du Christianisme, 1802, **by François René de Chateaubriand,** 1768–1848, introduced to French literature a mystical Christianity, which had a great influence on the French romantic writers.
The need for political freedom in Germany was the subject of the play *William Tell*, 1804, by the poet and dramatist **Johann Schiller,** 1759–1805.

The German romantic poets Brentano, 1778–1842, and **von Arnim,** 1781–1831, collected folk poems in *Des Knaben Wunderhorn*, 1805–08.
The lyric dramatic poetry of **Adam Oehlenschlager,** 1779–1850, was popular in Denmark.

The poetry of the Italian Ugo Foscolo, 1778–1827, extolled the past and the value of art as a permanent shrine to virtue.
The humanism of Johann Goethe, 1749–1832, was expressed in his play *Faust, Part* 1808.
Heinrich Kleist, 1777–1811, published *Penthesilea*, 1808.

Art and architecture

European art in the early 19th century saw a reaction to Neoclassicism and the beginnings of Romanticism, involving a shift from formal rules to an emphasis on the subjective—feelings, impressions, imagination—and a preference for fantasy, excess, and the poetic. The influence of Romanticism also inspired an interest in historical and foreign styles of architecture, while in painting it produced the freer technique and the more expressive use of color found in the work of Delacroix. The choice of subject matter also changed to include contemporary and historical scenes, which reflected the nationalist ideals of the time—a tendency heightened in France by the exotic career and lavish commissions of Napoleon. While Neoclassicism came to be rejected by artists in Western Europe, its influence spread elsewhere into Russia and the New World, where it dominated architecture.

The term "picturesque" was introduced in England at the end of the 18th century as an aesthetic category. Characterized by irregularity, variety, and roughness of texture, it had a decisive effect on landscape painting and architecture.
British industrial architecture had developed over the 18th century to include iron frame constructions, which were fireproof and functional.

The Greek revival in European architecture, *c.*1760–1830, was now at its height. Its essence was the exact reproduction of Greek models, which were admired for their simplicity and associated with the beginnings of civilization. It was predominantly used for public buildings.
In the United States, classic revival architecture was popularized by **Benjamin Latrobe,** 1764–1820.

Napoleon commissioned portraits and commemorative scenes to enhance his imperial image. Canvases presented an aura of magnificence with allusions to the Roman Empire as in "Napoleon as Emperor," 1806, by **Jean August Dominique Ingres,** 1780–1867, and *The Battle of Eylau*, 1808, by **Antoine Gros,** 1771–1835. Napoleonic architecture like the Paris Bourse, 1807, by **A. T. Brongriart,** 1739–1813, was similarly inspired.

Davidian ideals were questione in France by his pupils. Some, **Les Primitifs,** took inspiration from the Bible, Homer, and the Gaelic tales of Ossian. Others like **Anne-Louis Girodet,** 1767–1824, in his "Entombment of Atala," 1808, used unusual mystical subjects.
The investigation of the symbolic, mystical, and religious aspects of landscape took place primarily in Germany, with the work of **Caspar David Friedrich,** 1774–1840.

Music

Romanticism in European music began to replace classicism as personal expression in the arts took precedence over ideals of formal balance. But the first romantic composers, such as Ludwig van Beethoven, 1770–1827, and Carl von Weber, 1786–1826, were trained in classical techniques and brought restraint to bear on the new, sensuous style of music.

The piano repertory was rapidly extended by **Muzio Clementi,** 1752–1832, and Beethoven, as the instrument gained a greater range of notes and sound quality.

Short forms for the piano were being composed by **John Field,** 1782–1837, who wrote nocturnes, which would later be popularized by **Frédéric Chopin,** 1810–49.

Beethoven straddled the classical and romantic eras, extending the range of sonata form and composing works such as the *Coriolanus Overture*, 1807, directly inspired by literary ideas.

Program music, interpreting the events and moods of a specific story, emerged as a feature of romantic music, using evocativ sounds as in Beethoven's *Pastoral Symphony*, 1808.

Science and technology

Progress in technology and science in Europe divided between Britain and France. France became the center of pure science, while Britain forged ahead in industrial science. Although automation was invented in France, its potential was not fully exploited. Similarly, atomic theory was first proposed in England but was refined in Europe.

The most important technological innovation was that of powered transport in England and the US, which opened new areas of industrial expansion; in the same period gas lighting transformed city life. Many scientific discoveries, too, would have subsequent importance. Electrical science developed with the discovery of electromagnetism and would stimulate inquiry into the nature of matter as well as producing new sources of energy, while modern chemistry developed under the influence of Gay-Lussac and Avogadro. The study of fossils raised new questions about the age and origins of life.

The interference of light was shown, in 1801, by **Thomas Young,** 1773–1829, restoring the wave theory first put forward by Christiaan Huygens. Young also studied elasticity, giving his name to the tensile modulus, or scale of elasticity.
Automation using punched cards to control the production of silk fabric was invented in France, 1801, by **Joseph Marie Jacquard,** 1752–1834.
Ultra-violet light in the Sun's spectrum was discovered, 1801, by **Johann Ritter,** 1776–1810.

Jean de Lamarck, 1744–1829, a French naturalist, coined the term "biology" in 1802.
The first railroad locomotive was built in England by **Richard Trevithic,** 1771–1833, and first ran in 1804.
Screw-cutting machines and lathes were developed at the engineering works of the Englishman **Henry Maudslay,** 1771–1831, who invented the screw micrometer and schooled many fine engineers.

Gas lighting was introduced in European cities *c.* 1806.
The Clermont, built by **Robert Fulton,** 1765–1815, an American engineer, inaugurated the first regular steamboat service along the Hudson River in 1807, although a short-lived service had been run *c.* 1790.
The Geological Society of London was founded in 1807.

Potassium and sodium were discovered, 1806–07, by **Humphry Davy,** 1778–1829, an English chemist.
Jean Fourier, 1768–1830, a French mathematician, discovered that a complex wave is the sum of several simple waves.
The atomic theory, stating that the same elements have the same atoms and that a compound is made up of atoms of elements combined in fixed pro portions, was propounded in 1808 by **John Dalton,** 1766–1844.

810–1812

apoleon's empire reached its **eatest extent,** 1812, when ith Austria and Prussia he in- aded Russia. French forces ook Moscow, 1812, but were nable to sustain the Russian inter and were forced to retreat ith serious losses. **araguay and Venezuela** became dependent from Spain, 1811, arking the final collapse of panish imperial authority. **apoleon married Marie Louise** Austria in his search for an eir, 1810.

1812–1815

The Duke of Wellington, 1769–1852, led the Allied forces into Paris, 1814. Napoleon abdicated and was exiled. **The monarchy was restored** in Louis XVIII, *r.*1814–24. **The Congress of Vienna,** 1814–15, restored monarchs to the Austrian and Prussian thrones, and the kingdom of the Netherlands was founded as a buffer against France. **Britain** won definitive control of the **Cape of Good Hope,** 1814, on the route to India.

1815–1817

Napoleon returned from Elba and Austria, Britain, Prussia, and Russia formed a new alliance. Louis fled from Paris to return only after Napoleon's defeat at **Waterloo** and exile to St Helena, 1815. **The Holy Alliance** aimed to crush the spread of radicalism in Austria, Prussia, and Russia. **Prince Metternich,** 1773–1859, crushed similar aspirations in the German states. **Ferdinand I,** *r.*1815–25, regained the Italian throne.

1817–1820

The American and Canadian border was fixed in 1818. **Soldiers** killed 11 demonstrators in the **Peterloo Massacre** in England, 1819. **A revolt in Naples** against the despotism of Ferdinand I was crushed by Austrian forces in 1821. **The British founded Singapore** to rival Dutch Malacca as the center for Far Eastern trade. **Only Nepal, the Sikh and Sind states,** and Afghanistan were independent of British rule in India by 1818.

1820–1822

Ferdinand VII of Spain, *r.*1814–33, was captured by liberal rebels in 1820. **The nationalist Greek war** for independence from the Ottoman Empire began, 1821. The Great Powers intervened in 1827 and established a Greek kingdom in 1832. **Spain lost Mexico and Peru,** 1821, while Brazil became independent from Portugal, 1822. **Opium trade** between India and China flourished in the reign of **Hsüang Tung,** 1821–50.

1822–1825

A Spanish liberal revolt was crushed with French help, 1823. **The Monroe Doctrine,** 1823, asserted that the American continent could no longer be an arena for European colonial activity. **Britain surpassed other European countries** in her industrial and trading position, but agitation began for more *laissez-faire* trading policies. **The Anglo-Burmese wars** began in 1824, following Burmese aggression.

om 1810, **War Hawks** advocat- d war with Britain, which had een harassing American ship- ng. In 1812, Congress passed declaration of war.

In 1814 the British burned Washington. American resistance at Baltimore inspired "The Star-Spangled Banner" by **Francis Scott Key,** 1779–1843.

Unaware of the Treaty of Ghent, Gen. Andrew Jackson, 1767–1845, won an overwhelming victory at New Orleans in January 1815.

In the Adams-Onis Treaty, 1819, Spain gave the United States control of both East and West Florida. The Panic of 1819 hurt the US economy.

The Missouri Compromise of 1820 prohibited slavery north of latitude 36°30'. The American Colonization Society sent 88 free blacks to settle in Africa.

The Monroe Doctrine was enunciated, 1823, by **Pres. James Monroe,** 1758–1831. **The Erie Canal** was completed, 1825.

The Brighton Pavilion" by Nash

Lord Byron

The Peterloo Massacre

egel's **Science of Logic** was ublished in 1812–16. In it he eveloped a dialectical method reasoning–opposing a thesis ith its antithesis to establish a ynthesis–with the aim of re- ealing the nature of the Abso- te. Hegel believed history to e a dialectical progression to- ard the Absolute and consid- ed the Prussian state to be the ulmination of this dialectical ogression.

The conservative tradition in France found exponents in **Joseph de Maistre,** 1753–1821, and **Louis Bonald,** 1754–1840, who insisted on the supremacy of Christianity and the absolute rule of the Church and pope. De Maistre published his *Essay on Constitutions* in 1814, in which he used his facility for logical argument to oppose the progress of science, liberalism, and the empirical methods of the "philosophes," especially Voltaire.

The rising science of economics was systematized by **David Ricardo,** 1772–1823, in his *Principles of Political Economy and Taxation*, 1817, which aimed to set out the laws governing the division of the social product among the classes in society. The systematization of this work made him the leading exponent of the classical school in England, and he was influential both among *laissez-faire* economists and their opponents, such as Robert Owen and Karl Marx.

Jean Charles Sismondi, an early theorist of economic crisis, warned in his *New Principles of Political Economy*, 1819, against the effects of unregulated industrialism, predicting acute social conflict. In Germany, **Artur Schopenhauer,** 1788–1860, published *The World as Will and Idea* in 1819. His emphasis on man's will and irrational impulses prepared the way for the departure from the 18th-century idea of rational progress.

Thomas Erskine, 1788–1870, a Scottish theologian, in *Internal Evidence for the Truth of Christian Religion*, 1820, held that the meaning of Christianity lay in its conformity with man's spiritual and ethical needs. **Friedrich Schleiermacher,** 1768–1834, a German theologian and founder of modern Protestant theology, in *The Christian Faith*, 1821–22, saw religious feeling as a sense of absolute dependence and sin as a desire for independence.

The anti-union Combination Acts were repealed in Britain, 1824, after a campaign led by **Francis Place,** 1771–1854, and **Joseph Hume,** 1777–1855. Place, a follower of Malthus, advocated birth control as a means by which workers could limit their numbers to improve wages. **Leopold Ranke,** 1795–1886, a German historian, wrote *History of the Latin and Teutonic Nations, 1494–1514*, in 1824, seeking a history based on scientific methods.

adame de Staël, 1766–1817, rote *De L'Allemagne* in 1810, omparing French literature and ociety unfavorably with that of ermany. **e English middle classes** were ven perceptive scrutiny by **ne Austen,** 1775–1817, in *ense and Sensibility*, 1811, and ter *Pride and Prejudice*, 1813.

The English Romantic poet Percy Bysshe Shelley, 1792–1822, wrote his first major poem, *Queen Mab*, 1811–13. **The first historical novel** was the medieval romance *Waverley*, 1814, by **Sir Walter Scott,** 1771–1832. His evocations of the past influenced **James Fenimore Cooper,** 1789–1851. **Brothers Grimm** made their collection of folk tales, 1812–15.

Grotesque themes were studied by the German composer and author **Ernst Hoffmann,** 1776–1822, in his tales and in the novel *The Devil's Elixir*, 1813–15. **The psychological analysis** of a broken love affair is the subject of *Adolphe*, 1816, by **Benjamin Constant,** 1767–1830, an ardent liberal and a political journalist, closely aligned with the French Romantics.

The spirit of the Romantic movement was epitomized in the notorious life of **Lord Byron,** 1788–1824, and the tormented homeless Byronic hero became popular in European fiction. In contrast, his *Don Juan* (first two cantos, 1819), was a biting, unromanticized social satire. **William Hazlitt,** 1778–1830, commented on contemporary English life in astute essays.

Alphonse Lamartine, 1790–1869, moved from the private anguish of *Meditations*, 1820, to the mystical lyricism of *Harmonies Poëtiques*, 1830. **A search for eternal perfection** is the theme of *Prometheus Unbound*, 1820, by the English poet Shelley. His friend **John Keats,** 1795–1821, wrote rich, ornate narrative poetry, including the *Ode to a Nightingale*, 1819.

The Confessions of an English Opium Eater, 1822, was the autobiography of **Thomas De Quincey,** 1785–1859. **Thomas Peacock,** 1785–1866, skillfully used his satirical novels to attack English views, obsessions, and political dogmas.

e pastiches of Indian, Chinese, d Egyptian styles seen in the ince regent's Brighton Pavilion, om 1810, by the English archi- ct **John Nash,** 1752–1835, eflected the worldwide process exploration and colonization the European powers. **quasi-religious order,** the *Lu- asbrüder* was found in Vien- a, 1809, by **Friedrich Overbeck,** 789–1869, and **Frans Pforr,** 788–1812. They moved to ome in 1810 and became nown as the Nazarenes.

The work of **Francisco de Goya,** 1746–1828, combined objective reportage and a sense of personal horror at the Napoleonic Wars in "The Disasters of War," 1810–14. He later developed the new medium of lithography. In Russia, **Alexander I** commissioned classical buildings for St Petersburg and encouraged French Neoclassicism in all branches of the arts, particularly portraiture.

Neo-Renaissance architecture was developed in Germany by **Leo von Klenze,** 1784–1864. His Palais Leuchtenberg, Munich, 1816, is the first German example, although the style existed earlier in France. **German Neoclassical architecture** first developed after the fall of Napoleon, with the emphasis on purely Grecian forms seen in the Neue Wache, Berlin, 1816, by **Karl Friedrich Schinkel,** 1781–1841.

After 1816, when Dom João VI of Brazil had invited French architects, painters, and sculptors to Rio de Janeiro to "civilize" Creole taste, their neoclassical style dominated the arts for the next hundred years. **In France, Théodore Géricault,** 1791–1824, took contemporary events as the vehicle for his themes and used large canvases to strengthen their impact in, for example, "The Raft of the Medusa," 1817.

English Romantic portraiture with its emphasis on drama and psychological investigation was exemplified in the forceful works of **Sir Thomas Lawrence,** 1769–1830, whose portraits of the "Heads of State of Europe" in the Waterloo Chamber, **Windsor Castle,** 1818–20, celebrate the triumph over Napoleon.

Romantic tendencies in art were crystallized in the work of **Eugène Delacroix,** 1798–1863, where truth was no longer merely factual but a glimpse into man's soul. Delacroix set out to achieve this with the use of expressive color and an emphasis on mood and the poetic. His work marked a decisive shift in French painting away from the importance of form and stressed violence and drama, as in his "Massacre at Chios," 1824.

rchestral concerts became opular in London, Paris, and ienna as the middle classes egan to support music. The pa- on and his salon declined in fluence.

A greater variety of orchestral instruments allowed richer tone contrasts. There were few large orchestras, so many orchestral works were published as piano transcriptions.

Lieder, a German form of lyric song, was raised by **Franz Schubert,** 1797–1828, to new heights as his piano parts provided a counterpart to the voice echoing the mood of the lyric.

Conductors were required to marshal the expanded orchestra, as it could no longer be led by an instrumentalist. In 1820, **Ludwig Spohr,** 1784–1859, introduced the conductor's baton.

Opera centered on Paris. The light lyricism of the *Barber of Seville*, 1816, by **Gioacchino Rossini,** 1792–1868, gave way to the romanticism of **Carl von Weber's** *Der Freischutz*, 1821.

The symphony found new depths of expression, especially with **Beethoven,** as a personal creation requiring a large orchestra. His *Ninth Symphony*, 1823, is an example.

oseph Gay-Lussac, 1778–1850, French chemist, announced in 308 that that gases combine in ertain proportions by volume d suggested that the propor- ons are linked to the formula of e compound formed. Gay-Lus- ac's work also led to the cor- ct atomic weights of ele- ents. **Amadeo Avogadro,** 776–1856, an Italian, argued in 811 that equal volumes of gas- s at the same temperature and essure contain equal numbers molecules.

Georges Cuvier, 1769–1832, a French anatomist, broadened Linnaeus' classification to include phyla and fossils, thus founding paleontology. The hardness of materials was classified in 1812 by a German, Friedrich Mohs, 1773–1839. **Chemical symbols** as used today were introduced in 1814 by Jöns Berzelius, 1779–1848, a Swede, who later made a correct list of atomic weights. **Dark lines in the Sun's spectrum were identified,** 1814, by Joseph von Fraunhofer, 1787–1826.

The safety lamp was invented by **Humphry Davy** in 1815, to prevent explosions in mines. The optical experiments of **Jean Biot,** 1774–1862, after 1815, led to the founding of polarimetry. **The first geological map,** of England and Wales, was published, 1815, by **William Smith,** 1769–1839. **The single wire telegraph** was invented in 1816. **Photography** was born out of the experiments in 1816 of **Nocéphore Niepce,** 1765–1833.

Electromagnetism was found, 1820, by **Hans Oersted,** 1777–1851, who noticed that a compass needle was deflected by a wire carrying a current. He would later be the first to prepare aluminum, 1825.

André Ampère, 1775–1836, studied the effects of electric currents in motion, founding and naming the science of electrodynamics by 1822. He also invented the solenoid. **Thomas Seeback,** 1770–1831, a Russo-German physicist, invented the thermocouple, an instrument for measuring temperature as electricity, 1821.

The electromagnet, the first machine to use electricity, was made by **William Sturgeon,** 1783–1850, an English physicist. **Sadi Carnot,** 1796–1832, published *On the Motive Power of Fire*, 1824, in which he showed that only a fraction of the heat produced by burning fuel in an engine is converted into motion, which depends only on the temperature difference in the engine. This was the basis of modern thermodynamics.

Liberalism and nationalism 1825–1850

Principal events

The spread of industrialism from England to north Europe brought the rise of a solid middle class advocating liberal and nationalist ideas, as well as a new urban radicalism focused by regular economic booms and slumps. In spite of attempts to suppress them, these movements spread throughout Europe, culminating in the nationalist and radical revolts of 1848. At the time this was a failure but the ideals of 1848 would be realized later as Italy and Germany achieved unification and the old empires collapsed.

The United States expanded vigorously westward, her population and industry increasing, while European colonialism was most active in Asia. The impact of British culture was felt in India for the first time and the process of penetration of China began in earnest with the end of the Opium Wars, which forced China to open her ports to foreign trade.

1825–1827

Following a liberal **Decembrist revolt**, 1825, **Nicholas I**, *r.*1824–55, introduced repressive measures.

Charles X, *r.*1824–30, alienated bourgeois support in France by restoring to nobles land lost in the Revolution.

The British in India ended their titular subservience to Mogul rule, 1827.

The Javanese rebelled against Dutch rule but were put down.

1827–1830

Lord Bentinck, 1774–1839, built new canals and roads in India and prohibited the customs of suttee and thuggee.

Turkey recognized Greece's independence after British and Russian intervention, 1829.

Uruguay was established as an independent buffer state between Argentina and Brazil, 1828.

The Workingmen's party was established in the US, pledged to social reform.

1830–1832

The French liberal opposition expelled Charles X, replacing him with **Louis-Philippe**, pledged to rule with middle-class support, 1830. This sparked a liberal and nationalist revolt in Belgium, which became independent of the Netherlands.

Nationalist risings in Italy and Germany were unsuccessful.

The French established their authority in Algiers, 1830.

The Young Italy group was launched by **Giuseppe Mazzini**, 1805–72, in Italy in 1831.

1832–1835

Slavery was abolished throughout the British Empire, 1833.

The German customs union, completed in 1834, became the focus of German nationalism.

Regional opposition to the libera Spanish regime led to the **Carlis Wars**, 1833–39, in support of **Don Carlos.**

Louis-Philippe renounced his rac ical support and introduced strict censorship, 1835.

British trade with China increased after the East India Company's monopoly ended.

National events

The United States continued territorial expansion during this period, ultimately extending its boundaries to the Pacific Ocean. There was dispute over the Canadian and Mexican borders. Abolitionist sentiment intensified, and slavery became a heated domestic issue.

After the 1824 presidential election no candidate had a majority. The House of Representatives chose **John Quincy Adams**, 1767–1848, over **Andrew Jackson.**

The Democratic party was organized 1827. The doctrine of nullification was South Carolina's response to the Tariff of 1828.

In Virginia, Nat Turner, 1800–31, led a slave uprising (1831) that resulted in 60 white and more than 100 slave deaths. Slave codes became more rigid.

In 1832, Jackson threatened to enforce the tariff in response to South Carolina's nullification an vetoed the bill to recharter the Bank of the United States.

Stephenson's *Locomotion*, 1825

Simón Bolivar

Delacroix "1830 Revolution"

"View of Mount Fuji" by Hokusai

Religion and philosophy

Several European thinkers, principally in France, advocated the application of the observational, or "positive," methods used in the natural sciences to the study of social phenomena.

The growth of the industrial system stimulated much new and radical thought. Saint-Simon and, following him, Comte, argued that industrial society should be governed by a new "priesthood" trained in the positivist method, while the existing forms of social organization were criticized by utopian thinkers who looked forward to ideal societies free from inequality and injustice.

Marx and Engels, who were influenced by French utopianism as well as German idealism and British political economy, argued that in order to end the inequality and injustice of existing society there must be a working-class revolution.

A number of Adventist sects prophesying the return of Christ emerged during these years, especially in the US.

Henri de Saint-Simon, 1760–1825, in *New Christianity*, 1825, sought to combine the ideals of Christianity with science and a belief in industrialism to form a new religion of socialism based on a science of society. He advocated management of society by experts in the new social science, to aid welfare and progress. His theories were further developed by his onetime secretary, **Auguste Comte**, 1798–1857.

François Guizot, 1787–1874, published his *History of Civilisation in France*, 1829, a study of social institutions using empirical data and a historical approach.

James Mill, 1777–1836, in his *Analysis of the Human Mind*, 1829, developed Bentham's pleasure-pain doctrine in the field of psychology.

John Darby, 1800–82, set up the **Plymouth Brethren** sect in Ireland, 1830, emphasizing the second coming of Jesus Christ.

Mormonism was founded in New York State by Joseph Smith, 1805–44, in 1830, based on the *Book of Mormon*. Opposition to their enclosed community life would cause them to settle in Utah, 1847.

Modern Adventism was founded in the US by **William Miller**, 1782–1849, who began in 1831 to prophesy the imminent end of the world. The failure of his predictions produced many breakaway sects, including the **Seventh Day Adventists.**

The Oxford Movement within Anglicanism began, 1833, unde the leadership of **John Keble**, 1792–1866, and Cardinal **John Newman**, 1801–90. They sought to revive the ideals of th medieval Church and reintroduced elaborate rituals.

Félicité Lamennais, 1782–1854 a French Catholic priest, argued in *Thoughts of a Believer*, 1834 for the separation of Church anc state and attacked the papacy for its interference in politics.

Literature

While Romanticism spread to Russia with Lermontov and Gogol, its brooding introversion began to break down in Western Europe, and the political implications of its rebellion were explored. The Jung Deutschland group insisted on the political role of literature, and in France the realistic depiction of the past or of contemporary society became important new themes.

The social and nationalist commitment of these writers found expression in the revolutions of 1848, in which authors such as Hugo and Lamartine played an important role.

In England novelists explored social relationships. Dickens concentrated on the evil consequences of industrialization with a wealth of characterization equaled only by Balzac.

James Fenimore Cooper, 1789–1851, gained international fame with his historical novel *The Last of the Mohicans*, 1826, in which he portrayed the American Indians.

I Promessi Sposi, 1825–27, by the Italian **Alessandro Manzoni**, 1785–1873, is a love story set in 17th-century Italy with delicate Christian idealism.

The Cenacle group of poets was set up in Paris, 1827, by **Victor Hugo**, 1802–85, and **Sainte-Beuve**, 1804–69.

Hugo's *Odes et Ballades*, 1826, celebrated the theme of liberty. The romantic poetry of **Alfred de Musset**, 1810–57, and the stoical pessimism of **Alfred de Vigny**, 1797–1863, reflected French disillusionment in the post-Napoleonic era.

Social realism in the French novel began with the work of **Stendhal (Henri Beyle)**, 1783–1842. A soldier and critic, he wrote *Le Rouge et Le Noir*, 1830. **George Sand**, 1804–76, produced idealized novels such as *Indiana*, 1832, and **Prosper Merimée**, 1803–70, brought archeological exactness to the romantic novel.

The first great modern Russian writer, **Alexander Pushkin**, 1799–1837, broke down the archaic stiffness of the written style, and introduced realistic language. He used peasant folk songs in the poem *The Dead Princess*, 1834, and medieval history as the source for the novel *Eugene Onegin*, 1823–31 and the tragic drama *Boris Godunov*.

Art and architecture

Naturalism in painting—the devotion to truth to nature—received a special impetus from work in Britain where scientific advances and the Industrial Revolution affected art.

British landscapists such as John Constable studied natural effects in a scientific manner rather than composing classical panoramas, and French artists emulated his innovations.

The interest in history and in different historical styles continued throughout Europe and America. A large number of paintings of historical scenes was produced, but it is in architecture that the range of interest in different styles was clearest. Italian models remained a source for the style of secular public buildings but the Gothic revival received a new impetus.

England's new wealthy middle classes were beginning to impose their taste on painting and architecture, while rapid urbanization generated the need for new solutions in town planning.

The American ornithologist and painter **John James Audubon**, 1785–1851, published *The Birds of America*, from original drawings in England between 1827 and 1838.

Italian Renaissance architecture inspired the Travellers' Club, London, by **Charles Barry**, 1795–1860, an example of the neo-Renaissance style.

In France oil paints were sold in tubes for the first time *c.*1830–35, which made painting out of doors much easier.

A craze in France for things English known as *anglomanie* developed in the post-Napoleonic era. Watercolor painting became popular in Paris, where **Richard Parkes Bonington**, 1802–28, worked after 1820. British oil painting techniques were studied by French artists, especially after the exhibition of Constable's work in the Paris Salon of 1824, and **Delacroix** illustrated Byron's poem in his "The Execution of Doge Marino Faliero."

The School of Architecture, Berlin, 1832–35, by **Karl Friedrich Schinkel** was based on strict units of measurement, and the design used iron frame structures. It had vestiges of classical detail but came close to a "modern," simple, and functional style.

English industrial towns such as Manchester developed the back-to-back house as a solution to the housing needs generated by the Industrial Revolution.

In England, the taste and buying power of the new, wealthy, middle classes resulted in an increasing demand for genre and small-scale historical or romantic scenes with emphasis on nar rative, as in "Giving a Bite," 1834, by **William Mulready**, 1786–1863.

Japanese color printing reached its height in "The Thirty-six views of Mount Fuji," 1834–35 by **Hokusai** and the poetic "View of Kyoto," 1834, by **Ando Hiroshige**, 1797–1858.

Music

Romanticism evolved further in Europe, where composers came to consider music a kind of poetry that penetrated to the heart, ennobling the soul and stimulating the imagination. It was at times extravagant and replete with epic works and cult figures, stimulating growth in orchestration techniques and producing such new forms as the symphonic poem.

In Philadelphia, the first important music school was founded, 1825, by the Musical Fund Society.

The mouth organ, the Chinese sheng, came to Vienna in 1829.

Felix Mendelssohn, 1809–47, revived Bach's music in 1829 after a century of eclipse, giving it the status it enjoys today.

Hector Berlioz, 1803–69, made inspired use of the orchestra to express the extra-musical allusions of program music, as in his *Symphonie fantastique*, 1830, with its elaborate story line.

Frédéric Chopin, 1810–49, a Polish exile working mostly in Paris from 1831, wrote dazzling short pieces for piano in such forms as nocturne, mazurka, anc polonaise.

Science and technology

The rail system that grew up in Britain, providing cheap transport for labor and raw materials, proved a vital precondition for the expansion of any industrial society. The process of industrialization, however, brought more and more people into the cities and led to a severe worsening of the conditions of working people. In Bristol, England, the death rate doubled between 1831 and 1841, although advances in medicine and public health began to improve matters from 1840 onward. The discovery of asepsis was particularly important in lowering the child mortality rate.

In pure science the discovery of alternative geometries to that of Euclid prompted new inquiries into formerly accepted theories, clearing the way for Mach and Einstein.

The discovery of Brownian motion finally established the existence of unobservable particles, in this case molecules; an important step toward the eventual acceptance of atomic theory.

The first public steam railroad opened in 1825 between Stockton and Darlington in England. The first train was drawn by *Locomotion No. 1*, built by the British engineer **George Stephenson**, 1781–1848. **Robert Brown**, 1773–1858, a British botanist, observed the random motion of particles, **Brownian motion**, in 1827, thus proving that molecules exist.

Ohm's Law, relating current, voltage, and resistance, was laid down in 1827 by German physicist **Georg Ohm**, 1787–1854.

The polarimeter, which analyzes the passage of polarized light through matter, was developed in 1828 by British physicist **William Nicol**, 1768–1851.

Embryology was founded, 1828, by **Karl Baer**, 1792–1876.

Organic chemistry began with the synthesis of urea by German chemist **Friedrich Wöhler**, 1800–82, in 1828. He showed that organic substances do not always come from living things.

Non-Euclidean geometry was developed *c.*1829–30 by **Nikolai Lobachevski**, 1793–1856.

Screw threads were standardized, 1830, by the Briton **Sir Joseph Whitworth**, 1803–87, making mass production viable.

Electromagnetic induction was discovered, 1831, by a British physicist, **Michael Faraday**, 1791–1867. This discovery led to the electric generator. Faraday also formulated the laws of electrolysis in 1832.

The Principles of Geology, 1833 by **Sir Charles Lyell**, 1797–1875, showed that rocks evolve extremely slowly. **Karl Gauss**, 1777–1855, a German, devised 1833, a set of units for magnetism.

The Royal William, a Canadian vessel, was the first steamship to cross the Atlantic wholly under its own power, 1833.

With the building of the **Great Western** in 1838 by **I. K. Brunel**, 1806–59, transatlantic services became regular.

335–1837

e Boers of South Africa began **e Great Trek,** 1835, to find w territory free from British e. British attempts to unite its lonies of **Upper and Lower nada** led to revolt, 1837. **ctoria,** *r.*1837–1901, suc- eded to the British throne. **itain** attempted to intervene in rsia, 1834–38, to forestall ssian influence, but was re- lled by **Muhammed Shah,** 835–48.

e siege of the Alamo in San tonio, Tex., 1836, by Mexi- ns under **Santa Anna,** 1794– 76, ended with the massacre the Texans.

arles Dickens

obability theory and statistical ethods applied to social phe- mena by the Belgian **Adolphe uetelet,** 1796–1874, led to the scovery that the frequency of icide in a society was con- ant and therefore predictable. **lph Emerson,** 1803–82, an merican Unitarian, developed *Nature,* 1836, a belief called **anscendentalism,** proposing at spiritual exploration of one's ul in communion with nature d to the highest wisdom.

einrich Heine, 1797–1856, a erman poet and a member of **e Jung Deutschland** group, hich described romantic ideal- m and wanted all literature to ve a political role, wrote *Die omantische Schule* in Paris, 36.
acomo Leopardi, 1798–1837, ed the romantic theme of an's helplessness in the face nature, in *La Ginestra,* 1836.

merican primitive painting con- nued in the work of the Quaker inter **Edward Hicks,** 1780– 849, whose naive landscape ith animals, "The Peaceable ngdom," uses simple forms, at colors, and two dimensions. **ench romantic sculpture** ressed dramatic movement and eting gestures, poses, and pressions and was epitomized the "Marseillaise" on the Arc Triomphe, 1833–36, by **ançois Rude,** 1784–1855.

obert Schumann, 1810–56, as an arch-Romantic, especial- in his evocative piano music e *Carnaval,* 1834–35. He unded the avant-garde publica- n *Neue Zeitschrift fur Musik.*

obert Brown, 1773–1858, first scovered and named the nucle- s of a living cell.
harles Babbage, 1791–1871, a itish mathematician, de- eloped the principles of the echanical computer in the 330s.
he electric telegraph was pa- nted in Britain by **Sir Charles heatstone,** 1802–75.
he Colt pistol, the first repeat- g firearm, was patented, 835–36.

1837–1840

A working-class radical Chartist movement developed in England, stimulated by European economic depression.
China seized opium imports from India, provoking the **Opium Wars** with Britain, 1839.
British industrialists' attempts to introduce free trade led to the foundation of the **Anti-Corn Law League,** 1839.
Ieyoshi, *r.*1838–53, the Japanese shōgun, opposed mounting pressure for Occidental trade.

There was a major depression, 1837–43. Conflict over the New Brunswick-Maine border began, 1838, in the Aroostook River area.

California gold miners

The terms "sociology" and "positivism" were coined by the Frenchman **Auguste Comte,** 1798–1857. His *Course of Positive Philosophy,* 1830–42, argued for the use of positivist methods in social studies. He stated that man's thought had passed through the theological and metaphysical stages and reached the positivist stage. He divided sociology into statics, the study of the interdependence of social institutions, and dynamics, the study of change.

The prolific French novelist Honoré de Balzac, 1799–1850, wrote over 90 interconnecting novels and stories, 1829–43, set in Paris and the provinces in the 1820s, which he called *La Comédie Humaine.*

The Hudson River School of American landscape painters produced picturesque and romantic views of the eastern states, exemplified by **Thomas Cole,** 1801–48, and **Asher Durand,** 1796–1886.
An increased range of oil colors was introduced, including mauves, violets, bright greens, and intense yellows.

Mikhail Glinka, 1804–57, in such works as *A Life for the Tsar,* 1836, heralded the rise of a Russian national school, using folk music and inspired by the Napoleonic Wars.

The Morse code was invented, 1838, by **Samuel Morse.**
Stellar parallax was detected in 1838 by **Friedrich Bessel,** 1784–1846, encouraging astronomical interest beyond the solar system.
Vulcanization of rubber was discovered, 1839, by the American **Charles Goodyear,** 1800–60.
Theodor Schwann, 1810–82, and **Matthias Schleiden,** 1804–81, both German biologists, in 1839 first described the anatomy of animal and plant cells and cells' role in the organism.

1840–1842

Britain annexed **Natal,** 1843.
Upper and Lower Canada were united in 1840 and given responsible government.
The Straits Convention, 1841, among Russia, Britain, France, Austria, and Prussia, closed the Dardanelles and Bosporus to foreign shipping.
Frederick William IV of Prussia, *r.* 1840–61, encouraged German nationalism.
The Treaty of Nanking, 1842, opened Chinese ports to British trade.

The New York Tribune was founded by **Horace Greeley,** 1811–72, in 1840. The Webster-Ashburton Treaty, 1842, settled the US-Canadian border.

Ludwig Feuerbach, 1804–72, in *The Essence of Christianity,* 1841, advocated a humanistic atheism. His critique of Hegel and his claim that God is nothing other than a projection of human nature influenced Marx.
Alexis de Tocqueville, 1805–59, the first sociologist to examine the impact of democracy on nonpolitical institutions, held that democratic emphasis on equality might suppress individuality and lead to total conformity—a tyranny of the majority.

Mikhail Lermontov, 1814–41, stands at the beginning of Russia's golden age of prose. Pushkin's successor as poet, playwright, and novelist, he was directly influenced by Western literature, especially the work and the flamboyant romanticism of Lord Byron. His novel, *A Hero of Our Times,* on the tragic theme of a man without a purpose, appeared in 1840.

The Gothic Revival in Europe, which had begun *c.*1750 and was based on serious investigation of medieval sources, prompted the decision to build the **Houses of Parliament,** London, 1836–68, in a Gothic style, and the similar exploration of national Gothic styles in the rest of Europe.
Political cartoons reached a high level of sophistication in England in the work of **George Cruikshank,** 1792–1878, and in France with **Honoré Daumier.**

Vienna, in Ferdinand I's reign, 1835–48, was the center of popular dance music, exporting the Viennese waltz and works of the older **Johann Strauss,** 1804–49, to the rest of Europe.

Jean-Louis Agassiz, 1807–73, a Swiss naturalist, studied glaciers and showed, 1840, that an Ice Age had once occurred, producing glacial action that had helped to shape the land masses.
Anesthesia had its beginnings in 1842, when US surgeon **Crawford Long,** 1815–78, successfully operated on an etherized patient.

1842–1845

The persecution of Christians in Confucianist French Indochina led to French military involvement, 1840–50.
Sanitary reform and slum clearance were introduced in England in the 1840s.
The Anglo-Sikh wars broke out in India, 1845–48.
Texas was annexed by the United States in 1845.
Utopian socialism became popular in France among intellectuals and the working classes.

Texas was admitted to the Union, 1845, despite Mexican threats of war. Expansion after 1845 was justified by the doctrine of "Manifest Destiny."

Giuseppe Garibaldi

The Babi movement, which developed into the **Bahai** religion, was founded in Persia, 1844, by **Ali Muhammed,** 1819–50. It drew inspiration from diverse sources and emphasized the unity of mankind.
Sören Kierkegaard, 1813–55, a Danish religious philosopher, published *Either/Or,* 1843. Regarded as the founder of existentialism, he argued against rationalism and emphasized the need to make choices between ethical or aesthetic alternatives.

The fantastical and tormented aspects of Russian fiction stem from **Nikolai Gogol,** 1809–52. His novel *Dead Souls,* 1842, a moral satire on bureaucracy, centered on the career of a man who deals in dead serfs.
Adam Mickiewicz, 1798–1855, Poland's national poet, used themes of Lithuanian folklore in his vibrant epic works.

Joseph Turner, 1775–1851, in England was one of the first painters to celebrate contemporary technology. His "Rain, Steam, and Speed," 1844, proclaims the power of the machine in a diffuse, misty style suggesting the speed of the train.
The Barbizon School of French landscapists, including **Jean François Millet,** 1814–75, settled near Fontainebleau.
John Ruskin, 1819–1900, emphasized truth to nature in "Modern Painters."

Brass bands, especially in Germany, produced a popular music of their own. The cornet provided a high voice and became a virtuoso solo instrument.

The mechanical equivalent of heat was first measured and the principle of the conservation of energy put forward by **Julius von Mayer,** 1814–78, a German physicist, in 1842. The British physicist **James Joule,** 1818–89, and the German **Hermann Helmholtz,** 1821–94, established both with more thorough work *c.*1847.
The Great Britain, the first iron-hulled steamer powered by a screw propeller, crossed the Atlantic in 1843.

1845–1847

A potato famine in Ireland resulted in mass emigration to the United States, 1846–47.
The US invaded Mexico and occupied the capital in 1847, defeating Mexico after conflict over Texas, 1846–48.
Liberal hopes in Prussia were raised when the **Landtag** was called, 1847, by the king, who asked for funds to build railroads.
The accession of the liberal **Pope Pius IX,** *r.*1846–78, raised nationalist hopes in Italy.

An Anglo-American treaty settled the Oregon border, 1846. In the Mexican War, 1846–48, the United States acquired New Mexico, Texas, and California.

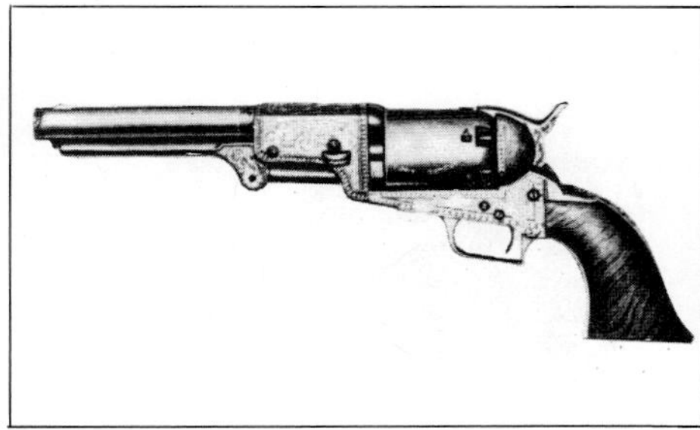

Colt Dragoon revolver, 1848

Pierre Proudhon, 1809–65, a French philosopher, held that "property is theft." His book *The Philosophy of Misery,* 1846, formulated anarchism as a political theory. Together with his fellow Frenchmen **Louis Blanc,** 1811–82, and **Louis Blanqui,** 1805–81, he called for an end to the capitalistic exploitation of labor and for a revolutionary change in the existing social and economic orders. These men participated in the revolt of 1848.

The English social novelist Charles Dickens, 1812–70, published one of his greatest novels, *Dombey and Son,* 1846–48, dealing with the Victorian family.
W. M. Thackeray, 1811–63, wrote his caustic attack on the false face of polite society, *Vanity Fair,* 1847–48, a satirical novel set on the eve of the Napoleonic wars.

Photography (daguerreotypes) and the style of early photographic portraits, where the subject had to maintain a still pose during the long exposure period, influenced such painters as **Ingres,** particularly in his portrait of "La Comtesse d'Haussonville," 1845.
Historical architecture spread in the US, as in Europe. The picturesque, Neo-Norman Smithsonian Institute in Washington, 1846, was built by **James Renwick, Jr.,** 1818–85.

Franz Liszt, 1811–86, a great piano virtuoso, toured the capitals of Europe, then retired from the concert stage.

Nitroglycerine was discovered, 1846, by the Italian chemist **Ascanio Sobrero.**
Neptune was discovered, 1846, by the German astronomer **Johann Galle,** 1812–1910.
Agriculture gained a scientific basis with the publication in the 1840s and 1850s of work by the German **Justus von Liebig,** 1803–73, showing how plants use vital elements in cycles.
The rotary printing press was invented in 1847 by the American **Richard Hoe,** 1812–86.

1847–1850

Britain annexed the Punjab and won Sikh loyalty, 1845–48.
An outburst of urban radicalism brought the expulsion of **Louis-Philippe** in France and the establishment of a republic, 1848.
Metternich resigned in Austria.
Hungary declared itself independent, and German and Italian nationalist movements emerged. By 1849, Austria had defeated the Italian revolt, and racial disputes split Hungary.
The gold rush in California opened up the West, 1848–50.

Gold, discovered at Sutter's Mill in the Sacramento Valley, 1848, brought *c.*80,000 adventurers to California, 1849. California became a state, 1850.

The Christadelphians, a pacifistic millennial adventist sect, was founded in 1848 in the US by **John Thomas,** 1805–71.
Karl Marx, 1818–83, and **Friedrich Engels,** 1820–95, wrote the *Communist Manifesto,* 1848, predicting the revolutionary overthrow of capitalism and its replacement by socialism. Marx saw history as a class struggle for ownership of society's material resources.

Powerful imagination and insight marked the works of the English novelists the **Brontë sisters. Emily,** 1818–48, wrote *Wuthering Heights,* 1847, an account of ferocious passions set against a raw elemental background. *Jane Eyre* by **Charlotte,** 1816–55, was published in the same year and *The Tenant of Wildfell Hall* by **Ann,** 1820–49, in 1848.

The Pre-Raphaelite Brotherhood was founded in England, 1848. Its painters sought a return to the purity and moral seriousness of 15th-century Italian art and rejected contemporary academic styles. Their work was characterized by great detail and the use of brilliant colors on a white ground as in "Awakening Conscience," 1852, by **William Holman Hunt,** 1827–1910, and "Christ in the House of his Parents," 1849, by **John Everett Millais,** 1829–96.

At the court of Weimar, 1848–61, Liszt supported young musicians, and originated the symphonic or tone poem, 1848–49.

Asepsis was demanded, 1847, by **Ignaz Semmelweis,** 1818–65, a Hungarian physician. He showed that childbed fever could be prevented if hospital doctors cleaned their hands regularly.
The St Lawrence Seaway was first opened in 1848.
Reinforced concrete was invented, 1849, by a French engineer, **Joseph Monier,** 1823–1906.
A telegraphic cable connection across the English Channel was laid in 1850.

Darwin and Marx 1850–1875

Principal events

The development of ruthlessly pragmatic political planning epitomized by the ministry of Bismarck in Prussia brought about the national unification of Italy and Germany, where the idealism of the 1848 revolutions had failed. Industrial expansion went hand in hand with cynical foreign policies, which with the demise of liberal ideals contributed to the growth of international tensions.

British imperial power was at its peak after the defeat of the Indian mutiny. Britain's economic supremacy, backed up by military strength, made it unchallengeable throughout the world.

The victory of the North in the US Civil War ended slavery and prepared the way for US industrial and political expansion, while the European powers extended their domination in Southeast Asia, and Japan set out to transform herself into a modern industrial society.

1850–1852

Napoleon III, *r.*1852–70, restored the French Empire after the upheavals of 1848.
The rights of national minorities were suppressed in the Austro-Hungarian Empire.
California became a free state in 1850, and a compromise was reached on slavery in the United States in 1850.
The vastly destructive T'ai-p'ing Rebellion broke out in China in 1851.
The English in India subdued Burma, 1851–53.

1852–1855

Russia's defeat in the Crimean War, 1854–56, checked her ambitions in eastern Europe.
The New York-Chicago rail link was completed, 1853.
The discovery by David Livingstone, 1813–73, of the Victoria Falls, 1855, sparked European exploration of the African interior.
Europe experienced an economic boom, 1852–56.
Camillo Cavour, 1810–61, began the industrialization of Piedmont in northern Italy.

1855–1857

After the Crimean War, the Black Sea was declared neutral and the virtual independence of Serbia recognized by the major European powers, 1856.
The Indian Mutiny, a series of mutinies by Sepoy troops and scattered popular uprisings against British rule, was ruthlessly suppressed, 1857–58.
John Brown, 1800–59, began organizing militant anti-slavery activity in the United States.

1857–1860

China was finally opened up by the treaties of Tientsin, 1858.
By the Government of India Act 1858, British rule in India was transferred to the crown. Administrative reforms and the building of railways followed.
Piedmont drove the Austrians from northern Italy, 1859.
The British raided Peking, 1860.
The Suez Canal construction was begun by de Lesseps, 1805–94.
Russia expanded at China's expense, 1858–60.

National events

The Antebellum period saw deepening differences between the pro- and antislavery states. With the election of Abraham Lincoln, 1809–65, the southern states withdrew from the Union. A bitter struggle took place, 1861–65, but following the Civil War the nation moved to achieve real unity.

California's admission as a free state, upset the balance of slave and free. **Henry Clay's** (1777–1852) Compromise of 1850 postponed the issue.

The Kansas-Nebraska Act, 1854, allowed popular sovereignty in those territories but did not prevent bloodshed. The Republican party was founded, 1854.

Dred Scott, *c.*1795–1858, a slave, took a suit for freedom to the Supreme Court, which declared the Missouri Compromise unconstitutional.

John Brown, 1800–59, was executed following a raid at Harpers Ferry, Va., 1859. Republican **Abraham Lincoln** was elected president, 1860.

Western and Atlantic Railroad: the *General*, 1855

Bessemer steel producing process

Indian Mutiny: massacre at Delhi

Religion and philosophy

The spread of industrialization provoked a major reassessment of moral, social, and political thought. Many Christians campaigned to relieve the worst aspects of urban poverty, and sociology developed tools to describe the changes in social relationships, while many political and moral philosophies grew up that rejected urbanization and capitalism, laying stress on personal withdrawal or social revolution. The latter was advocated in particular by Karl Marx whose work provided a radical attack on capitalist economics and stated that the victory of the proletariat over the bourgeoisie was a historical inevitability.

Darwin's theory of evolution proved as influential as the ideas of Marx, challenging many of the basic tenets of Christian belief and forcing the importance of scientific thought to the fore. Many attempts were made to apply his ideas to the political and cultural fields.

The T'ai-p'ing Rebellion in China, 1850, under the leadership of **Hung Hsiu-Chuan,** 1814–64, was a radical religious movement influenced by Protestant Christian teaching, which demanded the communalization of property, equal redistribution of land, and equality between men and women.
T. B. Macaulay, 1800–59, an English historian, published a *History of England* between 1848 and 1861, stressing the victory of liberalism since 1688.

Frederick Denison Maurice, 1805–72, the major theologian of 19th-century Anglicanism, published his *Theological Essays*, 1853. He helped to found the **Christian Socialist movement** in England, which tried to apply Christian ideals in an industrial society.
Henry Thoreau, 1817–62, an American, described **Transcendentalism** and his simple life in the midst of nature, in *Walden*, 1854.

Frédéric Le Play, 1806–82, a French sociologist, developed a technique of collating field data that influenced methods of statistical sampling in *European Workers*, 1855. He defined three basic family types, related to general social conditions.
Hippolyte Taine, 1828–93, a French historian, argued in *The French Philosophers* for the use of a scientific (positivist) method in the study of culture, 1857. He had a great influence on later 19th-century thought.

Charles Darwin, 1809–82, published *Origin of Species*, 1859 arousing opposition from the English Church because he contradicted Genesis and seemed to render the role of God in the creation superfluous. By implying that man stood at the pinnacle of evolutionary development Darwin's theory reinforced contemporary ideas of the inevitability of social progress. After defeat in the debate, the Church ceased to intervene in science.

Literature

As the realist novel produced the powerful and candid tragedy of Madame Bovary by Flaubert, new literary styles were also emerging in French poetry. Baudelaire's attempt to explore his inner self would lead to the symbolist movement to which reality beyond the poet's own imagination was irrelevant.

In Russia, Dostoevsky and Tolstoy were writing, and the moral, psychological, and political issues they explored recurred in the literature of the English Victorian novelists from Charles Dickens to George Eliot.

American literature reached maturity with the poetry of Whitman—a distinct contrast with contemporary European styles—and the strong prose of Melville's epic novel Moby Dick.

The American novelist Nathaniel Hawthorne, 1806–64, wrote *The Scarlet Letter*, 1850, and **Herman Melville** produced his allegorical *Moby Dick*, 1851, with an American delight in vigorous prose.
The Victorian Alfred Lord Tennyson, 1809–92, showed in his elegiac poem *In Memoriam*, 1850, verbal grace and awareness of moral dilemmas.

The fantastic and dream-inspired poems of *Les Chimères*, 1854, by **Gerard de Nerval,** 1808–55, would influence later symbolists.
The *poems* of **Matthew Arnold,** 1822–88, were an intellectual expression of Victorian unease as was the poetry of **Robert Browning,** 1812–89, whose dramatic monologues are full of human insight.

Walt Whitman, 1819–92, published his autobiographical *Leaves of Grass*, 1855.
Gustave Flaubert, 1821–80, published *Madame Bovary*, 1856.
Modern poetry began with *Les Fleurs du Mal*, 1857, by the Frenchman **Charles Baudelaire,** 1821–67.
Theophile Gautier, 1811–72, proclaimed the concept of art for art's sake, 1857.

Adalbert Stifter, 1805–68, wrote of the harmony of man and nature in *Der Nachsommer*.
Ivan Goncharov, 1812–91, wrote *Oblomov*, 1859, mocking the bankruptcy of intellectualism.

Art and architecture

The reaction against academic precepts, which ruled the bulk of official painting in Europe, began in earnest and took the form of the assertion that the subject matter of everyday life was worthy of art.

The Impressionists broke new ground with their revolutionary techniques for representing light and color, best seen in the works of Monet; while Realist painters like Courbet stated that art must have a social and political purpose. In the same period English art saw a distinct reaction against the aesthetics and values of industrial society with the work of the Pre-Raphaelites and the Arts and Crafts movement.

Town planning became a priority in the European capitals, and the use of cast iron revolutionized municipal architecture.

Trading contact with the East and the Meiji restoration in Japan brought an interpenetration of Eastern and Western art.

Realism reached its height in the works of **Gustave Courbet,** 1819–77, such as "The Stonebreakers," 1850.
Jean François Millet, 1814–75, created an ennobling picture of peasants in his canvas "The Sower," 1850.
The Pre-Raphaelite Brotherhood were defended by **John Ruskin,** 1851.
Prefabricated units of iron and glass were used by **Joseph Paxton,** 1803–65, in the Crystal Palace, London, 1851.

Honoré Daumier, 1808–79, painted children in "La Ronde," 1855.

Baron Haussmann, 1809–91, introduced squares, parks, and boulevards into Paris, 1851–68. His wide streets were designed to create impressive views and to ensure easy policing of the city center.
The New Building of the Louvre, 1852–57, and later the Paris Opera, 1861–74, illustrate the powerful Neo-Renaissance and Neo-Baroque forms that were key to the civic architecture of the Second Empire.

Landscapes by **Jean Baptiste Camille Corot,** 1796–1875, like "The Valley," 1855–60, anticipated the Impressionists with their use of muted colors and soft outlines.
The Arts and Crafts movement in England led by **William Morris,** 1834–96, and **Philip Webb,** 1831–1915, originated in a dissatisfaction with manufactured goods and a respect for the medieval craftsman. It produced wallpapers, furniture, tapestries and carpets usually by hand.

Music

Romantic ideals were reinforced in 1858 by Darwin's theory of evolution through the survival of the fittest, and confirmed the widely held view that man verges on perfection. The odd conclusion that art, like life, evolves from lower forms to higher led to an increasing distinction between serious and popular music, a distinction still prevalent in the West.

Musical forms still developed themes, much as the classics had done, but the work of composers such as **Liszt** gave music a mystical aura and set it apart from normal experience.

Late Romantic composers, such as **Richard Wagner,** 1813–83, and **Anton Bruckner,** 1824–96, aimed for grandeur by using large forces and a rubato (freer) beat to savor the sound.

Use of rubato tended to slow down performances and to produce rhythmic problems in large ensembles so that performances became dull and turgid.

Grand opera carried the Romantic ideal to a peak in the works of **Giuseppe Verdi,** 1813–1901 who in *Un Ballo in maschera*, 1859, evoked specific characters and moods.

Science and technology

Science and technology became more closely tied to the needs of industry in this period, especially in Germany where chemists produced dyes and explosives and in the United States where engineers enjoyed a high social status. The abolition of slavery in America and the rise of trade unionism in Europe both raised labor costs and so stimulated mechanization, while the Crimean War provided an incentive for the development of new and better kinds of steel.

While Darwin's theory of evolution, backed up by Mendel's researches into genetics, was the most popular scientific breakthrough, chemistry and astronomy both advanced dramatically with the development of spectroscopy in Germany and the application of the Doppler Effect. The former permitted many new elements to be discovered, while the latter, through the measurement of red-shift, produced more accurate estimates of the size of the known universe.

Entropy, following from the second law of thermodynamics, was conceived, 1850, by the German **Rudolf Clausius,** 1822–88.
The sewing machine was developed, 1851, by **Isaac Singer,** 1811–75, an American.
Physiology advanced with the work, *c.*1851, of the French scientist **Claude Bernard,** 1813–78.
The rotation of the Earth was demonstrated conclusively in 1851 by the French physicist **Jean Foucault,** 1819–68.

Symbolic logic was founded by **George Boole,** 1815–64, a British mathematician, with his *Laws of Thought*, 1854.

The first synthetic plastic material, later named celluloid, was patented in 1855 by the British chemist Alexander Parkes, 1813–90.
Mauve, the first artificial dye, was derived from aniline, 1856, by the British chemist **William Perkin,** 1838–1907. Production of the new synthetic substances stimulated the growth of modern organic chemistry.
Steel was produced cheaply in the converter patented in 1856 by the British metallurgist **Henry Bessemer,** 1813–98.

Atomic weights and chemical formulae were standardized by the Italian **Stanislao Cannizzaro,** 1826–1910, in 1858.
The principles of molecular structure were discovered by the German chemist **Friedrich von Stradonitz,** 1829–96, in 1858.
The theory of evolution was put forward in 1858–59 by the British naturalists **Charles Darwin,** 1809–82, and **Alfred Wallace,** 1823–1913.
The first oil well was struck near Titusville, Pennsylvania, in 1858.

60–1862

raham Lincoln, 1809–65, was cted president of the US on anti-slavery platform.
e Confederate states took Fort mter, 1861.
seppe Garibaldi, 1807–82, erated southern Italy from apolitan rule and gave it to dmont, uniting Italy, 1861.
exander II of Russia, *r.*1855– , emancipated the serfs in 61.
e French intervened in Mexico, 61, and installed Maximilian emperor, 1863.

uth Carolina seceded from the ion, 1860. In 1861, the Con- federate States of America mprised 11 states. Fort Sum- 's fall began the Civil War.

arles Darwin lampooned

rdinand Lassalle, 1825–64, ged German workers to seek versal suffrage, 1862. His ogram would form the basis of German Social Democratic rty established in 1869 in position to the revolutionary rxist International, and fore- adowed later social demo- tic and parliamentary vements.

impressionistic realist style sed on detailed social obser- ion was developed in France the brothers **Edmond** and **es de Goncourt,** 1822–96 and 30–70, in their *Journals.*
e realist novel in Russia pro- ced a varied account of the nflicts in Russian society.

stave Doré, 1832–83, illus- ted Dante's *Inferno,* 1861.
gène Emmanuel Viollet-le- c, 1814–79, in France, inter- eted Gothic architecture in ms of its structural principles d advocated new materials e iron, in his *Dictionary of ench Architecture,* 1858–75.
panese draftsmanship, flat panses of color and subject tter, strongly influenced the pressionists and later **Van gh** and **Gauguin.**

gro spirituals emerged in the as blacks took up the singing hool tradition of colonial nerica, but mixed with it a thmic work song style.

e open hearth process for the oduction of steel was de- oped in France, following the ention of the regenerative nace by **William Siemens,** 23–83, and **Frederick Sie- ens,** 1826–1904.
lloids were distinguished in 61 by the British chemist **omas Graham,** 1805–69. He o discovered osmosis.

1862–1865

An allied Western expedition participated in a violent civil war in Japan, 1864.
Rome remained under papal rule as a virtual protectorate of France.
Slavery was abolished and Lincoln assassinated, 1865.
Karl Marx, 1818–83, presided over the First International in London, 1864.
Christianity was spread in China by missionaries.

The Civil War ended at Appomattox Courthouse when Confederate **Gen. Robert E. Lee,** 1807–70, surrendered to Union Gen. **Ulysses S. Grant,** 1822–85.

Confederates in the Civil War

John Stuart Mill, 1806–73, an Englishman, attempted to create a political theory uniting the conditions of industrialism with basic tenets of human freedom. He argued in *Utilitarianism,* 1863, that what gives pleasure to man is good, while in *On Liberty,* 1859, he insisted that a man must be free to act as he wishes without disturbing the freedom of others. His political critique of English society brought him close to a socialist position.

The debate between Slavophiles and Westernizers was described in *Fathers and Sons* by **Ivan Turgenev,** 1818–83, an ardent Westernizer.
Count Leo Tolstoy, 1828–1910, the greatest exponent of the Russian realist novel, dealt in his epic *War and Peace,* 1865–72, with the Napoleonic Wars, combining a panoramic vision with acute analysis of character.

A turning point for modern painting was marked by the establishment in Paris in 1863 of the **Salon de Refusés,** which exhibited some of the 4,000 canvases rejected by the official Salon. It included works by **Camille Pissarro,** 1830–1903, **Paul Cézanne,** 1839–1906, **James McNeill Whistler,** 1834–1903, and **Edouard Manet,** 1832–83, whose "Déjeuner sur L'Herbe," of a naked woman enjoying a picnic with friends, created a sensation.

Faust, by **Charles Francis Gounod,** 1818–93, was produced in London, Dublin, and New York in 1863.

The first underground railway opened in London in 1863.
The Massachusetts Institute of Technology was founded, 1865.
Bacteriology was founded with the work of the French chemist **Louis Pasteur,** 1822–95, in the 1860s. Pasteur discovered that microorganisms cause fermentation and disease, and used sterilization to kill bacteria.
A submarine telegraphic cable was laid across the Atlantic from Ireland to Newfoundland, 1857–66.

1865–1867

After the defeat of Austria by Prussia in the war of 1866, the North German Confederation was set up.
American objections and opposition at home led to French withdrawal from Mexico, 1866.
The Dominion of Canada was established by the British North America Act, 1867.
The Dual Monarchy of Austria-Hungary was established, 1867—an unpopular compromise on the nationalist question.

The Fourteenth Amendment, 1866, granted blacks full citizenship. The Thirteenth Amendment, 1865, had prohibited slavery.

Karl Marx, 1818–83, published Vol. I of *Das Kapital,* 1867, providing a theoretical analysis of the workings of capitalism. He argued that industrial profits were made by exploiting the workers, but claimed that capitalism would plunge into chaos through its inner contradictions.
William Booth, 1829–1912, shocked at the extent of poverty and degradation in London, began his Evangelical ministry in 1865 and later founded the **Salvation Army.**

The Parnassians, a group of French poets including **Charles Marie Leconte de Lisle,** 1818–94, and later **Paul Verlaine,** 1844–96, rejected the emotionalism and loose forms of the Romantics and wrote strictly disciplined, detached verse following **Theophile Gautier.** Their name derived from the journal *Le Parnasse Contemporain,* first published in 1866.

Japanese prints were being collected in Paris in the 1860s and were exhibited at the Exposition Universelle, 1867. The influence of Japanese draftsmanship could be seen in Manet's "Portrait of Emile Zola," 1868, and in **Whistler's** "Princess of the Land of Porcelain," 1864.

Light opera centered on Paris and Vienna, with the theatrical humor of **Jacques Offenbach,** 1819–80, and the lavish settings of the younger **Johann Strauss,** 1825–99.

Genetics was founded with the publication, 1865, of the experiments of the Austrian botanist **Gregor Mendel,** 1822–84.
Dynamite was invented in 1866 by the Swedish inventor **Alfred Nobel,** 1833–96, who established the Nobel Prize.
Antiseptic surgery was introduced by the British physician **Lord Lister,** 1827–1912, by 1867. Following Pasteur's research into the nature of disease, he used carbolic acid to disinfect the operating theater.

1867–1870

Napoleon III instituted liberal reforms to quell growing opposition, but his empire collapsed in the face of a Prussian invasion, 1870
By 1870 the railway systems of France, England, and Belgium were virtually complete, stimulating heavy industry.
The victory of Mutsuhito, *r.*1868–1912, in Japan led to a policy of industrialization and an end to the shoguns.
Black suffrage was enforced in the United States, 1870.

Pres. Andrew Johnson, 1801–75, was impeached by the House but exonerated in the Senate, 1868. Wyoming territory granted women the vote, 1869.

Karl Marx

Papal infallibility was asserted by the first Vatican Council, 1869–70, which ruled that the pope or an ecumenical council of bishops was immune from error when pronouncing on matters of faith or morals. The pope's increased prestige resulting from this ruling partly compensated for the loss of the Papal States to Italy.
The classic statement of the case for women's suffrage was presented by **J. S. Mill** in *The Subjection of Women,* 1869.

The great novels of Fyodor Dostoevsky, 1821–81, including *Crime and Punishment,* 1866, *The Brothers Karamazov,* 1879–80, and *The Idiot,* 1868, study totalitarianism, the conflict between atheism and compassionate Christianity, and good and evil in man.
The English novelist Charles Dickens continued his prodigious output of social novels.

Mural painting in France was revived by **Pierre Puvis de Chavannes,** 1824–1898, whose monumental style and subdued colors seen in "Ludus Pro Patria", 1865–69, inspired the Symbolists of the 1880s. The effects of light out of doors on the surface of an object or figure were first captured and faithfully recorded by **Claude Monet,** 1840–1926, in his painting "Women in the Garden," 1866–70.

Wagner revolutionized opera, using a continuously moving harmonic structure over which leit motive identified dramatic elements. He believed opera should combine all the arts.

The typewriter was developed commercially after the 1867 invention of American **Christopher Sholes,** 1819–90. He was the first to use today's keyboard. The Periodic Table of the elements was devised by the Russian chemist **Dmitry Mendeleev,** 1834–1907, in 1869. From the table he predicted the properties of three new elements, all of which were found within twenty years.

1870–1872

A revolutionary commune set up in Paris, 1871, was ruthlessly suppressed. It rejected the authority of the French government after the surrender to Prussia.
Prussia's seizure of Alsace-Lorraine completed German unification, and a German Empire was proclaimed under **William I,** *r.*1861–88.
An American attempt to open up Korea failed, 1871–73, but Britain forced the Treaty of Pangkor on Malaya.

Railroad service linked Boston, Mass., to Oakland, Calif., 1870. Scandals rocked President Grant's administration.

William I acclaimed German emperor at Versailles

Bakunin 1814–76, a Russian anarchist, stressed the need for violent revolution to overthrow the state and allow the essential goodness of man to develop. His rejection of centralization and subordination to authority in favor of the free spirit of revolt led to his expulsion from the **International,** 1872, after conflicting with Marx.
Johann von Döllinger, a German theologian, 1799–1890, was excommunicated, 1871, for opposing the idea of infallibility.

George Eliot, the pseudonym of Mary Anne Evans, 1819–80, described the conflicts within English provincial society in *Middlemarch,* 1871–72.
The early French symbolist poets Arthur Rimbaud, 1859–91, and **Paul Verlaine,** 1844–96, aimed to devise a truly poetic visionary language; Rimbaud wrote *Une Saison en Enfer,* 1873.

Monet's painting, "Impression, Sunrise", 1872, exhibited in 1874 with works by **Pierre Auguste Renoir,** 1841–1919, **Alfred Sisley,** 1839–99, **Edgar Degas,** 1834–1917, **Pissarro,** and **Cézanne,** gave its name to the Impressionist movement with which these painters were associated. **Impressionism** abandoned traditional linear representation, aiming to capture the fleeting effects of light and color by using small dashes and strokes of color.

César Franck, 1822–90, a Belgian working in the classical tradition, attracted little attention in his lifetime but influenced an important group of younger French composers.

Light was shown to be an electromagnetic radiation by the British physicist **James Clerk-Maxwell,** 1831–79. He predicted other such radiations.

1872–1875

The conservative Third Republic was set up in France after the defeat of the Commune, in spite of repeated attempts to restore the monarchy.
Britain bought a decisive share in the **Suez Canal,** 1875, thus acquiring a quick route to India.
French power in Indochina, extended by Napoleon III, was confirmed, 1874.
The revelation of corruption in the Grant administration in the US resulted in financial panic and economic depression.

In 1873 a depression struck. Barbed wire influenced the development of the West after 1874, solving fencing problems of prairie settlers.

An upsurge of religious revivalism associated with the Temperance Movement, which saw alcohol as the cause of working-class degradation, was started in America and Britain by **D. L. Moody,** 1837–99.
Wilhelm Wundt, 1832–1920, a German who published *Principles of Physiological Psychology,* 1873–74, established experimental psychology. He sought to investigate by introspection the immediate experiences of consciousness.

Jules Laforgue, 1860–87, a symbolist, was one of the first French poets to use free verse.

The later Pre-Raphaelite style in England, best represented by the work of **Edward Burne-Jones,** 1833–98, like the "Briar Rose" series, 1871–90, later influenced the Symbolist movement.
London's first garden suburb, Bedford Park at Turnham Green, was designed by the Victorian architect and associate of **William Morris, Richard Norman Shaw,** 1831–1912, in 1875.

Johannes Brahms, 1833–97, carried on Beethoven's tradition especially in the symphony. Brahms' classical control of the emotional impulses in his music gives it a rich dramatic quality.

The Challenger expedition of 1872–76 founded oceanography. Intermolecular forces were calculated by **Johannes van der Walls,** 1837–1923, in 1873. He accurately described the behavior of real gases, using mathematical equations.

The age of imperialism 1875–1900

Principal events

Domination of the world outside the Americas lay with a few European states. Among them Britain was still the greatest imperial and industrial power, but Germany now increasingly challenged this position. The US also grew in strength and by 1900 overtook Britain in the production of basic industrial materials.

The emergence of a group of fixed alliances in Europe served to polarize foreign affairs and the Balkans, in particular, presented an inflammatory arena for international conflict.

Improvements in communications, however, and the quest for new bases of economic and political power shifted the focus of rivalries among the states to Africa and Oceania. Britain greatly extended its empire but the other European states, the US, and a newly modernized Japan also joined in the scramble. By 1899 all Asia was in the hands of Europe and China was in thrall to the West.

1875–1877

Britain bought the khedive's Suez Canal shares, 1875, and annexed South Africa, 1877.
The Slav nationalist forces in the Balkans erupted against Turkey, and the Bulgarian massacres, 1875, aroused a public outcry in Britain. Russia supported the insurgents, hoping to win new authority in the Balkans.
The Satsuma rebellion, 1877, led by conservative forces in Japan, failed to halt the tide of reform and new ideas.

1877–1880

After Russia's defeat of Turkey, 1878, Britain and Austria-Hungary intervened to check Russian ambitions, and the Powers met at the Congress of Berlin, 1878, to decide the future of the Balkans.
Germany and Austria-Hungary formed a Dual Alliance, 1879.
In Afghanistan Britain sought to secure her position in India against Russian expansion 1878–80.
Chile began her successful war against Bolivia and Peru, 1879.

1880–1882

British imperial expansion in Africa was checked by defeat in the Transvaal, 1881, but British occupation forces were installed in Egypt in 1882.
Under Bismarck, 1815–98, Germany aimed to build a solid European power structure, signing the **Three Emperors' Alliance** with Russia and Austria, 1881, and a similar alliance with Italy, 1882. At home, Bismarck introduced sickness benefits to help weaken the growing appeal of socialism.

1882–1885

Britain consolidated its positio on the Afghan border and in Egypt but was defeated by nat forces in the Sudan, 1885.
France took Indochina, 1884.
The Treaty of Berlin, 1884, de fined the rights of 14 Europea powers in Africa. This helped stop the scramble for colonies which could have led to a maj war.
Eastern Rumelia's union with Bulgaria, 1885, provoked war with Siberia, and Austria actec to save Serbia from invasion.

National events

The United States began to take its place among the great powers. Domestic issues included labor and Indian unrest. Financial difficulties following the Panic of 1893 continued for nearly five years before prosperity returned. Imperialist interests were manifested in the Spanish-American War.

Members of the terrorist organization, the Molly Maguires, were executed, 1876. Indians killed **Gen. George A. Custer,** 1839–76, at the Little Bighorn.

In 1878, the Knights of Labor, a secret group formed in 1869, became a national order. Open to both skilled and unskilled, it was the first successful US union.

From 1862–82, there were 200,000 Chinese immigrants. The Chinese Exclusion Act, 1882, banned Chinese workers for 10 years.

The Pendleton Act, 1883, required standardized exams for civil service jobs. New York City's Brooklyn Bridge was cor pleted, 1883.

Maxim machine gun

Paris Exhibition 1889: the Machine Hall

Queen Victoria

Religion and philosophy

Growing interest in the attempt to link social theory to biological evolutionism gave rise to more subtle sociological and anthropological studies in the English-speaking world. Drawing on the experience of colonial administration, men such as Tylor, Spencer, and Frazer developed the notion of a natural progression between "primitive" and "advanced" societies. Meanwhile in Vienna, Freud began to formulate influential ideas on the subconscious and human nature.

In philosophy the absolute idealism of Hegel found its first supporters in England with Bradley, while in the United States pragmatic thinkers such as William James argued that the truth of an idea depends on its social function.

The ideology of anti-Semitism grew up in the wake of heightened nationalist sentiment, while an evolutionary type of socialism grew more popular than its revolutionary counterpart.

Hinduism witnessed the rise of various reform movements in the 19th century under the impact of Western thought. Most important was that led by **Ramakrishna,** 1836–86, an extreme ascetic in the Vedanta tradition, who believed that all religions were essentially identical.
The Theosophical Society, which set out to foster the transmission of Eastern thought to the West, was founded in New York in 1875 by **Helena Blavatsky,** 1831–91.

The Jehovah's Witnesses, an evangelical movement believing in the second coming of Christ, was founded by **Charles Russell,** 1852–1916, in the United States.
Christian Science was founded in Boston by **Mary Baker Eddy,** 1821–1910, who rejected medicine and saw prayer as the only cure for illness.
Heinrich von Treitscke, 1834–96, fostered German nationalism in his *History of Germany in the 19th Century,* 1879–94.

A theory of social evolution was developed by the Englishman **Edward Tylor,** 1832–1917, in his *Anthropology,* 1881. Through studying primitive religion, he concluded that many existing social customs were "survivals" from earlier stages of development. Similar ideas were defended in America by **Lewis Morgan,** 1818–81, who developed the study of kinship systems.

In Russia, **Peter Kropotkin,** 1842–1921, was the leading theorist of the Anarchist move ment. In *Words of a Rebel,* 1884, he emphasized nonvio lence and argued that coopera tion rather than conflict was th basis of evolutionary progress.
The Fabian Society, founded in Britain, 1883–84, advocated a gradual evolution toward socialism.
The Zionist Movement held its first conference in Prussia in 1884 as anti-Semitism grew.

Literature

The pessimistic application of theories of evolution is found in Zola's naturalistic novels, which stressed the limitations on man's actions stemming from his inherited characteristics and the environment and portrayed the most sordid aspects of French lower-class life. In the same period English literature entered a more reflective stage, losing the exuberance of Dickens.

Nationalism still acted as a vital cultural stimulus, creating a school of national regeneration in Spain in reaction to the political weakness highlighted by the war with Cuba, and in Italy celebrating unification. In both, writers turned to their national classics for models. The first self-conscious Latin American school grew up asserting independence from European traditions.

English literature after 1875 saw a reaction to the confidence of the high Victorian era, reflected in the Decadent poetry of **Algernon Charles Swinburne,** 1837–1909. His sensual *Poems and Ballads* show traces of symbolist influences.
Gerard Manley Hopkins, 1844–89, described the tensions of his religious vision in lyrical, experimental poetry.

Realism in the theater was pioneered by the Norwegian **Henrik Ibsen,** 1828–1906, who dramatized social issues using ordinary conversation, as in *A Doll's House,* 1879. In England **G. B. Shaw,** 1856–1950, also attacked social complacency in plays enlivened by vivid characterization, satire, and wit such as *Mrs. Warren's Profession* and *The Devil's Disciple.*

Native American humor was found in *The Adventures of Huckleberry Finn* by **Mark Twain,** 1835–1910.
The meeting of the New World with the Old was explored by **Henry James,** 1843–1916, in *Portrait of a Lady,* 1881. He probed subtleties of character, temperament, and motive, as in *Washington Square* and the dazzling *The Golden Bowl.*

Naturalism in literature was ina gurated in France by **Emile Zola** 1840–1902, who explored deterministic notions of the rel tion between heredity and envi ronment and the casualties of urban society in the novels *Les Rougon Macquart,* 1871–93.
Guy de Maupassant, 1850–93, followed him in his novels and short stories such as *Boule de Suif.*

Art and architecture

A self-conscious and revolutionary avant-garde emerged in European art at the end of the 19th century. In France Van Gogh, Gauguin, and Cézanne, the major innovators of that time, developed their different styles out of their Impressionist origins. The Symbolists rejected the Impressionist vision, turning instead to the past and to the exotic imagery of the later English Pre-Raphaelites in which Art Nouveau, an essentially decorative style and the first non-historical style to win wide acceptance, also had roots. Beginning in Belgium and England, Art Nouveau owed its original character to a semi-abstract use of natural forms and had far-reaching effects in architecture and the applied arts.

Construction in metal became even more popular after the Paris exhibitions of 1878 and 1889, encouraged by the substitution of steel for iron, which also made possible the development of the skyscraper in the US.

A parallel to the Impressionist idea of forms dissolved in light appeared in the work of the greatest 19th-century sculptor, **Auguste Rodin,** 1840–1917, who produced his first free-standing figure, "Age of Bronze," in 1877.

Ballet girls, working girls, and cabaret artists were the subject matter for such works of **Edgar Degas** as "Scènes de Ballet," 1879. He worked in a great variety of media and was influenced by the action photographs of dancers and racing horses taken by **Muybridge.**
A Slavic revival in Russia reached its peak in the 1870s and 80s based on a careful documentation of national cultural history.

Official painting in England was represented by **Lawrence Alma-Tadema,** 1836–1912, and **Frederick Leighton,** 1830–96, who painted pseudo-classical scenes in a realistic though sentimental manner.
A move away from Impressionism was evident in the works of **Paul Cézanne,** 1839–1906, who achieved an almost abstract quality in such paintings as "L'Estaque," *c.*1882–85, with its emphasis on form, color, planes, and light.

Neo-Impressionism or **Pointillis** was developed by **Georges Seu rat,** 1859–91, **Paul Signac** 1863–1935, and **Camille Pis sarro,** 1830–1903. A reaction against the spontaneity of Im pressionism, it created the opti cal effect of light by means of dots of color, which were fuse by the eye into continuous tone
The Berlin Reichstag, 1884–94 and the **Victor Emmanuele II** monument in Rome, 1885–1911, used antique forms to create a sense of civic grandeu

Music

Romanticism began to decline as nationalism and impressionism became more important ideals in music. Meanwhile the future of American and European popular music was formed in the United States with the increasing appreciation of the rhythmic genius of black folk musicians and an awareness of the potential of the newly developed phonograph.

The origins of jazz and blues are found in the work songs that united poor blacks as they toiled in fields, and in gospel songs that united them in church.

Art songs were composed all over Europe, after decades of domination by German lieder writers. The form was finely worked by French composers like **Henri Duparc,** 1848–1933.

English light opera, notably the deft, tuneful creations of **W. S. Gilbert,** 1836–1911, and **Arthur Sullivan,** 1842–1900, became a craze throughout Europe, the US, and Australia.

National qualities appeared in 'serious music both out of patri tism, heard in **Bedřich Smetana** Czech *Ma Vlast,* 1874–75, and of exoticism, in **Alexis Emmanuel Chabrier's** *España,* 188

Science and technology

Germany now took the lead in the science-based industries as a result of the emphasis on science and technology in education and a political system that gave power to industry. It possessed a flourishing heavy industry, became the center of early automobile development, and led the field in medicine, now a preventive as well as a curative science, with the discovery of antibodies and of new drugs. Koch's work on tuberculosis was the most important advance. As a result of these technical discoveries combined with the widespread building of new hospitals, mortality rates dropped throughout western Europe. Other technological achievements that would alter society were the inventions of the telephone and phonograph.

Classical physics failed to explain discoveries made in radioactivity and the problem posed by the Michelson-Morley experiment, and entered a time of uncertainty that would only be resolved by Einstein's theory of relativity.

The telephone was patented in 1876 by the American inventor **Alexander Bell,** 1847–1922.
Bacteria were identified by methods of growing and staining cultures, developed from 1876 onward by the German bacteriologist **Robert Koch,** 1843–1910. He found the bacteria that cause tuberculosis, anthrax, and cholera.
The phonograph was invented in 1877 by the American inventor **Thomas Edison,** 1847–1931.

In 1879 **Edison** patented his incandescent light bulb. But in 1878, **Joseph Swan,** a British physicist, had patented the **first successful filament electric lamp.** In 1879–80 both Swan and Edison independently produced a practical light bulb.
Piezoelectricity, electricity produced by the compression of certain types of crystal, was discovered, 1880, by a Frenchman, **Pierre Curie,** 1859–1906.

The ether was proved not to exist by the experiments of the American physicists **Albert Michelson,** 1852–1931, and **Edward Morley,** 1838–1923, from 1881. This result led to the **theory of relativity.**
The electric trolley first ran in Berlin in 1881.
Cell division was described in 1882 by the German anatomist **Walther Flemming,** 1843–1905. Following Koch's work, **Pasteur** used attenuated bacteria to confer immunity to anthrax, 1881, and against rabies, 1885.

H. S. Maxim, 1840–1916, invented the **Maxim machine gun** in England, 1884.
The steam turbine was made in 1884 by the British engineer **Charles Parsons,** 1854–1931.
Motor transport was founded in 1885 with the invention of the automobile by **Karl Benz,** 1844–1929, a German enginee In the same year another Germa engineer, **Gottlieb Daimler,** 1834–1900, patented a gasolir engine that he used initially to power a motorcycle.

385–1887

e Canadian Pacific Railway s completed, 1885. American Indians were con- ed to reservations by 1887. e American Federation of La- was set up in 1886. rmany signed a Reinsurance eaty with Russia, 1887, to nimize the danger of war be- een them in the Balkans. tain, Italy, and Austria-Hungary reed to maintain the status o in the Mediterranean and the ar East, 1887.

1887–1890

The partition of Africa neared completion with Britain dominat ing the center and south. **In Japan, Emperor Meiji,** *r.*1867–1912, granted a Western style constitution. **In France** the war minister **Georges Boulanger,** 1837–91, attempted to seize power. **The US overtook Britain** in steel production by 1890. **The Social-Democratic party,** the most popular in Germany, was legalized, 1890.

1890–1892

In Germany, **Kaiser William II,** *r.*1888–1918, dismissed Bismarck in 1890 and let the treaty with Russia lapse. **The European alliance blocs** took shape. **The Triple Alliance** of Germany, Austria-Hungary, and Italy was renewed in 1891. Russia and France made a **Dual Alliance,** 1891. **Brazil** adopted a federal republican constitution, 1891. **In the US,** the **Populist party** grew out of agrarian protest at currency deflation.

1892–1895

In the victorious war against China, 1894–95, Japan gained Formosa and a free hand in Korea. The Powers' scramble for diplomatic and trading concessions in China began. **Sergei Witte,** 1849–1915, reformed Russian finances and stimulated industrialization and eastward expansion, 1890s. **The Dreyfus case,** 1894–99, revealed deep splits in French society between the liberal radicals and the Church and army.

1895–1897

After the abortive Jameson raid, 1895–96, Britain faced a crisis with the Boer Republics. **On the Nile, Lord Kitchener,** 1850–1916, began a campaign to reconquer the Sudan, 1896–98. In **Victoria's** Diamond Jubilee Year, 1897, British imperialism was at its peak. **France** aimed to consolidate the Saharan empire with a sphere of influence in Morocco. **Russia** threatened China, where the Powers gained territory and concessions, 1897–98.

1897–1900

In China, 1898, reactionary forces acted to stop the Westernizing **Hundred Days of Reform,** and an anti-foreign **"Boxer" Rebellion,** 1900, brought disruption and resulted in foreign intervention. **Britain** became entangled in the Boer War (1899–1902). **Faced with depression** the US raised its tariff wall, 1897, and joined in expansion overseas, fighting Spain, 1898, over **Cuba** and securing **Puerto Rico** and the **Philippines.**

---

muel Gompers, 1850–1924, s the first president of the nerican Federation of Labor, 86. The Haymarket Massacre curred in Chicago, 1886.

The Interstate Commerce Act was passed, 1887. There was a land rush in Oklahoma, 1889. In 1890, Congress passed the Sherman Antitrust Act.

In 1890, Indian desires to regain land were expressed in the ritual of the Ghost Dance. The Battle of Wounded Knee, 1890, ended the Ghost Dance War.

Wage reductions brought the violent Pullman Strike in Chicago, 1894, led by Socialist Eugene V. Debs, 1855–1926.

The "separate but equal" doctrine was established by the Supreme Court, 1896, in *Plessy v. Ferguson.* The Yukon Territory had a gold rush, 1897–98.

The Spanish-American War, 1898, triggered by the *Maine* sinking, brought new territories under US control. The Open Door Policy began in China, 1899.

ll at his telephone, 1892

Benz Velo motor car, 1896

Art nouveau: Horta interior

Leopard from Benin treasures

Sigmund Freud

---

edrich Nietzsche, 1844–1900, German, vehemently rejected ristianity, science, and con- mist moralities in *Beyond od and Evil,* 1886. **ouard Drumont;** 1844–1917, pularized anti-Semitism in *La ance Juive,* 1886. **rdinand Tönnies,** 1855–1936, e German sociologist, pub- hed *Community and Associa- n,* 1887, distinguishing "com- unities," involving moral con- nsus, from "associations," sed on self-interest.

James Frazer, 1854–1941, a British anthropologist, surveyed a great range of beliefs and customs in *The Golden Bough,* 1890. He claimed that there was a natural progression from magical, through religious, to scientific belief systems.

The Neo-classical school of economics was established by the Englishman **Alfred Marshall,** 1842–1924, in his *Principles of Economics,* 1890. He united the "classical" view that prices are determined by costs with the "marginalist" view of **W. S. Jevons,** 1835–82, that prices depend on the interaction of supply and demand. **Kang Yu-wei,** 1858–1927, advocated social equality in China and argued that Confucius had supported historical progress.

Herbert Spencer, 1820–1903, constructed and popularized a **comprehensive evolutionary theory** that saw all things as progressing from simplicity to complexity. His sociology, based on an analogy between societies and organisms, used the idea of the survival of the fittest. **F. H. Bradley,** 1846–1924, was an English proponent of Hegel. He argued that an idea's truth depended on its coherence with the set of ideas comprising the Absolute.

Philosophical pragmatism was expounded by the American psychologist **William James,** 1842–1910, in *The Will to Believe,* 1897. He argued that a belief was true if its acceptance aided the solution of practical problems. **Emile Durkheim,** 1858–1917, stirred French opinion with his sociological study *Suicide,* 1897, which attempted to link positivist social ideas with an interest in morality, which he saw as the basis of society.

Sigmund Freud, 1856–1939, elaborated the main tenets of psychoanalytic theory in *The Interpretation of Dreams,* 1900, developed in the course of clinical experience in Vienna. He divided the mind among the ego, id, and superego, and argued that psychological disorders stemmed from the repression of sexual urges in early life. His emphasis on the subconscious influenced later irrationalism. **H.S. Chamberlain,** 1855–1927, spread racist ideas in Germany.

---

mbolist poetry developed in ance with the *Poésies,* 1887, **Stéphane Mallarmé,** 42–98. He sought for an ideal rld, but one of the intellect d not the emotions. **aurice Maeterlinck,** 1862– 49, in Belgium, wrote sym- list plays. In Sweden **August rindberg,** 1849–1912, wrote ays such as *Miss Julie* in a turalist vein.

Italian nationalist ideas were voiced by **Giosuè Carducci,** 1835–1907. A scholar and anti-romantic, his *Odi Barbare* is a patriotic vision of Italy's glorious past and future destiny. **Verismo,** Italian realism, was developed by **Giovanni Verga,** 1840–1922, whose novels combined a perceptive study of the Sicilian class structure with the personal cares of *Mastro Don Gesualdo.*

In novels of English rural life such as *Tess of the D'Urbervilles,* 1891, **Thomas Hardy,** 1840–1928, expressed a pessimistic view of life in which man was swamped by cosmic ironies. **The English Decadent movement** is epitomized by *The Picture of Dorian Gray,* 1891, by Oscar Wilde, 1854–1900.

Knut Hamsun, 1859–1952, a Norwegian, condemned an overemphasis on social issues. **The stories and poems of Rudyard Kipling,** 1865–1936, examined the relationship between British and Indian culture. **H. G. Wells** pioneered science fiction in *The Time Machine.*

Russian realist drama reached its peak with the work of **Anton Chekhov,** 1860–1904, which had a huge effect on European drama, notably *Uncle Vanya* and *The Seagull.* Chekhov was also a masterly short story writer, able to convey pessimistic themes with a humorous twist. **The Greek poet Cavafy,** 1863–1933, wrote about the ironies of man's existence.

The height of the **Modernismo** movement in South America was realized in *Prosas Profanas* by the Nicaraguan poet **Rubén Dário,** 1867–1916. **The Generation of '98,** a group of Spanish intellectuals, set out to counteract Spanish apathy and revitalize Spanish culture. The group included the poet, philosopher, and novelist **Miguel Unamuno,** 1864–1936.

---

mbolist art, which developed er 1886, appealed to the agination and the senses. In ance its chief exponents were **stave Moreau,** 1826–98, ose paintings have a rich, vellike quality, and **Odilon don,** 1840–1916. **pressionist ideas** were taken England by **Wilson Steer,** 60–1942, and **Walter Sickert,** 60–1942, who set up the **w English Art Club,** 1886, in otest against pseudoclassical les.

Vincent van Gogh, 1853–90, a painter obsessed with the problems of expression, painted tormented landscapes and portraits using heightened color and a frenzied and turbulent style seen in "The Sower," 1888. **The Eiffel Tower** was constructed in 1889, demonstrating contemporary engineering skills.

Synthetism, characterized by strong flat colors in well-defined areas, was developed by **Paul Gauguin,** 1848–1903, in Tahiti. He influenced the **Nabis,** a group of French painters led by **Paul Serusier,** 1865–1927, who rejected Impressionism. **German Expressionism** can be seen in the works of the Norwegian painter **Edvard Munch,** 1863–1944, who expressed intense emotion in his "Frieze of Life," *c.*1890–1900.

Art Nouveau, an international decorative style using flat, flowing, and tendrillike forms, was popularized in England by the graphics of **Aubrey Beardsley,** 1872–98, from 1893, and the buildings of **Victor Horta,** 1861–1947, in Belgium. **Gothic forms and wild extravagant decoration** characterized the buildings of the Spanish architect **Antoni Gaudi,** 1856–1926. His church of **Sagrada Familia** in Barcelona, from 1893, is related to Art Nouveau.

The Vienna Sezession, set up to promote the Austrian form of Art Nouveau, 1897, was concerned mainly with interior design. **Gustav Klimt,** 1862–1918, was its leading exponent. **The English Vernacular style** of domestic architecture pioneered by **C. A. Voysey,** 1857–1941, emphasized natural materials and solid construction and developed many of the designs which became part of a modern (non-historical) European style.

A large collection of Benin art, the first African art well known in Europe, was brought back by a punitive expedition in 1897. **The Chicago school of architecture** pioneered a modern American public style, creating the skyscraper. The Schiesinger-Mayer store by **Louis Sullivan,** 1856–1924, begun in 1899, rose to nine floors and had detailing suggestive of Art Nouveau.

---

ssian music gained its national alities – lyricism, vitality, and lorful orchestration – in the rk of **Peter Tchaikovsky,** 40–93, and **Nikolai Rimsky- rsakov,** 1844–1908.

Symphonic traditions continued in Europe with vast works by **Anton Bruckner,** 1824–96, and **Gustav Mahler,** 1860–1911, who introduced folk elements.

National styles developed in the works of composers like **Jean Sibelius,** 1865–1957, in Finland and **Isaac Albéniz,** 1860–1909, in Spain.

Claude-Achille Debussy, 1862–1918, brought Impressionism to music. His intricate tone color and continuous form utilized exquisite harmony and a whole tone scale.

The American John Sousa, 1854–1932, wrote superb **marches** for marine bands, including *The Stars and Stripes Forever,* 1897.

Ragtime was played in the US in the 1890s by black pianists, notably by **Scott Joplin,** 1868–1917. The bright syncopation of the style overlaid European dance and march forms.

---

uminum could be produced onomically from 1886 by the ectrolytic process developed most at the same time by an nerican chemist, **Charles Hall,** 63–1914, and a French chem- , **Paul Héroult,** 1863–1914. **dio waves were produced** out 1887 by **Heinrich Hertz,** 57–94, a German physicist. **ison** set up a **research labora- y** at West Orange, N.J., 1887, th teams of inventors working gether systematically.

The pneumatic tire was invented in 1888 by the British veterinarian, **John Dunlop,** 1840–1921. **Photographic film** and paper were developed, 1884–88, by **George Eastman,** 1854–1932, an American inventor. Eastman's work made the moving picture, as well as still photography, a possibility.

Diphtheria antitoxin was isolated in 1892 by the German biologist **Paul Ehrlich,** 1854–1915.

The cinema was founded with the development of a good ciné camera and projector by the French inventors **Auguste Lumière,** 1862–1954, and his brother **Louis,** 1864–1948. The first public showing of their films took place in 1895. **X rays** were discovered, 1895, by the German physicist **Wilhelm Röentgen,** 1845–1923; they were soon used in medicine.

Radioactivity was discovered, 1896, by the French physicist **Antoine Becquerel,** 1852–1908. **The diesel engine** was invented by **Rudolf Diesel,** 1858–1913, and demonstrated in 1896. **The electron** was discovered in 1897 by the British physicist **J. J. Thomson,** 1856–1940. Thomson detected electrons in cathode rays and reasoned that all atoms contain electrons. **Malaria** was shown to be transmitted by the mosquito by the British physician **Sir Ronald Ross,** 1857–1932, in 1897.

The theoretical basis for space travel was provided by **Konstantin Tsiolkovsky,** 1857–1935. **Marie Curie,** 1867–1934, working with her husband **Pierre,** discovered polonium and radium in 1898. **Viruses** were discovered, 1898, by **Martinus Beijerinck,** 1851–1931. **Radioactivity** was found to include alpha rays and beta rays, in 1899 by a British physicist, **Ernest Rutherford,** 1871–1937. In 1913 he would use the rays to penetrate the atom.

Europe plunges into war 1900–1925

Principal events

World War I, arising from political and economic competition among the European Powers, dominated the period. In it, Europe suffered great losses in manpower and economic strength, while the United States and Japan won new political prestige. The need for organization on an unprecedented scale brought social and political upheaval in many countries. The old empires disappeared, leaving many new nationally based states, an embittered and dismembered Germany, and a communist Russia. Fear of socialism grew stronger and was linked with economic discontent to stimulate fascism in Italy.

The new location of power outside Europe and the rise of nationalism in India and China marked the transition from an international order based firmly on Europe to a world arena of politics, which would lead to widespread decolonization after World War I.

1900–1902

As France and Italy made an entente in 1902, weakening Italy's links with Germany. **Britain** emerged successfully from the **Boer War,** 1899–1902, and formed an alliance with **Japan.** This countered the Russian presence in **Manchuria** and encouraged Japan's expansionist ambitions in Asia.
The US Congress authorized the construction of the Panama Canal, appropriating $40,000,000, 1902.

1902–1905

The Entente Cordiale, 1904, of France and Britain settled the two powers' outstanding colonial disputes, especially in Egypt.
Japan firmly established her military power, defeating Russia in 1905 in Manchuria.
In defeat Russia was convulsed, 1905–06, with a revolution against tsarist autocracy by the industrial and intellectual classes.
Intervention by William II *r.*1888–1918, in Morocco, 1905, threatened French supremacy.

1905–1907

The Powers met at Algeçiras in 1906 to settle the Moroccan question in favor of France.
Tsarist rule in Russia was reimposed with only minor constitutional reforms.
Russia and Japan reached agreement over China in 1907.
Britain, France, and Spain agreed to oppose German naval expansion in the Mediterranean.
An Anglo-Russian Convention covered Persia, Afghanistan, and Tibet and brought Britain into Europe's power blocs.

1907–1910

Increasing Anglo-German comp tition was expressed in a race build warships.
With Russian agreement, Austr annexed Bosnia-Herzegovina ir 1908.
Nationalist unrest in Catalonia disrupted Spain, 1909.
The Powers intervened to prevent a Serbo-Austrian war.
India secured constitutional re forms in 1909.
The former Boer republics helped form a new dominion, t **Union of South Africa,** 1910.

National events

Technological advances affected labor and industry as well as business practices. The United States was fully recognized as a world power and fought in World War I. Social changes were underway, with temperance advocates, fundamentalist religious groups, and political reformers wielding influence.

Pres. William McKinley, 1843–1901, was assassinated. **J. P. Morgan,** 1837–1913, merged several firms into an industrial combination, US Steel.

Wilbur, 1867–1912, and **Orville,** 1871–1948, **Wright** flew the first airplane, 1903. The Industrial Workers of the World was founded by **Eugene V. Debs,** 1905.

Almost 700 people died in an earthquake and fire in San Francisco, 1906. In 1907, **George W. Goethals,** 1858–1928, directed Panama Canal construction.

The Model T Ford, designed by **Henry Ford,** 1863–1947, was sold in 1908. It was the first automobile made on an assemb line.

Wright Brothers' flight

Model T Ford

TO WIN
FREEDOM
FOR
WOMEN

Suffragettes, 1911

World War I: German skeleton in the trenches

Religion and philosophy

The philosophies of Bergson, Croce, Dilthey, and Husserl, stressing intuition and immediate sympathy as the basic method of understanding, contributed to the development of a concept of the human sciences distinct from the natural sciences.

Under their influence Max Weber investigated the motives as well as the causes of human action, notably the effect of religion on man's supposedly "rational" economic behavior. Russell and Wittgenstein, however, still took science and mathematics as the paradigm of knowledge in their work on the logical structure of language.

Psychoanalytic theory continued to explore the nature of the unconscious, but two of Freud's colleagues, Adler and Jung, criticized his insistence on the sexual basis of neuroses.

The Russian Revolution accentuated the socialist split between violence and the peaceful battle for working-class rights.

Vilfredo Pareto, 1848–1923, an Italian and a posivitist, wrote *The Socialist Systems,* 1902, a refutation of Marxist economics and sociology. He accepted the existence of class conflict but saw the process Marx described as a series of progressive revolutions as no more than the successive replacement of ruling elites by each other.
The Pentecostal Movement began in America *c.*1902.

Max Weber, 1864–1920, a German historian and sociologist, was concerned to combat the influential Marxist school of historical materialism. He opposed a simplistic belief in economic determinism and stressed the causal role of ideas in history.
In France, Maurice Barrès, 1862–1923, and **Charles Maurras,** 1868–1952, argued influentially for cultural unity, the supremacy of the state, and the primacy of the national interest.

Henri Bergson, 1859–1941, in *Creative Evolution,* 1907, stressed the importance of change through a creative life-force, in opposition to the static scientific view of nature. This view that intuition was superior to scientific or intellectual perception was echoed by **Wilhelm Dilthey,** 1833–1911, in Germany, to support an ethical relativism.
The Modernist Movement in Catholicism was condemned by Pope Pius X in 1907.

The German historian Friedrich Meinecke, 1862–1954, looked for a meaning within the histor cal process itself, but sought to avoid cultural relativism. His *Cosmopolitanism and the Natio State,* 1908, acknowledged the significance of the unification Germany but regretted the deat of the culture that preceded it.
Georges Sorel, 1847–1922, in *Reflections on Violence,* 1908, celebrated the use of violence and rejected all bourgeois values. He influenced Mussolini.

Literature

The need for new forms of self-expression able to encompass a growing awareness of the unconscious gave rise to many strong and individualistic movements in European literature. The surrealists evolved out of the symbolists, and their attempt to "trap" the subconscious in a spontaneous literary form broke down all restrictions of style.

In the English-speaking world a more formal school grew up with the modernist poets Pound and Eliot.

The German Expressionists were among the first to voice a lack of faith in society. Their prophecies were realized with World War I, the image of which haunted later writers.

Japan came into contact with Western realist and naturalist schools.

The Celtic literary Renaissance was a cultural reflection of Irish independence. Ancient legends were revived by **W. B. Yeats,** 1865–1939, **J. M. Synge,** 1871–1909, and **Sean O'Casey,** 1884–1964.
Revolution and man's capacity to withstand extremities dominate the novels of **Joseph Conrad,** 1857–1924, such as *Lord Jim,* 1900.

Impressionism, a German literary style that set out to describe complex emotional states by using symbolic imagery, is used in *Das Stundenbuch,* 1905, by **Rainer Marie Rilke,** 1875–1926.
James Joyce, 1882–1941, was self-consciously Irish but hostile to the Celtic Renaissance.

With the publication of *Kormichiye,* 1907, **Vyacheslav Ivanovich Ivanov,** 1866–1949, was acclaimed leader of the Russian Symbolist movement, which also included the poet **Alexander Blok,** 1880–1921.
Stefan George, 1868–1933, was influenced by Nietzsche in his desire to ennoble German culture with his esoteric poetry, such as *The Seventh Ring,* 1907.

Modern Japanese fiction began after 1905 with a powerful natu ralist school including **Shimazal Toson,** 1872–1943, and **Tayam Katai. Mori Ogai,** 1862–1922, reacted against their obsession with squalor in *Vita Sexualis,* 1909.
The American **Jack London,** 1876–1916, was stirred by social injustices to write popular tales and political tracts.

Art and architecture

Traditional forms and concepts of art were dramatically broken down between 1900 and 1925 as a variety of alternative aesthetic principles developed. In particular Cubism attempted to break away from the conventions of perspective that had ruled European art since the Renaissance, while Dadaism and Russian Constructivism aimed to destroy the distinction between art and life.

In architecture, too, definitive new styles emerged in the US and Europe with the publication of Frank Lloyd Wright's early designs and the establishment of the Bauhaus, both emphasizing asymmetry and plain surfaces.
The cinema transformed the whole scope of the visual arts, developing from the early popular experiments of 1900 to the politically motivated films of Eisenstein in Russia (where the Revolution stimulated artistic innovation in many fields), the dramas of Griffith, and the popular comedies of Chaplin.

In Paris **Pablo Picasso,** 1881–1973, began his Blue period, 1901–04, and his Rose period, 1905, producing lyrical, conventionally representational paintings.
The Intimiste painters Edouard Vuillard, 1868–1940, and **Pierre Bonnard,** 1867–1947, used Impressionist techniques in domestic scenes after 1900.

Cubism, rejecting traditional methods of portraying reality, began in 1907 with **Picasso's** "Demoiselles d'Avignon," 1907. Other Cubists include **Juan Gris,** 1887–1927, **Robert Delaunay,** 1885–1941, **Fernand Léger,** 1881–1955, and **Georges Braque,** 1882–1963.
A reaction in architecture against Art Nouveau produced the simple rectangular forms seen in the **Convalescent Home,** Vienna, 1903, by **Josef Hoffman,** 1870–1956.

The Fauvist period in painting, 1905–08, was characterized by the use of flat patterns and intense, unnatural colors. "Open Window, Collioure," 1905, by **Henri Matisse,** 1869–1954, is typical, as are the works from this period of **André Derain,** 1880–1954, **Maurice Vlaminck,** 1876–1958, and **Raoul Dufy,** 1877–1953.

In Germany the Expressionist painting of the **Die Brücke grou** 1905–13, distorted reality to produce a personal view of the world, depicting intense and painful emotions after the style of **Edvard Munch.** They were chiefly represented by **Emil Nolde,** 1867–1956.
The Italian Futurists produced work and manifestos that extolled the technological energy of modern life, from 1909.

Music

The Romantic tradition lingered on into the early twentieth century. Popular music began to make its mark, and many serious composers sought a radical break with the past while others turned to folk music for their inspiration. The radicalism in the arts that followed World War I produced a variety of new musical techniques as well as altering aesthetic principles.

Richard Strauss, 1864–1949, continued the romantic tradition with operas and tone poems in a grand Wagnerian style.

Giacomo Puccini, 1858–1924, brought Italian grand opera to a grand finale with such dramatic and melodic operas as *La Bohème,* 1896, *Tosca,* 1900, and *Madame Butterfly,* 1904.

Blues grew steadily more popular in the early 20th century in the United States. Their cross rhythms and varying intonation brought great expression to the simple *aab* 12-bar form.

New Orleans became the cradle of **jazz** as ragtime bands, using instruments left over from the Civil War, took up improvisation and developed into small traditional jazz bands.

Science and technology

Einstein's theories of relativity and Planck's quantum theory revealed a new picture of the ultimate workings of nature. Although Newton's theories still proved accurate enough for most predictions, Einstein held that there was no absolute motion, motion in respect of empty space. His relativity principle stated that motion must always appear as the relative motion of one object with respect to another. It related time, mass, and length to velocity and mass to energy, and provided a theoretical basis for the development of nuclear physics.

Although World War I stimulated research and technology in Europe, the impetus for scientific advance shifted to America. The invention of the electronic valve, which allowed the development of the radio transmitter to proceed, and the development of powered flight speeded up intercontinental communications, and the introduction of mass-produced cars revolutionized private transport.

Blood groups were first distinguished *c.*1900.
Gamma rays were discovered in radioactivity, 1900, by **Paul Villard,** 1860–1934.
The quantum theory that energy consists of indivisible units was proposed by **Max Planck,** 1858–1947, in 1900.
Guglielmo Marconi, 1874–1937, was the first to transmit radio signals across the Atlantic, in 1901.
The fingerprint system was introduced in Britain, 1901.

The first sustained flight by a power driven aircraft was made by **Wilbur** and **Orville Wright** in the US, 1903. **Detroit** became the center of the automobile industry, 1903.
The first electronic valve was made in 1904.
The special theory of relativity was published in 1905 by **Albert Einstein,** 1879–1955.

The cloud chamber, used in detecting the paths of atomic particles, was perfected, 1906, by **Charles Wilson,** 1869–1959.
The third law of thermodynamics, that absolute zero cannot be attained, was put forward in 1906.
Emil Fischer, 1852–1919, showed in 1907 that proteins are composed of amino acids—a vital step in molecular biology.
The first helicopter flew, 1907.

Ammonia was synthesized in 1908, enabling Germany to produce the first high explosives.
Chromosomes were established as the carriers of heredity, 190
Bakelite, a synthetic polymer used for making electric plugs, was invented in 1909. Its success stimulated the developmen of plastics.
Combine harvesters were common in the US by 1910.
Louis Bleriot made his first fligh in 1907 and flew across the English Channel, 1909.

10–1912
Mexico, Porfirio Diaz, 877–80, 1884–1911, was erthrown, and the US intered by occupying Vera Cruz. **e Triple Entente powers** of ance, Russia, and Britain made litary and naval agreements. ter the 1911 Agadir incident en the Germans sent a gunat to frighten the French, they untered German ambitions in orocco. **nationalist republic** was set up China in 1911 under **Sun Yat-n,** 1866–1925.

1912–1915
Austria's Archduke Franz Ferdinand, 1863–1914, was assassinated in June 1914 by Serbian nationalists, setting off events leading to world war. **By 1915** Germany and Austria, with Turkey and Bulgaria, were fighting against the Entente allies, with Italy and Japan. **Military operations** extended from the main "front" in France and Belgium to the Russian plains, the Balkans, the Middle East, and the German colonies in Africa.

1915–1917
Germany started a blockade of British shipping. The main naval battle at Jutland, 1916, was inconclusive. Germany's unrestricted submarine warfare (leading to the sinking of the **Lusitania** in 1915) provoked the US to enter the war, 1917. **The strain of war** brought revolution to Russia in 1917. The tsar abdicated, and **Bolshevik** forces led by **Lenin,** 1870–1924, won power and withdrew Russia from the war, after defeating the liberal government.

1917–1920
Britain, France, and the US defeated Germany in 1918. In the **Versailles Treaty,** 1919, inspired by the democratic ideals of **Woodrow Wilson,** 1856–1924, the US president, new ethnic Balkan states were established, and Turkey was partitioned. **War guilt** and indemnity were assigned to Germany, where an abortive revolution disrupted the new republic, 1919. **Wilson's League of Nations** was inaugurated in 1919 but without US participation.

1920–22
In Russia, reactionary forces with allied aid tried unsuccessfully to defeat the Bolsheviks. **Germany,** struggling against economic chaos after the loss of the major industrial centers, secured Soviet friendship in the **Treaty of Rapallo,** 1922. **Japan,** which had been granted Germany's rights in China by the Versailles Treaty, made peace with China, 1922. **Benito Mussolini,** 1883–1945, established fascist power in Italy in 1922.

1922–25
Germany countered France's occupation of the Ruhr, 1923–25, with passive resistance and suffered massive inflation, which destroyed the economic strength of the middle classes. **The Dawes plan,** 1924, eased the repayment schedule for German war reparations. **Kemal Ataturk,** 1881–1938, president of the new Turkish republic, began modernization of Turkish society, 1923. **The American economy** was booming.

e Progressive party, advocat- social reforms, was founded, 12. The federal government creased its antitrust activities.

The Panama Canal was officially opened in 1914, while World War I began in Europe. A German submarine torpedoed the *Lusitania,* 1915, with 128 US deaths.

US troops fought in the Mexican Border Campaign, 1916–17. In 1917 the United States entered World War I, and the Selective Service Act was passed.

Armistice ended World War I, 1918, and the United States, led by **Pres. Woodrow Wilson,** played a prominent role at Versailles Peace Conference, 1919.

In 1920 the 19th Amendment was ratified, giving women the vote, and the 18th Amendment, ratified in 1919, went into effect, establishing Prohibition.

Scandals marked the administration of **Pres. Warren G. Harding,** 1865–1923. In Tennessee, **John Scopes,** 1900–70, was convicted of teaching evolution.

bert Einstein

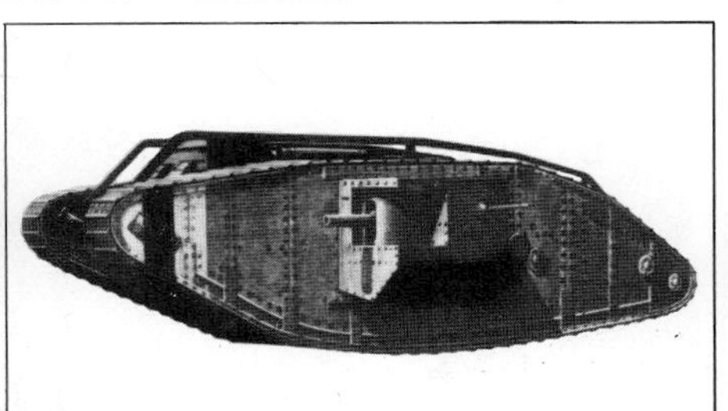
World War I tank, 1917

Russian Revolution: street scene in Petrograd, 1917

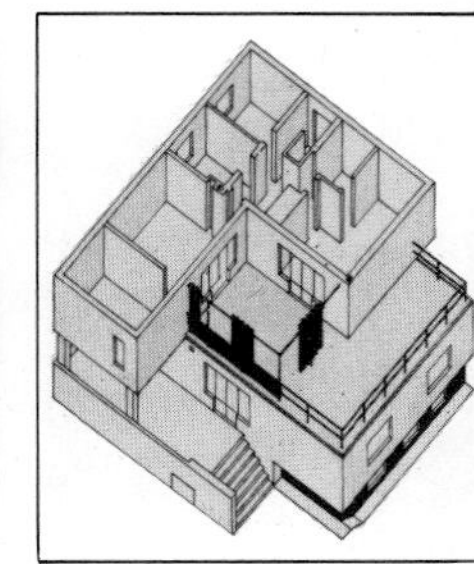
Bauhaus: house by Gropius

phisticated physics produced ientific theorists such as the strian **Ernst Mach,** 38–1916, and the Frenchman **nri Poincaré,** 1854–1912, o argued that unobservable tities like atoms should be garded only as useful postues about material nature. **enomenology** was founded by German philosopher **mund Husserl,** 1859–1938, o argued that true knowledge emmed from the imaginative alysis of direct experience.

Bertrand Russell, 1872–1970, the English philosopher and mathematician, applied empiricist principles to language, which he claimed to be constructed solely from sensory ideas and logic. In *Principia Mathematica,* 1910–13, he attempted, with **A. N. Whitehead,** 1861–1947, to derive mathematics from the axioms of logic. **Opposition to the war** led **Rosa Luxemburg,** 1871–1919, to found the left wing Spartacist party in Germany.

V. I. Lenin, 1870–1924, the Russian politician, argued in *The State and Revolution,* 1917, for a party of professional revolutionaries. **Freud's** emphasis on the sexual basis of psychiatric disorders led to the defection of two of his followers, **Carl Jung,** 1875–1961, and **Alfred Adler,** 1870–1937. Jung developed a theory of the collective unconscious, while Adler tried to derive a psychology from man's tendency to strive for perfection.

The British anthropologist Malinowski, 1884–1942, developed **functionalism,** 1914–18, in anthropology, studying social phenomena in terms of their function within an integrated social structure, in opposition to evolutionist anthropology. **Oswald Spengler,** 1880–1936, published *The Decline of the West,* 1918–22, claiming that Western civilization had ceased to be "creative" and had become concerned only with materialism.

The *Tractatus Logico-Philosophicus* of **Ludwig Wittgenstein,** 1889–1951, an Austrian living in London, was published in 1921; it argued that philosophy was an analytic, not a speculative, subject. **Aimee Semple McPherson,** 1890–1944, built the Angelus Temple in Los Angeles in 1922 and preached the religion of the foursquare gospel.

The Hungarian **Gyorgy Lukacs,** 1885–1971, a Marxist influenced by Hegel's idealism, wrote of the role of creative awareness in the development or revolutionary consciousness, in *History and Class-consciousness,* 1923. **Benedetto Croce,** 1866–1952, a historian who argued that the past could be understood only when seen in relation to current problems, became the spokesman for the opposition to Fascism in Italy after 1923.

e German Expressionists deribed visions of the collapse society. **George Heym,** 87–1912, prophesied a great r in *Umbra Vitae,* 1912, as did **orge Trakl,** 1887–1914.

Guillaume Appollinaire, 1880–1918, dominated the surrealist and avant-garde movements in Paris from 1913 until his death. He used random modes of expression in drama and initiated concrete poetry. **Ezra Pound,** 1885–1972, worked on his *Cantos* from 1914 until his death. His allusive, erudite style influenced many English poets.

The "literary revolution" in China in 1917 used the vernacular language in literature. **The English war poets** voiced their horror of mass warfare. **Rupert Brooke,** 1887–1915, and **Wilfred Owen,** 1893–1918, died while on duty. **Robert Graves,** 1895– , and **Siegfried Sassoon,** 1886–1967, also wrote about the period, both in prose and verse.

The Hindu writer **Rabindranath Tagore,** 1861–1941, translated the mystical *Gitanjali.* **Mohammed Iqbal,** 1873–1938, wrote in Urdu and Persian and voiced a growing resentment against the West, in India. **André Gide,** 1869–1951, kept his *Journals* from 1889–1949. **Hermann Hesse,** 1877–1962, wrote *Demian,* 1919.

The stream-of-consciousness technique was used by **Marcel Proust,** 1871–1922, to evoke the past in the long series of novels *À La Recherche du Temps Perdu,* 1913–27, and by **James Joyce,** 1882–1941, in *Ulysses,* 1922. This and *Finnegan's Wake,* 1939, are highly experimental, original, and questioning works.

Luigi Pirandello, 1867–1936, reflected the spiritual confusion of the postwar years in his play *Six Characters in Search of an Author,* 1921. **T. S. Eliot,** 1888–1965, wrote *The Waste Land,* 1922, a dense and highly literary meditation on the situation of modern man. **Franz Kafka,** 1883–1924, described man's spiritual bereavement in *The Trial,* 1925.

alytical Cubism, 1910–12, ncentrated on pure form, exuding interest in color. **Synetic Cubism,** 1912–14, inlved the construction of an age often by means of colge, such as the "Bottle of Anis l Mono," 1914, by **Juan Gris.** **r Blaue Reiter** group of Expresonist painters, 1911–14, used lor and abstract forms to cony spiritual realities and includ- **Wassily Kandinsky,** 1866–44, and **Paul Klee,** 1879–40.

Russian Constructivism, 1913–mid-20s, was initiated by **Vladmir Tatlin,** 1885–1953, and exploited the concept of Synthetic Cubism. Its emphasis was on abstract structures made of a variety of materials. Tatlin's "Constructions," 1913–14, were made of wood, metal, and glass. **The first long feature films** included the Italian *Cabiria,* 1914, and *The Birth of a Nation,* 1915, a drama about the US Civil War, directed by **D. W. Griffith,** 1880–1948.

The Dadaist movement developed in Zurich in 1916 in the work of **Jean (Hans) Arp,** 1887–1966, and **Tristan Tzara,** 1896–1963. It was deliberately "antiart" and aimed to outrage and scandalize a complacent society. Its chief exponent was **Marcel Duchamp,** 1887–1968, whose "Fountain," 1917, consisted of a urinal.
The films of **Charlie Chaplin,** 1889– , including *The Tramp,* 1915, won international acclaim.

The de Stijl group founded in Holland by **Theo van Doesburg,** 1883–1931, and **Piet Mondrian,** 1872–1944, developed their art and architecture based on spatial relationships. They used straight lines, right angles, and primary colors. **The Bauhaus school** of architecture, design, and craftsmanship was founded in Germany in 1919 by **Walter Gropius,** 1883–1969. It attempted to reconcile art and design with industrial techniques.

In France **Fernand Léger's** paintings reflected contemporary interest in machinery. His "Three Women," 1921, reduces figures to machinelike forms and uses metallic colors. **Frank Lloyd Wright,** 1869–1959, the greatest and most influential of US architects, designed the Imperial Hotel, Tokyo, 1919–22, using an entirely new anti-earthquake construction.

Architects in Europe such as **Walter Gropius, Mies van der Rohe,** 1886–1969, and **Le Corbusier,** 1887–1965, convinced of the need for streamlined, functional buildings, used the new media of concrete and glass to achieve a modern style epitomized in Gropius' design for the **Bauhaus,** 1925–26. **The Russian Revolution** stimulated experimental cinema, led by **Sergei Eisenstein,** 1898–1948, whose *Battleship Potemkin,* 1925, preached socialism.

e Ballets Russes of **Sergei aghilev,** 1872–1929, commisoned major works, such as **Igor ravinsky's** *Petrushka,* 1911, d **Maurice Ravel's** *Daphnis and hloe,* 1912.

The Rite of Spring, 1913, by **Stravinsky,** 1882–1971, gave new emphasis to the role of rhythm in serious music, using irregular meter and highly varied motifs.

Charles Ives, 1874–1954, became the first truly original US composer, working in several keys and rhythms at once, in many works such as his *Concord Sonata,* 1909–15.

Harmony reached a peak of complexity with **Stravinsky,** who worked in several keys simultaneously, and then split asunder in the keyless music of **Arnold Schoenberg** and **Béla Bartók.**

Bartók, 1881–1945, created a style marked by extreme dissonance and elegant melody, particularly in his six quartets, 1907–39. He collected and studied Hungarian folk music.

Twelve-note or serial music, created in 1924 by **Schoenberg,** 1874–1951, was based on an arbitrarily ordered series or row using the 12 notes of the chromatic (half tone) scale.

ectrical superconductivity was scovered in 1911. **uclear theory,** that the atom ntains a central nucleus, was nounced by **Lord Rutherford,** 371–1937, in 1911, in England. **tamins** were recognized as sential to health in 1906; their assification in 1911 stimulated etary studies. **ontinental drift,** the theory that e continents shift, was first oposed in 1912. **ellophane** was first manufactured in 1912.

The proton was recognized as the nucleus of the hydrogen atom by Lord Rutherford, in 1913. **Niels Bohr,** 1885–1962, showed, 1913, how changes in the electron orbits of the atom produce energy. **The Geiger counter** was used to measure radioactivity, 1913. **Atomic numbers** were determined by an X-ray method discovered in 1914. **The life cycle of stars** was determined by work done in 1914.

The general theory of relativity was published by Einstein in 1915. The theory explains how gravity affects light and how mass distorts space. **World War I stimulated technological advance** on both sides, particularly in weaponry and transport. **Tractors,** introduced by Ford in 1915, used the Diesel engine and led to greatly increased agricultural efficiency in the industrialized countries.

The first transatlantic flight was made, 1919, by the British aviators **Alcock and Brown.** The flight lasted almost 16 1/2 hours. **The first mass spectrograph** was developed in 1919. **The first commercial airplane** service, between London and Paris, was set up, 1919.

Diesel locomotives and rail cars came into use *c.*1920. The growing use of internal combustion engines led to a decline in the supremacy of coal as the major industrial fuel after 1910. **Radio broadcasting** on a regular basis began in the United States in 1920. **Insulin,** a hormone, was isolated in 1922 and first used in the treatment of diabetes. **The teleprinter** was developed in 1921, greatly speeding the transmission of long distance information.

Radioactive tracers, used for the determination of many biological reactions, were developed in 1923. **Electrons** were shown to behave as waves as well as particles, in 1922–24. This discovery made possible the invention of the electron microscope, in 1932. **External spiral galaxies** were found by Edwin Hubble, 1923. **Clarence Birdseye,** 1886–1956, experimented with quick-frozen foods commercially, 1924.

From depression to recovery 1925–1950

Principal events

The legacy of mistrust and depression following World War I brought a worldwide economic crisis at the end of the 1920s. The stronger industrial powers survived with the aid of new economic and social policies, but in Germany, where the obligation to pay war debts exacerbated the effects of national defeat, the Nazi regime, whose militarist ambitions in Europe would help to precipitate World War II, took power.

In the USSR a policy of forced industrialization was pursued under Stalin, destroying many of the ideals of the Revolution, while the basis for a communist China was laid after a long civil war. India won its independence, but only at the cost of partition.

World War II left Europe shattered and weak and Germany divided, with the capitalist and socialist blocs locked in a continuing, though ostensibly peaceful, struggle for power.

1925–1927

Chiang Kai-shek, 1887–1975, gained increasing control of the Kuomintang (nationalist party) in China. He captured Peking and unified the country, 1928, against Japanese expansion.
Germany joined the League of Nations, 1926, which hoped to bring peace by disarmament.
Fascist rule in Italy became increasingly authoritarian.
After Lenin's death, 1924, **Joseph Stalin,** 1879–1953, would begin forcible industrialization in Russia, 1928.

1927–1930

The Kellogg-Briand Pact was signed by 23 powers in 1928 to outlaw war.
The last allied forces left the Rhineland, 1929.
Leon Trotsky, 1879–1940, was exiled from Russia, 1929.
The Wall Street Crash, 1929, led to business depression in America, causing economic recession throughout Europe and a rise in left-wing activity.
Gandhi, 1869–1948, began a civil disobedience campaign against British rule in India.

1930–1932

The Round Table Conferences on India failed to satisfy nationalist demands, 1930.
The Hoover moratorium on war debts helped Europe to survive the depression, 1931, but the economic slump in Germany brought fighting between left- and right-wing groups.
Japan occupied Manchuria, 1931, after fears that trading with China would be cut.
A republic was set up in Spain, 1931, dominated by liberals and socialists.

1932–1935

Japan left the League of Natio
1933, after condemnation of h
action in Manchuria.
Adolf Hitler, 1889–1945, elec
ed German chancellor, set up a
Nazi dictatorship, 1933.
Franklin D. Roosevelt, 1882–
1945, introduced a New Deal c
social and economic reforms i
the US to end the slump, 1933
Stalin began a massive purge c
Russian party officials, 1935.
Civil war in China between the
left wing and nationalists led t
the Long March, 1934–35.

National events

The Wall Street crash of 1929 had a catastrophic effect on the United States. The economy came to a virtual halt, with unprecedented unemployment. The next decade was devoted to recovery. US attention then turned to Europe and the Pacific during World War II. Nuclear weapons changed the course of the war.

Charles Lindbergh, 1902–74, in 1927 landed his monoplane *The Spirit of St Louis,* in Paris, completing the first transatlantic solo flight.

A financial panic in 1929 resulted in a loss of $30,000,000,000 in stock values. The Wall Street crash led to unemployment and bank failures.

World War I veterans, numbering 17,000, converged on the capital to demand cash payment of bonuses. The "Bonus Army" was dispersed, 1932.

Pres. Franklin D. Roosevelt, 1882–1945, inaugurated in 1933 his New Deal, legislation designed to bring relief to ever phase of the economy.

Gandhi in Calcutta, 1925

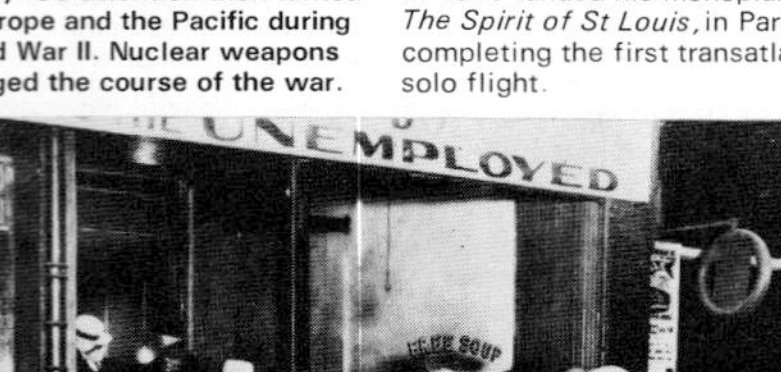
UNEMPLOYED

The Depression: soup kitchen in Chicago, 1930

LA GARRA DEL INVASOR ITALIANO PRETENDE ESCLAVIZARNOS

Spanish Civil War poster

Victims of Hitler's concentration camps

Religion and philosophy

Political thought was dominated by the conflict between the democratic ideal and its opponents on the left and right. Marxist political theory developed divergent trends as the Russian and Chinese revolutions took their course, but its influence in the West declined as supporters of liberalism rallied to oppose Fascism, with its ideological roots in 19th-century irrationalism. A new democratic philosophy, sustained by Keynes' economic theories of consumer prosperity, became linked with attempts to control political violence on a worldwide scale, marked by the founding of the United Nations.

The Christian Church came face to face with growing secularization in the industrialized countries and the problems of an emergent Third World.

Philosophy remained split between those primarily studying human consciousness and those who used a scientific model to understand reality.

The American J. B. Watson 1878–1958, developed behaviorist psychology in *Behaviorism,* 1925, seeking to explain behavior wholly in terms of responses to external stimuli.
In **Mein Kampf,** 1925–27, **Hitler** drew upon the ideas of **Gobineau,** 1816–82, who argued that the development of a civilization depends on racial superiority and purity, and requires military aggression. Hitler condemned democracy as based on invalid egalitarianism.

Existentialism was developed in Germany from Husserl's phenomenological ideas, by **Martin Heidegger,** 1889–1976, who was appointed professor of philosophy at Freiburg in 1928. He argued that authentic human existence consists in not being subordinated to the external world.
The word apartheid was first used to describe racial segregation in South Africa in 1929.

J. M. Keynes, 1883–1946, overthrew the neo-classical orthodoxy in economics with two books, *Treatise on Money,* 1930, and *The General Theory,* 1936. He stated that market forces that lowered wage rates would not cure economic depressions; production and investment would only increase if spending by consumers, business, and government went up. His theory influenced the New Deal and economic planning in the West until the 1970s.

Leon Trotsky, 1879–1940, a
Russian Marxist, argued for per
manent revolution in his *Histo*
of the Russian Revolution,
1932–33. He claimed that socialism in Russia could not sur
vive unless revolutions also toc
place in more advanced countries, and opposed Stalin's doctrine of socialism in one count
Gandhi organized *satyagraha*
(truth force) campaigns to fost
Indian nationalism by nonviolence and emphasized the value
of village life.

Literature

The insistent excavation of personal experience that had begun with the Romantics and reached a peak with the stream-of-consciousness writings of Proust and Joyce found new exponents in Virginia Woolf and the more consciously Freudian Surrealists. Much European writing of the interwar period, however, reflected a need to grasp the social issues of the time. Some, such as Camus, accepted the fact of social commitment while admitting the ultimate meaninglessness of existence. Others like Brecht developed new artistic forms to embody their political vision with a lesser emphasis on the individual. In the Third World, too, where writers were inspired by the ideal of national independence, a new, more confident literature emerged.

A major writer who met the requirements of socialist realism was **Mikhail Sholokhov,** 1905– , in his *Tales from the Don,* 1925.
The Bloomsbury Group in London included the novelist **E. M. Forster,** 1879–1970, and **Virginia Woolf,** 1882–1941, who used a personal style of imagery in *To the Lighthouse,* 1927.

D. H. Lawrence, 1885–1930, challenged the taboos of class and sex in novels such as *Lady Chatterley's Lover.* **John Cowper Powys,** 1872–1963, studied man in his environment, while **Malcolm Lowry,** 1909–57, wrote of his experiences in Mexico.
A group of left-wing poets in London in the 20s included **W. H. Auden,** 1907–73, and **Stephen Spender,** 1909–

A forerunner of the **Theater of the Absurd, Luigi Pirandello,** 1867–1936, explored the theme of mutual incomprehension.
American writing was richly varied, ranging from the southern novels of **William Faulkner,** 1897–1962, whose *Light in August* appeared 1932, to *The Grapes of Wrath* by **John Steinbeck,** 1902–68, treating the hardship of the depression.

"The Lost Generation," a group
of Americans in Paris in the
1920s and 1930s, included **F.
Scott Fitzgerald,** 1886–1940,
whose *Tender is the Night* was
an elegy for the American
Dream; the masculine **Ernest
Hemingway,** 1899–1961; **Gertrude Stein,** 1874–1946, an influential experimentalist; and
the less typical **Henry Miller,**
1891–

Art and architecture

In Europe before World War II there was increasing integration among art forms. Furniture design, painting, and architecture were developed by the de Stijl and Bauhaus groups. Formal developments in painting also affected architecture. By 1932 the new International Style had come into existence. The first Surrealist manifesto in 1924, with its emphasis on exploration of the unconscious, represented the culmination of the avant-garde movement which linked radical artistic and political ideas.

Many of the artistic movements of the postwar period found expression in the cinema, but the depression caused the collapse of the film industries of many European countries and introduced a period of Hollywood supremacy based on large studio organizations, which had the effect of suppressing much individual talent, and leading to the development of styles suited to a mass market that had little contact with the traditional arts.

Expressionist techniques were used by **Chaim Soutine,** 1893–1943, in "Page Boy at Maxim's," 1927, and by **Marc Chagall,** 1889– , in "Russian Wedding," 1925.
Expressionist cinema was developed by **Fritz Lang,** 1890–1976, in his vision of the future, *Metropolis,* 1926, while **Dali** explored surrealist cinema in *Le Chien Andalou,* 1928. *The Jazz Singer,* 1927, was the first talking picture.

Surrealism, founded in Paris, explored the reality of the subconscious. Its leading exponent was **Salvador Dali,** 1904– whose "Illuminated Pleasures," 1929, shows objects taken out of context and replaced in fantastic juxtapositions. Other important artists were **René Magritte,** 1898–1967, **Giorgio de Chirico,** 1888– , **Joan Miró,** 1893– , and **Max Ernst,** 1891–1976. **Ernst** and **André Masson,** 1896– , practiced automatism, a free-brush style.

The International Style in architecture, 1932, recognized a new and independent style that had emerged in the twenties. This was typified in the Villa Savoye, 1928–31, by **Le Corbusier,** with its white rectangular exterior and horizontal windows.
The individual style of the French painter **Georges Rouault,** 1871–1958, whose religious works achieve a stained glass quality, can be seen in his "Christ mocked by Soldiers," 1932.

**In Germany anti-Nazi artistic
expressions** by artists such as
Otto Dix, 1891–1969, **Georg
Grosz,** 1893–1959, **Max Beckmann,** 1884–1950, and **Oskar
Kokoschka,** 1886– , re-
sulted in either suppression or
exile for the artists concerned.
Socialist Realism was officially
adopted in the USSR under Sta
in in 1934, using an explicit,
academic style in order to convey clearly the message of the
dignity of the working classes.

Music

Serious music split into several mutually exclusive schools, most of which attracted few listeners or performers in spite of the spread of the radio and phonograph. However, these did help to broaden the audience for popular music, which, in various jazz forms and "musicals," flourished widely.

An English school, including **Frederick Delius,** 1862–1934, **Gustav Holst,** 1874–1934, and **Vaughan Williams,** 1872–1958, produced pastoral music after **Edward Elgar,** 1857–1934.

Louis Armstrong, 1900–71, created a solo style in jazz with his innovative trumpet improvisations of 1925–30.
Duke Ellington, 1899–1974, began an orchestral style in jazz.

Musical theater reached a peak of sophistication in the United States, with lavish shows and beautiful songs, notably by **George Gershwin,** 1898–1937, in *Porgy and Bess,* 1935.

Ionisation, 1931, by **Edgard Varèse,** 1885–1965, written sole
for percussion instruments,
showed that a piece of serious
music could be constructed
successfully using rhythm only

Science and technology

Economic depression and war hindered some areas of science while advancing others. In the West, steelmaking, engineering, and agricultural production fell during the thirties, but falling prices stimulated consumer industries, and aviation, radio, the car industry, and artificial fibers continued to develop. The USSR, too, was industrializing fast.

With the rise of Hitler, many nuclear physicists fled to America, where their research ensured that Germany's supremacy in physics was lost and that the Nazis would not be the first to possess nuclear weapons.

World War II made great use of science, both to destroy and to save lives. Electronics, radar, nuclear technology, jet aviation, and antibiotics were all products of the war.

In Britain important work was done in astronomy, exploring the implications of Einstein's theories to produce conflicting concepts of the origin of the universe.

Modern sound recording began with electric recording in 1925.
Liquid fuel rockets were first tested in America in 1926.
Wave mechanics, describing the wave motion of electrons, was founded by **Erwin Schrödinger,** 1887–1961, in 1926.
The Heisenberg uncertainty principle, that every observation has a degree of probability, was proposed in 1927.
The big bang theory of the origin of the universe was first put forward in 1927, by **Abbé Lemaître,** 1894–1966.

The anti-bacterial activity of penicillium mold was discovered, 1928, by **Alexander Fleming,** 1881–1955, but it was not made stable enough for medical use until 1943.
John Logie Baird invented a high speed mechanical scanning system, 1928, which led to the development of television.
The distance of galaxies was related to their speed of recession as measured by the red shift, 1929, by **Edwin Hubble** 1889–1953.

The cyclotron and other circular particle accelerators were developed from a working model made in America, *c.*1930.
Wallace Carothers, 1896–1937, invented **nylon** in 1931.
Radio astronomy began in 1931 with the detection of radio signals from outer space.
Deuterium, heavy hydrogen, was discovered in 1931.
The first nuclear reaction using an accelerator was activated in 1932.
Neutrons were discovered, 1932.

Skyscraper building in the US
was interrupted by the depression of the 1930s.
The first radioisotopes were pre
pared by **Frédéric Joliot-Curie,**
1900–58, and his wife **Irène,**
1897–1956, in 1934.
The meson, a sub-atomic particle, was predicted in 1935.

5–1937

governmental reforms of 5 in India again fell short of onalist demands.
solini invaded Abyssinia in 5 to satisfy fascist imperial itions. The League failed to vene effectively. **Hitler** re- arized the Rhineland, 1936. Mussolini proclaimed the **e-Berlin axis. A right-wing** after the Popular Front won elections led to civil war in n, 1936–39.
Japanese began their attack China in 1937.

1937–1940

Germany annexed Austria, 1938. Europe's powers met at **Munich,** 1938, to discuss German claims in Czechoslovakia, but failed to restrain Hitler. **German threats** to take Danzig in Poland resulted in Anglo-French intervention. **A European war** began in Sept. 1939.
Francisco Franco, 1892–1975, became dictator of Spain after defeating the republicans.
Japan had conquered most of eastern China by 1939.
Germany took France in 1940.

1940–1942

Germany waged a lightning war in the West, but failed to invade or destroy Britain, which fought at sea and in the air, and opposed Italy in north Africa.
In June 1941, Germany invaded Russia and drove the Red Army back to Moscow.
Japanese aggression in the Pacific, culminating in the attack on **Pearl Harbor,** Hawaii, 1941, brought the US into the war.
Hitler began the systematic genocide of the Jews, 1941.

1942–1945

In 1943 Russia stopped the Germans at Stalingrad, and Anglo-American forces took north Africa and invaded Italy.
Guerrilla action, especially in Yugoslavia and France, weakened Nazi control.
The invasion of Normandy by Britain and US in June 1944 opened a "second front," and Allied forces from east and west met on the Elbe in April 1945.
The Allies agreed on Soviet and Western spheres of influence at Yalta in 1945.

1945–1947

The US dropped two atomic bombs on Japan and ended the war in the Pacific, 1945.
The United Nations was formed in 1945.
The Truman doctrine, 1947, promised aid to non-communist countries, particularly Turkey and Greece.
Britain granted independence to India, 1947, which divided through religious conflict.
The Chinese communists were aided by Japan's defeat, controlling Manchuria by 1947.

1947–1950

The USSR blockaded Berlin, 1948–49, to isolate it from the west.
Zionists declared Israel's independence, 1948.
Mao Tse-tung, 1893–1976, set up the People's Republic of China, 1949.
The North Atlantic Treaty Organization provided for mutual assistance against aggression among the Western powers.
The socialist coup in Czechoslovakia, 1948, extended Soviet control of eastern Europe.

---

gress passed the Social Se- y Act, 1935, to provide re- ment benefits. Public works ects were a major part of the Deal.

President Roosevelt was unsuccessful in an attempt to expand the number of Supreme Court justices, 1937.

The United States entered the war after Pearl Harbor, Dec. 7, 1941. American-British war aims were defined by the Atlantic Charter, 1941.

In July 1945, an atomic bomb was tested at Alamogordo, N.M. In August, US pilots dropped atomic bombs on Hiroshima and Nagasaki, Japan.

The UN Charter was drafted and signed in San Francisco, 1945. The Atomic Energy Commission was established, 1946.

The United States participated in a massive airlift to blockaded Berlin. The North Atlantic Treaty Organization was founded, 1949.

170059

sserschmidt–262

Women munitions workers

Churchill, Roosevelt, and Stalin at Yalta

Atom bomb test

Vienna Circle, a group of osophers who met there, 2–36, including **Moritz lick,** 1882–1936, and **Rudolf nap,** formulated logical posi- sm, an empiricist philosophy anguage according to which statements that could be fied were meaningful.
e Pius XI, *r.*1922–39, con- ned fascism, 1931, and munism, 1937. He adopted endly attitude to Protestant ralism, although opposing *sez-faire* social policies.

Mao Tse-tung, 1893–1976, adapted Marxism-Leninism to Chinese conditions, and argued that the peasantry, as well as the industrial proletariat, could succeed in making a socialist revolution. Mao later maintained that socialism could only be reached by a permanent revolution to prevent the development of privilege. His studies in guerrilla warfare were important to his political success and influenced later Third World revolutionaries.

Phenomenology was developed in France by **Maurice Merleau-Ponty,** 1908–61, in *The Structure of Behavior,* 1942.
Oxfam was founded, 1942, to combat Third World poverty.
Dietrich Bonhoeffer, 1906–45, a German Protestant, argued that God is dead and sought a conception of Christianity relevant to a secular society.

Jean-Paul Sartre, 1905– , in *Being and Nothingness,* 1943, advanced the Existentialist claim that authentic existence requires the individual exercise of free choice.
Karl Popper, 1902– , an Austrian living in England, wrote *The Open Society and its Enemies,* 1944. He attacked the belief that there are general laws in history, which he saw as leading to totalitarian politics.

T. Adorno, 1903– , and **M. Horkheimer,** 1895– , of the Frankfurt School of Sociology, argued in *Dialectics of Enlightenment,* 1947, that true knowledge could only be achieved by a social revolution, which would liberate man from the idea that nature is independent of, and external to, him.

Martin Buber, 1878–1965, a Jewish thinker influenced by the mysticism of the Hasidic tradition in Judaism, advocated a direct, personal relationship of man with God, and praised the new *kibbutzim* in Israel as almost ideal socialist communities, in *Paths to Utopia,* 1947.
The World Council of Churches first met in 1948.
The welfare state, uniting private enterprise with state responsibility, took shape with the British National Health Service, 1948.

---

nish folk traditions and mod- cruelty were studied by **erico Garcia Lorca,** 1898– 6.
Germany an aesthetic and alist style was used by **mas Mann,** 1875–1955. His *eph and his Brothers,* 1933– explores the theme of exile. **ense of cultural collapse** in- ed **Robert Musil,** 1880– 2, to his Viennese novel *The n Without Qualities.*

Experimental epic theater was pioneered by the German Marxist **Bertolt Brecht,** 1898–1956.
Many foreign writers fought in the Spanish Civil War. **George Orwell,** 1903–50, described it in *Homage to Catalonia,* 1939.
Important English novelists dealing with traditional themes were **Graham Greene,** 1904– , **Aldous Huxley,** 1894–1963, and **Evelyn Waugh,** 1903–66.

The "negritude" movement, calling for black cultural identity, was initiated by **Leopold Senghor,** 1906–
Serious native American drama was created by **Eugene O'Neill,** 1888–1953, and **Tennessee Williams,** 1911– , who explored the frustrations of urban society. The plays of **Arthur Miller,** 1915– , deal with individual moral and political responsibility.

Salvatore Quasimodo, 1901–68, opposed **Fascism** in Italy in lyrical symbolist poetry.
The Makioka Sisters, 1943–48, by **Tanikaki Junichiro,** 1886–1965, owes much to Western realism.
Latin American literature flourished with the "poetry for simple people" of the Chilean **Pablo Neruda,** 1904–73, and the stories of **Jorge Luis Borges.**

In **Deaths and Entrances,** 1946, the exuberant imagery of the Welsh poet **Dylan Thomas,** 1914–53, is at its best.
Russia's history from 1900–30 was the subject of the humanistic novel *Doctor Zhivago,* by **Boris Pasternak,** 1890–1960.
Italy's leading novelists, **Cesare Pavese,** 1908–50, and **Alberto Moravia,** 1907– , both condemned modern estrangement.

Jean Paul Sartre, 1905– , gave existential philosophy a literary form in his war trilogy, *Les Chemins de la Liberté,* 1945–49. The existential dilemma also marks the feminist novels of **Simone de Beauvoir,** 1908–
Albert Camus, 1913–60, formulated his theories of **the absurd** in his novels and essays, notably *The Stranger,* 1942, and *The Plague,* 1947.

Nicholson, 1894– , one ritain's leading abstract art , achieved worldwide recog- on in the Cubist and Abstract exhibition, New York, 1936. rectangular, textured "White ef," 1936, is typical of his e at this time.
k Lloyd Wright, the American itect, produced two out- nding buildings—his famous **ing Water,** Bear Run, Pa., 6–37, and the **Johnson Wax inistrative buildings,** Racine, ., 1936–49.

One of **Picasso's finest paintings,** "Guernica," 1937, was prompted by the destruction of that Basque town by German bombers during the Spanish Civil War.
Hollywood won international supremacy in filmmaking during the Depression, using enormous casts in lavish productions such as *Gone with the Wind,* 1939.

American artists turned increasingly to the depiction of provincial life in a realistic style. "Nighthawks," 1942, by **Edward Hopper,** 1882–1967, records with formal precision the isolation of a city at night.
Hollywood cinema escaped the limitations of its genres (westerns, gangster films, and love stories) with *Citizen Kane,* 1941, directed by **Orson Welles,** 1915– , and *The Grapes of Wrath,* 1940, by **John Ford,** 1895–1973.

Official war artists in Britain, such as **Graham Sutherland,** 1903– , and **John Piper,** 1903– , recorded the devastating effects of the bombings.
Mies van der Rohe, in the US from 1938, designed during the war years the campus of the Illinois Institute of Technology, using cubic simplicity and perfect precision in details.

Emaciated single figures on wire frames characterized the work of the Swiss sculptor **Albert Giacometti,** 1901–66, such as "Man Pointing," 1947.
The British sculptor **Henry Moore,** 1898– , used his material to express natural forms in terms of stone or wood, as in "Three Standing Figures," 1947–48.
Italian neo-realist cinema relied on simple stories and untrained actors, as in *Open City,* 1946, by Roberto Rossellini, 1906–

Abstract Expressionism developed in the US after 1945, expressed in the drip paintings of **Jackson Pollock,** 1912–56, in the "black and white" paintings of **William de Kooning,** 1904– , and in the blurred expanses of rich colors in the work of **Mark Rothko,** 1903–70.
The Unité d'Habitation, 1946–52, by **Le Corbusier,** a huge block of 337 two-story apartments, was the first building to use rough cast concrete.

Neoclassic movement rein- rpreted classical form in mod- sound. Initiated by **Stravin-** , the style attracted **Sergei kofiev,** 1891–1953, and **Paul demith,** 1895–1963.

Serial music developed further with the work of **Alban Berg,** 1885–1935, and **Anton von Webern,** 1883–1945, eventually submitting all musical elements to mathematical procedures.

The swing era, 1935–45, dominated the popular music interest in the US, featuring such big bands as **Benny Goodman's,** playing highly arranged jazz with an energetic beat.

Glenn Miller, 1904–44, leader of the US Air Force Band in Europe, entertained troops with his distinctive "big band" saxophone sound.

Bebop, a complex form of jazz featuring virtuoso improvisation, emerged in 1945 as a reaction to the widely popular swing style. Its principal creator was **Charlie Parker,** 1920–55.

Radio and phonograph disseminated music to all developed countries, spreading new forms and styles so widely that national schools could no longer emerge.

---

v industries were developed scape the depression. In Brit- and the US, the new interest onsumer expenditure, com- ed with the completion of the ctricity supply, led to the wth of consumer durable in- tries, while in Germany road ding was encouraged.
citric acid cycle, which oc- s in bodily energy production, found in 1937.
eriments made by **Robert son-Watt,** 1892–1973, after 35 led to radar's invention.

The Graf Zeppelin (LZ 130) was built in 1938, the largest airship to be made. It ran on a regular transatlantic service.
The Volkswagen "Beetle," designed by **Porsche** to Hitler's requirements, was built, 1938.
Nuclear fission, developed as a source of energy in the US, was first achieved in 1939.
Einstein told the US president of the possibility of making an **atomic bomb,** 1939, to preempt German research.
Food-dehydration by vacuum-contact drying was developed.

Plutonium, the first artificial element, was made, 1940.
The first jet-powered aircraft flew in 1941, using an engine made by **Frank Whittle,** 1907–
The first nuclear reactor was built in 1942 in Chicago.
The German development of the **V2 rocket-bomb,** 1942, provided the basis for future rocket development. The war also brought improvements in electronics and medical equipment.

Large diameter pipelines facilitated the distribution of oil, 1943.
Penicillin was produced on a large scale from *Penicillium* mold in 1943.
DNA was shown to carry hereditary characteristics, 1944.
IBM produced a mechanical calculating machine, 1944.
DDT was discovered in 1939 and introduced as an insecticide, 1944, as synthetic fertilizers became available, leading to an increase in agricultural yields.

The first nuclear bombs were made in the US in 1945 and tested at Alamogordo, New Mexico, in 1945.
Britain's first atomic power station was built, 1947.
The sound barrier was broken by the Bell XI rocket-propelled American aircraft, 1947.
Radiocarbon dating, a method of accurately finding the ages of archeological discoveries, was perfected in 1947.

A Jaguar sports car, capable of 120mph (193kph) was put into production in 1948.
The "steady-state" theory of the universe was proposed by **H. Bondi** and **T. Gold,** 1948.
The transistor was invented in 1948. Its invention made possible the miniaturization of electronic equipment and combined with microcircuitry, the computer.
A United States step rocket sent a vehicle to a height of more than 240 miles in 1949.

The modern world 1950–1976

Principal events

The division of the world into two major power blocs after World War II was confused by a Sino-Soviet ideological split, and after a series of dangerous incidents between Russia and America in the 1950s and early 1960s the Cold War gave way to a period of official détente.

In spite of continuing imperialism by the major powers, whether militarily or by economic intervention, Third World liberation from European control accelerated, changing the composition of the United Nations as the newly independent African and Asian states have joined to force the industrialized countries to pay a higher price for raw materials.

Economic planning became increasingly worldwide with the rise of development economics and the attempt to control currency exchange rates. In the 1970s serious inflation spread to all the industrialized countries.

1950–1952

War between North and South Korea, which had its roots in the Communist triumph in China, produced UN intervention.

The Arab League powers formed a security pact and began a blockade of Israel, 1950.

No agreement on Germany's future was reached, but peace was made with Japan, 1951.

The US strengthened defense links with Japan and Formosa.

Six European powers joined a single **Coal and Steel Commission,** 1952.

1952–1955

Geneva conference, 1955, divided Vietnam into North and South after a Communist victory at **Dien Bien Phu** had forced the French forces to withdraw.

Opposition to British and French imperialism brought terrorist campaigns in Algeria, Kenya, Cyprus, and Malaya.

The USSR opposed the reunification of Germany, 1954, and the **Warsaw Pact** united the Soviet satellites in reaction to West Germany's incorporation in NATO, 1955.

1955–1957

The Soviet leader, Nikita Khrushchev, 1894–1971, denounced Stalinist principles, 1956; a Sino-Soviet split resulted. Soviet troops invaded **Hungary,** to crush a nationalist rising, 1956.

President Nasser, 1918–70, of Egypt, nationalized the Suez Canal Company, 1956, provoking Britain, France, and Israel to military intervention.

The Treaty of Rome, 1957, established the **Common Market** in Western Europe.

1957–1960

Discontent in France over th Algerian war brought **Charle Gaulle,** 1890–1970, to pow 1958.

China's Great Leap Forward, economic push in agricultur and industry, 1958, ended in economic chaos after the w drawal of Soviet aid, 1960.

World opinion was aroused b the Sharpeville massacre, 19

Fidel Castro, 1927– , a Marxist, controlled **Cuba,** 19

The Belgian Congo's indepe dence, 1960, led to anarchy

National events

The Cold War, which pitted the free world against the Communist bloc, intensified. The United States became embroiled in the Korean War and later the divisive Vietnam War. Domestic issues involved civil rights, student unrest, and the feminist movement. Political scandals rocked the country.

Pres. Harry S. Truman, 1884–1972, relieved **Gen. Douglas MacArthur,** 1880–1964, of command in the Far East, 1951.

In 1954, the Senate censured **Joseph McCarthy,** 1908–57. In *Brown* v. *Board of Education of Topeka,* 1954, the Supreme Court ruled against segregation.

The American Federation of Labor (AFL) and the Congress of Industrial Organizations (CIO) merged, 1955. Little Rock, Ark., schools desegregated, 1957.

The National Aeronautics anc Space Administration was es lished, 1958. The Civil Righ Act, 1960, focused on votin blacks.

Medevac in the Korean War

Le Corbusier: design

Fidel Castro

The Berlin Wall

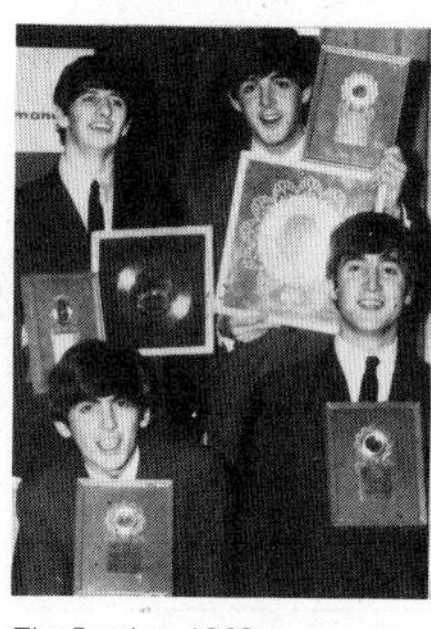

The Beatles, 1963

Nyerere of Tanzania

Religion and philosophy

American sociology was dominant in the West from World War II, expanding the use of surveys and other observational techniques into a major tool of government policy and developing in the work of Talcott Parsons a complex schema for the understanding of whole societies. Many of the general trends of thought seen in the industrialized countries also originated in the United States, whether in the work of theorists such as Marcuse, in the radical opposition to the Vietnam War, or in the hippie movement, with its complete rejection of political activism and search for increased personal awareness.

In the same period Third World theorists have produced an analysis of the processes and effects of colonialism and the means of eradicating it.

The Christian churches have tried to overcome some of their differences and in the Third World became linked with progressive social policies.

Frantz Fanon, 1925–61, a West Indian, analyzed the psychological and social repression of the black man in *Black Skin, White Masks,* 1952. He advocated an independent and socialist Third World.

Talcott Parsons, 1902– , an American, developed structural functional sociology in *The Social System,* setting out to construct a general model for societies, showing the interdependence of their institutions and emphasizing shared values.

Joseph McCarthy, 1908–57, led an American campaign against liberals and Marxists as a result of Cold War tension.

The Oxford School of Ordinary Language Philosophy, including **Gilbert Ryle,** 1900– , and **J. L. Austin,** 1911–60, followed Wittgenstein's later ideas. In *Dilemmas,* 1954, Ryle tried to show that problems in philosophy derive from conceptual confusion and would be resolved if we kept to the normal meaning of words.

Paul Tillich, 1886–1965, a Protestant, sought to fuse traditional religious values with a modern emphasis on individual responsibility in the *Dynamics of Faith,* 1956.

Noam Chomsky, 1928– , an American, revolutionized linguistics by analyzing the structure of language. He showed in *Syntactic Structures,* 1957, that grammatical speech depends upon a system of rules too complex to be learned by example.

Structuralism, the attempt to find basic patterns or "structures" for a scientific study c man, was developed by the Frenchman **Claude Levi-Strau** 1908– , in his *Structural A thropology,* 1958. **Michel Fou cault,** 1926– , applied this method to the history of idea **Jean Paul Sartre,** 1905– , t to link **Existentialism** and **Ma ism** in the *Critique of Dialect Reason,* 1960.

Literature

The rise of a worldwide reading public and the production of cheap and widely distributed books allowed the writer greater freedom of experimentation. Increasingly, confessional novels reflected a sense of the isolation of the individual, and the use of a journalistic approach to deal with contemporary events challenged the very concept of fiction, which traditionally required a distance between the author and his subject. At the same time the beat writers, in seeking to celebrate the spontaneous, questioned artistic form itself.

However, traditional literary forms remained the main vehicle for Third World writers, who set out to portray the conflicts aroused in the individual by the process of colonization.

The Theater of the Absurd, which saw man as a helpless creature in a meaningless universe, was explored by **Samuel Beckett,** 1906– , **Eugene Ionesco,** 1912– , and **Jean Genet,** 1910–

The "new novel," without form or plot, was developed in the work of **Alain Robbe-Grillet,** 1922– , and **Nathalie Sarraute,** 1902–

Black American writers gained status with *The Invisible Man,* by **Ralph Ellison,** 1914– , and the writings of **James Baldwin,** 1924– The Swiss dramatists **Max Frisch,** 1911– , and **Friedrich Dürrenmatt,** 1921– , and the Frenchman **Jean Anouilh, 1910–** , shared a preoccupation with the tragi-comic and grotesque aspects of life.

English drama was active in the 1950s. Disillusionment with contemporary Britain was vented by **John Osborne,** 1929– , in his play *Look Back in Anger,* 1956. **Harold Pinter,** 1930– wrote *The Room,* 1957, which he followed with *The Birthday Party,* 1958.

Arnold Wesker, 1932– , wrote socialist plays including *Roots,* 1958.

The work of Jack Kerouac, 1922–69, epitomized the out look of the American beat ge ation. Its writers included **Wi liam Burroughs,** 1914– , an **Henry Miller,** 1891– , and t poets **Allen Ginsberg,** 1926– and **Lawrence Ferlinghetti,** 1919– , all of whom sough "spontaneous living" and the means to express it.

Art and architecture

Although America still dominated the visual arts, the increasingly international nature of the market brought a new uniformity of style most clearly seen in architecture, with monumental concrete styles throughout the world.

In painting, attempts to explore the fundamentals of visual language produced an ever-simplified abstract style and the breakdown of traditional distinctions between the disciplines and even between art and life, while Pop art incorporated into art the mass-produced images of consumer society.

The emergence in many parts of the world, including South America, India, and eastern Europe, of the art film, aiming more at expression than at profit, challenged the domination of Hollywood and forced the adoption of new formal styles and greater individual freedom in American commercial cinema, as well as a more critical view of modern society.

Le Corbusier designed **Chandigarh,** the new capital of the Punjab, 1950, in rough cast concrete.

Skyscraper building in the US revived after World War II, with a new reliance on glass and steel, seen in Lever House, New York, 1952.

The growth of film festivals after 1945 led to a less commercial cinema, and brought the work of the Japanese **Kurosawa,** 1910– , and the Indian **Satyajit Ray,** 1921– , to the West.

"Brutalism" in architecture was a term coined, 1953, for a functional style which, for example, let electric ducts be seen.

Pier Luigi Nervi, 1891– , regarded as the most brilliant concrete designer of his age, helped design the UNESCO building in Paris, 1954–58.

The International Style in architecture can be seen, postwar, at its most elegant in the Rødovre Town Hall, Copenhagen, begun in 1955 by **Arne Jacobsen,** 1902–71.

Pop art emerged in London in 1956 in the works of **Richard Hamilton,** 1922– , **Peter Blake,** 1932– , and **Eduardo Paolozzi,** 1924– , using motifs from commercial art.

Hard-edge painting with large, clearly defined areas of bright color, was conceived in New York, 1958, and explored by **Ellsworth Kelly,** 1923–

Kinetic art made use of light and movement for its effects as in *Mobile,* 1958, by **Alexander Calder,** 1898–1976.

Brazilian architecture centerec on the building of a new capi **Brasilia.** Its cathedral, 1959, b **Oscar Niemeyer,** 1907– , us graceful curved concrete stru tures.

The New Wave of French cine emerged in 1959 in reaction t the clichés of Hollywood. *40 Blows,* 1959, by **François Truf faut,** 1932– , and *Breathles* by **Jean-Luc Godard,** 1930– introduced stylistic innovatior on a low budget.

Music

New elements appeared in Western music, stemming from new ways of producing sound and of organizing the music. The open texture of Eastern music began to make its mark in the West as Western music, in turn, reached the East. Rock music began simply in the 1950s and soon became highly creative.

Traditional methods lived on in the operas of **Benjamin Britten,** 1913–76, and the symphonies of **Dimitri Shostakovitch,** 1906–75, who created personal styles of music by conventional means.

John Cage, 1912– , pioneered a music in which the score is a set of directions delineating a musical process, giving much freedom to performers. His notorious *4' 3"*, 1952, is all silence.

Musique concrète widened musical horizons after World War II in France, involving a collage of sounds, both musical and natural, processed into a recording.

Rock music promoted a strong eight-note beat over a static harmony in popular music. At first played on guitars by grou with a lead singer, it later became far more complex.

Science and technology

Scientific institutions set up by governments or industries took over from the individual experimenter, as the scale on which scientific research is conducted mushroomed. The growth in prosperity in industrialized countries from 1945 was accompanied by a boom in technologically sophisticated goods available to the general public; in particular, electronic equipment was improved by miniaturization.

Much scientific research was related to the rival arms and space programs of the USSR and the US. But since the completion of the US Apollo Moon program, the emphasis in the US has shifted to the ecological problems that man must solve if he is to have a future on Earth. The hunt for new energy resources was stimulated by a rise in oil prices, and new foods were developed to help cope with expanding population. Small-scale technological innovations benefited Third World economies.

Magnetic recording developed during the 1950s. Modern sound and video recording as well as computer operations depend on storing electrical signals in the form of magnetic patterns according to principles discovered by the Danish inventor **Valdemar Poulsen,** 1869–1942, in 1898.

Soya-bean farming increased, *c.*1950, following a growing demand for vegetable oil during World War II.

The first hydrogen bomb was tested by the US in 1952.

The structure of DNA was found in 1953, leading to closer understanding of protein synthesis in the body and the inheritance of characteristics by the next generation.

Polio vaccine was developed, 1953–55.

Oral contraception followed from the investigations in the 1950s into the role that sex hormones play in reproduction.

The link between smoking and lung cancer was first proposed in 1952.

The neutrino, a fundamental particle predicted in 1931, was detected in 1956.

Nuclear power was first generated on a viable industrial scale in Britain from 1956.

Britain introduced a **Clean Air Act,** 1956, after 4,000 died in a London smog, 1952.

International Geophysical Year, an international venture to investigate the Earth, took place, 1957–58, and led to the first space shots.

Computers entered into comn cial use, 1955, and were com mon by 1960.

The first artificial satellite, Sp nik 1, was launched by the USSR in 1957.

Explorer 1, the first US satelli was launched, 1958, and dete ed radiation belts above the Earth.

Stereophonic records first became available in 1958.

The hovercraft was demonstra ed in 1959.

1960–1962
South Africa left the British Commonwealth, 1961, after Britain accepted the trend of decolonization in Africa, 1960.
The Russians built the Berlin Wall, 1961.
After **John F. Kennedy,** 1917–63, the US president, intervened in Cuba, 1961, Soviet missile supplies to Cuba provoked a world crisis, 1962. Kennedy supported the **Civil Rights Movement.**
Algeria won her independence.

1962–1965
The Nuclear Test Ban Treaty was signed by the US, USSR, and Britain, 1963, but China exploded her first bomb in 1964.
After Kennedy's assassination, Lyndon B. Johnson, 1908–73, signed civil rights bills and built up US forces in Vietnam to oppose the Communist rebels.
Britain granted independence to **Kenya,** 1963, and **Malawi,** 1964, but Rhodesia declared her own independence under white rule.

1965–1967
The Chinese Cultural Revolution aimed to weaken the bureaucracy and stimulate more public participation, 1966–68.
Growing American military activity in Vietnam failed to bring victory.
Biafran secessionist claims led to civil war in Nigeria.
Israel defeated the Arab states in the 1967 **Six Days War** and extended her frontiers.
France left NATO, 1966, to protest against American strength in Europe.

1967–1970
Student revolt in France, 1968, was echoed throughout Europe. After referendum defeat, 1969, de Gaulle resigned.
Soviet troops invaded Czechoslovakia to end liberal reforms.
Richard Nixon, 1913–   , resumed bombing North Vietnam, after peace talks and troop withdrawals, 1970.
Tanzania and Zambia secured Chinese support for a railroad linking the copper belt to the sea.

1970–1972
Massive balance of payments deficits forced a devaluation of the US currency, 1971.
China joined the UN, 1971.
Bangladesh was set up, 1971, after a civil war in Pakistan.
The EEC expanded to include Britain, Ireland, and Denmark.
Nixon visited China, 1972, and secured rapprochement with the Soviet Union.
Salvador Allende, 1908–73, a Marxist, was elected president of Chile, 1970, but was killed after a right-wing coup.

1972–1976
US troops left Vietnam, 1973.
The Arabs fought well in the October War, then forced up world oil prices to put pressure on Israel's western allies.
A coup in Portugal, 1974, led to revolution and the end of Portugal's empire in Africa.
Communists took control of South Vietnam and Cambodia, 1975.
China underwent extensive domestic changes in 1976 as **Premier Chou En-Lai** and chairman **Mao Tse-tung** died.

The attempted invasion at Bay of Pigs, 1961, involved US-supported Cuban nationals. The Peace Corps was founded, 1961.

Pres. John F. Kennedy, 1917–63, was assassinated in Dallas, 1963. **Pres. Lyndon B. Johnson,** 1908–73, initiated the War on Poverty, 1964.

A US military buildup in Vietnam, 1964–68, followed the Gulf of Tonkin Resolution. **Martin Luther King,** 1929–68, led a civil rights march, 1965, in Selma, Ala.

The intelligence ship Pueblo was seized by North Korea, 1968. Astronaut **Neil Armstrong,** 1930–   , walked on the moon's surface, 1969.

During a Vietnam War protest 4 college students were killed at Kent State University, Ohio, 1971. The Equal Rights Amendment was passed, 1972.

Scandals forced **Pres. Richard M. Nixon,** 1913–   , 1974, to resign. **Jimmy Carter,** 1924– defeated **Pres. Gerald R. Ford,** 1913–   , in 1976.

Riots in Washington after death of Martin Luther King, 1968

Ho Chi Minh

Apollo astronaut

Bangladesh famine victims

Prince Fahd of Saudi Arabia

R. D. Laing, 1927–   , studied schizophrenia in a personal rather than clinical way in *The Divided Self*, 1960, and developed a humanistic school of anti-psychology.
The Ecumenical Movement for Christian unity began in 1961–62 when the Eastern Orthodox and Catholic churches met with Protestants at the World Council of Churches, while the Vatican Council, 1962, tried to reconcile differences within Catholicism.

Herbert Marcuse, 1898–   , associated with the "Frankfurt" School of Sociology, argued in *One Dimensional Man*, 1964, that in modern industrial society there is a process of "repressive tolerance" that diverts the creative impulses in man by satisfying his material needs.
Julius Nyerere, president of Tanzania from 1964, set out to weaken Western influence by political non-alignment, to develop a village-based socialism, and to foster African nationalism.

The American Civil Rights Movement against racial intolerance of Negroes was led by **Martin Luther King,** 1929–68, who believed in the use of moral force. In the mid-60s, however, black leaders such as **Eldridge Cleaver** turned to violence.
The "flower-power" movement, originating with American students in 1967, sought awareness with the aid of mind-expanding drugs. A US counterculture grew up, based on communes and anarchism.

The radical student movement of 1968, originating in America and Europe in opposition to the Vietnam War, stressed individual liberation from the constraints of capitalism, influenced by Third World revolutionaries such as **Ché Guevara,** 1928–67, and the writings of **Marcuse.**
Pope Paul VI, *r.*1963–   , condemned the use of artificial methods of birth control, 1968, arousing widespread criticism.

Western religious groups stressing personal awareness included the "**Jesus freaks**" and the **Divine Light Mission,** which had Hindu elements.
The Conservation movement argued that continued industrial growth is incompatible with the preservation of the natural world and its resources.
Environmentalists predicted the imminent disappearance of natural resources.

The rapidly growing population of developing countries was the subject of a campaign, 1973–74, organized by **International Planned Parenthood Federation** to introduce birth control programs. The United Nations called 1975 **International Women's Year.**
The US Episcopal Church agreed to the ordination of women to the priesthood, 1976. The Korean **Sun Myung Moon** and his Unification Church continued to cause controversy, 1976.

The damaging effects of Western civilization in African culture were examined in the novels of **Chinua Achebe,** 1930–   , and the plays of **Wole Soyinka,** 1934–   , both Nigerians. The West Indian novelist **V. S. Naipaul,** 1932–   , wrote of poverty in Trinidad with delicate irony in *A House for Mr. Biswas*, 1961.

Postwar German society was explored in the writings of **Günter Grass,** 1927–   , and **Heinrich Böll,** 1917–   .
The American novel flourished in the works of **Saul Bellow,** 1915–   , **Philip Roth,** 1933– and **Norman Mailer,** 1923–   , who also satirized politics in a journalistic style.

South American literature reached the West with translations of established writers. The Colombian **Gabriel García Marquéz,** 1928–   , described the history of a family in a tropical town in *One Hundred Years of Solitude*, 1967.
Mexico's dual heritage of savagery and civilization was the theme of the surrealistic poetry of **Octavio Paz,** 1914–

Change of Skin by the Mexican **Carlos Fuentes,** 1928–   , was an "open novel" describing the fluctuations of experience.
Criticism of the Soviet regime in *Gulag Archipelago* led to the exile of **Alexander Solzhenitsyn,** 1918–
The Japanese postwar generation was described in the novels of **Yukio Mishima,** 1925–70.

Science fiction became increasingly popular, notably in the works of American writers **Kurt Vonnegut, Jr.,** 1922–   , **Isaac Asimov,** 1920–   , and **Ray Bradbury,** 1920–
Carlos Casteneda published his *Journey to Ixtlan*, the last of a series of accounts of his meetings with a Mexican shaman.

Traditional English drama was represented by **Tom Stoppard,** 1937–   , and **David Storey,** 1933–   , while in America **Edward Albee's,** 1928–   , *Seascape* won the Pulitzer Prize, 1975. The Nobel Prize for literature in 1976 went to **Saul Bellow.**
Formal experimentation in the theater produced the almost silent plays of **Samuel Beckett.**

Distorted human forms confined within a claustrophobic space characterized the work of the Briton **Francis Bacon,** 1910– seen in his "Red Figure," 1962.
A move toward formalism was seen in the dramatic use of curved concrete at the TWA buildings, Kennedy Airport, 1961, by **Eero Saarinen,** 1910–61.
Japanese architecture united traditional forms with the new materials of steel and concrete in the work of **Tange,** 1913–

Two exponents of **Op art,** who studied the effect of optical illusions juxtaposing colors and forms, were the Hungarian **Victor Vasarely,** 1908–   , and the Briton **Bridget Riley,** 1931–   .
Pop art in America in the 1960s took images from cartoon comics as in *Whaam*, 1963, by **Roy Lichtenstein,** 1923–   , and from commercial advertising in the work of **Andy Warhol,** 1930–
The Chinese sculpture "Rent Collection Yard," 1965, depicted the miseries of the empire.

The "Happening," the creation of an environment simulating the effects of hallucinatory drugs, often with rock music and shifting patterns of color, was pioneered in the US *c.*1965.
Realism in British painting was exemplified in the works of **Lucien Freud,** 1922–   , whose portraits and townscapes show detailed draftsmanship, and in the figure paintings of **David Hockney,** 1937–   , like "Peter getting out of Nick's pool," 1966.

A politically committed documentary style of filmmaking arose in Britain, seen in *Kes*, 1969, by the directors **Tony Garnett,** 1936–   , and **Kenneth Loach,** 1936–
Land Art and **"Arte Poyera,"** emerged in 1969 as an avant-garde movement that was concerned with art as assemblages of simple elements such as earth and rocks.

An exhibition in London and Paris of **Chinese art** treasures, including archeological discoveries made during the Cultural Revolution, restored cultural contacts between China and the West.
Conceptual art, practiced by **Barry Flanagan,** 1944–   , and **Keith Arnott,** 1931–   , in England, aimed to communicate through concepts rather than visual images.

An underground movement of abstract artists in the USSR attempted unsuccessfully to hold an open-air exhibition in Moscow, 1974.
The epic disaster film and kung fu and karate films became popular. Bulgarian-born artist **Christo Javacheff** created *Running Fence*, 24.5 miles of nylon fabric, in northern California, 1976.

Graphic notation of symbols to portray sound became widespread in the 1960s as composers sought new sounds and effects from electronic and conventional instruments.

Simplicity and space marked the experimental music of the 1960s. Composers like **Terry Riley,** 1935–   , used simple repeated phrases that overlap in ever-changing patterns.

The tape recorder, invented in 1942, made all kinds of artificial sound reproduction possible. It was used creatively in popular music, as in the song "Sergeant Pepper," 1967, by the **Beatles.**

Poet-musicians became popular in the late 1960s, singing their own often highly individual compositions. Most influential was **Bob Dylan,** 1941–

The synthesizer became a readily accessible instrument with the development of microelectronics. Its wide range of sounds may well spur future musical advances.

American theater saw the revivals of many musicals in the 1970s including *My Fair Lady*, *Porgy and Bess*, *Guys and Dolls*, and *Three Penny Opera*, 1976.

The bathyscape Trieste descended 7 mi(11 km) to the deepest part of the ocean, 1960.
The laser was invented in 1960, and used for precision cutting and optical surgery.
Tiros I, the first weather satellite, was placed in orbit by the United States in 1960.
Manned space flight began in 1961 with a one-orbit mission by the Soviet cosmonaut **Yuri Gagarin** 1934–68.
Telstar, the first communications satellite, was launched by the US in 1962.

Syncom, the first communications satellite that is constantly available for use, was put into orbit by the US in 1964.
Radiation at a wavelength of 7 centimeters was first detected from space in 1965, providing support for the big bang theory.
The development of integrated circuits in the 1960s brought new possibilities of miniaturization, stimulating the rise of the electronics industry in the US and making electronic equipment common in the West.

Plate tectonics developed as a theory to explain continental drift, from 1965.
Mariner 4, US space probe, flew past Mars in 1965 and sent back the first pictures of another planet.
The first heart transplant was performed in 1966.
Research into plant genetics and soil fertility led to the **Green Revolution** in many Third World countries, 1966–70, greatly increasing agricultural yields.

The Rance estuary power station in France, harnessing tidal energy, was set up, 1967. **DDT** was banned in the US, 1969, following concern about its harmful side-effects.
The first Moon landing was made in 1969 by members of the US Apollo 11 space mission. Space research facilitated **invisible light astronomy** and assisted **meteorology.** Spin-offs with industrial or domestic use included aluminum foil and teflon, convenient for cooking utensils.

Earth resource satellites were first launched by the US in 1971 to detect and map the world's resources.
A series of American space probes to look close-up at Mars, Jupiter, and Mercury began in 1971.
Germ warfare was banned by international convention, 1972.

The rise in oil prices, 1973, and limited nature of mineral fuel supplies stimulated research into **tidal, solar, and geophysical energy** as alternate sources.
A Soviet space probe took pictures of Venus; Soviet and US spacecraft linked in space, 1975. Unmanned Viking spacecraft on Mars tested for signs of life, 1976.
Supersonic US-Europe transport service began amid controversy, 1976.

CANDIDE,

OU

L'OPTIMISME,

TRADUIT DE L'ALLEMAND

DE

Mr. le Docteur RALPH.

Par M. de V.

M. DCC. LXVI.

The syxth booke.

How syr Launcelot and syr Lyonell departed fro ẏ courte for to seke aduentures. And how syr Lyonell lefte hym sleppynge and was taken. Ca.j.

How syr Ector folowed for to seke syr Launcelot/and how he was taken by

kynge Bagdemagus doughter/& how that he made his complaynte vnto her father. ca.vj.

How syr Launcelot behaued hym in a turneyment/and how he mette with syr Turquyne/ledynge with hym syr Gaherys. ca.vij.

How syr Launcelot & syr Turquyne fought togyder. ca.viij.

How syr Turquyne was slayne/and how syr Launcelot badde syr Gaherys to delyuer all the prysoners. ca.ix.

How syr Laũcelot rode with the damoysell/& how he slewe a knyght that distressed all ladyes/and also a vylayne that kepte a brydge. ca.x.

How syr Laũcelot slewe two gyauntes/and made a castell free. ca.xj.

How syr Launcelot rode dysguysed in syr kays harneys/and how he smote downe a knyght. ca.xij.

How syr Launcelot iusted agaynst foure knyghtes of the rounde table and ouerthrewe them. ca.xiij.

How syr Launcelot folowed a brachet in to a castell/where as he founde a deed knyght/and how he after was requyred of a damoysell for to hele her brother. ca.xiiij.

How that syr Launcelot came in to

FOUNDATION OF THE COMMONWEALTH
FEDERAL PARLIAMENT HOUSE
CANBERRA
1927
1/6
AUSTRALIA

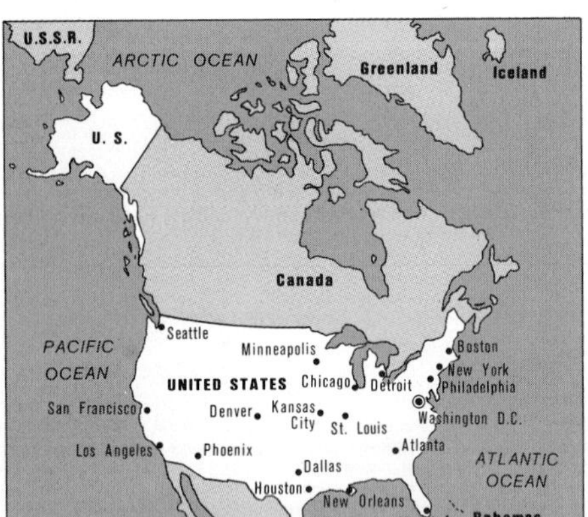

U.S.S.R.
ARCTIC OCEAN
Greenland
Iceland
U. S.
Canada
PACIFIC
OCEAN
Seattle
Minneapolis
Boston
New York
UNITED STATES
Chicago
Detroit
Philadelphia
San Francisco
Denver
Kansas City
St. Louis
Washington D.C.
Los Angeles
Phoenix
Atlanta
ATLANTIC
OCEAN
Dallas
Houston
New Orleans
Miami
Bahamas
0
1600 km
Mexico
Cuba
Haiti
Jamaica

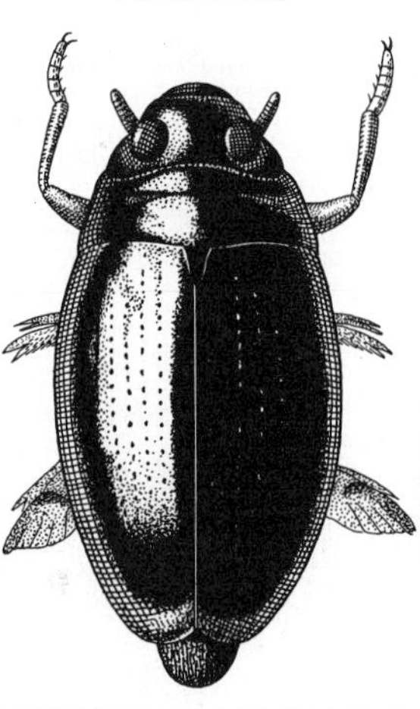

ALPHAPEDIA

Aachen (Aix-la-Chapelle), city in W West Germany, 40mi (64km) WSW of Cologne, near Belgian and Dutch borders; noted for hot sulfur baths used to treat rheumatism, gout, and skin disorders, also used by Romans in AD 1st century; probable birthplace of Charlemagne; site of medieval imperial diets and church councils. Taken by France 1794, city surrendered to Prussia 1815; occupied by Allies 1918–30; first major German city to fall to Allies in WWII (October 1944); important industrial center and railroad junction. Industries: steel, textiles, machinery, rubber goods. Pop. 176,781.

Aalto, Alvar (1899–1976), Finnish architect and furniture designer. His unique handling of floor levels and his use of natural materials and irregular forms can be seen in both his public buildings and private residences. His work includes the municipal library at Viipuri (1927–35), the sanitorium at Paimio (1929–33), the Baker House at the Massachusetts Institute of Technology (1947–48), Säynätsalo town hall group (1950–52), and Finlandia House, Helsinki (1971). His well-known furniture designs are characterized by curved strips of laminated wood.

Aarau, town in N Switzerland, on Aare River, 23mi (37km) W of Zurich at the foot of the Jura Mts; capital of Aargau canton; ruled by the Hapsburgs until taken by Bern 1415; became capital of Helvetic Republic 1798; site of cantonal library, Gothic church, 18th-century town hall, medieval towers. Industries: shoe manufacturing, electrical equipment, mathematical instruments. Founded 13th century. Pop. 16,881.

Aardvark, nocturnal, naked or sparsely haired mammal of central and southern Africa that lives on termites and ants picked up with its sticky foot-long (30cm) tongue. Length: to 5ft (1.5m); weight: to 150lbs (68kg). It is the only species in the order Tubulidentata. △540,548.

Aardwolf, rare nocturnal mammal that lives in open or bush country in Southern and East Africa. It has soft, black-striped yellow-gray underfur and coarse outer fur forming a crest along the back, and a long, bushy tail. It eats termites and other insects. Overall length: 26in (64cm). Family Hyaenidae; species *Proteles cristata.*

Aaron, in the Bible, older brother of Moses and first high priest of Israel. He acted as spokesman for Moses and performed many miracles. During Moses' stay on Mount Sinai, he built the golden calf and led in its worship. His tribe, the Levites, were priests of Israel.

Aaron, Henry Louis ("Hank") (1934–), US baseball player, b. Mobile. His major league career began in 1954 with the then Milwaukee (later Atlanta) Braves of the National League. In 1974 he surpassed Babe Ruth's major league career home run record of 714. He joined the Milwaukee Brewers in 1975 and set a lifetime home run record of 755 in 1976 before retiring as a player.

Abaca. *See* Manila Hemp.

Abacus, a mathematical tool used in Asia and the Middle East for solving problems of addition and subtraction. A simple device made up of beads strung on wire in units of 10, it has been used in various forms for thousands of years. The Chinese abacus dates from the 12th century. △1948.

Abadan, city in SW Iran, on Abadan Island in Persian Gulf; important center of Middle East oil; pipeline terminus; site of the first oil refinery (1913) built by the Anglo-Iranian Oil Company. Pop. 280,000.

Abalone, seashore gastropod mollusk with a single flattened spiral shell perforated by a row of respiratory holes, found on Mediterranean, E Atlantic, and Pacific shores and off coasts of S Africa and Australia. It has a large fleshy foot and sensory projections on the underside. Length: 12in (30cm). Family Haliotidae; species include *Haliotis rufescens.* △482.

Abandonment, In property law, the relinquishment of possession of property, as in throwing property away, losing it with no attempt to retrieve, or vacating it with no intent to return.

Abbadids, Moorish dynasty that ruled Seville, Spain, from 1023 to 1091. After the collapse of the Córdoba caliphate, the cadi of Seville proclaimed himself king as Abbad I in 1023. His son Abbad II succeeded him in 1042 and made Seville the strongest kingdom in southern Spain. His successor Abbad III, who became king in 1069, was a patron of the arts. He was overthrown and forced into exile in 1091 by the Almoravids. *See also* Almoravids.

Abbas I (1557–1628), shah of Persia (1586–1628), son of Mohammed Khudabanda. He stopped the Uzbeks, seized Ormuz (1622) and Baghdad (1623), founded the port of Bandar Abbas, erected great buildings at Esfahan, and left the Safawid dynasty strong.

Abbas II (1874–1944), khedive of Egypt (1892–1914), successor of Mohammed Tewfik. He ruled under the Ottoman Empire. From 1879 Lords Cromer and Kitchener governed with him, but the British deposed him in favor of his uncle, Hussein Kamil.

Abbas (died 652), uncle of the Prophet Mohammed and of the caliph Ali. A rich merchant in Mecca, he gave his name to the famous dynasty of Muslim caliphs, the Abbasid.

Abbasids, Muslim dynasty that held the caliphate from 750 to 1258. They traced their descent from Abbas, the uncle of Mohammed. The family came to power by defeating the Umayyads, who were exiled to Spain. The Abbasids moved the caliphate from Damascus to Baghdad, where it achieved great splendor, particularly under Harun al-Rashid and al-Mamun. After the family's downfall in 1258, one member escaped to Cairo, where the dynasty continued to be recognized until the 16th century. △1062.

Abbey, a complex of buildings that makes up a religious community, the center of which is the abbey church, and the whole of which is directed by an abbot or abbess. Since the fall of monasticism in England, often only the church remains. A famous example is Westminster Abbey.

Abbey Theatre, theater erected on Abbey St., Dublin (1904), by Annie E.F. Horniman to house the Irish National Theatre Society, presenting Irish actors in Irish plays. In 1924, with a government subsidy, the Abbey became the national theater of Ireland. Works by W.B. Yeats, Lady Gregory, J.M. Synge, and Sean O'Casey have been introduced there by such actors as Sara Allgood, Arthur Sinclair, and Barry Fitzgerald.

Abbott, Berenice (1898–), US photographer, b. Springfield, Ohio. Working in Paris, first as assistant to Man Ray, she made superb portraits of writers and artists of the 1920s. She began her celebrated studies of New York City in 1929. From 1958 she photographed scientific phenomena.

Abbott, George (1889–), American producer, playwright, director, and actor, b. Forestville, N.Y. Extraordinarily multitalented, beginning in 1926 with "Broadway," he wrote, directed, and produced a string of fast-paced hit shows spanning over 40 years. *Three Men on a Horse* (1935), *Boys from Syracuse* (1938), *Damn Yankees* (1955), and *A Funny Thing Happened on the Way to the Forum* (1961) exemplify his influence on US popular theater.

Abbott, (Sir) John (1821–93), lawyer, educator, and prime minister of Canada (1891–92). Dean of McGill Law School, he was a Conservative legislator ousted during the Pacific Scandal of 1873. In 1880 he was reelected to parliament and later succeeded John Macdonald as prime minister. *See also* Pacific Scandal of 1873.

Abbott and Costello, Bud Abbott (1895–1974), b. William Abbott in Atlantic City, N.J., and **Lou Costello** (1906–59), b. Louis Cristillo in Paterson, N.J., US vaudeville and film comedy team. Abbott was the straight man, and Costello was the rotund madcap in many films, including *Rio Rita* (1942) and *The Wistful Widow of Wagon Gap* (1948).

ABC Mediation, arbitration conducted by Argentina, Brazil and Chile to settle a dispute between Mexico and the United States when President Wilson landed Marines at Vera Cruz (1914).

Abd al-Hamid II (1842–1918), Ottoman sultan (1876–1909), nephew of Abd al-Aziz. He reigned after his brother, Murad V, became insane. He suspended the constitution, executing Midhat Pasha. Russia forced him to sign the Treaty of San Stefano (1878). He sought German aid to save the empire. A revolt of the Young Turks led to his ouster. Mohammed V succeeded. △1302.

Abd al-Malik (646–705), fifth Umayyad caliph (685–705), son of Marwan I. With Gen. al-Hajjaj, he defeated the rival caliph, Abdullah ibn-al-Zubayr, battled Byzantine forces, and united Islam. He reformed government and secured Arabic as the official language. Walid I succeeded. △1062.

Abd-al-Mumim (1094–1163), founder of the Almohad Empire, successor of Mohammed-ibn-Tumart. He conquered the Maghreb from the Almoravids, seizing the conquests of Roger II of Sicily in Africa as far as Tripoli. He united the Berbers; rebuilt Rabat, other ports, and towns; and was succeeded by his son, Abu Yaqub Yusuf.

Abd-el-Kader (1807–83), Algerian leader, emir of Mascara. He pushed the French and Turks from N Algeria, consolidating tribes and organizing resistance. In 1839 he began a holy war against the French. He and Abd-er-Rahman were defeated by Gen. Bugeaud at Isly (1844). Later he received the Grand Cross of the Legion of Honor for helping the Christians.

Abd-el-Krim (1885–1963), Rif leader in Morocco. In 1921–22 his Rif tribesmen captured Spanish outposts. In 1925 he attacked French Morocco and was defeated by combined French-Spanish troops. He surrendered in 1926, but escaped to Egypt to lead a new independence movement.

Abd er-Rahman I (died 788), first Umayyad emir of Córdoba (756–88). In 750 the Abbasids massacred his family in Damascus, but he escaped. He defeated Yusuf of Córdoba at Alameda (756). He united the Muslim tribes, checked the Frankish army of Charlemagne at Saragossa (778), and began the great mosque at Córdoba. Hisham I succeeded.

Abd er-Rahman III (891–961), Umayyad emir (912–29) and caliph (929–61) of Córdoba, successor of Abdullah. He reclaimed lost provinces, renovated his fleet, seized Ceuta, controlled Christian lands, and made Córdoba magnificent. Hakam II succeeded. △1078.

Abdomen, in vertebrates, that portion of the body between the chest and the pelvis, containing the abdominal cavity, and the abdominal viscera, including most of the digestive organs. In arthropods it is the posterior part of the body, containing the reproductive organs and part of the digestive system.

Abdul Baha, (Sir) (1844–1921), Persian religious leader, b. as Abbas Effendi. His chosen name means "Servant of Glory." He succeeded his father, Baha Ullah, as leader of the Bahai faith (1892–1921). He carried the Bahai message to Europe and the United States, winning many converts. *See also* Bahaism.

Abdul-Jabbar, Kareem (1947–), US basketball player, b. Lewis Alcindor in New York City. After an outstanding career at University of California, Los Angeles, where he led his team to three NCAA championships (1967–69), he joined the Milwaukee Bucks in the National Basketball Association (1969). Versatile and 7′3″ tall, he was considered his era's best player. He led the league in scoring (1971–72) and was named most valuable player three times (1971–72; 1974). He changed his name in 1970. In 1975, he was traded to the Los Angeles Lakers.

Abdullah (1882–1951), king of Jordan (1946–51), son of Hussein. In 1921, after aiding Britain in World War I, he became emir of Trans-Jordan. He lost control of Hejaz to Ibn Saud. In World War II he resisted the Axis. He fought Israel, annexed land, and signed an armistice (1949). He was assassinated in Jerusalem, and Talal ascended the throne.

Abdullah, (Sheikh) Mohammed (1905–), political leader of Muslims in Kashmir. He served as prime minister of Jammu and Kashmir after India's independence (1947–52) but was arrested in 1953 for advocating Kashmiri independence and was kept in protective custody almost continuously afterward.

Abel, in Genesis, second son of Adam and Eve, killed by his brother Cain. △810.

Abel, Niels Henrik (1802–29), Norwegian mathematician. After studying and working in Norway he later worked in France and Germany, where he generalized the binomial theorem and advanced the theory of elliptical functions.

Abelard, Peter (1079–1142), French philosopher, regarded as the founder of the University of Paris. In *Sic et Non (Yes and No)* he proposed reconciling discrepancies among Christian authorities through dialectic. His opponents advocated faith above logic and twice had him condemned as a heretic. He is best known for his tragic love affair with Héloise, for which he was attacked and emasculated. He became a monk; Héloise entered a convent.

Abe Lincoln in Illinois (1938), a drama by Robert Sherwood that portrays a very human Abraham Lincoln struggling to live the humble life he enjoys while at the same time taking a dignified stand for what he believes. The play, which won a Pulitzer Prize in 1939, also deals with the responsibilities of power in the face of certain war.

Aberdeen, town of Aberdeenshire, in NE Scotland: university and cathedral city: important docks and fish market. Industries: papermaking, shipbuilding, engineering, textiles. Pop. 182,006.

Aberdeen, town in NE Maryland, 29mi (47km) ENE of Baltimore; US Army's Aberdeen Proving Grounds and Army Chemical Center is just S; together they occupy 87,000 acres (35,235hectares). Industries: canning, shoes, rubber products. Named after Aberdeen, Scotland; Inc. 1892. Pop. (1970) 12,375.

Aberdeen, city in NE South Dakota; seat of Brown co; site of Northern State College (1899). Industries: flour, dairy products, trade center. Inc. 1882. Pop. (1970) 26,476.

Aberdeen Angus, jet black breed of beef cattle originally developed in Scotland. Small and naturally hornless, they yield excellent meat. Not as common as Shorthorn or Hereford breeds, they are gaining in popularity in the United States, Canada, New Zealand, and Argentina. *See also* Beef Cattle, Cattle. △372.

Aberhart, William (1878–1943), Canadian evangelist and Social Credit premier of Alberta (1935–43). A social reformer, he unsuccessfully attempted to initiate a policy of "social dividends" and to license banks. He instituted labor legislation and supported education and provincial autonomy.

Abernathy, Ralph (David) (1926–), US clergyman and civil rights leader, b. Linden, Ala. He succeeded Dr. Martin Luther King, Jr., as leader of the Southern Christian Leadership Conference upon King's assassination (1968) and continued to promote the nonviolent civil rights movement that King initiated. He organized the Montgomery bus boycott (1955) and the Poor People's March on Washington (1968). Abernathy was also chairman of the Atlanta branch of Operation Breadbasket, the economic arm of the SCLC. *See also* Southern Christian Leadership Conference.

Aberration, any of various defects in lens and mirror images arising when light is not incident at or near the center of the system. Spherical aberration occurs when rays from the object falling on the periphery of a lens or mirror are not brought to the same focal point as rays at the center; the image is thus blurred. Chromatic aberration occurs in lens images due to the different colors of the dispersed light being brought to different focal points; the image is thus falsely colored. △1522.

Aberration of Light, apparent slight change of position of a celestial object, such as a star, due to the effect of the orbital motion around the sun of the earth, and thus an observer, on the direction of arrival of the light. A telescope must be inclined by an angle of up to about 20″ to accommodate this. △1518.

Abidjan, capital city of the Ivory Coast, on the Ebrie Lagoon; popular tourist resort; site of the University of Abidjan (1963) and the Museum of the Ivory Coast; major center of communication, transportation, administration, commerce. Industries: soap, lumber, textiles, chemicals, beer. Pop. 285,000.

Abigail, two biblical figures, one being the wife of sheep and goat owner Nabal. She persuaded David not to retaliate for Nabal's refusal to give him a share of wool. She later became David's wife. The other was step sister of David, wife of Jether, and mother of Amasa.

Abilene, town in E central Kansas, on the Smokey Hill River, 90mi (145km) W of Topeka; seat of Dickinson co; important railroad shipping center of cattle 1867–71; end of the Chisholm Trail; childhood home of Dwight D. Eisenhower and site of the Eisenhower Museum. Industries: shipping, flour mills, creameries. Settled 1856; inc. 1869. Pop. (1970) 6,661.

Abilene, city in NW central Texas, 152mi (246km) WSW of Fort Worth; seat of Taylor co. Settled as a railway junction, it was named after Abilene, Kansas, because of the cattle driven there; site of Hardin-Simmons University (1891), Abilene Christian College (1906), and McMurry College (1923). Industries: agriculture, ranching, oil refining. Founded 1881; inc. 1882. Pop. (1970) 89,653.

Abington School District v. Schempp (1963), US Supreme Court case that ruled unconstitutional a law requiring bible readings in public schools, citing First Amendment restriction on laws "respecting an establishment of religion."

Ablation, in aerospace technology, the wearing away of the outer surface of a material by flaking, chipping, melting, or vaporization. Nose cones and leading edges of re-entry capsules and missiles are equipped with ablating material to remove excess heat. Good ablating materials such as quartz and teflon have low thermal conductivity, high melting points, high specific heat, and high heats of vaporization and fusion; they often create an insulating layer of vapor to protect the spacecraft further.

Ablation, in geology, a measure of glacial loss through melting, evaporation, wind erosion, or calving (formation of icebergs). Sometimes used in geomorphology to mean the loss of surface or rock by wind or water action.

Abnaki, or **Wabanaki,** tribe of Algonkian-speaking North American Indians of the Eastern Woodlands group. They inhabited NE New England, to which they apparently fled as refugees from English colonists. Later most of them went to New Brunswick, Canada, where their descendents live today. In history they were famous as the people who inhabited the fabled Norumbega.

Aardvark

Aberdeen, Scotland

Aberdeen Angus

Abidjan, Ivory Coast

Abnormal Psychology, division of psychology concerned with behavior disorders, eg, psychotic disorders such as schizophrenia, psychoneurotic problems such as phobias, personality disorders, and problems caused by brain damage or mental retardation. Unlike clinical psychology and psychiatry, abnormal psychology focuses on basic theory rather than on treatment. *See also* Clinical Psychology; Psychiatry. △760,764.

Abolitionism, 19th-century movement to end slavery in the United States. Although antislavery sentiment went back as far as the 1690s, when the Quakers began speaking out against it, the first antislavery society was not founded until 1775. Many other such societies were established during the Revolutionary War. The efforts of Thomas Jefferson resulted in the outlawing of slavery in the Northwest Territory (1787). The United States Constitution (1788) prohibited the slave trade. Several states passed legislation abolishing slavery in the 1780s. In 1808 the further importation of slaves was prohibited by Congress. In 1817 the American Colonization Society was formed to transport free blacks to a colony in Africa. This solution was denounced by Benjamin Lundy, William Lloyd Garrison and other influential abolitionists of this period. The Missouri Compromise (1820) prohibited new slave states above the 36°30′ north latitude. In 1833 the American Anti-Slavery Society was formed in Philadelphia. Active in this group were Arthur and Lewis Tappan, Theodore Dwight Weld and James G. Birney. The Underground Railroad, with such conductors as Harriet Tubman, helped fugitive slaves reach freedom. From the 1840s ex-slave Frederick Douglass was an abolitionist speaker. Efforts to elect abolitionist Birney president, as candidate of the Liberty party (1840, 1844), failed, as did the Free Soil party with former Pres. Martin Van Buren as candidate (1848). Sectional disputes intensified, and the Compromise of 1850 attempted to appease both North and South. Harriet Beecher Stowe's *Uncle Tom's Cabin* (1852) increased antislavery sentiment. During the 1850s the abolitionists concentrated on helping fugitive slaves. The Emancipation Proclamation (1863) weakened slavery, but it was not ended until the 13th Amendment to the US Constitution (1865). *See also* Free Soil Party; Garrison, William Lloyd; Missouri Compromise. △1276.

Abominable Snowman, legendary creature of the Himalayas. The Sherpa natives describe it as long-haired, able to walk erect, with apelike facial features. Several expeditions have attempted to find concrete evidence for the Yeti, as he is called by the Sherpas, but all have failed.

Abortion. △808.

Abraham, in the Bible, son of Terah and founder of Jewish nation. He was commanded by God to move to Canaan and transmit God's blessing to all people of the earth. Childless, his wife Sarah gave him her maid Hagar who bore Ishmael. A rivalry grew between the two women when Sarah bore Isaac several years later.

Abraham, Plains of, located in Quebec City, Canada, the site of the decisive battle of the French and Indian War. After the battle in 1759, during which generals Wolfe and Montcalm, the British and French commanders, were slain, the way was clear for British dominance in E Canada.

Abrahams, Peter (1919–), South African novelist. Although self-exiled at age 20 to England and later to Jamaica, he centered most of his novels around his homeland. *Mine Boy* (1946), *The Path of Thunder* (1948), and *Wild Conquest* (1950) all deal with particular problems of South Africa.

Abrams v. United States (1919), Supreme Court decision that upheld the espionage convictions of anti-World War I pamphleteers and broadened the "clear and present danger" doctrine first outlined in *Schenck* v. *United States*. *See also* Schenck v. United States.

Abrasion, in geology, mechanical wearing down of rock surface by wind, water, glacial movements, tides, or currents. *See also* Erosion. △262.

Abrasives, hard and rough substances used in grinding and polishing objects by abrading their surfaces. Some abrasives are used as fine powders, others in larger fragments with sharp, cutting edges. Most natural abrasives are minerals, eg diamond, garnet, emery, corundum, pumice, flint, and quartz. Crushed steel and powdered glass are also used. Synthetic abrasives include silicon carbide, aluminum oxide, and synthetic diamonds.

Abrasive Wheel, rotating disc of abrasive material or with abrasive material cemented to its outside surface. Modern tools grind to tolerances of 0.0001in (0.00025mm). Common operations are centerless grinding (where the rounded workpiece is smoothed between a grinding and a regulating wheel) and surface grinding of flat pieces. *See also* Abrasives.

Abruzzi, mountainous region in central Italy, on the Adriatic Sea; self-governing since 1965; capital is Aquila; comprised of the provinces of Chieti, Pescara, Teramo, and Aquila. Industries: textiles, food processing, agriculture, livestock. Pop. 1,205,142.

Absalom, several biblical figures, most notably the third son of David. He murdered his brother Ammon for the rape of their sister. Plotting to seize the throne that would soon be Solomon's, he was killed by David's general, Joab. Another was the father of Matthias and Jonathan.

Absalom, Absalom! (1936), novel by William Faulkner about the effects of the dynastic ambition of a white Southerner on his descendants, both white and black. It deals with Thomas Sutpen, his wife Ellen, her sister Rosa Coldfield, and Thomas' children, Henry and Judith, who are white, and Charles Bon, a mulatto. *See also* Faulkner, William.

Abscissa, distance of a point from the y axis in a Cartesian coordinate system; the x coordinate when the position of a point is expressed as the ordered pair (x,y).

Absent Without Leave (AWOL), administrative status of military personnel absent from their duty station without official permission. In the US Army, an individual who is AWOL over 30 days may be declared a deserter.

Absent Without Leave (1964), a novella by Heinrich Böll. It implicitly questions the values of modern society and asks how much validity they can have. The issue of duty is given an ironical treatment.

Absolute Advantage, situation in international trade in which a particular country is able to supply a product for sale at a lower cost than any other country. *See also* Comparative Advantage.

Absolute Zero, the temperature at which all parts of a system are at the lowest energy permitted by the laws of quantum mechanics. At this temperature (−273°C) the entropy of the system is also zero, although the total energy may be non-zero. The system has only one energy state available to it, and if isolated remains in that state forever. △1508, 1510, 1512.

Absolution, in religion, a formal act by a member of the clergy through which sins are forgiven, as in the sacrament of penance. The authority is derived from God, and grace is given to those qualified. It may be received following a private confession or a public ceremony.

Absolutism, government with unlimited power vested in one individual or group. First used to describe 18th-century European monarchies that claimed divine right to power. *See also* Divine Right.

Absorbent, substance with the power to absorb large quantities of other substances. Absorbents are usually porous materials: examples are activated charcoal and zeolites. They have many uses, including separating, purifying, decolorizing, and deodorizing.

Abstract Art, loosely used term commonly applied to 20th-century art styles. It has been used to cover two contrary schools. The first is the reduction or abstraction of natural forms to simpler, stylized ones, as in the works of Paul Klee, Paul Cézanne, and Jean Louis Forain. The second is the construction from non-representational basic forms of art objects that are intended to be appreciated for what they are, and not as representations. It can be subdivided into romantic and organic artists, including Wassily Kandinski, Joan Miró, Jean Arp, and Franz Kline, and classical and geometric artists, including Kazimir Malevich, Piet Mondrian, and Ben Nicholson. △1320.

Abstract Expressionism, US art movement most active in the late 1940s and early 1950s. It had worldwide acclaim and imitation. The paintings were generally large, abstract (with some figurative elements), asymmetrical in composition, with loose painterly brushwork and dramatic coloring. The artists laid great stress on the process of painting, some regarding it as a ritual. Stressing spontaneity and free expression, they revolted against prescribed technical procedures, traditional aesthetic canons, and the idea of a finished art product. They included Willem de Kooning, Jackson Pollock, Mark Rothko, and Robert Motherwell. △1372.

Abu al-Fida (1273–1331), Arab historian and ruler, b. Damascus. Governor (1310–20), then sultan (1320–31) of Hama (Syria), he is best known for his geography, *Location of the Countries* (1321), and *Abridgement of the History of Mankind* (1330), an Islamic history to 1329.

Abubacer. *See* Ibn-Tufayl.

Abu Bakr (573–634), first Muslim caliph, successor of Mohammed. His daughter, Aisha, married Mohammed, with whom he went on the Hegira. The Orthodox chiefs secured him as caliph (632). He subjugated the hostile tribes of Arabia with the help of Gen. Khalid ibn-al-Walid. He united the Arabian peninsula and urged conquests in Iraq, Persia, and Syria. He was instrumental in extending Islam as a world religion. In 634 Omar succeeded him. △1058, 1062.

Abu Dhabi, sheikdom on S coast of Persian Gulf; capital is Abu Dhabi. Founded by the Al Bu Falah family in the 18th century; signed a peace treaty with Great Britain 1820 and made a British protectorate 1892; became a member of the independent federation United Arab Emirates when it was formed in 1971. Main industry is oil, discovered 1958. Area: 26,000sq mi (67,340sq km). Pop. 46,375. *See also* United Arab Emirates.

Abulcasis, or Abul Kasim (*c.* 1013), Arab physician. His most important work was a textbook of surgery and medicine, *al-Tasrif,* which was divided into sections dealing with cautery, surgery, and fractures.

Abu-Simbel (Ipsambul or Abu Sunbul), village in S Egypt on the Nile River; site of two famous temples built by Ramesses II in the 13th century BC. In the early 1960s, the United Nations funded a project to cut up the huge statues of Ramesses II and the temples and move them inland, safe from the rising waters caused by the construction of the Aswan High Dam.

Abydos, ruined ancient city of Egypt, 50mi (80.5km) NW of Thebes; site of temples built from 1st to 25th dynasty. One of the temples contains tablets listing the names of ancient Egyptian rulers, which has aided in reconstructing the succession of Egyptian pharaohs. A famous temple of Osiris was built here by Ramesses II on top of another temple 2,000 years older.

Abydos, ancient city in Phrygia, Asia Minor, opposite Sestos at the narrowest point of the Dardanelles. Near here Xerxes I built a bridge of boats (480 BC), the Athenian fleet defeated the Spartan (411 BC), and Maslamah crossed his army (716–17).

Abyssal Animals, animals living at deepest ocean depths in low temperatures, darkness, and high pressure. They include crustaceans, fish, jellyfish, and squid. Adaptations for their environment include extended fins to detect food and warn of predators and expansible mouths, gullets, and stomachs to eat food as large as themselves. Usually gray or black and sometimes blind, they scavenge for fragments sinking from upper levels. △514, 626.

Abyssal Zone, the division of the ocean that begins at about the 2000-m (6,600-ft) depth and includes the rest of the deep ocean. The water temperature ranges from 41° to 30°F (5° to −1°C). The zone has no light so there are no seasons and no plants, but there are many forms of life like glass sponges, sea lilies, lamp shells, and grenadiers. The bottom is covered by deposits of biogenic oozes and non-biogenic sediments (red clays). △228.

Abyssinian Cat, exotic, short-haired domestic cat breed, probably developed from the Kaffir cat. It has a wedge-shaped head; green, gold or hazel almond-shaped eyes; broad-based pointed ears; and a long, tapered tail. Its ruddy brown or brick colored coat has black-tipped hairs. The Red variety lacks black pigment. *See also* Kaffir Cat.

Abzug, Bella (Savitsky) (1920–), former US Democratic congresswoman from New York (1970–76), b. New York City. She was a major critic of the war in Indochina and a leading proponent of women's rights. She was also legislative director for Women Strike for Peace (1961–70).

Acacia, evergreen shrubs and trees native to Australia and widely distributed in tropical or subtropical regions. They have small leaves and yellow or white flowers. Some species have thorns. Grown mainly as ornamentals, some are grown for gum arabic or other gums used in tanning, soap, and medicine. Height:

4–60ft (1.2–18m). Family Leguminosae; genus *Acacia*. △586.

Academic Freedom, right of teachers and students to work without improper interference from government or other external agencies. Like freedom of speech and the press, academic freedom is held to be essential to a democracy. The right is not absolute—it does not, for example, allow a teacher to utter or publish libel.

Académie Française, French literary academy. Established by Cardinal Richelieu in 1634, the Académie Française remains an influential institution. Its aim is to identify writing of literary distinction and to uphold the purity of the national language. Most of the great French writers have in the past belonged to the Académie. △1172.

Academies of Art. △1166.

Acadia, early term for what is now the Maritime Provinces of E Canada and the coastal region of N Maine. The area was first settled with Europeans in 1604 by Sieur De Monts. Early settlements such as Port Royal were attacked by British and colonial American forces over the issues of the fur trade and sea routes. In 1755 many of the French settlers were deported for refusing a loyalty oath to Britain. British dominance was complete by 1763, and the area developed profitable fishing and farming industries.

Acadia National Park, park in SE Maine; rugged coastal area comprised of Desert Island, Isle au Haut, and the S tip of Schoodic Peninsula. The park features rugged cliffs and the highest elevation on the E seaboard: Cadillac Mt, 1,530ft (467m). Area: 41,642acres (16,853hectares). Est. 1919.

Acanthocephala, phylum of spiny-headed parasitic worms once thought to be Nematodes. They are identified by a retractible spiny proboscis and an elongated, cylindrical body. The young are parasitic in insects and the adults in vertebrates, attaching themselves to the intestinal lining. Length: about 1ft (30.5cm). Species include *Echinorhyncus*.

Acanthus, thistlelike, perennial plant found in N South America, Africa, Mediterranean region, India, and Malaya. It has lobed leaves often spiny, and white or colored flower spikes. The 20 species include bear's breeches *(Acanthus mollis)*, with large, oval leaves and rose, white, or bronze flower spikes. Other species include *Justicia americana*, or water willow, with slender, willowlike leaves and pale violet or purple and white flower clusters. *A. spinosis*, with curled leaves, is the pattern for the ornamentation on the capital of the Corinthian column.

Acapulco, city in S Mexico, 190mi (306km) SSW of Mexico City, on the Pacific coast; winter resort noted for beautiful scenery, deep-sea fishing, lavish hotels, entertainment. It was an important port for 250 years linking Spain and the Philippines as "Manila Galleons" made annual trips to and from Manila. Coconuts and bananas are grown in area. Founded 1550 by Spanish. Pop. 174,378.

Acawai, or **Akawai,** tribe of Carib-speaking South American Indians inhabiting the riverine and interior areas of the Guianas. They are farmers, subsisting upon manioc, fishing, and extensive trading relations with other tribes. During the Colonial period they were the major suppliers of slaves to the Dutch and raided other less-aggressive tribes. *See also* Carib.

Accelerated Depreciation, in finance, a method used to depreciate the cost of an asset at a rate faster than the straight-line depreciation method. There are three methods of accelerated depreciation. They are the Sum of the Years Digit Method, Double Declining Balance Method, and Units of Production Method.

Acceleration, rate of change of velocity. *Average* acceleration $\bar{\mathbf{a}}$ of a body changing from velocity $\mathbf{v}_1$ to $\mathbf{v}_2$ in time t is $(\mathbf{v}_2 - \mathbf{v}_1)/t$. *Instantaneous* acceleration $\mathbf{a}$ is the value approached by $\bar{\mathbf{a}}$ as t becomes small. *See also* Velocity. △1492.

Accelerator, in economics, a more sophisticated form of the multiplier. According to this concept, as incomes are created and GNP levels increase, businessmen become more optimistic about the future and tend to increase their investment in new plant and equipment as well as planned inventory changes. This in turn further stimulates the increasing income levels, which results in an even higher GNP. *See also* Multiplier.

Accelerator, Electrostatic, type of particle accelerator in which a constant high voltage is applied between a pair of electrodes in an evacuated tube. Charged particles are accelerated in the electric field between the electrodes, gaining an energy eV, where e is the electron charge and V the applied voltage. The Van de Graaff generator (developed 1929) and the Cockcroft-Walton generator (1932) can be used as high-voltage sources. The energy of heavy ions can be doubled if two accelerators are used in tandem: negative ions are accelerated then stripped of some electrons; the resulting positive ions are accelerated by the second machine. *See also* Accelerators, Particle. △1484.

Accelerator, Field, type of particle accelerator in which charged particles are accelerated by use of alternating electric fields in an evacuated chamber. The particles must enter the high-frequency field as it begins increasing (negative particles) or decreasing (positive particles) for maximum energy increase. The path of the particles may be straight, as in linear accelerators, or curved, as in the cyclotron, synchrotron, and betatron. With a circular path the particles make many revolutions; the long path length allows greater energy increase. Magnetic fields are used to focus the particles into a narrow stable beam and to maintain the required curvature of the beam. As the particle velocity rises a relativistic increase in mass occurs. This causes beam instability in the cyclotron, limiting the final energy, but has been overcome in the high-energy synchrotron, betatron, and synchrocyclotron. △1484.

Accelerator, Particle, device in which charged elementary particles, such as electrons or protons, are accelerated to very high velocities and thus acquire very high energies. Accelerators have an evacuated chamber in which the particles move, acceleration being provided by motion in electric and magnetic fields. Electrostatic devices are relatively simple, having electrodes operating at a very high potential difference. In field accelerators an electric field produces the acceleration, the particles being kept in a stable narrow beam by magnetic fields. Accelerators are used in cancer treatment, in the production of radioactive isotopes for medicine, research, and technology, in sterilizing food, and so on. Very large expensive high-energy accelerators are used in nuclear physics to produce other particles, such as mesons, neutrinos, and antiparticles, by directing the accelerated beams at stationary targets or by causing two similar energetic beams to collide. The highest energies—hundreds of billions of electron volts (GeV)—are obtained with proton synchrotrons. Study of the reactions and decay processes of these particles provides information on nuclear forces and the basic nature of matter. *See also* Accelerator, Electrostatic; Accelerator, Field. △1484.

Accelerometer, a device to measure acceleration. A simple accelerometer is a plumb bob attached to the accelerating object—its angle with the vertical indicates the magnitude of the acceleration. A more sophisticated version, such as is used in ballistic missiles, is an electromechanical device that translates forces of acceleration into electrical current.

Acceptance of Goods, act that legally occurs when the seller delivers to the buyer physical possession of the goods and the buyer shows by his actions or words that he intends to accept them. Thus, use of a good, or further sale of it, or a statement that the good has been accepted constitutes acceptance of an oral offer to sell.

Acclimatization, adjustment of an organism to a new environment, climate or circumstances. It involves a gradual, natural change permitting an organism to exploit new regions. Plant and animal species acclimatize differently.

Accordion, musical instrument with organlike tone produced by air from a bellows vibrating reeds. The melody is played on a piano-type keyboard, with chordal accompaniment controlled by buttons. Invented (1822) by Friedrich Buschmann in Germany, the accordion is used in folk music of America, central Europe, and eastern Europe.

Account, in accounting, a device used to accumulate increases and decreases in particular balance-sheet items. A series of accounts forms a ledger.

Accounting, profession whose objective is to provide relevant financial information in a usable form in order that such groups as management, governmental units, and the investing public can make rational decisions.

Accra, capital city of Ghana, W Africa, on the Gulf of Guinea. Est. 17th century, around three fortresses: James Fort (British), Crèvecoeur (Dutch), and Chris-

Abruzzi, Italy

Acacia

Acanthus

Accra, Ghana

tiansburg Castle (Danish); taken by British in the 19th century; made capital of the Gold Coast Colony 1876; transportation and educational center; site of University of Ghana (1948) and the Defense Commission of the Organization of African Unity. Industries: textiles, food products, shoes, chemicals. Pop. 633,880.

Accretion, in geology, the building up of beaches and shorelines. Wave action and currents may add to some coastlines by transporting material from erosion zones. Deltas built up by river systems are accreted land created by the deposition of suspended materials. △260, 262.

Acculturation, that process of cultural change that occurs when one society meets another. There are two main types of acculturation. Free acculturation results from friendly interchange, and the acceptance of cultural change on the part of the changed society. Directed acculturation occurs when a society, through domination, forces another to change.

Acestes, in Vergil's *Aeneid,* a king of Sicily. Son of a Sicilian river god, Crimisius, and a Trojan woman, Segesta, he was the mythical founder of the city of Segesta. Aeneas was entertained by Acestes on his way to Italy and left many Trojans with him.

Acetaldehyde, colorless volatile flammable liquid (formula CH_3CHO) made by the partial oxidation of ethanol or catalytic oxidation of ethylene. Properties: sp. gr. 0.783; melt. pt. −185.8°F (−121°C); boil. pt. 69.44°F (20.8°C). *See also* Aldehyde.

Acetaminophen, ingredient used as a substitute for or in combination with aspirin in many over-the-counter drugs. It has fever-reducing and pain-killing properties.

Acetate, salt or ester of acetic acid; that is, a compound containing the ion CH_3COO^- or the group CH_3COO^-. Cellulose acetate is a material made by the action of acetic anhydride on cellulose. It is used in synthetic acetate fibers, in lacquers, and in acetate film.

Acetic Acid, colorless corrosive low-melting solid (formula CH_3COOH) made by the oxidation of ethanol, either by catalysis or by the action of bacteria. It is the active ingredient in vinegar, and has many uses in the organic chemicals industry. Properties: sp. gr. 1.049; melt. pt. 61.89°F (16.604°C); boil. pt. 244.4°F (117.9°C). *See also* Carboxylic Acid.

Acetone, colorless flammable sweet-smelling liquid (formula CH_3COCH_3) made by oxidizing isopropyl alcohol. It is a basic raw material for the manufacture of many organic chemicals and a widely used solvent. Properties: sp. gr. 0.79; melt. pt. −139.63°F (−95.35°C); boil pt. 133.16°F (56.2°C). △1562.

Acetophenetidin. *See* Phenacetin.

Acetylcholine, chemical compound released by certain nerve cells that serves as a transmitter in nerve conduction. Following stimulation of a nerve cell, acetylcholine is released at the point of contact (synapse) between it and the cell it innervates, causing that effector cell to act; such as stimulation of muscle contraction, or stimulating another nerve cell to conduct.

Acetyl Coenzyme A (Co A), acetyl derivative of coenzyme A, a sulfur-containing nucleotide, that is a precursor in the metabolism of fatty acids, carbohydrates, and proteins, being an important intermediate in the Krebs' cycle. Coenzyme A functions as a carrier of the 2-carbon acetyl group, which is attached to the sulfur group.

Acetylene, colorless flammable gaseous hydrocarbon (formula HC:CH), made by the action of water on calcium carbide or by breakdown of other hydrocarbons. It is used in high-temperature oxyacetylene cutting flames, and as a raw material for making some organic chemicals. Properties: melt. pt. −113.44°F (−80.8°C). △1558.

Achaean League, two confederations of Greek city-states formed in the area of the Peloponnesus called Achaea. The first, founded sometime in the 5th century BC for mutual protection against pirates, lasted through the 4th century BC. The second, founded in 280 BC to drive out the Macedonians, ended up warring with Sparta, siding with Rome in 198 BC. In 146 BC Rome subjugated and dissolved the league.

Achaemenids (*c.* 500–331 BC), Persian dynasty, descendants of Achaemenes who ruled in the province of Pars in SW Iran. The Greeks corrupted "Parsa" to "Persis" and used it for the whole kingdom. The rulers included Cyrus the Great, Cambyses, Smerdis, Darius I, Xerxes I, Artaxerxes I, Xerxes II, Sogdianus, Darius II, Artaxerxes II, Artaxerxes III, Arses, and Darius III, who was murdered fleeing from Alexander the Great (331 BC). △984.

Acheampong, Ignatius Kutu (1931–), Ghanaian chief of state (1972–). He joined Ghana's army in 1959 and in 1972 overthrew Kofi Abrefa Busia in a bloodless coup. As head of the Supreme Military Council he was generally conservative.

Achebe, Chinua (1930–), Nigerian writer. His novels deal primarily with a search for identity in modern Africa and with the effect of change on people's lives. *Things Fall Apart* (1958) depicts life in an African village before and after the arrival of missionaries.

Acheron, in Greek mythology, a river of the underworld. One of five rivers that surrounded Hades, the realm of Pluto. Charon carried the souls of the dead across either the Acheron or the Styx.

Acheson, Dean (1893–1971), US statesman, b. Middletown, Conn. After serving as assistant secretary of state (1941–45) and undersecretary (1945–47), he became secretary of state (1949–53) under President Truman. Strongly anti-communist, he helped develop such postwar policies as the Marshall Plan, the Truman Doctrine, and North Atlantic Treaty Organization (1949). He encouraged support for Nationalist China and UN involvement in Korea. His advice was sought by Presidents Kennedy, Johnson and Nixon. He wrote *Present at the Creation* (1969), which won a Pulitzer Prize (1970).

Achieved Status, in sociology, a person's position in a stratification system that has as its criteria certain attainable or controllable traits such as educational level, income, or marriage. *See also* Status; Stratification.

Achievement Test, test designed to measure how well an individual has learned a certain skill or certain information. School exams are achievement tests on specific subject matter.

Achernar, or **Alpha Eridani,** bluish-white main-sequence star in the constellation Eridanus. Characteristics: apparent mag. +0.47; absolute mag. −1.6; spectral type B5; distance 75 light-years.

Achilles, son of Peleus and Thetis; hero of Homer's *Iliad.* Achilles was the bravest and the greatest Greek hero of the Trojan war. Legend held him invulnerable from weapons because he had been dipped in the River Styx at birth, save for one heel by which he was held. Achilles chose to win glory and die young at Troy. During the fighting an arrow shot by Paris struck his heel, slaying him.

Achilles' Tendon, strong elastic band of connective tissue joining bone to muscle that connects the gastrocnemius muscle of the calf of the leg to the heel bone, or calcaneus.

Achomawi, tribe of North American Indians speaking a dialect of the Hokan language family. They inhabited the Pit River area in Shasta co, Calif., and are closely related to the Atsugewi. From a total of 3000 at the time of first contact, the tribe has dwindled to about 500 persons.

Acid, chemical compound containing hydrogen that can be replaced by a metal or other positive ion to form a salt. Acids dissociate in water to yield hydrogen ions (H^+): the solutions are corrosive, have a sharp taste, and give a red color to litmus indicator. Strong acids, such as hydrochloric acid (HCL), are fully dissociated into ions; weak acids, such as acetic acid (CH_3COOH), are partially dissociated. *See also* Base. △1520.

Acid Number, or value, number of milligrams of potassium hydroxide necessary to neutralize the free fatty acids in one gram of a specified substance. The acid number is used to measure the fatty acid content of fats, oils, etc.

Acidosis, abnormal condition in which the acid-base balance of the blood is upset, with the blood becoming too acidic (pH below 7). May be caused by kidney malfunction, diabetes, or other diseases. Symptoms include weakness and malaise.

Acid Rock. △1366.

ACLU. *See* American Civil Liberties Union.

Acmeism, movement in Russian poetry in the 1910s and 1920s led by N.S. Gumilev and S.M. Gorodetsky. The Acmeists, writing in a clear, precise style, rejected the mysticism and impressionism of the Symbolist movement. Acmeism produced several important poets, including Osip Mandelstam and Anna Akhmatova.

Acne, inflammatory disease of the sebaceous, or oil-producing, glands of the skin, probably caused by a hormonal imbalance and resulting in skin lesions ranging from mild blackheads and papules to infected cysts. It is extremely common at puberty, usually disappearing by 18, but sometimes persisting or periodically recurring in middle age, when a related disorder—acne rosacea—characterized by red blotchy (flushlike) acnelike lesions may occur. △724,790.

Acoma, Queres-speaking tribe of Pueblo Indians inhabiting a rock mesa 357ft (109m) high in Valencia, N.M.; the town name is Ako. First mentioned by Fray Marcos de Niza in 1539 as Acus, the town was entered by Coronado the following year. Next to Oraibi, it is regarded as the oldest continuously inhabited town in the United States. The tribe, noted for fine pottery, numbers approximately 2,000.

Aconcagua, mountain in W Argentina, in the Andes Mountains on Chilean border, 70mi (112km) WNW of Mendoza; highest peak in Western Hemisphere, 22,834ft (6,959m); first climbed by members of Fitzgerald expedition 1897.

Aconite, a flowering plant of the genus *Aconitum,* family Ranunculaceae, also called monkshood, friar's cap and wolfsbane. Its roots provide the alkaloid aconitine, which is used in modern times for medical purposes; in ancient times it was used as poison.

Acorn Worm, solitary, wormlike, marine animal found worldwide to depths of 10,000ft (3000m). The head-end of the burrowing or foraging adult has a proboscis and collar. Food is filtered from seawater entering the mouth and leaving through gill slits. Length: .75in–7.5ft (2cm–2.3m). A common genus is *Balanoglossus;* there are 100 species. Class Enteropneusta. △508.

Acosta, Gabriel (later Uriel) (*c.* 1591–1647), Portuguese theologian. A Roman Catholic convert to Judaism, he fled to Amsterdam. When excommunicated by the synagogue in Amsterdam for atheism, he recanted. In his *Autobiography* (1687), Acosta announced his preference for the "law of nature," or deism, over either Judaism or Christianity.

Acoustic Shielding, the deadening of unwanted sounds, usually by introducing sound-absorbing materials in the path of the sound waves. Sound enters a room in three ways: through the air, through the structure, or by the diaphragm action of floors, walls, and ceilings. Airborne sounds are absorbed by using thick and absorbent walls in which there are no cracks or ducts; doors and windows should fit tightly and be seated in rubber or felt liners. Windows should be double-glazed. Structure-born vibrations and diaphragm effects are reduced by using double walls with insulating material but as few ties as possible between them.

Acquired Characteristics, Inheritance of. △418.

Acre (Akko), seaport town in N Israel, on Bay of Acre, 10mi (16km) N of Haifa; Phoenician city captured by Arabs AD 638; ruled at different times by Egypt, Assyria, Persia, and Macedonia; from 1200–1291, it grew and prospered as center of Christian power. It was taken by British 1918; became part of Israel 1948; is center of Bahai religion. Industries: fishing, steel rolling. Pop. 33,900.

Acrilan, trademark for a kind of acrylic fiber, chiefly acrylonitrile, made by combining acetylene and hydrogen cyanide. Used extensively in the textile industry. *See also* Acrylic. △1620.

Acrobatics, Aircraft, aerial maneuvers involving abrupt changes in an aircraft's attitude or altitude that are not characteristic of normal flight. Variations and combinations of the climb, dive, loop, spin, and stall make up the acrobatic repertoire. Acrobatics are governed by federally enforced rules that prohibit demonstrations over densely populated areas, over crowds, below 1,500ft above the ground, when visibility is poor, or within Federal Airway limits.

Acromegaly, condition in which there is an overproduction of pituitary growth hormones in an adult, causing enlarged hands, feet, and facial features.

Acrophobia, irrational fear of high places, usually accompanied by obsessional thoughts of falling or jumping. Persons suffering from acrophobia often feel dizzy and nauseated (at times, nearly paralyzed) when they look down from a high place.

Acropolis, the rocky hill in the center of Athens, Greece, on which are located the Propylaea, the Parthenon, the Erectheum, and the Temple of Wingless Victory. Most of the architecture and sculpture was completed at the time of Cimon and Pericles and still stands, despite invasions and removal of its treasure to museums. △1002.

Acrostic, word-game in which words or phrases are formed from the first letter of the lines of a composition or a short poem. There are more complicated forms, such as double acrostic, using the first and last letters in the lines, or triple, which uses the first, last, and middle letters in the lines.

Acrylic, one of a group of synthetic, short-chain unsaturated carboxylic acid derivatives comprising many plastics and thermoplastic resins. Variations in reagents and processes of formation yield either hard and transparent, or soft and resilient products. Its transparency, toughness, and dimensional stability make it useful for molded structural parts, jewelry, adhesives, coating compounds, and textile fibers. △1620,1644.

Acrylic-Resin Paint, a synthetic plastic type of paint, in wide use since the 1960s. It dries rapidly and serves as a vehicle for any kind of pigment. It is capable of the transparent brilliance of water colors as well as the density of oil paints and stands up well under heat and humidity.

Actaeon. △838.

ACTH. *See* Adrenocorticotropic Hormone.

Actin, fibrillar protein involved in cellular contractile processes. It is most prevalent in muscle cells, where it reacts with myosin to form actomyosin. *See also* Actomyosin. △684.

Acting, representing a character in a performance on stage or before cameras. In ancient Greece acting had to be highly stylized because plays were performed in vast outdoor arenas. The actors (all male) wore platform sandals and large masks. The Romans held acting in low esteem; slaves performed farces. The tragedies of Seneca were written to be read aloud, not performed. Acting all but disappeared in Western Europe in the early Christian era. The first signs of revival were the crude religious pageants of the Middle Ages and the somewhat later trade guild pageants. The actors were all amateurs, members of the church or guild. Italy produced the first modern professional acting in the Commedia dell' arte, in which the players improvised situations based on standard plot outlines. Shakespeare's actors were professionals. Their style of acting was broad and exaggerated. During the Restoration period in England a more naturalistic style of acting evolved. Female roles were now played by women. The greatest impact on 20th-century acting was from the theories of the Russian director Konstantin Stanislavski. He encouraged the actor's total psychological identification with the character. The Actors' Studio, New York City, applied and expanded upon Stanislavski's theories in developing the method school of acting. Film and TV made new and different demands on actors, but offered new areas in which to work.

Actinide Elements, group of radioactive elements with atomic numbers from 89 to 103; actinium (89), thorium, protactinium, uranium, neptunium, plutonium, americium, curium, berkelium, californium, einsteinium, fermium, mendelevium, nobelium, and lawrencium (103). Each element is analogous to the corresponding lanthanide element (eg thorium is a close analogue of cerium). The most important member of the group is uranium, because of its use as a nuclear fuel; the transuranic elements (neptunium to lawrencium) do not occur in nature and only plutonium, because of its use in nuclear weapons, has any importance. △1552,1554.

Actinium, radioactive metallic element (Symbol Ac) of the actinide group, discovered first (1899) by André Debierne. It is found associated with uranium ores. Ac^{227}, a decay product of U^{235}, is a beta emitter. Properties: at. no. 89; sp. gr. 10.07 (calc.); melt. pt. 1922°F (1050°C); boil. pt. 5792°F(3200°C); most stable isotope Ac^{227} (half-life 21.6 yr). *See also* Actinide Elements.

Actinomycosis, fungus *(Actinomyces israelii)* infection, more common in men. Produces multiple, draining, pus-filled abscesses and sinus tracts, most often in the neck and face region, causing a "lumpy jaw" appearance, but also affecting other parts of the body. Treatment consists of draining abscesses and administering antimicrobial agents.

Action Painting. △1372.

Actium, Battle of (31 BC), naval clash in which the fleet of Octavian, commanded by Agrippa, defeated the fleets of Mark Antony and Cleopatra. Antony deserted his forces, and Octavian captured the majority of his ships. Antony's army surrendered a week later, making Octavian sole ruler of the Roman Empire.

Activated Complex. △1564.

Activated Sludge Reactor, sewage cleaning device used in many cities for removing harmful organic materials. Compressed air is introduced into tanks of waste water. This activates the sludge and adds large amounts of oxygen. Eventually a good balance of microorganisms is established. △1768.

Activation Energy. △1562,1564,1572.

Act of Congress, bill or resolution passed into law by both the US Senate and House of Representatives.

Act of Union (1841), legislation uniting French-speaking Lower Canada and English-speaking Upper Canada as proposed by Lord Durham. It gave equal representation to each sector. The subsequent council to Lord Sydenham, the governor, included both conservative and reform elements and established a parliament for the province that raised the issue of responsible self-government as opposed to British dominance. *See also* Lower Canada; Upper Canada.

Actomyosin, the complex of the proteins actin and myosin. This forms the basic unit of contraction in muscle cells.

Acton, John Emerich Edward Dalberg, 1st Baron (1834–1902), English historian, b. Italy. One of the most influential historians in Europe during the late 18th century, he never completed a book. While teaching at Cambridge University (1895–1902), however, he planned the *Cambridge Modern History* and his lectures and essays were collected in various volumes after his death. He was a Roman Catholic who was a strong liberal in religion and politics and an avid supporter of Liberal Prime Minister William Gladstone. Acton was a member of the House of Commons (1859–65) and received a peerage through Gladstone in 1869.

Acton, John Francis Edward (1736–1811), Neapolitan statesman, b. France of expatriate English parentage. After service in the French navy, he became commander of the naval forces of Tuscany, and in 1779 was called upon to reorganize the army and navy of Naples. Rising quickly in the government, he served as minister of finance and prime minister for extended periods between 1785 and 1806. Assisted by Emma, Lady Hamilton, he strengthened Naples' ties with England. He fled Naples for Sicily in 1806 upon Napoleon's conquest of the kingdom.

Acts of the Apostles, book of the New Testament, claims the same author as the Gospel of Luke. It was written for a believing community. Many see it written around 85 AD as a sequel. It covers the early church from Christ's resurrection through Paul's missionary work.

Actual Cash Value, referring to property, the replacement cost of the property less accumulated depreciation. *Replacement cost* is the amount of money required to replace damaged property with new materials at current prices. In insurance practice, "depreciation" connotes "economic" or true decrease in value, not the accounting definition. Most property insurance contracts agree to pay for the loss to the extent of the actual cash value of the damaged or destroyed property, a practice that reinforces the principle of indemnity.

Acupuncture. △748.

Adad, also **Hadad,** in Babylonian mythology, the rain god, bringer of storms, giver of waters, and protector of the harvest. In his role of war god he became the destroyer whose whirlwinds, thunderbolts, and droughts brought havoc to the enemy. In the Babylonian myth of the flood Adad appears as the storm god. With Sin and Shamash, he formed a powerful triangle of the pantheon.

Adalbert, Saint (956?–997), first bishop of Prague. He was elected bishop in 983 and came into increasing conflict with the ruling powers of Bohemia over what he saw as an insincere attitude toward the

Dean Acheson

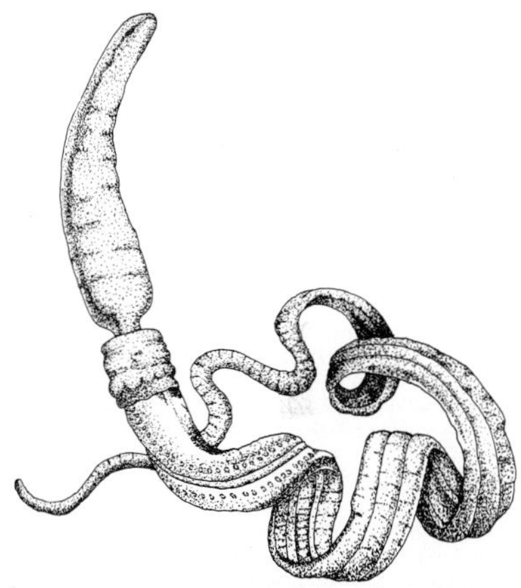

Acorn worm

Acre, Israel: Arab market

Acropolis

church. In 994 he left to become a missionary in Prussia, where he was murdered.

Adalbert (*c.* 1000–1072), German clergyman. He was a favorite of both Emperor Henry III, who appointed him archbishop of Hamburg-Bremen in 1043, and later of young Henry IV. His efforts to increase the power of the crown alienated the nobility and his centralizing ecclesiastical policies alienated many church officials. Their opposition forced his dismissal (1066) but he was reinstated by Henry IV (1069).

Adam, in the Bible, first man and progenitor of all mankind, created by God in his own image. He and his wife, Eve, were cast out of the Garden of Eden for sinning. They had three sons, Cain, Abel, and Seth. △810,844.

Adam, Robert (1728–92), Scottish architect and designer. He developed a refined neoclassical style that was highly influential in England and abroad. He designed interiors and furniture to harmonize with the exterior of his buildings. A notable example of his work is Luton Hoo mansion, Bedfordshire, England (1768–75).

Adams, Abigail (1744–1818), wife of Pres. John Adams and mother of Pres. John Quincy Adams, b. Abigail Smith at Weymouth, Mass. Very active in her husband's political career, her many letters have since become an important source for the history of US society. She strongly supported equal education for women and spoke out frequently against slavery.

Adams, Ansel (1902–), US photographer, b. San Francisco. Concentrating on the scenic grandeur of the Western United States, Adams has produced magnificent prints that are widely exhibited and reproduced. A cofounder of the *f*/64 group, he has been instrumental in forming museum and university photographic departments and is a celebrated teacher. He wrote the *Basic Photo-Books* series of technical manuals (1968).

Adams, Brooks (1848–1927), US historian, b. Quincy, Mass., a son of Charles Francis Adams and brother of Henry Adams, whom he influenced. His *Law of Civilization and Decay* (1895) held that civilizations rise and fall with the growth and decline of commerce and that the center of occidental civilization had steadily shifted westward. In *America's Economic Supremacy* (1900), he predicted the decline of Western Europe and proposed that within 50 years only the United States and Russia would be great powers.

Adams, Charles Francis (1807–86), US diplomat, son of John Quincy Adams and grandson of John Adams. He was appointed minister to London by Lincoln in 1861, and helped to hold England to neutrality in the US Civil War.

Adams, Henry (Brooks) (1838–1918), US author, b. Boston. A direct descendant of Presidents John Adams and John Quincy Adams, he was secretary to his father, Charles Francis Adams, Sr., first (1860–61) while the latter was in Congress and then (1861–68) when he was US minister to Britain. Returning to the United States, he taught history at Harvard University (1870–77). He resigned his teaching position and settled in Washington, D.C., devoting himself to writing. His works include the muckraking *Chapters of Erie* (articles written earlier with his brother Charles Francis Adams, Jr., and published in book form in 1886); *Democracy* (1880) and *Esther* (1884), topical novels; the monumental *History of the United States Under the Jefferson and Adams Administrations* (9 vols., 1889–91); *Mont-Saint-Michel and Chartres* (privately printed 1904, published 1913), reflections on medieval culture; *The Education of Henry Adams* (privately printed 1906, published 1918), a brilliant autobiographical work; and *The Degradation of the Democratic Dogma* (essays written earlier and published posthumously in 1919 by his brother Brooks Adams). His elegant but pessimistic theories of history and his ironic view of himself influenced writers of the 1920s.

Adams, James Truslow (1878–1949), US historian, b. Brooklyn. He began his career on the New York Stock Exchange (1900–1912), but later turned to writing. His *The Founding of New England* (1921) won the Pulitzer Prize for history. An economic conservative, he often called for a return to the "old-fashioned" virtues.

Adams, John (1735–1826), 2nd President of the United States, b. Braintree (now Quincy), Mass., graduate, Harvard, 1755. In 1764, he married Abigail Smith; they had five children, one of whom was John Quincy Adams. Adams practiced law in Braintree and Boston. He opposed the Stamp Act and became involved in anti-British politics, partly through the influence of his more radical cousin, Samuel Adams. After 1774, he was a member of the First and Second Continental Congresses, where he distinguished himself as a moderate revolutionist. He helped Thomas Jefferson draft the Declaration of Independence and sponsored George Washington as commander of the armed forces.

In 1777 he was sent as commissioner to France and spent most of the next decade in Europe. He was in France and the Netherlands during the Revolution and was one of the drafters of the Treaty of Paris (1783), which ended the war. In 1785 he became the first US minister to Great Britain, where he tried to reestablish normal trade relations. Frustrated in those efforts, he asked to be recalled in 1788.

In 1789, Adams was chosen vice president. His eight years in that office were distinguished but personally frustrating to him. Washington's administration, which began as nonpartisan, soon separated into factions. Adams acted as mediator between the conservative faction, led by Alexander Hamilton, and the liberal faction, led by Thomas Jefferson. Naturally a conservative, Adams moved closer to the conservative, or Federalist, faction. He was the Federalist candidate for president in 1796, running against Jefferson. Adams won by a small margin and Jefferson was elected vice president.

Adams's four years in office were marked by his efforts to steer a middle course between the pro-French faction of the Jeffersonians and the Federalists, who were violently anti-French. Only Adams's calm diplomacy (particularly in the XYZ Affair) avoided open war with France. His administration was not a popular success, however, and he was defeated for re-election by Jefferson. He retired to Quincy, where he died on July 5, 1826.

Career: First and Second Continental Congresses (1774–77); US commissioner and minister to France, the Netherlands, and Great Britain (1777–89); vice president (1789–97); president (1797–1801).

Adams, John Quincy (1767–1848), 6th president of the United States, b. Braintree (now Quincy), Mass., son of president John Adams and Abigail Smith Adams. As a young boy he accompanied his father on European diplomatic missions, and at the age of 14 he was secretary to the US minister to Russia. He graduated from Harvard in 1787 and read for the law. President Washington named him minister to the Netherlands in 1794. While in Europe he married Louisa Catherine Johnson; they had four children, one of whom was Charles Francis Adams (1807–86). In 1797 his father named him minister to Prussia. In 1803 he was elected to the US Senate as a Federalist. His independence alienated him from his party, however, and he resigned in 1808. He became minister to Russia in 1809, and in 1814 he was one of the commissioners that drew up the Treaty of Ghent, which ended the War of 1812. He became minister to Great Britain in 1815, and in 1817 President Monroe named him secretary of state. He is ranked as one of the most successful secretaries in US history; the Monroe Doctrine was his most enduring contribution. In the presidential election of 1824, Adams was the candidate of the almost extinct Federalists and ran against Andrew Jackson, Henry Clay, and William H. Crawford. Jackson polled the most votes, but the election was decided in the House of Representatives. Clay threw his support to Adams, who was elected. The Jacksonians charged them with a corrupt bargain, an accusation that only increased when Adams named Clay his secretary of state. Adams was not a natural politician; he had a cold and aloof personality, and he refused to enter into the political deals that were the norm of the era. As a result, his administration was not a successful one. He ran for reelection in 1828, again with Jackson as his opponent. The campaign was one of the dirtiest in US history, with both sides making unproved charges. Jackson won an overwhelming victory, and Adams retired, embittered, to Quincy. Three years later, however, he was elected to the House of Representatives, where he served with great distinction until his death at the age of 81.

Career: Minister to the Netherlands (1794–97), Prussia (1797–1800), Russia (1809–13), Great Britain (1815–17); US Senate (1803–08); secretary of state (1817–24); president (1825–29); US House of Representatives (1831–48).

Adams, Maude (1872–1953), US actress, b. Salt Lake City. A child star and leading lady to John Drew (1892–97), she charmingly portrayed J.M. Barrie heroines in *The Little Minister* (1897), *Quality Street* (1901), and *What Every Woman Knows* (1908). The first Peter Pan (1906), she was the most celebrated actress of her day, but sought seclusion in her private life.

Adams, Samuel (1722–1803), American Revolutionary patriot and signer of Declaration of Independence. b. Boston, Mass. As a member and clerk of the Massachusetts legislature (1765–74), he was the chief radical spokesman for revolution. He helped form the Sons of Liberty, the Committees of Correspondence, and led the 1765 Stamp Act protest and the Boston Tea Party (1773). He was a delegate to both sessions of the Continental Congress. △1218.

Adam's Apple, frontal protuberance in the neck, especially prominent in men, formed by the apex of the triangular-shaped larynx.

Adamson, Robert (1821–48), Scottish pioneer photographer. Working with David Octavius Hill from 1843 to 1848, he made celebrated calotypes of many prominent Scots and of Edinburgh and rural scenes.

Adams-Onís Treaty (1819), agreement between the United States and Spain, negotiated by Sec. of State John Quincy Adams and Spanish Minister Luis de Onís. Spain gave up its land east of the Mississippi River and its claims to the Oregon Territory and the United States assumed debts of $5,000,000 and gave up claims to Texas.

Adana, city in S Turkey, on Seyhan River; 30mi (48km) from Mediterranean coast; capital of Adana prov.; held by Egyptians 1832–40; scene of Armenian massacre 1909; occupied by French 1919–21. Industries: tobacco, textiles, grains, explosives. Founded *c.* 66 BC as Roman colony and military station. Pop. 351,700.

Adapa, mythological Babylonian hero. He was the fisherman son of the god of wisdom, Ea. Adapa was given the gift of great knowledge and intelligence by his father. When he was offered immortality by the sea gods in exchange for his knowledge, he refused, marking the fall of man.

Adaptation, the capacity of an organism or population of organisms to fit into its environment in such a way that it is able to continue to survive and reproduce itself. This capacity is usually achieved through development of characteristics that help the organism adapt; they are usually considered characteristics that can be inherited and passed on to successive generations. *See also* Adaptive Radiation. △408.

Adaptation, Social. Humans have learned to use technology to adapt to their physical world. They also have to learn behavior that will help them adjust to individuals and groups. Adaptation does not have to mean conforming but can be a give-and-take process between the person and other individuals and groups. △888, 892.

Adaptive Radiation, divergent adaptation, a simultaneous divergence of several populations of one parent type into different forms, each suited to a different environmental condition. If a species emerges and becomes distributed over several types of surroundings, the populations of each area may develop specialized features suited to the new environments. △582.

Addams, Charles Samuel (1912–), US cartoonist, b. Westfield, N.J. He is famous for his macabre drawings, seen most often in *The New Yorker* (from 1930s). His family of bizarre monsters was the basis of the popular television comedy program "The Addams Family." Collections of his work include *The Charles Addams Mother Goose* (1967).

Addams, Jane (1860–1935), US social reformer, b. Cedarville, Ill. She co-founded (1889) Hull House, a social settlement that served as a community center for the poor in Chicago, and was instrumental in the settlement movement across the country. Active in the women's suffrage movement, she was also co-recipient of the Nobel Peace prize (1931). Her works include *Twenty Years at Hull House* (1910), *A New Conscience and an Ancient Evil* (1912), and *The Second Twenty Years at Hull House* (1930).

Addax, large, powerful antelope found in the Sahara Desert. Grayish with black tuft on forehead, both sexes bear long, ribbed horns in open spiral. They have splayed hooves for moving on sand. Almost extinct due to hunting, it derives most of its water from succulent plants. Length: to 78in (2m); height: to 4ft (1.2m) at shoulder; weight: to 264lb (120kg). Family Bovidae; species *Addax maculatus.* △606.

Adderley, Cannonball (1928–75), US jazz alto saxophonist and bandleader, b. Julian Edwin Adderley in Tampa, Fla. He formed his own jazz group in the late 1950s with his brother Nat and later toured Japan and Europe. In the 1960s his jazz quintet became popular.

Addiction, use of drugs in such a way that they become essential to the individual. Characteristics of addiction usually include an overwhelming urge to continue taking the drug regardless of the means of obtaining it; a tendency to increase the dose; and a psychological and/or a physiological dependence. △730, 1446.

Addis Ababa (Addis Abeba), capital and largest city in Ethiopia; central section is 8,000ft (2,440m) above sea level; administrative and communications center; site of Haile Selassie I University (1950), National Theater and Library (1944), international airport; headquarters of Organization of African Unity. Founded 1887; scene of Italian-Ethiopian treaty (1896) that recognized Ethiopian independence; occupied by Italy 1936; liberated by British 1941. Industries: tanneries, textiles, breweries. Pop. 795,900.

Addison, Joseph (1672–1719), English poet, essayist, and politician. His essays, in the periodicals the *Tatler* (1709–11) and the *Spectator* (1711–12 and 1714) in which he collaborated with Richard Steele, cover literature, philosophy, politics, and morals. Addison wrote largely for the educated middle classes. His poetry includes the verse tragedy "Cato" (1713). *See also* Steele, Richard. △1188.

Addison, city in NE Illinois; suburb of Chicago; 6mi (10km) SW of O'Hare International Airport. Industries: foundries, heating equipment. Inc. 1894. Pop. (1970) 24,482.

Addison's Disease, condition in which there is decreased activity of the adrenal glands, resulting in skin bronzing, weakness, weight loss, digestive disturbances, and sometimes emotional changes. Usually successfully treated by cortisone administration. *See also* Adrenal Glands.

Addition, arithmetical operation signified by +, interpreted, for natural numbers, as the number of members of a set produced by combining other sets. The numbers added together are the addends; the result is the sum. *See also* Arithmetical Operations. △1446.

Ade, George (1866–1944), US author and playwright, b. Kentland, Ind. *Fables in Slang* (1899), told in the form of Aesop, but using a racy vernacular ending with a flip moral, made him famous. His best-known play was *The Sultan of Sulu* (1902), a comic opera.

Adelaide, town in Australia, at the mouth of the Torrens River on Gulf St. Vincent; capital of South Australia state; cultural and governmental center; site of the University of Adelaide (1874), Flinders University (1966), and the Natural History Museum (1895); noted for its churches and cathedrals; major port in South Australia. Exports: fruit, wine, wheat. Industries: machinery, chemicals, textiles, electronic equipment. Founded 1836; inc. 1840. Pop. 16,331.

Adélie Coast (Land), region in Wilkes Land, E Antarctica between George V Coast and Clarie Coast. Captain Jules Dumont d'Urville of France sighted the area (1840), and named it for his wife; Douglas Mawson, an Australian geologist explored it 1911–14 and 1929–31; under French rule from 1938. In 1955, the French Southern and Antarctic Territories were formed by combining Adélie Coast with several islands in Indian Ocean; site of meteorological-scientific bases since 1956. Area: 150,000sq mi (388,500sq km).

Aden, seaport city and capital of Democratic Republic of Yemen, on the Gulf of Aden, 100mi (161km) E of the Red Sea. A Roman trading port, its importance diminished with the discovery of the cape route around Africa to India (15th century); occupied by Ottoman Turks 1538 until *c.* 1839, when it was taken by Britain; governed until 1937 as part of India; made a free port 1850, greatly increasing its importance and trade with opening of Suez Canal 1869; made a crown colony 1935; surrounding territory became Aden Protectorate 1937; joined the British-sponsored Federation of South Arabia 1963; opposition by Aden nationalists, resulted in creation of the independent republic (1967), with Aden as capital since 1968. Industries: cigarettes, soap, oil refining, salt. Pop. 250,000.

Aden, Gulf of, W arm of Indian Ocean between Yemen and the Somali Republic, E Africa; connects with Red Sea on W via Bab al-Mandab; part of the Mediterranean Sea–Indian Ocean trade route. Length: 550mi (886km).

Adenauer, Konrad (1876–1967), German political figure. Lord high mayor of Cologne (1917–33), he was twice imprisoned by the Nazis. He helped create the Christian Democratic Union, the dominant postwar party, and was its leader (1946–66). In 1949 he was elected the first chancellor of the Federal Republic of Germany. As chancellor, he promoted German reconstruction, led Germany to membership in NATO (1955), campaigned for European unity and establishment of the Common Market. He resigned as chancellor in 1963. △1342.

Adenine, organic compound of the purine group, a group of nitrogen-containing compounds found in combined form in the nucleic acids.

Adenitis, inflammation of a gland or lymph node, occurring regionally, usually as a result of infection in a nearby organ or generalized as a result of a systemic disease.

Adenoids, mass of lymphoid tissue found in the upper part of the throat behind the nose. They can become infected, swollen, interfering with breathing and speaking, and are sometimes removed, often with the tonsils. △740.

Adenoma, type of tumor, often benign, with gland-like structure that occurs in glands such as the thyroid or pituitary.

Adenosine Triphosphate (ATP), nucleotide consisting of adenine, D-ribose, and three phosphate groups. Hydrolysis of ATP to give ADP (adenosine diphosphate) or AMP (adenosine monophosphate) and phosphate is accompanied by a large change in free energy. This hydrolysis is coupled to a phosphorylation reaction in biological systems to provide the energy needed for a number of processes. ATP is synthesized from ADP, for example in photosynthesis using energy derived from sunlight. △1572.

Adhesive, substance used for joining materials together. Many types of adhesive exist, including animal and vegetable products and synthetic resins. Adhesives are generally applied as colloidal sols, which change, in position, to gels holding the surfaces by cohesion and adhesion.

Adiabatic Process, process involving a thermodynamic change in a system, without any gain or loss of heat or mass into or out of the system, and resulting from the expansion or compression of the gas or fluid composing it. As a parcel of air rises in the atmosphere, for example, with decreasing pressure it expands and becomes cooler, and as an air parcel falls it is compressed and becomes warmer, without gaining or losing heat or mass from outside. △1502.

Adirondack Mountains, circular mountain group located in NE New York; extends from Mohawk Valley (S) to the St Lawrence River (N); site of many scenic lakes, gorges and waterfalls. Much of the area has been set aside as Adirondack State Park; noted famous resort areas, including Lake Placid and Lake George, are located here. Highest point is Mt Marcy, 5,344ft (1,630m).

Adjutant Stork, or Marabou, large scavenging bird found in Africa, India, and SE Asia, named for its militarylike gait. With white, black, and gray plumage and unattractive throat pouches, it feeds on carcasses. Length: 2–5ft (61–152 cm). Species *Leptoptilos dubius*.

Adler, Alfred (1870–1937), Austrian psychiatrist. After working with Sigmund Freud (1902–11), Adler broke with him to found his own school, "individual psychology." Contrary to Freud's emphasis on the sex drive, Adler postulated strivings for social success and power as fundamental in human motivation. Individuals develop problems and maladjustments when they cannot surmount feelings of inferiority acquired in childhood. Adler's concept of the "creative self" stressed the positive, active role the individual plays in shaping his own goals and personality. △774.

Adler, Dankmar (1844–1900), US architect, b. Germany. He first used his acoustical knowledge in designing the Central Music Hall in Chicago. In 1881 he went into partnership with Louis Sullivan, and the buildings they designed together, including the Auditorium (Chicago) and the Wainwright (St. Louis), reflected a new and modern architectural style.

Adler, Felix (1851–1933), US educator born in Germany. In 1857 he went to the United States, and in 1876 founded the nonsectarian Ethical Culture Society, or the Ethical Movement.

John Adams

Brady
N.Y.

John Quincy Adams

Samuel Adams

Adjutant stork

Adler, Larry (1914–), US harmonica player, b. Baltimore. He played with harmonica groups in the 1930s, then appeared in solo concerts, Hollywood films, and recordings. He has performed in many concerts, displaying unequaled virtuosity on his instrument and commissioning new works by composers including Vaughan Williams.

Adler, Luther (1903–), US actor, b. New York City. A scion of the Adler family, he acted with his parents in Yiddish theater, played many roles on Broadway and on tour (1922–30), worked with the Group Theater (1932–33), and returned to touring and Broadway (1940–64). He has also appeared in several films and in many TV dramas.

Adler, Stella (1902–), US actress, b. New York City. As a child, she acted with her parents in Yiddish theater, later starred on Broadway (1927–31), with the Group Theater (1931–39), and continues to act and direct. A student of Stanislavski, she has taught acting at the Stella Adler Theatre Studio in New York City since 1949.

Admetus, mythical king of Pharae, a city in Thessaly. He aroused the ire of Artemis, who ruled that he would die young. Apollo arranged his longevity if someone would die for him. Admetus's wife Alcestis took his place in death. However, Hercules went to her grave, outwrestled Death, and returned her to life.

Administrative Law, regulates the powers, procedures, and acts of administrative agencies of the executive branch of government. It applies to the organization, power, duties, and functions of these public agencies.

Admirable Crichton, The (1902), a comic satire by British playwright J.M. Barrie which examines the criteria for class distinctions. Crichton, a butler, is shipwrecked on an island with his employers. His skill and inventiveness quickly make him a leader, reversing the previous master-servant relationship.

Admiralty Islands, volcanic island group, NW of New Guinea in Bismarck Archipelago, SW Pacific Ocean; territory of New Guinea. Manus Island, largest of the group and site of the principal port Lorengau, is surrounded by approx. 40 smaller islands. Industries: pearls, copra. Discovered 1616 by Dutch seaman William Schouten. Area: approx. 800sq mi (2,072sq km). Pop. 21,588.

Admiralty Law. *See* Maritime Law.

Admixtures, in Construction. △1612.

Adobe Brick, structural blocks formed from a soil-clay of the same name in SW United States. Clay is mixed with water and straw, molded in blocks, and sun-dried. The bricks are excellent construction materials and have lasted millennia in arid climates.

Ado-Ekiti, city in SW Nigeria, 20mi (32km) SSW of Ilaro; taken by British 1894; site of phosphate deposits. Industries: cacao, indigo, dyeing, cotton weaving, palm oil, textiles, brick, poultry. Crops: yams, rice. Founded *c.* 15th century. Pop. 190,000.

Adolescence, life stage from puberty to the start of adulthood. As boys and girls move into their teens they experience rapid body changes and problems of emotional and social adjustment. *See also* Puberty. △790–792.

Adolf of Nassau (1250?–98), king of Germany (1292–98). He was elected successor to the Hapsburg Rudolf I in 1292, despite Rudolf's attempts to secure the crown for his son Albert. Adolf increased his lands and power so rapidly that the frightened electors deposed him in 1298 in favor of Albert I. Adolf was killed in the ensuing conflict.

Adonis, in Phoenician and Greek mythology, a youth loved by Aphrodite for his beauty. After Adonis was killed by a wild boar, Zeus allowed him to spend a third of the year with Aphrodite, a third with Persephone, queen of the underworld, and a third of his time as he wished.

Adoption, act of a person taking to himself as his child one who is not by fact or law his child. It is an institution or practice followed throughout the world, and in ancient times often involved the adoption of an adult male in order to continue a family line. Modern laws call for an investigation into the suitability of the proposed parent(s) and for the consent of a child over 12 or 14 years.

Adoration of the Lamb, The (Van Eyck). △1136.

Adoration of the Shepherds (Correggio). △1142.

Adoula, Cyrille (1922–), political leader in Zaire (formerly Republic of the Congo). In the independence movement he first supported Patrice Lumumba and then Joseph Kasavubu, holding cabinet posts. He was prime minister (1961–64) until succeeded by Moise Tshombe.

Adrenal Cortex. △690.

Adrenal Glands, pair of small, caplike, endocrine glands situated above the kidneys. Each consists of a cortex, or outer layer, and medulla, or inner part. Essential to human life, the cortex produces many steroids, including cortisone, that regulate the blood's salt and water balance and the function of certain white blood cells. The medulla produces two hormones: adrenaline (epinephrine), during emergency or stress, that increases the immediate energy supply, blood pressure, heart rate, and peripheral vasodilation; and noradrenaline (norepinephrine) that transmits nerve impulses and constricts peripheral vasodilation. △690.

Adrenaline, or epinephrine, chief hormone secreted by the adrenal medulla in man. It stimulates the nervous system, raises metabolism, increases cardiac rate and output, and increases blood pressure when released naturally or injected intravenously. When given as a drug it may have side effects such as anxiety, headache, dizziness, and weakness. It is often given to treat anaphylactic shock. *See also* Norepinephrine. △690.

Adrenal Medulla. △690.

Adrenocorticotropic Hormone (ACTH), protein hormone secreted by the anterior lobe of the pituitary. It stimulates the adrenal cortex to release steroid hormones. It is used to test adrenal function, and as an anti-inflammatory agent. △690.

Adrian I, Roman Catholic pope (772–95). Because of threats from the Lombards and their king, Desiderius, the pope sought help from Charlemagne. In 774, the Franks overcame the Lombards and Charlemagne increased the Papal States.

Adrian IV, Roman Catholic pope (1154–59), b. Nicholas Breakspear (*c.* 1100), the only English pope. In 1152 he served as a papal legate to Scandinavia and was successful in organizing the Church there. In 1155 he crowned emperor Frederick I Barbarossa, but relations with the emperor were not always amicable. In 1156 peace was made with Sicily and an alliance grew between the papacy and William I.

Adrian VI, Roman Catholic pope (1522–23), b. Adrian Florensz (1459) in the Netherlands; he was the most recent non-Italian pope. Advocating poverty and lacking funds of any amount, he curtailed elaborate celebrations in the Vatican. He was the first pope to encounter fully the Lutheran reform movement.

Adrian, Edgar Douglas (1889–), English physiologist. His important discoveries concerning the function of nerve cells, including the "all-or-none" law, earned him part of the 1932 Nobel Prize in physiology or medicine.

Adrian, city in SE Michigan, on the Raisin River; seat of Lenawee co; site of Adrian (1845) and Siena Heights (1919) colleges; in region known for chrysanthemums. Industries: paper goods, aircraft and automobile parts. Inc. 1836. Pop. (1970) 20,382.

Adrianople, Treaty of (1829), pact signed at Edirne (formerly Adrianople), Turkey, at the termination of the Russo-Ottoman War (1828–29). The treaty gave Russia the islands controlling the mouth of the Danube and the Black Sea coast of the Caucasus, and it opened the Dardanelles and Bosporus to Russian shipping.

Adriatic Sea, extension of the Mediterranean Sea, bordered by Italy (W) and Yugoslavia and Albania (E); extends 500mi (805km) SE from the Gulf of Trieste to the Strait of Otranto. Noted for clear, blue water and mild climate, it is a popular tourist region; Italian coast is low and straight, Yugoslav coast is rocky and indented, with many small islands. Width: 60–140mi (96–225km). Depth: 4,000ft (1,220m).

Adsorption, taking up by a solid or liquid of a gas or liquid in contact with it. The amounts adsorbed and the rate of adsorption depend on the nature of the structure exposed, the chemical identities and concentrations of the substances involved, and the temperature. Silica gel and active carbon can take up great volumes of gas.

Adult Education, programs for people older than the traditional school age. Some study to learn to read and write or to use the language of a new country. Others complete credits for high school or college diplomas. Many learn new skills or simply expand their general knowledge. In *continuing education,* people take refresher courses to keep up with developments in their fields. *See also* Extension Education.

Adventists, Christians concerned with the imminent Second Coming of Christ. Through him, the evil in the world will be destroyed. William Miller (1782–1849) formed the first organized movement in the United States in 1831. His followers were called Millerites or Second Adventists. Controversies over dates of the Coming led groups to split. *See also* Seventh-Day Adventists.

Advice and Consent, legislative power granted to the Senate by Article II, Section 2, of the US Constitution. The Senate must approve all presidential appointments and foreign treaties.

Aediles, magistrates of ancient Rome. The six aediles (three patricians and three plebeians), whose office lasted from 494 BC to AD *c.* 235, maintained public facilities, supervised public festivities, and enforced traffic and market regulations. △1014.

A.E.F. *See* American Expeditionary Force.

Aegean Sea, extension of the Mediterranean Sea between Greece and Turkey, bounded by Crete on the S; connected to the Black Sea and Sea of Marmara by the Dardanelles; contains many islands, mostly of Greece; in ancient times it was divided into the Thracian Sea, Icarian Sea, Myrtoan Sea, and Sea of Crete. Ancient name Archipelago now applies to any island group. Length: 400mi (644km). Width: 200mi (322km).

Aegis, in Greek mythology, the shield made for Jupiter by Vulcan. He carried thunder with it. Athena held it as a sign of authority when she went on missions for her father. In its center was the head of Medusa, which was said to have had the power of turning men to stone.

Aegisthus, in Greek legend, the son of Thyestes. Together they killed Atreus, king of Mycenae, father of Agamemnon and Menelaus. Aegisthus and his father held Mycenae until it was later recovered by Agamemnon. During the Trojan war Aegisthus seduced Agamemnon's wife, Clytemnestra, and murdered Agamemnon upon his return from Troy.

Aegyptopithecus. △646.

Aehrenthal, Count von Alois Lexa (1854–1912), statesman of Austria-Hungary. He served as ambassador to Romania (1895) and Russia (1899) before becoming foreign minister (1906–12). In this capacity he showed short-sightedness and substantial lack of ability, managing to alienate Italy, Russia, and most other European nations in the critical years before World War I.

Aemilianus (206?–253), Roman emperor. A general elected emperor by his soldiers, he ruled for only three months, before being assassinated by soldiers whose loyalty had shifted to Valerian.

Aemilian Way, ancient Roman road constructed by Marcus Aemilius Lepidus in 187 BC. An extension of the Flaminian Way, it began at Arminum (Rimini) and terminated at Placentia (Piacenza). Later lengthened to Mediolanum (Milan), it chiefly served the military.

Aeneas, in Greek mythology, the son of Anchises and Aphrodite. Active in the defense of Troy, he was removed by Poseidon from the city since he was destined to rule over the survivors of Troy. Aeneas led the Trojans westward to Italy. The Romans accepted Aeneas and his Trojan company as their ancestors.

Aeneid, poem written by the Roman poet Vergil between 30 and 19 BC. Written in 12 books, the *Aeneid* recounts the legendary founding of the town of Lavinium by the Trojan Aeneas. The *Aeneid* resembles the writings of Homer in both form and concepts: the first six books have been called "Vergil's *Odyssey*" and the last six, his *Iliad.* The two themes of Rome's destiny and human suffering are contained in the character of Aeneas who tries in spite of human limitations to fulfill the divine mission. The *Aeneid* was regarded by Romans as their national epic and the study of Vergil's works was widespread.

Aeolian Formation. *See* Eolian Formation.

Aeolians, ancient Greeks whose late Bronze Age members founded Lesbos and other settlements at the end of the second millennium BC. They were noted for genius in music and poetry.

Aeolis (Aeolia), ancient region in NW Asia Minor, extending from the entrance of the Hellespont (now the Dardanelles) on the Aegean Sea, to the Hermus River (now Gediz River) where Aeolian Greeks built cities before 1000 BC. Aeolis was considered a collective term for the cities rather than a geographical unit; the 12 southern cities formed the Aeolian League (8th century BC).

Aequi, ancient tribe in Italy. They expanded their territory from the central regions westward to occupy areas near modern Tivoli, Palestrina, and the Alban Hills. They returned to their original regions by 431 BC, allied with Rome, and attained Roman citizenship by the 1st century BC.

Aeration, artificial method of bringing air into direct contact with a fluid. Compressed air, furnishing oxygen to promote bacterial action, is blown into a reagent tank in the treatment of sewage. Aeration is also used in the fermentation and soft drink industries, as well as in the manufacture of penicillin and other antibiotics.

Aerial. *See* Antenna.

Aerial Reconnaissance. △1742.

Aerobe, an organism that can grow in the presence of free atmospheric oxygen. Some aerobes can live with or without oxygen and are called facultative anaerobes.

Aerodynamic Missile. *See* Cruise Missile.

Aerodynamics, science of air in motion and the forces acting on bodies, such as aircraft, in motion through the air. The designer of a flyable aircraft must consider four fundamental factors and their relationships: weight of the aircraft and load, lift to overcome the pull of gravity, drag or the forces that retard motion, and thrust, the driving force. Understanding of these forces is complicated by their non-uniform behavior in the various regimes of modern flight. △1496, 1718.

Aerolite. *See* Stony Meteorite.

Aeronaut. △1712.

Aeronautical Engineering, activity encompassing the design and construction of aircraft, their systems and performance in subsonic, supersonic, and hypersonic regimes of flight. By using such tools as the wind and shock tunnels, experimental evidence can be gathered on behavior of materials and designs as if in flight. Computers allow rapid solutions to theoretical problems that once could only be flight-tested. To understand new phenomena requires knowledge of thermodynamics, fluidics, and chemistry since flights in the hypersonic range involve physical and chemical changes not previously encountered by machines. Aeronautical engineering requires a comprehensive scientific background. *See also* Aerodynamics. △1496, 1718, 1744.

Aeronautics, science of the operation of aircraft. Airplanes, gliders, rotorcraft, and balloons share some principles of flight but are unique in others. Free balloons and dirigibles go aloft by displacing air with a gas or hot air. Free balloons have no means of propulsion, but dirigibles use aircraft engines. Rotorcraft utilize lift provided by a rotating wing or rotor. The helicopter propels itself forward by tilting the plane of rotation of its powered rotor, while the gyroplane or autogyro's rotor free-wheels, making it necessary to gain forward motion by using an engine-driven propeller. Gliders and airplanes use lifting wings. The glider dives for forward motion and lift. The airplane uses a second source of lift, the propeller, to pull itself forward, or moves in a reaction to the expulsion of hot gases. *See also* Aircraft. △1714–18.

Aeronomy, the study of the earth's upper atmosphere, including its composition, density, temperature, and chemical reactions, as recorded by sounding rockets and earth satellites. △212.

Aerosol, (1) suspension of liquid or solid particles in a gas. Mist comprises about 10^{15} water droplets suspended in a liter of air; airborne bacteria or dust (which we call smoke) are solid-based aerosols. (2) Pressurized spray container for packaging deodorant, insecticide, paint, etc. Fluorocarbons, often used as propellants in such aerosols, may be harmful to the ozone layer.

Aerospace Medicine, a division of medical science that studies the medical aspects and problems of human beings in space. An organization of medical personnel and scientists concerned with space study, called the Aerospace Medical Association (ASMA), was formed in the United States in 1959, as an outgrowth of the Aero Medical Association formed in 1929.

Aerostats. △1712.

Aeschylus (525–456 BC), Greek dramatist. The earliest known writer of tragedies whose plays exist in complete form, he was also the first to include more than one character in a play. Seven of his works survive: *The Suppliants, The Persians, The Seven Against Thebes, Prometheus Bound,* and the *Oresteia* trilogy *(Agamemnon, The Chöephoroe,* and *The Eumenides).* They are characterized by impressive language, and moral and religious themes. *See also* Oresteia. △998.

Aesculapius, in Greek mythology, son of Apollo and the nymph Coronis. The first physician, he became so skilled that he could restore the dead to life. In art he is portrayed as a strong youth bearing a serpent entwined around a staff.

Aesir, principal race of the Nordic gods. Three of these, Woden (Odin), Thor (Donar), and Tyr (Tiw), and a few others were the object of a cult that extended throughout the lands inhabited by the Teutons. Secondary to the Aesir was a race of Teutonic gods known as the Vanir.

Aesop (*c.* 620–560 BC), Greek fabulist. A former slave, he was the reputed creator of numerous short tales about animals, all illustrating human virtues and failings. Aesop supposedly died in Delphi, where he angered citizens and was thrown off a cliff. *See also* Fable.

Aesop's Fables, short animal tales designed to convey a moral lesson, eg *The Hare and the Tortoise* teaches "slow and steady wins the race," and *The Fox and the Crow* cautions against trusting flatterers. Ascribed by tradition to a slave in the 6th century BC, a collection of the tales accompanied by 185 "clear and lively woodcuts" was translated and printed by William Caxton in 1484.

Aesthetics, study of beauty and of standards of value in judging beauty, especially in art. The term was first used in the 18th century to describe a science whose object is beauty, although philosophizing about the arts dates from the writings of Plato and earlier. In the 18th century, G. W. F. Hegel employed the term in its present sense. In the 20th century, aesthetics has come to be regarded as a science independent of philosophy, studying works of art, human behavior toward art, and the enjoyment of art. △858.

Aethiopis Region. △76.

Aetolian League, a federal state organized from loose Greek tribes in 370 BC. It was normally hostile to Macedonia, but was Rome's first Greek ally. Later hostile to Rome, it was forced to be a subject ally in 189 BC.

Afanasiev, Aleksandr Nikolaevich (1826–71), Russian historian. Having written on all aspects of the Russian-Slavic tradition, he began in the middle of the century to write on folk mythology for several influential periodicals. Some of his more important works were *The Ancestor-House Demon* (1850), *The Sorcerer and the Witch* (1851), *Russian Satirical Journals 1769–1774* (1855), and in 1860, *Russian Folk Tales,* which was the first systematic study of Russian fairy tales.

Afars and the Issas, French Territory of the (formerly French Somaliland), autonomous territory of France, on NE coast of Africa near S entrance to the Red Sea. It is governed by a local president, council, and chamber of deputies. Djibouti is the capital.

In 1862, France obtained Obock on Somali Coast, gradually extended S to Djibouti in agreements with Afar and Issa chiefs. In 1896, France signed treaties with Britain, Italy, and Ethiopia defining boundaries of French Somaliland. From 1957 to 1967 the colony gained gradual autonomy; in 1967 it voted to remain a French possession and adapted its present name.

The majority of the inhabitants are members of the Afars and the less numerous Issas tribes. They frequently clash politically and economically. Less than 20% of population is European and Arab, with a few Ethiopians, Jews, and Indians. Most inhabitants are Muslims. Although French is the official language, Afar and Somali are primarily spoken. Nomadic life is followed by over half the population, who raise cattle,

Stella Adler

10

Aesop's fables

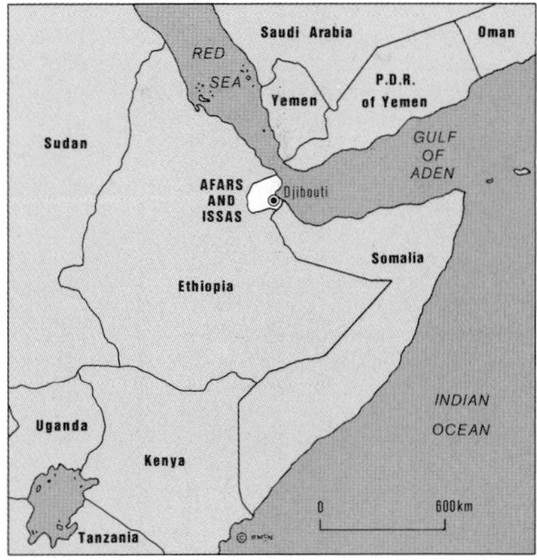

Saudi Arabia
Oman
RED SEA
Yemen
P.D.R. of Yemen
Sudan
GULF OF ADEN
AFARS AND ISSAS
Djibouti
Somalia
Ethiopia
INDIAN OCEAN
Uganda
Kenya
Tanzania
0
600km

Afars and Issas

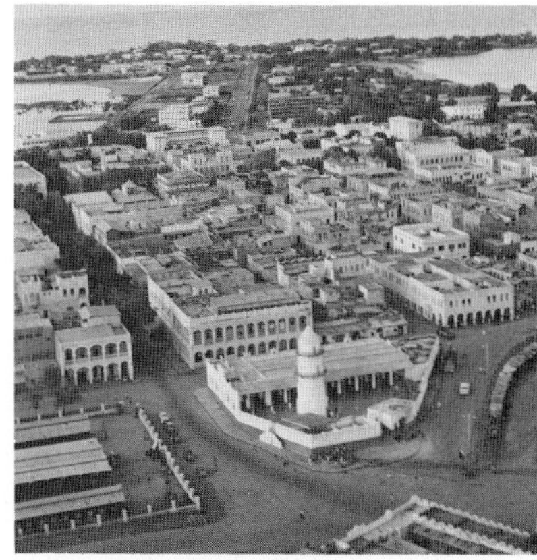

Djibouti, Afars and Isaas

sheep, goats, and donkeys. A very limited annual rainfall of 2–10in (51–254mm), in a country that is approximately 90% stony desert, allows for little agriculture; some dates are cultivated and a little market gardening is done. Industries include meat packing, salt, hides, skins. Temperatures range from 85°–125° F (29°–52°C). Pop. approx. 95,000. Area: approx. 8,880sq mi (23,000sq km).

Affenpinscher, small German "monkey dog" (toy group) known since the 17th century in Europe. This sturdy, terrier-type dog's rounded head, short-pointed muzzle, and small, pointed, erect ears accented by a prominent chin and bushy whiskers, moustache, and eyebrows give it a distinctive expression. The body is medium-length; legs are straight; and the tail is cut short and carried high. The black coat is hard, wiry, and short, except on the legs and face, where it is more shaggy. Average size: 8–10in (20–25cm) high at shoulder; 7–8lb (3–3.5kg). *See also* Toy Dog.

Affluent Society, The (1958), book on economics by John K. Galbraith. The author's theme, basically, is that in an advanced Western industrial society, a serious imbalance between the provision of public goods and private goods develops. According to Galbraith, as economic development progresses, more cars and leisure will necessarily mean more of such unwanted items as congestion and pollution. △1358.

Afghan Hound, aristocratic hunting dog (hound group) originating in Sinai Peninsula 4000–3000 BC and later established in Afghanistan. Aloof and dignified, it has a long, slender head and jaws; long, hanging ears; level back; arched loins; long, straight legs with large feet; and long, tapered tail with ring or curve at end. The thick, silky coat, which may be any color, is short and smooth on the back and longer over the rest of the dog. There is a long topknot on the head. Average size: 24–28in (61–71cm) high at shoulder; 50–60lb (22.6–27kg). *See also* Hound.

Afghanistan, Republic of, nation in W central Asia. Landlocked and mountainous, it has welcomed outsiders only recently. In the 1970s it is struggling to industrialize.

Land and Economy. Mountains of sedimentary rock over a metamorphic base separate N from S and cover 60% of the land. Peaks over 20,000ft (6,100m) rise in the E Hindu Kush. In the N, steppes slope down to the Amu Darya River; the S is covered by the Registan and other deserts (41,000sq mi; 106,190sq km). Arid in summer, cold in winter, the country has poor agricultural conditions, yet 80% of the people live by farming and herding. Minerals are difficult to find and mine. Small factories produce cloth and clothing, while families weave rugs and make pottery.

People. Local languages show most people to be descended from Persians, Tatars, and Mongols. Islam is the national religion, and the people belong mostly to the Sunnite sect. Many were once nomads, but today 90% lead a settled life, with 10% located in cities. Government programs bring education to more youngsters than religious schools once did, but only about 12% of the men and 6% of the women are literate.

Government. A republic (nearly a dictatorship) is maintained with military help. When finished, a new constitution will embrace Islamic and socialist concepts. Soviet influence is strong, but the government also accepts aid from Communist China and the United States.

History. Trade routes through the area in ancient times brought Persian (Iranian) traders, who gradually became dominant. The Pushtuns among them grew especially strong, although Arabs, Turks (Tatars), and Mongols left lasting influences. Afghans, descended from the Pushtuns, began to unite in the 17th century. The British exerted pressure from India in the 19th century, until they held control. After WWI, local tribes rebelled, and in 1921 Britain recognized the country as an independent monarchy. While King Mohammed Zahir Shah was in Europe (1973), Lt.-Gen. Mohammed Daud Khan seized power. Except for continual friction with Pakistan, Afghanistan remains neutral in world affairs or votes with Afro-Asian nations at the United Nations. Relations with Pakistan are complicated by Afghanistan's support of tribes in Pakistan.

PROFILE

Official name: Republic of Afghanistan
Area: 250,775sq mi (649,507sq km)
Population (1975): 19,300,000
Density, 77 per sq mi (30 per sq km)
Chief cities: Kabul, the capital; Kandahar,
Government: Head of state, Mohammed Daud Khan, president (seized power July 1973)
Gross national product (1973): $1,500,000,000
Trading partners (major): USSR, India

Africa, continent mostly in Eastern and Northern hemisphere straddling the equator. Of the continents, only Asia is larger.

Land. Africa forms a giant plateau between the Atlantic and Indian oceans. Its highest features include the Atlas and Ahaggar mts (NW), the Ethiopian Highlands (E), and the Drakensberg Mts (SE). Mt Kilimanjaro has the continent's highest peak, 19,340ft (5,899m). A huge sunken strip in the SE is known as the East African (or Great) Rift Valley. The Sahara, largest desert in the world, stretches across the N, covering more than 25% of the continent. The Kalahari and Namib are smaller deserts in the S and SW. Of islands near Africa, Madagascar (Malagasy Republic) is the world's fourth largest.

Lakes and Rivers. The Rift valley holds such major lakes as Rudolf, Nyasa, and Tanganyika; Lake Victoria, in the E, is Africa's largest, 26,828sq mi (69,485sq km); Lake Chad lies in the central N. The Nile, longest river in the world, 4,150mi (6,682km), flows from Lake Victoria. Other major rivers are the Niger, Congo, and Zambezi.

Climate and Vegetation. Only a N strip and the S end of Africa extend beyond the tropics. Much of the continent is hot and, outside the desert areas, humid. The strip along the equator receives more than 100in (254cm) of moisture a year in places, which helps produce a thick rain forest. The forest gives way to areas of acacia and brush and finally to grasslands, or savannas. The deserts receive little moisture, but grassy oases occur where springs and mountain streams provide water.

Animal Life. Ostriches live in the deserts, while vultures range over a wide area. The grasslands and brush support giraffes, rhinoceros, zebras, many types of antelopes, and lions. Elephants live from the plains to the forests, as do some giraffes, rhinoceros, zebras, many types of antelopes, and lions. Gorillas and chimpanzees remain in the jungles. Hippopotamuses are in the E rivers, and crocodiles remain numerous in places. Pythons are the largest snakes, but mambas and cobras are more dangerous to man.

People. The original inhabitants of Africa were dark-skinned peoples who hunted, fished, and gathered roots, fruits, and nuts. N of the Sahara, they were replaced by Arabs; S of the Sahara, Negroid types still predominate. Farming and herding support more than 85% of Africa's peoples. The pygmies of the rain forest continue as gatherers and hunters, as do the Bushmen and Hottentots of the SW deserts. The unusually tall Masai and Watusi of E Africa live by herding cattle and sheep.

Economy. The Arabs cultivate olives, figs, dates, and grains. Europeans have expanded agriculture below the Sahara, starting rubber, cocoa, coffee, and peanut plantations. Copper, bauxite, gold, and diamonds are mined. Various governments since the 1960s have nationalized some European-founded industries. Most rivers have cataracts suitable to run hydroelectric or industrial plants.

History. Egyptian civilization existed 6,000 years ago, and Phoenicians settled on Africa's Mediterranean coast about 1000 BC, but Roman forces later conquered them and Egypt. As Roman influence lessened, the kingdom of Ghana developed in W Africa. About AD 650, Arabs advanced W from the Arabian Peninsula. Below the Sahara, the Mali kingdom replaced that of Ghana during the 11th century. Portuguese began exploring the Atlantic coastline in the 15th century. Europeans came to seek gold and gems but between 1600–1800 captured blacks for the slave trade. The discovery of diamonds (1866) and gold (1886) in South Africa and the opening of the Suez Canal (1869) helped bring outsiders. During the late 19th century, European nations raced to build African empires. Most African countries have received independence since 1950. Communist and Western countries compete for influence, and powerful white groups fight to keep control of a few governments. △1116, 1212, 1268.

PROFILE

Area: 11,677,239sq mi (30,244,049sq km)
Largest nations: Sudan, Algeria, Zaire—each over 900,000sq mi (2,331,000sq km)
Population (1974 est.): 373,600,000
Density, 32 per sq mi (12 per sq km)
Most populous nations: Nigeria 79,760,000; Egypt, 37,500,000; Ethiopia, 28,000,000
Chief cities: Cairo, Egypt; Alexandria, Egypt; Kinshasa, Zaire; Casablanca, Morocco; Johannesburg, South Africa; Algiers, Algeria
Industries (major products): iron, steel, petroleum products, rubber, chemicals, fertilizers, textiles, foodstuffs
Agriculture (major products): dates, grapes, figs, wheat, corn, rice, barley, sorghum, cocoa, coffee, tea, vegetables, cotton
Minerals (major): gold, diamonds, bauxite, uranium, copper, iron ore, cobalt, manganese, coal, petroleum, natural gas

African Art. △974, 1214.

African Languages, languages spoken on the African continent. These include the Afro-Asiatic or Semitic languages in N and Ethiopia, such as Arabic, Cushitic, Berber. Others are the sub-Saharan, black, or Afro-African, which divided into three major families—Sudanic in central and E Africa, Niger-Kordofanian in equatorial, and Khoisan in the SW. English, Spanish, French, Portuguese, and Afrikaans show colonial presence. The original alphabets were non-Roman, but many were first rendered by Europeans into modified Roman with diacritics for unique sounds—clicks or tones.

African Methodist Episcopal Church, second largest Methodist group in the United States. Objecting to the church's racial discriminatory policy, a group withdrew from the Methodist Episcopal Church in 1787. The first AME church was dedicated in 1793 in Philadelphia. Richard Allen was the first bishop; formal organization followed in 1816. Its doctrines are those of traditional Methodist churches. There are approximately 1.1 million members. *See also* Methodist Church.

African Methodist Episcopal Zion Church, formed in 1796 by a group of black members of the John Street Church (Methodist Episcopal) in New York City who protested racial discrimination. The name was approved in 1848, and James Varick was the first bishop. The church spread rapidly throughout the northern states, and some churches developed in the South. Missionary activity and education are stressed. There are approximately 900,000 members.

African Violet, tropical African flowering house plant. The velvety, rounded leaves grow in spreading rosettes centered by purple or white blossoms with yellow stamens. Red stems and leaf undersides are common. Care: bright indirect light, warm temperature, humid air, well-drained soil (1 part potting soil, 2 parts peat moss, 1 part sand) kept barely moist with tepid water. Propagation is by leaf cuttings or crown divisions. Height: 4–6in (10–15cm). Family Gesneriaceae; genus *Saint paulia.*

African Wild Cat. *See* Kaffir Cat.

Afrikaners, or Boers, people of mainly Dutch descent inhabiting the Republic of South Africa. They first settled around the Cape in the 17th century and were joined by French Huguenot refugees. Tension between them and the British led first to the Great Trek (1835–40), in which the Afrikaners moved inland, establishing the Orange Free State and the Transvaal, and later to the Boer War (1899–1902), won by Britain. The Afrikaners control political power in South Africa, and their Calvinism and concern with "purity of blood" has led to the republic's policy of apartheid.

Afro-African Languages, languages native to the African continent and spoken by, or derived from, languages natively spoken by black African or Negroid peoples. The term is used sometimes to distinguish the three major families of sub-Saharan African languages from the Semitic or Afro-Asiatic languages of Arabic countries. Many black Africans speak Semitic tongues, and among themselves the three southern families differ at least as greatly as European and Oriental languages differ.

Afro-Asian Bloc, the countries of Africa and Asia when they act politically in concert (for example, in votes in the United Nations), but distinct from the Western powers or the Soviet bloc. *See also* Third World. △1352.

Afterbirth, the placenta and fetal membranes expelled from the uterus after childbirth. △704.

Afterimage, image formed as an aftereffect of staring at a bright spot or pattern. Often the color of the afterimage is the complement of the original stimulus. The "spots" one sees after a flashbulb fires are afterimages. △674.

Afternoon of a Faun, one-act ballet by Vaslav Nijinsky. △1368.

Agaja. △1212.

Aga Khan III (1877–1957), sultan and Imam of the Ismaili Muslim sect, son and successor (1885) of Aga Khan II. He founded the All-India Muslim League in support of British rule (1906), upgraded Muslim University (1920), and represented India at the World Disarmament Conference (1932) and at the League of

Nations (1932; 1934–37). Very wealthy, his thoroughbreds won the English Derby five times.

Agamemnon, Greek king of Mycenae, brother of Menelaus. He led the siege of Troy. When Troy fell Agamemnon returned home with his captive Cassandra, but was slain by his wife Clytemnestra and her lover Aegisthus. His death was avenged by his children Orestes and Electra.

Agar, complex substance extracted from certain seaweeds; a colloidal powder forming a rigid gel in solution. It is used as a thickening agent in ice cream, an emulsifier, adhesive, and support medium for growing bacterial cultures.

Agassiz, Alexander (1835–1910), US marine zoologist, b. Switzerland. He was influential in the development of modern systematic zoology, and made important studies of sea beds. In 1874 he succeeded his father, Louis, as curator of the Harvard Museum of Natural History, to which he also made major financial contributions.

Agassiz, John Louis Rodolphe (1807–1873), US naturalist, b. Switzerland. He worked to make science available to the public. Known also for his work in geology and ichthyology, Agassiz made significant studies in the classification of animals, especially fossil forms, and in the movement and distribution of glaciers. From 1836–1837 he explored glaciers, and in 1839 proved through experimentation that glaciers move. His *Études sur les glaciers* (1840) proposed the theory of an ice age, in which glaciers covered most of northern Europe. His general zoological classification, *Nomenclator Zoologicus* (1842–1846), aroused interest in the study of fossils and introduced order into what had been zoological chaos. He began lecturing and writing scientific essays in America in 1846, and in 1861 he became a US citizen.

Agassiz, Lake, glacial lake of ancient North America; about 700mi (1,130km) long by 200mi (320km) wide and covered parts of Saskatchewan, Ontario, Manitoba, North Dakota, and Minnesota. Formed by glacial blockage of various rivers, the lake existed as much as 2,000,000 years ago in the Pleistocene Epoch, and was named after Louis Agassiz in 1879.

Agate, a fine-grained variety of chalcedony, a silica mineral, that is essentially quartz. It occurs in bands of various colors, or blended in clouds or mosslike patterns. Semiprecious in quality, agate is frequently used for jewelry. *See also* Quartz.

Agave, short-stemmed, succulent flowering plant of the family Agavaceae found in tropical, subtropical, and temperate areas. All have narrow, lance-shaped leaves clustered at the plant base. Many have large flower clusters. The century plant *(Agave americana)* of SW North America is a well-known stemless plant with a 40-ft (12-m) stalk topped by a flower cluster. Each plant produces a flower spike once a year or less frequently, after which the leaves die, leaving the roots to produce a new plant. Other species are sisal hemp *(A. sisalana)* and the many species of yucca. Some species contain a sap that produces an intoxicant when fermented. There are fewer than 250 species in the wild, but many others are cultivated commercially or for decoration.

Agawam, town in S Massachusetts, on Connecticut and Westfield rivers; residential suburb of Springfield. Industries: farming, dairying, tobacco. Settled 1636; inc. 1855. Pop. (1970) 21,717.

Agee, James (1909–55), US author, b. Knoxville. A writer for *Fortune* magazine and a film critic for *Time* and *The Nation,* he also wrote poetry and novels. His works include *Let Us Now Praise Famous Men* (1941; with Walker Evans), a bitter account of sharecroppers in Alabama during the Depression, and *A Death in the Family* (1957). *See also* Death in the Family, A; Evans, Walker.

Age Grade, a system in which social status is determined by age groupings. As a person grows older, he or she periodically moves into a group with specified new positions and powers.

Agency for International Development (AID), US government agency that carries out assistance programs designed to help the peoples of certain less developed countries develop their human and economic resources, increase production capacities, and improve the quality of human life. It also promotes economic or political stability in friendly countries. Established by the Foreign Assistance Act of 1961 and subsequently amended.

Agency Shop, employment situation in which the worker need not be a member of a union before or after employment, but nevertheless must pay the recognized union in the plant an amount of money, usually equal to union dues. The idea is that the worker should pay part of the cost of union representation.

Age of Innocence, The (1920), novel of social criticism by Edith Wharton. Set in the 1870s in New York City, it attacks New York's fashionable society as represented in Newland Archer, the protagonist, who sacrifices an opportunity for a life of happiness with Ellen Olenska to fulfill the obligations of his society by marrying May Welland.

Agglomerate, coarse volcanic rock that includes both rounded and angular fragments in a finer matrix, thus combining the characteristics of conglomerates and breccias. Charles Lyell coined the term in 1831. *See also* Breccia; Conglomerate.

Agglutination, clumping of bacteria or red blood cells by antibodies that react with antigens on the cell surface. *See also* Antigen.

Aggregate, any building or construction material used to form concrete by mixing with cement, lime, gypsum, or other adhesive. It provides desirable qualities such as volume and resistance to wear. Examples are sand, crushed and broken stone, pebbles, and boiler ashes. Fine aggregates are used to make thin and smooth structural members; coarse aggregates are used for more massive elements.

Aggregate Consumption, total amount that consumers will spend on goods and services during the year. Economists assume that this amount will vary directly with the level of real GNP, stock of liquid assets, population size, and other variables. This aggregate consumption is a portion of GNP. *See also* Gross National Product.

Aggregate Demand, total demand for goods and services in the economy. It is composed of consumption (by households) plus investment (by business) plus government expenditures plus net exports (net foreign demand for goods and services; exports less imports). The dollar volume of aggregate demand depends upon the level of GNP, disposable income, and other aggregate measures of income and wealth as well as expectations about future economic conditions such as employment and inflation.

Aggregate Equilibrium, in macroeconomics, national income equilibrium for the economy. This equilibrium occurs when the level of operation of the economy is such that the total demand for goods and services equals the total or aggregate supply of goods and services. From this position, there is no tendency for prices to fall or rise or for producers to increase or decrease output.

Aggregation, treatment of a number of terms in a mathematical expression as a single unit, denoted by enclosing the terms in parentheses or placing a bar above them. Thus in $7(x^2 = 2)$ the whole term, $x^2 = 2$, is multiplied by 7.

Aggression, deliberate act that inflicts pain or suffering on another individual. Aggression in animals is regarded as instinctual by ethologists. The question of the origins of human aggression is controversial, however. Some regard it as instinctual; others, entirely learned; still others, as a mix. Modern psychologists suggest imitation as an important way children acquire aggressive behaviors. △784, 812.

Aggression, Social. △894.

Agincourt, village in N France, 33mi (53km) W of Arras; scene of defeat of French army by Henry V of England in 1415 during the Hundred Years War. Although the French were more heavily armored, English archers with longbows decimated the French ranks; battle is central to Shakespeare's *Henry V.*

Aging, Administration on, a division of the US Department of Health, Education and Welfare. It is involved with developing programs and legislation to assist and better the lives of the aging.

Aging, Human, changes, both physiological and psychological, that occur in individuals from the attainment of maturity until death. △802, 804.

Aglipay (y Labayán), Gregorio (1860–1940), Filipino clergyman; first bishop of the Philippine Independent Church. Ordained a Roman Catholic priest in 1888, he joined the Filipino revolutionary forces of Emilio Aguinaldo after the United States occupied the

Afghan hound

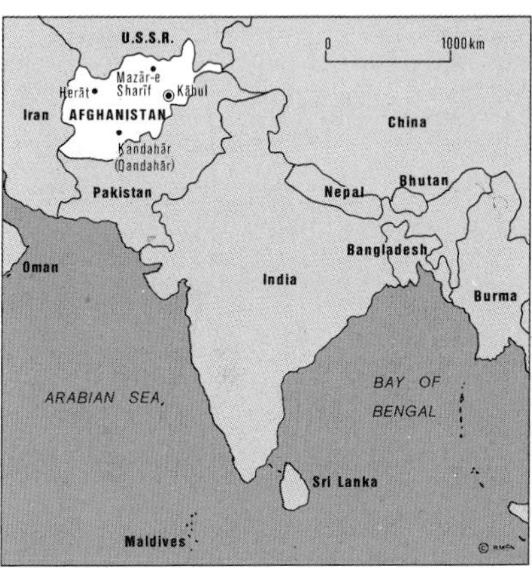
U.S.S.R.
0
1000km
Mazār-e Sharīf
Herāt
Kābul
Iran
AFGHANISTAN
China
Kandahār (Qandahār)
Pakistan
Nepal
Bhutan
Oman
Bangladesh
India
Burma
ARABIAN SEA
BAY OF BENGAL
Sri Lanka
Maldives

Afghanistan

Pamir, Afghanistan

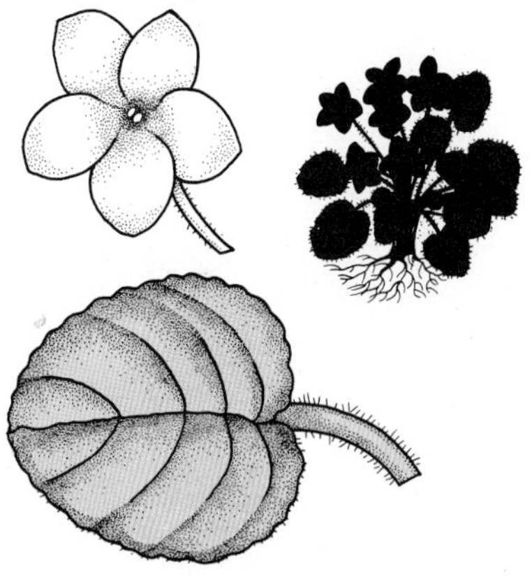

African violet

country (1898). Excommunicated by the Roman Catholic Church in 1902, he formed a national church and as supreme bishop Filipinized Roman Catholic practices. Membership reached approximately 1 million before his death.

Agnew, Spiro Theodore (1918–), US vice president, b. Baltimore, Md. He was elected chief executive of Baltimore co (1961) and governor of Maryland (1967). Richard M. Nixon's running mate on the Republican ticket (1968), Agnew served as vice-president (1969–73). His forceful, picturesque language made him a popular speaker. In 1973 he was indicted on bribery, conspiracy, and tax charges for actions he allegedly took while governor of Maryland. He pleaded no contest to charges of tax evasion and resigned on Oct. 10, 1973. He was subsequently disbarred (1974).

Agni, fire-god in Vedic mythology, revered as god of the home in his domestic aspect and appearing in lightning and the sun as a nature deity. He functioned as a messenger between men and the gods when he carried consumed offerings of the sacrificial altars to the heavens.

Agnosticism, theory of religious knowledge, associated with English rationalist Thomas Huxley (1825–95), that it is impossible either to demonstrate or to refute God's existence, on the basis of available evidence.

Agon. △1368.

Agoraphobia, morbid fear of open places, a term derived from the Greek *agora* (marketplace). Afflicted persons are apt to show signs of acute panic when alone in an open or public place.

Agouti, medium-sized, herbivorous rodent of Central and South America and West Indies. Hunted as food by man and other animals, they have short ears, long legs, tiny tails, and coarse fur that ranges from orange to brown to black. They sit erect when eating, holding food with their front paws. Family Dasyproctidae. *See also* Paca.

Agra, city in India, on Yamuna River. Established 1560 by Mogul emperor Akbar as the site for his capital; under reign of Shah Jahan, the Taj Mahal was built (1648) as the tomb and memorial to his wife Mumtaz Mahal; city's importance declined steadily when the Mogul empire moved its headquarters to Delhi (1658); annexed to British Empire (1802), it was capital of the North West prov. during the mid-19th century; site of Akbar's fort (1566) and tomb, the Pearl Mosque, and the Great Mosque—all magnificent examples of Mogul architecture. Industries: glass, shoes, textiles, tourism. Founded 1560. Pop. 5,000. *See also* Taj Mahal.

Agranulocytosis, acute and serious illness caused by chemicals or hypersensitivity to drugs in which infection-barrier granulocytes (a type of white blood cell) rapidly disappear, causing rapid and often overwhelming infection, usually starting at oral mucous membranes.

Agrarian Laws, Roman, legislation in ancient Rome by which public lands, usually confiscated from cities and states defeated in battle, were assigned to tenants. They were attempts to rectify the gross imbalance between lands held by the rich and the minimal share held by the poor. The principal enactments of these laws occurred in 367 BC, 233 BC, 133 BC, 123 BC, 82 BC, and 43 BC, but all of them were generally ignored or gotten around. The edict of Domitian (*c.* AD 82), granting public lands permanently to those who currently held them, kept them in the hands of the wealthy.

Agrarian, or **Agricultural, Revolution,** a change in attitudes and methods of farming that took place in England in the 18th century. With greater commerce came an increased market for food. Legal reallocation of land ownership (the "enclosure" movement) made for more compact and economical farms. Use of machinery, such as Jethro Tull's seed drill, began. Systems of crop rotation were instituted. Beginning before the industrial revolution, the transformation took over a century to complete and can be regarded both as a prelude to and a part of industrialization. △300.

Agrarian Socialism. △1268.

Agribusiness, the total agricultural industry, or sector, including producing farm products, processing them, and marketing the finished good, as well as production of agricultural machinery and supplies for the farm. △308.

Agricola, Gnaeus Julius (37–93), Roman general; conqueror and governor of Britain. As governor (*c.* 78–85), he Romanized Britain without oppression and expanded Roman influence to Wales and part of Scotland. His enlightened rule was described by Tacitus, his son-in-law.

Agricultural Adjustment Act (1933), New Deal legislation of President Franklin Roosevelt designed to increase the purchasing power of farmers by balancing production with consumption. It set up the Agricultural Adjustment Agency (AAA), which provided subsidies for lower production and penalized overproduction. The production control features of the AAA were declared unconstitutional (1936) by the US Supreme Court.

Agricultural Engineering, division of agricultural science including some mechanical engineering, construction, hydraulics, and soil mechanics. Engineering is responsible for irrigation, machine design, and changes in applications of various techniques.

Agricultural Research Service, US government agency of Department of Agriculture. Its basic mission is to provide the necessary knowledge and technology so the farmers can produce efficiently, conserve the environment, and meet the food and fiber needs of the US people. Est. 1953.

Agricultural Revolution. *See* Agrarian Revolution.

Agriculture, science of cultivating the soil and raising plant and animal foods necessary for human survival. Since Neolithic times (7000 BC), agriculture has been an essential way of life. Modern technology has raised farming from the self-survival level to a commercial level where a disproportionately small number of people feed almost the world's entire population. Areas improved by advanced technology include: irrigation, drainage, conservation, sanitation, plant and animal breeding, fertilization, pesticides, soil analysis, animal nutrient requirements, food preservation, and transportation. Biological and physical scientists and engineers are constantly developing new methods, raising production to an ever greater scale.

Mechanization, significant since the 18th century, has increased productivity, reduced manual labor, and replaced draft animals, in most countries, by machines. Specialization is the modern trend, with soil, climate, and topography determining the crop or animal raised: grain is raised on large, flat or rolling fields; truck farms and dairies are located adjacent to large cities for easier marketing; livestock is raised near its food source. △300–398, 304–320, 952.

Agriculture, Department of (USDA), US cabinet level department within the executive branch. It is directed by the secretary of agriculture, who is a cabinet member. It accumulates and makes available agricultural information. It engages in research, education, conservation, marketing, regulatory work, agricultural adjustment, surplus disposal, and rural development. The department's activities are primarily directed toward increasing the efficiency, production, and profit of the agricultural industry. Among its more important agencies are the Food and Nutrition Service, Soil Conservation Service, Forest Service, and Federal Crop Insurance Corporation. It was established in 1862.

Agrigento, formerly Girgenti; city in S Sicily, Italy; capital of Agrigento prov. It was founded *c.* 580 BC as Acragas or Akragas by Greek colonists from Gela; prospered until conquered by the Cathaginians in 406 BC; captured by Romans in 210 BC, and commerce improved. Greek ruins remain, including temples to Hera and Zeus. Industries: agricultural trade, mining. Pop. 51,682.

Agrippa, Marcus Vipsanius (63–12BC), Roman general, adviser to Roman emperor Augustus. After Caesar's death in 44 BC, Agrippa was influential in Augustus' attainment of the throne, commanding two naval battles in 36 BC against Sextus Pompeius and helping to defeat Mark Antony at Actium in 31 BC. Agrippa was appointed consul three times, married the emperor's daughter, and became heir-designate.

Agrippina I, Vipsania Agrippina (13 BC?-33 AD), daughter of Marcus Agrippa and Julia, the daughter of Roman Emperor Augustus. She married prince Germanicus, heir-designate to Emperor Tiberius. When Germanicus died, she suspected Tiberius, and engaged in several plots against him until she was banished in AD 19 to Pandateria, an island near Naples.

Agrippina II, Julia Agrippina (AD 15?–59), daughter of Vipsania Agrippina, and mother of Nero, who became a Roman emperor. When her uncle Claudius became emperor, she married him and persuaded him to name Nero as his heir-designate. In AD 54 she murdered Claudius, and Nero gained the throne. Nero had her killed in AD 59.

Agronomy, the science of improving methods of soil management in the interest of agriculture. The science revolves around studies of particular plants, soils, and the interrelationship of the two. Agronomy has resulted in disease-resistant plants, selective breeding, and chemical fertilizers.

Aguascalientes, city in central Mexico, 364mi (586km) NW of Mexico City; capital of Aguascalientes state; health resort, noted for mineral springs; built above ancient, advanced tunnel system of unknown origin. Industries: textiles, smelting, processed food. Founded 1575 as Spanish military base. Pop. 181,277.

Aguilar v. Texas (1964), US Supreme Court case in which the court declared that a search warrant was only valid when it had been issued by a magistrate who had studied an affidavit and determined there was a probable cause. The decision ruled out the use of hearsay evidence as a basis for a warrant.

Aguinaldo, Emilio (1869–1964), Filipino leader. Leader of the 1896 insurrection against Spain, he was exiled to Hong Kong, but returned with the outbreak of the Spanish-American War (1898) to fight for independence. He set up the Philippine Republic with himself as president, resisting the US occupation forces until 1901. After swearing allegiance to the United States, he retired to private life until 1935 when he ran unsuccessfully for the presidency. In 1945 he was accused of collaborating with the Japanese during World War II. After a brief imprisonment, he was released. In 1950 he became a member of the Philippine Council of State.

Ahab (died *c.* 853 BC), king of Israel (*c.* 874–853 BC), son and successor of Omri. He secured peace between his northern kingdom and Tyre by marrying Jezebel. With Benhadad he withstood Shalmaneser III at Karkar on the Orontes (*c.* 854 BC). Elijah told him to banish idols. He fought Benhadad for land east of Jordan and was killed. His son Ahaziah succeeded him.

Ahaz (died *c.* 727 BC), king of Judah (*c.* 735–725 BC), son of Jotham. With the aid of Tiglath-pileser III of Assyria, he beat back the forces of Pekah of Israel and Rezin of Damascus. The prophet Isaiah opposed his alliance with Assyria. His son Hezekiah succeeded him.

Ahidjo Ahmadou (1924–), first president of the United Republic of Cameroon. After serving in the territorial government of the French Cameroons, he managed to attain independence for his country (1960) and union with the new independent former British Cameroons (1961) while maintaining close ties with France. He forced the uniting of all political parties in 1966. Cameroon generally prospered under his leadership.

Ahmadabad, city in W India, on Sabarmati River; capital of Gujarat state; Mahatma Gandhi located his school for training freedom fighters at nearby Sabarmati Ashram; site of Indian National Congress headquarters; transportation and cultural center of the state, with numerous magnificent mosques, temples, and tombs; noted for its cotton. Founded 1412. Pop. 1,550,779.

Ahriman, or **Angra Mainyu,** Zoroastrian principle of evil and unrighteousness standing in opposition to the God, Ahura Mazda. Like God, Ahriman is pure spirit and has with him subsidiary evil spirits such as lust and heresy. Born of infinite time along with Ahura Mazda, nevertheless, Ahriman will be defeated. *See also* Ahura Mazda; Zoroastrianism. △846.

Ahura Mazda, in Zoroastrianism, the only God and creator. Later called Ohrmazd, Ahura Mazda was pure goodness. Evil was attributed to an opposing principle, Ahriman. Ahura Mazda will defeat Ahriman in the end. The six Bounteous Immortals springing from Ahura Mazda are godly aspects that can be shared in by righteous men. *See also* Ahriman; Zoroastrianism. △846, 984.

Ahvenanmaa Islands (Aland Islands), archipelago belonging to Finland, in the Baltic Sea, between Finland and Sweden; fewer than 100 of the 7,000 islands are habitable. Colonized by Sweden 12th century, they were ceded to Russia 1809; became part of Finland 1917; unsuccessfully petitioned at end of WWI to be returned to Sweden; made autonomous and neutral under Finland's sovereignty. Area: 581sq mi (1,505sq km). Pop. 21,010.

Ah, Wilderness! (1933), a nostalgic comedy by US playwright Eugene O'Neill which, unlike his searing drama, *Long Day's Journey into Night*, is a gentle, bittersweet look at a typical American small-town family. The play follows young Richard's halting initiation into adulthood, and observes the small domestic crises that make up the Miller family's daily life.

AID. *See* Agency for International Development.

Aïda (1871), tragic opera in four acts by Guiseppe Verdi, libretto in Italian by Verdi and Antonio Ghislanzoni, from a plot by Egyptologist Mariette Bey. The opera was commissioned for the opening of the Suez Canal (1869), but was not completed in time. The plot concerns an Egyptian hero, Rhadames (tenor), who spurns the hand of Princess Amneris (mezzo-soprano) for the love of an Ethiopian slave, Aïda (soprano). Jealousy and patriotism contribute to the death of the lovers, who are buried alive together. △1256.

Aid to Families with Dependent Children (AFDC), public assistance program in which government funds (usually state or local) are paid to low-income families that have dependent children. AFDC is the largest federally subsidized welfare program.

Aiken, Conrad (1889–1973), US poet, novelist, and critic, b. Savannah, Ga. His work includes *Selected Poems* (1929; Pulitzer Prize 1930), *Brownstone Eclogues and Other Poems* (1942), and *Ushant* (1952), an autobiography.

Aikido, martial art based on an ancient Japanese system of self-defense. Unlike some other martial art forms, where force is met with counter-force, Aikido employs the technique of avoiding action by giving way to an opponent's force, thereby causing the attacker to have a temporary loss of balance. Aikido also is used as a competitive fighting sport.

Ailanthus, or tree of heaven, paradise tree, Chinese sumac; deciduous, weedlike tree native to China but naturalized in America and Europe. It is tolerant of air pollution, thrives in any soil or climate, and resists most insects and diseases. The fern-shaped leaves grow to 3ft(9cm). Greenish-yellow male and female flowers are borne on separate trees. The nine species include *Ailanthus altissima*. Height: 50–75ft (15–23m). Family Simaroubaceae.

Aileron, hinged control surface on the outboard trailing edge of each wing of an airplane. By rotating the control wheel, the pilot deflects the ailerons down or up in opposite directions to increase or decrease lift, causing the airplane to roll or bank. △1718.

Ailey, Alvin (1931–), US modern dancer and choreographer, b. Rogers, Tex. He danced with Hanya Holm and the Martha Graham Company before forming the Alvin Ailey Dance Theatre in 1958, a primarily black, repertoire modern dance group, which has toured Australia, Africa, Southeast Asia, Europe, the Soviet Union, and the United States.

AIM. *See* American Indian Movement.

Aintab. *See* Gaziantep.

Ainu, aboriginal people, inhabiting Hokkaido (northern Japan) and Sakhalin, and formerly also found in the Kuril Islands. Racially distinct from the Japanese, Ainus possess certain Caucasoid features, notably profuse body and facial hair. Traditionally hunters, fishermen, and trappers, they practice animism and are famed for their bear cult.

Air Conditioning, process of controlling the flow, temperature, and humidity of air, at times including odor and dust removal, in homes, industry, and transportation facilities. Cooling and reduction of humidity is accomplished by refrigeration in summer. In winter the process is reversed by the injection of steam or warm water into heated air. Control of odors and dust is obtained through the use of air filters. Finally, air motion by fans ensures adequate removal of undesired air and replenishment with conditioned air.

Aircraft, machine that derives its lift from the reaction of the mass of air acted upon by fixed wings or rotor, or that rises as the result of being lighter than the surrounding air. Airplanes—heavier-than-air craft with fixed wings and engines—are classified on the basis of intended use, number of engines, type of landing gear, and wing configuration. Rotorcraft—the helicopter that uses a powered rotor for lift and thrust, and the gyroplane that uses a free-wheeling rotor and separate thrust engine—are a second category. Gliders—fixed-wing, powerless craft—comprise a third group; and lighter-than-air craft—rigid, semi-rigid—a fourth. △1714, 1716, 1718.

Aircraft, Military. △1742, 1744.

Aircraft Carrier, ship designed to carry aircraft and constructed so that aircraft can be launched from and landed on it. A modern nuclear carrier has a flight deck some 1000-ft (300-m) long. Weighing 75,000 tons and with a 4,500 man crew, a nuclear carrier can carry 90 aircraft and launch one per minute with each of four steam catapults. On the big carriers the landing deck is angled to port so that launching and landing operations may be carried on simultaneously. △1740.

Aircraft Engine, powerplant, single or in series, that provides energy to take off and maintain flight. Reciprocating engines in general use are gasoline fueled and air cooled. Jet engines that require special fuels are the turbojet and turbofan, which compress air before mixing fuel and utilize the expanding gas of combustion for propulsion. The simpler ramjet uses no compressor or turbine. △1626; 1716.

Air-cushion Landing System. △1676.

Air-Cushion Vehicle, often termed ground-effect vehicle or hovercraft; machine capable of hovering several inches to a few feet above ground or water and of motion forward, backward, or laterally. It accomplishes this by the use of power-driven fans rotating on vertical axes that force air through movable louvres to control direction. It is used as a recreation vehicle and has been experimented with by the military. △1682.

Airedale Terrier, working dog (terrier group) bred in northern England's Aire River Valley and brought to United States about 1881. Largest of the terriers, this wiry-coated, black and tan dog has a long, flat head squared off by chin whiskers. Ears are V-shaped and folded. Long straight legs appear massive because of their thick coat. The short tail is carried straight up. Standard size: 23in (58cm) high at shoulder; 45lb (20kg). *See also* Terriers.

Air Filter, device to remove dust and odors from air as part of the process of air conditioning. Filters may employ dry mechanical or wet viscous strainers, washers, or bubblers in which air is passed through a stream or container of water; and centrifugal or electrostatic separation.

Airfoil, any shape or surface such as a wing, tail, or propeller blades on an airplane that has as its major function the deflection of airflow to produce a pressure differential or lift. An airfoil typically has a leading and trailing edge, a chord, and upper and lower camber.

Air Force, Department of the, US government agency. It is responsible for providing an air force that is capable, in conjunction with the other armed forces, of preserving the peace and security of the United States. The department is separately organized under the authority, direction, and control of the secretary of defense. Est. 1947, subsequent legislation 1949.

Air Force, United States (USAF), one of the three major military services established under the Department of Defense in the National Security Act of 1947. It began as the Aeronautical Division of the Army in 1907, became the Aviation Section of the Signal Corps in 1914, the Air Service in 1918, the Army Air Corps in 1926, and the Army Air Forces in 1941. The United States has relied heavily on its air arm since World War I and in such non-war situations as the Berlin Airlift (1948–49) and the Cuban Missile Crisis of 1962.

Airframe, complete structure of an airplane without the power plant; consisting of wings, fuselage or body, tail assembly or empennage, and landing gear. Construction materials include metal, fabric, wood, and plastics in various combinations. *See also* Aircraft. △1714–18.

Airglow, faint permanent glow of the Earth's upper atmosphere resulting from the recombination of molecules, such as oxygen, nitrogen, and chemical impurities, that have been ionized during daytime by ultraviolet radiation from the sun and possibly by cosmic-ray and solar-wind particles.

Air Liquefier. △1502.

Airlock, the hermetically sealed passageway connecting airless environment (for example, outer space) with ship cabin or space station work area.

Agouti

Agra, India: Taj Mahal

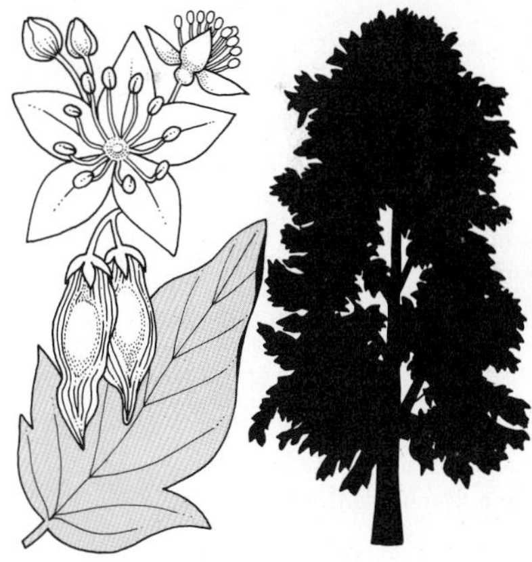

Ailanthus

Aircraft carrier: USS Nimitz

Entry is made through an outer door, which must be closed before inner door opens to preserve inner atmosphere.

Air Mass, a large body of the atmosphere nearly homogeneous horizontally in temperature, pressure, and vapor content and therefore in weather effects. High and low pressure zones on weather maps correspond to air masses, covering large areas horizontally although only a few miles vertically. Fronts, or frontal zones, occur between air masses, whose movement brings the weather. Air masses are often classified in terms of origin as polar (cold) or tropical (warm), maritime (wet, over oceans) or continental (dry, over land). *See also* Circulation, Atmospheric; Front, Weather.

Air Pollution, contamination of the atmosphere by any solid, liquid, or gaseous substances except for water. Natural pollutants include salt crystals from oceans, dust and gases from volcanoes, and pollen and spores from plants. Artificial pollutants include smokes and gases from industrial, automotive, municipal, and household activities.

Sources. In the United States, 60% of the air pollution is estimated to come from motor vehicles, 17% from industry and space heating, 14% from power plants, and 9% from incineration. Particularly harmful substances polluting air include carbon monoxide and dioxide, hydrocarbons, nitrogen and sulfur oxides, and fine smoke and dust particles, to all of which motor vehicles make a substantial contribution. Pollution often persists and accumulates with temperature inversions leading to pollution disasters, especially with fog.

Effects. Air pollution affects the health, particularly of those with respiratory difficulties like asthma, chronic bronchitis, and emphysema. Its economic costs are estimated at $10 billion a year in the United States alone. Many nations now have clean-air laws to prevent or diminish air pollution. *See also* Fluorocarbons; Inversion. △292.

Airport, tract of land upon which aircraft regularly take off and land. Airports generally contain facilites for storage, maintenance and fueling of aircraft, and some passenger facilities, but an airport can be a dirt strip with only a windsock. △1752.

Air Pressure, the pressure exerted by air, usually within an enclosed space. *See also* Atmospheric Pressure. △212.

Air Quality Act (1967), amendment to the Clean Air Act of 1963, which had begun federally supported studies of air pollution. The 1967 amendment called for the establishment of air quality control centers for regions where air pollution was a serious problem. In addition, the National Air Pollution Administration was required to publish information about pollutants and techniques that could be used to control them.

Airship, power-driven lighter-than-air craft able to control its direction of motion. A rigid airship or zeppelin maintains its form with a framework of girders covered by a rubber fabric. Nonrigids have no internal structure. Only the pressure of the contained helium maintains the shape. A semirigid airship utilizes a rigid or jointed keel to stiffen the rubberized envelope. △1712.

Airspace, within the United States considered to be volumes of the atmosphere bounded by specific altitudes and geographical limits for the purpose of regulating the flight of aircraft. It is divided into *controlled airspace,* where some or all aircraft are subject to air traffic control, and *uncontrolled airspace,* where federal authority is not exercised. *See also* Air Traffic Control. △1752.

Air Traffic Control, system of aircraft guidance to provide for safe, orderly movement. It consists of ground and local control, from the tower, concerned with traffic at the airport; arrival and departure control operating from radar rooms that directs stacking and separation and funnels traffic to or from the runways; and a system of en route control that allows controllers to "hand off" flights that reach the limits of their radar observation. △1752.

Aisha (611–678), the favorite of the 12 wives of the Prophet Mohammed, daughter of abu-Bakr. She married young, collected over 2000 sayings of Mohammed and his companions (hadiths), and incited an unsuccessful uprising against Ali. *See also* Mohammed.

Aisne, river in France; rises near Vaubecourt, flows NW and W from Argonne Forest to join Oise River near Compiègne. In WWI the plateau along the river near Craonne was scene of bitter trench warfare. Length: 175mi (282km).

Aix-en-Provence, city in SE France, 17mi (27km) N of Marseille near mineral springs; site of a popular spa, university (1409), 13th–14th-century Cathedral of Saint-Sauveur; cultural center; home of painter Paul Cézanne. Industries: wine making equipment, electrical apparatus, farming. Founded 123 BC by Romans. Pop. 89,566.

Aix-la-Chapelle, Treaty of (1748), diplomatic agreement between France and Britain ending the War of the Austrian Succession (1740–48) (known in America as King George's War). The treaty did little to settle the causes of the conflict as it simply called for the mutual restitution of conquests made during the war. *See also* Austrian Succession, War of the.

Ajaccio, seaport town and capital of Corsica, France, on the Gulf of Ajaccio, an inlet of Mediterranean Sea. Napoleon was born here and his home is a national museum; occupied by Italians in WWII. Industries: sardine fishing, shipbuilding, cigars, wax. Founded 1492 by Genoese colonists. Pop. 40,834.

Ajanta Caves. △1036.

Ajax, name given to two legendary heroes who fought on the Greek side during the Trojan war. The Greater Ajax was the son of Telamon, king of Salamis. The Lesser Ajax was the son of Oileus, king of Locris.

Ajax (*c.* 447 BC), Greek tragedy thought to be Sophocles' earliest surviving play. In it Ajax goes mad when the armor of Achilles is awarded to Odysseus instead of to him, angers the gods, and dies. Ajax is considered the hero of the work because he exemplifies the Greek code of honor.

Ajman ('Ujman), sheikdom in United Arab Emirates, in E Arabia, on the Persian Gulf; consists of the town of Ajman and two mountain villages. Formerly a British protectorate, it joined the United Arab Emirates 1971. Main industry is oil production. Area: approx. 100sq mi (259sq km). Pop. 4,245.

Ajmer, city in NW India; site where Jehangir received Sir Thomas Roe, first British ambassador to Mogul court, 1616; former capital of Ajmer-Merwara prov. and Ajmer state. Industries: agricultural trade, cotton mills, marble quarries. Founded 12th century as the capital of Chauhan dynasty of Rajputs. Pop. 269,233.

Ajuga, commonly called bugle or bugle-weed, a European perennial herbaceous plant of the mint family. It is widespread as a weed in North America but varieties are used for borders and in rock gardens.

Akan, African people who settled in Ghana, Togo, and the eastern Ivory Coast (*c.* 1000–1700). They have matrilineal clan groupings and ancestor worship; yams are the staple of their diet.

Akawai. *See* Acawai.

Akbar (1542–1605), Mogul emperor of India (1556–1605). Succeeding his father, he conquered Gujarat, Bengal, Kashmir, Sind, and Quandahar. He reformed the government, centralized the financial system, and won loyalty and unity among his non-Muslim people. △1202, 1204.

Akee. △340.

Akeley, Carl Ethan (1864–1926), US taxidermist, inventor, and explorer, b. Clarendon., N.Y. He invented methods of taxidermy that became standard museum practice. One of the first to make an attempt to display animals in their natural surroundings, he joined the American Museum of Natural History in New York City in 1909 and planned its famous African Hall.

Akhenaton (Ikhnaton) (*d.c.* 1362 BC), ancient Egyptian king of the 18th dynasty (*r.c.* 1379–1362 BC). He succeeded his father, Amenhotep III. His name at accession was Amenhotep IV. Renouncing the old gods, he introduced worship of the sun god, Aten, and established a new capital at Akhetaton (modern Tell-el-Amarna). After his death, however, Egypt rejected solar worship. His wife was Nefertiti. △972.

Akhmatova, Anna (1888–1966), pseud. of Anna Andreyevna Gorenko, Soviet poet. An Acmeist, her intense lyrics are best represented in the volumes *The Rosary* (1914) and *The Willow Tree* (1940). Although twice denounced (1946, 1957) for "bourgeois decadence," she remained an immensely popular poet in the Soviet Union.

Akiba ben Joseph (*c.* 50–135), Jewish rabbi and martyr in Palestine. He developed a new method of interpreting the Halakah, the Hebrew oral laws, and believed in the Messianic mission of Bar Cocheba, whom he supported in a revolt (132) against Roman Emperor Hadrian. He was imprisoned by the Romans and tortured to death.

Akihito (1933–), son of Emperor Hirohito, crown prince of Japan. After wide travel in foreign countries, he married a commoner, Michiko Shoda, in 1959, the first such marriage in the Japanese royal family. They have three children, the eldest born in 1960.

Akita, city in NW Honshu, Japan, on the Sea of Japan; capital of Akita prefecture; site of castle-fort (733) and university (1949); important export center. Akita prefecture contains the largest oil field and copper mines in Japan; agricultural region. Oil refining is the major industry. Crops: rice, tobacco, fruit. Pop. 235,873.

Akita, Japanese hunting dog (working group) bred in Akita prefecture in the 17th century; brought to United States in 1937 by Helen Keller. It has a broad, triangular head; small pointed, wide-set ears carried erect; a long body; muscular legs; and large, curled tail. The straight, harsh double coat of any color stands straight out and is shorter on head, legs, and ears. Average size: 20–27in (51–69cm) high at shoulder; 75–110lb (34–50kg). The Akita is considered a symbol of good health by Japanese and has been designated a national treasure by the Japanese government. *See also* Working Dog.

Akkad. △956.

Akron, city in NE Ohio, on Little Cuyahoga River, 35mi (56km) SE of Cleveland; seat of Summit co. Ohio and Erie Canal opened here in 1827 and spurred growth of area. Home of abolitionist John Brown is preserved as a museum. City has a dirigible airdock; site of world's first rubber factory, est 1869 by Dr. B. F. Goodrich, Institute of Rubber Research, and University of Akron (1913). Industries: rubber, plastics, transportation equipment. Settled *c.* 1825; inc. as village 1836; chartered as city 1865. Pop. (1970) 275,425.

Aksum. △1116.

Akure, city in S Nigeria; former independent Yoruba kingdom until 19th century, when it was taken by Benin; Britain took control of Akure 1894; site of agricultural school; marketing center for cacao. Chief industry is processed timber. Pop. 82,461.

Akutagawa, Ryunosuke (1892–1927), Japanese author. He is best known for his reinterpretations of traditional Japanese tales, vivid descriptions, and genius for the macabre. His major works include *Hana Rashomon* (1917) and *The Hell Screen* (1918).

Alabama, state in SE United States, in the Deep South's Cotton Belt. In the Civil War, it was one of the six original states of the Confederacy.

Land and Economy. Roughly the N half lies in the Appalachian Highlands, which have deposits of coal and other minerals; the remainder is in the Gulf Coastal Plain, which is crossed by the Black Belt, a wide strip of rich soil, valuable for farming. The Mobile River, flowing S to the Gulf of Mexico, and its tributaries, the Alabama and the Tombigbee, form the chief river system. On the Tennessee River in the N are three hydroelectric power dams and a Tennessee Valley Authority nuclear power plant. Traditionally agrarian, the economy has been altered by industrial growth concentrated in urban areas, where the majority of the population lives. Birmingham is a leading steel center.

People. The 19th-century settlers were immigrants from other states or black slaves who worked cotton plantations before the Civil War. The migration from rural areas to urban centers was long and slow.

Education and Research. There are about 60 institutions of higher education. The University of Alabama and Auburn University are state-supported. At Huntsville, NASA's George C. Marshall Space Flight Center is a focus of rocket and missile research.

History. Spanish explorers visited Alabama in the 16th century, but the first white settlers were the French, in 1701. Great Britain acquired the region from France in 1763 and ceded most of it to the United States after the American Revolution (1783). Some of the S, then part of Florida, was in Spanish hands until 1812. In 1817, the Territory of Alabama was created. Alabama seceded on Jan. 11, 1861; Montgomery was the first Confederate capital. Alabama was readmitted to the Union in June 1868. The state has been the scene of many civil rights demonstrations. In the late 1960s, Gov. George C. Wallace emerged as a potential US presidential candidate.

PROFILE

Admitted to Union: 1819; rank, 22nd
US Congressmen: Senate - 2; House of Representatives - 7
Population: 3,444,165 (1970); rank, 21st
Capital: Montgomery, pop. (1970) 133,386
Chief cities: Birmingham, 300,910; Mobile, 190,-026; Huntsville, 137,802
State Legislature: Senate, 35 members; House of Representatives, 106
Area: 51,609sq mi (133,667sq km); rank, 29th
Elevation: Highest, Cheaha Mt, 2407ft (734m); lowest, sea level
Industries (major products): iron and steel products, chemicals, processed foods, paper and paper products, textiles
Agriculture (major products): cotton, poultry, cattle
Minerals (major): coal, stone, petroleum
State nicknames: Heart of Dixie, Yellowhammer State
State motto: "We Dare Defend Our Rights"
State bird: Yellowhammer (Flicker)
State flower: Camellia
State tree: Southern Pine

Alabama, or **Alibamu,** Muskogean-speaking tribe of North American Indians. Their ancient home was the upper Alabama River; they moved around widely in the Southeast, eventually to Louisiana and Polk co, Tex., where their 500 descendants today inhabit a reservation area with the closely related Koasati.

Alabama Claims, demands by the US government for indemnity from Britain for damage done to Northern ships by the Confederate cruiser Alabama and other Confederate ships constructed and outfitted in England during the US Civil War. By the Treaty of Washington (May 1871), Britain agreed to submit the claims to arbitration. The United States was later awarded (1872) $15.5 million in gold for direct damages.

Alabaster, a compact, massive variety of gypsum, snow-white and translucent in nature. May be dyed or heated and made opaque. Used for statuary and ornaments for centuries. *See also* Gypsum.

Alacaluf, tribe of South American Indians occupying the Chilean archipelago along the coast from the Gulf of Peñas to the islands west of Tierra del Fuego. Subsisting almost entirely upon marine life, they apparently had little time to develop a pattern of civilization. Never more than 500, there are presently approximately 200 survivors.

Al-Alamein (El Alamein or **Al-'Alamayn),** village in N Egypt, 65mi (105km) W of Alexandria; Allied forces, led by British Gen. Bernard Montgomery, in November 1942 pushed Axis powers back across Libya into E Tunisia; this led to defeat of Axis efforts to take Alexandria and Suez Canal during WWII. △1338.

Alameda, city in W California, on island near E shore of San Francisco Bay, 6mi (10km) E of San Francisco; site of naval air base, commercial airports; Industries: manufacture of borax, aircraft parts, pumps. Inc. 1854. Pop. (1970) 70,968.

Alamo, mission building in San Antonio, called "the cradle of Texas liberty." Here, in February 1836, about 180 Texans, led by William Travis, Davy Crockett, and Jim Bowie, held out until overwhelmed by several thousand Mexicans under General Santa Anna on March 6. Six weeks later at San Jacinto, Texans went into battle shouting "Remember the Alamo." They then defeated Santa Anna's army in the final battle for Texas independence. △1274.

Alamogordo, city in SW New Mexico, 85mi (137km) NE of Sacramento, California; seat of Otero co; site of White Sands Missile Range, where the first atomic bomb was exploded June 16, 1945, and Holloman Air Force Base; trade center. Industries: lumber, tourism. Founded 1898; inc. 1912. Pop. (1970) 23,035.

Alanbrooke, Alan Francis Brooke, 1st Viscount (1883–1963), English military commander, b. France. As chief of the imperial general staff (1941–46), he directed British tactics against Germany and coordinated Anglo-American strategy with Eisenhower.

Al-Andalus. △1078.

Aland Island, largest of the Ahvenamaa Islands; possession of Finland, in the Baltic Sea between Finland and Sweden; main town and port is Maarianhamina. Industries: fishing, lumbering, farming.

Alanine, colorless soluble amino acid ($CH_3.CH.NH_2.COOH$). *See* Amino Acid.

Alarcón, Hernando de (fl. 16th century), Spanish navigator whose exploration proved that Lower California was a peninsula, not an island. He is also credited with being the first European to explore the Colorado River.

Alarcón, Pedro Antonio de (1833–91), Spanish novelist. His literary career reflected his transition from a staunch anticleric to a devout Roman Catholic. Wounded in the Moroccan campaign, he wrote a journal of his war experiences (1859–60) but gained international fame upon the publication of the short novel *The Three-Cornered Hat* (1874).

Alaric (*c.* 370–410), king of the Visigoths (395–410). His forces conquered Thrace, Macedonia, and Greece and occupied Epirus (395–96). He invaded Italy in 401 and 408 and engineered the siege (408) and sack (410) of Rome. The city was plundered relatively lightly, but the power of the Roman Empire was irredeemably diminished. He planned an invasion of Sicily and Africa, but his fleet was demolished in a storm. He died shortly thereafter. △1054.

Alaska, state in NW United States, separated from the continental United States by the province of British Columbia, Canada. It is the largest state in area and the smallest in population.

Land and Economy. About 25% of Alaska lies N of the Arctic Circle. The Alaska Range in the S central area includes the highest peaks in North America. The chief river is the Yukon, flowing E to W to the Bering Sea. The Aleutian Island chain, which has active volcanoes, extends 1,700mi (2,737km) SW and W. The Alexander Archipelago, containing hundreds of islands, is in the SE. Alaska's natural resources, especially fish, timber, and petroleum, are the base of its economy. Vast oil deposits in the Brooks Range in the N will be tapped by a pipeline which runs 800mi (1,288km) from Prudhoe Bay on the Arctic Ocean to Valdez on the S coast. Construction of the line brought thousands of workers to the state. Tourism is a major revenue source.

People. The population has more than tripled since WWII. Most people came from other parts of the United States. Their average age is younger than in other states. About 17% of the population is of Eskimo or Indian extraction.

Education and Research. There are nine institutions of higher education; some carry on research in meteorology and in testing materials and techniques under extreme climatic conditions.

History. Vitus Bering, a Danish navigator serving Russia, made the first recorded landing in July 1741. Russian hunters followed, and a monopoly company exported furs until wasteful slaughter of animals decimated the supply. The United States purchased Alaska from Russia on Oct. 18, 1867, for $7.2 million, less than 2 cents an acre. Fishing drew settlers, and after gold was discovered in the 1890s the population doubled in 10 years. Self-government was granted gradually but the first territorial legislature did not meet until 1913. In WWII, after Japanese forces occupied Attu and Kiska in the Aleutians, Alaska was developed as a major military area.

PROFILE

Admitted to Union: 1959; rank 49th
US Congressmen: Senate, 2; House of Representatives, 1
Population: 302,173 (1970); rank, 50th
Capital: Juneau, pop. (1970) 13,556
Chief cities: Anchorage, 48,081; Fairbanks, 22,640; Ketchikan, 6,994
State legislature: Senate, 20 members; House of Representatives, 40
Area: 586,400sq mi (1,518,776sq km); rank, 1st
Elevation: Highest, Mt McKinley, 20,320ft (6,198m); lowest, sea level
Industries (major products): processed foods (fish), forest products (pulp)
Minerals (major): petroleum, natural gas
State nickname: None
State motto: "North to the Future"
State bird: Yellow Ptarmigan
State fish: King Salmon
State flower: Forget-me-not
State tree: Sitka Spruce

Alaska Highway, road connecting Dawson Creek, British Columbia, with Fairbanks, Alaska; built by the United States April-November 1942 to link military installations in Alaska with US proper by protected land route. Length: 1,523mi (2,452m).

Alaskan Boundary Dispute (1902–03), dispute between the United States and Britain, representing Canada, over possession of the inlets between Alaska

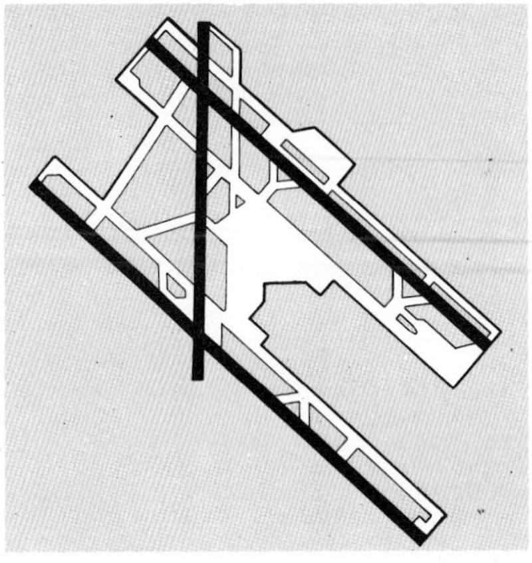

Airport, showing typical runway pattern (black)

Ajaccio, Corsica

Mobile, Alabama

Alaska: pipeline construction

and Canada after the Klondike gold strike. It was settled by a six-man panel in favor of the United States.

Alaskan Brown Bear, or Kodiak bear, omnivorous brown bear of Kodiak Island and adjacent areas on Alaskan mainland. Length: over 8ft (2.5m); weight: to 1715lb (772kg). Species *Ursus arctos.*

Alaskan Malamute, Arctic sled dog (working group) for pulling heavy freight; named after Eskimo tribe. This substantial dog has a broad head and large bulky muzzle; wedge-shaped ears erect at alert; brown, almond-shaped eyes; strong, compact body; straight, heavy-boned legs; and fox brush tail. The short to medium-length thick, coarse coat ranges from light gray to black with white. There is a characteristic face mask marking. Average size: 25in (64cm) high at shoulder; 85lb (38kg). *See also* Working Dog.

Alaska North Slope, lowland plain in N Alaska, between Brooks Range and Arctic Ocean; a frozen tundra during most of the year; petroleum reserves were discovered in late 1960s and developed in 1970s.

Alaska Purchase (1867), transfer of the Russian territory of Alaska to the United States for $7,200,000. Many Americans regarded Alaska as a frozen wasteland and the purchase was called "Seward's Folly" after Secretary of State William Seward, who negotiated the purchase.

Alaska Range, mountain range located in S central Alaska; extends in a semi-circular shape from the Alaska Peninsula to the Yukon. The highest point is Mt McKinley, 20,320ft (6,198m).

Alaungpaya, also known as Alompra or Aungzeya, meaning "the Victorious" (1711–60), king of Burma (1752–60). Of humble origins, Alaungpaya refused to become a vassal of the kingdom of Mon (in the Irrawaddy Delta) when the Burmese capital, Ava, was captured in 1752. Calling himself pretender to the throne, he organized Burmese resistance, recaptured Ava (1753), and took over (1757) the Mon capital, Pegu. He tried to conquer Siam (1760), but died with his army in retreat. The Alaungpaya dynasty he created held power until the British annexed Upper Burma in 1886.

Al Azhar, University of, university in Cairo, Egypt. It was founded in 972 and confers bachelors, masters, and doctors degrees in areas including theology, Islamic Law, business administration, and medicine.

Alba (or Alva), Fernando Alvarez de Toledo, Duke of (1508–82), Spanish general and regent of the Netherlands. He joined the Spanish army in 1524. In 1547 he was instrumental in the victory of Mühlberg over John Frederick, Elector of Saxony. In 1567, Philip II appointed him regent of Netherlands. He ruthlessly suppressed Protestant and nationalist opposition. Thousands of people, including Counts Egmont and Hoorn, were executed. In 1572 the Dutch rose up in armed rebellion. Alba was unable to quell it completely. He was recalled to Spain in 1573. After years of being out of favor, in 1580 he led a successful invasion of Portugal.

Albacete, city in SE Spain, on the La Mancha plain, approx. 140mi (225km) SE of Madrid; capital of Albacete prov.; site of 16th-century cathedral, archaeological museum, and ancient Moorish wall. Industries: cutlery, chemicals, saffron, wine, potatoes, grain, tiles. Pop. 93,233.

Albacore, long-finned tuna of warm seas. Cigar-shaped with a large tail sharply divided into two lobes, it has a long pectoral fin. A fast swimmer, it is an important commercial and game fish; albacore white meat is canned. Length: 3ft (91cm); weight: 40–80lbs. (18–36kg). Family Scombridae; species *Thunnus alalugna.* △626.

Alba Longa, city of ancient Latium near Lake Albano, 12mi (19km) SE of modern Rome; believed to have been built *c.* 1152 BC by Ascanius (son of Aeneas); reputedly Latium's most powerful city as head of Latin League, and mother city of Rome; traditional birthplace of Romulus and Remus; modern site of papal summer residence Castel Gandolfo, on Lake Albano. Only tombs (over 3,000 years old) remain of ancient city.

Albanel, Charles (1616–96), French missionary and explorer in Canada. In 1671 he was sent by Jean Talon, the first intendant of Quebec, to explore the Saguenay River and Hudson, Rupert, and James bays. Establishing profitable fur trading routes, he chronicled his travels in *The Jesuit Relations.*

Albani, (Madame) Emma (1852–1930), English soprano, b. Canada. She had her first public performance in 1869, made her English debut at Covent Garden in 1872, and her US debut at the Metropolitan Opera in 1890. She was a leading Wagnerian soprano of her day.

Albania (Shqipëri), People's Republic of, small independent nation of the Balkan Peninsula in SE Europe. Since WWII, Albania has been a Communist state. The country broke its ties with the Soviet Union in 1961 and became the first European country to ally itself closely with Communist China.

Land and Economy. Albania lies on the Adriatic Sea, bordered by Yugoslavia (N and E) and by Greece (S). The interior of the country consists of high mountain ranges and highland plateaus. In the N are the rugged, forbidding North Albanian Alps; the limestone surface rocks do not support good soil. The most fertile lands are found in the valleys of the S. Several W-flowing rivers drop through narrow, deeply cut valleys down to the coastal lowlands. Few Albanians live in these marshy coastal plains. Durres is the only notable seaport. The Soviet-styled economy is about evenly divided between agricultural production and industrialization. Substantial industrial progress has been achieved since WWII, and farm output has increased much faster than population. Foreign economic aid is required annually to offset deficits.

People. The population is exceptionally homogeneous; about 97% is of Albanian ethnic origin. The two major tribal groups are the Gegs of the N and the Tosks of the S. The Albanian language is spoken by both groups, but the dialect of the Tosks is the official language. All religious activities are strongly discouraged by the Communist government. Two-thirds of the people are Muslims of the Sunni and Bektashi sects; the remainder are Christians of the Eastern Orthodox and Roman Catholic churches. Nearly a million Albanians live in Yugoslavia.

Government. The constitution is styled on the Soviet model, and provides for a legislature (the People's Assembly), an executive branch (the Presidium), and an independent judiciary. True power lies, however, in the politburo and central committee of the Albanian Workers' party.

History. The Albanians are descended from the Illyrians, who settled the Balkan Peninsula in the pre-Christian era. For centuries the Albani tribe resisted the influence of the Romans and the Byzantines. The Turks gained control over the Albanians in the 15th century, and the Islamic religion penetrated all but the most mountainous regions. A national revival began in the 19th century and culminated in Albanian independence (1912). The Communist party, formed in WWII, with Enver Hoxha as its head, seized power in 1944. Albania became a client state of the Soviet Union. Hoxha and Mehmet Shehu dominated Albanian politics in subsequent years. Albania became a member of the United Nations in 1955. The break with the Soviet Union in 1961 caused severe damage to the country's economy. China sought to replace the Soviet Union as Albania's chief economic benefactor.

PROFILE

Official name: People's Republic of Albania
Area: 11,100sq mi (28,749sq km)
Population: 2,500,000; *Density,* 225 per sq mi (86 per sq km)
Chief cities: Tirana (capital); Durres; Shkoder
Government: Communist
Religion: Muslim, Eastern Orthodox
Language: Albanian (official)
Monetary unit: Lek
Gross national product: $1,100,000,000
Per capita income: $330
Industries (major products): food processing, textiles, petroleum products, cement
Agriculture (major products): corn, wheat, tobacco
Minerals (major): coal, chromium, copper
Trading partners (major): People's Republic of China, Czechoslovakia, Poland, East Germany

Albano, Lake (Albano Lago), lake in Italy, in the Alban Hills, SE of Rome; occupies an extinct volcanic crater; only outlet is a 1.75-mi (3.00-km) tunnel built by the Romans in 397 BC. Castel Gandolfo, papal residence, is located here. Area: 2sq mi (5sq km).

Albany, city in SW Georgia on Flint River; seat of Dougherty co; industrial and trade center for agricultural region. Crops: pecans, peanuts, cotton. Industries: airplane manufacturing, pharmaceuticals, meat packing, cotton milling. Inc. 1841. Pop. (1970) 72,623.

Albany, city and capital of New York, on the W bank of the Hudson River, 145mi (234km) N of New York City; seat of Albany co. Henry Hudson first visited the area in 1609 as he explored the river; Dutch traders built Fort Nassau here 1614, which was destroyed by flood 1617 and replaced by Fort Orange 1624; captured by English 1664 and renamed Albany; scene of 1754 Albany Congress; after the Revolutionary War, it replaced New York City as state capital (1797); site of Schuyler Mansion (1762), Ten Broeck Mansion (1798), Cherry Hill (1768, home of Van Rensselaer descendants until 1963), University of Albany (1844), state capitol (1871), and Albany Law School, Medical College, and College of Pharmacy. Industries: brewing, meat packing, chemicals, brushes, textiles. Settled 1614, 2nd-oldest permanent settlement in 13 colonies; inc. 1686. Pop. (1970) 114,873.

Albany Congress (1754), colonial conference to discuss Indian relations. Representatives from New Hampshire, Massachusetts, Rhode Island, Connecticut, New York, Pennsylvania, and Maryland met in Albany, N.Y., at British urging to gain the loyalty of the Iroquois Indians against the French. A treaty was negotiated. At this meeting Benjamin Franklin also proposed a Plan for Union of the colonies, which would have coordinated and centralized defense, Indian relations, and westward expansion. It was approved by the Congress but rejected by both Britain and the individual colonial governments.

Albany Regency, organization of Democratic party leaders in New York state, influential from 1820–48. It successfully controlled conventions and appointments until the defeat of Martin Van Buren's presidential bid (1848).

Albatross, large, oceanic bird of Southern Hemisphere famed for strong flying power. It has long, thick, hooked bill, short tail, webbed toes, long wings, and thick feathers. Known to eat ship throwaways, it feeds mainly on marine animals. After elaborate courtship, the females lay a single chalky egg in a small nest on an isolated island. Length: 4–11ft (122–335cm). Family Diomedeidae.

Albedo, the fraction of light or other radiation striking a surface or body, like the ground, that is reflected by it, the remainder being absorbed. Expressed as a percentage, bare ground has an average albedo of 10 to 20%, fresh snow 80 to 85%, and the whole earth, viewed from satellites, 36%.

Albee, Edward Franklin (1928–), US dramatist, b. Washington, D.C. His best known play is *Who's Afraid of Virginia Woolf?* (1962). Other of his clever, biting commentaries on American life include the one-act plays *The Zoo Story* (1959) and *The Sandbox* (1960), and the full-length plays *Tiny Alice* (1965), *A Delicate Balance* (1967, Pulitzer Prize), and *Seascape* (1975).

Albemarle Colony (1660), first English colony on Albemarle Sound, N.C. It was founded by Virginian and New England settlers and had a government independent of South Carolina.

Albemarle Sound, inlet of the Atlantic in NE North Carolina, 54mi (87km) long. Mostly fresh, shallow water, it is separated from the ocean by a long narrow island.

Alberoni, Giulio (1664–1752), Italian statesman who, after the War of Spanish Succession (1701–14), served until 1719 as de facto prime minister of Spain. He diminished Spanish aristocratic opposition to the monarchy, sought to drive Austrians from Italy, and worked to protect Spanish-US trade.

Albers, Josef (1888–1976), German painter, poet, and art teacher. He helped to develop color field painting and op art. He studied at the Bauhaus, and in 1933 he came to the United States. His most famous work, dealing with color relationships, is "Homage to the Square," a series of paintings begun in 1949. *See also* Color Field Painting; Op Art.

Albert I (1875–1934), king of Belgium (1909–34). Son of Philip, Count of Flanders, he succeeded his uncle, Leopold II, and restored confidence in the throne. In 1914 he led the Belgian resistance, holding the Germans while the Allied defense formed. He led the Belgian and French forces in the final general offensive through Belgium (1918). After the war, he devoted himself to the task of reconstruction.

Albert I (1250?–1308), king of Germany (1298–1308). He succeeded his father, Rudolf I, after the six-year reign of Adolf of Nassau, whom Albert deposed in 1298. He expanded his lands and Hapsburg rule through a war with the Rhenish electors, but was unsuccessful against Thuringia. He was assassinated by his nephew, John of Swabia.

Albert II (1397–1439), king of Germany (1438–39), king of Bohemia and Hungary (1438–39); founder of the Hapsburg German succession. He succeeded his father as Albert V, duke of Austria (1404–39), and as duke proved a capable reorganizer. His short reign as king was marked by unrest in Hungary and Bohemia and a war with the Turks in which he was killed.

Albert I, called Albert the Bear (1100–70), first margrave of Brandenburg (1150–70). His hold on Brandenburg was always tenuous, but he contributed greatly to the Christianizing and Germanizing of NE Germany.

Albert III, called Albert the Bold (1443–1500), Duke of Saxony. Founder of the Albertine line, he ruled Saxony jointly with his older brother, Ernest (1464–85). When the dominions were apportioned, Albert received eastern and western parts, including Meissen.

Albert, Carl Bert (1908–), former speaker of the US House of Representatives, b. North McAlester, Okla. Elected to the House in 1946, he became a prominent Democrat who was chosen majority whip, 1955; majority leader, 1962; and speaker, 1971. He retired in 1977.

Albert, Lake (Albert Nyanza), lake in E central Africa on the border between Zaire and Uganda. The Semliki River and the Victoria Nile empty into Lake Albert; the Albert Nile flows from it; discovered 1864 by Samuel Baker. Length: 100mi (161km); width: 19mi (31km); max. depth: 168ft (51m).

Alberta, province of W Canada, bordered on the S by the state of Montana.

Land and Economy. Except where the Rocky Mountain ranges lie along part of the W boundary, Alberta is part of the high plains of central North America, with a few hills and deep river valleys. The principal rivers are the Athabasca, Peace, Saskatchewan, and Milk. Lesser Slave Lake is the largest of the many lakes; Lake Louise, in the Rockies, is noted for its beauty. The fertile plains support vast wheat farming and livestock raising, and the oil and natural gas fields of central Alberta make a major contribution to the economy. Manufacturing is mostly concentrated in the areas of Edmonton and Calgary.

People. Settlement did not begin on a large scale until the late 19th century, when immigrants came from other Canadian provinces, the United States, and Europe. The character of the population stabilized, and now more than 80% was born in the province.

Education. The University of Alberta, at Edmonton, and the universities of Calgary and Lethbridge are the centers of higher education. There are a number of junior colleges.

History. The area was part of a huge territory granted in 1670 by Charles II of England to the Hudson's Bay Co., a fur-trading enterprise. In 1870 the government of Canada bought the region from the company. Farming pioneers arrived, and a transcontinental railroad was completed across the S part in 1885. The area was part of the North West Territories and was governed from the Canadian capital in Ottawa, but in 1882 this was divided into four districts, Alberta being one. In 1905 it was admitted to the Confederation as a province along with Saskatchewan. Natural gas was discovered as early as 1914, but rich oil fields found after WWII were a major stimulus to the economy.

PROFILE

Admitted to Confederation: Sept. 1, 1905; rank, 8th
National Parliament Representatives: Senate, 6; House of Commons, 19
Population: 1,600,000; rank, 4th
Capital: Edmonton, 434,116
Chief cities: Edmonton; Calgary, 400,154; Lethbridge, 40,706; Red Deer, 27,428
Provincial Legislature: Legislative Assembly, 75 members
Area: 255,285sq mi (661,188sq km); rank, 4th
Elevation: Highest, Mt Columbia, 12,294ft (3,750m); lowest, Slave River, 686ft (209m)
Industries (major products): petroleum products, processed foods (meat), chemicals, fabricated metals
Agriculture (major products): wheat, cattle, dairy products, hogs, poultry
Minerals (major): petroleum, natural gas, sulfur
Floral emblem: wild rose

Alberti, Leon Battista (1404–72), Italian scientist, architect, artist, and critic. He wrote influential treatises in Latin on architecture, painting, and sculpture. His major Italian work is the dialogue *On Family* (1434–42). He organized the Certame Coronario poetry contest of 1441. △1138.

Albert Nile, river in Uganda, the section of the Nile River that drains Lake Albert and flows N through NW Uganda; site of the Nimule Dam, part of Equatorial Nile Project to increase water power. Length: 130mi (209km).

Albert of Mecklenburg (*c.* 1340–1412), king of Sweden (1365–88), he succeeded Magnus Eriksson, last of the Folkungs. Swedish magnates objected to Albert's transfer of political power to German lords and enlisted the aid of Queen Margaret of Denmark and Norway, who defeated Albert's army in 1389, taking Albert prisoner.

Albert of Saxe-Coburg-Gotha (1819–61), prince consort of Queen Victoria. The son of Ernest I, duke of Saxe-Coburg-Gotha, Albert married his first cousin Victoria in 1840. Although at first unpopular in Britain because he was not English, he gradually gained acceptance through his promotion of science and the arts, his influence on diplomatic affairs, and his devotion to the queen. He suggested the International Exhibition of 1851. In world affairs he counseled for a restrained approach to the Trent Affair (1861), which helped to avoid a war with the United States.

Albertus Magnus (1206–80), German theologian. Exposed to Aristotle's philosophy at Padua, he became a Dominican (1223) and Bishop of Regensburg (1260). Albertus wrote *Books on the Sentences* and a *Summa Theologiae,* the second essentially repetitive of the Aristotelian Scholasticism of the first. Thomas Aquinas was one of his pupils. He was beatified in 1622.

Albi, town in S France, on Tarn River; capital of Tarn dept.; old part of city is called ville rouge for its red brick medieval buildings; 12th-13th-century religious movement of Albigenses was named for Albi; birthplace of artist Toulouse-Lautrec; site of museum that displays many of his paintings. Pop. 42,930.

Albigenses, followers of the Catharist heresy in southern France (Languedoc) during the 12th and 13th centuries who threatened the political power of the Roman Catholic Church. Pope Innocent III called for a crusade against them. The French crown used the crusade to conquer Languedoc in 1229. △1086.

Albinism, hereditary absence of pigment from the skin, hair, and eyes. The hair is snow white, and the eyes, which are often extremely sensitive to light, are pink with red pupils. In partial, or piebald, albinism, only certain areas are affected, producing white spotting or white forelock, for example. △724.

Alboin (died 573), Germanic Lombard king who conquered northern Italy. Coming from Noricum and Pannonia (now in Austria and Hungary), he led his people across the Alps to conquer north and central Byzantine Italy. He established Pavia as capital of the new Lombard kingdom (572).

Albumin, group of soluble proteins that occur in many animal tissues and fluids. Principal forms are egg albumin (ovalbumin), milk albumin (lactalbumin), and blood albumin (serum albumin). △718.

Albuminuria, presence of protein (serum albumin or globulin) in the urine. May result from poor posture, from eating certain foods, or from certain disease processes.

Albuquerque, Affonso de (1453–1515), Portuguese admiral and founder of the Portuguese empire in the East. He made his first trip to India in 1503 and went again in 1506, this time as governor. He explored the Madagascar and East African coasts and built forts throughout the East. He took control of Malacca, Calicut, the Malabar Coast, Ceylon, and Goa, which he made the Portuguese capital in the East (1510). The victim of political intrigue, he was recalled in 1515, but died before leaving Goa. △1122.

Albuquerque, city in W central New Mexico, on Upper Rio Grande River; seat of Bernalillo co; largest city in New Mexico. Founded by Spanish 1706, it served as a military post until 1870; newer city section was founded 1880; noted health resort. It is the site of Old Town Plaza (1706), Church of San Felipe de Nerí (1706), University of New Mexico (1889), University of Albuquerque (1940). Industries: nuclear research and development, food processing, railroad shops. Inc. 1890. Pop. (1970) 243,751.

Alcaeus (*c.* 600 BC), Greek lyric poet who wrote political songs, hymns, and love songs. He was widely imitated by Horace and others, but only fragments of his poems have survived.

Austria
Hungary
U.S.S.R.
Romania
Yugoslavia
ADRIATIC
SEA
BLACK
SEA
Bulgaria
Shkodër
ALBANIA
Italy
Tiranë
Vlorë
IONIAN
SEA
Greece
Turkey
MEDITERRANEAN SEA
0
400km
Albania

Albatross

Edward Albee

Edmonton, Alberta

Alcalá Zamora y Torres, Niceto (1877–1949), Spanish politician, president of Spain (1931–36). He was instrumental in overthrowing the monarchy in 1931 and was elected president of the Second Republic. A moderate whose policies pleased neither left nor right, he was forced out of office by the socialists in 1936 and went into exile.

Alcatraz Island, island in California, in San Francisco Bay, opposite the Golden Gate. Previously its rocky contour served as a fortification and federal penitentiary. It is now part of the Golden Gate Recreational Area.

Alcestis (438 BC), Greek tragedy by Euripides. The work is best known for its strong characterization of its noble heroine. Alcestis takes her husband's place in Hades so that he may live. Heracles brings her back alive, and husband and wife are reunited.

Alchemy, primitive form of chemistry practiced in Western Europe in the Middle Ages, popularly supposed to involve a search for the Philosopher's Stone—an agent capable of transmuting base metals into gold. In fact, alchemy was a more general study involving a combination of practical chemistry, astrology, philosophy, and mysticism, based on the concept of the unity of matter and analogous ideas of the unity of man with the universe. Similar movements existed in China and India. In Western Europe, alchemy was practiced from early Christian times until the 17th century. *See also* Paracelsus, Philippus Aureolus; Phlogiston Theory.

Alcibiades (450–404 BC), Athenian general and statesman, ward of Pericles, intimate of Socrates, related to Plato. After the disastrous Sicilian campaign which he inspired, he temporarily aided Sparta. Regaining position in Athens, he was defeated at Notium in 407. △994.

Alcman (*c.* 650 BC), chief lyric poet of Sparta. A former slave from Sardis, he is regarded as the founder of erotic poetry. He abandoned the hexameter and wrote in varied, simple meters. Among his known work, surviving in fragments, is the poem "Partheneion" (a choir song for girls), which was found in Egypt in 1855, on a 1st-century papyrus.

Alcmene, in Greek mythology, the mother of Hercules by Zeus. She was betrothed to Amphitryon, Prince of Thebes, who had avenged the death of her brothers. While he was away Zeus came to Alcmene disguised as Amphitryon. Iphicles was the son of Alcmene and Amphitryon.

Alcohol, member of a class of organic compounds characterized by the presence of a hydroxyl (-OH) group bound to a hydrocarbon group. Ethanol, C_2H_5OH, is the commonest example. Alcohols can be oxidized to aldehydes, as in $C_2H_5OH + O \rightarrow CH_3CHO$ (acetaldehyde). Further oxidation gives a carboxylic acid: $CH_3CHO + O \rightarrow CH_3COOH$ (acetic acid). They react with acids to give esters: thus, ethanol and acetic acid give ethyl acetate, $C_2H_5OH + CH_3COOH \rightarrow C_2H_5OOCCH_3$. Their systematic names are formed using the suffix -ol. △1504.

Alcohol, in Medicine. △744.

Alcohol, Ethyl. *See* Ethanol. △1558, 1562.

Alcohol, Methyl. *See* Methanol. △1572.

Alcoholics Anonymous, organization that seeks to help alcoholics help themselves, with the ultimate goal of rehabilitation. Founded in 1935, it has local autonomous groups in more than 90 countries. Membership is open to anyone who has the desire to stop drinking, and the group works on a shared-experience and help method.

Alcoholism, an illness marked by excessive use and preoccupation with alcohol that interferes with a person's health and ability to work and function in society. Extremely common, it is the number-one drug problem in many parts of the world. Alcohol is a depressant drug that produces changes in behavior even in moderate doses, but it is with repeated heavy use that serious problems occur. The illness develops insidiously and is sometimes hard to recognize, but signs such as frequent drunkenness, a great change in personality when drinking, a person's forgetting what he or she said or did when drinking, and sickness and problems at home or at work because of drinking signal the beginning of a serious problem. Alcoholism causes damage to many parts of the body and can result in cirrhosis of the liver, stomach and intestinal inflammation, and muscle damage as well as severe damage to the brain and nervous system, manifested by alcoholic blackouts, psychotic episodes and other illnesses. It is not known why some people become alcoholics, but a combination of psychological, hereditary, biochemical, familial, and cultural factors are probably interwoven to produce susceptibility. The illness is treated—very often successfully—in a variety of ways, many involving counseling or psychotherapy. Drugs that make a person physically sick immediately after taking alcohol are also sometimes used to produce alcohol aversion. △730.

Alcott, Amos Bronson (1799–1888), American philosopher, teacher, reformer, and important member of the New England Transcendentalists; b. near Wolcott, Conn. He established a series of progressive schools for children, the last of which was the Temple School in Boston, and was influential in founding the utopian community, Fruitlands, in Massachusetts. He was the father of the author Louisa May Alcott.

Alcott, Louisa May (1832–88), US author, b. Germantown, Pa. She is best known for her books for children. Her first published book was *Flower Fables* (1854), a collection of fairy stories. Family debts led her to write the autobiographical novel *Little Women* (1868). Its great success led her to write *An Old-Fashioned Girl* (1870), *Little Men* (1871), *Jo's Boys* (1886), and others.

Alcuin (735–804), scholar and cleric from Northumbria in Britain, trained at cathedral school at York. Invited to set up a palace school in court of Charlemagne, he became a central figure of the Carolingian Renaissance. His prolific writings include a corrected text of the Vulgate Bible. *See also* Carolingian Renaissance.

Aldebaran, or **Alpha Tauri,** red giant star in the constellation Taurus. Characteristics: apparent mag. +0.78; absolute mag. −0.2; spectral type K5; distance 65 light-years. △102.

Aldehyde, member of a class of organic compounds characterized by the presence of the group =CO:H. The simplest example is formaldehyde, HCOH, used as a preservative. Aldehydes can be made by oxidizing simple alcohols. They are generally reducing agents, being oxidized to carboxylic acids, and also form addition and condensation compounds with many reagents. Their systematic names are formed using the suffix -al (ethanal, CH_3CHO). *See also* Alcohol.

Alden, John (*c.* 1599–1687), American settler, b. England. A signer of the Mayflower Compact and organizer of Plymouth Colony, he settled in Duxbury, Mass. in 1627. Traditionally, he is known as the first Pilgrim to set foot on Plymouth Rock, and as the man who won the hand of Priscilla Mullens after first wooing her for his friend, Miles Standish, an event dramatized in Henry Wadsworth Longfellow's poem, "The Courtship of Miles Standish." He wed Priscilla in 1625 and they had 11 children. He served as the governor's assistant (1623–41, 1650–86), twice serving as deputy governor.

Alder, ornamental trees and shrubs of the birch family native to the Northern Hemisphere and W South America. They have toothed leaves and woody cones that remain on branches after nuts are released. The scaly bark is used in dyeing and the wood is used in bridges because it resists underwater rot. The red, speckled, and European alders are well-known species. They are short-lived trees and usually among the first to appear in denuded areas. There are 30 species. Family Betulaceae; genus *Alnus*. *See also* Birch.

Alderman, an elected or appointed member of a local legislative body that decides broad policies of municipal government. In more common usage aldermen are called council persons and are directly elected.

Aldhelm (Ealdhelm) (?639–709), English cleric and poet, saint of the Roman Catholic Church. He became abbot of Malmesbury *c.* 675 and first bishop of Sherborne in 705. He established numerous monasteries and churches.

Al-Din Bihzad, Kamal. △1064.

Aldosterone, mineralocorticoid hormone secreted by the adrenal cortex. It regulates the salt and water balance of the body.

Aldrich-Vreeland Currency Act (1908), emergency response to the 1907 Panic, it made temporary provisions for issuing bank notes based upon approved municipal securities and commercial paper, and provided for the formation of bank associations. It also provided for a National Monetary Commission to study banking conditions, which led to the Federal Reserve Act (1913). *See also* Currency Act (1900); Federal Reserve Act (1913).

Aldridge, Ira F(rederick) (*c.* 1805–67), US actor, b. New York City. Known as Black Roscius, he was esteemed as one of the finest actors of his time. After a triumphant London debut as Othello (1826), he went on to great fame in England and, after 1853, on the continent. He became an English citizen in 1863.

Aldrin, Edwin ("Buzz") (1930–), US astronaut, b. Glen Ridge, N.J. Aldrin piloted the Gemini XII orbital rendezvous space flight (November 1966) and the lunar module for the first lunar landing (July 1969). Following Neil Armstrong, he was the second man on the moon. △1724.

Aldrin, brown solid chlorinated naphthalene derivative (formula $C_{12}H_8Cl_6$) widely used as a contact insecticide. It is insoluble in water and is used as an emulsion or powder. It is also incorporated into plastic cable coverings to make them resistant to termites.

Ale. △350.

Alegría, Ciro (1909–67), Peruvian novelist. He is the outstanding writer of the *Indianista* (pro-Indian) novel. His best-known work is *Broad and Alien Is the World* (1941) which describes an Indian tribe's struggle in the face of the expropriation of their land by the white man. A social reform activist, he was jailed twice in Peru (1931,33) and exiled to Chile in 1934. He returned to Peru in 1948.

Aleichem, Shalom (1859–1916), pseud. of Solomon Rabinowitz, Yiddish novelist, dramatist, and short story writer. Born in Russia, he emigrated to the United States. He portrayed the oppressed Russian Jews with humor and compassion. His works include *The Old Country* (trans. 1946) and *The Milkman (Tevye)* (1945), adapted as the musical *Fiddler on the Roof* (1964). He helped found the Yiddish Art Theater and was influential in establishing Yiddish as a literary language.

Alemán, Miguel (1902–), Mexican president (1946–52) and the first candidate of the renamed Institutional Revolutionary Party (PRI). During his administration, PEMEX (the national petroleum monopoly) substantially increased production, the new University of Mexico campus was built, and transportation, communications, and mining industries grew dramatically.

Alemanni, or **Alamanni,** loose confederation of ancient Germanic tribes. First mentioned in 213 as unsuccessfully attacking the Romans between the Elbe and the Danube, by the 5th century they were settled in what is now Alsace, Baden, and NE Switzerland. In 496 they were defeated by Clovis I of the Franks, and by 536 they were completely subjugated to Frankish rule. They were converted to Christianity in the 7th century. From their name came the French and Spanish names for Germany: Allemagne and Allemania.

Alembert, Jean le Rond d' (1717–83), French mathematician, scientist, and writer who conducted important studies on fluid dynamics, celestial mechanics, and partial differential equations. In 1780 he published an eight-volume work on his mathematical studies. He also wrote articles for Diderot's *Encyclopédie,* which he helped to edit.

Alencar, José de (1829–77), Brazilian novelist, considered Brazil's first great prose writer. Best known for three novels about his country's Indians—*O Guarany* (1857), *Iracema* (1865), and *O sertanejo* (1876)—he has been praised for his vivid descriptions of Brazil's natural wonders but criticized for romanticizing the "noble savage." Also a lawyer and journalist, he became minister of justice in 1868.

Aleppo (Halab), second-largest city in Syria, approx. 70mi (113km) E of Mediterranean Sea; captured by Arabs from the Byzantines in AD 638; captured by Ottoman Turks (1517), became a great commercial center. Importance declined in late 19th century, after the completion of the Suez Canal; became part of Syria in 1924; site of 12th-century Byzantine citadel, the Great Mosque (715), university (1960) and institute of music; mentioned by Shakespeare in *Macbeth*. Industries: pistachio nuts, fruit, cotton, silk, cement. Pop. 639,000.

Alessandri Palma, Arturo (1868–1950), Chilean president. Elected in 1920, he was forced to resign in 1924, was recalled in March 1925 and was exiled again in October by the minister of war, Carlos Ibáñiz. Reelected in 1932, he was defeated in 1938 by Popular Front candidate Pedro Aguirre Cerda.

Aleut, distant branch of the Eskimo people occupying the Aleutian Peninsula and Shumagin Islands. They are divided into two major groups—the Unalaska and Atka. First discovered by Vitus Bering in 1741, they were forced into service as fur hunters and front-line attackers of other native peoples as far south as California. They numbered about 16,000, a number reduced to less than 1500 a century later due to brutal treatment. They were noted as excellent hunters of sea otters, blue foxes, and seals, and the women weave superb baskets of sea-grass. Today, approximately 5000 Aleut people live in scattered villages throughout SW Alaska. *See also* Eskimo.

Aleutian Islands, chain of volcanic islands, reaching from the Alaska Peninsula 1,200mi (1,932km) toward the USSR's Komandorski Islands. The main island groups are the Fox, Andreanof, Rat, and Near islands. The islands were discovered 1741 by the Danish explorer Vitus Bering for Russia and were purchased by the United States in 1867. The Japanese occupied some of the islands in WWII. Inhabited mainly by Eskimos, there is some agriculture, but the chief industries are fishing and fur hunting. Pop. (approx.) 8,000.

Aleutian Range, volcanic mountain system in S Alaska, on E Alaskan Peninsula, extends S to Aleutian Islands; site of Mt Katmai, 6,715ft (2,015m), and Katmai National Monument, a recreational facility in a volcanic area, including Valley of Ten Thousand Smokes. Length: approx. 700mi (1,127km).

Alewife, marine commercial fish found in N Atlantic and also landlocked in large freshwater lakes. Canned or salted as "river herring," it is gray-green with dark horizontal side stripes. Length: 15in (38.1cm); weight: 14oz (.4kg). Family Clupeidae; species *Pomolobus pseudoharengus.*

Alexander III, Roman Catholic pope (1159–81), b. Orlando Bandinelli. He was not the choice of Holy Roman Emperor Frederick I and an antipope, Victor IV, was elected. A schism persisted for 17 years, ending with the Lombard League victory over Frederick at the battle of Legano. Alexander decreed that the College of Cardinals be solely responsible for papal elections.

Alexander VI, Roman Catholic pope (1492–1503), b. Rodrigo Borgia (*c.*1431). Winning the papacy by promises and bribes, his reputation for poisoning his enemies grew with his drive for power. Many in the College of Cardinals were his relatives. He was more concerned with the arts and increasing the power of his office than with reform.

Alexander (886?–913), Byzantine emperor. He was co-ruler with his brother Leo VI for 26 years (886–912), and sole ruler for one (912–913). During the lifetime of Leo VI, Alexander, a pleasure-loving man, took little part in government. His tenure as sole ruler was disastrous, for he provoked a war with the Bulgars.

Alexander I (1777–1825), Russian tsar (1801–25). After repulsing Napoleon's attempt to conquer Russia (1812), he led his troops across Europe and into Paris (1814). During the first part of his reign, he introduced administrative and educational reforms with the advice of Mikhail Speranski. Later, however, under the influence of Alexis Ararchev, he instituted reactionary measures, including the establishment of military colonies. Under the influence of various mystical groups, he helped form the Holy Alliance with other European powers. He was named constitutional monarch of Poland in 1815 and also annexed Finland, Georgia and Bessarabia to Russia. △1178.

Alexander II (1818–81), Russian tsar (1855–81). He was known as the "Tsar Liberator" for his emancipation of the serfs in 1861. His reign saw the end of the Crimean War (1856), but under the influence of Pan-Slavism he warred with Turkey (1877–78) and gained much influence in the Balkans. He sold Alaska (1867), but expanded the eastern part of the empire. He brutally put down a revolt in Poland (1863). In 1881 he was assassinated by revolutionaries. △1286.

Alexander III (1845–94), Russian tsar (1881–94). Under the influence of Pobedonostsev, procurator of the Holy Synod, he introduced reactionary measures limiting local government; censorship of the press was enforced and arbitrary arrest and exile became common. Ethnic minorities were persecuted. In 1889, land captains appointed by the government limited the rights of the peasants. The three principles of orthodoxy, autocracy, and nationalism were the basis of his reign. Toward the end of his career, he formed an alliance with France. △1286.

Alexander I (1857–93), Bulgarian ruler (1878–86). A German prince of Battenberg and nephew of Tsar Alexander II of Russia, he was chosen by the Congress of Berlin in 1878 to rule the newly created principality of Bulgaria. Disputes over his ties with Russia led to his overthrow, kidnapping, restoration, and final abdication in 1886.

Alexander (1893–1920), king of Greece (1917–20) after the Allies forced the abdication of his father King Constantine. Premier Venizelos approved the entry of Greece into the war, gaining Smyrna and Thrace and hoping to form a "Greater Greece." Alexander died, from the bite of a pet monkey, before the plan could be carried out.

Alexander I ("The Fierce") (*c.* 1080–1124), king of Scotland (1107–24). He divided the kingdom (1107) with his younger brother David and married the daughter of his ally, Henry I of England.

Alexander II (1198–1249), king of Scotland (1214–49). He cultivated peace with England, fostered Norman institutions in Scotland, and extended royal authority.

Alexander III (1241–86), king of Scotland (1249–86). He repelled a Norwegian attack on the Western Isles (1263) and purchased the Norwegian possessions of Hebrides and Man (1266). He promoted peace with England and Norway and furthered Scottish unity, prosperity, and independence.

Alexander I (1888–1934), king of the Serbs, Croats, and Slovenes (1921–29) and king of Yugoslavia (1929–34). In his efforts to forge a united country from the rival national groups and ethnically divided political parties he created an autocratic police state. He was assassinated.

Alexander, Grover Cleveland (1887–1950), US baseball player. He set records for right-handed pitching. From 1911–30 he won 373 major league games and lost 208. He set a major league record for 16 shutouts in 33 victories in 1916. He played for the Philadelphia Phillies, the Chicago Cubs, and the St Louis Cardinals.

Alexander, Lloyd (1924–), US author of books for children, b. Philadelphia. He is noted for his chronicle of the imaginary land of Prydain: *The Book of Three* (1964), *The Black Cauldron* (1965), *The Castle of Llyr* (1966), *Taran Wanderer* (1967), and *The High King* (1968), which won the Newbery Medal for 1969.

Alexander Karageorgevich (1806–85), Serbian ruler. During his reign (1842–58) a new judicial system was introduced and the treaty of Paris (1856) gave support to Serbia's independence. His weak rule, however, caused him to be deposed by the national assembly.

Alexander Nevski (*c.* 1220–1263), Russian ruler and national hero, grand prince of Vladimir, the political center of Russia at this time. He paid voluntary tribute to the Mongols who in turn appointed him grand prince, after he had been prince of Novgorod (1238–52). He defeated the Swedes on the Neva (1240, hence the name "Nevski"), and the Teutonic Knights on Lake Peipus (1242). He was canonized in 1547.

Alexander of Tunis, Harold Rupert Leofric George, 1st Earl (1891–1969), English military commander. He directed the successful British offensive in Egypt and Libya (1942) and was Eisenhower's deputy in the victorious Tunisian campaign (1943) before becoming commander in chief of Allied forces in Italy. After the war he was governor-general of Canada (1946–52) and British minister of defense (1952–54).

Alexander Sarcophagus. △1002.

Alexander Severus, Marcus Aurelius (208?–235), Roman emperor (222–35). A boy of 14 when he came to power, he remained throughout his reign under the influence of his mother, Mamaea. As a military leader, he fought the newly established Persian Sassanid Empire (231–33), and restored the Roman frontier in the Near East. On the Rhine and Danube frontiers, he chose to buy peace from the Germans rather than to fight. His troops interpreted this policy as cowardice. They rebelled, killed Alexander and Mamaea, and plunged the empire into decades of military anarchy.

Alexander the Great (Alexander III of Macedonia) (356–323 BC), the greatest general in ancient history. Tutored by Aristotle, he took the throne at age 20, destroying rivals and consolidating power in Greece. In spring 334 he began the Persian expedition, conquering West Asia Minor and storming the

Alchemy

Louisa May Alcott

Aleppo, Syria: Byzantine citadel

Alewife

island of Tyre (332), his greatest military victory. He subdued Egypt and occupied Babylon, marching north in 330 to occupy Media and then conquering central Asia in 328. In 327 he invaded India. He then set about consolidating his empire but died of apparently natural causes at 32. Deified, a legend in his own time, he was buried in a golden coffin in Alexandria. △1004.

Alexander v. Holmes County Board of Education (1969), US Supreme Court decision declaring that desegregation plans to end dual school systems must be implemented "at once" following the guidelines of *Brown* v. *Board of Education* (1955). *See also* Brown v. Board of Education (1954);Brown v. Board of Education (1955).

Alexander's Feast (1697), second of John Dryden's odes for St. Cecilia's Day, describing a banquet celebrating Alexander's conquest of the Persian King Davius at which the poet and musician Timotheus plays upon the guest's passions, inciting them to destroy the city of Persepolis. Timotheus' skill is compared to that of Cecilia, the patron of music.

Alexandria (Al-Iskandariyah), chief port and 2nd-largest city in Egypt, on the W extremity of the Nile Delta, between Lake Maryut and Mediterranean Sea. Founded 332BC by Alexander the Great, it became part of the Roman Empire in 30BC. Muslims took over in AD642, and city declined until construction of the Mahmudiyah Canal in 1819 when trade revived and city began to flourish; site of university, several museums, zoological park, botanical gardens, and a 25,000-seat stadium; it is also Middle East headquarters for the World Health Organization. Industries: petroleum refining, textiles, paper, plastics. Pop. 2,032,000.

Alexandria, city in central Louisiana, 100mi (161km) NW of Baton Rouge; seat of Rapides Parish; burned by Union forces during Civil War; a commercial center for farming and forest region. Industries: brick, oil refining, chemicals, cotton ginning. Chartered 1832. Pop. (1970) 41,557.

Alexandria, city in N Virginia, 6mi (10km) S of Washington, D.C.; settled early 18th century; site of Carlyle House (1752); Gadsby's Tavern (1752) used by George Washington; Christ Church (1767). Industries: fertilizers, chemicals, machinery. Est 1748 by Virginia House of Burgesses; inc. 1779. Pop. (1970) 110,938.

Alexandrian Library, Egyptian library founded 290 BC by Ptolemy Soter of Alexandria and enriched by successive rulers. Destroyed by Saracen armies under Caliph Omar in 638, it is thought the collection reached 700,000 volumes.

Alexandrine, 12-syllable line in poetry. Its name is probably derived from French medieval poetry about Alexander the Great. The most noted use of alexandrine is in classical French tragedy. Famous occurrences in English are Drayton's *Polyolbion* (1613–22) and the last line of the stanza form used in Spenser's *The Faerie Queene* (1589; 1596).

Alexia. △864.

Alexis (1629–76), Russian tsar (1645–76). He established a new code of laws (1648). His war with Poland (1654–67) led to the reunification of the Ukraine with Russia. He suppressed a peasant rebellion led by Stenka Razin (1670–71) and supported Patriarch Nikon's church reforms. This led to the formation of the Old Believers, who refused to accept these reforms. Western culture began to influence the arts during his reign. △1178.

Alexis (1690–1718), son of Russia's Peter the Great. His mother was sent to a convent, and he was raised by aunts. Forced by his father to marry a German princess, he fled to Vienna. His father's envoys persuaded him to return. Accused of treason, and condemned to death, he died from torture before his planned execution.

Alexius I Comnenus (1048–1118), Byzantine emperor (1081–1118), founder of the Comnenian dynasty. This soldier-emperor came to the throne at a time when Byzantium was virtually destroyed, having lost vast territories to foreign invaders. During the 37 years of his reign, Alexius held off the Normans from their threatened attack on Constantinople; turned the force of the western armies of the First Crusade to his own advantage by using them to reconquer parts of Anatolia; and defeated the Patzinaks and Seljuk Turks. △1084.

Alexius II Comnenus (1168?–1183), Byzantine emperor (1180–83). The death of his father, Manuel I Comnenus, left 12-year-old Alexius the victim of unscrupulous adults. The unpopular regency of his Latin mother, Mary of Antioch, was overthrown by his uncle, Andronicus Comnenus. Andronicus, after having himself crowned as Alexius' co-emperor, had the boy strangled and his body thrown into the sea.

Alexius III Angelus (died 1210), Byzantine emperor (1195–1203), also known as Angelus Comnenus, sometimes surnamed Bambacoratius. Alexius gained the throne after deposing the rightful emperor, his brother Isaac II Angelus. An incompetent ruler, his neglect of foreign policy led to the rise of Byzantium's powerful Balkan rival, Tsar Kalojan of Bulgaria.

Alexius IV Angelus (died 1204), Byzantine emperor (1203–04). After the deposition of his father Isaac II Angelus, Alexius sought the help of western crusaders in order to regain the throne. With Venetian help, his father was restored and Alexius installed as co-ruler, but both were killed in the revolt of 1204.

Alexius V Ducas Mourtzuphlos (died 1204), Byzantine emperor (1204). He was the son-in-law of Alexius III Angelus, who gained the throne during the Constantinopolitan revolt of 1204, and lost it several months later when the city was captured by Latin soldiers of the Fourth Crusade.

Alfalfa, or lucerne, deep-rooted perennial plant native to Europe and naturalized in the United States. It has small leaflets and purple flower clusters. Valued for its ability to restore nitrogen to the soil, it is grown as fodder, pasture, and a cover crop. Height: 1–3ft (30–91cm). Family Leguminosae; species *Medicago sativa.*

Al-Farabi (873–950), Turkish Muslim philosopher. He was instrumental in distinguishing Islamic philosophy from theology. His major work, *The Virtuous City,* owes much to neo-Platonic thinking. His *Great Book of Music* is the most important premodern contribution to music theory.

Alfonso I (1112–85), first king of Portugal (1139–85). He was the son of Henry of Burgundy, count of Portugal. After his father's death (1112), his mother acted as regent until 1128, when Alfonso deposed her. He fought ceaselessly from about 1130 to 1139 against the kings of León and Castile and against the Moors. Upon conquering Lisbon in 1147, he styled himself king, a title later ratified by Castile and the pope. He was succeeded by his son Sancho I.

Alfonso III (1210–79), king of Portugal (1248–79). He was the son of Alfonso II and the brother of Sancho II, whom he succeeded. He seized power in 1245 after Sancho was deposed by the pope. He removed the last vestiges of Moorish power from Portugal and reached an agreement with the king of Castile, whose illegitimate daughter he married. Diniz, who succeeded Alfonso, was born of this union.

Alfonso V (1432–81), king of Portugal (1438–81). He was the son of Edward, whom he succeeded when he was six. His mother Queen Leonora and his uncle Dom Pedro fought a long battle over the regency. Pedro won but after Alfonso came of age in 1446 he came under the influence of Alfonso, Duke of Braganza. He made ill-fated attempts to win the crown of Castile; he was soundly defeated by Ferdinand and Isabella. Henry the Navigator made his explorations during his reign. He was succeeded by John II.

Alfonso VI (1643–83), king of Portugal (1656–83), son and successor of John IV. He was a mental defective, and his mother was regent until ousted by the count of Castelho Melhor. Alfonso's wife, Marie Françoise of Savoy, took his brother (later Peter II) as her lover and had her marriage to Alfonso annulled. She married Peter, and they took over as regents. Alfonso was exiled until his death, when he was succeeded by Peter.

Alfonso I (died 1134), Spanish king of Aragón and Navarre (1104–34). He succeeded his brother Peter I and fought with some success against the Moors. He married Urraca, Queen of Castile, and tried to usurp her lands. He was killed in a battle with her son Alfonso VII of Castile. Ramiro II succeeded him in Aragón, and Garcia IV succeeded him in Navarre.

Alfonso II (1152–96), Spanish king of Aragón (1162–96) and count of Barcelona (as Ramón Berenguer V, 1162–96). He also inherited Provence in 1166. He was the son of Petronilla of Aragón and Ramón Berenguer IV of Barcelona. He signed a peace treaty with Castile that recognized Aragonese rights in Valencia. He was succeeded in Aragón by Peter II and in Provence by a son.

Alfonso VI (*c.*1030–1109), Spanish king of León (1065–1109) and of Castile (1072–1109). He inherited León from his father, and after the assassination of his brother Sancho II of Castile, he took over that crown. He further consolidated his power in Spain by taking Galicia from his brother García in 1072. He made his capital city of Toledo a great cultural center. The exploits of El Cid took place during his reign.

Alfonso VII (1104–57), Spanish King of León and Castile (1126–57), son and successor of Urraca. He had himself crowned emperor at León in 1135. He won notable victories over the Moors at Córdoba (1146) and Almería (1147), but the cities were soon lost again to the Moors. At his death his lands were split: León to his son Ferdinand II and Castile to another son, Sancho III. △1078.

Alfonso VIII (1155–1214), Spanish king of Castile (1158–1214). He was the son of Sancho III, whom he succeeded at age three. After much fighting for the regency, he took control in 1166. He fought both Moors and fellow Christian kings. In 1212, however, he forged a coalition with the Christian kings and won an important victory over the Almohads. He married Eleanor, daughter of Henry I of England. Their son, Henry I, succeeded to the throne.

Alfonso X (1224–84), Spanish king of Castile and León (1252–84). He was the son and successor of Ferdinand II. He continued his father's wars against the Moors, but his chief ambition was to become Holy Roman emperor. A dissident group of German nobles named him anti-king (to Richard, Earl of Cromwell) but papal opposition kept him in Spain. Alfonso's credentials as a scholar were impressive; he wrote a landmark codification of the law and histories of Spain and the world. He was patron to Jewish, Moorish, and Christian scholars, philosophers, and scientists. In 1282, his son, Sancho IV, rebelled and took most of his kingdom away. Alfonso died two years later in Seville, his one remaining loyal city.

Alfonso XI (1311–50), Spanish king of Castile and León (1312–50). He was the son and successor of Ferdinand IV. Gibraltar was lost to the Moors during his reign, and he died in the attempt to recover it.

Alfonso XII (1857–85), king of Spain (1874–85). The son of Isabella II, he went into exile with her during the Carlist Wars. She abdicated in his favor in 1870, and in 1874 he was proclaimed king. His reign was marked by a considerable strengthening of the monarchy. He was succeeded by his son Alfonso XIII. *See also* Carlists.

Alfonso XIII (1886–1941), king of Spain (1886–1931). He was the posthumous son of Alfonso XII, and his mother Maria Christina acted as regent until 1902. Although personally popular, Alfonso was unable to cope with the various demands of Catalan and Basque nationalists, socialists, right-wingers, and republicans. In 1923 he turned to the right-wing dictator, Gen. Miguel Primo de Rivera. That government fell in 1930, and in 1931 Alfonso was forced to abdicate in favor of a republic.

Alfred (849–99), king of Wessex (871–99), called Alfred the Great. Warrior, scholar, and lawgiver, he saved Wessex from the Danes and laid the foundations of a united English kingdom. Youngest of four successively reigning sons of king Ethelwulf, he inherited a weak throne. After the Danish invasion of Wessex (878), he escaped to Athelney, returning a few weeks later to defeat the Danes at Edington and recover the kingdom. To strengthen Wessex against future attack, he built a fleet, constructed forts, and reorganized the army. He furthered political stability by publishing a code of laws, commissioned English translations of Christian Latin authors, encouraged scholarship, and founded schools.

Algae, a large and diverse group of essentially aquatic plants found in salt and fresh waters everywhere in the world. All algae make their own food by photosynthesis, and algae are the primary source of food for mollusks, fish, and other aquatic animals. Algae are directly important to man as a food (especially in Japan), as fertilizers, and as sources of agar, carrageenin, and alginic acid. Algae range in size from microscopic plants such as the green pond scums to huge brown kelps sometimes more than 150ft (46m) long. The smallest algae are variously shaped single-celled organisms, some of which can move about by means of whiplike "arms" called flagellae. Many single-celled algae cluster together in colonies. Larger many-celled algae—including the many familiar seaweeds—grow in a wide variety of shapes, including cords, ruffled sheets, and intricately branched structures resembling some land plants. However, even the most advanced algae do not have true roots, stems, and leaves like those of the higher plants. The chief kinds of algae are classified in five botanical divisions: blue-green algae (Cyanophyta), golden algae (Chrysophyta), brown algae (Phaeophyta), green algae (Chlorophyta), and red algae (Rhodophyta). *See also* Seaweed; Thallophyte. △568.

Algarve, southernmost province of Portugal; bounded by Baixo Alentejo prov. (N), Atlantic Ocean (S and W), and Guadiana River (E); capital is Faro. First occupied by Phoenicians, then Moors, who were overcome by Alfonso III in 1250. Products: fruits, tuna, and sardines. Area: 1,958sq mi (5,071sq km). Pop. 316,200.

Algebra, generalized form of arithmetic in which symbols replace numbers. Thus $3 + 5 = 8$ is a statement in arithmetic; $x + y = 8$ is one in algebra, involving variables x and y. Higher algebras also exist in which the entities are not necessarily numbers nor are the rules those of arithmetic. An example is Boolean algebra, which can be applied to sets (and also to logical propositions). It involves such concepts as the union and intersection of subsets of a given set. *See also* Mathematics. △1452–58.

Algebraic Fraction. *See* Fraction, Algebraic.

Algebraic Function, function that is expressible using algebraic terms and operations. For instance, $3x^3 + x$ is an algebraic function, as contrasted with log x, which is a transcendental function expressed by a convergent series. △1452.

Algebraic Operations, the operations of ordinary algebra: that is, the arithmetical operations addition, subtraction, multiplication, and division. Operations that involve infinite series and functions such as log x are not algebraic—they depend on the use of limits. The term *algebraic* is also applied to arithmetical operations carried out with due regard to sign. Thus, the algebraic sum of a and $-b$ is $a - b$, the algebraic product of $-a$ and $-b$ is $+ab$, etc. *See also* Arithmetical Operations. △1452.

Algeciras (Algeciros), seaport city in S Spain, on the Bay of Algecira in Andalusia; first Spanish town conquered by Moors, 711; taken by King Alfonso XI of Castile in 1344. Algeciras suffered much destruction during war between Moors and Spaniards; was rebuilt in 1704 by Spaniards; important resort area and port of entry from NW Africa. Pop. 81,662.

Alger, Horatio (1832–99), US author and minister who wrote more than 135 books for young boys on the theme of self help. The Horatio Alger hero became one who, through hard work, rose from rags to riches. His poor boys made good in such works as *Fame and Fortune, Struggling Upward,* and *Strive and Succeed.*

Algeria (Algérie), independent nation in North Africa. Influenced over the years by succeeding Arab and French colonization, this mostly Muslim country has nationalized land and industry. An army-backed regime rules the country.

Land and economy. Located in NW Africa, with 640mi (1025km) of coastline on the Mediterranean Sea between Tunisia and Morocco, neighbors include Libya (E), Niger (SE), Mali and Mauritania (SW). Two Atlas mountain chains determine its climate. In the N the Tellian chain runs parallel to the coast and is fertile with moderate climate and sufficient rain. The S Saharan range, a high plateau with less rainfall, separates the N from the Sahara Desert. Oil found in 1957 accounts for 70% of exports; natural gas is plentiful. Sixty percent of the population is engaged in agriculture, and a third of the national income is derived from its crops—cereals, fruits, wine, plus livestock and olive oil. The lack of skilled workers hindered production, and a system of worker-managed plants and farms was instituted (1967–71) to develop nationalized properties.

People. Descendants of invaders from Phoenicia, Rome, Arab lands, Turkey, and France, mixed with the indigenous Berber tribes, make up modern Algeria. Arabs brought their language, the official tongue, as well as their Islamic religion. There are about 50,000 foreign technicians and teachers in the country. There are some 45,000 Catholics, plus small Protestant and Catholic communities.

Government. A strong, central government controls the country, with policy making in the hands of the National Revolutionary Council. Rule is by decree.

History. Conquered by Carthage in 146BC, then Rome, and later the Arabs in the 7th century, the territory was colonized by France in 1830, and annexed as an overseas department with representation in the French assembly; control remained in French hands. The Algerian push for equal political rights led to a terrorist revolt in 1954 initiated by the Nationalist Liberation Front (FLN). In 1962, France signed the Evian accord providing for interim economic, cultural, and technical relations until a referendum on self-determination could be held. On July 1, 1962, the referendum was held and Algeria was declared independent. In 1963, Premier Ahmed Ben Bella was deposed in a bloodless coup by Col. Houari Boumedienne. The constitution was suspended.

PROFILE

Official name: Democratic and People's Republic of Algeria
Area: 919,590sq mi (2,381,738sq km)
Population: 16,800,000
Density: 18 per sq mi (7 per sq km)
Chief cities: Algiers (capital); Oran; Constantine
Government: Military
Religion: Islam
Language: Arabic
Monetary unit: Dinar
Gross national product: $8,800,000,000
Per capita income: $504
Industries: wine, olive oil, natural gas, petroleum products, leather goods
Agriculture: wheat, barley, corn, oats, flax, tobacco, olives, dates, citrus fruits, cattle
Minerals: oil, iron, zinc, lead, mercury, coal, copper
Trading partners: France (major), United States, European Common Market, USSR

Algiers (Alger or **Al-Jaza'ir),** city and capital of Algeria extends 10mi (16km) along W side of Algiers Bay; North Africa's chief port on the Mediterranean; first settled by Phoenicians, became a Roman colony (Icosium) 2nd century BC. Turks ruled 1518; base for Barbary pirates for 300 years; later became capital and trade center of French colony of Algeria; surrendered to Allies 1942; Algerian rebellion occurred 1954; independence was proclaimed 1962. City contains the National Library, university (1909), astronomical observatory, Jardin d'Essai Park, the Casbah (a 16th-century Turkish citadel), and the Great Mosque (1660). Industries: iron ore, flour, wine, tobacco, vegetables, paper, fishing, tourism. Pop. 897,352.

Alginates. △1574.

Algol. △110.

Algonkin, or **Algonquin,** large tribe that gave its name to the Algonkian language, distributed throughout North America. The Algonkin people occupied the Ottawa River area around AD 1600 at which time they numbered about 6000. They were driven from their home by the Iroquois and were eventually absorbed into other related tribes in Canada.

Algophobia, excessive fear of pain or hypersensitivity to it. *See also* Hypochondria.

Algorithm, a simple mathematical procedure of computation that involves computing columns of figures separately, and carrying or borrowing from one column to the next, or of positioning rows of figures in a rote manner so as to derive an answer by inspection. The procedure has been attacked because it rests upon mechanical procedures, rather than an understanding of an operation's logical structure.

Algren, Nelson (1909–), US fiction writer, b. Detroit. His works are usually realistic tales of small-time criminals such as the hero of *The Man with the Golden Arm* (1949). The novel is one of the best known dealing with drug addiction and won the National Book Award in 1950. Algren has also written short stories and other novels, including *A Walk on the Wild Side* (1956).

Alhambra, city in SW California, 5mi (8km) ENE of Los Angeles. Industries: aircraft parts, electronic equipment, air conditioners, steel tanks. Inc. 1903. Pop. (1970) 62,125.

Alhambra, Moorish palace and citadel overlooking Granada, Spain. Actually a series of buildings and gardens, the Alhambra was begun in 1248 by the Moorish rulers of Granada. It is the finest example of Moorish architecture in Spain and is regarded as one of the architectural masterpieces of the world. The buildings fell into disrepair after the expulsion of the Moors in 1492 but extensive restoration work has been done since the 19th century. △1078.

Ali (600?–61), fourth Muslim caliph (656–61), son of Abu Talib, the Prophet Mohammed's uncle. A faithful follower of the Prophet, Ali married his daughter Fatima and was expected to become caliph when he died. However, 3 other caliphs ruled, and 24 years passed before he succeeded Othman, another son-in-

Alfalfa

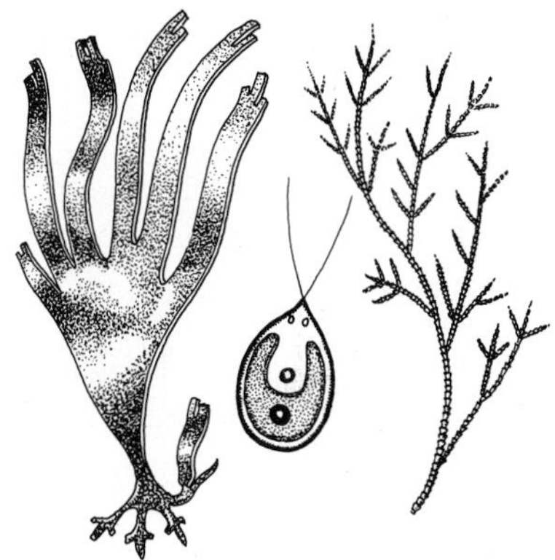

Algae

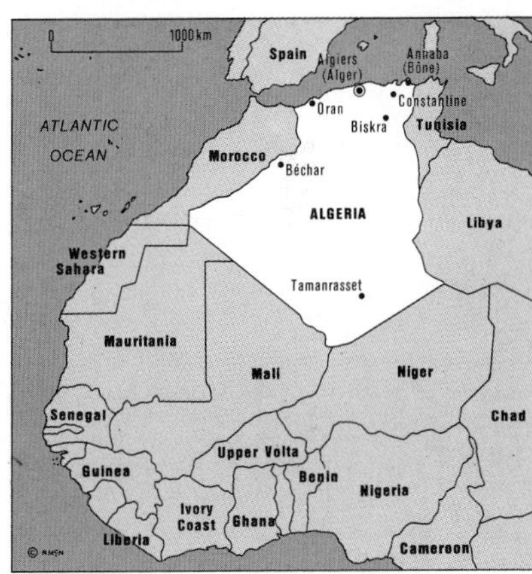
1000km
Spain
Algiers (Alger)
Annaba (Bône)
Oran
Constantine
Biskra
Tunisia
ATLANTIC OCEAN
Morocco
Béchar
ALGERIA
Libya
Western Sahara
Tamanrasset
Mauritania
Mali
Niger
Chad
Senegal
Upper Volta
Guinea
Benin
Nigeria
Ivory Coast
Ghana
Liberia
Cameroon

Algeria

Algiers, Algeria

law of Mohammed. Ali crushed a revolt in Iraq, but was not able to suppress Muawiyah, Mohammed's secretary who was now governor of Syria. When Ali was murdered by fanatics, his son Hasan succeeded him, but abdicated under pressure by Muawiyah. The division in Islam between the Sunni and the Shiites began at this time. Ali, his sons Hasan and Husain, and his wife Fatima are venerated by the Shiites who claim Ali was the rightful heir to Mohammed. △1062.

Alicante, city in SE Spain; capital of Alicante prov., former site of Roman naval base; scene of execution of José Antonio Primo de Rivera, Falangist leader (1936); important Mediterranean port. Exports: esparto, fruit, oil, wine, cereals. Industries: clay products, tobacco, textiles, automobile engines. Area: (prov.) 2,264sq mi (5,864sq km). Pop. (city) 184,716; (prov.) 920,105.

Ali, Muhammad (1942–), US boxer, b. Cassius Clay in Louisville, Ky. He won the Olympic light-heavyweight championship (1960) and then beat Sonny Liston for the world's heavyweight championship (1964) in Miami Beach, Fla. The World Boxing Association took away Ali's title (1967) after he refused induction into the US Army because of his religious beliefs. He was cleared of all charges (1970) by a US Supreme Court ruling and returned to the ring. He regained the world's title when he defeated George Foreman (1974) in Zaire. Ali's bouts with Joe Frazier were highlights in his career.

Alice, city in S Texas, 40mi (64km) W of Corpus Christi; seat of Jim Wells co; named for rancher Alice Kleberg. Industries: oil refining, livestock, farming. Settled 1886; inc. 1910. Pop. (1970) 20,121.

Alice's Adventures in Wonderland (1865), book by Lewis Carroll. In a carefully constructed world of nonsense, a young girl, Alice, encounters such characters as the White Rabbit, the Dodo, the Caterpillar, the Cheshire Cat, the March Hare, the Mad Hatter, and the Red Queen. Although scholars have debated the allegorical significance of these characters for years, they have remained marvelously resistant to adult interpretation.

Alien and Sedition Acts (1798), US legislation designed to curb criticism of the government. War with France seemed a real possibility, and critics of the Federalist party's policies were outspoken. Many of the severest critics were refugees from Europe. The Naturalization Act required 14 years residency for citizenship instead of the previous 5-year requirement. The Alien Act authorized the president to deport foreigners who were considered dangerous. The Alien Enemies Act enabled the deportation or confinement of foreign citizens during war. The most notorious was the Sedition Act, which was carried out in a partisan manner. It outlawed conspiracies against the government and allowed prosecution of those who wrote and published "false, scandalous or malicious" items against the government. Republicans attacked the laws and by 1802, only the Alien Enemies Act was still in force.

Alienation, in psychology, the state of being alienated or diverted from normal functions. The alienated person is estranged and withdrawn from contact with the real world. The term is also used in anthropology and sociology to indicate powerlessness or social isolation.

Alien Registration Act of 1940. *See* Smith Act.

Aligarh, city in N central India, between Ganges and Yamuna rivers; center of Muslim culture with establishment of Aligarh Muslim University (1920) and Aligarh Movement under Sayyid Ahmad Khan. The movement sought to teach Muslims participation in political life, resulting in separatist All-India Muslim League. Industries: cotton mills, agricultural market. Pop. 237,954.

Alimentary Canal, digestive tract that begins with the mouth cavity, continues into the esophagus to the stomach, small intestine, and large intestine, or colon, and ends at the anus. It is about 30ft (9m) long. *See also* Digestive System.

Alimony, divorce law, the compensation paid by one spouse to another for support after the divorce. Temporary alimony provides support to another for the duration of the divorce proceedings; permanent alimony pays for support thereafter.

Aliphatic Compound, any chemical compound of an organic class in which the atoms are not linked to form rings, including the alkanes, alkenes, and the alkynes. It is one of the major structural groups of organic molecules.

Aliquippa, industrial town in W Pennsylvania, on Ohio River, 19mi (31km) WNW of Pittsburgh. Industries: concrete, steelworks. Inc. 1894. Pop. (1970) 22,277.

Al Jizah. *See* Giza.

Al Kaid. △38.

Alkali, soluble substance that reacts with acids to make salts. Strong alkalis include the hydroxides of the alkali metals sodium, potassium, rubidium and cesium, as well as ammonium hydroxide, made when ammonia is dissolved in water. The carbonates of these metals and ammonium carbonate form weak alkalis.

Alkali Elements, univalent metals forming Group IA of the periodic table: lithium, sodium, potassium, rubidium, and cesium. They are all soft silvery-white metals, which rapidly tarnish in air and react violently with water to form solid hydroxides. The hydroxides are very soluble in water, forming strongly basic solutions. The electropositive properties and high reactivity of these elements is due to the single electron in their outer electron shells. △1564.

Alkaline-Earth Elements, bivalent metals forming Group IIA of the periodic table: beryllium, magnesium, calcium, strontium, barium, and radium. They are all light, soft, and highly reactive. All, except magnesium, react vigorously with cold water to form hydroxides. Magnesium will only react with hot water and its hydroxide is less soluble than those of the other alkaline earths. The oxides and hydroxides are strongly basic. Radium is important for its radioactivity. △1552.

Alkaloid, member of a class of complex nitrogen-containing organic compounds found in certain plants. Alkaloids are usually tertiary amines. They are often bitter and highly poisonous substances, important because of their physiological activity. Examples are atropine, codeine, morphine, nicotine, quinine, and strychnine.

Alkalosis, abnormal condition in which the acid-base balance of the blood is upset with the blood becoming too alkaline, or basic (pH above 7.45). It may result from acid loss in protracted vomiting, ingestion of alkalis, or kidney malfunction. Symptoms include irritability and neuromuscular hyperexcitability.

Al-Khwarizmi. △1440.

Al Kuwayt, seaport city in Kuwait, on Persian Gulf, in Asia; largest city in Kuwait; trade center with good harbor; site of university (1966). Main industry is petrochemicals. Pop. 80,008.

Alkyds, polyesters, generally of phthalic acid and glycerol. The solid resins are molded at high speed under low pressure and cured quickly. They are used widely in industrial products where insulating properties, strength, and stability over a wide range of voltage, temperature, and humidity are important. Examples are vacuum-tube bases and automotive ignition parts. *See also* Polyester.

Allah, Arabic name of God. The one and only God of Islam, Allah is the omnipresent and merciful rewarder. Unreserved surrender to Allah, as preached in the Koran, is the very heart of the Muslim faith. Beyond human conceptualization, Allah is at once formidable and benevolent. *See also* Islam; Koran. △846, 1058.

Allahabad, city in N central India, at junction of Yamuna and Ganges rivers; pilgrimage center because of Hindu belief that goddess Saraswati joined the two rivers at this point; site of Magh Mela fair, a religious celebration held every 12th year; site of University of Allahabad (1887), one of the oldest in India; agricultural trade center. Pop. 534,676.

Allan, (Sir) Hugh (1810–82), Canadian financier and shipbuilder, b. Scotland. In 1856 he founded the Allan Line of steamships and later helped plan the Canadian Pacific Railroad. His donation of $300,000 to the Conservative party of John Macdonald resulted in the Pacific Scandal of 1873. *See also* Pacific Scandal of 1873.

All'antica (In imitation of the Antique). △1134.

Allegheny Mountains, mountain range, extends from Pennsylvania through Maryland, Virginia, and West Virginia; contains large quantities of coal and timber. Highest point is Spruce Knob, W.Va., 4,860ft (1,482m).

Allegheny River, river with its source in N central Pennsylvania; flows NW to New York, then SW through Pennsylvania to Pittsburgh, where it meets the Monongahela and forms the Ohio River. Length: 325mi (523km).

Allegory, literary work in either prose or verse in which more than one level of meaning is expressed simultaneously. The fables of Aesop and of La Fontaine, which give human meaning to animal behaviors, are simple allegories. Other examples are the 15th-century anonymous play *Everyman;* 16th-century Edmund Spenser's *Faerie Queene;* 17th-century John Bunyan's *A Pilgrim's Progress.* Allegory can also be found in the works of John Dryden, Alexander Pope, and Jonathan Swift (18th-century); and in such later authors as Henry James, Franz Kafka, D.H. Lawrence, and William Faulkner.

Allegory of the Cave. △852.

Allegri, Antonio. *See* Correggio.

Allele, one of a pair of genes at the same location on a pair of chromosomes. *See* Genes.

Allen, Ethan (1738–89), US frontiersman and Revolutionary War soldier, b. Litchfield, Conn. He moved to the New Hampshire grants (now Vermont) in 1768 and became commander of the Green Mountain Boys, a volunteer militia. Allen and his troops, with sympathizers from Connecticut and Massachusetts, captured Fort Ticonderoga, May 10, 1775.

Allen, Fred (1894–1956), US humorist, b. John Florence Sullivan in Boston. He began his career as a vaudeville juggler, but became famous for his radio program, "The Fred Allen Show" (1932–49), on which he commented with dry humor on topical events. A highlight was his running "feud" with Jack Benny. On TV he appeared on "Judge for Yourself" (1953–54) and "What's My Line?" (1955–56).

Allenby, Edmund Henry Hynman, 1st Viscount (1861–1936), English military commander. A distinguished cavalry officer, he defeated the Turkish forces in Palestine and Syria (1917–18), capturing Jerusalem, Damascus, and Aleppo. He served as British high commissioner in Egypt (1919–25).

Allende Gossens, Salvador (1908–73), president of Chile (1970–73). He died in a military coup on Sept. 11, 1973. Candidate of the Popular Unity coalition, he was the first democratically elected Marxist head of state in Latin America. A medical doctor and active member of the Socialist party from its formation in 1933, he was senator from 1945 and unsuccessfully ran for the presidency in 1952, 1958, and 1964. △1354.

Allen Park, city in SE Michigan; suburb of Detroit. Industries: automobiles, tires, liquor. Settled early 19th century; inc. 1957. Pop. (1970) 40,747.

Allentown, city in E Pennsylvania on Lehigh River; seat of Lehigh co. The Liberty Bell was brought here for safekeeping in 1777; city was a munitions headquarters for Continental Army during Revolutionary War. In the Pennsylvania Dutch region, city is site of Muhlenberg College (1848), Cedar Crest College (1867), Allentown College of St Francis de Sales, and a branch of Pennsylvania State University. Industries: clothing, truck and bus bodies, beer. Founded 1762; inc. as borough 1811, as city 1867. Pop. 109,527.

Allergy, hypersensitive reaction exhibited to certain substances not normally considered distressing. Substances may include such diverse materials as pollen, animal dander, fungus, household dust, occasionally foods, and increasingly drugs, penicillin being a common allergen. The most typical allergic reactions are sneezing and reddening of eyes and mucous tissues (hay fever), wheezing and shortness of breath (asthma), and skin eruptions and itching (eczema). Certain childhood allergies, particularly to food, diminish with age; other allergies do not appear until adulthood. Although the tendency to allergic reactions is frequently hereditary, the specific allergy is not. In one family, a parent may react to pollen by sneezing, one child to dust by shortness of breath, another child to cat hair with eczema. Emotional state is apparently also a factor in the onset of some allergic reactions. In some cases, such as so-called penicillin shock in children, acute allergic reactions can be fatal. Treatment of allergic symptoms usually requires identification of the allergen, its removal from the environment if possible, or alternately a course of desensitization to the substance. Certain drugs are useful in relieving acute symptoms. *See also* Asthma; Eczema; Hay Fever. △112.

Alliance, city in NE Ohio, on Mahoning River, 55mi

(89km) SE of Cleveland. First settled in 1805 by Quakers from Virginia, it was a station on the Underground Railroad for escaping slaves. Industries: brick, tile, steel, rubber bands. Inc. 1889. Pop. (1970) 26,-547.

Alliance, in international relations, an agreement for furtherance of mutual or similar aims between states or other parties, usually arrived at by formal treaty. Related terms include pact, organization, league, and union. The North Atlantic Treaty Organization (NATO) is an alliance.

Alliance for Progress, multilateral program promoting economic and social development in Latin America initiated in 1961. The United States pledged $20 billion over a 10 year period. The Alliance has been described as noble and idealistic and as an attempt to counteract Fidel Castro's revolution in Cuba. Many regimes in Latin America were unwilling to take up the goals of the Alliance; nor did the United States supply the mechanisms that would have helped secure the goals. By 1971, the Alliance was virtually defunct. △1354.

Allied Powers. △1306, 1338.

Alligator, crocodilian similar to family Crocodylidae members, but it has a broader head and more obtuse snout. Each summer the female alligator lays 20–70 goose-sized eggs on shore in a mounded nest of leaves and mud and remains nearby to guard them. The American alligator (*Alligator mississipiensis*) is found only in SE United States. Length: to 19ft (6m). The almost extinct smaller Chinese alligator (*Alligator sinensis*) is restricted to the Yangtze-Kiang river basin. Length: to 6ft (1.8m). It has no webbing between its toes. Family Alligatoridae. *See also* Crocodile. △520.

Alligator Gar. △510.

Alliluyeva, Svetlana (1926–), Joseph Stalin's only daughter by his second wife, Nadezhda Alliluyeva. She was a teacher and translator in the Soviet Union. She defected to the West while in India in 1966, settling in the United States in 1967. She published her memoirs, *Twenty Letters to a Friend* (1967), and wrote an account of her experiences under diverse Soviet regimes, *Only One Year* (1969).

Alliteration, close repetition of consonant sounds within a line of verse or prose. Predominant in Old English poetry, then revived in the 14th century, alliteration is also found in some modern poetry: for example, in this line from W.H. Auden: "By the waters of waking I wept for the weeds."

Allium, bulbous herbs native to temperate to warm regions of the Northern Hemisphere. They are noted for their odor, characteristic of some species, such as garlic, onion, shallot, and chives. The leaves are mostly hollow and the small flowers grow in clusters. Often grown as ornamentals, the flowers are usually rose, lilac, purple, or white, with some reddish, yellowish, greenish, or blue. Family Liliaceae.

Allocation, in an economic system, process of deciding what will be produced and who will receive it, necessary because resources are limited. In a market economy such as the USA, price allocates goods on the basis of consumer income. Similarly, price also is the determining factor in the allocation of natural resources. In a nonmarket (command) economy, allocation is determined by some central authority.

Allori, Angelo. *See* Bronzino, Il.

Allosaurus, or **Antrodemus,** dinosaur that ranged North America during Late Jurassic-Early Cretaceous period. A biped with powerful hindlimbs and small, three-fingered clawed forelimbs. A hunting carnivore, it may have also been a scavenger. Length: to 35ft (10.5m); weight: 2 tons.

Allotrope, one of two or more distinct physical forms of an element, occurring in the liquid, gaseous, or, more usually, solid state. Examples are the existence of molecular oxygen and ozone, white and gray tin, and graphite, diamond, and other forms of carbon.

Allouez, Claude Jean (1622–89), French missionary in Canada. Ordained in 1655, he arrived in Quebec in 1658 and was named vicar general of the northwest regions. A colleague of Jacques Marquette, he traveled to the Great Lakes, converting Indians to Roman Catholicism and encouraging anti-Anglicanism. He wrote extensively about the Great Lakes region. He died in Michigan after living harmoniously with the Illinois Indians.

Alloy, a mixture of two or more metals. Alloys are generally hard and brittle and have a lower melting point than their constituents (those with the lowest melting point are called eutectic mixtures). Properties are frequently different from those of constituent elements and alloys may be considerably stronger than pure metals. Most are prepared by mixing when molten. Some mixtures, combining metal with another, non-metallic substance, such as in steel, are also referred to as alloys. △1600, 1612, 1562.

All Quiet on the Western Front (1929), novel by Erich Maria Remarque. It records in the dialogue of the average soldier the unheroic devastation and horrors of modern war and portrays the spiritual collapse of the post-war generation. The film version (1930) won two Academy Awards. △1370.

All Saints Day, in Christian churches, a day that celebrates all the saints of the church. The holiday is November 1 in the West and the first Sunday after Pentecost in the East. The festival was known as All Hallows in medieval England, and the eve of the day is celebrated in the United States as Halloween.

All Souls Day, in the Roman Catholic Church, a day that celebrates all of the departed souls. It is celebrated on November 2—or November 3 if the first date falls on a Sunday. It is believed that prayers for the departed will help prepare them for heaven.

Allspice, or **pimento**, aromatic tree native to West Indies, Mexico, and Central America. Small white flower clusters produce berry-like, brown, spicy fruits ¼in (6.4mm) in diameter and with the combined flavors of nutmeg, cloves, and cinnamon. They are dried and used as a spice, in perfumes, and in medicine. Height: to 40ft (12m); family Myrtaceae; species *Pimenta officinalis*. △356.

Allston, Washington (1779–1843), US painter, b. Waccamaw, S.C. The first important US Romantic painter, he was one of the first to make use of light and atmospheric color and to use nature as symbolic representation. His important works include *The Deluge* (1804) and *Moonlit Landscape* (1819).

Alluvium, general term that describes the sediments —sand, silt, and mud—deposited by flowing water along the banks, delta, or flood-plain of a river or stream. Fine-textured sediments that contain organic matter form soil.

Alma-Ata, formerly Vernyi or Vyernyi; largest city and capital of Kazakhstan, USSR, near China border; also capital of Alma-Ata oblast; site of Turkistan-Siberian rail terminus, two universities (1934 and 1945); commerce center. Industries: food processing, lumber, machinery, tobacco. Founded 1854 as Russian fortress. Pop. 730,000.

Almagro, Diego de. △1124.

Al Mansura (El Mansura), city in S Egypt, on Damietta River; capital of Daqahlîya governorate; scene of battle (1250) in which Crusaders, led by Louis IX (France), were defeated by Mameluke (Egypt). Industries: cotton, wool processing, dairying, woodworking. Pop. 212,300.

Almeria, city in SE Spain, on the Gulf of Almeria; capital of Almeria prov.; former Moorish naval base, taken by Christians 1489; site of Gothic cathedral, ruins of Moorish fort; important Mediterranean seaport. Exports: grapes, esparto, iron. Industries: chemicals, metalwork. Area: (prov.) 3,388sq mi (8,775sq km). Pop. (city) 114,510; (prov.) 375,004.

Almohads, Berber Muslim dynasty (1147–1269) in North Africa and Spain, followers of a monotheistic reform in Islam. Mohammed ibn-Tumart set about to purify Islam and oust the Almoravids. Later Abd-al-Mumim, Yusuf II, and Yakub I seized Morocco and Spain. In 1212 Alfonso VII of Castile routed them at Navas de Tolosa, and in 1269 their capital Marrakesh fell to the Merenid dynasty. △1078.

Almond, a tree, apparently native to S Asia, resembling the related peach, although larger and longer-living. The almond tree flowers around March north of the equator, and is grown widely. Leading exporters in the 1970s of nuts, almond oil, and meal were Italy, Spain, Morocco, Portugal, and Iran, in addition to the United States. Species *Prunus amygdalus*. *See also* Peach. △360.

Almoravids, Berber dynasty that ruled in Morocco and Moorish Spain in the 11th and 12th centuries. Yusuf ibn-Tashfin was the dynasty's greatest ruler. After conquering Morocco (*c.*1062), they founded Marrakesh. In 1086 Yusuf went to the aid of the petty

Ethan Allen

Alligator

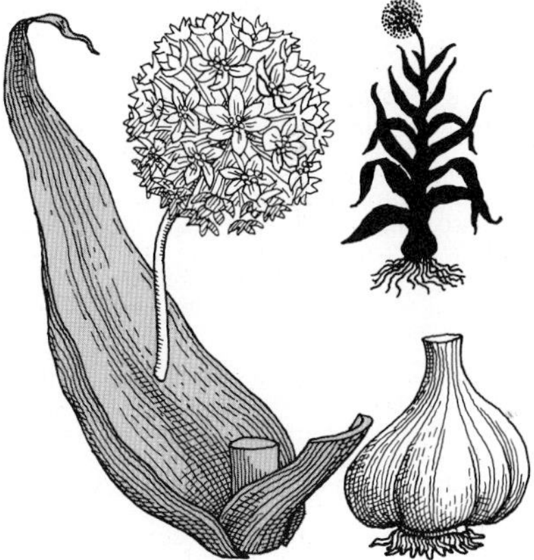

Allium

Allosaurus

Moorish kings in Spain. Shocked at the worldly Spanish Muslims, the puritanical Almoravids returned in 1090 and conquered virtually all of Muslim Spain. By 1107, however, Almoravid power was destroyed in both Morocco and Spain by the even more puritanical Almohads.

Aloe, a genus of African house plants that have fleshy leaves with spiny edges. They grow in dense rosettes and have drooping red or yellow flower clusters. Care: direct sunlight, well-drained soil (equal parts potting soil and sand) kept dry between waterings. Propagation is by suckers. Width: 4–10in (10–25cm). Family Liliaceae.

Alompra. *See* Alaungpaya.

Alopecia. *See* Baldness.

Alpaca. *See* Llama.

Alp Arslan (1029–72), sultan of the Seljuk Turks (1063–72). His conquest of Armenia and attacks on Syria, Cilicia, and Cappadocia severely weakened the military position of the Byzantine Empire. After a decisive victory over the Byzantines at the Battle of Manzikert (1071), Turkish domination of Asia Minor was assured.

Alpha Aquilae. *See* Altair.

Alpha Aurigae. *See* Capella.

Alphabet, writing system based, ideally, on the principle of one symbol for one phoneme. It was refined by the Greeks, but experimenting had been done from 1800 BC to 1300 BC. The alphabet allows a written language that makes the spread of information and culture possible and allows the storage of knowledge. The tools of writing greatly influenced the letter forms. △870.

Alpha Carinae. *See* Canopus.

Alpha Centauri, or **Rigil Kent,** binary star in the constellation Centaurus, and the nearest stellar system to the Sun. It has two components, Alpha Centauri A (yellow dwarf) and Alpha Centauri B (orange dwarf), orbited by a third faint companion, Proxima (red dwarf). Characteristics: apparent mag. 0.0 (A), +1.4 (B), +10.7 (Proxima); absolute mag. +4.4 (A), +5.8 (B), +15.1 (Proxima); spectral type G2 (A), K1 (B), M5 (Proxima); distance 4.3 light-years. *See also* Beta Centauri. △110, 134.

Alpha Rays, or **Alpha Particles,** stable, positively charged particles emitted spontaneously by certain radioactive isotopes (undergoing alpha decay), discovered by Pierre and Marie Curie and Ernest Rutherford and identified as nuclei of helium (two protons, two neutrons). Their penetrating power is low compared with that of beta particles but they cause intense ionization along their track. Their energy, characteristic of the emitting radioisotope, lies between 2 million and 12 million electronvolts. *See also* Radioactivity. △1480, 1554.

Alpha Waves, recording of one type of brain activity, which occurs when the subject is awake but relaxed, often with his eyes closed. Alpha activity is rhythmic with a typical 8 to 12 hertz wave. Alpha activity can be conditioned by positive reinforcement enabling some people to achieve a calm bodily state at will. *See also* Brain Waves. △820.

Alphonsus. △60.

Alphorn, or **Alpine Horn,** primitive musical instrument, a long wooden tube resting on the ground. Rossini used one of the typical herdsmen's melodies played on it in the overture to his opera *William Tell.*

Alpine Plants, small plants found on rocky slopes and mountain meadows above the treeline. They include Alpine forget-me-not *(Myosotis alpestris),* Drummond's willow *(Salix drummondiana),* Alpine harebell *(Campanula lasicarpa),* and others. The term is frequently applied to all mountain plants. Alpines, such as creeping juniper, are used chiefly in rock gardens. May be found at altitudes up to 5,000ft (1,525m).

Alpine Valley. △60.

Alps, mountain system of S central Europe, extends from Gulf of Genoa on the Mediterranean Sea to NW and W Yugoslavia. It occupies parts of Switzerland, Italy, France, Austria, Germany, and Yugoslavia; traversed by many gaps and passes. It is the origin of many geological terms associated with mountains and glaciers; noted for scenery, ski slopes, and lakes; year-round tourist attraction. Important source of hydroelectric power; it also provides grazing and farming land in its valleys. Highest peak is Mt Blanc, 15,771ft (4,810m). Length: 660mi (1,063km).

Alsace-Lorraine, region in E France composed of Bas-Rhin and Haut-Rhin depts.; territory of Belfort and Moselle. Bounded by Luxembourg (N), Germany (N and E), and Switzerland (S); separated from Germany by the Rhine River; region has been traditional source of friction between France and Germany. France lost region (except for Belfort) to Germany at end of Franco-Prussian War (1871); restored to France after WWI, lost again during WWII, and returned to France at end of war. Area is rich in iron ore, contains steel plants and textile mills. △1250.

Altadena, residential community in S California, in foothills of San Gabriel Mts, just N of Pasadena; noted for Christmas Tree Lane decorations at holiday time. Citrus fruits and avocados are grown, but most inhabitants work in Pasadena industries. Pop. (1970) 42,-380.

Altaic Languages, family of languages spoken by about 80 million people in Turkey, Iran, the Soviet Union, Mongolia, and parts of China. It consists of three branches: the Turkic languages, the Mongolian languages, and the Tungusic languages, a small group spoken in the Soviet Union and China. Turkish is the most important of the Altaic languages. They are named after the Altai Mountains where they are believed to have originated.

Altair, or **Alpha Aquilae,** the brightest star in the constellation Aquila; a white star of the first magnitude. Characteristics: apparent mag. +0.75; absolute mag. +2.1; spectral type A7; distance 16 light-years.

Altamira, Cave Paintings of (*c.* 14,000–9500 BC), paintings and engravings in prehistoric caves west of Santander, northern Spain. They were discovered in 1879 but not accepted as genuine until the early 20th century. The roof of the caves' lateral chamber is covered with animal paintings, including bison, boars, and horses, executed in vivid black, red, and violet, as well as eight engraved anthropomorphic figures and hand prints and outlines. △950, 1586.

Altdorfer, Albrecht (1480–1538), German painter and engraver. One of the first Europeans to paint nature scenes, he emphasized man's unity with and place in the natural world. *Battle of Alexander at Issus* (1529) is considered his masterpiece. △1144.

Alternating Current. *See* Current, Electric.

Alternation of Generations, two-generation cycle by which some plants reproduce. The asexual (sporophyte) form produces spores that in turn grow into the sexual (gametophyte) form. The gametophyte produces the egg cell (fern) or capsule (moss) that grows into another sporophyte. The moss gametophyte consists of the protonema, or moss plant. The fern gametophyte is the prothallus or familiar fern plant. *See also* Fern; Gametophyte; Moss.

Althing, Icelandic parliament and oldest European legislative assembly. It was first convened at Thingvellir, near Reykjavik, in 930. The 60 members (40 in the lower house and 20 in the upper house) are elected by proportional representation for four-year terms. The two houses act on occasion as a United Althing, as in 1944, when the assembly voted independence from Denmark.

Altitude, in astronomy, angular distance of a celestial body from the horizon, measured in degrees along a vertical circle passing through the body. Altitude and azimuth form a coordinate system for giving astronomical positions.

Altitude Sickness, deficiency of oxygen in the blood and tissues that occurs at high altitudes and produces symptoms such as dizziness, palpitations, headache, nosebleed, and nausea.

Alton, industrial city in SW Illinois, on Mississippi River, 4mi (6km) above mouth of Missouri River. Industries: steel, boats, tents. Founded 19th century as trading post. Inc. 1837. Pop. (1970) 39,700.

Altoona, city in central Pennsylvania, on E slopes of Allegheny Mts; laid out in 1849 as a switching point by Pennsylvania Railroad for trains crossing Alleghenies. Industries: shoes, clothing, machinery. Settled 1769; inc. 1868. Pop. (1970) 63,115.

Altruism, helping behavior that does not involve any selfish motives or obvious gain for the helper. Psychologists have identified several factors that may be important for the development of altruism, including the capacity for empathy and opportunities to observe altruistic models or parents.

Altruistic Suicide. △812.

Altus, city in SW Oklahoma, 70mi (113km) NW of Wichita Falls; seat of Jackson co; railroad junction and food processing center. Industries: canvas, metal, concrete products. Inc. 1907. Pop. (1970) 23,302.

Alum, any of several compounds, the most important of which medicinally are potassium or aluminum alum, used as astringents and styptics.

Alumina. △1598.

Aluminum, common metallic element (symbol Al) of group IIIA of the periodic table, first obtained in pure form by Friedrich Wöhler (1827). It is the most common metal in the earth's crust; the chief ore is bauxite (a hydrated oxide), from which the metal is extracted by electrolysis. Alloyed with other metals, it is extensively used in machined and molded articles, particularly where light materials are required, as in aircraft. Chemically it is a reactive metal, protected from oxidation by a passive layer of oxide. Properties: at. no. 13; at. wt. 26.9815; sp. gr. 2.699; melt. pt. 1220.38°F (660.21°C); boil. pt. 4473°F (2467°C); most common isotope Al^{27} (100%). △1554, 1566.

Aluminum Processing, the two-step process in the production of the pure metal from bauxite, its chief ore. Bauxite is first refined to obtain pure alumina (Al_2O_3), which is smelted to produce aluminum. The Bayer process, involving digestion, clarification, precipitation, and calcination is the most common refining process yielding half the original amount of ore. Smelting involves dissolving alumina in melted cryolite and passing a current through the mixture to yield pure aluminum and carbon dioxide (the Hall-Heroult process). *See also* Aluminum.

Alum Root. *See* Heuchera.

Alveolus (pl. Alveoli). △692.

Alyssum, wild flower native to Europe and found along roads and in waste lands of the United States. They have lance-shaped leaves, often covered with pale down and white or yellow flowers. Species include annual *Alyssum alyssoides;* perennial golden tuft *A. saxatile;* and biennial *A. petracum.* Height: 1–2ft (30–61cm). Family Cruciferae.

AM. *See* Amplitude Modulation.

AMA. *See* American Medical Association.

Amadeus (1845–90), king of Spain (1870–73). He was the duke of Aosta, the son of King Victor Emmanuel II of Italy. After Queen Isabella II of Spain was forced to abdicate in 1868, he was elected king by the Spanish Cortes. He accepted reluctantly, ruled three years, but abdicated readily in 1873 when the Carlist Wars broke out again.

Amadeus VIII (1383–1451), French count (from 1391) and duke (from 1416) of Savoy. As Felix V, he was the last of the antipopes (1439–49). Elected by the schismatic Council of Basel, he enjoyed little support and resigned after 10 years.

Amadis of Gaul, 13th- or 14th-century romance. The oldest extant version is a Spanish manuscript (*c.* 1508) by García Ordóñez de Montalvo, who derived the work from older manuscripts. The story is sometimes attributed to the Portuguese Vasco Lobiera (died 1403), and is similar in many respects to the earlier Arthurian romances of France and Germany. Amadis, illegitimate son of Perión, king of Gaul (Wales), is abandoned by his mother and is then rescued by a Scottish knight. He has a romance with Oriana, an English princess, and various knightly adventures with dragons, giants, etc.

Amado, Jorge (1912–), Brazilian novelist. His works, which abound in violence and stark realism, explore the plight of Brazil's poor. He occasionally writes lyrically about pastoral Brazil, but his main concern is poverty. *Sweat* (1934) and *Land of Violence* (1942) are typical.

Amagasaki, city in S Honshu, Japan, on Osaka Bay; site of 16th-century castle; damaged by US air raids 1945. Industries: iron, steel, chemicals, textiles. Pop. 553,696.

Amalfi, town in Italy, on N coast of Gulf of Salerno, 22mi (35km) SE of Naples; site of 11th-century church, Cathedral Sant Andrea; a 9th-century Italian aritime republic; popular seaside resort. Founded y Romans. Pop. 7,162.

malgam, solid or liquid alloy of mercury with other etals. Most metals will dissolve in mercury, although on is an exception. △1554.

malgamation, Ore, an old and still-used process of ecovering gold and silver from their ores by the use f mercury. The mercury forms an alloy (called amal-am) with the precious metals. This is then recovered nd processed to obtain the pure metal.

malric, two Latin kings of Jerusalem in the 12th entury. Amalric I of the Angevin dynasty ruled 163–74 and could not capture the Egyptian suze-ainty from Nureddin. Baldwin IV succeeded him. malric II ruled 1197–1205, claiming title from his iarriage to Isabella, eldest daughter of Amalric I. malric III succeeded him.

malthea. △86, 152.

mana Society, religious community in Iowa. ounded in Germany, the group was persecuted and ed to the United States in 1842. Seven villages in owa were settled in 1855. Specializing in wool and vood handicrafts, it is one of the most successful com-nunal communities.

manita, large genus of widely distributed mostly oisonous mushrooms. In contrast to common mush-ooms, amanitas usually have long stalks and have the rominent remains of a veil in a fleshy ring under the ap and at the bulbous base.

maranth, heavy-looking plant from tropics of E sia. Flowers, densely clustered in spikes or tassels, re often hidden by colorful foliage. Among 800 spe-ies is annual foxtail *Amaranthus caudatus* with a rimson-purple flower. Height: 1–3ft (30–90cm). amily Amarantaceae.

marillo, city in NW Texas, 65mi (105km) E of New Mexico in the Texas Panhandle; seat of Potter co; first vhite visitors were explorers with Francisco Coronado's expedition; settled after the Civil War, its conomy and population boomed with discovery of atural gas (1918) and oil (1921). Industries: gas, oil, rains, cattle. Inc. 1899. Pop. (1970) 127,010.

maryllis, any of more than 800 species of peren-ial herbs found mostly in the tropics and subtropics. All have bulbs or underground stems with narrow rasslike leaves and showy, lilylike flowers. The petals re attached to the seed receptacle and the fleshy ruits are kidney-shaped. Family Amaryllidaceae.

mati, family of Italian violinmakers in Cremona in he 16th and 17th centuries, including **Andrea** (*c.* 520–78), the founder of the Cremona school of vi-olinmaking, his two sons **Antonio** (*c.*1550–1638) and **Girolamo** (1551–1635), and Girolamo's son **Ni-olò** (1596–1684) and grandson **Girolamo** (1649–740).

Amazon, greatest river of South America, and 2nd ongest river in the world, draining the vast rain forest of N central South America. Its drainage basin in-cludes the N 75% of Brazil and substantial portions of Colombia, Ecuador, Guyana, Peru, and Venezuela. Carrying the greatest volume of water of any river in the world, the Amazon is the central artery of an ex-tensive river system; major tributaries are the Madeira, Purus, Juruá, Ucayeli, Marañon, Napa, Putu-mayo, Japurá, and Negro rivers; the Marañon is re-garded as the headstream of the Amazon proper. Al-though swampy flood banks accompany the river's path, the great Selvas (rain forest and drainage basin) s thickly vegetated terra firma, producing hardwoods and rubber, a region of approx. 2,053,318sq mi 5,318,094sq km) flanked by the Brazilian Highlands S), Andes Mts (W), and Guiana Highlands (N).

Cultivation of the region has been limited to the sporadic harvesting of natural products; lumbering has been hindered by the absence of pure stands of valuable woods, the rain forest encouraging growth of a wide variety of flora, side by side, across the entire region. The basin is sparsely inhabited, chiefly by Brazilians; the vast majority of these settlers reside along the floodbank, while a small Indian population lives and hunts in the greater expanses of the rain forest.

The Amazon is navigable as far W as Iquitos, Peru, or more than 2,000mi (3,220km) inland; the Brazil-ian government has begun a major program to de-velop the natural resources of the hinterland in step with the economically advanced E coast of Brazil. The river was first descended from Peru in 1541 by the Spaniard Francisco de Orellana. Length (including Marañon River, headstream): approx. 3,900mi (6,279km).

Amazonas, vast lowland region in N central South America, drained by the Amazon River system; bounded by the Pakaraima and Acarai Mts (N), Cordillera Oriental and Andes Mts (W), and Serra Das Pasecis and S Brazilian highlands (S); includes districts in S Venezuela, SE Colombia, N Peru, and central NW Brazil (largest). Total area of basin: over 750,000sq mi (1,942,500sq km).

Amazons, in Greek legend, a race of female warriors. They lived on the banks of the River Thermodon in Asia Minor. At the siege of Troy the Amazons fought as allies of the Trojans. Here their queen Penthesilia was slain by Achilles after she had killed many Greek warriors.

Ambala, city in N central India, between Sutlej and Yamuna rivers; site of excavations revealing pre-Aryan Harappa culture, the oldest prehistoric civilization known in India (*c.* 2500–1800 BC); trading center. Industries: grain market, sugar, glass. Pop. 87,750.

Ambassid. *See* Glass Fish.

Amber, hard, yellow-to-brown, translucent fossil resin, found in alluvial soils, in lignite beds, or on seashores, especially near the Baltic Sea, where large deposits represent extinct flora 50,000,000 years old. May be rods or irregular nodules. Fossil insects and plants found as inclusions. Deeply colored amber takes a fine polish and is prized as a gem. △244.

Amberfish, or **amberjack,** marine food and game fish found in tropical and subtropical waters. Fast swimming, this blunt-headed fish is blue and silver with bronze stripe along its side. The young have bright golden bands along the sides. Length: 5–6ft (1.5–1.8m); weight: 120lb (54kg). Family Carangidae; Species *Seriola dumerli.*

Ambergris, musky, gray, waxy substance formed in intestines of sperm whales, used in perfumes as a fixative for flower scents.

Ambler, Eric (1909–), English writer of espionage and criminal underworld stories, one of the best writers of his genre. His first well known work was *The Dark Frontier* (1936), followed by such titles as *Uncommon Danger* (1937), *Journey into Fear* (1940), *The Night-Comers* (1956), and *The Light of the Day* (1965).

Amblyopia, partial or sometimes total loss of vision in the absence of any signs of eye abnormality. It may be due to disease or to the ingestion of poisons.

Amboise, town in France on Loire River, 15mi (24km) E of Tours. Renaissance château with two towers stands over the town; once used by French kings, it later became a prison. A Huguenot conspiracy here in 1560 failed, but three years later the Edict of Amboise guaranteed religious freedom to Huguenot nobility and gentry; site of vineyards. Pop. 7,332.

Ambrose, Saint (*c.*340–97), bishop of Milan, who resisted imperial demands to surrender Milan's churches to the Arians. He refused to compromise his orthodox position, and acquired a reputation for administrative skill and eloquence. Augustine mentions Ambrose as instrumental in his own conversion. He was also the author of works on theology and ethics that greatly influenced the thought of the Western Church. △1028.

Ambrosia, in Greek and Roman mythology, magical substance eaten by gods. The gods kept their immortality by bathing in it or rubbing it into their skin. Without ambrosia a god became weak. A mortal who ate it became strong and immortal. Sometimes it was mixed with nectar as a drink.

Ambulatory Worship. △1080.

Ambystoma, North American mole salamander. Most hide underground except for breeding. Used in laboratories, they have a sturdy build and broad head. Length: to 13in (33cm). Best known of about 25 species are the marbled, spotted, and tiger salamanders. Family Ambystomidae. *See also* Salamander.

Amchitka Island, Aleutian island 69mi (111km) SE of Kiska Island off Alaska coast; site of underground nuclear testing in 1971. Length: 40mi (64km); width 2–5mi (3.6–8km).

Ameba, rhizopod protozoan that has constantly changing, irregular shape. Found in ponds, damp soil,

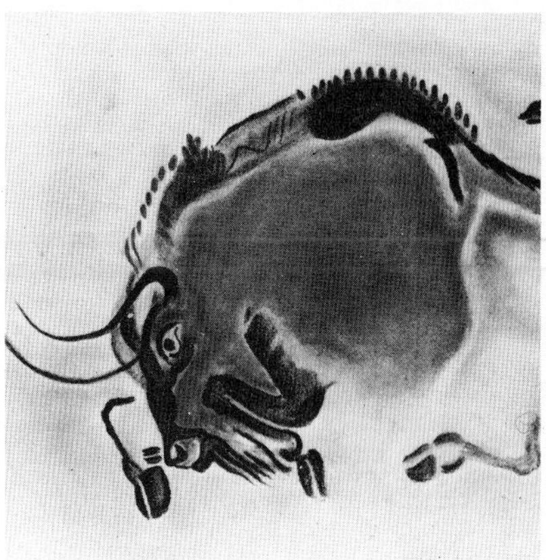

Altamira cave painting

Alyssum

Amberfish

Amboise, France

or animal intestinal tracts, it consists of a thin unit membrane covering, large nucleus, food and contractile vacuoles, and fat globules. It is almost transparent; reproduction is by fission. Length: to 0.1in (3mm). Class Rhizopoda (Sarcodina); species include common *Ameba proteus* and *Entameba histolytica*, which causes amebic dysentery. △458, 466.

Amebic Dysentery. *See* Dysentery.

Ameboid Motion, method of locomotion of amebas, other protozoa, and other animal cells, including white blood cells. When a cell area is stimulated, the outer tube of "gel" protoplasm extends outward in one direction forming a false foot, or pseudopod, and the inner liquid "sol" flows in that direction, carrying the whole cell with it.

Amendment, Constitutional, procedure to change or modify the US Constitution according to Article V of the document. Upon the recommendation of two-thirds of both houses of Congress, a proposed amendment may be submitted to the legislatures of the states or to special state conventions. Three-fourths of the states must approve in order for the amendment to be approved.

Amenemhat, four kings of ancient Egypt. In 2000 BC **Amenemhat I** (died *c.* 1960 BC) overthrew the nomarchs, centralized government, and founded the XII dynasty. His co-regent, Senusret I, succeeded. **Amenemhat II** (died 1903 BC) co-ruled with Senusret I (1938–35 BC), was king (1935–06 BC), and co-ruled with his son and successor, Senusret II. **Amenemhat III** (died 1801 BC) succeeded Senusret III, set up the first Nilometer, irrigated thousands of acres in the Faiyūm, but his successor, **Amenemhat IV** (died 1792 BC), let the dynasty decline. △960.

Amenhotep I, ancient Egyptian king of the XVIII dynasty (*r.* 1557–40 BC), successor of his father, Amasis I. He campaigned in Syria to the Euphrates and pushed the southern boundary to the second cataract. Thutmose I succeeded.

Amenhotep II, ancient Egyptian king (1448–20 BC), co-regent (1446–48 BC), son and successor of Thutmose III. He crushed an uprising in Syria, defended the frontier as far as the Euphrates, invaded Nubia, and erected temples to Amon at Karnak. Thutmose IV succeeded.

Amenhotep III, ancient Egyptian king (1417–1379 BC), and successor of his father, Thutmose IV. The XVIII dynasty peaked in his reign. Despite raids from the Bedouins and Hittites, he maintained peace throughout the empire. He built the 623-ft (190-m)-long Temple of Luxor, concluded the 1000-ft (305-m)-long Great Temple of Amon, promoted sculpture, and celebrated games. His wife, Queen Tiy, helped with state affairs. Akhenaton succeeded him.

Amenhotep IV. *See* Akhenaton.

Amenorrhea, absence of menstruation. Abnormal in a nonpregnant, nonlactating woman between the ages of puberty and menopause.

American Anti-Slavery Society, abolitionist group founded in Philadelphia (1833). The society was active in US politics and social life, sending ministers and printed material throughout the country to recruit members for the society and organize local groups. Influential figures in the group were William Lloyd Garrison and Arthur and Lewis Tappan.

American Bald Eagle. *See* Bald Eagle.

American Bar Association, organization whose members are attorneys admitted to the bar of any state in the United States. The association maintains a library and specialized committees varying from maritime law to "Education About Communism and Its Contrast with Liberty Under Law." Founded 1878. Members: about 160,000.

American Blue. *See* Russian Blue Cat.

American Buffalo. *See* Bison.

American Civil Liberties Union (ACLU), organization dedicated to defending "the rights of man set forth in the Declaration of Independence and the Constitution." Its activities vary from test court cases and opposition to repressive legislation to public protest on inroads of rights. It has defended people and organizations throughout the political spectrum, which has often made its activities controversial. The ACLU maintains a library and specialized committees, and its publications include *Civil Liberties.* Members: about 130,000. Founded 1920.

American Colonization Society, group founded by Robert Finley in 1817 to return free blacks to Africa for settlement. More than 11,000 blacks were transported to Sierra Leone and, after 1821, Monrovia, which became the Republic of Liberia (1847.) Leading forces of the society included James Monroe, James Madison, and John Marshall.

American Expeditionary Force (A.E.F.), World War I US army contingent sent to Europe (1918) under command of Maj. Gen. John J. Pershing. He preserved its identity and integrity when Allied field commanders wanted to integrate the US troops into the existing defense structure. The A.E.F. was a conscripted army led by professional soldiers.

American Farm Bureau Federation, agricultural organization, represented in 49 states of the United States and Puerto Rico with membership on a family basis. Its purpose is to analyze problems and formulate action to achieve educational improvement, economic opportunity, and social advancement for its members. Its publications include *Farm Bureau News* and *American Farmer.* Members: about 2,000,000. Founded 1919.

American Federation of Labor (AFL), US labor organization. It was founded of craft unions (skilled workers) consolidated into a single federation while each union maintained its autonomy. The AFL was organized in 1886 at a trades union convention in Columbus, Ohio. Samuel Gompers, its first president, served for 37 years (1886–1924). The AFL advocated strikes to gain goals of fair wages and hours, collective bargaining with employer and written contract. With decline of Knights of Labor, AFL grew into leading US union organization. It merged with the CIO in 1955. *See also* Gompers, Samuel.

American Federation of Labor and Congress of Industrial Organizations, The (AFL-CIO), US labor organization. It is a federation of over 125 national and international labor unions, combining both craft and industrial workers. Established in 1955, it combined in a merger the American Federation of Labor (AFL) and Congress of Industrial Organizations (CIO). The merger healed a 20-year breach between the two unions. George Meany was elected president. Although each union within the federation is fully autonomous, the ultimate governing body of the AFL-CIO is an Executive Council made up of the president, vice presidents, and secretary-treasurer, elected at its convention held every two years. *See also* American Federation of Labor; Congress of Industrial Organizations.

American Foxhound, versatile hunting dog (hound group) used in packs or individually to trail by scent; ancestors brought to US in 17th–18th centuries. It has a long, slightly domed head and square-cut muzzle; low-set, long, hanging ears; large hound eyes; a moderately long body with slightly arched loin; medium length legs; and slightly curved, brush tail. The close, hard coat can be any color. Average size: 22–25in (56–63.5cm) high at shoulder; 60–70lb (27–32kg). *See also* Hound.

American Fur Company, first US business monopoly, owned by John Jacob Astor. John Jay's Treaty of 1794 permitted US fur trading in the Pacific Northwest to compete with Montreal interests and the North West Company. Fort Astoria was set up in Oregon in 1805, where tea was traded for sea otter pelts. During the War of 1812 the United States was unable to defend Astoria, and Astor was forced to sell out to the North West Company in 1813. Fort Astoria reverted to US control in the 1840s when the fur trade had declined. *See Also* Astor, John Jacob; North West Company.

American Indian Movement (AIM), an organization of American Indians to promote the Indians' civil rights. In 1972 they took over the Bureau of Indian Affairs in Washington, D.C., to dramatize complaints that tribal councils were controlled by the Bureau. In 1973 members occupied the historic community of Wounded Knee, S. D., to point up demands for reform in tribal government and for revision of the framework in which Indians negotiate with the federal government.

American Library Association, founded in 1876 to promote the advancement of librarianship, it is the largest national association for libraries and librarians. It has about 35,000 members. Through committees, it accredits library schools and fosters library programs.

American Medical Association (AMA), a federation of 54 state and territorial medical associations, founded in 1847 for the promotion of medical standards of education and ethics. The AMA also dev
ops programs to provide scientific information to th
profession and health-education materials to the pu
lic. There were about 210,000 members in 1975.

American Republican Party, political party in th
pre-Civil War United States, it was opposed to foreig
ers and people of religions other than Protestant. *Se*
also Know-Nothing Party. △1276.

American Revolution (1775–81), conflict that e
tablished the independence of the 13 American col
nies from Britain.

Background. In 1760, King George III becam
king of England, and in 1763 the Peace of Par
ended the Seven Years War and in North America th
French and Indian War. The peace confirmed Britain
dominion of North America, as the French surren
ered Canada. Great Britain, faced with an expandin
empire and a large debt, sought to tax the coloni
and enforce existing trade laws. Writs of assistanc
(general search warrants), effective 1761, we
strongly opposed in Massachusetts. Following th
Sugar Act of 1764, British Parliament passed th
Stamp Act of 1765, which called for stamps on a
legal documents, newspapers, and cards. Colonis
protested against these measures, using "no taxatic
without representation" as a rallying cry, and Sons
Liberty groups were formed. Parliament repealed th
Stamp Act in 1766 but passed the Declaratory A
asserting the crown's right to legislate for the col
nies. The Townshend Acts of 1767 set a duty on in
ported tea, glass, and paper with the revenue to b
used to pay royal officials in the colonies. In 176
British troops arrived. Hatred for the troops in Bosto
erupted in a brawl March 1770, dubbed the Bosto
Massacre, in which five citizens were killed. Dutie
were dropped on all imports except tea. A truce co
tinued until the announcement in 1772 that Mass
chusetts officials would be paid by the crown, placir
them under British control. Unrest grew and in 1772
73, to keep in touch, committees of correspondenc
were formed in Massachusetts and other colonie
Aroused by the British Tea Act of 1773, designed t
aid financially the East India Co., colonists disguise
as Indians boarded ships in Boston harbor on Decen
ber 16 and dumped the tea. This resistance led t
disiplinary action through the Intolerable Acts, whic
closed the port of Boston, deprived Massachusetts
most of its rights, and provided that persons accuse
of a capital crime be tried in England. To enforc
these acts Gen. Thomas Gage, in charge of Britis
troops, was appointed the colony's governor. In re
sponse to the Intolerable Acts, the First Continent
Congress met in Philadelphia on Sept. 5, 1774. Th
colonial delegates rejected the Intolerable Acts an
set up the Continental Association, which provide
for nonimportation of all British goods and for none
portation to Britain.

War for Independence. In 1774 militia group
called Minutemen formed in the Boston area. Genera
Gage detailed British troops to destroy militia store
at Concord. Alerted, 77 armed Minutemen met th
British on April 19, 1775, on the Lexington Green. A
unidentified shot brought on the clash that kille
eight Americans. The British continued to Concord
destroyed supplies but were attacked by the militia a
Concord Bridge, and harassed by colonials on the re
turn march to Boston. Colonial reinforcements arrive
in Boston, and the town was soon under siege. Thes
troops before Boston became the Continental Army
and on June 15, the Second Continental Congres
made George Washington commander in chief. Be
fore his arrival in Cambridge on July 3, the Battle c
Bunker Hill took place on June 17. Americans wer
driven from their hasty entrenchments but inflicte
heavy losses on the British. On October 10, Gen. Wi
liam Howe replaced Gage as British commander. Th
British evacuated Boston on March 17, 1776, an
Washington proceeded to New York City. Durin
1775–76 the Americans waged an unsuccessful cam
paign against the British in Canada.

The Declaration of Independence, adopted on Jul
4, 1776, made the break with Britain decisive an
followed efforts to resolve differences with the crown
Militarily, the colonials did poorly, and after a series o
defeats Washington retreated from New York t
Pennsylvania. Crossing the Delaware River on Christ
mas 1776, he surprised and captured the British out
post at Trenton on December 26; on Jan. 3, 1777, h
defeated the British at Princeton, improving America
morale. The British, attempting to divide the colonies
mounted a three-pronged assault that focused or
New York State. Gen. John Burgoyne, descendin
along Lake Champlain from Canada, was to be joine
by Col. Barry St. Leger, advancing eastward in th
Mohawk Valley. They were to meet with Genera
Howe's forces moving N from New York City. The
strategy failed when Burgoyne was defeated and sur
rendered his army at Saratoga on Oct. 17, 1777, an
St. Leger had been defeated at Oriskany on August 6

A turning point in the war, it influenced France to recognize the colonies. Howe, instead of advancing up the Hudson, occupied Philadelphia. Washington's army, ill-fed and in rags, spent the winter of 1777–78 at Valley Forge, Penn., where they reorganized.

In 1778 the French alliance was signed. In June Sir Henry Clinton replaced Howe as commander of the British forces. On Dec. 29, the British captured Savannah, and the focus of the war shifted to the South. In 1779, Spain joined the war against England, and George Rogers Clark with his Virginians conquered the old Northwest. In 1780, General Cornwallis was given command of the southern campaign. On September 23, a plot of Benedict Arnold to surrender West Point to Clinton was revealed, but Arnold escaped. British control in South Carolina weakened, and in August 1781, Cornwallis was pushed to Yorktown, Va. The French fleet entered Chesapeake Bay and in September, Washington and the Comte de Rochambeau's French and American forces joined the Marquis de Lafayette at Williamsburg, Va. Finding himself bottled up, Cornwallis surrendered his army Oct. 19, 1781, ending the British military efforts in the United States. The remaining British troops stayed in New York City until the official end of the war on Sept. 3, 1783, when the Treaty of Paris was signed. *See also* individual battles and biographies; Boston Massacre; Continental Congress, First; Declaration of Independence; Intolerable Acts; Paris, Treaty of. △1218.

American River, river in N California, flows SW into the Sacramento River at Sacramento. Discovery of gold at Sutter's Mill on river in 1848 spurred California gold rush. Length: 30mi (48km).

American Saddle Horse, light horse breed for park or show riding developed in Kentucky, Tennessee, and Virginia for transportation over long distances. Known as a breed since 1891, this easy-riding horse has a refined head, long neck, short rounded back, and high-set tail. Colors are bay, brown, chestnut, gray, black, and golden. Height: 60–64in (152–163cm) at shoulder; weight: 1000–1200lb (450–545kg).

American Samoa, E part of Samoa island group in S Pacific Ocean; US territory; comprised of islands of Tituila (including capital, Pago Pago), Sand, Rose, Swains, and the Manua group. Under control of native chiefs until *c.* 1860, the islands were granted to United States 1899 by treaty with former co-administrators, Germany and Great Britain; a constitution (1960) allows local legislature. Exports: canned fish, copra, cacao, local crafts. Area: 76sq mi (197sq km). Pop. 27,769.

American Short-haired Cat, or domestic short-haired, domestic cat breed with a broad head, short face, powerful body, broad chest, strong legs, and thick tail. Its coat is short, fine, and dense. Color varieties are black, white, blue, cream, blue-cream, tortoiseshell, calico, and tabby.

American Staffordshire Terrier, well-muscled dog (terrier group) originally used as pit bull, or fighting dog. Brought to United States around 1870 as the Staffordshire Terrier, the heavier American version was registered as a separate breed in 1972. It has a powerful head, cropped or uncropped ears, deep chest, and short body. Legs are moderately long; the short tail tapers to a point; and the short, stiff coat can be any color or colors. Average size: 18–19in (46–48cm) high at shoulder. *See also* Terrier.

American System, formula advocated by Henry Clay and John C. Calhoun about 1824. Calling for high tariffs and highway construction, the policy also advocated the establishment of a national bank.

American Tobacco Case (1911), Supreme Court decision against the tobacco monopoly. The court declared only "undue" restraint of trade was forbidden. It allowed reorganization of the company and weakened the Sherman Antitrust Act.

American Water Spaniel, working gun dog (sporting group) developed in midwestern US. A dog that springs game and retrieves. It has a long head and square muzzle; long, low-set, lobular ears; sturdy body; medium-length legs; and a long, curved tail. The distinctive, closely curled coat is feathered on the legs and tail; colors are solid liver or dark chocolate. Average size: 15–18in (38–46cm) high at shoulder; 28–45lb (13–20.5kg). *See also* Sporting Dog.

Americium, radioactive metallic element (symbol Am), first of the actinide group, made by Glenn Seaborg and others by neutron bombardment of plutonium. Am^{241} is used as a source of gamma rays. Properties: at. no. 95; sp. gr. 13.67; melt. pt. 1821°F (995°C); boil. pt. 4725°F (2607°C); most stable isotope Am^{243} (7.37×10^3 yr). *See also* Actinide elements.

Ames, city in central Iowa, on the Skunk River, 28mi (45km) N of Des Moines; site of National Animal Disease Laboratory and Iowa State University of Science and Technology (1858). Industries: water treatment, electronic and water analysis equipment. Inc. 1870. Pop. (1970) 39,505.

Ames Room, demonstration devised by Adelbert Ames to show that past interactions between humans and their world exert an influence on their later perceptions. In the Ames room, one end of the far wall is nearer to the observer than the other end; the shape of that wall is also trapezoidal. Most viewers report a normal-looking room; however, two objects of equal size look unequal when placed at opposite ends of the far wall, eg two average-sized people are apparently transformed into a giant and a dwarf.

Amethyst, transparent, violet variety of crystallized quartz, containing more iron oxide than other varieties, found mainly in Brazil, Uruguay, Ontario and North Carolina. Valued as a semiprecious gem since ancient times. *See also* Quartz. △244.

Amhara. △1268.

Amharic, a language of the Semitic or Hamito-Semitic family. Original to the province of Amhara and Shoa, it has been the official language of Ethiopia since *c.* 1300 and has many words from the ancient Ghiz tongue, which was the official language at the time of the conversion to Christianity in 335. △974.

Amherst, Jeffrey (Baron) (1717–97), British general in America. During the last French and Indian War (1754–63), he was named commander-in-chief of British forces (1758). His victories included Louisbourg (1758), Crown Point and Ticonderoga (1759) and Montreal (1760). He was made a field marshal and baron after his conquest of Canada.

Amherst, city in W Massachusetts; named for Baron Jeffrey Amherst. Home of Emily Dickinson, Helen Hunt Jackson, Eugene Field, Robert Frost, and Noah Webster; site of Amherst College, Hampshire College, and University of Massachusetts. Inc. 1759. Pop. (1970) 126,331.

Amiens, city in France, on Somme River, 72mi (116km) N of Paris; known as Samarobriva in pre-Roman times; became part of French crown lands in 1185. Taken by Germany during Franco-Prussian War, WWI and WWII; site of 13th-century Cathedral of Notre Dame, the largest church in France and one of the finest examples of Gothic architecture. Industries: machinery, chemicals, textiles. Pop. 117,888.

Amiens, Treaty of (1802), diplomatic agreement between Britain, France, Spain, and the Netherlands inaugurating a 14-month interval of peace during the Napoleonic wars. France recovered most of her colonies but evacuated Naples. Britain withdrew from Egypt but retained Trinidad and Ceylon. The insecure peace ended in May 1803. △1226.

Amin, Idi (*c.*1925–), president of Uganda (1971–). He joined the British army in the colony of Uganda and became commander of independent Uganda's army in 1966. He staged a military coup in 1971, overthrowing Milton Obote. In 1972 he expelled about 80,000 Asian Ugandans. In the same year he also withstood a pro-Obote attack from Tanzania. He was elected president of the Organization of African Unity in 1975. Both his personal behavior and political policies have been flamboyant and erratic.

Amine, member of a class of organic compounds derived from ammonia by replacing hydrogen atoms with organic groups. Methylamine, CH_3NH_2, is a primary amine (one hydrogen replaced). Replacement of two hydrogens gives a secondary amine and three hydrogens gives a tertiary amine. Amines have a characteristic ammoniacle odor: they are produced in the putrefaction of organic matter. Like ammonia they are weakly basic. *See also* Alkaloid.

Amino Acid, acid containing at least one carboxyl group (-COOH) and at least one amino group (NH_2). These acids are of great biological importance as they link together to form proteins. They have the general formula $R{\cdot}CH(NH_2)COOH$ and link together to form the peptide structure -NH-CO- by condensation of the -NH_2 group of one acid and the -COOH of another. Proteins are cross-linked polypeptides consisting of hundreds or thousands of amino acids. Some 20 amino acids occur in proteins; not all organisms are able to synthesize all of them. Essential amino acids

American saddle horse

American Staffordshire terrier

American water spaniel

Idi Amin, left, with Pope Paul VI

are those that an organisms has to obtain ready-made from its environment. There are 8 such essential amino acids for man. △1570–74.

Amis, Kingsley (1922–), English novelist. He was a university teacher of English until 1963 and draws on this in his novels. His novels include *Lucky Jim* (1954), *That Certain Feeling* (1955), *Take a Girl Like You* (1960), *One Fat Englishman* (1963), and *Ending Up* (1974).

Amish, conservative Protestant sect, members of the old order Amish Mennonite Church. Descendants of the followers of Jakob Ammann, a 17th-century Mennonite leader who advocated strict community conformity, they started arriving in E Pennsylvania *c.* 1720. Today about 70,000 Amish are dispersed in 50 or so communities in the United States and Canada. They live as simply and self-sufficiently as possible, shunning modern conveniences such as electricity and automobiles. *See also* Mennonites.

Amistad Case. In 1839, slaves, led by a man named Cinque, overpowered their owners on the *Amistad*, a Spanish slave ship. The ship landed in the United States and Abolitionists forced the case to the Supreme Court, where former Pres. John Quincy Adams argued for the slaves, who were set free in 1841.

Amman, capital city of Jordan, 50mi (81km) ENE of Jerusalem. In Biblical times it was the chief city of the Ammonites and known as Rabbath Ammon; rebuilt in *c.*200 BC by Ptolemy II Philadelphus and renamed Philadelphia; prospered after 30 BC as part of the Roman Empire. Chosen as the capital in 1921, it is the administrative, commercial, and transportation center of Jordan; site of University of Jordan (1962). Industries: textiles, tobacco, cement, leather. Pop. 570,000.

Ammeter, instrument for measuring electric current. In the most accurate type (moving coil) for direct current, the current to be measured passes through a coil suspended in a magnetic field, causing deflection of a needle attached to the coil. The other main type (moving iron) can be used with both direct and alternating current. In this the coil is fixed and the passage of the current causes two pieces of soft iron to become magnetized; the mutual repulsion between them causes a needle to move.

Ammonia, colorless nonflammable pungent gas (formula NH_3) manufactured by the Haber Process. It is the most important nitrogen compound because of its production in fixing nitrogen for fertilizers. The gas dissolves in water to form an alkaline solution: ammonium salts contain the ion NH_4^+. Properties: melt. pt. −107.86°F (−77.7°C); boil pt. −28.03°F (−3.35°C). △1558, 1568.

Ammonium Cyanate. △1560.

Ammonoid, any of an extinct group of shelled cephalopod mollusks. They are believed to be descended from the nautiloids (of which the pearly nautilus is the only surviving form). Common as fossils in marine rocks of Devonian to Cretaceous ages, ammonoid shells are either straight or coiled and served as protective as well as hydrostatic devices that could be adjusted by varying the air pressure for different water depths. The many chambers of which each is composed are joined by highly convoluted walls that appear as complex suture lines on the surface. △564.

Ammons, A(rchie) R(andolf) (1926–), US poet, b. Whiteville Township, N. C. *Expressions of Sea Level* (1964), his second book of poems, received critical acclaim. In 1973 he won the National Book Award in poetry for his *Collected Poems: 1951–1971* (1972).

Ammons, Eugene ("Gene") (1925–1974), US jazz tenor saxophonist and bandleader. He played with Billy Eckstine, Jimmy Dale, and his own group in the 1940s. He led his own jazz groups since the early 1950s and composed many jazz numbers, the most popular of which was "Red Top" (1947).

Ammunition. △1734, 1738.

Amnesia, loss of memory; more particularly, partial or complete inability to recall. When the amnesia is selective (only certain unpleasant memories are eliminated), it is usually psychogenic. Organically caused amnesias are usually unrelated to specific details of experience. In retrograde amnesia memory loss extends back in time from the point of onset (eg, a head injury).

Amnesty, official act of pardon granted by the head of government to violators of a national law. Amnesty may be absolute or conditional. If absolute, it absolves the violator of all offenses. If conditional, it stipulates the offender must meet certain obligations to obtain the pardon.

Amniocentesis. △738.

Amniotic Fluid, liquid filling the amnionic cavity which protects the fetus from injury. This fluid is released at delivery when the membranes rupture.

Amorphous Substance, solid substance in which the atoms or molecules have no regular order. Amorphous substances are noncrystalline; the term does not refer to outward appearance but to internal structure. Charcoal, lamp black, and similar forms of carbon are examples. Glasses are also amorphous; characteristically they have no definite melting point but soften over a temperature range, and may be regarded as supercooled liquids. △1506.

Amortization, in accounting, the systematic allocation of costs associated with intangible assets over periods during which benefits might reasonably be expected to accrue. Such things as copyrights, patents, and goodwill are examples of intangibles possessing the ability to generate income over extended periods of time. Proper matching of revenues with costs associated with the development of these intangible assets thus requires amortization.

Amos, biblical author and third of the 12 minor prophets. During the reign of Uzziah, King of Judah (*c.* 8th century BC), he criticized the wickedness of the Hebrews.

Amoy (Xiamen, or **Hsia-men),** seaport city in SE China, on Amoy and Ku-lang islands on Formosa Strait. An important port, it flourished after being opened for foreign trade (1842); because of its proximity to Taiwan, it had great strategic importance after Communists took control of Chinese mainland (1949). Pop. 400,000.

Ampère, André-Marie (1775–1836), French physicist, mathematician and prodigy. He was professor of chemistry and physics at Bourg and later mathematics professor at Ecole Polytechnique in Paris. The founder of electrodynamics (now called electromagnetism), he performed numerous experiments with currents and magnetism. He was the first to derive electricity measuring techniques, and he also constructed the precursor of the galvanometer. Ampère's law is a mathematical description of the magnetic force between two electric currents. His name is also commemorated in the unit of electric current measurement (ampere). *See also* Electrodynamics.

Ampere. △1532.

Amphetamines, drugs that stimulate the central nervous system. They are used in medicine to treat certain psychiatric disorders, to depress appetite in certain weight-loss cases, and in special circumstances where temporary stimulation and prevention of fatigue are absolutely necessary. The drugs, including Benzedrine and Dexedrine, popularly known as "pep pills," are an increasing drug-abuse problem. After the immediate stimulating effects wear off, the user can experience fatigue and depression. The drugs can also cause apprehension, insomnia, dizziness, headache, digestive disturbances, confusion and even psychotic episodes and convulsions. A particularly severe form of amphetamine abuse involves injecting the amphetamine (then called "speed").

Amphibia, class of terrestrial to aquatic vertebrates between fish and reptile on the evolutionary scale. Amphibians have smooth, slimy, moist skin with a network of blood vessels to aid in respiration. Most adults have limbs with digits. Body temperature is determined by environment. Because amphibian eggs are shell-less, they are laid in water or humid surroundings to prevent drying out. There is generally an aquatic larval stage. All adults are carnivorous, but larvae are frequently herbivorous. The class consists of three living orders: Caudata—salamander and siren (sometimes sirens are classified separately as Trachystomata); Anura or Salientia—frog and toad; and Apoda—wormlike caecilian. There are about 2500 living amphibian species. △518, 524.

Amphibious Aircraft, aircraft capable of taking off and landing on water or land, with a combination of either retractable wheels and boat-shaped hull or auxiliary landing gear and pontoons or floats. Such aircraft are often used in pleasure flying and forestry. △1682.

Amphibious Warfare, the strategy and tactics of employing sea-launched land forces against coastal military objectives. Seaborne assaults are used to bypass enemy defenses and seize key objectives and often serve as the prelude to major overseas land campaigns. Specialized amphibious equipment ranges from large helicopter carriers and tank landing ships, to small amphibious vehicles and assault boats.

Amphibole, any of some 30 complex rock-forming mineral varieties characterized by their double-chain silicate (SiO_4) structure. They all contain water (as OH ions) and usually Ca,Mg,Fe. Found in igneous and metamorphic rocks. Form wedge-shaped fragments on cleavage. Orthorhombic or monoclinic crystals often needle-like or fibrous. Common varieties are hornblende, tremolite, actinolite and anthophyllite. Some varieties are used in commercial asbestos.

Amphioxus, or **lancelet,** marine, fish-shaped animal living in coarse gravel on warm sea bottoms. It has a well-developed notochord, but no enlarged head region or brain; segmented body muscles; a pharynx with gill slits; rudimentary eyes; and tentacles around its mouth to strain food from water. Length: to 3in (8cm). There are 25 species. Subphylum Cephalochordata; genus *Branchiostoma*. △508.

Amphipod, or **scud,** mainly marine crustaceans, though some are freshwater and a few, such as the beach flea, are semi-terrestrial. They have laterally compressed bodies and two compound eyes. Some are parasitic. Length: .125–5.5in (.32–14cm).

Amphisbaenid, cylindrical, mostly legless, burrowing reptile found in tropical America and Africa. They resemble earthworms having rings of scales around their bodies and tails. They have no external ear openings and no left lung. Only a few have short front legs. Length: 12in (30cm). The worm lizard *Rhineura floridana* is found in Florida. Formerly considered lizards, the 100 species are now classified as a Squamata suborder. Family Amphisbaenidae. *See also* Lizard.

Amphitrite, in Greek mythology, the goddess of the sea, wife of Poseidon. She fled to Atlas after refusing Poseidon's proposal of marriage, but was returned to Poseidon by a dolphin. As a reward, he transformed it into the constellation Dolphin.

Amphitryon. *See* Alcmene.

Ampicillin, an antibiotic. *See* Antibiotic.

Amplification. △1548.

Amplifier, device for increasing the voltage (voltage amplifier) or the current (power amplifier) of an electrical signal. In both cases the energy required to amplify the signal is obtained from a source other than the signal. The amplification device formerly used was the triode (or pentode) electron tube, but tubes have been almost completely replaced by the lighter, smaller, and more economical transistor.

Amplitude Modulation (AM), process in which a signal wave (the modulating wave) alters the intensity (amplitude) of a carrier wave, in order to transmit information. Sidebands are produced above and below the carrier frequency relative to the signal's value. △1794.

Amplitude, Wave. *See* Wave Amplitude.

Ampulla. △676.

Amritsar, city in NW India; capital of Amritsar district in Punjab state; est by Ram Das, 4th Sikh Guru. Guru Arjan built the Golden Temple, located in the middle of a lake, which attracts many Sikh pilgrims; center of Sikh empire and religion. Industries: carpets, textiles, embroideries. Founded 1577. Pop. 430,783.

Amsterdam, capital and largest city in Netherlands; divided by Amstel River and linked to the North Sea by the North Sea Canal. Dutch East India Co. (1602) brought the city to a peak in prosperity and a great influx of European refugees. Its commerce and importance declined with capture by French 1795 and British blockade during Napoleonic Wars; surrendered to Germany in WWII; site of church (1334), 16th-century city hall, Royal Palace, National Museum (1808), Rembrandt's house; Olympic Games (1928); seat of University of Amsterdam (1632), Free Reformed University (1880). Industries: exporting, fishing, diamond cutting, iron, steel, railroad cars, sugar and oil refining, food processing, chemicals, glass, paper, rubber, ships, cars, aircraft. Chartered *c.* 1300. Pop. 820,406.

Amsterdam, city in E central New York on Mohawk River. Nearby is Fort Johnson, home of British colonial leader William Johnson. Industries: carpets, rugs, clothing, novelties. Settled 1783; inc. 1885. Pop. (1970) 25,524.

AMU. *See* Atomic Mass Unit.

Amu Darya (Jayhun), chief river in central Asia; rises in Pamir Mts; flows NW down Hindu Kush slopes into plain below Termez, USSR; forms boundary between Tadzhik SSR and NE Afghanistan; flows W and NW through E Turkmen SSR and W of Uzbek SSR, into swampy delta at Aral Sea. Chief tributaries are Vakhsh, Kafirnigan, Surkhab (N), and Kundūz (S). Ancient name was Oxus; crossed by Alexander in 328 BC; navigable for 930mi (1,497km). Length: approx. 1,600mi (2,576km).

Amulet, object or emblem worn to ward off danger, ensure good fortune, or increase personal power. A rabbit's foot or St. Christopher's medal is an amulet. *See also* Fetish.

Amun, or **Amon,** ancient Egyptian deity of reproduction or of the animating force. He is represented as a ram or as a ram-headed man, or a goose or snake, and often as a crowned king. Amun was worshiped at Thebes in the 12th dynasty, then later as a powerful national god renamed Amun-Ra, identified with the sun. Amun's temples are at Luxor, Karnak, and Thebes. *See also* Amun-Ra. △972.

Amundsen, Roald (1872–1928), Norwegian explorer and discoverer of the South Pole. From 1903–06, he sailed through the Northwest Passage and, from his observations, was able to locate the exact position of the North Magnetic Pole. His next expedition took him to the Antarctic, and in December 1911, one month ahead of Captain Robert Scott, another explorer, he reached the South Pole. In his later years, he conducted an exploration of the north polar regions by air (1926). Throughout most of his life, Amundsen was a well-known lecturer and writer. His books include *North West Passage* (1908), *The South Pole* (1912), *The North East Passage* (1918–20), and *My Life as an Explorer* (1927).

Amun-Ra (Amun-Re), in 18th-dynasty Egypt, the national god, patronized by the pharaohs. Amun of Thebes became identified with the old sun god Ra, and emerged as Amon-Ra, only to be cast down when Akhenaton proclaimed worship of the single god Aton, the solar disk, as the state religion. *See also* Amun.

Amur (Hei-lung Chiang), river in NE Asia, at Soviet-Chinese border, formed by confluence of Shilka and Argun rivers; flows SE forming 1,000-mi (1,611-km) border between Manchuria and Soviet Union subdivisions, then flows NE, through Far Eastern USSR, before entering N end of Tatar Strait, of the Pacific. Chief ports are Soviet cities Khabarovsk, Komsomolsk, Nikolayevsk. Valley region was settled by Russians 1847. Length: approx. 1,800mi (2,898km).

Amylase, digestive enzyme secreted by the salivary glands (salivary amylase, or ptyalin) and the pancreas (pancreatic amylase, or amylopsin). It aids in digestion by breaking down starch into simple sugars. △694.

Amyotrophic Lateral Sclerosis, or Gehrig's disease, a disease of middle life primarily affecting men, with no known cause, brought to public attention by its affliction of baseball player Lou Gehrig. Symptoms are gradual weakness and atrophy of the muscles of the hands, then arms and legs, with some spasticity. There is no known treatment.

Anabaptists, ancestors of today's Baptists, active during the Middle Ages. Seeking to maintain the purity of the early Christian churches, they insisted on rebaptism, as infant baptism is not in accord with the New Testament. Scripture, rather than the church, was held supreme. For four centuries, Anabaptists grew in numbers in Europe. *See also* Baptists.

Anabasis, Xenophon's account in seven books of the Greek expedition under Cyrus the Younger against Artaxerxes of Persia, and the subsequent retreat and adventures of the Greek mercenaries (401–399 BC). △998.

Anableps, or four eyes, freshwater fish found from S Mexico to N South America. A band of skin divides its eyes into halves for simultaneous vision above and below the water surface. Young (1–5) are born alive at one time. Length: 6–8in (15–20cm). Family Anablepidae; species *Anableps.*

Anabolism, constructive metabolic process that turns food into living tissue in living organisms. *See also* Metabolism. △1572.

Anaconda, South American snake, related to the boa. It is mainly aquatic, a good climber, and feeds on mammals and birds near riverbanks. Color is olive-green with black blotches and rings. Length: to 25ft (7.6m). Family Boidae; species *Eunectes murinus.* △522.

Anacoustic Zone, or "zone of silence," the region above 100 miles altitude where distance between air molecules becomes greater than the wavelength of sound, so that no sound waves can be propagated. With increasing height, high-frequency (short-wavelength) sounds disappear first, and only lower tones can be heard.

Anacreon (*c.* 572–488 BC), Greek author. His main themes were wine, love, and merry living. Expressive in style, he wrote lyrics, elegies, and epigrams. Little of his work has survived, although he was often imitated.

Anaerobe, an organism that cannot grow in the presence of free atmospheric oxygen. Bacteria of this type are a problem in canning since they can grow under vacuum.

Anagram, a word or group of words whose letters have been transposed to produce other words, as "time" and "mite" from the word "emit." A sophisticated anagram would be a transposition of letters producing a word or phrase that bears some logical relation to the original.

Anaheim, city in S California, 16mi (26km) E of Long Beach; site of Disneyland, Anaheim Stadium and Convention Center; 8th most populous city in Calif. Industries: electronic equipment, fruit canning, greeting cards. Founded in 1857 by Germans; inc. 1870. Pop. (1970) 166,408.

Anahita. △984.

Anal Character, in psychoanalytic theory, a personality influenced by what happened in the second, or anal, stage of development, when the child's interests center around bowel movements. According to Sigmund Freud and others, conflicts at this stage may result in a holding-back, stingy and excessively orderly personality—or in one that has destructive, messy, disorderly traits.

Analgesic, drug that relieves pain. It may be narcotic, such as morphine or cocaine, or it may be non-narcotic, such as the commonly used aspirin and acetanilid and phenacetin compounds. △744.

Analog Computer, computer that solves scientific and technical problems by accepting a set of continuously varying quantities, which reflect variations in the physical quantities under consideration, and that manipulates them, usually electronically, as required. *See also* Computer, Electronic.

Analogy, in literature, a method of verbal comparison, from a term originally used by the Greeks to mean similarity in proportional relationships (as A is to B, so C is to D). It is a method used to heighten illumination, as in comparing a known thing or circumstance to another, or in defense in argumentation.

Analytic Geometry, or coordinate geometry, branch of geometry in which a position is represented by numbers in some coordinate system, and lines, curves, and surfaces can be represented by algebraic equations. The geometric properties can then be studied by the methods of algebra. It was first introduced by René Descartes in the 17th century; analytic geometry in Cartesian coordinate systems is also called Cartesian geometry. *See also* Mathematics. △1454, 1472.

Anamorphic Painting. △1472.

Anaphylactic Shock. *See* Anaphylaxis.

Anaphylaxis, or **anaphylactic shock,** an acute, serious allergic reaction that occurs after a person eats, inhales, or is injected with a substance (antigen), such as penicillin, insect venom, or certain foods, to which he has been previously sensitized and against which he has developed antibodies. Second exposure to the offending substance can lead to paleness, faintness, palpitations, hives, swelling, difficulty in breathing, and, if untreated, shock.

Anarchism, political theory that regards all forms of government as evil, coercive, and unnecessary. Anar-

Amman, Jordan

Amsterdam: Oude Schans Canal

Roald Amundsen

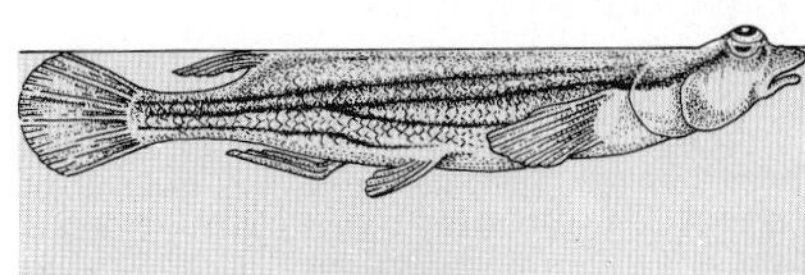

Anableps

chism advocates a social order based on liberty and voluntary cooperation. Zeno of Citium (*c.* 334–262 BC), the founder of stoicism, is regarded as the father of anarchism. In the 19th century Mikhail Bakunin advocated politically active, violent anarchism. Fear of anarchism, supposedly spread by foreign agitators, remained strong in the United States well into the 20th century. △1326.

Anastasia (*c.* 1901–?18), grand duchess of Russia, the youngest daughter of the last emperor, Nicholas II, presumably murdered together with other members of the royal family in July 1918. Since 1920, several women have claimed to be Anastasia, the legal heir to the Romanov fortune held in Swiss banks. None of the claimants has proven legitimate.

Anastasius I (430?–518), Byzantine emperor (491–518). Before accession to the throne, Anastasius had been a court official responsible for the improvement of the monetary system and for the reorganization of the tax collecting process. As emperor, his interest in financial management led to large increases in the state treasury. Anastasius' reign was characterized by numerous revolts.

Anastasius II (died 721), Byzantine emperor (713–15). A former civil servant brought to the throne by a military revolt, at his coronation he dropped his original name of Artemius and took that of his predecessor, Anastasius I, whom he wished to imitate. Civil war ended his brief reign, and Anastasius retired to a monastery.

Anat, chief West Semitic goddess of love and war, sister of the god Baal. She was noted for her ferocity in battle and her beauty. △978.

Anatolia. *See* Asia Minor.

Anatomy, that branch of biological science that studies the structure of an organism. The study of anatomy can be divided in several ways. On the basis of the size of the structures studied, there is gross anatomy, studying structures with the naked eye; microscopic anatomy, studying finer detail with a light microscope; submicroscopic anatomy, studying even finer structural detail with an electron microscope; and molecular anatomy, studying with sophisticated instruments the molecular makeup of structures. Microscopic and submicroscopic anatomy involve two closely related sciences: histology, the study of tissue that makes up a body organ, and cytology, the study of cells that make up a tissue. Anatomy can also be classified according to the organism or type of organism studied, for example, plant anatomy, invertebrate anatomy, vertebrate anatomy, human anatomy. Developmental anatomy, or embryology, is the study of the origin, development, and relationship of various body parts. The study of the structure of any body part is intimately connected with the function or activity of that organ, the study of which is physiology. *See also* Physiology. △662–695, 700–703.

Anatosaurus. *See* Trachodon.

Anaxagoras of Clazomene (*c.* 500–428 BC), Greek philosopher, the most important before Socrates. He was the teacher of Euripides, Pericles, and, possibly, Socrates. He believed that all matter was composed of "seeds" or minute particles. He explained the true cause of eclipses. Toward the end of his life he was exiled from Athens for his "impious" teaching that the sun was a white-hot stone and the moon was composed of earth and merely reflected the sun's rays.

Anaximander (611–547 BC), Greek scientist and philosopher credited as the author of the first geometric model of the universe. His fame rests chiefly on his doctrine of a single world-principle, the starting point and origin of the cosmic process, which he identified as *apeiron* or "the infinite." △1480.

Anaximenes, (fl.545 BC), member of the Milesian school of Greek philosophy, along with Anaximander and Thales. Attempting to resolve the problem of the origin and structure of the universe, he held the fundamental and most pervasive thing in the world to be air, which, being infinite, allows for the manifold processes of nature.

Ancestor Worship, worship and propitiation of the spirits of dead relatives. Ancestral spirits are worshiped to win benefits or avoid evils. Ancestor worship is based on the belief that spirits of the dead continue to live in the natural world and have the power to do good or evil. In the past, ancestor worship flourished in China, ancient Rome, and elsewhere, and it is still practiced in Melanesia. △1040.

Anchorage, seaport city, in S central Alaska, at head of Cook Inlet base of Kenai Peninsula, 470mi (757km) S of Fairbanks; state's oil supply center; location of army post, airport, salmon canneries; scene of severe earthquake (1964). Founded 1914. Pop. (1970) 48,081.

Anchovy, marine schooling fish found worldwide in temperate and tropical seas. Silvery fish with setback mouths, there are more than 100 species including the common Atlantic *Anchoa mitchilli.* Length: 5–9in (13–23cm). Family Engraulidae.

Ancient Mariner, The Rime of the (1798), by Samuel Taylor Coleridge, first published in *Lyrical Ballads.* Written in deceptively simple ballad style, the poem tells of a sailor who kills an albatross, the emblem of good luck, and brings the curse of nature upon himself and the crew.

Ancona, port city in central Italy, on the Adriatic Sea; capital of Ancona prov. Taken by Rome 2nd century BC, the city became a thriving port; it was under direct papal rule by 1532; French were dominant 1797–1816; became part of Italy 1860; allied bombing inflicted heavy damage during WWII. Industries: shipping, machinery, furniture. Founded *c.* 392 BC by Greeks from Syracuse. Pop. 108,326.

Ancre, Marquis d'. *See* Concini, Concino.

Andalusia, largest administrative region in S Spain, bounded by the Strait of Gibralter in the Mediterranean Sea (S), Portugal (W), Estremadura, New Castile, and Murcia provinces (N and E); divided into eight modern provinces 1833. Settled by Phoenicians 1100 BC, and taken by Romans 3rd century BC, it peaked under Moors 8th–13th centuries; fell to Nationalist forces during Spanish Civil War (1936–39). A popular resort area, it is a fertile region with large mineral deposits. Crops: wheat, corn, barley, grapes, olives, sugar, citrus fruit. Area: 33,675sq mi (87,218sq km). Pop. 5,971,277.

Andaman and Nicobar Islands, union territory in India, E of Bay of Bengal; island chain made up of the Andaman Islands (S) and Nicobar Islands (N); capital is Port Blair. The Andamans, consisting of about 175 islands, were used as British penal colony from 1858; the 19 Nicobar islands became a British possession in 1869. The two island groups were joined administratively in 1872 under British control until 1942 when occupied by Japan (1942–45); passed to India 1947. Exports: lumber, copra. Andaman Islands, area: 2,508sq mi (6,496sq km). Pop. 48,985. Nicobar Islands, area: 707sq mi (1,831sq km). Pop. 14,563.

Andaman Sea, branch of the Indian Ocean, in S Asia; bordered by Andaman and Nicobar Islands (W), Burma (N), Malay Peninsula (E), Sumatra (S); Rangoon, main port, is on the Gulf of Martaban, a NW inlet. Length: 600mi (966km). Width: 400mi (644km).

Andean Pact. △1352.

Andersen, Hans Christian (1805–75), Danish author of many fairy tales, notably "The Ugly Duckling," "The Little Mermaid," "Thumbelina," "The Swineherd," "The Emperor's New Clothes," "The Constant Tin Soldier," and "The Little Match Girl." The tales were first translated into English in 1846 by Mary Howitt, who called the book *Wonderful Stories for Children. See also* Fairy Tale.

Anderson, (Dame) Judith (1898–), Australian-born actress who, by 1924, had become famous for her portrayals of classical and modern roles. Made a dame of the British Empire in 1960, her stage roles include Lady Macbeth (her London debut, 1937, with Lawrence Olivier) and Medea (1947). On film she appeared in *Rebecca* (1940) and *Cat on a Hot Tin Roof* (1958).

Anderson, Marian (1902–), US contralto, b. Philadelphia. She established her reputation as a singer touring America and Europe in recitals (1925–35). Forbidden in 1939 by the Daughters of the American Revolution to perform at Constitution Hall, Washington, D.C., she was sponsored by Eleanor Roosevelt in a concert at the Lincoln Memorial. She made her Metropolitan Opera debut in 1955 as Ulrica in Verdi's *Un Ballo in Maschera,* marking the first appearance of a black singer in a leading role at the opera hall.

Anderson, Maxwell (1888–1959), US dramatist, b. Atlantic, Pa. At first a journalist, he turned full time to playwriting with the success of *What Price Glory?* (1924), an antiwar comedy written with Laurence Stallings. In 1933 he won a Pulitzer Prize for *Both Your Houses,* a satire on the US Congress. He wrote a number of plays in verse, most successfully *Winterset* (1935), a tragedy based on the Sacco-Vanzetti case, and *High Tor* (1937), a romantic comedy. He also wrote many historical dramas including *Elizabeth the Queen* (1930) and *Valley Forge* (1934). He wrote the librettos for the Kurt Weill musicals *Knickerbocker Holiday* (1938) and *Lost in the Stars* (1940).

Anderson, Robert (1805–71), Union general in the Civil War, b. near Louisville, Ky. In April 1861, he was a major commanding about 80 men at Ft. Sumter, S.C., when Confederates attacked and cut off relief from Washington, D.C. After withstanding a two-day bombardment (April 12–13), he had to surrender.

Anderson, Sherwood (1876–1941), US short story writer and novelist, b. Camden, Ohio. He wrote about life in the Midwest, achieving fame with *Winesburg, Ohio* (1919). Other works include *Dark Laughter* (1925) and *Beyond Desire* (1933).

Anderson, city in E central Indiana, 17mi (27km) WSW of Muncie, on the White River; seat of Madison co; natural gas discovered 1887; site of Anderson College (1917); rich farm area. Industries: automobile accessories, paper board products, Inc. 1865. Pop. (1970) 70,787.

Anderson, city in NW South Carolina; seat of Anderson co; commercial center for surrounding farms. Industries: textiles, sewing machines. Settled 17th century; inc. 1828. Pop. (1970) 27,556.

Andersonville Prison, historic prison in Andersonville, SW Georgia; used by the Confederacy to confine Union prisoners. Harsh conditions led to death of 12,000 soldiers. Est. 1970 as a national historic site. Area: 495 acres (200 hectares).

Andes, mountain range in South America, along Caribbean and Pacific coasts; extends through Venezuela, Colombia, Ecuador, Peru, Bolivia, Chile, and Argentina; one of the world's longest and highest mt ranges; formerly inhabited by the Incas. Aconcagua, in Argentina, is the highest peak, 22,835ft (6,965m). Hazardous air currents, rough terrain, and low temperatures have made transportation and communication extremely difficult. Most of its inhabitants have depended on subsistence farming and mineral products. Mineral exploitation is a major commercial concern of Andean countries. Length: 5,000mi (8,050km).

Andesite, named for a type of lava common in the Andes Mountains, an extrusive igneous rock similar to rhyolite in structure and similar to diorite in its composition. It contains feldspar and ferromagnesian minerals. *See also* Igneous Rocks.

Andorra, small state situated high in the E Pyrenees between France and Spain. Although the several high mountain valleys have poor soil, they support large flocks of sheep. The increasing tourist trade supplements the traditional livestock raising. Andorra La Vieja is the main town; the people are Catalan-speaking and Roman Catholic. Area: 179sq mi (464sq km). Pop. 20,550.

Andover, town in NE Massachusetts, 9mi (15km) E of Lowell; site of Phillips Academy (1778), Abbott Academy (1829), Benjamin Abbott Homestead (1685); Harriet Beecher Stowe is buried here; in 1832, Samuel Francis Smith wrote words to "America" here. Industries: rubber goods, guided missiles, chemicals, protective coatings. Founded 1643; inc. 1646. Pop. (1970) 23,695.

Andrássy, (Count) Gyula (1823–90), Hungarian statesman and diplomat. An ardent nationalist, he joined the abortive rebellion of 1848 against Austria and escaped execution by remaining in exile until 1857. When the dual monarchy was formed, he became first prime minister for Hungary (1867). From 1871 to 1879, he was minister of foreign affairs for the Austro-Hungarian Empire, which he represented at the Congress of Berlin in 1878. His plan for Austria, occupation of Bosnia and Herzegovina, was accepted by the powers. His son was also a Hungarian diplomat.

André, (Major) John (1751–80), English military officer executed by the Americans for working with Benedict Arnold during the Revolution. He was caught by American soldiers as he returned from negotiations with Arnold. Secret papers were found in his boot, and a board of American officers found him guilty of spying and condemned him to death by hanging.

Andrea da Firenze (*c.* 1337–77), Italian fresco painter, also known as Andrea di Bonaiuti. His work is marked by a narrative element and somewhat rigid composition. A follower of Giotto, Firenze's most im-

ortant works are in the church of Sta. Maria Novella
ı Florence.

.ndretti, Mario Gabriel (1940–), US automobile acer, b. Italy. He was a three-time winner of the US ›utomobile Club championship (1965–66; 1969) nd a winner of the Indianapolis 500 (1969).

Andrew, in the New Testament, son of Jonah, rother of Simon Peter, and one of the first disciples f Jesus.

.ndrić, Ivo (1892–1975), Yugoslav writer. He was nprisoned during World War I for nationalist political ctivities. Later he joined the Yugoslav diplomatic serice. He wrote short stories and poems but is best nown for his novels *The Bridge on the Drina* and *Bosnian Story* (both 1945). He was awarded the Nobel Prize for literature in 1961.

Androcles, Roman slave supposed to have lived *c.* .D 20, who ran away from his master and hid in a cave. He took a thorn from the paw of a suffering lion. Later Androcles faced the same lion in the Roman Arena. The lion recognized Androcles and refused to harm im.

Androgen, general name for masculinizing hornones secreted principally by the testes. *See also* Testosterone.

Andromeda, evergreen shrub of the heath family, with narrow leaves and pink, bell-shaped flowers. △32.

Andromeda Galaxy (M 31; NGC 224), great spiral galaxy in Andromeda, the nearest major external gal·xy to our own Milky Way system. It is larger than the Milky Way Galaxy, but resembles it closely, and also possesses satellite systems similar to the Magellanic Clouds. Distance 2,000,000 light years. *See also* Spiral Galaxy. △104, 112, 120.

Andronicus I Comnenus (1110?–1185), Byzantine emperor (1183–85). Andronicus attained the throne at the age of 65, after murdering his nephew Alexius II Comnenus and marrying the boy's 13-year-old widow Agnes-Anna, daughter of the French King Louis VII. Though his political goals were praiseworthy (he wished to reduce the power of the nobles and to minimize corruption in government), they were carried out with violence and brutality.

Andronicus II Palaeologus (1260–1332), Byzantine emperor (1282–1328). Andronicus inherited an exhausted empire, and his reign was characterized by military disaster, economic decline, and political catastrophe.

Andronicus III Palaeologus (1296?–1341), Byzantine emperor (1328–41). The revolt of Andronicus III against his grandfather Andronicus II (which gained the former his throne) was the first in a costly series of civil wars that hastened the internal collapse of the Byzantine Empire.

Andronicus IV Palaeologus, Byzantine emperor (1376–79). Andronicus gained the throne when, with the help of the Genoese, he deposed his father John V Palaeologus.

Andros, (Sir) Edmund (1637–1714), British colonial governor. He served as proprietary governor of New York (1674–81), and became the royal governor of the Dominion of New England (1686–89) ruling all the colonies north of New Jersey. He was also lieutenant governor of Virginia (1692–97).

Androsterone, steroid hormone with masculinizing effects. It is obtained from the testes and from male urine and controls the growth and function of male sexual organs and the production of secondary male sexual characteristics, such as the growth and distribution of hair.

Anechoic Chamber, or dead room, room designed to be echo-free so that it can be used in acoustic laboratories to measure sound reflection and transmission. The walls, floor, and ceiling must be insulated and all surfaces covered with an absorbent material, such as asbestos fiber, often over inward-pointing pyramid shapes to reduce reflection. To reduce standing waves the room is usually asymmetrical. *See also* Echo.

Anemia, an abnormal condition in which there is a decrease in the amount of the pigment hemoglobin in the red blood cells or a decrease in the number of red blood cells. Anemia may be caused by excessive blood loss, by a decrease in production of hemoglobin or red blood cells, or by excessive destruction of hemoglobin or red blood cells. Symptoms of anemia include fatigue, weakness, pallor, often vague gastrointestinal signs, and if the anemia is severe, faintness and palpitations. There are several types of anemia. In *iron-deficiency anemia* hemoglobin production is deficient because of a deficiency in the iron necessary for hemoglobin production. It is most commonly caused by chronic blood loss—from a minor disorder such as hemorrhoids or from serious diseases such as ulcers or cancer. *Pernicious anemia* is an impairment of the body's ability to absorb vitamin B_{12}, a vitamin necessary for normal red blood cell maturation. Deficiencies in other substances, such as folic acid or other B vitamins, may also decrease red blood cell production. In the *hemolytic anemias* there is excessive destruction of red blood cells. Such destruction may be due to hereditary abnormalities (such as sickle-cell anemia) or from nonhereditary conditions such as drug reactions or the production of antibodies to one's own red blood cells. Bone marrow is the site of red blood cell production and diseases of the bone marrow, due to radiation, drugs or chemicals, cancer, etc., may also produce anemia. *See also* Sickle-cell Anemia. △716.

Anemometer, an instrument using rotating cups, vanes, or propellers to measure the speed or force of the wind; wind or weather vanes indicate the direction from which the wind comes. △218.

Anemone, or pasqueflower, perennial plant found worldwide. It has sepals resembling petals and numerous stamens and pistils covering a central knob. Two or three deeply toothed leaves appear in a whorl midway up the stem. Many are wildflowers, including the North American wood anemone *(Anemone quinquefolia),* a low delicate plant with five sepals; Japanese anemone *(Anemone japonica),* an autumn-blooming species grown in gardens; and pasqueflower *(Anemone patens),* with large white or blue flowers appearing before the foliage. There are 150 species. Family Ranunculaceae. *See also* Buttercup.

Anesthesia, state of insensibility or loss of sensation produced by disease or various anesthetics used during surgical procedures. During general, or total, anesthesia the entire body becomes insensible and the individual sleeps; in local anesthesia only a specific part of the body is rendered insensible and the patient remains conscious. Local anesthetics, such as spinals, are injected into the spinal fluid and cause loss of sensation to part of the spinal area or the entire area below the injection level; nerve blocks affect only the pathway of a particular nerve; and others affect only small areas, such as the nose or bladder. Well-known anesthetic agents include nitrous oxide, a weak agent also called laughing gas; cyclopropane, a strong and widely used agent; ether and chloroform, volatile agents once widely used but now largely replaced; injected barbituate agents for short, relatively painless procedures; and relaxants for relaxing muscles for proper surgical manipulation. All anesthetic agents can produce undesirable and even dangerous effects and the choice, dose, and effects of each agent must be carefully considered for each patient. △752, 754.

Anesthesiology, branch of medicine involving the use of anesthetic agents to prevent pain during surgical and other procedures and care of the anesthetized patient. △752, 754.

Aneto, Pico de, highest peak in the Pyrenees in NE Spain, in the Maladeta group, S of the French border. Height: 11,168ft (3,406m).

Aneurysm, localized saclike enlargement of an artery, most commonly the aorta. It is caused by weakening of the artery wall and produces pain and pressure on surrounding tissues and hemorrhage if it ruptures. △722.

Angara, river in SE Siberian USSR; flows from SW end of Lake Baikal, N past Irkutsk and Bratsk, then W into Yenisei River. A source of hydroelectric power, river's large drainage basin has iron, coal, and gold deposits. River is also known as Upper Tunguska in its lower course. Length: approx. 1,150mi (1,852km).

Angel Falls, waterfall in SE Venezuela, in the Guiana Highlands; highest uninterrupted waterfall in world, 3,212ft (980m).

Angelfish, marine reef fish found in shallow tropical waters. Its deep body is laterally compressed and marked and colored brightly. Length: to 2ft (61cm). Family Chaetodontidae; species includes yellow and blue Queen *Holacanthus ciliaris.*

Angelico, Fra (1400–55), Italian painter, b. Guido di Pietro. His works of religious subjects, mostly tradi-

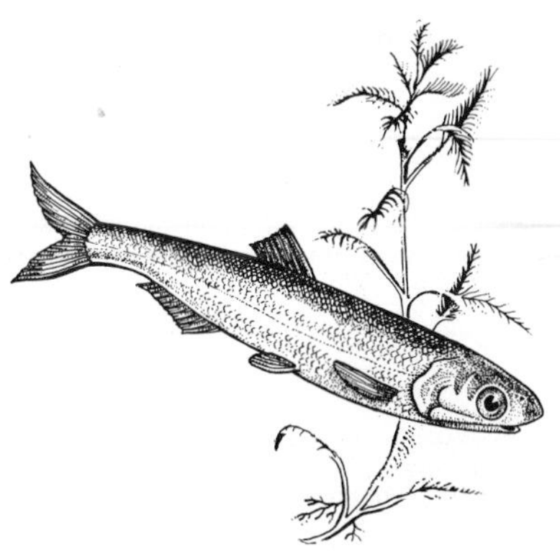

Anchovy

Marian Anderson

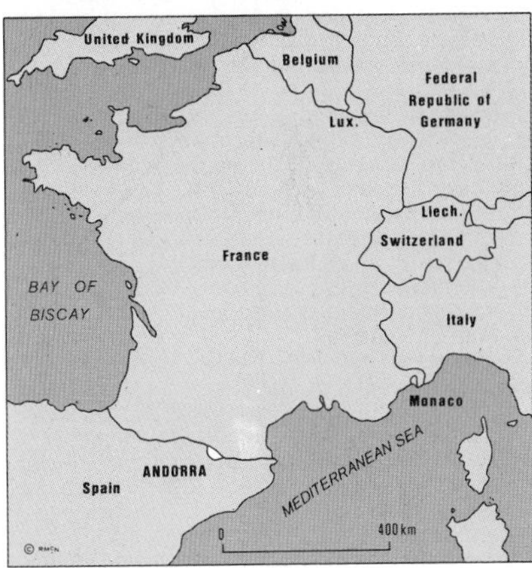
United Kingdom
Belgium
Federal Republic of Germany
Lux.
Liech.
Switzerland
France
BAY OF BISCAY
Italy
Monaco
ANDORRA
Spain
MEDITERRANEAN SEA
0
400km

Andorra

Angelfish

tional altarpieces, reflect a strong classical influence. He became a Dominican monk around 1421, and much of his work consisted of mural painting in the monastery of S. Marco in Florence, which he entered in 1439. His most famous work is a series of 35 paintings for the doors of a silver chest in the church of SS. Annunziata, Florence.

Angell, (Sir) Norman (1872–1967), English economist and worker for world peace, who was awarded the Nobel Peace Prize in 1933. His best known work is *The Great Illusion* (1910), an antiwar book which theorizes that if there were greater awareness of the economic ravages of war, fewer wars would be initiated.

Anger, human emotion ranging in intensity from annoyance to rage, usually evoked by a threatening but nonfeared stimulus, and often leading to aggression. *See also* Aggression; Emotion.

Angers, city in France, on the Marne River, 165mi (266km) SW of Paris; capital of Maine-et-Loire dept.; called Julio-Magus in Roman times. Invaded by Norse in 9th century, and by the English in 12th and 15th centuries; Huguenots took city in 1585; site of 12th-century Cathedral of St Maurice, and slate quarries. Industries: liqueur distillation, leather goods, rope. Pop. 128,533.

Angers Tapestries. △1104.

Angevins, medieval dynasty that became the Plantagenets, a line of English kings begun when Henry II (Count of Anjou) ascended the throne in 1154. The Angevins retained the crown until 1399.

Angina Pectoris, type of heart disease characterized by a distinctive anxiety-producing pain or feeling of tightness in the chest or back, often extending to the arm and sometimes to the jaw area or other parts of the body. It is often precipitated by walking outdoors, exposure to cold or wind, or emotional excitement. It is caused by a temporary decrease in blood and oxygen to a part of the heart, usually as a result of a narrowing or closure of a coronary artery. It is treated symptomatically, most often with nitroglycerine. Any underlying causes are corrected if possible. △716.

Angioma, common, localized lesion of the skin and underlying tissue caused by enlargement of blood or lymph vessels. So-called portwine stains and strawberry marks are types of angiomas.

Angiosperms, flowering plants that have seeds enclosed in an ovary. There are more than 250,000 species of angiosperms, including the majority of garden plants and most deciduous shrubs and trees. All existing seed-bearing plants are divided into two groups: angiosperms and gymnosperms (conifers and their relations), which have seeds borne on open scales. Angiosperms occur in every land area of the earth and are abundant in rivers and freshwater lakes. *See also* Gymnosperm.

Angkor, ancient site in NW Cambodia, covering an area of 40sq mi (104sq km); contains ruins of several capitals of the Khmer Empire, which flourished for six centuries; first capital founded by Yasovarman I, centered around the temple of Phnom Bak Kheng; site of the Angkor Wat (temple) complex (1113–50), one of the largest structures of worship in the world. Angkor Thom, the last capital (12th–13th centuries), centered around the Bayon, a Buddhist temple; site was abandoned 1434. Discovered by French 1860. △1114.

Angle, measure of the inclination of two straight lines or planes to each other. One complete revolution is divided into 360 degrees or 2π radians. One degree may be subdivided into 60 minutes, and one minute into 60 seconds. △1464.

Anglerfish, marine fish found in temperate and tropical seas. It is characterized by movable rod with lure (actually a modified ray of the dorsal fin) positioned on the head to attract prey. Most have a flattened head and wide mouth with hanging flaps of skin fringing the body. The 225 species include goosefish, monkfish, batfish, and frogfish. Order Lephiiformes. △510, 626.

Angles, a Germanic tribe from a district now called Angeln in Schleswig-Holstein. In the 5th century, with neighboring tribes, the Jutes and Saxons, they invaded England, settling in Mercia, Northumbria, East and Middle Anglia. Tacitus (1st century AD) described them as worshippers of the Scandinavian deity Nerthus. Bede, in *Ecclesiastical History* (731), described their conquest. The name England derives from their name (Angle-Land).

Anglesite, a sulfate mineral, lead sulfate ($PbSO_4$). Usually found together with cerussite in hydrothermal veins as an alternation product of galena. Orthorhombic system tabular or prismatic crystals; also massive or stalactitic. Colorless, white or gray; hardness 2.-5–3; sp gr 6.4.

Anglicanism, beliefs in accordance with the teachings of the Church of England. It has been identified as the "Anglican Communion" since the 19th century. Developing since Henry VIII's separation from the Roman Catholic Church (1534), it is based on scriptural and ecclesiastical authority. The governing function is episcopal, and worship is liturgical. Elements of both Roman Catholicism and Protestantism are contained in the theology.

Anglo-Japanese Alliance. △1272.

Anglo-Saxon Architecture (*fl.* 449–1066), architectural style found in several small churches in the southeast and north of England and characterized by long and short stonework, square apses, either aisles or side chambers called *porticus*, pilaster strips, and distinctive timber work. Anglo-Saxon architecture is difficult to distinguish from the Roman ruins it was often built on or from, and many wooden structures are lost. △1098.

Anglo-Saxon Chronicle, main source of British history of the Anglo-Saxon period. Compiled in the late 9th century, it traces the history of Britain from the Roman Conquest to the reign of Alfred the Great.

Anglo-Saxons, peoples of Germanic origin who settled in England beginning in the mid-5th century, supplanting the Celts. The term itself was first used in the early 9th century to distinguish the Saxon settlers in England from the Old Saxons of northern Germany. After the Norman Conquest (1066) "Anglo-Saxon" became synonymous with "English."

Angola, independent nation in W Africa. Also known as Portuguese West Africa until 1975 independence, it is a Bantu nation rich in oil, coffee, and diamonds. It has been torn by a nationalist civil war.

Land and economy. Located in both the equatorial and tropical climate zone, it is divided into two sections: Angola proper is S of the Congo River, bordered by Zaire (N and NW), Zambia (E), Namibia (South West Africa) (S), and the Atlantic Ocean (W). The exclave of Cabinda, a rain forest, is separated from Angola by Zaire. Central Angola is largely the Bie plateau, 3,000–5,000ft (915–1,525m) above sea level; hydroelectric power is generated by the plateau's falls and rapids. The Mocamedes Desert is in the S. Main rivers are the Cuanza and Cunene; Luanda and Lobito are the principal ports. Varying altitudes, cold ocean currents, and low rainfall result in a tropical N and semi-arid S. The most important economic development came with the 1966 discovery of oil off Cabinda and expansion of the Cassinga iron mines. Coffee is the main cash crop, and diamonds are a principal industry.

People. Angolans are almost entirely Bantu black Africans divided into four tribes: Ovimbundu (33%), Bankongo (24%), Kimbundu (25%), and Chokwe (8%). A version of Bantu is spoken by most tribes; Portuguese is common to the country. Roman Catholicism is the state religion; many tribes have their own beliefs. The literacy rate is 15%.

Government. Warfare has divided Angola into three insurrection groups: the Revolutionary Government of Angola in Exile, the Popular Movement for the Liberation of Angola, and the National Union for Total Independence of Angola.

History. Portuguese explorer Diego Cao landed in 1483, befriending the African kingdom. Portugal remained in power, with the exception of the 1641–48 Dutch occupation. Angola was a primary source of slaves for Brazilian plantations in the New World. After WWII nationalist Angolans sought autonomy, and uprisings continued until a new Portuguese government offered independence in 1975. Soviet-backed forces and Cubans overcame Western-backed factions. The savage civil war caused most of the whites to leave the country, the economy to decline, and a secession move by Cabinda. The country officially became independent on Nov. 11, 1975. By 1976 the Soviet-supported MPLA (Movemento Popular de Libertacão de Angola) controlled the government and most of the land area.

PROFILE

Official name: Angola
Area: 481,351sq mi (1,246,700sq km)
Population: 6,400,000
Density: 13per sq mi (5per sq km)
Chief cities: Luanda (capital); Nova Lisboa; Lobito
Government: Transitional (nationalist military parties)
Religion: Roman Catholic (state religion) and loc cults
Language: Portuguese (national)
Monetary unit: Escudo
Gross national product: $2,980,000,000
Per capita income: $492
Industries: food processing, bottling and brewin cement, glass, paper, cotton, footwear, soap
Agriculture: coffee, corn, sugar, cotton, wheat, t bacco, sisal, fish, cattle
Minerals: diamonds, petroleum, iron, copper, ma ganese, sulphur, phosphates
Trading partners: Portugal, Federal Republic of Ge many, United States, United Kingdom

Angola Pitta. △598.

Angora Cat, long-haired domestic cat breed wit round head, short body, short tail, and short, stron legs. It is also called Turkish and Ankara cat after i place of origin. Its large eyes are wide-set—one is blu and one is yellow. Not a Persian, its silky fine coat usually white. Smoke and Black varieties have yello eyes. A purebred Angora is usually deaf.

Angora Goat, domestic goat native to Turkey, no found worldwide. Its body is covered with long, silk hair (mohair) important in the textile industry. *Se also* Goat.

Angostura. *See* Ciudad Bolívar.

Angostura Bark, bark of a South American tre *Galipia officinalis,* known also as cusparia bark. It ha been used in the past to treat fevers, but is now use as an aromatic bitter.

Angra Mainyu. *See* Ahriman.

Angry Young Men, term applied to a group of Bri ish writers in the 1950s, taken from Leslie Allen Paul' autobiography *Angry Young Man* (1951) and popula ized through John Osborne's play *Look Back in An ger* (1956). All the writers and their heroes shared working- or lower-middle class background and a re bellious attitude toward British society. Besides Os borne, other writers identified with the group includ Kingsley Amis, John Braine, Alan Sillitoe, and Joh Wain.

Angstrom, Anders Jon (1814–74), Swedish astror omer and physicist, one of the founders of the scienc of spectroscopy. In 1861 he began to use the spectrc scope and photographic plates to study the solar sys tem. His experiments proved that the sun contain hydrogen, and in 1869 he was able to map the entir solar spectrum. Units of the wavelength of light ar named for him (angstrom unit).

Angstrom Unit, or Angstrom, unit of length, equa to 10^{-10} meter or 0.1 nanometer, used to express the wavelength of light and ultraviolet radiation, intera tomic and intermolecular distances, etc. Symbol: A △1502.

Anguilla, island in British West Indies; one of Lee ward Islands, 60mi (97km) NW of St Christopher; par of St Christopher Nevis-Anguilla group, associatec with Great Britain. Anguilla left the union in 1967 claiming political and economical discrimination, bu returned in 1971. Industries: tourism, livestock, min ing, fishing. Area: 35sq mi (91sq km). Pop. 6,000.

Angular Acceleration, rate of change of angula velocity. Average angular acceleration of a body whose angular velocity changes from ω_1 to ω_2 over a time t is $(\omega_2-\omega_1)/t$. Instantaneous angular accelera tion is value approached by ω as t becomes small. The direction of the angular acceleration vector is perpen dicular to the plane of motion. The tangential acceler ation a_T of a particle at a distance r from a fixed poin is directly proportional to the magnitude of its angular acceleration: $a_T = r\omega$.

Angular Distance, in astronomy, apparent distance on the celestial sphere between two celestial bodies measured along an arc of a great circle passing through them with the observer at the center. Angula distance of the Pointers (Ursa Major) is 5°.

Angular Momentum, the product of the moment of inertia I and angular velocity ω of a body or system of particles. Usually denoted by **L,** angular momentum is a vector quantity that is conserved (remains constant) at all times.

Angular Velocity, the rate of change of a body's angular position relative to a fixed point. Average angular velocity $\bar{\omega}$ of a body moving from angle θ_1 to θ_2 in time t is $(\theta_2 - \theta_1)/t$. Instantaneous angular velocity ω is the value approached by $\bar{\omega}$ in succeeding stants (mathematically, as t goes to zero). The direc-on associated with the angular velocity of a body is erpendicular to the plane of its motion. The speed of a body at a distance r from a fixed point is directly roportional to the magnitude ω of its angular veloc-y: $v = r\omega$. *See also* Velocity.

nhalt, historical region of central East Germany, E lower Harz Mountains; includes the present states Saxony and Brandenburg. Until 1918, when it ined the Weimar Republic, it was ruled by one of the ost ancient houses of Germany; a part of E Germany nce WWII.

nhinga. *See* Snakebird.

nhwei (Anhui), prov. in E central China divided by Van Mts into two areas: N is an extensive plain area ith limited agriculture due to cold winters; S has a ub-tropical climate and produces tea. Capital is ofei, 90mi (145km) W of Nanking. Industries: steel, on, coal, copper, rice, Hsuan paper, India ink. Area: 4,015sq mi (139,899sq km). Pop. 35,000,000.

nhydride, chemical compound derived from a spec-ed compound by abstraction of water. Thus sulfur ioxide, SO_3, is the anhydride of sulfuric acid: it reacts ith water thus, $SO_3 + H_2O \rightarrow H_2SO_4$. The organic nhydrides contain the group -CO-O-CO- and give car-oxylic acids with water: acetic anhydride, for exam-le, gives acetic acid thus, $CH_3CO{\cdot}O{\cdot}COCH_3 + H_2O \rightarrow CH_3COOH$. △1558.

nhydrite, a sulfate mineral, calcium sulfate ($CaSO_4$), sually found in sedimentary rocks associated with alt beds. Readily takes up water from gypsum. Crys-allizes in orthorhombic system, usually forming mas-ive deposits. Colorless when pure; glassy or pearly uster; hardness 3–3.5; sp gr 3. *See also* Gypsum.

niline, colorless oily liquid (formula $C_6H_5NH_2$) made y reduction of nitrobenzene. It is an important start-ng material for making organic compounds, particu-arly dyestuffs. Properties: sp. gr. 1.02; melt. pt. 0.66°F (−6.3°C); boil. pt. 363.43°F (184.13°C). *See lso* Amine. △1560.

nimal, living organism of the animal kingdom, dis-nguishable from members of the plant kingdom by haracteristics such as the power of locomotion, well-efined body shape, limited growth, and inability to roduce own food. Higher animals, such as the verte-rates, are easily distinguished from plants, but sim-ler forms are more difficult. Some one-celled organ-sms could be assigned to either category. Protozoa, ponges, jellyfish, segmented worms, arthropods, nollusks, echinoderms, and chordates are the major hyla.

nimal Behavior. △464, 536, 556–58.

nimal Classification, systematic grouping of ani-nals into categories based on shared characteristics. The first major classification was by Aristotle. The nethod now used was devised by Carolus Linnaeus, Swedish botanist, in the 1750s. All modern classifi-cation is based upon evolutionary relationships.

Of a two-part Latin name, the first part indicates genus, the second, species. A species is composed of animals capable of interbreeding in nature. A genus ncludes all similar and related species. The family takes in all like genera, and an order all related fami-ies. Similar orders are grouped in a class and related classes make up a phylum. Twenty separate phyla comprise the Animal Kingdom. For example, Dog: phylum Chordata; class Mammalia; order Carnivora; family Canidae; genus *Canis;* and species *familiaris. See also* Animal. △458.

Animal Farm (1946), allegorical fable by George Or-well about the Russian Revolution and the develop-ment of the Soviet Union. The animals of Manor Farm evict their brutal owners, are governed by pigs, and suffer increasingly under a police state.

Animal Husbandry, division of agriculture con-cerned with selection, breeding, production, manage-ment, and marketing of farm animals. The primary subjects of animal husbandry are beef and dairy cat-tle, hogs, sheep, horses, and poultry. Factors affecting animal husbandry include acreage, soil, market loca-tion, feed availability, state of markets, and climate. △370–372.

Animism, belief that the universe is filled with spirits capable of exerting a malignant or beneficial effect. Every natural object and phenomenon, whether tree, stream, or storm, is regarded as possessing life, con-sciousness, and a spirit. When animals and plants die their spirits live on, and, if an animal is killed improp-erly, its spirit can inflict harm. These beliefs are wide-spread in primitive religions. *See also* Fetish; Mana; Shaman; Taboo; Totem.

Anion. *See* Ion.

Anise, annual herb native to Egypt and widely cul-tivated for its small, ridged licorice-flavored seeds. It has small white flowers. Height: to 2.5ft (76cm). Fam-ily Umbelliferae; species *Pimpinella anisum. See also* Carrot.

Anjou, region and former province of W France, bounded N by Maine River, E by Touraine, SE by Saumurols, S by Poiton, and W by Brittany; under control of England in 1154, Italy in 1246, and a suc-cession of counts; Louis XI annexed it to French crown in 1480. An agricultural area known for its Vouvray and Saumur wines, it is watered by the Loire River.

Ankara, formerly Angora; capital city of Turkey and of Ankara prov., in W central Turkey, at junction of Cubuk and Ankara rivers; processing and agricultural trade center, on railroad line, especially noted for an-gora wool and mohair production; site of University of Ankara (1946), Middle East Technical University (1956), Hacettepe University (1967), and airport. An-cient town (Ancyra) was important commercial center, becoming Roman provincial capital (Galatia Prima); flourished under Augustus; captured by Tamerlane 1402. Ankara declined until establishment of Turkish national government there 1920. Industries: textiles, foodstuffs, cement and tiles, leather goods, metal works. Pop. 1,162,000.

Ankylosaurus, armored ornithischian dinosaurs of Cretaceous age (71–136 million years ago) of W United States and Canada. A low-set herbivore with short, massive legs and hooved feet, its leathery skin covering on its back and sides was armor-plated with bony nodules and plates arranged in geometric rows. Its tail ended in a bony club much like the head of a mace. Length: 15ft (5m); width: 6ft (1.8m); height: 4ft (1.2m). △570.

Ankylosis. △712.

Ann, Cape, peninsula on NE Massachusetts coast, 30mi (48km) NE of Boston; noted for tourist resorts, artist colonies of Rockport and Annisquam, and his-toric fishing village of Gloucester; Samuel de Cham-plain visited area 1605; settled 1623.

Annaba, formerly Bône; seaport and dept. capital in NE Algeria, at the E foot of the Edough Range. City was founded by Carthaginians, flourished as wealthy Roman port of Hippo Regius until *c.* AD 300 and was plundered by Vandals 431; rebuilt by Arabs in 7th century; center of Christianity and home of St Augus-tine, 396–430. Industries: phosphates, chemicals, cork, barley, ironworks. Pop. 150,161.

Anna Ivanovna (1693–1740), Russian tsarina (1730–40), daughter of Ivan V and niece of Peter the Great. She was called to the throne by a group of nobles. Her lover, Ernst Biron, influenced the reac-tionary policies of her reign. Political terror, German influence at court, and her oppression of the peasants made her an unpopular ruler.

Anna Karenina (1873–76), realist novel by Count Leo Tolstoi in which he explores the themes of mar-riage, social order, and responsibility. The passionate but adulterous and ultimately ruinous love affair be-tween Anna Karenina and Count Vronsky is con-trasted with the conventional marriage of Levin and Kitty.

Annales. △1028.

Annam (Anam), former kingdom on E coast of Indo-china, that now lies within the country of Vietnam; N boundary is 1954 demilitarized zone and dividing line of N and S Vietnam republics; extends 800mi (1,288km) on narrow strip between S China Sea (E) and Annamese Cordillera (W); capital was Hue. An-cient empire fell to China 214 BC and regained self-government; ruled by China AD 939–1428; French obtained missionary and trade agreements 1787, but disputes led to French seizure beginning 1858 and protectorate was est 1883–84. During WWII it was occupied by Japanese; in 1945 it became autono-mous state of Vietnam (comprised of Tonkin, Annam, and Cochin China); heavy and lengthy fighting cen-tered around Hue in 1968 Tet offensive of Vietnam War. Industries: textiles, rice, fish processing. Area: approx. 58,000sq mi (150,220sq km). △1378.

Annapolis, seaport city and capital of Maryland on S bank of Severn River 22mi (35km) SSE of Baltimore; seat of Anne Arundel co. Founded 1649 by Puritans from Virginia seeking asylum from religious persecu-

Angiosperm

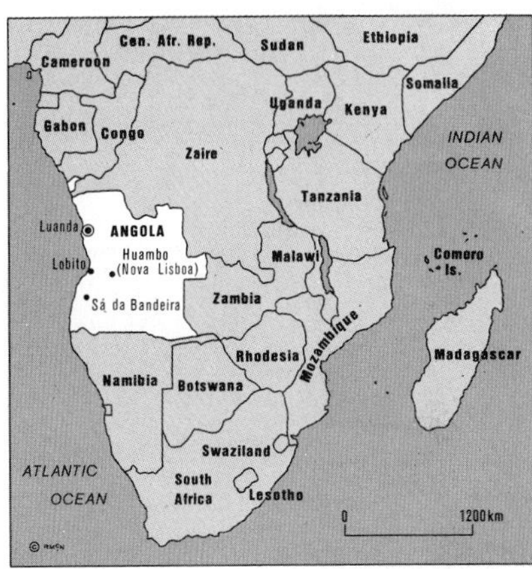
Cen. Afr. Rep.
Sudan
Ethiopia
Cameroon
Somalia
Gabon
Congo
Uganda
Kenya
Zaire
INDIAN OCEAN
Tanzania
Luanda
ANGOLA
Huambo (Nova Lisboa)
Lobito
Malawi
Comoro Is.
Sá da Bandeira
Zambia
Madagascar
Rhodesia
Mozambique
Namibia
Botswana
Swaziland
ATLANTIC OCEAN
South Africa
Lesotho
0
1200km

Angola

Anise

Ankylosaurus

tion, who est. (1650) a boatyard on the Severn River; served as temporary national capital (1783–84); scene of signing of the peace treaty with England (1784) ending Revolutionary War in Senate Chamber of the State House (still standing); site of St John's College (1696), US Naval Academy (1845), the Old Treasury (1695), Maryland's oldest building, and more than 80 pre-Revolutionary buildings. In 1965 the "old city" of Annapolis, laid out in 1696 when the colony's capital was moved here from St Mary's, was declared a national historic site. Industries: seafood packaging, boatyards, plastics, concrete products. Named Providence at founding 1649; changed to Annapolis 1695; chartered by Queen Anne 1708; inc. as city 1796. Pop. (1970) 29,592.

Annapolis Convention, conference called by the Virginia legislature inviting the 13 states of the US Confederation to meet in September 1786 in Annapolis, Md., to discuss common problems, particularly commerce and rival claims to western land. Only five states sent delegates. Disappointed, the reform-minded participants proposed another convention to meet at Philadelphia in May 1787.

Annapolis Royal, English name for Port Royal, French settlement in Canada. It was established in 1604 in southern Nova Scotia by Samuel de Champlain. The center of Sieur de Monts's fur trading monopoly, it was captured by the English in 1613, returned to the French in 1632, and finally taken for the British by colonial American forces in 1710. It served as a base for the settlement of Halifax.

Annapurna, mountain range in the Himalayan system, N central Nepal. Annapurna I (E) rises to 26,502ft (8,083m); it was scaled 1950 by French expedition led by Maurice Herzog; 11th-highest peak in the world. Annapurna II (W) rises to 26,041ft (7,943m).

Ann Arbor, city in S Michigan on the Huron River, 36mi (58km) W of Detroit; seat of Washtenaw co; research, educational, medical center; site of the University of Michigan (1817). Industries: computers, scientific instruments, automotive parts. Founded 1824 by pioneers from Virginia and New York; inc. 1851. Pop. (1970) 99,797.

Anne (1665–1714), queen of Great Britain and Ireland (1702–14). The second daughter of James II, she was the last reigning Stuart, and after the Act of Union (1707) first monarch of the united kingdom of England and Scotland. She was dependent on her successive favorites, Sarah, duchess of Marlborough, and Abigail Masham, but presided over an age of military success and cultural distinction. No child survived from her marriage (1683) with George, prince of Denmark. She was succeeded by George, elector of Hanover in 1714.

Anne, Princess (1950–), only daughter of Elizabeth II, fourth in line of succession to the throne; a noted competitive horsewoman. She married (1973) Lt. Mark Phillips.

Annealing, slow heating and cooling of a metal, alloy, or glass to release internal stresses, dislocations, or vacancies that may have been introduced during mechanical shaping such as rolling or extruding, to increase the material's workability and durability. Machine tools, wire, and sheet are annealed during manufacture.

Anne de Beaujeu, or **Anne of France** (1461–1522), eldest daughter of Louis XI of France and Charlotte of Savoy. Politically cunning, with her husband Pierre de Bourbon, seigneur de Beaujeu, she exercised much power during the early part of the reign of Charles VIII. She was responsible for arranging the marriage between Charles and Anne of Brittany.

Annelida, phylum of segmented worms. All have encircling grooves usually corresponding to internal partitions of the body. A digestive tube, nerves, and blood vessels run through the entire body, but each segment has its own set of excretory ducts. Annelids form an important part of the diet of many animals. There are more than 6000 species. The three main classes are Polychaeta, marine worms; Oligochaeta, freshwater or terrestrial worms; and Hirudinea or leeches. △458, 474.

Anne of Austria (1601–66), wife of Louis XIII of France, mother of Louis XIV. After her husband's death (1643), she ruled France as regent with Cardinal Mazarin until Louis XIV was crowned (1661).

Anne of Brittany (1477–1514), duchess of Brittany and Queen of France. Her second and third marriages, to Charles VIII and his successor, Louis XII, tied the province of Brittany to France.

Anne of Cleves (1515–57), fourth wife of Henry VIII. Her marriage (1540) was a political alliance joining Henry with the German Protestants, and was declared null after only six months. Pensioned by Henry, Anne remained in England until her death.

Annihilation, conversion of an elementary particle and its antiparticle, on collision, into radiation. The mass of the two particles is converted directly into energy in the form of gamma rays. An electron and positron annihilate to produce two gamma-ray photons, travelling in opposite directions to conserve momentum. Each has an energy of 0.51 MeV, which is equivalent to the rest mass of the electron or positron. △1484.

Anniston, city in NE Alabama, 65mi (105km) E of Birmingham; seat of Calhoun co; destroyed by Union forces 1865. Rebuilt as a private industrial village 1872, it was opened to public 1883. Industries: chemicals, iron pipes, machine parts, textiles. Settled 1863 as a supply depot for Confederate Army; inc. 1879. Pop. (1970) 31,533.

Annual, plants that complete their life cycle in one growing season. They are used in summer flower beds, window boxes, pots, or winter greenhouses. Popular garden annuals include zinnias, nasturtiums, sweet peas, and petunias. Some plants may be started indoors and others sown in place. Some self-seed, such as baby's breath and marigolds. *See also* Biennial; Perennial.

Annual Ring, or growth ring, concentric circles visible in cross-sections of woody stems or trunks. Representing the annual growth of the cambium layer, each ring consists of an inner spring (xylem) layer and an outer summer (phloem) layer. The growth of summer wood is thick-walled, providing contrast between the rings. Used to determine the approximate age of trees, the thickness of these rings reveals the environmental conditions during a tree's lifetime. △448.

Annular or Ring Eclipse. *See* Eclipse.

Anoa, or dwarf water buffalo, three smallest species of wild buffalo, native to Celebes and Philippines. The young are covered with yellow woolly hair; adults are almost hairless with black or brown skin blotched with white. Their short horns are straight and ringed. Height: to 41in (104cm) at shoulder. Family Bovidae; genus *Anoa*. *See also* Buffalo; Ox.

Anode, the positive electrode of an electrolytic cell or electron tube (sometimes called the *plate*). It is the electrode by which electrons leave a system. *See* Electrolysis. △1546–48, 1566.

Anodizing, the subjection of a metal such as aluminum or magnesium to electrolytic action by making it the anode of a cell, then coating the metal with a protective film.

Anole, arboreal lizard found in warm regions of North and South America and the West Indies. Enlarged finger and toe pads enable it to cling to surfaces. It is best known for its ability to change from brown to yellow and several shades of green. Males have an expandable dewlap. The familiar green anole, American chameleon, is found in S United States and Caribbean. Length: 5–18in (13–46cm). There are 200 species. Family Iguanidae; genus *Anolis*. *See also* Lizard. △522.

Anomalistic Period, time taken for a celestial body to make one complete revolution around another, starting and finishing at the same orbital point, such as perihelion or perigee. It is slightly longer than the sidereal period. For the Moon it equals 27.55455 days; for the Earth it is 365.25964 days.

Anomaly, a deviation from the expected value, as in "gravity anomaly." The gravity anomalies are the direct result of the deviation of the earth from the perfect theoretical ellipsoidal form. A meterological anomaly means a local reading of temperature or rainfall that differs from the expected. An oceanographic anomaly is an unexplained temperature or degree of salinity. △178.

Anonymity, protection of one's identity by means of a mask or some other form of secrecy, which has certain effects on one's behavior. In general, social psychologists have found that individuals are capable of more aggression, hostility, and apathy when their identities are not likely to be disclosed, as when bank robbers wear masks or members of the Ku Klux Kl wear sheets.

Anopheles Mosquito, bloodsucking arthropod, t principle vector of human malarias. The female nee a blood meal prior to laying its eggs, and during fee ing releases malaria organisms into the victim's bloo stream. △732.

Anorexia Nervosa, abnormal loss of appetite ar refusal to eat, occurring almost exclusively amor young women in their teens and twenties and prob bly of psychological origin. It results in emaciatio deficiency symptoms, amenorrhea, and other diso ders. △768.

Anorthosite, rock similar to gabbro, but made u almost entirely of plagioclase feldspar and containir little or no pyroxene. Anorthosite is an intrusive roc but its origin is uncertain. Large areas of this othe wise uncommon rock occur in New York, Minnesot Canada, Norway, and the Soviet Union. *See also* Ign ous Rock; Plagioclase.

Anouilh, Jean (1910–), French dramatist. noted playwright, his style is one of simplicity ar precision; his plays range from tragedy to comedy. H first play was *L'hermine* (1932). His notable work include *Traveler without Luggage* (1937), *Antigon* (1944), *The Waltz of the Toreadors* (1952), an *Becket* (1959).

Anoxia, general term for acute or chronic deficienc of oxygen in the tissues. It can occur at high altitude or as a result of underlying disease (eg, lung or hea malfunction) or toxic agents. Symptoms include tro bled breathing, rapid pulse, and cyanosis.

Anschluss, German word for the unification o Austria and Germany. Outlawed by treaty at the clos of World War I, expressly to limit the strength of Ge many, the Anschluss was nevertheless favored by Ge mans of all political persuasions, including Commu nists and Socialists as well as rightists. Unificatio finally took place through a show of force under Hitle (1938). The union was dissolved by the Allies in 194 and Austria again became an independent state. △ 1336.

Anshan (An-shan), city in Manchuria, China, 60m (97km) SW of Mukden. The hub of China's iron an steel production, iron mining dates from 10th century Industries: blast furnaces, cement, coke ovens, stee converters. Pop. 1,500,000.

Ansonia, city in S Connecticut, 8mi (13km) WNW o New Haven. Industries: copper, brass metals. Settle 1651; inc. 1893. Pop. (1970) 21,160.

Ant, insect of the order Hymenoptera. Representa tives range from 0.04 to 1.2in (1–30mm) in lengt and are found worldwide. They live as social insects feeding on plants, nectar, and other insects. Most rep resentatives are wingless, except at times of dispersal Family Formicidae. *See also* Army Ant; Carpente Ant; Fire Ant; Honey Ant.

Antabuse, drug that causes an abnormal physiologi cal reaction to alcohol. It is used in the treatment o alcoholism. *See also* Alcoholism.

Antaeus, in Greek mythology, the giant of Libya, the son of the sea god Poseidon and Gaea. All strangers passing through his land had to wrestle him, and since he derived strength when thrown by touching hi mother Gaea (Earth), he never lost. Hercules discov ered his secret and crushed him to death high off the ground.

Antakya, formerly Antioch; city in S Turkey, approx 20mi (32km) E of Mediterranean coast, on Orontes River; capital of Hatay prov.; founded *c.* 300 BC by Seleucus I; became commercial rival of Alexandria defeated by Pompey (64 BC); important Roman com mercial and cultural center; early Christian center conquered by Persians (538), Arabs (638), Byzantine Empire (969), Seljuk Turks (1085), army of the First Crusade (1098); severely damaged by earthquake 1872; transferred to Syria 1920; restored to Turkey 1939. Modern city occupies small part of ancient site remains of aqueduct, theater, castle, and thick walls still visible. Industries: olives, tobacco, cotton, grain. Pop. 57,855.

Antarctica, fifth-largest continent, surrounding the South Pole and surrounded by the Antarctic Ocean, which is actually the southernmost section of the Atlantic, Pacific, and Indian oceans. Almost entirely within the Antarctic Circle and perpetually snow-covered, it holds strategic and scientific interest for the rest of the world. No humans live permanently on

Antarctica. Scientists visit for purposes of research and exploration but leave when their work is accomplished.

Land. Shaped roughly like an open fan, with the Antarctic Peninsula as a handle, the continent is a snowy desert covering about 5,250,000sq mi (13,597,500sq km). The land is a high plateau, having an average elevation of 6,000ft (1,830m). Mountain ranges occur near the coasts. The interior, or South Polar Plateau, lies beneath about 8,000ft (2,440m) of snow, an accumulation of tens of thousands of years. Mineral deposits exist in the mountains, but exploiting them has not become practical. Coal may be plentiful, but the known deposits of copper, nickel, gold, and iron will not pay the expenses of unearthing and exporting them.

Seas and Glaciers. Most continents have lakes and rivers, but the rivers of Antarctica are frozen, inching toward the sea, and instead of lakes there are large bodies of water along the coasts. The great Beardmore Glacier creeps down from the South Polar Plateau and loses itself in the Ross Ice Shelf. This shelf of ice is that part of the Ross Sea that never thaws, and the Ross Sea is the part of the Antarctic Ocean that makes up the S extremity of the Pacific Ocean. The southernmost part of the Atlantic is that portion of the Antarctic Ocean known as the Weddell Sea.

Climate and Vegetation. Antarctica remains cold all year, with only a few coastal areas being free of snow or ice in summer—December to February. On most of the continent the temperature remains below freezing, and in August it has been recorded at nearly −130°F (−54°C). Precipitation generally amounts to only 7–15in (17.5–38cm) of snow a year, but melting is less than that, allowing a buildup over the centuries. Nevertheless, mosses manage to survive on rocks along the outer rim of the continent. Certain algae grow on the snow, while other algae appear in pools of fresh water when melting occurs.

Animal Life. The best known Antarctic animals are penguins, especially the emperor and Adélie. Whales, such as the blue and finback, live in the icy waters, as do a few species of hair seals.

History. Islands associated with the great S continent were sighted in the 18th century, and in 1820 Nathaniel Palmer, an American hunting fur seals, reached what is now called the Antarctic Peninsula. Explorers from several nations provided claims to sections of the continent for their countries, but the United States recognizes none of these. Charles Wilkes of the United States explored enough of the coast between 1838 and 1840 to prove a continent existed, and James Clark Ross of England made coastal maps about the same time. Toward the end of the 19th century, exploration reached inland until a race for the South Pole developed. Roald Amundsen of Norway won, reaching the pole on Dec. 14, 1911. The airplane brought a new era of exploration, and Richard E. Byrd of the United States became the best-known of the airborne polar explorers. In the 1970s scientists from a dozen nations studied the continent and its past. International treaties help control the activities on and around Antarctica.

Antarctic Circle, the southernmost parallel, 66.5° south of the equator, at which the sun neither sets on the day of summer solstice (December 22) nor rises on the day of winter solstice (June 21). *See also* Arctic Circle; Solstice.

Antarctic Current, a continuous eastward-moving ocean current encircling the earth around Antarctica. It moves the water from one ocean to another, a process completed every 1800 years.

Antares, or **Alpha Scorpii,** red supergiant star in the constellation Scorpius. It apparently has a smaller green companion orbiting it. Characteristics: apparent mag. 0.92; absolute mag. − 4.5; spectral type M1; distance 400 light-years. △102.

Anteater, usually nocturnal, toothless, insect-eating mammal that lives in forests of tropical America. It has a long tapered snout, a long sticky tongue for capturing insects, and long claws for ripping open ant and termite nests. Length: 7–60in (18–152cm). Family Myrmecophagidae. *See also* Edentate; Pangolin. △588.

Antelope, hollow-horned, bovid ruminants found throughout the Old World, except in Madagascar, Malaya, and Australasia; most occur in Africa. They range from rabbit-size to ox-size. Horns of varying shapes are borne by both sexes in some species, only males in others. All are two-horned except the chousingha or four-horned antelope. Most females bear a single young each year. Family Bovidae. *See also* Bovidae; Ruminant.

Antenna, or (especially in Britain) **aerial,** the part of a radio system from which the signal is radiated into space (transmitting antenna) or by which it is received from space (receiving antenna). The shape and structure of the antenna depend on the frequency of the radiation and the directional requirements of the system. For example, a beam antenna is required to transmit a radar beam while a simple wire may suffice for an amplitude-modulated radio receiver.

Anthony, or **Antony, Saint** (*c.* AD250–350), known as the first Christian monk. Born of Christian parents in Egypt, he withdrew into complete solitude to practice ascetic devotion at the age of 20. The monastic ideal, outlined in the *Life of St. Antony* attributed to St. Athanasius, attracted many. At his death Christian monasticism was well established.

Anthony, Susan Brownell (1820–1906), US reformer and woman suffragist, b. Adams, Mass. She organized the first woman's temperance association. In the 1850s, she lectured against slavery and for women's rights. After the Civil War, she opposed giving the vote to freed Negro men without enfranchising women and with Elizabeth Cady Stanton she organized the National Woman Suffrage Association (1869). It later became (1890) the National American Woman Suffrage Association and she was its president 1892–1900. *See also* Woman Suffrage.

Anthozoa, or flower animals, also called Actinozoa, a class of coelenterates characterized by columnar body, top mouth surrounded by tentacles, and bottom disc for sliding or holding. There is no medusa stage. Included are sea anemones, corals, and sea pens. Subphylum Cnidaria. △468.

Anthracnose, any of various fungal plant diseases that attack several important crops and are characterized by blisters or ulcerlike lesions of dead tissues, on fruit, leaves, and twigs. The lesions are often dark and sunken, or grayish with rust-colored edges. Spores of anthracnose fungi are commonly transmitted by insects, seeds, and rain.

Anthrax, contagious disease, chiefly of grass-eating mammals (but also affecting man, swine, dogs, and captive wild animals), caused by the microbe *Bacillus anthracis.* Animals catch the disease from contaminated feed and water and from certain insects in which the microbe may live for years. The symptoms of the fatal disease are staggering, bloody discharge, and convulsions. The disease can be prevented by vaccine and treated with arsenicals and antibiotics.

Anthropoid Apes, tailless primates including gibbons and larger great apes—orangutans, chimpanzees, and gorillas. Apes are the largest and—except for man—the most intelligent primates. Family Pongidae. *See also* Primates. △554.

Anthropoidea, suborder of primates including monkeys, apes, and human beings. Anthropoids have flatter, more manlike faces and larger brains and are larger size than prosimian primates. *See also* Primates. △554.

Anthropology, science of man in his physical and sociocultural aspects. It is concerned with the whole chronological and geographic range of human societies. However, there has been an emphasis on microstudies of small autonomous (frequently pre-literate) groups since to explore the range of human physical and sociocultural diversity it is important to examine societies whose isolation implies an original group of institutions. Modern anthropology stems from the first half of the 19th century when the first systematic racial classification was made and an interest in cultural evolutionism followed the publication in 1859 of Darwin's *Origin of Species. See also* Ethnography; Ethnology; Anthropology, Cultural; Anthropology, Physical; Anthropology, Social. △646–60, 874–82.

Anthropology, Applied, study used in any situation where it is useful for people making decisions about a community to know something about the population for which they are responsible. Such a situation has normally arisen with the study of third-world societies subject to the rule of Western administrations. Hence the phrase "anthropology is the child of colonialism." Applied anthropology is now mainly concerned with development programs. *See also* Anthropology. △646–60, 874–82.

Anthropology, Cultural, study concerned with depicting the character of various cultures, and the similarities and differences between them. This branch of anthropology is concerned with all cultures whether simple or complex and its methodology entails a holistic view, field work, comparative analysis (both within the society and cross-culturally), and a tendency to base theoretical models on empirical

REGINA ANNA D. G. ANGLIÆ SCOTIÆ FR. ET HIBERNIÆ
Queen Anne

Antelope

Susan B. Anthony

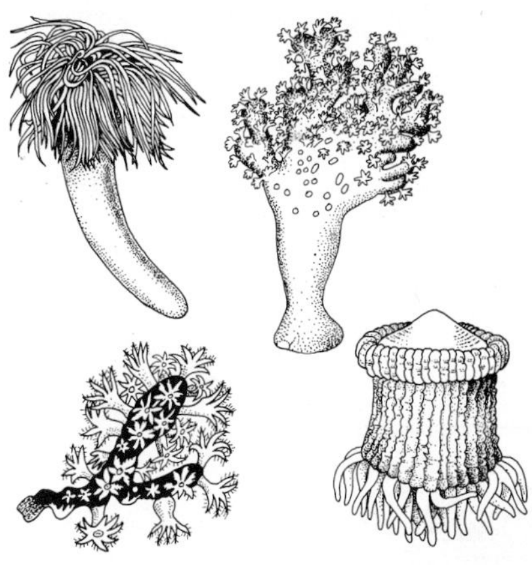
Anthozoa

data rather than vice versa. *See also* Anthropology; Culture. △646–60, 874–82.

Anthropology, Physical, basically biological discipline linked traditionally with the behavioral science of anthropology. It emerged from the zoological and taxonomic studies of the 18th century as an interest in racial differentiation. In the 19th century this was extended into a concern with the fossil origin of man and his evolution (hence the links with archeology). With recent discoveries in genetics, physical anthropology could be described as human biology. *See also* Anthropology.

Anthropology, Social, branch of anthropology concerned with social relationships, especially those which are institutionalized into regular behavior. These include ritual, religion, kinship, marriage, economics, and political organization. Anthropologists are constantly adding information to assimilate ethnographic data in the hope of analyzing social structure and process in a society. Among present day anthropologists there is an increasing interest in structural models and comparative analysis. See also Anthropology; Ethnography; Ethnology.

Anti-aircraft Artillery, ground-based weapons employed against aircraft in flight. Until the end of World War II the term referred to cannon, although during the war the Germans tested rockets and increasingly since then the term has referred to surface-to-air missiles (or rockets). Flak, the German term for anti-aircraft shrapnel, was very effective in World War II, Korea, and Vietnam. △1734.

Antibes, resort town in S France, on the Riviera, 11mi (18km) SW of Nice. Founded by Greek colonists, it was called Antipolis; contains ruins of a later Roman settlement and 16th–17th-century fortifications. Industries: tourism, oranges, olives, wines, perfumes. Founded 340 BC. Pop. 47,547.

Antibiotic, a chemical produced by a microorganism—for example, by specific strains of certain bacteria or molds—that is capable, in dilute solutions, of stopping the growth of or destroying bacteria and some other disease-causing microorganisms. The introduction of antibiotics, since about the time of World War II, has revolutionized medical science, making possible the control and in some cases the virtual elimination of once widespread and often fatal diseases, including typhoid, plague, cholera, and tuberculosis.

Antibiotics are selective—that is, effective against only specific microorganisms; those effective against a large number of microorganisms are known as broad-spectrum antibiotics. Antibiotics in general are bacteriostatic, inhibiting the growth of sensitive bacteria. Some others dissolve or kill sensitive bacteria. Some important antibiotics are penicillin, the first widely used antibiotic, effective against many staphylococcal infections, including bronchitis and tonsillitis; streptomycin, effective against tuberculosis, and some lung, liver, and urinary infections; and the tetracyclines, effective against many bacterial and rickettsial infections. Some bacteria, once sensitive to certain antibiotics, have become resistant to them, posing a serious threat to continued antibiotic therapy and giving impetus to a constant search for new antibiotics. △746, 1570.

Antibody, or immunoglobulin, globular protein of the blood that reacts specifically with foreign substances or organisms that enter an animal, rendering it immune to them. Preformed antibodies can be injected for immediate protection, for example, injection of tetanus antitoxin. △738, 740, 1570.

Anticline, in geology, an upward fold in sedimentary rocks that results in a tilting of the stratifications. In a simple anticline, the oldest rocks are domed at the center of the formation; the newer layers of sedimentary deposition are layered over the dome. *See also* Folding. △250, 252.

Anticoagulant, substance that prevents or counteracts coagulation, or clotting. Heparin is a commonly used blood anticoagulant.

Anticyclone. △214, 218.

Anti-depressant. △770.

Antidiuretic, an agent that inhibits the discharge of urine from the body. An antidiuretic hormone (ADH)—vasopressin—is secreted by the posterior pituitary gland and acts to increase water retention by the kidneys.

Antidote, remedy or other agent used to counter the effects of a poison. Antidotes are specific, depending on the poison ingested.

Antietam, Battle of (Sept. 16–17, 1862), Civil War engagement, also known as Sharpsburg, fought in Sharpsburg, Md. Gen. George McClellan's 75,000 Union soldiers made five assaults on Gen. Robert E. Lee's 40,000 Confederates. Each side lost over 12,000 men. Neither side won, but Lee was forced to give up his Maryland campaign and retreat to Virginia. △1276.

Anti-Federalist Party (Republicans), organized in 1792 to oppose the proposed Constitution, mainly on the grounds that it gave the central government too much power. Anti-Federalist support came mostly from the back country and agricultural sections. Anti-Federalist leaders included Richard Henry Lee and Patrick Henry of Virginia and George Clinton of New York.

Antifreeze, substance dissolved in a liquid to lower its melting point and thus prevent it freezing in cold weather. The antifreeze used in car radiators is usually ethylene glycol (ethane diol, HOC_2H_4OH), to which is added corrosion inhibitors and antifoaming agents. △1562.

Antigen, any substance or organism which, when injected into the body, induces the formation of antibodies that will react specifically with that antigen. *See also* Antibody. △740.

Antigone, in Greek mythology, daughter of Oedipus and Jocasta, king and queen of Thebes. She accompanied Oedipus until his death, tried to prevent her brother Polynices from attacking Thebes, and committed suicide after she was condemned to death by Creon for defying his prohibition against burying Polynices. Sophocles' tragedy *Antigone* (*c.* 442 BC) is notable for its noble characterization of its heroine.

Antigonus I (*c.* 382–301 BC), general of Alexander the Great. He was governor of Phrygia (333 BC). In the struggles over the regency, he defeated Perdiccas with the aid of Ptolemy I, Antipater, and Craterus. He controlled Mesopotamia, Syria, and Asia Minor. At Salamis (306 BC) he defeated his prior ally, Ptolemy I, but at Ipsus (301 BC) he was defeated and slain by Seleucus and Lysimachus, despite help from his son, Demetrius I.

Antigua, island in British West Indies, in Leeward Islands group; named for a Spanish church; occupied by both French and Spanish; it was colonized by British in 1632; slavery was abolished in 1834; made self-governing 1967. Antigua is a coral and volcanic island with natural harbors; site of U S seaplane base. Discovered 1493 by Christopher Columbus. Industries: cotton, fruit, vegetables. Pop. 54,304.

Antihistamine, drug that counteracts or otherwise prevents the effects of histamine, a natural substance released by the body in response to injury or more often as part of an allergic reaction, which produces symptoms such as sneezing, runny nose, burning eyes.

Anti-Lebanon Mountains (Al-Jabal ash Shargi), mountain range along E coast of Lebanon. Highest peak is Mt Hermon, 9,232ft (2,816m). Part of the range forms the Lebanon-Syria border.

Antilochus, in Greek legend, king of Pylos, the son of Nestor. In saving his father's life during the Trojan War, he was killed by Memnon, king of the Ethiopians. He thus fulfilled the prophecy, "Beware of an Ethiopian."

Antilogarithms, numbers having specified numbers as their logarithm. Thus the antilogarithm (or antilog) of 0.4771 is 3, because log 3 = 0.4771 (to 4 places of decimals). *See also* Logarithms. △1456.

Anti-Masonic Party, first third party in the United States formed after the disappearance in 1826 of William Morgan, who had revealed the secrets of the Freemasons. The Anti-Masons were opposed to secret societies and staunchly supported freedom of the press. In 1831, in Baltimore, they held the first national nominating convention and issued the first written platform of any US party. After 1836 the party declined and was eventually absorbed by the Whigs.

Antimatter, matter identical to ordinary particles in all except charge. Antiparticles such as positrons (the antielectron), antiprotons, and antineutrons, are produced in many reactions but instantly collide with other particles and disappear. Since the photon is its own antiparticle, the possibility exists that distant stars or galaxies are made up of antimatter.

Antimissile Missile, or **antiballistic missile (ABM),** a defensive missile designed to intercept and destroy incoming ballistic missiles. Its usefulness i questionable because of short warning times, hig speeds of attack missiles, the possibility of decoys and the need to limit warhead size for explosions ove a nation's own territory. *See also* Ballistic Missile.

Anti-Monopoly Party, minor party organized in Ch cago in 1884. Its program included demands for graduated income tax, establishment of a departme of labor, assistance to farmers, and federal regulatio of monopolies in interstate commerce. After 1888 the Anti-Monopoly party joined the Greenback Labo party under the name of the People's party.

Antimony, toxic metallic element (symbol Sb) o group V of the periodic table, known from early times Commonest ore is stibnite (a sulfide). It is used i some alloys, particularly in hardening lead for batter ies, type metal, etc. The element has two allotropes a silvery metallic form and an amorphous gray form. Properties: at. no. 51; at. wt. 121.75; sp. gr 6.684; melt. pt. 1,166.9°F (630.5°C); boil. pt. 2,984°F (1,640°C); most common isotope Sb^{121} (57.25%).

Antioch. *See* Antakya.

Antioch, city in W California, near the mouth of the Sacramento River; agricultural processing and shipping center. Industries: canneries, lumber mills, steel works. Settled 1849; inc. 1890. Pop. (1970) 28,060

Antiochus II (died 247BC), king of Syria (*c.* 261–247 BC), successor of Antiochus I. He set aside Laodice and married Berenice, the daughter of Ptolemy II thus securing peace and recovering territory. At his death Seleucus II and Berenice fought for the throne Berenice was murdered and a war with Ptolemy III her brother, ensued.

Antiochus III, the Great (242–187 BC), king of Syria (223–187 BC), son of Seleucus II. After his defeat a Rafa (217 BC) by Ptolemy IV, he invaded Egypt (212–202 BC), seizing land from Ptolemy V with the help of Philip V of Macedon. He recaptured Palestine, Asia Minor, and the Thracian Cheronese. The Romans overwhelmed him at Thermopylae (191 BC) and a Magnesia (190 BC). The rebuilt Seleucid empire shrank when he gave up all possessions west of the Taurus. Seleucus IV succeeded him.

Antiope, in Greek legend, two figures. One was the mother of Amphion and Zethis by Zeus. The other was the wife of Theseus and the daughter of a queen of the Amazons and Ares, god of war.

Antioxidant, chemical additive designed to reduce oxidation. Antioxidants are used to prevent fatty foods becoming rancid, deterioration of rubber, formation of gums in gasoline, etc. Most are organic amines and phenols, functioning by terminating the free-radical chain reaction causing oxidation. Sulfur dioxide and ascorbic acid are often used as antioxidants for foodstuffs.

Antiparticles. *See* Elementary Particles and Antiparticles.

Antiperspirant. △1814.

Antiphanes (408?–?334BC), Greek playwright. A leading writer of comedy, he wrote 260 plays, including parodies of myths. His style is based on wit, charm, and elegance. His plays include *Creation of Man, Sappho,* and *As Much Again.*

Antipope, one who falsely claims to be pope, or whose election to pope was later declared unsanctioned by the Roman Catholic Church. Clement III (Guibert of Ravenna), Benedict III (Pedro de Luna), and Felix V (Amadeus VIII) were among the 36 antipopes.

Anti-Price Discrimination Act. *See* Robinson-Patman Act (1936).

Anti-Saloon League, most powerful of all Prohibition groups, it was founded (1893) to campaign against the corner saloon which, members felt, was impairing the efficiency of the working class. It spurred considerable state legislation outlawing alcohol. *See also* Prohibition.

Anti-Semitism, prejudice against Jews. Since ancient times, Jews were persecuted for religious reasons. They refused to worship idols or emperors. Almost from the beginning of the Christian era they were accused of being Christ's crucifiers. Denied access to other professions, Jews of the Middle Ages turned to moneylending and other professions looked upon with contempt, thus inadvertently adding economic prejudice. The growing nationalism of the nineeenth century further isolated the Jews who now ecame looked upon as racially separate or inferior. Tyrants such as Tsar Alexander II of Russia in the late 9th century and Adolf Hitler in the 20th century drew upon all these separate currents of anti-Semitism to strengthen their own positions. After World War II, anti-Zionism among the Arabs and the Soviet Union added a new, political dimension to anti-Semitism. △1332.

Antiseptic, substance that destroys disease-causing and other organisms on the surface of the body. Most are toxic if taken internally. Among the commonly used antiseptics are alcohol, iodine, and chlorine. △752.

Antitank Weapons. △1734, 1736.

Antitoxin, antibody produced by the body in response to toxins. They are specific and neutralize the toxin. Antitoxin serums are used to treat and prevent bacterial diseases, such as tetanus and diphtheria.

Antler, bony outgrowth on the skull of male deer shed annually. In temperate-zone species, antlers begin to grow in early summer. They are soft, well supplied with blood, and covered with thin, velvety skin. Later, the blood recedes and the dried skin is rubbed off. Antlers then serve as sexual ornaments and weapons until shed the following spring. First-year males grow short spikes. More branches (points) are added each year until maturity is reached. *See also* Deer; Horn.

Ant Lion, or **doodlebug,** larvae of ant lion fly, found worldwide, with larger ones in the tropics. They have large, sickle-shaped jaws and dig conical pits in dry sand or dust, feeding on ants that fall in. Adults are soft-bodied with 2.8–7in (7–18cm), finely veined wings. Family Myrmeleontidae. *See also* Lacewing; Neuroptera.

Antofagasta, city in N Chile, on the Pacific Ocean; capital of Antofagasta prov.; founded 1870 by Chileans to utilize nitrates in the Desert of Atacoma. The War of the Pacific began in 1879 when Chilean troops moved into the city; Bolivia relinquished both city and province to Chile after the war. Industries: copper, nitrates, foundries, ore refineries. Pop. 125,081.

Antonescu, Ion (1882–1946), Romanian general, leader of the Iron Guards. After alternating periods of imprisonment and office holding, he was appointed premier (1940) at Germany's insistence, and in 1941 he set up a military dictatorship, forcing the abdication of King Carol II. Antonescu suppressed all opposition, modeling his regime on that of Germany. He aided the German invasion of Russia in 1941 and later declared war on the United States and England. Arrested during King Michael's coup in September 1944, he was executed as a war criminal in 1946.

Antoniadi, E.N. △62.

Antoninus Pius (86–161 AD), Roman emperor (138–61). The adopted son of Hadrian, he was made consul (120) and later sent as proconsul to Asia. His peaceful reign saw the promotion of art and science, the construction of public works and fine buildings, legal reform, and new provisions for orphans. In Britain Agricola built the Wall of Antoninus (142–43). Antoninus' constant companion was his wife's nephew, Marcus Aurelius, who eventually became emperor himself. △1020.

Antonioni, Michelangelo (1912–), Italian filmmaker. He helped inaugurate the new realism in film making after World War II. His first feature film was *Cronaca di un amore* (1950). *L'Avventura* (1959) brought him recognition. Other important works include *The Red Desert* (1964), and *Blow-Up* (1966). *Zabriskie Point* (1969) was a commercial and critical failure.

Antony, Marc (*c.* 83–30 BC), Roman military and political leader. In spite of his wild youth, he proved an able soldier. Julius Caesar had him appointed a quaestor in 52 BC and a tribune in 49 BC. He fought with Caesar against Pompey at the battle of Pharsala (48 BC). After Caesar's assassination (44 BC), Antony roused the populace against the conspirators and drove them from Rome. His relations with Octavian were uneasy, but he was finally given control over Asia after defeating the last of the conspirators at Philippi in 42 BC. He then met and fell in love with Cleopatra. In 40 BC he married Octavian's sister, Octavia, as a peace gesture, but by 37 BC he had deserted her and was living openly with Cleopatra in Alexandria. In 36 BC he married Cleopatra. Octavian stripped him of his authority and sent a fleet to destroy him. Antony and Cleopatra's fleets were defeated off Actium in 31 BC. Antony killed himself upon Octavian's entry into Alexandria. △1018.

Antony and Cleopatra (*c.* 1606), a tragedy by William Shakespeare in which Antony, one of Rome's great triumvirate, is bewitched by the charms of Cleopatra, Queen of Egypt. His obsession with her causes him to neglect his country and antagonize his allies, and finally costs him his power and his life. Like many Elizabethan plays, the drama deals with the dangers of pride.

Antrodemus. *See* Allosaurus.

Antwerp (Antwerpen, Anvers), port city in N Belgium, on the Scheldt River, 23mi (37km) N of Brussels; capital of Antwerp prov. Antwerp rose to commercial prominence in the 15th century as English merchants moved their headquarters here; it was the seat of the world's first stock exchange (1460). Its commercial importance was influenced by the closing of the Scheldt River by the Treaty of Westphalia (1648) and its reopening (*c.* 1803) and improvement by Napoleon I; by 1863, Antwerp was considered one of the world's major ports; site of State University Center (1965), Royal Museum of Fine Arts (1880–90), zoological gardens, 14th-century Cathedral of Notre Dame, ancient city walls. Industries: oil refining, food processing, shipyards, diamond cutting. Chartered 1291. Pop. 226,570.

Antwerp School, school of painting that developed *c.*1480 and continued into the 17th century, inspired by the rise of capitalism and humanism. Strongly influenced by Italian painting, it used rich, warm tones in intimate paintings. Brueghel the elder, Rubens, and Van Dyck are representative artists. △1144.

Anu, in Assyro-Babylonian mythology, the supreme god of the pantheon, chief of the triad of the sons of Anshar, Anu, Ea, and Enlil. Anu is the sky-god, enthroned in heaven as the ruler of destiny, and the creator of spirits and demons from cold and rain and darkness. Anu ruled with Bel as the two principle Mesopotamian deities.

Anubis, jackal-headed god of the ancient Egyptians. △832.

Anura. △518.

Anxiety, emotional state marked by apprehension or dread in which a specific focus is usually lacking. Anxiety is manifested by restlessness, rapid heart beat, tremor, sweating, and irregular breathing (sometimes accompanied by a feeling of constriction or suffocation). △760, 766.

Anzio, town in central Italy, on the Tyrrhenian Sea. According to legend it was founded by Anteias; favorite resort of Romans by 341 BC; birthplace of Caligula and Nero; Greek statue of Apollo of Belvedere is among ruins of Nero's villa; Allied landing site January 1944. Industries: tourism, fishing. Pop. 22,108.

ANZUS Pact (Australia-New Zealand-United States Treaty Organization), defensive alliance organized by the United States in 1951 in response to waning British power, the Korean War, and fear of a Soviet threat in the Pacific.

Aorta, the largest artery in the body. Oxygenated blood passes from the heart's left ventricle through a set of semilunar valves to the aorta. Just outside the heart, the aorta curves into an aortic arch and branches to form the arteries that carry the oxygenated blood to all parts of the body except to the lungs. *See also* Artery; Heart. △688.

Aoudad, or **Barbary Sheep,** wild sheep found in N African rocky hills and now introduced into SW United States. It has a uniform reddish-brown coat and long, soft mane on throat and chest. Both sexes have large, backward-pointed horns. It can be crossbred with domestic goats. Length: to 75in (1.9m). Family Bovidae; species *Ammotragus lervia. See also* Sheep.

Apache, an Athabascan-speaking tribe of North American Indians inhabiting Arizona, New Mexico, and Oklahoma. Divided into four primary bands—the White Mountain, San Carlos, Jicarilla, and Mescalero —they migrated from the Northwest about 1000 AD with the Navajo but separated to form a distinct tribal group. They retained their earlier nomadic raiding customs, which brought them into military conflict with the Mexicans and US citizens, notably under Cochise and Geronimo. They lived in brush wickiup dwellings and are noted for their basketry. The total population is approximately 15,000.

Antietam: national battlefield site

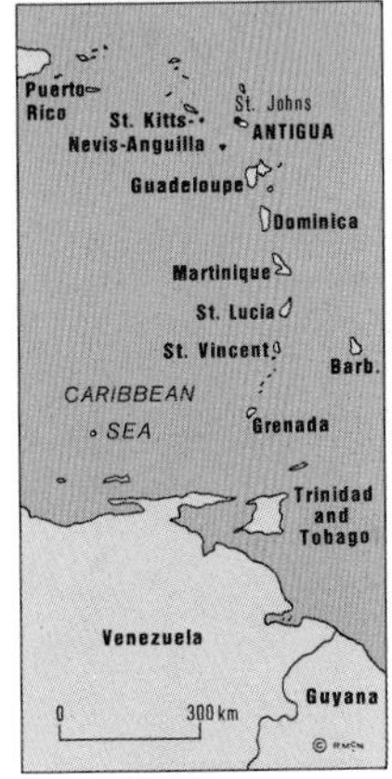
Puerto Rico
St. Kitts-Nevis-Anguilla
St. Johns
ANTIGUA
Guadeloupe
Dominica
Martinique
St. Lucia
St. Vincent
Barb.
CARIBBEAN SEA
Grenada
Trinidad and Tobago
Venezuela
Guyana
0
300 km

Antigua, British West Indies

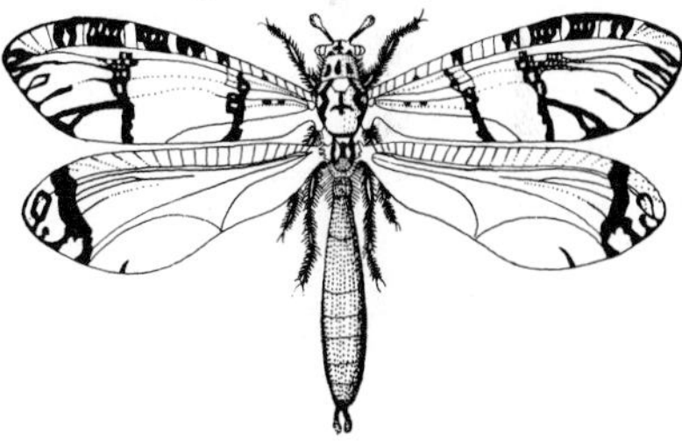

Ant lion

Aoudad

Apache Wars, series of battles in Arizona, New Mexico, Texas, and Oklahoma between Apache Indians and whites. One Indian leader, Cochise, made peace in 1872, but another, Geronimo, fought until 1886. Atrocities occurred on both sides.

Apalachicola National Forest, park in the SW corner of the Panhandle of Florida, has numerous lakes and three large rivers stocked with fish. Area: 1,000sq mi (2,590sq km).

Apartheid, the Republic of South Africa's policy of racial separation. Meaning "apartness" in Afrikaans, the policy was made official by Daniel F. Malan after his Nationalist party took power in 1948. Based on the doctrine of white supremacy, apartheid severely limits all aspects of the lives of South Africa's blacks (70% of the population), holding them in economic and political subservience. South Africa left the British Commonwealth in 1961 in response to antiapartheid pressures. △816.

Apatite, a phosphate mineral, calcium phosphate with hydroxyl, fluorine, and chlorine. Found in igneous rocks and sedimentary deposits. Hexagonal system prismatic or tabular crystals; also in granular aggregates or massive crusts. White, if pure, but often green, brown, yellow or blue; hardness 5, sp gr 3.-1–3.4. Frequently beautiful as a gem, but usually too soft for cutting and polishing. Varieties called asparagus stone (green) or moroxite (blue) are gems.

Apennines (Appennino), mountain range extending length of Italian peninsula; a continuation of the Pennine Alps. Unselective deforestation over the years has caused deep erosion and landslides; site of numerous hydroelectric plants, sheep and goat grazing. Highest point is Mt. Corno, 9,560ft (2,916m). Length: 840mi (1,352km).

Aperture, part of a lens or mirror system in an optical instrument through which light can pass. In a telescope it is the clear diameter of the main mirror or objective lens and controls the instrument's light-gathering power.

Apex, in astronomy, point on the celestial sphere, located in the constellation Hercules, toward which the sun appears to be moving. As the sun slowly orbits the galactic center, nearby stars, as seen from the earth, appear to move away from it due to the sun's relative velocity.

Aphasia, condition usually associated with an organic brain disorder involving the loss or impairment of ability to communicate through language. May involve loss of ability to communicate by speech, writing, or symbols or the inability to comprehend language. Often clinically expressed through vague and confused speech. *See also* Brain Disorders. △722.

Aphid, or plant louse, soft-bodied insect found worldwide. It transmits virus diseases of plants. Winged or wingless, these insects suck plant juices and are often found in large numbers in one location. Females reproduce with or without mating, resulting in one to several generations per year. Length: to 0.2in (5mm). Family Aphididae. *See also* Homoptera.

Aphid Lion. *See* Lacewing.

Aphorism, concise sentence expressing an important truth. Hippocrates published his famous series of precepts under the title *Aphorisms.* One of these, translated later by Chaucer, is: "The life so short, the craft so long to learn."

Aphrodite, Greek goddess of love, beauty, and fruitfulness. Identified by the Romans as Venus. Daughter of Zeus and Dione. Her husband was designated as Hephaestus (Vulcan), although she loved many gods and legendary mortals. Among these were Mars, Adonis, whose death left her brokenhearted, and Anchises, who was the father of Aeneas. Statues of her include Venus de Milo (Paris) and Aphrodite of Cnidus (Rome).

Apia, capital and chief port of Western Samoa, on N coast of Upolu Island; UN trust territory until 1962, when Samoa became independent country; site of geophysical observatory and agricultural college. Industries: cacao, coffee, lumber, handcrafts. Pop. 30,-593.

Apocalyptic Literature, a literary genre, most prevalent in Judaic and Christian works from about 200 BC to 200 AD, which incorporated great acts of God along with overwhelming catastrophies such as plagues or famines. The works were popular among religiously persecuted groups, and showed the forces of God winning for the faithful.

Apocrypha, certain writings of the Old Testament not considered canonical by Jews and Protestants but generally included in the Roman Catholic canon. The Apocrypha consists of the following books: First Esdras, Second Esdras, Tobit, Judith, Wisdom, Ecclesiasticus, Baruch, the Prayer of Manasses, First Maccabees, Second Maccabees. Also included are the following parts of books: Esther 10.4 to 16.24 and Daniel 3.24–90, 13, and 14. In Roman Catholic bibles, these works are considered deuterocanonical, except for First and Second Esdras (numbered Third and Fourth Esdras in Catholic bibles) and the Prayer of Manasses. Those works are considered pseudoepigraphical and are usually placed in an index at the end of the Old Testament. The term "apocryphal" is also sometimes used to identify certain spurious New Testament writings. *See also* New Testament; Old Testament.

Apogee, point in the orbit about the earth of the moon or an artificial satellite, at which the body is farthest from the earth. *See also* Perigee. △98.

Apollinaire, Guillaume (1880–1918), originally named Guillaume de Kostrowitzky, French poet, writer, and art critic. A leading figure in avant-garde circles, he championed Cubism and Futurism and contributed to several literary journals. His poetry, varying from the lyrical to the modernist, includes *Alcools* (1913) and the typographically experimental *Calligrammes* (1918). Other works are a collection of short stories, *L'Hérésiarque et cie* (1910), and a play, *Les Mamelles de Tirésias* (1918).

Apollo, Greek god, second to Zeus. Deity of the sun, archery, agriculture, patron of farmers, poets, physicians, founder of cities, and giver of laws. He was the son of Zeus and Leto, twin to Artemis. In the Trojan war he sided with Troy, sending a plague against the Greeks. In art and sculpture he is represented as a partially draped figure with a bow and quiver, shepherd's crook, sometimes accompanied by an animal sacred to him. △832.

Apollo and Daphne (Bernini). △1162.

Apollo Fountain. △1144.

Apollo Lunar Surface Experimental Package (ALSEP). △54.

Apollonia, ancient district in Illyria near the modern town of Fier, Albania, founded by the Corinthians in the 6th century BC; during the time of the Roman Republic it was a prosperous seat of culture and philosophy, a link on the Via Egnatia between Brindisi and Greece.

Apollonius of Rhodes (3rd century BC), Greek poet. Born in Alexandria, Apollonius spent his later life in Rhodes. A pupil of Callimachus, he disagreed with the views of his teacher on epic poetry. Apollonius is best known as author of the epic poem *Argonautica.*

Apollo Program, US project to send men to the Moon. Initiated in May 1961 by President John Kennedy, it achieved its objective on July 21, 1969, when Neil Armstrong set foot on the lunar surface. The program terminated with the successful Apollo-Soyuz linkup in space during July 1975, having placed over 30 astronauts in space and 12 on the Moon. △54, 142, 1724.

Apoplexy. *See* Stroke.

Apostle, in Christianity, the 12 original disciples of Jesus. The term was extended to include the major missionaries of the early church, including Paul and Barnabas, and later missionaries, including Patrick of Ireland, to previously pagan nations. △1026.

Apostles' Creed, a formulated expression of beliefs used in Western Christianity as far back as the 2nd century. The creed is not the work of the apostles. Simple in form, it deals with the three persons of the Trinity.

Apostolic Succession, doctrine in Orthodox, Roman Catholic, and Anglican churches that the ministry is continued from the apostles of Christ. The basis of the historical church is guaranteed continuity usually in the rank of bishop.

Apotheosis, act of deifying a human being. The Greeks elevated founders of cities and colonies to the status of gods after death. The Romans deified Romulus, Caesar, Augustus, and others. After Christianity became the official religion of the Roman Empire, emperors could not be deified.

Appalachian Mountains, mountain system extending from E Canada SW to Alabama. Includes the White Mts, Green Mts, Catskills, Alleghenies, Blue Ridge, and Cumberland Mts. The highest point is Mt Mitchell in Yancey co, N.C., 6,684ft (2,039m).

Appaloosa, western breed of horse developed by the Nez Percé Indians of NW United States. A strong backed horse, it is bay, chestnut, black, or gray with a distinctive white mark over loin, rump, and hip containing spots of body color. Tail and mane are thin. Height: at least 56in (142cm) at shoulder; weight 1100lb (495kg).

Apparent Magnitude. *See* Magnitude.

Apparent Movement, or illusory movement, phi phenomenon, or the marquee effect, occurs when two or more stimuli are turned on and off in rapid succession; if they are lights, a spot of light appears to jump from one location to another. Motion pictures, which are really a series of sequential still pictures, are an example of apparent movement. △672.

Appeals, Courts of, system directly beneath the US Supreme Court, created (1891) to relieve work load of Supreme Court. There are 11 Courts of Appeals, 1 in the District of Columbia and 10 circuits distributed throughout the United States. Each court has from three to nine judges but cases are generally heard before three judges. There is no original jurisdiction. Appeals are brought from administrative agencies and the US Tax Court and District Courts. Most often they act as courts of last resort.

Appeasement, policy where one government grants unilateral concessions to another to forestall a political, economic, or military threat. Appeasement of Germany at Munich (1938) at the expense of Czechoslovakia is considered a classic example. △1336.

Appendicitis, inflammation of the appendix probably caused by obstruction of the organ. Symptoms include general abdominal distress, followed by more severe pain in the lower right abdomen. Nausea and vomiting usually follow. Acute appendicitis is usually treated only by surgical removal of the appendix. A ruptured appendix can cause peritonitis and death. *See also* Peritonitis.

Appendix, small, fingerlike organ located near the junction of the small and large intestines, usually in the lower right quarter of the abdomen. It has no known function but often becomes inflamed, necessitating surgical removal.

Appenzell, canton in NE Switzerland; originally ruled by the abbots of St. Gallen. It united with Swabian cities 1377; protected by Swiss confederation 1411, became member 1513; divided into two half-cantons (1597), Appenzell Inner Rhodes (Catholic) and Appenzell Outer Rhodes (Protestant); noted for scenic beauty, intricate embroidery and lace. Area: 161sq mi (417sq km). Pop. 62,147.

Appian Way, ancient military road in Italy, constructed 312 BC by the censor Appius Claudius Caecus. It was the chief highway to Greece and the East, connecting Rome with Capua; later extended to Beneventum, Tarentum and Brundisium; portions remain today. A new, parallel Appian Way was built in 1784. Length: approx. 350mi (564km).

Apple, common name for the most widely cultivated fruit tree of temperate climates. Derived from the *Malus pumila* native to SE Europe and SW Asia, apples are propagated by budding or grafting. More than 7,000 varieties have been recorded in the United States alone. From the flowers, which require cross-pollination to produce a desirable fruit, the fleshy fruit develops in a variety of sizes, shapes and acidities; generally roundish, 2–4in (5–10cm) in diameter and some shade of yellow, green, or red. A mature tree may yield up to 30 bushels of fruit in a single growing season. Of the total world production, Europe produces 50% to 60% of the annual crop with the United States adding another 16% to 20%. Japan, Korea, China, India, Australia, New Zealand, Argentina and Chile are also important producers. More than 80% of the U S annual crop is used as fresh fruit; less than 10% is used for vinegar, juice, jelly, and apple butter; almost 10% is canned. Family Rosaceae. △338.

Applegate, Jesse (1811–88), US frontiersman, b. Kentucky. He was a surveyor, cattleman, writer, and teacher. In 1843 he led a wagon train to Oregon, and then again in 1845 when he settled there, establishing a ranch at Yoncalla. He reorganized the territorial government and united the British and American settlers in Oregon. He supported the Union and Lincoln the Civil War, writing newspaper essays in their vor. His *A Day with the Cow Column* (published 34) recounted his experiences on the Oregon Trail.

pple Maggot, or railroad worm, black and yellow , 0.16 to 0.24in (4–6mm) long, with spotted wings. is a serious pest of apples and blueberries through-t North America. The larvae leave brown trails rough the inside of the fruit. Family Tephritidae, ecies *Rhagoletis pomonella*. *See also* Diptera.

ppleseed, Johnny (*c* 1774–1845), b. John Chap-an in Leominster, Mass., US folk hero who planted ple orchards throughout the midwestern United ates. In 1840 he settled in a cabin near Mansfield, hio, but continued, as he did in his youth, to travel ındreds of miles to scatter apple seeds. Stories of his ndliness and his understanding of animals spread ıtil he was a legend in his own lifetime.

ppleton, city in E Wisconsin, on Fox River, 105mi 69km) NW of Milwaukee; seat of Outagamie co; site first US hydroelectric plant (1882); Lawrence Uni-ersity (1847). Industries: paper products, farm tools, nned goods. Settled 1833; inc. 1857. Pop. (1970) 7,143.

pplied Mathematics, study of physical henomena using mathematical methods. In one ense the subject is simply the application of mathe-atical tools in science or engineering. More gener-ly, it is a body of knowledge and theory with a math-matical structure including the abstract entities and rmal rules of 'pure' mathematics together with phys-al measurable quantities and physical laws. It in-udes such topics as mechanics, fluid mechanics, sta-stics, quantum theory, and relativity theory. *See also* athematics.

pplied Psychology, use of psychological theory in elds as diverse as the design of spacecraft, classroom arning, industrial relations, personnel counseling, onsumer education, military training, and mental ealth.

ppliqué. *See* Embroidery.

ppointment, Presidential, power granted in rticle II, Section 2, of the US Constitution per-itting the president to fill offices in the executive nd judicial branches of the national government, ne regulatory agencies, and armed forces. Some ajor positions, such as Supreme Court justices nd cabinet members, must be approved by the enate.

ppomattox, town in Virginia, 18mi (29km) E of ynchburg; near Appomattox Court House National istorical Park; seat of Appomattox co; nearby is site f Gen. Lee's surrender to Union forces under Gen. rant (Apr. 9, 1865). Industries: tobacco marketing, ımber, flour milling, batteries, clothes. Inc. 1925. op. (1970) 1,400.

ppomattox River, river in SE Virginia; rises in Ap-omattox co; flows E to the James River at Hopewell. ength: 137mi (221km).

ppreciation, increase in the market value of an sset, usually only that increase that was not the result f any activity on the part of the current owner, eg, a ome may appreciate while one lives in it regardless f any improvements made or not made.

pprenticeship, learning a craft or trade from a killed worker in exchange for assisting in the work for specified time period. Known since ancient times, he practice became highly structured in medieval urope under the supervision of the guilds. Today, pprenticeship programs sponsored by unions or pro-essional organizations are regulated by governmen-al agencies.

Appropriation, legislative method of setting apart money for a particular use. In the US Congress, appro-priation bills generally originate in the House of Rep-esentatives. The influential House Appropriations Committee and its many subcommittees are the prin-cipal architects of the appropriations measures.

Apricot, a stone-fruit tree cultivated throughout tem-perate regions, thought to have originated in China. Large, spreading trees with dark green leaves and white blossoms bear the yellow or yellowish-orange fruit that is eaten fresh or preserved. Species *Prunus armeniaca*. △338.

April, fourth month of the year. The name may be derived from the Latin word *aperire* ("to open"). It has 30 days. The birthstone is the diamond.

Apse, in architecture, a semicircular or polygonal space for a choir or at the end of an aisle; in a church or temple it may hold an altar or statues.

Apteryx. *See* Kiwi.

Aptheker v. Secretary of State (1964), US Supreme Court case declaring that a law denying passports to members of registered Communist organizations was unconstitutional. The court said that the law was too broad and indiscriminate and restricted the right to travel implicit in the First Amendment.

Aptitude Test, test designed to predict how well an individual will perform on some task or job. Scholastic aptitude tests assess abilities related to successful performance in school; vocation aptitude tests measure abilities related to skills involved in specific occupations. The latter are used in vocational counseling.

Apuleius, Lucius (*c.*125–170), Roman writer. His prose narrative *The Golden Ass* (or *Metamorphoses*) is the only classical Latin novel that has survived in its entirety. He also wrote philosophical treatises influenced by Neoplatonism and Eastern mysticism. *See also* Golden Ass, The. △1028.

Aqaba, Gulf of, NE arm of the Red Sea between the Sinai Peninsula, Egypt, and Saudi Arabia; entrance is through the Strait of Tiran. Gulf has played important role in Arab-Israeli conflicts; it was blockaded by Arabs 1949–56, and again in 1967 when Israel held strategic points along Strait of Tiran to guarantee open passage for ships. Length: 100mi (161km).

Aquaculture. *See* Fish Culture.

Aquamarine. See Beryl.

Aquarium, vessel for keeping fish in captivity, ranging from small bowls to large public aquariums. Fish were kept in captivity as early as 2500 BC in Sumeria, and ancient Romans kept marine fish in large pools connected to the sea. Indoor aquariums were developed by Sung Dynasty (960–1278) Chinese who kept goldfish in porcelain vessels. The earliest large public aquarium was the Fish House at Regent's Park, London, in 1850. The New York Aquarium opened in 1896. There are now about 100 large aquariums in the United States, including the Marinelands in Florida and California. Home aquariums usually hold 10–15 gal (38–57l) of water. Equipment such as thermostatic heater, air pump, filter, plants, and sand or gravel is needed to provide proper balance between fish, water, oxygen, and temperature. *See also* Tropical Fish.

Aquarius, or the Water Bearer, equatorial constellation situated on the ecliptic between Capricornus and Pisces; the eleventh sign of the zodiac. It contains the Saturn Nebula (NGC 7000), the globular cluster M2 (NGC 7089), and the Helix Nebula (NGC 7293). Brightest star Beta Aquarii. Astrological sign for the period Jan. 20–Feb. 18. △136, 826.

Aquatic Animals, animals living in water, including minute zooplankton, crustaceans, fish, and mammals. Physical factors affecting their growth include temperature, light intensity, and available carbon dioxide, oxygen, and dissolved materials. △550,552.

Aquatic Mammal, mammal that spends all or most of its life in water. They evolved from land-living ancestors. Some, notably whales (including dolphins and porpoises) and sirenians, have adapted completely to a life in water and no longer leave the water to breed. Their forelimbs are modified into flippers and they have lost their hind limbs and developed a tail fin. Seals are almost as adapted for aquatic life as whales but retain functional hind limbs and leave the water to breed. Other partially aquatic mammals include the beaver, muskrat, and water rat (rodent); otter (carnivore); and water shrew and desman (insectivore).

Aquatic Plant. *See* Hydrophyte.

Aquatint, type of etching that produces transparent tones. The copper plate, bitten by acid through a porous ground of granulated resin, becomes textured, and produces a speckled tone when printed. *See also* Printmaking.

Aqueduct, man-made water conveyor used to transport a stream of water across a valley, operating with the force of gravity or with the pressure of the water. △1762.

Aqueous Solution, solution in which water is the solvent. Water dissolves many polar substances, that is, ionic compounds and covalent compounds with

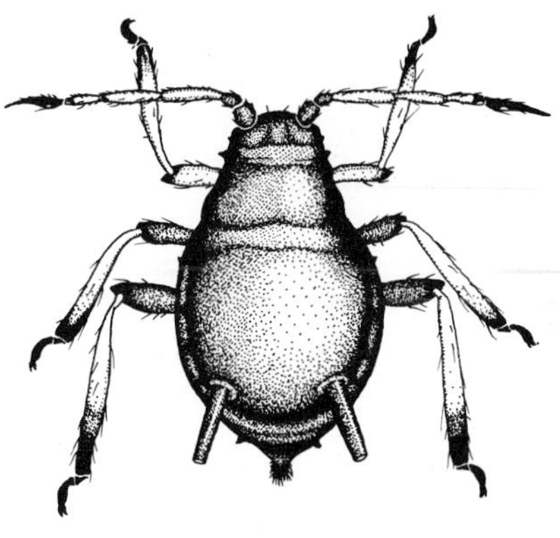

Aphid

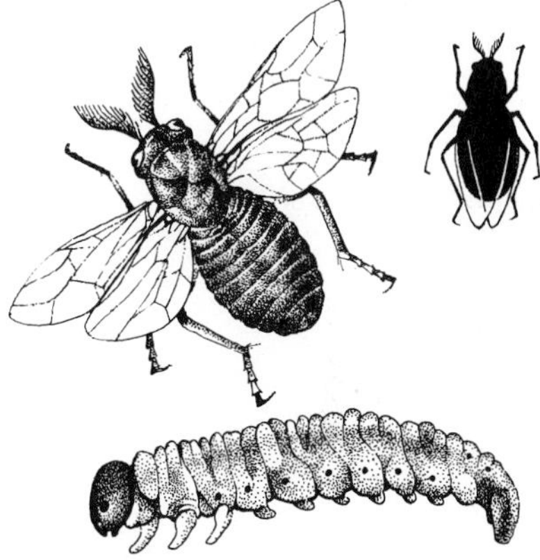

Apple maggot

Appomattox Court House: Lee surrenders to Grant

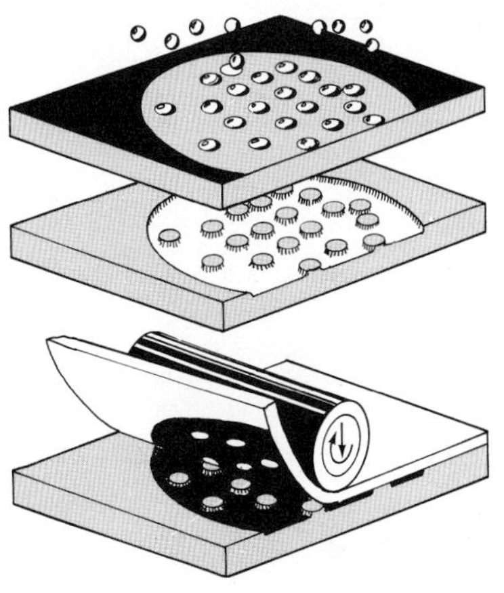

Aquatint

molecular dipoles, because the water molecules themselves are polar, with negative charge on the oxygen atom. They tend to cluster around positive ions (solvation), making the solution energetically favorable. *See also* Electrolytic Solution.

Aqueous Tension. △1504.

Aqueteague. *See* Weakfish.

Aquifer, an underground formation that is an economically significant water source. An aquifer might be sand or gravel, or any other type of permeable rock layer that holds and delivers water to streams, springs, or wells. The water source may be glacial and the aquifer system may be extensive. *See also* Hydrology; Water Table. △254.

Aquinas, Thomas (*c.*1225–74), Roman Catholic theologian, philosopher, and saint. He joined the Dominican order, followed Albertus Magnus to Paris in 1245, and thereafter refused ecclesiastical dignities in order to preach and work on his *Summa Theologica* (1266–73). Revelation, he argued, could not conflict with reason, and while separate, they rested on the one absolute Truth. In the *Summa Catholicae Fidei contra Gentiles,* he defined theology as the queen of the sciences. The *Summa* was to systematize all human knowledge by reconciling Aristotle and Christianity. Philosophically, he maintained the real existence of Universals. Aquinas was canonized in 1323. △856, 1088.

Aquitaine, historical region of SW France; Toulouse was the capital. Under the Romans it was called Aquitania and became an integral part of the Roman Empire, including all land between Pyrenees Mts and Garonne River. The Romans were followed by the Visigoths and then the Franks. Independent for a time, it belonged to France and then England until early 13th century when all but Gascony (S part) was returned to France. At end of Hundred Years War in 1453 all of Aquitania was inc. into France. △1096.

Aquitania. △1020.

Arab, peoples of many nationalities found predominantly in the Middle East and North Africa, who share a common heritage in the religion of Islam and their language (Arabic). The majority of the population is either agriculturalist or city-dwelling; the remainder practice pastoralism, raising camels, sheep, and goats. The patriarchal family is the basic social unit in a strongly traditionalist culture that has been little affected by external influences, although wealth from oil is bringing rapid modernization.

Arabia, peninsular region in SW Asia, bordered by Persian Gulf (E), Arabian Sea (S), Syrian Desert (N), and Red Sea (W); unified by Muslims in 7th century; dominated by Ottoman Turks after 1517. Husayn led successful revolt against the Turks and founded independent state in Hejaz region. The Saud family defeated Husayn in a violent siege and founded Saudi Arabia in 1925. Great Britain held protectorates, but after WWII British influence declined greatly and other independent states emerged in the region. Area: 1,000,000sq mi (2,590,000sq km). Pop. 17,-000,000.

Arabian, oldest horse breed, developed for endurance in the Arabian deserts. Source of all light horse breeds, this slender horse has a refined head, deep quarters, and short back with one less lumbar and one or two less tail vertebrae than other breeds. Its sleek coat is bay, gray, chestnut, black, or white, with black skin and white marks only on head and legs. Height: 56–61in (142–155cm) at shoulder; weight: 850–1100lb (385–500kg).

Arabian Desert, mountainous desert in E Egypt bordered by Nile Valley (W), Red Sea and Gulf of Suez (E); extends along E coast of Egypt, merging with Nubian Desert in S. Oil is produced in N; granite, sandstone, and porphyry found in the mountains are used for building stones. Nomadic tribes inhabit the desert; site of 3rd-century monastery of St Anthony. Area: 86,000sq mi (222,740sq km).

Arabian Nights, The, also called **A Thousand and One Nights** and originally **Alf Layla Wa Layla,** tales of a variety of origins—Arab legends, Indian and Persian fairy tales, and Egyptian love stories—compiled in written form as long ago as the 15th century in the colloquial Arabic language from the oral tradition. In the Western versions Scheherazade tells one tale nightly of such heroes as Aladdin, Ali Baba, or Sinbad to postpone her death by her master's hand. The tales throw some light on Arabic life in the 9th through 16th centuries.

Arabian Sea, NW arm of Indian Ocean, bordered by Somalia and Arabian Peninsula (W), India and Malabar Coast (E), Indian Ocean (S). Two main branches are off to the NW: Gulf of Aden connecting with Red Sea, and Gulf of Oman joining with Persian Gulf. Indus River is the largest river emptying into the sea; major medieval trade route between Arab kingdoms and Chinese empire passed through Arabian Sea and Persian Gulf. Length: 1,800mi (2,898km).

Arabic, a Semitic language. Classical Arabic is the language of the Moslem scriptures, the Koran. With many colloquial variations, the written form is understood in all Moslem countries across North Africa to Iraq. Original to the Arabian Peninsula, it spread with Islamic conquests in the 7th and 8th centuries. Estimated number of speakers now is 90 million. △866.

Arabic Numeral, one of the symbols 0, 1, 2, 3, 4, 5, 6, 7, 8, and 9, used in the common notation for writing numbers in the decimal system. *See also* Numeral. △1448.

Arab-Israeli Wars (1948–49, 1956, 1967, 1973–74). Tension and armed conflict between Israel and the Arab States have existed since 1920, when Britain received a League of Nations mandate for Palestine. The first full-scale war was set off by Israeli independence on May 14, 1948. From 1945–1948 the Israelis had made substantial gains against Palestinian Arabs. The 1948–49 war clearly showed the Arab opposition to Israeli independence, on territory the Arabs considered as theirs. During 1948 Arab troops from Egypt, Iraq, Lebanon, Syria, and Transjordan (modern Jordan) invaded Israel. Initial gains by the Arabs were soon halted and a cease-fire was established on Jan. 7, 1949. From 1949 to 1956 truce was enforced by UN security forces. In October 1956 the Israeli armed forces under the direction of Moshe Dayan launched an attack into the Sinai Peninsula. Israel was supported by France and Britain, who were alarmed by the nationalization of the Suez Canal. International opinion forced a cease-fire in November; Israel surrendered territorial gains after it had been guaranteed access to the Gulf of Aqaba on its southern border. In 1967, Egyptian President Nasser closed the Gulf of Aqaba to Israel, and in retaliation Israel launched a massive air attack, and in the ensuing Six Day War Israel captured the Sinai Peninsula, the Golan Heights on the Syrian border, and the Old City of Jerusalem. Intermittent hostilities continued until 1973, when the Arab states began active preparations for war. Egyptian and Syrian forces attacked on Oct. 6, 1973, on Yom Kippur, a Jewish holiday. Israel managed to push back Egypt and Syria only after losing many men and much equipment. A tentative cease-fire was established by October 25, but fighting continued until 1974. The basic problems between Israel and the Arab states remained unresolved. △1380.

Arab League, name given to the League of Arab States formed in 1945 to give a collective political voice to the Arab nations. Members include Egypt, Syria, Lebanon, Iraq, Jordan, Sudan, Algeria, Kuwait, Saudi Arabia, Libya, Morocco, Tunisia, Yemen, Peoples Democratic Republic of Yemen, Qatar, and the Palestinian Arabs. The most important attempts have been made by the league in terms of Arab economic life. In 1953 they set up an Arab Telecommunications Union. In 1954 a postal union was organized and in 1959 a financial organization (Arab bank) was developed. The Arab Common Market was formed in 1965 and opened to all Arab members in 1973. Political unity, however, has been hampered by a split among the members concerning pro-Western activities. △1350.

Arachnida, worldwide class of arthropods including spiders, ticks, mites, scorpions, and harvestmen. All have four pairs of jointed legs, two body regions (cephalothorax and abdomen), and chelicerate jaws. They lack antennae and wings. *See also* Harvestman; Mite; Scorpion; Spider; Tick.

Arafat, granite hill in Saudi Arabia, 15mi (24km) SE of Mecca; ancient pagan sanctuary associated with many legends; site of annual pilgrimage, pulpit from which the Khutbal (pilgrimage address) is given.

Arafat, Yasir (1929–), leader of the Palestine Liberation Organization (PLO), one of the first Palestinians to advocate guerrilla war against Israel. In 1974 he was recognized by Arab leaders as the "sole legitimate representative of the Palestinian people."

Aragón, region in NE Spain, bordered by the Pyrenees Mts (N), the Iberian Mts (S), Catalonia (E), and Old Castile (W); formerly part of ancient Roman province of Hispania Tarraconensis. In 1479 the Kingdom of Aragon became part of Spain; Aragón retained own government, currency, and military forces u the 18th century; agricultural region. Crops: grap wheat, sugar beets. Industries: textiles, chemica iron, marble, limestone. Area: 18,382sq (47,609sq km). Pop. 1,152,708. △1078.

Aragonite, a carbonate mineral, calcium carbona ($CaCO_3$), formed under special conditions, generally caverns and hot springs. Readily converts to calc (another mineral of $CaCO_3$). Orthorhombic syste groups of needle-like crystals or massive depos twinning common. Glassy white; hardness 3.5–4; gr 2.9.

Aral Sea (Aral'skoje More), formerly Khorezm skoye More; 4th-largest inland body of water in t world, in central Asian USSR, in SW Kazakhstan a NW Uzbekstan; has no outlet, many small islands; f by rivers Syr Darya (NE) and Amu Darya (S); genera shallow and only slightly saline, indicating geograp ically recent separation from Caspian Sea, 175 (282km) to the E. Population along shores is spars concentrated mostly in NE Aralsk-Kazalinsk. Settl by Russians in 1840s. Area: approx. 26,000sq (67,340sq km).

Aram. △980.

Aramaic, Biblical Semitic language, the original la guage of parts of the Old Testament. After the Baby nian captivity, it was the common written and spok language of the Middle East until replaced by Arab. Minor dialects persist.

Aran Islands, group of three small islands in Nort ern Ireland, at entrance to Galway Bay. Chief islan are Inishmore, Inishman, Inisheer; site of pre-Christi ruins. Area: 18sq mi (47sq km). Pop. 2,269.

Arapaho, Algonkian-speaking tribe of North Ame can Indians. Their original home was in the Red Riv valley; they moved across the Missouri River and sp into two groups. After the Treaty of Medicine Lodg (1847) one group joined the Southern Cheyennes Oklahoma, while the northern band went onto Wir River Reservation with the Shoshone. A Plains trib they joined with the Cheyenne in raiding migratin white settlers. Their population today is approx mately 3000.

Arapaima. △618.

Ararat, Mount (Büyük Ağri Daği), mountain in extremity of Turkey, 10mi (16km) from Iranian borde 20mi (32km) from USSR; has two extinct volcan peaks; named for 9th century BC kingdom founde there; earthquake (1840) destroyed last settlemen traditional landing place of Noah's Ark (Genesis 8:4 boundary treaties with Russia (1921) and Iran (193 locate mountain completely in Turkey; first climbe by Friedrich Parrot 1829. Great Ararat rises 17,000 (5,185m); Little Ararat rises 13,000ft (3,965m).

Araucaria, genus of evergreen tree native to th Southern Hemisphere. They have scale-like leave whorled branches, and seed-bearing cones. Famil Pinaceae. *See also* Norfolk Island Pine, Monkey Pu zle Tree.

Arawakan, a family of American Indian language spoken in northern South America, mainly in Co lombia, Venezuela, and Peru, but also in Brazi Guyana, and Surinam. Taino, an Arawakan languag now extinct, was once the dominant language of th islands in the Caribbean. The English word "hurr cane" comes from this language.

Arbitrage, process whereby currency, securities goods, or gold are purchased in one country's marke and sold in another market for a profit, which is poss ble when there are differences among the exchang rates or interest rates in various countries. *See als* Exchange Rate.

Arbitration, settling disputes by seeking and accept ing third-party decisions. Arbitration is rarely compul sory; success is dependent upon both parties to th dispute accepting the arbitrator's decision. In th United States, the American Arbitration Associatior founded 1926, provides professional arbitrators t settle labor-management disputes. The United Na tions International Court of Justice has had limite success in arbitrating disputes between nations.

Arboriculture, scientific cultivation of trees an shrubs used for decoration and shade. Aspects o growth studied include pruning; transplanting; tre removal; treatment of wounds, cavities, and othe damage; controlling insects; and diagnosing ailments Early Egyptians were the first to transplant trees prop ly and correct treatments of wounds were known in ncient Greece. Arboriculture includes growing timer trees (silviculture) and fruit trees (pomology). △ 64; 366.

rborvitae, common name for six species of the enus *Thuja*, a resinous, evergreen conifer of the Cyress family (Cupressaceae) native to North America nd E Asia. It grows in the form of trees or shrubs, with hin outer bark, fibrous inner bark, and a characteriscally flattened branch.

rbutus, trees and tall shrubs native to the Mediteranean region and W North America. They have dark reen, leathery leaves, and reddish brown bark. The rn-shaped flowers are white, red, or pink, and the trawberry-like fruit is red or orange. Family Ericaeae.

rc (geometric), portion of a curve. For a circle, the ength *(s)* of an arc is the product of the angle (θ) it ubtends at the center, measured in radians, and the adius *(r)*: that is, $s = r\theta$.

Arcadia, ancient region in Peloponnesus, Greece; ompletely surrounded by mountains. Chief city, Megalopolis, was center of political activity and capial of the Arcadian Confederacy; destroyed during Greek War of Independence (1821–29). Founded 370BC.

Arcadia, city in S California, 13mi (21km) ENE of Los Angeles; site of Santa Anita racetrack. Industries: aerospace, optical goods, cameras. Inc. 1903. Pop. 1970) 42,237.

Arcadius (377?–408), first Eastern Roman emperor 395–408). After the death of Theodosius I, the Roman Empire was split between his sons into sepaate states; the East ruled by Arcadius; the West ruled by his brother Honorius. Neither brother was a strong uler. During Arcadius' reign the government was controlled by the praetorian prefect Rufinus and later by various military leaders and the Empress Eudoxia.

Arch, in construction, a rigid, upward curved span between two points of support, usually functioning in the bearing of great weight, as in a bridge or ceiling. The triumphal arches of the Romans are an example of arch use for decoration, rather than support. True arches have been used for at least 6,000 years; uncurved arches, with one large stone leaning on another, have neolithic origins.

Archaeopteryx, first known bird, it was preserved in Jurassic deposits in Europe. Raven-sized and fully feathered, its skeleton resembled a reptile's rather than a modern bird's. It had no beak, but jaws with teeth. It was capable only of weak, flapping flight. △ 570,572.

Archangel (Archangel'sk), city in Russian SFSR, USSR; capital of Archangel'sk oblast; port at head of Dvina Gulf and Northern Dvina delta; contains large harbor (often ice-bound); site of monastery of Archangel Michael (1685–99). City was opened to European trade *c.* 1600 by Boris Godunov, and it prospered as only Russian port until 1703; received Allied convoys during WWII. Industries: shipbuilding, lumber milling, paper production. Settled 10th century by Northmen. Pop. 343,000.

Archangel Raphael and Tobias, The (Stoss). △ 1136.

Arch Bridge, a bridge that uses arched spans to bear the weight of the bridge superstructure as well as its load. Arch bridges thrust outward as well as down at the ends and are said to be under compression. Arch bridges date back at least 2000 years to still-standing Roman edifices. △1756–58.

Archelon. △572.

Archeology, scientific study of former human life and activities through material remains (fossils, artifacts, buildings). Archeologists' work includes: retrieval of the remains from the ground or seabed; recording and interpreting the circumstances in which objects were found (their level in the soil, association with other objects); thorough examination and description of their finds; and hence the building up of a picture of the culture that produced the objects. In the study of cultures that developed the art of writing, written remains supplement other material, but archeology increasingly relies on the aid of various scientific techniques to increase knowledge about the past. △1292.

Archer, The. *See* Sagittarius.

Archerfish, fish found in brackish waters of SE Asia and Australia. It is yellowish-green to brown with dark markings and catches insect prey by spitting water "bullets." Length:to 8in (20cm). Family Toxotidae; 5 species including *Toxotes jaculatrix.*

Archery, sport involving the use of a bow and arrow. The object is to accumulate points by shooting a specified number of arrows in a target that consists of five concentric circles, the innermost circle being the "bull's-eye." Other than target-shooting, the three other divisions of archery are field, flight, and crossbow. Archery was the prime military weapon used before the advent of gunpowder and was revived as a sport in England in 1676 by Charles II. Its popularity grew after the Grand National Archery Association, the sport's first governing body, was formed in England in 1861. △930.

Arches National Park, region in SE Utah, overlooking Colorado River Gorge; includes unusual giant sandstone arches, windows, pinnacles, and spires; landscape arch forms a natural bridge more than 100ft (31m) high and 291ft (89m) long. Authorized 1929. Area: 82,953acres (33,596hectares).

Archimedes (287–212 BC), Greek mathematician and inventor. He is known for his studies in geometry, physics, hydrostatics, and mechanics. He is credited with discovering the principle (Archimedes' principle) that an object immersed in fluid will lose in weight an amount equal to the weight of the fluid displaced. He also invented a mechanical device (Archimedes' screw) that raises water and calculated the value of π. Several legends surround his life, one of which is that he discovered Archimedes' principle while sitting in his bath watching the water his body displaced. It is said that he ran all the way home shouting "Eureka!" (I have found it), forgetting even to dress. His works include *On the Sphere and Cylinder, On Spirals, On Floating Bodies,* and *On the Method of Mechanical Theorems.* △1006, 1438, 1488, 1448, 1496.

Archimedes' Principle, the observation that a body in a fluid is buoyed up by a force equal to the weight of the displaced fluid. The principle is said to have occurred to Archimedes in his bath as he puzzled over how to tell a golden crown from one alloyed with silver. △1496, 1504.

Archimedes' Screw, a machine used for raising water, thought to have been invented by Archimedes in the 3rd century BC. The most common form of the machine is a cylindrical pipe enclosing a helix, inclined at a 45° angle to the horizontal with its lower end in the water. When the machine rotates, water moves up through the pipe.

Archipelago, a sea or a marine area in which many islands are clustered, or the islands themselves. *See also* Atoll; Coral Reef.

Archipenko, Alexander (1887–1964), US sculptor and painter, b. Russia. His revolutionary works include the first sculpted collage, the famous *Medranos* (1912), and the changeable, motor-driven painting *Archipentura* (1924).

Architecture. A work of architecture is a stable construction that meets the practical and aesthetic needs of a civilized people. Both an art and a technique, its quality is a determining factor of that society's quality of life. △1258, 1298, 1322.

Architrave, in classic architecture, the beam that is the lowest piece in the entablature (the architrave, frieze, and cornice), above the colonnade of a building and below the roof. Although very plain in Doric architecture, other styles compose it of several horizontal layers and bands.

Archives, documentary materials accumulated by an institution and preserved for their historical and literary value. The concept of archives located independently of a library reached full development during the French Revolution.

Arch of Constantine. △1024.

Archons, leaders in Athens and other Athens-influenced cities. At first elected for life, they later (683 BC) were elected annually as magistrates, but lost power after the sweeping reforms of 487 BC.

Arctic, Area N of the Arctic Circle (lat. 66° 30′ N); includes the Arctic Ocean, Greenland, and the northernmost regions of Asia, Europe, and North America. These lands partially surround the ice-covered Arctic Ocean and vary from low coastal plains to high ice plateaus and mountains; most of the area is

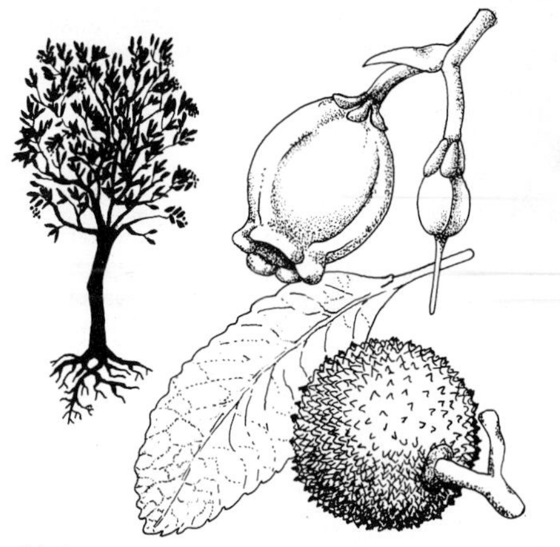

Arbutus

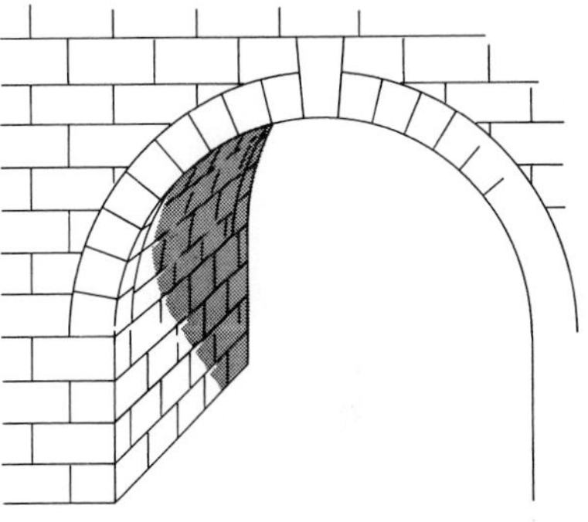

Arch

Archer fish

Archimedes' principle

dominated by tundra, poorly drained lowlands. Sparsely populated, the region has been inhabited for centuries by people mainly of the Mongoloid race. The main groups include the Eskimo of Greenland, North America, and E Siberia, the Samoyeds of W USSR, the Chukchi of E USSR, and the Lapps of Europe. Hunting, fishing, reindeer herding, and handcrafts are the chief sources of support. Various Arctic regions contain vast resources of minerals; however, most are inaccessible. The Arctic regions of the USSR are the most developed. The Arctic regions were first explored by Norsemen (9th–12th centuries); exploration continued in the 16th and 17th centuries by the Dutch and English in search of the Northwest or Northeast Passage to the Orient. The English navigators Henry Hudson discovered the Hudson Bay in 1610 and William Baffin explored Baffin Bay in 1616. Russian exploration was led by the Danish navigator Vitus Bering, who discovered the Bering Straits 1728. British naval officer John Franklin, lost in an Arctic expedition (1845–48), is credited with the discovery of the Northwest Passage. US exploration began 1850; the first official US scientific expedition was 1881–82; US explorer Robert E. Peary was the first man to reach the North Pole (1909). The first air flight over the North Pole was accomplished by US explorers Richard E. Byrd and Floyd Bennett and Norwegian explorer Roald Amundsen. The USSR established the first drifting scientific station (1937). During WWII the US Air Force set up several air bases and meteorological stations in Alaska, Canada, and Greenland. The US atomic-powered submarine, the Nautilus, accomplished the first submerged crossing of the North Pole (1958).

Arctic Circle, the northernmost parallel, 66.5° north of the equator, at which the sun neither sets on the day of summer solstice (June 21) nor rises on the day of winter solstice (December 22). *See also* Antarctic Circle; Solstice.

Arctic Ocean, ocean N of Arctic Circle, between North America and Eurasia; almost totally landlocked, bordered by Greenland (SW), Canada and Alaska (NW), USSR (N and NE), Norway (SE); connected to Pacific Ocean by Bering Strait, and to Atlantic Ocean by Davis Strait and Greenland Sea. The smallest ocean, it includes Barents, Beaufort, Chukchi, Greenland, and Norwegian seas. There is animal life (plankton) in all Arctic water and polar bears, seals, and gulls up to 88° N. Area: 5,400,000sq mi (13,986,000sq km).

Arctic Tern, seabird whose migrations are longest of any bird—from summer breeding areas in the far north to wintering areas in Antarctica. It has gray, black, and white feathers and a bright bill and feet. Gregarious, it nests in colonies and lays eggs (1–4) in a sandy scrape nest. Length: 17in (43cm). Species *Sterna paradisaea*. △528.

Arcturus, or **Alpha Boötis,** red giant star in the constellation Boötes. Characteristics: apparent mag. −0.06; absolute mag. −0.3; spectral type K2; distance 36 light-years.

Ard. △304.

Arden, city in N central California. Pop. (1970) 82,492.

Ardennes (Forest of Ardennes), wooded plateau area in SE Belgium, N Luxembourg, and Ardennes dept in N France, E and S of Meuse River. Chief cities are Liège and Namur; scene of heavy fighting in both world wars, especially in the Battle of the Bulge, Dec. 1944–Jan. 1945. A well-preserved forest, wild game is abundant and cleared areas support farming and grazing. Population is sparse.

Ardmore, city in S Oklahoma, 100mi (161km) S of Oklahoma City; seat of Carter co; site of Carter Seminary, federal school for Indians. Industries: oil refining, food processing, fiber glass, sportswear. Settled 1887; inc. 1898. Pop. (1970) 20,881.

Area, measure of the amount of surface of a plane figure or body; given in square units (cm^2, in^2, etc). The area of a rectangle of sides *a* and *b* is *ab*; the areas of triangles and other polygons can be determined using trigonometry. Areas of curved figures and surfaces can be determined by using integral calculus. △1466.

Arendt, Hannah (1906–75), US political scientist, b. Germany. She was research director for the Conference on Jewish Relations (1944–46) and executive director of Jewish Cultural Reconstruction (1949–52). She was the first woman appointed to a full professorship at Princeton University (1959). Among her works studying contemporary totalitarianism and racism are *The Origins of Totalitarianism* (1951), *The Human Condition* (1958), *Eichmann in Jerusalem* (1963), and *Crises of the Republic* (1972).

Areola. △686.

Ares, Greek god of war (Roman, Mars). He was the son of Zeus and Hera and the lover of Aphrodite. Ares' activities were making war and love. In the Trojan war he sided with the Trojans, whose leader, Hector, he favored with his personal protection. Among his offspring were Fear, Rout, and Cynus, who was slain by Hercules. In art Ares is often represented as a stalwart figure armed with a helmet, shield, and spear.

Arezzo, city in central Italy; capital of Arezzo prov. in Tuscany. Former Etruscan town of Arretium, it became a Roman military station famous for Arretine red clay vases; birthplace of Petrarch and Vasari; site of numerous 14th-century houses and palaces, an Etruscan museum, cathedral (1286–1510); agricultural trade and transportation center. Industries: textiles, leather goods. Pop. 84,839.

Argali, or **Marco Polo sheep,** wild sheep native to the mountains of Cen. Asia. The largest of all sheep, it has 75-in (1.9-m) curved horns. Height: 4ft (1.2m) at shoulder; weight: 300lb (135kg). Family Bovidae; species *Ovis ammon*. *See also* Sheep.

Argenteuil, city in N France, on the Seine River; developed around a 7th-century convent, which was destroyed during the French Revolution; site of shrine in Saint-Denis Basilica (1866) containing the Seamless Tunic, traditionally believed worn by Christ. Industries: metalworks, furniture, airplane and railroad parts, chemicals. Pop. 90,480.

Argentina, republic in South America occupying most of S part of the continent. In the Americas only Canada, the United States, and Brazil are larger. Most people, Spanish-speaking and Roman Catholic, come from European backgrounds. In some ways underdeveloped, Argentina prospers when labor and political unrest and weather permit.

Land and Economy. The Andes stretch down W Argentina, separating it from Chile. Several peaks reach above 20,000ft (6,100m), and Aconcagua is the highest mountain in the Americas, 22,834ft (6,964m). N Argentina has a hot, humid savanna area, the Chaco, covered with grasses and occasional trees. Central Argentina is the plains, or pampas, region where livestock and cereal grains thrive in the temperate climate. S Argentina, cold and mountainous, is sheep country. Numerous rivers border or cross Argentina, with the Paraná and Uruguay joining to form a wide estuary, the Rio de la Plata. Minerals, largely unexploited, occur in the mountains. The country is second to Venezuela among petroleum producers of Latin America and has large natural gas pockets. During WWI and II, Argentina industrialized but still imports many manufactured goods. Exports, including beef, are mainly agricultural.

People. Wandering Indian tribes occupied the land until Spaniards drove them out or mixed with and absorbed them. A large mestizo population resulted; these people of mixed blood became the gauchos, or cowboys, of the pampas. Late in the 19th century Europeans—Italians, Spaniards, and Germans, particularly—flocked to the country. Their descendants and the mestizos have gradually lost much of their separate identities. About 68% of the people lives in urban areas, with more than 35% in Buenos Aires.

Government. The constitution is patterned on that of the United States. It requires citizens over 18 to vote, and they elect the president and vice president —who must be native-born Roman Catholics—and members of the Senate and Chamber of Deputies by secret ballot. The governments of the 22 provinces are clearly subordinate to the central government.

History. Under the viceroyalty of Peru, Argentina suffered by being distant from Lima, but in 1776 Spain formed the viceroyalty of La Plata with headquarters in Buenos Aires. When Napoleon went to war with Spain in 1808, independence movements spread, and Argentina became free in 1816. Political coups caused turmoil throughout Argentine history. In 1946, Col. Juan Perón, after gaining popularity with labor, won the presidency. He became a dictator, but in 1955 the army overthrew him. From exile he rebuilt his strength and regained the presidency in 1973, with his third wife, Isabel, as vice president. He died in 1974, and she became Latin America's first woman president, but a financial scandal, inflation, and guerrilla warfare weakened her regime, and she was removed from power in 1976.

PROFILE

Official name: Argentine Republic
Area: 1,100,000sq mi (2,849,000sq km)
Population (1975): 25,400,000
Density, 23per sq mi (9per sq km)
Chief cities: Buenos Aires (capital); Rosario; Córdob
Government: Head of state, Jorge Videla, preside
Gross national product (1973 est): $27,750,000,000
Per capita income (1973): $1,200.
Industries (major products): iron, steel, cars, machinery, petroleum products.
Agriculture (major products): beef, wheat, cor grapes, sorghum, oats, wool.
Minerals (major): petroleum, natural gas, lead, zin tin, manganese, iron, copper, beryl.
Trading partners (major): European Common Market, Brazil, United States.

Arginine, essential amino acid ($NH_2C(NH)NH(CH_2)_3CH{\cdot}NH_2{\cdot}COOH$). *See* Amino Acid.

Argolis, district in Greece in NE Peloponnesus extending to city of Argos; in Greek mythology Kin Pelops established a powerful kingdom in Argos; h ancestors included Agamemnon and Atreus; note home of the Argives, Greeks of great wealth and cu ture (*c.* 2,000 BC).

Argon, gaseous nonmetallic element (symbol Ar) c the noble-gas group, discovered (1894) by Lord Ray leigh and Sir William Ramsay. Argon is present in th Earth's atmosphere (0.94% by volume) and is ob tained by the fractionation of liquid air. It is use in electric-light bulbs, fluorescent tubes, arc welc ing, and semiconductor preparation. The elemer forms no compounds. Properties: at. no. 18; at. wt 39.948; density 1.7837 g dm^{-3}; melt. pt. −308.6°F (−189.2°C); boil. pt. −302.3°F (−185.7°C); mos common isotope Ar^{40} (99.6%). *See also* Noble Gases. △1552.

Argonaut, predaceous, ocean-dwelling cephalopo mollusk found worldwide. Related to the octopus, i has eight suckered arms. Two of the female's arms are modified to secrete a coiled, paper-thin, ridged shel that is actually an egg case. The shell-less male has a specialized tentacle (hectocotyles) to hold sperm. I detaches and independently crawls into female's mantle. Female length: 6m (15.2cm); shell length: 8in (20.3cm). Male length: 1in (2.5cm). The paper nauti lus *(Argonauta argo)* is best known of the six species Family Argonautidae. *See also* Cephalopod. △482.

Argonauts, in Greek legend, 50 heroes who sailec the ship *Argo* to Colchis, a kingdom at the easterr end of the Black Sea, in search of the Golden Fleece Their leader was Jason, husband of Medea. Many ad ventures and tragedies characterized their wander ings. The Golden Fleece symbolized a kingdom prom ised Jason when he returned with it.

Argus, name of several figures in Greek legend. One was a giant with 100 eyes, half of which remained open at all times. Another Argus was the shipbuilder who built the ship *Argo* for Jason and became a crew member.

Argus Pheasant, peacocklike pheasant of Malaya and Borneo, frequently seen in zoos and parks. The inner-wing feathers are broadened, elongated, and marked with round, colorful eyespots. At mating time, the male clears a forest floor site and performs a courtship display, elevating his wing feathers to form reflectors on either side of his back. Length: 6ft (1.8m). Species *Argusianus argus*. *See also* Pheasant.

Argyll, Archibald Campbell, 1st Duke of (1651?–1703), Scottish leader. Unsuccessful in winning James II's favor, he became a supporter of William and Mary, formally offering them the Scottish crown in 1689. Although he played no personal role, his regiment was responsible for the massacre of the rebellious MacDonalds at Glencoe in 1692. *See also* Glencoe, Massacre of.

Argyll, Archibald Campbell, 8th Earl and 1st Marquess of (1598–61), Scottish leader. His concern for an independent, Presbyterian Scotland caused him to change sides frequently during the English Civil War. After gaining some concessions from Charles I in 1641, he actively sided with Parliament, leading an army against Royalist forces. But the execution of Charles I in 1649 turned him against Cromwell. In 1651 he crowned Charles II King of Scotland. When the Scottish invasion of England in 1652 on behalf of Charles II failed, Argyll returned to the Commonwealth side. After the successful restoration of Charles II in 1660, Argyll was arrested and executed for treason.

Aria, in music, a solo song with instrumental accompaniment; also a lyrical instrumental piece. It is an important element of opera, and is also found in cantatas and oratorios. The term originated in the 17th entury when Giulio Caccini published a series of ongs with continuous accompaniment, which he ermed arie (singular, aria).

riadne. △836, 1028.

rianism, theological stance heretical to Christianity ased on the teachings of Arius (*c.*250–336). Arius aught that Christ was a created being, and not divine. ince the Son had a definite beginning, he is mortal, nd as such can have no direct knowledge of God. The ouncil of Nicaea (325) condemned Arianism. *See lso* Nicaea, Councils of. △1052, 1054.

rias, Arnulfo (1897–), President of Panama. He as elected in 1939 and overthrown in 1941. ledged to oppose US intervention in Panamanian ffairs, he seized power in 1949 but was ousted in 951. Following an unsuccessful bid for the presiency in 1964, he won the 1968 contest but reained in power for only 10 days, before being overrown once more by the military.

riel, satellite of Uranus. △88.

Aries, or **the Ram,** northern constellation situated n the ecliptic and lying southeast of Triangulum. As he first sign of the Zodiac, it formerly contained the irst Point of Aries, the intersection of the ecliptic and he equator marking the vernal equinox. Owing to recession this has now shifted westward into Pisces. Brightest star: Alpha Arietis (Hamal). Astrological sign or the period Mar. 21–Apr. 19. △132, 826.

Ariosto, Lodovico (1474–1533), Italian Renaissance poet and dramatist. He was forced by economic esponsibilities into work as a statesman, diplomat, and administrator for the d'Este family. His plays were he first to imitate Latin comedy in the vernacular. His most famous work is the epic poem *Orlando Furioso* 1532).

Aristarchus. △40, 60, 1006.

Aristocracy, system in which a privileged class exercises political control over society. Historically, the term describes a hereditary nobility. Its contemporary usage includes any ruling group or class, especially those characterized by wealth.

Aristophanes (*c.* 448–380 BC), Greek writer of comedies. Eleven of his more than 40 plays survive; they are the only extant comedies from his time. All follow the same basic plan: realistic characters become involved in absurd situations. Graceful choral lyrics frame caustic personal attacks. A conservative, Aristophanes attacked Euripides' innovations in drama, Socrates' philosophical radicalism, and Athens' expansionist policies. His most noted plays are *The Clouds* (423), *The Birds* (414), *Lysistrata* (411), and *The Frogs* (405). △998.

Aristotle (384–322 BC), Greek philosopher, Plato's disciple for 19 years. After Plato's death, he opened his first school in Asia Minor. Having educated Philip of Macedon's son Alexander between 343 and 334 BC, Aristotle returned to Athens to open a school in the Lyceum. Upon Alexander's death (323), Aristotle, accused of impiety, fled to Euboea where he died a year later. Moving away from Plato's theory of the Forms, he developed the theory of the Unmoved Mover. Among his works are *De Anima, Metaphysics,* and *Nicomachean Ethics.* △852, 854, 858, 1088.

Arithmetic, simple calculations and reckoning using numbers and such operations as addition, subtraction, multiplication, and division. The study of arithmetic usually involves learning procedures for operations such as long division, extraction of square roots, etc. More fundamental study of the integers is a branch of higher mathematics—number theory. *See also* Mathematics. △1446–48.

Arithmetical Operations, the commonly used operations of arithmetic: addition, subtraction, multiplication, and division. The procedures of arithmetic were put on a formal axiomatic basis by Guiseppe Peano in the late 19th century. Using certain postulates, including that there is a unique natural number, 1, it is possible to give formal definition of the set of natural numbers and the arithmetical operations. Thus, addition is interpretable in terms of combining sets: in $2 + 7 = 9$, 9 is the cardinal number of a set produced by combining sets of 2 and 7. Multiplication can be thought of as repeated additions: subtraction and division are the inverse operations of addition and multiplication. The operations can be extended to negative, rational, and irrational numbers. △1446.

Arithmetic Mean, or average, number obtained from a set of numbers by dividing their sum by the number of members in the set. Thus for numbers a, b, c, and d, the arithmetic mean is $(a + b + c + d)/4$. *See also* Geometric Mean.

Arithmetic Progression, sequence of numbers in which each term is produced by adding a constant term to the preceding one. Thus it has the form a, $a + d$, $a + 2d$, . . . An example is the progression 1, 3, 5, etc. Here d is called the common difference. The sum of such a progression, $a + (a + d) + (a + 2d) + \ldots$, is an arithmetic series. For n terms it has a value $n/2[2a + (n-1)d]$. △1456.

Arius (*c.*250–336), an heretical priest, noted for his asceticism. He supported a subordinationist teaching about the person and nature of Christ: the Son is a perfect creature, but inferior to the Father and less than divine. In 325 the Council of Nicaea condemned him.

Arizona, state in SW United States, bordered on the S by Mexico.

Land and Economy. The Colorado Plateau, at elevations of 4500 – 10,000ft (1,373 – 3,050m) occupies the N part of the state. It is cut by many steep canyons, notably the Grand Canyon of the Colorado River, which is a national park. The Colorado is the principal river, flowing about 700mi (1127km) through the state and along its W boundary. Hoover Dam in the NW created Lake Mead for irrigation and water supply to distant points. Other scenic landmarks are Monument Valley, the Painted Desert, and the Petrified Forest. The Mexican Highlands, a mountain mass running NW to SE, separates the plateau from the Sonoran Desert region in the SW and S. Arizona's mineral resources and its grazing and farming land have long been mainstays of the economy. Mining and agriculture are still important, but since the 1950s manufacturing has been the most profitable sector. Tourism is a major source of income.

People. Between 1950 and 1970, Arizona's population more than doubled, and in the 1970s its annual growth rate was more than 35%; new residents came from all parts of the United States. Arizona is a popular retirement region because of its healthful climate. Nearly 80% of the population is classed as urban. Arizona has more Indians than any other state, remnants of the 15 aboriginal tribes.

Education and Research. There are nine institutions of higher education. The Lowell Observatory at Flagstaff and the Kitt Peak National Observatory at Tucson are leading centers of astronomical research.

History. Spanish explorers visited the region in 1539–40, and Jesuit missionaries taught the Indians after 1690. The area became part of Mexico, which kept it after winning independence from Spain in 1821. At the end of the Mexican War (1848), Mexico ceded most of the present state to the United States and in 1853 land in the SW was acquired from Mexico by the Gadsden Purchase. Arizona became a US territory in 1863. Major growth of the state came after WWII, which started an industrial boom.

PROFILE

Admitted to Union: 1912; rank, 48th
US Congressmen: Senate - 2; House of Representatives - 4
Population: 1,772,482 (1970); rank, 33rd
Capital: Phoenix, pop. 501,562 (1970)
Chief cities: Tucson, 262,933; Scottsdale, 67,823; Tempe, 63,550
State legislature: Senate, 30 members; House of Representatives, 60
Area: 113,909sq mi (295,024sq km); rank, 6th
Elevation: Highest, Humphreys Peak, 12,670ft (3864m); lowest, 100ft (31m) on Colorado River
Industries (major products): machinery (electrical, non-electrical), electronic components
Agriculture (major products): cotton, citrus fruits, cattle, sheep
Minerals (major): copper, gold, silver, molybdenum
State nickname: Grand Canyon State
State motto: Ditat Deus (God Enriches)
State bird: Cactus Wren
State flower: Saguaro Cactus Blossom
State tree: Paloverde

Ark, Noah's, according to Genesis 6:14–16, the floating house Noah was ordered to build and live in with his family and one pair of all living creatures during the Flood. 450ft (137m) long and 75ft (22.8m) wide, it was believed to have come to final rest on Mount Ararat. *See also* Ararat. △838.

Arkansas, state in the S central United States; one of the 11 Confederate states in the Civil War.

Land and Economy. In the E and S the land is low, providing excellent soil for farming, while rugged hills of moderate height mark the W and N. All the drainage flows into the Mississippi River, which forms the

Arctic tern

Peru
Bolivia
Brazil
Paraguay
PACIFIC OCEAN
Salta
San Miguel de Tucumán
Corrientes
Córdoba
Mendoza
Rosario
Uruguay
Chile
Buenos Aires
ARGENTINA
Mar del Plata
Bahía Blanca
ATLANTIC OCEAN
Comodoro Rivadavia
0
700km

Argentina

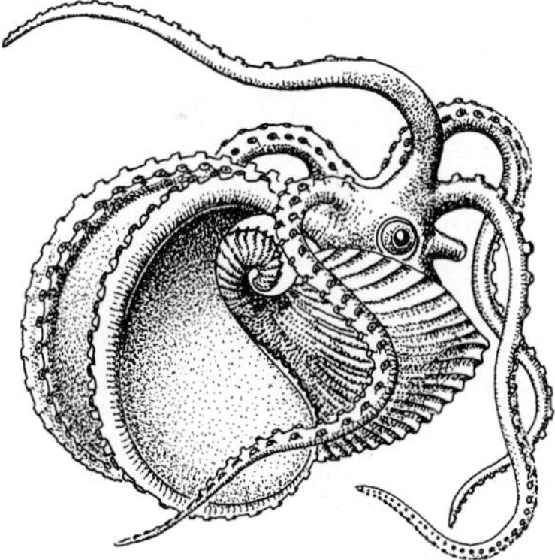

Argonaut

Arizona: Agate Bridge, Petrified Forest National Park

E boundary. The state's principal river is the Arkansas, flowing SE across the central area. Forests are extensive and contribute largely to the economy. Agriculture is important, but manufacturing is expanding. Hot Springs National Park is a major attraction in the tourist industry.

People. Most residents are descended from immigrants who moved westward from the S Atlantic states after 1815. A rural way of life in isolated communities prevailed generally until after WWII, but by 1970 half the population was classed as urban.

Education. There are more than 20 institutions of higher education. The University of Arkansas is state-supported, and there are seven state colleges.

History. Spaniards visited the region in 1541, and by 1673 Frenchmen descended the Mississippi as far as the Arkansas River. In 1682 the Sieur de la Salle claimed all the Mississippi valley for France. Four years later the French made a settlement, later called Arkansas Post, on the lower Arkansas River. Their missionaries and traders were active until 1762, when France ceded the area to Spain. Returned to France in 1800, it passed to the United States by the Louisiana Purchase in 1803. It was made part of Missouri Territory in 1812 and became a separate territory in 1819. Arkansas was the 9th state to secede and join the Confederacy in 1861. It rejoined the Union in 1868. Development of the state's resources proceeded slowly until the 1950s.

PROFILE

Admitted to Union: 1836; rank, 25th
US Congressmen: Senate - 2; House of Representatives - 4
Population: 1,923,295 (1970); rank, 32nd
Capital: Little Rock, 132,483 (1970)
Chief cities: Fort Smith, 62,802; North Little Rock, 60,040; Pine Bluff, 57,389
State legislature: Senate, 35 members; House of Representatives, 100
Area: 53,104sq mi (137,539sq km); rank, 27th
Elevation: Highest, Magazine Mt, 2823ft (861m); lowest, Ouachita River, 55ft (17m)
Industries (major products): wood products, chemicals, processed aluminum ore
Agriculture (major products): cotton, poultry, rice, timber
Minerals (major): bauxite (aluminum ore), petroleum, natural gas
State nickname: Land of Opportunity
State motto: Regnat Populus (The People Rule)
State bird: Mockingbird
State flower: Apple Blossom
State tree: Shortleaf Pine

Arkansas Post, village in SE central Arkansas on Arkansas River; site of the first white settlement in Arkansas; served as capital of Arkansas Territory (1819–21); nearby is Arkansas Post National Memorial. Founded by the French in 1686 as a trading post. Pop. 15.

Arkansas River, river with its source in central Colorado; flows E through Kansas and SE across the NE corner of Oklahoma, SE to Arkansas, emptying into the Mississippi River in SE Arkansas. Length: 1,450mi (2,335km).

Ark of the Covenant, according to Jewish tradition, the portable wooden gold-adorned chest containing the two stone tablets on which the Ten Commandments were inscribed. Regarded as the most sacred shrine of ancient Israel, it symbolized God's covenant with His chosen people. Only the high priest could look upon it; no one could touch it. The tabernacle built by King Solomon to house it was destroyed in 586 BC and no further record of the original Ark remains. In today's synagogues, the Holy Ark is a closet or recess in which the congregation's sacred scrolls are kept. △844.

Arkwright, (Sir) Richard (1732–92), English textile industrialist and inventor. His use of power machinery and the factory production system was innovative. In 1764 he began work on his spinning frame, which he patented in 1769.

Arles, town in S France, on Rhone River 45mi (72km) NW of Marseille. Romans called it Arelate and connected it to the Mediterranean Sea by canal in 103 BC; counts of Savoy and King Charles VI of France acquired it in 14th century; contains remains of a 2nd-century Roman amphitheatre, now used for bullfights, and 12th–14th century Montmajour abbey. Industries: boat building, metal working, sulfur refining. Pop. 45,744.

Arlington, town in E Massachusetts; suburb of Boston; scene of bitter fighting following battles of Lexington and Concord (1775); site of Jason Russell house furnished in 17th- and 18th-century antiques. Settled 1630; inc. 1807. Pop. (1970) 53,524.

Arlington, city in N Texas, 13mi (21km) E of Fort Worth; site of University of Texas at Arlington (1895). Industries: automobiles, rubber products, machinery. Founded 1876; inc. 1883. Pop. (1970) 89,723.

Arlington, city in N Virginia, across Potomac River from Washington, D.C.; site of Arlington National Cemetery, Tomb of the Unknown Soldier, the Pentagon, and Marymount College (1950). Originally a part of the District of Columbia, it was made a co of Virginia in 1847. Pop. (1970) 174,284.

Arlington Heights, city in NE Illinois; NW suburb of Chicago; race track is nearby. Industries: publishing, nursery farming. Pop. (1970) 64,884.

Arlington National Cemetery, national cemetery in Virginia, opposite Washington, D.C., on the S bank of the Potomac River; former estate of Robert E. Lee; site of Tomb of the Unknown Soldier, memorial amphitheater, and graves of many servicemen and prominent Americans. Area: 408acres (165hectares). Est. 1864.

Arm, technically, that part of the body comprised of the upper part of the limb extending from the shoulder joint to the elbow. In popular usage the term has come to mean both the arm and the forearm.

Armada, Spanish, fleet sent in 1588 by the Catholic Philip II of Spain against the Protestant Elizabeth I of England. The Armada, under the command of the Duke of Medina Sidonia, consisted of 130 ships. It sailed up the English Channel, where it was met by a fast, modern English fleet. Badly beaten in the fight and hampered by the weather, the Armada was unable to land in England. It tried to get back to Spain by sailing around Scotland. Storms destroyed it, and its survivors were forced to surrender. The destruction of the Armada marked the decline of Spanish power and the consequent rise of English power.

Armadillo, nocturnal mammal found from Texas to Argentina. Noted for the armor of bony plates that protects its back and sides; when attacked, some species roll into a ball so that no vulnerable parts are exposed. It eats insects, carrion, and plants. Length: 5–40in (12.7–101cm). Family Dasypodidae. △588.

Armageddon, from the Hebrew *har megiddo,* "hill of Megiddo"; according to Revelation 16:16, the place where the final battle between the demonic kings of the earth and the forces of God will be fought at the end of the world. The strategically situated Palestinian city of Megiddo was historically the scene of many battles in Biblical times.

Armagnac, region in SW France; formerly part of old province of Gascony; agricultural area, famous for brandy. Once part of the Roman Empire, it became a countship in the 10th century; annexed by France 1607.

Armagnacs, faction that supported the duke of Orleans in the early 15th-century civil war in France. Led by Bernard VII, Count of Armagnac, they opposed John, Duke of Burgundy, who collaborated with the English invaders in this phase of the Hundred Years' War. *See also* Hundred Years' War.

Armature, in Mechanics. △1540.

Armenia, ancient kingdom of W Asia, now divided between Iran, Turkey, and USSR; centered in the mountainous region SE of Black Sea and SW of Caspian Sea; the Euphrates and Araks rivers have their sources in this historical political battlefield. Strategically located between Europe and Asia, it has been the scene of repeated battles for more than 3,000 years. It enjoyed prosperity under Tigranes the Great 95–56 BC; under Roman and Byzantine rule until AD 1046 when it fell to Turkey; ravaged by Mongol forces (13th century); divided between Ottomans and Persia (1620), the latter part coming under Russian rule 1828–29; Turkish Armenians' fight for independence began in 1894 and culminated in almost total destruction of Armenian population by 1915. Armenia's declaration of independence (1917) was opposed by Russia and Turkey. Russo-Turkish Treaty (1921) established present boundaries.

Armenian Language, Indo-European language spoken in the Armenian, Georgian, and Azerbaijan Soviet Socialist Republics and in parts of Turkey, central Europe, and North and South America. It is the single remaining survivor of a distinct part of the Indo-European language group.

Armenian Soviet Socialist Republic, smallest co stituent republic of USSR, in the S Caucasus Mts. R public occupies E part of ancient Armenia; borde Georgian SSR (N), Iran (S), Azerbaijan SSR (E), ar Turkey (W); a mountainous region, it rises to 13,43 (4,097m) at Mt Aragats. Yerevan is capital; oth major cities are Leninakan and Kirovakan. Araks ar its tributary Razdan are the chief rivers; Lake Seva has fishing industry; Araks valley is agricultural regio Products: cotton, fruit, rice, tobacco. Area: appro 11,500sq mi (29,785sq km). Est. 1921; made a co stituent republic 1936. Pop. 2,493,000.

Arminianism, liberal Calvinism mixed with huma ism, named after its founder, Jacobus Arminiu (1560–1609). Reason and faith should not be contr dictory. The sacraments are merely signs of unio and Christ's death is only an example of God's punis ment of sin. It was later to influence the developme of deism and pietism.

Arminius (18 BC?–21 AD), German tribal leader, chi of the Cherusci. In 9 AD he surprised and destroyed Roman army under Varus advancing in the Teutobur Forest. Never again did the Romans attempt to co quer German lands E of the Rhine. Praised by Tacitu he became a folk hero (his name in the German form Hermann) to 19th-century German nationalists.

Armistead, Lewis Addison (1817–63), Confede ate general in the Civil War, b. New Bern, N.C. H fought for the United States (1831–61) in the Mexica War and on the western frontier, but in 1861 resigne his commission to command a North Virginia reg ment. He was killed in the Battle of Gettysburg.

Armistice, World War I. △1308.

Armor, (1) Protective clothing and headgear usuall made of metal or thick leather used to prevent injur to warriors in battle. Employed since antiquity, bod armor, except for the helmet, ceased to be of use i Europe in the 17th century. (2) Metal plating on war ships or armored vehicles that is at least stron enough to deflect small arms fire. Warships were firs armored in the mid-19th century, vehicles durin World War I. (3) Military units having a high concen tration of armored vehicles such as tanks, armore personnel carriers, and mechanized artillery. △1592 1726.

Armored Car. △1736.

Armored Personnel Carrier. △1736.

Armory Show, international exhibition of moder art held at the 69th Armory, New York City, Feb 17–March 15, 1913. It later traveled to Chicago an Boston. Originally the show was intended to exhibi radical US artists, but the European section created a greater controversy. The show introduced Impres sionism, Post-Impressionism, Fauvism, and Cubism t the less aesthetically developed US viewers. It force US artists to discard academicism and was the beginning of modern art in the United States.

Armour, Philip Danforth (1832–1901), US industrialist, b. Stockbridge, N.Y. He pioneered in the Chicago meat-packing industry, using in-plant slaughtering, refrigerated railroad cars, and national distribution. With his brother he started Armour & Co. in 1870.

Arms, Right to Bear, provision of the Second Amendment of the US Constitution that allows citizens to keep and bear arms for their own defense. The provision specifically permits the establishment of state militias. It is often cited by opponents to gun control laws.

Arms Control, activity undertaken by powerful nations to prevent one from destroying the other in warfare, especially with nuclear weapons. The nations attempt to maintain a balance of power by regulating each other's stockpiling of weapons. Not the same as "disarmament," which means to give up or reduce the military establishment of a nation. △1344, 1390.

Armstrong, Henry (1912–), US boxer, b. Henry Jackson in Columbia, Miss. He held the world's featherweight championship (1937–38), lightweight championship (1938–39), and welterweight championship (1938–40). He was elected to the Hall of Fame in 1954.

Armstrong, (Daniel) Louis (1900–71), US jazz trumpeter, singer, and bandleader, b. New Orleans. "Satchmo" rose to prominence in the 1920s in Chicago and in Harlem cabarets. After that he made numerous world tours, appeared in films, and made many recordings with other jazz musicians and bands.

His unique, gruff vocal style produced several hit recordings including "Hello Dolly" (1964). △1366.

Armstrong, Neil (Alden) (1930–), US astronaut, b. Wapokoneta, Ohio. He was the first man to walk on the moon (July 21, 1969). Selected a NASA astronaut in 1962, he was the command pilot for the Gemini XIII orbital flight. △56, 1724.

Armstrong, William H(oward) (1914–), US author of children's books, b. Lexington, Va. He is best known for *Sounder*, the story of a black sharecropper's family in the South during the Depression. This book was awarded the Newbery Medal for 1970. Other works include *Barefoot in the Grass* (1970) and *Sour Land* (1971).

Army, Department of, division of the Department of Defense. It is charged with providing support for national and international policy and for US security by planning, directing, and reviewing the military and civil operation of the Department of the Army. This includes the organization, training, and equipping of US land forces for prompt and sustained combat operation. Est. 1789, amended by subsequent legislation in 1947, 1949.

Army, United States, the ground service of the US armed forces. It consists of approximately 785,000 personnel under the president, who is commander in chief of the armed forces, and the general supervision of the secretary of the army and his advisor, the Army chief of staff, who is the Army's highest ranking officer. The Army chief of staff is a member of the Joint Chiefs of Staff. The department of the Army is charged with the organization, training, and equipping of these forces, but not their military employment. The army also provides assistance in disaster relief, conducts research into weapons development, carries on training at civilian colleges, and administers the US Military Academy at West Point, among other services. The Army has 16 active divisions and helps to maintain 8 National Guard and 12 reserved divisions; major overseas commands are the Seventh Army in Europe and the Eighth Army in Korea. The Continental Army existed from 1775, but the first regular standing was authorized by Congress in 1785. The war department was established in 1789. The department of war became the department of the Army in 1947, and in 1949 it became a part of the Department of Defense. The US Army has taken part in all major wars between the War of 1812 and the Vietnam conflict. A draft was occasionally employed and was used in peacetime after World War II. In 1973, Congress established an all-volunteer Army. *See also* Defense, Department of; Joint Chiefs of Staff.

Army Ant, or **Driver Ant,** highly predaceous, tropical and subtropical ant found in both hemispheres. Ranging in size from 0.13 to 1.75in (3.25–43.75mm) in length, they move en masse hunting for food and migrating. Family Formicidae. Subfamily Dorylinae. *See also* Ant; Hymenoptera.

Armyworm, moth caterpillar that travels in hordes, destroying crops as they go. The best known armyworm is the orange-, brown-, and yellow-striped *Pseudaletia unipuncta*. Length: 1.5in (38mm). Outbreaks of this caterpillar occur annually east of the Rocky Mountains in the United States. Family Noctuidae.

Arnica, a large genus of perennials of the composite family, native to the Northern Hemisphere. It has daisylike flower heads. *Arnica montana* was formerly used for treating sprains.

Arno, river in Italy; rises in the Apennines Mts; flows W to the Ligurian Sea below Pisa; site of flood control works, some planned by Leonardo da Vinci; failed to prevent serious flooding of Florence in 1966, which resulted in major damage to city's art treasures. Length: 150mi (242km).

Arnold, Benedict (1741–1801), Revolutionary War officer and traitor, b. Norwich, Conn. He was placed in command of Philadelphia after being wounded at the battle of Saratoga. In 1780, he was given command of West Point, a fort he proposed to deliver to the British for a sum of money. The plan failed, and Arnold fled. He was made a brigadier general by the British and led raids on New London, Conn., and Virginia. He died in London.

Arnold, Henry Harley (1886–1950), US general, known as "Hap," b. Gladwyne, Pa. He graduated from West Point in 1907 and was assigned to the aviation division of the Signal Corps in 1911, receiving his flying instructions from Orville Wright. He became chief of the US Army Air Corps (1938) and chief of the US Army Air Forces in 1942. In 1944 he was promoted to five-star general. A long time advocate of a separate Air Force, he became the first five-star general of the new branch in 1949.

Arnold, Matthew (1822–1888), English poet and critic. The son of Thomas Arnold, he held the Oxford chair in poetry (1857–67). His writings include literary criticism, such as *Essays in Criticism* (series 1, 1865; series 2, 1888), and social commentary, such as *Culture and Anarchy* (1869). His poems include "Sohrab and Rustum" and "The Scholar Gypsy" (1853) and "Thyrsis" and "Dover Beach" (1867). *See also* △1240.

Arnolfini Wedding, The (Van Eyck). △1136.

Arnulf (*c.* 850–99), king of the East Franks (887–99); last Carolingian Holy Roman emperor (896–99). He gained the kingdom of the East Franks by defeating his uncle Emperor Charles III. He decisively defeated the Norsemen at Louvain in 891. He invaded Italy (894), captured Rome (895), and was crowned Holy Roman Emperor there (896).

Aromatic Compound, organic chemical compound that contains atoms of carbon joined to form a ring-shaped molecule.

Aroostook River, river in N Maine and Canada, rises in Piscataquis co; flows NE across New Brunswick, Canada, and empties into the St John River E of Fort Fairfield, Me. Length: 140mi (225km).

Aroostook War (1838–39), Canadian dispute over the Maine-New Brunswick boundary. The Aroostook Valley was claimed by both Canada and the United States, and a conflict arose over Canadian lumber operations in the area. In 1839 a contingent of 50 Maine militia men also moved into the valley. Fighting was threatened, but Gen. Winfield Scott negotiated a truce, and the dispute was submitted to a commission. It was settled by the Webster-Ashburton Treaty (1842). *See also* Webster-Ashburton Treaty.

Arp, Hans Jean (1887–1966), French sculptor, painter, and poet. He was a pioneer in the field of abstract art and a leader in European avant-garde movements in the first half of the 20th century. In Zurich during World War I he was a founder of the Dada movement and in the 1920s joined the Surrealists. He first sculpted in the early 1930s. His works are marked with a simple exuberance, of which *Mountain, Table, Anchors, Navel* (1925) and *Human Concretion* (1935) are typical examples. *See also* Abstract Art; Dada; Surrealism. △1318, 1320.

Árpád (died 907), semi-legendary Magyar chief, national hero of Hungary, founder of the Árpád dynasty. In 895 the invading Magyars under Árpád seized control of Pannonia. Árpád conquered Moravia, raided the Italian peninsula, and also attacked Germany. During constant wars with the Bulgarians and Walachians, he greatly extended his territory. By 896, the Magyars controlled what is now called Hungary.

Árpád, name of dynasty that ruled Hungary, first as dukes (889–1001), thereafter as kings. The first crowned king of this line was Stephen I in 1001. The line became extinct with the death of Andrew III in 1301.

Arras, town in N France, on the Scarpe River, 25mi (40km) SW of Lille; capital of Pas-de-Calais dept. A wealthy banking and weaving town during Middle Ages; became part of French crown lands in 1659 by Treaty of Pyrenees. Industries: oil works, metalworking, brewing. Settled during Roman times. Pop. 49,144.

Arras, Union of (1579), pact signed by the Walloon (southern, Roman Catholic, French-speaking) provinces of the Low Countries that separated them from the northern, Protestant provinces, which in response formed the Union of Utrecht. Although the Union of Arras signed a separate peace treaty with their Spanish overlords, they were soon reconquered. The signatories of the Union of Arras formed the basis of present-day Belgium and Luxembourg; the Union of Utrecht signatories formed the basis of the Netherlands.

Arrest, the act of placing a person in custody or under restraint, most usually because he is suspected of committing or has committed a crime. In civil proceedings, an arrest is made for the purpose of holding a person to a demand made against him.

Arrhenius, Svante August (1859–1927), Swedish chemist and physicist, awarded a Nobel Prize in 1903

Arkansas: the Ozarks

Louis Armstrong

Army ant

Benedict Arnold

for his theory of electrolytic dissociation. His later work was concerned with reaction rates, the physical chemistry of biological processes, the structure of the universe and the revelation that light exerts pressure.

Arrhythmia, an irregularity in the pace or force of the heartbeat. Various abnormalities include atrial tachycardia (fast heartbeat), atrial flutter, and atrial fibrillation, in which there is erratic and ineffective atrial contraction. In the course of normal activity, the heart rate of a healthy person will have some variety.

Arrowhead, or swamp potato, marsh plant found in tropical and temperate America. Its leaves are arrow-shaped and flowers are small, white, and cup-shaped on long stems. Species include common arrowhead *Sagittaria latifolia*. Family Alismataceae. △452.

Arrowroot, tropical and subtropical perennial plant found in wet habitats of North and South America. Leaves are lance-shaped and flowers are usually white. Among 350 species are West Indian *Maranta arundinacea* whose rhizomes yield an easily digested starch. Family Marantaceae. △332.

Arrowsmith (1925), novel by Sinclair Lewis about the efforts of Martin Arrowsmith, a dedicated doctor, to avoid the commercialism that pervades medicine and devote himself to research.

Arrowworm, wormlike, marine invertebrate common in warm waters. They are transparent and dart-shaped with thin fins and pairs of spiny hooks for jaws. They eat plankton and small animals. Length: 0.1–4in (3mm–10cm). There are 50 species. Phylum Chaetognatha. △506.

Arsenal, a repository or magazine of arms, materiel, and munitions for land, air, or naval warfare. The term also can refer to a building used for training troops or the place where military equipment, arms, and munitions are manufactured.

Arsenic, toxic metalloid element (symbol As) of group V of the periodic table, probably obtained by Albertus Magnus (1250). Chief ores are realgar and orpiment (both sulfides) and mispickel (arsenopyrite, FeSAs). Arsenic is used for hardening lead and in semiconductors. Two allotropes are known: a gray metallic form and a yellow nonmetallic form. Properties: at. no. 33; at. wt. 74.9216; melt. pt. 1503°F (817°C); sublimes 1135°F (613°C); most common isotope As^{75} (100%).

Arson, crime, the intentional burning of the property of another. In most places arson is divided into degrees, with the heaviest punishment meted for actions which endanger life.

Arsenopyrite, a sulfide mineral, iron arsenide-sulfide (FeAsS); the major ore of arsenic. Found with precious metal ores in high-temperature veins. Monoclinic system prismatic crystals or granular masses. Metallic white-gray; hardness 5.5–6; sp gr 6.

Artaxerxes I, king of Persia (465–424 BC) under the Achaemenid dynasty. Later weaknesses of the Persian Empire were attributed to his reign as there were many uprisings in the provinces while he was king. He authorized the revival of Judaism as well as many cultural exchanges between Greece and Persia. △984.

Artaxerxes II, king of Persia (404–359 BC), he was the son and successor of Darius II. Artaxerxes relied heavily on his officials to rule the land. His reign was troubled by an assassination attempt by his brother Cyrus and by revolts by his satraps.

Artaxerxes III, king of Persia (359–338 BC) who gained the throne by murdering his brother's family. His reign was marked by terror. In 342 BC he succeeded in strengthening the Persian Empire by destroying Sidon. He was poisoned by his minister Bagoas in 338 BC and was succeeded by his son Arses (replaced by Darius III in 336 BC).

Art Deco, decorative style, also known as *moderne*. First promoted in Paris in 1925, it flourished in the late 1920s through the 1930s. It sought to create for mass production sleek, linear decorative and industrial designs expressive of modern technology. Glass, semi-precious stones, and man-made materials such as ferro-concrete and plastics were favored.

Artemis, Greek goddess, daughter of Zeus and Leto, twin sister of Apollo (Roman, Diana). She was a virgin who assisted in childbirth and protected the young of humans and animals. She was goddess of the hunt, deity of light, associated with the moon.

Arteriography. △750.

Arterioles. △662.

Arteriosclerosis, several diseases of the arteries, including atherosclerosis, the most common form. It is caused by deposits of fatty materials and sometimes calcium on the arterial walls, narrowing the passage for blood, with the calcium also decreasing elasticity of the arteries. There are usually no overt symptoms until the disease in well advanced. Serious cases can lead to coronary disturbance, in which case symptoms may include exrcruciating chest pains radiating to the arms or neck (angina pectoris). So-called senile forgetfulness or confusion may occur if brain vessels are involved. There is evidence that predisposition to the disease is hereditary and that it is more likely to strike cigarette smokers, sedentary persons, or those with high-fat diets. Prevention and control of arteriosclerosis through low fat/low cholesterol diet and exercise is currently favored. If an aneurysm or obstruction in the artery is identifiable, surgery may be indicated. Anticoagulant drugs are sometimes effective on a short-term basis. See also Aneurysm; Angina Pectoris; Atherosclerosis. △716.

Artery, a blood vessel that carries blood away from the heart. The pulmonary artery carries deoxygenated blood to the lungs, but all other arteries carry oxygenated, usually bright red, blood to the various tissues of the body. Artery walls are thick, elastic, and muscular, and they pulsate as they carry blood through the body. They are protected and usually embedded in muscle; a cut artery is serious, causing quick blood loss. △688.

Artesian Water, results from a formation in which an aquifer exists between layers of impervious rock. The water in the aquifer is under sufficient pressure to rise to the surface wherever possible. It does so naturally in bubbling springs or in dug wells that need no pumping. The name indicates the region in France (Artois) where such wells exist. *See also* Aquifer; Hydrology. △254.

Arthritis, an inflammation of the joints. Its most common form, rheumatoid arthritis, occurs most frequently in middle-aged women. The cause is unknown, although physical and emotional stress may trigger symptoms. Symptoms may begin with aching and stiffness developing into pain in the joints affected. Persons with chronic rheumatoid arthritis may show swelling of hands and wrists, perhaps deformities of hands and fingers. The disease is rarely totally disabling. Treatment includes prescribed exercise, particularly of the affected joints, diet, rest, and salicylates (aspirin) to reduce pain. The most severe cases may require surgery or other types of medication. Other forms of arthritis may result from staphylococcal or gonococcal infection. *See also* Rheumatism. △720.

Arthropod, members of the largest animal phylum, Arthropoda. Living forms include crustaceans, arachnids, centipedes, millipedes, and insects. The more than 800,000 species are thought to have evolved from annelids. All have a hard outer skin of chitin that is attached to the musculature on the inside. The body is divided into segments, modified among different groups, with each segment originally carrying a pair of jointed legs for walking or swimming. They have well-developed digestive, circulatory, and nervous systems. Landforms use tracheae for respiration. △484–502.

Arthur, Chester Alan (1830–86), 21st President of the United States, b. Fairfield, Vt.; graduate, Union College, 1848. In 1859 he married Ellen Lewis Herndon; they had three children. A lawyer in New York City, Arthur became a faithful lieutenant of Roscoe Conkling, the Republican state boss. In 1871, President Grant named Arthur collector of customs for New York, a powerful patronage-dispensing office. He was removed in 1878 by President Hayes, thereby setting off a bitter dispute between Conklin's Stalwarts and the Half-Breeds, or supporters of James G. Blaine. The two factions stalemated the 1880 Republican convention. They finally compromised by naming James A. Garfield for president and Arthur for vice president. The ticket won the election with a narrow popular majority.

In July 1881, Garfield was shot by an assassin. He died on Sept. 19 and Arthur became President. His administration belied his background as a party hack. It was honest and efficient and made a serious effort to reform the spoils system. He was denied renomination in 1884 by his party, which nominated Blaine.

Career: collector of customs, port of New York (1871–78); vice president (1881); President (1881–85).

Arthur, semilegendary British king said to have united British tribes against the invading Saxons after the Roman withdrawal. He is usually considered as having lived in the 6th century, although this is not borne out by the *Anglo-Saxon Chronicle*. He became the focus for many medieval legends and romances and became an important figure in English literature.

Arthurian Romance, in literature, the numerous medieval stories based on the largely apocryphal life of King Arthur of Britain and his knights. Arthur was probably a real chieftain who flourished in the 6th century. He is mentioned in several ancient chronicles. His feats combine the courage of a human general and the mystical powers of a god. An early written form of the legend appears in the *Historia* of Geoffrey of Monmouth (12th century). It was developed further by the Norman writer Wace (12th century). The legend also spread to France, where it was popularized in the writings of Chrétien de Troyes (12th century). A major Arthurian work is Thomas Malory's *Morte d'Arthur* (1485). Modern works have also been based on the legend.

Artichoke, or globe artichoke, tall, thistlelike perennial plant native to the Mediterranean region, widely grown in warm regions for the large, edible, immature flower heads. It has spiny, lobed or fernlike leaves and its flowers, if allowed to mature, are blue or white. Height: 3–5ft (0.9–1.5m). Family Compositae; species *Cynara scolymus*.

Article 15, section of the Uniform Code of Military Justice that allows non-judicial punishment for minor offenses to be given by the offender's military commander. Military personnel may refuse punishment by Article 15 and demand trial by court martial; punishment by Article 15, however, is not considered a criminal conviction. *See also* Court Martial.

Articles of Confederation (1781–89), the first constitution of the United States. This document formally joined the 13 colonies for the first time under a central government. The Articles, proposed by Richard Henry Lee and drafted by a committee headed by John Dickinson, were in force until superseded by the US Constitution in 1789. Submitted to the Continental Congress in 1776 and adopted the next year, the Articles were not ratified by all the states until 1781. There was controversy over whether each state would be represented by one delegate or would be represented according to population and whether taxation would be based on population or land value. There was also much dispute over the disposition of the western lands. In the final form, the Articles gave each state one vote, based taxes on the value of surveyed land, and prevented the US government from interfering with a state's western territory. The US government provided for in the Articles of Confederation was weak because it lacked the power to tax, to force the states to obey its laws, or to regulate trade. The desire for a stronger government led to the Constitutional Convention of 1787. *See also* Constitution of the United States.

Artificial Gravity. *See* Gravity, Artificial.

Artificial Insemination, the induction of semen without sexual intercourse by using an instrument to inject seminal fluid into the vagina or uterus. Among the first successful insemination experiments on mammals were those of Italian physiologist Lazzaro Spallanzani (1729–99). The artificial impregnation of livestock makes available proven sires at low cost. In human reproduction the semen may be from the husband of the woman inseminated or from an anonymous donor. △370, 372.

Artificial Kidney, a popular term for a device operating outside the body that removes from the blood the substances ordinarily removed by a properly functioning natural kidney and excreted in the urine. *See also* Dialysis. △728.

Artificial Limb, a man-made limb or segment thereof used to replace a limb or part of a limb lost by amputation and often to perform its functions. △752.

Artificial Respiration. △758.

Artificial Satellite. *See* Satellite, Artificial.

Artificial Sweetener. *See* Sweetener, Artificial.

Artillery, projectile-firing weapons with a carriage or mount. An artillery piece is generally one of four types —gun, howitzer, mortar, or missile launcher. Modern artillery is classified according to caliber ranging from under 120mm for light artillery, to over 210mm for very heavy. The exact origin of artillery is unknown, although it appears to have been used in Europe and the Near East in the 14th century. Used by the Turks to take Constantinople in 1453, it became an important weapon in the 15th century. Advances in the 19th century, including smokeless powder, elongated shells, rifling, and rapid-fire breach loading, made artillery indispensable on the battlefield. △1732–34, 1738.

Artiodactyla, order of mammals characterized by hoofs with an even number (2 or 4) of toes. It includes giraffes, hippopotamuses, deer, cattle, hogs, sheep, goats, camels, and water buffaloes. Mostly of Old World origin, artiodactyls are now found worldwide. They range in size from the 8-lb (3.6-kg) mouse deer to the 4.5-ton hippopotamus.

Artist, The (Gericault). △1228.

Art Nouveau, decorative art movement that spread throughout Western Europe and, to some extent, to the United States from the 1880s to about 1910. Architecture, painting, sculpture, graphic arts, furniture, textiles, and jewelry were all influenced by the style's fluid, undulating lines; symbolic themes; and exotic, dreamlike designs. Some of the most successful practitioners of art nouveau were architect Antonio Gaudi, one of the most original artists of the movement; Hector Guimard, who designed the entrances to the Paris *métro;* René Lalique, jewelry designer; Louis Tiffany, glassware designer; Alphonse Mucha and Aubrey Beardsley, graphic designers and artists.

Art Nouveau Architecture. △1298.

Artois, province in N France bordering Flanders (E). First ruled by the dukes of Flanders, the wealthy province passed to France in 1180. Subsequently under Burgundian and then Hapsburg rule, Artois was retaken by France in 1659. △1096.

Aruba, island in Netherlands Antilles, off the coast of NW Venezuela. Industries: tourism, phosphates, oil refining. Area: 69sq mi (179sq km). Pop. 59,813.

Arum, flowering succulent plants, native to Europe. The wild and cultivated species have large, veiny leaves and dense flowers on a short stem surrounded by a spathe. Complex natural insect traps are formed by these flowers. These plants contain calcium oxalate that produces a burning sensation in the mouth and throat when eaten. Common species are the jack-in-the-pulpit, calla lily, skunk cabbage, and philodendron. Family Araceae.

Arvada, town in NE central Colorado; W suburb of Denver. Inc. 1904. Pop. (1970) 46,814.

Arzachel. △60.

Asbestos, fibrous naturally occurring mineral used in insulating and fireproofing materials. Asbestos is used in the form of wool, fabric, and various asbestos-cement compounds. Several types exist; they are varieties of amphibole, pyroxene, and chrysotile minerals. The form known as blue asbestos (amosite) has certain advantages over the other white forms, but can cause a serious lung condition (asbestosis).

Asbestos Processing, obtaining of a fire-resistant mineral fiber from certain kinds of quarried asbestos rocks, chiefly those containing the chrysotile variety of the serpentine group of minerals. Fibers are freed by crushing the rock and separated by a blowing process. Only fibers at least 0.4in (1cm) long are used in combination with cotton for spinning into yarn. Shorter lengths are used for millboard and building materials.

Ascension Island, volcanic island in S Atlantic Ocean, midway between Africa and South America; governed by British Colony of St Helena; discovered 1501 by Portuguese explorer João da Nova; site of US missile and satellite tracking station; only settlement is Georgetown. Pop. 1,363.

Asceticism, self-denial of bodily pleasures and worldly pursuits indulged in for religious purposes, typically to heighten spiritual awareness. It is practiced in some form in most religions, and in Christianity it is regarded as an imitation of Christ. The commonest form of ascetic discipline—and the form most often practiced by lay persons—is fasting. △812.

Asch, Sholem (1880–1957), Yiddish novelist, b. Poland. He emigrated to the United States in 1909, helped free Yiddish literature from Jewish esotericism. His works include the play *The God of Vengeance* (1907), the novel *A Village* (1904), and the trilogy *The Nazarene* (1939), *The Apostle* (1943), and *Mary* (1949). He settled in Israel in 1956.

Asclepius. *See* Aesculapius.

Ascomycetes. △426.

Ascorbic Acid. *See* Vitamin C.

Asen, name of medieval Bulgarian dynasty (1186–1258). **John,** or Ivan, **Asen I** (died 1196) and his brother **Peter** (died 1197) were boyars from Tirnovo who rose against Byzantium in 1185 and established the second Bulgarian empire. Both were murdered by rival boyars, and rule was assumed by their younger brother **Kaloyan,** or **Yoannitsa** (*r.* 1197–1207). Continuing to raid Serbia, Kaloyan made peace with Byzantium in 1201. Taking advantage of the Fourth Crusade's capture of Constantinople in 1204, he broke with the Eastern Orthodox Church, accepted the primacy of the Pope, and was crowned by a papal legate. He extended his territory over all of western Macedonia before his murder in 1207. **John,** or Ivan, **Asen II** (1218–41), son of John Asen I. His mild and benevolent reign marked the height of the 2nd Bulgarian Empire. John added Epirus, Macedonia, Serbia, and part of Albania to his realm. In 1232 a break with the papacy left the Bulgarian Church independent. The Asen dynasty ended with **Kaliman I** (*r.* 1241–46), **Michael Asen** (*r.* 1246–57), and **Kaliman II** (*r.* 1257–58).

Asepsis. △752.

Asexual Reproduction, reproduction of organisms characterized by the lack of meiosis and fusion of two gamete nuclei. It occurs in several forms: fission (bacteria, protozoa); budding (hydra); spore formation (yeast); vegetative reproduction (strawberries); regeneration (planaria); and parthenogenesis (honeybees).

Asgard, in Scandinavian mythology, the domain of the gods. The Aesir resided here in splendid mansions. Chief of these was Valhalla, home of Woden, where the heroes slain in battle were carried in triumph.

Ash, genus of deciduous trees found in northern temperate regions. The wood is elastic, strong, and shock resistant, used for tool handles, baseball bats. About one-half of the 70 species are American, including *Fraxinus americana,* the white ash, found from Nova Scotia to Texas; black ash, *F. nigra;* and the green ash, *F. pennsylvanica lanceolata.* Others are manna ash, *F. ornus,* the flowering ash of southern Europe and Asia Minor, and the European ash, *F. excelsior,* which grows to 140ft (43m) tall. Family Oleaceae. △594.

Ash, or volcanic ash, fine particles of lava thrown up by a volcanic explosion. The cone of compound volcanoes consists of built-up layers of ash and lava.

Ashanti, Negroid people of S and central Ghana. In the 18th century they established a powerful empire, based on trade in slaves with the Dutch and British. Conflicts with the British throughout the 19th century were finally resolved in 1902, when the Ashanti territories were declared a British Crown colony. Ashanti society is matrilineal and traditionally agricultural, plantain, bananas, manioc, yams, and cocoa being the chief crops. Ashantis bear allegiance to a paramount chief, whose capital is at Kumasi and who is advised by his mother or sister. Ashanti religion is animist and includes ancestor-worship; their crafts include weaving.

Ashcan School (*c.* 1907), group of US painters, also called The Eight, who revolted against the National Academy and aestheticism and painted realistic city scenes (including ashcans) and ordinary people. They included Robert Henri, George Luks, William Glackens.

Ashe, Arthur Robert (1943–), US tennis player, b. Richmond. He has won the US (1968) and Australian (1970) singles championships. Noted for his serve, he was among the 10 top-ranked US players from 1963. In 1975 he won the World Championship Tennis (WCT) title and the Wimbledon tournament.

Asher ben Yehiel, also known as Rosh (*c.* 1250–1327), Jewish spiritual leader. Leader of the Jews of Germany, he moved to Spain in 1303 and was appointed the chief rabbi of Toledo. Although he encouraged scientific study, he opposed the study of philosophy, which he saw as challenging the study of Torah.

Chester Alan Arthur

Artichoke

Artiodactyl: kob antelope

Arthur Ashe

Asheville, city in W North Carolina, 100mi (161km) WNW of Charlotte, on the Swannanoa River near Great Smoky Mts National Park; site of Vanderbilt estate, Colburn Mineral Museum, Asheville-Biltmore College (1927); birthplace of Thomas Wolfe. Industries: tourism, tobacco processing, lumber, electronic equipment, textiles, glass. Founded 1794; inc. 1797; chartered as city 1835. Pop. (1970) 57,681.

Ashikaga, or **Muromachi,** period of Japanese history (1338–1573), named after Takauji Ashikaga (1305–58), who was appointed Shogun (generalissimo) by the emperor in 1338. His descendants ruled firmly from 1392–1467, the rest of the period being largely a time of civil war. △1048, 1210.

Ashkenazim, Jews who originally settled in NW Europe, as distinguished from the Sephardim, Jews who settled in Spain and Portugal.

Ashkenazy, Vladimir (1937–), Soviet pianist. He studied at the Central Music School of Moscow and the Moscow State Conservatory. In 1956 he won first prize in the Queen Elizabeth Piano Competition in Brussels, and in 1962 he shared first prize with John Ogdon in the prestigious Tchaikovsky Piano Competition in Moscow.

Ashkhabad (Aschabad), formerly Poltoralsk; city in central Asian USSR, near Iranian border; capital of Turkmen SSR; fertile oasis region; site of university (1950), museum, agricultural, medical, and teachers' colleges; crossed by Trans-Caspian Railroad. Industries: vineyards, orchards, cotton, silk, motion pictures. Founded 1881 as fortress (Askhabad). Pop. 253,000.

Ashland, industrial city in NE Kentucky, on the Ohio River; retail, wholesale, and shipping center. Settled 1815; inc. 1870. Pop. 29,245.

Ashoka, emperor of India (*c.* 274–136 BC). His reign is known from engravings on rocks and from traditions in Sanskrit literature. He was referred to as Piyadassi, "benevolent aspect." One of his edicts suppressed a royal hunt and stressed the sanctity of animal life. He was a lay Buddhist and his son converted Ceylon, present day Sri Lanka, to that faith. △986.

Ashqelon, town in Israel, 38mi (61km) WSW of Jerusalem; produces citrus fruits, cotton. Nearby are ruins of ancient Ashkelon. Founded 1949; pop. 40,-100.

Ashtabula, city in NE Ohio, on Lake Erie at mouth of Ashtabula River; port of entry on St Lawrence Seaway. Industries: chemicals, fiberglass, farm tools. Settled 1803; inc. 1831. Pop. (1970) 24,313.

Ashtart. *See* Astarte.

Ashton, (Sir) Frederick (1906–), English choreographer, b. Ecuador. He joined the Sadler's Wells Ballet in London (1935), now the Royal Ballet, and was its chief choreographer until 1963 and director (1963–70). His classics, *Cinderella* (1948), *Ondine* (1958), *La Fille Mal Gardée* (1960), and many other works have been performed by major ballet companies around the world. △1368.

Ashton-Warner, Sylvia (1905–), British teacher and author who was influential in developing many progressive educational methods. Works recounting teaching experiences with the Maori and in US schools include *Teacher* (1963) and *Spearpoint: Teacher in America* (1972). Novels include *Spinster* (1958) and *Bell Call* (1964).

Ashur, national god of the Assyrians. A god of battle, depicted as eagle-headed and winged, usually combined with the solar disk surmounted by a warrior, he is identified with Baal of the city of Ashur, a storm god, and has similarities to Jahweh of the early Israelites.

Ashurbanipal, or **Assurbanipal,** king of Assyria (669–627 BC). Noted as the last great king of Assyria, under his reign Assyria reached its highest level in art, architecture, literature, and science, although the period was beset with warfare. He abandoned control of the Nile Valley in 654 BC, but conquered several Phoenician cities and suppressed a Babylonian revolt led by his half-brother (648 BC), slaughtering many inhabitants in retaliation. By 639 BC the Elamite kingdom had been absorbed by Assyria. Ashurbanipal assembled the first systematically organized library in the Near East. More than 20,000 tablets and fragments of the library, the chief sources of knowledge of ancient Mesopotamia, are now in the British Museum. Constant warfare so weakened his empire that his two sons, who ruled briefly after his death, could not preserve it. Assyria succumbed to the Medes and the Persians a few years later. △954, 980.

Ashurbanipal II (died *c.* 859 BC), King of Assyria (883–859 BC), often called Ashurnazirpal II. He was credited with helping to establish a more centralized Assyrian state with the use of governors to rule the western regions of the empire. △980.

Ashwander v. Tennessee Valley Authority (1936), US Supreme Court case in which an Alabama power company employee tried to block the sale of company land to the TVA on the grounds that TVA, established by the federal government, was an unconstitutional agency. The court avoided the constitutional question and ruled only that the contract between TVA and the company was valid. The case is noted for Justice Louis Brandeis' opinion, which outlined what he believed to be the functions of the court.

Asia, largest continent of the world, entirely in the Eastern Hemisphere. It extends above the Arctic Circle and, at Singapore, almost to the equator, with much of Indonesia and smaller islands lying below that line.

Land. Asia is separated from Europe by an imaginary line along the Ural Mountains, Caspian Sea, Caucasus Mountains, and Black Sea. Its vast area includes some barely habitable regions—the frozen N; the Arabian and central deserts, of which the Gobi is one of the largest in the world, est at 500,000sq mi (1,295,000sq km); and the world's tallest mountains, including the Himalaya, Karakoram, and Kunlun. The highest peak is Everest, at 29,028ft (8,854m).

Lakes and Rivers. Major lakes fall mostly across the center of Asia and include the Caspian—partly in Europe—the Aral Sea, and lakes Balkhash and Baikal. Many rivers flow from the mountains, with the Yangtze being Asia's longest, 3,434mi (5,526m); others are the Lena, Mekong, Yellow, Indus, Brahmaputra, and Ganges.

Climate and Vegetation. Asia experiences temperature extremes, with warm days and cold nights, hot summers and cold winters. In the S peninsulas the climate is hot and, except in Arabia, moist. Coniferous forests cover much of the N 25% of the continent, while tropical rain forests thrive in the S central, SE, and island regions. Steppe areas border the central mountain and desert sections, and grasslands occur in E Asia.

Animal Life. Monkeys are numerous, but unique apes are the orangutan of SE islands and the gibbon of Malaysia. Probably best-loved is China's giant panda, which is related to the raccoon. Less exotic mammals include bears, wolves, leopards, tigers, camels, and elephants. Ducks, quail, owls, vultures, doves, wrens, and hundreds of other birds abound. Nests of cliff swallows are collected for bird's-nest soup, and mynas can be taught to imitate speech. Dangerous reptiles include crocodiles, kraits, cobras, and pythons.

Economy. Agriculture is important to most countries. Rice forms the major crop in the E and S, while wheat and barley grow to the W and N. China and Japan are highly industrialized, with India and Turkey becoming steadily more so. Petroleum supports several Arabian lands.

People. Asia, with half the world's population, has many peoples, sometimes classed in two major categories. The Mongoloid peoples live in the E half of Asia; the Caucasians, whether light-skinned (as in parts of the USSR), dark-skinned (as in India), or in between (as in the Arab lands), inhabit the W half. Major languages are Indo-Aryan, Sino-Tibetan, Ural-Altaic, Malayan, and Semitic. Hinduism has the most adherents, followed by Islam, Confucianism, Buddhism, Shintoism, Christianity, Taoism, and Judaism.

History. About 3000 BC the Sumerians developed a type of character-figure writing (cuneiform), and in another 1,500 years the Phoenicians developed an alphabet. Between 600 and 500 BC both Buddha and Confucius flourished, and the Persian Empire came into existence. Early in the 7th century AD, China became the world's most advanced region, and the Arabs began to spread Islam. To free the Holy Land from Islamic control, Europeans launched numerous Crusades, which brought about an increased knowledge of and interest in Asia. Genghis Khan controlled much of Asia before his death in 1227, and his grandson Kublai Khan encouraged the arts as well as war. In the mid-15th century, Turks replaced remnants of the Roman Empire with the Ottoman Empire. After Vasco da Gama reached India, and Ferdinand Magellan proved that man could sail round the globe, Asia's isolation began to end. The British, French, Dutch, Spanish, and Portuguese gained footholds, which started crumbling when the Spanish-American War took the Philippines out of European control. Japan proved itself a world power in the Russo-Japanese War early in the 20th century and continued on a path of belligerency until its defeat in WWII. Asian history since then has involved independence for colonial regions, and communist-free world confrontations with no clear-cut victories.

PROFILE

Area: 17,000,000sq mi (44,030,000sq km)
Largest nations: USSR, Asian (6,500,000sq mi, 16,835,000sq km); China, communist (3,700,000 sq mi; 9,583,000sq km); and India (1,200,000sq mi; 3,108,000sq km)
Population: 2,200,000,000
Density, 130per sq mi (50per sq km). *Most populous nations,* China, communist, 830,000,000; India, 700,000,000; Japan, 120,000,000
Chief cities: Tokyo, Japan; Shanghai, China; Peking, China; Bombay, India; Djakarta, Indonesia, 5,100,-000; Hong Kong, 4,200,000
Industries (major products): chemicals, machinery, iron, steel, textiles, ships
Agriculture (major products): rice, wheat, barley, fruits, sugar cane, cotton, rubber
Minerals (major): petroleum, tin, bauxite, copper, iron ore, antimony, gem stones, coal

Asia Minor (Anatolia), great peninsula of extreme W Asia, bordered by Black Sea (N), Mediterranean (S), and Aegean Sea (W); the famous waterway comprised of the straits of Bosporus and Dardanelles passes through this region, and with the Taurus Mts in the S and Anatolian Plateau spreading through the remainder of the area, it comprises most of Turkey; the scene of political struggles since ancient times.

Asian Literature, creative writings from the peoples of Asia. It can be separated into five divisions: (1) the ancient Middle East; (2) the Arabic and Persian literatures that followed in the area of the ancient Middle East and also went beyond it; (3) India; (4) China and Japan; and (5) Southeast Asia. There is no overall unifying characteristic of Asian literature.

The Hebrew Old Testament makes the literature of the ancient Middle East the most important to the Western world. In Arabic literature lyric poetry, such as the verses in the Koran, is the most significant form. The Persians were known for their epic poetry. In Indian writing religious feelings predominate; the mundane and the secular are linked. The Hindu epic *Mahabharata* typifies this fact. Chinese literature emphasizes philosophy as expressed in lyric poetry. The anthology *Shih Ching* is an example. Poetry and drama have dominated in Japan; brevity, as in 17-syllable *haiku,* is the soul of wisdom in Japanese poetry. Southeast Asia has the most diverse literature.

Asian Pika. △608.

Asimov, Isaac (1920–), US author, especially noted as a science-fiction writer, b. Russia. While serving in various academic positions, he wrote more than 40 science-fiction works. He also authored *The Intelligent Man's Guide to Science* (2v., 1960), which covers in essay form all of science for the layman, and has written widely on scientific subjects.

Asmara (Asmera), city in N Ethiopia, 40mi (64km) SW of Mesewa; capital of Eritrea prov.; occupied by Italy 1889; capital of Italian colony 1936–1941, when it was captured by British; became part of Ethiopia 1962; site of University of Asmara (1958); fertile region where fruits, vegetables, coffee and oil seeds are grown. Industries: breweries, ceramics, textiles. Pop. 218,360.

Asmodeus, Prince of Demons in Hebrew mythology. In Talmudic literature he was the adversary of King Solomon, who compelled him to help build the temple in Jerusalem. Asmodeus later borrowed Solomon's magic ring, with which he flung the king into a faraway land, assumed his shape, reigned in his stead, and committed the sins attributed by scripture to Solomon.

Asp, or asp viper, S European viper characterized by an upturned snout. It varies in color, but is mostly brown-red with dark spots. It feeds on rodents, birds, lizards, and earthworms and is aggressive when disturbed. The asp Cleopatra used to commit suicide was probably another species of N African viper or Egyptian cobra. Length: to 30in(76cm). Family Viperidae; species *Vipera aspis. See also* Viper.

Asparagine, white crystalline soluble amino acid ($NH_2CO{\cdot}CH_2CH{\cdot}NH_2{\cdot}COOH$) that occurs in leguminous plants. *See* Amino Acid.

Asparagus, perennial plants primarily native to Africa. They have tuberous or fleshy roots, scale-like leaves, small greenish flowers, and are grown for their decorative greenery or as a garden vegetable. *Asparagus officinalis,* an erect perennial of Europe and Asia, is grown widely in the United States for its edible, tender shoots. Family Liliaceae.

Asparagus Fern, house plant native to S Africa with feathery foliage growing on long, cascading stems, upright plumes, or horizontal triangular branchlets. Care: bright indirect light, barely moist soil (equal parts loam, peat moss, sand). Propagation is by root division or seeds. Family Liliaceae; genus *Asparagus.*

Aspartic Acid, white crystalline amino acid ($COOH \cdot CH_2 \cdot CH \cdot NH_2 \cdot COOH$) that occurs in sugar beets. *See* Amino Acid.

Aspects, in Astronomy. △826.

Aspen, town in W central Colorado, on Rolling Fork River; seat of Pitkin co; winter resort; site of Castle Peak, Snowmass Mountain, and Aspen Institute for Humanistic Studies, which sponsors annual Aspen Music Festival. Founded 1878 as silver mining camp; inc. 1881. Pop. (1970) 2,437.

Aspen, several trees *(Populus)* of the willow family, known for their oval leaves that quake in even gentle breezes, owing to their slender, flattened petioles. Native to temperate Eurasia, North Africa, and North America, they grow to 90ft (27m).

Asphalt, naturally occurring black or brown semisolid bitumens, used mainly for road covering and roofing. Asphalts are found in deposits in many parts of the world, including Trinidad, Venezuela, and in Alabama and Texas. They were probably produced by chemical change of mineral oils and consist of colloidal suspensions of coal-like material in heavy oil.

Asphyxiation, cause of death resulting from lack of oxygen in air breathed. Common causes of asphyxiation are drowning and smoke inhalation.

Aspidistra, or cast-iron plant, a genus of durable house plants native to China with arching, oval leaves. Care: indirect light, barely moist soil (equal parts loam, peat moss, sand). Propagation is by root division. Height: to 3ft (91cm). Family Liliaceae.

Aspiration Level, in psychology, the goal a person will set for himself in a particular situation, influenced by his knowledge of his capabilities in relation to the difficulty involved in attaining the goal. △812.

Aspirin, or **acetylsalicylic acid,** white crystalline substance made from salicylic acid; an extensively used antipyretic and analgesic drug taken for headache, rheumatic pain, fever, etc. △744, 1560.

Asquith, Herbert Henry. *See* Oxford and Asquith, Herbert Henry Asquith, 1st Earl of.

Ass, wild equine found in African and Asian desert and mountain areas. Smaller than the horse, it has a short mane and tail, large ears, small hooves, and dorsal stripes. It brays instead of neighing. Gestation period is 12 months; one colt is born. Male is called a jack; female a jennet or jenny. The three African races (species *Equus asinus*) are Nubian (now extinct), North African, and the rare Somali. Height: 3–4.5ft (91.5–137cm) at shoulder. Asian races, *Equars hemion,* are the Kiang, Ghorkar, and Onager. Family Equidae. *See also* Kiang; Onager.

Assad, Hafez al (1928–), president of Syria. He attended the Syrian Military Academy and rose through the ranks to become a general. He was minister of defense (1965–70). After a coup d'état in 1970 he became president.

Assam, state in NE India, almost cut off from the main body of India by Bangladesh (SW) and Nepal (W); capital is Shillong; ruled by Ahom empire 1400–1825; passed to Britain 1826 through the Treaty of Yandabo; became self-governing province 1937; provided home for Hindu refugees from Muslim East Pakistan 1959–60, 1971. Industries: tea, rice, sugar cane, timber, oil. Area: 30,000sq mi (77,700sq km). Pop. 14,857,314.

Assassin, secret Muslim sect founded *c.*1090 by Hasan ibn-al-Sabbah. It quickly gained control of the Muslim world by spreading terror. The members were organized into two classes with the highest class as devotees. They were used as instruments of assassination, sometimes sacrificing their own lives. The order was noted in the tales of Marco Polo and the crusaders, who brought the term "assassin" to Europe. It derives from the alleged use of hashish by terrorists seeking ecstatic visions. △1112.

Assassin Bug, large, often brightly colored bug found worldwide. Most species feed on other insects but some feed on man and rodents. Length: 0.25–1.33in (6–34mm). Family Reduviidae. *See also* Kissing bug.

Assateague Island, a 37-mile (60-km) barrier island, in SE Maryland and N part of E peninsula, Virginia; separates Chincoteague Bay from the Atlantic Ocean. Area: 28sq mi (73sq km).

Assemblies of God, largest Pentecostal religious sect in the United States, founded by preachers of the Church of God in Hot Springs, Ark., in 1914. In 1916 it was incorporated and titled General Council of Assemblies of God. There are about 600,000 members at present. *See also* Pentecostalism.

Assembly Line. △1660.

Assimilation, a blending of cultures that occurs when different groups live closely together and merge their ways of life. European immigrants to the United States in the 19th and early 20th centuries became assimilated. They adopted American ways but also added some of their customs and attitudes to American life style. *See also* Pluralism.

Assiniboine Indians, nomadic North American Indian tribe. Their language was Siouan, and they were related to the Dakotas, although they migrated westward from Minnesota to Saskatchewan and the Lake Winnepeg area. Their culture is that of the Plains Indians. They were peaceful trading partners of the Hudson's Bay Company, and their trade helped to destroy the French monopoly among tribes of that region. Today they are about 5,000 in number, with 4,000 on reservations in Montana and 1,000 living in Canada.

Assiniboine River, river in S Canada; rises in S Saskatchewan prov.; flows SE into Manitoba then E into the Red River at Winnipeg; valley is a leading wheat-growing region. Named for Assiniboine Indians. Length: 590mi (950km).

Assisi, town in central Italy, overlooking the Tiber and Topino rivers; developed from ancient town of Asisium; birthplace of St Francis; site of medieval castle, cathedral (1140), and the famous St Francis' Basilica. Industries: manufacturing, tourism. Pop. 24,755.

Associationism, doctrine in psychology and philosophy that describes the content of consciousness (thinking, learning, memory) as ideas (memories of sensory impressions) linked together by certain associative principles. Commonly cited principles are temporal contiguity (ideas occurring close together in time become associated), similarity (similar ideas become associated), and frequency (ideas that occur together repeatedly become associated). The doctrine began with British empiricist philosophers such as John Locke and George Berkeley and was furthered by David Hartley, Thomas Brown, and J.S. Mill in the 19th century. Many of the doctrine's principles, most notably temporal contiguity, have influenced learning theory in psychology. △778.

Associationism, economic philosophy based on the concept that free associations between people in cooperative enterprises would be the best way to achieve the goals of socialism. Charles Fourier, Robert Owen, and Louis Blanc were leading proponents of associationism.

Associative Law, rule of combination in mathematics in which the result of two or more operations on terms does not depend on the way in which they are grouped. Thus, normal addition and multiplication of numbers follows the associative law, since $a + (b + c) = (a + b) + c$, and $a \times (b \times c) = (a \times b) \times c$. △1446.

Assonance, imperfect rhyme, where the stressed vowels in the words agree, but the consonants do not. Examples are: "hulks, exults"; "penitent, reticence"; "neck, met." Commonly found in medieval ballads, assonance has also been used as a literary device by such poets as John Milton, Alfred Tennyson, Gerard Manley Hopkins, and Dylan Thomas.

Assumption. *See* Postulate.

Assumption, generally accepted principle on which a subject is built. *See also* Postulate. △1462.

Assyria, ancient empire of the Middle East. It took its name from the city of Assur, or Ashur, which was located on the Tigris River near the modern city of Mosul, Iraq. At its height, the Assyrian Empire comprised the modern nations of Iraq, Syria, Jordan, Israel, and Egypt; and it included parts of Saudi Arabia,

Asp

Aspen, Colorado

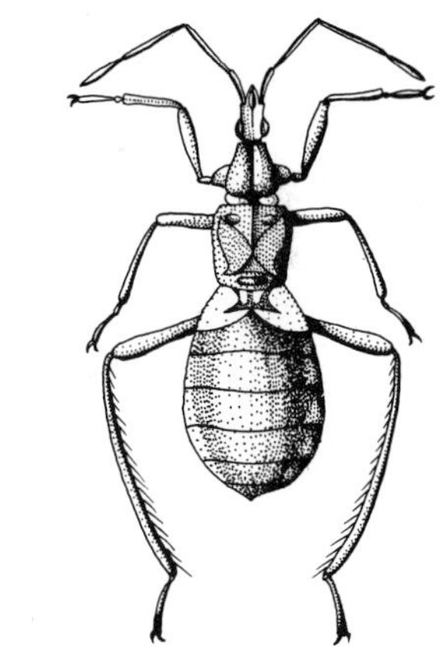

Assassin bug

Assisi, Italy

Armenia, and Asia Minor (Turkey). The Assyrian Empire had its beginning in the 3rd millennium BC, reached its zenith between the 9th and 7th centuries BC, and thereafter went into swift decline. In 612 BC its capital city, Nineveh, was captured by a combined force of Medes, Babylonians, and Scythians, and Assyria lost its hegemony. Later Assyria was absorbed into the Persian Empire.

The Assyrians were a Semitic people who adapted parts of the Babylonian and Hittite religions; their chief god was Ashur, and their kings were regarded as deities. The Assyrians gradually increased their power until the 12th century BC, when their first great king, Tiglath-pilesar I (died *c.* 1077 BC), conquered Babylonia and parts of Armenia and Asia Minor. In the 9th century Ashurnazirpal II further expanded the empire and established efficient control over the conquered territories. An exceedingly warlike people, the Assyrians continued to increase their territories under such rulers as Shalmaneser III (died 824 BC), Tiglath-Pilesar III (died 727 BC), Sargon (died 705 BC), Sennacherib (died 681 BC), and Esar-Haddon (died 669 BC).

Ashurbanipal (died 627 BC) was the last great Assyrian king. Under his rule Assyrian art—particularly its great bas-relief sculpture—and Assyrian learning reached their greatest development. The luxuriance of Ashurbanipal's court at Nineveh was of legendary proportions. The cost of maintaining his huge armies, added to the sumptousness of his court, fatally weakened the empire. Two of his sons ruled briefly after his death, but with the capture of Nineveh in 612 BC, the empire fell into ruin. △954, 956, 980.

Assyrian Architecture (*fl.* 1250–612 BC), architectural style derived from Babylonian architecture. Temples and ziggurats were significant structures, but palaces became even more important. The Assyrians used multicolored ornamental brickwork, and the high plinths or dados at the bases of their buildings were often carved with low-relief sculpture. Interiors were similarly decorated with continuous friezes. The cities of Ashur, Ninevah, Nimrud, and Khorsabad were the sites of the greatest Assyrian palaces. △954.

Assyro-Babylonian Mythology, described a cosmic order of heaven, earth, and an underworld and populated it with some 4000 deities and demons to direct the physical and spiritual activities of the world. The complex stories dealing with the Mesopotamian pantheon are generally regarded as literary entertainments or interesting explanations of natural occurrences and religious rituals, having little effect on the daily lives or religious activities of the people. As in the later state religion of the Greeks of the Golden Age, the mythology is an important part of the culture in the arts, but is not an integral part of the liturgy of the priests or church.

Astaire, Fred (1899–), US dancer and film star, b. Frederick Austerlitz in Omaha, Nebr. Teamed with his sister, Adele, in vaudeville until she retired in 1933, he starred with Ginger Rogers in a number of 1930s musical films noted for elegance and exuberance. His major films include *The Gay Divorcee* (1934), *Top Hat* (1935), *Swing Time* (1936), *Royal Wedding* (1951), *Funny Face* (1956), and the drama *On the Beach* (1959).

Astarte, also Ashtart or Ashtoreth, Phoenician goddess of fertility and love, equivalent to Ishtar of the Assyro-Babylonians and Aphrodite of the Greeks. She is represented by a crescent, perhaps symbolic of the moon or the horns of a cow. The dove, gazelle, and myrtle were sacred to her. △978.

Astatine, radioactive element (symbol At) of the halogen group, first made (1940) by bombarding bismuth with alpha particles. It is made only in trace amounts. Properties: at. no. 85; melt. pt. 482°F (250°C); boil. pt. 662°F (350°C); most stable isotope At^{210} (half-life 8.3hr). *See also* Halogen elements.

Aster, a genus of mostly perennial, leafy-stemmed plants native to the Americas and Eurasia. Popular garden plants, asters usually bear daisylike flowers in clusters. The outer rays are white, blue, pink or purple and the inner disks are yellow, turning darker with age. Family Compositae.

Asteroid, minor planet or planetoid, any of several thousand small celestial objects orbiting the sun in the region between Mars and Jupiter. Ranging in diameter from only a few kilometers to several hundred, asteroids may be the remains of a planet that broke up or failed to attain a stable existence. *See also* Ceres. △78.

Asthenic Reaction, or neurasthenia, outdated term meaning "a state of nervous weakness." The syndrome was characterized by complaints of weakness and fatigue, diffuse pain, irritability, and insomnia. The term is at times used interchangeably with hypochondria. △814.

Asthenosphere, portion of the earth's upper mantle extending from 60–120mi (97–193km) below the surface. *See also* Crust, Earth; Mantle. △166.

Asthma, recurring seizures of shortness of breath or breathlessness accompanied by wheezing or whistling sound. Difficulty in breathing is caused by the inability to force air out of the lungs; inhalation is not impaired. Asthma is designated as cardiac, non-allergic bronchial, and allergic bronchial, the last by far the most common. Some hereditary factors are attached to allergic bronchial asthma. Bronchial attacks may be excited by allergens such as pollen, molds, and dust, less frequently by foods and drugs. Acute attacks frequently occur at night, may be prolonged and culminate in coughing and expectoration of sputum. Drugs are sometimes prescribed to contain acute attacks, but elimination of, or desensitization to, stimulus is the treatment of choice. *See also* Allergy. △714; 768.

Astigmatism. △674.

Astor, John Jacob (1763–1848), US merchant and fur trader, b. Germany. Arriving penniless in the United States, Astor became a successful businessman in New York City and then went into the China trade. In 1808 he founded the American Fur Co. and after the War of 1812 developed a monopoly on the US fur trade. He retired from the fur trade in 1834 and concentrated on land investment.

Astor, Nancy Witcher (Langhorne), Viscountess (1879–1964), British politician, the first woman elected to the House of Commons, serving 1919–45, b. United States. A Conservative, she advocated temperance, educational reform, women's and children's welfare. In the 1930s, she and her husband William Waldorf Astor became, at their estate Clivedon, the center of a group of influential proponents of appeasement toward Nazi Germany.

Astoria, port city in NW Oregon, 70mi (113km) NW of Portland on Columbia River; seat of Clatsop co. Nearby Fort Clatsop was the winter headquarters for Lewis and Clark 1805–06. Industries: fishing, lumber, agriculture, tourism. Founded 1811 by John J. Astor's Pacific Fur Co., the first permanent US settlement on W coast; inc. 1876. Pop. (1970) 10,244.

Astrakhan (Astrachan), port city in SE European USSR; on Caspian Sea and Voly River delta, approx. 800mi (1,288km) SE of Moscow; capital of Astrakhan oblast; site of USSR's largest fisheries; a railroad, airline, oil shipping, and trade center; site of walled kremlin (*c.* 1550). City developed in the 13th century under Mongols; near site of ancient Khazar city of Itil (8th–10th centuries); Tartar stronghold until capture 1554–56 by Ivan IV (the Terrible); in 1917–20 civil war the city remained in Russian hands, becoming a base for Caspian Sea conquest of 1920. Exports: oil, rice, timber, fruit. Pop. 411,000.

Astraphobia, excessive fear of storms, thunder, and lightning that cause a feeling of personal vulnerability or impending disaster.

Astrobiology. *See* Exobiology.

Astrodynamics, the practical application of celestial mechanics, ballistics, mathematical perturbation theory, and observation reduction to the determination, prediction, and correction of orbits and trajectories in space. A branch of astronautics.

Astrogeology, study of rocks, craters, and other surface features of the Moon, Mars, and other planets. Includes on site and laboratory studies of Moon rocks, seismological data (Moon only), photographic mappings, magnetic field measurements, and micrometeorite data. △54.

Astrolabe. △40, 1442.

Astrology, pseudoscientific study of the influence supposedly exercised by celestial bodies upon the lives of men. Originating in Babylon some 3000 years ago, it sought by means of essentially arbitrary rules to work out man's personal fate according to the motions and positions of the Sun, Moon, and planets at the time of his birth. For this purpose, accurate observational records began to be kept, which eventually provided the impetus for transforming the superstition of astrology into the exact science of astronomy. △826.

Astrometry, branch of astronomy concerned mainly with the determination of the position and motion of celestial bodies. △40, 126.

Astronaut (Russian: Cosmonaut), person who navigates or rides in a space vehicle; also, a person selected for a training program to fly in space vehicles. Most astronauts are former test pilots. The first man in space was Yuri Gagarin, Soviet Union, 1961. The first man on the Moon was Neil Armstrong, United States, 1969. The first woman in space was Valentina Tereshkova, Soviet Union, June 16, 1963. △54, 142, 1724.

Astronautics, or astronautical engineering, the practical study of the principles of space flight. Astronautics includes astrodynamics, propulsion theory, astrogeology, astrobiology, communications principles, and the design, materials analysis, guidance, and control of spacecraft. △142.

Astronomical Unit (symbol A.U.), astronomical unit of length used for distance measurements within the solar system, equal to the mean distance of the Earth from the Sun. 1 A.U. is equal to 92.957 million mi (149.60 million km).

Astronomy, branch of science that has been studied since ancient times and is now concerned with the universe and its contents in terms of the relative motions of celestial bodies, their positions on the celestial sphere, physical and chemical structure, evolution, the phenomena occurring on them, etc. The main branches are celestial mechanics, astrophysics, cosmology, and astrometry. Waves of all regions of the electromagnetic spectrum can now be studied either with ground-based instruments or, where no atmospheric window exists, by observations and measurements made from satellites, space probes, and rockets. These instruments include telescopes, associated photographic and spectrographic equipment, and other detecting and analyzing devices, which are often coupled to a computer in order to process measurements and other information rapidly. △38, 1478.

Astronomy, Gamma-Ray, branch of astronomy concerned with the study of gamma rays from space. Gamma rays cannot penetrate the Earth's atmosphere and must therefore be detected by equipment carried in satellites, etc. The Sun is the principal source of gamma rays.

Astronomy, Infrared, branch of astronomy concerned with detecting infrared (IR) waves from space, determining their source, and studying the IR spectrum of such sources. Most IR radiation is absorbed by the Earth's atmosphere apart from a few narrow long-wavelength bands and the band adjacent to the visible region; thus most studies must be made from satellites, rockets, or balloons. The Sun is an important IR source. Thousands of other IR sources are now known. These are mainly stars with low surface temperatures, some of which are only in an early development stage. Very strong IR sources exist in Cygnus, the Orion Nebula and at the galactic center. IR techniques are used to study planetary atmospheres, stellar evolution, galactic structure, and in many other fields. △46.

Astronomy, Optical, oldest branch of astronomy, in which reflecting and refracting telescopes and other optical equipment are used in detecting and studying light sources in the universe. Sources include celestial bodies, such as the planets and their satellites, that reflect light from a nearby star and bodies, such as stars and star systems (galaxies), that emit light. The entire visible spectrum can penetrate the Earth's atmosphere for ground-based telescopic studies. However, due to atmospheric disturbances, pollution, background light from the night sky, clouds, etc, observatories are often in mountainous or other isolated regions and many observations are made from satellites, space probes, and high-flying aircraft.

Astronomy, Radar, branch of astronomy in which radar pulses reflected back to Earth from celestial bodies inside the solar system are studied for information concerning the distance from Earth of the bodies, their orbital motion, and large surface features. △40.

Astronomy, Radio, relatively new branch of astronomy in which radio telescopes and other equipment are used to detect radio waves from space and determine their source and energy spectrum. Radio wavelengths of about 8mm to over 20m can pass through the Earth's atmosphere without ionospheric reflection. Radio astronomy studies this wavelength band and the resulting view of the radio universe differs from that of the visible universe, although radio sources can often be identified with visible light sources. The most powerful radio sources include the Sun; interstellar clouds of hot hydrogen, such as the Orion Nebula; discrete sources, mainly supernova remnants and pulsars, such as the Crab Nebula; quasars; and radio galaxies. There is also a weak isotropic background radio emission centered on the 21cm emission of hydrogen. △4,6, 96, 124.

Astronomy, Ultraviolet, branch of astronomy concerned with detecting ultraviolet (UV) waves from space, determining their source, and studying the UV spectrum of such sources. An atmospheric window exists for high-wavelength UV waves (200–400 nanometers), which can thus be studied from the ground. Lower wavelengths must be studied from satellites and rockets. The Sun is an important UV source; other discrete sources include the Orion Nebula and the intense Wolf-Rayet stars. △46,108.

Astronomy, X-ray, branch of astronomy concerned with detecting X-rays from space, determining their source, and studying the spectrum of X-ray energies emitted. X-rays are absorbed by the Earth's atmosphere so that detecting instruments, such as Geiger counters and specially designed telescopes, must be carried in satellites or rockets. X-ray sources include the Sun, whose emission originates mainly in the corona, and the Crab Nebula. Other Galactic sources occur in the constellations Scorpio, Cygnus, and Centaurus. Extragalactic sources include the radio source Cygnus A and the radio galaxy M87 in Virgo. △46, 108.

Astrophysics, branch of astronomy concerned with the physical and chemical nature of stars and other celestial bodies and with their evolution. Many branches of science, including nuclear physics, plasma physics, relativity, and spectroscopy, are used in predicting properties and features of celestial bodies and in interpreting the information obtained from astronomical studies in all sections of the electromagnetic spectrum. △56, 48.

Asturias, Miguel Angel (1899–1974), Guatemalan novelist. He won the Nobel Prize for literature in 1967. His most famous novel, *El Señor Presidente* (1946), condemns dictatorship. It was based on conditions in his own country but has been praised for its universality. In it he criticizes the change from a rural, natural world to an urbanized community dominated by a dictator. Among his other novels are *Hombres de maíz* (1949), about the takeover of Indian land for maize-growing profits, and a trilogy criticizing US economic control of banana plantations.

Asturias, former kingdom in northwestern Spain, coextensive with the modern Oviedo province. The indigenous Iberian people were conquered by the Romans in the 2nd century BC. When the Moors overran Spain in the 8th century, the Christian nobles fled to the Asturian mountains. One of them, Pelayo, founded (*c.* 718) the kingdom of Asturias; it was from this first Christian kingdom that the gradual reconquest of Spain began. In the 10th century it became the kingdom of Asturias and León, and three centuries later it became part of the kingdom of Castile. △ 1078.

Asunción, capital and largest city of Paraguay, in S Paraguay, on E bank of Paraguay River at the junction with Pilcomayo River; chief river port and administrative, industrial, and cultural center of Paraguay; site of Pantéon Nacional (tomb for national heroes), La Encarnación (church), National University (1889), Catholic University (1960); scene of "comuneros" rebellion against Spanish rule 1731; occupied by Brazil 1868–76. Industries: meat packing, textiles, food products. Founded 1536 as trade outpost and Jesuit mission. Pop. 385,000.

Aswan, city in SE Egypt, on the E bank of the Nile River just below Lake Nasser and the Aswan High Dam which impounds it; capital of Aswan governorate. An ancient Egyptian settlement called Syene, meaning "market place," the city was of strategic importance to the Egyptians and Greeks because it controlled shipping and communication from above the first cataract of the Nile. The modern city is a commercial and tourist center that has benefited greatly from the construction of the Aswan High Dam (completed 1970). Although some archeological treasures were lost in the impounding of Lake Nasser, the temples of Abu-Simpel were saved; the rocky terrain is the site of ancient Egyptian and Greek temples and monuments. Industries: steel, textiles, tourism. Pop. 206,300.

Aswan High Dam, 5mi (8km) S of the Aswan Dam in Egypt, constructed (1960–70) after a delay over water rights with Sudan. A 310-mi (500-km) long artificial lake, Lake Nasser, was created by the dam's construction and has expanded both Egypt and the Sudan agriculturally. Some 100,000 people and archeological treasures had to be moved to make way for the lake. The dam, of earth, clay, and rock, is 3mi (4.8km) long and 364ft (111m) high. △1764.

As You Like It (*c.* 1599), a comedy by William Shakespeare about the wicked Duke Frederick and his brother, Duke Senior. Banished from power, Duke Senior establishes a new court under nature's laws in the Forest of Arden. The intricate plot resolves both a star-crossed love affair as well as the political feud.

Atabrine, quinacrine hydrochloride, an antimalarial drug. It is a yellow, bitter compound.

Atahualpa (1500–33), Incan ruler of Peru. The son of Huayna Capac, he fought for control of the Incan realm with Huáscar, his half-brother, whom he defeated in 1532, the year Francisco Pizarro arrived in northern Peru. Atahualpa later was taken prisoner by Pizarro and executed. △1124.

Atamasco Lily, or **zephyr lily,** North American bulb plant growing wild in wet woods and clearings. The large waxy flower faces upward and is pink or white. Leaves are long, slim, and channeled. Height: 6–15in (15–38cm). Family Amaryllidaceae; species *Zephyranthes atamasco.*

Atatürk, Kemal (1881–1938), Turkish leader and founder of modern Turkey. As a youth he joined the Young Turks, a liberal movement that sought to establish a government independent of Ottoman rule. He fought against the Italians in Tripolitania (1911) and served with distinction in World War I. In 1919 he organized the Turkish Nationalist party in E. Anatolia and formed an army. In 1919 he announced the aims of an independent Turkish state and in 1921–22 he expelled the Greeks from Anatolia. He abolished the sultanate (1922) and proclaimed the republic in 1923. Elected president in 1923 and reelected in 1927, 1931, and 1935, he instituted reforms touching on virtually every aspect of national life.

Atchafalaya River, river in S Louisiana; rises in Avoyelles parish; flows S to Atchafalaya Bay. Length: 170mi (274km).

Atget, Eugène (1857–1927), French photographer, former sailor and actor. At 42 Atget began to produce his vast, complex portraits of Paris and its environs. His powerful, serene images of street scenes, people, parks, and sculpture gardens form a unique vision of a vanished era. Berenice Abbott obtained world acclaim for Atget's work after his death.

Athabasca Lake, lake in W central Canada, on N Alberta-Saskatchewan border; 4th-largest lake in Canada; drains into the Slave River. Fort Chipewyan built in 1788 is preserved at W end of lake; gold and uranium deposits nearby. Area: 3,120sq mi (8,081sq km).

Athabascan, or **Athapascan,** also known as Slave Indians, tribe and language family of North American Indians inhabiting NW Canada. They were forced north to the Great Slave Lake and Fort Nelson by the Cree. Their common name, Slave, derives from the domination and forced labor exacted by the Cree. The Athabascan tribe has always been closely linked to the Chipewyan people, and some authorities regard the two as one extended group. Today some 25,000 Athabascan Indians live in NW Canada. The Athabascan language, which derives from the tribe, covers the largest geographical area of all North American Indian groups; speakers extend from the Cree in Canada to the Tolowa and Hupa in California and the Navajo and Apache of the Southwest. No accurate count exists, but the Athabascan-speaking tribes of North America would probably approximate well over 250,000.

Athabasca River, river in Alberta, Canada; rises in the Rocky Mts in SW Alberta; flows NE then N, empties into Lake Athabasca. Since mid-1960s synthetic crude oil has been produced from sands along shore. Length: 765mi (1,232km).

Athanasian Creed, a Christian profession of faith that explains the teachings of the church on the Trinity and the incarnation. It is accepted as the authoritative profession in the Roman Catholic and Anglican churches.

Athanasius, Saint (*c.* 297–373), Christian theologian, Doctor of the Church. As patriarch of Alexandria, he confuted the Arians—and Arius himself—both during and after the Council of Nicaea (325). In *Discourses against the Arians* (357) he represented the Trinity as composed of three Persons in one Nature. During the tumultuous Arian controversy, when he

Fred Astaire with Cyd Charisse

Aster

Astrology

Asunción, Paraguay

was twice forced into exile, he steadfastly upheld the Nicene Creed and maintained thereby the essential divinity of Christ. He is no longer credited with writing the Athanasian Creed. Feast: May 2. *See also* Arianism; Nicene Creed.

Atheism, a system of thought developed around the denial of God's existence. Atheism, so defined, first appeared during the Enlightenment, the age of reason. In ancient Greece, it meant refusal to worship the state deities.

Athelstan (*c.* 895–939), king of England. King of the Mercians and the West Saxons, he gained Northumbria and invaded Scotland. By his decisive victory over the Scots, Danes, and Welsh at Brunanburh (937), he confirmed his rule over most of England.

Athena, Greek goddess of war and crafts (Roman, Minerva). She was born fully grown and armed from the head of Zeus. As the goddess of war, she aided the Greeks in the Trojan War. As goddess of crafts, she inspired the ship *Argo* and the wooden horse by Epius. Athens was named in her honor. △832.

Athens (Athínai), capital city of Greece, SW of Saronic Gulf; capital of Attica department. The ancient city built on the Acropolis was the greatest center of art and culture in Greece; gained significant power during Persian Wars (500–449 BC); city prospered from 468 to 429 BC under Cimon and Pericles, during which time Aeschylus, Sophocles, Euripides, and Socrates produced their finest work; defeated by Sparta in the Peloponnesian Wars (431–404 BC). Under Alexander the Great, Athens gained some independence; it declined under Roman control (from 228 BC). After Greek War of Independence (1821–30), Athens regained former standing as a cultural and commercial center. Most noted artistic treasures are the Parthenon (432 BC), a temple to Athena; Parthenos, a Doric structure created by Ictinus and Callicrates; the Erechtheum (408 BC), a temple of Athena, Poseidon, and Erechtheus; and the Theater of Dionysus (*c.* 500 BC), the oldest Greek theater. Modern Athens and its port of Piraeus form a major transportation and economic hub of the Mediterranean. Industries: shipbuilding, paper mills, machinery, textiles, breweries, chemicals, glass, tourism. Pop. 867,023. △992.

Athens, city in NE Georgia, on Oconee River; seat of Clarke co; site of University of Georgia (1801) and classic pre-Civil War homes. Industries: textiles, dairy products, poultry processing, transformers. Inc. 1801. Pop. (1970) 44,342.

Athens, city in SE Ohio, on bluffs overlooking Hocking River; seat of Athens co; site of Ohio University (1804), first college in the Northwest Territory. Industries: midget automobiles, scooters, building materials. Settled *c.* 1797; inc. 1912. Pop. (1970) 24,168.

Atherosclerosis, most common form of arterial disease. An early stage of arteriosclerosis, it is a thickening of artery walls. *See also* Arteriosclerosis. △716.

Athlete's Foot, a contagious, fungus-caused infection usually appearing first between the last two toes. Itching, macerated skin and blisters are usual symptoms. △724.

Áthos, Mount, mountain peak in NE Greece, on S Athos peninsula. Inhabited since 9th century by an independent community of monks of St Basil; made theocratic republic 1927 and placed under Greek suzerainty. Height: approx. 6,670ft (2,034m).

Atkinson, (Justin) Brooks (1894–), US drama critic, b. Melrose, Mass. He began reviewing plays on the *Boston Evening Transcript* (1919), became literary editor (1922), then drama critic (1925) for the *New York Times,* where he remained for 30 years. During World War II he was war correspondent in Chungking, China, then news correspondent in Moscow. He was awarded a Pulitzer Prize for journalism (1947) and is the only drama critic to have a theater named for him (New York City). He has written many books on US literature and natural history as well as dozens of volumes on the theater, among them *Broadway Scrapbook* (1947), *Tuesdays and Fridays* (1963), *Brief Chronicles* (1966), and *Broadway* (1970).

Atlanta, industrial city in NW central Georgia; state capital; seat of Fulton co; distribution, commercial, cultural, and financial capital of the SE United States. The land was ceded to Georgia 1821 by Creek Indians and was settled 1833; by 1837, it was founded as the town at the end of the Western and Atlantic Railroad line and named Terminus; served as a Confederate supply depot and communications center during the Civil War; on Sept. 2, 1864, it fell to Gen. Sherman who devastated the city by fire on November 15. The city was rapidly rebuilt into an important industrial and commercial center; it was made temporary state capital 1868 and, by popular vote, permanent capital 1877. In the 20th century, Atlanta grew to become one of the major US cities; it was one of the first southern cities to desegregate its schools successfully; Maynard Jackson was installed as Atlanta's first black mayor in 1974. It is the site of capitol building (1899), city hall (1929), Cyclorama Building, High Museum of Art, Oakland Cemetery, Fort Walker, Atlanta Campaign National Historic Site, Kennesaw Mt National Battlefield Park, grave of Martin Luther King, Jr., many government, military, and business institutions, Atlanta Stadium (1966) hosting the professional football team, Atlanta Falcons, and baseball team, Atlanta Braves. Among its educational institutions are Emory University (1836), Georgia Institute of Technology (1885), Atlanta University (1865), Morehouse College (1867), and Georgia State University (1913). Industries: textiles, furniture, chemicals, glass, paper, lumber, iron and steel, leather, electronics, aluminum, candy, farm equipment, flour, automobile and aircraft assembly, printing, publishing, food processing. Inc. 1843 as Marthasville; renamed Atlanta 1845; reinc. 1847. Pop. (1970) 497,421.

Atlantic, Battle of the. △1338.

Atlantic Charter (Aug.14, 1941), agreement between Winston Churchill and Franklin D. Roosevelt outlining the common aims of their governments in international affairs. They renounced territorial aggrandizement and called for self-determination for all people in selecting their governments. Among other points, they called for freedom of the seas, the abandonment of force in foreign policy, and greater international cooperation in improving worldwide economic and social conditions to free all people from fear and want.

Atlantic City, city in SE New Jersey, 60mi (97km) SE of Philadelphia, on Absecon Island; built on a 10mi (16km) sandbar in Atlantic Ocean; developed after railroad was constructed in 1854; site of 4-mi (6-km) boardwalk (1896); modern convention and tourist center. Settled 1790 as a fishing village; inc. 1854. Pop. (1970) 47,859.

Atlantic Intercoastal Waterway, system of inland waterways along the Atlantic coast from Cape Cod, Mass., to Florida Bay. Main points are Trenton, N.J.; Norfolk, Va.; Beaufort, N.C.; Jacksonville, Fla.; and Miami, Fla.

Atlantic Ocean, second largest of the world's oceans, separates North and South America from Europe and Africa. Divided into the N Atlantic and S Atlantic at about 5°N latitude, it has two separate current systems; N system circulates clockwise; S counterclockwise. Area: 32,000,000sq mi (82,880,000sq km). Width: approx. 2,500mi (4,025km). Length: approx. 8,000mi (12,880km). Greatest known depth: Milwaukee Deep, in the Puerto Rican trench, 30,246ft (9,225m).

Atlantis, legendary island in the Atlantic Ocean, W of the Rock of Gibraltar. Plato wrote about Atlantis in his dialogues (the "Timaeus" and the "Critias") and described their highly developed society before the island was destroyed by an earthquake and overtaken by the sea. The name Atlantis is synonymous with Utopia, and groups trying to discover the island's site are continually active.

Atlantosaurus. △570.

Atlas, in Greek mythology, the son of the Titan Iapetus and the nymph Clymene and brother of Prometheus. According to Homer, he was a marine being who supported the pillars that divided heaven and earth. According to Hesiod, he was one who, having warred against Zeus, was condemned to hold up the heavens. △682.

Atlas, collection of maps or charts, usually found in book form, and often containing pictures, indexes of placenames, and facts of interest. It may be world or regional, and contain such information as climate, boundaries, geology, history, and population. The term comes from the custom of placing a picture of the Greek god Atlas holding up the earth in the frontispiece of books of maps.

Atlas and Axis. △682.

Atlas Mountains, mountain system in NW Africa; extends 1,500mi (2,415km) from the coast of SW Morocco to the coast of N Tunisia; consisting of several ranges, the highest peak, Toubkal, 13,671ft (4,170m), is found in the Grand Atlas range in W Morocco; rich in minerals, the mountains have fertile, well-watered farmland on the N and drier, grass-covered slopes on the S.

Atmosphere, the whole envelope of air, composed of a variety of gases, surrounding the earth or other celestial body and held to it by gravitational attraction. The physics, chemistry, and dynamics of atmospheric processes are studied in the attempt to understand, predict, and control events affecting weather, climates, and pollution. *Composition.* A mixture of the heavier gases in the atmosphere lies near the earth. About 95% of the atmosphere by mass is below the 15-mi (25-km) altitude. Dry air is composed largely of nitrogen (78.1%), oxygen (20.9%), and about 0.9% of inert argon gas, with varying amounts of water vapor added near the earth. The remaining 0.1% of the atmosphere consists of traces of carbon monoxide and dioxide, other pollutants like sulfur and nitric dioxides, and more inert gases like krypton, xenon, and the fluorocarbons. Further from the earth are lighter gases like atomic oxygen, helium, and hydrogen. *Atmospheric shells.* The atmosphere can be conceived as a series of concentric shells in which the earth is nested. In the shell nearest the earth, the troposphere, ranging up 5 to 7mi (8 to 11km) above the surface, the mixture of the air's gases and dust with water vapor creates all the clouds, precipitation, and weather. The colder stratosphere, the next shell, from 5 to 25mi (8 to 40km), contains the jet streams, clear conditions, and ozone concentrated in its upper regions. Above, to a height of 50mi (80km), is the mesosphere, in which many chemical reactions occur, powered by sunlight. The temperature climbs steadily in the thermosphere above, which gives way to the exosphere at about 185mi (300km), from which helium and hydrogen may dart off into space. The ionosphere, the shell of ions or charged particles affected by the magnetic field, ranges from about 30mi (48km) out into the Van Allen belts. △212.

Atmospheric Pressure, the pressure exerted by the atmosphere because of its gravitational attraction to the earth or other body, measured by barometers and usually expressed in units of inches (or millimeters) of mercury. Standard atmospheric pressure at sea level is 29.92 inches (760 millimeters) of mercury, and the column of air above each square inch of earth's surface weighs about 14.7 pounds (6.7kg). With an atmosphere composed largely of carbon dioxide, the surface atmospheric pressure of Venus is 95 times that of the earth. △212.

Atoll, ring of coral rising from the ocean floor in warm areas of strong sunlight. Most atolls are built on the top of submarine volcanoes that have been eroded. The coral that is above sea level is usually surrounded on the ocean side by a reef of submerged coral, which on larger atolls may have other tiny islands in among the underwater formations. △202,268.

Atom, smallest particle of matter that can take part in a chemical reaction, every element having its own characteristic atoms. The atom, once thought indivisible, consists of a tiny central positively charged nucleus, identified by Ernest Rutherford (1911), around which orbit electrons. The number of electrons in an atom (atomic number) and their configuration determines its chemical properties. The nucleus contains tightly packed protons and neutrons, the number of protons equaling the electron number in a neutral atom. Removal of an atomic electron produces a charged ion. The orbits of the electrons were first described in the (Niels) Bohr atom (1913), using quantum mechanics. An electron of a particular energy can only occupy one of a number of permitted orbits, termed energy levels. Given sufficient energy an electron can jump from one energy level to a higher one. It can also return to a lower level, emitting radiant energy in the form of a photon of a specific frequency. Wave mechanics has since modified the concept of fixed orbits. *See also* Nucleus, Cell. △1478–84, 1556.

Atomic Battery, or **nuclear battery,** device that converts energy from radioactive particles into electrical current. Common sources include tritium (H_3) and Krypton-85, both emitters of beta particles.

Atomic Bomb. *See* Nuclear Weapon.

Atomic Clock, the most accurate device for measuring time, based on atomic or molecular events of known frequency (the reciprocal of time). In the cesium clock, used to define the second, the frequency used is that of the radiation (9,192,631,770 hertz) absorbed when cesium-133 atoms change between two different energy states in a magnetic field. The accuracy is better than one part in 10^{13}. In the ammonia clock the frequency of vibration (23,870 Hz) of the nitrogen atom is used. △1658.

Atomic Energy. *See* Nuclear Energy.

Atomic Energy Commission, a civilian commission established (1946) to regulate and control all phases of the nuclear energy program, removing this authority from the War Department. The five-member board, appointed by the president and approved by the Senate, is supervised by the Congressional Joint Committee on Atomic Energy. In 1954, private industry began to participate in the development of peaceful uses of atomic energy. In 1975 the Atomic Energy Commission was replaced with the Energy Research and Development Administration and Nuclear Regulatory Commission.

Atomic Mass Number, or nucleon number, the total number of protons and neutrons (nucleons) in the nucleus of a particular atom. The isotopes of an element have different mass numbers although their atomic numbers are identical.

Atomic Mass Unit (AMU), unit of mass, used to express atomic weights, defined since 1961 as 1/12th the mass of the most abundant isotope of carbon, carbon-12 (6 electrons, 12 protons + neutrons). It is equal to 1.6605×10^{-27} kg.

Atomic Number, number of protons in the nucleus of a neutral atom of an element or number of electrons moving around that nucleus. It determines the chemical properties of an element and its position in the periodic table. Isotopes of an element all have the same atomic number. △1550, 1552.

Atomic Pile (nuclear reactor). △1484, 1502, 1550.

Atomic Power, status achieved by several countries through the development of atomic weapons. The United States, the Soviet Union, Britain, and France are acknowledged atomic powers. The People's Republic of China is approaching that status. India, Israel, and several other countries have the potential to develop nuclear weapons. Before a country can be classified as an atomic power, however, its technology, production capability, and delivery systems all must be evaluated.

Atomic Radius, radius of an atom when it can be considered as if it were a small hard sphere. Thus, effective radii of atoms can be measured from experiments on probabilities of atomic collisions. In fact, most of the volume occupied by an atom is "empty space," and the electron distribution can be described only by a probability. No absolute geometric meaning can be given to the atomic radius; its value depends on the circumstances in which it is used. For example, radii can be ascribed to atoms in different types of chemical bond. △1480, 1550.

Atomic Spectrum, spectrum of sharp lines characteristic of the element involved and produced by the radiation emitted when electrons jump between energy levels of the atom. *See also* Atom.

Atomic Structure. △1480, 1484, 1550.

Atomic Weapons, International Control of, international attempt to curtail development, testing, spread, and use of nuclear weapons. *See* SALT Agreements.

Atomic Weight, the average mass of the atoms in a particular specimen of an element (usually taken to be the natural isotope composition), given in atomic mass units. It is the ratio of the mass of the atom in question to 1/12th the mass of the carbon-12 atom. △1550, 1552.

Atonality, in music, the practice of organizing a composition in terms of timbre and rhythm and the 12 tones of the chromatic scale without reference to a tonal center, as in Arnold Schoenberg's *Pierrot Lunaire* (1912).

Atonement, in religion, process by which a sinner moves toward union with God, through prayer, sacrifice, and the cleansing of one's deeds and thoughts. It is a theme that is apparent in some form in most religions, modern and ancient.

ATP. *See* Adenosine Triphosphate.

Atrium, interior court of a Roman house, partially roofed, onto which the dwelling rooms opened. The term is also applied to the entrance court of early Christian churches. △1016.

Atrophy, in medicine, refers to the shrinking of a cell, tissue, or organ. It may be associated with a number of pathological conditions, most commonly muscular diseases.

Atropine, poisonous alkaloid (formula $C_{17}H_{23}O_3N$) obtained from certain solanaceous plants, such as *Atropa belladona* (deadly nightshade). It is used medically as an anti-spasmodic, and for dilating the pupil of the eye.

Atsina, also called Gros Ventres, Algonkin-speaking tribe of North American Indians who were once part of the Arapaho. They occupied the Milk and Missouri rivers from Montana N into Saskatchewan. They were never a large tribe, and the present population, all of whom live on Fort Belknap Reservation, is approximately 2250.

Attalus III Philometer (*c.* 170–133 BC), king of Pergamum (138–133 BC). He foresaw Roman expansion and bequeathed his kingdom to Rome. His legacy caused violent dissension in the Roman assembly when Tiberius Gracchus proposed that Attalus' wealth be used to finance agrarian reforms. In the resultant strife Tiberius and many followers were killed.

Attention Span, number of stimuli that the senses receive or the duration of attention during a time interval.

Attica (Attiki), department in central Greece, bounded by the Aegean Sea (E), Saronic Gulf (S), Gulf of Cornith (W), Euboea Island and Voiotia dept. (N); capital city is Athens. According to legend, Cecrops, a mythical king, divided the region into 12 independent colonies, united by Theseus under administrative control of Athens (700 BC); Cleisthenes, a politician of Athens, reformed the aristocratic rule, classifying people into 10 tribes based on topographical divisions. Industries: lead mining, marble quarrying, cattle, shipping, tourism. Area: 1,305sq mi (3,375sq km). Pop. 2,060,000. *See also* Athens.

Attila (*c.* 406–53), known as the Scourge of God, king of the Huns (434–53), coruler with his elder brother Bleda until he murdered him in 445. Theodosius II, Roman emperor of the East, was compelled to pay him tribute. Nevertheless, Attila invaded the Balkan peninsula (441–43), destroying cities and demanding and receiving a threefold increase in his tribute. After Emperor Valentinian III of the West refused to pay tribute Attila invaded Gaul (451). Allied with the Ostrogoths and Vandals, he fought a great battle at Châlons-sur-Marne against the Roman general Aëtius who was supported by the Visigoths. Attila suffered heavy losses but was still able to invade Italy the next year. He was met at the gates of Rome by Pope Leo I whose majestic presence is said to have prevented the city's destruction. With his army suffering from disease and lack of provisions, he recrossed the Alps and died before he could once again invade Italy. △1054.

Attis, Greek shepherd who was loved by Cybele, goddess of the earth, fertility, and wild nature. In a jealous rage Cybele caused Attis to lose his senses. In this deranged state Attis castrated himself and died. Cybele transformed him into a pine tree, which became sacred to her. She changed his blood into violets.

Attitude, Spacecraft, orientation with respect to a given set of axes. Three variables specify attitude: *pitch,* the angle with the horizontal made by the long axis of the spacecraft; *yaw,* the angle through which the bow turns left or right of the "forward" direction; and *roll,* the angle of rotation about the long axis.

Attitudes, sets of beliefs, values, and feelings in an individual that are consistent across different situations and circumstances. Studies of attitudes in social psychology have focused primarily on the process of attitude change, especially under circumstances where the individual is confronted with persuasion. The effectiveness of a persuasive attempt depends on many factors, including the believability of the source (persuader), the nature of the persuasive message (eg, whether strong arguments come first or last), and personality characteristics of the receiver or target of the persuasive attempt (eg, older subjects are usually less gullible). Of special concern to both sociologists and psychologists are prejudice and discrimination, cases in which increased knowledge of attitude formation and change might benefit society. △896.

Attleboro, city in SE Massachusetts, near Rhode Island. Industries: jewelry (since 1780), silverware, scientific instruments. Settled 1634; inc. 1914. Pop. (1970) 32,907.

Attlee, Clement (Richard), 1st Earl (1883–1967), English politician, prime minister (1945–51). His experience as a social worker in London's East End convinced him to dedicate his life to social improvement

Athens, Greece

Mount Athos, Greece: monastery

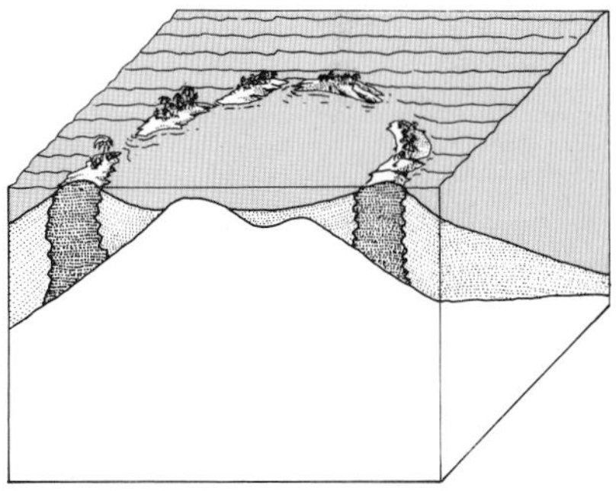

Atoll

Attica, Greece

through politics. He joined the Fabian Society (1907) and the Labour party (1908). First elected to Parliament in 1922, he served the first (1924) Labour government and the second (1929–31) becoming postmaster general. In 1935 he became leader of the Labour party. He served in Winston Churchill's wartime coalition government (1940–45) and became prime minister himself with the 1945 Labour victory. Under his leadership, the Bank of England, all utilities, the railroads, and the coal and iron and steel industries were nationalized. The National Health Service and other social reforms were instituted. India, Pakistan, Burma, Ceylon, and Palestine were granted their independence. The Labour party was narrowly defeated in 1951. Attlee continued as head of the party in opposition until his retirement in 1955.

Attorney General of the United States, chief US law officer. He heads the US department of justice and is a cabinet member. The attorney general represents the country in legal matters and gives advice and opinions to the president and to the heads of the executive departments when requested. The office was established in 1789. *See also* Justice, Department of.

Attucks, Crispus (1723?–70), American patriotic figure, supposedly a fugitive slave who had worked 20 years as a merchant seaman. Unarmed seamen and Boston dockworkers were taunting British troops guarding customs officers when the troops opened fire, killing Attucks and four others in the "Boston Massacre."

Atum, ancient Egyptian deity pictured as a human being and identified with the sun god Re. Atum was the god of creation according to the priests of Heliopolis, an important religious center of Egypt. △834, 972.

Auburn, city in E Alabama, in Lee co; location of Auburn University (1857). Industries: textiles, tires. Founded 1836. Pop. (1970) 22,767.

Auburn, city in W central New York, at outlet of Owasco Lake in Finger Lakes region. Homes of William H. Seward and Harriet Tubman are preserved here. Industries: rope, shoes, rugs. Inc. 1848. Pop. (1970) 34,599.

Auburn, city in NW Washington, 15mi (24km) NE of Tacoma; originally named Slaughter for a hero of Indian wars. Industries: metal, lumber, pottery. Founded 1887; inc. 1914. Pop. (1970) 21,817.

Auckland, largest city in New Zealand, on an isthmus of NW North Island; chief port and capital of Auckland prov.; served as capital of New Zealand 1841–1865 and now is chief base of New Zealand's navy; site of the War Memorial Museum, University of Auckland (1882), many extinct volcanoes. Industries: shipyards, canneries, chemicals. Pop. 151,900.

Auden, W(ystan) H(ugh) (1907–73), US author, b. England. His works encompass social and political commentary. He went to the United States in 1939 and from 1956–61 taught poetry at Oxford University. His works, showing great technical skill, include *The Age of Anxiety* (1947; Pulitzer Prize, 1948).

Audio Track. △1800.

Audit, investigation of a company's accounting procedures. Either firms independent of the company to be audited or internal personnel may undertake an audit, depending upon the firm's objective. Corporations with outstanding stock held by the public are required to retain the services of independent certified public accountants for periodic audits, to ensure that the financial statements issued by the corporation are in compliance with "generally accepted accounting procedures."

Auditory Canal. △676.

Auditory Nerve, the eighth cranial nerve. It transmits sound impulses from the cochlea of the inner ear to the auditory cortex of the brain. It also functions in the maintenance of balance. *See also* Cranial Nerves.

Audubon, John James (1785–1851), US ornithologist and artist, b. Les Cayes, Santo Domingo (now Haiti). He painted all of the species of birds in the United States known in the early 19th century. He met with little success in the United States, supporting himself by sidewalk portraiture. In 1826 he sent his work to Europe, where it was published as *The Birds of America* in four volumes (1827–38). After publication Audubon became a great success and proceeded to publish *Ornithological Biography* (5 vols., 1831–39) and *A Synopsis of the Birds of North America* (1839). Today Audubon's works remain both popular and respected for their beauty and accuracy.

Auerbach, Red (1917–), US basketball coach and executive, b. Arnold Auerbach in New York City. A president and general manager of the Boston Celtics in the National Basketball Association, he was also their coach (1949–66) and won nine championships (1957,1959–66). He was also coach of the Washington Capitols in the Basketball Association of America (1946–49).

Augean Stables, in Greek legend, a series of filthy stalls belonging to King Augeas of Elis. As one of his 12 labors Hercules had to clean them in one day. He diverted the waters of the Alpheus and Peneus rivers through the stables, washing away all the filth. The expression is a synonym for a dirty or untidy place.

Augite. *See* Pyroxene. △240.

Augsburg, city in S West Germany, on the Lech River; a free imperial city in 1276; became a prosperous banking and commercial center in 15th and 16th centuries; Augsburg Confessions (1530), a basic profession of Lutheran beliefs, were presented to Imperial Diet here; noted for cathedral started in 994, a 17th-century town hall, and 16th-century Fuggerie (residence for poor). Industries: textiles, clothing, motor vehicles. Founded *c.* 15 BC by Romans. Pop. 212,963.

Augsburg, League of, alliance formed in 1686 by the Roman Catholic and Protestant enemies of the French King Louis XIV. Composed of Spain, Sweden, the Holy Roman Empire, and a number of lesser states, its formation under Emperor Leopold I was a reaction to France's encroachment on the lands bordering the Holy Roman Empire. Following the French attack on the Palatinate in 1688, a new coalition against the French, the Grand Alliance, was formed in 1689 by Austria, England and the Netherlands; Savoy and Spain joined later. *See also* Grand Alliance, the War of.

Augsburg, Peace of, agreement reached by the Diet of the Holy Roman Empire meeting in Augsburg, Germany, on Sept. 25, 1555, that ended the conflict between Roman Catholics and Lutherans within the empire. It was the first permanent legal recognition of Lutheranism in Germany. Each prince was to decide whether Roman Catholicism or Lutheranism was to be practiced in his lands. Dissenters were allowed to sell their lands and move. Free cities and imperial cities were open to both Catholics and Lutherans. The rights of other Protestant sects, including Calvinists, were not considered. △1152.

Augsburg Confessions, summation of the Lutheran faith, formulated in 1530. Martin Luther and Philipp Melanchthon collaborated on its development. First presented to the Holy Roman Emperor Charles V, it was given to theologians of the Roman Catholic church for consideration; they renounced it. A bond among Lutheran churches, it became a model for later statements of religious beliefs. Its moderate language and temperate tone showed loyalty to Christian traditions.

August, eighth month of the year. Named after the Roman Emperor Augustus, it has 31 days. The birthstone is the sardonyx or carnelian.

Augusta, city at head of navigation of Savannah River in E Georgia; seat of Richmond co; resort area, scene of annual Masters golf tournament; trade center; former capital of Georgia (1785–95). Industries: brick and clay products, textiles, chemicals, wood and paper products. Settled 1735; inc. 1798. Pop. 59,-864.

Augusta, capital city in S central Maine, on Kennebec River, 35mi (56km) from the Atlantic Ocean; site of Plymouth Colony trading post, Fort Western (1628; a museum since 1754); capitol was designed by Charles Bulfinch; site of James G. Blaine's 19th-century home, now governor's mansion. A dam built across the Kennebec River 1837 converted Augusta from a shipping center to a manufacturing city. Industries: tourism, lumber, shoes, textiles, paper products. Inc. 1797; chartered as city 1849. Pop. (1970) 21,-945.

Augustine, Saint (354–430), Christian theologian and philosopher. Augustine's *Confessions* gives us an intimate psychological self-portrait of a spirit in search of ultimate purpose. This he believed he found in his conversion to Christianity (386), which took place only after worldly and philosophical confusion. As bishop of Hippo (North Africa) from 396–430, he defended Roman Catholic orthodoxy against the Manichaeans, the Donatists and the Pelagians. According to the doctrine of his *Enchiridion* (421), he tended to emphasize the corruption of human will, and the freedom of the divine gift of grace. The *City of God* (426), perhaps his most enduring work, was a model of Christian apologetic literature. Of the Four Fathers of the Latin Church, which also included Ambrose, Jerome and Gregory, Augustine is considered the greatest.

Augustus, Gaius Julius Caesar Octavianus (Octavian) (63 BC–AD 14), first Roman emperor (27 BC–AD 14). The adopted son of Julius Caesar, he went to Rome after Caesar's assassination in 44 BC to avenge his death. He secured the consulship and made an alliance with Anthony and Lepidus, the Second Triumvirate, which defeated his enemies. At Philippi (42 BC) Anthony and he defeated Brutus and Cassius. With Agrippa's aid, he beat Pompeius (36 BC) on the Mediterranean. At the battle of Actium (30 BC) Agrippa's victory over Anthony consolidated power of Octavian at Rome. In 29 BC the Senate voted him emperor. The title "Augustus" was conferred upon him in 27 BC, but he called himself "the first citizen." As emperor, he sought no more conquests and fostered colonization. He reorganized the empire, made taxation more equitable; rebuilt roads, temples, and the Forum; took general censuses; set up good fire, police, and military protection; and encouraged art, literature, and education. His only defeat occurred when his legions under Varus were massacred by the German troops of Arminius (AD 9).

His reign is called the Augustan Age, the time of Vergil, Ovid, Livy, Horace, Maecenas. Roman civilization developed under his world peace *(Pax Romana)*. Tiberius, his stepson, succeeded him. △1018, 1020.

Augustus II, called the Strong (1670–1733), German-born king of Poland (1697–1704, 1709–33); elector of Saxony as Frederick Augustus I (1694–1733). An alliance with Peter the Great of Russia against the Swedish Charles XII brought Augustus to the Polish throne. He was forced to give up the crown to Stanislas I Leszcznski in 1704. Civil war (1704–09) and invasion by Charles XII weakened the Polish state. Augustus was restored to the throne after Peter the Great defeated Sweden at the battle of Poltava in 1709, but Russia became even more dominant in Polish affairs.

Augustus III (1696–1763), king of Poland (1734–63) and, as Frederick Augustus II, elector of Saxony (1734–63). Russia and Austria forced Augustus on the Poles at the end of the War of the Polish Succession in 1734. As a result, Augustus was little more than a Russian puppet.

Auk, squat-bodied seabird of colder Northern Hemisphere coastlines. The flightless great auk *(Pinguinus impennis)*, called the Atlantic penguin, became extinct in the 19th century; height: 30in (76cm). The razor-billed auk is typical of living species. Family Alcidae. *See also* Razor-billed Auk.

Aulos, ancient double-reed wind instrument of Asian origin, producing a romantic, sensual tone like a shrill oboe. It was used extensively in classical Greek music. △998.

Aurangzeb (1618–1707), last of the great Mogul emperors of India (1658–1707). In 1658 he had his father, Shah Jahan, imprisoned and crowned himself emperor. In the first part of his reign, he strengthened his empire; under him the empire reached its apex. Toward the end of his reign, however, he alienated many of his people, especially the Hindus and the Deccan. △1202.

Aurelia. △470.

Aurelian (Lucius Domitius Aurelianus) (212?–75), Roman emperor (270–75). His victories against the Germanic invaders of Italy, his reconquest of Palmyra, and his recovery of Gaul and Britain earned him the title of "Restorer of the World." In Rome he established the Unconquered Sun God as the protective deity of the empire. △1030.

Aureomycin, an antibiotic. *See* Antibiotic.

Auricle, also known as atrium, each of the upper two chambers of the four-chambered heart. They are comparatively thin-walled since they only pump blood down into the muscular ventricles of the heart. *See also* Heart.

Auriga, or **the Charioteer,** northern constellation situated northeast of Taurus. Auriga contains several open clusters, including M36 (NGC 1960). Brightest star Alpha Aurigae (Capella). △110, 132.

Aurignacian Period. △652.

Auriol, Vincent (1884–1966), French socialist, principal founder of the Fourth Republic, president (1947–54). He entered parliament in 1914 and served as minister of finance under Léon Blum (1936–37). During World War II, he fought in the Resistance and then joined Charles de Gaulle's government in exile.

Aurochs, or **Urus,** extinct wild ox, the longhaired ancestor of modern domesticated cattle. Once found throughout forests of Africa, Europe and SW Asia, it became extinct in 1627. Back-breeding experiments in Germany have produced an animal resembling ancient species. Family Bovidae; species *Bos primigenius.*

Aurora, suburban city in NE central Colorado, 5mi (8km) E of Denver in Adams and Arapahoe cos. Inc. 1903. Pop. (1970) 74,974.

Aurora, city in NE Illinois, 37mi (60km) W of Chicago; site of Aurora College (1893). Industries: chemicals, glass, transportation equipment. Inc. 1857. Pop. (1970) 74,182.

Aurora, a sporadic radiant display appearing in shifting, colored rays, streamers, or draperies in the night sky. Most frequent in zones around the earth's poles and called aurora borealis to the north and aurora australis to the south, auroras are caused by interactions of charged particles from the sun with the earth's magnetic field. △96.

Ausable Chasm, gorge in NE New York; formed by the Ausable River; site of thundering waterfalls including Rainbow Falls at the S end. Length: 2mi (3km); width: 20–50ft (6–15m).

Austen, Jane (1775–1817), English novelist. A clergyman's daughter, she led an uneventful life but wrote six novels of great craftsmanship, insight, and wit: *Sense and Sensibility* (1811), *Pride and Prejudice* (1813), *Mansfield Park* (1814), *Emma* (1816), *Persuasion* (1818), and *Northanger Abbey* (1818). *See also* individual novels.

Austerlitz, Battle of. △1226.

Austin, John (1790–1859), English jurist. He systemized philosopher Jeremy Bentham's legal ideas and founded the analytical school of jurisprudence. He was a professor of jurisprudence at University College, London (1826–32), and a member of the Criminal Law Commission (1833). His greatest work was *Province of Jurisprudence Determined* (1832).

Austin, Moses (1761–1821), US pioneer, b. Durham, Conn. He was a miner in Virginia, Missouri, and the Spanish territories. He received a grant in 1821 to settle 300 families in what was to become Texas. When he died, his son Stephen took over the grant.

Austin, Stephen (1793–1836), US pioneer, b. Wythe County, Va. On his father's death in 1821, he took up his father's grant in the Spanish territory that was to become Texas. He settled the first English-speaking colony there and was followed by many other successful colonists. Mexico opposed this colonization, and Austin went to Mexico City to argue his case, but was arrested. On his return in 1835, he became a leader in the fight for Texas independence.

Austin, city in S central Texas, 75mi (121km) NE of San Antonio, on both sides of the Colorado River; capital of Texas and seat of Travis co; served as capital of the Republic of Texas 1839, which was temporarily moved to Houston 1842–45 because of insurgent Mexican occupation of San Antonio and Indian invasions; after Texas was admitted to the United States 1845, it served as temporary capital until 1870 when it was made the permanent seat of government. Austin's industrial growth was spurred 1934 with the harnessing of the Colorado River for hydroelectricity and the initiation of flood control projects. It is the site of the capitol building (1885), old land office (1857), governor's mansion (1856), French embassy (1840), and home of author O. Henry; educational institutions include University of Texas (1881); nearby are many recreational facilities and Bergstrom Air Force Base; convention center; commercial and distribution center for diversified farming region. Industries: electronics, glass, furniture, food processing, bricks, tiles, machinery, wood and metal products. Settled 1835 as Waterloo; inc. 1839 and renamed in honor of Stephen F. Austin. Pop. (1970) 251,808.

Australasia, geographical term for the islands of New Zealand, New Guinea, and Australia, in the S Pacific Ocean; sometimes used synonomously with Oceania, including the Malay Archipelago and Polynesia to the NE.

Australia, independent nation in the S Pacific Ocean occupying the continent of Australia. First settled by the British, it has received large influxes of immigrants since WWII. The standard of living is among the highest in the world.

Land and Economy. The smallest, most arid continent, it is located below the SE Asian archipelago, bisected by the Tropic of Capricorn and bounded on the E by the Pacific Ocean, W by the Indian Ocean, and includes the State of Tasmania. Most of the country is a low plateau with a flat and arid center. Its 12,000-mi (19,320-km) coast contains the Great Barrier Reef, largest coral reef in the world. The SE section is 500,000sq mi (1,295,000sq km) of fertile plain. The low ranges (Great Dividing Range and Australian Alps) mainly parallel the E coast with moderate chains in the W and central sections. Most are rounded foothills with no glaciers and little snow. The highest is Mt Kosciusko, 7,316ft (2,231m). Darling, its longest river, has been dry for as long as 18 months. Rainfall is sufficient on the E coast, the SE and SW; the interior receives less than 10in (26cm) annually. Water supply and conservation are continuous problems. An unpredictable climate results from its latitude and long coastline exposed to the tradewinds. Although agriculture accounts for most of its export income, there has been rapid industrial growth. About 35% of the work force is in manufacturing, 11% in agriculture. Wool and meat are major products. Australia produces 30% of the world's wool supply and is the largest exporter of beef, second of lamb. Over half of its large wheat crop is exported. Mineral exports have been rising, especially since the 1965 discovery of iron ore. Oil and gas were found 1965–68 and uranium 1972–74. By 1971 iron ore replaced wool as the leading single export.

People. Until 1788 there were 350,000 aborigines in the country. As European, predominantly British, settlements grew, indigenous peoples declined. Now each state is responsible for those in its region. Many Chinese came before the 1901 restriction act, and since WWII, 2,300,000 immigrants, 50% British and many from central European countries, have entered. Two-thirds of the population is in the SE (New South Wales and Victoria), one-third in Sydney and Melbourne. English is the official language. Literacy is 98.5%.

Government. Fully independent within the British Commonwealth, Australia is governed by a prime minister, the leader of the majority party in the elected House of Representatives, and an elected, bicameral parliament. Its three main parties are Australian Labor party (trade unions), Liberal party (business), and Country party (agriculture).

History. Early discovery of Australia was delayed by the colossal size of the Pacific Ocean. In 1577, Sir Francis Drake, looking for spices and trade, turned N to Peru. It was not until 1605–06 that Dutch explorer William Jansz sailed close to Queensland; he was probably the first European to see the coast, which he described as desolate, with black savages. In 1642, Abel Janszoon Tasman circumnavigated the continent, reaching Tasmania and New Zealand. Englishman James Cook, sailing around Cape Horn in 1768, was the first European to reach the E coast, and in 1770, finding it favorable for settlement, he took possession for Britain. Many early settlers were convicts; 19th-century policy emancipated them, and immigration was encouraged. Six colonies were created: New South Wales (1823), Tasmania (1825), Western Australia (1838), Southern Australia (1842), Victoria (1851), and Queensland (1859). These were united under the Commonwealth of Australia Act of 1900. The first parliament met in 1901. The Statute of Westminster Adoption Act of 1942 gave Australia complete autonomy. △1260.

PROFILE

Official name: Commonwealth of Australia
Area: 2,967,909sq mi (7,686,884sq km)
Population: 12,755,638
Density: 5 per sq mi (2 per sq km)
Chief cities: Canberra (capital); Sydney; Melbourne; Adelaide; Brisbane
Government: Republic
Religion: Anglican, 35%; Catholic, 25%; Methodist, 10% (no state religion)
Language: English
Monetary unit: Australian dollar
Gross national product: $73,500,000,000
Per capita income: $3,998
Industries: wool, iron, steel, textiles, electrical and radio equipment, drugs, chemicals, metal products, aircraft, ships, automobiles, meat products, machinery
Agriculture: cattle, sheep, wheat, fruits, sugar
Minerals: uranium, coal, gold, copper, iron, silver, lead, tin, bauxite, petroleum, gas, nickel

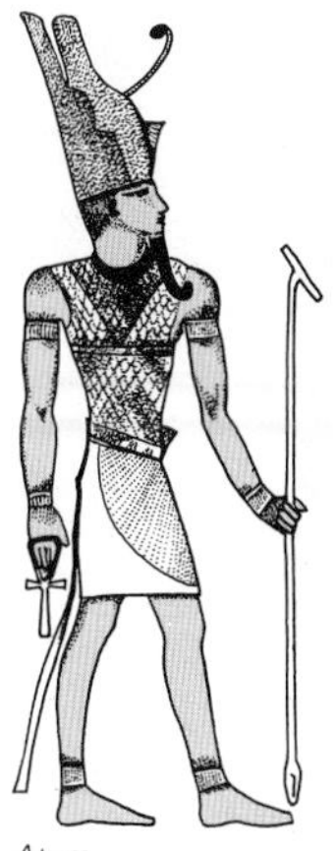
Atum

Aurochs

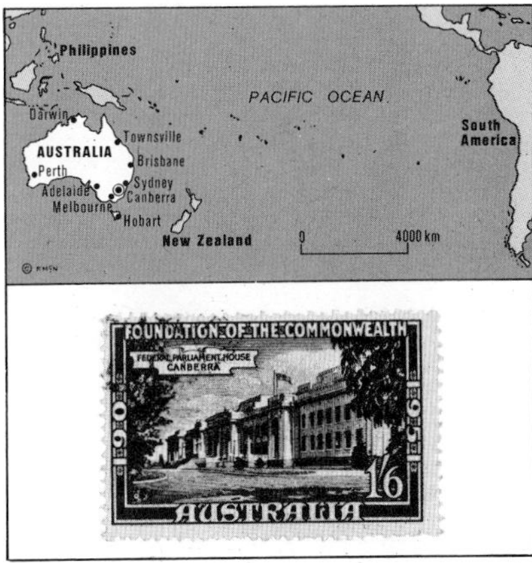
Philippines
PACIFIC OCEAN
Darwin
AUSTRALIA
Townsville
Brisbane
Perth
Sydney
Adelaide
Canberra
Melbourne
Hobart
New Zealand
South America
0
4000 km
FOUNDATION OF THE COMMONWEALTH
FEDERAL PARLIAMENT HOUSE CANBERRA
1/6
AUSTRALIA
Australia

Australia: Sydney Opera House

Trading partners: United Kingdom, United States, Japan, People's Republic of China

Australian Aborigines (officially: Native Australians), peoples who inhabited Australia prior to European settlement. Decimated by the early European settlers, they number under 45,000 in some 500 tribes. They are traditionally nomadic, living by hunting and gathering in small scattered groups. Their society is patrilineal, and polygamy is widespread, as is both male and female circumcision, the latter playing an important part in initiation ceremonies. Their culture is traditionally rich in carving and painting and their religion includes a remarkable and diverse mythology. △880.

Australian Alps, mountain range in Victoria and New South Wales, SE Australia; part of Great Dividing Range, which forms the watershed between the Murray River system and streams flowing into the Tasman Sea; site of numerous resort areas and forest reserves; first explored 1839–40. Highest peak is Mt Kosciusko, 7,316ft (2,231m), highest point in Australia.

Australian Antarctic Territory, external territory of Australia in Antarctica, including all territory and islands (except Adélie Land). Claimed 1933. Area: 2,360,000sq mi (6,112,400sq km).

Australian Ballot, method developed in Australia in the 1850s for choosing candidates for public office. It ensures public funding, proper preparation and handling of votes, and, most importantly, secrecy in the electoral process.

Australian Cattle Dog, herding dog, also called Australian heeler because it herds livestock by nipping their heels. This dog has a V-shaped head and prick ears. The body is covered with a short, harsh coat colored mottled blue with tan or red speckle. Average size: 18–20in (46–51cm) high at shoulder; 33lb (15kg).

Australia-New Zealand-United States Treaty Organization. *See* ANZUS Pact.

Australian Kelpie, herding dog, also called Australian collie. It has a V-shaped head, prick ears, almond-shaped eyes, and brush tail. The short, dense coat can be solid black, red, fawn, liver, smoke blue, black and tan, or red and tan. Average size: 18–20in (46–51cm) high at shoulder; 30lb (13.5kg).

Australian Terrier, small working dog (terrier group) bred from first English dogs shipped to Australia. This rugged dog has a long, flat head topped by a light-colored topknot and pricked, pointed ears. The body is low-set; legs are short; and the docked tail is carried up. The Aussie's rough coat is 2.5in (6cm) long; color is blue-black or silver-black with tan, sandy, or red. Average size: 10in (25cm) high at shoulder; 12–14lb (5–6kg). *See also* Terrier.

Australoid Race, one of the major human racial groupings, often subdivided into pygmy (Negrito) and full-sized peoples. Full-sized Australoids have heavy skin pigmentation; large jaws and prominent brow ridges; wavy to curly hair; and hair distribution and stature similar to Caucasoids. The term usually covers the Australian and Tasmanian aborigines and associated populations. *See also* Negrito Subrace.

Australopithecus, or "southern ape," name given to race of extinct near-men whose fossilized bones, dating back to about 3,000,000 years ago, have been found in South Africa. The Australopithecines had teeth more human than ape-like, and like man could move and stand fully erect without the help of their arms. They are therefore classified as hominids (men), and are possibly direct ancestors of modern man. *See also* Pithecanthropus. △648.

Austrasia, Germanic N and E part of the Frankish kingdom during the Merovingian period of French history. Divided into the semi-independent regions of Austrasia, Neustria, and Burgundy in the 6th and 7th centuries, the lands were reunited under the Austrasian Pepin family just in time to ward off the Arab crossing of the Pyrenees. From this new foundation sprang the Carolingian empire of Charlemagne.

Austria, Republic of, nation in central Europe. It was once the center of an extensive empire under the royal house of Hapsburgs. Vienna, the capital, is one of the world's great cities.

Land and Economy. About 70% of Austria lies in the E Alps. The mountains, composed primarily of crystalline rock and limestone, comprise three longitudinal ranges: the Northern Limestone Alps, the Central Alps, and the Southern Limestone Alps. The highest peak is the Grossglockner, 12,461ft (3,801m). The rivers Inn, Salzach, and Enns flow N into the Danube. The Drava River drains the S mountains. Austria's spectacular mountain scenery attracts tourists and sports enthusiasts from all over the world. The Austrian economy is that of a prosperous modern industrial nation. Large industrial concentrations have developed around the cities of Vienna, Linz, and Graz. Austria is landlocked; its chief waterway is the Danube, and the most fertile lands lie in the Danubian Plain. The nation's largest industrial firms, commercial banks, oil and heavy industry concerns were nationalized by the government in 1946.

People. The Austrians are descended from a variety of peoples, including Germans, Slavs, and Mediterraneans. The people are 98% German-speaking; the various dialects are related to the Bavarian group of dialects. Almost 90% of the people is Roman Catholic, while 6% is Protestant. The majority lives in the city and works in industry. One-fifth of the entire population lives in Vienna.

Government. The constitution separates the federal government into executive, legislative, and judiciary branches. Power is wielded chiefly by the legislature—the Federal Assembly; this body consists of the Federal Council (Bundesrat) and the National Council (Nationalrat). The head of government is the chancellor. He and his ministry are responsible to the National Council. Austria's major political parties are the Socialist party and the more conservative People's party.

History. The founding of Austria—or *Österreich,* the "eastern realm"—is generally traced to Otto I, 10th-century emperor of the Holy Roman Empire. Vienna became the capital in 1140. After 1278, Austria became identified with the powerful House of Hapsburg. The Austrian branch of the Hapsburgs united with the crowns of Hungary and Bohemia, establishing what later became the Austrian Empire. In 1867 the dual monarchy of Austria-Hungary was created; it lasted until WWI. In 1918 the Hapsburgs were overthrown and Austria was est. as a republic. Germany seized Austria in 1938, uniting the two countries. Defeated in WWII, Austria was partitioned into four zones by the Allies. Austria became a member of the United Nations in 1955, the year the Allies ended their occupation.

PROFILE

Official name: Republic of Austria
Area: 32,375sq mi (83,851sq km)
Population: 7,459,000
Density: 230per sq mi (89per sq km)
Chief cities: Vienna (capital), 1,614,300; Graz, 248,500; Linz, 202,800; Salzburg, 128,800
Government: Federal republic
Religion (major group): Roman Catholic
Language (official): German
Monetary unit: Schilling
Gross national product: $27,887,000,000
Per capita income (1973): $3,222
Industries (major products): chemical products, heavy machinery, vehicles, textiles, electrical equipment
Agriculture (major products): wheat, rye, potatoes, dairy products
Minerals (major): lignite, graphite, iron, copper, magnesite, natural gas
Trading partners (major): West Germany, Italy, Switzerland, Great Britain

Austrian Empire, all lands controlled by the Hapsburg dynasty, beginning in 1804, when Holy Roman Emperor Francis II, reacting to Napoleon I's assumption of the title of emperor, proclaimed himself Francis I, emperor of Austria. Under Francis I and Metternich, the Austrian empire successfully thwarted change at home and encouraged peace abroad. Nationalist movements and calls for constitutional government were ignored until the 1848 revolution in Paris touched off similar revolts throughout the empire—in Vienna, Bohemia, Hungary, and the Italian provinces. They were put down and a constitution enacted (but never put into effect).

Under Prince Felix Schwarzenberg and Emperor Francis Joseph, authoritarian rule continued until Austria's humiliating war with Prussia in 1866. Loss of land and prestige forced the emperor to negotiate with the Hungarian nationalist leaders, and the compromise or *Ausgleich* of 1867 was worked out. Thereafter the term "empire of Austria" was applied only to the non-Hungarian Hapsburg territories, and the area as a whole was called the Austro-Hungarian or Dual Monarchy. *See also* Austro-Hungary; Austro-Prussian War.

Austrian Succession, War of the (1740–48), name for what was actually several related wars: the war for the Austrian succession itself, in which France supported Spain's claim to part of the Hapsburg domains; the first and second Silesian Wars, in which Frederick II of Prussia took Silesia from Austria; and the war between France and Britain over colonial possessions (known as King George's War). *See also* King George's War.

Austro-Hungary (1867–1918), reorganization of the Austrian Empire as the dual monarchy of the Empire of Austria and the Kingdom of Hungary. After its defeat in the Austro-Prussian War (1866), Austria was compelled to grant greater autonomy to Hungary. The *Ausgleich,* or compromise, of 1867 created the dual monarchy. The Emperor of Austria and the King of Hungary would be the same person, but each nation would have its own parliament and premier and control its internal affairs. Only foreign affairs would be controlled by a central government. The *Ausgleich* did not take into consideration the nationalistic desires of Slavic, Italian, and other minorities, nor did it please Hungarians who wanted complete autonomy or Austrians who would have preferred a realignment with other German states. The death of the first Emperor-King, Francis Joseph, in 1916 and serious setbacks in the war led to the inevitable collapse of the dual monarchy. Czechoslovakia and Hungary declared their independence in 1918, Emperor Charles abdicated, and Austria was declared a republic. △1232.

Austronesian Languages, or Malayo-Polynesian languages, include Malay, Indonesian, Tagalog, Malagasy, and numerous other languages spoken in Indonesia, the Philippines, New Guinea, and the islands of the Pacific Ocean. There are four branches: Indonesian, Melanesian (which includes Fijian), Micronesian (which includes Chamorro, spoken on Guam), and the Polynesian languages, which include Maori, Tongan, Tahitian, and Samoan. There are about 175 million speakers in all.

Austro-Prussian War (1866), conflict with Prussia and Italy allied against Austria, also known as Seven Weeks War. Prussian Chancellor Bismarck triggered the war in order to assure Prussia's supremacy in Germany and to remove Austria from the confederation of German states. The administration of Schleswig-Holstein, held in part by both nations, was used by Bismarck as an excuse for the war. Austria was defeated at Königgrätz and was forced to leave the German Confederation and to cede Venetia to Italy. △1250.

Authoritarianism, political philosophy that concentrates power in the hands of a person or small group not responsible to the people. Authoritarian systems deify the state and are based on antidemocratic principles. Classic examples are Germany under Hitler, Italy under Mussolini, and Spain under Franco.

Authoritarian Personality, or **Authoritarianism,** in psychology, a personality characterized by tendencies toward unquestioning obedience to authority figures, a desire for obedience from others, rigid thinking, and hostility toward outgroups. *See also* Attitudes; Prejudice.

Autism, Infantile, disorder of young children characterized by failure to relate to others, failure to use language normally, and ritualistic behavior such as playing for hours with one toy. The autistic child seems to withdraw into a private world. The causes of autism are not known, but some experts believe such children have a disorder that affects their ability to understand language and to form concepts.

Autistic Thinking, thought disorder common to schizophrenics, especially children, that involves self-directed thinking (thinking directed toward imagined satisfaction), as opposed to reasoning, which leads to action. Everyone indulges in autistic thinking (eg, daydreams) but total dependence on this form of gratification is abnormal.

Autocracy. △902.

Autogyro. △1720.

Autoimmune Disease, any one of a group of disorders caused by antibodies produced specifically to direct attacks against the body's own tissues. One such disease in which autoimmunity is believed involved is systemic lupus erythematosus (SLE), an inflammation of the connective tissue occuring most often in young women. The occasional presence of so-called auto-antibodies in an individual does not necessarily indicate autoimmune disease. Treatment depends on the target of the attack.

Autolycus, in Greek mythology, son of the Greek god Hermes and mortal Chione. He received from his father the gift of rendering what he touched invisible. In this way he was able to commit numerous thefts until one day Sisyphus, whose oxen he had stolen, caught him.

utomatic Control System. △1670.

utomatic Writing, (1) in clinical psychology and sychiatry, a symptom of disturbed functioning: the dividual writes something without being con-iously aware of what he is writing or even that he is riting. (2) in spiritualistic encounters, a supposed ay that departed souls may communicate with the ving, that is by causing a living person to write a essage in the spirit's own handwriting. *See also* arapsychology.

utomobile. The first automobile was built by the renchman N.J. Cugnot in 1769. Cugnot's vehicle as steam-powered, designed to haul artillery, and chieved about 2mph (3.2kph). In 1862, J.J.E. Lenoir uilt the first gas-fueled internal combustion two-roke engine. In 1876, German inventor N.A. Otto uilt the first four-stroke engine, the prototype of odern automobile engines. By 1885 Karl Benz and ottlieb Daimler had founded an automobile industry Germany. Seven years later, the Duryea brothers, J. ranklin and Charles, created the first American gaso-ne-powered auto; it achieved 10mph (16kph). By 910 there were some 80 manufacturers in North merica, but not until 1913, when Henry Ford intro-uced mass-production techniques, was production ommercially feasible for the mass market.

utomobile Insurance, insurance designed to over one or more of the following: *liability,* protec-on for the insured against loss arising out of his legal ability when his automobile injures others or dam-ges their property; *medical services,* payment for the edical expenses of the insured and any passengers hose injuries are automobile-related; *physical dam-ge,* coverage for damages or loss to automobile; and *ninsured motorists,* coverage for the insured if in-ured by a driver who carries no liability insurance and ho was at fault. In states with "no fault" automobile nsurance plans, coverage may include all of the bove plus the insured's lost wages and other direct xpenses resulting from an automobile accident.

utomobile Racing, sport involving the use of spe-ially designed cars. The sport originated in France in 894 and has since developed into one of the most opular spectator attractions in the world, with sev-ral varieties of races using special types of cars. hese races include Grand Prix, stock car, drag, sports ar, and midget. Most popular worldwide is the Grand rix circuit, which includes about 20 drivers who com-ete annually in tracks in several countries for the orld's driving championship. In the United States, ne most popular event is the Indianapolis 500, an nnual race that began in 1911. △930.

Indianapolis 500 Winners

ear	Winner
940	Wilbur Shaw
941	Floyd Davis, Mauri Rose
946	George Robson
947	Mauri Rose
948	Mauri Rose
949	Bill Holland
950	Johnnie Parsons
951	Lee Wallard
952	Troy Ruttman
953	Bill Vukovich
954	Bill Vukovich
955	Bob Sweikert
956	Pat Flaherty
957	Sam Hanks
958	Jimmy Bryan
959	Rodger Ward
960	Jim Rathmann
961	A. J. Foyt
962	Rodger Ward
963	Parnelli Jones
964	A. J. Foyt
1965	Jim Clark
1966	Graham Hill
1967	A. J. Foyt
1968	Bobby Unser
1969	Mario Andretti
970	Al Unser
1971	Al Unser
1972	Mark Donohue
1973	Gordon Johncock
1974	Johnny Rutherford
1975	Bobby Unser
1976	Johnny Rutherford

Automobile Safety. △1698.

Autonomic Nervous System, portion of the ner-vous system that is entirely efferent in action and that experiences widespread effects during emotional epi-sodes. It includes both central and peripheral nervous system elements, and its actions affect the glands and organs of the body. It is subdivided into the *sympathetic nervous system,* which predominates during periods of strong emotion (eg, anger or fright), and the *parasympathetic nervous system,* which predominates during periods of relative emotional calm. △664.

Autopilot, Aircraft. △1670.

Autumnal Equinox, equinox occurring when the sun crosses the celestial equator, moving toward the southern hemisphere, on about September 23. The crossing point on the equator is the First Point of Libra, now actually situated in the constellation Virgo, which is diametrically opposite the First Point of Aries. *See also* Equinox.

Auvergne, region and former prov. of S France, now divided into depts of Puy-de-Dôme and Cantal. In Roman times it was conquered by Julius Caesar after the fall of the Gallic leader Vercingetorix. It has a scenic chain of inactive volcanoes running N to S, and many examples of Romanesque architecture. △1096.

Auxin, plant hormone produced in growing tips of roots and stems. Auxins accelerate plant growth by stimulating cell enlargement and interacting with other hormones. Actions include cell elongation in response to geotropism and phototropism; cambial growth; fruit drop and leaf fall; and plant part dominance. Types include natural indoleacetic acid and synthetic auxins used commercially. *See also* Gibberellin. △430, 448.

Avalanche, tumbling down of a mass of snow. An avalanche is most likely on a hill of slope greater than 35°. The snow that moves may be dry, from recent snowfall; wet, thawed, or wet with rain; or slab, wind-packed, wind-driven snow. Any steep slope with 12in (30cm) or more of new snow may avalanche as a result of weather change or slope disturbance due to vibration. △262.

Avars, Mongolian people who settled near the Volga River about 461. While one group remained there, another moved into the Danube River basin in the 6th century, occupying Dacia, what is now modern-day Romania. Their domain extended from the Volga to the Baltic Sea, and they exacted huge tributes from the Byzantine Empire during this time. The Avars were finally crushed by Charlemagne in 795.

Avatar, a "descent" or incarnation of God. The original idea was that from time to time God manifests himself in order to restore virtue. In Hindu tradition, Vishnu had ten important avatars. Avatars appear also in Buddhist and Jain traditions. △1034.

Avellaneda, formerly Barracas al Sud; port city in E Argentina; suburb of Buenos Aires; capital of Avellaneda district; major industrial and rail center; port section is called Doc Sud. Industries: meat packing, grain processing, oil refining, woolens, chemicals. Pop. 337,538.

Avempace, or **Ibn-Bajjah** (*d.* 1138), Islamic philosopher. Learned in medicine, mathematics, and astronomy, his most noted treatise was "The Rule of the Solitary," dealing with the formation of the ideal state, which, seeking realization of each individual's full potential, would best be modeled on the solitary man's discipline.

Avenarius, Richard (1843–96), German philosopher, b. Paris. An advocate of pure experience, Avenarius embraced extreme nominalism and "the given" as self-sufficient. His chief works are *Philosophy as Thoughts of the World according to Least Action* (1876) and *Critic of Pure Experience* (1888–90).

Average, in statistics, the one score that most typifies an entire set of scores. It may be the arithmetic mean of the scores (the sum of the scores divided by their number), the mode (the one score that occurs most often), or the median (the score that divides the set of scores into upper and lower halves). Most often the "average" is the arithmetic mean.

Averrhoës, medieval Latin name for Abu-al-Walid Ibn Rushd (1126–98), foremost Islamic philosopher in Spain. Appointed *qadi,* or judge, in Seville in 1169 and later in Córdoba, he became physician to the Caliph of Marrakesh in 1182. Banished (1184–99) to a small village near Seville for advocating reason over religion, he returned to favor shortly before his death. His major work, *Incoherence of the Incoherence,* defends Neoplatonism and Aristotle. △852, 858.

Aversion Therapy, or aversive conditioning, use of learning or conditioning procedures to develop aversive responses to certain situations or to unwanted

Australian kelpie

Australian terrier

Belgium
Ger. Dem. Rep.
Poland
Lux.
Federal Republic of Germany
Czechoslovakia
France
Linz
Vienna (Wien)
Salzburg
AUSTRIA
Liech.
Innsbruck
Graz
Switzerland
Hungary
Italy
Yugoslavia
ADRIATIC SEA
0
200km

Austria

Linz, Austria

habits. The therapy consists of pairing a noxious stimulus such as an electric shock or bad-tasting substance with the performance of the unwanted behavior (eg, overeating or smoking) until an aversion to that behavior is developed. △772.

Aviary, enclosure, usually spacious enough for flight, for the observation and/or breeding of captive birds. It is generally made of wire-mesh. Large flight cages are usually found in zoos, though private homes sometimes have a room or porch set aside. Natural planted surroundings are preferred, although difficult to maintain. △638.

Avicenna, Latin name of Abu Ali Ibn Sina (980–1037), influential Persian philosopher and physician. A royal physician to Persian princes, he attempted to reconcile his own Neo-Platonic mysticism with Islamic doctrine. Among his many works are the *Shifa (Recovery),* a collection of treatises on Aristotelian logic, metaphysics, and natural science, and the *Canon,* a medical compendium. △852, 858.

Avignon, city in SE France, 50mi (81km) NNW of Marseilles at the confluence of the Rhone and Durance rivers. A thriving city under Roman rule, it declined in the 5th and 6th centuries. In 1316 work on the Papal Palace was begun. The massive, fortress-type palace has a great hall with incomparable acoustics, gardens, and beautifully carved tomb of John XXII, with its Romanesque cathedral, Notre Dame des Doms. Papacy held Avignon until 1791 when it was annexed to France. Industries: wine, grain, leather. Pop. 86,096.

Avignon, School of, school of painting that originated with the move of the Papal Court to Avignon, France (1309–77). Artists such as Simone Martini of Siena followed the popes to France, spreading Italian trecento art to northern Europe. The greatest product of this school was the anonymous *Pietà* in Villeneuve-les-Avignon (*c.* 1460).

Ávila, city in central Spain, on Adaja River, 53mi (85km) WNW of Madrid; capital city of Ávila prov., religious center noted for medieval architecture, including Cathedral of San Salvador, Basilica of San Vicente, and 11th-century wall; birthplace of St Teresa. City was taken from the Moors in 1088 by Alfonso VI of León and Castile. Industries: flour milling, tanning, woolen goods. Area: (prov.) 3,110sq mi (8,055sq km). Pop. (city) 31,000; (prov.) 203,798.

Aviz, dynasty that ruled Portugal from 1385 to 1580. It was founded by John I, who was grand master of Aviz, a knightly order. The dynasty's rule coincided with the most glorious period of Portuguese history. Its last ruler was Henry the cardinal-king.

Avocado, fruit of the avocado tree that is green to dark purple and pear-shaped. Its soft, greenish flesh surrounds a single large seed and has a nutty flavor; weight: to 4lb (2kg). Or, many varieties of a single species *(Persea americana)* of a tall or spreading tree with elliptical leaves native to Mexico, Central America, and W South America, cultivated worldwide.

Avocet, graceful, long-legged, black-patterned, white wading bird. It sweeps its long, upcurved bill through shallow water for food. It performs a mass courtship rite that includes specific head movements. Spotted, olive eggs (4) are laid in a rootlet-lined ground scrape, usually near water. Length: 18in (44cm). Genus *Recurvirostra.*

Avogadro, (Lorenzo Romano) Amedeo, Conte di Quaregna e Ceretto (1776–1856), Italian physicist and chemist. Avogadro's law, stating that equal volumes of gases at the same pressure and temperature contain the same number of molecules, led him to hypothesize that nitrogen and oxygen are diatomic molecules (an idea accepted after his death). △1502.

Avogadro's Number, or **Avogadro's Constant,** a constant (symbol *L*) equal to 6.022×10^{-23} /mol, giving the number of atoms or molecules present in one mole of a substance. It is both the ratio of the universal gas constant to Boltzmann's constant and of Faraday's constant to the charge of the electron. *See also* Mole. △1502.

Avon River, either of two rivers in England. Bristol, or Lower Avon, rises in Cotswold Hills, Gloucestershire, and flows S and W through Bristol to enter Severn Estuary at Avonmouth. Length: 75mi (121km). Warwickshire, or Upper Avon, rises in Northamptonshire, and flows SW through Stratford-on-Avon to join Severn River at Tewkesbury. Length: 96mi (155km).

Avranches, town in NW France, 8mi (13km) NE of Mont St Michel. A stone marker designates the spot where the English King Henry II made amends to papal representatives in 1172 for the murder of Thomas à Becket. Industries: farming, fishing, livestock raising. Founded as Roman military station. Pop. 9,775.

Awakened Conscience, The. △1252.

Awami League, formerly (1949–70) major opposition party of Pakistan; since 1971, major party of Bangladesh (former East Pakistan); renamed Awami Peasants' and Workers' League of Bangladesh (1975). Led by Sheikh Mujibur Rahman from 1953 to his death in a military coup in 1975, from 1966 the party advocated a federation government for Pakistan that would give more autonomy to East Pakistan. In 1970 the party won a majority of the legislature, but the government canceled the election and outlawed the party. Civil war broke out in early 1971 and East Pakistan won its independence, becoming Bangladesh.

Awl. △1602.

AWOL. *See* Absent Without Leave.

Axelrod, Julius (1912–), US pharmacologist, b. New York City. He shared the 1970 Nobel Prize in physiology or medicine with Ulf Svante von Euler and Sir Bernard Katz for their work on the chemistry of nerve-impulse transmission. Axelrod discovered how the neurotransmitter noradrenaline is inactivated after it has performed its work.

Axiom, accepted assumption used as a basis for deductive reasoning. *See* Axiomatic Method; Postulate. △1462.

Axiomatic Method, method of mathematical reasoning based on logical deduction from assumptions (axioms). The method is fundamental to the philosophy of modern mathematics; it was used by the Greeks and formalized early this century by the great German mathematician David Hilbert. In an axiomatic system certain undefined entities (terms) are taken and described by a set of axioms. Other, often unsuspected, relationships (theorems) are then deduced by logical reasoning. Seen in this light, mathematics is a purely abstract system with no connection with the physical world. Applications of mathematics are those in which objects or measurements in the physical world can be identified with the terms of the system. For instance, the points, lines, and angles of Euclidean geometry are connected by postulates, and theorems, such as the Pythagorean theorem, can then be deduced. This geometry describes measurements of position, distance, and angle in space. △1462.

Axis, in Anatomy. △682.

Axis, in astronomy, imaginary line about which a planet or star rotates and which passes through the poles of the body. The time taken for one complete rotation gives the length of day on that planet. △ 1468.

Axis Deer, or **chital, hog deer,** small deer native to India, Indochina, and Philippine Islands. They are bright reddish- or yellowish-brown with white spots and have three-tined antlers. Hog deer are stockier than the others. Indian axis deer congregate in herds of 100 or more. Length: to 5ft (1.5m); weight: to 1000lb (450kg). Family Cervidae; genus *Axis. See also* Deer.

Axis Powers, term applied to Germany and Italy after they signed the Rome-Berlin Axis in October 1936 and to Japan, which joined them in the Tripartite Pact (Sept. 27, 1940). Minor Axis powers were Hungary and Romania (1940) and Bulgaria (1941). △1338.

Axolotl, common name of neotenic ambystomid salamander of W United States and Mexico. They are stout bodied with finned tail and well-developed gills. Length: to 14in (35.6cm). Family Ambystomidae. △ 518.

Axon, that part of a nerve cell, or neuron, that carries a nerve impulse beyond and away from the cell body, carrying, for example, an impulse for movement to a muscle. There is only one axon per neuron. The axon is often long and usually unbranched. Its central part, or axis cylinder, is surrounded with a fatty, pearly myelin sheath (white matter) in all peripheral nerves and in all central nerves, except those of the brain and spinal cord. Those in peripheral nerves are covered by an additional delicate sheath, a neurillemma, that functions to regenerate damaged nerves. *See also* Neuron. △664.

Axum, Kingdom of. △974.

Aye-Aye, small, primitive, squirrellike primate c Madagascar's bamboo forests. Nocturnal and tree dwelling, it is dark brown to black and has long, na row, bony fingers with claws. Its diet includes insects fruit, and other plant foods. Length: 16in (40.6cm excluding tail. Species *Daubentonia madagascaren sis.*

Ayers Rock, rock in SW Northern Territory, Aus tralia. The largest monolith in the world, it is ova shaped and composed of a composite mass of clasti sedimentary rock; included in Ayers Rock-Mt Olga Na tional Park (est. 1958). Discovered by Sir Henry Ayer (1872). Height: 1,143ft (349m). Length: 4mi (6km) Width: 1.5mi (2.4km).

Aymará, major tribe of South American Indians, oc cupying the highlands of Bolivia and Peru. By 150(they were brought into the Inca Empire, subsequently being overcome by the Spanish in 1542. The Aymará instigated a revolt in 1780 in which they unsuccess fully sought to overthrow the Spaniards. Their culture is marked by excellence in textiles, pottery, and metal work. Today the Aymará population is approximately 600,000.

Aymé, Marcel (1902–67), French novelist. His nov els, such as *The Green Mare* (1933) and *The Secre Stream* (1936), combine fantasy and satire, as do his witty short stories, such as *Across Paris and Othe Stories* (1958). He also wrote children's books, including *Les Contes du Chat Perché* (1939).

Ayo. △390.

Ayrshire, common breed of dairy cattle originally from Scotland, introduced widely in Canada and to a lesser extent in the United States, South Africa, and New Zealand. Medium-sized and gracefully built, they are predominantly red, brown, and white, with black markings. Their milk production is below Holsteins' but greater in butterfat content. *See also* Dairy Cattle; Dairy Farming. △372.

Ayub Khan, Mohammad (1907–74), military leader and president of Pakistan (1958–69). After a military career that began in 1928 as an officer in the British Indian Army, he became commander in chief of the Pakistani army in 1951. Between 1954–56, he was defense minister. In 1958 a military coup made him ruler of the country. He was chosen president by referendum in 1960 and again in 1965 under a new constitution. Although Pakistan had made economic progress under Ayub Khan, student riots over suffrage restrictions and continuing disputes with India over Jammu and Kashmir forced his resignation in 1969.

Azalea, shrubs and small trees native to temperate regions of Asia and North America. Mostly deciduous, they have leathery leaves, and showy, funnel-shaped flowers of red, pink, magenta, orange, yellow, and white, sometimes variegated. Family Ericaceae; genus *Rhododendron. See also* Rhododendron.

Azaña, Manuel (1880–1940), Spanish politician. He was premier (1931–33, 1936) in the republic and was elected president in 1936. He was the titular head of the Loyalists during the Spanish Civil War but did not play an important part.

Azande, Negroid people of the Sudan, Zaire, and the central African Republic, speaking a Chari-Nile language. Their patrilineal, polygynous society is highly skilled in crafts such as metal and woodwork, and is noted for its amalgam of widely divergent ethnic minorities. Azande religion is totemic and includes ancestor worship; it is believed that a man has two souls, one of which at death becomes a totemic animal for the clan.

Azerbaijan Soviet Socialist Republic (Azerbajdžanskaja), constituent republic in SE European USSR, in E Transcaucasia; bordered by Dagestan Autonomous Republic (N), Iran and the Aras River (S), Caspian Sea (E), and Armenian Republic (W). Baku is the capital and major industrial center. The republic includes Nakhichevan Autonomous Republic and Nagorno Karabakh Autonomous Oblast; site of Baku University, Azerbaijan Academy of Sciences. Region was known to ancients as Albania, and was dominated by Arabs, Turks, and Mongols; ceded by Persia to Russia (1813, 1828). After Bolshevik Revolution, Azerbaijan joined Armenia and Georgia to form anti-Bolshevik group; proclaimed independence but was taken by Red Army 1920. Soviet rule was est and region became member of Transcaucasian SFSR 1922; became separate constituent republic 1936. Industries: chemicals, building materials, carpets, agriculture, oil and other mineral processing. Area: 33,436sq mi (86,599sq km). Pop. 5,111,000.

Azimuth, angle between the vertical plane on which a celestial body is located and the plane of the meridian. It is measured, in astronomy, eastward from the north point of the observer's horizon and in navigation and surveying westward from the south point. Altitude and azimuth form a coordinate system for giving astronomical position. △180.

Azores, island group of Portugal in N Atlantic Ocean, approx. 900mi (1,450km) W of Portugal; includes three island groups of nine main islands: Sao Miguel and Santa Maria (E); Terceira, Graciosa, Sao Jorge, Faial, and Pico (center); Flores and Corvo (W). Crops: grapes, tea, pineapples, oranges, grains, tobacco, vegetables. Industries: tourism, wine, basket weaving, pottery. First visited by Portuguese 1427–37; settled 1450. Pop. 336,100.

Azov, Sea of (Azovskoye More), N arm of Black Sea, between Ukrainian SSR (N) and Rostov oblast and Krasnodar Krai (E); Crimea is SW; connected with Black Sea by Kerch Strait; narrows in NE to form Gulf of Taganrog. A shallow sea with only slight salinity, it is fed by the Don, Mius, Kalmius (N), Yeya, and Kuban rivers (E). Fishing center is on its E coast. Area: 14,520sq mi (37,607sq km).

Aztec, Indian civilization that rose to a position of dominance in the central valley of Mexico (*c.* 1450). A warlike group with an excellent military organization, the Nahua, or Aztecs, settled near the western shore of Lake Texcoco (*c.* 1325). They established a tribute-collecting empire, which included most of modern Mexico and went as far south as Guatemala. Their state was theocratic, placing emphasis on a number of deities; worship included human sacrifice. At the time of the Spanish conquest, Aztec society was in the process of changing from a clan-based system to a highly stratified one based on the exploitation of labor. Using the discontent of the satellite tribes, Hernán Cortés was able to recruit the Indian allies necessary for his defeat of the Aztecs in 1521. △1118, 1124.

Aztec Architecture was based on that of the cultures they subdued, especially that of the Toltecs. The Aztecs excelled in engineering. Their capital, Tenochtitlán (1325), built on an island, depended on dikes, causeways, and canals. It stood for 200 years. △1118.

Aztec Ruins National Monument, historic area in NW New Mexico; contains 12th-century ruins of Pueblo Indian town; erroneously named by early colonizers, who believed the ruins to be of Aztec origin. Area: 27 acres (11 hectares). Est. 1923.

Azurite, a carbonate mineral, basic copper carbonate. Found in oxidized portion of copper ore veins, often as earthy material with malachite. Hardness 3.-5–4; sp gr 3.77–3.89. Crystal brilliant and transparent blue, too soft for good gemstone. Used by ancients as pigment in wall painting.

Azusa, city in S California, 18mi (29km) ENE of Los Angeles; site of Azusa Pacific College (1899) and Citrus College. Industries: aircraft components, citrus fruit, electronic equipment, bicycles, distilling. Inc. 1898. Pop. (1970) 25,217.

Avignon, France: papal palace

Aye-aye

B

Baade, Walter (1893–1960), US astronomer, b. Schröttinghausen, Germany. He discovered the asteroid Hidalgo (1920), and held positions at German and US observatories, carrying out investigations into extragalactic systems. His research on stellar populations and Cepheid variable stars was especially noteworthy.

Baal, Phoenician god of fertility. Second in importance to El, he was identified with the Greek god Zeus. Every seven years Baal would fight Mot, god of sterility. If Baal won, there would be seven years of good harvests; if Mot won, there would be seven years of famine.

Baalbek (Ba'labakk), town in E Lebanon, 35mi (56km) NW of Damascus. An early Phoenician settlement, Greeks occupied it 331 BC and renamed it Heliopolis (city of the sun); colonized by the Romans 1st century BC. Noted for Greek and Roman architecture, it is site of Temple of Jupiter built during Nero's reign (AD 54–68) and the Temple of Bacchus (AD 100). Pop. 11,700.

Ba'ath Party, political party in Syria and Iraq, founded in 1941. Its major objectives are socialism and pan-Arabism. From 1963 the Ba'ath party has been the only legal political party in Syria. Splintering in the party caused frequent changes in government. In 1970 Hafez al Assad became prime minister. In Iraq the party also came into power in 1963 when Abdal Arif became president. A coup in 1968 brought in Ba'ath general Ahmad Hassan as president.

Babbage, Charles (1792–1871), British mathematician, professor at Cambridge. He worked out the first actuarial tables and planned a calculating machine, the forerunner of the modern computer, the construction of which he failed to complete. △1672.

Babbitt, Milton (1916–), US composer, musicologist, and teacher, b. Philadelphia. A student of Roger Sessions', he was also educated in mathematics, which has contributed to his thinking and writing. Babbitt has been very influential as a theorist and teacher. His early efforts involved analyzing and systematizing 12-tone music. His compositions include vocal music and three string quartets.

Babbitt (1922), novel by Sinclair Lewis about George Babbitt, a Midwestern businessman, city promoter, and diehard Republican who begins to reevaluate his life. After a brief fling against the deadening conformity that surrounds him, he again becomes a "good citizen."

Babbitt Metal, any alloy containing a high tin content as well as copper and antimony, specifically an alloy invented by Isaac Babbitt in 1839 as bearing material for steam engines. Some or most of the tin content may be replaced by lead.

Babel, Tower of, according to Genesis 11:1–9, a tall building built in the Babylonian city of Babel to reach heaven. God made the workers' speech incomprehensible to one another, scattered them over the earth, and thus stopped the building of the tower. △816.

Babenberg, Austrian dynasty (976–1246). Leopold I was the first Babenberg margrave of Austria. In 1156, Emperor Frederick Barbarossa raised the status of Austria to a duchy. In 1246, Duke Frederick II died childless. The Babenbergs had extended the domain of Austria eastward.

Baber (1483–1530), first Mogul ruler of India (1526–30). He became ruler of Fergana, a principality in C Asia in 1495. He struggled with various relatives for Samarkand but lost all holdings and settled in Kabul, from where he gained control of Delhi and Agra, establishing Mogul rule in India. △1202.

Babeuf, François Emile (1760–97), called "Gracchus," political activist in the French Revolution. He supported land reform and the Constitution of 1793. He was guillotined by the Directory after an at-

Azalea

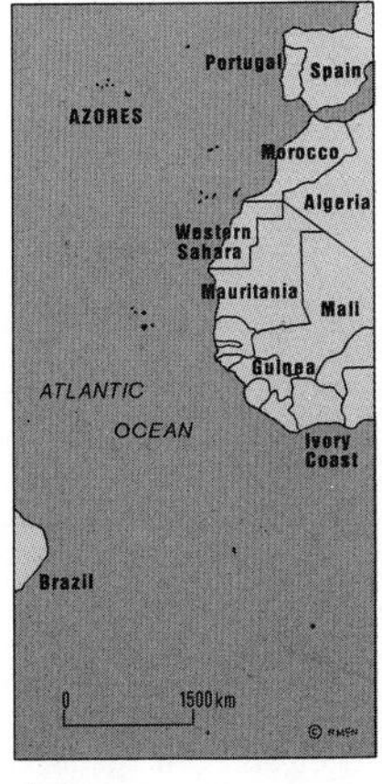

Portugal
Spain
AZORES
Morocco
Algeria
Western Sahara
Mauritania
Mali
Guinea
ATLANTIC
OCEAN
Ivory Coast
Brazil
0
1500km

Azores

tempted insurrection. His *Manifesto of Equals* (1796), favoring the use of secrecy and force, influenced later socialists.

Babington, Anthony (1561–86), English conspirator. In 1586 he led Babington's Plot, a conspiracy against Elizabeth I, aiming to replace her with Mary, Queen of Scots, thereby restoring Catholicism to England. The plot failed, and he was executed.

Babism, Muslim religious sect founded in 1844 in Persia by Sayyid Ali Mohammed, the self-proclaimed prophet Bab (gate). Drawing on the teachings of all existing branches of Islam, the Babists believed in the imminent coming of the Promised One. In 1848 the Babists declared their secession from Islam and rose up against the new shah. Their revolt was crushed and Ali Mohammed was executed (1850). The remaining Babists fled to Constantinople in 1863. In 1868 the sect split into factions disputing the leadership.

Babi Yar (1961), poem by Yevgeny Yevtushenko evoking the horror of the Nazi massacre of 34,000 Jews at Kiev and attacking continuing anti-Semitism.

Baboon, large African monkey with doglike face. They have cheek pouches for carrying food, and males have huge canine teeth up to 2in (5cm) long. The buttocks have callouslike pads surrounded by brilliantly colored naked skin. Walking on all fours, they are day-active, ground dwellers that travel in families and larger troops led by old males, usually in open, rocky country. They eat a wide variety of plant foods, insects, and other small animals. Baboons are aggressive fighters, and several old males can usually fight off a leopard—probably their main enemy. Weight: 30–90lb (14–41kg). Genus *Chaeropithecus* (or *Papio*). *See also* Monkey. △558.

Babylon, an ancient city of Mesopotamia located on the Euphrates River about 55mi (89km) S of present-day Baghdad. Settled since prehistoric times, it was made the capital of Babylonia by Hammurabi in the 18th century BC. The city was completely destroyed in 689 BC by the Assyrians under Sennacherib. After restoration it flourished and became noted for its hanging gardens, one of the seven wonders of the world, and its sensual living. In 275 BC the city was abandoned when the Seleucid dynasty built a new capital at Seleucia. △954, 958.

Babylonia, ancient empire of Mesopotamia. City states, including Ur and Lagash, existed in the area since the 3rd millennium BC. The first empire centered in the city of Babylon was est. by Hammurabi *c.* 1955–13 BC. Toward the end of the 18th century BC the city was sacked by the Hittites, and early in the next century the empire was taken over by the Kassites, an originally nomadic people from Elam. The first Babylonian empire fell to the Assyrians *c.* 722–626 BC. Nabopolassar reestablished an independent Babylonia in 625 BC. With the Persians and Medes as allies, he captured the Assyrian capital, Nineveh. In 538 BC the second Babylonian empire fell to the Persians. △954, 958.

Babylonian and Neo-Babylonian Architecture, architectural style that flourished from 3000 to 1250 BC and whose chief buildings were temples. As architectural complexes developed around them, the temples were generally raised on platforms. Cities developed from several temple groups, and the elevation of the central temple formed a ziggurat ("holy mountain"). The city of Babylon included the colored and glazed Ishtar Gate, Nebuchadnezzar's citadel palace, and the famous Hanging Gardens. △954, 958.

Babylonian Captivity (586–538BC), period from the fall of Jerusalem when Jewish leaders were deported to Babylon until the fall of Babylon itself to the Persians and the return of the Jews to Israel.

Babylonian Captivity (1309–77), exile of popes at Avignon. As choice of the French king, Pope Clement V set up court in Avignon, a papal see in French territory, beginning a line of French popes under the influence of the king. The term, first used metaphorically by the Italian scholar Petrarch, is a reference to the 48-year-long Babylonian captivity of the Jews from the period of the fall of Jerusalem (586 BC) to the return of the Jews to Israel (538 BC). The papal court returned to Rome with Pope Gregory XI in 1377, but two French antipopes, Clement VII and Benedict XIII, lived at Avignon during the Great Schism (1378–1417).

Baccarat, French card game, popular in gambling casinos. The game involves a banker and two players. Each player, including the banker, receives two cards with an option for a third. The object of the game is to hold two or three cards that count nine or as close to nine as possible. Picture cards count nothing and the first digit is disregarded from all totals above nine.

Bacchae (405 BC), Greek tragedy by Euripides. Dionysus assumes human form, causing grief and confusion to those on earth. The play is notable for its provocative religious and mystical qualities.

Bacchanalia, festivals in ancient Greece in honor of Bacchus. They were marked by much drinking and revelry and were often riotous and licentious. The celebrants, known as Bacchantes, originally were women, but later men were included. They wore fawn skins, ivy on their heads, and carried pine cone–topped staffs. △836.

Bacchus, Roman god of wine, similar to the Greek god Dionysus. He was the son of Jupiter and Semele. Reared by nymphs, shepherds, and satyrs, he learned the secrets of cultivating grapes and making wine. His worship led to riotous revelry and debauchery. △344.

Bach, (Baron) Alexander von (1813–93), Austrian political figure. Although he originally supported the Revolution of 1848, he joined the government after its suppression, becoming first minister of justice (1848) then minister of interior (1849–59). He initiated the Bach System, a policy of centralized rule designed to thwart nationalism and to encourage Germanization. In 1855 he signed a concordat with the Roman Catholic Church, giving it extensive rights within the Austro-Hungarian Empire. He was dismissed from his influential office after defeat in the war with Italy and was appointed ambassador to the Vatican (1859–67).

Bach, Johann Sebastian (1685–1750), German Baroque composer. He held a series of successive court positions as organist and music director and had 20 children, four of whom were also composers. Though only a few of his works were published during his lifetime, Bach brought contrapuntal forms to their highest expression and is unequaled in his ability to interweave melodies with the highly constrictive rules of Baroque harmony and counterpoint. His greatest works include masterpieces for the organ (chorale preludes, fugues, toccatas, etc); the six *Brandenburg Concertos* for chamber orchestra; over 200 cantatas; church music, such as the *Mass in B Minor;* violin sonatas; harpsichord and violin concertos; and numerous works for the harpsichord, such as *The Well-Tempered Clavier,* six *Partitas,* and *The Art of the Fugue,* incomplete at his death. △1196.

Bachelor's Button, or cornflower, popular, hardy garden annual grown almost worldwide. It has gray-green foliage and blue, purple, pink, or white flowers. Height: 3ft (0.9m). Family Compositae; species *Centaurea cyanus.* △424.

Bach System (1849–59), administrative policy for Hungary introduced by Alexander von Bach, Austro-Hungarian minister of the interior, after the failure of the rebellion of 1848. The constitution of 1848 was suspended in 1851, and Hungary lost its historical identity. It was ruled from Vienna by officials and broken into five administrative "governments." A rigorous program of Germanization was employed to discourage further nationalist uprisings.

Bacillus, genus of aerobic, gram-positive, spore-forming bacteria present in the soil. One species, *B. anthracis,* causes anthrax pathogenic to man. *See also* Bacteria.

Bacitracin, antibiotic effective against many disease-causing microorganisms but of somewhat limited use because of certain toxic properties.

Backgammon, game of strategy and luck usually involving two players. There is a specially marked board divided into two halves, each containing 12 alternately colored points. Each player receives 15 disks that are arranged in a predetermined order (US version) on the boards. Each move is determined by the throw of dice, and the first player to successfully move all 15 pieces around the board into his "home" or "inner board," and then off the board, wins the game.

Bacon, Francis (1561–1626), English philosopher and statesman. He rose swiftly under James I, being appointed attorney general (1613); lord keeper (1617)—a post his father, Nicholas, had held under Elizabeth I; and finally lord chancellor (1618). But he was forced to resign his offices (1621), charged with venality. Neither official responsibilities nor dismissal impeded his philosophical effort to break the hold of Aristotelian logic in favor of an inductive empiricism. Nature, he affirmed, could be understood only by systematic experimentation, and controlled only by being understood. He entertained the notion of cataloging all useful knowledge in his *Advancement of Learning* (1605) and *Novum Organum* (1620). *The New Atlantis* (1627) discusses his philosophy as practiced in an imaginary nation. △1294, 1780.

Bacon, Francis (1910–), British painter, b. Dublin. His satiric works emphasize the repulsive, horrible aspects of human life. His works often mimic religious art, as in his variations of the Velázquez portrait of Pope Innocent X and his Black Triptychs—three triptychs on the suicide of his closest friend. △1294, 1780.

Bacon, Roger (*c.* 1214–94), English philosopher and scientist. Under the influence of Robert Grosseteste at Oxford, he studied languages, mathematics, alchemy, and astronomy. Writing the *Opus majus (Major Work)* for Pope Clement IV, he urged that extensive studies of these areas be included in university curriculums. Clement died before acting on this proposal. △1438.

Bacon. △376.

Bacon's Rebellion (1676), revolt led by Virginia colonist Nathaniel Bacon to protest the autocratic colonial government and the lack of protection from Indian raids. Bacon carried out successful raids against the Indians and burned Jamestown when Gov. William Berkeley tried to stop the rebellion. Rebellion ended after Bacon died from fever.

Bacteria, one-celled microscopic organisms of the plant kingdom (class Schizomycetes) that are capable of free living since they possess all the metabolic processes necessary for growth and reproduction. They are present virtually everywhere, and some can live even in the absence of free oxygen. They can be classified according to (1) shape: cocci (round or oval), bacilli (rod shaped); and spirilla (curved rods); (2) need for oxygen; (3) ability to take up Gram's stain (gram negative or positive); and (4) ability to utilize various metabolites. Some bacteria form spores, hardened protective cases, which permit them to survive harsh environments, even for centuries. Bacteria are a major cause of human disease, and many ways to control them have been devised. Common protective measures include sterilization with high heat (121°C), such as pasteurization to kill pathogenic bacteria in milk, and exposure to chemical disinfectants. Some bacteria and yeasts produce compounds that kill other bacteria, and these have been isolated and used as antibiotics, such as penicillin. The body can produce antibodies to some bacteria to kill them. Not all bacteria are pathogenic; some are useful in such processes as the production of cheese, alcoholic beverages, and drugs. △422, 1574.

Bacteriology, branch of microbiology that studies the characteristics and action of bacteria.

Bacteriophage, a virus that infects bacteria, a so-called phage or bacterial virus. The virus is used to study the chemical processes of heredity.

Badajoz, city in SW Spain, on the Guadiana River, near Portuguese border; capital of Badajoz prov.; an ancient fortress city that flourished under Moorish rule; site of ruins of Moorish citadel and 13th-century cathedral; important trade center. Area: (prov.) 8,360sq mi (21,652sq km). Pop. (city) 101,710; (prov.) 687,599.

Bad Axe, Battle of (1832), battle in the Black Hawk War, near the mouth of Wisconsin's Bad Axe River, in which the Indians under Black Hawk were badly defeated by US troops.

Baden-Baden, town in SW West Germany, 18mi (29km) SW of Karlsruhe in the Black Forest; site of 3rd-century Roman garrison, Roman mineral bath remains. Now a health resort and spa, it has many hotels, villas, walks, and parks. Pop. 39,074.

Baden-Powell of Gilwell, Robert Stephenson Smyth Baden-Powell, 1st Baron (1857–1941), British soldier and founder of the Scout movement. He held Mafeking against the Boers (1899–1900). From 1910, he devoted himself to the Scout movement.

Baden-Württemberg, state in SW West Germany; capital is Stuttgart; bordered by Switzerland (S), France and Rhineland-Palatinate (W), Hesse (N), and Bavaria (E); agriculture and livestock are important, but industry is major occupation; site of the universities of Freiburg and Heidelberg; popular tourist resort, location of Baden-Baden spas. Industries: machinery, textiles, motor vehicles, glass. Area:

3,803sq mi (35,750sq km). Formed 1952. Pop. 3,959,700.

Badger, burrowing, nocturnal mammals found in Eurasia, North America, and Africa. They have flattened, stocky bodies with short legs and tails. Carnivores, they also eat insects and plants. Eurasian badgers *(Meles meles)* are the largest and have gray bodies with black and white striped heads. American badgers *(Taxidea taxus)* are smaller and have gray-brown to red fur with a white head stripe. Length: 16–28in (40.6–71cm); weight: 22–44lb (10–20kg). Family Mustelidae.

Bad Godesberg, part of the city of Bonn in W West Germany, on the Rhine River; site of the 13th-century Godesberg Castle, Redoute mansion (1790); popular 18th-century spa; scene of Godesberg Conference, meeting place of Adolf Hitler and Neville Chamberlain (1938). Formerly an independent city, inc. into Bonn 1969. Pop. 73,512.

Badlands, horizontally bedded sediment in an arid or semi-arid area. The infrequent and heavy rains cause rapid runoff and the result is severe erosion. The terrain is characterized by steep gullies and almost no vegetation. *See also* Desert; Erosion. △260.

Badlands National Monument, scenic area in SW South Dakota; preserves the natural rugged beauty of this region. Area: 170sq mi (440sq km). Est. 1929.

Badminton, game for two to four persons. It is the national sport of Malaysia, Singapore, and Indonesia, and is popular in the United States and Canada. It enjoyed popularity in England in the 1870s after it was brought over from India (where it was called *poona*), and the rules were changed. The game is similar to tennis, and the object is to volley, with light rackets, a shuttlecock or bird (a cork base to which feathers are attached) until it is missed by an opponent or hit out of bounds. The court used for singles (indoors and out) is 17 by 44 feet (5.2 by 13.4m); for doubles it is 20 by 44 feet (6.1 by 13.4m). The net is 5 feet (1.5m) high in the center.

Badoglio, Pietro (1871–1956), Italian general and statesman. Chief of Italian general staff in World War I, he led Italians at the armistice talks. Chief of staff again in 1925 and field marshal in 1926, in 1940 he resigned as chief of staff. He headed the government that took power after Mussolini's downfall and arranged the armistice with the Allies (Sept. 3, 1943).

Baedeker, Karl (1801–59), German publisher, best known for a series of guidebooks to various cities which aimed to eliminate the need for guided tours. The first French editions appeared in 1846; English editions appeared in 1861.

Baekeland, Leo Hendrik (1863–1944), US chemist, b. Belgium. He invented a type of photographic paper capable of being developed under artificial light. He also invented the first of the thermosetting plastics—Bakelite—a substance that led to the development of the plastics industry.

Baer, Maxmillian Adelbert "Max" (1909–1959), US boxer, b. Omaha, Nebr. He beat Primo Carnera (1934) for the world's heavyweight championship in Long Island City, N. Y., and lost it in the same arena to James J. Braddock (1935). He was elected to the Hall of Fame in 1968.

Baeyer, Johann Friedrich Wilhelm Adolph von (1835–1917), German organic research chemist. He was awarded a Nobel Prize in 1905 for his synthesis of indigo. He also investigated uric acid derivations, discovered the phthalein dyes, and devised a "strain" theory to account for the stability and conformation of five-membered and six-membered carbon rings.

Baez, Joan (1941–), US folk singer, b. New York City. She attended Boston University and first appeared in coffee houses (1958–60). In the 1960s she toured US colleges and Europe, made many recordings, and appeared at Carnegie Hall three times. She was well known as a Vietnam War protester in the 1960s.

Baffin, William (1584–1622), English navigator and explorer. From 1612–16, he led several expeditions in search of the Northwest Passage, one of which led to the discovery of the bay between Greenland and Canada (since named for him). He was the first to determine longitude at sea by using lunar observation.

Baffin Island, largest and easternmost island in the Canadian Arctic Archipelago of the Northwest Territory; separated from Labrador by Hudson Strait; 5th-largest island in the world; mostly mountainous terrain. Population is almost entirely Eskimo. S area visited 1576–78 by Martin Frobisher, English explorer. Named for William Baffin who visited N part of island in 1616. Length: 1,000mi (1,610km). Width: 500mi (805km). Pop. 3,387.

Bagehot, Walter (1826–77), British economist and writer. Trained as a lawyer, Bagehot was a banker (1852–58) and an influential editor of *The Economist* (1860–77). His *Lombard Street* (1873) inaugurated the modern theory of central banking.

Baggataway. *See* Lacrosse.

Baghdad, capital city of Iraq, on the Tigris River; est 762 as capital of Abbaside caliphate, it grew to be a cultural and financial center. Hub of caravan trade between India, Persia, and the West; destroyed by the Mongols 1258; in the early 20th century Iraq gained independence from Turks, and Baghdad became capital (1921); modern administrative, transportation, and educational center. Industries: oil refineries, textiles, gold and silverware, food processing. Pop. 2,183,760.

Baghdad Railway, rail line linking Europe and the Middle East. In 1902 a German firm was granted permission by the Ottoman Empire to extend the line through Turkey to Baghdad. Great Britain and France objected to this "Berlin to Baghdad" linkup, seeing it as a threat to their own imperialist interests in the Middle East. They sought every means possible of stopping the construction. The resulting tension was a contributing factor to the hostility leading up to World War I.

Bagot, (Sir) Charles (1781–1843), British colonial administrator. A career diplomat, he was minister to France (1814) and to the United States (1815–20). He helped negotiate the Rush-Bagot Convention (1817). He was appointed by Robert Peel in 1841 to the post of Canadian governor-general, an office he held until his death. He cooperated with Louis Lafontaine and Robert Baldwin in establishing a representative government in Canada.

Bagpipe, musical instrument with reed pipes connected to a windbag held under the arm and filled by mouth or bellows. Chanter pipes have finger holes for melody, with drone pipes producing monotone accompaniment. Bagpipes, originating in Greece or Asia, are associated with Scotland and Ireland but are also played elsewhere in rural Europe.

Bagworm, moth caterpillar that partially conceals itself in a cocoon of silk strands and leaf and twig bits. The common bagworm *(Thyridopteryx ephemeraeformis)* attacks trees and shrubs, especially arbovitae and cedar. Family Psychidae.

Baha'ism, religion founded (1863) by Bahaullah as an outgrowth of Babism. Headquartered in Haifa, Israel, this rapidly growing religion has centers throughout the world. Baha'ism seeks world peace through the unification of all religions. It stresses a simple life dedicated to serving others. It recognizes Bahaullah as the latest prophet of God. *See also* Babism; Bahaullah.

Bahamas, Commonwealth of the, independent archipelago in Atlantic Ocean, SE of Florida and NE of Cuba. It is comprised of 700 islands, 2,000 cays, and numerous coral reefs stretching over a 700-mi (1,127-km) area.

The rocky terrain of the islands provides little chance for agricultural development. The subtropical climate averages between 70–90°F (21–32°C). Tourism is the mainstay of the economy; commercial fishing, salt, rum, cement, oil refining, and handicrafts are important industries, of which large amounts are exported. There is an international airport at Nassau, the capital of the Bahamas, on New Providence Island.

Of the native population, over 90% is African or of mixed Afro-European stock. The majority lives on New Providence Island, in or near Nassau, earning a living from the tourist, fishing, or handicraft industries. The Church of England is the predominant religion with a see at Nassau since 1861. Education is compulsory between ages 6 and 14; Queens College is in Nassau.

Ruled as a crown colony since the 18th century, the Bahamian political parties demanded a degree of independence in 1962; by 1963, a new constitution was drawn up providing for a cabinet form of government. In 1973, the Bahamas became an independent nation; the monarch of England and governor-general remain titular heads of state; a prime minister rules as head of government.

San Salvador Island is traditionally believed to be the first stop of Christopher Columbus in his quest of

Baboon

Johann Sebastian Bach

Francis Bacon

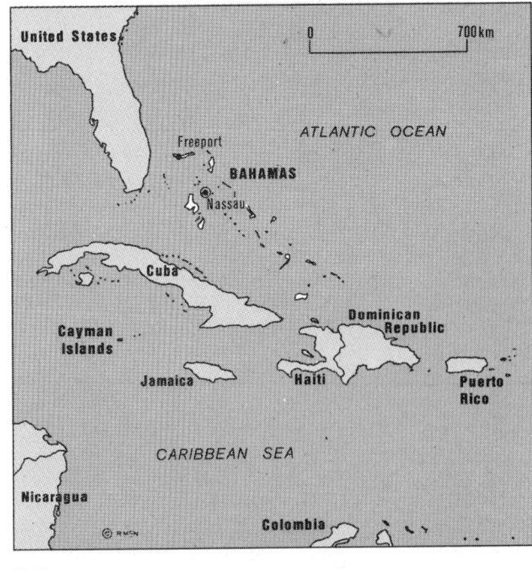
United States
0
700km
ATLANTIC OCEAN
Freeport
BAHAMAS
Nassau
Cuba
Cayman Islands
Dominican Republic
Jamaica
Haiti
Puerto Rico
CARIBBEAN SEA
Nicaragua
Colombia
Bahamas

the New World (1492). Partially settled by England's Eleutherian Adventurers (1648), the islands' development was hampered by numerous pirate and buccaneer bases. Charles II granted the islands to six lords proprietors of Carolina in 1670; this proved unsuccessful because of numerous pirate and Spanish attacks. The British crown, represented by Capt. Woodes Rogers, assumed complete and direct control by 1729, expelling militants and restoring civil order. Held briefly by Spain (1782) during American War of Independence, the islands were given back to England by the Treaty of Versailles (1783) in exchange for E Florida. In 1834, the lords proprietors had relinquished all their authority to the crown and slavery was abolished. The Bahamas were used extensively during WWII by both American and British forces for training and air bases.

PROFILE

Official name: Commonwealth of the Bahama Islands
Area: 5,380sq mi (13,934sq km)
Population: 168,812
Chief islands: Grand Bahama, Abaco, Eleuthera, New Providence, Andros, Cat, San Salvador (Watlings), Exuma, Long, Crooked, Acklins, Mayaguana, Inagua
Religion: Church of England
Language: English (official)
Monetary unit: Bahamian dollar

Bahaullah (1817–92), Persian religious leader, b. Mirza Husayn Ali Nuri, founder of Baha'ism. He became a Babist in 1850 and suffered with them in their persecution. In 1863 he broke with the Babists, declaring himself Bahaullah ("The Glory of Allah"), the Promised One foretold by Bab. His work, the *Katabi Ikan (The Book of Certitude)* is the Baha'i holy book. *See also* Babism; Baha'ism.

Bahia, state in E central Brazil; capital is Salvador. Industries: minerals, cattle, carnuba wax, lumber, cacao, tobacco, sugar distilling, cotton milling. Area: 216,612sq mi (561,025sq km). Declared province of Brazil 1823, state 1889. Pop. 7,420,906.

Bahrain (Al-Bahrayn), island state in the Persian Gulf off the coast of Saudi Arabia. The economy is dependent upon petroleum. The nation consists of the islands of Bahrain, Sitrah, Al-Muharraq, Umm Na' sān, and about 30 smaller ones. The terrain is generally flat and only on the main island does the altitude rise above 330ft (100m). Summers are hot and humid, and most rainfall is limited to the cooler winter months. Soils are fertile once irrigated; because of the lack of surface water much of the supply has to be raised by artesian wells. In the irrigated areas fruit and vegetables are the main crops; livestock is unimportant. Although Bahrain has produced petroleum from oilfields in the center of Bahrain Island for over 40 years it derives most of its income from refining Saudi oil that is piped from Dhahran to Sitrah. Traditional industries of dhow building and pearling are being replaced by industries serving a more affluent populace. Two major developments of the 1970s have been the smelting of bauxite and the development of Mīnā' Salmān as a free port for the S Persian Gulf. The country is ruled by a royal family assisted by a cabinet; in 1972 a constitution was drafted.

History. Bahrain was conquered by the Muslims in 7th century, by the Portuguese in 16th century, and by Persians in 17th. In 1861, Bahrain became a British Protectorate, and until 1971, Britain was responsible for its defense and foreign affairs. Since 1782 the Al Khalifah family has ruled the state.

PROFILE

Official Name: Bahrain
Area: 240sq mi (622sq km).
Population: (1971) 216,078.
Density: 134 per sq mi (347 per sq km).
Chief cities: Manama (capital), 89,729; Al-Muharraq, 41,143.
Government: Head of state, Sheikh Isa bin Sulman Al Khalifah.
Religion: Islam
Gross national product: (1973) $390,000,000.
Trading partners (major): Japan, Saudi Arabia.

Baia. *See* Baiae.

Baiae (Baia), ancient city in SW Italy, W of Naples; site of modern village of Baia. The Romans enjoyed its climate and thermal springs; Julius Caesar and Nero built villas here. Malaria outbreak caused its abandonment in 1500.

Baikal (Baykal, Bajkal), Lake, Asia's largest fresh water lake and world's deepest lake, in S Siberia, USSR, near Mongolian border, chiefly within Buryat ASSR; fed by Barguzin, Selenga, and many other rivers. Angara River is sole outlet; bordered by mountain ranges Baikal (W), Barguzin (E), Khamar-Daban (S). Contains 27 islands, has moderating influence on climate of the region; site of large hydroelectric project. Its center section reaches depth of 5,710ft (1,742m). Length: 395mi (636km). Width: (max.) 49mi (79km).

Baile Átha Cliath. *See* Dublin.

Bailey, F(rancis) Lee (1933–), US lawyer, b. Waltham, Mass. Renowned criminal lawyer, he won an acquittal in the retrial of Dr. Samuel H. Sheppard, who had been convicted of the 1954 murder of his wife (1966). He defended Albert DeSalvo, the confessed Boston Strangler (1966–67), and was chief counsel for Patricia Hearst, the kidnapped newspaper heiress, convicted of bank robbery in 1976. He co-authored *The Defense Never Rests* (1972).

Bailey, James Anthony (1847–1906), circus impresario. Born James A. McGinnis in Detroit, Bailey became an advance agent for Robinson & Lake Circus at the age of 13. In 1872 he became partner in Cooper & Bailey, which merged with competitor P.T. Barnum's in 1881. After Barnum's death in 1891, Bailey became the sole leader of the Barnum and Bailey Circus.

Bailey, Liberty Hyde (1858–1954), US botanist, b. South Haven, Mich. He helped to establish horticulture as an applied science through the systematic study of cultivated plants. His work had an important influence on the development of genetics and plant pathology. He founded and directed the Bailey Hortorium at Cornell University, Ithaca, N.Y. (1904–13), and published 700 scientific papers and 66 books, including two significant encyclopedic works.

Bailment, legal condition in which one person (bailee) has physical possession of personal property that belongs to another person (bailor). The bailee assumes certain responsibilities for the care and protection of the property until such time as it must be returned.

Baird, Spencer Fullerton (1823–87), US naturalist and vertebrate zoologist, b. Reading, Pa. He was a leading authority on North American birds and mammals. Largely through his efforts the US Commission of Fish and Fisheries was established in 1871. His work on fish culture at Woods Hole, Mass., made his laboratory there world famous.

Bait Pricing, offering of a good for sale at a low price, with the expectation that the customer will not in fact purchase the item. Bait pricing occurs when an automobile dealer advertises the lowest priced model, fully expecting customers will purchase the higher priced ones.

Baja California (Lower California), peninsula in NW Mexico, extends 800mi (1,288km) SSE between Mexico and the United States; S half is the territory of Baja California Sur; N half comprises the state of Baja California, which has the highest standard of living in Mexico; most important crop is long-staple cotton; main industry is the assembling of imported materials. Discovered 1535 by the Spanish; separated from Alta California, United States, 1772; formation of Baja state 1951. Pop. (state) 854,561; (territory) 123,786.

Bajazet, or **Beyazid, I** (1347–1403), Ottoman sultan (1389–1402). After conquering the local rulers of E Anatolia and defeating the forces of the Holy Roman Emperor Sigismund of Hungary at Nicopolis (1396), he besieged Constantinople (1402). The siege was interrupted by the invasion of Tamerlane, whose forces defeated his at Ankara (1402). He died Tamerlane's prisoner.

Bajazet, or **Beyazid, II** (1447–1513), Ottoman sultan (1481–1512). Noted for developing Ottoman culture rather than power, he rebuilt Constantinople after the earthquake (1509) but lost Cilicia to the Mamelukes in a war (1488–91) and Cyprus to Venice (1489), with which he also warred unsuccessfully (1499–1502). In 1510 civil war broke out between his sons, and in 1512 he abdicated in favor of one of them, Selim.

Bakelite, trade name for a thermosetting resin consisting of phenol or cresol condensed with formaldehyde; used for insulating purposes and in making plastic products. The trade name is also applicable to a wide range of thermoplastic resins. Named after L. H. Baekeland. △1618.

Baker, Josephine (1906–75), US singer and dancer, b. St. Louis. After traveling to Paris as the star of *La Revue Nègre* (1925), she stayed to become a successful entertainer in Parisian music halls. She became a French citizen. Known as the "Dark Star" of the Folies Bergère, her performances in a G-string ornamented with bananas caused a sensation.

Baker, Mount, mountain in NW Washington, one of the peaks in the Cascade Range. Some volcanic activity occurred in the 1970s. Height: 10,778ft (3,287m). Also a peak in N Colorado. Height: 12,406ft (3,784m).

Baker Island, small atoll in central Pacific Ocean near the equator, SW of Hawaii. Discovered 1832 by US Capt. Michael Baker; became US Territory 1936. Area: 1sq mi (2.6 sq km).

Bakersfield, city in S central California, at the S end of the San Joaquin valley; seat of Kern co; gold discovered in 1885 and petroleum in 1889; important oil refining center. Industries: plastics, drugs, processed foods. Inc. 1898. Pop. (1970) 69,515.

Baker v. Carr (1962), landmark US Supreme Court decision holding that apportionment of state legislatures and redistricting to assure proper representation were proper issues to be decided in federal courts. The court overruled *Colegrove* v. *Green* (1946) and limited the "political question" doctrine to cases involving separation of powers questions and deference to the executive.

Baking Powder, mixture used in baking as a substitute for yeast. Baking powders generally contain sodium bicarbonate mixed with an acid constituent such as tartaric acid, cream of tartar, or calcium phosphate, so that carbon dioxide is produced, thus giving a spongy texture during baking.

Bakongo. *See* Kongo.

Bakr, Ahmad Hassan al (1914–), Iraqi political figure. He was forced to resign as an officer in the army in 1958 because of his political activity. In 1963 he served briefly as prime minister when the Ba'ath party temporarily seized power. In 1968 he became president after a more successful coup.

Baku, city and capital of Azerbaijan (Azerbajdžanskaja) SSR, USSR; important oil shipping port on W coast of Caspian Sea. City encircles Baku Bay and is a major Soviet industrial and cultural center. Commercial oil production began in the 1870s and now the port handles tremendous volume of oil and oil products shipping. City is site of Azerbaijan Academy of Sciences, cultural institutions, 13th-century fortress of Bad-Kube, 11th-century mosque, 12th-century Maiden's Tower. Baku was trade and craft center in medieval times; prospered under Shirvan Shahs 15th century; Persians ruled 1509–1723; annexed by Russia 1806. Pop. 1,261,000.

Bakunin, Mikhail (1814–76), Russian political philosopher. He was converted to violent revolution while in Paris (1848), and was active in radical politics. His position, known as revolutionary anarchism, repudiates all forms of governmental authority as fundamentally at variance with human freedom and dignity. In *God and the State* (1882) Bakunin recognized natural law alone as consistent with liberty. *See also* Anarchism. △1288, 1326.

Bakwanga. *See* Mbuji-Mayi.

BAL (British Anti-Lewisite), oily liquid used as an antidote for poisoning caused by organic arsenic compounds and heavy metals, including mercury and gold.

Balaam, in the Bible, Midianite prophet called by Balek, king of Moab, to curse the Israelites wandering in the wilderness. Commanded by an angel of God, through his donkey, he blessed them instead.

Ba'labakk. *See* Baalbek.

Balaguer, Joaquín (1906–), Dominican Republic lawyer, diplomat, and president (1960–62; 1966–). Exiled in 1962, he returned and defeated Juan Bosch (1966). He was elected by plebiscite in 1970 and again in 1974 after a violent campaign in which three of the four opposition candidates withdrew from the race.

Balakirev, Mili Alekseyevich (1837–1910), Russian composer. One of the "Russian Five" dedicated to advancing Russian nationalism in 19th-century music, his best-known compositions are *Islamey* (begun in 1866, but not completed until 1882) and incidental music to *King Lear* (1858–61). △1246.

Balaklava (Balaclava), section of city of Sevastopol,

n Ukrainian SSR, USSR; site of ancient Greek city. A medieval Genoese settlement, it was taken by Turks 1475. Balaklava was scene of charge of the Light Brigade (1854) during Crimean War. Industries: limestone quarrying, fishing, health resort. Inc. 1957 into Sevastopol. Pop. 5,000.

Balaklava, Battle of (1854), inconclusive action fought during the Crimean War by English, French, and Turkish troops resisting a Russian attack on their supply port of Balaklava. It is famous for the gallant but disastrous charge of Lord Cardigan's Light Brigade of cavalry.

Balanced Budget, situation in which tax revenues are equal to government expenditures, eliminating the need for discretionary fiscal policy in controlling the economy. Keynesians oppose the balanced budget principle.

Balance of Payments, overall surplus or deficit that occurs as a result of the exchange of all goods and services between countries. A country with a balance of payments deficit incurs a debt that will require that arrangements be made for future payment or the exchange of gold between countries. Balance of payments deficits, if continual, can be a serious problem, because they will cause an outflow of gold. Such a drain in turn leads to pressure for devaluation in order to correct the deficit situation. A country with a balance of payments surplus is in a favorable position, but it may be under international pressure to revalue (ie, lower the price of gold) in order to adjust the imbalance. △940, 1384.

Balance of Power, system in international affairs in which nations seek to keep peace and order by maintaining an approximate equilibrium of power among rivals, thereby preventing any single one from having a marked advantage.

Balance of Trade, surplus or deficit incurred by a country; the difference between the sum of its imports and the sum of its exports.

Balanchine, George (1904–), US ballet dancer and choreographer, b. Georgi Balanchivadze in Russia. Trained at the Imperial Ballet School, St Petersburg, he left Russia in 1924 and became a principal dancer and choreographer for Diaghilev's Ballets Russes in Paris. He moved to the United States in 1933 and was director of the Metropolitan Opera ballet (1934–37). A founder of the School of American Ballet (1934), he became the first artistic director of the New York City Ballet in 1948. Works he has choreographed include *The Prodigal Son* (1929), *The Nutcracker* (1954), *Don Quixote* (1965) and *Slaughter on Tenth Avenue* for the musical *On Your Toes* (1936). △1368.

Balaton, Lake, lake in W Hungary, 55mi (89km) SW of Budapest; many shoreline resorts; largest lake in central Europe. Area: 232sq mi (601sq km).

Balboa, Vasco Núñez de (*c.*1475–1519), Spanish conquistador and discoverer of the Pacific Ocean. He went to Hispaniola in 1500 and in 1510 to Darién (Panama), where he ousted its governor, Martín Fernández de Enciso, and took control. With a group of Indians he crossed the isthmus and discovered, in September 1513, the Pacific. Before that news reached Spain, the king dispatched Pedro Arias de Ávila to take charge of Darién. Arias had treason charges brought against Balboa and had him executed in 1519.

Balboa, port town in Panama Canal Zone, on the Gulf of Panama, Pacific Ocean; suburb of Panama city; administrative headquarters for Panama Canal Zone; site of US naval base. Pop. 2,568.

Bald Cypress, deciduous tree growing in shallow water in SE United States. They have woody growth (knees) on the roots that grow above water and lose their feathery, light green needles in autumn. Height: to 15ft (4.6m). Family Taxodiaceae; species *Taxodium distichum.*

Bald Eagle, or **American Bald Eagle,** large eagle, also the national emblem of the United States, found along North American wetlands particularly in Alaska and Florida. A sea eagle, it feeds on fish and small animals. It is brown with a white head and tail and yellow bill. Although protected by law since 1940 (1953 in Alaska), it readily succumbs to pesticides and is now endangered. Length: 40in (102cm). Species *Haliaetus leucocephalus. See also* Eagle.

Balder, Scandinavian God of sunlight, beauty, brightness, and wisdom, the son of Woden and Frigg. Through the treachery of Loki, god of evil, Balder was killed by an arrow made of mistletoe. Of all the Aesir, pantheon of the gods in Asgard, he was the fairest and most amiable.

Baldness, or **Alopecia,** the absence of hair from the skin where hair normally is present. Causes include hereditary disease, old age, nutritional deficiencies, and pregnancy. In some cases, hair will grow back normally; in others, loss is permanent. Premature baldness, loss of hair in late adolesence or early adulthood, occurs most often in males and is believed hereditary.

Baldwin, James (1924–), US author, b. New York City. A novelist, essayist, and playwright, he was born in Harlem, where he preached in storefront churches as a youth. He lived in Paris (1948–56). His works deal with race relations and with sexuality. They include the novel *Go Tell It on the Mountain* (1953); the books of essays *Notes of a Native Son* (1955), *Nobody Knows My Name* (1961), and *The Fire Next Time* (1963); and the play *Blues for Mister Charlie* (1964). △1374.

Baldwin, Robert (1804–58), Canadian statesman. A leader of the movement for representative, cabinet government for Canada. With Louis LaFontaine (representing the French of lower Canada), he shared the first premiership of united Canada (1841–43). They were returned to power (1847–51). He advocated cooperation between French and British Canadians, organized an effective system of municipal government for Ontario, reorganized the court system, and secularized the University of Toronto.

Baldwin, Stanley, 1st Earl Baldwin of Bewdley (1867–1947), British Conservative statesman. He ran the family iron business until elected to Parliament (1908). He became chancellor of the exchequer (1922–23), and although his handling of the US debt was criticized, he succeeded Bonar Law as prime minister (1923–24). Becoming prime minister again (1924–29), he weathered the general strike (1926). While prime minister for the third time (1935–37), he had to deal with the abdication crisis (1936).

Baldwin I (1171–1205), count of Flanders and Hainaut, first Latin emperor of Constantinople (1204–05). After the capture of Constantinople from the Byzantine Christians by the western armies of the Fourth Crusade and the partition of the territories formerly held by the Byzantine Empire, Baldwin was elected ruler of the newly formed Latin state. He remodeled the empire along Western feudal lines. His empire was invaded by the Bulgars, and he was captured and slain by them. He was succeeded by his brother Henry.

Baldwin II (1217–73), last Latin emperor of Constantinople (1228–61). He was overthrown by Michael Palaeologus who restored the Byzantine Empire. Baldwin fled to exile in the West.

Baldwin I (1058–1118), king of Jerusalem (1100–18). A military leader of the First Crusade (1096–99), he demanded and received the crown of Jerusalem in 1100. He consolidated and strengthened the Latin states of the Middle East.

Baldwin II (died 1131), king of Jerusalem (1118–31). His cousin, Baldwin I, appointed him Count of Edessa (1100–18). He was captured by the Seljuk Turks in 1104 and held until ransomed in 1108. He then recaptured Edessa from his regent, Tancred. He was again captured by the Turks (1123–24) while king of Jerusalem. After release, he expanded his kingdom. He was succeeded by his son-in-law, Fulk of Anjou.

Baldwin, town in SW Pennsylvania; suburb of Pittsburgh; bituminous coal region. Industries: tools, metal goods, wood products. Inc. 1952. Pop. 26,729.

Baldwin Park, city in S California; suburb of Los Angeles. Settled 1870; inc. 1956. Pop. (1970) 47,285.

Bale. *See* Basel.

Balearic Islands, resort islands in the W Mediterranean, off the coast of Spain; comprises Baleares prov., Spain; capital is Palma; formerly occupied by Iberians, Phoenicians, Greeks, Carthaginians, Romans, and Byzantines. The Moors established an independent kingdom in the 11th century, and its pirate inhabitants harassed Mediterranean coastal cities. The chief islands are Minorca, Ibiza, and Majorca. Industries: tourism, silver filigree, olive oil, wine, fruit. Area: 1,936sq mi (5,014sq km). Pop. (city) 234,098; (prov.) 558,287.

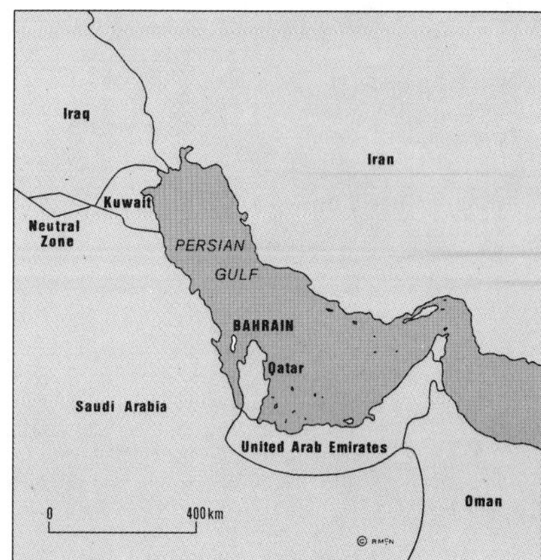
Iraq
Iran
Kuwait
Neutral Zone
PERSIAN
GULF
BAHRAIN
Qatar
Saudi Arabia
United Arab Emirates
Oman
0
400km

Bahrain

George Balanchine

Bald eagle

James Baldwin

Balenciaga, Cristóbal (1895–1972), Spanish fashion designer. He designed elegant clothes for celebrities. In the 1950s he designed the chemise, or sack dress, in reaction to Christian Dior's New Look. It enjoyed some success and led to the revival of other looks of the 1920s.

Balfour, Arthur James Balfour, 1st Earl of (1848–1930), British Conservative statesman. His time as prime minister (1902–05) was marked by party friction. He was an energetic leader of the opposition (1906–11) and first lord of the admiralty (1915–16). In 1917 he issued the Balfour Declaration in favor of founding a Jewish nation in Palestine. He played a major role in postwar European agreements.

Balfour Declaration, letter written by British Foreign Secretary Arthur Balfour to the British Zionist Federation in 1917 pledging cooperation for the settlement of Jews in Palestine. Jews were admitted when the area, a province of the Ottoman Empire, became a British mandate after World War I. In 1948 British forces withdrew and the state of Israel was proclaimed.

Bali, island province of Indonesia, off E tip of Java between Bali Sea and Indian Ocean; capital is Denpasar. Under Javanese control from AD 1000, it was a Dutch possession 1908–1949; occupied by Japanese during WWII; center of Majaphit Hinduism religion and culture; famous for natural beauty and native culture; popular tourist resort. Industries: rice, cassava, copra, meat processing. Area: 2,171sq mi (5,623sq km). Pop. 2,247,000.

Baliol, John de (1249–1315), King of Scotland. His claim to the Scottish throne was upheld by Edward I of England, who claimed feudal overlordship of Scotland as a consequence (1291). Baliol quarreled with Edward, invaded England (1296), but was captured. Liberated (1299), he died in retirement in Normandy.

Balkan Entente. △1302, 1304.

Balkan Mountains, major mountain range of Balkan Peninsula in Bulgaria; extends from E Yugoslavia through central Bulgaria to the Black Sea; constitutes a continuation of the Carpathian Mts. Rich in minerals, serves as climatic barrier for inland region; includes Shipka Pass at an altitude of approx. 4,000ft (1,220m). Highest peak is Botev, 7,794ft (2377m).

Balkan States, group of countries in SE Europe, on the Balkan Peninsula, consisting of Albania, Bulgaria, Greece, Romania, Turkey, and Yugoslavia.

Balkan Wars (1912–13), two successive wars involving Balkan powers. In the first, the members of the Balkan League (Serbia, Bulgaria, Greece, and Montenegro) won most of the Ottoman Empire's European territory. In the second, Serbia, Greece, and Romania quarreled with Bulgaria over the distribution of conquests in Macedonia. △1302.

Balkhash (Balchas), industrial city in SE Kazakh SSR, USSR, on N shore of Balkhash Lake; center of copper smelting industry; rail terminus. Founded 1929 as Bertys; renamed 1937. Pop. 77,000.

Balkhash, Lake (Balchaš, Ozero), lake in SE Kazakh SSR, USSR; extends approx. 100mi (161km) from Chinese border, from Kazakh Hills (NE) to desert steppes (SW); lake has no outlet. Chief inlet is fresh water Ili River, thus W half of lake is fresh water, with salinity increasing toward E. Area: 6,562sq mi (16,996sq km). Depth (avg.): 20ft (6m).

Ball, Lucille (1911–), US comedienne, b. Jamestown, N.Y. She began her career as a showgirl in New York City, then went to Hollywood, making her film debut in *Roman Scandals* (1931). She appeared in over 70 more films. But her greatest success came in the TV series "I Love Lucy," in which she costarred with her then husband Desi Arnaz. It became the longest running series in television (1951–57). Desilu Productions, which produced the program, became the largest television production studio. After her divorce from Arnaz in 1960, she appeared on "The Lucy Show" (1961–68).

Balla, Giacomo (1871–1958), Italian artist. In Rome he was influenced by the poet Emilio Filippo Tommaso Marinetti, who founded the futurist literary movement. Balla, adopting futurism, urged artists to use art as a means to change Italy's culture through the acceptance of science and technology. His works, which emphasize movement and abstraction, include *The Street Light—Study of Light* (1909) and *Dynamism of Dog on a Leash* (1912). *See also* Futurism.

Ballad, narrative poem of strong rhythm and simple language, suitable for singing. Ballads are of two types: folk and literary. Early folk ballads, such as "Barbara Allen" and "Lord Randal," were anonymous, transmitted orally in song, and altered as repeated from generation to generation, resulting in many versions of the same story. Literary ballads are later poets' skilled imitations of the anonymous popular form. An example is Samuel Taylor Coleridge's "The Rime of the Ancient Mariner."

Ballade, poem comprised of three stanzas of seven or eight lines each, concluding with an envoy addressed to a prominent person, which serves as a summary or dedication. The same line ends each stanza and the envoy. Only three or four rhymes recur. Derived from Old French poetry, the ballade form is exemplified in "Ballade to Queen Elizabeth" by Henry Austin Dobson.

Ball-and-Socket. △682.

Ballet, theatrical art form in which stylized dancing to music conveys a story or theme. It evolved from Renaissance court spectacles. The first formal ballet, *La Ballet Comique de la Reine,* was performed at the French court of Catherine de Medicis in 1581. Thoinot Arbeau wrote the first treatise on ballet, *Orchésographie* (1588). Louis XIV, who himself performed in ballet, founded the French Royal Ballet Academy in 1661. The first ballet for public performance was not commissioned until early in the 18th century. Jean Georges Noverre was the most influential choreographer and theorist of the 18th century. His *Lettres sur la Danse et les Ballets* (1760) insisted that meaningless gestures and masks be replaced by a more naturalistic style. The performance of *La Sylphide* in Paris (1832) set the model for the romantic ballets of the 19th century. Toward the end of the 19th century Russian ballet began emphasizing technique and virtuosity. In 1909, Sergei Diaghilev and his Ballets Russes revolutionized ballet with dynamic choreography and dancing. The mid-20th century saw a melding of elements of classical ballet and modern dancing. △1194, 1368.

Ballet Comique de la Reine, La, ballet by Baldassario Belgiojoso produced in 1581, the first ballet as we know the art form today. A lavish spectacle, it lasted five hours and cost 3.6 million gold francs. The libretto was published and used as one of the first books on ballet.

Ballet Folklorico, national dance company of Mexico. Founded (1952) and directed by Amalia Hernandez, its dances combine elements of the American Indian and Spanish cultures with modern dance techniques.

Ballet Russe de Monte Carlo, the name of several ballet companies that succeeded the Diaghilev Ballets Russes, which disbanded after Sergei Diaghilev's death in 1929. Under the management of René Blum and Col. Vasili de Basil from 1932, who vied for control, the company toured the United States under impresario Sol Hurok's sponsorship. In 1938 Léonide Massine and Blum formed a new, separate company. George Balanchine and Michel Fokine, among others, have been associated with this company. *See also* Diaghilev, Sergei.

Ballets Russes, dance company founded in 1909 in Paris by Sergei Diaghilev with Michel Fokine as chief choreographer. The company revitalized and reshaped ballet by bringing together some of the greatest, most innovative dancers (Anna Pavlova, Nijinsky), choreographers (Léonide Massine, Bronislava Nijinska, George Balanchine), composers (Stravinsky, Debussy, Richard Strauss), and artists as set and costume designers (Picasso, Chagall, Matisse). The company disbanded after Diaghilev's death in 1929, but many of its members then joined the Ballet Russe de Monte Carlo.

Ballinger-Pinchot Controversy (1909–11). Richard Ballinger, President Taft's secretary of the interior, doubted the legality of the Theodore Roosevelt administration's removing waterpower sites from public entry and reopened the lands. Gifford Pinchot, forest service chief, accused Ballinger of catering to private business and was fired by Taft. The controversy split the Republican party. *See also* Pinchot, Gifford.

Ballista, large crossbowlike firing device used by the Romans and other ancient armies to hurl rocks and other missiles at enemy formations and fortifications. △1732.

Ballistic Missile, self-propelled missile that traverses most of its trajectory in the earth's outer atmosphere under the influence of gravity alone. Ballistic missiles equipped with thermonuclear warheads and dispersed in ground-based hardened silos or in nuclear submarines are the supreme military weapon of modern times. *See also* Intercontinental Ballistic Missile; Intermediate Range Ballistic Missile; Missile.

Ballistics, study of projectile motion. *Exterior* ballistics includes the study of gravitational forces, atmospheric friction, variation of the direction and strength of the gravitational field with height, variation of the temperature and density of the atmosphere with height, curvature of the earth's surface, and change in the velocity of sound with altitude. *Interior* ballistics deals with events inside the gun barrel or rocket engine: propulsion systems, gas pressure changes, effect of spinning (rifling) on stability, and strength of materials.

Balloon, bag of tough, light material filled with heated air or buoyant gas, lighter than air so as to rise and float in the atmosphere. It is non-powered and flies only where the wind takes it. Balloons have been used for meteorology, communications, military observation, upper-air research, and for sport flying. △1712.

Balloon Fish. *See* Porcupine Fish.

Ballooning, sport in which participants ascend and travel in a basket-like gondola suspended from a balloon filled with hot air or hydrogen. The basic principle of the hot-air balloon, first tried out successfully in 1783 in France by two brothers, Joseph and Jacques Etienne Montgolfier, is to heat the air inside the balloon. As the heated air expands, it becomes lighter than the surrounding air and tends to rise. The use of hydrogen for ballooning was begun in 1766 by Henry Cavendish, who showed that hydrogen was seven times lighter than air.

In 1783, the first manned flight with a hot-air balloon was achieved by Pilatre de Rozier. Later on in the year, three men successfully made the first ascent with a hydrogen-filled balloon. Ballooning reached the height of its popularity in the early part of the 20th century with such notable events as the annual James Gordon Bennett Cup race. Although declining in popularity after World War II, the sport enjoyed a resurgence in the 1970s with the application of modern techniques.

Ballot, object used to cast a vote. The word derives from the Italian *ballotta,* "little ball." Since 5th-century BC Athens, balls were used to cast votes: white for yes, black for no. Today, the usual ballot, a sheet of paper, is being replaced by the voting machine.

Ballot, Australian, form of ballot first introduced in Victoria, Australia, in 1857. The names of all candidates are printed on a single ballot that has been prepared by the government. Voting is in secret and supervised by a nonpartisan or bipartisan committee.

Balsa, evergreen tree native to tropical America. Its light, buoyant wood is used for rafts and airplane models. Leaves are heart-shaped and the whitish or greenish flowers are bisexual. Height: to 80ft (24m). Family Bombacaceae; species *Ochroma lagopus. See also* Kapok.

Balsam, aromatic resin obtained from plants. Or, healing preparations, especially those with benzoic and cinnamic acid added to the resin. Or, balsam-yielding trees, such as the balsam fir and balsam poplar. Also numerous species of tropical succulent plants of the family Balsaminaceae that are sprawling, waterside forms with thin leaves and pendent flowers. *Impatiens* is the most common North American genus.

Balsam Fir, evergreen tree native to NE North America. It has flat needles and 2.5in (6.3cm) cones. It is often grown for pulpwood and Christmas trees. Height: to 70ft (21.3m). Family Pinaceae; species *Abies balsamea.*

Baltic Sea, arm of the Atlantic Ocean in N Europe, connected with the North Sea by Kattegat and Skagerrak; bordered by Denmark, Sweden, Finland, USSR, Poland, East Germany, and West Germany. The Kiel Canal links the Baltic to the North Sea and the White Sea; Baltic Canal links it to the White Sea; partially frozen in the winter. Area: 160,000sq mi (414,400sq km).

Baltimore, Barons of. *See* Calvert, Cecilius; Calvert, Charles; Calvert, George.

Baltimore, David (1938–), US microbiologist, b. New York City. He shared the 1975 Nobel Prize in physiology or medicine for his work on the "interaction between tumor viruses and the genetic material of the cell." Working independently of colaureate Howard Temin, he proved the existence of reverse transcriptase, the enzyme necessary for viral genetic information to be incorporated into an animal cell.

Baltimore, major US seaport city, in N central Maryland, 40mi (64km) NE of Washington, D.C., on the Patapsco River estuary; largest city in Maryland. Acquired by the Maryland legislature 1729, it developed into a shipbuilding center and major exporter of flour and tobacco. Baltimore served as the meeting place for the Continental Congress (December 1776–March 1777) during the British occupation of Philadelphia in the American Revolution, and inspired Francis Scott Key to write "The Star Spangled Banner" during the British bombardment of Fort McHenry (Sept. 13–14, 1814); it flourished during both world wars as demand for ships and industrial produce increased. It is the site of the home and grave of Edgar Allen Poe, Lee-Jackson Memorial, Pimlico racetrack, Westminster Church, Municipal Museum (1813), Flag House Museum, Lexington Market (1803), Fort McHenry National Monument (est. 1939), Cathedral of the Assumption of the Blessed Virgin (1806, 1st U.S. Roman Catholic cathedral), London Park and Baltimore National cemeteries, Washington Monument (1815, earliest memorial to George Washington); and home of National Football League's Baltimore Colts and American Baseball League's Baltimore Orioles. Numerous institutions of higher education including Johns Hopkins University (1876). Industries: steel, shipbuilding, shipyards, aerospace, electrical insulators, chemicals, copper and sugar refining, printing, publishing. Settled mid-17th century by the Barons of Baltimore; town est. 1729; inc. 1745 as town, 1797 as city. Pop. (1970) 905,759.

Baltimore Oriole, American songbird named because its colors are the same as the coat of arms of the Baltimore family, founders of Maryland. The male has black head, neck, back, and wings and orange breast, rump, and outer tail feathers. Females, olive above and yellow below, build long slender weed-and-bark nests slung from twigs in a high tree. Length: to 8in (20cm). Species *Icterus galbula*.

Baluchistan, region and province in central and SW Pakistan, bordering Iran (W), Afghanistan (N), and the Arabian Sea (S); terrain is hilly and arid, inhabited by few nomadic tribes. Region was ruled by Arabs 7th–10th centuries; made British dependency 1876, became part of Pakistan 1947–48. Exports: natural gas, salt, fish. Area: approx 134,000sq mi (347,060sq km). Pop. 1,483,999.

Baluchitherium, extinct genus of giant rhinoceros believed to have been the largest land mammal ever to have existed, and known from fossil deposits of Late Oligocene and Early Miocene age in Asia. △574.

Balzac, Honoré de (1799–1850), French novelist. Balzac began writing thrillers in a Paris attic before his spectacular failure as a publisher. His first success was *Les Chouans* (1829), and many great novels followed in his grand scheme *The Human Comedy*. They include *Eugénie Grandet* (1833), *Le Père Goriot* (1835), and *La Cousine Bette* (1847). △1238.

Bamako, picturesque capital city of Mali, on the Niger River, 90mi (145km) NE of the Guinea border; site of schools of medicine, administration, and engineering; leading center of Muslim learning 11th–15th centuries; occupied by French 1883; made capital of French Sudan 1908. Industries: shipping, textiles, meat, metal products. Pop. 387,650.

Bambara, Negroid people of the upper Niger valley in the Mali Republic. Their patrilineal society has no central organization. Livelihood is generally based on subsistence farming, although cash crops such as cotton and peanuts are also grown. They are proficient in wood and metal sculpturing. They achieved political hegemony at two periods—in the early 17th century and again in the mid-18th century—but are now largely intermingled with other peoples of the region.

Bamberg, city in West Germany on Regnitz River, 31mi (50km) N of Nürnberg; capital of powerful ecclesiastic state 1007–1802, when it joined Bavaria; site of 12th-century church, bishops' palaces (1571–76), observatory. Industries: textiles, machinery, beer. Pop. 69,303.

Bamboo, tall, treelike grass found worldwide in tropical and subtropical regions, mostly in SE Asia. The hollow, woody stems grow in branching clusters from a thick rhizome and the leaves are stalked blades. It is used for construction materials and household implements. Some bamboo sprouts are eaten. The pulp and fiber go into paper production. Height to 120ft (37m). There are 1000 species. Family Gramineae; subfamily Bambusoidae. *See also* Grass. △452; 454.

Banana, long, curved, yellow or reddish fruit of the banana plant consumed worldwide. It has soft, creamy flesh. Or, treelike plant found in tropical areas worldwide. It is propagated from sprouts growing from the perennial root or rhizome. The large annual stem is topped with a crown of long, broad leaves. A spike of yellow, clustered flowers grows from the crown center. This spike bends downward and becomes bunches of 50–150 fruits or hands of 10–20. After fruiting, the plants die. Those used for cooking are called plantain. Height: to 40ft (12m). Over 100 varieties are cultivated. Family Musaceae; genus *Musa*. *See also* Plantain.

Banaras. *See* Varanasi.

Bancroft, George (1800–91), US diplomat and historian, b. Worcester, Mass. A Jacksonian Democrat, he was appointed secretary of the Navy (1845) and established the US Naval Academy at Annapolis, Md. He served as minister to England (1846–49) and to Germany (1867–74), where he became a personal friend of Chancellor Bismarck. His comprehensive *History of the United States* (10 vols., 1834–74) analyzed the country's origins and development.

Band, a group of musicians playing primarily woodwind, percussion, and brass instruments, or a specifically designated group of instruments, as in a string band or brass band. Famous bandmasters and composers, such as Patrick S. Gilmore and John P. Sousa, helped to elevate the quality of the band in the United States.

Banda, Hastings (Kamuzu) (*c.* 1902–), president of Malawi (1966–). He studied medicine in the United States and practiced in England before returning to Africa (1953). He became a nationalist political leader, guiding Nyasaland to independence as Malawi and to membership in the British Commonwealth (1964) and establishing an autocratic presidency (1966). He was criticized by other black African leaders for dealing with South Africa.

Bandaranaike, Sirimavo (Ratwatte Dias) (1916–), prime minister of Sri Lanka (formerly Ceylon). She became the world's first female prime minister in 1960, after her husband, the former premier, was assassinated in the previous year. Her Sri Lanka Freedom party was defeated in 1965, but returned to power in 1970. In 1971 she put down an uprising led by the Marxist People's Liberation Front. In 1972 a new constitution was adopted and the country's name was officially changed to Sri Lanka. Under Mrs. Bandaranaike, the nation has pursued socialist and neutralist policies.

Bandaranaike, Solomon West Ridgeway Dias (1899–1959), Prime Minister of Ceylon from 1956–1959. He made Sinhalese the official language and founded the Sri Lanka Freedom party, which united the nationalists and socialists.

Banda Sea, section of the Pacific Ocean, surrounded by the Malay Islands, Indonesia, linking the Indian and Pacific Oceans; bounded by Buru and Ceram (N), Kai and Aru (E), Tanimbar Islands (S), Timor (SW), Celebes (NW). Length: 600mi (966km). Width: 300mi (483km).

Banded Seal. △610.

Banded Sea Snake. △524.

Bandelier National Monument, historic area in N New Mexico; contains prehistoric ruins of Pueblo Indian dwellings. Est. 1916. Area: 29,661acres (12,013hectares).

Bandinelli, Baccio (or Bartolommeo) (1493–1560), Italian sculptor. His best work is a bas-relief of 88 apostles, prophets, and saints in the Cathedral of Florence. He was a rival of Michelangelo.

Band Spectrum. *See* Spectrum.

Bandung, city in Indonesia, 110mi (177km) SE of Djakarta; capital of West Java prov.; scene of historic Asian-African Conference (1955), Nuclear Research Center (1964). Industries: food processing, canning, tea, quinine, textiles. Founded 1810. Pop. 1,114,000.

Bandung Conference (1955), meeting in Bandung, Indonesia, of representatives of 28 nonaligned countries of Africa and Asia and China to show united opposition to colonialism and to gain recognition for the "Third World." *See also* Third World. △1352.

Balsam

Baltimore oriole

Honoré de Balzac

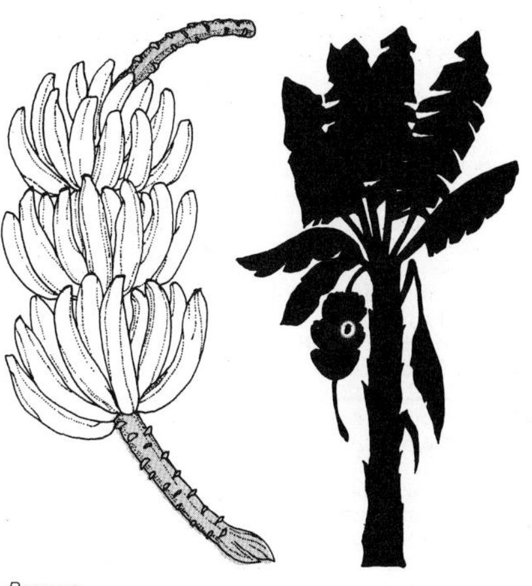

Banana

Bandura, Arthur. △784.

Band Waves. △1794, 1796.

Baneberry, any of about 10 species of perennial plants (genus *Actaea*) of the buttercup family found throughout the temperate Northern Hemisphere. All have poisonous berries appearing in fall. The North American white baneberry *(A. alba)* has sharply toothed leaflets and white berries with black eyes. Height: to 2ft (61cm).

Banff, town in SW Alberta, Canada, on the Bow River in the Rocky Mts; noted for Indian and natural history exhibits and summer fine arts school conducted by the University of Alberta; popular resort town. Pop. 896.

Bangalore (Bangalur), city in S central India, 180mi (290km) W of Madras; capital of Mysore state; est 1537 by Mysore dynasty, it was besieged and occupied by Hyder Ali (1758) but later restored to former rulers by British defeat (1791) of Tippoo Sahib, Hyder Ali's son. Britain ruled Mysore 1831–81, retaining Bangalore as military headquarters until 1947; 5th-largest city in India; industrial and transportation center. Pop. 1,041,900.

Bangkok (Krung Thep), capital city of Thailand, on the Chao Phraya river, 25mi (40km) above the Gulf of Siam; capital of Phra Nakhon prov. Commercial, financial, transportation, and cultural center; hub of major rice-growing region; site of Grand Palace walls, Wat Phra Kaew (royal Buddhist temple), several universities, national theater and museum; headquarters of UN Economic Commission for Asia and the Far East. The capital of Siam and stronghold against Burmese until destroyed 1767; capital changed to Thon Buri (1769) until King Rama I renamed Bangkok capital in 1782. Industries: textiles, food processing, sawmills, oil refining, shipyards. Pop. 2,132,000.

Bangladesh (Bengal Nation), independent nation in Asia. It is a low-lying plain formed by the Ganges and Brahmaputra rivers. Its monsoon climate, which gives it the highest rainfall in the world, and its location in the cyclone belt combine to produce devastating floods; a weak economy has generated periodic famine.

Land and Economy: The world's eighth-most populous nation, it is bisected by the Tropic of Cancer. Its coastline borders the Bay of Bengal with India and Burma adjacent. Raw jute and jute manufacture account for 90% of foreign earnings. Offshore oil was found in 1974. Although over 80% of the people are farmers and rice is the major crop, the country is not self-sufficient in food; it depends on foreign aid. Land productivity, disease, famine, and the birth rate are long-term problems. It is estimated that the present population of 73,700,000 will rise to 175,000,000 by the year 2000.

People: 98% of the people are Bengali and speak Bengali, the official language; the rest include Urdu-speaking Muslim immigrants from India and tribal units. Islam is the religion of 85% of the people with the balance made up of Hindus, Buddhists, Christians, and animists. The literacy rate is 20%.

Government: A 1972 constitution was based on nationalism, secularism, socialism, and democracy, and on a parliament with power in the hands of the prime minister.

History: A melting pot of Dravidians, Aryans, Mongolians, Arabs, Persians, and Turks, the region of Bangladesh was ruled by Hindu and Buddhist dynasties until the British assumed control in the 18th century. In 1947, India and Pakistan gained independence. Pakistan was divided into two sections, East and West, two areas nearly 1,000 miles (1,610km) apart. In the mid-1960s, Sheikh Mujibur Rahman emerged as the spokesman for East Pakistan autonomy. President of the Awami League, he was jailed for civil disobedience and fled to India, where in 1971 he organized a provisional government. Bengali forces defeated Pakistan, and on March 16, 1971, Bangladesh emerged as a nation. Mujibur Rahman was killed in a 1975 coup d'état.

PROFILE

Official name: People's Republic of Bangladesh
Area: 55,126sq mi (142,776sq km)
Population: 73,700,000
Density: 1,360per sq mi (525per sq km)
Chief cities: Dacca (capital); Khulna; Chittagong
Government: Military decree
Religion: Islam
Language: Bengali
Monetary unit: Taka
Gross national product: $7,730,000,000
Per capita income: $100
Industries (major products): jute products, cotton textiles, wood products, processed foods
Agriculture (major products): jute, rice, sugar cane, tea, oilseeds, fish, forests, cotton
Trading partners (major): India

Bangor, city in S Maine, at the confluence of Penobscot and Kenduskeag rivers. Settled 1769 as Sunbury, it was occupied by British during War of 1812; important port of entry. Industries: tourism, shoes, paper, tools, lumber, printing. Inc. as town 1791, as city 1834. Pop. (1970) 33,168.

Bangui, capital city of Central African Republic; a port on the Ubangi River, near the Zaire border; nation's chief port of international trade. Industries: textiles, food products, shoes, beer, soap. Founded 1889 by French. Pop. (including suburbs) 238,579.

Bangweulu (Bangweolo), lake and swamp area in NE Zambia, central Africa. Swamps are formed by flooding of lower Chambezi River, which enters the lake from E; commercial fishing area; visited by David Livingstone 1868. Area (lake and swamps): approx. 3,800sq mi (9,842sq km).

Banjo, musical instrument with from four to nine strings; drum-like body; and long, fretted neck, strummed with pick. Probably of Arabic or Spanish origin, it was brought to America by slaves.

Banjul. *See* Bathurst.

Bankhead, Tallulah Brockman (1903–68), US stage and screen actress, b. Huntsville, Ala., whose performance in Lillian Hellman's *The Little Foxes* (1939) and Thornton Wilder's *The Skin of Our Teeth* (1944) won for her the prestigious New York Drama Critics' Circle Award.

Bankhead, William Brockman (1874–1940), speaker of the US House of Representatives, 1936–40, and father of Tallulah, b. Moscow, Ala. In the House from 1917 until his death, he also served as majority leader. He was an advocate of New Deal measures.

Banking, Aircraft. △1718.

Banking System, in the United States, consists of the Federal Reserve System; the commercial banking system, which includes nearly 14,000 individual banks of various sizes; various regulatory government agencies; financial intermediaries; and, in a sense, the federal government itself. The banking system is a service-oriented business that provides to individuals and businesses the services of holding money, facilitating an easy means of payment, providing loans, and providing stability to the financial sector. The banking system facilitates exchange through the use of demand deposits, and the wide acceptance of these demand deposits as a means of payment enhances exchange of goods and services. △934, 1126.

Bank of England, England's central banking institution, founded in 1694 and situated in Threadneedle Street, City of London. Nationalized in 1944, it regulates foreign exchange, issues bank notes, advises the government on monetary matters, and acts as the government's financial agent.

Bank of the United States, First (1791–1811), national bank established under Alexander Hamilton's plan to put the United States on a solid economic basis. The bank conducted business for the government. It was soundly operated, but state banking interests defeated its rechartering.

Bank of the United States, Second, national bank chartered in 1816. This bank, modeled on Alexander Hamilton's First Bank, was chartered by Congress although there was much opposition to giving it the power to establish local branches that would compete with state-chartered banks. Maryland unsuccessfully carried its challenge to the Supreme Court in the case of *McCulloch* v. *Maryland* (1819). President Andrew Jackson opposed the bank and vetoed its rechartering, so it went out of existence in 1836.

Bankruptcy, legal procedure whereby a business may be liquidated under the direction of the court system. A bankruptcy petition is normally filed only when a business determines that its obligations so far outweigh its net worth and future opportunities that it will be impossible for the business to survive.

Banks, Ernest (1931–), US baseball player, b. Dallas. Known as a home run hitter (512), he spent his entire career with the Chicago Cubs (1953–71).

Banks, (Sir) Joseph (1743–1820), English explorer and naturalist. He is better known for his patronage and promotion of the sciences than for his own work. His home served as a meeting place for scientists and the exchange of ideas, and as president of the Royal Society he cultivated interchange with scientists throughout the world. As honorary director of the Royal Botanical Gardens at Kew, he was responsible for sending many botanical collectors on international expeditions.

Banneker, Benjamin (1731–1806), US scientist, b. Elliott, Md. He was a mathematician, astronomer, surveyor, and clock-maker. In 1791 he became the first black presidential appointee when George Washington appointed him to the District of Columbia Commission to survey the site of the new capital.

Bannister, Roger (Gilbert) (1929–), English athlete. An Oxford graduate, he was the first man to run the mile in less than four minutes. He accomplished the feat on May 6, 1954, in a time of 3 minutes, 59.4 seconds. He received his medical degree at St. Mary's Hospital Medical School (1954) and subsequently became a well-known physician and government sports advisor.

Bannock, a Shoshonean-speaking tribe that broke off from the Northern Paiute and settled in SE Idaho where they acquired many Nez Percé and Shoshoni traits. They are primarily noted for their role in the Bannock War of 1878. The bulk of the tribe—some 500 individuals—share Fort Hall, Idaho, with the Shoshoni tribe.

Bannockburn, town in central Scotland, scene of battle (1314) in which Robert Bruce defeated the English under Edward II. Pop. 3,887.

Bantam Books, Inc. v. Sullivan (1963), US Supreme Court case in which the court outlawed the circulation of "blacklists" by state anti-pornography commissions. The court said the lists constituted "prior restraints," condemned in *Near* v. *Minnesota* (1931).

Banteng. △582.

Banting, (Sir) Frederick Grant (1891–1941), Canadian physician. He shared the 1923 Nobel Prize in physiology or medicine for his work in extracting the hormone insulin from the pancreas, thus making it possible to give insulin to diabetes mellitus sufferers.

Bantu Languages, languages variously grouped with the Benue-Niger or Niger-Kordofanian families of African languages. They form the largest group of languages spoken from the Congo Basin to South Africa. Swahili or Kingwana is the most widely used of these. With Lingala, Zulu, Luganda, and others they total over 30 million speakers. △880.

Banyan, evergreen tree of E India whose branches send down aerial shoots that take root, forming new trunks. These trunks of a single tree can cover an area up to 2000ft (610m) in circumference. It has dark green, oval leaves and produces small, round fruits. Height: to 100ft (30m). Family Moraceae; species *Ficus benghalensis.*

Baobab, tropical tree native to Africa, Madagascar, and N Australia. It has a stout trunk containing water storage tissue, and short, stubby branches with sparse foliage. Fiber from its bark is used in making rope. Its gourdlike fruit has edible pulp. Height: to 75ft (23m); trunk diameter: 30ft (9m). Family Bombacaceae; species *Adansonia digitata.* △586.

Bao Dai (1913–), emperor of Annam (1932–45), chief of state of Vietnam (1949–55), b. Nguyen Vinh Thuy. He cooperated with the Vichy French and Japanese during World War II. He resigned in 1945 when the Viet Minh nationalists under Ho Chi Minh gained control of Indochina. When the French regained control, they appointed him head of a united Vietnam (1949). After the French defeat and partition in 1954, the monarchy was abolished (1955) and Bao Dai went into exile.

Baptism. △830, 1026.

Baptistry, part of a church or related separate building used for baptism. Based on the early baptistry in the Lateran basilica at Rome, many were octagonal. Baptistries remained even after immersion was no longer practiced. △1104, 1134.

Baptists, members of a Protestant denomination who profess a personal religion based on the principle of religious liberty. With no official creed and no hierarchy, individual churches are autonomous. Historically, they developed from the Reformation Anabaptists. They continue to practice baptism of believers only through immersion. Insisting on freedom of thought and expression, they developed a democratic government. The Baptist World Alliance, an advisory group, convenes every five years. Baptists comprise one-third of Protestants in the United States. *See also* Anabaptists.

Bar, a unit of pressure, corresponding to the pressure of a column of mercury one meter high. Atmospheric pressure is about .76 bars, or 760 millibars. A millibar is also called a torr, after the Italian Torricelli, an early inventor of the barometer. △268.

Bar, Confederation of (1768), patriotic Polish anti-Russian association of Catholic nobles. After Protestants and Greek Orthodox Catholics were granted equal rights with Polish Catholics, the confederation led an uprising that eventually led to civil war, and, in 1772, the first partition of Poland.

Barabbas, in the New Testament, convicted felon in prison at the time of Jesus' trial before Pilate. The people, given a choice of which prisoner to set free, convinced Pilate Barabbas should be released and Jesus crucified.

Baranof Island, island off SE Alaska, W Alexander Archipelago. It is named for Russian trader Aleksandr Baranov. Area: 1,597sq mi (4,136sq km).

Baranov, Aleksandr Andreevich (1746–1819), Russian fur trader in Alaska. After heading an earlier Russian fur trading company in the Kodiak Islands, Baranov became (1799) head of the Russian-American Company. He greatly expanded Russian penetration of North America—eventually establishing posts as far south as Fort Ross, north of San Francisco—and brought great profits to the company.

Barataria Bay, inlet off SE Louisiana; Grand and Grand Terre islands stand between it and Gulf of Mexico; source of shrimp, muskrat furs, sulfur, oil.

Barb, light horse breed native to Barbary region of N Africa. Introduced in England by King Charles II (reigned 1660–85) to develop racing thoroughbreds, it is similar to the Arabian but has a more rugged physique. *See also* Arabian.

Barbados, island state in West Indies, in Windward Islands group, E of St Vincent: Settled by British 1627; member of Organization of American States, Caribbean Free Trade Area, and the United Nations. Industries: tourism, sugar cane, molasses, rum, fishing. Highest point is Mount Hillaly, 1,104ft (336m). Pop. 238,141.

Barbari, Jacopo de (1440–1516), Venetian painter and engraver. Barbari was consulted by Dürer on style and influenced Dürer's work. Barbari was one of the first, possibly the first, to paint a signed and dated pure still life, which included a dead partridge, gauntlets, and an arrow. His work included engravings on copper, etchings, and woodcuts. Two famed etchings are *Judith* and *Dying Cleopatra.*

Barbarians. △1008, 1054, 1074.

Barbarosa (1466?–1546), Ottoman naval commander, b. as Khair ed-Din. In 1518 he seized Algiers from Spain for the Ottoman Empire. Later he gained all the Barbary States. He continued to harass European shipping in the Mediterranean. He was admiral of the Ottoman fleet (1533–44).

Barbary Ape, tailless, yellowish-brown, apelike monkey native to Algeria, Morocco, and Gibraltar. It is the size of a small dog. The Gibralter Barbary apes are the only wild monkeys in Europe. Species *Macaca sylvana. See also* Macaque.

Barbary Coast, waterfront section of San Francisco, California; known for corruption that flourished during 1890–1917; named after the notorious Barbary Coast of North Africa.

Barbary Sheep. *See* Aoudad.

Barbary States, coastal region in N Africa, consisting of Tripoli, Tunisia, Algeria, and Morocco; part of Libya until Roman domination in AD 42; independent Muslim states 7th–15th centuries; pirate states under Turkish control (16th–19th centuries), notorious for Mediterranean raids. Several wars reduced their power, and France gained control of Algeria, Morocco, and Tunisia by 1912. Now independent states: Libya (1951), Morocco and Tunisia (1956), Algeria (1962).

Barbed Wire, a form of fencing patented (1867) by Joseph F. Glidden. First marketed in 1874, the metal wire had barbs spaced every few inches. This simple product changed the history of the west by allowing the fencing of cattle ranges to contain livestock and prevent damage to property by cattle.

Barbel, or Barb, freshwater fish of W Asia and S central Europe. A game and food fish, it has an elongated body, flattened underside, and two pairs of fleshy mouth whiskers. Length: 19.7–35.4in (50–90cm); Weight: to 49lb (22kg). Family Cyprinidae; species *Barbus barbus.*

Barbels. △516.

Barber, Samuel (1910–), US composer, b. West Chester, Pa. Using a basically conservative, post-Romantic style, Barber has composed works in many forms, including chamber music; two symphonies; a *Piano Concerto* (1963, Pulitzer Prize 1963); and two operas, *Vanessa* (1956, Pulitzer Prize 1956) and *Antony and Cleopatra* (1966). *See also* Romantic Music.

Barberini Family, aristocratic Roman family founded upon the merchant wealth of Francesco Barberini (1528–1600). **Maffeo Barberini** (1568–1644) was elected Pope Urban VIII (1623) and made cardinals of his nephew Francesco, his brother Antonio the Elder, and another nephew Antonio the Younger (patron of Baroque artist Bernini). Church offices and strategic marriages into the Colonna family and to Francesco II of Modena increased the family's power. The dynasty died out in 1736.

Barber of Seville, The (1816), 3-act comic opera by Gioacchino Antonio Rossini, Italian libretto by Cesare Sterbini, after Pierre Beaumarchais' play satirizing aristocratic foibles. Performed first in Rome, it was a failure, but had a successful performance in New York (1819). Figaro (baritone) is a clever, boastful barber of 17th-century Spain who helps Count Almaviva (tenor) to win Rosina (soprano) in spite of the efforts of her guardian Bartolo (bass) to marry her for her dowry. △1256.

Barberry, thorny shrub widespread in northern temperate regions. Leaves and small, yellow flowers appear at same time in spring. The small, red fruit is a favorite of birds. Height: 7ft (2m). Among the 300 species are the American *Berberis canadensis,* European *B. vulgaris,* and Japanese *B. thunbergii.* Family Berberidaceae.

Barberton, city in NE Ohio, on Tuscarawas River; suburb of Akron; contains Lake Anna. Industries: automobile tires, rubber products. Inc. 1892. Pop. (1970) 33,052.

Barbet, brightly colored tropical bird, related to the toucan and honeyguide, known for its annoying sounds. They are stocky, coarse looking birds, with heavy bills, beardlike bristles, and short legs. They feed mainly on fruit. They excavate a cavity in a tree limb leading to a chamber where white eggs (2–5) are laid. Length: 4–13in (10–33cm). Family Capitonidae.

Barbirolli, (Sir) John (1899–1970), English conductor. He conducted the New York Philharmonic (1937–42) and then the Hallé Orchestra, Manchester, England. He was especially known for his interpretations of English composers.

Barbiturates, drugs used to induce sleep or sedation. Among the common barbiturates are phenobarbital, secobarbital (Seconal), pentobarbital (Nembutal). When taken in prescribed doses, they are safe, effective medical agents, but barbiturates are also dangerous drugs: in large doses they are addictive, and when combined with other drugs such as alcohol or tranquilizers can produce unexpected unconsciousness and death.

Barbizon School, school of painting that derives its name from a village 30 miles southeast of Paris near the forest of Fontainebleau. A group of artists, led by Théodore Rousseau, gathered there (*c.*1830–80) to discuss art and to paint what was simple and commonplace in nature. Many artists visited. Millet, Courbet, Daumier, and Corot were inspired to do searching landscapes there.

Barbour, John (*c.*1316–1395), Scottish poet. About 1375 he wrote *The Bruce,* Scottish literature's earliest epic, describing Scotland's fight for independence from England. It combines patriotic sentiment with historical accuracy.

Barcelona, seaport city in NE Spain, between Besos and Llobregat rivers on the Mediterranean Sea, 385mi (620km) NE of Madrid; capital of Barcelona prov. In 1714 Philip V of Spain captured the city;

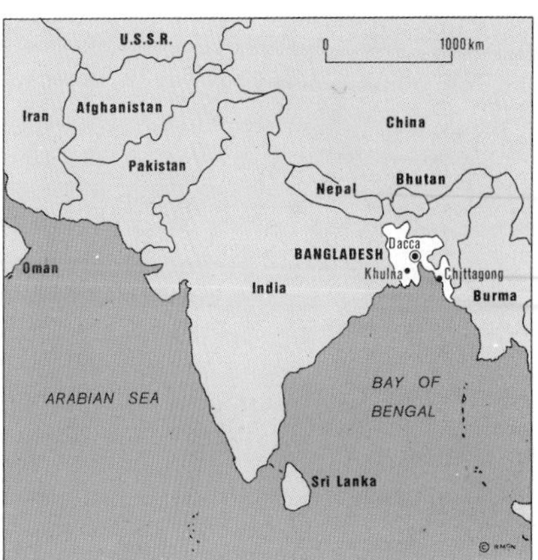
U.S.S.R.
0
1000km
Iran
Afghanistan
China
Pakistan
Nepal
Bhutan
Oman
BANGLADESH
Dacca
Khulna
Chittagong
India
Burma
ARABIAN SEA
BAY OF BENGAL
Sri Lanka
Bangladesh

Bangui, Central African Republic

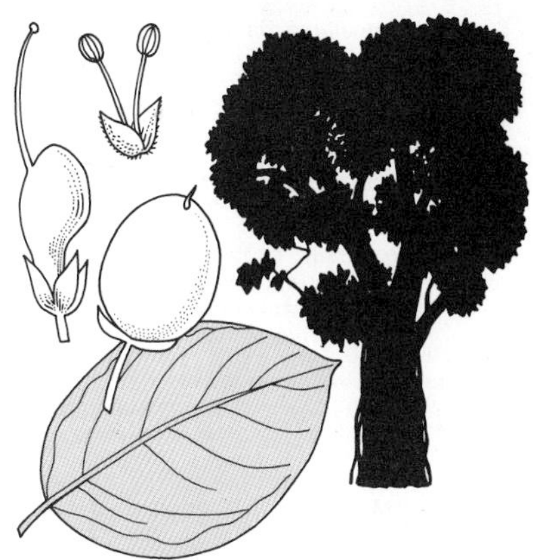
Banyan

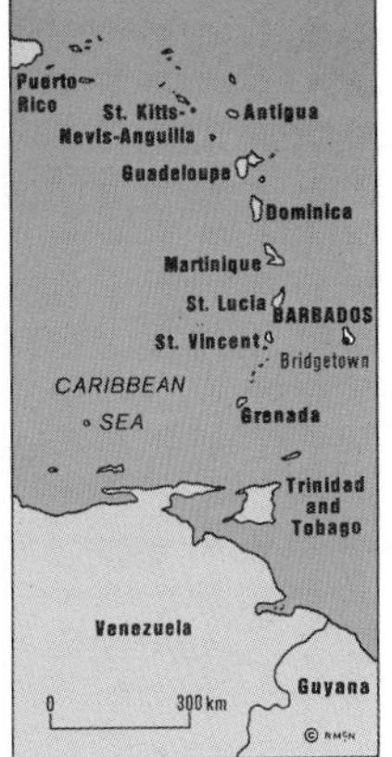
Puerto Rico
St. Kitts-Nevis-Anguilla
Antigua
Guadeloupe
Dominica
Martinique
St. Lucia
BARBADOS
St. Vincent
Bridgetown
CARIBBEAN SEA
Grenada
Trinidad and Tobago
Venezuela
0
300km
Guyana
Barbados

taken by French during Napoleonic Wars (1808–13). Barcelona has been the center of anarchist and separatist movements since 19th century. Industries: breweries, sawmills, furniture, petroleum. Founded 3rd century BC by Carthaginian Barca family. Pop. 1,745,142.

Barchan Dune, cresent-shaped sand hill that is built up in regions of limited sand and where the wind is constant in velocity and direction. Barchans occur fairly frequently on riverbanks and, as a result of constant wind, move fairly rapidly, particularly the smaller ones. *See also* Desert; Dune. △266.

Bar Cocheba, Simon (died 135), leader of the rebellion of the Jewish community against the Romans in Jerusalem in 132–135. At first successful, he was finally slain in battle.

Bardstown, city in central Kentucky; seat of Nelson co; site of early missionary work; preserves the house where Steven Foster wrote "My Old Kentucky Home." Industries: distilleries, lumber. Settled 1778; inc. 1788. Pop. (1970) 5,816.

Bareilly, city in N India; capital of Bareilly district; became a British possession (1801); site of Bareilly College (1837). Industries: sugar, cotton, furniture, rope. Founded 1537. Pop. 334,064.

Barents, Willem (died 1597), Dutch navigator and explorer. He commanded several expeditions in search of a Northeast Passage. The arctic sea northeast of Scandinavia bears his name.

Barents Sea, part of Arctic Ocean, E of USSR and N of Norway; named for Dutch navigator Willem Barents. Main ports of Murmansk and Vardø are ice-free.

Barge, flat-bottomed boat used to transport cargo in inland waterways. Originally, goods were moved on unpowered (dumb) barges pulled by horses along towpaths. With the advent of powered barges, whole assemblies of interconnected powered and dumb barges were used on natural waterways. Today, barges that can carry 10,000 tons are towed by high-powered tugs for short voyages.

Bargello, Italian national art museum, Florence. It originated as the Palazzo del Podestà in 1255, and was converted into a prison in 1574 and into a museum in 1857–65. It is known for important Renaissance sculptures including Davids by Michelangelo, Donatello, and Verrocchio; bronzes by Cellini and Pollaiuolo; Giotto's portrait of Dante; and terra-cottas by Della Robbia.

Bar Harbor, town in SE Maine, on Mt Desert Island; popular resort site; Acadia National Park is nearby. Settled 1763; inc. 1796. Pop. (1970) 3,716.

Bari, port city in S Italy; capital of Bari prov. and Apulia region; an important Roman colony, it was later ruled by Saracens, Byzantines, Normans, Germans, and Venetians; embarkation point for Crusaders; joined Italy 1860; site of 11th-century cathedral, Norman castle, and archeological museum. Industries: food processing, oil refining, boatbuilding, textiles. Pop. 348,914.

Barite, a sulfate mineral, barium sulfate ($BaSO_4$). In sedimentary rocks and as gangue material in ore veins in limestone. Orthorhombic system tabular crystals or masses. Radiating clusters of crystals are called "barite roses." Colorless, white or yellow; hardness 3–3.5; sp gr 4.5. △242.

Barium, common metallic element (symbol Ba) of the alkaline-earth group, discovered 1808 by Sir Humphrey Davy. Chief sources are heavy spar (sulfate) and witherite (carbonate). The barium atoms are opaque to X rays, and barium sulfate is taken internally to permit X-ray examination of the intestines. Properties: at. no. 56; at. wt. 137.34; sp. gr. 3.5; melt. pt. 1337°F (726°C); boil. pt. 2984°F (1641°C); most common isotope Ba^{138} (71.66%). *See also* Alkaline-earth Elements.

Bark, outer protective covering of a woody plant stem. It is made up of several layers. As food-conducting cells die, they become the inner layer. The cork layer, waxy and waterproof, is the thickest layer and hardens into the tough, often-fissured outer covering. Lenticels, spongy areas, allow the stem to breathe. In smooth-barked trees, the cork layer is active for the life of the tree; in rough-barked trees, the outer cork layer dies and cracks as the stem diameter increases. *See also* Cork. △448.

Bark Beetle, or engraver beetle, small brown to black beetle that tunnels through inner bark and wood of trees. The tunnels of some form species-characteristic, engraving-like patterns. Family Scolytidae.

Barkentine. △1678.

Barkley, Alben William (1877–1956), US vice president and political leader, b. Graves co, Ky. He served as a US representative (1913–27) and senator (1927–49; 1954–56) and was instrumental in securing passage of New Deal legislation. He was also Senate majority leader (1937–47). Under Pres. Harry Truman, he was vice president (1949–53).

Barley, cereal grass, native to Asia and Ethiopia, widely cultivated since 5000 BC. Three cultivated species are: *Hordeum vulgare,* favored in United States; *H. distichum,* commonly grown in Europe; and *H. irregulare,* or irregular barley, grown in Ethiopia. Barley is used as food for humans and animals, and in making malt beverages. Family Gramineae. *See also* Grass. △326.

Barlow, Joel (1754–1812), US author and diplomat, b. Redding, Conn. He attended Yale University, where he became a member of the Connecticut Wits. After 1789 his work, including *The Conspiracy of Kings* (1792; verse) and *Advice to Privileged Orders* (1792; prose), reflected his sympathy with the liberal ideas of the French Revolution. Among his other works are *Hasty Pudding* (1793), a poem in praise of New England cornmeal, and *The Columbiad* (1807), an epic poem. *See also* Connecticut Wits.

Bar Mitzvah, Jewish ceremony in which a young male (traditionally 13 years and 1 day) is initiated into the adult religious community by reading from the Torah as part of the worship service. A parallel ceremony, the Bat Mitzvah, for girls has been introduced in some synagogues and temples. △790.

Barnabus, Christian apostle of the first century, originally named Joseph. Barnabus accompanied Paul (Saul) on two proselytizing missions to Cyprus and the European mainland. A rift developed between the two religious leaders; Paul replaced Barnabus as head of the Antioch church.

Barnacle, sessile crustacean living mostly on rocks and floating timber. Some are commensal on whales, turtles, and fish. There are also parasitic species. The free-swimming larvae settle permanently on their heads and their carapace becomes covered with a number of calcareous plates. The shrimplike adult stands on its head and uses its feet to kick food into its mouth. Two main types are those with stalks (goose barnacles) and those without stalks (acorn barnacles). There are 800 living species. Subclass Cirripedia. *See also* Crustacean. △622.

Barnard, Christian (1922–), South African surgeon. On Dec. 3, 1967, he was the first to perform a human heart transplant and in 1974 he was the first to implant a second heart in a patient and to link the circulations of the two hearts so they worked together as one.

Barnard, Edward Emerson (1857–1923), US astronomer, b. Nashville, Tenn. He is chiefly known as an acute observer and pioneer in astronomical photography. He discovered comets, catalogued dark nebulae, and made observations of the red dwarf star now bearing his name.

Barnard, Henry (1811–1900), US educator. As an official in Connecticut and Rhode Island, he worked to improve the schools and to provide free public education. He was the first US commissioner of education (1867–70).

Barnard's Star, red dwarf star in the constellation Ophiuchus. It was discovered by US astronomer E. E. Barnard in 1916, and is remarkable for having the greatest proper motion of any star so far observed. A companion body, perhaps an orbiting planet, with a mass 15 times that of Jupiter, was detected near it in 1963. Characteristics: apparent mag. 9.5; absolute mag. 13.2; spectral type M5; distance 6.0 light-years. △156.

Barnaul, city in Russian SFSR, USSR, on Ob River; capital of Altai Krai; industrial and trade center serving surrounding agricultural and mining area; site of agricultural and teachers' colleges. Founded 1738. Pop. 459,000.

Barnburners, group of radical Democrats in New York state in the 1840s, later split between the Free-Soilers and regular Democrats.

Barnegat Bay, arm of Atlantic Ocean along E coast of New Jersey; entered by Barnegat Inlet between Long Beach Island and Island Beach Peninsula; site of several resorts. Length: 30mi (48km).

Barn Owl, owl with a heart-shaped, monkeylike face and long legs mostly found in the Eastern Hemisphere. The widely distributed common barn owl *(Tyto alba)* lives in old buildings where its acute hearing helps it locate rodents and other prey in total darkness; other barn owls hunt during the day, except the nocturnal bay owl *(Phodilus badius)* of Asian forests. Family Tytonidae. *See also* Owl.

Barn Swallow, swift-flying, highly migratory swallow, commonly summering in the Northern Hemisphere and wintering in S Southern Hemisphere. It is generally steel blue above, chestnut to salmon to white below, and has a deeply forked tail. It feeds on insects and builds a mud-and-straw, feather-lined nest in a barn or other building for its brown- or purple-spotted white eggs (4–6). Length: 6–7in (15–17.5cm). Species *Hirundo rustica.*

Barnum, Phineas Taylor (1810–91), US showman and promoter, b. Bethel, Conn. A superb publicist, he established (1842) the American Museum in New York City, where he presented the dwarf Tom Thumb, a bearded lady, and other "freaks." In 1850 he brought Jenny Lind to the United States for a concert tour. After a temporary retirement from show business, he opened (1871) in Brooklyn, N.Y., his circus, billed as "The Greatest Show on Earth." He later merged (1881) with a rival to form Barnum and Bailey.

Baroda, city in W India, between Mahi and Narbada rivers; headquarters of the Gaikwars (18th century) who enhanced it with gardens and picturesque buildings; site of Baroda University (1949) and the State Museum and Picture Gallery (1894). Industries: cotton textiles, chemicals, pottery. Pop. 404,229.

Baroja y Nessi, Pío (1872–1956), Spanish novelist. He gained recognition for his bitter, humorous, and pessimistic novels portraying down-and-out characters moving in a colorful but meaningless world. His works included *The Tree of Knowledge* (1911) and *Memoirs of a Man of Action* (1913–35).

Barometer, an instrument for measuring atmospheric pressure in order to predict probable local weather changes resulting from approaching fronts and air masses. Mercury and aneroid barometers are two basic types, and barographs are barometers recording changes in atmospheric pressure. *See also* Atmospheric Pressure. △1496, 1656.

Barons' War (1263–67), struggle between Henry III of England and his barons. Breaking his pledge to rule through a council of barons (1261), Henry provoked war (1263). Rejecting arbitration by Louis IX of France, the barons, under Simon de Montfort, defeated Henry at Lewes (1264) and summoned a parliament (1265). The royalists' victory at Evesham (1265) eventually ensured the barons' submission without securing their constitutional aims.

Baroque Architecture, architecture characterized by exuberant decoration, curvaceous forms, an emphasis on grand or superhuman scale, and a sense of movement. It flourished in the 17th and early 18th centuries and changed character according to the country in which it was used. Many buildings were designed to evoke a specific emotional response from those who entered. In the 18th century in England, France, and Italy a greater sense of restraint and classicism prevailed; for these exceptions the term "Baroque Classicism" is used. △1162–64.

Baroque Art, style of art from late 16th to early 18th centuries, between Mannerism and Rococo. The term is from the French, meaning odd or curious, and until the 19th century, Baroque art was thought of as absurd and grotesque. Italian Baroque is generally divided into three periods: Early (from 1585), High (from 1625), and Late (1675–1715). The style is characterized by a concern for balance and wholeness. To achieve a unified effect, parts of a large painting are subordinate to the whole, and paintings and sculpture are subordinate to the building they decorate.

Baroque art is also known for its high technical virtuosity and its reproduction of reality, ie, in the color and texture of an object. It is dynamic and attempts to involve the spectator in a specific dramatic moment. Strong opposites are evident, eg, light against dark, mass against void, and strong diagonals and curves. The aim is for the total effect, and often tricks of scene painting, such as false perspective and *trompe l'oeil,* are used to produce it. The sculpture and architecture of Bernini dominated High Baroque. His masterpieces include the Piazza before St. Peter's and his marble group "Ecstasy of St. Teresa." In painting, Cortona's "The Rape of the Sabines" and his famous ceilings exemplify the style. Rubens, Rembrandt, Van Dyck, Velázquez, and Murillo painted in the Baroque style. △1162–64.

Baroque Music, music composed from roughly 1600 to 1750. The period is notable for the development of contrapuntal (polyphonic) music culminating in the masterpieces of J. S. Bach and Handel, the development of opera, oratorio, and cantata featuring solo singers, and the emergence of many purely instrumental forms of music such as the fugue, sonata, concerto, suite, toccata, passacaglia, and chaconne. Many composer-musicians were employed and patronized by royal courts of Europe. Some of the other major composers of this period include Monteverdi, Vivaldi, and Scarlatti from Italy, Lully, Couperin, and Rameau from France, Buxtehude and Telemann from Germany, and Purcell from England. Though German by birth, Handel spent much of his highly successful career in England. *See also* Cantata; Opera; Oratorio; Polyphony.

Barotseland (Western Province), historical region in W Zambia, central Africa; bordered by Angola (W) and Caprivi Strip of South West Africa (S); Mongu is the capital. Zambezi River drains the prov.; primarily savanna grassland, it is a livestock- and grain-raising area, with some teak forest. In 1911 region became prov. of British protectorate of Northern Rhodesia; called Western Province after Zambian independence 1964. Area: 63,000sq mi (163,170sq km). Pop. 410,-087.

Barqah. *See* Cyrenaica.

Barque, standard merchant ship in the North Atlantic during the second half of the 19th century, characterized by two square-rigged masts and a third with fore-and-aft sails.

Barracouta, or snoek, atun, South African mackerel, commercial food fish found in tropical and temperate marine waters. A snake (deep-sea) mackerel, it has a laterally compressed body, elongated lower jaw, and two dorsal fins. Length: 3.3ft (lm); weight: 8.8–13.2lb (4–6kg). Family Gempylidae; species *Thyrsites atun.*

Barracuda, marine fish found in tropical Atlantic and Pacific. Known to attack man, it has a large mouth with razor sharp teeth; its olive green body is elongated. Length: to 6ft. (183cm.); weight: 3–50lbs.(1.4–23kg.). Family Sphyraenidae; species 20, including Great *Sphyraena barracuda.* △510.

Barranquilla, city and port in N Colombia, on Magdalena River; capital of Atlántico dept. In 1935 the river channel was deepened to accommodate ocean-going vessels; rich agricultural region; site of two universities. Industries: canneries, flour mills, petrochemicals. Founded 1629. Pop. 656,100.

Barras, Paul, Vicomte de (1755–1829), French leader, important member of the Directory during the Revolution, 1795–99. He influenced Napoleon's rise to power. Napoleon became suspicious of him, however, and intermittently kept Barras out of France.

Barre, city in N central Vermont, 7mi (11km) SSE of Montpelier; statue of Scottish poet Robert Burns; winter resort. Industries: granite quarries, tool manufacturing. Settled 1788; inc. as city 1894. Pop: (1970) 10,209.

Barred Owl, North American owl with barred, brown plumage and a strident call. Length: 1.3–1.7ft (40–52cm). Species *Strix varia. See also* Owl.

Barred Spiral Galaxy, type of spiral galaxy in which the arms extend from opposite sides of an elongated central section resembling a bar. Barred spiral galaxies are graded in three groups, SBa to SBc, according to increasing openness of their spiral arms. *See also* Galaxy; Spiral Galaxy. △122.

Barrel Cactus, barrel-shaped cactus of North America. Most have stout, hooked spines and obvious ribs. Flowers, varying in color, are usually fragrant. Many smaller species with showy blooms are kept as houseplants. Family Cactaceae; genera *Ferocactus*—height: to 10ft (3m)—and *Echinocactus*—height: to 2ft (61cm). *See also* Cactus.

Barrel Organ, mechanical musical instrument developed in 15th-century Holland. Pins on a rotating drum control organ pipes fed from a wind chest. Mozart wrote three compositions for it; a portable modification, the hurdy-gurdy, is used by street musicians.

Barrett, David (1930–), premier of British Columbia (1972–75). A social worker, he entered the provincial legislature as a member of the New Democratic party in 1963. His election as premier in 1972 ended 20 years of conservative Social Credit party rule. His policy of socialist reforms was rejected electorally in 1975.

Barrie, (Sir) James Matthew (1860–1937), Scottish dramatist and novelist. His novel, *The Little Minister* (1891), established his reputation as a novelist, but after the production of his play *Walker, London* (1892) he devoted himself to the theater, writing mostly light dramas. *Peter Pan* (1904), *Dear Brutus* (1917), and *Mary Rose* (1920) were sentimental fantasies for children. Among his other plays were *The Professor's Love Story* (1895), *Quality Street* (1903), *The Admirable Crichton* (1903), and *What Every Woman Knows* (1908).

Barrier Reef, a long narrow coral reef lying roughly parallel to the shore but separated from it by a large deep lagoon. The Great Barrier Reef of Australia is the most famous.

Barrow, Errol (1920–), economist, lawyer, and prime minister of Barbados (1966–). Co-founder of the Democratic Labour party and the island's chief executive (1961–66), he was elected prime minister when Barbados became a sovereign state and member of the British Commonwealth.

Barrow, village in Alaska; the northernmost US community, it is 9mi (14km) SW of Point Barrow. US Navy operates Arctic Research Laboratory nearby. Whaling is chief industry. Pop. (1970) 2,104.

Barry, Philip (1896–1949), US dramatist, b. Rochester, N.Y. His successful high comedies, often touched with fantasy, portray individualistic characters in complex social situations, as in *The Philadelphia Story* (1939). Barry, who studied playwriting under George P. Baker, also wrote *White Wings* (1926), *Holiday* (1928), *Hotel Universe* (1930), and *The Animal Kingdom* (1932).

Barrymores, acting family, known as the "royal family of the American stage." **Maurice** (1847–1905) was the patriarch of the clan, b. Herbert Blythe in Agra, India. He gave up a career in law to be an actor, making his stage debut in a London production of *London Assurance* (1872). In 1875 he went to the United States where he joined Augustin Daly's stock company and married Georgiana Drew, daughter of a US acting family. Their children—**Lionel** (1878–1954), **Ethel** (1879–1959), and **John** (1882–1942)—all b. Philadelphia, were raised in the tradition of the theater. Lionel made his debut at age 6. At 15 he returned to the stage in Sheridan's *The Rivals.* After studying painting in Paris for 3 years he starred in *Peter Ibbitson* (1917), *The Copperhead* (1918), and *The Jest* (1919). He won an Academy Award for *Free Soul* (1931). He made many films and starred in the "Dr. Kildare" series on radio and film. Ethel made her stage debut at age 14, after giving up plans to be a pianist. Her stage roles included *A Doll's House* (1905), *Trelawney of the Wells* (1911), and *The Corn Is Green* (1942). She won an Academy Award for *None but the Lonely Heart* (1944). John, known as the "Great Profile," made his stage debut at 11 in *Magda.* After a long and successful stage career that covered modern and classical roles, he went to Hollywood where he starred in *Beau Brummel* (1924), *Don Juan* (1926), *Grand Hotel* (1932), and *Dinner at Eight* (1933). The three Barrymore children co-starred in *Rasputin and the Empress* (1932).

Barter, exchange of one good or service for another without the benefit of money as a medium of exchange. A barter agreement among countries calls for exchange of stated amounts of goods.

Bartered Bride, The (1866), 3-act comic opera with orchestral overture and folk dances, by Bedřich Smetana, Czech libretto by Karel Sabina. First produced as an operetta with dialogue, it was later enlarged. Bohemian villagers Hans and Wenzel (tenors) and Marie (soprano) contend with their families and the comic marriage broker Kezal (bass). The first important Bohemian opera, it is the foundation on which Bohemian national music rests. It established Smetana as the first "national" Bohemian composer.

Barth, Heinrich. △1268.

Barth, John (1930–), US author, b. Cambridge, Md. A professor of English, he has written several novels. His works are complex and imaginative. They include *The End of the Road* (1958), *The Sot-Weed Factor* (1960), *Giles Goat-Boy* (1966), and *Chimera* (1972), three novellas for which Barth won the 1973 National Book Award in fiction.

Barn owl

P.T. Barnum

Barracuda

Ethel and John Barrymore

Barth, Karl (1886–1968), Swiss theologian. A leading thinker of 20th-century Protestantism, he tried to lead theology back to principles of the Reformation and to emphasize the revelation of God through Jesus Christ. His school has been called dialectical theology or theology of the word. In 1935 he was deported from Germany for his anti-Nazi stance. His works include *Epistle to the Romans* (1918) and the four-volume *Church Dogmatics* (1932–62).

Barthé, Richmond (1901–), US sculptor, b. St. Louis. He studied at the Art Institute of Chicago and received many honors for his work, which includes "West Indian Girl," "Toussaint L'Ouverture," and "Head of a Tortured Negro."

Bartholdi, Frédéric Auguste (1834–1904), French sculptor. He is well known for the Statue of Liberty in New York Harbor, dedicated in 1886. His best work is the "Lion of Belfort" in Belfort, France.

Bartholomew, according to the New Testament, one of the 12 apostles of Christ. It has been conjectured that he might be identical with Nathanael.

Bartlesville, city in NE Oklahoma, 40mi (64km) N of Tulsa on Caney River; seat of Washington co; site of Bartlesville Wesleyan College (1910), and oil and natural gas wells. Industries: oil refining, smelting. Founded 1877; inc. 1897. Pop. (1970) 29,683.

Bartlett, Josiah (1729–95), American patriot and a signer of the Declaration of Independence, b. Amesbury, Mass. After a successful medical practice, he served variously as chief justice of the New Hampshire superior court (1788–90), chief executive of the state, and then governor (1793–94).

Bartlett, Neil. △1558.

Bartók, Béla (1881–1945), Hungarian composer. With Zoltán Kodály, Bartok amassed a definitive collection of Hungarian folk music that became the basis of many of his compositions. His early works exhibited a preference for dissonance and avoided sentimentality. Later works display more attention to melody and a mastery of orchestration. His orchestral works contain a number of masterpieces including *Music for Strings, Percussion, and Celesta* (1936), *Violin Concerto No. 2* (1938), and *Concerto for Orchestra* (1943). His six string quartets have been regarded as the finest since Beethoven. He was also a piano virtuoso and composed many piano pieces, including *Mikrokosmos*, a six-volume set of progressive piano pieces. *See also* Kodály, Zoltán. △1364.

Bartolommeo, Fra (1475–1517), Italian painter, b. Bartolommeo di Pagolo del Fattorino. Painting religious subjects in a conservative style, he continued to work in the High Renaissance style after Mannerism had come into its own. His important works include *Jonah* and *Isaiah*, both in the Uffizi, Florence. *See also* Renaissance Art.

Barton, Benjamin Smith (1766–1815), US naturalist, b. Lancaster, Pa. He authored many important books on botany, including *Elements of Botany* (1803), the first US textbook on botany.

Barton, Clara (Clarissa Harlowe) (1821–1912), US educator and humanitarian, b. Oxford, Mass. She taught school (1836–54) before establishing a very successful free school in New Jersey. During the Civil War she traveled with the Union Army to nurse the wounded, provide supplies, and search for the missing. She went abroad (1869) to do similar work in the Franco-Prussian War with the International Red Cross. When she returned to the United States, she founded the American National Red Cross (1881) and campaigned for US ratification of the Geneva Convention (1882). She was responsible for the "American Amendment" at the Geneva Convention (1884), which provided for the Red Cross to be active in peacetime emergency work, such as natural disasters.

Bartram, John (1699–1777), colonial American botanist, b. Darby, Pa. The first in North America to hybridize flowering plants, Bartram traveled the American colonies extensively, often with his son William, collecting plant specimens. He established botanical gardens near Philadelphia that were internationally famous.

Baruch, the personal scribe used by the biblical prophet Jeremiah in transcribing his first and second scrolls. Baruch went into hiding with Jeremiah after the prophesies were read to Jehoiakim, king of Judah, who burned them. God ordered the scrolls rewritten. His name was given to the Book of Baruch.

Baruch, Bernard Mannes (1870–1965), US financier and government adviser, b. Camden, S.C. A securities expert and speculator, he became a millionaire before age 30. As chairman of the War Industries Board (1918–19), he exercised great power over the US economy. He was an economic adviser at the Versailles Conference after WWI and to all US presidents until his death. As US representative to the United Nations Atomic Energy Commission, he presented a plan for international control of atomic energy (1946) that was vetoed by the USSR.

Baryon, member of a subgroup of hadrons, all of which have half-integral spin. They include the proton and neutron (nucleons) and the long-lived hyperons. A quantum number, the baryon number, may be assigned as +1 for baryons, −1 for antibaryons, and 0 for mesons. In any nuclear reaction the baryon number must remain constant: baryons cannot be created or destroyed except in pairs of baryons and antibaryons. *See also* Hadron; Meson; Quark.

Baryshnikov, Mikhail (1948–), international ballet dancer. He was a member of the Kirov Ballet in Leningrad from 1967 until he defected from the USSR in 1974. He has toured Australia and Europe and frequently performs with the American Ballet Theatre.

Basalt, hard, fine-grained igneous rock, which may be intrusive or extrusive. The most common rock found in volcanic lava, its color can be dark green, brown, dark gray, or black. Its composition is chiefly plagioclase, feldspar, and pyroxene, and it often has a glassy appearance. *See also* Igneous Rocks; Plagioclase. △228,246.

Base, chemical compound that can react with an acid to form a salt (and water). Most bases are oxides or hydroxides of metals or are compounds, such as ammonia, that yield hydroxide ions in water. Soluble bases are also called alkalis. Bases give solutions that contain hydroxide ions (OH^-) and give a blue color to litmus paper. Strong bases, such as caustic soda (NaOH), are fully dissociated into ions; weak bases, such as ammonia (NH_3), are partially dissociated in solution. *See also* Acid.

Base (geometric), side opposite the vertex of a triangle from which an altitude is drawn. The area of a triangle is one half the product of the base and the height. *See also* Triangle. △1448, 1464.

Baseball, sport popular in the United States (where it is the national game), Japan, the Caribbean, and Latin America. The top US professional teams are divided into the American and National Leagues. It is played by two opposing teams of nine players each—a pitcher, catcher, four infielders, and three outfielders.

Rules. Except for a 1973 American League ruling that allows a designated hitter to bat for the pitcher without having to play the field, players may not return to the game once they are replaced. There are usually four umpires in a game who rule on all aspects of play. A regulation game is divided into nine innings; each team having three outs in an inning and runs being scored each time a player completes a circuit of four bases. Games tied at the end of nine innings are played until there is a winner, except for curfew limits or rain delays, in which case the game, from the point it ended, is rescheduled. The home team always bats last, except if it is leading after the visitors have completed their half of the ninth inning, in which case it has won the game, and there is no need to bat. In the United States, the two leagues are the American and National. The American League of 14 teams is composed of the Baltimore Orioles, Boston Red Sox, California Angels, Chicago White Sox, Cleveland Indians, Detroit Tigers, Oakland Athletics, Kansas City Royals, Minnesota Twins, Milwaukee Brewers, New York Yankees, Seattle Mariners, Texas Rangers, and Toronto Bluejays. The National League of 12 teams is composed of the Atlanta Braves, Chicago Cubs, Cincinnati Reds, Houston Astros, Los Angeles Dodgers, Montreal Expos, New York Mets, Philadelphia Phillies, Pittsburgh Pirates, St. Louis Cardinals, San Diego Padres, and San Francisco Giants. The teams in each league are divided into two divisions. Each team plays a 162-game schedule, and the winner of each division competes in a best-three-out-of-five playoff series. The winners then compete in a World Series (held annually since 1905), a best-four-out-of-seven series, to decide the champion.

History. Baseball is believed to have its roots in the English game of rounders, played in the 19th century. Although credit is given to Abner Doubleday for inventing baseball in Cooperstown, N.Y. (the site of the Baseball Hall of Fame), in 1839, the claim is refuted by some authorities. In 1846, Alexander J. Cartwright, a surveyor, established a set of rules and the guidelines to the playing field, which included having the bases 90 feet (27.4m) apart. The game was further enhanced by a set of playing rules written in 1858 by Henry Chadwick.

After the Civil War, when the game was popular with Union soldiers, the first professional team, the Cincinnati Red Stockings, began playing in 1869. Their success led to the formation of the first professional league, the National Association, which began in 1871 and gave way to the National League in 1876. Other professional leagues were formed, but none survived except for the American League, which began play as a major league in 1901.

WORLD SERIES WINNERS

Year	Winner	Games Won	Games Lost
1903*	Boston (AL)	5	3
1905	New York (NL)	4	1
1906	Chicago (AL)	4	2
1907	Chicago (NL)	4	0
1908	Chicago (NL)	4	1
1909	Pittsburgh (NL)	4	3
1910	Philadelphia (AL)	4	1
1911	Philadelphia (AL)	4	2
1912	Boston (AL)	4	3
1913	Philadelphia (AL)	4	1
1914	Boston (NL)	4	0
1915	Boston (AL)	4	1
1916	Boston (AL)	4	1
1917	Chicago (AL)	4	2
1918	Boston (AL)	4	2
1919*	Cincinnati (NL)	5	3
1920*	Cleveland (AL)	5	2
1921*	New York (NL)	5	3
1922	New York (NL)	4	0
1923	New York (AL)	4	2
1924	Washington (AL)	4	3
1925	Pittsburgh (NL)	4	3
1926	St. Louis (NL)	4	3
1927	New York (AL)	4	0
1928	New York (AL)	4	0
1929	Philadelphia (AL)	4	1
1930	Philadelphia (AL)	4	2
1931	St. Louis (NL)	4	3
1932	New York (AL)	4	0
1933	New York (NL)	4	1
1934	St. Louis (NL)	4	3
1935	Detroit (AL)	4	2
1936	New York (AL)	4	2
1937	New York (AL)	4	1
1938	New York (AL)	4	0
1939	New York (AL)	4	0
1940	Cincinnati (NL)	4	3
1941	New York (AL)	4	1
1942	St. Louis (NL)	4	1
1943	New York (AL)	4	1
1944	St. Louis (NL)	4	2
1945	Detroit (AL)	4	3
1946	St. Louis (NL)	4	3
1947	New York (AL)	4	3
1948	Cleveland (AL)	4	2
1949	New York (AL)	4	1
1950	New York (AL)	4	0
1951	New York (AL)	4	2
1952	New York (AL)	4	3
1953	New York (AL)	4	2
1954	New York (NL)	4	0
1955	Brooklyn (NL)	4	3
1956	New York (AL)	4	3
1957	Milwaukee (NL)	4	3
1958	New York (AL)	4	3
1959	Los Angeles (NL)	4	2
1960	Pittsburgh (NL)	4	3
1961	New York (AL)	4	1
1962	New York (AL)	4	3
1963	Los Angeles (NL)	4	0
1964	St. Louis (NL)	4	3
1965	Los Angeles (NL)	4	3
1966	Baltimore (AL)	4	0
1967	St. Louis (NL)	4	3
1968	Detroit (AL)	4	3
1969	New York (NL)	4	1
1970	Baltimore (AL)	4	1
1971	Pittsburgh (NL)	4	3
1972	Oakland (AL)	4	3
1973	Oakland (AL)	4	3
1974	Oakland (AL)	4	1
1975	Cincinnati (NL)	4	3
1976	Cincinnati (NL)	4	0

*nine-game World Series

BASEBALL HALL OF FAME

1936
Tyrus R. Cobb
Walter P. Johnson
Christopher Mathewson
George H. (Babe) Ruth
John P. (Honus) Wagner

1937
Morgan G. Bulkely

Byron B. (Ban) Johnson
Napoleon (Larry) Lajoie
Cornelius McGillicuddy (Connie Mack)
John J. McGraw
Tristram E. Speaker
George Wright
Denton T. (Cy) Young
1938
Grover C. Alexander
Alexander J. Cartwright, Jr.
Henry Chadwick
1939
Adrian C. (Cap) Anson
Charles A. Comisky
Edward T. Collins
William A. Cummings
William B. Ewing
Henry L. (Lou) Gehrig
William H. Keeler
Charles (Hoss) Radbourne
George H. Sisler
Albert G. Spalding
1942
Rogers Hornsby
1944
Kenesaw M. Landis
1945
Roger P. Bresnahan
Dennis Brouthers
Frederick C. Clarke
James J. Collins
Edward J. Delahanty
Hugh Duffy
Hugh A. Jennings
Michael J. Kelly
James H. O'Rourke
Wilbert Robinson
1946
Jesse C. Burkett
Frank L. Chance
John D. Chesbro
John J. Evers
Clark C. Griffith
Thomas F. McCarthy
Joseph J. McGinnity
Edward S. Plank
Joseph B. Tinker
George E. (Rube) Waddell
Edward A. Walsh
1947
Gordon S. (Mickey) Cochrane
Frank F. Frisch
Robert M. (Lefty) Grove
Carl O. Hubbell
1948
Herbert J. Pennock
Harold J. (Pie) Traynor
1949
Mordecai P. Brown
Charles L. Gehringer
Charles A. Nichols
1951
James E. Foxx
Melvin T. Ott
1952
Harry E. Heilmann
Paul G. Waner
1953
Edward G. Barrow
Charles A. (Chief) Bender
Thomas H. Connolly
Jay Hanna (Dizzy) Dean
William J. Klem
Aloysius H. Simmons
Rhoderick J. (Bobby) Wallace
William H. (Harry) Wright
1954
William M. Dickey
Walter J. Maranville
William H. Terry
1955
Joseph P. DiMaggio
Charles L. (Gabby) Hartnett
Theodore A. Lyons
Arthur C. (Dazzy) Vance
1956
Joseph E. Cronin
Henry B. Greenberg
1957
Samuel E. Crawford
Joseph V. McCarthy
1959
Zachariah D. Wheat
1961
Max G. Carey
William R. Hamilton
1962
Robert W. A. Feller
William B. McKechnie
Jack R. Robinson
Edd J. Roush
1963
John Clarkson
Elmer Flick
Samuel Rice
Eppa Jeptho Rixey
1964
Lucius (Luke) Appling
Urban (Red) Faber
Burleigh Grimes
Timothy Keefe
Henry (Heinie) Manush
John Montgomery Ward
Miller Huggins
1965
James F. Pud Galvin
1966
Charles D. (Casey) Stengel
Theodore (Ted) Williams
1967
Branch Rickey
Charles (Red) Ruffing
Lloyd Waner
1968
Hazen (Kiki) Cuyler
Leon (Goose) Goslin
Joe (Ducky) Medwick
1969
Roy Campanella
Stan Coveleski
Waite Hoyt
Stan (The Man) Musial
1970
Lou Boudreau
Earle Combs
Ford F. Frick
Jesse Haines
1971
David (Beauty) Bancroft
Jacob (Eagle Eye) Beckley
Charles (Chick) Hafey
Harry B. Hooper
Joseph J. Kelley
Richard (Rube) Marquard
Leroy (Satchel) Paige
George Weiss
1972
Lawrence (Yogi) Berra
Vernon (Lefty) Gomez
Will Harridge
Sanford (Sandy) Koufax
Early (Gus) Wynn
Ross (Pep) Youngs
1973
Roberto Walker Clemente
William G. (Billy) Evans
Monfred (Monte) Irvin
George Lange Kelly
Warren Edward Spahn
Michael F. (Mickey) Welch
1974
James (Cool Papa) Bell
James L. (Sunny Jim) Bottomley
John (Jocko) Conlan
Edward C. (Whitey) Ford
Mickey Charles Mantle
Samuel L. Thompson
1975
Howard Earl Averill
Stanley Raymond Harris
William Jennings (Billy) Herman
Ralph McPherran Kiner
William Julius Johnson
1976
Oscar Charleston
Roger Connor
Cal Hubbard
Bob Lemon
Fred Lindstrom
Robin Roberts

Basel (Bâle, or **Basle),** city in NW Switzerland, on the Rhine River; capital of Basel canton; joined the Swiss Confederation 1501; site of cathedral where Erasmus is buried, medieval gates, 16th-century town hall, 15th-century university, and annual Swiss Industries Fair. Industries: publishing, silk textiles, food produce, metal goods. Pop. 212,857.

Basel, Council of, Roman Catholic Church council convoked at Basel in 1431. It instituted church reforms and conciliated the Hussites in Bohemia. Conflict with Pope Eugene IV over conciliar authority led the pope to denounce the council in 1437. In 1439, the council declared Eugene deposed and chose an antipope, Amadeus of Savoy, as Pope Felix V. Felix resigned in 1449 and the council was dissolved.

Basement Rock. △276.

Basenji, ancient, deerlike, barkless hunting dog (hound group) originating in central Africa. It has a flat

Clara Barton

Bernard Baruch

Baseball

Basel, Switzerland

head with rounded muzzle and wrinkled forehead; small, pointed erect ears; and almond-shaped eyes. The short body is deep-chested; legs are long and strong; and the high-set tail is curled tightly over to the side. Its short, silky coat can be chestnut red, black, or tan. Feet, chest, and tip of tail are white. Average size: 17in (43cm) high at shoulder; 24lb (11kg). *See also* Hound.

Basho, Matsuo (1644–94), Japanese poet. He was responsible for the development and popularity of the three-line haiku poem. Influenced by Buddhism, his poems used the speech of commoners. *The Narrow Road of Oku* (1689) was his final work. *See also* Haiku.

Basic English, a simplified form of English developed between 1925 and 1930 by the British scholar Charles Kay Ogden. Its vocabulary consists of only 850 words, of which 600 are nouns, 150 are adjectives, and only 18 are verbs. It is simple to learn, yet at the same time adequate for conveying information and ideas.

Basie, Count (1904–), US jazz bandleader, pianist, and composer, b. William Bassie in Red Bank, N.J. He played with bands in the 1920s and 30s, forming his own in 1935. His band made a steady ascent through the 1960s to the heights of popularity and made numerous recordings. Many of Basie's compositions, including *One O'Clock Jump,* have been played by other jazz musicians. Basie also played with Benny Goodman's sextet, and appeared many times on the radio and in films.

Basil, common name for *Ocimum basilicum,* an annual of the tropics. An aromatic herb of the mint family with white or purple flowers, its dried leaves are used for seasoning. △358.

Basil I, Byzantine emperor (*r.* 867–86) and founder of the Macedonian dynasty. The son of a provincial peasant, Basil was befriended by Emperor Michael III, who assisted him in his rise to power. After Michael designated him as co-emperor, Basil had his former patron murdered and assumed sole power in Byzantium. Basil's most effective policies concerned the conversion of the Bulgars to Orthodox Christianity rather than to Roman Catholicism; military campaigns against the Paulician religious sect in Asia Minor; and an attempted revision of Roman legal codes.

Basil II (958?–1025), Byzantine emperor (976–1025), surnamed Bulgaroctonus ("Bulgar-slayer"). One of Byzantium's ablest rulers, Basil presided over the apogee of the empire. He is best known for his military victory over the Bulgarian tsar Samuel in 1014, which brought the entire Balkan peninsula under Byzantine control. During Basil's reign, the empire's sphere of influence was further enlarged by the conversion of Kievan Russia to Orthodox Christianity. △1056.

Basilar Membrane. △676.

Basilica, Roman, long halls used as commercial markets and courtrooms, related in plan to the Greek temple. Basilicas were typically rectangular, with colonnades and one or more apses. The earliest examples date from the 2nd century BC and were next to the Forum.

Basilica Church, the earliest type of Christian church, first erected *c.* 312 AD under Constantine. A long colonnaded hall, with altar at the east end and entrance at the west, was characteristic. Plain exteriors contrasted with richly decorated interiors. △1060.

Basilisk, semi-aquatic lizard found in trees near streams of tropical America. It has a compressed greenish body, whiplike tail, crest on its back, and an inflatable pouch on its head. It can run over water in a two-legged fashion, and eats plants and insects. Length: to 20in (51cm). Family Iguanidae; genus *Basiliscus.* △520.

Basin, Oceanic, one of two major provinces of the deep ocean floor, lying at over 2km (1.2mi) in depth. The mid-ocean ridges is the other province. Together they constitute 56% of the earth's surface. The deep ocean basin is underlain by a thin crust, about 7km (4.3mi) thick, and is covered by thin sediment and dotted by low abyssal hills. △250.

Basketball, fast-action ball game, most popular in the United States, where it is played professionally. It is also played extensively in Europe, Latin America, and Asia. It is played by two teams of five persons each, usually indoors, on a court a maximum of 94 feet (28.7m) in length and 50 feet (15.2m) in width. At each end of the court is a backboard to which a metal ring is attached, 18 inches (45.7cm) in diameter and 10 feet (3m) above the floor. Bottomless netting is usually attached to the rim. The five players consists of two guards, two forwards, and a center, with free substitution permitted.

Rules. Players may pass, dribble, roll, or throw the ball, but may not run with it. The object is to advance the ball to the team's own basket and attempt to score by shooting the ball through the top of the basket. Each field goal counts two points, and free throws (shots taken as the result of penalties) count as one point. Professionals, who play four 12-minute quarters, are allowed to commit six fouls before being eliminated from a game. Collegians, who play two 20-minute halves, are allowed five fouls. If a contest ends in a tie, five-minute quarters are played until the deadlock is broken.

History. Basketball was invented in 1891 by Dr. James Naismith, a physical education instructor at the YMCA college in Springfield, Mass. Professional basketball began in 1896 in New York City, but did not reach its popularity as a spectator sport until 1954, when the game was greatly enhanced by the "24-second rule" (professional only), requiring that a team shoot within 24 seconds or lose possession of the ball. The most popular major basketball league today is the National Basketball Association, which began in 1949 with the merger of the National Basketball League and the Basketball Association of America. Another major league, the American Basketball Association, was formed in 1961. Four of its teams were incorporated into the NBA in 1976, and the rest disbanded. The game is a major sport at colleges and high schools in the United States. The most popular of all post-season collegiate tournaments is the National Collegiate Athletic Association championships, begun in 1939. The sport has been a part of the Olympic Games since 1936. △930.

BASKETBALL HALL OF FAME

Teams

First Team	1959
Original Celtics	1959
Buffalo Germans	1961
Renaissance	1963

Coaches, Players, Contributors

1959
Allen, Dr. F.C. (Phog)
Carlson, Dr. H. Clifford
Gulick, Dr. Luther H.
Hickox, Edward J.
Hyatt, Charles
Kennedy, Matthew P.
Luisetti, Angelo (Hank)
Meanwell, Dr. Walter
Mikan, George L.
Morgan, Ralph
Naismith, Dr. James
Olsen, Harold G.
Schommer, John J.
Stagg, Amos Alonzo
Tower, Oswald

1960
Blood, Ernest A.
Hanson, Victor
Hepbron, George T.
Kearney, Frank W.
Lambert, Ward L.
McCracken, Branch
Macaulay, C. Edward
Murphy, Charles (Stretch)
Porter, H. V.
Wooden, John

1961
Borgmann, Bennie
DeBernardi, Forrest S.
Hoyt, George
Keogan, George E.
Kurland, Robert
O'Brien, John J.
Phillip, Andy
Quigley, Ernest C.
Roosma, Col. John S.
Sachs, Leonard
Schabinger, Arthur A.
Steinmetz, Christian
Toby, David
Trester, Arthur L.
Wachter, Edward A.
Walsh, David

1962
McCracken, Jack
Morgenweck, Frank
Page, H.O.
Reid, William A.
Sedran, Barney
St. John, Lynn W.
Thompson, John A. (Cat)

1963
Gruenig, Robert (Ace)

1964
Bunn, John W.
Foster, Harold (Bud)
Holman, Nat
Irish, Ned
Jones, R. Williams
Loeffler, Kenneth D.
Russell, John (Honey)

1965
Brown, Walter A.
Hinckle, Paul D. (Tony)
Hobson, Howard
Mokray, William G.

1966
Dean, Everett S.
Lapchick, Joe

1967
Bee, Clair F.
Cann, Howard G.
Gill, Amory T. (Slats)
Julian, Alvin F. (Doggie)

1968
Auerbach, Arnold J. (Red)
Dehnert, Henry G. (Dutch)
Iba, Henry P. (Hank)
Rupp, Adolph F.
Taylor, Charles H. (Chuck)

1969
Carnevale, Ben
Davies, Robert

1970
Cousy, Robert J.
Pettit, Robert L.
Saperstein, Abe

1971
Diddle, Edgar A.
Douglas, Robert L.
Endacott, Paul
Friedman, Max (Marty)
Gottlieb, Edward
Wells, Clifford

1972
Beckman, John
Drake, Bruce
Lonborg, Arthur C. (Dutch)
Ripley, Elmer H.
Schayes, Adolph
Wooden, John R.

1973
Fisher, Harry A.
Podoloff, Maurice
Schmidt, Ernest J.

1974
Brennan, Joseph
Liston, Emil S.
Russell, William (Bill)
Vandivier, Robert (Fuzzy)

1975
Gola, Tom
Krause, Edward (Moose)
Litwack, Harry
Sharman, Bill

NBA CHAMPIONS

1947	Philadelphia
1948	Baltimore
1949	Minneapolis
1950	Minneapolis
1951	Rochester
1952	Minneapolis
1953	Minneapolis
1954	Minneapolis
1955	Syracuse
1956	Philadelphia
1957	Boston
1958	St. Louis
1959	Boston
1960	Boston
1961	Boston
1962	Boston
1963	Boston
1964	Boston
1965	Boston
1966	Boston
1967	Philadelphia
1968	Boston
1969	Boston
1970	New York
1971	Milwaukee
1972	Los Angeles
1973	New York
1974	Boston
1975	Golden State
1976	Boston

Basket Plant, small, colorful, trailing plant in hanging container. Used indoors and outdoors, the usual container is a wire basket lined with sphagnum moss, filled with soil, and planted with plants such as ivy or fuchsia. Outdoor baskets, containing plants such as creeping juniper, should be set on the ground and mulched in winter. Basket plants dry out faster than other potted plants and must be watered frequently.

Basket Star. △504.

Basking Shark. △626.

Basques, people inhabiting N Spain and SW France in the W foothills of the Pyrenees, numbering approximately 900,000. They are of unknown origin, and their language has no known relationship with any other language. Traditionally farmers, shipbuilders, and sailors, they possess a fierce independence which has led to several bloody clashes with the Spanish government. △866.

Basra (Al-Basrah), port city in Iraq, on the Shatt al-Arab River; capital of Basra prov: second in importance to Baghdad during Abbasid dynasty (750–1258); destroyed by Mongols 13th century and rebuilt 8mi (13km) from original site. Under Ottoman Empire (17th century), it was opened as a port to European traders; harbor was renovated by British in WWI and used as a supply route to Russia during WWII. Industries: oil, grains. Exports: dates. Founded 638. Pop. 313,327.

Bass, Sam (1851–78), US bandit, b. Indiana. He went to Texas when he was 17 and led a band of bank and train robbers but was considered a "good" badman because he was supposed to have given so much of his loot to worthy poor people. One of his own men betrayed him to the Texas Rangers, and he was killed at Round Rock in a shootout. There are songs and stories about his generosity and a legend of his buried treasure. He is known as the Robin Hood of Texas.

Bass, marine and freshwater food and game fish. The marine striped bass *(Roccus saxatilis)* is found along the Atlantic coast of North America and is a major game fish. Length: 6ft (183cm); weight: 125lb (56kg). Smallmouth bass *(Micropterus dolomieu)* and largemouth bass *(Micropterus salmoides)* are found in North American fresh waters. Weight: 12–25lb (5–11kg). The black bass *(Centropristis striatus)* is a valuable food fish. Length: to 2ft (61cm); weight: 8lb (3.5kg). Another marine bass, the channel bass or red drum *(Sciaenops ocellata)*, is an important food and game fish of the American Atlantic. Length: 5ft (152.4cm); weight: 75lb (34kg). Order Perciformes.

Bassano, Jacopo (*c.* 1517–92), Italian painter, b. Jacopo da Ponte. Of the late Renaissance Venetian school, he primarily adopted the styles of other artists. After 1540 he was heavily influenced by the Florentine and Roman Mannerists. His work, extensive and varied, included religious subjects, landscapes, and scenes of daily life. Notable works include *Flight into Egypt* (1536) and *Adoration of the Shepherds* (1568). *See also* Renaissance Art.

Bass Clarinet, woodwind musical instrument (sometimes metal) ranging 3 octaves, one below the B*b* clarinet. It has a single-reed mouthpiece bent horizontally and a bell bent upward. It is used in symphony orchestras. *See also* Clarinet.

Basse Dance, court dance that originated in Italy during the 14th century. Usually the first dance performed at a ball, it was comprised of small, gliding steps performed in a long column by couples holding hands. It was replaced by the pavane around 1650.

Basse-taille. △1608.

Basse Terre, town in British West Indies, on St Kitts Island in Leeward Islands group; capital of St Kitts-Nevis; commercial center. Founded 1627. Pop. 14,-133.

Basse-Terre, seaport town in French West Indies; capital of French dept. of Guadeloupe; important import-export center serving surrounding agricultural region. Founded 1643. Pop. 15,458.

Basset Horn, musical instrument resembling a bass clarinet without the horizontal mouthpiece. It was used by Mozart in *The Magic Flute* and *The Marriage of Figaro* and by Richard Strauss in *Salome* and *Electra*. It is usually replaced today by the alto clarinet. *See also* Bass Clarinet; Clarinet.

Basset Hound, hunting dog (hound group) originating in France several centuries ago. It has a large, domed head; deep, heavy muzzle; hanging lips; and dewlaps. The low-set, very long ears hang in folds; eyes are sad. A long, level body is set on short, heavy-boned legs; the long tail is carried up. Coat is hard and short; colors are white, tan, and black. Skin is loose and elastic. Average size: 12–15in (30–38cm) high at shoulder; 25–50lb (11–23kg). The basset is used for trailing game by scent over rough terrain. *See also* Hound.

Bassoon, main bass instrument of symphony orchestra woodwinds, with a range of 3 octaves corresponding to the cello. It has a double-reed mouthpiece and a conical bore, the tube bending back on itself to reduce length. Bassoons are used extensively in modern symphonic and chamber music. △1244.

Bass Strait, channel in SE Australia connecting the Indian Ocean and the Tasman Sea; Melbourne is on its NW coast; important fishing industry. Discovered by George Bass (1798). Length: 185mi (266km). Width: 80–150mi (129–241km).

Basswood. *See* Linden.

Bast, also Bastet and Pasht, ancient Egyptian goddess of the city of Bubastis, depicted as a lion-headed woman crowned with the solar disk and sacred asp, or as a cat-headed goddess with the sistrum, or ritual rattle. In the latter form she is Pasht, the personification of life and fecundity. Two festivals were held in her honor, one at Bubastis and the second and lesser at Memphis.

Bastille, 14th-century fort and prison in Paris. Because political prisoners were traditionally incarcerated there, it became a symbol of royal oppression. On July 14, 1789, a Parisian mob stormed it, captured the ammunition stored there, and released its prisoners (only seven, none of them political). Its governor was killed, its troops surrendered, and the fort was destroyed. This action marked the beginning of the French Revolution, and its anniversary (July 14) is celebrated as the major French holiday. △1224.

Bastion Fort. △1732.

Bastogne, town in SE Belgium, 23mi (37km) N of Arlon; held by US troops during the Battle of the Bulge (1944) when Germans were driven back (1945); highway and railroad junction. Pop. 6,694.

Basutoland. *See* Lesotho.

Bat, only mammal that can fly rather than glide. Bats are nocturnal and found in all tropical and temperate regions. Most are brown, gray, or black. The bat's wing is formed by a sheet of skin stretched over a frame of greatly elongated "arm" and "hand" bones. Bats are able to fly and hunt in complete darkness by a kind of sonar, which uses echoes of the bat's own supersonic squeaks to locate obstacles and prey. Many bats live largely on insects, some are carnivorous, some live on flower nectar and pollen, and one group—the flying foxes—subsists on fruit. They are generally small, ranging in length from 0.75–15in (2–38cm). The 178 genera of bats make up the order Chiroptera. △546.

Bataan, province of the Philippines, on peninsula of Luzon Island, extending S from W central coast, shielding Manila Bay from South China Sea. Densely forested on W side, population is concentrated along E bay; scene of heavy fighting during WWII between American-Philippine forces and Japanese forces. Crops: rice, sugar cane. Pop. 214,131.

Batan (Batanese Islands), island group between Luzon Island, Philippines, and Formosa Island; the northernmost prov. of the Philippines, is comprised mainly of Zitberat, Y'ami, and Batan islands; capital is Basco, on Batan Island. Industries: sugar cane, rice, coal mining. Area: 80sq mi (207sq km). Pop. 11,425.

Batavi, or **Batavians,** Germanic tribe living in the Rhine-Meuse delta area of what is now Netherlands about the time of Christ. Noted as warriors, they served in the Roman army. About 70 AD, Claudius Civilis led them in an unsuccessful revolt against Roman rule. In the 4th century they were displaced by the Salian Franks.

Batavian Republic (1795–1806), name for the Netherlands after its conquest by the French. The principal accomplishment of the republic was the beginning of social and political modernization. In 1806 it became the Kingdom of Holland, ruled by Louis Bonaparte.

Bateson, William (1861–1926), English biologist. He founded and named the science of genetics. His experiments served as a foundation for the modern understanding of heredity. Bateson translated much of Gregor Mendel's pioneering work on plant mutation and was instrumental in bringing it recognition as

Basenji

Basilisk

Basketball

Basset hound

well as extending, through his own experiments, Mendel's theories to animals. △420.

Batfish, bottom-dwelling, marine angler fish of W Atlantic and E Pacific. Flat-bodied and scaleless, it has large armlike pectoral fins. Length: to 15in (38.1cm). Family Ogocephalidae; species 60, including short-nosed *Ogocephalus nasutus*. *See also* Anglerfish.

Bath, city in SW England, on the River Avon, 10mi (16km) SE of Bristol. Hot springs discovered here by Romans in 1st century have been used to treat rheumatism, arthritis, and gout. In the 18th century the city became a fashionable resort area, and appeared in much contemporary British literature; fine examples of Georgian architecture remain; site of homes of Admiral Nelson, William Pitt, Charles Dickens. Each June the Bath Festival features music, drama, sports. Industries: printing, electrical engineering, paint, tourism, soap. Chartered 1189. Pop. 84,760.

Batholith, huge mass of igneous material that reaches the earth's surface. A batholith is so considered if it has an exposed surface of about 40 sq mi (104 sq km). It may have been originally an intrusive igneous structure, which eventually became surface material as a result of erosion. △246.

Báthory, name of noble Hungarian family. Its most notable member was Stephen Báthory, king of Poland (1575–86), and a famous soldier. Stephen's brother Christoph succeeded him as prince of Transylvania (1576–81) and invited the Jesuits to give religious instruction in his domain. Christoph's son Sigismund (1572–1613) fought the Turks in 1588; abdicated in favor of Emperor Rudolf (1598) but later tried to regain his realm. Stephen's son, Gabriel, known for his cruelty, was driven from the country and murdered in 1613. Elizabeth, the last of the family (died 1614), is reputed to have murdered young girls so she could bathe in their blood. *See also* Stephen Báthory.

Baths, public bathing facilities. At first they were probably related to religious ritual. Baths existed in ancient Egypt and the Indus River Valley. The classical Greeks built elaborate public baths. These were copied and further embellished with mosaics and gilt details by the Romans. Water was brought by aqueduct from reservoirs and heated in pipes. The grandest Roman baths, now in ruin, were built by three emperors: Titus (80), Caracalla (212–35), and Diocletian (302). Even more richly designed baths were built later in Islamic nations, including the baths of the Alhambra in Granada, Spain, built in the 14th century. △1016.

Bathsheba, in the Bible, wife of Uriah the Hittite and, later, wife of David, who arranged Uriah's death in battle. Solomon was one of her sons by David.

Baths of Caracalla, Roman baths (thermae) built at Rome (211–17 AD). The huge enclosure included gardens, a stadium, and lecture rooms as well as the *tepidarium* (warm lounge), *caldarium* (hot room), and *frigidarium* (cooling room with open-air swimming pool). △1024.

Bathurst (Banjul), capital of the Republic of Gambia, W Africa, in W Gambia on St Mary's Island where Gambia River enters the Atlantic Ocean; port and economic center of Gambia. Industries: peanut processing, shipping of skins, hides, beeswax. Founded 1816 by British as a trading post. Pop. 36,570.

Bathymetric Chart, a map that shows the topography of the sea bottom. Contour lines connect all known and extrapolated points at the same depth below sea-level. Data are obtained by sounding techniques, especially echo sounding, sonar, and underwater television. *See also* Sonar.

Bathysphere. △238.

Bathythermograph, a record made by a device attached to a research platform and used to measure water temperatures at various depths. △236.

Batik, technique for decorating textiles by covering with molten wax the portions of a design that are to remain undyed, dyeing the exposed area, removing the wax, rewaxing, and redyeing. The process is repeated for each color desired. The technique was originally developed in Malaya.

Batista (y Zaldívar), Fulgenico (1901–73), Cuban political leader. A sergeant in the army, he led a successful coup in 1933. From then until 1940 he ruled through figurehead presidents. In 1940 he was elected president. He retired in 1944 and moved to Florida, where he had major investments. A 1952 military coup brought him back into power. His rule was ruthless; corruption was blatant and even the pretense of democratic institutions was dropped. In 1959 he was overthrown by Fidel Castro. Batista went into exile, living splendidly in Estoril, Portugal.

Bat Mitzvah. *See* Bar Mitzvah.

Baton Rouge, capital city of Louisiana, in SE central section, on the Mississippi River, 78mi (126km) WNW of New Orleans; seat of East Baton Rouge parish; farthest-inland deep water port on the Gulf of Mexico; ceded to Britain by France 1763, and to United States with Louisiana Purchase (1803); site of large petrochemical complex, Louisiana State University, and Southern University. Industries: natural gas, chemicals, plastics, wood products. Settled 1719; inc. 1817; became capital 1849. Pop. (1970) 165,963.

Battambang (Batdambang), town in W Cambodia; capital of Battambang prov.; ceded to Thailand by Cambodia 1809; to French Indo-China 1907; back to Cambodia 1946; market center in major rice-producing area. Pop. 38,846.

Battani, al-, Latin name Albategnius (*c.* 850–929), Arab astronomer and mathematician, well known throughout Europe in his own time. He corrected some of Ptolemy's observations, including that for the length of the year. *On Stellar Motion* was published in 1537.

Battenberg, German princely family. In the 19th century, the titles prince and princess of Battenberg were bestowed on the morganatic grandchildren of the grand duke of Hesse-Darmstadt. One of them, Louis Battenberg (1854–1921), became an English admiral, was created marquess of Milford Haven, and married a granddaughter of Queen Victoria. During World War I, the English branch of the Battenbergs anglicized the name to Mountbatten. Prince Philip, Duke of Edinburgh, is a Mountbatten.

Battery, a collection of cells that convert different types of energy, usually chemical, into direct current electrical energy. Primary batteries, such as those in a flashlight, cannot be re-charged, unlike storage batteries, which are re-charged when a current in the reverse direction restores the original chemical state. The lead and sulfuric acid battery, used in the automobile, is most common. △1542, 1566, 1794.

Battle Act (1951), legislation that stated that any nation shipping war materials to Soviet-dominated countries could lose US aid. This act reinforced the policies stated in the Truman Doctrine.

Battle Creek, city in S Michigan, 110mi (176km) W of Detroit, at the confluence of Kalamazoo and Battle Creek rivers; site of Dr. John H. Kellogg's Battle Creek Sanitarium (1866), now the Battle Creek Health Center; known for cereals and biscuits. Industries: farm equipment, valves, pumps. Settled 1831; inc. 1859. Pop. (1970) 38,931.

Battle of. . . . *See* second part of name.

Battleship, most powerful type of naval warship during the late 19th and early 20th centuries, displacing from 10,000 to over 75,000 tons. Battleships combined the thickest armor and the most powerful naval guns. In addition to their main armament, housed in huge armored turrets, most were armed with smaller batteries for combating lighter enemy warships, and, later, automatic weapons for protection against aircraft. During World War II the striking power of the battleship was surpassed by that of the aircraft carrier. The few surviving battleships are limited to amphibious support missions. *See also* Aircraft Carrier. △1740.

Batu Khan (died 1255), Mongol leader who defeated Russia in 1240 and also controlled Hungary, Poland, and Bohemia. His invasion was made easier by the lack of unity among the Russian rulers. He planned to invade Europe, but returned to the East to choose a successor to head the Mongol empire (1241). △1112.

Batumi (Batum), seaport city in SW Georgian SSR, USSR, on the Black Sea; capital of Adzhar ASSR; major port and trade center, near Turkish border; site of oil pipeline and Soviet naval base. City was site of ancient Greek colony of Batis; medieval hold of Georgia; possession of Turks 16th century–1878, when it was annexed to Russia. Industries: oil refining and shipping, food processing, engineering works. Pop. 101,000.

Bat Yam, city in W central Israel, on the Mediterranean Sea; suburb of Tel Aviv-Jaffa; industrial and tourist center. Industries: printing, publishing. Pop. 83,500.

Baudelaire, Charles (1821–67), French poet and critic, precursor of Symbolist poetry. He contributed to reviews and translated Edgar Allan Poe. Baudelaire was charged with obscenity on the publication of his volume of poetry *Les Fleurs du Mal* (1857). His critical works include *Curiosités esthétiques* (1868) and *L'Art Romantique* (1869). △1240.

Baudouin (1930–), king of Belgium (1951–). He succeeded his unpopular father, Leopold III, who abdicated in his favor. He granted independence to the Belgian Congo (1960) and encouraged the formation of the Common Market.

Baugh, Samuel Adrian ("Sammy") (1914–), US football player, b. Temple, Tex. He was a quarterback known for his accurate passes. He played for the Washington Redskins (1937–52) and led them to two National Football League championships (1937, 1942). He coached the New York Titans (1960–61) and the Houston Oilers (1964) in the American Football League. He was elected to the Football Hall of Fame in 1963.

Bauhaus, school for architects and artists founded at Weimar, Germany, in 1919 by Walter Gropius. Such diverse talents as Marcel Breuer, Paul Klee, Wassily Kandinsky, Lázló Moholy-Nagy, and Ludwig Mies van der Rohe worked together to produce a distinctly modern approach to design. The Bauhaus style emphasized craftsmanship and its architecture, in particular, was severely functional. The Bauhaus, which moved to Dessau in 1925, aroused opposition from the traditionalists, and it was closed by the Nazis in 1933. Most of its members moved to the United States, where Chicago became the center of the Bauhaus style. △1298, 1320.

Bauhin, Gaspard (1560–1624), Swiss anatomist and botanist. He gave a scientific binomial system of classification to anatomy and botany and was the first to describe the ileocecal valve (Bauhin's valve) between the large and small intestines.

Bauhinia, genus of evergreen shrubs, trees, and woody climbing vines, native to tropical and subtropical areas of the world. They are grown for their showy flowers and foliage. Family Leguminosae.

Baumgarten, Alexander Gottlieb (1714–62), German philosopher, considered a disciple of Christian Wolff. His ambitious system is now chiefly remembered for the *Aesthetica* (1739). Beauty, according to Baumgarten, involved the sensuous recognition of perfection. The word "aesthetics," in its modern use, was of his coinage. *See also* Aesthetics.

Bavaria (Bayern), largest state of West Germany; bounded by East Germany (N), Hesse and Baden-Württemberg (W), Austria (S), Czechoslovakia (E); Munich is the capital. Part of Roman Empire until 5th century; taken by Charlemagne 788; part of Holy Roman Empire 10th century; ruled by Wittelsbach family 1180–1918, who joined it to Second German Empire in 1871; became republic 1918; constitution was abolished 1933; came under W Germany as state of Bavaria 1946; agricultural region. Industries: tourism, glass, porcelain, Bavarian beer. Area: 27,239sq mi (70,549sq km). Pop. 10,603,200.

Bavarian Succession, War of the (1778–79), conflict between Austria and Prussia. Charles Theodore of the Palatinate, who succeeded Maximilian III Joseph as elector of Bavaria, ceded Lower Bavaria and part of the Palatinate to Austria. His heir, Charles of Zweibrücken, influenced by Frederick II of Prussia, protested the transfer. War was declared, but there were only a few skirmishes. By the Treaty of Teschen (1779) Austria renounced its claims to Bavaria, but retained the Innviertel, a small region on its border.

Bayamón, town in NE central Puerto Rico; first municipality in Puerto Rico to be settled; industrial and residential suburb of San Juan. Crops: coffee, tobacco, fruit, sugar. Founded 1772. Pop. (municipality) 154,440; (town) 146,363.

Bayberry, North American shrub with evergreen, aromatic leaves, naked flowers, and small fruits covered with a greenish-white wax used in making bayberry candles and perfumed soap. Height: to 35ft (11m). Family Myricaceae; species *Myrica cenifera*.

Bayazid. *See* Bajazet.

Bay City, city in E Michigan, 15mi (24km) N of Saginaw on the Saginaw River; seat of Bay co; noted for Indian relics; important shipping and marketing point for large agricultural area; port of entry, handling Great Lakes shipping. Founded 1836; inc. 1865. Pop. (1970) 49,449.

Bayeux Tapestry (11th–12th century), actually an embroidery, in the Bayeux Museum, Bayeux, France. Depicting in more than 70 scenes the Norman Conquest of England (1066), it is 230ft by 20in (70m by 51cm). Traditionally it is attributed to Queen Matilda, wife of William the Conqueror, but is probably of a somewhat later date. As well as a fine work of art, it is an important source of the costuming and military history of the time.

Bayle, Pierre (1647–1706), French philosopher. Forced into exile, he taught philosophy at Rotterdam (1680). He argued against superstition in *Thoughts on the Comet* (1682) and advocated toleration and Pyrrhonian skepticism in the erudite *Historical and Critical Dictionary* (1697–1706). The French Enlightenment claimed Bayle's critical approach to tradition as an inspiration. *See also* Enlightenment.

Baylor, Elgin (1934–), US basketball player, b. Washington, D.C. He played for Minneapolis (later Los Angeles) (1958–72) in the National Basketball Association and scored 23,149 points in his career as an outstanding forward.

Bay of Pigs Invasion (1961), an unsuccessful effort by Cuban exiles to overthrow Premier Fidel Castro by invading the south coast of Cuba near the Bay of Pigs. About 1500 Cubans, trained, equipped, and transported by the United States, were involved. President Kennedy, after an initial denial, accepted US responsibility for the invasion attempt. △1352.

Bayonne, port town in SW France, at confluence of Nive and Adour rivers, near Bay of Biscay. Taken by English in 1199; French since 1451. A citadel dating from 1633–1707 overlooks the harbor and city. Industries: shipbuilding, distilling, chocolates. Pop. 42,-743.

Bayonne, city in NE New Jersey, on a 3-mi (5-km) peninsula between New York Bay and Newark Bay; site of huge oil refineries (since 1875), US naval supply depot. Industries: chemicals, metal products, textiles, yacht building. First visited by Henry Hudson in 1609; settled by Dutch and English 1656; inc. 1869. Pop. (1970) 72,743.

Bayonne Decree (1808), order issued by Napoleon to seize all US ships in French-controlled ports. It was issued in the wake of the US embargo acts.

Bayou, a lake or sluggish stagnant stream, with an almost imperceptible current, that follows a winding course through alluvial lowlands, coastal swamps, marshes, or river deltas. The term is localized to the lower Mississippi River basin.

Bayreuth, city in S West Germany, 41mi (66km) NE of Nürnberg, on Roter Main River; belonged to branch of the Hohenzollern family (1248–1791); taken by Prussia 1791; ceded to Bavaria 1810; scene of annual Bayreuth Festival of Wagnerian music held in Festspielhaus (opera house designed by Wagner). Industries: textiles, metals, machinery. Founded 1194. Pop. 63,530.

Baytown, city in SE Texas, 22mi (35km) ESE of Houston; location of shipyard dating to Civil War. Industries: oil, rubber products, petrochemicals. Settled 1864. Pop. (1970) 43,980.

Bazaine, François Achille (1811–88), French military officer and marshal of France. He served in the Crimean War (1854–56) and in Mexico (1863). Created marshal in 1864, he commanded French troops in the Franco-Prussian War (1870–71). His incompetence led to the disaster at Sedan, in which Emperor Napoleon III and his army were captured. Convicted of treason in 1873—for intrigues with the Germans during the war—Bazaine escaped and lived thereafter in exile. *See also* Franco-Prussian War.

Bazille, Jean-Frédéric (1841–70), French painter. A patron and member of the Impressionists, he was influential to that movement's growth. He worked with Monet and Renoir and gained his first success with his *Family Reunion*, shown in the Paris Salon of 1868. He died in the Franco-Prussian War. *See also* Impressionism.

BCG, or **Bacillus Calmette-Guerin,** a vaccine against tuberculosis, named for its discoverers, the French bacteriologists Albert Calmette and Camille Guerin.

Beach, Rex (Ellingwood) (1877–1949), US novelist, b. Atwood, Mich. He is best known for *The Spoilers* (1906) and other adventure novels about the Klondike, many of which were made into films.

Beach, the gently sloping zone of the shore, covered by sediment, sand, or pebbles, that extends from the low-water line to the limit of highest storm waves. The sediment is derived from erosion or river alluvium. Waves washing on the beach move the sediment back and forth so the heavier pebbles remain on the beach and the sand works down into the water. △622.

Beach Flea, or sand hopper, semi-terrestrial amphipod crustacean that hides in burrows in wet sand or in seaweed. Its legs are modified for hopping. Length: to 1in (2.5cm). Family Talitudidae. △622.

Beach Grass, perennial grass found on sandy coasts of Europe, N Africa, and North America. It grows in tufts, has rolled, spikelike leaves, and long, cylindrical flower clusters. Because the tough underground stems spread, it is planted to combat beach erosion. Height: to 3ft (91cm). Family Gramineae; genus *Ammophila*. *See also* Grass.

Beacon, Aircraft, low frequency and medium frequency radio transmission. The location of the radio transmitter is indicated on navigation charts. A pilot is able to fly to the transmitter, or he can use it to determine his position by checking indications on his automatic direction finder. △1752.

Beaded Lizard. *See* Gila Monster.

Beadle, George Wells (1903–), US biologist, b. Wahoo, Nebr. Studying mutations in the bread mold *neurospora*, he and Edward Tatum found that genes are responsible for enzyme synthesis and that these enzymes control each step of all biochemical reactions occurring in an organism. For this discovery he shared the 1958 Nobel Prize in physiology or medicine.

Beagle, hunting dog (hound group) used in packs to chase and follow small game. Of ancient origin; modern breed dates from mid-19th-century England. One of the most popular breeds, it has a long, slightly domed head with a medium-length, square-cut muzzle. Low-set, hanging ears are long and broad; the wide-set, large eyes have a soft expression. A short-backed, muscular body is set on medium-length legs. The brush tail is carried up. The white, tan, and black coat is close and hard. Average size: two varieties—to 13in (33cm) high at shoulder; and over 13in but not over 15in (38cm); 20–40lb (9–18kg). *See also* Hound.

Beak, or bill, horny or stiff animal mouthparts that are projecting or pointed. Beaks are found among cephalopods, some insects, some fish, and all egg-laying mammals, turtles, and birds. Bird bills are adapted to many functions: grasping, preening, seed cracking, piercing, tearing, sieving, nectar-sipping, stabbing, and display. △528.

Beaked Whale, small to medium toothed whale with distinct beak. Ranging from solitary to gregarious, they make rapid deep dives for food fish and cephalopods. Length: 13–43 ft (4–13m). Family, Hyperoodontiade. *See also* Whale.

Beam Bridge. △1758.

Beam Trawls. △386.

Bean, Roy (*c.* 1825–1903), US frontier judge, b. Mason co, Ky. He went to California in 1847, then to Chihuahua, Mexico, where he ran a trading post. He was chased out of Mexico for cattle rustling. During the Civil War he joined a band of Confederate irregulars. After the war he followed the construction camps of the Southern Pacific Railroad, working as a saloonkeeper and a gambler. In 1882 he settled in Vinegaroon, Tex., which he had renamed Langtry after the English actress Lily Langtry. He had himself appointed justice of the peace and held court in his saloon. Known as the "only law West of the Pecos," he kept order in his court with his six-guns and dispensed harsh, bizarre, but often appropriate sentences.

Bean, plants grown for their edible seeds and seed pods, including broad, string, snap, kidney, and scarlet runner beans. The broad bean *(Vicia faba)* is native to Asia, and is grown mainly in Canada and Europe as fodder. The string bean *(Phaseolus vulgaris)* is native to tropical South America and is common in the United States. There are several varieties cultivated. Its long pod or kidney-shaped seeds are eaten as vegetables. *Phaseolus vulgaris humilis* is a bush type. Both types have varieties of yellow, green, or wax

Bath, England

Bathurst, Gambia

ET FVG

Bayeaux tapestry: detail

Beagle

pods. The scarlet runner *(Phaseolus coccineus)* has scarlet, rather than white or lilac, flowers and shorter, broader seeds. Family Leguminosae. *See also* Lima Bean; Soybean.

Bear, large, omnivorous, and nocturnal mammals with stocky bodies, thick coarse fur, and short tails. Bears are native to the Americas and Eurasia. The sun bear is the smallest, the Alaskan brown bear the largest. They have poor sight, fair hearing, and an excellent sense of smell. Except for the fish- and seal-eating polar bear, they eat a wide variety of plant and animal foods. They often kill their prey with a powerful blow by the forepaw. In cold regions, all except the polar bear spend most of the winter hibernating. Length: 4–10ft (1.2–3m); weight: 100–1715lb (45–780kg). Order Carnivora; family Ursidae; there are 6 species. △550.

Beardtongue. *See* Pentstemon.

Bear Flag Revolt (1846), uprising by US settlers in California. During the Mexican War, a group of US emigrants in Mexico's territory of California proclaimed the Republic of California at Sonoma in June and raised the "bear flag," which showed a grizzly bear facing a red star. The republic lasted until US troops arrived in July and replaced the bear flag with the American.

Bear Grass. *See* Camass.

Bearings, the supporting elements, usually of specially resistant metals, that permit connected members of machines to rotate or move in a straight line relative to one another without allowing them to separate in the direction in which the load is applied. To minimize friction, surfaces of bearings are generally lubricated. The surfaces may also be separated by balls confined to a race (ball bearings) or by rollers (roller bearings).

Béarn, historical region of SW France, in the Pyrenees; formerly part of Roman Aquitania; now part of Pyrénées-Atlantiques dept. In the 6th century Bearn was controlled by Gascony; it became a county in the 9th century. In 1290 Béarn passed to the count of Foix, who became king of Navarre; in 1484 it passed to the house of Albret. In 1620 Béarn was united with the French crown, administered by the parliament of Navarre. Main industry is cattle breeding.

Bear River, river in SE Idaho and N Utah; rises in the Uinta Mts in N Utah; flows N to Wyoming, turns NW to Idaho, bends S to Utah and empties into the Great Salt Lake. Length: approx. 350mi (564km).

Beat Generation, term referring to a group of US writers in the 1950s who rejected middle-class values and commercialism. Originally centered in New York, where many of them first met, the group included poets Allen Ginsberg, Gregory Corso, and Lawrence Ferlinghetti and novelists Jack Kerouac and William Burroughs. When Ferlinghetti moved to San Francisco, his City Lights Press became publisher to many of the Beat writers.

Beatification, act in the Roman Catholic Church by which the pope authorizes the public veneration of a deceased individual. It is a step toward canonization. The title "Blessed" is given.

Beatitudes, group of blessings spoken by Jesus at the opening of the Sermon on the Mount, as recorded most fully in Matthew 5:3–12.

Beatles. △1366.

Beauchamp, Pierre (1636–1705), French dancer at the Académie Royale de Musique, Paris. He is famous for naming the five positions of classic ballet (1700), which form the basis of ballet technique. △1194.

Beaufort, Henry (*c.* 1374–1447), English statesman and prelate, illegitimate son of John of Gaunt. As chancellor to Henry IV and Henry V, Beaufort considerably influenced English domestic and foreign policy. Guardian of Henry VI (1422), he controlled England in the 1430's, and endeavored to conclude peace with France. As bishop of Winchester from 1404 he completed the cathedral.

Beaufort, Margaret, Countess of Richmond and Derby (1443–1509), English heiress, patroness of learning. By Edmund Tudor, Earl of Richmond (married 1455), she became the mother of the future Henry VII.

Beaufort Sea, part of the Arctic Ocean NE of Alaska, W of Arctic Archipelago; first explored by Canadian Vilhjalmur Stefansson (1915). Maximum depth: approx. 15,000ft (4,575m).

Beaufort Wind Scale, a scale of numbers from 0 to 17 corresponding to stages in wind force and speed, with names and descriptions of the resultant land or sea effects. The Beaufort number 0 means calm, wind less than 1 mile per hour, with smoke rising vertically. Beaufort 3 means light breeze, 8–12 miles per hour, with leaves in constant motion. Beaufort 11 is storm, 64–72 miles per hour, and Beaufort 12–17 is hurricane, 73–136+ miles per hour with devastation.

Beauharnais, Alexandre, Vicomte de (1760–94), French general who served in the American Revolution. In 1789 he was a deputy of the nobility in the revolutionary French States-General. As commander of the army of the Rhine in 1793, he was held responsible for the surrender at Mainz and was guillotined. His wife, Josephine, later married Napoleon.

Beauharnais, Eugène de (1781–1824), French general, son of Napoleon's wife Josephine. A lieutenant of his stepfather at the battles of Marengo and Lützen, he was later adopted by Napoleon and made (1805) viceroy of Italy. After Napoleon's downfall, he lived in Bavaria as the duke of Leuchtenberg.

Beauharnais, Joséphine de. *See* Josephine.

Beauharnois, Marquis de (Charles de la Boische) (1670–1749), governor of French Canada (1726–46). A successful naval commandant, he attempted to improve relations with Canadian Indians, thus falling out with the intendant, Claude-Thomas Dupuy. He backed Pierre de Vérendryes' explorations and rose to a lieutenant-general after his retirement from politics.

Beaujolais, former province of France on W bank of Saône River, north of Lyon; formed around the small village of Beaujeu; Lyon is the industrial hub of this area. Known for Beaujolais wine.

Beaumarchais, Pierre Augustin Caron de (1732–99), French dramatist whose related plays *The Barber of Seville* (1775) and *The Marriage of Figaro* (1784) were made into operas by Rossini and Mozart respectively. A cosmopolitan adventurer, Beaumarchais satirized the court society into which he had married. *See also* Barber of Seville, The; Marriage of Figaro, The.

Beaumont, (Sir) Francis (1584–1616), English dramatist who in collaboration with John Fletcher from about 1606 to 1616 produced romantic tragicomedies, including *The Knight of the Burning Pestle, Philaster, A Maid's Tragedy, A King and No King,* and *The Scornful Lady* (1613). Although contemporaries of Shakespeare, Beaumont and Fletcher were more influenced by Ben Jonson.

Beaumont, William (1785–1853), US surgeon, b. Lebanon, Conn. He gained valuable knowledge of the functioning of the human stomach through a series of experiments he performed on the stomach of Alexis St. Martin, who, as the result of a gunshot wound, had a small opening into his body over his stomach that provided Beaumont with a unique opportunity to study stomach action.

Beaumont, port city in SE Texas, 73mi (118km) E of Houston; seat of Jefferson co; first settlers were French and Spanish fur trappers and explorers; population boom occurred in 1901 after discovery of oil. Industries: oil refining, paper, lumbering, sulfur, rice milling. Settled 1835; inc. 1881. Pop. (1970) 115,-919.

Beauregard, Pierre Gustave Toutant de (1818–93), Confederate Civil War general, b. near New Orleans, La. He served in the Mexican War and was superintendent of West Point when war broke out in 1861. On April 14, 1861, he forced the Union surrender of Ft. Sumter, S.C., in the first action of the war. He also served as a commander at Bull Run (1861), at Shiloh (1862), and in the Carolinas (1864–65). He was active in Louisiana government after the war.

Beauvais, town in France, 42mi (68km) NW of Paris. It was noted for making Gobelin tapestries; the factory was destroyed in WWII and never rebuilt; site of the unfinished cathedral of St Pierre. Industries: building materials, machinery, blankets. Founded by Romans. Pop. 46,777.

Beauvais Cathedral. △1104.

Beauvoir, Simone de (1908–), French novelist and essayist. *She Came to Stay* (1943) and *The Mandarins* (1954) are portraits of the Existentialist intellectual circle of which she was a member and of her close companion, Jean-Paul Sartre. Her best known work remains the lengthy feminist essay *The Second Sex* (1949). Other significant works include *The Prime of Life* (1960), *A Very Easy Death* (1964), and *The Coming of Age* (1972).

Beaux-Arts, Ecole des. △1252.

Beaver, large rodent with fine brown to black fur, webbed hind feet, and a broad scaly tail; lives in streams and lakes of Europe and North America. Although the flesh is edible, beavers are hunted mostly for their fur which, after the coarse hairs have been removed, is highly valuable. Beavers eat parts of trees, shrubs, and plants. They build lodges of trees and branches above water level and construct dams and canals of stones, sticks, and mud. Length: to 4ft (1.2m); weight: to 70lb (32kg). Species *Castor fiber.* △592.

Beaverbrook, (William) Max(well) Aitken, 1st Baron (1879–1964), Canadian born British politician and proprietor of mass-circulation newspapers. A successful financier by 1907, he moved to England entered Parliament (1910). He gained control of the *Daily Express* (1916) and the *Evening Standard* (1923), founded the *Sunday Express* (1918) and invigorated popular journalism. In 1936 he tried to prevent Edward VIII's abdication, and in WWII he was a minister in Churchill's cabinet. A fervent imperialist, he backed the Suez campaign in 1956 and opposed Britain's bid to join the European Economic Community.

Beccaria, César de (1738–94), Italian philosopher and criminologist. Author of *On Crime and Punishments* (1764), advocating penal reform and creation of an enlightened judicial code.

Bechet, Sidney (1897–1959), US jazz clarinetist, saxophonist, and composer, b. New Orleans. He toured the United States in various groups (1912–19) and then toured Europe, giving concerts in all the European capitals. Between 1928–38, he played with the Noble Sissle Band and wrote music for the lyricist Noble Sissle.

Beck, Józef (1894–1944), Polish statesman. He served as a colonel in Pilsudski's Polish legion in World War I, and as military attaché in Paris (1922–23). As foreign minister (1932–39) he rejected Hitler's demands for concessions in the Polish Corridor and Danzig with greater firmness than the leaders of Austria and Czechoslovakia. On April 6, 1939, he signed the alliance with Great Britain that would bring her into World War II six months later in Poland's defense.

Beck, Martin (1868–1940), US theatrical producer and manager, b. Germany. Head of the Radio-Keith-Orpheum circuit of vaudeville houses. He originated the booking system of the circuit, and built several theaters, including the Martin Beck in New York City.

Becket, Thomas à (1118?–70), English clergyman and statesman. A friend of Henry II, he was appointed chancellor of England (1155) and vigorously pursued the interests of the crown. In 1162 he became archbishop of Canterbury. Resigning the chancellorship that year, he thenceforth devoted his energies exclusively to church affairs. Bitter conflict with Henry over clerical privileges and the independence of ecclesiastical courts followed, and Becket fled from England seeking papal support. Returning unsubdued to Canterbury after six years' exile, he was murdered there by four of Henry's knights. He was acclaimed a martyr and canonized (1173).

Beckett, Samuel (1906–), Irish novelist and playwright. Living in Paris since 1937, he writes in both English and French. His bleak mastery of theater of the absurd is shown in such plays as *Waiting for Godot* (1956), *Endgame* (1957), *Krapp's Last Tape* (1958), and *Not I* (1973). He is concerned with alienated individual consciousness in his novels, such as *Murphy* (1938), *Malone Dies* (1951), *Molloy* (1951), and *Watt* (1953). He received the Nobel Prize for literature in 1969. *See also* Theater of the Absurd.

Becklin's Object. △106.

Beckmann, Max (1884–1950), German expressionist painter. His work is unique in its constricted treatment of space, primitive angular forms, vividness of color, and the staring intensity of its faces. Condemned as a decadent artist in 1933, Beckmann left Germany in 1938 and settled in the United States. His most famous works are nine triptyches painted after 1932, among them the monumental *Departure* in the Museum of Modern Art, New York City.

Becknell, William (1796?–1865), US trader and explorer, b. Amherst co, Va. He established the trading route known as the Sante Fe Trail (1821–22), which was used for 50 years and immortalized in legend. In 1834 he settled in Texas.

Beckwith, Julia Catherine (1796–1867), Canadian author. Her romance, *St. Ursula's Convent; or The Nun of Canada* (2 vols., 1824), was the first novel written by a native-born, English-speaking Canadian and published in Canada. It was written while the author was in her teens.

Beckwourth, James P(ierson) (1798–1867), US Western pioneer guide, b. Fredericksburg, Va. He traveled throughout the West with fur trappers, lived with the Crow Indians, and served as an army guide. He discovered Beckwourth Pass in the Sierra Nevadas in 1860.

Becquerel, Antoine Henri (1852–1908), French physicist. He was professor of physics at the Paris Museum of Natural History (a post held by his father and grandfather before him) and later at the Ecole Polytechnique. He is remembered for his accidental discovery of radioactivity in uranium salts, for which he shared a Nobel Prize (1903) with Pierre and Marie Curie. His other work was concerned with the rotation of the plane of polarized light in a magnetic field. △1480–82.

Bed Bug, broad, flat, wingless bug found worldwide. It feeds by sucking blood from birds, animals, and man. Length: to 0.25in (6mm). Family Cimicidae; species *Cimex lectularius.*

Bede (*c.* 673–735), called the Venerable Bede, monk and scholar from Northumbria in Britain who spent his entire life in the monastery of Jarrow near Whitby. The most important of his many works on science, grammar, history, and theology is the *Ecclesiastical History of the English Nation,* which covers the period from Caesar's conquest to 731.

Bedford, John of Lancaster, Duke of (1389–1435), third son of Henry IV of England. Lieutenant of England during much of Henry V's absence in France, he became regent of France and protector of England (1422). He administered France justly and was successful in the renewed fighting after 1427 but failed at the siege of Orléans (1429). He was responsible for Joan of Arc's execution (1431).

Bedford Hours. △1106.

Bedlam, institution for the insane, founded as the priory of St. Mary of Bethlehem, London (1247), converted *c.*1400 to a hospital, and incorporated as a royal foundation (1547). The word "Bedlam" is a corruption of "Bethlehem." △762.

Bedlington Terrier, graceful, lamblike breed of dog (terrier group) established 1870, brought to United States about 1890. First called gypsy's dog, the Bedlington terrier has a pear-shaped head; filbert-shaped, hanging ears; long legs; and a gracefully curved 9–11 in (23–28cm) tail. The coat, usually trimmed to 1in (2.5cm) for show, can be blue, liver, blue and tan, liver and tan, sandy, or sandy and tan. Average size: 16.5in (42cm) high at shoulder; 17–23lb (8–11kg). *See also* Terrier.

Bedouin, nomadic people of Arab culture and Muslim faith, inhabiting the deserts of the Middle East. Traditionally they live in tents, moving with their herds of camels, goats, sheep, or sometimes cattle across vast areas of arid land in pursuit of the sparse grazing. Their society is patrilineal and they are proverbial for their hospitality, honesty, and fierce independence and courage. Although true Bedouin despise manual labor and city life, many have succumbed to 20th-century economic pressures and taken up employment in the towns.

Bedsheet Ballot, US political term used to describe a long ballot that includes, besides a list of candidates, assorted propositions or referenda.

Bedsore, ulcerous sore caused by prolonged pressure against the skin, occurring most often in bedridden patients. Bedsores may be prevented by cleanliness and relief of pressure.

Bed-wetting, or enuresis, the unintentional voiding of urine at night by children. Protracted enuresis may be due to delayed maturation of bladder capacity or control, and often disappears with maturity. True enuresis appears to be more closely related to a child's general health and emotional state than to organic dysfunction, hence successful treatment is increasingly oriented to careful planning and patience on the part of parents. Drugs or psychiatric treatment are occasionally prescribed.

Bee, any member of the insect Superfamily Apoidea. They are distinguished from other members of the Order Hymenoptera by the presence of specially adapted hairs, which allow for the collection of pollen. They all feed their young honey and pollen, rather than animal food. The body is usually quite hairy and the hairs are multi-branched or plumose. Honey and bumblebees are social insects forming colonies; many other bees are solitary. Found worldwide, they are important pollinators, with some living in other bees' colonies. *See also* Bumblebee; Carpenter Bee; Honeybee. △498.

Beebe, Charles William (1877–1962), US naturalist and explorer, b. Brooklyn, N.Y. He was curator of ornithology (1899–1919) and director of tropical research (1919–52) at the New York Zoological Society. He led many scientific explorations in Central and South America, the West Indies, and the Orient. His numerous books, including *Galapagos* (1923), *Beneath Tropic Seas* (1928), and *Unseen Life of New York* (1953), combined meticulous scholarship with literary style.

Beech, deciduous tree native to the northern hemisphere. All have wide-spreading branches, smooth gray bark, and alternate, coarse-toothed, green leaves. Male flowers hang from thin stems and pairs of female flowers hang on hairy stems and develop into triangular, edible nuts enclosed by burs. The American beech *(Fagus grandifolia)* is an important timber tree used for furniture and tool handles; height: 80ft (24m). There are 10 species. Family Fagaceae.

Beecham, (Sir) Thomas (1879–1961), English conductor. He founded the New Symphony Orchestra in 1905, the Royal Philharmonic in 1919, and the London Symphony in 1932, becoming its permanent conductor. He introduced the operas of Richard Strauss into England and was widely known as an interpreter of such composers as Frederick Delius and Jean Sibelius.

Beechcraft. △1716.

Beecher, Henry Ward (1813–87), US clergyman, b. Litchfield, Conn. Claiming to be the recipient of special revelation, he became a passionate preacher. Of wide influence, he campaigned against slavery and for woman suffrage. He edited the *Independent,* a Congregational journal, and later, the *Christian Union.*

Beecher, Lyman (1775–1863), US Presbyterian clergyman, b. New Haven, Conn. He was pastor at Litchfield, Conn. (1810–26) and Boston (1826–32), and was president of Lane Theological Seminary (1832–52). He was noted for his sermons on temperance and against slavery. Among his children were Henry Ward Beecher and Harriet Beecher Stowe.

Bee Eater, tropical Eastern Hemisphere bird that swoops to catch its favorite prey, bees and wasps. They have long curved beaks; bright, often greenish, plumage; and long tails. They nest in large colonies and build tunnels to their egg chambers where white eggs (2–5) are laid and incubated by both parents. Length: 6–15in (15–38cm). Family Meropidae.

Beef. △372, 378.

Beefalo. △398.

Beef Cattle, breeds of domesticated cattle raised primarily for meat. Larger than dairy cattle, they are chunky and rectangular in appearance and convert most of their food into flesh. Beef production includes three distinct agricultural types: breeding, ranching, and feeding. Some farmers do all three, but the modern trend is toward specialization. Breeds include Aberdeen Angus, Brahman, Charolais, Hereford, Longhorn, and Shorthorn. *See also* Animal Husbandry; Cattle. △302, 372.

Bee Fly, gray to black fly, 0.6 to 1in (15–25mm) long, found worldwide. The adult feeds on flower nectar; the larvae are parasitic on other insects. Family Bombyliidae, genus *Bombylius. See also* Diptera.

Beefsteak Fungus, a species of arboreal mushroom, *Fistulina hepatica,* also called ox-tongue or poor man's beefsteak, that is common on hardwoods, especially oak. Wedge-shaped, it has a cap 2–10in (5–25cm) broad with spore-bearing tubes on the underside. When present, the stem is horizontal. Young beefsteak fungi look and feel like meat; the flesh oozes red juice. It is edible and mycophagists rate it from fair to good.

Beaver

Henri Becquerel

Bee

Henry Ward Beecher

Beef Trust, combination of large meat-packing companies formed in 1902. The National Packing Co. was formed by G.F. Swift, J.O. Armour, and Edward Morris to gain control of Midwestern packing houses. The government was unanimously upheld in its anti-trust prosecution by the Supreme Court in *Swift and Company* v. *United States* (1905), but the trust was not broken up until 1920.

Beekeeping. △342.

Beer, alcoholic beverage produced by brewing and fermentation of a cereal extract (malt), which is flavored with a bitter substance (hops). Ingredients also include water, sugar, and yeast. The alcohol content of beer ranges from about 1.5 to 8.3 grams per cc. Among the types of beer are ales, which are pale or brown in color; stouts, very dark brown and bitter; and porter, a sweeter stout. Beer is especially popular in the United States, Great Britain, and Germany. △350.

Beerbohm, Max (1872–1956), English caricaturist and drama critic. His writings are collected in *A Christmas Garland* (1895), parodies of contemporary novelists (*The Works of Max Beerbohm* [1896]), and *Around Theatre* (1930; 1953). He also wrote a novel, *Zuleika Dobson* (1911), an ironic fantasy set in Oxford.

Beers, Clifford W(hittingham) (1876–1943), US pioneer in the treatment of the mentally disturbed, b. New Haven. A former mental patient, Beers wrote *A Mind That Found Itself* (1908), which portrays the mentally disturbed as sick people who could be treated. He founded the American Foundation for Mental Hygiene in 1928.

Be'er Sheva' (Beersheba), city in S Israel, 45mi (72km) SW of Jerusalem; capital of Southern District; site of oracle, important during Biblical times; controlled by Britain 1922–47; site of Negev Institute for Arid Zone Research; industrial, commercial, educational, and transportation center. Industries: chemicals, glass. Pop. 77,400.

Beet, vegetable originating in Europe and parts of Asia. It is cultivated in most cool areas. Its leaves are green or red, and edible but it is grown for the thick, red or gold root. Beets should have sandy loam in a sunny area. Some varieties are eaten as a vegetable, others are a source of sugar, and some are used as fodder. Family Chenopodiaceae; species *Beta vulgaris*. *See also* Sugar Beet.

Beethoven, Ludwig van (1770–1827), German composer, b. Bonn. A virtuoso pianist, Beethoven gradually became deaf, making a concert career impossible. Despite his deafness, he composed many masterpieces that place him in the forefront of all composers. He is often regarded as the last Classical and the first Romantic composer. He was a master of orchestral form.

His early works are in the classic tradition of Haydn and Mozart, with whom he studied. His middle period (1801–1814), despite increasing deafness, produced his Third and Fifth symphonies, the "Emperor" *Piano Concerto No. 5*, the *Violin Concerto*, and the "Appassionata" *Piano Sonata No. 23*. In his last period, composing in total deafness, Beethoven produced his last five string quartets, the *Missa Solemnis*, and the Ninth Symphony, which many critics regard as the greatest symphony ever composed, and which was the first symphony to use singers and a chorus. His one opera, *Fidelio* (1805, revised 1814), is also highly regarded. △1246.

Beetle, insects characterized by horny front wings that serve as protective covers for the membranous hind wings and are not used in flight. They are widely distributed on every continent except Antarctica. Most beetles live on land, but some are aquatic. They are usually stout-bodied, and their mouthparts are adapted for biting and chewing. Poor flyers, exoskeletons give them protection against bodily injury and drying up, a serious problem for most insects. Beetles are the most numerous group of insects, and over 300,000 species have been described. Most feed on plants, some are predators of small animals, including other insects, and some are scavengers. Beetles undergo complete metamorphosis. Their larvae, called grubs, usually have three pairs of legs, but grubs of weevils or snout beetles are legless. Unlike caterpillars, grubs have distinct heads, usually dark in color. Length: 0.02–7.5in (0.5mm–19cm). Order Coleoptera. *See also* Insect. △500.

Beggar's Opera, The, opera with libretto by John Gay and popular music of the day arranged by J.C. Pepusch, first performed in England in 1728. It was very popular in its time, is one of the few successful "ballad" operas, and formed the basis of the 20th-century comic opera *The Threepenny Opera* (1928).

Beggar-ticks, stick-tight or bur marigold, plants in the genera *Bidens* and *Desmodium* with prickly seed pods that catch on fur or clothing. They usually grow wild. Height 2–8ft (0.6–2.4m). Family Compositae.

Begonia, family of plants, shrubs, or trees native to tropical America and SE Asia. Those popular as house plants have various sized and shaped leaves; white, pink, or red flowers; and often hairy stems. There are three types: rex with ornamental leaves of green, red, and silver combinations; rhizomatus with fleshy, creeping stems and glossy leaves; and basket with trailing stems and brightly colored leaves. Male and female flowers are separate but on the same plant. Care: bright indirect sunlight, humid air, well-drained soil (equal parts loam, peat moss, perlite, sand). Propagation is by stem and leaf cuttings or division of rhizomes. Family Begoniaceae; genus *Begonia*. △324.

Behan, Brendan (1923–64), Irish writer. His play *The Quare Fellow* (1954) was based on his experiences of Borstal (reformatory) prison and the Irish Republican Army, as was the prose, autobiographical novel *Borstal Boy* (1958). His next play, *The Hostage* (1958), was typically uninhibited. He started, but did not finish, a third, *Richard's Cork Leg*.

Behavioral Ecology, study of the interactions between an ecological environment and the behavior that takes place within it. Drawing on biology, behavioral ecologists study such topics as the ways an organism adapts to its habitat, as well as human behavior in various settings. *See also* Ecology; Ethology.

Behaviorism, school of psychology that emphasizes studying observable acts using the methods of the natural sciences, particularly laboratory experiments. Early behaviorists objected to explanations of behavior that involved references to mind, will, or feelings. They studied actions that could be observed objectively, measured, and counted. Behaviorists try to explain learning as simple conditioning. Leading American behaviorists are John B. Watson and B.F. Skinner. △768, 772.

Behavior Modification, or Behavior Therapy, treatment of psychological disorders by using principles and methods from learning theory. Such treatment assumes that abnormal or undesirable behavior is learned, as are other behaviors, through conditioning and reinforcement. Therapy is designed to reward and encourage desirable, constructive behaviors while unwanted or abnormal behaviors are ignored or punished. For example, an overaggressive child's behavior might be modified as follows: when the child behaves destructively, isolate him (a time-out period); reward constructive behavior (quietness, cooperation) with praise, affection, or even candy immediately after the behavior occurs; punish intolerable instances of aggression with withdrawal of privileges. Behavior therapy is used to treat such diverse problems as alcoholism, juvenile delinquency, and the behaviors of the mentally retarded and behaviorally disturbed. *See also* Behaviorism; Learning Theory; Reinforcement.

Behistun (Bisitun), ancient town in W Iran, 22mi (35km) E of Kermānshāhan; site of cuneiform inscriptions carved on monument of Darius the Great, limestone cliffs above the town; Henry Rawlinson climbed the cliffs in 1835 to copy and decipher the texts, called "The Rosetta Stone of Asia."

Behring, Emil Adolph von (1854–1917), German bacteriologist and pioneer immunologist. In 1901 he was awarded the first Nobel Prize in physiology or medicine for his work on serum therapy, especially for developing a diphtheria antitoxin.

Behrman, S(amuel) N(athaniel) (1893–1973), US dramatist, b. Worcester, Mass. He excelled in the brilliant dialogue of high comedy, as in *The Second Man* (1927), *End of Summer* (1936), *Wine of Choice* (1938), an adaptation of *Amphitryon 38* (1938), *No Time for Comedy* (1939), an adaptation of Franz Werfel's *Jacobowsky and the Colonel* (1944), *Fanny* (1954, with Joshua Logan), and *Lord Pengo* (1962).

Beida (Zawiyat al-Bayda), town in NE Libya, NE of Benghazi, in the Al-Jabal al-Akhdar plateau; site of the tomb of Raweifi ibn Thabit, Muslim holy man and companion to the prophet Mohammed; site of Islamic university, and administrative offices. Pop. 12,799.

Beiderbecke, Bix (1903–31), US jazz cornetist, pianist, bandleader, and composer, b. Leon Beiderbecke in Davenport, Iowa. He played with many jazz bands including Paul Whiteman's (1928–30). He composed "Davenport Blues" (1925) and "In the Mist" (1927).

Beijing. *See* Peking.

Beira, seaport city in E central Mozambique, on Mozambique Channel; capital of Manica e Sofala district; developed 1891 as a railroad terminus into interior; major trade and commercial center; tourist resort. Pop. 58,970.

Beirut (Bayrut), capital city of Lebanon, on the E shore of the Mediterranean Sea; was ancient Phoenician city of Berytus; prospered in 1500 BC as a trade center and later as an important commercial colony of the Roman Empire and site of a prominent law school (AD 3). City was captured by the Arabs 635 and by the Ottoman Turks 1516; taken by France in WWI (1918); extensively damaged in 1975–76 civil war; major center of trade, culture, finance; site of Lebanese, French, American, and Arab universities. Industries: shipping, food processing, textiles. Pop. 131,500.

Beirut, American University of, university in Beirut, Lebanon. It was founded in 1866 as Syrian Protestant College, and acquired its present name in 1920. The university confers bachelors, masters, and doctors degrees. Major areas of study include architecture, nursing, engineering, and agriculture.

Békésy, Georg von (1899–), US physicist, b. Hungary. As director of the Hungarian Telephone System Research Laboratory (1923–46), he worked on problems of communication and the mechanics of human hearing. At Harvard University (1949–66) he carried on his research on the cochlea of the ear. For this research he received a Nobel Prize in physiology or medicine (1961). Extending his studies to other senses, he developed a unified picture of the role of sensory and nervous processes in perception.

Bel. *See* Decibel.

Belafonte, Harry (1927–), US singer and actor, b. New York City. He often appeared on Broadway, and in films and television specials, many of which he produced himself. He gained fame with his calypso recordings and was a civil rights activist who worked closely with Martin Luther King, Jr.

Belalcázar, Sebastián de. *See* Benalcázar, Sebastián de.

Belasco, David (1854–1931), US actor, producer, and playwright, b. David Valasco in San Francisco. He was responsible for innovations in scenic realism, stage lighting, and nondeclamatory acting styles. His sentimental melodramas *Madame Butterfly* (1900) and *The Girl of the Golden West* (1905) became Puccini operas. His Belasco Theater (1907) produced hundreds of plays, encouraging US writers and developing such performers as Mrs. Leslie Carter, David Warfield, and Ina Claire.

Belém, seaport city in N Brazil, on Pará River, 90mi (145km) from Atlantic Ocean; capital of Pará state; site of governor's palace (1762), and Belém University of Pará (1957). Industries: sawmills, shipyards, brick. Exports: rubber, Brazil nuts, pepper. Founded 1615. Pop. 565,097.

Belfast, capital and largest city of Northern Ireland, at the mouth of the River Lagan on Belfast Lough; seat of County Antrim. It is the site of a Norman castle, Cathedral of Ste Anne, Queens University (1845), Victoria College (1854), National Museum and Art Gallery; scene of much fighting between Catholics and Protestants since the 19th century; noted as center of Irish linen industry. Industries: tobacco, food processing, shipbuilding, textiles, aircraft. Founded 1177; inc. 1613 by James I of England; became capital of Northern Ireland 1920. Pop. 358,991.

Belgae, Germanic and Celtic tribes who banded together about 2000 years ago and lived in what is now Belgium, the Netherlands, Germany, and northern France. The German tribes overcame and mixed with the Celts, producing a nation that Julius Caesar called the bravest of the Gauls. Caesar conquered them in 57 BC. Many Belgae crossed over to and settled in Britain.

Belgian, draft horse breed developed in Belgium from Flemish type horse and introduced in the United States in 1886. A patient, powerful horse, it has a massive, wide, deep and low-set body. Colors are bay, chestnut, and roan, all with flaxen mane and tail and white face blaze. Height 62–68in (157–173cm) at shoulder; weight: 1900–2200lb (855–990kg).

Belgian Malinois, sheepherding dog (working

group) bred in Belgium about 1898. A square, elegant dog, it has a flat head with pointed muzzle; triangular, erect ears; deep-chested, level-backed body; straight, medium-length legs; and long tail. The short, straight coat, colored rich fawn to mahogany, is longer around the neck, on the tail, and on back of thighs. Average size: 22–26in (56–66cm) high at shoulder; 50–60lb (23–27kg). *See also* Working Dog.

Belgian Sheepdog, sheepherding dog (working group) developed in Belgium 1891–98 and also called Gronendael. It has a flat head with pointed muzzle; triangular, erect ears; level, firm body; medium-length, straight legs; and long tail. Its abundant black coat is long and straight with shorter hair on head, ears, and lower legs. Average size: 21–26in (53–66cm) high at shoulder; 50–60lb (22.5–27kg). *See also* Working Dog.

Belgian Tervuren, shepherd dog (working group) bred in Belgium about 1885. It has a long head with pointed muzzle; erect, triangular ears; level back; medium-length, straight legs; and long tail. The long, harsh coat is shorter on head, ears, and lower legs. Color is rich fawn to russet mahogany with black overlay and face mask. Average size: 22–26in (56–66cm) high at the shoulder; 50–60lb (22.5–27kg). *See also* Working Dog.

Belgium (Belgique, or **België), Kingdom of,** a small, densely populated nation of W Europe. The people are of Flemish, French, and German background; all three languages are in current usage. The country, which is a constitutional monarchy, has one of the world's most highly developed economies.

Land and Economy. Belgium is a country of coastal lowlands and gently undulating plains rising to the hills of the Ardennes in the S. Flanders, the coastal area bordering the North Sea, is a flat, moist plain traversed by many rivers and canals. Belgium's central plain, lying between Flanders and the Meuse River, is a fertile farming region; most industry is situated here, as is a majority of the country's population. The Ardennes is a rocky, wooded plateau unsuitable for farming. The climate is maritime, with damp, foggy winters and mild summers. Industry is focused in the cities along the Scheldt and Meuse rivers; both are important coal regions. For centuries, Belgium has been famed for its textiles, linens, and lace. Other important industries include chemical, coal, metallurgical, glassware, furniture, and sugar refining. The economy depends upon extensive importation of raw materials, and foreign export markets for its manufactured products. Only 7% of the population is engaged in agriculture. Antwerp and Ghent are major European seaports.

People. Belgians may be divided roughly into two major language-groups. N of Brussels the people are mostly Flemings; the official language is Flemish, which is similar to Dutch. The Belgians of the S are called Walloons; the official language, Walloon, is a dialect of French. The city of Brussels is officially bilingual. The country is overwhelmingly Roman Catholic.

Government. The king is the head of state and commander-in-chief of the armed forces. The ministers of government are leaders of the dominant party in parliament, and are appointed by the king. Government policy is carried out by the prime minister and his cabinet. The leading political parties are the Social Christian, Socialist, and Liberal. Voting in national elections is compulsory for all Belgians 21 years and older.

History. During the Middle Ages many textile manufacturing and trade centers developed in the area that is now Belgium. The French united the small states of the region in the 14th century, and included them in the duchy of Burgundy. After 1477, the Austrian and Spanish branches of Hapsburgs controlled the area for more than 300 years. Belgium and the Netherlands were united after the Congress of Vienna (1815). The Belgians revolted and founded a constitutional monarchy 1831 under Prince Leopold of Saxe-Coburg. Belgium colonized Africa's Congo region in the 19th century. In both world wars the country was overrun and occupied by German forces. It joined the North Atlantic Treaty Organization (NATO) in 1949. Belgium was instrumental in conceiving and forming the European Economic Community.

PROFILE

Official name: Belgium, Kingdom of
Area: 11,781 sq mi (30,513sq km)
Population: 9,800,000
Density: 832per sq mi (321per sq km)
Chief cities: Brussels (capital); Antwerp; Ghent
Government: constitutional monarchy
Religion (major): Roman Catholic
Languages: Flemish, French, German
Monetary unit: Belgian franc
Gross national product: $53,300,000,000
Industries (major products): chemicals, glass, textiles
Agriculture (major products): wheat, barley, sugar beets, potatoes
Minerals (major): coal, iron, copper
Trading partners (major): West Germany, France, Netherlands, United States

Belgrade (Beograd), capital city of Yugoslavia, at the junction of the Sava and Danube rivers; settled by Celts, Illyrians, and Romans. In 1929 it became part of Yugoslavia, and suffered much damage during German occupation in WWII; center of cultural, economic, and political activities of Yugoslavia; site of 16th-century Darjah Mosque, museums, palaces, and Serbian Academy of Science. Industries: chemicals, metals, machine tools, textiles. Pop. 741,613.

Belgrano, Manuel (1770–1820), Argentine independence leader. He participated in the Revolution of 1810 and led Argentine forces against Paraguay (1811). As general of the army, he defeated royalist forces in 1812 and 1814. At the Congress of Tucumán (1816), he recommended an Inca monarchy for Argentina.

Belisarius (505–65), Byzantine general. Under Emperor Justinian I, Belisarius waged important campaigns against the Germanic tribes which threatened Byzantium on its western frontiers. He subjugated the Vandals in northern Africa, and the Ostrogoths in Italy, taking the Ostrogothic capital of Ravenna in 540. On the eastern frontier, his campaign against the Persians was unsuccessful. △1056.

Belize (British Honduras), self-governing British colony in Central America, bounded by the Caribbean Sea (E), Mexico (N), and Guatemala (S and W). The terrain is mostly low with swampland along the coast, rising inland to the country's highest point, Victoria Peak, approx. 3,700ft (1,130m), and heavily forested in S regions. The main industry is timber, followed by fishing and tourism. Only a small portion of the land is farmed. Chief products include: sugar cane, citrus fruits, coconuts, maize, rice, yams, and beans. The people, predominantly English-speaking, are of black African descent and are concentrated around Belmopan, the capital, and Belize, the principal port. Spanish-speaking Mayan Indian descendants live in northern regions. Originally part of the Mayan civilization, the area was settled *c.* 1638 by British logcutters from Jamaica. Constantly contested by Spain until 1798, it came under the administration of Jamaica, 1862–84. Belize adopted a new constitution in 1960 and gained internal self-government in 1964. Guatemala, which has claimed Belize since 1821, restated its claim of sovereignty in 1975; however, the United Nations reaffirmed its position preserving the territory of the colony and its right to complete internal self-government. Its constitution provides for a parliamentary system, headed by a prime minister, and a bicameral legislature.

PROFILE

Official name: Colony of Belize
Area: 8,866sq mi (22,963sq km)
Population: 119,645
Chief cities: Belmopan (capital), Belize
Government: Self-governing colony (United Kingdom)
Language: English

Belize, town in Belize, Central America; 50mi (81km) NW of Belmopan; formerly the country's capital, now the largest city and principal port; almost totally destroyed in a hurricane (1961). Industries: sawmilling, rice hulling; trade center for lumber, fruit, coconuts. Pop. 39,257.

Bell, Alexander Graham (1847–1922), US inventor of the telephone and educator of the deaf, b. Scotland. He was educated at Edinburgh and London and worked with his father, inventor of the Visible Speech System for educating the deaf. The family moved to Canada in 1870, and Bell began teaching his father's system in New England. He opened a training school in Boston in 1872 and taught speech at Boston University from 1873–77. His work in the transmission of sound by electricity led to the first demonstration of the telephone in 1876. He founded the Bell Telephone Co. in 1877. Among his other inventions were the photophone, an instrument for transmitting sound by light vibrations (1880), and the wax cylinder record for phonographs.

Bell, city in S California, 5mi (8km) S of Los Angeles; suburban community with small businesses. Inc. 1927. Pop. (1970) 21,836.

Belladonna, poisonous herb *(Atropa belladonna)* that has a sap used medicinally to enlarge the pupil of the eye and whose roots and leaves contain the antispasmodic pain-relieving drug atropine. *See also* Atropine.

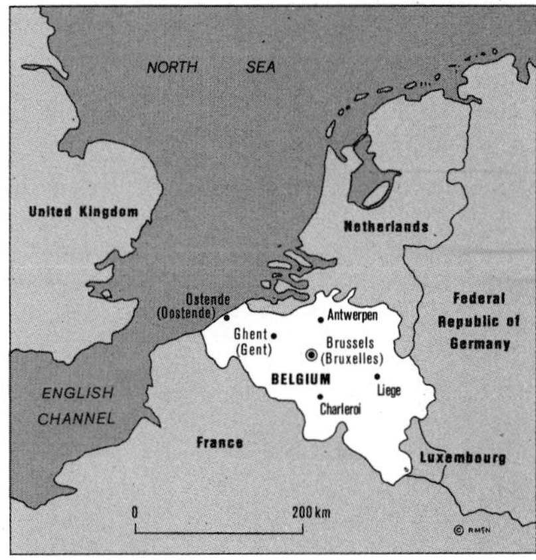
NORTH SEA
United Kingdom
Netherlands
Ostende
(Oostende)
Ghent
(Gent)
Antwerpen
Brussels
(Bruxelles)
BELGIUM
Liege
Charleroi
Federal
Republic of
Germany
ENGLISH
CHANNEL
France
Luxembourg
0
200km

Belgium

Brussels, Belgium: Maison du Roi

Belgrade, Yugoslavia

Alexander Graham Bell

Belladonna Lily, South African bulb plant cultivated for its fragrant rose-pink flowers. Family Amaryllioacene species *Amaryllis belladonna.*

Bellamy, Edward (1850–1898), US author, b. Chicopee Falls, Mass. Best known for *Looking Backward: 2000–1887* (1888), a utopian novel prophesying a new social and economic order. The popularity of the novel inspired the founding of clubs and magazines to discuss and advance Bellamy's ideas.

Bellbird, tropical American cotinga with a loud bell-like call. The black-winged bellbird *(Procnias averano)* of Trinidad and N South America has fleshy growths hanging from its chin and throat. The Central American three-wattled bellbird *(Procnias tricarunculata)* has whiplike wattles around its bill.

Belleau Wood, Battle of (June 2–July 7, 1918), World War I Allied victory in France in which the US 2nd Division, spearheaded by its Marine brigade, checked German attacks west of Château-Thierry. The Americans counterattacked and recaptured the village of Bouresches and the southern edge of Belleau Wood.

Belle Fourche River, river in NE Wyoming and W South Dakota; rises in NE Wyoming, flows NE into Cheyenne River in South Dakota. Length: approx. 350mi (564km).

Belle Isle, Strait of, channel in Canada separating Newfoundland and SE Labrador; ice-locked November–June; northernmost entrance to the Gulf of St. Lawrence. Length: 35mi (56km). Width: 15mi (24km).

Bellerophon, in Greek legend, the son of Glaucus, king of Corinth and grandson of Sisyphus. Iobates sent him to slay the fire breathing dragon Chimera. On his way Bellerophon captured and tamed the winged horse Pegasus, and by riding above the dragon he was able to kill it with bow and arrows.

Belleville, city in SW Illinois, 14mi (23km) SE of E St Louis; seat of St Clairio. Scott Air Force Base is nearby. Industries: coal mining, stoves, stencil machines, beer. Inc. 1819. Pop. (1970) 41,699.

Belleville, town in NE New Jersey, on Passaic River, 4mi (6km) N of Newark; originally called "Second River Section" of Newark, formed separate town 1839. Industries: water purifiers, electrical equipment, tools. Settled by Dutch (1680); inc. 1910. Pop. (1970) 37,629.

Bellevue, city in E Nebraska, on Missouri River, 10mi (16km) S of Omaha; oldest settlement in Nebraska; capital of former Nebraska Territory (1854); site of Strategic Aerospace Museum. Principal industry is meat packing. Founded as a trading post 1823; inc. 1855. Pop. (1970) 21,953.

Bellevue, city in W Washington, on Lake Washington; E suburb of Seattle; population increased with the completion of the Floating Bridge to Seattle. Industries: electronic components, concrete, prefabricated homes. Settled 1880; inc. 1953. Pop. (1970) 61,102.

Bellflower, city in S California, N of Long Beach; suburban community with truck farms and small businesses. Inc. 1957. Pop. (1970) 51,454.

Bellflower, annual, perennial, or biennial plants native to northern temperate regions and tropical mountains and now cultivated in gardens. All have bell-shaped flowers of white, blue, or pink, alternate leaves, and milky sap. Well-known are the blue, biennial Canterbury bells *(Campanula medium)* and tall *Campanula americana* found in moist woodlands of the United States; height: to 6ft (1.8m). There are 300 species. Family Campanulaceae.

Bell Gardens, city in S California, NW of Downey; suburb of Los Angeles. Industries: electrical equipment, paper manufacturing. Inc. 1961. Pop. (1970) 29,308.

Bellingham, city in NW Washington, 18mi (29km) S of Canadian border, on Puget Sound; formed from combination of four towns in 1903. Industries: farming, lumber, fishing, processed foods. Founded 1852; inc. 1904. Pop. (1970) 39,375.

Bellini, Gentile (*c.* 1429–1507), Italian painter. The brother of Giovanni, he was more prominent in his lifetime than his brother. His paintings for two charitable foundations in Venice, full of portraits and views of the city, became the prototypes in the genre.

Bellini, Giovanni (*c.* 1430–1516), Italian painter. He was the genius of the Venetian High Renaissance and the greatest of the Venetian Madonna painters. In his early works, executed in the family workshop, his treatment of nature was precise and realistic, in 15th-century fashion, but it gradually became poetic and monumental, as did his handling of color and light. He frequently included landscapes as background, as in his portraits of the Doges. In his graceful, gentle allegorical paintings and his altarpieces (such as that for San Giobbi), he often used architectural settings, within which the figures were bathed in light and atmosphere. In *St. Jerome,* one of his later, highly innovative works, the saint is seated in a landscape and seen through an arch before which the other life-sized figures stand. The greatest teacher of his generation, his pupils included Giorgione, Titian, Palma Vecchio, and Sebastiano del Piombo. In midcareer he began using oils instead of tempura, thereby establishing their predominance in Venetian painting. △1138.

Bellini, Vincenzo (1801–1835), Italian composer of bel canto operas, most notably *Norma* and *La Sonnambula* (both in 1831) and *I Puritani* (1835). △ 1246.

Belloc, (Joseph) Hilaire (Pierre) (1870–1953), English author, b. France. A versatile writer, he is remembered chiefly for his light verse, especially *Cautionary Tales* (1907). He wrote several satirical novels in collaboration with G.K. Chesterton. He was an earnest Catholic and a Liberal member of Parliament (1906–10).

Bellow, Saul (1915–), US author, b. Lachine, Canada. Reared in Chicago, he taught English and creative writing at various universities. A novelist, short story writer, and playwright, his first novel, *The Dangling Man,* appeared in 1944. Subsequent novels include *The Adventures of Augie March* (1953), *Henderson the Rain King* (1959), *Herzog* (1964), and *Mr. Sammler's Planet* (1970). Bellow won three National Book Awards for fiction (1954, 1965, 1971) and was awarded the 1976 Nobel Prize in literature.

Bellows, George (1882–1925), US illustrator and painter, b. Columbus, Ohio. A member of the Ashcan School, he painted many fine portraits, as well as depictions of prize fights, street scenes, prayer meetings, and rallies. *See also* Ashcan School.

Bell's Palsy, form of neuritis characterized by complete paralysis of one side of the face. Recovery may be spontaneous; surgery is indicated rarely.

Bellwood, city in NE Illinois, 15mi (24km) W of Chicago. Industries: hardware, iron castings, lift trucks. Founded after Civil War; inc. 1900. Pop. (1970) 22,096.

Bellwort, perennial woodland plant native to Canada and the United States. They have fleshy root stalks, light green leaves, and yellow, bell-shaped flowers. Family Liliaceae; genus *Uvularia.*

Belmont, city in W California, 10mi (16km) SSE of San Francisco; site of College of Notre Dame (1851). Settled 1851; inc. 1926. Pop. (1970) 23,667.

Belmopan, capital of Belize, 41mi (66km) SW of city of Belize. Made capital 1970. Pop. 1,000.

Belo Horizonte, city in E Brazil, 200mi (322km) N of Rio de Janeiro; capital of Minas Gerais state; first planned city in South America; site of University of Minas Gerais (1927), and the Catholic University of Minas Gerais (1959). Industries: mineral ores, diamonds, textiles, iron, steel. Founded 1897. Pop. 1,106,722.

Beloit, city in S Wisconsin, on Rock River, 70mi (113km) SW of Milwaukee. Industries: diesel engines, generators, shoes. Founded 1837; inc. 1857. Pop. (1970) 35,729.

Belorussian (Belorusskaja) Soviet Socialist Republic (White Russia), constituent republic in W central European USSR; bordered by Lithuanian and Latvian republics (N), the Ukraine (S), Russian Soviet Federal Socialists Republic (E), Poland (W). Since 1944, Belorussian SSR comprises 12 oblasts; population is 80% Belorussian, 20% Russian, Polish, and Jewish. Minsk is capital. Region was colonized by East Slavic tribes 5th–8th centuries; passed to Russia 1772, 1793. The republic proclaimed independence 1918 but was taken by Red Army 1919; site of Soviet-Polish War 1919–20. Treaty of Riga (1921) gave W part to Poland and E part to USSR (1922); W section was inc. into USSR 1939. Only the Ukrainian Republic and Belorussia of the 15 union republics of USSR have separate UN seats. Industries: lumber, potatoes, grains, flax, sugar beets, electrical equipment, textiles, chemicals. Area: 80,154sq mi (207,599sq km). Pop. 9,003,000.

Belshazzar, in the Bible, son of Nebuchadnezzar and last king of Babylon. Daniel prophesied the conquering of Babylon by Cyrus and Belshazzar was slain the same night.

Beluga, or white whale, small, toothed Arctic whale that is milky white when mature. It preys on fish, squid, and crustaceans and is, in turn, prey for killer whales. Its curlewlike cry is easily audible. Length: to 17ft (5m). Species: *Delphinapterus leucas. See also* Whale. △552.

Bemba, Negroid warrior people of NE Zambia, Zaire, and Rhodesia. Their society is traditionally matrilineal, based on subsistence agriculture, and characterized by an absence of craft skills and material possessions. Many of the males now find employment as migrant laborers in the copper mines.

Bemelmans, Ludwig (1898–1962), US humorist, b. Austria. He came to the United States in 1914. His witty books, which he illustrated himself, are based on his experiences in the hotel and restaurant business. They include *Madeline* (1939), *Hotel Bemelmans* (1946), and *Dirty Eddie* (1947).

Benalcázar, or **Belalcázar, Sebastián de** (*c.* 1479–1551), Spanish conquistador. He accompanied Christopher Columbus on his third voyage (1498) and joined Francisco Pizarro in the conquest of Peru (1532). He founded several settlements in Colombia and searched for El Dorado. In 1541 he became governor of Popayán province. Long involved in political intrigues, in 1550 he was convicted of killing a rival conquistador, but he died before his appeal could be heard.

Benares. *See* Varanasi.

Ben Bella, Ahmed (1919–), Algerian political figure. After service in the French army in World War II, he joined the movement for Algerian independence from France. Imprisoned (1950), he escaped (1952). After helping found the *Front de Libération Nationale* (1954) to wage armed struggle, he was imprisoned again (1956–62). Independence won (1962), he was elected president. He sponsored reforms but was overthrown in a coup (1965).

Bench, Johnny (Lee) (1947–), US baseball player, b. Oklahoma City. A catcher, he joined the Cincinnati Reds in 1967. In 1975, he helped lead the team to its first World Series win since 1940.

Benchley, Peter (1940–), US author, b. New York City. A reporter and magazine writer, he wrote *Jaws* (1974), an immensely popular novel about a shark that terrorizes a resort community, and *The Deep* (1976).

Benchley, Robert (1889–1945), US humorist, b. Worcester, Mass. A drama critic for *Life* (1920–29) and the *New Yorker* (1929–40), he also wrote and acted in a number of witty short films and performed on radio. His books include *Of All Things* (1921), *Pluck and Luck* (1925), *The Treasurer's Report* (1930), *From Bed to Worse* (1934), and *Benchley Beside Himself* (1943).

Benchmark. △180.

Bender-Gestalt Test, in psychology, a test devised by Lamatta Bender to aid in the diagnosis of mental and neurological disorders. The subject is instructed to copy, as accurately as possible, a series of nine geometrical designs. The test is indicative of a child's visual-motor level of maturation and may detect evidence of organic brain dysfunction as well as personality problems.

Bends, or decompression sickness, nitrogen saturation of the tissues brought on by an increase, followed by a swift decrease, in atmospheric pressure. It is most common in divers and tunnel workers. Symptoms are pains in the joints, particularly the knees. Treatment consists of proper decompression and recompression procedures, and administration of oxygen.

Benedict, Ruth Fulton (1887–1948), US anthropologist whose theories of culture and personality were influential. She conducted extensive fieldwork among the southwest Indian tribes of the United States, as well as with the Serrano of California and the Canadian Blackfoot. Her best known work is *Patterns of Culture* (1934) which described cultural behavior patterns. Other works include *Zuni Mythology*

(1935), and *The Chrysanthemum and the Sword* (1946), a work on Japan.

Benedict XI, Roman Catholic pope (1303–04), b. Niccolo Boccasini (*c.*1240). A member of the Benedictine order, he was made a cardinal in 1298 and served on missions to England and France. He was noted for his sanctity and administrative abilities. In 1638, he was beatified by Pope Clement XII.

Benedict XIII, antipope (1394–1423), b. Pedro de Luna (*c.*1328). He was elected antipope mainly on his promise to end the Great Schism, but failed to do so. *See also* Great Schism.

Benedict XIV, Roman Catholic pope (1740–58), b. Prospero Lambertini (1675). He was concerned with improving the living conditions of all classes of people. He attempted to improve the church spiritually and politically.

Benedict XV, Roman Catholic pope (1914–22), b. Giacomo della Chiesa (1854). During World War I, he strived for peace among nations, stressing pacifist idealism. He tried to unite all Roman Catholics, made changes in the Curia, and published a new Code of Canon Law.

Benedictines, Roman Catholic monastic order founded in the 6th century by St. Benedict. The first monastery was at Monte Cassino, Italy. Benedictine monasteries, which follow St. Benedict's rule, later spread all over the world. △1086.

Benelux Economic Union, European economic union, forerunner of the European Common Market. The 50-year treaty creating this economic union of Belgium, the Netherlands, and Luxembourg was signed in 1958 to replace an earlier customs union formed in 1948. The treaty went into effect Nov. 1, 1960. △1356.

Beneš, Eduard (1884–1948), Czechoslovak statesman. A disciple of Tomaš Masaryk, he actively promoted Czech independence during World War I and became the first foreign minister of the newly created state (1918–35). He was delegate to the Paris peace conference; member of the council of the League of Nations; chief proponent of the Little Entente. Beneš was elected president of Czechoslovakia in 1935. After resigning in Sept. 1938 to protest German occupation of the Sudetenland, he headed the Czech government-in-exile from London. He returned in 1945; was reelected president in 1946; but resigned in 1948 after the Communist takeover.

Benét, Stephen Vincent (1898–1943), US author, b. Bethlehem, Pa. Noted for his poetry and short stories, he won a Pulitzer Prize in 1929 for his epic poem, *John Brown's Body* (1928). His brother, William Rose Benét, was also a writer.

Benevento, city in SW Italy, NE of Naples; capital of Benevento prov. Est. as Malies by the Samnites, it was an important Roman town on the Appian Way. Manfred, King of Naples and Italy, was killed here 1266; site of Lombard-Saracenic cathedral and Trajan's Arch (Porta Aurea). Industries: agricultural machinery, optical instruments, bricks. Pop. 59,578.

Bengal, region in India, partitioned in 1947, including West Bengal state, India, and Bangladesh, and combined delta of the Ganges and Brahmaputra rivers; ruled by King Gopala (AD 750) who founded Pal dynasty, spreading Buddhism and prosperity through region; followed by Senas, a Hindu people, in the late 11th century; invaded by Mohammed Khalji in 12th century, who reorganized region under Muslims; Akbar, Mongol emperor, ruled from 1576, when Bengal became the richest region in empire. Conquered by British 1757, it became center of British Indian Empire with Calcutta as capital city; made an autonomous region (1937) with present boundaries secured in 1947. Area: 77,442sq mi (200,575sq km).

Bengal, Bay of, NE inlet of the Indian Ocean, bounded by India and Sri Lanka (W), India and Pakistan (N), Burma (E), Indian Ocean (S); many principal rivers empty into the Bay, including Ganges, Brahmaputra, Kirstna, Mahanadi; major ports on its shores are: Madras, Calcutta, Akyab, Chittagong, Visakhapatnam, Trincomalee. Length: approx. 1,300mi (2,093km). Width: 1,000mi (1,610km).

Bengali, a major language of the Indian subcontinent. It is spoken by virtually all of the 75 million inhabitants of Bangladesh, and by 45 million more in the Indian province of East Bengal. Bengali belongs to the Indic branch of the Indo-European family of languages. In number of speakers it ranks sixth or seventh in the world. △866.

Benghazi (Banghazi), city in Libya, on the NE shore of the Gulf of Sidra, 400mi (644km) E of Tripoli; city has been conquered and ruled by the Romans, Vandals, Byzantines, Arabs, and Turks (16th century to 1911); the Italians, using Benghazi as a colonizing headquarters in the 1930s, developed it into a seaport, naval and air base, and WWII supply base. One of the two capital cities in Libya, it is commercial and industrial center for Cyrenaica prov. Industries: shipping, construction, oil, food processing. Founded by the Greeks 6th century BC. Pop. 170,000.

Benguela (Benguella), city in W Angola, Africa; S of Lobito on Atlantic Ocean; capital of Benguela prov.; site of railroad built in 1920's. Produces and exports sisal, corn, sugar, coffee. Founded 1617. Pop. 35,-162.

Ben-Gurion, David (1886–1973), Israeli political figure, prime minister (1948–53, 1955–61, 1961–63), b. as David Green in Poland. Ben-Gurion was the prime figure in the establishment of the state of Israel. He emigrated to Palestine (1906). Expelled by the Turks during World War I, he returned when the British took control. Encouraging Jewish immigration in the 1920s and 1930s in the hopes of bringing about a Jewish national homeland, he became (1935) head of the Zionist Executive, a worldwide organization. Though he called for the Jews of Palestine to fight for independence (1939), he cooperated with the British during World War II.

After the war he led the struggle against the British until independence (1948), then became the new state's first prime minister and led it through a war with Arab states (1948–49). After resigning (1953), he returned to the government as defense minister (1953) and soon became prime minister again (1955), leading Israel through another conflict with the Arabs (1956). Resigning (1961), he quickly returned to the premiership. After retiring (1963), he continued his political involvement, forming a splinter party from the dominant Mapai party, which he had helped found (1929) and led. His books include *Rebirth and Destiny of Israel* (1954), *Israel: Years of Challenge* (1965), and *Memoirs* (1970). △1380.

Ben-Hur (1880), popular novel by Lew Wallace about the rise of Christianity. It is narrated by Judah Ben-Hur, a Jew wrongly accused by Messala, a former friend, of attempting to murder the Roman governor of Judea. He is sent to the galleys for life, and his mother and sister are imprisoned. He escapes to revenge himself on Messala by defeating him in a chariot race and to rescue his mother and sister, now lepers. All three convert to Christianity after the women's disease is cured by Christ. The most notable film version was produced in 1926 and reissued with sound in 1931. Directed by Fred Niblo, it starred Ramon Novarro and Francis X. Bushman.

Benin, independent nation of E Africa, formerly called Dahomey. Once a French protectorate, it is a country of 40 ethnic tribal groups and a low-level economy.

Land and Economy. Located in the bulge on the S side of W Africa, Benin is bordered by Nigeria, Toga, Upper Volta, and Niger, with 75 mi (121km) on the Gulf of Guinea. The coast is hot and humid, and there are two rainy and two dry seasons; average annual rainfall is 32in (813mm). Benin has three plateaus, one fertile, another of bare rocks, and a third with streams flowing to the Volta and Niger rivers and including the Atakora range. The E section is a plain. Subsistence agriculture is the economic base. Half of exports were palm products or cotton.

People. The leading class in Benin is composed of male-line descendants of the Aja (Fons, or Dahomey) who had established the early kingdom. Trained for civil service by the French, they are the best educated; literacy is 25% among school-age children. In the N are the nomadic Fulani and the Somba tribe, hunters with no political organization; E are Baribas. 90% of the population is rural, and 65% practices animist religion. French is the common language.

Government. Although the 1970 charter provided for a three-member presidential council to govern until 1976, it was toppled in 1972 by Maj. Mathieu Kereku.

History. Benin's history dates back to three principalities—Allada, Porto-Novo, and Dahomey—in the S area who were being pushed by the N Kingdom of Abomey in the 16th century. Dahomey was the most aggressive, pushing N and selling slaves. In 1863 the king of Porto-Novo sought French protection. By 1892 France had subjugated all groups and made them protectorates as French West Africa. The 1956 Overseas Reform Act expanded civil rights, and in 1960 the country became independent as Dahomey. The official name was changed to Benin in 1976. Economic and regional rivalries have caused numerous

Bellflower

Saul Bellow

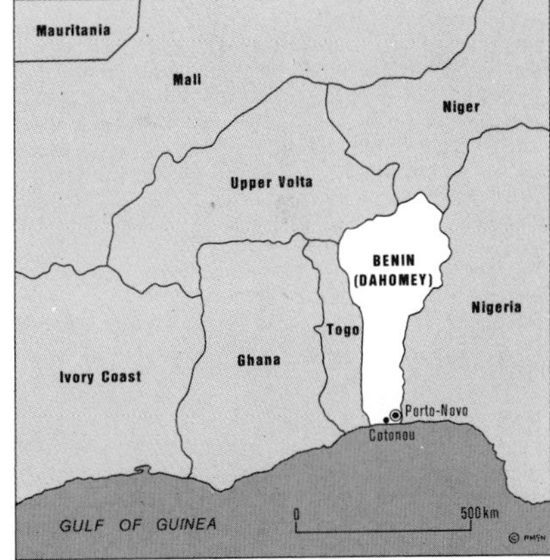
Mauritania
Mali
Niger
Upper Volta
BENIN
(DAHOMEY)
Nigeria
Togo
Ghana
Ivory Coast
Porto-Novo
Cotonou
GULF OF GUINEA
0
500km

Benin

Benin: Ganvie

military coup d'états and changes of government since 1960.

PROFILE

Official name: Benin
Area: 43,483sq mi (112,621sq km)
Population: 3,100,000
Density: 60per sq mi (23per sq km)
Chief cities: Porto-Novo (capital); Cotonou
Government: Military
Religion: Animist, Christian, and Moslem
Language: French (official)
Monetary unit: CFA franc
Gross national product: $348,000,000
Per capita income: $122
Industries: peanuts, cotton, bicycles
Agriculture: peanuts, cotton, coffee, tobacco, palm oil
Minerals: petroleum
Trading partners: France (major), European Common Market, United States, Canada

Benin, Kingdom of, West African state from *c.* 1400–1897. It established friendly relations with Portugal, sending an ambassador in the 16th century, and carrying out an extensive trade in pepper, cloth, ivory, palm products, and slaves. Benin was subjugated by Great Britain in 1897–98 and is now a part of Nigeria. △1212, 1214.

Benin Art. △1214.

Benin City, city in S Nigeria, 150mi (242km) E of Lagos, on a branch of the Benin River; capital of Mid-Western state; an administrative, trade, and cultural center during 13th–18th centuries; excavations have uncovered art treasures of this period. Industries: rubber processing, mining, lumber, yams, coconut palms. Pop. 116,774.

Benitoite, a ring silicate mineral, barium titanium silicate, found only in San Benito County, Calif. Hexagonal system tabular, triangular crystals. Glassy blue to white; hardness 6–6.5; sp gr 3.6. Valuable gemstone when transparent, without flaws, and of good color.

Benjamin, in Genesis, youngest son of Jacob, born to Rachel who died during childbirth. His tribe settled between Judah and Ephraim. According to the New Testament, the apostle Paul descended from this tribe.

Benjamin, Judah Philip (1811–84), Confederate statesman, b. St. Thomas. A lawyer, he served (1853–61) as US Senator from Louisiana. During the Civil War, he was attorney general (1861), secretary of war (1861–62), and secretary of state (1862–65) of the Confederacy. After the South's defeat, he escaped to England where he was a prominent lawyer.

Bennett, James Gordon (1795–1872), US reporter, editor, and publisher who founded the New York *Herald*, b. Scotland. He developed national news coverage for the New York *Courier* and *Enquirer* before founding the *Herald* in 1835. His innovations included financial, sports, and society reporting, critical reviews, and extensive use of telegraphed reports from correspondents.

Bennett, Richard Bedford (1870–1947), Canadian politician. In 1927 he became leader of the Conservative party. As prime minister (1930–35), he advocated preferential tariff agreements within the British Commonwealth and met with partial success at the 1932 Imperial Economic Conference at Ottawa. He led the Conservative opposition until his retirement from politics in 1938.

Bennett's Comet. △90.

Ben Nevis, mountain in W Scotland, in Inverness-shire, near Fort William, overlooking Glen Nevis; highest point in the British Isles, 4,406ft (1,344m).

Bennigsen, Rudolph von (1824–1902), German political leader. From Hanover, he was a cofounder of the Nationalverein (1859), which advocated a united, democratic Germany. In 1867 he helped found the National Liberal party and served as its president until 1898. He served in the German Reichstag (1871–82, 1888–97), as its president 1873–79.

Benning, Fort, US Army installation in W Georgia; largest infantry camp in the United States. Est. 1918. Area: 97,000acres (39,285hectares).

Bennington, town in SW Vermont, 31mi (50km) W of Brattleboro; seat of Bennington Co; headquarters of Ethan Allen and the Green Mountain Boys; scene of British defeat by Americans in 1777; location of Bennington College (1925). Industries: agriculture, plastics, paper, electronical equipment. Pop. (1970) 7,950.

Bennington, Battle of (Aug. 16, 1777), American Revolutionary War battle in which British forces, under Col. F. Baume, were defeated by American forces under Gen. John Stark while attempting to seize needed supplies in Vermont. The defeat marked the beginning of British Gen. Burgoyne's defeat and was a turning point in the war.

Benny, Jack (1894–1975), US comedian, b. Benjamin Kubelsky in Waukegan, Ill. He began in vaudeville at the age of 17, using a violin (which he had studied seriously) as a comic prop. "The Jack Benny Show" ran on radio 1932–55 and on TV 1950–65. He also appeared in films. He was known for his delayed, deadpan delivery and his pretended vanity (he was always 39) and stinginess.

Bent, William (1809–69), US frontiersman, b. St. Louis. With his brother Charles he established Bent's Fort, Colorado, as a trading post in 1832. He was the state's first permanent white settler. He served as a scout in the Mexican War.

Bentham, Jeremy (1748–1832), English philosopher, jurist, and social reformer. Trained as a lawyer but never practicing, Bentham developed the theory of utilitarianism based on the premise that "the greatest happiness of the greatest number" should be the object of individual and government action. This philosophy was spelled out in his *Introduction to the Principles of Morals and Legislation* (1789). His followers were responsible for much of England's early reform legislation. *See also* Utilitarianism. △860.

Benthic Division, all of the ocean bottom from the high-tide line to the greatest depths. It is divided into two main systems, the littoral and the deep-sea. The littoral system is divided into eulittoral and sublittoral zones and the deep-sea into the bathyal and abyssal zones.

Benthos, the forms of life on the ocean floor. They include sessile animals like sponges and barnacles, creeping forms like crabs and snails, and burrowing ones like clams and worms. The term "benthos" is also applied to the deepest part of the ocean. *See also* Benthic Division. △624, 626.

Bentivoglio, Italian dynasty that controlled Bologna in the late 15th century. They rose to power as propapist Guelf leaders. After two family attempts to seize power in the early 15th century, Annibale became virtual lord of the city (1443–45). Assassinated, he was succeeded by Sante (died 1463) who clarified Bolognese independence of the papacy and allied with Milanese Sforzas. In the early 1500s, the family, driven from Bologna, settled in Ferrara.

Bentley. △1694.

Benton, Thomas Hart (1889–1975), US painter, b. Neosho, Mo. He was a leader of the regionalist movement and was famous for his paintings of rural and small-town life and for his many murals (including those for the Truman Library in Independence, Mo.). He was also the teacher of Jackson Pollock.

Benton v. Maryland (1969), US Supreme Court decision overruling *Palko* v. *Connecticut* (1937) and declaring that the double jeopardy provision of the Fifth Amendment is applicable to state proceedings. *See also* Palko v. Connecticut (1937).

Benz, Karl (1844–1929), German pioneer of the internal combustion engine. After some success with an earlier two-stroke engine, Benz built a four-stroke in 1885 that, first applied to a tricycle, achieved great success when installed in a four-wheel vehicle in 1893. Benz was the first to make and sell light, self-propelled vehicles built to a standardized pattern. Hundreds of vehicles had been built by the turn of the century.

Benzedrine. *See* Amphetamine.

Benzene, colorless volatile sweet-smelling flammable liquid hydrocarbon (formula C_6H_6) obtained in petroleum refining. Benzene is the simplest aromatic hydrocarbon having a structure containing a hexagonal ring of unsaturated carbon atoms (benzene ring). It is a raw material for manufacturing many organic chemicals and is also a useful solvent. Properties: sp. gr. 0.879; melt. pt. 41.9°F (5.5°C); boil. pt. 176.18°F (80.1°C). △1556, 1560–62.

Benzoic Acid, colorless crystalline weak carboxylic acid (formula C_6H_5COOH) made from toluene. Properties: sp. gr. 1.266 (at 15°C); melt. pt. 252.32°F (122.4°C); boil. pt. 480.2 (249°C).

Ben-Zvi, Itzhak (1884–1963), Israeli political figure, president (1952–63); b. Isaac Shimshelevich in the Ukraine. Fleeing Russia, he settled in Palestine (1907). There he worked with David Ben-Gurion and other Zionist leaders to create the institutions basic to the formation of the state of Israel, including Histadrut, the dominant labor organization, and the Mapai party, the leading political force. At Israel's independence (1948) he became a member of parliament and was elected president in 1952, serving until his death.

Beograd. *See* Belgrade.

Beothuk, now-extinct people once inhabiting Newfoundland, perhaps the first Indians seen by white explorers. They were noted for their custom of painting their bodies with red ochre. Only a handful survived among the English colonists, and in time these apparently crossed the Belle Isle Strait and became intermixed with the Naskapi.

Beowulf (?8th century), Old English epic poem. It tells how the murderous monster Grendel terrorizes King Hrothgar's Danish domains until Beowulf, a Swedish prince, kills it by tearing off its arm. Grendel's mother seeks revenge, but Beowulf kills her in an underwater battle. Fifty years later the aged Beowulf, now king of Sweden, fights and slays a fire-breathing dragon, but dies of his wounds.

The poem's unknown author used already ancient material—the gloomy folklore, violent history, and harsh morality of the pagan Germanic peoples before their migration to England—to construct a lyrical tragedy infused with the newer and gentler sentiments of Christianity. It is written in long, alliterative lines with four strongly emphasized syllables. Metaphors are frequently used, but similes are rare.

Berbers, Caucasoid African people, believed to originate from the E Mediterranean, who constitute the basic population of Morocco, Algeria, and Tunisia. Their traditional livelihood is by subsistence farming, the chief crops being grain, vegetables, and fruit, with some animal husbandry, especially among the nomadic tribes. Typical Berber houses are single-story, built of stone, with a few small windows to minimize heat penetration. Each village or nomadic tribe is governed by decisions taken at meetings which all respectable and healthy adult men attend.

Berchtesgaden, town in West Germany, 10mi (16km) S of Salzburg, Austria, in the Bavarian Alps. Salt mined since the 12th century; site of Adolf Hitler's villa retreat, Berghof (1938); bombed by Allies Mar. 1945; popular resort. Pop. 4,500.

Berchtold, (Count) Leopold von (1863–1942), Austro-Hungarian statesman. As foreign minister (1912–15), he was responsible for the ultimatum sent to Serbia (1914) after the assassination of Archduke Francis Ferdinand at Sarajevo, which was the immediate cause of World War I. △1304.

Berea, city in NE Ohio; suburb of Cleveland; site of Baldwin-Wallace College (1845). Industries: farm implements, greenhouses. Inc. 1850. Pop. 22,396.

Berengar I (died 924), king of Italy from 888 and crowned Holy Roman Emperor by Pope John X in 915. Founder of a line of 9th–11th century princes, he had a career of shifting fortunes against local nobles, invading Magyars (899), and French armies. He was finally murdered by one of his own men.

Berengar II (*c.* 900–966), self-styled king of Italy (950–61) and protagonist in the career of Otto the Great. When Berengar attacked Pope John XII, Otto came to pope's defense and was crowned Holy Roman Emperor (962). Subsequent negotiations between John and Berengar ended in Otto deposing John and imprisoning Berengar.

Berenson, Bernard (1865–1959), US art critic, b. Vilnius, Lithuania. He was taken to the United States as a child. An authority on Italian Renaissance art, he published a number of books on the subject. For most of his life he lived in Italy at his home, I Tatti (willed to Harvard University), a gathering place for intellectuals.

Berg, Alban (1885–1935), Austrian composer. A student of Arnold Schoenberg, Berg composed his relatively few works in a complex, highly individualized style based on Schoenberg's 12-tone system. His opera *Wozzeck* (1923) is regarded as one of the masterpieces of 20th-century opera. He also composed a *Violin Concerto* (1935) and began another opera,

Lulu, which was unfinished at his death. △1256, 1364.

Bergama, town in W Turkey, 50mi (81km) N of İzmir; site of ancient Greek city (Mysia); former capital of Pergamum kingdom (3rd century BC); political and cultural center of the East for nearly four centuries; early center of Christianity; commercial center under Byzantine and Ottoman empires. Industries: carpets, iron, silver and copper mining. Crops: tobacco, olives. Pop. 24,121.

Bergamo, city in N Italy; capital of Bergamo prov. Est. by Gauls, it became a Roman town; destroyed by Attila; joined Italy 1859; site of Romanesque cathedral, baptistry (1340). Industries: textiles, cement. Pop. 124,626.

Bergen, port city in SW Norway, on the North Sea; capital of Hordaland co; 3rd-largest city in Norway; industrial and cultural center; site of University of Bergen (1948), National Theater (1850), several museums and art galleries, Rosencrantz Tower (1562), Haakonshallen (13th-century Viking hall). Industries: shipbuilding, electrical equipment, textiles, processed fish. Founded in the 11th century, Bergen was Norway's chief city and the residence of several medieval kings. Pop. 115,590.

Bergenfield, town in NE New Jersey, 15mi (24km) E of Paterson; site of Old South Church (1799). Industries: pharmaceuticals, machinery, clothing. Pop. (1970) 29,000.

Bergman, (Ernst) Ingmar (1918–), Swedish stage and film writer-director. With a versatile company of artists and a strong personal vision, he has created dark allegories, sex satires, and complex studies of human relationships. His major films include *The Seventh Seal* (1956), *Wild Strawberries* (1957), *The Virgin Spring* (1959), *Persona* (1965), *Scenes from a Marriage* (1974), and *The Magic Flute* (1975). △1370.

Bergman, Ingrid (1915–), Swedish actress whose acclaimed stage performances—*Joan of Lorraine* (1946), *Liliom* (1940), and *Anna Christie* (1941)—led to a long and varied film career in Hollywood. She won Academy Awards for *Gaslight* (1944), *Anastasia* (1956), and *Murder on the Orient Express* (1974).

Bergschrund, either one deep and wide crevasse in a glacier, or a series of parallel and narrow ones. The breaks are produced by tension within the ice, often at the point where the moving ice separated from the immobile or apron ice. The formation is more common in old or retreating glaciers. △262.

Bergson, Henri (1859–1941), French philosopher of evolution. He saw the world as a struggle between man's life force (élan vital) and the material. Man perceives the material through the use of his intellect while the life force is perceived through intuition. It is through intuition that one perceives the reality of time. He received the Nobel Prize for literature in 1927. Among his many works are *Time and Free Will* (1889), *Laughter* (1901), *Creative Evolution* (1907), and *The Creative Mind* (1934).

Beria, Lavrenti Pavlovich (1899–1953), head of the Soviet Secret Police (NKVD). His revolutionary activity began in Georgia. In 1921 he was appointed security police chief in Georgia. As NKVD head in 1938, he took part in Stalin's purges and controlled labor camps. When Stalin died in 1953, he was arrested and secretly executed for treason. △1344.

Beriberi, disease caused by deficiency of Vitamin B_1 and other vitamins, frequently brought on by a diet of polished rice. Symptoms are weakness of legs, then arms. Therapeutic doses of B complex vitamins are the treatment.

Bering (Beringa) Island, island in E USSR, in SW Bering Sea, off the coast of Kamchatka peninsula; largest of the Komandorski group; flat and barren lands suffer severe windstorms; named for Vitus Bering, Danish navigator who served Russia and died here 1741; chief town is Nikolskoye. Width: approx. 15mi (24km). Length: approx. 55mi (89km).

Bering Sea, northernmost reach of Pacific Ocean, bounded by Siberia (NW), Alaska (NE), and separated from the Pacific Ocean by the Aleutian Island chain; connected with Arctic Ocean via the Bering Strait; ice-locked in winter months. Exploration for Russia by Danish navigator Vitus Bering in early 18th century led to international recognition of great fur-seal resource. Sale of Alaska to the United States in 1867 precipitated the Fur-Seal Controversy (1881). Area: approx. 878,000sq mi (2,274,020sq km).

Bering Sea Fur-Seal Controversy, dispute between various nations, mainly the United States and Britain and Canada, concerning control of the eastern Bering Sea and its lucrative fur-seal trade. After 1867 US hunters endangered the seal population of the region by overhunting. In 1881 US citizens demanded control of the entire region, seized British ships, and weakened Canadian commercial interests. In 1893 an international board of arbitration ruled in favor of the British. An agreement in 1911 among Britain, Japan, Russia, and the United States limited hunting and made concessions to Canadian interests.

Bering Strait, strait at N extreme of Bering Sea, separating W Alaska from extreme E Siberia and connecting Bering Sea (S) with the Arctic Ocean (N); named after Vitus Bering, Danish explorer who served Russia. Width: approx. 55mi (89km).

Berkeley, George (1685–1753), Irish philosopher and churchman. Educated at Trinity College, Dublin, Berkeley wrote his important *Principles of Human Knowledge* (1710), soon popularized in *Three Dialogues Between Hylas and Philonous* (1713). His radical empiricism failed to convince readers that experience is composed of bundles of ideas alone. No more successful were various American projects (1720–31), including a projected college for American Indians. He was created Anglican Bishop of Cloyne (1734–53) and pursued his criticisms of materialism and exposed logical errors in mathematics in the *Analyst* (1734), and *Siris* (1744). *See also* Empiricism; Materialism.

Berkeley, city in W California, N of Oakland; originally a land grant from Spain to Peralta family in 1820; annexed to the United States 1853 and named Oceanview; name changed in 1866 to Berkeley; site of Armstrong College (1918), the University of California (1868), Lawrence Radiation Laboratory (atomic research), Lawrence Hall of Science. Industries: food processing, chemicals, metal products. Founded 1853; inc. 1878. Pop. (1970) 116,716.

Berkeley, Busby. △1362.

Berkelium, radioactive metallic element (symbol Bk) of the actinide group, first made (1949) by alpha-particle bombardment of Am^{241}. Properties: at. no. 97; most stable isotope Bk^{247} (1.4×10^3 yr). *See also* Actinide Elements.

Berkley, residential city in SE Michigan; suburb of Detroit; 12mi (19km) SSE Pontiac. Inc. 1932. Pop. (1970) 21,879.

Berkshire Festivals, summer musical festivals founded in 1934, and since held at Tanglewood, Mass., with the Boston Symphony Orchestra. In 1940 the Berkshire Music Center was founded. The Berkshire Festivals are the most widely known of such events in North America and serve as a proving ground for many talented and aspiring but unknown musicians.

Berkshire Hills, series of low mountains with forests, lakes, and streams in W Massachusetts. Highest point is Mt Greylock, 3,491ft (1,065m).

Berle, Adolf Augustus, Jr. (1895–1971), US lawyer, b. Boston. He became one of Franklin D. Roosevelt's Brain Trust as a specialist in corporation law. In 1936, he was a delegate to the Inter-American Conference at Buenos Aires. He was Assistant Secretary of State (1938–44) and later an advisor to President Kennedy.

Berle, Milton (1908–), US comedian, b. Milton Berlinger in New York City. He began his career in vaudeville and appeared in Broadway shows and films. His pioneer television series, "The Texaco Star Hour" (1948–53), won him the nicknames "Mr. Television" and "Uncle Miltie."

Berlin, Irving (1888–), US composer of musicals and over 1000 popular songs, b. Israel Baline in Russia. His successful Broadway musicals include *Annie Get Your Gun* (1946) and *Call Me Madam* (1950). Two highly successful films are *Easter Parade* (1948) and *White Christmas* (1954). His many popular songs include "Alexander's Ragtime Band," "White Christmas," and "God Bless America."

Berlin, city in East Germany, on the Spree and Havel rivers; former capital of Germany. Core of the city developed from two Wendish villages of Berlin and Kölln which merged in 1307. It was nearly destroyed in the Thirty Years' War (1618–48) but was rebuilt. In the 17th century a canal connecting the Oder and Spree rivers helped it as a great trading center; it developed as an 18th-century industrial center and in

Beowulf

Bergen, Norway

Ingmar Bergman

Irving Berlin

1871 became the capital of the German Republic. Before its virtual destruction in WWII, it was the 2nd-largest city in Europe and 5th-largest in the world.

In July 1945, Berlin was divided into four sectors: British, French, US, and Russian. Tension and distrust between Russia and the three Western powers resulted in Berlin Blockade by Russia in 1948. Massive US airlift made the blockade ineffective, and it was lifted in 1949. After this, the Russians organized the Democratic Republic of Germany (East Germany) with East Berlin as its capital. In 1951, West Berlin became one of the states of the German Federal Republic (West Germany). Further tension between the United States and Russia developed during the East Berlin rebellion of 1953 and led to the erection (1961) of East Germany's Berlin Wall, which was an attempt to stem the flow of refugees out of East Berlin. *See also* Berlin, East; Berlin, West.

Berlin, Conference of (1884–85), meeting of the major European nations, the United States, and Turkey in Berlin to discuss the problems of West African colonization and arrange for free trade along the Niger and Congo rivers. The conference affirmed British claims on Nigeria and Belgian claims on the Congo, but other agreements on trade and political neutrality proved untenable in the years to follow.

Berlin, Congress of (1878), meeting of European states after the Russo-Turkish war, which Russia won. It overrode the Treaty of San Stefano by which Russia had received large areas in the Caucasus and gained independence for Serbia, Montenegro, and Bulgaria, and semi-independence for Bosnia and Hercegovina. At the congress, German chancellor Otto von Bismarck established the Treaty of Berlin, which limited Russia's naval power, divided Bulgaria, and allowed Austria-Hungary to occupy Bosnia and Hercegovina △1232, 1298–1300.

Berlin, East, city and capital of East Germany; site of state opera, Humboldt University (formerly Frederick William University), and St. Hedwig's Cathedral. On the site of the Royal Palace is Marx-Engels Square. In the Soviet Military Cemetery is a massive statue of a Soviet soldier, built partly from the remains of Hitler's Chancellery. A fine zoo and many museums are also here. Moscow-designed apartment buildings line Karl Marx Allee, the sector's showcase. Erection of the Berlin Wall in 1961 put the famous Brandenburg Gate totally in Soviet zone. Industries: clothing, electrical goods, chemicals. Pop. 1,085,441.

Berlin, West, city and state of West Germany, more than 100mi (161km) inside East Germany. The main street, Kurfürstendamm, runs through the heart of city, and contains cafés, theaters, hotels, and night clubs; site of Tiergarten Park, Olympic Stadium, Dahlem Gallery, Benjamin Franklin Hall, and Dahlem Free University (1948). Industries: electrical goods, clothing, machinery, foodstuffs. Pop. 2,130,900.

Berlin Airlift (1948–49), an operation put into effect by the United States and Great Britain after the USSR closed all roads and rail lines between West Germany and Berlin, cutting off supply routes to the city. The 11-month airlift, in 272,264 flights, provided basic necessities to blockaded Berlin. △1342.

Berlin Decree (1806), act by Napoleon directed against the British blockade of European ports. It placed Britain under a French blockade.

Berlin Wall, barrier built between East and West Berlin by the East Germans (1961). The fortified and heavily guarded wall cut off movement and communication between West Berlin and the rest of East Germany except at official crossing sites. △1346.

Berlioz, Hector (1803–1869), French Romantic composer who astounded his contemporaries with innovative orchestral writing in such works as *Symphonie fantastique* (1830), *Harold in Italy,* for viola and orchestra (1834), and *Roméo et Juliette* (1839). He also wrote grandiose, operas, including *Les Troyens* (1859). *See also* Romanticism in Music. △1246.

Bermuda, formerly Somers Islands; 300 islets and islands constituting British crown colony, 570mi (918km) SE of Cape Hatteras, North Carolina; includes larger islands of St George, Somerset, Bermuda, and Ireland; capital is Hamilton, on Bermuda Island. It became part of the crown in 1684 and was granted internal self-government in 1968; site of U.S. naval and air force base. Industries: tourism, perfume, ship repairing, pharmaceuticals, textiles, cut flowers. Area: 21sq mi (54sq km). Pop. 53,000.

Bermuda Grass, perennial grass native to the Mediterranean region and grown in North America as lawn and pasture grass. It has short, flat leaves, flower spikes at stem tips, and creeping rhizomes. Height: to 16in (40cm). Family Gramineae; species *Cynodon dactylon.*

Bern, capital city of Switzerland, on Aare River, 59mi (95km) SW of Zurich; capital of Bern canton; became part of Swiss Confederation in 1353; accepted the Reformation in 1528; during French Revolutionary Wars, Bern was occupied by French troops (1798); noted for medieval architecture, 15th-century town hall, Gothic cathedral, and university. Industries: precision instruments, chemicals, chocolate, tourism. Founded 1191 as military post. Pop. 162,405.

Bernadette of Lourdes (1844–79), b. Bernadette Soubirous. The daughter of a poor French miller, she began to see visions of the Virgin Mary (1858), who revealed to her the healing shrine of Lourdes. In 1866 she became a member of the Sisters of Notre Dame at Nevers. △748.

Bernadotte, (Count) Folke (1895–1948), Swedish diplomat. In June 1948, as head of the Swedish Red Cross, he was appointed UN mediator to negotiate a truce between the newly created state of Israel and the Arab countries. On Sept. 17, while negotiating a permanent armistice, he was killed by Israeli partisans in Jerusalem.

Bernadotte Dynasty, family of Béarn, France. In 1810 Jean Baptiste Bernadotte (1763?–1844) was chosen crown prince to succeed the childless Charles XIII of Sweden who had adopted him. The son of a Franch lawyer, he rose from the ranks in Napoleon's army. Under his leadership Sweden acquired Norway from Denmark. He became King Charles XIV in 1818, founding the present Swedish dynasty. King Carl XVI Gustav, Sweden's king, is the seventh ruler of the Bernadotte dynasty.

Bernard, Claude (1813–78), French physiologist. He defined the role of the pancreas in digestion, the glycogenic function of the liver, and the regulation of blood supply by vasomotor nerves.

Bernard of Clairvaux (1091–1153), French mystic and religious leader. He was abbot of the Cistercian monastery of Clairvaux (1115–53). Under his direction, nearly 100 new monasteries were founded. In 1130 he became a churchman of international importance during a contested papal election and afterward became an adviser to several popes. He actively fought heresy and advocated the Second Crusade (1146). His devotion to the Virgin Mary and the Infant Christ greatly influenced his contemporaries and the future direction of the Roman Catholic Church. △ 1086.

Bernese Mountain Dog, Swiss draft dog and pet (working group) brought to Switzerland 2000 years ago by Roman soldiers. A hardy dog, it has a flat head with strong muzzle, hanging lips, and dewlaps; short, compact body; sturdy legs; and thick, medium length tail. The silky, long, slightly wavy coat is jet black with russet brown and white marks. Average size: 23–27.5in (58.5–70cm) high at shoulder; 50–70lb (23–32kg). *See also* Working Dog.

Bernhard of Lippe-Biesterfeld (1911–), prince consort of the Netherlands, married Juliana of Orange in 1937; became prince consort when she became queen in 1948.

Bernhard of Saxe-Weimar, Duke (1604–39), Protestant general in the Thirty Years War. He took command of the Swedish army during the battle of Lützen (Nov. 6, 1632) after King Gustavus II was killed in battle, and won an important victory. In 1633 he won the battle of Regensburg but was defeated by imperial forces at Nördlingen in 1634. His army went into French service in 1635 and scored important victories, climaxed by the capture of Breisach in 1638. He died suddenly of a fever the next year. *See also* Thirty Years War.

Bernhardt, Sarah (1844–1923), original name Rosine Bernard, French actress of legendary international stature, known as the greatest tragedienne of her day. Her superb potrayals in *King Lear* (1867), *Ruy Blas* (1867), *Phèdre* (1874), and *Hernani* (1877) earned her the title "divine Sarah." She also toured Europe and the United States, managed the Theatre Sarah Bernhardt in Paris (1899) where she played Hamlet, made two silent films (1912), and continued acting even after a leg amputation (1914).

Bernini, Gianlorenzo (1598–1680), Italian architect and sculptor. He dominated sculpture in his time, but his reputation failed when the Baroque style went out of favor. It has since been regained. Early portraits—psychological studies—include the "Vigevano" bust (1617–18), the "Montoya" bust (*c.* 1621), and "Bellarmine" bust (1622). Later works, including "Francis I d'Este" (1650–51) and "Louis XIV" (1665), represent portrait bust in the ultimate Baroque style.

His architectural work was largely executed in his later career, and many of his most important plans and designs were never executed. In 1637 he designed the facade towers for St. Peter's, Rome, but the project ended in disaster because of technical problems and nearly ruined his career. His design for the square of St. Peter's (1662–64) is a masterpiece. He was commissioned to design the new Louvre in 1665, but the plan, though influential, was never realized. He designed several churches, including S. Andrea al Quirinale in Rome (1658–70), the Palazzo di Montecitorio (1650), and the S. Maria dell' Assunzione in Arrica (1662–64). His artistic aim, to express the mysteries of the Catholic religion with artistic clarity, is best realized in the sculpture "Ecstasy of St. Theresa" (1645–52) in Santa Maria della Vittoria, Rome. *See also* Baroque Art. △1162, 1164.

Bernoulli, Daniel (1700–82), Swiss mathematician and member of a famous family of mathematicians. His book on hydrodynamics indicated that fluid pressure decreases as the velocity of fluid flow increases. This statement is Bernoulli's Equation. He also attempted the first statement of the kinetic theory of gases. △1496.

Bernoulli's Equation, the relation between the work done on a moving liquid by pressure forces and its change in kinetic and potential energy. Generally stated in the form $p + \frac{1}{2} v^2 + gy =$ constant, where p is the pressure, v the velocity, g the density, and y the height of the fluid at any point. The equation makes it possible to measure the velocity of a liquid by measuring its pressure at two points, as with a manometer or Pitot tube. △1496.

Bernstein, Basil. △890.

Bernstein, Leonard (1918–), US conductor, composer, and pianist, b. Lawrence, Mass. He debuted in 1943 and was associated with the New York Philharmonic Orchestra as a conductor (1955–58) and as music director (1958–69), after which he devoted a great deal of time to composing and writing. During his tenure with the New York Philharmonic he became well known and popular both as a conductor and as a musician. His compositions include three symphonies, ballets, and music for the Broadway shows *Candide* (1956) and *West Side Story* (1957).

Berra, Yogi (1925–), US baseball player, b. Lawrence Peter Berra in St. Louis. A catcher and hitter, he played for the New York Yankees (1946–63) and the New York Mets (1965). He compiled 358 home runs, a record for a catcher. He also managed the Yankees (1964) and the Mets (1972–75). He was elected to the Baseball Hall of Fame in 1972.

Berry, Charles Ferdinand, duc de (1778–1820), French nobleman, second son of Charles X. During the French Revolution, he served in the royalist army of the Prince de Condé. From 1801–14, he was in exile in England. Returning to France during the reign of Louis XVIII, he was assassinated by a group trying to kill off all Bourbon claimants to the throne. His widow, Marie Caroline Ferdinande Louise, duchess de Berry, later tried to claim the throne for his son.

Berry, Jean de France, duc de (1340–1416), French prince during Hundred Years' War and a generous patron of the arts. His heavy taxation to support the wars led to a peasant revolt in 1381; however, he counseled for peace. His art treasures included tapestries and notable illuminated manuscripts.

Berry, historic region and former prov. in central France; originally a settlement of the Bituriges Cubi, part of Roman Aquitance, it was purchased by French Crown 1101; made a duchy 1360; returned to France 1601; a prov. until 1789, when France was divided into depts.; cattle farming region; chief city is Bourges.

Berry, small, fleshy fruit containing many seeds. It consists of an outer skin, fleshy middle, and inner membrane enclosing the seeds. Often juicy and edible, a true berry comes from a flower ovary with petals attached underneath (superior ovary). Berries include tomato, grape, eggplant, and red pepper; citrus fruits are modified berries. False berries are fruits formed from the matured ovary wall and other flower parts, often the floral tube. They can be distinguished from true berries by flower remnants left on the fruit (cranberry). △360.

Berthelot, Pierre Eugène Marcellin (1827–1907), French chemist. By synthesizing a number of organic compounds, including natural fats, ethyl alcohol, methyl alcohol, benzene, and methane, he destroyed the spurious distinction between the organic and inorganic. In the 1860s he did important work in thermochemistry, including the invention of a calorimeter, used to measure chemical reaction heat. In 1895 he was appointed foreign secretary.

Berthier, Louis Alexandre, Prince de Wagram (1753–1815), Napoleon's trusted assistant and chief of staff of the Grande Armée, sovereign prince of Neuchâtel. He fought during the American and French revolutions, Napoleon's first reign (when he acquired his titles), and served Louis XVIII until Napoleon's reappearance.

Berthollet, Claude Louis, Comte (1748–1822), French chemist. He discovered the structure of ammonia, showed the bleaching ability of chlorine, and predicted the law of mass action, though his views were ignored on this subject. He was made a senator and a count by Napoleon.

Bertillon Measurement, system of measuring human physical characteristics (eg length of middle finger), evolved originally by Alphonse Bertillon (1853–1914) for criminal identification, and now used extensively by physical anthropologists. △918.

Berwyn, residential city in NE Illinois, 10mi (16km) W of downtown Chicago; located on the Chicago Sanitary and Ship Canal. Inc. 1891. Pop. (1970) 52,502.

Beryl, a ring silicate mineral, beryllium aluminum silicate. Hexagonal system, usually prismatic hexagonal crystals; glassy white, blue, yellow, green, pink; hardness 8; sp gr 2.6–2.8. Gemstone varieties are aquamarine (pale blue-green) from Brazil; emerald (deep green) from Colombia; and morganite (pink) from Madagascar. Cut stones have little brilliance, but are valued for intense color. △240.

Beryllium, metallic element (symbol Be) of the alkaline-earth group, first isolated (1828) by Friedrich Wöhler. It occurs in many minerals including aquamarine and emerald (both forms of beryl). The metal is used in certain alloys that combine lightness with rigidity. Beryllium and its oxide are also used as moderators in nuclear reactors. Properties: at. no. 4; at. wt. 9.01218; sp. gr. 1.85; melt. pt. 2332°F (1279°C); boil. pt. 5378°F (2972°C); most common isotope Be^9 (100%). *See also* Alkaline-earth Elements. △1554.

Berzelius, Baron Jöns Jakob (1779–1848), Swedish chemist, one of the founders of modern chemistry. His accomplishments include the discovery of the elements cerium, selenium, and thorium; the isolation of the elements silicon, zirconium, and titanium; the determination of atomic weights; and the devising of a modern system of chemical symbols. He prepared the first table of atomic weights, and he contributed to the founding of the radical theory. *See also* Periodic Table.

Besançon, city in E France, at the foot of the Jura Mountains; contains ruins of a Roman arch, aqueduct, and theater; became part of France 1676. University of Besançon opened 1691. Industries: textiles, food processing, clock- and watchmaking. Pop. 113,000.

Besant, Annie (1847–1933), English theosophist and social reformer. A supporter of birth control and free thought, she joined the Theosophical Society in 1889, serving as its president from 1907 until her death. She lived for many years in India, where she established (1898) the Central Hindu College at Benares. She was later active in the movement for Indian self-government and was president of the Indian National Congress in 1917. She wrote many books on theosophy. *See also* Theosophy.

Bessarabia, historical region in SW European USSR; primarily in Moldavian SSR and the Ukraine, it forms passageway from Russia to Danube valley. Kishinev is capital. Greek colonists settled Black Sea coast 7th century BC; site of Roman colony Dacia until *c.* AD 4th century when Goths, Huns, Avars, and Magyars invaded; by 7th century Slavs had settled in the region. Kievan Russians held control 9th–11th centuries; it was included in Moldavia 1367; ceded to Russia 1812; proclaimed autonomous republic 1917; renounced Soviet ties 1918 and declared independent Moldavian republic (united with Romania); forced to inc. into USSR 1940 (confirmed 1947). Crops: grapes, grains, tobacco, sugar beets, fruit. Area: 17,600sq mi (45,584sq km).

Bessel, Friedrich Wilhelm (1784–1846), German mathematician and astronomer. A self-taught astronomer, by the age of 26 he was appointed by Frederick William III of Prussia to build an observatory at Königsberg, where he remained for the rest of his life as director. In 1818 he produced a new star catalogue and in 1838 he measured the parallax of 61 Cygni, giving the first measurement of a star's distance. He worked out the general method of mathematical analysis involving the functions that bear his name.

Bessemer, city in N central Alabama, 10mi (16km) SW of Birmingham. Industries: lumber, steel. Settled 1887. Pop. (1970) 33,428.

Bessemer Process, the first method for mass-producing steel. Carbon and other impurities are removed from molten pig-iron with a blast of air forced through the molten metal in a Bessemer converter. After most carbon is removed, some is restored to desired proportions, along with manganese, with the addition of ferromanganese when the metal is poured into a large ladle. Ingot molds are then filled with the steel from the ladle. Invention of the process is credited to Henry Bessemer, an English engineer who obtained the first patent in 1855, and to William Kelly, an American inventor whose patent was issued in 1857. △1236, 1284, 1594.

Best, Charles Herbert (1899–), Canadian physiologist, b. W. Pembroke, Me. He participated in the discovery of insulin in 1921 with F.G. Banting. From 1929–65 he was head of the department of physiology at the University of Toronto and chief of the Banting-Best department of medical research after Banting's death (1941).

Beta Centauri, or **Agena,** or **Hadar,** bluish-white giant star in the constellation Centaurus. It is associated with a 9th-magnitude companion. Characteristics: apparent mag. 0.61; absolute mag. −4.3; spectral type B1; distance 300 light-years. △110.

Beta Crucis, or **Mimosa,** blue-white subgiant star in the constellation Crux (Southern Cross). Characteristics: apparent mag. +1.28; absolute mag. −4.0; spectral type B0; distance 370 light-years.

Beta Decay. △1484.

Betancourt, Rómulo (1908–), Venezuelan lawyer, economist, and president (1959–63). Founder of the reformist Democratic Action (AD) party and president of a junta that governed from 1945–47, he was elected president in 1958 after living 10 years in exile.

Beta Rays, or **Beta Particles,** particles emitted spontaneously by certain radioactive isotopes (undergoing beta decay), discovered and identified as energetic electrons by Antoine Becquerel (1876). They cause ionization along their path and have fairly high penetrating power. Their energy, ranging from 0.003 million to 13 million electronvolts, is characteristic of the emitting isotope. Beta decay results from the breakdown of a neutron in the nucleus to a proton, an electron, and an antineutrino. *See also* Radioactivity. △1480.

Betatron, field accelerator in which electrons move in a circle inside a toroidal vacuum chamber. Acceleration is induced by the changing magnetic flux of an electromagnet. Energies can reach 300 MeV.

Betelgeuse, or Alpha Orionis, red supergiant star and the second-brightest star in the constellation Orion. It is a pulsating variable whose diameter fluctuates between 330 and 460 solar diameters. Characteristics: apparent mag. +0.85 (mean); absolute mag. −5.5 (mean); spectral type M2; distance 650 light-years.

Betel Nut Palm, also areca, tall slender palm tree native to Malaya; planted throughout Southeast Asia and the Pacific islands. Height: to 100ft (30.5m). It has small feather-shaped leaves. Its seeds are chewed as a stimulant or narcotic. Family Palmaceae, species *Areca catechu.*

Bethany (Al-'Ayzariyah), town in Jordan, 2mi (3km) E of Jerusalem, at foot of Mt of Olives; Biblical home of Mary, Martha, Lazarus; traditional site of the Ascension of Jesus and Jesus' raising of Lazarus from the dead.

Bethany, city in central Oklahoma, 7mi (11km) W of Oklahoma City. Industries: feed and flour milling, cotton ginning. Inc. 1910. Pop. (1970) 21,785.

Bethe, Hans Albrecht (1906–), US nuclear physicist, b. Strassburg, Germany (now Strassbourg,

Hamilton, Bermuda

Bern, Switzerland

Bernese mountain dog

Leonard Bernstein

France). He helped to develop the atomic bomb, although his major scientific contribution has been in the field of stellar energy processes. He determined the source from which the sun and stars derive their energy. He was honored in 1961 with the Fermi award for his work with atomic energy, and in 1967 with a Nobel Prize for his work on stellar energy production and his contributions to the nuclear reaction theory.

Bethel (Baytin), archeological site and village in Jordan, 11mi (18km) N of Jerusalem; as city of ancient Palestine it preceded Jerusalem as a Jewish shrine; traditional site of Jacob's dream of ladder reaching to heaven; occupied by Israel 1967.

Bethel, manufacturing town in SW Connecticut; former home of showman P.T. Barnum; site of Gen. Israel Putnam's memorial campground and museum. Industries: electronic components, chemicals. Settled *c.* 1700; inc. 1855. Pop. (1970) 10,945.

Bethel, town in SW Pennsylvania, S of Pittsburgh; site of Fort Couch during Revolutionary War. First Presbyterian Church W of Allegheny Mts was founded here 1776. Chief industry is coal mining. Inc. 1950. Pop. (1970) 34,791.

Bethesda, city in W central Maryland, 7mi (11km) from Washington, D.C.; site of research center of National Institutes of Health (1939), Naval Medical Center (1942), and National Cancer Institute. Settled in late 17th century by Scottish, English, and Irish, it was named for the Bethesda Presbyterian Church, which they built in 1820. Pop. (1970) 71,621.

Bethlehem (Bayt Lahm), town in Jordan, 5mi (8km) SSW of Jerusalem; traditional birthplace of Jesus Christ; early home of King David; site of Biblical massacre of the Innocents (Matt. 2:16) and Church of the Nativity built by Constantine (AD 326), oldest Christian church still in use. Under Ottoman Empire 1571–1915, and then part of British Palestine mandate until 1948, it was inc. into Jordan 1950; occupied by Israelis since 1967 war. Tourism and sale of religious souvenirs are principal industries. Pop. 16,313.

Bethlehem, city in E Pennsylvania on the Lehigh River, 5mi (8km) E of Allentown; site of Lehigh University (1865), Moravian College (1807). Bach Choir performs here at annual festival. Industries: steel, cement. Settled 1740 by Moravians; inc. 1917. Pop. (1970) 72,686.

Bethlen, (Count) Stephen (1874–1947), Hungarian statesman. After a short period of Communist rule, Hungary achieved a degree of political stability under Bethlen, who was appointed premier by Regent Horthy in 1921, an office he held until 1931. Bethlen persuaded the League of Nations to help with financial reconstruction (1923), but economic conditions worsened. Active in party politics 1931–35, Bethlen retired in 1939.

Beth-shan, or Beth-shean, ancient town at the meeting of the Valley of Israel with the Jordan River Valley. Settled *c.* 4000 BC, it was an Egyptian outpost from the 15th–12th centuries BC and later a Philistine town until conquered by the Israelites at the time of David. During Hellenistic times it was an important center of the Decapolis, a league of cities. It was taken by the Romans in 64 BC. Later it became the capital of a prov. of the Byzantine Empire. It declined after being conquered by the Arabs in AD 636 and was renamed Beisan.

Bethune, Mary McLeod (1875–1955), US educator, b. Mayesville, S.C. The daughter of former slaves, she began teaching in 1895. In 1904 she established the Daytona Normal and Industrial Institute for Negro Girls in Florida. In 1923 it became Bethune-Cookman College, of which she was president until 1942. Active in national affairs, she founded the National Council of Negro Women and was director of Negro affairs in the National Youth Administration (1936–44).

Beti, Mongo (1932–), pseud. of Alexandre Biyidi, African novelist, b. Cameroon. An important figure in the Negritude movement, he explores modern African life and the effects of colonialism, often through satire. Among his works are *The Poor Christ of Bomba* (1956), *Mission to Kala* (1958), and *King Lazarus* (1960).

Betjeman, John (1906–), English poet. He became Poet Laureate in 1971. His verse, traditional in form, was concerned with the details and oddities of English domestic life. *Summoned by Bells* (1960) was a verse autobiography of his early years. He was also a noted authority on Victorian and Edwardian architecture.

Betony, common name for colorful herbs of the mint family including *Stachys grandiflora* and *S. officinalis.* Flowers of this perennial from Asia Minor are white or purple arranged in showy clusters.

Bet Sh'ean, town in NE Israel, in Jordan River valley, 18mi (29km) SE of Nazareth; excavations have revealed settlements (*c.* 3,000–2,000 BC); important center in the 18th and 19th Egyptian dynasties; mentioned in the Bible as Beth-shan; one of ten cities of Decapolis; taken by Arabs AD 636; some early structures remain. Modern town was settled 1949 by Israelis. Produces textiles. Pop. 11,900.

Bettelheim, Bruno (1903–), US psychologist, b. Vienna, Austria. He applied the psychoanalytic approach to emotionally disturbed children, detailing the roles that parents play in the development of their children's personalities. His books include *Love Is Not Enough* (1950) and *The Empty Fortress* (1967).

Bettendorf, city in E Iowa, on Mississippi River 5mi (8km) E of Davenport; named for W.P. Bettendorf who est. railroad equipment business here in 1902. Industries: foundry products, railroad equipment, farm equipment. Settled 1840; inc. as town 1903, as city 1922. Pop. (1970) 22,126.

Bevan, Aneurin (1897–1960), British socialist statesman. An active trade unionist, he became a Labour member of Parliament (1929) and gradually assumed leadership of the Labour party left wing, whose views he expressed in the *Tribune,* which he edited (1940–45). As minister of health (1945–51), he inaugurated the National Health Service. His book *In Place of Fear* was published in 1952.

Bevatron, an elementary-particle accelerator, similar to a synchrotron, that accelerates particles into the billion-electron-volt (BeV) range. *See also* Synchrotron.

Beverly, city in NE Massachusetts, on Massachusetts Bay; site of Endicott Junior College (1939) and North Shore Community College (1965); in 1775 the schooner *Hannah* was outfitted and commissioned here by Gen. George Washington as the first ship of the US Navy. Industries: electronic tubes, shoes. Settled before 1630; inc. as town 1668, as city 1894. Pop. (1970) 38,348.

Beverly Hills, city in S California, entirely surrounded by Los Angeles; famous as home of movie and television stars. Inc. 1914. Pop. (1970) 33,416.

Bevin, Ernest (1884–1951), British trade unionist and socialist statesman. Organizer of the Dockers' Union (1910–21) and general secretary of the Transport and General Workers' Union (1921–40), Bevin planned the general strike (1926) and later criticized Labour's failure to overcome unemployment. He was minister of Labour and National Service (1940–45), and as foreign secretary (1945–51) he assisted in Europe's economic recovery and helped establish the North Atlantic Treaty Organization.

Beyazid. *See* Bajazet.

Beyle, Marie Henri (1783–1842). *See* Stendhal.

Bezique, card game for two or more players. Most popular is the two-handed version that is played with 64 cards. Bezique for three requires a 96 card pack and for four a 128 card pack. The game was developed in France and England in the 1860s and was the principal inspiration for pinochle. The cards in each suit rank ace, 10, king, queen, jack, 9, 8, 7. The twos to the sixes are disregarded. Each player is dealt eight cards; another card is turned up to establish trump. A player other than the dealer leads and the others follow, playing any card they desire. Cards are drawn from the deck after each trick. The highest card or trump wins the trick, and the game continues until all cards, from the hand and deck, have been played.

Bhagavad Gita, or "The Song of the Lord," popular episode in the sixth book of the Hindu epic, the *Mahabharata.* Probably composed shortly before the Christian era, the Gita presents Krishna as the Supreme God who, if worshiped, will save men. The Gita begins with a battle between two related but hostile clans. The archer Arjuna, seeking his relatives in the opposing army, hesitates until Krishna reminds him of his duty to fight. Devotion and faith toward the Lord is the central theme. *See also* Hinduism; Krishna; Mahabharata. △848.

Bhakal (Sheep). △608.

Bhakti. △1036.

Bhavnagar (Bhaunagar), city in W India, on Gulf of Cambay (Khambhat); chief port of Kathiawar Peninsula; capital of former princely state of Bhaunagar; site of two colleges of Gujarat University. Industries: textiles, bricks, tiles. Exports: cotton, grain, oilseeds. Founded 1723. Pop. 222,462.

Bhumibol (or Phumiphon) Adulyadej (1927–), king of Thailand (1946–) as Rama IX. Born and educated in the United States, his powers are ceremonial.

Bhutan, a monarchy with an advisory council and 130-member national assembly. Located in the Himalayas, on NE border of India, it is bounded by Tibet and China (N), Assam and India (E), Assam and West Bengal (S), and Sikkim and Tibet (W). The official capital is Thimbu; traditional capital is Punakka.

Eight high mountain ranges, including the Himalayas, cross the country; the highest peak is Kula Kangri, 24,784ft (7,559m). Torrential annual rain storms, with an average fall of 200–250in (508–635cm), are recorded.

The people of Bhutan are predominantly Bhutias. Their religion is a form of Buddhism closely related to Tibetan Buddhism. The language, basically Tibetan, is Dzongka. They are mainly farmers of small plots; rice is the chief crop. Yaks, pigs, sheep, cattle, and tanguns (a breed of pony) are raised. Handicrafts of metal, wood, and leather are produced.

In the 9th century the original inhabitants of Bhutan were conquered by Tibetan soldiers who ultimately became the present Bhutians. China took the country in 1720; in 1772 relations with Britain began, and in 1864, Britain occupied part of S Bhutan; portions were annexed to India in 1865. By a 1910 treaty Britain agreed that it would subsidize Bhutan and manage its foreign affairs. When India gained its independence in 1949, it assumed Britain's role with Bhutan, while Bhutan managed its own internal affairs. A Chinese threat to the country in the 1960s caused India to close the Tibetan-Bhutanese border, and Bhutan built up a small army. In 1971, Bhutan joined the United Nations.

Government is conducted by a monarch and small advisory council. In 1954 a national assembly was formed; 25% of its 130 members is appointed by the king; the remainder is composed of village headmen, elected for five-year terms. The present ruler is Singhi Wangchuk, who succeeded his father in 1974.

PROFILE

Official name: Bhutan
Area: 18,147sq mi (47,001sq km)
Population: 1,300,000
Chief cities: Thimbu (official capital); Punakha (traditional capital); Paro Dzong
Religion: Buddhism
Language: Dzongka

Bhutto, Zulfikar Ali (1928–), Pakistani political leader. A protégé of Ayub Khan, he held several cabinet posts between 1958–63 before becoming foreign minister. Critical of the agreement ending the war with India, he left the government and formed the opposition Pakistan People's party (1967). After the 1970 election he refused to cooperate with Mujibur Rahman's Awami League, which had won a majority in the legislature. Civil war resulted. After Bangladesh (East Pakistan) gained independence, Bhutto became president of what remained of Pakistan (1971). Under a new constitution (1973), he became prime minister.

Biafra, former state in W Africa, formed from East-Central, South-Eastern, and River states of Nigeria. After it was est May 30, 1967, by Ibos, all economic aid was cut off by Nigeria. War broke out July, 1967; overwhelmed by numerous Nigerian attacks, Biafra's land size was reduced, oil fields (its main source of income) were lost, and its people suffered high casualties; secessionist attempt ended Jan. 15, 1970, when Biafra was reincorporated into Nigeria.

Biafra, Bight of, wide bay off coasts of Cameroon and Equatorial Guinea, W Africa; in E part of Gulf of Guinea; contains island of Fernando Pó.

Bialystok, city in NE Poland, approx. 100mi (161km) NE of Warsaw; capital of Bialystok prov.; manufacturing center. Industries: metal, textiles. Founded 1310. Pop. 166,600.

Biard, Pierre (1567–1622), French missionary in Canada. A Jesuit, he accompanied Père Masse and Jean de Poutrincourt to Acadia in 1611. His colony at St Sauveur des Monts (Bar Harbor) was destroyed by Samuel Argall acting on a commission from the governor of Virginia. Biard was returned to France, where he wrote *Relation de la Nouvelle France* (1616), while defending himself against charges of collaboration with Argall.

Biarritz, town in SW France, near Spanish border on Bay of Biscay. Native population is Basque; popular resort area since 1838 with mild climate, mineral waters, and beaches. Pop. 26,750.

Biathlon, sport that involves skiing and target shooting, popular in Scandinavia. Each competitor is required to ski 20 kilometers (12.4 miles), stopping four times during the race to fire at a fixed target with a rifle. A miss results in penalty time being added to the race time. The competitor with the lowest corrected time wins.

Bible, sacred scriptures of Judaism and Christianity. It is regarded as the source of divine revelation and of prescriptions and prohibitions for moral living. The Hebrew Bible, or Old Testament, excluding the Apocrypha, is accepted as sacred by both Jews and Christians. The Roman Catholic Church and Eastern Orthodox Church each accept parts of the Apocrypha as sacred, while Jews and Protestants do not. The New Testament is accepted as sacred only by Christians. *See also* Apocrypha; New Testament; Old Testament. △1130,1152. Following is a list of the books of the Bible.

Books of the Bible
(King James Version)
Old Testament

Genesis	Ecclesiastes
Exodus	Song of Solomon
Leviticus	Isaiah
Numbers	Jeremiah
Deuteronomy	Lamentations
Joshua	Ezekiel
Judges	Daniel
Ruth	Hosea
I Samuel	Joel
II Samuel	Amos
I Kings	Obadiah
II Kings	Jonah
I Chronicles	Micah
II Chronicles	Nahum
Ezra	Habakkuk
Nehemiah	Zephaniah
Esther	Haggai
Job	Zechariah
Psalms	Malachi
Proverbs	

New Testament

Matthew	I Timothy
Mark	II Timothy
Luke	Titus
John	Philemon
Acts	Hebrews
Romans	James
I Corinthians	I Peter
II Corinthians	II Peter
Galatians	I John
Ephesians	II John
Philippians	III John
Colossians	Jude
I Thessalonians	Revelation
II Thessalonians	

Bibliography, system of listing books, described and arranged for easy reference and study. Swiss naturalist Konrad von Gesner (1516–65) is credited with the first modern bibliography, *Universal Bibliography,* a listing of all living and deceased Latin, Greek, and Hebrew writers, published in 1545.

Bibliothèque Nationale, national library of France, located in Paris. The oldest in the world still in existence, it dates from the reign of Charles V (1364–80). First opened to the public in 1692, it receives a copy of every publication printed in France. The library is divided into nine departments, including books, coins, maps, and manuscripts.

Bibracte, former stronghold of Gaul atop Mt Beuvray in central France, 13mi (21km) WSW of Autu; scene of defeat of Helvetii by Caesar, 58 BC. Augustus moved population from Bibracte to Augustodunum, now Autun.

Bicameral System, legislative system having two chambers or branches. Its origin dates back to the House of Commons and House of Lords in the English Parliament. Bicameralism refers to the structure of the legislature, not its method of operation.

Biceps. △682.

Bichir, primitive bony fish found in African fresh waters. Elongated with large horny scales, it has 5–18 flaglike finlets along its back and a two-part swim bladder for breathing air at the water surface. Length: 2–3ft (61–91cm). There are 11 species including Congo *Polypterus weeksi*. Family Polypteridae. *See also* Osteichthyes.

Bichon Frise, French-Belgian dog (nonsporting group) descended from water spaniel. Popular in ancient times as item of barter; common street or circus dog in 1880s. It has a broad, round head; longish muzzle; and pronounced nose. Ears are dropped; a long body is set on strong-boned legs; and the tail is curved to lie over the back. The long, silky, loosely curled coat gives the dog a powder puff appearance; colors are solid white or white with cream, apricot, or gray. Average size: 8–12in (20.5–30.5cm) high at shoulder. *See also* Nonsporting Dog.

Bicycle, a light, two-wheeled steerable vehicle, propelled by human power, first made by Karl von Drais in Germany (1816) and developed as an important means of transportation and recreation in many countries. Englishman J.K. Starley demonstrated the first successful chain drive in 1885. Today most bicycles have a "diamond frame" invented in 1893, coaster or friction brakes, a drive system providing 1 to 18 possible ratios, inflatable tires, light-weight alloy wheels, and myriad accessories. △1688.

Bicycle Racing, sport, most popular in Europe and the United States, involving a variety of events, from the sprint to the internationally known Tour de France (begun in 1903), where the world's best cyclists compete annually in a road race more than 2,000 miles (3,220km) long. Racing in the United States was most popular during the 1920s and 1930s, when Madison Square Garden in New York City held six-day races. The sport in the United States suffered with the advent of the automobile and, unlike Europe, is only now conducted on an amateur level. Bicycle racing, a regular event at the Olympic Games, first blossomed with the invention of the pneumatic tire in 1888 by John Dunlop, an English veterinary surgeon.

Bicycle Thief (1947), Italian film. Among the foremost examples of postwar cinema realism, this film was directed by Vittorio De Sica from a screenplay by Cesare Zavattini. It featured nonprofessional actors in a carefully structured story of a poor man's search for the bicycle he needs for his job.

Bidault, Georges (1899–), French political leader. He is known for his leadership of the underground resistance movement during World War II. Following the war he headed the provisional government (1946). He served as coalition premier 1949–50 and was later minister of defense and foreign minister. He founded (1958) the Christian Democratic party, which opposed Charles de Gaulle's Algerian independence plan. He lived in exile in Brazil, returning to France in 1968. △1342.

Biddle, John (1615–62), founder of English Unitarianism. His *Twelve Arguments Drawn Out of Scripture* (1644) denied the trinitarian doctrine. Biddle was arrested in 1645 and the book was publicly burned in 1647. In 1654 he was exiled to the Scilly Islands for publishing *Two-fold Catechism.* He returned to the mainland in 1658, was arrested again in 1662, and died in prison.

Biddle, Nicholas (1786–1844), US financier, b. Philadelphia. After serving in US legations abroad and in the US Congress, Biddle became the president of the Bank of the United States in 1822. His strong management of the bank led to attacks on him and the bank by Pres. Andrew Jackson's followers, but he served until its charter expired in 1839.

Bidwell, John (1819–1900), US rancher and political figure, b. Chautauqua co, N.Y. He traveled to California with the first wagon train to leave Independence, Mo., in 1841. He worked at Sutter's Fort and then found gold on the Feather River. He bought a huge ranch and became a leading rancher. He served in the California legislature and militia and US House of Representatives. He ran for president on the Prohibition party ticket in 1892.

Biedermeier Style, a phase of German art (1816–48) characterized by simplicity, orderliness, and sober realism. The name is derived from a humorous literary character, a symbol of middle-class conservatism. Furniture of this style was well designed, using local materials and naturalistic stenciled decorations.

Biela's Comet. △92.

Bien-hoa, manufacturing city in S Vietnam, 20mi (32km) NNE of Saigon; former capital of Cambodia; site of US air base in Vietnam war. Pop. 82,506.

Biennial, plant that lives two years, producing flowers and seeds the second year. Some biennial

Bethlehem, Jordan

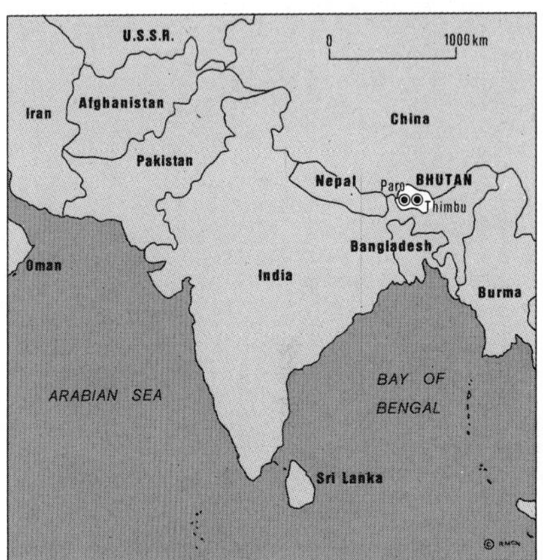
U.S.S.R.
0
1000km
Iran
Afghanistan
China
Pakistan
Nepal
BHUTAN
Paro
Thimbu
Bangladesh
Oman
India
Burma
ARABIAN SEA
BAY OF
BENGAL
Sri Lanka

Bhutan

Bichon frise

Bicycle

seeds planted in early spring will blossom that same year. Most biennials are sown from June to August and bloom the following year. Popular garden biennials include foxglove, Canterbury bells, and wallflower. Some biennial garden plants seem perennial because they reseed themselves. *See also* Annual; Perennial.

Bienville, Jean Baptiste Le Moyné, Sieur de (1680–1768), French colonizer of Louisiana, b. Canada. In 1698, he accompanied his brother, Sieur d'Iberville, from Canada to the mouth of the Mississippi River. He founded Mobile (1710) and New Orleans (1718) and was the governor of Louisiana (1701–12, 1717–26, 1733–43).

Bierce, Ambrose (Gwinett) (1842–?1914), US journalist, short story writer, and poet, b. Meggs co, Ohio. He wrote a well-known newspaper column "The Prattler," a mixture of literary gossip, epigrams, and short stories. His fame rests on three volumes of collected stories and other writings: *In the Midst of Life*, *Can Such Things Be?* (1893), and *The Devil's Dictionary* (1906). One of his most noted stories is "An Occurrence at Owl Creek Bridge." Bierce was known for a great, and often cruel, wit. He disappeared into war-torn Mexico, and his fate is unknown.

Bigamy, in English and US law, criminal offense of entering into a second marriage when a first marriage is still in effect. Bigamy is also the state of a man having two wives or a woman two husbands.

Bigard, Barney (1906–), US jazz clarinetist, b. Leon Albany Bigard in New Orleans. He was one of the soloists with Duke Ellington's Band (1928–42) and with Louis Armstrong's All Stars (1947–55). In 1961–62 he toured Europe and Africa.

Big-Bang Theory of Universe, cosmological theory postulating that at some time in the past all the matter of the universe was concentrated at near infinite density at one point and was subsequently hurled in all directions at great velocity by a cataclysmic explosion. Matter, evolved into galaxies, nebulae, etc, is still receding but with time the velocity has decreased. The universe thus has a finite size and age. The recently discovered microwave cosmic background radiation is thought to be the remnant radiation of the big bang and is thus evidence for this theory. *See also* Hubble Constant. △122,126.

Big Bend National Park, park in W Texas; features spectacular mountain and desert scenery and a wide variety of geological structures. The park is a triangle formed by a large bend in the flow of the Rio Grande River. Area: 708,221acres (286,830hectares). Est. 1935.

Big Dipper. *See* Ursa Major.

Big Four, term applied to the World War II Allies, the United States, Great Britain, and the USSR and China. The term was also applied to the leaders of those countries, President Franklin D. Roosevelt, Prime Minister Winston Churchill, Premier Joseph Stalin, and President Chiang Kai-shek.

Bighorn Mountains, mountain range in N central Wyoming, reaching 120mi (193km) into S Montana, E of the Bighorn River; contains Bighorn National Forest. Highest point is Cloud Peak, 13,175ft (4,018m).

Bighorn Sheep, or Rocky Mountain sheep, wild sheep, native to mountains of W North America, closely related to Siberian forms. Living in herds of about 50, their great climbing ability is aided by elastic foot pads. The largest curved horns so far measured reached 50in (1.3m). Height: 3.5ft (1.07m) at shoulder; weight: up to 300lb (136kg). Family Bovidae; species *Ovis canadensis*. *See also* Sheep.

Bignonia, a genus of woody vines native to North America and Japan that have small disks at ends of tendrils for climbing, compound leaves, and showy, yellow or reddish tubular flowers. The cross vine or trumpet flower *(B. capreolata)* grows in S United States. Family Bignoniaceae.

Big Sioux River, river in South Dakota; rises in NE South Dakota, flows SE to form South Dakota-Iowa boundary, and empties into the Missouri River in SE South Dakota. Length: 420mi (676km).

Big Spring, city in NW Texas, 78mi (126km) NW of San Angelo; seat of Howard co; site of Webb Air Force Base. Industries: chemicals, fertilizer, oil. Pop. (1970) 28,735.

Big Stick Diplomacy, US foreign policy in the early 1900s developed by Pres. Theodore Roosevelt, who said, "Speak softly and carry a big stick." The 1903 Skagway settlement of an Alaskan boundary dispute with Canada after the 1896 Klondike gold rush was a victory for the policy.

Bihár, state in NE India; bordered by Nepal (N), West Bengal state (E), Orissa and Madhya Pradesh states (S), Uttar Pradesh state (W); capital is Patna. Known in ancient times as Magadha, it was center of the Maurya (4th and 3rd centuries BC) and Gupta (AD 4th and 5th centuries) dynasties; drained by Ganges River, it is a rich agricultural area and produces a majority of the country's mica, coal, copper, and iron ore. Area: 67,198sq mi (174,043sq km). Pop. 56,387,296.

Bikel, Theodore (1924–), US folksinger and actor, b. Austria. In addition to doing concerts, recordings, and television shows, he has appeared on stage in *The Sound of Music* (1959–61) and in many films, including *My Fair Lady* (1964) and *The Russians Are Coming, the Russians Are Coming* (1966). He hosted a radio show (1958–63).

Bikini Atoll, formerly Escholtz Island; group of about 30 islets in W central Pacific Ocean; part of Ralik Chain (Marshall Islands), US-administered UN trust territory; scene of US atomic and hydrogen bomb tests 1946–1958; island was declared safe for habitation 1969. Area: 2sq mi (5sq km).

Bilateralism, agreement between two states to jointly pursue common interests. Bilateral agreements pertain to political, military, economic, technical, and cultural matters. Mutual benefit is generally the key to such agreements. Accordingly, agreements involve both great and small powers.

Bilateral Monopoly, market situation in which there is a pure monopoly on both the buyer's and seller's side, ie, there is a single purchaser of a good and a single seller of this good. An example of a bilateral monopoly would be a union selling the services of its workers to only one employer.

Bilbao, city in N Spain on the Nervión River, near the Bay of Biscay; capital city of Vizcaya prov.; important commercial center and seaport. Industries: chemicals, steel, shipbuilding. Founded *c.* 1300. Pop. 410,490.

Bilbo, Theodore Gilmore (1877–1947), US senator (1935–47), b. Pearl River co, Miss. A lawyer, he was a state senator (1908–12), lieutenant governor (1912–16) and governor (1916–20; 1928–32) of Mississippi before entering the Senate. He won popular support through his demagogic appeals to racism and white supremacy in the South.

Bildungsroman, German "educational novel," of which the prototype is Goethe's *Wilhelm Meister*, where an artistic temperament is taught by experience how to come to terms with reality. Gottfried Keller's *Der Grüne Heinrich* (1854–55) is the last direct example, while Thomas Mann's *The Magic Mountain* (1924) is a good example of an ironical parody of this traditional form.

Bile, complex mixture of substances secreted by the liver, stored in the gall bladder, and released into the intestine, where it aids in the absorptive process during digestion. △694.

Bile Acids, group of steroid acids present in bile. In man the commonest is cholic acid ($C_{24}H_{40}O_5$), which is conjugated by its carboxyl group to the amino groups of the amino acids glycine and taurine. The bile acids are emulsifiers for fats and fat-soluble vitamins, thus promoting their absorption by the intestine.

Bilharzia. △732.

Bilirubin, reddish-yellow bile pigment. It consists of a breakdown product of hemoglobin conjugated to glucuronic acid for excretion.

Bill, draft of a proposed law. It requires legislative action before it can become law. A bill before either house of the US Congress requires the approval of both houses to become a law.

Billbug, weevil that is pest of grasses and cereal crops. They have long snouts, or bills. The common corn billbug (genus *Sphenophorus*) is best known. Family Curculionidae.

Billerica, residential town in E Massachusetts, on Concord River. Industries: textiles, building materials, farming. Settled 1637; inc. 1655. Pop. (1970) 31,648.

Billiards, game most popular in the United States and England. It has several variations, played either with 3 balls (billiards) or 15 balls (pocket billiards). In billiards the standard table is 6 by 12 feet (1.8 by 3.66m), with 6 pockets (English) or no pockets (United States), where scoring is by caroms only. Pocket billiards is the more popular game in the United States. The table is 9 by 4.5 feet (2.7 by 1.4m), with 6 pockets. A cue ball is used along with 15 consecutively numbered balls. The object is to make a continuous run of 14 balls, leaving the 15th on the table. The 14 balls are then racked again, and the ball that remained from the previous game is used to scatter the racked balls. Players shoot until they miss sinking a ball, and the first player to score 150 points (one point for each ball) is the winner.

Billings, city in S central Montana, on Yellowstone River; seat of Yellowstone co; site of Eastern Montana College (1927), Rocky Mountain College (1883); nearby are Custer National Forest and Yellowstone National Park, and Inscription Cave (discovered 1937), containing ancient Indian writings. The Yellowstone Museum has Indian artifacts and relics of the area's history. Industries: oil refining, sugar refining, meat packing, flour milling, vegetable canning. Founded 1882 during construction of Northern Pacific Railroad; inc. 1885. Pop. (1970) 61,581.

Billion Dollar Congress, the 51st Congress, elected in 1882. It was named for its habit of representing special interests by granting them large sums of money and public privileges.

Bill of Exchange, unconditional written order from one party to another calling on him to pay on demand, or at some specified future date, a sum of money to some particular person, or to bearer. A check is a bill of exchange. △1126.

Bill of Rights, name given to the first 10 amendments to the US Constitution. These amendments were passed by Congress and ratified by the states in 1791, only four years after the signing of the Constitution. They were added because many in the United States feared tyranny by the new government, and several states were willing to ratify the Constitution only after George Washington promised to add such a list of liberties. Among the protections of the Bill of Rights are the freedom of worship, of speech, of the press, and of assembly; the right to bear arms; freedom from unreasonable search and seizure; the right to a speedy trial by jury; and protection from self-incrimination. Powers not granted specifically to the federal government were reserved for the states. *See also* Constitution of the United States. △1218.

Bill of Rights (1689), British statute enshrining the constitutional principles established after James II's abdication (1688) and accepted by William and Mary as a condition of their ascending the throne. It excluded Roman Catholics from the succession, set out the subject's political and civil rights, and effectively guaranteed parliamentary supremacy over the crown.

Billy Budd, novella by Herman Melville written shortly before his death in 1891 but not published until 1924. The symbolic, tragic story takes place aboard a British man-of-war in 1797. Billy Budd, an innocent young sailor, becomes the victim of the hatred of Claggart, the evil master-at-arms. Billy accidentally kills Claggart in reaction to a plot by Claggart against him. Captain Vere, commander of the ship, sympathizes with Billy but feels he has no choice but to hang him.

Billy the Kid (1859–81), US outlaw, also known as William H. Bonney, b. Henry McCarty in New York City. He moved to New Mexico in 1873 with his mother and stepfather. After killing a man in 1877, he took the alias William H. Bonney. In 1878 he killed a sheriff and led a gang of cattle rustlers. He was captured in 1880, tried, and sentenced to death. He admitted to 21 murders. He escaped jail, but was caught and killed by Sheriff Pat F. Garrett of Lincoln co, N. Mex.

Biloxi, city in SE Mississippi, on small peninsula between Biloxi Bay and Mississippi Sound on the Gulf of Mexico. New Biloxi was founded in 1719 and was the capital of French Louisiana until 1722, when New Orleans replaced it; site of "Beauvoir," last home of Jefferson Davis (1852–54), the Biloxi Light House (1848), and Ship Island (off the coast), a Union Fort in the Civil War. Industries: tourism, fishing, boatbuilding. Inc. 1896. Pop. (1970) 48,486.

Bimetallism, policy of defining the money of a country in terms of two metals, usually gold and silver, making each of them legal tender, and defining each of them in terms of the other. Bimetallism has not worked well and has not been used in recent years because the value of the metals changes with respect to each other.

Binary Star, stellar system consisting of two separate stars orbiting around a common center of gravity. Visual binaries are those whose component stars can be distinguished with the naked eye or through a telescope; spectroscopic binaries are visually unresolvable but show redshifts and blueshifts in their spectra as the individual stars move toward or away from the observer. *See also* Double Star; Eclipsing Variable. △110, 156.

Binary System. △1672.

Binary Theory. △48.

Binding Energy, energy that must be supplied to an atomic nucleus in order to split it into its constituent nucleons (neutrons and protons). A nucleus must be supplied with its binding energy before it will undergo fission (except in the case of radioactive decay). The mass of a nucleus is slightly less than the mass of its constituent particles. According to Einstein's law, $E = mc^2$, this difference in mass is equivalent to the energy released when the nucleons bind together. This is the energy source of the hydrogen bomb and the fusion reactor. *See also* Fission, Nuclear. △1482–84.

Binet, Alfred (1857–1911), French psychologist. He established the first French psychology laboratory (1889) and the first French psychology journal (1895). His greatest achievement was devising the first successful, practical intelligence tests (1905), which profoundly influenced the measurement of abilities in psychology and education the world over. *See also* Intelligence Testing; Stanford-Binet Scales. △778.

Bingham, George Caleb (1811–79), US painter, b. Augusta co, Va. Largely self-taught, he is best known for his genre Missouri scenes, as exemplified in *Shooting for the Beef* (1850) and *Fur Traders Descending the Missouri* (1845), considered his best, and certainly most famous, work.

Bingham, Hiram (1875–1956), US explorer-archeologist, b. Honolulu. His discovery, in 1911, of the Inca mountain city of Machu Picchu in the Peruvian Andes helped historians to retell the story of Peru before the Spanish conquest. He led numerous expeditions to South America to study Inca ruins and described his adventures in such works as *Inca Land* (1922), *Machu Picchu* (1930), and *Lost City of the Incas* (1948). He also served as governor of Connecticut (1925) and was a US senator (1925–33).

Binghamton, city in S central New York at the confluence of the Chenango and Susquehanna rivers. Harpur College of the State University of New York is here. Industries: shoes, electronic equipment. Inc. 1867. Pop. (1970) 64,123.

Bingo, board game, similar to lotto, usually played by a large group for cash prizes. Each player purchases one or more boards with each board containing five columns (B–I–N–G–O) with a total of numbers (between 1 and 75). The center portion of the board has an empty or "free space." Small balls, numbered to 75, are put in a box, and randomly selected. The first player to fill in five spaces in a row, either vertically, horizontally, or diagonally, wins the game.

Binoculars, optical instrument, for use with both eyes simultaneously, that produces a magnified image of a distant object or scene. It consists of a pair of identical telescopes, one for each eye, both containing an objective and eyepiece lens and a system, usually of prisms, to form an erect image. △1518.

Binomial Nomenclature, scientific system of giving each organism a two-part, Latin name. The first part is the genus and the second part the species, for example, *Homo sapiens* is the binomial name for humans. This system was developed by Swedish botanist Carolus Linnaeus in the 18th century. △408.

Binomial Theorem, rule for expanding an expression of the form $(x + y)^n$, where n is a positive integer, as a series. This is given by $x^n + n\,x^{n-1}y + \frac{n(n-1)}{2}\,x^{n-2}y^2 + \frac{n(n-1)(n-2)}{3!}\,x^{n-3}y^3 \ldots y^n$. If n is not a positive whole number the series becomes infinite (the binomial series).

Biochemistry, study of the chemical compounds and reactions occurring in living matter. It includes the isolation and identification of natural products of plants and animals—fats, proteins, hormones, enzymes, etc.—together with study of the complex reactions of these in metabolism. △1570.

Biodegradability, property of a substance that allows microorganisms to break it down into stable, simple compounds such as water and carbon dioxide. This property is utilized in refuse disposal.

Bioelectricity, electricity originating in living plants or animals. Different electrical potentials are built up within the organism. Bioelectricity caused by ionic separation across a membrane is associated with nerve impulses and muscle contractions.

Bioengineering, science of applying engineering techniques to the problems of medicine and biology. Also, the engineering of devices to aid or replace defective or insufficient body organs, for example, artificial limbs and hearing aids.

Biofeedback, from "biological feedback," monitoring of internal bodily states by using sensitive electronic instruments. People are trained to control internal functioning through operant conditioning. Using biofeedback, people can learn to consciously control their heart rate, blood pressure, and brain-wave patterns. The method holds promise for treating headaches, hypertension, and other problems related to the activities of the autonomic nervous system. *See also* Autonomic Nervous System. △748, 818.

Biogenetic Law, or recapitulation theory, principle that the stages that an organism goes through during embryonic development reflect the stages of that organism's evolutionary development.

Biological Clock, internal system in organisms that relates behavior to certain rhythms. Functions, such as growth, feeding, or reproduction, coincide with certain external events, including day and night, tides, and seasons. This innate sense of timing makes some animals feed during the day when food is available and they can see best. These "clocks" seem to be set by environmental conditions, but if organisms are isolated from these conditions, they still function according to the usual rhythm. If conditions change gradually, the organisms adjust their behavior gradually.

Biology, study or science of life, including botany, zoology, ecology, morphology, physiology, cytology, histology, genetics, embryology, and microbiology. These sciences deal with life and living things, including origin, history, makeup, development, function, and relationships of living things to each other and their environment. Biology is also the study of how life perpetuates itself and the differences between the living and not living.

Bioluminescence, production of light, without heat, by living organisms. Its biological function is varied: in some species (fireflies) it is a recognition signal in mating; in others (squids) it is a method of diverting predators for protection; and in many deep-sea fish it is simply a form of illumination. The light-emitting substance (luciferin) in most species is an organic molecule that emits light when it is oxidized by molecular oxygen in the presence of an enzyme (luciferase). Each species has different forms of luciferin and luciferase. Some jellyfish do not require an enzyme, light being emitted by a protein (photoprotein) when it is acted upon, in some species, by a calcium ion, in others, by molecular oxygen. △514, 626.

Biome, extensive community of animals and plants whose makeup is determined by soil and climatic conditions. Characteristically, there is distinctive, dominant vegetation, such as tundra, desert, or jungle. △580.

Biophysics, study of biological problems in terms of the laws and techniques of physics. Subjects studied include: the structure and function of such complex biological molecules as proteins and nucleic acids using X-ray diffraction methods; the conduction of electricity by nerves in terms of the action potentials created by the flow of sodium and potassium across the sheaths of nerve fibers; the transport of molecules across cell membranes using radioactive tracers and other physical methods; muscle contraction using electron microscopy and X-ray diffraction; energy transformations in living organisms; and the function of hormones in the body using radioisotopes as tracers. Applied biophysics is concerned with the design of biomedical instruments as well as the diagnosis and treatment of cancer using scanning techniques and radiotherapy.

Biosociology, the study of the interactions between the biological makeup of human beings and their social behavior. Such questions as the following are studied: How important are the physical characteristics a person is born with? How do they affect learning to get along with others? Are some abilities largely

Bighorn sheep

Bilbao, Spain

Billy the Kid

George Caleb Bingham

inherited or learned? *See also* Behavioral Ecology; Ethology.

Biosphere, or zone of life, portion of the earth from its crust to the surrounding atmosphere, encompassing all living organisms. It is self-sufficient except for energy and extends a few miles above and below sea level.

Biotin. *See* Vitamin H.

Biotin, member of the vitamin B complex (formula $C_{10}H_{16}O_3N_2S$) that occurs in small quantities in most cells. *See* Vitamin.

Biotite, one of the mica group of common rock-forming minerals. It is potassium and magnesium-iron aluminum silicate [$K(Fe,Mg)_2$ $(Si_3Al)O_{10}$ $(OH)_2$]. Common in igneous and metamorphic rocks. Monoclinic system tabular prismatic crystals, grains and scaly masses. Splits into elastic sheets. Black, dark green or brown; glassy. *See also* Mica.

Birch, any of about 40 species (genus *Betula*) of trees and shrubs native to cooler areas of the Northern Hemisphere. The smooth, resinous bark peels off in papery sheets. The double-toothed leaves are oval or triangular with blunt bases and arranged alternately on branches. The male catkins droop while smaller female catkins stand upright and develop into conelike clusters with tiny one-seeded nuts. Some well-known species are gray, sweet, and yellow birch. The American white or paper birch *(Betula papyrifera)* has clear white striped bark that peels naturally. It was formerly used for canoes and wigwam coverings by Indians. Height: to 80ft (24m). Family Betulaceae.

Bird, 8600 species of feathered vertebrates occupying every conceivable habitat from deserts and tropics to polar wastes. They are warm-blooded and have forelimbs modified to wings, hindlimbs for walking, and jaws elongated into a toothless beak. They lay eggs in nests, incubate the eggs, and care for young. They feed on seeds, nectar, fruit, and carrion and hunt insects and large prey. Sight is the dominant sense, with smell being the poorest. Size ranges from the 2.5in (6.4cm) bee hummingbird to the royal albatross with a wingspread of 11.5ft (3.5m), and the 8ft (2.4m) tall ostrich. Several extinct flightless birds were even bigger. Of the 27 orders, the perching birds include more species than all others combined.

The bird body is constructed primarily for flight with all its parts modified accordingly. There are several flightless groups of large land birds: ostrich, rhea, emu, cassowary, kiwi, and penguin. Flightless members of typically flighted groups also occur, such as the rail and cormorant. Birds are descended from thecodont reptiles with the first fossil bird, *Archaeopteryx*, dating from late Jurassic times. Class Aves. △526–538.

Bird Banding, practice of ringing a bird's leg with a light aluminum band for identification. Birds are released after banding. This practice is helpful in unravelling bird migration and distribution, life spans, and territorial requirements. Ornithologists share records on a worldwide basis. *See also* Ornithology.

Bird House, construction that provides a ready-made nest or nesting cavity for birds. Individual box houses with openings of varying size are good for titmice, chickadees, wrens, nuthatches, flickers, and some owls. Apartment house types attract colonies of purple martins. Open houses with bracket sides, bottom shelves, and roofs are good for phoebes, robins, and barn swallows. Depending on the species, bird houses should be placed 5–15ft (1.5–4.6m) above ground, in partial shade, and in a location protected from cats.

Bird Migration, periodic movement from one climatic zone or region to another, usually for feeding or breeding purposes. Few birds remain in the same locality for the entire year. They generally gather in flocks before migrating and use the colder part of their range for breeding. Distances traveled range from the Arctic tern's 22,000-mile (35,400-km) annual flight from pole to pole to the short altitudinal and local movements of tropical species. Migration is triggered by internal drives tied to the reproductive cycle and keyed by changes in day length, temperature, and food supply. Directional clues used during migratory journeys include innate factors, use of the sun and stars as a compass, and geographic features. △532.

Bird of Paradise, brightly colored, ornately plumed, perching bird of N Australia, New Guinea forests, and nearby areas. They generally have stocky bodies, rounded wings, short legs, and squarish tails. The males' plumes—wirelike, twisted, threadlike, or pennantlike—are black, orange, red, yellow, blue, or green and become erect during elaborate courtship displays and rituals. Pinkish streaked eggs (1–2) are laid in a cup-shaped nest of twigs, stems, and leaves on a branch. Length: 5–40in (12.5–102cm). Family Paradisaeidae.

Bird-of-Paradise Flower, ornamental plant native to S Africa. It grows from rhizomes and has stiff, leathery, oblong leaves. The flowers are brilliant orange and blue held in a boat-shaped, green bract. Height: to 5ft (1.5m). Family Musaceae; species *Strelitzia reginae*. △452.

Birds, The (414 BC), Greek comedy by Aristophanes. Disgusted with their world, a group of men persuade the birds to create a city halfway between heaven and earth in which they will have complete control of gods and men. An amusing fantasy, it illustrates man's eternal search for an ideal society.

Bird Sanctuary, area set aside for the shelter and protection of birds. Long-range management of proper food supplies and suitable nesting sites is essential. Gardens, woodlots, and orchards are suitable for songbirds; fields and pastures for game birds; marshlands, ponds, and lakes for waterfowl.

Birdseye, Clarence (1886–1956), US industrialist and inventor who developed a technique for deep-freezing foods, b. Brooklyn, N.Y. He began experimenting with freezing food in 1917 and had frozen fish on the market in 1925. He was one of the founders of General Foods Corp., held over 300 patents, and worked successfully to reduce drastically the time required to freeze foods.

Bird's-nest Fungus. △426.

Bird Spider. △490.

Birmingham, city in NW England; 2nd-largest British city; known for manufacture of cheap goods known as "Brummagem ware." Industries: cars, bicycles, chemicals, electrical equipment, chocolate (in suburb Bournville), guns, machine tools, plastic goods. Pop. 1,013,366.

Birmingham, industrial city and port of entry in N central Alabama, in Jones Valley; seat of Jefferson co; largest city in Alabama. Originally a cotton-growing area, it was founded 1871 by Elyton Land Co. in conjunction with Louisville and Nashville Railroad. It is the site of Samford University (1842), Birmingham-Southern College (1856), Daniel Payne College (1889), Miles College (1907). Industries: iron, steel, metalworking, fabricated metals, construction and transportation equipment. Inc. 1871. Pop. (1970) 300,910.

Birmingham, city in SE Michigan; suburb of Detroit, on the River Rouge. Settled 1819; inc. 1933. Pop. (1970) 26,170.

Birney, James Gillespie (1792–1857), US abolitionist, b. Danville, Ky. A slave owner turned reformer, he worked for the colonization of Liberia and worked in the American Anti-Slavery Society. A believer in political action, he ran for president as the Liberty party candidate (1840–44).

Birth Adjustments, problems of newborn infants who suddenly need to breathe, to adapt to a new temperature, to be fed through the mouth, and to eliminate through bladder and intestine. *See also* Birth Trauma.

Birth Control Pill, also often called Oral Contraceptive, a pill containing estrogen and progesterone hormones that prevents ovulation and thus the possibility of pregnancy. A widely used method of birth control, it has been associated with some serious and some minor side effects and should be prescribed on an individual basis. △706.

Birthmark, or nevus, an area of pigment, usually red, purple, yellow, or brown, appearing on the skin at birth or shortly after. Some are caused by concentrations of melanin, others (strawberry marks) by raised blood vessels. Most birthmarks fade or disappear with maturity.

Birth of a Nation, The (1915), US film. This Civil War melodrama was directed by D. W. Griffith who adapted the script with Frank Woods from two Thomas Dixon novels. The 12-reel film incorporated many technical innovations that were widely adopted later. It brought world renown to its star Lillian Gish. The film's sympathetic treatment of the early Ku Klux Klan caused Griffith to be characterized as a bigot. △1316.

Birth Order, sequence of birth of children in a family. Psychologists have studied the effects of birth order on personality development, noting, for example, that parents may be overanxious with the first and over-spoiling with the youngest. Parent attitudes are more important than birth order itself. △776.

Birth Rate, statistical system for determining the number of births in a given area, age group, socioeconomic stratum, or time period. The most common type is the crude birth rate, or the number of births per 1000 population per year.

Birth Rites, ceremonies (symbolic action accompanied by ritualistic speech) performed at the birth of a child. These serve both to celebrate a safe birth and to stress the fact that the child is a member of the society presenting the rite. The ceremonies usually involve relations with the spiritual world and are of virtually universal distribution (for example, christening in Western societies). *See also* Rites of Passage.

Birthstone, a gemstone associated with the month of one's birth and worn as a talisman. January, garnet; February, amethyst, March, bloodstone or aquamarine; April, diamond; May, emerald or agate; June, pearl or moonstone; July, ruby or onyx; August, sardonyx or carnelian; September, sapphire; October, opal, tourmaline, or beryl; November, topaz; December, turquoise, ruby, or zircon. △244.

Birth Trauma, theory that neurotic anxiety can be explained as a result of the shock experienced by an infant during birth, when it passes from the safe environment of the uterus into the more dangerous world outside. *See also* Birth Adjustments.

Biscay, Bay of, inlet of Atlantic Ocean, SW of France and N of Spain; noted for strong currents and sudden, violent storms. Chief ports: Bilbao, San Sebastián, Santander in Spain; Bayonne, Brest, La Rochelle, Saint-Nazaire in France. Resort area is along French coast; site of important sardine fishing grounds.

Biscayne Bay, inlet of the Atlantic Ocean on the E coast of Dade co, SE Florida. Miami is on its NW shore and the island of Biscayne Key is on the NE. Biscayne National Monument at S end of bay. Shallow, narrow inlet is 40mi (64km) long.

Bisection, Angle, geometrical construction to cut an angle into two equal parts. An arc is drawn, with its center at the vertex, cutting the sides of the angle at two points. Two arcs of equal radius are then drawn from these points, and a straight line drawn from their point of intersection to the vertex, thus bisecting the angle.

Bishop, Elizabeth (1911–), US poet, b. Worcester, Mass. Her poetry is disciplined and descriptive. She won the Pulitzer Prize in poetry for *Poems: North and South—A Cola Spring* (1955). Other works include *The Complete Poems* (1969).

Bishop, title for a rank within the ministry of the Christian church. Duties of the bishop include the general control of a particular diocese.

Bishops' Wars (1639, 1640), campaigns by Charles I of England against the Scots. Charles aimed to strengthen episcopacy by imposing English church ritual on Scotland; the 1638 Covenant pledged the Scots to defend presbyterianism. By the treaty of Ripon (1640), Charles was forced to pay an indemnity to the invading Scots.

Bismarck, Otto von (1815–98), German statesman. Born into a wealthy Prussian family, he dedicated his life to building, by any means, a strong, unified Germany under Prussian leadership. He entered the Prussian parliament in 1847 and served until he was appointed Prussian minister to the German diet (1851–59). Between 1859–62 he was ambassador to Russia and, in 1862, ambassador to France. In 1862 William I named him premier of Prussia. He quickly dissolved the parliament and expanded the army. In 1864, jointly with Austria, he seized Schleswig-Holstein from Denmark in a brief war. In 1866 he forced Austria into the Austro-Prussian (Seven Weeks) War. Austria was discredited as Prussia's rival among the German states, Schleswig-Holstein was granted outright to Prussia, and the Northern German Confederation was formed. Bismarck then turned to uniting the German states against France. Victory in the Franco-Prussian War (1870–71) brought the southern German states into the Prussian-led confederation. In 1871 William I was proclaimed German emperor and Bismarck the first chancellor. Bismarck now turned to alliances rather than wars to foster German interests. In 1872 he formed the Three Emperors' League with Austro-Hungary and Russia. He presided over the

1878 Congress of Berlin, which established spheres of influence in the Balkans, and the 1884 Berlin Conference that did the same for Africa. In 1879 he dissolved the Three Emperors' League by forming the Triple Alliance with Austro-Hungary and Italy. His one major failure was his 1871–78 *Kulturkampf* campaign against the Roman Catholic Church and the Catholic Center party. He dealt more successfully with the socialists. When repressive measures instituted in 1878 failed, he himself introduced sweeping social reforms. Between 1883–87, Germany became the first nation to institute a comprehensive social security system and to establish child and woman labor laws. Throughout his years as chancellor, Bismarck encouraged industrialization at home and colonization overseas. He found it difficult to work with William II, who came to power in 1888. In 1890 the "Iron Chancellor" was forced to resign and went into retirement. △1250, 1300.

Bismarck, city and capital of North Dakota, in S central part of state over-looking Missouri River; seat of Burleigh co. Lewis and Clark stayed near here 1804–05. Camp Greeley (later Fort Hancock) was built in 1872 to protect workers on Northern Pacific Railroad. Industries: livestock raising, dairying, woodworking. Inc. 1873. Pop. (1970) 34,703.

Bismarck Archipelago, volcanic island group off NE New Guinea, SW Pacific Ocean; comprised of New Britain (largest), New Ireland, Lavongai, Admiralty Islands, Duke of York Islands, Massau Islands, Vitu Islands, and many smaller islands. Australia administered the archipelago as a part of UN Trust Territory of New Guinea from 1947 until 1975 when it became a part of Papua New Guinea. Products: shellfish, coconuts. Founded 1616. Area: 19,173sq mi (49,658sq km). Pop. 176,471.

Bismuth, metallic element (symbol Bi) of group V of the periodic table, first identified as a separate element in 1753. The chief ores are bismite (oxide) and bismuth glance (sulfide). Bismuth expands when it solidifies, a property exploited in several bismuth alloys used in making castings. Properties: at no. 83; at. wt. 208.9806; sp. gr. 9.75; melt. pt. 520°F (271.3°C); boil. pt. 2840°F (1561°C); most common isotope Bi^{209} (100%).

Bison, two species of wild oxen formerly ranging grasslands and open woodlands over most of North America and all of Europe. Once numbering in millions, the American bison is now almost extinct in the wild. The Wisent (European Bison) was reduced to two herds by the 18th century. Both are now found in parks. Head, neck, and shoulder hair is long and shaggy with a beard on the chin and shorter hair on the rest of the body. They have heavy heads, short necks, humped shoulders, short, upcurving horns. The American is more massive and shaggier than the European. Length: to 137in (3.5m); height: to 117in (3m); weight: to 2970lb (1336kg). Family Bovidae; species American *Bison bison*, Wisent *Bison bonasus*. *See also* Buffalo.

Bissau (Bissao), largest city in Guinea-Bissau, W Africa, on Bissau Island; former colonial capital (1942–74); administrative and military center. Founded 1687 by Portuguese as fortified post and trade center; a free port since 1869. Crops: palm oil, peanuts, copra, hardwoods, rubber. Pop. 62,101.

Bithynia, ancient region of NW Asia Minor. Originally occupied by Thracians, it was inc. into the Persian Empire by Cyrus the Great in the 6th century BC. The Bithynians never submitted to Alexander the Great or his successor. It evolved into a strong, independent kingdom until several weak leaders led to its rapid decline. In 74 BC, according to the will of its last king, Nicomedes IV, it became a Roman province. △1020.

Bitter Lakes, two lakes in NE Egypt; Great Bitter and Little Bitter Lakes, connected and crossed by Suez Canal. Located in ancient bed of Red Sea.

Bitterling, freshwater fish native to Asia Minor and central Europe. Deep-bodied, its fin rays are not true spines. Female deposits eggs into mantle cavities of clams and mussels for breeding. Length: to 3.5in (8.9cm). Family Cyprinidae; species *Rhodeus sericeus*.

Bittern, solitary heronlike wading bird found in marshes around the world. Heavy-bodied, it is brownish with streaks and spots and easily hides itself in swamplands. During mating, males snap their bills and make gulping noises. The female lays white or brownish eggs (3–6). Length: 10in–3ft (25–91cm). Family Ardeidae.

Bitterroot, perennial native to mountainous North America from Montana to British Columbia and south into California, with fleshy leaves, short stalks and red blossoms. The starchy root was a food of the American Indian. Family Portulacaceae; species *Lewisia rediviva*.

Bitterroot Range, range of the Rocky Mts reaching along the Idaho-Montana border. Length: approx. 300mi (483km). Discovered in 1804–05 by Lewis and Clark Expedition. Highest point is Scott Peak, 11,393ft (3,475m).

Bittersweet, woody climbing plant found in moist thickets. The entire plant is toxic. The pointed leaves have a lobe at the base on each side; the violet or purple flowers produce coral red berries. Height: to 12ft (3.7m). Family Solanaceae; species *Solanum dulcamara*.

Bivalve, 20,000 living species of mollusks. Characteristically their soft parts are enclosed by two hinged shells (valves) closed by powerful muscles. Most are marine but there are many freshwater forms. The majority burrow in mud or sand; some attach themselves to solid objects; and many bore into wood or rocks. Included are clams, cockles, scallops, oysters, mussels, and lucines. They are headless and have a hatchet-shaped foot for digging and sometimes eyes lining the mantle edge. Usually two siphons circulate water for extracting food particles. Sexes are generally separate, but some are hermaphroditic. Classification varies but is usually based on variations of gill arrangement. Length: 1/6in–4ft (2mm–1.2m). Class Pelecypoda. *See also* Mollusk. △478.

Bizerte (Binzert or Bizerta), fortified city and seaport in N Tunisia, N Africa, on Mediterranean Sea. Northernmost city in Africa, it has harbor with channel to Lake of Bizerte; site of German base in WWII and French naval base to 1963. Industries: fish processing, olive oil, flour mills, oil refining, cement, brick and tile production, ship repair. Founded by Phoenicians. Pop. 51,708.

Bizet, Georges (1838–75), French romantic composer. His opera *Carmen* (1875), though unsuccessful when first performed, has become one of the most popular operas ever. Bizet also composed other operas and two successful orchestral pieces, a *Symphony in C* (1855) and the *L'Arlesienne Suites* (1872). △1246, 1256.

Bjerknes, Vilhelm F. (1862–1951), Norwegian physicist who laid the groundwork for a revolution in weather forecasting by applying theories of fluid forces and motions to the circulation of the atmosphere with the development of air masses, fronts, and cyclones.

Björling, Jussi (1907–60), Swedish tenor. He studied at the Stockholm Conservatory and the Royal Opera School and made his debut in 1930. He appeared in over 50 roles in leading opera houses of Europe and the United States, his most famous roles being in the Italian and French operatic repertoire.

Bjørnson, Bjørnstjerne (1832–1910), Norwegian poet, novelist, and dramatist. A great public figure and prolific writer, his works included the novels *Trust and Trial* (1857) and *The Heritage of the Kurts* (1884), the plays *Lame Hulda* (1858) and *The Bankrupt* (1874), and *Poems and Songs* (1870). He lectured throughout Europe and was awarded the Nobel prize for literature in 1903.

Black, Davidson. △650.

Black, Hugo (LaFayette) (1886–1971), US jurist and senator, b. Harlan, Ala. A US Senator from Alabama (1927–37), he sponsored the Wages and Hours bill (1937), investigated merchant-marine subsidies (1933) and vigorously supported New Deal legislation. Appointed an associate justice of the US Supreme Court in 1937, he favored a broad interpretation of the Constitution, and wrote numerous dissents defending civil rights and liberties. In the late 1960s, however, he voted to uphold state criminal laws.

Black, Joseph (1728–99), Scottish chemist and physicist. He became professor of medicine at Glasgow and later of chemistry at Edinburgh. Rediscovering "fixed air" (carbon dioxide), he discovered that this gas is produced by respiration, burning of charcoal, and fermentation; that it behaves as an acid; and that it is probably found in the atmosphere. He founded the theory of latent heat and investigated the concept of specific heat but was unable to fit them into place because of his belief in the phlogiston theory. He also invented a form of ice calorimeter. *See also* Phlogiston Theory.

Bird of paradise

Otto von Bismarck

Bison

Hugo Black

Black and Tan Coonhound, hunting dog (hound group) used to trail possum and raccoon by scent. A descendant of the 11th-century English Talbot hound, it has an oval-shaped head and long, square muzzle; low-set hanging ears; a level-backed body; medium-length, straight legs; and long tail carried freely. The short, dense, coal black coat is marked with rich tan. Standard size: 25–27in (63.5–68.5cm) high at shoulder; 70–85lb (32–38kg). *See also* Hound.

Black and Tan Terrier. *See* Manchester Terrier.

Black Ape, or Celebes ape, Celebes crested macaque, tailless, tree-dwelling, medium-sized monkey found chiefly on N Celebes Island. It has a small crest of hair and is mostly black or dark brown. Species *Cynopithecus niger. See also* Monkey.

Black Bass, black sea bass, or sea bass, marine food fish found well offshore in N Atlantic. Length: 2ft (61cm); Weight: to 8lb (3.6kg). Family Serranidae; species *Centropristis striatus. See also* Bass. △392.

Black Bear, bear found in North America and Asia. The American black bear lives in forested areas from Canada to C Mexico. It is usually black and eats a wide variety of plant and animal foods, including carrion. It is usually timid and avoids man. Length: 5–6ft (1.5–1.8m); weight: 265–330lb (120–150kg). Species *Euarctos americanus*. The Asiatic black bear lives in bush or forest areas of E and S Asia. Smaller than the American black bear, it has a white crescent marking on the chest. It is aggressive and sometimes kills livestock and humans. Species *Selenarctos thibetanos. See also* Bear.

Blackbeard (died 1718), English pirate, b. Edward Teach. In 1716 he began attacking shipping off the West Indies, the Spanish Main, and the coasts of Carolina and Virginia. His career ended when his 40-gun warship, *Queen Anne's Revenge,* was attacked by two sloops sent by the governor of Virginia, and he was killed.

Black Beauty (1877), a children's book by Anna Sewell. A sentimental story of a horse passing from owner to owner in 19th-century England, this popular book started the trend in children's literature toward stories about pets and wild creatures.

Black Belt, rich, low-lying farm land area—5,000sq mi (12,950sq km) located in Alabama and Mississippi. An underlayer of soft limestone is responsible for the black clayey soil's fertility. A prosperous cotton-growing area, livestock and diversified farming have become prominent since 1970.

Black Belt, in judo, grade given to those who have proven certain fighting ability. There are five black belt ratings, progressing from 1st to 5th Dan (degree).

Blackberry, or bramble, fruit-bearing bushes, native to the northern temperate regions. Having erect or trailing prickly stems and leaves of oval, toothed leaflets, the blossoms are white, pink, or red, and the edible berries are black or dark red. Family Rosaceae; genus *Rubus.*

Blackbird, American bird, the male having black or blackish plumage. The typical red-winged blackbird *(Agelaius phoeniceus)* has a straight bill, long pointed wings, and rounded tail. They feed on insects and sometimes, in flocks, become crop pests. Nesting in colonies, the female builds a nest for the eggs (2–7) and the male helps care for the young. Length: 8–10in (20–25cm). Family Icteridae.

Blackbody, an ideal body that absorbs all incident radiation and reflects none. Such a body would look black; hence the name. The study of blackbodies has been an extremely important part of the history of physics. Wien's Law, Stefan's Law, and Planck's Law of Blackbody Radiation grew out of this study, as did Planck's discovery of quantum mechanics.

Blackbuck, or Indian antelope, medium-sized, long-horned antelope native to the open plains of India. Females and young are fawn colored and males are dark, becoming almost black at maturity. Underparts are white with white on muzzle and around eyes. Only males carry long, annulated, spiral horns. They are hunted for sport by trained cheetahs. Length: to 47in (1.2m); height: to 32in (81cm) at shoulder. Family Bovidae; species *Antilope cervicapra.*

Black Canyon of the Gunnison National Monument, deep, narrow canyon in W Colorado, eroded by the Gunnison River; named for the dark sided canyon walls. Est. as park 1933. Area: 13,667 acres (5,535hectares).

Black Codes (1865–66), laws passed in former Confederate states restricting the civil and political rights of newly freed blacks. In addition to providing for segregation of public facilities, the laws restricted the blacks' freedom of employment, freedom of movement, right to own land, and freedom to testify in court. The Black Codes were later repealed by radical Republican state governments.

Black Death, an outbreak of plague, thought to be bubonic plague, which ravaged most of Western Europe during the 14th century and at 10-year intervals throughout the Middle Ages. Carried by the infected fleas of the black rat, the plague came west from Kaffa, a grain port in the Crimea, in 1346. It had reached England and Italy by 1348 and Germany, Scandinavia, and Poland by 1349–50. The Black Death took about one third of the population of Europe in the first three years, and perhaps a total of half before the worst epidemics ceased. The results were a widespread decline in morality, a decline in the achievements of monasteries, political discontent, a labor shortage, and in Germany, the massacre of thousands of Jews, who were blamed for the plague. *See also* Bubonic Plague. △1102.

Black-eyed Susan, or yellow daisy, annual or biennial North American plant. It has hairy leaves and daisylike flowers with golden-yellow rays and purplish-brown disks. Height: 3ft (0.9m). Family Compositae; species *Rudbeckia hirta.*

Blackface Sheep. △376.

Black-figure Technique. △1000.

Blackfish, or tautog, marine food and game fish of the North Atlantic. It is black or greenish. Length: to 3ft (91.5cm); weight: 22lb (10kg). Family Labridae; species *Tautoga onitis.*

Black Fly, or buffalo gnat, yellow to gray, blood sucking fly, 0.04 to 0.2in. (1–5mm) long, found in north temperate and subarctic areas. The larvae are found in fast-running water. Some diseases are carried by this fly, but the bite alone may be severe enough to disable a man. Family Simuliidae. *See also* Diptera.

Blackfoot, or Blackfeet, one of the largest and most warlike North American Indian tribes; actually a confederation of three Algonquian-speaking subdivisions: the Siksika, or Blackfoot proper; the Kainah; and the Pikuni. Their nomadic Plains traits were intensified with the acquisition of the horse. They originally occupied a vast area in Saskatchewan, Alberta and N Montana and are among the few Indians still occupying their old homelands. Today there are approximately 6250 Blackfoot in the United States and 3500 in Canada.

Black Forest (Schwarzwald), heavily forested mountain range in SW West Germany, between Rhine and Neckar rivers to Swiss border; source of Danube and Neckar rivers with many lakes and mineral springs. Range is a popular tourist attraction, famous for cuckoo clocks and music boxes. Industries: lumbering, cattle. Highest peak is Feldberg, approx. 4,898ft (1,494m). Length: 90mi (145km).

Black Friday (Sept. 24, 1869), day of financial panic in the United States. Jay Gould and James Fisk, two unscrupulous financiers, attempted to corner the gold market and drove the price of gold up. When the US government sold $4 million of its gold reserve, the price of gold fell and many speculators were ruined. *See also* Fisk, James; Gould, Jay.

Black Gum. *See* Tupelo.

Black Hawk War (1832), war between the Sac and Fox Indians and the United States. Black Hawk was a Sac chief who opposed the forced treaty of 1831. Fighting bravely against superior numbers of US volunteers, Black Hawk was finally defeated at the Battle of Bad Axe (1832).

Blackhead, or comedo, plug of fatty matter blocking a pore, usually on the face.

Black Hills, mountain cluster in W South Dakota and NE Wyoming; named for the dark pines that appear black from afar. Gold was discovered (1874) by an exploratory mission led by General Custer; site of Homestake Mine, largest U.S. gold mine; uranium, mica, silver, and feldspar are also mined. Tourist areas include 2 national forests, Wind Cave National Park, Custer State Park, Jewel Cave National Monument, and Mt Rushmore National Memorial. Highest peak is Harvey Peak, S. Dak., 7,242ft (2,209m). *See also* Mount Rushmore.

Black Hole, postulated end-product of the total gravitational collapse of a massive star into itself following exhaustion of its nuclear fuel, the collapsed matter inside being crushed to unimaginably high density. It is an empty region of totally distorted space that acts as a center of gravitational attraction; matter is drawn toward it and once inside cannot escape. Its boundary (the event horizon) is a demarcation line, rather than a material surface, defining the area from which no matter, light, or other radiation can escape. Suspected but unconfirmed black holes include Cygnus-XI. △108.

Blackjack, card game for two or more players, using a regular deck. Each player, including the dealer, receives two cards; the dealer's second card is turned face up. The object is to get more points than the dealer but less than 22. Aces count as 11 or 1, picture cards as 10, and all others count their face value. All players may take additional cards, but any total over 21 automatically loses. The dealer may not take any cards if his two-card total is 17 or extra cards add up to 17. If the dealer's total is 16, or reaches 16, he must take an additional card.

Blacklists, a labor practice in which certain people are excluded from employment. During the late 19th and early 20th centuries, blacklisting was sometimes used by employers against those employees who were union organizers or agitators, preventing them from gaining employment in a particular industry. It was also practiced during the 1940s and 1950s to boycott entertainers thought to have been associated with the Communist party.

Black-mantled Goshawk. △538.

Blackmore, R(ichard) D(oddridge) (1825–1900), English novelist and poet, studied law. His best-known novel is *Lorna Doone* (1869).

Black Mountain Poets, designation for writers affiliated with Black Mountain College in North Carolina in the 1950s. There the writers came under the influence of Charles Olson. Among the poets, in addition to Olson, are Robert Creeley, Robert Duncan, Denise Levertov, and Joel Oppenheimer.

Blackmun, Harry A(ndrew) (1908–), US jurist and lawyer, b. Nashville, Ill. A practicing attorney (1934–59), law instructor, and Mayo Clinic counsel (1950–59) he was appointed in 1959 to the US Circuit Court of Appeals. In 1970 he was nominated an associate justice of the US Supreme Court by Richard Nixon. Blackmun's nomination was confirmed unanimously in June 1970. He is considered moderately liberal on civil rights issues and a conservative on matters of criminal law.

Black Muslims, US religious movement, officially called the Nation of Islam, founded in Detroit in 1930 by W. D. Fard. After Fard's disappearance in 1934, Elijah Muhammad took over leadership and moved to Chicago. The Muslims adhere strictly to the Koran's moral codes, forbidding alcohol, drugs, gambling, and smoking. Women are subservient to men. The Muslims maintain their own schools, farms, and businesses, living as independently as possible from the larger society. In the 1960s, Malcolm X carried the Muslim message to a larger, more sophisticated audience. Suspended from the church in 1963, he was assassinated in 1965. Muhammed Ali is a leading lay spokesman for the movement. Total membership is kept secret. Elijah Muhammad died in 1975 and was succeeded by his son Wallace, who called for radical changes in the movement, including the welcoming of whites into the movement and the promotion of women to leadership positions.

Black Oak, North American timber tree with lobed, reddish leaves and dark, blocky bark. Height: to 80ft (24m). Family Fagaceae; species *Quercus velutina.*

Blackout, Physiological, total obscuration of vision encountered by test pilots and astronauts during heavy acceleration; caused by insufficient oxygen supply to the eye. Blackout is the opposite of *redout,* a reddish haze caused by engorged blood vessels in the eye, which is encountered at zero-g or negative-g conditions.

Blackpool, city in NW England, on Irish Sea coast, 28mi (45km) N of Liverpool; vacation resort, attracting 8,000,000 visitors annually; Noted for illuminations and 520ft (157m) tower. Pop. 151,311.

Black Sea, inland sea between Europe and Asia, connected to the Aegean Sea by the Bosporus, Sea of Marmara, and the Dardanelles; surrounded by USSR (N and E), Turkey (S), Bulgaria and Romania (W). It is a major USSR sea outlet, yielding large quantities of anchovies, carp, mullet, bream, and gobies. Area: 159,600sq mi (413,364sq km).

Black Shirts, members of the Italian Fascist party formed in March 1919. The movement adopted black shirts as a uniform and swore devotion to Benito Mussolini. *See also* Fascism; Mussolini, Benito.

Blacksmith, one who works in iron with a forge. Those making metal into tools and other objects by heating in a forge and hammering on an anvil were important in 19th-century building construction when many wrought-iron structures were made. △1592.

Black Snake, or black rat snake, wide-ranging North American rat snake, also called pilot or mountain black snake. A good climber, it is shiny black, sometimes with small, light spots between scales, and has a paler belly. Length: to 6ft (183cm). Family Colubridae; species *Elaphe obsoleta*. *See also* Colubrid.

Black Spot, any of various plant diseases, mostly caused by fungi, that form black spots on leaves, including apple scab, apple anthracnose, peach scab, and black spot of roses. Rose black spot, caused by the fungus *Diplocarpon rosae*, is the worst rose disease in North America.

Blackstone, (Sir) William (1723–80), English jurist and legal scholar. As a fellow of All Souls College at Oxford (1753), he introduced the first law curriculum in an English university and became the first Vinerian Professor of Law at Oxford (1758). Elected to Parliament (1761), he was the first solicitor-general to Queen Charlotte Sophia (1763). He was knighted and appointed a Justice of the Common Pleas in the same year (1770). His book *Commentaries on the Laws of England* still serves as the foundation for much of the English and US legal practice.

Blacktail Deer. △556.

Black Theater, a dramatic genre that deals exclusively with the black experience and which seeks to develop and express a unique black aesthetic. The movement emerged during the militant 1960s in the United States with such playwrights as LeRoi Jones, Charles Gordone, and Ed Bullins. The plays in this genre are often statements of racial pride and identity.

Black Volta (Volta Noire), chief headstream of the Volta River in W Africa; rises in Upper Volta, flows S to join the White Volta River, forming the Volta River; forms part of W boundary of Ghana. Length: 840mi (1,352km).

Black Walnut, deciduous tree *Juglans nigra* of the walnut family growing to 150ft (46m). A native of E and Central United States, it is grown for ornament, timber, and nuts.

Blackwell, Elizabeth (1821–1910), US physician, b. England. In 1847, she began to study medicine at the Geneva Medical School in New York after being denied admission to several other schools. She graduated (1849) at the head of her class, becoming the first woman doctor in the United States. She pioneered in obtaining medical education for women in the United States and established the New York Infirmary (1857) which combined health services and medical training. In 1869 she emigrated to England to continue her teaching and writing.

Black Widow Spider, American black spider with red markings, often hour-glass shaped, underneath. It is poisonous, resulting in symptoms similar to appendicitis. The female eats its mate and bites. The male does not bite or feed. Several closely related species are found worldwide. Length: to 0.6in (15mm). Family Theridiidae; species *Latrodectus mactans*. *See also* Spider.

Bladder, Urinary, a large pouch in which urine is stored. Urine, a kidney secretion containing waste products and water extracted from the blood, is passed through two narrow tubes, the ureters, to the bladder, where it is stored until the pressure becomes too great and nervous impulses signal that the bladder has to be emptied. Urine leaves the bladder through the urethra. △694.

Bladderwort, matlike, aquatic plant found in bogs or ponds. It has feathery, threadlike leaves with small bladders. Upright stems bear purple or dark pink flowers. Species include purple *Utricularia purpurea* and butterwort *Pinguicula*. Family Lentibulariaceae. △444.

Bladensburg, town in S central Maryland; residential suburb of Washington, D.C.; scene of battle Aug. 24, 1814, in which British defeated Americans and proceeded to Washington to burn many public buildings. Chartered 1742; inc. 1854. Pop. (1970) 7,488.

Blaine, James Gillespie (1830–93), US public official, *b.* West Brownsville, Pa. An influential Maine Republican, he served as a state legislator (1858–62), a congressman (1863–76), speaker of the house (1869–75), and US senator (1876–81). He ran for president in 1884 but lost the election to the Democratic candidate, Grover Cleveland, partly because of the defection of reform Republicans (Mugwumps). He served as secretary of state (1881; 1889–92).

Blaine, city in SE Minnesota; suburb of Minneapolis; organized as a township in 1877 and named for Sen. James G. Blaine. Chief industry is construction. Inc. 1964. Pop. (1970) 20,640.

Blair, Francis Preston (1791–1876), US journalist, b. Abingdon, Va. A supporter of Andrew Jackson and a member of Jackson's kitchen cabinet, he founded the pro-Jackson Washington *Globe* in 1830 and published it until 1845. He opposed slavery and was instrumental in establishing the Republican party. After the Civil War, however, he returned to the Democratic party.

Blair, James (1655–1743), American clergyman and educator, b. Scotland. He came to Virginia in 1685. In 1693 he obtained a charter for the College of William and Mary, of which he was president until his death. From 1694 he was a member of the Virginia Council, and as its president, was governor of the colony in 1740–41.

Blake, William (1757–1827), English poet, painter, and engraver. He was apprenticed to an engraver (1772) and studied at the Royal Academy (1778). A friend of William Godwin and Thomas Paine, he supported the French Revolution. His work is characterized by the prophetic and mystical visions he experienced. *Poetical Sketches* (1783) was followed by *Songs of Innocence* (1789), *The Marriage of Heaven and Hell* (1790), and *Songs of Experience* (1794). His prophetic books, portraying his private mythologies, include *The Book of Urizen* (1794), *The Four Zoas* (1797), *Milton* and *Jerusalem* (1804). In addition to his own works, Blake illustrated *The Book of Job* and Dante's *Divine Comedy*. △1228.

Blakewell, Robert (1725–95), British agriculturist who revolutionized sheep and cattle breeding in England by methodical selection and inbreeding. One of the first to breed both cattle and sheep for meat, his farm was a famous example of early scientific management in agriculture.

Blanc, Louis (1811–82), French Socialist leader and historian, b. Spain. He originated the phrase adopted by Karl Marx "to each according to his needs, from each according to his abilities." His involvement in the Revolution of 1848 forced him into exile where he wrote a 12-volume history of the French Revolution. He returned to France in 1871 and was elected to the Chamber of Deputies.

Blanc, Mont, highest peak in the Alps, and the 2nd-highest peak in Europe; on the French-Italian border; scaled in 1786; popular resort area. The 7-mi (11-km) Mt Blanc tunnel is cut through its base. Height: 15,771ft (4,810m).

Blanche of Castile (1187?–1252), queen of France. She was the granddaughter of Eleanor of Aquitaine and Henry II of England. Her marriage to Louis VIII (1200) was meant to reconcile the Capets and the Plantagenets. She became queen in 1223 and served as regent for her son Louis IX (1226–36, 1248–52), and co-regent with another son Alphonse (1250–52).

Blanching, bleaching plant parts by protection from sun to improve color and texture, usually for vegetables. Celery is blanched by mounding earth around the stalks. Endive and cauliflower are blanched by tying the outside leaves over the heads.

Blanda, George F. (1927–), US football player, b. Youngwood, Pa. Considered the game's "ageless wonder," he began his career in 1949, and was still active in the late 1970s. He held a host of records in the National Football League, and as a quarterback and kicker, he scored over 2000 points.

Bland-Allison Act (1878), legislation providing for the purchase and coinage of silver by the secretary of the treasury. The original form, introduced by Richard P. Bland, called for unlimited coinage and was opposed by the bankers. William B. Allison suggested a compromise that limited the coinage, and this version was passed.

Black bear

Harry Blackmun

Black widow spider

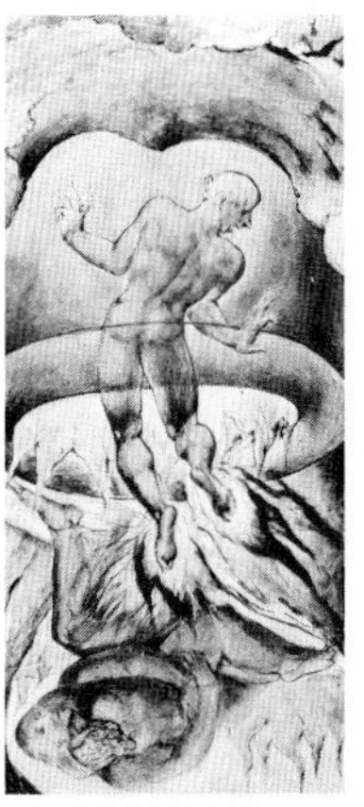

Drawing by William Blake from Dante's Inferno

Blank Verse, unrhymed verse, especially iambic pentameter or unrhymed heroic; widely used in English dramatic and epic poetry. The Earl of Surrey introduced blank verse into England in the 16th century with his translation of the *Aeneid.* The form was used by Christopher Marlowe, William Shakespeare, John Milton, William Wordsworth, and Alfred Tennyson, among others. *See also* Iamb.

Blantyre, city in S Malawi, SE Africa, in the Shire Highlands; commercial center of Malawi. Industries: textiles, cement, food processing. Founded 1876; merged with Limbe to form one city 1956. Pop. 169,-000.

Blarney, village in SW Republic of Ireland, in central Cork. It is noted for 15th-century castle containing the Blarney Stone, said to endow anyone who kisses it with "the blarney" (fluent persuasive speech). Pop. 932.

Blasco Ibáñez, Vicente (1867–1928), Spanish novelist. Most of his novels dealt with rural communities of his native Valencia and barely concealed his political opinions, which eventually forced him to emigrate. His best works are *The Cabin* (1898) and *Reeds and Mud* (1902). He later sacrificed good writing for easy money and popularity, as in *Blood and Sand* (1908). His war novel, *The Four Horsemen of the Apocalypse* (1916), made him world famous.

Blast Furnace, smelting furnace in which iron ore is made into pig iron; it is also used in smelting other metals, such as copper, lead, and tin. A blast of compressed air, supplied from the bottom of the furnace, provides combustion for smelting the ore. The furnace used in iron production is usually a cylindrical steel structure, narrow at the top and bottom. As the metal becomes molten, it sinks to the bottom where it is tapped. △1584.

Blastocyst. △700.

Blastomycosis, infectious, fungus-caused disease usually centered in the lungs, which can spread to the skin. Untreated, it may be fatal.

Blastula, embryo at the developmental stage that consists of a hollow, cavity (blastocoele) surrounded by one or more spherical layers of cells. Commonly called the hollow ball of cells stage, it follows the morula stage in embryonic development.

Blaue Reiter. △1294.

Bleach, substance used to remove the color from textiles, paper, etc. Most bleaches act by oxidizing the pigment. Chlorine, or compounds such as calcium and sodium hypochlorites, are commonly used. Other oxidizing bleaches are hydrogen peroxide, used for hair, and sodium perborate. For some applications reducing agents, such as sulfur dioxide, are employed. △1558.

Bleeder's Disease. *See* Hemophilia.

Bleeding. *See* Hemorrhaging.

Bleeding Heart, ornamental perennial plant with feathery leaves, arched stems, and clusters of heart-shaped, rose-red flowers. Height: to 2ft (60cm). Family Fumariaceae; species *Dicentra spectabilis.*

Bleeding Kansas, name given to Kansas just before the Civil War. In 1854, Kansas Territory was opened by the US government. Settlers swarmed in to decide by referendum if Kansas would be a slave or a "free soil" territory. After bloody conflict an uneasy peace was est in 1856. Kansas became a free state in 1861.

Blenheim, village in S West Germany, on Danube River, 23mi (37km) NNW of Augsburg; scene of English victory over French and Bavarians in War of Spanish Succession. (1704). Pop. 900.

Blennerhassett, Harman (1765–1831), US conspirator, b. Hampshire, England. He went to the United States in 1796 and settled on an island in the Ohio River, where he built a mansion. He became a friend of Aaron Burr and advanced him funds for a planned invasion of Mexico (1805). Blennerhassett was arrested for conspiracy in 1806, but was later released.

Blenny, marine fish of shallow and offshore waters of all tropical and temperate seas. Scaleless, with a long dorsal fin, it is olive green with varicolored markings. Length: to 4in (10.2cm). Family Blenniidae; species 300, including fringehead *Blennius tentacularis.*

Blepharitis, inflammation of the border of the eyelid, sometimes accompanied by ulceration and discharge.

Blériot, Louis (1872–1936), French aircraft designer and aviator who was the first man to fly across the English Channel (1909). The flight from Calais to Dover took 37 minutes. As a designer Blériot was responsible for a number of design innovations, including a system by which the pilot could operate elevators and ailerons by remote control. In World War I he built the noted SPAD fighters. △1714.

Bleuler, Paul Eugen (1857–1939), Swiss psychiatrist, pioneer in the diagnosis and treatment of psychoses. He coined the term *schizophrenia* and, unlike his predecessors, attributed the symptoms to psychological rather than physiological origins.

Blewit and Wood Blewit. △428.

Bligh, William (1754–1817), British admiral. Captain of HMS *Bounty* (1787), Bligh survived the famous mutiny (1789), sailing nearly 4,000 miles (6,400km) in the ship's longboat. After service at Camperdown (1797) and Copenhagen (1801) he was governor of New South Wales (1805–08).

Blight, a term applied either to the yellowing, browning, and withering of plant tissues caused by various diseases, or to the diseases themselves. Blights may be caused by microorganisms, such as bacteria and fungi, or by environmental factors such as drought. Common blights induced by microorganisms include fire blight and bean blight, caused by bacteria, and spinach blight (mosaic), caused by a virus. Blight diseases typically affect leaves more severely than other plant parts. Control of blight depends on its cause. Blights caused by microorganisms, for example, are controlled by good sanitation; by growing blight-resistant varieties; and by spraying with various fungicides and antibiotics.

Blindfish, or Blind Cave Fish, freshwater fish found mainly in cave waters of North America. Usually white, it ranges from being blind, with no or imperfect eyes, to having sight. Length: to 3in (7.6cm). Family Characidae; species includes Mexican *Astyanax jordani* and Family Amblyopsidae; species Ozark *Amblyopsis rosae.*

Blindness, in the United States is defined as corrected vision not exceeding 20/200 on the standard Snellen eye chart. Blindness occurs most frequently in persons over 55, with the greatest percentage caused by senile cataract (clouding of the lens) and glaucoma (hardening of the eye due to pressure within the eyeball). Other causes of blindness include infectious disease such as tuberculosis, measles, or syphilis; diseases such as diabetes; nutritional deficiencies; injuries; and congenital anomalies, which include inherited defects. Blindness as a result of disease and accident is being reduced rapidly with progress in research, early diagnosis, and accident prevention programs. Education for the blind includes not only Braille reading and guide dog training, but also active sports, and classes and vocational training aimed at enabling the visually impaired to function as independently as possible in sighted society.

Blind Snake, burrowing, wormlike, termite-eating, legless reptile with rudimentary eyes. They have vestiges of pelvic girdles. The Typhlopidae (blind snakes) found worldwide tropically are considered legless lizards. The Leptotyphlopidae (slender blind snakes) range from S Central United States to Argentina and are also found in Africa and Asia. Length: 4–12in (102–305mm). *See also* Lizard; Reptile; Snake. △524.

Blind Spot, small area of the retina of the eye where there is no visual reception. It is the area where optic nerve processes converge and where blood vessels enter and leave the eye. △674.

Bliss, Fort, US army post in El Paso, W Texas; extends into New Mexico; site of missile and aircraft research and training center. Area: approx. 50sq mi (130sq km). Est. 1849 to protect gold miners and mines in area. Pop. 34,000.

Blister Beetle, medium-sized, cylindrical-bodied beetle that secretes blister-producing cantharidin. Formerly used as a diuretic and aphrodisiac, cantharidin was made from the dried European blister beetle known as the Spanish fly *(Lytta vesicatoria).* Family Meloidae.

Blitzkrieg, (from German, "lightning war"), mode of warfare characterized by a sudden, overwhelming attack with powerful force. The blitzkrieg tactic was effectively used by the German forces in their invasion of Poland in September 1939.

Blixen, Karen. *See* Dinesen, Isak.

BL Lacertae. △124.

Bloc, legislative group organized to foster special interests or to obstruct legislative action. In international politics, the term describes a coalition of states with shared interests.

Bloch, Konrad Emil (1912–), US biochemist, b. Germany. He studied fat metabolism, in particular how cholesterol is synthesized in the body. He shared the 1964 Nobel Prize in physiology or medicine with Feodor Lynen.

Blockade, military tactic aimed at closing ports to commerce or obstructing communications and movement in and out of a territory. In international relations, a blockade is considered a legitimate action in warfare.

Block and Tackle. *See* Pulleys and Hoists.

Block Island, island in the Atlantic Ocean approx. 9mi (14km) S of Point Judith, Rhode Island; site of two lighthouses; fishing and resorts. Visited in 1614 by Dutch navigator Adrian Block, settled 1661; coextensive with town of New Shoreham, Inc. 1672. Area: 11sq mi (28sq km). Pop. (1970) 489.

Block Mountain, an uplift that is the result of block faulting. This is one type of fault in which the crustal portions of the earth are broken into structural blocks of different elevations and positions. *See also* Orogeny. △252.

Bloc Voting, practice among legislators or delegates of uniting to advance or obstruct legislative action. Bloc voting is also used by groups in support of an issue or candidate.

Bloemfontein, city and judicial capital of Republic of South Africa, 295mi (475km) W of Durban; capital of Orange Free State province; seat of appellate division of the Supreme Court. Dutch farmers settled in area early 19th century; site of modern city was selected as a fort by Major Douglass Warden 1846; major educational center with two US observatories nearby; site of University of Orange Free State (1855). Industries: furniture, glassware, metal works. Founded 1846. Pop. 146,200.

Blois. △1096.

Blois, town in N central France on Loire River; capital of Loir-et-Cher dept. In 10th century the counts of Blois were most powerful feudal lords of France; town was a favorite royal residence. Industries: wheat, vegetables, wine. Pop. 42,264.

Blood, a fluid tissue composed of plasma in which are suspended several types of individual cells. Blood volume in a healthy individual is about 5.8 qts (5.5 liters) of which 54% is plasma, and 46% is composed of cells. Blood transports oxygen, water, nutrients, body metabolites, and internal secretions, and contains all the factors necessary for clotting. The blood cells fall into two major classes: erythrocytes or red blood cells, and leukocytes or white blood cells. The red blood cells carry oxygen; the white blood cells serve as scavengers which phagocytose foreign objects, such as bacteria and cellular debris that may be present in the blood stream. Normal red cells count is about 4.8–5.4 million per cubic centimeter, while the normal white count is about 5000 cells per cubic centimeter. Platelets, small disks filled with granules, which participate in blood clotting, are also present in numbers around 2–3,000,000 per cubic centimeter. Disease states exist in which one or more of the constituents are present in abnormal amounts; for example, too few red cells as in anemia, or too many white cells as in leukemia. △688.

Blood Clotting, a protective physiological mechanism to prevent loss of blood due to injury or other causes of hemorrhage. A tight fibrous meshwork forms at the site of injury through a complex series of interrelated reactions involving about 20 blood-borne factors. At the injury site, platelets gather, releasing thromboplastin, which converts prothrombin to thrombin; thrombin is involved in splitting fibrinogen to fibrin, which polymerizes with other fibrin molecules to form a clot, plugging the break. Normal clotting time is 8 to 15 minutes. Hemophilia is the congenital absence of one of these factors, resulting in excess bleeding. Abnormal clot formation blocking a vessel is called thrombosis. △740.

Blood Feud. △882.

Bloodhound, hunting dog (hound group) that trails by scent; known as early as 3rd century in Europe. Evidence uncovered by the bloodhound is acceptable in courts of law. It has a long, tapering, narrow head with loose, hanging lips and wrinkled skin. The low-set ears are very long and hang in folds; eyes are deep-set. The strong-backed body is set on large, muscular legs; a long, tapering tail is carried up. The short coat can be black, red and tan, or tawny. Average size: 25–27in (63.5–68.5cm) high at shoulder; 80–110lb (36.5–50kg). *See also* Hound.

Blood Plasma. *See* Plasma.

Blood Poisoning, or **Bacteremia,** the prolonged invasion of the bloodstream with pathogenic bacteria. Symptoms may include a relatively sudden onset of chills and fever, nausea, vomiting, change in the character of a wound, skin eruptions. Bacteria may enter through lesions in the skin or follow an infectious disease. Antibiotics are the usual treatment.

Blood Pressure, the pressure exerted on the walls of the arteries by the blood; a function of the elastic resistance of the artery (diastolic pressure) and cardiac output (systolic pressure). An average adult pressure is 120/80 mm Hg. systolic/diastolic pressure.

Bloodroot, plant found in the fertile woods of E United States. A low-growing perennial, the white or pink blooms appear before the leaves. Its alkaloid, sanguinarine, is used in medicine. Family Papaveraceae; species *Sanguinaria canadensis.*

Blood Tests. △702.

Blood Type. Erythrocytes, or red blood cells, are grouped into several types because of genetically determined antigens located on their surface. For example, the ABO system consists of four major types: A or B, A and B, or neither (O), depending on the presence or absence of these factors. Knowledge of blood type is important with respect to transfusions and tissue or organ transplants; and has medico-legal uses, especially in assignment of paternity. △688.

Blood Vessel, closed tubelike processes that carry blood throughout the body. There are three major types of blood vessels: arteries, which carry blood away from the heart; veins, which carry blood to the heart; and capillaries, the smallest blood vessels, where gases and dissolved substances diffuse in and out of the blood. *See also* Artery; Capillary; Vein. △688.

Bloody Assizes (1685), trials held in the West Country of England following the Duke of Monmouth's rebellion (1685). Judge Jeffreys, who presided, conducted the trials with notorious severity, sentencing over 300 people to be hanged, about 800 to transportation, and hundreds more to flogging, imprisonment, or fines.

Bloomer, Amelia Jenks (1818–94), US women's rights campaigner, b. Homer, N.Y. She founded (1848) and edited the *Lily,* the first US magazine for women, and wrote articles on education, unjust marriage laws and female suffrage. As part of her campaign for the emancipation of women she popularized the full trousers that became known as "bloomers."

Bloomfield, town in NE New Jersey, 4mi (6km) NNW of Newark; served as Revolutionary War supply point; site of Bloomfield College (1868). Industries: pharmaceuticals, petrochemicals, electrical equipment. Settled 1660; inc. 1900. Pop. (1970) 52,059.

Bloomington, city in central Illinois, 35mi (56km) ESE of Peoria; seat of McLean co; site of Illinois Wesleyan University (1850), and burial place of Adlai E. Stevenson. Industries: hybrid corn, dairying, coal mining. Inc. 1839. Pop. (1970) 39,992.

Bloomington, city in S central Indiana, 45mi (72km) SW of Indianapolis; seat of Monroe Co. A heavily forested region, it also has limestone quarries; site of Indiana University (1820). Inc. 1878. Pop. (1970) 42,890.

Bloomington, city in SE Minnesota; suburb adjacent to Minneapolis; business center. Industries: electronics, computers, farm equipment. Inc. 1953. Pop. (1970) 81,970.

Bloomsbury Group, British intellectual group that met in the homes of members in the Bloomsbury Square area of London between 1904–39. It included Clive and Vanessa Bell, E. M. Forster, Roger Fry, John Maynard Keynes, Lytton Strachey, and Leonard and Virginia Woolf. The group's philosophy, "the creation and enjoyment of aesthetic experience," was influenced by the philosopher G. E. Moore.

Blount, William (1749–1800), US political leader, b. Edgecombe co, N.C. He was a member of the Continental Congress and a delegate to the Federal Constitutional Convention. From 1790–96 he was governor of the territory south of the Ohio River (Tennessee) and superintendent of Indian affairs there. He was the first US senator from the new state of Tennessee (1796) but was expelled from the Senate for participating in a plot to aid the British in obtaining Spanish Florida and Louisiana.

Blowfish. *See* Puffer.

Blowfly, greenbottle fly, or bluebottle fly, black, blue, or green fly, 0.25 to 0.45in (6–11mm) long, found worldwide. The larvae usually feed on dead animals or meat-containing garbage. This fly's habits resemble those of the housefly. Family Calliphoridae. *See also* Housefly.

Blowgun, or blowpipe, weapon consisting of a tube through which a pellet or poisoned dart is ejected by force of breath. It is widely used by South and Central American and Southeast Asian people for hunting small game, and is highly efficient in forest zones, and where accuracy is valued above range.

Blücher, Vasili Konstantinovich (1889–1938?), marshall of the Soviet Union. He joined the revolutionary movement in 1910, became commander in chief in the Far East (1921), and military adviser to the revolutionary government in China (1924–27). Said to have opposed Stalin, he disappeared in 1938.

Bluebell, or harebell, blue bellflower developed in England and widely cultivated in gardens. Other unrelated plants are also called bluebells. Height: 6–20in (15–51cm). Family Campanulaceae; species *Campanula rotundifolia.*

Blueberry, deciduous evergreen shrub native to E North America. There are two types: the cultivated highbush, grown commercially, prefers acid, damp soil; the wild lowbush prefers sandy, acid soil. Family Ericaceae; genus *Vaccinium.*

Bluebird, North American thrush found in open woodlands and cultivated areas feeding on insects, often in orchards and farmyards. They have thin bills, stocky bodies, and forked tails. Males are bluish above and females grayish. Pale blue eggs (4–6) are laid in a grass-and-weed-lined nest in a hole in a tree or fence post. Length: 7in (17.8cm). Genus *Sialia.*

Bluebonnet, or Texas bluebonnet, annual wildflower of Texas, easily grown in United States. It has blue flower spikes and blooms in late spring. Height: to 1ft (30cm). Family Leguminosae; species *Lupinus subcarnosus.*

Blue-Collar Worker, a person involved in physical labor that results in the production of goods and services. Factory workers and farmers are blue-collar workers.

Blue Crab, swimming food crab prized along Atlantic and Gulf coasts. They are scavengers in brackish water near mouths of rivers. The body extends on each side to a long, sharp spine. After molting, the shell is soft. Its last pair of legs is flat and oarlike. Length: 6in (15cm). Family Portunidae; species *Callinectes sapidus. See also* Crustacean; Decapod.

Blue Cross, a private health insurance organization established as a nonprofit prepayment plan that indemnifies the hospital or attending physician on the basis of services performed. Both group and individual memberships are available. Blue Cross plans operate independent of one another in different parts of the country and arrange contracts with specific hospitals in their areas of jurisdiction.

Bluefish, schooling marine food and game fish found throughout tropical and temperate seas, except the C and E Pacific. Fished commercially, it is blue-green with a black blotch on each side. Length: to 4ft (121.9cm); weight: to 27lb (12.2kg). Family Pomatomidae; species *Pomatomus saltatrix.*

Bluegill, or bluegill sunfish, North American freshwater fish found in still water lakes and ponds. Ice-fished in winter, it is marked by 5–7 vertical bars on each side. Length: to 15in (38.1cm); Weight: 41lb (1.8kg). Family Centrachidae; species *Lepomis macrochirus.*

Blue-green Algae, widely distributed group of primi-

Bleeding heart

Bloodhound

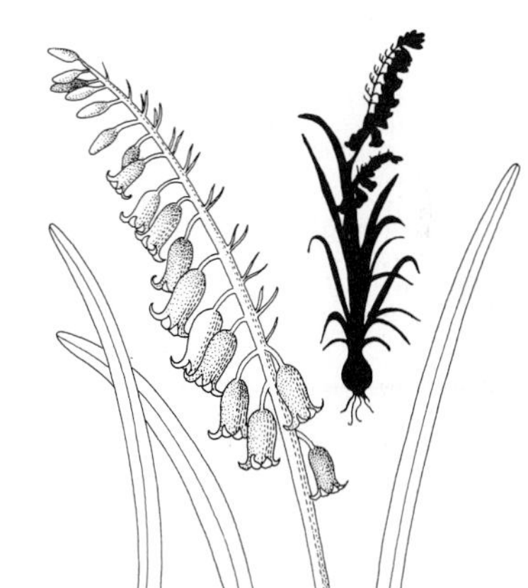

Bluebell

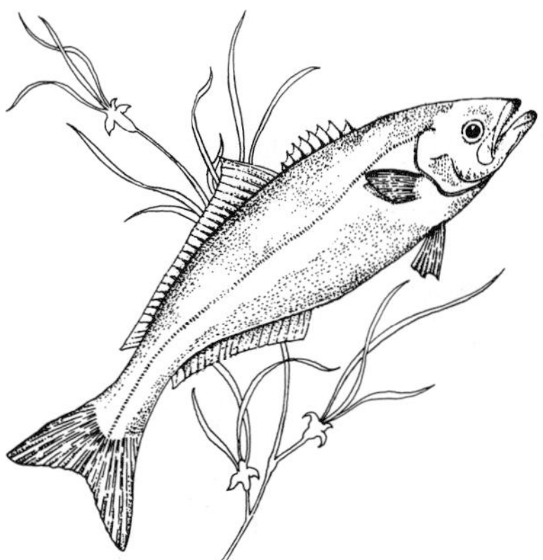

Bluefish

tive microscopic algae (division Cyanophyta) found in virtually every environment, including oceans, barren rocks, glaciers, and hot springs. The characteristic blue-green color results from the presence of a blue pigment in addition to green chlorophyll. Dense growths of blue-green algae produce the "blooms" that give eutrophic ponds and lakes a muddy green color. In existence for more than 2 billion years, some are single cells, others occur in threadlike rows of cells. All lack a definite nucleus. They resemble bacteria.

Blue Island, city in NE Illinois, 15mi (24km) S of downtown Chicago on Calumet Sag Channel; site of railroad terminal, yards and workshops. Industries: lumber, barrels, wire, tile. Inc. 1843. Pop. (1970) 22,-958.

Blue Jay, E North American bird known for its loud "jay-jay" call. It has a large head crest, rounded wings, long tail, and bright blue, black, and white plumage. It builds a bulky nest, high above ground in dense evergreen thickets, for its olivey eggs (3–6). Length: 10–12in (25–30cm). Species *Cyanocitta cristata.*

Blue-line Pipe Fish. △516.

Blue Mold. △426.

Blue Nile, (Al-Bahr Al-Azraq), river in NW Ethiopia; rises in Lake Tana, flows S and W into the Sudan, merging with White Nile to form the Nile River; site of Roseires and Sennar dams, built for irrigation. Length: 1,000mi (1,610km). *See also* Nile.

Blueprint, a photographic reproduction (using cyanide salts) with white lines against a blue background, frequently employed in drafting. The paper is coated with a solution of ammonium ferric citrate and potassium ferricyanide and exposed to intense light under the transparent sheet of material to be copied. When washed, the copy emerges, stable to light.

Blue Racer. △520.

Blue Rider (Blaue Reiter), loosely organized group of artists formed in Munich, Germany, in 1911 by the abstract expressionist Wasily Kandinski. Influenced by cubism, the group tried to stress in their paintings inner impulses and to provoke a personal response from their viewers. The group included Aleksey von Jawlensky, Paul Klee, Franz Marc, and August Macke. △1294.

Blue Ridge Mountains, E and SE range of the Appalachian Mountains, extending from S Pennsylvania into Georgia, includes Black Mountains, Unaka Mountains, Great Smoky Mountains, and South Mountain. A narrow ridge 10mi wide (16km) in N, widens to 70mi (113km) in North Carolina. Heavily forested with few lakes; people live in valleys on small farms. Site of Great Smoky Mountains National Park in North Carolina and Shenandoah National Park in Virginia; Appalachian Trail takes hikers across top of range. Industries: timbering, apple growing, tourism. Highest peak is Mount Mitchell, N.C., 6,684ft (2,039m).

Blues, style of jazz-folk music that developed in the late 19th century and that was first popularized in the United States by W.C. Handy. A blues song typically involves 12 measures, in a minor key, with flatted 3rd and 7th chords (the "blue" notes). Blues songs are often slow and sad, expressing despair for a lost lover. Blues songs were a large part of early American jazz and still influence many jazz and folk artists today. △1366.

Blue Shark. △510.

Blue Shield, a surgical expense insurance plan organized similarly to the Blue Cross plan and often operated in conjunction with it. Coverage is for medical, surgical, and various ancillary services.

Blue Sky Law, name given to legislation designed to protect investors from unscrupulous sellers of highly speculative stock ("the blue sky").

Bluet, or Quaker ladies, small tufted, perennial plant native to North America with small leaves and white or blue flowers. Family Rubiaceae; species *Houstonia caerulea.*

Blue Trunk Fish. △514.

Blue Whale, slate-blue whalebone whale hunted almost to extinction. It summers in the arctic and Antarctica and winters in warmer seas. The largest animal that ever lived, its 4-ton tongue is as large as an elephant. Length: to 100ft (30m); weight: 150 tons. Species *Sibbaldus musculus.*

Blum, Leon (1872–1950), French statesman and political leader. He served in the Chamber of Deputies (1919–40) as a leader of the Socialist party where he introduced sweeping social reforms. He was premier (1935, 1936–37) and vice premier (1938–39), leading the opposition to the Munich Pact. Interned by the Vichy government (1941–45) he was released by the Allies. He headed the caretaker government (1946–47) prior to the elections held by the new Fourth Republic.

Blumenbach, Johann Friedrich (1752–1840), German physiologist and comparative anatomist, often called the father of physical anthropology. His research in the measurement of craniums suggested for the first time the importance of utilizing comparative anatomy in the study of human history. Blumenbach proposed five families of man: Caucasian, Mongolian, Malayan, Ethiopian, and American.

Blyden, Edward Wilmot (1832–1912), educator and author, b. St. Thomas, West Indies. Unable to gain admission to a US college because he was black, he emigrated to Liberia, attended school there, and became president of Liberia College (1880). He held several government posts and was a principal colonizer of Liberia. His books include *Liberia's Offering* (1873).

Blytheville, city in NE Arkansas, 5mi (8km) S of Missouri border; seat of Mississippi co; trade center for agricultural products. Settled 1853; inc. 1891. Pop. (1970) 24,752.

B'nai B'rith, Jewish service organization, founded in New York City in 1843. Open to any Jew who follows its precepts of love and brotherhood, its name means "sons of the Covenant." It is the oldest and largest Jewish service organization in the world, with over half a million members. It sponsors the Hillel Foundation on college campuses and combats anti-Semitism through the Anti-Defamation League (founded 1913).

Bnei Brak (Bene Beraq), city in W central Israel; suburb of Tel Aviv-Jaffa. Industries: textiles, diamond cutting and polishing. Pop. 72,100.

Boa, constricting snake mostly restricted to the New World. All bear their young live. The boa constrictor *(Constrictor constrictor)* of American tropics grows to 12ft (3.7m). Smaller species are the iridescent rainbow boa and emerald tree boa. Most are arboreal but some are subterranean. The rosy boa and rubber boa of W United States are small, terrestrial forms. Family Boidae.

Boadicea (died 62 AD), British queen of the Iceni in East Britain. She was the wife of King Prasutagus, who, on his death, left his daughters and the Roman emperor as co-heirs. The Romans seized his domain and Boadicea led a revolt against them. Defeated, she took poison. The name more properly appears as Bonduca and Boudicca.

Boas, Franz (1858–1942), US anthropologist, first professor of anthropology at Columbia University (1899–1936), b. Germany. He was a scholar of the cultures and languages of the American Indians, of statistical physical anthropology, and of descriptive and theoretical linguistics. Important works include *Primitive Art* (1927), *Anthropology and Modern Life* (rev. ed. 1932), *The Mind of Primitive Man* (rev. ed. 1938), and *Race and Democratic Society* (1945), a collection of essays.

Boating, sport, popular world-wide, that includes yachting, motorboating, rowing (crew racing), canoeing and iceboating. Races are held with each type of craft, and rowing, yachting, and canoeing are included in the Olympic Games. The most prominent boating competitions include the International Challenge Cup (canoe sailing), the International Team Trophy (power cruisers), the Harmsworth Trophy and Gold Cup (motorboating), the Ice Yacht Challenge Pennant of America (iceboating), and the America Cup races (yachting).

Boat Lily. △454.

Boaz, in the Bible, Bethlehemite related to Naomi's husband Elimelech. He married their daughter-in-law Ruth, inheriting her deceased husband's estates.

Bobcat, or wild cat, red lynx, vicious, short-tailed cat found throughout swamp, forest, and chaparral areas of United States, S Canada, and Central America. Its reddish-brown coat has black spots and underparts are white. The gestation period is 50–60 days and 2–4 young are born. It feeds on rodents and jack rabbits. Length: body—25–30in (63.5–76.2cm); tail—5in (12.7cm). Family Felidae; species *Lynx rufus. See also* Cat; Lynx.

Bobolink, American songbird that nests in Canada and N United States and winters in S South America. Males have a tawny neck, buff back, and black underparts. Females lay brown-spotted eggs (4–6) in a simple ground nest. Length: to 7in (17.8cm). Species *Dolichonyx oryzivorus.*

Bobsledding, one of the fastest and most dangerous of winter sports. Two- or four-men teams ride in an open steel-bodied vehicle with sledlike runners on an icy, snow-covered downhill course that is steeply banked with twisting inclines. The competition bobsled, for a four-man crew, weighs 489 pounds (220kg), and 356 pounds (160kg) for the two-man crew. Bobsledding, which followed tobogganing, was developed at St. Moritz, Switzerland, in the late 19th century and was first included in the winter Olympic Games in 1924. The only bobsled course in the United States is at Mt. Van Hoevenberg in Lake Placid, New York, site of the 1932 winter Olympic Games. *See also* Tobogganing.

Bobwhite. *See* Quail.

Boca Raton, residential coastal city of SE Florida, 17mi (27km) N of Ft Lauderdale, in Palm Beach co. Home of Florida Atlantic University and US Air Force radar training center. Established 1924; inc. 1925. Pop. (1970) 28,506.

Boccaccio, Giovanni (1313–75), Italian poet and prose writer. His first work, the *Filocopo,* is sometimes considered the first European novel, but he is best known for the *Decameron* and for *Fiammetta,* the partly autobiographical story of a young man's first love affair. He knew and imitated the older Dante, and with his friend Francesco Petrarch he is considered one of the founders of the Italian Renaissance. *See also* Decameron. △1100.

Boccanera, wealthy Genoese family of the 13th & 14th centuries remembered for roles in so-called democratic revolts of 1257 and 1339. Guglielmo became "captain of the people," which meant virtual dictator, after his 1257 victory against the old aristocracy, but he was overthrown by nobles in 1262. Simone, elected first Genoese doge after the "popular" revolt of 1339, was deposed and fled to Pisa in 1344. He returned with Visconti aid in 1356 and was supposedly poisoned in 1363.

Boccie, a ball game, popular in Italy and in Italian communities throughout South America, Australia, and the United States. It can be played indoors or outdoors, uses a playing area that averages 60 by 10 feet (18 by 3m), with boarded sides and ends. The surface is covered with sand or soil. There are two to four players on a team, and four balls for each team. After a smaller wooden ball (jack) is thrown toward the end of the enclosure, the players, in turn, try to bring their ball to a position closest to the jack, by throwing the ball underhand. A player may use the side boards or any surface of the playing area in an attempt to move their opponent's ball away from the jack or to protect the position of his ball. One point is awarded for each ball that is closer to the jack than an opponent's. A game is 12 points.

Boccie was played in ancient Rome. The English version, called *bowles,* was played in the 12th century, and the German game, *keglers,* began in the 14th century. The game is governed by the Unione Federazioni Italiane Bocce, founded in Turin in 1898.

Boccioni, Umberto (1882–1916), Italian painter and sculptor. One of the strategists of the futurist group, he was its only sculptor. His works emphasized motorization and movement of planes in space. His bronzes include "The Mother" (1911); his paintings, "The City Rises" (1910) and "Elasticity" (1912). *See also* Futurism.

Bochum, city in West Germany, 10mi (16km) E of Essen; site of church (1599), Ruhr University (1965), planetarium (1964); commercial and transportation center. Industries: steel, iron, automotive, textiles, chemicals, machinery. Chartered 1321. Pop. 346,-010.

Bock, Hieronymus (*c.* 1480–1554), German botanist. Often considered the founder of modern botany, he constructed a system of plant classification based on physical characteristics. His description of German plants, *Neu Kreutterbuch* (1539), was a vast improvement on earlier herbals.

Bodenheim, Maxwell (1893–1954), US author, b. Hermanville, Miss. From his early twenties, he lived in New York City, in Greenwich Village. He wrote poetry nd novels. His works include *Minna and Myself* 1918), *Against This Age* (1925), and *Bringing Jazz* 1930), poetry; and *Blackguard* (1923), *Replenishing Jessica* (1925), and *Virtuous Girl* (1930), novels.

Bode's Law, empirical numerical relationship for the mean distances of the planets from the sun. It is named for German astronomer Johann Bode, who popularized it in the late 18th century. If the number 4 is added to 0, 3, 6, 12, 24, 48, 96, 192, and each sum is divided by 10, the figure arrived at is the mean distance in astronomical units of the planets from the sun beginning with Mercury and including the asteroid belt. The law works for those planets known in the 18th century. It does not work for Neptune and Pluto, discovered in the 19th century.

Bodhista, bodhisatta, or bodhisatva, in Hinayana Buddhism, an individual who is about to reach Nirvana, such as Gautama prior to his enlightenment. In Mahayana Buddhism, this is an individual on the verge of enlightenment who delays his salvation in order to help mankind. *See also* Buddhism; Nirvana.

Bodin, Jean (1530–96), French political philosopher. His most important political work was *Six livres de la république* (1576), a political and economic analysis of the state. In it, Bodin proposed a strong hereditary monarchy with restraints only on the monarch's power of taxation.

Bodleian Library, founded in 1602 at the University of Oxford in England. It served as a deposit library for 150 years until the British Museum opened. Its collection has grown to 2.5 million volumes and, in the central and dependent libraries, can accommodate 17,000 readers.

Bodoni, Giambattista (1740–1813), Italian printer, one of the originators of the first modern, Roman style, type face. He published editions of Homer, Vergil and Horace in the new type face. His editions were considered particularly elegant, although there were numerous typographical errors.

Body Image. △818.

Body Language, communication of feelings and attitudes by means of bodily gestures, postures, and positions. Such gestures may be conscious and deliberate (eg, a clenched fist) or unconscious (eg, drooping shoulders indicating despondency). △814, 862.

Boeotia, department in central Greece, bounded by Attica, Megaris, Gulf of Corinth (S), Phocis (W and NW), Atlantic channel and the Euripos (E), and Locres Opuntia (N); capital is Levádhia; site of 19th-century excavations by Heinrich Schliemann, revealing the Treasury of Minyas (1250 BC). The Boeotian League (7th century BC), headed by Thebes, defeated the Spartans; and Thebes dominated until destroyed by Alexander the Great 336 BC. Area: 1,225sq mi (3,173sq mi). Pop. 114,288.

Boer, Dutch word meaning farmer. Name used to identify Dutch- and Huguenot-descended inhabitants of the Republic of South Africa. More correctly called Afrikaner. *See also* Afrikaners. △1268.

Boer War, or **South African War** (1899–1902), conflict between Britain and the Transvaal (South African Republic) and Orange Free State. The British had gradually laid claim to South African lands in the 19th century, and their mining operations and control of commerce created great resentment among the Boers, white residents of Dutch, German, and Huguenot descent. War broke out in late 1899. After initial victories the Boer forces were repeatedly defeated by the reinforced British. Failing at conventional warfare, the Boers carried out an extensive guerrilla campaign that the British crushed with concentration camps and dragnets. An uneasy truce was arranged (Treaty of Vereeniging, 1902), and the Union of South Africa was formed in 1910. △1268.

Boethius (Anicius Manlius Severinus) (*c.* 475–525), Roman statesman and philosopher under the Emperor Theodoric. He attempted to eliminate governmental corruption, but was finally imprisoned on a charge of conspiracy. In prison at Ticinum, where he was subsequently tortured and executed, he wrote *On the Consolation of Philosophy,* a dialogue based on Neoplatonist and Aristotelian principles. *See also* Neoplatonism.

Bogardus, James (1800–74), US architect, b. Catskill, N.Y. He was one of the first to use cast iron in the facades of buildings, important in the development of steel frame construction. In 1848 he built a factory in New York City, itself with cast iron frame, to build prefabricated cast iron frames for other buildings. One of his best known works still standing is the Iron Building in New York City. △1258.

Bogart, Humphrey (DeForest) (1899–1957), US film actor, b. New York City. He is acclaimed for roles requiring a complex of qualities: toughness, cynicism, sexual magnetism, heroic integrity, and honor. His films include *The Petrified Forest* (1936), *The Maltese Falcon* (1941), *Casablanca* (1942), *The Big Sleep* (1946), *Treasure of the Sierra Madre* (1948), *The African Queen* (1951), for which he won an Academy Award as best actor, and *The Caine Mutiny* (1954).

Bog Cotton. △452.

Bogomils, 10–15th century heretical Christian sect, founded by Bogomil, a priest. This starkly ascetic group originated in Bulgaria *c.* 950, spread to other Slavic countries and to France, influencing the Albigensian heresy. Bogomils believed that the power of evil (Satan, God's first and fallen son) or materialism was uppermost in the world but with the redeeming help of God's second son (Christ), this bondage could be broken and evil destroyed. Called the "Beloved of God," these "Old Believers" comprised the bulk of Christians in Bulgaria, despite continued persecution.

Bogomolets, Aleksandr Aleksandrovich (1881–1946), Russian physiologist and pathologist. He claimed to have discovered a potion to combat the diseases of old age and to prolong life. The preparation was supposedly utilized in healing the wounds of Russian soldiers in World War II. In 1930 he was elected head of the All-Ukranian Academy of Sciences.

Bogotá, capital city of Colombia; in central Colombia, 300mi (483km) N of the equator. Known as "Athens of the South," it is a cultural, educational, and financial center of Colombia; has fine examples of Spanish colonial architecture. Founded 1538 by the Spanish near the center of a Chibcha Indian culture; in 1830 it became the capital of New Granada, later called Colombia. Industries: tobacco products, sugar, flour, textiles. Pop. 1,966,341.

Bohemia, historic region, now refers to W Czechoslovakia. From 950–1526 it was part of the Holy Roman Empire; under the rule of the Hapsburgs, it became part of Austria-Hungary (1526). It secured its independence following WWI, becoming the core of the new country of Czechoslovakia. Munich Pact (1938) removed the Sudetanland from Czechoslovakia and annexed it to Germany; the pre-1938 boundaries were restored in 1945. Made a prov. of Czechoslovakia 1945, it was dissolved in 1949, and rezoned 1968. △1074, 1154.

Bohemund I (*c.* 1056–1111), Norman Crusader, prince of Antioch (1099–1111). Christened "Marc," he became known by his nickname, the name of a legendary giant. Son of Robert Guiscard, he fought with him against the Byzantine Empire (1081–85). Later he obtained S Apulia after a war against his brother. In 1096 he joined the First Crusade and played a key role in the capture of Antioch (1098), then became its prince. He was held captive by the Turks (1100–03) but was released and married the daughter of the king of France. Warring against the Byzantines, he was defeated (1108). Defeated again, by the Muslims in 1109, he remained away from Antioch until his death.

Böhm-Bawerk, Eugen von (1851–1914), Austrian economist whose main contribution was in the area of interest and capital. Böhm-Bawerk was critical of socialism, because he believed capital, like labor, was a scarce productive resource, and should be paid accordingly.

Bohr, Niels (1885–1962), Danish physicist. He worked with J.J. Thomson and Ernest Rutherford before being appointed professor at the University of Copenhagen. He used the quantum theory to explain the structure of the atom. He escaped from German-occupied Denmark (1943) and helped to develop the atom bomb in the United States. After the war he returned to Copenhagen and worked for international cooperation. He was awarded a Nobel Prize in physics in 1922 for his work on atomic structure. *See also* Quantum Theory. △1480, 1484.

Boiardo, Matteo Maria (1434–94), Italian poet. An aristocrat who enjoyed the patronage of the dukes of Este, his uncompleted epic *Orlando Innamorato* revived the Italian epic, chiefly by inspiring Ludovico Ariosto. His *Three Books on Love* (1499) for Antonia Caprara is among the best lyric poetry of the age.

Boileau-Despréaux, Nicolas (1636–1711), French poet and critic. In *L'Art Poétique* (1674), he expounded classical standards for poetry, and his criti-

Boa constrictor

Franz Boas

Bogotá, Colombia

Niels Bohr

cisms gained him both friends and enemies. He was appointed historiographer to Louis XIV in 1677. △1172.

Boiler. △1628–30.

Boiling Point, the temperature at which a substance changes phase from liquid to vapor or gas. △1504.

Boise, capital and largest city of Idaho, in valley of the Boise River; seat of Ada co; trade center for agricultural region of SW Idaho and E Oregon. Crops: sugar beets, potatoes, alfalfa, onions. Industries: steel, sheet metal, furniture, electrical equipment, lumber products. Founded 1863 as supply center for gold miners; inc. 1864; reinc. 1961 to annex suburbs. Pop. (1970) 74,990.

Boise River, river in SW Idaho, formed from three forks that rise in the Sawtooth Mts and flow together approx. 15mi (24km) E of Boise, then W past Boise to Snake River at Oregon line. The river is used in Idaho irrigation projects. Length of river from point of convergence is 60mi (97km).

Bola, or bolas, missile hunting weapon of South American Indians, consisting of three or more stone balls held together with thongs, and thrown in such a manner as to entangle the legs of the prey. The bola is used predominantly in the open country of the Patagonian and Pampas zones.

Bolas Spider. △488.

Boleslav I, called the Mighty (died 1025), Polish ruler (992–1025), first to be crowned king of Poland (1025). Starting from a small principality on the Vistula River, he established Polish dominion from the Oder and Neisse rivers to the Dnieper and from Western Pomerania to the Carpathian Mountains. Bohemia recognized him as a duke (1003). The Christian church was firmly established. At his death, Poland was one of the strongest states of Europe. △1074.

Boleslav II, called the Bold (*c.*1039–83), king of Poland (1058–79), succeeding his father Casimir I. Opposing the power of the Holy Roman Empire, he asserted Polish influence in Bohemia and Hungary and in 1069 he took Kiev. In 1079 he had the Bishop of Cracow (St Stanislas) executed for rebellion. He in turn was excommunicated by the pope and deposed by his brother Ladislas Herman. He died in exile in Hungary.

Boleslav III, called the Wry-Mouthed (1086–1138), king of Poland (1102–38). He warred against Bohemia, Hungary, and Kiev. He defeated an invasion of Poland by Holy Roman Emperor Henry V (1109) and regained and Christianized Pomerania.

Boleslav IV (1127–73), king of Poland (1146–73). During his ineffectual reign, the Holy Roman Empire conquered the entire area along the Baltic Sea west of the Vistula River. Emperor Frederick Barbarossa forced Boleslav's complete submission in 1157.

Boleslav V, called the Chaste (1221–79), king of Poland (1227–79). During his reign the Mongols invaded and devastated Poland (1237–41). The kingdom was left divided into a number of independent, warring principalities. Large numbers of Jews, escaping persecution in western Europe, settled in Poland.

Boletus, a genus of terrestrial mushrooms whose spore-bearing parts are tubes instead of gills. They have a fleshy central stem and cap. Of the many species, several are edible. Poisonous ones either turn blue when bruised, have red tube mouths, or both.

Boleyn, Anne (1507–36), second wife of Henry VIII of England. Henry, who was tiring of Queen Catherine of Aragon and wanted a male heir, became infatuated with her. The pope's refusal to grant a divorce led to Henry's break with Rome. The archbishop of Canterbury annulled his marriage to Catherine and he married Anne (1533). Anne gave birth to the future Queen Elizabeth but no sons. Henry, tiring of her, had her beheaded on charges of adultery and incest.

Bolger, Ray(mond Wallace) (1904–), US dancer and actor, b. Boston. He was best known for his role as the Strawman in the film *The Wizard of Oz* (1939). Among his credits are the musical *On Your Toes* (1936), and the ballet *Slaughter on Tenth Avenue.*

Bolide, or fireball, large unusually bright meteor.

Bolingbroke, Henry St. John, Viscount (1678–1751), English political philosopher and statesman. A Tory member of Parliament (1701), he achieved power under Queen Anne (1713) but continued in opposition during the Hanoverian succession. His *Idea of a Patriot King* (1749) was thought to have influenced the "philosophes," to whom his skepticism presumably appealed. *See also* Philosophes.

Bolingbroke, Viscount. *See* Saint John, Henry.

Bolívar, Simón (1783–1830), the central figure in the South American independence movement in both its political and military phases. He took part in the ferment that arose in Latin America following the Napoleonic invasion of Spain, and was instrumental in the creation of two short-lived republican governments in Venezuela (1810–14). Twice defeated by royalist forces, Bolívar went into exile (1815), but returned to the mainland the next year. By 1819 he had achieved some successes on the battlefield in eastern and southern Venezuela. In that year, Gran Colombia was created and Bolívar became its president. Military victories in Peru, Bolivia, and Ecuador followed. At a time when sovereignty was becoming a reality, Bolívar no longer believed that a system founded on representative and republican principles was feasible. He came to feel that Latin America was unprepared for democratic government. In the end, Bolívar became completely disillusioned, believing America to be ungovernable. △1234.

Bolivar. *See* Ciudad Bolívar.

Bolivia, Republic of, landlocked nation in W central South America, with extremes in altitude, climate, and wealth.

Land and Economy. Bolivia has three regions: mountains in the center and along the W border; a great plateau—the altiplano—stretching between them; and a N and E plains area (68% of the country). The Bolivian Andes contain deposits of tin and silver, major supports of the economy. The altiplano has an average altitude of 12,000ft (3,660m), and, although cold and dry, provides the best living conditions. There Indians raise potatoes, beans, and cereal grains. Entirely in the S tropics, Bolivia has hot, humid lowlands in the N and E, and in the SE has a share of the dry Gran Chaco prairie. Oil from the S should prove of great value. La Paz, seat of most government functions, has textile, footwear, and other light industries, while the second city, Cochabamba, produces foodstuffs and cigarettes. Sucre, the official capital, is the judicial center.

People. About 55% of the people are Indians of the Quechua and Aymara tribes, and another 31% are of Spanish and Indian blood. The whites, Spanish-speaking and Catholic, control government, mining, and industry, while the mestizos perform labor duties and farm; the Indians, mostly illiterate, live by farming.

Government. Formally a republic with a president, Senate, and Chamber of Deputies elected by all adults, Bolivia has been ruled by the military since 1971, with free elections postponed until 1980. The legislature was suspended in 1969.

History. Tiahuanaco Indians settled beside Lake Titicaca, highest major lake in the world, about the time of Christ. Later, the Incas ruled the region for 200 years, until the Spanish arrived in the 1530s. Bolivian rebellions against Spain started in the 18th century, but independence came only in 1825 when Antonio José de Sucre defeated the Europeans. Bolivia's borders developed as the country split from Peru (1839), lost land leading to the Pacific to Chile (1883), and lost a war with Paraguay (1935) over the Chaco. In the 1970s, Bolivia is trying to win assistance from the Organization of American States in regaining a corridor to the sea, and accepts aid from Brazil, Argentina, and Venezuela.

PROFILE

Official name: Republic of Bolivia
Area: 424,163sq mi (1,098,581sq km)
Population: 5,400,000
Density, 13per sq mi (5per sq km)
Chief cities: Sucre, official capital; La Paz, seat of government
Government: Head of state, Hugo Banzer Suárez, president (took power August 1971)
Gross national product: $1,700,000,000
Trading partners (major): Brazil, Argentina

Böll, Heinrich (1917–), German novelist and short-story writer. His works include *Where Were You, Adam?* (1950), *Acquainted with the Night* (1953), *The Clown* (1963), *Absent Without Leave* (1964), and *Group Portrait with Lady* (1971). A concern for catholic authenticity pervaded his work, but his humorously satirical short stories were perhaps his finest achievement. Böll won the Nobel Prize for literature in 1972.

Bollandists, Flemish Jesuits named for Jean Bolland, first editor of the *Acta sanctorum,* lives of Roman Catholic saints, the first volume of which appeared in 1643. The Bollandists were his collaborators and successors in producing the lives.

Bolling v. Sharpe (1954), US Supreme Court decision. It held that racial segregation in Washington, D.C., schools was so unjustifiable as to violate the due process clause of the Fifth Amendment as it embodies concepts of equal protection of the law.

Boll Weevil, small, gray, long-snouted beetle common in Mexico and SE and SC United States. Adults and larvae feed on the cotton plant, especially the bolls, and are serious crop pests. There are usually 4–6 generations each year. Species *Anthonomus grandis. See also* Weevil.

Bollworm, or pink bollworm, caterpillar destructive to cotton in many parts of the world. The bollworm is pinkish or cream colored. Besides attacking green cotton bolls, it feeds on okra, hollyhock, hibiscus, and related plants. Length: 0.5in (12mm). Species *Pectinophora gossypiella.*

Bologna, city in N central Italy, at foot of Apennines; capital of Bologna prov. and Emilia-Romagna region. The ancient Etruscan town of Felsina, it became a free commune 12th century; site of 11th-century university, Church of San Petronio (1390), and the Palazzo Comunale (13th, 15th, 16th centuries); transportation center. Industries: chemicals, food processing, electric motors. Pop. 488,510.

Bolsheviks, group led by V.I. Lenin that obtained a brief majority in the early 20th-century Russian Social Democratic party, but then lost power to the Mensheviks. In the 1917 November Revolution, however, the Bolsheviks played such an important role that the revolution carries their name. By 1918 the break with the Mensheviks was total and the Bolsheviks formed the Russian Communist party. The Bolsheviks stressed absolute party loyalty and were generally hesitant to compromise on any issue. △1310.

Bolshevism. △904, 1310.

Bolshoi Opera, leading Russian opera house, founded in 1780 in Moscow and housed in its present building since 1825. The company performs mostly Russian repertory and a few foreign operas translated into Russian. The Bolshoi has premiered most of the great Russian operas ever composed. The opera company visited the Western Hemisphere for the first time in 1967 when it performed at the Exposition in Montreal.

Bolshoi Theater Ballet, based in Moscow, one of the largest and most famous ballet companies of the USSR. Their school held its first classes in 1773 and has trained many of Russia's most famous dancers. The Bolshoi is known for its exquisite and elaborate productions of classical and modern Soviet ballets. Its most famous works are *Giselle, Cinderella, Red Poppy,* and *Romeo and Juliet.* Among its most noted choreographers have been Marius Petipa, Alexander Gorsky, and Michel Fokine.

Bol'šoj Kavkaz. *See* Caucasus.

Bolton, city in NW England, 11mi (18km) NW of Manchester; spinning frame (1769) and spinning mule (1779) were invented here. Industries: textiles, chemicals. Pop. 153,977.

Boltwood, Bertram. △276.

Bolzano (Bozen), city in N Italy; capital of Bolzano prov.; important regional commercial center since the Middle Ages; it became Italian 1918. Heavily damaged in WWII, many landmarks remain, including the cathedral, 14th-century Franciscan church, and medieval houses. Industries: tourism, engineering, textiles, wine. Pop. 103,479.

Boma, port city in W Zaire, equatorial Africa, on Congo estuary, 60mi (96km) E of Atlantic Ocean; commercial center; capital of Congo Free State (1887–1908) and of Belgian Congo until 1923. Exports: lumber, cacao, bananas. Founded as slave market in 16th century. Pop. 79,230.

Bomb, an explosive that is planted (mine), concealed (booby trap), thrown (grenade), projected (mortar shell), flown (buzz bomb). It is most frequently an explosive dropped (aerial bomb) such as atomic bomb, or fragmentation bomb. △1746, 1810.

Bomb, Volcanic, piece of solid material ejected by a volcano and cooled. It is greater than 32mm in diameter. *See also* Volcano.

Bombardier Beetle, ground beetle found in North

America and Europe. It fights off predators by bombarding them with an irritating gas. Each discharge of gas makes a sound like a tiny popgun. Genus *Brachinus.*

Bombay, largest city in India; capital of Maharashtra state; located on an island off W coast, it is second only to Calcutta as India's leading port. It was ceded to England by Portugal 1661 as part of Catherine Braganza's dowry to Charles II; annexed by East India Co. 1708; dock and transportation facilities expanded in late 19th century; after 1941, population grew due to immigration and increasing birth rate. City was enlarged through rezoning 1951; cultural, educational, trade, and financial center; site of University of Bombay (1857), Indian Institute of Technology (1958). Industries: chemicals, textiles. Exports: cotton, manganese. Founded 1534. Pop. 5,700,358.

Bomb Calorimeter, type of calorimeter used for measuring heats of combustion, consisting of a sealed vessel in which the sample is burned in oxygen. The heat change is calculated from the temperature rise. *See also* Calorimeter. △1550.

Bona Dea, Roman deity of fruitfulness in earth and in women, also known as Damia. Women celebrated her cult with a mysterious festival forbidden to men. The dedication day of her temple was May 1.

Bonald, (Vicomte) Louis de (1754–1840), French political philosopher. A reactionary advocate of monarchy and unalterably opposed to revolution, he was the author of a counter-revolutionary political system in *Theory of Political Power* (1796) and *Analytical Essay on Natural Laws* (1801). △1290.

Bonaparte, family of Italian origin living in Corsica (also spelled Buonaparte). **Carlo** (1746–85), a lawyer, and **Maria Letizia Ramolina** (1750–1836), known as Madame Mère, were parents of a large family whose members were raised to distinction by their second and famous son, Napoleon I. **Joseph** (1768–1844), the eldest son, became king of Spain (1808–13). **Charles Lucien Jules Laurent** (1775–1840), the third son, known as Prince Canino, opposed Napoleon's despotic rule and lived in exile in Italy. **Maria Anna Elisa (Elisa)** (1777–1870) became Duchess of Tuscany. **Louis** (1778–1846) was created King of Holland in 1806. He married Hortense de Beauharnais. Their son became Napoleon III. **Maria Paulina (Pauline)** (1780–1825) was first married to General LeClerc and later to Prince Camillo Borghese. **Carolina (Caroline)** (1782–1839) married Joachim Murat, a marshal of France, who became king of Naples. *See also* Napoleon I; Napoleon II; Napoleon III. △1226.

Bonaparte, Joseph (1768–1844), king of Spain, b. Corsica. He was the eldest brother of Napoleon I. He participated in the Italian campaign (1797) and later served as diplomat for the First Republic of France. Napoleon made him king of Naples (1806), and he was appointed king of Spain in 1808, serving until 1813. After Napoleon's defeat at Waterloo, he resided in the United States (1815–32). △1234.

Bonaparte, Louis (1778–1846), King of Holland (1806–10), brother of Napoleon Bonaparte and father of Charles Louis Napoleon, later Napoleon III of France. He accompanied his brother in the Italian and Egyptian campaigns. Became a general in 1804; governor of Paris 1805. Forced by Napoleon to take the Dutch throne, he worked to restore the economy and promote the welfare of the Dutch, but the French Continental System was ruinous to Dutch trade. Napoleon felt he was too lenient and the conflict led Louis to abdicate (1810). He assumed the title of Comte de St-Leu. Holland was annexed to France.

Bonaparte, Napoleon. *See* Napoleon I.

Bonapartism, domestic reforms and governmental centralization carried out by Napoleon Bonaparte (1769–1821) during his rule in France. △1226.

Bonaventure (*c.* 1217–74), Italian theologian and Roman Catholic saint. In 1254 he became head of the Franciscan school in Paris. In 1257 he was elected minister general of the order. Three varieties of theology, he claimed, correspond to 3 stages of mind in the consideration of God: the senses, reason, and last, pure mind. Unlike Aquinas, he did not favor Aristotelianism, but rather a more mystical and Platonic turn of mind is clear in his *Itinerary of Mind and God.* △1088.

Bond, Ionic. *See* Ionic Bond. △1554–56, 1562.

Bonds, promissory notes guaranteeing the repayment of a specific amount of money on a particular date at a particular fixed rate of interest. Bonds may be issued by corporations, states, cities, or the federal government. The quality of the bond and the interest rate paid on it will be determined by the length of time the loan will be outstanding and the risk involved. Thus the federal government would normally pay a lower rate of interest on its bonds than would cities because US bonds are relatively risk-free. A very healthy corporation could normally pay a lower interest rate than a less secure business.

Bonds, Chemical. *See* Chemical Bonds. △1570.

Bône, *see* Annaba.

Bone, a type of connective tissue that forms the framework, or skeleton, of the body, protects the internal organs, serves as lever for muscles, stores calcium and phosphorus, and in its marrow produces red and white blood cells. Bone is surrounded by membrane, the periosteum, the outer layer of which serves for the attachment of ligaments, tendons, and muscles; the inner layer contains osteoblasts for bone growth. Bone itself is composed of a strong, dense, outer compact layer and a lighter, porous, inner spongy layer that contains the bone marrow. All bone contains a hard, calcium-containing matrix, which is arranged in layers, or lamellae, that are generally arranged concentrically around a Haversian canal, a canal containing a blood vessel. Bone cells, or osteocysts, each in a space called a lacuna, occur between lamellae and are linked to one another and to the blood vessels by canaliculi. Bone formation is called ossification. *See also* Skeletal System. △662, 682.

Bone China, white, translucent ceramic ware developed in England in the 19th century, with a body of kaolin, china stone, and bone ash, prized for its pure white color, thinness, and translucence.

Bonefish, marine game fish found in shallow, warm waters. A bottom feeder, it has a pointed head covered with thick cartilage, a receding mouth, and silvery coloring. Length: 3.5ft (106.7cm); Weight: 18lb (8.2kg). Family Albulidae; species *Albula vulpes, Dixonia hemoptera.*

Bongo, large Central African antelope living in dense, humid forests. Both sexes carry spirally twisted horns. It has a reddish coat with vertical white stripes along its sides, erect mane and large ears. Height: to 55in (1.4m) at shoulder; weight: to 484lb (220kg) Family Bovidae; species *Boocerus Taurotragus eurycerus.* △598.

Bonheur, Rosa (1822–99), French painter and sculptor. She was best known and very popular in her time for her sympathetic and accurate depictions of animals. She first exhibited at the Paris Salon of 1841 with two animal paintings and later with sculpture. Her works include *The Horse Fair* (1853).

Boniface (*c.* 680–754), English missionary, a Roman Catholic saint. Called the Apostle of Germany, he left England in 716 to convert the pagan Germans. For his success he was rewarded with the Archbishopric of Mainzin (745). In 754, however, he was martyred by pagans in Friesland. △1052.

Boniface VIII, Roman Catholic pope (1294–1303) b. Benedetto Gaetani (1235). To bring order to Rome and prevent schism, he imprisoned his predecessor, Celestine V. He offered the first plenary indulgence for all who made a pilgrimage to Rome in 1300.

Boniface IX, Roman Catholic pope (1389–1404) b. Pietro Tomacelli (*c.* 1345). Elected pope during the Great Schism, he excommunicated Clement VII, the antipope. He tried, unsuccessfully, to strengthen Rome's position during the schism. He decreed the feast of the Visitation.

Bonifacio, historic seaport in S Corsica, France, on Strait of Bonifacio; site of citadel built by Bonifacio I, count of Tuscany, and Pisan-style 12th-13th century church. Industries: fishing, olive oil, cork. Founded *c.* 828. Pop. 2,146.

Bonito, marine tuna found in all warm and temperate waters, usually in large schools. Canned commercially, it is blue-black and silver. Length: to 3ft (91cm); Weight: 12lb (5.4kg). Family Scombridae; species includes *Bonito bonite.* △392.

Bonn, capital city of Federal Republic of Germany (West Germany), on the Rhine River, 13 mi (21km) S of Cologne; residence of electors of Cologne (1238–1794); awarded to Prussia by Congress of Vienna (1815); site of 11th-century Romanesque cathedral, Poppelsdorf Castle (1715–30), Rathas (city hall,

Anne Boleyn

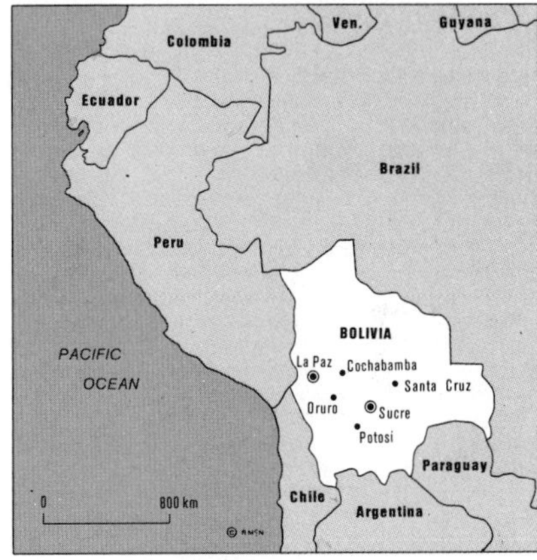
Colombia
Ven.
Guyana
Ecuador
Brazil
Peru
BOLIVIA
PACIFIC
OCEAN
La Paz
Cochabamba
Santa Cruz
Oruro
Sucre
Potosi
Paraguay
0
800 km
Chile
Argentina

Bolivia

Heinrich Boll

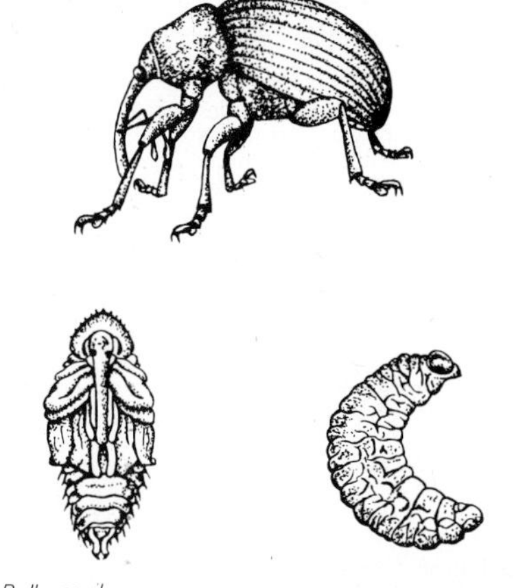

Boll weevil

1837) university (1786); birthplace of Beethoven; chosen as capital of West German state 1949. Industries: publishing, aluminum, electrical materials, stoneware, chemicals, insurance. Founded AD 1st century as Roman camp. Pop. 138,012.

Bonnard, Pierre (1867–1947), French painter. His early work, mainly of domestic scenes, was in the style of Paul Gauguin and Paul Sérusier. He received favorable reviews for his entries in the Salon des independents, Paris, in 1891, and a year later, for *The Terrasse Family*. Other notable works include *Luncheon* (1927) and his masterpiece, *Figure Before a Fireplace* (1917).

Bonneville Dam, Columbia River dam on Washington-Oregon border; constructed 1933–43 by US Corps of Engineers, used for hydroelectricity and flood control. Length: 2,690ft (820m). Height: 197ft (60m).

Bonneville Salt Flats, flat, barren salt land in NW Utah; part of the bed of Pleistocene Lake Bonneville; scene of auto racing and speed trials. Area: approx. 100sq mi (259sq km).

Bonney, William H. *See* Billy the Kid.

Bonnie Prince Charlie. *See* Stuart, Charles Edward.

Bonsai, Japanese gardening art of dwarfing woody plants and shrubs by pruning and restraining root growth. True bonsai are outdoor plants and need a dormant period during winter. Bonsai plants are most easily formed from plants with a substantial, tapering trunk, naturally twisted branches, and small leaves. The tree or shrub is shaped so the lower trunk is bare of branches; the middle is bare in front; and the top is surrounded. Branch shape is controlled by wiring. Container shape should complement. Practiced for centuries in the Orient, bonsai has been popular in the United States since World War II. △448.

Bontemps, Arna W(endell) (1902–73), US writer, b. Alexandria, La. First identified with the Harlem Renaissance of the 1920s, he wrote extensively on the black experience. His works include poetry; novels: *God Sends Sunday* (1931), *Black Thunder* (1935); children's books; many biographies; and anthologies of black poetry, music, folklore, and slave narratives.

Bonus Army (1932), group of unemployed veterans that marched on Washington D.C. and demanded cash payment of bonus certificates. The 17,000 veterans camped out during June and July until President Hoover sent regular troops under Douglas MacArthur to disperse them. In 1936, the veterans were given cashable bonds. △1324.

Booby, seabird found in colonies on tropical and subtropical islands. They have bright faces, long necks, cone-shaped bills, and webbed feet. Expert fliers, they dive for fish. Most lay 2–3 eggs. Length: 26–40in (65–100cm). Genus *Sula*.

Book Binding. △1778.

Booker T. Washington National Monument, site in Hales Ford, SW Virginia; preserves the birthplace and childhood home of this educator and social reformer. He developed Tuskegee Institute into one of the leading centers of black education. Area: 218acres (88hectares). Est. 1956.

Book Louse, or bookworm, transparent to white, usually wingless insect found worldwide. It feeds on molds in dusty places with high temperature and humidity, such as shelves, books, and behind loose wallpaper. Length: to 0.04in (1mm). Family Liposcelidae; genus *Liposcelis*.

Book of Common Prayer, official service book for the Church of England. First prepared in 1549 under the direction of Archbishop Thomas Cranmer to simplify the services of the recently formed church. Many editions and revisions have been issued since the first text.

Book of Hours. △1106.

Book of Mormon, The, sacred work of the Church of Jesus Christ of Latter-Day Saints (Mormons). Mormons hold it in equal esteem with the Bible. First published in 1830, it is supposedly the translation of golden tablets revealed to Joseph Smith, the church's founder, by the angel Moroni in Palmyra, N.Y. It tells the story of a Hebrew tribe that sailed to America (*c.* 600 BC) across the Pacific and then split into two groups. One group, the Lamanites, lost their beliefs and became savages. They were the ancestors of the American Indians. The others, the Nephites, developed a great culture. Jesus Christ appeared among them, and his teachings and the history of the tribe were written down by the prophet Mormon and his son Moroni on the gold tablets. The Lamanites, however, eventually destroyed the Nephites (*c.* AD 400). Smith claimed that he returned the tablets to the angel after showing them to 11 witnesses. *See also* Mormons.

Book of the Dead, a collection of Old Egyptian texts dating from the 16th century BC and after. The papyrus texts, which were of many different kinds, were placed in the tombs of the dead in order to help them combat the dangers of the underworld. △972.

Book Value, in accounting, the net value of a particular item as carried on a company's accounting records. For example, acquisition costs of a particular asset less its accumulated depreciation would equal its book value.

Boolean Algebra. *See* Algebra. △1458.

Boomerang, missile weapon, evolved by the Australian aborigines for hunting and warfare. Essentially a modified throwing stick, the boomerang is shaped with a pronounced curve or angle, enabling the skilled thrower to make it describe a circle in the air and return to him. Non-returning boomerangs are also found.

Boone, Daniel (1734–1820), US trailblazer and pioneer, b. Oley Township, Pa. In 1775, Boone blazed the Wilderness Road and founded Boonesboro in Kentucky. During the Revolution, he was captured by Indians. He escaped in 1778 and reached Boonesboro in time to prevent its capture. He lost his Kentucky lands because of faulty titles, and then moved to Missouri, where he again lost his land, but Congress restored part of it.

Boonesboro, historic village in E central Kentucky on Kentucky River; named after Daniel Boone who in 1775 built a fort used as region's seat of government; due to numerous Indian attacks, the settlement was abandoned.

Booster Shot, a supplemental dose of a vaccine given to maintain immunity against a specific disease.

Booth, Edwin Thomas (1833–93), US actor, b. near Bel Air, Md. Booth was born into a prominent family of actors and made his debut in 1849. He specialized in Shakespearean roles and was considered one of the finest Hamlets of his time. He frequently appeared on the New York stage (1862–73), and in 1869 built the Booth Theatre, which went bankrupt after five years despite its splendid productions. He was among the first US actors to win international recognition, touring Europe (1880–82). In 1889 he founded the Players' Club. He was elected to the American Hall of Fame in 1925. His brother John Wilkes Booth assassinated Pres. Abraham Lincoln.

Booth, John Wilkes (1838–65), US actor and assassin of President Lincoln, b. Bel Air, Md. A successful actor who often appeared with his brothers Edwin and Junius Brutus, he was a Confederate sympathizer. On April 14, 1865, at Ford's Theater in Washington, D.C., he fatally shot President Lincoln, who died shortly thereafter. Unsuccessful attempts on the lives of members of Lincoln's cabinet were made by co-conspirators. Booth escaped but was trapped in a barn, where he died. The assassination infuriated the North and contributed to the severity of Reconstruction. △1276.

Booth, William (1829–1912), English religious leader, founder (1878) and first general of the Salvation Army. *See also* Salvation Army.

Boothia Peninsula, peninsula in Northwest Territory, Canada; northernmost part of North American mainland. Almost uninhabited, it was discovered and explored by British explorer John Ross 1829–33. Area: 12,483sq mi (32,331sq km).

Borage, hairy, annual herb, native to the E Mediterranean region and cultivated in Europe and North America for bee-feeding, salads, and flavoring. It has rough, oblong leaves and drooping clusters of bright blue flowers. Height: to 2ft (60cm). Family Boraginaceae; species *Borago officinalis*.

Borah, William Edgar (1865–1940), US senator from Idaho (1907–1940), b. Fairfield, Ill. He supported the direct election of senators, income tax, and eight-hour day, but opposed women's suffrage and child labor laws. A leading prohibitionist and strong isolationist, he was one of the leaders of the fight against US entry into the League of Nations. He chaired the Senate Foreign Relations Committee during 1924–33.

Borate, one of a class of inorganic compounds that are salts of boric acid (H_3BO_3) or of more complex oxyacids of boron. Many borate minerals exist: the most important are borax, colemanite, and kernite, all used as sources of boron compounds.

Borax, the most common borate mineral, hydrous sodium borate. Occurs in large deposits in dried-up salt lakes in arid regions. Monoclinic system prismatic crystals, crusts and masses. Colorless or white; transparent or opaque; hardness 2–2.5; sp gr 1.7. Many commercial uses such as in ceramics, in agricultural chemicals, as water softener.

Borchert, Wolfgang (1921–1947), German short-story writer, dramatist, and poet. His highly sensitive poems and prose sketches, *On That Tuesday* (1947) and *The Dandelion* (1947), vividly and uniquely record a young man's disillusion with post-war Germany. His best known work, the play *The Man Outside* (1947), portrays with grotesque imagery the isolation of those returning from war.

Bordeaux, seaport city in SW France, on the W bank of the Garonne River; capital of Gironde dept. Although 60mi (97km) from open ocean, it is an excellent deepwater port. In 4th century it was a thriving metropolis of the Roman province of Aquitania Secunda; the English held it 1154–1453 and developed its trade; site of 18th-century buildings, vestige of a 3rd-century Roman amphitheatre and the Gothic cathedral of St. André; famous for wines and brandies. Industries: shipbuilding, textiles, soap, glass, beer. Pop. 266,662.

Borden, Lizzie (Andrew) (1860–1927), US figure in a murder case, b. Fall River, Mass. She is known because of the mutilation murder of her father and stepmother in 1892. She was acquitted in a sensational trial, but many books were written about the case and she became a part of folklore.

Borden, (Sir) Robert Laird (1854–1937), Canadian prime minister (1911–20). A lawyer, historian, and educator, he headed the Conservative party after 1901. Borden worked for civil service reform, public telephone and telegraph ownership, and imperial preferential trade, while attacking economic reliance on the United States. He cooperated with Henri Bourassa's nationalist faction, railroad interests, and industrialists, and he represented Canada at the Washington Disarmament Conference (1921) and the League of Nations. He wrote extensively on Canada's history, constitution, and jurisprudence.

Border Collie, oldest sheepherding purebred dog with great speed and strength. The head is similar to that of the old-fashioned collie with a slightly blunted, short muzzle and broad skull. The black or black and white coat is wavy and can be long or short. Average size: 18in (45.5 cm) high at shoulder; 45lb (20.5kg). *See also* Collie.

Border Ruffians, name given to pro-slavery men in the Missouri-Kansas area who fought against anti-slavery forces in Kansas Territory.

Border States, those slave-holding states where there was strong anti-slavery sentiment, including Delaware, Kentucky, Maryland and Missouri, and West Virginia, which remained in the Union. They were called border states because they shared a border with the Confederate States. President Abraham Lincoln, anxious not to lose these states to the South, excluded them from the Emancipation Proclamation (1863). △1276.

Border Terrier, working dog (terrier group) purebred since the 18th century in the border country of northern England and Scotland. The border terrier's hunting ability is shown in its otter-shaped head; straight, muscular legs; and narrow body. Ears are V-shaped, dropped forward. The short tail is carried up. The short, dense, harsh coat is blue and tan, grizzle and tan, or red. Average size: 12in (30cm) high at shoulder; 13–15lb (6–7kg). *See also* Terrier.

Bordet, Jules Jean Baptiste Vincent (1870–1961), Belgian bacteriologist and immunologist. He was awarded the 1919 Nobel Prize in physiology or medicine for his development of the complement fixation test, an important diagnostic tool in immunology.

Bore, Tidal, a turbulent, wall-like wave of water that rushes up a narrowing estuary, bay, or tidal river. It seems to be caused by a combination of the incoming tidal wave, the slope and shape of the channel, and the river flow. △226.

Boreal Forest, wooded zone with a cold, dry climate and poor sandy soil, including the Northern Hemisphere just below the Arctic tundra, high mountain regions, and SE United States. It is characterized by the predominance of coniferous trees such as pine, fir, spruce, and hemlock.

Borges, Jorge Luis (1899–), Argentine writer, the best-known Argentine author of the 20th century. His huge output of work has become a frame of reference for all Latin American writers. Most famous for his short stories—including the collections *El hacedor* (1960) and *El informe de Brodie* (1970)—he also wrote books of poetry and essays. His stories often use elaborate puzzles to dramatize what he believes is the extreme difficulty of achieving knowledge. Despite this skepticism, he writes with humor and awe about our attempts to unravel life's mysteries. △ 1376.

Borghese, noble Italian dynasty, originating in 13th-century Siena and moving to Rome in the 1500s. **Camillo** became Pope Paul V (1605). His nephew **Scipione Caffarelli**, a cardinal (died 1633, patron of artist Bernini), was responsible for the construction of the Villa Borghese. Other family members furthered dynastic wealth by obtaining principalities and marrying into the Orsini and Aldobrandini families. **Camillo** (1775–1832) won infamy by selling the Borghese art collection to his brother-in-law, Napoleon.

Borgia, family, notorious in 15th- and 16th-century Italian politics. From Spain the family went to Rome with first Borgia pope, **Calixtus III** (1455–58). His nephew **Rodrigo** became **Pope Alexander VI** (1492) and was the father of the infamous **Cesare** (*c.*1475–1507) and **Lucrezia** (1480–1519). By alliances with the French, use of papal influences, strategic marriages, and treachery, the family sought political control over the Papal states and throughout central Italy. Alexander's death in 1502, Cesare's illness at the same time, and the election of Borgia enemy Giuliano della Rovere as Pope Julius II conspired to defeat Borgia aspirations.

Borgia, Cesare (*c.*1475–1507), major figure in Italian politics while his father was Pope Alexander VI. In 1498 he secured French military assistance for an assault on central Italy. His ruthlessness in the successful campaigns through 1502 won him the reputation that caused Machiavelli to cite him as the example of the new "prince." His political fortunes collapsed with Alexander's death (1502), his own illness, and the election of a Borgia enemy as Pope Julius II.

Borgia, Lucrezia (1480–1519), daughter of Pope Alexander VI and sister of Cesare Borgia. Her 1493 marriage to Giovanni Sforza, lord of Pesaro, was annulled by Alexander in 1497 when the alliance it had created proved unworkable. The 1498 marriage to Alfonso, nephew of Alfonso II of Naples, ended with Alfonso's murder by Cesare's henchman when that tie threatened the alliance with France. After the collapse of Borgia aspirations in 1503, she lived the art patron's quiet life at the court of Ferrara with husband, Alfonso d'Este.

Borglum, (John) Gutzon (1871–1941), US sculptor, b. Bear Lake, Idaho. His technical expertise is not always evident, due to the size of his work. His best-known works include a bust of Christian IX in Denmark, "Lincoln" in Newark, N.J., and a head of Lincoln in the Capitol Rotunda in Washington, D.C. His last project was the carving of the heads of Washington, Jefferson, Lincoln, and Theodore Roosevelt in the side of a cliff at Mt. Rushmore, S.D. This work was completed by his son Lincoln Borglum.

Boric Acid, also known as orthoboric acid or boracic acid, H_3BO_3, a white crystalline compound. It is weakly acidic and water soluble. It occurs naturally in the hot lagoons of Tuscany, Italy. Boric acid is used as a mild antiseptic, particularly when diluted in water, as an eyewash. It is also used as the solid in dusting powders.

Boring Machine, device for making accurate and smoothly finished holes in metal objects. Drilled holes are enlarged with a cutting bore, generally tipped with steel, carbide, or diamond, and gripped in an adjustable boring head attached to a rotating spindle. The work-holding table can usually be moved in two perpendicular directions so that holes can be spaced accurately.

Boriquén, or **Borinquén,** Arawak-speaking tribe of prehistoric American Indians originally occupying Puerto Rico. Related to the Taíno, they were killed off or enslaved by the Carib and later by Spanish invaders. At one time their population exceeded 10,000 persons.

Boris I (*r.* 852–89, died 907), czar of Bulgaria. In 865 Boris was converted to Christianity and imposed baptism on his subjects. After the failure of negotiations with the pope to create an archbishopric in Bulgaria, Boris accepted the primacy of the Eastern Orthodox Church (870). He ended his life in a monastery and is venerated as a saint.

Boris III (1894–1943), czar of Bulgaria (1918–43). Following his father's abdication, Boris ruled as a constitutional monarch for 15 years, becoming dictator in 1934. Returning from a meeting with Hitler, who wanted Bulgaria to declare war on the USSR, Boris died under mysterious circumstances.

Boris Godunov (1874), opera in prologue and four acts by Modest Mussorgsky, Russian libretto by the composer based on Alexander Pushkin's play and Nikolai Karamzin's histories. Of several versions, Nicolai Rimsky-Korsakov's orchestration is the best known, although Mussorgsky's original scoring is being revived. The plot is a series of scenes from Russian history (1598–1605). △1256.

Borlaug, Norman Ernest (1914–), US agronomist, b. Cresco, Iowa. He was awarded the Nobel Peace Prize in 1970 for his accomplishments in the "green revolution," developing an improved wheat seed and a higher-yielding rice.

Bormann, Martin (1900–45), German National Socialist leader. He joined the Nazi party in 1925 and was important in the party hierarchy. In 1941 he succeeded Rudolf Hess as depty fuehrer. Although reported dead in 1945, he was sentenced to death in absentia by the Nuremberg war crimes tribunal. In 1973 the West German government declared him dead, a suicide in 1945, when his skeleton was identified.

Born, Max (1882–1970), British physicist, b. Breslau, Germany. A physics professor at Gottingen University, he left Germany in 1933 and went to Great Britain, where he later became professor at the University of Edinburgh. For his work in quantum mechanics, the basis of atomic and nuclear physics, he received the 1954 Nobel Prize.

Borneo, island in the Malay Archipelago, SE Asia. Largely undeveloped, Borneo is the world's 3rd-largest island, divided into four political regions: Sarawak state (W) and Sabah state (N) are Malaysian; Brunei state (NW) is a British protectorate; Kalimantan state (E, central, and S) which covers 70% of the island, is part of Indonesia. Borneo was colonized by Chinese in the 7th century, followed by Malays; Spanish, Portuguese, Dutch, and English trade started in the 16th and 17th centuries; by 1888, Sabah, Brunei, and Sarawak were declared British protectorates; the remainder were claimed by Dutch; present divisions were fixed in 1963. Industries: agriculture, forestry, fishing, oil and coal extraction. Area: 287,000sq mi (743,330sq km). Pop. 6,800,000.

Bornholm, island group in extreme E Denmark, in the Baltic Sea. After Germany's surrender in May, 1945, German forces made a desperate stand here, but Soviet troops forced their surrender. Bornholm is largest island. Industries: farming, fishing, handicrafts. Pop. 47,241.

Bornite, or peacock ore, a sulfide mineral, copper iron sulfide (Cu_5FeS_4); common copper ore in intrusive igneous rocks and metamorphic rocks. Cubic system, rarely as crystals, frequently in masses. Bronze with purple iridescent tarnish; metallic; opaque; hardness 3; sp gr 5.

Bornu (Kanen-Bornu). △1116.

Borobudur, ruins of a Buddhist monument in central Java, built under the Sailendra dynasty around 800. The work is formed by the stupa (a relic mound), the mandala (ritual diagrams), and the temple mountain, all forms in Indian Gupta religious art.

Borodin, Aleksandr (1834–87), Russian composer. He was one of the "Russian Five," composers who promoted Russian nationalism in music in the 19th century. His most popular work is the *Polovtsian Dances* from his opera *Prince Igor* (begun 1869). He also composed three symphonies. △1246.

Borodino, town in Russian SFSR, USSR, on the Kolocha River, 70mi (113km) WSW of Moscow; battlefield site of 1812 Napoleonic Wars where Russians under Mikhail Kutuzov were defeated, thus opening Moscow to Napoleon's army.

Boron, nonmetallic element (symbol B) of group III of the periodic table, first isolated (1807) by Sir

Daniel Boone

John Wilkes Booth

Borage

Aleksandr Borodin

Humphry Davy. It occurs in several minerals, notably borax and the chief ore, kernite. Amorphous boron, an impure powder, is made by reducing the oxide with magnesium. Pure boron is obtained as a hard crystalline material by decomposing boron tribromide vapor on a hot metal filament. The element is used in semiconductor devices and the stable isotope B^{10} is a good neutron absorber, used in nuclear reactors and particle counters. Properties: at. no. 5; at. wt. 10.81; sp. gr. 2.34 (cryst.), 2.37 (amorph.); melt. pt. 4172°F (2300°C); most common isotope B^{11} (80.22%). △1554.

Borromeo, Carlo (1538–84), Italian church reformer and Roman Catholic saint. He was created cardinal by his uncle Pius IV (1560), and then Archbishop of Milan. His tenure was remarkable for administrative and spiritual reform. He lived simply, insisted on an educated clergy, and urged the reconvening of the Council of Trent. During the plague of 1576–78 he heroically administered to the needs of the populace.

Borromini, Francesco (1599–1667), Italian architect. His Baroque palace and church designs were based on geometric modules rather than on the proportions of the human body and had tremendous influence in Italy and northern Europe. A notable example of his work is S. Carlo alle Quattro Fontane in Rome (begun 1634).

Borstal System, British method for rehabilitation of juvenile offenders, ages 16–21. The system derives its name from the first institution, which was established for boys, at Borstal, England, in 1902. It emphasizes training, residential-type living, and individual attention. The system was later extended to girls.

Borzoi, hunting dog (hound group) that relies on sight and speed; also called Russian wolfhound. An elegant dog dating from 17th-century Russia, it has a slightly domed, long, narrow head; long, powerful jaws; small, fine ears laid back on the neck; a deep but narrow-chested body; gracefully curved back; long legs; and a long, curved tail. The long, silky coat is flat, wavy, or curly; it is short and smooth on the head, ears, and front of legs. The coat can be any color. Average size: 26–31in (66–81cm) high at shoulder; 75–105lb (34–47.5kg). *See also* Hound.

Bosch, Jerome (Hieronymus van Aeken) (*c.* 1450–1516), Flemish painter. He portrayed fantastic creatures in strange worlds. His archaic and highly individualistic style is explained in part by his artistic isolation and his adherence to heretic Protestant sects. His concern with the evils that constantly beset mankind is depicted in *Garden of Earthly Delights;* his anti-Church attitude, in *Adoration of the Kings. Hay-Wain* is a good example of his style—flat figures in rich dress in a panoramic view. △1144.

Bosch, Karl (or Carl) (1874–1940), German industrial chemist who adapted Fritz Haber's ammonia synthesizing method to an industrial scale. His work involved finding usable metallic catalysts to achieve this high-pressure synthesis. His invention of the Bosch process (in which water gas and steam at high temperatures are passed over a catalyst) aided in the large scale preparation of hydrogen. Bosch was awarded a 1931 Nobel Prize (jointly with Friedrich Bergius) for his high-pressure methods.

Bose, (Sir) Jagadis Chandra (1858–1937), Indian plant physiologist and physicist. He invented highly sensitive tools capable of detecting tissue responses of plants to external stimuli. His automatic recorder, which regulated very slight movements, allowed him to demonstrate feeling in plants and to anticipate parallelism between plant and animal tissue.

Bosmon's Potto. △554.

Bosnia, constituent republic in central Yugoslavia on the Sava River; comprises the regions of Bosnia (N) and Hercegovina (S), in the Dinaric Alps; Sarajevo is the capital. First settled by the Serbs, became powerful independent country by the 12th century; taken by Turks in 1463, then ruled by Hungary, Germany, and finally Yugoslavia in 1946. Industries: lumber, corn, tobacco, cotton, wheat, grapes, copper, iron ore, lignite, manganese, hydroelectricity. Area: 19,741sq mi (51,129sq km). Pop. 3,742,852.

Bosnia and Hercegovina. △1232, 1302.

Bosporus, narrow strait joining Sea of Marmara with Black Sea, separating European and Asian Turkey; scenic banks are lined with villas and old castles; important strategic and commercial passage; controlled by Turks since 1452; refortified after Montreux Convention of 1936. Length: 19mi (30km). With Dardanelles Strait at SW end of Sea of Marmara, Bosporus creates a water route from the Black Sea to the Aegean Sea. *See also* Dardanelles.

Bossier City, city in NW Louisiana, across the Red River from Shreveport; site of ruins of Confederate Fort Smith; Barksby Air Force Base nearby; center of large oil- and gas-producing area. Inc. 1907. Pop. (1970) 41,595.

Bossuet, Jacques Bénigne (1627–1704), French theologian. He became the most respected preacher at the court of Louis XIV. His *Politics drawn from Holy Scripture* (1709) advocated the divine right of kings. He vigorously opposed both Jansenism and Pietism in favor of moderate and traditional Catholicism. *See also* Jansenism; Pietist.

Boston, seaport city and capital of Massachusetts, in E part of state at mouth of Charles and Mystic rivers on Massachusetts Bay; seat of Suffolk co; largest city in New England. Founded 1630 by John Winthrop and Puritans as the main colony of the Massachusetts Bay Co., it was named for the town in Lincolnshire, England. Seeking religious freedom, the colony soon developed into a stronghold of Puritanism and a leader in the opposition to Britain's taxation and trade restrictions; it was the scene of several events leading to the outbreak of the American Revolution: the Boston Massacre (March 5, 1770), the Boston Tea Party (Dec. 16, 1773), and the Battle of Bunker Hill (June 17, 1775). Boston contains the 17th-century home of Paul Revere, Old North Church (1723), Old South Meetinghouse (1729), Faneuil Hall (1742), and the Old State House (1748). It was the birthplace of US Unitarianism at King's Chapel (1785) and is the site of the mother church of Christian Science (1894); the YMCA was started here (1851) seven years after it was founded in Britain; the Roman Catholic Archdiocese of Boston is the 2nd-largest in the United States; from 1830–65 city was center of an abolitionist movement.

A noted educational center, Boston is the site of the Boston Public Latin School (1635), and of numerous colleges, including Mass. College of Pharmacy (1823), Boston University (1839), Mass. State College at Boston (1852), New England Conservatory of Music (1867), Mass. College of Art (1873), Burdett College (1879), Emerson College (1880), Wheelock College (1889), Northeastern University (1898), Wentworth Institute (1904), Simmons College (1899), Suffolk University (1906), Emmanuel College (1919). Harvard University (1636), Tufts University (1858), Brandeis University (1848), Radcliffe College (1879), and Mass. Institute of Technology (1860) are nearby. Cultural facilities include the Boston Museum of the Fine Arts, the Isabella Stewart Gardner Museum, Boston Public Library, and Boston Symphony Orchestra. Leading medical centers and research facilities are here; Boston is also the home of the Red Sox (American League baseball team), the Celtics (National Basketball Association team), and the Bruins (National Hockey League team). Industries: apparel, chemicals, publishing, shipbuilding, electronic equipment, fishing, wool processing. Inc. as city 1822. Pop. (1970) 641,071.

Boston, Siege of (1775–76), Revolutionary War conflict. British troops in Boston were surrounded by American colonial forces. The siege began in April 1775 when the British retreated to Boston after the battles at Lexington and Concord. It ended in March 1776 when American troops, under the command of George Washington, captured Dorchester Heights and the British under Gen. William Howe evacuated Boston and sailed to Nova Scotia.

Boston Associates, group of Massachusetts investors headed by Francis Cabot Lowell. At Waltham, Mass. (1814), the group built the first US factory to combine all the operations necessary to turn raw cotton into finished cloth.

Boston Massacre (1770), riot by American colonists angered over the quartering of troops in private homes. It was put down by British soldiers and resulted in the death of five civilians, including Crispus Attucks. The riot was used as a propaganda device by Sam Adams. The soldiers were tried for murder, defended by John Adams, and acquitted. △1218.

Boston News-Letter, first successful American newspaper, published 1704–1776. Founded by John Campbell, it was edited by him until 1722. In 1708 the first illustration in a colonial newspaper appeared in it.

Boston Port Act (1774), one of the Coercive Acts, it closed Boston to trade until restitution had been made for the tea destroyed in the Boston Tea Party. *See also* Boston Tea Party.

Boston Tea Party (1773), protest by a group of Bostonians, disguised as Indians, against the Tea Act and the policy of "taxation without representation." Tea from ships was thrown into Boston harbor after Gov. Thomas Hutchinson refused to let the ships return to England without unloading. *See also* Tea Act. △1218.

Boston Terrier, native American breed (nonsporting group) bred in Boston about 1870 from English bulldog and white English terrier. Its square head is flat on top. The muzzle is square, short, and wide. Ears are natural bat shape or cropped. Large eyes are wide-set. The short body is wide-chested. Wide-set legs are medium-long. The short, low-set tail is either straight or screw-shaped. Characteristic coloring of the short, smooth, fine coat is brindle with a specific pattern of white marks. Average size: three classes—under 15lb (7kg); 15–20lb (7–9kg); 20–25lb (9–11.5kg). *See also* Nonsporting Dog.

Boswell, James (1740–95), Scottish biographer and author. He traveled widely in Europe, meeting Voltaire and Jean Jacques Rousseau. His early works include *Account of Corsica* (1768) and *Journal of a Tour to the Hebrides* (1785), an account of his travels with Samuel Johnson. A friend of Johnson and fellow member of the Literary Club, his *Life of Johnson* (2 vols., 1791) is one of the greatest English biographies.

Bosworth Field, English battleground 12 miles (19.3km) W of Leicester, site of the concluding battle of the Wars of the Roses (1485). There the Lancastrians, under the future Henry VII, defeated and killed the Yorkist Richard III.

Botanical Garden, large garden preserve for display, research, and teaching purposes. Wild and cultivated plants from all climates are maintained outdoors and in greenhouses. Although organized gardens date from ancient Rome, the first botanical gardens were est during the Middle Ages. In the 16th century, gardens existed in Pisa, Bologna, Padua, and Leiden. Aromatic and medicinal herbs were arranged in rows and still exist in the Botanical Garden of Padua. The first US botanical garden was est. by John Bartram in Philadelphia in 1728. Famous botanical gardens include the Royal Botanical Gardens in Kew (near London) est. 1759; Botanical Gardens of Berlin-Dahlem 1646; and Botanical Gardens in Schönbrunn, Vienna 1753.

Botany, the study of plant life. It includes the classification, structure, physiology, reproduction, and evolution of plants; also plants in relation to their environment and the economic aspects of their use by man. The chief subdivisions of botany are taxonomy, morphology, physiology, and genetics. Plants have always been important to man and necessary to human life. Primitive man depended on plant life for food, warmth, and shelter. Man learned to cultivate wild plants and discovered those that would grow from seed and those that were weeds. He studied plant composition, proper breeding methods, and treatment of diseases. As botanists learned more about plants, they began to catalog all known plants instead of only those with medicinal virtures. The first authentic work in botany is credited to Theophrastus, a pupil of Aristotle, about 300 BC. △424–56.

Botany Bay, bay of the Tasman Sea in New South Wales, Australia; discovered by Capt. James Cook in 1700. Fed by the Georges and Woronora rivers, it is about 5mi (8km) across and 1mi (1.6km) wide at its mouth.

Botfly, warble fly or cattle grub, stout black and white to gray fly, 0.35 to 0.7in (9–18mm) long, an ectoparasite of many animals; found worldwide. The larvae enter through small wounds and grow under the skin. Damage to the skin is caused by infection of the exit hole. Family Oestridae. *See also* Diptera.

Bothnia, Gulf of, chief arm of the Baltic Sea; north of Ahvenanmaa Islands, between Sweden (W) and Finland (E); freezes part of the year; contains lumber shipping ports. Length: approx. 400mi (644km). Width: 50–150mi (8–241km).

Bothwell, James Hepburn, 4th Earl of (?1535–78), Scottish nobleman, third husband of Mary, Queen of Scots. He made many enemies in Scotland's turbulent politics but won the queen's affection by loyally supporting her. When her husband Lord Darnley was murdered (1567), Bothwell was implicated; nevertheless, Mary married him. The nobles rebelled, and Bothwell fled abroad. He died insane in a Danish prison.

Botswana, Republic of, formerly Bechuanaland Protectorate; republic in S Africa bounded by Namibia (N and W), Rhodesia (NE), Republic of South Africa (S and SE). It was the first British high commission territory to attain independence (1966); the main legislature is a National Assembly, headed by President Seretse Khama.

The terrain is a tableland rising to a mean elevation of 3,300ft (1,007m). In the S and SW the enormous Kalahari Desert expands N into bush lands. The Okavango River basin, located in the NW, has industrial potential as source for an irrigation project. Although varying from N to S, the average annual rainfall is 18in (457mm), and the climate is subtropical. Only 4% of the land is used for agricultural purposes (corn, sorghum, peanuts); the economy is dependent upon cattle export, inhabitants' work in the mines, and industries of Rhodesia and the Republic of South Africa. Botswana has developed its copper and diamond industries since their discovery in 1969–70.

The majority of Botswana's population belongs to its eight principal tribes: Bamangwato, Bakwena, Bangwaketse, Batawana, Bakgatla, Bamalete, Barolong, Batlokwa. These people are mainly pastoral, with low literacy rates and health standards. Most industrial workers are of European descent and are mainly from South Africa. Christianity and tribal beliefs constitute the main religions. English is the official language, with Tswana as the main African language.

Until its independence in 1966, Botswana was ruled as a British protectorate. Its government was headed by a British resident commissioner who was responsible to the high commissioner; advisory councils were added later. Seretse Khama founded the Bechuanaland Democratic party in the 1960s and was made its first president; he was made president of the new Republic of Botswana in 1966. A British protectorate was est. in the N in 1884–85 at the insistence of the Botswana tribes as a safeguard against occupation by Boers and Matabeles. British Bechuanaland was est. the same year, as a crown colony lying S of the Molopo River. Ten years later the S area was annexed to Cape of Good Hope colony, with the N region remaining a protectorate until its independence in 1966.

PROFILE

Official name: Republic of Botswana
Area: 231,804sq mi (600,372sq km)
Population: 700,000
Chief cities: Gaborone (capital); Serowe; Kanye; Molepolole
Religion: Tribal, Christianity
Language: English (official), Tswana
Monetary unit: South African rand

Botticelli, Sandro (*c.* 1445–1510), Italian painter. Influenced by Piero Pollaiuolo, he worked with him on a series of *Seven Virtues* (1470; Uffizi, Florence). In Florence he was patronized by the leading families, including the Medicis, whose portraits he included in *Adoration of the Magi* (Uffizi, Florence). In 1481 he went to Rome to assist in the decoration of the Sistine Chapel. After his return to Florence, he painted a number of mythological pictures, including *Birth of Venus* and *Pallas Subduing a Centaur* (both, Uffizi, Florence). He is known for his masterful use of color, graceful lines, and poignant themes. △1138.

Bottle-nosed Whale, beaked whale found in Atlantic waters. Its nose resembles the neck of a bottle and it usually travels in small groups. Length: 30ft (9m). Species *Hyperoodon ampullatus* (N Atlantic); *Hyperoodon planifrons* (S Atlantic). *See also* Beaked Whale; Whale. △552.

Botulism, form of food poisoning caused by a bacterial toxin so lethal that death can occur within hours, apparently from respiratory paralysis. Early symptoms include lassitude, disturbance of vision, sometimes though not always with nausea and vomiting. The most frequent source of botulism is home-canned foods. Hospitalization is necessary.

Boucher, François (1703–70), French painter, decorator, and engraver. A follower of the Rococo style of the Louis XV period, he was immensely popular and widely imitated all over Europe. He painted historical, mythological, genre, and landscape works, executing over 1,000 paintings, 10,000 drawings, and 180 engravings, of which the Wallace Collection of London holds the largest part. *See also* Rococo. △1190.

Boucicault, Dion(ysius Lardner) (1822–90), Irish actor and dramatist. Living in London and New York, he wrote numerous romantic melodramas, such as *The Colleen Bawn* (1860). In *The Octoroon* (1859) he attempted a serious stage treatment of an American black theme, creating a popular standard piece for touring American repertory companies.

Boucicaut Master. △1146.

Bougainville, largest island of Solomon Island group, in W Pacific Ocean, E of New Guinea; territory of Papua, New Guinea. The Emperor Mountains run through the middle section; contains rich soil, many harbors. Discovered 1768 by Louis de Bougainville, the island was under German control 1882, taken by Australia 1914, occupied by Japan during WWII, and retaken by Australia 1945. Crops: coconuts, coffee, cacao. Exports: copra, rubber. Area: 3,880sq mi (10,049sq km). Pop. 70,000.

Bougainville, Louis Antoine de (1729–1811), French navigator. An army veteran of the French and Indian Wars, in 1753 he joined the navy and commanded the first French naval force to circumnavigate the globe (1766–69). Later, Napoleon I named him a senator and count of the Empire. △1260.

Bougainvillea, tropical, flowering woody vine often grown as garden plant in warm climates. Its inconspicuous flowers have showy purple or red bracts. It was named after explorer Louis de Bougainville who collected it near Rio de Janiero. Family Nyctaginaceae; species *Bougainvillea spectabilis.*

Bouguer Anomaly, the observation that the gravity measured on a great rock mass, such as a mountain range, is greater than the average. This is due to the gravitational force exerted by the rock mass itself. △178.

Bouillon, Frédéric Maurice de la Tour d'Auvergne, duc de (1605–52), French general, the son of Henri de Bouillon and the brother of Marshal Turenne. He entered the service of Louis XIII in 1635. For his part in the Cinq Mars conspiracy (1642) he was forced to give up Sedan. He later took part in the Fronde against Cardinal Mazarin (1649).

Bouillon, Henri de la Tour d'Auvergne, vicomte de Turenne, duc de (1555–1623), French marshal and Protestant leader, the first of his family to become duke of Bouillon. He helped Henry of Navarre obtain the French throne as King Henry IV, but was later involved in a conspiracy against him (1602).

Bouillon, town in SE Belgium, on the Semois River near the French border; named 1088 for crusader Godfrey of Bouillon, who made it the capital of a duchy; it was held by the La Marck family until 1594, when it was transferred to the French. Pop. 2,949.

Boulanger, Georges Ernest Jean Marie (1837–91), French general and minister. Supported by the Bonapartists and royalists, he became a serious threat to the republican government in the 1880s. He committed suicide after being deported.

Boulanger, Nadia (1887–), French music teacher and composer. She has taught many significant 20th-century composers including Aaron Copland, Walter Piston, and Virgil Thomson.

Boulder, city in N central Colorado, seat of Boulder co, 25mi (40km) NW of Denver; site of University of Colorado (1876) and National Bureau of Standards. Industries: tourism, space research, agriculture, mining. Settled 1858; inc. 1871. Pop. (1970) 66,870.

Boulder Fern, or hayscented fern, lacy, North American fern of dry woodlands and open pastures. The brittle, yellowish-green fronds have haylike aroma. It has a slender, rapidly growing rootstock. Height: to 3ft (9km). Family Cyatheaceae; species *Dennstaedtia punctilobula.*

Boulenger's Arrow Poison Frog. △524.

Boulle, Pierre (1912–), French novelist and short-story writer. His wartime experiences, fighting for the Free French in Indochina, provided the background for the novel *Bridge on the River Kwai* (1952). Boulle's other novels included *The Face of a Hero* (1953) and *Planet of the Apes* (1963).

Boulogne-sur-Mer, seaport town in France, on the English Channel; one of the leading fishing ports of France; in AD 53 the Romans sailed from here to conquer Britain. During WWI it was a British base, and during WWII it was a German submarine base. Industries: canning, shipbuilding. Pop. 49,276.

Boumedienne, Houari (1925?–), Algerian political figure, b. as Mohammed Boukharouba. In the Algerian war for independence from France, he commanded guerrilla forces around Oran (1955–60) under the name Boumedienne and then became chief of staff of the rebel army (1960–62). He served as minister of defense and vice president from the achievement of independence (1962) to the coup (1965) in which he overthrew President Ben Bella, his former ally, and became leader of the country himself.

Boston, Massachusetts: Christian Science Center

Boston terrier

Angola
Zambia
Mozambique
Rhodesia
Namibia
Serowe
BOTSWANA
Gaborone
Kanye
Swaziland
South Africa
Lesotho
INDIAN OCEAN
0
800 km

Botswana

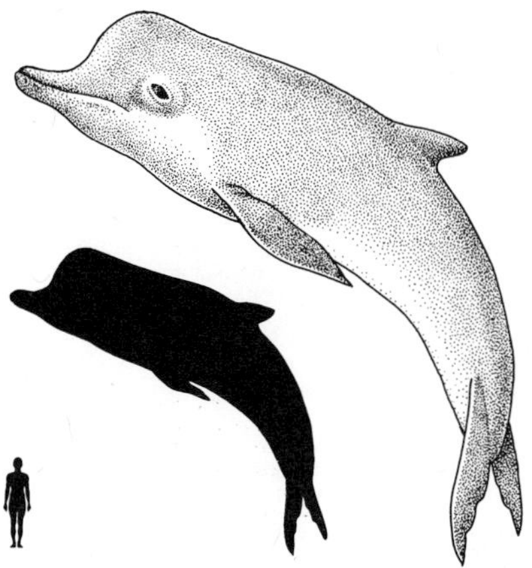

Bottle-nosed whale

In foreign policy he has maintained a strong anti-Israel position.

Bouncing Bet, common name for a herbaceous plant of the pink family, native to Europe and W Asia and naturalized in North America. The stocky upright perennial growing to about 3ft (91cm) bears clusters of large pink or white blooms in late summer. Family Caryophyllaceae; species *Saponaria officinalis. See also* Pink.

Boundary-layer Flow, the behavior of a fluid in the region immediately next to a solid body immersed in the fluid. In this region, layers of the fluid "slide" over one another, and the measure of this internal friction, viscosity, becomes the determining characteristic of the flow.

Bound Brook, town in N central New Jersey, on Raritan River; site of American Revolutionary War battle (1777) where American forces were defeated by British under Cornwallis. Industries: flowers, chemicals, textiles. Settled 1681; inc. 1891. Pop. (1970) 10,263.

Bountiful, city in N central Utah; N suburb of Salt Lake City. Founded 1847 by Mormons; inc. 1892. Pop. (1970) 27,956.

Bourbon, Antoine de (1518–62), duc de Vendôme, king of Navarre (1555–62). Through his marriage (1548) to Jeanne d'Albret, heiress of Navarre, he became king of Navarre. He converted to Protestantism and was an important Huguenot leader. He later reembraced Roman Catholicism. His son, Henry III of Navarre, became the first Bourbon king of France as Henry IV.

Bourbon, Charles, duc de (1490–1527), constable of France, imperial general. He became constable in 1515. Conflict with King Francis I led him to leave French service in 1522 and ally himself with Holy Roman Emperor Charles V. He subsequently fought against France and defeated the French at Pavia (1525). He was killed in battle in 1527.

Bourbon, House of, European dynastic family, the various branches of which were longtime rulers of France, Spain, and several independent Italian states. The Bourbons were descendants of the Capetians, the royal family that ruled France from 987 to 1328. In 1272, Robert of Clermont, a descendant of Louis IX, married Beatrice of Bourbon, a great heiress, and their son Louis was created duc de Bourbon in 1327. The ducal title continued until 1527 when the Bourbon lands were seized by the crown and the title eliminated. In the meantime, a cadet branch, the Bourbon-Vendôme line, was adding important fiefs to its holdings, including the kingdom of Navarre. Thus, when Henry of Navarre became king of France as Henry IV in 1589, the Bourbons became France's ruling family. They continued to rule until the French Revolution. Two members of the family, Louis XVIII and Charles X, ruled during the Bourbon Restoration (1814–30) and Louis Philippe, who ruled from 1830–48, was of the Bourbon-Orleans line, a cadet branch. Descendants of that line continued to be pretenders to the French crown.

The Bourbons became the ruling family of Spain in 1700 when Philip V, grandson of Louis XIV of France, assumed the throne, an act that brought on the War of the Spanish Succession. Except for brief periods, his descendants continued to rule Spain until 1931, when the Second Republic was declared. The republic, in turn, was replaced by the Nationalist government of Francisco Franco. His hand-picked successor, Juan Carlos I, who became king upon Franco's death (1975), was a Bourbon. The Bourbon rulers of Naples, the Two Sicilies, and Parma were all descended from the Spanish Bourbons. △1182.

Bourbonnais, former territory in central France, most of which corresponds to the present dept. of Allier. It was gradually put together by the counts of Bourbon, who became known as the Archimbaud dynasty. One of their members, Beatrice of Bourbon, married Robert (1256–1318), son of Louis IX of France, and thus gave the name "Bourbon" to the French royal family. Bourbon became a duchy in 1327 and was attached to the French crown in 1531.

Bourgeois Gentleman (1670), satirical comedy by French dramatist Molière about M. Jourdain, a wealthy bourgeois whose desire to be considered a gentleman becomes an obsession and finally a delusion. The play contains Molière's typical social satire as well as brilliantly realized characters.

Bourgeoisie, the middle class. Originally it referred to the artisans and craftsmen who lived in medieval French towns. The Industrial Revolution greatly increased their number and importance. They divided into the *haute bourgeoisie* (captains of industry and bankers) and the *petite bourgeoisie* (managers and tradesmen). Karl Marx credited the bourgeoisie with being instrumental in overthrowing feudalism but condemned them as reactionary capitalists who held down the proletariat. Among many intellectuals, especially those who were once called bohemian, the bourgeoisie is stereotyped as selfish, materialistic, mediocre, and unimaginative.

Bourges, city in central France, 122mi (195km) S of Paris; capital of Cher dept. Caesar captured it 52 BC; it later became the capital of the Roman prov. of Aquitania Prima; a medieval trade, banking, and financial center; site of 13th-century Cathedral of St Etienne. Town is now a market center for the surrounding agricultural area. Pop. 70,814.

Bourguiba, Habib (*c.*1903–), Tunisian political figure, president (1957–). In 1934 he founded the Neo-Destour party. In the next two decades he was often imprisoned by the French rulers of Tunisia for his nationalist activities. During his years of liberty he traveled abroad several times promoting the cause of Tunisian independence. In 1954 he began the negotiations that culminated in independence in 1956. Premier (1956–57), he deposed the bey and became the president (1957). In foreign policy he has favored negotiations between the Arab states and Israel. In 1974 he agreed to a plan for merger of Tunisia and Libya, but the plan has not been acted upon.

Bourke-White, Margaret (1906–71), US photojournalist, *b.* New York City. On the staffs of *Time, Fortune,* and *Life* magazines, she produced dramatic photo-essays on a great variety of subjects, including the rural South of the 1930s, the Italian and Russian campaigns of World War II, concentration camp victims, the Korean War, South Africa, India, modern industrial technology, and world political leaders.

Bouvier des Flandres, a cattle-driving dog (working group) bred in southwestern Flanders and northern France. A powerful dog, it has a medium-long, flat head; arched brow; and wide, deep muzzle. The high-set, erect ears are cropped to points. The body is short; the legs appear heavy because of coat; the high-set tail is docked. The fawn to black coat is rough and unkempt with characteristic eyebrows, mustache, and beard. Average size: 23.5–27.5in (59.5–70cm) high at shoulder; 60–70lb (27–32kg). *See also* Working Dog.

Bovet, Daniele (1907–), Italian pharmacologist, b. Switzerland. He was awarded the 1957 Nobel Prize in physiology or medicine for his pioneering work on the development of antihistamines and the muscle relaxants used in surgery. He also studied the bacteria-killing property of prontosil, a compound containing sulfanilamide.

Bovidae, family of horned ruminants consisting of 49 genera and about 115 species that are found worldwide. They feed on grass or other plants and most are gregarious and nomadic. Included are antelopes, buffalo, cattle, goat, and sheep. The earliest fossil record of this family is from Miocene times.

Bow, Clara (1905–65), US silent film star, b. Brooklyn, N.Y. Known as the "It" girl, she was a vivacious comedienne who personified the flapper in *Dancing Mothers, Mantrap* (1926), *It* (1927), and *The Wild Party* (1929). Her much publicized wild personal life and difficulty in adjusting to sound films led to a sharp decline in her popularity and her early retirement.

Bow (in weaponry). △1726, 1732.

Bow and Arrow, missile weapon comprising a length of wood, horn, etc., flexed and held in tension by a string, and a pointed shaft, usually flighted with feathers and tipped. Developed probably in the Upper Paleolithic, the bow and arrow is still almost universally used by primitive communities for hunting and warfare. The weapon's efficacy is often increased by steeping the arrowheads in poison. *See also* Archery.

Bowditch, Nathaniel (1773–1838), American navigator and mathematician, b. Salem, Mass. After five sea voyages he wrote *The New American Practical Navigator* (1802), a revision and correction of an English work. He later was an insurance actuary, but continued to write on astronomy. He translated Pierre Laplace's *Mécanique céleste (Celestial Mechanics),* 1829–39.

Bowdler, Thomas (1754–1825), English editor. He is noted for his expurgated version of Shakespeare, *The Family Shakespeare,* which first appeared in 1818. He also published an expurgated edition of Gibbon's *History of the Decline and Fall of the Roman Empire* (1826). The term *bowdlerize,* meaning to omit indelicate sections, is derived from his name.

Bowdoin, James (1726–90), American political leader, b. Boston. A prosperous merchant and landowner, he was active in the Massachusetts government before and during the American Revolution, and served on the state constitutional convention in 1779. He was governor of Massachusetts (1785–87) and suppressed Shay's Rebellion. Bowdoin College is named for him.

Bowel. *See* Colon.

Bowell, (Sir) Mackenzie (1823–1917), prime minister of Canada (1894–96), b. England. He rose from humble origins to become minister of customs, colonel of militia, prime minister, and opposition leader of the Conservatives (1896–1906).

Bowerbird, forest bird of New Guinea and Australia. The male builds a complicated and brightly ornamented bower to attract the female. After mating, the female lays her eggs (1–3) in a cup-shaped nest. Adults, mainly terrestrial, have short wings and legs and variously colored plumage. Length: 10–15in (25–38cm). Family Ptilonorhynchidae.

Bowery, The, an area of Lower Manhattan in New York City. Name was taken from the street that runs from Chatham Square to Cooper Square and parallels much of Broadway. During latter part of 19th century it had many fine theaters; later became a collecting point for derelicts. Since 1960 efforts have been made to rid area of slums and provide shelter for those in need. It was originally knowns as Bouwerie Lane, from Governor Peter Stuyvesant's nearby farm (bouwerie).

Bowfin, or mudfish, dogfish, gringle, grindle, primitive bony fish found in fresh waters of E United States and Canada. Its long cylindrical body has a characteristic long spineless dorsal fin. The head is covered with bony plates, the body with heavy scales. A well-developed swim bladder enables it to survive for 24 hours out of water. Family Amiidae; Species *Amia calva. See also* Osteichthyes.

Bowie, James (*c.*1796–1836), US frontiersman and hero of the Texas Revolution, b. Logan, Ky. He moved to Texas from Louisiana in 1828 and married the daughter of the Mexican vice governor. But by 1832 he had joined the US colonists who opposed the Mexican government. Appointed a colonel in the Texas army (1835), he fought in several battles before being killed at the Alamo. The invention of the bowie knife has been attributed to him.

Bowie, residential city in W central Maryland; site of Woodward Mansion (*c.*1743), now city hall, and Bowie State College (1867). Inc. 1916. Pop. (1970) 35,028.

Bowling, indoor sport in which a ball is rolled down a wooden alley in an attempt to knock down a set of maple pins. The most popular form of the game, which includes duckpins, rubberband duckpins, and candlepins, is tenpins, played with a large, heavy ball and ten 15-inch (38.10cm) pins set up in a triangular form at the target end of the alley. A regulation alley measures 41 to 42 inches (104–107cm) and 60 feet (18.3m) from the foul line to the center of the headpin. The ball, which has two to three finger holes, weighs from 10 to 16 pounds (4.5 to 7.2kg).

A game is divided into 10 frames, with a maximum of 2 throws for each frame. Each downed pin counts as one point. Knocking all the pins down on the first ball is called a strike and scores 10 points plus the total of the next two throws. Toppling all the pins on the second ball is called a spare and scores 10 points plus the total of the next throw. The highest score possible is 300, made by 12 consecutive strikes.

History. Bowling, which existed as early as 5200 BC, was introduced in the United States by the Dutch in the 19th century. The sport began to flourish in the 1950s with the introduction of the automatic pinsetter. The American Bowling Congress, formed in 1895, includes over 5,000,000 members.

Bowling Green, industrial city in SW Kentucky, 95mi (153km) SW of Louisville; seat of Warren co; agriculture area. Industries: meat packing, tobacco processing, tool and die making. Founded 1789. Pop. (1970) 36,253.

Bowling Green, city in NW Ohio, 19mi (31km) SSW of Toledo; seat of Wood co; site of Bowling Green State University (1910); a fertile, agricultural area; oil wells nearby. Industries: meat packing, cut glass, metals. Inc. 1855. Pop. (1970) 21,760.

Box, evergreen tree or shrub found in tropical and temperate regions in Europe, North America, and W Asia. The shrub is popular for topiary and box lumber is used for musical instruments. It has dark green, oval glossy leaves and pale brown ridged bark. One female flower is surrounded by several male flowers; none have petals. The 100 species include English or common *Buxus semepervirens* and larger *Buxus balearica* that grows to 80ft (24m).

Boxcar. △1708.

Box Elder, deciduous tree native to temperate North America. A rapidly growing tree, its leaves are oblong and pointed. The flowers are yellowish-green with different sexes on separate trees. Height: to 70ft (21m). Family Aceraceae; species *Acer negundo.*

Boxer, German police dog (working group) originally used for bullbaiting and dogfighting; named for its fighting style of using paws like man boxing. A sturdy, square-built dog, it has a slightly arched head and square muzzle with lower jaw protruding, wrinkles, and black mask. High-set, erect ears are cropped to points. A short body is set on medium-long straight legs. The docked tail is carried up. A short, shiny coat is fawn and brindle. Average size: 21–25in (53.5–63.5cm) high at shoulder; 60–75lb (27–34kg). *See also* Working Dog.

Boxer Rebellion (1900), violent Chinese uprising to oust all foreigners from China. Forces led by secret society of Boxers (Righteous and Harmonious Fists) that murdered Europeans and Chinese Christians besieged Peking's foreign legation enclave for two months. An eight-nation expeditionary force put down the uprising, and in 1901 a treaty was signed allowing the stationing of troops in China and the resumption of trade.

Boxing, sport of fist fighting, also known as pugilism and prize fighting. It is a contest between two participants in a roped-in square (ring). The ring area measures from 18 to 24 feet square (5.5 to 7m), and extends two to three feet (.61 to .91m) beyond the ropes. The surface is padded and covered with canvas, and three ropes, supported to posts at each corner, form the ring's boundaries. Boxers, who fight according to weight, are classified into eight divisions. These are flyweight (112lb, 50kg), bantamweight (118lb, 85kg), featherweight (126lb, 57kg), lightweight (135lb, 60.7kg), welterweight (147lb, 66.1kg), middleweight (160lb, 72kg), light-heavyweight (175lb, 79kg), and heavyweight (unlimited). For amateurs, a light-welterweight (139lb, 63kg), and light-middleweight (156lb, 70kg) class is included. Boxers wear trunks with a protective cup underneath, a fitted mouthpiece, high soft-soled shoes, and leather gloves. Professional fighters use 8-ounce (227-gram) gloves, and amateurs use 12-ounce (340-gram) gloves. Professional bouts can be 4, 6, 8, 10, 12, or 15 rounds of 3 minutes duration with a 1-minute rest in-between. Amateur bouts are scheduled for three rounds of two minutes each. A fight is enforced by a referee in the ring, and ends when there is a knockdown (where a boxer is unable to get to his feet by the count of 10), or a technical knockout (one fighter is too seriously injured to continue). If both fighters finish the scheduled rounds, a decision is awarded by the officials, usually the referee and two judges

History. Boxing, one of the oldest athletic endeavors, dates from 4000 BC. The more modern form of boxing emerged in England in 1719 where the contestants fought without gloves. The bare-knuckle era came to a close in 1889 when the boxing rules introduced in 1865 by John Sholto Douglas, 8th Marquis of Queensbury, were standardized.

HEAVYWEIGHT CHAMPIONS

1882–92	John L. Sullivan
1892–97	James J. Corbett
1897–99	Robert Fitzsimmons
1899–1905	James J. Jeffries
1905–06	Marvin Hart
1906–08	Tommy Burns
1908–15	Jack Johnson
1915–19	Jess Willard
1919–26	Jack Dempsey
1926–28	Gene Tunney
1928–30	Vacant
1930–32	Max Schmeling
1932	Jack Sharkey
1933	Primo Carnera
1934	Max Baer
1935–37	James J. Braddock
1937–49	Joe Louis
1949–51	Ezzard Charles
1951–52	Joe Walcott
1952–56	Rocky Marciano
1956–59	Floyd Patterson
1959	Ingemar Johansson
1960–62	Floyd Patterson
1962–67	Cassius Clay (Muhammad Ali)
1970–73	Joe Frazier
1973–74	George Foreman
1974–	Muhammad Ali

Box Lacrosse, a fast action game, popular in Canada and similar to lacrosse. It is played by two teams of 6 persons each in a boarded-in area—indoors or out—not less that 60–90 feet (18.3–27.4m) wide by 160–200 feet (48.8–61m) long. Each team defends a goal (4ft; 1.2m wide) centered at each end of the playing area. The rules are similar to (field) lacrosse, except that the ball may be played off the surrounding boards. The game was introduced in Australia in 1930. *See also* Lacrosse.

Box Turtle, turtle native to United States and Mexico with a hinge across the undershell, enabling front and back portions to close completely against the upper shell. All species have domed shells. They are terrestrial and eat animal and vegetable matter. Length: 5–6in (127–153mm). Family Emydidae; genus *Terrapene. See also* Turtle.

Boyars, higher nobility of Russia until Peter the Great, who abolished the title. The most influential members belonged to a council that advised the tsar in affairs of state. During the medieval period, the boyars struggled to take power from the princes. In reaction, Ivan the Terrible attacked the boyars in the 16th century and confiscated their estates. By the 17th century their power had declined. △1176–78.

Boycott, attempt to change a policy or practice by refusing to deal with the originator of the policy. The term originated in 1880 when Irish tenant farmers refused to work for, supply, or speak with a man named Charles Boycott who was an agent of their landlord. A labor strike is technically a form of boycott. A *primary boycott* is directed against the party with whom the dispute exists; a *secondary boycott* is directed at a third party (eg, one of a manufacturer's suppliers) to get him to bring pressure on the first party. Secondary boycotts in labor disputes are illegal under the Taft-Hartley Act (1947).

Boyd, Belle (1844–1900), Confederate spy, b. Martinsburg, Va. (now W. Va.). A code expert, she kept the Southern army informed of Union troop movements in the Shenandoah Valley. Caught three times, she married the man who held her in custody, Sam Wylde Hardinge, and they fled to England in 1864. She wrote *Belle Boyd in Camp and Prison* (1865) and returned to the United States to give dramatic lectures on her experiences.

Boyle, Richard, 1st Earl of Cork (1566–1643), English settler in Ireland. He settled in Ireland in 1588, acquiring vast estates including Walter Raleigh's (1602). Employing English settlers, he improved the land, built mills, established new towns, ironworks and other industries. In 1629 he was appointed a lord justice of Ireland and in 1631 he became Ireland's Lord high treasurer. Between 1633–41, he struggled with Thomas Wentworth, Earl of Strafford, lord deputy of Ireland, for influence at court and in Ireland. He finally triumphed over Strafford. Two of his sons were Robert Boyle, the scientist, and Roger Boyle, 1st Earl of Orrey.

Boyle, Robert (1627–91), English scientist, often regarded as the father of chemistry, and an advocate of the experimental approach to science. Working at Oxford, with Robert Hooke as his assistant, he made an efficient vacuum pump with which he was able to establish that the volume of a gas is inversely proportional to its pressure at a constant temperature. He freed experimental science from much alchemical superstition, introducing the modern concept of an element (which forms compounds). He worked to characterize acids and alkalies, and he showed the importance of air in sound propagation. After leaving Oxford he moved to London, becoming a founding fellow of the Royal Society. △1502.

Boyle's Law, the observation that the volume of a gas at constant temperature is inversely proportional to the pressure. First stated by Robert Boyle around 1660, the discovery was spurred by Boyle's invention of a vacuum pump allowing him to reduce pressures to levels never before achieved. Boyle's Law is a special case of the Ideal Gas Law: $pV = NkT$. *See also* Ideal Gas Law. △1502, 1514.

Boyne River, river in E Republic of Ireland; rises in Bog of Allen in Kildare, and flows NNE through Meath into Irish Sea below Drogheda; scene of Battle of the Boyne (1690) fought 3mi (5km) W of Drogheda. Length: 70mi (113km).

Bouncing bet

Bourges, France

Clara Bow

Boxer

Boy Scouts, a world-wide organization for boys which stresses outdoor knowledge and good citizenship and operates without racial, religious, political, or class distinction. The Boy Scouts are divided into community groups called troops, which are subdivided into patrols. Scouts can advance through several grades and can earn merit badges for proficiency in various activities. There are three classes of scouts: tenderfoot, first and second class. The Cub Scouts and Explorer Scouts are affiliated organizations for boys under 12 and older teenagers respectively. The organization was founded in Great Britain in 1908 by Sir Robert Baden-Powell. It was incorporated in the United States in 1910, and headed by James E. West, 1911–43. Its US publications include: *Boy's Life, Scouting Magazine,* and *Exploring Magazine.*

Boysenberry, perennial bramble, related to loganberries but hardier and more productive, having a larger, less acidic berry. Most berries are frozen and shipped, but some are eaten fresh, canned, or made into preserves. Family Rosaceae; genus *Rubus. See also* Loganberry.

Boys Town, village in E Nebraska, W of Omaha; famous community for orphaned or abandoned boys; governed by the residents, it is a non-profit organization run entirely on contributions. Founded 1917 by Father Edward J. Flanagan; inc. 1936. Pop. (1970) 989.

Bozeman, John M. (1835–67), US explorer, b. in Georgia. He moved west in search of gold. In 1862–63 he found a new route west, the Bozeman Trail, crossing the Continental Divide at what came to be known as Bozeman Pass. The land belonged to the Sioux, however, and Bozeman and his partner barely escaped alive. It was several years before the pass came into general use. The Sioux, led by Red Cloud, fought the building of a road at the pass and massacres resulted. Bozeman was himself killed by Indians three years after founding Bozeman, Mont.

Bozeman, city in SW Montana, 75mi (121km) ESE of Butte; seat of Gallatin co; nearby is Bozeman Pass on Bozeman Trail, used by gold prospectors who were rerouted by Indian attacks; it later became an important cattle route; site of Montana State University (1893). Industries: wheat, barley, cattle. Pop. (1970) 18,670.

Bozeman Trail, path from Julesburg, Col., to Virginia City, SW Montana. This was a short-cut discovered by John M. Bozeman, a pioneer of the early west. After 1877 it became an important cattle route.

Brabant, ancient duchy covering area in S Netherlands and N Belgium; independent in 12th century, became part of Netherlands in 19th century. Settled in 5th century by Franks.

Brachiopoda, or lamp shell, small animal phylum identified by two-valved shell, a stalk in some species, and a characteristic ciliated lophophore—a tentacle-like organ used for feeding. Similar in appearance to bivalve mollusks, the brachipod valves are dorsal and ventral rather than right and left. Reproduction is sexual. Among some 260 species are *Lingula* (oldest known animal genus) and *Terebratulina.* △506.

Brachioradialis. △684.

Brachiosaurus, giant vegetarian sauropod dinosaur living in North America and E Africa during Jurassic times. It was unique, having larger forelimbs than hind limbs. This was probably a useful adaptation for standing in water with only its nostrils, on top of its head, above the surface. It was the heaviest of all dinosaurs. Weight: 80ton (72t). *See also* Sauropoda.

Brachyceratops. △572.

Bracken, or brake fern, weedy fern *(Pteridium aquilinum)* found in temperate and tropical areas throughout the world. It has a perennial black rootstock that extends underground and sends up 15-ft (4.-6m) fronds at intervals. The leaves are coarse, triangular, and used as fodder.

Bracket Fungus, or **Shelf Fungus,** any of a large family (Polyporaceae) of common arboreal fungi that have spore-bearing tubes under the cap. Bracket fungi are usually hard and leathery or woodlike and have no stems. They often cover old logs and their parasitic activity may kill living trees. Some are edible when young.

Bract, modified leaf found on a flower stalk or the flower base. Bracts are usually small and scalelike. In some species they are large and brightly colored as in the dogwood and poinsettia.

Bradbury, Ray Douglas (1920–), US science-fiction writer, b. Waukegan, Ill. He used his genre to make mankind aware of its shortcomings and to demonstrate the value of culture. He wrote many excellent short stories, but he is best known for his novels, *Martian Chronicles* (1950), *The Illustrated Man* (1951), and *Fahrenheit 451* (1953). △1778.

Braddock, Edward (1695–1755), British military commander. He was given command of all British forces in North America in 1755 against the French. He cut the first road westward from Cumberland, Md., through the Allegheny mountains. Leading a force to attack Ft. Duquesne (Pittsburgh, Pa.), he was mortally wounded during an ambush by French and Indians near Duquesne.

Braddock, James Joseph ("James J.") (1905–1974), US boxer, b. New York City. He won the world's heavyweight championship by beating Max Baer (1935) in Long Island City, N.Y., and lost the title to Joe Louis (1937) in Chicago. He was elected to the Boxing Hall of Fame (1964).

Bradenton, winter resort city on W Florida peninsula, 11mi (18km) N of Sarasota; seat of Manatee co; shipping point for citrus fruits. Est. 1850; inc. 1903. Pop. (1970) 21,040.

Bradford, William (1590–1657), colonial governor and signer of Mayflower Compact. A Pilgrim, he came to America on the Mayflower (1620), and was elected governor of Plymouth Colony (1621), serving almost continually until his death. He helped draw up a body of laws for the colony (1636) and provided firm leadership through difficult times. His *History of Plimoth Plantation, 1620–46,* is the basis for all accounts of the Plymouth Colony. *See also* Mayflower Compact; Pilgrims; Plymouth Colony.

Bradford, city in N England, in Aire Valley, 9mi (14km) W of Leeds; former center of Yorkshire woolen industry. Industries: textiles and textile machinery. Pop. 293,756.

Bradley, Bill (1943–), US basketball player, b. Crystal City, Mo. A three-time All-American at Princeton (1963–65), he was a Rhodes Scholar at Oxford (1965–67), before joining the New York Knicks in the National Basketball Association in 1967.

Bradley, Francis Herbert (1846–1924), English philosopher. Bradley's idealism was Hegelian by inspiration. *Appearance and Reality* (1893) contained his famous theory of "the degrees of truth." Dialectic analysis distinguishes his *Principles of Logic* (1883).

Bradley, James. △1522.

Bradley, Omar Nelson (1893–), US general, b. Clark, Mo. He graduated from the US Military Academy and later taught there. In World War II he commanded the II Corps in North Africa and the invasion of Sicily (1943), led the 1st Army in the Normandy invasion (1944), and took over the 12th Army Group in Germany (1944). After the war, he served as chief of staff of the US Army (1948–49) and was appointed first chairman of the joint chiefs (1949–53). He retired from the military in 1953.

Bradstreet, Anne (Dudley) (1612–72), colonial American poet, b. Northampton, England. She came to the Massachusetts Bay Colony in 1630 with her husband Simon who became governor. Her poems were published in 1650 in England under the title *The Tenth Muse Lately Sprung Up in America.* Some of her poems are well regarded for their view of colonial New England and its people.

Brady, James Buchanan (Diamond Jim) (1856–1917), US financier, b. New York City. A salesman for railway supplies, and a successful financier, he made a fortune and was called Diamond Jim for the numerous diamonds and other precious stones that he owned. He endowed the James Buchanan Brady Urological Institute at Johns Hopkins in Baltimore.

Brady, Mathew B. (1823–96), pioneer US photographer, b. Warren co, N.Y. After studying daguerreotypy with Samuel F.B. Morse, he became the leading US portraitist of his day. President Lincoln was a frequent subject. Brady organized a staff of photographers to make a record of the Civil War when that conflict broke out. Much of his work is in the Library of Congress. He died alone and forgotten in a hospital charity ward.

Bradycardia, arrhythmic heartbeat defined by a pulse of less than 60 per minute. Sometimes associated with hemorrhaging, it is also common in healthy athletes.

Braganza, dynasty that ruled Portugal from 1640 until the monarchy was abolished in 1910; a collateral branch ruled as emperors of Brazil from 1822 to 1889. The dynasty was founded by the Duke of Braganza, who ruled (1640–56) as John IV. During the Napoleonic Wars, the royal family fled to Brazil, then a Portuguese colony. When Brazil declared its independence in 1822, it was ruled by Pedro I, the son of John VI of Portugal. The monarchy was overthrown in 1889.

Bragg, Braxton (1817–76), Confederate general, b. Warrenton, N.C. He served in the US army until 1856. At the outbreak of the Civil War in 1861 he joined the Confederate army. He commanded the army of Tennessee and won the battle of Chickamauga (1863), but was forced to retreat from Tennessee. He was relieved of his command in Dec. 1863 and was adviser to President Davis (1864–65).

Bragg, (Sir) William Henry (1862–1942), English physicist. With his son, William Lawrence, he worked on the determination of crystal structure by X-ray diffraction and was responsible for Bragg's law. He was awarded a Nobel Prize in 1915 jointly with his son.

Bragg, (Sir) William Lawrence (1890–1971), English physicist, b. Australia. With his father, William Henry, he worked on the determination of crystal structure by X-ray diffraction and was awarded a Nobel Prize for this work in 1915 jointly with his father.

Bragg, Fort, US Army base in E North Carolina, N of Fayetteville. Founded in 1918 as an artillery post, it is now principal airborne training center and site of Special Warfare School; includes Pope Air Force Base. In 1865 it was scene of battle of Monroe's Crossroads. Area: 11,136acres (4,510hectares).

Brahe, Tycho (1546–1601), Danish astronomer. Educated in law at Copenhagen and Leipzig, he became interested in astronomy and devoted himself to improving observational techniques, later building an observatory on the island of Ven (1576). The most accurate observer of his time, he discovered a nova (1572) and did much to advance the Copernican theory. His calculations were later used by Johannes Kepler. △38,1160.

Brahma, creator god in Hinduism. First mentioned in the *Brahmanas,* he is one of the three gods in the Trimurti. Although Brahma is equal to the gods Vishnu and Shiva, he has not been the object of a special devotional cult, and there is only one temple devoted to him, at Pushkar in India. *See also* Brahmanas. △846.

Brahman, highest ranking hereditary group of the traditional Indian caste system. Their ancient function was as priests and religious leaders. Brahmans took their status from their seer progenitors who in Hindu belief gained supernatural powers through piety and learning. △846.

Brahmanas, texts produced by Indian priestly class, the Brahmans, that, following the early poetic phase of the celebration of ancient Vedic rites (*c.*1500–*c.* 900 BC), sought to interpret the ceremonial rituals in prose. They were produced *c.*900–*c.*700 BC. The later portions of the *Brahmanas* introduce more philosophical concepts of attaining revelation through meditation.

Brahman Cattle. *See* Zebu. △372.

Brahmanism, an Indian religion characterized by acceptance of the *Veda* as divine revelation. The *Brahmanas,* the major texts of this religion, are the ritualistic books comprising the greater portion of Vedic literature. As Brahmanism developed, the *Upanishads* became important texts also. With time, deities of post-Vedic origin were worshiped and the influence of Brahman priests diminished. A newer, popular form of Brahmanism emerged. "Hinduism" is the customary term for this modern phase of development. *See also* Hinduism; Upanishads; Veda.

Brahmaputra, important river in SE Asia; rises as the Matsang River in N Himalayan Mts, Tibet; flows across SE Tibet as Tsangpo River; continues S to Assam, India, as the Dihang River. It becomes known as Brahmaputra from Sadiya S to Bangaladesh where it joins the Jamuna River, sharing the Ganges Delta in the Bay of Bengal. Length: 1,800mi (2,900km); navigable for last 800mi (1,288km).

Brahms, Johannes (1833–1897), German romantic composer. Encouraged by his friends Robert and Clara Schumann, he began to earn his living as a composer at age 30. He followed classical models of form and was a master of contrapuntal harmony. He composed in all major musical forms except opera. Among his greatest works are the *German Requiem* (1868), the *Variations on a Theme of Haydn* (1873), the *Violin Concerto in D* (1878), and two piano concertos. His songs, including *Schicksalslied* (1868), and chamber music are also highly regarded. His first symphony did not appear until 1876, but was followed by three others. They are among the finest symphonies of the Romantic period. *See also* Romanticism in Music. △1246.

Braided Stream, an old riverbed that has gradually created a network or series of interconnected channels or braids. Or, a river fed by meltwater, carrying considerable suspended material from the parent glacier.

Braille, Louis (1809–52), French inventor of the Braille system of reading for the sightless, who was himself blinded at the age of three. While a scholar, and later a teacher, at the Institute of Blind Youth in Paris, Braille developed a system of embossed dots to enable the blind to read by touch. This was published first in 1829, and a more complete form appeared in 1837. In 1932, a form known as Standard English Braille became accepted for worldwide use.

Brain, principal structure of the central nervous system, composed primarily of neurons and their supporting cells. The human brain is about the size of two clenched fists held tightly together, and it is distinguishable by an extremely convoluted outer covering or cortex. The brain develops from a structure called the neural tube and when fully developed it retains hollow recesses (ventricles) to circulate cerebrospinal fluid. The cortex is an elaborate thickening at the front of the "tube"; a second thickening further back forms the cerebellum. The forward area, the forebrain, is followed by the midbrain and the hindbrain. These areas are covered by the cerebral cortex, which has identifiable features called lobes (frontal, temporal, parietal, and occipital), each of which is associated with one or more behaviors, eg, sight.

In addition to regulating observable behavior, the brain governs the organ systems of the body. It is now known that there is no one center in the brain for activity; brain functions are much more complex and usually involve many diffuse relationships. *See also* individual parts of the brain; Central Nervous System. △662, 666–68.

Brain Damage, term used to describe the cause of almost any loose set of symptoms, such as disturbances of speech or movement, which might have roots in injury to the brain. It is most often connected to children who exhibit physical or social symptoms of retardation. Causes may be related to delayed or incomplete brain development, brain trauma suffered during or after birth, psychiatric or social disturbances, or diseases such as epilepsy. Treatment depends on accurate diagnosis. *See also* Cerebral Palsy; Epilepsy.

Brain Disorders, mental disturbances in which the central feature is an impairment of brain tissue function. They should be distinguished from functional, or psychogenic, mental disturbances in which the primary cause does not involve an impairment of brain function. Brain disorders are associated with impairment of memory, orientation, comprehension, and judgment, and also by shallowness of emotional expression. These symptoms may vary widely in severity depending mostly upon the extent of underlying brain impairment. Secondary personality changes are often observed in these disorders, depending upon such factors as the strength and type of personality and the amount of psychological and social stress present.

Organic brain disorders are divided into acute and chronic types depending upon the reversibility of the brain function disturbance. Acute disorders are temporary and generally the result of a disruption of brain function rather than the destruction of brain tissue, as in the chronic disorders. Acute brain disorders may be caused by such things as infection, drug or alcohol intoxication, and brain trauma. Chronic brain disorders include such things as congenital defects, hereditary diseases, senility, and brain damage. *See also* Brain Damage; Senility. △722.

Brain Storage, in psychology, the capacity of the mind (brain) to store information (memories). The term is most often used in physiological theories of changes that occur in the brain when information is learned. *See also* Memory. △670.

Braintree, town in E Massachusetts, 10mi (16km) S of Boston; birthplace of Gen. Sylvanus Thayer (1785), superintendent of West Point, and founder of Thayer Academy; his home is an historical center and museum. Industries: abrasives, metal and rubber products. Settled 1625; inc. 1640. Pop. (1970) 35,050.

Brain Trust, group of advisors to Pres. Franklin D. Roosevelt. An unofficial cabinet, it was instrumental during the early years of the New Deal (1933–35) in developing social and economic policies. Prominent brain-trusters included Raymond Moley, Adolf A. Berle, Jr., and Rexford G. Tugwell.

Brainwashing, technique used to alter a person's basic beliefs and attitudes without the person's consent. Such techniques involve attempts to render a victim's beliefs so useless that he substitutes new values and beliefs for the old ones. Specific procedures have included removal from peer group, starvation and physical abuse, threats of death, and forced confessions and self-recriminations—all designed to make a captive dependent on his captors and receptive to new ideas. Acceptance of the new ideas is rewarded. Brainwashing has different effects on different individuals. A person's background may enable him to withstand substantial stress, as revealed by Korean War POWs.

Brain Waves, output of the electrical activity of selected areas of the brain. A brain-wave recording is called an electroencephalogram (EEG), which is taken by placing electrodes on the scalp, amplifying their output, and recording the result. Typical EEG patterns correspond to several activity or consciousness states; eg, alpha activity is registered by persons who are resting but conscious. This activity can be conditioned through positive reinforcement, with the reinforcer simply a light that goes on when alpha activity occurs. △820.

Braking, Atmospheric, drag exerted on a vehicle as it reenters the earth's atmosphere and encounters increased air densities. This friction slows and heats the vehicle. Orbital calculations and materials design are influenced by this factor. It includes the concept of "skipping" into and out of the atmosphere repeatedly to slow down safely.

Bramante, Donato (1444–1514), Italian painter and architect. His Roman buildings, eg, Sta. Maria dele Pace and the circular Tempietto of S. Pietro, stand as classic examples of High Renaissance style. His most important work is the basilica of St. Peter's, Rome. △1140.

Brampton, town in S Ontario, Canada, 21mi (34km) NW of Toronto; seat of Peel co; noted for greenhouses; important dairy region. Industries: automobiles, optical goods, soap. Inc. 1873. Pop. 41,238.

Bran, skin or husk of grains of wheat, rye, or other cereal grasses. It is separated from the kernels and used for animal feed and for roughage in the human diet. *See also* Grass.

Branching, growth extension of vascular plants. A branch, developing from the stem, consists of the branchlet, previous year's growth, and the twig, new growth. The terminal bud at the twig end forms a new twig during the next growing season, as do lateral buds in leaf axils along the twig. Types of branching include: tillering—branches produced from the plant base (cereals and grasses); ex-current—single main shaft and smaller, lateral branches (conifers); deliquescent—spreading branches (deciduous trees); and columnar—unbranched stem (coconut and palms).

Brancusi, Constantin (1876–1957), French sculptor. His primitive style is revealed in a series of wooden sculptures begun in 1914, which include "Prodigal Son" (1914), "Sorceress" (1916), and "Chimera" (1918). In 1919, his controversial "Bird in Space" was not permitted to enter the United States as a work of art but instead was taxed on its value as raw metal. This decision was later reversed in a suit filed by Brancusi, and the sculpture is now housed in the Museum of Modern Art, New York City. Other works include "The Kiss" (1908), "Prometheus" (1911), "Sculpture for the Blind" (1924; Philadelphia Museum of Art), and "Flying Turtle" (1943).

Brand, Hennig. △1554.

Brandeis, Louis D(embitz) (1856–1941), US jurist and lawyer, b. Louisville, Ky. A Boston lawyer (1879–1916) known as the "people's attorney," he opposed high utility rates and railroad monopolies, supported wages-and-hours laws and inexpensive life insurance. An advisor to President Wilson, he was instrumental in creating the Federal Reserve Act (1913) and Clayton Anti-Trust Act (1914). His appointment as associate justice of the US Supreme Court (1916–39) aroused much criticism. The first Jew to sit on that

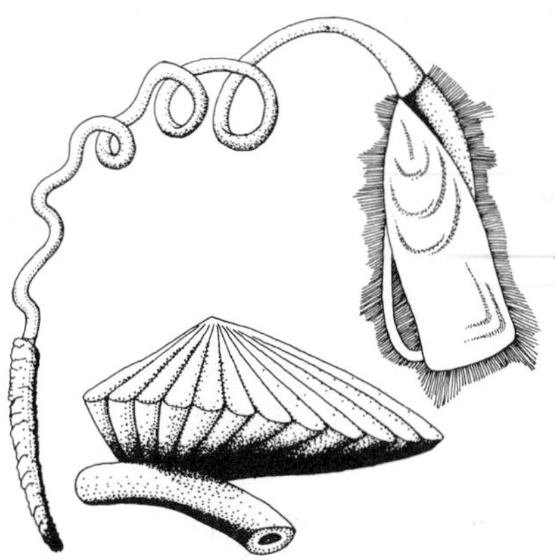

Brachiopoda

William Henry Bragg

Johannes Brahms

Louis Brandeis

court, he was noted for his dissents favoring civil liberties and social welfare legislation and for his use of sociological facts to support his opinion. His opinion in *Whitney* v. *California* (1927) is considered a milestone in the defense of unpopular expression.

Brandenburg, former state in NE Germany, now part of East Germany. It formed the nucleus for the kingdom of Prussia; Berlin and Potsdam are the chief cities. The March of Brandenburg, as it was called, was founded in 1134 by Albert I the Bear, who brought in settlers from the lower Rhineland. It came under the rule of the Hohenzollerns in 1411, and in 1417 Frederick I became the first elector of Brandenburg. Joachim II, who ruled 1535–71, converted to Lutheranism. Frederick William the Great Elector ruled 1640–88 and greatly increased its territory. His successor, Frederick II, became the first king of Prussia in 1701. *See also* Hohenzollern Dynasty.

Brandenburg, port city in central East Germany, on Havel River, 38mi (61km) SW of Berlin. Present city evolved from the 1715 union of a Wendish village founded in 1170 on S bank of Havel and a German settlement founded in 1196 on N bank. A third part of the town is on an island in the river and is the site of a 12th–14th-century cathedral. Industries: steel, tractors, textiles. Pop. 93,660.

Branding. *See* Cattle Brands.

Brandon, town in SW Manitoba, Canada, 127mi (204km) W of Winnipeg; overlooks the Assiniboine River; site of provincial fair and Brandon University (1899). Founded 1879; inc. 1882. Pop. 30,832.

Brandt, Willy (1913–), German statesman, b. Herbert Frahm. A member of the Social Democratic party, he fled to Norway and then to Sweden during the Nazi reign. It was while in exile that he adopted Willy Brandt as a pseudonym. He returned to Germany after World War II and was elected mayor of West Berlin in 1957. In 1969 he became chancellor of West Germany. He initiated a program of cooperation with the Communist bloc nations. In 1971 he was awarded the Nobel Peace prize. He resigned in 1974 after a close aide was exposed as an East German spy. △1390.

Brandywine Battlefield, historic site on Brandywine Creek, in SE Pennsylvania; scene of Revolutionary War battle (Sept. 11, 1777) in which Americans under George Washington were defeated by British under General Howe.

Branford, town in S Connecticut, on Long Island Sound; site of Swain-Harrison House (1680). Industries: iron fittings, concrete forms, wire. Settled 1644 by colonizers from Wethersfield; named for Brentford, England; inc. 1930. Pop. (1970) 20,444.

Brannan, Samuel (1819–89), US businessman and political figure, b. Saco, Me. A printer, he became a Mormon and in 1846 led a party of Mormon settlers by ship to Yerba Buena, which became San Francisco. There he published the *California Star,* the first newspaper in San Francisco; built a flour mill; and ran the store at Sutter's Fort. In 1850 he was elected to San Francisco's City Council and formed a fire-fighting unit and the first Committee of Vigilance to fight crime.

Brant, Joseph (1742–1807), Mohawk Indian chief. He served under Sir William Johnson in the French and Indian War and in Pontiac's Rebellion. He attended Moor's Charity School for Indians in Lebanon, Ct. (1761–63) and became an Anglican convert and missionary. He was commissioned a captain in the British Army in 1775 and fought on the British side in the American Revolution. He led the Indian contingent at the Battle of Oriskany (1777) and led the raid on Cherry Valley (1778) and other forays that terrorized the Mohawk Valley. After the war he moved to Ontario. He translated the Anglican Book of Common Prayer and the Gospel of Mark into Mohawk.

Brant, Sebastian (1457–1521), German satirical writer and poet. He is noted primarily for his long moral satire *Narrenschiff* (1494), which was to initiate a trend in 16th-century Europe. His other works include several Latin translations and theoretical musings on the lives of the saints.

Brant, Northern Hemisphere coastal bay marine goose with stocky, dark-colored body, white collar, and rump feathers. It feeds on roots and shellfish and nests in the far north, laying white eggs (3–5). Length: 2ft (0.6m); weight: 3lb (1.4kg). Genus *Branta*. △612.

Brantford, city in SE Ontario, Canada, approx. 60mi (97km) SE of Toronto, on the Grand River; named for Mohawk Indian chief Joseph Brant who est the Six Nations of the Iroquois tribes here 1784, for which organization the city is still headquarters; home of Alexander Graham Bell. Industries: agricultural and construction equipment, machinery, truck bodies, lumber, paper, furniture. Pop. 62,853.

Branting, Karl Hjalmar (1860–1925), Swedish statesman, the first Social Democrat elected to the Riksdag, 1896. Editor of *Socialdemokraten;* finance minister (1917); premier (1920, 1921–23, 1924–25). An outstanding leader in social and welfare reforms, he was a delegate to the League of Nations and was awarded the Nobel Peace prize in 1921.

Braque, Georges (1882–1963), French painter, printmaker, and sculptor. He was a pioneer of modern art. His earliest work precurses cubism (*Large Nude, Landscape at L'Estague, Houses at L'Estague,* 1907–09). *Head of a Woman* (1909) and *Violin and Palette* (1909–10) are transitional works between early and analytic cubism, which influenced later modern art. Later he moved to collages, and after World War I his style became flatter and his color stronger (*The Table,* 1918). *Woman with a Mandolin* (1937) typifies his more diverse style of the 1930s and 40s, while *The Echo* (1956) shows the brighter colors of his later work. *See also* Cubism. △1296.

Brasidas (died 422 BC), Spartan general who saved Megara from Athens and won other important victories in the Peloponnesian Wars. Thucydides thought him unusually flexible, for a Spartan. He died at Aphipolis fighting an Athenian force under Cleon.

Brasília, capital of Brazil; city is in W central Brazil, 580mi (934km) NW of Rio de Janeiro. Constitution of 1891 referred to moving the capital inland from Rio de Janeiro, but it was not until 1956 that construction was begun; in 1957 city was laid out in shape of an airplane by Lúcio Costa, Brazilian architect; extremely modern public buildings were designed by Oscar Niemeyer. In 1960 the capital was formally moved; site of presidential palace, cathedral, university. Pop. 272,002.

Brass, an alloy of copper and zinc. Often small amounts of other metals, such as tin, are added to make the alloy more resistant to corrosion. Brass is yellow in color. It is used for plumbing and lighting fixtures, electrical fittings, and ornamental metalwork.

Brasses, type of gravestone consisting of an engraved, rectangular brass sheet mounted on a polished stone slab. A two-dimensional figure of the deceased was engraved on the brass against a hatched background. This form of funeral monument was introduced into Western Europe early in the 13th century, and the greatest number of brasses (over 7000) have survived in England. They are an important source of information on medieval English armor and costumes. △1214.

Brassica, genus of 40 species of plants, including mustard, cabbage, cauliflower, broccoli, and turnip. They have flower clusters at the plant top, long, beaded seedpods, and leaves with thick midribs. Charlock *(Brassica kaber)* is bristly with lobed leaves; height 1–2ft (30.5–61cm). Field Mustard *(B. rapa)* is a succulent plant with gray-green, lobed leaves; height: 24–32in (61–81.3cm). *B. japonica* is the source of edible mustard greens. Family Cruciferae.

Brătianu, name of family of prominent Romanian political leaders. **Ion** (1822–91) participated in the uprising against Russian and Turkish rule in 1848. He opposed the dictatorial rule in 1856 of Alexandru Cuza, forced his abdication, and helped elect Prince Charles of Hohenzollern as king. He was premier (1867–68; 1876–88). His brother **Dmitrie** (1818–92) succeeded him in office. His sons were leaders of the Liberal party. **Ion** (1864–1927), who represented wealthy, conservative interests, was premier several times (1909–11; 1913–18; Dec. 1918–Sept. 1919; 1922–26; June-Sept. 1927). Ion acted as a near dictator after 1922. He was succeeded by his brother **Vintilă** (1867–1930), who was forced out of office in 1928.

Bratislava, city in S central Czechoslovakia, on W bank of Danube River, 30mi (48km) E of Vienna; capital of Slovakia, became part of Hungarian kingdom after 10th century, and part of Czechoslovakia in 1918. Now a shipping and manufacturing center, it has a pipeline carrying oil from USSR. Pop. 285,905.

Bratsk, city in E Siberian Russian SFSR, USSR; comprised of eight settlements separated by forests on the Angara River; site of enormous hydroelectric plant and ruins of Cossack watchtowers. Industries: metallurgy, cellulose, construction. Founded 1631 by Cossacks. Pop. 155,000.

Braun, Eva (1912–45), mistress of Adolf Hitler. A photographer's assistant, she met Hitler about 1936 and lived with him thereafter. So far as is known, she never exercised any political influence. She and Hitler were married in Berlin the day before they committed suicide together.

Braun, Wernher von. *See* Von Braun, Wernher.

Brave New World (1932), satiric novel by Aldous Huxley. The novel presents a future totalitarian society with technologically developed leisure industries, genetic manipulation, and sterile promiscuity.

Braxton, Carter (1736–97), a signer of the Declaration of Independence, b. Newington, Va. He furnished ships for the Revolutionary War, and was a member of the Continental Congress (1775–76; 1777–83; 1785) and also served in the Virginia Council of State (1786–91; 1794).

Brazil (Brasil), Federative Republic of, largest nation of South America and third-largest in the Western Hemisphere. A country of sophisticated cities and primitive jungle areas, it lures tourists and fortune seekers in spite of inflation, political turmoil, and civil unrest.

Land and Economy. About 65% of Brazil is a high plateau of crystalline and stratified rocks sloping W toward the Paraguay River and N to the Amazon. The Amazon basin, covered with a thick rain forest, stretches along the equator and forms the major lowland. Near the Atlantic coast the Brazilian Highlands rise to more than 9,000ft (2,745m). The most N part of Brazil is in the Guiana Highlands. A wealth of minerals—iron ore, manganese, lead, gem stones, marble—waits to be extracted. About 60% of the people raise cereal grains or help on large ranches, and coffee and other plantations. Manufacturing has developed since WWII, although heavy machinery, fuels, and some other goods are imported.

People. Some Indians of the Amazon and the high mountains keep their individuality, but those of the central plateau have mixed with Europeans, as have descendants of blacks brought as slaves. Perhaps 60% of the people are of European, especially Portuguese, descent, and 35% have mixed blood. Portuguese is the major language, and more than 90% of the population is Roman Catholic. School expansion and adult education in the 1960s reduced illiteracy, but about 40% of the people still cannot read or write.

Government. Formally a republic with a president, Senate, and Chamber of Deputies, Brazil came under military control in 1964.

History. The Portuguese claimed Brazil in 1500 and started settlements after 1530. During Europe's Napoleonic Wars the Portuguese royal family escaped to Rio de Janeiro. Some members remained to rule when peace returned to Europe and, to prevent local unrest, declared Brazil's independence in 1822. Dom Pedro II held the Brazilian throne for half a century. Turmoil following the abolition of slavery led to the Emperor's departure for Europe in 1889, when Brazil became a republic. Since then civil strife and political upheavals have alternated with short periods of peaceful progress. Ernesto Geisel became the country's first Protestant president in 1974. He faced problems of civil unrest, opposition from the Church, inflation of 30% to 40% a year, and air and water pollution as a result of industrialization.

PROFILE

Official name: Federative Republic of Brazil
Area: 3,286,478sq mi (8,511,965sq km)
Population (1975 est): 109,700,000
Chief cities: Brasília, the capital; São Paulo; Rio de Janeiro
Government: Head of state, Ernesto Geisel, president (took office March 1974)
Gross national product: $70,000,000,000
Per capita income: $700
Industries (major products): foodstuffs, textiles, cars, lumber, paper, drugs
Agriculture (major products): coffee, corn, wheat, cacao, tobacco, sugar cane, fruits
Minerals (major): iron ore, manganese, lead, zirconium, diamonds, oil
Trading partners: United States, European Common Market, Argentina, Venezuela

Brazil Current, warm current of S Atlantic Ocean; a branch of S Equatorial current; flows S along E coast of South America.

Brazilian Highlands, region in E Brazil, S of Guiana Highlands; landforms are separated by two river systems, the Paraná-Paraguay and the Amazon. The highest peak in Brazil, Pico da Bandeira, 9,482ft (2,892m), lies in the SE section.

Brazil Nut, seed of an evergreen South American tree found particularly along the Amazon River and Rio Negro. It has 2-ft (61-cm) leathery leaves and grows to 150ft(46m) tall. Cream yellow flowers produce a thick-walled fruit 4–6in (10.2–15.2cm) in diameter. Inside the fruit are 12–25 large, 3-sided seeds—the Brazil nut of commerce. Family Myrtaceae; species *Bertholletia excelsa.*

Brazing, process in which metallic parts are joined by the fusion of alloys that have lower melting points than the parts themselves. The filler material is either pre-placed or fed into the joint as the parts are heated. Brazed joints are highly reliable and used extensively in the rocket and aircraft industry.

Brazos River, river in central Texas; formed by the confluence of the Salt Fork and Double Mountain Fork in N Texas; flows SE into the Gulf of Mexico. Length: 840mi (1,352km).

Brazza, Pierre Paul François Camille Savorgnan de (1852–1905), French explorer, b. near Rome, Italy. He explored the Ogowe River in West Africa for the French government in the late 1870s and 1880s. He founded Brazzaville (Congo) and established a French protectorate over the kingdom of Makoko. From 1886–98 he was governor general of the French Congo.

Brazzaville, capital and largest city of the Republic of the Congo, Africa, on Stanley Pool on the Congo River; former capital of French Equatorial Africa (1910–1958); and a base of the Free French forces during WWII; a major port on the Congo River; connects by rail to the country's main seaport, Pointe-Noire. Industries: beverages, tanning, construction, textiles, tobacco. Founded 1880 by the French explorer Savorgnan de Brazza. Pop. 175,000.

Breach of Contract, in legal terms, occurs when one of the contracting parties fails to perform in accordance with the terms of the contract. When one party breaches the contract, the other has the legal right to treat his own obligation under the contract as discharged. In addition, the damaged party has right to damages or to specific performance.

Bread. △328.

Bread Mold, any of several hundred species of fungi (order Mucorales) found in soil and organic matter that have distinctive, usually black, spores. The familiar species, *Rhizopus nigricans,* forms a dense wooly growth on bread, fruits, and vegetables.

Breadroot, or Indian breadroot, perennial plant native to the prairies of W North America. It has an edible tuberous root, small oval leaves, and blue and whitish flower spikes. Height: to 1.5ft (46cm). Family Leguminosae; species *Psoralea esculenta.*

Breakbone Fever. *See* Dengue.

Break-even Analysis, technique for determining at what point the firm's costs equal its revenue. The break-even point is a zero-profit position for the firm. Break-even analysis may be shown either graphically or by numerical analysis.

Breakwater. △1760.

Bream, freshwater minnow of E and N Europe. Fished commercially in the Baltic Sea region, its high-set body is black and silver. Length: 19.7–27.6in (50–70cm). Weight: 8.8–13.2lb (4–6kg). Family Cyprinidae; species *Abramis brama.* △390, 616.

Breast, either of a pair of glandular organs that in the female produce and secrete milk to nourish newborn young. In the male they are rudimentary and nonfunctional. The human female breast, which develops during adolescence, is made up of about 20 irregularly shaped lobes separated by connective tissue and fat tissue. Lactiferous ducts lead from each lobe to the nipple, a small cone-shaped structure in the center of the breast, surrounded by an areola, a pigmented area that is pinkish before pregnancy, brownish after. *See also* Lactation. △686.

Breastbone. *See* Sternum.

Breath Holding, a common response to stress in children under the age of four, associated with violent crying and temper tantrums. Since it produces a lack of oxygen, breath holding can lead to dizziness and fainting. Children rarely engage in breath holding after age six.

Breathing, or respiration, a two-stage process during which oxygen-laden air is drawn into the lungs by contraction of muscles of the chest wall which expand the lungs; upon relaxation, the lungs recoil, expelling carbon dioxide–laden air. *See also* Respiratory System.

Brébeuf, (St.) Jean de (1593–1649), missionary and patron saint of Canada, b. France. Ordained a Jesuit in 1623, Brébeuf traveled extensively after 1625 among the Hurons of Georgian Bay and Lake Huron. Caught between the British and Indians, he was tortured to death by the Iroquois. His translations from the Hurons are found in *The Jesuit Relations.* He was canonized in 1930.

Breccia, general term that describes a rock formed by the cementation of sharp-angled fragments in a matrix of a material that may be different from or similar to that of the fragments. Their origin varies. Some are formed in fault zones, some in talus slopes, and others are volcanic in origin.

Brecht, Bertolt (1898–1956), German dramatist, b. as Eugen Berthold Friedrich Brecht. Among his notable works, most depicting a world of struggle and suffering in a uniquely bittersweet manner, are: *In the Jungle of Cities* (1923), *Edward II* (1924), *A Man's a Man* (1926), *The Threepenny Opera* (with music by Kurt Weill, 1928), *The Rise and Fall of the City of Mahogonny* (with music by Kurt Weill, 1930), *St. Joan of the Stockyards* (1932), *The Seven Deadly Sins of the Petty Bourgeoisie* (with choreography by George Balanchine and music by Kurt Weill, 1933), *The Private Life of the Master Race* (1937), *Mother Courage and Her Children* (with music by Paul Dessau, 1941), *The Good Woman of Setzuan* (with music by Paul Dessau, 1943), *Galileo* (English version, 1947), *The Caucasian Chalk Circle* (1st version, with music by Paul Dessau, 1948), *Schweyk in the Second World War* (with music by Hans Eisler, 1956), and *The Resistible Rise of Arturo Ui* (published posthumously, 1957).

After Hitler came to power (1933), Brecht lived abroad, first in Scandinavia, then in the United States. After appearing under subpoena before the House Un-American Activities Committee (1947), he returned to Europe, first to Switzerland, then to East Berlin. There he directed the Berliner Ensemble and tested his dramatic theories, such as the *Verfremdungs-Effekt* (alienation or distancing effect, devices reminding the audience that the theater is not reality). His plays move from realism to expressionism in what he called epic theater, an attempt to merge social with aesthetic concerns.

Breckinridge, John Cabell (1821–75), US vice president, b. Lexington, Ky. He was a major in the Mexican War and a congressman (1851) until elected vice president under James Buchanan (1856). Defeated as a pro-slavery presidential candidate in 1860 by Abraham Lincoln, he became a Confederate general and secretary of war in Jefferson Davis' cabinet (1865).

Breckman, Max. △1294.

Brecknockshire (Breconshire or Brycheiniog), former co in SE Wales; since 1974 part of Powys co; mountainous, with Brecon Beacons in S. Co town is Brecon.

Breda, city in S Netherlands, 14mi (23km) W of Tilburg, on Merk River; site of Compromise of Breda (1566) marking Dutch rebellion against Philip II of Spain and the Inquisition. Industries: fruit canning, textiles, machinery. Chartered 1252. Pop. 121,209.

Breech Birth. △704.

Breeder Reactor, a nuclear fission reactor in which more fissile material is produced than is consumed. *See* Fission Reactor. △1482, 1638.

Breeding, changing or promoting certain genetic characteristics through careful selection and combination of the parent stock. Breeding may be a crossing or inbreeding to produce the desired type of offspring. △416.

Breed's Hill, low hill on Boston's Charlestown peninsula, where the Battle of Bunker Hill was fought on June 17, 1775. American troops, sent to Bunker Hill, entrenched several hundred yards S at Breed's Hill, where they inflicted heavy losses on the British. *See also* Bunker Hill, Battle of.

Bregenz (Brigantium), city in W Austria, at E end of Lake Constance (Bodensee), 78mi (126km) WNW of Innsbruck; capital of Vorarlberg prov.; lake harbor and tourist resort. Industries: chemicals, electronic equipment, textiles. Settled by Celts. Pop. 24,078.

Brasília, Brazil: hotel district

Bratislava, Czechoslovakia

CARIBBEAN SEA
Panama
Venezuela
French Guiana
ATLANTIC
Colombia
Guyana
Sur.
Ecuador
Manaus
Belém
OCEAN
Fortaleza
Natal
Recife
BRAZIL
Peru
Maceió
Salvador
Brasília
Goiânia
Bolivia
Belo Horizonte
Vitória
PACIFIC
São Paulo
Rio de Janeiro
Paraguay
Santos
OCEAN
Curitiba
Argentina
Pôrto Alegre
0
1600km
Chile
Uruguay
Brazil

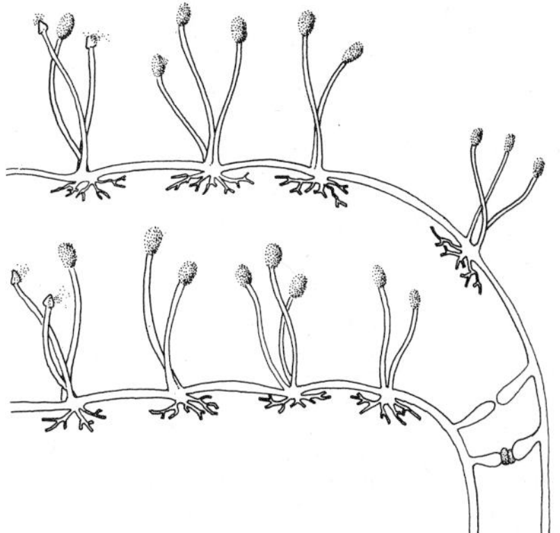
Bread mold

Breisgau, historic region in SW West Germany, E of the Rhine River and NE of Basel, Switzerland; region was held successively from Middle Ages by the Dukes of Zähringen, the counts of Kyberg and Urach, and the Hapsburgs; ceded to duchy at Baden 1810 and became part of state of Baden-Württemberg 1951. The region was autonomous and wealthy in 18th century, at which time its area was approx. 1,000sq mi (2,590sq km).

Breitenfeld, village in East Germany, 6mi (10km) N of Leipzig; scene of two important battles of the Thirty Years' War (1618–1648), Sept. 17, 1631, and Nov. 2, 1642; both were Swedish victories over forces of the Holy Roman Empire.

Bremen, port city in N West Germany on Weser River; capital of state of Bremen est. 1947; virtually independent until 18th century; part of French empire 1810–13; joined North German Confederation 1866; site of WWII naval base. Industries: food processing, beer, textiles, iron, steel, shipbuilding. Founded *c.* 782. Pop. 606,500.

Bremerhaven, seaport city in W Germany, on the N bank of Weser River as it flows into the North Sea; first regular ship service between United States and continental Europe was est. here 1847; West Germany's largest fishing port. Founded 1827; inc. 1851. Pop. 149,250.

Bremerton, city in W Washington, 15mi (24km) SW of Seattle, on Puget Sound; named for William Bremer who founded the townsite and est. the Puget Sound Naval shipyard, the most important industry in the city. Founded 1891; inc. 1901. Pop. (1970) 35,307.

Bren Gun. △1730.

Brennan, William J(oseph), Jr. (1906–), US jurist, b. Newark, N.J. A judge of the New Jersey Superior Court (1949–50) and the New Jersey Supreme Court (1952–56), he was appointed an ad interim associate justice of the US Supreme Court by Eisenhower in 1956. His appointment was confirmed by the Senate in March 1957. Considered a moderate liberal and a civil rights advocate, his opinion in *New York Times* v. *Sullivan* (1966) limited the scope of state libel laws. He also defended civil liberties in his opinions on the law of obscenity.

Brenner Pass, lowest of main Alpine passes, connecting Bolzano, Italy, with Innsbruck, Austria. The first road to traverse Alps was built across this pass 1772. During WWII, Hitler and Mussolini met here several times. Elevation: 4,495ft (1,371m). Length: 59mi (95km).

Brescia, city in N Italy; capital of Brescia prov. Sacked by Attila 452, it repeatedly changed rulers, passing to Austria 1814, and joining with Italy 1859. The city contains the Roman bronze *Winged Victory,* the 13th-century Broletto, and the Loggia (15th-16th century); transportation and agricultural center. Industries: firearms, vehicles, textiles. Pop. 204,369.

Breslau. See Wrocaw.

Brest, seaport city on Atlantic coast of France, near tip of Brittany; contains an excellent natural harbor and the chief French naval base on the Atlantic Ocean. During WWII, Germany had a huge submarine base here; site of a national engineering school. Industries: electronic equipment, clothing. Pop. 154,-023.

Brest, formerly Brest-Litovsk; city in Belorussian (Belorusskaja) SSR, USSR; capital of Brest oblast; river transport center at confluence of Bug and Muchavec rivers; site of teachers college, signing of Polish Orthodox and Roman Catholic church union (1596). Founded 1017 by East Slavs; conquered 1241 by Mongols, 1319 by Lithuania; under Polish rule 1569; sacked by Swedes 1657; annexed by Russia 1795; under Polish rule 1919–39, then returned to Russia. Industries: food processing, lumbering, textiles. Pop. 122,000.

Brest-Litovsk, Treaty of (1918), peace treaty between Russia and Germany in World War I. The terms were harsh, and Russia had to give up its Baltic provinces and the Ukraine. Trotsky was against signing the treaty, but the Germans increased their offensive and, fearing the new Bolshevik state would be destroyed, Lenin accepted the terms. The treaty was annulled by the Soviets after Germany was defeated. △1310.

Bretigny, Treaty of (1360), diplomatic agreement between England and France. Edward III of England abandoned his claim to the French throne. In return his vast holdings in southwestern France were freed from French sovereignty. The treaty was soon broken on both sides, and the Hundred Years War resumed.

Breton, André (1896–1966), French poet and theorist. A founder of the Surrealist movement, he wrote many essays on the subject, such as *Manifeste du Surréalisme* (1924) and *Le Surréalisme et la peinture* (1928). His fictional works, including a partly autobiographical novel *Nadja* (1928), *Les vases communicants* (1932), *L'Amour fou* (1937), and *Poèmes* (1948), reflect Surrealist theories. *See also* Surrealism. △1318, 1376.

Breton, Nicholas (*c.* 1545–*c.*1626), English poet and satirist. A prolific writer in several genres, his works include *Wit's Trenchmour* (1597), a prose dialogue on angling, and lyrics published in *England's Helicon* (1600).

Breton, language spoken in Brittany, on the northwest coast of France. A Celtic language, it is most closely related to Welsh, the area where it was originally spoken. It is rapidly dying out in favor of French. △866.

Bretton Woods Conference (1944), United Nations' Monetary and Financial Conference meeting at Bretton Woods, N.H. Representatives of the 44 United Nations agreed to establish the International Monetary Fund and the International Bank for Reconstruction and Development. △1384.

Breuer, Josef (1842–1925), Austrian physiologist, associate of Sigmund Freud. Breuer's discovery that, under hypnosis, neurotic patients would reveal unconscious feelings, and their symptoms would disappear, became a seminal discovery for the psychoanalytic movement and inspired Freud to pursue further his researches into the unconscious.

Breuer, Marcel (1902–), US architect and designer, b. Hungary. He studied and taught at the Bauhaus from 1920 to 1928, during which time he designed his famous tubular steel chair. In 1937 he went to Harvard University to teach architecture. A leading exponent of the International style, he practiced with Walter Gropius (1938–41), combining Bauhaus internationalism with New England regionalism in several houses, including his own at Lincoln, Mass. (1939). He also designed the UNESCO Building, Paris (1953–58; with Pier Nervi and Bernard Zehrfuss), St. John's Abbey, Collegeville, Minn. (1953–61), and the Whitney Museum of American Art, New York City (completed 1966).

Brewing. *See* Fermentation. △358.

Brewster, William (1567–1644), pilgrim religious leader, signatory of the Mayflower Compact. He withdrew from the Anglican church (1606) forming the Separatists, who, due to persecution, fled from England to Holland (1608), where they became known as Pilgrims. He returned to England to help organize the Pilgrim migration on the *Mayflower* 1620. He was a leader of the church at Plymouth and influential in management of the colony. *See also* Mayflower Compact.

Brezhnev, Leonid (1906–), Soviet political leader. He was active in the Ukrainian Communist party after 1931, and in 1935 he graduated from the Dneprodzerzhinsk Metallurgical Institute as an engineer. He rose steadily in party posts, and in 1952 he became secretary to the central committee of the Soviet Communist party. In 1957 he became a member of the presidium (later politburo) of the central committee. He helped plan the downfall of Nikita Khrushchev in 1964 and soon emerged as one of the two chief rulers of the Soviet Union, sharing power with Alexei N. Kosygin. Brezhnev was named first secretary and Kosygin was premier. Brezhnev's power steadily eclipsed that of Kosygin, however, and by the late 1960s, Brezhnev was acknowledged as the sole ruler, although Kosygin remained as premier. Brezhnev's tenure in office was marked by a vigorous foreign policy. In 1968 he sent Soviet troops into Czechoslovakia to put down an uprising. That action caused him to enunciate the "Brezhnev doctrine," which stated the Soviet intention of intervening in the domestic affairs of any of the Soviet bloc countries if Communism became threatened there. He pursued a policy of détente with the West, particularly with the United States, and signed various treaties and trade agreements with the Western powers. At the same time he pursued an aggressive policy furthering Soviet—and Communist—interests in Africa and the Middle East. Soviet relations with the Communist government of China continued to deteriorate under his leadership. △1344.

Brian Boru (926–1014), king of Ireland (1002–14). Originally a clan princeling in Munster, he unified all Ireland. He was murdered after winning a great victory over the Norse at Clontarf. Norse power in Ireland was destroyed forever, but Ireland fell into chaos with Brian Boru's death.

Briand, Aristide (1862–1932), French statesman. A lawyer, he entered the Chamber of Deputies (1902) as a Socialist and helped to draft the law (1905) for the separation of the Roman Catholic Church and the state. He first became premier in 1909–10 and was also premier in WWI (1915–17). An advocate of peace and internationalism, he was awarded the Nobel Peace prize (1926). As foreign minister 1925–32, he was the author of the Locarno Pact (1925) and the Kellogg-Briand Pact (1928). *See also* Kellogg-Briand Pact.

Briard, French sheep dog (working group) dating from at least 12th century. It has a long, wide head and muzzle; high-set, thick ears carried flat against the head or cropped; deep- and broad-chested body; strong-boned legs; and long tail carried with a crook at the end. The long coat is coarse and hard and can be any uniform color but white. Average size: 22–27in (56–68.5cm) at shoulder; 70–80lb (32–36.5kg). *See also* Working Dog.

Brice, Fanny (1891–1951), US singer and comedienne, b. New York City. While in vaudeville, she was discovered by Florenz Ziegfeld and joined his "Follies." Also known for her radio presentations of the spoiled brat "Baby Snooks," her life and stage career form the basis for the 1964 musical comedy *Funny Girl.*

Brick, any baked or fired, rectangular or prismatic, mass of clay used for construction. Sun dried brick was used 5000 years ago in Egypt and Babylonia. The modern US building brick measures 2¼ × 3¾ × 8in (5.7 × 9.5 × 20.3cm). It is made from ground clay in machines that either mold bricks or cut off an extruded section of stiff clay to make a complete brick. It is then conveyed into a continuously operating kiln. △1582, 1610.

Bridge, any structure providing a continual passage over a body of water, roadway, or valley for man, vehicles, pipelines or power transmission lines. Bridges are prehistoric in origin, the first probably being logs that fell across a desired path. Today, bridges come in a great variety of forms, depending upon span, function and area—moveable bridges, pontoon bridges, overpasses, causeways, aqueducts, suspension bridges and cantilever bridges. △1584, 1704.

Bridge, card game for four players with a regular deck. It is derived from whist and is one of the most popular card games in the English-speaking world. The game has several versions, but the most popular since 1925 is contract bridge. This version is, except for the scoring, the same as auction bridge, in which each player bids for the right to name trump. With the four players pairing off into partners, the entire deck is dealt (13 cards per player) and the bidding begins. After the bid is won, the partner of the player who won the bid lays his hand face up on the table. The bidder then plays off this hand and his own to try to win the number of tricks bid plus six other tricks. The cards rank from ace down to two; in bidding, suits rank spades, hearts, diamonds, and clubs. Cards must be played in order of suit, and then with trump.

Bridge, in dentistry, a partial denture held in place by anchorage of various sorts to adjacent teeth. Depending on the situation it may be permanently installed or removable. Usually, only one or several teeth in a series are artificially replaced in this manner. △756.

Bridge on the River Kwai (1952), novel by Pierre Boulle, set in a Japanese prisoner-of-war camp in Siam in World War II. The British prisoners are forced to build a bridge of strategic importance, which only their obsessed colonel attempts to do efficiently. The film adaptation (1957), directed by David Lean and starring Alec Guinness, was extremely successful.

Bridgeport, city in SW Connecticut, 17mi (27km) SW of New Haven, on Long Island Sound; port of entry and chief industrial city in Connecticut. Industries: electrical appliances, firearms, helicopters. Settled 1639, grew as a fishing community; inc. 1836. Pop. (1970) 156,542.

Bridger, James ("Jim") (1804–81), US fur trader, hunter, trapper, b. Richmond, Va. He discovered the Great Salt Lake (1824), South Pass through the Rockies, and the area now Yellowstone Park. In 1843 he built Fort Bridger in southwest Wyoming to supply the settlers traveling on the Oregon Trail. He helped plan stagecoach routes, scouted for the army against the Indians, and then in 1857 against the Mormons.

Bridger, Fort, village and early US trading post in SW Wyoming, approx. 30mi (48km) E of Evanston; James Bridger, American frontiersman, est trading post here 1843; it was subsequently used as US army fort 1858–90; now a state park.

Bridges, Calvin Blackman (1889–1938), US geneticist, b. Schuyler Falls, N.Y. He helped to prove the chromosomal basis of heredity and sex. Work with Thomas Hunt Morgan on the fruit fly *(Drosophila)* proved that heritable variations were traced to observable changes in the chromosomes. These experiments resulted in the construction of "gene maps," which proved the chromosome theory of heredity.

Bridgeton, city in S New Jersey, on Cohansey River; seat of Cumberland co; site of New Jersey Liberty Bell, which rang on July 7, 1776, calling citizens to hear the Declaration of Independence; has several 18th-century buildings. Industries: food processing, clothing, fertilizer. Settled 1686; inc. 1865. Pop. (1970) 20,435.

Bridgman, Elijah Coleman (1801–61), US missionary, b. Belchertown, Mass. He was the first American Protestant missionary to China. He arrived in 1829 and remained through life, winning the trust of the Chinese. He founded and managed the *Chinese Repository* and translated the New Testament into Chinese (published 1862).

Bridgman, Laura (1829–89), first US blind, deaf mute to be successfully educated, b. Hanover, N.H. As a child, she was put under the care of Dr. S.G. Howe of the Perkins Institute in South Boston. He taught her with the aid of an alphabet similar to Braille, which he devised. As a grown woman, she was a sewing teacher at the Institute.

Bridgman, Percy Williams (1882–1961), US physicist, b. Cambridge, Mass.. Working in the field of high pressures, he designed equipment capable of withstanding increasingly higher pressures. He was thus able to investigate new solid forms, which in turn yielded new information on processes and substances deep within the earth. He received the 1946 Nobel Prize for his work in the high-pressure field. Working as a consultant researcher for General Electric, he formed synthetic diamonds by the utilization of high-temperature and high-pressure combinations.

Brie, historical region in N central France, E of Paris; in Middle Ages it comprised a county; located mainly in Seine-et-Marne dept., it is famous for vineyards and Brie cheese.

Brienne, formerly a county in NE France, 23mi (37km) NNE of Troyes; held by Brienne family 10th–18th century, whose most famous member was the Crusader John of Brienne (1148–1237), King of Jerusalem (1210–25).

Brig, 18th-century development of the brigantine, slightly larger and with three to four sails on each of two main masts.

Brigantine, small, two-masted sailing ship appearing in the 17th century. △1678.

Brighton, city in S England, on the English Channel, 48mi (77km) S of London; popular holiday resort. City was popularized in the 19th century when the Prince Regent's royal pavilion was rebuilt here (1817). Pop. 166,081.

Bright's Disease, term no longer in widespread use describing any of several kidney diseases characterized by albumin in the urine.

Brigid, Saint (453–523), Irish holy woman. The city of Kildare, according to legend, takes its name from Saint Brigid's cell, which she established in an oak tree, hence Kil-dara, "the church of the oak." She is said to have performed numerous miracles and is recognized as one of the patron saints of Ireland.

Brillat-Savarin, Anthelme (1755–1826), French author on gastronomy. A lawyer, he was a member of the National Assembly in the French Revolution, but fled during the Reign of Terror and spent time in Switzerland, the Netherlands, and the United States. He wrote *Physiologie du goût* (1825); tr. *Physiology of Taste* (1825), an amusing work on dining.

Brindisi, city in S Italy; capital of Brindisi prov.; a Roman naval station; Virgil died here 19 BC. Conquered by Normans 1071; one of major embarkation ports for Crusaders; site of Roman column marking terminus of Appian Way, and medieval castle of Frederick II; commercial center. Industries: food processing, chemicals, wine. Pop. 80,357.

Brine Shrimp, small branchiopod crustacean related to fairy shrimp and found in salt lakes throughout the world. It can live in high concentrations of brine and swims belly-up. It has no carapace and has stalked, compound eyes and a long tail. Length: 0.5in (13mm). *See also* Crustacean; Fairy Shrimp.

Briod. △328.

Brisbane, (Sir) Thomas Makdougall (1773–1860), British astronomer and colonial administrator. He served in the British army for many years. He was governor of New South Wales (1821–25) in Australia, there establishing an observatory near Sydney in 1822. He founded another observatory in Scotland in 1841. Brisbane, Australia, is named for him.

Brisbane, seaport city in E Australia, on the Brisbane River; capital of Queensland state; site of Renaissance-style Parliament House (1869), University of Queensland (1909); major shipping and rail center. Exports: wool, meat, sugar, coal. Industries: oil refineries, food processing, textiles, shipbuilding, automotive assembly. Settled 1824 as a penal colony; became capital in 1859. Pop. 703,000.

Brissot de Warville, Jacques Pierre (1754–93), French journalist and revolutionist. He founded the Amis des Noirs, a society for the prevention of slave trade. He edited *Patriote francais* (for the people), and when he aligned himself with the Girondists, it became the Girondist publication. Sentenced to death following war with Austria, which he had helped to foment, he was executed in 1793.

Bristle Tail. *See* Silverfish.

Bristleworm. △974.

Bristol, city in SW England, on the River Avon, 7mi (11km) from mouth of Bristol channel; important seaport since the 12th century; site of Brunel's Clifton Suspension Bridge (1845), crossing the Avon NW of Bristol. Imports: wine, fruit, grain, tobacco. Industries: aircraft, footwear, tobacco, chocolate, chemical products. Pop. 425,203.

Bristol, industrial city in N Connecticut, 15mi (24km) SW of Hartford; site of American Clock and Watch Museum. Industries: clock-making, tools. Settled 1727; inc. 1911. Pop. (1970) 55,487.

Bristol, town in E Rhode Island, 16mi (26km) SE of Providence on Narragansett Bay; seat of Bristol co; scene of King Philip's War (1675–76); site of Herreshoff boat yards (1863), where many America's Cup champions have been built, and Roger Williams College (1919). Industries: yachts, rubber products, wire, cable. Settled 1669; inc. 1681. Pop. (1970) 17,860.

Bristol, city in Tennessee, on Virginia border; site of Shelby's fort used by Daniel Boone. The state line is in the middle of a street dividing Bristol, Tennessee, from Bristol, Virginia; cities united as an industrial unit; transportation and processing center. Inc. 1890. Pop. (1970) 20,064.

Britain. *See* Great Britain.

Britain, Battle of (August-October, 1940), the German air offensive against Britain. Saturation bombing of military installations, factories and land and sea transportation sites by the Luftwaffe was to be a prelude to a German invasion. Britain resisted valiantly, destroying over 1500 German bombers, and invasion plans were abandoned. △1338.

Britannia Metal, alloy primarily of tin (94%) with a small amount of copper (1%) and antimony (5%). Britannia metal is silver white in color and similar to pewter and is used widely in making domestic tableware, such as silverware, teapots, and other items.

British Cameroons, area in W Africa. Once a German protectorate, it came under the League of Nations in 1919 and then under the United Nations before its N and S peoples voted (1961) to join Nigeria and Cameroon, respectively.

British Columbia, prov. in W Canada, on the Pacific Ocean, bordered on the S by the states of Washington, Idaho, and Montana, and in the extreme NW by the state of Alaska.

Land and Economy. British Columbia is mountain-

Bremen, West Germany

Brest, France

Leonid Brezhnev

STORE FOR MEN
AND
WHO SHOP FOR MEN
SUMMER
SUITS

Brisbane, Australia

ous; many ranges of the Rocky Mts run S to N, with deep river valleys among them. The Pacific coastline is broken by inlets with hundreds of islands, of which Vancouver Island in the SW is the most important. Vast forests cover much of the country and yield the timber that is a mainstay of the economy. Commercial fishing is a major industry along the coast. Manufacturing is centered in the cities of the SW; agriculture is largely confined to the valleys. The mountain and coast scenery attracts a profitable tourist trade.

People. The cities of the S and the S end of Vancouver Island contain more than 70% of the pop. The majority came from other Canadian provinces, and trace their origins primarily to the British Isles.

Education. There are three universities supported by the prov.—the University of British Columbia, at Vancouver; Simon Fraser University at Burnaby, a Vancouver suburb; and the University of Victoria. Notre Dame University at Nelson is a Roman Catholic institution.

History. Capt. James Cook of Britain landed on the coast in 1778. Russians and Spaniards sought to exploit the fur trade, and in 1794 the British government sent Capt. George Vancouver to take possession of the land. Other British explorers pushed W from Canada, and the region came to be called New Caledonia. In 1846, the S boundary with the United States was fixed, and in 1849 Vancouver Island became a British colony. It was united with New Caledonia as British Columbia in 1866. The prov. developed steadily after the first transcontinental railroad was completed in 1885.

PROFILE

Admitted to confederation: July 20, 1871; rank, 6th
National Parliament representatives: Senate, 6; House of Commons, 23
Population: 2,462,000 (1971); rank, 3rd
Capital: Victoria, 60,897 (1971)
Chief cities: Vancouver, 422,278; Victoria; New Westminster, 42,083
Provincial legislature: Legislative Assembly, 55 members
Area: 366,255sq mi (948,600sq km); rank, 3rd
Elevation: Highest, 15,300ft (4,663m), Mt Fairweather; lowest, sea level
Industries (major products): lumber, paper and pulp, processed foods
Agriculture (major products): cattle, poultry, vegetables, fruits
Minerals (major): copper, asbestos, coal, gold, silver, lead, zinc
Floral emblem: flowering dogwood

British East Africa, a term used for the African countries of Kenya, Tanganyika, Uganda, and Zanzibar (now united with Tanganyika as Tanzania), all once under the British Empire.

British Empire, overseas territories ruled by Great Britain. The empire originated in the late 16th century with the commercial activities of the chartered companies, eg, the British East India Company. *The First Empire.* Commercial ventures (sugar and tobacco plantations), missionary activities, and slave trading led to creation of British colonies in the Caribbean and N America in the 17th century. Loss of thirteen American colonies led to the demise of the First Empire (1783) and transfer of control of the colonies from the crown to Parliament. *The Second Empire.* British expansion was renewed in the 19th century and colonies were acquired in the Far East, Australia, Africa, and elsewhere. By World War I, the empire included about one-fourth of the world's pop. and land surface. A trend toward self-government ultimately resulted in independence for most colonies and the formation of the Commonwealth of Nations. *See also* Commonwealth of Nations. △1260–62, 1266.

British Empiricism, philosophical position initially associated in the 17th and 18th centuries with John Locke, George Berkeley, and David Hume. Empiricism identifies experience as the sole source of knowledge of phenomena; it denies the existence of innate ideas and the possibility of demonstrating the certainty of synthetic propositions; and it holds that universals are reducible to sense data. This data refines reality in time and space as the realm to which rational belief is confined. △1264, 1332.

British Guiana. *See* Guyana, Republic of.

British Honduras. *See* Belize.

British Indian Ocean Territory, island colony in Indian Ocean, composed of Chagos Archipelago, Farquhar Atoll, Desroches Island, Aldabra Islands; est. 1965 by Britain in an effort to remain in a strategic position between Africa and Asia. Industries: coconuts, fishing. Area: 31sq mi (80sq km). Pop. 560.

British Isles. *See* Great Britain.

British Museum, English art museum, London. Established by an Act of Parliament as a storehouse of knowledge for the benefit of the "learned and curious," it was opened in 1759. Its original purpose was historical and scientific rather than aesthetic. The nucleus of the original collection was donated by Sir Hans Sloane in 1753. Later additions included the Rosetta Stone and the Phrygian and Elgin Marbles. The Museum comprises the National Museum of Archaeology, the Department of Ethnology, the Museum of Natural History, and the Department of Prints and Drawings, which houses an album of Dürer's drawings, works by Rembrandt and Rubens, a sketchbook by Bellini, 20 drawings by Michelangelo, and 20,000 drawings by Turner.

British North America Act (1867), legislation of the British parliament creating the Dominion of Canada from the provinces of Nova Scotia, New Brunswick, and Canada. The act provided for a constitution, a bicameral parliament, the reestablishment of Ontario and Quebec as separate provinces, and a legal system for Canada. Education and property law were left to the provinces, with the central government to control foreign policy and criminal law.

British Somaliland, British protectorate in E Africa. Formed in 1884–87, it was united with Italian Somaliland as the independent state of Somali in 1960.

British Thermal Unit (BTU), the amount of heat energy necessary to raise the temperature of a pound of water from 63°F to 64°F. One BTU is the equivalent of 778.3 foot-pounds, 252 calories, or 1055 joules.

British West Indies, island group in the West Indies, between the Caribbean Sea (W), Gulf of Mexico (NW), and Atlantic Ocean (E). Group includes: Cayman Islands, the Turks and Caicos Islands, British Leeward Islands, British Virgin Islands, British Windward Islands, and Barbados. In 1958, ten British territories formed the West Indies Federation; it dissolved as members began to proclaim independence (1961–62). West Indies Associated States (1967) including Antigua, Saint Kitts, Nevis, Dominica, Grenada, Saint Lucia, Saint Vincent, are voluntarily associated with Great Britain, and are internally self-governing.

Brittany (Bretagne), region and former prov. in NW France, jutting into Atlantic Ocean and bounded on N by English Channel. Prehistoric megaliths (huge stones) indicate an ancient race may have inhabited the area *c.* 2500–1800BC; earliest known people were Celts from British Isles (*c.* 8th century BC.). Romans conquered the area 56BC, withdrew in the 5th and 6th centuries. From 10th century Brittany was involved in a series of battles with England or France until 1532 when it became part of France. Industries: tourism, fishing, farming, orchards. △1096.

Brittany Spaniel, gun dog (sporting group) bred in France; of ancient lineage; first tailless specimen bred about 100 years ago. This rugged but graceful dog has a medium-length head and muzzle, tapering to a fawn, tan, or pink nose. The short, leafy ears are set high and lie flat; legs are long and graceful; and the tail, when present, is docked. The dense, flat coat is dark orange and white and lightly feathered on the legs. Average size: 17.5–20.5in (44.5–52cm) high at shoulder; 30–40lb (13.5–18kg). *See also* Sporting Dog.

Britten, Benjamin (1913–76), English composer. Although he composed in all forms, Britten was primarily known for his operas, which rank him as the foremost English opera composer of the 20th century. His operas include *Peter Grimes* (1945), *The Rape of Lucretia* (1946), *Albert Herring* (1947), *A Midsummer Night's Dream* (1960), and *Death in Venice* (1973). His most popular nonoperatic work was the *Young Person's Guide to the Orchestra* (1946), a set of variations displaying the different sounds of the orchestra. △1364.

Brittle Star, or serpent star, marine echinoderm with small central disc body and long, sinuous arms, which break off easily and are reproduced by regeneration. Class Ophiuroidea; species include phosphorescent *Amphipholis* and a small *Ophiactis.* △504, 626.

Brno (Brunn), city in central Czechoslovakia, 115mi (185km) SE of Prague; site of Gothic Cathedral of St Paul and 13th-century castle; scene of a yearly international trade fair. Industries: armaments, machinery. Founded 10th century. Pop. 335,918.

Broadbill, stocky, brightly colored bird of tropical Africa and Asia. With a flattened bill, short neck and legs, and strong feet, it feeds mainly on insects and other small animals. The female lays spotted white eggs (2–4) in a woven root-and-grass nest suspended over water. Length: 5–11in (12–28cm). Family Eurylaimidae.

Broadcast Channels, bands of carrier wave frequencies within which an individual transmitter is allowed to broadcast its message. The conventional radio channel is 10 kilocycles wide, while a television band has a width of 6 megacycles. △1794–96.

Broadside, single sheet of paper printed on one side. Popular ballads of the 16th and 17th centuries were printed on broadsides for sale in public places where they were also sung or recited.

Broadway, a major thoroughfare in New York City that began as the principle N-S street of New Amsterdam. It runs from the S tip of Manhattan to the N city limit in the Bronx. It passes through the Wall Street financial district, the major merchandising centers at Union (14th Street), and Herald (34th Street) squares. N of Times Square (42nd Street), it is known as the "Great White Way" because of the many lights illuminating theater and movie marquees. Between 64th and 67th streets it is bordered by Lincoln Center for the Performing Arts; between 113th and 121st street it passes Columbia University.

Broccoli, variety of cauliflower with large, lobed leaves and thick stems. Tiny green or purple flowers form 9-in (23-cm) compact heads that are eaten. It matures in 60–70 days. Family Cruciferae; species *Brassica oleracea.*

Brock, (Sir) Isaac (1769–1812), Canadian military leader, b. England. After serving in Europe Brock moved to Canada in 1802, established Fort George in Quebec Province, and rose to lieutenant governor of Upper Canada. A brilliant strategist in the War of 1812, he defeated US Gen. William Hull at Detroit and died in the battle at Queenston Heights in 1812.

Brock, Lou (is Clark) (1936–), US baseball player, b. El Dorado, Ark. He set a major league record by stealing 118 bases in 1974. He began his career with the Chicago Cubs (1961) and was traded in 1964 to the St. Louis Cardinals.

Brocket Deer, or càriacu, small deer ranging from S Mexico to Paraguay. Stout with slender limbs and an arched back, they are timid and live alone or in pairs in wooded areas. Their antlers are usually simple spikes. Length: to 3ft (91cm); weight: to 46lb (21kg). Family Cervidae; genus *Mazama;* There are 10 species. △602.

Brockton, city in E Massachusetts; historic museum, junior college. Industries: shoes, textiles, machinery. Settled *c.* 1700, it was part of Bridgewater until 1821; inc. 1881. Pop. (1970) 89,040.

Brod, Max (1884–1968), Austrian Czech novelist, critic, and philosopher, important for his discovery of Franz Kafka and the posthumous publication of Kafka's *Collected Writings* (1935–37). A Zionist, he went to Israel in 1939. His fiction includes *The Redemption of Tycho Brahe* (1916) and *Reubeni, Prince of the Jews* (1925).

Broederlam, Melchior. △1136.

Broglie, Jacques Victor Albert, 4th Duc de Broglie (1821–1901), French statesman. He was elected to French Academy (1856). He held government positions including membership in the national assembly (1871), ambassador to London (1871–72), premier (1873–74) and minister of justice (1877). He was a liberal monarchist leader in the Senate. He wrote numerous history books and articles.

Broglie, (Prince) Louis Victor de (1892–), French physicist. He became professor of physics at the University of Paris. He is responsible for the concept that all elementary particles have an associated wave and for the formula that predicts this wavelength. With Erwin Schrödinger he later developed the form of quantum mechanics called wave mechanics, for which he was awarded a Nobel Prize in 1929. △1480.

Broglie Family, French noble family. They were naturalized French subjects originating from Italy. The Broglies had distinguished military careers in Louis XIV's armies and the diplomatic corps. **François Marie II** (1671–1745), 1st Duc de Broglie, led Louis XIV's armies in Flanders, Germany, Italy. He was made marshall of France (1734). **Victor** (1785–1870), 3rd Duc de Broglie, was a distinguished statesman, serving as minister of the interior and foreign affairs and president of the council (1835).

Bromeliad, any of 2,000 species of tropical American plants of the family Bromeliaceae (order Bromeliales); some of which are epiphytic, some terrestrial herbs, some subshrubs. All have basal leaves and flowers in dense spikes, panicles, or heads with large bracts. Most familiar of the family are the pineapple *(Ananas comosus)* and Spanish moss *(Tillandsia usneoides).*

Bromfield, Louis (1896–1956), US novelist, playwright, and essayist, b. Mansfield, Ohio. Primarily noted for his early fiction, his novels include *The Green Bay Tree* (1924), *Possession* (1925), *Early Autumn* (1926; Pulitzer Prize 1927), *A Good Woman* (1927), and *The Rains Came* (1937). Later work includes nonfiction about his farm, Malabar, in Ohio.

Bromide, salt of hydrobromic acid, or an organic compound containing bromide. The bromides of ammonium, sodium, potassium, and certain other metals are used medically as sedatives. Silver bromide is light-sensitive and is used in photography.

Bromine, nonmetallic element (symbol Br) of the halogen group, first isolated in 1826. It is extracted by treating sea water or natural brines with chlorine. The element is a red-brown volatile liquid used in making a range of commercially useful compounds. Chemically it resembles chlorine but is less reactive. Properties: at. no. 35; at. wt. 79.904; sp. gr. 3.12; melt. pt. 19.04°F (−7.2°C); boil. pt. 137.8°F (58.78°C); most common isotope Br^{79} (50.54%). *See also* Halogen Elements. △1552, 1568.

Bronchi (sing. bronchus), the two branches into which the trachea (windpipe) divides, with one branch leading to each lung. The bronchi divide treelike into smaller and smaller branches, called bronchioles, as they spread through the lung. They eventually open into the lung's air sacs and alveoli where the gases of air and blood are exchanged. *See also* Lungs. △692.

Bronchiectasis, enlargement of one or more bronchial tubes usually resulting from bronchitis or tuberculosis. Symptoms are coughing and copious expectoration.

Bronchioles. △690.

Bronchitis, inflammation of the bronchial tubes caused most frequently by irritation of the lungs from chemicals or pollutants or by disease. Symptoms include coughing and expectoration of mucus. Medication relieves symptoms; a warm, dry climate improves the condition. △714.

Bronk, Detlev Wulf (1897–1975), US biophysicist and medical administrator, b. New York City. A pioneer in electromicroscopic monitoring of the human nervous system, he was president of Johns Hopkins University (1949–53). In 1953 he became head of Rockefeller Institute for Medical Research, which in 1965 became Rockefeller University, a school for graduate studies.

Brontë, Anne (1820–49), English novelist. The youngest of the Brontë sisters, she became a governess, an experience reflected in *Agnes Grey* (1847). Her other novel is *The Tenant of Wildfell Hall* (1848).

Brontë, Charlotte (1816–55), English novelist. Her personal life was unhappy. She was born into genteel poverty; her mother, four sisters, (two of them, Emily and Anne, also novelists), and dissolute brother died early; her love for a married man was unrequited; she died in childbirth within a year of her marriage. Her four novels—*The Professor* (written 1846, published 1857), *Jane Eyre* (1847), *Shirley* (1849), and *Villette* (1853)—are works of remarkable passion and imagination. *See also* Jane Eyre.

Brontë, Emily (1818–48), English novelist and poet. She was the sister of Charlotte and Anne Brontë, also novelists. Her love for her native Yorkshire moors and her insight into human passion are manifested in her poetry and in her only novel, *Wuthering Heights* (1847).

Brontosaurus, or Apatosaurus, best-known of huge North American sauropods of Jurassic times (136–190 million years ago). Supported on four elephantine limbs and bearing a long neck and tail, this giant had a small head with feeble, peglike teeth that probably served for shoveling in soft, aquatic vegetation. Length: 80ft (24m); weight: over 40 tons. *See also* Sauropoda. △572.

Brontotherium. △410.

Bronx, The, residential borough of New York City, N.Y., on S end of a peninsula bordered by the Hudson River (W), Harlem River (SW), East River (S), Long Island Sound (E); connected to boroughs of Manhattan and Queens by a network of bridges. Site of numerous educational institutions, the Bronx Zoo, and Yankee Stadium. Founded by Jonas Bronck for the Dutch West India Co. 1641. Inc. as part of New York City 1898. Pop. (1970) 1,472,216.

Bronze, traditionally an alloy of copper and tin containing no more than 33% tin. It has long been used in art for sculpting. Other substances are often added, such as aluminum (aircraft parts, tubing), silicon (marine hardware, chemical equipment) and phosphor (springs, electrical parts). Bronze is noted for its strength, hardness, resistance to corrosion, and malleability. △1588, 1596, 1600.

Bronze Age, period from the early fourth millennium BC onward, in which man learned to make bronze artifacts and to use the wheel and the ox-drawn plow. The resulting growth of technology and trade occasioned the rise of the first civilizations in Sumer and Egypt. *See also* Iron Age. △1588.

Bronze Sculpture, sculpture of bronze. Bronze is strong, enduring, and has great tensile strength, a desirable property in sculpture, making possible free extension or protrusion of unsupported parts of a figure and permitting a large mass to be balanced on a narrow base. Bronze can convey the effect of plastic (modeling), glyptic (carving), or toreutic (metalworking), depending upon the nature of the original. For example, Renaissance and modern bronzes reflect a plastic technique because they are cast from originals modeled in clay. Early Greek bronzes reflect a glyptic technique because their originals were carved wood.

There are two main types of cast objects, solid and hollow. In primitive cultures solid casts were used, but this is only effective for small objects. The invention of hollow casting allowed for the production of monumental works, lighter in weight, and for free-standing parts to be cast separately and then assembled. In solid casting a model of the object is executed in wax, which is then coated with clay. Firing hardens the clay mold and melts the wax model, which flows out. Molten bronze, which is poured into the mold, cools, and when the clay mold is broken, the bronze cast is free. The cast is then perfected by chasing, reworking small details, and polishing. There are two methods of hollow casting: the *cire-perdue* or "lost-wax" process and sand casting. The former is used for art; the latter, primarily in industry and for small pieces of large works. In the *cire-perdue* method, the wax model must be hollow, so it is produced on a core of clay. The clay core is attached to an outer clay mold by iron bars so it remains in place when the wax model is melted out. The space once occupied by wax is now filled with molten bronze. Large casts are made in pieces and attached later. The final removal and reworking is the same as for solid casts. Cellini used the original model to make an intermediate plaster mold that could be used to make many wax models. Thus many reproductions or replicas could be made from one model.

When bronze is exposed to air it develops a patina, a hard protecting surface. A natural patina, taking many years, forms from copper carbonate (light greenish) or copper sulfate (brownish black). Often an artificial patina is produced by the sculptor. Bronze casting is extremely old, going back to the third millennium BC and bronze has been a popular medium for art throughout history. Some master bronze sculptors include Donatello, Ghiberti, Cellini, Verrocchio, Rodin, Epstein, Brancusi, and Lipchitz. Chinese and Japanese bronzes are equally noteworthy.

Bronzino, Il, pseud. of Angelo Allori (1502–72), Italian painter. He was leader of the second generation mannerist style, marked by elegance and grace. He had a strong impact on the development of portraiture. His works include *Young Man with the Lute* (1540) and *Ascension* (1552). *See also* Mannerism.

Brooke, Alan Francis. *See* Alanbrooke, 1st Viscount.

Brooke, Edward William (1919–), US Senator, b. Washington, D.C. He was admitted to the Massachusetts bar in 1948, elected attorney general of Massachusetts in 1963, and in 1967 became the first black senator since Reconstruction. He was reelected in 1972. A Republican, he is author of *The Challenge of Change* (1966). He served on the President's Commission on Civil Disorders (1967) and in 1970 was instrumental in defeating confirmation of G. Harold Carswell to the US Supreme Court.

Brooke, L(eonard) Leslie (1862–1940), English author and illustrator of children's picture books. At the

Vancouver, British Columbia

Benjamin Britten

Brno, Czechoslovakia

Louis Victor de Broglie

turn of the 20th century, he helped establish the genre with *Johnny Crow's Garden, The Story of the Three Little Bears, The Story of the Three Little Pigs,* and others.

Brooke, Rupert (Chawner) (1887–1915), English poet. The patriotism of his early war poems and his good looks made him a contemporary legend, though both his criticism and poetry suggest a more complex personality than the naïve hero. He died on a hospital ship without having experienced actual warfare.

Brookeborough, Basil Stanlake Brooke, 1st Viscount (1888–1973), prime minister of Northern Ireland (1943–63). He was elected to the Northern Ireland Parliament (1929) and served as provincial minister of agriculture (1933–41) and of commerce (1941–45) before becoming prime minister. He developed the economy and improved relations with the Republic of Ireland, although he was an uncompromising supporter of Northern Ireland's inclusion in Great Britain.

Brook Farm, utopian community, founded 1841 in W Roxbury, Mass. Led by George Ripley, a former Unitarian minister, members tried to combine thinking with working and to give equal pay to all; many famous people of the time participated, including Nathaniel Hawthorne, Charles Dana, Ralph Waldo Emerson; experiment was abandoned in 1847 due to unproductive land and lack of water power for industries. Original farm started with 15 members, 200 acres (81 hectares), and 4 buildings; site is now marked by a bronze plaque.

Brookfield, village in NE Illinois, 13mi (21km) W of Chicago; site of Brookfield Zoo. Inc. 1893 as Grossdale; present name was adopted 1905. Pop. (1970) 20,284.

Brookfield, residential city in SE Wisconsin, on Fox River, 12mi (19km) W of Milwaukee; suburb of Milwaukee, with light industries. Inc. 1954. Pop. (1970) 32,140.

Brookline, residential town in E Massachusetts; suburb of Boston; birthplace of President John F. Kennedy, now a national historic site; site of antique auto museum and Hebrew College. Settled 1630s; inc. 1705. Pop. (1970) 58,689.

Brooklyn, borough of New York City, New York; seat of and coextensive with Kings co. in SW extremity of Long Island; separated by East River from Manhattan, to which it is connected by the Brooklyn (1883), Manhattan (1909), and Williamsburg (1903) bridges, subway tunnels, and the vehicular Brooklyn-Battery Tunnel; it is connected to Staten Island by the Verrazano-Narrows Bridge (1964). Brooklyn was scene of Revolutionary War Battle of Long Island during which British Tories defeated the patriots and gained control of Long Island, Aug. 27, 1776. The borough is the site of Brooklyn College (1930), Packer Collegiate Institute (1845), Pratt Institute (1887), Long Island University (1926), St Francis College (1858), St Joseph's College for Women (1916), New York City Community College of Applied Arts and Sciences (1946), Kingsborough Community College (1963), Prospect Park, Marine Park, and Coney Island. Industries: shipbuilding, brewing, paint, varnish, building equipment. First sighted 1524 by Giovanni da Verrazano, Florentine navigator; founded by Dutch and Walloons (1636–37). First settlement in 1645 was called Breuckelen; inc. as village 1816, as city 1834; became borough 1898. Area: 71sq mi (184sq km). Pop. (1970) 2,601,852.

Brooklyn Center, city in E Minnesota, on Mississippi River; suburb of Minneapolis. First settled in 1840s as a farm trading center; inc. 1911. Pop. (1970) 35,173.

Brooklyn Park, city in SE Minnesota, 2mi (3km) W of Mississippi River and 9mi (14km) NW of Minneapolis. Inc. 1954. Pop. (1970) 26,230.

Brook Park, city in NE Ohio; SW suburb of Cleveland. Chief industry is dairy products. Inc. 1914. Pop. (1970) 30,774.

Brooks, Gwendolyn (1917–), U.S. poet, b. Topeka, Kan. The first black woman to win the Pulitzer Prize (for *Annie Allen* in 1949), she writes sensitively of Northern ghetto life. Her verse was collected in *The World of Gwendolyn Brooks* (1970).

Brooks, Van Wyck (1886–1963), US literary critic, b. Plainfield, N.J. His first book, *The Wine of the Puritans,* a critique of the American Puritan heritage, was published in 1909. This critique was developed further in *America's Coming-of-Age* (1915), *The Ordeal of Mark Twain* (1920), and *The Pilgrimage of Henry James* (1925). Later works shifted from critiques of American culture to appreciations of it. Such works include *Emerson and Others* (1927) and the series *Makers and Finders* (1936–1952), the first volume of which, *The Flowering of New England,* won a Pulitzer Prize in 1937.

Brooks Range, mountain range across N Alaska, from Kotzebue Sound to the border of Canada; separates Arctic Ocean coastal plain from the Yukon basin; barren, rugged, uninhabited. Highest peak is Mt Michelson 9,239ft (2,818m).

Brook Trout. *See* Char.

Broomcorn, cultivated variety of sorghum. The tall grass panides are used for brooms and brushes. *See also* Sorghum.

Brothers Karamazov, The (1879–80), psychological novel by Fyodor Dostoevski, about Fyodor Karamazov and his four sons; Dimitri, a good-for-nothing, Ivan, an atheistic intellectual, Alyosha, who is studying for the priesthood under the elder, Zossima, and the illegitimate Smerdyakov, an epileptic. Their relationships become increasingly complex—Fyodor and Dimitri both love Grushenka, while Ivan loves Dimitri's betrothed, Katerina. The drama lies in the murder of the father by the sons, symbolizing man's revolt against his heavenly father.

Brougham, Henry Peter, 1st Baron Brougham and Vaux (1778–1868), British political figure, b. Scotland. In the House of Commons (1810–12, 1815–30) he fought for press freedom, the abolition of slavery, legal reform, and public education. As chancellor (1830–34), he reformed legal procedure and helped pass the Reform Act (1832). He was a founder of the University of London (1828) and designed the brougham carriage.

Broun, (Matthew) Heywood (Campbell) (1888–1939), US newspaper columnist and labor organizer, b. Brooklyn, N.Y. Author of a popular syndicated column, "It Seems to Me," during the 1920s and 1930s. He helped to found the American Newspaper Guild (1933), the first successful union for editorial workers.

Brouwer, Adriaen (*c.* 1605–38), Flemish painter. Influential in the development of Dutch and Flemish painting, he is noted for his depictions of peasant life and for his humorous treatment of figures sleeping, drinking, smoking, and fighting (eg. *The Smokers,* Metropolitan Museum of Art, New York City). △1168.

Brown, Charles Brockden (1771–1810), US author, b. Philadelphia. Considered one of the first Americans for whom writing was a profession, he gained acclaim for his Gothic romances. Probably his best-known novel was *Wieland* (1798), about a man who hears God command him to murder his family. Other works include *Ormond* (1799), *Arthur Mervyn* (1799–1800), *Edgar Huntly* (1799), *Clara Howard* (1801), and *Jane Talbot* (1801).

Brown, George (1818–80), Canadian journalist and statesman, b. Scotland. Brown emigrated to Canada in 1843, starting the Toronto *Banner* in that year and the reform political weekly *Toronto Globe* in 1844. In parliament (1857–65) he was anti-French and anti-Roman Catholic, argued for proportional representation of Canada East and Canada West, and campaigned for a confederation of British North American provinces. An enemy of trade with the United States, he refused knighthood and a senate seat. He was murdered by an employee.

Brown, Helen Gurley (1922–), US author and editor, b. Green Forest, Ark. An advertising copywriter for many years, she gained notoriety with her book *Sex and the Single Girl* (1962). In 1966 she became editor of *Cosmopolitan* magazine and transformed the failing publication into a sleek monthly directed at the unmarried working woman.

Brown, James Nathaniel "Jimmy" (1936–), US football player, b. St. Simons Island, Ga. Known as an outstanding running back, he had a career total of 12,312 yards (10,558m). He played for the Cleveland Browns in the National Football League (1957–65) and scored 126 touchdowns. After his retirement, he became a film actor.

Brown, John (1800–59), US anti-slavery crusader, b. Torrington, Conn. He led the Pottawatomie Massacre (1856) in Kansas in which five alleged slaveowners were killed. In an attempt to provoke a slave rebellion in Virginia he raided a government arsenal at Harper's Ferry in October 1859, but he was captured by a company of marines commanded by Robert E. Lee. After being tried for insurrection, treason, and murder, he was convicted and hanged at Charlestown (now in W. Va.) on Dec. 2, 1859.

Brown, John Mason (1900–69), US author, lecturer, and critic, b. Louisville, Ky. He specifically educated himself for a career in theater criticism by going to the theater as a youth and by studying drama at Harvard. He became drama critic for *Theatre Arts* (1924–28), then the New York *Evening Post* (1929–41). A charter member of the New York Drama Critics Circle (1935), he was its president for four years. He was drama critic for the New York *World-Telegram* (1941–42) and the *Saturday Review* (1944–55). Among his many books on the theater are *Two on the Aisle* (1938), *As They Appear* (1952), *Through These Men* (1956), and *Dramatis Personae* (1963).

Brown, Marcia (1918–), US author and illustrator of children's books, b. Rochester, N.Y. She has twice won the Caldecott Medal. *Cinderella,* translated anew from the French and illustrated in pastels, won in 1955. *Once a Mouse . . . A Fable Cut in Wood,* illustrated by woodcuts of bold design, won the award in 1962.

Brown, Mordecai Peter Centennial ("Three Finger") (1876–1948), US baseball player, b. Nyesville, Ind. He pitched 229 winning games (1903–16) and recorded one of the lowest career earned run averages in history (2.06). He was elected to the Baseball Hall of Fame in 1949.

Brown, Paul Eugene (1908–), US football coach, b. Norwalk, Ohio. One of pro football's most successful coaches, he formed and coached the Cleveland Browns in the former All-American Football Conference (1946–50) and won the league's championship all four years. He coached the same Cleveland team in the National Football League (1950–62) and also coached the Cincinnati Bengals (1968–75).

Brown, Robert (1773–1858), Scottish botanist. He went on an expedition to Australia (1801–05) and returned to England with valuable botanical collections. He described the flora of Australia in *Prodomus florae Novae Hollandiae et Insulae Van Diemen* (1810), a classic of systematic botany. In 1831 he described and named the nucleus of the plant cell, one of his pioneering observations. He is best known for establishing, in *A Brief Account of Microscopical Observations* (1829), that minute particles suspended in a liquid or gas are continuously in motion. This movement has since been called "Brownian movement." *See also* Brownian Movement.

Brown, Sterling Allen (1901–), US writer and authority on black literature, b. Washington, D.C. His works include *The Negro in American Fiction* (1937), *Negro Poetry and Drama* (1937), and *The Negro Caravan* (1941).

Brown, William Wells (1816–84), US writer, b. Lexington, Ky. A former slave, he escaped to Europe where he wrote novels, plays, and histories of his people, including *Narrative of William Brown, Fugitive Slave* (1847), *Clotel, Or, The President's Daughter* (1852), and *The Black Man, His Antecedents, His Genius, and His Achievements* (1863).

Brown Algae, a group of almost exclusively marine algae (division Phaeophyta) that includes the largest seaweeds, the kelps, some of which are more than 150ft (46m) long. Like familiar higher plants but unlike most other algae, brown algae have complex structures including rootlike holdfasts to anchor them to the ocean floor; air-filled bladders to help them float; and other organs resembling stems and leaves. △432.

Brown Bear, brown colored bears including the grizzly and Alaskan brown, or Kodiak, bears. Originally found in most of Eurasia and W North America, they are now rare except in Alaska and Canada. The largest of all bears, some are carnivores, some herbivores, and some omnivores. Length: over 8ft (2.4m); weight: 300–1,715lb (135–772kg). Species *Ursus arctos. See also* Bear. △592.

Brownian Movement, rapid and random movement of particles suspended in a fluid, observable up to a particle size of 3×10^{-3}mm, caused by the thermal kinetic energy of its environment. The diffusion of pollutants through the atmosphere, and the movement of "holes" (minute regions of positive electrical charge) through a semiconductor are examples. △1502.

Browning, Elizabeth Barrett (1806–61), English poet. The wife of Robert Browning, she lived in Florence from 1847. She began writing poetry at an early age. *The Battle of Marathon* was published privately in 1820 and was followed by *The Seraphim and Other Poems* (1838) and *A Drama of Exile* (1845). The 1850 edition of her poetry included *Sonnets from the Portuguese. Aurora Leigh* (1856) was her last important poem.

Browning, Robert (1812–89), English poet. He is noted for his use of the dramatic monologue, as in "My Last Duchess" and "Soliloquy of the Spanish Cloister," both published in *Bells and Pomegranates* (1846). While living in London (1832–46), he wrote the volumes *Paracelsus* (1835), *Sordello* (1840), and other works as well as *Bells and Pomegranates*, a collection that also includes the narrative poem "Pippa Passes" and the dramatic lyric "Home Thoughts from Abroad." In 1846 he married Elizabeth Barrett and moved to Italy, where he lived until she died in 1861. While there he published the volumes *Christmas-Eve and Easter Day* (1854) and *Men and Women* (1855), which includes "Love Among the Ruins" and "Fra Lippo Lippi." Returning to London, he became popular with *Dramatis Personae* (1864) and *The Ring and the Book* (1864–69), a series of dramatic dialogues that many consider his masterpiece. His later works include *Dramatic Idyls* (2 vols., 1879–80). △1268.

Brown Kiwi. △526.

Brown Rot, any of various chiefly fungal plant diseases characterized by decay and browning of tissues. The worst cause of brown rot is the fungus *Monilivia fructicola*, which attacks peaches and other stone fruits after harvesting.

Brown Snake, wide-ranging North American Secretive snake. Dekay's snake of NE United States lives in moist woods, swamps, and city parks and lots. Brownish with two parallel rows of black spots down its back, its young have a yellow collar. Length: to 13in (33cm). Family Colubridae; species *Storeria dekayi. See also* Snake.

Brownsville, port city in S Texas, 25mi (40km) W of Gulf of Mexico; seat of Cameron co; est. as a military post by Gen. Zachary Taylor, who named it Fort Brown for Major Jacob Brown. Industries: food processing, chemicals, fishing. Founded 1846. Pop. (1970) 52,522.

Brown Swiss, rugged breed of dairy cattle originally from the mountains of Switzerland. Found in the United States, they are more common in Italy, Austria, and Hungary. Brown, they sometimes have a gray stripe along the back. They produce more milk than Ayrshires but the butterfat content is the same. One of the oldest breeds, it was once also used for meat and as a draft animal. *See also* Dairy Cattle. △372.

Brown-tail Moth, tussock moth caterpillar that is a serious pest of many fruit and deciduous shade trees, especially in the New England states, New Brunswick, and Nova Scotia. It is dark brown and hairy, with tufts of white hairs along each side. Length: 1.5in (38mm). Species *Nygmia Phaeorrhoea.*

Brown v. Board of Education (of Topeka) (1954), landmark US Supreme Court decision that overturned the "separate but equal" doctrine of public education established in *Plessy v. Ferguson* (1896). The court, led by Chief Justice Earl Warren, declared that racial segregation in schools "deprived the children of the minority group of equal educational opportunities" and found separate facilities to be "inherently unequal" and in violation of the Constitution's equal protection clause. This decision gave impetus to the later civil rights movement of the 1960s.

Brown v. Board of Education (1955), US Supreme Court decision that sought to implement the desegregation ruling of *Brown v. Board of Education of Topeka* (1954). The court declared that local courts had to fashion equitable remedies to fit local circumstances and instructed them to do so "with all deliberate speed." *See also* Brown v. Board of Education of Topeka (1954).

Brubeck, David (Warren) ("Dave") (1920–), US jazz pianist and composer, b. Concord, Calif. In 1951 the Dave Brubeck Quartet was formed, consisting of Brubeck, Paul Desmond (alto sax), Joe Morello (drums), and Eugene Wright (bass). This group enjoyed tremendous acclaim and popularity in the 1960s. Brubeck also composed music, including cantatas and orchestral works.

Bruce, Blanche Kelso (1841–98), US political figure, b. Farmville, Va. He was a US Senator from Mississippi (1875–81), the first black to serve a full term. He fought for the civil rights of blacks, Indians, and Asians in the United States and served as Register of the Treasury Department (1881, 85–89) and as Recorder of Deeds (1889).

Bruce, Edward (died 1318), Scottish king of Ireland (1315–18). He helped his brother, Robert I, become Scotland's king. In Ireland he led the Irish against their English overlords, before being killed in battle.

Brucellosis, or undulant fever, disease passed from animal to man often in unpasteurized milk; often fatal if undiagnosed. Symptoms include headache, weakness, remittent fever. Pasteurization of milk and destruction of infected animals have made the disease rare. △736

Bruch, Max. △1246.

Brucite, a secondary hydroxide mineral, magnesium hydroxide [$Mg(OH)_2$], derived from periclase (MgO). In marbles and serpentine metamorphic rocks. Hexagonal system plates and fibrous masses. Pearly white to red; transparent and waxy; hardness 2.5; sp gr 2.4.

Brücke, Die, loose association of German painters, founded in Dresden (1905) by Ernst Kirchner, Karl Schmidt-Rottluff, and Erich Heckel. They thought of their art as a bridge between the current academic style of painting and a freer style of expression. Using broken lines, angular forms, and intense colors, they produced emotionally expressive woodcuts and paintings. △1294.

Bruckner, Anton (1824–1896), Austrian Romantic composer. An intensely religious man, Bruckner composed mostly religious works and nine symphonies infused with religious feeling. Closer in style to the symphonies of Schubert than to those of Beethoven, Bruckner's symphonies contain scherzos second only to those found in Beethoven's symphonies, and his last three symphonies were major achievements of Romantic music. *See also* Romanticism in Music.

Brueghel, Jan the Elder (1568–1625), Flemish painter. He painted religious and mythological subjects, landscapes, and still lifes in the Mannerist style. His early work borrowed subjects from his father (Pieter the Elder) and other contemporaries. Later and more original works include a painting of the "Four Elements" (*c.* 1609) and an exquisite landscape, "Village Street" (1611). *See also* Mannerism.

Brueghel, Pieter the Elder (Peasant Brueghel) (*c.* 1525–69), Flemish painter. He was one of the greatest of Netherlandish painters, whose style, untouched by the conventional, was nearly impressionistic. He was a great artist of action and movement, and his works depict generalized forms often with a satirical approach. His work developed most obviously in his treatment of the landscape. Early works use the landscape solely as background, transitional works separate the foreground from middleground, and later works develop the landscape into a unified whole, with fewer and smaller figures present. An example of his early work is "Children's Games"; "Peasant Wedding" is in his mature style. His paintings fall into roughly three categories, all of which overlap—the fantasy or allegory, the genre, and the Biblical. Representative paintings include, respectively, "Fall of the Rebel Angels" (1562), "Return of the Herd," and "Massacre of the Innocents." △1144.

Brueghel, Pieter the Younger (1564–1638), Flemish painter. His country and religious works are sometimes copied from, and always in the tradition of, his father (Pieter the Elder). His nickname "Hell" derived from his depictions of hell.

Bruges (Brugge), city in NW Belgium, 55mi (89km) WNW of Brussels; capital of West Flanders prov.; 14th-century commercial and financial center of N Europe; dukes of Burgundy resided here and founded Order of Golden Fleece (1429). City is built on a network of canals, for which the city is called "City of Bridges." Industries: shipbuilding, food processing, tourism. Founded 865. Pop. 51,303.

Brûlé, Etienne (1591–1633), Canadian explorer, b. France. Brûlé came to Quebec with Samuel de Champlain in 1608. In the next 20 years he explored the Great Lakes and Georgian Bay, guiding French expeditions and befriending the Hurons, who, nevertheless, killed and cannibalized him in 1633.

Brummell, George Bryan (1778–1840), English social dandy called Beau Brummell; noted for his wit and style of dress. As a close friend of the prince of Wales (later George IV), Brummell greatly influenced English men's fashions. Gambling debts caused him to flee to

Brooklyn Museum

John Brown

Brown bear

Brown Swiss

France, where he lived in poverty and died insane in an asylum at Caen.

Brundage, Avery (1887–1975), US sportsman, b. Detroit. He was a staunch advocate of keeping "professionalism" out of amateur sports, and served as president of the International Olympic Committee (1952–72).

Brunei, sultanate in N Bornea, SE Asia; under British protection; capital is Bandar Seri Begauan; influenced by Chinese (10th–11th centuries); Brunei kings ruled island 15th–16th centuries; their power diminished during trade with western European nations; by 1888, it was ruled by Britain; in 1963 Brunei became a protectorate with sultan's power reinstated. Oil was discovered 1929, and the island now enjoys highest standard of living in SE Asia. Area: 2,226sq mi (5,765sq km). Pop. 135,665.

Brunel, (Sir) Marc Isambard (1769–1849), British engineer, b. France. A refugee from the French Revolution, he came to New York City in 1793 and was chief engineer of New York. He went to England in 1799, where he invented machinery for making ships' blocks. He was responsible for the construction of the Thames Tunnel (1825–43) and was knighted in 1841.

Brunelleschi, Filippo (1377–1446), Italian architect. His systematic use of perspective and his engineering skill made completion of the octagonal ribbed dome of the Florence Cathedral possible. His other architectural achievements include Ospedale degl' Innocenti and the Church of San Lorenzo, both in Florence. △1134.

Bruner, Jerome S(eymour) (1915–), US psychologist, b. New York City. Bruner's work in child and educational psychology has emphasized how children develop their thinking capacities as they interact with the environment.

Brunhild, a beautiful princess in ancient Germanic literature. She was a Valkyrie, who Odin banished from Valhalla for disobeying his rule. On earth, she could only marry a man stronger than herself. Siegfried fulfilled this condition, but wooed her for another. When Brunhild discovered this trickery, Siegfried was killed.

Brunner, Emil (1889–1966), Swiss theologian. A professor of systematic theology at Zurich (1924–53), in his *Mediator* (1927) he presents Christ in the language of dialectical theology and sees revelation as a personal experience. Other works include *Christianity and Civilization* (1948–49) and *Dogmatics* (1946–60).

Bruno, Giordano (1548–1600), Italian philosopher. A fierce opponent of Aristoteleanism and a supporter of the doctrines of Copernicus, his religious attitude of extreme pantheistic immanentism was developed in his two Italian treatises. In his later Latin treatises he modified this position somewhat. Nevertheless, he was censured for unorthodoxy and burned at the stake. He had considerable influence on Spinoza, Leibniz, Descartes, and Schelling. *See also* Pantheism.

Brunswick, city in E West Germany on Oker River, 90mi (145km) SSE of Hamburg; capital of Lower Saxony state; site of crossroads of ancient trade routes, St Balsius Cathedral (1173–94), and Dankwarderode fortress (1175), technical university; member of Hanseatic League (13th century). Industries: pianos, optical equipment, food products, printing. Founded 861; made city 12th century. Pop. 225,621.

Brunswick, town in S Maine, on Casco Bay; site of Bowdoin College (1794) where Nathaniel Hawthorne and Henry Wadsworth Longfellow were students; Longfellow later taught here; Harriet Beecher Stowe wrote *Uncle Tom's Cabin* here. Industries: shoes, clothing, tourism. Settled 1628; inc. 1739. Pop. (1970) 16,195.

Brussels (Bruxelles), city in central Belgium, 26mi (42km) S of Antwerp; capital of Belgium, and of Brabant prov. Est. as a military post in the 10th century, it prospered and became the center of the wool industry; capital of Netherlands (1530) under Hapsburg empire; scene of World's Fair (1958). Industries: textiles, chemicals, electrical equipment, brewing. Founded *c.* 900. Pop. 161,089.

Brussels Griffon, small, distinctive Belgian dog (toy group) derived from the Affenpinsoher and the Belgian street dog. It has an upturned, black nose set between prominent eyes, a domed forehead, and protruding chin. Small, high-set ears are cropped or natural. The body is short; legs are medium-length and wide-set; the docked tail is held high. There are two types of coat: rough (wiry, but not shaggy, with a fringe around the face) and smooth. Colors are reddish brown and black or solid black. Average size: 8in (20cm) high at shoulder; 8–10lb (3.5–4.5kg). *See also* Toy Dog.

Brussels Sprouts, cabbage-related plant first grown in Belgium. Leaves grow from the top of a thick, erect stalk and stem buds develop into miniature, globular heads that are eaten as a vegetable. It matures in 85–90 days. Height: 22in (55.9cm). Family Cruciferae; species *Brassica oleracea gemmifera.*

Brut (*c.* 1205), early Middle English verse history of Britain by Layamon from the supposed arrival of Brutus, son of Aeneas, to the time of Cadwalader (*c.* 689). Based on the works of Geoffrey of Monmouth and Robert Wace, the *Brut* contains the earliest mention in English of King Arthur, King Lear, and Cymbeline. It is the first significant work in Middle English.

Brutalism, in Architecture. △1322.

Brutus, Lucius Junius (*fl.* late 6th century BC), a founder of the Roman Republic. He led the Romans in the expulsion of the last Tarquin king (510 BC) after the rape of his kinswoman Lucrece by the king's son. He is reputed to have executed his own two sons for plotting to restore the Tarquins.

Brutus, Marcus Junius (*c.* 85–42 BC), Roman political figure, one of the principal assassins of Julius Caesar. First siding with Pompey, he was forgiven by Caesar and made governor of Cisalpine Gaul (46 BC). He turned against Caesar after the murder of Cato, his uncle. After Caesar's murder (44 BC), he went to Greece, where he raised an army and with Cassius engaged in battle with Marc Antony and Octavian. Defeated at Philippi (42 BC), he committed suicide.

Bryan, William Jennings (1860–1925), US lawyer and politician, b. Salem, Ill. A former Democratic Congressman (1891–95) and a leading advocate of the free coinage of silver, Bryan made the "Cross of Gold" speech at the 1896 Democratic convention which won him the presidential nomination; he lost to William McKinley. Nominated again in 1900, he ran on a chiefly anti-imperialist platform and was again defeated by McKinley. He was defeated in his third try in 1908 by William Howard Taft. He helped Woodrow Wilson win the Democratic nomination in 1912 and became Wilson's secretary of state. He resigned in 1915, believing Wilson's foreign policy to be leading the country into World War I.

In his later years, Bryan became a religious fundamentalist. He favored prohibition and opposed the teaching of evolution. He acted as prosecuting attorney in the Scopes "monkey" trial in 1925, opposing Clarence Darrow, who was attorney for the defense. Bryan won the case but died five days after its conclusion. *See also* Free Silver; Scopes Trial.

Bryan, city in E central Texas, 72mi (116km) SSE of Waco; seat of Brazos co; cotton plantation area. Industries: farming, aluminum, laboratory research equipment. Inc. 1872. Pop. (1970) 33,719.

Bryansk (Br'ansk), formerly Debryansk; city in Russian SSR, USSR, on the Desna River; capital of Bryansk oblast; site of 17th-century cathedral and monastery; annexed to Moscow 1503; held by Germans 1941–43. Industries: flour, lumber, iron, cement. Founded 1146. Pop. 318,000.

Bryant, William Cullen (1794–1878), US poet and editor, b. Cummington, Mass. He began to write poetry as a youth; his first book of *Poems* appeared in 1821. It contained some of his most famous verse, including *Thanatopsis* and "To a Waterfowl." Although he studied and practiced law, he dropped it in 1825 when he became coeditor of *New York Review.* In 1826 he began working for the New York *Evening Post,* soon rising to editor (1829) and part-owner. Under his leadership the *Post* emerged as a powerful liberal organ, advocating abolition and free trade. Bryant also continued to write poetry, primarily nature poetry. Later volumes of his work include *The Fountain* (1842), *A Forest Hymn* (1860), and *Thirty Poems* (1864).

Bryce Canyon National Park, park in SW Utah. It contains very colorful and unusual erosional forms. In horseshoe-shaped amphitheaters along the Paunsaugunt Plateau stand highly colored and grotesque pinnacles, walls, and spires. Area: 36,010acres (14,-584 hectares). Est. 1928.

Bryophyte, a group of small green plants (division Bryophyta) consisting of the mosses and liverworts. Bryophytes grow on damp surfaces exposed to light, including rocks and tree bark, and are found in nearly every land habitat from the Arctic to the Antarctic. They lack specialized tissues for transporting water, minerals, and food; instead, these materials diffuse slowly from cell to cell through the plant. In the typical bryophyte life cycle a relatively conspicuous green sexual stage alternates with an inconspicuous non-green asexual (spore-bearing) stage that is dependent on the sexual stage for food. *See also* Alternation of Generations. △436.

Bryozoa, phylum of moss animals, also called sea mats and corallines. These plantlike, marine animals live in branching colonies. Each animal has a protective case, U-shaped digestive tract, and ciliated feeding tentacles. The body is formed of two cell layers. Reproduction is by budding. Species include *Alcyonidium;* length: 11.8in (300mm) and *Bugula;* length: 2.8in (70mm).

Bubastis, ancient city in the Nile Delta of Egypt. Dating back to the VI dynasty (2420–2258 BC), it gained importance when the pharaohs of the XIX dynasty (1320–1200 BC) moved their capital to the Delta. Bubastis itself served as capital during the XXII (945–745 BC) and XXIII (745–718 BC) dynasties. The city declined following the second Persian conquest (343 BC). It was noted as the center of worship of the cat-headed (or lion-headed) goddess Bast. According to Herodotus, it also held an annual Saturnalia.

Bubble Chamber, instrument for detecting and identifying charged particles, such as the proton. It consists of a large chamber in which a liquid, usually hydrogen or helium, is kept just above its boiling point by pressure. Any energetic ionizing particle passing through the liquid will ionize it. If the pressure is suddenly reduced, allowing the liquid to reach its boiling point, a line of tiny bubbles begins to form along this ionized path. These tracks are photographed before the pressure is restored, particles being identified by the nature of the tracks, their curvature in an applied magnetic field, and by the tracks of their decay products. *See also* Cloud Chamber. △1504.

Buber, Martin (1878–1965), Jewish philosopher, theologian, and political activist, b. Vienna. An early, ardent Zionist, from 1901 he edited *Die Welt,* the Zionist weekly. He edited *Der Jude,* the leading journal of German-speaking Jewish intellectuals (1916–24). He defiantly opposed the Nazis in Germany until forced to migrate to Palestine in 1938, where he became a professor of social philosophy at Hebrew University. His most important published work is *I and Thou* (1923), which discusses the relationship between man and God.

Bubonic Plague, disease usually transmitted to humans by fleas from rats. Symptoms include chills and fever, followed by vomiting, diarrhea, headache, and inflammation and swelling of lymph nodes, especially in the region of the groin. Sanitation is the preventive measure. △732.

Bucaramanga, commercial city in N central Colombia, in the E Andes highlands; many colonial monuments. Crops: coffee, tobacco, cacao. Founded 1622. Pop. 249,998.

Bucephalus, horse of Alexander the Great. It accompanied Alexander on his major campaigns. When Bucephalus died (326 BC) in India, Alexander had him buried on the banks of the Hydaspes River (now Jhelum River) and built the city of Bucephalia in his memory. The city was across from the modern city of Jhelum in Pakistan.

Buchanan, James (1791–1868), 15th President of the United States, b. near Mercersburg, Pa.; graduate, Dickinson College, 1809. He never married. A Pennsylvania lawyer, he began his political career as a Federalist and later became a conservative Democrat.

A strong secretary of state under President Polk, he settled the Oregon dispute with Great Britain, but the dispute with Mexico over Texas resulted in the Mexican War. In 1853, President Pierce named him minister to Great Britain. While in that post, he negotiated the ill-fated Ostend Manifesto, which would have authorized the United States to take Cuba by force if necessary.

As the Democratic presidential candidate in 1857, he was the narrow winner over John C. Fremont, the Republican, and Millard Fillmore, the candidate of the Whigs and Know-Nothings. His presidency was marked by the rising animosity between the proslavery and the antislavery states. His attempt to maintain the "sacred balance" between North and South pleased no one, and the South moved closer and closer to secession. He reluctantly supported the federal garrison at Fort Sumter because of his fear that it would precipitate war. He was right: the Civil War began only weeks after he left office.

Career: House of Representatives, 1821–31; Minister to Russia, 1832–34 and Great Britain 1853–56; U.S. Senate, 1834–45; Secretary of State, 1845–49; President, 1857–61.

Bucharest (Bucuresti), capital and largest city of Romania, on Dimbovita River; became capital 1862; occupied by Germans 1916–18; under Nazi control 1940–44; site of 17th-century Metropolitan Church, theaters, museums, two universities, and seat of patriarch of Romanian Orthodox Church; major industrial and communications center. Industries: food processing, textiles, chemicals, automobiles, metal working, oil refining. Founded 15th century as fortress. Pop. 1,475,050.

Buchenwald, village in SW East Germany near Weimar. It was the site of one of the most notorious German concentration camps for the imprisonment of Jews, est. 1937 by the Nazis; taken in April 1945 by US troops, who found extreme examples of starvation and torture.

Buchner, Edward (1860–1917), German biochemist. He became professor at Berlin, Breslau, and finally at Würzburg, having been awarded a Nobel Prize in 1907 for his work on fermentation. His work indicated that it was not the actual yeast cells, but rather the enzymes contained within them, that actively caused alcoholic sugar fermentation. He was killed in World War I. *See also* Fermentation.

Buck, Pearl (1892–1973), U.S. novelist, b. Hillsboro, W.Va. The daughter of missionaries, she was raised in China, which is the setting for many of her novels. A prolific writer, her first book appeared in 1930. The following year *The Good Earth* was published. A novel about Chinese peasants, it won her the Pulitzer Prize in 1932. Other works include *Sons* (1932), *The Mother* (1934), *A House Divided* (1935), and *Dragon Seed* (1942). In 1938 she was awarded the Nobel Prize in literature.

Bucket Dredge. △1664.

Buckeye. *See* Horse Chestnut.

Buckingham, Edward Stafford, 3rd Duke of. *See* Stafford, Edward, 3rd Duke of Buckingham.

Buckingham, George Villiers, 1st Duke of (1592–1628), English courtier. As James I's favorite from 1614 he became rich and influential; he also dominated Charles I. His diplomatic and military missions to Spain and France (1623–27) were disasters, largely because of his incompetence and insolence. Parliament's two attempts to impeach him (1626,1628) were blocked by Charles I. He was assassinated by a disgruntled soldier.

Buckingham, George Villiers, 2nd Duke of, (1628–87), English courtier and political figure. He was educated with Charles I's sons and supported the Royalists in the Civil War (1642–48). Charming, rich, and unprincipled, he glittered in Restoration England, writing drama and poetry, patronizing the arts and sciences, and intriguing in politics. He was a privy councillor (1662–74) and then a major opposition figure (1675–80).

Buckingham, Henry Stafford, 2nd Duke of. *See* Stafford, Henry, 2nd Duke of Buckingham.

Buckingham, Humphrey Stafford, 1st Duke of. *See* Stafford, Humphrey, 1st Duke of Buckingham.

Buckingham Palace, London residence of British sovereigns since 1837. Formerly belonging to the dukes of Buckingham, it was purchased by George III (1761) and remodeled by the architect John Nash in 1825 into a 600-room palace. Sir Aston Webb redesigned the east front in 1913. The celebrated changing of the guard takes place daily when the sovereign is in residence.

Buckley, William F., Jr. (1925–), US journalist, b. New York City. He was the editor and founder of *The National Review* (1955). He is noted for his syndicated newspaper column and his television discussion show. His books include *Man, God, and Yale* (1951), *The Unmaking of a Mayor* (1966), and *Four Reformists—A Guide for the Seventies* (1973).

Buckner, Simon Bolivar (1823–1914), Confederate officer and US public official, b. Hart co, Ky. At the outbreak of the Civil War he initially supported Kentucky neutrality, but later joined the Confederate army. Taken prisoner in 1862 he was soon exchanged. After the war he was editor of the Louisville *Courier* and from 1887–91 was governor of Kentucky.

Buckwheat, dicotyledonous grain plant native to Asia and cultivated worldwide and well adapted to cool and arid places. This grain is important as poultry and livestock food. Bees make a dark honey of its pollen. Common buckwheat *(Fagopyrum esculentum)* is branched and has swollen sheaths where heart-shaped leaves are attached; white bisexual flowers; and triangular seeds enclosed by brown rind. Height: to 3ft (1m). Tartarian buckwheat *(F. tataricum)* has seeds with toothed edges. Its flour, unsatisfactory for bread, is used in pancakes. Hulled kernels are called groats. Family Polygonaceae.

Bucyrus, city in N Ohio, 58mi (93km) N of Columbus; seat of Crawford co. Industries: machinery, rubber hose, fluorescent lights. Settled 1818; inc. 1886. Pop. (1970) 13,111.

Budapest, capital city of Hungary, on the Danube River; formed by inc. of Buda and Pest, 1872. Buda became the capital of Hungary 1361; by 1800, Buda's importance was waning and Pest became Hungary's more important city. After union of two cities, Budapest became one of two capitals of Austro-Hungarian monarchy; by 1917 it was Hungary's leading commercial center as well as its cultural hub. In 1918 it was declared capital of independent country of Hungary; Russia seized control 1948; city was scene of unsuccessful uprising against Russian control in 1956: Industries: flour milling, iron and steel products, tourism. Settled AD100 by Romans. Pop. 1,940,212.

Buddenbrooks (1901), novel by Thomas Mann (with his elder brother Heinrich). Showing the influences of Friedrich Nietzsche and Richard Wagner, the story depicts the decline of a wealthy merchant family, caused by an increase in spiritual and artistic refinement and culminates in the death of the last heir.

Buddha, name given to Siddhartha Gautama (*c.* 563–*c.* 483 BC), the founder of Buddhism. Buddha, in Sanskrit, means "the enlightened one." Born into a noble family of the Himalayan foothills, at the age of 29 he left his family to become a wandering ascetic. After six years of meditation and fasting, he obtained enlightenment while seated under the holy tree Bodh Gaya. For the rest of his life he traveled throughout N India preaching his message. *See also* Buddhism. △988.

Buddhism, religion founded in India *c.* 528 by Siddhartha Gautama, the Buddha. Buddhism is based on Four Noble Truths: existence is suffering; the cause of suffering is craving and attachment; cessation of suffering is possible through Nirvana; Nirvana is attained through the Eightfold Path, which consists of the proper views, resolve, speech, action, livelihood, effort, mindfulness, and concentration. Today there are more than 160 million Buddhists in the world, concentrated most heavily in Burma, Ceylon, Indochina, and Japan. △988.

Budding, or gemmation, form of asexual reproduction that produces a new organism from an outgrowth of the parent. Buds break from the parent (hydra) or remain attached. Several freshwater sponges form gemmules (internal buds) that escape from the parent during unfavorable conditions and open to form new sponges when conditions are favorable. △468.

Budding, in horticulture, grafting buds on woody plants to produce more vigorous plants or to dwarf, particularly in stone fruit trees. It is done with varieties of the same, or closely related, species. A bud and small piece of bark are cut from a shoot of new growth and inserted into a T-shaped cut on the understock with the bud touching the cambium layer. It is then tied in place. Budding is most successful when done in spring. △324.

Budge, Don (1915–), US tennis player, b. John Donald Budge in Oakland, Calif. He won the US and British singles title (1937–38) and in 1938 scored a grand slam by also winning the French and Australian championships.

Budgerigar. *See* Parakeet.

Buena Park, city in S California, W of Anaheim; most important industry is tourism; site of Knott's Berry Farm and a wax museum of movie stars. Inc. 1953. Pop. (1970) 63,646.

Buena Vista, Battle of (Feb. 1847), Mexican War battle, in which US troops under Gen. Zachary Taylor were attacked by General Santa Anna's Mexican

Brussels, Belgium

William Jennings Bryan

James Buchanan

Bucharest, Romania: Satalui Open Air Museum

army. After two indecisive days, Santa Anna withdrew, giving the United States control of northern Mexico.

Buenos Aires, capital of Argentina, in E central Argentina, on estuary of the Río de la Plata, 150mi (242km) W of Atlantic Ocean. Colonized 1536 by Pedro de Mendoza who named it Santa María del Buen Aire; he abandoned it because of indian attacks; refounded by Juan de Garay 1580. In 1854, a constitution was drawn up, and Buenos Aires began challenging other provinces for control of the government. In 1880, city was detached from Buenos Aires prov. and set up as a separate federal district and capital of Argentina; political, commercial, industrial center; site of University of Buenos Aires (1821). Industries: tourism, textiles, meat processing, flour mills, metal works. Pop. 2,972,453.

Buerger's Disease, inflammation of arteries and veins often accompanied by thrombosis. Causes are unknown although men 20–45 are most susceptible. Symptoms are numbness, tingling, pain. Treatment is rest and exercise. *See also* Thrombosis.

Buffalo, industrial city and port of entry in W New York, on E shore of Lake Erie; seat of Erie co. Settled 1803 by Holland Land Co., its industrial growth was spurred as W terminus of newly opened Erie Canal (1825); scene of assassination of President McKinley at 1901 Pan-American Exposition and of inaugural oath of Theodore Roosevelt. It is site of McKinley Monument, Theodore Roosevelt Inaugural National Historic Site, Albright-Knox Art Gallery, Canisius College (1870), D'Youville College (1908), State University of New York at Buffalo (1867). Industries: flour milling, automobiles, chemicals, railroad shops. Inc. 1832. Pop. (1970) 462,768.

Buffalo, common name for several wild or domesticated oxen of Asia and Africa. It is a misnomer for American bison. Family Bovidae. *See also* Anoa; Ox; Water Buffalo.

Buffalo Fish, freshwater fish found in large rivers of the Mississippi Valley. Brownish to bluish-green, this sucker is a bottom feeder. Length: 10in–3ft. (25–90cm); weight: average 2–3lbs (0.9–1.4 kg), many are 20–30lbs (9–14kg). Family Catostomidae; species: bigmouth *Ictiobus cyprinellus*, smallmouth *Ictiobus bubalus*.

Buffer Solution, solution to which a moderate quantity of a strong acid or a strong base can be added without making a significant change to the pH. Buffer solutions usually consist of a mixture of a weak acid and one of its salts, a mixture of an acid salt and its normal salt, or a mixture of two acid salts.

Buffon, Georges Louis Leclerc, Comte de (1707–88), French naturalist. From 1739 as keeper of the Jardin du Roi (now Jardin des Plantes) in Paris he began to collect data for the monumental *Histoire naturelle, générale, et particulière* (44 vols., 1749–1804), a popular compendium of natural history interspersed with his speculations, some of which anticipate Charles Darwin's theories. △408,418.

Buganda, region of SE Uganda, E Africa. Inhabitants are mainly of Ganda tribe; enjoys rich soil and good climate. Area: 25,631sq mi (66,384sq km). △1116, 1212.

Bugle, brass wind instrument resembling a small trumpet without valves, capable only of natural tones (C-F-A-C). Because its penetrating tones carry great distances, it is used for military signaling, as in call to arms, reveille, retreat, and taps. *See also* Trumpet.

Bug River, two rivers in E Europe. Southern Bug River rises in hills of Ukrainian SSR, USSR, flows SE to Black Sea and is navigable for less than 100mi (161km). Length: 530mi (853km). Western Bug River rises in hills ENE of Zoluchev, in Ukrainian SSR, USSR, flows NW to Brest, forming part of Soviet-Polish border, and is navigable for 300mi (483km). Length: 484mi (779km).

Bujumbura, formerly Usumbura; capital city and chief port of Burundi and Bujumbura prov., SE central Africa, on tip of Lake Tanganyika in W Burundi; administrative, commercial, and manufacturing center; site of University of Bujumbura (1961), airport. Est. as German military post 1897, city was made capital of Belgian Ruanda-Urundi after WWI; remained capital when Burundi proclaimed independence 1962. Industries: tourism, textile, soap, agricultural products. Pop. 70,000.

Bukavu, formerly Costermansville; port city in E Zaire, Equatorial Africa, at S end of Lake Kivu; capital of Kivu region; administrative and trade center. Industries: food processing, tourism. Founded 1901. Pop. 183,025.

Bukhara (Buchara), city in W Uzbek SSR, USSR; capital of Bukhara oblast; site of 10th-century mausoleum of Ismail Samanid, minaret of Kalyan (1127), the Ulugbek (1417–18), oldest Muslim school in central Asia. City was under Arabs 7th-9th century when it became Islamic center; capital of Persian Samanid state 10th century; under Turks and Mongols 12th-15th centuries; made a protectorate of Russia 1868. Industries: natural silk, natural gas, handicrafts, textiles, rugs. Pop. 119,000.

Bukharin, Nikolai Ivanovich (1888–1938), Soviet Communist theoretician. He joined the Bolsheviks in 1906 and was deported in 1911. In Cracow he collaborated with Lenin on the newspaper *Pravda*. He returned to Russia in 1917, opposed the Brest-Litovsk Treaty, and supported Stalin's position in 1924 against rapid industrialization. In 1937, he was accused of being a Trotskyite. He was executed in the 1938 purges. △1310.

Bukovina, historic region in NE Romania, extending into W Ukrainian SSR; gained by Romania through terms of the treaty of St Germain (1919) and the treaty of Sevres (1920). The Romanian Peace treaty of 1947 awarded N Bukovina to the Russians. In WWII many Jews of the Bukovina region were annihilated. Resources include timber, petroleum, salt, manganese, copper, iron. Grain and livestock are raised. Area: 4,031sq mi (10,440sq km).

Bulawayo, city in SW Rhodesia, central S Africa, 240mi (384km) SW of Salisbury; site of a Matabelle revolt (1896); nearby are 18th-century ruins of Khami; 2nd-largest city in Rhodesia, and major industrial center. Industries: textiles, motor vehicles, cement. Founded by British 1893. Pop. 70,000.

Bulb, underground bud that produces a plant. It consists of a short, underground stem and enlarged, fleshy leaf scales. Food is stored in the scales, which are layered in a series of rings (onion) or loosely attached to the stem (some lilies). Bulbs produce smaller bulbs in the axils of the outer leaf scales. When mature, these offsets can be planted, producing new flowering-sized bulbs. △452.

Bulbul, noisy songbird of tropical and subtropical Africa and Asia. They have rounded wings and long, dull-colored plumage with some having crests. They feed on fruits and insects. The female lays spotted white or pink eggs (2–4) in a cup-shaped nest in a tree or bush. Length: 7in (17.5cm). Family Pycnonotidae.

Bulfinch, Charles (1763–1844), US architect, b. Boston. He is particularly noted for his public buildings, including the State House in Boston; University Hall at Harvard, Cambridge, Mass; and Massachusetts General Hospital, Boston. From 1818–30 he completed the building of the Capitol in Washington, D.C.

Bulgakov, Sergei (Nikolayevich) (1871–1944), Russian economist and theologian. As a student he rejected religion and became a Marxist economist. He wrote *Capitalism and Agriculture* (1901) and *Philosophy and Economics* (1912). He returned to the church, becoming a priest in 1918. His reconversion is discussed in *The Unfading Light* (1917). He was expelled from the Soviet Union in 1923 and became dean of the Russian Orthodox Theological Institute of Paris. His theological viewpoint, called sophiology, was concerned with creation and the unity of all. Major theological works include *The Comforter* (1936) and *Wisdom of God* (1937).

Bulganin, Nikolai (1895–1975), prime minister of the USSR (1937–38). During World War II, he was deputy commissar for defense. He later became defense minister (1947–49; 1953–55). He rose from being just a Central Committee member to become a member of the Presidium (1948). He was expelled from the Presidium for opposing Krushchev in 1958. △1344.

Bulgaria (Bâlgarija), People's Republic of, nation of the Balkan Peninsula in SE Europe. Since WWII, the country has been one of the Communist bloc nations under the domination of the Soviet Union. Bulgaria was part of the Ottoman Empire for 500 years. The Bulgarian language is a Slavic tongue.

Land and Economy. The Balkan Mts traverse the country from W to E, dividing Bulgaria into two separate geographic regions. N of the mountains lies the Danube Plain, a tableland of limestone and loess reaching N to the Danube River. S of the Balkan range lies the extensively farmed Maritsa Valley. Sofia, the capital city, is situated in the mountains in W central Bulgaria, with convenient access to both the Danube and Maritsa regions. Bulgaria has one of the least developed economies in Europe. The Communist regime which gained power after WWII established a centrally planned, Soviet-style economy. Agriculture was collectivized, and the chief emphasis was put on developing industry. The pattern of foreign exports shifted steadily from farm to manufactured products. In its effort to develop necessary electric power and heavy industry, consumer goods were neglected. Living standards remained low. Bulgaria receives substantial economic assistance from the Soviet Union.

People. The Bulgars who invaded and settled what is now Bulgaria in the 7th century were a non-Slavic people. Today's Bulgarian tongue derives not from the Bulgars but from the Slavs they conquered and by whom they were assimilated. The Bulgarian language is written in the Cyrillic alphabet. Most Bulgarians belong to the Bulgarian Orthodox Church. A minority of less than 10% is Muslim. As elsewhere, there is a constant movement in the population from the farming villages to the manufacturing centers.

Government. Bulgaria styles itself a people's republic, but the Bulgarian Communist party wields dictatorial power in the country. A national assembly elected by the people functions only to approve party policies and decrees. The national assembly elects from its members a presidium, of which the chairman is given the title of president.

History. In the early Middle Ages the Bulgarian kingdom became a powerful state, reaching from the Black Sea to the Adriatic. A golden age of art and culture culminated with the rule of the 10th-century Bulgarian emperor Simeon I. The Ottoman Turks conquered Bulgaria 1396 and ruled for five centuries. The beginnings of modern Bulgaria are traced to demands for political independence in the 19th century. In WWI, Bulgaria allied with Germany, hoping to regain lost territories in the Balkans. Defeated, Bulgaria suffered economic and political crises through the 1920s and 1930s. Economic progress was achieved with Germany's help in the 1930s; the two nations were allied in WWII. The Soviet Union invaded Bulgaria in 1944. Two years later a Communist regime was established, with Georgi Dimitrov as premier.

PROFILE

Official name: People's Republic of Bulgaria
Area: 42,823sq mi (110,912sq km)
Population (1974): 8,800,000
Density: 205per sq mi (79per sq km)
Chief cities: Sofia (capital); Plovdiv; Varna
Government: Communist
Religion: Bulgarian Orthodox Church
Language: Bulgarian (official)
Monetary unit: Lev
Gross national product: $13,000,000,000
Per capita income: $690
Industries (major products): steel, cement, fertilizer, textiles
Agriculture (major products): wheat, corn, tobacco, barley, sugar beets
Minerals (major): iron ore, copper, lead, zinc, petroleum
Trading partners (major): Soviet Union, East Germany, Italy

Bulgars, Turaien people living on the Black Sea. Part of their population moved to present day Bulgaria and, in the 9th century, the rest emigrated to the Volga region, which later became a major Russian economic center in the Middle Ages. They adopted the Moslem faith and were ruled by the Mongols in the 13th century. At the beginning of the 15th century, they became subjects of the Muscovite state.

Bulge, Battle of the, final German offensive in World War II. The US lines were thin along the border of France and Germany when the Germans launched an attack in December 1944. US forces rallied, holding at Bastogne, and the Germans were thrown back. △1338.

Bull, The. *See* Taurus.

Bullard, (Sir) Edward C(risp) (1907–), English geophysicist. He is noted for his work in geomagnetism, especially his theory of the geomagnetic dynamo, based on convective motion within the earth's core.

Bulldog, English bullbaiting breed (nonsporting group) several centuries old. No longer a vicious fighter, its distinctive large head has a short, turned-up muzzle; large nose set between the eyes; projecting lower jaw; and hanging lips. High-set ears fold over and back. The large body has muscular shoulders; broad chest; and short, stout legs. The short tail is straight or screw-shaped and carried low. A short, straight, fine coat can be a red or other color brindle; solid white, red, or fawn; or piebald. Skin is soft and loose. Average size: 13–15in (33–38cm) at shoulder; 50lb (22.5kg). *See also* Nonsporting Dog.

Bulldog Ant. △502.

Bulldozer, a tractor fitted with ground-gripping tracks and a large vertical blade at the front; used for leveling ground, clearing debris, and removing boulders. △1664.

Bullet. △1728, 1810.

Bullfighting, sport popular in Mexico, Columbia, Peru, Venezuela, Ecuador, and Spain, where it is the national sport. A bullfight usually includes six bulls and three matadors, who are assigned two bulls each on the basis of a lot chosen the morning of the fight. Each matador, whose role it is to kill the bull, has five assistants. These include two picadors, who are mounted on armored horses, and three *peones* or *banderilleras.* A bullfight takes place in three stages so that the bull can be sufficiently weakened (his head hanging low) so a clean kill can be made. In the first stage, the picadors stab the bull four times with their lances *(pics)* (this number varies according to the condition of the bull) to weaken the charging bull. The *peones* then come out and, while on the run, plant the banderillas (barbed sticks) on the withers of the bull behind the neck muscles, a maneuver to anger the bull so that it will charge the matador. The matador then enters the arena with a sword and small red cape (muleta). Before attempting to kill the bull—by thrusting the sword into the bull's heart through the top of the neck—the matador makes several daring passes with his muleta. Depending upon the matador's performance, he may be awarded the tail or ears of the bull.

Bullfrog, or American bullfrog, aquatic frog, native to the United States, living in lakes and ponds. It is green or green with brown markings above. It has a loud, bass voice and is famous for its jumping ability. Length: to 8in(20cm). Family Ranidae; species *Rana catesbiana. See also* Frog.

Bullhead, freshwater catfish originally found throughout E United States. Now farmed as food, it has been introduced in Europe and Hawaii. It has four pairs of fleshy mouth whiskers and a square tail. Length: to 24in (61cm); weight: to 8lb (3.6kg). Family Ictaluridae; species include yellow *Ictalurus natalis* and brown *Ictalurus nebulosus.*

Bullmastiff, guard and watchdog (working group) developed in England from a cross of 60% mastiff and 40% bulldog; also called gamekeeper's night dog. A powerful dog, it has a large head with broad, deep muzzle, wrinkles, and hanging lips. V-shaped ears are carried close to the cheeks; body is compact; wide-set legs are straight and well-boned; the tapered tail is set high. A short, dense coat is red, fawn, or brindle. Average size: 25–27in (63.5–68.5cm) high at shoulder; 110–130lb (50–59kg). *See also* Working Dog.

Bull Moose Party. *See* Progressive Party.

Bull Run, First Battle of (July 21, 1861), Civil War engagement, also called Manassas, fought near Manassas, Va., not far from Washington D.C. Undertrained Union troops commanded by Gen. Irvin McDowell, at first successful, were eventually routed by Confederate troops under Gen. P.G.T. Beauregard, reinforced by Gen. Thomas J. Jackson, who earned his nickname "Stonewall" at the battle. △1276.

Bull Run, Second Battle of (Aug. 28–30, 1862), Civil War battle, also called Manassas. On the old battleground of 1861, 48,000 Confederates under Gen. Robert E. Lee beat 75,000 Union soldiers under Gen. John Pope, so that once more, Lee threatened Washington D.C. Union losses were 16,000 to the Confederates' 9000. Pope was dismissed as commander of the Union army, and Gen. George McClellan, the former commander, was given command again.

Bull Snake, nonpoisonous snake found in Central and W United States and Mexico. Its powerful body is yellow marked with dark splotches. It kills by constriction. Length: to 5ft (1.5m). Family Colubridae; species *Pituophis melanoleucus. See also* Snake △584.

Bull Terrier, a sport dog (terrier group) recognized in two varieties—the white ("White Cavalier") and the colored. In the past this strongly built, active dog was used in dog pits and for bear baiting. Its large, oval head has a characteristic downface profile; ears are small and erect; the dark eyes are sunken and triangular. The bull terrier has a broad-chested body; big-boned legs; and a short tapering tail. A short, flat, harsh coat is pure white in the white variety and any color but white in the colored. Average size: 19–23in (48.5–56cm) high at shoulder, 30–36lb (135–165kg). *See also* Terrier.

Bülow, Bernhard, Prince von (1849–1929), German statesman and imperial chancellor from 1900–09. A careful conservative in domestic affairs, his facile mobility in foreign affairs heightened European tensions before World War I. He was forced to resign in 1909 because of imperial disfavor.

Bülow, Friedrich Wilhelm, Freiherr von (1755–1816), Prussian general. In the Napoleonic Wars he defeated the French at Luckau, Grossbeeren, and Dennewitz (for which he was made a count) in 1813. He also participated in the victory at Leipzig (1813) and in the Waterloo campaign in 1815.

Bulrush, grasslike herbs *(Scirpus)* of the sedge family. Growing to 9ft (2.7m), their stalks are tipped with headlike clusters of flowers. They prefer damp, boggy places of Europe, Africa, and North America.

Bultmann, Rudolf (Karl) (1884–1976), German theologian. He is one of the most controversial and influential New Testament scholars of the 20th century. His existentialist interpretations, which systematically demythologize the New Testament, are found in *The Theology of the New Testament* (1951). △1388.

Bulwer-Lytton, Edward George, 1st Baron Lytton (1803–73), English author and politician. A prolific writer in many genres, his work, including the novels *Pelham* (1828), *Eugene Aram* (1832), *The Last Days of Pompeii* (1834), and *The Coming Race* (1871), is often overly rhetorical. He was also a member of Parliament (1831–41, 1852–68).

Bumblebee, robust, black and yellow to orange bee, usually 0.75in (19mm) or more in length. It usually builds its nest in deserted mouse or bird nests. Found worldwide, they are important pollinators of clover, due to their very long tongues. Family Apidae, tribe Bombini. *See also* Bee.

Bunche, Ralph Johnson (1904–71), US statesman, b. Detroit. He headed the political science department at Howard University from 1929 until World War II, when he became chief research analyst for the Office of Strategic Services. Following two years in the State Department (1944–46) he joined the United Nations as director of the trusteeship division. As secretary of the Palestine Commission, he brought peace to the Holy Land, for which he was awarded the Nobel Peace Prize (1950). In 1957 he became UN undersecretary for special political affairs. From 1967 until his death, he was undersecretary general of the United Nations.

Bundesrat, upper house of the West German and Austrian parliaments. In West Germany, it is composed of voting representatives elected by the 10 federal states and of non-voting West Berliners, serving four-year terms. The Bundesrat acts on measures sent from the Bundestag, the lower house. Historically, the Bundesrat acted as the chief executive organ of the German Confederation (1815–66). *See also* Bundestag.

Bundestag, 496-member lower house of the West German parliament, responsible for initiating legislation, ratifying the most important treaties, and electing the West German chancellor. With an equal number of representatives from the state parliaments, the Bundestag elects the federal president. There are also 22 non-voting members from West Berlin. *See also* Bundesrat.

Bunin, Ivan A(lekseevich) (1870–1953), Russian writer. Opposed to the 1917 revolution, he left Russia and settled in France. Influenced by Turgenev, his works lament the passing of the old Russian order. They include the novel *The Village* (1910) and the short story "The Gentleman from San Francisco" (1916). He was awarded the Nobel Prize for literature in 1933.

Bunker Hill, Battle of, Revolutionary War battle that took place on June 17, 1775, on Boston's Charlestown peninsula. The first major battle of the Revolution, it actually was fought south of Bunker Hill on Breed's Hill, where the Americans built hasty fortifications. Technically defeated, the Americans earned a moral victory by inflicting heavy losses on the British. △1218.

Bunsen, Robert Wilhelm (1811–99), German chemist, professor at Marburg and later at Heidelberg. His early work on organic arsenicals caused him

Buenos Aires, Argentina

Poland
Union of Soviet Socialist Republics
Czechoslovakia
Hungary
Romania
Yugoslavia
Ruse
Varna
BLACK SEA
BULGARIA
Sofia
(Sofija)
Burgas
Plovdiv
Albania
Turkey
Greece
IONIAN SEA
0
400km

Bulgaria

Bullfrog

Ralph Bunche

the loss of an eye in an explosion and also severe poisoning. When he recovered he widened his scope, designing several calorimeters, a carbon-zinc electric cell (Bunsen cell), a grease-spot photometer, and contributed to the development of the gas burner associated with his name. He discovered an arsenic poisoning antidote, and studied the properties of magnesium. With his assistant Gustav Kirchhoff, he devised the science of spectroscopy, using it to discover two new elements (cesium and rubidium).

Bunsen Burner, gas burner widely used in science laboratories. It is named for its inventor, Robert W. Bunsen. The burner is a 5-in (13-cm) upright tube, usually of brass, attached to a gas source. It has an adjustable valve at its base to admit air. The flame is smokeless and intense.

Bunshaft, Gordon (1909–), US architect, b. Buffalo, N.Y. Chief designer for the architectural firm Skidmore, Owings, and Merrill, he designed Lever House, New York (1952), a glass curtain-walled skyscraper that created an international style. Other buildings include Connecticut General Life Insurance headquarters, Bloomfield, Ohio (1957), Beinecke Rare Book and Manuscript Library, Yale University (1963), and the Johnson Library, University of Texas, Austin (1971). △1322.

Bunting, brightly colored finch found almost worldwide. These birds with canarylike bills build cup-shaped nests for pale spotted eggs (2–6). Males of the New World genus *Passerina* are brightly colored; length 5in (12.5cm). Females are smaller and duller. Buntings of the Old World genus *Emberiza* are slightly larger and dull colored with streaks. The circumpolar snow bunting *(Plectrophenax nivalis nivalis)* is almost white. Family Fringillidae.

Buñuel, Luis (1900–), Spanish filmmaker working outside Spain. His films were concerned with unmasking religious and social hypocrisies by means of surrealist comic vision. Among his major works were *Un Chien Andalou* (1928), *Viridiana* (1961), *Belle de Jour* (1967), *The Discreet Charm of the Bourgeoisie* (1972), and *The Phantom of Liberty* (1974). *See also* Surrealism.

Bunyan, John (1628–88), English preacher and author. A Parliamentarian soldier during the English Civil War, he became a Puritan minister in 1655 and twice suffered imprisonment for his nonconformist religious activities. His writings, popular and colloquial in style, include *Grace Abounding* (1666), and *The Pilgrim's Progress* (1678). *See also* Pilgrim's Progress, The. △1852.

Bunyan, Paul, US folk hero. Tales of the giant lumberjack and his Blue ox, Babe, appeared in the mid-19th century lumber camps, telling of a giant able to cut miles of trees with a swing of his ax and crediting him with the creation of the Rocky Mountains and the Grand Canyon. Babe helped shape the land by drinking rivers dry.

Buoyancy, the upward force experienced by an object in a fluid. The object actually encounters pressure from all sides, but the pressure on its lower part is greatest because of the increasing depth of the fluid. Thus the resultant of all these forces is a force acting upward. This upward force is equal to the weight of the water displaced. *See also* Archimedes' Principle. △1496.

Burbages, The, Elizabethan actors. James (died 1597), one of earl of Leicester's players, built the first English playhouse, The Theatre, in Shoreditch (1596). His son, Richard (1567?–1619), excelled as an actor in the tragedies of Shakespeare and Jonson. In 1598 he and his brother Cuthbert moved The Theatre to Bankside and, taking Shakespeare as a partner, founded the famous Globe Theatre.

Burbank, Luther (1849–1926), US horticulturist, b. Lancaster, Mass. Through the scientific development of numerous useful varieties of fruits, grains, and flowers, he helped to elevate plant breeding to a modern science. On his world famous experimental farm in Santa Rosa, Calif., Burbank utilized revolutionary breeding methods to develop more than 800 new strains and varieties of plants, including 113 new varieties of plums and prunes, 10 new berries, and 50 varieties of lilies. His method, which consisted of obtaining good seedlings by gathering multiple crosses of foreign and native strains that were then grafted onto mature plants, allowed for a speedy assessment of hybrid characteristics, aiding both the study of genetics and the development of plants for commercial use.

Burbank, city in S California, 10mi (16km) NW of Los Angeles; site of movie and television studios; chief industry is aircraft manufacture. Inc. 1911. Pop. (1970) 88,871.

Burbot, freshwater codfish found around the North Pole to Eurasia and North America; also in Great Lakes. A slender fish, it spawns in winter. Length: to 32in (81.3cm); weight: 12lb (514kg). Family Gadidae; species *Lota lota*. △516.

Burbridge (née Peachey), (Eleanor) Margaret (*c.* 1925–), English astronomer. She was professor of astronomy at the University of California, San Diego, from 1965, and director of the Royal Observatory, Greenwich (1972–73). With her husband Geoffrey, she contributed significantly to the study of quasars.

Burdock, weedy herb found throughout Europe, North Africa, and North America. It has large, basal leaves and thistlelike purple flowerheads covered by stiff, hooked bracts. The common or lesser burdock, *Arctium minus*, is a biennial with reddish-purple flowers. Height: to 9ft(2.7m). Family Compositae.

Burdwan, city in NE India, on Damodar River; site of ancient temples and palaces. Industries: rice and oilseed milling, trade center, tools, cutlery. Pop. 152,-239.

Bureaucracy, body of appointive government officials who implement and often influence public policy. Characterized by an administrative hierarchy resembling a pyramid, bureaucracies are ranked from the top down, according to responsibilities, duties, and qualifications. Bureaucracy is popularly associated with "red tape" and with functioning by rigid and arbitrary routine. △904, 928.

Buret. △1568.

Burger, Warren Earl (1907–), chief justice of the US Supreme Court (1969–), b. St. Paul, Minn. In 1931 he received a law degree and began practicing and teaching law. He was assistant attorney general in charge of the civil division of the department of justice (1953–56). He served as judge of US Court of Appeals in Washington, D.C. (1956–69) and was then appointed by Pres. Richard M. Nixon as chief justice of the Supreme Court (1969). Before the appointment, he was active in criminal law reform and critical of many Warren Court decisions on criminal cases. A conservative, his court has restrained and at times reversed liberal decisions of the Warren Court. In *Harris* v. *New York* (1971) the Court reversed *Miranda* v. *Arizona,* thereby legalizing the use of a suspect's statement, made while in police custody, for trial purposes. The ruling on the Federal Election Campaign Act of 1974 (1976) upheld most of the act, but stated that the commission that would administer federal political-matching funds must be appointed by the president rather than Congress.

Burgess, Anthony (John Burgess Wilson) (1917–), English novelist and critic. Malaya, where he lived (1954–59), is the setting for a trilogy—*Time for a Tiger* (1956), *The Enemy in the Blanket* (1957), and *Beds in the East* (1959). In later novels he shows an interest in projecting social trends in linguistic effects, and in religious symbolism, as in *A Clockwork Orange* (1962).

Burghley, William Cecil, 1st Baron (1520–98). *See* Cecil, William, 1st Baron Burghley.

Burgos, city in N Spain, 130mi (209km) N of Madrid; capital of Burgos prov.; capital of kingdom of Castile (9th-16th centuries); home and burial place of El Cid; served as capital of Gen. Francisco Franco's regime during Civil War (1936–39); site of Gothic cathedral (1221), Church of San Esteban, and Arco de Santa Maria; important trade and tourist center. Industries: fabrics, soap, furniture, shoes, wine. Founded 884. Pop. 119,915.

Burgoyne, John (1722–92), British general during the Revolutionary War. He served in Boston (1775) and Canada (1776). Campaigning in New York State, he secured Crown Point and Ft. Ticonderoga, but was forced to surrender his forces at Saratoga, Oct. 17, 1777. △1218.

Burgundy, historical region of France that now includes depts. of Yonne, Côte-d'Or, Saône-et-Loire, Ain, and Nièvra; contains numerous medieval Romanesque churches; Dijon is its historical capital. A rich agricultural region, it has been known for its wine since 50 BC. Burgundy's golden age began in 1361 when France's John II made his son, Philip the Bold, duke of Burgundy. These dukes dominated French politics in the early 15th century. Their last reigning duke, Charles the Bold, unsuccessfully challenged power of Louis XI in 1465; Burgundy as a state ceased to exist after 1477 when Louis XI made it part of the crown lands. △1096.

Burgundy, School of, group of Flemish panel painters and miniaturists who worked at Dijon between 1390 and 1420. Their work was intended for Chartreuse de Champmol near Dijon, but their style of realism remained Flemish. The master of Flemalle and the Van Eyck brothers have their roots here. △1136

Burial Rites. △652, 990.

Burke, Edmund (1729–97), Irish political figure and author. He became secretary to British prime minister Rockingham and entered Parliament (1765). He attacked increasing royal power and supported the parliamentary process. With Charles J. Fox he sought wiser treatment for the Catholics and Americans. As forces' paymaster (1782–83) he reduced crown patronage. He instigated the impeachment of Warren Hastings in an attempt to reform India's government (1788). Burke believed in liberty based on order, with change being gradual. His *Reflections on the Revolution in France* (1790) shows his horror at the radicalism of the French Revolution, and he broke with Fox over the reform question (1791). △898, 1218, 1288.

Burlesque, in the United States, a type of popular entertainment accenting sex and comedy and devised by Michael Bennett Leavitt (1865). The peak in its popularity was the 1900s and it spawned dozens of famous comics and singers. After World War I, to compete with films, it introduced the striptease. Though all but faded from existence, elements exist in other forms of popular entertainment.

Burlingame, suburban city in W California, on the W shore of San Francisco Bay; named for US diplomat Anson Burlingame; site of Russell College (1928). Founded 1868; inc. 1908. Pop. (1970) 27,320.

Burlington, city in SE Iowa, built on four hills overlooking the Mississippi River; seat of Des Moines co; site of Zebulon Pike's fort (1805); shipping center. Industries: farming, explosives, tractors. Settled 1832; inc. 1836. Pop. (1970) 32,366.

Burlington, city in N central North Carolina, 18mi (29km) E of Greensboro; site of Elon College. Industries: textiles, hosiery, yarn. Inc. 1893. Pop. (1970) 35,930.

Burlington, city in NW Vermont, on Lake Champlain; seat of Chittenden co; scene of British naval attack in War of 1812; birthplace of John Dewey; burial place of Ethan Allen. Largest city in the state, it is site of University of Vermont and Trinity College. Industries: metallurgy, missile parts, textiles, wood products. Settled 1773; inc. 1865. Pop. (1970) 38,633.

Burma (Myanma), an isolated socialist republic in Asia. Its greatest asset is its mineral wealth. The famous WWII Burma Road supply line to China from 1938–42 ran through the country.

Land and economy. Circled by barriers of imposing mountain ranges to the N, E, and W (Saramati is 15,000ft (4,575m) above sea level), Burma has been isolated from outside contact; its forests and rivers have discouraged travel within the country. The Irrawaddy River is its economic lifeline and major transportation system. Rangoon is its chief port. Burma's monsoon climate results in yearly rainfall of 30in (76cm) in the central dry zone to 200in (508cm) on the coast. An agricultural country, it once led the world in rice exports, but shifting world markets have lowered sales. Exports are ore, precious stones, lumber. The chief import is industrial machinery.

People. Burmans comprise the main ethnic unit with smaller groups of Karens, Chins, and Kachins. Eighty-five percent practice Thervada Buddhism. Burmese is the principal language. Education is free from primary school to college. Traditional Buddhist schools exist in the rural areas. Literacy is 64%.

Government. Burma is ruled by military decree. Army officers and civilians constitute the ruling body, the Union Revolutionary Council.

History. Kublai Khan's Mongols invaded in 1287 and started centuries of warring dynasties until 1824, when Burma was annexed to British India. In 1937 a constitution allowed some self-government. Occupied by the Japanese in WWII, it suffered great devastation until 1945 when the Japanese were defeated and Burma became a parliamentary democracy. In 1962, Gen. Ne Win grabbed power from elected premier U Nu and set Burma on a socialist path with a neutral foreign policy. Uprisings by Communist guerrillas and pressures from ethnic minorities are its most pressing problems.

PROFILE

Official name: Socialist Republic of the Union of Burma
Area: 261,789sq mi (678,034sq km)
Population: 31,200,000; *Density:* 119per sq mi (46per sq km)
Chief cities: Rangoon (capital); Mandalay; Moulmein
Government: Socialist republic
Religion: Buddhist (major)
Language: Burmese
Monetary unit: Kyat
Gross national product: $2,800,000,000
Per capita income: $82
Industries: processed food, textiles, tobacco, and wood products
Agriculture: rice, cotton, teak, rubber, sesame, millet
Minerals: petroleum, lead, silver, tin, tungsten, zinc, rubies, sapphires, jade
Trading partners: United States, United Kingdom, Japan, European Common Market

Burma Road, major ground transportation route into Nationalist China during World War II. Closed by Japanese pressure, the road from the railhead at Lashio, Burma, to Siakwan in Yunnan prov., China, was reopened by Allied forces in 1945. Until then China's links with the outside were primarily by air.

Burmese, the official language of Burma, spoken by about three-fourths of the population, or some 25 million people. It belongs to the Tibeto-Burman branch of the Sino-Tibetan family of languages.

Burmese Cat, short-haired domestic cat breed developed in the United States during the 1930s. Not an oriental type, it has a round head, yellow or gold almond-shaped eyes, wide-set ears, and a thick, muscular body. The flat, satinlike coat of this dainty, affectionate cat is solid sable brown. Varieties are Blue and Champagne.

Burnet, (Sir) Frank Macfarlane (1899–), Australian virologist and immunologist. He shared the 1960 Nobel Prize in physiology or medicine with Peter Medawar for their discovery of acquired immunological tolerance. Burnet also studied the multiplication of bacterial viruses and antibody formation.

Burnet, Gilbert (1643–1715), British churchman and historian. An advisor to William and Mary, he was appointed bishop of Salisbury by them. His *History of the Reformation in England* (3 vols., 1679–1714), based on original sources, and his *History of His Own Time* (published 1723–24) are invaluable studies of 17th-century Britain. His *Exposition of the 39 Articles* (1699) advocated a more open theology for the Church of England.

Burnet, common name for perennials native to the north temperate zone. The leaves, comprised of serrated leaflets, are sometimes used in salads when young. Small individual flowers are bunched along tall spikes. Conspicuously long stamens give the spikes a feathery look. The American burnet grows to 5ft (1.5m.). Family Rosaceae; genus *Sanguisarba.*

Burnett, Frances (Eliza Hodgson) (1849–1924), US author, b. England. She is most noted for *Little Lord Fauntleroy* (1886), a rags-to-riches tale. She is also remembered for her last children's book, *The Secret Garden* (1911).

Burnett, W(illiam) R(iley) (1899–), US author, b. Springfield, Ohio. His novels about such types as gangsters and prizefighters include *Little Caesar* (1929), which was made into a film starring Edward G. Robinson (1930), *Dark Hazard* (1944), and *The Asphalt Jungle* (1949).

Burney, Fanny (1752–1840), English novelist and diarist. Her most successful novel *Evelina* (1778) was followed by *Camilla* (1796) and *The Wanderer* (1814). Her diaries and letters vividly describe contemporary life. △1188.

Burnham, Daniel (Hudson) (1846–1912), US architect, b. Henderson, N.Y. With partner John Wellborn Root he was an important influence in the development of Chicago's commercial architecture, designing such buildings as the Rookery (1886) and the Reliance Building (1890), which utilized steel-frame construction. Burnham also designed the Flatiron Building in New York City (1901), and Union Station in Washington, D.C. (1909). Burnham's famous plan for the city of Chicago (1907–09) provided for the preservation of wooded areas and parklands in anticipation of large-scale development and population increases. He also prepared plans for several other cities in the United States and the Philippines.

Burnham, Forbes (1923–), prime minister of Guiana (1964–). Founder of the People's National Congress (1955), Burnham was chief executive when British Guiana attained independence (1966) and became a republic (1970). His party increased its electoral majority in the 1973 contest.

Burns, George (1896–), US comedian, b. New York City. With his wife Gracie Allen, he starred in vaudeville, on radio and on TV's *Burns and Allen Show* (1950–58). In 1975 he received an Academy Award for *The Sunshine Boys,* a film with Walter Matthau.

Burns, Robert (1759–96), the national poet of Scotland. The son of a tenant farmer, he began to write poetry in 1783. In 1786 he published *Poems, Chiefly in the Scottish Dialect* to raise money to emigrate to Jamaica. The huge success of this volume led him to change his plans and move to Edinburgh, where he became the chief attraction of literary and social circles. A second, expanded edition of his poems appeared in 1787. In 1788 he left Edinburgh, married, and settled on a farm in Ellisland where he remained until 1791, when he obtained a post in the excise office at Dumfries. He died after an attack of rheumatic fever. In his poetry he combined Scottish dialect and folk idiom with the craftmanship of the finest British poets. He added new vitality to English poetry, which had grown stilted. He wrote nearly 300 songs set to ancient Scottish airs, including "Auld Lang Syne," "Flow Gently, Sweet Afton," and "Comin' Thro' the Rye." His lyric poems, such as "To a Mouse" and "To a Louse," were often satiric, yet playful, as were such longer poems as "The Cotter's Saturday Night" and "Tam o'Shanter."

Burns, damage to body tissue by heat, chemicals, electricity, or radiation. First-degree burns involve only the superficial skin, second- and third-degree burns penetrate progressively deeper. Treatment includes relief of pain, control of infection, prevention of shock. △724, 758.

Burnside, Ambrose Everett (1824–81), Union Civil War general, b. Liberty, Ind. He participated in the Battle of Bull Run (1861). He led the Army of the Potomac in the Union defeat at Fredericksburg (1862). He was relieved of command of IX Corp following Petersburg (1864). After the war, he was governor of Rhode Island and US senator (1875–81).

Burr, Aaron (1756–1836), vice president of the United States, b. Newark. A Revolutionary War veteran and senator from New York (1791–97), he ran for vice president on Thomas Jefferson's Democratic-Republican ticket in 1800. Burr and Jefferson were tied in the electoral college but Jefferson was elected president with Alexander Hamilton's support. Hamilton's public attacks on Burr led to a duel in which Burr killed Hamilton (1804). His political career ended by this duel, Burr engaged with Gen. James Wilkenson in an apparent conspiracy to establish an independent republic in the Southwest. He was tried for treason but was acquitted (1807) and spent the rest of his career practicing law.

Burro, Spanish word for ass, small domesticated ass used as a pack animal in SW United States and in Mexico. A long-eared, sturdy animal derived from the Nubian wild ass, it is brown, gray, or black. Many are now feral. Family Equidae; species *Equus asinus asinus. See also* Ass.

Burroughs, Edgar Rice (1875–1950), US author of adventure novels, b. Chicago. A prolific writer, he is noted for the Tarzan books, a series of 23 jungle novels, the first of which was *Tarzan of the Apes* (1914). Motion pictures and comic books based on the Tarzan novels were enormously successful. Burroughs also wrote romances about life on other planets, which were early examples of science fiction.

Burroughs, William (1914–), US novelist, b. St. Louis. Regarded as a founder of the Beat Generation; his most prominent work, *Naked Lunch* (1959), deals in part with his addiction to heroin. Other works, experimental in style, include *The Ticket That Exploded* (1967) and *The Wild Boys* (1971). *See also* Beat Generation.

Burrows, Abe (1910–), US playwright, director, and humorist, b. New York City. He wrote many radio and TV shows, such as "Duffy's Tavern" (1941–45) and "Abe Burrows Almanac" (1950). He also appeared on radio and TV as well as in theaters and nightclubs. He wrote Broadway plays (*Can Can,* 1953; *Say, Darling,* 1958) and directed his own and others'.

Luther Burbank

Warren Burger

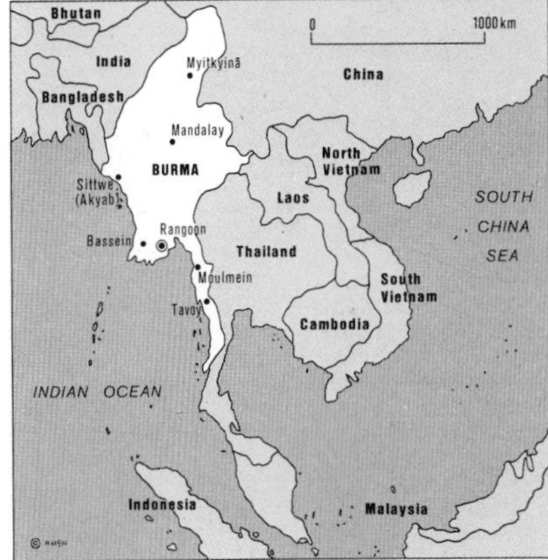
Bhutan
0
1000km
India
Myitkyinā
China
Bangladesh
Mandalay
North
Vietnam
BURMA
Sittwe
(Akyab)
Laos
SOUTH
CHINA
SEA
Rangoon
Bassein
Thailand
Moulmein
South
Vietnam
Tavoy
Cambodia
INDIAN OCEAN
Indonesia
Malaysia

Burma

Burnet

He received the N.Y. Drama Critics Award as co-author of *Guys and Dolls* (1951) and *How to Succeed in Business Without Really Trying* (1961), for which he was also awarded a Pulitzer Prize and a Tony Award. Among his other works are a song "The Girl with the Three Blue Eyes" and the screenplay for *Solid Gold Cadillac* (1956).

Bursa, formerly Brusa, city in NW Turkey, approx. 13mi (21km) SE of Sea of Marmara; capital of Bursa prov.; ancient city of Prusa founded by King Prusias; now a rail terminus and trade center. Industries: textiles (especially silk), carpets, tiles, tobacco, rice, grains. Pop. 275,900.

Bursae. △682.

Bursitis, inflammation of a sac or cavity usually near a joint. Cause may be injury or disease. It is characterized by pain, swelling, limited motion.

Burton, Harold H(itz) (1888–1964), US jurist, mayor of Cleveland (1935–40) and US senator from Ohio (1941–45), b. Jamaica Plain, Mass. He was appointed associate justice of the US Supreme Court in 1945, where he shared the views of judges Vinson and Frankfurter favoring judicial restraint, the loyalty oath, and other civil liberty restrictions. He did, however, side with the liberal wing on civil rights decisions, most notably *Brown* v. *Board of Education* (1954). After retiring in 1958, he served occasionally on the court of appeals in Washington, D.C.

Burton, Richard (1925–), Welsh actor. Noted for his distinctive speaking voice, he is most noted for his performances in dramatic roles. His major British roles include appearances in the Shakespearean repertory with the Royal Shakespeare Theatre and the Old Vic Company. His US successes include *Camelot* (1961), *Hamlet* (1964), *Equus* (1976) on Broadway; his films include *The Robe* (1953), *Cleopatra* (1962), *Who's Afraid of Virginia Woolf?* (1966). He was married to the actress Elizabeth Taylor.

Burton, (Sir) Richard Francis (1821–90), English explorer and specialist on the Orient. In 1853, disguised as an Afghan pilgrim, he made a pilgrimage to Medina and Mecca, being one of the first Europeans to visit those cities. On his second trip to East Africa with John Speke in 1858, he discovered Lake Tanganyika. From 1861 until his death, he served in the British diplomatic service. The author of more than 30 travel books, he was best known for his translation of the Oriental tales, the "Arabian Nights." △874.

Burundi, republic in E central Africa, headed by a president, bordered by Rwanda (N), Tanzania (E), Lake Tanganyika (SW), and Zaire (W). The capital is Bujumbura. Located near the equator, the country has two wet and two dry seasons with an annual rainfall of 31–57in (79–145cm); prolonged droughts have often resulted in serious famines. The lowlands of the W (Ruzizi River Valley and E shore of Lake Tanganyika) rise rapidly into mountains from 7,000–9,000ft (2,135–2,745m) and then fall into lower plateaus of 4,500–6,000ft (1,373–1,830m), where most of the population is concentrated. A predominantly agricultural economy (41% of land is arable) supports widespread subsistence farming. Coffee is the main export crop; cotton and tea are also exported; some cattle are raised. Cassiterite (tin) is the chief mineral. The Hutu or Bahutu comprise 86% of population and are mainly farmers. The Tutsi (Watutsi) are cattle raisers and warriors and account for 12% of inhabitants; they are socially above the Hutu. Elementary schools enroll about 40% of children in this age group; few go on to secondary or college education.

In the 19th century the country was ruled by a king (Tutsi). Burundi and Rwanda joined German East Africa in 1890. Germany actually began to rule in 1897. During WWI Belgium occupied the country, and in 1919 the League of Nations made it a Belgian mandate. In 1946 it became a UN trust territory, and in 1962 it became independent. Since then it has suffered many power struggles between Hutu and Tutsi. A new constitution was adopted in 1970, but fighting broke out shortly afterward, resulting in death for many Hutus.

PROFILE

Official name: Republic of Burundi
Area: 10,747sq mi (27,835sq km)
Population: 3,800,000
Chief cities: Bujumbura (capital); Gitega
Religion: Christianity and tribal
Language: Kirundi and French
Monetary unit: Franc

Bury Bible. △1082.

Burying Beetle, or carrion beetle, medium-sized beetle found in all temperate regions. They bury and lay their eggs in dead mice, frogs, birds, and other small animals. Genus *Necrophorus.*

Bury Saint Edmunds, market town in S England; farming region. St Edmund, last king of the Angles, was buried here 903. Industries: sugar refining, brewing, agricultural machinery. Pop. 25,629.

Bus. △1686, 1700.

Bush, Vannevar (1890–1974), US electrical engineer, b. Everett, Mass. From 1932–38 he was vice president and dean of engineering at Massachusetts Institute of Technology. He headed the World War II Office of Scientific Research and Development, overseeing the initial stages of the atom bomb project. From 1938–55 he was president of the Carnegie Institute of Washington.

Bush Baby, or galago, primitive squirrellike primate of African forests and bushlands. They are usually gray or brown with a white stripe between the eyes. Bush babies are gregarious, nocturnal, tree dwellers, often domesticated as pets. Genera *Galago, Euoticus. See also* Primates. △554.

Bush Ballad, early Australian verse celebrating the exploits of the common people. It has been called the first true Australian literary form. Sometimes sung, bush ballads are simple and often crude but mirror a vital, independent society.

Bushbuck. *See* Kudu, Nyala, Sitatunga, and Bushbuck.

Bush Cat. *See* Serval.

Bushido, or Way of the Samurai, a code of conduct in Japan not unlike the chivalric codes of European knights. It stressed complete loyalty to one's master, bravery, and a hard spartan life-style. Unlike European knights, however, Samurai were encouraged to take pride in their literary and educational accomplishments.

Bushmaster, largest New World pit viper, found in Central America and N South America. It has large venom glands and long fangs and is gray and brown with a bold diamond pattern. Length: to 12ft (3.7m). Family Crotalidae; species *Lachesis muta. See also* Pit Viper.

Bushmen, or San, Khoisan-speaking people of southern Africa; characteristically of short stature, with a leathery yellowish skin and large buttocks. Until recently they had a hunting and gathering culture, with little value for material possessions. However, only a few thousand still follow traditional ways, mostly in the Kalahari region; others have become assimilated into white and Bantu agricultural society as hired laborers. △660, 878.

Bushrangers, bandits who terrorized the Australian outback in the 19th century. Many were escaped convicts, others were adventurers who after 1850 attacked gold convoys. The notorious Kelly gang was wiped out in 1880.

Business Cycles, patterned movements of the economy consisting of recurring periods of prosperity and recession. Normally measured by the industrial production of the economy, a business cycle may be divided into four phases: depression, recovery, prosperity, and recession. Depression is the turning point of the lower portion of the business cycle; prosperity is the turning point of the upper portion. Recession and depression are usually associated with rising unemployment and decreases in consumer buying power. Recovery and prosperity are normally associated with low unemployment, expanding consumer purchasing power, and rising prices. The short-run business cycle consists of seasonal fluctuations in the economy as well as short periods of expansion and contraction. The long-run business cycle involves major movement of the economy over many years.

Bussing. △1360.

Bustamante, William Alexander (1884–), prime minister of Jamaica (1962–67), founder and president of the Jamaica Labour party (1943). As leader of the opposition (1955–62), he favored Jamaica's withdrawal from the West Indies Federation. He became Jamaica's first prime minister in 1962.

Bustard, shy, heavy-bodied, ostrichlike bird of Eastern Hemisphere grasslands and semideserts that flies strongly and runs swiftly. It has a thick bill, a long neck and legs, gray or brown plummage with white spots on top and black spots below. It feeds on small animals, and lays eggs (1–5) in a ground depression. Height: 14.5–52in (37–132cm). Family Otididae. △384.

Butadiene (1,3-butadiene), gaseous flammable hydrocarbon (formula $CH_2{:}CHCH{:}CH_2$) made from butenes or by cracking naphtha. It is copolymerized with styrene to produce synthetic rubbers. Properties: sp. gr. 0.62; melt. pt. −164.03°F (−108.91°C); boil. pt. 24.06°F (−4.41°C).

Butane, gaseous flammable colorless hydrocarbon (C_4H_{10}), obtained as a byproduct of petroleum refining. It is used as a fuel gas and in the manufacture of synthetic rubber. Properties: melt. pt. −217.03°F (−138.35°C); boil. pt. 31.1°F (−0.5°C).

Butcherbird. *See* Shrike.

Butler, James, 12th Earl and 1st Duke of Ormonde. *See* Ormonde, James Butler, 12th Earl and 1st Duke of.

Butler, Joseph. △860.

Butler, Samuel (1835–1902), English satiric novelist, scientific writer, and translator. Emigrated to New Zealand in 1859. Returning to England, he wrote *Erewhon* (1872), *The Way of All Flesh* (1903), travel books, articles on Homer, and several works opposing Darwin's theory of evolution.

Butt, Isaac (1813–79), Irish political figure. Initially a conservative lawyer and member of Parliament, he became increasingly nationalistic because of the failures of British rule in Ireland. He demanded land reform and led the Home Rule movement in Parliament (1870) until supplanted by Charles Stewart Parnell. *See also* Home Rule.

Butte, city in SW Montana, in plateau of Rocky Mts; seat of Silver Bow co; site of Montana College of Mineral Science and Technology (1893), headquarters of Deer Lodge National Forest. Industries: silver, copper, and manganese mining. Founded 1864; inc. as town 1876; as city 1879. Pop. 23,368.

Butte, hard rock remnant covering soft sediment in an arid region. When wind and water erosion wear away softer rock on the slopes of a hill, the resulting formation is a columnar structure with nearly vertical sides. △260.

Butter. △374.

Buttercup, or crowfoot, herbaceous flowering plant distributed worldwide. Numerous stamens and pistils form a button or bushy cluster at the flower center and leaves are palmate and deeply cut. The common buttercup *(Ranunculus acris),* found in fields and meadows, is an erect, hairy plant with glossy yellow flowers. Height: to 3ft (91cm). Family Ranunculaceae.

Butterfish, marine commercial fish found along Atlantic and Pacific coasts. A favorite sport fish for panfrying, it is silvery-gray or blue with dark spots. Length: 12in (30.5cm); weight: 1.25lb (0.57kg). Family Stromateidae; species includes Atlantic *Peprilus triacanthus* and California pompano *Peprilus simillimus.*

Butterfly, day-active, usually brightly colored insect. The butterfly is distinguished from the moth by its slender body and knobbed antennae. It holds its wings vertically when at rest. Order Lepidoptera; family Papilionoidea. *See also* Lepidoptera. △492, 502.

Butterfly Fish, tropical marine fish found around coral in shallow waters. A popular aquarium fish, it has a disc-shaped, compressed body with extended snout. Colors and patterns are bright and varied. Length: 6–8in (15.2–20.3cm). Family Chaetodontidae; species includes common *Chaetodon ocellatus.* △514.

Butternut, a deciduous tree *Juglans cinerea* of the Walnut family, native to E North America, growing to 90ft (27m). The fruit is ovalish, and the nut is furrowed, oily, and sweet.

Butterwort, any of a large group (genus *Pinguicula* of the family Lentibulariaceae) of carnivorous bog plants that capture and digest insects in a sticky secretion ("butter") on their leaves. Butterworts are stemless and bear single white, purple, or yellow flowers on a leafless stalk.

Button, Richard Totten ("Dick") (1929–), US figure skater, b. Englewood, N. J. He was 16 when he won the US senior figure skating championship. He held the world's title (1948–52) and won two Olympic gold medals (1948,1952).

Buttonwood. *See* Sycamore.

Buttress. △1094, 1056.

Butz, Earl (Lauer) (1909–), US educator and cabinet member, b. Albion, Ind. An instructor of agricultural economics at Purdue University (1935–54), he was appointed assistant secretary of agriculture by President Eisenhower (1954–59). Dean of agriculture at Purdue (1957–67), he then became dean of continuing education until 1971, when appointed secretary of agriculture by President Nixon. He resigned in 1976 after public protest of some racially offensive remarks.

Buzzard, slow-moving hawk with broad, rounded wings, fan-shaped tail, sharp hooked beak, and sharp talons. The common European buzzard *(Buteo buteo)* is brown above and mottled with white below. North American representatives include the red-shouldered hawk *(Buteo lineatus)* and red-tailed hawk *(Buteo jamaicensis)*. In the Western Hemisphere the term "buzzard" is often used for the turkey vulture *(Cathartes aura)*. Length: 23–32in (59–81cm). Genus *Buteo*.

Byng, John (1704–57), British admiral, shot for neglect of duty. In 1756, just before the Seven Years' War, he was sent to protect Britain's base on the Mediterranean island of Minorca but failed to drive off an attacking French fleet. Believing himself seriously outgunned and outmanned, he withdrew to Gibraltar, where he was court-martialled, found guilty, and given the mandatory death sentence. Despite a recommendation for mercy, Byng was shot to appease the enraged public.

Byrd, Harry Flood (1887–1966), US public official, b. Martinsburg, W. Va. A Democrat, he served as governor of Virginia (1926–30) and was US senator from Virginia (1933–65). He was a conservative Southerner and opposed liberal measures. For many years he was head of the Senate finance committee.

Byrd, Richard Evelyn (1888–1957), naval officer and polar explorer, b. Winchester, Va. He entered the Navy (1912), retired (1916), and was recalled and trained as an aviator (1917). With copilot Floyd Bennett, he led the first flight over South Pole (1926) and the first of five North Pole expeditions (1928). He spent five months alone in Antarctica (1934), publishing experiences in *Alone* (1938). His last Antarctic trip (1955–56) was in preparation for US participation in the International Geophysical Year.

Byrd, William (1543–1623), English musician, who became the greatest composer of the Elizabethan period. A lifelong Roman Catholic, Byrd was appointed by Elizabeth I to be joint organist of the Chapel Royal with Thomas Tallis, whom he succeeded (1585). With Tallis, he was granted a monopoly to print music. Byrd was master of all the musical forms of his day, important for his madrigals, the body of distinguished church music that he wrote for both Catholic and Anglican services.

Byrnes, James F(rancis) (1879–1972), US lawyer and statesman, b. Charleston, S.C. A US congressman (1911–25) and senator (1931–41) from South Carolina, appointed associate justice of the US Supreme Court by Franklin D. Roosevelt in 1941, he resigned in 1942 to direct the Office of Economic Stabilization. US secretary of state (1945–47) and delegate to the UN (1953), he was governor of South Carolina (1951–55), advocating segregation and states' rights.

Byron, George Gordon Noel Byron, 6th Baron (1788–1824), English poet. Lord Byron is as much remembered for his flamboyant, romantic life as for his poetry. He was born with a club foot and as a child suffered poverty and abuse from his unstable mother. At the age of 10, he inherited the title and estates of a great-uncle. His first collection of poems, published in 1807, was badly received; but with *English Bards and Scotch Reviewers* (1809), a satirical work, his reputation was made. In 1812 he published the first of two cantos of *Childe Harold's Pilgrimage*. It was a brilliant success, and Byron immediately became the literary and social lion of London. Identified with the romantic, idealistic hero of his poem, Byron was widely regarded as the personification of the romantic poet; the term "Byronic hero" was coined as much to describe him as the protagonists of his poems. Byron embarked on a series of love affairs, most notoriously one with Lady Caroline Lamb, wife of William Lamb (later Lord Melbourne). He apparently also had homosexual affairs and a liaison with his half sister. In 1815 he married Annabella Milbanke, but the marriage lasted only a year, primarily because of the rumors of Byron's varied sex life. The scandals of his personal life increased, and Byron left England for Italy.

Despite a life of dissipation in Italy and Switzerland, Byron produced a large body of work, including Cantos III and IV of *Childe Harold* (1816, 1817), *The Prisoner of Chillon* (1816), *Beppo* (1818), *Mazeppa* (1819), and *Don Juan* (1819–24). He became interested in the cause of the Greek independence fighters against Turkish domination. He went to Greece to fight with them but contracted brain fever and died shortly after his arrival. In his own day, Byron was highly regarded as a lyric poet and was ranked with Percy Bysshe Shelley and John Keats as the great trio of English Romanticism. Modern critics, however, tend to regard his satirical works more highly than his lyrical poems. *Don Juan* is generally regarded as his masterpiece. △1222,1240.

Bystander Apathy, failure of bystanders to become involved enough to protect the welfare of people who are in trouble. Social psychologists have shown that such bystanders may not be "apathetic" at all, but rather may not act because they fear reprisals or injury to themselves. What a bystander will do or not do depends on many factors and is not easily predictable.

Byzantine Architecture, architecture characterized by the use of the dome to cover polygonal and square churches, baptistries, and tombs and dating from the 5th century. The plan is typically central rather than longitudinal, and the central dome, surrounded by groupings of smaller or semi-domes, is supported by means of pendentives. Construction is of brick arranged in decorative patterns and mortar. Interiors are faced with marble slabs, colored glass mosaics, gold leaf, and fresco decoration. Typically the head and shoulders of Christ are depicted in the dome, the four Evangelists in the pendentives, and the Virgin and Child in the east-facing apse. Byzantine architecture remained unusually conservative for more than a thousand years and influenced church building in Russia, Italy, Greece, and elsewhere. △1056,1060.

Byzantine Art. △1060.

Byzantine Empire, known also as the East Roman Empire, or Medieval Greek Empire. The history of the Byzantine Empire spanned the long period from AD 330 when its capital city of Constantinople was est. by the Roman Emperor Constantine the Great, to the year 1453, when the same city was captured by the Ottoman Turks.

Location. Constantinople, a well-fortified city on the Bosporus, commanded one of the most important routes between the European and Asian continents. The city was the heart of the empire, whose outer boundaries were constantly changing, as it annexed foreign territories and was in turn invaded. It generally comprised large parts of Anatolia, or Asia Minor, and the Balkans, as well as (during periods of expansion) S Italy and Ravenna, Greece, Syria, Egypt, and portions of Spain and the N African coast.

Culture. Though the Byzantines considered themselves the heirs of the Roman Empire (and referred to themselves as Romans), their society was a mixture of many elements. The traditions of imperial Rome shaped their governmental institutions; the language and customs of classical Greece molded their cultural life; and Orthodox Christianity determined their religion.

Government and History. The Byzantine state was, in theory, a continuation of the Roman Empire. While the Roman Empire in the West had fallen into decline after the Germanic invasions, imperial traditions remained in effect in the East. The Emperor Justinian I (r.527–65) reconquered the territory of the old Roman Empire, and codified the Roman law. Under the Heraclian emperors (610–717), the empire defeated its Persian enemies, but also saw the rise of the Arab threat. During the age of the Iconoclastic Controversy (717–867), the Isaurian and Amorian rulers dealt with severe internal crises. The Macedonian epoch (867–1081) is known as the Golden Age of the Byzantine Empire, for it was a time of territorial consolidation and cultural flowering. The emperors of the Comnenian and Angelian dynasties (1081–1204) witnessed both an expansion of Byzantine power and the threatening advance of the crusading armies of W Europe. The crusaders ruled Byzantium during the dominion of the Latin Empire of Constantinople (1204–61). Michael VIII, restorer of the Greek Empire, founded the Palaeologan dynasty (1261–1453). When, in 1453, Constantinople fell to the Turkish forces of Sultan Muhammad II, the Byzantine Empire came to an end. △1056.

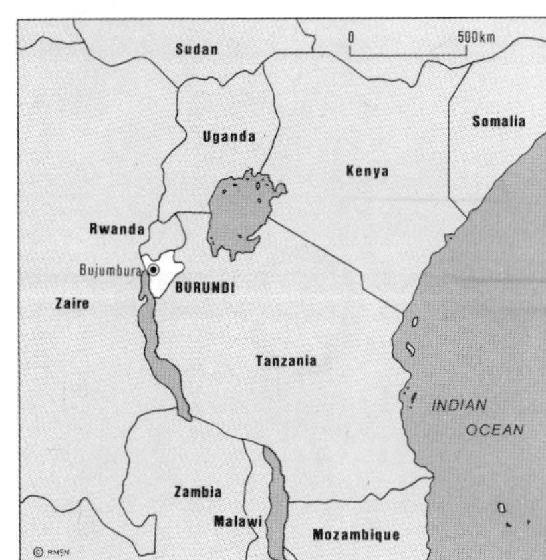
Sudan
0
500km
Somalia
Uganda
Kenya
Rwanda
Bujumbura
BURUNDI
Zaire
Tanzania
INDIAN
OCEAN
Zambia
Malawi
Mozambique
Burundi

Bush baby

Richard Byrd

George Byron

C

CAB. *See* Civil Aeronautics Board.

Cabal, advisers to Charles II of England during the period 1667–73. Chosen by the king to replace the earl of Clarendon, who had been impeached as lord chancellor, the initials of the five members—Clifford, Arlington, Buckingham, Ashley Cooper, Lauderdale—spelled "cabal." They plotted with the king to bring about religious toleration for Dissenters (including Catholics) against the wishes of Parliament. However, the 1672 Declaration of Indulgence produced an uproar causing all high-ranking Catholics (including two in the Cabal) to resign, thus ending the Cabal.

Cabala, or Kabbala, form of Jewish mysticism. It holds that every word, letter, number, even accent of the Bible contains mysteries to be interpreted. The earliest extant cabalist work is the *Sefir Yezirah* (Book of Creation), dating from about the 3rd century AD This work contains monologues attributed to Abraham to which numeralogy was applied to explain creation. Cabalism spread throughout Europe in the 13th century and is still practiced by some Hasidic Jews. △844.

Cabaret Theater, a form of entertainment, usually held in a cafe setting, characterized by intimate rapport between entertainer and audience and simple production values, and often producing satire and avant-garde humor. In pre-Hitler Germany it was linked with advanced politics and art and influenced the works of Bertolt Brecht.

Cabbage, vegetable cultivated for over 2000 years. Its large, green or reddish-purple leaves have fleshy midribs and form round, compact heads; diameter: 6–9in (15.2–22.9cm); weight: 4–6lb (1.8–2.7kg). A cool weather crop, it matures in 60–75 days. If grown during hot weather, it often goes to seed. Chinese cabbage *(Brassica pekinensis)* has a milder taste and 18in (45.7cm) cylindrical heads. Family Cruciferae; species *Brassica oleracea capitata.*

Cabbage Palm, several palms whose young leaves are eaten as a vegetable. Among them are cabbage palmetto *(Sabal palmetto),* a 90ft (27m) tall palm native to SE United States; *Roystonea oleracea,* also called palmiste, a 120ft (37m) tall West Indian palm; and the Australian *Livistona australis,* which grows to 80ft (24m). Family Palmaceae.

Cabécar, small tribe of Talamancan-speaking American Indians occupying the Talamanca Plain and Sixaola River in Costa Rica. A major tribe in pre-Columbian times, they were conquered by the Bribri and have become intermixed with the latter. Their population is possibly 700.

Cabeiri, or **Kabeiroi,** minor spirits in Greek mythology, often associated with underground fires (as in volcanoes) and with metal working. Myths about them are conflicting. For example, the Cabeiri of Lemnos were said to be sons and helpers of Hephaestus, god of fire and blacksmith of the gods. The Cabeiri of Samothrace were said to be sons of Zeus and Calliope.

Cabell, James Branch (1879–1958), US novelist and critic, b. Richmond, Va. He wrote fantasy-adventures set in the mythical country of Poictesme during the Middle Ages. His works suggest that man's hope for the future lies in aestheticism.

Cabeza de Vaca, Álvar Núñez (*c.*1490–*c.*1557), Spanish explorer. Leaving Spain in 1527, he was shipwrecked the following year off the Texas coast. He and three other survivors were the first Europeans to explore the American Southwest, as recorded in his *The Shipwrecked Men* (1542). His *Comentarios* (1555) recounts hardships endured in South America, where he served unsuccessfully as governor of Paraguay (1541–42) and opened a trail from Brazil to Paraguay.

Cabildo, the municipal council, the lowest stage of the administrative hierarchy in colonial Spanish America. Also called *ayuntamiento,* the cabildo performed normal, routine functions. A defender of community interests before outside authorities, it was the only colonial institution that retained a measure of autonomy from royal prerogatives.

Cabinda (Kabinda), port town in Angola, SW Africa, 35mi (56km) N of Congo River; capital of Cabinda, an autonomous Angolan district. Exports: palm, timber, oil, cacao. Pop. 13,499.

Cabinet, body of official advisers to a nation's chief executive; usually the heads of the government's administrative departments. Its power differs in various political systems. In the United States, it exercises only the authority the president chooses to give it. △902,906,1358.

Cabinet Government, system in which the legislature establishes the administrative government and provides the leadership. The chief executive is usually a prime minister selected by the party with a majority in the legislature. The system originated in 18th-century England with the development of parliamentary supremacy and party government. △902.

Cabinetmaking, skill of furniture-making and interior woodwork finishing. Cabinetmaking reached its height in the 18th century, the golden age of furniture design, under the masters Thomas Chippendale, George Hepplewhite, Thomas Sheraton, the Adam brothers, and Duncan Phyfe, an immigrant from Scotland working in America. Cabinets can be divided into a large number of classes according to their shape, style, period, and country of origin, but their common characteristics are that they contain a series of drawers and pigeonholes. In its rudimentary form the cabinet was an oblong box, with or without feet, small enough to rest on a table, filled with drawers and closed with doors, and used for safeguarding jewels, precious stones, and money. During the Renaissance cabinets became more elaborate and architectural until they became one of the most sumptuous pieces in the household.

The basis of the cabinet was wood, carved, polished, or inlaid, sometimes embellished with ivory, tortoiseshell, and cut and polished precious stones. Doors and drawers were sometimes painted with classical or mythological scenes. During the 16th and 17th centuries a popular form actually recreated a tiny palatial interior behind folding doors. Armoires, which consisted of two pieces, one on top of the other, originated with the Flemish cabinetmakers and spread to France and England. A glass-fronted cabinet for china and glass was highly favored by the English during the Georgian period.

Cabin in the Sky, musical play with lyrics by John LaTouche, music by Vernon Duke, and book by Lynn Root, first produced on Broadway in 1940 and made into a film in 1943. It featured an all-black cast and several popular songs, including the title song and "Taking a Chance on Love."

Cable, George Washington (1844–1925), US short story writer and novelist, b. New Orleans. A leader of the local color movement, a number of his stories of Louisiana appeared in a collection, *Old Creole Days* (1879). His novels include *The Grandissimes* (1880), about early 19th-century Louisiana, *Madame Delphine* (1881), and *Bonaventure* (1888). *See also* Local Color.

Cable, in Communications. △1790.

Cable Television, generally refers to community antenna television. CATV does not broadcast, but picks up signals at a central antenna and delivers them to individual subscribers via coaxial cables. Originally designed for areas with poor reception and no local station, cable TV, run by private franchise, now serves to increase the variety of local viewing by transmitting channels brought by microwave relay.

Cable (car) Tramway. △1700.

Cabot, George (1752–1823), US merchant and politician, b. Salem, Mass. After college he went to sea as a captain in a family-owned vessel. He served in both houses of Congress (1791–96) and refused the secretaryship of the navy. Cabot was one of the Essex Junto, a Federalist group of rich New Englanders who opposed the War of 1812 at the Hartford Convention (1814).

Cabot, John (c.1450–98), navigator and explorer, b. Giovanni Caboto in Italy. He was employed by Henry VII and sailed in the *Mathew* from Bristol in search of a western route to India. He landed at Cape Breton Island or Newfoundland (1497). On his second voyage (1498) he presumably reached Greenland and sailed on to Chesapeake Bay. His discovery served as the basis of English claims in North America.

Cabot, Sebastian (*c.* 1476–1557), Italian navigator and explorer. The son of John Cabot, he explored the Americas for England and Spain. He founded and directed the expeditions of the Merchant Adventurers of London, which initiated Russian-English commerce with a treaty.

Cabral, Luis de Almeida (1929–), Guinea-Bissau political figure, b. Cape Verde Islands. He founded the African party for the Independence of Guinea and Cape Verde with his brother Amilcar in 1956 and worked for it until Guinea-Bissau became independent in 1974 and he became its first president.

Cabral, Pedro Álvares (*c.* 1467–*c.* 1520), Portuguese navigator. In 1500 King Manuel sent him with a fleet of ships to the East Indies. Unaccountably, he sailed westward and discovered Brazil, which he claimed for Portugal.

Cabrillo, Juan Rodríguez (died 1543), Portuguese explorer in Spanish service. He discovered California (1542) while exploring the west coast of Mexico. He landed at Point Loma Head, San Diego Bay (now in Cabrillo National Monument), then sailed up to San Francisco Bay.

Cabrillo National Monument, memorial in S California, on San Diego Bay; dedicated to Juan Rodriguez Cabrillo, discoverer of California (1542). Est 1913. Area: 123acres (50hectares).

Cacao, or chocolate tree, tropical and subtropical evergreen tree found in South and Central America. Its seeds are the source of chocolate and cocoa. It has long, leathery, oval leaves and yellow flower clusters, and reddish, woody fruits, each containing about 50 flat cacao beans. Height: 40ft(12m). Family Sterculiaceae; species *Theobroma cacao.* △354.

Caceres, Andrés Avelino (1836–1923?), Peruvian military hero during the War of the Pacific against

Chile (1879–83), and president (1886–90, 1894–95). He was thwarted in his attempt to impose a military dictatorship in 1894.

Cáceres, city in W central Spain, on Cáceres River; capital of Cáceres prov.; site of many Roman and Moorish remains. Industries: cloth, pottery, leather, stock raising, wine. Area: (prov.) 7,701sq mi (19,946sq km). Pop. (city) 56,064; (prov.) 457,777.

Cacomistle, or ring-tailed cat, nocturnal, omnivorous member of the raccoon family native to SW United States and Mexico. Agile tree-climbers, they have gray to brown fur with black bands on bushy tails. They make good pets, being especially good rat hunters. Length: 14.5in (36.8cm); weight: to 2.5lb. (1.1kg). Family Procyonidae; species *Bassariscus astutus* (or *Jentinkia sumichrasti*).

Cactus, dicotyledonous succulents found throughout the Western Hemisphere, the majority in hot, arid regions. These leafless plants are thick, fleshy, and spiny. The swollen green joints of the stem function as leaves. A layer of wax over the stem helps control evaporation of moisture and roots are adapted to absorb water. Large cuplike blossoms have many stamens and stigmas in the center. Some well known species are barrel cactus, saguaro, prickly pear, and cereus. There are over 1000 species. Family Cactaceae.

Caddis Fly, mothlike insect found worldwide. It is an important fish food. Adults have long antennae and hold their wings tentlike. The larvae are found in ponds and streams, building cases or nets to live in. Length: 1in (25mm). Order Trichoptera.

Caddo, language family and confederation of related US Indian tribes once occupying the region of Louisiana, Arkansas, Texas, and Oklahoma. They were closely related to the Natchitoches, Adai, Hasinai, and Eyeish peoples, all of whom are now extinct. About 1,000 members of the various Caddoan bands live on the Witchita Reservation in SW Oklahoma.

Cade, Jack (died 1450), Irish rebel who led the 1450 disturbance in Kent and Sussex (Cade's Rebellion) against Henry VI. Claiming to be a Mortimer, cousin of the Duke of York, and captain of Kent, he issued a manifesto listing administrative reforms, and in May and June marched with 40,000 followers on London. They maintained order for two days, and then began pillaging the city. Cade, with a price on his head, escaped but was killed in Sussex.

Cadillac, (Sieur) Antoine de la Mothe (1658–1730), French colonial adminstrator. Arriving in Canada (1683), he engaged in Indian fighting (1684–87), and commanded the post at Michilimackinac (1694–97). He founded Detroit (1701) and served as its commandant (1704–10). He was governor of Louisiana (1713–16) until he fell into political disfavor and was imprisoned briefly in the Bastille.

Cadillac, city in W Michigan, 70mi (113km) N of Grand Rapids, on Cadillac and Mitchell lakes; named for Antoine de la Mothe Cadillac, colonial explorer who founded Detroit; site of Manistee and Huron national forests. Industries: forestry, rubber products, tourism. Settled 1871; inc. 1877. Pop. (1970) 9,990.

Cádiz, seaport city in SW Spain, on the Bay of Cádiz; capital of Cádiz prov. Conquered by Carthaginians, Romans, Goths, Moors; Columbus departed from Cádiz in his 2nd journey to the New World (1495); site of 13th-century cathedral, art and archaeological museums, tomb of composer Manuel de Falla. Industries: chemicals, paper, textiles, salt, shipbuilding, fishing. Founded 1100 BC by Phoenicians. Pop. 135,743.

Cádiz, Gulf of, wide inlet of Atlantic Ocean, on SW coast of Spain; extends for 200mi (322km) from Cape Saint Vincent, Portugal, SE to Gibralter; the Guadalquivir and Guadiana rivers flow into it.

Cadmium, metallic element (symbol Cd) of group IIB of the periodic table, first isolated (1817) by Friedrich Stromeyer. It is found in greenockite (sulfide) but the chief source is as a by-product in the extraction of zinc. Its main use is as a protective electroplated coating. Chemically it resembles zinc. Properties: at. no. 48; at. wt. 112.4; sp. gr. 8.65; melt. pt. 609.6°F (320.9°C); boil. pt. 1409°F (765°C); most common isotope Cd^{114} (28.86%).

Cadmus, in Greek mythology, a prince of Phoenicia. Cadmus and his brothers were sent to find their sister Europa, who had been carried off by Zeus. After a fruitless search, Cadmus founded and settled in a town he named after himself. After eight years of proving himself to the gods, he was crowned king of Cadmia, later called Thebes.

Cadogan, William, First Earl of Cadogan (1675–1726), Irish military officer and diplomat. A trusted ally of the Duke of Marlborough, he served as quartermaster general (1702–11), leading the march to Bavaria (Blenheim, 1704) and to the battle of Oudenarde in 1708. After an exile of three years (1711–14), he held several diplomatic posts under George I, encouraging the Hanoverian succession. He gained his peerage after putting down the Scottish insurrection of 1715–16.

Caduceus, in classical times, a herald's wand or staff, a badge showing that the bearer was a sacred person not to be molested. Its original form was in all probability a straight branch from the top of which two twigs grew. These twigs were then pulled back and twined around the branch. Later the twigs were represented as snakes. Thus the caduceus is often snake-entwined.

Caecilian, limbless, underground burrowing amphibian resembling oversized earthworm, found in Central and South America, Asia, and Africa. Possessing minute, often useless, eyes, it has a sensory tentacle in a groove above the nose on each side of the head. The male has an organ for internal fertilization of the female. There are live-bearing and egg-laying species. Length: to 4.5ft (1.4m). There are 75 species. Order Gymnophiona; family Caeciliidae. *See also* Amphibia. △518.

Caecum, blind end or pouch at the junction of the small and large intestines and to which is attached the appendix. *See also* Colon. △694.

Caedmon (*fl.* 670), earliest-known English poet. According to Bede, he was an illiterate herdsman of Whitby Abbey who was commanded in a vision to turn the scriptures into poetry. Although credited with many other Old English poems, his sole surviving work is probably the brief "Hymn to Creation."

Caen, city and port in N France, on the Orne River; capital of Calvados dept.; important since 11th century, when William the Conqueror resided here. Many architectural masterpieces were destroyed in WWII; its university (1432) was rebuilt, and the 11th-century Abbaye Aux Hommes (burial place of William the Conqueror), Abbaye aux Dames, and Church of St Nicholas were preserved. Industries: iron ore mining, textiles, automobiles, electronic gear. Pop. 110,262.

Caernarvon (Caernarfon), historic town in NW Wales, on Menai Strait; formerly county town of Caernarvonshire, which became part of Gwynedd in 1974; site of Roman fortress ruins (AD 70–80); castle built by Edward I (1283) in which his son Edward II (or Edward of Carnarvon) was born 1284. He was crowned first Prince of Wales here in 1301; Princes of Wales are now invested here. Industries: tourism, slate exporting, oil importing. Pop. 9,253.

Caesar, (Gaius) Julius (*c.* 104–44 BC), Roman general and political figure. Of patrician birth, he married Cornelia, daughter of Cinna, a colleague of Marius, popular party leader who granted Caesar a priesthood (87 BC) that was later proscribed by Sulla (82 BC). After Sulla's death Ceasar became military tribune and leader of the popular party against the Senate. As pontifex maximus (63 BC) he directed reforms that resulted in the Julian calendar. He fought in Spain, returning to form the First Triumvirate (60 BC) with Pompey and Crassus. An effective mediator, he instituted agrarian reforms, created a plebeian-patrician coalition, and successfully waged the Gallic Wars (58–49 BC), emerging as one of history's greatest military commanders. He secured Roman dominance of Gaul and Britain.

When his rivalry with Pompey caused the Senate to demand that he dissolve his army, he refused and crossed the Rubicon River to engage in civil war. He defeated Pompey's forces at Pharsalus (48 BC) and, pursuing Pompey to Egypt, met Cleopatra, who later bore him a son. He conquered Pharnaces II of Pontus and wrote of the victory "Veni, vidi, vici" ("I came, I saw, I conquered"). Returning to Rome, he became dictator but refused royal title. Resentment against him mounted, and he was assassinated in the senate on the Ides of March (44 BC) in a conspiracy led by Cassius and Marcus Brutus. He bequeathed his wealth and power to his grandnephew Octavian, who, with Mark Antony, avenged his murder. Historians debate Caesar's character but laud his military genius, statesmanship, and writings, *The Gallic Wars* and *Civil War*. △1018.

Caesar and Cleopatra (1899), 5-act comedy by George Bernard Shaw, based on Plutarch's *Life of*

GIOVANNI CABOTTO VENEZIANO
John Cabot

Sebastian Cabot

Cacomistle

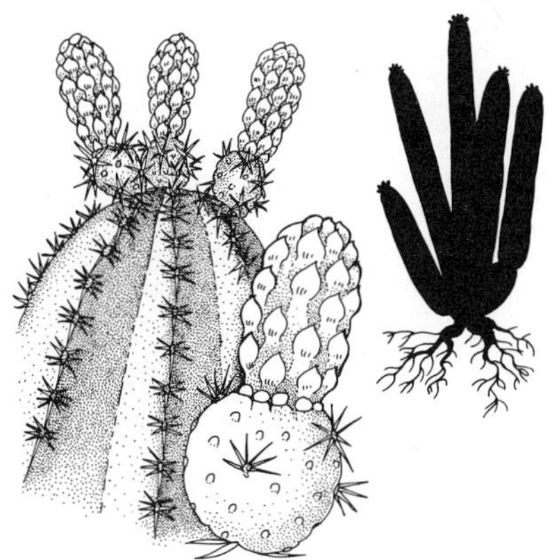
Cactus

Caesar, first presented in 1901. Presenting Cleopatra as a 16-year-old schoolgirl who has herself rolled in a rug and carried to the apartment of a middle-aged Caesar, Shaw's play differs in its characterization from others using the same theme.

Caesarea, ancient city in Israel, on Mediterranean Sea, 22mi (35km) S of Haifa; was a Roman capital in Palestine, given to King Herod by Octavian 30 BC; site of St Paul's imprisonment AD 57–59; scene of massacre of Jews demanding Roman citizenship AD 66; fortified 1251 by Louis IX; destroyed by Saracens 1291; noted for ancient Roman theater.

Caesium. *See* Cesium.

Caesura, pause in a line of verse, occuring near the middle and generally indicating a pause in the meaning. The caesura is found in Greek and Latin prosody as well as in English-language prosody.

Caetano, Marcello (1906–), Portuguese statesman. A noted lawyer, he helped set up the corporate government of dictator António de Oliveira Salazar in 1933. He was prime minister (1968–74) after Salazar was incapacitated by a stroke. He went into exile after the 1974 military coup.

Caffeine, a stimulant found in several plants, used in many common beverages, including coffee, tea, cola drinks, and in some medicines.

Cage, John (1912–), US composer, b. Los Angeles. His daring experiments and innovations received attention (eg, pianos "prepared" with objects on their strings to alter pitch and tone; adding chance events to music). Compositions for prepared piano include *Bachanale* (1938) and *Sonatas and Interludes* (1946–48). △1364.

Cage Birds, birds kept as pets in cages, including finches, especially many varieties of singing and show canaries; parrot group, especially parakeets; and mynah, valued for its mimicking ability.

Cagliari, port city in Sardinia, Italy; capital of Cagliari prov. and of Sardinia region. Founded by Phoenicians, it was independent in the Middle Ages; vital naval and air bases on island were destroyed by Allied bombing in WWII. Historical landmarks include Roman amphitheater, Cathedral of St Cecilia (1257–1312), 5th- and 6th-century Christian church. Exports: lead, zinc, salt. Industries: agriculture, salt extraction, cement. Pop. 219,852.

Cagney, James (1904–), U.S. actor, b. New York City. After high school, he entered the theater as a dancer in choruses in vaudeville. He became a Broadway success in *Maggie the Magnificent* (1929) and in *Penny Arcade* (1930). His film role in *Public Enemy* (1930) launched his film career with Warner Brothers, playing the invincible gangster who held the sympathy of his audience. His portrayal of George M. Cohan in *Yankee Doodle Dandy* in 1942 won him an Academy Award.

Caguas, city in E central Puerto Rico; fertile agricultural area; major industrial center. Industries: sugar refining, textiles, coffee. Pop. 62,807.

Cahokia, village in SW Illinois, on the Mississippi River; first permanent settlement in Illinois, est 1699 as French mission; site of several 18th-century buildings, and Parks College of Aeronautical Engineering. Inc. 1927. Pop. (1970) 20,469.

Cahokia Mounds, large prehistoric American earthworks, situated in Illinois, and named after the Cahokia tribe who inhabited the vicinity in historic times. The mounds are in a group of about 85, the highest 100ft (30.5m) taking the form of a quadrangular pyramid with a massive adjoining platform.

Caillaux, Joseph Marie Auguste (1863–1944), French statesman. As premier (1911–12) he arranged a controversial settlement with Germany over the Agadir crisis in Morocco. His wife shot and killed the editor of *Le Figaro* in 1914 (over allegations the newspaper had made about Caillaux). Caillaux resigned as finance minister to defend her, and she was acquitted. He was imprisoned as a pacifist in World War I but returned to power briefly as finance minister again in 1925.

Caiman, or cayman, alligatorlike reptile of Central and South America. Most abundant are the spectacled caimans with curved ridges of bone connecting the eye sockets. The black caiman *(Melanosuchus niger)* is the largest, reaching a length of 15ft (4.6m). Smooth-fronted caimans are the smallest and have especially heavy armor. Family Alligatoridae. *See also* Alligator.

Cain, in Genesis, firstborn son of Adam and Eve and brother of Abel. Because God accepted Abel's offering in preference to his own, Cain murdered Abel in anger. Banished to the wilderness, he and his family lived thereafter as nomads. △810.

Cain, James M(allahan) (1892), US author, b. Annapolis. His realistic novels about criminals and other seamy characters include *The Postman Always Rings Twice* (1934), *Double Indemnity* (1936), *Mildred Pierce* (1941), and *Three of a Kind* (1943).

Caine Mutiny, The (1951), novel by Herman Wouk. It deals with a mutiny against a paranoid captain on a US minesweeper and the subsequent court-martial of an officer involved in the mutiny. It was dramatized as *The Caine Mutiny Court-Martial* (1954) and made into a film.

Cairn Terrier, small working dog (terrier group) bred in Scotland and first shown in United States in 1916. Used to rout fox and badgers, the cairn has a short, broad head, small pointed and erect ears; a medium-long, level body; short legs; and a short tail carried up. Its hard, weather-resistant coat is any color but white. Its ears, muzzle, and tail tip are darker than the coat. Average size: 10in (25cm) high at shoulder; 14lb (6.3kg). *See also* Terrier.

Cairo, capital city of Egypt; a port on the Nile River; includes two islands in the Nile, Zamalik and Rawdah, linked to the mainland by bridges. Cairo was founded AD 969 and includes Old Cairo, a Roman fortress city. Built on high ground to avoid Nile floods, it flourished and replaced Alexandria as the capital in 1863; site of the sphinx and pyramids of Giza (dating from 3,000 BC), over 400 museums, temples, palaces, and mosques. Industries: tourism, textiles, iron, steel, sugar refining, cigarettes. Pop. 4,961,000.

Caisson, a watertight structure or chamber used in excavation or construction. It accommodates workmen underwater and also facilitates removal of excavated materials. Frequently used in underwater tunnels, where it acts as a shell for the building of a foundation. Open caissons or pneumatic caissons using air pressure to support the excavation may be used.

Cajetan (1469–1534), Italian theologian, b. as Tommaso de Vio. Appointed a cardinal in 1517, he was papal legate to Germany (1518–19) where he attempted to reconcile Martin Luther and the Catholic Church. He strongly opposed Henry VIII's divorce from Catherine of Aragon. His commentaries on the *Summa Theologica* of Thomas Aquinas are still considered to be authoritative.

Calabria, region of S Italy, comprising the "toe" of the Italian "boot"; includes the provinces of Catanzaro, Cosenza, and Reggio di Calabria; capital is Catanzaro. Region was center of Greek colonization; fortunes declined under Roman rule; it was repeatedly invaded; conquered by Giuseppe Garibaldi 1860. Economic development has been slow due to the rugged terrain, poor communications, earthquakes, and feudal landholding conditions. Industries: hydroelectric power, agriculture, livestock, quarrying. Area: 5,822sq mi (15,079sq km). Pop. 2,067,154.

Caladium, genus of tropical American plants commonly grown for their brilliantly colored, variegated, arrow-shaped leaves. Leaf colors combine green, red, pink, silver, and white. It grows from a tuberous rhizome (underground stem) that can be stored. Family Aracea.

Calah, ancient city in Assyria, S of Ninevah, founded 13th century BC by Shalmaneser I. It is the same city as Nimrud. In 880 BC it was used as the capital of Assyria by Ashurnasirpal II; and is mentioned in the Book of Genesis. Excavations have uncovered palaces of Ashurnasirpal II and Shalmaneser III, ivories, sculpture, and the black obelisk of Shalmaneser III.

Calais, city in N France, on the Strait of Dover. A major commercial center and seaport since Middle Ages, it fell into English hands in 1347; a Rodin monument commemorates the legend of six burghers who offered their lives to save the town; city was returned to French rule 1558. Industries: lace making, chemicals, paper. Pop. 74,634.

Calamine, a pinkish, odorless powder of zinc oxide and some ferric oxide, dissolved in mineral oils and used in skin ointments to treat such disorders as chicken pox, poison ivy, and skin rashes.

Calamity Jane (1857–1903), US frontier figure, b. as Martha Jane Canary in Princeton, Mo. After working in mining and railroad camps in Montana and other western states, she became associated with the US Cavalry as a guide and scout in the Black Hills area. She was in Deadwood, S.D., during the gold rush there in the latter half of the 1870s. Dime novels presented her as a crusader against evil romantically attached to Wild Bill Hickok. In actuality she was a heavy-drinking, rough-and-tumble character who wore men's clothing and was expert with a rifle and on a horse. There is no evidence for the Hickok attachment. Drifting around the West, she married (1891) a man named Clinton Burke, but he soon left her. She then appeared in Wild West shows. There are various explanations for her nickname. One is that it stemmed from her hard-luck experiences. Another is that it came from her help to victims of misfortune. Another is that she warned people that to offend her was to "court calamity."

Calcination, process of heating solids to high temperatures, but below their fusion point, in order to remove volatile substances, oxidize a portion of their mass (roasting), or render them friable. Lead, zinc, calcium, copper, and iron ores calcine to agglomerated oxides, which may be used as colored pigments or as intermediates in metal extraction.

Calcite, a carbonate mineral, calcium carbonate ($CaCO_3$). Found in all types of occurrences and with all classes of rocks. It is the main constituent of limestone. Hexagonal system varied crystals from rare tabular to prismatic or needlelike, also microcrystalline to coarse. Glassy white, fluoresces red, pink, yellow; hardness 3; sp gr 2.7. Transparent variety used in optical instruments. △240.

Calcium, common metallic element (symbol Ca) of the alkaline-earth group, first isolated (1808) by Sir Humphry Davy. It occurs in many rocks and minerals, notably limestone (carbonate) and gypsum (sulfate), and in bone. The metal has few commercial applications but calcium compounds are widely used. Chemically it is a reactive element, combining readily with oxygen, nitrogen, and other nonmetals. Properties: at. no. 20; at. wt. 40.08; sp. gr. 1.55; melt. pt. 1.558 °F (848°C); boil. pt. 2709°F (1487°C); most common isotope Ca^{40} (96.95%). *See also* Alkaline-Earth Elements.

Calcium Carbonate, white insoluble compound (formula $CaCO_3$) that occurs as marble, chalk, limestone, calcite, etc. It is used in the manufacture of cement and lime, and as a constituent of antacids and dentifrices. Properties: sp. gr. 1.49–1.66 (calcite); decomposes at 1648°F (898°C).

Calculators, Desk. △1672.

Calculus, branch of higher mathematics involving the operations of differentiation and integration. Calculus is often considered to have two parts—differential calculus and integral calculus—both concerned with the limiting values of a function as a variable tends to approach zero. Differential calculus enables the calculation of the rate at which one quantity changes with respect to another. It is used in finding slopes of curves, velocities, accelerations, etc. Integral calculus is used in finding the areas enclosed by curves, and in solving related problems. *See also* Mathematics. △1460.

Calculus, a "stone," often a calcium compound, usually in the urinary system. Excruciating pain is the chief symptom. Spontaneous expulsion is frequent.

Calcutta, city in E India; capital of West Bengal state; 2nd-largest city and chief port in India; former capital of British India (1773–1912); site of the Maidan (a park with statues of famous men), St Paul's Cathedral, Ochterlony Monument, the Kalighat (a Hindu temple). Calcutta is the world's largest jute-milling center; transportation hub. Industries: electrical equipment, cotton textiles, food processing. Exports: mineral ores, tea, hides, chemicals. Founded *c.* 1690. Pop. 3,158,838.

Caldecott, Randolph (1846–86), English illustrator of children's books. The popularity of his illustrations of Washington Irving's books led to his being asked to illustrate a pair of children's books in color: *The House That Jack Built* and *John Gilpin,* based on William Cowper's ballad, both published in 1878. Caldecott followed these with 14 other titles. The Caldecott Medal has been awarded annually since 1938 to the artist of the most distinguished US-published illustrated book for children.

Calder, Alexander Stirling (1870–1945), US sculptor, b. Philadelphia. Winner of many prizes and awards, he was a prolific worker, covering a wide range of subjects. He was the creator of archways, sundials, memorials, fountains, and portrait busts.

Calder, Alexander (1898–1976), US sculptor, b. Philadelphia. He gained recognition with his miniature circus and toys made of wire and wood, which he exhibited at the Salon des Humoristes, Paris, 1927. In 1926 he executed his first wire sculpture, "Josephine Baker." Influenced by Joan Miró and Pieter Mondrian he created the mobile, a kinetic sculpture with parts that move either by motors or air currents. His first mobile was "Dancing Torpedo Shape." The term *mobile* was given to Calder's moving sculptures by Marcel Duchamp; Jean Arp coined the term *stabile* to apply to similar work that did not move. In later years, Calder became increasingly occupied with monumental stabiles, such as "Ticket Window" (1965; Lincoln Center for the Performing Arts, New York City) and "Man," executed for the 1967 Montreal Expo.

Calder, Frank (1877–1943), Canadian ice hockey executive, b. Scotland. He was the National Hockey League's president from the league's formation (1917) until his death. The Calder Trophy, given annually to the outstanding rookie, is named for him.

Caldera, volcanic basin, usually large and shallow, the result of subsidence of a volcanic summit. This is due to the migration of magma under the earth's crust. Caldera of extinct volcanoes, if fed by snow, springs, or ice, may become crater lakes. △176.

Calderón Bridge, battle-site near Guadalajara, Mexico where Gen. Calleja, commanding 6000 royalists, defeated the 36,000 supporters of Miguel Hidalgo on Jan. 16–17, 1811. Hidalgo's movement was irreparably damaged.

Caldwell, Erskine (1903–), US author, b. Coweta co, Ga. His novels and short stories about the South often deal with people down on their luck and are noted for their mixture of humor, sex, and violence. His works include the novels *Tobacco Road* (1932) and *God's Little Acre* (1933), a number of other novels, and several collections of short stories.

Caldwell, (Janet) Taylor (1900–), US novelist, b. England. She attended the University of Buffalo and began her writing career with her second husband, Marcus Reback, as her coauthor. Her carefully plotted novels include *Dynasty of Death* (1938), *Devil's Advocate* (1952), *Dear and Glorious Physician* (1959), and *Glory and the Lightning* (1974).

Calendar, a system by which the beginning and the divisions of the civil year are fixed. Days, weeks, and months are arranged in a definite order. Divisions are based on the movements of the earth and the appearances of the sun and moon. Ancient lunar calendars, based on the number of days between two full moons (29½ days), resulted in a lunar year of 354 days. In modern calendars, months are approximately one-twelfth of a solar year (365¼ days).

Calgary, city in SW Alberta, Canada, at the junction of the Box and Elbow rivers; site of the University of Calgary (1945) and Provincial Institute of Technology and Art (1916); industrial and commercial center. Industries: grain elevators, flour mills, livestock, wheat, lumber, brick, cement, oil refineries. Founded in 1875 as Northwest Mounted Police post; inc. 1893; government reorganized 1952. Pop. 400,154.

Calhoun, John Caldwell (1782–1850), US vice president and political leader, b. Abbeville District, S.C. After serving in the House of Representatives (1811–17), he was secretary of war (1817–25) under Pres. James Monroe. He was vice president (1825–32), under John Quincy Adams and Andrew Jackson, resigning over the nullification issue. Calhoun was elected to the Senate immediately and served there, except for a brief period as secretary of state under Pres. John Tyler (1844–45), until 1850. A staunch advocate of slavery, states' rights and nullification, he strongly influenced the South in the course that led to the Civil War.

Cali, city in W Colombia on Cali River; capital of Valle dept.; damaged in 1885 by earthquake. Cauca Valley Authority (1954) was established to develop flood control, land reclamation, and electric power; site of old aqueduct, cathedral, and two universities. Industries: tourism, tires, tobacco, textiles, paper. Founded 1536. Pop. 950,500.

Caliche, as used in Mexico and SW United States, gravel and sand pounded together with carbonate. This formation is frequently found over gold-bearing rock. Another name for this type of impervious formation is calcrete.

Calicut (Kozhikode), seaport city in S India, on the Arabian Sea; capital of the Kozhikode district. Visited by Vasco de Gama 1498, it developed into European trading center with post est. by British East India Co. 1664; calico cloth (named for the city) was first exported to England in 17th century; ceded to Britain 1792, who held it until 1947, when India declared independence. Exports: coconuts, coffee, tea, spices, rubber, lumber. Pop. 330,225.

California, state in W United States, situated on the Pacific Ocean, the largest state in population and the 3rd-largest in area.

Land and Economy. In the W, the low Coast Ranges run N and S, paralleling the high Sierra Nevada in the E. Between these ranges lies the fertile Central Valley, drained by the Sacramento and San Joaquin rivers. In the SE are broad desert areas; the N is mountainous. With an all-year growing season and vast irrigation projects, the state is a leader in many crops. It also ranks high in commercial fisheries. Forests covering about 40% of the land support an important lumber industry. Mineral deposits include a variety of ores valuable in manufacturing, which is the largest sector of the economy. California factories make aircraft, aerospace equipment, electronic components, missiles, automobiles, communications equipment, chemical and petroleum products, cement, paper, and fibers. A year-round tourist industry is important to the state.

People. Between the 1950 and 1970 censuses, the population nearly doubled. About 90% of the people live in urban areas. Approximately the same proportion were born in the United States, with the remainder coming largely from Mexico, Canada, the British Isles, China, and Japan.

Education and Research. The University of California, with many branches, is world-famous. Among notable privately endowed institutions are Stanford University, California Institute of Technology, and the University of Southern California. There are more than 200 institutions of higher education. The Lick, Mt Wilson, and Palomar observatories are leaders in astronomical research. Other important facilities are the Scripps Institution of Oceanography and the Lawrence Radiation Laboratory.

History. Spanish sailors explored the coast in 1542, but the first settlement was in 1769, when Spaniards from Mexico founded a mission at San Diego. Other missions and military posts were established, and California was joined to Mexico, then a Spanish colony. The lands of the 21 Franciscan missions were broken up by law, and land grants created huge cattle ranches. Settlers came from the United States, and in 1846, early in the Mexican War, US forces occupied California, which was ceded to the United States at the war's end. After gold was discovered in 1848, the Gold Rush swelled the population from 15,000 to 250,000 in four years. In November 1849 the people voted California into the Union without approval of Congress, which did not come until Sept. 9, 1850. The opening of the Union Pacific Railroad in 1868 brought an era of great expansion. During and immediately after WWII the spread of manufacturing plants speeded the shift of economic emphasis from agriculture to industry.

PROFILE

Admitted to Union: 1850; rank, 31st
US Congressmen: Senate—2; House of Representatives—43
Population: 19,953,134 (1970); rank, 1st
Capital: Sacramento, 257,105 (1970)
Chief cities: Los Angeles, 2,809,596; San Francisco, 715,674; San Diego, 697,027
State legislature: Senate, 40 members; Assembly, 80
Area: 158,693sq mi (411,015sq km); rank, 3d
Elevation: Highest, Mt Whitney, 14,494ft (4421m); Lowest, Death Valley, 282ft (86m) below sea level
Industries (major products): transportation equipment, processed foods, machinery (electrical and non-electrical), ordnance, metal products
Agriculture (major products): fruits, vegetables, nuts, poultry, cattle, dairy products
Minerals (major): petroleum, borax, asbestos
State nickname: Golden State (unofficial)
State motto: Eureka (I Have Found It)
State bird: Valley Quail
State flower: Golden Poppy
State tree: Redwood

California, University of, state university in California. It was founded as a land grant institution at Oakland in 1868. The university system is composed of nine campuses located throughout the state. Undergraduate study is offered at eight campuses: Berkeley, Davis, Irvine, Los Angeles, Riverside, San Diego, Santa Barbara, and Santa Cruz. It also operates university extension and agricultural extension services.

Cairo, Egypt

Calamity Jane

John C. Calhoun

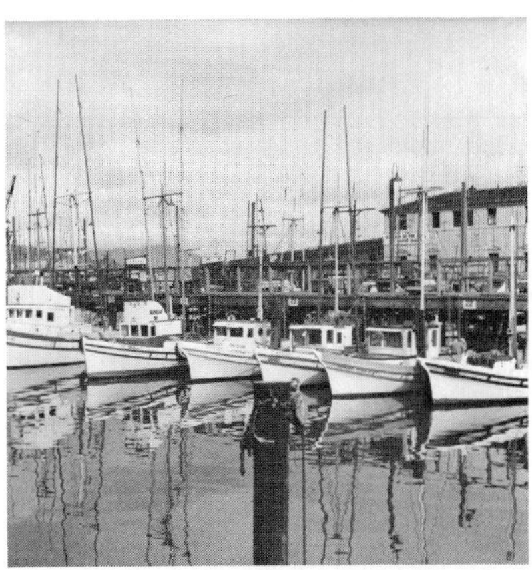

San Francisco, California: Fisherman's Wharf

California Current, Pacific Ocean current; flows S along W coast of North America; part of clockwise current of the entire North Pacific, carrying cool waters from the North Pacific current.

California Fan Palm, also desert palm of California, a stout-trunked palm native to the Colorado desert and cultivated as a decorative tree in California and Europe. Found in groves or clumps, its tall trunk is covered with a thick mat of dead leaves; leaves are fan-shaped and the black berry fruits were used as food by American Indians. Height: 50–75ft (15–23m). Family Palmaceae; species *Washingtonia filifera.*

California Institute of Technology, private university in Pasadena, Calif. Originally Throop Polytechnic Institute, it confers bachelors, masters, and doctors degrees. Major areas of study include engineering, sciences, marine biology, humanities, and social sciences.

Californium, radioactive metallic element (symbol Cf) of the actinide group, first made (1950) at the University of California, Berkeley, by alpha-particle bombardment of Cm^{242}. Properties: at. no. 98; most stable isotope Cf^{251} (8000yr). *See also* Transuranium Elements.

Caligula, Gaius Caesar (12–41), Roman emperor (37–41), nephew of Tiberius. The Senate and army made him emperor over the grandson of Tiberius. He became mentally disturbed, and his reign was cruel and absurd. His soldiers killed him and made Claudius I emperor. △1020.

Caliph, ruler of the Muslim community. Upon Mohammed's death in 632, Abu Bakr was designated the first Khalifat rasul-Allah ("successor of the Messenger of God"), or Caliph, by popular vote in Medina. Through the years, the center of the Caliphate was moved often. In 1517 the Ottoman sultan Selim I seized the title for himself and his dynasty. The Turkish republic abolished the title in 1924.

Caliphate. △1058, 1062.

Calixtus I, Roman Catholic pope (217–22), and saint. Rising from slavery, his leniency with adulterers, murderers, and other sinners was condemned but became important in forming the church's penance doctrine.

Calixtus II, Roman Catholic pope (1119–24), b. the son of a French count of Burgundy. A spokesman for reformers within the church, he sponsored Gregorian reforms and opposed lay investiture. In 1122, he signed the Concordat of Worms achieving a compromise on this issue with Holy Roman Emperor Henry V.

Calixtus III, Roman Catholic pope (1455–58), b. Alonso de Borja (1378) in Spain. His only notable achievement was a crusade against the Turks. His practice of nepotism gave the Borgia family its prominence in Italy.

Calla Lily, flowering plant native to S Africa and cultivated widely in greenhouses and as a house plant. The flower consists of a white showy spathe and yellow spadix. Height: to 2.5ft (76cm). Family Araceae; species *Zantedeschia elliottiana.*

Callao, seaport city on central W coast of Peru, approx. 8mi (13km) W of Lima. Center of international commerce, greater Callao is a province with departmental status. Industries: flour milling, brewing, sugar refining. Founded 1537 by Francisco Pizarro, the original city was destroyed by tidal wave and earthquake 1746. Pop. (greater Callao prov.) 320,700; (city) 196,919.

Callas, Maria (1923–), US soprano, b. New York City. She studied at the Athens Conservatory and made her debut in Verona in 1947. From 1950–58 she was a principal soprano at the La Scala Opera House, Milan, Italy, establishing her reputation as a leading singing actress. She made her Metropolitan Opera debut in 1956 in *Norma.* Noted for her stormy personality, she made infrequent appearances after 1960.

Calles, Plutarco Elías (1877–1945), president of Mexico (1924–28). During his administration the Bank of Mexico, agrarian and cooperative associations, and the first military college in Latin America were founded. His anti-clerical policy fomented the Cristero Revolt which was suppressed. Through the National Revolutionary party (PNR), he wielded considerable political power during the Portes Gil, Ortíz Rubio, and Rodríguez administrations, but was exiled by Cárdenas in 1936.

Callicrates, Greek architect in Athens, 5th century BC. Together with Ictinus, he erected the Parthenon (447–432 BC). He also designed the Temple of Athena Nike.

Calligraphy, art of fine writing. It differs from lettering, which uses mechanical aids such as the rule, compass, and square. Calligraphy is free hand, with a certain style, and with the components in proportion to each other and to the whole. In Europe there was a marked difference between the hands used for literary works, generally called uncials, rounded, easily inscribed letters, and those used for documents and letters, called cursive, which were more practical, regularized, and handsome. Within these classes several distinct styles were employed side by side. These distinctions are apparent in extant Greek examples. Fragments on papyrus from the 3rd century BC show a variety of cursive hands. Documents from the 2nd and 1st centuries BC show less breadth and spaciousness than the earlier samples, and the letters are rounder and more uniform in size. Several different types of Greek uncials were used in Roman times; among these was the "biblical hand," whose letters were square, heavy, upright, with thick and thin strokes well distinguished. This became the prevalent type of uncial during the Byzantine period. By this time papyrus had been replaced by vellum. During the 8th century the minuscule superseded the uncial for ordinary, commercial purposes. The Latin alphabet, used in calligraphy, developed like the Greek. Square or "rustic" capitals were used for literary works; a cursive form, which developed into uncial and minuscule cursive, was used for letter writing and documents. The minuscule cursive became the basis for medieval church and commercial writing, varying from nation to nation, and according to the purpose. Special hands were used by different classes, such as clerks, public scriveners, and notaries, and by papal and other chanceries. Intentional complexity was developed to prevent forgeries. During the Renaissance handbooks on calligraphy were developed, and from the 17th century, as English commerce spread, so did the English writing style. The 20th century has witnessed a revival of interest in the art of fine writing. △1208.

Callimachus (*c.*300–240 BC), Greek poet. Born in Cyrene, Callimachus was the most important Greek poet of the Hellenistic period. Among the best-known of his works were the *Aetia,* or *Causes,* a discussion of the origins of myths, legends, and rituals; and the *Lock of Berenice,* a celebration of the Egyptian Queen Berenice.

Callimachus, Athenian commander at the battle of Marathon (490 BC). He accepted Miltiades' decisive plan to meet the Persians in the field and was killed in the last stages of the battle.

Calliope, steam-operated musical instrument with a series of pipes or whistles played on a keyboard. Invented in America (*c.*1880) and named for the Greek Muse of Eloquence, it was often mounted on circus parade wagons.

Callisthenes of Olynthus (360?–?328 B.C.), Greek philosopher and historian. A nephew of Aristotle, he was chosen as historian of Alexander the Great's Asiatic expedition. He criticized Alexander's adoption of Oriental customs, was accused of plotting against him, and died in prison. He is considered the first historian to refer to the story of Alexander's divine birth. His works include a history of Greece from 387–357 and a history of the Phocian War.

Callisto, satellite of Jupiter; one of the Galilean satellites. Diameter 2795mi (4500km); mean distance from planet 1,168,000mi (1,881,000km); mean sidereal period 16.69 days. △86.

Callistratus (died 355 BC), Athenian orator. Best known for his speech of 366, which is supposed to have inspired the orator Demosthenes. He also commanded Athenian forces sent to intervene in fighting between Thebes and Sparta in 378. He was later condemned, exiled to Macedonia, and then executed for Spartan sympathies. Callistratus was also the name of a mid-2nd century BC Greek author of commentaries on poets.

Call of the Wild The, (1903), adventure novel by Jack London about the great dog Buck and his conflicts with man and nature as he proceeds farther and farther north on a kind of odyssey. When his last master is killed, Buck responds to nature's call and joins a wolf pack, though he often seemed more human than animal.

Calloway, Cab(ell) (1907–); US orchestra leader and singer, b. Rochester, N.Y. Known for his improvisational jazz singing, the "King of Hi-De-Ho" did recordings, radio shows, and nightclub work. The scat-singer of "Minnie the Moocher," he also appeared in *Stormy Weather* (1943) with Lena Horne. In 1952–54 he toured in *Porgy and Bess,* playing Sportin' Life.

Callus, hard, thickened area of skin usually at a place on hands or feet where pressure is continual. A callus may be removed by chemicals or friction.

Caloric Theory of Heat. *See* Heat.

Calorie, the amount of heat necessary to raise one kilogram of water at atmospheric pressure from a temperature of 14.5°C to 15.5°C. The small calorie, written without a capital, is that amount of heat necessary to raise a gram of water through that temperature interval. Thus the Calorie is 1,000 times the size of the calorie. △1508.

Calorimeter, a device that measures the heat energy of a substance. The calorimeter consists of an insulated container filled with fluid, a stirrer, and a thermometer. When a known amount of the heated substance is placed in the calorimeter, it loses heat to the liquid. The stirrer distributes this heat evenly and the temperature change determines the heat energy of the substance.

Caloris Basin. △62.

Calpurnia (*fl.* 1st century BC), Roman noblewoman. A member of the prominent Piso family, she was Julius Caesar's last wife (married 59 BC). She is mentioned in Plutarch and appears as a character in Shakespeare's *Julius Caesar.*

Calumet City, city in NE Illinois; suburb of Chicago. Industries: steelworks, meat packing, chemicals. Settled 1868; inc. 1911. Pop. (1970) 33,107.

Calvary, place where Jesus was crucified. Called Calvary by John, both Luke and Matthew refer to the site as Golgotha. The location has most often been thought to be near the Church of the Holy Sepulchre in Jerusalem, but a small hill called "Gordon's Calvary" has also been proposed as the actual site.

Calvert, Cecilius, 2nd Baron Baltimore (*c.* 1605–75), first proprietor of Maryland. He acquired the grant to the colony of Maryland (1632) after the death of his father, George Calvert. He was an absentee ruler, governing by deputies. A Roman Catholic, he managed to retain the colony through the Puritan Revolution in England, passing control to his son Charles.

Calvert, Charles, 3rd Baron Baltimore (1637–1715), second proprietor of Maryland. He was sent to Maryland by father, Cecilius, as a deputy governor (1661). He became proprietor after his father's death (1675). A Roman Catholic in a predominantly Protestant Maryland, he was autocratic and suppressed a revolt (1676). He went to England (1684) to debate a boundary controversy with William Penn. His charter was overthrown by a Protestant revolt (1689) and he never returned.

Calvert, George, 1st Baron Baltimore (*c.*1580–1632), English statesman. He resigned as secretary of state (1625) when he announced his conversion to Roman Catholicism; he was made a baron the same year. Member of the Virginia Company and the Council for New England, he was granted Avalon in Newfoundland (1623) as a colony. He was dissatisfied over the severe climate and French emnity so he was granted the territory of Maryland (1632). He died before the charter was issued, and the grant passed on to his son, Cecilius.

Calvin, John (1509–64), French theologian, a key figure of the Protestant Reformation; b. as Jean Chauvin. He first prepared for a career in the Catholic Church but then turned to the study of law and, later, the classics. Around 1533 he converted to Protestantism and began work on his *Institutes of the Christian Religion* (published 1536). In this work, frequently revised and expanded, he presented the basics of what came to be known as Calvinism. To avoid persecution, he traveled in France, Italy, and Switzerland. In 1536 he was persuaded to stay in Geneva, Switzerland, and advance the Reformation there. He began a thoroughgoing, austere revamping of the life of the city. Opposition to him emerged, and he was banished in 1538, but he was welcomed back in 1541 and remained there until his death. In 1541 his *Ecclesiastical Ordinances* provided a framework for church and civic life in what came to be called the "Protestant Rome." Regulation of conduct in Geneva was extended to all areas of life. Economic development was promoted by emphasis on such virtues as thrift, industry, sobriety, and responsibility. Supposed witches and heretics (such as Michael Servetus, who was burned at the stake in 1553) were persecuted. Education was promoted. Calvin split with the Lutherans over the nature of the sacrament of the Lord's Supper and vigorously trained many French refugees to act as missionary pastors to that country. He also intrigued with various French nobles in the events that led to the Wars of Religion (1562–98). By the time of his death the brilliant and charismatic Calvin saw the beginnings of the great impact his doctrines were to have thoroughout Western Europe. △1152.

Calvinism, doctrines and attitudes derived from or strongly influenced by Protestant theologian John Calvin (1509–64) and advanced by the churches (Reformed and Presbyterian) established in his tradition. The term is used in several senses, ranging from the narrowly specific to the broadly general, from the theological and moral to the social and psychological. Rejecting papal authority and relying on the Bible as the source of religious truth, Calvinism stresses the utter sovereignty of God and the predestination of every person either to election—by irresistible grace—to bliss in harmony with God or to damnation in separation from him. It politically subordinates state to church and cultivates austere morality, family piety, business enterprise, education, and science.

The development of these doctrines, particularly predestination, and the rejection of consubstantiation regarding the sacrament of the Last Supper caused a split in Protestantism between the Lutheran church and what became the Reformed and Presbyterian churches. Jacobus Arminius (1560–1609) later posed an important challenge to Calvinism over the question of predestination, and his views were adopted by the Methodists and most Baptists. The influence of Calvinism spread rapidly, particularly in Switzerland, France, The Netherlands, England, Scotland, and what became the United States, and it had profound impact on the course of Western cultural history. In Britain and the United States it was part of the Puritan movement. Among important figures in its spread and development were John Knox (1505–72) in Scotland and Jonathan Edwards (1703–58) in what became the United States. △1152–5.

Calvo Doctrine, the nonintervention policy named for the Argentine jurist Carlos Calvo who in 1869 articulated the idea that no nation had the right to exercise diplomatic pressure or armed force against another nation in order to collect debts owed its citizens.

Calypso, in Greek mythology, the daughter of Atlas and Tethys. She reigned over the mythical island of Ogyaria. When Odysseus landed on the island during a storm, she kept him there for seven years. She bore him three sons, Latinus, Nausthinous, and Nausinous. Finally, Hermes was sent by Zeus, king of the gods, to have Odysseus released.

Camagüey, formerly Puerto Príncipe; city in E central Cuba; capital of Camagüey prov.; important agricultural trade center. Industries: exotic woods, cattle raising. Founded 1514. Pop. 178,600.

Camaldolites (Congregation of the Monk Hermits of Camaldoli), Roman Catholic religious order. They were founded as an offshoot of the Benedictines by St. Romuald at Camaldoli in Italy about 1012 during the monastic reform movement of that time. The order ideally sought to combine hermitages and monasteries, but separate establishments of each type were also made. The Camaldolites have a history of both scholarship and evangelization. They operate about 30 establishments today.

Camara, Helder (Archbishop). △1388.

Camargo, Marie. △1194.

Camass, or bear grass, hardy, North American plant. The familiar camassia has long thin leaves, blue or white flowers, and edible bulbs. It grows from British Columbia to California. Family Liliaceae.

Cambacérès, Jean Jacques Régis de (1753–1824), French political leader. He urged moderation during the French Revolution and later supported Napoleon. Despite opposition to Napoleon's aggressive policies he became archchancellor (1804) and duke of Parma (1808).

Cambium, layer of formative cells, only one cell thick, in woody plant stems and roots. This layer manufactures cells from spring until frost, increasing the diameter of the woody stem. It is located between the mature wood and bark, providing a zone of weakness enabling the bark to be peeled off. △448.

Cambodia, independent nation in SE Asia. Once an advanced artistic civilization, then part of French Indochina, it has been buffeted by the SE Asian war. The Khmer Rouge, the Communist military forces, took control in 1975, and a new constitution was adopted in 1976.

Land and Economy. With Laos and Vietnam, Cambodia was once part of French Indochina. It is dependent on rice fields in the level central area formed by the Mekong River basin. Bordered by Thailand, Laos, Vietnam, and the Gulf of Thailand, its SE is covered with mountains and forests. The climate is tropical monsoon. Before WWII the economy was based on rice farming in a 75,000sq mi (200,000sq km) area, plus fishing and forestry. Since the war, the economy has suffered. Exports of rice and rubber have dropped in spite of crash programs, forcing urban dwellers to work in the paddies.

People. Cambodians are descended from the Khmer, S Indian settlers who intermarried with Mongoloid tribes. Ethnic minorities include Chinese, Vietnamese, Cham-Malays, and Burmese. Hinayana Buddhism is the main religion, Khmer the common language. Monastery schools for primary education were always prevalent, and since independence secondary education has been open to almost all. Literacy is 85%.

Government and History. The 1976 constitution provides for a republic with a legislative assembly of 150 members.

A vassal of the Funan empire (AD100–500), Cambodian lineage also includes Indian migrants from the sub-continent. Wealth came from rice and caravan trade tolls. In 802, Jayavarman took the throne, inaugurating a period of great art and architecture in a civilization still seen in the ruins of Angkor, the ancient capital. In 1863, France was asked to provide protectorate status to Cambodia, and in 1953 Cambodia declared its independence. US-Vietnam warfare increased tensions on the country, and in 1970 Gen. Lon Nol took power from Prince Norodom Sihanouk. The country became the Khmer Republic, heavily dependent on US military and economic aid. On April 17, 1975 the Khmer Rouge (Communist National United Front) assumed authority under Khieu Samphan. Prince Sihanouk became titular head of the government, but he resigned in 1976.

PROFILE

Official name: Democratic Cambodia
Area: 69,898sq mi (181,036sq km)
Population: 8,100,000; *Density:* 104 per sq mi (40 per sq km)
Chief cities: Phnom Penh (capital), 393,995
Government: Communist
Religion: Buddhism
Language: Khmer
Monetary unit: Riel
Gross national product: $680,000,000
Per capita income: $81
Industries: textiles, paper, oil products, plywood, tobacco products
Agriculture: forests, fish, rice, rubber, maize, palm sugar, cotton, silk, cattle, tobacco, oil seeds, sweet potatoes
Minerals: iron, copper, manganese, gold, oil
Trading partners: Japan, Singapore, China, France, Hong Kong

Cambon, Jules Martin (1845–1935), French diplomat. Son of the French revolutionary Joseph Cambon and brother of French ambassador Pierre Paul Cambon, he was mediator between the United States and Spain in the Spanish-American War negotiations and a leading negotiator at Versailles in 1919. He served as French ambassador to Washington (1897–1902), Madrid (1902–07), and Berlin (1907–14) and was also governor general of Algeria (1891–97).

Cambon, Pierre Joseph, known as Joseph Cambon (1754?–1820), French revolutionary. Known primarily as a specialist in public finance, he managed and tried to stabilize national finances during the Revolution. He also served in the legislative assembly (1791), convention (1792), and committee for public safety (1793). After encouraging the downfall of Robespierre, he retired in 1795. He was banished during the Bourbon Restoration in 1815.

Cambrian Period, the oldest period of the Paleozoic Era, lasting from about 570 million to 500 million years ago. It is the earliest geological system containing a large assortment of fossils. All the animal phyla, with the exception of the vertebrates, are represented in the seas. The land was barren. The most common forms were trilobites, brachiopods, sponges, and snails. Plant life consisted of seaweeds. *See also* Geologic time; Paleozoic Era. △276, 564, 568.

Cambridge, city in E England, on River Cam, 48mi (77km) NE of London; important medieval river port;

Callao, Peru

Calligraphy

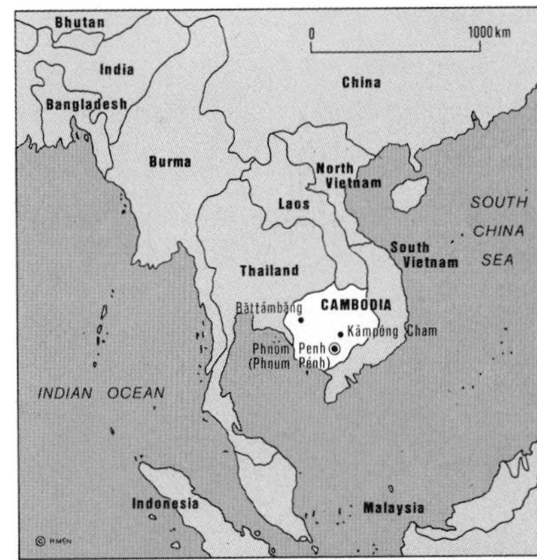

Bhutan
India
Bangladesh
0
1000km
China
Burma
North Vietnam
Laos
SOUTH CHINA SEA
South Vietnam
Thailand
Battambang
CAMBODIA
Kâmpóng Cham
Phnom Penh
(Phnum Pénh)
INDIAN OCEAN
Indonesia
Malaysia

Cambodia

Cambodia: Angkorwat

noted for 12th-century university containing many buildings of historic and architectural value. Industries: printing, cement, electronics. Pop. 98,519.

Cambridge, city in E Massachusetts, across the Charles River from Boston; seat of Middlesex co; site of Harvard University (1636), Radcliffe College (1879), Massachusetts Institute of Technology (1859), and Lesley College (1909); noted for Craig House (1759), Cooper-Frost-Austin house (*c.*1657), Episcopal Church (1761). Industries: printing, publishing, electronics, scientific instruments. Settled 1630; inc. 1846. Pop. (1970) 100,361.

Cambridge Platonists, group of Cambridge philosophers and theologians who advocated a revival of Neo-Platonism in the 17th century, especially Ralph Cudworth and Henry More. They claimed that the mind, or "Candle of the Lord," could achieve mystic union with God by virtue of eternal and immutable ideas. *See also* Neoplatonism.

Cambyses II (*d.* 522 BC), son of Cyrus the Great and King of Persia (529–522 BC), his main achievement was the conquest of Egypt. His other campaigns failed and turned him from a benevolent to a harsh ruler. He died in battle in Syria. △984.

Camden, city in W New Jersey, on Delaware River opposite Philadelphia, Pennsylvania; seat of Camden co; developed around railroad (1834) into a commercial and shipbuilding center; home of Walt Whitman (1873–92). Industries: soup, pens, paper, wood products, electric and electronic goods. Settled *c.* 1681; inc. 1828. Pop. (1970) 102,551.

Camel, large, even-toed, cud-chewing, hoofed mammal. They are covered with dense shaggy brown or gray wool. Their broad, two-toed, padded feet, heavy eyelashes, and hairs in ears protect against sand. They are indispensible beasts of burden in desert areas, being able to survive on minimum food and water and to carry large loads. The one-humped dromedary, native from India to N Africa, is no longer found in the wild. The two-humped Bactrian, native to Chinese Turkistan and Mongolia, is widely domesticated in other areas. The dromedary is taller because of its longer legs, reaching 6.5ft (2.0m) at shoulder. Family Camelidae; genus *Camelus*. *See also* Artiodactyla; Ruminant. △606.

Camel, Bactrian. △1742.

Camel, Dromedary. △1742.

Camel, Sopwith. △1742.

Camellia, evergreen trees or shrubs native to Japan and popular as garden plants. They have oval, dark green leaves and waxy, roselike flowers of pink, red, white, or rose. Family Theaceae; species *Camellia japonica*.

Camelops. △576.

Camelot, in English mythology, the place where King Arthur of England held his court. The popular legend found its way into Tennyson's *The Idylls of the King* which, in turn, produced several other books, movies, and the Lerner and Loewe musical, *Camelot*.

Camel Spider. △604.

Cameos, ornamental jewelry consisting of a carved stone such as onyx, sardonyx, or agate, usually circular or oval, affixed to a background of a different color. The decoration, usually white, is carved in raised relief. Cameos were a very common form of jewelry in the ancient world, and great care was used in choosing stones consisting of several variegated strata. Interest in them was revived in the Renaissance and continues to the present.

Camera, optical device of varying complexity for taking photographs, consisting essentially of a light-tight box in which photographic film can be positioned. Light from the scene being photographed is focused by a lens system onto the film when a shutter is opened for a brief period. The amount of light falling on the film is controlled by the shutter speed, often variable, and by the diameter of the lens (aperture), which can also often be varied using an adjustable diaphragm. A viewfinder indicates what will appear on the photograph. Many cameras also have a rangefinder, enabling a focused image to be produced for a given object distance, and a built-in exposure meter, used to determine correct combination of shutter speed and aperture for the prevailing light conditions. △1518, 1784–86.

Camera Lucida, apparatus for drawing and copying in perspective, developed in 1812 by W. H. Wollaston. A prism is set between the draftsman's eye and the paper in such a way that light is reflected from the object he is copying onto the paper.

Camera Obscura, optical apparatus consisting of a darkened chamber into which light is admitted through a convex lens. A portable version of this was used by 17th- and 18th-century artists to trace scenes from nature. By the 19th century it was reduced to a box, fitted with a lens and mirror, placed on a tripod, and surrounded by black curtains. It eventually developed into the modern camera.

Cameroon (Cameroun), Federal Republic of, nation in W Africa, extending from Gulf of Guinea approx. 700mi (1,125km) NE to Lake Chad. There are five major geographical regions. The coastal plain extends 10–50mi (16–81km) inland from the sea to the forest region; the climate is one of extreme heat and humidity, with an annual rainfall of over 360in (914cm). The mountain region of W Cameroon extends N to the edge of Lake Chad; this region has a mild climate with fertile soil; it is the site of Mt Cameroon, the highest peak in W Africa, rising to 13,354ft (4,073m). The inland forest plateau is less humid than the coastal plain; it produces cacao, bananas, palm oil, rubber and hardwood. The Adamawa plateau region forms a barrier between the N and S. The N Savanna plain extends from the Adamawa plateau region to Lake Chad; little rainfall and high temperatures produce little vegetation.

Cameroon's economy depends almost entirely on subsistance farming. About 80% of the population lives in E Cameroon. There are over 150 different ethnic groups. The major ethnic groups of E Cameroon are the Fulani and Kirdi (N), and Bamiléké, Bulu, Bamoun, Ewondo, Beti, Douala, Bassa (S). W Cameroon ethnic groups include the Bakweri, Douala, Nigerians, Ibo, Ibibio, Ijaw, Ekoi, and Edo. Approx. 60% of all Cameroonians follow tribal animism; 22% Roman Catholic and Protestant; 14% Muslim. There are two educational systems: W Cameroon is modeled after the British system, and E Cameroon is based on the French system. In the S most school age children attend classes; in the N, more isolated region, only a little over 10% attends school. Cameroon has teacher training and technical education institutions. The Federal University in Yaoundé has an enrollment of over 1,000 students.

In 1961 the constitution of Cameroon became official, and an independent federation was formed; in May of the same year Ahmadou Ahidjo was elected president by the National Assembly. The Cameroonian National Assembly is elected for a five-year term by universal suffrage. The assembly is made up of 50 members, 40 from E Cameroon, and 10 from the W. The president appoints the prime minister and cabinet; each province has a legislative assembly, which is headed by a premier who is appointed by the president.

Before gaining independence, Cameroon had a history of foreign domination. The region was discovered in the 15th century by the Portuguese, but the Germans first est a protectorate of Cameroon 1884–1914. During WWI the territory was occupied by both British and French troops and was subsequently divided between the two nations as mandates under the League of Nations. After WWII, Cameroon became a UN trust territory governed by France. An independence movement of the radical Union des Populations du Cameroon (UPC) led to Cameroon's development into an autonomous state in 1957. Three years later Cameroon achieved complete independence.

PROFILE

Official name: Federal Republic of Cameroon (Cameroon)
Area: 183,569sq mi (475,444sq km)
Population: 6,400,000
Chief cities: Yaoundé (capital), Douala, Edéa
Government: Constitutional republic, with elected national assembly
Religion: Animism (major); Christianity, Islam
Language: French, English (official)
Monetary unit: Franc CFA

Camisards, French Protestants of the Cévennes region who rebelled against Louis XIV (1702) after being systematically persecuted. Though small in number, they were at first successful under their leader, Jean Cavalier, but by 1711 their force was diminished and Protestantism had all but disappeared in France.

Camões, Luis Vaz de (1524–80), Portuguese epic and lyric poet. A courtier and soldier, he served in North Africa, where he lost an eye, and India (1553–70). In 1572, after returning to Lisbon, he published *Os Lusíadas,* regarded ever since as the Portuguese national epic. He also wrote fine love lyrics in Portuguese and a few comic dramas.

Camomile, or chamomile, any of several plants of the genera *Anthemis* and *Matricaria*. Flowers of the perennial European camomile are used to make a medicinal tea. This plant is also a popular groundcover. *M. chamomilla* is the annual false camomile. Family Compositae.

Camouflage, in military science, technique used to conceal personnel and equipment from observation by making them blend with their natural surroundings. Examples are nets used to break up angular silhouettes and colors reflecting local environments.

Camp, Walter (Chauncey) (1859–1925), US football expert, b. New Britain, Conn. He is considered the father of US football and had a leading role in the development and shaping of modern rules. He wrote over 30 books on football and physical fitness and originated (1889), with Caspar W. Whitney, the practice of choosing All-American teams.

Campaign, Political, effort conducted by groups or parties to secure election of a candidate or candidates, or adoption of a program. Political campaign styles differ depending on the political system, but the goals are similar. Typically, campaigns require a large degree of organization, strategy, communications, and funding to succeed.

Campanella, Roy (1921–), US baseball player, b. Philadelphia. A catcher, he played for the Brooklyn Dodgers (1948–57). His career was terminated by an off-season car accident. He won the National League's Most Valuable Player Award three times (1951, 1953, 1955) and was elected to the Baseball Hall of Fame in 1969.

Campania, region in S Italy, on Tyrrhenian Sea; includes provinces of Anellino, Benevento, Caserta, Napoli, and Salerno. Capital is Naples. Settled by Greeks and Etruscans, it prospered under Roman rule (4th century BC); conquered by Goths, Byzantines, Lombards, Normans; merged with Italy 1860. Chiefly mountainous; fertile plains produce fruit, grain, wine. Industries: metallurgy, chemicals, textiles, shipbuilding, tourism. Area: 5,249sq mi (13,595sq km). Pop. 5,132,860.

Campanile, bell tower, often near but not attached to a church. They originated in the 6th century, and were the first church spires in Europe. A notable example is the campanile in Piazza San Marco, Venice.

Campbell, Archibald, Earl of Argyll. *See* Argyll, 8th Earl and 1st Marquess of.

Campbell, John Wood, Jr. (1910–) (pseuds. Don A. Stuart, Karl van Kampen), US science-fiction writer and editor, b. Newark, NJ. He began writing for publication as a college student and continued his prodigious output until age 28, when he became an editor. He wrote only sporadically thereafter.

Campbell, (Sir) Malcolm (1885–1948), English automobile and speedboat racer. He was the first man to reach a speed of 300mph (483kph), which he accomplished in his famed automobile *Bluebird* at the Bonneville (Utah) Salt Flats (1935). He then turned to speedboats and set a record by reaching 141mph (227km/h) (1939). He was knighted in 1931.

Campbell, (Mrs) Patrick, born Beatrice Stella Tanner (1865–1940), English actress for whom G.B. Shaw wrote the part of Eliza Doolittle in *Pygmalion* (1912). A distinguished actress, she and Shaw had a platonic affair recorded in a volume of letters later used as the basis for the play *Dear Liar* (1970).

Campbell, Robert (1808–94), Canadian fur trader and explorer, b. Scotland. He worked for the Hudson's Bay Company exploring the Mackenzie River and established posts at Pelfy Banks (1846), Fort Selkirk (1848), and Fort Chipewyan (1856). *See also* Hudson's Bay Company.

Campbell, city in W California, SW of San Jose; main industry is fruit and vegetable processing. Founded 1885; inc. 1952. Pop. (1970) 24,770.

Campbell-Bannerman, (Sir) Henry (1836–1908), British prime minister (1905–08), b. Scotland. Entering Parliament (1868), he held minor posts before becoming war secretary (1886) and reforming his department. As Liberal leader, he formed a strong reforming government (1905–08) before ill health forced his retirement.

Campbell River, village in SW British Columbia, Canada, on E shore of Vancouver Island, at the mouth of the Campbell River; site of John Hart Hydroelectric Project. Industries: lumbering, paper. Pop. 7,825.

Campbell-Stokes Recorder. △216, 218.

Campeche, seaport in SE Mexico, on W coast of Yucatán Peninsula, on Gulf of Campeche; capital of Campeche state; site of pre-Colombian town. Exports: cotton, sugar cane, cigars, hides, tobacco. Industries: cigars, chocolate, tanning, distilling, shoes. Spain landed 1517; founded 1540. Pop. 59,627.

Camp Fire Girls, US organization for girls (ages 6–18), founded in 1910 by Luther Halsey Gulick and other educators "to stimulate and aid in the formation of habits making for health and character." The girls are divided into four groups: Blue Birds (6–8), Camp Fire Girls (9–11), Junior Hi Camp Fire Girls (12–13), and Horizon Clubs (14–18). Publications include *The Camp Fire Girl.* Membership: about 600,000.

Camphor Tree, evergreen tree native to Taiwan, Japan, China, Java, Sumatra, and Brazil. Camphor is obtained from its wood by distillation. Family Lauraceae; species *Cinnamomum camphora.*

Campin, Robert. △1136.

Campinas, city in SE Brazil, 57mi (92km) NW of São Paulo. Industries: sugar refining, metal casting, coffee processing. Pop. 252,145.

Campion, Edmund (1540–81), English clergyman. Although he had strong Roman Catholic leanings, he became an Anglican deacon in 1568. While in Dublin, he wrote a *History of Ireland* (1571). He went to Europe in 1571 and was ordained a Catholic priest in 1578. In 1580 he returned to England to minister to the Catholics there, who were forbidden to practice their religion. He made many conversions. His pamphlet *Decem rationes* (1581) against the Protestants created a sensation. Arrested and tortured on the rack, he refused to recant his religious convictions. Condemned on trumped-up charges of treason, he was hanged, drawn, and quartered. He was beatified by the Catholic Church in 1886.

Campion, common name for the over 500 species of the large genus *Silene* of the pink family. Found mainly near the Mediterranean, certain species grow in central Europe and Great Britain.

Campobello, island in SW New Brunswick, Canada, at the entrance of Passamaquoddy Bay just off the coast of Maine; connected to Lubec, Me., by the Roosevelt Memorial Bridge (1962). Pres. Franklin D. Roosevelt maintained a summer home here; since 1964, administered by a joint US–Canadian Commission as an international park. Area: 2,722acres (1,102hectares).

Cam Ranh Bay, inlet of S China Sea, on E coast of S central Vietnam, between Phan Rang and Nha Trang; site of former French naval base and largest US base during Vietnam War. Length: 10mi (16km). Width: 20mi (32km).

Camus, Albert (1913–60), French novelist, playwright, and essayist, born in Algeria. After working in avant-garde theater and journalism, he became one of the leaders of the French Resistance. He achieved recognition with his first novel *The Stranger* (1942). Despite the recurrent themes of "the absurd" and mankind's powerlessness in his novels *The Plague* (1947) and *The Fall* (1956), and in essays (*The Rebel,* 1951), he committed himself to humanitarian values and received the Nobel Prize for literature in 1957.

Cana (Cana of Galilee), village in Israel, approx. 4mi (6km) NE of Nazareth; where Christ reportedly performed his first miracle by turning water into wine at a wedding.

Canaanites, Biblical name of the people who inhabited Palestine, lower Syria, and Lebanon, dating to the 3rd millennium BC. They occupied the ancient maritime territory of Phoenicia and were known as Phoenicians, the Greek word for "purple," because of their famous Tyrian purple dye acquired from shellfish.

Canada, independent nation in North America. A country rich in minerals and agriculture, it was settled by the French and English and became an independent Commonwealth country with a government patterned on the US federal system.

Land and Economy. The 2nd-largest country in the world (after the USSR), Canada occupies the N half of the North American continent, stretching E and W from the Atlantic to Pacific oceans, N from the 49th parallel to the North Pole, including all the islands in the Arctic Ocean from W of Greenland to Alaska. It is divided into 10 provinces, which are (E–W): Newfoundland, Nova Scotia, Prince Edward Island, New Brunswick, Quebec, Ontario, Manitoba, Saskatchewan, Alberta, and British Columbia. Two territories—Northwest Territories and Yukon Territory—are in the NW. The outstanding geological feature is the Canadian Shield, a 1,850,000-sq-mi (4,791,500-sq-km) arc of Pre-Cambrian rock from Labrador around Hudson Bay to the Arctic islands. The Shield, site of once great mountain chains worn down and covered by the sea, contains valuable minerals—gold, silver, platinum, copper, nickel, cobalt, iron and zinc—making Canada one of the most important mining countries in the world. The Shield's N portion is a treeless plain with permanently frozen subsoil; in its S section are forests. Extending from the Shield's W border to the Canadian Rockies are prairies more than 800mi (1,288km) wide that yield wheat, the dominant crop, and are centers of livestock raising. W Canada is a land of mountains with fishing, agriculture, and lumbering the principal industries. The E provinces provide rich farm lands, forests, coal mines, and major fishing sources along the long coastline. Source of a route into the interior for early settlers, the St Lawrence-Great Lakes area is the most populous section of Canada as well as its economic and political center. It contains over 60% of the population. Abundant minerals have made Canada the world leader in the production of silver, nickel, potash, and zinc; second in gypsum, asbestos, uranium, and sulfur; third in gold, lead, and platinum; fourth in magnesium and fifth in copper. Timber is also valuable, and Canada is a world leader in newsprint production. The growth of manufacturing during the 1950s and 1960s changed Canada from a rural society to an industrial and urban country. Farming employs 7% of the working population. Mechanization has made it possible to export 30%–40% of its total agricultural production, accounting for 11% of total exports. Wheat is particularly important. Of the total fishing catch, 75% is exported.

People. Canada's indigenous Indians and Eskimos are descendants of the Mongoloid tribes who took the NW route from Asia across the Bering Strait 15,000–20,000 years ago. The Arctic region contains about 12,000 Eskimos. Today, 44% of the population is British, coming mainly from the United Kingdom. About 30% is French, descended from the colonists who came to Canada in the 17th and 18th centuries. During the American Revolution many British loyalists fled to Canada from the United States, and after 1900 waves of immigrants from Germany, the Ukraine, and Italy settled on the prairie farmlands or the urban centers. Native Indians have been increasing in number, accounting for over 210,000, mostly living in the prairie states. During periods of US prosperity, emigration has brought Canadians S to work in the industrial cities. Forty-six percent of the population is Roman Catholic with the coalition United Church of Canada next (20%). Literacy is almost 100%.

Government. In its role as a member of the Commonwealth of Nations, Canada is both a constitutional monarchy and a democracy. Internally, there is a federal structure of the 10 provinces and 2 territories. The British monarch names a governor general who serves as symbol of the association with the Commonwealth. Parliament is divided into two houses. Members of the Senate are appointed by the governor general on the advice of the prime minister. Members of the House of Commons are elected. The executive branch includes a cabinet, headed by the prime minister, who is the leader of the party in power.

History. Rivalry between the French and the English marked Canada's early development. John Cabot, sailing for England, reached Newfoundland in 1497 and claimed possession for King Henry VII. In 1534, French explorer Jacques Cartier planted the French flag on the Gaspé Peninsula, and in 1604, Samuel de Champlain established the first French colony, Port Royal, in Nova Scotia; four years later he founded what is now the city of Quebec. French navigators traveled the St Lawrence and Hudson rivers, claiming large interior lands for France. Traders and missionaries penetrated the interior, and French officials made peace with the Indians, thus encouraging French immigration. Seeking a share of the lucrative fur trade, the British in 1670 est the Hudson's Bay Co. Continental war between France and England extended to the New World, and the 1759 defeat of French commander Montcalm brought the fall of Quebec; the 1763 Treaty of Paris gave Canada to Britain. In 1791 a constitutional act divided Canada into two sections—an English portion in what is now Ontario and a French portion in what is now Quebec. The next 40 years were marked by trade and expansion. Alexander Mackenzie, the first white man to cross the continent, reached the Arctic in 1789 and the Pacific in 1793. The United States invaded Canada during the War of 1812, which ended in a stalemate with the

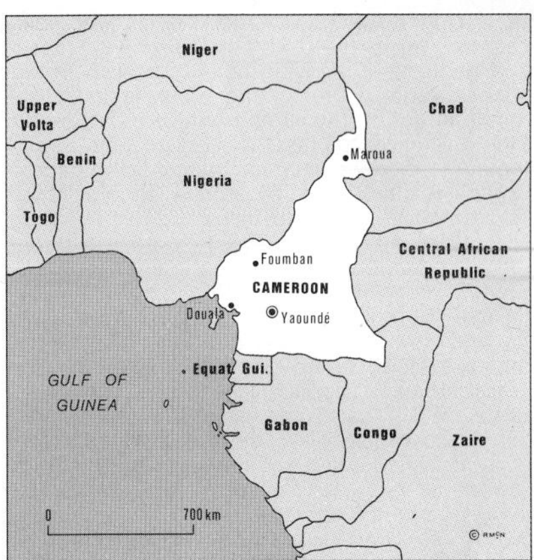

Niger
Upper Volta
Chad
Benin
Maroua
Nigeria
Togo
Central African Republic
Foumban
CAMEROON
Douala
Yaoundé
GULF OF GUINEA
Equat. Gui.
Gabon
Congo
Zaire
0
700km

Cameroon

Albert Camus

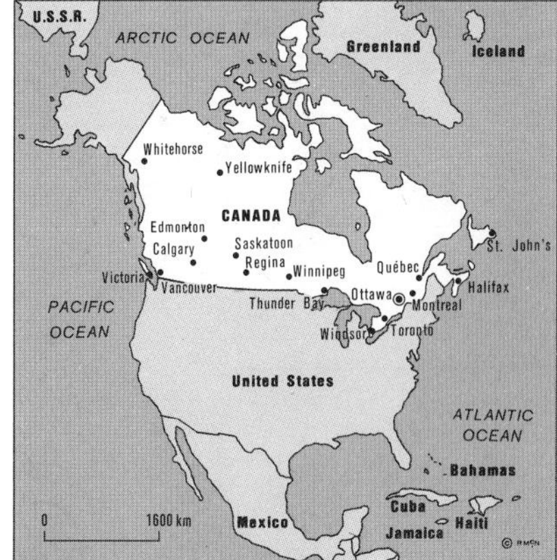

U.S.S.R.
ARCTIC OCEAN
Greenland
Iceland
Whitehorse
Yellowknife
CANADA
Edmonton
Calgary
Saskatoon
Regina
Winnipeg
Québec
St. John's
Victoria
Vancouver
Thunder Bay
Ottawa
Montreal
Halifax
Windsor
Toronto
PACIFIC OCEAN
United States
ATLANTIC OCEAN
Bahamas
Cuba
Haiti
Jamaica
Mexico
0
1600 km

Canada

Canada: Jasper National Park, Alberta

Treaty of Ghent. French Canadians demanded political reform, and in 1840 Upper and Lower Canada were joined and self-government approved. Border questions between the United States and Canada were settled during the same period when the 49th parallel was accepted as the demarcation line. A movement to join the isolated colonies spread across the continent was spurred by promises to build a railway system linking the provinces and to provide future protection against US invasion, especially during the Civil War, when there was anti-British feeling in the United States. In 1867 the British North America Act joined four provinces—Quebec, Ontario, Nova Scotia, and New Brunswick—and provided for a parliamentary system. In 1869 Canada bought land from the Hudson Bay Co., carving out of it the provinces of Manitoba (1870), Saskatchewan (1905), and Alberta (1905). Encouraged by a transcontinental railway promise, British Columbia joined the union in 1871 and Prince Edward Island in 1873. The last addition came in 1948 when Newfoundland became Canada's 10th province. Outstanding leaders during the drive for independence and the early years of confederation included John A. Macdonald, Wilfrid Laurier, and William Lyon Mackenzie King. Canada joined the Allies in WWII and after the war became a member of the United Nations. The Liberal party has dominated politics since the early 1960s, with first Lester Pearson and, from 1968, Pierre Elliott Trudeau as prime minister.

PROFILE

Official name: Canada
Area: 3,851,809sq mi (9,976,185sq km)
Population: 22,737,000
Density: 6per sq mi (2.3per sq km)
Chief cities: Ottawa (capital); Montreal; Toronto; Edmonton
Government: Constitutional monarchy with parliamentary system of government
Religion: Roman Catholic (major), Anglican
Language: English, French
Monetary unit: Canadian dollar
Gross national product: $150,300,000,000
Per capita income: $5,372
Industries: pulp and paper, petroleum products, iron, steel, motor vehicles, aircraft, machinery, chemicals, aluminum, fish canning
Agriculture: wheat, barley, oats, rye, potatoes, fish, cattle, forests
Minerals: oil, iron ore, gold, silver, platinum, copper, nickel, cobalt, zinc
Trading partners: United States, Japan, United Kingdom

Following is a list of the prime ministers of Canada.

PRIME MINISTERS OF CANADA	
John A. McDonald	1867–73
Alexander Mackenzie	1873–78
John A. McDonald	1878–91
John J.C. Abbot	1891–92
John S.D. Thompson	1892–94
Mackenzie Bowell	1894–96
Charles Tupper	1896
Wilfrid Laurier	1896–1911
Robert L. Borden	1911–20
Arthur Meighen	1920–21
W. L. Mackenzie King	1921–26
Arthur Meighen	1926
W. L. Mackenzie King	1926–30
Richard B. Bennett	1930–35
W. L. Mackenzie King	1935–48
Louis Stephen St. Laurent	1948–57
John George Diefenbaker	1957–63
Lester B. Pearson	1963–68
Pierre Elliott Trudeau	1968–

Canada Company, land-settlement company, chartered in 1826 to attract settlers to Upper Canada and to help repay debts from the War of 1812. John Galt was charged with the sale of 1,400,000 acres (567,000 hectares) of crown lands to industry. Effective in promoting colonization, the company operated until the 1950s.

Canada East, official title of Lower Canada after 1841. In 1867 the area was designated as Quebec. *See also* Lower Canada.

Canada First Movement, nationalist Canadian political movement. Arising slowly after the Act of Union (1867), it received its name from a speech given in Toronto in 1871 by W. A. Foster. Its short-lived journal the *Nation* was pro-independence and influenced the formation of the Canadian National Association and the Northwest Emigration Aid Society.

Canada Goose, North American wild goose found in wide ranging habitats, grazing on grasses or feeding on aquatic vegetation in streams and ponds. It has white cheek pouches and a long black neck. Nesting on stream banks or tundra, it lays white eggs (4–10). Length: 23–40in (58–100cm); weight: 3–14lb (1 1/3–6 1/3kg). Species *Branta canadensis*. *See also* Goose.

Canada Lynx, short-tailed cat found in forest swamp areas of Canada, Alaska, and NW United States. A valuable fur mammal, it has large feet and tufted ears and long thick fur that is grayish mottled with brown, white cheek hair, and black ear marks. The gestation period is 62 days and 1–4 young are born. It feeds on hares, rodents, and birds. Length: body—32–36in (81–91cm); tail—4in (10.2cm); weight: 15–30lb (6.7–13.5kg).

Canada West, official title of Upper Canada after 1841. In 1867 the area was designated as Ontario. *See also* Upper Canada.

Canadian Pacific Railway, transcontinental railroad system in Canada. Privately owned, it stretches from Halifax, Nova Scotia, to Vancouver, British Columbia. It grew out of an agreement in 1871 between the Canadian federal government and British Columbia in which the federal government promised to build a transcontinental line if British Columbia joined the Canadian confederation. Construction was begun by the government but, following a political scandal (Pacific Scandal) and other difficulties, it was turned over to a private syndicate in 1880. The main line from Montreal to the Pacific coast was completed in 1885. *See also* Pacific Scandal.

Canadian Pondweed. △452.

Canadian River, river in SW United States; flows from S Colorado S and E across NE New Mexico and NW Texas to Arkansas River in Oklahoma. In mid-19th century river valley was part of pioneers' Fort Smith-Santa Fe Trail. Length: 906mi (1,459km).

Canadian Shield (Laurentian Highlands), great plateau of Canada, roughly outlining the Hudson Bay; extends from the Mackenzie River basin SE through S Ontario and S Quebec (passing through Great Lakes region of N central America), and NE to the Labrador Sea; this large geographic formation is characterized by numerous lakes and rivers and coniferous forests.

Canal, artificial waterway constructed for irrigation, drainage, navigation or in conjunction with hydroelectric dams. Many canals serve multiple purposes. The construction of canals is ancient; 4000 years ago, Nahrwn, 400ft (122m) wide and 200mi (322km) long, was built in ancient Mesopotamia. The longest canal able to accommodate large ships today connects the Baltic and White Seas in the USSR; it is 141mi (227km) long.

Canal Boat, flat-bottomed craft used on canalized natural inland waterways and artificial canals to transport goods. Barges are the best-known. With the enlargement of formerly inadequate canal lock systems, large powered barges are economical transport units, especially in Europe.

Canal Engineering. △1762.

Canaletto (1697–1768), Italian painter, b. Giovanni Antonio Canal. A landscapist, he is most famous for his views of Venice. He was very popular in the 1720s and 30s, especially with visiting Englishmen. He executed four views of Venice for Stephano Conti of Lucca (1725–26) and a large group of Roman scenes in the 1740s. After 1745 he went to England, where he painted many popular London views and landscapes.

Canalo. △68.

Canary, popular cage bird found wild in the Azores and Canary and Madeira islands. These yellowish finches feed on fruits, seeds, and insects and lay spotted greenish-blue eggs in cup-shaped nests. The pure yellow varieties are larger than the wild canaries, and have been domesticated since the 16th century. They are taught various songs by exposing them to recordings. They breed poorly in captivity. Family Fringillidae; species *Serinus canarius*.

Canary Current, cold current of N Atlantic Ocean; flows SW from Spain along NW coast of Africa; joins North Equatorial current at approx. 20° N latitude.

Canary Islands, an island group in the N Atlantic Ocean, approx. 70mi (113km) off the NW coast of Africa. The Canary Islands constitute two provinces of Spain: Las Palmas, consisting of Gran Canaria, Lanzarote, Fuerteventura, Graciosa, Montana Clara, Alegranza, Roque de Ester, Roque del Oeste, Las Isla de Lobos; and Santa Cruz de Tenerife, consisting of Tenerife, La Palma, Gomera, Hierro. The chief cities are Santa Cruz de la Palma and Las Palmas. The area is 2,808sq mi (7,273sq km).

The islands are mountainous, warm, with little rainfall; efficient irrigation allows the development of numerous crops, including bananas, sugarcane, tobacco, tomatoes, nuts, citrus fruits, grapes, and vegetables. The islands' economy is based on the export of agricultural goods. A great quantity of grapes are grown for the manufacture and export of wine. Fishing, fish canning and salting are major industries. Because of the mild climate and beautiful scenery the tourist industry is growing rapidly.

The inhabitants are mostly Spanish immigrants; the original inhabitants, called Guanches, are believed to be of Berber stock. The Guanches have been entirely absorbed by the Spanish settlement.

In 1402 French explorer Jean de Bethencourt attempted unsuccessfully to conquer the islands. Henry III of Castile came to his aid, naming Bethencourt king of the islands, answerable only to Spain. In 1936, Francisco Franco began his revolt against the Spanish republic from the islands. Pop. 1,170,224.

Canasta, card game for two to six players. The game, a branch of the rummy family, is generally played by two sets of partners using two standard decks. The object is to accumulate points through various melding methods, similar to rummy. The cards have different point values, and 3000 points is usually the total needed to win. *See also* Rummy.

Canaveral, Cape, low sandy promontory extending E into Atlantic Ocean in E Florida; site of NASA's John F. Kennedy Manned Space Flight Center, main US launch site for space flights and long-range missiles; Patuck Air Force Base is nearby.

Canberra, capital city of Australia, in Australian Capital Territory, SE New South Wales, 155mi (248km) SW of Sydney on the Molonglo River. Settled *c.* 1824, it was chosen 1908 as the new site of Australia's capital. Designed 1911 by Chicago architect, Walter Burley Griffin, construction began 1913 but was interrupted by WWI and the Depression; by 1927, the capital and some governmental agencies were moved to Canberra; the first meeting of Parliament was held 1947. The transfer of nongovernmental activities to the area greatly spurred the city's development and construction increased with the est of National Capital Planning Commission (1958). By 1960s, Canberra was Australia's largest inland city. It is the site of Australian National University (1946), Canberra University College (1929), Royal Military College, Mt Stromlo Observatory, Parliament House, Yarralumla House (residence of governor-general), The Lodge (home of prime minister), Australian-American Memorial, and approx. 40 international embassies. The federal government is the major employer of Canberra's residents; tourism is a major industry. Pop. 133,100.

Canberra Bomber. △1744.

Canby, Henry Seidel (1878–1961), US author, b. Wilmington, Del. He taught at Yale University for many years and was a founder (1924) of the *Saturday Review of Literature* (now *Saturday Review*). He also wrote several critical studies, including *Thoreau* (1939) and *Whitman* (1943).

Cancer, unchecked growth of tissue spreading through the body, frequently causing death unless diagnosed and treated early. It may occur in virtually any organ, with prostate cancer most frequent in men over 65, breast and cervical cancer most frequent in women. No specific cause of cancer has been determined, although irritants such as smoke may act as triggers to certain types of cancer. Treatment can be surgical, chemical, by radiation, or some combination of these. *See also* Carcinoma; Leukemia; Sarcoma. △712,750.

Cancer, or the Crab, northern constellation situated on the ecliptic between Gemini and Leo; the fourth sign of the zodiac. It contains two open clusters: M44, the Praesepe or Beehive Nebula (NGC 2632), and M67 (NGC 2682). Brightest star Beta Cancri. Astrological sign for the period June 22–July 22. △130, 826.

Candela, or new candle, basic unit of luminous intensity defined as the luminous intensity of a black body of surface area 1/60 square centimeter at the temperature of freezing platinum (1,769°C) and at atmospheric pressure. Symbol cd.

Candelabra Tree. △586.

Candia. *See* Iraklion.

Candida, 3-act drama by George Bernard Shaw. Published in Shaw's book *Plays, Pleasant and Unpleasant* (1898), its first public London performance was in 1904. Candida, wife of clergyman James Morell, is worshipped by poet Eugene Marchbanks, young friend of the family. Forced to choose between them, Candida chooses Morell, the weaker of the two, because he needs her more.

Candide (1759), short novel by Voltaire written as a satire of optimistic philosophical theories. A farcical yet horrific tale, it recounts the adventures of Candide, who has been taught to be thoroughly optimistic about life by his tutor, Pangloss. His journeys are beset by disaster and misfortune, but he relentlessly pursues his ideal in the form of the baron's daughter Cunégonde, who eventually adds to his disillusionment. △1188.

Candlewood. *See* Ocotillo.

Candytuft, annual and perennial plants native to Spain and popular garden flowers. They have large, domelike clusters of white, red, or violet flowers. Species include annual rocket candytuft *(Iberis saxitilis)*; annual candytuft *(I. umbellata)*; and perennial evergreen candytuft *(I. sempervirens)*. Height: to 18in (45.7cm). Family Cruciferae.

Cane, a grasslike plant *(Arundinaria gigantea)* growing in SW United States. With flat 1-ft (30-cm) leaves, it can grow to 25ft (7.6m) in damp swampy areas.

Cane Mills. △342.

Canidae, or dog family, chiefly meat-eating mammals that typically have long muzzles, large canine teeth, long legs, long tail, and blunt claws that cannot be retracted. It includes domestic and wild dogs, coyotes, wolves, jackals, and foxes. It is represented everywhere except Antarctica. Order Carnivora.

Canis Major, or the Great Dog, southern constellation situated south of Monoceros. It contains the bright open cluster M41 (NGC 2287). Brightest star Alpha Canis Majoris (Sirius).

Canker, ulcerous sore, especially around the mouth and lips. Causes may be from injury, allergy, or hormonal reaction. Healing is usually spontaneous.

Cankerworm, two small, slender moth caterpillars that feed on tree leaves. The spring *Paleacrita vernata* which also feeds on fruits, and the fall *Alsophila pometaria* are in the measuring worm family (Geometridae).

Canna, or Indian shot, flowering plant native to tropical America and Asia. Grown as an ornamental, it has large red, pink, yellow, or white flowers and large, broad leaves. Height: 1.5–5ft (46–152cm). Among 50 species is *Canna indica.* Family Cannaceae. △452.

Cannabis. *See* Hemp.

Cannae, ancient town in SE Italy, on the Ofanto River, between modern Barletta and Canosa; site of crushing defeat in 216 BC of Roman army by the Carthaginians under Hannibal. The Roman consul Lucius Aemilius Paulus died in the battle.

Cannel, or **Cannel Coal.** *See* Coal. △282.

Cannes, resort city in SE France on French Riviera, 18mi (29km) SW of Nice; site of 16th- and 17th-century churches in the old part of city; scene of international film festival held each spring. Industries: textiles, shipbuilding. Pop. 67,152.

Cannibalism, eating human flesh as food or for ritual purposes. The practice was once very widespread and still exists in New Guinea and elsewhere. People are eaten to satisfy vengeance or hunger or as a means of acquiring their strength and powers.

Canning, George (1770–1827), English political figure. A follower of the younger Pitt, he entered Parliament in 1793 and was undersecretary for foreign affairs (1796–99), treasurer of the navy (1804–06), and foreign minister (1807–10). He resigned as foreign minister after bitter rivalry, including a duel, with Viscount Castlereagh. As president of the board of control for India (1816–20), he followed reform policies. After Castlereagh's death, he became foreign minister again (1822–27). A conservative himself, by supporting free trade and liberal movements abroad, he shrewdly advanced Britain's interests. After his maneuverings in Latin America provoked the Monroe Doctrine, he stirred up British prejudice against the United States. On the domestic scene he innovated by deliberately appealing outside Parliament for public support for his policies. He became prime minister four months before his death.

Canning. △396.

Cannizzaro, Stanislao (1826–1910), Italian chemist, professor, and legislator who demonstrated the importance of atomic weights in chemical calculations. In 1853 he discovered the Cannizzaro reaction in which an aldehyde is converted to equal amounts of the salt of an acid and an alcohol. He was responsible for the amplification and application of Avogadro's law to atomic theory, and for distinguishing between atomic and molecular weights. *See also* Avogadro's Number.

Cannon, Joseph G. (1836–1926), Republican congressman (1873–91; 1893–1913; 1915–23), b. New Garden, N.C. Known as "Uncle Joe," Cannon was Speaker of the House (1903–11) who ruled with an iron hand, appointing all committees. He chaired the Rules Committee that determined priority of bills and created the arbitrary and partisan control of procedure called "Cannonism." Attempts to oust him (1909–10) failed, causing serious party rifts.

Cannon, Walter B(radford) (1871–1945), US physiologist, b. Prairie du Chien, Wis. He studied the regulations of hunger and thirst in animals, introduced the term homeostasis to describe the ability of an organism to maintain its internal environment, and proposed a theory of emotion that placed the seat of emotions in the thalamus of the brain.

Cannon, cast metal tube used to fire and aim missiles propelled by the explosion of gunpowder in the cylinder. Cannon were first used in the 14th century. Major improvements in the 19th century included steel tubes, more powerful chemical propellants, breech-loading mechanisms, and standardized parts. By World War I, recoil devices were employed to absorb the shock of firing. *See also* Artillery; Howitzer. △1732–1734.

Cano, Juan Sebastián del (*c.* 1460–1526), Spanish navigator who was first to circumnavigate the globe. He commanded one of five vessels in Magellan's famous expedition and assumed control in 1521 after Magellan's death, returning to Spain in 1522. △1122

Canoe, narrow, double-ended, shallow draft boat, propelled by paddles or sail, different forms of which are used on inland and offshore waters by communities all over the world. Canoes range in size from boats easily portable by one man to Maori "war canoes" 60ft (18m) long.

Canon Law, body of ecclesiastical law. In the Roman Catholic church, it is based on custom and regulations set forth by the founders of Christianity, with later additions of decrees of councils and popes and bishops. The most recent compilation of canon law, known as Codex juris canonici, was completed in 1918. It encompasses general universal laws, as well as local diocesan laws, and supersedes all prior compilations. A further revision, initiated in 1959, is now in progress.

Canopus, or Alpha Carinae, the second brightest star visible from earth. Canopus is a yellowish supergiant. Characteristics: apparent mag. −0.71; absolute mag. −5.5; spectral type FO; distance 300 light-years. △134.

Canova, Antonio (1757–1822), Italian sculptor. A foremost neoclassical artist, his works include "Eurydice" (1773; Louvre, Paris), "Orpheus" (1776; Louvre, Paris), "Venus Victrix" (1804; Borghese Gallery, Rome), and the "Amor and Psyche" group (Louvre, Paris). Called to Paris in the early 1800s by Napoleon, he executed a bust of Napoleon from life, in addition to a number of other Napoleonic statues. △1198.

Cantaloupe, or muskmelon, trailing annual vine native to S Asia. Many varieties are cultivated in North America. It has roundish, hairy leaves and small, yellow flowers. The musky, netted fruit is globelike with yellow, white, or red flesh. The true cantaloupe *(Cucumis melo cantalupensis)* has a scaly rind unfamiliar to most people. Family Cucurbitaceae; species *Cucumis melo reticulatus. See also* Melon.

Cantata, musical work consisting of several pieces or movements sung by vocalists and chorus, often accompanied by an orchestra. Cantatas were composed mainly in the Baroque period by such masters as Alessandro Scarlatti, Rameau, and J.S. Bach, who composed over 200, most of them with religious texts. *See also* Baroque Music.

Canal

Canberra, Australia

Candytuft

Cannes, France

Canterbury, Archbishop of, primate of all England according to the doctrines of the Church of England. Residing in Canterbury, Kent, the archbishop also maintains a seat in Lambeth Palace, London. The archbishopric was established when Pope Gregory I sent (597) St Augustine to England on a mission to convert the Anglo-Saxons. During the Reformation, Archbishop Thomas Cranmer accepted the English crown's decision (1534) to make the English monarch, not the pope, head of the Church of England. Although no longer considered the head of all the separate dioceses in England, the archbishop presides as senior bishop over the Lambeth Conferences, which are held every 10 years by the Anglican communities.

ARCHBISHOPS OF CANTERBURY

Augustine	601–04
Lawrence (or Laurentius)	604–19
Mellitus	619–24
Justus	624–27
Honorius	627–53
Deusdedit	655–64
Theodore	668–90
Brihtwald (or Beorhtweald)	692–731
Tatwin (or Taetwine)	731–34
Nothhelm	735–39
Cuthbert	740–60
Breguwine (or Bregowine)	761–64
Jaenbeorht (or Lambert, etc)	765–92
Ethelhard (or Aethelheard)	793–805
Wulfred	805–32
Feologeld (or Feolgild)	832
Ceolnoth	833–70
Ethelred (or Aethelred)	870–89
Plegmund (or Plegemund)	890–914
Aethelhelm	914–23
Wulfhelm	923–42
Odo (or Oda)	942–58
Aelfsige	959
Beorhthelm	959
Dunstan	960–88
Ethelgar (or Aethelgar)	988–90
Sigeric	990–94
Aelfric	995–1005
Aelfheah (or Alphege)	1005–12
Lyfing	1013–20
Ethelnoth (or Aethelnoth)	1020–38
Eadsige	1038–50
Robert of Jumièges	1051–52
Stigand	1052–70
Lanfranc	1070–89
Anselm	1093–1109
Ralph d'Escures (or Ralph de Turbine)	1114–22
William of Corbeil	1123–36
Theobald	1138–61
Thomas à Becket	1162–70
Richard	1174–84
Baldwin	1184–90
Hubert Walter	1193–1205
Stephen Langton	1207–28
Richard le Grant (or Richard of Wethershed)	1229–31
Edmund Rich	1233–40
Boniface of Savoy	1245–70
Robert Kilwardby	1273–78
John Peckham	1279–92
Robert de Winchelsea	1293–1313
Walter Reynolds	1313–27
Simon Meopham	1328–33
John de Stratford	1333–48
Thomas Bradwardine	1349
Simon Islip	1349–66
Simon Langham	1366–68
William Whittlesey (or Wittlesey)	1368–74
Simon of Sudbury	1375–81
William Courtenay	1381–96
Thomas Arundel	1396–1414
Henry Chichele (or Chicheley)	1414–43
John Stafford	1443–52
John Kempe	1452–54
Thomas Bourchier	1454–86
John Morton	1486–1500
Henry Dean	1501–03
William Warham	1504–32
Thomas Cranmer	1533–56
Reginald Pole	1556–58
Matthew Parker	1559–75
Edmund Grindal	1576–83
John Whitgift	1583–1604
Richard Bancroft	1604–10
George Abbot	1611–33
William Laud	1633–45
William Juxon	1660–63
Gilbert Sheldon	1663–77
William Sancroft	1678–91
John Tillotson	1691–94
Thomas Tenison	1695–1715
William Wake	1716–37
John Potter	1737–47
Thomas Herring	1747–57
Matthew Hutton	1757–58
Thomas Secker	1758–68
Frederick Cornwallis	1768–83
John Moore	1783–1805
Charles Manners Sutton	1805–28
William Howley	1828–48
John Bird Sumner	1848–62
Charles Thomas Longley	1862–68
Archibald Campbell Tait	1868–82
Edward White Benson	1883–96
Frederick Temple	1896–1902
Randall Thomas Davidson	1903–28
Cosmo Gordon Lang	1928–42
William Temple	1942–44
Geoffrey Francis Fisher	1945–61
Arthur Michael Ramsey	1961–74
Frederick Donald Coggan	1974–

Canterbury, cathedral city in SE England, on River Stour; market town trading in grain and hops. The present cathedral, built 11th-15th centuries, replaced St Augustine Abbey and a later cathedral that burned; it is the seat of the archbishop and primate of the Anglican Church. Murder of Thomas à Becket (1170) occurred in the cathedral and is commemorated by a tablet; after his canonization, Canterbury became a major pilgrimage center. Geoffrey Chaucer's *Canterbury Tales* (14th century) deal with these pilgrims. The 15th-century tower of the cathedral is 235ft (72m) high. City is also site of University of Kent at Canterbury (1964). Tourism is the chief industry. Founded AD 43. Pop. 33,157.

Canterbury Bells, biennial bellflower native to S Europe and widely cultivated. It has large spikes of cup-shaped pink, blue, or white flowers. Family Campanulaceae; species *Campanula medium. See also* Bellflower.

Canterbury Cathedral. △1104.

Canterbury Tales, The (*c.* 1388–1400), collection of narrative poems by Geoffrey Chaucer, each purporting to be told by one of a party of pilgrims to Canterbury. The pilgrims are described in a vivid "Prologue." The tales range from the courtly "The Knight's Tale" to the bawdy "The Miller's Tale," from the charming "The Nun's Priest's Tale" to the exuberant characterizations by narration in "The Wife of Bath's Tale" and "The Pardoner's Tale." △1100.

Cantigas de Santa Maria. △1078.

Cantilever (1) a projecting beam that is rigidly supported at one end with force applied at the free end, as in a diving board. Used in constructing balconies. (2) A bridge supported by two projecting beams, joined in the center by a connecting member and supported on piers and anchored by counterbalancing members. △1758.

Cantilever Bridge, form of girder bridge, characterized by a span that can be considered as two half-beams effectively anchored at one end and meeting (unsupported) in the middle. The Quebec Bridge (1918) has a main cantilever span 1,800ft (550m) long where it crosses the St Lawrence River. △1758.

Canto, major division of a long poem, such as the cantos comprising Dante's *Divine Comedy,* Edmund Spenser's *Faerie Queene,* and Lord Byron's *Don Juan.*

Canton (Guangzhou), largest city and port in S China, on Pearl River, 95mi (153km) from Hong Kong; capital of Kwangtung prov. From 300 BC, when it was conquered by the first emperor of the Ch'in dynasty, it has been an important trading port. It served as the headquarters (1911) of the revolutionary movement and the Nationalist party and as site of the Whampoa Military Academy, est 1924 and directed by Chiang Kai-shek; the Republic of China was declared here (1920s). Industries: textiles, paper, rubber products, shipbuilding, sugar refining, iron and steel production, furniture. Pop. 2,300,000.

Canton, city in E central Ohio, 20mi (32km) SSE of Akron; seat of Stark co; site of Malone College (1892), Walsh College (1960); was the home of President William McKinley who is buried here in National McKinley Memorial (1907). Industries: water softening equipment, forgings, steel, office equipment. Inc. 1854. Pop. (1970) 110,053.

Cantonese, one of the major dialects of Chinese. Within the Chinese People's Republic it is spoken by about 50 million people, mainly in the extreme southern provinces of Kwangtung and Kwangsi. It is also the dialect spoken by most Chinese in Southeast Asia and in the United States. △866.

Catonsville Nine, group of Roman Catholic anti-war protesters, led by Daniel and Philip Berrigan, who in May 1968 destroyed draft files in Catonsville, Md., to protest US military involvement in Indochina.

Cantor, Eddie (1892–1964), US comedian and singer, B. Edward Israel Iskowitz in New York City. He headlined in Ziegfeld's "Follies" (1916–19), and in the musicals *Kid Boots* (1923–26) and *Banjo Eyes* (1941). Known for singing "If You Knew Susie," "Dinah," "Toot, Toot, Tootsie," and "Ain't She Sweet," he also appeared in films, in a popular radio series, and on television.

Cantor, singer who performs in a religious service. He may lead a choir or the congregation or sing the service himself in response to the rabbi, priest, or minister.

Cantos, The, long poetic work by Ezra Pound. Begun in 1915, it was intended to consist of 120 poems, or "cantos," of which a few remained unfinished at the time of Pound's death in 1972. Complex, erudite, and allusive, *The Cantos* is epic in scope, sweeping through the history of civilization (especially China, Renaissance Italy, and the United States) and ranging from the intensely lyrical and personal to the public and didactic. Much about the events of Pound's own life and his views on the arts and political economy is incorporated as are fragments from many literatures and even musical notes and Chinese characters. Particularly important for the work is material from the *Odyssey,* Ovid's *Metamorphoses,* and the *Divine Comedy.* The general theme of *The Cantos* is the search for exemplars of beauty and order.

Canute II (?994–1035), king of Denmark (1014–28), Mercia (1016), England (1017–35), and Norway (1028–29). He accompanied his father, Sweyn, on the Danish invasion of England (1013). After his father's death (1014) he withdrew to Denmark and was accepted as joint king with his brother until 1018, when he became sole king. He invaded England again (1015) and divided it (1016) with the English king Edmund Ironside. He was accepted as king of the whole country in 1017 after Edmund's death. His rule over England was a just and peaceful one. He restored the church to high position and codified English law. He also worked for good relations with Normandy, Aquitaine, and the Holy Roman Empire. His reign in Scandinavia was more turbulent. He conquered Norway (1028), made one son king of Denmark (1028), and made another son king of Norway (1029). Toward the end of his life he led an army into Scotland to stop Scottish invasions.

Canute IV (1043?–1086) "The Holy," king of Denmark (1080–86) and patron saint. A harsh king, he levied heavy taxes to benefit the church. Planning to invade England, he forced the peasants to mobilize but they rebelled, killing him at the Church of St. Alban at Odense. He was canonized in 1099. Feast: Jan. 19.

Canute VI (1163–1202), king of Denmark (1182–1202). The eldest son of Waldemar I, he was crowned in 1170 at age 7 as co-regent to his father and became king in 1182. During his 20-year reign, Denmark made progress and became more independent of Germany. Archbishop Absalon's military victories enabled Canute to style himself "king of the Danes and Wends."

Canvasback Duck, North American diving duck that is a prized game bird. It has a chestnut head and neck, pale gray back, and black breast and tail. It lays large, greenish eggs (10). Length: 2ft (61cm); weight: 3lb (1.4kg). Species *Aythya valisneria. See also* Duck.

Canvassing Board, electoral body responsible for official vote-counts, tabulations, and certifications during elections. It operates on the city, county, and state levels and is usually bipartisan.

Canyon, deep, narrow depression in the earth's crust, either on land where it is the result of water erosion by a youthful river moving through arid terrain, or marine where its origin is not as clear. It may be the same as the canyon on land with subsidence of the entire riverbed and surrounding terrain or the result of marine currents, particularly turbidity currents. △228, 260.

Canyon de Chelly National Monument, park in NE Arizona; contains ruins of Indian villages (350–1300), cliff dwellings and Mummy Cave. Area: 83,840acres (33,955hectares). Est. 1931.

Canyonlands National Park, park in SE Utah. It is a geological paradise of spires, rocks, and mesas rising more than 7,800ft (2,379m); site of Indian petroglyphs (*c.*1000 years old). Area: 337,258acres 136,589hectares). Est. 1964.

Capa, Robert (1913–54), US war photographer, b. André Friedmann in Hungary. From 1936 in Spain until his death from a land mine in Indochina, Capa portrayed the horror of war and its effect on soldiers and civilians.

Capacitance, or electrical capacity, ability of a capacitor to store electrical charge when there is a potential difference between its plates. The capacitance, C, of a capacitor is equal to the charge, Q, on either plate divided by the voltage between the plates, V; or $C = Q/V$. It is measured in farads. △1544.

Capacitor, or condenser, electrical device having the property of capacitance and consisting of a system of conductors (plates) separated by an insulator (dielectric). Simplest form has two parallel metal plates, each of area A, separated by a distance, d, which is filled with a dielectric of permittivity $\mathbf{E}$. The capacitance, C, is equal to $A\mathbf{E}/d$. △1544.

Cape Breton Island, rocky island in NE Nova Scotia, Canada; separated from the mainland by the Strait of Canso; site of Cape Breton Highlands National Park, numerous summer resorts, and North Barren, highest peak in Nova Scotia. Industries: lumbering, fishing, coal mining, pulp. Ceded from French to British 1763. Pop. 166,943.

Cape Buffalo, several races of large oxen, native to Africa south of the Sahara Desert. Brown to black, their hair is thick on the young, sparse on adults. Horns, recurved, meet at bases over the forehead, forming a helmet. It can run 35mph (56kph). Considered the most dangerous African game animal, its numbers have been greatly reduced because of hunting. Height: to 59in (150cm) at shoulder; weight: to 2000lb (900kg). Family Bovidae; species *Syncerus caffer. See also* Buffalo; Ox. △586.

Cape Coast, city in S Ghana, W Africa, 75mi (121km) WSW of Accra; capital of Central Region; capital of the Gold Coast until replaced by Accra (1877). Industries: fishing, export trade. Settled 1610 by Portuguese. Pop. 51,764.

Cape Cod, sandy peninsula in SE Massachusetts, extends into the Atlantic Ocean in a hook shape, forming Cape Cod Bay; glacial origin. Presently a popular resort area, it was originally a haven for fishing, whaling, and salt making. The area facing the Atlantic is now major part of Cape Cod National Seashore.

Cape Cod National Seashore Recreational Area, land on Cape Cod, Mass; est 1961 by US government to preserve natural scenic beauty of peninsula. Extending from Chatham to Provincetown, it includes beautiful beaches, nature trails, guided walks, and historic sites, including Marconi's first wireless station in United States. Area: 44,660acres (18,087hectares).

Cape Colony, a colony founded by the British in 1806. The area was first occupied by black Africans and Boers and subsequently became a province of the Republic of South Africa. *See also* Cape Province.

Cape Fear River, river in central and SE North Carolina; formed by the confluence of the Deep and Haw rivers; flows to Atlantic. Length: 202mi (325km).

Cape Girardeau, city in SE Missouri, overlooking the Mississippi River; occupied by Union Forces during Civil War; site of Fort D (1861), Southeast Missouri State University (1873); trade and distribution center. Inc. 1843. Pop. 31,282.

Cape Hatteras National Seashore Recreational Area, area of beaches and sand dunes on the Atlantic Ocean in E North Carolina; made up of Hatteras, Bodie, and Ocracoke islands. First national seashore in the United States, site of Cape Hatteras Lighthouse (1870). Authorized 1937. Area: 28,500acres (11,542hectares).

Cape Horn, southernmost point in South America; sighted by Francis Drake in 1578; first rounded in 1616 by Willem Cornelis van Schouten; known for vicious westerly gales; clipper ship trade route to California in the 1850s.

Capek, Karel (1890–1938), Czech novelist, playwright, and essayist. After studying philosophy, he became a journalist. His works chiefly portrayed man's struggle against fate, especially in a scientific world. His writings included *R.U.R.*, a play about robots (1920), and the novel *War with the Newts* (1936).

Capelin, smelt-like, schooling, marine fish found in Arctic and N Pacific. It is distinguished by long anal fin and tufted growths along its sides. Length: 5.9–7.9in (15–20cm). Family Salmonidae; species *Mallotus villosus.*

Capella, or Alpha Aurigae, spectroscopic binary star in the constellation Auriga, both of whose components are yellow giants. Characteristics: apparent mag. +0.09 (combined); absolute mag. +0.12 (Capella A), +0.37 (Capella B); spectral type G8 (Capella A), GO (Capella B); distance 45 light-years.

Cape Province, formerly Cape Colony; cape and province in the Republic of South Africa, bordered by Indian Ocean (SE) and Atlantic Ocean (W); unofficially known as Cape of Good Hope. Slaves were imported in 1658; however the British abolished slavery in 1834, 20 years after the cape was ceded to Britain. Diamonds were discovered in 1867. Parliamentary government est. 1872; joined with Union of South Africa in 1910; site of Stellenbosch, Cape Town, Rhodes, and Fort Hare universities. Industries: wool, diamonds, wine, asbestos. Area: 278,465sq mi (721,224sq km). Pop. 6,199,634.

Capercaillie, largest grouse of European evergreen forests. It is valued as a game bird. The male is mostly black with green reflections, red wattles over the eyes, and some white patches. The smaller female is brownish and lays yellowish eggs (5–8) in a ground-scrape nest after the male performs a trancelike courtship dance. They feed on vegetable matter. Length: 3ft (90cm). Species *Tetrao urogallus.*

Capet, surname given to King Hugh of France and his descendants (987–1328). Although originally an elective monarchy, the throne was passed from father to son for 15 generations by having the eldest son crowned during his father's lifetime. The Capetians gradually extended their rule from the two counties of Paris and Orleans to the whole of France. Philip Augustus, who reigned from 1180 to 1223, laid the foundations for the French monarchy by dispossessing the English king of Normandy, Anjou, and Maine. The dynasty's prestige was enhanced by the just reign of Louis IX. △1096.

Capetians, French royal family forming the third dynasty, it began with Hugh Capet, Duke of Francia, in 987 and ended with Charles IV in 1328, providing France with a total of 15 kings. Hugh Capet was elected king after the death of Louis V, the last of the Carolingians. The House of Capet effected alliance with the Church; dominance over the feudal forces, thus extending the king's rule over the entire country; and the beginnings of an administrative system. It was succeeded by Philip VI of the House of Valois.

Cape Town, capital city of the Republic of South Africa, and capital of Cape prov.; at the foot of the Table Mts. It is the site of Union Parliament, a 17th-century castle, and the National Historic Museum. Noted educational and tourist center, it includes the University of Cape Town, Stellenbosch University, and Table Mt aerial cableway. Industries: clothing, engineering equipment, motor vehicles. Pop. 691,-296.

Cape Verde (Cabo Verde), island republic in E Atlantic Ocean, approx. 300mi (483km) W of Dakar, Senegal (W Africa). Formerly an overseas province of Portugal, the island group became independent on June 5, 1975, through the efforts of the African Party for the Independence of Guinea and Cape Verde, which is now the controlling party in the government. The archipelago is comprised of about 15 islands and islets, which are divided into two groups: the Windward Islands (N), including Boa Vista, Sal, São Nicolau, Santa Luzia, São Vicento, Santo Antão, Ilhéu Branco, and Ilhéu Raso; and the Leeward Islands (S), including São Tiago (the largest), Maio, Fogo, Brava, and the Ilheus do Rombo. Capital is Praia, on S São Tiago island.

The islands are of volcanic origin and are generally mountainous, containing deposits of coal and salt, important to the group's economy. Inhabitants are primarily Portuguese and African. The literacy rate is comparatively high and many Cape Verdian males leave the islands to work in Portugal or Africa. Mining, fishing, and farming are the chief occupations, but agricultural output of cash crops (coffee, tobacco, sugar cane, oranges, sisal, peanuts) has been hindered by recurrent droughts, including a severe one in 1975. Discovered 1455 by Alvise Ca Da Mosto serving Prince Henry of Portugal, the archipelago became part of Portugal in 1495 and was administered as a separate province of Portugal until its independence.

Canterbury, England

Canton, China

Cape Town, South Africa

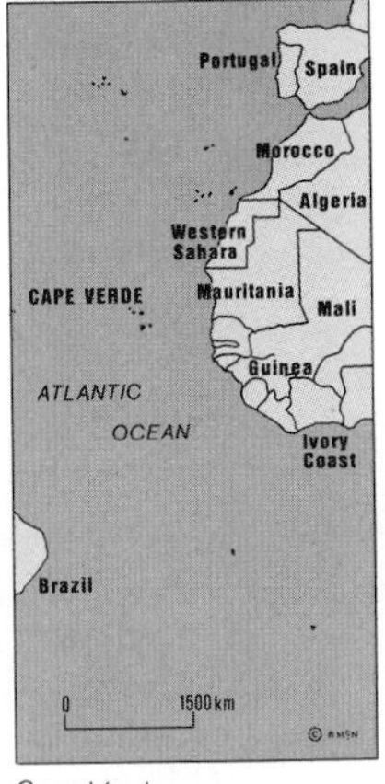
Portugal
Spain
Morocco
Algeria
Western Sahara
CAPE VERDE
Mauritania
Mali
Guinea
ATLANTIC
OCEAN
Ivory Coast
Brazil
0
1500km
Cape Verde

PROFILE

Official name: Cape Verde
Area: 1,557sq mi (4,033sq km)
Population: 300,000
Chief cities: Praia (capital); Mindelo
Religion: Roman Catholic
Language: Portuguese
Monetary unit: escudo
Gross national product: $40,000,000.

Cape Verde Peninsula, peninsula in Republic of Senegal; westernmost projection of Africa. Discovered *c.* 1445 by Portuguese Navigator, Joao Fernandes; mostly dunes, limestone cliffs and marshes. Dakar, capital of Senegal, is on its S coast.

Cap-Haïtien, seaport town in N Haiti, West Indies, 95mi (153km) N of Port-au-Prince; capital of Nord dept.; settled by French, it served as capital of colonial Haiti 1697–1770; occupied 1791 by forces of Toussaint L'Overture, rebel slave leader; 1811–1820 was capital of kingdom of Henri Christophe who built the Sans Souci Palace and Citadelle La Ferrière, still standing. Exports: coffee, sugar. Pop. 44,123.

Capillarity, the elevation or depression of a liquid in a small open tube, called a capillary tube, inserted in the liquid. Capillarity is caused by the surface tension forces between the liquid and the tube material. *See also* Surface Tension. △1504.

Capillary, the smallest blood vessel in the body. The walls of capillaries consist of a single cell layer through which oxygen diffuses from the blood and carbon dioxide and dissolved wastes diffuse into the blood, turning it from its arterial bright red to its venous dark purplish.

Capital, in accounting, the obligation a business enterprise has to its owners. Capital includes not only the owner's contribution but also profits retained within the business for future use. △934.

Capital, in economics, factor of production that includes plant and machinery used in the production process. The rate of return on capital is normally referred to as the interest rate. Capital is fixed in the short run in that new plants and new equipment cannot be obtained in a specific short-run period. Capital is normally provided through the sale of stocks and bonds or other forms of debt.

Capital Gain, the difference between the buying price for a capital asset and a higher selling price. If a stock is purchased for $100 and is later sold for $120, a $20 capital gain has occurred. *Long-term* capital gains occur if the asset has been held more than six months. They are taxed at a more favorable rate than *short-term* capital gains in which the asset is held less than six months. The time requirements have been changed to 9 months for 1977 and to 12 months from 1978 on.

Capitalism, economic system characterized by private ownership of the means of production and by dependence upon the profit motive and the market direction of productive efforts. In a capitalistic system the owners of productive resources, by trying always to maximize the income earned by them, presumably ensure that the most effective use is made of all resources. As each resource owner searches for higher returns from his resources, he is forced to use them in the way consumers in general want them used, for this is the only way he can earn the maximum return. Under capitalism, government plays a relatively small part in the economy, regulating more than controlling. Producers and consumers are free to make most economic choices. △902.

Capital Punishment, punishment of death for a person convicted of a criminal act. A United Nations' survey conducted in 1975 revealed that 103 of the 135 member states retained capital punishment. No one was executed in the United States from 1967 until 1977. After protracted litigation and circus-like publicity, convicted murderer Gary Gilmore was executed by a Utah firing squad to end the suspension of capital punishment in the United States.

Capitol, building in Washington, D.C., in which the US Congress convenes. President Washington laid the cornerstone in 1793. William Thornton was the original architect. Congress first met in the partially completed building in 1800. In 1814 it was burned to the ground by the British. Its restoration was supervised by Benjamin Latrobe and then Charles Bulfinch, who saw its completion in 1830. Under the direction of Thomas U. Walter it was greatly enlarged (1851–65), with the addition of the extended House and Senate wings and central dome. The building is approximately 750ft (229m) long and 350ft (107m) wide, with the dome reaching a height of 288ft (88m).

Capitol Reef National Park, park in S central Utah; named for a dome-shaped whitecap rock along the Fremont River; the park features a 60-mi (97-km) uplift of sandstone cliffs with highly colored sedimentary formations dissected by narrow high walled gorges. Area: 254,242acres (102,968hectares). Est. 1937.

Capone, Al(phonse) (1899–1947), US gangster of the Prohibition era, b. Italy. He grew up in Brooklyn, N.Y. First a bodyguard to Johnny Torrio, Capone inherited the former's crime empire. In 1927, Capone's wealth was about $27,000,000, most derived from illegal liquor. He was eventually convicted of income tax evasion (1931) and imprisoned.

Caporetto, Battle of. △1306.

Capote, Truman (1924–), US author, b. New Orleans. His first novel, *Other Voices, Other Rooms,* appeared in 1948. Other works include a novella, *Breakfast at Tiffany's* (1958), *The Grass Harp* (1951), and *In Cold Blood* (1965), with which Capote stated he had introduced a new literary genre, the nonfiction novel.

Cappadocia, ancient plateau region of Asia Minor (modern E central Turkey); cuneiform tablets found at Kültepe record Assyria-Asia Minor trade before 1800 BC; part of Persian Empire (6th century BC); semi-independent kingdom (*c.* 225 BC); annexed as Roman province AD 17; early Christian center (AD 1st century).

Capra, Frank (1897–), US film director, b. Italy. He was noted for his comedies, eg *Platinum Blonde* (1931), *It Happened One Night* (1934), and *You Can't Take It With You* (1938). During World War II he directed propaganda films. Postwar films included *A Hole in the Head* (1959) and *A Pocketful of Miracles* (1961).

Capri, Island of (Isola Di Capri), island in Bay of Naples, Italy. A favored Roman resort, the Roman Emperor Augustus resided here; it passed from French to British rule several times during the Napoleonic Wars; was returned to Kingdom of the Two Sicilies 1813. The Blue Grotto, a famous cavern on the coast, was rediscovered in 1826; site of ruins of two medieval castles. Industries: tourism, agriculture, fishing. Area: 4sq mi (10sq km). Pop. 7,725.

Capricornus, or the Sea Goat, southern constellation situated on the ecliptic between Sagittarius and Aquarius; the tenth sign of the zodiac. Usually referred to as Capricorn only for astrological purposes, this constellation contains the faint globular cluster M30 (NGC 7099). Brightest star: Delta Capricorni (Deneb Algiedi), an eclipsing binary. Astrological sign for the period Dec. 22–Jan. 19. △136, 826.

Caprivi (de Caprara de Montecucoli), Count Leo von (1831–99), German military and political leader. A distinguished army officer in the Franco-Prussian War, he served as chief of the admiralty (1883–88), reorganizing the navy. He succeeded Bismarck as chancellor (1890–94). He abrogated the antisocialist law and reduced the length of military service. These actions alienated conservatives as did his favoring of industrial growth over agriculture.

Caprivi Strip, narrow strip of land in NE South West Africa, bounded by Botswana (S), Zambia and Angola (N); named in honor of German Chancellor Leo von Caprivi, who wanted the land as outlet to Zambezi River; desert climate; some farming is done in the easternmost section of the strip, where the Zambezi River is used for irrigation. Length: 300mi (483km). Width: 50mi (81km).

Capsule, Spacecraft, the portion housing the astronauts or scientific payload of the mission. The capsule must be designed to withstand the heat, acceleration, shocks, vibration, spinning or tumbling, radiation, meteoritic impacts, vacuum and low temperatures of space while maintaining a stable environment for the passengers and instruments. The capsule contains the spacecraft controls, portholes, instruments to monitor the physical activities of the crew, TV cameras, ventilators, and hand grips. Capsules have double walls to protect against meteorites and highly reflecting exteriors. △142, 1724.

Captains Courageous (1897), adventure novel by Rudyard Kipling. Set among the fishermen of the Newfoundland Grand Bank, it tells of the exploits that transform millionaire's son Harvey Cheyne on the fishing ship *We're Here.*

Capua, town in S Italy, destroyed by Saracens AD 84[illegible] and rebuilt on site of ancient Casilinum 856; until 1860 it was part of Kingdom of Naples; scene of WWII action; site of Norman castle (1050) and castle towers of Emperor Frederick II (1239). Industries: munitions, chemicals, sugar. Pop. 19,176.

Capuchin, also cebus or ring-tailed monkey, small monkey found from Honduras to N Argentina. Generally brown, yellowish, or gray, they are day-active tree dwellers. Omnivorous but preferring fruit, they are the most common pet monkeys in the United States and Europe. Species white-faced *Cebus capucinus,* weeper *C. apella,* white-fronted *C. albifrons,* black capped *C. nigrivittatus. See also* Monkey. △602.

Capuchins, a Roman Catholic religious order, begun by Matteo da Bascio in 1525 as a reform movement of the Franciscans. The pointed hood (in Italian *capuccino*) of their habit provided them with their name. They also wear beards. The order is a strict one emphasizing austerity. They played an important role in the Counter-Reformation, particularly in preaching and in foreign missions. In 1619 they were constituted an independent order, the Order of Friars Minor Capuchin. In 1622 they were instrumental in founding the Congregation of the Propagation of the Faith in Rome. One of the largest Catholic orders, they number about 15,000 friars today.

Capulin Mountain National Monument, historic area in NE New Mexico; contains cinder cone of an extinct volcano. Est. 1916. Area: 775acres (314hectares).

Capybara, largest living rodent, native to Central and South America. Semi-aquatic with webbed feet, it is big-bodied, short-legged, tiny-tailed, and nearly hairless. Length: 4ft (1.2m); weight: 110lb (50kg). Species *Hydrochoerus Lydrochaeris.* △546, 602.

Carabac. *See* Water Buffalo.

Caracal, or Persian lynx, short-haired, long-eared carnivore of the cat family native to Africa and parts of Asia and India. Mainly nocturnal, caracals are quick and agile. They have slender, red-furred bodies and pointed ears tipped with black tufts. Length: 2.5ft(76cm); weight: to 40lb(18kg). Family Felidae; species *Felis caracal.*

Caracalla, Marcus Aurelius Antoninus (188–217 AD), Roman emperor (211–17). The son of Septimius Severus, he earned his name because he wore a Gallic tunic *(caracalla).* He resented sharing rule with his brother, Geta, whom he murdered along with 20,000 of Geta's supporters. He pacified the German frontier, planned further Persian conquests, and extended Roman citizenship to all free male inhabitants of the empire (212) in order to increase the income tax. He erected the Baths of Caracalla. Macrinus killed him in Asia and succeeded him as emperor.

Caracara, agile, diurnal bird of prey related to falcon found from S United States through South America. They are black and white and eat carrion and live animals. Length: 20–25in. (50–62.5cm). Family Falconidae.

Caracas, capital city of Venezuela, on Guaire River; under Spanish control until 1821; city almost destroyed by earthquake (1812); birthplace of Simón Bolívar, leader of revolts against Spain; site of Central University of Venezuela (1725), Plaza Bolívar, official center of city, equestrian statue of Simón Bolívar, and colonial cathedral (1614); oil boom in 1950s spurred city's growth. Industries: automobiles, oil, breweries, rubber goods. Founded 1567. Pop. 1,625,000.

Caracul. *See* Karakul.

Caramanlis, Constantine (1907–), prime minister of Greece. A lawyer, he entered parliament in 1935 and served in cabinet posts after World War II. He became prime minister in 1955, promoting industrialization and a pro-West foreign policy, resigning in 1963 after quarreling with King Paul and going into exile. He returned in 1974 after seven years of military rule, forming a civilian government and scoring an impressive election victory.

Caravaggio, Michelangelo Merisi da (1573–1610), Italian painter. His realistic and naturalistic style was in direct contrast to the late Mannerist style of his day. He attracted many admirers and followers for a time, but the movement died out after 1620, by which time his influence had been felt throughout Europe. His early works include the *Calling of St Matthew* and the *Martyrdom of St Matthew, Boy with a Basket of Fruit,* and *The Fortune Teller. Rest on the Flight into Egypt* (*c.*1590–95) demonstrates Caravaggio's earlier graceful, lyrical, and delicate style, while *Raising of Lazarus* (1609) is typical of his later realistic style, marked by emotional intensity and angular drawing. Caravaggio's artistic manipulation of light enables his works to suggest a spirituality and religious feeling that his otherwise realistic rendering would deny. △1162.

Caraway, biennial herb native to Eurasia and cultivated for its small, brown, crescent seedlike fruit that is used for flavoring foods. It has feathery leaves and white flowers. Family Umbelliferae; species *Carum carvi.*

Carbide, inorganic compound of carbon with a more electropositive element. Boron and silicon both form hard carbides used as abrasives. Many transition metals also form carbides, in which the carbon atoms occupy interstitial positions in the metal lattice. Some electropositive metals form ionic carbon compounds. The best known is calcium carbide (CaC_2), which reacts with water to give acetylene.

Carbohydrate, organic compound of carbon, hydrogen and oxygen, in which the last two have the same proportions as in water. The simplest carbohydrates are the sugars, usually with five or six carbon atoms in each molecule. Glucose and fructose are naturally occurring sugars with the formula $C_6H_{12}O_6$, but with different structures. One molecule of each combines with loss of water to make cane sugar ($C_{12}H_{22}O_{11}$). Starch and cellulose have hundreds of glucose molecules linked together, in long lines in cellulose but branching in starch. *See also* Saccharide. △1570, 1572.

Carbolic Acid, solution of phenol (C_6H_5OH) in water, used as a disinfectant.

Carbon, common nonmetallic element (symbol C) of group IV of the periodic table, known from earliest times. There are two crystalline allotropes; graphite, a soft black slippery solid, and diamond, a very hard gemstone. Various amorphous forms of carbon also exist. Industrial diamonds are used in rock drills and in cutting and polishing tools. Graphite is a solid lubricant and is also employed in electrodes, crucibles, and lead pencils. Amorphous carbon has many uses including as a pigment for inks, filler for rubber, and absorbent for decolorizing and deodorizing. Chemically carbon is notable for the vast number of compounds it forms with hydrogen and other nonmetals. Properties: at. no. 6; at. wt. 12.011; sp. gr. 1.9-2.3 (graphite), 3.15-3.53 (diamond); melt. pt. 6422°F (approx.) (3550°C); sublimes 6093°F (3367°C); most common isotope C^{12} (98.89%). △1554–60, 1568–70.

Carbonaceous Chondrite, a special kind of rare stony meteorite. *See also* Stony Meteorite.

Carbonari, early-19th-century members of Italian secret society advocating liberal, nationalist position. Opposed to conservative regimes imposed on Italy after the Council of Vienna (1815), they were a bourgeois ideological model for Giuseppe Mazzini's Young Italy movement, which was to be important to the Risorgimento at mid-century.

Carbonates. △1568.

Carbon Black, finely divided form of carbon made by incomplete combustion of natural gas or petroleum oil. It is used in both natural and synthetic rubber and in printing inks. Properties: sp. gr. 1.8–2.1; boil. pt. 7592°F (4200°C).

Carbon Cycle, circulation of carbon in the biosphere. Atmospheric carbon dioxide is changed to carbohydrates by plants during photosynthesis. Animals eat the plants and return carbon dioxide to the atmosphere by defecation and decomposition.

Carbondale, city in SW Illinois; site of Southern Illinois University (1874); Memorial Day was first celebrated here in 1868; railway and trade center for a coal mining and farming area. Inc. 1869. Pop. (1970) 22,816.

Carbon Dioxide, colorless odorless gas (formula CO_2) that occurs in the atmosphere (0.03%) and as a product of combustion of fossil fuels. In its solid form (dry ice) it is used to refrigerate foods, etc.; as a gas it is used in carbonated beverages, as a fire extinguisher, and to provide an inert atmosphere in welding. Properties: density 1.98 kg dm^{-3}; melt. pt. (5.2 atm) -69.9°F (-56.6°C); sublimes -109.5°F (−78.5°C). △1564, 1568, 1570–72.

Carbon Dwarf Star, very late type of red dwarf star belonging to either of two spectral classes designated N and R. The absorption lines in the spectra of these stars are due chiefly to carbon compounds and the surface temperatures involved range downward from about 2600°K to 1700°K. △100.

Carbon 14. △276.

Carboniferous Period, the fifth geologic division of the Paleozoic Era, lasting from 345 to 280 million years ago. Often divided into two periods: the Mississippian and the Pennsylvanian. It is called the "Age of Coal" because of extensive swampy forests that turned into most of today's coal deposits. Amphibians flourished and the first reptiles appeared. Land snails, scorpions, spiders, giant archaic dragonflies and cockroaches were common. Marine life including sea lilies and sharks abounded in warm, shallow inland seas; lobefins, lungfishes, and numerous primitive rayfinned fishes lived in fresh water. *See also* Geologic Time; Paleozoic Era. △276, 562, 568.

Carbon Microphone. △1792.

Carbon Monoxide, colorless odorless highly poisonous gas (formula CO) formed during the incomplete combustion of fossil fuels and occuring in coal gas and the exhaust gas of internal-combustion engines. It is used in producer gas, in metallurgy, and in the manufacture of chemicals. Properties: density 1.25 kg dm^{-3}; melt. pt. −326°F (−199°C); boil. pt. −312.7°F (−191.5°C).

Carbon Tetrachloride, colorless nonflammable liquid with characteristic odor (formula CCl_4) prepared by the chlorination of methane or the catalytic reaction of carbon disulfide and chlorine. It is used as a refrigerant, insecticide, degreaser, and dry cleaning fluid. Properties: sp. gr. 1.59; melt. pt. −9.4°F (−23°C); boil. pt. 170.2°F (76.8°C). △1568.

Carborundum, trade name for silicon carbide (SiC) abrasives and refractories prepared by heating silica (SiO_2) with carbon in an electric furnace. It is used in grinding wheels, abrasive grains and powders, and valve-grinding compounds, and in refractory bricks and blocks. Nearly as hard as diamond, it slowly oxidizes at temperatures above 1,832°F (1,000°C).

Carboxylic Acid, member of a class of organic compounds containing the group CO·OH. The commonest example is acetic acid, CH_3COOH, present in vinegar. Carboxylic acids can be made by oxidizing an alcohol (an intermediate aldehyde is produced). Generally, they are weakly acidic; like other acids they form salts with bases and esters with alcohols. Esters of high-molecular weight carboxylic acids, such as stearic, lauric, and oleic acids, are present in animal and vegetable fats; for this reason carboxylic acids are often called fatty acids. The systematic names are formed using the suffix -oic (ethanoic acid, CH_3COOH). *See also* Alcohol. △1574.

Carboxyls. △1570.

Carburetor, device used in gasoline-powered internal-combustion engines to vaporize and mix fuel with air and inject the mixture into the engine inlet airstream in the correct ratio for proper combustion. Generally steady speed requires a ratio of 15:1 air to fuel. Richer ratios of 10:1 air to fuel are necessary for starting cold engines.

Carcassonne, town in S France, on Aude River, 57mi (92km) SE of Toulouse; capital of Aude dept. Originally fortified by the Romans in 1st century BC, old part of town is hilltop medieval fortress; Visigoths built towers in 6th century that are still intact; fortifications were added in 12th century. New city across river is a farm trading center. Industries: tourism, textiles, shoes, rubber. Pop. 43,616.

Carcinogen, substance or agent that causes cancer. Carcinogens include chemical agents, radiation, and some viruses. Many different chemical carcinogens have been identified in laboratory animals and a smaller number are definitely established for man. For example, beta-naphthylamine causes bladder cancer among workers in the dyestuffs industry, coal tar and coal-tar derivatives produce skin cancer, and carcinogenic hydrocarbons in tobacco smoke cause lung cancer.

Carcinoma, one of two major forms of cancer, a malignant growth of epithelial cells, which can push into surrounding tissues. *See also* Cancer; Sarcoma.

Cardamine, or bitter cress, genus of herb found in wet areas. The leaves, round or featherlike, are borne on long stalks; flower clusters are white and rose or purple; and seedpods are long and narrow. Species include spring cress *(C. bulbosa)*—height: to 18in

Truman Capote

Al Capone (left) *with detective*

Capuchin

Constantine Caramanlis

(45.7cm); mountain water cress *(C. rotundifolia); and* cuckooflower *(C. pratensis).* Family Cruciferae.

Cardamom, herb from tropical India. A thick plant, it has white flowers with yellow and blue striped edges. The seeds are used as a spice and in medicine. Height: to 10ft (3m). Family Zingiberaceae; species *Elettaria cardamom.*

Cárdenas, Lázaro (1895–1970), president of Mexico (1934–40), whose previous experience included the governorship of Michoacán and cabinet posts. Far to the left of his predecessors in office, Cárdenas accelerated the distribution of communal lands, expropriated oil properties (1938), and encouraged labor unionism.

Cardiac Cycle, process by which the heart pumps blood. Blood enters the heart while it is relaxed (diastole), filling the atria and ventricles. Contraction (systole) of the ventricles forces blood out of the heart. At the end of this contraction, the ventricles again relax, and the heart starts to fill again, readying for the next cycle. *See also* Circulatory System; Heart. △688.

Cardiff (Caerdydd), capital of Wales, and major port, in South Glamorgan on Severn estuary at mouths of rivers Taff, Rhymney, and Ely; seat of university college of South Wales and Monmouthshire (1893); site of 11th-century castle; administrative center for Mid and South Glamorgan. Industries: steel, shipbuilding, motor components, cigars, paper, chemicals, brewing. Pop. 278,221.

Cardigan Welsh Corgi, guard and cattle dog (working group) brought to British Isles over 3000 years ago by Celts. Related to the dachshund, it has a wide, flat head with medium-length, tapered muzzle; large, wide-set, erect ears, rounded at tips; long, strong body; short, slightly bowed legs; and long fox brush tail. The moderately long coat can be red, sable, black, tricolor, or blue merle—all with white marks. Average size: 12in (30.5cm) high at shoulder; 15–25lb (7–11.5kg). *See also* Working Dog.

Cardinal, rank in the hierarchy of the clergy of the Roman Catholic Church. Ranked after the Pope, most are bishops, nominated as cardinals by the Pope. The title of "Eminence" is used to refer to a Cardinal. With administrative functions, they reside in Rome unless they are bishops of foreign dioceses. A new pope is elected by the College of Cardinals. *See also* Cardinals, College of.

Cardinal, or redbird, North American songbird with a pleasant, clear, whistlelike song. The male has bright red plumage and crest and a thick orange-red bill. The female is duller in color. They feed on seeds, fruits, and insects. A loose, cup-shaped nest, lined with fine grass and hair, holds the pale blue, heavily spotted eggs (4) incubated by the female. The male helps feed the young. Length: to 9in (23cm). Family Fringillidae; species *Richmondena cardinalis.*

Cardinal Number, number expressing the content of a set but not the order of its members. Thus 6 is a cardinal number in "6 books". Two sets have the same cardinal number if their members can be put in one-to-one correspondence—a concept that allows the idea of cardinal numbers of infinite sets. The set of integers is said to have cardinal number X (aleph-null). The set of all real numbers cannot be put into one-to-one correspondence with aleph-null and is a "larger" infinite set. Other higher sets can be constructed leading to arithmetic of transfinite numbers.

Cardinals, College of, also known as the Sacred College, group of cardinals serving as advisors and counsellors to the pope. It is ranked highly in the Roman Curia, after the pope. During a vacancy in the papal office, the College of Cardinals controls the church and elects the new pope.

Cardiology, branch of medicine that deals with the diagnosis and treatment of the diseases and disorders of the heart and vascular system. △716.

Cardozo, Benjamin Nathan (1870–1938), US jurist, b. New York City. In 1891 he was admitted to the bar and (1913) was elected to the New York Supreme Court. He was appointed by Herbert Hoover to the Supreme Court. He served as an associate justice (1932–38). Considered a liberal, he strove to simplify the law and to create an intermediary department between the legislature and the courts. His decisions on New Deal legislation were extremely influential.

Cardozo, Francis Louis (1837–1903), US public official, b. Charleston, S.C. He served as secretary of state and treasurer in South Carolina state government during Reconstruction. Later he was pastor of Temple Street Congregational Church in New Haven, Conn.

Carducci, Bartolommeo (1560–1608) and **Vincenzo** (1568?–1638), Italian painters. These brothers went to Spain in 1585. Bartolommeo painted frescoes in the Escorial library and altarpieces in the church of San Felipe el Real, introducing the Baroque style to Spain. Vincenzo painted *The Martyrdom of St. Andrew* in Toledo Cathedral and a series of paintings for El Paular monastery. He also wrote *De las Excelencias de la Pintura* (1633).

Carducci, Giosue. △1240.

Carey Act (1894), US law authorizing the president to grant land to the Western states on the condition that it be irrigated. The states were to sell land to settlers, who were required to cultivate at least 20 acres (8 hectares). The act was largely ineffective.

Cargo Cult, millenarian religious and political movement in parts of Melanesia where natives have been suddenly confronted by white civilization. They expect their ancestors to return in planes or ships laden with modern goods and to free them from white control and the need to work. As part of the cult they prepare runways and landing areas for the expected cargoes.

Caria, ancient division of Asia Minor, in SW part of modern Turkey; ruled by Lydia (6th century) then Persia; conquered 334 BC by Alexander and later Syria, became part of Roman province 125 BC.

Cariama. *See* Seriema.

Carib, group of American Indians, relatively few in number, scattered over a large area of N South America. They speak dozens of related but different languages often loosely referred to as Carib, but more accurately known as the Cariban languages.

Caribbean Sea, extension of N Atlantic Ocean, bounded by South America, Central America, and the West Indies; location of 12 independent island republics. Main tributary rivers are: Magdalana and Atrato of Columbia; San Juan Grande and Coco of Nicaragua; and Motagua of Guatamala. Sea is crossed by international shipping lanes to Panama Canal. Area: 750,000sq mi (1,942,500sq km).

Cariboo Mountains, mountain range in E British Columbia, Canada, separated from main range of Rocky Mts by upper Fraser River; W foothills were scene of 1860 gold rush. Length: approx. 200mi (322km). Highest peak is Mt Sir Wilfred Laurier, 11,750ft (3,584m).

Caribou, or reindeer, large deer inhabiting N Canada, Alaska, E Siberia, Greenland, and Arctic Eurasia. Their thick coats have woolly underfur and the broad hooves can be splayed out for support in snow. Both males and females have antlers. Male antlers are long, sweeping beams with forward projecting brow tines. Gregarious, some formerly assembled in herds of thousands for fall migration. Some types are now almost extinct. They mate in September and October. The gestation period is eight months with 1–2 calves born. They eat grasses, sedges, leaves, lichens, and mosses. Height: 4ft(1.2m) at shoulder; weight: to 700lb (320kg). Family Cervidae; genus *Rangifer. See also* Deer. △548, 592.

Caricature, art history term meaning a charged or loaded portrait. The caricaturist attempts to convey the essence of his subject in a comic likeness. More generally, the term is used to denote a pictorial burlesque or ludicrous representation. The word and genre first appeared in the late 16th century. Bernini was a master caricaturist. Hogarth attempted to distinguish between depiction of character, his forte, and comic likeness, but the two traditions merged. Daumier, the 19th-century French political caricaturist, was a great master. In the 20th century many popular graphic artists have combined caricature with social and political satire.

Caries, Dental. *See* Cavity, dental.

Carina, or the Keel, extensive southern constellation situated south of Vela and Puppis. It contains the Keyhole Nebula (NGC 3372). Brightest star Alpha Carinae (Canopus). △134.

Carleton, Guy, 1st Baron Dorchester (1724–1808), British military figure and colonial administrator, b. Ireland. Entering the British army in 1742, he saw service in North America during the French and Indian War, including at the Battle of the Plains of Abraham (1759). He became lieutenant governor of Quebec in 1766 and governor in 1768. He conciliated the French-Canadians, and his policies were confirmed by the Quebec Act passed by the British Parliament (1774). As British military commander in Canada in 1775, he defeated the Quebec campaign (1775–76) of the Americans in the Revolutionary War. Clashes with British officials then led to his retirement and departure from Canada (1778). In 1782, however, he returned as commander in chief of British forces in Canada. He was named a baron and governor in chief of British North America in 1786. Serving as governor until 1796, he advocated the federation of all British colonies in North America and promoted the Constitution Act of 1791.

Carlisle, borough in S Pennsylvania, 19mi (31km) W of Harrisburg; seat of Cumberland co; station on Underground Railway before Civil War; site of Dickinson College (1773), US Army War College (1951), First Presbyterian Church (1757), and grave of Molly Pitcher, Revolutionary War heroine. Industries: steel, shoes, rugs, quartz crystals. Founded 1751 on land formerly belonging to William Penn; inc. 1782. Pop. (1970) 18,079.

Carlisle, Charles Howard, Earl of (1629–85), English statesman, member of the powerful Howard family. He joined the commonwealth cause in the Civil War, and served in many capacities during Cromwell's rule, in the executive, in the army, and in parliament. He regained favor after the Restoration, was given several titles and military positions, and served as ambassador to Russia, Sweden, and Denmark (1663–64). He was governor of Jamaica (1677–81).

Carlisle, Frederick Howard, 5th Earl of. *See* Howard, Frederick, 5th Earl of Carlisle.

Carlists, Spanish faction that favored the royal claims of Don Carlos (1788–1855) and his successors. When Ferdinand VII left the throne (1833) to his daughter, Isabella II, rather than his brother Carlos, civil war broke out. Isabella's forces finally won in 1840. Carlist sentiments persisted, however, and several uprisings (1860, 1869, 1872) failed, but the Carlists seized considerable territory in 1873. That uprising was ended in 1876, but Carlist sentiments—and Carlist pretenders—have persisted to the present.

Carloman, name of several members of the Frankish Carolingian dynasty, including **Carloman** (715–54), mayor of the palace of Austrasia; **Carloman** (828–880), king of Bavaria and Italy; and **Carloman** (died 884), who became sole ruler of the realm. △1066.

Carlos, or Don Carlos (1545–68), Spanish crown prince, son of Philip II and Maria of Portugal. He was engaged to Elizabeth of Valois, daughter of the King of France, but she married his father instead. Although Carlos has been romanticized—particularly in Schiller's play and Verdi's opera—evidence indicates that he was mentally deranged and possibly homicidal. Philip kept him in prison, where he died.

Carlos, or Don Carlos (1788–1855), Spanish prince and pretender to the throne. His elder brother Ferdinand VII changed Spanish law so that his daughter Isabella II could succeed him, which she did in 1833. Carlos was then proclaimed king by his partisans, known as Carlists, and civil war ensued. Isabella won in 1840, and Carlos went into exile. In 1845 he resigned his pretensions in favor of his son Don Carlos II. *See also* Carlists.

Carlsbad. *See* Karlovy Vary.

Carlsbad, city in SE New Mexico, on Pecos River; seat of Eddy co. Carlsbad reclamation project begun in 1906 has formed lakes, canals and ditches that serve 20,000acres (8,100hectares). Nearby is Carlsbad Caverns, a national park. Industries: mining, ranching, tourism. Inc. 1918. Pop. (1970) 21,297.

Carlsbad Caverns National Park, park in SE New Mexico. A series of limestone caves, 60,000,000 years old, are the largest yet discovered. The caverns are characterized by magnificent stalagmite and stalactite formations, and countless bats that swarm in the evenings, except in winter. Still not totally explored. Area: 46,753acres (18,935hectares). Est. 1930.

Carlyle, Thomas (1795–1881), Scottish philosopher, critic, and historian. An early study of German Romantics led to his translation of Goethe's *Wilhelm Meister* (1824). His most successful work, *Sartor Resartus* (1833–34), combined philosophy and autobiography. His histories include *The French Revolution* (3 vols. 1837), and a study of Frederick II of Prussia (6 vols. 1858–65). He was antidemocratic n his political thought and sought strong heroes or leaders, as expressed in a series of lectures *On Heroes, Hero Worship, and the Heroic in History* (1841).

Carmel, Mount, mountain ridge in NW Israel; extends 15mi (24km) from Esdraelon plain to Mediterranean Sea; home of the prehistoric Carmel man, a link between Neanderthal and modern man; associated with biblical prophets Elijah and Elisha; grapes for Mt Carmel wine are grown here; site of many monasteries and Jewish kibbutzim; Order of Carmelites founded here AD 1156. Height: 1,789ft (546m).

Carmelites, the "Order of Our Lady of Mount Carmel;" religious order founded by St Berthold in Palestine in 1154. The order of Carmelite Sisters was founded in 1452. The primitive rule of poverty, vegetarianism, and solitude, established by Albert of Vercelli in 1209, was revitalized in the "Teresian Reform" of St Teresa in the 16th century. Missionary work is stressed.

Carmen (1875), opera in 4 acts by Georges Bizet, French libretto by Henri Meilhac and Ludovic Halévy, after Prosper Mérimée's novel. The title role is for mezzo-soprano but is sometimes sung by soprano or contralto. Carmen, a femme fatale, induces Don José (tenor), a corporal of the guard, to join the gypsy smugglers, then deserts him for the toreador Escamillo (baritone) and meets her tragic death at the hands of Don José. △1256.

Carmichael, Stokely (1941–), US black activist, b. Trinidad. As chairman of the Student Nonviolent Coordinating Committee (1966), he popularized the term "black power." He joined the more militant Black Panther party (1967) and served as its prime minister until 1969. He left the Panthers in protest of their associations with white radicals and lived in self-imposed exile in Africa until 1972 when he returned to the United States. He married singer Miriam Makeba.

Carmina Burana, a manuscript collection of popular Latin songs from a 12th-century monastery in Bavaria. Probably composed and perpetuated by minstrels and students, many of the songs or poems tell of gambling and drinking, but some have moral or religious subjects. During the 18th-century, several translations were published in Europe, and the lyrics were set to music by Carl Orff in 1935.

Carnallite. △1554.

Carnap, Rudolph (1891–1970), German philosopher. A member of the Vienna Circle and recognized as a founder of logical positivism, he came to the United States from Europe in 1936. Coeditor of the *Journal of Unified Science* (formerly *Erkenntnis*) with Hans Reichenbach, he wrote extensively on the theory of probability, theory of knowledge, mathematical logic, and the philosophy of science. *See also* Logical Positivism.

Carnarvon, Henry Howard Molyneux Herbert, 4th Earl of. *See* Herbert, Henry Howard Molyneux, 4th Earl of Carnarvon.

Carnation, popular name for a perennial of European origin, now widely grown in greenhouses. A slender-stemmed herbaceous plant that grows to 5ft (1.5m), the carnation blooms from October to June. Each plant produces 18 to 24 blooms ranging in color from white to yellow, pink and red. In some varieties the petals are variegated. Carnations are grown commercially for cut flowers. Family Caryophyllaceae; species *Dianthus caryophyllus.*

Carnegie, Andrew (1835–1919), US industrialist and philanthropist, b. Scotland. He came to the United States as a boy and at 16 he became one of the first US telegraph operators, working for the Pennsylvania Railroad for 12 years (1853–65). Foreseeing the demand for iron and steel, he left the railroad and started the Keystone Bridge Works, and from 1873 he concentrated on steel. He bought oil fields, a railway, and steamships and by 1901, when his Carnegie Steel Co. was sold for $250 million to the US Steel Co. combine, it was producing 25% of the steel sold in the United States. He endowed 2,500 libraries and donated more than $350 million to foundations. In 1900 he founded the Carnegie Institute of Technology in Pittsburgh and in 1902 the Carnegie Institution of Washington, D.C. △1278.

Carnegie Hall, music theater in New York City, opened in 1892 and named after philanthropist Andrew Carnegie, one of its chief benefactors. Until 1962, when the first halls of Lincoln Center opened, it was the home of most symphony concerts in New York City. It is world famous as a concert hall where the greatest popular and classical musical artists from all over the world often perform. It has excellent acoustics and seats about 3,000 people.

Carnegie Institute, US art museum in Pittsburgh. The museum (est. 1896) houses a special collection of paintings by Pittsburgh artists, along with collections of oriental ivories, bronzes, sculpture, jades, paintings, and textiles. It also contains European and American decorative arts, paintings, sculpture, drawings, and prints; 19th to early 20th-century French artists; and European furniture, porcelain, and silver.

Carnera, Primo (1906–1967), Italian boxer. Standing over 6ft 5in (195.6cm) tall and weighing 260lbs(117kg), he was the biggest man ever to win the world's heavyweight championship (1933) when he defeated Jack Sharkey in Long Island City, N.Y. He lost the title in the same arena to Max Baer (1934).

Carnic Alps (Alpi Carniche, Karnische Alpen), mountain range of the Eastern Alps, between S Austria and NE Italy, in Carniola region; year-round resort area. Highest peak is Mt Kellerwand, 9,217ft (2,811m).

Carnivora, an order of about 274 living species of mammals found worldwide (except for the Antarctic and some oceanic islands). They probably arose from insectivores during the Paleocene. Most are carnivorous, having teeth adapted for eating flesh, a simple stomach and short intestine, clawed toes, and a well-developed brain. The clavicles (collar bones) are lacking or are vestigial. Some of the best known are cats, dogs, bears, hyenas, weasels, raccoons, civets, and seals.

Carnivorous Plant. *See* Insectivorous Plant.

Carnot, (Lazare) Hippolyte (1801–88), French politician. A republican who sided with the revolutionary radicals of the 1848 February Revolution, he served as minister of education in its first provisional government. A member of the national assembly (1864–69), he became a life senator in 1875. He was the son of L. N. M. Carnot (scientist and statesman) and father of Sadi Carnot (4th president, 3rd Republic).

Carnot, Nicolas Léonard Sadi (1796–1832), French army officer and engineer. His major work, *Réflexions sur la puissance motrice du feu* (1824), provided the first theoretical background to the steam engine and introduced the concepts of reversible cycles and the second law of thermodynamics. He died of cholera at the age of 36 and his work was forgotten until it was revived by Lord Kelvin in 1848.

Carnot, Sadi (1837–94), French political leader, president of the Third Republic (1887–94). After quashing the antirepublican movement by supporting the arrest of Gen. Georges Boulanger, he successfully defended the regime during the Panama Canal scandal (1892). He was stabbed to death by an Italian anarchist.

Carnot Cycle, the steps gone through by a heat engine (such as a steam or gasoline engine) that transform heat energy into mechanical work. All such engines extract heat at high temperature from some reservoir (the boiler or the gasoline); use the expansion of gases at that temperature to perform work such as moving a piston; and then reject waste heat into another reservoir, such as the atmosphere, at lower temperature. This process is often diagrammed on a pressure-volume graph. Such graphs allow comparison of the efficiencies of widely differing types of engines. △1510.

Carnotite, a secondary vanadate mineral, potassium uranium vanadate, an ore of uranium and radium important for atomic energy. Occurs in the Colorado Plateau, Australia, and Congo as yellow-green crusts or cavity fillings in sandstone and in fossilized wood. Finely crystalline (probably orthorhombic), dull or earthy; sp gr 3–5.

Carol I (1839–1914), prince of Romania (1866–81); first king (1881–1914). He aided Russia in the first Russo-Turkish War, 1877–78. Romanian independence and Carol's sovereignty were recognized by the Congress of Berlin in 1878; Carol was crowned in 1881. Romania was neutral during the First Balkan War (1912), but in the second it joined Serbia and Greece against Bulgaria. As a result, Romania became, by 1913, the strongest Balkan power. Carol preserved the neutrality of Romania at the start of World War I, but sympathized with the Germans.

Carol II (1893–1953), king of Romania (1930–40),

Caricature: John Wayne in True Grit

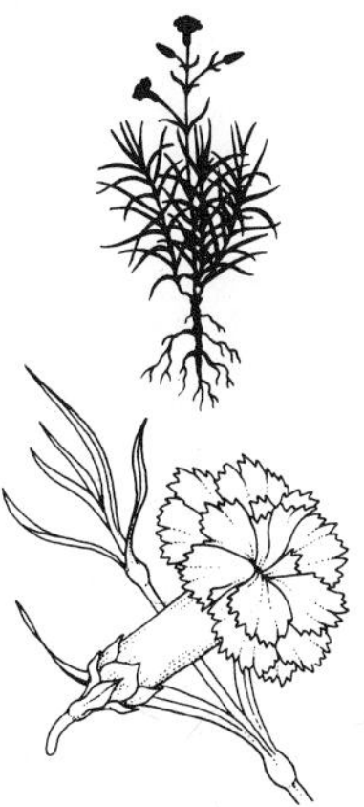

Carnation

Andrew Carnegie

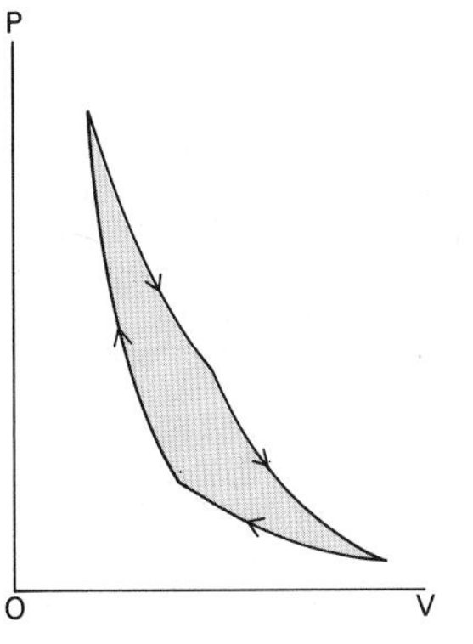
P
O
V

Carnot cycle

grandnephew of Carol I. His 1917 morganatic marriage to Mme. Zizi Lambrino ended in divorce, and in 1921 he married Helen, a princess of Greece. In 1925 he renounced the throne to move to Paris with his mistress Magda Lupescu. He returned in 1930 and supplanted his son Michael as king, despite opposition of the Liberals and economic crisis conditions. Carol II supported the Romanian Fascist party. Anti-Jewish laws and rigid censorship were part of his program to become dictator, but German pressure forced him to abdicate in favor of his son Michael in 1940, leaving the real power in the hands of the dictator, Ion Antonescu.

Caroline Affair (1837), United States-Canadian altercation. In 1837, Canadian rebels, under William Lyon Mackenzie, took refuge on Navy Island, in the Niagara River. A US boat, the *Caroline*, which supplied the rebels, was captured, set on fire and sent over Niagara Falls by Canada's Capt. Andrew Drew. One US citizen was killed. The controversy's arbitration led to the Webster-Ashburton Treaty. *See also* Rebellion of 1837; Webster-Ashburton Treaty.

Caroline Islands, archipelago of more than 900 volcanic islands, coral islets, and reefs in W Pacific Ocean, N of the equator; part of US Trust Territory of the Pacific Islands since 1947; larger islands include Palau, Ponape, Truk, and Yap. Fishing is the main occupation; most natives are Micronesians. Exports: cacao, tapioca, dried bonito. Area: 830sq mi (2,150sq km). Pop. 66,900.

Caroline of Brunswick (1768–1821), queen of George IV of Britain. They were separated for most of their marriage, but on George's accession (1820) she claimed her rank of queen. The government introduced a divorce bill, but Caroline won public sympathy, the case was abandoned, and she retained her title, although she was prevented from entering Westminster Cathedral to attend his coronation.

Carolingian Renaissance, cultural revival in France and Italy under the encouragement of the Emperor Charlemagne (742–814). Having enlarged and enriched the Frankish kingdom and organized an efficient government, the illiterate monarch was able to gather notable educators and artists from all over his kingdom and beyond, including the British teacher Alcuin of York, who helped him found a palace school at Aachen. He promoted Catholicism, art, and learning by founding abbeys and encouraging church building. As the first Roman emperor in the West in over 300 years, he imposed a new culture in Europe, combining Christian, Roman, and Frankish elements. Although his renaissance declined along with his empire after his death, its influence remained until the later Middle Ages. △1080.

Carolingians, dynasty that governed in France from 751 to 987; in Germany from 751 to 911; and in Italy, sporadically, from 774 to 901. Their alliance with the popes and their strong administrative ability enabled the Carolingians to rule new kingdoms, transforming Europe from a group of tribes into feudal monarchies. Their empire was at its peak under Charlemagne, who was crowned "Emperor of the Romans" in 800. △1066, 1070–72.

Carotene, plant pigment with vitamin A activity; obtained from fruits and vegetables in the diet and converted by the eye into visual pigment, necessary for sight.

Carotenoid, one of a group of fat-soluble plant pigments ranging in color from yellow to red. Carotenoids also occur in some animal fats. They include three isomers of carotene, a red pigment that is converted in the liver into vitamin A.

Carothers, Wallace Hume (1896–1937), US chemist, b. Burlington, Iowa, who discovered the synthetic fiber now called nylon. He committed suicide before seeing its enormous success. *See also* Nylon.

Carotid Artery. △688.

Carousel, musical play by Richard Rodgers and Oscar Hammerstein II, originally appearing on Broadway in 1945 and based on Ferenc Molnar's play *Liliom.* It contains several successful songs including "If I Loved You" and "June Is Bustin' Out All Over" and was made into a successful motion picture in 1955.

Carp, freshwater food fish found in temperate waters. Farmed in Japan for low-cost protein, it has four fleshy mouth whiskers and is brownish or golden. Length: to 40in (101.6cm); Weight: 60lb (27.2kg). Family Cyprinidae; species includes common *Cyprinus carpio* and Asiatic grass carp *Ctenophrynogodon idella.*

Carpathian Mountains, mountain range in central and E Europe, beginning in E Czechoslovakia and extending NE to Polish-Czechoslovakian border; Northern Carpathians (Beskids and Tatra) run E along border and SE through W Ukraine, USSR; Southern Carpathians (Transylvania Alps) continue SW to Danube River; sparsely settled except for valleys in S regions. Industries: lumbering, mining, tourism. Highest peak is Gerlachovka, 8,737ft (2,665m) in Northern Carpathians. Length: 950mi (1,530km).

Carpenter, Malcolm Scott (1925–), US astronaut and naval officer who, in the Aurora 7, was the second American to make an orbital space flight (May 24, 1962), circling the earth three times. In 1965 he left the space program to lead teams in Sealab II, an experiment in living and working under the Pacific. Carpenter helped inaugurate Sealab III in 1967, then in 1969 retired from naval duty.

Carpenter Ant, large black ant, 0.25 to 0.75in (6.35 to 19mm) long, that makes its home in galleries in damp wood. It feeds on honeydew from aphids and not the wood in which it lives. It is found worldwide. Family Formicidae; Genus *Camponotus.*

Carpenter Bee, yellow and black to metallic bee, 0.25 to 1in (6–25mm) long, found worldwide. It makes its nest in plant stems or wood. The larger ones resemble bumblebees. Family Apidae, Subfamily Xylocopinae. *See also* Bee.

Carpentersville, village in NE Illinois on the Fox River, 38mi (61km) NW of Chicago. Industries: pumps, plowshares, steel specialties. Inc. 1887. Pop. (1970) 24,059.

Carpentier, Georges (1894–1975), French boxer. He was the world's light-heavyweight champion (1920–22). He lost a heavyweight championship bout to Jack Dempsey (1921) at Boyle's Thirty Acres, Jersey City, N.J., in the sport's first $1,000,000 gate. He was elected to the Boxing Hall of Fame in 1964.

Carpentry, the craft and trade of cutting, working, and joining lumber for structural and functional purposes. Involved are basic house construction, the building of staircases, windows and doors, and furniture-making and decorative woodwork. Many specialized tools and techniques have been developed over the centuries.

Carpetbaggers, epithet used after the US Civil War to refer to Northern whites affiliated with the Republican party who went to the South to participate in Reconstruction. The name referred to the carpetbag in which these people often carried their belongings. △1278.

Carpet Beetle, small beetle whose larvae feed on rugs, upholstery, stored clothing, and other textile products. The best protection against them is frequent and thorough housecleaning. Genera *Anthrenus* and *Attagenus.*

Carpet Sweeper. △1820.

Carra, Carlo. △1296.

Carracci, Agostino (1557–1602), Italian printmaker and painter. His work was influential in the Bolognese reform movement, which led to the classicist trend of 17th-century painting in Rome. His works include *Communion of St. Francis* (*c.*1581), *Pluto* (1592), *The Communion of St. Jerome* (*c.*1594), and *Galatea* (1597–99). His brother Annibale and cousin Lodovico were also artists.

Carracci, Annibale (1560–1609), Italian fresco painter. His work includes influential frescoes in the Farnese Gallery (1597–1604), *Crucifixion* (1583), *Crucifixion* (1594), and the Baroque-styled works *Beaneater* and *Resurrection.* He was the brother of the artist Agostino Carracci and cousin of the artist Lodovico Carracci.

Carracci, Lodovico (1555–1619), Italian painter. He dominated the artistic scene in Bologna as leader of the Carracci Academy, which included his cousins Agostino and Annibale Carracci. He made a strong contribution to Baroque art through such works as *Bargellini Madonna* (1588), *Preaching of St. John the Baptist* (1592), and *The Crucifixion* (1614) *See also* Baroque Art.

Carrack, small wooden sailing ship first appearing in the Middle Ages and characterized by one or two large square-rigged main masts, one or two smaller lateen mizzen or rear masts, and a rear rudder. One example was the *Santa Maria* of Christopher Columbus. △1678.

Carranza, Venustiano (1859–1920), as first chief c the constitutionalist army during the Mexican Revolu tion, he defeated Huerta (1914). Interim president i 1915, he allowed the Pershing expedition to pursu Villa, resulting in the US occupation of Veracru Elected president in 1917, he was unable to impos a civilian successor. Carranza was murdered in a vi lage in Puebla in 1920.

Carrara, formerly Apuania; city in central Italy; site o renowned marble quarries, used by Michelangelo Notable landmarks include Pisan-style 12–14th-cer tury cathedral, 13th-century castle. Chief industry i the production and exportation of marble. Pop. 66 821.

Carrel, Alexis (1873–1944), US surgeon, b. France He was awarded the 1912 Nobel Prize in physiolog or medicine for his development of a technique fo sewing blood vessels end to end. He also contribute to tissue culture research. △802.

Carrera Blanco, Luis (1903–73), Spanish admira and political leader. He fought on the Nationalist sid in the Spanish Civil War and was associated with th Francisco Franco regime from the beginning. In 197 he was named premier and was widely expected t succeed Franco. But in December 1973 he was assas sinated, apparently by Basque nationalists.

Carrera Brothers, José Miguel (1785–1821), Juar José (1782–1818), Luis (1791–1818), Chilean inde pendence leaders and political rivals of Bernard O'Higgins. José Miguel became de facto president o Chile in 1811 and again in 1814. Juan José and Lui were executed by firing squad in 1818; José Migue in 1821.

Carriages. △1686.

Carrier, in disease, any person, who in apparen good health harbors a disease that does not affec him, yet upon accidental contact, the disease can b transmitted with resultant full-blown infection. △ 1792–94, 1800.

Carrier Pigeon, a homing pigeon; any domestic pi geon used for racing or carrying messages and trainec to return to its loft by being released at gradually increased distances. The name is also given to a breec of large pigeons with long wings, bare skin about the eyes, and a greatly developed cere, the fleshy cover ing at the base of the bill.

Carriers, in Electronics. △1546.

Carrier Wave, a high frequency electromagnetic wave modulated by sound or light signals in wireless transmission. The length and frequency of its carrier wave identifies each individual transmitter, so that a receiver can be tuned to its channel. To prevent interference, transmitter carrier waves are normally separated by clear channels of 10 kc frequency. △1794

Carroll, Lewis (1832–98), pseud. of Charles Lutwidge Dodgson; English mathematician, photographer, and novelist. He is especially remembered for *Alice's Adventures in Wonderland* (1865) and its sequel, *Through the Looking-Glass* (1872), which have attracted much serious scholarly criticism as well as being popular children's classics. *See also* Alice's Adventures in Wonderland.

Carronade. △1738.

Carrot, a single species *(Daucus carota)* of herbaceous plant native to Afghanistan and cultivated widely. It has an edible taproot that is white, yellow, purple, or orange. It has fernlike leaves sheathed at the base and white, flat-topped flower clusters. Other members of the carrot family (Umbelliferae) are parsley, celery, anise, dill, caraway, and poison hemlock.

Carson, Kit (1809–68), US trapper, guide, and soldier; b. as Christopher Carson in Madison co, Ky. Raised in Missouri, in 1826 he ran away to Taos, N.M. He then made his living as a trapper, hunter, and guide throughout the Rockies and Sierras. He achieved fame for his work as guide for John C. Frémont's expeditions (1842–46) and was with Frémont in California when the Bear Flag Revolt took place in 1846. During the Mexican War he carried dispatches for Frémont and Gen. Stephen Kearny. In 1853 he was US Indian agent at Taos and in 1861 he became a colonel in the army and fought against Confederate and Indian forces. At the end of the war he was made a brigadier general and commanded at Fort Garland in Colorado (1866–67). In 1868 he was named superintendent of Indian affairs for Colorado Territory.

Carson, Rachel Louise (1907–1964), US biologist and science writer, b. Springdale, Pa. She is best known for her widely popular and influential books on pollution, wild life, and the sea. She made her career with the US Bureau of Fisheries, now the US Fish and Wildlife Service. In 1951 she published *The Sea Around Us*, a natural history of the sea, which subsequently won a National Book Award. *Silent Spring* (1962), about the dangers of pollution, had worldwide impact. Other works include *Under the Sea-Wind* (1941) and *The Edge of the Sea* (1955).

Carson, city in S California; suburb of Los Angeles; site of California State College (Dominguez Hills). Industries: oil refining, paper products, fabricated metals. Inc. 1968. Pop. (1970) 71,150.

Carson City, capital of Nevada, 30mi (48km) S of Reno; coextensive with Ormsby co; founded as Eagle Station (1851), renamed for Kit Carson; experienced population and financial boom with the discovery of the Comstock Lode (1859); site of a branch of US Mint (1870–93), which houses a natural science and history museum. Industries: tourism, gambling. Inc. 1875. Pop. (1970) 15,468.

Cartagena, city and port in NW Colombia, on the Bay of Cartagena in the Caribbean Sea; good harbor; important city of Spanish America in the 17th century; became part of Colombia 1821. Principal oil port of Colombia; site of university (1824). Industries: oil refining, sugar, tobacco, hides, textiles, tourism. Founded 1533. Pop. 256,598.

Cartagena, major seaport city in SE Spain, on the Mediterranean Sea; Moors captured the city in the 8th century; recaptured by Spaniards in 13th century; destroyed by Francis Drake in 1585; site of medieval Castillo de la Concepción, and modern naval base. Industries: shipbuilding, lead, zinc, iron. Founded *c.* 255 BC by Carthaginians. Pop. 146,904.

Carte, Richard D'Oyly. *See* D'Oyly Carte, Richard.

Cartel, formal agreement among the producers of a good to fix the market price and to divide the market among the participants. Cartels ordinarily result in higher prices to consumers and extra profits for sellers. Unless specifically exempted, cartels are illegal in the United States. *See also* Sherman Antitrust Act.

Carter, Howard. △1348.

Carter, James Earl, Jr. (Jimmy) (1924–), 39th president of the United States (1977–), b. Plains, Ga. Carter attended the US Naval Academy, from which he graduated in 1946. He entered the Navy and was assigned to the nuclear submarine program under Adm. Hyman Rickover. In 1946 he married Rosalynn Smith; they had three sons and one daughter. Upon the death of his father in 1953, Carter resigned from the Navy and returned to Plains, where he took over the family peanut farming and processing business.

Carter served in the Georgia state senate, and in 1966 he entered the Democratic primary for governor. He was defeated but four years later he won both the Democratic primary and the general election. He attracted nationwide attention when, in his inaugural address on Jan. 12, 1971, he called for an end to racial discrimination in Georgia. As governor he continued to attract attention as a prime example of the "new politics" in the South. His four-year administration was noted for improved race relations, a streamlined state bureaucracy, and general fiscal conservatism.

Deciding to run for the presidency, Carter entered all the state primaries in 1976. He won the early ones, thereby establishing himself as the front runner among the large field of Democratic candidates. He continued to solidify his lead, and by the time the Democratic Convention met in July, he had enough delegates to win the nomination on the first ballot. He chose Sen. Walter F. Mondale as his running mate. The Carter-Mondale ticket won over the Republican team of Gerald Ford and Robert Dole.

Career: governor of Georgia (1971–75); president (1977–).

Carteret, (Sir) George (c.1610–80), British proprietor in America. In England, he was a naval officer and a Royalist supporter, for which the king gave him a grant to American lands "to be called New Jersey." He was one of the eight original proprietors of Carolina (1663) and joint proprietor with Lord Berkeley of the province of New Jersey (1664). He also served as deputy treasurer of Ireland (1667–73).

Carteret, Philip (1639–82), British governor in America. Commissioned by his cousin George Carteret, he became governor of New Jersey province (1664) and instituted a legislative assembly (1668). When the province was divided in 1676, he was governor of East Jersey (1676–82).

Carteret, town in NE New Jersey, opposite Staten Island, NY, 11mi (18km) S of Newark. Industries: oil and copper refineries, steel mills, paints. Inc. 1906. Pop. (1970) 23,137.

Cartesian, doctrine of the 17th-century French philosopher René Descartes. Cartesians agreed with Descartes that all human knowledge could be established with mathematical certainty on the basis of indubitable first truths. The thinking self alone, working on its own clear and distinct ideas, could create a world. Matter (extended substance) and mind (thinking substance) constituted the fullness of reality, while the former, always in motion, was the sole object of scientific study. *See also* Cogito Ergo Sum; Descartes, René; Rationalism. △856.

Cartesian Coordinate System, coordinate system in which the position of a point is specified by its distances from intersecting lines (the axes). In the simplest type—rectangular coordinates in two dimensions—two axes are used at right angles: the y axis and the x axis. The position of a point is then given by a pair of numbers (x,y). The abscissa, x, is the point's distance from the y axis, measured along the x axis, and the ordinate, y, is the distance from the x axis. The axes in such a system need not be at right angles. In three dimensions three axes are used, and a point has three coordinates, x, y, and z. *See also* Coordinate System. △1458.

Carthage, ancient seaport in N Africa, on tip of peninsula in Bay of Tunis; founded by Phoenician colonists, 9th century B.C.; fought the Punic Wars against Rome. Carthage was destroyed during the Third Punic War 149–146 B.C. Rebuilt by Caesar in 44 BC, it was the capital of the Vandals (439–533 AD), and was nearly destroyed by the Arabs (698). Louis IX (St. Louis) of France died there in 1270 of plague while on a crusade. △978, 1012.

Carthusians, Christian religious order founded by St Bruno in 1084 at the Grande Chartreuse monastery near Grenoble, France. A strictly contemplative order, the monks are vowed to silence and solitude. The order includes nuns. △1086.

Cartier, (Sir) George Étienne (1814–73), premier of Canada (1857–62). Cartier sided with the rebels against the British administration in 1837 and was forced to hide in the United States. He represented Montreal in the Legislative Assembly (1848–73) and was provincial secretary and attorney general, becoming premier in the Cartier-Macdonald administration. He encouraged railroad interests and helped French Canadians accept federation at the Quebec Conference of 1864.

Cartier, Jacques (1491–1557), French explorer. Born of a wealthy family, Cartier probably accompanied Verrazano to New France in 1524. In 1534 he was sent by Francis I to find a northwest passage to the Spice Islands. He explored the Gulf of St. Lawrence, Newfoundland, New Brunswick, and, in a second voyage (1535), Quebec and Montreal. He established good relations with the Indians but lost favor with the French court. In 1541 he helped found a colony at Cap Rouge and then devoted the rest of his life to exploration and description of Canada, decimating his personal fortune.

Cartilage, a flexible supporting tissue composed of a nonliving matrix within which are living cartilage cells. Cartilage is comparatively soft. In man the ends of some bones and the nose, the ears, and the windpipe, remain cartilaginous throughout life. △682.

Cartography, the ancient art and science of representing all or a portion of the earth's surface to some kind of scale, usually drawn or printed on a flat surface through the use of various kinds of projections. There are many kinds of maps, the most common being topographical. In civil engineering planning, relief maps are the clearest method for demonstrating the three-dimensional nature of the terrain. *See also* Map. △180.

Cartoon, preparatory drawing for a tapestry, oil painting, fresco, or stained-glass window. The design, drawn in chalk, charcoal, pencil, or, in the case of the weaver's cartoon, in full color, was transferred by tracing with a stylus or pounding charcoal dust through tiny holes. The present use of *cartoon* as a humorous drawing is derived from a 19th-century competition for fresco designs for Parliament parodied in *Punch*.

Cartridges, in Sound Recording. △1798.

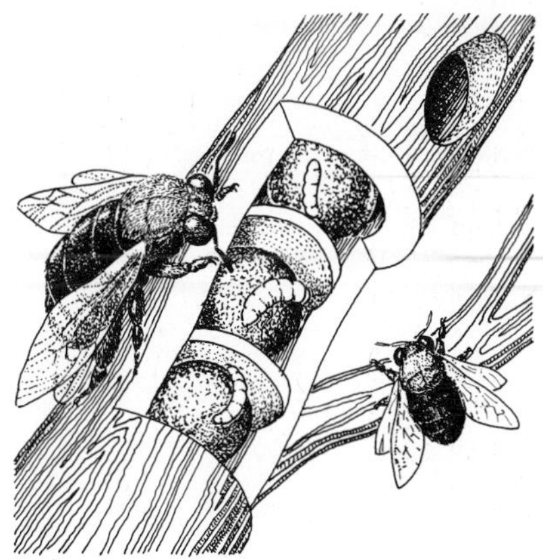

Carpenter bee

Carrara, Italy

Carrier pigeon

Jimmy Carter

Cartwright, Alexander Joy, Jr. (1820–92), US baseball organizer, b. New York City. Responsible for organizing the first baseball game ever played (1846), Cartwright, a surveyor, also established the 90-foot distance between bases and the use of nine men on a side. He was elected to the Baseball Hall of Fame in 1938.

Cartwright, (Sir) Richard John (1835–1912), Canadian historian and politician. A banker, he was elected to Parliament as a Conservative (1863) but in 1878 joined the Liberals. He was minister of finance (1873–78) in Alexander Mackenzie's administration, and minister of trade and finance (1896–1911) in Wilfred Laurier's administration, supporting trade with the United States.

Carus, Carl Gustav. △1242.

Caruso, Enrico (1873–1921), Italian tenor, one of the most famous operatic singers of all time. He made his debut in Naples in 1894, and his fame began in 1902 when he sang at Monte Carlo. After his US debut at the Metropolitan Opera in 1903 in Verdi's *Rigoletto*, he remained at the Metropolitan for 17 years. He earned the Metropolitan much success and money, singing about 50 different roles and becoming the most acclaimed and highest paid singer in the world. He also appeared in the leading European opera houses and made many phonograph recordings.

Carver, George Washington (1864–1943), American agricultural chemist and experimenter, b. Diamond Grove, Mo. He is best known for his scientific research on the peanut, from which he derived more than 300 products. Born a slave, he attended Simpson College in Iowa and received a master's degree in science from Iowa State Agricultural College. In 1896 he became head of the department of agriculture at Tuskegee Institute in Alabama, where he devoted his research to developing products that might be utilized by the South, whose lands had been ravaged by the one crop system. He developed products from the peanut, sweet potato, and soy bean. His primary intent was to aid impoverished farmers, which he did in part through extensive lecture tours.

Cary, (Arthur) Joyce (Lunel) (1888–1957), British novelist, b. Northern Ireland. He left Oxford University to study art. His experiences in colonial political service in Nigeria (1913–20) are reflected in *Mister Johnson* (1939). He also wrote two trilogies, the first of which contains *The Horse's Mouth* (1944), his most famous novel.

Casablanca (Dar-el-Beida), seaport and largest city in Morocco, on W coast, on the Atlantic Ocean; subtropical climate; commercial, industrial and export center for approx. 60% of Morocco's trade. Built on site of ancient city of Anfa, which was destroyed by Portuguese 1468; occupied by French 1907; site of conference between Prime Minister Churchill and President Roosevelt, Jan. 1943. Industries: cement, chemicals, textiles, tobacco, food processing. Pop. 1,-395,000.

Casablanca Conference (January 1943), meeting of US Pres. Franklin Roosevelt and British Prime Minister Churchill at Casablanca, North Africa. The Allied leaders pledged to fight until the Axis forces surrendered unconditionally.

Casadesus, Robert (1899–1973), French pianist and composer. After winning many prizes early in his career, he taught piano classes in the United States from 1934 to 1947. He was one of the great French pianists of his generation, often appearing with his wife, pianist Gaby Casadesus. He also composed many piano works.

Casa Grande Ruins National Monument, park in S Arizona; preserves an excavated Indian Pueblo containing a huge 600-year-old building. Area: 473acres (192hectares). Est. 1892.

Casals, Pablo (1876–1973), Spanish cellist and conductor. He organized his own orchestra in Barcelona in 1919, directed the Prades Music Festivals in southern France from 1950, and organized the annual Casals Festival in Puerto Rico starting in 1957. His virtuoso playing influenced many other cellists.

Casanova, or **Casanova de Seingalt, Giovanni Jacopo** (1725–98), Italian adventurer and author. He studied for the priesthood but was expelled for immoral conduct; after serving as secretary to a Roman cardinal and serving in the Venetian army, he traveled throughout Europe, gaining a reputation for gambling, spying, and womanizing. Imprisoned in Venice (1755) he escaped and returned to Paris where his amorous deeds and charm led to financial and social success. He served as a spy for the Venetian Inquisition (1774–82) and retired as librarian for Count von Waldstein in Bohemia. His memoirs are world famous.

Cascade Range, mountain range in W United States; extends from NE California N across Oregon and Washington into Canada; site of Cascade Tunnel, 8mi (13km) railroad tunnel, longest in North America. Crater Lake National Park and Lake Chelan National Recreation area are in Cascades. Highest peak is Mt Ranier, 14,410ft (4,395m).

Case, the classification of nouns and pronouns according to their use in a sentence. The noun or pronoun is in the nominative case when it is used as the subject or subjective complement; it is in the objective (accusative) case when it is used as the direct or indirect object of a verb or preposition; it is in the possessive case when it indicates ownership or relationship.

Casein Paint, a surface finish made up of colors ground into a solution of casein, a mild protein, used for 800 years as a binder and adhesive. Since the early 20th century refined ready-made casein paints have come into wide use. They furnish a moderate impasto, cannot be fused like oil paints, but can be glazed or overpainted.

Casement, (Sir) Roger (David) (1864–1916), Irish political figure. As a British consul (1895–1912), he gained international fame by exposing exploitation of natives in the Congo and Peru. During World War I he sought German assistance for Irish independence. After he landed in Ireland from a German submarine, the British government executed him for treason. In an attempt to destroy his reputation, British agents circulated what purported to be his diary accounts of homosexual encounters. It has never been established whether the accounts were genuine.

Cashel, town in S Republic of Ireland; noted for Rock of Cashel and ruins where Kings of Munster were once crowned. Pop. 2,693.

Cashew, evergreen tree *(Anacardium occidentale)* of the sumac family, native to the West Indies. Growing to 40ft (12m), it has longish leaves and yellow-pink flowers. The kernel of the nut is popular for eating. Its gum is sometimes used in varnish.

Cashmere Goat. *See* Kashmir Goat.

Casimir I, called the Peaceful (1015–58), king of Poland (1040–58). Faced with a revolt of the nobles, he fled to Hungary, losing Kraków and Gniezno to the duke of Bohemia. In 1041, Holy Roman Emperor Henry III helped him to regain his territory, and Christianity was restored. Casimir was forced to give up his royal title and became a grand duke.

Casimir II, called the Just (1138–94), King of Poland (1177–94), son of Boleslav III. He was practically elected by the magnates who extracted privileges from him. The clergy also obtained concessions (1180). Casimir promulgated laws protecting the peasants and established a Polish senate.

Casimir III, called the Great (1309–70), king of Poland (1333–70), son of Ladislas I and last of the Piast dynasty. His enlightened rule encouraged education and the spread of culture. He also Westernized administration and published a new legal code. He added Galacia to his domain (1340), while abandoning Silesia and Pomerania. Called the "Peasants' King," he improved their conditions. German and Jewish refugees were protected. In 1364, the University of Cracow was established.

Casimir IV (1427–92), king of Poland (1447–92). The greatest cultural heights were reached during his reign. Casimir conducted a successful 13-year war against the Teutonic Knights (1454–66) and acquired West Prussia, Pomerania, and other lands from them by the terms of the 2nd peace of Thorn (1466). In 1467, he founded the Polish Sejm, or diet.

Casino, card game played by two to four players with a standard 52–card deck. The object of the game is to take the greatest number of cards and the greatest number of spades by either matching cards that are played on the table or by building upon the cards played on the table (placing a two on a seven for an eventual pickup with a nine).

Casper, city in N central Wyoming; seat of Natrona co; population boomed with discovery of oil 1890. Industries: oil refining, meat packing. Founded 1888; inc. 1889. Pop. (1970) 39,361.

Caspian Sea, shallow salt lake primarily in USSR; extreme S portion is on Iranian border; world's largest inland body of water; water level fluctuates according to evaporation and tributaries' conditions; mainly fed by the Volga River, also receives the Ural, Emba, Kura and Terek rivers; has no outlet. Chief USSR ports are Baku, an oil center, and Astrachan. An important trade route for centuries, it was a medieval Mongol-Baltic route for Asian goods; transportation and shipping route; supports fisheries and sealeries. Area: 144,000sq mi (372,960sq km).

Cass, Lewis (1782–1866) US political leader, b. Exeter, N.H. A lawyer, he was governor from 1813–31 of the Michigan Territory. Andrew Jackson appointed him secretary of war (1831–36) and he served until he was named US minister to France. As a Senator (1845–48), he supported annexation of Texas and Oregon, resigning in 1848 to run unsuccessfully as Democratic candidate for president. He served again in the Senate (1849–57) until he became secretary of state under President Buchanan (1857–60).

Cassander (*c.* 358–297 BC), king of Macedonia (316–297 BC), son of Antipater. He joined Alexander in Asia in 324. They disliked one another, but the tradition that he murdered Alexander is false although he did slay Alexander's mother, son, and widow. After Antipater's death, he tried to hold Macedonia and Greece against Antigonus' efforts to reunite Alexander's empire and defeated him in the Battle of Ipsus (301 BC).

Cassandra, in classical mythology, a Trojan skilled in the art of prophecy, but condemned by Apollo never to be taken seriously. Her warning that the Greeks would capture Troy went unheeded. She was raped by the Greek soldier Ajax, carried off by Agamemnon, and murdered by Clytemnestra and Aegisthus.

Cassatt, Mary (1845–1926), US painter and printmaker, b. Allegheny City, Pa. Influenced by Degas, her work generally depicts social and domestic scenes, most often involving fashionable women and children. Her works, also influenced by Oriental art, include the notable *The Morning Toilet* (1886), *The Lady at the Tea Table* (1885), and *Woman Sewing* (1886).

Cassava, or manioc, tapioca plant *(Manihot esculenta)*, a woody shrub or herb of the spurge family. A native of Brazil, it grows to 9ft (2.7m), and has small clustered flowers. The tuberous roots are poisonous, but when the juice is expelled, they become edible and are used for food.

Cassette Recorder. △1798.

Cassini, Giovanni Domenico (1625–1712), French astronomer, born in Italy. In France from 1669, he is chiefly remembered for being the first to detect the dark cleft between Saturn's two outer rings (Cassini's Division). He also discovered four of Saturn's moons. △84.

Cassini's Division. △84.

Cassino, formerly San Germano; town in central Italy, on the Rapido River; built on ancient (866) Volsci town of Casinum; site of Monte Cassino (Benedictine abbey) which was medieval center of arts and learning; scene of savage fighting 1944 in which town and monastery were destroyed; later rebuilt; agricultural and commercial center. Chief industry is toys. Pop. 25,088.

Cassiodorus (*c.* 487–583), Roman statesman and cleric who founded a monastery at Vivarium, where he collected a library and taught his monks to copy Latin manuscripts. He played an important role in the preservation of classical culture and scholarship during the early monastic period in western Europe, a task later passed on to the Benedictines.

Cassiopeia, northern circumpolar constellation situated in the Milky Way north of Andromeda and characterized by the W shape of its five most conspicuous stars. In addition to several clusters and variables, Cassiopeia contains two radio sources: Cassiopeia A, the remains of a supernova of 1700, and Cassiopeia B, the remnant of Tycho Brahe's supernova of 1572. △100, 132.

Cassiterite, an oxide mineral, tin oxide (SnO_2); the major ore of tin. Mined from placer deposits chiefly in Malay peninsula. Also in pegmatites and high-temperature veins. Tetragonal short prismatic crystals; often twinned, or masses and radiating fibres. Transluent black, yellow or white; hardness 6–7; sp gr 7. △242.

Cassites. *See* Kassites.

Cassius Longinus, Gaius (died 42 BC), Roman general and political figure, leader of the assassins of Julius Caesar. A bitter, ascetic man of distinguished family, he campaigned under Crassus in Parthia (53 BC), saving the remnants of the defeated army. Siding with Pompey against Caesar, he was pardoned and promised the governorship of Syria. After organizing with Marcus Brutus the successful conspiracy against Caesar (44 BC), he fled to Macedonia where he and Brutus engaged in battle at Philippi (42 BC) with Mark Antony and Octavian, who sought to avenge Caesar's murder. Cassius committed suicide, erroneously believing the battle to be lost.

Cassowary, huge, powerful, flightless bird of rain forests of New Guinea, N Australia, and nearby islands. Adult has coarse black plumage, horny growth on a brightly colored head, short bill and legs, and sharp claws. The male incubates green eggs (3–8) in a platform nest on the forest floor. Length: 52–65in (1.3–1.6m); weight: 40lb (63kg) or more. Species *Casuarius casuarius.* △526.

Castagno, Andrea del (c.1423–57), Italian painter, b. Andrea di Bartolo di Bargilla. He studied with Filippo Lippi and was first influenced by Masacio, then by Donatello and Uccello. He was noted for his naturalistic treatment of religious subjects. His best works include a portrait of Niccolò da Tolentino on a horse (1456) in the cathedral of Florence and "The Youthful David" on a shield (1450–57) now in the National Gallery of Art, Washington, D.C.

Castanets, percussion instrument producing clicking sounds with two pairs of hinged hardwood shells attached to the player's thumbs. They are often played by Spanish dancers, often to guitar accompaniment.

Caste, a formal, rigid system of social stratification based on factors beyond individual control (eg, race, sex, or religious heritage) and sanctioned by tradition. This kind of system is called *ascriptive* because the individual is born into his or her position and cannot change it. The Hindu caste system in India and South Africa's apartheid are contemporary examples. *See also* Stratification. △890, 896.

Castel Gandolfo, town in central Italy, on Lake Albano; became realm of Holy See 1608; summer residence of Pope. The Villa Barberini houses the Vatican observatory. Industries: peaches, wine, fish. Pop. 4,623.

Castello Branco, Humberto (1900–67), president of Brazil (1964–67). As army chief-of-staff, he coordinated the coup against the Goulart administration (March 1964). His belief in executive authority is reflected in the constitution of 1967.

Castelnuovo-Tedesco, Mario (1895–1968), Italian composer who emigrated to the United States in 1933. He composed in many forms, including songs, opera, concertos, chamber music, and solo piano and guitar music (*Guitar Concerto in D,* 1939).

Cast Fossil. △560.

Castiglione, Baldassare (1478–1529), Italian Renaissance diplomat and writer. Noted for his book *Il Cortegiano,* he was very active as a diplomat, serving at the court of Urbino (1507–13) and then with the papal court. He ended his career as papal nuncio to Charles V in Spain. *See also* Il Cortegiano.

Castiglione, Giovanni Benedetto (1616–70), Italian painter and printmaker. He was the leading 17th-century Italian follower of the Dutch school as well as first known practitioner of monotype, or single-print technique. He was also among the first to make chiaroscuro woodcuts. △1208.

Castile, New, provincial region in Spain; captured by Castilian kings from Moors (1212). New Castile includes the provinces of Madrid, Toledo, Guadalajara, Cuenca, and Ciudad Real. Philip II made Madrid the capital of Spain in 1561. Chief products are olive oil and grapes. Pop. 5,164,026.

Castile, Old, provincial region in Spain; former county of the kingdom of Leon, ruled by Castilian kings. Castile and Aragón were united in 1479 by Isabella I of Castile and Ferdinand II of Aragón. Old Castile includes the provinces of Ávila, Logroño, Santander, Burgos, Segovia, Soria, Valladolid, and Palencia. Severe climate and poor soil allow only limited grain growing and sheep raising. Pop. 2,135,788.

Castillo de San Marcos National Monument, national park in St Augustine, Florida; preserves the oldest land fortress (1672) of continental United States. Area: 20acres (8hectares). Est 1924.

Casting, Metal, forming metal materials by permitting molten metal to fill and solidify in molds of desired shapes. Most castings are made by pouring metal in sand and clay molds. Specialized processes, such as plastic molding, composite molding, investment casting (or lost wax process), and die casting permit greater dimensional accuracy, smoother surfaces, and finer detail. △1588.

Cast Iron, a general term that includes a number of irons, especially gray irons and pig irons (those directly out of the blast furnace). They cover a wide range of iron-carbon-silicon alloys containing from 1.7 to 4.5% carbon along with varying amounts of other elements. Gray iron (so-called because its fracture looks grayish) is the most widely used for casting automobile blocks, machinery parts, hollow ware, and many other products. *See also* Casting, Metal. △1584, 1592–94.

Cast Iron Architecture. Used in European structures since 1779, cast iron became most important with the development by James Bogardus of prefabricated iron skeletal frames in the latter 19th century. Cast iron architecture prefigured the skyscraper developed by the Chicago School, although steel became its main material. △1258, 1298.

Castle, team of US ballroom dancers. **Vernon** (1887–1918), b. Vernon Castle Bythe in England and **Irene (Foote)** (1893–1969), b. New Rochelle, N.Y. Married in 1911, they popularized ballroom dancing with their exhibition performances in the United States and Europe prior to World War I. They made famous the Castlewalk, Castle Polka, Fox Trot, Maxixe, Tango, and Hesitation Waltz. Castle House, their New York City teaching studio, made 20th-century social dancing fashionable. They are co-authors of *The Modern Dance* (1914), a book on ballroom dancing. Vernon Castle was killed during an air training session in World War I.

Castle, a fortified residence of a king or noble in the Middle Ages. Built of earth or masonry, located on a site dominating its environs and usually surrounded by a water filled moat, castles were enclosed by high walls protecting those inside from attack or siege. Castles could be of regular or irregular shape, but almost all had common architectural elements for defensive purposes. Turrets were usually found at the angles of the wall and occasionally interspersed along the exterior walls. The walls were built thick enough to withstand bombardment and wide enough at the top to allow the defenders to group and maneuver behind the protection afforded by the parapets that capped them. Inside the walls were the residence, the stables, the arsenal, and the storage space for the daily provisions. △1098.

Castle Architecture, architecture resulting from the combination of feudal residences with fortresses, developed in the 9th century. Built on a defensible height, the main tower or keep was surrounded by a masonry palisade and a ditch. The main entrance was protected by drawbridge and portcullis. Later, fortifications were doubled by a second surrounding wall flanked by towers. The discovery of gunpowder ended the military usefulness of castle architecture. △1082, 1098, 1592.

Castlebar, market town in NW Republic of Ireland, at E end of Castlebar Lough; site of Irish-French victory over British (1798) known as the "Races of Castlebar"; agricultural area. Pop. 5,970.

Castlereagh, Robert Stewart, 2nd Viscount (1769–1822), British diplomat and politician, b. Ireland. While chief secretary of Ireland (1799–1801), he helped secure the passage of the Act of Union with Great Britain (1800). As British war secretary (1805–06, 1807–09), he opposed Napoleon vigorously but had to resign after a duel with George Canning, his great political rival. Castlereagh was a brilliant foreign secretary (1812–22), backing Wellington in war and helping secure a long-term peace in Europe at the Congress of Vienna (1814–15). △1230.

Castor and Pollux, in Greek and Roman legend, twin sons of Leda. The twins were inseparable; after Castor's death Pollux refused immortality. They were transformed into the constellation Gemini.

Enrico Caruso

George Washington Carver

Cassowary

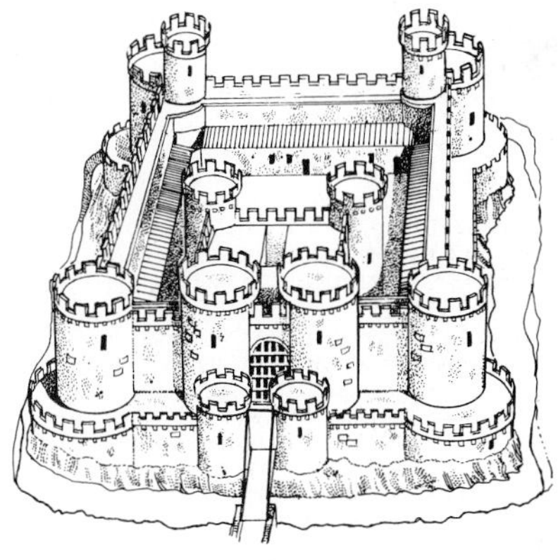

Castle

Castor Oil, a viscous, yellowish oil from the castor bean plant, sometimes used as a cathartic and for many industrial uses.

Castro, Fidel (1927–), Cuban revolutionary leader and prime minister (1959–). Protesting Fulgencio Batista's seizure of power (1952), Castro led an armed attack on the Moncada military barracks (July 26, 1953). Unsuccessful, Castro was captured and sentenced to 15 years in prison. Granted an amnesty in 1955, he went to Mexico, learned guerrilla tactics, and began his association with Che Guevara. Castro returned to Cuba in 1956 and set up his headquarters in the Sierra Maestra Mts. When the Batista regime collapsed in 1958, Castro capitalized on the power-vacuum and became de facto head of state. Within a few months he had consolidated his position and was able to rule without the support of traditional political groups. Pledged to the radical transformation of Cuban society, he declared himself a Marxist-Leninist in 1961. △1352, 1354.

Castro Valley, residential area in W California, 19mi (31km) SE of San Francisco; originally a section of a Mexican land grant made to Don Guillermo Castro 1841. Pop. (1970) 44,760.

Cat, carnivorous mammals found on all continents except Australia and ranging in size from the common housecat to the Siberian tiger. Most cats walk on their toes and have short, rounded skulls; meat-eating teeth; and sharp retractile sickle-shaped claws. They have five toes on each front foot and four on each back foot. They have good nocturnal vision, acute hearing, and a well-developed sense of equilibrium. Most cats are nocturnal and solitary. The gestation period is about three months and 1–6 blind, helpless young are born.

Cats are descended from the same general evolutionary stock as civets and mongooses; the extinct sabertoothed cat appeared about 38 million years ago. Modern cats are classified into two main groups. The small felids—*Felini*— include 15 genera with 28 species ranging from the familiar domestic cat to the puma. The big felids—*Pantherini*— developed from the small cats. They include two genera: *Uncia* (snow leopard) and *Panthera,* with four species (leopard, jaguar, tiger, and lion). The throat anatomy of big cats enables them to roar.

The domestic cat *(Felis domesticus)* developed in Asia, Africa, and Europe, possibly from the Kaffir cat and the European wildcat. It was domesticated by the Egyptians and Indians sometime before 3000BC and was brought West by Phoenician sailors. Domestic breeds are divided into two groups: short-hairs, which include American, foreign or exotic, and Manx breeds; and longhairs, which include Persian and Angora breeds. Family Felidae.

Catacombs, early Christian (and some Jewish) subterranean cemeteries, often used as refuges from persecution and as shrines. The extensive catacombs of Rome are best known, but remains of others have been found in Europe, N Africa, and Turkey. Built between the 1st and 5th centuries, those in Rome are a complex of layered corridors as deep as 60ft (18m) below ground with burial niches, vaults, and rooms along the sides covered with inscribed tablets. Some were decorated with fresco. Plundered during the barbarian invasions, they were later largely forgotten until rediscovered in 1578. They are now maintained by the Vatican.

Catalan, Romance language spoken mainly in northeastern Spain (in the area known as Catalonia), but also in the Balearic Islands, Andorra, and southern France. There are about 6 million speakers in all.

Catalepsy, condition in which parts of the body remain in any position in which they are placed. Causes may be organic, psychological, or the result of hypnosis.

Cataloging, Library, process of listing and describing a library's collection, enabling users to know what the library contains. Book catalogs, originally used, have been replaced by card catalogs, categorized by subject, author, or both.

Catalonia, region in NE Spain, extends from French border S to Mediterranean Sea; includes Barcelona, Gerona, Lérida, and Tarragona. United with Aragón in 1137, Catalonia kept its own laws and language; became an important medieval trade center; declined after union of Castile and Aragón (1479); became a 20th-century center for the anarchist movement; site of several medieval castles. Industries: tourism, automobiles, airplanes, textiles. Crops: grapes, olives, cereals. Area: 12,332sq mi (31,940sq km). Pop. 5,-122,567.

Catalpa, ornamental American and Asiatic tree that has large, heart-shaped leaves and showy white or purple flowers. The beanlike fruit pods contain many seeds. The common catalpa *(Catalpa bignonioides)* is sometimes called Indian bean. Height: to 60ft (18m). Family Bignoniaceae.

Catalysis, modification of the rate of a chemical reaction, by the addition of a substance, termed a catalyst, which is not consumed in the reaction. Catalytic action can reveal the reaction mechanism; many industrial processes rely on catalysis to accelerate reactions and occasionally to inhibit undesirable ones. Development of life forms is impossible without catalysis, for a series of strikingly specific-acting enzymes select and follow just one of a large number of metabolic pathways, acting much faster than nonbiological catalysts.

Catalyst, chemical compound that accelerates or inhibits the rate of a chemical reaction without itself being consumed. Inhibitors are commonly antioxidants, often used to prevent degradation of organic compounds, especially in air. Metals or their compounds catalyze by absorbing gases to their surface, forming intermediates that readily react to form the desired product, then product-forming while regenerating the original catalytic surface. △1564, 1572–74.

Catalytic Converter, an antipollution device used for internal combustion engines. It consists of a bed of catalytic agents through which flows the gaseous exhaust of fuel combustion. Converters located in mufflers reduce harmful unburned hydrocarbons and carbon monoxide. These converters are adversely affected by tetraethyl lead found in some gasolines. △1698.

Catalytic Cracking, *See* Cracking.

Catamaran, a swift, bridged-over, two-hulled craft, equipped with sails, popular in sport sailing. Originally, a raft of Indian and Indonesian waters developed for cargo carrying and for long voyages by Melanesian and Polynesian peoples.

Catania (Catana), port city in E Sicily, Italy, at foot of Mt Etna; capital of Catania prov.; ancient Catana was founded by Greeks 729 BC, and repeatedly invaded; it suffered devastating volcanic eruption 1669, earthquake 1693; city was rebuilt 18th century; site of Greek and Roman ruins, Norman Cathedral (1091), first Sicilian university (1434). Industries: chemicals, sulphur, textiles. Pop. 409,088.

Catapult. △1732.

Cataract, opacity of the lens of the eye usually a result of degenerative changes in old age or disease such as diabetes. Symptoms are gradual but painless loss of vision. The cataract may be removed surgically and corrective lenses prescribed.

Catastrophism, geological term used by Georges Buffon (1707–88). Looking at fossil evidence of extinct animals, he believed that changes in Earth and its plants and animals came about only as a result of violent activities which destroyed all preceding life. Subsequent forms were thought to be new creations.

Catatonic. △760.

Catawba, one of the most powerful southern Siouan tribes of North American Indians, originally living in North Carolina and Tennessee. They were active on the colonists' side during the Revolution and as a reward were given land in York and Lancaster counties in South Carolina, where about 350 now reside; a few moved to Oklahoma. They are noted for their pottery and basketry.

Catboat, a broad-beamed, shallow-draft sailboat with a single mast placed forward and carrying a single large sail extended by a long boom; generally with a centerboard and very popular in sport sailing.

Cat Brier. *See* Greenbrier.

Catch Basin. △1768.

Catcher in the Rye (1951), novel by J.D. Salinger. It deals with several days in the life of Holden Caulfield, a teenage boy who is unable to cope with the hypocrisy and phoniness that he sees around him.

Catch-22 (1961), novel by Joseph Heller. Set on a Mediterranean island during World War II, the book juxtaposes farce and realism to produce a funny but harrowing picture of the insanity of war and modern society.

Catecholamine Theory of Depression. △770.

Category, in Logic. △854.

Caterpillar, wormlike larva of a butterfly or mot Caterpillars have segmented bodies, short antenna simple eyes, chewing mouthparts, and 5–8 pairs legs, some with hooks or claws. Most have a few sca tered hairs, but some are woolly looking. Nearly a feed on plants and plant products and many are se ous farm and garden pests. *See also* Lepidoptera. 498.

Catfish, freshwater and marine fish found worldwid in tropical and subtropical waters. Characterized b fleshy whiskers on the upper jaw, they are scaleles and some species have venomous spines. Length: t 4ft (121.9cm); Weight: 57lb (25.6kg). Order Silur formes (also Cyriniformes); families include Sea, Ma rine, Electric, North American Freshwater, Clarii (Walking), Long-whiskered, and Upsidedown.

Cathar Heresy. △1084.

Catharsis, in psychology, expression of represse feelings during the treatment of neurotic disorders Sigmund Freud and Josef Breuer pioneered the "Ca thartic Method," in which hypnotized patients wer encouraged to remember and tell about represse experiences. Though Freud later abandoned hypnc sis, he retained the basic form of psychoanalytic trea ment.

Cathedral Architecture. The early churches wer basilicas. During the 11th and 12th centuries, mas sive domed and vaulted Romanesque architectur predominated. The great Gothic cathedrals of th 13th, 14th, and 15th centuries had ribbed vaults pointed arches, and windows of stained glass tha contributed to the sense of lightness and soarin space. *See also* Gothic Architecture; Romanesque Ar chitecture. △1080–82, 1092.

Cather, Willa (1873–1947), US novelist and short story writer, b. Winchester, Va. When a child, he family settled in Red Cloud, Nebr. She grew up amon the immigrant farmers who became the subject c many of her books. She graduated from the University of Nebraska (1895) and served as managing editor o *McClure's Magazine* in New York (1908–12). He fiction incorporates the pioneer traits she knew sc well: love of the land, loyalty to family, ties to the past and the constant struggle with nature. Operatinc within this framework in books usually set in the Mid west or Southwest, she created quiet works filled with strong characters who make life a noble thing. He novels include *O Pioneers!* (1913), *My Antonia* (1918), *A Lost Lady* (1923), *The Professor's House* (1925), and *Death Comes for the Archbishop* (1927)

Catherine I (1684–1727), tsarina of Russia. Origi nally a Lithuanian peasant, she became the mistress of Prince Menshikov and later the mistress of Tsar Peter I (Peter the Great). She adopted Orthodoxy, and in 1712 became Peter's wife. In 1724, she was crowned tsarina and reigned after Peter's death, al though Menshikov was the actual ruler. During her reign, the Academy of Sciences was opened (1725) and the Supreme Privy Council was established.

Catherine II (1729–96), tsarina of Russia (1762–96). A German princess, she married Peter III in 1762. His mismanagement of government and his bad treatment of her led Catherine to organize a rebellion that ended in Peter's assassination. She was crowned tsarina in 1762. At the beginning of her reign, she was a liberal monarch and called meetings to discuss reforms. Threatened by the radical sentiments of the French Revolution, however, she became a reactionary. She imposed serfdom in the Ukraine, took part in the division of Poland among Russia, Prussia, and Austria (1795), cruelly suppressed the Pugachev Rebellion of 1773, and increased the privileges of the gentry in the Charter of 1785. A patroness of the arts, she corresponded with the French writers Voltaire and Diderot, wrote satires, and built palaces. △1178,-1180.

Catherine de Médicis (1519–89), queen of France. The daughter of Lorenzo de' Médici, she became queen of France (1547) as Henry II's consort. Perpetually threatened by various factions, she clung to power by trying to set rival groups against each other, or by attempting conciliation. Her tolerance of the Protestant Huguenots eventually gave way to dependence on the Roman Catholic Guise party, whose growing power she failed to control. She exerted great power during the reign of her son Charles IX (1560–74) and had some influence over her youngest son, Henry III (reigned 1574–89). △1154.

Catherine of Aragon (1485–1536), Spanish-born first queen of Henry VIII of England, whom she married in 1509. Their only living child was a daughter. Henry, wanting a male heir, used her former marriage (1501–02) to his brother Arthur as a pretext for divorce. Archbishop Cranmer declared their marriage null (1533). Despite continued harassment, Catherine refused to accept the Act of Succession (1534). This law placed the children of Henry's second wife, Anne Boleyn, in line to the throne.

Catherine of Siena (1347–80), Roman Catholic saint. She took orders in 1364, and was supposed to have received the *stigmata* or impression of Christ's wounds. Active politically, Catherine encouraged Pope Gregory XI to return to Rome from Avignon (1377).

Catherine of Valois (1401–37), queen of France, also called Catherine of France. The daughter of Charles VI of France, she became queen of England upon her marriage to King Henry V, according to the terms of the Treaty of Troyes (1420). A son, the future Henry VI, was born the next year, and in 1422 Henry V died. She then married Owen Tudor, and their son Edmund, Duke of Richmond, was the father of Henry VII, the first Tudor king.

Cathode, the negative electrode of an electrolytic cell or electron tube. It is the electrode from which electrons enter a system. *See* Electrolysis; Electron Tube. △1566.

Cathode Rays, radiation emitted by the cathode of an electron tube containing a low-pressure gas. The rays were identified (1897) by J. J. Thomson as streams of charged particles whose charge-to-mass ratio indicated an unknown extremely lightweight elementary particle, later called the electron. The electrons are emitted from the cathode as a result of the impact of positive gas ions formed in the tube.

Cathode Ray Tube, a type of vacuum tube used as a television picture tube and an oscilloscope. An electron gun shoots a beam of electrons, focused by a grid. This strikes a fluorescent screen to produce a spot of light. An electrostatic or magnetic field deflects the beam to particular spots on the screen. In a television picture tube, the deflecting plates are controlled by the incoming picture signals. △1796.

Catholic Church. *See* Roman Catholic Church.

Cation. *See* Ion.

Catkin, drooping, scaly spike of unisexual flowers without petals, such as the pussy willow or poplar. This deciduous flower cluster is also typical of birches and some beeches.

Catlin, George (1796–1872), U.S. painter, b. Wilkes-Barre, Pa. His pictures of Indian life are invaluable both to art and to history. Produced in the years 1832–37, his paintings show 45 different tribal groups. Many are now exhibited in the Catlin Gallery of the National Museum, Washington, D.C.

Cat Nation. *See* Erie Indians.

Catnip, or catmint, common name for *Nepeta cataria,* an aromatic herb of the mint family. Introduced from Europe, it grows wild in North America. Cats are attracted to this perennial and are excited by its aroma.

Cato (the Elder), Marcus Porcius (234–149 BC), Roman statesman, orator, and writer. He served as an officer in the Second Punic War (191 BC). He held many important posts in Rome beginning in 204 BC, culminating in his appointment as censor in 184. As censor he worked to restore the old ideals of Rome—courage, honesty, and simple living. Cato urged the destruction of Carthage and lived to see the Third Punic War begin. His *On Agriculture* (*c.*160 BC) is the earliest fully extant Latin literary work. Fragments of his *Origines,* the first Latin history of Rome, remain.

Cato (the Younger), Marcus Porcius Cato Uticensis (95–46 BC), Roman patriot. Great-grandson of Cato the Elder, his support of Republican government and his opposition to Caesar led to the foundation of the first triumvirate. Military tribune of Macedonia (67) and quaestor (65), he was tribune (62) and praetor (54). He favored Pompey against Caesar in 49 and when news of Caesar's victory reached him in Utica, he committed suicide in preference to surrender to Caesar.

Cat Scratch Disease, probably a virus-caused disease contracted through the scratch of an apparently healthy cat, rarely another animal. Symptoms begin with small pustule; fever, headache, lymph involvement follows. Recovery is slow.

Cat's Eye *See* Chrysoberyl.

Catskill Mountains, plateau of the Appalachian system in SE New York, on the W bank of the Hudson River. Highest peak is Slide Mt, 4,204ft (1,282m). Area of Rip Van Winkle legend, it abounds in forests, streams, and lakes; popular resort area near New York City metropolitan area.

Catt, Carrie Chapman Lane (1859–1947), U.S. reformer and suffragette, b. Ripon, Wis. Raised on the frontier, she moved to New York after her second marriage. She joined the National American Women Suffrage Association and became its president in 1900. Her "Winning Plan" meant working for suffrage through local political parties. Catt was also a founder of the Daughters of the American Revolution (DAR).

Cattail, tall marsh plants with long, erect leaves and stiff stems bearing fuzzy, brown, cylindrical flower spikes. The leaves of some species are used in making baskets or matting. Height: 3–9ft(1–3m). Species include common *Typha latifola.* Family Typhaceae.

Cattaneo, Carlo (1810–69), Italian philosopher. After leading the unsuccessful Milanese insurrection (1848), he spent most of his life in Lugano, Switzerland. He edited the influential journal *Il Politecnico* (1839–44, 1860–63). His view of history emphasized the importance of scientific inquiry to society's well-being and the importance of thought as social action. He held that human history could be understood through a social psychology supported by scientific method.

Cattell, James M(cKeen) (1860–1944), US psychologist, b. Easton, Pa. He pioneered in measuring intelligence. He was the first president of the American Psychological Association (1895).

Cattle, large ruminant mammals of the original Old World genus *Bos.* Included are domesticated cattle *(Bos taurus),* and domesticated zebu *(Bos indicus).* Other members are the wild and domesticated yak of Central Asia, the wild gaur and domesticated gayal of S Asia, and the wild banteng and koupray of Indochina. Young cattle are calves; females are heifers until they give birth and are then cows; males are bulls. Castrated males raised for beef are steers and when raised as draft animals, oxen. Horns, sometimes only on males, are permanent, hollow, and unbranched. The cheek teeth are high-crowned for grazing. A thick pad replaces the upper front teeth. In the wild, cattle congregate in small herds. They are raised primarily for meat and milk. Leather, glue, gelatin, and fertilizer are by-products. Before farm machinery, draft oxen were essential to agriculture. Cattle were domesticated about 8000 years ago in Anatolia. Height: 39–78in (1–2m) at shoulder; weight: 1100–2200lb (500–1000kg). *See also* Auroch; Beef Cattle; Dairy Cattle; Water Buffalo.

Cattle Brands, any of various marks made on the skin of cattle to permit easily recognizable identification. In the past, this was done with a hot iron stamp attached to a long handle. By pressing the burning iron against the thigh of a cow, the resulting scar made the pattern of the stamp. Today, branding is done with chemicals, tattooing, paint, tags, and notching. The practice of branding is 4000 years old, with its origin in Egypt.

Cattleya, tropical American, epiphytic orchid popular with florists and amateur gardeners. The large, showy flowers have two petals and a large lip surrounding the flower center. Colors range from white with yellow velvety markings to deep purple. Leaves are lance-shaped. There are 40 species and many varieties, including the white nun *(Cattleya skinnerii)* and the Brazilian *C. labiata* having up to seven flowers on each stem. Height: to 18in (45.7cm). Family Orchidaceae.

Catton, (Charles) Bruce (1899–), US historian, b. Petoskey, Mich. A specialist in Civil War history, he stresses the individual in history rather than nations, thus bringing the reader closer to the event. He won the Pulitzer Prize for *A Stillness at Appomattox* (1953).

Catullus, Gaius Valerius (died 54 BC), Roman poet. Of a wealthy family, Catullus spent most of his short life in Rome, where he became part of the literary society and attended the salon of Clodia. The beautiful Clodia was the most important influence of Catullus' life and the "Lesbia" of his most famous poems. His longer works are the poems *Attis* and *The Mar-*

Fidel Castro

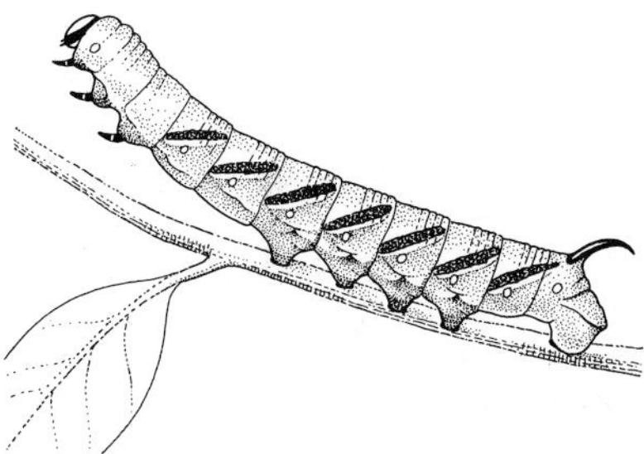
Caterpillar

Cathedral: Salisbury, England

Catherine of Aragon

riage of Peleus and Thetis, but he is best known for his short love lyrics. *See also* Attis. △1028.

Catulus, Gaius Lutatius (*fl.* 3rd century BC), Roman consul. In 241 BC he led the fleet that defeated the Carthaginians at the Battle of the Aegates Islands that ended the First Punic War.

CATV. *See* Community Antenna Television.

Cauca, river in W Colombia; rises in the Andes Mts, flows N to Magdalena River; lower course is navigable. Coffee is grown in its fertile valley. Length: 600mi (966km).

Caucasian Languages, family of languages, numbering about 40, spoken by over 5 million people in a small area of the Soviet Union between the Black and the Caspian seas. Georgian is the most important of these languages, accounting for over half of all the speakers. Others include Kabardian, Adygei, Abkhazian, Chechen, Ingush, Avar, Lezgin, and Dargin.

Caucasoid Race, one of the major human racial groupings. Physical characteristics include light skin pigmentation; narrow, high-bridged noses; hair varying between straight and curly; heavy body hair; and high incidence of the Rh-negative blood type. Since 1500 AD, Caucasoids have spread from their European, Near Eastern, and North African homelands, displacing aboriginal populations in many parts of the world. △658.

Caucasus (Bol'voj Kavkaz), mountain system and region in SE European USSR, extends from Kuban River mouth on Black Sea SE to Apsheron Peninsula on the Caspian Sea. System includes two major regions: North Caucasia (steppes) and Transcaucasia; forms a natural barrier between Asia and Europe. The Georgian Military Road, Mamison and Daryal passes, and Ossetian Military Road are major traversing routes; major cities include Yerevan, Grozny, Baku (oil pipeline origin), Tbilisi, Ordzhonikidze. The range has been scene of invasions and migrations of Persians, Khazars, Arabs, Huns, Mongols, and Russians. Source of oil, iron, manganese, hydroelectric power; site of several tourist resorts along the Black Sea coast. Crops: cotton, fruits, grain. Highest peak is Mt Elbrus, 18,481ft (5,637m). Length: 750mi (1,208km).

Cauchon, Pierre (c.1371–1442), French bishop. As bishop of Beauvais, he presided over the trial of Joan of Arc who was captured in his diocese in 1430. Since he had been councilor of English King Henry VI and his regent in France, the Duke of Bedford, since 1422, he served English interests at the trial by obscuring the political aspects with inquisitorial procedure. He became bishop of Lisieux in 1432 and participated in the anti-papist Council of Basel in 1435.

Caucus, private meeting of political party members to select candidates, assess issues, or plan a campaign. In a legislative caucus, party members discuss leadership positions, issues, policies, and strategies.

Caudillo, type of political leader prevalent in Latin America during the 19th century. A civilian-on-horseback, he was supported by a paramilitary force. The aim of the caudillo band was to gain wealth; the tactic usually violence. Some caudillos dominated only very small areas; others an entire nation.

Cauliflower, plant of the cabbage family with a short, thick stem and large, lobed leaves. White or purplish flower clusters form tightly compressed 8in (20cm) heads that are eaten as a vegetable. In the garden, the heads are blanched, or kept white, by tying outer leaves over the head; some varieties are self-blanching, having leaves that grow over the head. It matures in 50–80 days. Family Cruciferae; species *Brassica oleracea italica.*

Cauliflower Fungus. △428.

Caustic Soda. *See* Sodium Hydroxide.

Cauto River, longest river in Cuba; rises in Sierra Maestra; flows NW and W to Caribbean Sea, N of Manzanillo; navigable for small vessels. Length: 150mi (242km).

Cavafy, Constantine (1863–1933), properly Konstantínos Pétrou Kavafis, b. Alexandria, Egypt, influential Greek poet. His poetry, mostly written after middle age, benefited from his love of English and French literature and expressed his skeptical opposition to traditional values, such as Christianity.

Cavalcanti, Guido (*c.* 1250–1300), Italian lyric poet. A contemporary and personal friend of Dante, he is mentioned in the *Inferno* and in the dedication of the *Vita Nuova.* Although he was a philosopher and dialectician and treated love as an abstract and impersonal principle, he was often personal and expressive in his poetry. His most famous poem is "Donna mi Prega" ("A Lady Begs Me"). *See also* Dante Alighieri.

Cavalier, Jean (c1681–1740), French Huguenot general. At the age of 20, this baker of Anduze became the leader of the camisards, the white-shirted guerrillas who fought the army of Louis XIV for three years during the Huguenot revolt in Cévennes. He surrendered to Villars in 1704, and the revolt gradually ended. Cavalier served Savoy and then sailed to England where he became governor of the Isle of Wight.

Cavalier King Charles Spaniel, small hunting dog based on the 16th-century toy spaniel popular during the reign of England's Charles II and featured in paintings of the time. The modern breed, not considered a toy, has a flat skull with a short, tapered muzzle; wide-set ears and eyes; and a square, deep-chested body. The long, silky coat is black with tan marks or solid red. Average size: 12in (30.5cm) high at shoulder; 10–18lb (4.5–8kg). *See also* Spaniel.

Cavalier Poets, group of 17th-century English lyric poets, most of whom were courtiers at the court of Charles I and disciples of Ben Jonson. Their poetry is witty, amorous, and often bawdy. The leading cavalier poets were Robert Herrick, Thomas Carew, John Suckling, and Richard Lovelace.

Cavally, river in W Africa; rises in the Man Mts in W Ivory Coast; empties into the Gulf of Guinea; forms a section of the boundary between the Ivory Coast and Liberia. Length: 320mi (515km).

Cave, Edward (1691–1754), English printer and publisher, who produced the first modern English magazine. He wrote and published *The Gentleman's Magazine* (1731–54), a collection of news and political essays. One of his writers was Samuel Johnson.

Cave, a natural underground cavity, with an opening to the surface formed by ground water, underground streams, and ocean waves. The study of caves, called speleology, includes cave geology, hydrology, anthropology, and biology. △256.

Cave Barb. △514.

Cavell, Edith (1865–1915), English nurse. She established modern nursing in Belgium and later was killed by the Germans for aiding and sheltering Allied soldiers during World War I, an execution that aroused public outcry throughout much of the world.

Cavendish, George (1500–61), English biographer, best known for his *Life of Cardinal Wolsey* (1557). Cavendish was an assistant to Wolsey, the chief minister of Henry VIII, from 1527 to 1530, a position that gave him the opportunity to write a first-hand account of the political and religious aspects of the Henrican Reformation.

Cavendish, Henry (1731–1810), English physicist and chemist. He discovered hydrogen and the composition of water, determined the composition of air, and estimated the Earth's mass and density by a method called the Cavendish experiment. He also determined nitric acid composition, the specific gravity of carbon dioxide and hydrogen, and stated the inverse square law for the interaction of charged particles. The Cavendish Laboratory at Cambridge is named after him. △1490.

Cavendish, William, Duke of Newcastle. *See* Newcastle, William Cavendish, Duke of.

Cavendish, William, 1st Duke of Devonshire. *See* Devonshire, William Cavendish, 1st Duke of.

Cavity, Dental, a localized wearing away of a tooth, beginning at the surface and progressing inward to the pulp. Microorganisms acting on sugars and starches and producing an excess of acid are believed to be the underlying cause. Prevention and treatment include proper diet, cleaning of teeth and filling of existing cavities. △756.

Cavour, Camillo Benso, Conte di (1810–61), Italian (Piedmontese) statesman instrumental in uniting Italy under Savoy rule. A 19th-century liberal dedicated to liberty, progress, and moderation, he first was prime minister to Victor Emmanuel II in 1852. From 1856–60 he engineered Italian liberation from Austrian domination (with French aid), then the expulsion of the French from southern Italy (with Giuseppe Garibaldi's forces), and, finally, the neutralization of Garibaldi's influence in liberated regions. This allowed formation of kingdom of Italy in March 1861, three months before his death. △1250.

Cavy, South American rodents from which guinea pigs are descended. Most are small (under 2.2lb or 1kg), dark, nocturnal plant-eaters with short legs and no tail, but the Patagonian cavy has long legs and weighs up to 33lb (16kg). Family Caviidae. *See also* Guinea Pig. △588.

Cawnpore. *See* Kanpur.

Caxton, William (1422–1491), the first English printer. He set up his printing press in 1476 at Westminster. He published over 100 books, 24 of them his own translations from French.

Cayenne, capital city of French Guiana, N central South America, on Cayenne Island in Cayenne River. Devil's Island is off the NW coast; site of Pasteur Institute (1940). Industries: sawmills, rum, gold. Founded by French 1664. Pop. 19,668.

Cayley, Sir George (1773–1857), English inventor who founded the science of aerodynamics and pioneered in aerial navigation. He built the first successful glider able to carry a man and developed the basic form of the modern airplane. He also founded the Regent Street Polytechnic Institute in London, invented the caterpillar tractor, and did research in scientific education and in land reclamation.

Cayman Islands, islands in British West Indies, 200mi (322km) NW of Jamaica, in NW Caribbean Sea; includes Grand Cayman, Little Cayman, and Cayman Brac. Capital is Georgetown on Grand Cayman. Industries: tourism, turtle and shark fishing, shipbuilding, coconuts, lumber. Discovered 1503 by Christopher Columbus; colonized 1734. Pop. 10,652.

Cayuga, major branch of the Five Nations of the Iroquois Confederacy, originally living around Lake Cayuga, N.Y., and Grand River in Ontario, Canada. The Cayuga joined the British during the Revolution and afterwards became widely scattered into Ohio, Wisconsin, and Oklahoma, where they joined the Seneca. Today there are approximately 550 in Oklahoma and 400 Cayuga in New York.

Cayuga Lake, lake in W central New York; longest of the Finger Lakes. At S end of lake is Taughaunock Falls with a drop of 215ft (66m). Along shore of lake are Wells College and Cornell University. Area: 38mi (61km) long by 1–3.5mi (1.6–5.6km) wide.

CCC. *See* Civilian Conservation Corps.

Ceauşescu, Nicolae (1918–), Romanian Communist party leader and statesman. Under a collective leadership with Ion Maurer and Chivu Stoica from 1961 Romania's growth rate was the highest in Eastern Europe. The country cooperated fully with the Soviet Union, and the land was collectivized. Beginning in 1965, under his leadership as Communist party secretary, economic problems with the USSR caused a resurgence of Romanian nationalist spirit. In 1965 Ceauşescu succeeded as chief of the party upon the death of Premier Gheorghiu-Dej, and in 1967 he became president of the council (or chief of state) as well. He was formally designated president in 1974.

Cebu, city in central Philippines, on central E coast of Cebu Island; capital of Cebu prov. A mountain range extends length of the island; rich agricultural area; site of oldest Spanish settlement in the Philippines (1565), Southwestern University (1950). Industries: hemp, tobacco, corn, sugar cane, rice, coconuts, coal. Discovered 1521 by Ferdinand Magellan. Pop. 342,-116.

Cebus Monkey. *See* Capuchin.

Cecil, Lord (Edward Christian) David (1902–), English biographer and literary critic, best-known for his two-volume study of Lord Melbourne. Much of his writing was an outgrowth of his lectures at Oxford, where he was Goldsmith's professor of English literature (1948–70).

Cecil, Robert. *See* Salisbury, 1st Earl of; Salisbury, 3rd Marquess of.

Cecil, (Edgar Algernon) Robert, first Viscount Cecil of Chelwood (1864–1958), English statesman. A Conservative member of Parliament (1906–23), he won the 1937 Nobel Peace Prize. After holding posts of undersecretary (1915) and assistant secretary of state (1918) and minister of blockade (1916), he helped draft the League of Nations covenant, was president of the League of Nations Union (1923–45), and represented Britain at several disarmament conferences.

Works include *The Way of Peace* (1928) and *A Real Peace* (1941).

Cecil, William, 1st Baron Burghley (1520–98), chief minister of Elizabeth I of England. He was secretary of state (1550–53) under Edward VI but failed to win Mary's favor. On Mary's death Elizabeth made him again secretary of state (1558–72) and then lord high treasurer (1572–98). An able administrator, he helped the queen steer a moderate course between Catholicism and extreme Protestantism. He was an invaluable link between the queen and Parliament. In 1587 he was responsible for ordering the execution of Mary, Queen of Scots.

Cecilia, Saint (died 230?), patron saint of music and the blind. Her festival is celebrated on November 22. According to her legend, she converted her husband to Christianity and was martyred with him. She was reputed to accompany her devotions with music.

Cecropia Moth, large North American moth that is dark reddish-brown. It has no mouthparts and lives only the few days needed to mate and lay eggs. Cecropia caterpillars feed on tree and shrub leaves. Wing span: to 6in (15cm). Family Saturniidae; species *Hyalaphora cecropia*. *See also* Moth.

Cecrops, in Greek mythology, the founder of Athens. Cecrops, possessor of a man's body and a snake's tail, became the first king of Attica. He brought 12 Greek cities under his control, made Athena the patron deity, and acknowledged Zeus as the supreme god.

Cedar, evergreen tree native to North Africa and Asia, and grown in warmer temperate regions worldwide. They have clustered needlelike leaves, oblong cones, and fragrant, durable wood. They are popular lawn trees. Height: 40–200ft (12–61m). Family Pinaceae; genus *Cedrus*.

Cedar Falls, city in NE Iowa, 6mi (10km) W of Waterloo, on the Cedar River; site of University of Northern Iowa (1876). Industries: pumps, golfing equipment, farm machinery. Inc. 1854. Pop. (1970) 29,597.

Cedar Rapids, city in E central Iowa, 105mi (169km) ENE of Des Moines; seat of Linn co; named for rapids on the Cedar River; site of Coe College (1851), Mount Mercy College (1875), and an art museum with a collection of works by Grant Wood. City is one of Iowa's chief industrial and commercial centers. Industries: cereals, machinery, paper, pharmaceuticals. Settled 1838; inc. as town 1849, as city 1856. Pop. (1970) 110,642.

Cedar Waxwing, small North American bird with red, waxy-looking flight feathers. It has brownish plumage, black eye patches, and a yellow-tipped tail. Migrating in large, compact flocks, it feeds on berries and blossoms. The female lays pale bluish-gray eggs (3–5) in a cup-shaped, twig-and-grass nest in a tree. Length: 8in (20cm). Species *Bombycilla cedrorum*.

CEEB. *See* College Entrance Examination Board.

Celadon, semi-transparent bluish or grayish-green glazes used in Chinese and Korean ceramics. Noteworthy are the celadon wares of the Sung period (10th–13th centuries). *See also* Porcelain. △1044.

Celandine, erect, branched herb, common in Britain and America. The plant has yellow sap, serrated leaves, and yellow flowers of about 1in (2.5cm) wide. Family Papaveraceae; species *Chelidonium majus*.

Celebes Sea, part of the Pacific Ocean between Philippines and Indonesia, SE Asia; bounded by Sulu Archipelago and Mindanao Island (N), Sangihe Island (E), Celebes Island (S), Borneo (W). Area: 165,000sq mi (427,350sq km).

Celery, biennial plant native to Europe and widely cultivated for its long stalks used as a vegetable or salad. Its seedlike fruits are used as food flavoring and in medicine. It has white flowers. Family Umbelliferae; species *Apium graveolens*.

Celesta, percussion instrument resembling a glockenspiel and played by keyboard, with a range from middle C up 4 octaves. Invented by Auguste Mustel in Paris (1868), its clear, tinkling tones were first used in symphonic orchestration by Tchaikovsky in "Dance of the Sugar Plum Fairy," from the *Nutcracker Suite* (1892). *See also* Glockenspiel.

Celestial Equator, great circle on the celestial sphere, lying midway between the celestial poles in the same plane as the earth's equator. △130.

Celestial Mechanics, branch of astronomy concerned with the relative motions of celestial bodies that are associated in systems, such as the solar system or a binary star system, by gravitational fields. First developed by Isaac Newton in the 17th century on the basis of Kepler's laws and the law of gravitation, celestial mechanics (rather than general relativity) is usually sufficient to calculate the various factors determining the motion of planets, satellites, comets, stars, and galaxies around a center of gravitational attraction. △38.

Celestial Poles. △130.

Celestial Sphere, imaginary sphere of infinite radius used for defining the positions of celestial bodies as seen from Earth, which lies at the center of the sphere. The sphere rotates, once in 24 hours, about a line that is an extension of the Earth's axis. The position of a celestial body is the point at which a radial line through the body meets the surface of the sphere. It is given quantitatively in terms of coordinates, such as declination and right ascension or altitude and azimuth, referred to great circles on the sphere, such as the celestial equator, horizon, or ecliptic.

Celestine V, Roman Catholic pope (1294) and saint, b. Pietro di Murrone (c. 1215). A Benedictine monk, he was never in Rome as pope and became the first pope to abdicate when he was unable to adapt to the papacy. He was canonized by Pope Clement V in 1313.

Celestite, a sulfate mineral, strontium sulfate ($SrSO_4$), with distinctive pale blue, orthorhombic system tabular or elongate crystals. Chiefly in sedimentary rocks, also as gangue material in ore veins. Sometimes in fibrous veins and fine-grained deposits. Glassy white to pale blue; hardness 3–3.5; sp gr 4.

Celiac Disease, intestinal disturbance caused by intolerance to wheat and rye products. Symptoms include depression, abdominal distention, soft stools.

Cell, smallest unit of life that can exist and sustain itself independently. All living things are made up of one or more cells. Most cells are composed of a surrounding membrane, interior, jellylike cytoplasm, and nucleus. Usually, cells reproduce, grow, and metabolize within their membranes. Cells can be an entire organism or specialized units, as in muscles or nerves. Cytoplasm is the source of origin of organelles having specialized functions. Endoplasmic reticulum (ER), microscopic layers of enfolded membrane, is found throughout the cytoplasm. There are two types of ER: rough, containing ribosomes composed of protein and RNA, and smooth, that appears as a series of tubules.

Blue-green algae and bacteria cells do not have nuclei. Instead, these cells have large chromosomes floating in the cytoplasm. Vacuoles, found mostly in plant cells, are membrane-bound sacs of liquid and dissolved solids that maintain the water balance within the cell. Food vacuoles accomplish digestion. Other organelles include the mitochondria, Golgi apparatus, lysosomes, and granules. Most plant cells also contain chloroplasts. △412.

Cell, Battery. △1532, 1542, 1546.

Cell Division, cell increase making it possible for an organism to grow. In some body parts, including lower skin layers, intestinal lining, and blood cells, this process continues throughout an individual's life. *See also* Mitosis.

Celler-Kefauver Act (1950), US act that amended section 7 of the Clayton Act (1914). The amendment prohibits any merger that substantially lessens competition in any line of commerce in any part of the country. It specifically closes the "asset loophole" contained in the Clayton Act, which had permitted anticompetitive mergers that were accomplished by asset acquisition because it only specifically covered certain stock acquisition mergers.

Cellini, Benvenuto (1500–71), Italian goldsmith, sculptor, and author of a famous *Autobiography* (1558–62). As proud and unscrupulous as he was talented, he was often involved in brawls and scandals and was twice imprisoned. His best-known work as a goldsmith was an elaborate saltcellar for Francis I of France (1543). His "Nymph of Fontainebleau" (1543–44) a bronze relief, is the high point of the art of the School of Fontainebleau. He began to work with free-standing sculpture in 1545; his "Perseus and the Head of Medusa" is one of that craft's greatest achievements. △1150.

Cello or (Violoncello), second largest of violin family

Caucasus Mountains, USSR

Cavy

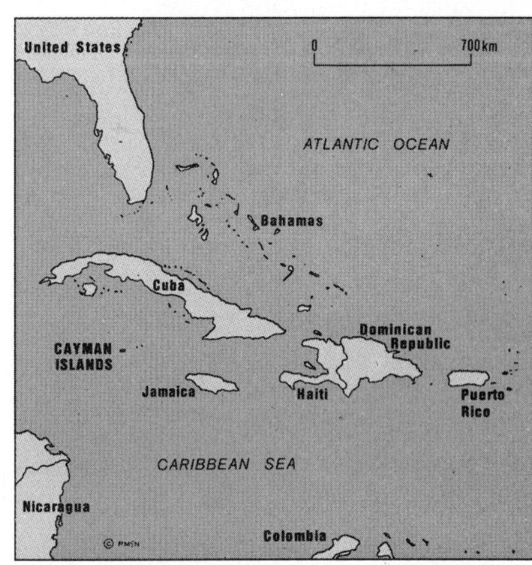

United States
0
700km
ATLANTIC OCEAN
Bahamas
Cuba
Dominican Republic
CAYMAN ISLANDS
Jamaica
Haiti
Puerto Rico
CARIBBEAN SEA
Nicaragua
Colombia

Cayman Islands

Cedar waxwing

of musical instruments, with a soft, mellow tone, one octave below the viola, and a range of 2½ octaves. The seated player, using a bow, holds the cello vertically, supporting it with his knees. Developed in the 16th century by Amati, cellos are used in symphony orchestras, string ensembles, and as solo instruments, notably by Pablo Casals. △1244.

Cellophane, flexible, transparent film made of regenerated cellulose and used mostly as a wrapping material. It is made by dissolving wood pulp or other plant material in an alkali, and then neutralizing the alkaline solvent with an acid. The precipitate is impregnated with glycerine, dried, and cut into sheets.

Cells, Electrochemical, devices from which electricity is obtained as a result of a chemical reaction. A cell consists of two electrodes (a positive anode and a negative cathode) immersed in a solution (electrolyte). The chemical reaction takes place between the electrolyte and one of the electrodes. In a primary cell, current is produced directly as a result of chemical action, whereas in a secondary cell (battery) the chemical reaction is reversible and the cell can be charged by passing a current through it. △1566.

Celluloid, a cheap, hard, synthetic plastic invented in 1870 and made by mixing cellulose nitrate with pigments and fillers in a solution of camphor or alcohol. When heated, the resulting compound is pliable and moldable. Highly flammable, it has been superseded by other plastics. △1618.

Cellulose, fibrous carbohydrate providing the structural framework of plant cell walls. The most abundant organic compound in the world, it is made up of glucose subunits. It is economically important as plant fibers (cotton), lumber, and wood pulp, and is obtained by treating wood to dissolve everything but the cellulose and is used in manufacturing paper products, rayon, and celluloid. △430, 448, 694.

Cellulose Acetate. △1620.

Cellulose Nitrate. *See* Nitrocellulose.

Cellulose Plastics, any of numerous thermoplastic (plastic when reheated) derivatives of the plant substance cellulose. Included are cellulose nitrate (or nitrocellulose), used in explosives and propellants; various cellulose acetates for making textile fibers and packaging films; and ethyl cellulose, used in the manufacture of shock-resistant materials. △1608, 1618.

Celsius, Anders (1701–44), Swedish astronomer noted for inventing the Celsius, or centigrade, thermometer (1742). He also published a collection of observations of the aurora borealis (1733). △1508.

Celsus, Aulus Cornelius (1st century AD), Roman encyclopedist, author of a comprehensive work covering several topics. Only the section dealing with medicine survived. *De medicina* is the most complete Roman medical text extant. Most of what is known about Hellenistic medical practices is based on Celsus' description.

Celtic Art. △1050.

Celtic Culture. △1008.

Celtic Languages, group of languages spoken in parts of Great Britain, Ireland, and France, forming a subdivision of the Indo-European family. There are two branches: the Brythonic, which includes Welsh, Breton, and the extinct language Cornish; and Goidelic, which includes Gaelic and Manx, of the Isle of Man, which died out only recently. The Celtic languages were dominant in Britain until the 5th century AD when they began to be supplanted by the Germanic dialects of the invading Anglo-Saxons. △866.

Celtic Mythology, stories of local deities of the Celtic tribes who were scattered throughout continental Europe and the British Isles. Each tribe had an omnipotent god, similar in attributes to Dagda, who possessed all-embracing power and whose cauldron was always full, signifying abundance. The world that the gods inhabited was seen in the myths as a reflection of the world of men. Female divinities seem to have been identified more closely with nature or with a local topographical feature.

Celtis, Conradus Proctucius (1459–1508), German scholar, also known as Konrad Celtes. He was named Germany's first poet laureate by Frederick III in 1487. Celtis held teaching posts at several European universities and founded a number of literary societies. His lively poetry included *Amores* and an unfinished epic on Theodoric, the German leader who conquered Italy, AD 471–526.

Celts, group of people originating in Europe, chiefly in what is now Germany. There were many Celtic tribes, or peoples, speaking related languages as they spread from Germany and France to Belgium, Ireland, Scotland, and Wales. They also invaded Italy, Bohemia, and Russia. They were called Keltoi by the Greeks and Gauls by the Romans after Julius Caesar, whose war against them in 58 BC ended Celtic independence on the European continent. Celtic culture was rural, the economy largely local except for rather sophisticated metal production. Celtic religious and cultural leaders, called druids, practiced magic and Celtic ritual. Celtic culture and language can still be traced in Ireland, Scotland, Wales, and Britanny. △ 990, 1008, 1050.

Cement, a fabricated substance that hardens and becomes adhesive after being applied in a plastic mass. In engineering, cement refers to a fine powder, consisting of gypsum, lime, plaster, or portland cement. Used to bind sand and gravel to form concrete, to unite structures, and to coat surfaces as a protection from chemicals. △1612.

Cement, Portland, a binding material used in concrete and mortar. It is made by heating a mixture of crushed chalk and clay to form a clinker, which is then crushed and packed into bags. When water is added to cement, it recrystallizes, the interlocking crystals of calcium silicate and calcium aluminate forming a hard mass on drying. △1612.

Cementum. △756.

Cenci, Beatrice (1577–99), Italian noblewoman and literary heroine. One of the 12 children of Francesco Cenci's first marriage, she along with her brothers plotted his death in 1598 after he remarried and treated the family cruelly. At her trial, Beatrice claimed (apparently falsely) that her father had attempted incest, but she and her two brothers were convicted and executed. Her story formed the basis for Shelley's *The Cenci* (1819) and Guerrazzi's *Beatrice Cenci* (1854). She traditionally is believed to be the subject of Guido Reni's painting in the Barberini Palace, Rome.

Cenis, Mont, pass on French-Italian border; one of the great invasion routes of Italian history; site of one of world's longest railroad tunnels, the first through the Alps, constructed 1857–70, connecting Turin, Italy, with Chambéry, France. Altitude: 6,831ft (2,083m).

Cenozoic Era, most recent major division of geologic time, beginning about 65 million years ago and extending through the present, called the Age of Mammals. It is subdivided into the Tertiary and Quaternary periods. It is the period during which the modern world with its characteristic geographical features and plants and animals developed. *See also* Geologic Time. △276, 576.

Censors, two magistrates of ancient Rome. They were elected for a five-year term to take the census (for taxation and military purposes); oversee public works, finance, and morals; and fill senate vacancies. The office lasted from 443 BC to the reign of Domitian (AD 81–96). △1014.

Censorship, the system whereby the government claims the right to protect the public interest by influencing the release of any item of mass communication, such as books, newspapers, movies, and plays. Censorship can take on two forms; one where the government discourages or suppresses printed material, and one whereby the press is used as an instrument of the government, with the press required to print anything provided by the government. In the United States, the First Amendment forbids abridgement of freedom of the press. A recent case pertaining to this was *New York Times* v. *United States* (Pentagon Papers).

Census, survey conducted by a national government to collect facts about the society it governs. In addition to ascertaining up-to-date population counts, most censuses also seek information about marital status, age and sex of citizens, numbers of children, occupation, education, housing, and spoken language. The government may use this information as a basis for policy-making.

Census, Bureau of, US government agency established in 1902 as part of the Department of Commerce. In 1972 the bureau combined with the Office of Business Economics to form the Social and Economic Statistics Administration. It serves as a center for compiling, analyzing, and publishing a broad range of general-purpose statistics dealing with economic, social, and demographic data in the United States. *See also* Census, United States.

Census, United States, official count of the nation's population and statistical tabulation of age, sex, employment, and other data. The census has been carried out every 10 years, beginning in 1790 as called for by Article 1, Section 2, of the Constitution. Census data determines the number of representatives alloted to each state in the House of Representatives and is useful for governmental planning.

Centaur, in Greek mythology, one of a race of beings part horse and part man. They were the children of the Lapith king Ixion. △832.

Centaurus, or the Centaur, extensive southern constellation situated north of Crux and Carina and containing the sun's nearest stellar neighbors, the stars of the Alpha Centauri system. The bright star Beta and the globular cluster Omega are also prominent. △ 134.

Center of Gravity, point in or near a body or system of bodies through which passes the resultant force of all the gravitational forces acting on each particle of the body or system. It is thus the point at which the weight of the body may be considered to act. In a uniform gravitational field it is the same as the center of mass. △178, 1488.

Center of Mass, the point in space associated with a rigid body or system of particles such that the acceleration of this point multiplied by the total mass of the system equals the sum of all the forces acting on the system. Isaac Newton first verified his law of gravity by assuming the earth and moon to attract each other as though they were point masses located at their centers.

Centigrade, a term for the temperature scale having 100 divisions between the freezing point of water (0 degrees) and boiling point (100 degrees). Now replaced by the term "Celsius" after the inventor of the scale. *See also* Temperature Scales. △1500.

Centimeter, unit of length defined as one hundredth part of a meter. *See* Weights and Measures.

Centipede, or hundred-legger, invertebrate animal found worldwide. Red to brown, they have one pair of legs per body segment, one pair of antennae, and little or no sight. Predacious, they feed mostly on other arthropods, but some inflict a painful bite. Living in dark places, they find their prey by touch and smell. Length: 1.2–6in (3–17mm). Class Chilopoda. *See also* Myriapoda.

CENTO. *See* Central Treaty Organization.

Central, Cordillera, mountain range of the Andes in Colombia; one of three parallel systems: Oriental, Central, and Occidental. Highest peak is 19,020ft (5,801m).

Central, Massif. *See* Massif Central.

Central African Empire, formerly Central African Republic, landlocked nation in central Africa, governed by an emperor. Bounded by Chad (N), Sudan (E), Zaire and Congo Republic (S), and Cameroon (W). The country is a great, well-watered plateau covered by savanna, except for an area of dense tropical forests (S) and a semi-desert area (NE). It has a humid climate with annual rainfall of 70in (178cm) in the Ubangi (Oubangui) River Valley, and 31in (79cm) in NE semi-desert. Subsistence agriculture provides the primary livelihood. Coffee and cotton are chief cash crops; peanuts, timber, and rubber are also exported. Only 2% of land is cultivated. Approximately 90% of the population lives in rural areas. The country has no dominant tribe; most of the inhabitants migrated into the area during past 200 years to escape the slave trade. The four main ethnic groups are Azande, Yakoma, Sango, and Banziri. French is the official language, but Sango is spoken in all areas. The literacy rate is between 5% and 10%; about 45% of elementary-age school children attend school.

The French first occupied the area in 1887; in 1894 the colony of Ubangi-Shari was formed; it was administratively united with Chad in 1906 and made part of French Equatorial Africa in 1910. Forced labor by concessionaires to whom France had leased the territory led to rebellions in 1928, 1935, and 1946. Ubangi-Shari supported the Free French in WWII. At the end of the war France's attitude toward her colonies altered and they were given representation in French parliament. The first responsible government was created in 1957. In 1958 the colony voted to ecome a self-governing republic within the French ommunity, and its name became Central African Reublic. In 1960 it declared its independence, but the ext six years saw a deterioration in the economy, and orruption and increasing inefficiency under President David Dacko. As the result of a bloodless coup ec. 31, 1966–Jan. 1, 1967, Col. Jean-Bedel Bokassa ook over the presidency, abrogated the constitution, nd dissolved the National Assembly. In 1976, okassa adopted an Islamic name, transformed the epublic into an empire, and proclaimed himself Emeror Bokassa I.

PROFILE

Official name: Central African Empire
Area: 240,535sq mi (622,986sq km)
Population: 1,600,000
Chief cities: Bangui (capital); Bouar; Carnot
Religion: Tribal, Christian, Islam
Language: French (official), Sango
Monetary Unit: Franc CFA

Central America, geographical term for the narrow strip of land that connects North America to South America and divides the Caribbean Sea from the Pacific Ocean; it consists of Guatemala, El Salvador, Honduras, Nicaragua, Costa Rica, Belize, Panama. Highly developed by the Mayas, the region (excluding Panama) was conquered and ruled by the Spanish from the 16th century until 1839 when the confederation broke up and independent states were formed. The terrain is mostly mountainous; climate is tropical. The area enjoys an economic, ethnic, and geological unity; Spanish is the main language. Crops: bananas, coffee, cotton. Area: 276,400sq mi (715,876sq km).

Central American Common Market (CACM), an association for the economic integration of the five nations of the area. The Treaty of Central American Economic Integration, signed by the states between 1960 and 1963, projected a five-year goal for achieving the desired ends. Nationalism and balance of payments deficits have impeded success.

Central Bank, institution that regulates and sets policy for a nation's banking system. The US central bank is the federal reserve system. *See also* Federal Reserve System. △934.

Central Intelligence Agency (CIA), government agency established to coordinate intelligence activities of the several government departments and agencies in the interest of national security in the United States. The CIA works in an advisory capacity to the National Security Council in matters of national security. The agency has no police, subpoena, or law enforcement powers or internal security functions. The National Security Council may direct the CIA to perform other functions related to security. In the mid-1970s the CIA was attacked for abusing its powers, particularly in violating the restrictions against its operation within the United States. Founded 1947.

Central Nervous System (CNS), portion of the nervous system encased by the bony skull and spinal column, ie, the brain and the spinal cord.

Central Powers, the World War I coalition of Germany, Austria-Hungary, Bulgaria, and Turkey that fought the Allied Powers of Britain, France, Belgium, Russia, and, later, the United States. △1306.

Central Tendency, method of summarizing large groups of data into meaningful statistics. The basic measures of central tendency are the arithmetic mean, the median, and the mode. Each measure is useful under certain conditions, but the most commonly used is the arithmetic mean. *See also* Frequency Distribution.

Central Treaty Organization (CENTO), mutual security system made up of Turkey, Iran, Pakistan, and Britain, established 1955. The United States is a full member of some CENTO committees and has observer status at council meetings. CENTO headquarters are in Ankara, Turkey, moved from Baghdad (1958) when Iraq withdrew from membership and the name was changed from Baghdad Pact in 1959.

Centrifugal Force, the apparent (but nonexistent) outward force felt by a person in curvilinear motion. For example, a bus turning left causes a passenger to experience a "force" to the right, but it is simply his own tendency to continue in a straight line conflicting with the bus' leftward acceleration. △1490, 1494.

Centrifuge, a mechanical device, usually a rapidly spun container, using centrifugal force to separate substances of varying density. Used in draining water (as in a washing machine), separating cream from milk, blood cells from whole blood, sugar from syrup and many other laboratory and industrial purposes. △1494.

Centriole, dense body forming central portion of the centrosome near the nucleus of a cell. It occurs in all cells except those of angiosperms and the sperm cells of ferns and gymnosperms. During mitosis and meiosis, centrioles divide before the rest of the cell, moving to either pole of the cell and forming the spindle.

Centripetal Force, the inward force on an object constraining it to move in a curvilinear path. The sun's gravitational force is also the centripetal force causing the earth's nearly circular motion. A mass m traveling with velocity v in an arc of a circle of radius r is acted upon by a centripetal force $F = mv^2/r$. △1494.

Centurion, military officer of ancient Rome. The commander of 1/60 part of a Roman legion, or 100 men, he usually rose from footsoldier and was well paid to maintain discipline. The 60 centurions of a legion were organized into 10 cohorts of six, chief among which was the first cohort.

Cèpe. △428.

Cephalic Index, measurement of the head, used in physical anthropology. The maximum width of the skull is divided by the maximum length, and the result expressed as a percentage: the classifications are dolichocephalic (long-headed; under 75%); mesocephalic, or mesaticephalic (medium; 75–80%); brachycephalic (short-headed; over 80%). △660.

Cephalopod, predatory marine mollusk (including squid, cuttlefish, nautilus, octopus) having eight or more arms surrounding the mouth. Each has a well-developed nervous system permitting great speed and alertness; large eyes with image-forming ability equalling vertebrates'; and a mouth with a parrotlike beak. Most squirt inky fluid to confuse attackers. They move by jet-stream propulsion, squirting water from their mantle edge. Their heavily yolked eggs develop into larval young, resembling adults. The extinct ammonoids and belemnoids were once common cephalopods. There are 600 living species. *See also* Mollusk. △480.

Cepheid Variable, type of regular pulsating variable star whose maximum luminosity is directly proportional to the time it takes to pass from one maximum brightness to the next. These objects, whose prototype is the star Delta Cephei in the northern constellation Cepheus, are generally very reliable in their light variations, thus allowing their distances to be very accurately measured. Classical Cepheids, of Population 1, have periods of one to fifty days. Their discovery in external galaxies has been a major aid in determining intergalactic distances. *See also* RR Lyrae Variable. △112,120.

Ceramics, in art, objects made of moistened clay that have been shaped and then baked. Earthenware, terra-cotta, brick, tile, faience, majolica, stoneware, and porcelain are all ceramics. The clay consists largely of aluminum silicates derived from weathered rock or occuring in natural deposits and may contain iron oxide, sand, bone ash, grog (crushed pottery), petuntse (china stone), steatite, mica, or powdered flint, which are used to create different kinds of pottery and porcelain.

Clay may be shaped by hand, using a coil or slab technique, a mold, or a potter's wheel. Ceramic ware is ornamented by clay inlays, by relief modeling on the surface, or by incised, stamped, or impressed designs. A creamy mixture of clay and water (slip) can be used to coat the ware. After drying, ceramic ware is baked in a kiln, until it has hardened into its "biscuit" stage. Glaze, a silicate preparation applied to the clay surface and fused to it during firing, is used to make the pottery nonporous and to give it a smooth, colorful, decorative surface.

Primitive cultures of Africa, America, and the Pacific, as well as ancient Egypt and neolithic communities of Europe, were all familiar with terra-cotta vessels. In ancient Egypt they developed a faience with a glaze, and Mesopotamia and Persia used large architectural tiles with colorful glazes. In the 6th and 5th centuries BC the Greeks developed red, black, and white glazed pottery with figures and scenes on it, while the Romans used relief decoration on theirs. Persian, Syrian, and Turkish pottery with colorful glazes continued to be produced after the fall of Rome. In Spain, lusterware, the first sophisticated ceramics of the modern era, was produced by the 9th-century Moors. Italian majolica, Dutch delft, German Meissen, and English Wedgewood were further refinements of the product. Chinese porcelain dates from the T'ang dynasty, and Chinese stoneware goes back to about 3000 BC. In the 20th century there has been renewed interest in folk pottery. △1208.

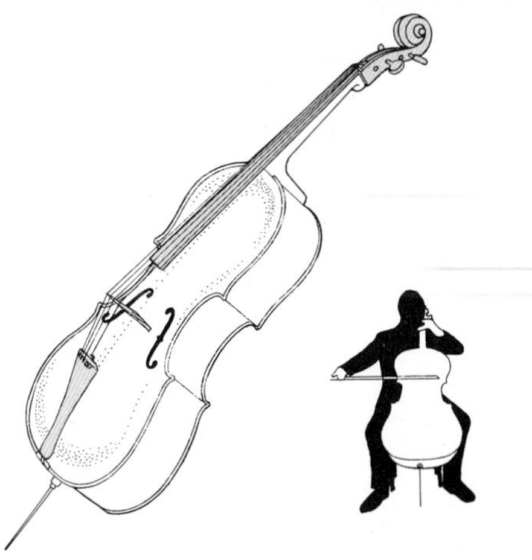

Cello

Cement

Niger
0
800km
Chad
Nigeria
Sudan
Ethiopia
CENTRAL
AFRICAN
REPUBLIC
• Bambari
Bouar
Bangui
Cameroon
Equat.
Gui.
Uganda
Kenya
Gabon
Congo
Zaire
Rwanda
Burundi
Tanzania
ATLANTIC
OCEAN
Angola
Zambia
Malawi

Central African Empire (formerly Republic)

Ceramics

Ceramics, in technology, articles made from inorganic compounds formed in a plastic condition and hardened by heating in a furnace. Earthenware is a porous ceramic made from kaolin, ball clay, and crushed flint. Porcelain is made from kaolin and feldspar, and heated to a higher temperature. It is nonporous and translucent. Special ceramics are made from pure aluminum oxide, silicon carbide, titanates, and other compounds.

Ceram (Seram) Sea, a section of W Pacific Ocean in central Moluccas, Indonesia, N of Banda Sea and S of Moluccas Sea. Area: approx. 20,000sq mi (51,800sq km).

Ceratopsians. △570, 572.

Ceratosaurus. △408.

Cerberus, in Greek mythology, a dog who guarded the entrance to Hades. He is represented as having three to fifty heads. △832.

Cerdan, Marcel (1922–1949), French boxer, b. Algeria. He won the world's middleweight championship (1948) from Tony Zale. He lost it (1949) to Jake LaMotta. On his return to the United States to fight LaMotta in a rematch, he was killed in a plane crash in the Azores.

Cerdic (died 534), Anglo-Saxon king. According to tradition, he landed near Southampton from Germany (495), fought the Britons, and founded the kingdom of Wessex (519).

Cereal, any grain of the grass family (Poaceae), used for food, including wheat, corn, rice, rye, oats, and barley. Cereals are the principal food source for the world's population, directly or indirectly as feed for livestock.

Cerebellum, a part of the brain, often known as the "little brain." Somewhat butterfly shaped, the cerebellum is divided into two hemispheres, marked by parallel grooves. The cerebellum is concerned mainly with coordination of muscular activity, regulating muscle tone for proper posture and balance, and regulating voluntary muscular movements. It also modifies cerebral cortex activity. *See also* Brain. △664–66

Cerebral Cortex, covering structure of the brain, most highly developed in humans, which suggests that it governs the higher nerve activity usually termed the human intellect. The cortex has intricate connections with most other neural structures in the body. △666.

Cerebral Hemorrhage, rupture of a blood vessel in the brain usually caused by arteriosclerosis, less often by injury or disease. Symptoms are headache, vomiting, then coma. Extensive hemorrhage is fatal; recovery from minor hemorrhage may take months. △722.

Cerebral Palsy, disease caused by damage to the brain. The damage may result from disease or injury before birth, from difficulties during childbirth, or, in later life, from infection, circulatory diseases, or head injury. Symptoms include spastic movements of arms and legs, and sometimes convulsions. Signs of mental retardation, which accompany the disease in about one-third of the cases, may reflect difficulty in communication rather than acute retardation. Treatment includes speech and muscle training and use of orthopedic devices.

Cerebrospinal Fluid, fluid found in the subarachnoid space, between the arachnoid and the pia mater layers of the meninges, the membranes that protect the brain and spinal cord from shocks. A sample of the fluid taken by means of a spinal tap aids in the diagnosis of diseases affecting the meninges. *See also* Meninges.

Cerebrum, one of the major divisions of the brain, and that part that makes the human brain so different in activity and appearance from the brains of other animals. It is divided into two dome-shaped parts, the cerebral hemispheres, each of which is divided into four lobes: frontal, parietal, temporal, and occipital. Each hemisphere is made up of an outer dark grayish layer (gray matter) known as the cerebral cortex; cortical white matter, made up of nerve fibers; and gray basal ganglia that connect with other portions of the cerebrum and with other parts of the brain. The cerebral cortex, which is convoluted to increase its surface area, is the basis of the brain's intellectual capacity, the seat of learning and memory, and a center for associative functions, for many sensory perceptions, and for many motor activities. *See also* Brain. △664–66.

Cerenkov, Pavel Alekseevich (1904–), Russian physicist. Working at the Institute of Physics of the Soviet Academy of Science, he discovered that light is emitted by charged particles traveling at very high speeds, a phenomenon known as the Cerenkov effect. He was awarded a Nobel Prize in 1958 jointly with I.M. Frank and I.Y. Tamm. △1522.

Cerenkov Radiation, bluish light emitted in a cone when energetic particles travel through a transparent medium of fairly high refractive index (such as water) at a speed that exceeds the velocity of light in that medium. △1522.

Ceres, in Roman mythology, goddess of food plants. She was often worshipped with the god Cerus.

Ceres, largest of the asteroids; the first to be sighted, discovered (1801) by Giuseppi Piazzi. Diameter 750mi (1200km); mean distance from Sun 257,000,000mi (413,770,000km); mean sidereal period 4.6 yr. △78.

Cereus, cactus native to West Indies and E South America and found throughout North and South America. Its stems are long, cylindrical, ribbed, and may be treelike or trailing. The night-blooming cereus, found in Arizona, New Mexico, and Texas, is usually drab though it produces magnificent fragrant white flowers that open for only one night. It is often kept as a house plant. Height: to 8ft (2.4m). There are 25 species. Family Cactaceae; genus *Cereus*.

Cerium, metallic element (symbol Ce) of the lanthanide group, first isolated in 1803. Chief ore is monazite (phosphate). It is used in pyrophoric alloys and in catalysts and the oxide is used in incandescent mantles. Properties: at. no. 58; at. wt. 140.120; sp. gr. 6.7; melt. pt. 1463°F (795°C); boil. pt. 278°F (3468°C); most common isotope Ce^{140} (88.48%). *See also* Lanthanide Elements.

Cerletti, Ugo. △770.

Cerré, Jean Gabriel (1734–1805), US fur trader, b. Canada. He established himself as a trader in Kaskaskia, Ill. Both sides sought his help in the American Revolution. George Rogers Clark's capture of his trading post resulted in Cerré's acceptance of US citizenship and a magistrate's position under the military. After the war Cerré moved to French-held St. Louis.

Certificate of Deposit, certificate issued by a commercial bank for a specific face amount and at a specified interest rate and time period. Certificates of deposit are negotiable instruments. The interest paid on certificates of deposit is normally greater than that paid on regular time deposits.

Certified Check, regular check drawn on a bank by a depositor and certified by the bank before payment is made on it. The bank, in effect, certifies that the check will be honored when it is presented for payment.

Certosa de Pavia, Gothic style Carthusian monastery founded in 1396 near Pavia by Duke Gian Galeazzo Visconti of Milan to serve as his family's mausoleum. The complex was begun under the Viscontis and completed under the Sforzas. The monastery, which was completed around 1450, is known for the rich terra cotta decorations in its two cloisters.

Cerumen. *See* Ear Wax.

Cervantes, Miguel de (1547–1616), Spanish novelist, poet, and dramatist. He went to Italy in 1569, in the service of a cardinal, was wounded in the Battle of Lepanto in 1571. While returning to Spain in 1575, he was captured and kept as a slave in Algiers. He was ransomed in 1580 and settled in Madrid. Cervantes' works include *La Galatea* (1585), *Don Quixote de la Mancha* (1605; 1615), and *Novelas Ejemplares* (1613). *See also* Don Quixote de la Mancha.

Cervera y Topete, Pascual (1839–1909), Spanish admiral, Count of Jerez, Marquis of Santa Ana. Minister of marine in 1892, he sailed at the head of the Spanish fleet May 19, 1898, to fight the Americans in the Spanish-American War. When he reached the harbor at Santiago, Cuba, he tried to run the American blockade; his ships were surrounded and sunk. Upon defeat he remarked, "Spain prefers honor without ships to ships without honor." Taken prisoner, he was returned to Spain (September 1898).

Cervix. △700.

Césaire, Aimé (1913–), West Indian poet, b. Martinique. He wrote in French and introduced the term Négritude in his *Return to My Native Land* (1939). He was active politically in Martinique and through his poetry espoused the recovery of black dignity. *See also* Négritude.

Cesalpino, Andrea (1519–1603), Italian physiologist and botanist. His *De plantis* (1583) was one of the first attempts to classify plants according to their flowers and fruits.

Cesarean Section. △704.

Cesium, or caesium, rare metallic element of the alkali-metal group, discovered in 1860. Chief ore is pollucite (silicate). Cesium has few commercial uses. Chemically it is an extremely reactive electropositive element. The decay rate of the isotope Cs^{133} is used in defining the second. Properties: at. no. 55; at. wt. 132.9055; sp. gr. 1.87; melt. pt. 83.30°F (28.5°C); boil. pt. 1274°F (690.0°C); most common isotope Cs^{133} (100%). *See also* Alkali Elements; Atomic Clock.

Cetacea, order of mammals comprised of whales, including porpoise, dolphin, and the narwhal. △552.

Cetinje, town in Yugoslavia, 19mi (31km) SE of Kotor; site of tombs of Montenegro rulers, and royal palace. Founded 1485 by Ivan the Black of Montenegro. Pop. 12,500.

Cetus. △112, 136.

Ceuta, Spanish city in N Morocco, on the Strait of Gibraltar; a territory of Spain since 1580 and part of Cadiz prov. Built by the Phoenicians, it was in turn held by Carthaginians, Romans, Vandals, Byzantines, Arabs, and Portuguese. Forming one of the Pillars of Hercules, it is an important refueling port for ships. Industries: shipping, fishing, food processing. Pop. 67,187.

Cevennes, mountain range in S France, W of Rhône River, extends NE and SW from St Etienne to Canal du Midi, which separates the range from the Pyrenees. Mulberry, olive, and chestnut trees grow on the slopes. Highest peak is Mt Mézenc, 5,753ft (1,755m).

Cézanne, Paul (1839–1906), French painter. In 1861 he went to Paris to study art, where he met Camille Pissarro, who strongly influenced his development. He exhibited with the first Impressionist show of 1874: *House of the Hanged Man* (1873–74; Louvre, Paris) is characteristic of his Impressionist period. He later separated himself from the Impressionists, trying to paint what he saw in simple geometric shapes, using color and distortion, as in *The Card Players* (1890–92; S. C. Clark Collection, New York City). His portraits, such as *Madame Cézanne* (c. 1885; S. S. and V. White College, Ardmore, Pa.), are also geometrical studies. The *Bathers* (1898–1905; Philadelphia Museum of Art) incorporates a number of his methods of dealing with perspective. Cézanne is one of the most important influences on 20th–century art. △1254, 1294.

CGS System, system of units based on the centimeter, the gram, and the second. *See* Weights and Measures.

Chaadyev, Piotr Yakovlevich (1794–1856), Russian philosopher. His idealistic philosophy stressed the importance of unity at all levels, the immorality of egoism, the idea of Russia's divine mission, and the importance of Christianity for understanding history. An aristocratic army officer in his early years, he traveled in Europe (1823–26) and then wrote eight *Philosophical Letters* expressing his views. When the first of these was published in 1836, its criticisms of Russian institutions for isolating the country from the West and Roman Catholicism caused him to be declared insane and forbidden to publish more. He remained in Moscow, however, in contact with other intellectuals. His work touched off the controversy between Westernizers and Slavophiles, with both of whom he had affinities.

Chaban-Delmas, Jacques (Michel-Pierre) (1915–), French politician. A liberal Gaullist, he was French prime minister from June 1969 to July 1972, when he resigned under criticism for liberal domestic reforms and charges of possible tax evasion. He was prominent in the Resistance during World War II, overseeing all Resistance military operations in occupied France. A deputy in the national assembly from 1946, he was minister of public works (1954), minister of state (1956–57), minister of national defense (1957–58), and president of the national assembly (1958–69).

Chabanel, Noël (1613–49), French Jesuit missionary in America who worked among the Huron Indians and was captured and killed by Iroquois. He and other such missionaries were canonized as the Martyrs of North America (1930).

Chacabuco, Battle of (Feb. 12, 1817), the first major engagement in the War of Independence against Spain led by José de San Martín after he crossed the Andes from Argentina to Chile. The royalists withdrew with heavy losses from the Santiago area.

Chachalaca, noisy, long-tailed game bird found in brushlands and forest edges of S United States and Central and South America. These brownish, chicken-like birds may be a potential future meat source. The female lays white eggs (2) in a stick-and-leaf nest in a low tree. Length: 19.75in (50cm); weight: 1lb (0.5kg). Genus *Ortalis.*

Chacma, black-faced, dark-furred baboon of E and S Africa. Species *Chaeropithecus ursinus. See also* Baboon.

Chaco, lowland plain in S central South America, having three principal divisions: Chaco Boreal in N Paraguay and S Bolivia; Chaco Central in NE Argentina; Chaco Austral in central Argentina. Most inhabitants reside in Argentine cities of Formosa and Resistencia. Industries: lumbering, cattle grazing, oil prospecting, tannin extraction. Area: 300,000sq mi (777,000sq km). Pop. 500,000.

Chaco Canyon National Monument, historic area in NW New Mexico; contains Pueblo Indian ruins dating from the peak of their civilization (900–1000). Est. 1907. Area: 21,509acres (8,711hectares).

Chaco War, conflict between Paraguay and Bolivia over possession of the Chaco (1932–35). Bolivia, landlocked as a result of territory lost during the War of the Pacific, sought a route to the sea via the Rio de la Plata. The war cost 50,000 Bolivian and 35,000 Paraguayan lives. Most of the disputed territory was ceded to Paraguay by the 1938 peace treaty.

Chad, republic in N central Africa, completely landlocked; governed by a president. Capital is Ndjamena (formerly Fort Lamy). Bounded by Central African Republic (S), Sudan (E), Libya (N), and Cameroon, Niger, and Nigeria (W), it is 900mi (1,449km) from the nearest seaport. Almost entire N half of country is desert with an annual rainfall of approximately 8in (20cm). There is little human life here except for nomads. Below this a steppe zone with a rainfall of 30in (76cm) has more vegetation; palm trees thrive. This area slopes toward Lake Chad (W) where cattle are raised. The highest population concentration is in the semi-tropical savanna region in the S. Annual rainfall is 35–48in (89–22cm), and there is farming and fishing. From the late 1960s–1974 Chad suffered a severe drought, as did much of W Africa.

The people of the N region are predominantly Muslim tribes of Bedouin Arabs, Fulani, Tuareg, and Wadaians; herding is their main occupation. The S part of Chad has a predominantly black African population of Saras, Massa, and Moudang; they are mainly animists with some Christians. Agriculture is their main occupation. Hostile feelings between these two distinct civilizations have often erupted in violence. Cotton accounts for 80% of Chad's exports; peanuts are the only other cash crop. Trade is chiefly with France.

The history of Chad has been traced by archaeological findings to the beginning of the Christian era; by the AD 4th century it was an important trading center. Various tribes attempted to take it, and by the 12th century a kingdom of Kanem existed within Chad. From the 16th–19th century it was controlled by Kanem and Bornu. Dissension during the 19th century weakened the states; foreign exploration of the area had begun and by 1913 Chad was conquered by France. In 1920 it was made a colony within the federation of French Equatorial Africa. After WWII it was granted its own territorial assembly and given representation in French parliament. In 1960 it became an independent republic.

By 1965 a one party system controlled the country and in 1966 a guerrilla war broke out. President Ngarta Tombalbaye requested French assistance under a defense pact with that country. The French withdrew in 1971 and warfare ceased in 1973. Tombalbaye was assassinated in 1975 and was succeeded by Felix Malloum.

PROFILE

Official name: Republic of Chad
Area: 495,754sq mi (1,284,000sq km)
Population: 4,000,000
Chief cities: Ndjamena, formerly Fort Lamy (capital); Moundou; Fort-Archambault
Religion: Islam, animism, Christianity
Language: French (official)
Monetary unit: Franc CFA

Chad, Lake, lake in N central Africa; mainly in the Republic of Chad, partly in Nigeria, Cameroon, and Niger. Chief tributary is the Chari River. Depth (max): 25ft (7.6m). Depending on the season, surface of lake varies from 4,000–10,000sq mi (10,360–25,900sq km).

Chadic Languages, large sub-group of Afro-Asiatic or Semitic-related languages. They are found in N area of Nigeria and E to Republic of Chad. Hausa (Haoussa) is the largest member of this group. Unlike other Semitic-related African tongues, these, because of interaction with languages to south, are tone languages.

Chadwick, Florence May (1918–), US swimmer, b. San Diego, Calif. She was the first woman to swim the English Channel both ways. She broke the time record for swimming the Santa Catalina Channel and also crossed the Straits of Gibralter, the Dardanelles, and the Bosporous in record swimming time.

Chadwick, George Whitefield (1854–1931), U.S. composer, b. Lowell, Mass. He studied at the New England Conservatory, Boston, and in Leipzig and Munich, and taught at the New England Conservatory, of which he was director (1897–1931). He taught composition to many composers. He appeared frequently as guest conductor of orchestras, and also composed traditional music.

Chadwick, Henry (1824–1908), US baseball writer, b. England. He wrote the game's first rule book (1858). A pioneer in his field, he was elected to the Baseball Hall of Fame in 1938.

Chadwick, Sir James (1891–1974), English physicist. In 1932 he discovered the neutron by bombarding beryllium with alpha particles. For this work he was awarded a Nobel Prize in 1935. *See also* Neutron.

Chaeronea, ruined ancient city in E central Greece, NW of Thebes; scene of Philip II of Macedon's defeat of the united forces of Thebes and Athens (338BC); the massacre of the Thebans by Alexander, Philip's son; and Sulla's victory over the army of Mithridates VI of Pontus (86BC).

Chaetognatha, a phylum of about 50 species of marine invertebrates known as arrowworms. *See* Arrowworm.

Chagall, Marc (1887–), French painter, b. Russia. In 1910, he went to Paris from Russia. His paintings, often dreamlike with floating figures, are full of Russian folk lore and Jewish symbolism and are said to have influenced the Surrealists. His most recent work has been abstract designs for stained-glass windows and architectural decoration, including 12 stained-glass windows symbolizing the tribes of Israel (1962) in the Hadassah-Hebrew University Medical Center synagogue in Jerusalem and two vast murals (1966) for the Metropolitan Opera House, New York City, representing the sources and triumph of music.

Chaga's Disease, infectious disease transmitted by a protozoan parasite, *Trypanosoma cruzi,* in insect feces, primarily in South and Central America. Swelling at entry point (often the eye), fever and malaise are early symptoms; heart involvement is typical of the chronic form. △732.

Chagatai. *See* Jagatai.

Chain, Ernst Boris (1906–), English biochemist, b. Germany. He shared the 1945 Nobel Prize in physiology or medicine for his part in "the discovery of penicillin and its therapeutic effect." Chain, working with Howard Florey and Alexander Fleming, helped to isolate and prepare penicillin for large-scale production. *See also* Florey, Howard. △746.

Chaining, in psychology, an operant conditioning procedure in which an organism is taught to perform specific behaviors in a particular sequence or "chain"; eg, a dog is taught to roll over, sit up, and beg. Normally the last behavior (eg, begging) must be learned first because reinforcement guides the learning process. *See also* Operant Conditioning. △778.

Chain Mail. △1726.

Chain Reaction, a self-sustaining molecular or nuclear reaction in which the products of the reaction are required to sustain the reaction. *See* Fission, Nuclear. △1482, 1638.

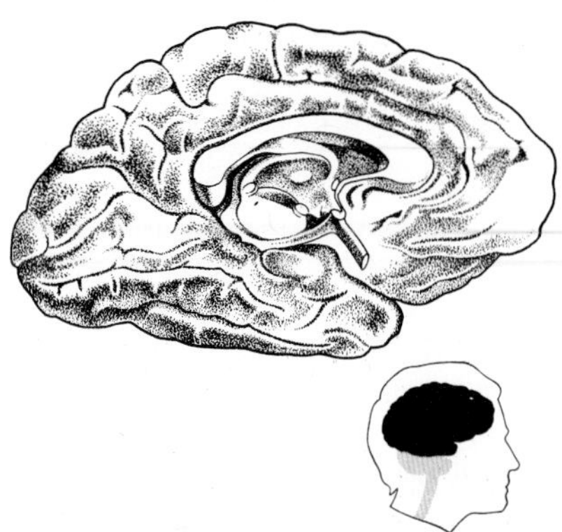

Cerebrum

Cervantes' Don Quixote and Sancho Panza

Chachalaca

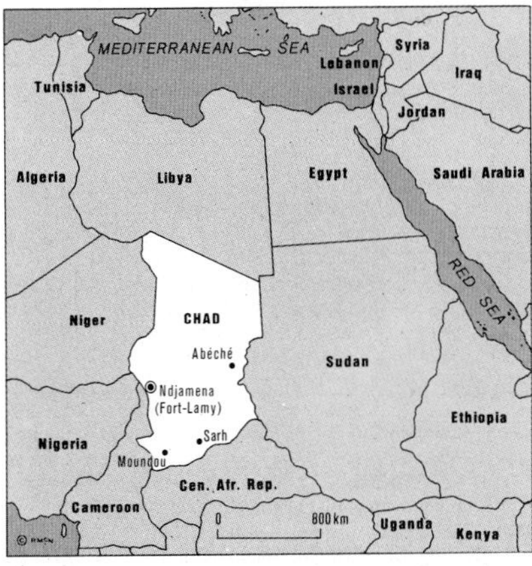
MEDITERRANEAN SEA
Syria
Lebanon
Israel
Iraq
Tunisia
Jordan
Algeria
Libya
Egypt
Saudi Arabia
RED SEA
Niger
CHAD
Abéché
Sudan
Ndjamena
(Fort-Lamy)
Ethiopia
Sarh
Nigeria
Moundou
Cen. Afr. Rep.
Cameroon
0
800km
Uganda
Kenya

Chad

Chalcedon, ancient Greek city in Bithynia, on the E shore of the Bosporus opposite ancient Byzantium (now Istanbul). Its site is now occupied by Kadikoy, Turkey. It was founded by Greeks from Megara (*c.* 680 BC) shortly before the founding of Byzantium; because its site was clearly less desirable than that of Byzantium, it was dubbed the "city of the blind." It vacillated between Spartan and Athenian interests, was ruled for a time by Persia, became part of Alexander the Great's empire, and came under Roman domination in 197 BC. Mithridates VI of Pontus inflicted a notable defeat on the Romans at Chalcedon in 73 BC. Frequently attacked by barbarians thereafter, it was the site of the Christian church's Council of Chalcedon in AD 451. It fell to Persia again in 616 and was destroyed by the Turks in 1075.

Chalcedony, fine-grained variety of quartz used by gem engravers and cut and polished as ornamental. Well-known varieties are agate (common, semiprecious; occurring in colored bands), bloodstone (dark green with bits of red jasper throughout), carnelian (translucent dark red with hematite dispersions), flint (opaque black, due to carbon inclusions), jasper (opaque and usually red due to a mixture of hematite), and onyx (striped).

Chalcidice (Khalkidhikí), department and peninsula in NE Greece forming three fingers in the Aegean Sea: Kassandra (W), Sithonia (central), Athos (E); originally inhabited by Thracians, Greeks est colonies 8th and 7th centuries BC; subsequently conquered by Macedonia and Rome. Industries: magnesite mining, agriculture, beehives. Pop. 75,582.

Chalcid Wasp, dark colored wasp, 0.08 to 0.12 in (2–3mm) long, with some less than 0.02 in (0.5mm); found worldwide. Most of the larvae are parasitic on other insect eggs and larvae. Superfamily Chalcidoidea. *See also* Hymenoptera.

Chalcis (Khalkís), town in E Greece, on Euboea Island; capital of Euboea prefecture; important commercial city of ancient Euboea, its residents founded settlements in Sicily, Italy, Macedonia, and Chalcidice; defeated by Athens 446 BC; annexed to Macedonia 338 BC; occupied by Venice AD 1209; besieged by Turks 1470; came under Greece 1830; Aristotle died here 332 BC. Industries: trade, soap, cement. Pop. 36,381.

Chalcocite, a sulfide mineral, copper sulfide (Cu_2S), and one of the chalcocite group, which also includes acanthite and stromeyerite. A major ore of copper found mainly in sulfur deposits. Orthorhombic system granular masses, or rare prismatic crystals, sometimes twinned. Metallic, dark gray, easily cut; hardness 2.-5–3; sp gr 5.8.

Chalcolithic Age. *See* Copper Age.

Chalcopyrite, a sulfide mineral, copper iron sulfide ($CuFeS_2$); the most important copper ore. In sulfide veins and in igneous and contact metamorphic rocks. Tetragonal system sphenoidal or tetrahedral crystals, often twinned, and as masses. Brittle, metallic, brass-colored, opaque. Hardness 3.5–4; sp gr 4.3. △240.

Chaliapin, Fyodor Ivanovitch (1873–1938), Russian operatic bass. Already one of the most famous singing actors of his day, he made his Western debut at La Scala in Milan in 1901 and at the Metropolitan Opera in New York City in 1907. His differences with the Soviet government caused him to leave Russia in 1921 when he returned to the Metropolitan. He was particularly noted for his role in Musorgski's *Boris Godunov.* △1256.

Chalk, natural calcium carbonate ($CaCO_3$) formed from the shells of minute marine organisms. It varies in properties and appearance, pure forms, such as calcite, containing up to 99% calcium carbonate. Blackboard chalk consists of calcium sulfate.

Challenger Expedition, first oceanographic expedition to circle the globe. The voyage of the 2300-ton steam corvette H.M.S. *Challenger* began December 1872, lasted till May 1876, and collected data that filled 50 large volumes, written by 76 authors over a 23-year period. Nearly every ocean was sounded and almost 4500 new species of animals were collected. △228, 236.

Challens, Mary. *See* Renault, Mary.

Chalmers, Thomas (1780–1847), Scottish churchman. He was a leader in the formation of the Free Church of Scotland (1843), which grew out of dissent within the Established Church over state interference in church matters.

Chalmette National Historical Park, region in SE Louisiana; site of a portion of the Battle of New Orleans in War of 1812. Authorized as park 1939. Area: 142acres (58hectares).

Chalôns-sur-Marne, city in NE France, on the Marne River, 95mi (153km) NE of Paris; capital of Marne dept.; scene of 451 defeat of Attila and the Huns by Actius; site of 13th-century Cathedral of St Etienne. Industries: champagne, wallpaper, electrodes, beer. Pop. 50,764.

Chalukya, south Indian dynasty that ruled in the Deccan intermittently from 543 to 1200. The dynasty was founded by Pulakesian I and held power until 757; it returned in *c.* 973 and ruled until 1189 when the kingdom was divided. The last Chalukya king died in 1200.

Chambered Nautilus. *See* Nautilus.

Chamberlain, (Sir) (Joseph) Austen (1863–1937), English political figure. The son of Joseph Chamberlain and half brother of Neville Chamberlain, he entered upon a 45-year Parliamentary career in 1892. He was postmaster general (1902), chancellor of the exchequer (1903–05, 1919–21), secretary of state for India (1915–17), a member of the war cabinet (1918–19), lord privy seal (1921–22), Conservative party leader (1921–22), foreign secretary (1925–29), and first lord of the admiralty (1931). As foreign secretary he was one of the main architects of the Locarno Pact of 1925 by which France, Germany, and Belgium accepted their existing frontiers and Britain and France agreed to guarantee these frontiers. He received the 1925 Nobel Peace Prize (with Charles G. Dawes) for his work on the pact.

Chamberlain, Joseph (1836–1914), English political figure. A successful business career led to his election (1873) as reform mayor of Birmingham. He left that post after being elected to Parliament (1876). He served as Liberal president of the board of trade (1880–85) and president of the local government board (1886) but resigned (1886) and joined the Liberal-Unionists, who opposed Prime Minister Gladstone's home rule proposals for Ireland. As colonial secretary (1895–1903) in the Conservative/Liberal-Unionist government (1895–1906), Chamberlain advocated both social reform and a vigorous colonial policy. He was held responsible for the events that led to the Boer War (1899–1902). He resigned his post in 1903 to campaign for a tariff policy giving preference to products from British Empire countries. His advocacy of a departure from Britain's traditional policy of free trade split the Conservative/Liberal-Unionist bloc and led to its removal from office in 1906. That same year he suffered a stroke that incapacitated him until his death. △1300.

Chamberlain, Joshua Lawrence (1828–1914), US general, b. Brewer, Me. Educated at Bowdoin, he was a Medal of Honor recipient for his defense of Little Round Top in the battle of Gettysburg. At the war's end he was a major general. He was governor of Maine (1866–70) and president of Bowdoin College (1871–83).

Chamberlain, (Arthur) Neville (1869–1940), English political figure. He was a son of Joseph Chamberlain and half-brother of Austen. From business he turned to municipal politics (1911) and entered Parliament as a Conservative (1918). From 1922 he held government posts whenever the Conservatives ruled, eventually becoming prime minister (1937–40). He sought peace through negotiation and by appeasing Hitler and Mussolini while Britain rearmed. German successes at the beginning of World War II brought about his resignation (1940).

Chamberlain, Owen (1920–), US physicist, b. San Francisco. After working on the development of the atom bomb, he became professor of physics at the University of California, Berkeley. With Emilio Segrè, using the Bevatron accelerator, he confirmed the existence of the antiproton, for which they were awarded a Nobel Prize for physics in 1959.

Chamberlain, Wilton Norman "Wilt" (1936–), US basketball player, b. Philadelphia. The greatest offensive player in pro basketball history, with a career total of 31,419 points and a 50.4 scoring average in the 1961–62 season. He played in the National Basketball Association for Philadelphia (1960–62, 1965–68), San Francisco (1963–65), and Los Angeles (1969–73).

Chamber Music, music in which one person plays each part, as opposed to orchestral music, where several people play each part. The number of players determines the name of the group. For example, a trio is composed of three players, a quartet of four players. Much chamber music is for string instruments only. In general, the emphasis is on the group's performance as a whole rather than on that of any individual player. △1196,1244.

Chambers, Ephraim. △1780.

Chambord, Henri Charles Ferdinand Marie Dieudonne d'Artois, Comte de (1820–83), pretender to the French throne, and last male heir of the senior branch of the Bourbons. His grandfather, Charles X, abdicated in his favor after the revolution of 1830, but Louis Philippe seized the crown instead. Many attempts to restore Chambord to the monarchy collapsed because of his refusal to compromise.

Chameleon, arboreal lizard found chiefly in Madagascar, Africa, and Asia. The common chameleon *(Chamaeleo chamaeleon)* ranges into Spain. It is characterized by its ability to change color. The compressed body has a curled, prehensile tail and bulging eyes that move independently. Many species have a helmet or horn on the head. They are egg-laying as well as live-bearing and eat insects and small birds. Length: 7–24in (17–60cm). There are 80 species. Family Chamaeleontidae. *See also* Lizard. △520.

Chamois, nimble, goatlike ruminant inhabiting mountain ranges in Europe and Asia Minor. Close-set horns with backward hooked ends are worn by both sexes. It has coarse brown fur. Females and young gather in herds. Its skin is made into the familiar polishing chamois. Length: to 50in (1.3m); weight: 55–110lb (25–50kg). Family Bovidae; species *Rupicapra rupicapra.*

Chamomile. *See* Camomile.

Champagne, district of France, E of Paris, consisting mainly of Aube, Marne, Haute-Marne, and Ardennes depts. Major city is Reims where early French kings were crowned. Trade fairs in the 11th-13th centuries made the district a center of European trade and finance; scene of heavy fighting during WWI along Marne River. Area is rather arid and produces most of the world's champagne. △1096.

Champaign, city in E central Illinois; founded 1855 when the Illinois Central Railroad came through; site of University of Illinois at Urbana-Champaign (1867); fertile farm area. Industries: metal products, electrical equipment, academic apparel. Inc. 1860. Pop. (1970) 56,532.

Champlain, Samuel de (1567–1635), French explorer, founder of New France (Canada). In 1603 he went on an exploring and fur-trading expedition to the Gulf of St. Lawrence, where he explored the St. Lawrence River as far as the Lachine Rapids. He later (1604–07) led settlers to Port Royal (now Annapolis Royal, Nova Scotia) and explored the Atlantic coast from Nova Scotia to Martha's Vineyard, discovering Mt Desert Island and the larger Maine rivers. As lieutenant governor of New France, Champlain founded Quebec in 1608. He explored northern New York State, where he discovered Lake Champlain in 1609. He also explored the Ottawa River (1613) and the Great Lakes (1615). He served as governor of New France from 1633–35. △1216.

Champlain, Lake, lake separating New York State and Vermont, extending into Quebec, Canada; connects to the Hudson River by Champlain division of Barge Canal and serves as a link in the Hudson-St Lawrence waterway. Discovered by Samuel de Champlain 1609, scene of many historic battles in French and Indian Wars, American Revolution (including a naval conflict 1776), and the defeat of British in War of 1812 by Thomas MacDonough. Many resorts are on the lake making use of it for swimming, fishing, boating, and winter sports. Plattsburgh, NY, and Burlington, Vt, are its largest cities. Area: 490sq mi (1269sq km).

Champollion, Jean François (1790–1832), French Egyptologist. The first conservator of Egyptian antiquities for the Louvre, he is generally considered the creator of Egyptology. He was the leading figure in decoding the Rosetta Stone, the key to all Egyptian hieroglyphics.

Ch'an Buddhism. *See* Zen.

Chance, Frank Leroy (1877–1924), US baseball player, b. Fresno, Calif. He was the first baseman on the Chicago Cubs' famed "Tinker-to-Evers-to-Chance" double-play combination. He was elected to the Baseball Hall of Fame in 1946.

Chance, in Probability. △1476.

Chancellorsville, Battle of (May 2–4, 1863), Civil War battle on the edge of the Virginia Wilderness, ended in defeat for Union Gen. Joseph Hooker after Confederate Commander Gen. Robert E. Lee sent Gen. Thomas J. "Stonewall" Jackson in a forced march to surprise the Union rear. Lee lost fewer than 13,000 to Hooker's 17,000, but his greatest loss was Jackson, accidentally killed by a Confederate patrol.

Chan Chan, capital of the Chimu kingdom on the northern coast of Peru, which reached the height of its power between AD 1400 and 1450. Extensive adobe ruins remain. Chan Chan was the administrative center of the agricultural Chimu economy. After the Inca conquest (*c.* 1464), Chan Chan became an Inca provincial capital. △1120.

Chandelle, in aviation, a maximum-performance climbing turn with a 180° change in direction. It is used as a training maneuver to demonstrate coordination, speed sense, and planning since it requires arrival at the opposite heading as the bank becomes zero and the airspeed is just above the stall. *See also* Stall, Aircraft.

Chandigarh, city in NW India, at foot of Siwalik Hills; capital of Punjab and Haryana states. One of India's planned cities, designed by Swiss architect Le Corbusier, it was built up in the 1950s; seat of Punjab University (1947), site of garden of Pinjora, replica of Srinigar's Shalimar gardens. Pop. 256,979.

Chandler, Albert Benjamin ("Happy") (1898–), US statesman and baseball executive, b. Corydon, Ky. A Commissioner of Baseball (1945–51), Chandler was also a US Senator and governor of Kentucky (1935–39; 1955–59).

Chandler, Raymond Thornton (1888–1959), U.S. author, b. Chicago. His detective novels, featuring the tough private eye Philip Marlowe, include *The Big Sleep* (1939), *Farewell, My Lovely* (1940), *The Little Sister* (1949), and *The Long Goodbye* (1953). *See also* Detective Story.

Chandragupta (321?–296 BC), founder of the Maurya Empire, the first great empire of India. He seized the throne of Magadha kingdom from the Nanda dynasty and extended their holdings to include much of northern India. He is believed to be the Sandrocottos of Greek literature of the time of Alexander the Great. △986.

Chandragupta I (*r.* AD 320–335), Indian emperor. He inherited his kingdom from Ghatotkacha. He enlarged it through marriage to a princess of north Bihar. He was the first Indian ruler to use the title of emperor.

Chandragupta II (*reigned c.* 380–414), emperor of northern India. Grandson of Chandragupta I, he increased his holdings southward through the marriage of his daughter to the Vakataka king Rudrasena II. △1034.

Chanel, Gabrielle (Coco) (1883?–1971), French fashion designer. She revolutionized women's fashion beginning in the 1920s with a straight, simple, uncorseted line and many elements of her designs borrowed from men's clothing. She is associated with short hair, costume jewelry, the Chanel suit, jersey dresses, bell-bottom pants, trench coats, and Chanel #5 perfume.

Chaney, Lon (1883–1930), US silent film actor, b. Colorado Springs, Colo. The son of deaf-mutes, Chaney was a brilliant mime noted for complex disguises in horror films. His major films included *The Penalty* (1920), *The Hunchback of Notre Dame* (1923), *The Unholy Three* (1925), and *The Phantom of the Opera* (1925). His son, Lon Chaney, Jr., also became a film actor.

Chang. *See* Yangtze River.

Changchun, city in central Manchuria, NE China; capital of Kirin prov.; site of first automobile plant in China. Industries: agricultural products, machinery, textiles, food processing. Pop. 1,500,000.

Chang Tang, arid desert plateau in central and N Tibet, W China, bounded by Trans-Himalayas (S) and Kunlunshanma (N); contains many fresh and saline lakes. Area: 210,000sq mi (543,900sq km).

Channel Islands, group of islands in SW end of English Channel, 30mi (48km) off W coast of France. Part of United Kingdom, the main islands are Jersey, Guernsey, Alderney, and Sark. Main towns are St Helier, Jersey, and St Peter Port, Guernsey. Group constitutes a popular holiday resort with mild climate and fertile soil. Industries: farming, tourism, fishing. Exports: agricultural and dairy products. Area: 75sq mi (194sq km). Pop. 125,243.

Channel Islands National Monument, area off the coast of S California, including Anacaps and Santa Barbara islands; known for sea lion herds, fossils, and marine life. Est. 1938. Area: 18,167 acres (7,358hectares).

Channing, Edward (1856–1931), US historian, b. Dorchester, Mass. A pupil of Henry Adams at Harvard, he remained there and helped develop the graduate curriculum. He wrote *A History of the United States* (6 vol., 1905–25) for which he won a Pulitzer Prize (1926). Other works include *A Student's History of the United States* (1898) and *The Jeffersonian System 1801–1811* (1906).

Channing, William Ellery (1780–1842), US clergyman, b. Newport, R.I. Ordained a Congregationalist minister, from 1803 to his death he was pastor of the Federal Street Church in Boston. He became leader of those within Congregationalism who were turning away from Calvinism. His sermon *Unitarian Christianity* (1819) led to his recognition as one of the founders of Unitarianism. In 1820 he organized a conference of ministers that became the American Unitarian Association in 1825.

Chanson de Roland, French epic by an unknown author of the late 11th century, which describes the defeat of Charlemagne's rear guard at Roncevaux pass in the Pyrenees on Aug. 15, 778. Because of the treachery of Ganelon, the king's main forces do not arrive in time to save Roland (Hrodlandus, Margrave of Brittany). As in the typical *chansons de geste* (songs of great deeds), the poem alters historical fact in order to develop the personal and tragic elements of a situation. The structure consists of 10-syllable lines grouped in *laisses,* which all end in the same assonance. *See also* Chansons de Geste; Charlemagne. △1100.

Chansons de Geste, Old French epic poems of the 11th through 13th centuries, generally dealing with the military campaigns of Charlemagne and his lieutenants. These anonymously written narratives describe imaginary events in the lives of William of Orange, Girart de Rosillon, Roland, and others. *Chanson de Roland* is perhaps the best known of the works.

Chanterelle, a genus of medium-sized fleshy terrestrial mushrooms (Cantharellaceae), most of which are edible, especially *C. cibarius,* which has long been highly prized. It has an orange, funnel shaped cap with prominent gills continuing down the stem.

Chanukah. *See* Hanukkah.

Chanzy, Antoine Eugène Alfred (1823–83), French general and statesman. As commander of the Second Army of the Loire, Chanzy was defeated at Le Mans in 1871. He served as governor general in Algeria (1873); and after standing unsuccessfully for election in 1879 for president, he served as ambassador to St. Petersburg (1879–81).

Chao K'uang-yin (died 976), founder of the Chinese Sung dynasty (960–1279). He was a scholarly general who eliminated regional military control, established a paid army, and laid the basis for three centuries of cultural flourishing in Sung China. △1042.

Chaos, in early Greek cosmology, the representation of the emptiness of the universe and the darkness of the Underworld.

Chapala, Lake, largest lake in Mexico, 30mi (48km) S and SE of Guadalajara; resort noted for scenery and fishing. Area: 651sq mi (1,686sq km).

Chapbook, a forerunner of the inexpensive book or magazine. The chapbook was a cheap pamphlet that was sold by a chapman (peddler) between the 15th and 18th centuries. These small books were pulp fiction, newsletters, comics, and easy-to-read Bible stories, all designed for the common taste and education.

Chapel Hill, residential town in central North Carolina, at the edge of the Piedmont region, 11mi (18km) WSW of Durham; site of University of North Carolina (1789). Founded 1792; inc. 1851. Pop. (1970) 25,537.

Chaplin, Charlie (1889–), English actor and filmmaker, b. Charles Spencer Chaplin. Widely rated the greatest comedian of the silent era and a brilliant

Chalcis, Greece

Neville Chamberlain

Chameleon

Champagne, France

mime, he toured the United States with a pantomime troupe in 1910 and worked for Keystone Studios (1914–16). In his short films, including *Tillie's Punctured Romance* (1914), *The Immigrant* (1917), and *A Dog's Life* (1918), he developed the Tramp—a jaunty, wistful, often pathetic soul in baggy pants, bowler, and moustache. In 1919, with D. W. Griffith, Mary Pickford, and Douglas Fairbanks, Sr., he founded United Artists Films, an independent production company. Among Chaplin's major features were *The Kid* (1920), *The Gold Rush* (1924), *The Circus* (1928), *City Lights* (1931), *Modern Times* (1936), *The Great Dictator* (1940), *Monsieur Verdoux* (1947), and *Limelight* (1952). Attacked for his politics and personal behavior, he left the United States in 1952 to settle in Switzerland. △1316.

Chapman, Frank Michler (1864–1945), US ornithologist, b. Englewood, N.J. He is best known for his extensive studies of North and South American birds. In 1894 he became associate editor of *Auk*, and in 1899 he founded and edited *Bird-Lore*. He was associate curator (1888–1908) and then curator (1908–42) of ornithology for the American Museum of Natural History in New York City.

Chapman, George (*c.*1559–1634), English poet and dramatist. He completed Marlowe's *Hero and Leander* (1598). His works include the poem *The Shadow of Night* (1594), the plays *The Blind Beggar of Alexandria* (1596) and *Bussy D'Ambois* (1607), and famous translations of Homer's *Illiad* (1611), and *Odyssey* (1614). *See also* Hero and Leander.

Chapman, Maria Weston (1806–85), US reformer, b. Weymouth, Mass. She followed her husband's parents into the antislavery movement. She wrote and edited *Right and Wrong*, assisted Lloyd Garrison (1834), editor of the *Liberator*, and authored antislavery pamphlets, songs, hymns, and articles. She edited an autobiography of Harriet Martineau (1877).

Chapultepec, national park in central Mexico, SW of Mexico City, in rocky hill region; site of 18th-century castle; favorite resort area of Maximillian; stronghold during Mexican War, fell to United States (Sept. 8, 1847); scene of Inter-American conference (Feb. 21–Mar. 8, 1945) that passed Act of Chapultepec, a wartime tactic to insure assistance and solidarity in the Western Hemisphere.

Char, or brook trout, freshwater game fish found in coastal streams and isolated lakes in E North America and parts of Europe. It is speckled with buff or red spots and has white borders on ventral and anal fins. Length: to 31in (79cm); weight: 15lb (6.8kg). Family Salmonidae; species Arctic char *Salvelimus alpinus*, brook trout *Salvelimus fontinalis*. *See also* Osteichthyes. △390.

Characin, or characid, freshwater tropical fish found from Texas to lower South America and in Africa. Popular home aquarium fish, characins have slender to fairly deep bodies and beautiful colorations. Length: 1in–5ft (2.5–152.4cm); Weight: to 125lb (56.7kg). Family Characidae; 1,000 species including silver dollar fish, piranha, neon tetra, and headstander.

Charbray. *See* Zebu.

Charcot, Jean Baptiste Étienne August (1867–1936), French explorer and physician. Son of the famous psychiatrist Jean Martin Charcot, he led two Antarctic expeditions. During the first (1903–05), he found that the Bismarck Strait connected with the sea east of the Graham coast; he also mapped the Palmer Peninsula's west coast. He tried to reach the South Pole in his 1908–10 expedition. He drowned when his ship *Pourquoi-Pas?* was wrecked off Iceland.

Charcot, Jean Martin (1825–1893), French physician, the "father of neurology." He did classic studies of hypnosis and hysteria and was teacher to Pierre Janet and Sigmund Freud. His work centered on how behavioral symptoms of patients related to diseases of the nervous system. △748, 762.

Chardin, Jean-Baptiste Siméon (1699–1779), French painter. His paintings were careful, quiet, but always fresh and lively. He sold his work very cheaply and made many copies of popular pictures. Paintings of middle-class life were a fad in his lifetime, but he gave them up to go back to still-life pictures and finally to portraits painted with pastels. △1190.

Chariot (Hittite). △976.

Charioteer, The. *See* Auriga.

Charisma. △890.

Charismatic Renewal. △1388.

Charlemagne (742–814), king of the Franks, (768–814) and Holy Roman emperor (800–814). The eldest son of Pepin the Short, he inherited Neustria, the northwestern half of the Frankish kingdom, in 768 and annexed the other half upon his brother Carloman's death (771). Responding to threats against Rome and his own sovereignty, he led two armies into Italy and captured the Lombard throne (773). In reprisal to constant Saxon raids, he began a long (772–785) and brutal conquest of Saxony, finally securing it for Christianity and Frankish law. He also deposed the disloyal duke of Bavaria and defeated the Avars of the middle Danube (791–96,804), adding new lands to his empire. By 811 he had established the Spanish March, a Christian refuge in northern Spain. He was coronated emperor by Pope Leo III (800). A man of great power and enthusiasm, he initiated the intellectual, artistic, and ecclesiastical awakening known as the Carolingian Renaissance. His empire, though lacking sufficient economic and political structure to maintain unity after his death, had combined the Germanic peoples for the first time. He was canonized in 1165. △1066, 1070.

Charles II (Charles the Bald) (823–77), king of the West Franks (843–77) and Holy Roman emperor (875–77). He was the son of Emperor Louis I. Louis' elder sons revolted against Charles' kingdom. Lothair I was defeated at Fontenoy (841) by Charles and his brother Louis the German. The Treaty of Verdun (843) made Charles king of the West Franks. At the death of Emperor Louis II, Charles secured the imperial crown and was Holy Roman Emperor (875–77). *See also* Verdun, Treaty of.

Charles III (Charles the Fat) (839–88), Holy Roman emperor (881–87) and king of France (884–87) as Charles II, great-grandson of Charlemagne. He almost succeeded in reuniting Charlemagne's empire, but failed because of ill health.

Charles IV (1316–78), Holy Roman emperor (1355–78) and king of Bohemia (1347–78). Supported by Pope Clement VI, he was elected antiking to Holy Roman Emperor Louis IV in 1346. Louis died in 1347, and Charles was elected German king (emperor-elect). Crowned emperor by the papal legate in 1355, Charles brought to an end the long dispute between emperor and pope. He ruled from Prague, where his rule brought Bohemia into its golden age. He founded Charles University, the oldest in central Europe, in 1348. In 1356 he issued the Golden Bull, which greatly increased the power of the emperor. He was succeeded by his son, Wenceslaus. *See also* Golden Bull; Holy Roman Empire.

Charles V (1500–58), Holy Roman emperor (1519–58) and king of Spain as Charles I (1516–56). From his father, Philip I of Castile, he inherited the Netherlands in 1506. He grew up in Flanders, where he was born, under the guidance of his regent-aunt Margaret of Austria. He inherited Spain, Naples, Sicily, and Sardinia from his grandfather Ferdinand II in 1516. In 1517 he arrived for the first time in Spain, where he appointed foreign favorites to court positions and greatly increased taxes. He bribed the electors of the Holy Roman Empire into naming him (1520) successor to his grandfather Emperor Maximilian I. He left Spain for Germany in 1520, hoping to establish a universal empire. But his attempt failed, primarily because of three counterforces: the ambitions of Francis I of France in Italy, the threats of the Ottoman Turks, and the Protestant Reformation in Germany. Peace was made with France in 1529, but the long war had led to revolts in Spain (Comuneros, 1520–21), and by the Protestants in Germany (Sickingen's revolt, 1522–23; Peasants' War, 1524–26). Charles was able to hold off the Ottomans but was unable to push them back. Although in the Edict of Worms (1521) he had declared Martin Luther and his followers to be outlaws, the Protestants grew stronger. Charles became a leader of the Catholic Reformation as formulated at the Council of Trent (1545). As early as 1521, Charles had begun sharing rule of his vast empire with his brother Ferdinand, king of Bohemia and Hungary. He gave Ferdinand increasing power in Germany and returned to Spain in 1531. In 1554 and 1555 he ceded his Italian possessions and the Netherlands to his son Philip. He entered the monastery of Yuste, Spain, in 1556, ceding Spain to Philip. In 1558 he officially abdicated as Holy Roman emperor to be succeeded by Ferdinand. △1152.

Charles VI (1685–1740), Holy Roman emperor (1711–40) and king of Hungary, as Charles III. After an unsuccessful attempt to ascend to the Spanish throne that precipitated the War of the Spanish Succession, he became Holy Roman emperor. Retiring to his Austrian possessions, he lost much of his land in wars. He was able to secure his daughter Maria Theresa's succession only with much difficulty. He was the last of the Hapsburg male line.

Charles VII (1697–1745), Holy Roman emperor (1742–45) and elector of Bavaria (1726–45). Married to the niece of Emperor Charles VI, he spent his later years in a war contesting the succession of Maria Theresa, daughter of Charles VI, to the Austrian possessions of the Hapsburgs.

Charles I (1887–1922), Austrian emperor (1916–18), and king (as Charles IV) of Hungary (1916–18), the last Hapsburg ruler. Grandnephew of Emperor Francis Joseph, on accession to the throne he sought a separate peace with the Allies and tried to hold the crumbling empire together. In 1918, Hungary and Czechoslovakia declared their independence, Charles abdicated and went into Swiss exile. In 1921 he twice attempted to regain the Hungarian throne. He was arrested and deported to Madeira, where he died.

Charles I (1600–49), king of England, Scotland, and Ireland (1625–49). Charles made an unpopular marriage in 1625 to Catholic Henrietta Maria of France. Until 1628 he was dominated by the 1st duke of Buckingham, who commanded an inglorious war against France (1626–30). Because it failed to finance the war, Charles dissolved Parliament three times in four years. In 1628 it forced him to assent to the Petition of Right, which, among other things, prohibited taxation without Parliament's consent. Charles then ruled without a parliament (1629–40). His arbitrary exactions antagonized the landed class and his High Church policies enraged the Scots, who revolted (1639). Almost bankrupt, Charles called the Short Parliament and then the Long Parliament in 1640. The latter gained many reforms and impeached his chief advisers.

In the Grand Remonstrance (1641) Parliament summarized the grievances against the king. Civil war broke out in 1642. With Scottish aid, the forces of Parliament crushed the king's troops at Naseby (1645) and Charles surrendered. Charles's intrigues during his imprisonment led to a second civil war in 1648, but Cromwell's army triumphed, and Charles was tried and beheaded. △1156.

Charles II (1630–85), king of England, Scotland, and Ireland (1660–85). Charles fled to France after his father's defeat in 1646. After his father's execution Charles was proclaimed king of Scots, and he unsuccessfully invaded England (1650–51). Thereafter Charles was in exile until Cromwell's death; he was proclaimed king of England in 1660.

In 1662 Charles issued the Declaration of Indulgence, which freed nonconformist Protestants and Catholics from interference, but Parliament forced him to withdraw it. He also attempted to circumvent Parliament's foreign policy by making secret agreements with Louis XIV of France and accepting covert subsidies from him. Titus Oates's accusations of a Popish Plot created national hysteria (1678–80), during which many Catholics were forced out of office. Charles dissolved the Parliament that passed the Habeas Corpus Act (1679) and successfully staved off Parliament's attempts to introduce bills preventing James, his brother and a professed Catholic, from succeeding to the throne, the Exclusion Crisis (1680–81). (Charles had married Catharine of Braganza in 1662, but they had no children.) Threatened by assassination in the Rye House Plot (1683), Charles died of a stroke in 1685. △1156.

Charles III, called **Charles the Simple** (879–929), king of France (893–923). Son of Louis II, he was excluded from succession as an infant. Nevertheless he was crowned king by a party of nobles and prelates in 879. After the death of Eudes, Count of Paris, in 898, his rule was undisputed. In 911 he made peace with the Norse invaders. By the Treaty of Saint-Clair-Sur-Epte, he ceded Normandy to them but gained Lorraine. He was deposed and imprisoned in 923, to be succeeded by Raoul of Burgundy.

Charles IV, called **Charles the Fair** (1294–1328), king of France (1322–28), successor of his brother Philip V. He increased royal revenues by debasing the coinage and levying taxes. He invaded Guienne (1324), a possession of England, and in 1327 England ceded most of the province to Charles and paid a large indemnity. The last king of the Capetian dynasty, he was succeeded by Philip VI of the Valois line.

Charles V, called **Charles the Wise** (1337–80), king of France (1364–80). An able ruler, he regained most of the territory previously lost to the English; stabilized the coinage; and took a stand against marauding free companies; strengthened royal authority; introduced standing army, powerful navy, fiscal re-arms; established royal library; built Bastille. Placed severe economic burden on country through lack of practical budgeting. Succeeded by his son Charles VI.

Charles VI, called **Charles the Well-beloved or Charles the Mad** (1368–1422), king of France 1380–1422). Until 1388 he was controlled by his uncle Philip the Bold of Burgundy, whose policies drained the treasury and provoked uprisings. After ruling effectively for four years, Charles suffered the first of recurrent attacks of insanity. Philip and Louis d'Orleans, the king's brother, fought over control of the kingdom. Philip had Louis murdered in 1407 and allied himself with Henry V of England. Charles was compelled to sign the Treaty of Troyes (1420), which recognized Henry V as his successor.

Charles VII, called **the Well-Served** (1403–61), king of France (1422–61). The son of Charles VI, he reigned at the end of the Hundred Years' War. Excluded from throne by Treaty of Troyes; however, took power (1422) when Charles VI died. Ruled south of the Loire; Henry V of England controlled the north. Joan of Arc and Arthur III, Duke of Brittany, were two of his followers in the war against England. He was crowned (1429) at Rheims. Treaty of Arras (1435) won Burgundy as ally in 1440. A truce with England was signed, and England finally withdrew from Guienne (1453). He established heavy taxation, a standing army, and a permanent land tax. He was succeeded by his son Louis XI.

Charles VIII (1470–98), king of France (1483–98). He succeeded his father Louis XI and was originally controlled by his sister Anne de Beaujeu and her husband. But after 1491 he ruled on his own. He was obsessed with gaining the kingdom of Naples. In 1494 he invaded Italy, and in 1495 he entered Naples. But he was forced to retreat. The only positive result was the introduction of knowledge of the Italian Renaissance into France. He was succeeded by his cousin Louis XII.

Charles IX (1550–74), king of France (1560–74). His mother Catherine de Médicis became regent when at the age of 10 he succeeded his brother Francis II, although her authority temporarily waned when in 1571 the young king fell under the influence of Gaspard de Coligny, leader of the Huguenots. Coligny and thousands of his followers were slain in the St Bartholomew's Day Massacre (1572), ordered by Charles at the instigation of his mother. He was succeeded by his brother Henry III.

Charles X (1757–1836), king of France (1824–30). Brother of Louis XVI and Louis XVIII, he fled France at the outbreak of the French Revolution in 1789. He remained in England until the Bourbon restoration (1814). He opposed the moderate policies of Louis XVIII. After the assassination of his son in 1820, his reactionary forces triumphed. Shortly after his accession, he signed a law (1825) indemnifying émigrés for land confiscated during the Revolution. In 1830 he dissolved the liberal chamber of deputies and issued the July Ordinance, which restricted suffrage and press freedom and dissolved the newly elected chamber. The people rose up in arms and Charles was forced to abdicate and flee. He designated his grandson Henry as successor, but the Duc d'Orléans, Louis Philippe, was selected.

Charles I, or **Charles Robert of Anjou** (1288–1342), king of Hungary (1308–42). Elected by the diet (1308), he was the founder of Anjou dynasty in Hungary. He restored order, encouraged trade and the expansion of cities, and acquired Bosnia and Serbia. He also imposed the first direct tax. His marriage to the sister of Casimir III of Poland ensured the succession of his son Louis to the Polish throne.

Charles I (1226–85), king of Naples and of the Two Sicilies (1266–85), son of Louis VIII of France and Blanche of Castile. This prince, noted for restless ambition and harsh administration, was offered the throne by Pope Innocent IV and became one of the most powerful European rulers.

Charles III (1345–86), king of Naples (1381–86) and (Charles II) of Hungary (1385–86). A member of the Hungarian branch of the Angevin dynasty, with help of Pope Urban VI and by murder he triumphed over French claimant to Neapolitan throne, Louis of Anjou.

Charles I (1863–1908), king of Portugal (1889–1908). He was the son and successor of Louis I. Unable to compete with British and German power in Africa, Charles was criticized at home for giving into their demands. After a revolt in 1906, he set up a military dictatorship. That resulted in another revolt in which Charles and the heir apparent were assassinated. His second son, Manuel II, succeeded to the throne.

Charles I, king of Spain. *See* Charles V, Holy Roman emperor.

Charles II (1661–1700), king of Spain, Naples, and Sicily (1665–1700). He was the son and successor of Philip IV, and the last of the Spanish Hapsburgs. He was mentally incompetent and reigned under the regency of his mother, Mariana of Austria, and his illegitimate half-brother, John of Austria. During Charles's reign, Spain was greatly weakened by the War of Devolution and the War of the Grand Alliance. His death—and his will naming Philip of Anjou as his heir—set off the War of the Spanish Succession. *See also* Devolution, War of; Grand Alliance, War of; Spanish Succession, War of.

Charles III (1716–88), king of Spain (1759–88) and of Naples and Sicily (1735–59), the son of Philip V and Elizabeth Farnese. He conquered (1734) Naples and Sicily in the War of the Polish Succession and inherited the Spanish crown in 1759 from his half-brother Ferdinand VI. He then turned over Naples and Sicily to his son Ferdinand, who ruled as Ferdinand I of the Two Sicilies. Charles was a highly competent ruler. His reign was marked by the gaining of Louisiana from the French in 1763 and by the expulsion of the Jesuits in 1767. He was succeeded by his son Charles IV. △1180.

Charles IV (1748–1819), king of Spain (1788–1808), son and successor of Charles III. Unable to cope with the upheavals of Napoleon Bonaparte, Charles virtually turned over the government to his wife Maria Luisa and her lover Manuel de Godoy. Godoy formed an alliance with France, but Spain was nevertheless occupied by French troops in the Peninsular War. Charles was forced to abdicate in favor of his son Ferdinand VII, who in turn was forced from the throne by Napoleon. *See also* Godoy, Manuel de; Maria Luisa.

Charles IX (1550–1611), king of Sweden (1604–11). The third son of Gustav I, he led a rebellion against his brother Eric XIV and opposed his brother John III's Catholicism. At John's death he became regent (1599–1604) and established Lutheranism. John's Catholic son Sigismund III, king of Poland, claimed the throne but was formally deposed. Charles's reign was marked by constant war due to his efforts to secure Swedish sovereignty of the Arctic coast.

Charles X (1622–60), king of Sweden (1654–60). He ascended the throne when his cousin Queen Christina abdicated in his favor. His efforts to complete Swedish dominion of the Baltic resulted in a reign of military activity. He invaded Poland unsuccessfully and twice invaded Denmark, crossing the frozen sea. He established the natural frontiers in Scandinavia, recovering the S provinces of Sweden from Denmark, and died during efforts to negotiate a peace with European powers in 1660. He was succeeded by his son, Charles XI.

Charles XI (1655–97), king of Sweden (1660–97). He was not a soldier like his father, Charles X, whom he succeeded in 1660, but his courage during the Battle of Lund (1676) resulted in victory over the Danes. His marriage to Princess Ulrica of Denmark further cemented Scandinavian relations. He was uneducated, but became a strong monarch, strengthening Sweden financially, improving armaments, judicial processes, church government, art and science. He was succeeded by his son, Charles XII.

Charles XII, (1682–1718), king of Sweden (1697–1718). His father Charles XI supervised his education, training him in all aspects of administration. Given full sovereignty in 1697, he was a military hero, defeating Denmark, Russia, and Poland in The Great Northern War. His invasion of Russia (1708) was hampered by an unusually severe winter. Defeated, he fled to Turkey. Sweden's power was strengthened by his early victories, but his endless wars exhausted Sweden's resources. Invading Norway he was shot, possibly assassinated, at Fredriksten in 1718. His sister Ulrica Eleanor succeeded him.

Charles XIII (1748–1818), king of Sweden (1809–10) and Norway (1814–18). After his brother Gustav III was assassinated in 1792, Charles became regent and when his nephew Gustav IV abdicated in 1809, he became king, accepting a new constitution of limited monarchy. He ceded Finland to Russia and signed treaties with Denmark and France. He became king of Norway in 1814. Marshal Bernadotte succeeded him in Sweden as Charles XIV in 1810.

Charles XIV John (1763–1844), king of Sweden

Charlie Chaplin

Chapultepec, Mexico

Char

Charles II of England

(1810–44). French by birth, his original name was Jean Baptiste Bernadotte. He fought in the French Revolution and was made a marshal of Napoleón. He was chosen by the Swedish legislature in 1810 to succeed Charles XIII, who had no heirs. By the Treaty of Kiel he forced Denmark to cede Norway to Sweden, and he became king of Norway as Charles III John (1818–44). He joined the Allies against Napoleon at the Battle of Leipzig in 1814. His subsequent reign brought peace and prosperity to Sweden.

Charles XV (1826–72), king of Sweden and Norway (1858–72). On the death of his father, Oscar I, in 1859 he became king, instituting reforms in communal, ecclesiastical, and criminal laws. He created a bicameral parliament and advocated "Scandinavianism," which sought political union of the three northern kingdoms, but he failed to keep his promise of military help to Denmark in the Schleswig-Holstein Affair. A popular king, he was an amateur painter and a poet.

Charles XVI Gustav (1946–), king of Sweden (1973–). Known as Carl, he ascended the throne after the death of his grandfather, King Gustav VI. His father, Prince Gustav Adolf, was killed in an air crash in 1947. A descendant of Marshal Bernadotte, he was a constitutional monarch with no political power and was an environmentalist, knowledgeable on international affairs, labor and industry. In 1976, his plans to marry Silva Sommerlath, a West German commoner, were made public, and he visited the United States.

Charles, Prince of Wales (1948–), eldest son of Elizabeth II of Great Britain, heir to the British throne. Educated at Cambridge University (1967–70), he trained as an air force pilot before becoming a naval officer (1971–76). He was invested with the title Prince of Wales in 1969.

Charles, called **Charles the Bold** (1433–77), last reigning duke of Burgundy (1467–77), son and successor of Philip the Good. Aligned with England by marriage to Margaret, Edward IV's sister (1468), he was ruler of the Low Countries, Luxembourg, Burgundy, and Franche-Comte. He continued to conquer lands separating his possessions. He seized Lorraine in 1475, thereby alienating the Swiss, whom he subsequently attacked. He was defeated and killed by the Swiss in 1477. Continually at war with France throughout his reign, Burgundy's resistance to that country ended with his death.

Charles III, called **Charles the Great** (1543–1608), duke of Lorraine (1545–1608). He was brought up in the French court under the influence of Henry II. He returned to Lorraine in 1560 and reformed the legal system and the calendar, and promoted economic growth. He disputed the claim of the Protestant Henry IV to the French throne. German Protestants supporting Henry invaded Lorraine in 1587 and Henry declared war in 1592. Hostilities ceased in 1594 when Henry converted to Catholicism.

Charles IV (1604–75), duke of Lorraine. He succeeded to the duchy in 1634, but because of French domination and the turmoil of the Thirty Years War, he often was out of power. France invaded Lorraine in 1633 and forced Charles to abdicate to his brother in 1634. He regained the duchy in 1641 but lost it again in 1648. He was imprisoned by the Spanish (1654–59). Louis XIV restored him to Lorraine in 1661, but had him removed for the last time in 1670. △1096.

Charles V (1643–90), duke of Lorraine. Although he succeeded to his title in 1675, Louis XIV refused to allow him to rule. He was twice a candidate for the Polish crown (1669, 1674). From 1664 he served in the army of the Holy Roman Empire, commanding the imperial forces in the third Dutch War (1672–78) and in the defense of Vienna against the Turks (1683). △1128,1152.

Charles, Ezzard (Mack) (1921–1975), US boxer, b. Lawrenceville, Ga. The National Boxing Association named Charles the world's heavyweight champion when he beat Jersey Joe Walcott (1949) in Chicago, after Joe Louis' retirement (1949). Charles won the title outright (1950) in New York City after he beat Louis, who came out of retirement. He lost the title to Walcott (1951) in Pittsburgh, Pa., and was elected to the Hall of Fame in 1970.

Charles, Jacques Alexandre César (1746–1823), French physicist, inventor, and mathematician who was the first to use a hydrogen balloon. He discovered the law relating the expansion of a gas to its temperature rise. Gay-Lussac published this work some 15 years after Charles's discovery and it is alternately known as Charles's law or Gay-Lussac's law. He is credited with inventing a thermometric hydrometer and improving Fahrenheit's aerometer and Gravesande's hydrometer.

Charles, Ray (1932–), US singer and pianist, b. Ray Charles Robinson in Albany, Ga. Blind since age six, he played and sang with various bands until his first hit recording "I Got a Woman" (1955), which launched him into stardom. He has recorded many albums and has been highly successful as a blues and popular singer.

Charles Albert (1798–1849), king of Sardinia-Piedmont (1831–49). He came to power when Charles Felix, last of the main Savoy line, died. Charles Albert granted a more liberal constitution. In support of Italian unity, he tried to drive the Austrians out of Lombardy and Venetia but was defeated (1849) and renounced his throne in favor of his son Victor Emmanuel II. △1248.

Charles Augustus (1757–1828), duke of Saxe-Weimar-Eisenach (1758–1828) and grand duke after 1815. Through his alliance with Frederick II of Prussia he achieved great influence in German affairs. He fought against Napoleon I in the Napoleonic Wars, but his duchy was forced to enter the Confederation of the Rhine in 1806. An important member of the Congress of Vienna, he was raised to the rank of grand duke by that body. He was a great patron of the arts; Goethe and Schiller were under his protection.

Charles Darnay, character in Charles Dickens' *A Tale of Two Cities.* A refugee from the French Revolution, he renounces his title and marries Lucie Manette.

Charles Emmanuel I (1562–1630), duke of Savoy (1580–1630). Throughout his career he alternated his allegiance between France and Spain; during the Thirty Years' War he first fought with the enemies of the Hapsburgs, but then went over to the Spanish side (1627), where he suffered military defeat.

Charles Emmanuel II (1634–75), duke of Savoy (1638–75). Because he became duke at age 4, his mother, Christine of Bourbon, sister of Louis XIII of France, acted as his regent—thus closely tying Savoy's policies to France's. Upon Christine's death (1663) Charles Emmanuel assumed governorship of Savoy but remained strongly dominated by Louis XIV and French policy.

Charles Emmanuel III (1701–73), duke of Savoy and king (Charles Emmanuel I) of Sardinia (1730–73). Siding with France and Spain in the War of Polish Succession, he defeated the Austrians at Guastalla (1734) and obtained Novara and Tortona (1738). In the War of Austrian Succession (1740–48) he sided against Spain and in the Treaty of Aix-la-Chapelle (1748) received Vigevano.

Charles' Law, the observation that the volume of a gas at constant pressure is directly proportional to its temperature. Discovered by the French scientist Jacques Charles around 1787, the law is a special case of the Ideal Gas Law. *See also* Boyle's Law; Ideal Gas Law.

Charles Martel (688–741), Frankish ruler, natural son of Pepin of Heristal, grandfather of Charlemagne. Upon the death of his father (714), he seized control of Austrasia and Neustria. He later conquered Burgundy, Aquitaine, and Provence and subjugated many German tribes across the Rhine. In 732 at Tours he halted the advance of the Muslims from Spain. He divided his kingdom between his sons Pepin the Short and Carloman. △1066.

Charles of Lorraine (1712–80), prince of Lorraine, brother-in-law of Austrian Empress Maria Theresa. He joined the Austrian army in 1736 and campaigned against the Turks (1737–39) and fought in the War of the Austrian Succession (1740–48). He served as governor of the Austrian Netherlands (1648–57, 1663–80), ruling with uncommon fairness. During the Seven Years War (1756–63), he led the Austrian forces until his defeat by the Prussians at Leuther in December 1757.

Charles of Valois (1270–1325), French prince. The father of Philip VI, the first Valois king, Charles was also count of Anjou and Maine by marriage and son-in-law to Baldwin II, the last Latin emperor at Constantinople. Charles' father was Philip III and his older brother was Philip IV; however, his claims on both the eastern and western crowns were unsuccessful and he made his reputation as a soldier.

Charleston, port city in SE South Carolina; seat of Charleston co; William Sayle and a group of English colonists settled nearby in 1670 at Albemarle Poin later for better defense they moved to Oyster Poin and made their capital Charles Town, which wa named for King Charles II, and served as capital unt 1790. The first Civil War engagement was here a Fort Sumter; site of the First Ordinance of Secessio (1860). Points of interest include the Dock Stree Theater (1736), one of the first in the country; Colleg of Charleston 1770; Fireproof Buildings (1826 Charleston Museum (1773); Slave Market Museum Industries: foreign trade, chemicals, steel, tourism Founded 1680; inc. 1783. Pop. (1970) 66,945.

Charleston, capital city of West Virginia, in W cen tral part of state at junction of Elk and Kanawha rivers seat of Kanawha co; city grew around Fort Lee; home of Daniel Boone. Industries: chemicals, glass, meta timber, oil, coal. Founded 1788; inc. 1794. Pop (1970) 71,505.

Charleston, popular US dance of the 1920s. Origi nated by southern blacks around the turn of the 20th century, it was used in vaudeville and musical shows It was one of the first "Jitterbug" dances.

Charlevoix, Pierre Francois Xavier de (1682–1761), Canadian historian and explorer, b. France. He canoed up the St. Lawrence in 1721 to the Great Lakes and eventually reached New Orleans. He wrote the first general history of Canada (1744) and edited *Memoires de Trevoux,* a Jesuit journal.

Charlotte, city in S North Carolina; state's largest city and capital of Mecklenbourg co; site of two universities and three colleges; birthplace of Pres. James K. Polk; distribution center for agricultural products. Industries: cotton products, farm implements, oil refining, chemicals. Settled *c.* 1748; inc. 1768; occupied by British 1780. Pop. (1970) 241,178.

Charlotte Amalie, seaport and capital of the US Virgin Islands, on St Thomas Island; Danish architecture. Pop. 12,372.

Charlottesville, city in central Virginia, 70 mi (113km) W of Richmond; seat of Albemarle co; named for Queen Charlotte of Britain; site of University of Virginia (1819); Monticello, Thomas Jefferson's home; Ash Lawn, James Monroe's home. Industries: publishing, research, textiles. Founded 1762; inc. 1888. Pop. (1970) 38,880.

Charlottetown, capital of Prince Edward Island, Canada, in center of island overlooking Hillsborough Bay; site of University of Prince Edward Island (1969); major commercial and transportation center. Industries: food processing, fishing, tourism. Founded by French 1720; became capital 1765; inc. 1855. Pop. 18,631.

Charolais, creamy white breed of beef cattle, originally developed in France. In the United States it is sometimes crossbred with zebu. *See also* Beef Cattle; Zebu. △372.

Charterhouse of Parma (1839), novel by Stendhal, narrating the adventures of Fabrizio del Dongo. His aunt, Sanseverina, sponsors him in a church career. After Fabrizio becomes archbishop of Parma, he has an affair with Clélia Conti who has earlier helped him escape from prison. The tragic death of their son and Clélia's death is followed by Fabrizio's retirement to a monastery (the Charterhouse) and death.

Charter Oak, white oak tree in Hartford, Conn., the traditional hiding place for the Connecticut charter when autocratic Gov. Edmund Andros of New England demanded its surrender in 1687. The tree was destroyed by a storm in 1856.

Charter of Liberties (1701), document written by William Penn. It established government for Pennsylvania and Delaware. It provided for a common government, separately appointed councils and elected assemblies. Religious freedom was assured. *See also* Frame of Government.

Chartism, British working-class movement for social and political reform, 1838–48. The Chartists sought the enactment of William Lovett's People's Charter, which called for the democratization of the ballot. Racked by factional disputes and unable to capitalize on the continental revolutions of 1848, the movement collapsed when plans to resettle industrial workers in the countryside failed. △1288, 1326.

Chartres, town in NW France, on the Eure River, 50mi (81km) SW of Paris; capital of Eure-et-Loir dept.; rich farming area. In ancient times Druids assembled here; early Christians built a basilica in 4th century on site now occupied by the 12th-13th century Gothic

Cathedral of Notre Dame, whose stained glass and superb sculptures make it one of Europe's finest structures. Industries: woolens, leather, hosiery, radio and television parts. Pop. 34,469. △1094.

Charybdis, in Greek mythology, a whirlpool that dwelled opposite the monster Scylla in a Sicilian sea; the daughter of Poseidon and Earth. She had stolen the oxen of Hercules, for which Zeus changed her into a whirlpool whose vortex swallowed up ships, but failed to capture that of Odysseus. *See also* Scylla and Charybdis.

Chase, Mary Ellen (1887–1973), US author, b. Blue Hill, Me. She taught English at Smith College (1918–55) and is known for her fiction and biographical writings. Her most notable works include *A Goodly Heritage* (1932), *Mary Peters* (1934), *Silas Crockett* (1935), *A Goodly Fellowship* (1939), and *The White Gate* (1954).

Chase, Salmon Portland (1808–73), chief justice of the US Supreme Court (1864–73), b. Cornish, NH. He is known as the defender of fugitive slaves. He organized the Liberty party (1841) and was founder of the Free-Soil party (1848). He served as US Senator (1849–55, 1860), and governor of Ohio (1855–59). He was secretary of the treasury (1861–64), during which time he supported the National Banking Act (1863). He was appointed chief justice by President Lincoln, succeeding Roger Taney. As chief justice, Chase reorganized the federal courts in the South, and presided over the Jefferson Davis trial (1867) and the Senate impeachment proceedings against President Johnson (1868). His dissenting opinion in the Slaughterhouse Cases (1873) became a position of the courts about the restrictive clause of the 14th Amendment. He also presided over *Hepburn* v. *Griswold* (1870), which made legal tender unconstitutional. The decision was reversed in the Legal Tender Cases (1871) despite his dissenting view.

Chase, Samuel (1741–1811), US jurist, b. Somerset co., Maryland. A signer of the Declaration of Independence and Maryland General Assemblyman (1764–84), he was appointed an associate justice of the US Supreme Court in 1796. A Federalist, impeached in 1804 for his conduct at the trials of two Jeffersonians, he won acquittal on the ground that holding opposing political views is not misconduct.

Chase, Stuart (1888–), US economist, b. Somesworth, N.H. Educated at the Massachusetts Institute of Technology and Harvard, he worked as an accountant, investigator for the Federal Trade Commission (1917–22), and as a consultant to Labor Unions (1922). He founded the Consumers Union and wrote *Tragedy of Waste* (1925), *Your Money's Worth* (1927) *A New Deal* (1932), *Rich Land Poor Land* (1936), and *Tyranny of Words* (1938).

Chat, several species of warblers, including the North American yellow-breasted chat *(Icteria virens)* known for its mimicking ability, and the red-breasted chat *(Granatellus venustus)* of Central America. *See also* Warbler.

Chateau Architecture, fortified seigneurial residence that was the French equivalent of the English castle in medieval times. In the 15th century changes in methods of warfare and in the feudal system made the heavily fortified chateau obsolete. Lightly fortified, luxurious country houses, such as Amboise, Blois, Chambord, and Chenonceaux, mark the transition between medieval fortress and country mansion. △1106, 1146, 1166, 1190.

Chateaubriand, François-René, Vicomte de (1768–1848), the dominant literary figure of his generation and the founder of French Romanticism. For him, nature was savage and beautiful, man primitive and good, and God omnipotent and benevolent. A trip to the United States in 1791 influenced his writing; the landscapes and people he encountered in the wilds of America gave vent to his vivid imagination, reflected in works such as *Atala* (1801) and *Le génie du Christianisme* (1802).

Château de Chambord. △1146.

Château de Gaillon. △1146.

Chateauguay, Battle of (1813), engagement in the War of 1812, in which 4000 US soldiers under Wade Hampton moved against 1600 French Canadian troops who were defending access to Montreal. The attack was repulsed by the Canadians with minimal bloodshed.

Châteauroux, town in central France on the Indre River; capital of Indre dept.; grew around 10th-century castle built by lords of Déols; castle was replaced in 15th century by Chateau Raoul, which still stands. Industries: woolens, paper, agricultural machinery. Pop. 49,138.

Château Thierry, town in France, on E bank of Marne River, 47mi (76km) ENE of Paris; built on the side of a hill with ruins of old castle Thierry, reputedly built by Charles Martel. Jean de la Fontaine was born here 1621; his home is a museum. Industries: stone quarrying, musical instruments, yarn. Pop. 11,049.

Chatham, William Pitt, Ist Earl of. *See* Pitt, William, Ist Earl of Chatham.

Chatham, town in SW Ontario, Canada, 65mi (105km) SW of London, on Thames River; commercial center of agricultural district. Founded 1835. Pop. 34,601.

Chattahoochee River, river in Georgia, Alabama, and Florida; rises in NE Georgia, flows SW to Alabama border, S to Florida border, forming Lake Seminole. Length: 436mi (702km).

Chattanooga, city in E Tennessee, on Tennessee River; seat of Hamilton co; originally a Cherokee territory, it later became a trading center called Ross' Landing; served as a Union military base during Civil War and was the scene of many battles including the Chattanooga and Chickamauga campaigns; since 1935, it has been headquarters of the Tennessee Valley Authority. Industries: iron, steel, processed foods, synthetics, tourism. Settled 1835; inc. 1839. Pop. (1970) 119,082.

Chattanooga Campaign (October-November 1863). In the Western campaigns of the Civil War, the railroad center of Chattanooga, Tenn., was a key to Union progress west toward the Mississippi River and south into Georgia. After a long campaign, Gen. William S. Rosecrans gained the city but later was besieged there and had to be rescued by Gen. Ulysses S. Grant. △1276.

Chatterji, Bankim Chandra (1838–94), Indian novelist, the father of the novel in Bengali. He was a prolific writer, his central theme being the struggle against Muslim oppression. His "Hail to Thee, Mother" became the anthem of the Hindu Indians.

Chatterton, Thomas (1752–70), English poet and forger of antiquities. His poverty and lack of literary recognition led him to suicide at seventeen, by which time he had written satire, comic opera, pseudo-archaic history, and excellent poetry purporting to be composed by Thomas Rowley, an imaginary Elizabethan monk. △1222.

Chaucer, Geoffrey (*c.*1340–1400), the greatest of English medieval poets, strongly influenced by contemporaneous French and Italian writers. Born in London the son of a wine merchant, he served at court and on diplomatic missions before being appointed controller of customs in London (1374–86). His writings are remarkable for their range, narrative sense, power of characterization, and humor. They include *The Book of the Duchess, The House of Fame, The Parliament of Fowls, Troilus and Criseyde,* and *The Canterbury Tales. See also* individual works. △1100.

Chaus, or jungle cat, swamp lynx, striped yellowish to brownish cat found in scrub and mountain areas of S Asia, the Middle East, and NE Africa. Long-legged, it will interbreed with the domestic cat. Length: body—23.6–29.5in (60–75cm); tail—9.8–13.8in (25–35cm). Family Felidae; species *Felis chaus. See also* Cat.

Chautauqua, US adult education movement that flourished in the latter part of the 19th century. The name comes from Lake Chautauqua, N.Y., where summer courses began in 1874. At the height of the movement, more than 100 centers and many traveling groups offered popular education and entertainment to millions.

Chautauqua Lake, lake in W New York, near Lake Erie. Grapes and other fruits are grown here; resort area. Length: 18mi (29km). Width: 1–3mi (1.6–4.8km).

Chavez, Cesar Estrada (1927–), US labor leader, b. Yuma, Ariz. Born of Mexican-American parents, Chavez migrated to California as a field worker. He organized field workers (1962) into the National Farm Workers Association (NFWA). In 1966 the NFWA merged with the Agricultural Workers Organizing Committee of the AFL-CIO, becoming the United Farm Workers Organizing Committee. In 1968–70 he led a successful national boycott of California grapes,

Charolais

Salmon P. Chase

Château

Caucer 1400

Geoffrey Chaucer

and later a lettuce boycott. In the mid-1970s disputes over farm-laborer representation continued.

Chavín, one of the earliest prehistoric culture periods in South America, lasting from *c.* 1000 to 200 BC Named for the Chavín de Huántar in N Peru, these people developed excellent stone sculpture, the earliest gold work yet found in the Americas, as well as some of the most remarkable ceramics, judged both by technology and esthetic form.

Checheno-Ingush (Ceceno-Ingusskaja) Autonomous Soviet Socialist Republic, administrative district in SE European USSR, in the N Caucasus; capital is Grozny. Formed in 1936 by merging the Chechen and Ingush autonomous areas, it was dissolved 1943–44 because of German collaboration in WWII; reunited 1957. Chief rivers are the Terek and Sunzha; whose valleys are the main source of agricultural products; Grozny oil field is a major source of Soviet oil; 40% of population is urban. Industries: oil refining, food processing, chemicals, oil field equipment, wine, cognac, fruit canning. Area: 7,452sq mi (19,301sq km). Pop. 1,065,000.

Checkerberry. *See* Wintergreen.

Checkers, game for two players. It originated in Europe in the 16th century. Each player uses 12 pieces (either red or black) and sets them on the board in a predetermined order. The board consists of 64 alternately colored squares (either red and black or white and black). All play is from the black squares. The players sit opposite one another and alternate in moving their pieces forward. Pieces are captured by jumping over opposing pieces, and the game ends when all of a player's pieces are removed from the board.

Checks and Balances, division of power provided for in the US Constitution among the legislative, executive, and judicial branches of government to ensure that no one has domination over the other two. △ 902, 906.

Cheektowaga, city in W New York, E of Buffalo. Pop. (1970) 113,844.

Cheese. △370, 374.

Cheetah, or hunting leopard, spotted cat found in hot, arid areas of Africa, Middle East, and India. A long-legged cat with blunt, nonretractable claws, its coat is tawny brown with round black spots. Capable of running over 55mph (88.5kph), it hunts gazelles and antelope by sight. Its gestation period is 90–95 days and 1–8 young are born. Length: body—55–59in (140–150cm); tail—23.6–31.5in (60–80cm); weight: 132lb (60kg). Family Felidae; subfamily Acinonchinae. Species include Asian *Acinonyx venatica;* African *Acinonyx jubatus,* and the striped *Acinonyx rex. See also* Cat. △606.

Cheever, John (1912–), US author, b. Quincy, Mass. A short story writer and novelist, his works deal with suburbanites. Among his novels are *The Wapshot Chronicle* (1957), *The Wapshot Scandal* (1964), and *Bullet Park* (1969).

Chefoo (Yantai, or Yen-tai), port city in E China, on N coast of the Shantung Peninsula; important fishing port, opened to foreign trade 1862; scene of Chefoo Convention (1876) which est. new Chinese ports for foreign trade. Pop. 180,000.

Chekiang, smallest province in E China, on E China Sea, including the Choushan archipelago; capital is Hangchow, the royal capital under the Southern Sung dynasty (12th–13th centuries); birthplace of Chiang Kai-shek, Nationalist Chinese leader. Industries: agriculture (in the N plain region), fishing (on the coast and in the archipelago), silk, food processing. Area: 39,305sq mi (101,800sq km). Pop. 31,000,000.

Chekov, or **Chekhov, Anton Pavlovich** (1860–1904), Russian playwright whose theatrical realism evolved with the Moscow Art Theatre under Constantin Stanislavski. Chekhov depicted the frustrations of Russian society in the final years of tsarism. The characters of *The Sea Gull* (1896), *Uncle Vanya* (1899), *The Three Sisters* (1900), and, especially, *The Cherry Orchard* (1904) were created with such validity that they bridged the Bolshevik Revolution and remain favorites of Soviet theater and elsewhere. △ 1240.

Chelan Lake, lake in N central Washington; largest natural lake in state; outlet at S end of lake flows into Columbia River. Length: 55mi (89km). Width: approx. 2mi (3km).

Chelation, chemical reaction in which a single organic compound, termed a chelating agent, binds itself to a metal ion at more than one point. Tartaric acid, $(HO_2CCHOH)_2$, and ethylenediamine, $(H_2NCH_2)_2$, are chelating agents. Such ligands are used as extractants in chemical separations and widely affect molecular environments such as hemoglobin in life processes.

Chelmsford, town in NE Massachusetts, 22mi (35km) NW of Boston; site of Fiske House (1790) and Unitarian Church (1840); nearby is Billerica State Forest. Industries: textiles, electronics, granite quarrying. Settled 1650; inc. 1655. Pop. (1970) 31,432.

Chelonia. △520.

Chelsea, city in E Massachusetts; suburb of Boston; scene of the battle of Chelsea Creek (1775); site of Cary-Bellingham house (1659). Industries: electrical machinery, shoes, paint. Settled 1624; inc. as town 1739, as city 1857. Pop. (1970) 30,625.

Chelseaware, the porcelain produced at the prominent Chelsea factory in London between about 1745 and 1770, when the operations were transferred to Derby. The earliest examples copied naturalistic silver forms such as a crayfish saltshaker. From 1750, Meissen and Sèvres influence was felt. Among items produced were cleverly designed small bottles and boxes known as "Chelsea toys."

Chelyabinsk (Cel'abinsk), industrial city in Russian SFSR, USSR, on Mias River; capital of Chelyabinsk oblast; metallurgical and industrial center; resettlement area for emigrants to Siberia in 19th century. Industries: food processing, iron, steel, textiles, chemicals. Founded 1658; chartered 1745. Pop. 874,000.

Chembini. △1196.

Chemical Analysis. △1568.

Chemical Bonds, forces holding atoms together in chemical compounds. In an isolated atom the electrons move around the positive nuclei. When atoms come together to form compounds, the total electrons move in the combined field of the nuclei, and a more stable configuration is produced (that is, one of lower energy). Usually chemists treat the forces between atoms as individual linkages between pairs of atoms. These are the chemical bonds, which are classified according to the way the electrons are distributed. A covalent bond is formed by sharing a pair of electrons between two atoms; when the electron pair is supplied by one of the atoms the link is a coordinate bond. Ionic bonds are produced by transfer of electrons to form ions, which bind by electrostatic attraction. In ionic, and to a lesser extent, coordinate bonds there is an unequal distribution of charge between the atoms. Such bonds are said to be polar. A bond produced by sharing one electron pair, or by transfer of one electron, is a single bond. Double and triple bonds can also form. In compounds it is often possible to assign an energy to a bond—equal to the energy to separate two parts of the molecule. This is the bond energy. *See also* Covalent Bond; Hydrogen Bond; Ionic Bond; Valence. △1554–58.

Chemical Elements. △1552–54.

Chemical Equation, representation of a chemical reaction, using symbols for the atoms of the elements. The equation shows how the atoms are rearranged as a result of the reaction: eg, $2H_2 + O_2 = 2H_2O$ is the equation representing the formation of water from hydrogen and oxygen. A knowledge of atomic weights enables the equation to be used to calculate the proportions in which the substances will react. In this example, 4 kg $[2 \times (1 + 1)]$ of hydrogen react with 32 kg $(16 + 16)$ of oxygen to form 36 kg of water (at. wt. O=16, H=1).

Chemical Equilibrium, state of a reversible reaction when the concentrations of products and reactants are constant with time. The initial rate of a chemical reaction falls off as the concentrations of reactants decrease and the build-up of products causes the rate of the reverse reaction to increase. Equilibrium is the steady state occurring when these two rates are equal and reaction has apparently ceased. *See also* Equilibrium Constant. △1504.

Chemical Kinetics, branch of chemistry concerned with the measurement and study of reaction rate and its dependence on factors such as concentration and temperature. The term is also applied to the behavior of a particular reaction. △1502.

Chemical Nomenclature. Until the end of the 18th century the names of substances gave no indication of their composition. J. J. Berzelius (1779–1848) proposed the system now used, in which the name of a compound indicates the elements it contains and sometimes in what proportions. The naming of the elements themselves has been somewhat haphazard—some from Greek (eg iodine and chlorine), some from mythology (eg thorium and niobium), etc.

When two elements combine to form a compound the name of the second element is modified to end in *-ide* (hydrogen chloride). When more than one compound can be formed from the same elements a numerical suffix is used (eg carbon monoxide, carbon dioxide). The naming of chemical compounds (especially in organic chemistry) is now a precise discipline and many older names have been modified to comply with modern rules.

Chemical Reaction, process in which one or more chemical substances are converted into other substances. Reactions involve the formation or breaking of chemical bonds as the starting materials (the reactants) change into the final substances (the products). These changes characterize the mechanism of the reaction, which may be simple or may involve a complex sequence of steps. *See also* Chemical Equilibrium; Chemical Kinetics; Endothermic Reaction; Exothermic Reaction. △1480,1554, 1560, 1568.

Chemical Stimulation of the Brain, technique in which chemicals (drugs) are introduced directly into the brain to stimulate local populations of brain cells or to test the effect of a drug on brain tissue. The substance may be injected into the brain, or a permanent dispensing device (cannula) may be implanted.

Chemical Symbols. The alchemists used symbols for some of the elements and John Dalton (1766–1844) devised a more extensive system. However, these have all been abandoned in favor of the system devised by J. J. Berzelius in 1811. In this system letters, or pairs of letters, are used to represent the atoms of an element (eg O for oxygen). Not all elements can be represented by their initial letters (11 elements start with the letter C), some require two letters (eg Cl for chlorine and Cd for cadmium). Several elements have symbols based on their Latin names, eg Na for sodium (natrium). △1484.

Chemical Warfare, employment of chemical weapons, such as poisonous gases, defoliants and herbicides, over large areas. △1746.

Chemistry, branch of physical science concerned with the formation of compounds by chemical elements and with the structures and reactions of such compounds. Chemistry is essentially concerned with the electrons in atoms, in particular with the way atoms form chemical bonds. Nuclear properties and reactions are the province of physics.

The subject grew out of alchemy in the 17th and 18th centuries. Today it is a vast body of knowledge with a number of subdivisions. The main classification is into organic chemistry, the study of carbon compounds, and inorganic chemistry, the study of compounds of the other elements. Physical chemistry is concerned with the physical properties and behavior of compounds.

Chemistry is of immense commercial importance. Industrial chemistry, including chemical engineering, involves the study and development of equipment and processes for making useful chemicals and products, including fertilizers, cosmetics, explosives, pharmaceuticals, dyestuffs, paints, synthetic resins and fibers, and plastics. *See also* Alchemy; Biochemistry. △1550.

Chemotherapy, treatment of a disease by systematic drugs that specifically kill or impair disease-producing organisms in the body without damaging the patient. The term is often used to describe the treatment of cancer by drugs. Generally, it is the use of any drug to treat any disease. The concept of specific drug treatment was first introduced in the early 1900s by German bacteriologist Paul Ehrlich and greatly advanced after the mid-1930s with the development of sulfa drugs, antibiotics, and other modern drugs. △ 746, 770.

Chemurgy, the development of new chemical products for industry from organic raw materials, especially those of agricultural origin.

Chenab, one of "Five Rivers" of the Punjab, India; rises in the Indian Himalayas, flows through Jammu Kashmir and W central Punjab, Pakistan, to unite with the Sutlej to form the Panjnad River; supports extensive canal and irrigation systems. Length: 599mi (964km).

Chen-Chiang (Chinkiang, Zhenjiang), city in E

China, on S bank of Yangtze River, 43mi (69km) NE of Nanking. First opened to foreign trade in 1859, it was a British concession until 1927, when it was returned to China; served as capital of Kiangsu prov. from 1928–49; site of Kiangsu medical college. Industries: silk, vinegar, paper products, tobacco, rice and flour milling. Pop. 250,000.

Chengchow. *See* Zhengzhou.

Chengdu (Chengtu), city in S central China, near Ching Kiang River, 170mi (274km) NW of Chungking; capital of Szechwan prov.; site of US air base 1944–45, university (1931), irrigation system over 2,000 years old; agricultural trade center. Industries: iron, steel, machinery, silk. Pop. 2,000,000.

Ch'eng I, or **Ch'eng Yi** (1033–1107), Chinese philosopher, founder of the Neo-Confucian School of Reason *(li)*, which has been characterized as the school of "Platonic realism." He was originally a student of Chou Tun-i, and his work was given definite expression by Chu Hsi. *See also* Chu Hsi.

Cheng-te (Chengteh, or Chengde), city in NE China, on Luan River 110mi (177km) NE of Peking; former summer capital of Ch'ing Dynasty (1644–1911); site of many parks, lakes, palaces, and pavilions; distribution center for pharmaceuticals, lumber products, fruits. Pop. 2,000,000.

Chengtu. *See* Chengdu.

Chennault, Claire Lee (1890–1958), US Air Force general, b. Commerce, Tex. He was the leader of the Flying Tigers, a volunteer air corps set up to aid China. After serving in World War I, he trained pilots until his first retirement (1937). As advisor to Chiang Kai-shek (1937), he formed the Flying Tigers, putting his ideas on tactical air power to the test. He was made brigadier general (1942) and major general (1943).

Chenonceaux, village in W central France, on the Cher River; site of Renaissance chateau (1515–22) occupied by Diane de Poitiers and then by Catherine de Médicis; in 1560 Catherine added wing spanning river; setting and gardens of chateau are outstanding. Pop. 285.

Chen Tu-hsiu (1879–1942), Chinese political leader. One of the founders of the Chinese literary renaissance of 1917, he helped found the Chinese Communist party, which he led from 1921–27. He was deposed by Mao Tse-tung in 1927, arrested in 1933, and pardoned in 1937. △1270.

Cheops. *See* Khufu.

Cherbourg, seaport in NW France, on English Channel, on N shore of Cotentin Peninsula. Founded as a Roman outpost, it was under English control periodically until 18th century; severely damaged during German occupation in WWII. Modern city is naval base, trade center, and seaside resort. Pop. 38,243.

Cherchell (Cherchel), town and port in N Algeria, on the Mediterranean Sea. Ancient city (Iol) was founded by Carthaginians; made capital of Mauretania 25 BC and renamed Caesarea. Important center of Greco-Roman culture after being taken by Rome AD 42 and it declined after being sacked by Vandals in 5th century; site of many Roman ruins, including baths and an amphitheater. Pop. 11,667.

Chernigov (Cernigov), port city in Ukrainian SSR, USSR, on Desna River; capital of Chernigov oblast. A Lithuanian city in 14th century, it passed to Russia in 16th century; under Polish rule part of 17th century; site of Spasski Cathedral and the Church of the Assumption in the Yelets Monastery (both 11th century). Industries: footwear, flour, textiles, musical instruments. Founded c. 907. Pop. 159,000.

Chernov, Viktor (1876–1952), Russian revolutionary, one of the founders (1902) of the Socialist Revolutionary party. After the overthrow of the tsar in 1917, he served as minister of agriculture in the Kerensky government. He briefly headed the constitutional assembly that tried to rule after the downfall of Kerensky in 1918. An anti-Bolshevik, he joined the White Russians in the east and tried to establish a moderate government in Samara. It was taken over by the right-wing forces of Admiral Kolchak. He went into exile in 1921 and lived thereafter in Europe and the United States.

Chernovtsy (Cernovcy), city in Ukrainian SSR, USSR, on Prut River, near Romanian border; capital of Chernovtsy oblast; cultural, commercial and industrial center; important Moldavian center in 14th century; occupied by Austria by 1775; part of Romania 1918–40; annexed to Russia in 1940. When it was occupied during WWII by Germans, Jewish population was executed. Industries: textiles, machines, wood processing, food preserving. Pop. 187,000.

Chernyshevsky, Nikolai Gavrilovich (1828–89), Russian writer. A follower of French socialists and the nihilists, he was convicted of revolutionary activities in 1862 and exiled to Siberia until 1883. While there he wrote historical works and political novels, including *What Is to Be Done* (1863), which presented utopian schemes of social revolution.

Cherokee, second largest tribe of North American Indians; members of the great Iroquoian language family. They migrated south into the Appalachian region around Tennessee, Georgia, and the Carolinas. Smallpox introduced by white settlers caused the deaths of over one-half of the tribe. The Cherokee sided with the British during the Revolution, and as a result were forced to move west over the tragic Trail of Tears, further reducing their population. Today approximately 45,000 live in Oklahoma, while about 15,000 still remain in North Carolina, descendants of those few Indians who escaped into the hills. Another 15,000 reside throughout the United States. There are almost no full-blooded Cherokee today.

Cherry, widely grown fruit tree of the temperate regions, probably native to W Asia and E Europe. Three types of cherry trees, bearing the sweet, sour, or duke cherries, are grown for their edible fruit, which is almost globular, about 1in (2.5cm) in diameter and yellow to red to almost black in color. Sweet cherries are eaten fresh. All types are canned or frozen. The wood is prized for the manufacture of furniture. Family Rosaceae; genus *Prunus.* △338.

Cherry Laurel, any of various evergreen shrubs native to SE Europe and grown ornamentally in the United States. Reaching to 18ft (5.4m), they have glossy leaves and white flowers. Family Rosaceae; genus *Prunus.*

Cherry Orchard, The (1904), 4-act drama, last and best known play of Anton Chekhov. At its premiere in the Moscow Art Theatre (1904), the author's wife Olga Knipper created the role of aristocrat Mme. Ranevskaya. A bankrupt family, symbol of decaying czarist society, fails to save its estate as their cherry orchard is cleared for commercial housing by new owner Lopakhin, enterprising son of a serf.

Chert, impure, brittle type of flint. A cryptocrystalline variety of silica, its color can be white, yellow, gray,or brown. It occurs mainly in limestones and dolomites, and its origin is unknown.

Chesapeake, city in SE Virginia; scene of the Battle of Great Bridge (1775); formed by union of South Norfolk with Norfolk co. 1963. Industries: farming, fertilizer, lumber, steel equipment. Inc. 1963. Pop. (1970) 89,580.

Chesapeake and Leopard Incident (1807), incident in which the *Chesapeake,* a US frigate, was stopped near US territorial waters by the British ship *Leopard,* whose commander claimed the right to search for British deserters. US commander James Barron refused. The British then fired on the *Chesapeake* and impressed 4 seamen, including 2 Americans.

Chesapeake Bay, inlet of the Atlantic Ocean in Virginia (S) and Maryland (N) at the mouth of the Susquehanna River; divides the Delmarva Peninsula from E Maryland and E Virginia; fed by Patuxent, Rappahannock, James, and Chester rivers. Part of intercoastal waterway, it is linked to Delaware River by the Chesapeake and Delaware Canal. First permanent English settlement in present-day United States was at Jamestown, Virginia, on Chesapeake Bay (1607); in 1608 John Smith explored and charted the bay. US Naval Academy was built at Annapolis 1845. Baltimore, on the Patapsco River, arm of the bay, is Maryland's largest city. Length: 193mi (311km). Width: 3–30mi (5–48km).

Chesapeake Bay Bridge-Tunnel. △1754.

Chesapeake Retriever, water-loving hunting dog (sporting group) developed from English stock shipwrecked off the Maryland coast. The head is broad with a short, pointed muzzle. Small ears hang loose, and yellowish eyes are wide-set. A medium-length body is slightly higher in the hindquarters; feet are webbed; and the tail is 12–15in (30.5–38cm) long. The thick, short dark brown to deadgrass color coat is particularly water- and cold-resistant. Average size: 23–26in (58.5–66cm) high at shoulder; 65–75lb (29.5–34kg). *See also* Sporting Dog.

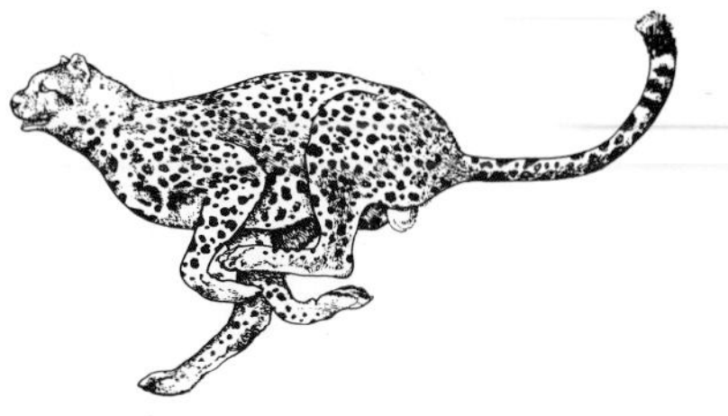

Cheetah

Chekiang province, China

Anton Chekov

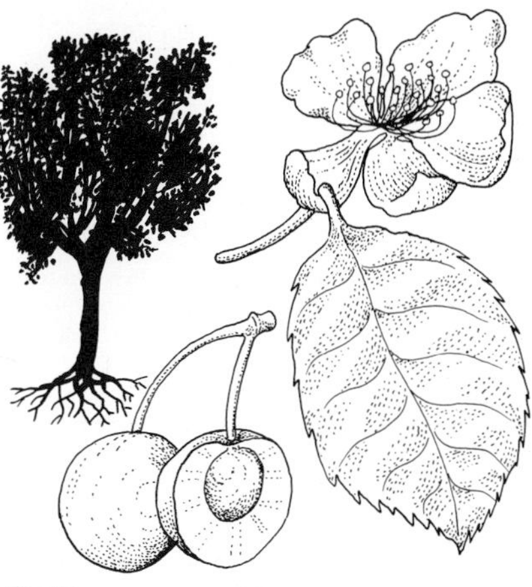

Cherry

Chesnutt, Charles Waddell (1858–1932), educator considered the first US black novelist of stature; b. Cleveland, Ohio. His novels, such as *The Marrow of Tradition* (1901), deal with racial prejudice and its consequences. He is best known, however, for *The Conjure Woman* (1899), a book of short stories about incidents of slavery told in Southern black dialect by an old gardener to his Northern employers.

Chess, board game for two players. Play is conducted on a square board of 64 alternately colored squares. Each player receives 16 chessmen, of one color. There are 8 pawns, 2 knights, 2 bishops, 2 rooks (or castles), 1 queen, and 1 king. The pieces are arranged in a predetermined order on the board, and each piece has a designated order of movement. The game is "pure" in that no luck or dice are involved. The object of the game is to trap, or checkmate, the opponent's king. It is believed that a version of the modern game originated in India in the 6th century.

Chester, port city in SE Pennsylvania, 14mi (22km) SW of Philadelphia on Delaware River; industrial and commercial center; site of Pennsylvania Military College (1821), Penn-Morton College, Crozer Theological Seminary (1867), Caleb Pusey House (1683), noted as the oldest English house in the state, Old Court House (1724), Pennsylvania's oldest civic building. Industries: shipbuilding, steel, automobiles, pharmaceuticals, electronics, oil refining, paper, textiles, chemicals. Settled 1644 by Swedish and Dutch settlers; inc. 1866. Pop. (1970) 56,331.

Chesterton, G(ilbert) K(eith) (1874–1936), English essayist, novelist, and poet. His Father Brown stories, concerning the detective work of a wordly wise priest, first appeared in 1911. He wrote many essays on social and political themes. His novels include *The Napoleon of Notting Hill* (1904) and *The Man Who Was Thursday* (1908). He became a Roman Catholic in 1922, after which he published *St. Francis of Assisi* (1923) and *St. Thomas Aquinas* (1933).

Chestnut, deciduous tree native to temperate areas of the northern hemisphere. It has lance-shaped leaves and furrowed bark. Male flowers hang in long catkins and female flowers are solitary or clustered at base of catkins. The prickly husked fruits open to reveal 2–3 nuts. The American chestnut *(Castanea dentata)*, once common, has been almost wiped out by blight. Other species bearing single-nut fruits are called chinquapin. There are four species. Family Fagaceae. *See also* Chinquapin.

Chestnut Blight, a highly destructive disease that has nearly wiped out the American chestnut. The blight is caused by a fungus *(Endothia parasitica)* that produces cankers in the vital cambium layer of the stem and branches. Chinese and Japanese chestnuts are resistant to the disease.

Chevalier, Maurice (1888–1972), French singer and actor. A star of the French music halls, he first appeared in the United States in the operetta *Dédé* (1921). His manner was breezy and casual, he almost always appeared in a jauntily tipped straw hat to sing songs such as "Louise" and "Mimi." Among his films were the musicals *Gigi* (1958), *Can-Can* (1960), and *Fanny* (1961).

Cheviot Hills, range running SW-NE along English-Scottish border. Highest point is The Cheviot, 2,676ft (816m), in Northumberland. Length: 35mi (56km).

Chevreuse, Marie de Rohan-Montbazon, Duchesse de (1600–79), French political figure. An intimate of Anne of Austria, wife of Louis XIII and regent of her son Louis XIV, she was exiled (1626–28) for intriguing against Cardinal Richelieu. Abroad she conspired with Charles I of England and Charles IV of Lorraine. On the death of Louis XIII, she returned to favor. At first she conspired against Cardinal Mazarin, but finally became his ally.

Chevrotain, or mouse deer, small, even-toed, hoofed mammal from C Africa and SE Asia. Resembling deer, they have small, hornless heads, pointed snouts, and slim legs. Most are brown with white spots and stripes. The males have small upper tusks. Height: 14in (35cm) at shoulder; family Tragulidae; genera *Hyemosuchus* and *Tragulus;* there are 7 species. △548,598.

Chevy Chase, town in W central Maryland, residential suburb of Washington, D.C., developed on and around estate, known as Cheivy Chace, of Joseph Belt (1690–1761). Inc. 1914. Pop. (1970) 16,424.

Cheyenne, capital city of Wyoming, 10mi (16km) N of Colorado border; seat of Laramie co; a leading town in the Old West, frequented by Calamity Jane, Buffalo Bill, and Wild Bill Hickock. Industries: packing plants, oil refineries. Founded 1867 by officers of US Army and Union Pacific Railroad; inc. 1869. Pop. (1970) 40,914.

Cheyenne, large Algonquian-speaking North American Indian tribe whose home was originally in Minnesota but who spread into the Red River region, the Platte, and into Wyoming. In the mid-18th century they allied with the Arapaho; about the same time they split evenly into the Northern and Southern Cheyenne. The Northern Cheyenne now live in Montana, around Tongue River, numbering about 2000; the Southern group made peace with their earlier enemies the Kiowa and settled in Oklahoma, where approximately 3500 Cheyenne-Arapaho now live. *See also* Arapaho.

Cheyenne River, river in Wyoming and South Dakota; rises in E Wyoming, flows to South Dakota and turns NE, entering the Missouri River in central South Dakota. Length: 527mi (848km).

Chiang Ch'ing (1914–), the fourth wife of Chinese Communist leader Mao Tse-tung. A former Shanghai movie actress, she joined Mao in Yenan during the war against Japan. She emerged from relative obscurity in the 1960s to become a high-ranking party official and the leader of the Cultural Revolution faction. After Mao's death (1976), she came under strong political attack.

Chiang Ching-kuo (1909–), prime minister of Nationalist China and elder son of Chiang Kai-shek, whom he succeeded as Taiwan's leader in 1975. Ching-kuo returned to China after spending 12 years in the Soviet Union and rose rapidly in the Nationalist government, becoming prime minister in 1972.

Chiang Kai-shek (1887–1975), key political leader in 20th-century China. He was head of the Nationalist Party (Kuomintang) and government from 1928 until his death. Successor to Sun Yat-sen, Chiang was a Japanese-trained military officer and the first commandant of the Whampoa Military Academy, whose graduates helped form his political power base. He consolidated his power from 1928, fighting rebellious warlords and opposing the Communists. During war with Japan (1937–45) he emerged as one of the "big four" global leaders. He was elected president of China in 1948 under a post-war constitution and retained the position after his government retreated to Taiwan in 1949. He married Soong Mei-ling in 1927 and became a Christian. △1328.

Chiaroscuro, art term for the opposition of light and dark in painting and graphics. Rembrandt and Caravaggio were skilled in its use.

Chiastolite, variety of andalusite, aluminum silicate (Al_2OSiO_4), found in metamorphic rocks. Orthorhombic system elongated prismatic crystals, which in cross-section show a black cross on a gray ground. Hardness 7.5; sp gr 3.1–3.2.

Chiba, city in Japan, on Tokyo Bay; capital of Chiba prefecture; important agricultural region; site of 8th-century Buddist temple, university (1949). Industries: textiles, paper. Pop. 482,133.

Chibcha, or Muisca, a late prehistoric culture in South America occupying the departments of Cundinamarca and Boyacá in Colombia; Bogotá and Tunja were the major centers. Between 1000–1541, when the Spaniards conquered the region, these people developed remarkable city-states; and with a total population of about 750,000 inhabitants, were one of the few to equal the Inca in political sophistication. Artistically, however, they produced inferior pottery, and their weaving and goldsmithing were inferior to that of their neighbors. The legend of El Dorado comes from the Chibcha custom of the king annually diving into Lake Guatavita covered with gold dust, which washed off in a sacrifical ceremony. In modern times, Chibcha refers to a contemporary American Indian language family whose speakers inhabit southern Panama and northern Colombia.

Chicago, city in NE Illinois, on SW shore of Lake Michigan; seat of Cook co and 2nd-largest US city, major industrial, commercial, cultural, and shipping center of the Midwest. A trading post under Jean Baptiste Point du Sable and John Kinzie in the late 1700s, it was site of Fort Dearborn military post 1803; with the construction of the Erie Canal and railroads, Chicago attracted more settlers. The River and Harbors Convention of 1847 attracted businessmen from outside the city; such as Cyrus McCormick, a manufacturer of farm equipment; settlers were put to work in newly established retail houses such as Marshall Field and Co., in the stockyards of Gurdon S. Hubbard's meat packing industry, and food processing plants. The city was the scene of the Chicago Fire (Oct. 8–10, 1871), the Haymarket Riot (labor uprising, 1886), and the Pullman Strike (1894). Chicago's Columbia Exposition (1893) introduced such contemporary ideas as electric transit systems and the "skyscrapers" of architects Louis H. Sullivan and Frank Lloyd Wright. Chicago became a noted cultural center in the late 19th and early 20th centuries, with the establishment of the Chicago Symphony Orchestra, a city opera company, and literary magazines. Chicago contains the largest railroad terminal in the world, and O'Hare International Airport, busiest US commercial airport; home of several professional sports teams: Chicago Cubs and Chicago White Sox (baseball), Chicago Bears (football), Chicago Black Hawks (hockey), and the Chicago Bulls (basketball); site of McCormick Place, convention center, Merchandise Mart, Museum of Science and Industry, Art Institute of Chicago, the Newberry Library, and the Library of International Relations; colleges include the University of Chicago (1890), Northwestern University (1851), University of Illinois (1946), Loyola University (1869), Chicago State University. Industries: steel, chemicals, machinery, plastics, furniture, metalworking, food processing. Inc. 1837. Pop. (1970) 3,369,359.

Chicago, University of, university in Chicago. It was founded through gifts of John D. Rockefeller. Under its first president, William R. Harper (1891–1906), the university attained academic prominence. Major areas of study include biological sciences, education, library science, theology, and humanities.

Chicago Heights, city in NE Illinois, S of Chicago; site of Prairie State College. Industries: steel, automobile bodies, castings, railroad cars. Settled 1830; inc. 1901. Pop. (1970) 40,900.

Chicago River, short river in Chicago, Illinois, formed in downtown area by confluence of North Branch and South Branch. Since 1930 it flows via Chicago Sanitary and Ship Canal to Des Plaines River; prior to 1930 it flowed E from its point of convergence to Lake Michigan; the change in course forced Chicago to build sewage treatment plants. Length: (N Branch) 24mi (39km); S Branch) 10mi (16km).

Chicago School of Architecture, late 19th-century US development of commercial building design that used the principle of metal framing to achieve great height in buildings. The all-steel skeleton, first employed here, became the standard method of skyscraper construction. Dankmar Adler, Louis Sullivan, Daniel Burnham, John Root, William Holabird, and Martin Roche were the main practitioners.

Chicanos, term used by Mexican-Americans to describe themselves. The term stems from the Aztec word "Meshicano." The term became popular in the late 1960s as a result of Cesar Chavez's efforts to organize migrant Mexican farm workers and also as a result of a 1967 land dispute that sought to have much of the southwestern United States returned to its original Mexican owners.

Chichén Itzá, chief city and shrine of the combined Toltec and Maya peoples in Yucatán, Mexico, between AD 11th and 13th centuries. Remains include temple-pyramids, an astronomical observatory, and a sacrificial well. After 1200 Chichén Itzá lost its preeminence to nearby Mayapan. Period of occupation *c.*600–1450.

Chichester, cathedral city in S England, 13mi (21km) NE of Portsmouth; market town for agriculture and livestock; many Roman architectural remains; site of Norman cathedral (begun 1090). Pop. 20,547.

Ch'i-ch'i-ha-erh (Qiqihaer, or Tsitsihar), city and port in China, on Nen River near Great Khingan Mts. Industries: locomotives, machine tools, paper products, cement. Founded 1691. Pop. 1,500,000.

Chichimec, name applied to the scattered, heterogeneous groups of Indians living to the north and west of the Toltec and Aztec empires of central Mexico. Hunters and warriors, they successfully resisted Aztec and Spanish domination.

Chickadee, any of several North American titmice whose calls resemble a whistled "chick-a-dee." Chickadees are small and plump, with short, rounded wings, stubby bills, dark caps and bibs, and light cheeks. The typical black-capped chickadee *(Parus atricapillus)* of E North America is an active, easily tamed bird that feeds on seeds and insects. It grows to about 5in (13cm). Its nests—often in tree stumps—hold 5 to 9 brown-speckled white eggs that hatch in 12 days. Family Paridae; genus *Parus. See also* Titmouse.

Chickahominy, river in W Virginia; rises NW of Richmond; flows SE to its mouth on lower James River; scene of intense fighting in Civil War. Length: approx. 0mi (145km).

Chickamauga, Battle of (Sept. 19–20, 1863), Civil War battle in Georgia near Chattanooga, Tenn. Confederate Gen. Braxton Bragg defeated Union Gen. William S. Rosecrans. Union Gen. George H. Thomas won the name "Rock of Chickamauga" for his stand there.

Chickamauga and Chattanooga National Military Park, historical site in NW Georgia and SE Tennessee, preserves the campaign areas of the Battle of Chickamauga (1863). Authorized 1890. Area: sq mi (8sq km) in Tennessee; 10sq mi (26sq km) in Georgia.

Chickasaw, small, fiercely independent and warlike North American Indian tribe closely related to the Muskhogean-speaking Choctaw, occupying N Mississippi-Tennessee lands from Memphis into neighboring Alabama. They were far more important in history than their numbers indicate; allied with the English, they were hostile to the French and Spanish but quite friendly with Americans. Being slaveholders, during the Civil War they joined the Confederacy with their Choctaw brothers, for which they were punished severely by the loss of their lands. About 6000 now live in Oklahoma.

Chicken, most important domesticated bird in the world. It is the major source of eggs and an important meat source, supporting a specialized and widespread food industry. Chickens are also raised for exhibitions and scientific use. These light-skeletoned birds have short weak wings, strong legs, chin wattles, and a head comb. Males are known as cocks; females as hens; and castrated males as capons. Various breeds have been developed for particular use. Some, such as Rhode Island, Wyandotte, and Plymouth Rock, are raised for meat and eggs. Others, such as White Plymouth Rock, Cornish, and Rock Cornish, mainly supply meat. The White Leghorn is an excellent egg producer. Miniature bantams, the long-tailed Japanese Yokohama, and others are raised for ornament. Species *Gallus domesticus.*

Chicken Pox, or varicella, contagious virus-caused disease usually of children. Early symptoms are mild headache, low fever, general malaise, followed within a day by small blisters surrounded by redness usually visible first on the torso. Recovery is rapid with little or no scarring. Antihistamine is often prescribed to relieve itching. △724.

Chick-pea, also dwarf pea, garbanzo, chich, gram; bushy annual cultivated from antiquity in S Europe and Asia for its pealike seeds, it is now also grown in Africa and the Americas. Seeds are eaten boiled or roasted; sometimes ground as a coffee substitute. Family Leguminosae; species *Cicer arietinum.* △330.

Chickweed, common name for a spreading annual, native to Europe and naturalized throughout temperate regions. Its drooping stems grow to about 12in (30cm). Having opposite oblong leaves about 2.5in (6cm) long, the smaller white flowers are about 0.5in (1.3cm) wide. Chickweed is a garden weed in North America. Family Caryophyllaceae; species *Stellaria media.*

Chicle, a natural gum, available in reddish-brown pieces and consisting of the coagulated milky juice of the sapodilla *(Achras zapota),* a fruit tree of tropical America. First tried as a substitute for rubber, chicle became the chief ingredient of chewing gum by the end of the 19th century. In the 1940s it began to be replaced by synthetics and now has little commercial value.

Chicopee, city in SW Massachusetts, at the confluence of the Chicopee and Connecticut rivers. Industries: rubber products, sporting goods, firearms, and machinery. Settled 1641; inc. 1890. Pop. (1970) 66,-76.

Chicory, perennial weedy plant. Its leaves are used cooked or as salad greens and the fleshy roots are ground for mixing with or substituting for coffee. Chicory has bright blue, daisylike flowers. When grown only for its leaves, plant tops are cut off, forcing it to produce a leafy head that is sometimes called French endive. Height: 6ft (1.8m). Family Compositae; species *Chichorium intybus.*

Chicoutimi, town in SE Quebec, Canada, on Saguenay River, 120mi (193km) N of Quebec City; site of branch of University of Quebec (1969). Industries: farming, aluminum, paper, lumber. Founded 1676 as Jesuit mission; inc. 1676. Pop. 32,990.

Chiem (Chiemsee) Lake, largest lake in West Germany, 40mi (64km) ESE of Munich; outlet is Alz River. Contains three islands; the largest is site of a palace imitating Versailles, built in late 19th century by Louis II of Bavaria. Area: 31sq mi (80sq km).

Ch'ien Lung (1711–99), fourth Manchu emperor of China (1736–96). The Ch'ien Lung emperor helped China to the apex of its power under the Manchus, taking Tibet (1751) and other regions. He also encouraged literature and art, and brought China into closer contact with Europe and into a period of unmatched prosperity during which the population more than doubled. △1206.

Chigger, also called harvest mite, or red bug, tiny, red larva of some kinds of mites found worldwide. Adults lay eggs on plants and hatched larvae find a host animal or human, in whom their bites cause a severe rash and itching. Length: 0.01in (.25mm). Order Acarina; family Trombiculidae. *See also* Mite.

Chihuahua, largest state in Mexico, on North-Mexican Plateau; climate and terrain vary from cool mountains (W), mild (central), to arid desert (E); city of Chihuahua, the capital of the state, is site of beautiful colonial cathedral and is famous breeding center for miniature Mexican dogs named after city. Industries: zinc, lead, copper, gold mining, forestry, livestock raising, tourism, beans, cotton, coats, potatoes, fruit. Founded (state) 1560 as Spanish settlement; (city) 1700. Area: (state) 95,400sq mi (247,086sq km). Pop. (state) 1,730,012; (city) 363,850.

Chihuahua, tiny terrierlike dog (toy group) descended from the 9th-century Techichi, dog of the Central American Toltec Indians. It has an appledome skull; short, pointed nose; large, wide-set eyes; and large, erect ears. The level-backed body is set on straight legs with small feet. The long, sickle-shaped tail is held in a loop over the back. There are two types of coat: the smooth is soft, close, and glossy with a ruff on the neck; the long is flat or slightly curly, feathered on the feet and legs, with a large ruff around the neck and plumed tail. Coat may be any color. Average size: 5in (12.5cm) high at shoulder; to 6lb (2.5kg). *See also* Toy Dog.

Chikamatsu Monzaemon (1653–1725), Japanese dramatist, b. as Sugimori Nobumori. Writing mainly for the puppet theater, Chikamatsu wrote over 160 plays and is perhaps the greatest Japanese dramatist. His writings were mostly historical romances and domestic tragedies, including *The Love Suicides at Amijima* (1703) and *The Battles of Coxinga* (1715), which are still performed today.

Child, (Sir) John (died 1690), English colonial official. The first person to control all of the East India Company's Indian factories (1686–90), his use of military power to gain territory for the company and his unscrupulous behavior led to rebellion and war. He was deputy-governor of Bombay (1679–81) and president of Surat (1682–90). Child engaged in war with the Mogul emperor of Delhi and when Child's province, Surat, was seized, his removal was one of the peace conditions.

Child, Lydia Maria (1802–80), US author and reformer, b. Medford, Mass. During 1826–34 she edited *Juvenile Miscellany,* the first US children's periodical. An ardent abolitionist, she wrote *Appeal in Favor of That Class of Americans Called Africans* (1833) and edited the *National Anti-Slavery Standard* (1841–49). She was also an advocate of woman suffrage.

Childbirth. △704.

Child Development, study of the changes that occur in children from conception to adolescence. First called child psychology, the field first focused on such topics as weaning, feeding schedules, and toilet training. The scope is now broader, including all factors—hereditary and environmental, physical and emotional—that interact as children grow up. *See also* Developmental Psychology. △778–789.

Childe, V(ere) Gordon (1892–1957), Australian prehistorian. His study of the cultures of the Western world in the second and third millennia BC led to *The Danube in Prehistory* (1929). Other influential works include *Man Makes Himself* (1937) and *The Dawn of European Civilization* (1925). △884.

Childebert I (died 558), Frankish king (511–58). On the death of his father, Clovis I, he received a portion of the kingdom, along with his three brothers. His

Chess

Maurice Chevalier

President and Madame Chiang Kai-shek

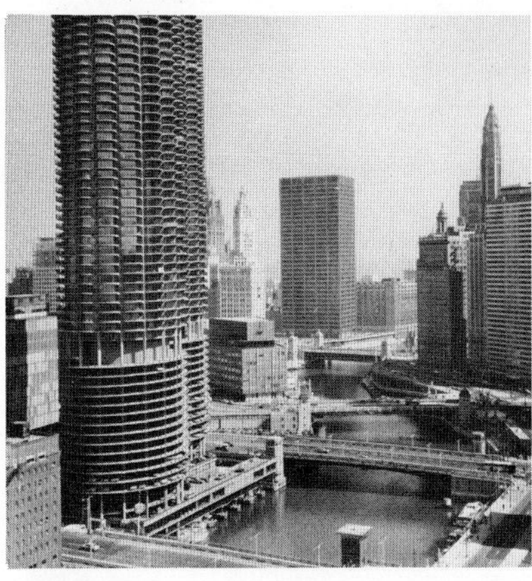
Chicago, Illinois

capital was Paris. On the death of his brother, Clodomir (524), he and his brother Clotair I portioned his land. In 534, Childebert and Clotair conquered Burgundy and Provence. He attacked but failed to capture Spain (542).

Childebert III (died 711), Frankish king (696–711). He was one of the last rulers of Merovingian dynasty. Throughout his reign real power was held by the mayors of the palace, the Carolingians.

Childe Harold's Pilgrimage (1812–18), autobiographical, romantic poem by Lord Byron, divided into 4 cantos, in Spenserian stanzas. The poem tells of a young man's disillusionment with his easy life and his subsequent wanderings through Europe.

Childeric I (436–81), king of the Salian Franks (458–81). With Roman aid he defeated the Visigoths at Orléans (463). He later defeated the Saxons and the Alemanni. He was succeeded by his son, Clovis I. In 1653 his tomb was found at his capital near Tournai, Belgium.

Childeric II (653?–673), king of Austrasia (660–673). He was the last Merovingian king to attempt to rule independently of the Carolingian mayors of the palace. He seized Neustria and Burgundy from the mayors but was assassinated in the same year.

Childeric III Frankish king (*r.* 741–751), last of Merovingians. Rule was entirely subject to control of the mayors of the palace, the Carolingians. Pepin the Short deposed Childeric (751).

Child Labor, employment of children under a specified age. Once common in the United States, it has been forbidden by federal law since the 1938 Fair Labor Standards Act. Earlier, several states had tried to prevent child labor but were not permitted to do so by the Supreme Court. On other occasions the Court declared laws passed by the Congress unconstitutional. The 1938 law makes it legal for chidlern to begin work at age 16 in most industries and businesses engaged in interstate commerce. In particularly dangerous work situations, the minimum employment age is 18 years. Some exceptions to the law exist. The states generally set a minimum age of 14 to 18 years. △1220, 1236.

Child Marriage, marriage in which one or both participants are children. Since sexual and romantic attachments are obviously low in such a case, the marriage is usually arranged so as to provide an economic and social link between two families or groups. *See also* Marriage.

Child Psychiatry, study and treatment of childhood behavioral disorders, including childhood schizophrenia, early infantile autism, adjustment reactions of childhood, mental retardation, and learning disabilities.

Child Psychology. *See* Child Development; Developmental Psychology.

Children of Jesus. △1388.

Children's Crusade (1212), movement to regain the Holy Land from the Muslims. The crusade was preached by two 12-year-old boys, Stephen of France and Nicholas of Germany. Encouraged by beliefs in angelic guidance and miracles, thousands of boys and girls, followed by bands of adult vagabonds, headed toward Marseilles, intending to cross the Mediterranean to Palestine. Although Pope Innocent III tried to end the crusade, some of the German children actually reached the Holy Land, where they disappeared. The French children were offered free transportation to Jerusalem by Hugh the Iron and William of Posquères, who took them instead to Africa and sold them as slaves.

Children's Literature, in English-speaking countries, emerged as a distinct form in the 18th century. John Newbery, an English author, was the first serious publisher of children's books. He published a collection of Mother Goose rhymes in 1765. (A translation of Charles Perrault's *Tales of Mother Goose* had appeared in 1729). Newbery also published *A Pretty Little Pocket Book* (1744) and *Little Goody Two Shoes* (1765). In the 19th century, romanticism encouraged the creation of works for children, including the folk tales of the brothers Grimm and the fairy stories of Hans Christian Andersen. With Edmund Evans's improvements in color printing methods (1865), picture books flourished, as did the great illustrators, Kate Greenaway, Randolph Caldecott, Howard Pyle, and Arthur Rackham. Many 19th-century works of fantasy and adventure—Robert Louis Stevenson's *Treasure Island* (1880), Lewis Carroll's *Alice's Adventures in Wonderland* (1865), and *Through the Looking Glass* (1872), Louisa May Alcott's *Little Women* (1868), and Mark Twain's *Adventures of Huckleberry Finn* (1885)—are still popular with children and adults. In the 20th century the output of children's literature has been huge. In the United States, the Newbery Medal is awarded for outstanding children's books; the Caldecott Medal, for the best picture book. The Carnegie and Greenaway Medals are awarded in Great Britain.

Chile, Republic of, nation in SW South America. Sometimes considered the most European of Latin American countries, it has suffered relatively few political upheavals and is known for encouraging the arts.

Land and Economy. Long (about 2,500mi; 4,025km) and narrow (average width, about 110mi; 177km), Chile occupies a plain between the Pacific Ocean and the Andes, where some peaks reach above 20,000ft (6,100m). The Atacama Desert, containing nitrate and copper deposits, occupies about 70,000sq mi (181,300sq km) of the N. Chile's central zone provides rich soils, but they must be irrigated to produce wheat, alfalfa, corn, beans, peas, and fruits. S Chile is wet and cold. Broken into a maze of islands and peninsulas, it produces petroleum and lumber, and offers good sheep-raising country.

People. Mostly mestizos and European—Spaniards, Britains, Germans—the people speak Spanish and are about 90% literate. The Mapuche (Araucanian) Indians make up less than 2% of the population and live mainly in the S. Most people belong to the Roman Catholic church, although many attend irregularly. About 65% live in urban communities.

Government. According to its constitution, Chile should have a president and a two-house legislature elected by citizens 21 and over who can read and write. But in 1973, the military overthrew the leftist government that had won control in 1970, disbanded the legislature, and ordered all political parties to become inactive.

History. In the mid-1500s, Pedro de Valdivia founded settlements in Chile and encouraged colonists to come there. José de San Martín and Bernardo O'Higgins defeated the Spanish in Chile in 1818 and guaranteed the country independence. By winning a victory over Bolivia and Peru in 1883, Chile gained the Atacama Desert. In 1938 the people elected a left-of-center president, Pedro Aguirre Cerda, and from then on gradually moved further left. Salvador Allende was elected president in 1970 and was Latin America's first freely elected Marxist chief of state. His nationalization of industries, conservative position, and a disintegrating economy all contributed to the military coup in 1973 that resulted in his death.

PROFILE

Official name: Republic of Chile
Area: 292,250sq mi (756,928sq km)
Population: 9,910,000
Density: 37per sq mi (18per sq km)
Chief cities: Santiago, the capital; Valparaiso
Government: Head of state, Gen. Augusto Pinochet Ugarte, president (took power Sept. 1973)
Monetary unit: Peso (replacing the escudo in 1975)
Gross national product: $7,940,000,000
Per capita income: $800
Industries (major products): iron and steel, petroleum products, foodstuffs
Agriculture (major products): wheat, sugar beets, potatoes, corn, rice, fruits
Minerals (major): copper, nitrates, iron ore, petroleum, cobalt, coal, zinc
Trading partners (major): United States, European Common Market, Argentina

Chili, hot red pepper raised commercially in Mexico and SW United States. Also called cayenne pepper, it is an annual with ovate leaves and white or greenish-white flowers that produce seedpods. When dried, this pod is ground into a condiment. Height: 1–6ft (30–82cm). Family Solanaceae; species *Capsicum frutescens.*

Chillicothe, city in S Ohio, 45mi (72km) S of Columbus; seat of Ross co.; former capital of old Northwest Territory (1800). Industries: shoes, paper. Inc. 1802. Pop. (1970) 24,842.

Chilperic I (539–84), Frankish king of the Merovingian dynasty (561–84). Ruthless in tactic and desire, he was embroiled in fraternal wars from his father's death (561) to his assassination (584).

Chilperic II (*c.* 675–721), king of Neustria (715–20) and Austrasia (719–20). As a Merovingian, he first legitimized the Neustrian power of Ragenfrid, then the Frankish kingdom of Charles Martel.

Chiltern Hills, range of chalk hills in S central E gland, extending NE from Goring Gap in the Tham Valley, through Oxfordshire, Buckinghamshire, ar Bedfordshire, to the East Anglian heights; former densely wooded, yielding beech for furniture. Highe point is Coombe Hill, 852ft (260m). Length: 55r (89km).

Chimera. △832.

Chimaera, or **ratfish,** also rabbit fish, elephant fis ghost shark, cartilaginous, deep water fish with sho nose, long poison spine at dorsal fin, and ratlike ta Its liver oil is used in precision equipment. Length: 3 (91.4cm); weight: 35lb (16kg). Family Chimaerida species, about 28 including Pacific *Hydrolagus colle See also* Chondrichthyes. △510.

Chimbote, port city on coast of W central Peru, a prox. 250mi (403km) NNW of Lima; suffered sever damage in 1970 earthquake. Industries: steel, fishin fish meal. Pop. 97,100.

Chimkent (Čimkent), city in S Kazakh SSR (Centra Asian) USSR, in W foothills of Tien Shan Mts; capita of Chimkent oblast; industrial center on Turkistar Siberian railway; site of teachers' college and mu seum; founded 12th century as caravan center on Sil Road to China; Russia gained control 1864. Indus tries: fruit canning, lead smelting, natural gas, chem cal and lead works. Pop. 247,000.

Chimney Swift, small, sooty brown bird with lon tapering wings that breeds in E and C North America It attaches its nest with gluey saliva to an inside vert cal chimney wall. It feeds on insects. The female lay white glossy eggs (4–5). They migrate with thei young to Central and South America for the winte Length: 6–12in. (15–30cm). Species *Chaetur pelagica.*

Chimpanzee, gregarious, intelligent great ape c tropical Africa. Chimpanzees are mostly black an powerfully built. A smaller chimpanzee of the Congc region is sometimes classified as separate species Chimpanzees often nest in trees but spend most wak ing time on ground searching for fruits and nuts. They are quite communicative and, in captivity, have learned a limited human vocabulary. Height: 4.5f (1.3m); weight: 150lb (68kg). Species *Pan tro glodytes,* Congo *Pan paniscus. See also* Primates. △ 558.

Chimu, Indian civilization of northern coastal Peru (*c.* AD 1000–1470). △1118, 1120.

China, History of, dates back more than 3,000 years. Skeletal fragments and pottery shards found in the 1923 excavations of limestone hills SW of Peking pointed to the existence of human life in the area 500,000 years ago; 20,000 years ago evidence of modern man appeared. With marked ethnic and regional differences, an authentic, persistent culture appeared to develop from within the area in a pattern of exalted culture, invasion by barbarians leading to a period of decay and decline, and another high cultural plane once the invaders were expelled. The first recorded dynasty was the Shang (*c.* 1600–1030 BC) with royal houses, carvings on stone, and script. Evidence of merchants first appeared in the Chou dynasty (1030–221 BC). Iron was used, astronomy analyzed, music developed, and Confucius lived. In the Ch'in dynasty (221–207 BC) the first centralized government was organized by an emperor, who burned antagonistic books, and the Great Wall was built. The peaceful Han dynasty (202 BC–AD 221) rivaled Rome in wealth, power, and prestige. Foreign trade flourished; Buddhism emerged; and astronomy and literature were studied. Warfare, invasions, and Taoism appeared from 220–581, followed by a period of construction within the country in the Sui period (581–618). The first historical encyclopedia, scientific studies, and the only female emperor in Chinese history came in the T'ang dynasty (618–906). Printing emerged in the politically chaotic years of 907–960, and the Sung dynasty (960–1279) developed civil service examinations, paper currency, modern cities, trading ships, gunpowder, political parties, and the magnetic needle. Kublai Khan, founder of the Yuan dynasty (1264–1368), continued intellectual advances and building. Marco Polo wrote of his reign. A decline at the close of the Yuan period continued into the Ming dynasty (1368–1644); despots suppressed opposition. Paintings, porcelains, and rugs were produced, and Roman Catholic missionaries introduced Western culture. Conquest of China by Manchu peoples brought the Chi'ing (Manchu) dynasty (1644–1911), a period of European imperialist expansion to seek raw materials and markets for products and to obtain opium. The United States promoted the Open

Door Policy, giving all nations equal access to China's trade. In the Boxer Uprising (1900) anti-Western Chinese attempted unsuccessfully to oust all foreigners. Reforms to save China by overthrowing the Manchus came too late. In 1911 the emperor abdicated. A republic was established with Sun Yat-sen its first president but in 1912 Sun resigned in favor of Yuan Shih-K'ai, whose repressive policies outlawed Sun's radical Kuomintang party. In 1921 Sun set up a rival government in Canton with aid from the newly formed Chinese Communist party and the USSR. Chiang Kai-shek led the Kuomintang army in victory, but then reversed Sun's policy of cooperation with the Communists and executed many leaders. In 1928, Chiang organized a Nationalist government in Nanking and received foreign recognition. The rival Communist government was set up in the early 1930s in Kiangsi; however, Chiang's opposition forced them on a Long March (1934) to Shensi prov. where they reorganized and spread their philosophy among the peasants. Mao Tse-tung emerged as their leader. At the end of World War II, full scale war broke out between the hostile factions as they fought for territory evacuated by the Japanese. Inflation, official corruption, and famine weakened the Nationalists and support shifted to the Communists. Peking fell to them in January 1949. Other major cities followed, and on Oct. 1, 1949, the Communists proclaimed a central people's government. The Nationalist government moved to Taiwan. *See also* China, People's Republic of; China, Republic of. △968, 1038–44, 1206, 1270, 1348.

China (Zhongguo), People's Republic of, independent nation in Asia, also known as Communist China. With 22 provinces and 5 autonomous regions, China contains 20% of the world's population. It has passed through domestic and foreign wars to the present Communist government.

Land and Economy. There are fertile plains and deltas in the E watered by three great rivers (Yangtze, Yellow, and Si). Mountains separate it from Manchuria and Mongolia on the N; the Himalayas are to the S. China is the third-largest country in the world. It is the world's largest producer of rice and the third-largest coal producer. Eighty percent of its trade is with free-world countries, with major imports of machinery, fertilizer, and grains and exports of raw materials, agricultural products, and textiles.

People. The largest ethnic group is Han Chinese (94%), and the national language is the Peking dialect of Mandarin Chinese. Religion has been discouraged by the state. In pre-Communist China there were Buddhists, Confucianists, Taoists, Muslims, and Roman Catholics. Two major goals have been control of population growth and the expansion of education.

Government. The Constitution of the People's Republic (1954) theoretically provides that power be shared by the National People's Congress, its standing committee, and the party chairman. In fact, government reins are held by the Communist party structure.

History. In the 1920s, when China was an unstable republic, Chiang Kai-shek organized the country under a coalition of Nationalists, Soviet advisors, and the Communists, an association lasting until 1927 when Chiang drove the Communists out. This precipitated the 1934–35 Long March to Shensi prov. where the Communists reorganized, spread their philosophy, and in 1949 defeated Chiang, who fled to Taiwan. On Oct. 1, 1949, the People's Republic of China was born under the leadership of Chairman Mao Tse-tung.

Under Chairman Mao and Premier Chou En-lai, China long remained isolated from world economic and diplomatic affairs, although it took possession of Tibet (1950) and fought in the Korean War. The Cultural Revolution of the late 1960s sought to revitalize revolutionary policies and was indicative of internal power struggles. China's admission to the United Nations in place of Taiwan (1971) showed China's increased importance in world affairs. The deaths of Mao and Chou, in 1976, led to internal disputes, with moderates Hua Kuo-feng and Teng Hsiao-ping emerging as the new leaders and discrediting left-wing elements led by Mao's widow, Chiang Ch'ing. △1348, 1352.

PROFILE

Official name: People's Republic of China
Area: 3,691,502sq mi (9,560,990sq km)
Population: 830,000,000
Density: 223per sq mi (89per sq km)
Chief cities: Peking (capital); Shanghai; Tientsin; Wuhan; Canton; Chunking; Shenyang
Government: One-party Communist people's republic
Religion: Buddhism, Confucianism, Taoism, Roman Catholics. The state discourages organized religion.
Languages: Mandarin Chinese (national)
Monetary unit: Yuan
Gross national product: $172,000,000,000
Industries: electronics, pharmaceuticals, iron, steel, textiles, fertilizer, machinery, oil products
Agriculture: rice, wheat, sugar, cotton, sorghum, corn, tobacco, soybeans, tea, fish, hemp, cattle, jute
Minerals: coal, iron ore, tin, antimony, tungsten, molybdenum, salt, oil
Trading partners: Japan, Federal Republic of Germany, Hong Kong, United Kingdom, Singapore

China, Republic of (Taiwan), independent nation, also known as Nationalist China, primarily on the island of Taiwan, 90mi (145km) off SE coast of mainland China. The government was established by Gen. Chaing Kai-shek's Kuomintang government in 1948 after Communists captured the mainland.

Land and Economy. Taiwan, 240mi (386km) long, also includes the Pescadores Island, Quemoy, and Matsu. Mountains cover the E; the W is fertile and cultivated. The climate is semi-tropical, and the country is in the typhoon and earthquake belt. Light manufacturing has replaced agriculture as the dominant factor in the economy.

People. The Taiwanese are descended from migrating mainlanders, aboriginal Philippine tribes, and over 2,000,000 who came from mainland China since 1949. Mandarin is taught in schools, and Buddhism-Taoism is the principal religion. Literacy is 84%.

Government. The 1947 constitution provided for elected National Assembly. After Chiang Kai-shek's death in 1975 power passed to his son, Chiang Ching-kuo.

History. Migrations came from the mainland in the 17th century, the Dutch (1624–61), several Chinese warring dynasties, and in 1895 the Japanese. The republic has administered the island since the Japanese surrendered at the end of WWII. Taiwan's international position declined in the 1970s with the loss of its UN seat to mainland China in 1971 and the increasing diplomatic recognition of the Communist regime. However, the economy continued strong, and hopes of decreased tension with the mainland grew after Chiang Kai-shek's death, in 1975.

PROFILE

Official name: Republic of China
Area: 13,562sq mi (35,126sq km)
Population: 16,000,000
Density: 1,173per sq mi (452per sq km)
Chief city: Taipei (capital)
Government: Republic
Religion: Buddhism, Taoism
Language: Mandarin (taught in schools), Amoy and Hakka dialects
Monetary unit: Taiwan dollar
Gross national product: $9,400,000,000
Per capita income: $663
Industries: textiles, clothing, electrical appliances and equipment, processed foods, chemicals, machinery, metal products
Agriculture: rice, tea, sugar, sweet potatoes, jute, camphor, bananas, fish
Minerals: gold, silver, copper, coal
Trading partners: United States, South Korea, Canada, Latin America, Australia, European Common Market

China Clay, or kaolin, a fine white clay from weathered aluminous minerals that contain kaolinite as principal constituent. It remains white after firing and is used chiefly in manufacturing fine ceramics.

Chinaware, any ceramic ware with a china clay (kaolin) base, typically a fine thin ware fired at higher temperatures than earthenware, therefore nonporous and nonplastic.

Chinch Bug, black insect, 0.17 to 0.2in (4.25–5mm) long, with white wings and red legs; a serious pest of grass, corn, wheat, and other grain in the eastern and central United States. Family Lygaeidae; species *Blissus leucopterus*. *See also* Hemiptera.

Chinchilla, small, soft-furred rodents native to South America that were hunted almost to extinction and are now bred in captivity for their fur, the most expensive of all animal skins. The fur is long and silky, silver to brown or blue gray with darker outer hairs, dense, and soft to the touch. Length: 9–15in (23–38cm); weight: 1–2lb (500–1000g). Family Chinchillidae.

Ch'in Dynasty (221–207 BC), the totalitarian state that unified all of China into a centralized area of control. It is noted for the building of the Great Wall and is infamous for the burning of books (213 BC) and persecution of scholars. It made legalist philosophy the basis for governmental control over the population. The English name for China stems from this time. *See also* Tsin Dynasty. △1038.

Chinese, language spoken by about 95% of the pop-

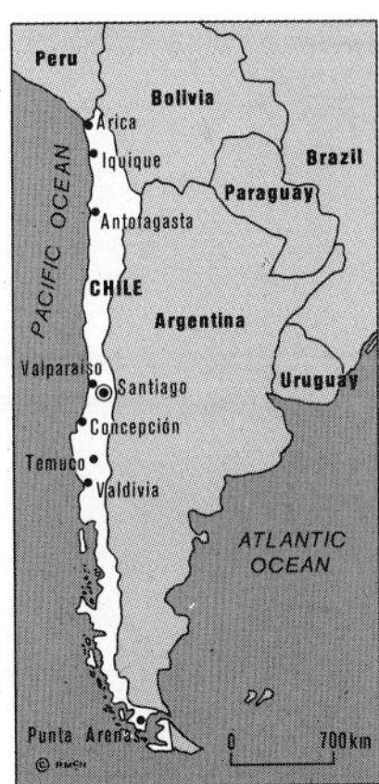
Peru
Bolivia
Arica
Iquique
Brazil
Paraguay
PACIFIC OCEAN
Antofagasta
CHILE
Argentina
Valparaiso
Santiago
Uruguay
Concepción
Temuco
Valdivia
ATLANTIC OCEAN
Punta Arenas
0
700km
Chile

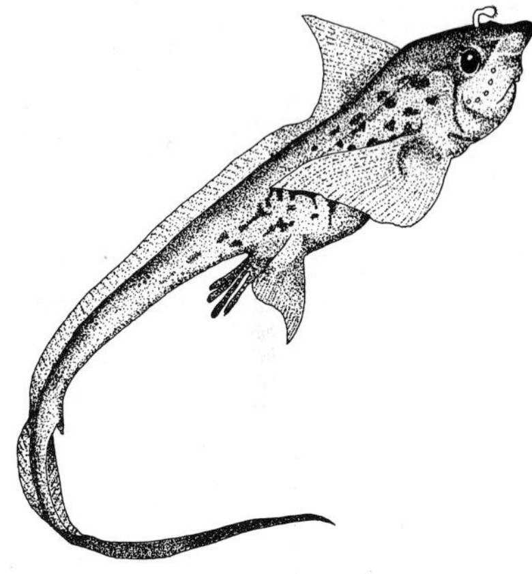
Chimaera

U.S.S.R.
Harbin (Haerbin)
Mongolia
Changchun
Shenyang (Mukden)
Peking (Beijing)
Korea
Urumchi (Wulumuqi)
Kashgar (Kashi)
Huhehot (Huhehaote)
Tientsin (Tianjin)
Taiyuan
Tsingtao (Qingdao)
Lanchou (Lanzhou)
Sian (Xi'an)
Nanking (Nanjing)
Japan
CHINA
Shanghai
Wuhan
Lhasa (Lasa)
Nepal
Chengtu (Chengdu)
Chungking (Chongqing)
Hangchou (Hangzhou)
India
Bhutan
Kunming
Canton (Guangzhou)
Taiwan
Bangladesh
Burma
PHILIPPINE SEA
Laos
Haikou
North Vietnam
BAY OF BENGAL
Thailand
Philippines
0
1000 km
Camb.
South Vietnam
People's Republic of China

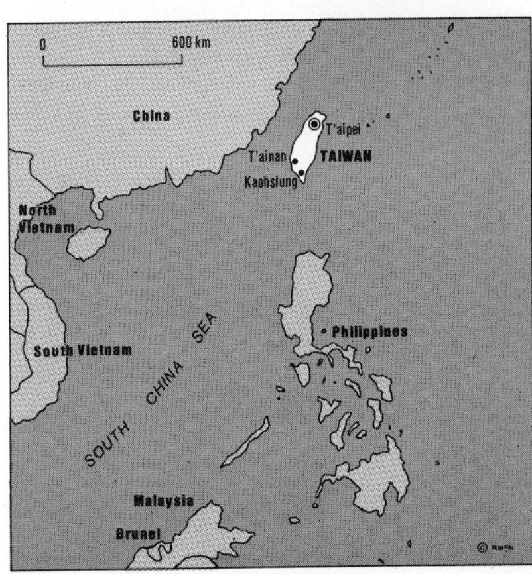
0
600 km
China
T'aipei
T'ainan
TAIWAN
Kaohsiung
North Vietnam
SOUTH CHINA SEA
Philippines
South Vietnam
Malaysia
Brunei
Republic of China (Taiwan)

ulation of China and by many millions more in Taiwan, Hong Kong, Southeast Asia, and other countries. There are six major dialects, which are not mutually intelligible, of which the most important is Mandarin, spoken by about two-thirds of the population. Chinese is written in ideographs, which number in the thousands and date back several thousand years. It has twice as many speakers as any other language in the world.

Chinese Architecture, architectural style that as early as the neolithic period used columns, not walls, to support roofs, faced houses south, and used bright colors. The characteristic Chinese roof with wide overhang and upturned eaves was probably developed in the Chou period (1027–*c.* 256BC). The ground plan of temples and palaces—a walled complex with central axis—was established in the Han dynasty (202 BC–AD 220). In the same period, the practice of building residential units around a central courtyard containing an elaborately planned garden became standard. The pagoda derives from Buddhist influences, notably the Indian stupa, and dates from the 6th century. △1040, 1044, 1208.

Chinese Art. △1044.

Chinese Exclusion, series of laws to limit Chinese immigration into the United States. Skilled and unskilled Chinese laborers were barred from entering the United States by the Chinese Exclusion Act of 1882. Subsequent laws continued this policy, which was supported by labor leaders on racist and economic grounds. In 1943 Congress established an annual quota of 105 for immigration from China. The national origins quota system ended in the 1960s.

Chinese Lantern Plant, or winter cherry, perennial plant native to Japan and widely cultivated in gardens. The creeping stems bear large, ovate, long-stalked leaves and small white flowers that produce a red berry surrounded by a papery, lanternlike red calyx. Height: to 2ft (61cm). Family Solanaceae; species *Physalis.*

Chinese Literature. The oldest Chinese writing of any kind is found in the Shang dynasty (*c.* 1600–*c.* 1030 BC), but the oldest literature comes from the Chou dynasty (*c.* 1030–221 BC). This period produced the canonical writings of Confucianism: the Five Classics, including the first poetry anthology *Shih ching* (Classic of Odes); and the Four Books, containing doctrinal writings, such as *The Book of Mencius.* Traditionally attributed to Confucius (*c.* 551–479 BC), the *Shih ching* was probably in existence before his time. Also in this era Lao-tzu supposedly founded Taoism, a religious-magical reaction to the moral-political emphasis of Confucianism. During the Han dynasty (206 BC–AD 220), *fu* flourished; they were elaborate prose poems praising the dynasty. The golden age of Chinese literature arrived in the T'ang dynasty (618–907). Li Po, Wang Wei, and Tu Fu were the outstanding poets. In the Sung dynasty (960–1279) the novel, often historical, and the drama, stressing conflicts such as filial versus national loyalty, came into being. But the lyric poem has been the dominant form in Chinese literature. It is normally philosophical but with a quietness of tone and an emphasis on simple, routine experiences. In the first half of the 20th century the literature became greatly modernized. Under the Communists, strict censorship was imposed. △1038, 1042–44.

Chinese Music dates back at least 4000 years. Its importance was emphasized by Confucius (551–479 BC) and again later by the emperors of the Han Dynasty (206 BC–AD 220). During the T'ang Dynasty (618–906) and the Sung Dynasty (960–1279), Chinese music entered its classical period; orchestras of 300 or more instruments were commonly used for ritual and court music. The Chinese tonal system is based on fifths. Chinese music may be generally classified into four types: sacred music, chamber music, folk music, and operatic music. Instruments used include those made of bamboo and wood, as well as metal bells and stone chimes.

Chinese Restaurant Syndrome (CRS), group of symptoms including severe headache, weakness and muscular tingling believed caused by monosodium glutamate, used liberally in Chinese restaurant food. Bed rest is indicated. CRS in children may produce convulsions.

Ch'ing Dynasty (1644–1911), also known as Manchu Dynasty, last great dynasty in China. The Manchus were tungusic tribesmen who invaded and took over Ming Dynasty China, keeping traditional Chinese patterns of rule but maintaining garrisons and separate quarters for themselves. They gradually became sinicized and provided China with a period of stability and prosperity until disrupted by Western imperialism. They were overthrown when the Chinese republic was founded. △1206.

Ch'ingtao (Qingdao, or Tsingtao), port city in E China, on Yellow Sea. Germany occupied city 1897 in retaliation for murder of two German missionaries by Chinese; leased as part of Kiaochow prov. from 1898 for 99 years. Modern city was constructed 1898–1914; Japan held it 1914–22 and 1938–45; site of US naval base 1945–49, when it fell to communists; seat of Shantung University (1926). Industries: textiles, food processing, tobacco, paper, diesel locomotives. Pop. 1,900,000.

Chingtto. △1206.

Chinkiang. *See* Chen-Chiang.

Chino, city in S California, 30mi (48km) E of Los Angeles; site of state prison; business and processing hub for regional dairy and agricultural farms. Industries: mobile homes, textiles. Founded 1887; inc. 1910. Pop. (1970) 20,411.

Chinoiserie, European style of furniture and the decorative arts that reflected fanciful and poetic notions of China based on exports of Chinese ceramics, textiles, and travelers' tales. Jean Henri Riesener created furniture in this style for the French court in the late 18th century. △1208.

Chinook, or Flathead (from their custom of deforming infant's heads as a beauty mark), American Indians living along the Pacific coast from the mouth of the Columbia River north to Grays Harbor in Washington. Though numbering less than 1000, the Chinook traveled widely and their language was used by many Indians and whites during the settlement period. Approximately 400 Chinook live on the Quinault and Warm Springs Reservations.

Chinook, the name used for foehn winds on the lee or downwind side of the Rocky Mountains. *See also* Winds.

Chinquapin, deciduous tree native to United States and China. It has hairy leaves and twigs and single-seeded fruits. There are six species. Family Fagaceae; genus *Castanea.* Or, evergreen trees and shrubs native to E Asia and W United States. Family Fagaceae; genus *Castanopsis. See also* Chestnut.

Chintz. △1204.

Chios (Khios), island in E Greece, W of Turkey, in Aegean Sea; colonized by Ionians and occupied by Persians 494–79 BC; joined Delian League 478 BC; flourished under Byzantines AD 1st century; passed to Constantinople, Genoese, Ottomans, finally to Greece (1912); traditional birthplace of Homer. Industries: sheep and goats, figs, olives, marble quarries. Area: 350sq mi (907sq km). Pop. 53,942.

Chi Particles. *See* Quark.

Chipmunk, small, ground-dwelling squirrel native to North America and Asia. They carry food (nuts, berries, seeds) in cheek pouches and store it underground. Color varies but most are brown with one or more black-bordered, light stripes. Active tree-climbers in summer, they sleep much of the winter. Length: 5–6in (13–15cm) excluding tail. Family Sciuridae; genera *Eutamias* and *Tamias.*

Chippawa, village in S Ontario, Canada, just above Niagara Falls; scene of American victory (1814) during War of 1812. Chief industry is manufacturing of artificial abrasives. Founded 1783 by United Empire Loyalists. Pop. 3,877.

Chippendale, Thomas (1718?–1779), English furniture designer and maker whose fame came not so much from his own works, although he was one of the great English craftsmen, as from the wide circulation of *The Gentleman and Cabinet-Maker's Director . . . ,* a trade catalogue illustrating the designs of his shop.

Chippewa, known in Canada as Ojibwa, the largest Algonquian-speaking tribe of North American Indians, inhabiting a region from Lake Superior and Lake Huron west to Turtle Mountain, North Dakota. The Chippewa drove the Sioux west onto the Plains, drove the Fox south, and repulsed the Iroquois. They were always a large tribe and today about 55,000 live along the United States-Canada border. In error, Longfellow based his poem Hiawatha upon Chippewa legend, even though the major character was Iroquois.

Chiricahua National Monument, park in SE Arizona; unusually shaped rock formations. Area: 10,645acres (4,311hectares). Est. 1924.

Chirico, Giorgio de (1888–), Greek-born Italian painter. Best known for disturbing landscapes and still lifes, mostly done before World War I, Chirico used exaggerated perspective in depicting empty and almost lifeless city spaces. Chirico founded "metaphysical painting," but later repudiated all modern art and studied the subjects and techniques of academic art. △1318.

Chiropractic, a type of medical practice based on the theory that the nervous system integrates all of the body's functions, including defense against disease, and that when the nervous system is impaired in any way—by, for example, "nerve interference" caused by even a slightly misplaced vertebra or other musculoskeletal part—there is decreased resistance to disease and pain. Chiropractors aim to remove nerve interference by manipulations of the musculoskeletal parts, particularly in the spinal region.

Chiru, or Tibetan antelope, medium-sized, slim-legged antelope native to plateaus of Tibet and considered sacred by Mongols. Its short, woolly hair is pale fawn with darker face and front of legs. Long, black, high-rising horns are carried only by males. It digs a deep depression as a shelter. Length: to 55in. (1.4m); height: to 32in (81cm) at shoulder. Family Bovidae; species *Fantholops hodgsoni. See also* Ruminant.

Chisholm, Shirley (1924–), first black US congresswoman. A Democrat, she was elected to represent a section of Brooklyn where she was born. A specialist in early education and child welfare, she served in the New York state assembly before being elected to Congress in 1968. She wrote two books: *Unbought and Unbossed* (1970) and *The Good Fight* (1973).

Chisholm v. Georgia (1793), first important US Supreme Court decision in which the court upheld the right of a citizen of one state to sue the government of another state. Strong opposition to this ruling led to the adoption of the 11th Amendment (1798), which overturned the decision.

Chisolm, Jesse (1806?–?68), US trader. Half Cherokee Indian, he had a trading post near Wichita, Kan. In 1866 he drove a wagon train through Indian Territory (Oklahoma) from Texas to Kansas, and the route he took became the Chisolm Trail, over which Texas longhorn cattle were driven to Kansas shipping points.

Chisum, John Simpson (1824–84), US cattleman, b. Hardeman co, Tenn. The family moved to Texas where Chisum worked at several trades and then entered cattle ranching. He moved to New Mexico where he amassed land and sufficient stock to be the largest single cattle owner in the United States. In 1880 he worked with Pat Garrett to bring law to the frontier.

Chital. *See* Axis Deer.

Chitimacha, tribe of Tunica-speaking North American Indians inhabiting the Grand River, Grand Lake, and Bayou Teche region in Louisiana. A strong tribe, they held off the French for many years. Today some 375 live around Charenton, La. Chitimacha basketry is highly prized for its color and intricacy of design.

Chitin. △494, 1574.

Chiton, or coat of mail, simple mollusk found creeping on rocks along marine shores. Bilaterally symmetrical, its upper surface has eight overlapping shells; underneath are a large fleshy foot, degenerate head with mouth, gills, and mantle. Length: to 12in (30.5cm). Class Amphineura (or Polyplacophora); family Chitonidae; species include giant Pacific *Amicula stelleri.* △476.

Chittagong, city in Bangladesh, S Asia, on Karnaphuli River; principal port of country and capital of Chittagong division; conquered 1666 by nawab of Bengal; ceded 1760 to British East India Co. Port facilities damaged 1971 in Indo-Pakistani War. Industries: jute, tea, oil, engineering works. Pop. 437,200.

Chittenden, Thomas (1730–97), first governor of Vermont, b. Guilford, Conn. He held a number of local offices before moving to a land grant on the Winooski River in Vermont. He worked for Vermont's statehood and served as governor (1778–79; 1790–97).

Ch'iu Ying (fl.1522–60), Chinese painter. One of the "Four Masters" of the Ming dynasty, Ch'iu Ying is traditionally said to have excelled in the execution of detail in the style of the blue-and-green school; he was also a master of ink drawings. Authentication of the many works attributed to Ch'iu Ying has been difficult.

Chivalry, code of ethics and behavior for knights in Western Europe between about the 11th and the 14th centuries. The term comes from the French word for knighthood, *chevalerie,* and the code was generally established by the 13th century. Combining Christian virtues and barbarian ferocity, a knight was expected to show unflinching courage, a passion for adventure, devotion to a lady of his choice, fair play, loyalty, generosity, and uprightness. He was expected to defend his lord, his lady, the Holy Church, and Christendom, as well as provide protection and show compassion for the weak and the injured. Although these virtues were probably rare in reality, the literature of the Middle Ages abounds with embodiments of the ideal. △1098.

Chives, perennial herb that smells like an onion, but does not have bulbous roots. The long hollow leaves have an onion-like flavor and are used as a seasoning. The flowers grow in rose-purple clusters. Family Liliaceae; species *Allium schoenoprasum.*

Chloral Hydrate, drug that in therapeutic doses produces natural-like sleep but with repeated use becomes addictive. Mixed with alcohol (as in a "Mickey Finn") or taken in large doses, it is dangerous and can result in death.

Chloramphenicol, widely known under the trade name Chloromycetin, an antibiotic effective against many disease-causing microorganisms. It should be used very cautiously because it can produce serious blood cell loss.

Chlorate, salt of chloric acid, containing the ion ClO_3^-. Chlorate salts are good oxidizing agents and sources of elemental oxygen. Sodium and potassium chlorates are used in explosives and also as weedkillers.

Chloride, salt of hydrochloric acid, or an organic compound containing chlorine. The best known example is common table salt, sodium chloride (NaCl).

Chloride Ion. △1506.

Chlorination, Water, process of adding chlorine in liquid form to water supplies for purposes of purification. Chlorine is also sometimes used as an initial process in sewage treatment facilities to eliminate odors. △1768.

Chlorine, common nonmetallic element (symbol Cl) of the halogen group, first discovered (1774) by Swedish chemist K.W. Scheele. It occurs in common salt (NaCl), carnallite, and sylvite. The element, a greenish-yellow gas which is extracted by electrolysis of brine, is extensively used in purifying drinking water, making wood pulp, and in the manufacture of a vast range of compounds. Chemically it is a reactive element, combining with most metals. Properties: at. no. 17; at. wt. 35.453; sp. gr. 3.214 g dm^{-3}; melt. pt. −149.76°F (−100.98°C); boil. pt. −30.28°F (−34.6°C); most common isotope Cl^{35} (75.53%). *See also* Halogen Elements. △1566, 1568.

Chloroform, colorless volatile sweet-smelling liquid (formula $CHCl_3$) prepared by the chlorination of methane or the action of bleaching powder on acetone, acetaldehyde, or ethanol. It is used in the manufacture of fluorocarbons, as an insecticide, solvent, and anesthetic. Properties: sp gr 1.48; melt. pt. −82.3°F (−63.5°C); boil. pt. 142.2−F (61.2°C). △1562.

Chloromycetin. *See* Chloramphenicol.

Chlorophyll, one of a group of pigments present in the chloroplasts of plants that absorb light for photosynthesis. Chlorophylls are responsible for the green color of plants; in some plants, however, the green color may be masked by the presence of other photosynthetic pigments. There are several types: chlorophyll A (formula $C_{55}H_{72}O_5N_4Mg$) is present in all photosynthetic plants except bacteria; chlorophyll B ($C_{55}H_{70}O_6N_4Mg$) occurs in higher plants and green algae; and chlorophylls C and D are present in some algae. △1572.

Chloroplast, the microscopic green structure within a plant cell in which photosynthesis takes place. The chloroplast is enclosed in a double membrane. Two pigments providing the green color (chlorophyll A and chlorophyll B) absorb the light energy that converts to chemical energy.

Chloroquine, synthetic drug used mainly to treat malaria.

Chlorosis, in plant pathology, a yellowing or blanching of leaves of green plants caused by deficiencies of minerals, especially magnesium or potassium, or by plant parasites.

Chlorpromazine, widely known under trade name Thorazine, a synthetic drug, first developed as an antinauseant, but subsequently found to tranquilize, or calm, the central nervous system. Considered a major tranquilizer, it is used under close medical supervision in the treatment of schizophrenia and cases of severe anxiety or other mental illnesses. △770.

Chlorpropamide, generic name for drug used as an oral agent in the control of diabetes. It is often known under trade name Diabinese.

Choanichthyes, subclaess of bony fish containing Crossopterygii (Coelacanth) and Dipnoi (lungfish). Most common during the Devonian period (345–395 million years ago), most members of this group are now extinct. They are characterized by bony skeleton, paired fins with a central skeletal axis, nostrils opening through the face and into the mouth, and a well-developed air bladder. Members of this group provided the evolutionary stock for amphibians. Class Osteichthyes. △566.

Choate, Joseph Hodges (1832–1917), US lawyer, b. Salem, Mass. He served in the *Alabama* claims case, argued the constitutionality of the income tax law before the US Supreme Court, and served on the committee that removed Boss Tweed from office in New York City. His activities in foreign affairs included ambassadorship to Great Britain (1899–1905) and chairmanship of the US delegation to the Hague Conference (1907).

Choctaw, one of the largest tribes of Muskhogean-speaking North American Indians, located in SE Mississippi and part of Alabama. An agricultural people closely related to the Chickasaw, they were generally at peace with the settlers, and remained neutral during the Revolution. As large slave-owners, they supported the South during the Civil War. A majority of the Choctaw moved to Oklahoma in 1830, where some 40,000 of their descendents still reside. *See also* Chickasaw.

Choiseul, Etienne Francois, Duc de (1719–85), French statesman. He fought with distinction in the War of Austrian Succession (1740–48), then entered the diplomatic service under Mme. de Pompadour's patronage. He served as ambassador to Rome (1754–57) and to Austria (1757–58), where he negotiated the marriage between Marie Antoinette and the future Louis XVI. As minister of foreign affairs (1758–70), he negotiated the Family Compact of 1761 between France, Spain, and other Bourbon rulers and the Treaty of Paris (1763) ending the Seven Years War. He annexed Lorraine in 1766 and Corsica in 1768. He supported the publication of the Encyclopédie in 1759 and aided suppression of the Jesuits in 1764. He was dismissed from court in 1770, mainly at the instigation of Mme. Du Barry.

Choking, condition in the throat that occurs when air flow to the lungs is partially or completely blocked by something in the throat, voice box, or windpipe, or by an irritating gas causing a reflex stopping of breathing.

Chola, south Indian dynasty. The Cholas established a kingdom in the areas around Tenjore and Tiruchirapalli and attacked Ceylon in the 2nd century, but were soon submerged by neighboring peoples. They rose again in the 9th century. Rajaraja I (*r.* 985–1014) and Rajendra I (*r.* 1014–44) extended their empire in India and attacked Ceylon. Rajendra I also organized a great naval expedition that attacked the Srivijaya empire in Sumatra. After this war the Chola empire dominated much of India, Ceylon, Southeast Asia, and what is now Indonesia. Revolts reduced the power of the empire in succeeding years, and the dynasty ended in 1279. Social and economic life and Hindu culture flourished under the Cholas, who built great monuments, temples, and irrigation systems. Village assemblies played an important role in local government in their state. △1034

Cholecystitis, an inflammation of the gall bladder, most often associated with gallstones. In mild forms it produces indigestion, sometimes with nausea and vomiting, after eating fried or greasy foods. Severe or acute attacks usually require removal of the stone.

Cholera, acute disease caused by the bacteria *Vibrio cholerae* and occurring in epidemic form in tropical

Chios, Greece

Chiru

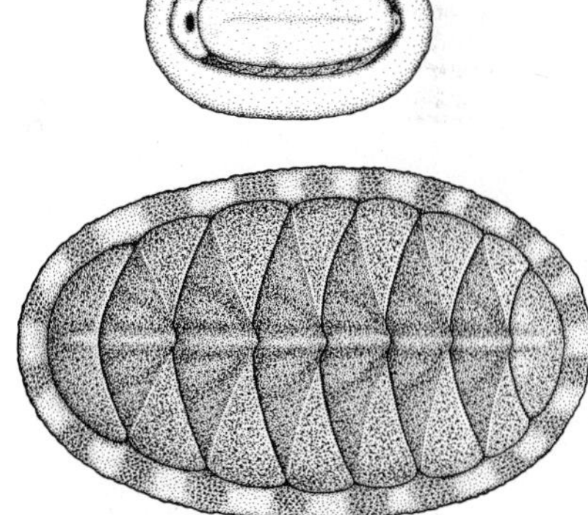
Chiton

Chives

and subtropical areas with poor sanitation. Produces almost continuous, watery diarrhea, often accompanied by vomiting and muscle cramps; leads to severe dehydration. If untreated, more than half the victims die; but adequate care, including fluid replacement and antibiotics, can result in a very high recovery rate. △732,734.

Cholesterol, white waxy sterol ($C_{27}H_{45}OH$) that occurs in plasma, blood cells, egg yolk, bile, etc, and is an important constituent of cell membranes. A diet rich in animal products may produce excess cholesterol in the blood, which is suspected of being a contributory factor in cardiovascular disease. △1570.

Choline, one of the B vitamins; necessary for the synthesis of fatty acids by the liver. Dietary sources are egg yolk, and some vegetable oils.

Cholinesterase, enzyme that breaks down the nerve transmitter acetylcholine at the nerve synapse. *See also* Acetylcholine.

Cholla, cactus characterized by cylindrical joints, native to North and South America. The tree cholla has loose, branching joints that cling to passers-by; height to 12ft (4m). The cane cholla has spectacular red flowers and persistent yellow fruit; height: to 8ft (2.5m). The Christmas cholla has clusters of olive-sized, red fruits that ripen in December; height: to 3ft (1m). Family Cactaceae; genus *Opuntia. See also* Opuntia.

Cholula (Cholula de Rivadabia), town in E central Mexico, 6mi (10km) W of Puebla; ancient center of Toltec and Aztec civilizations; city conquered and destroyed, and Indians massacred by Hernando Cortés (1519); site of ruins of famous pyramid Teocali de Cholula, sacred worship place to the Aztec god Quetzalcoatl, and several churches; popular tourist spot. Pop. 12,833.

Chomsky, (Avram) Noam (1928–), US linguist, b. Philadelphia. His book *Syntactic Structures* (1957) and other writings have revolutionized modern linguistic theory. His ideas have also had considerable impact on psychologists concerned with the analysis of language acquisition. Chomsky and others believe that the human capacity for language is partially innate, in contrast to the view of behaviorists. *See also* Behaviorism, Linguistics. △776.

Chondrichthyes, class of cartilaginous fish including Elasmobranchs (shark, ray, and skate) and Holocephali (chimaera). These marine fish have cartilaginous skeletons, well-developed lower jaw, paired fins, separate gill openings, no air bladder, bony teeth, and placoid scales. Fertilization is internal; males have specialized pelvic fins or claspers. The chimaera is intermediate in development between sharks and bony fish. It has separate anal and urogenital openings and the upper jaw is fused to the cranium, as in bony fish. Chondrichthyes developed during the late Devonian period (345 million years ago). There are about 600 living species. △510, 512.

Chondrule, spheroidal body, usually under 1/10in (3mm) embedded in a ground mass and common to chondrite stony meteorites. *See* Stony Meteorite.

Ch'ŏngjin, city in NE North Korea, on the Sea of Japan; controlled in the 1930s by Japan, which developed the Musan iron mines; severely damaged during the Korean War (1950–53). Industries: iron, steel, sardines. Pop. 265,000.

Chŏnju, city in South Korea, 120mi (193km) S of Seoul; burial place of the founder of the Yi dynasty; richest rice-growing and most densely populated region in South Korea. Industries: fans, paper, ginger. Pop. 262,816.

Chopin, Frédéric (1810–1849), composer and pianist, b. Poland of Polish and French parents. After 1831 he lived in Paris and had a long love affair with George Sand. Chopin is regarded as one of the greatest composers for the piano. His music is highly melodic, lyrical, romantic, and original, and important in the development of piano techniques. Although he composed two piano concertos and three piano sonatas, his best-known works are numerous short pieces—ballades, etudes, nocturnes, waltzes, preludes, impromptus. Polish nationalism inspired his mazurkas and polonaises. △1246.

Chopin, Kate O'Flaherty (1851–1904), US author, b. St. Louis. She lived on a plantation, and when her husband died she returned to St. Louis. Her fiction is based on plantation people and includes *Bayou Folk* (1894), *A Night in Acadie* (1897), and *The Awakening* (1899). Her understanding of the feminine psyche was controversial at the time, and it was not until the 1960s that her literary prowess was recognized.

Chord, in music, the simultaneous occurrence of three or more musical tones of different pitch. How notes are distributed and spaced within a chord is called chording. Depending on the placement of notes, chords can be broken down into the categories anomalous, characteristic, common, inverted, or transient. The study of harmony involves the functions of the various chords and classifies them as dominant, subdominant, and the diminished 7th, among others.

Chordate, vertebrates and some marine animals characterized by a rodlike, cartilaginous, supporting structure called a notochord at some point in their life cycle. Other shared features are gill slits, hollow nerve cord along the back, bilaterally symmetrical body, and segmented muscles and nerves. Chordates are subdivided into three subphyla: urochordates—tunicate or seasquirt; cephalochordates—amphioxus; and vertebrates that have a notochord surrounded and replaced by bony or cartilaginous vertebrae. Hemichordates are wormlike marine animals (acorn worm and pterobranch) sometimes classified as chordates but generally put in a separate phylum. Phylum Chordata. *See also* Acorn Worm; Amphioxus; Tunicate; Vertebrate. △508.

Chorea, any of several diseases involving involuntary jerking movements of parts of the body. One form, Sydenham's chorea, or St. Vitus dance, occurs in children, more often in girls, and is characterized by irregular muscular movements and abrupt jerks. Usually accompanied by an emotional disorder, it is self-limiting, usually subsiding in a few weeks or months. It may be associated with rheumatic fever. Another form of chorea, Huntington's chorea, is a rare hereditary disease that starts in early middle life with jerky motions and lack of coordination and gradually progresses with mental deterioration, emotional outbursts, and grotesque movements occurring, and finally death. Other rarer forms of chorea may occur during serious illnesses or may be present at birth.

Chorus, term derived from the Greek work *choros,* meaning a sacred dance with singing. A chorus is a group of singers who perform choral music in operas, oratorios, or concerts. Large church choirs are called choruses. Most modern choral music is written for four-part harmony.

Choryphopon. △576.

Chou Dynasty (1122–221 BC), longest and most famous of Chinese dynasties, noted for its achievements in government, literature, philosophy, and art. The founder, Wu Wang, overthrew the Shang dynasty. During the Spring and Autumn period (722–481 BC), Confucius and Lao Tze founded schools of thought that gave thrust to all subsequent Chinese culture. It was an age when Chinese culture expanded throughout most of present-day China. △1038.

Chou En-lai (1898–1976), the leading international spokesman and prime minister of the People's Republic of China from its founding in 1949 until his death. Educated in Japan and Europe, he rose to high position in the Communist party at an early age and remained its most skilled negotiator and international contact man. He participated in the famous Long March and represented the Communists in Chungking during World War II. His negotiating skills played a crucial role in the eventual Communist victory in China.

Choukoutienian Culture. △650.

Chouteau, (René) Auguste (1749–1829), US fur trader and political figure, b. New Orleans. He served as clerk with Pierre de Laclède, with whom he is credited with founding (1764) the trading post that became St. Louis. After Laclède's death (1778) he became the leading figure of the St. Louis area and controlled with his half brother the important trade with the Osage Indians. After the Louisiana Territory was acquired by the United States (1803), he held a number of political offices, serving as judge, justice of the peace, president of the St. Louis Board of trustees, colonel of militia, Missouri legislator, and US commissioner for various treaties with the Indians.

Chouteau, (Jean) Pierre (1758–1849), US fur trader and political figure, b. New Orleans. With his half brother René Auguste Chouteau, he controlled the important trade with the Osage Indians. In 1804 he became US agent for all Indian tribes west of the Mississippi. He was also a captain and major of militia, justice of the peace, and one of the first trustees of St. Louis. He founded the first permanent white settlement in Oklahoma.

Chouteau, Pierre, Jr. (1789–1865), US businessman, b. St. Louis. Son of Jean Pierre Chouteau and brother of Auguste Pierre Chouteau, he early became active in the fur trade with other members of his family. He eventually became head of the American Fur Co. and also engaged in many other business enterprises.

Chow Chow, ancient Chinese hunting dog (nonsporting group) brought to West in 1780. The only dog to have a blue-black tongue, its massive head has a short, broad muzzle and full, hanging lips. The small, erect ears tilt forward slightly. A short, compact body is set on heavy-boned legs. The tail is carried close to the back. The dense, coarse coat of any color stands straight out and forms a large ruff around the neck. Average size: 18–20 in (45.5–51cm) high at shoulder; 50–60lb. (23–27kg). *See also* Nonsporting Dog.

Chrétien de Troyes, romance writer of northern France (fl. *c.* 1160–1190), noted for his tales of King Arthur and his knights. Besides a number of translations of Latin poems, he wrote at least seven romances, including *Lancelot, Ywain,* and *Perceval.* Although he derived his subject matter from oral tradition and written sources, his contributions to romance literature include elaboration of plot structure and character development.

Christ. *See* Jesus Christ.

Christ, Churches of, once known as Campbellites, originated in the United States in 1811 by Alexander Campbell. An outgrowth of the Disciples of Christ, it derives unity from the Bible, the only basis of faith. It is a movement back to Scripture. There are about 2,400,000 members. *See also* Disciples of Christ.

Christchurch, city on E South Island, New Zealand, at N base of Banks Peninsula; site of University of Canterbury (1873), and Christ's College School of Arts (1882). Industries: fertilizer, rubber, woolens, electrical goods, furniture. Founded 1850 as a Church of England settlement. Pop. 165,086.

Christian I (1426–81), king of Denmark (1448–81), Norway (1450–81), and Sweden (1457–64). A weak king with a vast empire including Schleswig-Holstein, his control of Sweden ended with military defeat and the Treaty of Kalmar, 1472.

Christian II, called "the Cruel" (1481–1559), king of Denmark and Norway (1513–23) and of Sweden (1520–21). A revolt ended his harsh reign in Sweden, and Gustavus Vasa became king. Danish nobles hated Christian's reforms favoring the middle classes and rebelled. Frederick I seized the Danish throne. Christian attempted to retake control of Norway (1531–32), but was captured and imprisoned for the rest of his life.

Christian III (1503–59), king of Denmark and Norway (1534–59). The son of Frederick I, Christian was elected king in 1534. He established Lutheranism in Denmark in 1536, broke the power of the Hanseatic League, and instituted social and educational reforms.

Christian IV (1577–1648), king of Denmark and Norway (1588–1648), the son of Frederick II. Despite the costly Kalmar War (1611–13) with Sweden and his failure in the Thirty Years War (1618–48), his reign was one of cultural and commercial growth.

Christian V (1646–99), king of Denmark and Norway (1670–99), son of Frederick III. Although a weak despot, his minister Griffenfeld made him absolute monarch. A statute book, *Christian V's Danish Law,* replaced old provincial laws.

Christian VI (1699–1746), king of Denmark and Norway. The son of Frederick IV, he was crowned in 1730. A Pietist, he forbade theaters but built an extravagant palace. In 1733 he instituted *Stavnbandet,* a form of serfdom favoring land owners.

Christian VII (1749–1808), king of Denmark and Norway (1766–1808), son of Frederick V. Mentally ill, his physician Johann Struensee controlled the government 1770–72, ousting minister Johann Bernstorff. Struensee's autocratic methods aroused opposition, and he was arrested and executed in 1772. Christian's son and successor, Frederick VI, acted as regent from 1784.

Christian VIII (1786–1848), king of Denmark (1839–48). Elected king of Norway (1814) he was driven out after refusing a union with Sweden the same year. After succeeding his cousin Frederick VI of Denmark, he rejected demands for a new constitution and other liberal programs.

Christian IX (1818–1906), king of Denmark (1863–1906). He succeeded Frederick VII and was a constitutional monarch. He lost Schleswig-Holstein in a war with Prussia and Austria in 1864. During his reign socialism spread and the constitution was revised.

Christian X (1870–1947), king of Denmark (1912–47) and Iceland (1919–44). He succeeded Frederick VIII. During his reign universal suffrage was established (1915) and social welfare policies were consolidated. He tried to remain neutral during WWI and heroically defied the Germans during occupation, 1940–45.

Christian, Charles "Charlie" (1919–42), US jazz guitarist, b. Dallas, Tex. In the 1930s he played with his brother's band, then led his own band, and eventually played with Benny Goodman's band (1939–41). He helped develop the jazz style called "bebop" (now called "bop").

Christian Architecture, Early, architectural period (330–800) dominated by the basilica churches. Commonly erected over the burial place of the saint to whom the church was dedicated, they synthesize the features and materials of earlier Roman buildings, secular and sacred. Typically, closely spaced columns support a simple entablature, or more widely spaced columns carry semi-circular arches up to the sanctuary and apse. △1050.

Christianity, religion based on belief in Jesus Christ as the Son of God. God revealed himself to man through Christ, who is seen as a prophet. Numerous Christologies, or theological understandings of Christ, have been developed. The historical reality of his life is understood, although treated differently in relation to the understanding of Christ as divine. Through his redemptive act, salvation is possible for man to attain. Different churches vary on the process of salvation.

Christianity is an historical religion, based on Judaism but shaped by the Western world. The first division within Christianity was that between the Eastern and Western churches. During the 16th century, the Reformation in England, which began as a reform within the church, led to the development of Protestantism. The major Christian divisions are Orthodox, Roman Catholicism, and Protestantism. Ecumenical movements today are attempting to unite the Christian churches in an effort to make Christianity an active, positive force in the world. *See also* Protestantism; Roman Catholic Church. △844, 1026, 1052, 1264.

Christian Science, religious movement founded by the American Mary Baker Eddy (1821–1910). Its followers believe that mankind's physical and moral problems can be solved by means of prayer. Instruction is based on the Bible and Mrs. Eddy's book *Science and Health with Key to the Scriptures.* Divine Mind is used as a synonym for God, and man, as the "image and likeness of God," is regarded as the complete and flawless manifestation of this Mind.

Christiansted, port city of St Croix, in the US Virgin Islands, West Indies. Industries: rum, sugar, tourism. Founded 1733. Pop. 2,966.

Christie, (Dame) Agatha (Miller) (1891–1976), English author. A prolific and popular writer of detective stories, her novels have intricate plots and are often set in an upper-class setting in England. Her most famous characters are Hercule Poirot, a cunning but eccentric Belgian detective, and Miss Jane Marple, an elderly English village spinster-sleuth. Her novels include: *The Mysterious Affair at Styles* (1920), which introduced Poirot; *The Murder of Roger Ackroyd* (1926), considered a classic of the detective genre; *Murder at the Vicarage* (1930), which introduced Marple; *Murder on the Orient Express* (1934); *And Then There Were None* (1940); and *Curtain* (1975), ending the Poirot series. She also wrote plays, including *The Mousetrap* (1952) and *Witness for the Prosecution* (1953). *The Mousetrap* holds a world's record for the longest continuous run at one theatre (from 1952). Some romantic novels by her appeared under the name Mary Westmacott.

Christina (1626–89), queen of Sweden (1644–54). Age six at her father Gustavus II's death, she was under a regency headed by Chancellor Axel Oxenstierna who gave her political instruction. A scholarly woman, she encouraged literature and science, but her jealousy of Oxenstierna, her capricious foreign policy, strong anti-Protestant views, her extravagance and her refusal to marry, led to her abdication in favor of her cousin Charles, later Charles X.

Christmas, religious celebration commemorating the birth of Jesus Christ. It is celebrated on December 25 in the West.

Christmas Cactus, Brazilian hybrid cactus widely cultivated for its striking flowers. In the wild, this cactus grows on trees or shrubs but produces its own food. It is pollinated by hummingbirds. A popular house plant, it needs more moisture and less sun than other cactus. Family Cactaceae; genus *Schlumbergera.*

Christmas Carol, A (1843), sentimental story by Charles Dickens. Ebenezer Scrooge, a miser who thinks Christmas is an unnecessary expense, is converted by horrific visions of his past, present, and future. His subsequent generosity saves the life of Tiny Tim, the crippled son of his clerk, Bob Cratchit.

Christmas Fern, North American evergreen fern common on rocky slopes, wooded streambanks, and in swamps. Its lustrous, tapering, green leaves cascade from a central rootstock. Height: to 2.5ft (76cm). Family Aspleniaceae; species *Polystichum acrostichoides. See also* Fern.

Christmas Island, largest atoll in Pacific Ocean, S of Hawaii and N of the equator; in Line Islands; discovered 1777 by Capt. James Cook; annexed by Britain 1888; site of nuclear tests by Britain (1950s) and United States (1962); sovereignty claimed by Britain and United States. Area: 222sq mi (575sq km). Pop. 477.

Christophe, Henri (1767–1820), Haitian revolutionary leader, president (1807–11), and king (1811–20). Born a free black on the island of Grenada, he participated in the armed struggle against the French and fought a civil war with the partisans of the mulatto Pétion. Christophe ordered the construction of the Citadelle, a fort overlooking present-day Cap Haitien, which cost 20,000 Haitian lives.

Christopher, Saint, patron of ferrymen. A vast quantity of legend has grown up about this early martyr, who possibly perished during Decius' persecution, *c.* 250. One legend has it that he took up carrying travelers across a river as a work of charity, among whom was Christ in the form of a child. He is considered to be a legendary figure and is no longer officially recognized as a saint by the Roman Catholic Church.

Chromatography. △1562, 1568.

Chromite, an oxide mineral, ferrous chromic oxide ($FeCr_2O_4$) and the only ore of chromium. Separates early from magma when igneous rocks first form. Cubic system octahedral crystals and granular masses. Weakly magnetic; black, metallic and opaque; hardness 5.5; sp gr 5.1. △278.

Chromium, metallic element (symbol Cr) of the first transition series, first isolated in 1798. Chief ore is chromite ($FeO.CrO_3$). Chromium is a dull gray metal but takes a high polish and is extensively used as an electroplated coating. It is also an ingredient of many special steels. Properties: at. no. 24; at. wt. 51.996; sp. gr. 7.19; melt. pt. 3434°F (1890°C); boil. pt. 4500°F (2,482°C); most common isotope Cr^{52} (83.76%). *See also* Transition Elements.

Chromosomal Aberration, any abnormality in the chromosomes of a cell, such as a variation in the normal number or a change in the normal arrangement of the genetic material, which may produce an unexpected characteristic. One controversial genetic theory states, for example, that males with an extra Y chromosome (XYY) tend to exhibit criminal, violent, and antisocial behavior. Many geneticists, however, feel there is not enough evidence to establish a definite causal relationship between this genetic defect and deviance. △914.

Chromosomes, threadlike bundles in the nuclei of the cells of bodies of organisms, containing the genes that determine the heredity of an individual. Chromosomes are arranged in pairs, and the number of pairs is constant within a given species. Humans normally have 46, arranged in 23 pairs; one of each pair is passed on to offspring during reproduction. *See also* Heredity. △416, 420.

Chromosphere, region of the sun's atmosphere closest to the solar surface (photosphere), extending upward for some 3100mi (5000km) and increasing in temperature from 4000°K to 1,000,000°K. The chromosphere merges into the tenuous corona and is the source of many solar phenomena, including flares, prominences, and spicules. *See also* Sun. △96.

Chronicle Plays, a form of historical drama popular in England during the 1590s which used *The Chronicles of England, Scotland, and Ireland* by Raphael Holinshed (1577, 1587) as a principal source. Usually

Cholla

Frederick Chopin

Chow Chow

Charles Dickens' Christmas Carol

patriotic, the form includes Marlowe's *Edward II* and Shakespeare's *Richard* and *Henry* plays.

Chronicles, two historical books of the Old Testament. Called Paralipomenon in the Douai Bible, the two books can be divided into four sections: a lengthy genealogy from Adam to Saul; the fall of Saul and accession of David, with some instructions on worship; the reign of Solomon; the history of Judah from the division of the kingdom to the fall of Jerusalem and the Babylonian exile.

Chronometer, a portable time piece, usually having a detent escapement and compensation balance, beating half-seconds, for keeping accurate time. The atomic clock is the most precise instrument to date. *See also* Atomic Clock.

Chrysalis, intermediate or pupa stage in the life cycle of all true butterflies (except the satyr and panessian). It hangs, without a cocoon, on a silk pad from a stalk. *See also* Butterfly; Lepidoptera; Pupa. △494, 498.

Chrysanthemum, large genus of annual and perennial plants native to temperate Eurasia. Centuries of selective breeding have modified the original plain daisylike flowers. Most species, such as the florists' chrysanthemum *(C. morifolium)*, have striking large white, yellow, bronze, pink, or red flower heads. Family Compositae.

Chrysler, Walter Percy (1875–1940), US industrialist, b. Wamego, Kan. He began his career as a railroad machinist. By 1912 he was in the automobile business, first as manager and then president of Buick works. He reorganized the Maxwell Corp. (1920), became its head, and changed its name to Chrysler Corp. The company prospered and added Dodge, Plymouth, and DeSoto lines.

Chrysoberyl, an oxide mineral, beryllium aluminum oxide ($BeAl_2O_4$). Found in beryllium-rich pegmatite dikes. Orthorhombic system rare crystals, prismatic or tabular. Transparent green, yellow, or brown; hardness 8.5; sp gr 3.69. Gem varieties are cat's eye and alexandrite. Bright yellow-green is most highly valued.

Chrysostum, Saint John (*c.* 345–407), theologian and Roman Catholic saint. He celebrated his conversion to Christianity (*c.* 368) by 10 years of solitary asceticism. Although consecrated archbishop of Constantinople (398), he continued to live with monastic symplicity. He offended the emperor and earned the veneration of the crowd by reviling his superiors for moral reprobation; he was banished in 404. Chrysostum is the author of voluminous homilies, commentaries, and letters.

Chuang-tzŭ (365?–290? BC), Chinese philosopher. His book is one of the most important works in Taoism. Preaching detachment from worldly desires, its quiet, contemplative outlook has strongly influenced the Chinese character.

Chub, freshwater carp found in flowing waters. It has a large head, wide mouth, and is gray-brown. Length: 4–12in (10–31cm). Family Cyprinidae; species includes *Hybopsis gracilis, Leuciscus cephalus.* Also, marine schooling fish found in warm seas, oval-shaped with a small mouth and bright colors. Family Kyphosidae; species yellow *Kyphosus incisor* and Bermuda *Kyphesus secatrix.* △390.

Chuckwalla, flattened, desert-dwelling lizard of SW North America. It is dull-colored with loose side folds of skin and sometimes has red blotches or a banded tail. It eats creosote leaves, hides in rocky crevices, and inflates its body when threatened. Length: to 20in (50cm). Family Iguanidae; species *Sauromalus obesus. See also* Iguana.

Chuck-Will's-Widow, bird of E United States known for its nocturnal "chuck-will-widow" call. It has reddish-brown feathers marked with black and the male has white tail patches. It feeds mainly on insects. The female lays pinkish eggs (2) in dead leaves on the ground. Length: 12in (30cm). Species *Caprimulgus carolinensis.*

Chugach Mountains, range in S Alaska; extends from Cook Inlet E to W St Elias Mts; site of Chugach National Forest; highest peak is Mt Marcus Baker, 13,250ft (4,041m). Length: approx. 300mi (480m).

Chu Hsi (1130–1200), Neo-Confucian thinker, best known for his commentaries on the central Confucian texts, the *Four Books.* Chu's philosophy is a systematic summation of the Neo-Confucian school before his time. A noted statesman, Chu preferred the role of teacher and his lectures at the White Deer Grotto brought fame to the nearby Confucian University. *See also* Confucianism.

Chukchi, Paleo-Asiatic-speaking people, who inhabit the Chukchi peninsula in NE Soviet Union. They are divided into the seminomadic reindeer herders of the tundra, and a sedentary coastal group who practice fishing. △1590.

Chukchi Sea, part of Arctic Ocean, lies N of Bering Strait between Asia and North America, bounded W by Wrangel Island, S by NE Siberia, and NW by Alaska; distinguishable from the Arctic Ocean only by its oceanographic qualities (it is more saline); navigable August-September.

Chulalongkorn, Somdeth Phra Paraminda Maha (1853–1910), king of Siam as Rama V (1868–1910). He abolished slavery and the feudal system, modernized the courts, built railroads, and advanced education and technology. Educated in Europe himself, he appointed many Europeans to government posts. He often was in conflict with the French in neighboring Indochina who coveted his territory.

Chula Vista, city in S California, S of San Diego. Industries: citrus fruits, vegetables, aircraft parts, textiles. Inc. 1911. Pop. (1970) 67,901.

Ch'unch'ŏn, city in South Korea, on the Pukhan River, 45mi (72km) NE of Seoul; agricultural area. Crops: soybean, rice, millet. Pop. 122,672.

Chungking (Ch'ung-ching, Chongqing), city in S China, at junction of the Yangtze and Chialing rivers; former headquarters of the ancient Kingdom of Pa, overtaken by the state of Chin 4th century BC; wartime capital of China 1937–45 after Nanking was beseiged during Japanese invasion; transportation and shipping center. Industries: chemicals, steel, iron, silk, cotton textiles, plastics. Pop. 3,500,000.

Churches of God, US Protestant Pentecostal religious sect. It grew out of the Later Rain revival that began in the Great Smokey Mountains in 1886 under the leadership of R.G. Spurling and W.F. Bryant. They preached that a second rain of gifts of the Holy Spirit similar to the first Pentecostal would occur. Members practice speaking in tongues. There have been many splits in the church since its founding. Today about half a million people are members of various Churches of God sects.

Churchill, (Lord) Randolph Henry Spencer (1849–95), English political figure, father of Winston Churchill. He entered Parliament (1874) as a Conservative but attacked the Conservative old guard and campaigned for "Tory democracy." He became secretary of state for India (1885–86) and chancellor of the exchequer (1886). In an unsuccessful bid for more power, he resigned from office (1886) but returned to Parliament in 1892 and attacked William Gladstone's plans for Irish Home Rule.

Churchill, Sarah Jennings, Duchess of Marlborough. *See* Marlborough, Sarah Jennings Churchill, Duchess of.

Churchill, Winston (1871–1947), US novelist, b. St. Louis. He graduated from the US Naval Academy (1895), but pursued a literary career. Best known today for his historical novels; in his own day, for novels attacking corruption. *Richard Carvel* (1899), a novel of the American Revolution, and *The Crisis* (1901), a novel of the Civil War, are his most popular works.

Churchill, (Sir) Winston (Leonard Spencer) (1874–1965), English political figure and author, Britain's prime minister (1940–45, 1951–55). The son of Lord Randolph Churchill and Jennie Jerome, an American, he became a cavalry officer (1895). He served in campaigns in India (1896–98) and the Sudan (1898) and established a reputation as an author with his accounts of them. As a reporter in South Africa he was captured (1899) by the Boers but escaped and gained public attention that assisted in his election to the British Parliament in 1900 as a Conservative. Switching to the Liberals in 1904 to support free trade, he became undersecretary of state for the colonies (1906–08), president of the Board of Trade (1908–10), and home secretary (1910–11). As home secretary he suppressed labor unrest but also promoted social reforms. As first lord of the admiralty (1911–15), he expanded the British navy in preparation for war. The failure of the Dardanelles Campaign (1915), which he had strongly supported, brought about his resignation and return to active military service (1915–16).

He returned to political office as minister of munitions (1917–18), secretary of state for war and for air (1918–21), and colonial secretary (1921–22). As war secretary he insisted on British intervention against the Bolsheviks in Russia. As colonial secretary he promoted the formation of new Arab states while supporting a Jewish national homeland in Palestine and helped negotiate the establishment of the Irish Free State. Defeated in the election of 1922, he turned to writing his *The World Crisis* (5 vol., 1923–29), a history of World War I. He entered Parliament again in 1924, serving as Conservative chancellor of the exchequer (1924–29). As chancellor, he worsened economic conditions by returning Britain to the gold standard (1925), an act that contributed to the general strike of 1926. Out of office from 1929 to 1939, he continued in the public eye through his writings, his opposition to Indian nationalism, and his support of Edward VIII, and, above all, for his warnings of the danger posed by Nazi Germany.

The coming of World War II brought him back to government, first as first lord of the admiralty (1939–40) and then as prime minister (1940–45) and minister of defense (1940–45). An inspiring orator and phrasemaker, he proved a brilliant war leader as he mobilized Britain with "blood, toil, tears, and sweat" to meet its "finest hour," the dark days of the Battle of Britain. He established particularly close ties with US President Roosevelt; became the principal architect of the "grand alliance" among the United States, Britain, and the Soviet Union after 1941; and attended a series of vital international conferences at Casablanca, Teheran, Cairo, Quebec, and Yalta.

Shortly after the defeat of Germany in 1945, the Conservatives were defeated at the polls by the Labour party. Churchill then turned to warning against Communist expansion (coining the phrase "Iron Curtain" in 1946) and writing his highly regarded *The Second World War* (6 vol., 1948–53). Once more prime minister (1951–55) he ended rationing and the nationalization of the steel and auto industries but retained most of Labour's socialistic reforms and sought to maintain a special relationship between the United States and Britain. In 1953 he received the Nobel Prize in literature. He resigned his office in 1955 and then published another major historical work, *A History of the English-Speaking Peoples* (4 vol., 1956–58).

Churchill River, formerly Hamilton River, river in Newfoundland, Canada; rises in Ashuanipi Lake, in SW Labrador; flows through a series of lakes to the Atlantic Ocean, near Rigolet; large hydroelectric power station at Churchill Falls (300ft; 92m). Length: 600mi (966km).

Churchill River, river in NW Saskatchewan, Canada; flows from Methy Lake W to N through several lakes, into Hudson Bay at Churchill, N Manitoba; location of former fur trade route; hydroelectric power plant on upper course. Length: 1,000mi (1,610km).

Church of Christ, Scientist, or **Christian Science,** Protestant religion founded by Mary Baker Eddy (1821–1910) in Boston in 1879. Faith healing is central, as health is considered a spiritual reality. Membership totals are not published. *See also* Christian Science; Faith Healing.

Church Theater, drama that is either staged in or sponsored by a church. In the Middle Ages the Catholic Church was instrumental in reviving popular interest in drama, staging mystery and miracle plays as a means of both instruction and inspirational entertainment. With the Reformation, church participation in drama ceased, and not until the 20th century, with the 1929 Canterbury Festival of Music and Drama, did drama re-establish a place in religion. △1086.

Churn, a device for making butter. The old farm style dash churn consisted of a wooden cylindrical tub and lid with a wood plunger that was manually raised and dropped. Modern industrial churns are huge, barrel-shaped containers that agitate until all fat globules clump together to form butter. The remaining liquid, buttermilk, is drained off.

Churriguera, José Benito de (1665–1725), Spanish architect after whom a style of baroque, "Churrigueresque," is named. One of a family of artists who worked together in Madrid and Salamanca, José Churriguera combined the grand baroque of Rome with forms from local wood sculpture to produce an exuberant style characterized by twisted columns and ornate stucco decoration. His work was highly influential in Spain and the colonies and imitations were often done by less judicious and skillful workers. Thus "Churrigueresque" is often used inaccurately to mean vulgar baroque.

Churrigueresque Style, extravagant Baroque architecture and ornamentation in Spain and Spanish America. It takes its name from José de Churriguera nd his family, 17th-century Spanish architects and ecorators. Churrigueresque was actually a term of pprobrium coined by neoclassical detractors.

:hu-ta (Pa-ta Shan-jen) (*c.*1626–1705), Chinese ainter. Said to have been a descendant of the impe-al Ming family, Chu-ta became a Buddhist monk, amous for eccentricity, if not insanity and drunken-ess. His bizarre behavior is reflected in his paintings; mall studies of birds, fishes, and animals, often mis-hapen and touched with human qualities, and land-capes with an air of mystery. Works by Chu-ta are in e Freer Gallery, Washington, D.C., and the British Auseum. △1208.

:hyle, a fine emulsion of neutral fats found in lymph essels in the intestine, which results from absorption f fats during digestion.

:hyme, the mixture of partially digested food and igestive juices present in the stomach during the igestive process. △694.

:hymotrypsin. △694.

:IA. *See* Central Intelligence Agency.

:iano, Galeazzo, conte di Cortelazzo (1903–44), alian statesman and fascist leader. In 1922 he took art in the Fascist March on Rome and in 1930 mar-ed Benito Mussolini's daughter Edda. He was instru-ental in Italy's entry into World War II (1940). Differ-g with Mussolini on foreign policy, he was a member f a plot to oust Mussolini (1943) and was turned over y the Germans to Italian fascists, who executed him.

:iardi, John (1916–), US poet and literary critic, b. oston. He has written for both adults and children. is works include some 25 volumes of poetry, eg *I 1et a Man* (1961), *The Man Who Sang the Sillies* 961), both for children, and an excellent translation Dante's *Divine Comedy* (1954, 1961).

:icada, or 17-year locust, or dog-day cicada, large, ylike insect found worldwide. A true locust makes a ud sound by rubbing a pair of plates on its abdomen ogether. Females lay eggs in tree twigs, often caus-g damage to the twigs. The dog-day cicada appear nnually in July and August. The 17-year locust or eriodical cicada appear every 13–17 years. Cicada rvae spend from 2 to 17 years in the ground feeding n roots. Length: to 2in (30mm). Family Cicadidae.

icero, Marcus Tullius, or **Tully** (106–43 BC), oman political figure, philosopher, and orator. A ader of the senate, he exposed Catiline's conspiracy nd prosecuted his supporters. Although he opposed ulius Caesar he took no part in his assassination. He ttacked Marc Antony in the senate. When Octavian ame to power, Antony persuaded him to have Cicero xecuted. Among his greatest speeches were *Ora-ons Against Catiline* and the *Phillipics*, defenses of e republic in answer to Marc Antony. His Stoic philo-ophical works include *De Amicitia* (On Friendship) nd *De officius* (On Duty). He wrote a number of works n rhetoric. His many letters are a rich source of infor-ation on Roman life and politics.

icero, Quintus Tullius (*c.*102–43 BC), Roman com-ander. The younger brother of Marcus Tullius Ci-ero, he was propraetor of the province of Asia (*c.*60) and fought in Gaul in 54. He was proscribed along ith his brother after Caesar's assassination, joined ith Marcus Brutus, fled, and was executed. △1028.

icero, town in NE Illinois; suburb of Chicago; has ver 150 factories in approx. 2sq mi (5sq km). Indus-ies: communication and electronic equipment, print-g presses, rubber goods. Founded 1857. Pop. 970) 67,058.

ichlids. △514.

id, The (died 1099) (Spanish: El Cid Campeador, he lord champion"), Spanish national hero. His real ame was Rodrigo, or Ruy, Díaz de Vivar. A knight in e service of the Christian kings of Castile and Na-rre, he distinguished himself in wars against the oors. In 1081, however, he was banished by Alfonso I and went into service of the Moorish king of aragoza. Later he conquered Valencia and Murcia om the Moors and ruled them until his death. His eeds have been much romanticized in Spanish leg-nd and literature. Pierre Corneille based his tragedy *e Cid* on him. △1078.

igarette Lighter. △1816.

ilia. △700.

iliata, class of protozoa found in fresh water, characterized by hairlike cilia used for locomotion and food collecting. Orders include the Holotrichs with cilia over the entire body *(Paramecium)*; Spirotrichs with fused cilia around the mouth *(Stentor)*; and Peritrichs, with cilia around the mouth and stalk for attachment *(Vorticella)*. △466.

Cilicia, ancient area of SE Asia Minor (now in Turkey), between the Taurus Mts and the Mediterranean. It was dominated in succession by Assyria, Persia, Greece, Rome, Byzantium, the Arabs, Armenia, the Mamelukes, the Ottomans, finally becoming part of modern Turkey. △1020.

Cimabue, Giovanni, properly Cenni di Pepo (*c.* 1240–*c.*1302), Italian painter who was an important transitional figure between the Byzantine style of painting and the great Florentine school of the 14th century. His best-known work is *Madonna and Child Enthroned with Angels and Prophets* now in the Uffizi Gallery, Florence. Much of Cimabue's work has been damaged by time or accident. The frescoes at the Church of St Francis at Assisi and the mosaics at the Cathedral of Pisa are in poor condition and the great *Crucifixion* at Santa Croce was severely damaged in the Florentine flood of 1966. Little is known of his life; he is said to have been the teacher of Giotto.

Cimarron, Territory of, now the panhandle of Oklahoma; in 1887 attempt was made by squatters and other settlers to est. it as an independent territory. In 1888–89 droughts, dust storms, and availability of homestead sites elsewhere created a decline in population. In 1890, Congress made it part of Oklahoma Territory.

Cimarron River, river in the central and SW United States; rises in E New Mexico, flows across SW Kansas and Oklahoma into the Arkansas River. Length: approx. 500mi (805km).

Cimbri, ancient Germanic tribe. The Cimbri fought successfully against Rome (113 BC) in Illyricum and later migrated to Gaul and Spain. They joined with the Teutones to take Italy but were vanquished by Roman forces under Marius and Catulus at Vercellae in 101 BC.

Cimon (507?–449 BC), Athenian statesman and soldier, his numerous military and political successes made him leader of the aristocrats opposing Themistocles and later Pericles. His greatest military success was destroying the Persian fleet *c.*466 BC.

Cinchona, trees native to the Andes Mountains and grown in South America, Indonesia, and Zaire. They are a source of quinine. Family Rubiaceae.

Cincinnati, city and port of entry in SW Ohio, across the Ohio River from Covington, Ky.; seat of Hamilton co; 3rd-largest city in Ohio. Originally named Losantiville, it grew around Fort Washington, est 1789 by the US government to quell indian attacks; in 1790, its name was changed to Cincinnati (after the Revolutionary War Society of Cincinnati) and made co seat; served as first seat of Northwest Territory legislature. Known as the "Queen City" of the West, development was spurred by steamboat trade on Ohio River and the completion of the Miami Canal (1827), making the city a shipping center for farm products and meat. Before the Civil War, it was a terminus on the Underground Railroad. In order to compete with the growing cities of Chicago and St Louis, Cincinnati built its own railroad (1880) connecting with Chattanooga, Tenn.; it is still the only US city to own and lease its own railroad. It was scene of Cincinnati riots (1884), a result of corruption in politics and law enforcement; the reform movement won the 1924 election, ending the era of boss control. Cincinnati is the site of the Taft Museum (1820), Tyler Davidson Fountain (1871), Cincinnati Zoological Garden (1875), Eden Park; birthplace of President William H. Taft. Notable educational institutions include University of Cincinnati (1819), Ohio College of Applied Science (1828), Xavier College (1831), Hebrew Union College (1875). Industries: machine tools, soap products, playing cards, brewing, meat packing, cosmetics, automobiles, truck bodies, aircraft engines, radar, machinery, metal goods, furniture, candy, mattresses. Founded 1788; inc. 1802 as town, 1819 as city. Pop. (1970) 452,524.

Cincinnatus Lucius, or Titus Quinctius (*c.*519–438 BC), legendary Roman hero. Consul in 460, he was named dictator by the Senate in 458. He left his farm, defeated the Aequians in 16 days, and then renounced his post to return to his farm. According to legend, he was again called to the dictatorship in 439 to put down the traitor Spurius Melius.

Cinder Cone, truncated, conical structure composed

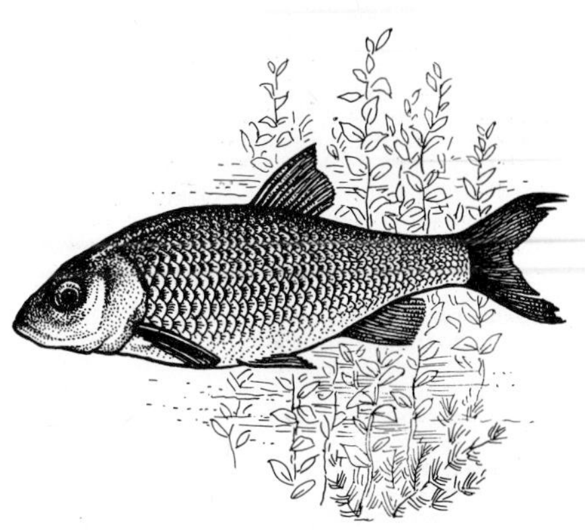

Chub

Winston Churchill

Churn

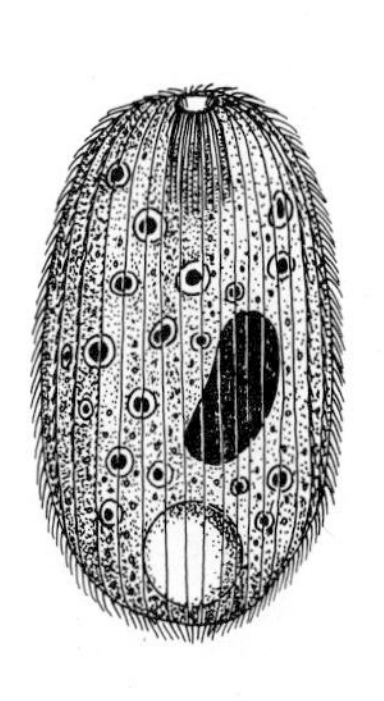

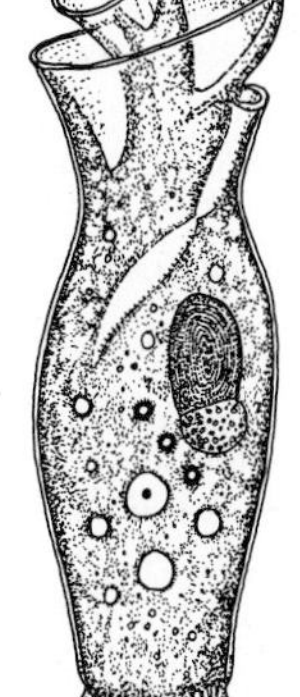

Ciliata

largely of unconsolidated volcanic material, mostly ash. The cinder cone is a characteristic of a volcano that produces large amounts of gas and ash rather than lava and is tall rather than broad.

Cinderella, heroine of a folktale of international derivation. More than 500 versions of the story are known in Europe alone. All the stories involve a youngest daughter who is badly treated by a jealous stepmother and stepsisters, helped by a supernatural person, and married by a rich prince.

Cineraria, or florist's cineraria, perennial hothouse plant native to the Canary Islands. It has heart-shaped leaves and large clusters of white, pink, blue, or purple daisylike flowers. Family Compositae; species *Senecio cruentus*. *See also* Dusty Miller.

Cingulate Gyrus, protuberance or ridge between depressions on the surface of the cerebral cortex, part of the limbic system. *See also* Limbic System. △666.

Cinna, Lucius Cornelius (*c.*130–84 BC), Roman political figure. After service in the Social War (90–88 BC), he became consul (87 BC). After Sulla left Rome for the war against Mithridates VI, Cinna repealed Sulla's laws and proposed full civil equality for the new Roman citizens of Italy. Conservatives allied with his fellow consul Gnaeus Octavius to expel Cinna from Rome. Cinna then allied with Marius, Sulla's rival, captured Rome and massacred Sulla's followers. After the death of Marius (86 BC) Cinna directed affairs, holding the consulship until his death. He suppressed dissent but instituted economic reforms and extended the franchise to all inhabitants of Italy. In 84 BC he mobilized to resist the returning Sulla, but his troops mutinied and killed him.

Cinnabar, a sulfide mineral, mercuric sulfide(MgS) and the major ore of mercury. Found in hydrothermal veins and volcanic deposits. Rhombohedral system columnar or prismatic crystals, often twinned, and as granular masses. Red; brilliant to dull; hardness 2–2.5; sp gr 8.1.

Cinnabar Moth. △502.

Cinnamon, light brown spice made from the dried inner bark of the cinnamon tree. Its delicate aroma and sweet flavor make it a common ingredient in baked foods. Once worth its weight in gold, it was also valued for religious rites and witchcraft. Or, a bushy evergreen tree native to India and Burma and now cultivated in West Indies and South America. Family Lauraceae; species *Cinnamomum zeylandicum*.

Cinnamon Fern, common North American fern found in wet places. Its woolly, cinnamon-colored, spore-bearing fronds are not as tall as the separately produced broad foliage fronds. It grows in bouquet-like clusters. It is a popular greenhouse plant. Height: to 4ft (120cm). Family Osmundaceae; species *Osmunda cinnamomea*. *See also* Fern.

Cinque, Joseph (1811–52), leader of a slave revolt aboard the Spanish ship *Amistad* in 1839, b. Sierra Leone. *See also* Amistad Case.

Cinquefoil, any of various annual and perennial plants and shrubs, native to the temperate and arctic regions. The leaves are composed of three leaflets, and the small white, yellow, or red flowers consist of five petals. Family Rosaceae; genus *Potentilla*. △444.

Cinque Ports, association of ports in SE England. The grouping of Dover, Hastings, Hythe, Romney, and Sandwich began under the Anglo-Saxons and was expanded by the Norman kings, who granted privileges in return for the ports providing ships during wartime. The association reached its height during the Hundred Years' War (1337–1453). After Henry VIII founded the royal navy, the ports' power declined.

CIO. *See* Congress of Industrial Organizations.

Circadian-Diurnal Rhythm. △760.

Circassians, Muslim people native to the Caucasus Mountains. During the 19th century, they unsuccessfully resisted the Russian government's attempt to take over the Caucasus. They often figure in Russian literature, such as in Lermontov's *Hero of Our Times*.

Circe, in Greek legend, daughter of Helios and Perse. Known for her evil spells, she was able to change humans into wolves, lions, and swine. When Odysseus' ship landed on her island, all his men were turned into swine. Odysseus, protected by moly, a magic herb, forced Circe to restore his men to human form.

Circle, plane geometric figure that is the locus of points equidistant from a fixed point (the center). This distance is the radius (r). The area of a circle is πr^2 and its perimeter (circumference) is $2\pi r$. *See also* Conic. △1462.

Circuit, Electric, system of electric conductors and electronic components connected together so that they form a continuously conducting path. In modern electronic devices, circuits are often printed in copper onto a plastic card (printed circuit) to which the transistors, capacitors, and other elements are soldered. In even smaller devices, a chip of semiconductor is treated in such a way that it consists of a number of components connected together. △1532, 1536, 1542–44.

Circuit Breaker, an automatic switch in an electrical circuit that functions as a fuse, opening the circuit if abnormal conditions, such as overloads, occur. It is not destroyed in operation and can be reclosed (reset). Circuit breakers on transmission lines are controlled by precise relays that locate failures and cause only the needed breakers to operate, thus isolating a specific section. △1532, 1650.

Circuit Court, court whose territorial jurisdiction extends over several counties or districts. A former system of US courts, they were abolished by the Judicial Code 1911, and their original jurisdiction was given to district courts. They were principal trial courts of all federal matters except those specially delegated to district courts.

Circular Flow of Income, model of the economic system that depicts the relationships or flow of money and economic goods throughout the economy. As goods are produced by the business sector, they flow to the consumer sector. In return for such goods, the business is paid money. A circular flow also occurs with the factors of production. Land, labor, and capital flow from the consumers who own these resources to business firms that use them to produce goods. In return for the factors of production, the consumer sector is paid wages or income.

The exchange of goods produced by businesses for dollars from the consumer is accomplished through use of the market mechanism of supply and demand. Through supply and demand, the price of the goods as well as the quantity produced is determined.

Circulation, Atmospheric, the patterns of average flow of the atmosphere around the earth by means of which heat is transferred from zones with a surplus, like the tropics, to zones of heat deficit, like the poles. Explanations of the poleward circulation are found in convective cells, supplemented by large-scale eddies involving planetary waves, cyclones and anticyclones, low-pressure troughs, and high-pressure ridges. The eddies also take part in the longitudinal atmospheric circulation around the earth, with the earth's rotation maintaining easterly winds toward the equator and westerlies toward the poles. Narrow jet streams blow swiftly over middle latitudes, usually toward the west in the lower stratosphere, and move further poleward during the summer. Both poleward and longitudinal circulations are stronger in the winter than in the summer hemisphere. *See also* Cyclone; Easterlies; Hadley Cell; Jet Stream; Westerlies. △214.

Circulation, Blood. △688.

Circulatory System, the transportation system of the body, transporting oxygen and digested food to tissues throughout the body and carrying carbon dioxide and other waste materials to organs that remove wastes from the body. The circulatory system consists of closed blood vessels that carry the blood throughout the body propelled by the pumping action of the heart. In mammals, birds, and some reptiles there are two circulatory systems: the pulmonary (lung) circulation and the systemic (bodily) circulation, intimately related. In the circulation, blood enters the lungs, where it picks up oxygen and gives off carbon dioxide. The freshly oxygenated blood then flows through the pulmonary vein to the left auricle of the heart, then to the left ventricle, from which it is pumped through valves into the aorta, the largest artery in the body. The aorta branches into a network of arteries and finally capillaries, carrying oxygen to all parts of the body (including the heart itself). The blood picks up waste products in the capillaries, which join to form venules and eventually veins leading to one main vessel, the vena cava, which returns the deoxygenated blood to the heart's right auricle. The blood enters the right ventricle, from which it is pumped through the pulmonary artery to the lungs. *See also* Heart. △688.

Circumcision, operation of cutting away the whole or part of the foreskin of the penis. There is a wide ethnic incidence of circumcision as a ritual, where it signifies either the formal introduction of a male int his group or the achievement of status. *See also* Puberty Rites.

Circumference, measure of the distance around closed curve. For a circle it is equal to $2\pi r$, where is the radius. △1462.

Circumpolar Star, any star that remains above th horizon during the entire 360 degrees of daily travel △38.

Circumstantial Evidence. △912.

Circus Maximus, the oldest and largest of th Roman stadia used for horse and chariot races, it wa 2,000ft (610m) long, 650ft (198m) wide, and seate 250,000 spectators. Erected, traditionally, in the 6th century BC by Tarquin the younger, first Etruscan kin of Rome, it was substantially rebuilt and made an important resort by Julius Caesar. It no longer stands.

Cirque, bowl-shaped, eroded area around a snow bank or a glacier. The eroded area is usually cut int the bedrock by repeated freezing and thawing or may be the result of glacial movement. Cirque lake are water-filled formations, often fed by the retreatin glacier that created them. *See also* Erosion; Glaciology. △262.

Cirrhosis, serious disease in which bands of fibrou tissue form in the liver. The liver becomes hard, bloo flow through the organ is impaired, and some live cells die. Cirrhosis of the liver is one of the most common causes of death among middle-aged people. It i usually associated with alcoholism but may also b caused by certain tropical fungal food contaminant and occasionally as a result of viral hepatitis or som rare disorders. Generally a loss of appetite and general weakness are followed by signs of liver impair ment: jaundice, spidery skin marks, tendency t bleed, and, in men, a loss of sexual functioning. Earl treatment, particularly in alcohol-induced cases i which cessation of alcohol intake occurs, can arres development of the disease. Otherwise, blood vessel leading to the liver become engorged, sometime rupturing, and the liver no longer detoxifies harmfu intestinal material, leading to serious, hard-to-trea and often fatal consequences. △730.

Cirripedia. *See* Barnacle.

Cisalpine Gaul, ancient region of Gaul in presen day Italy. The name is derived from the Latin "on th side of the Alps." Divided into Cispadane Gaul ("th side of the Po River") and Transpadane Gaul, it wa settled by the Gauls, 5th century BC, and then con quered (222 BC) and assimilated by the Romans Julius Caesar granted its inhabitants Roman citizer ship 49 BC.

Cisalpine Republic, N Italian state set up by Napo leon (1797) as a French dependency. It united th Italian states from Lombardy to Emilia for the first tim in modern history. In 1805 it became the kingdom c Italy.

Cispadane Republic, government of the Italian re gion of Emilia est by Napoleon Bonaparte in ear 1797, with its constitution based on that of Bologna On July 17, 1797, Napoleon merged it with the Cisa pine Republic.

Cistercians, religious order of White Monk founded by St Robert of Molesmes in 1098, based o ideals of strict and primitive Benedictinism. A clois tered community dedicated to prayer and adoratio the Cistercians were noted agricultural pioneers an sheepherders. The 17th century brought the Stric Observance reform, whose supporters are popular known as Trappists. △1086.

Cithara. *See* Kithara.

Citizen Kane (1941), US film. Produced and directe by Orson Welles from Herman J. Mankiewicz screenplay and photographed by Gregg Toland, th film described the career of a newspaper tycoo markedly similar to William Randolph Hearst. starred Welles, Everett Sloane, Joseph Cotton, an Agnes Moorehead. Abounding in cinematic innov tions, it remains one of the most gripping films in th medium's history. △1370.

Citizen's Band, one of two narrow radio-frequenc bands reserved by the Federal Communications Cor mission for use by US citizens for low-power rad transmissions. A license is required for use of a ci zen's band radio, but no procedural regulations a enforced. Protocols between communicators a loosely based on standardized police radio codes b adapted to the special interests using the frequencies, such as motor vehicle operators, farmers, and fishermen. From 1977, 40 channels were available on citizen's band radios in the United States.

Citizenship, relationship in which a person is a member of a state, by birth or naturalization, and owes allegiance to it. Citizenship carries with it certain rights and duties. Modern countries determine the requirements for citizenship. The United States, for example, generally supports the rule of *jus soli,* and anyone born in the United States is a citizen. The United States also accepts children born abroad of US parents as citizens during their minority and they may retain citizenship if they fulfill certain conditions. △886.

Citric Acid, colorless crystalline solid (formula $C_6H_8O_7$) having a sour taste and occurring free in lemons and limes. It is used for flavoring, in effervescent salts, and as a mordant. Properties: sp gr 1.54; melt. pt. 307.4°F (153°C). △1572.

Citric Acid Cycle. *See* Krebs' Cycle.

Citrus Fruits, important fruits of the genus *Citrus* in the rue family. These include the orange, lime, lemon, grapefruit, kumquat, and tangerine. These subtropical trees or shrubs are widely cultivated wherever they can get plenty of sun and moisture. The flowers are usually white, waxy, and fragrant. The fruit is usually ovoid with a thick, aromatic rind. The interior is pulpy and juicy and is divided into segments that contain the seeds. Most citrus fruits contain a high amount of vitamin C.

City, in the United States, a term applied to municipalities governed under a charter granted by the state. In general, a political unit with a large, centralized population. △898, 904, 992, 996.

City of God, The, religious and philosophical work by Augustine of Hippo. Begun about two years after the Visigoths sacked Rome in 410 and completed in 426, it was a reply to charges that the influence of Christianity had caused the city's fall. The first 10 of the work's 22 books held that vices within the empire rather than Christianity brought about Rome's collapse. The remaining books elaborate an important Christian philosophy of history. In this view history from the fall of Adam to the end of time is seen as the development of two opposing powers, the city of God and the city of the world, a place of conflict and confusion. To one or the other of these cities all mankind must eventually belong. After the Last Judgment the city of God becomes Heaven and the city of the world Hell.

City-state, self-governing political unit comprised of an independent city and its adjacent hinterland. Historically, city-states have existed during three periods: the ancient city-states of Mesopotamia and Greece; those of Medieval and Renaissance Europe; and, to a limited extent, in the modern world. They represent an effective form of political organization to achieve physical and economic protection. Many, like ancient Athens and medieval Florence, flourished as commercial and cultural centers. They sometimes banded together to form maritime leagues or alliances for trading and protection. Although the nation-state is today the dominant political unit, several city-states persist as anomalies in the contemporary world. The most notable is Singapore.

Ciudad Bolívar, formerly Angostura; city and port in E Venezuela; capital of Bolivar state, on Orinoco River; site of longest suspension bridge in South America, the Angostura, 2,336ft (712m) long. Industries: wood products, leather. Founded 1764 as Angostura. Pop. 109,605.

Ciudad Delicias, city in N Mexico, 45mi (72km) SE of Chihuahua; fertile agricultural valley region, watered by irrigation system of Conchos River. Industries: cotton, sugar cane, corn, tobacco, cattle, dairying. Pop. 64,385.

Ciudad Juárez, city in N Mexico, on the Rio Grande; connected by bridge to El Paso, Tex.; site of Mission of Our Lady of Guadalupe (1659), and Museum of Art and History; named for Mexican President Benito Juárez (1888); commercial center. Industries: tourism, textiles. Pop. 436,054.

Ciudad Madero, city in E Mexico, N of Tampico; important center of petroleum industries. Pop. 89,994.

Ciudad Mante, city in NE Mexico, 80mi (129km) NW of Tampico; agricultural center. Industries: livestock, canning, copper mining, tanning, sugar refining, distilling. Pop. 79,130.

Ciudad Obregón, city in NW Mexico, 65mi (105km) SE of Guaymas; agricultural region. Industries: livestock, vegetables, flour milling, canning, copper mining. Pop. 138,506.

Ciudad Victoria, city in E central Mexico, 135mi (217km) NW of Tampico; agricultural and trading center; site of university (1956). Industries: mining, sugar cane, citrus fruit, livestock, tanning, textiles. Founded 1750. Pop. 94,304.

Civet, or **Civet Cat,** small, savage, catlike animal found in Africa, Asia, and S Europe. Related to the genet and mongoose, it has a small head and narrow body set on long legs. Its coat is brindled gray with black stripes and spots. The substance known as civet is a fatty secretion of the animal's scent glands, once important as a perfume base. Length: body—28in (7cm), tail—14in (35cm). Family Viverridae; species five, including African *Viverra civetta* and Asian *V. civettictis.* △550, 598.

Civic Repertory Theater, a theater founded in New York City by actress Eva Le Gallienne. For seven years (1926–33) the theater offered productions of Shakespeare, Shaw, Chekhov, and Ibsen with top-priced tickets at $1.50. Others involved included Burgess Meredith and Nazimova.

Civil Aeronautics Board (CAB), US government agency. It has broad authority to promote and regulate the civil air transport industry within the United States and between the United States and foreign countries in the interest of US foreign and domestic commerce, the postal service, and national defense. Founded 1938.

Civil Defense, civilian governmental effort to handle emergencies and disasters both in time of war and peace. In the United States, it includes cooperation among the federal, state, and local governments in the sponsoring of educational programs, the storing of supplies and equipment, and the establishment of a nationwide communications system for emergencies.

Civil Disobedience, passive resistance to law or authority, usually associated with an act of conscience. The term originated with Henry Thoreau's essay "Resistance to Civil Government," (1849) in which he argued that disobeying a law is preferable to disobeying one's own conscience. It was associated in India with the nationalist supporters of Mohandas K. Gandhi and in the United States with the followers of Martin Luther King, Jr.

Civil Engineering, the field of engineering that deals with the creation, improvement, and protection of the communal environment, providing facilities for living, industry, and transportation, including large buildings, roads, bridges, canals, railroad lines, airports, water-supply systems, dams, harbors, docks, aquaducts, tunnels, and other constructions. Civil engineering requires a thorough knowledge of surveying, construction, material properties, soil properties, and hydraulics. Important divisions of the field are architectural, irrigation, transportation, soil and foundation, geodetic, hydraulic and coastal, and ocean engineering. △1612.

Civilian Catastrophe Reaction, gross stress reaction associated with a natural disaster such as an earthquake or tornado, similar to that of *traumatic neurosis.* Catastrophe victims may be unable to concentrate, stare, have nightmares, lose appetite, suffer mood disturbances and various other signs of anxiety. This reaction gradually subsides during the weeks following the disaster though traces of it may linger for years. *See also* Traumatic Neurosis.

Civilian Conservation Corps (CCC), US organization established in 1933 to provide employment for young men 18–25 during the Depression. Over 2,000,000 men in 1,500 camps were engaged in conservation work doing useful outdoor work such as reforestation, flood control, and road construction.

Civilization, Process of. △884–86.

Civil Law, legal system derived from Roman Law prevalent in continental Europe and in the Western Hemisphere in Louisiana, Quebec Province, and Latin America. It is distinguished from common law, the system generally adhered to in England and English-speaking countries. Civil law is based on a system of codes, the most famous of which is the Napoleonic Code (1804), and decisions are precisely worked out from general basic principles *a priori;* that is, the civil

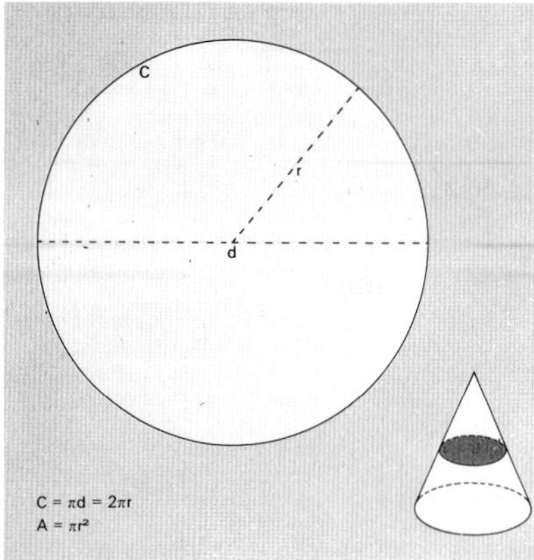
c
r
d
C = πd = 2πr
A = πr²
Circle

Circus Maximus

Cirque: Rocky Mountains

Orson Welles (left) *and Joseph Cotton in* Citizen Kane

law judge is bound by the conditions of the written law and not by previous judicial interpretation. Civil law influences common law in the areas of jurisprudence, admiralty, testamentary and domestic relations, and is the basis for the system of equity. In common usage, the term civil law means regulations governing private legal affairs, and contrasts with public law and criminal law. *See also* Common Law; Law; Roman Law. △908–10.

Civil Liberties *See* Civil Rights and Liberties.

Civil Rights, Commission on, US federal commission that investigates complaints alleging that citizens are being deprived of their right to vote because of their race, color, religion, sex, or national origin, or, in the case of federal elections, by fraudulent practices. It appraises the laws and policies of the federal government and submits reports of its activities, findings, and recommendations to the president and Congress.

Civil Rights Act of 1866, law passed April 1866 over President Andrew Johnson's veto. It gave blacks citizenship and extended civil rights to all persons born in the United States (except Indians). *See also* Civil Rights Act of 1870.

Civil Rights Act of 1870, US law passed to reenact the Civil Rights Act of 1866, which was considered to be of dubious constitutionality. The 1870 law was declared unconstitutional by the US Supreme Court in 1883. *See also* Civil Rights Act of 1866.

Civil Rights Act of 1875, US law passed to outlaw discrimination in public places because of race or previous servitude. The act was declared unconstitutional by the Supreme Court (1883–85), which stated that the 14th Amendment, the constitutional basis of the act, protected individual rights against infringement by the states, not by other individuals.

Civil Rights Acts (1957, 1960, 1964, 1968), US legislation. The first of these acts established the Civil Rights Commission to investigate violations of the 15th Amendment. The 1960 Civil Rights Act enabled court-appointed federal officials to protect black voting rights. An act of violence to obstruct a court order became a federal offense. The Civil Rights Act of 1964, the strongest civil rights legislation since the Civil War, established as law equal rights for all citizens in voting, education, public accommodations, and in federally assisted programs. In 1968, a civil rights act was passed guaranteeing equal treatment in housing and real estate to all citizens.

Civil Rights and Liberties, basic individual rights and freedoms protected against infringement by government. In the United States, they include the rights to freedom of speech, press, religion, and assembly, as well as the rights to property and equal treatment under law. The US heritage stems from a series of English documents: the Magna Carta (1215); the Petition of Right (1628); and the Bill of Rights (1689). Together with the US Constitution (particularly the first 10 amendments) and the civil rights acts, they represent the basis for US civil rights and liberties. *See also* Civil Rights Acts.

Civil Rights Cases (1883), US Supreme Court decision that declared the Civil Rights Act of 1875 void. The court ruled that the 14th Amendment applied to "state action" only and did not prohibit discrimination by private individuals. This decision was overruled by subsequent legislation and broad judicial interpretation of "state action." *See also* Civil Rights Act of 1875.

Civil Service. △906.

Civil Service Commission, US federal agency. It was established in 1883 to create a merit system for appointments to federal jobs, rather than personal preference or political considerations. Selection is made by competitive exam, administered by the commission. The commission also is responsible for job classification, pay, tenure, training, labor management relations, insurance programs, and retirement for federal employees. △906.

Civil War, American (1861–65), conflict between the North (the Union) and 11 southern states (the Confederacy), sometimes known as the War Between the States. Its immediate cause was the secession of the southern states from the Union; northerners regarded the Union as indivisible, and the war was fought to resolve that issue. The more general cause was the question of slavery, an institution well established in the southern states but one that abolitionists were determined should not be extended to the new western states. Sectional differences between North and South, particularly economic ones, were at least as old as the nation, but by the 1850s slavery, abolition, and states' rights had created schisms that, despite efforts at compromise, seemed insoluble. Politically, the two sides had polarized: Northern abolitionists had coalesced into the new Republican party and southern states' righters remained in the Democratic party. The election in 1860 of the Republican candidate, Abraham Lincoln, was the virtual assurance of southern secession from the Union. On Dec. 20, 1860, South Carolina left the Union, quickly followed by Texas, Mississippi, Georgia, Florida, Louisiana, and Alabama. North Carolina, Virginia, Tennessee, and Arkansas seceded later. There was, in addition, secessionist sentiment in the border states, but all of them eventually stayed in the Union.

The war began on April 12, 1861, when South Carolina fired on Fort Sumter, the federal installation in Charleston harbor. Lincoln, newly inaugurated, recognized that as an act of war, and the battle was joined. The Confederate capital was established at Richmond, Va., and the Union army's first objective was to take that city. In the attempt, however—in the first Battle of Bull Run (July 21, 1861)—Confederate troops scored a victory. Lincoln was forced to begin his long search for a military commander who would measure up to the able southern generals, particularly Robert E. Lee and Stonewall Jackson. The search finally ended with Ulysses S. Grant, who became commander of the West in October 1863 and supreme commander in March 1864. His ablest lieutenant was William T. Sherman.

In the meantime, the Confederates continued to pile up victories. Lee, replacing the wounded Joseph E. Johnston, won the Peninsular Campaign (April–June 1862). Stonewall Jackson carried off a brilliant campaign in the Shenandoah Valley (March–June 1862) and went on to win the Seven Days battle (June–July 1862) and the Second Battle of Bull Run (August 1862). Union superiority in both numbers and in material was beginning to be felt, however, and Union troops checked Lee's army in the Antietam campaign (September 1862), the battle of Fredericksburg (Dec. 13, 1862), and twice at Chancellorsville (December 1862 and May 1863). The Union victory in the Gettysburg campaign (June–July 1863) is generally considered the turning point of the war. By that time the vastly superior northern navy had effectively blockaded southern ports, thereby denying the Confederacy much needed trade with Europe. It was from such trade that the South had depended for much of its war materials. The war in the West took on increasing importance. Union strategy was to win the war by dividing the South, which was to be accomplished by taking control of the Mississippi, Tennessee, and Cumberland rivers. The first big Union victory was at Fort Donelson, on the Tennessee, on Feb. 16, 1862. General Grant was the Union commander. The Battle of Shiloh (April 1862) was less conclusive. Grant won a signal victory in the Vicksburg campaign (November 1862–July 1863), which, combined with the fall of Memphis (June 1862), gave the Union control of virtually all of the Mississippi. Confederate troops, under Braxton Bragg, almost defeated the Union forces in the Chattanooga campaign (November 1863), but the superior forces of the Union saved the day. By the end of 1863, Tennessee was restored to the Union.

In March 1864 Grant went east to become supreme commander. He confronted Lee's army in the Wilderness campaign (May–June 1864) and began the long siege of Petersburg, Va., the defense of which was vital to the survival of Richmond. General Sherman, meanwhile, won the Battle of Atlanta and began his destructive march through Georgia to the sea. He conquered Savannah in December 1864. He then moved north and won the battle of Five Forks (April 1, 1865), the last major battle of the war. That victory cut off the southern retreat route for Confederate troops in Richmond. Petersburg fell two days later, and Richmond was no longer defensible. Realizing the desperation of his position, Lee surrendered to Grant at Appomattox Courthouse on April 9, 1865. Other southern commanders quickly capitulated, and the war was over.

By almost any criterion, the Civil War was the most destructive in US history. The casualties were greater than those of any other war, and the physical destruction of the countryside was unprecedented. It caused the economic ruin of the South, and the Reconstruction policies after the war poisoned the relations between North and South for a century. The war, and Reconstruction, left a legacy of racial bitterness between white and black. *See also* Abolitionism; Reconstruction; Slavery; individual battles and leaders. △1276.

Civil War, English (1642–48), conflict arising out of the struggle between Charles I and Parliament. When Charles ruled without Parliament (1629–40), divisions between the court and the people over religion, taxation, rights, and foreign policy were increased. A Scottish revolt against church policy compelled Charles to summon the Long Parliament (1640) to raise funds. The Parliament impeached the king's closest advisers and in the Grand Remonstrance (1641) demanded church reform and greater parliamentary power. The king responded by attempting to arrest John Pym and other parliamentary leaders (1642). The king and parliament raised opposing armies.

The king and his royalist supporters held the north and west until the Scots joined the parliamentarians and defeated him at Marston Moor (1644). Parliament organized the New Model Army, making Oliver Cromwell second-in-command. The Royalists were decisively defeated at Naseby (1645) and Charles surrendered (1646). He escaped from custody (1647), formed an alliance with the Scots and began the Second Civil War (1648). The king's forces were swiftly defeated by Cromwell's army. Parliament, now firmly controlled by Cromwell, tried Charles and executed him for treason (1649). A Commonwealth, with Cromwell as leader, was declared. △1156.

Civil War, Spanish (1936–39), conflict between the Loyalists and Nationalists for control of Spain. Both sides began as loose alliances: the Loyalists, so-called because they were loyal to the government of the Second Republic, consisted of republicans, socialists, Communists, and Basque and Catalonian separatists. The Nationalists comprised the right-wing professional army, the more conservative faction of the Roman Catholic Church, monarchists, Carlists, and the great landowners.

The causes of the war began in 1931, when the monarchy was abolished and the Second Republic was instituted. The government made attempts to reform Spanish institutions and customs. Church and state were separated; land reform was begun; and military influence was controlled. All these measures were upsetting to the traditionalist forces of Spain, including the church, the landed interests, and the military.

The actual war began in July 1936, with an uprising of the Spanish army in Morocco. The commander there, Francisco Franco, soon emerged as the leader of the Nationalist side. The Nationalists quickly took control of the north of Spain, while the Loyalists held Madrid, Catalonia, and much of the south. Fighting, including aerial bombing of civilians, was intense and great suffering resulted.

Nazi Germany and Fascist Italy gave aid to the Nationalist forces, including both troops and supplies. The democracies, on the other hand, maintained strict neutrality, leaving only the Soviet Union to come to the aid of the Loyalists, which greatly strengthened the Communists within the Loyalist ranks. International brigades, mostly under Communist control, were formed and fought on the side of the Loyalists. The Nationalists made steady progress throughout 1937 and in late 1938 began a major assault on Catalonia. When Barcelona fell in January 1939, the Loyalist cause was doomed. On March 27, 1939, the Nationalists entered Madrid, and the war was over. More than 1,000,000 Spaniards had been killed, and more than 250,000 were forced into exile. △1324.

Civil Works Administration (CWA), organization created by executive order of Pres. Franklin D. Roosevelt (1933–34) to provide emergency employment. The CWA, under Harry Hopkins, put 4,000,000 men to work on civic improvement.

Civitavecchia, town in W central Italy, on Tyrrhenian Sea; chief port for Rome; sacked by Saracens 828; Pope Leo IV built walled mountain town 854; old site rebuilt under papal protection. Final construction of citadel was supervised by Michelangelo; site of naval arsenal built by Bernini 1508. Industries: cement, metallurgical works. Pop. 42,570.

Clair, René (1898–), French filmmaker. His early work owes a debt to Surrealism. Complex comic characterization is emphasized in his later films, including *The Italian Straw Hat* (1928), *A Nous la Liberté* (1931), *The Flame of New Orleans* (1941), *Les Belles de nuit* (1952), and *Les Fêtes galantes* (1965). *See also* Surrealism.

Clairvoyance, the supernatural or extrasensory power to see objects or events actually removed in time and space from the observer, a form of extrasensory perception or ESP. *See also* Parapsychology; Precognition. △824.

Clam, bivalve mollusk found mainly in marine waters. It is usually partially buried in sand or mud with its shells slightly open for feeding. With a large foot fo burrowing, its flat body lies between two muscles for closing the shells and is covered by the mantle and has in- and out-current openings, elongated into siphons in some species. Class Pelecypoda. The largest species is Tridacna; Length: 5ft (152cm); Weight: 500lb (225kg). Edible clams include *Venus mercenaria*, quahog or hard shell clam of Atlantic coast, and *Mya arenaria*, the soft shell or gaper clam. △482.

Clam Worm. *See* Nereis.

Clan, unilineal descent group, in which kinship is recognized either through the male line (patrilineal) or through the female line (matrilineal). *See also* Kinship; Matriarchy; Patriarchy. △882.

Claremont, city in S California; site of Claremont College (1946), Pomona College (1887), and Scripps College (1926); suburban city with small businesses. Inc. 1907. Pop. (1970) 23,464.

Clarence, George, Duke of (1449–78), younger brother of Edward IV of England, b. Ireland. He joined his father-in-law, the earl of Warwick, in revolt against Edward (1469–70), but later rejoined his brother (1471). In 1478 he was accused of treason and murdered in the Tower of London before he stood trial.

Clarendon, Edward Hyde, 1st Earl of (1609–74), English statesman and historian. Initially critical of Charles I, he became a leading royal adviser (1641) and later worked for the Restoration. As Charles II's chief minister, his moderation made him unpopular. Forced into exile (1667), he wrote his *History of the Rebellion* about the English Civil War.

Clarendon, Constitutions of (1164), 16 articles issued by Henry II of England, limiting temporal and judicial powers of the church. The article requiring clerics convicted in church courts to be surrendered to secular courts for punishment was especially controversial. Archbishop Thomas à Becket initially accepted the articles, but later repudiated them. The ensuing quarrel led to Becket's murder.

Clarendon Code, four English statutes passed (1661–65) under Charles II's minister Clarendon to strengthen the established church. Nonconformist worship was hampered by restrictions on the size of gatherings and the movement of ministers. Municipal and church officers were required to be professed Anglicans. These laws reduced the strength of the Nonconformists, especially the Presbyterians.

Clarinet, woodwind musical instrument of ancient Asian origin, with end-blown cylindrical wood pipe and single-reed mouthpiece, commonly pitched B*b* (also A), with alto clarinet E*b*. Utilized for flexibility and tonal quality variations in different registers, it has a range of 3 1/2 octaves, from D below middle C. It has been used in symphony orchestras since the early 19th century and in jazz since around 1920. △1244.

Clark, Champ, full name James Beauchamp Clark (1850–1921), US congressman, b. Anderson co, Ky. He sat in the House (1893–95, 1897–1921) and was speaker (1911–19). A prominent party leader, he almost won the Democratic presidential nomination in 1912.

Clark, George Rogers (1752–1818), American Revolutionary general, b. Albemarle County, Va. A militia captain in Lord Dunmore's War (1774), Clark was given a commission in the Virginia militia during the revolution by Gov. Patrick Henry. In 1778, he took the offensive in the Northwest Territory. After suffering great hardships, he and his men defeated the British at Kaskaskia, Ill. (1778), and Vincennes, Ind. (1779).

Clark, Kenneth B(ancroft) (1914–), US psychologist and educator, b. Panama Canal Zone. Professor of psychology at City College of New York from 1942, his study of racial discrimination was cited by the Supreme Court in its 1954 school desegregation decision. His books include *Prejudice and Your Child* (1955) and *Dark Ghetto* (1965).

Clark, (Sir) Kenneth McKenzie (1903–), English art historian. A professor at Oxford, he was director of the National Gallery in London (1934–45) and chairman of the Arts Council on Great Britain (1955–60). His writings include *Leonardo da Vinci* (2d ed. 1952), *Rembrandt and the Italian Renaissance* (1966), and *The Romantic Rebellion* (1974). His television lecture series *Civilisation*, a cultural survey, was extremely popular.

Clark, Mark Wayne (1896–), US general, b. Madison Barracks, N.Y. He graduated from West Point (1917) and fought in France in World War I. During World War II he took command of the US ground forces in Europe (1942) and the 5th Army (1943) during the Italian campaign. He led the US forces in occupied Austria and became supreme commander of the UN forces in Korea (1952). After his retirement from the army (1953), he was president of The Citadel (1954–66).

Clark, Ramsey (1927–), US lawyer and political leader, b. Dallas. In the Dept. of Justice (1961–66) he was assistant attorney general and deputy attorney general. He served as attorney general in 1966–67 under Pres. Lyndon Johnson. He was strongly in favor of civil rights and an outspoken opponent of the Vietnam War. In 1974 he was an unsuccessful Democratic candidate for the Senate from New York. His books include *Crime in America* (1970) and, with Roy Wilkins, *Search and Destroy* (1972).

Clark, Tom C(ampbell) (1899–), US jurist and lawyer, b. Dallas, Texas. A US Justice Department attorney (1937–45), he became US attorney general in 1945, and in 1949 was appointed an associate justice of the US Supreme Court. A civil rights advocate noted for his opinion upholding the provisions of the Civil Rights Act of 1964 requiring desegregation of public accommodations, he retired in 1967 when his son, Ramsey Clark, became attorney general.

Clark, William (1770–1838), US explorer who, with Meriwether Lewis, led an expedition of the Northwest Territory (1803–06), b. Caroline co, Va. In 1813 he became governor of Missouri Territory; from 1821 he served as superintendent of Indian affairs. *See also* Lewis and Clark Expedition.

Clark, William Andrews (1839–1925), US financier and senator, b. Cornellsville, Penn. He went to the Colorado gold fields but made his fortune in provisioning, mail service, banking, and organizing mining companies. He became a power in timber and utilities. He aided in the move to Montana statehood and served as a US senator (1899–1900, 1901–07). His art collection is now in the Corcoran Gallery in Washington, D.C.

Clark, William Smith (1826–1886), US educator, b. Ashfield, Mass. After serving in the Union Army and the Massachusetts General Court (1864–67), he helped found Amherst Agricultural College (1867) (now University of Massachusetts). He served as president (1867–79) and professor of chemistry and botany; then as consultant (1876–77) in the establishment of Imperial College of Agriculture in Sapporo, Japan.

Clark & McCullough, US comedy team: **Bobby Clark** (1888–1960) and **Paul McCullough** (1883–1936), both b. Springfield, Ohio. With a bouncing cane, trick cigar, and raccoon coat, they appeared together in musicals such as *The Ramblers* (1926) and *Strike Up the Band* (1930) during their 36 year partnership.

Clarke, Arthur Charles (1917–), English science-fiction writer. He is noted for the solid scientific background in his works; many of the scientific predictions in his novels have become realities. His novels include *Childhood's End* (1953), *A Fall of Moondust* (1961), and *Voices from the Sky* (1965). The film *2001: A Space Odyssey* (1968) was based on his short story "The Sentinel."

Clark Memorandum (1928), restated the Monroe Doctrine within terms of self-preservation without giving up US hegemony. Essentially noninterventionist, it inaugurated cordial inter-American relations, culminating in the Latin American Conferences of the 1930s.

Clarksburg, city in N West Virginia, on West Fork River; seat of Harrison co; served as Union supply base during Civil War; birthplace of Stonewall Jackson. Industries: mining, oil, glass. Inc. 1785. Pop. (1970) 24,684.

Clarksdale, city in NW Mississippi, on the Sunflower River; cotton processing and distributing center. Industries: paper, conveyor belts, house trailers. Inc. 1882. Pop. (1970) 21,763.

Clarksville, city in NW Tennessee; seat of Montgomery co; site of Austin Peay State University. Industries: agriculture, cattle raising, tobacco, meat packing. Inc. 1855. Pop. (1970) 31,719.

Class, Social, a system of social stratification that organizes groups of people on the basis of shared characteristics. Social scientists have long argued about the basis for class distinctions. Socialist thinkers believe capital and access to the means of production are the basic factors; others state that status is crucial;

American Civil War: Union troops at Petersburg, Virginia

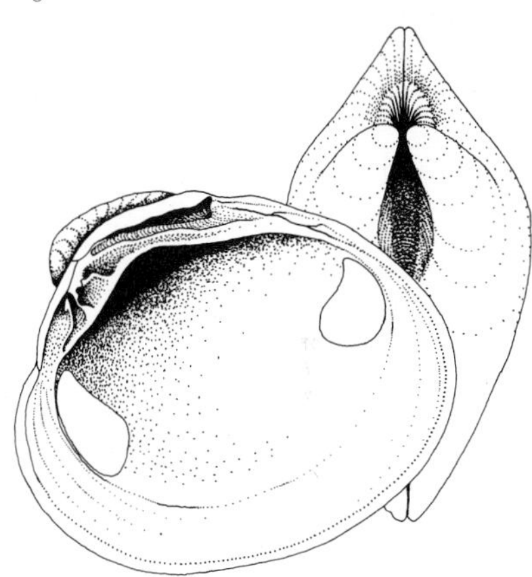

Clam

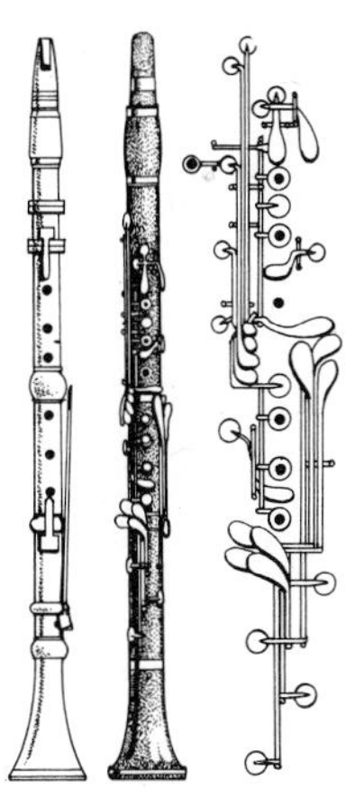

Clarinet

George Rogers Clark

a third group claims a group's relationship to political power determines its class position. The concept of social class is fundamental to the understanding of social organization. *See also* Status; Stratification; △890, 1016.

Class Action, suit brought by one or more members of a class for themselves or in behalf of themselves and other persons similarly situated. Class action suits were popular means of redress used by consumer and environmental groups in the United States until 1974, when the Supreme Court limited the circumstances whereby class action suits could be considered.

Classical Conditioning. *See* Pavlovian Conditioning.

Classical Music, music composed from roughly 1750 to 1820. At this time musical styles were characterized by emotional restraint, the dominance of homophonic methods (ie, melodies with accompaniment), and clear structures and forms underlying the music. During this period instrumental music crystallized into the forms of concerto, sonata, symphony, and string quartet. The piano became the most popular keyboard instrument, replacing the harpsichord. The greatest composers of this period—all from Vienna—were Haydn, Mozart, Beethoven, and Schubert, who are among the greatest who have ever lived. Also important in this period were reformations in opera introduced by Gluck. *See also* Opera; Polyphony.

Classicism in Art, art history term used to describe both an aesthetic attitude and an artistic tradition. The artistic tradition refers to the classical antiquity of Greece and Rome, its art, literature, and criticism, and the subsequent periods that looked back to Greece and Rome for their prototypes, viz., Carolingian Revival, Renaissance, and neoclassicism. The aesthetic use of the term suggests the classical characteristics of clarity, order, balance, unity, symmetry, and dignity. The concept is also used in a comparative sense to describe those works that exhibit the salient features of a given style. △1166.

Classic Revival, art and architecture in the style of the ancient Greeks and Romans. In general, the style reflects a simplicity, harmony, and balance. The Italian Renaissance and the neoclassic style in England and the United States in the early 19th century are examples of classic revival.

Classification, Biological, or taxonomy, organization of plants and animals into categories based on similarities of appearance, structure, evolution, or habit. The categories, ranging from the most inclusive to the exclusive, are kingdom, phylum, class, order, family, genus, species, and sometimes variety. There are also subphyla, subfamilies, etc., in some categories. *See also* Taxonomy. △408, 458, 592.

Classification, Library, process of organizing materials in a collection according to a system. Widespread interest in classification developed during the late 19th century, a period of great growth for libraries. The Dewey Decimal System is the most used worldwide.

Classification of Animals. *See* Animal Classification.

Claude, Albert (1899–), US cell biologist, b. Luxembourg. He was awarded part of the 1974 Nobel Prize in physiology or medicine for his pioneering use of the electron microscope to study the detailed anatomy of the cell. He discovered two cell organelles—the mitochondrion and the endoplasmic reticulum.

Claudianus, Claudius (*c.* 370–404), last important Latin poet in the classical tradition. An Alexandrian, Claudianus came to Italy and mastered Latin. His poems, falling into three groups, include panegyrics along with the mythological epic *De raptu Proserpinae.*

Claudius I (10 BC–AD 54), Roman emperor (41–54), son of Drusus, nephew of Tiberius. He was the first emperor chosen by the army, a situation that angered the Senate. He made conquests in Germany, added Britain as a province of Rome (43), absorbed Mauritania, Thrace, and Judea into the empire, and built the harbor at Ostia and the Claudian aqueduct. His wives and enemies maligned his ability. Agrippina, his fourth wife, poisoned him and secured the emperorship for her own son by a former marriage, Nero.

Clausel (or Clauzel), Bertrand, Count (1772–1842), French soldier. Clausel served in the Napoleonic Wars in Spain (1810–13); he backed Napoleon during the One Hundred Days and was made marshall of France for subduing the Bordeaux royalists. When the Bourbons returned, he was condemned to death; he spent 1815–20 in the United States. When he returned to France, he devoted himself to promoting the colonization of Algeria and was governor general of Algeria (1835–37).

Clausius, Rudolf Julius Emanuel (1822–88), German physicist. He is regarded as the founder of thermodynamics and, using the work of Carnot, was the first to state explicitly the second law. He also introduced the concept of entropy.

Clavell, James (1924–), US author, b. England. He went to the United States in 1953 and worked as a film writer, director, and producer. He has written several popular novels, including *King Rat* (1962), *Tai-pan* (1966), and *Shōgun* (1975).

Claves, Cuban musical instrument consisting of two round hardwood sticks beaten together to produce a percussion accompaniment for popular and folk tunes.

Clavichord, earliest stringed musical instrument with mechanical action controlled by a keyboard. Introduced in the 12th century, it was used extensively from the 16th to 18th century. J. S. Bach composed his series "The Well-Tempered Clavier" (1722) for this instrument with its soft, delicate, expressive tone. △1132.

Clavicle, or collarbone, thin slightly curved bone attached by ligaments to the top of the sternum. The collarbone and shoulder blade make up the shoulder, or pectoral girdle, linking the arm to the axis of the body. △682.

Clavier, generic term for stringed musical instruments played with a keyboard, such as the harpsichord, Clavichord, and later the pianoforte.

Clavius. △52.

Clay, Cassius. *See* Ali, Muhammad.

Clay, Clement Claiborne (1816–82), US political figure, b. Huntsville, Ala. He served in the US Senate (1853–61) and the Confederate Senate. Clay spent a year in Canada (1864) trying to negotiate a peace with the Union and on his way home was accused of complicity in the plot to kill Abraham Lincoln. He spent a year in Fortress Monroe and was then freed.

Clay, Henry (1777–1852), US statesman, b. Hanover co, Va. A lawyer, he practiced in Lexington, Ky., after 1797. He served in both the US House of Representatives (1811–14; 1815–21; 1823–25), where he was several times speaker, and in the US Senate (1831–42; 1849–52). He was one of the "war hawks" who favored the War of 1812. He ran for president in 1824, and when the election went to the House of Representatives, he threw his support to John Quincy Adams, who was elected. When Adams named Clay secretary of state (1825–29), the charge of "corrupt bargain" was widely made. One of the founders of the Whig party, he ran against Andrew Jackson, a bitter political enemy, in 1832. He continued to oppose the Jacksonians in Congress. He ran for president again in 1844 as a Whig but was defeated by James Polk. Clay's last years in the Senate were spent trying to work out a compromise between the slave-owning states of the South and the free northern states. The Compromise of 1850 was one result of those efforts. *See also* Compromise of 1850; War of 1812; Whigs.

Clay, group of aluminum silicate rocks of various compositions, including kaolinite and halloysite, usually mixed with some quartz, calcite, or gypsum. It is formed by the weathering of granite or other igneous rocks containing feldspar. Soft when wet, it hardens on firing and is used to make pottery, stoneware, tiles, bricks, and molds, and as a filler for paper, rubber, and paint. △248.

Clayton Anti-Trust Act (1914), US legislation to strengthen the Sherman Anti-Trust Act (1890). It prohibited corporate practices not previously covered, including price discrimination, interlocking directorates, tying contracts, and holding stock in competitive firms. It exempted trade unions from restraint of trade clauses.

Clayton-Bulwer Treaty (April 1850), agreement between the United States and Great Britain negotiated by Sec. of State John M. Clayton and Sir Henry Bulwer. Among the treaty's provisions were joint control and protection of any ship canal that might be built in Central America, guaranteed neutrality and security of such a canal, and pledges not to occupy or colonize any part of Central America.

Clean Air Amendments (1970), measures designed to speed up the pace of air cleanup programs begun in the 1960s by making the Environmental Protection Agency (EPA) responsible for all air pollution control functions. The EPA was ordered to develop programs for the prevention and control of air pollution and it was given power to designate as Air Quality Control Regions any areas where air pollution was a serious problem. The 1970 measures gave individual citizens power to initiate action against polluters, including US government agencies. Resistance from industry and local governments, however, has weakened the act's strength.

Cleaner, Metal. △1562.

Cleanthes (*c.* 331–232 BC), Greek philosopher. A disciple of Zeno of Citium, he was the second head of the Stoic school. Of the fragments of his works that survive, the principal one is the philosophical poem "Hymn to Zeus." More than did Zeno, he stressed the transcendency of God. *See also* Stoicism.

Clear-air Turbulence (CAT), the turbulence encountered by aircraft at high altitudes, often associated with the jet stream, even though the atmosphere is devoid of clouds.

Clear and Present Danger, imprecisely defined legal doctrine enunciated by the Supreme Court in *Schenck* v. *United States* (1919). It held that freedom of speech could be restricted if words or circumstances created a clear and present danger to national interests. It ended, for a time, free criticism of public policies and was used primarily against Communists. *See also* Schenck *v.* United States (1919).

Clearing, in banking, settlement of claims and charges by banks against each other. The claims are submitted to a central agency (clearinghouse) where settlement is made without the actual transfer of cash. The claims themselves, usually consisting of checks and promissory notes, are called clearings. Commerce between nations is cleared through central banks; stock and commodity exchanges also use the system.

Clearinghouse, institution established by businesses engaged in similar activities to facilitate transactions among them. Bank clearinghouses, for example, aid in the exchange of checks, drafts, notes, etc. In industry or trade, a clearinghouse is a building in which the products of two or more companies are combined for distribution or sale.

Clear Lake, either of two lakes in California: 1) A fresh water lake in W California, 80mi (130km) N of San Francisco; largest within the state; recreational area. Length: 25mi (40km). Width: 1–10mi (2–16km). 2) A vast reservoir in NE California, 10mi (16km) S of Oregon border; the Lost River flows out of it NW to Oregon.

Clearwater, residential city, W Florida peninsula, 18mi (29km) NW of St Petersburg; seat of Pinellas co. Industries: citrus fruits, fishing. Settled as Clear Water Harbor in 1841; inc. 1891. Pop. (1970) 52,074.

Clearwing Moth, small, day-flying moth that has transparent hindwings and looks like a wasp. Clearwing caterpillars bore into the roots and stems of trees and shrubs. Family Aegeriidae. *See also* Moth.

Cleaver, Eldridge (1935–), US black militant and author, b. Leroy Eldridge Cleaver in Wabbaseka, Ark. He began a series of prison terms (1954–66) and became a convert to the Black Muslim faith. He described his experiences in *Soul on Ice* (1968) and lectured extensively. Former minister of information for the Black Panther party, he fled the United States in 1968 to avoid returning to jail for a parole violation. In 1975 he surrendered to FBI agents in New York City, reaffirming his allegiance to the United States.

Cleburne, Patrick Ronayne (1828–64), Confederate general in the Civil War, b. Ireland. He settled in Arkansas (1849) and after the secession of that state became a colonel. His successes at Shiloh; Richmond, Ky.; and Perryville earned him major general's rank (1862). He was in the fighting at Chickamauga, Missionary Ridge, and Atlanta and was killed at Franklin, Tenn.

Cleft Palate, congenital deformity in which there is an opening in the palate, or roof of the mouth, causing direct communication between the nasal and mouth cavities. It is often associated with harelip, an opening of the upper lip. Cleft palate results from a defect in embryonic development and can range in severity from a small opening to complete separation of the alates and opening of part of the gum tissue. Normal eatment includes special feeding for the first year, en surgical correction of the deformity, followed by pecial dental care and speech therapy if necessary. 756.

leisthenes, the name of two Greek statesmen. The st was tyrant of Athens *c.* 600–580 BC; the second, s grandson, was in power 508–506, completely nanging the administrative divisions of Athens and aving behind the state power of ostracism. He is ought of as the creator of Athenian democracy. △ 96.

leistogamous Flower, small, closed self-fertilizing owers. Cleistogamous fertilization takes place within flower that does not open. It ensures seed producon when normal cross-pollination fails. Sweet violet, xalis, and impatiens are examples.

leland, John (1709–89), English novelist. Freuently destitute, Cleland wrote *Fanny Hill* (1748–9) to save himself, he claimed, from starving. His her works include the novel *Memoirs of a Coxcomb* 751) and the play *Titus Vespasian* (1755). *See also* anny Hill.

lematis, genus of about 250 species of perennial, ostly climbing shrub found worldwide. Many have tractive flowers or flower clusters. Leaves are usuly compound. Well-known species are woodbine nd old-man's-beard. Family Ranunculaceae.

lemenceau, Georges (1841–1929), French political figure. While a medical student in Paris he helped und and wrote for republican journals and was jailed riefly in 1862 for these activities. Between 1865–869 he lived in the United States. Shortly after rerning to France he participated in the founding of e Third Republic. He served in the chamber of depues from 1876 to 1893. He was also highly influential rough newspaper articles he wrote. Having made any powerful enemies, he was defeated for reelecon in 1893. He then dedicated himself to journalism r the next decade. He was an early, ardent defender f Alfred Dreyfus. In 1902 he was elected to the sene and in 1906 became premier. As premier he seted the first Moroccan crisis, enforced the new w separating church and state, and strengthened rance's alliance with Great Britain. He broke with the ocialists over his harsh measures against striking iners. His cabinet fell in 1909. Back in the senate he tacked Germany and urged military preparedness. November 1917 he formed a coalition government at restored French morale and led to victory. Repreenting France at the Paris Peace Conference he ashed with Woodrow Wilson over concern for ench security. His government was defeated in 920 and he retired from the senate. △1308.

lemens, Samuel Langhorne. *See* Twain, Mark.

lement I, Roman Catholic pope (88?–97?) and int. His primary concern was church organization. e remained under constant observation by civil auorities until his martyrdom for refusing to pledge legiance to the Roman emperor.

lement III (*c.* 1110), antipope, b. Guibert of avenna. Chancellor of the Holy Roman Empire in aly (1057–63), he supported Emperor Henry IV in s struggles against the papacy. When in 1080 Pope regory VII excommunicated Henry, Guibert sumoned a council that declared Pope Gregory disosed and named Guibert as his successor. Backed up y Henry's troops, Guibert entered Rome in 1083 and as enthroned as Pope Clement III in 1084.

lement III, Roman Catholic pope (1187–91), b. aolo Scolari. After the fall of Jerusalem to Saladin in 187, he preached the Third Crusade. He made the cottish church dependent on Rome (1188).

lement IV, Roman Catholic pope (1265–68), b. uy le Gros Foulques in France (*c.* 1200). An adviser King Louis IX, he entered the church after his wife's eath. He served as a papal legate to England, Wales, nd Ireland, and was elected pope while in England n a diplomatic mission. He stressed papal authority, oping to lessen that of local monarchs in religious atters.

lement V, Roman Catholic pope (1305–14), b. Berand de Got (*c.* 1264). He was crowned pope at Lyons nd lived his entire life in France, creating French ontrol in the College of Cardinals. He ignored herees, refusing to employ the courts of Inquisition.

lement VI, Roman Catholic pope (1342–52), b. erre Roger de Beaufort (*c.* 1291) in France. He was crowned in Avignon, and despite bishops' protests he declared that all churches and offices were responsible to the pope. The Plague (Black Death) struck during his reign.

Clement VII, antipope (1378–94) during the Great Schism. He had served as a papal legate under Pope Gregory XI. He remained convinced of the legitimacy of his election as pope. *See also* Great Schism.

Clement VII, Roman Catholic pope (1523–34), b. Giulio de Medici (1478). Unable to deal with the growing Protestant Reformation, he achieved little church reform.

Clement VIII, Roman Catholic pope (1592–1605), b. Ippolito Aldobrandini (1536). Noted for piety and moral integrity, he displayed concern for the poor and the purity of the church and reformed the church's religious orders. He encouraged peace between Spain and France.

Clement XI, Roman Catholic pope (1700–21), b. Giovanni Francesco Albani. He encouraged missionary work but limited the use of indigenous or local customs in missions. Jansenism was influential during the papacy. *See also* Jansenism.

Clement XIV (1705–74), Roman Catholic pope (1769–74), b. Giovanni Ganganelli. A Franciscan, his sympathies were with the Jesuit order, but as pope, he suppressed the Jesuits in 1773 for the sake of peace with European princes determined to destroy them.

Clemente, Roberto (Walker) (1934–1972), US baseball player, b. Carolina, P.R. He compiled over 3000 hits in his 18-year major league career. He died in an airplane crash while en route with supplies to the earthquake victims of Managua, Nicaragua. He was elected to the Baseball Hall of Fame in 1973.

Clementi, Muzio. △1196.

Clement of Alexandria (150?–?220), Greek church father. His full name was Titus Flavius Clemens. He studied in Alexandria, Egypt, where he founded a school that became a center of learning. Several writings have survived, including his *Hortatory Address to the Greeks*, the *Paedagogue*, the treatise *Who Is the Rich Man That Shall Be Saved?*, and the *Hypotyposes*. For Clement, Christian truth is joined to Greek philosophy while his work paves the way for specifically Christian doctrine.

Cleomenes III (died 219 BC), Spartan king (235–219 BC). The son of Leonidas II, this ambitious king wanted to become leader of the Achaean League and re-create a society of aristocrats. His resources, however, were not sufficient to achieve this aim. He fought the Achaean League and Macedonia from 225–222 and after his defeat fled to Egypt where he was imprisoned. He escaped in 219 and tried to raise a revolt in Alexandria; when it failed he committed suicide.

Cleon (died 422 BC), Athenian politician. In 425 BC, after the death of Pericles, he spurned Sparta's peace proposals and continued the Peloponnesian War. An unprincipled demagogue and uneven soldier, he sought his own power and glory and was killed at Anphipolis fighting the Spartan Brasidas. △994.

Cleopatra (69–30 BC), queen of Egypt (51–30 BC). In 48 BC, with the aid of Julius Caesar, she overthrew her husband-brother coruler Ptolemy XII. She became Caesar's mistress, followed him to Rome, and bore him a son, Caesarion. After Caesar's assassination (44 BC), she fled Rome. She won the affections of Marc Antony and with him returned triumphantly to Egypt (42 BC). In 36 BC they were married. This outraged Octavian Caesar; he decided to destroy them. In 31 BC Antony and Cleopatra's fleets were destroyed at Actium. They fled back to Alexandria where Antony killed himself. Cleopatra surrendered to Octavian, but was unable to win him over. She killed herself with an asp. △1018.

Clepsydra. △1658.

Clermont, Robert Fulton's steamship that sailed from New York City to Albany in 32 hours in August 1807. △1859.

Clermont-Ferrand, capital city of Puy-de-Dôme dept. in S central France; scene of council in 1095 that initiated the Crusades. Industries: rubber goods, chemicals, linen, machinery. Founded by Romans. Pop. 148,896.

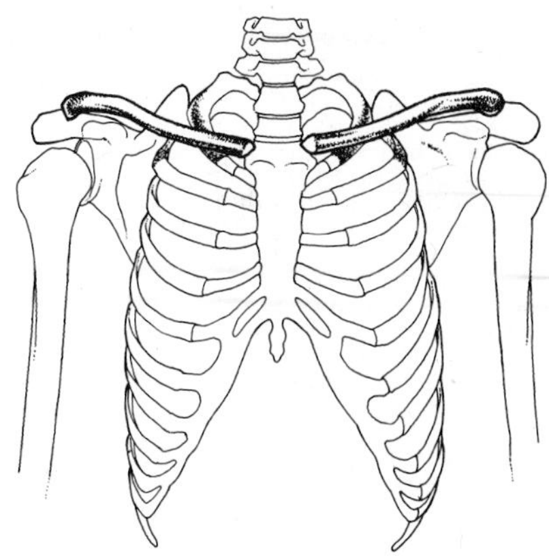

Clavicle

Henry Clay

Clearwing moth

Georges Clemenceau (left) at the front, World War I

Cleveland, (Stephen) Grover (1837–1908), 22nd and 24th President of the United States, b. Caldwell, N.J. In 1886 he married Frances Folsom; they had five children. A lawyer in Buffalo, N.Y., Cleveland was elected mayor of that city (1881). His reputation as a reformer led to his nomination and election as Democratic governor of New York. He quickly achieved a national reputation, and the Democrats chose him as their presidential candidate (1884). He won a narrow victory over James G. Blaine.

His first term was marked by an attempt to reform the civil service and by his advocacy of a low tariff; both issues had strong opponents in both parties. He ran for re-election in 1888 but was narrowly defeated by Benjamin Harrison, the Republican candidate and an advocate of a high tariff.

In 1892, he was nominated again, and this time he decisively defeated Harrison. The Panic of 1893 raised the issue of free coinage of silver, which was supported by the radical or free-silver Democrats. An economic conservative, Cleveland opposed free coinage and secured the repeal of the Sherman Silver Purchase Act, which enraged the radical Democrats. In 1894, he broke the Pullman Strike in Chicago by the use of federal troops. The free-silver Democrats prevailed at the 1896 convention and nominated William Jennings Bryan.

He was essentially a moderate in foreign policy. Cleveland broadened the interpretation of the Monroe Doctrine in the Venezuela Boundary Dispute with Great Britain. He refused to annex Hawaii after a US-backed faction overthrew the monarchy, and he discouraged those who wanted to take Cuba from Spain.

Career: Mayor, Buffalo, N.Y., 1881; New York Governor, 1883–85; President, 1885–89, 1893–97.

Cleveland, city and port of entry in NE Ohio, at mouth of Cuyahoga River on Lake Erie; seat of Cuyahoga co; largest city in Ohio. A leading ore port and Great Lakes shipping point, it is also an iron and steel center; site of Case Western Reserve University (1826), John Carroll University (1886), Cleveland State University (1923), Cuyahoga Community College (1963), and the Cleveland Institute of Art and the Fine Arts Garden; home of the Cleveland Symphony Orchestra, and Play House (1916), which operates three repertory theaters; parks total 2,000acres (800hectares) and include a large zoo; the city's *Plain Dealer* newspaper is nationally known. John D. Rockefeller was educated in Cleveland and started his oil dynasty here in 1870 by forming Standard Oil Co. The National Aeronautics and Space Administration maintains a large research center here. Industries: chemicals, oil refining, garments, food processing. Founded 1796 by Moses Cleaveland; chartered as city 1836. Pop. (1970) 750,879.

Cleveland, city in SE Tennessee; seat of Bradley co; administrative headquarters for Cherokee National Forest; site of Lee College. Inc. 1838. Pop.(1970) 20,651.

Cleveland Bay, light horse breed developed in Cleveland district of Yorkshire, England, for riding, driving, and farm use. Large for a light horse, it is always solid bay with black legs. Height: 64in (160cm) at shoulder; weight: 1150–1400lb (521.6–635kg).

Cleveland Heights, city in N Ohio; E suburb of Cleveland; just W of city are Case Western Reserve University (1826), Cleveland Museum of Art, and Ursuline College (1871). Inc. 1921. Pop. (1970) 60,767.

Cliburn, Van (1937–), US pianist, *b.* Shreveport, La. He was the first US citizen to win the prestigious Tchaikovsky Piano Competition in Moscow (1958). Since that time he has received acclaim as a piano virtuoso.

Click Beetle, or skipjack, snapping beetle, beetle that turns over by snapping its body and throwing itself into the air. It makes an audible click in the process. Its long, cylindrical larvae are called wireworms. Family Elateridae. *See also* Wireworm.

Cliff Dwellers, Pueblo Indians of the US Southwest, who lived in masonry houses built into the sides of cliffs (about AD 1000). Hand-hewn stone bricks and adobe mortar were the main construction materials. Ceilings had large crossbeams placed on laths of small branches, plastered over. Buildings were four to five stories high with each story set back, making terraces. By the end of the 13th century, the Pueblos had left their cliff dwellings for small villages further south. *See also* Mesa Verde; Pueblo Indians.

Clifford, Clark McAdams (1906–), US cabinet member, b. Fort Scott, Kan. He served in the Navy in World War II and was appointed a naval aide (1946–50) by President Truman helping significantly to formulate the Truman Doctrine (1947). He also helped plan President Truman's campaign strategy in 1948. He advised John F. Kennedy (1961–63), then served President Johnson on the Foreign Intelligence Advisory (1963) and as secretary of defense (1968–69).

Clifton, city in NE New Jersey on Passaic River, 9mi (14km) N of Newark. Industries: steel, textiles, chemicals, electronics. Settled 1640 as fur trading post; inc. 1895. Pop. (1970) 82,437.

Climate, the totality of weather behavior over periods of decades or centuries, investigated by climatologists. Macroclimates cover broad climatic regions around the globe; microclimates involve climatic conditions of a small area like a lawn or a field. Solar radiations reaching the earth vary with the seasons over broad regions, determining the torrid (tropical), temperate, and frigid (polar), or similar, climatic zones. Land and sea characteristics, like mountain ranges and ocean currents, as well as the general atmospheric circulation contribute also to the mean temperatures and precipitation, as well as vegetative cover, that defines smaller climatic regions. W. Köppen's climate classification, for example, basically involves mean temperature, precipitation, and vegetative distributions as affected by these other factors. C. W. Thornthwaite's analysis of climates emphasizes the measurement of potential evapotranspiration, the amount of moisture, if available, removed from the land by both evaporation from surfaces and transpiration by plants. *See also* Climate Control; Weather. △220.

Climate Control, the prediction and control of climatic changes. Evidence over thousands of years from tree rings, Earth strata, pollen counts, and Greenland and Antarctic ice cores, from many past glaciations, and even from weather data of the last 100 years has indicated vast changes in climates. Some evidence exists of a worldwide warming during the first four decades of this century, since followed by a cooling trend. But the causes, single or multiple, for these changes are as yet undetermined. They have been attributed variously to variations in solar output, in Earth's orbital path or axis of rotation, in the Earth's atmosphere (caused by changes in amount of volcanic or meteoric dust or carbon dioxide or ozone), in ocean currents, or in snow cover or vegetation cover. Until climatic changes can be explained, climates cannot be controlled, although changes have been proposed employing such techniques as shifting ocean currents or melting polar ice by darkening it. *See also* Climate; Weather Modification. △220.

Climatic Zone. △220.

Climatology, the study by scientists (climatologists) of the earth's climates with the aim of identifying their conditions, including characteristic temperature, pressure, winds, precipitation, and vegetation, and eventually determining their causes and ultimate control. *See also* Meteorology. △220.

Climb, Aircraft. △1718.

Climbing Fern, or Hartford fern, delicate North American fern with 3ft (91cm) vinelike leaves in rows on a twining stem. Sterile leaflets are palmately lobed and sporiferous leaflets are forked. Family Schizaeaceaea; species *Lygodium palmatum. See also* Fern.

Climbing Perch, tropical freshwater fish found in SE Asia. Not a true perch, it is popular with home aquarists. It is gray-brown or green and uses extended gill covers to "walk" on land for short distances. Length: to 10in (25.4cm). Family Anabantidae; species *Anabas testudineus.*

Clingmans Dome, mountain in the Great Smoky Mts, on the North Carolina-Tennessee border; highest peak in Tennessee, 6,662ft (2,032m).

Clinical Psychology, field psychology concerned with diagnosis and treatment of behavior disorders, from failures in adjustment to severe mental illness. Clinical psychologists may work with psychiatrists, but they are not required to have medical degrees. *See also* Abnormal Psychology; Psychiatry.

Clinton, De Witt (1769–1828), US statesman, b. Little Britain, N.Y. He was a successful mayor of New York City (1803–15) and in 1812, he ran for president but lost to James Madison. As governor of New York (1817–21; 1825–28), he worked for political, social, educational, and religious reforms. He was responsible for the construction of the Erie Canal (1817–25), and the Champlain-Hudson Canal.

Clinton, George (1739–1812), US statesman, b. Little Britain, N.Y. An early patriot and delegate to the Second Continental Congress, he signed the Declara tion of Independence. He was briefly a brigadier ger eral in the Revolution and then was elected governc of New York (1777). He served to 1795 and late supported Thomas Jefferson, whose vice presider he became in 1804. Reelected in 1808, he died i office.

Clinton, (Sir) Henry (1738?–95), English genera Sent to the American colonies in 1775, he serve under Generals Howe and Burgoyne at Boston in Ma and Bunker Hill in June; he participated in the Battl of Long Island in August 1776. In 1778 he succeede Howe as commander-in-chief and in 1780 capture Charleston and the southern army. He resigned h post in 1782 and two years later served as governc of Gibralter. His son, Sir Henry Clinton (1771–1829 was one of Wellington's favorite officers, serving i the Peninsular War (1811) and at Waterloo (1815).

Clinton, city in E central Iowa, on the Mississipp River; site of Mt St Clare College (1895), Eastern low Community College (1929). Industries: corn and live stock processing, iron works, machine shops. Inc 1859. Pop. (1970) 34,719.

Clipper Ship, three-masted commercial vessel bui during the first half of the 19th century primarily fc speed, and characterized by a long slim hull and man sails. One of the fastest, the American *Flying Clouc* sailed from New York to San Francisco via Cape Hor in 89 days. △1678.

Clique, a small group without a formal purpose c organization, held together by shared interests an feelings of confidence. Adolescents often hav cliques, in addition to belonging to organized club: societies, or gangs.

Clitoris. △700.

Clive, Robert, Baron Clive of Plassey (1725–74 English soldier and colonial administrator. He went t India as an official of the British East India Compan in 1843. He was taken prisoner when Madras wa recaptured by the Bengalese in 1746, but escape He used guerrilla tactics to take and hold Arcot in th struggle between the French and British East Ind companies (1751). Appointed governor of Fort S David (1755), in 1757 he recaptured Calcutta an defeated the Bengalese at the Battle of Plassey. H governed Bengal until 1760, when he returned t England. He was governor of Bengal again 1765–6 but had to return to England to answer charges c embezzling state funds. He was acquitted by Parli ment in 1772. △1202.

Cloaca, common cavity into which intestinal, urinar and genital tracts open in fish, reptiles, birds, an some primitive mammals.

Clock. △1658.

Clock, Atomic. *See* Atomic Clock.

Clodius, Publius (93?–52 BC), Roman demagogu and tribune. Elected tribune in 59 BC, he was consi ered a "creature of Caesar" as he organized gangste to fight the mobs of Pompey and Milo. He exiled C cero because he had prosecuted Clodius in 6 Clodius was killed by Milo's men, but these gang wa opened the path for war between Caesar and Pon pey.

Cloisonné, type of enameling technique used in By antine art. It reached its apex in Western art durin the 10th and 11th centuries. The design is cor structed out of wires soldered to a plate, and the cel (cloisons) thus formed are filled with a colored vitr ous paste which, when fired, turns into colored glas △1208, 1608.

Cloister, an uncovered quadrangle surrounded by covered walk. An open colonnade forms the side the walk facing the quadrangle; the other side bounded by the inner walls of surrounding building Notable examples are at Oxford University and S John Lateran Church, Rome. △1080.

Cloisters, The, museum in Fort Tryon Park in Ne York City that houses part of the medieval collectic of the Metropolitan Museum of Art. Donated by Joh D. Rockefeller, Jr., the building consists of five medi val monasteries from S France, including the 12t century chapter house from Notre-Dame-de-Pontau Among the works in the art collection are the Flemis Merode Altarpiece, the 15th-century Unicorn tape tries, as well as numerous sculptures, frescoes, tape tries, enamels, and decorative objects.

Clone, the set of plants obtained from a single orig

al parent, through some means of vegetative propagation such as budding, grafting, or taking cuttings. In nimals, asexual reproduction of one parent often oduces a set of individuals that form a clone. △324.

lontarf, town in E Republic of Ireland, on N shore f Dublin Bay; suburb of Dublin. Irish forces under rian Boru defeated the Danes here 1014; site of lontarf Castle (1835).

losed Circuit Television, different from usual teleasting in that closed circuit transmissions are made ver cables rather than by airwaves. Closed circuit ograms will not interfere with regular telecasts and an be seen only on television sets that are connected ith the cable network.

losed Shop, requirement that membership in a bor organization is a precondition of employment. lthough outlawed by the Taft-Hartley Act (1947), the formal situation where only union members are red to work in a shop is not uncommon. *See also* pen Shop.

losing Costs, costs involved in the purchase of a ome or other property, excluding the price itself.

lostridium Thermohydrosulfuricum. △1574.

losure. *See* Cloture Rule.

lotaire I (*c.* 497–561), Frankish king. On the death f his father, Clovis I, in 511 he received a share of the ankish kingdom with his capital at Soissons. In 524 e divided the share of his deceased brother Clodomir ith another brother Childebert I. In 531 he conuered and divided Thuringia with his brother Theooric. He and Childebert seized and divided Burgundy 534. Their attack against the Visigoths of Spain was epulsed (542). Clotaire became the sole king of the anks after the death of Theodoric's heir (555) and f Childebert (558).

lotaire II (died 629), Frankish king. He succeeded s father, Chilperic I, as king of Neustria (584). Upon e death of his cousin Theodoric II (613), he became ng of Austrasia, thus becoming king of all the anks. In 614 he had to make concessions to the obles, including the establishment of the position of ayor of the palace, that would in the long run deroy the power of the Frankish kings.

lothes Moth, small moth whose larva attacks oolen fabrics, furs, and leather. The most destructive f the three species is the case-making *Tinea pelonella.* It builds and lives in a small portable case. amily Tineidae. *See also* Moth.

loture Rule (1917), rule in the Senate that calls for one-hour limit on speeches if, after petition preented by at least 16 senators, there is an affirmative vo-thirds vote of those present and voting. Repeatdly challenged as encouraging not discouraging filiusters, cloture has rarely been approved by the Sene.

loud, a visible mass of tiny water droplets or ice articles in the atmosphere, formed by condensation f water vapor around condensation nuclei. Other ouds may consist of dust or smoke particles dense nough to be visible. Clouds are classified in many oups by meteorologists according to their appearnce and formation. Cirrus clouds are white and filmy curly, usually high in altitude and formed of ice ystals. Cumulus clouds are white, piled-up masses of ouds at low or middle altitudes, with flat bases and ounded outlines above. Stratus clouds are relatively w, gray clouds stretched out horizontally in layers. imbostratus clouds are dark and gray, accompanied sually by precipitation. Cumulonimbus clouds are exeptionally dense with a flat base, developing rapidly ertically with an anvil head or plume to form the miliar thundercloud yielding lightning, thunder, and sually heavy precipitation, sometimes hail. *See also* ondensation. △214–16.

loud Chamber, or **Expansion Chamber,** instruent for detecting and identifying charged particles, ich as the proton, based on a device invented by C. . Wilson (1895). It consists of a chamber containing aturated gas or air. If the gas is cooled quickly by diabatic expansion, any energetic ionizing particle assing through the gas will leave a line of droplets ong its path. The liquid drops form on the ions left the wake of the particle. Particles can be identified y the nature of the tracks, their curvature in an apied magnetic field, and by the tracks produced by ecay products. *See also* Bubble Chamber. △1478.

louded Leopard, small, rare cat found in forests of dia, SE Asia, Sumatra, and Borneo. A nocturnal prowler, its coat is ochre yellow marked with dark stripes and spots. It is an expert climber and has the longest canine teeth of any cat. The gestation period is 90 days and 2–4 young are born. Length: body—29.5–41.4in (75–105cm); tail—27.5–35.4in (70–90cm); weight: 50lb (23kg). Family Felidae; species *Leo nebulosa.*

Clouds, The (423 BC), Greek comedy by Aristophanes. It satirizes Socrates. There has been much controversy over whether the portrayal of Socrates is an accurate one.

Cloud Seeding, the technique of adding particles to clouds to alter their natural development, usually to initiate or increase their precipitation. Granulated solid carbon dioxide and silver iodide crystals have been used to promote the formation of precipitation in clouds by providing condensation nuclei. Mixed results have been obtained from many cloud-seeding experiments, and the technique is not yet under predictable control. *See also* Weather Modification.

Clove, aromatic, evergreen tree native to the Molucca Islands and the source of the cloves of commerce. Small purple flower clusters are dried to produce cloves. Height: to 40ft (12m). Family Myrtaceae; species *Eugenia aromatica.* △356.

Clover, generally low growing annual, biennial, and perennial plants. Primarily native to temperate and warm regions of the Northern Hemisphere. The leaves have three leaflets, seldom four, and the dense flower clusters are white, red, purple, pink, or yellow. Clover nectar is used by bees for making honey. These plants restore nitrogen to the soil and are used for forage and in lawn seed mixtures. Family Leguminosae; genus *Trifolium.*

Clovis I, or Chlodowech (465–511), Salian king of the Frankish kingdom that dominated much of western Europe in the early Middle Ages. Clovis invoked the aid of his wife Clotilda's god during a battle near Cologne. Victorious, he and his troops were baptized. He divided his kingdom among his sons shortly before his death. △1052–54, 1096.

Clovis II (632–57), Merovingian Frankish king of Neustria and Burgundy. The son of Dagobert I, he reigned from the age of five, but was controlled by Erchinoald, mayor of the palace.

Clovis III (682–95), Merovingian king of Neustria and Burgundy. His rule marked the end of the Merovingians' power; his kingdom was actually controlled by Pepin II, Carolingian mayor of the palace of Austrasia.

Clovis, city in E New Mexico, near Texas border; center of livestock and irrigated farm area. Cannon Air Force Base is nearby; site of annual fair and rodeo. Inc. 1909. Pop. (1970) 28,945.

Clownfish, or clown triggerfish, marine fish found in shallow Indo-Pacific waters. It has a compressed body, leathery skin, a spine in its dorsal fin, and has blue and green streaks on black, with an orange mouth. Family Balistidae; species *Balistoides conspicillium, Balistoides niger.* Also orange, brown, and white Indo-Pacific damselfish. Length: to 6in (15.2cm). Family Pomacentridae; species *Amphiprion percula.* △516.

Clubfoot, congenital deformity in which the foot twists inward and downward, looking somewhat like a club. It occurs in about one out of 1000 births, usually in males. It can be corrected by placing the foot in casts to make its position normal or by surgical intervention. In a few cases clubfoot occurs after birth as the result of neurological or muscular disease.

Club Moss, any of about 200 species (genus *Lycopodium,* order Lycopodiales) of small evergreen seedless plants, which, unlike the more primitive true mosses, have specialized tissues for transporting water, food, and minerals. The stems of some species are erect, while those of other species (the ground pines) creep along the ground and bear erect branches.

Cluj, city in NW central Romania, on Someşul River in Transylvania; formerly part of Austria-Hungary, became Romanian in 1920; noted for 14th-century Gothic church and botanical gardens. Industries: chemicals, electrical equipment, machinery. Founded 12th century by German colonists. Pop. 202,715.

Clumber Spaniel, slow-working finder and retriever breed of dog (sporting group) originally bred in England by Duke of Newcastle at Clumber Park. A sedate, heavy-looking dog with a thoughtful expression,

Grover Cleveland

Cleveland bay

Clipper ship

Clover

it has a massive head with upper lips overhanging the lower jaw. Long, broad ears hang close to the head. The long, low body is set on short, heavy legs. The tail is carried low. A silky, feathered coat is lemon or orange with white. Average size: about 17in (43cm) high at shoulder; 55–65lb (25–29.5kg). *See also* Sporting Dog.

Cluniac Order, or **Order of Cluny,** Roman Catholic religious order. Founded by William the Pious, Duke of Aquitaine, in 910 at the Monastery of Cluny near Mâcon, France, it was known almost from its beginning for its high standards, reflected in strict Benedictine rule, stress on splendid and solemn worship, importance of personal spiritual life, and sound economics with independent lay control. Its influence spread throughout southern France and Italy, reaching its height in the 12th century. The monastery at Cluny survived until 1790.

Cluny, town in E central France, in Saône-et-Loire dept.; noted for Benedictine Abbey of Cluny and for Cluny lace. Founded 910 by St Berno, a Burgundian monk. Pop. 4,412.

Cluster, Galaxy. *See* Galaxy Cluster.

Cluster, Stellar, any of innumerable collections of gravitationally associated stars occurring within galaxies. Stellar clusters are of two main types: open, or galactic, clusters and globular clusters. Open clusters, usually found in the spiral arms of galaxies, consist of up to several thousand young stars belonging to Population I; globular clusters, much more concentrated, are found in the halo surrounding the centers of galaxies and consist of old Population II stars running into the millions. △116.

Cluster Variable. *See* RR Lyrae Variable.

Clutch, Automobile, any device placed between the rotatable parts of the engine and the input-shaft for quickly connecting or disconnecting motor and drive mechanism. Temporary disengagement of the motor is essential during the shifting of transmission gear ratios.

Clyde River, river in Scotland; rises in Southern Uplands; flows NE, then NW, passing over the Falls of Clyde near Lanark, and widening into the Firth of Clyde at Dumbarton; noted for shipbuilding yards below Glasgow. Length: 106mi (171km).

Clydesdale, draft horse breed developed in Clyde River Valley, Scotland, from Flemish and English horses. It was introduced in the United States during the 1870s. A massive horse with distinctive style and action, it has characteristic long hair below its knees. Colors are bay or brown with white marks. Height: 64–68in (163–173cm) at shoulder; weight: 1700–1900lb (710–860kg).

Clymer, George (1739–1813), American patriot and a signer of the Declaration of Independence and the US Constitution, b. Philadelphia, Pa. A successful merchant, he attended the Continental Congress (1776–78; 1780–83) and later worked to promote penal reform in Pennsylvania.

Clytemnestra, wife of Agamemnon, Greek king of Mycenae, who led the siege of Troy. After the fall of Troy, Agamemnon returned home with his captive Cassandra, where he was slain by Clytemnestra and her lover Aegisthus. The Greek poet Aeschylus attributes the murder to Clytemnestra alone. The murder was avenged by Agamemnon's son Orestes.

Cnidaria, or **Coelenterata,** a phylum consisting of about 9000 species of aquatic invertebrates. Included are corals, hydras, jellyfish, sea anemones, sea pens, sea fans, and sea whips.

Cnidus (Cnidos), ancient Greek city of Caria, SW Asia, on tip of Resadiye Peninsula, Turkey; independent city and member of Dorian Hexapolis; ruled by Persians 540 BC; noted for wealth, temples, and statues; important trade center; site of a medical school and the statue Aphrodite by Praxiteles.

Cnossus. *See* Knossos.

CNS. *See* Central Nervous System.

Coachwhip Snake, or whipsnake, slender agile snake ranging from United States to N South America. It varies in color but is frequently brown and striped or cross-barred. Unrelated species in Asia and Australia are also called whipsnakes. Length: to 5ft (1.5cm). Family Colubridae; genus *Masticophis*. *See also* Colubrid.

Coal, a blackish rock composed of petrified vegetable matter, used as a fuel. In the Carboniferous and Tertiary Periods, vegetation subsided in swamp regions to form peat (a low grade fuel) bogs. Sedimentary deposits covered the bog, applying pressure, resulting in various kinds of coal. Coal is classified by fixed carbon content and by petrologic components. Lignite, bituminous coal, and anthracite coal show increasing carbon content; high carbon content results in better fuel. Petrologic components are called macerals, organic counterparts to the minerals in inorganic rock. Cannel coal is derived from microspores and is used in stoves and fireplaces. △282, 286, 1640.

Coalescence. △216.

Coal Fish. *See* Pollack.

Coalition, alliance of groups, parties, or states that serves the mutual political interests of its participants. In democratic countries with multiparty systems, coalitions are frequently formed by political parties or groups that seek to govern but alone do not have a majority in the representative assembly. △902.

Coal Mining, the process of removing coal from an excavation, or mine, carried on as a basic worldwide industry. Two principal systems are used: surface (strip) mining, a form of quarrying used when the seam of coal is near the surface; and underground (deep) mining, in which the seam is reached through shafts or tunnels. Power machines have replaced traditional hand tools. Although 3,000,000,000 metric tons are mined annually worldwide there are sufficient reserves to assure the future of the industry. △282–86, 1640.

Coal Tar. △1560.

Coanda Wall-attachment Effect. △1496.

Coast and Geodetic Survey, agency of the US department of the interior. It studies coastal areas and measures the areas and shape of tracts of land and the curvature, shape, and dimensions of the earth.

Coast Guard, US, branch of the armed forces. It is within the department of transportation, but operates as part of the Navy in time of war or when the president directs. Peacetime missions include search and rescue at sea, marine law enforcement, safety and environmental protection, and navigation assistance (buoys, lightships, beacons, etc). The Coast Guard operates over 250 ships, 160 aircraft, and 2,000 small craft with 37,000 military and 6,000 civilian personnel. It was established in 1790 as the Revenue Marine, an agency to enforce maritime law, and was administered by the treasury department. It was later renamed the Revenue Cutter Service and (1915) then became the Coast Guard. In 1939 control of the Lighthouse Service was added and in 1942 it took over functions of the Bureau of Marine Inspection and Navigation. It became a component of the department of transportation in 1967.

Coastlines. △268.

Coast Ranges, mountain ranges paralleling the Pacific coast of North America, from S California, N through Oregon and Washington into British Columbia and Alaska; composed of folded and sometimes faulted sedimentary rocks; the faults have caused earthquakes in California. Some S valley areas are cultivated for grapes, fruit, and vegetables; in the N, they are an important source of redwood, spruce, and Douglas fir trees.

Coati, or Coatimundi, 3 species of raccoonlike rodents of the SW United States and South America. Most have long, slender brown to black bodies (although some are orange-red) with long tapering snouts and long ringed tails. Coatis forage in groups on the ground or in trees for plant and animal food. Length: 50in (127cm); weight: 25lb (11.3kg). Family Procyonidae. △602.

Coat of Mail Shells. △476.

Coatzacoalcos, city in SE Mexico, on Gulf of Campeche, 134mi (216km) SE of Veracruz. Industries: petroleum, lumber, canning, soap. Pop. 108,818.

Coaxial Cable, device for the simultaneous transmission and strengthening of multiple radio, television, and telephone signals. The cable may house 20 or more coaxials, each a copper wire suspended in a tube. △1792.

Cobalt, metallic element (symbol Co) of the first transition series, discovered about 1735. It is found i cobaltite (CoAsS) and smaltite (arsenide), but the bu is obtained as a by-product during the processing c other ores. The metal is used in high-temperatur steels. It is a ferromagnetic element and a constituer of certain magnetic alloys. Co^{60} (half-life 5.26yr) is a artificial isotope used as a source of gamma rays i radiotherapy, tracer studies, etc. Properties: at. nc 27; at. wt. 58.9332; sp gr 8.9; melt. pt. 2723° (1495°C); boil. pt. 5198°F (2870°C); most commo isotope Co^{59} (100%). *See also* Transition Element △1554, 1572.

Cobb, Lee J. (1911–76), US actor, b. Lee Jacob i New York City. Beginning as actor/director at th Pasadena Playhouse in the early 1930s, he acted wit the Group Theater, New York City, from 1935, pe forming in Clifford Odets' *Waiting for Lefty* (1935 *Thunder Rock* (1939), and *Golden Boy* (1937), whic he also played in the film version (1939). Durin World War II he was with the California Radio Produc tion Unit of the US Army Air Corps, and following th war he gave his best-known stage performance, po traying Willy Loman in *Death of a Salesman* (1949 He appeared in many films, including *Exodus* (1960 *Our Man Flint* (1965), and *Lawman* (1971). He als appeared on TV from 1960.

Cobb, Ty(rus Raymond) (1886–1961), US baseba player, b. Narrows, Ga. Cobb played for the Detro Tigers (1904–26) and the Philadelphia Athletic (1926–30), compiling a record 4191 hits and 89 stolen bases. He was the first elected member of th Baseball Hall of Fame (1936).

Cobden, Richard (1804–65), English statesmar economist, and businessman. Cofounder of the Ant Corn Law League (1838), he served in parliamer (1841–57, 1859–65) as champion of free trade. H opposed imperialist foreign policies and supporte the North in the American Civil War.

Coblenz (Koblenz), city in W West Germany, at cor fluence of the Rhine and Moselle rivers, 56mi (90km SE of Cologne. Founded in 9th century BC as a Roma camp, it was later a residence of Frankish kings; fror 10th to late 18th century it was held by archbishop of Trier. During WWII, 80% of city was destroyed; sit of Church of St Castor (built 836 and rebuilt 1200 and 11th-century fortress of Ehrenbreitsen. Industrie pianos, furniture, textiles. Pop. 105,648.

Cobra, poisonous snake found worldwide. It has in movable, hollow or grooved venom-conducting fang in the front upper jaw. Included are coral snake mambas, kraits, and true cobras. Family Elapida Also, several large snakes capable of spreading the neck skin into a hood. The king cobra or hamadrya *(Ophiophagus hannah)* of SE Asia is the larges length to 18ft (5.5m). Several African and Asian sp cies can spit venom into enemies' eyes. △520.

Cobrafish. *See* Lionfish.

Cocaine, white crystalline alkaloid extracted fro the leaves of the coca plant. It is used in the form c its hydrochloride as a local anesthetic but as a dange ous habit forming drug it is strictly controlled.

Coccidiodomycosis, a fungus *(Coccidioides immiti* infection, occurring mainly in the southwester United States and western South America. Produce cough, fever, and aches but often disappears spo taneously. In more severe cases abscesses form unde the skin. If the infection spreads and is untreate death can occur.

Coccyx, the end of the vertebral column in mar formed by the fusion of four small vertebrae. △68

Cochin China (Cochinchine), historical region Vietnam, including greater part of South Vietnam. is bounded by Cambodia (NW), Annam region of Vie nam (NE), South China Sea (SE), Gulf of Siam (SW This flat alluvial plain of the Mekong River delta is on of the world's foremost rice-producing areas; fishing an important industry. Ceded by Annam to France 1862 by terms of Treaty of Saigon; became part c French Indochina 1887; inc. into Vietnam 1949; b came part of South Vietnam 1954. *See also* Vietnar △1378.

Cochineal, soft-bodied, scale insect found in Mexic and SW United States. Females have red bodies ar feed on prickly pear cactus. Until about 1875, crir son dye was produced from the dried female bodie Length: ⅛in (3mm). Family Dactylopiidae; specie *Dactylopius coccus.*

Cochise (*c.*1815–1874), chief of the Chiricahua A

aches. In 1861 the US Army captured him for a crime he did not commit, killing five of his relatives. He escaped and then led his tribe in war against settlers and the military in Arizona for 11 years. Concurrently, a war of extermination was being raged against his people. Cochise was befriended by Thomas Jeffords and through him made a treaty with Gen. Oliver Otis Howard that created a reservation of the chief's native territory. He lived peacefully on the reservation until his death, after which the treaty was broken and his people were moved from their land.

Cochlea. △676.

Cockatoo, large parrot with elongated, erectile crest. Most live in Australia, SW Asia, and nearby islands. They are mostly white, tinged with pink or yellow. They favor treetops, laying white eggs (1–4) in a tree hole nest, and feed on fruit and seeds. Length: 15in (38cm). Family Psittacidae.

Cockburn, (Sir) George (1772–1853), English admiral. After presiding over the capitulation of Martinique to Britain (1809), he was second in command (1813–14) in the War of 1812 and participated in the capture of Washington, D.C. In 1815 he carried out Napoleon's sentence of deportation and was governor of St. Helena (1815–16). He became admiral (1837), senior naval lord (1841), and admiral of the fleet (1851).

Cockchafer. △500, 594.

Cockcroft, (Sir) John Douglas (1897–1967), English physicist whose research dealt with particle acceleration in an electric field. Working with Ernest Walton, he constructed a voltage multiplier capable of accelerating protons to higher energy levels. The Cockcroft-Walton generator was utilized in the disintegration of lithium atoms by bombarding them with protons. The 1951 Nobel Prize was awarded to both men for their use of particle accelerators to study atomic nuclei. Cockcroft also contributed to the development of the atomic bomb.

Cockcroft-Walton Generator, device in which a high constant voltage is obtained by multiplying a low alternating voltage using a circuit of rectifiers and capacitors. *See also* Accelerators, Electrostatic.

Cocker Spaniel, capable gun dog (sporting group) named for proficiency in flushing woodcock. It has a rounded head and broad, square muzzle; the well-feathered ears are long and set at eye level. The sturdy, compact body is set on straight, strongly boned legs; the tail is docked. A well-feathered, flat coat is black, black and tan, parti-colored, or any other solid color. Average size: 14–15in (35.5–38cm) high at shoulder; about 25lb (11.5kg). *See also* Sporting Dog.

Cockfighting, sport, popular in Latin America and Asia, in which two gamecocks are pitted against each other in a fight. The gamecocks—bred for fighting—are placed in a small circular pit. To enhance the action, metal spurs are sometimes attached to the bird's natural spurs. The match goes on until one of the gamecocks refuses to fight or is killed. The sport has its origins in ancient Persia, Greece, and Rome and is still practiced where it is legal in some areas of the United States.

Cockle, bivalve mollusk found in marine waters. Its varicolored, heart-shaped shell has strong, radiating ribs. Many are edible. Length: 2–3in (50.8–76.2mm). Class Pelecypoda; family Cardiidae; species include *Cardium aculeatum*.

Cock-of-the-rock, fruit-eating, brightly colored, parrotlike bird of tropical South America. Its large, erect crest almost hides its bill. After group courtship dances, females lay eggs (2) in a mud-and-stick nest near a cave entrance. The golden cock-of-the-rock is orange-gold with black markings. The Peruvian species is red with black wings and tail. Length: to 12in (30cm). Genus *Rupicola*.

Cockroach, or roach, croton bug, insect with long feelers and flat, soft body found worldwide, though most are tropical. Its head is hidden under a shield (pronotum) and it may be winged or wingless. Living in dark, damp places indoors or outside, some species are serious household pests. Length: ½–2in (13–50mm). Order Blattaria. *See also* Orthoptera.

Cocoa. △354.

Coconut Oil, semisolid fat with a characteristic odor, consisting principally of the glyceride of lauric acid ($CH_3(CH_2)_{10}COOH$). It is extracted from pressed boiled coconut meat and used to manufacture soaps, vegetable fats, candles, and cosmetics. Properties: sp gr 0.92; melt. pt. 68–82°F (20–28°C).

Coconut Palm, or copra palm, tall palm native to the seashores of the Indo-Pacific and the Pacific coast of South America; most important commercially of all the palms. To 100ft (30.5m) tall, it has a leaning trunk and a crown of feather-shaped leaves each about 20ft (6.1m) long. Flower clusters have separate male and female flowers; the fruit, the familiar coconut, ripens in 10 to 12 months. The dried meat of the coconut is copra, the valuable commercial product that is the source of coconut oil used in the manufacture of margarine, soap, and cooking oil. Family Palmaceae; species *Cocos nucifera*.

Cocoon, case or wrapping produced by larval forms of animals, such as moths and earthworms, for the resting or pupal stage in their life cycle. Some spiders spin a cocoon that protects their eggs. *See also* Chrysalis; Moth; Pupa.

Cocos Islands, group of 27 small coral islands in Indian Ocean, SW of Java and Sumatra; discovered by Capt. William Keeling 1609; a protectorate of Australia since 1955. Exports: copra, coconuts. Area: 5sq mi (13sq km). Pop. 611.

Cocteau, Jean (1889–1963), French writer and painter who worked in ballet, theater, opera, and film. An immensely prolific and versatile artist, Cocteau was influenced by avant-garde movements but never belonged to any group. He is probably best known for his plays, including *Les Enfants terribles* (1929), dramatized from his novel, and for his films, many of which are also adaptations of his novels and plays. They include *Blood of a Poet* (1933), *La Belle et la Bête* (1946), and *Orphée* (1949).

Cod, bottom-dwelling marine fish found in cold to temperate waters, mainly in Northern Hemisphere. A valuable food fish, it is shades of gray, green, brown, or red, with a speckled pattern. Other members of the cod family are haddock, pollock, tomcod, and burbot. Length: to 6ft (182.8cm); Weight: to 211lb (95.8kg); average to 25lb (11.3kg). Family Gadidae; species: 150, including Atlantic *Gadus morhua* and Pacific *Gadus macrocephalus*.

Coddington, William (1601–78), US colonist, b. England. He was one of the commissioners of the Massachusetts Bay Company (1630), but his defense of Anne Hutchinson caused him to move first to Providence, then to what is now Portsmouth (1638). He helped to found Newport (1639). He was governor of Newport (1640) and several times magistrate of the Rhode Island colonies (1674, 1675, 1678).

Code. *See* Cryptography.

Code, Broadcast, in communications, a voluntary guide established by the National Association of Broadcasters (NAB) for self-censorship by broadcasters in the use of commercials and other programming. Networks also self-regulate affiliates.

Codeine, white crystalline alkaloid extracted from opium by the methylation of morphine. It is used in medicine as an analgesic and in the treatment of coughs. *See also* Opium. △744.

Code Napoléon (1804), French civil code that, with revisions, is still operative. Until the code was enacted, the French were subject to widely diversified laws, based on Roman law, customs, and royal decrees; marriage and family life were controlled almost entirely by the Roman Catholic Church's canon laws. Social breakdowns resulting from the French Revolution necessitated codification. The code was intended to conform only to the dictates of reason. It prohibited social inequalities and freed civilian institutions from the Church's control, permitting freedom of person and contract and upholding the inviolability of private property. △1226.

Codex. △872.

Codling Moth, small, grayish moth whose larva is one of the most destructive insect pests of apples. This brown-headed, pinkish-white caterpillar is the main cause of wormy apples. Species *Carpocapsa pomonella*. *See also* Moth.

Cod Liver Oil, an oil rich in vitamins A and D obtained from the livers of cod. It is used to prevent rickets in children and for other nutritional purposes.

Codreanu, Corneliu Zelea- (*c.* 1899–1938), Romanian fascist leader. He founded the anti-Semitic National Christian League in 1923, was arrested for political activity in 1924, and murdered the police

Clumber spaniel

Coblenz, West Germany

Sir John Cockcroft

Coconut palm

prefect upon his release. He was tried and acquitted for this in 1925. In 1928 he combined his organization with another to form the terrorist Iron Guard; he later sided with Nazi Germany. In 1938 he was arrested for plotting against the government and was shot by the police.

Cody, William Frederick ("Buffalo Bill") (1846–1917), US frontiersman, scout, and showman, b. Davenport, Iowa. At 14 he rode for the Pony Express and served as scout during the Civil War. Ned Buntline made Cody famous in his semi-fictional dime novels about his exploits, including killing 4280 buffalo in a 17-month period. In 1872, Cody played the lead in his own touring Wild West show. In 1883 he organized the "Wild West" exhibition, with Annie Oakley and Chief Sitting Bull among his star performers.

Coeducation, teaching male and female students in the same classes. In ancient and medieval times, girls were taught separately, if at all. In Europe boys and girls began to attend the same elementary classes after the Reformation. By 1900 most US elementary schools were coeducational but many high schools and colleges were not. The coeducation movement grew in the 20th century as part of the drive for women's rights, and the practice is now widely accepted.

Coefficient, term multiplying a specified unknown in an algebraic expression. Thus, in $5xy$, 5 is the coefficient of xy and $5x$ is the coefficient of y.

Coefficient of Expansion. *See* Expansion, Coefficient of.

Coefficient of Friction. *See* Friction, Coefficient of.

Coelacanth, or latimeria, bony fish, thought to be extinct for over 300,000,000 years, then found in deep marine waters near the Comoro Islands off Africa in 1939. This steel-blue fish has fins at the end of fin stalks; hollow fin spines; heavy bony plates under the throat; and a cartilaginous skeleton. Length: 5ft (1.5m); weight: 127lbs (57.6kg). Order Coelacanthini; species *Latimeria chalumnae*. △510.

Coelenterate, aquatic phylum of animals characterized by having the digestive cavity as the main body cavity. It represents the first animal group to reach the tissue level of organization. They are radially symmetrical, jellylike and have a nerve net and one body opening. Reproduction, which is sexual and asexual, includes polyp and medusa forms in the life cycle; regeneration also occurs. The almost 10,000 known species include jellyfish, sea anemone, coral, comb jellies, and hydroids. △468.

Coelostat. △94.

Coenzyme, a nonprotein molecule, usually containing a vitamin and phosphorus. When combined with an apoenzyme, a protein molecule, it activates an enzyme.

Coercion, legal concept involving compulsion and constraint. Coercion is the direct or positive application of physical force to compel a person to act against his will (actual coercion, in legal terms) or where one party is constrained by subjugation to another to do something he would not do if he were not subjugated (implied coercion).

Coercive Acts (1774). *See* Intolerable Acts.

Coeur, Jacques (*c.* 1395–1456), French merchant and official. After making a fortune in trade, Coeur served under Charles VII from 1436, controlling state financial affairs and instituting monetary reforms. In addition, he used his own resources to support France against England in Normandy. He was imprisoned on false charges (1451–55), but escaped and served under Pope Calixtus III. △1126.

Coeur d'Alene, city in N Idaho, 32mi (52km) E of Spokane, Washington; developed after 1882 discovery of silver and lead deposits; site of junior college. Industries: mining, farming, lumbering. Pop. (1970) 16,228.

Coffee, tree or shrub native to tropical Africa and Asia and cultivated in tropical South America. They have white or cream flowers and long leaves. The beanlike seeds are ground to make coffee, a drink popular worldwide. Height: to 15ft (4.6m). Family Rubiaceae; genus *Coffea*. △354.

Coffin, Henry Sloane (1877–1954), US clergyman, b. New York City. One of the most important spiritual leaders of Presbyterianism during the first half of the 20th century, he was pastor of New York's Madison Avenue Church (1905–26) and president of Union Theological Seminary (1926–45). A liberal theologian and social thinker, he favored reunion of the northern and southern Presbyterian churches and union with the Episcopal Church. He opposed racial discrimination and favored an equitable sharing of economic goods among the people of the world. His major works include *The Greed of Jesus* (1907) and *Religion Yesterday and Today* (1940).

Coffin, Levi (1789–1877), US abolitionist, b. New Garden, N.C. He was the only son in a Quaker family. He lived and prospered in Indiana, where he was identified with the Underground Railroad. He spent his last years working to help black freedmen.

Coffin, R(obert) P(eter) Tristram (1892–1955), US author, b. Brunswick, Me. Primarily a poet, he wrote many books of verse about his native state. His works include *Strange Holiness* (1935; Pulitzer Prize 1936), *Maine Ballads* (1938), and *Selected Poems* (1955).

Coggan, Frederick Donald (1909–), archbishop of Canterbury who succeeded Arthur Ramsey on the latter's retirement in 1974. Coggan began as curate in a working-class church in London, and later served in academic positions in London and Toronto. He was made bishop of Bradford in 1956 and archbishop of York in 1961. He is known for his liberal views on racial and sexual liberty.

Cogito Ergo Sum, (Lat., I think, therefore I am). In his *Meditations* (II), the French philosopher René Descartes attempted to establish his own existence by reference to the act of thinking itself. What thinks must exist in order to think, whatever else may be doubted. Upon this intuitively necessary truth, he wished to devise an entire body of knowledge, newly founded on the certain basis of reason rather than on authority or sense, and therefore free of inherited error. *See also* Cartesian; Descartes, René; Rationalism. △856.

Cognac, town in W France, on Charente River, 23mi (37km) W of Angoulême. Francis I was born here 1494. It was a Huguenot stronghold in 16th century; cognac was first manufactured in the 17th century. Pop. 22,062.

Cognitive Development Theory, theory in developmental psychology concerned with growth in the processes of perceiving, thinking, and knowing. Swiss psychologist Jean Piaget holds that cognitive processes develop through four stages from birth to adult status. During the first stage the child is most concerned with objects around him. Not until the final stage can a person make full use of symbols and logic. Jerome Bruner, an American, believes the course of development is more flexible than Piaget contends. △778, 788.

Cognitive Psychology, broad area concerned with perceiving, thinking, and knowing—eg, how individuals perceive information by sight or hearing, how they organize and store what they have perceived, how they remember and use information, how they use language and images. *See also* Cognitive Development Theory.

Cohan, George M(ichael) (1878–1942), US entertainer, songwriter, and playwright, b. Providence, RI. Brought up in a family of vaudeville performers, Cohan opened his own theater in New York City in 1911. He wrote such popular musical shows as *Forty-five Minutes from Broadway* (1906) and *The Song and Dance Man* (1923), and such popular songs as "Over There," "You're a Grand Old Flag," "Give My Regards to Broadway," and "I'm a Yankee Doodle Dandy."

Coherence Theory, in Logic. △854.

Cohesion, the attraction of molecules of a substance for each other.

Cohn, Ferdinand Julius (1828–98), German botanist. One of the founders of bacteriology as a separate science, his studies of algae and fungi began in 1868, and he published *Contributions to the Biology of Plants* in 1870. He conducted extensive research into lower plants, including bacteria, which he recognized as plants and attempted to classify. *See also* Bacteriology.

Coimbatore, city in S India, on Noyil River; occupies strategic position on E entrance to Palghat Gap, the only break in W coastal mountains for 900mi (1,449km); site of ancient Hindu pagoda of Perur. Industries: cotton, tanneries, coffee, sugar. Pop. 405,-592.

Coimbra, city in W central Portugal; capital of Coimbra district; regional trade center; site of Roman and Moorish ruins, a 12th-century cathedral, University of Coimbra (1260). Pop. 108,046.

Coke, (Sir) Edward (1552–1634), English jurist. As attorney general, he prosecuted the Earl of Essex, Sir Walter Raleigh, and the Gunpowder Plotters (1600–05). A chief justice of Common Pleas (1606), he protected the common law from crown encroachment. He presided over the King's Bench (1613) but was removed by James I (1616). Afterward, he served on both the Privy Council and the Court of the Star Chamber. Elected to Parliament (1620), he became leader of the party that opposed many of the king's policies. He led The Great Protestation (1621), for which he was briefly imprisoned (1621–22). He was the principal author of the *Petition of Right* (1628). His work, *Institutes* (1628–44), includes his famous analysis, *Coke Upon Littleton*.

Coke Processing, the production of a solid residue useful in metallurgy and home heating, from coal. Certain types of bituminous coal are heated to about 2192°F (1200°C) out of contact with air until most of the volatile constituents have been driven off. What remains is carbon with small amounts of other elements and coal minerals. *See also* Coal. △1640.

Col, high, narrow mountain pass that may be the intersection of two cirques or a high point between two mountain valleys. *See also* Cirque.

Colbert, Claudette, professional name of Lily Chauchoin (1905–), US actress, b. Paris, France. She started on Broadway under contract to producer Al Woods. With the advent of sound films, Paramount Studios bought her contract. She starred in many films, winning an Academy Award for her role in *It Happened One Night* (1934). She was in C.B. DeMille's *The Sign of the Cross* and *Cleopatra*, and by 1936 was Paramount's highest paid star.

Colbert, Jean Baptiste (1619–83), French minister of finance to Louis XIV. Having plotted the conviction and imprisonment of finance minister Nicolas Fouquet, Colbert dominated a newly created council of finance. He became controller general (1665), reforming the taille (a major tax) and terminating the financiers' plunder of the treasury. His efforts to increase France's international trade and to reorganize industry helped France to dominate Europe. His powers grew to include control of the navy, and he strongly influenced the country's cultural and intellectual life. △1170.

Colchester, city in SE England, on Colne River, 53mi (85km) NE of London; market town for agricultural and horticultural district. The first Roman colony in Britain settled here AD 43. Industries: chemicals, agricultural engineering, footwear. Pop. 76,145.

Colchis, ancient country in the Caucasus on the E side of the Black Sea (now part of the Georgian Republic of the USSR). In Greek legend it was the home of Medea, where Jason and the Argonauts stole the Golden Fleece. It was dominated successively by Persia, Greece, and Rome, and later became the focus of hostility between Byzantium and Persia (AD 6th century).

Cold, Common, very common, mild, contagious viral infection of the upper respiratory tract. More prevalent in cold months, colds usually occur in adults about two or three times a year, but more frequently in children and adults in close contact with children. A cold is caused by a virus, mostly a rhinovirus or enterovirus, with susceptibility perhaps increased by such factors as chilling, and is easily spread from person to person. Symptoms include obstruction and inflammation of the nose, sore throat, cough, hoarseness. The disease is self-limiting, usually disappearing within 10 days. There is no treatment for the common cold. Fever-reducing drugs, pain-relieving drugs, and decongestants may relieve symptoms and bring comfort. Antibiotics have not been found to be effective but may be given in cases where an accompanying bacterial infection is present.

Colden, Cadwallader (1688–1776), American writer and political leader, b. Ireland. After completing medical studies, he emigrated to America (1710). He wrote on a variety of subjects including botany, physics, and philosophy, and he was one of the leading intellectuals in the colonies. His best known work is *History of the Five Indian Nations Depending on the Province of New York* (1727). As lieutenant governor of New York (1761–76), he was unpopular for his loyalist position on the Stamp Act (1765).

Cold Frame, wood or concrete structure covered with glass or plastic doors and used outdoors to extend the plant growing season. Heated by the sun, it is used to force bulbs, harden off seedlings started indoors, and protect seeds from heavy rains and animals. During winter, the frame can protect perennials, and be used to root shrub seedlings, and cold treat seeds and bulbs.

Cold Harbor, Battle of (June 3, 1864). Civil War engagement at Cold Harbor, Va., where Union Gen. Ulysses S. Grant lost 7,000 men in less than an hour during one attack on Gen. Robert E. Lee's entrenched Confederate troops. Confederate casualties numbered 1,500.

Cold Sore, also called fever blister, a small sore, often found around the lips, sometimes on the cheeks, ears, or genitals. It first appears as a tiny fluid-filled blister on a red skin patch, sometimes becomes pus-filled, and then dries up, leaving a yellowish or brownish crust for a week or two. Caused by a virus—herpes simplex—it is often associated with a cold, sometimes with other febrile diseases, sunburn, and menstruation.

Cold War, post-World War II political, ideological, and economic confrontation between the Soviet Union and the United States and their respective allies. Serious crises resulted from this situation, including the Berlin blockade (1948–49), and the Korean conflict (1950–53). Each side viewed the other with suspicion and considered world domination the primary goal of its adversary. Mutual distrust and tension characterized the period. △1342, 1390.

Cole, George Douglas Howard (1889–1959), English economist and writer. A professor at Oxford (1944–57), he was noted for founding guild socialism. He later returned to his original Fabianism and was chairman of the Fabian Society (1939–46). His many works include *A Short History of the British Working Class* (1927) and *The British Common People* (1939). With his wife Margaret he also authored several detective stories.

Cole, Nat "King" (1919–65), US singer and pianist, b. Nathaniel Adams Cole in Montgomery, Ala. He was a jazz pianist in the King Cole Trio (starting 1939), but in the 1950s he achieved popularity as a singer of many hit songs, including "Unforgettable," "Mona Lisa," and "Nature Boy." He appeared in films, and in 1960 he toured internationally as a solo artist.

Cole, Thomas (1801–48), US landscape painter, b. England. A founder of the Hudson River school, Cole was fascinated by the American landscape. Early success allowed him to live in Catskill, N.Y., a region that inspired him. His large, romantic, lyric paintings, such as *The Voyage of Life*, are major works. *See also* Hudson River School.

Coleman, James S(amuel) (1926–), US sociologist, b. Bedford, Ind. Coleman's work has been in the areas of educational sociology, processes of collective decision making, and community conflict. He has also contributed to the development of mathematical sociology. His books include *Union Democracy* (1956), *Community Conflict* (1957), *Introduction to Mathematical Sociology* (1964), and *Equality of Educational Opportunity* (1966), which he coauthored and which has become known as the Coleman Report.

Coleoptera, the largest order of insects (over 250,000 species), comprising the beetles and weevils. All have a front pair of wings not used for flight that are rigid and serve as a protective covering for the delicate flight wings and upper abdomen. Mouthparts are of the chewing type. Larvae are grubs that pass into an inactive pupal stage before maturing. Species vary in size from minute forms that live within spore tubes of fungi to Goliath beetles to 4in (10cm) long. Some are destructive pests of crops, while others (such as the ladybugs) are valuable to man. *See also* Beetle; Weevil. △500.

Coleridge, Samuel Taylor (1772–1834), English Romantic poet and critic. Although he devoted most of his literary life to criticism, political journalism, and philosophy, he is chiefly remembered today as the author of the poems "The Rime of the Ancient Mariner," "Kubla Khan," and "Christabel." His poetry is noted for its rich imagery and exotic settings. In 1798 he and William Wordsworth published *Lyrical Ballads*, a collection of their poems that is generally considered the real beginning of the Romantic movement in English poetry. His greatest critical work, *Biographia Literaria* (1817), documents the critical theories of Romanticism. His criticisms of Shakespeare were highly influential in his day, as were his writings on German metaphysical philosophy. △1240.

Colette (Sidonie Gabrielle) (1873–1954), French novelist. Her first works, including the *Claudine* series (1900–04), were published under her first husband's pseudonym, Willy. Her novels, most of which contain strong autobiographical elements, were written in an exuberant style. Among her best-known works are *Chéri* (1920), *The Last of Chéri* (1926), and *Gigi* (1945).

Coleus, genus of bushy house or garden plant native to Africa and Indonesia, with oval, serrated leaves of reddish, green, or yellow combinations. Flowers are inconspicuous. Care: bright light, barely moist soil (equal parts of loam, peat moss, sand). Propagation is by stem cuttings or seeds. Height: to 30in (76cm). Family Labiatae.

Colfax, Schuyler (1823–85), US vice president (1869–73), b. New York City. A Republican party leader in Indiana, he was a US representative (1855–69) before becoming vice president. He was discredited in the Crédit Mobilier scandal.

Colgate, William (1783–1857), US manufacturer, b. England. He rose from being an apprentice to a New York soapmaker to owning his own factory (1847). With his son, he branched into the perfume business (1850). Colgate supported a small academy in Hamilton, N.Y., which was later named Colgate University.

Colic, spasmodic, cramplike pain in the abdomen usually becoming intense, subsiding, and then recurring. It may occur in the gall bladder (biliary colic), kidney or ureter (renal colic), intestines (intestinal colic), or in some other abdominal organ. △718.

Coligny, Gaspard II de, Seigneur de Châtillon (1519–72), French admiral (1552), Huguenot leader. Announcing his support in 1560, Coligny became the sole leader of the Huguenots (1569) and was responsible for the Peace of Saint-Germain (1570). His suggestion to Charles IX that both sides fight against Spain angered Catherine de Médicis and François de Lorraine, Spanish allies. Catherine ordered Coligny's assassination; unsuccessful, she warned Charles of retaliation. The king demanded the Huguenot leaders' deaths, and Coligny was beaten and decapitated during the St Bartholomew's Day Massacre.

Colima, small state in W central Mexico, on the Pacific Ocean; formed by the foothills of the Sierra Madre Occidental and 70mi (113km) of coastal lowlands; economy based mainly on agriculture, fishing, mining. Colima, capital city, is commercial and agricultural center of state; site of colonial cathedral and state university. Industries: food processing, tanning, tobacco, shoes, leatherware. Founded (city) 1522; (state) 1824. Area: (state) 2,106sq mi (5,455sq km). Pop. (city) 72,074; (state) 240,235.

Colitis, inflammation of the lining of the colon, or large intestine, that produces bowel changes, usually diarrhea and cramplike pains. It may be acute, caused by infection; or chronic, often due to an emotional problem. In severe chronic ulcerative colitis, the colon lining ulcerates and bleeds. △718.

Collage, pictorial technique in which all kinds of objects, chosen for their symbolic value, are pasted onto a painted background. It was begun by Georges Braque (1911) and used by Picasso and Max Ernst. Collage differs from papier collé in which objects are chosen for shape and texture alone. △1294, 1316.

Collagen, a protein substance that is the main constituent of bones, tendons, cartilage, connective tissue, and skin. It produces gelatin when boiled. △682, 1574.

Collagen Diseases, any of several diseases marked by an abnormal change in the makeup of the body's connective tissues. Included in the group are systemic lupus erythematosus (SLE), often called lupus; scleroderma; dermatomyositis; rheumatic fever; and rheumatoid arthritis.

Collar Bone. *See* Clavicle.

Collared Lizard, big-headed, long-tailed lizard of SW United States and Mexico. Able to run on its hind legs, it is yellowish-green and brown with two black nape bands and light back spots. It eats smaller lizards and insects. Length: to 14in (35.5cm). Family Iguanidae; species *Crotaphytus collaris*.

Collateral, the assets that are put up by a borrower to secure a loan. Most financial institutions will not provide unsecured loans but require collateral.

Collective Bargaining, process through which

Buffalo Bill Cody

Coimbra, Portugal

Colchester, England

Coleus

wages and other conditions of employment are determined in the unionized firm. Representatives of the workers and the owners meet to make offers on a labor agreement that is to remain in force for a specified period. Over the years the process has changed as the issues have grown more complex. An agreement may be several hundred pages in length, cover almost anything, and require the opinions of countless experts on both sides. If an agreement is not reached, a strike or lockout results.

Collective Farms, large agricultural tracts in the USSR that are worked by a community of peasants who share in the profits in proportion to the labor each one contributes. Collectivization of private farms was begun in 1929 and by 1934, 71% of all peasant lands had been collectivized. In 1949 the smaller collectives were consolidated into larger ones. Under Khrushchev, the peasants were given the responsibility for maintaining the farm machinery as well as the land itself. △1312.

Collective Security, method by which nations aim at preventing aggression by pledging mutual support in case of attack. Most collective-security agreements are regional in scope (eg, the Organization of American States, the Warsaw Pact), although the founders of the United Nations hoped that it would become a global, collective security arrangement.

Collectivism, political and economic doctrine that advocates public control and ownership of the means of production and distribution. Similar to but more rigorous than classic socialism, it stresses central planning and overall coordination of economic life. Collectivism, to some degree, exists in both socialist and communist countries. △1312.

Collectivization, agricultural policy initiated in the USSR in the early years of communism and in China after the communist takeover. Modernization of agriculture required larger land units than the existing peasant plots. Small holdings were brought together (collected) to make large-scale farming possible and to bring agriculture under control of the state.

College, in a broad sense, any educational institution above the high school level. The term may also mean: a separate undergraduate school; the undergraduate division of a university; or a professional school, such as a teachers college. *See also* Junior College; Land-Grant College.

College Entrance Examination Board (CEEB), US organization established in 1900 to help in selecting applicants for college. One division of the CEEB, the Educational Testing Service, administers the Scholastic Aptitude Test (SAT) and achievement tests to large numbers of applicants. SAT scores are one important factor in deciding who will be admitted to college.

College Park, city in W central Maryland, 7 mi (11km) NE of Washington, D.C.; site of the main campus of the University of Maryland (1807); present economy closely tied to university research institute and electronics manufacturing. Settled 1745; inc. 1945. Pop. (1970) 26,156.

Collembola. △492.

Collie, sheepherding dog (working group) bred from Scots shepherd and drover dogs in the mid-19th century. Popular in United States since 1880, it has a lean, wedge-shaped head; small, triangular ears held ¾ erect at alert; almond-shaped eyes; a long, muscular body; straight, medium length legs; and a long tail. The rough-coated variety has a long, straight, harsh coat, except on head and legs, where it is short. The smooth variety has a short, hard coat. Colors are sable and white; black, white, and tan; mottled blue-gray and black with white; and white. Average size: 22–26in (56–66cm) high at shoulder; 50–75lb (23–34kg). *See also* Working Dog.

Collier, Arthur (1680–1732), English philosopher. In his principal work, *Clavis Universalis, or New Inquiry after Truth* (1713), Collier advocated a form of idealism, similar to that held by George Berkeley. Both deny the independent existence of an external world (to be is to be perceived). *See also* Berkeley, George; Idealism.

Collingwood, Robin George (1889–1943), English philosopher and historian. At first an idealist who developed a philosophy of special sciences, he rejected idealism from 1937. In a major early work, *Speculum Mentis* (1924), he developed a system based on five forms of experience and the degree of truth in each, with art as the lowest and philosophy as the only form to yield truth. In *The New Leviathan* (1942), he views all expression as linguistic; the mind-end is consciousness and all acts of consciousness are also linguistic. His other works include *Religion and Philosophy* (1916) and *The Principles of Art* (1938).

Collins, Michael (1890–1922), Irish revolutionary. He fought in the Easter Rising (1916) and helped establish the Irish assembly (1918). He became intelligence director for the Sinn Fein and helped negotiate self-government for southern Ireland (1921). He was killed in the ensuing civil war. *See also* Sinn Fein. △1314.

Collins, (William) Wilkie (1824–89), English novelist who made important contributions to the development of the genre of the detective novel in books such as *The Woman in White* (1860) and *The Moonstone* (1868). He collaborated with Charles Dickens in writing many stories, including "The Wreck of the *Golden Mary.*" Collins was a master of intrigue and suspense and a technical innovator of narrative form.

Collodi, Carlo (1826–90), Italian journalist and newspaper editor, b. Carlo Lorenzini. The founder of two satirical journals, he is remembered as the author of the classic children's story *Pinocchio* (1880; English translation 1892), a tale of a marionette turned into a boy.

Colloid, substance composed of fine particles which can be readily dispersed in a continuous phase. A solid dispersed in a liquid is termed a sol, a solid or a liquid in a gas an aerosol, a liquid in a liquid an emulsion, and a gas in either a liquid or a solid a foam. Chemists identify three main types: reversible, irreversible, and association colloids. Reversible colloids—including cellulose, proteins, hemoglobin, nylon, polystyrene, and vulcanized rubber—form true solutions, subject to the physical laws of nature, spontaneously formed when a dry colloid and a dispersion medium are brought together. Irreversible colloids—including gelatin, cheese, dough, milk, and clay—cannot be dismantled to their original components and require additional stabilizing compounds, usually adsorbed ions. Sols (dilute suspensions), emulsions, aerosols, foams, and pastes (concentrated suspensions) are irreversible colloidal suspensions. Soaps, detergents, and some dyes are examples of association colloids which have spontaneously aggregated to form stable larger molecules called micelles, which have hydrophobic centers and hydrophilic surfaces. △1562.

Colloidal Condensation, preparative technique for irreversible sols similar to precipitation. A supersaturated solution may be carefully condensed so that a large number of small particles are produced rather than a crystallization into large agglomerates. Electrodialysis has been used to agitate and control the deposition.

Colloidal Dispersion, preparative technique for a colloidal system such as an emulsion or a foam. Emulsions are stabilized by an emulsifying agent, such as proteins or clay; foam is stabilized by a foaming agent. Oil-in-water emulsions are used in polishes, cosmetic preparations, and foodstuffs such as margarine and mayonnaise. Meringue and fire-fighting preparations are examples of foams.

Colloidal Particle, a solid or liquid droplet of 10^{-6} to 10^{-2} mm diameter composed of an aggregate of molecules or a single giant molecule. Such particles may be formed by breaking down macroscopic particles by mechanical or chemical (known as peptizing) dissociation or by preparing a supersaturated solution, which then aggregates.

Collusion, practice of all (or some) of the firms that comprise a given industry whereby they substitute cooperation for independent action. A cartel is a form of collusion. Collusion usually involves rigging market prices so that the participants obtain more profits.

Colman, Ronald (1891–1958), English actor. In 1920 he went to New York, where he was discovered playing a supporting role in the Broadway production of *La Tendresse.* Colman was given the leading male part opposite Lillian Gish in *White Sister* and was an instant success. He was signed by Sam Goldwyn, and starred, usually as a lover, in many films, both silent and sound. He was best known for his performance in *Arrowsmith.*

Colobus, or guereza, large, black and white, thumbless monkeys of equatorial Africa. Their long, silky fur was once used to trim women's coats. They are day-active tree dwellers that feed chiefly on leaves. The three species include *Colobus polykomos,* with a bushy white tail and striking white body markings. *See also* Monkey. △554, 598.

Cologne (Köln), city in W West Germany on the Rhine River, 25mi (40km) S of Düsseldorf. Romans est. a fortress here AD 50 and it remained in their control until 5th century. It was made an archbishopric by Charlemagne in 785. It declined toward end of Middle Ages and was ceded to Prussia in 1815; site of Cologne cathedral (started 1248, completed 1880), and Gurzenich, a Renaissance patrician's house; agricultural, commercial, tourist center. Industries: chemicals, textiles, banking, insurance, eau de cologne. Pop. 860,818.

Cologne Cathedral. △1094.

Colomb, Michel. △1146.

Colombia, nation in NW South America. A land of mountains and tropical lowlands, it has vast uninhabited areas. People of one region distrust people from others, helping to keep the country backward.

Land and Economy. The Andes, with peaks of nearly 19,000ft (5,795m), cover the NW third of the country and provide coal, platinum, and petroleum. Coffee from the mountains accounts for about 50% of export sales. The E and S slope down to such major rivers as the Orinoco, Putumayo, and Amazon. Between the mountains and equatorial lowlands, grassy plains provide good beef-cattle lands. Sugar cane, cotton, tobacco, and bananas grow well in Colombia.

People. Nearly 70% of Colombians have mixed blood, and many of these mestizos take an active part in public life. Another 20% of the population is of European descent, while Indians and blacks make up the remaining 10%. In the 20th century people have moved to the cities, and about 75% of the population is urbanized. Spanish is the official language, and Roman Catholicism the state religion. About 35% of the people can neither read nor write.

Government. The constitution calls for a president who cannot succeed himself, a senate, and a chamber of representatives. The Liberal and Conservative parties are the most powerful, and in the late 1970s the Conservatives seemed to be stronger. Liberal president Alfonso López Michelsen found many of his reforms blocked by the opposition.

History. Colombia, called New Granada by the Spanish when they made settlements on the Caribbean coast in the 1520s, took its present name in honor of Christopher Columbus after it gained independence in 1819. Simón Bolívar's Gran Colombia originally included Venezuela and Ecuador, which broke free in 1830, and Panama, which gained its independence with US help in 1903. Political strife in the 1950s led to an agreement whereby Conservatives and Liberals alternately held the presidency until 1974. The open political campaign of 1974 produced a decisive victory for the Liberals. △1120.

PROFILE

Official name: Republic of Colombia
Area: 440,000sq mi (1,139,600sq km)
Population: 25,900,000
Chief cities: Bogotá, capital; Medellín
Government: Head of state, Alfonso López Michelsen, president (elected 1974)
Gross national product: $10,590,000,000
Industries (major products): textiles, foodstuffs, iron, steel, petroleum products

Colombo, largest city and capital of Sri Lanka; a port on the Indian Ocean; inhabited by Muslims in the AD 8th century, followed by the Portuguese in 16th century and Dutch in 17th. Taken by the British 1796, it became Sri Lanka's chief port and capital; site of Allied naval base during WWII, several churches, mosques, Buddhist and Hindu temples, the University of Sri Lanka, and several colleges. Industries: ivory carving, gem cutting, tobacco processing, textiles, oil refining. Pop. 582,767.

Colón, city in W central Cuba, 27mi (43km) SE of Cardenas; located on Central Highway; railroad hub; site of polytechnic school. Industries: poultry, cattle, sugar cane, honey, tobacco, fruit. Pop. 84,100.

Colón, largest city and port in E Panama, at Caribbean mouth of Panama Canal; important commercial and free trade center. Founded 1850 as Aspinwall; name changed 1890. Pop. 95,308.

Colon, the large intestine, that part of the digestive tract that extends from the small intestine to the anus. Separated from the small intestine at the colic valve, it begins at a blind pouch, the caecum, and then passes upward (the ascending colon) along the right side of the abdomen, then across (the transverse colon) and then downward (the descending colon) along the left side, at the end of which it makes an S-shaped curve (the sigmoid colon) and opens into the rectum where stiff folds hold the contents until defecation takes place. The colon functions to absorb ater from the digested food material and to allow cterial action for the formation of feces. *See also* gestive System. △694.

olonial Insects. △464, 498.

olonialism, a control by one country over a depen- ɘnt area or people. Although it is associated with odern political history, the practice is ancient. In 'estern colonial history, economic, political, military, ıltural, and psychological factors all have been in- ɔlved. In the post–World War II era, the term came connote exploitation. *See also* Imperialism; △ ?18, 1260–62, 1280, 1304, 1350.

olonnade, a series of columns at regular intervals. 'hen in front of a building, a colonnade is called a ɔrtico. A colonnade surrounding a building or an ɔen court within a building is called a peristyle. The ɜrthenon at Athens is an example of a peristyle.

olonna Family, one of the most powerful Roman milies. They were descended from the 10th-century ɔunts of Tusculum and took their name from a village the Alban hills. The first Colonna was Pietro (*c.*)64); by the 13th century they had gained a position wealth and power. Important members include ɔpe Martin V, several cardinals, and generals, states- en, and scholars, including Vittoria (*c.* 1492–1547), poet who was the center of a group of famous artists cluding Michelangelo.

olony, in biology, group of similar animals or plants ving together for mutual benefit. Individuals perform e or varied functions and may be structurally sepa- ted or united. △464, 498.

olophon, a method in early printed works by which e printer detailed his role in the creation of the book ɜually in a paragraph at the end. It has since come mean a printer's identification or statement of the pestyle used, paper, and possible crafts employed.

olophony. *See* Rosin.

olor, sensation experienced when light of sufficient ightness and of a particular wavelength strikes the tina of the eye. Normal daylight (white light) is com- ɔsed of a spectrum of pure colors, each of which has different wavelength. The colors can be placed in ven bands, red, orange, yellow, green, blue, indigo, ıd violet, of decreasing wavelength, one band gradu- ing into the next. A pure spectral color is called a ɹe. If the color is not pure but contains some white is desaturated and is called a tint. Saturation is the ɜgree to which a color departs from white and ap- oaches a pure hue. A color also has luminosity, or ightness, which determines its shade.

Colors can be mixed to produce other colors. Any lor can be obtained by mixing the right proportions three primary colors. Mixing paints and mixing the me colored lights produce different colors: red and een light mix to produce yellow; red and green ɜint mix to produce brown. Colored lights combine an additive process; paints and pigments combine a subtractive process. △1516.

olorado, state in the W central United States, the ghest in the nation, with an average elevation of 800ft (2074m).

Land and Economy. The N to S ranges of the ɔcky Mts, with more than 50 peaks over 14,000ft 270m), traverse the W half. Their crests form the ɔntinental Divide. The rest of the state is covered by e W portion of the Great Plains, grazing and farming nd. Major rivers rise in the state—the Colorado, Rio rande, Arkansas, North Platte, and South Platte. ɔlorado's economy has been dominated succes- vely by mining, agriculture, and manufacturing. uge reserves of petroleum, natural gas, and coal main. Irrigation made possible the varied agricul- re of the plains. Food processing is the state's lead- g industry. Manufacture of ordnance and other mili- ry material in government plants is important. The cilities for year-round recreation make tourism a ajor aspect of the economy.

People. More than 75% of the population resides urban areas in a strip N and S of Denver in the nter of the state. Less than 5% were born outside e United States, but only approx. 50% were born in ɔlorado.

Education. There are about 30 institutions of gher education. The US Air Force Academy is near ɔlorado Springs. The small town of Aspen, once a ining community, has developed as a cultural cen- r, which features a music school and festival each ar.

History. The United States acquired the E part of ɔlorado from France by the Louisiana Purchase of 803. The remainder was ceded by Mexico in 1848 after the Mexican War. Discovery of gold and silver spurred immigration from other states, and Colorado became a territory in 1861. Building of railroads after 1870 expanded the population rapidly. WWI stimulated agriculture, and WWII shifted the economic emphasis to manufacturing.

PROFILE

Admitted to Union: Aug. 1, 1876; rank, 38th
US Congressmen: Senate, 2; House of Representatives, 5
Population: 2,207,259 (1970); rank, 30th
Capital: Denver, 514,678 (1970)
Chief cities: Denver, Colorado Springs, 135,060; Pueblo, 97,453
State Legislature: Senate, 35 members; House of Representatives, 65
Area: 104,247sq mi (270,000sq km); rank, 8th
Elevation: Highest, Mt Elbert, 14,431ft (4401m); Lowest, 3350ft (1022m), Arkansas River on Kansas border
Industries (major products): processed food, machinery, electronics, metals
Agriculture (major products): sugar beets, cattle, sheep, wheat, corn, fruit
Minerals (major): molybdenum, tin, vanadium, tungsten, uranium, lead, zinc, oil shales
State nickname: Centennial State
State motto: Nil Sine Numine (Nothing Without the Deity)
State bird: Lark Bunting
State flower: Rocky Mountain Columbine
State tree: Colorado Blue Spruce

Colorado Potato Beetle, or potato beetle, potato bug, small, oval beetle that is a major pest of potato plants and other members of the potato family, including the tomato and eggplant. Adults are shaped the same as ladybugs but are twice as long and are yellow with 10 lengthwise, black stripes. Species *Leptinotarsa decemlineata.*

Colorado River, major river of the SW United States; rises in N Colorado, flows generally SW into the Gulf of California, passing through the Grand Canyon. Length: 1,450mi (2,335km).

Colorado Springs, residential city in E central Colorado, seat of El Paso co, at the foot of Pikes Peak; resort city; location of trade center for Cripple Creek gold field, US Air Force Academy. Founded 1871; inc. 1878. Pop. (1970) 135,060.

Colorado Tick Fever, tick-borne virus disease prevalent in the western United States. It produces chills, fever, photophobia, headache, body aches, nausea, and vomiting for about two days, then subsides for a day or two, only to recur for another day or two, after which it usually disappears completely.

Color Blindness, general term for several disorders of color vision. The most common form involves red-green vision, a hereditary defect affecting males almost exclusively, in which the person does not see red or green. A much less common defect, yellow-blue color blindness, is usually the result of disease. Monochromatism is a very rare inherited disorder in which the person sees only black, white, and gray. △674.

Color Field Painting, style of American painting in which the picture surface is a continuous plane with figure and ground given equal value. Color is liberated from any limitation imposed by internal forms or structure, and the spectator is engulfed in the intensity of the optical effects and the emotional impact. The style was prevalent in the late 1940s, late 1950s, and early 1960s; Barnett Newman was its chief exponent.

Color Television. △1796.

Color Vision, ability to discriminate light based upon its wavelength. It is mediated entirely by the three types of cone cells of the retina. Each type of cone cell is maximally sensitive to a particular part of the spectrum. Color is also determined by other factors, such as contrast and adaptation. The rod cells of the periphery do not register color vision. *See also* Vision. △674.

Colosseum, large amphitheater in Rome built AD 72–80 by the Emperor Vespasian and his sons Titus and Domitian. Oval in shape, 620 × 513ft (189 × 156m), 157ft (48m) high, and seating 45,000, it was used for gladiatorial contests. Much of the structure remains, despite partial dismantling during the Renaissance and damage from earthquakes. △1022.

Colossians, New Testament epistle written by the apostle Paul during his first captivity in Rome. Addressed to the Christians at Colossae, it warns of the

Collie

Cologne, West Germany

Jamaica
Haiti
CARIBBEAN SEA
Barranquilla
Cartagena
Costa Rica
Cucuta
Venezuela
Panama
Medellin
Manizales
Bucaramanga
Guyana
Bogotá
Cali
COLOMBIA
PACIFIC OCEAN
Ecuador
Brazil
Peru
0
1000km

Colombia

Colorado: Great Sand Dunes National Monument

semi-Judaistic and Oriental philosophy that was corrupting their simple faith and questioning the eternalness of Jesus.

Colostrum, the first milk produced by the mammary gland immediately following parturition; it is nonnutritive compared to later milk secretion.

Colt, Samuel (1814–62), American inventor of the Colt revolver, b. Hartford, Conn. A single-barreled firearm with an automatic revolving set of chambers, brought into successive alignment, the Colt was patented in Europe in 1835 and in the United States in 1836. Colt also invented the submarine battery and utilized the first telegraph cable underwater. He established his own plant in Hartford (1847) at the site of the present Colt plant. He developed the first assembly-line procedure.

Colton, city in SE California, 3mi (5km) S of San Bernadino; shipping center. Settled *c.* 1875 with the building of Southern Pacific Railroad through the area. Pop. (1970) 20,016.

Colts Foot. △444.

Colubrid, term for snakes of the family Colubridae. It includes about 80% of the world's snakes. Their habitats vary from terrestial to aquatic to arboreal, with a few species being subterranean. Most are medium to small sized. They all lack any trace of pelvic girdles or hind limbs and have no left lung. The few that are rear-fanged, capable of conducting poison from venom glands, are relatively harmless to man, but some such as the boomslang can cause fatalities. Racers, water, garter and rat snakes are included in the 2,000 species. *See also* Snake.

Colugo. *See* Flying Lemur.

Columba, Saint (521–97), Irish missionary. He became a priest (*c.* 551) and founded two important monasteries, including Iona (563). From his seat as abbot of Iona, he continued to pursue the conversion of northern Scotland. △1052, 1056.

Columbia, city in central Missouri, 27mi (43km) N of Jefferson City; site of University of Missouri, Stephens College; a farm and coal area; medical center. Inc. 1826. Pop. (1970) 58,804.

Columbia, capital and largest city of South Carolina; seat of Richland co. Founded as state capital 1786, it was nearly destroyed in Civil War; childhood home of Woodrow Wilson; site of University of South Carolina (1801), Columbia College (1854), Allen University (1870), Benedict College (1870), Woodrow Wilson Museum, many antebellum houses. Industries: textiles, printing, electronic equipment. Inc. 1854. Pop. (1970) 113,542.

Columbia, city in central Tennessee, on Duck River; seat of Maury co; preserves James K. Polk House (1816). Industries: cattle raising, tobacco, shipping. Inc. 1817. Pop. (1970) 21,471.

Columbia Heights, city in E Minnesota, 5mi (8km) E of Mississippi River; suburb of Minneapolis. Inc. 1921. Pop. (1970) 23,837.

Columbia Plateau, region in NW United States, between Cascade and Rocky Mt ranges; extends over Oregon, Idaho, Washington; serves as major source of hydroelectric power, and important agricultural and grazing region. It is underlaid with deposits of lava more than 10,000ft (3,050m) thick, and sedimentary rock; site of Craters of the Moon National Monument, and of Snake River. Area: approx. 100,000sq mi (259,000sq km).

Columbia River, river in SW Canada and NW United States; flows from Columbia Lake in British Columbia through Washington and Oregon, and empties into the Pacific Ocean N of Portland; commands one of the largest drainage basins on the continent. Area: approx. 259,000sq mi (670,810sq km). Length: 1,214mi (1,955km).

Columbia University, university in New York City. It was established in 1754 as King's College, and its name was changed to Columbia College in 1784. It became Columbia University in 1912. Columbia confers bachelors, masters, and doctors degrees. Major areas of study include geology, engineering, architecture, medicine, and the arts.

Columbine, perennial herbaceous plant native to cool parts of the Northern Hemisphere. It has five-petaled, spurred flowers and notched leaflets. There are 100 species including the North American columbine *(Aquilegia canadensis)* with drooping red bells, found in rocky woods; height: to 2ft (61cm). Family Ranunculaceae.

Columbium. *See* Niobium.

Columbus, Christopher (1451–1506), Italian explorer in the service of Spain, discoverer of America. He was a seaman and in 1476 went into Portuguese service. By about 1480 he had become a master mariner. He became convinced that the Orient could be reached by sailing west. Unable to gain the sponsorship of the Portuguese, he went to Spain about 1484. Finally, Ferdinand and Isabella agreed to sponsor him and, on Aug. 3, 1492, he set out with his three ships, the *Niña*, the *Pinta*, and the *Santa María*.

After more than two months at sea, land was sighted on Oct. 12, 1492; it was one of the Bahamas (probably Watlings Island). Convinced he had found the East Indies, Columbus called the natives Indians. After exploring nearby islands, he returned to Spain in great triumph.

Columbus made a second voyage in 1493 and explored Hispaniola, Cuba, Jamaica, and the Venezuelan coast. He returned to Spain in 1496 to justify his administration (there had been none of the expected "riches of the Orient"). He returned to the colonies in 1498. In 1500, Spain sent a governor to the New World; he had Columbus arrested and returned to Spain in chains. Columbus recouped his fortunes enough, however, to finance one last voyage to America. It was not successful, and he died in 1506 in Spain, neglected and poverty stricken, but still convinced that he had discovered the western route to the East. △1122.

Columbus, city in W Georgia, at head of navigation of Chattahoochee River; seat of Muscogee co; 2nd-largest city in Georgia; industrial and shipping center; important Confederate industrial city. Industries: textiles, iron, food processing, lumber, chemicals, furniture, concrete. Settled 1828. Pop. (1970) 155,028.

Columbus, city in S central Indiana, on the E fork of White River; seat of Bartholomew co. During Civil War it was a Union depot. Industries: electrical components, diesel engines. Inc. 1821. Pop. (1970) 26,457.

Columbus, city in NE Mississippi, on the Tombigbee River; site of antebellum homes, Mississippi State College for Women, Columbus Air Force Base. Industries: dairying, cotton, timber, livestock, marble works. Inc. 1821. Pop. (1970) 25,795.

Columbus, city and capital of Ohio, in the central part of state on the Scioto River, 97mi (156km) NE of Cincinnati; seat of Franklin co. During Civil War, Camp Jackson (now Fort Hayes) served as a recruit collection point, and a Union arsenal was built in 1863; also site of Camp Chase, a Civil War prison. Columbus is the site of Ohio State University (1870), Capital University (1850), Bliss College (1899), Franklin University (1902), Ohio Dominican College (1911), Ohio Technical College (1952), the State Capitol, and the Gallery of Fine Arts (1878). The Battelle Memorial Institute (1929), the largest private research organization of its kind in the world, conducts scientific, technological, and economic research; the Orton Ceramics Foundation, the Chemical Abstracts Service, and Ohio State University research facilities have established this city as a leading research and scientific center. Industries: machinery, fabricated metal, printing, publishing, glassware, refrigerators. Founded as state capital 1812; inc. as city 1834. Pop. (1970) 540,025.

Columella, Lucius Junius Moderatus, 1st-century Roman soldier and farmer. Taking up farming in Italy, he wrote on agriculture in hopes of spurring interest in the simpler life. His second and more complete book on rural life, *De Re Rustica,* has survived.

Column, in architecture, a vertical post, supporting part of a building. A column may be free-standing, with a capital, base, and shaft, or it may be partly attached to a wall, in which case it is called an engaged column. A rostral column is a type of triumphal column from which projected the prows of captured ships to commemorate naval victories. Triumphal columns such as the Roman Trajan's Column had narrative reliefs to depict battle victories. Annulated columns, which are clustered together by rings or bands, were popular in medieval England.

Coly. *See* Mousebird.

Coma, state of unconsciousness caused by a temporary or permanent injury to the brain. It may be caused by a head injury, severe intracranial infection, lack of blood supply to the brain, or other causes.

Coma Berenices, or Berenice's Hair, northern constellation situated between Leo and Boötes and nor of Virgo. It has few bright stars but numerous galaxi and galaxy clusters. The north galactic pole is locat in Coma.

Comalcalco, city in SE Mexico, approx. 26mi (42k NW of Villahermosa, on Río Seco; agricultural cent produces rice, coffee, fruit, lumber; site of maj Mayan ruins. Pop. 71,651.

Comanche, a major Shoshonean-speaking Americ Indian tribe who apparently separated from the p ent Shoshoni in the distant past and migrated from Wyoming into Kansas. With the attraction of Mexic horses drawing them south, they raided farther a farther, until they became widely known and fear throughout Texas and Mexico. Numbering at mc 15,000, they were famous as daring horsemen a for introducing the horse to the Northern Plai tribes. Approximately 3500 Comanche people li on reservations in SW Oklahoma today.

Combat Neurosis, form of traumatic neurosis th develops under conditions of military combat, usua after injury or a close escape from it. Sleep distu ances, loss of appetite, mood disturbances, anxie and strong feelings of personal vulnerability usua occur. Symptoms often diminish dramatically wh the individual is removed from battle only to retu again when he reenters combat. *See also* Traumat Neurosis.

Combine, complex agricultural machine that cu threshes, cleans, and gathers cereal crops. Mode combines are self-powered and designed to cut or the top, fruited section, or head, of a cereal stalk, be the head to release the grain, separate the grain fro the chaff, and direct the grain into an attached gra tank. △310.

Combustion, fast chemical reaction emitting he and light, commonly involving oxygen. In solids a liquids the reaction speed may be controlled both the rate of oxygen flow to the surface, and by ca lysts. Industrial techniques harness this energy in t design of combustion chambers and furnaces. Exp sions and detonations are examples of rapid combu tion. *See also* Spontaneous Combustion. △156 1572.

COMECON. *See* Council for Economic Mutual A sistance.

Comédie-Française, French national theat founded in 1680. It is still organized according to charter granted by Louis XIV and revised by Nap leon. There are two kinds of members: *pensionnair* chosen on the basis of audition, and *societaire,* which the *pensionnaire* can be elevated only up the death, retirement, or resignation of a *societair* Over the years there have been many disputes b tween actors and management, but the organizati continues to produce excellent theater.

Comedy, one of the two types of drama. It diffe from tragedy in a lightness of style as opposed to t seriousness of tragedy, by objectivity of perspecti rather than the intensely personal viewpoint of tra edy, and usually has a happy ending. It originated early Greek fertility rites and, in modern usage, refe to any humorous play.

Comedy of Errors, The, (?1592), 5-act farce by W liam Shakespeare. Written in blank verse, it is an ear Shakespeare play, perhaps his first. It is also his sho est. Recent scholars dispute its previously accept 1592 date of composition, assigning it a much earli date. Its first known performance was at Grey's Ir (1594). The "Errors" in the title are mistakes in ide tity, as twin brothers, both named Antipholus, w their twin servants both named Dromio, separated a shipwreck during their infancy, come together in plot full of comic confusion.

Comenius, John Amos (1592–1670), Czech re gious leader and educational reformer, who fluenced the growth of modern education. Comeni believed in education for all children, girls as well boys. His best-known book, *Orbis Sensualum Pict* (The Visible World), used many pictures and relat Latin to the student's native tongue—both innov tions at the time.

Comet, small body orbiting the Sun, often in a ve elliptical long-period orbit, and probably composed ice and rocky material. Partial vaporization near t Sun produces a luminous dusty gaseous envelo (coma) and a characteristic luminous tail, up to m lions of miles long, that swings around so that it ways points away from the Sun. Comets might pos bly be ejected, by stellar perturbation, into the so system from a distant region (Oort's cloud) around the Sun and might finally disintegrate to produce meteors. △90.

Cominform (Communist Information Bureau), organization established in 1947 to provide information to and coordinate the Communist parties of the USSR, Bulgaria, Czechoslovakia, Hungary, Poland, Romania, Yugoslavia, France, and Italy. It replaced the Comintern, which had been abolished in 1943. Due to problems between the USSR and Yugoslavia, the latter was expelled in 1948. The organization was dissolved in 1956.

Comintern. *See* Communist International.

Comiskey, Charles Albert (1858–1931), US baseball player and executive, b. Chicago. The founder of the Chicago White Sox (1900), he was also a player (1882–94) and a manager (1883, 1885–94). He was elected to the Baseball Hall of Fame in 1939.

Comitia, assembly of citizens in ancient Rome. The early Comitia Curiata was drawn from the three tribes to elect officials and inaugurate priests. The later Comitia Centuriata, mainly patricians, elected officials, made laws, and declared war. Its lawmaking function was taken over by the Comitia Tribunata in the 3rd century BC. The Comitia ended with the establishment of the empire. △1014.

Commager, Henry Steele (1902–), US historian and educator, b. Pittsburgh, Pa. His most successful works are *The American Mind* (1950), a treatment of the social problems of the late 1800s, and *The Growth of the American Republic* (1930), a highly successful textbook he wrote with Samuel Eliot Morison.

Command Economy, authoritarian socialist economy that uses "commands" flowing from some agency (rather than "dollar votes" flowing from the market) to direct the productive resources to different uses. A requirement for a command economy is that government either owns the means of production or has effective control of them.

Commedia dell' Arte, a style of Italian Renaissance comedy performed on rough stages erected in the streets. The plays were comic and improvised—there were no scripts, but plot outlines or scenarios—and often crude and coarse. An extremely popular form, the Commedia produced several now-familiar stock characters: Harlequin (the clown); The Capitano (a braggart soldier); Pantalone (the deceived father or cuckolded husband); and Colombina (a feisty maid).

Commerce, Department of, a US government department that fosters, serves, and promotes the nation's economic development and technological advancement through activities that encourage and assist states, regions, communities, industries, and firms. Its agencies include the Bureau of the Census, Office of Business Economics, Patent Office, and National Bureau of Standards. Founded 1903 as Department of Commerce and Labor; became separate department 1913.

Commercial Bank, banking institution providing services to individuals and businesses within the US economy, primarily by creating and maintaining demand deposits. There are about 14,000 nationally or state chartered US commercial banks. Many are members of the federal reserve system.

Commercial Law, body of laws governing business transactions except those relating to carriage of goods (maritime law). An outgrowth of Roman *jus gentium,* it was revived during the Renaissance and administered by special courts in principal trading cities. "Merchant Law," a term applied to the principles of procedure and doctrine, evolved into effective municipal laws. These were incorporated into English common law in the 18th century and then were adopted in the United States. Commercial law influenced the formation of the laws of admiralty, negotiable paper, and of sales. *See also* Roman Law.

Committee on Public Information, headed by journalist George Creel, created a week after United States entry into World War I. Arranged voluntary press censorship and executed a broad ranging propaganda campaign against Germans, representing them as devils with agents everywhere. Its emotionalism contributed to growing national hysteria against pacifists and dissenters.

Committees of Correspondence, committees formed by towns and villages before and during the American Revolution to coordinate activities against the British. The first committee was formed in Boston (1772).

Commodity Market, market organized by traders in which promises of immediate and future delivery are made. The commodities themselves are not brought to the market place; only contracts for those commodities are sold. Commodity markets deal in items that are subject to sampling and grading, such as grains, sugar, coffee, tea, cotton, wool, rubber, and copper.

Commodus (161–92), Roman emperor (180–192), son of Marcus Aurelius. He amused himself in organizing contests between cripples, fighting as a gladiator, worshiping Mithra, and living in luxury. He raised soldiers' pay 25% and wished to rename Rome after himself. His irresponsible rule helped collapse the western provinces of the empire. He was murdered, and Pertinax followed as ruler. *See also* Mithra. △1020.

Common Carrier, any company that undertakes, for hire, the carrying of goods, persons, or messages, treating its entire clientele without individual preference and being responsible for all losses and injuries. The term applies to public utilities, such as trains, buses, motor freight, planes, pipeline operators, and telephone-telegraph agencies.

Common Cause, US nationwide, nonpartisan citizens' lobby working for legislative action and for political reform, founded by John W. Gardner in 1970. Within a year after it began, the organization had 215,000 dues-paying members, a permanent staff of 50, and several hundred volunteers working on national and local issues.

Common Denominator. *See* Denominator, Common.

Common Field Mushroom. △428.

Common Law, system of legal jurisprudence developed in England and adopted in most English speaking countries. Distinguished from civil law, which is a codified system based on statutes, its chief characteristics are judicial precedents, trial by jury, and the doctrine of the supremacy of law. Named for the king's court, "common to the whole realm," rather than local or manorial courts, it dates back to the Constitutions of Clarendon (1164), which limited jurisdiction of ecclesiastical courts and established supremacy of the king's courts. A basis of the US legal system, rules and principles established before the colonization of America are considered binding, but later English decisions have only "persuasive authority" in the United States. Recently, the courts, unable to keep pace with social developments, especially in areas of commercial, administrative, and criminal law, replaced much of common law with statutes. Equity jurisprudence was devised to ease hardships due to the inflexibility of some rules of common law and are now judged in the same courts as suits of law. *See also* Civil Law; Law; Roman Law.

Common Market. *See* European Economic Community.

Common Mold (Mucor). △426.

Commons, J(ohn) R(ogers) (1862–1945), US economist, b. Hollandsburg, Ohio. A teacher at the University of Wisconsin (1904–32), he became a leading US labor economist and a spokesman for social and economic reform. In his *A Documentary History of American Industrial Society* (10 vol., 1910–11) and *History of Labor in the United States* (4 vol., 1919–35), he advanced a theory of the evolution of the American labor movement. In *Legal Foundations of Capitalism* (1924) and *Institutional Economics* (1934), he emphasized the importance of group controls or rules for orderly individual action. He also drafted much of the legislation that made Wisconsin a model of reform in such areas as civil service, public utility and railroad regulation, workmen's compensation, and unemployment insurance.

Commons, House of, lower elective house of the British Parliament. *See* Parliament, British.

Common Sense, pamphlet written in January 1776 by Thomas Paine. The first clear call for American independence from Britain, it attacked the British monarchy as chiefly responsible for the restrictive acts against the colonists. △1218.

Common Stock, or ordinary stock, represents owners' equity in the corporation. Common stock is divided into shares and issued in the form of certificates.

Columbine

CHRISTOPHORVS COLVMBVS LIGVR INDIARV PRIM' INVET A 1492

Christopher Columbus

Combine

Commedia dell'arte

Holders of common stock may vote at stockholders' meetings. *See also* Stock.

Commonwealth (1649–60), British republic established after Charles I's execution (1649). It was dominated by Oliver Cromwell and the army, but no stable form of government could be evolved. On Cromwell's death (1658) England fell into chaos and the monarchy was restored (1660). △1332.

Commonwealth of Nations, free association of states, consisting of Britain and independent countries once her dependencies. It has developed from the British Empire in the 20th century and stresses cultural and economic cooperation. The British sovereign is head of the Commonwealth, and those members that are dominions, such as Canada, recognize her as their queen. Other members, including India, are republics.

Commune, in social science, a community of people who choose to live together for a shared purpose. In the 19th century many communes were formed to try to put utopian socialist ideals into practice. In the 1960s hippies and others formed communes that were intended to be cooperative, self-supporting, and free of certain values held by the dominant society. △1360.

Commune of Paris (1871), Parisian insurrection against the French government. After the collapse of the Second Empire (1870), the royalist National Assembly was elected (1871). Republican Paris, fearing a reinstatement of the monarchy, formed the Commune government in opposition to the Assembly. The Commune was crushed when government troops entered Paris on the first day of *la semaine sanglante* (bloody week), during which 20,000 insurrectionists were slain. △1288, 1300.

Communication, Nonverbal, communication by means other than spoken or written language, as by postures, gestures, and facial expressions. Actors convey shades of meaning by the way they walk, stand, use their hands, or direct their gaze. People in general consciously or unconsciously use body language. △ 862.

Communications Act (1934), US law to provide for the regulation of the communication media. The act established the Federal Communications Commission (FCC) to supervise the telephone, telegraph, and radio industries. Television was put under the FCC later.

Communications Satellite Corp. (COMSAT), corporation created in 1962 under US government control to operate an international satellite communications system. Stock is held equally by the public and by private companies, including AT&T, IT&T, RCA, and Western Union International.

Communism, political and economic system in which the major means of production and distribution are held in common. In purer forms of communism, all property, including housing, is held collectively. Although forms of communism have existed throughout history, in modern usage the term "Communism" is ordinarily used to describe the economic system advanced by Karl Marx in *Das Kapital* and put into effect in Russia by V.I. Lenin and in China by Mao Tse-tung. As political theory, Communism shares most of the tenets of socialism, and no strict dividing line between the two can be fixed. Both are contrasted to the system of free enterprise and private property known as capitalism.

The origins of communism can be traced to early tribal life. Hunting lands, fishing waters, and early farming plots were looked upon as community assets; such private rights as existed extended only to personal property. Plato's *Republic* (4th century BC) describes a Utopian communist society. Early Jewish sects, such as the Essenes, were communistically organized, as were many early Christian communities; communistic settlements continued to exist among the Christian sects until the 19th century, when such communistic settlements as Oneida, New Harmony, and Amana were founded.

Modern communism, however, is a product of the 19th century. Secret revolutionary societies were founded in Italy, France, and Germany; their purpose was to overthrow the established order and institute a new, propertyless society. Louis Blanc and Louis Auguste Blanqui, both French, were communist theorizers who were also political activists involved in the Revolution of 1848. That year, 1848, also saw the publication of *The Communist Manifesto* by Karl Marx and Friedrich Engels. That work set forth the basic theories of Marxist communism. According to Marxism, a communistic society is historically inevitable; capitalism, because of its emphasis on higher and higher profits, would eventually so reduce the condition of the workers (the individual proletariat) that they would rise up, overthrow the capitalists, and establish a classless society (the dictatorship of the proletariat). Marx's general philosophy of the class struggle, known as dialectical materialism, was fully set forth in his major work *Das Kapital* (1867–85). It is considered the bible of modern Communist parties, and all factions consider themselves the true interpreters of Marx's philosophy.

The history of Communism in the 20th century, despite its foundation on the work of a single man, has been one of incessant infighting and factionalization. In 1903 the Russian Communist party split into two factions, the Mensheviks and the Bolsheviks. The more radical wing, the Bolsheviks, advocated a violent overthrow of the government and the establishment of a socialist state that would transcend national boundaries and eventually become worldwide. Under the leadership of V.I. Lenin, the Bolsheviks were successful in transforming the government that was set up after the Russian Revolution of 1917 into a full fledged Communist state, the first in history. Upon Lenin's death in 1924, the Russian Communist party split between the followers of Joseph Stalin and Leon Trotsky. The Stalinists won and purged the Trotskyites from the party; those who were not executed went into exile, as did Trotsky himself. Stalin remained dictator of Russia for the rest of his life, and Communism both in Russia and in the rest of the world was a reflection of his policies. The Comintern and the Cominform were formed as instruments to coordinate the policies of national Communist parties around the world. Only the schismatic branches of Communism, such as the Trotskyites, remained independent of Moscow. At the end of World War II, the victorious Soviet armies were in occupation in most of E Europe. In each country these occupation forces left behind a fully functioning Communist government, and all the nations of E Europe became in effect puppet governments of the Soviet Union. The old Marxist dream of an international Communist state seemed possible.

In 1948, however, the Communist government of Yugoslavia, under Marshal Tito, broke away from the Soviet Union and pursued an independent course. In 1949 the People's Republic of China was proclaimed, thereby putting the world's most populous country under Communism and creating a potential rival to Soviet hegemony. The Soviet Union and China maintained close relations until the mid-1950s; after that, continual differences between the two nations made a unified Communism impossible. During the same period, the Communist parties of the West began exhibiting more and more independence and the Communist countries of E Europe, while continuing to be tied to the USSR both militarily and economically, exhibited an independence unheard of in the days of Stalinist monolithic Communism. *See also* Capitalism; Marx, Karl; Socialism. △902, 1308–10.

Communism, Primitive, a label for the way of life of some small preliterate groups that shared whatever property they had and cooperated closely to survive. This pattern existed long before the development of modern communist ideology.

Communism Peak (Kommunizma, Pik), formerly Stalin Peak or Garmo Peak; peak in SE Tadzhik SSR, USSR, in the Pamirs region; highest peak in USSR. Height: 24,590ft (7,500m).

Communist International, or Comintern, also known as the Third International, Communist organization. It was founded by V.I. Lenin in Moscow (1919) because he feared that the Second International might have a resurgence under noncommunist leadership and he wished to claim leadership of the world socialist movement. The Comintern demanded obedience to its decisions and expelled all dissidents, thus alienating potential support among European socialists. In order to placate its allies in World War II, the Soviet Union abolished the Comintern (1943). △ 1310.

Communist Manifesto (1848), work by Karl Marx and Friedrich Engels. Essentially it states that economic factors determine social relations. The authors call upon the workers to substitute communism for the inequitable system of capitalism.

Communist Party. △1310.

Communist Party, Chinese, political organization established in July 1921 by Li Ta-chao and Ch'en Tu-hsiu. The party was strengthened by its alliance (1924) with Chiang Kai-shek's Kuomintang, but was virtually shattered when the Communists were expelled from Chiang's group in 1927. Mao Tse-tung was the guiding force in revitalizing the party in the early 1930s. Under his leadership, which was solidified during the "Long March" from Kiangsi to Yenan (1934–35), the party revised the Soviet proletariat-based model to fit the peasant-oriented economy of China and achieved total power in China (1949). △ 1328, 1348.

Communist Party of America, radical party organized in 1919 to represent the interest of workers, farmers, and the lower middle class. Its program evolved from open revolutionary objectives to so-called "popular front" socialist goals. The party was strongest in 1932 when it polled 102,991 votes in the presidential election. In 1940, following the passage of the Voorhis Act, the party severed its connection with the Communist International and began to lose strength. Subsequently, the Smith Act (1940), the McCarran Act (1950), and the Communist Control Act (1954) drastically reduced its rights and possible influence. *See also* Smith Act.

Communist Party of the Soviet Union, official party of the USSR. It wields all effective political power in the Soviet Union and, as the oldest Communist party in the world, it has considerable influence over the Communist parties in other countries. It has about 15,000,000 members, or less than 5% of the total Soviet population. The party is organized into almost 400,000 local units, called cells, in every part of the Soviet Union. Party organization parallels the hierarchy of the local government administration; it is an organization that assures party control of every level of government. Usually, each party cell consists of a nucleus of full-time, paid cadre and a membership consisting mostly of the government bureaucracy. In addition, there are party cells in all other Soviet institutions, such as the school system and the armed forces; and cells operate in all factories, collective farms, newspapers, and in the entertainment business. Thus the Communist party maintains control over every aspect of life in the Soviet Union. Each party unit has a ruling body called a presidium headed by a first secretary. The local units meet periodically in party congresses. At the national party congress, the central committee is chosen. It, in turn, elects the presidium (formerly politburo), which is the highest ruling body of the Soviet Communist party. The general secretary of the presidium is, in effect, the actual head of the Soviet government.

The Soviet Communist party traces its origins to an organization founded in 1893 by G.V. Plekhanov. In 1903 the party split into the Bolshevik and Menshevik factions. The Bolsheviks, under V.I. Lenin, triumphed after the Russian Revolution of 1917 and became the ruling force in the Soviet Union. After Lenin's death in 1924, the party came under the control of Joseph Stalin. Stalin brought the party under his strict personal control, and the party trials and purges of the 1930s were the methods by which Stalin liquidated all opposition within the party and the nation. Thousands were executed and many more imprisoned or exiled. After Stalin's death in 1953, party membership was broadened and steps taken to assure collective leadership of party affairs. Nikita Khrushchev became the leading figure and led the party in an extensive "destalinization" program. His personal power increased, but in 1964 he was suddenly removed from power. A collective leadership replaced him with Aleksei Kosygin and Leonid Brezhnev occupying the leading positions. They jointly ruled over party and governmental affairs until about 1970, when Brezhnev, as general secretary, emerged as the dominant figure. *See also* Communism; Lenin, Vladimir Ilyitch. △1310, 1312.

Communist Party v. Subversive Activities Control Board (SACB) (1961), US Supreme Court case upholding the right of the SACB to require the Communist party to register. Prior to this decision, the court had ruled that individual party members need not register.

Community, in social science, a grouping of people, usually in one place and with a feeling of belonging together. A community is larger than the other basic unit, the family. Examples of communities are hunting and gathering bands of early men, farming villages, and modern cities. Within cities there are many communities in the sense of people with shared jobs or interests or backgrounds, held together by interdependent needs.

Community Antenna Television (CATV), system in which cables connect a central antenna to numerous television receivers, providing a wide range of commercial programs telecast by distant stations. Subscribers do not need separate antennas, but pay monthly fees for the cable service. CATV began about 1950.

Community College. *See* Junior College.

Community Psychology, specialized subdivision of

linical psychology that studies individuals' adaptaon to a community and the community's need for hange.

ommutation of Sentence, change in punishment educing severity. Commutation does not eradicate uilt and may be put into effect without the consent f the prisoner. Commutation is neither a pardon which terminates punishment) nor a reprieve (the emporary witholding of sentence or the temporary uspension of execution).

ommutative Law, rule of combination in mathenatics in which an operation on two terms is independent of the order of the terms. Thus, normal addition nd multiplication of numbers is commutative, since $\times b = b \times a$, and $a + b = b + a$. Vector multilication, on the other hand, does not obey the comnutative law. △1446.

omnenus, Byzantine family of possible Italian oriin, it reached its height of importance in the 10th-2th centuries, providing six Byzantine emperors 057–1185), statesmen, and authors (such as Anna omnena, 1083–*c.* 1150, a historian). The family also upplied all the emperors of Trebizond (1204–1461), vith the last one, David Comnenus, executed in 1462 y Mohammed II. There were some attempts to link he Bonaparte family with a Corsican branch of the omnenus family, but no basis was found for such a onnection. △1060.

omo, city in N Italy, at SW end of Lake Como; capial of Como prov.; defeated by Rome 196 BC; it beame a free commune in the 11th century; liberated y Garibaldi 1859; Mussolini was executed here 945. Landmarks include 14th–18th-century Cathedral of St Maria Maggiore, and Church of St Caroforo. Industries: silk, tourism. Pop. 93,199.

omo, Lake (Lago Di Como), lake in N Italy, fed by dda River and many other sources; outlet is at Lecco; esort area. Area: 56sq mi (145sq km).

omoro (Comores) Islands, independent republic ff the E coast of Africa, between Mozambique and Malagasy Republic; it is an archipelago in the Indian Ocean at the N entrance to the Mozambique Channel. our major islands and many small islands, all of volanic origin, make up the archipelago. The islands are nountainous with fertile soil; the highest point is Mt arthala, 7,746ft (2,363m), an active volcano on Grand Comoro, the largest island; Anjouan, Mayotte, nd Moheli are the other major islands. Moroni, on Grand Comoro, serves as the capital and is the largest ity.

The climate is tropical with a dry season from May hrough October. Agriculture is the chief industry; 5% of land is in plantation ownership, often foreign. oconuts are grown on rich lowlands, and upland rice n the higher, erosion plagued lands. Vanilla, copra, ocoa, and sisal are major crops and exports; rice, nachinery, and petroleum are imported. The people re mainly African with some Arabs and Indians. rench, Arabic, and Swahili are spoken. Most of the eople are Muslims.

From 1841 to 1909, France gradually acquired the slands; during WWII they were occupied by British roops. France granted the islands administrative auonomy within the French Union 1946, and in 1958 he territorial assembly voted to remain in the French Republic as an Overseas Territory. In 1968 internal utonomy was achieved; a referendum in December 974 resulted in 94% of electorate approving indeendence from France, which was made official on uly 6, 1975. The United Nations accepted the omoro Islands as its 143rd member in 1975. The overnment is headed by a triumvirate led by Ali Soiih.

PROFILE

Official name: Comoro Islands
Area: 838sq mi (2,170sq km)
Population: 291,000
Chief cities: Moroni (capital); Mutsamudu; Fomboni
Religion: Muslim
Language: French, Arabic, Swahili

ompanys, Luis (1883–1940), Spanish politician. A eader of the Catalan Esquerra, a leftist group favoring Catalan autonomy, he was a member of the republian Cortes (1932–33) and minister of marine. As rime minister of the separatist Catalan government n 1934 he was arrested; he then served as president f the Catalan state (1936–38) during the Civil War. He was tried and executed by the Franco regime.

ompany Union, labor organization formed by a ompany for its employees. Since the passage of the National Labor Relations Act of 1935, many company nions have been found to be in violation of the section prohibiting company influence, control, or domination of a union.

Comparative Advantage, in international trade, condition that exists when a country is able to produce a product relatively more cheaply than other products. If one country has a comparative advantage in product A and another country has a comparative advantage in product B, the countries are able to trade good A for B to the advantage of both. △940.

Comparative Psychology, field that compares the behaviors of various animal species. Comparative psychologists study animals to learn more about all species and to aid their understanding of human behavior. *See also* Ethology.

Comparative Statistics, in economics, used to analyze the movement from one equilibrium position to another. This analysis therefore involves no movement of time but simply allows for comparison of two or more time period equilibrium positions. *See also* Market Equilibrium.

Comparator, a measuring device used to inspect a part for deviation from a specified value, normally by direct matching or comparing with a master part against preset tolerances. The decision to accept or reject a part may be done by an operator or, in some cases, the comparator makes the decision automatically.

Compass, Drawing, instrument used in geometrical constructions to draw circles and mark off equal lengths. Formed of two pointed legs so joined that one may be kept fixed at a point while the other (generally having a pencil point) is turned around it at the desired distance.

Compass, Magnetic, direction-finding instrument consisting of a magnetized needle centrally pivoted so that it rotates in a horizontal plane and is free to align itself with the earth's magnetic field. It therefore points along the magnetic meridians to the magnetic north pole. The needle moves above a card marked with the points of the compass or the magnet may be attached to the card, which itself rotates. △1534.

Compass, Marine, a large magnetic compass used on ships. It consists of parallel magnetic needles attached to the underside of a graduated compass card, which is centrally pivoted in a glass-covered bowl. The bowl, filled with alcohol and water, is supported on gimbals and retains balance despite the ship's rolling.

Compass Jellyfish. △470.

Competition, in economics, degree of competitiveness or rivalry in a market situation. Competition is advantageous to the consumer since it promotes lower prices and higher output levels. The degree of competition within a particular market is usually strongly related to the number of firms within that market or to the degree of monopoly power held by the firm or firms within the industry.

Compiègne, town in N central France, 45mi (72km) NE of Paris, on the banks of the Oise River; scene of Joan of Arc's capture by the Burgundians May 24, 1430; site of elaborate 15th-century palace and beautiful adjoining forests and parks. Armistice ending WWI was signed Nov. 11, 1918, in a railroad car in the Compiègne forest. Industries: tires, chemicals, glass. Founded as Roman outpost. Pop. 29,700.

Compleat Angler, The (1653), discourse on fishing by Izaak Walton in the form of a dialogue between Piscator (Fisherman), Venator (Hunter), and Auceps (Falconer). A unique literary work, it combines humor, pastoral description, verse, and practical instruction.

Complementary Colors, two spectral colors, such as yellow and blue or red and greenish-blue, that can be mixed to form white light. *See also* Color.

Complex Ion. *See* Ion, Complex.

Complex Number. *See* Number, Complex. △1448.

Composite Family, a group (Compositae) of nearly 20,000 different plant species in which the so-called flower is actually a composite flower head made up of a cluster of many, usually tiny, individual flowers. In a typical composite, the daisy, the flower head has a central yellow disk, consisting of a cluster of tiny male and female flowers lacking visible petals. The outer ring of female ray flowers has relatively large white petals. In composites such as the dandelion and endive, the flower head consists entirely of ray flowers. Others, such as thistles, consist entirely of disk

Como, Italy

Cen. Afr. Rep.
Sudan
Ethiopia
Cameroon
Somalia
Gabon
Congo
Uganda
Kenya
Zaire
INDIAN OCEAN
Tanzania
COMORO ISLANDS
Malawi
Angola
Zambia
Mozambique
Rhodesia
Madagascar
Namibia
Botswana
Swaziland
ATLANTIC OCEAN
South Africa
Lesotho
0
1200km

Comoro Islands

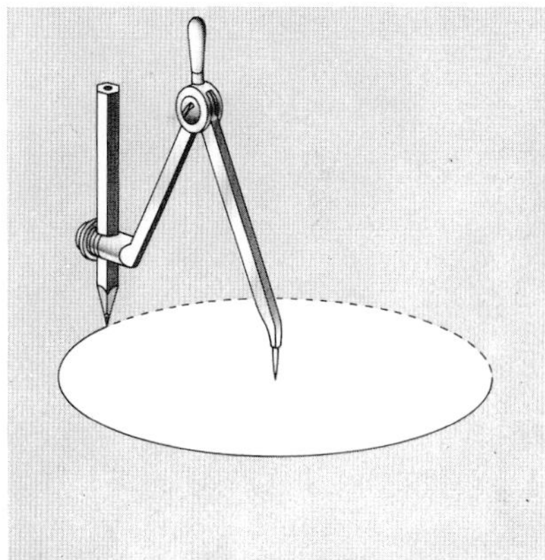

Compass (drawing)

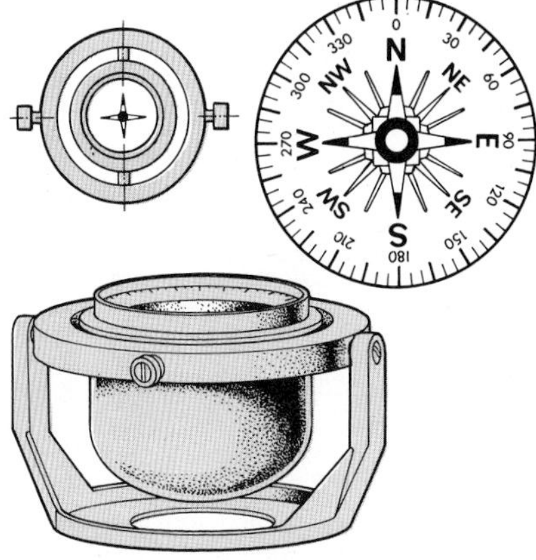
N
NE
E
SE
S
SW
W
NW
0
30
60
90
120
150
180
210
240
270
300
330

Compass (marine)

flowers. Composites comprise the largest plant family and have great variety of form and size. They are important to man as a source of food, and garden flowers. △444.

Compost, mass of rotted animal and plant matter used as a fertilizer. When properly prepared, with nitrogen added during decomposition, it is crumbly and free of noxious odor and does not compete with plants for nitrogen. Large amounts must be used to compensate for relatively low nutrient content (when compared with artificial fertilizers), but soil structure is greatly improved after several seasons of composting. *See also* Fertilizers. △320.

Compound, substance formed by chemical combinations of two or more elements. Compounds are produced by rearrangement of the electrons orbiting the combining atoms, and usually have quite different properties from those of their constituent elements. Ionic compounds have ionic bonds—they are simply collections of oppositely charged ions in which no distinct molecules exist. Covalent bonding produces two types of compound. In one, covalent compounds, a solid is formed in which the bonds extend throughout the crystal. Such compounds are hard and high-melting: boron nitride is a typical example. More commonly, molecular compounds are formed, in which groups of atoms are bound in distinct molecules. Such compounds tend to be low-melting, volatile, and soluble in nonpolar solvents. *See also* Element; Molecule. △1506, 1552, 1556–58.

Compound Eye, eye made up of hundreds or thousands of simple eyes, each having light-sensitive cells, nerve fibers, and corneal lens. It is found in insects and most other arthropods.

Compound Interest, interest that is earned not only on the principal but also on the accumulated interest of prior time periods. Simple interest is interest only on principal. *See also* Interest Rates.

Compressed Gas. △1502.

Compresser, Air, machine that decreases the volume of a quantity of air while increasing its pressure, creating great potential force. Used in motors and tools, such as pneumatic hammers, paint sprayers, and sandblasters. △1486.

Compression, Engine, in an internal-combustion engine, the pressure applied to a fuel-air mixture by a rising piston in a cyclinder. Compression is measured as a ratio of piston displacement and combustion-chamber volume.

Compromise of 1850, set of balanced resolutions by Sen. Henry Clay (Ky.) to prevent civil war. The US Congress agreed to admit California as a free state, organize New Mexico and Utah as territories without mention of slavery, provide for a tougher fugitive slave law, abolish the slave trade in Washington, D.C., and assume the Texas national debt.

Compromise of 1877, US political bargain in which Southern Congressmen were promised the withdrawal of federal troops from the South in exchange for supporting the election of Republican Rutherford B. Hayes as president. The agreement ended Reconstruction.

Compsoenathus. △572.

Compton, Arthur Holly (1892–1962), US physicist, b. Wooster, Ohio. He was appointed head of the physics department at Washington University, later moving to the University of Chicago. He worked in the field of X rays and discovered the scattering process (Compton scattering) for which he was awarded a Nobel Prize in 1927 jointly with C.T.R. Wilson. As head of the early phase of the Manhattan Project, he helped create the first sustained nuclear chain reaction.

Compton, Karl Taylor (1887–1954), US physicist, b. Wooster, Ohio, brother of A.H. Compton. An outstanding researcher (crystallography, ionization, photoelectricity), he was a Princeton professor (1915–30) and president of the Massachusetts Institute of Technology (1930–48).

Compton, city in S California, 13mi (21km) S of Los Angeles; residential suburb for Los Angeles and Long Beach; site of Compton College (1927). Industries: aircraft, electronics, oil, steel. Inc. 1888. Pop. (1970) 78,611.

Compton-Burnett, (Dame) Ivy (1892–1969), English novelist. Her novels, written mainly in dialogue, take place in upper-middle-class society in Edwardian England. They include *Pastors and Masters* (1925), *A House and its Head* (1935), *The Present and the Past* (1953), and *Mother and Son* (1955).

Compton Effect, or **Scattering,** scattering of electromagnetic radiation (X rays or gamma rays) by electrons, with consequent slight decrease in frequency of the scattered radiation (that is, loss of energy). The effect first described by A.H. Compton can be explained by considering the radiation to be a stream of photons.

Compulsive Personality, personality trait disturbance marked by obsessive concerns and rigid, ritualistic behaviors, making for an inhibited, orderly, stubborn, and relatively unemotional individual. Such people have an inordinate capacity for work and an inability to relax and enjoy life. There is no room for spontaneity; everything is planned and fitted into its proper place.

Compulsory Testimony Act. *See* Immunity Act.

Computer. △1584, 1660, 1672–74, 1710.

Computer, Digital, mechanism capable of calculating mathematical problems or manipulating data, usually at high speeds, in accordance with processing instructions and routines either permanently built into or temporarily stored within the computer. In the process of data manipulation or mathematical computation, the computer compares, combines, or otherwise relates facts and figures, producing logical conclusions or recording facts in a prescribed way. Often compared with a human brain because of its decision-making ability, a computer is fundamentally limited to operate in the manner by which it is programmed by a human being. The main elements of a computer are: (1) central processor, (2) data input device, (3) data output device, and (4) facilities for storing instructions and data.

Computer, Electronic, electronic machine that accepts and processes information and supplies results in a desired form. The most widely used and versatile type is the digital computer that manipulates large quantities of information at high speed according to a set of instructions (a program) written in any of various prescribed forms (programming languages). Information fed into the system must be in a discrete form, consisting only of numbers, characters, and symbols, that are converted internally into binary form—combinations of digits comprising only ones and zeros. Both input data and program are stored in the computer memory and can be accessed when required.

The central processing unit of the computer performs operations on the data according to the program instructions. These operations include arithmetical addition, subtraction, multiplication, and division and also logical operations involving decision making on the basis of comparison of input or processed data. The final results are then output in a variety of ways, usually in printed or graphic form or as a display on a screen. Unlike the digital computer, which is basically a counting machine, the analog computer is a measuring device. The hybrid computer is a combination of these two in which the continuously variable input of an analog computer is converted into a set of discrete information for much more rapid and sophisticated digital processing. △1672–74, 1782.

Computer Assisted Instruction (CAI), method of instruction featuring interaction of student with computer. Intended to relieve human teachers of routine tasks, it is an economical means of reducing instructional staff. The student is sequentially led by computer through a programmed lesson, including information presentation, testing, evaluation, and, if necessary, a similar repetitive review. A new lesson is begun after mastery of the previous lesson. Data terminals, including visual displays, are the means for student/computer dialog. Some CAI systems allow further dialogs, with students initiating inquiries and computers responding to the limit of the stored data and inherent decision-making process of the program. △1674.

Computer Language, a set of words and rules to enable a human being to communicate with a computer. Languages are normally classified into two categories: (1) machine languages having semantics (meaning), which are the specific, detailed computer instructions, and (2) higher level languages, having both semantics and syntax (sentence structure or pattern formation), which are readily understood by the human computer programmer. The latter languages are reduced to machine language by the compiler, assembler, or translator device that serves as an interface device between the programmer and the computer.

The higher level languages can be further classifie into: (1) Problem-oriented languages (such as STRES for structural engineering), in which the programm need not know much of computer operation or cor puter solution methods. The problem is described the specialized language of the user. 2) Procedur oriented languages, which describe the input, outpu and logical functioning of the program. FORTRA and BASIC are most commonly used. The proble must be described by the input to the translator an the programmer must know the method of comput tion. (3) Assembly languages or symbolic machir languages used as mechanical aids in writing actu computer instructions and highly dependent on th specific computer used. △1674.

Computer Memory. *See* Memory, Computer.

COMSAT. *See* Communications Satellite Corp.

Comte, Auguste (1798–1857), French philosophe The founder of positivism, Comte's basic system is th law of the three stages—theological, metaphysica and positive—that represent the development of th human race. In the first two stages the human min is finding causes to explain phenomena, while in th third, explanation of a phenomenon is found in a lav Comte saw philosophy as a coordination of all th sciences with the purpose of improving the huma race, and he founded the Religion of Humanity fulfill this purpose. His philosophy was a major infl ence on British thinkers, particularly J.S. Mill an Frederic Harrison. His major works include *Positi Philosophy* (1830–42) and *Positive Polity* (1851–54 △888, 1290.

Comuneros, partisans in the Spanish War Comunidades (1520–22). Led by Juan López d Padilla, a nobleman of Toledo, they marched again the regular troops of the regent Adrian of Utrecht ar Charles V. In all, 15 cities joined the municipal counc of Toledo in seeking administrative reforms. Howeve popular support turned the movement into a clas revolution. The *comuneros* were defeated at Villal (1521), their leaders executed, and all rebellious citie subdued.

Conakry, capital city of Guinea, W Africa, o Toumbo Island, in Atlantic Ocean; site of Polytechni Institute of Conakry (1963) and international airpor a major port and deep water harbor, it is the admini trative, commercial, and economic center of Guine terminus of country's only railroad. Exports: ores, agr cultural products. Founded 1890. Pop. 197,267.

Conant, James Bryant (1893–), US chemist, di lomat, and educator, b. Dorchester, Mass. He was professor of chemistry (1916–33) and president Harvard University (1933–53). He served as US hig commissioner (1953–55) then ambassador to We Germany (1955–57). In 1957 he began an elabora study of American education. His writings includ *Modern Science and Modern Man* (1952), *Educatic and Liberty* (1953), *Slums and Suburbs* (1961), *Scie tific Principles and Moral Conduct* (1967), and h autobiography, *My Several Lives* (1970).

Conant, Roger (1592?–1679), US colonist, b. E gland. He emigrated to New England in 1623. H lack of religious orthodoxy led to his moving to Nar tasket (1624–25). Later he founded Salem (1626). H served as governor of new colonies and in the co ony's general court.

Concentration Camps, centers where people "undesirable" political, racial, or military persuasio are placed for detainment, punishment, slave labo and extermination. Used by the Spanish during th Cuban rebellion of 1895, by the British during th Boer War, and by many totalitarian regimes, concen tration camps were used extensively by Nazi Ge many. They were also employed by the Soviet Unio

Concepción, city in S central Chile; capital of Co cepción prov. Founded 1550 by Pedro de Valdivi the conqueror of Chile; destroyed by earthquake many times and severely damaged in 1960. Indu tries: glass, textiles, sugar, hides, steel. Pop. 185,22

Conception, the implantation of the blastocyst in th uterine wall. In humans it occurs 6–7 days followin fertilization, which takes place in the fallopian tube It marks the start of pregnancy. △700.

Concept Learning, the formation of an abstractio of an aspect of a group of objects or events commo to all of them. Concept learning enables a person t classify his experiences. Concepts themselves may b abstract or concrete; any object may belong to mor than one concept.

According to Jean Piaget, concept learning corresponds to maturation stages. Children begin learning concepts through visual experiences with objects. As the child matures, he learns to distinguish among more abstract properties. The ability to conceptualize is increased by the variety of sensory stimuli that are available to the child; hence, an advantaged child may exhibit a higher level of thinking than a disadvantaged child of the same age and intelligence. △778.

Conceptualism, philosophical theory in which the universal is found in the particular. A position between nominalism (which analyzes universals into particulars) and realism (in which universals are real apart from all particulars), conceptualism includes both universals and particulars. Essentially, it holds that the mind is the individual that universalizes by experiencing particulars, finding common factors in them, and then conceptualizing these common factors as universals. One example is the "concrete universal" of Hegelians, in which the mind is the concrete individual capable of grasping the meaning of universals. △852.

Concertina, musical instrument developed *c.* 1830. A compact, hexagonal accordion with studs on both sides, it was preferred in England and was used by 19th-century sailors to accompany sea chanties. The Argentine version is the Bandoneon. *See also* Accordion.

Concerto, musical work for an instrumental soloist accompanied by orchestra and usually designed to show off the performer's technical skill on his instrument. Concertos usually have three parts or movements, the first and last following the form of a sonata. The concertos of such composers as Beethoven, Grieg, Tchaikovsky, and Rachmaninoff are among the most popular of all classical music works.

Conch, gastropod mollusk found worldwide in warm seas. It has a large spiraled shell. Types include true conchs *(Strombus);* spider conchs *(Lambis),* and deep water *Tibia* shells. Length: 4–12in (10.2–30.5cm). Class Gastropoda; family Strombidae. △482, 1686.

Conciliation, form of third-party intervention in a dispute, labor or otherwise. The conciliator does not express an opinion about the possible terms of agreement, but acts as a go-between to keep the discussion going. Mediation is a form of conciliation, but the mediator may make suggestions for settlement.

Concini, Concino (died 1617), also known as Marquis d'Ancre, Florentine-born adventurer, marshal and chief minister of France early in reign of Louis XIII (from 1613). Arriving in France (1600) with the Florentine Marie de Medici (who married Henri IV and later was regent for Louis XIII), he was her chief advisor and brought the future Cardinal Richelieu into government. He was assassinated.

Concord, city in W central California, NNE of Berkeley; center of oil and farming region; manufactures electronic equipment. Settled 1852; inc. 1905. Pop. (1970) 85,164.

Concord, town in E Massachusetts, 19mi (31km) NW of Boston on Concord River; scene of historic Revolutionary War battle of Concord and neighboring Lexington, Apr. 19, 1775. British forces were sent from Boston to destroy ammunition and supplies stockpiled in Concord; the Minute Men courageously checked the British advance at the North Bridge. The battle is commemorated by Daniel C. French's bronze Minute Man statue and the Minute Man National Historic Park (est 1959). Concord developed as a literary center mid-19th century, and the homes of such famous residents as Ralph Waldo Emerson, Henry David Thoreau, Nathaniel Hawthorne, Louisa May and A. Bronson Alcott are preserved as museums; site of Antiquarian Museum, Old Manse (1769) built by Emerson's grandfather, Walden Pond, and area where Ephraim Bull developed the concord grape. Industries: electronic and wood products, furniture, iron, precision machinery, tourism, fruit, poultry. Settled 1635. Pop. (1970) 16,148.

Concord, capital city of New Hampshire, in S central section, on Merrimack River 15mi (24km) N of Manchester; seat of Merrimack co. Industrial and financial center, it was the scene of New Hampshire's ratification of the Constitution as the ninth and deciding state on June 21, 1788; noted in 19th century for manufacture of Concord stagecoaches; site of St Paul's School, New Hampshire Technical Institute (1961), last home of President Franklin Pierce (1857–60, now a museum); birthplace of Mary Baker Eddy. Quarries N of city produce famous white Concord granite used for building the Library of Congress, Museum of Modern Art in New York City, and the New Hampshire state house (1819). Industries: leather, granite quarrying, electrical equipment, printing. Founded as trading post 1660; settled in 1727; inc. 1733 by Massachusetts as Rumford, by New Hampshire as Concord 1765, as town 1784, as city 1853; designated capital 1808. Pop. (1970) 30,022.

Concordat of 1801, agreement concluded between Napoleon and Pope Pius VII on July 16, 1801. It established the Roman Catholic church as the religion of the majority of French people; the state was to pay the salaries of the bishops and some priests, and France's first consul had the right to nominate bishops to be confirmed by the Pope. Napoleon wanted the concordat to win over the clergy and so disarm the royalists and also to gain the support of Belgium and the Rhineland. The Pope, although he did not want to alienate the royalists, wanted the French army in Rome as protection. Napoleon's publication of the Organic Articles and his claims of the supremacy of the emperor over the Pope made it difficult to implement the agreement. Napoleon regarded the concordat annulled on Feb. 23, 1812, although it remained in force formally in France until Dec. 6, 1905, with passage of the bill separating church and state.

Concorde. △1716.

Concordia, in Roman mythology, goddess that personified the union of citizens. She had a temple near the Forum and was represented on coins as holding a cornucopia and olive branch.

Concrete, a hard, strong building material composed of a cementing material, such as Portland cement, and an aggregate of minerals (sand and gravel or broken rock) mixed with water. *See also* Cement. △1610–12.

Concubinage, cohabitation of a man and woman not married to each other. Concubinage is usually a socially recognized relationship into which a couple enters instead of marriage, or which exists in addition to the man's marriage. In most legal systems children of such a union cannot inherit property as of right. *See also* Harem.

Concurrent Majority, political theory that important social and political issues require more than a simple majority for a law to become effective. According to the theory, all important factions within a constituency must generally concur before legislation is passed. It was first espoused by John C. Calhoun about 1810 in the South Carolina legislature where the diametrically opposed economic interests of the planters and the dirt farmers clashed. It was later used by Calhoun and other pro-slavery southerners as the philosophic basis for preventing the North from outlawing slavery in the South.

Concussion, temporary brain malfunction due to a blow to the head. It is manifested by loss of consciousness for a few seconds or minutes, and later by intermittent headache and brief giddiness or difficulty in concentrating. Treatment consists of rest and close observation to ensure that no serious head injuries are present.

Condé, House of (1530–1830), junior branch of the House of Bourbon. Notables of the line included the first prince, **Louis I de Bourbon** (1530–69), a Huguenot leader; he signed the Peace of Longjumeau (1568). His son, **Henry I** (1552–88), was also a Huguenot leader. The third prince was **Henry II** (1588–1646), a Catholic. Arrested for blackmail and sedition (1616), he was later rewarded for loyalty to Louis XIII. **Louis II, the Great Condé** (1621–86), was the last leader of the Fronde uprisings (1648–53). He became one of Louis XIV's greatest generals. **Louis Joseph de Bourbon** (1736–1818) fought in the Seven Years' War and supported the monarchy after the French Revolution. When his son **Louis Henri Joseph** (1756–1830), the ninth prince, was found hanged, the line ended.

Condensation, deposition of a solid or liquid from its vapor onto a cool surface, occurring when the gaseous vapor pressure exceeds that of its liquid or solid phase. Condensation occurs in pure air that is supersaturated with moisture; in the atmosphere dispersed dust particles can attract moisture when the relative humidity is less than 100%.

Condensation, Colloidal. *See* Colloidal Condensation.

Condensation Nucleus, a small solid or liquid particle, like dust, on which water vapor in the atmosphere begins to condense in tiny water droplets or ice crystals with cloud formation. △216.

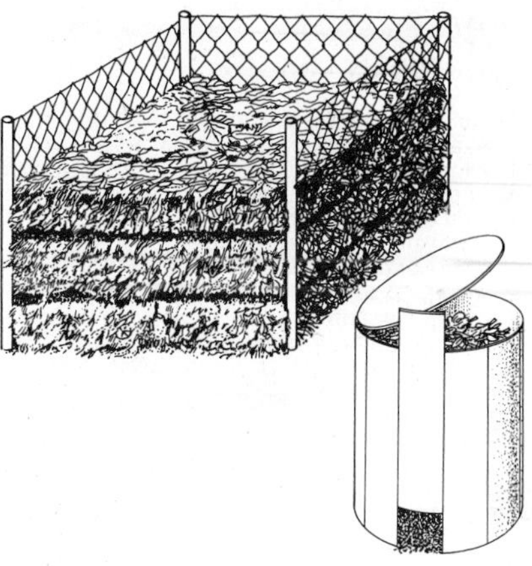

Compost

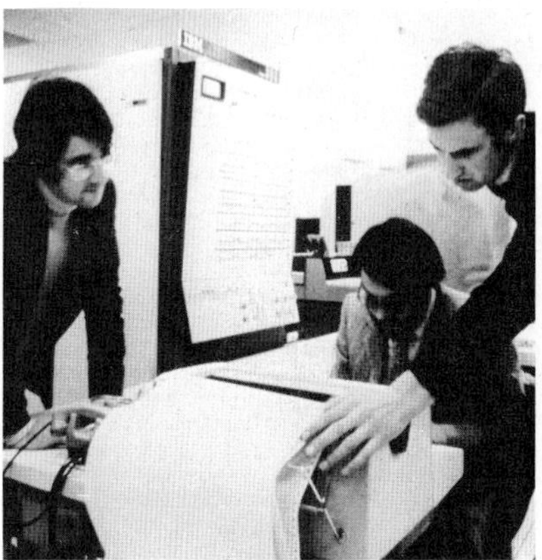

Computers

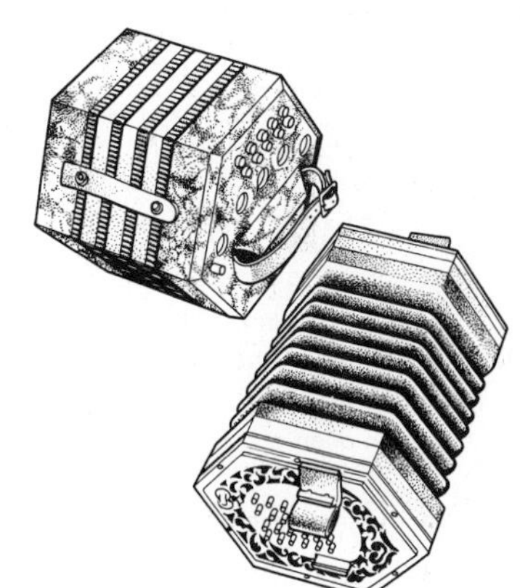

Concertina

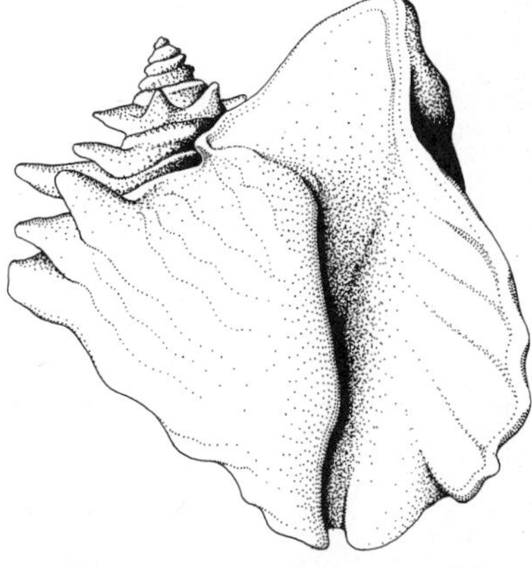

Conch

Condenser. *See* Capacitor.

Condenser, Steam. △1630.

Condillac, Étienne Bonnet de (1715–80), French philosopher. Condillac was the most eminent member of the school of sensationalists, believing that human understanding can be reduced to the articulation and comparison of sensations derived from experience. A strong Lockean influence pervades his *Treatise on Systems* (1746) and *Treatise on Sensation* (1754).

Conditioned Response, in psychology, any behavior learned through procedures of operant or Pavlovian conditioning. *See also* Operant Conditioning; Pavlovian Conditioning. △772.

Conditioning. *See* Operant Conditioning; Pavlovian Conditioning. △772.

Condon, Edward U(hler) (1902–74), US physicist, b. Alamogordo, N.M. A former director of the National Bureau of Standards, he also applied quantum mechanics to investigations of the atom and its nucleus. He was an investigator of flying saucers and he wrote a controversial report on UFOs.

Condor, American vulture that typically soars in search of carrion. The Andean condor *(Vultur gryphus)* of mountainous W South America is glossy black with a reddish head and neck. The almost extinct Californian condor *(Gymnogyps californianus)*, gray-brown with an orange head and red neck, is limited to the San Joaquin Valley of California. Length: 3.5–4.5ft (1–1.4m); wingspan: to 12ft (3.7m); weight: to 25lb (11.3kg).

Condorcet, Marie Jean Antoine Nicholas de Caritat, Marquis de (1743–94), French philosopher and mathematician noted for his *Essay on the Calculus of Probabilities* (1785), which systematized that study. He influenced 19th-century thought with his idea of the indefinite progress of man in his *Sketch for a Historical Picture of the Progress of the Human Mind* (1795). Condorcet was president of the legislative assembly (1792), where he promoted a system of educational reforms. Arrested during the Reign of Terror, he died in prison.

Condottieri, leaders of mercenary armies hired to fight numerous wars among 14th- to 16th-century Italian states. Their armies were largely made up of foreigners, and they themselves were often non-Italian. By the late 14th century Italian *condottieri* began conquering principalities for themselves. Famous among *condottieri* were the Englishman John Hawkwood (late 14th century) and Francesco Sforza (who won Milan in 1450).

Conductance, reciprocal of resistance in a direct current circuit; resistance divided by the square of impedance in an alternating current circuit. It is measured in siemens.

Conduction, the transfer of heat from molecule to molecule within a body. If an iron rod is placed in a flame, the heat energy received at one end causes increased vibratory motion of the molecules in that end. By bumping into molecules further along the rod, the increased motion is passed along to them, and finally the end not in the flame grows hot. △1508.

Conductivity, Electrolytic, passage of an electric current through an electrolyte. Electrovalent compounds (acids, bases, and salts) in solution break up into positively and negatively charged ions (for example, $NaCl \rightarrow Na^+ + Cl^-$); the ions carry the current through the solution. The electrolytic conductivity (κ) is the ratio of the current density to the field strength.

Conductor, substance or body having a relatively low electrical resistance. Metals are the best conductors, as a large number of free electrons are available to provide a current, when they flow in one direction. The resistance of a metallic conductor increases with temperature as the vibrations of lattice atoms increase, hindering the motion of the electrons. △1530–32.

Conductor, Orchestra. △1244.

Cone, scaly fruit- or seed-bearing vessel of plants, such as fir, pine, spruce, club mosses, and horsetails. It is made up of scales, varying in number, shape, and size, which separate to release seeds developed at the base. Generally, cones are woody at maturity.

Cone, solid geometric figure swept out by a line (the generator) that joins a point moving in a closed curve in a plane, to a fixed point (the vertex) outside the plane. In a right circular cone the vertex lies above the center of a circle (the base), and the cone's generators join the vertex to points on the circle. Such a cone has a volume $1/3\pi r^2h$ and a curved surface area πrs, where h is the vertical height, s the slant height, and r the radius of the base. △1454, 1466.

Cone Shell, gastropod mollusk found in tropical seas, particularly Indo-Pacific. Having heavy, cone-shaped shell with vivid marks and colors, some species can inflict serious or fatal stings. Length: 1–3in (25.4–76.2mm). Family Conidae; 500 species, including rare *Conus dominicanus*. △482.

Confederate Constitution, adopted on Feb. 9, 1861, by the Confederate States of America in Montgomery, Ala. Nearly identical to the US Constitution, it differed in that it emphasized states' rights and the right to hold slaves.

Confederate States of America (CSA). The government formed in February 1861, by the first 6 states that seceded from the United States. South Carolina was the first state to secede (December, 1860), followed by Mississippi, Florida, Alabama, Georgia, and Louisiana. Texas, Virginia, Arkansas, North Carolina, and Tennessee joined the CSA soon after. There were also Confederate governments in Kentucky and Missouri. Jefferson Davis was elected president, and a constitution recognizing slavery and state sovereignty was adopted. The capital, located originally at Montgomery, was later moved to Richmond. The government dissolved with the war's end in April 1865. △1276.

Confederation, Articles of. *See* Articles of Confederation.

Confederation of Canada, union of Canada after the British North America Act (1867). Under confederation, Canada assumed powers of tariff, taxation, defense, and criminal law. Confederation paved the way for the inclusion in Canada of British Columbia (1871), Prince Edward Island (1873), and Newfoundland (1949). *See also* British North America Act.

Confederation of the Rhine, alliance of German states proposed by Napoleon in January 1806. Agreed to by 16 German princes in July 1806, they renounced their attachment to the Holy Roman Empire, placed themselves under the protection of Napoleon, and pledged 63,000 men to his army. Eventually, the Confederation included Bavaria, Baden, Saxony, Württemberg, Westphalia, Hesse-Darmstadt, and most of the minor states, many of which joined at Napoleon's defeat of the Prussian army on Oct. 14, 1806. A device to control the German princes, the alliance broke apart after Napoleon's defeat in Russia (1812–13).

Configuration, Electron, the particular pattern of electrons occupying the shells and subshells of an atom. The electron configuration is usually written in a notation using 1, 2, 3, etc. for the principal shell and *s, p, d,* and *f* for the subshell. The number of electrons is written as a superscript. For example, the configuration of the helium atom is $1s^2$; that of the chromium atom is $1s^22s^22p^63s^23p^64s^23d^4$. △1480, 1550–52, 1560.

Conformity, in geology, the undisturbed, continuous layering of sediments in even strata with no evidence of folding, faulting, or intrusion of new materials, or erosion or wind or water change. *See also* Unconformity. △272.

Confucianism, philosophy that dominated China until the early 20th century. In 1970, it had an estimated 370,000,000 followers, mainly in Asia. It is based on the *Analects,* sayings attributed to Confucius (*c.* 551–479 BC). At first strictly an ethical system for the proper management of society, it acquired quasi-religious characteristics. In the 1st century AD shrines were erected where sacrifices were offered to Confucius, a practice continuing to the 20th century. After the religions of Taoism and Buddhism eclipsed Confucianism in the 3rd to 7th centuries, neo-Confucianism placed the early precepts on a metaphysical basis. Man is seen as potentially the most perfect form of *li,* the ultimate embodiment of good. Confucianism stresses the responsibility of sovereign to subject, of family members to each other, and of friend to friend. Politically, it acted to preserve the existing order, upholding the status of the mandarins, Confucian literati who ran the Chinese bureaucracy. When the monarchy was overthrown (1911–12) Confucian institutions were ended, but since the Communist revolution in China (1949), many traditional Confucian elements have apparently been incorporated in Maoism.

Confucius (551–479 BC), founder of Confucianism. Born in the Chinese province of Lu of aristocratic ancestry, he was an excellent scholar, athlete, and musician. He opened a school where the sons of wealthy families studied for careers of government service. Tradition holds that he became prime minister of Lu but was framed by dishonest officials and resigned in shame. Wandering throughout China for 30 years, he sought a return to the morality in politics of the early Chou dynasty. He never found real support and returning to Lu in 484 BC, he spent his last years engaged in scholarship. He died disappointed, not realizing the high regard later generations would give his ideas. Although many of his writings were lost, some of his teachings are recorded in the *Analects. See also* Confucianism. △860, 1040.

Conger Eel, marine fish found worldwide in shallow warm and temperate waters. Its serpentine body is grayish, sometimes with a reddish tint. A food fish in Europe and Japan, it spawns in deep water. Length: to 8ft (244cm); Weight: 12lb (5.4kg). Family Congridae; species 100, including *Conger oceanicus.*

Conglomerate, in geology, sedimentary rock formed of rounded pebbles bound in a finer matrix. Formerly called "pudding stone," conglomerates are commonly formed along beaches, rivers, or as glacial drift. In glacial tillite the rounded particles may range from pebbles to huge boulders. *See also* Sedimentary Rocks.

Conglomerate Merger, in its pure form, the combination of companies producing totally unrelated products, for example, the merger of ITT and Sheraton Hotels. *Product extension conglomerate mergers* occur when two companies producing complementary products combine. A *conglomerate product-extension merger* occurs when two companies selling the same product in separated markets combine. A merger between a milk company in Maryland and a milk company in California would be a merger of this type.

Congo, People's Republic of, independent nation in W central Africa. A self-proclaimed scientific socialist state, it gained independence from France in 1960. A low-level economy makes it dependent on imports and foreign aid.

Land and economy. Situated on the equator, it is bordered by Gabon, Cameroon, the Central African Republic, Zaire, Cabinda, and the Atlantic Ocean. Topographical regions include the coastal plain, S central Niari valley (the most fertile area), central Bateke Plateau, and the N Congo River basin. The climate is tropical. Subsistence farmers on 2% of the land raise corn, bananas, rice, peanuts, fruits, chickens, and goats. Cash crops are sugar cane, coffee, and tobacco. Potash is the most valuable mineral; oil drilling has begun.

People: Fifteen ethnic groups divided into 75 tribes comprise most of the population; in addition there are about 12,000 Europeans, mostly French, in the country. French is the official language. Christianity is the dominant religion. Literacy is estimated at 20%.

Government. Although the 1970 constitution placed power in the Congolese Labor party and made the party leader head of state, it provided no tenure for the office. The executive branch is named by the president, and there is no provision for a legislature.

History. Originally three tribal kingdoms dominated by the slave trade, the region came under French protection in 1883. By 1958 it had become an autonomous member of the French community in Africa, and in 1960 it achieved independence. Abbe Fulbert Youlou, its first president, was deposed in a 1963 coup. Scientific socialism was proclaimed by the next president, Alphonse Massamba Debat. His term ended with a 1968 military coup; Capt. Marien Ngoubi took power and proclaimed Africa's first "People's Republic."

PROFILE

Official name: People's Republic of the Congo
Area: 132,046sq mi (341,999sq km)
Population: 1,031,000
Density: 8per sq mi (3per sq km)
Chief cities: Brazzaville (capital); Pointe Noire
Government: Socialist
Religion: Christian, animist
Language: French
Monetary unit: CFA francs
Gross national product: $425,000,000
Per capita income: $423
Industries: wood products, flour, sugar, brewing, cement, textiles
Agriculture: cocoa, bananas, peanuts, sugar cane, tobacco, forests
Minerals: potash, petroleum, natural gas, forests
Trading partners: France, Federal Republic of Germany, People's Republic of China, USSR

Congo (Zaire), largest river in central Africa, flows from Zambia to the Atlantic Ocean; divided into 4 sections: Upper Congo, the main headstream; Middle Congo, slow-moving and narrow; Lower Congo, beginning at Stanley Pool outlet; and the Estuary, final portion entering the Atlantic Ocean. River forms an excellent system of navigable waterways and hydroelectrical development. Largest drainage basin in Africa: 1,600,000sq mi (4,144,000sq km). Length: 2,900mi (4,669km).

Congo Snake, or Congo Eel, blind salamander found in lowland areas of S United States. Its blue-black, elongated body has tiny limbs, a pointed head, and lungs; it has no tongue or gills. It spawns every other year. Length: to 3.3ft (1m). Family Amphiumidae; species: *Amphiuma means, Amphiuma tridactylum, Amphiuma pholeter.*

Congregational Church, known in the United States as the United Church of Christ, developed in the 17th century, as a non-conformist offspring of the Church of England. Stressing freedom of conscience and the independence of each congregation in scriptural interpretation, the church was particularly successful with American colonies. Congregationalists have been prominent in the ecumenical movement. The church has about two million members in the United States, with a lesser following in England and Wales.

Congregationalism, Christian church organization in which each local church is autonomous and independent; also called at various times Brownists, Separatists, Independents. Congregationalism is based on the belief that, according to Scripture, Christ is the head of the church and all members are God's priests. Modern Congregationalism began about 1550. Congregationalists were prominent in Oliver Cromwell's English army and government in the mid-17th century and were a major political force in the American colonies, settling Plymouth Colony in 1620 and establishing Harvard College in 1636. As the modern United Church of Christ with a membership of 2,000,000, Congregationalism occupies a position between Presbyterianism and the Baptists.

Congressman-at-Large, representative elected to the US Congress on a statewide or "at large" basis rather than in a single-member congressional district. Such elections are authorized in cases of reapportionment.

Congress of Industrial Organizations (CIO), US labor organization. It was originally the Committee for Industrial Organizations formed (1935) within the American Federation of Labor to unionize workers in the mass production industries. The AFL ordered the Committee to disband in 1936. It was expelled (1937) from the AFL with 10 unions and in 1938 became the Congress of Industrial Organizations. The CIO scored organizational success gaining steel, auto, textile, rubber, electric, and mine workers. John L. Lewis was the CIO's first president, resigning in 1940. It merged with the AFL in 1955.

Congress of Racial Equality (CORE), US interracial organization. Founded in 1942 by James Farmer, CORE employed sit-ins, picketing, and boycotting tactics to combat discrimination in employment. It gained national recognition with the "Freedom Rides" in the Deep South (1961). It became more militant in its approach to racial problems after Farmer was succeeded by Floyd McKissick in 1966. By 1970, it had more than 70,000 members in more than 180 local groups.

Congress of the United States, the legislative branch of the federal government. It was created by Article I, Section 1 of the US Constitution: "All legislative Powers herein granted shall be vested in a Congress of the United States, which shall consist of a Senate and House of Representatives." The first meeting of Congress took place in 1789 in New York City. The Senate is composed of two elected members from each state who serve 6-year terms. One third of the Senate is elected every 2 years. The House of Representatives is comprised of 435 elected members who serve 2-year terms. The number of representatives from each state is determined by population. Both senators and representatives must be residents of the state from which they are chosen. A senator must be at least 30 years old and a citizen for at least 9 years, a representative must be at least 25, and citizen for at least 7 years. A resident commissioner from Puerto Rico (4-year term), and delegates from Guam, the Virgin Islands, and the District of Columbia elected for 2-year terms complete the composition of Congress. The commissioner and delegates do not have voting powers in Congress or in the committees to which they are assigned. The presiding officer in the Senate is the vice president, and the House elects a speaker to preside. The preparation and consideration of legislation is largely accomplished by the 17 standing committees in the Senate and the 21 in the House of Representatives. There are additional commissions and committees, some of which are composed of members from both Houses. Powers of Congress include the right to assess and collect taxes (chief power), regulate commerce, coin money, declare war, propose Constitutional amendments, establish post offices and post roads, establish lower courts, raise and maintain an army and navy, and "to make all Laws which shall be necessary and proper for carrying into execution the foregoing powers, and all other powers vested by this Constitution in the Government of the United States or in any Department or Officer thereof." Legislation must be passed by both Houses and be signed by the president to become law. The House initiates all tax bills and has the power to impeach the president. The Senate can approve treaties and presidential appointments and tries the president if he is impeached. The Constitution requires that Congress meet at least once every year, and the president may call special sessions. △906.

Congreve, William (1670–1729), English dramatist who wrote comedies of manners such as *Love for Love* (1695) and *The Way of the World* (1700). He became manager of the Haymarket Theatre in London in 1707.

Congruence, equivalence of shape and size. Two congruent geometric figures will coincide exactly when superimposed.

Conic, or conic section, curve found by the intersection of a plane with a cone. Depending upon the angle at which the cone is cut, the conic section can be a circle, ellipse, parabola, or hyperbola. A conic may alternatively be defined as the locus of a point that moves so that the ratio of its distances from a fixed point (the focus) and a fixed line (the directrix) is constant. This ratio is called the eccentricity (symbol: e): $e = 1$ gives a parabola, $e > 1$ an hyperbola, $e < 1$ an ellipse. A circle is the limiting case of an ellipse with $e = 0$. △1454.

Conic Projection. △180.

Conifers, cone-bearing trees, usually evergreen, such as pine, fir, hemlock, spruce, redwood, and cedar. They are a major plant resource of North America, furnishing building materials (softwoods), pulpwood, and other products. Classified as gymnosperms, conifers lack showy flowers, but foliage detail, cones, and color give them an ornamental quality. Order Coniferales. Eight families are usually recognized.

Conjugation, in biology, sexual reproduction by fusion of identical gametes. It is characteristic of certain simple animals and lower plants. In spirogyra algae, a temporary conjugation tube is a passageway for the contents of one cell to enter another. Ciliate protozoans adhere to one another and nuclear material is exchanged through a temporary fusion area. △422.

Conjugation, in astronomy, celestial configuration characterized by a coincidence in the longitudes of two celestial objects, usually two planets or a planet and the Sun, as viewed from the Earth. Inferior conjunction occurs when either Mercury or Venus lies between the Earth and the Sun; superior conjunction occurs when they lie on the opposite side of the Sun to the Earth. △38.

Conjunction, logical proposition produced by joining two simple propositions by *and*. An example is the proposition "Bill is boring and Bill is conceited"; it is true only if both parts are separately true. The conjunction of two simple propositions, P and Q, is written $P \wedge Q$, read "P and Q."

Conjunctivitis, inflammation of the conjunctiva, the mucous membrane lining of the eyelid. It can be caused by infection, usually bacterial, by exposure to irritants, or by allergy, and produces watery, burning, and itching eyelids. The acute contagious form is known as pink-eye.

Conkling, Roscoe (1829–88), US political leader, b. Albany, N.Y. A US representative (1859–63; 1865–67) and senator (1867–81), he controlled the Republican party in New York and, with it, party patronage. He was a leader of the "stalwart" Republicans, who opposed civil service reform. In 1881, he resigned from the Senate in protest against losing control of patronage.

Connally, John Bowden (1917–), US public offi-

Condor

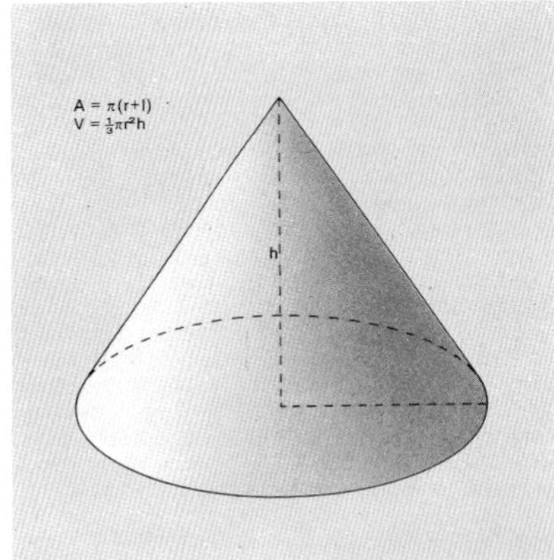
A = π(r+l)
V = ⅓πr²h
h

Cone

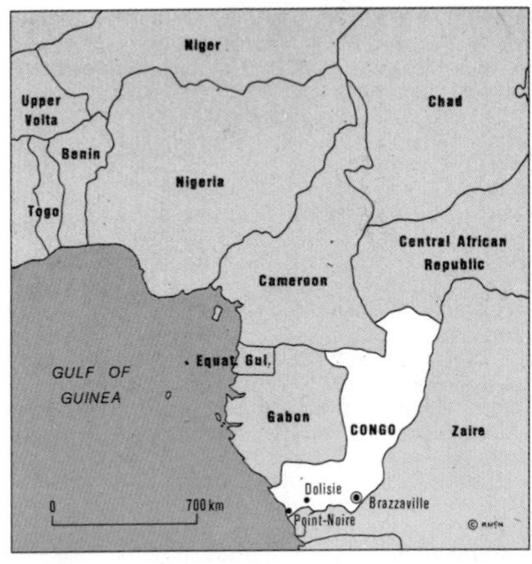
Niger
Upper Volta
Chad
Benin
Nigeria
Togo
Central African Republic
Cameroon
GULF OF GUINEA
Equat. Gui.
Gabon
CONGO
Zaire
Dolisie
Brazzaville
Point-Noire
0
700km

Congo

Congo River, Zaire

cial, b. Floresville, Tex. He was secretary of the navy (1961) but resigned (1962) to run successfully for governor of Texas. When President Kennedy was assassinated, Connally was riding in the same car and was wounded. Although a Democrat, he was appointed President Nixon's secretary of the treasury (1971) but later he became a Republican and resigned to work on Nixon's reelection campaign. He served as special aide to the president during the Watergate Affair. He left the White House soon after that and was later acquitted of a bribery charge related to the 1972 election.

Connecticut, state in the NE United States, in the New England region.

Land and Economy. A narrow plain lies along the shore of Long Island Sound in the S. In the W and E, hill ridges run N and S, with the highest in the NW corner. The Connecticut River Valley between the ridges is fertile farmland. Other major rivers are the Housatonic (W) and the Thames (E). In earlier days, Connecticut was known as a maker of small machines, and manufacturing is the heart of the economy. Defense contracts, including building nuclear submarines, are important. Hartford is the nation's foremost insurance center.

People. In the 19th century, Connecticut received thousands of immigrants from Europe, creating a mixture of nationalities and races, but by the late 20th century about 90% of its people were born in the United States. More than 75% live in urban areas. Thousands of residents in the SW section commute to jobs in New York City.

Education. Yale University, founded in 1701, is at New Haven. The University of Connecticut's principal campus is at Storrs. Trinity College, Wesleyan University, and Connecticut College are leading privately-endowed schools. There are about 50 institutions of higher education. The US Coast Guard Academy is at New London.

History. The first permanent settlements were made in the Connecticut River Valley around Hartford by English from E Massachusetts. Others were established along Long Island Sound, and in 1662 the colony received a charter from Charles II of England. When the American Revolution began, the colony had nearly 200,000 inhabitants. After the war, many migrated to neighboring states or to lands in the Middle West, but later the state's growing light industry drew new residents. In each of the country's major wars, Connecticut was a prime supplier of arms, munitions, and tools. In 1974, Ella T. Grasso was elected governor, the first woman governor in the United States to be elected governor in her own right.

PROFILE

Admitted to Union: Jan. 9, 1788; 5th of the 13 original states to ratify the US Constitution
US Congressmen: Senate, 2; House of Representatives, 6
Population: 3,032,217 (1970); rank, 24th
Capital: Hartford, 158,017 (1970)
Chief cities: Hartford; Bridgeport, 156,542; New Haven, 137,707
State Legislature: Senate, 36; House of Representatives, 151
Area: 5,009sq mi (12,973sq km); rank, 48th
Elevation: Highest, 2,380ft (726m), on Mt Frissell; lowest, sea level
Industries (major products): aircraft engines and parts, helicopters, industrial machinery, household appliances, hardware, silverware
Agriculture (major products): milk, poultry, tobacco
Minerals (major): stone, sand, gravel, clay
State Nickname: Constitution State
State Motto: Qui transtulit, sustinet (He who transplants, sustains)
State Bird: Robin
State Flower: Mountain laurel
State tree: White oak

Connecticut Compromise (1787), compromise at Philadelphia Constitutional Convention between large states, which favored representation based on population (Virginia Plan), and small states, which wanted equal representation regardless of size (New Jersey Plan). Proposed by Oliver Ellsworth of Connecticut, the plan was incorporated into the Constitution and included representation by population (House of Representatives) and equal representation for the states (Senate).

Connecticut River, river in New England; rises in Connecticut Lakes, in N New Hampshire; as it flows S, it forms a natural border between New Hampshire and Vermont; continues through W central Massachusetts and central Connecticut to empty into Long Island Sound near Old Saybrook; it has 23 tributaries and is used chiefly in the production of hydroelectricity and irrigation. Discovered 1614 by Adrian Block, Dutch explorer. Length: 407mi (655km).

Connecticut Wits, writers in Hartford, Conn. at the turn of the 18th century, who jointly produced satirical verse reflecting their conservative, Federalist political views. Joel Barlow, John Trumbull, Timothy Dwight, and David Humphreys, among others, were members of the group, which was also known as the Hartford Wits. Their work, which appeared in contemporary periodicals, included *The Anarchiad* (1786–87), *The Echo* (1791–1805), and *The Political Greenhouse* (1799).

Connective Tissue, bodily tissue that maintains the body's form and holds it together. Composed of cells, protein fibers, and carbohydrate substance. Bones, ligaments, cartilage, and skin are all connective tissue.

Connelly, Marc(us) Cook (1890–), US dramatist, b. McKeesport, Pa. He began his career in collaboration with George S. Kaufman on *To The Ladies* (1922), one of many successful comedies. Writing independently he won a Pulitzer Prize for *The Green Pastures* (1930), a humorous dramatization of Biblical tales interpreted in the Southern black folk idiom.

Connolly, Maureen ("Little Mo") (1934–69), US tennis player, *b.* San Diego, Calif. At 16, she became the youngest player to win the US national singles, a title she later successfully defended (1952–53). She won the Wimbledon championship (1952–54) and, in 1953 won the grand slam of tennis by capturing the French and Australian championships, the other two major world titles. After breaking her leg in a riding accident (1955), she was forced to retire.

Connors, James Scott "Jimmy" (1952–), US tennis player, b. East St. Louis, Ill. He won the US, British, and Australian singles championship (1974) and the British (1973) and US (1975) doubles title with Ilie Nastase. His challenge matches on television against other stars stimulated interest in tennis.

Conodont, any of numerous kinds of toothlike microfossils composed of calcium phosphate and occurring in marine deposits of Paleozoic and early Mesozoic ages. Their origin is uncertain. They have been thought to be polychaete jaw parts, the radular teeth of mollusks, the copulatory structures of nematodes, and even of algal derivation. They have been classified in great detail and are used extensively in stratigraphy.

Conon (died *c.* 390 BC), Athenian admiral who used Persian sea power to devastate the Spartan fleet at Cnidos (394 BC).

Conquistador, Spaniard who participated in the conquest of the New World; a professional or semiprofessional soldier, usually from Castile. △1124.

Conrad I (died 918), German king (911–18); uncrowned as Holy Roman emperor. With little support from the nobility, he failed, after a brutal struggle, to maintain the Carolingian tradition in the East Frankish kingdom. He was succeeded by his rival Henry, Duke of Saxony (Henry I).

Conrad II (*c.* 990–1039), Holy Roman emperor (1027–39), first of the Salian dynasty. He was elected German king (emperor-elect) in 1024 but was opposed by a powerful combination of forces. He won and was crowned emperor in 1027. Opposition continued, but Conrad consolidated his power and left a prosperous and powerful throne to his son, Henry II. △1072.

Conrad III (1093–1152), first German king (1138–52) of the Hohenstaufen dynasty. He was crowned antiking to Holy Roman Emperor Lothair II in 1127 and was excommunicated by the pope. He later submitted to Lothair and was crowned German king (emperor-elect) after Lothair's death. His main opposition came from Henry the Proud and then his son Henry the Lion. From this fight arose the two great Italian factions, the Guelphs and the Ghibellines. Conrad was never crowned emperor but was succeeded by his nephew, who ruled as Frederick I. *See also* Hohenstaufen Dynasty; Holy Roman Empire.

Conrad IV (1228–54), German king (1237–54) and king of Sicily and Jerusalem (1250–54). The son of Holy Roman Emperor Frederick II of the Hohenstaufen dynasty, he was elected German king (emperor-elect) in 1237, replacing his elder brother. He joined with his father in fighting the papacy, mostly over Italian territories. Pope Innocent IV deposed Frederick in 1245 and named an antiking to replace Conrad in 1246. Germany was plunged into war. Conrad inherited Sicily and Jerusalem upon Frederick's death in 1250 but was never crowned emperor. *See also* Hohenstaufen Dynasty; Holy Roman Empire.

Conrad, Joseph (1857–1924), British novelist, b. Teodor Józef Konrad Korzeniowski in Poland. His years as a ship's officer in Asian, African, and Latin American waters suggested the exotic settings of many of his novels. His works include *Almayer's Folly* (1895), *An Outcast of the Islands* (1896), *The Nigger of the 'Narcissus'* (1897), *Lord Jim* (1900), *Typhoon* (1903), *Nostromo* (1904), *The Secret Agent* (1907), *Under Western Eyes* (1911), *Victory* (1915), and the short novel *The Heart of Darkness* (1902). Conrad deals with the psychological conflicts that confront men in extreme situations.

Conradin, also **Conrad V,** (1252–68), last of the German Hohenstaufen dynasty, the son of Conrad IV. He was the anti-papal (Ghibelline) claimant to the throne of the Two Sicilies. He was executed in Naples attempting to recover Sicily from Charles I of Anjou.

Conscience, the element of a personality that signals "right" or "wrong" about a thought or a deed. In many respects, the psychoanalytic concept of the superego is the same as conscience. *See also* Superego. △786.

Conscientious Objector, person who refuses to serve in the armed forces because of religious, ethical, or philosophical convictions. Traditionally in the United States, members of certain religious sects (e.g. Quakers, Jehovah's Witnesses) have been excused from combat duty although they have generally been expected to serve in non-combat roles. Persons who objected to a particular war on political grounds (e.g. Copperheads in the Civil War) have not generally been considered conscientious objectors and have not been excused from conscription. The Selective Service Act of 1948 specifically excused only objectors who were members of a pacifistic religious body, but in 1970 the Supreme Court ruled that persons with deeply held moral convictions must be excused also. Conscientious objectors became a major issue during the Vietnam War, when more than 100,000 men for a variety of reasons refused to be drafted. Many of them left the country to avoid prosecution.

Consciousness, an awareness or perception of an inward psychological fact. The concept was defined in 1690 by John Locke. Initially consciousness was considered separate and different from the material substance of the physical world. Behaviorists refer consciousness to awareness and responsiveness as contrasted with their lack during sleep or coma. Today levels of consciousness are correlated with brain waves measured on an electroencephalograph. *See also* Brain Waves.

Consensus, in social science, agreement by a majority on issues, rules, or procedures. It does not mean absence of debate. In a democracy public opinion about parties and candidates changes, but there is consensus on basic policies. Politicians try to manipulate opinion to form a consensus favorable to them. The breakdown of consensus is called "cleavage."

Consent, Popular, fundamental principle of the democratic system, which holds that government is based on the consent of the governed, a concept originated by John Locke. *See also* Locke, John. △898.

Conservation, Laws of, physical laws stating that some property of a closed system is unchanged by changes in the system. The most important are the laws of conservation of matter and of energy. The former states that matter cannot be created or destroyed; the total mass remains constant when chemical changes occur. The total energy of a system also remains the same; energy is simply converted from one form into another. In fact mass and energy are interconvertible according to the equation $E = mc^2$. What is conserved is the total mass and its equivalent in energy. The two classical laws are approximate cases of a law of conservation of mass-energy. △1564.

Conservation Law, Nuclear, in a nuclear interaction, the total charge, spin, or other specific quantum number of the interacting particles must equal that of the resulting particles. In strong interactions all quantum numbers are conserved. In weak interactions several of the laws break down, notably that for parity.

Conservation of Energy, Law of. *See* Conservation, Laws of.

Conservation of Matter, Law of. *See* Conservation, Laws of.

Conservation of Momentum. △1492.

Conservatism, political philosophy that favors the preservation of traditional institutions and practices. The conservative, basically distrustful of politics, believes that human attitudes and behavior cannot be improved through legislation. He strongly opposes too much governmental regulation. He believes social change should be gradual and occur within a historical framework. Created as a reaction to the ideas of the Enlightenment, conservatism relies on habit and experience, not pure reason, as the basis for social order. △1288.

Conservative Party, Britain's major right-wing political party. Under Sir Robert Peel it developed from the Tory party in the 1830s to protect the interests of both landowners and industry and defend law and order. Disraeli reorganized the party, committing it to democracy and social reform as well as conservatism (1870s). The Liberal decline (1920s) allowed the Conservatives to dominate the interwar years, and the World War II coalition was led by Winston Churchill, the Conservative leader. The postwar party followed moderate policies, although it swung to the right after 1970. Conservative membership is traditionally middle-class and its MPs are mostly businessmen, lawyers, and landowners; nevertheless, it enjoys fairly strong working-class support. The party organization consists of the Parliamentary party, which elects the leader, the National Union of Conservative Associations, and the Central Office.

Conshelf. △230.

Considérant, Victor Prosper (1809–93), French socialist. A supporter of Fourier's philosophy of communal socialism, he became leader of the movement at François Fourier's death (1837) and edited the journal *Phalange* and the daily *La Democratie pacifique* (1843). A declared republican in 1848, he formed the Democratic and Socialist Committee in 1849 and joined the call for insurrection. He was accused of treason and fled to Belgium and then Texas, where he established a socialist commune, La Réunion. He returned to France in 1869 and rather than standing for Parliament, worked on finding scientific bases for establishing the ideal commune. His works include *La Destinée sociale* (1834–38).

Consort, in Music. △1244.

Conspicuous Consumption, term introduced in *The Theory of the Leisure Class* (1899), by Thorstein Veblen to describe ostentatious wealth. According to Veblen, some goods are consumed mainly to impress others with the owner's wealth rather than to satisfy any basic need.

Constable, John (1776–1837), English painter whose work, together with that of his contemporary, J.W. Turner, was the precursor of the Impressionist movement. Although Constable also painted portraits of considerable interest, his landscapes of the English countryside began the turn toward naturalism and direct observation of nature. Constable studied at the Royal Academy and copied from Claude Lorrain and Ruisdael. He worked at reproducing the effects of clouds and light on water—often using broken color and thick impasto texture. His first success came when *The Hay Wain* (1821) and *View on the Stour* (1822) were shown at the Paris Salon of 1824 and were acclaimed by French romantic artists, especially Delacroix. Constable was neglected in England until 1890 when the small oils on which his large works were based were shown to the public. These are much admired today; most are in the Victoria and Albert Museum. Other museums with major paintings are the National Gallery, London, and the Metropolitan Museum and Frick Collection, New York. △1242.

Constance, Council of (1414–18), gathering of Roman Catholic prelates convoked by Antipope John XXIII in 1413 to end the Great Schism between Rome (Pope Gregory XII) and Avignon (Pope Benedict XIII) and to deal with several heresies (notably those of Jan Hus). The council, which was held at the cathedral of Constance in Germany, favored the resignation of all three "popes." Gregory XII resigned, but John XXIII fled and was returned as a prisoner. The council was reconvoked in 1415, and Benedict XIII was deposed in 1417. The election of Martin V in 1417 during the council ended the Great Schism. Jan Hus was condemned and burned as a heretic. *See also* Great Schism; Hus, Jan.

Constance, Lake, lake bordering on Austria, West Germany, and Switzerland; fed and drained by the Rhine River; divides into two arms near the city of Constance; contains remains of prehistoric lake dwellings. Local industries include fruit growing, wine, fishing. Area: 208sq mi (539sq km).

Constans, Flavius Julius (323?–350), Roman emperor (337–350). The youngest son of Constantine the Great, he shared the title of Augustus with his two brothers. After the death of his brother Constantine II (340), Constans controlled both the central and western dioceses of the empire.

Constant, number or symbol that has a fixed value in an algebraic expression. *See* Variable.

Constanta, chief seaport city in Romania, on the Black Sea; taken by Rome 72 BC; named in 4th century by Constantine; major trade center; site of naval base, marine biology station, many mosques, synagogues, statue of Ovid, Roman and Byzantine ruins, and Orthodox cathedral. Industries: exporting grain, lumber, petroleum. Founded 7th century BC as a Greek colony. Pop. 172,464.

Constantine I, or **Constantine the Great** (280–337), Roman emperor (305–337). In 312 at the Battle of the Milvian Bridge Constantine defeated his rival Maxentius and was declared senior Augustus of the Roman Empire. The victory had religious as well as political implications. Before the battle Constantine had appealed to the God of the Christians for help against the pagan forces of Maxentius; he regarded his victory as the answer to this appeal. Though born and educated a pagan, he was sympathetic to the Christian Church, perhaps seeing in it a means of unifying his people. In 313 Constantine and coemperor Licinius issued the Edict of Milan, which granted Christians freedom of worship and restored properties that had been confiscated from their churches. In 324 he defeated Licinius and became sole Roman emperor. He established a new capital, or a second Rome, at Constantinople in 330. In 325 he convened the First Council of Nicaea to deal with Arianism. △1030, 1056.

Constantine II (317?–340), Roman emperor (337–40), b. Flavius Claudius Constantinus. The eldest son of Constantine the Great, he shared the title of Augustus with his two brothers. His portion was the Western Empire. He ruled it only briefly, however, for he was killed in battle after invading his brother Constans' Eastern realm.

Constantine III (612?–41), Byzantine emperor (*r.* 641), designated co-ruler with his half-brother Heraclonas by their father Heraclius. This partnership, one of the notable instances in Roman and Byzantine history of rule by coemperors, was terminated by Constantine's early death.

Constantine IV (648–85), Byzantine emperor (*r.* 668–85). Under his leadership, the westward advance of the Arabs was decisively halted. The defeat of the Arab forces at Constantinople in 678 saved not only the Byzantine Empire, but also prevented an Arab invasion of Europe.

Constantine V (719–75), Byzantine emperor (*r.* 741–75). Slanderously nicknamed Copronymous ("Dungname"), by his ecclesiastical opponents, this powerful iconoclastic emperor fought the defenders of the images with both theological arguments and political force. He is known especially for repressive measures against the monasteries. Constantine was an effective military commander, and under his leadership Byzantium's Arab and Bulgar enemies were defeated. *See also* Iconoclastic Controversy.

Constantine VI (771–797?) Byzantine emperor (*r.* 780–97). Constantine inherited the throne at the age of 10, when his mother Irene was named regent and coemperor. Constantine and Irene waged a continual and bitter struggle for power, which ended with Constantine's blinding (at the order of his mother) and death at the age of 27.

Constantine VII Porphyrogenitus (905–59), Byzantine emperor (*r.* 912–59) and scholar. Constantine was a patron of arts and scholarship and was himself the author of two important political works. *On the Administration of the Empire* was a manual of foreign diplomacy intended for the guidance of his son, and *On the Ceremonies of the Byzantine Court* was a handbook written in order to maintain the imperial court ceremonial.

Constantine VIII (960?–1028), Byzantine emperor (*r.* 1025–28). Brother and successor of Emperor Basil

John Connally

Connecticut

Jimmy Connors

Constanta, Romania

II, Constantine was an old man when he inherited the throne, and was little interested in affairs of state.

Constantine IX Monomachus (1000–55), Byzantine emperor (*r.* 1042–55). A member of the civil aristocracy, Constantine was named emperor when he became the third husband of the 64-year-old Empress Zoë. He was an ineffectual ruler, and did little to improve the Byzantine state. It was during Constantine's reign that the schism between the Eastern and Western Churches occurred (1054).

Constantine X Ducas (1007–67), Byzantine emperor (*r.* 1059–67). A member of the civil nobility of Constantinople, Constantine favored the civil service and neglected the army. As a result, the military position of the empire was severely weakened.

Constantine XI (Palaeologus) (1404–53), Byzantine emperor (*r.* 1448–53). Formerly Despot of Morea, Constantine was the last emperor of Byzantium. He was killed fighting against the Turkish forces of Murad II during the seige and ultimate capture of Constantinople.

Constantine I (1868–1923), king of Greece (1913–17; 1920–22). Married to sister of William II of Germany, he was pro-German during World War I. His premier, Eleutherios Venizelos, was pro-Allies, and Constantine left Greece in 1917 when it joined the Allies, but was recalled at his son Alexander's death (1920). There was a military revolt in 1922. He abdicated and died in exile.

Constantine II (1940–), king of Greece. Married to Anne Marie of Denmark, he became king in 1964. In a political crisis of 1965–66 he dismissed the prime minister. After a successful military coup and an unsuccessful counter-coup (1967), Constantine II left Greece for exile in Rome. The monarchy was abolished in Greece (1973).

Constantine, ancient Cirta, fortified city in NE Algeria, on Rhumel River; capital of Constantine dept.; founded as Sarim Batim by Carthaginians; was trade center and capital of Numidia and wealthy grain port under Romans; destroyed AD 311 and rebuilt by Constantine. A major inland city, it contains a university and a Muslim school. Industries: agricultural produce, textiles, leather goods, tourism. Pop. 240,672.

Constantine Nikolaevich (1827–92), Russian grand duke. Second son of Czar Nicholas I and brother of Czar Alexander II, he was commander of the Russian fleet in the Baltic during the Crimean War and governor general of Poland (1862–63). He was two times president of the imperial council (1865, 1878), but was held under suspicion after the accession of Alexander II and was dismissed in 1882 for holding revolutionary views.

Constantine (Konstantin) Pavlovich (1779–1831), Russian grand duke. The second son of Czar Paul I and brother of Czars Alexander I and Nicholas I, he was raised by his grandmother Catherine the Great to be emperor of the Eastern Empire once her Greek project to re-establish the Byzantine empire was successful. Instead, he became commander-in-chief of Poland (1815). He secretly renounced his claim to the throne (1822) in order to divorce his wife and marry a Polish countess. The confusion this produced led to the 1825 Decembrist uprising. The severity of his rule in Poland led to the 1830 uprising.

Constantinople, capital city of the Byzantine Empire. In AD 330 the Roman Emperor Constantine the Great established a "Second Rome" on the site of the old Greek colony of Byzantium. Its location on the Hellespont was strategic, for it lay at the meeting point of Europe and Asia. For over 1000 years, until its capture by the Ottoman Turks in 1453 (and the subsequent change of its name to Istanbul), Constantinople was the hub of the Byzantine world. *See also* Istanbul. △1030, 1056.

Constantinople, First Council of (381), gathering of Christian bishops and other representatives. It was convoked by Emperor Theodosius I to unite the Eastern Church; there were no Western bishops or Roman legates present. Council decrees granted Constantinople honorary precedence over all churches but Rome, condemned Appolinarianism (the doctrine that Christ had human body but divine spirit), and upheld the doctrine of Christ's humanity. Although it is of a later date, the Nicene Creed is traditionally associated with this council.

Constantinople, Second Council of or Fifth General Council (533), gathering of Christian bishops and other representatives. Convoked by Emperor Justinian and attended almost entirely by Eastern bishops, the council met to decide the controversy of the Three Chapters regarding Nestorianism (the doctrine that two separate persons, one divine and one human, were contained in Christ). The council condemned this doctrine and upheld the position that Christ was one person who was simultaneously both God and Man. Pope Virgilius and the council were not in entire agreement on the matter, but he finally accepted the council version.

Constantinople, Third Council of or Sixth General Council (680), gathering of Christian bishops and other representatives. It was convoked by Emperor Constantine to decide the Eastern Church Monothelite controversy (heresy confessing only one will in Christ). The Rome Synod, convened the same year by Pope Agatho, affirmed the doctrine of two wills—divine and human—in Christ and sent this decision to the council. The council declared the Monotheletics heretical and rejected the physical unity of two wills in Christ. It did, however, admit a moral unity of these wills.

Constantinople, Fourth Council or Eighth General Council (869–70), gathering of Christian bishops and other representatives. It was convoked to decide the Photian Schism between the Greek and Latin Churches. The controversy began when Ignatius was deposed as patriarch of Constantinople (858) and replaced by Photius. The pope in Rome maintained that Photius was the true patriarch, and his intervention in Eastern Church affairs was resented by Constantinople, which was also in dispute with Rome over the question of authority in Bulgaria. In 867 the Fourth Council confirmed the reinstatement of Ignatius, an action supported by the pope, thus briefly restoring harmony between East and West.

Constantinople, Latin Empire of. On April 13, 1204, the western armies of the Fourth Crusade captured the city of Constantinople and divided the former Byzantine territories among themselves. Western European feudal organizations were imposed upon some of the newly-formed states, and Constantinople was placed under the control of Baldwin, Count of Flanders. The Latin Empire ended when, in 1261, the Greek Empire was restored by Michael Palaeologus.

Constantius I (c.250–306), Roman emperor (305–06). A general, he was appointed caesar (subemperor) in 292 after defeating Carausius. In 296 he put down a rebellion in Britain and in 298 defeated the Alemanni in Gaul. When Diocletian and Maximian abdicated in 305, he became emperor of the West. He was succeeded by his son Constantine I.

Constant Value, a national income account adjusted for fluctuating prices in an effort to measure GNP with stable dollars, ie, dollars of constant purchasing power. Since current GNP uses the current dollar, GNP figures taken over time may prove misleading. With constant value, the quantity of output in two years, eg, 1966 and 1976, are both valued using the price level in 1966. Then the effect of any inflation is eliminated and the constant value figures for 1966 and 1976 accurately reflect quantity differences. The same concept applied to a person's salary gives this result: 1966 income was $10,000 and 1976 income is $20,000. If the price level has doubled, the person's constant value income is the same in both years. *See also* Gross National Product.

Constellation, any of the recognized patterns formed by groupings of conspicuous stars as viewed from earth. Constellations are optical effects caused by perspective, and the mutual proximity of their component stars is essentially illusory. Groupings visible in northern and equatorial regions have long-established names derived by ancient astronomers from animals and mythological figures; southern constellations, however, remained unknown until discovered by European navigators during the 16th and 17th centuries. These latter tend to be named after objects connected with navigation, seafaring, and science. △128.

Constellations of the Zodiac. △128, 826.

Constitution, USS, famous 44-gun US frigate, known as "Old Ironsides." It was launched in 1797 and made naval history in its successful battle against the British ship *Guerrière* in the War of 1812. It was saved from scrapping when Oliver Wendell Holmes's poem "Old Ironsides" (1830) extolled its war record. The *Constitution* was rebuilt in 1833, served as a naval academy school ship and has been docked in Boston since 1897.

Constitutional Act of 1791. Instituted by British Prime Minister William Pitt, the act divided French and English Canada, creating a system of government dominated by an appointed executive branch. The elected Legislative Assembly dealt only with local issues. Dissatisfaction with the form of government led to the Rebellion of 1837 and to the Durham Report (1839) reforms. *See also* Durham Report; Rebellion of 1837.

Constitutional Construction, legal interpretation of the US Constitution. It generally takes two basic forms. In the *strict* view, the Constitution is a rigid document that can be altered only by formal amendment. The *flexible* view sees the Constitution as an adaptable document that must be reinterpreted as times and conditions change.

Constitutional Convention (1787). *See* Constitution of the United States.

Constitutional Government, government based on a set of principles embodied in a document whose authority stems directly from the consent of those governed. A written constitution was a distinct US departure from the largely unwritten legal code that long had been the foundation for many European governments. The US Constitution created a federalist form of government, with authority shared by the nation and states. The Constitution is a legal instrument, regarded as supreme law, guaranteeing basic civil rights and resources should such rights be violated. It has proved to be highly flexible, adapting to new conditions through interpretation and amendment. △906.

Constitutionalism. △900.

Constitutional Law, as understood in the United States, refers to the body of legal principles arising from interpretation and application of the constitution (federal or state) by courts empowered to judge cases involving the constitutionality of legislative acts. The power of the judiciary to pass on acts of other branches of government is implied from the federal Constitution, as stated in the opinion of Chief Justice Marshall in *Marbury* v. *Madison* (1803). Constitutional law, in this sense, does not exist in England since there is no written constitution; English courts do not have power over acts of Parliament, for parliamentary supremacy is a fundamental principle of the unwritten English constitution. △908–10.

Constitutional Types, or somatotypes, classifications of different types of human bodies, and the general theory that there is a relationship between body types and personality traits. Ernest Kretschmer devised the first such theory in the 19th century, but the foremost system is that of William H. Sheldon, who identified three major types of physique: *endomorphy,* characterized by a round, fat, flabby appearance; *mesomorphy,* athletic and muscular; and *ectomorphy,* frail and thin. Though psychologists have not accepted the alleged relationships that these types have to personality, Sheldon's system does provide a convenient way of measuring and classifying body types. △814.

Constitutional Union Party (National Constitutional Union), minor political party organized in 1860 to support Sen. James Bell (Tennessee) for president. Composed mostly of former Whigs, the party declared "no political principle other than the Constitution of the country, the union of the states, and the enforcement of the laws." In the election, votes for Bell helped fragment opposition to victor Abraham Lincoln.

Constitution of the United States, the formal statement of the US system of government. Written in 1787 and ratified in 1788, it replaced the Articles of Confederation and took effect in 1789.

At the end of the Revolutionary War the United States was a weak confederation of 13 states. The divergent interests of the separate states and the unrest on the Western frontier created fear that the Union would not survive. In 1786 at the Annapolis Convention, James Madison and Alexander Hamilton led representatives of five states meeting to settle problems of interstate commerce. Finding that commerce was bound up with many other issues, they called for a meeting of all states to discuss the problems facing the states. The result was the Constitutional Convention, which met in Philadelphia in 1787.

The state legislatures sent their best men to the convention, which met from May 25 to September 17—George Washington, James Madison, and George Mason came from Virginia; Rufus King and Elbridge Gerry from Massachusetts; Roger Sherman and Oliver Ellsworth from Connecticut; Hamilton from New York;

Benjamin Franklin, James Wilson, Gouverneur Morris, and Robert Morris from Pennsylvania; William Paterson from New Jersey; John Rutledge and Charles Pinckney from South Carolina. Only Rhode Island was not represented. The only important men missing were Thomas Jefferson, John Jay, and John Adams, who were representing the United States abroad. George Washington was elected president of the convention, which opened in Independence Hall.

Framing of the Constitution. Madison, the principal architect of the Constitution, was a nationalist, favoring a strong central government of three branches—executive, judiciary, and legislative. He offered the Virginia, or large-state, plan, which provided for legislative-representation based on population, and this was countered by the New Jersey, or small-state, plan which provided for each state to be represented equally. The result was the Connecticut Compromise, keeping the outline of Madison's plan but creating a two-house legislature: the Senate with equal representation of all states and the House of Representatives apportioned according to population. From the New Jersey plan came the key feature that the Constitution should be the supreme law of the land, binding on all states and enforced by all courts. The document adopted by the Constitutional Convention was a short one, laying the ground work for a strong central government with Madison's three branches but not trying to cover every possible eventuality. It is composed of a Preamble, seven articles, and 26 amendments.

Ratification and Amendments. The Constitution had to be ratified by 9 of the 13 states before it could become law. In some states there was strong opposition, led by anti-Federalists who feared a powerful central government. Among the most prominent was Patrick Henry in Virginia. Only by convincing oratory —particularly by Madison in Virginia and Hamilton in New York—were the wavering states won over and the Constitution ratified.

In 1791 the first 10 amendments, known as the Bill of Rights, were added to provide more protection for individuals. With these and other amendments, the Constitution has served to hold together the large and diverse nation while protecting the rights of the people. The Constitution's preamble states the reasons for adopting a constitution. Article I deals with such matters as the powers of Congress, the composition of the House and Senate and election to them, and restrictions upon the powers of the states. Article II covers the presidency, including election and powers, while Article III outlines the powers and responsibilities of the judiciary. Article IV describes relations between states and the admission of new states. Article V details how amendments to the Constitution shall be made; Article VI states the authority of the Constitution; and Article VII says that nine states will have to ratify the Constitution before it becomes effective.

The first 10 amendments to the Constitution, known as the Bill of Rights, were adopted in 1791. The First Amendment guaranteed freedom of religion, speech, press, and assembly. The Second guaranteed the right to bear arms, while the Third protected citizens against soldiers being quartered in private homes. The Fourth Amendment guarded the public from unreasonable search and seizure, and the Fifth protected accused persons from self-incrimination. The Sixth guaranteed a speedy trial, the Seventh trial by jury, and the Eighth protection from cruel and unusual punishment. The Ninth and Tenth said that the people retained rights not delegated to the federal or state authorities.

The next amendment (XI, 1795) prohibited a citizen of one state from suing another state government. Amendment XII (1804) set up separate ballots for electing the president and vice president. The Civil War Amendments (XIII, 1861; XIV, 1868; XV, 1870) outlawed slavery, declared all people born or naturalized in the United States citizens, and declared that the right to vote could not be denied because of color. Amendment XVI (1913) gave the Congress the right to enact personal income taxes. Popular election of US senators was established by Amendment XVII (1913). Prohibition, enacted by Amendment XVIII (1919), was repealed by Amendment XXI (1933). Women received the right to vote by Amendment XIX (1920). Amendment XXII (1951) limited the length of time a person may be president, and Amendment XXV (1967) set procedures for filling vice-presidential and presidential vacancies. Amendment XXIII (1961) gave District of Columbia residents the right to vote for president. The poll tax was prohibited by Amendment XXIV (1964). The voting age was lowered to age 18 by Amendment XXVI (1971). Amendment XXVII, barring discrimination based on sex, went to the states for ratification in 1972. *See also* Bill of Rights; Connecticut Compromise; New Jersey Plan; Virginia Plan. △1218.

Following is the text of the Constitution of the United States:

THE CONSTITUTION
of the
UNITED STATES OF AMERICA

We the People of the United States, in Order to form a more perfect Union, establish Justice, insure domestic Tranquility, provide for the common defence, promote the general Welfare, and secure the Blessings of Liberty to ourselves and our Posterity, do ordain and establish this Constitution for the United States of America.

ARTICLE I.

Section 1. All legislative Powers herein granted shall be vested in a Congress of the United States, which shall consist of a Senate and House of Representatives.

Section 2. The House of Representatives shall be composed of Members chosen every second Year by the People of the several States, and the Electors in each State shall have the Qualifications requisite for Electors of the most numerous Branch of the State Legislature.

No Person shall be a Representative who shall not have attained to the Age of twenty five Years, and been seven Years a Citizen of the United States, and who shall not, when elected, be an Inhabitant of that State in which he shall be chosen.

Representatives and direct Taxes shall be apportioned among the several States which may be included within this Union, according to their respective Numbers, which shall be determined by adding to the whole Number of free Persons, including those bound to Service for a Term of Years, and excluding Indians not taxed, three fifths of all other Persons. The actual Enumeration shall be made within three Years after the first Meeting of the Congress of the United States, and within every subsequent Term of ten Years, in such Manner as they shall by Law direct. The Number of Representatives shall not exceed one for every thirty Thousand, but each State shall have at Least one Representative; and until such enumeration shall be made, the State of New Hampshire shall be entitled to chuse three, Massachusetts eight, Rhode-Island and Providence Plantations one, Connecticut five, New-York six, New Jersey four, Pennsylvania eight, Delaware one, Maryland six, Virginia ten, North Carolina five, South Carolina five, and Georgia three.

When vacancies happen in the Representation from any State, the Executive Authority thereof shall issue Writs of Election to fill such Vacancies.

The House of Representatives shall chuse their Speaker and other Officers; and shall have the sole Power of Impeachment.

Section 3. The Senate of the United States shall be composed of two Senators from each State, chosen by the Legislature thereof, for six Years; and each Senator shall have one Vote.

Immediately after they shall be assembled in Consequence of the first Election, they shall be divided as equally as may be into three Classes. The Seats of the Senators of the first Class shall be vacated at the Expiration of the second Year, of the second Class at the Expiration of the fourth Year, and of the third Class at the Expiration of the sixth Year, so that one third may be chosen every second Year; and if Vacancies happen by Resignation, or otherwise, during the Recess of the Legislature of any State, the Executive thereof may make temporary Appointments until the next Meeting of the Legislature, which shall then fill such Vacancies.

No Person shall be a Senator who shall not have attained to the Age of thirty Years, and been nine Years a Citizen of the United States, and who shall not, when elected, be an Inhabitant of that State for which he shall be chosen.

The Vice President of the United States shall be President of the Senate, but shall have no Vote, unless they be equally divided.

The Senate shall chuse their other Officers, and also a President pro tempore, in the Absence of the Vice President, or when he shall exercise the Office of President of the United States.

The Senate shall have the sole Power to try all Impeachments. When sitting for that Purpose, they shall be on Oath or Affirmation. When the President of the United States is tried, the Chief Justice shall preside: And no Person shall be convicted without the Concurrence of two thirds of the Members present.

Judgment in Cases of Impeachment shall not extend further than to removal from Office, and disqualification to hold and enjoy any Office of honor, Trust or Profit under the United States: but the Party convicted shall nevertheless be liable and subject to Indictment, Trial, Judgment and Punishment, according to Law.

Section 4. The Times, Places and Manner of holding Elections for Senators and Representatives, shall be prescribed in each State by the Legislature thereof; but the Congress may at any time by Law make or

John Dickinson

Benjamin Franklin

Alexander Hamilton

Rufus King

alter such Regulations, except as to the Places of chusing Senators.

The Congress shall assemble at least once in every Year, and such Meeting shall be on the first Monday in December, unless they shall by Law appoint a different Day.

SECTION 5. Each House shall be the Judge of the Elections, Returns and Qualifications of its own Members, and a Majority of each shall constitute a Quorum to do Business; but a smaller Number may adjourn from day to day, and may be authorized to compel the Attendance of absent Members, in such Manner, and under such Penalties as each House may provide.

Each House may determine the Rules of its Proceedings, punish its Members for disorderly Behaviour, and, with the Concurrence of two thirds, expel a Member.

Each House shall keep a Journal of its Proceedings, and from time to time publish the same, excepting such Parts as may in their Judgment require Secrecy; and the Yeas and Nays of the Members of either House on any question shall, at the Desire of one fifth of those Present, be entered on the Journal.

Neither House, during the Session of Congress, shall, without the Consent of the other, adjourn for more than three days, nor to any other Place than that in which the two Houses shall be sitting.

SECTION 6. The Senators and Representatives shall receive a Compensation for their Services, to be ascertained by Law, and paid out of the Treasury of the United States. They shall in all Cases, except Treason, Felony and Breach of the Peace, be privileged from Arrest during their Attendance at the Session of their respective Houses, and in going to and returning from the same; and for any Speech or Debate in either House, they shall not be questioned in any other Place.

No Senator or Representative shall, during the Time for which he was elected, be appointed to any civil Office under the Authority of the United States, which shall have been created, or the Emoluments whereof shall have been encreased during such time; and no Person holding any Office under the United States, shall be a Member of either House during his Continuance in Office.

SECTION 7. All Bills for raising Revenue shall originate in the House of Representatives; but the Senate may propose or concur with Amendments as on other Bills.

Every Bill which shall have passed the House of Representatives and the Senate, shall, before it become a Law, be presented to the President of the United States; If he approve he shall sign it, but if not he shall return it, with his Objections to that House in which it shall have originated, who shall enter the Objections at large on their Journal, and proceed to reconsider it. If after such Reconsideration two thirds of that House shall agree to pass the Bill, it shall be sent, together with the Objections, to the other House, by which it shall likewise be reconsidered, and if approved by two thirds of that House, it shall become a Law. But in all such Cases the Votes of both Houses shall be determined by Yeas and Nays, and the Names of the Persons voting for and against the Bill shall be entered on the Journal of each House respectively. If any Bill shall not be returned by the President within ten Days (Sundays excepted) after it shall have been presented to him, the Same shall be a Law, in like Manner as if he had signed it, unless the Congress by their Adjournment prevent its Return, in which Case it shall not be a Law.

Every Order, Resolution, or Vote to which the Concurrence of the Senate and House of Representatives may be necessary (except on a question of Adjournment) shall be presented to the President of the United States; and before the Same shall take Effect, shall be approved by him, or being disapproved by him, shall be repassed by two thirds of the Senate and House of Representatives, according to the Rules and Limitations prescribed in the Case of a Bill.

SECTION 8. The Congress shall have Power To lay and collect Taxes, Duties, Imposts and Excises, to pay the Debts and provide for the common Defence and general Welfare of the United States; but all Duties, Imposts and Excises shall be uniform throughout the United States;

To Borrow Money on the Credit of the United States;

To regulate Commerce with foreign Nations, and among the several States, and with the Indian Tribes;

To establish an uniform Rule of Naturalization, and uniform Laws on the subject of Bankruptcies throughout the United States;

To coin Money, regulate the Value thereof, and of foreign Coin, and fix the Standard of Weights and Measures;

To provide for the Punishment of counterfeiting the Securities and current Coin of the United States;

To establish Post Offices and post Roads;

To promote the Progress of Science and useful Arts, by securing for limited Times to Authors and Inventors the exclusive Right to their respective Writings and Discoveries;

To constitute Tribunals inferior to the supreme Court;

To define and punish Piracies and Felonies committed on the high Seas, and Offences against the Law of Nations;

To declare War, grant Letters of Marque and Reprisal, and make Rules concerning Captures on Land and Water;

To raise and support Armies, but no Appropriation of Money to that Use shall be for a longer Term than two Years;

To provide and maintain a Navy;

To make Rules for the Government and Regulation of the land and naval Forces;

To provide for calling forth the Militia to execute the Laws of the Union, suppress Insurrections and repel Invasions;

To provide for organizing, arming, and disciplining the Militia, and for governing such Part of them as may be employed in the Service of the United States, reserving to the States respectively, the Appointment of the Officers, and the Authority of training the Militia according to the discipline prescribed by Congress;

To exercise exclusive Legislation in all Cases whatsoever, over such District (not exceeding ten Miles square) as may, by Cession of particular States, and the Acceptance of Congress, become the Seat of the Government of the United States, and to exercise like Authority over all Places purchased by the Consent of the Legislature of the State in which the Same shall be for the Erection of Forts, Magazines, Arsenals, dock-Yards, and other needful Buildings;—And

To make all Laws which shall be necessary and proper for carrying into Execution the foregoing Powers, and all other Powers vested by this Constitution in the Government of the United States, or in any Department or Officer thereof.

SECTION 9. The Migration or Importation of such Persons as any of the States now existing shall think proper to admit, shall not be prohibited by the Congress prior to the Year one thousand eight hundred and eight, but a Tax or duty may be imposed on such Importation, not exceeding ten dollars for each Person.

The Privilege of the Writ of Habeas Corpus shall not be suspended, unless when in Cases of Rebellion or Invasion the public Safety may require it.

No Bill of Attainder or ex post facto Law shall be passed.

No Capitation, or other direct, Tax shall be laid, unless in Proportion to the Census or Enumeration herein before directed to be taken.

No Tax or Duty shall be laid on Articles exported from any State.

No Preference shall be given by any Regulation of Commerce or Revenue to the Ports of one State over those of another: nor shall Vessels bound to, or from, one State, be obliged to enter, clear, or pay Duties in another.

No Money shall be drawn from the Treasury, but in Consequence of Appropriations made by Law; and a regular Statement and Account of the Receipts and Expenditures of all public Money shall be published from time to time.

No Title of Nobility shall be granted by the United States: And no Person holding any Office of Profit or Trust under them, shall, without the Consent of Congress, accept of any present, Emolument, Office, or Title, of any kind whatever, from any King, Prince, or foreign State.

SECTION 10. No State shall enter into any Treaty, Alliance, or Confederation; grant Letters of Marque and Reprisal; coin Money; emit Bills of Credit; make any Thing but gold and silver Coin a Tender in Payment of Debts; pass any Bill of Attainder, ex post facto Law, or Law impairing the Obligation of Contracts, or grant any Title of Nobility.

No State shall, without the Consent of the Congress, lay any Imposts or Duties on Imports or Exports, except what may be absolutely necessary for executing its inspection Laws: and the net Produce of all Duties and Imposts, laid by any State on Imports or Exports, shall be for the Use of the Treasury of the United States; and all such Laws shall be subject to the Revision and Controul of the Congress.

No State shall, without the Consent of Congress, lay any Duty of Tonnage, keep Troops, or Ships of War in time of Peace, enter into any Agreement or Compact with another State, or with a foreign Power, or engage in War, unless actually invaded, or in such imminent Danger as will not admit of delay.

ARTICLE II.

SECTION 1. The executive Power shall be vested in a President of the United States of America. He shall hold his Office during the Term of four Years, and, together with the Vice President, chosen for the same term, be elected, as follows

Each State shall appoint, in such Manner as the Legislature thereof may direct, a Number of Electors, equal to the whole Number of Senators and Representatives to which the State may be entitled in the Congress: but no Senator or Representative, or Person holding an Office of Trust or Profit under the United States, shall be appointed an Elector.

The Electors shall meet in their respective States, and vote by Ballot for two Persons, of whom one at least shall not be an Inhabitant of the same State with themselves. And they shall make a List of all the Persons voted for, and of the Number of Votes for each; which List they shall sign and certify, and transmit sealed to the Seat of the Government of the United States, directed to the President of the Senate. The President of the Senate shall, in the Presence of the Senate and House of Representatives, open all the Certificates, and the Votes shall then be counted. The Person having the greatest Number of Votes shall be the President, if such Number be a Majority of the whole Number of Electors appointed; and if there be more than one who have such Majority, and have an equal Number of Votes, then the House of Representatives shall immediately chuse by Ballot one of them for President; and if no Person have a Majority, then from the five highest on the List the said House shall in like Manner chuse the President. But in chusing the President, the Votes shall be taken by States, the Representation from each State having one Vote; A quorum for this Purpose shall consist of a Member or Members from two thirds of the States, and a Majority of all the States shall be necessary to a Choice. In every Case, after the Choice of the President, the Person having the greatest Number of Votes of the Electors shall be the Vice President. But if there should remain two or more who have equal Votes, the Senate shall chuse from them by Ballot the Vice President.

The Congress may determine the Time of chusing the Electors, and the Day on which they shall give their Votes; which Day shall be the same throughout the United States.

No Person except a natural born Citizen, or a Citizen of the United States, at the time of the Adoption of this Constitution, shall be eligible to the Office of President; neither shall any Person be eligible to that Office who shall not have attained to the Age of thirty five Years, and been fourteen Years a Resident within the United States.

In Case of the Removal of the President from Office, or of his Death, Resignation, or Inability to discharge the Powers and Duties of the said Office, the Same shall devolve on the Vice President, and the Congress may by Law provide for the Case of Removal, Death, Resignation or Inability, both of the President and Vice President, declaring what Officer shall then act as President, and such Officer shall act accordingly, until the Disability be removed, or a President shall be elected.

The President shall, at stated Times, receive for his Services, a Compensation, which shall neither be encreased nor diminished during the Period for which he shall have been elected, and he shall not receive within that Period any other Emolument from the United States, or any of them.

Before he enter on the Execution of his Office, he shall take the following Oath or Affirmation:—"I do solemnly swear (or affirm) that I will faithfully execute the Office of President of the United States, and will to the best of my Ability, preserve, protect and defend the Constitution of the United States."

SECTION 2. The President shall be Commander in Chief of the Army and Navy of the United States, and of the Militia of the several States, when called into the actual Service of the United States; he may require the Opinion in writing, of the principal Officer in each of the executive Departments, upon any Subject relating to the Duties of their respective Offices, and he shall have Power to grant Reprieves and Pardons for Offences against the United States, except in Cases of Impeachment.

He shall have Power, by and with the Advice and Consent of the Senate, to make Treaties, provided two thirds of the Senators present concur; and he shall nominate, and by and with the Advice and Consent of the Senate, shall appoint Ambassadors, other public Ministers and Consuls, Judges of the supreme Court, and all other Officers of the United States, whose Appointments are not herein otherwise provided for, and which shall be established by Law: but the Congress may by Law vest the Appointment of such inferior Officers, as they think proper, in the President alone, in the Courts of Law, or in the Heads of Departments.

The President shall have Power to fill up all Vacancies that may happen during the Recess of the Senate, by granting Commissions which shall expire at the End of their next Session.

SECTION 3. He shall from time to time give to the Congress Information of the State of the Union, and recommend to their Consideration such Measures as he shall judge necessary and expedient; he may, on extraordinary Occasions, convene both Houses, or either of them, and in Case of Disagreement between them, with Respect to the Time of Adjournment, he may adjourn them to such Time as he shall think proper; he shall receive Ambassadors and other public Ministers; he shall take Care that the Laws be faithfully executed, and shall Commission all the Officers of the United States.

SECTION 4. The President, Vice President and all civil Officers of the United States, shall be removed from Office on Impeachment for, and Conviction of, Treason, Bribery, or other High Crimes and Misdemeanors.

ARTICLE III.

SECTION 1. The judicial Power of the United States, shall be vested in one supreme Court, and in such inferior Courts as the Congress may from time to time ordain and establish. The Judges, both of the supreme and inferior Courts, shall hold their Offices during good Behaviour, and shall, at stated Times, receive for their Services a Compensation, which shall not be diminished during their Continuance in Office.

SECTION 2. The judicial Power shall extend to all Cases, in Law and Equity, arising under this Constitution, the Laws of the United States, and Treaties made, or which shall be made, under their Authority; —to all Cases affecting Ambassadors, other public Ministers and Consuls;—to all Cases of admiralty and maritime Jurisdiction;—to Controversies to which the United States shall be a Party;—to Controversies between two or more States;—between a State and Citizens of another State;—between Citizens of different States;—between Citizens of the same State claiming Lands under Grants of different States, and between a State, or the Citizens thereof, and foreign States, Citizens or Subjects.

In all Cases affecting Ambassadors, other public Ministers and Consuls, and those in which a State shall be Party, the supreme Court shall have original Jurisdiction. In all the other Cases before mentioned, the supreme Court shall have appellate Jurisdiction, both as to Law and Fact, with such Exceptions, and under such Regulations as the Congress shall make.

The Trial of all Crimes, except in Cases of Impeachment, shall be by Jury; and such Trial shall be held in the State where the said Crimes shall have been committed; but when not committed within any State, the Trial shall be at such Place or Places as the Congress may by Law have directed.

SECTION 3. Treason against the United States, shall consist only in levying War against them, or in adhering to their Enemies, giving them Aid and Comfort. No Person shall be convicted of Treason unless on the Testimony of two Witnesses to the same overt Act, or on Confession in open Court.

The Congress shall have Power to declare the Punishment of Treason, but no Attainder of Treason shall work Corruption of Blood, or Forfeiture except during the Life of the Person attainted.

ARTICLE IV.

SECTION 1. Full Faith and Credit shall be given in each State to the public Acts, Records, and judicial Proceedings of every other State. And the Congress may by general Laws prescribe the Manner in which such Acts, Records and Proceedings shall be proved, and the Effect thereof.

SECTION 2. The Citizens of each State shall be entitled to all Privileges and Immunities of Citizens in the several States.

A Person charged in any State with Treason, Felony, or other Crime, who shall flee from Justice, and be found in another State, shall on Demand of the executive Authority of the State from which he fled, be delivered up, to be removed to the State having Jurisdiction of the Crime.

No Person held to Service or Labour in one State, under the Laws thereof, escaping into another, shall, in Consequence of any Law or Regulation therein, be discharged from such Service or Labour, but shall be delivered up on Claim of the Party to whom such Service or Labour may be due.

SECTION 3. New States may be admitted by the Congress into this Union; but no new State shall be formed or erected within the Jurisdiction of any other State; nor any State be formed by the Junction of two or more States, or Parts of States, without the Consent of the Legislatures of the States concerned as well as of the Congress.

The Congress shall have Power to dispose of and make all needful Rules and Regulations respecting the Territory or other Property belonging to the United States; and nothing in this Constitution shall be so construed as to Prejudice any Claims of the United States, or of any particular State.

SECTION 4. The United States shall guarantee to every State in this Union a Republican Form of Government, and shall protect each of them against Invasion; and on Application of the Legislature, or of the Executive (when the Legislature cannot be convened) against domestic Violence.

ARTICLE V.

The Congress, whenever two thirds of both Houses shall deem it necessary, shall propose Amendments to this Constitution, or, on the Application of the Legislatures of two thirds of the several States, shall call a Convention for proposing Amendments, which, in either Case, shall be valid to all Intents and Purposes, as Part of this Constitution, when ratified by the Legislatures of three fourths of the several States, or by Conventions in three fourths thereof, as the one or the other Mode of Ratification may be proposed by the Congress; Provided that no Amendment which may be made prior to the Year One thousand eight hundred and eight shall in any Manner affect the first and fourth Clauses in the Ninth Section of the first Article; and that no State, without its Consent, shall be deprived of its equal Suffrage in the Senate.

ARTICLE VI.

All Debts contracted and Engagements entered into, before the Adoption of this Constitution, shall be as valid against the United States under this Constitution, as under the Confederation.

This Constitution, and the Laws of the United States which shall be made in Pursuance thereof; and all Treaties made, or which shall be made, under the Authority of the United States, shall be the supreme Law of the Land; and the Judges in every State shall be bound thereby, any Thing in the Constitution or Laws of any State to the Contrary notwithstanding.

The Senators and Representatives before mentioned, and the Members of the several State Legislatures, and all executive and judicial Officers, both of the United States and of the several States, shall be bound by Oath or Affirmation, to support this Constitution; but no religious Test shall ever be required as a Qualification to any Office or public Trust under the United States.

ARTICLE VII.

The Ratification of the Conventions of nine States, shall be sufficient for the Establishment of this Constitution between the States so ratifying the Same.

DONE in Convention by the Unanimous Consent of the States present the Seventeenth Day of September in the Year of our Lord one thousand seven hundred and Eighty seven and of the Independence of the United States of America the Twelfth IN WITNESS WHEREOF We have hereunto subscribed our Names,

G^o WASHINGTON—*Presid^t.*
and deputy from Virginia

Attest WILLIAM JACKSON *Secretary*

Delaware
GEO: READ
GUNNING BEDFORD jun
JOHN DICKINSON
RICHARD BASSETT
JACO: BROOM
Maryland
JAMES MCHENRY
DAN OF ST THOS. JENIFER
DANL CARROLL
Virginia
JOHN BLAIR
JAMES MADISON Jr.
North Carolina
WM. BLOUNT
RICHD. DOBBS SPAIGHT.
HU WILLIAMSON
South Carolina
J. RUTLEDGE
CHARLES COTESWORTH PINCKNEY
CHARLES PINCKNEY
PIERCE BUTLER.
Georgia
WILLIAM FEW
ABR BALDWIN
New Hampshire
JOHN LANGDON
NICHOLAS GILMAN
Massachusetts
NATHANIEL GORHAM
RUFUS KING
Connecticut
WM. SAML. JOHNSON
ROGER SHERMAN
New York
ALEXANDER HAMILTON
New Jersey
WIL.: LIVINGSTON
DAVID BREARLEY.
WM. PATERSON.
JONA: DAYTON
Pennsylvania
B FRANKLIN

William Livingston

Gouverneur Morris

Robert Morris

William Paterson

Constitution of the United States

THOMAS MIFFLIN
ROBT MORRIS
GEO. CLYMER
THOS. FITZSIMONS
JARED INGERSOLL
JAMES WILSON
GOUV MORRIS

Amendment I

Congress shall make no law respecting an establishment of religion, or prohibiting the free exercise thereof; or abridging the freedom of speech, or of the press; or the right of the people peaceably to assemble, and to petition the Government for a redress of grievances.

Amendment II

A well regulated Militia, being necessary to the security of a free State, the right of the people to keep and bear Arms, shall not be infringed.

Amendment III

No Soldier shall, in time of peace, be quartered in any house, without the consent of the Owner, nor in time of war, but in a manner to be prescribed by law.

Amendment IV

The right of the people to be secure in their persons, houses, papers, and effects, against unreasonable searches and seizures, shall not be violated, and no Warrants shall issue, but upon probable cause, supported by Oath or affirmation, and particularly describing the place to be searched, and the persons or things to be seized.

Amendment V

No person shall be held to answer for a capital, or otherwise infamous crime, unless on a presentment or indictment of a Grand Jury, except in cases arising in the land or naval forces, or in the Militia, when in actual service in time of War or public danger; nor shall any person be subject for the same offence to be twice put in jeopardy of life or limb; nor shall be compelled in any criminal case to be a witness against himself, nor be deprived of life, liberty, or property, without due process of law; nor shall private property be taken for public use, without just compensation.

Amendment VI

In all criminal prosecutions, the accused shall enjoy the right to a speedy and public trial, by an impartial jury of the State and district wherein the crime shall have been committed, which district shall have been previously ascertained by law, and to be informed of the nature and cause of the accusation; to be confronted with the witnesses against him; to have compulsory process for obtaining witnesses in his favor, and to have the Assistance of Counsel for his defence.

Amendment VII

In Suits at common law, where the value in controversy shall exceed twenty dollars, the right of trial by jury shall be preserved, and no fact tried by a jury, shall be otherwise reexamined in any Court of the United States, than according to the rules of the common law.

Amendment VIII

Excessive bail shall not be required, nor excessive fines imposed, nor cruel and unusual punishments inflicted.

Amendment IX

The enumeration in the Constitution, of certain rights, shall not be construed to deny or disparage others retained by the people.

Amendment X

The powers not delegated to the United States by the Constitution, nor prohibited by it to the States, are reserved to the States respectively, or to the people.

Amendment XI
(Adopted Jan. 8, 1798)

The Judicial power of the United States shall not be construed to extend to any suit in law or equity, commenced or prosecuted against one of the United States by Citizens of another State, or by Citizens or Subjects of any Foreign State.

Amendment XII
(Adopted Sept. 25, 1804)

The Electors shall meet in their respective states and vote by ballot for President and Vice-President, one of whom, at least, shall not be an inhabitant of the same state with themselves; they shall name in their ballots the person voted for as President, and in distinct ballots the person voted for as Vice-President, and they shall make distinct lists of all persons voted for as President, and of all persons voted for as Vice-President, and of the number of votes for each, which lists they shall sign and certify, and transmit sealed to the seat of the government of the United States, directed to the President of the Senate;—The President of the Senate shall, in presence of the Senate and House of Representatives, open all the certificates and the votes shall then be counted;—The person having the greatest number of votes for President, shall be the President, if such number be a majority of the whole number of Electors appointed; and if no person have such majority, then from the persons having the highest numbers not exceeding three on the list of those voted for as President, the House of Representatives shall choose immediately, by ballot, the President. But in choosing the President, the votes shall be taken by states, the representation from each state having one vote; a quorum for this purpose shall consist of a member or members from two-thirds of the states, and a majority of all the states shall be necessary to a choice. And if the House of Representatives shall not choose a President whenever the right of choice shall devolve upon them, before the fourth day of March next following, then the Vice-President shall act as President, as in the case of the death or other constitutional disability of the President.—The person having the greatest number of votes as Vice-President, shall be the Vice-President, if such number be a majority of the whole number of Electors appointed, and if no person have a majority, then from the two highest numbers on the list, the Senate shall choose the Vice-President; a quorum for the purpose shall consist of two-thirds of the whole number of Senators, and a majority of the whole number shall be necessary to a choice. But no person constitutionally ineligible to the office of President shall be eligible to that of Vice-President of the United States.

Amendment XIII
(Adopted Dec. 18, 1865)

SECTION 1. Neither slavery nor involuntary servitude, except as a punishment for crime whereof the party shall have been duly convicted, shall exist within the United States, or any place subject to their jurisdiction.

SECTION 2. Congress shall have power to enforce this article by appropriate legislation.

Amendment XIV
(Adopted July 28, 1868)

SECTION 1. All persons born or naturalized in the United States, and subject to the jurisdiction thereof, are citizens of the United States and of the State wherein they reside. No State shall make or enforce any law which shall abridge the privileges or immunities of citizens of the United States; nor shall any State deprive any person of life, liberty, or property, without due process of law; nor deny to any person within its jurisdiction the equal protection of the laws.

SECTION 2. Representatives shall be apportioned among the several States according to their respective numbers, counting the whole number of persons in each State, excluding Indians not taxed. But when the right to vote at any election for the choice of electors for President and Vice-President of the United States, Representatives in Congress, the Executive and Judicial officers of a State, or the members of the Legislature thereof, is denied to any of the male inhabitants of such State, being twenty-one years of age, and citizens of the United States, or in any way abridged, except for participation in rebellion, or other crime, the basis of representation therein shall be reduced in the proportion which the number of such male citizens shall bear to the whole number of male citizens twenty-one years of age in such State.

SECTION 3. No person shall be a Senator or Representative in Congress, or elector of President and Vice-President, or hold any office, civil or military, under the United States, or under any State, who, having previously taken an oath, as a member of Congress, or as an officer of the United States, or as a member of any State legislature, or as an executive or judicial officer of any State, to support the Constitution of the United States, shall have engaged in insurrection or rebellion against the same, or given aid or comfort to the enemies thereof. But Congress may by a vote of two-thirds of each House, remove such disability.

SECTION 4. The validity of the public debt of the United States, authorized by law, including debts incurred for payment of pensions and bounties for services in suppressing insurrection or rebellion, shall not be questioned. But neither the United States nor any State shall assume or pay any debt or obligation incurred in aid of insurrection or rebellion against the United States, or any claim for the loss or emancipation of any slave; but all such debts, obligations and claims shall be held illegal and void.

SECTION 5. The Congress shall have power to enforce, by appropriate legislation, the provisions of this article.

Amendment XV
(Adopted March 30, 1870)

SECTION 1. The right of citizens of the United States to vote shall not be denied or abridged by the United States or by any State on account of race, color, or previous condition of servitude.

SECTION 2. The Congress shall have power to enforce this article by appropriate legislation.

Amendment XVI
(Adopted Feb. 25, 1913)

The Congress shall have power to lay and collect taxes on incomes, from whatever source derived, without apportionment among the several States, and without regard to any census or enumeration.

Amendment XVII
(Adopted May 31, 1913)

The Senate of the United States shall be composed of two Senators from each State, elected by the people thereof, for six years; and each Senator shall have one vote. The electors in each State shall have the qualifications requisite for electors of the most numerous branch of the State legislatures.

When vacancies happen in the representation of any State in the Senate, the executive authority of such State shall issue writs of election to fill such vacancies: *Provided,* That the legislature of any State may empower the executive thereof to make temporary appointments until the people fill the vacancies by election as the legislature may direct.

This amendment shall not be so construed as to affect the election or term of any Senator chosen before it becomes valid as part of the Constitution.

Amendment XVIII
(Adopted Jan. 29, 1919)

SECTION 1. After one year from the ratification of this article the manufacture, sale, or transportation of intoxicating liquors within, the importation thereof into, or the exportation thereof from the United States and all territory subject to the jurisdiction thereof for beverage purposes is hereby prohibited.

SECTION 2. The Congress and the several States shall have concurrent power to enforce this article by appropriate legislation.

SECTION 3. This article shall be inoperative unless it shall have been ratified as an amendment to the Constitution by the legislatures of the several States, as provided in the Constitution, within seven years from the date of the submission hereof to the States by the Congress.

Amendment XIX
(Adopted Aug. 26, 1920)

The right of citizens of the United States to vote shall not be denied or abridged by the United States or by any State on account of sex.

Congress shall have power to enforce this article by appropriate legislation.

Amendment XX
(Adopted Feb. 6, 1933)

SECTION 1. The terms of the President and Vice President shall end at noon on the 20th day of January, and the terms of Senators and Representatives at noon on the 3d day of January, of the years in which such terms would have ended if this article had not been ratified; and the terms of their successors shall then begin.

SECTION 2. The Congress shall assemble at least once in every year, and such meeting shall begin at noon on the 3d day of January, unless they shall by law appoint a different day.

SECTION 3. If, at the time fixed for the beginning of the term of the President, the President elect shall have died, the Vice President elect shall become President. If a President shall not have been chosen before the time fixed for the beginning of his term, or if the President elect shall have failed to qualify, then the Vice President elect shall act as President until a President shall have qualified; and the Congress may by law provide for the case wherein neither a President elect nor a Vice President elect shall have qualified, declaring who shall then act as President, or the manner in which one who is to act shall be selected, and such person shall act accordingly until a President or Vice President shall have qualified.

SECTION 4. The Congress may by law provide for the case of the death of any of the persons from whom the House of Representatives may choose a President whenever the right of choice shall have devolved upon them, and for the case of the death of any of the persons from whom the Senate may choose a Vice President whenever the right of choice shall have devolved upon them.

SECTION 5. Sections 1 and 2 shall take effect on the 15th day of October following the ratification of this article.

SECTION 6. This article shall be inoperative unless it shall have been ratified as an amendment to the Constitution by the legislatures of three-fourths of the several States within seven years from the date of its submission.

Amendment XXI
(Adopted Dec. 5, 1933)

SECTION 1. The eighteenth article of amendment to the Constitution of the United States is hereby repealed.

SECTION 2. The transportation or importation into any State, Territory, or possession of the United States for delivery or use therein of intoxicating liquors, in violation of the laws thereof, is hereby prohibited.

SECTION 3. This article shall be inoperative unless it shall have been ratified as an amendment to the Constitution by conventions in the several States, as provided in the Constitution, within seven years from the date of the submission hereof to the States by the Congress.

Amendment XXII
(Adopted Feb. 27, 1951)

SECTION 1. No person shall be elected to the office of the President more than twice, and no person who has held the office of President, or acted as President, for more than two years of a term to which some other person was elected President shall be elected to the office of the President more than once. But this Article shall not apply to any person holding the office of President when this Article was proposed by the Congress, and shall not prevent any person who may be holding the office of President, or acting as President, during the term within which this Article becomes operative from holding the office of President or acting as President during the remainder of such term.

SECTION 2. This article shall be inoperative unless it shall have been ratified as an amendment to the Constitution by the legislatures of three-fourths of the several States within seven years from the date of its submission to the States by the Congress.

Amendment XXIII
(Adopted Mar. 29, 1961)

SECTION 1. The District constituting the seat of Government of the United States shall appoint in such manner as the Congress may direct:

A number of electors of President and Vice President equal to the whole number of Senators and Representatives in Congress to which the District would be entitled if it were a State, but in no event more than the least populous State; they shall be in addition to those appointed by the States, but they shall be considered, for the purposes of the election of President and Vice President, to be electors appointed by a State; and they shall meet in the District and perform such duties as provided by the twelfth article of amendment.

SECTION 2. The Congress shall have power to enforce this article by appropriate legislation.

Amendment XXIV
(Adopted Jan. 23, 1964)

SECTION 1. The right of citizens of the United States to vote in any primary or other election for President or Vice President, for electors for President or Vice President, or for Senator or Representative in Congress, shall not be denied or abridged by the United States or any State by reason of failure to pay any poll tax or other tax.

SECTION 2. The Congress shall have power to enforce this article by appropriate legislation.

Amendment XXV
(Adopted Feb. 10, 1967)

SECTION 1. In case of the removal of the President from office or his death or resignation, the Vice President shall become President.

SECTION 2. Whenever there is a vacancy in the office of the Vice President, the President shall nominate a Vice President who shall take the office upon confirmation by a majority vote of both houses of Congress.

SECTION 3. Whenever the President transmits to the President pro tempore of the Senate and the Speaker of the House of Representatives his written declaration that he is unable to discharge the powers and duties of his office, and until he transmits to them a written declaration to the contrary, such powers and duties shall be discharged by the Vice President as Acting President.

SECTION 4. Whenever the Vice President and a majority of either the principal officers of the executive departments or of such other body as Congress may by law provide, transmit to the President pro tempore of the Senate and the Speaker of the House of Representatives their written declaration that the President is unable to discharge the powers and duties of his office, the Vice President shall immediately assume the powers and duties of the office as Acting President.

Thereafter, when the President transmits to the President pro tempore of the Senate and the Speaker of the House of Representatives his written declaration that no inability exists, he shall resume the powers and duties of his office unless the Vice President and a majority of either the principal officers of the executive departments or of such other body as Congress may by law provide, transmit within four days to the President pro tempore of the Senate and the Speaker of the House of Representatives their written declaration that the President is unable to discharge the powers and duties of his office. Thereupon Congress shall decide the issue, assembling within 48 hours for that purpose if not in session. If the Congress, within 21 days after receipt of the latter written declaration, or, if Congress is not in session, within 21 days after Congress is required to assemble, determines by two-thirds vote of both houses that the President is unable to discharge the powers and duties of his office, the Vice President shall continue to discharge the same as Acting President; otherwise, the President shall resume the powers and duties of his office.

Amendment XXVI
(Adopted June 30, 1971)

SECTION 1. The right of citizens of the United States, who are eighteen years of age or older, to vote shall not be denied or abridged by the United States or any state on account of age.

SECTION 2. The Congress shall have the power to enforce this article by appropriate legislation.

Construction Engineering, a division of civil engineering responsible for preparing the site, directing the placement of materials, and organizing personnel and equipment. △1612.

Constructivism, abstract movement in sculpture dating from 1913 when Vladimir Taitlin created the first free geometric constructions in space. Antoine Pevsner and Naum Gabo issued the manifesto of the style in 1920, when they published the *Realist Manifesto,* explaining their aesthetic interest in movement in space using materials of the machine age. The constructivist aesthetic influenced modern architecture and sculpture. △1320.

Consubstantiation, Christian doctrine stating that after the words of consecration in Communion the substances of bread and wine remain along with the body and blood of Christ. The doctrine is opposed to that of transubstantiation. *See also* Transubstantiation.

Consular Service, corps of government agents stationed abroad concerned with commercial activities and with providing certain essential services for their own nationals living in foreign countries. Consular officials are not diplomatic representatives; their role is established by bilateral treaty and not by international law as is the case for the diplomatic service.

Consulate (1799–1804), name given to the French Republic's government while under Napoleon Bonaparte's control. It consisted of a three-house legislature and a three-consul executive branch, but was actually dominated completely by Bonaparte.

Consuls, two chief magistrates of ancient Rome. Said to have been established in 510 BC, the traditional date for the expulsion of the king, the consuls were elected annually by the Comitia Centuriata to administer civil and military matters. After 367 BC, one consul was a patrician, the other a plebeian. Each had veto power over the other. Under the empire the title was merely honorary.

Consulting Psychology, special field of psychology that studies problems and offers professional help to people in business, industry, schools, colleges, government, etc. *See also* Industrial Psychology.

Consumer Affairs, Office of, a division of the US Department of Health, Education and Welfare, formerly the President's Committee on Consumer Interests. The executive agency handles consumers' complaints, encourages research, and distributes information of interest to consumers. It is the coordinating agency for all federal activity in the field of consumer protection.

Consumer Determinism, in economics, the concept that the consumer in a market economy has the ability to control or determine his economic life. The consumer is able to purchase the goods and services available at existing market prices according to his income.

Consumer Equilibrium, in economics, satisfaction level or position from which the consumer would tend

Charles Cotesworth Pinckney

John Rutledge

Roger Sherman

George Washington

not to move. The consumer may be in equilibrium when the combination of goods and services he purchases provides the highest possible utility level.

Consumer Price Index (CPI), most commonly used indicator of the general price level. The CPI is a retail price index that is determined by comparing prices of a basket of goods in a given year to the price of the same goods in a base year. Currently, the 1967–68 period is used as the base for computing the Consumer Price Index, ie, it is considered 100.00. Thus the CPI for 1974 was 154.3. *See also* Wholesale Price Index.

Consumer Protection, movement designed to protect consumer interests and encourage more responsible producers. It gained great impetus in the 1960s and 1970s, largely through the investigative efforts of Ralph Nader. The consumer movement stresses the importance of an educated buying public as protection against inferior merchandise and false advertising and works to increase and strengthen consumer protection laws. *See also* Nader, Ralph.

Consumer's Union of the United States (CU), organization, "to provide for consumers, information and counsel relating to consumer goods and services." It also gives information and assistance on the expenditure of the family income and initiates and cooperates with individual and group consumerism efforts. It publishes *Consumer Reports,* a monthly magazine. Founded 1936.

Consumption Function, foundation of macroeconomic theory, indicates the relationship between consumption and changes in the level of income. When consumers' incomes rise, they will spend a proportion of this new income on consumption goods. In addition, consumption will depend upon such things as interest rates and accumulated wealth.

Contact Dermatitis, acute or chronic inflammation of the skin produced by contact with a certain natural or synthetic substance—for example, wool, poison ivy, detergent—usually appearing as skin redness, swelling, sometimes oozing vesicle formation, accompanied by itching. Treatment consists of removal of the offending agent and application of symptomatically bland compresses and of corticosteroids if necessary. *See also* Allergy.

Contact Lenses. △674.

Container Ship. △1680.

Container Transportation, late 1960s development, chiefly in ocean shipping, that has greatly speeded cargo-moving. Ships have compartments above and below decks to hold large containers. In port, the containers are loaded and unloaded with specialized automated equipment. Usually, filled containers leave the factory by truck, are loaded onto railroad cars, and then onto a ship. △1680.

Containment Policy, US strategic policy following World War II aimed at curbing Soviet expansion. It was officially initiated with the Truman Doctrine of 1947, which extended military and economic aid to Turkey and Greece to counteract Communist influence.

Contarini, noble Venetian family, dating from at least 7th century, that gave Venice eight doges and many important statesmen and scholars. Domenico was the first Contarini doge (1043–71), and Andrea (r. 1367–82) patriotically donated his wealth to the state. Gasparo (1483–1542) was a humanist scholar, diplomat, theologian, and cardinal. Other Contarini notables were Ambrogio (d. 1499), a great traveler; Giovanni (d. 1603), a painter; and Marco (d. 1689), a patron of music.

Contempt of Congress, citation for interference with, or disrespect for, congressional authority. A witness called before a congressional investigating committee who is deemed uncooperative may be held in contempt and is liable to prosecution.

Conti Family, younger branch of French royal family in the Bourbon House of Condé. The family began its continuous line with **Armand de Bourbon, Prince de Conti** (1629–66); he took the name from the town of Conti, located near Amiens. The line ended with **Louis François Joseph de Bourbon** (1734–1814), who was exiled after the French Revolution.

Continent, land mass, measured in millions of square miles, that rises to some considerable height above sea level. The continents, which float on plates that make up the earth's crust, do not end at the water line but extend to the limits of the continental shelves. These extensions of the land masses are submerged, continous territories and many offshore islands are highlands whose valleys are under water.

Continental Congress, First (1774), meeting of delegates from all the American colonies except Georgia. It created a unified resistance to the Coercive Acts and the Quebec Act. The Congress issued a Declaration of Rights and Grievances, adopted the Suffolk Resolves, and agreed on economic sanctions against Britain. An association was formed to oversee the commercial boycott of Britain. The delegates agreed to meet again in 1775 if the grievances were not redressed. *See also* Quebec Act. △1218.

Continental Congress, Second (1775), convention of colonial delegates principally to plan defense against Britain. It opened on May 10 in Independence Hall in Philadelphia shortly after the battles of Lexington and Concord. The Congress appointed George Washington commander of the Continental Army, tabled a reconciliation plan proposed by Lord North, opened ports in defiance of the Navigation Acts, and sent a diplomatic representative to France. Finally, on July 4, 1776, Congress adopted the Declaration of Independence, severing the colonies from Britain. The Congress continued to meet in different cities as the federal legislature until 1789. △1218.

Continental Divide, a line of separation running the length of a continent; determines to which side of the continent waters flow; in United States and Canada it determines whether they drain into the Pacific or Atlantic oceans; the line generally follows the crestline of the Rocky Mts: In South America, it follows the W portion of the Andes Mts.

Continental Drift, a theory which proposes that at one time all present-day land masses were joined in one supercontinent, Pangaea, but that about 200,000,000 years ago it broke up and the resulting land masses, roughly the continents of today, began to move over the earth's surface. The idea was first suggested in 1912 by a German meteorologist Alfred Wegener but the theory lay dormant until 1960 when H.H. Hess, using new evidences—radioactive dating, seafloor spreading, and magnetic field reversal—revived it. The theory explains the existence of similar mountain chains and strata and similar animal orders and plant genera found on different continents, as well as other zoological and geological anomalies. *See also* Plate Tectonics. △172, 410.

Continental Rise, the part of the continental margin that lies between the continental slope and the abyssal plain. It is a gentle incline and consists of sedimentary debris that slumps down from the shelf and slope above. △228.

Continental Shelf, the nearly flat part of the continental margin between the shoreline and the continental slope. The shelves lie at a depth of 200m (656ft) and have an average width of 60km (37mi). Economically important, they produce about 90% of the world's marine food resources, a fifth of the total world production of petroleum and natural gas, and $200,000,000 of sand and gravel. △228.

Continental Slope, the relatively steep slope of the continental margin that lies between the continental shelf and the continental rise and that leads down into deep water. The slope marks the outward edge of the continental crust where it meets the oceanic crust. △228.

Continuous Casting. △1594.

Contour Farming, practice of tilling moderately sloping land along lines of equal elevation, to prevent excessive runoff and reduce loss from surface erosion. It also aids in conserving water in the furrows.

Contrabassoon, or double bassoon, woodwind musical instrument pitched one octave below the bassoon. Used in symphony orchestras, it is the largest member of the oboe family. Its tube is 16ft (4.9m) long, doubled on itself four times, with the bell directed downward.

Contract, agreement between parties that can be legally enforced. The contract creates rights and obligations, and if the obligations are not satisfied, they can be enforced by a court order. Before an agreement can be a contract, five elements must be present. It must be between competent parties; they must have reached mutual assent; the bargain must be legal; consideration must be involved; and the agreement must be in the proper form. △910.

Contract Labor Law (1885), legislation designed to prevent importation of cheap labor. The law forbade immigration of laborers under contract and prepayment of passage of aliens, excluding professionals and skilled and domestic labor. In 1891, 1907, and 1917 the act was amended. △910.

Contralto, the lowest of the three types of female or boys' voices. The other types are mezzosoprano and soprano. A man singing in this range is called a countertenor.

Control Grid. △1548.

Control Rocket, small rocket engine used to make fine adjustments to the craft's attitude or orbit. *Attitude control jets* use compressed gas to alter the craft's orientation. *Vernier engines* make adjustments to the craft's speed to change its orbit.

Control Systems, means by which a process is made to conform to prescribed instructions, either by maintaining the values of certain parameters at a constant level or by making them change according to a predetermined plan. Control systems may be mechanical, electromechanical, electronic, fluidic (operated by liquid or gas pressure), or a combination of any of these means. All systems depend on either feed forward (such as a cutting tool that follows the shape of a model) or on feedback (a governor that reduces the input of fuel to an engine when the power exceeds a certain level). Many of the more complex systems used in industry are computer controlled. *See also* Electronic Control Systems. △1670.

Convection, transfer of heat by fluid currents, as in the warming of a room by air currents past the radiators. *See also* Heat Transfer. △1508.

Convection Cell, an organized circular flow of fluid, such as air or water, based on thermal changes in density and gravitational attraction, with updrafts away from the heat source and subsidence in the cooler outer regions, involved in the formation of clouds in the atmosphere.

Convergence, in mathematics, property of an infinite series (or sequence) of having a finite limiting value. Thus, for the series $1 + \frac{1}{2} + \frac{1}{2}^2 + \frac{1}{2}^3 \ldots$ the sum of the first two terms is 1.5, the first three 1.75, the first four 1.875, and as more and more terms are taken it approaches the limit 2. Such a series is said to converge. *See also* Divergence.

Convergence Theory, in social science, the theory that capitalist and socialist industrialized societies are tending to become more alike. The theory holds, for example, that technology is the greatest influence on social structure; that many decisions are made by managers, who have similar outlooks whether they work for capitalist or socialist employers; and that features of capitalism such as class distinctions are breaking down.

Convergent Evolution, the tendency of several different species to resemble each other, and to evolve and develop similar characteristics in the effort to adapt to a limited environment. △420, 574.

Converging Lens. *See* Lens.

Converse, Frederick Shepherd (1871–1940), US composer, b. Newton, Mass. He studied at Harvard and at the Royal Conservatory in Munich, where his *Symphony in D Minor* was played at his graduation. He taught composition at Harvard and harmony at the New England Conservatory, and wrote numerous compositions, among them his one-act opera *The Pipe of Desire.* This was the first US opera ever given at the Metropolitan Opera in New York City.

Convertible Currency, currency that can be exchanged for other currencies for any purpose and without penalty. In order for a currency to be convertible, it must be defined in terms of an accepted standard of value, eg gold, under a pure gold standard. *See also* Exchange Rates. △1384.

Convulsion, a bodily malfunction in which violent, involuntary spasms of the voluntary muscles occur, sometimes accompanied by loss of consciousness. May be symptomatic of several diseases.

Conway, Thomas (1735–1800), Irish-French general who went to America with other French officers during the Revolution. He served at Brandywine and Germantown and is remembered for his part in the Conway Cabal. By 1778, abandoned by his congressional friends, he rejoined the French army and saw service in French India. He fought for the royalists in the French Revolution and died in exile in England.

Conway Cabal, in US history, a plot in 1777 named

ter Thomas Conway. The group plotted to remove George Washington as commander and replace him with Horatio Gates. The plot failed and actually strengthened Washington's position as commander-in-chief. After investigation, it was discovered that Conway was accused unfairly and the alleged plot was not instigated by him.

Cook, David J. (1840–1907), US law enforcement officer, b. near LaPorte, Ind. He is best known as founder of Volunteer Rocky Mountain Detective Association. He had a long career as a marshal and sheriff in the Denver area and was arbiter in the Leadville, Col., mine strike in 1880.

Cook, Frederick Albert (1865–1940), US explorer and physician, b. Callicoon Depot, N.Y. In 1891 he was surgeon of the Peary arctic voyage; in 1879, surgeon of the Belgian antarctic voyage. During one of his own expeditions (1907–09), he claimed to have discovered the North Pole. At first hailed as a hero, he was later discredited when his claim was rejected. Imprisoned in 1923 for participating in an oil swindle, he was released in 1930 and pardoned in 1940.

Cook, James (1728–79), English naval officer and explorer. In 1768–71, Cook led a scientific voyage to Tahiti to observe the transit of Venus. He next surveyed the coast of New Zealand, taking formal possession of parts. He then charted the eastern coast of Australia, naming it New South Wales and claiming it for England. On a second expedition to the South Pacific (1772–75), Cook mapped much of the Southern Hemisphere and sailed farther south than anyone before him. On his last voyage (1776) he discovered the Sandwich (Hawaiian) Islands. △874, 1186, 1260.

Cook, Thomas (1808–92), English founder of world-wide tourist agency, Thomas Cook & Son. At first a missionary and temperance meeting organizer, he began to arrange group tours for temperance organizations (1841–44). He opened his own firm in 1845, providing his customers with railroad discounts and travel guides. He first offered foreign tours in 1850, the grand tour of Europe in 1856, and the first around-the-world tour in 1872.

Cook, Mount, New Zealand's highest peak, in Southern Alps in Tasman National Park, W central South Island. Height: 12,349ft (3,766m).

Cooke, Jay (1821–1905), US banker and financier, b. Sandusky, Ohio. Jay Cooke and Company, formed in 1861, was one of the country's best known banking houses. It supported the federal treasury during the Civil War. Its failure (1873) from railway speculation prompted general panic. Cooke later recovered his fortune in Western mining.

Cooke, Terrence (James) (1921–), US clergyman, b. New York City. In 1968 he was appointed Roman Catholic Archbishop of New York. He shared the conservatism of his predecessor, Cardinal Spellman, in theology and liturgy but was more progressive in social and political matters. He was named a Cardinal in 1969.

Cook Islands, island group in S Pacific Ocean, SE of Samoa; comprised of two major groups, the Northern Cook Islands (Manihiki Islands), and the Lower or Southern Cook Islands; self-governing, with foreign relations conducted through New Zealand. Industries: farming, fishing. Discovered 1773 by Capt. James Cook. Area: 90sq mi (233sq km). Pop. 22,000.

Cooley, Charles Horton (1864–1929), US sociologist, b. Ann Arbor. Holding a degree in economics, Cooley taught sociology at the University of Michigan (1892–1929). He is best known for his theory of the "looking-glass self," the theory that people define themselves by how others define them. He wrote *Human Nature and Social Order* (1902), *Social Organization* (1909), and *Social Process* (1918).

Cooley's Anemia. *See* Thalassemia.

Coolidge, (John) Calvin (1872–1933), 30th President of the United States, b. Plymouth, Vt.; graduate, Amherst College, 1895. In 1905 he married Grace Goodhue; they had two sons. A lawyer who practiced in Northampton, Mass., he became active in Republican politics and was elected to numerous local and state offices. In 1916, he was elected lieutenant governor of Massachusetts; two years later he was elected governor. He gained national attention in 1919 by his strong action against striking policemen in Boston. In 1920 he became the Republican vice-presidential candidate, running with Warren G. Harding. The Harding-Coolidge ticket won an overwhelming victory. Harding died suddenly on Aug. 2, 1923, and Coolidge succeeded him. His first task was cleaning up the scandals of the Harding administration. He fashioned a conservative, business-oriented administration. The country was prosperous, and he was easily elected to a full term in 1924. In foreign affairs, his administration was marked by adroit diplomacy. A laconic man, known as "Silent Cal," he never explained his reasons for not choosing to run for reelection in 1928.

Career: Massachusetts Lieutenant Governor, 1916–19; Massachusetts Governor, 1919–21; Vice President, 1921–23; President, 1923–29.

Coolidge, William David (1873–1975), US physicist, b. Hudson, Mass. He developed a method for drawing tungsten into filaments for light bulbs and radio tubes. He built a tube (Coolidge tube) capable of producing accurate radiation amounts. He also devised portable X-ray units and worked on construction techniques for industrial quality control. He devised the first successful submarine-detection system with Irving Langmuir, and he also did work on the atomic bomb project.

Coon, Carleton Stevens (1904–), US anthropologist, b. Wakefield, Mass. He made important archeological discoveries in North Africa and the Middle East. He published many works on the development of human races, including *Origin of Races* (1962), which was controversial because of his views on the evolution of different races.

Coon Rapids, city in E Minnesota, on the Mississippi River; suburb of Minneapolis-St Paul; site of Anoka-Ramsey State Junior College (1965). Industries: plastics, metallurgy, aerospace research. Inc. 1952. Pop. (1970) 30,505.

Cooper, Anthony Ashley, 1st Earl of Shaftesbury. *See* Shaftesbury, Anthony Ashley Cooper, 1st Earl of.

Cooper, Anthony Ashley, 7th Earl of Shaftesbury. *See* Shaftesbury, Anthony Ashley Cooper, 7th Earl of.

Cooper, Gary (1901–61), US film star, b. Frank James Cooper in Helena, Mont. He was idolized for his portrayal of virile, taciturn, honest, and courageous Western heroes. His films included *Nevada* (1927), *The Virginian* (1929), *Morocco* (1930), *Sergeant York* (1941), and *High Noon* (1952). △1362.

Cooper, James Fenimore (1789–1851), US author, b. Burlington, N.J. Raised in northern New York State, he drew on his background to produce a series of novels about the New York frontier. After a brief stint in the navy, he settled down as a gentleman farmer. In 1820 his first book, *Precaution,* a rather conventional novel of manners, appeared. With the publication of *The Spy* (1821), a novel of the American Revolution, he gained attention. His most successful works were the romantic novels of frontier life known as the Leather-Stocking Tales. *The Pioneers,* the first of these, appeared in 1823. The others were *The Last of the Mohicans* (1826), *The Prairie* (1827), *The Pathfinder* (1840), and *The Deerslayer* (1841). In addition to this series, other novels include *The Pilot* (1823), a story of the sea, *The Red Rover* (1828), and the Littlepage trilogy—*Satanstoe* (1845), *The Chainbearer* (1845), and *The Redskins* (1846). A political conservative, Cooper's social criticism included *The American Democrat* (1838). He also wrote *A History of the Navy of the United States* (1839). From 1833 he lived at his home in Cooperstown in upstate New York. *See also* Leather-Stocking Tales, The. △1374.

Cooper, Peter (1791–1883), US industrialist and inventor, b. New York City. He made his fortunes in ironworks, transportation, trans-ocean telegraphy, and manufacturing. His philanthropies were all based on the idea of education for the common man. To further this aim he founded a free institute, Cooper Union, and underwrote lectures and libraries. A popular figure, he was also an abolitionist, civic reformer, and the Greenback party's unsuccessful presidential candidate (1876).

Cooper, Thomas (1759–1839), US scientist, b. England. He was both a Pennsylvania judge and professor of chemistry at Dickinson College. His opposition to the Alien and Sedition Acts led to six months imprisonment in 1800. He taught and was president of South Carolina College (1820–33). He was also editor of *South Carolina Statutes at Large.*

Cooperative Commonwealth Federation, Canadian political party, formed in 1932 from a coalition of labor and socialist groups. Espousing a mild form of socialism, it was successful mostly in the western provinces. In 1961, the name was changed to the New Democratic party.

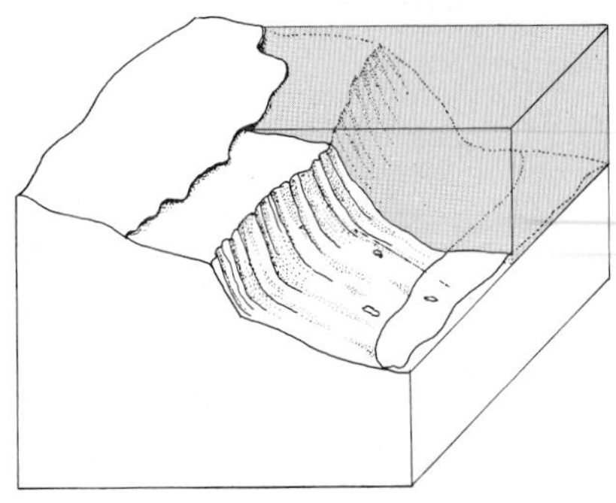

Continental shelf

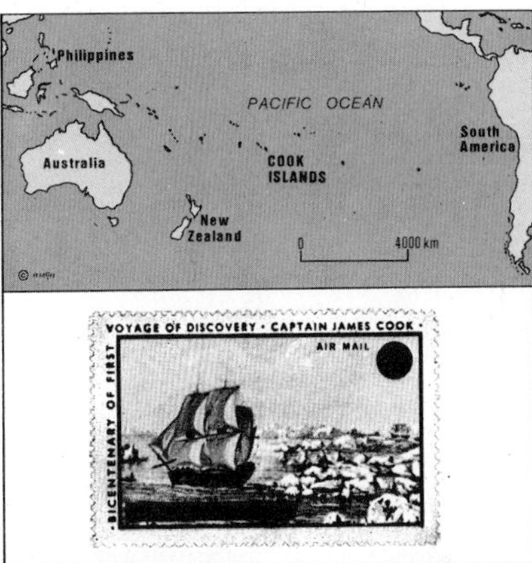
Philippines
PACIFIC OCEAN
Australia
COOK ISLANDS
South America
New Zealand
0
4000 km
VOYAGE OF DISCOVERY • CAPTAIN JAMES COOK •
AIR MAIL
BICENTENARY OF FIRST

Cook Islands

Calvin Coolidge

James Fenimore Cooper

Cooperative Farming, organizing of farmers for improved marketing, purchasing, and credit benefits. Three-quarters of the farmers in the United States belong to cooperatives. △306–08.

Cooperative Federalism, joint efforts by the federal, state, and local governments to solve common problems. The most conspicuous examples of this approach are the grants-in-aid programs, which provide federal funds, administered by the states, for hospital construction, old age pensions, urban renewal projects, and related works.

Cooperative Societies, nonprofit, voluntary business groups owned and operated by their membership. Consumers' cooperatives distribute goods directly from producer to consumer. Elimination of the middleman plus large-quantity group purchases reduce costs substantially. Producers' cooperatives serve the marketing needs of farmers and growers.

Cooper's Hawk, North American hawk. It is gray above with a rusty barred chest and tail. The female is much larger than the male. Length: 20in (51cm). Species *Accipiter cooperi*. *See also* Hawk.

Cooperstown, village in E New York, 59mi (95km) W of Albany; seat of Otsego co. Located at the S end of Lake Otsego, it is the setting for James Fenimore Cooper's "Leather-Stocking Tales"; he refers to the lake as "Glimmerglass." National Baseball Museum and Hall of Fame are here; New York State Historical Association has its headquarters at Fenimore house; also here is Farmers' Museum. A resort community, it was founded by William Cooper (1785), father of James Fenimore Cooper. Inc. 1807. Pop. (1970) 2,403.

Coordinate Geometry. *See* Analytic Geometry. △1454, 1472.

Coordinate System, reference system used to locate a point in space. A point can be defined by numbers representing distances or angles measured from lines or points of reference. Thus, in a Cartesian coordinate system, a point is defined by distances from intersecting axes. In a polar coordinate system, distance from a fixed point is used together with angular distance from a reference line. In general, two numbers are required to define a position in a plane; three numbers are required in three-dimensional space. In a coordinate system, curves or surfaces can be represented by algebraic functions, thus allowing geometric properties to be studied by algebraic methods. *See also* Cartesian Coordinate System. △1458.

Coordination Complex, type of compound in which one or more groups or molecules form coordinate bonds to a central metal atom, usually a transition metal. The complex may involve formation of a complex ion, or may be a neutral molecule as in nickel tetracarbonyl, $Ni(CO)_4$. The coordinating species are known as ligands. Inorganic chemistry is mainly concerned with the study of such compounds; some, such as heme and chlorophyll, have biochemical importance. *See also* Ion, Complex.

Coos Bay, port city in SW Oregon, on Coos Bay, an inlet of Pacific Ocean. Siuslaw National Forest is nearby; site of Southwestern Oregon Community College (1961); important lumber shipping port. Industries: fisheries, lumber milling, fish canning, tourism. Founded 1854 as Marshfield; inc. 1874; renamed 1944. Pop. (1970) 13,466.

Coot, aquatic bird of freshwater marshes. Sluggish, but a strong swimmer and diver, it feeds in or near water and lays buff-colored, brown-spotted eggs (8–12) on floating reed nests. The American coot, or mudhen, is slate gray with white bill and green legs and feet. Length: 13–16in (33–41cm). Species *Fulica*.

Cope, Edward Drinker (1840–97), US paleontologist who discovered about 1000 US species of extinct animals, particularly those of the Tertiary Period. He also revived the Lamarckian theory of evolution. *The Vertebrata of the Cretaceous Formations of the West* (1875) and *The Vertebrata of the Tertiary Formations of the West* (1883) are standard references.

Copenhagen (København), capital of Denmark, on E Sjaelland and N Amager islands in the Øresund; a trading and fishing center by early 11th century, a university was founded in 1479; became the capital in 1443; occupied by Germans in WWII; site of Amalienborg Square, enclosed by four 18th-century palaces, which has been royal residence since 1794, 17th-century stock exchange building, Cathedral of Our Lady built *c.* 1209 and rebuilt early 19th century, Tivoli Gardens (1843). Industries: furniture, Copenhagenware, iron foundries, shipyards. Pop. 625,678.

Copepod, marine and freshwater crustaceans. Some are parasitic on aquatic animals, especially fish. Their segmented, cylindrical bodies have a single median eye and no carapace. Length: 0.02–0.08in (0.5–2mm); length of parasitic forms may be over 1ft (30.5cm). There are 7500 species. Subclass Copepoda. *See also* Crustacean. △486.

Copernican Theory. △38.

Copernicus, Nicolaus (Mikotaj Kopernik) (1473–1543), Polish cleric and astronomer. His treatise *De Revolutionibus Orbium Caelestium* (1543) expounded the Copernican system and laid the foundations of modern astronomy. By assuming the earth's diurnal rotation and postulating a Sun-centered universe, he challenged both ancient science and religious dogma. △38, 1442.

Copland, Aaron (1900–), US composer, b. Brooklyn, N.Y. He is especially known for his works combining American folk elements and melodies with 20th-century symphonic techniques. His popular ballets include *Billy the Kid* (1938), *Rodeo* (1942), and *Appalachian Spring* (1944, Pulitzer Prize, 1945). Less well known has been Copland's experimentation with serial techniques (eg, *Piano Fantasy*, 1957). He also wrote *A Lincoln Portrait* (1942) and *Canticle of Freedom* (1955) and film music.

Copley, John Singleton (1738–1815), US painter of portraits and historical scenes, b. Boston. The finest portrait painter of the colonial period, Copley had little academic training and was a working artist at 15. His extraordinary abilities as a draftsman and colorist made him successful in his 20s. Copley's portraits are marked by realistic detail, such as the use of objects from the sitter's life. Settling in England about 1775, he continued to do portraits and began producing large historical paintings of contemporary events in modern dress. Although these won both critical and popular esteem, Copley's reputation is based on the early American portraits, which are unique in their vigor and immediacy. Many of the finest *(Paul Revere, John Hancock)* are in the Museum of Fine Arts, Boston.

Coppelia, ballet in three acts by Arthur Saint-Léon; music by Léo Delibes. First produced in Paris in 1870, it is famous for introducing folk dance into ballet.

Copper, metallic element (symbol Cu) of the first transition series, known from earliest times. It occurs native and in several ores including cuprite (an oxide), malachite, and chalcopyrite (a sulfide). The metal is extracted by smelting and purified by electrolysis. It is a good thermal and electrical conductor, second only to silver, and is extensively used in boilers, pipes, and electrical equipment. It is also used in alloys such as bronze and brass. The sulfate is an important agricultural poison. Chemically it tarnishes in air, oxidizes at high temperatures, and is attacked only by oxidizing acids. Properties: at. no. 29; at. wt. 63.546; sp gr 8.96; melt. pt. 1981°F (1083°C); boil. pt. 4703°F (2595°C); most common isotope Cu^{63} (69.09%). *See also* Transition Elements. △1588, 1596, 1600.

Copper Age, or chalcolithic age, period in which man discovered how to extract copper by heating its ore with charcoal. This art was known in the Middle East before 3500 BC. A subsequent important development was the alloying of copper with tin to produce bronze. *See also* Bronze Age. △1588.

Copperhead, poisonous pit viper, closely related to the water moccasin found in E and Central United States. It likes rocky, wooded areas in the north and swamps in the south. It has a coppery head and chestnut bands on a brown body. It is unaggressive. Length: to 36in (91cm). Family Viperidae; species *Agkistrodon contortrix*. *See also* Pit-viper.

Copperheads (also called Butternuts or Peace Democrats), term used in the 1860s (originally in *The New York Tribune*) to describe Democrats who favored the restoration of the Union by negotiation rather than by war. Although Lincoln took strong measures against the Copperheads, they won considerable support in Illinois, Indiana, and Ohio until the end of the Civil War.

Copper Plating. △1566.

Copper Sulfate. △1558.

Copra Palm. *See* Coconut Palm.

Coprates Rift Valley. △70.

Coprolite. △560.

Coptic Church, the Christian church in Egypt an Ethiopia, claiming St. Mark the Evangelist as its fou der. After the Council of Chalcedon in 451, it officiall became Monophysite. In the 19th century, it was ent tled Coptic Orthodox, to distinguish it from Easter and Roman rites. Arabic is now used in its service The church is democratically organized with approx mately 2.6 million members.

Copyright, exclusive right to the publication, sale, c production of a work granted by the government to it creator for a specified time period. Copyrights protec written works, art works, plays, motion pictures, etc from unauthorized use. Most western nations sub scribe to the Universal Copyright Convention, whic affords a reciprocal protective arrangement.

Copyright Office, agency within the Library of Cor gress. Its responsibilities include the copyrighting c subjects such as books, periodicals, dramatic and mu sical compositions, maps, works of art, photography prints, or labels used for articles of merchandise, mc tion pictures, and sound recordings. Founded 1870

Coquina Clam, wedge-shaped clam found in warn seas. Also called butterfly or pompano shell, it varie in color. Length: 0.75in (19.1mm). Class Pelecypoda family Donacidae; species include *Donax variabilis.*

Coral. △468.

Coral, colonial coelenterate found in cold to tropica marine waters. Characterized by limestone skeleton secreted by each animal polyp. Reef building coral are found only in waters above 70°F (21.1°C). Sof corals secrete a fleshy material; horny corals (sea fans secrete fan shaped supports; and stony corals secrete limestone cups. Reef length: 0.25in (6.4mm) to hun dreds of miles. Class Anthozoa. △270, 564.

Coral Fish, or reef fish, brilliantly colored, bony tropi cal fish found among coral reefs and formations. They are usually flat-bodied and round, with a large tail anc short fins. Many have poison spines. They can swim ir any position. Included are butterfly, angel, cardinal damsel, and parrot fish. △514.

Coral Gables, residential city in SE Florida, on Bis cayne Bay, 5mi (8km) SW of Miami. Superb example of a planned city; site of University of Miami (1925) Inc. 1925. Pop. (1970) 42,494.

Coral Reef, biogenic or organic mass of rock consist ing of corals and other calcium carbonate secreting animals. Such reefs grow in warm, shallow marine areas. The growth of reefs is strongly influenced by the prevailing currents and temperatures of the sur rounding seawater. The main types of reefs are fring ing and barrier. The former is attached to a landmass which eventually sinks leaving the barrier reef as the only visible land. △268, 624.

Coral Sea, arm of the SW Pacific Ocean, between E coast of Australia, Melanesia (NW), and New Zealand (SW); N part becomes Solomon Sea, S part becomes Tasman Sea; scene of US victory over Japanese 1942.

Coral Sea, Battle of (May 1942), World War II naval and air battle in the southwest Pacific. The US Navy inflicted heavy losses on the Japanese fleet and checked Japan's progress toward Australia.

Coral Snake, American and SE Asian colorfully banded poisonous snake. They have short fangs and potent venom. New World species, gaudily ringed in red, yellow, and black, range from S United States to Argentina and include the eastern coral snake *(Micrurus fulvius)*. It is secretive and feeds on snakes, lizards, and frogs. There are numerous snakes that mimic coral snakes. Length: to 24in (61cm). Family Elapidae. *See also* Snake.

Corbett, James John ("Gentleman Jim") (1866–1933), US boxer, b. San Francisco, Calif. He won the world's heavyweight championship from John L. Sullivan (1892) in New Orleans, La., in the first heavyweight match ever fought with gloves. He lost the title to Bob Fitzsimmons (1897) in Carson City, Nev.

Corbin, Margaret (1751–1800), American Revolutionary, b. Franklin co, Pa., who followed her soldier husband into battle. She served as the only woman in the Invalid Regiment (1776–83), stationed at West Point, and was awarded a Congressional pension.

Corcoran, William Wilson (1798–1888), US art collector and financier, b. Baltimore, Md. He donated the Corcoran Gallery of Art in Washington, D.C., which houses his collection, consisting chiefly of US painting from colonial times to his death. The present classical revival museum building dates from 1897. In

1840 Corcoran formed the banking firm of Corcoran and Riggs and made his fortune by successfully selling US treasury bonds to London. In 1854 he retired to devote himself to his many philanthropic concerns.

Corday, Charlotte (1768–93) French patriot. A noblewoman with the full name Marie Anne Charlotte Corday d'Armont, she stabbed the Jacobin Jean Paul Marat to death in his bath on July 13, 1793, and was guillotined on July 17. Influenced by the ideas of "antique heroism" (Plutarch), Voltaire, and the Abbé Raynal, she supported the principles of the French Revolution but not the Reign of Terror. When Marat decided there should be 200,000 more victims, she decided to kill him rather than Maximilien Robespierre.

Cordillera Blanca, lofty arm of the Andes Mts. in N central Peru. Mostly in Ancash dept., range extends NNW to SSE between the Cordillera Central (E) and the Cordillera Negra (W). Length: approx. 200mi (322km). Highest peak is Nevado Huascarán, 22,205ft (6,772m).

Córdoba, city in central Argentina, 387mi (623km) NW of Buenos Aires; capital of Córdoba district; site of National University of Córdoba (1613). Industries: cement, leather, glass, textiles. Founded by Jerónimo Luis de Cabrera 1573. Pop. 580,015.

Córdoba, city in E Mexico, 55mi (89km) WSW of Veracruz; contains excellent preservations of colonial buildings; scene of Treaty of Córdoba (1821) establishing Mexican independence; important agricultural center. Industries: coffee, tobacco, sugar cane, textiles, tanning, lumber, tobacco. Founded 1618. Pop. 78,495.

Córdoba, city in S Spain, on the Guadalquivir River; capital of Córdoba prov.; ruled by Iberians, Romans, Visigoths, and Moors; flourished under the rule of Caliph Abd er-Rahman III. In 1236 Ferdinand III of Castile captured Córdoba and imposed a new language and Christian culture on the city; site of 8th-century mosque, Roman bridge, and fine art museum. Industries: bronze, copper, chemicals, electrical fittings, fruit. Area: (prov.) 5,297sq mi (13,719sq km). Pop. (city) 235,632; (prov.) 724,116.

Córdoba Caliphate, Muslim monarchy established in Córdoba, Spain, in the 10th century. When the Umayyad caliphate was deposed in Damascus in 750, one member of the family, Abd er-Rahman I, fled to Spain, where he became emir of Córdoba. Abd er-Rahman III assumed the title of caliph. The Umayyads ruled until 1031 as caliphs. *See also* Caliph; Umayyads. △1078.

CORE. *See* Congress of Racial Equality.

Core (Drilling), a cylindrical rock sample that has been gathered by some sort of drilling device; on land usually by a rotary drill, from the sea often by a metal cylinder with a cutter on the bottom that is driven in by force. The core is used to identify the various layers in the rock or sediment. △170.

Core, Earth, the interior of Earth under the Mohorovicic discontinuity. Information concerning the composition of the core is obtained from seismic measurements. The core may be a plasma, compressed material, in which the electrons have been pushed toward the nuclei of the atoms of the material. Layers exist in the core. The outer one is relatively liquid, the inner is incompressible and probably solid iron with admixture of nickel and some other lighter element still unidentified. *See also* Mantle; Moho. △166.

Corelli, Arcangelo. △1196.

Coreopsis, a large genus of annual and perennial plants cultivated for their daisylike flower heads. A popular annual is the tall golden coreopsis *(C. grandiflora),* with yellow rays and a reddish-brown center. Height: to 3ft (91cm). Family Compositae.

Corfu (Kérkira), island in NW Greece; 2nd-largest of the Ionian group; with Paxos Island forms a department of Greece; Corfu is the capital; scene of first recorded naval battle 665 BC, with Corinth for possession of Epidamnus; allied with Athens 433 BC against Corinth; held by Romans 229 BC–AD 336, when it fell to the Byzantines; occupied by Venetians 1386–1797; under British protection 1815–64, when it passed to Greece; site of "Pact of Corfu" (1917), uniting Serbia, Croatia, and Slovenia; occupied by Germany during WWII. Industries: olives, olive oil, fruit, livestock, wine, tourism, fishing. Area: 229sq mi (593sq km). Pop. 97,412.

Cori, Carl Ferdinand (1896–), US biochemist, b. Czechoslovakia, came to US 1922, naturalized 1928. He shared the 1947 Nobel Prize in physiology and medicine with his wife Gerty Theresa (1896–1957), for their discovery of how the chemical energy of glycogen, a carbohydrate stored in the liver and muscle, is broken down into a form that can be used by the body.

Coriander, a single species, *Coriandrum sativum,* of annual herb native to Europe and Asia Minor and widely cultivated for its aromatic seeds used for food flavoring. It has a hollow stem, divided leaves, and pink or white flowers. Height: to 3ft (91cm). Family Umbelliferae.

Corinth (Korinthos), city in NE Peloponnesus, Greece, at the SW end of the Isthmus of Corinth; 3mi (5km) NE of site of the ancient city of Corinth, destroyed by earthquake (1858); capital of Corinthia dept. Inhabited since Neolithic period (5,500 BC); it was ruled by Bacchiad kings 8th-7th centuries BC, Syracuse and Corcyra 700 BC; prospered as major trade and commercial state 620–500 BC; fought with Sparta during the Peloponnesian War (431–404 BC) and with Athens, Thebes, and Argos against Sparta during Corinthian War (395–387 BC); joined Achaean League 243 BC to fight against Romans, who destroyed city 146 BC. Rebuilt 44 BC by Caesar, Corinth became capital of Achaea; passed from Venetian rule AD 1682–1715 to Turks 1715–1822, and then became part of Greece. Ruins of old Corinth include temple of Apollo, marketplace, amphitheater. Present city is a transportation center. Trading of olives, raisins, wine are important industries. Pop. 15,892. △992.

Corinth, city in NE Mississippi, near Tennessee border; seat of Alcorn co; scene of heavy fighting Oct. 3–4, 1862 when Union forces under Gen. William Rosecrans defeated Confederates under Gen. Earl Van Dorn. Industries: telephone equipment, textiles, clothing, dairy products. Founded 1855. Pop. (1970) 11,581.

Corinth, Isthmus of, isthmus in Greece, between the Gulf of Corinth and Saronic Gulf; connects central Greece with the Peloponnesus; crossed by 17th-century Corinth canal; connects the Adriatic and Ionian seas; site of remnants of ancient Isthmian Wall (restored 3rd-6th centuries AD), for the defense of Peloponnesus; sanctuary of Poseidon. Width: approx. 7mi (11km). Length: approx. 20mi (32km).

Corinthian Order, latest and most ornate of the classical orders of architecture, developed by the Greeks in the 4th century BC, but used more extensively in Roman architecture. The shaft is slender, and the capital is elaborately carved. *See also* Orders of Architecture. △1002.

Corinthians, two New Testament epistles of St. Paul written to the Christian church in Corinth, a wealthy, vice-ridden city. He discusses the problems of false apostles and immorality. The first letter was written when he was leaving Ephesus, the second from Macedonia.

Corinthian War (395–87 BC), war between Corinth and Sparta. The Corinthian democrats became angry because Sparta, an ally in the Peloponnesian War, refused to destroy the defeated Athens. Corinth then allied with Athens, Argos, and Thebes and declared war on Sparta in midsummer of 395. The indecisive Battle of the Stockade (393) was fought at the Corinthian city walls with dissenting Corinthian aristocrats fighting along with the Spartans. Fighting ended with the Peace of 387, the aristocrats returned to Corinth, and Corinth rejoined the Spartan League.

Coriolanus (1607), 5-act tragedy by William Shakespeare, after Plutarch's *Life of Coriolanus.* Roman hero Coriolanus, a candidate for consulship, is banished by a mob raised by jealous tribunes. He turns for aid to Aufidius, Rome's enemy and his own personal foe, and they march against Rome. The pleas of his mother, Volumnia, dissuade him from his purpose. Rome is saved but Coriolanus is killed by Aufidius.

Coriolis, Gaspard Gustave de (1792–1843), French theoretical physicist who explained the effect of the earth's rotation on objects moving above its surface in terms of the force or effect bearing his name. *See also* Coriolis Force. △214.

Coriolis Force or **Effect,** an apparent force on particles or objects like winds, clouds, or aircraft moving in the atmosphere, due to the rotation of the earth under them, such that the particle's motion is deflected toward the right in the Northern Hemisphere and toward the left in the Southern, but the particle's speed is unaffected. The direction of water whirling around a drain demonstrates this force. △214, 224.

Copenhagen, Denmark

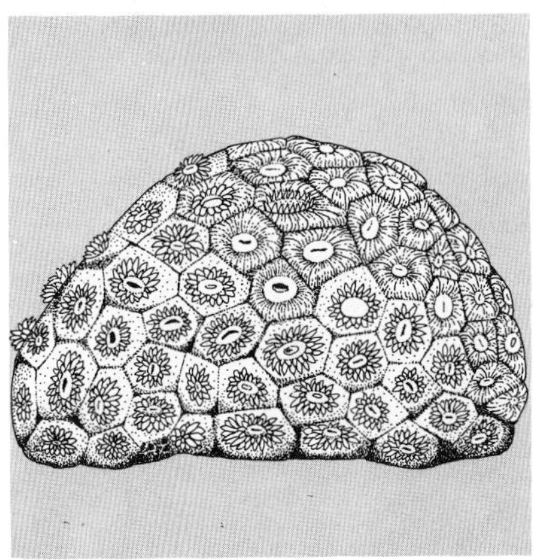

Coral

Cordoba, Spain

Corinth, Greece

Cork (Corcaigh), seaport in SE Republic of Ireland, at mouth of Lee River; seat of County Cork. Settlement developed around a monastery founded by St Finbar in 7th century. In 9th century Danes occupied city and walled it. Danes were driven out 1172. Oliver Cromwell occupied Cork in 1649 and Duke of Marlborough in 1690. Many public buildings were destroyed in nationalist uprisings in 1920; site of 18th-century St Anne's Church, 19th-century St Patrick's Church, and University College of Cork (1845). Industries: brewing, distilling, tires, fertilizers, woolen goods, motor vehicle assembly, bacon curing. Pop. 128,235.

Cork, protective outer layer of bark on woody plant stems. Cork insulates against severe temperature changes and retards water loss. Commercial cork is obtained from the cork oak *(Quercus suber),* an evergreen native to the Mediterranean area. Grown commercially in Spain, Algeria, and Portugal, the trees are stripped of their corky, thick outer bark every 8–10 years. Height: 60ft (18.3m).

Corm, fleshy, underground stem that produces a plant. Corms have more stem tissue and fewer leaf scales than bulbs. New corms are produced on top of old corms that last one growing season. Examples are gladiolus, tuberous begonia, and crocus. △324.

Cormorant, aquatic, ducklike bird found in coastal and inland waters throughout the world. It has a hooked bill; blackish metallic plumage; long, stiff tail, and webbed feet. Pale blue or green chalky eggs (2–4) are laid in stick-and-seaweed nests on the ground or in trees. Cormorants are used to catch fish in the Orient. Their excrement is the fertilizer guano. Length: 20–40in (51–101cm). Species *Phalacrocoracidae.* △534.

Corn, a single species *(Zea mays)* of tall, annual cereal grass native to the New World and introduced worldwide. It has stout, erect, solid stems with narrow leaves. Male flowers are born in a tassel; pollen from the tassel falls onto elongated silks at ends of ears and germinates. The mature ear bears 1000 seeds on a hard cob. Each ear is enclosed in leaves called husks. Commercial classifications are dent, flint, flour, sweet, and popcorn. Hybridizing has resulted in superior strains. It is used as food for humans and livestock. Manufactured products derived from it are numerous. It is also called maize and Indian corn. Family Gramineae. △326.

Corn, in medicine, an elevated painful thickening of the skin at a point of sustained pressure or pinching, most often occurring on a toe as the result of improperly fitting shoes.

Cornea, part of the sclera, or outer layer of the eye, that forms a transparent protective bulge over the iris. △674.

Corn Earworm, or cotton bollworm, noctuid moth caterpillar that is a serious crop pest in North and South America. It attacks many plants, and is a major pest of cotton and corn. Species *Heliothis zea.*

Corneille, Pierre (1606–84), major French classical dramatist. His plays include the tragedy *Médée* (1635), the epic *Le Cid* (1637), and a comedy *Le Menteur* (1643). He was elected to the French Academy (1647).

Cornell, Ezra (1807–74), US philanthropist, b. Bronx, N.Y. He moved to Ithaca (1828) and was active in local politics and real estate dealings. His interest in plant and animal breeding led to intensive farming and his early interest in the telegraph made him a millionaire. He was chief stockholder of Western Union Telegraph (1855). As a state legislator, he and Andrew White founded Cornell University (1865).

Cornell, Katharine (1898–1974), US actress, b. Berlin, Germany, who was one of the first performers to form a repertory company. She and her husband, Guthrie McClintic, produced several plays in which she starred, including *The Barretts of Wimpole Street* (1931), *St. Joan* (1936), *Antony and Cleopatra* (1947), and *Dear Liar* (1960).

Cornet, musical instrument similar to a shortened trumpet. It was used by 19th-century French and Italian composers, by Stravinsky in *Petrouchka* (1911), and in early jazz by King Oliver (*c.*1909). Its tone is more subdued than the trumpet's. *See also* Trumpet.

Cornflower. *See* Bachelor's Button.

Cornharvest, The (August). △1144.

Cornish, Samuel (1790–1859), US reformer and journalist. He participated actively in the American Anti-Slavery Society, and edited, with John B. Russwurm, *Freedom's Journal* (1827), the first black newspaper.

Corn Laws, British laws regulating grain trade in farmers' interests, especially in 18th-19th centuries. The Napoleonic Wars increased grain prices and caused food riots. The Anti-Corn Law League was formed (1838) to promote free trade and cheap food. After the Irish famine, parliament repealed the Corn Laws (1846).

Corn Plant. *See* Dracaena.

Cornplanter (1746?–1836), Seneca Indian chief who signed treaties with the United States and generally promoted peaceful relations between the United States and the Indians. Cornplanter was also known as John Abeel (O'Bail). He opposed John Sullivan's campaign against the Iroquois at first. Eventually the federal government granted him land and an annuity.

Cornwall, county in SW England, forming a peninsula bounded by Atlantic Ocean, English Channel, and Devonshire, and terminating in Lands End. Terrain consists of rocky indented coast with hills and moors inland; drained by Camel, Fowey, Tamar, and Fal rivers; tourist center with mild climate. Chief towns are Bodmin, Truro, St Austell, Camborne-Redruth. Area: (including Scilly Isles) 1,356sq mi (3,512sq km). Pop. (including Scilly Isles) 379,892.

Cornwallis, Charles Cornwallis, 1st Marquis (1738–1805), English soldier and administrator. At first a successful commander in the American Revolution, he was forced to surrender at Yorktown (1781). As governor-general of India (1786–93, 1805), he reformed the administration, law, and army and suppressed Tipu Sahib's revolt. Cornwallis was viceroy of Ireland (1798–1801), where he defeated the 1798 revolt and French invasion and carried through reforms and parliamentary union with Britain. △1218.

Cornwell, David. *See* LeCarré, John.

Corollary, theorem that follows so obviously from the proof of some other theorem that no, or almost no, proof is necessary. A by-product of another theorem.

Coromandel Coast, rugged coastline of SE India, extending from Point Calimere to Krishna River; the rough seas on coast during monsoon season are a major shipping hazard. Madras, Cuddalore, and Nellore are among the major cities. Length: 450mi (725km).

Corona, city in S California, 12mi (19km) SW of San Bernardino; E of Cleveland National Forest. Industries: processing citrus fruits, plywood, mobile homes. Settled 1898; inc. 1906. Pop. (1970) 27,519.

Corona, outer atmosphere of the sun, visible as a pearly halo during a total eclipse. It extends outward from about 3100m (4991km) above the solar surface (photosphere) and consists chiefly of highly ionized hydrogen, nickel, calcium, and iron atoms at a temperature of 1,000,000°K or more. *See also* Sun. △96, 98.

Corona Borealis, or the Northern Crown, northern constellation situated east of Boötes. It contains several binaries and variables, including the recurrent nova T Coronae Borealis and the irregular variable R Coronae Borealis. △130.

Coronado, Francisco Vásquez de (*c.*1510–54), Spanish explorer. He went to Mexico in 1535, and in 1540 he headed an expedition to locate the seven cities of Cibola, reported to be the repositories of untold wealth. He explored the western coast of Mexico, discovered the Colorado River, the Grand Canyon, followed the route of the Rio Grande eastward, and then headed north through the Texas Panhandle, Oklahoma, and eastern Kansas. His discoveries were impressive, but he found no gold.

Coronado, city in S California, across bay from San Diego; site of naval air station and amphibious base; Hotel del Coronado is a state monument. Inc. 1890. Pop. (1970) 20,910.

Coronal Hole, low-density low-temperature region in the Sun's corona, first observed in 1973, from which X-ray emission is apparently minimal. Such regions appear on X-ray photographs as dark extensive areas, often originating near the Sun's poles. They are associated with disturbances in the solar wind. △98.

Coronary Heart Disease, disease of the coronary blood vessels, particularly the aorta and arteries supplying blood to the heart tissue. The term is also occasionally used to refer to any heart disease. △716.

Coronary Occlusion, blocking of a coronary blood vessel, especially of a coronary artery supplying blood to the heart tissue. The occlusion almost always is caused by a thrombus, or blood clot, in the artery. △716.

Coronary Thrombosis, blood clot in an artery to the heart, preventing blood and with it oxygen and nutrients from reaching that part of the heart supplied by the artery. This phenomenon, known commonly as a "heart attack," may cause injury to the heart tissue or death. △716.

Coronograph, telescope for viewing the Sun's corona during daylight, at which time it is normally invisible. Mounted at a high altitude, it consists basically of a high-quality dust free optical system and a filter (Lyot filter) through which only a very narrow wavelength band can pass. Thus individual emission lines of the coronal spectrum can be viewed without being obscured by the much more intense radiation from the Sun's surface. △980.

Corot, Jean Baptiste Camille (1796–1875), French painter of landscapes and portraits, one of the most important 19th-century artists. Trained academically, Corot traveled widely, making small oil sketches on the spot and later producing large salon paintings based on them. Critical evaluation of Corot's immense output has varied. His misty landscapes, highly popular in his time, were once considered his best work; later critics prefer the oil sketches and portraits.

Corporate State, concept of government where workers and employers from similar industries are organized into corporations, which, together with other corporations, select representatives who determine national policy. Fascist Italy adopted features of the corporate state, with Benito Mussolini setting himself up as the final arbitrator of differences among the various corporate units.

Corporation, business organization that is legally a separate entity, which gives it limited liability as compared to a proprietorship or partnership. The owners, or stockholders, are not individually responsible for the legal dealings of the corporation, except to the extent of their holdings. The corporation form is most usual in large organizations.

Corps of Engineers, division of the US Department of the Army. Its responsibilities include engineering works such as major dams, reservoirs, levees, harbors, and many other structures for the benefit of the public. Founded 1824.

Corpus Christi, port city in S Texas, on Corpus Christi Bay, 200mi (322km) SW of Houston; seat of Nueces co; bay discovered in 16th century by Alonso de Pineda, Spanish explorer, on Corpus Christi Day; more permanent settlement occurred in 1839 when Col. H.L. Kinney est a trading post; population and financial boom came with the discovery of oil in early 20th century. Industries: oil refining, chemicals, fishing, natural gas. Inc. 1852. Pop. (1970) 204,525.

Corpus Luteum. △700.

Corrasion, the mechanical erosion of shores or stream banks whereby rocks and soil are removed or worn away by glaciers, wind, running water, or wave activity. △268.

Correggio, real name Antonio Allegri da Correggio (*c.*1490–1534), Italian painter born in Correggio. A major Renaissance artist whose works foreshadow the Baroque, Correggio painted mainly in Parma. In frescoes, especially those at the Parma cathedral, he produced brilliant spatial compositions, and daring, though anatomically exact, foreshortening effects. Like the frescoes, his paintings are marked by striking composition and sophisticated play of light and color. Among major works in museums is "Adoration of the Child" in the Uffizi, Florence. △1142.

Correggio, town in N central Italy, 8mi (13km) NE of Reggio; former seat of principality of the da Correggio family 12th–17th century; site of 16th-century palace; birthplace of painter Antonio Allegri, called Correggio after the town; agricultural area. Industries: cheese, wine, sausage, pharmaceuticals. Pop. 20,062.

Corregidor, small island at mouth of Manila Bay, Philippines. Known as "the Rock," it was fortified by Spain 18th century; taken by United States in 1898, it became Fort Mills. An Allied stronghold during

WWII, it surrendered to Japanese, May 1942; was retaken by US troops February 1945; annexed to Philippines 1947. Area: 2sq mi (5sq km).

Correlation, in geology, relating fossils and structures found in one stratum with those found in an analogous layer in a different locale. *See also* Paleontology. △274,276.

Correlation, in statistics, a number that summarizes the direction and degree of relationship between two dimensions or variables. Correlations range between 0 (no relationship) and 1.00 (a perfect relationship), and may be positive (as one variable increases, so does the other) or negative (as one variable increases, the other decreases). When two variables are highly correlated, as is IQ with school achievement, one may be used to predict the other. Thus, IQ tests have traditionally been used in American schools to predict likelihood of success in school. *See also* Intelligence Testing; Statistics.

Correspondence, property of two geometric figures in which angles, lines, and points in one bear a similar relationship to angles, lines, and points in another. △854.

Correspondence School, institution offering home study courses. Typically the student receives study materials by mail and sends his completed assignments back for grading. Lectures may be given over radio or television. Many universities as well as special schools offer courses in nearly every field. A few unscrupulous organizations try to sell worthless degrees by mail.

Corroboree. △594.

Corrosion, slow gradual chemical attack on the surfaces of solids, especially metals and alloys, by a moist environment. Tarnishing in air is not serious, but electrolytic corrosion underground, where anaerobic bacterial action may occur, and under moist conditions, can produce deep and dangerous structural decay. Materials are protected by plating, painting, or cathodic protection. △1566.

Corrupt Practices Acts, US state and federal laws enacted after 1890 aimed at eliminating campaign and election abuses. The Corrupt Practices Act of 1925 limited primary and general election expenses for congressional candidates, made disclosures of election expenses mandatory, outlawed fraudulent practices, and put controls on certain organizations such as corporations. By 1952, all the states had laws of this type, though, for various reasons, they have not always been enforced.

Corryvreckan (Corrievreckan), Gulf of, channel off W Scotland, between Jura and Scarba; site of whirlpool around rock that rises to within 15ft (4.5m) of surface.

Corsica (Corse), mountainous island in the Mediterranean Sea, about 105mi (170km) SE of French coast. Until 1768, when France purchased all rights to the island, it was under control of a series of Italian rulers, having been a Roman colony 3rd century BC-AD 5th century; Napoleon was born here 1769. In 1794, Britain took over the island, but Napoleon retrieved it for France; briefly occupied by British (1814 and 1815) and Germans (1942 and 1943). Capital is Ajaccio. Industries: sheep raising, wine and cheese making, tourism. Area: 3,367 square miles (8,721sq km). Pop. 269,830.

Corsini, important Italian family that, from 1244, contributed 56 priors (chief executives) and 8 *gonfalonieri* (supreme magistrates) to the Florentine Republic. Andrea Corsini (1302–73), prior of Florence and bishop of Fiesole, was canonized in 1629. Filippo Corsini (1334–1421) was made count palatinate in 1371 by Emperor Charles IV. Another Corsini, Lorenzo, became Pope Clement XII in 1730, and his nephew Bartolomeo was made prince of Sismano (1731) and a grandee of Spain (1732).

Corso, Gregory (1930–), US author, b. New York City. A poet of the Beat Generation, his volumes of verse include *The Vestal Lady on Brattle* (1955), *Gasoline* (1958), *Bomb* (1958), and *Elegiac Feelings American* (1970). *See also* Beat Generation.

Cortés, Hernando (Hernán Cortez) (1485–1547), central figure in the Spanish conquest and colonization of Mexico, a prominent planter of Cuba who had been in America since 1504. Under the patronage of Diego de Velásquez, Cortés sailed for the mainland with 700 men in 1518. He declared himself independent of Velásquez, gave himself the official standing and legal authority to colonize, and marched inland toward the Aztec capital. Converting many Indians into allies of his cause, Cortés was able to capture Tenochtitlán in 1521. Cortés' personal power, symbolized by his titles and estates, gradually was eroded by the Crown. He died in Spain, but his remains were transferred to Mexico in 1566. △1124.

Cortes, the legislature of Spain. Its members are not popularly elected but are named by various agencies of government. The Cortes has little power; it is used chiefly to ratify executive orders. Local cortes (Spanish meaning "courts") were established in Spain in the 12th and 13th centuries as various regions were reconquered from the Moors. Their power waned as the strength of the monarchy grew.

Cortex. △666.

Cortisone, adrenal cortex hormone essential for carbohydrate, protein, and fat metabolism; kidney function; and disease resistance. Synthetic cortisone is used to treat adrenal insufficiency, rheumatoid arthritis, and some other inflammatory diseases. It can cause serious side effects.

Corundum, an oxide mineral, aluminum oxide (Al_2O_3). Found in igneous, pegmatitic, and metamorphic rocks; rhombohedral system pyramidal or prismatic crystals and granular masses. Translucent to transparent in many hues; hardness 9; sp gr 4. Next to diamond, hardest natural substance. Gemstone varieties are sapphire and ruby. Star sapphires reflect light in six-pointed star. Also used in watches and motors. △244.

Corvallis, city in W Oregon on Willamette River, 28mi (45km) SSW of Salem; seat of Benton co; site of forestry research center and headquarters for Siuslaw National Forest; food processing center for fertile agricultural area. Inc. 1857. Pop. 35,153.

Cosecant, ratio of the length of the hypotenuse to the length of the side opposite to an acute angle in a right-angled triangle. The cosecant of angle A is usually abbreviated "cosec A," and is equal to the reciprocal of its sine. *See also* Trigonometric Functions. △1464.

Cosenza, city in S Italy; capital of Cosenza prov.; site of many rebellions for Italian independence; town damaged by earthquakes 18th, 19th, 20th centuries; site of restored Romanesque cathedral, Norman castle, and medieval churches. Industries: agriculture, furniture, wool. Pop. 101,908.

Cosgrave, Liam (1920–), Irish lawyer and politician. Elected to the Dail Eireann (1943), for the Fine Gael party, he was external affairs minister (1954–57), becoming party leader (1965) and prime minister (1973).

Cosgrave, William Thomas (1880–1965), Irish nationalist. He fought in the 1916 rebellion against Britain and helped win independence. Cosgrave was president of the Irish Free State (1922–32) and founded the moderate Fine Gael party.

Cosine, ratio of the length of the side adjacent to an acute angle to the length of the hypotenuse in a right-angled triangle. The cosine of angle A is usually abbreviated "cos A." *See also* Trigonometric Functions. △1464.

Cosmic Dust, very fine particles of solid matter in any part of the universe, including meteoric dust and interstellar matter that absorbs starlight and forms nebulae of dark matter in galaxies. Spherical dust particles, about .002in (.05mm) in diameter, found in certain marine sediments, are thought to be the remains of some 5,000 tons of cosmic dust falling on the earth each year.

Cosmic Rays, high-energy particle radiation that consists mainly of protons and also heavier nuclei, neutrinos, and photons and originates in space, possibly from stellar explosions and eruptions. On entering the earth's atmosphere the particles collide and react with oxygen, nitrogen, and other atoms and molecules and large numbers of other elementary particles are produced. These include pions and their decay products (muons, neutrinos, and photons) and also electrons and positrons. These particles can be detected by surface or balloon-borne instruments or by tracks in photographic emulsions. △1484.

Cosmology, branch of astronomy concerned with the origin, evolution, and future characteristics of the universe as a whole, its dimensions, structure, and other features. Once considered the province of theology and philosophy, it is now a science based on

Cormorant

Cornwall, England

Cortisone crystals (in polarized light)

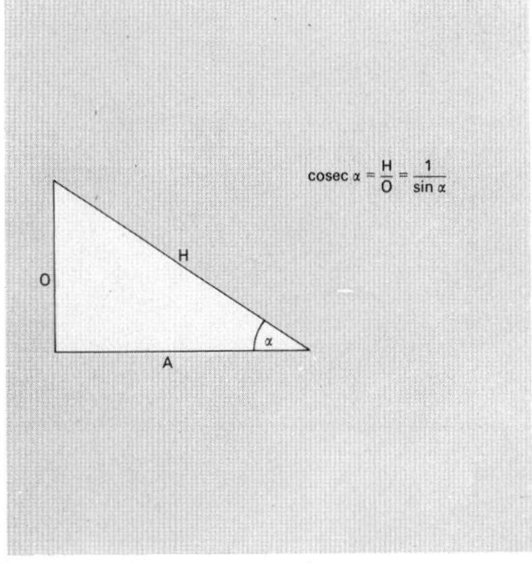
cosec α = H/O = 1/sin α
H
O
A
α

Cosecant

theoretical physics and mathematics. Experimental data, as in the form of galactic red shifts and the isotropic microwave background radiation, is now available for testing the various cosmological theories including the big-bang theory, with the associated oscillating theory, and the steady-state theory. However, the validity of the laws of physics and the nonvariability of physical constants throughout the unimaginable dimensions and time scale of the universe cannot necessarily be assumed. △48, 126.

Cosmos, a genus of showy late-flowering annual and perennial plants native to tropical America but easily grown in temperate climates. They have fernlike leaves and variously colored ray flowers. The common garden annual *C. bipinnatus*, has single or double flower heads shading from white to red. Height: 4–6ft (1.2–1.8m). Family Compositae.

Cossa, Baldassare (?1370–1419), Antipope John XXIII (1410–15). Elected antipope by the Council of Pisa, he convoked the Council of Constance in 1414 to end the Great Schism. The Council called for his resignation along with the other papal contenders: Gregory XII (Rome) and Benedict XIII (Avignon). He fled the council but was brought back and forced to resign. He was imprisoned until 1418 when he acknowledged Martin V as pope. *See also* Great Schism.

Cossacks, runaway serfs who settled in southern Russia prior to the 16th century. The name is Turkic for "free warriors." The Cossacks held land in common and were governed by village assemblies headed by a hetman, or leader. A militaristic people, they conquered Siberia in the 16th century and took part in the rebellions of Stenka Razin and Pugachev in the 17th and 18th centuries. In the 19th century, their privileges were curtailed by the czar and they were used to suppress revolutions. During the civil war between the Reds and the Whites after the Communist Revolution (1917), they supported the Whites. They strongly resisted collectivization and were suppressed by Stalin.

Costa Brava, coastal strip in NE Spain, near French border, on the Mediterranean; important tourist resort since WWII.

Costa e Silva, Artur da (1902–69), president of Brazil (1967–69). The senior army general supporting the overthrow of João Goulart (1964), he was war minister in the cabinet of Humberto Castello Branco. He dismissed the congress that elected him president and ruled by decree.

Costa Gomes, Francisco da (1914–), Portuguese army officer and politician. He served as chairman of the joint chiefs of staff in the regime of Marcello Caetano. He was one of the army officers that overthrew the Caetano government in 1974 and installed António Spínola as president. When leftist army officers forced Spínola out in September 1974, Costa Gomes replaced him as president until 1976.

Costa Mesa, city in S California, SSW of Santa Ana; site of Orange Coast College (1947) and Southern California College (1920). Industries: boatbuilding, plastics, electronic equipment. Inc. 1953. Pop. (1970) 72,660.

Costa Rica, nation in S Central America. Second-smallest of the countries between Mexico and South America, it carries influence out of proportion to its size and small population.

Land and Economy. Mountains run the length of the country, with some peaks reaching above 12,000ft (3,660m). They may contain large mineral deposits, but mining is not extensive. Plains exist along the coasts and in the N and NW, the latter region being good for cattle ranches. Farms reach far up mountain slopes, with extensive cultivation of sugar cane, coffee, cocoa, rice, and bananas. Costa Rica is a nation of small landholdings rather than of large estates.

People. Early settlers drove out the Indian peoples and modern Costa Rica, except for blacks in port cities, has a population mainly of Spanish descent. About 90% is literate and 95% belongs to the Roman Catholic church.

Government. A republic, Costa Rica has a president, two vice presidents, and a one-house legislature. All citizens 21 and over have had the vote since 1949. Several political parties exist, but the Communist party has been outlawed.

History. Christopher Columbus reached Costa Rica ("rich coast") in 1502, and during colonial times it was a province of Guatemala. Although it gained independence from Spain in 1821, Costa Rica came under Mexican control for a short period and then belonged to the United Provinces of Central America until that collapsed in 1838. It has generally rejected union with neighboring countries but joined the Central American Common Market, launched in 1958 and made active in the 1960s.

PROFILE

Official name: Republic of Costa Rica
Area: 19,650sq mi (50,894sq km)
Population: 2,000,000
Chief cities: San José, the capital; Alajuela
Government: Head of state, Daniel Oduber Quirós, president (elected 1974)

Cost-Benefit Analysis, in economics, analytical tool used to determine the worthiness of a particular project or to compare various projects. Cost-benefit ratios are computed by first determining the dollar cost of the project and then determining the dollar benefit that will be received by the proposer. If two projects are in competition for the available resources, the one with the lower cost-benefit ratio would be considered more economically feasible. △1460.

Costermansville. *See* Bukavu.

Cost of Living. Since World War II, the Bureau of Labor Statistics (BLS) has measured the cost of living (money necessary to purchase a certain level of goods and services) for an urban worker's family of four persons. However, in the mid-1960s, two other budgets were added, and the BLS now publishes annually lower, intermediate, and upper level family budget costs. These are not poverty budgets, but range from "modest but adequate" to "comfortable."

Cost-Push Inflation. △938.

Costume, Theatrical, clothing worn by actors during a performance. Early theatrical costume was closely related to religious ceremony and tended to be highly symbolic. The Greek theater employed costumes to depict a comedy or a tragedy. During the Middle Ages costumes of the actors were usually the contemporary dress of the times and had little if anything to do with the period of the play. Gradually an effort was made toward historical accuracy; more authentic detail was employed as designs were simplified. Realistic costume design has become an integral part of the entire production.

Cotangent, ratio of the length of the side adjacent to an acute angle to the length of the side opposite to the angle in a right-angled triangle. The cotangent of angle A is usually abbreviated "cot A," and is equal to the reciprocal of its tangent. *See also* Trigonometric Functions. △1464.

Cotinga, mostly brightly colored and bizarrely ornamented tropical birds, such as cock-of-the-rock and umbrella bird. There are some plain and dull-colored species. Family Cotingidae. *See also* Bellbird; Cock-of-the-rock; Umbrella Bird.

Cotonou, city in S Benin (Dahomey), W Africa, approx. 20mi (32km) W of Porto Novo; former capital and largest city in Benin; main port, railroad terminus, shipping center. Pop. 208,000.

Cottian Alps, mountain range N of Maritime Alps, between France and Italy. Highest peak is Mt Viso, 12,602ft (3,844m).

Cotton, perennial and annual shrubby plant native to tropical regions of the world. Although some species can be treelike or ornamental, most cotton is grown for the fibers that develop in the seeds and are made into fabric. The leaves are lobed and flowers are yellow, white, pink, or purple. *Gossypium hirsutum*, or upland cotton, is a tropical American variety grown commercially in the S United States. Cotton needs a long, warm growing season, with ample moisture, except at harvest time. Family Malvaceae.

Cotton Bollworm. *See* Corn Earworm.

Cotton Gin, a machine used for separation of lint from seed. Eli Whitney's invention of 1793, which replaced hand separation, could clean 50lb (22kg) per day and revolutionized the cotton industry.

Cottonmouth. *See* Water Moccasin.

Cottontail, small rabbit with a fluffy white tail. It lives in widely varying habitats from S Canada to Argentina and is brownish with light underparts. Length: 10–17in (25–43cm). Genus Sylvilagus. *See also* Rabbit. △540.

Cotton-top Marmoset. △554.

Cottonwood, a tree *Populus deltoides* of the willow family, native to E North America, growing to 90ft (27m). It has heart-shaped quaking leaves. The seeds have a cotton-like coat, from which the name is derived.

Coty, René (1882–1962), president of the Fourth French Republic (1954–59). Unable to ease France's political turmoil, Coty resigned under threat of a coup d'état during the Algerian crisis.

Coudé Telescope. △42.

Coughlin, Charles Edward (1891–), US Roman Catholic priest, b. Canada. Known as the "radio priest," he eventually introduced political views into his sermons, and in 1934 helped to form the Union party to oppose President Franklin D. Roosevelt's re-election. Coughlin's sentiments became increasing anti-Semitic and pro-fascist, and he was finally silenced by his superiors (1942).

Coulomb, Charles Augustin de (1736–1806), French physicist. After serving as a military engineer in the West Indies, he returned to Paris shortly before the Revolution. His invention of the torsion balance led to his experiments in electrostatics and the discovery of the inverse square law that bears his name. The unit of electric charge is named after him. *See also* Coulomb's Law.

Coulomb's Law, the force, F, between two point charges, Q_1 and Q_2, is proportional to the product of the magnitude of the charges and inversely proportional to the square of the distance, d, between them. Usually stated as: $F = Q_1Q_2/4\pi \mathbf{E}d^2$, where $\mathbf{E}$ is the absolute permittivity of the intervening space.

Coumadin, trade name for a widely used anticoagulant drug (Warfarin).

Council, Ecumenical, or General Council, formal meeting of Christian bishops and other representatives from throughout the world to define church doctrine and discipline. The last council of all the Christians, before the East-West schism, was in Nicaea (787). Roman Catholic councils must be convened by the pope. Council decrees confirmed by the pope are then considered infallible. There have been 21 Roman Catholic councils, the most recent being Vatican II, convoked in 1962 by John XXIII and concluded by Paul VI.

Council Bluffs, city in SW Iowa, on the bluffs overlooking the Missouri River; site of Union Pacific Railroad E terminus (1863); supply point for California gold rush (1849–50); now a trading center for large agricultural region. Industries: cast iron pipes, grain elevators. Settled by Mormons 1846; inc. 1853. Pop. (1970) 60,348.

Council for Economic Mutual Assistance (COMECON), trade organization formed in 1949 by the USSR and six East European Communist nations in response to the Marshall Plan in Western Europe. Besides the USSR, Bulgaria, Czechoslovakia, Hungary, Poland, Romania, Albania, and E. Germany were the initial members, with Cuba joining in 1972. Instead of setting up one large market, the council established a series of bilateral trade agreements but provided for no uniform price system, thus hindering economic development. △1342, 1346.

Council for New England, trading and colonization company formed as the Virginia Company of Plymouth, England under a royal charter (1606). Financial failures forced reorganization (1620), which provided land patents to the Plymouth Colony (1621, 1630), and Massachusetts Bay Colony (1628).

Counseling Psychology, specialty that applies psychology to such varied matters as planning school courses, choosing careers, and dealing with social or marital problems. Counseling psychologists usually do not treat problems as serious as mental illness; these are left to the clinical psychologist. △774.

Counterculture, a term coined in the 1960s for the way of life of young people who reject conventions about work, property, dress, sexual behavior, and other patterns. △1360.

Counterpoint, the weaving together of two or more carefully controlled melodic lines. The pitches of the lines must result in harmonic sounds, whether dissonant or consonant, at regular rhythmic points. The melodic lines need not move in the same direction at the same time. There are three main types of counterpoint. The first is the cantus firmus type in which a new melody is added to an already existing tune, as in a descant. The second type is vertible, or double counterpoint, in which two melodies, neither of which is complete in itself, fit together. In this type, the top and bottom melodies may be exchanged. The third type is canon, or imitative counterpoint, in which the same melody is repeated by starting again at various points throughout the work, as in a round.

Counter-Reformation, revival of the spiritual and theological life of the Roman Catholic Church in Europe during the 16th and 17th centuries. It began as a reaction to the Protestant Reformation. Led by humanists, scholasticism was encouraged and a renewed prestige was achieved for the papacy and the church. Bishops' duties were reformed, and new monastic orders appeared, including the Capuchins and Jesuits. Founded by Ignatius Loyola, the Jesuits led the reform movement. Spanish mysticism flourished and encouraged an improved sense of spirituality. The Council of Trent (1545–63) achieved needed reforms in doctrine. △1154.

Count of Monte Cristo, The (1844), novel by Alexandre Dumas père. Edmond Dantes, a young sailor, is imprisoned for 14 years in the Château d'If and is befriended by the Abbé Faria who dies leaving Dantes his fortune. Escaping disguised as Faria's corpse, he finds the money and uses it to avenge himself on his enemies.

Country and Western Music, popular music associated with rural south and western culture in the United States. The music typically features lyrics about romance or sorrow and instrumental music played by stringed instruments such as the guitar, banjo, or fiddle. Its roots are in English folk ballads introduced into the United States. It became increasingly popular in the 1970s. △1366.

Couperin, François (1668–1733), French Baroque composer, called "le Grand" to distinguish him from others in his musical family. He composed many pieces for the organ and harpsichord that subsequently influenced J. S. Bach. △1196.

Couplet, two consecutive lines of rhyming verse usually the same in length and meter. A closed couplet is one that is complete in logic and grammar. *See also* Heroic Couplet.

Coupling, a mechanical fastening connecting shafts together for power transmission. A flexible coupling is used to compensate for misalignment of shaft axes and mispositioning of shaft centerline; a rigid coupling is used for maximum power transfer with minimum misalignment. △1488.

Courbet, Gustave (1819–77), French painter of portraits and landscapes, leader of the 19th-century French school of realists. Largely self-taught by his studies of great works in the Louvre, Courbet rejected traditional theories of subject matter and treatment. A highly-gifted craftsman, he followed his own inclination in art and politics. His monumental treatments of scenes from peasants' lives shocked many but won praise from critics like Baudelaire. His political activity forced him into exile (1873) from France. Major collections of Courbet's work are in the Louvre, Paris, and the Metropolitan, New York. △1252.

Court, Margaret Smith (1942–), Australian tennis player. She won the US (1962; 1965; 1969–70; 1973), British (1963; 1965; 1970), Australian (1960–66; 1969–71), and French (1962; 1964; 1969–70) singles championships.

Court Ballet. △1194.

Court Dances, popular form of social entertainment for the European aristocracy from the Middle Ages through the 19th century. Most of the dances were refined versions of peasant dances. Some of the most frequently performed were the Basse Danse, Gaillard, Gavotte, Gigue, Minuet, and Pavane.

Court Martial, judicial trial proceedings in the US armed forces. In summary courts martial, the court acts as judge, jury, and both trial and defense counsel; in special and general courts martial, juries and counsels are present. Summary courts martial consider minor offenses and sentences are limited to confinement for one month and loss of two-thirds of a month's pay. An accused may object to a summary court martial and request a general or special type. *See also* Uniform Code of Military Justice.

Court of Versailles, at Versailles Louis XIV had built for himself a magnificent new court, attracting nobles with his pageantry and extravagance, and thus removing them from their home sources of power. They kept, however, their privileges and exemptions from taxation. For more than 50 years Louis XIV was the symbol of France's greatness and potentially disastrous extravagance.

Court Packing Bill (1937), attempt by Pres. Franklin D. Roosevelt to gain the authority to add six justices to the US Supreme Court, thereby changing its composition. The nation denounced the proposal, and Congress rejected the bill.

Courtrai (Kortrijk), town in NW Belgium, 16mi (26km) NNW of Tournai; site of Battle of the Golden Spurs (1302). Manufacture of linen and lace is the main industry. Pop. 45,138.

Courts, tribunals established by governments to decide controversies brought before them in the proper manner and to impose punishment for wrongdoing or to remedy a damage. There are courts at each governmental level, and in the USA all courts are finally subject to the Supreme Court's decisions. △912.

Courtship, period before marriage in which a man woos a woman. In many societies this does not only involve the participants emotionally but includes an exchange of gifts; these are often presented to her parents as well. In many cases where marriage is arranged (as in India) there is no contact between the couple. *See also* Marriage. △794.

Courtship of Miles Standish, The (1858), narrative poem by Henry Wadsworth Longfellow set in colonial America. Miles Standish, captain of the Plymouth colony, sends his friend John Alden to woo Priscilla Mullins for him. John and Priscilla fall in love, and Miles feels betrayed. Eventually, however, the friends are reconciled.

Court Tennis, game, played on an indoor court with four surrounding walls 30 feet (9.1m) high, a ball, and 16-ounce (453-gram) 27-inch (69cm) rackets. The singles court is 78 feet (23.8m) long and 27 feet (8.2m) wide; the doubles court is the same length but 36 feet (11m) wide. A center net is supported by two three-foot (.91m) posts. The object of the game is to place the ball over the net and play the surface of the floor, the walls, and the ceiling in an attempt to put the ball out of the reach of an opponent. The scoring, which is complicated, consists of winning a certain number of sets. Popular with French and English royalty and the forerunner of most modern racket games, court tennis was introduced in the United States in 1876. The most prominent tournament is the World Open.

Cousteau, Jacques Yves (1910–), French oceanographer. Best known as the co-inventor (with Emile Gagnan) of the Aqua-Lung—an independent diving unit permitting divers underwater mobility—he also invented a process of underwater television and conducted a series of undersea living experiments (Conshelf I–III, 1962–65). His famous research ship *Calypso* made expeditions from 1950, many of which were filmed by Cousteau for television and motion pictures. His books include *The Silent World* (1953).

Cousy, Robert Joseph "Bob" (1928–), US basketball player, b. New York City. He played for the Boston Celtics (1951–63) and was considered one of the game's finest backcourt men. He played in 12 All-Star games and had a professional coaching career that included the Cincinnati Royals (1970) and the Kansas City-Omaha Kings (1971–74).

Couzens, James (1872–1936), US industrial leader, b. Canada. A Ford Motor Company executive, he was in charge of sales and advocated the $5.00-a-day minimum wage. Leaving Ford in 1915, he became Detroit's Republican mayor (1919–22), then Michigan's senator (1922–36).

Covalence. *See* Valence.

Covalent Bond, type of chemical bond in which two atoms share a pair of electrons; both electrons move in the combined field of the two nuclei. Most compounds having covalent bonds have discrete molecules. They tend to be low melting and soluble in nonpolar solvents. *See also* Chemical Bonds. △1506, 1554–58.

Covenanters, 17th-century Scots who entered agreements to defend Presbyterianism. When Charles I attempted to impose Episcopalianism, many Scots subscribed to the National Covenant (1638) and successfully resisted him. By the Solemn League and Covenant (1643) they helped England's parliament against Charles in return for religious concessions. The Covenanters suffered persecution between the Restoration (1660) and the Glorious Revolution (1688).

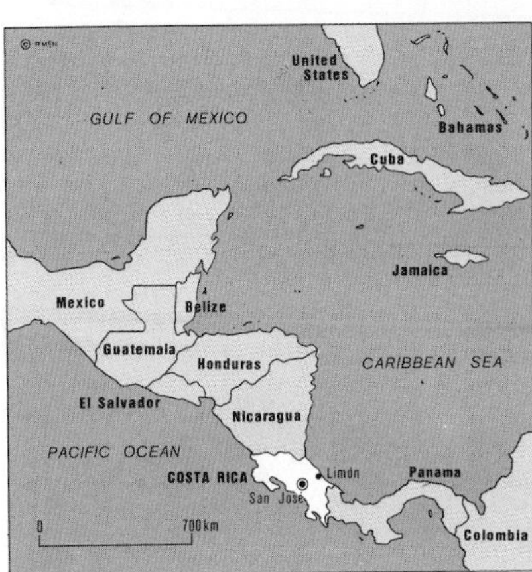
United States
GULF OF MEXICO
Bahamas
Cuba
Jamaica
Mexico
Belize
Guatemala
Honduras
CARIBBEAN SEA
El Salvador
Nicaragua
PACIFIC OCEAN
COSTA RICA
Limón
San José
Panama
0
700km
Colombia
Costa Rica

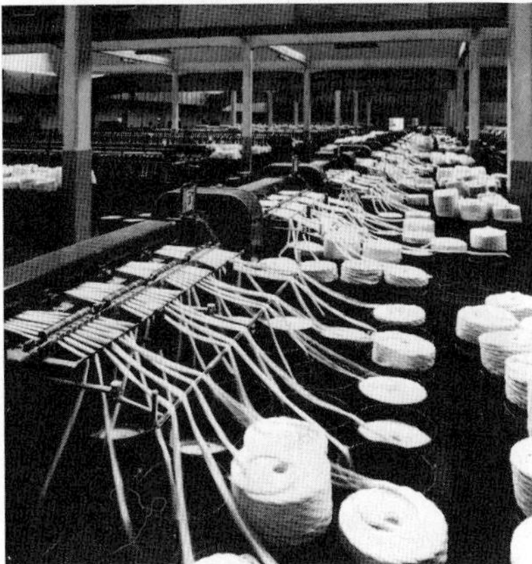
Cotton: textile manufacturing

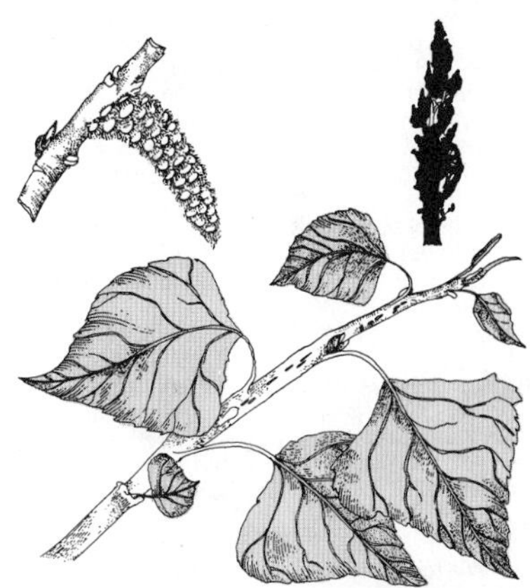
Cottonwood

Gustave Courbet: self-portrait

Covent Garden, leading opera house of England, founded in 1732 in the heart of a produce market in London, located in its present building since 1858. In the late 19th century the opera company achieved world fame as the home of many great singing stars such as Lilli Lehmann, Nellie Melba, and the De Reszkes. After a decline in the early 20th century, Covent Garden again became one of the world's foremost opera houses under the direction of Rafael Kubelik (1955–58), Georg Solti (1958–69), and Colin Davis (from 1971).

Coventry, city in central England, 16mi (26km) SE of Birmingham. An important weaving center in the Middle Ages, the city was severely damaged in WWII. Industries: cars, bicycles, machinery, electrical equipment, rayon, hosiery. Pop. 334,839.

Coverdale, Miles (1488–1569), English Bible translator. He published the first English translation of the Bible in 1535 and was a principal collaborator in the *Great Bible* (1539). △1148.

Covered Wagon, The (1923), US film. A pioneer of the western genre, it set the standard for a host of imitations. Adapted by Jack Cunningham from a novel by Emerson Hough, it was directed by James Cruze, photographed by Karl Brown, and edited by Dorothy Arzner.

Covina, city in S California, 20mi (32km) E of Los Angeles. Industries: fruit processing, medical supplies, fabricated metals. Settled 1842; inc. 1901. Pop. (1970) 30,380.

Covington, city located at confluence of Licking and Ohio rivers in N Kentucky; seat of Kenton co; named for Gen. Leonard Covington, War of 1812 hero. Industries: machine tools, freight cars, prison equipment. Inc. 1834. Pop. (1970) 52,535.

Coward, (Sir) Noel (Pierce) (1899–1973), English playwright, composer, and performer. In show business from an early age, he first attracted notice as a playwright with his drama *The Vortex* (1924). He is most noted, however, for his highly polished comedies, including *Hay Fever* (1925), *Fallen Angels* (1925), *Easy Virtue* (1925), *Bitter Sweet* (1929), *Private Lives* (1930), *Design for Living* (1932), *Conversation Piece* (1934), *Tonight at 8:30* (a group of nine one-act plays performed in various groups of three, 1936), *Present Laughter* (1939), and *Blithe Spirit* (1942). Other popular works written by him include *Cavalcade* (1931), a patriotic play; *In Which We Serve* (1942), a patriotic film; and *Brief Encounter* (1946), a film. He also composed hundreds of songs, including "Mad Dogs and Englishmen" and "Mad About the Boy," performing many of them in cabaret and revues.

Cowbird, blackbirdlike North and South American bird that follows cattle herds, sometimes picking ticks off the cattle. A nest parasite, the female lays her eggs in the nest of another species, often removing its eggs first. Length: 8in (20cm). Family Icteridae.

Cowfish, or trunkfish, bony marine fish found on both sides of the tropical Atlantic. Its triangular body has netlike markings and spines projecting from the top of the head. Scales are fused. Length: to 18in (45.7cm). Family Ostraciidae; species *Acanthostracion quadricornis.*

Cowley, Malcolm (1898–), US author, b. Belsano, Pa. He lived in France in the 1920s and wrote about American intellectuals there in *Exile's Return* (1934). He also wrote poetry and criticism and was an editor of the *New Republic* (1929–44).

Cowpea, or Black-eyed Pea, bushy, annual plant native to Asia. It has edible 8–12 in (20–30cm) pods but is grown mainly as a cover crop or for cattle feed. Family Leguminosae; species *Vigna sinensis.*

Cowper, William (1731–1800), English poet and hymn writer. Subject to intermittent depressive mania, he wrote a variety of prose and poetry, such as the long blank-verse poem *The Task* (1783), during his lucid periods.

Cowper's Glands. △700.

Cowpox, virus-caused contagious disease of cows that produces a skin eruption on the teats and udder. Cowpox pus was used by Edward Jenner to develop a vaccine against smallpox, a serious disease probably caused by the same virus. △1186.

Cowrie, or cowry, gastropod mollusk identified by ovoid, polished shell with toothed opening and varied markings. Length: 0.33–3.5in (8.3–88.9mm). Family Cypraeidae; 200 species, including map cowry *Cypraea mappa.*

Cowslip. *See* Marsh Marigold.

Cox, James Middleton (1870–1957), US political leader and newspaper publisher, b. near Jacksonburg, Ohio. A successful journalist, he entered politics as a mild reformer and served as a US Representative (1909–13) and Ohio governor (1913–15; 1917–21). The Democratic presidential candidate in 1920, he ran with Franklin D. Roosevelt and lost to Warren G. Harding. He then returned to journalism. His autobiography, *Journey Through My Years,* was published in 1946.

Coxey's Army, group of about 500 unemployed US workers led by Jacob S. Coxey of Ohio, who marched to Washington, D.C. in the spring of 1894 to demand federal relief through a government-financed public works program and the issuance of large amounts of paper money. The group disbanded when Coxey and other leaders were arrested for trespassing on the US Capitol. Other armies of unemployed also went to Washington during the same period.

Coyoacán, federal district in central Mexico, 6mi (10km) S of Mexico City; site of old Cortés palace, first seat of Spanish government. Pop. 338,850.

Coyote, medium-sized wild dog, resembling a small wolf, originally native to W North America. They have moved into many eastern areas formerly inhabited by wolves, including New England. Usually grayish-brown, they have pointed muzzles, big ears, and bushy tails. Their diet consists mainly of rabbits, rodents, and carrion, but they prey occasionally on domestic animals. Species *Canis latrans. See also* Canidae.

Coypu, large aquatic rodent, also known as nutria, native to South America, that now also lives in North America and Europe, both wild and on fur farms. Coypus have brown outer fur and soft gray underfur that is commercially valuable. Weight: 18lb (8kg). Species *Myocastor coypu.*

Cozens, John Robert. △1242.

CPI. *See* Consumer Price Index.

Crab, flattened, triangular, or oval decapod crustacean covered with a hard shell. Primarily marine, some crabs are found in fresh water and a few are terrestrial. Their short abdomen, often called a tail, is bent under. A pair of large foreclaws, a pair of movable eyestalks, and segmented mouth are characteristic. Crabs usually move sideways. Many crabs are edible. Size: pea-sized–12ft (3.7m) from leg tip to opposite leg tip. Some of the 4,500 species are parasitic. Order Decapoda. *See also* Crustacean; Decapod. △490.

Crab Apple, small sour fruit produced by certain apple trees. The various species grow in North America and Asia. The fruit is used in making preserves and jelly. The name also refers to small, hardy horticultural forms of apple trees. Family Rosaceae; genus *Malus.* △338.

Crabeater Seal. △624.

Crab Grass, weedy annual grass native to Europe and naturalized in the United States. The blades are coarse, hairy, and rough. It bears spreading purple flower spikes and spreads rapidly. Although sometimes cultivated for hay and pasturage, it is considered a noxious weed. It can be eliminated from lawns by uprooting or poisoning. Height: to 3ft (1m). Family Gramineae; genus *Digitaria.*

Crab Nebula, bright emission nebula in the constellation Taurus, the still expanding remnant of a supernova first observed by Chinese and Japanese astronomers in July 1054. Having a structure characterized by gaseous filaments, the Crab is a powerful radio and X-ray source, with a pulsar located at its center. △104–06.

Crab Spider, webless spider that moves sideways like a crab and is found worldwide. Red to brown, they hide on flowers and grab their prey as it comes to feed. Length: to 0.8in (20mm). Family Thomisidae. *See also* Spider.

Cracking, treatment of the raw products of the first distillation of oil refining, so as to break up the hydrocarbons into smaller molecules by the controlled use of heat, catalysts, and often pressure. The cracking of petroleum yields heavy oils, gasoline, and such gases as ethane, ethylene, and propylene, which are used in the manufacture of plastics, textiles, detergents, and agricultural chemicals.

Cracow. *See* Krakow.

Craft Unions, organizations formed by the skilled workers in the crafts. Membership is usually limited to those in the trade. Usually conservatively oriented, most craft unions have apprenticeship programs to train new members, which have the additional effect of monitoring entry into the brotherhood.

Craigie, Sir William Alexander (1867–1957), Scottish lexicographer and philologist, specializing in Scandinavian languages and English. He was joint editor of the Oxford English Dictionary (1901–33), then professor at the University of Chicago, where he was chief editor of *The Dictionary of American English.* His works include *Icelandic Sagas* (1913) and *A Study of American English* (1927).

Craiova, city in S Romania, 112mi (180km) W of Bucharest; capital of Oltenia region, on the Jiul River; site of university (1966) and church of St Demetrius (1652); rich agricultural region with deposits of coal, oil, natural gas. Industries: electrical equipment, food processing. Pop. 175,454.

Crake. △618.

Cram, Ralph Adams (1863–1942), US architect and writer, b. Hampton Falls, N.H. An authority on Gothic architecture and exponent of the Gothic revival in the United States, he designed the graduate college and chapel at Princeton University (Princeton, N.J.) and buildings for the US Military Academy at West Point, Rice University, and several other academic institutions. With his partner F.W. Ferguson he took part in the reconstruction of the Cathedral of St. John the Divine, New York City, changing its style from Romanesque to late Gothic. He was also the author of many books on architecture, including *The End of Democracy* (1937).

Cramp, involuntary persistent contraction of a muscle producing sharp pain. It may occur in almost any muscle as a result of overexertion such as can occur in athletics, chronic strain, or from normal physiological causes such as menstruation.

Cranach, or **Kranach, Lucas, the Elder** (1472–1553), German painter and engraver. Court painter to the electors of Saxony and a close friend and follower of Martin Luther, Cranach painted portraits and religious and mythological scenes. Cranach used female nudes in an erotic way new to German art. Among his best-known works are *Eve* (Uffizi, Florence) and *The Judgement of Paris* (Metropolitan, New York). △810.

Cranberry, evergreen shrub or small tree grown mostly in the US. They have oval leaves, pink or whitish flowers, and red, sour fruit. *Vaccinium macrocarpon,* American cranberry, is grown commercially in Massachusetts, New Jersey, and Wisconsin. Family Ericaceae. △360.

Crandall, Prudence (1803–90), US educator, b. Hopkinton, R.I. She is known for her attempt to educate black girls. She accepted a black child in her school, but her attempt to run a school only for black girls led to Connecticut's "Black Laws" (1833), which called for local approval of such a school. The case went to court but she was forced out. The Black Laws were repealed in 1838.

Crane, Hart (1899–1932), US poet, b. Harold Hart Crane in Garrettsville, Ohio. Acclaimed as one of the most brilliant and creative 20th-century American poets, he published his first volume, *White Buildings,* in 1926. His major work, *The Bridge* (1930), is a series of related poems in which New York City's Brooklyn Bridge serves as a mystical symbol of the creative power of civilization. After a life plagued by problems, Crane jumped from a ship on a return trip to the United States from Mexico.

Crane, Stephen (1871–1900), US novelist, short story writer, poet, and war correspondent, b. Newark, N.J. He is best known for *The Red Badge of Courage* (1895), a realistic study of the mind of a soldier in the Civil War. Initially a subject of critical controversy, the work has since become an influential classic. *Maggie: A Girl of the Streets* (1893) is a study of urban squalor. His "The Open Boat" (in *The Open Boat and Other Tales of Adventure,* 1898) is considered one of the finest short stories in the English language. Other works include *The Black Rider* (1895) and *War Is Kind* (1899), volumes of verse, *The Monster and Other Stories* (1899), and *Whilomville Stories* (1900).

Crane, large marsh bird found around the world.

Long-legged, they have brownish, grayish, or white plumage with bright ornamental heads. They fly with long necks straight and feed on almost anything. After courtship dances, the female lays eggs (2) in a bulky plant-material nest on the ground or above water. Height: 30–60in (76–152cm). Family Gruidae. △630.

Crane Fly, long-legged fly resembling the mosquito. This brown to gray insect, ranging from 0.25 to 1.25in (6.35–31.75mm) in length, is found worldwide in damp areas. The larvae are aquatic or semi-aquatic and feed on decaying vegetable matter. Family Tipulidae. *See also* Diptera.

Cranes. △1654, 1666.

Cranesbill, common name for geranium. *See also* Geranium; Pelargonium.

Cranial Nerves, twelve nerves that arise from the brain and are numbered according to the site of origin in the brain. The olfactory nerve (I), is concerned with smell; the optic (II), with vision; the oculomotor, trochlear, and abducens (III, IV, VI), with the movement of certain muscles of the eye; the trigeminal (V), with sensation in parts of the face and with movement of jaw muscles in chewing; the facial (VII), with the sense of taste and with face, scalp, ear, and neck muscle movement, and salivary gland secretion; the auditory (VIII), with hearing and balance; the glossopharyngeal (IX), with taste, touch, and temperature in mouth area organs, pharynx muscle movement, and salivary gland secretion; the vagus (X), known as the "wanderer," with muscle movement in the larynx and pharynx, stimulation of gastric and pancreatic secretion, and movement of autonomic muscles of heart, bronchi, esophagus, stomach, small intestine, and other organs; the accessory (XI), with muscle movement in neck, shoulder, and arm region; and the hypoglossal (XII), with tongue muscle movement.

Cranium, or brain case, dome-shaped, solid, hard bone structure that surrounds and protects the brain. It is made up of eight bones: one frontal, two parietal, two temporal, one occipital, one sphenoid, and one ethmoid. △682.

Cranmer, Thomas (1489–1556), English prelate and reformer. A distinguished theologian, he was appointed Archbishop of Canterbury by King Henry VIII (1533) and divorced Henry from Catherine of Aragon despite papal opposition. Cranmer promoted the English Reformation, encouraging the translation and dissemination of the *Great Bible* (1538) and compiling the first Book of Common Prayer (1548). After Mary's accession (1553), Cranmer was tried, deposed, and burnt at the stake.

Cranston, city in N Rhode Island, on the Pawtuxet River, 5mi (8km) S of Providence; named after colonial Gov. Samuel Cranston. Industries: machinery, chemicals, textiles, beer. Inc. as town 1754, as city 1910. Pop. (1970) 74,287.

Crassula Falcata. △446.

Crassus, Marcus Licinius (*c.* 115–53 BC), Roman political figure. He commanded part of Sulla's victorious forces in 83 BC and amassed a vast personal fortune in property. Raising a private army, he suppressed the slave rebellion led by Spartacus (71 BC). Crassus served as consul with his rival Pompey, and in 60 BC Julius Caesar formed with them the first triumvirate. After another joint consulship with Pompey (55 BC), Crassus became governor of Syria. He was killed fighting the Parthians at Carrhae. △1018.

Crater, depression or pit of large size usually with steep sides. The crater may be the result of a meteor impact or more likely the summit of a volcanic cone. △92,176.

Crater, Lunar, any of several thousand circular formations on the moon's surface, produced by volcanic activity or, in some cases, by meteoric impact. Craters range in size from tiny depressions to vast walled plains and high ring mountains. Small craters often appear in chains along rills, and many large craters have associated central peaks within them. △56–60.

Crater Lake National Park, located in the Cascade Range in SW Oregon. The park features Crater Lake, the second deepest lake in North America. The waters of the lake were formed by precipitation and are maintained solely by rain and snow; there is no outlet. Crater Lake is known for the intense blue color of the water. Park area: 160,290acres (64,917hectares). Lake area: 20sq miles (52sq km). Est. 1902.

Craters of the Moon National Monument, park in SE central Idaho, near Arco; preserves volcanic phenomena, with unusual landscape effects. Area: 53,545acres (21,686hectares). Est. 1924.

Crates, name of four different Greek philosophers: Crates of Thebes (4th century BC), cynic disciple of Diogenes; Crates of Athens (3rd century BC), philosopher, head of the Old Academy; Crates of Mallus (2nd century BC), Stoic philosopher and grammarian; Crates of Tarsus (2nd century BC), Academic philosopher.

Crates The Cynic, 4th century BC Theban philosopher. A disciple of Diogenes, Crates donated the profits of his wealth to his fellow-citizens, and traveled about with his wife Hipparchia, preaching voluntary poverty.

Cratinus (*c.* 510–422 BC), Greek poet and playwright. Despite his reputation as a great comic poet, he was portrayed as a drunkard in Aristophanes' play *The Knight.* Cratinus retaliated by winning first prize for his play *Wine Flask* (423 BC) in a competition in which Aristophanes' *The Clouds* placed third.

Crawford, Francis Marion (1854–1909), US novelist, b. Italy, who argued that fiction ought to avoid realistic representation and instead devote itself to entertainment. His first work, *Mr. Isaacs, A Tale of Modern India* (1882), was followed by more than 40 others, all of which deal with various countries in which Crawford lived.

Crawford, Thomas (1814–57), US sculptor, b. New York City. He studied in Rome and brought a neoclassical style to his art. His most famous works are his equestrian rendering of *George Washington* in Richmond, Va., and his enormous *Freedom* statue on top of the dome of the US capitol.

Crayfish, edible decapod crustaceans found in freshwater rivers and streams of temperate regions, with a few saltwater species. Smaller than lobsters, they burrow into stream banks and feed on animal and vegetable matter. Some cave-dwelling species are blind. Length: to about 6in (15cm). Families Astacidae (Northern Hemisphere), Parastacidae (Southern Hemisphere), Austroastacidae (Australia). *See also* Crustacean; Decapod. △486.

Crazy Horse (died 1877), Indian name, Jashunca-Uitco, Indian chief of the Oglala Sioux. He defeated Gen. George Crook at the Rosebud River (June 17, 1876) and assisted chief Sitting Bull in the massacre of Gen. George Custer's force at the Little Big Horn (June 25). He was shot while resisting imprisonment for allegedly planning a revolt.

Creatine, amino acid found mostly in the muscle tissues of vertebrates (and some invertebrates). It is important to energy production. The alleged anti-cancer agent, Krebiozen, is a creatine.

Crécy (Crécy-en-Ponthieu), village in N France; scene of the first major battle of the Hundred Years War, Aug. 26, 1346. Though greatly outnumbered, King Edward III and the English won the battle through their use of the longbow, firm discipline, and greater mobility. The French were hampered by their use of the crossbow and heavy armor. Victory enabled the English to take Calais.

Credi, Lorenzo di (*c.* 1458–1537), Italian painter and sculptor. A fellow-student with Leonardo da Vinci in the school of Andrea del Verrocchio, Lorenzo painted mostly religious subjects. His best-known work is *The Annunciation* in the Uffizi Gallery, Florence.

Credit, Letter of, document issued by a bank allowing the holder to draw upon an amount of money at some other institution. Liability is assumed by the issuing bank. There are several types of letters of credit; the document itself contains the terms limiting negotiability. Widely used in international commercial transactions, travelers' checks are also a type of letter of credit.

Crédit Mobilier, US construction company involved in a financial scandal. Organized (1864) by Oakes Ames, a US Representative and Union Pacific Railroad stockholder, it gained vast profits from contracts with Union Pacific, which had received federal funds. Ames bribed members of Congress to prevent an investigation. When the scandal broke in 1872, it ruined the reputations of Ames and other officials.

Credit Union, an association organized for the purpose of making loans available to its members. The cooperative obtains funds by selling shares to its

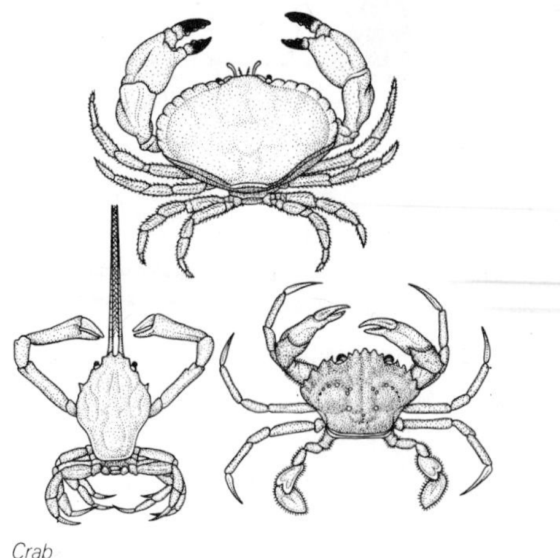

Crab

Cranberry

Crane

Crayfish

members; shares are sold at fixed rates and members may buy as many shares as they wish. Credit unions are nonprofit organizations; all earnings made from the low-interest rate collected on loans are paid to the members as dividends.

Cree, one of the largest divisions of the Algonquian language family of North American Indians, ranging from James Bay to the Saskatchewan River in Canada. The tribe split into the Plains Cree and the Woodlands Cree, each reflecting the culture of the area. Like the closely related Chippewa, the Cree served as guides and hunters for French and British traders and were a lifeline of the Hudson's Bay Company for decades. At one time numbering over 20,000, at least half that number still survive in Canada, mostly living on reserves in Manitoba.

Creek, a confederation of tribes speaking the Muskhogean tongue, and thus more properly known as Muskhogean Indians. One of the largest tribal groups living in SE United States, they ranged from coastal Georgia into Alabama, Florida, and Mississippi. Following the Creek Wars of 1813–14, they were removed to Oklahoma, where some 15,000 descendants now live; approximately 5000 are scattered throughout the Southeast. These people had a greater effect upon the settlement of the SE Gulf Coast than any other tribe, and their political skills are regarded as second only to those of the Iroquois.

Creek War (1813–14), conflict between the Creek Indians of Alabama, Georgia, and N Florida and the white settlers. Instigated by the British, chief Red Eagle and his warriors massacred over 500 whites at Fort Mims (1813). The Creek nation was thoroughly defeated by Gen. Andrew Jackson at the battle of Horseshoe Bend. Jackson pardoned Red Eagle, but the Creeks had to cede much of their land, and later were moved to the Indian territory (later, Oklahoma).

Creeping Jenny. *See* Moneywort.

Creeping Thistle. △446.

Crémazie, Joseph Octave (1822–79), Canadian poet, known as the father of French-Canadian poetry. He was a founder of the Mouvement littéraire de Québec (c.1852), a group that stimulated French-Canadian literary development. His patriotic poems include "Le vieux soldat canadien" (1855), about an old soldier who awaits the return of the French.

Cremona, city in N Italy; capital of Cremona prov.; Virgil attended school here; medieval center of learning; site of a Renaissance school of painting; 12th-century cathedral and the Torazzo (13th-century bell tower); violins were made here 16th-18th century by Amati and Stradivari families; agricultural and dairy center. Industries: farming machinery, silk textiles, bricks. Founded 218 BC by Romans. Pop. 80,798.

Creole, pidgin language that eventually becomes the mother tongue of a speech community. Examples are Haitian Creole, based on French, and numerous other French creoles spoken in the Caribbean, Louisiana, Mauritius, and elsewhere. Papiamento, based on Spanish, is spoken in the Netherlands Antilles, while a number of Portuguese creoles are spoken in western Africa.

Crepuscolari, (the twilight poets), early 20th-century school of Italian poets, characterized by unrhetorical melancholy and rumination. The foremost exponents were **Guido Gozzano** (1883–1916) and **Sergio Corazinni** (1885–1907), who shared a similar ironic detachment in describing decadence.

Crerar, Henry Duncan Graham (1888–1965), Canadian soldier and diplomat. A brilliant artillery tactitian in World War I, he organized the militia and was chief of general staff in World War II. He represented Canada in several postwar peace conferences.

Cresap, Michael (1742–75), American frontier soldier, b. Allegany co, Md. He held a claim in the Northwest Territory and was accused (1774) of starting Lord Dunsmore's War by killing the family of a friendly Indian chief. At the start of the American Revolution, Cresap raised a rifle company, marched to Boston in record time, and died of exhaustion.

Cress, various pungent-leaved plants, including rock cress *(Arabis)* with purple or pink flowers; winter cress *(Barbarea)* with yellow flowers; yellow cresses *(Rorippa)*; and bitter cresses *(Cardamine)*. Family Cruciferae.

Cressy, Hugh Paulinus de (1605–74), English churchman. He converted to Roman Catholicism while in Rome in 1646, then became a Benedictine monk (1649). He returned to England in 1660 and became chaplain to Queen Catherine of Braganza, wife of Charles II. He edited the works of several Counter-Reformation mystics. His *Church History of Brittany, or England* (1668) was an early attempt at objective church history.

Crested-tailed Marsupial Mouse. △544.

Cretaceous Period, the last period of the Mesozoic Era, lasting from 135 to about 65,000,000 years ago. Dinosaurs flourished until the end of this period, when they became extinct. The first true placental and marsupial mammals appeared and modern flowering plants were common. A great continental sea crossed North America from Alaska to the Gulf of Mexico. The Rocky Mountains had their origin. *See also* Geologic Time; Mesozoic Era. △276.

Crete (Kret, Kriti), the largest island of Greece, in E Mediterranean Sea, SSE of the Greek mainland. The chief cities are Canea and Candia. Crete has a mountainous terrain, with rolling country. Sheep and goats are raised in the uplands, making Crete a main producer of wool, hides, cheese, and goat's milk. Mild climate and adequate rainfall support cultivation of cereals, grapes, carob, olives, and oranges. Crete produces olive oil, wine, leather, and handicrafts. Cretans have strong ties with Greece; however, the people possess a unique diction, nomenclature, and physique. The people are overwhelmingly Greek Orthodox, under the supervision of the archbishop of Athens.

Crete's impressive history began in the Neolithic period, Early and Middle Bronze Age. Cretan society was far more advanced than any contemporary European civilization. Minoan art and architecture flourished from 1600 BC. Knossos was destroyed along with other leading Crete cities, apparently by some natural disaster. Crete's importance declined, and the Greek mainland became dominant. After 1125 BC the Dorians controlled Crete, setting up a hundred independent political units in which the male Dorians held power and created an oligarchic type of constitution. During the 9th century BC, it was important as a trade route from the Near East; it adopted the Phoenician alphabet and developed the art of finely painted pottery. In the 3rd century BC the island accepted the unstable protection of Macedon and became a notorious pirate center. Crete was conquered by Rome 68–67 BC and later came under Byzantine rule. In AD 826 Arab domination brought slave raiding and piracy by Arab seamen. In 1669, Crete fell to an oppressive Turkish reign; Cretan resentment caused numerous uprisings against the government. In 1898 foreign intervention forced Turkey to evacuate Crete, which became an autonomous state under Turkish sovereignty, governed by a high commission of Britain, France, Russia, and Italy. In 1908, Cretans proclaimed union with Greece; this union was confirmed by the Treaty of London 1913. Area: 3,186sq mi (8,256sq km). Pop. 483,075.

Cretinism, disorder present at birth or beginning in early childhood in which a deficiency of thyroid hormones produces retarded physical and mental development. Symptoms include high birth weight, large tongue, thick skin, potbelly appearance, sleepiness, failure to grow and develop. Treatment consists of administration of thyroid hormones.

Crevasse, deep opening in a glacier. It is the result of stress within the glacier or the movement of the glacier over uneven terrain. △262.

Crèvecoeur, J. Hector St John (1735–1813), b. Michel-Guillaume Jean de Crèvecoeur; French-American naturalist-author who, after emigrating to Canada and settling eventually in the United States, wrote about life in the New World. He farmed until the Revolutionary War. In 1780, he returned to France. His famous book, *Letters from an American Farmer* (1782), which described the rural life of the period, was published in London. Returning to America in 1783, Crèvecoeur wrote articles on agriculture and medicine. From 1790 he lived in France.

Crew Racing. *See* Rowing.

Cribbage, card game for two players. A standard 52 card deck is used along with a cribbage board (scoring device). Each player receives six cards and discards two into a separate pile called the "crib." Cards in the hand are played alternately, and there are different point values for various combinations. A replacement card is taken from the deck for each card played. Picture cards and 10s count at 10 points, aces as 1 each, and the other cards their face value. The object is to reach 31 points or as close as possible without exceeding the total. After each game, the two other cards, or "crib" are used to add additional points to the score. Generally, 121 points are needed to win the match.

Crib Death. *See* Sudden Infant Death Syndrome.

Crichton, Michael (1942–), US author, b. Chicago. While a medical student, he published six novels and won the 1968 Mystery Writers of America Award for *A Case of Need* (1968). Other novels include *The Andromeda Strain* (1969), *The Terminal Man* (1972), and *The Great Train Robbery* (1975).

Crick, Francis H(arry Compton) (1916–), English biophysicist. He received (with James Watson and Maurice Wilkins) the 1962 Nobel Prize for medicine or physiology for assisting in the discovery of the molecular structure of deoxyribonucleic acid (DNA).

Cricket, brown to black bug with long antennae and hind legs adapted for jumping; found worldwide. The field and house crickets are the best known of this family. The males produce a chirping sound. Length: 0.3–2in (7.6–51mm). Family Gryllidae. *See also* Mole Cricket.

Cricket, a game popular in Great Britain and other Commonwealth nations, the national summer sport of England, where it originated in the Middle Ages. It is played by 2 teams of 11 persons each on a field about 525 feet by 550 feet (160m × 168m). A game, which may take several days to complete, consists of one or two innings. In an inning all the men of a team bat once in a fixed order; the team scoring the most runs wins. Except for serious injury, no substitutions are allowed. Batsmen and wicketkeepers (catchers) wear gloves, and the fielders are positioned in non-fixed positions around the outlying areas of wickets. The game evolves around two wickets, which are placed near the middle of the field, 66 feet (20.1m) apart. A wicket is made of 3 wooden stumps 28 inches high (71.1cm) with 2 small wooden crosspieces (bails), balanced in grooves in the stumps. At each wicket stands a batsman who uses a cane-handled, paddle-shaped bat. The bowler, who stands at one of the wickets, has six to eight throws to retire the batsman. Runs are scored each time a batsman exchanges wickets with his partner; on a long hit he may score as many as six runs. The pitcher delivers the hard, leather-covered ball, overarm with a stiff arm action, usually on a bounce. If he does not retire the batsman after the alloted pitches, another bowler (a starting fielder) begins the next series of pitches from the opposite wicket. A batter is retired in a number of ways. Some are technical, but the most common are if the bowler breaks the bails of the wicket on the pitch, if the batsman flies out, or if the fielders retrieve the ball and knock down the bails before the batsman reaches the wicket.

Crime. △914–21.

Crime and Punishment (1866), novel by Fyodor Dostoevsky. It examines the nature of crime and guilt. Raskolnikov, a penniless St. Petersburg student, kills an old pawnbroker for her money. Surprised in the act by the pawnbroker's sister, he also kills her and flees without the money. Confessing his crimes to Sonia, a girl driven to prostitution, he is overheard and blackmailed. He eventually gives himself up and is exiled to Siberia.

Crimean War (1853–56), war fought by Britain, France, and Turkey against Russia. Russian ambitions in the Middle East aroused British and French fears. When Russia claimed a protectorate over Orthodox Christians in Turkey and occupied Turkish dependencies, Britain and France declared war and sent troops to the Crimean Peninsula (1854). Bad administration and leadership led to the pointless Charge of the Light Brigade and thousands of deaths through disease and lack of supplies. Military efforts centered on Sevastopol, which Russia surrendered in 1855. Peace was reached at the Congress of Paris (1856). An important consequence was the diplomatic isolation of Austria; the war also demonstrated to Britain and Russia the need for military reform. △1232.

Criminal Law, branch of law "which defines crimes, treats of their nature, and provides for their punishment." The three elements of criminal law are: an offense must be committed against the public and prosecuted by the state, as distinguished from a tort, or violation of a private right; the act must be a specified crime according to the criminal code; that code must state a definite punishment for the crime charged. Crimes can be classified as *mala in se*, immoral or wrong in themselves, such as murder, rape, arson; or *mala prohibita*, those acts not morally wrong but prohibited by statute for infringing on the rights of others, such as disturbing the peace. They are graded by their gravity as treason, felony, and misdemeanor. In the United States, criminal law consists of statutory and common law, though there is a lessening importance of common law. Each state, as well as the federal government has its own criminal code of law; there are no common law crimes against the US federal government. △910.

Criminology, subdivision of sociology that is concerned with the general processes of making laws, breaking laws, and reacting to the breaking of laws. The three principal divisions of criminology are: *sociology of law,* an attempt to scientifically analyze the conditions under which criminal laws develop; *criminal etiology,* an attempt to scientifically analyze the causes of crime; and *penology,* which is concerned with the control of crime. *See also* Law; Penology. △914–22.

Crinoid, primitive class of marine echinoderms, the only class having an upward-directed mouth, which is located with the other main organs in a small central disc. Long feathery arms surround it. It is spineless with tube feet used for respiration. Class Crinoidea. *See also* Feather Star, Sea Lily. △272, 504, 560.

Crinum Lily, tropical bulb plant with long, narrow, evergreen leaves and fragrant flowers that are trumpet or star-shaped. The swamp *Crinum americanum* and grand *Crinum asiaticum* have white flowers and are cultivated in S United States. Family Amaryllidaceae.

Cripps, (Sir Richard) Stafford (1889–1952), British socialist politician. He joined the Labour party as solicitor-general (1930–31) and entered parliament (1931). For cooperating with communists against fascism, he was expelled from the Labour party (1939). Churchill made him ambassador to Russia (1940–42) and minister of aircraft production (1942–45). Readmitted to the Labour party (1945), Cripps held economic appointments. As chancellor of the exchequer (1947–50) he pursued a rigid austerity program.

Critias (450–403 BC), Athenian politician and writer, pupil of Socrates. Exiled during the Peloponnesian Wars for favoring Sparta, he returned to become one of the cruelest of the "30 tyrants" and was killed when the exiled democrats returned.

Critical Mass, minimum mass of fissile material required in a fission bomb to sustain a chain reaction. *See* Fission, Nuclear. △1482.

Critical Periods, in psychology, stages of development in which important learning must take place if it is to be effective. For example, dogs will not be suitable as pets unless they get used to people before they are four months old. Some psychologists believe children are particularly prone to develop behavior problems if they do not have close mother attachments in infancy.

Critical Point, the temperature and pressure above which a liquid and its vapor phase can no longer coexist. If a substance is slowly compressed at temperatures and pressures above the critical point it seems to change gradually from gas to liquid, rather than suddenly separating into two phases.

Crittenden, John Jordan (1787–1863), US lawyer and statesman, b. near Versailles, Ky. He was senator from Kentucky (1817–19, 1835–41, 1842–48, and 1855–61). He served as attorney general under Pres. Benjamin Harrison (1841) and Millard Filmore (1850–53). His "Crittenden's propositions" of 1860 sought to reach a compromise on slavery with the southern states and prevent war, but it was defeated.

Croaker, or hardhead, marine fish found in shallow tropical and temperate waters. A commercial and sporting fish, it is silver with brown bars on its sides. It uses its air bladder and attached muscles to make croaking and drumming sounds. Length: to 20in (50.8cm); weight: 4lb (1.8kg). Family Sciaenidae; species include Atlantic *Micropogon undulatus.*

Croatia (Hrvatska), federal unit and republic in NW Yugoslavia; includes Croatia proper, Slavonia, Dalmatia, and major part of Istria. A former kingdom, Croatia fell under the rule of Hungary 1091; after the fall of Austro-Hungarian Empire in 1918, a kingdom was formed by Serbs, Croats, and Slovenes; political conflicts resulted in the assassination of Stefan Radie, leader of the Croatian Peasant party; his successor formed a separate Croatian state. In 1945, Croatia became a Yugoslav republic. Industries: lumber, coal, petroleum, iron ore, tourism. Pop. 4,422,564. △1232.

Croce, Benedetto (1866–1952), Italian philosopher and historian. His *Philosophy of the Spirit* (1902–17) is concerned with aesthetics, logic and linguistics, ethics, and historiography. He was an Italian senator (1910–20) and minister of education (1920–21). An anti-Fascist, he retired from politics when Mussolini came to power, not returning until 1943 when he became head of the Liberal party. Historical works include *A History of Italy, 1871–1915* (1927) and *History as the Story of Liberty* (1938).

Crockett, David (1786–1836), US frontiersman, b. Green co, Tenn. He served under Andrew Jackson in the Creek Wars (1813–14). He served in the Tennessee legislature (1821–26) and the US Congress (1827–31, 1833–35). A Whig, he opposed the policies of Jackson and the Democrats. He shrewdly cultivated the image of a rough frontiersman. Three books about his life, including *A Narrative of the Life of David Crockett* (1834), supposedly of his authorship were probably not written by him. He moved to Texas in 1835 after not being reelected and died fighting at the Alamo.

Crocodile, flesh-eating, lizardlike reptile found in warm parts of every continent except Europe. Most crocodiles have a longer, more pointed snout than members of the alligator family. All lay hard-shelled eggs in nests. Length: to 23ft (7m). The Asian salt water crocodile *(Crocodylus porosus)* is a man-eater. The American crocodile lives in brackish and salt water around Ecuador, Mexico, the West Indies, and Florida. There are about 15 species including two dwarf species in Africa. Family Crocodylidae. *See also* Reptile. △520.

Crocodile Bird, or Egyptian plover, African bird that feeds on insects, often those infesting crocodiles. It is gray, black, and white, with greenish markings. Dark-speckled, cream eggs (2–3) are buried in the sand. Length: 9in (23cm). Species *Pluvianus aegyptius.*

Crocodile River. *See* Limpopo.

Crocus, hardy perennial flowering plant native to Eurasia and widely cultivated. It is low-growing with a single tubular flower and grasslike leaves arising from an underground corm. It blooms in early spring or fall. Saffron crocus is a popular autumn variety and yellow cloth-of-gold crocus is an early spring favorite. There are 75 species. Family Iridaceae; genus *Crocus.*

Croesus, last King of Lydia (*r.* 560–546 BC). Wealthy and friendly to the Greeks, he was overthrown by Cyrus the Great.

Cro-Magnon Man, tall, erect Upper Paleolithic race of man, probably the earliest representatives of *Homo sapiens* in Europe, where they settled between 40,000 and 30,000 years ago. Cultures such as the Aurignacian, for which Cro-Magnon Man was responsible, were distinguished by the manufacture of varied and sophisticated stone tools, as well as bone, horn, and ivory artifacts. Cro-Magnon artists produced the cave paintings of France and northern Spain. *See also* Paleolithic Age. △652.

Cromer, Evelyn Baring, Earl of (1841–1917), English administrator and diplomat. His negotiations for the Anglo-French settlement of 1904 regarding Egypt and his 24-year rule as consul general in Egypt had a marked influence on the development of the modern state of Egypt. He favored extensive development of railways, agriculture, and irrigation at the expense of political and intellectual progress. Eventually these policies led to his unpopularity and resignation. He wrote *Modern Egypt* (1908) and *Political and Literary Essays* (1908–16).

Cromwell, Oliver (1599–1658), Lord Protector of England, Scotland, and Ireland (1653–58), Puritan soldier and politician. A country landowner, he opposed Charles I in parliament and became a successful parliamentarian officer in the Civil War (1642–48), rising to second-in-command. In the subsequent turmoil he supported the army against parliament and the Presbyterians, and helped bring about the king's execution. He brutally suppressed revolts in Ireland, but showed clemency to the Scottish Covenanters, whom he also defeated (1649–51). More differences between parliament and the army led Cromwell to dissolve parliament and become Lord Protector, head of a military dictatorship (1653). His domestic policy now increased religious toleration and legal and administrative reforms. Backed by a powerful army and navy, his foreign policy supported British trade and colonization. When he died, the government quickly collapsed under his son and successor Richard. *See also* Charles I; Civil War, English; Cromwell, Richard. △1156.

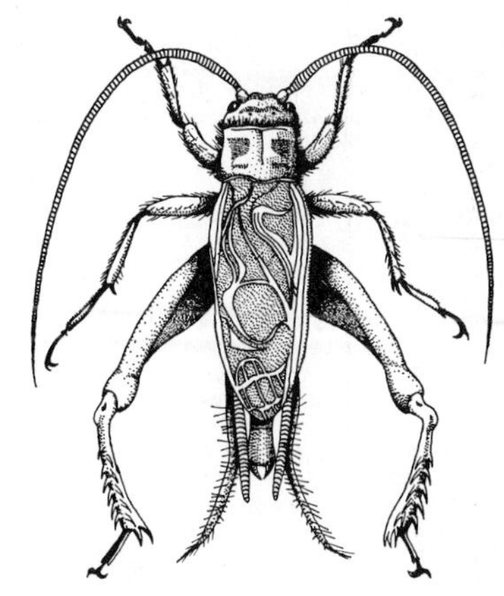

Cricket

David Crockett

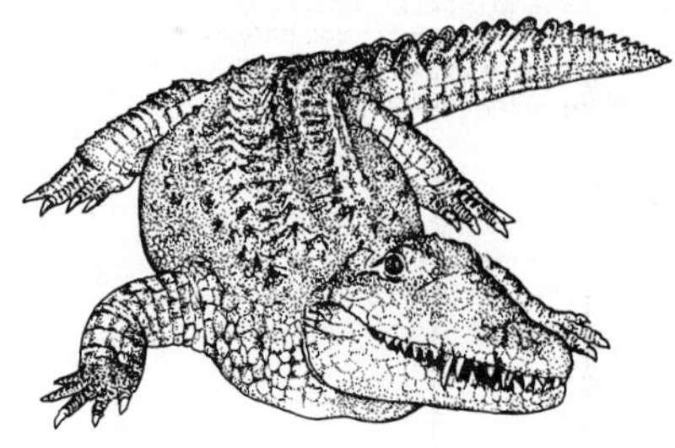

Crocodile

Crocus

Cromwell, Richard (1626–1712), Lord Protector of England (1658–59). Oliver Cromwell's son and successor, Richard was an able officer but an incapable ruler. Ousted from power after eight months, he spent 20 years in exile before returning to live quietly at Cheshunt.

Cromwell, Thomas, Earl of Essex, (1485–1540), English administrator and royal adviser. In Cardinal Wolsey's service Cromwell attracted Henry VIII's attention. His suggestion that the king become head of the church in England (1532) was rewarded with major offices and great wealth. He dissolved the monasteries and directed the Reformation until Henry had him executed for supposed treason.

Cronin, A(rchibald) J(oseph) (1896–), Scottish novelist. He was a medical inspector of mines and physician until the success of his first work, *Hatter's Castle* (1931) allowed him to devote all of his time to writing popular, melodramatic novels. Cronin based some of his plots on his own experiences, including *The Citadel* (1937), which dealt with the life of a mining company doctor. Other works included *The Keys of the Kingdom* (1941), *The Judas Tree* (1961), and *Pocketful of Rye* (1969).

Cronkite, Walter Leland, Jr. (1916–), US journalist and commentator, b. St. Joseph, Mo. While a student at the University of Texas (1933–35) he worked as a reporter for the *Houston Post* and for the Scripps-Howard syndicate. In 1939 he joined United Press (UP) and was attached to both foreign and US news bureaus. During World War II he wrote eyewitness accounts of events at the front and afterward covered the Nuremberg trials. He was UP bureau chief in Moscow (1946–48). In 1950 he joined the CBS news staff, serving as moderator and commentator for programs presenting news analysis and current events. He became anchorman for CBS News and, as such, won a Peabody public-service award in 1963.

Cronus, in Greek mythology, the youngest son of Uranus and Gaea. Cronus castrated his father at the instigation of his mother and became head of a new dynasty. By his sister Rhea he was the father of Hades, Poseidon, Zeus, Hestia, Demeter, and Hera.

Crook, George (1829–90), US Army officer, b. Dayton, Ohio. He spent his early career in the Pacific Northwest. He served in the Civil War and in the Indian Wars. He fought the Sioux and led the action against the Apache and their leader, Geronimo. He was promoted to brigadier general (1873) and made commander of the department of the Platte (1875). From 1888, he was major general in command of the division of the Missouri.

Crookes, (Sir) William (1832–1919), English scientist. After lecturing in chemistry at Chester College, he inherited a fortune, which enabled him to devote himself to private research. His high-vacuum research led to the invention of the radiometer and the Crookes tube, which led to the discovery of X rays. He was the first to suggest that cathode rays consist of negatively charged particles. He discovered the element thallium and was a well-known spiritualist.

Crop Rotation, practice of growing different crops on the same field, usually in a specified order. A legume sod crop is often included in the sequence. This protects and improves the soil and reduces erosion. Rotated crops generally complement each other, each providing nutrients required by the other. △304, 320.

Croquet, lawn game, popular in Great Britain and the United States, in which wooden balls are hit with wooden mallets through a series of 9 or 10 wire arches. The first player to complete the series and hit the posts placed at each end of the field wins. Croquet was developed in France in the 17th century. The US game, called Roque, was devised in 1899 and uses a different course layout.

Crosby, Bing (1904–), US popular singer and actor, b. Harry Lillis Crosby in Tacoma, Wash. For over 30 years he was one of the most popular singers in the United States. In 1944 he won an Academy Award for the film *Going My Way.* His recording of Irving Berlin's "White Christmas" is the all-time best-selling record.

Crossbill, forest finch of the N Northern Hemisphere. Varying in color, it has a heavy, curved, scissorlike bill used to pry seeds from evergreen cones. Bluish spotted eggs (4–5) are laid in a twig-and-grass nest. Length: 6in (15cm). Genus *Loxia.*

Crossbow. △1726, 1732.

Crossbreeding, outbreeding, the crossing or mixing of two unlike parents to produce a hybrid, for example, crossing a horse and a donkey to produce a mule. △416.

Cross of Gold Speech (1896), pro-silver speech by Sen. William Jennings Bryan of Nebraska. The speech, advocating the free coinage of silver, was delivered before the Democratic Convention (July 8) and was so powerful that Bryan gained the party's nomination for president.

Crossopterygian, lobefinned fish group extinct for 75 million years except for the coelacanth. It resembles elasmobranchs and terrestrial vertebrates, foreshadowing the latter. Fossil forms show fins in transition to extremities for locomotion, and trunks and tails similar to those of amphibians. The group flourished during the Devonian Period about 400,000,000 years ago and provided the evolutionary stock for land vertebrates. Subclass Choanichthyes. △566.

Cross-pollination, transfer of pollen from the flower of one plant to a flower on another plant. The result of cross pollination is a genetic mix, or hybrid.

Croswell Case (1803), US court case involving Harry Croswell, a New York newspaper editor who was accused of libeling President Jefferson. He was convicted of libel and later appealed the decision with the aid of Alexander Hamilton as his counsel. Hamilton argued for freedom of the press, even if it involved high officials. The conviction was sustained, but in 1805 Hamilton's proposal was made law in New York State. It was used until 1964, when the *New York Times* v. *Sullivan* Supreme Court case expanded freedom of the press.

Croton, genus of tropical plants native to Australia and islands of the South Pacific. *C. variegatum pictum* is the most popular, with long leaves variegated with green, red, yellow, and white. It grows to 6ft (1.8m).

Croup, respiratory disorder most common in young children caused by an inflammation of the larynx (voice box). Croup can be triggered by bacterial or viral infection, local irritation, or allergy, and is characterized by a harsh, strident-sounding cough. Treatment depends on the cause. Steam inhalation is often helpful.

Crouse, Russel (1893–1966), US dramatist and journalist, b. Findlay, Ohio. He collaborated with Howard Lindsay on the long-running domestic comedy *Life With Father* (1939), adapted from the Clarence Day novel, and on *State of the Union* (1945; Pulitzer Prize 1946). Crouse also produced Broadway musicals.

Crow, large tribe of Siouan-speaking American Indians who early separated from the Hidatsa. They migrated into the Rocky Mountain region from the Missouri River, and today occupy a large reservation area in Montana. They are noted for their physical stature and fine costume; the Crow women are among the most artistic of Plains Indians. The present population of 4500 is divided into the Mountain and River Crow. *See also* Hidatsa.

Crow, large, black birds found in woodlands and farm areas worldwide except in polar regions, South America, and some Pacific islands. The American crow *Corvus brachyrhynchos,* attains a length of 20in (50cm) and a wingspread of 3ft (91cm). Living in large flocks, they feed on plant and animal matter and carrion. They can be crop pests. Considered intelligent, they can sometimes be taught to repeat phrases. Their stick-and-twig nests are built in tall trees for the greenish eggs (3–8). Family Corvidae.

Crowfoot. *see* Buttercup.

Crown, in dentistry, an artificial covering substitute for the natural crown of the tooth, or the portion that protrudes beyond the gum. Crowns are used in dental practice when teeth are chipped or broken but otherwise solidly rooted and healthy. They are also employed for anchorage when constructing bridges or replace missing teeth. *See also* Bridge. △756.

Crown Gall, a cancerlike growth that occurs on a wide variety of broadleaved plants, including peaches, apples, roses, raspberries, and sugar beets. The gall, caused by the bacterium *Agrobacterium tumefaciens,* typically forms at the affected plant's crown—the point where the plant emerges from the soil.

Crown of Thorns, spiny, shrubby house plant native to Madagascar with small leaves and clusters of red flowers. Care: bright light, soil (equal parts of potting soil, sand) kept dry between waterings. Propagation is by stem cuttings. Height: to 3ft (91cm). Family Euphorbiaceae; species *Euphorbia splendens.*

CRS. *See* Chinese Restaurant Syndrome.

Crucible Process, a process for making fine tool and high-speed steel. Carbon steel is melted in fire-clay crucibles in order to make a homogeneous high-quality metal. Coke fires were initially used (1740), but were replaced (1870) by the Siemens regenerative gas furnace that could heat 100 crucibles at a time to temperatures over 3100°F (1700°C). Electric furnaces are now employed.

Crucifer. △444.

Cruikshank, George (1792–1878), English illustrator and cartoonist. In addition to political and theatrical work, Cruikshank drew illustrations for more than 850 books. The best known are those done for Dickens' *Sketches by Boz* and *Oliver Twist.* △1644.

Cruise Missile, or aerodynamic missile, self-propelled missile traveling in the lower atmosphere under constant powered flight. It may be rocket- or jet-powered, eg the German V-1 during World War II. Unlike ballistic missiles, cruise missiles must be aerodynamically designed to minimize atmospheric drag. *See also* Ballistic Missile.

Cruiser, major naval warship displacing 5–10,000 tons, usually serving as a general-purpose combat ship, often taking the place of the more costly battleship. *See also* Battleship.

Crusades (1095–1272), series of military expeditions undertaken by Western European Christians to recover the Holy Land from the Muslims. In 1095 at the Council of Clermont, Pope Urban II urged Christians to go to war to save the Holy Sepulcher, which had been despoiled by the Seljuk Turks who controlled Jerusalem. He promised that the journey would count as full penance. From crosses distributed at the meeting the name Crusade evolved. Peter the Hermit and others spread the message throughout Europe.

Peasants Crusade (1095–96). Even before the first sanctioned crusade could get underway, several thousand French peasants that had set out toward Jerusalem had sacked Belgrade. German peasants turned to attacking Jews and had to be dispersed by the king of Hungary. When the remnants of these two groups reached Constantinople they were quickly shipped across to Jerusalem and easily defeated by the Turks.

First Crusade (1096–99). An organized army under Bishop Ademar and Count Raymond IV of Toulouse captured Nicea (1097), Antioch (1098), and, finally, Jerusalem (1099). Godfrey of Bouillon was elected the first ruler of the Latin Kingdom of Jerusalem.

Second Crusade (1147–49). Preached by Bernard of Clairvaux after the fall of Edessa (1144) to the Turks, it failed in its goal of capturing Damascus.

Third Crusade (1189–91). It followed the fall of Jerusalem (1187) to Saladin. Richard I of England was able to work out a truce with Saladin that allowed Christian access to the Holy Sepulcher.

Fourth Crusade (1202–04). It never reached the Holy Land. Instead it fought with the Venetians against Hungary and in 1204 sacked Constantinople, overthrowing the Byzantine Empire and establishing the Latin Empire of Constantinople.

Children's Crusade (1212). Led by a French peasant boy, Stephen of Cloyes, thousands of children embarked from Marseilles and other ports only to be sold into slavery or to die of hunger or disease.

Fifth Crusade (1218–21). It struck at Egypt with little success.

Sixth Crusade (1228–29). The only nonmilitary Crusade, it was led by Holy Roman Emperor Frederick II. He was able to negotiate a truce with the Muslims that restored some Christian control.

Seventh (1248–50) and **Eighth** (1270) **Crusades.** Both led by Louis IX of France with little success. The Eighth was called off when Louis died in Tunisia.

Ninth Crusade (1271–72). Led by Prince Edward (later Edward I) of England, little was accomplished. The last Latin Kingdom (city state) in the Near East, Acre, fell to the Muslims in 1291. △1084, 1098.

Crust, Earth, the visible cover or what is sometimes called the silicic phase of Earth. The crust is that part of the planet from the Moho to the outer limit of the core. The silicic rocks are less dense and float on the denser mantle. △166.

Crustacean, any of a large class (26,000 species) of invertebrate animals in the phylum Arthropoda. Included are the familiar decapods (crabs, lobsters, shrimps, and crayfish), isopods (pill bugs, woodlice), cirripedes (barnacles), and a multitude of other forms, most of which are not distinguished by popular names. The majority of crustaceans are aquatic, either marine or freshwater (although a few are semi-terrestrial). They breathe through gills or the body surface. There are two pairs of antennalike appendages in front of the mouth and at least three pairs of appendages behind the mouth that act as jaws. All have the typical exoskeleton of arthropods. They include some of the largest as well as the smallest arthropods, ranging from the giant Japanese spider crab, 12ft (3.7m) wide with limbs extended, to the water fleas, under 0.01 in (.25mm) in length. △486.

Crux, Crux Australis, or the Southern Cross, prominent southern constellation whose four brightest stars, Alpha (Acrux), Beta, Gamma, and Delta, form the famous southward-pointing cross. The constellation contains the Coal Sack, a dark nebula easily discernible against the background of the Milky Way, and the open cluster NGC 4755 or Kappa Crucis (named the Jewel Box by Sir John Herschel). △134.

Cryogenics, the study of physics at very low temperatures. Some materials exhibit highly unusual properties at temperatures within a few degrees of absolute zero: they become super conducting (that is, they can carry an electrical current indefinitely) or "creep" over boundaries, apparently defying the laws of gravity. Such behavior is intensively studied, partly because the low temperatures and small number of energy states involved allow fuller understanding of quantum mechanical principles, and partly for potential applications of immense value.

Cryolite, a halide mineral, sodium-aluminum fluoride (Na_3AlF_6). In pegmatite dikes (Greenland has the only large deposit). Used in aluminum processing. Monoclinic system granular masses or occasional cubic, frequently twinned, crystals. Icy-looking or brown or red; brittle; hardness 2.5; sp gr 3.

Cryosurgery, surgery carried on at a very low temperature in which a freezing probe replaces a cutting edge. It is particularly effective in treating Parkinson's disease and tonsillitis.

Cryptococcosis, serious fungus *(Cryptococcus neoformans)* infection, usually occurring in middle age, more often in men. It affects the central nervous system, including the membranes of the brain, and sometimes the lungs, skin, and other organs.

Cryptogam, early botanical term for plant that bears no flowers or seeds, reproducing by spores. It included mosses, liverworts, and ferns. Conifers and angiosperms were called phanerogams.

Cryptography, "hidden writing," also called cryptology. Cryptography involves use of codes and ciphers for safe transmission of secret messages; also involves cryptanalysis, or ways of decoding such messages. The difference between codes and ciphers is primarily technical. In general, ciphers use substitutions for single letters, whereas codes use substitutions (usually 5-letter groups) for whole words, phrases, or sentences. For economy, codes are used commercially with the aid of easily obtainable commercial code books. Modern computers are helpful to the cryptanalyst, but cannot always break code or cipher systems without the aid of human experts.

Crystal, city in SE central Minnesota, 4mi (6km) W of Mississippi River; suburb of Minneapolis and part of the Minneapolis-St Paul metropolitan area. Inc. 1960. Pop. (1970) 30,295.

Crystal, a solid with a repetitive lattice-like structure. Most solids are crystalline, although some, like glass and asphalt, are amorphous. Crystals exhibit many types of atomic symmetries: cubic (table salt), planar (mica), and over two hundred other arrangements. Macroscopic crystals belong to 32 symmetry classes, which can be grouped into seven crystal systems: triclinic, monoclinic, orthorhombic, trigonal, hexagonal, tetragonal, and isometric. For a given type of crystal, the angles between its planar faces and edges are always the same, no matter how it is broken or reduced. This observation, first made in the 17th century by Nicolaus Steno of Denmark, is the First Law of Crystallography. In all the crystal systems except the isometric, light travels at different velocities along different axes of the crystal because of the differing distances between atoms; thus it will be refracted at different angles and appear to be doubled on leaving the crystal. Such crystals (eg, calcite) are birefringent. △240–44, 1506, 1558.

Crystal Lattice, three-dimensional arrangement of atoms, ions, or molecules in a crystalline substance. The term is sometimes used in a more restricted sense to denote the abstraction of the pattern of points on which the atoms, ions, or molecules are located. △1504–06, 1562.

Crystallization, process whereby atoms, ions, or molecules aggregate themselves in a regular repeating arrangement, either from the dissolved or pure liquid state, often initiated by supersaturation, to form a solid or oriented liquid crystal with specific physical properties. Crystallization is an important laboratory and industrial technique for purifying (and separating) compounds. △1504, 1562.

Crystallography, the study of crystal structure by X ray diffraction. Coherent waves will be diffracted, or reinforced in some directions and weakened in others, by striking regularly recurring obstacles of the proper spacing. In crystalline solids this spacing is of the order of a few Ångstroms. Since X rays have wavelengths of comparable size, they are diffracted by the crystals. Knowing the wavelength of the X rays and measuring the angles at which they are strengthened and weakened allows crystallographers to calculate the three-dimensional structures of the crystals. Conversely, a knowledge of the crystal structure allows the wavelengths of unknown X ray sources to be measured. The first great crystallographer, who did his work when both X rays and crystal structure were little understood, was Max von Laue; Sir William Bragg also made important contributions to theory. △240–44, 1506.

Crystal Optics, optical properties of crystals. Transmission of light by crystals differs from transmission by glass in that the refractive index may depend on direction (crystals are not, in general, isotropic). Uniaxial crystals (belonging to the tetragonal, hexagonal, and rhombohedral systems) have two principal refractive indices and display double refraction. Biaxial crystals (orthorhombic, monoclinic, triclinic) have three principal refractive indices. Information on crystal structure can often be obtained by microscopic investigation in polarized light. *See also* Polarization of Light. △ 1506.

Crystal Palace, first building of its size (408×1850ft; 124×564m) made of glass and iron. Designed for the 1851 International Exhibition in London by Sir Joseph Paxton, it was prefabricated and was assembled at the site. Developed by Paxton's work in greenhouse construction, it directly affected train-station design.

Crystal Structure. *See* Crystal.

Csonka, Lawrence R. "Larry" (1946–), US football player, b. Stow, Ohio. A power runner, he played with Miami in the National Football League (1969–74) and Memphis in the World Football League (1974–75) before joining the New York Giants (1976). In 1974, he was selected the most valuable player in the Super Bowl.

CU. *See* Consumer's Union of the United States.

Cuauhtémoc (*c.*1495–1525), last Aztec ruler of Mexico, unsuccessfully defended Tenochtitlán against Cortés' siege of the capital. Four years later, while on an expedition to Honduras with Cortés, Cuauhtémoc was implicated in a plot to kill the Spaniards and was executed.

Cuautla, city in S central Mexico, approx. 18mi (29km) SE of Cuernavaca in Cuautla River Valley; scene of 1812 heroic defense by patriot armies against Spanish forces; site of resort and hot springs. Industries: tourism, rice, sugar cane. Pop. 67,869.

Cuba, Republic of, independent nation, on the largest island in the West Indies, 90mi (144km) S of Florida. Since 1959 it has been under the control of Fidel Castro, a left-wing revolutionary. Cuba's economic mainstay is sugar.

Land and economy. Situated entirely in the Tropic Zone, Cuba is in the trade winds belt; its climate is semi-tropical. The island extends 745mi (1,199km) E-W, its width is 22–125m (35–201km). Its 2,500mi (4,025km) coastline includes Havana and Guantanamo harbors, two of the best in the world. About 60% of Cuba is flat to rolling with many fertile valleys. It contains three mountain ranges, the highest being Sierra Maestra. Despite a high level of support and economic investment from the Soviet Union, Cuba's economy has remained essentially stagnant since 1959. It is estimated that from 1959–70, the real per capita GNP declined 9% while other Latin-American countries increased by 24%. Agriculture is the basis of the economy, especially the cultivation and refining of sugar, which accounts for 80% of export earnings.

Walter Cronkite

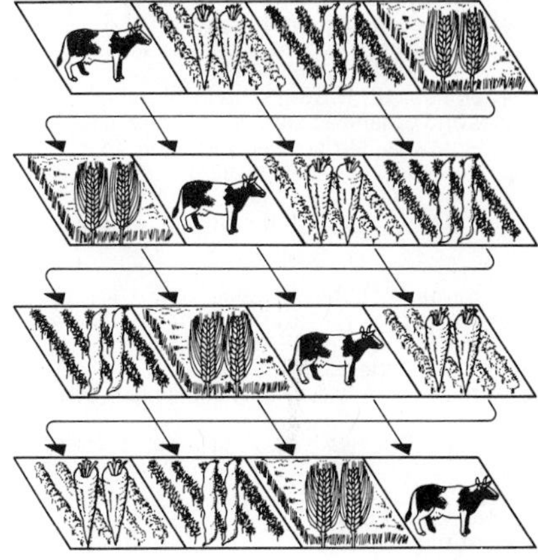
Crop rotation

Crossbill

Crow

Cuba imports an estimated 40% of its food requirements.

People. Ethnically, the Cuban population is derived from Europe, Africa, Asia, and from the Indians who lived on the island when Christopher Columbus discovered it. Spanish is the official language, and literacy is reported at 95%. Compulsory education was established in 1961. Roman Catholicism is the religion of 85% of the people, although African faiths, Judaism, and Protestant sects are represented.

Government. Cuba, with only one legal party—the Communist party—has been ruled by decree since 1959, although authority is nominally vested in the cabinet.

History. Cuba was discovered and claimed for Spain by Christopher Columbus in 1492; for years Havana served as Spain's crossroad commercial seaport to its colonies. In 1850 Cuban planters started an independence movement, a struggle that precipitated the Ten Years' War (1868) and a general uprising in 1895. The United States supported the revolutionaries after the *USS Maine* was blown up in Havana harbor. In 1898, Spain relinquished its hold on Cuba. An army revolt, led by Gen. Fulgencio Batista in 1933, made him the leading power in the country, and in 1952 he seized the presidency. Opposition to his corrupt regime became apparent, and in 1953 a young lawyer, Fidel Castro, began a guerrilla action against Batista, who quit on Jan. 1, 1959. Castro became premier on Feb. 16, 1959. He nationalized banks and industries and organized state farms under a left-wing government with strong backing from the Soviet Union. On April 17, 1961 about 1,400 Cubans, trained in the United States, landed at the Bay of Pigs in a vain effort to regain the island.

PROFILE

Official name: Republic of Cuba
Area: 44,218sq mi (114,525sq km)
Population (1975 est): 9,500,000
Density: 214.8per sq mi (82.9per sq km)
Chief cities: Havana (capital); Camaguey; Santiago de Cuba
Government: Premier Fidel Castro Ruz, premier
Religion: Roman Catholic
Language: Spanish
Monetary unit: Peso
Gross national product: $3,400,000,000
Per capita income: $388
Industries (major): sugar products, textiles, chemicals
Agriculture: sugar cane, tobacco, rice, citrus fruits, sweet potatoes
Minerals: iron, copper, salt, manganese
Trading partners: Soviet Union (major), Communist China, Czechoslovakia

Cuban Missile Crisis (1962), United States-USSR confrontation over the installation of Soviet rockets in Cuba. US reconnaissance planes first discovered the rockets, which were capable of carrying nuclear warheads to almost anywhere in the Western Hemisphere. This action challenged both the Monroe Doctrine and President Kennedy's warnings to Russia and Cuba against making Cuba an offensive military base. The United States alerted the armed forces and blockaded Cuba. Soviet Premier Khrushchev, after receiving assurances that the United States would not invade the island, dismantled the missile bases. △1390.

Cube, result of multiplying a given number together three times. Thus the cube of *a* is $a \times a \times a$, written a^3. △1466.

Cube Root, number that must be multiplied together three times to give a specified number. For example, the cube root of 27 is 3, since $3 \times 3 \times 3 = 27$. Cube roots are written in the form $\sqrt[3]{27}$ or $27^{1/3}$.

Cubic Equation, equation of the third degree; that is, one in which the highest power of the unknown is 3. An example is $2x^3 + x^2 + 7 = 0$. Cubic equations have three roots, two of which may be imaginary.

Cubism, innovative movement in 20th-century painting, originating with Pablo Picasso and Georges Braque and joined by Juan Gris, Fernand Léger, Jean Metzinger, Albert Gleizes, and others. Cubism, a term coined by art critic Louis Vauxcelles, was a conscious reaction to the French Romanticism of Ferdinand Delacroix, the sensuous appeal of the Impressionists, and the decorative color of the Fauves, and was a return to the classical tradition of Ingres. Still life was the subject matter, seen as a composition of quasi-geometric forms without atmosphere and light, with restricted colors, verging toward the monochromatic, and without movement. Natural perspective was abandoned, and a new perspective of overlapping, interlocking, semitransparent planes was used in an attempt to present the solidity and volume of the object two-dimensionally, from many different aspects simultaneously. Cubism falls into three phases: the Paul Cézanne phase (1907–09), so-called because of his influence and that of black sculpture and primitive art; the analytical phase (1910–12), which showed an increasing breakdown of form and a use of simultaneity, showing a fragmented object displayed from all angles and open from inside; and the synthetic phase (1913–14), developed by Gris, which discarded imitation completely and sought to recreate the object by means of "emblems" similar to a metaphor in a poem. Gris did not distort the object but painted an analogous construction. Picasso's *Les Demoiselles d'Avignon* is regarded as the source picture of cubism. △1296.

Cuckoo, widely distributed forest bird. Common species are the ani, roadrunners, and coucal. True Old World cuckoos are generally brownish with a few species being brightly colored. They feed on small animals. A brood parasite, the female removes one egg of another species and lays her egg—often a match in color—in the nest. Soon after the cuckoo chick has hatched, it throws out the other's eggs and any young that may have hatched. It is then fed by the foster mother. Length: 6–24in (15–61cm). Family Cuclidae.

Cucumber, trailing, annual vine originally from tropical Africa and S Asia. It has yellowish flowers and the fruit is eaten raw or pickled. It needs a warm climate and is sensitive to frost and pests. Family Cucurbitaceae; species *Cucumis sativus.*

Cudahy, city in SE Wisconsin, on Lake Michigan, 7mi (11km) S of Milwaukee. Industries: meat packing, iron and steel products. Founded 1892 by John and Patrick Cudahy, meat packing scions. Inc. 1906. Pop. (1970) 22,078.

Cueing, in communication, a way one person can convey intents or wishes by hints. He can use words, as by an indirect mention of a topic he wants to talk about. Or he can use nonverbal means, as by turning toward someone when he wants to talk. *See also* Communication, Nonverbal.

Cuenca, city in S central Ecuador; called "marble city" because of many notable buildings. Among richest agricultural areas in Andes, it is also the commercial center of Ecuador. Founded 1557. Pop. 77,300.

Cuernavaca, town in S central Mexico, 37mi (60km) S of Mexico City; site of palace and 1st Mexican sugar refinery, both built by Hernán Cortés (1535), popular resort of Cacahuamilpa Caverns, university (1938). Industries: brewery, tobacco, cement, paper. Pop. 44,278.

Cuffe, Paul (1759–1815), US seaman and philanthropist, b. Cuttyhunk Is., Mass. A self-made man, by 1795 he owned a fleet of whaling ships. In 1815 he sailed nine black families to Sierra Leone, but died before he could bring more. He also founded schools for blacks in Massachusetts.

Cukor, George (1899–), US stage and film director, b. New York City. He is noted for stylish comedies and literary dramas. His major films include *Camille* (1936), *The Women* (1939), *The Philadelphia Story* (1940), *Born Yesterday* (1950), and *A Star is Born* (1954). Many of his films featured Katharine Hepburn (often teamed with Spencer Tracy).

Culbertson, Ely (1891–1955), US bridge expert, b. Romania. The son of an American oilman, he began a lifetime study of bridge during his education in Geneva. He married Josephine Murphy, another bridge expert and their well-publicized games against other bridge stars popularized the game. Culbertson was US bridge team captain on several occasions. His writings include articles and columns on bridge.

Culiacán, city in NW Mexico, 30mi (48km) from Pacific coast; headquarters of Francisco Coronado's expedition up the Gulf of California (1540). Industries: leather, textiles, lumber, mining, corn, tobacco, sugar cane, cotton. Founded 1531 by Nuño Guzmán. Pop. 358,812.

Cullen, Countee (1903–46), US poet, b. New York City. A major figure of the Harlem Renaissance, his poetry includes *Color* (1925) and *The Ballad of the Brown Girl* (1928). *See also* Harlem Renaissance.

Culpeper, Nicholas. △742.

Culpeper, Thomas (1635–89), US royal governor, a favorite of Charles II, received all of Virginia as a 30-year grant. He ruled as governor (1682–83), attempting to swindle the colonists by paying wages in his own coinage. He was returned to England and convicted of corruption. His daughter, Catherine Fairfax was his heir.

Culpeper's Rebellion, in US history, an uprising by North Carolina colonists against the British crown. In 1677 John Culpeper, a surveyor, led the colonists in a protest against British trade policies, which the colonists considered discriminatory. The colonists jailed the British governor and named Culpeper governor. He ruled until 1679, when the British reasserted authority. It is regarded as the first popular uprising in the American colonies.

Cultivator, agricultural implement used to chop or uproot weeds and loosen the soil in fields of crops. Cultivator is a general term applied to a myriad of implements that vary according to the crop, the development of the crop, and the soil. △310.

Cultural Lag, in anthropology, period of delay that occurs when an innovation that produces changes in some aspects of a culture requires adjustments in related areas in that culture. *See also* Culture.

Cultural Relativism, concept in anthropology that holds that the effects of a culture trait are relative to the rest of the culture. Particular practices in one culture fit in with the norms and values of that culture. Wife purchase, for example, may fit in a culture where values and institutions are in accord with it, but it will conflict with the values of other cultures.

Culture, in anthropology, all knowledge that is acquired by man by virtue of his membership in a society. A culture incorporates all the shared knowledge, expectations, and beliefs of a group. Culture in general distinguishes men from animals since only man can pass on accumulated knowledge due to his mastery of language and other symbolic systems. Only man develops and uses culture consistently in the form of tools. *See also* Anthropology, Cultural.

Culture-Fair Test, in psychology, an ability test that is not unfair to minority or ethnic groups. Traditional IQ tests have been criticized for their dependence on standard English for test instructions and questions. Culture-fair tests use pictures or symbols that give no one an advantage because of his or her linguistic or ethnic background. *See also* Intelligence Testing. △778.

Culver City, city in S California, SW of Los Angeles; center of motion picture industry since 1915. Industries: electronic and aerospace equipment. Inc. 1917. Pop. (1970) 34,526.

Cumae (Cuma), ancient town in SW Italy, W of Naples; thought to be oldest Greek colony in Italy or Sicily, founded about 750 BC; successfully repulsed the Etruscans; defeated by Samnites 5th century BC; under Roman control 338 BC; fortunes declined, and the town disappeared in AD 13th century; site has Greek and Roman ruins as well as cavern where the Cumaean Sibyl pronounced her prophesies.

Cumberland, city in NW Maryland, on the Potomac River; seat of Allegany co; site of Fort Cumberland (1755). Industries: coal mining, iron, steel, missile components. Inc. 1850. Pop. (1970) 29,724.

Cumberland Falls. *See* Great Falls.

Cumberland Gap, a mountain gap near the meeting point of Virginia, Kentucky, and Tennessee. It was discovered in 1850 and the Wilderness Road ran through it.

Cumberland Gap National Historical Park, region in the Cumberland Gap at junction of Virginia, Kentucky, and Tennessee borders; the Wilderness Road, forged by Daniel Boone, traverses the gap. Area: 20,176acres (8,171hectares). Est. 1940.

Cumberland River, river in Kentucky and Tennessee; rises in Cumberland Plateau in E Kentucky, flows SW through Kentucky and Tennessee to Nashville, turns NW to meet the Ohio River near Paducah, Ky. River's development for hydroelectric power and flood control is under jurisdiction of the Tennessee Valley Authority. Series of locks and canals make most of the river navigable for small craft. Barges move cargoes of petroleum, steel, chemicals, food, sand, gravel. Fort Donelson was built by Confederacy on the Cumberland River to protect Nashville, Tenn. U.S. Grant took the fort February 1862. Length: 687mi (1,106km).

Cumbria, county in NW England, formed 1974 from the former counties of Cumberland and Westmorland, and from parts of Lancashire and Yorkshire. It is bounded N by Solway Firth and W by Irish Sea; contains Lake District. Industries: agriculture, dairy farming, tourism. Administrative center is Carlisle. Area: 2,609sq mi (6,757sq km). Pop. 476,133.

Cumbrian Mountains, mountain range in NW England; extends through Cumberland, Westmorland, and N Lancashire; contains highest peak in England, Scafell Pike, 3,210ft (979m).

Cumin, a single species, *Cumin cyminum*, of annual herb native to the Middle East and widely cultivated for its seedlike fruit used as a food flavoring. It has a branching stem and small pink and white flowers. Height: to 6in (15cm). Family Umbelliferae.

cummings, e. e. (1894–1962), US poet, b. Edward Estlin Cummings in Cambridge, Mass. His first work, *The Enormous Room* (1922) was a novel. His poetry, usually exhibiting either sentimental emotion or cynical realism or a combination of both, is characterized by unconventional typography, spelling, and punctuation as well as other innovations. His verse includes *Tulips and Chimneys* (1923), *No Thanks* (1935), and *Poems, 1923–1954* (1954).

Cumulonimbus. △214.

Cunard, (Sir) Samuel (1787–1865), Canadian businessman. From a mercantile family, he showed early business aptitude and by 1838 owned 40 ships and monopolized several lucrative mail routes. His British and North American Royal Mail Steam Packet Company (1840) became the Cunard Line in 1878. After 1859, Cunard retired to England.

Cuneiform, most significant writing system in the ancient Near East. Used in the last three millenniums BC, it combined logographic and syllabic forms in wedge shaped pictographs. It also included numbers. △870–72.

Cunner, small marine food fish found in the North Atlantic. Related to the wrasse, it is brown, olive green, blue, or reddish. Length: to 17in (43cm); weight: 3lb (1.4kg). Family Labridae; species *Tautogolabrus adspersus* (American), *Crenilabrus melops* (English). *See also* Osteichthyes.

Cunobelinus. *See* Cymbeline.

Cup Fungus. △426.

Cupid, in Roman mythology, a winged boy armed with a bow and arrow. He is the equivalent of the Greek god Eros. Although primarily known for shooting arrows of passion, the Romans represented him as the pleasant sleep of death or a beneficent spirit.

Cuprite, or ruby copper, a secondary oxide mineral, cuprous oxide (Cu_2O). Found in oxidation zones of copper sulfide veins. Cubic system octahedral, dodecahedral, and cubic crystals and earthy masses. Red to black, brittle, translucent; hardness 3.5–4; sp gr 6.

Curaçao, largest island in Netherland Antilles in Dutch West Indies, in Caribbean Sea; contains natural bay, 18th-century Dutch-style houses, and pontoon bridge across St Anna Bay. Majority of inhabitants are descended from African slaves imported during the 17th and 18th centuries; original Arawak Indians are extinct. Capital is Willemstad. Industries: tourism, cement, tiles, paint, shipbuilding. Length: 36mi (58km). Width: 6mi (10km). Pop. 143,800.

Curare, dark brown resinous poisonous extract obtained from various tropical South American trees of the genera *Chondodendron* and *Strychnos*. It contains many alkaloids, notably D-tubocurarine, which is used as a muscle relaxant. It is used on the poisoned arrows of South American Indians. △744.

Curassow, large, crested, long-tailed, turkeylike game bird of Central and South American tropical forests. It feeds on forest matter and insects. The female lays white eggs (2–3) in a stick-and-leaf nest near the ground. These birds are considered a potential future meat source. Length: 20–40in (50–100cm). Family Cracidae, genera *Crax* and *Mitu*.

Curculio, small weevil with snouts, especially nut weevils and the plum curculio *(Conotrachelus nenuphar)*, a pest of plums, cherries, peaches, apricots, and apples. Family Curculionidae. *See also* Weevil.

Curia, political division of ancient Rome. It was composed of patrician and plebeian family units. Military service and electoral function came to be based on the curia. The term later came to refer to public meeting places. In medieval Europe it was used for the court. The modern papal court is still called the Curia.

Curie, Pierre and Marie Sklodowska. Pierre (1859–1906), a French physicist, became a professor at the Sorbonne. His early work concerned the electric and magnetic properties of crystals; he enunciated Curie's law relating magnetism and temperature. After marrying (1895) the Polish Marie Sklodowska (1867–1934), he joined in her work on radioactivity. Together they discovered radium and polonium in 1898 and were awarded a Nobel Prize in 1903 jointly with A.H. Becquerel. After Pierre's death in a road accident, Marie succeeded to his chair and received a second Nobel Prize (for chemistry) in 1911. △1482.

Curie, unit (symbol Ci) used to measure the activity of a radioactive substance, that is, the number of atoms that disintegrate in unit time. One curie is defined as 3.7×10^{10} disintegrations per second, roughly the activity of one gram of radium.

Curing. △380.

Curium, radioactive metallic element (symbol Cm) of the actinide group, first made (1940) by Glenn Seaborg and others by alpha-particle bombardment of Pu^{239}. Properties: at. no. 96; sp gr 13.5 (calc); melt. pt. 2444°F (1340°C); most stable isotope Cm^{244} (half-life 1.6×10^7yr). *See also* Transuranium Elements.

Curled Dock. △446.

Curlew, long-legged shorebird with long down-curved bill and mottled brown plumage. Often migrating long distances, it lives in open areas near water, feeds on small animals, insects, and seeds, and nests on the ground, laying 2–4 eggs. Length: 24in (61cm). Genus *Numenius*.

Curley, James Michael (1874–1958), US political figure, b. Boston. He was mayor of Boston five times (1914–18, 1922–26, 1930–34, 1937–39, 1946–50). Three of those terms preceded his term as governor of Massachusetts (1935–37). He served in Congress (1911–14, 1943–46). Convicted in 1946 of mail fraud, he served five months in jail. His sentence was commuted by President Truman and he completed his last term as mayor.

Curling, game that is the major winter sport of Scotland. It is also popular in Canada and the N United States. It may have originated as early as the 16th century. The game is played by two teams of four persons each on an ice surface 138ft (42m) long by 14ft (4.3m) wide. Each player has two circular stones —dished on bottom and top and having a top handle for the player's grip—which weigh from 40–44 pounds (18–20kg). Players are also provided with a crampit, or spiked metal plate, to get a foothold in the ice, and a broom to sweep the ice in front of the swerving stone. At each end of the ice is a circular target with an area in the center known as the "tee." The ice is sprinkled with water to make it pebbly. While a player sends his stone toward the tee, another player sweeps the surface in front to give the stone a smoother surface on which to ride. Each player delivers two stones, alternately with his opponent. One point is counted for each stone of one side that is closest to the tee. A game is 10 or 12 rounds (16 stones per round).

Curly-Coated Retriever, breed of dog (sporting group) unsurpassed as water retriever and one of the oldest retriever breeds. Brought to the US in 1907, this steady dog has a long head and jaw; small, close ears; short muscular body; long legs; and a short, straight, pointed tail. Its black or liver coat is crisply curled. Average size: 23in (58cm) high at shoulder; 65lb (29kg). *See also* Sporting Dog.

Currant, hardy, primarily deciduous shrub *(Ribes)* of the saxifrage family, native to cooler temperate regions of the Northern Hemisphere and South America. Their red or white fruit is eaten fresh or in preserves. *See also* Gooseberry.

Currency Act, or **Gold Standard Act** (1900), US legislation, passed after a long controversy, that established gold as the currency standard, reduced minimum requirements for bank capital, and extended the issuance of bank notes. It helped precipitate a financial crisis in 1907.

Currency Issue, general debate in the United States after the Civil War between supporters of hard money (backed by specie) and soft money (greenbacks, not backed by specie). Supporters of the Ohio Idea, a soft money plan, were repudiated in 1869 with the Public Credit Act providing for payment of government debt in gold.

Current Asset, in accounting, an asset that is ex-

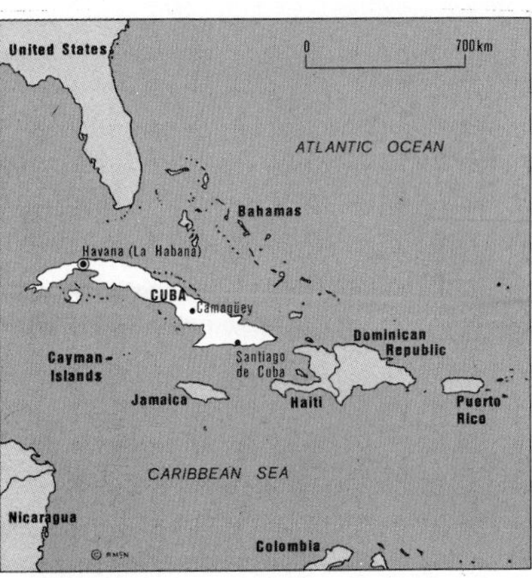
United States
0
700km
ATLANTIC OCEAN
Bahamas
Havana (La Habana)
CUBA
Camagüey
Cayman-
Islands
Santiago
de Cuba
Dominican
Republic
Jamaica
Haiti
Puerto
Rico
CARIBBEAN SEA
Nicaragua
Colombia
Cuba

Cumberland Gap National Park, Kentucky

e e cummings

Marie and Pierre Curie

pected to be used up within the particular company's operating cycle. Examples of current assets include ordinary trade receivables, cash, government securities held on a short-term basis, and trade inventories.

Current, Electric, rate of flow of electric charge through a conductor. Measured in amperes—a flow of some 10^{18} electrons per second being equivalent to one ampere. Direct current (D.C.) flows continuously in one direction, whereas alternating current reverses direction periodically. In the United States the power supply has a frequency (number of complete cycles) of 60 cycles per second (hertz), in the United Kingdom it is 50 hertz. The magnitude of an alternating current, I, at any instant, t, after the start of the cycle is given by: $I = Im \sin(2\pi ft)$, where f is the frequency, and Im is the maximum current. △1532, 1536, 1540–44.

Currents, Oceanic, broad slow drifts of water moving in a given direction. Surface currents flow around a gyre, clockwise in the Northern Hemisphere and counterclockwise in the Southern. Waters in a current are warmed at the equator, driven along by the prevailing surface winds, and then rotated partly by deflection at a coastline and partly by the Coriolis force. Oceans also have deep currents (density currents) caused by temperature and salinity variations. *See also* Coriolis Force; Gyre. △224.

Currier & Ives, 19th-century US firm of lithographers who published hand-colored prints of great commercial popularity and historic interest. Nathaniel Currier (1813–88) founded the business in New York about 1836 and became partners with James Merritt Ives (1824–95) in 1857. The company produced over 7000 lithographs of current events, rural and city scenes, sports, and still lifes.

Cursor Mundi (*c.* 1300), English poem of unknown authorship. Its 24,000 lines, written in a northern English dialect, tell the history of the world from creation to doomsday and are based somewhat on the English poet Caedmon's (died *c.* 680) paraphrase of Genesis. The first four books of the poem cover the events from creation to Solomon's successors; Book 5, the early lives of Mary and Jesus; Book 6, the later life of Jesus and the Apostles; and Book 7, the Last Judgment.

Curtis, Charles (1860–1936), US political leader, b. Indian Territory near Topeka, Kan. A lawyer, he served as a Republican in the House of Representatives (1893–1907) and Senate (1907–13, 1915–29), where he was party whip in the 1920s. He was vice president under Pres. Herbert Hoover (1929–33).

Curtis, Cyrus Hermann Kotzschmar (1850–1933), US publisher of *The Ladies Home Journal*, b. Portland, Me. He founded the Curtis Publishing Co. (1890). *The Ladies Home Journal* was a branch of the *Peoples Ledger Tribune* and *Farmer of Philadelphia* (1872), Curtis' first periodical. He also purchased *The Saturday Evening Post* (1897), which he quickly brought to fame. Eventually he purchased several other newspapers, including the New York *Evening Post* and the Philadelphia *Inquirer*, but none of these publications did as well as his magazines. He is also well known for his substantial contributions to charitable organizations.

Curtis, Samuel Ryan (1805–66), US soldier and engineer, b. Champlain, N.Y. After graduating from West Point (1831) he served as a civil engineer for road and river development projects. He served as a colonel in the war with Mexico and as a major general (1862) in the Civil War. He was also involved in negotiating treaties with the Indians (1865–66) and recorded the construction of the Union Pacific Railroad.

Curtiss, Glenn Hammond (1878–1930), US aviator, b. Hammondsport, N.Y. He began, as did the Wrights, building bicycles. By 1908 he was a member of the Aerial Experiment Association (AEA) and won a trophy for the first US flight of more than 1mi (1.6km). He built planes during World War I and his JN-4 or Jenny was a well-known trainer. Curtiss' company and that of the Wrights, after long patent rights lawsuits, merged to become the Curtiss-Wright Corporation.

Curtius, Quintus, early Roman historian, probably living and writing under Claudius. Nothing further is known of this man beyond his principal work, the *History of Alexander the Great.* This book represents the earliest example of Latin prose of non-Roman orientation.

Curvature of the Spine, abnormal deviation in the position of the spine, which normally has four gentle curves. There are three major types: scoliosis, or lateral curvature, which can be due to bad posture or to a prebirth abnormality; lordosis, an accentuation of the inward curve of the neck region or more commonly of the lower back region resulting in a swayback appearance; and kyphosis, an accentuation of the outward curve of the chest region, which in severe form can result in a hunchback appearance. *See also* Lordosis.

Curvilinear Function. △1452.

Curzon Line, demarcated by the League of Nations in 1919, established the Polish eastern frontier and awarded the city of Vilna to Lithuania and large areas to Russia. Poles invaded the USSR and recovered the territory. The Yalta Conference of 1945 recognized the Curzon line, however.

Curzon of Kedleston, George Nathaniel Curzon, 1st Marquess (1859–1925), English Conservative statesman. He entered parliament (1885) and traveled widely in the East before becoming viceroy of India (1899–1905). There he carried out many reforms before his resignation was engineered. Curzon served in the war cabinet (1915–19) and became foreign secretary (1919–24). △1266.

Cush, Kingdom of. *See* Kush, Kingdom of.

Cushing, Harvey (1869–1939), US surgeon, b. Cleveland, Ohio. His pioneering techniques for surgery on the brain and spinal cord helped advance neurosurgery. He also first described the syndrome produced by oversecretion of adrenal hormones that is now known as Cushing's syndrome.

Cushing's Syndrome, rare disease characterized by obesity of the body trunk, facial redness, and in women an increase in body hair and menstrual disturbances. The disease is often associated with high blood pressure, diabetes mellitus, brittle bones, and psychological disturbances. It is caused by an excessive amount of adrenal hormones, which can be produced by a tumor or some other cause, and occasionally by the administration of the drug cortisone. Treatment depends on the cause. △726.

Cushman, Pauline (1835–93), US actress and Union spy in the Civil War, b. New Orleans. While with an acting troup she was recruited by the Union. Cushman was eventually caught and sentenced to hang. She was freed by the Union takeover of Shelbyville, Tenn., and became a famous figure in the North as an actress and lecturer.

Cusk, bottom-dwelling marine fish found on both sides of the North Atlantic. A commercial fish, it is gray, red-brown, or pale yellow and has a long dorsal fin. Length: 3.5ft (106.7cm); weight: 27lb (12.2kg). Family Gadidae; species *Brosme brosme.*

Custard Apple, family of partially evergreen trees native to the Old World and grown in tropical and subtropical America. Leaves are lance-shaped, and yellow flowers produce large, red to brown, heart-shaped fruits with sweet, edible, custard-like pulp. Height: to 30ft (9m). Of the many species *Annona cherimolia*, the cherimoya, is most important. Family Annonaceae. *See also* Papaw. 340.

Custer, George Armstrong (1839–76), US military officer, b. New Rumley, Ohio. He graduated last in his West Point class (1861), but during the Civil War he became a major general in the Union army (1864). He was returned to a lower rank after the war. A striking figure, he went West to fight Indians after the Civil War and was made acting commander of the 7th Cavalry (1866). Court-martialed for disobeying orders, he was suspended from the service for a year (1867). When he returned, he led his men to a decisive victory over the Cheyenne chief Black Kettle at Washita River (1868). In 1876 he was sent to round up hostile Sioux and Cheyenne who were to meet with Sitting Bull. Outmaneuvered by the Indians, he was killed and his command wiped out in the Battle of Little Bighorn.

Custer Battlefield National Monument, historic area in SE Montana; site of Custer's Last Stand (June 25–26, 1876); a monument marks the graves of those killed during the battle. Authorized 1879. Area: 765acres (310hectares).

Custom, in anthropology and sociology, a pattern of habitual behavior characteristic of a particular group of people. For example: eating turkey on the last Thursday of each November is a custom in the United States. Customs are transmitted from generation to generation as the core of a group's culture, but they are not biologically determined and are basically impermanent. Customs tend to be maintained for longer periods in nonindustrial than in industrial societies. When customs are formally established in the religious or moral sphere, they lead to systems of ethics. When formally established as rights or duties, they lead to systems of laws. △896.

Customs Court, federal court having sole jurisdiction over decisions arising under tariff laws. With a presiding judge and eight judges, its sessions are held in New York City, and decisions can be appealed to US Court of Customs and Patent Appeals.

Cutaneous Senses. *See* Skin Senses.

Cuthbert (died 760), Archbishop of Canterbury (740–60), whose accomplishments include persuading King Ethelbald to confirm the privilege of the churches of Kent, bringing the conduct of the English church closer to that of the church at Rome, and establishing Christ Church, Canterbury, the burial place of archbishops, and hence the most important church in England.

Cuticle, horny outer layer of skin, popularly the skin around the fingers and toenails. *See also* Epidermis. △686.

Cutler, Manasseh (1742–1823), US cleric, b. Killingly, Conn. He was a founder of the Ohio Company the agency that colonized the Ohio Valley. Cutler helped draft the Ordinance of 1787, which brought law to the region once known as the Northwest Territory.

Cuttack, city in E India, on Manhanadi delta; capital of Orissa state; under Hindus, Moguls, and Marathas (during 16th and 17th centuries); transportation center with canal network. Industries: steel, glass, paper, flour milling, tobacco. Founded 925. Pop. 204,356.

Cutter, a small, fast-sailing boat with a single mast rigged fore and aft, carrying a mainsail and at least two headsails. Traditionally, the deep and narrow hull has a raking stern, a vertical stem, and a long bowsprit. *See also* Sloop.

Cutting, a piece of a plant used to start a complete new plant of the same kind. Like other methods of vegetative (asexual) propagation, cuttings have the advantage of producing plants that are genetically identical to the parent plants. Cuttings are most commonly taken from young stems, although leaves and pieces of root are used to propagate certain plants. The type of care required depends on the nature of the cutting. Cuttings of woody twigs, including apple and grape, are usually taken during the winter and stored under cool moist conditions until spring, when they are planted in soil to develop the root systems that will enable the cutting to develop into new plants.

Cutting Tools. △1602.

Cuttlefish. *See* Squid.

Cutworm, nocturnal moth caterpillar that feeds on plants, often cutting through the stems at ground level. They are dull-colored. Length: to 2in (5cm). Family Noctuidae.

Cuvier, Georges, (Baron de) (1769–1832), French geologist and zoologist, a founder of the disciplines of comparative anatomy and paleontology. His scheme of classification stressed the form of organs and their correlation within the body. He applied this system of classification to fossils and came to reject the theory of the gradual development of the earth and animals, favoring instead a theory of catastrophic changes.

Cuvillies (or Cuvilles), François de, the Elder (1698–1767), French architect and decorator. In Munich he was in the service of Maximilian Emanuel, elector of Bavaria. In 1745 he became first architect to the court. His rich, decorative interiors were greatly influenced by the French rococo style. Among his many works are the Amalienburg hunting pavilion of the Nymphenburg Palace, the gardens and buildings of the Munich Residenz, the Antiquarium, and the Opera. His last work was the facade of the Theatinerkirche. △1190.

Cuyahoga Falls, city in NE Ohio, on Cuyahoga River, 5mi (8km) N of Akron. Industries: machinery, rubber products, tools, paper products. Inc. 1920. Pop. (1970) 49,678.

Cuyahoga River, river in Ohio; rises in NE Ohio, flows SW then N, empties into Lake Erie at Cleveland. Length: approx. 100mi (161km).

Cuza, Alexandru Ioan (1820–73), Romanian ruler, prince of Walachia and Moldavia. After the Russian defeat in the Crimean War, the Turkish sultan recognized Cuza, who was a fairly unknown colonel but had been elected prince in 1859. In 1862 the union of the two principalities was permitted and the resulting entity called Romania. Cuza's domestic reforms included emancipation of the peasantry and establishment of institutions of higher learning. Scandals in Cuza's private life led to his overthrow in 1866. △1232.

Cuzco, city in S central Peru, 350mi (564km) SE of Lima; capital of Cuzco dept.; agricultural trade center. Ancient capital of Inca Empire, it is center of archeological research in South America; nearby sites include the fortress of Sacsahuaman, Inca terraces at Pisac, and the Inca city of Machu Picchu. Founded *c.* AD 1100; at height of development (1500) empire extended from Argentina (S) to Colombia (N); fell to Spaniards 1533. Pop. 105,400.

CWA. *See* Civil Works Administration.

Cyanide, salt or ester of hydrocyanic acid (HCN). They are all intensely poisonous, the most important, sodium cyanide (NaCN), is used in electroplating, the heat treatment of metals, and as an insecticide. △1572.

Cyanocobalamin. *See* Vitamin B_{12}.

Cybele, in Greek mythology, the goddess of caverns. She personified the earth in its primitive state and was worshiped on the tops of mountains. She exercised dominion over the wild beasts who formed part of her retinue.

Cybernetics, mathematical theory for optimizing control and communication systems originated by the US mathematician Norbert Weiner in 1948. The theory covers a number of disciplines including computers, learning theory, physiology of the nervous system, servomechanisms, automatic control systems, and the theory of communications. It enables comparison to be made between the problems of control, communication, and feedback of information in biological and engineering systems and has been successfully applied to the design of automated factory processes. △1670.

Cycad, also called sago-palm, family of primitive, seed-bearing, palmlike shrub and tree; found in tropical and subtropical regions. These plants flourished 125–150 million years ago. Feathery leaves crown a stout, columnar stem. Leaves of most species are poisonous. An edible starch is made from the pith of some. Most of the 90 surviving species are under 20ft (6.1m) tall and include *Dion spinulosum* of the Mexican rain forest and the Cuban corcho *Microcycas calocoma* that produces 2-ft (0.6-m) cones. Family Cycadaceae. △440.

Cyclades (Kiklâdhes), large island group off S Greece, in S Aegean Sea; dept. of Greece; capital is Hermoupolis. Name was derived from Greek "kyklos," meaning cluster, because the islands encircle island of Delos. During Middle Ages, most of the islands were inc. into the Venetian Duchy of the Archipelago; annexed to Greece 1832. Islands are very mountainous, and rich in mineral deposits. Industries: tourism, mining, agriculture. Area: 993sq mi (2,572sq km). Pop. 86,084.

Cyclamates, white odorless soluble crystalline salts, calcium cyclamate $(C_6H_{11}NHSO_3)_2(Ca \cdot 2H_2O)$ and sodium cyclamate $(C_6H_{11}NHSO_3Na)$, with a very sweet taste. They have about 30 times the sweetening power of sucrose.

Cyclamen, genus of 20 species of low-growing perennial herbs, native to Central Europe and the Mediterranean region and grown widely by florists. They have tuberous roots, and heart- or kidney-shaped leaves, often marbled or ribbed. The drooping blooms are white, pink, lilac or crimson. Family Primulaceae.

Cycle in electricity, series of changes through which an alternating current passes. Starting from zero it rises through a sine wave to a maximum, declines sinusoidally to zero, declines similarly to a minimum, and climbs back to zero again. The frequency of the current is the number of such cycles in one second. This is measured in hertz (cycles per second). △1544.

Cyclohexane. △1558.

Cycloid. △1454.

Cyclometer. △1538.

Cyclone, a system of winds or storm that rotates inward around a center of low atmospheric pressure, counterclockwise in the Northern Hemisphere and clockwise in the Southern Hemisphere, the opposite of anticyclones centered in high-pressure areas. Tropical cyclones, originating near the equator, give rise to hurricanes when strong enough. Although having the same spiral motions, cyclones are distinguished from small-scale systems like tornadoes and waterspouts. *See also* Tornado. △214.

Cyclopedia. △1780.

Cyclopropane, colorless gas used as an anesthetic during surgery.

Cyclops, common freshwater predatory copepod crustacean. Transparent and bullet-shaped, it is named for its large median eye. Gravid females carry two large egg sacs. Length: under 1/16in (1.6mm). *See also* Copepod; Crustacean. △486.

Cyclops, various figures in Greek mythology. According to Homer, they were one-eyed cannibal giants in Sicily. In Hesiod, they were Arges, Brontes, and Steropes, the three sons of Heaven and Earth. Cyclops were considered by later authors to be the workmen of Haphaestus, who made the thunderbolt that killed Asclepius.

Cyclostome, or cyclostomata, class of jawless fish including lamprey and hagfish, found in temperate-to-cold waters of Northern and Southern hemispheres at depths of 98.4–3280.8 ft. (30–1000m). These fish have jawless sucking mouths with sharp teeth and no bones, scales, paired fins, or sympathetic nervous systems. Their eellike bodies are supported by cartilage and an unsegmented notochord (skeletal rod). Respiration is through gill pouches. Fertilization is external. There are about 45 species of Cyclostomes. △508.

Cyclothymic Personality, personality pattern disturbance in which mood fluctuations of sadness and elation are common in a normally extroverted and outgoing person. This lifelong personality pattern is highly resistant to change with life experience or therapy. Though the moodiness may at times be severe, disturbances of cognitive functioning or of orientation to reality rarely occur.

Cyclotron, earliest field accelerator (1932) in which charged particles describe a spiral path inside two evacuated D-shaped chambers at right angles to a fixed magnetic field. A high-frequency electric field between the chambers accelerates the particles each time they cross the gap, the radius of the path increasing with velocity. The beam is deflected out of the device by a second electric field. Maximum energy is about 25 MeV. *See also* Synchrocyclotron. △1486.

Cygnus, the Swan, or the Northern Cross, extensive northern constellation situated between Draco and Pegasus and including five conspicuous stars in the shape of a cross. Cygnus contains the open cluster M39 (NGC 7092) and two important radio sources, Cygnus A and the Cygnus Loop. Brightest star Alpha Cygni (Deneb). △110, 130.

Cygnus Loop, composite bright nebula located in the constellation Cygnus. It is made up of several separately catalogued portions, including the Veil Nebula (NGC 6992/5), and appears as wispy filaments forming roughly circular arcs. The Cygnus Loop is an ancient supernova remnant and a powerful source of radio waves and X rays. △106.

Cylinder, solid figure or surface formed by rotating a rectangle about one side as axis. If the vertical height is h and the radius of the base r, then the volume is $\pi r^2 h$ and the curved surface area $2\pi rh$. △1466.

Cylinder, Engine, one of the cylindrical chambers in internal combustion engines. Inside each, a piston is impelled by the pressure of the expansive force of combusting fuel and, in 4-stroke engines, by the recoil of another piston.

Cylon, Athenian noble who tried but failed to establish tyranny in Athens (632 BC) by seizing the Acropolis. Many of his men were executed on the sacred altar of Athena, a highly sacrilegious and scandalous event.

Cymbal, saucer-shaped, concave percussion instrument of brass, usually without definite pitch. It is played by clashing together a pair held in both hands, or by striking a suspended cymbal with a beater. Introduced with Turkish martial music (*c.* 1750), it is used in symphonic and jazz works.

General George Custer

Cuzco, Peru

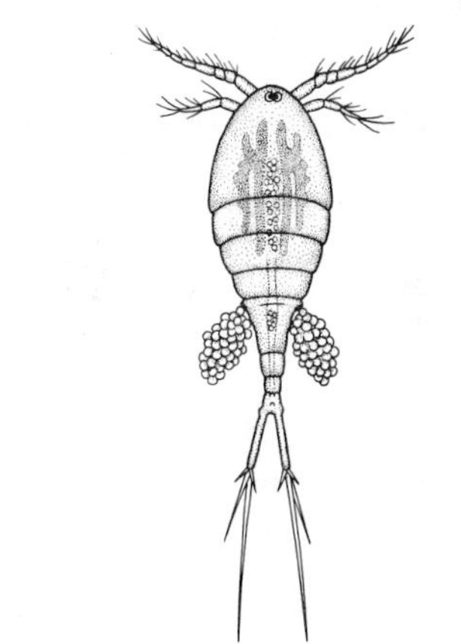

Cyclops

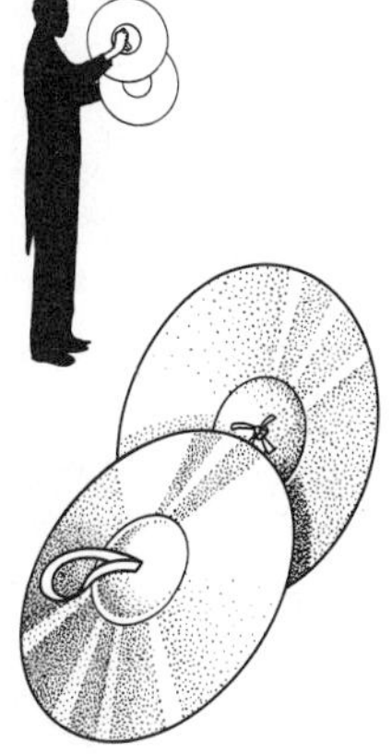

Cymbals

Cymbeline, or Cunobelinus, (died *c.* AD40), ancient British king. Inheriting the chieftainship of the Catuvellauni from his father, he established his capital at Colchester. Shakespeare used his name but invented his history in *Cymbeline*.

Cymbeline (1610), 5-act play by William Shakespeare. Based on Holinshed's *Chronicles* and Boccaccio's *Decameron*, the play is quasihistorical. King Cymbeline of ancient Britain banishes Posthumus for marrying Cymbeline's daughter Imogen against the king's wishes. Through trickery Posthumus loses a wager on Imogen's fidelity with the crafty Lachimo and sends to have Imogen killed, but she escapes. In the course of Cymbeline's preparations for a war against Rome, the complications of the plot are resolved.

Cymbidium, orchid native to tropical Asia. An epiphyte (grows on other plants), it is generally ivory white or dull purple. There are 70 species and several thousand horticultural hybrids. Among them is *Cymbidium hookerianum*, which has a large green flower with a yellow and purple-spotted large lower petal or lip. Family Orchidaceae.

Cynewulf (*fl.* 800), English poet. Presumed author of *Elene, Fates of the Apostles, The Ascension*, and *Juliana*, because the manuscript of these poems are "signed" *Cynewulf* in runic characters. Internal evidence suggests he was a priest in Mercia or Northumbria in the north of England. Cynewulf's work shows a clarity of narrative unusual in Old English poetry.

Cypress, city in S California, 9mi (14km) NE of Long Beach. Inc. 1956. Pop. (1970) 31,894.

Cypress, evergreen tree native to North America and Eurasia. They have scalelike leaves, roundish cones, a distinctive symmetrical shape, and prefer warmer climates. Height: 20–150ft (6–46m). Family Cupressaceae; genus *Cupressus*.

Cypripedium, or lady's slipper, moccasin flower; orchid found in bogs and swamps of North America, China, and Europe. The lowest petal, or lip, is large, slipperlike, and colored pink, yellow, or white. The leaves are broad and shiny. Species include *Cypripedium acaule*, lady's slipper; *C. reginae*, moccasin flower; and *C. arietinum*, the ram's head. Height: to 3ft (0.9m). Family Orchidaceae.

Cyprus, Republic of, an island nation in the E Mediterranean Sea. The Cypriot population is made up mostly of Greeks (78%) and Turks (18%). The two groups have inhabited the island for centuries, living for the most part under foreign domination. Established as an independent republic in 1960, Cyprus continued to be marked by internal strife between its Greek and Turkish citizens.

Land and Economy. The Troodos Mts occupy the S and W half of the island. Except for a narrow coastal mountain range in the N, the rest of Cyprus consists of fertile lowlands, sometimes called the Mesaorian Plain. The climate of Cyprus is typical of the Mediterranean area, with mild winters and hot, dry summers. The economy depends for its stability on agriculture, which employs about one-third of the Cypriot work force. Agriculture also supplies raw materials to local industry and accounts for half of all exports. The per capita income of Cyprus is the highest in the E Mediterranean, except for Israel.

People. The Greek Cypriots trace their ancestry back to Mycenaean Greek settlements in the 2nd millennium BC The ancestors of of the Turkish Cypriots arrived after the Turkish conquest of Cyprus in 1571. Both groups are fiercely exclusive. The Greeks are Christians belonging to the Cyprus Orthodox Church, while the Turks are Muslims. There is no intermarriage and very little socializing between the two groups. Consequently, no sense of national unity or purpose has developed. Many Cypriots speak both Greek and Turkish, and the English language is in widespread use. For both groups, the extended family is the main social unit.

Government. The constitution provides for a president elected by the Greek majority, a vice-president elected by the Turkish minority, and a house of representatives that is 70% Greek and 30% Turkish. The constitution is the law of the republic and guarantees the rights of all Cypriots. Archbishop Makarios served as first president of the republic. In 1960, Great Britain, Greece, and Turkey agreed to serve as guarantors of Cypriot security, either unilaterally or collectively.

History. For nearly 3,000 years Cyprus has been controlled by the dominant power in the area, from the ancient Phoenicians to the British of modern times. After three centuries of Turkish administration, Cyprus was leased from Turkey by the British in 1878. Great Britain annexed Cyprus at the start of WWI. The Greek Cypriots had for years demanded union with Greece; the campaign increased in violence after WWII. In the 1950s, Greek Cypriot guerrillas carried out attacks on the British military. The governments of Greece and Turkey negotiated a settlement in Zurich in 1959, which was then approved by the British. The republic was est Aug. 16, 1960. Intercommunal fighting broke out sporadically in the 1960s. UN troops were installed in 1964; however, severe conflicts followed when Greece injected troops of its own in 1967. Tension abated as Greece and Turkey reconciled differences, but Turkey then invaded the island in 1974. The action was condemned internationally, but Turkish forces remained on the island, ostensibly to protect the Turkish minority.

PROFILE

Official name: Republic of Cyprus
Area: 3,572sq mi (9,251sq km)
Population: 659,000
Density: 176per sq mi (68per sq km)
Chief cities: Nicosia (capital); Limassol; Famagusta
Government: Republic
Religion: Eastern Orthodox, Muslim
Language: Greek and Turkish (both official)
Monetary unit: Cyprus pound
Gross national product: $400,000,000
Per capita income (1971): $650
Industries (major products): cotton, rayon, shoes, soap
Agriculture (major products): wheat, barley, potatoes, citrus fruit
Minerals (major): iron pyrites, asbestos, copper
Trading partners (major): United Kingdom

Cyrankiewicz, Józef (1911–), Polish politician and premier (1947–52, 1954–70). Secretary of the Socialist party in Cracow in 1935, Cyrankiewicz was taken prisoner by the Germans in 1939, escaped and organized a resistance movement, but was sent to Auschwitz in 1941. He succeeded Boleslaw Bierut as premier in 1954.

Cyrano de Bergerac, Savinien (1619–55), French writer. He became renowned for his free thinking, humor, and burlesque romances. His works included two prose fantasies, *Journey to the Moon* (1656) and *The Comical Tale of the States and Empires of the Sun* (1662), published posthumously. He was the model for Edmond Rostand's Cyrano.

Cyrano de Bergerac (1897), 5-act drama by Edmond Rostand. First performed in Paris, it remains popular today and has been made into a film (1950) and a TV play (1975). Cyrano, afflicted with an enormous nose, writes love letters to Roxane for his handsome friend Christian, although he loves her himself. When Christian is killed in battle, Roxane enters a convent. She finds out about Cyrano's love for her years later on the day he is killed by an enemy.

Cyrenaica (Barqah), easternmost section of Libya, formerly a province (1951–63); colonized by the Greeks 7th century BC and taken by Rome 96 BC, it formed part of the Ottoman Empire after 16th century; was colonized by Italians in 1930s; scene of many WWII battles. Industries: oil, citrus fruit, sheep and goat raising. Area: 330,258sq mi (855,368sq km). Pop. 350,024.

Cyrenaic School, a school of hedonistic philosophy founded by Aristippus (*fl.* late 4th and early 3rd century BC). Maintaining that happiness lies not in slavery to, but in mastery over, pleasure, this school disappeared before the advance of Epicureanism.

Cyrene (Shahhat), ancient city in NE Libya, 6mi (10km) from Marsa Susa; founded 630 BC under the Greek dynasty of Battus I as the capital of Cyrenaica; annexed to Persian Empire 525 BC, to Egypt 322 BC, and to Rome 96 BC; conquered by Arabs AD 642. Libyan excavations have uncovered many ruins, notably the temples of Apollo and Zeus. Pop. 6,266.

Cyrene, in Greek mythology, queen of Cyrene, mother by Apollo of Aristaeus and Idmon. Apollo fell in love with Cyrene when he saw her wrestle a lion that had attacked her father's flock. She was also the mother by Ares of Diomedes and Thrace.

Cyrus the Great (*c.* 600–529 BC), king of Persia, founder of the Achaemenid dynasty and the Persian empire. He took over Media, defeated and captured king Croesus of Lydia (c 546 BC), and captured Babylon (538 BC) and the Greek cities in Asia Minor. He delivered the Jews from their captivity, giving them Palestine to rule. He failed to conquer Egypt under Amasis II. In the Bible, he is called God's appointed servant (Isaiah 40–48). While fighting the Massagets, a tribe northwest of the Caspian, he was defeated and killed. His son, Cambyses, succeeded him. △984.

Cyrus the Younger (*c.* 424–401 BC), Persian satrap, son of Darius II. After plotting unsuccessfully to kill his brother Artaxerxes II, king of Persia, he hired Greek mercenaries, who helped him defeat the king at Cunaxa. Cyrus, however, died in battle. The retreat of the Ten Thousand (mercenaries) under Clearchus, Spartan ruler of Byzantium, is told in Xenophon's *Anabasis*.

Cyst, abnormal growth in the form of a sac that contains solid or liquid material produced by the cells in the walls of the sac. It may occur in a glandular organ, such as breast or prostate, or in the skin.

Cysteine, crystalline amino acid (formula $HS{\cdot}CH_2{\cdot}NH_2{\cdot}COOH$) that occurs in most proteins. *See* Amino Acid. △1574.

Cystic Fibrosis, hereditary disease, first appearing in childhood, in which the body produces abnormally thick mucus that often obstructs the breathing passages, causing chronic lung disease. There is also a deficiency of pancreatic enzymes and an abnormally high salt concentration in the sweat. There is no cure; the disease is treated with antibiotics, salt replacement, and special diet to reduce the need for pancreatic enzymes, but is often fatal in childhood.

Cystitis, acute or chronic infection of the urinary bladder, more common in women, usually caused by bacteria. Symptoms include frequency of urination, burning during and after voiding, difficulty in voiding, low back pain, and slight fever. Treatment consists of antibiotics and increased fluid intake.

Cytochrome. △1574.

Cytology, biological study of living cells, including structure, function, and significance. △412.

Cytoplasm, jellylike, non-particulate matter within a cell membrane, exclusive of the nucleus. *See also* Cell. △412.

Cytosine, a base (nonacid) that is one of the components of deoxyribonucleic and ribonucleic acid (DNA, RNA).

Czartoryski, noble Polish family of Lithuanian origin. Early members of the family were hostile to Poland. By the end of the 16th century, however, they had begun to view the Polish-Lithuanian union favorably, and by the 18th century, under the Saxon kings, they virtually ruled Poland.

Czartoryski, Adam Jerzy (1770–1861), Polish political figure, the most renowned member of his prominent family. Seeking the restoration of his family's property confiscated in an insurrection against Russia (1794), he became an adviser to the future Czar Alexander I (r.1801–25), with whom he later became disillusioned. He was deputy foreign minister of Russia (1802–04), foreign minister (1804–06), Polish spokesman at the Congress of Vienna (1815), and member of the executive council (1815–30). He became president of the revolutionary government of Poland during the insurrection of 1830 and went into exile in Paris in 1831 after the suppression of the revolt by the Russians. His residence was the political center of Polish exiles until his death.

Czartoryski, Adam Kazimierz (1734–1823), Polish nobleman. The son of Fryderyk Michal Czartoryski, he became a publisher and minister of education for Poland—the first such minister in the world—and made his palace at Pulawy a center of cultural life. His son was Adam Jerzy Czartoryski.

Czartoryski, Aleksander August (1697–1782), Polish nobleman. The son of Kazimierz Czartoryski and brother of Fryderyk Michal Czartoryski (1696–1775), he was governor of Ruthenia. When his and his brother's attempts to reform the Polish constitution failed, he became politically estranged from King Augustus III. After the death of Augustus (1763), he and his brother gained the support of Russia's Catherine II and made their nephew Stanislas Augustus Poniatowski king.

Czartoryski, Wladyslaw (1828–94), Polish political figure and archivist. The son of Adam Jerzy Czartoryski, he sought to carry on his father's work for Polish independence by serving as chief representative abroad of the Polish revolutionary government during the anti-Russian insurrection of 1863. He founded the important Czartoryski Museum in Cracow in 1876.

Czech, language spoken in the western and central two-thirds of Czechoslovakia—the areas known as Bohemia and Moravia—by about 10 million people. A Slavic language, it is closely related to Slovak, spoken in the eastern third of the country.

Czechoslovakia, nation in central Europe, member of the Communist Bloc. The country was formed in 1918 of the former Austro-Hungarian provinces of Bohemia, Moravia, Slovakia, and Ruthenia. The Czechs occupy the W area, Bohemia and Moravia, while the Slovaks inhabit the E. The Czechs and Slovaks have a common ancestry and language and were reunited with the formation of the Czechoslovak Republic.

Land and Economy. The historic province of Bohemia is a fertile plain nearly encircled by the Ore Mts and the Moravian Hills. Prague lies in the center of this important region. Moravia, also in the W, is a fertile lowland area extending to the Carpathian Mts of Slovakia. The country's industry is well-developed, and employs about 60% of the entire work force. Heavy industry is dominant, as in the production of iron and steel, heavy machinery, and motor vehicles. All industry is nationalized. Prague has an international airport. Bratislava, the capital of Slovakia, has developed as a port on the Danube River. Czechoslovakia is the most prosperous country in E Europe.

People. The population is about 65% Czech and the rest Slovak. The Czech and Slovak languages have separate cultural histories and literatures but are mutually intelligible. The language is Slavonic. More than 80% of the population of the country is Roman Catholic. The Communist regime confiscated church property in 1949, and subsequently discouraged all church activities. The majority of Czechoslovaks today still live in small communities.

Government. The constitution of 1960 provides for a legislature, the National Assembly, elected by the people. The president of the republic is chosen by the assembly, and in turn appoints the premier and his cabinet. The entire government, however, is controlled by the Communist party through its large central committee and 21-member presidium.

History. The Slavs who settled the land in the AD 5th century developed the Moravian empire. Slovakia was conquered AD 900 and ruled by the Magyars (Hungarians) for 1,000 years. Bohemia was a kingdom within the Holy Roman Empire, and later the Austrian Empire. Czech nationalism developed in the 19th century. When Austria-Hungary collapsed in 1918, Czechoslovakia was established as an independent country with T. G. Masaryk as president. In 1938–39, Britain and France permitted Nazi Germany to seize the country. Eduard Beneš returned with his government-in-exile in 1945 when the Allied armies liberated Czechoslovakia. The Communist party gained control in 1948. The government took over all phases of Czech life—farming, business, industry, churches, and schools. Under Alexander Dubček, the government introduced a series of liberal anti-Soviet reforms in 1968. The Soviet Union and its allies—Poland, East Germany, Hungary, and Bulgaria—interfered militarily and ousted Dubček.

PROFILE

Official name: Czechoslovak Socialist Republic
Area: 49,365sq mi (127,855sq km)
Population: 14,634,747
Density: 296per sq mi (114per sq km)
Chief cities: Prague (capital); Brno; Bratislava
Government: Communist
Religion: Roman Catholic 65%; Protestant 35%
Language: Czechoslovak
Monetary unit: Koruna
Gross national product: $41,200,000,000.
Industries (major products): machinery, chemicals, textiles, military equipment
Agriculture (major products): wheat, barley, potatoes, sugar beets
Minerals (major): coal, iron ore, graphite, copper
Trading partners (major): Soviet Union, East Germany, Poland, West Germany

Czerny. △1196.

Czestochowa, city in S Poland, on Warta River, approx. 125mi (201km) SW of Warsaw; site of ancient monastery on Jasna Gosa (Mountain of Light) containing image of the Virgin painted by St Luke (14th century), which was successfully defended against Sweden (1655, 1702) and became a symbol of national strength and unity. City was taken by Germany in WWI and WWII. Industries: iron works, textiles, paper mills. Pop. 187,600.

Czolgosz, Leon (1873–1901), US anarchist, b. Detroit, Mich. He shot and mortally wounded President McKinley (Sept. 6, 1901) at the Pan-American Exposition in Buffalo, N.Y. Czolgosz was immediately apprehended and later executed.

Czuczor, Gergely (1800–66), Hungarian philologist and poet. He helped compile a dictionary of his native language that was published in 1861. Czuczor, a Benedictine monk, was imprisoned for writing *The Alarm* (1848), a poem that exhorted Hungarians to cast off Austrian rule.

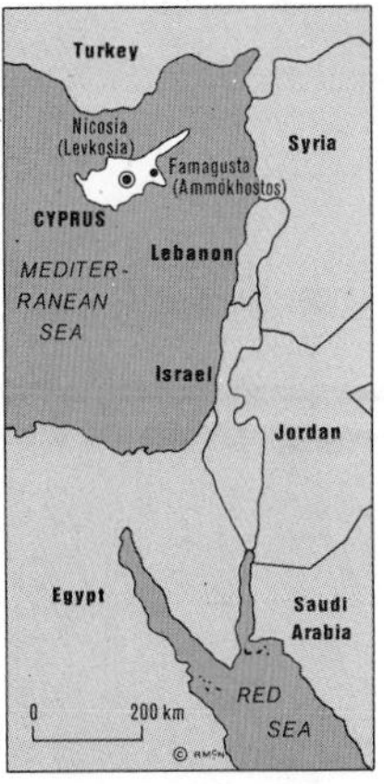
Turkey
Nicosia
(Levkosia)
Famagusta
(Ammokhostos)
Syria
CYPRUS
Lebanon
MEDITER-
RANEAN
SEA
Israel
Jordan
Egypt
Saudi
Arabia
RED
SEA
0
200 km
Cyprus

Cyrenaica, Libya

Denmark
BALTIC SEA
U.S.S.R.
German
Democratic
Republic
Poland
Prague
(Praha)
Federal
Republic of
Germany
Pilsen
(Plzeň)
Ostrava
Brno
CZECHOSLOVAKIA
Košice
Bratislava
Liech.
Austria
Hungary
Romania
Italy
Yugoslavia
0
400 km
Czechoslovakia

D

Dab. △516.

Dabag, among the ancient Serbs, the supreme god, the same as the Slavic god Svetovid. Dabag was originally represented as the god of the underworld and depicted as a wolf. He also ruled the herd and protected mines and metals. With the advent of Christianity he became the adversary of God, Svetovid, or the devil, who is today called Daba.

Dabrowski, Jan Henryk (English form Dombrowski) (1755–1818), Polish general. After serving in the 1792 and 1794 campaigns against Russia, he allied with France, forming the Polish legion for Napoleon (1798). He fought in Italy (1801), against Austria (1807), and in the 1812–13 Russian campaigns. After Napoleon's defeat, Dabrowski was appointed general of the cavalry and senator palatine of Poland (1815).

Dacca, port city and capital of Bangladesh, 80mi (129km) NE of Khulna, just W of Meghna River; scene of Pakistani surrender to Indian troops in 1971; location of University of Dacca and University of Engineering and Technology. Industries: jute, carpets, boatbuilding, textiles, soap, rubber goods, jewelry. Pop. 362,006.

Dace, freshwater fish found in S and E United States. A minnow with a large head and mouth, its sides are marked with a red stripe bordered by two darker stripes. Length: to 11.8in (30cm). Family Cyprinidae; genera include *Phoxinus, Chrosomus,* and *Leuciscus.*

Dachshund, German hunting dog (hound group) used to follow badgers to earth; one of the most popular breeds. Its head is tapered and long; rounded, hanging ears are set near the top of the head. The long body is set on short legs; a medium-long tail is carried in line with the back. There are three varieties of coat: short-haired, wire-haired, and long-haired; colors include solid red; black, chocolate, gray, or white with tan marks; and dappled. Average size: 5–9in (13–23cm) high at shoulder; 5–20lb (2–9kg). *See also* Hound.

Dacia, ancient kingdom comprising the heartland of present-day Romania. King Decebalus of Dacia heroically fought off the Romans until defeated by Trajan in 106. Roads, bridges, and a great wall were built by the Romans, who evacuated the province in 270 when faced by barbarian invasions. Latin speech was preserved, however. While the area was under Bulgarian rule, Christianity was introduced during the 9th century. △1020.

Dacron, man-made, long-chain polyester fiber made from glycol and terephthalic acid. It has high elastic recovery and low moisture absorption and is not combustible, but melts at about 500°F (260°C). Used extensively in rope and in permanent-press fabrics. △1620.

Dada or **Dadaism,** movement in literature and the visual arts, which was started in Zurich in 1916 by a group of international artists, including Tristan Tzara, Marcel Janco, Richard Huelsenbeck, Hugo Ball, Jean (Hans) Arp, and others. The group, repelled by war and bored with the prevalent cubist art styles, promulgated complete nihilism, satire, and disgust with and ridicule of civilization. Emphasis was given to the illogical or absurd, and the importance of chance in artistic creation was exaggerated. Adherents of the movement participated in antisocial behavior designed to shock a complacent public. No specific artistic style evolved, but Arp tried to develop the cubist techniques of montage and collage. △1318.

Daddy-longlegs. *See* Harvestman.

Daedalus, in Greek mythology, architect and sculptor. In order to escape from King Minos' disfavor, Daedalus made wings of feathers and wax for himself and his son Icarus. Icarus' wings melted when he flew too close to the sun. He fell into the Icarian sea and drowned.

Daffodil. *See* Narcissus.

Dagger-sword (Hittite). △1592.

Dagobert I (died 639), Merovingian king of the Franks (628–39). He maintained the conquests of his father, Clotaire II.

Daguerre, Louis Jacques Mandé (1787–1851), French painter and inventor of daguerreotypy, an early process whereby a delicate photographic image is produced on a silver-coated copper plate developed with iodine vapor. A painter of stage sets, in 1829 he joined Nicéphore Niepce in photographic experiments. Their process was announced and ceded to the public in 1839 at the same time that William Fox Talbot announced calotypy in England. △1784.

Dahlberg, Erik, Count (1625–1703), Swedish soldier, architect, and graphic artist who distinguished himself as a military engineer in Sweden's war with Denmark (1676–79) and later in the Great Northern War (1700–22). He was responsible for the construction and rebuilding of many forts. His best-known work is the architectural illustrations for *Sweden Ancient and Modern* published 1717.

Dahlia, genus of popular, late-blooming, tender, tuberous-rooted perennial plants, native to mountainous areas of Mexico and Guatemala. They range from low-growing dwarfs to "trees" more than 20ft (6m) tall. The common or garden dahlia *(D. pinnata)* has been developed into more than 2,000 varieties with a wide range of flower head forms—usually white, yellow, red, purple, or bicolored. Height: 4–5ft (1.2–1.5m). Family Compositae. △446.

Dahlia Anemone. △468.

Dahomey, nation in W Africa. *See* Benin.

Daigo II. △1210.

Daimler, Gottlieb. △1692.

Daimyo, local leaders in Japan who came to power with the decline of the central government during the feudalistic Ashikaga period. They maintained their power through military strength, like the European feudal barons.

Dairy Cattle, varieties or breeds of domesticated cattle raised mainly for milk production. Cows have large udders and convert most of their food into milk far in excess of that needed for nursing calves. Farmers wean calves a few days after birth; females are raised as replacement stock, most males butchered for meat. Dairy breeds are specialized to produce either a great volume of milk or milk rich in butterfat. The most common dairy breeds are: Holstein, Jersey, Guernsey, Ayrshire, and Brown Swiss. Family Bovidae; species *Bos taurus. See also* Cattle; Dairy Farming. △372.

Dairy Farming, production of milk and its products. Through management of dairy cows and cultivation of feed crops, an efficient kind of farming is carried on, with manure replacing nutrients taken from soil by food crops. Modern dairying with cows fed from silage reduces the seasonal aspects. US dairy breeds include Holstein, Guernsey, Jersey, Ayrshire, Brown Swiss, and Shorthorn. △370–372.

Dairy Products. △372–74.

Daisy, any of several members of the compositae family, especially the oxeye daisy *(Chrysanthemum leucanthemum),* a hardy Eurasian perennial widely naturalized in North America. It has 2in (5cm) flowers with yellow central disks and white ray flowers. Height: 1–3ft (31–92cm). △444.

Dakar, capital and largest city in Senegal, W Africa, on S tip of Cape Vert, on Atlantic coast; grew rapidly after the completion of railroad leading to Senegal River 1855; site of Roman Catholic cathedral and presidential palace; a modern city with excellent educational and medical facilities, including Pasteur Institute. Industries: peanut oil, sugar refining, fertilizers, cement. Founded 1857 as French fort; named capital of Senegal 1958. Pop. 580,000.

Dakota Indians, more commonly known as Sioux, North American Indian tribe now inhabiting the northern plains, mainly North and South Dakota, and eastern Montana, where they migrated from Minnesota, Wisconsin, and Iowa. The tribe has three major divisions: the Santee Dakota, Yankton Dakota, and Teton Dakota. They were noted for their military prowess, and were one of the largest tribes of Indians. Their culture is regarded as the typical "Indian" form in the United States. The present population is approximately 40,000 Sioux living in United States, plus another 5,000 in Canada.

Daladier, Edouard (1884–1970), French statesman, Radical party leader, and minister of war. Prime minister in 1933, 1934, and in 1938–40, he signed the Munich pact in 1938 and declared war on Germany a year later. Impounded by the Vichy government and deported to Germany, he later opposed the Indochina war.

Dalai Lama, ruler of the Yellow Hat sect of Tibetan Buddhism. The Grand Lama of the Yellow Hat monastery at Lhasa was given the title Dalai, meaning "ocean" or "measureless," in the 16th century. The spiritual as well as temporal leader of his people, he was thought to be an incarnation of Avalokita, the Mahayana Bodhista of compassion and mercy. *See also* Lama; Lamaism.

Dale, Henry Hallett (1875–1968), English physiologist. He shared the 1936 Nobel Prize in physiology or medicine with Otto Loewi for discoveries relating to the chemical transmission of nerve impulses. Dale found that the chemical acetylcholine served to transmit nerve impulses across the tiny gap from one nerve cell to another.

Daley, Richard Joseph (1902–76), US political figure, b. Chicago. He served as mayor of Chicago (1955–76). He figured prominently in national politics in 1960 when he brought Chicago into the Democratic column in a close election and in 1968 when he stamped out protest demonstrations during the presidential convention.

Dalhousie, James Andrew Broun Ramsay, Marquis of (1812–60), British administrator. Also Lord Ramsay upon the death of his brother, he was governor-general of India (1847–56). In addition to acquiring territories such as Punjab, Jhansi, and Nagpur, he expanded the railroad, roads, and telegraph; develped trade and agriculture; and opened irrigation works. As president of the British Board of Trade (1845), he established regulations for the railroad system.

Dali, Salvador (1904–), Spanish artist whose achievements have been attended by enormous personal publicity. His style, a blend of meticulous realism and hallucinatory transformations of form and space, made him an influential Surrealist. His paintings are in major Western museums. Dali has also designed jewelry, fabrics, furniture, and stage decor. He collaborated on *Le Chien Andalou,* a classic film. A noted book illustrator, he has also written two autobiographies. △1318.

Dallapiccola, Luigi (1904–75), Italian composer. He studied with German and Austrian masters and was also influenced by Monteverdi. An innovative musician, he used the 12-tone system of Schoenberg in his compositions from 1939 on. His choral *Canti di prigonea* and opera *Il prigionero* gained him an international reputation. In 1956 he became professor of composition at Queens College, New York.

Dallas, city in NE Texas, the state's second largest city, and the Southwest's leading commercial, financial, and transportation center; seat of Dallas co. Dallas-Fort Worth Regional Airport, opened 1974, is the world's largest commercial airport. City is headquarters of many major US oil firms; three-fourths of all known US oil reserves are located within 500mi (805km) of Dallas. The Big D, as local residents call it, is also noted as a fashion center.

Cotton, cattle, and oil spurred the city's growth since it was first settled in the 1840s. Discovery of the giant East Texas Oil Field in 1930 led to further expansion. While on a visit to Dallas on Nov. 22, 1963, President John F. Kennedy was assassinated. Today the city is one of the fastest growing in the nation. Major schools: Southern Methodist University; University of Dallas; University of Texas, Dallas. Industries: oil refining, women's clothing, aircraft, missile parts, electronic equipment, cotton-processing machinery.

Dallas has several noted museums and cultural institutions, including the Dallas Theater Center, designed by Frank Lloyd Wright. The city boasts two professional football teams, the Dallas Cowboys and the Texas Rangers. Its famed Cotton Bowl stadium features a playoff between two top college football teams each New Year's Day. Inc. 1856 as town, 1871 as city. Pop. (1970) 844,401.

Dalling and Bulwer, William Henry Lytton Earle Bulwer, Baron (1801–72), English author and diplomat. He served in the army, various embassies, and parliament. He was one of the signers of the Clayton-Bulwer treaty (1850), which paved the way for international agreements establishing a Central American canal. This occurred while he was ambassador to the United States. His writings include *An Autumn in Greece* (1826), *France: Social, Literary, and Political* (1834–36), *Historical Characters* (1867), and *Lord Byron* (1835).

Dalmatia, region of Yugoslavia, between Bosnia and Herzegovina and Adriatic Sea. An important Roman province 1st–5th centuries, it became part of Byzantine Empire 6th century; taken by the Hapsburg Empire 1815; after WWII, became part of the federal republic of Croatia under Yugoslav government. Industries: shipbuilding, fishing, textiles, chemicals, wine, olive oil. Area: 4,916sq mi (12,732sq km). △1302.

Dalmatian, versatile, ancient breed of dog (non-sporting group) and only coaching dog; best known as firehouse, English coach, or Plum-pudding dog. It has a long, flat-skulled head with long muzzle; dark, golden, or blue eyes; high-set, thin ears close to the head; powerful body; strong legs; and long, tapered, curved tail. Its distinctive short, hard coat has a pure white ground with small black or liver spots. Average size: 19–23in (48–58cm) high at shoulder; 35–50lb (16–22.5kg).

Dalton, Hugh, Baron Dalton of Forest and Frith (1887–1962), English statesman. A Labour member of Parliament from 1924, he nationalized the Bank of England while he was chancellor of the exchequer (1945–47). He also was undersecretary in the foreign office (1929–31), minister of economic warfare (1940–42), president of the board of trade (1942–45), and minister of town and country planning (1950). He was the author of *Call Back Yesterday* (1953) and *High Tide and After* (1962).

Dalton, John (1766–1844), English chemist and physicist and one of the fathers of modern physical science. His early interest in meteorology yielded important information on the trade winds, the cause of rain, and the Aurora Borealis. He described color blindness (sometimes called Daltonism) based on his own experiences and those of his brother. His study of gases led to Dalton's law of partial pressures (the sum of the pressure of each gas equals the total pressure of a mixture of these gases), and to his idea that as temperature rises, gases expand. His atomic theory states that each element is made up of indestructible, identical, small particles, and he constructed an atomic weights table. △1480, 1484, 1550.

Dalton, Robert (1867–92), US bandit, b. Cass co, Mo. In 1888 he was a US marshal in Indian Territory, but he killed his rival in a love affair and he and his brothers Emmet and Grattan began their lives as thieves and train robbers. They were very successful until they went to Coffeyville, Kan., and the townspeople struck back. Emmet was the only survivor, and he went to prison.

Dalton's Law, the statement that the pressure exerted by each gas in a mixture of gases does not depend on the pressures of the other gases, provided no chemical reaction occurs.

Daly City, city in W California, suburb of San Francisco; est. 1906 by homeless victims of the San Francisco earthquake. Inc. 1911. Pop. (1970) 66,922.

Dam, Henrik (1895–1976), Danish biologist who shared (with E.H. Doisy) the 1943 Nobel Prize in physiology or medicine for his discovery of vitamin K, the fat-soluble vitamin needed for blood clotting.

Dam, a barrier built across a stream, river, estuary, or section of ocean to confine or check the flow of water for irrigation, flood control or power generation. Dams date back at least as far as the Egyptian civilization of 3500 years ago. Common types are gravity, arch, buttress, and embankment dams. The highest dam is the USSR's Nurek, 1030 ft (314m) high. The Fort Peck Dam in Montana has a record volume of 125,000,000 cu yd (95,000,000 cu m). △634, 1764.

Damanhur, city in N Egypt, in Nile River delta, 37mi (59km) ESE of Alexandria; site of ancient city of Hermopolis Parva; communications center and cotton market. Pop. 161,400.

Damas, Léon (1912–), Guinean poet. An early supporter of negritude, he studied in Paris, where he became André Gide's protégé. His collections of verse, *Black Label* (1956), *African Songs of Love, War, Grief and Abuse* (1961), and *Pigments* (1962) are sensitive portrayals of village life. *See also* Negritude.

Damascus (Dimasho, or Ash Sham), capital and largest city of Syria, in SW Syria on the Barada River E of the Anti-Lebanon Mts; administrative, financial, and communications center; site of the Citadel (originally Roman, rebuilt 13th century), Umayyad Mosque (8th century), church of St John the Baptist (4th century), several mosques, Syrian University (1923), National Museum. Inhabited since prehistoric times, it is believed to be the oldest continuously occupied city in the world. An ancient Egyptian and Biblical city; became independent Aramaean Kingdom *c.* 1000 BC; occupied by Babylonians, Persians, Greeks, and Romans; scene of many battles during Crusades; under Ottoman Turks (1516–1918) until occupied by British and taken by French (1920) and made part of French mandate of Syria; made capital of Syria 1961. Industries: textiles (damask fabrics), glass, sugar, cement, furniture. Pop. 835,000.

Damasus I, Roman Catholic pope (366–84), and saint, born in Spain. His election was challenged by the Arian Ursinus who was elected antipope. Both were consecrated by bishops and two factions developed. Eventually Emperor Valentian I expelled Ursinus. Damasus asserted that a pope could be tried by only ecclesiastical courts. Under him, Jerome produced a revised Latin Bible.

Damavand (Demavend), volcanic mountain peak in N Iran, 35mi (56km) NE of Tehran; highest point in Iran, 18,934ft (5,775m); rich in mineral deposits, especially sulfur.

D'Amboise, Jacques (1934–), US dancer and choreographer, b. Dedham, Mass. He joined the New York City Ballet (1953) and has performed on Broadway and television. His own works include *The Chase* (1963), *Quatour* (1964), and *Irish Fantasy* (1964).

Damietta (Dumyat), city in N Egypt, on Lake Manzala near the Mediterranean. Dimity, a sheer cotton fabric, was first made here; commercial center. Indus-

Dakar, Senegal

Richard Daley

Dalmatian

John Dalton

tries: cotton, glass, processed rice and fish. Pop. 98,000.

Damocles, in Greek mythology, a courtier of Dionysius of Syracuse (Sicily). His eulogies of Dionysius made him a well-known figure at court. At a banquet, Damocles noticed a sword hanging by a fragile thread above his head. He was thus made to realize that the wealth and power he coveted did not bring happiness and might well be ephemeral.

Damon and Pythias, models of friendship in Roman legend. The legend is based on Pythias' plotting against the tyrant Dionysius of Syracuse (*c.* 430–367 BC). He was condemned to death, but Damon agreed to take his place until the day of his execution so Pythias could return home to settle his affairs. He returned on the day of his execution, and Dionysius was so impressed with the loyalty of the two that he pardoned Pythias.

Dampier, William (1652–1715), English navigator and buccaneer. An adventurous early career included a buccaneering expedition against Spanish America and a trip across the Pacific, after which he was marooned. Sent by England in 1699 to explore the South Seas, he explored the coasts of Australia, discovered New Guinea and gave his name to Dampier Archipelago and Dampier Strait. He later piloted two commercial voyages, one which marooned Alexander Selkirk. △1260.

Damping-Off, a fungus disease of seeds or seedling plants. In the most striking form—postemergence damping-off—young seedlings topple over as a result of stem rot at the soil line. Damping-off fungi may also invade a seed before it sprouts (germination failure) or attack a seedling before it reaches the soil surface (preemergence damping-off).

Damrosch, Walter (1862–1950), US conductor, b. Germany. He was a major influence on American musical culture. In 1885 he took over the Metropolitan Opera in New York City and established its reputation by recruiting important singers. He later conducted for the New York Philharmonic and the New York Symphony Society, which merged with the Philharmonic in 1928. From 1926 to 1950 he conducted radio broadcasts of classical music.

Damselfish, any of 250 species of small marine fishes, found mostly in the tropical waters of the Atlantic and Indo-Pacific oceans. To 6in (15cm) long, brilliantly colored, deep-bodied, usually with a forked tail. Unlike most fish, it has a single nostril on each side. Family Pomacentridae.

Damson, tree and fruit of any of various species *(Prunus)* grown in the north temperate zone. The small trees seldom exceed 20ft (6m). The fruit, called a drupe, is fleshy and one-seeded, varying from yellow to red to purple in color, and is eaten fresh, or dried or preserved. Family Rosaceae.

Dan, in Genesis, fifth son of Jacob, born to Bilhah. His tribe settled north of Judah near the Mediterranean Sea.

Dana, Charles Anderson (1819–97), US newspaper editor, b. Hinsdale, N.H. In 1868 he became editor and owner of the New York *Sun* and is noted for setting and maintaining a high standard within his paper, thereby setting an example for other publications. He also openly criticized the corruption in President Grant's administration, and denounced labor unions and civil service reforms. Among his works are *The Art of Newspaper Making* (1895), *Eastern Journeys* (1898), and *Recollections of the Civil War* (1898).

Dana, Francis (1743–1811), US political figure, b. Charlestown, Mass. He was a member of John Adams' mission to Paris in 1779. Dana sat in the Continental Congress (1776–78) and spent two years at the Russian court (1781–83) as an unrecognized envoy. He later served on the Massachusetts supreme court (1785–1806).

Dana, James Dwight (1813–95), US naturalist, b. Utica, N.Y., known for his work in mineralogy and zoology. He also presented practical theories of mountain building, volcanoes, and origins of continents. His book *A System of Mineralogy* (1837) remains a standard.

Dana, John Cotton (1856–1929), US librarian and author. He had no formal training in librarianship but reorganized the Denver Public Library and Newark Library where he served as librarian. His book, *Library Primer,* written in 1896 and updated in later editions, is a standard textbook in library science.

Dana, Richard Henry (1815–82), US author, b. Cambridge, Mass. He shipped as a common sailor on the brig *Pilgrim* (1834) around Cape Horn to California and back. From that experience came *Two Years Before the Mast* (1840), a classic in American literature of the sea. One of the founders of the Free Soil party, he later became active in the Republican party.

Danaë, in Greek mythology, the daughter of Acrisius. She was the mother by Zeus of Perseus, who killed his grandfather and the Gorgon.

Da-Nang, formerly Tourane; one of chief cities of Vietnam; contains port on S China Sea; commercial shipping, rail connections, airport, copper, gold, and coal deposits are nearby. First European settlers landed at Da-Nang Bay 1535; it was ceded to France by Annam 1787; site of huge US military base during Vietnam War. Pop. 334,200.

Danbury, city in SW Connecticut, 20mi (32km) NW of Bridgeport, in Fairfield co. Industries: hats, electronics. Settled 1685; inc. 1889. Pop. (1970) 50,781.

Danbury Hatters' Case *(Loewe* v. *Lawlor),* brought before the US Supreme Court in 1908 by D.E. Loewe and Co. of Danbury, Ct., who sued the local union of the United Hatters of North America for calling a nationwide boycott. The Supreme Court, citing provisions of the Sherman Anti-Trust Act outlawing secondary boycotts, decided in favor of the plaintiff. Members of the local union were fined $250,000.

Danby, Thomas Osborne, Earl of, (1631–1712), (subsequently Marquess of Carmarthen, Duke of Leeds), English Tory politican. He achieved high office through patronage and financial ability, becoming Charles II's treasurer and chief minister (1673–78). He built up an Anglican court party in Parliament, but was imprisoned (1679–84). Danby organized Tory support for William and Mary; he helped them gain Britain's crown and became their chief minister (1690–95).

Dance, English word derived from Old High German *danson,* to drag or stretch. Dancing is the art of ordered body movements coupled with leaps and measured steps that dates back to the beginning of man. The dancer moves through a predetermined space to the accompaniment of musical instruments or voice. From early man to the present, dance has been a means to communicate emotions, rituals, entertainment, or as a form of popular expression.

Dance of Death, macabre gyrations of the risen dead. In the Middle Ages popular belief had it that the dead rose up at night to dance over their graves to lure the curious and unsuspecting near and to dance them to their death. This superstition was reinforced with stylized dance pageants, paintings, and illustrations depicting the dance and its equalizing nature.

Dancer, Stanley (1927–), US harness racing driver and trainer, b. New Egypt, N.J. Considered one of the best drivers in the sport, he became in 1964 the first driver to win $1,000,000 in purses in one year.

Dandelion, hardy, yellow-flowered, Eurasian perennial plant widely established as a lawn weed in North America. Its deeply notched leaves are sometimes gathered, or specially grown, for salad or cooked greens. The flower heads are occasionally used in making wine. Family Compositae; species *Taraxacum officinale.* △446.

Dandie Dinmont Terrier, Scots hunting dog (terrier group). Purebred since 1700, its name is from a character in Sir Walter Scott's *Guy Mannering* (1815). The Dandie's massive skull is topped by a distinctive topknot. Large eyes are hazel; ears hanging. Its long body has a downward curve in the back; the legs are short; and the 8–10in tail (20.3–25.4cm) is curved up. Its pepper or mustard-colored coat is hard but not wiry and about 2in (5cm) long. Average size: 8–11in (20.3–28cm) high at shoulder; 18–24lb (8–11kg). *See also* Terrier.

Dandolo Family, Venetian family that became rich and powerful by the 11th century, was at its height in the 12th–14th centuries, and held high offices in Venetian government until the fall of the republic. Prominent members included **Enrico** (*c.* 1108–1205), doge of Venice who took Constantinople in 1204; **Giovanni** (doge, 1280–89); **Francesco** (doge, 1328–39); and the last Dandolo doge **Andrea** (doge, 1343–54), who joined the crusade against the Turks (1343–46) and also fought Genoa (1348–54).

Dandruff, dead scalp skin that appears as white o yellowish flakes in the hair. It is made noticeable b oiliness and dense growth of hair, and is sometime increased by inflammation, commonly seborrheic de matitis.

Dane, Clemence (1888–1965), pseud. of Winifre Ashton, English novelist and playwright. She inaugu rated her literary career with the publication *Reg ment of Women* (1917), a fictional account of teach ers at a girls' school. Dane wrote detective stories plays, essays, and biography in addition to her popu lar novels.

Danegeld, land tax levied in medieval England. Orig nally levied (991) to buy off Danish raiders, the tax wa continued until 1162, largely as a source of royal rev enue.

Danelaw, areas of northern and eastern England i the early Middle Ages in which Scandinavian custom ary law prevailed. In the 9th century land between th Thames and Tees rivers was overrun and settled b Danes who had their own legal code, different from Anglo-Saxon law. The Danelaw persisted for severa centuries; it had a large free peasantry.

Danforth, Thomas (1703–86), US pewterer, b Taunton, Mass. He opened a copper and pewter sho in Norwich, Conn. in 1733 and was an active pewtere until 1773. His prolific output was of high quality; h followed the English style of marking his pewter. Hi descendants, the Danforths and the Boardmans, ca ried on the tradition of the most notable pewtering family in America.

Dangerfield, Thomas (1650–85), English crimina He sought to profit from the "Popish Plot" hysteri (1678–79) by informing. Dangerfield accused Catho lics of plotting to kill the king and Whig leaders bu was pilloried for perjury and died from a bystander's blow.

Daniel, biblical prophet and book bearing his name The book, probably written in the 2nd century BC relates events in Daniel's life (6th century BC) during Babylonian captivity and his visions. Daniel interprets Nebuchadnezzar's dreams, reads the handwriting on the wall at Belshazzar's feast, and escapes from the lion's den. This book is an early example of apocalyp tic literature.

Daniel, Peter V(ivian) (1784–1860), US jurist, b Stafford co., Va. He was a government official in Vir ginia (1812–35) and then served on the US Distric Court (1836–41). A Jeffersonian who championed the cause of states' rights, he was appointed an associate justice of the US Supreme Court in 1841 and sat unti his death. His opinions were noted for eloquence o style.

Daniels, Josephus (1862–1948), US newspaper man and public official, b. Washington, N.C. He was secretary of the Navy in Wilson's cabinet. There, he worked to upgrade the education of enlisted person nel. Daniels edited several papers which eventually became the Raleigh *News and Observer.* He managed the presidential campaigns for Bryan (1908) and Wilson (1912) and was ambassador to Mexico (1933–41). His works include *Life of Woodrow Wilson* (1924), *Tar Heel Editor* (1939), *The Wilson Era* (2 vol., 1944–46), and *Shirt Sleeve Diplomat* (1947).

Danish, the official language of Denmark, spoken by virtually all of the country's 5,000,000 inhabitants, and also in Greenland and the Faroe Islands. A Germanic language, it is very similar to Norwegian and is also intelligible to speakers of Swedish.

D'Annunzio, Gabriele (1863–1938), Italian poet, novelist, and playwright. His flamboyant rhetoric greatly influenced Italian poetry of the early 20th century. His poems include *Alcyone* (1904) and his best-known novels are *The Triumph of Death* (1896) and *The Child of Pleasure* (1898). In the novel *The Flame of Life* (1900), he portrayed his mistress, the actress Eleonora Duse. He became a national hero when he seized and ruled Fiume (Trieste) from 1919 to 1921. △1240, 1332.

Dante Alighieri (1265–1321), Italian poet famous for the *Divine Comedy,* written in terza rima. Orphaned in adolescence, he married Gemma Donati. He became one of the rulers of the city-state of Florence, and was responsible for the exile of his brother-in-law and that of his best friend, Guido Cavalcanti. Later, Dante was exiled and wrote his inspired and majestic works under the patronage of various nobles until he died in poverty in Ravenna. Other works include *La Vita nuova* (The New Life), Convivio (Banquet), *De monarchia* (On Monarchy), and *De Vulgare* *eloquentia,* a treatise appealing for the use of the vernacular in literature. *See also* Cavalcanti, Guido; *Divine Comedy; Terza Rima.* △1100.

Danton, Georges Jacques (1759–94), French statesman and controversial official of the revolution. He played the role of moderate in the turbulent 1790s, seeking conciliation between the Girondists and Montagnards. Leader of the Jacobins (1793) and a member of the Committee of Public Safety, he was arrested during the Reign of Terror and guillotined, an act that began the fall of the Revolutionary government.

Dantonists, followers of Georges Jacques Danton (1759–94), one of the leaders of the French Revolution. Danton was briefly head of state of the new Republic but came to fear the excesses of the Reign of Terror, during which he was imprisoned and guillotined.

Danube River, second-longest European river; rises in Black Forest of W Germany, flows NE then SE, entering Austria at Passau; continues, forming border between Czechoslovakia and Hungary, flows S into Yugoslavia, then SE and E to form part of Romania-Bulgaria boundary; continues N across SE Romania and E into the Black Sea. It was made an international waterway by Treaty of Versailles (1919), and is presently under control of the Danube Commission, headquartered in Budapest, Hungary. Length: approx. 1,776mi (2,859m).

Danville, city in E Illinois, 120mi (193km) S of Chicago; seat of Vermilion co; former site of a Kickapoo Indian village. Industries: agriculture (corn and soybeans), trading stamps, coal mining. Inc. 1869. Pop. 42,570.

Danville, city in S central Virginia, on Dan River; used as a Confederate military complex during Civil War; site of Sutherlin Mansion; large textile industry. Founded 1793; inc. 1870. Pop. (1970) 46,391.

Danzig. *See* Gdansk.

Daoud Khan, Sandar Mohammed (1908–), Afghanistan military and political figure. He served as prime minister (1953–63) under Emir Mohammed Zahir Shah. He then returned to the army, where he became a lieutenant general. In 1973 he overthrew Zahir Shah, proclaimed Afghanistan a republic, and had himself appointed president and prime minister.

Daphne, a nymph in Greek mythology. Apollo, struck by one of Eros' gold-tipped arrows, fell in love with Daphne. Daphne, however, shot with one of Eros' leaden-points, scorned all men. To protect her from Apollo, the gods transformed Daphne into a laurel tree. Thereafter, Apollo wore a laurel branch on his head as a symbol of his love and grief.

Daphnia, or water flea, minute, flea-shaped crustacean living in freshwater worldwide. It has four to six pairs of legs and is an important food source for aquatic life. Length: to 0.12in (3mm). Order Branchipoda; group Cladocera.

Daphnis, in Greek mythology, the inventor of pastoral poetry. The son of Hermes (Mercury) and a nymph, Daphnis was taught by Pan to be a minstrel to Apollo. Daphnis pledged his love to the jealous nymph Nomeia, but was seduced by the nymph Chimaera. Nomeia blinded him for his unfaithfulness.

Da Ponte, Lorenzo (1749–1838), Italian scholar, b. Emanuele Conegliano. He wrote some 36 librettos including those for Mozart's *The Marriage of Figaro, Don Giovanni,* and *Così fan tutte.* After a period of exile in Vienna and London, Da Ponte emigrated (1805) to the United States where he became a respected teacher and promoter of Italian language and culture.

Dapsang. *See* Godwin-Austen.

DAR. *See* Daughters of the American Revolution.

Dardanelles, narrow strait separating NW Turkey and Gallipoli Peninsula. Ancient name was Hellespont; scene of crossing of Xerxes I (480 BC) and Alexander the Great (334 BC); site of Allied campaign WWI (1915). With the Bosporus Strait, Dardanelles creates a water route from the Black Sea through Sea of Marmara to Aegean Sea; it is the only passage to Mediterranean Sea for Russian fleet. Length: 38mi (61km). Width: 1–4mi (2–6km). *See also* Bosporus.

Dardanus, son of Zeus and Electra and ancestor of the Trojans. Dardanus, according to Greek legend, married Bateia, the daughter of Teucer, the first king of Troy. He succeeded Teucer and applied the name Dardania to the entire region. Dardanus placed the Palladium, an image sacred to the goddess Athena, in Troy; Athena, in gratitude, protected the state from its enemies.

Dare, Virginia (1587–?), first English child born in America, in the Roanoke Island Colony. The granddaughter of Roanoke Gov. John White, she disappeared after an Indian attack. Her fate, and that of the rest of the colony, are unknown. *See also* Roanoke Island Colony.

Dar-el-Beida. *See* Casablanca.

Dar es Salaam (Daressalam), capital city of Tanzania, in central E Tanzania, on shore of Indian Ocean, S of Zanzibar Channel; major commercial, industrial, and administrative center of Tanzania; site of several colleges. Industries: textiles, clothing, building materials, oil. Exports: agricultural products, diamonds, minerals. Founded 1862 by sultan of Zanzibar. Pop. 272,-515.

Darien, residential town in SW Connecticut, on Long Island Sound; site of the Mather Homestead (1778); a majority of its inhabitants commute to New York City. Settled 1640; inc. 1820. Pop. (1970) 20,411.

Darien, the first important Spanish settlement in Central America, founded in 1509. The region, modern Panama, was the principal base for the exploration of the mainland between 1511 and 1519.

Darien Scheme (1695–1700), unsuccessful Scottish project to colonize the Isthmus of Panama and control its trade. The Scots, opposed by the English government, invested heavily. The failure of the settlements demonstrated Scotland's commercial weakness as a small state and helped secure the Act of Union (1707) with England.

Darío, Rubén (1867–1916), Nicaraguan poet. The father of the *Modernista* movement, he exerted a liberating influence on Latin American writers. His poems embraced many subjects, including doubts and loss of faith, the struggle to find harmony in contradictions, and the exotic. His finest book of verse, *Songs of Life and Hope* (1905), is noted for its universality and eloquence. He is regarded by many as the most outstanding poet who ever wrote in Spanish.

Darius I, called "the Great" (c.558–486 BC), Achamenid king of Persia. Troubled by revolts, particularly in Babylon, he restored order by dividing the empire into provinces, allowing some local autonomy and tolerating religious diversity. He also fixed an annual taxation, developed commerce, campaigned to consolidate his frontiers, built roads, and connected the Nile to the Red Sea by canal. His desire to punish the Greeks for their part in the Ionian revolt (499–494) led to his defeat at Marathon in 490. △992, 1004.

Darius II (died 404 BC), king of Persia (423–404 BC), son of Artaxerxes I. He killed Sogdianus, who had murdered Xerxes II, and claimed the throne. He lost Egypt but crushed uprisings and revived Persian power in Greece. Artaxerxes II followed.

Darius III (*c.*380–330 BC), king of Persia (336–330 BC). He murdered the eunuch Bagoas, who had reared him and put him on the throne after poisoning Artaxerxes III and Arses. He was defeated at Isus (333 BC) and Gaugamela (331 BC) by Alexander the Great. He fled to Ecbatana, the capital of Media, and then to Bactria (NE Afghanistan), where the satrap Bessus killed him and battled Alexander.

Dark Adaptation, shift in functional dominance from cone cells to rod cells in the retina as overall illumination is reduced. The complete process takes 35–40 minutes. Thus humans find it difficult to see when they enter a dark room but experience improved vision with time. *See also* Vision.

Dark Ages, term frequently used to describe the period of European history between the fall of Rome (*c.*395–410) and the Norman Conquest in England (1066) or the reign of Charlemagne in France (*c.* 800). The term has become somewhat obsolete as scholars learn more about this period. Although the 4th through the 11th centuries in Europe were characterized by great social and political upheavals, the migrations and conquests of the Germanic tribes made possible the merging of their tribal culture with classical culture, a merger that forms the basis of modern European society. Also significant in this period are the conversion of the West to Christianity, the preservation of classical learning, and the creation of uniquely Christian art and literary forms.

Dance of death

Dandie Dinmont terrier

Gabriele D'Annunzio

Dante Alighieri

Darlan, Jean Louis Xavier François (1881–1942), French admiral. He was made commander in chief of the French navy in 1939 and of all the armed forces in 1942. At the Allied invasion of North Africa, he ordered the French to halt opposition; cooperated with General Eisenhower before he was slain by a French royalist.

Darling, Jay Norwood (1876–1962), US editorial cartoonist, b. Norwood, Mich. Known as "Ding" Darling, he won Pulitzer Prizes in 1924 and 1943. Darling moved from Iowa to New York in 1911 to join a syndicate associated with the New York *Globe*, but he returned to his former employer, the Des Moines *Register*, two years later.

Darling, river in SE Australia; rises in S Queensland and N and W New South Wales; flows SW into Murray River; navigable in rainy seasons. Length: 1,702mi (2,740km).

Darmstadt, city in central West Germany, 12mi (19km) E of Rhine River. Alstadt (Old Town) part of town dates back to Middle Ages. Neustadt (New Town), built in late 18th and early 19th centuries, is well-planned community W of original settlement. City was severely damaged in WWII. Industries: chemicals, steel, machinery. Pop. 141,884.

Darnley, Henry Stuart, or **Stewart, Lord** (1545–67), Scottish noble, second husband of Mary, Queen of Scots. Educated in England, he was a claimant to the English succession. He returned to Scotland (1565) to marry Queen Mary. Weak and vicious, Darnley was involved in the murder of Mary's aide Rizzio (1566). Mary then became party to Darnley's murder at Kirk o'Field, one of her houses.

Darrow, Clarence Seward (1857–1938), US lawyer and labor advocate b. Kinsman, Ohio. He defended Eugene V. Debs (1894) following the Pullman strike. In the Woodworkers case (1898), he won for labor the legal right to strike. He successfully defended William Haywood (1903), accused of assassinating former Idaho Gov. Frank Steunenberg. He achieved further fame in the Loeb-Leopold murder case (1924) and in the Scopes "monkey" trial (1925), successfully opposing William Jennings Bryan. He wrote *Crime, Its Cause and Treatment* (1922).

Darter, freshwater fish of temperate North American waters east of Rocky Mountains. Brilliantly colored, it is bottom-dwelling. Length: 1–9in (2.5–23cm); average 2–2.75in (5–7cm). Family Percidae; species 100, including Johnnydarter *Etheostoma nigrum*.

Dartmoor, moorland region in SW England, in S Devon with isolated granite masses; est. as a national park 1951; source of principal rivers of Devon; site of prison at Princetown built 1806 for French captives; now a convict prison. Area: 365sq mi (945sq km). Highest point is High Willhays, 2,039ft (622m).

Dartmouth, city in S Nova Scotia, Canada; on Halifax harbor opposite Halifax; site of oceanographic institute. Industries: oil refining, electronic equipment, breweries, ship building. Founded 1750. Pop. 64,002.

Dartmouth College v. Woodward (1819), US Supreme Court decision interpreting the contract clause of the Constitution. The Court held that a corporate charter was a contract with which state laws could not interfere. This ruling greatly aided the early growth of capitalism and big business in the United States.

Darts, a game particularly popular in the United States and Great Britain, developed in England in the 15th century. It is played with 3 weighted wooden or metal darts 5–6in (12.7–15.2cm) long. The darts are thrown at a board, 18 inches (45.7cm) in diameter. Indoors, players stand 9ft (2.7m) away. Outdoors, they stand 20–30ft (6.1–9.1m) away. There are several variations of play, as well as types of targets. The object in the 20-point board is to start with a certain score (201, 301, 501, 1001), according to the number of players, and to reach zero by subtracting the amount of points scored from the number indicated.

Daru, Pierre Antoine, Comte (1767–1829), French general, statesman, and historian. As a trusted ally of Napoleon, he became intendant-general of the Grande Armée in 1805 and defeated the Prussian army late that year. After arranging the Prussian indemnity payments, he was minister of state (1811), minister of war (1813), and minister of state during the Hundred Days (1815). He was made a member of the chamber of peers by Louis XVIII (1819). His works include *Histoire de la République de Venise* (1819–21); *Astronomie* (1830).

Darwin, Charles (Robert) (1809–82), English naturalist, b. Shrewsbury. He proposed a biological theory of natural selection as a mechanism of organic change in his monumental *The Origin of Species* (1859). Popularly credited with originating the theory of evolution, Darwin in fact owed much of his theory to the work of others, but utilized fine research ability in merging his own thought with various tentative theories and suggestions already on record.

In 1831 he served as naturalist on the government ship *Beagle*, which surveyed the South American coast, and he returned to the region in 1836 consumed with an interest in animal variations and their causes. He was influenced in his study by the work of a contemporary, Edward Blyth, who suggested that nature selected and preserved the best-adapted species in a given environment and who recognized the possibility of organic change to be implicit in the theory.

After 20 years of research, the development of several theories by Alfred Russel Wallace spurred Darwin's presentation of his own theories at a meeting of the Linnaean Society in 1858. Publication of *The Origin of Species* followed. It proposed three factors responsible for changes in the plant and animal world: variation (the tendency of each organism to vary in some degree from the parent), a conservative heredity factor that limits the degree of variation, and natural selection, which results in the perpetuation of those organisms best fitted to survive. Darwin elaborated his theory in a number of later works, notably *The Descent of Man* (1871). *See also* Evolution; Natural Selection. △418, 768, 1186.

Darwin, Erasmus (1731–1802), English physician, grandfather of Charles Darwin. His *Zoonomia, or the Laws of Organic Life* (1794–96) advanced the theory of evolution.

Darwin, seaport in Australia, at the entrance to Port Darwin; headquarters of the Allies in N Australia during WWII; bombed by the Japanese 1942. Cyclone Tracy (December 1974) destroyed 90% of the city; 5-year reconstruction plan includes housing construction that will withstand cyclone-force winds. Its harbor is the major shipping depot for the sparsely populated and undeveloped N region. Founded 1869. Pop. 21,617.

Darwinism, theory of the origin and evolution of the species as developed by Charles Darwin and presented in *The Origin of Species* (1859). Darwin viewed life as a constant competitive struggle in which some members of the species possessed certain advantageous traits. These characteristics were passed down through generations by a process termed "natural selection," strengthening the species and enabling survival of the fittest. *See also* Darwin, Charles Robert. △418–20, 1282, 1290.

Darwin's Finches, term applied to the finches of the Galapagos Islands that Charles Darwin carefully observed while on his voyage on the *Beagle*. These observations overthrew Darwin's belief in the immutability of species and were seminal to his development of the theory of evolution. Darwin noted that all the finches on the various islands of the Galapagos group were closely related to a species of finch found on the mainland of South America and were all quite similar to one another—but with some differences from island to island. Studying further, he found that the differences could be correlated with the feeding habits of the different varieties of finches—with, for example, finches with powerful beaks eating large seeds, finches with small beaks eating smaller seeds, finches with fine beaks eating insects—and that the feeding habits were an adaptation to the particular environment of the species. These observations, combined with geological observations and other biological data, led Darwin to formulate a theory of evolution based on the idea of natural selection working on the variability within species to favor the better adapted to the environment. *See also* Adaptive Radiation; Natural Selection.

Data Processing, systematic sequence of operations performed on data, especially by a computer or other electronic or electromechanical device, in order to process new information, revise or update existing information stored in the system, as on magnetic tape, punch cards, or microfiche, or extract information from the system. The data can be in the form of numerical values, scientific or technical facts or measurements, lists of names, places, book titles, etc., with associated relevant information. The main processing operations performed by a computer are arithmetical addition, subtraction, multiplication, and division, and logical operations, which involve decision making on the basis of comparison of data, as in the operation: if condition *a* holds then follow programmed instruction P; if *a* does not hold then follow instruction Q. *See also* Computer, Electronic. △1672–74.

Date Palm, stout-trunked palm *Phoenix dactylifera* native to desert oases of North Africa east to India. One of the most important palms commercially, it is cultivated in the SW United States. It has feather-shaped, gray-green leaves; large flower clusters produce the date fruit of commerce. The wild date palm, *P. sylvestris*, is native to India; its fruits are not edible. Height: to 100ft (30.5m); family Palmaceae. △452.

Dating, Radioactive, any of several methods using the laws of radioactive decay to assess the very considerable ages of archeological remains, fossils, rocks, and of the earth itself. The specimens must contain a very long-lived radioisotope of known half-life, which, together with a measurement of the ratio of radioisotope to a stable isotope (usually the decay product), gives the age. In potassium-argon dating, the ratio of potassium-40 (half-life 1.26×10^{98} yr) to its stable decay product argon-40 gives ages over ten million years. In rubidium-strontium dating the ratio rubidium-87 (5×10^{10} yr) to its stable product strontium-87 gives ages up to several billion years. In radiocarbon dating the proportion of carbon-14 (5730 yr) to stable carbon-12 absorbed into once-living matter (wood, etc) gives ages up to several thousand years. △276.

Daubigny, Charles François (1817–1878), French landscape painter and etcher. A working artist at 17, Daubigny exhibited at the Salon at 21. An open-air painter, often classified as a Barbizon artist, Daubigny had a houseboat studio for over 30 years. His atmospheric oils of the Seine and Oise river areas are in the great museums of the West.

Daugava. *See* Dvina.

Daugavpils, formerly Dvinsk; city in E Latvian SSR, USSR, on the Dvina River, approx. 85mi (137km) NNE of Vilnius; commercial and industrial center; founded 1274 by Livonian kings; ceded to Russia 1772 by kingdom of Lithuania and Poland. Industries: food and grain processing, textiles, lumber, iron. Pop. 101,000.

Daughters of the American Revolution (DAR), patriotic society founded in 1890 whose members are female, lineal descendents of activists in the cause of American independence. The DAR was chartered by the US Congress in 1896. There are 2,900 local chapters and approximately 187,000 members.

Daumier, Honoré (1808–79), French lithographer, painter, and sculptor, one of the great social satirists. He worked for lawyers and booksellers before studying art and contributing lithographs, often lampoons of political figures, to magazines. For many of these he made terra-cotta models. He was jailed for six months in 1832 for a caricature of Louis Phillipe. His output was prodigious—more than 4,000 lithographs and 200 canvases. His work, always focused on humanity, is well represented in museums.

Dauphiné, French province, now occupied by the departments of Drôme Isère, and Haute-Alpes. Created by the Dauphin family's gradual addition of lands to the countship of Viennois, this land and the title dauphin were sold to Charles V of France in 1349 and annexed to France in 1457 as a result of disputes over its independence within the royal family. Revolts in 1789 made Dauphiné one of the birthplaces of the French Revolution. △1096

Davao, seaport and largest city on Mindanao island, Philippines; capital of Davao Del Norte prov.; commercial center; site of university (1965). Exports: abaca, plywood, copra, rice, tobacco. Founded 1849. Pop. 148,424.

Davenport, city in E central Iowa, on the Mississippi River; treaty ending Black Hawk War (1832) signed here; site of first railroad bridge to span Mississippi River (1856); commercial and rail center. Industries: shipping, cereal, aluminum, farm and railroad equipment. Founded 1835; inc. 1836. Pop. (1970) 98,469.

David (Donatello). △1134.

David (*c.* 1040–970 BC), king of Israel (*c.* 1010–970 BC); son of Jesse and father of Solomon; successor of Saul. The Old Testament narrates his conquest of the Philistines, particularly the giant Goliath; his friendship with Jonathan, son of Saul; and the rebellion, reconciliation, and death of his son, Absalom. He unified the Jewish tribes and moved the capital from Hebron to Jerusalem. His descendants held the kingdom until 586 BC. Many Psalms are ascribed to him. △982.

David I (1084–1153), king of Scotland (1124–53). b. Carlisle. His marriage to the countess of Northampton involved him in English politics and he fought for Matilda against King Stephen (1138). He introduced Anglo-Norman feudalism into Scotland, where he reorganized the church and administration and built many castles.

David II (1324–71), king of Scotland (1329–71). Exiled after the defeat by Edward III at Halidon Hill (1333), he fought the English in France and Britain until captured (1346). Released (1357) for a ransom he could not pay, he became dependent on the English king.

David, or **Dewi, Saint** (*c.* 520–600), patron saint of Wales. Traditionally he played an important part in two Welsh synods and founded many churches in South Wales.

David, Gerard or **Gheerardt** (*c.* 1460–1523), Flemish painter whose work was not widely known until the 19th century. Experts disagree on the number of authentic paintings. Though influenced by van Eyck and van der Weyden, David has an austere grace that is distinctive. Among his works are *Madonna Enthroned* (Louvre, Paris) and *Annunciation* (Metropolitan Museum, N.Y.).

David, Jacques-Louis (1748–1825), French painter of historical scenes and portraits. As leader of the neoclassical movement, David had a great effect on art and fashion. Influenced by Poussin and Greek and Roman art, David's work was involved with his Jacobin views and support of Napoleon. Among many major works are *Death of Marat* (Museum of Modern Art, Brussels), *Mme. Récamier* (Louvre, Paris), and *Death of Socrates* (Metropolitan Museum, N.Y.). △1198.

David Copperfield (1850), semiautobiographical novel by Charles Dickens that he called his "favorite child." Copperfield retrospectively relates his adventures, misfortunes, and eventual success and happiness. The novel contains many vivid characters, such as Micawber, Uriah Heep, Barkis, and Mrs. Gummidge.

Davidson, Jo (1883–1952), US sculptor, b. New York City. He studied in New York and Paris. He made more than 300 portrait busts of prominent figures, including Woodrow Wilson, David Ben-Gurion, Gandhi, Franklin D. Roosevelt, and Tito. His realistically rendered works were usually done in bronze, marble, or terra cotta.

Davidson, Thomas (1840–1900), US philosopher and educator, b. Scotland. Although he emigrated to the United States in 1867, on a visit to London in 1883 he founded the Fellowship of the New Life, out of which the Fabian Society developed. He established lecture classes in New York City for workers and a summer school at his home in the Adirondacks in New York. His many books include *Aristotle and Ancient Educational Ideals* (1892) and *History of Education* (1900). *See also* Fabian Society.

David with the Head of Goliath (Caravaggio). △1162.

Davies, Arthur Bowen (1862–1928), US painter and lithographer, b. Utica, N.Y. His own work was romantic though he was a member of "the Eight," also called the "ashcan school." President of the Society of Independent Artists, he organized the 1913 Armory Show, which introduced modern art to the United States.

Davies, Joseph Edward (1876–1958), US diplomat, b. Watertown, Wis. He was a member of the Federal Trade Commission (1915–16) and best known for his ambassadorial posts. He was US envoy to the Soviet Union (1936–38). He described his experience in *Mission to Moscow* (1941). He also represented the United States in Belgium and Luxembourg (1938–40) and served as chairman of the War Relief Control Board (1942–46).

Davies, (Sir) Louis Henry (1845–1924), chief justice of Canada's Supreme Court (1918–24). A Liberal, Davies sat in the House of Commons (1882–1901), was minister of marine and fisheries, and was premier of Prince Edward Island before joining the Supreme Court (1901).

Davies, William Henry (1871–1940), Welsh poet. After living as a tramp in Britain and the United States, he wrote his *Autobiography of a Super-Tramp* (1907) while living in a London rooming house. Thereafter he wrote many volumes of simple, sincere, unaffected verse.

Davis, Alexander Jackson (1803–92), US architect, b. New York City. With Ithiel Town he designed many public buildings in the Greek Revival style, notably the US Customs House in New York City and the capitol buildings of Indiana, North Carolina, Illinois, and Ohio.

Davis, Benjamin Oliver, Sr. (1877–1970), US army officer, b. Washington, D.C. The first black to achieve the rank of brigadier general in the US Army (1940), Davis had made his way through the ranks. He retired in 1948.

Davis, Benjamin Oliver, Jr. (1912–), US Air Force officer, b. Washington, D.C. He was the first black graduate of West Point and became the first black general in the US Air Force. After his retirement from the Air Force in 1970 he served as assistant transportation secretary in charge of the force of federal marshals empowered to prevent airplane hijacking.

Davis, Bette (1908–), US film actress, b. Ruth Elizabeth Davis in Lowell, Mass. She is well known for her intense roles in such films as *Of Human Bondage* (1934), *Dangerous* (1935), *The Petrified Forest* (1936), *Jezebel* (1938), *The Old Maid* (1939), *The Little Foxes* (1941), and *All About Eve* (1950).

Davis, Charles Henry (1807–77), US naval officer, b. Boston. He was involved in the Union's defeat of the Confederacy's Mississippi River fleet. He rose to rear admiral's rank. He later served in the bureau of navigation (1862–65) and as superintendant of the Naval Observatory (1865–67, 1874–77).

Davis, David (1815–82), US jurist b. Cecil co, Md. He was instrumental in Abraham Lincoln's presidential nomination and served as Lincoln's campaign manager. An associate justice of the US Supreme Court (1862–77), his opinion in *Ex Parte Milligan* (1866) limited the scope of military courts. He was a US Senator from Illinois (1877–83).

Davis, Glenn (1924–), US football player, b. Claremont, Calif. He won fame with Army (1943–46), where he starred with Doc Blanchard as a running back. He won the Heisman Trophy (1946) and was a three-time All-American (1944–46). He also played in the National Football League with Los Angeles (1950–51).

Davis, Jefferson (1808–89), President of the Confederate States of America (1861–65), b. Todd co, Ky. He was elected to the House of Representatives (1845) but resigned to fight in the Mexican War (1846). After the war he entered the Senate (1847–51) and then served as Pres. Franklin Pierce's secretary of war (1853–57). Reelected senator (1857), he resigned when Mississippi seceded from the Union, and became president of the Confederate States of America, a position he held until the end of the Civil War. He served two years in prison and was indicted for treason (1866) but never tried. He refused to seek amnesty after the war. △1276.

Davis, or **Davys, John** (1550–1605), Canadian explorer, b. England. He made three voyages in search of a northwest passage (1585–87), and he explored the Davis Strait, Cumberland Gulf, and Baffin Bay. He also fought against the Spanish Armada and invented the Davis quadrant.

Davis, John Wesley (1799–1859), speaker of the US House of Representatives during part of the Mexican War, 1845–47, b. New Holland, Pa. He was also commissioner to China, 1848–50, and governor of Oregon Territory, 1853–54.

Davis, Miles (Dewey, Jr.) (1926–), US jazz trumpeter and bandleader, b. Alton, Ill. In the 1940s he worked with such jazz artists as Billy Eckstine and Charles Parker. From 1950 he led his own jazz combo with his arranger, Gil Evans. His muted, introspective style has influenced many other jazz musicians.

Davis, Ossie (1917–), US actor, director, and playwright, b. Cogdell, Ga. He first performed on Broadway in *Jeb* (1946), where he met his future wife, actress Ruby Dee. Other plays he appeared in include *No Time for Sergeants* (1956), *Jamaica* (1957), *A Raisin in the Sun* (1959), and his own play *Purlie Victorious* (1961). He directed the film *Cotton Comes to Harlem* (1970) and wrote a number of TV scripts. He has appeared frequently on TV, often with his wife Ruby Dee.

Davis, Paulina Wright (1813–76), US suffragist, b. Bloomfield, N.Y. She lectured on anatomy and physi-

Clarence Darrow

Charles Darwin

Benjamin O. Davis, Sr.

Jefferson Davis

ology for women and was instrumental in opening the medical fields to them. She founded the first women's rights newspaper, *Una* (1853) and wrote *A History of the National Women's Rights Movement* (1871).

Davis, Richard Harding (1864–1916), US journalist, b. Philadelphia. He began his career in 1886 and joined *Harper's Weekly* in 1890. He is best known for his first hand accounts as a war correspondant in the Cuban Revolution, the Spanish-American War, the South African War, and World War I. His other works include *Soldiers of Fortune* (1897), *The Dictator* (1904), and *Miss Civilization* (1906).

Davis, city in central California, 15mi (24km) W of Sacramento; site of University of California at Davis (1908). Industries: canned foods, steel products. Settled 1850; inc. 1917. Pop. (1970) 23,488.

Davis Resolutions. Introduced by Sen. Jefferson Davis (Miss.) in opposition to the ideas of Sen. Stephen Douglas (Ill.), these resolutions presented the Southern point of view in the 1860 Democratic convention. Neither side was strong enough to carry the convention and the result was a split party that ran two candidates, Douglas and John C. Breckinridge.

Davitt, Michael (1846–1906), Irish nationalist. Son of an evicted peasant, he became a Fenian and was imprisoned (1870). Released (1877), he founded the Land League to help tenants against absentee landlords (1879). He favored nationalizing land and gradually came to oppose the policies of Charles Parnell. △1312.

Davy, (Sir) Humphry (1778–1829), English chemist who isolated potassium, sodium, and the alkaline-earth metals by the application of electrolysis to the decomposition of chemical compounds. He is credited with preparing nitrous oxide, calcium, and boron, discovering chlorine and two chlorine oxides, and providing an explanation for chlorine's bleaching action. He showed that diamonds are a form of carbon and that acidic properties are due to hydrogen, and he invented a safe miners' lamp (the Davy Lamp). △ 1566.

Dawes, Charles Gates (1865–1951), US political leader, b. Marietta, Ohio. He was a lawyer and banker, who served as comptroller of the currency under Republican Pres. William McKinley. His effectiveness as an administrator in France in World War I led to his appointment as the first US budget director (1921). In 1923 he headed the financial commission that drew up the Dawes Plan (1924) to restructure the German economy, for which he received the Nobel Prize (1925). Under Pres. Calvin Coolidge he was vice president (1925–29) and then served in posts under Pres. Herbert Hoover.

Dawes, Henry Laurens (1816–1903), US political figure, b. Cummington, Mass. He spent 36 years in the US Congress (1857–93). He had served in both houses of the Massachusetts legislature before his federal service. His achievements include establishment of the weather service, the completion of the Washington Monument, and the Dawes Act (1887), which provided for land grants to Indians.

Dawes, William, Jr. (1745–99), American patriot, b. Boston. A volunteer dispatch rider, he rode from Boston to Lexington and Concord on April 18, 1775, to warn the colonists of the arrival of British troops. En route he met with Paul Revere and was joined by Dr. Sam Prescott, who also helped warn the people.

Dawes Act (1887), named for Senator Henry L. Dawes (Mass.), ended the Indian reservation system in the United States. Lands held in common by the tribes were surveyed and parcelled out to individual, resident Indians. All Indians were to become citizens of the United States in 1924, at which time they could lawfully sell the property allotted to them.

Dawes Commission, board appointed by President Cleveland in 1893 to negotiate with the Five Civilized Nations living in Oklahoma. The Dawes Act of 1887 had not applied to the Cherokee, Creek, Choctaw, Chickasaw, and Seminole Indian tribes. The commission compiled a list of Indians and surveyed and allotted tribal lands. The commission was disbanded in 1905.

Dawes Plan (1924), US financial plan developed by Charles G. Dawes to collect and distribute World War I payments. It established a schedule of payments that Germany could bear and arranged for a $200 million gold loan by US bankers to the German government to stabilize German currency.

Dawson (Dawson City), town in W Yukon Territory, Canada, at the junction of the Yukon and Klondike rivers, 50mi (80km) E of the Alaskan border; boom town during Yukon gold rush, 1896, with a population of 15,000 to 20,000; capital of Yukon Territory 1898–1951; named 1887. Pop. 745.

Day, Benjamin Henry (1810–89), US journalist, b. Springfield, Mass. He is known as the founder (1833) of the New York *Sun*, the first successful penny paper. Later, his magazine *Brother Jonathan* was the first illustrated weekly in the United States (1842).

Day, Clarence Shepard (1874–1935), US author, b. New York City. He entered his family's brokerage business, served in the Navy and is best known for stories of his youth. He wrote *Life With Father* (1935) and *Life With Mother* (1937), which were the basis of the Lindsay-Crouse play, *This Simian World* (1920), and *Scenes from the Mesozoic* (1935), which he also illustrated.

Dayananda Sarasvati (1824–83), Indian religious figure, b. as Mula Sankara. Discontented with the condition of Hinduism in his day, he became the major spokesman for a return to the authority of the Vedas, the earliest and most sacred scriptures of India. He condemned idol worship, child marriage, and the low status of women and advocated remarriage of widows, study of the Vedas by members of all castes, and the founding of charitable and educational institutions. He founded the Arya Samaj (Society of Nobles) in 1875 to propagate his views.

Daydreaming, form of autistic thinking, it is nonobjective and self-directed, unrealistic but gratifying. Daydreaming can be a withdrawal reaction, a psychological defense mechanism that allows the individual to retreat into a fantasy world of gratification that he cannot attain in the real world. Unless carried to extremes, daydreaming is a normal activity and serves an important function in temporarily mastering or dealing with frustration. *See also* Autistic Thinking.

Daylight Saving Time, a system of producing an additional period of daylight in the evening, by setting clocks one or two hours ahead; used in the United States and much of Europe since World War I. The system was adopted as a fuel conservation measure, as less electricity is needed. Customarily, clocks are set ahead in spring and back again to local standard time in the fall.

Dayflower, any plant of the genus *Commelina* whose blue or purple flowers wilt after one day. They have jointed, creeping stems, and lance-shaped leaves. Family Commelinaceae.

Day-Lewis, C(ecil) (1904–72), Irish poet and critic. His concern for social justice and left causes is evident in his poetry, particularly that which relates to the Spanish Civil War. His poetry includes *Transitional Poem* (1929), *The Magnetic Mountain* (1933), *Overtures to Death* (1938), and *Selected Poems* (1967). *The Poetic Image* (1947) is his most important critical work. He was England's poet laureate (1968–72).

Day Lily, widely cultivated herbaceous perennial plant native to temperate regions of Central Europe, E Asia, and Japan and found wild on roadsides of E United States. It has long thin leaves and lilylike, yellow to reddish-orange flowers that open for one day. Family Liliaceae; genus *Hemerocallis*.

Dayton, city in W Ohio, on Great Miami River, 45mi (72km) NNE of Cincinnati; seat of Montgomery co; growth came with extension of canals 1830–40 and railroads in 1850s; cash register business began here in 1880; site of University of Dayton (1850), Wright State University (1964), home of Wilbur and Orville Wright, and Wright Patterson Air Force Base. Industries: refrigerators, cash registers, paper, computing scales. Settled 1796; inc. 1805. Pop. (1970) 243,-601.

Daytona Beach, resort in E Florida, 92mi (148km) SSE of Jacksonville; noted for hard, white, 25mi (40km) long beach. Settled 1870; inc. 1876; mainland and resort sections consolidated in 1926. Pop. (1970) 45,327.

Dazhbog. △838.

D-Day (June 6, 1944), the first day of the Allied invasion of Europe in Normandy, France. The Allies commanded by Gen. Dwight D. Eisenhower landed on beaches between Cherbourg and Le Havre. Despite heavy losses, they held their beachheads and pushed the Germans back. Within a year, the war in Europe was over. △1338.

DDT, Dichlorodiphenyltrichloroethane, a colorless crystalline organic halogen compound, first used as an insecticide in 1939 against the Colorado potato beetle. It acts as a contact poison, disorganizing the nervous system, and is effective against mosquitoes, fleas, moths, beetles, and other destructive insects. Many species, however, develop resistant populations and birds and fishes, feeding on affected insects, suffer toxic effects. All but essential uses of DDT were banned in the United States in 1971. △318.

Deadfall, kind of primitive trap, especially for large game, constructed so that a heavy weight falls upon the intended victim, either killing it or leaving it disabled and prey to the hunters.

Dead Leaf Butterfly, or Leaf Butterfly, tropical butterfly of S Asia and E Indies. When a dead leaf butterfly rests on a twig, its folded wings look like withered leaves. Genus *Kallima*. *See also* Butterfly. △ 502.

Deadly Amanita. *See* Death Cup.

Deadly Nightshade, also belladonna, devil's herb, sleeping nightshade; fatally poisonous, perennial herb native to S Europe and Asia, rare in the United States. Flowers are bell-shaped, purplish, and 1in (2.5cm) long; the fruit is a shiny black berry. The plant has been cultivated for a medicinal supply of the alkaloids scopolamine and atropine, obtained from the roots and leaves. Family Solanaceae; species *Atropa belladonna*.

Dead Reckoning, a navigational position-finding method that determines the position of a ship or aircraft without the help of celestial observation. Calculations are made from the records of the course and distance already covered and provisions are made for estimated drift. Dead reckoning permits the navigator to plot his location and to plan his course and speed.

Dead Sea (Al-Bahr al-Mayyit), salt lake on border between Jordan and Israel; water is supplied by the Jordan River and several smaller streams and springs; historically known by many other names (The Sea, Eastern Sea, Sea of Araba); cities of Sodom and Gomorrah believed to lie under S end; contains large quantities of common salt, potassium, bromine, sodium, chlorine, sulfate, calcium magnesium. Area: 360sq mi (932sq km). Depth: (avg.) 1,000ft (305m).

Dead Sea Scrolls, manuscripts and papyri discovered in 1947 and later in caves and ruins along the Dead Sea, primarily around Qumran. These documents, written in Hebrew or Aramaic, most between 100 BC–50 AD are of importance to scholars, providing valuable information about the relation of early Christianity to Judaism. They include most of the Old Testament, many apocryphal and pseudographical works, Biblical commentaries, and documents that shed light on the history of the time. △872,1026.

Deadwood, town in Black Hills of N South Dakota; seat of Lawrence co. Wild Bill Hickok and Calamity Jane are buried here. Industries: tourism, lumber. Settled 1876; inc. 1881. Pop. (1970) 2,409.

Deafness, a lack of the sense of hearing. The *congenitally* deaf are born deaf; the *adventitiously* deaf are born with normal hearing but lose it later in life. There are three major types of deafness: (1) Conductive hearing loss, the most prevalent, in which there is interference with the transmission of sound to sense organs in middle or inner ear, often as a result of childhood infection and high fever or development of bony abnormalities later in life. (2) Sensory-neural hearing loss, usually occurring at birth due to intrauterine infection, Rh incompatibility effects, or other neural damage, or developing in late life as a result of vascular degeneration and advancing age. (3) Central hearing loss or abnormality in the central nervous system, occurring from brain damage or disease or various psychogenic disorders.

The treatment of deafness depends on its cause and ranges from removal of impacted wax and administration of drugs to combat infection to delicate surgical and microsurgical procedures that can, for example, correct some congenital malformations and bony growths. Electronic hearing aids that amplify sound help many hard-of-hearing, and the use of sign language and speech reading or lip reading techniques help the deaf function in normal life. Gallaudet College in Washington, D.C., is the only liberal arts college in the world exclusively for the deaf. △676.

Deak, Ferencz (1803–76), Hungarian political leader. A leader of the Liberal Reform party, he served in the Hungarian legislature (1833–36, 1839–40). He supported the revolution of 1848, drawing up the liberal March Laws, but resigned as Minister of Justice n opposition to Kossuth's more radical programs. After Kossuth's fall in 1849, Deak became the leader of the Hungarian nationalists. In 1867 he was instrumental in drawing up the Ausgleich (compromise) that established the Dual Monarchy.

Dean, Dizzy (1911–1974), US baseball player, b. Jay Hanna Dean in Lucas, Ark. A pitcher in the 1930s, Dean won 150 games with the St. Louis Cardinals until he suffered an injury in the All-Star Game (1937). He was elected to the Baseball Hall of Fame in 1953.

Dean, James (1931–55), US actor, b. Marion, Ind. In 1953 he played the restless son in the film adaptation of John Steinbeck's novel *East of Eden,* and in 1954 he appeared as a misunderstood drag-racing teenager in *Rebel Without a Cause.* Killed in an automobile crash before the release of his final film *Giant,* he became a cult hero, mourned greatly by the young.

Deane, Silas (1737–89), US diplomat, *b.* Groton, Conn. During the Revolution, he arranged an alliance with France (1778) and served as a delegate to the Continental Congress (1774–76).

Dearborn, Henry (1751–1829), US general, b. Hampton, N.H. He distinguished himself in many Revolutionary War battles from Bunker Hill to the British surrender at Yorktown. He marched against Quebec and served in the Saratoga, Valley Forge, and Monmouth campaigns.

Dearborn, city in SE Michigan, on the River Rouge, adjoining Detroit; home of the Ford Motor Co.; site of Greenfield Village, birthplace of Henry Ford, and his estate, Fair Lane, deeded to the University of Michigan in 1956. Industries: automobiles, bricks, tools, dies, metal products. Settled 1795; inc. 1925. Pop. (1970) 104,199.

Dearborn Heights, city in SE Michigan, 8mi (13km) E of Detroit. Pop. (1970) 80,069.

Death, the end of the body's physical life, a concern of specialists in many fields. Doctors and public health officers study causes of death, death rates, and longevity. Lawyers have to define death in legal terms, not always a simple matter. A current medical-legal-ethical controversy involves the "right to die" for the hopelessly ill. Funeral and burial customs are important parts of social and religious life. Philosophers and theologians discuss life after bodily death. Doctors and psychologists join in a new field called thanatology to study the behavior of the dying and those around them. △806–08.

Death Cup, also called death cap or deadly amanita, a very poisonous, though rare, mushroom *(Amanita phalloides)* found in wooded areas. Typically it has an olive-green cap, though it may be white or yellow. The distinguishing marks include the remains of the veil in which young death cups are enclosed—an inverted cap under the true cap and a fleshy cup at the bulbous base. The toxin takes at least 8 hours to show an effect, after which time it may cause agonizing pain and severe liver damage often ending in death.

Death in Venice (1911), novella by Thomas Mann, about Gustav von Aschenbach, a great writer, who is unable to survive creatively in a bourgeois environment. This conflict is complicated by his homosexual feelings for a beautiful young boy he meets in Venice. The author used the affinity of genius and disease to symbolize the decay of Western art.

Death of a Salesman (1949), 2-act drama by Arthur Miller. First performed in New York, it won a Pulitzer Prize, Tony Award, and New York Drama Critics' Circle Award. It was also made into a film (1951). Salesman Willy Loman, dedicated to the idea that to be well-liked will bring success, finds instead that it has led to failure for himself and his two sons, while a neighbor boy he had always disliked became successful. Unable to face the breakup of his world, he kills himself so his family can have his insurance money.

Death Rate, statistical system for determining the frequency of death in a population. The most common type is the crude death rate, or the number of deaths per 1000 population per year. △734.

Death Rites, rites that accompany the passage of a person from the realm of the living to that of the dead. Though these are often accompanied by mourning this is not always the case, as among certain South American Indians. Symbolic action and speech on burial is a common form of death rite, which can last for a few minutes or for several weeks. *See also* Rites of Passage. △806.

Death's-Head Moth, large European hawk moth that has markings suggestive of a human skull on the upper surface of its thorax. Species *Acherontia atropos. See also* Hawk Moth.

Death in the Family, A (1957), novel by James Agee. Published posthumously, it is a semiautobiographical story about a family whose life is shattered by the father's untimely death. The novel was dramatized in 1960 as *All the Way Home.*

Death Valley, large desert in E California, almost surrounded by high mountains, Panamint Range (W) and Armagosa Range (E); contains the lowest point in the Western Hemisphere, 282ft (86m) below sea level. Named in 1849 by goldseekers who were lost attempting to cross it and survived only by climbing the steep Panamint Mts. Hottest summer temperatures in US occur here, up to 134°F (56.7°C). Gold and silver were mined in 1850s; borax was mined in large quantities in late 19th century and taken out by 20-mule teams. Death Valley National Monument contains the entire valley and is administered by National Park Service. Highest peak is Telescope Peak in Panamints, 11,049ft (3,370m). Area: 1,907,760 acres (772,643hectares).

Deathwatch Beetle, small beetle that tunnels through wood and, especially in old houses, produces a faint ticking sound once thought to presage a death in a family. The sound is actually made by the animal bumping its head against the wood, and is the mating signal of the female beetle. Family Anobiidae; species *Xestobium rufovillosum.*

DeBakey, Michael Ellis (1908–), US surgeon who pioneered surgical techniques for treatment of circulatory disorders. In 1966, DeBakey implanted the first mechanical device into a human chest to assist the heart. He had already devised the roller pump (1932), a part of the machinery used in open-heart surgery and developed a method of grafting frozen blood vessels to replace those that were diseased as a correction of aortic aneurisms; later (1956), he replaced the grafts with plastic tubing.

Debentures, bonds that have no mortgage backing. Debentures are promises to pay a particular amount of money on a specific date at a certain rate of interest. The security of a debenture depends solely upon the financial well-being of the corporation or agency that issues it.

Debrecen, city in E Hungary, 137mi (220km) E of Budapest; site of Reformed Church serving as the stronghold of Hungarian Protestantism (16th century); city sometimes referred to as "The Calvinist Rome." Louis Kossuth proclaimed Hungary's independence here (1849). Industries: processed food, farm machinery, railroad cars. Pop. 115,122.

Debs, Eugene Victor (1855–1926), US labor organizer, b. Terre Haute, Ind. In 1884 he was elected to the Indiana legislature. He helped establish and was president of American Railway Union (1893–97). He organized the Social Democratic party of America (1898) and was five times its presidential candidate (1900–20). He was one of the founders of the Industrial Workers of the World (IWW). He was imprisoned during the Pullman Strike (1894) and for violation of Espionage Act (1918). △1326.

DeBusschere, David Albert (1940–), US basketball player and executive, b. Detroit. He played for the Detroit Pistons of the National Basketball Association (1962–69); was player-coach (1964–67), and played for the New York Knicks (1969–74). He was general manager of the New York Nets in the American Basketball Association for 1974–75 and he then was named ABA commissioner (1975–76). He was also a pitcher for the Chicago White Sox in the American League (1962–63).

Debussy, Claude Achille (1862–1918), French composer, founder of the Impressionistic movement in music. Contrary to the trends of his time, Debussy wrote highly original music that was delicate, soft, and suggestive rather than emotional and bombastic. He influenced many composers to turn away from the dominant styles of the 19th century to explore new possibilities of orchestral color and form. Many critics mark Debussy's *Prélude à l'après-midi d'un Faune* (1894) as the beginning of 20th-century music. His orchestral works include *Nocturnes* (1899), *La Mer* (1905), and *Images* (1909). His piano works, among the most important in the piano literature, include the *Suite Bergamasque* (1905, containing the famous "Clair de Lune"), two books of *Images* (1905–07), two books of *Preludes* (1910, 1913), and 12 *Etudes* (1915). His one opera is *Pelléas et Mélisande* (1902). △1364.

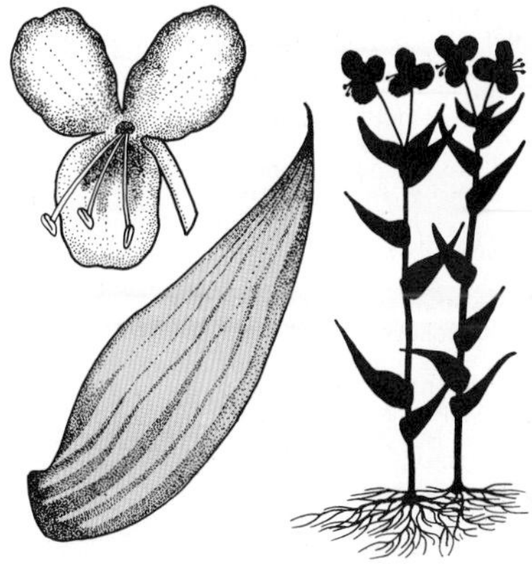

Dayflower

D-day: Dwight D. Eisenhower with troops

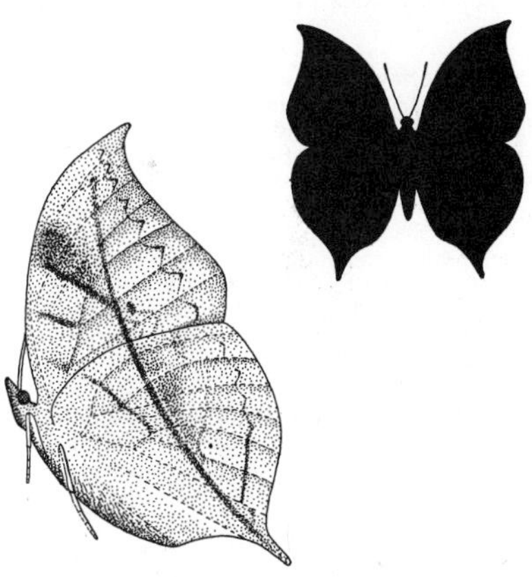

Dead leaf butterfly

Eugene V. Debs

Debye, Peter Joseph Wilhelm (1884–1966), Dutch-American physical chemist who showed that the ionization of the charged atoms of salts in solution is complete. In 1936 he was awarded a Nobel Prize for his work on molecular dipoles and his investigations of X rays and the scattering of light in gases. He emigrated to the United States in 1940 and was appointed professor at Cornell University.

Decaborane. △1558.

Decadents, term applied to writers of the late 19th century who believed in art's freedom from social and moral restraints. Influenced by Charles Baudelaire, French decadents included the poets Paul Verlaine, Stéphane Mallarmé, and Arthur Rimbaud, and the novelist Joris Huysman. Verlaine contributed to the review *Le Décadent* (1886–89). English decadents include Oscar Wilde, Ernest Dowson, and Lionel Johnson. Much of the work of the English writers was first published in *The Yellow Book* (1894–97). *See also* individual authors.

Decameron, collection of 100 stories written in 1351–53 by the Italian Giovanni Boccaccio. The stories are set within a frame story about ten young men and women who meet in a church in Florence in 1348 when the Black Death is sweeping the city. Partly to escape the infection and partly for amusement, they flee to a villa in the hills of Fiesole, where they pass the time for ten days telling one another anecdotes, fabliaux, and fairy tales, many of them bawdy. The same type of frame story is later used by Chaucer in the *Canterbury Tales* and is a popular motif in both medieval and modern literature. △1100.

Decapod, crustacean order of 8,500 species including shrimp, lobster, and crab. Most are marine, some are found in fresh water. Some crabs are amphibious and some terrestrial. All have eight pairs of legs, the first three pairs modified for feeding, the remaining five are for motion. *See also* Crustacean. △486.

Decathlon, series of 10 different track and field events. It takes place over a two-day period and is considered the most demanding of all athletic events. On the first day the individual must compete in a 100-meter race, long jump, shot put, high jump, and a 400-meter race. The second day includes the 110-meter hurdles, discus, pole vault, javelin, and 1500-meter race. It is an Olympic Games event.

Decatur, Stephen (1779–1820), US naval captain, b. Sinepuxent, Md. Active in the campaigns against pirates in Tripoli (1804) and Algiers (1815), he commanded a fleet against the British in the War of 1812. He was noted for his toast "Our country, right or wrong!"

Decatur, industrial city in N Alabama, 75mi (121km) N of Birmingham in Morgan co; the city was enlarged by annexing Albany (formerly New Decatur) and Fairview (1927). Industries: chemicals, auto parts. Settled 1820; inc. 1826. Pop. (1970) 38,044.

Decatur, residential city in NW Georgia; seat of DeKalb co; suburb of Atlanta; site of Agnes Scott College (1889); named for Commodore Stephen Decatur. Inc. 1823. Pop. (1970) 21,943.

Decatur, city in central Illinois, on the Sangamon River; seat of Macon co; here in 1860 Lincoln received his first endorsement for the presidency at the state Republican convention; site of Millikin University; major railroad center; agricultural area. Industries: chemicals, electronic components, glass, brass products. Inc. 1839. Pop. (1970) 90,397.

Decay, or rot, partial or complete deterioration of a substance caused by natural changes. Plant rot, caused by soil-borne bacteria and fungi, affects any plant part making it spongy, watery, hard, or dry. △1550.

Decay, Radioactive. *See* Radioactivity. △1482.

Deccan, peninsular plateau region in central India, between Narmada and Krishna rivers; surrounded by many mountain ranges; N Deccan was long a source of conflict between the S Dravidian and N Aryan inhabitants; by 232 BC Aryan culture had reached all of India. N end of the plateau has rich volcanic soil and produces cotton, grains; in the S there are coffee and tea plantations.

December, twelfth month of the year. Its name comes in part from the Latin for "ten" because it was the last month of the old ten-month calendar. It has 31 days. The birthstone is the ruby, turquoise, or zircon.

Decembrists, Russians, including many officers and noblemen, who staged a revolt in December 1825. They were members of the Northern Society, a secret political society demanding representative democracy. On December 14, 3,000 troops led by the Decembrists gathered in Senate Square in St. Petersburg. These troops were not well organized, and Czar Nicholas I quickly suppressed their revolt. Several Decembrists were executed, while others were sent into exile in Siberia.

Decemvir, a commission of ten officials in Rome. One such commission was the Decemviri Sacris Faciundus, which supervised the Sibylline Books, the games of Apollo, and the secular games.

Decibel (dB), logarithmic unit (one tenth of a bel) for comparing two power levels; frequently used for expressing the intensity of a sound in terms of some reference level. The intensity (I_1) of a sound is expressed in decibels as $10\log_{10}(I_1/I_2)$, where I_2 is usually the threshold intensity of a note of the same frequency. The perceived noise decibel (PN dB) is the sound pressure in decibels above a datum level of 2×10^{-5} pascal of a band of random noise. △1498.

Deciduous Forest, leaf-dropping forest or forest belt found scattered east of the Rocky Mountains in the United States, below Scandinavia throughout Europe, and in most of China and Japan. These forests usually include maple, oak, elm, beech, birch, hickory, ash, and other trees. △594.

Decimal System, commonly used system of writing numbers using a base ten and the Arabic numerals 0–9. It is a positional number system, each position to the left representing an extra power of ten. Thus, 6,741 is $(6 \times 10^3) + (7 \times 10^2) + (4 \times 10^1) + (1 \times 10^0)$. Note that $10^0 = 1$. Decimal fractions are represented by negative powers of ten placed to the right of a decimal point. Thus, 3.145 is $3 + (1 \times 10^{-1}) + (4 \times 10^{-2}) + (5 \times 10^{-3})$, or $3 + 1/10 + 4/100 + 5/1000$. △1448.

Decius (Gaius Messius Quintus Trajanus) (201–51), Roman emperor (249–51). Hoping to strengthen the state religion, Decius was responsible for the especially cruel and methodical persecution of Christians in the empire. △1030.

Declaration of Independence, historic document adopted by Second Continental Congress (July 4, 1776) in which the 13 American colonies justified their separation from Britain. The Congress adopted a resolution of independence, and a committee of five was appointed to draw up a formal document. Thomas Jefferson, John Adams, and Benjamin Franklin drew up the basic outline for the declaration, and Thomas Jefferson wrote it. It was presented to the Congress on June 28 and adopted on July 4, with a few changes. The formal signing took place on August 2. The Declaration states the necessity of government having the consent of the governed, of government's responsibility to the people. The colonies' grievances against the British crown are outlined. In conclusion, the colonies declared themselves free of Britain and united under a single government. Following is the text of the Declaration of Independence. △1218.

IN CONGRESS, JULY 4, 1776
THE UNANIMOUS DECLARATION OF THE THIRTEEN UNITED STATES OF AMERICA,

WHEN in the Course of human events, it becomes necessary for one people to dissolve the political bands which have connected them with another, and to assume among the powers of the earth, the separate and equal station to which the Laws of Nature and of Nature's God entitle them, a decent respect to the opinions of mankind requires that they should declare the causes which impel them to the separation.

We hold these truths to be self-evident, that all men are created equal, that they are endowed by their Creator with certain unalienable Rights, that among these are Life, Liberty and the pursuit of Happiness. That to secure these rights, Governments are instituted among Men, deriving their just powers from the consent of the governed. That whenever any Form of Government becomes destructive of these ends, it is the Right of the People to alter or to abolish it, and to institute new Government, laying its foundation on such principles, and organizing its powers in such form, as to them shall seem most likely to effect their Safety and Happiness. Prudence, indeed, will dictate that Governments long established should not be changed for light and transient causes; and accordingly all experience hath shewn, that mankind are more disposed to suffer, while evils are sufferable, than to right themselves by abolishing the forms to which they are accustomed. But when a long train of abuses and usurpations, pursuing invariably the same Object, evinces a design to reduce them under absolute Despotism, it is their right, it is their duty, to throw off such Government, and to provide new Guards for their future security. Such has been the patient sufferance of these Colonies; and such is now the necessity which constrains them to alter their former Systems of Government. The history of the present King of Great Britain is a history of repeated injuries and usurpations, all having in direct object the establishment of an absolute Tyranny over these States. To prove this, let Facts be submitted to a candid world:

He has refused his Assent to Laws, the most wholesome and necessary for the public good.

He has forbidden his Governors to pass Laws of immediate and pressing importance, unless suspended in their operation till his Assent should be obtained; and when so suspended, he has utterly neglected to attend to them.

He has refused to pass other Laws for the accommodation of large districts of people, unless those people would relinquish the right of Representation in the Legislature, a right inestimable to them and formidable to tyrants only.

He has called together legislative bodies at places unusual, uncomfortable, and distant from the depository of their public Records, for the sole purpose of fatiguing them into compliance with his measures.

He has dissolved Representative Houses repeatedly, for opposing with manly firmness his invasions on the rights of the people.

He has refused for a long time, after such dissolutions, to cause others to be elected; whereby the Legislative powers, incapable of Annihilation, have returned to the People at large for their exercise; the State remaining in the mean time exposed to all the dangers of invasion from without, and convulsions within.

He has endeavoured to prevent the population of these States; for that purpose obstructing the Laws for Naturalization of Foreigners; refusing to pass others to encourage their migrations hither, and raising the conditions of new Appropriations of Lands.

He has obstructed the Administration of Justice, by refusing his Assent to Laws for establishing Judiciary powers.

He has made Judges dependent on his Will alone for the tenure of their offices, and the amount and payment of their salaries.

He has erected a multitude of New Offices, and sent hither swarms of Officers to harass our people, and eat out their substance.

He has kept among us, in times of peace, Standing Armies, without the Consent of our legislatures.

He has affected to render the Military independent of and superior to the Civil power.

He has combined with others to subject us to a jurisdiction foreign to our constitution, and unacknowledged by our laws; giving his Assent to their Acts of pretended Legislation:

For quartering large bodies of armed troops among us:

For protecting them, by a mock Trial, from punishment for any Murders which they should commit on the Inhabitants of these States:

For cutting off our Trade with all parts of the world:

For imposing Taxes on us without our Consent:

For depriving us in many cases of the benefits of Trial by Jury:

For transporting us beyond Seas to be tried for pretended offences:

For abolishing the free System of English Laws in a neighbouring Province, establishing therein an Arbitrary government, and enlarging its Boundaries so as to render it at once an example and fit instrument for introducing the same absolute rule into these Colonies:

For taking away our Charters, abolishing our most valuable Laws and altering fundamentally the Forms of our Governments:

For suspending our own Legislatures, and declaring themselves invested with power to legislate for us in all cases whatsoever.

He has abdicated Government here by declaring us out of his Protection and waging War against us.

He has plundered our seas, ravaged our Coasts, burnt our towns, and destroyed the lives of our people.

He is at this time transporting large Armies of foreign Mercenaries to compleat the works of death, desolation and tyranny, already begun with circumstances of Cruelty & perfidy scarcely paralleled in the most barbarous ages, and totally unworthy the Head of a civilized nation.

He has constrained our fellow Citizens taken Captive on the high Seas to bear Arms against their Country, to become the executioners of their friends and Brethren, or to fall themselves by their Hands.

He has excited domestic insurrections amongst us, and has endeavoured to bring on the inhabitants of our frontiers, the merciless Indian Savages, whose known rule of warfare is an undistinguished destruction of all ages, sexes and conditions.

In every stage of these Oppressions We have Petitioned for Redress in the most humble terms. Our repeated Petitions have been answered only by repeated injury. A Prince, whose character is thus marked by every act which may define a Tyrant, is unfit to be the ruler of a free people.

Nor have We been wanting in attentions to our Brittish brethren. We have warned them from time to time of attempts by their legislature to extend an unwarrantable jurisdiction over us. We have reminded them of the circumstances of our emigration and settlement here. We have appealed to their native justice and magnanimity, and we have conjured them by the ties of our common kindred to disavow these usurpations, which would inevitably interrupt our connections and correspondence. They too have been deaf to the voice of justice and of consanguinity. We must, therefore, acquiesce in the necessity, which denounces our Separation, and hold them, as we hold the rest of mankind, Enemies in War, in Peace Friends.

WE, THEREFORE the Representatives of the UNITED STATES OF AMERICA, in General Congress, Assembled, appealing to the Supreme Judge of the world for the rectitude of our intentions, do, in the Name and by Authority of the good People of these Colonies, solemnly publish and declare, That these United Colonies are and of Right ought to be FREE AND INDEPENDENT STATES, that they are Absolved from all Allegiance to the British Crown, and that all political connection between them and the State of Great Britain, is and ought to be totally dissolved; and that as FREE AND INDEPENDENT STATES, they have full Power to levy War, conclude Peace, contract Alliances, establish Commerce, and to do all other Acts and Things which Independent states may of right do. AND for the support of this Declaration, with a firm reliance on the protection of divine Providence, we mutually pledge to each other our Lives, our Fortunes and our sacred Honor.

John Hancock
Button Gwinnett
Lyman Hall
Geo. Walton
Wm. Hooper
Joseph Hewes
John Penn
Edward Rutledge
Thos. Heyward, Jr.
Thomas Lynch, Jr.
Arthur Middleton
Samuel Chase
Wm. Paca
Thos. Stone
Charles Carroll
of Carollton
George Wythe
Richard Henry Lee
Th. Jefferson
Benj. Harrison
Thos. Nelson, Jr.
Francis Lightfoot Lee
Carter Braxton
Robt. Morris
Benjamin Rush
Benj. Franklin
John Morton
Geo. Clymer

Jas. Smith
Geo. Taylor
James Wilson
Geo. Ross
Caesar Rodney
Geo. Read
Tho. M:Kean
Wm. Floyd
Phil. Livingston
Frans. Lewis
Lewis Morris
Richd. Stockton
Jno. Witherspoon
Fras. Hopkinson
John Hart
Abra. Clark
Josiah Bartlett
Wm. Whipple
Saml. Adams
John Adams
Robt. Treat Paine
Elbridge Gerry
Step. Hopkins
William Ellery
Roger Sherman
Sam. Huntington
Wm. Williams
Oliver Wolcott
Matthew Thornton

Declaration of the Rights of Man and Citizen (1789), statement of the principles of the French Revolution. It was adopted by the Constituent Assembly on Aug. 26, 1789, accepted by Louis XVI on October 5, and included in the constitution of 1791. Influenced by the US Declaration of Independence and the ideas of Jean Jacques Rousseau, it established the sovereignty of the people and the restrictions for social consideration embodied in "liberty, equality, and fraternity." The Rights of Man was a powerful influence in 19th century democratic and socialist movements.

Declaratory Act, law in which Britain's Parliament, after repeal of the Stamp Act (1766), asserted its right to tax the American colonies. △1218.

Declination, angular distance of a celestial body north or south of the celestial equator (north is positive, south is negative), thus measured in degrees along a line passing through the body and the celestial poles. Declination and right ascension form a coordinate system referred to the celestial equator. △138.

Declination, Magnetic, the angle between the magnetic lines of force and the meridians of latitude. Declination is measured in degrees east or west of the magnetic north, which is the spot pointed to by a compass. The lines of equal declination are isogonic lines, the line of zero declination is the agonic line. △168.

Decolonization. △1332, 1350.

Decomposition, natural degradation of organic matter into simpler substances. Organisms of decay are usually bacteria and fungi. △580.

Decompression Chamber. △238.

Decorated Style, term used to describe the middle phase of Gothic architecture in England from about 1270 to 1350. Characteristic of the style was the use of vaulted portals and richly designed windows using narrow strips of stone in bar tracery, such as at Exeter Cathedral. Ribs in the vaults of portals became more delicate.

Decorated Triggerfish. △516.

Découpage, form of collage in which surfaces are decorated with paper cutouts or similar material and then permanently preserved by painting or gluing. The technique is simple and has gained popularity as an easily accessible art form.

Dedham, town in E Massachusetts, on the Charles River; seat of Norfolk co; site of Fairbanks House (1636), and first public school in America (1649); scene of the Sacco-Vanzetti trial (1921) in Norfolk co courthouse; Horace Mann practiced law here. Industries: electronics, industrial research. Settled 1635; inc. 1636. Pop. (1970) 26,938.

Deductive Logic, method of inference in which a conclusion follows necessarily from one or more given premises; this is in contrast to induction. Although originally generalized from Aristotle's "syllogism," today a syllogism is only one special case of deduction. *See also* Inductive Logic; Syllogism. △854.

Dee, John. △822.

Deed, a signed written document that immediately transfers ownership of land from one existing person, the grantor, to another, the grantee. The transfer is also known as a conveyance, and the terms are used interchangeably.

Deep Scattering Layer (DSL), a "phantom" sound-reflecting layer in the ocean water. Various layers that can be detected during the day by sound-detecting devices disappear at night. Small deep-dwelling fish that feed on the water surface at night may be the cause.

Deep-sea Drilling Project (Project Mohole), a US scientific program sponsored by the National Science Foundation to obtain a core from the mantle of the earth by drilling through the crust, abandoned in 1966. (The moho, or base of the crust, is thinnest under deep oceans.) The core was expected to carry a continuous fossil and sediment record of the earth's history.

Deer, slim, even-toed, long-legged, hoofed, ruminant mammals. There are 17 genera of 53 species distributed in the Americas, Eurasia, NW Africa, Japan, Philippine Islands, and Indonesia. They have been introduced in Australia, New Zealand, New Guinea, and Hawaii. Deer eat grass, bark, twigs, and young shoots. Their habitat is varied and includes forests, arctic tundra, desert, open bush and swamps.

The musk deer is the smallest, the moose the largest. They are mostly brownish and young are often spotted. In some species this spotting is retained into adulthood. Most males bear antlers. During the mating season, males fight fiercely over a harem. Temperate species mate in late fall or winter. The gestation period is 160 days in musk deer and 10 months in the Eurasian roe deer, with usually 1–2 young born. Most deer gather in groups. The family is known to have existed since the Oligocene Epoch. Length: 2.5–9.5ft (0.8–3m); weight: 201–1760lb (90–792kg). Family Cervidae. *See also* Artiodactyla; Ruminant. △548.

Deer Fly, or Gadfly, fly, closely related to the horsefly, found worldwide. This 0.28 to 0.4in (7–10mm) fly has a brown or black body with dark wing markings. The female gives a painful bite and is known to transmit anthrax, tularemia, and loa loa. Family Tabanidae, species *Chrysops app.* and *Tabanus spp. See also* Horsefly.

Deerslayer, The (1841), novel by James Fenimore Cooper about Natty Bumppo, a young hunter living among the Delaware Indians in New York State during the French and Indian Wars and his efforts to help the Hutter family against the Iroquois. The book is one of

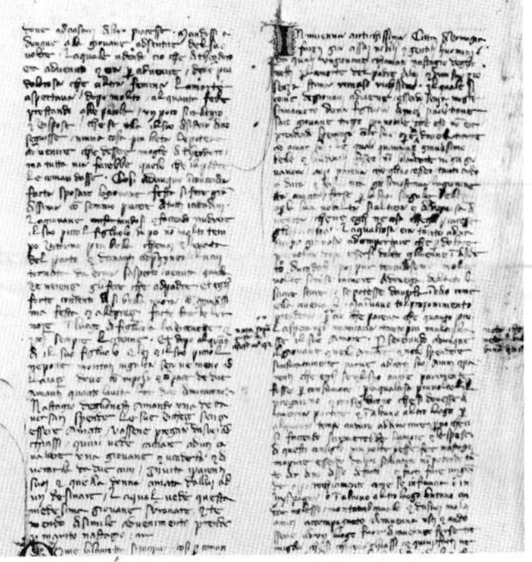

Boccaccio's Decameron

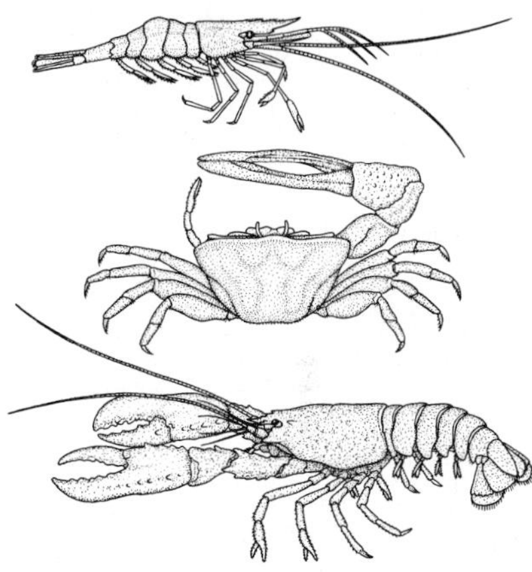

Decapoda

Deep Sea Drilling Project: core sample

Deer

the Leather-Stocking Tales. *See also* Leather-Stocking Tales, The.

De Facto Segregation, segregationist practices supported by custom rather than law. An example is the "neighborhood" school with a racially segregated student population.

Defenestration of Prague (May 1618), an event that marked the beginning of the Thirty Years War. During the Reformation, Catholic Hapsburg supporters persecuted the Protestants. Angry Czechs threw two Hapsburg representatives out of castle window into a moat.

Defense, Department of (DOD), US, cabinet-level department within the executive branch. It is directed by the secretary of defense who is a cabinet member. The defense department is responsible for all agencies concerned with national security and consists, in addition to secretary of defense, the Joint Chiefs of Staff, the service departments, and the operational military commands. The secretary of defense, with the president, is responsible for all operational military activities, providing civilian control for the Army, Navy, and Air Force. The DOD was originally established as the war department in 1789. In 1947, the National Security Act brought the three branches of the military forces together under the National Military Establishment, which in 1949 was renamed the department of defense. *See also* Joint Chiefs of Staff; Air Force, US; Army, US; Navy, US; and Marine Corps, US.

Defense Department Reorganization Act (1958), US act passed under President Eisenhower, it changed the organization of the Department of Defense by eliminating ambiguities in command authority and centralizing research and engineering within the department. With this bill, the secretary of each of the armed services became responsible to the secretary of defense.

Defense Mechanism, in psychology, any method that an individual uses (unconsciously) to ward off anxiety caused by unpleasant thoughts or desires. Such mechanisms were first described by Freud in 1894. In their extreme forms, defense mechanisms can be symptomatic of mental disturbance, especially neuroses. However, to some extent all of us use them daily, when we rationalize mistakes, deny faults, or intellectualize unpleasant emotions.

Deficit Finance, government borrowing of funds from future tax revenues in order to finance current purchases of goods and services. This is accomplished through the Treasury Department's sale of government securities. If the government does not have a balanced budget, it must engage in deficit financing. *See also* Balanced Budget.

Deflation, falling prices, the opposite of inflation. Deflation normally occurs during a recession or depression, and it can be measured by the price indexes in the same way that inflation is measured. Excess capacity of the productive facilities within the economy usually is the cause of deflation. Excess capacity leads to an excess supply condition in which suppliers wish to supply more goods at full employment than consumers wish to buy. *See also* Inflation. △1322.

Defoe, Daniel (1660?–1731), English journalist and novelist. He joined the Duke of Monmouth's rebellion (1685) and William III's army (1688). He supported the foreign king in the poem *The True-born Englishman* (1701) and was imprisoned for his pamphlet "The Shortest Way with Dissenters" (1702). His works include *Robinson Crusoe* (1719), *Moll Flanders* (1722), *A Journal of the Plague Year* (1722), and *Roxana* (1724). △1184, 1188.

De Forest, Lee (1873–1961), US inventor who developed the audion tube (1907), a device that made live radio broadcasting possible. It remained the key component of radio, television, radar, telephone, and computer systems until the transistor was invented in 1947.

Degas, (Hilaire Germain) Edgar (1834–1917), French painter and sculptor. Classically trained and a lifelong admirer of Ingres, Degas was a perfectionist whose achievement was to combine the discipline of classic art with the immediacy of the modern. His early work reflects his studies of the masters. After meeting Manet and Zola, he showed his work at the Impressionists' exhibitions. Sharing their interest in everyday life, he began painting ballet, cafe, and racing scenes. A brilliant draftsman influenced by Japanese prints and photography, he introduced unusual angles and off-center composition into his carefully planned work. To master movement, he made sculptures of dancers and horses. His use of color and light, always subtle, became concentrated in the late pastels. In his lifetime only one work, *The Cotton Exchange at New Orleans,* was sold to a museum and his rank as one of the greatest French artists was not known until his work was auctioned after his death. His work is in major museums. △1254.

De Gasperi, Alcide (1881–1954), Italian politician and prime minister. Born in the region of Trento under Austrian rule, in his early political years he worked for Trentino reunification with Italy. Strongly anti-Fascist, he was imprisoned twice in the 1920s. Active in the resistance during World War II, after the war he was secretary of the Christian Democratic party and prime minister (1945–53).

De Gaulle, Charles André Joseph Marie (1890–1970), French general, president (1959–69), and celebrated patriot. A graduate of the Ecole Spéciale Militaire of Saint-Cyr, he fought in World War I and was wounded and captured in 1916. He later fought against the Bolsheviks in Poland, graduated from the Ecole Supérieur de Guerre in 1924, and served in the occupation of the Rhineland and in Lebanon. A proponent of a mechanized professional army, he was made brigadier general in charge of the 4th Armored Division in 1940. When the Vichy government was created, he went to England as the self-declared head of the French resistance and was sentenced to death by court-martial in France. He was later head of the French Committee of National Liberation in Algiers. After the war, he made two partially successful attempts to reorganize French government (1945–46) and following a period of retirement was elected president of the Fifth Republic in 1958. He settled the Algerian crisis, saw France become a nuclear power, and withdrew from NATO in 1966. He resigned after the refusal of his suggested reforms in 1969. △1356.

Degeneration, evolutionary regression. The loss of a function or structure causing a higher form to revert to a lower form.

Degradation, in geology, wearing away or general reduction or erosion of Earth. The carrying off of rocky material by wind, water, or ice are degradative processes. Downcutting of a stream as it cuts its channel is also degradation. Otherwise, the denudation of slopes or the transportation of material is classed as degradation. *See also* Denudation; Erosion.

Degree, unit of angular measure equal to one three hundred and sixtieth of a complete revolution. One degree is written 1°, and can be divided into 60 parts called minutes (′), which may in turn be divided into 60 parts called seconds (″). 360 degrees are equal to 2π radians.

Degree, Academic, title showing that a person has completed a course of college study. The associate's degree, such as associate in arts (A.A.) or science (A.S.), is granted by a junior college after completion of two years. The bachelor's degree, such as B.A. or B.S., is awarded after four (sometimes three) years of college. The master's degree, such as M.A. or M.S., requires one or more years of study above the bachelor level. The doctorate—for example, doctor of philosophy (Ph.D.)—requires several years of graduate study plus a dissertation. Professional degrees, such as the M.D. for medicine, show that a person has completed the courses required for his field. Honorary degrees do not require study but are rewards for fame or public service.

Degree Day, a unit of the departure of the average outdoor daily temperature from a standard, such as 65°F (18°C), used in measuring fuel-consumption requirements.

Degree of Arc, angular measure equal to 180th part of the angle subtended by a semicircular arc at the center of the circle. It is measured in degrees, minutes, and seconds, where 60 seconds equal one minute and 60 minutes equal one degree. In astronomy 15 degrees of arc (15°) is equal to one hour of right ascension.

DeHaven, Edwin Jesse (1816–65), US explorer, b. Philadelphia. As an acting master in the US Navy, he sailed on the Wilkes expedition to Antarctica (1839). In 1850 he led a sailing expedition in an unsuccessful search for the lost English explorer Sir John Franklin; while caught in drifting arctic ice, he discovered new territory later named Grinnell Land.

Dehydration, loss of water from a solid, liquid, or gas by physical or chemical means, hastened by the presence of a catalyst, by heat, or by a dehydrating agent, such as sulfuric acid. Dehydration is an old established method of food preservation whereby the growth of predative microorganisms is inhibited.

Deimos, smaller of Mars' two satellites, discovered (1877) by Asaph Hall. Diameter 7.5mi (12km); mean distance from planet 14,600mi (23,500km); mean sidereal period 1.26 days. △76.

Deindividuation, in social science, the behavior of those persons in groups who lose their sense of individual identity and responsibility. They may go along with the crowd in failing to help someone in trouble, or they may join in mob violence. *See also* Anonymity.

Deinotherium. △574.

Deirdre, a tragic figure in Irish mythology. Conchobar, the king of Ulster, kidnapped the beautiful Deirdre with the intention of marrying her, but she fled with Naoise to Scotland. Shortly after returning to Ulster, Naoise and his two brothers were murdered; Deirdre died of grief.

Deism, religious belief or form of theism restricting God's action to an initial act of creation, after which He retired to consider the excellence of his work. Deists held that the natural creation is regulated by law and inscribed with perfect moral principles. Many "philosophes," for example Voltaire and G.E. Lessing, were Deists. *See also* Philosophes.

Déjà Vu (French, literally "already seen"), the experience or feeling that one has encountered the same situation on some previous occasion when, in reality, the situation is a new one. Psychologists explain such experiences by concluding that the situation is probably very similar to some previously experienced situation that can no longer be consciously remembered. △824.

De Jure Segregation, segregationist practices supported by existing laws. Despite federal civil rights legislation, discrimination in housing, employment, and education is still practiced.

DeKalb, city in N Illinois, 60mi (97km) W of Chicago. Barbed wire was first manufactured here in 1870s; site of Northern Illinois University (1895). Industries: wire, hybrid seed corn. Inc. 1877. Pop. (1970) 32,949.

Dekker, Thomas (1572–1632), English dramatist best known for his comedy *The Shoemaker's Holiday* (1599). He also wrote *The Gull's Hornbook* (1609), a satirical pamphlet containing incidental details of the London theater of his day.

De Kooning, Willem (1904–), US painter, b. Holland; an important abstract expressionist. After studying in Europe, de Kooning went to the United States in 1926. He did free-lance work, including work on a mural under Fernand Léger. He also did murals for the Federal Arts Project. De Kooning began painting abstractions, mainly portraits, in the 1930s but did not have a one-man show until 1948. Though influenced by Picasso and Gorky, de Kooning's paintings are distinctive and original. Marked by organic shapes in harsh colors or white on black, they are done in energetic, almost violent brushwork. His first critical and popular success came in the mid-1950s with the series of paintings called *Woman.* A leader of the New York, or action, school, de Kooning continued to alternate between abstractions and further investigations of the *Woman* theme. His work is in private collections and major museums of modern art.

de la Cierva, Juan. △1720.

Delacroix, (Ferdinand Victor) Eugène (1798–1863), French painter, a leader of the romantic movement. His masterly composition and brilliant use of color have influenced modern painting since his time. Delacroix considered becoming a writer, and his *Intimate Journals* and *Correspondence* are important descriptions of the life of a painter involved in intellectual life. Classically trained, he also studied the works of the masters. He knew the English painter Constable and admired Byron, Shakespeare, Scott, and Goethe. Delacroix's first success came with large historical paintings such as *The Massacre at Chios* and *The Death of Sardanapalus* (both, Louvre, Paris) that are notable for sensuous and violent subject matter as well as technical excellence. His enormous output included portraits, religious and allegorical studies, and hunting and Oriental scenes. Delacroix also made lithographs and painted major murals for King Louis Phillipe. △1228.

de la Mare, Walter (1873–1956), English poet, short story writer, and anthologist. He worked as a clerk for the Standard Oil Company until 1936, when he received a government pension. His poems have great power to suggest mystery and eeriness. His collections of poems include *Songs of Childhood* (1902), *Peacock Pie* (1913), and *Poems for Children* (1930). Of his poetry anthologies, *Come Hither* (1923) is outstanding. His prose includes the novel *Memoirs of a Midget* (1921) and the collection of stories *On the Edge* (1930). He also wrote imaginative stories for children.

Delany, Martin R(obinson) (1812–85), US journalist, physician, and political figure, b. Charles Town, Va. (now W.Va.). In Pittsburgh in 1843 he founded the weekly *Mystery*, which publicized grievances of women and blacks. In 1852 he received a medical degree from Harvard University, and during the Civil War he served as an army surgeon, becoming (1865) the first black to receive a regular commission in the US Army. After serving in the Freedmen's Bureau (1865–67), he became a judge in Charleston, S.C.

Delaunay, Robert (1885–1941), French painter. An artist of the Cubist style, he exhibited with the Munich Blue Rider Group. Central to his work is the use of color to define structure.

Delaware, state in the E United States on the Atlantic Ocean and Delaware Bay, about midway between New York City and Washington, D.C.

Land and Economy. Delaware occupies the N portion of the Delmarva Peninsula between the Atlantic Ocean and Chesapeake Bay; parts of Maryland and Virginia lie to the S. Most of the state is a coastal plain; the higher elevations are in the extreme N. The Delaware River, which carries a great volume of shipping to the port of Philadelphia, forms part of the E boundary. Manufacturing, principally in the Wilmington area, center of the huge E.I. du Pont de Nemours chemical industry, is the mainstay of the economy. Wilmington also contains the home offices of many large corporations. Agricultural production, chiefly poultry raising, is centered in the central and S sections. Shellfishing is important along Delaware Bay.

People. Migration from other states has been significant; only about 3% of the population is foreign-born, but only about 50% was born in the state. A little over 70% resides in urban areas.

Education and Culture. The University of Delaware is at Newark and there are six other institutions of higher education. Notable museums are the Henry Francis du Pont Winterthur Museum near Wilmington, which displays the history of American decorative arts in a number of period rooms, and the Hagley Museum, which emphasizes the history of US industry.

History. The first permanent white settlement was made by Swedes at Fort Christina (Wilmington) in 1638. Called New Sweden, it spread N and S along the Delaware River. In 1655 the Dutch conquered New Sweden and added the land to their colony of New Netherland. The English seized New Netherland in 1664, naming it New York, and the Delaware area remained part of that colony until 1682, when the Duke of York ceded it to William Penn to give his new colony of Pennsylvania a seacoast. In 1704, Penn allowed the three "Lower Counties" to elect an assembly of their own, which functioned as a separate colonial government, although the governor of Pennsylvania was nominally its governor. In the final voting on the Declaration of Independence in July 1776, Caesar Rodney, one of Delaware's three delegates, cast the deciding ballot. Delaware's ratification of the US Constitution came less than three months after the document was finished. The state remained loyal to the Union in the Civil War. Manufacturing development began in 1802 with the establishment of the du Pont gunpowder mill, the first unit of the diversified du Pont industries.

PROFILE

Admitted to Union: Dec. 7, 1787, first of the 13 original states to ratify the US Constitution
US Congressmen: Senate, 2; House of Representatives, 1
Population: 548,104 (1970); rank, 46th
Capital: Dover, 17,488 (1970)
Chief cities: Wilmington, 80,386; Newark, 21,298
State Legislature: Senate, 21; House of Representatives, 41
Area: 2,057sq mi (5,328sq km); rank, 49th
Elevation: Highest, 442ft (135m), near Centerville; lowest, sea level
Industries (major products): chemicals, processed foods, metal products, machinery, textiles
Agriculture (major products): broiler chickens, cattle, corn, vegetables
Minerals (major): sand, gravel
State nicknames: First State, Diamond State
State motto: Liberty and Independence
State bird: Blue hen chicken
State flower: Peach blossom
State tree: American holly

Delaware Indians, named for Lord De la Warr, this tribe of Algonkin-speaking North American Indians call themselves *Lenni-Lenape*, meaning "real men." The tribe, divided into three major divisions, the Unami, Munsi, and Unalachtigo, lived in New Jersey, Long Island, E Pennsylvania, and N Delaware. Originally numbering about 8,000 persons, most of the Delaware were forced to move in the early 19th century to Indian Territory (now Oklahoma) where about 2,000 live today.

Delaware River, river in New York, New Jersey, and Pennsylvania; rises in the Catskill Mts of SE New York; its East and West branches meet at Hancock, New York; flows SE along New York-Pennsylvania border to Port Jervis then between New Jersey and Pennsylvania S to Delaware Bay. It cuts through Kittatinny Mts forming Delaware Water Gap near Stroudsburg, Pa. At Trenton, New Jersey, it becomes navigable and travels through a highly industrialized area that creates serious pollution problems. Second only to the Mississippi River in annual freight tonnage carried, its upper course furnishes water power through a series of dams and reservoirs that also provide flood control and water to municipalities. River is connected to Chesapeake Bay by the 19mi (30km) Chesapeake and Delaware Canal. Scene of Washington's crossing from Pennsylvania to fight at Battle of Trenton Dec. 25, 1776. Length: 280mi (450km).

Delaware Water Gap, scenic gorge on the Pennsylvania-New Jersey line; cuts through the Kittatinny ridge of the Appalachian Mts; site of the Delaware Water Gap National Recreation Area, which includes the gap, parts of the mountain ridge, several islands, and 40mi (64km) of river bank.

De la Warr, Thomas West, Baron (1577–1618), colonial governor of Virginia. A member of Parliament (1597), he was also a soldier, and the first governor of the Jamestown Colony (1610–11). When he arrived the colonists were discouraged and ready to leave, but under his authority the colony was strengthened. A state (Delaware), river, and bay are named after him.

Delbrück, Max (1906–), US biologist, b. Germany. He shared the 1969 Nobel Prize in physiology or medicine for his discovery that bacterial viruses reproduce sexually, thus showing that genetic recombination occurs.

Del City, city in central Oklahoma, 4mi (6km) E of Oklahoma City. Tinker Air Force Base is SW of city. Industries: wheat, cotton, oil. Nearby Midway was annexed to Del in 1963. Pop. (1970) 27,133.

Delderfield, Ronald Frederick (1912–73), English novelist. He began his career as a playwright and newspaperman. His most famous work was a trilogy dealing with life in the English countryside at the end of the Victorian era: *God is an Englishman* (1970); *Theirs Was the Kingdom* (1971); *Give Us This Day* (1973). All were best-selling narrative accounts of England's transformation from an agricultural to an industrial society as seen from the perspective of a single family.

Deledda, Grazia (1875–1936), Italian novelist. Her novels, the best known of which is *Ashes* (1904), are usually dominated by the rugged landscape of her native Sardinia and the struggle of its simple, passionate people against their tragic destiny. She won the Nobel Prize for literature in 1926.

Delegated or Enumerated Powers, powers granted to Congress in Article I, Section 8 of the Constitution including the authority to impose and collect taxes, borrow money, regulate commerce at home and abroad, and to declare war. Section 8 also sets forth the implied powers of Congress. *See also* Elastic Clause; Implied Powers.

Delft, city in SW Netherlands; formerly an important commercial center until the 17th century when it was replaced by Rotterdam; center of ceramics industry; site of 13th-century Gothic church, 15th-century Gothic church (Nieuwe Kerk), which contains the tombs of William the Silent and Hugo Grotius, 17th-century town hall, technical university; scene of the assasination of William the Silent (1584). Industries: Delftware (pottery), china, tiles. Founded 11th century. Chartered 1246. Pop. 83,698.

Delhi, capital city of India, on Yamuna River; partitioned into Old Delhi, New Delhi, and Union Territory of Delhi. Old Delhi is the commercial part of the city; New Delhi, planned by English architects, is the administrative center; Old and New Delhi are on sites

Degas: self portrait in oil

Charles De Gaulle: liberation of Paris, 1945

Dover, Delaware: Governor's House

Delftware tiles

containing remnants of at least seven cities, some dating back almost 2,000 years. Delhi was held by English 1803–1947; capital of British India 1912, replacing Calcutta; New Delhi became the official capital in 1937 and remained so after the independence of India (1947). Points of interest include Rashtrapate Bhavan, presidential palace; Jami Masjid, India's largest mosque; the marble Red Fort; and National Museum. Most of Delhi's industries are from Old Delhi: cotton textiles, jewelry, clothing, shoes, handicrafts, tourism. Pop. 3,772,457.

Delhi Sultanate (1192–1398), powerful Muslim state in India. Mohammed of Ghor defeated the Hindus at Taraori in 1192, establishing the sultanate, which lasted until the Mogul Empire was established. It included five successive dynasties, the Slave, Khaljis, Tughluqs, Sayyis, and Lodis. Thirty-three different sultans ruled during this time. Under Mohammed ibn Tughluq (1325–51) the sultanate reached its largest area. Tamerlane (Timur) invaded in 1399, and anarchy followed. The Muslims formed separate states, and there was no attempt at forming a unified government, which led to eventual domination by the Mogul empire. △1202.

d'Elhuyar, Don Juan. △1554.

Delian League, confederacy of Greek city-states formed to conduct war on Persia, 478–404 BC. Though League policy theoretically was decided by an assembly in which each member state was considered equal, Athens (which provided the largest fleet) came to dominate the League. By the time peace was concluded with Persia in 449 BC, the League was nothing less than the Athenian empire. △994.

Délibes, Leo. △1246.

Delilah, biblical Philistine courtesan loved by Samson. She discovered his long hair was the source of his great strength and cut it off, betraying him to the enemy. △840.

Delinquency, Juvenile, crimes committed by youths and all other acts that come under the jurisdiction of juvenile courts. A youth may be defined in widely varying ways, with the lower limit being 7 or 8 and the upper limit, 15, 16, 18, or 21. "Delinquent" acts include those that the law would class as crimes if committed by an adult. Also included are such loosely defined acts as incorrigibility or vagrancy. The original purpose of the special laws and courts for youthful offenders was to spare them the stigma of being processed by criminal courts. Social scientists have sought the causes of juvenile delinquency in personal maladjustments and in society's failures. △790, 914, 916.

Delirium Tremens, serious condition occurring most often when alcohol is abruptly withdrawn from an alcoholic, occasionally as a reaction to barbiturates or other drugs. It produces tremor, loss of appetite, terrifying dreams, various mental and nervous-system disturbances, and if severe, delirium. In some 10% of cases, death occurs. △730.

Delisle, Guillaume (1675–1726), French scientist. The first scientific cartographer and one of the founders of modern geography, he used astronomical observations and accurate measurements to compile the 90 or so maps he published during his lifetime. His first important work—maps of the continents and a globe—was published in 1700. He was premier geographer to the king in 1718 and tutored the young Louis XV. His brother was the French astronomer Joseph Nicholas Delisle.

de Lôme Letter (1898), private correspondence written by Dupuy de Lôme, Spanish minister to the United States, to a Cuban friend. The letter, characterizing Pres. McKinley as weak and two-faced, was stolen and published in the New York *Journal*. This incident increased US sentiment against Spain just before the Spanish-American War.

De Long, George Washington (1844–81), US naval officer and explorer. After an arctic voyage in 1873, De Long again set sail in 1879 for arctic research. His ship was soon caught in a polar ice pack and drifted until 1881 when it was crushed. De Long was one of 14 survivors to reach Siberia, only to die there of cold and starvation. Three years after his ship sank, several items belonging to his crew were found on an ice floe off Greenland's coast, supporting the theory of a transarctic drift.

Delorme, or **de l'Orme, Philibert** (1515?–70), French architect. He studied in Rome and in 1547 was commissioned by Diane de Poitiers to build her chateau at Anet. Under Henry II, he was appointed superintendant of buildings. At Henry's death, he was dismissed by Catherine de Médicis and then wrote two books with illustrations of many of his buildings, which no longer exist. Only parts of the chateau at Anet and the tomb of Francis I at St. Denis survive. A most influential artist, he was known for his introduction of classical forms into French architecture.

Delos (Dhilos), smallest island in Cyclades (Kikladhes) group, Greece, in S Aegean Sea; by Greek legend, considered the center of the islands and birthplace of Apollo and Artemis; appointed treasurer of the Delian League 478–454 BC. Declared a free port by Rome (166 BC), it prospered as an important shipping and slave center; destroyed during Mithridatic Wars (87 BC). French excavations since 1877 have uncovered remains of temples, theaters, commercial buildings.

Delphi, ancient city-state in Greece, 6mi (10km) from Mt Parnassus. The Delphic Oracle, est *c.* 8th century BC, became the most famous oracle and sacred sanctuary in ancient Greece; legend says the priestess Pythia entered the Temple of Apollo from which she received the prophecy, which was recorded by priests and used to guide important state decisions. The temple was sacked by the Romans; Theodosius I closed the oracle 390 AD with the onset of Christianity; site of the Amphictyonic League, the religious organization of the city-states that established the Pythian Games. French excavations (1892) revealed the artifacts.

Delphic Oracle. △994.

Delphinium, or larkspur, any of about 250 species of herbaceous plant native to temperate parts of the Northern Hemisphere. They have buttercuplike leaves and loosely clustered, blue or white, spurred flowers. Spring larkspur *(Delphinium tricorne)* and tall larkspur *(D. exaltatum)* are common wildflowers. Rocket larkspur *(D. ajacis)* has finely cut leaves and is frequently cultivated. Family Ranunculaceae.

Del Rio, city in W Texas, on Rio Grande, across from Ciudad Acuña, Mexico; site of international bridge to Mexico. Industries: farming, cattle, fruit. Founded 1868; inc. 1911. Pop. (1970) 21,330.

Delta, a fan-shaped body of alluvium deposited at the mouth of a river. A delta occurs when a river drops more sediment than waves, tides, or currents can remove. The term was introduced in the 5th century BC by Herodotus to describe the land at the mouth of the Nile River which resembled the Greek letter △, delta. △258, 270.

Delta Geminorum. △88.

Deluge, The, story of the Great Flood. In one of its earliest pre-Biblical versions, reconstructed from a broken clay tablet from Mesopotamia, some of the gods decide to destroy mankind. But one of them, Enki, thinking this harsh, counsels a mortal, Ziusadra, to build a boat to save the seed of mankind. The flood lasted for seven days; then the sun shone and the earth reappeared. The gods, pleased with his obedience, made Ziusadra immortal. *See also* Noah.

Delusion, false, irrational belief or thought. People suffering from paranoia may have delusions of grandeur, persecution, etc. Those who have delusions of grandeur are convinced that they have an important identity (God, Napoleon, Gandhi) and can be totally out of contact with reality, that is, psychotic. *See also* Paranoiad Personality. △760, 764.

Demand, in economics, the schedule of prices and the quantities that would be purchased by consumers at those prices. For most goods, the normal relationship between price and quantity is inverse, that is, as the price of the good increases, the quantity demanded by consumers declines. The demand for a good is determined by a number of factors, however, including purchaser's income, price of competing goods, and consumer tastes and preferences.

Demand Curve, graphic representation of relationship between prices and quantity demanded. It slopes downward to the right, indicating that consumers will increase the quantity of the good purchased as prices fall.

Demand Shift, in economics, a change in the demand curve at all prices. Thus a different quantity would be purchased at every possible price. Demand shifts may occur because of changes in consumer income, in tastes and preferences, or in the price of substitute goods. *See also* Demand Curve.

Demand Theory, in economics, the body of knowledge and theory relating to consumers' demands for goods and services. Demand theory makes assumptions concerning the logic of consumers' desires and the consumers' preferences for higher utility levels. From these assumptions, economists have developed a theory of behavior. It can be logically shown that the consumer will prefer more of a good at a lower price than at a higher price. It can be shown also that the consumer will react differently to price changes in different goods, depending upon the elasticity of demand.

Dementia Praecox, term used by Emil Kraepelin at the turn of the century to describe what is now called schizophrenia. Literally, it means irreversible mental deterioration *(dementia)* in a young person *(praecox)*. *See also* Kraepelin, Emil. △764.

Demerol, trademark for a synthetic morphine, used widely as a painkiller.

Demeter, in Greek mythology, the goddess of corn, health, and marriage. She was the daughter of Cronus and Rhea and a sister of Zeus. △832, 838.

Demetrius I (*c.* 336–283 BC), king of Macedonia (294–283 BC). Named Demetrius Poliorcetes ("taker of cities"), this son of Antigonus I ruled Greece (293–289). He freed Athens and Megara in 307, defeated Ptolemy in 306, besieged Rhodes in 305–04, and suffered defeat at Ipsus in 301. He invaded Asia in 287 but was forced to surrender to Seleucus I in 285.

Demetrius II (*c.* 278–229 BC), king of Macedonia (239–229 BC). The son of Antigonus II Gonatus, he was defeated in the Demetrian War against the Achaeans and the Aetolian League. He was the father of Philip V of Macedon.

Demetrius I Soter (187–150 BC), king of Syria (162–150 BC). Sent as a hostage to Rome during the reign of his father, Seleucus III, he saw his kingdom usurped by his uncle Antiochus IV (175 BC), then by his cousin Antiochus V. In 162 BC, aided by the Greek historian Polybius, he escaped from Rome, killed his cousin, and gained the throne. He crushed the revolt of Timarchus in Babylon and attempted to subdue the Maccabees in Jerusalem. He was killed battling against the pretender Alexander Balas.

Demetrius II Nicator (161–125 BC), king of Syria, son of Demetrius I. With the help of Ptolemy VI he seized power from Alexander Balas (146 BC). He was captured and imprisoned by the Parthians (141 BC). He retook the throne in 128 BC, ousting the usurper Tryphon, governor of Antioch. He was slain at Tyre while fighting the Egyptians.

De Mille, Agnes (George), (1909–), US dancer and choreographer, b. New York City. Between 1927–40 she appeared with dance companies in the United States and Europe. Her choreography for the Broadway musical *Oklahoma* (1943) elevated musical dance numbers to an integral part of the plot and a serious art form. She went on to choreograph many other musicals, including *Carousel* (1945), *Brigadoon* (1947), *Gentlemen Prefer Blondes* (1949), *Paint Your Wagon* (1951), and *Come Summer* (1969). She also created ballets that combined classical and modern elements, including *Rodeo* (1942) and *Fall River Legend* (1948).

De Mille, Cecil B(lount) (1881–1959), US film producer and director, b. Ashfield, Mass. He is noted for lavish dramatic spectacles. With his first film, *The Squaw Man* (1913), he established Hollywood as the US film-production capital. He brought stage actors and techniques to film and stabilized the length of feature films. DeMille evinced an unerring assessment of public taste: His Biblical epics—*The Ten Commandments* (two versions, 1923, 1956) and *King of Kings* (1926)—combine a Victorian moral tone with graphic sexuality. Other major films include *Forbidden Fruit* (1921), *Union Pacific* (1939), and *The Greatest Show on Earth* (1953), which won him an Academy Award for best director.

Democracy, political system in which authority is rooted in the consent of the governed. In one form the will of the people is expressed indirectly, through elected representatives. Democracy stresses that all men are endowed with basic civil rights. In the United States, executive, legislative, and judicial branches of government are separated and a system of checks and balances exists to curtail their power. Fixed periodic elections are conducted to insure that government is ultimately responsible to the electorate. △898–904.

Democratic Party, US political party, the descendant of the Anti-Federalist and Democratic-Republican parties. From Thomas Jefferson's election in 1800 through James Buchanan's election in 1856, the party was strong, gathering its support mainly from farmers, small businessmen, and the professional classes. In this period, Democrats opposed a central bank, protective tariffs, and internal improvements at federal expense. Southern planters in the party promoted expansionism, which led the United States to war with Mexico (1846). Party strength declined after the Civil War until 1932, when Franklin D. Roosevelt was elected. After that, it remained strong until 1952. In 1960, Democratic candidate John F. Kennedy won the presidential election beginning "the New Frontier" era that stressed US world responsibilities for peace and economic growth at home. Lyndon B. Johnson succeeded Kennedy with an ambitious program of domestic legislation. In the 1976 elections, the Democratic candidate, Jimmy Carter, was elected president. *See also* Democratic-Republican Party. △276, 1358.

Democratic-Republican Party, US political party, originally called the Anti-Federalist party, or Republicans. Led by Thomas Jefferson, James Madison, and James Monroe, the party opposed strong central government and Alexander Hamilton's economic policies. It supported the French Revolution, advocated an agrarian democracy, strict construction of the Constitution, and other measures to minimize aristocratic control of government. *See also* Anti-Federalist Party; Democratic Party.

Democratic-Republicans (Jacksonian), a group within the Democratic-Republican party that supported Andrew Jackson. They were opponents of John Quincy Adams and Henry Clay in the election of 1828. The party had split after Adams' election in 1824. Unlike Thomas Jefferson, who favored minimal government, Jackson believed in the necessity of a strong federal government to curb predatory interests. After Jackson's election this group became known as the Democratic party. *See also* Democratic Party.

Democritus of Adbera (*c.* 460–*c.* 370 BC), Greek philosopher. Although none of his books survive, he is best remembered for his atomic theory. He suggested that all matter consisted of tiny, indivisible particles; that various atoms differed physically; and that atoms' motions were determined by laws of nature, not the actions of gods. He also stated that the Milky Way consisted of a large mass of tiny stars. △1480, 1550.

Demographic Transition Theory, or theory of the vital revolution, social theory stating that populations increase and decrease in relation to the degree of social development. In premodern societies, death and birth rates are high. Modernization decreases the death rate, but not the birth rate, causing a temporary acceleration in population growth. With more advanced development, the birth rate also drops and population growth stabilizes.

Demography, term introduced in 1855 by the Frenchman Achille Guillard for the scientific study of human populations, their changes, movements, size, distributions, structures, and developments. The study may be said to have begun with the work of Englishman John Graunt who published the first mortality table (1662). Demographic methods are primarily statistical and quantitative, and they are used by government and business for ascertaining public needs. *See also* Population.

Demonetization, ending the practice whereby the value of a nation's currency is defined by precious metal. Monetary metal, metal coins, and paper money no longer are freely convertible. The reform became widespread after World War I. Demonetization also refers to the withdrawal from circulation of certain kinds of currency, which then cease to be considered legal tender.

Demosthenes (384–322 BC), Athenian orator and statesman. He achieved fame as a public speaker after struggling to overcome physical disabilities. He devoted his life to speaking and fighting on behalf of the Greek states in their resistance to Philip of Macedon. His works include the *Philippics* and *On the Crown.* △994, 998, 1004.

Demotic, in Writing. △870.

Dempsey, Jack (1895–), US boxer, b. William Harrison Dempsey in Manassa, Colo. He won the world's title from Jess Willard (1919) in Toledo, and lost it to Gene Tunney (1926) in Chicago. In a rematch with Tunney (1927), he lost after flooring Tunney because he did not go immediately to a neutral corner, which delayed the start of the referee's count. He was elected to the Boxing Hall of Fame in 1954.

Demulcent, a soothing, generally oily or mucilaginous substance used to relieve pain in inflamed or irritated mucous surface.

Dendrite, that part of a nerve cell, or neuron, that carries impulses to the cell body; for example, impulses from sense organs to the cell body. Dendrites are often short and branching, and there may be more than one per neuron. *See also* Neuron. △664, 668.

Dendrobium, genus of orchid native to SE Asia and popular as a cultivated plant. It has inconspicuous leaves and showy flowers with an unpleasant scent. The 900 species include *D. nobile* that has white to deep purple flowers with purple centers. Height: to 3ft (91cm). Family Orchidaceae.

Dendrochronology, annual measurement of time by examination of growth rings in trees. This data can be related to wood used in structures, and to the hydrology of the region where it grew, thus fixing points in the climatic history of a particular area. Chronology based on the bristlecomb pine, a particularly long-lived tree, extends back over 7000 years. △276.

Deneb, or Alpha Cygni, remote and very luminous white supergiant star in the constellation Cygnus. Characteristics: apparent mag. +1.26; absolute mag. −7.0; spectral type A2; distance 1500 light-years.

Dengue, contagious virus disease transmitted by the *Aedes aegypti* mosquito. Occurring in epidemic form in the tropics and in the warm months in temperate areas, it produces fever, headache, and fatigue, followed by severe back pain, muscle aching, and the appearance of a reddish rash. Recovery usually follows, and second attacks are rare.

Denikin, Anton Ivanovich (1872–1947), Russian general. After serving in World War I, he became (1918) chief of staff for the Provisional government but was shortly dismissed. He and Gen. Lavr Kornilov staged a revolt against the Provisional government, and he was arrested. He escaped after the Bolsheviks seized power and became commander of the White forces in the Russian Civil War. Defeated by Bolshevik troops in 1920, he left for Constantinople. He lived in France from 1926. △1310.

Denis, king of Portugal. See Diniz.

Denis, Saint (3rd century? AD), patron saint of France. According to tradition, he was the first bishop of Paris and was martyred on Montmartre. He is often represented carrying his severed head in his hands. His feast day is October 9.

Denison, city in NE Texas, 65mi (105km) N of Dallas, near Oaklahoma border; birthplace of President Dwight D. Eisenhower; distribution center for grain and dairy products. Industries: food processing, cotton textiles. Inc. 1873. Pop. (1970) 24,923.

Denitrification, process that reduces nitrites or nitrates to yield nitrites, nitrogen oxides, ammonia, or free nitrogen. Denitrifying bacteria change the nitrogen of ammonia into free nitrogen that enters the atmosphere or soil. *See also* Nitrogen Cycle.

Denizli, city in SW Turkey, on tributary of Menderes River; capital of Denizli prov.; site of ruins of ancient Greek cities Laodicea ad Lycum and Hierapolis; early Christian center and site of one of "Seven Churches of Asia Minor." Industries: tourism, grain, cotton, tobacco. Founded *c.* 200 BC by Antiochus II. Pop. 83,600.

Denmark, independent kingdom in N Europe situated at the entrance to the Baltic Sea. The country covers most of the Jutland Peninsula and includes the islands of the Danish archipelago. Greenland and the Faeroe Islands are integral parts of Denmark.

Land and Economy. Denmark is a country of low-lying plains consisting mostly of clay and sands deposited in the glacial era. After the Ice Age, the area comprised a continuous land-bridge connecting the Jutland and Scandinavian peninsulas. Subsequent flooding created the present-day fjords and straits. Denmark has a temperate maritime climate, with mild summers and cloudy, humid winters. Although lacking coal, hydroelectric power, and most mineral resources, the economy of Denmark is nonetheless highly industrialized. The industries range from iron, steel, and shipbuilding to a broad range of consumer products. Denmark is also known for its fine porcelains, textiles, and furniture. Only about 8% of

Delphi, Greece

Delphinium

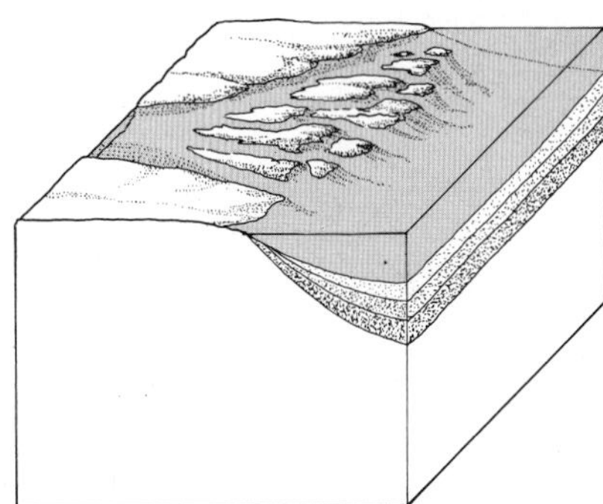
Delta

Cecil B. De Mille

the people are engaged in agriculture. Copenhagen is the leading port and manufacturing center.

People. The Danes are a Scandinavian people, closely related to Norwegians and Swedes, and trace their ancestry to Germanic tribes that moved into the area in the early Christian era. The official language is Danish, a Germanic tongue. The people are entitled to complete religious freedom, but the Evangelical Lutheran Church is the official church of Denmark. About 97% of the Danes are members of this church. Nearly 75% of the people live in urban communities.

Government. Denmark is a constitutional monarchy. Succession to the throne is hereditary, and the ruling monarch must be a member of the national church. Executive power lies with the monarch, while legislative power is shared by the monarch and a parliament (Folketing). In executive matters the monarch exercises authority through government ministers. Major international obligations cannot be assumed without the approval of the Folketing, which may also force the resignation of any, or all, of the monarch's ministers. The major political parties are the Social Democrats, Agrarians, and Conservatives.

History. Denmark first appears in recorded history with the rise of marauding Danish Vikings in the 8th century AD. King Harold Bluetooth Christianized Denmark in the 10th century. Under Canute II, the Danish kingdom extended over Norway and, for a brief period, all of England. Denmark and Norway were united until the 19th century. As an ally of Napoleonic France, Denmark was forced in 1815 to cede Norway to Sweden. A liberal constitution, approved in 1849, abolished absolute power and created a parliament. Denmark was neutral in WWI, but was invaded and conquered by Nazi Germany in WWII (April 1940). The war caused severe economic difficulties. US financial aid assisted in the post-war industrial recovery. Denmark joined the United Nations in 1945, and later became a member of the North Atlantic Treaty Organization (NATO). Since 1972, it has belonged to the European Economic Community. *See also* Faeroe Islands; Greenland.

PROFILE

Official name: Denmark, Kingdom of
Area: 16,629sq mi (43,069sq km)
Population: 5,000,000
Density: 301per sq mi (116per sq km)
Chief cities: Copenhagen (capital); Aarhus; Odense
Government: constitutional monarchy
Religion (major): Evangelical Lutheran Church
Language: Danish (official)
Monetary unit: Krone
Gross national product: $26,800,000,000
Per capita income: $3,400
Industries (major products): food processing, furniture, diesel engines, electrical products
Agriculture (major products): dairy products, hogs, beef, barley
Minerals (major): lignite
Trading partners (major): United Kingdom, Sweden, West Germany, United States

Dennis v. United States (1951), US Supreme Court case upholding the Smith Act conviction of a Communist party official for contempt. The court declared that free speech principles do not preclude a state from punishing anyone who advocates the overthrow of the government by force or violence. *See also* Smith Act.

Denominator, Common, number that is a multiple of the denominators of two or more specified fractions. Thus for 2/3 and 1/7, the (least) common denominator is 21, allowing the fractions to be put in the forms 14/21 and 3/21, for addition, etc. △1446.

Denonville, Jacques René de Brisay, Marquis de (1642–1710), governor of New France (1685–89), b. France. A career soldier, he fought the Iroquois and laid waste to Seneca lands, strengthened Fort Frontenac, and kept peace among conflicting Canadian factions.

Densitometer, instrument for measuring the optical transmission or reflection (optical density) of a material, such as a photographic film or plate. It can be used in spectroscopy to determine the positions of spectral lines and bands and to measure their relative densities, and thus intensities.

Density, the mass per unit volume of a substance. The density of a solid or liquid is normally constant over a wide range of temperatures and pressures. This fact was used to establish the unit of mass (the gram) in the metric system—the density of water was taken to be one gram per cubic centimeter. The density of a gas, however, depends strongly on both pressure and temperature. △1502, 1504.

Dental Hygiene, the prevention, through education and treatment, of tooth decay and gum disease. In dentists' offices, specially trained dental hygienists remove deposits and stains from teeth and may apply fluorides. They also advise on diet and nutrition. Education departments sometimes employ personnel to explain the importance and techniques of oral hygiene to children. △756.

Dentine. △756.

Dentistry, the profession concerned with the care and treatment of the oral cavity, particularly the teeth and their supporting tissue. Besides general practice, dentistry includes such specialties as oral surgery, prosthodontics, periodontics, orthodontics, pedodontics, and public health. Scientific dentistry started in the 16th and 17th centuries in Germany and France when it became recognized as a separate profession; university courses were initiated and dental textbooks were published. Before that time barbers had performed most dental services. Today the practice of dentistry is strictly controlled; there are special educational requirements and licensing procedures in all countries. △756.

Dentition, the type, number and arrangement of teeth. In adult man, there are 32 teeth: in each jaw are 4 incisors; 2 canines; 4 premolars, or bicuspids; 4 back molars; and finally at about 18 years of age, 2 wisdom teeth. Man's teeth cut, grind, and tear food and are not adapted to any particular type of diet. *See also* Tooth.

Denton, city in N central Texas, 38 mi (61km) NW of Dallas; seat of Denton co; named for John B. Denton, lawyer and minister killed by Indians. Industries: processed food, plastics. Founded 1855; inc. 1866. Pop. (1970) 39,874.

D'Entrecasteaux, volcanic island group in SW Pacific Ocean, off SE coast of New Guinea; administered by Papua and New Guinea; group consists of Fergusson (largest), Goodenough, and Normanby islands. Dobu is chief settlement. Named for French navigator Antoine d'Entrecasteaux, who discovered the archipelago 1793. Area: 1,200sq mi (3,118sq km). Pop. 32,336.

Denture, artificial substitute for all the teeth in the upper or lower jaw; usually made of plastic and occasionally reinforced with metal. The retention of such a prosthetic device depends on the firmness of the underlying tissues and the adhesion provided by the saliva of the mouth. When well-fitted and designed, it can improve natural appearance. A partial denture is called a bridge. △756.

Denudation, in geology, all the processes that result in either wearing away or lowering of the Earth's surface. In a narrow sense, denudation may be synonymous with erosion; however, erosion, mass wasting, transportation, are all considered to be processes resulting in denudation. *See also* Erosion.

Denver, capital and largest city of Colorado, in N central Colorado, at foot of Rocky Mts on South Platte River; seat of Denver co. It served as territorial capital 1867; prosperity was greatly spurred with the discovery of gold and silver (1870s and 1880s), and the building of the Denver Pacific Railroad (1870); site of capital building (19th century), many government agencies including the US Mint; Denver Art Museum, Boettcher Botanical Gardens; University of Denver (1864), Loretto Heights College (1891), Regis College (1877), Temple Buell College (1909), Rockmont College (1914); many resort and recreational areas set in the surrounding beautiful scenery; processing, shipping, and distribution center for agricultural area. Industries: aerospace, electronics, rubber goods, luggage, tourism, mining, livestock, meat packing, railroad shops, food processing. Founded 1860 with inc. of Auraria and two other villages, and named in honor of Kansas territorial governor James W. Denver; inc. 1861. Pop. (1970) 514,678.

Deoxyribonucleic Acid (DNA), molecule found in chromosomes and viruses that is resposibile for storing the genetic code. It consists of two long chain polynucleotides shaped like a twisted rope ladder, the sides of which consists of sugar-phosphate chains and the rungs of linked nitrogenous bases. The sugar is 2-deoxy-D-ribose and the four bases are adenine, cytosine, guanine, and thymine. The genetic code is stored by the sequence of the bases, three bases coding for one amino acid. *See also* Nucleic Acids. △1570–74.

Dependence, in psychology, the extent to which an individual needs other people in order to function, as opposed to independence, functioning on one's own. Infants are totally dependent on their parents for satisfying basic survival needs, but most children progress toward some degree of independence as they grow

Dependent Variable. *See* Variable.

Depersonalization, in psychology and psychiatry, a state in which a person feels detached from his own reality or body, and the actions of oneself as well as of others are perceived as dreamlike and unreal. It is a symptom of some serious mental disorders such as the schizophrenic reactions and other psychoses. △760.

DePew, Chauncey Mitchell (1834–1928), US political figure, b. Peekskill, N.Y. He is best known for his membership on the board of the New York Central (1882–1928) and its affiliated railroads. He was general counsel for the Vanderbilt railroads (1866) and served them during the period of great rail expansion. He was New York senator (1899–1911). A popular speaker, he published an autobiography, *Memories of Eighty Years* (1922).

DePew, city in W central New York; suburb of Buffalo; named for Chauncey M. DePew, railroad executive and US senator. Industries: printing, chemicals, steel stampings. Inc. 1894. Pop. (1970) 22,158.

Depletion, a special form of depreciation referring to the exhaustion of nonreplaceable natural resources, eg, oil, minerals, or natural gas, as they are exploited for human use. Depletion is usually figured as the percentage of the estimated reserves of the resource that has been used up, ie, mined or pumped.

Deposition, in geology, layering or placing any material in a constructive process. The accumulation of sediment, ore deposits, and organic material by any natural agent that would result in stratification of rock-forming material is deposition. △258.

Depreciation, decline in the value of an asset as it is spread over its economic life. Depreciation covers the decrease in value or usefulness because of use, age, or exposure to the elements but does not cover unexpected losses due to accident or natural disaster. It is a way of measuring an asset's actual cost and actual value to the owner, either a firm or an individual. In the United States deduction for depreciation of an asset may be taken as a business expense in determining taxable income.

Depression, bottom of the business cycle. Depression is associated with high unemployment levels, excess capacity, seriously decreased purchasing power for consumers, and lack of business expansion, encouraged by pessimism. Government influence tends to be more effective in curing a depression than in dampening the inflation caused by prosperity. *See also* Business Cycle. △764, 766, 1324.

Depression, emotional state marked by sadness, dejection, feelings of guilt and worthlessness and self-blame. In severe depressions psychomotor retardation can lead to a near stupor. Depressions are often accompanied by physical complaints, including loss of appetite, insomnia, and inertia. Social withdrawal and reality distortion are also usually present.

Depression, Great, in US history, the severe economic crisis that afflicted the country in the 1930s. It was part of a worldwide downturn in economic activity. The Great Depression is generally thought to have begun with the collapse of the stock market in October 1929 and not to have finally ended until about 1940, when increased defense spending strengthened the economy.

Economists differ as to the relative importance of the various causes of the Great Depression, which was both more serious and longer lasting than the usual downturn in the business cycle. Among those causes were the economic dislocations brought about by World War I, the unbridled stock market speculations of the 1920s, the easy credit money that produced more industrial production than consumers were able to purchase, a prosperity that was unequally shared (farmers and workers did not take part in it to the extent that other segments of the economy did), and the protectionist trade policies of a series of conservative Republican administrations that denied foreign markets for US products. The stock market crash of October 1929 was especially wrenching to the economy; it was estimated that $30,000,000,000 was lost in stock values during the crash week. Since a large part of stock speculation was done on margin, or credit, the collapse had a devastating effect on the nation's banking system and, to a lesser extent, on foreign banks that had helped to finance the speculation. Bank failures became commonplace. Whereas 659 banks failed in 1929 (already a high figure, as had been the case throughout the 1920s), 1,352 ailed in 1930 and 2,294 in 1931. Virtually any set of statistics proves that the depression was of a much greater magnitude than the ordinary business downturn. Unemployment, which had been at 1,500,000 persons in 1929, jumped to 4,000,000 in 1930 and continued to increase until it reached 13,000,000 in 1932 (almost one-third of the work force). The gross national product fell by almost 50%: from $104,000,000,000 in 1929 to $58,500,000,000 in 1932. Automobile production fell from 5,500,000 cars in 1929 to 1,500,000 in 1932.

Herbert Hoover, who became president only months before the crash, was slow to respond to the downslide. Surrounded by economic conservatives, he tended to a laissez-faire attitude, believing that conditions would right themselves. The Hawley-Smoot Tariff Act, passed by the Republican Congress in 1930 and signed by Hoover, had the effect of helping to spread the US depression worldwide. It brought U.S. tariffs to an all-time high, causing 25 other nations to raise theirs in retaliation. International trade fell alarmingly as a result. Despite his belief in the basic soundness of the economy, Hoover instituted several antidepression measures, including a large public works program and the Reconstruction Finance Corporation. After the Democrats won control of Congress in the 1930 election, there was an upswing of federal programs.

In 1932 the Democrats nominated Franklin D. Roosevelt for president; his campaign promised an active federal program that would bring a "new deal" to the American People. He won an overwhelming victory, and from the date of his inauguration in 1933, the history of the Great Depression mirrored that of his New Deal, which was designed to end it. In Europe, perhaps the most devastating effect of the depression was the emergence of Adolf Hitler and the Nazi party from the ruins of the German economy. *See also* New Deal. △1324.

Depressive Reaction, a neurotic or psychotic disorder that has as its primary characteristic severe depression. A *neurotic depressive reaction* is a disorder that occurs when an individual experiences a disturbing event, eg loss of a loved one. He or she typically withdraws, feels helpless and worthless, and may be unable to cope with daily life. Although this disorder responds to treatment with drugs and the support of sympathetic people, it may sometimes develop into a *psychotic depressive reaction.* Individuals with this severe disorder may lose contact with reality and threaten and attempt suicide. Although such behavior is similar to that of manic-depressives, there is no elated manic stage. Electroshock and psychotherapy are sometimes used to treat psychotic depressive reaction. *See also* Depression; Manic-Depressive Psychosis.

DeQuincey, Thomas (1785–1859), English essayist and critic. DeQuincey led an unsettled life after leaving Oxford, where he first took opium. His *Confessions of an English Opium Eater* (1822) made him famous.

Depretis, Agostino (1813–87), Italian political leader and a leftist leader of the Risorgimento (the mid-century movement for Italian unification). The head of various national government ministries from 1862, by 1873 he was the leader of the left. He was prime minister 1876–78, 1878–79, 1881–87.

Deptford Pink. △444.

Depth Charge, explosive cannister detonated underwater at predetermined depths and used by naval vessels and aircraft to destroy submerged submarines.

Depth Perception, ability to localize the position of objects in three-dimensional space. Even though the retina is two-dimensional, information about depth is created in the retinal image. These "depth cues" include such factors as linear perspective and relative size. Physiological information, such as ocular convergence, is also important. △674.

Derailleur Gear. △1688.

Derain, André (1880–1954), French painter. An artist of the fauvist style, he characterized his prolific landscapes with brilliant color, swift curves, and spontaneous lines. His later style was influenced by Italian masters, and his subjects became precisely drawn in subdued colors. *See also* Fauvism. △1294.

Derby, Edward George Geoffrey Smith Stanley, 14th Earl of (1799–1869), English Conservative statesman and orator. At first a Whig, he gradually became leader of the Protectionists, whom he rallied, and was eventually recognized as Conservative leader (1851). As prime minister (1852, 1858–59, 1866–68) he passed the electoral Reform Act (1867) and ensured Disraeli's succession.

Derby, Thomas Stanley, 1st Earl of (1435–1504), English noble. At Bosworth Field (1485) he commanded a large force which he withheld from aiding Richard III. After the battle he crowned his stepson, the victorious Henry VII, and was made earl.

Derby, city in N central England, on Derwent River, 37mi (60km) NE of Birmingham; important railway junction. England's first silk mill was built here 1719. Industries: railway engineering, aircraft engines, textiles, electrical equipment, porcelain, paints, hosiery. Pop. 219,348.

Derby Day. △1252.

Derich Born (Holbein). △1144.

Derivative, rate of change of a mathematical function with respect to a change in the independent variable. The derivative is an expression of the instantaneous rate of change of the function: in general it is itself a function of the variable. A common example is in obtaining velocities and accelerations. An object moves a distance x in time t, according to the equation $x = at^2$. In such motion the velocity increases with time (the object accelerates). The expression dx/dt, called the first derivative of distance with respect to time, is equal to the velocity of the object. For the example it equals 2 at. The result is obtained by considering a small time interval δt, over which the average velocity is $\delta x/\delta t$, and taking the limit of this as t becomes vanishingly small. The second derivative, written d^2x/dt^2, is equal to the acceleration. Derivatives can similarly be used to find the slope of a curve at a particular point. *See also* Calculus; Differential Equation; Limit.

Dermaptera. △492.

Dermatitis, an inflammation of the skin that in acute form produces redness, itching, and blister formation or oozing and in chronic form thickening and darkening of the skin and scales. In *contact dermatitis,* contact with a particular substance—such as soap or poison ivy—produces the reaction. In *atopic dermatitis* (often associated with hay fever and asthma) excessive dryness occurs and redness at the neck and elbow and knee bends. In *stasis dermatitis,* heavy pigmentation and sometimes ulcers develop on the inner sides of lower legs as result of poor circulation. In *neurodermatitis,* there is no known cause except the patient's repeating rubbing and scratching of the area. The term is also sometimes used for eczema. *See also* Eczema. △686.

Dermatology, branch of medicine that deals with the diagnosis and treatment of skin diseases and disorders. △686, 724.

Dermis, the inner of the two main layers of the skin. Also known as the true skin, the dermis is made up of connective tissue fibers that give strength and toughness. It is richly supplied with blood vessels and contains many nerve endings, sensory organs of touch, and numerous glands. △686.

Dern, George Henry (1872–1936), US politician, mining executive and public official, b. near Scribner, Nebr. He was the co-inventor of the Holt-Dern ore roaster, was governor of Utah (1925–32), and served as President Roosevelt's secretary of war (1933–36), when the post included the administration of the work corps created under the unemployment relief act of 1933. He was the author of the Workmen's Compensation Law, the Corrupt Practices Act and the State Mineral Land Leasing law.

Derry. *See* Londonderry.

Dervish, member of a Muslim religious fraternity, similar to a Christian monk. Central to dervish devotion is the *Dhikr* or "remembering" of God, often attained through a hypnotic or ecstatic trance.

DES. *See* Diethylstilbestrol.

Desai, Morarji (Ranchodji) (1896–), Indian political figure. After entering the civil service in 1919, he resigned in 1930 to devote himself to the movement for Indian independence. He was jailed by the British several times for his activities. After independence (1947), he was minister of finance (1958–63, 1967–69), and deputy prime minister (1967–69). From 1969 he was an opponent of Prime Minister Indira Gandhi.

Desalination. △1562.

0
400 km
NORTH SEA
DENMARK
Ålborg
Århus
Sweden
Odense
Copenhagen (København)
BALTIC SEA
Neth.
Belgium
Federal Republic of Germany
German Democratic Republic
Poland
Lux.
Czechoslovakia
France
Austria
Switzerland
Liech.
Hungary

Denmark

Copenhagen, Denmark: Tivoli Gardens

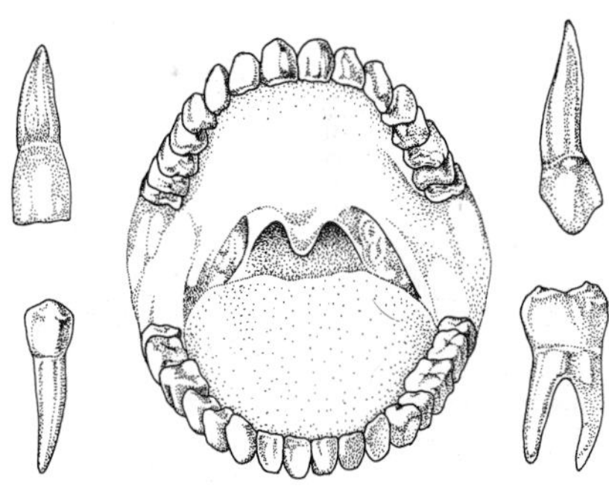

Dentition: (clockwise from lower left) *biscuspid, incisor, canine, molar*

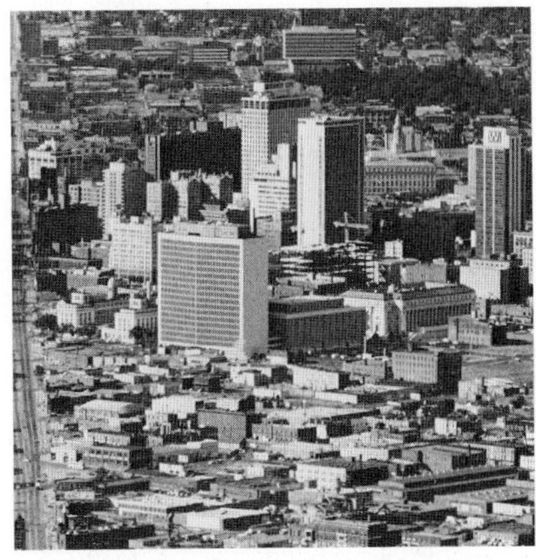

Denver, Colorado

Descartes, René (1596–1650), French philosopher and mathematician. He received a Jesuit education and saw military service (1612–21). Thereafter he retired to pursue scientific and philosophical inquiries. He founded analytic geometry and contributed to geometrical optics in the treatise that prefaced the *Discourse on Method* (1637). Here, and in his *Meditations*, Descartes introduced modern metaphysics, as the work of deduction and intuition. Mind, he held, was essentially separate from matter, which was extended, inert substance. Mind knows matter only through ideas, whose clarity and distinctness, guaranteed by God, confers truth. Descartes died in Sweden, shortly after accepting the invitation of Queen Christina to join her intellecual court. *See also* Cartesian; Cogito Ergo Sum; Rationalism. △856, 858, 1184.

Deschutes River, river in central and N Oregon; rises in Cascade Range; flows N to Columbia River; source of power and irrigation. Length: 240mi (386km).

Desegregation, ending laws or customs that separate people on such grounds as sex, age, race, or religion. *See also* Integration.

Desensitization, process in which a person allergic to a certain substance or substances is subjected to injection of the allergen, or offending substance, in a series of gradually increasing dosages in hope of desensitizing or decreasing the person's sensitivity to the substance. *See also* Allergy. △772.

Desert, arid region of any latitude typified by scant, intermittent rainfall and little vegetation. Since erosion is a great influence, more important in arid as compared to more humid regions, the landforms of any desert are unique. The region can be classified as young, mature, or old, depending on the extent of the remains of the mountain and stream features it once had. *See also* Butte; Degradation. △266, 590, 604–06.

Desert Palm of California. *See* California Fan Palm.

De Sica, Vittorio (1901–74), Italian film director and actor. He is noted for his use of nonprofessional actors in biting, realistic drama. His major directing credits are *Bicycle Thieves* (1947), *Umberto D* (1952), *Indiscretion* (1952), *Two Women* (1961), and *A Brief Vacation* (1974). He acted in *General Della Rovere* (1959).

Desiderius (AD 8th century), last Lombard king (756–74) and father-in-law of Charlemagne. When Desiderius threatened papal territory and his sovereignty, Charlemagne rejected his wife and in 774 captured the Lombard throne.

Desman, aquatic, molelike mammal that eats insects, mollusks, and fish. It has a flexible tubular snout, webbed hind feet, and vertically flattened scaly tail. The Russian *Desmana moschata* has red-brown fur that is commercially valuable. *Galemys pyrenaicus*, found in the Pyrenees, is smaller and lighter in color. Length: body—to 8in (215mm); tail—to 8in (215mm). Family Talpidae.

De Smet, Pierre Jean (1801–70), Belgian Jesuit missionary, and founder of many missions in the American West. He made numerous trips to Europe to raise funds for his work. De Smet was a mediator trusted by the Indians; he helped in negotiation with Sitting Bull, chief of the Sioux (1869). De Smet depicted the Indians in *Western Missions and Missionaries* (1859) and *New Indian Sketches* (1863).

Desmid, any of a group of tiny single-celled green algae (order Desmidiales) that live in fresh water and are characterized by perforations in their cell walls and highly symmetrical shapes resembling those of diatoms. They differ from diatoms chiefly in their lack of a silica skeleton. Some form colonies. *See also* Green Algae.

Des Moines, capital city of Iowa, in the center of the state near the confluence of the Des Moines and Racoon rivers; site of Iowa State Fair Grounds, Drake University (1881), Grand Valley College (1896), the Des Moines Art Center, Des Moines Symphony. Damaged by severe flooding 1954, the city is now protected by dams and reservoirs. Industries: insurance, publishing, plastics, chemicals, outdoor clothing. Founded as Fort Des Moines 1843; inc. 1851; chartered as city 1857; made capital 1858. Pop. (1970) 201,404.

Des Moines River, unnavigable river in NW central Iowa, formed by junction of E and W forks in Humboldt co; flows SE across Iowa; empties into Mississippi River at Keokuk; used for hydroelectric power. Length: 327mi (526km).

Desmoulins, Camille (1760–94), pamphleteer and journalist in the French Revolution. His writings and speeches did much to further the revolutionary cause. A critic of the new government, he became alligned with Jacques Danton and was guillotined.

De Soto, Hernando (*c.* 1500–42), Spanish explorer. Commissioned by Emperor Charles V to conquer the North American mainland, De Soto left Spain in 1539 and landed on the Florida coast. He set off by land in search of gold and silver. His travels took him through Georgia, the Carolinas, Tennessee, and Alabama, but he found no riches. A second trip took his expedition to the Mississippi River; they were probably the first white men to see it. He traveled up the Arkansas River into Oklahoma and then returned to the Mississippi, where he died. His men buried him in the river and explored Texas. Eventually they followed the Mississippi to the Gulf of Mexico. Remnants of the group turned up at Veracruz, Mexico, in 1543.

Des Plaines, city in NE Illinois, on Des Plaines River; suburb of Chicago; site of O'Hare International Airport and Glenview Naval Air Station. Industries: radio parts, electrical equipment, greenhouse specialties. Inc. 1925. Pop. 57,239.

Despotism, absolute or autocratic rule by an individual, without legal sanction or popular consent. The term dates from ancient Greece and has been applied to dictatorial systems under which power was tyrannically and arbitrarily imposed and personal freedoms severely curtailed. The 18th century has been called the "Age of Enlightened Despotism," when a number of rulers exercised absolute power with the rationale that their regimes sought the betterment of the governed.

Dessalines, Jean Jacques (1785–1806), Haitian revolutionary and leader of the independence movement after the capture of Toussaint. Dessalines drove out the French (1803), declared independence (1804) and changed the country's name from St. Domingue to Haiti. He became Emperor Jacques and ruled with nobility (1804–06). A national hero, he is considered the father of Haitian independence.

Destroying Angel, a species of very poisonous mushroom *(Amanita virosa)* common to wooded areas. It is all white with a scaly stem that has a frayed ring under the cap. It, like death cups, is often fatal.

Destructive Distillation, *See* Distillation.

Detached Calm, in Sculpture. △1002.

Detective Story, type of narrative fiction that follows this pattern: crime committed (usually murder); clues gathered and interpreted; criminal exposed in a climactic scene. An early example popular in England and the United States was William Goodwin's *Adventures of Caleb Williams* (1794). In the 19th century the police novel evolved, in England based upon the activities of Scotland Yard and in France based on *Memoires* by François Eugène Vidocq. In 1841 Edgar Allan Poe established the genre of the detective story in the United States with *The Murders in the Rue Morgue*.

Détente, in International Relations. △1390.

Detergent, any substance used for cleansing. Strictly speaking, detergents include both soaps and synthetic detergents (syndets), which have molecules that possess a long hydrocarbon chain attached to an ionized group. The hydrocarbon chain attaches to grease and other nonpolar substances; the ionized group has an affinity for water. Substances of this type lower surface tension (that is, they are surface active). The term is often used in the more restricted sense of synthetic detergents, of which there are several types; the commonest are salts of organic sulfonic acids. Domestic detergents often contain additives such as colorants, perfume, bleach, and optical brighteners. *See also* Soap. △1504, 1562.

Detergent Pollution, essentially a product of domestic use. Until the advent of biodegradable detergents, this was a considerable and visible problem. High phosphate detergents aggravate conditions in streams and contribute to algal bloom.

Determinant, a square array of numbers associated with a value that is the algebraic sum of all the products that can be formed by using as factors an element from each column in succession (each from a different row). The signs of the products may be positive or negative depending upon whether the number of changes in the rows necessary to restore them to natural order is even or odd. Determinants are used extensively to solve systems of equations.

Determinism, philosophical doctrine that every event can be explained as a result of earlier events. Everything has a cause; no event is purely accidental. What seems to be free choice can be explained if all its antecedents are known. Psychologists recognize a number of determining (if not rigidly controlling) factors in behavior—eg, constitution, health, attitudes, conflicts, and social pressures. △858.

Detonator, a device using sensitive chemicals (initiating explosives) to blast charges of less sensitive compounds (high explosives). The detonating charge is housed in a thin-walled metal or plastic, waterproof capsule. Detonators may be exploded electrically or by igniting a fuse. △1810.

Detroit, city and port in SE Michigan, on Detroit River just W of Lake St Clair; seat of Wayne co; most populous city in state. Antoine de la Mothe Cadillac founded French fort and trading post here 1701 named Fort Pontchartrain; captured by British 1760, it was held during a long siege by Pontiac; used as British control center during the American Revolution; it was surrendered to United States by terms of Jay's Treaty 1796. Detroit served as territorial then state capital 1805–1847; it was severely burned in 1805 and rebuilt to resemble Washington D.C. Lost to Britain in War of 1812, it was retaken by US forces under William Henry Harrison in 1813. Detroit contains University of Detroit (1877), Detroit Institute of Technology (1891), Marygrove College (1910), Wayne State University (1933), Mercy College of Detroit (1941), Detroit Bible College (1945), and Michigan Lutheran College (1962). The Ambassador International Bridge (world's longest international suspension bridge) and a vehicular tunnel connect Detroit with Windsor, Ontario; site of Fort Wayne (1841–51), now a military museum; Belle Isle, a park in the Detroit River containing gardens, a conservatory, children's zoo, and an aquarium; and the Detroit Institute of Arts.

Detroit is the headquarters of General Motors Corp., Chrysler Corp., Ford Motor Co., and the United Automobile Workers Union, one of the world's largest unions. Detroit is a leading Great Lakes shipping and rail center. Industries: steel, pharmaceuticals, food processing, metal stamping, machine tools, tires, paint, wire goods, automobiles and parts, ball bearings, calculators. Inc. as village 1815, as city 1824. Pop. (1970) 1,512,893.

Deuterium, isotope (symbol D) of hydrogen whose nuclei contain a neutron in addition to a proton. Every million hydrogen atoms in nature contain about 156 deuterium atoms. Deuterium occurs in water as D_2O (heavy water), from which it is obtained by fractional electrolysis. Heavy water is used as a moderator in some fission reactors and it could become a fuel in fusion reactors. Properties: mass no. 2; atomic mass 2.0147. △1482, 1550, 1552.

Deuteron, nucleus of a deuterium atom, consisting of one proton and one neutron. *See* Deuterium. △1482.

Deuteronomy, biblical book, fifth and last book of the Pentateuch consisting of discourses delivered by Moses shortly before he died. It explains the laws laid down by the previous books, Genesis, Exodus, Leviticus, and Numbers. *See also* Pentateuch.

Deva, the all-encompassing word for god in the Vedas, the earliest religious texts of India. There were 33 of these gods, 11 for each of the three world categories—sky, air, and earth. Some of the nature gods of Vedic poems appear in present-day Hinduism; they include Surya (the sun) and Varuna (the sky).

De Valera, Eamon (1882–1975), Irish statesman, b. New York City. Active in Ireland's effort toward independence, after the Easter Rebellion of 1916 he was elected president of the Sinn Fein party while imprisoned in England. Opposing W. T. Cosgrave's Free Irish State ministry, he founded the Fianna Fail party in 1924 and succeeded Cosgrave in 1932. He continued as head of Ireland's government with only two brief interruptions until 1959, when he became president of the Republic of Ireland. He retired in 1973. △1314.

De Valois, Ninette. △1368.

Devaluation, reduction in value of a country's currency relative to gold. Countries use gold as the international unit of exchange. Devaluation is in effect a decrease in the value of the country's currency relative to all other countries' currencies, which means that a particular country's products become cheaper for other countries to purchase. It also becomes more expensive for the country that has devalued to purchase products from other countries. Thus, with devaluation, imports become more expensive and exports become cheaper. Devaluation is thus often used to rectify a balance of payments deficit.

Developmental Psychology, study of behavior as it changes through all life stages, from the uterus through birth, childhood, adolescence, the middle years, and old age. Behavior is affected by the interaction of physical growth, maturation (eg, changes in the activity of sex glands), and learning. Psychologists study normal growth, change, and self-actualization, as well as life-stage related problems. *See also* Adolescence; Aging; Child Development. △776, 802.

De Vere, Aubrey Thomas (1814–1902), Irish poet, critic, and essayist. Friend of Tennyson, Wordsworth, and Cardinal Newman, converted to Roman Catholicism (1851). His poetry, in the romantic style, includes *Waldenses* (1842) and *Legends of St. Patrick* (1872).

Devi or **Mahadevi,** in Hindu mythology and religion, the great goddess, consort of Siva, daughter of Himavat. In this aspect she is represented as beautiful and adorned with jewels. In her darker aspect as Chandi, Bhairavi, Durga, or Kali, she is frightful with attributes of death, the noose, iron hook, and prayer book. *See also* Durga; Kali.

Deviance, in the social sciences, anything that departs from or conflicts with the standard norm. Deviant behavior is atypical behavior that departs from socially or culturally accepted patterns. In considering both "deviation" and "norm," social scientists take into consideration the group context within which the "deviance" is noted. For instance, members of a teenage gang would consider behavior that showed respect for law "deviant." △888, 890, 892, 914–16.

Deviated Septum, an abnormality of the muscular wall, or septum, separating the nasal cavities. Such an abnormality can interfere with normal nasal functioning and breathing.

Deviation, in statistics, the difference between any one of a set of numerical values and the mean of the set. If the values are bunched together around the mean, the deviations of the various values will tend to be small. If they are widely dispersed, the deviations will tend to be large.

Devilfish, or manta, devil ray, horned ray, flat-bodied elasmobranch found in tropical and temperate marine waters. A surface feeder, it is a food and game fish in some areas. Its disclike body may be blue, black, or brown and has two slender feeding fins at the head and a poison tail spine. Width: 4–20ft (1.2–6.1m); weight: to 3502lb (1576kg). There are four genera. Family Mobulidae. *See also* Chondrichthyes; Ray. △510.

Devil Pupfish. △516.

Devil's Island (Île du Diable), smallest and southernmost of the Îles de Salut in the Caribbean Sea, off the coast of French Guiana. French penal colony, 1852–1938.

Devils Postpile National Monument, monument in E central California; noted for columns of volcanic rock. Est 1911. Area: 798 acres (323hectares).

Devils Tower National Monument, tower of columnar rock in NE Wyoming, on the Belle Fourche River; formed from volcanic intrusion of igneous rocks; first US national monument (1906). Height: 865ft (264m).

Devolution, War of (1667–68), conflict over the Spanish Netherlands. When Marie Thérèse, daughter of the king of Spain, married Louis XIV of France (1660), she signed away her rights to the Spanish Netherlands in return for a large dowry. The dowry was never paid, and Louis used that as a pretext for invading the territory. French troops won an easy victory, but the United Provinces formed the Triple Alliance with England and Sweden, which in turn forced the return of much of the territory to Spain by the Treaty of Aix-La-Chapelle. *See also* Aix-La-Chapelle, Treaty of; Triple Alliance. △1170.

Devon (Devonshire), county in SW England, bounded by English Channel and N by Bristol Channel; hilly in E, NE, S, and Dartmoor; drained by Exe, Tamar, Dart, and Teign rivers. Chief towns are Exeter, Plymouth, and Torbay. Industries: dairy products, cider, tourism, engineering. Area: 2,612sq mi (6,765sq km). Pop. 896,245.

Devon Cattle, dual-purpose breed of horned, dark red domesticated cattle. Originally developed in Devonshire, England, they have been introduced in the United States and Argentina. Yields of milk and meat are fair. *See also* Beef Cattle; Cattle.

Devonian Period, the fourth oldest period of the Paleozoic Era, lasting from 400 to 350 million years ago. It is called the Age of Fishes. Numerous marine and freshwater remains include jawless fishes, placoderms, and forerunners of today's bony and cartilaginous fishes. The first land vertebrate, the amphibian *Ichthyostega*, appeared. Land arthropods included scorpions, mites, spiders, and the first insects. Land plants consisted of tall club mosses, scouring rushes, and ferns. *See also* Geologic Time; Paleozoic Era. △276, 566.

Devonshire, William Cavendish, 1st duke of (1641–1707), English statesman. He entered parliament in 1661 and played an active and daring role as opponent of the court of Charles II. He withdrew from the post of privy councilor in 1679 in protest against the Roman Catholic interest and aided in the impeachment of royal officials. He opposed James II's rule, and encouraged the accession of the Protestant William of Orange in 1688.

De Voto, Bernard (1897–1955), US author, b. Ogden, Utah. From 1935 until his death he wrote a column for *Harper's* magazine. He was literary editor of Mark Twain's estate and wrote studies of Twain (1932; 1942). He also wrote history and won a Pulitzer Prize in 1948 for his study of the Rocky Mountain fur trade, *Across the Wide Missouri* (1947).

de Vries, Adriaen. △1150.

De Vries, Hugo (1848–1935), Dutch botanist. He introduced the concept of mutation into the study of genetics. In 1900 along with Karl Correns and William Bateson, he rediscovered Gregor Mendel's works on heredity. His *Mutation Theorie* (1901–03) influenced later concepts of the role of mutation in evolution. △420.

Dew, water vapor condensed directly on grass and other surfaces near the ground. *See also* Precipitation.

Dewar, (Sir) James (1842–1923), Scottish chemist and physicist who was involved in extremely-low-temperature research. He built a device that produced liquid oxygen. He also constructed Dewar flasks (household varieties are Thermos bottles), which were capable of storing low-temperature liquid oxygen for longer periods than was previously possible. He liquified and solidified hydrogen. The first practical smokeless powder, cordite, was jointly developed by Sir Frederick Abel and Dewar.

Dewey, George (1837–1917), US admiral, Spanish-American War hero, b. Montpelier, Vt. He served in the Civil War and became a commodore in 1896. When the Spanish-American War began (1898) Dewey sailed for the Philippines. On May 1 he entered Manila Bay after midnight and defeated the Spanish fleet at dawn with only 8 US men wounded. He was promoted to Admiral of the Navy (1899), the highest rank ever held by a US naval officer.

Dewey, John (1859–1952), US educator, philosopher, and psychologist, b. Burlington, Vt. While he was a professor at the University of Chicago (1894–1904), he founded (1896) the Laboratory School to experiment with educational methods. He joined the faculty of Columbia University (1904) and taught there until 1930. A chief founder of Functionalism, Dewey strove to make the social sciences deal with the practical problems of education and mental disturbances. His theories about "learning-by-doing" and individualized instruction had profound impact on US educational practices and the development of applied psychology. His books include *The School and Society* (1899) and *Experience and Education* (1938).

Dewey, Melvil (1851–1931), pioneer US librarian. He created the Dewey Decimal System, a means of classifying books by divisions of the number 10. He established the first library training school at Columbia College where he was librarian (1883–88) and was a founder of the American Library Association (1876). △1782.

Dewey, Thomas Edmund (1902–71), US lawyer and politician, b. Owosso, Mich. As special investigator of organized crime (1935–37) and district attorney

Desman

Detroit, Michigan

Devon cattle

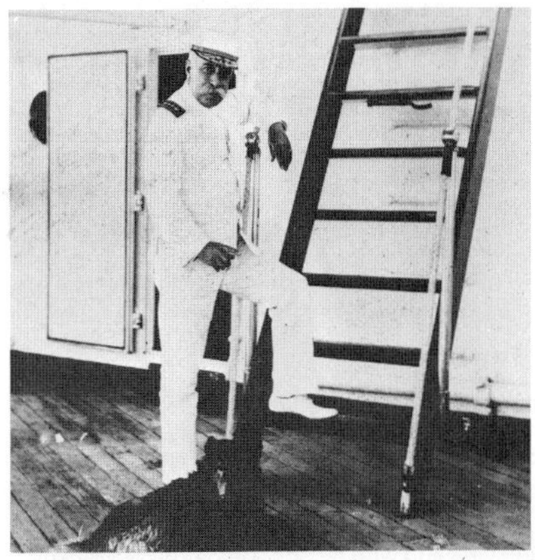

Admiral George Dewey

(1937) in New York City, he gained national fame as a racket buster. He became New York governor (1942) and two years later he ran unsuccessfully for president against Franklin Roosevelt. He was re-elected governor (1946, 1950). In 1948, he was favored in the presidential race but was edged out by Harry S. Truman.

Dewey Decimal System, means of classifying books created by Melvil Dewey in 1876. The system is based on the number 10 used decimally. It is popular because of its subject currency and simplicity. There have been only 18 revisions in the system. △1782.

Dew Point, the temperature at which a vapor begins to condense, as water vapor in the air condenses into cloud when the air becomes saturated with the vapor.

Dexedrine. *See* Amphetamine.

Dextran, stable, water-soluble polysaccharide used as a substitute or extender for blood plasma in treatment for shock.

Dharma, sacred law or duty in Hindu tradition. Virtue lies in following one's Dharma, the first of the four man's ends. One's Dharma varies with one's caste and stage in life. In Buddhism the Dharma is the doctrine of Buddha; in Jainism the Dharma is The Good as the principle of motion. *See also* Hinduism.

Dhaulagiri, Mount, seventh-highest peak in the world, in the Himalayan system, N central Nepal; first climbed 1960 by Swiss expedition led by Max Eiselin; the Ganges, Gandak, and Ghagura rivers rise on its slopes. Height: 26,810ft (8,177m).

Dhole, rare, medium-sized, yellowish- to brownish-gray wild dog native to Central and E Asia. It preys chiefly on rodents and other small mammals, but packs are known to attack deer and other large mammals and may even drive tigers from their prey. Length: 30–40in (76–102cm); weight: 30–46lb (14–21kg). Family Canidae; species *Cuon alpinus. See also* Canidae.

Dhow, a sharp-bowed Arab sailing craft, with one or two masts with slanting triangular sails (lateen rigging), used in the Indian Ocean and the Red Sea. In the larger kinds, called baggals, the mainsail is much larger than the mizzensail.

Diabetes Insipidus, a disorder in which there is extreme thirst and excessive output of very dilute urine caused by decreased secretion of the hormone vasopressin (caused by brain tumor or disease, or unknown reason, or occasionally by kidney disease) and which, if untreated—by appropriate medication to decrease urine output—can lead to fall in blood volume, shock, dehydration, and even death.

Diabetes Mellitus, a common metabolic disorder in which the body's inability to obtain and use adequate amounts of the hormone insulin results in disease characterized by inability to handle carbohydrates. It may also affect many other body organs and functions. Susceptibility to diabetes mellitus is inherited but the disease usually develops with obesity, pregnancy, menopause, infection, or severe emotional stress and is slightly more common in females. A nonhereditary form is produced by cancer of the pancreas. Insulin is normally secreted by islets in the pancreas. In juvenile diabetes, the pancreas is diseased, too little insulin is produced, and severe symptoms result. In maturity, or adult-onset (after 40) diabetes mellitus, the effectiveness and speed of release of insulin from the pancreas is often disturbed, producing minor, or in some cases, almost no, symptoms. In diabetes mellitus, the body cannot handle the sugar end-products of carbohydrate metabolism and convert them to energy compounds. The excess sugar is excreted in urine and signs such as frequent urination, dry mouth, extreme thirst, weakness, weight loss, and blurred vision can result. Diagnosis depends on urine and blood tests as well as special glucose-tolerance tests. The disease cannot be cured but can be treated with carbohydrate-limited diet, exercise, and administration of drugs—either insulin injection or synthetic oral drugs—to lower blood-sugar levels. △726.

Diabinese. *See* Chlorpropamide.

Diadochi, generals and administrators who fought over Alexander the Great's empire after his death (323 BC). Perdiccas, supported by Eumenes, lost the regency in battle (321 BC) to Antipater, allied with Antigonus I, Ptolemy I, and Craterus (who was slain). After Antipater's death (319 BC) Antigonus I declared himself king and with his son, Demetrius of Macedon, tried to rebuild the empire but was defeated and slain by Seleucus I and Lysimachus at Ipsus (301 BC). Later Demetrius overthrew Cassander, son of Antipater. After Seleucus I defeated Lysimachus (281 BC) the empire and power were divided among the sons of Ptolemy I, Antigonus I, and Seleucus I.

Diaghilev, Sergei (1872–1929), Russian ballet producer. In 1909 he founded the Ballets Russes in Paris. With Michel Fokine he brought together some of the greatest dancers: Anna Pavlova, Nijinsky; choreographers: Léonide Massine, Bronislava Nijinska, George Balanchine; composers: Stravinsky, Debussy, Richard Strauss; and artists as set and costume designers: Picasso, Chagall, Matisse, to revitalize and reshape ballet choreography and stage production. △1368.

Dial, The (July 1840–April 1844), quarterly magazine of literature, philosophy, and religion published by the New England Transcendentalists. Until 1842, Margaret Fuller was its editor; Ralph Waldo Emerson succeeded her. Contributors included Emerson, Henry David Thoreau, Bronson Alcott, Charles Pearce Cranch, and Jones Very. *See also* Transcendentalism.

Dialect, a regional variety of a language, distinguished from other varieties by features of pronunciation, grammar, and vocabulary. Dialectical differences may be relatively slight (as in the case of dialects of American English), or they may be sufficiently great (as in Italian and Chinese) that mutual comprehension becomes difficult or even impossible. △866.

Dialectical Logic, philosophical concept of G. W.F. Hegel (1770–1831). Hegel argued that ordinary logic, governed by the law of contradiction, is static and lifeless. In the *Science of Logic* (1814–16) he claimed to satisfy the need for a dynamic method, whose three moments of thesis, antithesis, and synthesis, both canceled and preserved the irreconcilable. Logic was to be dialectical, or a process (movement) of resolution by means of conflict of opposing categories; in short, thought was as "living" as organic nature itself. *See also* Dialectical Materialism.

Dialectical Materialism, philosophy according to Karl Marx (1818–83). Marx agreed with Georg Hegel that the course of history was logically dialectical, that is, change occurred in terms of the opposition of thesis, antithesis, and synthesis. Marx believed that Hegel was wrong, however, to define the subject of dialectics as spirit or reason. For Marx, the proper dialectical subject was material, sensuous experience. Mind (soul, reason) was at most derived from material or social realities. *See also* Dialectical Logic; Marx, Karl.

Dialysis, process for separating a colloid from a dissolved substance by virtue of their different rates of diffusion through a semipermeable membrane. In the artificial kidney the unwanted (smaller) molecules diffuse away into the dialysate. Electrodialysis employs a direct electric current to accelerate the process, especially useful for isolating proteins. △728.

Diamond, a native element, carbon (C). Found in volcanic pipes and in alluvial deposits. Cubic system generally octahedral crystals. Brilliant, transparent to transluscent, colorless and many hues, depending on impurities; hardness 10; sp gr 3.5. Hardness, brilliance, and fire make diamonds unsurpassed as gems. Weighted in carats (0–200 gm) and in points (1/100 carat). Largest mines in South Africa and Brazil. About 20% suitable for gem use; others used in industry. △244, 1506, 1556.

Diamondback Terrapin, brackish water turtle, native to US Atlantic and Gulf coasts. Famous as a food delicacy, it is named for its grooved and ridged carapace plate. Female length: to 9in (23cm); male length: to 5in (13cm). Family Emydidae; species *Malaclemys terrapin. See also* Turtle.

Diamond Head, cape at SE end of Oahu Island, Hawaii; an extinct volcano, it is scenic area and tourist attraction; conditionally approved by US Department of Interior as national landmark; Fort Rutgers military reservation is here. Height: 761ft (232m).

Diamond Necklace Affair, incident at the court of France's Louis XVI in 1785. Deceived by the Comtesse de la Motte, and thinking he could regain Marie Antoinette's favor, Cardinal de Rohan purchased an expensive diamond necklace in the queen's name, which the comtesse stole. The cardinal's unfair treatment before and after his exoneration was held as proof of royal despotism, and indirectly contributed to causes of the French Revolution.

Diana, in Roman mythology, the goddess of woodlands and domestic animals. She was worshipped at her temple on the Aventine as the sister of Apollo. She was a special goddess of women because of her associations as a fertility deity. She was also the protector of slaves.

Diana Monkey, W African guenon with a white beard, throat, and upper chest. *See also* Guenon. △598.

Diana of Ephesus. △836.

Diane de France (1538–1619), daughter of Henry II of France. Legitimized in 1547, she exercised considerable political influence in the courts of Henry III and Henry IV. She was made Duchess of Angoulême in 1582.

Diane de Poitiers, duchesse de Valentinois (1499–1566), mistress and virtual queen of the young Henry II of France. His love for her, as well as her beauty and vivacity, overshadowed the real queen, Catherine de Médicis, witchcraft being one of the rumored means by which Diane maintained her appeal.

Diaphragm, muscular sheet that separates the thoracic, or chest, cavity from the abdominal cavity. It is a characteristic feature of mammals. △692.

Diaphragm, in Contraception. △706.

Diarrhea, the frequent elimination of more or less loose, watery stools, often accompanied by cramps and gas pains. Diarrhea is a symptom, caused by a functional disorder, such as spastic colitis and its accompanying emotional stress, fatigue, food allergy, or lack of vitamins; by an inflammation; by a generalized body disorder such as kidney disturbance or thyroid gland overfunction; or by infections of the lower bowel caused by bacteria, viruses, or other agents. A mild short attack of diarrhea is not serious and can be treated by bland diet; more severe and longer lasting attacks and those accompanied by fever and other signs should be treated by a physician.

Dias, Bartolomeu (or **Bartholomew Diaz**) (c.1457-1500), Portuguese navigator, the first European to round the Cape of Good Hope. In 1487, under the commission of King John II of Portugal, Dias sailed three ships around the African continent, thereby opening the route to India. He was part of the expedition of Pedro Alvares Cabral (1500) that discovered Brazil, but went down with his ship shortly after leaving Portugal.

Diaspora, the Jewish communities outside Palestine or Israel. Numbers of Jews were sent into exile by the Assyrian conquest (722 BC) and the Babylonian conquest (586 BC). Although Cyrus the Great allowed Jews to return from Babylonia in 538 BC, part of the Jewish exiles remained behind. In the 3rd century BC significant Jewish communities existed in Alexandria, Egypt, and Antioch, Syria. By the period of the destruction of Jerusalem by the Romans (AD 70) and their defeat of Bar Kokba's revolt (AD 135), the Diaspora had spread throughout the Near and Middle East and North Africa and to Rome itself. By then Diaspora Jews far outnumbered those within Palestine, a situation that continues today, but their religious and cultural center remained the Holy Land. The Diaspora gradually extended until it reached from England to China and India, and then, in more recent centuries, throughout the whole world.

Diastole, the time of the cardiac cycle during which the heart muscle is relaxed, and is filling with blood. *See also* Heart.

Diastrophism, an overall term encompassing all the processes of large-scale changes in the earth's crust. Intrusion and metamorphism are considered divisions of diastrophism as are the large movements that produce mountain ranges, ocean basins, and continents. On occasion, diastrophism formerly was used to describe a localized event. It is now reserved to detail large-scale phenomena only.

Diathermy, a form of physical therapy in which heat is generated in tissues by means of high-frequency electric currents of various wavelengths. Three forms are in wide use: shortwave, ultrasound, and microwave. Diathermy can be used to warm (in relief of muscle soreness) or to destroy tissues (as a surgical adjunct).

Diatom, any of a group of tiny to microscopic single-celled algae (class Bacillariophyceae) that are characterized by a shell-like cell wall of silica. The shell, or frustule, consists of two halves that fit together like the top and bottom of a shoe box. Diatom shells occur in a wide variety of highly symmetrical shapes. They live in nearly every environment that has water and is exposed to sunlight, including virtually all bodies of salt and fresh water and even soil, damp rocks, and tree bark.

Diatomaceous Earth, sediment formed from the skeletons of diatoms, microscopic marine plants. The deposits are pure silica and often form large, thick beds on the ocean bottom.

Diatomic. △1556.

Diaz, Bartholomew. *See* Dias, Bartolomeu.

Díaz, Porfirio (1830–1915), president of Mexico (1876–80, 1884–1911). After twice failing to unseat President Juárez, but succeeding against Lerdo in 1876, Díaz retained power for 30 years in a country where political instability and frequent changes of government had marked the first half century of independence. The rural aristocracy, urban middle class, church, intellectuals, and foreign economic interests supported the regime. Growing opposition crystallized under Francisco Madero in 1911; Díaz resigned and sailed for France.

Díaz Ordaz, Gustavo (1911–), president of Mexico (1964–70), whose term of office was marked by political unrest. The student demonstrations during the 1968 Olympiad were violently suppressed by the army.

Dickens, Charles (John Huffam) (1812–70), English novelist. Immensely popular in his own time, he remains to this day the most widely read novelist in the English language. He created many memorable comic characters in his novels while at the same time attacking social injustices. He spent his childhood in Chatham and London where his father held minor posts in the navy. At the age of 12 he went to work in a shoe-black factory when his father was thrown into debtors' prison. At 17 he became a court stenographer and less than two years later a parliamentary reporter. In 1833 he began contributing sketches on London life, signed Boz, to periodicals. The best of these were collected and published as *Sketches by Boz* (1836). Their favorable reception led to the publication of *Pickwick Papers* (1836–37), which was highly successful. Dickens would continue to write for the rest of his life. Most of his novels first appeared in installments in periodicals. He himself edited two major periodicals: *Household Words* (1850–59) and *All the Year Round* (1858–70). His early novels were *Oliver Twist* (1838), *Nicholas Nickleby* (1839), *The Old Curiosity Shop* (1841), and *Barnaby Rudge* (1841). *Martin Chuzzlewit* (1843) drew upon impressions he received of the United States on a visit in 1842. *A Christmas Carol,* the first and most successful of his holiday stories, appeared in 1843. Between 1844–46 he lived in Italy and Switzerland. *Dombey and Sons* appeared in 1848, followed by *David Copperfield* (1850), his own favorite novel and his most autobiographical work. The 1850s also saw the publication of *Bleak House* (1853), *Hard Times* (1854), *Little Dorrit* (1857), and his only historical novel, *A Tale of Two Cities* (1859). In 1856 he moved to his last permanent home, Gad's Hill Place, Kent. In 1858 he separated from his wife of 22 years, who had bore him 10 children. He was linked romantically with Ellen Ternan, a young actress. *Great Expectations,* considered by many critics to be his finest novel, appeared in 1861. His last completed novel was *Our Mutual Friends* (1865). In 1867–68 he made a triumphant US tour, giving dramatic readings from his works. He died of a stroke in 1870 before completing *The Mystery of Edwin Drood.* He was buried in the Poets Corner of Westminster Abbey. △1238.

Dickey, James (1923–), US author, b. Atlanta. He worked in advertising before devoting himself full-time to writing. An autobiographical poet, his works include *Drowning with Others* (1962), *Helmets* (1964), and *Buckdancer's Choice* (1965; National Book Award 1966). He also wrote *Deliverance* (1969), a novel that was made into a film.

Dickinson, Emily (1830–86), US poet, b. Amherst, Mass. She is generally considered one of the outstanding poets produced by the United States. Although only a few of her poems were published during her lifetime, more than 1000 were found in her bureau after her death and published over time.

According to her first biographer, she was "a social creature in the highest sense" from age 18 to 23, but at 23 she began to retreat into herself and was a recluse by 1870, the family catching only occasional glimpses of her as she moved quietly about the house. Biographers do not agree on the reasons for her withdrawal, but she did find a world of her own, a world of beauty and suggestion and sometimes of death in simple things—a stone, a glance, a bee, a bobolink. Her poetry employs sharp phrases and rich stanzas with intimated rhyme to display her emotions, her love of nature, and her sense of eternity.

Dickinson, John (1732–1808), US patriot, b. Talbot co, Md. His political writings, collectively known as *Farmers Letters* (1767), influenced the Revolutionary cause while Dickinson himself held to the hope of reconciliation with the Crown. Although he did not sign the Declaration, he fought in the war. Dickinson was executive officer of both Delaware (1781–82) and Pennsylvania (1782–85). At the Constitutional Convention (1787) he championed the small states and signed the Constitution as a representative from Delaware.

Dickinson, Jonathan (1688–1747), American clergyman and educator, b. Hatfield, Mass. A leading Presbyterian and preacher during the Great Awakening, he obtained a charter for the College of New Jersey (later Princeton University) in 1746 and opened the school in his own home in Elizabeth in 1747. He served briefly as the school's first president.

Dicotyledons, larger of the two subclasses of flowering plants, angiosperms, characterized by two seed leaves (cotyledons) in the seed embryo. Plant leaves are usually net-veined and flower parts are in fours or fives. The smaller subclass is monocotyledon. This system of angiosperm classification has been used since the late 17th century. The majority of common garden plants are dicotyledons. *See also* Angiosperm, Monoctyledon. △444–46.

Dictatorship, absolute rule by an individual or group without consent of the governed. Under the Roman republic, a dictator might be appointed for a limited period during an emergency. All power resides in the dictator, with representative assemblies either abolished or existing as showcases. Personal freedoms are severely limited; censorship is enforced; education is tightly controlled; and perhaps most significantly, legal restraints on governmental authority are abolished. △902, 1334–36.

Dictatorship of the Proletariat, stage that Karl Marx felt must precede introduction of pure communism and during which all remaining capitalistic thoughts and attitudes would be weeded out. In this stage the state owns the means of production and directs the production of goods and services. The few capitalistic procedures (eg, wage payment based on productivity) that survive to this stage are dying out.

Diction, the selection of words with awareness of their effectiveness and appropriateness. The manner in which words are used constitutes style. Diction refers to the choice of words. There are four levels of usage—formal, informal, colloquial, and slang. Diction also refers to distinctness of pronunciation.

Dictionary. △1780.

Dictum, a remark, statement, or observation referring to a case. Gratis dictum is the voluntary offering of information. Simplex dictum is a statement that is made without proof. Obiter dictum is a remark made by a judge in reference to the interpretation and application of the law.

Dictyoptera. △492.

Dicumarol, trademark name for dicoumarin, an anticoagulant used to reduce and retard blood clots.

Didactic Literature, creative works primarily intended to instruct their readers or audience in some thesis or doctrine. Such works are distinguished from purely imaginative ones, which are presented as ends in themselves. A didactic work may present direct statements with proofs and examples or use various imaginative devices to translate its points into narratives or dramatic terms. Great didactic works from the ancient world include Hesiod's *Works and Days,* Lucretius' *De rerum natura,* and Vergil's *Georgics.* Most medieval literature, including Dante's *Divine Comedy,* and much Renaissance literature, including Spenser's *Faerie Queene* and Milton's *Paradise Lost,* have strong didactic elements. Didactic writing flourished in the 18th and 19th centuries, with Pope's *Essay on Man* and *Essay on Criticism* being outstanding examples. The "art for art's sake" movement in the 19th and 20th centuries is a reaction against didacticism.

Didelot, Charles. △1194.

Diderot, Denis (1713–84), French philosopher and man of letters. He assumed direction of the French *Encyclopedia* (1751) soon after incarceration for irreligious writings (1749). *On the Interpretation of Nature* (1754) and *D'Alembert's Dream* (1760) reveal Dide-

Thomas Dewey

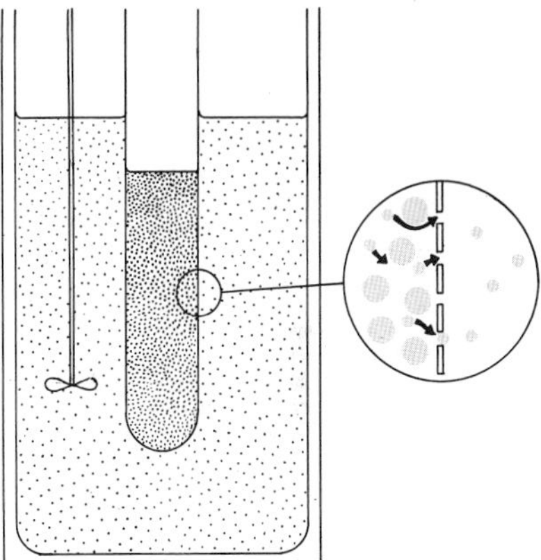

Dialysis

Charles Dickens

Emily Dickinson

rot's scientific materialism, and *Jacques the Fatalist* and *Rameau's Nephew* illustrate his determinism. Also noteworthy were Diderot's contributions to art and literary criticism. He represented a radical phase of the French Enlightenment. *See also* Enlightenment; Materialism. △1780.

Dido, in Greek mythology, the founder of Carthage, daughter of the Tyrian king Mutto, sister of Pygmalion, widow of Acerbas. Dido committed suicide to escape marriage to Iambas, a local chieftain.

Didrikson, (Mildred) Babe (1914–1956), US athlete, b. Port Arthur, Tex. Outstanding in track she won two events in the 1932 Olympics. She turned her attention to golf from 1934 and won wide press notices under her new name of, Babe Didrikson Zaharias, following her marriage (1938) to George Zaharias, a wrestler. She was the first American to win the British amateur title (1947) and won three US Women's Opens (1948, 1950, 1954). She also excelled in a number of other sports.

Diefenbaker, John George (1895–), Canadian political leader. A homesteader and lawyer in Saskatchewan, he developed a reputation for oratory and foreign affairs expertise. He was elected to the House of Commons (1940) and served as the Progressive-Conservative prime minister (1957–63). He was opposition leader in commons (1963–67).

Dieffenbachia, or dumbcane, erect, evergreen plant native to tropical America. Large, stalked leaves with variegated veins grow near the plant top. Leaf veins are light green, yellow, or white. They are commonly grown as house plants. If the poisonous leaves or fleshy stem are chewed, temporary speechlessness results. Height: to 6ft (1.8m). Family Araceae; genus *Dieffenbachia. See also* Arum.

Diegueño, a confederation of Yuman-speaking North American Indians often commonly termed Mission Indians. The Diegueño proper take their name from Mission San Diego in S California. They were famous for the strong resistance they offered the early Spanish settlers and missionaries. Once numbering perhaps 3,000 persons, today about 700 survivors occupy a small area near San Diego.

Dieldrin, brown solid chlorinated naphthalene derivative ($C_{12}H_8OCl_6$) widely used as a contact insecticide and prepared by the oxidation of aldrin with peracids. It is insoluble in water and used as an emulsion or powder.

Dielectric, insulator, especially one that separates two conductors, as in a capacitor. The permittivity of a dielectric is a measure of the extent to which it can resist the flow of charge. The dielectric strength (usually measured in V/mm) is the maximum field that the dielectric can withstand without breaking down. △1544.

Diem, Ngo Dinh (1901–63), prime minister of South Vietnam (1954–63). A nationalist, opposed to both the Communists and the French, he was appointed premier of South Vietnam by Emperor Bao Dai in 1954. The following year the monarchy was abolished and Diem became the sole ruler. At first he received strong US support. Corruption, favoritism of Roman Catholics over the Buddhist majority, and setbacks in the war against the Communists led to growing discontent at home. With covert US support, dissident generals staged a coup in 1963. Diem was murdered during the fighting. △1378.

Dien Bien Phu, town in Vietnam, near Laotian border, occupied by the French in 1953 to cut supply lines of the Viet Minh. After a 55-day battle during which the Viet Minh under Gen. Vo Nguyen Giap surrounded the French, the French, under Christian de Castries, finally surrendered. The Vietnamese victory ended a fight begun in 1946 to drive the French from Vietnam. The ensuing peace agreement granted North Vietnam to the Viet Minh and independence to Laos, Cambodia, and South Vietnam. △1378.

Diesel Engine, an internal combustion engine in which air is compressed to a temperature sufficiently high to ignite fuel injected directly into the cylinders. There combustion and resulting expansion actuate pistons. Pressure creates the necessary heat to ignite the air-fuel mixture rather than the system found in gasoline engines. △1626, 1632.

Diesel Fuel, a petroleum product heavier than kerosene but lighter than heating oil, used to power diesel engines in trucks, buses, trains, and ships. Unlike gasolines, diesel fuels burn unevenly. They are graded against standardized mixtures of hexadecane and alpha methylnaphthalane to establish a cetane number. A cetane number of about 50 is desirable.

Diet, in Health. △696, 736, 802.

Diet, legislative assembly or administrative council, principally important in German history. Charles IV established the diet of the Holy Roman Empire by his Golden Bull of 1356. The diet comprised three estates—the electors (of the Holy Roman Emperor), other lay and church nobility, and representatives of the imperial cities—each of which met separately. Approval by each estate and the consent of the emperor were requred on all matters. The most important of the diet's infrequent assemblies were at Nuremburg (1467), Worms (1521), and Augsburg (1530). After the Treaty of Westphalia ended the Thirty Years' War in 1648, the diet lost its legislative character, becoming instead an ambassadorial conference and finally dissolving in 1806 with the breakup of the empire. The term was retained for the legislatures of later German governments and, at times, for those of Austria, Hungary, Poland, Sweden, Denmark, Switzerland, and Japan (which still uses the term). △1272.

Dietary Laws, instructions, either secular or religious, which involve what foods may or may not be consumed under certain conditions. Such laws are one of the many ways a social group maintains its identity. Many Hindus, for example, practice vegetarianism, and Muslims undertake ritual fasting. In Judaism, such laws are called *Kashrut.* They prohibit certain foods entirely and indicate that others must be prepared in a certain way. The term *kosher* signifies foods that are "fit."

Diethylstilbestrol, a synthetic estrogen used as a drug commonly known as DES. Diethylstilbestrol has been used in cattle feeding as a growth stimulant and in humans in a "morning after" contraceptive pill and in the 1950s as an agent to prevent miscarriage. The drug has, however, been found to have cancer-causing potential and its use is now strictly limited.

Dietrich, Marlene (1902–), US film star and cabaret singer, b. Maria Magdalena von Losch, in Germany. Her glamorous image evolved in films directed by Josef von Sternberg, such as *The Blue Angel* (1930) and *Blonde Venus* (1932). Other notable films included *Destry Rides Again* (1939) and *Rancho Notorious* (1952).

Difference. *See* Subtraction.

Differential, small change occurring in the value of a mathematical expression as a result of a small change in a variable. More formally, if $f(x)$ is a function of x, the differential of the function, written df, is given by df $= f'(x)\,dx$, where $f'(x)$ is the derivative of $f'(x)$. The differential of a function is useful in obtaining the results of small changes. For example, if the rate r of a chemical reaction is related to concentration c by the equation $r = 5c^2$, the derivative dr is equal to $10\,cdc$. A small change in the value of c, from 6 to 6.01 say, produces a small change in r, obtained by putting $c = 6$ and $dc = 0.01$; thus $dr = 0.6$.

Differential, Automobile. △1696.

Differential Calculus. *See* Calculus.

Differential Equation, equation containing derivatives. For example, the equation $dN/dt = AN$, where N is the number of people in the population, t the time, and A a constant, is a highly simplified equation for population growth. dN/dt, the derivative of population with respect to time, is the rate at which population increases. According to the equation this is proportional to the population: that is, the higher the population, the faster it grows. Differential equations are solved by integration. In this example the result is $N = N_0\,e^{At}$, where N_0 is the initial value. *See also* Calculus; Derivative; Partial Differential Equation.

Differentiation, in Calculus. △1460.

Differentation, Magnetic. △278.

Diffraction, slight spreading of a light beam into the shadow region when the light travels through a narrow opening or past the edge of an obstacle. It results from the failure of light to travel in straight lines and is a consequence of the wave nature of light. Diffraction patterns can be observed on a screen behind the object: with a circular object or aperture light and dark concentric rings are seen; with a slit, wire, or straight edge there are light and dark bands. Fresnel diffraction occurs with a simple arrangement of light source and diffracting object. In Fraunhofer diffraction a parallel beam of light falls on the object and the diffraction patterns are focused onto the screen by a lens. Fraunhofer diffraction is less mathematically complex than Fresnel diffraction and can provide information on the wavelength of the light.

Other waves, including sound and radio waves and X rays, undergo a similar spreading when traveling through apertures or past obstacles. This accounts for the audibility of sound around corners and the propagation of radio waves over the curved surface of the earth. △1520.

Diffraction Grating, optical device for producing spectra by diffraction of light. In one form a light beam is diffracted by passing it through a flat glass plate on which very closely spaced parallel equidistant lines have been ruled. *See also* Diffraction. △1520.

Diffraction, Wave. *See* Diffraction.

Diffusion, spontaneous flow of a substance in a mixture from regions of high concentration to regions of low concentration, resulting from the random motion of the individual atoms or molecules. Diffusion apparently ceases when there is no longer a concentration gradient. Its rate increases with temperature. The process occurs quickly in gases, more slowly in liquids, and extremely slowly in solids. △1502, 1564.

Digby, (Sir) Kenelm (1603–65), English diplomat, scientist, and writer. A Royalist, he defended Charles II in Paris (1641) and was chancellor to his queen (1644). He was exiled in 1643 for his conduct in the Great Rebellion and again in 1649. Among his scientific discoveries was his announcement that oxygen is necessary for plant life (1661); many of his other "discoveries" are not highly regarded now. He was one of the first members of the Royal Society (1663) and friend of Descartes and Sir Thomas Browne.

Digestion, process of breaking down food molecules into forms that can be absorbed by an organism. Digestion occurs by means of physical agents (teeth) and chemical agents (enzymes). This process provides nutrients and energy to keep an organism alive.

Digestive System, that organ system of the body concerned with the digestion of foodstuffs. It is also known as the alimentary system. It begins with the mouth cavity, which includes teeth, tongue, and salivary glands; and continues into the pharynx, which connects with the esophagus, or gullet, that carries food into the stomach. The stomach opens into the small intestine, which then opens into the large intestine, or colon. After food is swallowed it is pushed through the roughly 30ft (9m) of the digestive tract by rhythmic muscle contractions and relaxations known as peristalsis. On its journey the food is transformed into liquid that can be absorbed by the tissues of the body; specifically, the carbohydrates are changed to glucose; the proteins to amino acids; and the fats to fatty acids and glycerol. The indigestible parts are eventually eliminated from the body in a mass (feces) through the rectum, at the end of the colon. △694.

Digger Indians, contemptuous term applied by 19th-century white settlers to several Indian tribes in California, Utah, and Nevada who lived on acorns, herbs, and camass roots. *See also* Paiute Indians.

Digger Wasp. △464.

Digit. *See* Numeral. △1448.

Digital Clocks. △1668.

Digital Computer, computer that accepts input in discrete form, as numbers or characters, rather than in continuously variable form and processes it in the form of digits. *See also* Computer, Electronic. △1672.

Digitalis, drug obtained from the leaves of the purple foxglove plant that is used to treat heart disease. It increases contractions of the heart muscles and slows the cardiac rate.

Digitalis Purpurea. △1560.

Digital Signal, digits representing zeros and ones, transmitted by radio and translated by computer into dots of various shades to produce pictures similar to half-tone newspaper photographs. △1792.

Dijon, city in E France; capital of Côte-d'Or dept. An ancient city, it flourished in the 11th century when rulers of Burgundy made it their royal residence; site of Dijon University (1722), Cathedral of St Bénigne, and 13th-century Church of Notre Dame. Exports: Burgundy wine, mustard, cassis. Pop. 145,357.

Dik-dik, tiny African antelope with soft, yellow-gray to reddish hair and tuft of fur on forehead. Ringed horns are carried only by males. They may live in large groups, families, or singly. The name is derived from its call. Length: to 26in (66cm); height: to 16in (41cm) at shoulder; weight: to 11lb (5kg). Family Bovidae; genus *Madoqua. See also* Antelope. △586.

Dike, an intrusion of igneous rock whose surfaces are very different from those of the adjoining materials. Dikes are usually vertical and the pattern they exhibit is a reflection of the stress fractures of the bedrock that they have intruded. *See also* Igneous Rock; Intrusion. △176, 246.

Dike, in engineering, any barrier or embankment, usually constructed of earth, designed to confine or control water. Dikes are used in reclaiming land from the sea by sedimentation, as practiced in the Netherlands, and are also of value as a control against river flooding (called artificial levees in that case).

di Lasso, Orlando. △1132.

Dill, a single species, *Anethum graveolens*, of aromatic annual herb native to Europe and widely cultivated for its small, oval, seedlike fruit and feathery leaves used for flavoring food. Family Umbelliferae.

Dillinger, John (1903–34), US criminal, b. Indianapolis, Ind. He spent most of his adult years in various prisons. A 13-month rampage of robbing banks and escaping across state lines led to strengthening of both interstate police efforts and the Federal Bureau of Investigation (FBI). Dillinger was trapped in Chicago and killed by federal agents.

Dillon, Clarence Douglas (1909–), US public official, b. Switzerland. A member of the N.Y. Stock Exchange at the age of 22, he was in international finance from the start of his working life. He served as US ambassador to France (1953–57) and undersecretary of economic affairs (1957–59) and state (1959–61) during the Eisenhower administration. Appointed Kennedy's secretary of treasury (1961), Dillon reshaped international trade policies.

DiMaggio, Joseph Paul ("Joe"), (1914–), US baseball player, b. Martinez, Calif. A hitter and center fielder for the New York Yankees (1936–42; 1946–51), DiMaggio hit in a record 56 consecutive games in 1941 and had a lifetime .325 batting average. He was elected to the Baseball Hall of Fame in 1955.

Dime Novel, fast-paced, thrilling novels, first sold in 1860 and popular through the 1890s, whose subject matter was mainly the American Revolution, the frontier, or the Civil War. Originally sold for 10 cents by the firm of Beadle and Adams, they sold by the thousands throughout the country. Series about Deadwood Dick by Edward Wheeler, and Nick Carter by several authors, were among the best. After 1880 the appearance of poor imitations, pulp magazines, comic strips, and other serialized stories significantly lowered the dime novel's popularity.

Dimensional Analysis. △1450.

Dimethys. △1558.

Dimetrodon, early mammallike reptile called pelycosaur found in North America during the Early and Middle Permian Period (225–280 million years ago). It was carnivorous, with sharp, differentiated teeth. The "sail fin" on its back, composed of elongated spines from the vertebral column, may have served for temperature regulation. Length: 10ft (3m). *See also* Pelycosaur. △568.

Diminishing Returns, Law of, or the law of increasing costs, states that as more and more of a variable input (eg, labor) is added to the production process, while all other factors are held constant, the addition to total output per unit will begin to decline after some point. While the first unit of labor, for example, might produce ten units of output, the second unit of labor may only produce eight units of output; the third, only six units, etc. While the total output tends to increase, the marginal output (addition to total output) will decline after some point. △936.

Dinaric Alps, SE division of Eastern Alps in Yugoslavia, along E coast of Adriatic Sea; joins Alpine system in the N; extends from Istria to Albania; contains many peaks over 8,000ft (2,400m). Length: 400mi (644km).

Dinaric Subrace, subdivision of the Caucasoid race, characterized by tall stature, swarthy skin, usually black hair and eyes, large straight noses, and flattened occipital regions of the skull. Dinarids form almost the entire Serbian population and predominate in Romania.

D'Indy, Vincent. △1246.

Dinesen, Isak (1885–1962), pseud. of Karen, Baroness Blixen-Finecke, Danish writer. Her life on a coffee plantation in Kenya (1914–31) was recounted in *Out of Africa* (1938). Her collections of short stories include *Seven Gothic Tales* (1934), *Winter's Tales* (1943), and *Shadows on the Grass* (1961).

Dingo, yellowish-brown, medium-sized wild dog of Australia. It is thought to be a descendant of domestic dogs introduced by aborigines several thousand years ago. It preys mostly on rabbits and other small mammals, but sometimes attacks sheep and cattle. Height: 24in (61cm) high at shoulder. Family Canidae; species *Canis dingo. See also* Canidae. △590.

Dinichthus. △566.

Diniz, or **Denis** (1261–1325), king of Portugal (1279–1325), son and successor of Alfonso III. A scholar and a poet, Diniz founded the University of Coimbra. As king he encouraged agriculture and commerce and strengthened royal power by checking the wealth of the church and by confiscating the property of the Knights Templar. He was married to St. Elizabeth of Portugal, who mediated the conflicts between Diniz and his son, who succeeded him as Alfonso IV.

Dinocerata, or uintathere, archaic North American mammals of early Tertiary times. Ponderous and short-limbed, many bore short horns and males had powerful tusks. Advanced forms reached rhinoceros proportion.

Dinosaur, extinct reptiles that dominated life on land during Mesozoic era. They first appeared during the Triassic period and became extinct during Cretaceous period. Bipedal carnivores had tearing jaws and sharp teeth; herbivores were usually four-footed and sometimes extremely heavy. No single explanation of their extinction suffices. Many geologic and climatic changes occurred and perhaps these specialized reptiles were unable to adapt. No modern descendents exist. Two orders existed: Saurischia and Ornithischia, both descended from Triassic thecodonts. Length: 2–90ft (0.6–27m). △410, 570, 572.

Dinosaur National Monument, area in NE Utah and NW Colorado; site of fossils of prehistoric reptiles embedded in sand and clay, covered by sediment; beds uplifted and exposed by erosion; largest known Brontosaurus remains found here. Est 1915. Area: 206,663acres, (83,699hectares).

Diocletian(us Caius Aurelius Valerius) (245–313), Roman emperor (284–305), *b.* Dalmatia. Of humble birth, he rose through the ranks of the army and was proclaimed emperor by his troops. In order to hold the empire together and to administer it more efficiently, he appointed Maximian Augustus (coemperor) in 286 and appointed Constantius I and Galerius as caesars (subemperors) in 293, thus establishing the Tetrarchy. During his reign, Britain was restored to the empire (296) and the Persians were subjugated (298). The Edict of Diocletian (301) attempted to regulate prices and wages but created economic chaos. Diocletian ordered the last major persecution of Christians, beginning in 303. In 305 he retired to his palace in Dalmatia. △1030, 1056.

Diocletian, Palace of, Roman palace-fortress, built 295–305 at Split, Yugoslavia, by the Emperor Diocletian. △1024.

Diode, electronic device with only two electrodes, used mainly as a rectifier. The semiconductor diode, which has largely replaced the electron-tube device, has a single p-n junction. It allows current to flow when, say, a positive voltage is applied with only a very small current flowing in the reverse (negative) voltage direction. *See also* Electron Tube; Semiconductor. △1546–48.

Diogenes (412?–323 BC), Greek Cynic philosopher. Nicknamed the "Dog" by his own contemporaries because of his eccentric public behavior, he is best known as the philosopher who lived in a tub and carried a lantern around Athens at midday searching for an honest man. He went to Athens when young, studied under Antisthenes, and was later captured and sold into slavery at Corinth (his owner freed him). He believed only in practical good as the means to truth; freedom could be achieved by reducing needs to the barest minimum and happiness by returning to nature.

Diogenes of Apollonia (2nd half of 5th century BC), Greek philosopher. A natural philosopher who studied and taught in Athens during a transitional period of Greek thought, he tried to combine ancient ideas

Babe Didrikson

Marlene Dietrich in Blue Angel

Dike

Isak Dinesen

with the new biological observations. Influenced by Anaxagoras, he proposed that all things in the world are modifications of air, and further that this common harmony of air was due to an all-encompassing intelligence. He went on to explain perception by using the properties of air. His major works include *On Nature* and the lost treatises *Meteorology, Nature of Man*, and *Against the Sophists*.

Diomede Islands, two islands in the Bering Strait; Big Diomede (Ratmanov) is a possession of USSR; Little Diomede belongs to the United States; between the two islands passes the USSR-US boundary and the international date line. Discovered Aug. 16, 1728 (St Diomede's Day) by Vitus Bering.

Diomedes, two figures in Greek mythology. One the king of the Thracian Bistones owned man-eating horses. Conquered by Hercules, Diomedes was fed to them. The other was the son of Tydeus and a leader in the Trojan War. He founded Arpi in Apulia.

Dione, satellite of Saturn. △86.

Dionysius of Halicarnassus (1st century BC), Greek orator and historian. Dionysius taught Greek rhetoric at Rome (30–8 BC), and was author of the *Antiquitates Romanae*, a history of Rome written in elaborate rhetorical style.

Dionysius the Areopagite (1st century AD), first bishop of Athens, a Catholic saint. As described in Acts 17:15–34, Dionysius was converted to Christianity as he heard Paul preach the sermon of "the unknown God" on the Hill of Mars (Areopagus) in Athens. He was martyred about AD 95. He is often confused with the Pseudo-Dionysius (*c.* 500) who forged mystical writings in the name of Dionysius the Areopagite. These writings provided a system of the cosmos and emphasized a union between God and soul and the progressive deification of man. They had an important influence on both the Eastern and Western churches until the 16th century, when their authenticity was contested.

Dionysius the Elder (*c.* 430–367 BC), tyrant of Syracuse (405–367). Perhaps the most powerful Greek until Alexander the Great, this despotic and cruel ruler's ambitions were to spread Hellenism beyond the boundaries of the city. To this end, he tried to form an empire in Lower Italy by driving Carthage away (405–404, 398–382, 383–378, 368) and seizing Rhegium (387), Caulonia, and Croton (379). He then displaced the populations within his control to mix the people. A supporter of the arts and an erstwhile playwright, he once sold Plato as a slave.

Dionysius the Younger (*c.* 368–*c.* 344 BC), tyrant of Syracuse. Son of Dionysius I, he succeeded him in 367 and reigned until 357 when he was driven from Syracuse by Dion. He became tyrant of Locri and then returned to rule Syracuse until 344; he was driven out the second time by Timoleon. Although Dionysius was a cruel and uneducated ruler, Plato wanted to set up the ideal state under him.

Dionysus, in Greek mythology, the god of fruitfulness and wine, the son of Zeus and Semele. He was worshipped by women in orgiastic and secretive rites. △836, 844.

Diorite, deep-seated igneous rock, similar to granite in its texture, but made up mainly of plagioclase feldspar and hornblende, biotite or augite. It is usually gray or dull green. △246.

Dioscorides Pedanius (*c.* 60 AD), Greek botanist, physician, and pharmacologist. He wrote *De materia medica*, the oldest known text on drugs and their use. It included detailed plant descriptions and information on the specific use, dose, and administration of plant-derived drugs.

Dip, in geology, the angle between the maximum slope of a surface and the horizontal. This angle is a measure of the tipping and faulting that disrupts the layers of sedimentary rocks. In geomorphology, dip also means a low place or depression in the land surface. △274.

Diphilus (*fl. c.* 360 BC), Greek playwright. A writer of comedy, he wrote 100 plays, 60 of which survive. Some of his lively plays had mythological themes. He was imitated by Plautus and Terence, and many of his plays were later redone by the Romans.

Diphtheria, an acute, contagious infection, chiefly affecting children, once epidemic throughout the world. The bacteria *Corynebacterium diphtheriae*, often entering through the upper respiratory tract, releases exotoxin that produces symptoms of fever, chills, malaise, mild sore throat, brassy cough, and thick coating of the upper respiratory tract with dead cells and bacteria. The body responds by producing antitoxin and recovery usually follows. Complications, including impaired function of the heart and peripheral nerves, may occur temporarily. Routine immunization of children with diphtheria toxoid confers immunity.

Diplococcus, genus of bacteria characterized by gram-positive, rod-shaped cells that grow in pairs. It causes pneumococcal pneumonia and is treated with antibiotics and penicillin. *See also* Bacteria. △566.

Diplodocus, sauropod dinosaur of North America of the Jurassic period (136–190,000,000 years ago). It was proportionately more slender than other sauropods with an especially long neck and tail. This swamp-dwelling vegetarian was longer than any known dinosaur. Length: to 90ft (27m). *See also* Sauropoda. △410.

Diplomacy, practice of conducting negotiations between nations. Nations maintain agents—diplomats—abroad to represent them in dealings with foreign states. The diplomat also regularly prepares reports for his government on the economic, political, and military affairs of his host country. Major powers generally exchange ambassadors. When an ambassador is not present, a chargé d'affaires will conduct diplomatic relations. Members of the corps advance through the merit system, although ambassadors are appointed. *See also* Embassy; Foreign Service.

Diplomatic Immunity, protection extended to members of the diplomatic corps in the form of exemption from search, arrest, or prosecution in their host country. Visiting diplomats also are further exempt from customs regulations. The embassy or legation building is considered extraterritorial, a status conferring additional protection.

Diplopia, double vision, a disorder of vision that can result from various diseases or from the action of certain drugs on the central nervous system.

Diplura. △492.

Dipnoi. *See* Lungfish.

Dipole, Molecular, separation of electric charge in a molecule. In a covalent bond between different atoms the electron pair is not equally shared between the two atoms. Thus, in hydrogen chloride, HCl, the electrons are attracted toward the more electronegative chlorine atom, giving it a partial negative charge and leaving an equal positive charge on the hydrogen atom. Such dipoles contribute to the chemical properties of molecules.

Dipper, widely distributed bird found in or near fast-flowing mountain streams where it swims and dives, feeding on aquatic invertebrates and small fish. It has a thin straight bill, short wings and tail, and grayish or brownish plumage. It builds a large, domed, grass-and-moss-lined nest, often behind a waterfall, for its white eggs (4–5). Length: 6.5in (16.5cm). Genus *Cinclus*.

Dipsomania, an insatiable, often periodic, craving for alcoholic beverages. *See also* Alcoholism.

Diptera, the order of true flies. They are distinguished from other insects by having soft bodies and one pair of wings, with the other pair reduced to knob-like halteres. They have a complete life cycle—egg, larva, pupa, and adult—with the larva being wormlike. This group includes several important pests. Mosquitoes, horseflies, houseflies, black flies, and others either attack man and animals or carry diseases. The Hessian fly, apple maggot, and others attack crops. The bee flies and robber flies, on the other hand, are beneficial, attacking several pest insects. △492.

Dipterus. △410, 568.

Diptrotodont. △544.

Dirac, Paul Adrien Maurice (1902–), English physicist who devised a new version of quantum mechanics. His equation (the Dirac equation) combines relativity and quantum-mechanical descriptions of electron properties, resulting in accurate values and relating them to fundamental principles. He was awarded the Nobel Prize for physics (1933) and the medal of the Royal Society (1952). △1484.

Direct Current. *See* Current, Electric.

Direct Democracy, system, also known as "pure democracy," in which citizens govern themselves directly, not through representatives. Once practiced in ancient Greece, it survives today in the New England town meeting. △904.

Directorate. △1224.

Directory The, (1795–99), set up by the constitution of the year III in revolutionary France, was a governing body including a legislature, judiciary, treasury, and executive, each largely independent of the other, representing the many diverse political viewpoints of France from 1795 to 1799. The five executive directors were able to maintain power only by a careful balancing of countervailing forces and the use, in emergencies, of the military. This large and effective army, greatly successful under the command of Napoleon, was the instrument of a coup in 1797, establishing a dictatorship dependent on the victories of war and setting the stage for Napoleon's rule in 1799.

Dirksen, Everett McKinley (1896–1969), US political figure, b. Pekin, Ill. He was an influential leader in the US Senate (1950–69). He began his senate career as a conservative, and was minority leader two years later. He is best known as the Senate's architect of the Civil Rights Act (1964) and the Voting Rights Act (1965). He was noted as a magnificent orator.

Disarmament, reduction of weaponry and armies. Efforts to achieve international disarmament have focused on limiting the nuclear arms race between the United States and the Soviet Union. In 1963, nuclear weapons in outer space were banned. A nuclear nonproliferation treaty was signed in 1972, which also marked the start of the Strategic Arms Limitation Talks (SALT). △1308.

Disc Cam. △1652.

Discharge Petition, US congressional petition signed by 218 House members, requesting withdrawal of a proposed bill from committee consideration. Few attempts at discharge have been successful.

Discharge Tube. △1526.

Disciples of Christ, American religious denomination, deriving all its beliefs from the New Testament. Protestant in background, it strives to return to the purity of the Scriptures. Originating in the religious revival movements in 19th century frontier America, there is no single founder and no creed but Christ. There are approximately 1,200,000 members.

Disclosure of Information Act (1966), US bill signed by President Johnson in an attempt to make government records more accessible to the public. The act did not become law, and was superseded by the Freedom of Information Act (1967). *See also* Freedom of Information Act.

Disconformity, the hiatus or eroded surface between two layers of rock. The time interval represented by the hiatus is more difficult to estimate than the rate of deposition of a layer. However, it is a necessary factor in determining the age of rock formations. *See also* Unconformity. △270, 668.

Discount Rate, rate of interest that the federal reserve banks charge to member commercial banks for discounting loans. In effect, this involves loaning money to the commercial banks, and is one way the federal reserve controls the money supply. If the Federal Reserve Board raises the discount rate, commercial banks will be forced to increase their lending rate.

Discrimination, prejudicial treatment of an individual or group on the basis of race, religion, ethnic background, sex, or age. In the broader, public sense, discrimination may take the form of housing restrictions, segregated community facilities, and limited employment and educational opportunities. △894.

Disease, an impairment of health or abnormal functioning of an organism, affecting the entire organism or one organ or system of the body. Disease may be acute, producing severe symptoms for a short time; chronic, lasting a long time; or recurrent, with symptoms returning periodically. There are many types and causes of disease: infectious diseases, caused by harmful bacteria, viruses, or other agents; hereditary and metabolic diseases; diseases of growth and development; diseases of the immunological system; neoplastic (tumor-producing) diseases; nutritional diseases; endocrine (hormonal) diseases; diseases due to particular physical agents, for example, lead poisoning; circulatory diseases; and mental diseases.

Treatment depends on the cause and course of the disease, but in general, may be symptomatic, relieving symptoms but not necessarily combating the cause of the disease; or may be specific drug therapy, attempting to cure the underlying cause of the disease. Surgery is also sometimes a method of treatment, as is radiation therapy, physical therapy, and psychotherapy.

Disease prevention involves eradication of disease-producing organisms, vaccines to confer immunity against disease, public health measures, and careful medical care and checkups. △710–32.

Dish Garden, miniature garden of slow-growing foliage plants in a shallow dish or tray. Planted in coarse gravel covered with garden loam and sand or peat moss, it is not a long-lasting arrangement. Plants suited to dish gardens are cactus, seedling evergreens, and small ferns and succulents. The Japanese garden art of sakei is the creation of miniature landscapes in a tray using rocks for mountains, moss for grass, and miniature evergreens.

Disinfectant. △1558.

Disjunction, logical proposition produced by joining two simple propositions by the word *or.* An example is the proposition "John is intelligent or John is modest"; it is false if both parts are separately false, otherwise it is true. This is the inclusive disjunction—the type used in mathematics—in which the proposition is true if *both* components are true. In ordinary speech a second type, the exclusive disjunction, is also used expressing an alternative between the two components. The disjunction of two simple propositions, P and Q, is written $P \vee Q$, read *"P* or *Q."*

Dislocation. △720.

Dislocations of Atoms. △1506.

Dismal Swamp, area in SE Virginia and NE North Carolina; extends approx. 40mi (64km) from Suffolk, Va., to Elizabeth City, N.C. Dense forests, undergrowth, and peat bogs attract sportsmen and naturalists; a canal for small pleasure craft from Norfolk to Elizabeth City opened in 1828; in center of swamp is Lake Drummond, 18sq mi (46sq km). George Washington owned and surveyed part of swamp in 1763. Previously covering an area of 2,200sq mi (5,700sq km), it is now approx. 600sq mi (1,554sq km) in size.

Disney, Walt(er Elias) (1901–66), US film animator and studio executive, b. Chicago. His cartoon features, animal, fantasy, and adventure films are internationally renowned. His first success, *Steamboat Willie* (1928), was the first cartoon to use sound. It featured Mickey Mouse, who became the world's most famous cartoon character, rivaled only by another Disney character, Donald Duck. Among his studio's best-loved films are *Snow White and the Seven Dwarfs* (1938), *Fantasia* (1940), *Dumbo* (1941), *Treasure Island* (1950), *The Living Desert* (1953), and *Mary Poppins* (1964). In 1955 the innovative amusement park, Disneyland, opened in Anaheim, Calif.

Disneyland, large amusement park in Anaheim, SE California; designed by Walt Disney; transportation provided by monorail, stagecoach, keel boats, and log rafts; includes historical and fairyland reproductions, and industrial exhibits. Opened 1955. Area: over 160acres (65hectares).

Disney World, a large amusement park 16mi (26km) NW of Orlando, Florida; opened in 1971; one of Florida's leading tourist attractions.

Dispersion, Colloidal. *See* Colloidal Dispersion.

Dispersion, Wave. *See* Wave Dispersion.

Displaced Persons, Europeans left homeless after World War II. They at first entered the United States under limited quotas, but later under a President Truman directive, 42,000 persons were admitted. By June 1948, visas were authorized for 205,000, including 3,000 nonquota orphans. The issuance of visas was extended through 1951.

Displacement, in geology, the relative movements of two adjacent groups of rock in relation to each other. Displacement is spoken of in terms of the direction of change and the specific amount of the movement. Lateral displacement is described as strike slip and strike separation whereas vertical displacement is known as dip slip and dip separation. *See also* Faulting; Folding.

Displacement, in physics, replacement of one atom in a compound by an atom of a different element. *See also* Substitution.

Displacement, in psychology, defense mechanism in which there is a psychological shift in meaning, reference, or emotional emphasis from a more to a less disturbing focus. A common form of this mechanism is in the displacement of anger, eg, when a mother, angry at her husband, begins to shout at her child. *See also* Defense Mechanism.

Display, in non-verbal Communications. △862.

Disposable Personal Income, in national income measurement, aggregate measure of the income available for the household sector to spend for consumption or to save. Disposable personal income includes an individual's earned income plus transfer payments from the government less taxes. Disposable income has generally grown rapidly since World War II. *See also* Transfer Payments.

Disraeli, Benjamin, 1st Earl of Beaconsfield (1804–81), English Conservative statesman and writer. He was a novelist before entering Parliament (1837), where he dominated the romantic Young England Tories and helped overthrow Robert Peel after the Corn Laws were repealed (1846). As Conservative leader in the Commons, Disraeli helped Lord Derby reunite the party, was several times chancellor of the exchequer, and piloted an electoral reform act (1867) through Parliament. On Derby's retirement, Disraeli became prime minister (1868). Prime minister for a second time (1874–80) he passed social reform legislation. An imperialist, he secured Britain's half-share in the Suez Canal, and at the Congress of Berlin (1878), he forced Russia to surrender Turkish lands, annexing Cyprus for Britain. His health failing, Disraeli was defeated by his Liberal rival, William Gladstone (1880). *See also* Gladstone, William; Peel, Sir Robert. △1302.

D'Israeli, Isaac (1766–1848), English author, the father of Benjamin Disraeli. D'Israeli is best-known for his six-volume *Curiosities of Literature* (1791–1834), a collection of essays and anecdotes on 18th-century history and literature. D'Israeli also wrote poetry, novels, and biography. His study of Charles I (five vols., 1828–31) earned him an honorary degree from Oxford University.

Dissenters. *See* Nonconformists.

Dissociation, splitting apart or separating of specific contents of consciousness, or dividing experience into independent regions. In the *dissociative reaction* considerable personality disorganization is reflected in such symptoms as fugue state, depersonalization, amnesia, and sleepwalking. Dissociated states of awareness tend to alternate with one another in consciousness. △914.

Distemper, dangerous contagious disease of young dogs, similar to influenza in humans. Distemper is an airborne viral disease, often complicated by secondary bacterial infections. Symptoms are fever, shivering, discharges, pneumonia, convulsions, spasm, and paralysis. No cures are known, although multiple vaccinations are a preventative. Wild canines, raccoons, and members of the weasel family are also susceptible.

Distillation, evaporation and recondensation process carried out on a liquid at controlled pressures in apparatus comprising a still, a condenser, and a receiver. In destructive distillation the product(s) of decomposition are collected. In fractional distillation various liquid mixtures or fractions are collected depending on their boiling points. In rectification (a type of fractional distillation widely used as a separation procedure in the petroleum industry), where the condenser comprises a series of plates to facilitate liquid–vapor equilibrium, relatively pure products may be collected from a liquid mixture. △352.

Distribution, in economics, portion of the total amount of the goods and services a society produces that each individual or group receives. Sometimes called personal distribution or income distribution in order to distinguish it from the marketing of commodities (physical distribution), it has been an important aspect of economic analysis since Adam Smith focused on the issue in the 18th century.

Distributive Law, rule of combination in mathematics in which a specified operation applied to a combination of terms is equal to the combination of the operation applied to each individual term. Thus, in algebra and arithmetic $3 \times (2 + 1) = (3 \times 2) + (3 \times 1)$; the multiplication is distributed over addition. △1446.

Distributor, Engine, an electrical device for distributing the secondary current from the induction coil. This current has to be directed to the various spark plugs of a multicylinder, gasoline internal combustion engine in their proper firing order. △1632.

Diplodocus

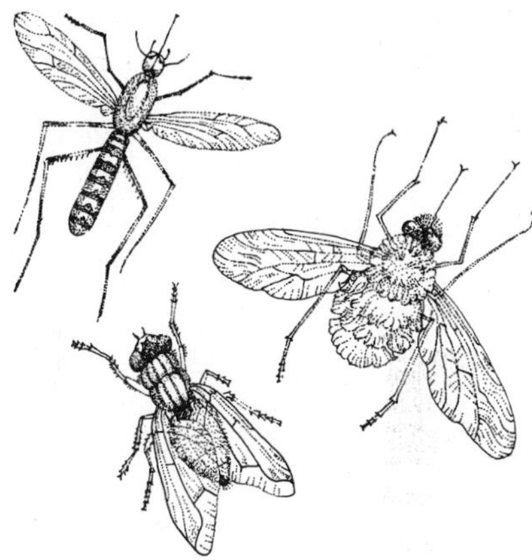

Diptera

Walt Disney

Benjamin Disraeli

District Court, lowest US federal court with original jurisdiction over such matters as admiralty, maritime, bankruptcy, penal, and criminal matters. There is at least one in each state. Each is presided over by one judge, except in cases involving injunctions against federal or state laws on questions of constitutionality where three judges preside. From these decisions, there is direct appeal to Supreme Court. Where one judge presides, appeals are made to the Courts of Appeals.

Dithyramb, irregular poem or chant of a wild or inspired nature. Dithyrambs are primarily identified with ancient Greece. There they originated as improvised choral lyrics sung at banquets in honor of Dionysus, the god of wine. Later other gods were honored, and dithyrambs became important parts of theatrical presentations and great festivals. The dithyramb began to achieve literary distinction with the poet Arion around 600 BC. He developed them for regular choruses with formal presentations. Lasus of Hermione, (*c.*525 BC) was the most famous composer of dithyrambs. Simonides, Pindar, Bacchylides, Philoxenus, and Timotheus also composed them. Dithyrambs gradually used more and more startling linguistic and musical devices. They eventually died out in their classical form in the 2nd century AD. Aristotle maintained that Greek tragedy developed out of the dithyramb. True dithyrambs have been rare since ancient times, but it has been said that Dryden's *Alexander's Feast* (1697) and T.S. Eliott's *The Waste Land* (1922) are among poems containing dithyrambic elements.

Ditmars, Raymond Lee (1876–1942), U.S. naturalist, b. Newark, N.J. He published many popular books on the biology of reptiles. Curator of reptiles (1899–1910) and of mammals (1910–1942) for the New York Zoological Park, he wrote *The Reptile Book* (1907), *Snakes of the World* (1931), and other works.

Diuretic, drug used to increase the flow of urine and, usually, its salt content. Diuretics are used to treat edema, an over-accumulation of fluid caused by congestive heart failure or other diseases, and abnormal kidney function.

Diver. *See* Loon.

Divergence, property of an infinite series (or sequence) of not having a finite limiting value. Such a series is said to diverge. The harmonic series, $1 + \frac{1}{2} + 1/3 + \frac{1}{4}, \ldots,$ is an example of a divergent series. *See also* Convergence.

Diverging Lens. *See* Lens.

Diverticulitis, an inflammation of diverticula, small intestinal wall outpouchings, frequently caused by fecal matter obstructing the neck of the pouch. Symptoms include lower left side pain, cramps, nausea, vomiting, sometimes fever, malaise, alternating constipation and diarrhea. If untreated (with antispasmodics, antibiotics, and bland diet) abcess, hemorrhage, and intestinal wall performation can occur, with surgery indicated. △718.

Dividend, in terms of insurance, a return in part of the premium on participating insurance to reflect the difference between the premium charged and the actual losses, expense, and investment performance experienced by the insurance company. Such premiums are usually calculated in such a way as to provide some margin over the anticipated cost of the insurance protection.

Divination, foretelling the future or discovering what is unknown by understanding various signs. Divination is a form of magic with worldwide distribution. Signs of the future are very often thought to be found in the entrails of animals that are especially sacrificed. Other techniques include casting lots and palmistry. Divination assumes revelation or association between the natural world and human affairs. △822.

Divine, Father (*c.* 1882–1965), US clergyman, b. probably as George Baker in Savannah, Ga. Originally a revival preacher among Southern blacks, he moved to New York State about 1915, founded the Peace Mission Movement, and adopted the name Father Divine. The movement grew rapidly, largely in New York City and Philadelphia, and eventually encompassed some 500,000. Divine used the large sums of money donated to him by his followers to help support black-owned businesses. His movement declined sharply after his death.

Divine Comedy (*c.*1307–21), allegorical, narrative poem by Dante Alighieri. Through this work Dante established Tuscan as the literary language of Italy. It is divided into three parts, *Inferno, Purgatorio,* and *Paradiso* and consists of the author's imaginary tour of Hell, Purgatory, and Heaven. He meets his contemporaries, historical figures, and characters from mythology, the Bible, and classical literature. It is written in terza rima, a complex verse form.

Relying on both pagan and Christian descriptions of the afterlife, Dante divides the three worlds into multiple levels; each soul is carefully placed in his proper level and is punished according to the nature of his sins on earth. Although concerned with his intellectual and religious feelings about man's life on earth and his relationship to God, Dante also uses the allegorical medium to vent his own personal rivalries and political opinions. *See also* Terza Rima. △1100.

Divine Right of Kings, political theory, popular in 16th and 17th centuries, that anointed kings derive absolute and irresistible authority directly from God. Law is an instrument of grace, not a contrivance of human wisdom, so that the king is answerable only to God and is above all promulgated laws, including his own. △898.

Diving, water sport in which acrobatic maneuvers are performed off a springboard or highboard. The several types of competition include the 1- and 3-meter springboards and the 5-, 7.5-, and 10-meter firm highboards. The judging, based on points, is complicated and depends not only on the difficulty of the dive but also on the diver's movement at the start, his technique and grace of the flight, and his entry into the water. All world diving is governed by the Fédération Internationale de Natation Amateur, organized in 1908.

Diving Beetle, or predaceous diving beetle, medium-sized, aquatic beetle found in ponds over most of the world. The adult and larva prey on insects, tadpoles, and small fish. Diving beetles have long hind legs adapted for swimming and threadlike antennae. Family Dytiscidae. △616.

Diving Bell, Halley. △238.

Diving Birds, widely differing birds that typically dive —some shallowly, others deeply—for food. Loons are the most adept divers. Others include grebes, albatrosses, diving petrels, tropic birds, pelicans, boobies, cormorants, some ducks and geese, jacana, dippers, and kingfishers. *See also* individual birds.

Division, arithmetical operation signified by ÷, interpreted as the inverse of multiplication. The quotient of two numbers, $a \div b$, is the number that must be multiplied by b to give a. a is called the dividend and b the divisor. Quotients can also be written as fractions. *See also* Arithmetical Operations. △1446.

Divisionism, Italian version of neo-Impressionism which emerged in the late 1880s and 1890s and was practiced by Segantini, Previati, and Pelliza da Valpedo. This movement led to futurism and espoused the technique of juxtaposing small strokes of pure color directly on the canvas and allowing the eye of the viewer to blend them at a distance rather than first mixing the colors on the palette. *See also* Pointillism. △1294.

Division of Labor, plan of production in which each individual or group of workers specializes in a single phase of the production process. The performance of one, or a limited number of operations, is characteristic of contemporary mass production in both capitalistic and socialistic economies. The specialization of machines is a closely related aspect.

Divorce, legal dissolution of a valid marriage. Social scientists view divorce as the most constant of all major social problems. Statistics show that the United States has the highest divorce rate of the developed societies; however, the divorce rate of several European countries has actually increased faster in recent years. The US divorce rate steadily increased from the mid-19th century until the end of WWII. Since then it has fluctuated, and the rate of increase has slowed; however, social changes such as improved job opportunities for women, accelerated urbanization, greater mobility, and other factors, indicate the long-term pattern of US divorce rate is upward. The legislative power on divorce is maintained by state rather than the federal government, and state divorce policies are varied.

Dix, Dorothea (Lynde) (1802–87), US pioneer in the treatment of the mentally ill, b. Hampden, Maine. She exposed the inhumane treatment of the insane and inspired legislation resulting in patients being treated in state mental hospitals rather than confined to prisons.

Dix, John Adams (1798–1879), US political figure and soldier, b. Boscawen, N.H. After serving in the War of 1812, he began a political career and was US senator from New York (1845–49). He was president of both the Union and Pacific and Erie railroads before becoming secretary of the treasury under President Buchanan (1861). He served as a major general in the Union Army during the Civil War. Appointed US minister to France (1866–69), he was also governor of New York (1873–74).

Dix, Fort, US Army reservation in central New Jersey. Largest Army training center in country in WWII, it is now a major induction, discharge, and overseas transfer point. Area: 32,000acres (12,960hectares). Founded 1917 as Camp Dix.

Dixieland, style of jazz music originating in New Orleans in the early 1900s and featuring popular melodies, lively rhythms, and a generally cheerful sound. *See also* Jazz. △1366.

Dixon, Jeane. △822.

Djakarta, capital city of Indonesia, on NW coast of Java; originally a trading post and fort; severely damaged by earthquake 1699; became capital of Indonesia after recognition of its independence by Dutch, Dec. 29, 1949. An administrative, cultural, and educational center, Djakarta is site of University of Indonesia (1950). Industries: iron foundries, printing, sawmills. Exports: rubber, tea, quinine. Founded 1619 by Dutch Jan Pieterszoon Coen. Pop. 4,576,-009.

Djawa. *See* Java.

Djawa, Laut. *See* Java Sea.

Djibouti (Jibuti), capital city of French Territory of Afars and Issas, Africa; on the S shore of the Gulf of Tadjura, S of the Bab el Kandeb Strait; site of Ethiopian railroad terminus; trade center. Founded 1888; named capital 1892, free port 1949. Pop. 62,000.

Djilas, Milovan (1911–), Yugoslav political writer and political leader. A Communist party official and one of Tito's leading cabinet ministers, he was involved in the assertion of independence from the Kremlin in 1948, but his outspoken criticism of Tito's regime especially in the foreign press, ended his political career (1954). *The New Class: An Analysis of the Communist System* was published in 1957, leading to his arrest. He was released in 1966 but subsequently clashed with the government over his views.

Dmitri (died 1606), pretender to the throne of Russia, b. as Yury Otrepyev. After Tsar Feodor I died in 1598, Otrepyev, then a monk, claimed to be Dmitri, Feodor's son and heir to the throne of Russia. The real Dmitri had died in 1591. Boris Godunov, however, became tsar. In 1603 Otrepyev went to Lithuania, where he obtained support to invade Moscow in 1604. Boris Godunov died in 1605, and Dmitri was proclaimed tsar after bringing about the death of Feodor II, son of Boris. Dmitri's Polish advisers and pro-Polish policies alienated the Russians, and in 1606 Dmitri Vasily Shuysky led a revolt in which Dmitri was murdered.

DNA. *See* Deoxyribonucleic Acid.

Dnepr (Dnieper), river in Ukranian SSR, USSR; rises in Valdai Hills, W of Moscow; flows S through Belorussia, the Ukraine, and cities of Smolensk, Mogilev, Kiev, Cherkassy, Kremenchug, Dnepropetrovsk, Zaporozhye, Nikopol, Kherson, into Black Sea. The 3rd-longest river in Europe, it contains the Dreproges Dam (1932), which made river navigable for entire course; Dnepr is linked by canal to western Bug River; site of hydroelectric stations. Length: 1,430mi (2,300km).

Dneprodzerzhinsk (Dneprodzeržinsk), formerly Kamenskoye; city in Ukrainian SSR, USSR, on Dnepr River. Industries: metallurgy, iron, steel, chemicals, cement, tools. Founded c.1750. Pop. 227,000.

Dnepropetrovsk, city in Ukrainian SSR, USSR, on the Dnepr River; capital of Dnepropetrovsk oblast; site of state university, technical schools, agricultural and teachers' colleges, museums. Industries: iron, steel, food processing, chemicals, heavy machinery. Founded 1787 by G.A. Potemkin for Catherine II; named for Ukrainian Bolshevik, Petrovski (1926). Pop. 903,000.

Dnestr (Dniester), river in Ukrainian SSR, USSR; rises in N slopes of Carpathian Mts; flows SE to Black Sea SW of Odessa; part of its course forms Ukrainian-Moldavian republic borders; irregular water levels hamper navigation; site of hydroelectric station; frontier delineation between USSR and Romania 1918–1940. Length: 845mi (1,360km). Basin area: 27,800sq mi (72,000sq km).

Dnieper River. *See* Dnepr.

Dniester River. *See* Dnestr.

Doberman Pinscher, elegant guard and police dog (working group) bred in Germany about 1890. A square-built dog, it has a long, blunt, wedge-shaped head; cropped, erect ears; deep chest; short, firm back and broad loin and hips; straight, medium-length legs; and docked tail. The smooth, hard, short coat is black, red, blue, or fawn—all with rust marks. Average size: 24–28 in (61–71cm) high at shoulder; 60–75lb (27–34kg). *See also* Working Dog.

Dobruja (Dobrudja), historic region in SE Romania and NE Bulgaria, located S of Danube River along Black Sea coastline; became part of Romania after second Balkan War (1913). S Dobruja given to Bulgaria by German-imposed treaty of Craiova (1940). Inhabitants include Tatars, Romanians, Turks, and Bulgarians. The region is mainly agricultural; grapes, grains, and sheep are raised. Area: 9,000sq mi (23,310sq km).

Dobzhansky, Theodosius (1900–75), US geneticist and authority on human evolution, b. Russia. He was influential in the development of population genetics as a separate study. Educated in Russia, he taught there and then in the United States. He became a US citizen in 1936. His writings include *Genetics and the Origin of Species* (1937), *Mankind Evolving* (1962), and *Genetics of the Evolutionary Process* (1970).

Docetism, heresy in Christianity. Docetism (from the Greek "to seem") was the doctrine that Christ did not have a material human body but rather was a phantasmal human and that his birth, death, and other earthly manifestations were merely illusions. This belief, regarded as the first Christian heresy, reached its height with the 2nd century Gnostics. The first to use the name "Docetist" was Serapion, bishop of Antioch (190–203). *See also* Gnosticism.

Dock, any of over 100 species (genus *Rumex*) of flowering plants native to North America and Europe, with oblong or lance-shaped leaves and many small, scaly brown flowers. Most are considered weeds, but some are cultivated for their edible leaves or as ornamentals. Family Polygonaceae.

d' Ockeghem, Jean. △1132.

Doctorow, E(dgar) L(awrence) (1931–), US author, b. New York City. His novels include *Welcome to Hard Times* (1960), *The Book of Daniel* (1971), and *Ragtime* (1975), a novel about the United States at the turn of the century.

Dodder, leafless, parasitic, twining herb with threadlike stems. Usually straw-colored or orange, with many small yellow flowers, the plant attaches to the stem of a larger plant, releases its contact with the ground, and attaches its roots to the host. Species include *Cuscuta pentagona,* or field dodder. Family Convolvulaceae. △444.

Dodecanese (Dhodhekanisos), island group in Greece, in the SE Aegean Sea, between W Turkey and E Crete; capital is Rhodes; conquered and ruled since 1600 BC by many nations and groups, including Athens, Sparta, Rome, Venice, Crusaders, Knights of St John. Under Turkish control 1500–1912, it was seized by Italy 1912 and passed to Greece 1947.

Dodge, Grenville Mellan (1831–1916), US military officer and engineer, b. Danvers, Mass. A major general in the Civil War, he was Republican representative from Iowa (1867–69) and served as chief engineer of the Union Pacific Railroad (1866–70). Dodge and William Horne later built a railroad in Cuba (1899–1903). He headed the Dodge Commission whose investigations of the causes of the Spanish-American War (1898–1900) resulted in massive reorganization of the US Army.

Dodge, Mary Mapes (1831–1905), US editor and author of works for children, b. Mary Elizabeth Dodge in New York City. From 1873 to 1905 she edited *St. Nicholas,* a children's magazine that attracted major authors and artists of the day. She also wrote the classic *Hans Brinker, or the Silver Skates.*

Dodge City, city in SW Kansas, on Arkansas River; seat of Ford co; established near Fort Dodge on Santa Fe Trail, it became a cowboy town; Wyatt Earp and Bat Masterson were among its marshalls. Industries: farm tools, shipping. Founded 1872; inc. 1875. Pop.(1970) 14,127.

Dodgson, Charles Lutwidge. *See* Carroll, Lewis.

Dodo, extinct, flightless bird that lived on the Mascarene Islands in the Indian Ocean. The last dodo died about 1800. The true dodo *(Raphus cucullatus)* of Mauritius Island and the similar Réunion solitaire *(Raphus solitarius)* were heavy-bodied with large heads and large hooked bills. Weight: to 50lb (23kg). The Rodriguez or solitaire dodo *(Pezophaps solitaria)* was smaller, with a straight bill and knobbed wings.

Dodsworth (1929), novel by Sinclair Lewis about a middle-aged American, Sam Dodsworth, whose marriage breaks up after he is confronted with his wife's shallowness as they travel together in Europe.

Doedicorus. △574.

Doenitz, Karl (1891–), German naval officer. He entered the submarine service in 1916 and in World War II was commander of the submarine fleet until 1943. He then became grand admiral and commander in chief of the German navy until 1945, when Hitler named him as his successor to the Reich. He submitted the German surrender in 1945 and was sentenced to 10 years in prison by the Nuremberg tribunal in 1945.

Doesburg, Theo van (1883–1931), Dutch painter, writer, and critic. He was a founder of the influential art review *de Stijl* in 1917. His art developed from Cubism, and he eventually limited himself to geometric compositions of black and white combined with primary colors. *See also* Cubism.

Dog, mammal closely related to the jackal, wolf, and wild dog. It has a slender, muscular body; long head with slender snout and triangular ears; small paws with five toes on the forefeet and four on the hind; non-retractile claws; and well-developed canine teeth. The dog walks on its toes with the heel, or hock, off the ground. Smell is the dog's most important sense and its hearing is acute. The gestation period is 49–70 days and one or more helpless young are born.

Dogs developed from the tree-dwelling miacis, that lived 40–50 million years ago, through intermediate forms to tomarctus, that lived 15 million years ago. The dog was domesticated 15,000 years ago. There are 400 breeds; the oldest is the Saluki, in existence for 7,000 years. Dog breeds are classified into sporting, hound, terrier, working, toy, and non-sporting groups. Length: body—13.4–53.2in (34–135cm); tail—4.3–21.3in (11–54cm); weight: 3.3–165.31lb (1.5–74kg). Family Canidae; species *Canis familiaris. See also* individual breeds. Following is a list of dog breeds recognized by the American Kennel Club, organized by major groups.

Dog Breeds

Sporting Dogs
- Pointer
- Pointer, German Shorthaired
- Pointer, German Wirehaired
- Retriever, Chesapeake Bay
- Retriever, Curly-Coated
- Retriever, Flat-Coated
- Retriever, Golden
- Retriever, Labrador
- Setter, English
- Setter, Golden
- Setter, Irish
- Spaniel, American Water
- Spaniel, Brittany
- Spaniel, Clumber
- Spaniel, Cocker
- Spaniel, English Cocker
- Spaniel, English Springer
- Spaniel, Field
- Spaniel, Irish Water
- Spaniel, Sussex
- Spaniel, Welsh Springer
- Vizla
- Weimaraner
- Wirehaired Pointing Griffon

Hounds
- Afghan Hound
- Basenji
- Basset Hound
- Beagle
- Black and Tan Coonhound
- Bloodhound
- Borzoi
- Dachshund
- Foxhound, American
- Foxhound, English
- Greyhound
- Harrier

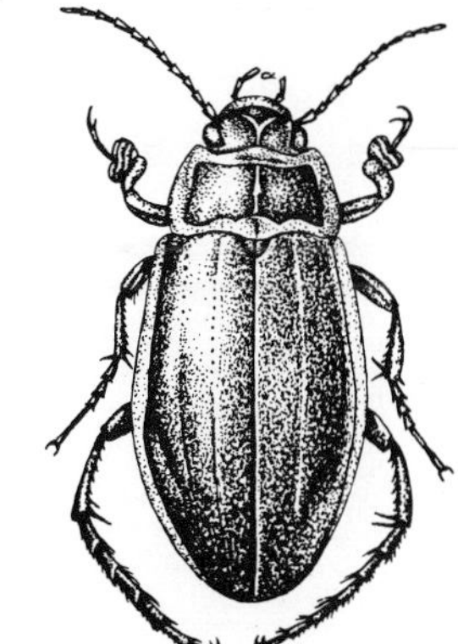
Diving beetle

Dorothea Dix

Djakarta, Indonesia

Dnepr River, USSR

Irish Wolfhound
Norwegian Elkhound
Otter Hound
Rhodesian Ridgeback
Saluki
Scottish Deerhound
Whippet
Working Dogs
Akita
Alaskan Malamute
Belgian Malinois
Belgian Sheepdog
Belgian Tervuren
Bernese Mountain Dog
Bouvier des Flandres
Boxer
Briard
Bullmastiff
Collie
Doberman Pinscher
German Shepherd
Giant Schnauzer
Great Dane
Great Pyrenees
Komondor
Kuvasz
Mastiff
Newfoundland
Old English Sheepdog
Puli
Rottweiler
St. Bernard
Samoyed
Shetland Sheepdog
Siberian Husky
Standard Schnauzer
Welsh Corgi, Cardigan
Welsh Corgi, Pembroke
Terriers
Airedale Terrier
American Staffordshire Terrier
Australian Terrier
Border Terrier
Cairn Terrier
Dandie Dinmont Terrier
Fox Terrier
Irish Terrier
Kerry Blue Terrier
Lakeland Terrier
Manchester Terrier
Miniature Schnauzer
Norwich Terrier
Scottish Terrier
Sealyham Terrier
Skye Terrier
Soft-Coated Wheaten Terrier
Staffordshire Bull Terrier
Welsh Terrier
West Highland White Terrier
Toys
Affenpinscher
Brussels Griffon
Chihuahua
English Toy Spaniel
Italian Greyhound
Japanese Spaniel
Maltese
Manchester Terrier (toy)
Miniature Pinscher
Papillon
Pekingese
Pomeranian
Poodle (toy)
Pug
Shih Tzu
Silky Terrier
Yorkshire Terrier
Non-Sporting Dogs
Bichon Frise
Boston Terrier
Bulldog
Chow Chow
Dalmation
French Bulldog
Keeshond
Lhasa Apso
Poodle
Schipperke
Tibetan Terrier

Dogbane, N American tall, branched perennial plant with fibrous stems and milky poisonous sap. They bear loose clusters of small, white or pink, bell-shaped flowers. Indian hemp *(Apocynum cannabinum)* was formerly grown for cordage fiber. Family Apocynaceae.

Dogfish, shark found worldwide in marine waters. Generally grayish with white spots, they have no anal fin. They are usually divided into two groups: spiny dogs with a stout, sharp spine in front of each dorsal fin and spineless dogs that lack a spine in front of the second dorsal fin. Length: 4ft (1.2m); weight: 20lb (9kg). The spineless Greenland shark is 21ft (6.4m) long. Suborder Squaloidei. *See also* Chondrichthyes; Sharks. △392, 510.

Doggerel, trivial verse, written for comic or burlesque effect, loosely styled, irregular in meter, often badly written. The word can be used as a term of abuse.

Dog-headed Water Snake. △524.

Dogon, Negroid people whose traditional ancestral dwellings are in remote cave-villages in the Hombori Mountains of the Mali Republic. Their patrilineal village society is based on subsistence agriculture, principal foods being millet and sorghum. Their religion is notable for its abstract concepts and a powerful creation myth.

Dog Racing, sport, popular in some parts of the United States. Greyhounds are kept in an enclosed chute and then released to chase a mechanical rabbit, which rides on an electric rail around the track. Parimutual betting is conducted in the few states that permit this type of racing. The dogs are classified on a scale from E upwards, and continuing losses at the E level disqualifies the animal from further competition. The sport, which dates from ancient times, began to grow in popularity with the introduction in 1919 of the mechanical rabbit, prior to which real rabbits were used. The sport was introduced in Great Britain in the 19th century and was called "coursing." The chase included live game such as deer, foxes, and hares. The first track in the United States was Derby Lane, built in 1925 in St. Petersburg, Fla.

Dog Shows, competition to determine the best class of canine in a certain breed. It is a popular attraction in the United States and elsewhere in the world. The American Kennel Club (AKC) recognizes 118 breeds divided into 6 basic categories: sporting dogs, terriers, working dogs, hounds, toys, and non-sporting dogs. The judging rules, which are complicated, differ from breed to breed. The most prestigious of all US competitions is the Westminster Kennel Club Show, where all entries, including puppies, must be previous blue ribbon winners in a show sponsored by the AKC.

Dogtooth Violet, bulbous perennial plant native to Europe and Asia. The stalked leaves are blotchy and reddish-brown and the flowers are rose to purple. Family Liliaceae; species *Erythronium dens-canis.*

Dogwood, any of several small trees and shrubs in the genus *Cornus* of the dogwood family (Cornaceae). The best known species is the flowering dogwood *(C. florida),* native to E North American forests from S Canada to Florida. In the wild, flowering dogwoods are graceful, sparsely leaved inhabitants of the dimly lit understory of deciduous forests. Their small flowers, enclosed by four large, petallike, white bracts, bloom before the leaves open.

Doldrums, a nautical term for the region over the ocean near the equator characterized by calms, light and variable winds, and squalls, and corresponding approximately with the equatorial trough, a belt of low pressure around the equator.

Dole, Robert Joseph (1923–), US political leader, b. Russell, Kansas. He served with distinction in World War II and was severely wounded. After the war he was elected as a Republican to the Kansas legislature. In 1960 he was elected to the US House of Representatives. He served there until 1969, when he entered the US Senate, where he became known as a conservative and highly partisan Republican. He served as Republican national chairman (1971–73) and was a vigorous defender of Richard Nixon during the Watergate scandal. Later, however, he criticized Nixon's role in the affair. In 1976, Pres. Gerald Ford chose Dole as his running mate in the 1976 presidential campaign.

Dole, Sanford (1844–1926), US statesman, b. Honolulu, Hawaii, son of missionary parents. He studied law at Williams College and then led demands for democratic government in Hawaii. When a revolutionary group overthrew the queen in 1893, he refused to comply with Pres. Grover Cleveland's demand for her restoration. As first president of the republic (1894–1898) he pressed for US annexation, which came in 1898. Dole was the territory's first governor (1900–03).

Dolerite. △246.

Dolichosoma. △566.

Dollar Diplomacy, term used to describe US policy of military and economic interference in Latin American affairs in the early 1900s. A number of Caribbean countries (Dominican Republic, Cuba, Haiti, Honduras, Costa Rica, and Nicaragua) were, at various time, heavily in debt to certain European governments. The United States intervened, citing the threat of European encroachment in the western hemisphere and the need to safeguard US investments in these countries.

Dollfus, Audouin (-Charles) (1924–), French astronomer, known as a pioneer in high-altitude observation from balloons. An expert in planetary studies, he discovered Janus, the 10th satellite of Saturn, in 1966.

Dollfuss, Englebert (1892–1934), Austrian Chancellor (1932–34). A Christian Socialist, he became chancellor at a time when the country was close to economic collapse and threatened by external and internal enemies. In 1932 he obtained a much needed international loan by agreeing not to form a customs union with Germany. In 1933 he dissolved the National Socialist party, which had been calling for union with Nazi Germany. In February 1934 he crushed the Social Democratic party and in April assumed dictatorial powers. He was assassinated on July 25 by Austrian Nazis who were attempting to seize power.

Döllinger, Johann Joseph Ignaz von (1799–1890), German theologian. Professor of church history at the University of Munich (1826–73), he refused to accept the doctrine of the infallibility of the pope promulgated by the Vatican Council in 1870. For his opposition he was excommunicated in 1871. He became a leader in the formation of the Old Catholics, an independent German Catholic church.

Doll's House, A (1879), 4-act drama by Henrik Ibsen. There have been many successful productions of this first important social drama dealing with the problem of women's freedom. Its longest Broadway run was in 1937. It has also been produced on film and for TV. Although Nora escapes the legal consequences of forging her father's name on a check to keep her husband, she is forced to face the realities of her domestic life. Realizing that her husband had been keeping her as a doll, Nora leaves him to establish her own identity.

Dolomite, a sedimentary rock, probably formed by the alteration of limestone by seawater. Also, carbonate mineral, calcium-magnesium carbonate [$CaMg(CO_3)_2$], found in dolomite rocks and metamorphosed rocks. Calcite-like rhombohedral system prismatic crystals, often intergrown, are found in hydrothermal veins. Pearly-white or pink; hardness 3.5–4; sp gr 2.8.

Dolomites (Dolomiti or Dolomiten), part of Italian Alps, in NE Italy; formed of dolomitic limestone and shaped by erosion; first climbed by English in 19th century; landslides caused Vaiont Dam to overflow in 1963 killing 2,000 in nearby Longarone. Highest peak is the Marmolada, 10,964ft (3,342m).

Dolphin, small, toothed whale having distinct beak and slender body. Larger than the porpoise, it is the fastest and most agile and playful of whales. In captivity, the highly intelligent, bottle-nosed dolphin readily learns complicated routines. Length: to 14ft (4.3m). Family Delphinidae; species *Tursiops truncatus.* △552.

Dolton, town in NE Illinois, on Calumet River, S of Chicago; truck farming area. Industries: glass, chemicals, paper bags. Inc. 1892. Pop. (1970) 25,937.

Domagk, Gerhardt (1895–1964), German chemist. In 1927 he was made director of the research institute of the I.G. Farben industrial works. He is known for his discovery of the drug prontosil, the forerunner of sulfanilamide, the first of the "wonder drugs" used to combat infectious diseases. He was awarded the Nobel Prize in medicine and physiology in 1939 for his discovery. △746.

Domain, set of values possible for the independent variable of a function. Thus for a function $f(x)$ the domain is the set of values of x for which $f(x)$ is real.

Domain, in Magnetism. △1534–36.

Dome, Lunar, any of several broad-based low mountains on the surface of the moon, often characterized by crater pits on their summits. △52.

Domenichino (Zampieri) (1581–1641), Italian

painter and architect. In 1602 he worked with Annibale Carraci on the Farnese Palace. Between 1621–23 he was chief Vatican architect. He became a leading painter of the early Baroque style. His landscape paintings, including *The Hunt of Diana* and *Landscape with St. John Baptizing*, had a profound influence on Nicolas Poussin and Claude Lorrain.

Dome of the Rock. △1062.

Domesday Book, also called Doomsday Book, two-volume census ordered by William the Conqueror and compiled (1085–86) to assess the economic facts of his kingdom so that he might levy a higher Danegeld. Now located in the Record Office, London, it records the ownership and value of all lands at the time of the survey and also at their bestowal and at the time of Edward the Confessor; the value of crops, cattle, etc. is also included along with the social status of the owners. A special edition of the Domesday Book (so-called because no one could escape inclusion) was published in 1783. △1076.

Domestic Gas. △1560.

Dominance, in genetics, the tendency of one characteristic of a heterozygous pair of alleles to manifest itself over another. For example, if an offspring has one allele each for brown eyes and blue eyes, the brown-eyed allele will dominate and manifest itself over the blue. *See also* Heredity. △416.

Dominance Relationships, or pecking orders, systems of status within social groups in which different individuals are ranked or ordered in terms of status or "dominance." Most such systems in animal societies are based on strength or aggressiveness. In human societies, status depends more on the acquisition of possessions, wealth, or prestige. △464.

Dominic (1170?–1221), Spanish churchman, a Roman Catholic saint, and founder of the Dominicans, b. Domingo de Gúzman. In 1203 Pope Innocent III sent him to S France to preach to the Albigenes. In 1215 he founded the Dominicans, who were pledged to poverty and dedicated to study and preaching.

Dominica, largest island of Windward Islands, West Indies, in the Caribbean Sea, between Guadeloupe and Martinique islands; capital and chief port is Roseau; population is largely descended from African slaves; small Carib Indian community remains. Dominica was captured by the French 1778; returned to Great Britain 1783; inc. with Leeward Islands 1833; member of West Indies Federation 1958–62; became self-governing state 1967. Crops: copra, bananas, cocoa, coconuts, tobacco, spices. Discovered 1493 by Columbus. Area: 290sq mi (750sq km). Pop. 70,302.

Dominican Republic, independent republic on the E two-thirds of Hispaniola Island, West Indies; it shares the island with the Republic of Haiti (W). The terrain is generally rugged, traversed E-W by the Cordillera Central mountain system, rising to its max. height at Pico Duarte, 10,490ft (3,197m), the highest peak in the West Indies. To both the N and S of this system are smaller, less-elevated ranges. The most fertile area of the country, the Cibao, lies in the NW between two mountain ranges and is drained by the Yuna and Yaque del Norte rivers.

Agriculture dominates the economic activity of the Dominican Republic; sugar, coffee, cacao, and tobacco are the major exported crops. For mainland consumption, tobacco, fruits, vegetables, rice, corn, and tomatoes are cultivated. Dominating the manufactures are textiles, glassware, metal products, paint, and cement. Cattle raising is an important growing industry, as is the mining of bauxite and nickel. In 1973 the Dominican Republic was the world's 15th-largest producer of bauxite and 7th-largest producer of nickel. The majority of the population lives in rural farm areas or urban ghettos where the literacy rate is low. The University of Santo Domingo, the oldest in the Americas, was founded 1538 by the Spanish; there is also the Pedro Henríquez-Urena University and Catholic University. There are many fine examples of colonial architecture in Santo Domingo, among them the cathedral housing Christopher Columbus' remains.

The island was discovered 1492 by Christopher Columbus, who established the first settlement in the New World at Isabella (1493) and by 1496 had founded Santo Domingo as Spain's capital in the West Indies. By 1697, Spain had ceded the W portion of the island, known as Saint Domingue, to France by the Treaty of Ryswick, causing great economic hardship for Santo Domingo. In 1795 the island was once again reunited by the Treaty of Basel and ruled by French-Haitian administration, under Toussaint L'Overture. Haiti declared its independence in 1804 and included Santo Domingo within its borders. The Dominicans revolted against this domination in 1843 and declared the independent nation of the Dominican Republic. Spain regained domination in 1861 but withdrew for the last time in 1865 after political upheavals. The United States gained control of Dominican customs 1905–1941 because of the country's foreign debts. The presence of US Marines was resented by Dominican nationalists, and they were withdrawn in 1924. With the 1930 election came the military dictatorship of Rafael Leonidas Trujillo Molina, who stabilized the economy, but the government grew corrupt. In 1960 he was censured by the Organization of American States (OAS), and a year later was assassinated. The first free election was held in 1962 electing Juan Bosch as president. His reign lasted less than one year; he was overthrown in a military coup d'etat. In 1966, Joaquín Balaguer was elected president; he was reelected in 1970 and 1974.

PROFILE

Official name: República Dominicana
Area: 18,703sq mi (48,440sq km)
Population: 4,011,589
Chief cities: Santo Domingo (capital); Santiago; San Francisco de Macorís; San Pedro de Macorís
Religion: Roman Catholic
Language: Spanish
Monetary unit: Peso

Dominicans, Roman Catholic religious order. Known officially as the Order of Friars Preachers and often informally as Black Friars, they were founded by St. Dominic in 1215. They were the first Catholic religious order to have preaching doctrine as their primary task and the first to accept members into the order as a whole ready to be sent anywhere, rather than into autonomous houses. The order provided houses of study at centers of learning, and under the leadership of Albertus Magnus (died 1280) and Thomas Aquinas (1225–74) rapidly became prominent in the intellectual life of the church. They vigorously propagated Thomism and have often been called on to provide official theologians. They preached against the Albigensians, Moors, and Jews; evangelized from Scandinavia to India and later throughout the world; and were placed in charge of the Inquisition. The order includes both men and women. Their habit is white with a black mantle. They have sought to popularize the saying of the rosary, and they wear rosaries on their belts. △1086.

Dominion, self-governing member of the British Commonwealth of Nations. Some dominions recognize the British monarch as titular sovereign while others do not. Dominion status confers trade, technical assistance, and military aid preferences. Dominions are independent nations which freely cooperate. No formal ties, except for a secretariat, exist with Britain.

Dominion Day, national holiday in Canada (July 1). It commemorates the establishment of the Dominion of Canada on July 1, 1867, uniting Nova Scotia, New Brunswick, and Upper and Lower Canada.

Dominoes, game played with rectangular pieces. The standard game uses 28 pieces. Each piece is divided into halves, each half containing from 0 to 6 dots in every combination—0-0, 1-1, 1-0, etc. The dominoes are played one at a time, and must be placed next to a domino that has a corresponding number. Each time a combination of the outer halves totals 5 or multiples of 5, the player receives a similar score.

Domino Theory, tenet of US foreign policy formulated after World War II; often applied to Southeast Asia. It is based on the thesis that if one country falls to Communist rule, its neighbors will inevitably succumb as well. The domino theory was one reason for US involvement in Vietnam and was subscribed to by the successive administrations of Presidents Eisenhower, Kennedy, Johnson, and Nixon.

Domitian (51–96), Roman emperor (81–96), second son of Vespasian. Despite holding no high posts, he succeeded Titus to the throne. Though his rule was at first orderly, he gave way to his cruel, tyrannical nature. He recalled Agricola from Britain, overpowered the Senate, and ruled like an absolute monarch. His repressive politics led to plots against him and a reign of terror. His wife, Domitia, arranged his assassination. The Senate chose Nerva as emperor to show its right to name the emperor.

Don, river in Ukrainian SSR, USSR; rises S of Moscow in mid-Russian Uplands, SE of Tula; flows S then SW to Sea of Azov. Rostov-na-Donu (Rostov-on-Don) is major port city; annual floods are controlled by Tsim-

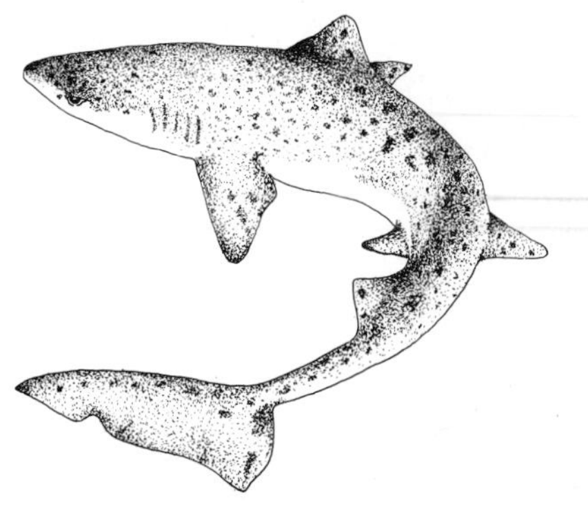

Dogfish

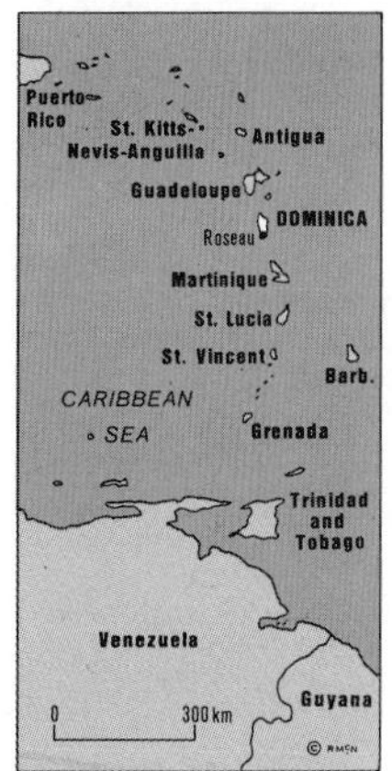
Puerto Rico
St. Kitts
Antigua
Nevis-Anguilla
Guadeloupe
DOMINICA
Roseau
Martinique
St. Lucia
St. Vincent
Barb.
CARIBBEAN SEA
Grenada
Trinidad and Tobago
Venezuela
0
300km
Guyana

Dominica

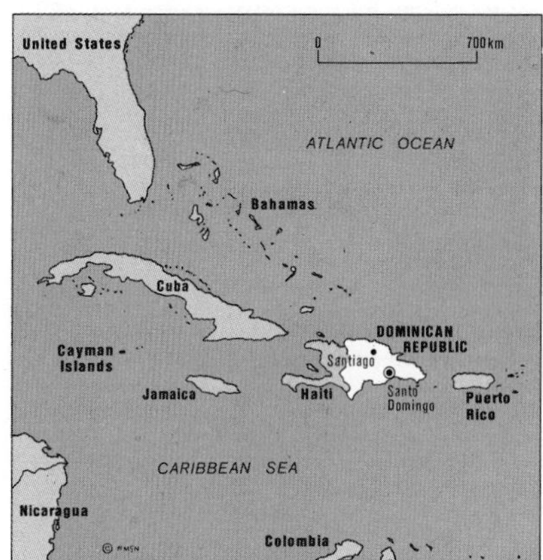
United States
0
700km
ATLANTIC OCEAN
Bahamas
Cuba
DOMINICAN REPUBLIC
Cayman Islands
Santiago
Jamaica
Haiti
Santo Domingo
Puerto Rico
CARIBBEAN SEA
Nicaragua
Colombia

Dominican Republic

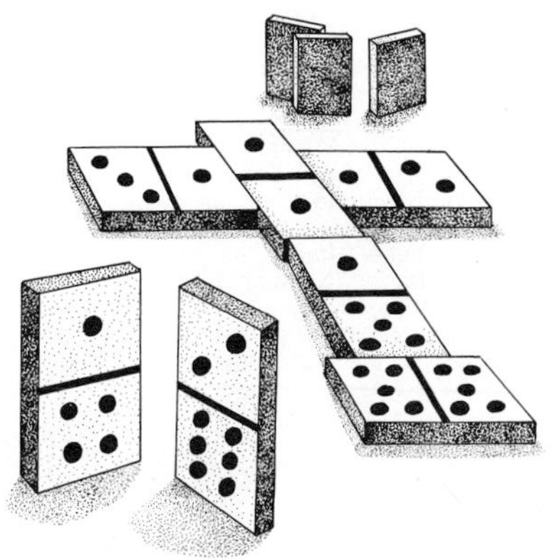

Dominoes

lyansk Reservoir. River is navigable for 850mi (1,370km); shipping route for grain, lumber, and coal; fisheries in lower course. Donets River is major tributary; Don Basin lies between Volga River (E) and Dnepr River (W). Area of Basin: 160,000sq mi (414,400sq km). Length: 1,200mi (1,930km).

Donald Bane, Scottish king, the first of a succession of weak kings to rule after the death of Malcolm III (1093). As Malcolm's brother he was supported in his claims to the throne, and he successfully seized Edinburgh Castle. He was unseated by Duncan II, but returned after Duncan's murder, only to be unseated by Edgar in 1097.

Donatello (*c.*1386–1466), Italian sculptor, b. Donato di Niccolò di Betto Bardi. He worked in Florence, and much of his work shows the influence of the Gothic tradition. For example, his wooden statue "Mary Magdalen" (1455), in the Baptistery, Florence, reflects the expressive and emotional qualities of this style. His "Zuccone" prophet (*c.*1420), in the Florentine campanile shows his use of realism in its portrayal of an ugly subject. He usually worked in bronze and marble. His realistic style extended from his numerous heroic-type free-standing sculptures to his flat reliefs. In these marble low reliefs, he showed a remarkable mastery of perspective and light and shadow. He received many commissions, among which were the Gates of Paradise doors for the Baptistery in Florence. *See also* Gothic Art. △1134

Donati's Comet. △90.

Donets (Northern Donets), river in Ukrainian SSR, USSR; rises in mid-Russian uplands, NE of Belgorod, flows SE to the Don River; lower course is navigable; tributaries are Oskol, Aidar, Lugan rivers. Length: 650mi (1,046km).

Donets (Donbas) Basin, major industrial region in Ukranian SSR, USSR, N of Sea of Azov and SW of Donets River; area is primarily in Donetsk and Voroshilovgrad oblasts, extending E into Rostov oblast; supplies up to 50% of USSR's coal and steel. Area: 10,000sq mi (25,900sq km).

Donetsk (Doneck), formerly Yuzovka or Stalino; city in Ukrainian SSR, USSR, on Kalmius River; capital of Donetsk oblast; largest city in Donets Basin; industrial and coal mining area; site of university, mining school, coal research institute, theater; developed after 1870 founding of ironworks by Scottish entrepreneur John Hughes. Industries: iron, steel, chemicals. Pop. 879,-000.

Donizetti, Gaetano (1797–1848), Italian operatic composer. He wrote 67 operas, both comic and serious. His most popular operas, include *L'Elisir d'Amore* (1832), *Lucia di Lammermoor* (1835), *Roberto Devereux* (1837), *La Fille du Régiment* (1840), and *Don Pasquale* (1843). △1246.

Donkey, or ass, domesticated equine derived from Nubian wild ass of Africa. A hardy saddle and pack animal, it is small and has long ears. Known since 4000 BC, it is also used to produce mules. Height: 3–5ft (1–1.5m) at shoulder. Breeds include Poiton, Spanish Giant, and Savoy. Family Equidae; species *Equus asinus asinus.*

Donnagel, trade name of drug (really a combination of agents) used as an antidiarrheal agent.

Donne, John (c.1571–1631), English poet and cleric. Raised a Roman Catholic, but converted to Anglicanism, he was ordained in 1615 after years of poverty. In 1621 he became dean of St Paul's Cathedral, London, where his sermons attracted much attention. Although widely known in his lifetime, the poems for which he is now famous were not published until 1633. Noted for their wit, extravagant imagery, and passion, they include love poems, satires, and religious sonnets. *See also* Metaphysical Poetry. △1148.

Donner Party, California-bound group who traveled overland from Illinois using a little-used route south of the Great Salt Lake (Utah). The party camped at Truckee Lake, Utah, in November 1846 where they were caught in the early snows in the Sierra Nevada Mountains. They escaped starvation by eating the flesh of those who died. Of the 87 members of the party, 47 survived.

Donnybrook, town in E Republic of Ireland; suburb of Dublin; famous for its annual fair, begun in 1204 but condemned in 1855 for unruliness and violence.

Donovan, William Joseph (1883–1959), US lawyer and military officer, b. Buffalo, N.Y. He served in World War I, winning the Congressional Medal of Honor. In World War II, Donovan organized the Office of Strategic Services (OSS) and headed it 1942–45. It was later reorganized as the Central Intelligence Agency. Donovan was US Ambassador to Thailand (1953–54).

Don Quixote de la Mancha (1605, 1615), novel by Miguel De Cervantes, published in two parts, initially intended to be a burlesque of chivalric romances. The author combined tragedy and comedy in his portrayal of the adventures of an elderly country gentleman, Don Quixote, and a peasant, Sancho Panza. Don Quixote is an avid reader of chivalric romances and, like a knight of old, sets out to redress the world's wrong.

Dooley, Thomas Anthony (1927–61), US physician and author who helped focus public attention on problems in Southeast Asia. As a naval officer in Vietnam (1954), he helped to evacuate refugees. In 1958, Dooley helped to found The Medical International Corporation (MEDICO), providing doctors and hospital facilities to underdeveloped nations. His books include *Deliver Us from Evil* (1956), *The Edge of Tomorrow* (1958), and *The Night They Burned the Mountain* (1960).

Doomsday Book. *See* Domesday Book.

Doppelganger, ghostly counterpart of a person; a double, invisible to others, that haunts him throughout his life.

Doppler, Christian Johann (1803–53), Austrian physicist and mathematician who is remembered as the discoverer of the Doppler effect, which is the change in the observed wave frequency caused by motion of the source and/or receiver of the wave. This effect is utilized in radiolocation, sonar, and astronomy. △126.

Doppler Effect, change in frequency of a wave, usually a sound or light wave, when there is relative motion between wave source and observer; the change depends on the velocities of the wave, source, and observer. With a sound wave the effect is demonstrated by the drop in pitch of a vehicle's siren as the vehicle passes the observer, the velocity of approach suddenly changing to a velocity of recession. With a light wave the source or observer velocity must be very large for an appreciable effect to occur, as when light is received from a rapidly receding galaxy with its spectral lines shifted toward the red end of the spectrum. *See also* Red Shift. △126.

Dorado, tropical offshore marine fish. A favored sport fish, it has a squarish head, forked tail, and long dorsal fin with 65 rays. Its silvery, blue, and yellow colors change when it is taken from the water. Length: 5ft (152.4cm); Weight: 67lb (30.4kg). Family Coryphaenidae; species: common *Coryphaena hippurus,* pompano dolphin *Coryphaena equisetus.*

Dorado, or the Swordfish, southern circumpolar constellation. It has no stars brighter than the third magnitude but is easily discerned because it contains most of the Large Magellanic Cloud.

Dorat, Jean (1508–88), French teacher and poet. His humanist ideas and knowledge of classical literature greatly influenced the doctrines of the Pléiad. He wrote Latin poems, some in imitation of Pindar. *See also* Pléiad.

Dorati, Antal (1906–), US; conductor, b. Hungary. He conducted the Minneapolis Symphony Orchestra (1949–60). Chief conductor of the Royal Philharmonic, Stockholm, from 1966, he became music director of the National Symphony Orchestra, Washington, D.C., in 1970.

Dorchester Company, fishing and mercantile company of Dorchester, England. It abandoned its permanent settlement at Cape Ann, Mass. (1626), feeling it was unprofitable. Governor Conant remained and moved to Salem, the original site for Massachusetts Bay Colony (1629).

Dordogne, river in SW France, formed by convergence of Dor and Dogne rivers; famous vineyards along its 293mi (471km) course.

Dordrecht, city in SW Netherlands, 12mi (19km) ESE of Rotterdam, on Meuse River; industrial and shipping center. Founded 1008; chartered 1200. Pop. 101,-736.

Doré, Gustave (1833–83), French illustrator, painter, and sculptor. Known best for his engraved book illustrations, he illustrated editions of Dante's *Inferno* (1861), *Don Quixote* (1862), and the Bible (1865). Many of these engravings depict grotesque and bizarre scenes. △810, 1172.

Doria, Andrea (1468–1560), Genoese admiral and statesman. In the service of the Hapsburg Emperor Charles V, he freed Genoa (1528) from the French and then became virtually absolute ruler of the city, reforming its constitution, which remained unchanged until 1798. Although he remained active in Genoese affairs, he continued until the end of his life to aid the Emperor against both the French and the Turks.

Dorians, peoples who settled in north Greece *c.*200 BC. About 900 years later they conquered Mycenae, starting a 300-year "dark age" of Greek culture. They were later responsible for developing city-states and dominated classical Greek military achievement. △992.

Doric Order, earliest of the five classical orders of architecture, used originally by the Greeks and imitated by the Romans. The Doric column generally has no base. Its shaft is thick and broadly fluted; its capital is simple and unornamented. *See also* Orders of Architecture. △1002.

Dormancy, temporary state of inaction or reduced metabolism. Animals may go dormant by hibernating. Plant seeds cease to grow or develop. An organism can return to a fully active state when conditions, such as temperature, moisture, or day length, change.

Dormouse, mouse size, squirrel-like rodent of Eurasia and Africa that hibernates in winter. Most dormice are active at night and sleep by day. They eat nuts, fruit, seeds, insects, eggs, and tiny animals. Length: 4–8in (10–20cm) excluding tail. Family Gliridae. △594.

Dorr's Rebellion (1841–42), a revolt protesting injustices in the Rhode Island state constitution, which restricted voting privileges to landowners and their oldest sons. Led by Thomas Wilson Dorr, the insurrectionists seized the statehouse and declared Dorr governor. The state militia was brought into action, the rebels dispersed, and Dorr was jailed. A new constitution was adopted (1843).

Dorset, county in SW England, bounded by English Channel(s). It is traversed W to E by North Dorset Downs and by South Dorset Downs near coast; drained by Frome and Stour rivers. Chief towns are Dorchester, Bournemouth, Poole, and Weymouth. Industries: tourism, agriculture, quarrying. Area: 973sq mi (2,520sq km). Pop. 361,213.

Dorset Spider Crab. △490.

Dortmund, city in W West Germany; a port on the Dortmund-Ems Canal; commercially important during Middle Ages; site of the Reinold church (begun in 13th century). Industries: iron smelting, steel, beer. Founded in 9th century. Pop. 647,047.

Dory, a small, narrow boat, about 20ft (6m) long, for fishing. It has pointed ends, high flaring sides and a flat bottom. Engines, sails, or oars are used for power.

Dos Passos, John (1896–1970), US novelist, b. Chicago. His work reflects his social conscience. His first novel, *Three Soldiers,* appeared in 1921. Subsequently, he began to develop the innovative techniques that characterize his trilogy, *U.S.A.* (1937). These include stream-of-consciousness writing and the use of contemporary headlines and biographies of prominent Americans in the novels.

Dostoevsky, Fyodor (Mikhailovich) (1821–81), Russian novelist. After writing *Poor Folk* (1846) and *The Double* (1846), he joined a revolutionary group, was arrested, and sentenced to death (1849). Reprieved at the last minute, he was sentenced to four years' hard labor in Siberia. He married (1857) and returned to St. Petersburg, where he edited several journals with his brother Mikhail and wrote *Notes from the Underground* (1864). After *Crime and Punishment* (1866) appeared, he married his secretary, Anna, and left Russia to escape creditors. While abroad, he wrote *The Idiot* (1868–69) and *The Possessed* (1871–72). His last major work was *The Brothers Karamazov* (1879–80). △1238.

Dothan, ancient city in central Palestine, in uplands NE of Samaria; ruins have been partially excavated. Here Joseph was sold into slavery by his brothers.

Dothan, city in SE Alabama, 15mi (24km) N of Floridian border; seat of Houston co; scene of annual nationwide peanut festival; site of nuclear power plant, George C. Wallace Junior College (1965); industrial and commercial center. Industries: hosiery, cotton processing, peanut oil, lumber products, farm machinery. Settled and inc. 1885. Pop. (1970) 36,-733.

Dou, Gerard (1613–75), Dutch painter. Although a student of Rembrandt (1628–31), Dou's paintings generally do not show his influence. His most popular works are highly detailed, small-scale scenes of everyday life.

Douai, town in N France, on the Scarpe River, 19mi (30km) S of Lille; became part of France 1713. At its Roman Catholic college, the Old Testament of the Douay Bible was prepared in 1609. Industries: wire, springs, boilers. Pop. 49,187.

Douala (Duala), chief seaport city in Cameroon, W equatorial Africa, on Bight of Biafra; taken from Germans 1914. Industries: brewing, metalworking, textiles. Pop. 250,000.

Douay Bible, first English translation of the Bible authorized by the Roman Catholic Church. Gregory Martin, an Oxford scholar living in exile, was the main translator. The translation is based on the Latin Vulgate. The New Testament was published in Reims in 1582; the Old Testament at Douai in 1609–10. It was revised in 1750 by Richard Challoner.

Double Bass Viol, largest stringed instrument, usually with four strings tuned in fourths (E-A-D-G) and played one octave below the musical notation. Resembling smaller violins but with sloping shoulders, the double bass is held vertically, with the player standing behind, commonly using a bow for classical music, but plucking the strings in jazz where it is primarily a percussion instrument.

Doubleday, Abner (1819–93), US soldier, b. Ballston Spa, N.Y. An army general and a Civil War hero, he is given credit for being the "inventor of baseball," a claim disputed by most historians.

Double Galaxy, stellar system consisting of two adjacent galaxies orbiting around a common center, rather like a binary star. The components are often linked by tenuous bridges of intergalactic matter. Multiple galaxies also exist, comprising several component members. *See also* Binary Star. △104.

Double Jeopardy, the prosecution of one person for the same offense more than once. A provision of the Fifth Amendment to the US Constitution usually bars such an action.

Double Star, star that appears single when viewed with the naked eye but is in reality two stars seen very close together. Double stars are either gravitationally associated binaries or simply the results of optical effects involving two completely separate objects that happen to lie in or near the same line of sight. *See also* Binary Star. △110.

Double Vision. *See* Diplopia.

Dougga, village in Tunisia, 68mi (109km) SW of Tunis; site of ruins of ancient city of Thugga; includes a Punic Mausoleum (2nd century BC), Roman forum, arches, theater, and a temple built 2nd century AD by Marcus Aurelius in honor of Jupiter, Juno, and Minerva; attracts many tourists.

Doughty, Thomas (1793–1856), US painter, b. Philadelphia. He was an early member of the Hudson River School of landscape painters. His works include "In Nature's Wonderland" (1835); *See also* Hudson River School.

Douglas, noted Scottish family traceable from the 12th century. The descendants of Sir William de Douglas were powerful landowners based at Douglasdale, Lanarkshire. As earls of Douglas (1358–1488) and earls of Angus (1389–1761), branches of the family played important roles in Scottish affairs, providing bishops and regents.

Douglas, Aaron (1899–), US painter, b. Topeka, Kans. His murals of the history and culture of US blacks are at Bennett College, Greensboro, N.C., and Fisk University, Nashville, Tenn. He also illustrated many books, including James Weldon Johnson's *God's Trombones* (1927).

Douglas, Archibald, 3rd Earl of Douglas (1328?–1400?), Scottish soldier and diplomat. Also called Douglas the Grim, the Black Douglas, Lord of Galloway. The illegitimate son of Sir James Douglas (the Good), he was constable of Edinburgh (1361), ambassador to France for David II of Scotland (1369) and to renew the Franco-Scots alliance (1371). In 1389–91 his diplomatic mission was to gain the inclusion of Scotland in the peace between England and France.

Douglas, Archibald, 4th Earl of Douglas (1369?–1424), Scottish noble. Captured by Hotspur (1402), he joined the victors against Henry IV of England at Shrewsbury (1403) but was again captured. Ransomed, he fought the English in the north and in France. He was created duke of Touraine (1423) but was killed at Verneuil by the duke of Bedford.

Douglas, Archibald, 5th Earl of Douglas (1391?–1439), Scottish noble. He fought against the English in France (1421), and conducted James I back to Scotland from his English captivity (1424), later becoming lieutenant-general of Scotland (1437–39).

Douglas, Archibald, 6th Earl of Angus (1489?–1557) Scottish noble. He married Margaret Tudor, sister of Henry VIII of England and mother of James V, boy-king of Scotland, (1514). With Henry's aid Angus ruled Scotland (1526–28), but when James asserted himself, Angus was exiled (1529–42). On James' death, Angus returned and helped repel the English invasions (1547–48).

Douglas, Gavin (*c.*1475–1522), Scottish poet, instrumental in the emergence of Scots as a language distinct from English or Gaelic. One of the most proficient medieval poets, Douglas completed a rhymed-couplet version of Vergil's *Aeneid* in Scots (1513), the first translation of a classical poem into an English-based language.

Douglas, (Sir) Howard (1776–1861), British military officer. A career soldier, he served in the Peninsular War (1808–12). He was governor of New Brunswick (1823–31), at a time when the border with Maine was in dispute. He prepared the British case when that boundary dispute was submitted to arbitration, wrote on political and military topics, and ended his career as an educator.

Douglas, (Sir) James (1803–77), Canadian fur trader and political leader, b. British Guiana. Working for the Hudson's Bay Company (1821–58), he established Forts Connolly (1827) and Victoria (1842). He served as governor of Vancouver Island (1851–63) and of British Columbia (1858–63). In his term of office, Douglas argued with the elected legislature but maintained a firm rule of law during the Yukon Gold Rush of 1858. He developed Vancouver as a center of western commerce and has been called "the Father of British Columbia."

Douglas, Lloyd C(assel) (1877–1951), US author, b. Columbia City, Ind. A Lutheran clergyman, he wrote a number of novels, including *Magnificent Obsession* (1929). Several of his novels were historical ones based on the New Testament. Among the latter are *The Robe* (1942) and *The Big Fisherman* (1949).

Douglas, Stephen Arnold (1813–61), US political leader, b. Brandon, Vt. He was secretary of state of Illinois (1840–41) and served in the US House of Representatives (1843–47). Known as the "Little Giant," he was a senator (1847–61). While in Congress, he championed western expansion, popular sovereignty, and sponsored the Kansas-Nebraska Act (1854). He ran for the Senate against Abraham Lincoln (1858), when the Lincoln-Douglas debates took place. In 1860 he again opposed Lincoln, this time as the Democratic nominee for president. *See also* Kansas-Nebraska Act; Lincoln-Douglas Debates.

Douglas, William O(rville) (1898–), US Supreme Court member and conservationist, b. Maine, Minn. He was chairman of the Securities and Exchange Commission (1936–39), when he was appointed to the Supreme Court in 1939. Along with Justice Hugo Black, he wrote numerous dissents in the 1940s and 1950s in support of civil liberties, including his eloquent defense of free speech in *Dennis v. United States* (1951), an anti-Communist case. He also wrote the majority opinion in *Griswold v. Connecticut* (1962), which struck down anti-birth control legislation. He retired in 1975 after serving for the longest period in the court's history.

Douglas Aircraft. △1714.

Douglas Fir, evergreen tree native to NW United States and Canada. It is an important timber pine, and is also grown in the E United States as an ornamental. Height: to 300ft (91m). Family Pinaceae; species *Pseudotsuga taxifolia.*

Douglas-Home, Sir Alec (1903–), British Conservative politician. Entering Parliament (1931), he became Neville Chamberlain's parliamentary private

John Donne

Fyodor Dostoevsky

Stephen A. Douglas

William O. Douglas

secretary (1937–39) and subsequently held ministerial posts. Although a lord (14th Earl of Home, from 1951), he became foreign secretary (1960–63), but had to renounce his peerage to become prime minister (1963–64). He was created a life peer (Baron Home of the Hirsel) in 1974.

Douglass, David (*c.* 1720–86), US actor-manager, b. England. He emigrated to Jamaica (*c.* 1750). Coming to America in 1758, he established theaters in New York; Philadelphia; Newport, R.I.; Perth Amboy, N.J., and Charleston, S.C. In 1766 he built America's first permanent theater, the Southwark, in Philadelphia, where the first professional play by an American, *The Prince of Parthia* by Thomas Godfrey, was produced (1767).

Douglass, Frederick (1817–95), US abolitionist and social reformer, b. Tuckahoe, Md. An escaped slave, he became a popular lecturer for the Massachusetts Anti-Slavery Society and earned enough money to purchase his freedom. He began (1847) publication of an abolitionist paper, *North Star*. He helped recruit black soldiers during the Civil War, and after the war he held several government posts, including minister to Haiti (1889–91).

Doukhobours, or **Dukhobors,** a Russian-Canadian religious sect. The name means literally "spirit-wrestlers." The Doukhobours originated in 18th-century Russia, preaching the inherent goodness of man without the intercession of organized religion. Persecution in Russia drove them to Saskatchewan in 1899, where they lived communally, shunning tobacco, alcohol, and meat. Despite public opposition to their pacifism, the sect flourished as farmers there and in British Columbia. The Sons of Freedom, a militant wing, do not permit their children to attend public school, but many Doukhobours have become absorbed into the Canadian population.

Doum Palm, also doom palm, branched-trunk palm native to upper Egypt and the Sudan. Sacred to ancient Egyptians, it has fan-shaped leaves borne in clusters at the end of each branch. Fruits are edible and have a gingerbread flavor. Height: to 30ft (9.1m); family Palmaceae; species *Hyphaene theobaica*.

Douris (active *c.* 500 BC), Athenian vase painter. His many extant works show great draftsmanship and often dramatic tales. Examples are at the Louvre, Paris, and the Metropolitan Museum of Art, New York City.

Douro (Duero), river in Spain and Portugal; rises in mountainous N central Spain; flows W across Spain to form part of NE border of Portugal (W central border of Spain); continues through Portugal to its mouth on the Atlantic, 2mi (3km) S of Porto; supports hydroelectric power plants along Portuguese stretch of the river. Length: 556mi (895km).

Douroucouli, or night monkey, gray, squirrel-sized monkey found from Nicaragua to NE Argentina. It is a night-active tree dweller and eats fruit and insects. Species *Aotus trivirgatus*. *See also* Monkey.

Dove, cooing, plump-bodied bird found worldwide except in polar and subpolar areas and on some isolated islands. These pigeon-related birds have small heads, short legs, and dense, variously colored plumage. They feed mostly on vegetable matter and build flimsy stick platform nests in a tree or on the ground for the pale white eggs (1–2). Both parents incubate the eggs and feed the young. A special substance, "pigeon's milk," is produced in the parents' crops during incubation and fed to the fledglings. Length: 6–30in (15–76cm). Family Columbidae.

Dover, town in SE England, on Strait of Dover (strait connecting English Channel and North Sea). One of the Cinque Ports (confederation of SE coastal towns 11th–14th centuries organized to protect England before Navy was created) and important seaport. Pop. 34,395.

Dover, capital city of Delaware, on the St Jones River, 45mi (72km) S of Wilmington; shipping and canning center for the surrounding farm and fruit-growing region; site of Dover Air Force Base; contains fine examples of Georgian architecture. Industries: gelatin food products, synthetic polymers, adhesives, latex, resins, chemicals. City laid out 1717; made state capital 1777; inc. 1929. Pop. (1970) 17,488.

Dover, city in SE New Hampshire, on Bellamy, Salmon Falls, and Cocheco rivers; site of 1812 cotton factory, and garrison house from late 1600s. Industries: shoes, printing presses, farm equipment. Settled 1633; inc. 1855. Pop. (1970) 20,850.

Dovzhenko, Aleksandr (1894–1956), Soviet film director and writer. He joined Odessa Studios in 1926 and directed the lyrical *Zvenigord* (1928). His *Arsenal* (1929), a realistic study of revolution, and the tragic drama *Earth* (1930) are considered his greatest works. Pressure by Stalin influenced *Aerograd* (1935) and *Shchors* (1939) and preceded official censure. Dovzhenko's wartime documentaries were released as the work of Julia Solntseva, his wife and collaborator.

Dowland, John (1563–1626), English composer of songs and lute music. △1132.

Downers Grove, city in NE Illinois, 21mi (35km) W of Chicago; site of George Williams College, operated by the YMCA. Industries: plastics, electrical components, scientific instruments. Inc. 1873. Pop. (1970) 32,751.

Downey, city in S California, SE of Los Angeles; suburban community for the Los Angeles and Long Beach areas. Industries: metallurgy, rubber, aerospace, chemicals. Inc. 1957. Pop. (1970) 88,445.

Downpatrick, town in E Northern Ireland, approx. 15mi (24km) SE of Belfast; St Patrick is thought to have founded a church here *c.* 440, and Ireland's three great saints (Patrick, Columba, and Bridget) were long thought to be buried here; other early religious structures remain. Industries: textiles, grains, sheep. Pop. 8,401.

Downs, North and South, two chalk hill ranges in SE England, running parallel and separated by The Weald, a valley approx. 30mi (48km) wide; the North Downs extend SE approx. 100mi (160km) from S outskirts of London, to Kent near the coast; the South Downs extend approx. 65mi (105km) from E Hampshire through W Sussex to E Sussex, near Brighton. The ranges, especially the South, are noted sheep pasturing areas.

Down's Syndrome. *See* Mongolism.

Doyle, (Sir) Arthur Conan (1859–1930), British novelist. He was a physician before writing the detective novel *A Study in Scarlet* (1887), featuring character Sherlock Holmes. Other Sherlock Holmes stories are collected as *Adventures of Sherlock Holmes* (1891) and *The Memoirs of Sherlock Holmes* (1893). Holmes was revived by popular demand in *The Return of Sherlock Holmes* (1904). Among his other works were *The Lost World* (1912), featuring the eccentric scientific explorer Professor Challenger, and *The White Company* (1890). In later life he became interested in spiritualism.

D'Oyly Carte, Richard (1844–1901), English impresario associated with the operas of Sir William S. Gilbert and Sir Arthur Sullivan. He founded the Savoy Theatre in London (1881)—the first to be lighted electrically—for the purpose of producing Gilbert and Sullivan's works. The company is still in existence.

DPT Injection, vaccination against diphtheria, pertussis, and tetanus routinely given all children.

Dracaena, or dragon tree, corn plant, genus of house plant with stalklike trunk and long, arching leaves of green streaked with white, red, or gold. In its native Africa it grows to 60ft (18.3m). There are also shrubby varieties. Care: bright indirect light, soil (equal parts loam, peat moss, sand) kept moist. Propagation is by stem cuttings and sections or air layering. Height: to 8ft (2.5m). Family Agavaceae.

Drachenfels, peak in the Siebenbirge range, W West Germany, on the E bank of Rhine River. According to legend it is site of Siegfried's slaying of the dragon; the Drachenburg, a fortress now in ruins, was built here in 1117 by Archbishop Frederick I of Cologne. Drachenfels is German for "dragon's rock." Height: 1,053ft (321m).

Draco, or the Dragon, northern circumpolar constellation situated north of Cygnus and surrounding Ursa Minor. Brightest star Gamma Draconis (Etamin). △130.

Dracon, one of six men elected by the archons of Athens to pass laws. In 621 BC he drew up laws famous for their severity and for allowing the city to settle intra-family disputes. Death was specified even for minor crimes. Most of his laws, except those for homicide and differentiating premeditated and involuntary crime, were repealed by Solon.

Draft Riots, outbreaks against conscription in the Civil War. Both the Confederacy (in 1862) and the Union (in 1863) passed laws to draft men into their armies. Riots against such laws occurred in the North, the worst in July 1863 in New York City, where over 1,000 were killed or injured.

Drag Car Racing, a form of automobile racing, most popular in the United States. Specially designed cars about 13ft (4m) in length and weighing around 1,300lbs (585kg) are used. The front wheels are narrower than the back wheels. The driver is seated behind the two larger wheels, and the engine—capable of up to 1,300 horsepower—is exposed and placed toward the middle of the vehicle. Competitions, usually at a quarter-mile (0.4km) distance, are in three to eight (two-car) elimination heats. Speeds have reached 270 miles per hour (434.5km per hour), and parachutes are used to slow the vehicle down.

Dragger, any fishing boat equipped to operate a dragnet, that is, an open conical net designed to be drawn along the bottom.

Drago, Luis Mariá (1859–1921), Argentine diplomat. Minister for foreign affairs (1902–03) and a member of the Hague Tribunal, he was the author of the Drago Doctrine put before the Hague Conference in 1907. In reaction to the intervention of Great Britain, Italy, and Germany in Venezuela, the doctrine stated that European powers could not intervene with arms to collect public debts of American states. The conference, however, decided to adopt the less stringent Porter proposition, which called for arbitration of claims but did not rule out force.

Dragon. △832.

Dragon Tree. *See* Dracaena.

Drainage System, collective description of the streams, lakes, and other surface manifestations of water and its removal from a particular region. Another term for the region that contributes water to a stream and its tributary waters is a drainage region. Two adjacent regions are separated by a divide. *See also* Hydrology. △260.

Drake, Sir Francis (1540–96), English sailor and adventurer. A brilliant seaman, he won fame and fortune raiding Spanish shipping and colonies in the Caribbean (1570–73). In the *Golden Hind* Drake sailed west around the world (1577–80), plundering Spanish ports and ships in the Pacific. Queen Elizabeth I knighted him (1581) and he became mayor of Plymouth (1582). Further raids against Spain and her colonies increased his wealth and fame (1585–87). Drake's seamanship and daring contributed greatly to the defeat of the Spanish Armada (1588). His last expedition was less successful and he died of dysentery in the West Indies.

Drama. *See* Theater.

Dramamine, trade name of drug (dimenhydrinate) used chiefly to treat motion sickness and other disorders manifested by vertigo and nausea.

Drapeau, Jean (1916–), mayor of Montreal (1954–). A lawyer and educator, Drapeau organized the Montreal Civic party (1960) and was elected in a series of landslides. He ran on a platform of civic beautification and industrial development and was instrumental in building the Place des Artes, Metro, and Expo '67 and in having the 1976 summer Olympics held in Montreal.

Draper, John William (1811–82), US chemist who pioneered in spectral analysis and in photography. He took the first photos of the moon (1839) and was among the first to use the daguerreotype process.

Draper, Ruth (1884–1956), US actress, b. New York City. She gained international fame for her dramatic monologues, which she authored. A gifted mimic, she was able to create, on a bare stage with few props, the impression of conversing with several invisible companions. She made her acting debut at the Aeolian Hall, London.

Drava River, river in Austria and Yugoslavia; rises in Carnic Alps; flows E through Austria into Yugoslavia; empties into the Danube; forms part of Yugoslav-Hungarian border. Length: approx. 450mi (725km).

Dravidian Languages, family of languages spoken in the southern third of India by nearly 150,000,000 people. The four major Dravidian languages are Telugu, Tamil, Kannada (Kanarese), and Malayalam. Tamil is also spoken in Sri Lanka. Another Dravidian language, Brahui, is spoken in Pakistan. The Dravidian languages were probably spoken throughout most of India until its speakers were driven south by the invading Indo-Europeans about 1000 BC.

Dravidian Literature. The cultural center of Dravidian literature was the ancient city of Madura. During the first three centuries of the Christian era, Tamil literature attained its golden age. *Kural* of the weaver Tiruvalluvar, an allegory about wisdom, wealth and pleasure, was one of the most popular works in Tamil. The *Tiruvāchegam* of Mānikkar Vāchagar was also famous, and its aphorisms were widely quoted. The works of the 12 Ālvārs, or saints, of whom the best known are Tiru-mangai and the female saint, Andāl (*c.* AD 800) helped to make Dravidian literature unique.

Drawbridge, or bascule. △1758.

Drawing, trace left by chalk, crayon, charcoal, pen, or pencil on a surface; specifically in art history, representations or patterns sketched on paper. In ancient Egypt sketches were drawn with a brush on potsherds. During the Middle Ages drawing as an autonomous technique was mainly restricted to the pattern book used in workshops. In the 14th century the first independent drawings on paper appeared, and the techniques then used in modeling by hatching and highlighting with white were described by Cennino. Pisanello (Antonio Pisano) drew from nature for the purpose of study.

Drawing achieved independence as a means of artistic expression with Leonardo da Vinci. He considered his sketches like the rough drafts of poems; his unfinished drawings were used to suggest fresh ideas for major works. Raphael was influenced by him and was considered a great natural draftsman. Michelangelo's drawing technique of close-hatching resembled the chisel. He supposedly destroyed most of his sketches, not wanting the public to view the evidence of his labors.

At this time Giorgio Vasari collected drawings to keep a record of the various styles of the artists. In the Academy of the Carraccis drawing was systematically cultivated. Among north Italians, Jacopo da Pontormo and Tintoretto produced great drawings. In northern Europe, Albrecht Dürer was known for his vast and varied drawings and Pieter Brueghel for his studies of Genre figures and landscapes. Rembrandt, John Ruskin and the Pre-Raphaelites, Vincent van Gogh, Henri Matisse, Paul Klee, and Pablo Picasso were all interested in the art of drawing, as were the sculptors François Rodin and Aristide Maillol.

Dreadnought, H.M.S., one of the first of a new class of British battleships launched in 1906, larger and faster than its predecessors, with turbine engines and a main armament of large-caliber guns. These changes enabled battleships to direct fire over long ranges and reduce the danger of torpedo attack. *See also* Battleship. △1740.

Dreams. *See* Sleep and Dreams.

Dredger, any fishing vessel fitted with dredges (usually attached to outriggers) that rake up mollusks, crustaceans, or other catch from the sea-bottom. Simple dredges used in shallow water are long, pronged sticks with attached collecting bags. Deep-sea dredges are operated by research vessels at depths of up to 3,300ft (1000m).

Dredging, a method of surface mining employing a floating barge with a boom at one or both ends and usually a concentrating plant in the hull. The dredge is sunk into the bottom and bucket-lines continuously excavate materials which are screened and washed to obtain heavy minerals. *See also* Placer Mining. △ 242, 278.

Dred Scott v. Sanford (1857), US Supreme Court case holding that the Missouri Compromise, which freed slaves in certain territories, was unconstitutional and that slaves were not to be considered "citizens" and could not claim rights established and protected under the Constitution. Abraham Lincoln openly criticized this ruling and called for its overturn in his presidential campaign. *See also* Missouri Compromise.

Dreiser, Theodore (Herman Albert) (1871–1945), US author, b. Terre Haute, Ind. After working on various newspapers in the Midwest, he moved (1894) to New York City, where he made his living as a writer and editor on magazines before turning to creative writing fulltime in 1911. He became one of the foremost exponents of naturalism in American writing. His long, brooding but compassionate novels depicted man as the victim of biology, economics, society, and chance and probed the nature of modern urban, industrialized society in America.

His first novel, *Sister Carrie* (1900), was given only limited circulation by its publisher because of its alleged immorality. Dreiser had frequent clashes with censorship in his career. His second novel, *Jennie Gerhardt* (1911), like *Sister Carrie*, explores the life of a "fallen woman." His Cowperwood Trilogy, *The Financier* (1912), *The Titan* (1914), and *The Stoic* (1947), explores the life of a business magnate. *The Genius* (1915) and its sequel, *The Bulwark* (1946), explore the life of an artist. His greatest work, the novel *An American Tragedy* (1925), depicts a poor young man driven to murder by the dream of success.

Drepanaspis. △566.

Dresden, city in SE East Germany, on the Elbe River, 100mi (161km) SE of Berlin; capital of Dresden district. It was almost destroyed in WWII. Dresden china has been famous since the 18th century. Industries: optical instruments, chemicals, clothing. Settled by Germans 13th century. Pop. 501,508.

Dresden, Battle of (Aug. 26–27, 1813), Napoleon's last significant victory. This defeat of Prussian, Russian, and Austrian forces was accomplished in part by the French troops and artillery's exceptional mobility.

Drew, US theatrical family, founded by **John** (1827–62), b. Ireland, and **Louisa Lane Drew** (1820–97), b. England. Married in Albany (1850), the couple went to Philadelphia the following year, where John Drew became co-manager (1853) with William Wheatley, of the Arch Street Theater. John embarked on a tour to England, California, and Australia in 1860. During his absence Louisa accepted the managership of the theater, a position she held for 30 years, although after the first eight years she spent a good deal of her time touring with Joseph Jefferson (chiefly in *The Rivals*) until her retirement in 1892. Three of their children attained success on the stage. **Georgiana** (1856–93), after one season with Augustin Daly's Fifth Avenue company in New York (1875), became a noted supporting actress until her death at 37. She married Maurice Barrymore (1875) and became the mother of Lionel, Ethel, and John Barrymore, all of whom were noted actors. **John Drew II** (1853–1927), also began with the Fifth Avenue company, left to join Edwin Booth's company, where he played Rosencrantz in *Hamlet*. He rejoined Daly's company (1879–92), then joined Charles Frohman's Empire stock company, where he rose to stardom playing polished, sophisticated roles. Sidney Drew, adopted son of John and Louisa, also was an actor.

Drew, Charles R(ichard) (1904–50), US physician, b. Washington, D.C. His research at the Columbia Medical Center in the late 1930s led to the discovery that blood plasma could replace whole blood transfusions. During World War II he supervised the American Red Cross blood-donor project even though he was not allowed to donate blood himself because he was black. His continuing protest led to a change in policy. The Red Cross accepted donations from blacks; however, they kept them in a separate bank for black recipients only.

Drew, Daniel (1797–1879), US financier, b. Carmel, N.Y. In 1844 he moved from the steamboat business to Wall Street to become a trader in railroad stock and a stock manipulator. Known for his unscrupulous business practices, he successfully battled Cornelius Vanderbilt for the Erie Railroad (1866–68) in the "Erie War." In "Black Friday" (1859) and the panic of 1873, his fortune was wiped out. He founded Drew Theological Seminary, Madison, N.J.

Dreyer, Carl Theodor (1889–1968), Danish motion picture director. Internationally famous, he was known for his pictures that featured prolonged close-up character exploration rather than rapid action. His themes often centered around religion and the supernatural, often involving the conflict between good and evil. He made numerous silent films, most notably *The Passion of Joan of Arc* (1928). He also directed films with sound.

Dreyfus Affair. The affair began with the court martial of Alfred Dreyfus, a French army officer and a Jew, for treason in 1894. Convicted under scanty evidence of sending military information to the Germans, Captain Dreyfus was deported for life. His case became the focus of ardent anti-Semitism and nationalism on one side and a growing anti-military revisionist movement by his supporters. Demands to reopen the case by such Dreyfus supporters as Emile Zola increased, especially as evidence incriminating a Major Esterhazy was suppressed and covered up. Finally Colonel Henry, an accomplice, confessed to the forgeries and committed suicide. Dreyfus was given clemency (1899), but it was not until 1906 that he was fully cleared. The affair stifled French anti-Semitism but opened political and social divisions that troubled France for decades. △1300.

Drift, in geology, gradual change in the landmass, related to creep. In oceanography it indicates the

Sir Arthur Conan Doyle

Dracaena

S.T FRAN...
DRAECK

Sir Francis Drake

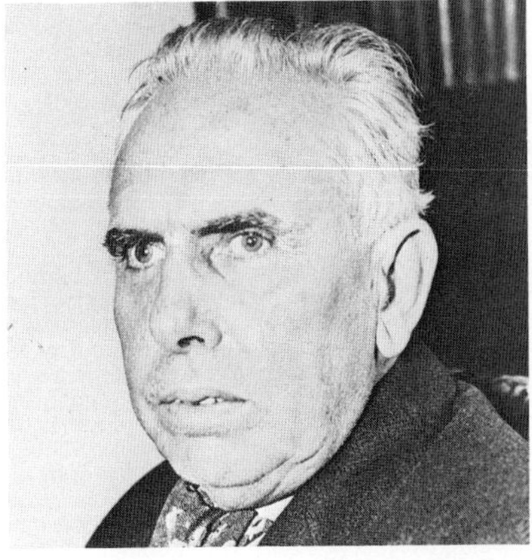

Theodore Dreiser

slow oceanic circulation, and sedimentary drift is a general description of surface debris, which is either river or glacier-carried. It may also indicate an accumulation such as a snowdrift or sanddrift. Continental drift is the movement of continents (tectonics).

Drift Tube. △1484.

Drill, large, gregarious, ground-foraging monkey found in rain forests of C W Africa. It has a doglike muzzle and huge teeth. Length: 32in (82cm). Species *Mandrillus leucophaeus. See also* Baboon; Mandrill.

Drilling Machine, or **Drill Press,** power tool for making holes. A vise holds the workpiece into which a drill held in a rotating spindle is fed. Spindle-speed can be varied. Depending on the final product, machines with either single or multiple spindles are used. Special tapping attachments can produce threaded holes. △1606.

Drilling Ship. △170.

Drina River, river in Yugoslavia, formed at the confluence of the Tara and Piva rivers, 8mi (13km) NE of Maglic Peak; receives Cotina and Lim rivers; supports hydroelectric plant at Zvornick; navigable for 206mi (331km). Length: 285mi (459km).

Drip Irrigation. △314.

Drip Paintings. △1320.

Drive, basic biological need of an organism that motivates it to achieve satisfaction, eg, hunger "drives" an organism to find food. Drive is a fundamental concept in the psychology of motivation and an important principle in learning theory and psychoanalytic theory. △812.

Drive-Reduction Theory, in psychology, assumption that satisfying a basic biological need or drive is necessary for learning to occur. The theory's foremost advocate was Clark Hull during the 1930s and 1940s. Applied primarily to the behavior of animals, it was graudally superseded by more diverse and complex learning theories. *See also* Drive.

Drogheda (Droichead Atha), town in NE Republic of Ireland, in S Louth, 4mi (6km) from mouth of Boyne River. Danes controlled town in 10th century; in 1394, Irish princes surrendered to Richard II. Oliver Cromwell stormed Drogheda in 1649 and killed most of the inhabitants. Battle of Boyne was fought near here in 1690, and town surrendered to William III. Industries: textiles, brewing, engineering, cement, fertilizers, cattle export. Pop. 19,744.

Drone. △498.

Dropsy. *See* Edema.

Drought, a condition that occurs when evaporation and transpiration exceed precipitation for considerable periods. Four kinds are recognized: permanent, typical of arid and semi-arid regions; seasonal, in climates with a well-defined dry and rainy season; unpredictable, an abnormal failure of expected rainfall; and invisible, when even frequent showers do not restore sufficient moisture lost to evaporation.

Drowning, one of the leading causes of accidental death, suffocation caused by water or other liquid in the lungs, depriving the body of needed oxygen. At first, breathing rate and depth increases, heartbeat increases, and neck veins become prominent as the body fights for oxygen. If submersion continues, however, within short time—5 minutes—breathing ceases and death can result unless prompt first aid, including artificial respiration, is given. Drowning usually occurs in deep water but can occur in few inches of water, even in a bathtub.

Drug, a chemical agent used therapeutically to cure a disease or correct a disorder. Drugs may be obtained from plant, animal, or mineral sources, but most today are synthetic. Some drugs are chemotherapeutic agents, fighting infection by acting on disease-causing organisms, either killing or immobilizing them. Included in this group are the antibiotics, the sulfa drugs, and the antimalarial, antituberculosis, antiviral, and antifungal agents. Other drugs are pharmacodynamic, affecting various systems of the body. Digitalis, a common example of such an agent, increases heart muscle contraction. Other drugs may be used in diagnosis, prevention, or other ways. Drugs are commonly administered orally, topically, or by injection. Dosage, effectiveness, speed of action, possible toxicity vary with the particular drug and the individual being treated. *See also* Pharmacology. △730, 746, 770, 1558, 1560.

Drug Abuse and Addiction. △730.

Druids, pre-Christian Celtic priests in ancient Britain, Ireland, and Gaul, suppressed by Rome. The earliest Druidic records date from the 3rd century BC, but the Druids probably existed far earlier. They conducted a strongly ritualistic religion and were also a powerful political influence. △1050.

Drum, primitive, universal, percussion instrument, generally a hollow cylinder or vessel with skins stretched across openings, and struck with hands or beaters. Brought from Asia by the Crusaders, drums appeared in European orchestras with Turkish band instruments about 1750. Symphony orchestras use the snare (side or military) drum, a shallow cylinder with two skin heads, the lower crossed by strings (snares); the tenor (field) drum, a deeper tube with two heads; the larger bass drum, beaten with padded mallets; the timpani (kettledrum), with a single, tunable head; and the tambourine, a shallow, single-headed drum with metal jingles set loosely around the rim. Jazz bands use drums extensively, often for solos. *See also* Timpani. △1500.

Drumfish, or croaker, tropical and temperate marine fish found in brackish or fresh water. It uses its air bladder and attached muscles to make drumming sounds. The American freshwater drum, or Thunder-pumper *(Aplodinotus grunniens)* is found in lakes and streams from Canada to Guatemala. The marine black drum *(Pogonias cromis)* grows to 4ft (121.9cm), weights up to 146lb (65.7kg). Family Sciaenidae.

Drumlin, hill created by a glacier out of either debris or bedrock. Drumlins usually occur in groups. They are ellipsoidal in shape and the long axis is parallel to the movement of the parent glacier. The head end points toward the retreating glacier and is steeper and higher than the tapering tail. *See also* Deposition. △262.

Drupe, or stone fruit, any fruit with a thin skin, fleshy pulp, and hard stone or pit enclosing a single seed. Drupes are usually produced by flowers with petals attached beneath the ovary (superior ovary). Examples are plum, cherry, peach, olive, almond, and coconut. △452.

Drury Lane Theatre, London's oldest theater still in use. It was built in 1663 and known as the Theatre Royal, on Bridges St. Rebuilt in 1674 by Christopher Wren after being completely destroyed by fire, it is the most famous playhouse in London.

Druses, or Druzes, religious sect of the Near East. An offspring of the Ismaili Muslims, it includes elements of belief from other religions. The Druses originated in the reign of Caliph al-Hakim (996–1021). Al-Hakim claimed to be divine, and a cult grew up about him. The Druses are a continuation of this cult. Their name comes from al-Darazi, the first to proclaim the cult publicly. The man who gave form to the Druse faith was Hamza Ibn Ali. Stressing pure monotheism, he maintained that al-Hakim would live in hiding until he came for the Last Judgment but also emphasized the possibilities of direct communication with divinity as a living presence. The Druses are secretive about their beliefs and rituals. They allow no conversion or intermarriage and divide members of the faith itself into two groups, those fully initiated into its tenets (less than 10% of the total) and those not so initiated. Persecuted in Egypt, the Druse community was able to sustain itself only in the mountains of what is now Syria, Lebanon, Jordan, and Israel. They number about 370,000.

Dryads, in Greek mythology, forest nymphs who guarded trees. They carried axes to punish those who harmed the trees they protected.

Dry Cell, zinc casing filled with chemical paste surrounding a carbon rod. The rod is a positive electrode, the zinc casing a negative. Chemical reaction provides the source of electricity that flows whenever the carbon-zinc circuit is closed. A flashlight switch, for instance, closes the circuit and produces current for the light.

Dryden, John (1631–1700), English poet and playwright. He produced his *Heroic Stanzas* on Cromwell's death in 1659, followed by *Astraea Redux,* praising Charles II, in 1660. As Poet Laureate (1668–88) Dryden wrote numerous fine plays, poems, and essays. After embracing Catholicism (1687), he lost his post. His poems include *Annus Mirabilis* (1667), *Absalom and Achitophel* (1681), *Mac Flecknoe* (1682), *The Hind and the Panther* (1687), and *Alexander's Feast* (1697). His most noted plays are *All for Love* (1678) and *Marriage à la mode* (1673).

Dry Dock, any structure in dock areas that can be closed off and pumped free of water. Ships are floated in and left resting on props at the bottom of the dry dock. Repairs or maintenance can proceed on otherwise unapproachable parts of the vessel. △1680.

Dry Farming, production of crops in semiarid areas without irrigation. Wheat, sorghum, and beans are successful dry crops, highly dependent upon soil management for availability of moisture and supply of nutrients. It is made possible by the fallow system, in which land is plowed and tilled but left unseeded for one growing season. △314.

Dryinid Wasp. △502.

Dryopithecus, several species of extinct apelike primates, representative of the dryopithecines, the group believed to be the basal stock of both modern apes and men. Widespread in Europe, Africa, and Asia during late Miocene and Pliocene times. *Dryopithecus* itself is thought to be ancestral to chimpanzees and gorillas. Another drypithecine, *Ramapithecus* (of 12,000,000 years ago) is believed to be at the base of hominid evolution. △646.

Dry Tortugas, group of seven islands in SW Florida, at entrance to Gulf of Mexico; site of Fort Jefferson National Monument (est. 1935), federal bird sanctuary (est. 1908); virtually uninhabited due to nonexistence of fresh water (hence its name). Discovered 1513 by Ponce de León; annexed to United States with Florida 1819. Area: 75sq mi (194sq km).

DSL. *See* Deep Scattering Layer.

Dual Alliance, in European History. △1300.

Dualism, doctrine in philosophy and metaphysics that recognizes two basic and mutually independent principles, such as mind and matter, body and soul, or good and evil. Characterized by precise definition of concepts, dualism contrasts with monism, in which reality has a single ultimate nature. Both Plato and Descartes were dualists, but more modern philosophers, influenced by the discoveries of modern science, have tended more toward monism.

Duality, in Geometry. △1462.

Dubai (Dubayy), independent state, one of seven states forming the federation of United Arab Emirates, in E Arabia, on the Persian Gulf. A dependency of Abu Dhabi until 1833, it became a British protectorate in the 19th century; it was at war with Abu Dhabi from 1945–48; oil was discovered in the early 1960s. Chief industry is oil production. Capital is Dubai. Area: approx. 1,500sq mi (3,888sq km). Pop. 59,092.

Du Barry, Marie Jeanne Bécu, Comtesse (1743–93), French adventuress. She was mistress of, among others, Jean du Barry, who facilitated her rise under the false title of comtesse du Barry, eventually engineering, through a marriage to his brother, her acceptance as last mistress of Louis XV of France. A great patron of the arts and normally politically inactive, she was executed by the Revolutionary tribunal for associations with the British and her aid to the émigrés.

Dubawnt Lake, lake in N central Canada, in Northwest Territories. Dubawnt River flows through it. Located N of tree line, it is ice-bound most of year. One of Canada's largest lakes, it covers 1,600sq mi (4,144sq km).

Dubček, Alexander (1921–), Czechoslovak Communist party secretary, leader of liberal reform movement during the late 1960s. He earned enthusiastic national support with his statement: "Let the struggle of ideas begin." The Soviets, however, viewed the reform program as a threat to their economic domination of the country and on Aug. 20, 1968, Warsaw Pact military forces occupied Czechoslovakia. A purge of party leaders followed and Dubček lost his post. △1344.

Du Bellay, Guillaume, Seigneur de Langey (1491–1543), French diplomat and writer. Important as one of Francis I's most competent diplomats and antagonist of Emperor Charles V, he executed the Treaty of Cambrai. He went to England (1529–30) and helped Henry VIII obtain his divorce; from 1532–36 he worked to unite the German princes in opposition to Emperor Charles V. He was governor of Turin (1537–39) and of Piedmont (1539–42). A friend of prominent writers of the time, including Rabelais, he wrote *Ogdoades* and *Epitome de l'Antiquité des Gaules et de France* (1556).

Dubhe. △38.

Dubinsky, David (1892–), US labor leader, b. Poland. He immigrated to the United States in 1911. He was known for his leadership of the International Ladies Garment Workers Union (ILGWU). He became the secretary-treasurer of the bankrupt union (1929) and president in 1932 (until retirement in 1966). He expelled the Communists, increased membership, and bargained successfully leading to industry stabilization and increased benefits for the workers. He was also vice-president of the AFL (1934–36; 1945–55) and the AFL-CIO (1955–69). He was a founder of the American Labor party (1936), and New York's Liberal party (1944).

Dublin, capital of Republic of Ireland, at mouth of Liffey River on Dublin Bay; seat of County Dublin; commercial center and seaport. A Danish town until 1014 when defeated by Brian Boru, it returned to Danish control but in 1170 Richard Strongbow took Dublin for the English, and it became center of English authority in Ireland. Ravaged by religious wars 1640–90, improvement in city's fortunes occurred in 18th century. Strikes beginning in 1913 finally ended in Easter Rebellion of 1916; site of Christ Church Cathedral (1053), St Patrick's Cathedral (1192), St Audoen's Arch (1215, gate from town's walls), Trinity College (1591), University College (1908), and Abbey Theatre (1904); birthplace of Oscar Wilde (1854), George Bernard Shaw (1856), James Joyce (1882). Jonathan Swift served as dean of St Patrick's for 30 years and is buried there. Industries: brewing, distilling, clothing, footwear, textiles, fertilizers. Pop. 566,-034.

Dubois, (Marie) Eugène (François Thomas) (1858–1940), Dutch anatomist and geneticist. He discovered the remains of Java man in 1890 while excavating caves on the islands of Sumatra and Java. After finding a skull cap, a thighbone, and evidence of apelike features, Dubois published his findings and returned to Europe, where he became professor of geology at the University of Amsterdam in 1895. *See also* Java Man. △650.

Du Bois, W.E.B. (1868–1963), educator, author, and black leader, b. William Edward Burghardt Du Bois in Great Barrington, Mass. He taught economics and history at Atlanta University (1896–1910), and founded the Niagara movement (1909) that later became the National Association for Advancement of Colored People. He was the editor of the group's magazine, *Crisis* (1910–32). He urged liberation of African colonies at several Pan African conferences (1900–27), and was co-chairman, with Kwame Nkrumah, of the fifth Pan African congress (1945). He became a communist (1961) and emigrated to Ghana (1962) where he died. His writings include *The Souls of Black Folk* (1903) and *Color and Democracy* (1945).

Dubrovnik, seaport town in Yugoslavia, in Dalmatia, on the Adriatic Sea; built by Greek refugees, became part of Byzantine Empire 867; site of 14th-century mint, cloisters, Franciscan and Dominican monasteries; sponsors an annual music festival; tourist center. Products: wood, grapes, cheese, olives. Pop. 26,000.

Dubuffet, Jean (1901–), French painter and sculptor. After several years in business, Dubuffet began his art career in 1942. Among his best-known works are assemblages of glass, sand, rope, and other junk arranged into crude shapes, which he called *pâtes.* He also collected the work of psychotics and others who were untrained and called it *art brut* (raw art).

Dubuque, city in NE Iowa, on the Mississippi River opposite Wisconsin-Illinois state line; seat of Dubuque co; named for Julien Dubuque, lead miner (1788); growth was rapid after Black Hawk War (1832); site of University of Dubuque (1852), Clarke College (1843); a rich farming area and trading center. Industries: meat packing, metal and woodworking. Settled 1833 (oldest Iowa city); inc. 1841. Pop. (1970) 62,309.

Duccio di Buoninsegna (*c.*1255–1319), Italian painter. Duccio was the first great painter of the Sienese School. In his works he added naturalness and lyricism to rigid Byzantine figures. His two major surviving works are the *Rucellai Madonna* (commissioned 1285, Uffizi Gallery, Florence) and the Maestà altarpiece done for Siena Cathedral (1308–11), panels of which can be seen at several museums in Europe and the United States.

Duchamp, Marcel (1887–1968), French painter. Influenced by Paul Cézanne, he later turned to the Cubist and Futurist styles, causing a sensation at the 1913 New York Armory Show with his *Nude Descending a Staircase.* After World War I he became a founder of the Dada movement in New York. He was also the inventor of "ready-made" art, treating commonplace objects as works of art; and he constructed many nonfunctional machines. *See also* Dada. △1318.

Duck, worldwide waterfowl valued as game and domesticated for their eggs and meat, rich in iron and B vitamins. They nest in cool areas and migrate to warm areas over winter. All have long necks, short legs, webbed feet, varied color, and dense plumage underlaid by down, and waterproof feathers. Males, or drakes, are usually brighter.

Dabbling ducks feed from the water surface; others dive for food. All strain seeds, aquatic insects, crustaceans, and mollusks from the water with their flat bills. Most engage in complex courtship, lay a large clutch, and are flightless during a post-breeding molt. Ducks are divided into eight tribes: whistling, or tree, duck; sheldrake; dabbling river duck; perching duck; diving pochard; sea duck; stiff-tailed duck; and torrent duck. Length: 1–2ft (30–60cm); weight: to 16lb (7.2kg). Family Anatidae. △534.

Duckpins *See* Bowling.

Duckweed, a family (Lemnaceae) of 4 genera and 40 species of tiny, aquatic, monocotyledonous, rootless flowering plants. The flowers are almost invisible; there are no leaves. The Watermeal *(Walffia arrhiza)* is the smallest of all flowering plants.

Duclos, Jacques (1896–1975), French politician. A member of the central committee of the French Communist party from 1920 and the Communist International from 1936, he was elected deputy from 1926–32, 1936–40, and 1945–58. From 1959, he was senator for Seine. A critic of De Gaulle, he compared De Gaulle's authoritarianism and desire for power with that of Napoleon III in *De Napoléon III à de Gaulle* (1964).

Ductless Gland. *See* Endocrine System.

Dudley, city in W central England, 10mi (16km) NW of Birmingham. Industries: coal mining, wrought iron products, boilers, chains, tiles, bricks. Pop. 185,535.

Duel, prearranged armed contest between two persons with deadly weapons. Believed to have originated during battles among medieval Germanic tribes, the duel became a judicial practice. This declined in the 16th century when duels became associated with knighthood and chivalry. The purpose was usually not to kill, but to draw blood. The 19th century saw a revival of duels especially in Germany among university students. In the United States, Alexander Hamilton was killed in the famous duel with Aaron Burr (1804). Adverse public opinion has made dueling illegal in most countries.

Duesenberg. △1694.

Duff, (Sir) Lyman Poore (1865–1955), Canadian jurist. A successful lawyer in Toronto, he joined the Supreme Courts of British Columbia (1904) and became a Canadian Supreme Court judge (1906). He was chief justice of Canada (1933–44).

Duffy, (Sir) Charles Gavan (1816–1903), Irish-Australian statesman and writer. He helped found and edit the *Nation* (1842), the organ of the Young Ireland movement; served in Parliament (1852–55); and was tried for his political activities. He emigrated to Australia and in Victoria became minister of public works (1857), minister of lands (1858, 1862), prime minister (1871–73), and speaker of the legislative assembly (1877). He returned to Europe (1880) and in 1891 became the first president of the Irish Literary Society. He wrote *Ballad Poetry of Ireland* (1845), *Young Ireland—1840–50* (1880–83), and *Conversations with Thomas Carlyle* (1892).

Dufy, Raoul (1877–1953), French painter. An Impressionist, Dufy converted to the Fauvist style early in his career about 1905 under the influence of Henri Matisse. His style changed again about 1909 while he was with Georges Braque at L'Estaque. He developed a bright, decorative, calligraphic style well suited to his subjects, such as racing and boating scenes. He also did textile designs and book illustrations. *See also* Fauvism.

Dugong, or sea cow, large plant-eating aquatic mammal found in shallow coastal waters of Africa, Asia, and Australia. Gray and hairless, they have no hind legs and their forelegs have been modified into weak flippers. Length: 12ft (3.6m); weight: 600lb (270kg). Species *Dugong dugon.* △540, 548.

Du Guesclin, Bertrand (*c.*1320–80), French soldier and constable. France's leading soldier of the time, he

Drury Lane Theatre

Dublin, Ireland

W.E.B. Du Bois

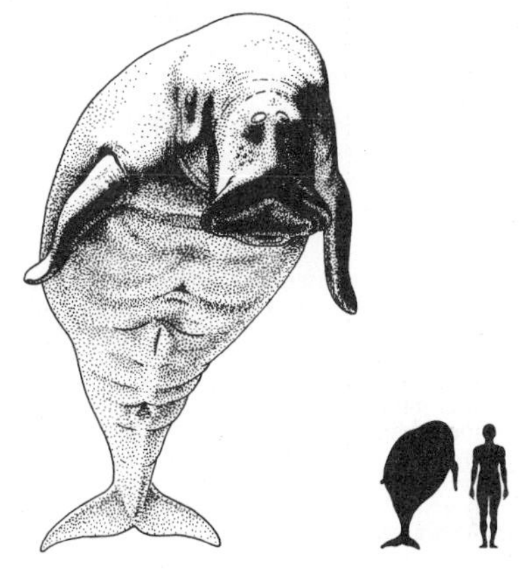

Dugong

reorganized the French army to use sieges and guerrilla tactics to defeat the English. Twice taken prisoner by the English, and twice ransomed, he defeated Peter the Cruel in Spain and put the crown of Castile on Henry of Trastamara (1369). Under Charles V, he freed southern and western France from the English (1370–79).

Duhamel, Georges (1884–1966), French playwright and novelist. A member of the Abbaye group, his works reflect its desire for human unity and fraternity. *Civilisation: 1914–17* (1918) won the Prix Goncourt in 1918. He is best known for the novel series *Cycle de Salavin* (1920–32) and the *Pasquier Chronicles* (1933–45). He was elected to the Académie Française in 1936.

Duiker, or duikerbok, small sub-Saharan African antelope usually found in scrubland. The female is larger than the male and occasionally carries stunted horns: male horns are short and spiky. It is gray to reddish yellow. Height: to 26in (66cm) at shoulder; weight: to 37lb (17kg). Family Bovidae; species *Sylvicapra grimmia*. △598.

Duisburg, city in W West Germany, at confluence of Rhine and Ruhr rivers. Center of German armaments industry, it suffered extensive damage in WWII. Industries: textiles, chemicals, metal products. Founded 9th century. Pop. 460,517.

Duke of York Islands, group of 13 coral islands in SW Pacific, in the Bismarck Archipelago, between NE New Britain Island and SW New Ireland Island; part of Papua New Guinea. Largest island is Duke of York. Area: 23sq mi (60sq km). Pop. 5,870.

Dulcimer, medieval stringed instrument originally Persian, with a flat, triangular sounding board and 10 or more strings struck with hand-held hammers. It is the prototype of the pantaleon and cimbalon. In early America the zither was called a dulcimer.

Dulles, Allen Welsh (1893–1969), US diplomat, b. Watertown, N.Y. He was the first director of the Central Intelligence Agency (1953–61). He is the author of *The Craft of Intelligence* (1963) and *Secret Surrender* (1966). He had served in the diplomatic service from 1916, on the Peace Commission, and in the State Department. He returned to government in World War II in the Office of Strategic Services, which became the Central Intelligence Service.

Dulles, John Foster (1888–1959), US political leader, b. Washington, D.C. He held diplomatic posts under Presidents Woodrow Wilson, Franklin D. Roosevelt, and Harry Truman. He helped to form the United Nations at the San Francisco Conference (1945) and was US delegate there (1945–49). He served as Pres. Dwight D. Eisenhower's secretary of state (1953–59), favoring a policy of "containing" Communism. △1352.

Dulong, Pierre-Louis (1785–1838), French chemist and physicist. After training in medicine he became assistant to Berthollet, finally being appointed professor at the École Polytechnique. He discovered the explosive nitrogen trichloride, and in 1819 he helped formulate Dulong and Petit's law of specific heats, which aided in the determination of atomic weights. His other studies involved the refracting power and the specific heat of gases.

Dulse, any of a group of fairly large red seaweeds (genus *Rhodymenia*, especially *R. palmata*), that are used as a food condiment. Dulses grow chiefly in cold northern seas. *See also* Red Algae.

Duluth, Daniel Greysolon, Sieur (1636–1710), Canadian explorer. A soldier, he emigrated from France to Canada in 1675 and worked as a fur trader. He explored Lake Superior (1678), founded Fort St Joseph (1686), and was commandant of Fort Frontenac (1690–96). He established trading relations with the Sioux and wrote an account of his travels. He gave his name to the city of Duluth, which he founded as a fort in 1679.

Duluth, city in NE Minnesota, at W edge of Lake Superior, 140mi (225km) NE of Minneapolis; seat of St. Louis co. Area visited by Sieur Duluth, a French voyager (1679); the W terminus of the St Lawrence Seaway, it is near rich iron ore ranges and wheat fields; tourist center. Industries: meat packing, publishing, electronics manufacturing. Trading post est 1792. City founded 1856; inc. 1870. Pop. (1970) 100,578.

Dumas, Alexandre (1802–70), French novelist and dramatist. His success began with his numerous romantic historical plays, such as *La Tour de Nesle* (1832). He is best remembered now for the swashbuckling historical novels *The Three Musketeers* (1844) and *The Count of Monte Cristo* (1845). △1238.

Dumas, Alexandre (1824–95), French dramatist and novelist. The illegitimate son *(fils)* of Alexandre Dumas *père*, his first great success was *La Dame aux Camélias* (1852), a realistic view of the demi-monde milieu of Paris. His didactic later plays, such as *Les Idées de Madame Aubray* (1867), provoked changes in French social laws.

Du Maurier, Daphne (1907–), English novelist, granddaughter of George Du Maurier. She also wrote plays, short stories, and a biography of Branwell Brontë. Her popular novels include *The Loving Spirit* (1931), *Jamaica Inn* (1936), *Rebecca* (1938), *Frenchman's Creek* (1941), and *The Glass Blowers* (1963).

Du Maurier, George (1834–96), English novelist, poet, and artist, b. France. His major novels, based on early memories of France, are *Peter Ibbetson* (1891) and *Trilby* (1894). His illustrations, which appeared in *Punch* and *Cornhill Magazine*, recreate the mild social satire of the novels.

Dumbarton Oaks Conference (1944), meeting held near Washington, D.C., by representatives of the United States, Great Britain, USSR, and China. The six-week meeting resulted in a plan for an international coalition to preserve world peace after World War II. The organizational structure, agreed upon at that meeting, became the basis for the United Nation's charter adopted the next year.

Dumbcane. *See* Dieffenbachia.

Dumfries, town in S Scotland, on the Nith River; amalgamated with Maxwelltown 1929; seat of Dumfriesshire. Robert Burns died and was buried here 1796; his house is now a museum. Industries: knitwear, hosiery, chemicals. Pop. 29,384.

Dumont, borough in NE New Jersey; residential suburb of Hackensack. Settled by Dutch 1677; inc. 1894. Pop. (1970) 20,155.

Dumont d'Urville, Jules Sébastien César (1790–1842), French explorer. After making coastal surveys of Australia (1826–29), he sailed to Antarctica (1837–40) where he discovered Joinville Island and Adélie Land. An admiral in the French navy, he led two expeditions around the world in the ships *Astrolabe* (1826–29) and *Zélée* (1837–40). He described his voyages and supplied maps in a 49-volume work.

Dumouriez, Charles François (1739–1823), French general. During the French Revolution he was initially a Jacobin and then became allied with the Girondins in forcing a war on Austria. After a number of victories and defeats, he prepared to overthrow the French government, but his army left him and he deserted to the Austrians (1793). He later lived in exile in England (1804–23).

Dumuzi, ancient Mesopotamian king of the city of Erech who was worshiped as a fertility god after his death. A ritual reenactment of the marriage of Dumuzi and Inanna, the patron deity of Erech, was held each New Year's day. As late as the 6th century BC Jews knew him as Tammuz and recounted the story of his descent into the underworld, identifying this with the annual withering of vegetation.

Dunant, Jean Henri (1828–1910), Swiss philanthropist. A founder of the Red Cross and recipient of the first Nobel Peace prize (1901) with Frédéric Passy, he donated his entire fortune to a campaign to secure relief for wartime wounded. He was responsible for the Geneva Convention of 1864, which set down wartime rules and established the International Red Cross.

Dunbar, Paul Laurence (1872–1906), US author, b. Dayton, Ohio. His poems written in the dialect of black people earned him the title "poet of his race." He demonstrated a facility for a mixture of sadness and humor in *Lyrics of Lowly Life* (1896) about Southern black life before the Civil War. Three of his four novels, however, are about white characters.

Duncan I (died 1040), king of the Scots, son of Cronan, lay abbot of Dunkeld, and grandson of Malcolm II. He was killed in 1040 by Macbeth for reasons unclear to historians. Two of his sons, Malcolm III Canmore and Donald Bane, were later kings of the Scots.

Duncan II (died 1094), king of Scotland, eldest son of Malcolm III. His father gave him as a hostage to William the Conquerer, and Duncan was knighted in Normandy in 1087. When his father died and his uncle Donald Bane was elected king, Duncan led a force of English and Normans and captured the throne. His followers were driven out, however, and he was killed the following year.

Duncan, Isadora (1878–1927), US dancer, b. San Francisco, who achieved fame first in Europe with her dances based on Greek classical art. She was one of the greatest influences on modern dance chiefly because of her innovative and pioneering expressions of feeling. She was noted for her Greek costumes with many scarves draped about her neck. She died in a tragic accident when a scarf she was wearing caught in a wheel of a car in which she was riding and strangled her. Her autobiography is *My Life* (1926–27). △1368.

Dundalk, city in NE Maryland, on the Patapsco River. City was in path of British march on Washington in War of 1812. Industries: steel; radio, electronic, and automotive parts; yachts. Inc. 1946. Pop. (1970) 85,377.

Dundee, city in E Scotland, on N shore of the Firth of Tay; important port and university town. Industries: jute, linen, heavy engineering, lumber, shipbuilding. Pop. 181,842.

Dune, hill or ridge of windblown particles, most often sand. Dunes are found wherever wind flow is obstructed and sandy particles that it carried are deposited. Dunes occur in a variety of shapes depending on the direction of the wind, whether or not it is constant, and the surrounding landforms, which affect direction and velocity. △266.

Dunedin, city and port in New Zealand, on SE coast of South Island at head of Otago Harbor; site of first university in New Zealand, University of Otago (1869). Industries: iron, brass, clothing, shoes. Founded 1848 as a Free Church of Scotland settlement. Pop. 82,700.

Dunes, Battle of the (June 4, 1658), fought on the dunes of Dunkerque (Dunkirk) between French troops under the Vicomte de Turenne aided by English Cromwellian troops and Spanish troops led by Don John of Austria allied with English royalists under the Duke of York. The Spanish army was defeated according to the plan of French Prime Minister Mazarin, who wanted to force Spain into the "grand marriage" alliance of Louis XIV and the Spanish Infanta.

Dung Beetle, or tumblebug, small to medium-sized scarab beetle that feeds on dung. Some species form balls of dung as food for their larvae. The balls may be tumbled, or rolled, some distance before being buried in the ground. Family Scarabaeidae. *See also* Scarab Beetle. △492, 498

Dunham, Katherine (1914–), US dancer and choreographer, b. Chicago. In 1945 she founded the Katherine Dunham Dance Company and the Katherine Dunham School of Cultural Arts in New York City. Her choreography is based on ethnic ritual, folk stories, and the everyday life of blacks in Africa, the Caribbean, and the United States.

Dunkirk (Dunkerque), city in N France, on Strait of Dover, 44mi (71km) NW of Lille. Evacuation of Allied troops from here May 29–June 2, 1940, was caused by German breakthrough to the English Channel. It is a leading French port and one of the major iron and steel areas of W Europe. Founded in 7th century; came under French rule 1662. Pop. 74,362.

Dunkirk Evacuation (1940), evacuation of 338,000 British, French, and other Allied troops from Dunkirk, France, to England after the initial German breakthrough in World War II. These forces, trapped against the English Channel, abandoned their equipment, and were transported in 220 naval and over 660 other vessels, many of them civilian (May 29–June 2). △1338.

Dunmore, John Murray, Earl of, (1732–1809), British colonial governor. He was governor of New York (1770) and Virginia (1771–75). He led the Indian campaign (1774) known as Lord Dunmore's War in the Ohio region. Expelled as Virginia governor at the start of the Revolution, he served as governor of the Bahamas (1787–96).

Dunne, Finley Peter (1867–1936), US journalist and humorist, b. Chicago. He was the author of a series of books in which Mr. Dooley, an Irish saloonkeeper, comments upon current events and the social scene. Dunne first created Dooley for the Chicago *Post*. His books include *Mr. Dooley in Peace and War* (1898) and *Mr. Dooley on Making a Will* (1919).

Duns Scotus, John (1265–1308). Scottish theologian and scholastic philosopher. A member of the Franciscan order, he was ordained in 1291 and subsequently lectured at Cambridge, Oxford, and Paris. His principal works were his commentaries on the works of Peter Lombard. His philosophy came to be called Scotism. *See also* Lombard, Peter; Scholasticism. △858.

Dunstan, Saint (910–88). English monk who became counsellor to King Edmund of Wessex, and made important religious reforms as abbot of Glastonbury. He was driven into exile in Flanders under Edwig, but when Edgar became king he was made archbishop of Canterbury (959–88). He is important for his reforms of monasticism, rebuilding churches, and furthering education.

Dunster, Henry (1617–59). American educator and first president of Harvard, b. England. Almost immediately after emigrating to New England (1640), he was appointed president of the newly founded school. He tried to pattern Harvard after English secondary education, but his Baptist leanings caused his resignation (1654). He went on to be pastor of Scituate, Mass. (1654–59).

Duodenum, first section of the small intestine shaped like a horseshoe. The pyloric sphincter separates it from the stomach. Alkaline bile and pancreatic juices enter the duodenum and mix with intestinal secretions to aid in digestion. △694.

Duplessis, Maurice Le Noblet (1890–1959), premier of Quebec (1936–39; 1944–59). A lawyer, he was elected to Parliament in 1927 and became Conservative party leader 1933–35. He founded the Union Nationale party which was nationalist, antilabor and pro-farmer. He ran Quebec autocratically and almost single-handedly.

Du Pont de Nemours, Eleuthère Irénée (1771–1834), US industrialist, b. France. He was the founder of the huge, diversified chemical company, and family empire. With his father **Pierre Samuel Du Pont de Nemours** (1739–1817), he came to the United States (1799). They started a business backed by French government capital, producing high-quality gunpowder near Wilmington, Del. (1804). Du Pont prospered during the War of 1812 and made a fortune. He was director of the Second Bank of the United States in Philadelphia. The company, E. I. Du Pont de Nemours and Co., continued under his sons and grandsons.

Duprat, Antoine (1463–1535), French cardinal and statesman. As chancellor of France appointed by Francis I, he arranged the Concordat of Bologna (1516) with Pope Leo X, establishing the power of the French king over the French church. A patron of the arts, he later became archbishop of Sens (1525), cardinal (1527), and papal legate (1530).

Duquesne, Fort, French fort built 1754 during French and Indian War, on site of present day Pittsburgh; because of its strategic location, it was scene of several attempts by British and colonials of Virginia to capture it; in 1758 French burned the fort and retreated; Virginia and Pennsylvania soldiers built the first Fort Pitt nearby.

Dura (Europus), ancient city of Syria, on the Euphrates River. Founded *c.* 300 BC, it was abandoned *c.* AD 257; site has yielded many valuable archaeological remains of Mesopotamia from Hellenistic to Roman times. Present village of Salihiye is here.

Durand, Asher Brown (1796–1886), US engraver and painter, b. Jefferson Village, N.J. Famous for his engravings of John Trumbull's "The Signing of the Declaration of Independence," he was also prominent in the Hudson River School of landscape painters. *See also* Hudson River School.

Durango (Victoria de Durango), state in NW Mexico, in the fertile valley of the Nazas River; highly developed agriculturally; vast plains in middle region provide excellent pastures and mountainous N regions are rich in minerals. Durango, the capital city, is major commercial center for the state; noted for 18th-century cathedral and government palace. Industries: lumber, mining, grain, cotton, sugar cane, tobacco, tanneries, foundries, textiles. Area: (state) 46,196sq mi (119,648sq km). Founded (city) 1556; (state) 1824. Pop. (city) 192,934; (state) 919,381.

Durante, Jimmy (1893–), US comedian, b. James Francis Durante in New York City. The "Schnozzola" worked in vaudeville, theater, films, records, radio, and television. A member of the nightclub team Clayton, Jackson, & Durante (1923–30), he appeared in the plays *Get-Rich-Quick Wallingford* (1932) and *Jumbo* (1935), and in the film version of *Jumbo* (1962).

Durban, formerly Port Natal; chief port of South Africa, on N shore of Natal Bay, 300mi (483km) SE of Johannesburg; scene of 1908–09 national convention, initiating the 1910 Union of South Africa; site of University of Durban (1960), University of Natal (1949), and Durban Museum; busiest port of South Africa, and important industrial center. Exports: sugar, oranges, pineapples, wool, coal, maize. Industries: petroleum, textiles, automobiles, paint, sugar refining. Settled 1824. Pop. 495,458.

Dürer, Albrecht (1471–1528), German engraver, designer of woodcuts, and painter. Son of a goldsmith, Dürer at the age of 15 was apprenticed to Nuremberg painter and book illustrator Michael Wolgemuth. After traveling throughout Germany and to Italy in the early 1490s, he returned to live permanently in Nuremberg.

In his workshop he produced paintings, engravings, and woodcuts, forms in which he had acquired immense technical skill. He was influenced by the engravings of Martin Schongauer and the art of Mantegna. He spent much of 1505 and 1506 in Venice, seeing the High Renaissance there firsthand. By this time he had become well established and received several commissions for altarpieces. For the Emperor Maximilian he designed a huge woodcut, *Triumphal Arch.* A convert to Protestantism, he had deep and often troubled feelings about religion that are frequently apparent in his art. His studies of the ideal proportions of the human body and of perspective are also evident in his works. In 1526 he presented Nuremberg with *Four Apostles* that reflects his religious and theoretical thinking. His other well-known works include *Self-Portrait* (1493) and *Knight, Death, and Devil* (1513). △1144.

D'Urfé, Honoré (1567–1625), French novelist. Of noble birth, he was best known for his long prose romance *Astrée* (1607–1619), a pastoral novel inspired by earlier Spanish and Italian pastorals, in which he delicately and lucidly idealized love. △1172.

D'Urfey, Thomas (1653–1723), English Restoration dramatist and songwriter. He published three collections of his songs (1683–85), which were put to music by eminent composers. His early plays tended to be farcical and his later ones more sentimental. They are considered forerunners of the ballad opera.

Durga, in the Hindu pantheon, the wife of Siva. Depicted as a 10-armed goddess, she is both destructive and beneficent but is worshiped today as a warrior against evil. Her festival, which occurs in September or October is the occasion for family reunions. △1036.

Durgapur, city in E central India, on the Damodar River. Dams on river furnish hydroelectric power to area. Industries: iron, steel, coal. Pop. 206,638.

Durham, John George Lambton, 1st Earl of (1792–1840), English Whig statesman. A radical, he promoted reform in Britain, and served briefly as governor-general of Canada (1838). He produced a report (1839) recommending internal self-government for Canada, which became the basis of British policy there. △1332.

Durham, city in N central North Carolina in Piedmont area; seat of Durham co. After the Civil War James B. Duke and other tobacco industrialists developed the area; Duke University was founded here 1838. In 1959 the 5,000-acre (2,025-hectare) Research Triangle Park opened. Industries: textiles, hosiery, cigarettes. Settled 1750; inc. 1869. Pop. (1970) 95,438.

Durham Cathedral. △1082.

Durham Report (1839), report on Canada, written after the Rebellion of 1837 by John George Lambton, Earl of Durham. Durham was sent to Canada (1838) as governor-general following much discontent there. Holding that position only briefly, he wrote the influential *Report on the Affairs of British North America* (1839) which promulgated union of Lower and Upper Canada, internal self-government, and the extension of the British cabinet system to Canada. Anti-French in sentiment, the report stressed the need for British immigration and spurred the reform movement that led to the Act of Union of 1841.

Durkheim, Emile (1858–1917), French sociologist, one of the founders of modern sociology. Educated in Germany and France, he taught at the University of Bordeaux and at the Sorbonne in Paris. Influenced by the positivism of Comte, Durkheim is credited with

John Foster Dulles

Alexandre Dumas (fils)

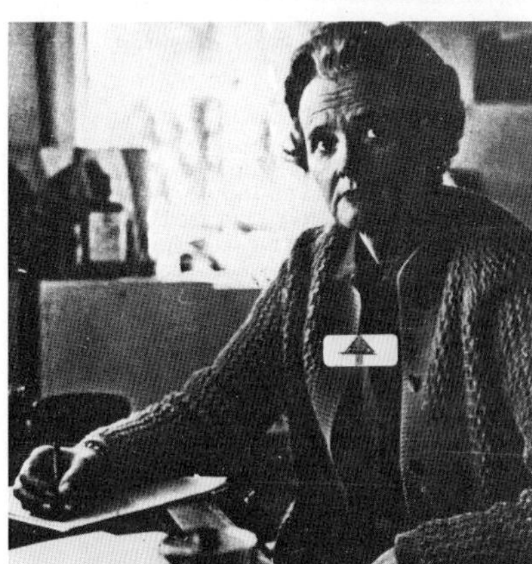

Daphne Du Maurier

Isadora Duncan

laying the framework for the analysis of social systems. His main works are *The Division of Labor in Society* (1893), *The Rules of the Sociological Method* (1894), *Suicide* (1897), and *The Elementary Forms of Religious Life* (1912). △888.

Duroc. △376.

Durocher, Leo (Ernest) (1906–), US baseball player and manager, b. W. Springfield, Mass. One of the game's most colorful and controversial figures, he was a player for 17 years and a manager for 25 years with several National League teams. Durocher was suspended for a year (1947) as the result of a public dispute with Larry MacPhail, then co-owner of the New York Yankees.

Durrell, Lawrence (George) (1912–), British author, b. India. After attending a number of schools in India and England and working at odd jobs, he began to travel widely. The novel *The Black Book*, expressing an atmosphere of moral decadence, was published in 1938. From 1941 to 1958 he held various British official and diplomatic posts. The short story collections *Esprit de Corps* (1958) and *Stiff Upper Lip* (1959) spoof diplomatic life and describe places where he lived. His masterpiece is *The Alexandria Quartet*, a novel published in four parts—*Justine* (1957), *Balthazar* (1958), *Mountolive* (1958), and *Clea* (1960). Other novels include *Tunc* (1968), *Numquam* (1970), *Monsieur* (1975). He also wrote several volumes of poetry.

Durrës (Durazzo), city in W Albania, on coast of Adriatic Sea; capital of Durrës prov. Albania's major port. Exports: grain, olive oil, tobacco. Founded 625 BC as a joint colony of Corcyra and Corinth; population is largely Muslim. Pop. 53,800.

Dursley Peterson Bicycle. △1688.

DuSable Jean (1745?–1818), US pioneer, b. Haiti. He built a trading post between the Chicago and Des Plaines rivers in 1775 around which the city of Chicago developed. He also managed posts at Michigan City and Port Huron.

Dusan, or **Dushan, Stefan** (1308–55), ruler of medieval Serbia. He promulgated a new code of laws (1349–54) and extended his dominions into Macedonia, Albania, and Greece, proclaiming himself emperor of the Serbs and Greeks in 1346. He died suddenly while planning an attack on Constantinople.

Dušanbe. *See* Dushanbe.

Duse, Eleanora (1859–1924), Italian actress. She made her debut at the age of four in *Les Miserables;* at 14 she played Juliet. Known for her beautiful use of her hands and her scorn for the use of make-up and corsets, she played all over the world in such plays as *Théodora, La Locandiera,* and *La Dame aux Camélias.* She introduced several plays of Gabriele d'Annunzio, and also gave notable performances in works of Ibsen *(Ghosts, Lady from the Sea)* and James Huneker *(Iconoclasts).* Her health forced her retirement before World War I, but she later gave special matinees in London (1923) and eight performances at the Metropolitan Opera House in New York City. She died in Pittsburgh while on tour.

Dushanbe (Dušanbe), formerly Stalinabad; city and capital of Tadzhik SSR, USSR, at the foot of the Gissar Mts; industrial, trade and transport center; site of Tadzhik University and Academy of Sciences (1951). Industries: cotton milling, leather goods, food processing. Founded 1925. Pop. 400,000.

Dussek, Jan Ladislav (1760–1812), Bohemian pianist and composer. △1196.

Düsseldorf, city in W West Germany, at confluence of Rhine and Düssel rivers; a cultural center. In 14th-16th centuries it was capital and residence of dukes of Berg; became part of Prussia in 1815; occupied by France 1921–25. Industries: chemicals, textiles, iron, steel. Founded in 13th century. Pop. 650,377.

Dust, Galactic, dust found in the outer arms of spiral galaxies. It seems to be made up of minute particles, perhaps of graphite and ice. *See also* Interstellar Matter; Nebula; Star.

Dust Bowl, name applied to an area of about 100,000,000 acres (40,500,000 hectares) of the Great Plains in the United States, where there has been much wind erosion damage. Due to drought, overplanting, and mismanagement, much of the topsoil was blown away in the 1930s. Subsequent government soil conservation programs, such as crop rotation, terracing and strip planting, reduced damage.

Dust Devil, a brief, small-scale whirlwind containing sand or dust and ranging from 10 to 100ft (3 to 30m) in diameter.

Dust Storm, or duster, a violent storm laden with fine dust picked up by high winds sweeping a drought or arid region. *See also* Sandstorm. △216.

Dusty Miller, plants with stems and leaves covered with fine, whitish hairs. *Senecio cineraria* is a 2–2½ft (61–76cm) perennial with flat-topped clusters of cream or yellow flowers, grown mainly for its woolly-white foliage. Family Compositae.

Dutch, the official language of the Netherlands, spoken by virtually all of the country's 13 million inhabitants, and also in the Netherlands Antilles and in Surinam (the former Dutch Guiana). Dutch is a Germanic language and thus belongs to the Indo-European family. △866.

Dutch East India Company (1602–1798), trading company chartered by the Dutch government. It was given extensive political and military authority to protect and control trade in Asia. It was one of the world's first joint-stock companies. One of the most successful of the many European trading companies, at one time it had a monopoly on all Dutch trade from Africa east to South America. Driving out British and Portuguese traders, it monopolized the rich Spice Islands trade. It established Batavia (Djakarta), Indonesia (1619) as its heaquarters and founded a colony at the Cape of Good Hope in southern Africa (1652). The company was nationalized in 1798. △1158, 1200, 1260.

Dutch Elm Disease, a serious fungus disease that has caused the destruction of many thousands of American elms. The disease-causing fungus *(Ceratocystis ulmi)* plugs water-conducting tissues, causing wilting of leaves and usually the eventual death of the tree. The fungus is transmitted from tree to tree by bark beetles and underground through the root systems of adjacent trees. The disease can be controlled by strict sanitation procedures, including prompt removal of seriously infected trees, spraying to kill the bark beetles, and fungicide treatment.

Dutchman's-breeches, perennial wildflower native from Nova Scotia to Kansas. It has clusters of yellow-tipped white flowers with widely separated spurs (breeches). Height: to 10in (25cm). Family Fumariacea; species *Dicentra cucullaria.*

Dutchman's-Pipe, woody, perennial vine found in woods of NE North America. The leaves are heart-shaped, and purple and white flowers are are U-shaped with flaring mouths. Length: 30ft(9m). Family Aristolochiaceae; species *Aristolochia durior.*

Dutch Wars, three 17th-century Anglo-Dutch naval conflicts arising from commercial rivalry. The first war (1652–54) stemmed from efforts to exclude the Dutch from England's trade. England, although more successful in the fighting, was exhausted, and the peace treaty was inconclusive. The second war (1664–67) followed England's seizure of New Amsterdam (New York). The Dutch inflicted heavy losses and England had to modify her trade laws, but by the Treaty of Breda (1667) both sides kept their colonial conquests. The third war (1672–78) arose from French ambitions in the Low Countries. France invaded the Netherlands with English support but the Dutch were victorious at sea and stemmed the French advance on land. England made peace (1674) and the war ended with French territorial gains in the Spanish Netherlands and Dutch trade gains.

Dutch West India Company (1621–1791), trading company chartered by the Dutch government to control trade on Atlantic coasts of America and Africa. The company's original activities involved slave trading and harassing the Spanish fleet as much as normal trade. Although unable to wrest Brazil from the Portuguese (it ceased its efforts in 1661), the company did found settlements in the Caribbean and establish New Netherland (now New York and New Jersey), which was lost to England in the 1660s. Afterward the company confined itself mainly to the African slave trade.

Duvalier, François (1907–71), president of Haiti (1957–71), whose prominence as a public health specialist was a springboard to politics. Elected, he declared himself president-for-life and used voodoo worship and the feared Tontons Macoutes (an extralegal vigilante group) to cement the dictatorship. He died of a stroke and was succeeded by his son.

Duve, Christian René de (1917–), Belgian cell biologist who was awarded part of the 1974 Nobel Prize in physiology or medicine for his contributions to a detailed description of the structure and function of the cell and its parts. Analysis of biochemical activity in a cell led him to discover the lysosome, an organelle that acts as the "stomach of the cell."

Duveen, Joseph, Baron Duveen of Millbank (1869–1939), English art dealer, influential in determining art tastes during his lifetime, especially in the United States, where his business was eventually headquartered in New York. Duveen began art dealing at an early age, particularly in works of the old masters, and helped many millionaires build their collections. For building a wing at the National Gallery, London, and a wing for the Elgin marbles at the British Museum, he was knighted (1919). Made a baronet (1926), he was raised to the peerage (1933).

Dvina, Northern, river in N Russian SFSR, USSR, formed at confluence of Sukhona and Yug rivers; flows N, turns NE into Dvina Bay of White Sea near Archangel'sk where delta is formed, connects with Volga-Baltic Waterway by Sukhona River and Northern Dvina canal. Length: 465mi (750km).

Dvina (Daugava), Western, river in Ukrainian SSR, USSR; rises in Valdai Hills, flows S and W through Belorussia and Latvia republics to delta at Gulf of Riga of Baltic Sea. Riga is main port. River is navigable in lower course; two dams are at Latvia; supports hydroelectric stations; connects by canal with Berezina and Dnepr rivers. Length: 635mi (1,022km).

Dvorak, Antonin (1841–1904), Czech Romantic composer. Dvorak adapted the spirit of Czech nationalism and folk music to a classically oriented style influenced by Brahms and Wagner. He composed in every form, but is especially known for his orchestral works, which include nine symphonies, two sets of *Slavonic Dances,* and a number of overtures and symphonic poems. His *Cello Concerto* (1895) is regarded as one of the supreme achievements in that form. He lived in the United States (1892–94), a stay that inspired his most popular work, the *Symphony No. 9* ("From the New World") (1893) and his "American" *String Quartet No. 6. See also* Romanticism in Music. △1246.

Dwarf Galago. △554.

Dwarfism, condition in which a person is much below normal size and lacks the ability for normal growth. Dwarfism is associated with several inherited disorders including mongolism, Turner's syndrome, and achondroplasia, a condition in which there is normal mentality, normal trunk and short arms and legs; and can also be acquired as a result of chronic kidney disease, cystic fibrosis, and potentially treatable pituitary gland malfunction in which too little growth hormone is secreted. △726.

Dwarf Pea. *See* Chick-pea.

Dwarf Star, low-magnitude star appearing in the main sequence of the Hertzsprung-Russell diagram. Dwarfs belong to the spectral classes G, K, and M, and are characterized by small diameter and very high density in comparison to giant stars of the same spectral types. They are also about 10 magnitudes fainter. △100.

Dwight, Timothy (1752–1817), US author and educator, b. Northampton, Mass. A minister at Greenfield Hill, Conn., he wrote *Greenfield Hill* (1794), a pastoral poem imitative of Oliver Goldsmith and Thomas Gray. He was a member of the Connecticut Wits and contributed to their writings. From 1795 until his death he was president of Yale University. *See also* Connecticut Wits.

Dye, substance used to impart color to textiles, hair, wood, etc. Dyes are classified according to the way they are applied, which in turn depends on the fiber to be colored. Direct dyes can be applied directly to the fabric; they are acidic or basic compounds that bind to fibers such as wool and silk. Indirect dyes, used for cotton, need a mordant (a compound such as aluminum hydroxide or tannic acid), which is first applied to the cloth and forms a colored precipitate with the dyestuff. Vat dyes are insoluble substances that are first reduced to a colorless soluble form that is reoxidized in the fiber. Ingrain dyes are made on the fibers by chemical reaction. △1560.

Dylan, Bob (1941–), US singer and composer, b. Robert Zimmerman in Duluth, Minn. He taught himself to play the guitar, piano, autoharp, and harmonica and became very popular on concert tours and in recordings from 1960. One of the originators of the folk-rock style of popular music, he has composed many songs, eg "Blowin' in the Wind" and "The Times They Are A-Changing." △1366.

Dynamics, in economics, change or changes occurring in economic conditions over a period of time. Dynamics is often used in equilibrium analysis in order to see the movement of the economic situation over time. Dynamics is also important in simulation models where changes affect the relationship through the movement over time. △936.

Dynamite, a solid, blasting explosive that contains nitroglycerin incorporated in an absorbant base, such as charcoal. Shock-resistant, but easily detonated by heat or percussion, it is used in mining, quarrying, and engineering. Invented in the 19th century by Alfred Nobel. △1810.

Dynamo. △1540.

Dynamometer, an electrical rotating device used to measure the output torque of rotating machinery; acting as an electric brake, generator, or motor, depending on the device under test. Direct readings are obtainable from an attached scale.

Dyne, the unit of force in the metric centimeter-gram-second (cgs) system of units. One dyne is the force that gives a mass of one gram an acceleration of one centimeter per second per second. One newton equals 100,000 dynes.

Dynel, trademark for an acrylic fiber (of the polyvinyl chloride, or PVL, type) made from vinyl chloride and acrylonitrile. Characterized by great resistance to burning, it is used extensively for yarns and fabrics.

Dysentery, an infectious disease characterized by frequent loose stools, intestinal bleeding, and in severe cases, intestinal ulceration. Spread by fecal-contaminated food and water, it often occurs in epidemic form in crowded areas with poor sanitation and in particular in tropical areas. One type, caused by bacteria (usually *Shigella*), is usually treated with antibiotics. The other type, caused by ameba *(Endamoeba histolytica),* is harder to treat; the ameba sometimes occurs in cyst form and produces chronic dysentery, characterized by intermittent diarrhea and other often mild symptoms.

Dysfunction, distinction in the highly refined sociological theory of structural functionalism that means any function, or consequence of a social system, that lessens the system's adaptation to its setting, thereby reducing its ability to survive. *See also* Structural Functionalism. △1360.

Dyslexia, a term variously defined but generally used to mean marked difficulty in learning to read. Often used for persons who habitually reverse the letters of words (reading "was" for "saw"), letters themselves ("b" for "d"), or perceive letters upside down. The causes—brain damage, other neurological problems, environmental factors—are disputed, as are modes of treatment. △768.

Dysmenorrhea, painful menstruation, distinct from normal functional menstrual discomfort or premenstrual tension. It can occur shortly after menarche (primary) or later in life (secondary), and is characterized by cramplike pain in the lower abdomen, sometimes radiating to the back and thighs.

Dysprosium, metallic element (symbol Dy) of the Lanthide group, first identified in 1886 by Lecoq de Boisbaudran. Chief ores are monazite (phosphate) and bastnasite (fluorocarbonate). The element has few commercial uses. Properties: at. no. 66; at. wt. 162.5; sp. gr. 8.56 (25°C); melt. pt. 2565°F (1407°C); boil. pt. 4235°F (2335°C); most common isotope Dy^{164} (28.18%). *See also* Lanthanide Elements.

Dzerzhinsk (Dzerzinsk), formerly Chernorech, then Rastyapino; city in Russian SFSR, USSR, on Oka River; industrial center named (1929) for Soviet secret service founder Felix Dzerzhinsky. Industries: textiles, chemicals, engineering works. Pop. 228,000.

Dzhambul (Dzambul), formerly Aulie Ata; city in SE Kazakh SSR, USSR, on Talas River; capital of Dzhambul oblast. Founded in 7th century, city was ruled by Arabs and became capital of Karakhan State 10th–12th centuries; annexed to Russia 1864. Industries: sugar refining, fruit canning, chemicals, metal and leather products. Pop. 205,000.

Dzungaria (Zhuangaerpendi), arid region in NW China, between Tien Shan and Altai mts; ruled by Dzungars, a Mongol tribe, in the 17th century; overtaken by Chinese in 1850s; 35% of the population is nomadic; oil discovered in 1955 brought railway transportation and further development of the area. Pop. 1,500,000.

Eleanora Duse

Düsseldorf, West Germany

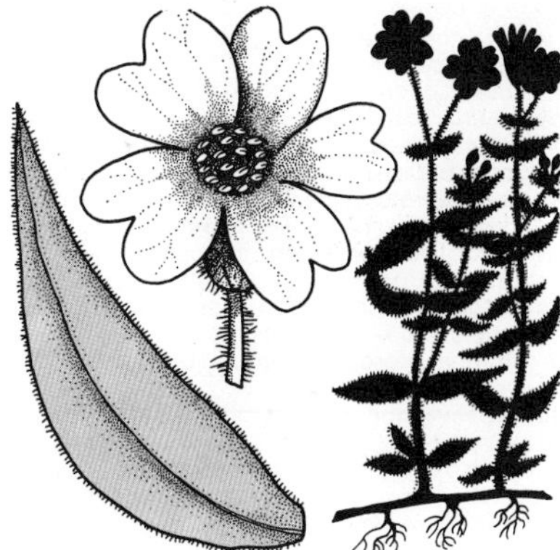
Dusty miller

Ea, or **Enki,** in Mesopotamian mythology, the god of freshwater, son of the sea goddess Nammu. He gave kings their wisdom and artisans their skill. At the creation, Ea was responsible for the details of organization of the world, providing water, seed, and animals and appointing subordinate deities to watch over them. △838.

Eadmer or **Edmer of Canterbury** (*c.* 1055–1124), English monk in Canterbury. An Anglo-Saxon by birth, Eadmer is known as friend and confidant of Anselm of Canterbury, and as a writer on historical and religious subjects. His most important writings were a history of Britain from the time of the Norman Conquest to 1120 *(Historia novorum),* biographies of Anselm and other English saints, and a tract on the conception of the Virgin Mary.

Eadred. *See* Edred.

Eads, James Buchanan (1820–87), US engineer and inventor, b. Lawrenceburg, Ind. A self-taught man, his formal education ended when he was 13. Inventing and using the diving bell to salvage sunken steamboats and their cargoes, he formed the first ship salvaging business on the Mississippi (1842). Early in the Civil War (1861), he built a fleet of armor-clad gunboats in 65 days to patrol the Mississippi. He succeeded, after other engineers failed, in building a bridge over the Mississippi at St Louis (1867–74). The largest bridge at that time, it was named for him. He designed a jetty system, forcing the Mississippi to dredge its own channel into the Gulf of Mexico (1875–79).

Eagels, Jeanne (1894–1929), US actress, b. Kansas City, Mo. She began her acting career in a touring tent show, then played small roles on the stage and in films until her most successful role as Sadie Thompson in *Rain* (1922). She also appeared on stage in *Her Card board Lover* (1927), and in several films, including *Woman and Sin* (1927), *Jealousy* and *The Letter* (both 1929), before her early death.

Eagle, widespread strong, flesh-eating, diurnal birds of prey. Sea and fishing eagles, including the bald and stellar eagles, are large birds, frequenting seacoasts where they dive for fish and feed on other small animals and carrion. Old World serpent eagles, including harriers, are stocky reptile-eating birds. The large harpy eagles inhabit tropical forests and the booted eagles with feathered legs, including true eagles *(Aq-*

Antonin Dvorak

uila), are open country predators. They have long hooked bills, broad wings, and powerful toes with long curved claws, and are usually brownish, black, or gray with light or white markings. They nest high on seacoasts or island mountains, building massive grass-and-leaf-lined stick nests, called aeries. These nests are often used for many years. Light brown eggs (1–2) are laid. Several species are endangered as a result of hunting, pesticide poisoning, and a low reproduction rate. Length: 16–40in (41–102cm). Family Falconidae. *See also* Falcon.

Eagleton, Thomas Francis (1929–), US Senator b. St. Louis, Mo. Picked by Senator George McGovern as the Democratic vice-presidential candidate in 1972, he was forced to withdraw after news accounts revealed he had been treated for depression.

Eakins, Thomas (1844–1916), US painter, b. Philadelphia. After studying art and anatomy in Philadelphia, Eakins went to Paris (1866–70) where he developed his precise, realistic style. On his return to Philadelphia he taught at the Pennsylvania Academy of Fine Arts (1870–86). He had to resign from this position because of his insistence on using live nude models.

Most famous for his portraits, he insisted on portraying reality, so that many of them are not flattering, although they are often penetrating. He was also a photographer and sculptor. Among his many famous works are "The Gross Clinic" (1875), which created a scandal because of its realism; "The Chess Players" (1876), both at the Metropolitan Museum of Art, New York City; and "The Biglon Brothers" (1873), National Gallery, Washington, D.C. △1252.

Eames, Charles (1907–), US architect and industrial designer, b. St.Louis. Educated at Washington University School of Architecture, Eames is best known for designing chairs made of molded plywood and plastic. He has also designed toys and houses and created films. Much of his work has been done in collaboration with his wife, Ray Kaiser.

Ear, specialized sense organ of hearing. It converts sound waves to nerve impulses that are carried to the brain and also maintains a sense of orientation and equilibrium. In most mammals the ear consists of the outer ear, middle ear, and inner ear. The visible outer ear contains the ear canal that carries sound waves to the eardrum, a flexible, thin membrane separating the outer and middle ears. The middle ear is an air-filled passage connected to the pharynx by the Eustachian tube, and to the inner ear by three tiny bones, the hammer (maleus), anvil (incus), and stirrup (stapes). These bones conduct sound vibrations to the oval window, a thin membrane leading to the inner ear. The inner ear, or labyrinth, contains the spiral-shaped cochlea and organ of Corti, the essential hearing organ. Sound vibrates a membrane lining the cochlea, causing thousands of feathery hairs in the organ of Corti to bend. These vibrations merge into the acoustic nerve that transmits nerve impulses to the brain. The inner ear also contains three semicircular canals and the utricle and saccule sacs that function to maintain orientation and equilibrium. △676.

Earache, pain in the ear that can be caused by wax accumulation, a foreign body in the ear, referred pain from teeth, mouth, or jaw, but is most often produced by infection of the middle ear or of the auditory canal. Treatment depends on the cause.

Earhart, Amelia (1898–1937), US aviator, b. Atchison, Kan. The first woman to cross the Atlantic as a passenger in 1928, she became the first woman pilot to make solo flights across the Atlantic (1932) and from Honolulu to Oakland, Calif. (1935). In an attempt to fly around the world, she disappeared between New Guinea and Howland Island in the Pacific (1937).

Early, Jubal (1816–94), Confederate Civil War general, b. Franklin County, Va. A colonel at the First Battle of Bull Run, he was promoted to general and served in every campaign of Lee's Army of Northern Virginia. In 1864, he nearly captured Washington, D.C.

Early Bird Satellite, world's first commercial communications satellite. Launched April 6, 1965, to link North America and Europe. *See also* Communications Satellite Corporation.

Early Technology. △1582.

Earp, Wyatt (Berry Stapp) (1848–1929), US law enforcement officer, b. Monmouth, Ill. Raised in Iowa, he was a sheriff, stagecoach driver, surveyor, and railroad construction worker. In 1879 he went to the silver mining camp at Tombstone, Ariz., as the deputy sheriff. In 1881 he and his two brothers took part in the famous gunfight at the O.K. Corral. He also served as US marshal in Dodge City and Wichita, Kansas.

Earth, third planet from the sun, with one natural satellite, the moon. The Earth has outer radiation belts, an oxygen-rich atmosphere, and a lithosphere, or solid crust, beneath which is the mantle and the outer and inner core. Mean distance from the sun, 92,900,000mi (149,569,000km); mass, 5.976×10^{27}g; volume, 1.083×10^{27}cu cm; equatorial radius, 3,963,221mi (6,378,188km); polar radius, 3,949,921mi (6,380,785km); rotation period, 23hr 56min; period of sidereal revolution, 1.00004 years; composition in order of abundance, oxygen, silicon, aluminum, iron, magnesium, calcium, sodium and potassium, titanium, phosphorous, hydrogen. *See also* Solar System. △66, 162–65.

Earth Balls △428.

Earthenware, vessels and other utensils or ornaments made of clay, fired at relatively low temperatures, resulting in porous, opaque, non-ringing pieces.

Earthlight. *See* Earthshine.

Earthquake, a number of rapid, consecutive, elastic waves in Earth. A major quake is usually preceded by a few foreshocks (small quakes) and followed by many minor aftershocks. The source of a quake may be shallow or up to 430mi (692km) deep. The shallow quakes are thought to be the rapid release of slowly accumulated strain along fault lines extending over a wide region. The rupture of a fault and the friction between faulting rock surfaces produces the elastic waves. The origin of the slowly accumulated strain is not known. *See also* Seismology. △174.

Earthquake Prediction, the part of seismology dealing with the projection of possible quakes and their magnitude and location using past history of a region and measurement of the buildup of the strains in it and the time of the buildup. *See also* Seismology. △174.

Earthshine, or earthlight, phenomenon observed during the crescent phase of the Moon, whereby the darkened portion of the lunar disk is illuminated by an ashen light reflected onto it by the Earth. △182.

Earthside, Lunar, face of the moon that is permanently turned toward the earth. Gravitational effects of the earth on the moon slowed down and ultimately captured the moon's axial rotation. The lunar earthside exhibits numerous and varied surface features, including several large maria. *See also* Farside, Lunar; Mare. △52, 58.

Earthworm, terrestrial and semi-terrestrial annelids having cylindrical, segmented bodies covered with tiny bristles. Most are a uniform red, pink, or brown. They are mainly subterraenean in moist soil. Their burrowing loosens and aerates soil, making it fertile. Most are hermaphroditic. Worms are eaten by many animals. Tropical species are largest. Length: 2in–11ft (5cm–33m). The four families include several hundred species. Class Oligochaeta. *See also* Annelida. △474.

Ear Wax, or Cerumen, a brown, waxy substance secreted by glands in the outer ear. It serves to protect skin from dessication, and presumably entrance of insects. △676, 686.

Earwig, slender, brownish-black insect found in dark, damp areas. Some have a pair of forceps on the end of the abdomen. Two suborders, found in Malaya and South Africa, are ectoparasites of bats and rodents. Order Dermaptera. △492, 496.

East Anglia, eastern England, centered on counties of Norfolk and Suffolk, formerly an Anglo-Saxon kingdom, founded *c.* 600 AD It was usually dependent on other kingdoms until the Danish invasion (9th century). After 917 East Anglia became an earldom of Anglo-Saxon England.

East Bengal, region on Bay of Bengal; included in East Pakistan (1947); became part of Bangladesh (1971). The population is mainly Muslim. Area: 44,514sq mi (115,291sq km).

Eastbourne, city in S England, on English Channel at foot of S Downs, 3mi (5km) SW of Beachy Head; vacation resort. Pop. 70,495.

East Chicago, city in NW Indiana, on Lake Michigan, 18mi (29km) SE of Chicago. Industries: oil refining, steel, chemicals. Inc. 1889. Pop. (1970) 46,982.

East China Sea, N branch of the China Sea, bordered by Korea and Japan (N), E China (W), Taiwan (S), and the Ryukyu Islands (E). Area: approx. 482,300sq mi (1,249,157sq km). Depth (max.): approx. 15,000ft (4,575m).

East Cleveland, city in NE Ohio; site of General Electric lamp factory and electrical research laboratories. Inc. 1911. Pop. (1970) 34,600.

East Detroit, city in SE Michigan, 10mi (16km) NE of Detroit. Industries: structural steel, tools. Inc. 1925 as Halfway Village; renamed and inc. as city 1929. Pop. (1970) 45,920.

Easter, the central Christian feast, celebrating the resurrection of Christ on the third day after his crucifixion. In the West it is celebrated between March 22–April 25, on whichever Sunday follows the first full moon on or after March 21 (the vernal equinox).

Easter Island (Pascua, Isla de), island in S Pacific Ocean, about 2,000mi (3,220km) off W coast of Chile, to which it was annexed 1888. Inhabited mostly by Polynesian farmers, the island is famous for its hieroglyphs and formidable statues carved in stone standing up to 40ft (12m) tall. Chile has named the island an historic monument. Discovered Easter Day, 1722, by Dutch seaman Jakob Roggeven. Area: 46sq mi (119sq km). Pop. 1,135.

Easterlies, any broad currents or persistent patterns of winds from the east, such as the tropical easterlies or trade winds and the equatorial and polar easterlies. The trade winds occur in the northern and southern margins of the tropics during the summer and cover most of the tropics during winter. *See also* Westerlies.

Easter Lily, bulbous house plant native to Formosa with large, white, trumpet-shaped, fragrant flowers and narrow, arching leaves. Care: bright indirect light, moist soil. Propagation is by offsets or seeds. Height: to 3ft (92cm). Family Liliaceae; species *Lilium longiflorum.*

Eastern Orthodox Church, a community of over 125,000,000 Christians, located primarily in the Soviet Union, Eastern Europe, and the Middle East. They share the same form of worship and episcopal organization, but each Orthodox church has its own national head. Iconography is prominent, as well as elaborate ritual. The clergy may be married prior to ordination. There is no central governing body, and they reject the jurisdiction of the Roman pope, the principal point dividing the Eastern Orthodox from the Roman Catholics. When Constantine, the emperor who first made Christianity lawful throughout the Roman Empire, moved his capital to Byzantium (later Constantinople, now Istanbul) in 330, a culture separate from Rome developed. Conflicts grew between the Eastern patriarchs and the bishop in Rome. The schism that developed in the 11th century was made irreparable when Crusaders invaded Constantinople (1204). Attempts at reconciliation in 1274 and 1439 failed. In 1962 several Orthodox observers attended the second Council of the Vatican. The following year the Eastern Orthodox churches agreed to open a dialogue with Rome. △1176–78.

Eastern Rite, teachings of those Eastern churches that have maintained a link with the Roman Catholic Church. The Eastern rite differs in liturgical practices from the Latin rite. These churches, divided into national groups, are under the jurisdiction of the Holy See in Rome. *See also* Latin Rite.

Easter Rebellion, Irish uprising against the British. △1314.

East Goths. *See* Ostrogoths.

East Hartford, town in E central Connecticut, opposite Hartford on Connecticut River. A colonial manufacturing center, it was site of first US powder mill (1775). Industries: airplane engines, steel fabrication, paper, bottling works. Settled 1639; inc. 1783. Pop. (1970) 57,583.

East Haven, residential town in S Connecticut; E suburb of New Haven; includes Lake Saltonstall, site of state's first iron mill. Inc. 1785. Pop. (1970) 25,-120.

East India Company (1600–1874), British trading company and political organization in India. Founded for the East Indian spice trade, it was forced by Dutch competition to concentrate on India, where it gradually won a monopoly and political supremacy. The British government assumed its political direction (1773, 1784). When the company lost its monopoly

(1813–33), it served as an administrative agency until abolished. △1202.

East India Company, Dutch. △1260.

East India Company, French, a government-controlled business founded in 1664 under Louis XIV for trade with the Eastern world. Growing, but never financially sound, the company became involved in Indian political intrigue and conflicts with the British and, defeated by the British under Robert Clive, dissolved by the time of the French Revolution. △1200.

East Jersey, one of two proprietorships formed in colony of New Jersey after English seized New Netherland. Defined by the Quintipartite Deed of 1676 as the northeastern portion of New Jersey, East Jersey was ruled by Sir George Carteret until 1680 when it was purchased by a group of small proprietors. East Jersey enjoyed freedom of conscience and had a heterogeneous society. East and West Jersey were reunited (1702) into one royal province. *See also* West Jersey.

East Lansing, city in S central Michigan, on Red Cedar River, 5mi (8km) E of Lansing; site of Michigan State University (1855), first US state agricultural college. Surrounding farm area produces sugar beets, grain, livestock. Settled 1849; inc. 1907. Pop. (1970) 47,540.

East Lothian, co in SE Scotland, E of Edinburgh, between the Firth of Forth and Lammermuir Hills; co seat is Haddington; chief river is Tyne. Area's S uplands are pasture and woodlands; coastal plains are farmed; site of castles of Dirleton, Tantallon, and Hailes. Oliver Cromwell defeated Scots at Dunbar 1650. Area: 267sq mi (692sq km). Pop. 55,891.

Eastman, George (1854–1932), US photographic inventor and manufacturer, b. Waterville, N.Y. He introduced machine-coated plates (1879), paper roll film (1884), celluloid roll film and the Kodak camera (1888), and daylight-loading film (1891), thereby creating the basic materials for still and motion picture photography. He founded the Eastman Kodak Co. in 1892. △1784.

Eastman, Max (1883–1969), US author, b. Canandaigua, N.Y. A leading leftist, he was an editor of *The Masses* (1913–17) and *The Liberator* (1918–22). In addition to numerous political works, he wrote several works on the psychology of literature, including *The Enjoyment of Poetry* (1913) and *The Enjoyment of Laughter* (1936). His autobiography *Love and Revolution* appeared in 1965.

East Meadow, residential city in SE New York, on W Long Island, 23mi (37km) E of New York city. Pop. (1970) 46,352.

Easton, city in E Pennsylvania, at confluence of Delaware and Lehigh rivers; seat of Northampton co; site of First United Church of Christ (1776), and Lafayette College (1826). Industries: paper products, electronic equipment, steel. Founded 1751 by Thomas Penn; inc. 1886. Pop. (1970) 30,256.

East Orange, city in NE New Jersey, adjacent to Newark, it is also suburb of New York City; site of Upsala College (1893). Industries: hydrants, waterworks supplies, insurance. Settled 1678, city was part of Orange until 1863; chartered as city 1899. Pop. (1970) 75,471.

East Paterson, borough in NE corner of New Jersey, 2mi (3km) SE of Paterson. Industries: television receiving communications equipment. Inc. 1916. Pop. (1970) 20,511.

East Point, city in NW central Georgia, 7mi (11km) SSW of Atlanta in Fulton co. Main industry is textiles. Inc. 1887. Pop. (1970) 39,315.

East Providence, city in E Rhode Island, on Providence and Seekonk rivers. Originally part of Massachusetts, it was annexed to Rhode Island 1862; site of Bradley Hospital, one of world's first children's neuropsychiatric facilities. Industries: metal products, chemicals, jewelry, oil storage. Inc. 1958. Pop. (1970) 48,207.

East Prussia, former province of Prussia, in NE Germany. Bordered by Poland and Lithuania (S and E), it extended to Memel and Baltic Sea (N and NE); lowlying, heavily-wooded area; controlled by Teutonic Knights and Poland 13th-17th centuries; in 1701 Frederik III of Brandenburg was crowned King of Prussia, uniting E Prussia with Prussia. Since 1945 East Prussia has been divided between Soviet Union (N) and Poland (S). Industries: lumbering, shipbuilding, fishing, stock raising. Area: 14,283sq mi (36,993sq km). Pop. 2,500,000.

East River, strait in New York City, SE New York; connects Long Island Sound (N) with New York Bay (S). Manhattan Island forms W shore and borough of Queens and the Bronx on Long Island forms the E shore. Length: 16mi (26km). Width: 600–4,000ft (183–1,220m).

East Saint Louis, city in SW Illinois, on the Mississippi River, opposite St Louis, Missouri, to which it is connected by four bridges; site of Cahokia Courthouse (1837), oldest courthouse W of Allegheny Mts. Industries: brick, tile, machinery, gasoline. Founded 1795 as Illinoistown; inc. 1865. Pop. (1970) 69,996.

Eaton, John Henry (1790–1856), lawyer, politician and diplomat, b. Halifax, N.C. After representing Tennessee in the US Senate (1818–29), he was appointed secretary of war by Pres. Jackson, whose daughter had been his first wife. He resigned from the cabinet in 1831 after his second marriage to Peggy O'Neill, a woman considered socially unacceptable by the other cabinet wives. He was governor of Florida (1834–36) and minister to Spain (1836–40).

Eaton, Peggy (*c.*1796–1879), US social figure, b. Washington, D.C. Born Margaret O'Neill, she was the wife of John Henry Eaton, secretary of war under Pres. Andrew Jackson. Because her father was a tavern owner, she was not accepted in Washington society and was snubbed especially by the wife of Vice President John C. Calhoun. President Jackson's attempt to help her split the cabinet.

Eaton Affair (1831), social boycott against the wife of John Eaton, secretary of war in President Andrew Jackson's cabinet. Eaton's wife Peggy was defended by Jackson and Secretary of State Martin Van Buren and snubbed by Vice-President John C. Calhoun and others in Washington society. The situation led to the resignations of Eaton and Van Buren and, finally to Jackson's appointment of a new, stronger, and more harmonious cabinet.

Eau Claire, city in W central Wisconsin, at confluence of Eau Claire and Chippewa rivers; seat of Eau Claire co; developed around sawmills built on Eau Claire River (1800s). Industries: paper, dairying, tires, defense products. Inc. 1872. Pop. (1970) 44,619.

Eban, Abba (Solomon) (1915–), Israeli diplomat, b. Aubrey Solomon Eban in South Africa. Raised in England, he served in the British army in the Middle East during World War II. Working for the Jewish Agency for Palestine after the war, he helped maintain relations with the British in the period before the founding (1948) of the state of Israel. In 1947 he began his diplomatic career as a liaison officer of the US Special Committee on Palestine. He was Israel's first permanent UN representative (1949–59) and during that time also served as ambassador to the United States. After being elected a Mapai (Labor party) member of the Israeli parliament in 1959, he served as minister of education and culture (1960–63), deputy prime minister (1963–65), and foreign minister (1966–74).

Ebbinghaus, Hermann (1850–1909), German psychologist whose work *On Memory* (1885) founded the scientific study of memory. Using himself as a subject for his research, he described in detail the process of learning, remembering, and forgetting of verbal materials. He also founded the first German psychology journal in 1890.

Ebionites, literally, "poor men," a sect of ascetic Jewish Christians who flourished from the 2nd to 4th centuries east of the Jordan River. Outside the mainstream of Christianity, they held property in common, believed poverty basic to Christianity, stressed Christ's humanity rather than divinity, emphasized Mosaic law, and used only the Gospel of St. Matthew as scripture. There were two divisions: the Pharisaic Ebionites, who stressed Mosaic law, and the Essenic Ebionites, who tended more toward Gnosticism.

Eboli, town in S Italy, near ruins of ancient Eburum; medieval section is on hillside overlooking modern section on the Piána del Sele; site of Romanesque basilica and castle of the Colonna family; agricultural center: Industries: olive oil, dairy products. Pop. 27,-168.

Ebony, hard, fine-grained, dark heartwood of various Asian and African trees of the genus *Diospyros* in the ebony family (Ebenaceae). The major commercial source of ebony is the macassar ebony *(D. ebenum)* of S India and Malaysia. Ebony is prized for woodcarving and cabinet work.

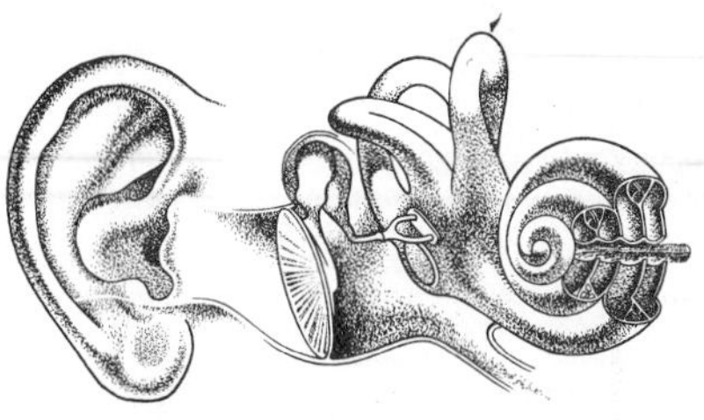

Ear

Amelia Earhart

Easter Island carving

George Eastman

Eboué, Félix Adolphe Sylvestre (1884–1944), French colonial administrator, served in various African positions before his appointment as governor of Chad (1938–40) and governor general of French Equatorial Africa (1940–44), in which capacity he aided De Gaulle's Free French. Always respectful of African traditions, Eboué was the first black man to be buried as a French hero.

Ebro, river in NE Spain; rises in Cantabrian Mts; flows SE into the Mediterranean Sea, below Tortosa; scene of Spanish Civil War battle (1938) fought along banks. Supplies energy for 50% of Spain's hydroelectricity. Length: approx. 575mi (926km).

Eccentricity (symbol *e*), number defining the form of a conic section: *e* less than 1 is an ellipse; $e = 0$ is a circle; $e = 1$ is a parabola; *e* greater than 1 is a hyperbola. For an ellipse it is the ratio of the distance between the foci to the length of the major axis. It is one of the elements determining the orbit of a celestial body.

Ecclesiastes, biblical book of aphorisms written by one called "the Preacher," thought to be Solomon. The author dwells on vanity in all things and expresses skepticism about the state of the world: "One generation passeth away, and another generation cometh: but the earth abideth forever." He exhorts his readers to "Fear God, and keep his commandments: for that is the whole duty of man."

Ecclesiasticus, book of the Apocrypha. The work of Jesus ben Sira, a teacher in Jerusalem, *c.* 190 BC, it follows the tradition of Jewish wisdom literature.

Ecgberht. *See* Egbert.

Echeverría Álvarez, Luis (1922–), president of Mexico (1970–76), sponsored a new federal agrarian reform law. A moderate on domestic issues, he articulated a bold foreign policy in support of Fidel Castro's Cuba and Salvador Allende's Chile.

Echidna, or spiny anteater, any of two species of egg-laying, burrowing, nocturnal mammals that compose the family Tachyglossidae (order Monotremata) found in New Guinea, Australia, and Tasmania. It is stocky, to 30in (76cm) long, with spines as well as hair on the upper parts, and has a small mouth and an extensible tongue. The female lays a single egg and transfers it to a pouch. △544.

Echinoderm, phylum of spiny-skinned marine invertebrate animals related to same evolutionary stock that produced Chordates. They are radially symmetrical with five axes and have calcareous skeletal plates in their skin. Their hollow body cavity (coelom) includes a water vascular system and tube feet. Reproduction is sexual, and a bilaterally symmetrical larva resembling that of Chordates is produced; regeneration also occurs. The 5700 species include sea urchins, sea cucumbers, and starfish. △504.

Echo, in Greek mythology, an Oread or mountain nymph. She was deprived of speech except to repeat the last words of others as a punishment for helping Zeus to deceive his wife Hera. Echo faded to just a voice, when Narcissus spurned her love.

Echo, sound reflected from a surface so that it returns to the source and is heard after a silent interval of 0.1 seconds or more. This minimum time for differentiating the echo from the original sound implies a path difference of about 32 yards (30m). High notes provide a better echo than low notes. Echoes are useful in echo-sounding devices but are objectionable in auditoriums, where they are eliminated by using absorbent material on the walls and avoiding curved surfaces that can focus echoes like a mirror. *See also* Anechoic Chamber; Underwater Sound. △1498.

Echolocation, system of orientation in some animals, such as whales and bats. They emit high frequency sound waves and determine position by the returning echoes. △512, 546.

Echo Sounder, device that sends sound pulses through water to the sea bottom where they are reflected back to a ship's hull or platform and detected. Continuous recordings provide a profile of the bottom by translating the time needed for the echo to return to the detector. △236.

ECHO Viruses, a group of viruses found in the feces of apparently healthy individuals, resulting in the inappropriate name Enteric Cytopathogenic Human Orphan. There are 28 types of these RNA-containing viruses. They are known to cause diseases such as aseptic meningitis, skin rashes, enteritis, and diarrhea. ECHO 28 is the common cold virus.

Eck, Johann Maier von (1486–1543), German theologian, defender of the papacy against German reformers. He publicly debated Martin Luther in 1519, then obtained the 1520 papal bull condemning him. He drafted the 1530 refutation of Lutherism as defined by the Augsburg Confession.

Eclampsia, a rare disorder occurring in the last 10 weeks of pregnancy, characterized by high blood pressure, swelling, excessive weight gain, convulsions, and albumin in the urine. The cause is unknown. Treatment includes various drugs to control the symptoms. Delivery may be hastened or caesarean section performed.

Eclecticism, in philosophy, the combination of elements from different systems of thought without resolving conflicts among the systems. The method was favored by Roman philosophers, including Cicero; some Renaissance thinkers; and 19th century philosophers led by Victor Cousin, who coined the term.

Eclipse, temporary concealment of one celestial body by another. The term usually signifies the obscuration of the Sun (solar eclipse) or Moon (lunar eclipse), as viewed from the Earth. Both lunar and solar eclipses may be either total or partial but solar eclipses may also be annular. An annular, or ring, eclipse occurs when the new Moon is too far away from the Earth to mask the Sun's disk completely. *See also* Eclipse, Lunar; Eclipse, Solar; Eclipsing Variable Star. △52, 98.

Eclipse, Lunar, temporary partial or total obscuration of the Moon occurring when the full Moon passes into the shadow of the Earth. During a lunar eclipse, which occupies several hours from start to finish, the Moon is sometimes seen to have a reddish color as a result of receiving sunlight scattered by the Earth's atmosphere. △52.

Eclipse, Solar, temporary obscuration of the Sun caused when the new Moon passes directly between the Sun and the Earth, casting its swiftly moving shadow over part of the daylight side of our planet (the zone of totality). During a total solar eclipse the Moon's dark body exactly blots out the Sun's disk, affording a fleeting glimpse of the corona. Occasionally, however, annular, or ring, eclipses occur. *See also* Eclipse. △98.

Eclipsing Variable, or binary, regular variable star in which the light variations are due to the fact that the star is a binary having a bright component associated with a darker companion. The two stars regularly pass in front of each other and are at maximum brightness only when they are seen shining together. The prototype of the best-known class of eclipsing variables is Beta Persei (Algol). △110.

Ecliptic, great circle on the celestial sphere, inclined at 23½° to the celestial equator, that is the yearly path of the Sun as seen from Earth or the Earth's orbit as seen from the Sun. The ecliptic plane thus passes through the centers of both Earth and Sun. The planets are always located near the ecliptic.

Eclogues, or "Selections," sometimes called *Bucolics* or "Pastoral Poems," ten poems written by 1st-century BC poet Vergil, modeled on the *Idylls* of Greek poet Theocritus. As in Vergil's other works, there is a great sympathy for suffering.

Ecological System. *See* Ecosystem.

Ecology, or environmental biology, bionomics, biological study of relationships between living things and their environments. It is also involved with interactions of organism groups to each other and their surroundings. △578–80.

Econometrics, quantitative branch of economics, involves the application of statistics to economic problems. Ordinarily, econometrics involves using computer programs to seek solutions to real-world economic problems.

Economic Opportunity Act (1964), created the Office of Economic Opportunity (OEO) to eliminate the causes of poverty through training programs such as the Job Corps, and by direct assistance to people living in substandard conditions. VISTA was the agency created by the Economic Opportunity Act and was responsible for recruiting and training volunteers to help staff the anti-poverty programs.

Economics, study of how individuals in a particular society choose to allocate scarce resources in order to produce goods that are demanded by that society. It involves the study of the methods used in producing the goods in order to obtain maximum efficiency in the use of the scarce resources. Economics also involves the process of deciding how goods are distributed to various individuals and groups within a society as well as dealing with the study of economic growth within the society. The society must somehow provide for future wants as well as for present needs and must allocate goods in such a way that future needs will be met. △936.

Economic Systems, elements in a society that answer these questions: What should be produced? How is it to be produced? and For whom is it to be produced? Economists distinguish between systems that are characterized by private ownership of producer goods and market control over the system and those that are characterized by some authoritarian structure where economic decisions are made by planning agencies. The USA is often cited as an example of the free enterprise, market (capitalistic) system, while the USSR is often called a command (communistic) system, where producer goods are owned by the government, or by some agency of the government. *See also* Capitalism; Communism; Socialism. △902.

Economies of Scale, decreasing unit costs as plants expand operations, usually resulting from the increased efficiency associated with producing more output. The expanded firm may now be able to take advantage of technological conditions that were impossible at the smaller scale of operation or it may be able to hire more specialized workers. Economies of scale do not always occur as the firm expands. The firm may reach a size beyond which expansion is no longer desirable.

Ecosphere. △66.

Ecosystem, or ecological system, community of living things and its environment. It is self-sustaining only if it recycles elements, has a constant energy source, and can incorporate energy into organic compounds and pass it from organism to organism. △580.

ECT. *See* Electroconvulsive Therapy.

Ecuador, Republic of, independent nation on the NW coast of South America. It is governed by an army junta. Fish and oil (found in 1972) are its chief exports.

Land and economy. The Andes Mts divide the country into three areas: costa, hot, humid lowlands; Sierra, temperate highlands, and Oriente, tropical lowlands. In addition to coffee, fish, and bananas, oil exports were started in 1972. Deposits of copper, iron, lead, and coal are still largely untapped.

People. Population is made up of 40% Indians, 40% mixed bloods (mestizo), 10% Spanish descendents, and 10% blacks. The majority are subsistence farmers. Most of the people are Roman Catholic. Primary education is compulsory, and the literacy rate is 60%.

Government. Political parties are loose groups lacking clear programs. Under the present regime, legislation is enacted by decree, supreme court justices are appointed by the president, and lower-level justice is by military-civilian tribunals. One of Ecuador's main foreign policy problems is the defense of its 200mi (322km) of fisheries jurisdiction off the Pacific coast. Ecuador is a member of the United Nations, Organization of American States, and Andean Common Market.

History. Spanish conquistadores subjugated the Inca Empire in 1532 and incorporated it into the viceroyalty of New Granada until 1822, when Simon Bolivar led a successful fight for independence. Instability characterized political life from independence until after WWII. Galo Plaza Lasso, elected president in 1948, was the first president since 1925 to finish his term (1948–52). José Velasco Ibarra was president three times from 1952. In 1972 he was ousted by Gen. Guillermo Rodgriguez Lara's military regime.

PROFILE

Official name: Republic of Ecuador
Area: 109,483sq mi (283,561sq km)
Population: 7,100,000
Density: 65 per sq mi (25 per sq km)
Chief cities: Quito (capital); Guayaquil
Government: Military Junta
Religion: Roman Catholic
Language: Spanish
Monetary unit: Sucre
Gross national product: $3,200,000,000
Per capita income: $371
Industries (major): processed foods, textiles, cement, petroleum products
Agriculture: bananas, coffee, cacao, rice, sugar cane, cotton
Trading partners: United States, Japan, Federal Republic of Germany

Ecumenical Council. △1086.

Ecumenism, movement toward unity among different churches. With Vatican Council II (1962–65), the term became widely known. Churches are all to recognize the universal aspects of religion and to assume a more noticeable role in the modern world. Through discussions and joint projects, a common ground is sought amid the diversity of denominations. △388.

Eczema, form of chronic dermatitis characterized by redness, oozing, blisters, itching. It can be caused by contact with a substance to which the skin has been sensitized, such as poison ivy or detergent. More generalized eczema may occur with no identifiable cause, usually in persons with histories of allergies. Treatment is with local medication. *See also* Allergy; Dermatitis. △724.

Eddington, (Sir) Arthur Stanley (1882–1944), English scientist involved in the fields of mathematics, relativity, cosmology, and astronomy. While professor of astronomy at Cambridge, he worked on the structure of stars. He also made significant and pioneering contributions to the general theory of relativity, and was an eloquent popularizer of science.

Eddy, Mary Baker (1821–1910), founder of the Christian Science Church, b. Bow, N.H. Subject to convulsions, she sought a cure through both physical and mental healing. She discovered the spiritual and philosophical system of Christian Science in 1866 while reading the Bible after a serious fall. Her book *Science and Health* (1875) explains the Christian Science system. The Church of Christ, Scientist was chartered in 1879. Mary Baker Eddy also founded the *Christian Science Journal* (1883), The Christian Science Publishing Society (1898), and the *Christian Science Monitor* (1908). *See also* Christian Science.

Eddy Current, current induced in a conductor when subjected to a varying magnetic field. Eddy currents cause a loss of energy in a.c. generators and motors; the reaction between the eddy currents in a moving conductor and the field in which it moves retards the motion of the conductor. △1538.

Ede, city in E Netherlands, in Gelderland prov. Industries: yarn, pianos, metallurgy. Pop. 71,952.

Edelman, Gerald M(aurice) (1929–), US molecular biologist, b. New York City. He shared the 1972 Nobel Prize in physiology or medicine for his work on unraveling the chemical structure of the antibody gamma globulin. The determination of the structure of gamma globulin was essential to other research on how antibodies function in the immune system to recognize and destroy invaders in the body.

Edelweiss, small perennial plant native to the Alps and other high Eurasian mountains. It has white, downy leaves and its small yellow flower heads are enclosed in whitish bracts. Family Compositae; species *Leontopodium alpinum*. △608.

Edema, or dropsy, abnormal accumulation of fluid in spaces between cells of body tissues. It is frequently associated with liver or kidney disturbance, pregnancy, and heart failure.

Eden, (Sir) Anthony, Earl of Avon (1897–1977), English Conservative politician. He resigned as foreign secretary (1938) in protest against appeasement but re-entered the cabinet during World War II and served again as foreign secretary (1939–45, 1951–55). He promoted the Anglo-Soviet war alliance, the establishment of the United Nations, and France's withdrawal from Indochina. As prime minister (1955–57) he ordered British troops into Suez; the resulting crisis led to his resignation.

Eden, in the Bible, garden created by God as the home of Adam and Eve, until they were banished for eating the forbidden fruit from the tree of knowledge. △810.

Edentate, small group of mammals (order Edentata) found from Kansas to Patagonia. The roughly 30 species include the armadillos, sloths, and anteaters. Although "edentate" means "toothless," only the anteaters truly fit this description. △546.

Ederle, Gertrude (Caroline) (1907–), US swimmer, b. New York City. She shared a gold medal as a member of the US women's relay swimming team in the 1924 Olympics. In 1926 she was the first woman to swim the English Channel, crossing from Cap Gris-Nez, France, to Dover, England, in 14hr 31min, breaking the previous record by 1hr 59min.

Edessa (Edhessa) town in NW Greece; capital of Pella dept.; served as ancient capital of Macedonian kings; Philip II was assassinated here 336 BC; trade center. Industries: textiles, tobacco, cotton. Pop. 16,521.

Edgar (943?–75), English king. His reign (959–75) was peaceful and prosperous. He supported the church and St. Dunstan's monastic reforms, systematized naval defense, and allowed autonomy to the Danes in return for their loyalty.

Edgehill. △1156.

Edina, town in SE central Minnesota. Area has 60 lakes and large amount of park land. Industries: electronic and computer equipment. Inc. 1888; village of Morningside was annexed 1966. Pop. (1970) 44,046.

Edinburgh, (Prince) Philip (Mountbatten), Duke of (1921–), husband of Queen Elizabeth II of Great Britain and Ireland, b. Corfu, Greece. He served as a British naval officer (1939–52), rising to the rank of commander before his wife ascended the throne and he became prince consort.

Edinburgh, capital city and port of Scotland, on S shore of Firth of Forth, 40mi (64km) E of Glasgow on both banks of the Clyde River; Capital of Scotland since 14th century. Leith serves as its seaport; birthplace of Sir Walter Scott (1771). John Knox lived here; his home (1556) still stands; site of University of Edinburgh (1582), Heriot-Watt University (1966), Royal Scottish Museum, and National Museum of Antiquities. At Edinburgh Castle the annual tattoo is held. Holyrood Abbey (1128) and Holyrood Palace (built *c.* 1500 by James IV) are here. Mary Queen of Scots lived in Holyrood Palace 1561–67; here she married Lord Darnley, saw her secretary David Rizzio murdered, and finally married the Earl of Bothwell; statue to Sir Walter Scott stands in the East Princes Street Gardens. His death in 1832 marked the end of Edinburgh's golden age that began in the middle of the 18th century. Industries: brewing, distilling, printing, electronics, rubber, tourism. Pop. 453,422.

Edirne (Adrianople), fortified city in NW Turkey, 130mi (209km) NW of Istanbul, at the confluence of Maritsa and Tundzha rivers; capital of Edirne prov.; regional agricultural market and manufacturing center; site of mosque of Selim II (1574), and palace ruins. Founded by Hadrian *c.* AD 125, city fell to Visigoths 378; passed to Turks 1361; taken by Russia 1829–79; restored to Turkey 1923. Industries: cotton, silk, cheese, grain, fruit, tobacco, leather, soap, cattle. Pop. 46,091.

Edison, Thomas Alva (1847–1931), US inventor, b. Milan, Ohio. The most productive inventor of his time, he received over 1,000 patents for practical applications of scientific principles. Self-educated, he spent most of his childhood in Port Huron, Mich., and became a railroad newsboy at 12 and a telegraph operator at 16. He patented his first invention, an electronic vote recorder, in 1869. With money made from an improved stock-ticker system, he set up his own plant in 1871 in Newark, N.J., where besides manufacturing he developed automatic telegraph transmitters and receivers and (1874) a quadruplex telegraphic transmittal system. In 1876 he discontinued manufacturing to set up in Menlo Park, N.J., the first US industrial research laboratory. There he developed the carbon telephone transmitter (1877–78); the phonograph (1877–78); and the first commercially successful incandescent lamp (1879), for which he developed a complete distribution system—from dynamos to household sockets. He moved his laboratory to large, modern quarters in West Orange, N.J., in 1887. There he developed the mimeograph, dictating machines, the fluoroscope, early motion picture cameras and projectors, and an iron-alkaline storage battery. In 1883 he discovered the Edison effect, which would later form the basis of the electron tube. In 1889 he formed the Edison Electric Light Company, which through mergers became General Electric in 1892. During World War I he headed the US Navy consulting board on ship defenses and helped to develop the manufacture of previously imported chemicals, including carbolic acid. Late in life he attempted to develop a practical rubber substitute. △1278.

Edmer of Canterbury. *See* Eadmer of Canterbury.

Edmonton, capital city of Alberta, Canada, on the North Saskatchewan River; trade center for the surrounding agricultural area; site of Edmonton House, 19th-century trading post, University of Alberta (1906); petrochemical center since the 1947 discovery of oil. Industries: oil refining, meat packing. Est 1795 as a Hudson's Bay Co. trading post. Pop. 434,116.

Jamaica
Haiti
CARIBBEAN SEA
Costa Rica
Panama
Venezuela
Guyana
PACIFIC OCEAN
Colombia
Quito
ECUADOR
Ambato
Guayaquil
Cuenca
Brazil
Peru
0
1000km
Ecuador

Mary Baker Eddy

Edinburgh, Scotland

Thomas A. Edison

Edmund (921?–46), English king. Succeeding his half-brother Athelstan as king (939), he reconquered northern England from the Vikings. During his reign a monastic revival began. He was murdered by a banished robber.

Edmund Ironside (981?–1016), English king. On the death of his father, Ethelred the Unready, Edmund was proclaimed king (1016). Edmund won several victories over the rival claimant, the Dane Canute, before Canute defeated him. The two divided England, and Edmund ruled Wessex until his death. *See also* Canute.

Edmund Rich, Saint (1175?–1240), English ecclesiastic and scholar. Renowned as a teacher at Oxford, he preached the Sixth Crusade in England (1227) and became Archbishop of Canterbury (1234–40). He opposed King Henry III's favoritism toward foreign counselors and eventually withdrew to France to become a monk. He was canonized *c.* 1249.

EDP. *See* Electronic Data Processing.

Edred, or Eadred, (died 955), English king. Crowned in 946 he strove successfully to keep Northumbria in England and supported the monastic revival.

Education, the ways a society informs and instructs its members. Before the first formal schools, family and group members taught children basic survival skills as well as cultural traditions. Modern formal education is an enormous enterprise, yet the early influences of the family and the informal education of the mass media are also crucial parts of learning. *See* such articles as Adult Education; Degree, Academic; Elementary School; High School; Teaching Machine; University.

Educational Psychology, branch of psychology focusing on learners and learning. Educational psychologists study child development, the learning process, teacher-student relationships, and ways of measuring abilities and achievement.

Educational Television (ETV), system of television channels reserved by the Federal Communications Commission for educational and cultural programs. Without commercial advertising, they are financed by private industry foundations, government grants, local stations, and viewers. Most ETV stations are part of the National Educational Television (NET) network.

Education of Henry Adams, The (1907), autobiographical study by Henry Adams. Emphasizing themes of failure and discontinuity, Adams presents himself as a figure struggling to understand his times. The book is a record both of Adams' sensitive personality and his "dynamic" theory of history.

Edward I (1239–1307), king of England. He won influence and fame suppressing the baronial revolt (1263–65) against his father, Henry III, and crusading (1270–72). Succeeding his father (1272), he carried out important administrative, judicial, and financial reforms, which increased royal power and weakened feudalism. By summoning frequent parliaments and including commoners in them, he contributed greatly to Parliament's development. Edward conquered Wales and incorporated it into England (1275–95). Although he also conquered Scotland in 1296, the remainder of his reign was occupied with Scottish revolts.

Edward II (1284–1327), king of England. As king (from 1307), Edward's general inability and reliance on favorites alienated his barons, who increasingly took control of England, especially after the Scots decisively defeated him at Bannockburn (1314). He regained control (1322) only to rely on new favorites and alienate his queen, Isabella, who became mistress of an exiled baron. These two invaded England (1326) and deposed and murdered Edward. *See also* Isabella; Mortimer, Roger de.

Edward III (1312–77), king of England. Succeeding Edward II in 1327, he unsuccessfully tried to conquer Scotland. His claim to the French throne (1340) led to the Hundred Years' War. Despite brilliant military successes at Crécy (1346), Calais (1347), and Poitiers (1356), Edward was forced to renounce his claims at the Treaty of Bretigny (1360). During his reign, much important anti-papal and commercial legislation was enacted, the role of Parliament increased, and the Black Death caused considerable economic and social changes. Edward's later years were overshadowed by his sons' quarrels and territorial losses. *See also* Bretigny, Treaty of; Edward the Black Prince.

Edward IV (1442–83), king of England. Heir of the House of York, he defeated the rival Lancastrians, supporters of Henry VI, and became king (1461). Initially his ally, the Earl of Warwick, ruled England, but Edward gradually assumed more authority. Warwick deposed Edward and reinstated Henry (1470), but Edward obtained help from Burgundy and crushed his enemies (1471). He re-established order and began important administrative reforms.

Edward V (1470–83), king of England. He succeeded his father, Edward IV, in April 1483, with his uncle Richard as regent. Richard imprisoned Edward and his younger brother and, proclaiming them illegitimate, made himself king as Richard III. The two boys were murdered, probably in August 1483. *See also* Richard III.

Edward VI (1537–53), king of England and Ireland, and only legitimate son of Henry VIII. An intelligent boy, he was a gifted student and a fanatical Protestant. During his reign (1547–53) leading Protestants came to England and his regents continued the English Reformation. His uncle, the duke of Somerset, ruled initially as lord protector but he was overthrown by the duke of Northumberland (1549) and executed (1552). Northumberland persuaded Edward to appoint Lady Jane Grey (Northumberland's daughter-in-law) heiress to the throne.

Edward VII, (1841–1910), king of Great Britain and Ireland. The eldest son of Queen Victoria, he was excluded from government affairs by his mother, but was allowed to pay official visits and perform minor functions. He turned his energies to social life, travel, and sport, and was involved in several scandals. As king (1901–10) he restored court pageantry and became very popular. He attempted to maintain European peace through personal contacts between rulers and contributed noticeably to the growth of the Anglo-French alliance.

Edward VIII (1894–1972), king of Great Britain and Ireland, subsequently duke of Windsor. In World War I he served on the army staff. He was a popular royal heir, but becoming king in 1936 he decided to marry an American divorcee, and had to abdicate. During World War II he was governor of the Bahamas.

Edward (Idi Amin Dada), **Lake,** lake in central Africa, on Zaire-Uganda border; discovered 1889 by Henry Stanley; connected to Nile River by Semliki River. Area: 830sq mi (2,150sq km).

Edwards, Harry. △748.

Edwards, Jonathan (1703–58), American minister and theologian, b. East Windsor, Conn. As a powerful young preacher in Northhampton, Mass. (1729–50), he gained a wide following. With his Calvinist themes of predestination and man's dependence on God, he brought about a religious revival called the Great Awakening, which he chronicled in *A Faithful Narrative of the Surprising Work of God* (1737). His fierce sermons, like "Sinners in the Hands of an Angry God," argued against any change in the strict Calvinist creed. He was appointed president of the College of New Jersey at Princeton a few months before he died. △860.

Edwards v. South Carolina (1963), US Supreme Court case reversing the breach of peace convictions of a group of demonstrators that had gathered peaceably at the state capitol. The court upheld their right to so express their views peacefully.

Edward the Black Prince (1330–76), outstanding English general, eldest son of Edward III. He distinguished himself in France at Crécy (1346) and led the English to victory at Poitiers (1356). As his father's viceroy in Aquitaine (1363–71), he proved an incapable ruler, despite further military success in Spain (1367) and brutal measures at Limoges (1370).

Edward the Confessor (1003?–1066), English king. The Anglo-Saxon heir, he was made king (1042) by Earl Godwin of Wessex, who dominated England. Godwin's power was weakened by Edward's Norman favorites, and Godwin's family was exiled (1051). Returning (1053), Godwin and his son Harold became the effective rulers, and Edward devoted himself to religion.

Edward the Elder (died 924), king of Wessex (899–924). He was the son of Alfred the Great and is supposed to have ruled jointly with his father. His reign saw the power and territory of Wessex extended at the expense of the Danes and other English kingdoms.

Edward the Martyr (died 978), king of England (c.963–78). He was popularly regarded as a saint after his murder, which may have been the responsibility of his stepmother Aelfrida.

Edwin (d. 633), king of Northumbria (616–33). He became a Christian in 627, and his reign was important for the spread of Christianity. He died defeated in battle by a Welsh king Cadwallon and the heathen King Penda of Mercia.

Edwy (died 959), king of Wessex (955–59). His reign is noted for his quarrel with Dunstan, who was subsequently exiled. He was succeeded by his younger brother Edgar.

Eel, marine and freshwater fish found worldwide in shallow temperate and tropical waters. They have snakelike bodies, no scales, dorsal and anal fins continuous with the tail, and an air bladder connected to throat. All spawn and die in the sea; American and European eels in the Sargassum Sea. Eggs develop into ribbonlike larva, the leptocephalus; then into the elver or glass eel; and finally into the adult. Length: to 10ft (305cm). Families include Freshwater, Spaghetti or Moray, Conger, and Snake eels. Order Anguilliformes.

Eel Grass, flowering plant that grows under water. It has long, grasslike leaves and spikes of inconspicuous flowers. Family Potamogetonacae; species *Zostera marina.* △620.

Effectors, or motor neurons, specialized output cells that activate the voluntary muscles of the body. Effector impulses originate in the brain and result in the often complex and delicate muscle activity called behavior.

Egan, Patrick (1841–1919), Irish nationalist and US politician, b. Ireland. An active member of the Irish Land League, he emigrated to the US (1883) to avoid arrest. There he gained political prominence, first as a Republican and then, after 1896, as a Democrat. He served as US ambassador to Chile (1888–93).

Egbert or **Ecgberht** (died 839), king of Wessex (802–39) and ruler over all the other English kingdoms in the course of his reign. In 828 he defeated Beornwulf of Mercia, and he or his son Ethelwulf conquered other kingdoms thereafter. He also made a perpetual alliance with the church of Canterbury.

Egg, or **ovum,** reproductive cell of female animals surrounded by protective jelly, albumen, shell, chorion, egg case, or membrane depending upon species. Egg functions are: supply food reserve in the form of a yolk for embryo; supply nucleus containing half the chromosomes of future embryo; supply almost all the cytoplasm upon union with the sperm. The amount of yolk in an egg depends on when the embryo actively begins to feed. Bird and insect eggs have a large yolk, mammalian eggs a much smaller one. The lifespan of a mature human egg is 12–24 hours, sea urchin eggs—40 hours, most invertebrates, amphibians, and fish—minutes. △530, 700.

Eggplant, shrublike plant of the nightshade family, native to Africa or India; until the 20th century grown mainly as an ornamental. The leaves are large and the 2in (5.1cm)-wide violet flowers produce a berry fruit ranging from a small egg-shape to a large pear-shape. Height: 2–3ft (61–92cm). Species: cultivated *Solanum melongena;* wild *S. incanum.*

Eggs. △382.

Egmont, Lamoral, Count of (1522–68), Flemish general and statesman. In the service of Philip II of Spain he defeated the French at Saint-Quentin (1557) and Gravelines (1559). Although himself a Catholic, he protested the Spanish persecution of Protestants in the Low Countries. In 1566 he took his protest, to no avail, to the king in Spain. The new Spanish governor of the Low Countries, the Duke of Alba, had Count Egmont and Count Hoorn arrested on false charges of treason in 1567 and publically beheaded in 1568. This led to open revolt in the Low Countries.

Ego, in psychoanalysis, the conscious level of personality that deals with the real world. According to Sigmund Freud, the child is first driven by the impulses of the id. The ego develops as he learns to live with others and balance the demands of the id and of the superego (which sets standards and ideals). *See also* Id; Superego. △786, 812.

Egret, white heron of temperate and tropical wetlands known for its plumes, once popular for decorating hats. They are long-legged, long-necked, slenderbodied wading birds with daggerlike bills. They feed on small animals, nest in rookeries, and lay pale bluish eggs (3–6) in a platform nest on the ground or in a tree. Height: 20–40in (51–102cm). Genus *Egretta.*

Egypt (Misr), an independent nation in the Middle East. The ancient land of the Pharoahs, it is now a republic with limited economic resources.

Land and economy. Mostly a rainless, arid desert, Egypt is located in the NE corner of Africa bordered on the N by the Mediterranean Sea, W by Libya, S by the Sudan, and E by the Red Sea, Gulf of Suez, and Israel. Geographically, it is divided into four regions. The Nile Valley and delta provide 10,000sq mi (25,900sq km) under cultivation, a total that is expected to be increased by irrigation from the Aswan Dam. The W and S deserts and the E desert, along the Red Sea and the Nile, are high plateaus of rugged hills and mountain peaks. Its climate is temperate. The highest peak is Mt Catherine in the Sinai 8,652ft (2,639m) above sea level; the lowest is the Qattara Depression, 400ft (120m) below sea level, in the W desert. The economy is basically agricultural, with half the labor force engaged in land production; maximum land holding is limited to 100acres (40hectares) per family. Cotton is the principal crop and accounts for 50% of total earnings. Oil, major industries, and public utilities have been nationalized. Although the economy suffered a decline after the 1967 and 1973 wars with Israel, it has begun to recover. Revenue from the Suez Canal is increasing. Alexandria is the chief port.

People. The most heavily-populated country in the Arab world, 99% of the people live in the Nile Valley and delta, which have a population density of 2,500per sq mi (965per sq km). In the rural regions, the farmers (fellahin) are descended from Arab settlers who mixed with the indigenous pre-Islamic tribes after the Muslim invasion. The cosmopolitan cities of Cairo and Alexandria are attracting more rural dwellers as industrial jobs become available. Sunni Islam is the principal religion (90%). Arabic is the official language; literacy is 35%. With disease under control, life expectancy has risen to 53 years and the growing population is one of Egypt's major problems.

Government. The 1971 constitution set up a strong presidential-type government with authority in the elected president. When the elected unicameral People's Assembly is not in session, the president may rule by decree.

History. Egypt fell under Roman domination in 58 BC when the Ptolemies (Cleopatra) used Julius Caeser and Marc Antony to regain domination of their dynasty. Rome annexed Egypt and killed the last Ptolomy. In succeeding years Egypt came under Persian rule (616–28), followed by the Arabs (639–42), who introduced the Islam religion. In the 10th century the ruling Fatamids founded Cairo (969). In 1250 militant Mamelukes seized control; they were unseated by the Ottoman Turks in 1517. The modern state of Egypt began with the 1805 rule of Muhammed Ali, a political, social, and economic reformer. In 1856, Suez Canal building costs plunged Egypt into debt and opened the door to British intervention, occupation of Cairo, and protectorate status in WWI. Nationalism grew, and in 1922 a parliamentary kingdom under British domination was established. The final struggle between the Wafd nationalists and the king, Farouk, came in 1952 when Gen. Muhammed Naguib led an uprising and became premier. Farouk abdicated, and Egypt was declared a republic on June 18, 1953. Strong man of the revolt, Gen. Gamal Abdal Nasser deposed Naguib and became president. Opposition to the existence of Israel was the rallying cry for Egyptians, and in October 1956 Nasser barred Israel from use of the nationalized Suez Canal. Israeli forces invaded the Sinai peninsula, Britain and France bombed the canal, and the war was over on November 7. In 1967, Egypt took over the Gaza Strip and closed the Gulf of Aqaba to Israeli shipping. In the Six-Day War that followed, Israel captured Gaza and the E bank of the Suez. A UN cease-fire ended hostilities; a peace-keeping force was placed in the area. Nasser was succeeded in 1970 by Anwar al-Sadat, whose nationalistic policies were partly responsible for the 1973 Arab-Israeli War. *See also* Arab-Israeli Wars; Egypt, History of. △972.

PROFILE

Official name: Arab Republic of Egypt
Area: 386,660sq mi (1,001,449sq km)
Population: 37,500,000
Density: 97per sq mi (37per sq km)
Chief cities: Cairo (capital); Alexandria; Giza; Suez
Government: Republic (one-party system)
Religion: Islam
Language: Arabic (official)
Monetary unit: Egyptian pound
Gross national product: $17,900,000,000
Per capita income: $259
Industries: chemicals, steel, cement, fertilizer, film, electrical instruments, textiles
Agriculture: cotton, fruit, olives, cereals, sugar cane, vegetables
Minerals: petroleum, phosphate, salt, iron, manganese, gold, gypsum, titanium
Trading partners: communist countries, United States

Egypt, Ancient, civilization that flourished along the Nile River in NW Africa from before 3400 BC until 30 BC, when the last Egyptian king, Ptolemy XIV, was put to death by order of Octavian (later Roman Emperor Augustus), and Egypt was annexed to Rome. As a result of the extensive scholarship of Egyptologists of the 19th and 20th centuries, a considerable body of information exists on Egyptian history, even from the earliest periods. Traditionally, Egyptian history is separated into five periods: the Old Kingdom (or Old Empire); the First Intermediate Period; the Middle Kingdom (or Middle Empire): the Second Intermediate Period; and the New Kingdom (or New Empire). The individual dynasties are numbered, generally in Roman numerals, from I through XXX.

The kingdoms of Upper Egypt and Lower Egypt were united in about 3100 BC by Menes, King of Upper Egypt, and he founded the first Egyptian dynasty. From the beginning, a form of theocracy is believed to have existed, with the king, or pharaoh, regarded as divine. Elaborate burial rites and tombs, from which so much modern knowledge of Egypt derives, also developed early. By the beginning of the II dynasty, about 2890 BC, considerable trade existed between Egypt and the Sinai; the Egyptians possibly traded as far north as the Black Sea. The Old Kingdom began in the III dynasty, during 2686 BC. Khufu (or Cheops), founder of the IV dynasty, ruled *c.* 2600, built the great pyramid at Gizeh (al Jizah). His successors Kahfre (who is believed to be represented as the face of the Sphinx) and Menkaure built the other pyramids at Gizeh. Pepi II of the VI dynasty, who ruled from *c.* 2294–*c.* 2188, organized the caravan trade with Nubia, the Sudan, and Punt. The capital probably was at Memphis. During the VI dynasty, priests and local governors, whose office became hereditary, achieved great power at the expense of the king. The Old Kingdom disintegrated in about 2181 BC. Complete power passed to the provinces. No central records were kept, resulting in a period of historical obscurity.

During the first Intermediate Period, the capital was moved to Heracleopolis, where the weak rulers of the IX and X dynasties resided. Some central authority was restored when Intef, a Theban noble, proclaimed himself king in 2134 and founded the XI dynasty. The capital was moved to Thebes, center for the worship of the god Amon.

The Middle Kingdom (c.2050–1786 BC) The great rulers of the XII dynasty brought the Egyptian kingdom to its highest flowering. Amenemhat I, founder of the dynasty in about 1891, centralized power at Thebes by reducing the long powerful nobles to a feudal status. He and his successors reestablished the old trade routes, reopened mines, and extended the Egyptian border to the Second Cataract of the Nile. They irrigated al Fayyum, thereby greatly increasing the amount of arable land. They built forts along the Nile and constructed a canal that bypassed the First Cataract. Great building projects were carried out; among the most impressive was the great temple of Amon at Karnak. A uniform writing system was adopted, and Egyptian literature reached its peak.

The XII dynasty—and the Middle Kingdom—came to an end in 1786, when the country was invaded and conquered by the Hyksos. The Hyksos were a Semitic people from Syria. Their weapons, new to Egypt, included the horse-drawn war chariot, the bronze sword, and the composite bow (made of wood, sinew, and horn). The Hyksos ruled Egypt during the Second Intermediate Period and founded the XIII–XVII dynasties. They adapted themselves readily to Egyptian culture but introduced Oriental deities into the Egyptian religion; artifacts of the period also show Oriental influence.

The New Kingdom. Began about 1570 BC when the Hyksos were expelled by an Egyptian general who assumed the throne as Amasis I and founded the XVIII dynasty. His son and successor was Amenhotep I, who continued his father's military victories by reconquering Nubia, which had been allied with the Hyksos. He also invaded Syria. Thutmose I, who became king *c.* 1504, extended Egypt's border to the Third Cataract and subdued Syria as far as the Euphrates River. Thutmose III, who assumed sole power in 1468 BC, brought the empire of the New Kingdom to its zenith by conquering territories east of the Euphrates and by extending Egyptian power below the Third Cataract. The conquests of the kings of the XVIII, XIX, and XX dynasties brought unprecedented wealth into Egypt, including thousands of slaves. Great tombs and temples were built, the most spectacular of which were located in the Valley of the Kings, across the Nile from Thebes. The tomb of Tutankhamen, a king of the XVIII dynasty, was discovered in 1922 and has been a source of much information about Egypt of the New Kingdom.

Amenhotep IV, who ruled *c.* 1375–58, changed his

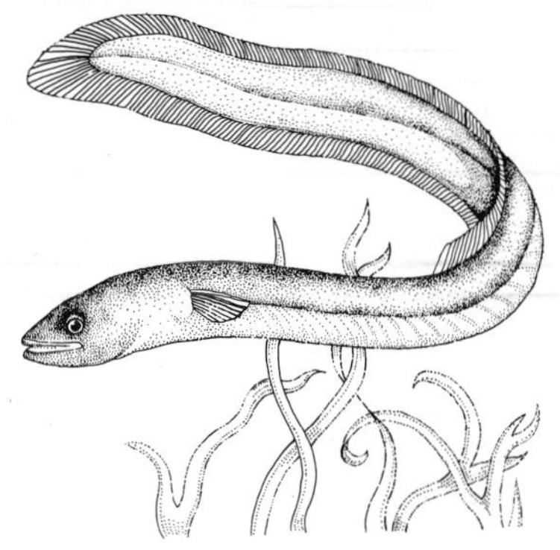
Eel

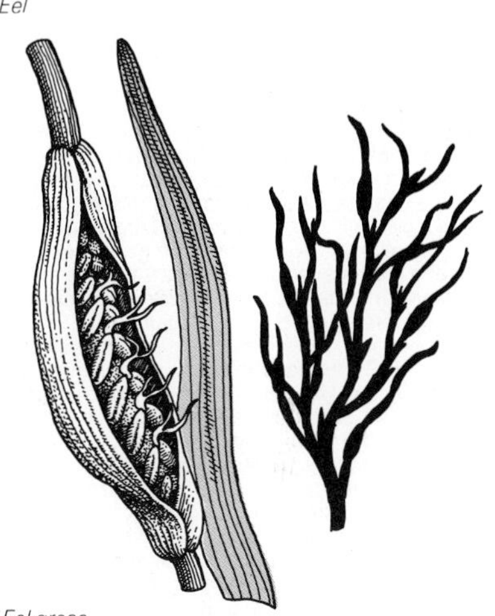
Eel grass

Egret

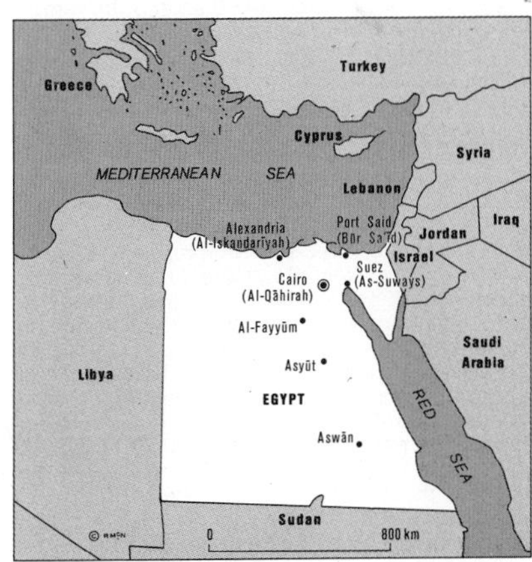
Turkey
Greece
Cyprus
Syria
MEDITERRANEAN SEA
Lebanon
Iraq
Alexandria
(Al-Iskandarīyah)
Port Said
(Būr Saʽīd)
Jordan
Israel
Suez
(As-Suways)
Cairo
(Al-Qāhirah)
Al-Fayyūm
Saudi
Arabia
Asyūt
Libya
EGYPT
RED SEA
Aswān
Sudan
0
800 km
Egypt

name to Ikhnaton in honor of the sun god Aton. He attempted to institute a monotheism with Aton as the sole god, established a new capital at Akhetaton in honor of Aton, and directed all royal artists and architects to works honoring the sun god. His lack of interest in non-religious affairs was costly; Nubia and Syria were lost during his reign. His successors ruled over a greatly weakened and reduced empire. Even his religious reforms did not survive him; a conservative priesthood restored the old polytheism at his death. Ramesses I founded the XIX dynasty in about 1320 and his successors gradually rebuilt the empire until it reached the splendor of Ramesses II. Some of the greatest wonders of Egypt were built under his reign, including Abu Simbel, the Ramesseum, and temples at Luxor and Karnak. He also carried on a long war against the Hittites, a war that only ended when he married (1267) a Hittite princess.

The wars with the Hittites weakened Egypt and a series of ineffectual rulers followed Ramesses II, who ruled with his wife, Queen Tiy. After them, the New Kingdom declined, and foreign influence was increasingly felt in the country. The capital was moved to Tanis in 1085, marking the end of the New Kingdom. The Tanite (or XXI) dynasty was replaced by the Libyan dynasty, which ruled from Bubastis. It was replaced by Nubian conquerors, who founded the XXII dynasty. The capital was moved to Saïs in 712, and the country fell under Assyrian domination. In 525 the Persians took control until 405, when the Egyptians revolted, and the last native dynasties appeared. Unable to reestablish Egypt's former grandeur, the new ruling class fell to the armies of Alexander the Great in 332. Alexander founded the great port city of Alexandria and moved the Egyptian capital there. After Alexander's death his empire was divided among his generals and Ptolemy became the ruler of Egypt as Ptolemy I. Under him and his successors, known as the Ptolemies, Alexandria became the greatest city in the Hellenistic world. It was a great center of learning and its library was a legendary repository of ancient and modern manuscripts. The Ptolemies maintained a powerful empire for two centuries, and Egypt under them was the greatest of the Hellenistic nations. Roman power was on the ascendancy, however, and when Ptolemy XI asked Pompey and his Roman army for aid in 58, it marked the end of Egyptian independence; Pompey restored him to the throne but he became a Roman puppet. His daughter Cleopatra tried to assert her independence by her celebrated machinations with Julius Caesar and Marc Antony, but she was defeated and committed suicide. Her son Ptolemy XIV (whose father probably was Julius Caesar) was the last Ptolemy to rule; he was put to death at the age of 13 by Octavian (later Emperor Augustus). From that time, Egypt became a province of Rome and was ruled directly from there. △960, 972, 980, 984.

Egyptian Architecture, architecture developed before 3000 BC and characterized by post and lintel construction, massive walls covered with hieroglyphic and pictorial carving, flat roofs, and such structures as the pyramid, mastaba, obelisk, and steeply battered pylon. Houses were built of clay or baked bricks. Tombs and temples reproduced features of domestic architecture but on a massive scale using permanent materials. A prominent example of Old Kingdom (2680–2258 BC) architecture is the funeral complex at Saqqara built by Imhotep for King Zoser, which consists of a 200-foot-high stepped pyramid surrounded by a columned processional hall and niched limestone wall. Middle Kingdom tombs at Bani Hasan (1991–1786 BC) were carved from the rock cliffs on the banks of the Nile. Examples of New Kingdom architecture are the massive mortuary temple of Queen Hatsheput at Deir el Bahari (1480 BC) and the temple of Amon at Karnac (1570–1085 BC). △960, 972.

Egyptian Art, the artistic and architectural works of ancient Egypt, usually classified according to the ancient dynasties as follows: In the Old Kingdom period (*c.* 2686–2181 BC) works were chiefly relief sculpture and painting characterized by front and side views of the human figure, flat color tones, symmetry in sculpture, and minimal suggested movement (static figures). Relief decorated private tombs and temples and portrayed the daily life of the subjects. Statues were realistic. A great architect of this period was Imhotep. Painting was subordinate to sculpture. In the Middle Kingdom period (2050–1786 BC) art became increasingly formalized and less realistic. There was little relief sculpture and more painting, jewelry work, and figurines. The New Kingdom (*c.* 1570–1085 BC) saw greater boldness of design. Art and technique reached its peak in this period in the realistic portrayal of the family life of the pharoah Ikhnaton and his family, including the famous bust of Queen Nefertiti in Berlin. Art of the Saite period (8th century BC) returned to the simpler modes of the earlier Old Kingdom.

Ancient Egyptian architecture was characterized by massively thick walls, flat stone roofs, and relatively few columns. Belief in life after death led to the construction of huge, permanent temples and tombs. With the decline of Egyptian power during the Ptolemaic dynasty, the distinctive Egyptian art styles declined and gave way to dominance by Greek and Roman forms. △960, 972.

Egyptian Mythology. The polytheistic mythology associated with Egypt developed when small agricultural communities, each with its own local deities, were united under the pharoahs. In the melding, some gods and their stories were identified with others and some joined into families to form the vast pantheon, producing a multiplicity of myths that explained the same phenomenon. Each religious center, meaning virtually every city, had its own creation myth justifying itself as the center of existence. Although there is an account of the Flood there is no Eden in the myths, no past Golden Age or prediction of the end of the world to come, reflecting the relatively stable society that existed under the pharoahs. △834, 972.

Egyptian Privet. *See* Henna.

Ehrenburg, Ilya (Grigoryevich) (1891–1967), Soviet novelist and journalist. He lived in Western Europe (1908–17, 1921–40), working as a journalist for several Russian newspapers. His novels, introducing Western European trends into Soviet literature, include the satiric *Julio Jurenito* (1921), *The Storm* (1948), and *The Thaw* (1954). He has also written essays on Stendhal and Chekhov and six volumes of memoirs *Men, Years, Life* (1960–64).

Ehrlich, Paul (1854–1915), German bacteriologist. He shared the 1908 Nobel Prize in physiology or medicine for his work on immunity, which included diphtheria antitoxin studies and the development of basic standards and methods for studying toxins and antitoxins. His subsequent search for a "magic bullet" against disease and his discovery of salvarsan, a chemical effective against syphilis microorganisms, introduced the modern era of chemotherapy (a term he coined). △746.

Eichmann, Adolf (1906–62), Austrian Nazi, head of the Gestapo's Jewish section in World War II. He supervised the Nazi policies of deportation, slave labor, torture, medical experimentation, and mass murder in the concentration camps, which led to the death of some 6,000,000 Jews during the war. Escaping to Argentina (1945), he was abducted by Israelis (1960) and executed in Israel for his crimes against humanity.

Eider Duck, large sea duck found in northern areas of Europe, Asia, and North America. Its down is used for pillows and quilts. Genus *Somateria. See also* Duck.

Eidetic Imagery, or photographic memory, capacity to obtain purely mental images that are so vivid that the person having them can describe them in detail. Few people have the ability to form eidetic images.

Eiffel, Alexandre Gustave (1832–1923), French engineer who established metal as an architectural material. His Eiffel Tower, built for the 1889 Paris Exhibition, was the world's tallest structure until 1930. He also designed the Bon Marché store in Paris and was the engineer for the frame of the Statue of Liberty. △1298.

Eiger, mountain peak in S central Switzerland, in the Burnese Alps. Height: 13,025ft (3,973m).

Eight, The, group of American painters formed in 1907. *See* Ashcan School.

Eight Masters of T'ang and Sung, the term traditionally used in Chinese schools for eight outstanding prose writers during the T'ang (618–906) and Sung (960–1279) dynasties. During the T'ang, Han Yü (768–824) and Liu Tsung-Yüan (773–819) instituted a return to the simpler style of several centuries earlier. Six other masters furthered this reform during the Sung. They were: Ou-yang Hsiu, Wang An-shih, Su Shih, Su Hsün, Su Chê, and Tsêng Kung.

Eijkman, Christiaan (1858–1930), Dutch medical researcher and physician. He shared the 1929 Nobel Prize in physiology or medicine "for his discovery of the antineuritic vitamin." Eijkman was the first to recognize a dietary deficiency disease, demonstrating that beriberi was produced by a lack of a certain dietary substance, later identified as vitamin B_1.

Einaudi, Luigi (1874–1961), Italian economist and statesman, was president of Italy (1948–1955). In the years immediately after World War II he was governor of the Bank of Italy and designer of Italy's postwar program of monetary stabilization. In 1948 he became Italy's first elected president.

Eindhoven, industrial city in S Netherlands, approx. 55mi (89km) SE of Rotterdam. Industries: electrical equipment, textiles, steel. Founded 1232. Pop. 188,831.

Einhard, (*c.* 770–840), historian of the medieval Frankish Empire. Born in Germany, in the valley of the Main River, Einhard became a teacher in Fulda, and later an important scholar and diplomat at the court of Charlemagne. Einhard is best known as author of the *Life of Charlemagne (Vita Caroli Magni),* the most influential biography of the Middle Ages.

Einstein, Albert (1879–1955), German-American physicist, b. Ulm, Germany. He published three important theoretical papers: the first concerned the application of quantum theory to photoelectricity (for which he was awarded a Nobel Prize in 1921), the second contained a mathematical analysis of the Brownian motion, and the third contained the first publication of the special theory of relativity—a paper that completely revolutionized physics and led to the atomic bomb, through its equation of mass and energy. In 1915 Einstein produced his general theory of relativity, which has far-reaching implications in astronomy. Being a Jew, he left Germany when Hitler came to power, spending the rest of his life in the United States, becoming a US citizen in 1940. He wrote to President Roosevelt in 1939 advocating research on the atom bomb, but after the war he worked devotedly for peace. Element 99 (einsteinium) is named after him. *See also* Quantum Theory; Relativity Theory. △1524.

Einsteinium, radioactive metallic element (symbol Es) of the actinide group, first identified in 1952 as a decay product of U^{235} produced in the first large hydrogen-bomb explosion. Properties: at. no. 99; most stable isotope Es^{254} (half-life 276 days). *See also* Transuranium Elements.

Einthoven, Willem (1860–1927), Dutch physiologist. He was awarded the 1924 Nobel Prize in physiology or medicine for his work on the string galvanometer, the mechanism for the electrocardiogram, an extremely important diagnostic tool.

Eire. *See* **Ireland, Republic of.**

Eisenach, city in East Germany, 31mi (50km) W of Erfurt. German Socialist Democratic party founded here 1869; site of 12th-century churches of St Nicholas and St George, house where Johann Sebastian Bach was born (now museum), and 18th-century castle. Industries: agricultural machinery, electrical equipment, motor vehicles. Founded late 12th century. Pop. 50,777.

Eisenhower, Dwight David (1890–1969), 34th president of the United States, b. Denison, Texas, graduate, West Point, 1915. In 1916 he married Mamie Doud; they had two sons. A professional soldier whose career spanned World Wars I and II, he rose slowly in rank in the peace-time army between those wars. By the beginning of World War II, he had reached the rank of colonel. He gained the attention of Gen. George C. Marshall and was given increasingly important assignments. He commanded the invasion of North Africa in 1942, where he showed a mastery of military planning and logistics. More importantly, he displayed a great gift for getting the various Allied military commanders to work together. In 1944, he assumed command of the entire Allied military operation in Europe. He planned Operation Overlord, the invasion of France, which began on D Day, June 6, 1944, when the largest military force ever assembled in history landed on the beaches of Normandy. By the time Germany surrendered on May 7, 1944, Eisenhower—by now a five-star general—was the most famous hero of the war.

He returned to the United States as army chief of staff. He was approached by both political parties to run for president; instead, he became president of Columbia University (1948). In 1950, at President Truman's request, he returned to Europe as NATO commander. He resigned that position in 1952 to run for the Republican presidential nomination.

After a close fight with Senator Robert A. Taft, he won the nomination. He chose Richard M. Nixon as his running mate. He easily defeated his Democratic opponent, Adlai E. Stevenson, Jr., and soon fulfilled his campaign pledge of ending the Korean War. He continued Truman's internationalist policies but adopted a more conservative, pro-business domestic program. He suffered a major heart attack in 1955 but recovered and ran for re-election in 1956, again against Stevenson. He and Nixon won by an even greater landslide than in 1952.

His second term was plagued by both domestic and foreign problems. In 1957, he used federal troops to force school integration in Little Rock, Ark., and in 1958, he sent US Marines to Lebanon. In 1959 a summit meeting with the Soviet Union was cancelled after a US spy plane was shot down over Russia. In 1961 relations with Cuba were broken. Despite all those setbacks, he left office in 1961 still one of the most popular presidents in US history.

Career: US Army, 1915–52; Columbia University president, 1948–52; president, 1953–61. △1358.

Eisenstein, Sergei (1898–1948), Soviet film director, technical innovator, and theorist. Able to complete only six films in 25 years, he remains one of the most influential artists in the history of the medium. He developed a strong intellectual and aesthetic style, enhanced by creative editing. His films are *Strike* (1924), *The Battleship Potemkin* (1925), *October*, (or *Ten Days That Shook the World* 1927), *The General Line* (1928), *Que Viva Mexico* (unfinished, 1931), *Alexander Nevsky* (1938), and *Ivan the Terrible* (two of three parts completed, 1942–46).

Eisner, Kurt (1867–1919), German statesman and writer. A socialist, he opposed German involvement in World War I. Proclaiming the new republic of Bavaria after the war, he became its first prime minister but was murdered a few months later.

Eitoku, Kano (1543–90), Japanese painter. Probably trained by his grandfather Motonobu, he is best known for his decorative works of gigantic forms painted on gold-leaf backgrounds. The rulers Nobunaga and Hideyoshi were among his patrons. △1048.

Ejido, Mexican "community land," distributed according to Indian practices from the time before Spanish domination. Reinstated by the constitution of 1917, this system gave land back to the villages, where some of it was divided into family plots. Since farming on such a small scale is inefficient, best results have been obtained through community land-use.

El. For other cities beginning with "el," see second part of name.

El Alamein. *See* Al-Alamein.

Eland, largest, oxlike African antelope. Giant or Derby eland of Central Africa has more massive horns than common eland of Central and S Africa. Common eland is uniformly gray; Derby is tan with black neck with white band at base. Both sexes carry heavy, spiralled horns. Gregarious and slow-moving, they are good jumpers. They have been trained to harness, but now are greatly reduced in number. Length: to 117in (3m); height: to 70in (1.8m) at shoulder; weight: to 1980lb (900kg). Family Bovidae; species giant or derby *Taurotragus derbianus,* common *Taurotragus oryx. See also* Antelope. △548.

Elasmosaurus. △572.

Elastic Cartilage △682.

Elastic Clause, Paragraph 18, Article I, Section 8, of the Constitution, setting forth the implied powers of Congress "to make all laws which shall be necessary and proper for carrying into execution the foregoing. . . ."

Elasticity, the study of the changes in shape or volume of solids, liquids, or gases subjected to external forces. The ratio of the forces to the cross-sectional area of the body is called stress; the body's change in shape is called strain; and the ratio of the stress to the strain is called an elastic modulus of the material. *See also* Strain; Stress.

Elasticity of Demand, measure of the responsiveness of consumers to price change. It is found by dividing the percentage *change in quantity* demanded by the percentage change in price. If there were a 10% price increase in the good and the quantity demanded of the good decreased by 10%, the elasticity would be unitary. If the percentage change in quantity demanded exceeded 10%, the good could be said to have an *elastic demand,* that is, a fairly small change in price elicited a relatively large change in demand. If the percentage change in quantity is less than 10%, the good could be said to have an *inelastic demand.* △936.

Elasticity of Molecules. △1506.

Elastomer, any of a variety of plastic, rubberlike substances with the physical properties of natural rubber, used in tires and other products. Important are copolymers in which the main molecular chain is composed of carbon atoms, usually based on petroleum derivatives (Buna S, Buna N, butyl rubber). Polysulfide rubbers (thiokols) and silicones are other elastomers. △1618.

Elat, seaport town in S Israel, on Gulf of Aqaba; site of pipeline terminal to Haifa, constructed 1960. Industries: fishing, diamond polishing, tourism. Pop. 14,600.

Elba (Isola d'Elba), Italian island in Tyrrhenian Sea; largest of Tuscan Archipelago; chief port and town is Portoferraio, on N coast. Island is mountainous, and is a major supplier of Italy's iron ore, mined since Etruscan and Roman times; site of exile of Napoleon I (1814–15); his villa still remains. Industries: fisheries, wine, iron ore, tourism. Area: 86sq mi (223sq km). Pop. 27,602.

Elbe River, river in central Europe; rises in Krknoše Mts of NW Czechoslovakia, flows across Czechoslovakia into East Germany, NW through central East Germany, across West Germany and into the North Sea at Cuxhaven, West Germany. In 1945 river was made part of demarcation line between East and West Germany. It is navigable for 525mi (845km). Length: 725mi (1,167km).

Elbert, Mount, mountain peak in central Colorado, in Sawatch Range of the Rocky Mt system; highest peak in the state and the US Rocky Mts, 14,433ft (4,402m).

Elbrus (Elborus), Mount (Gora El'Brus), two peaks in the Caucasus Mts, Russian SFSR, USSR; formed by two extinct volcanoes; W peak is highest in Europe, 18,481ft (5,637m). E peak is 18,356ft (5,599m) high.

Elburz Mountains (Alborz, Reshteh-ye Kūhhā-ye), narrow mountain group in N Iran, along SW and S coasts of the Caspian Sea; divides the dry inland plateau from the agriculturally rich lowlands; contains Mt Damāvand, highest peak in Iran, 18,934ft (5,774m). Length: 600mi (966km).

El Cajon, city in S California, E of San Diego; site of Grossmont College (1961). Industries: electronic equipment, missile parts, metal products. Inc. 1912. Pop. (1970) 52,273.

El Cerrito, city in W California, 6mi (10km) N of Oakland. Inc. 1917. Pop. (1970) 25,190.

Elche, city in SE Spain; scene of annual mystery play; site of Greek, Roman, and Arabic ruins. Industries: leather, dates, soap, palm oil. Pop. 122,663.

El Cordobés (1936–), Spanish bullfighter, *b.* Manuel Bénitez Pérez. Rising to national fame in the 1960s, he became the highest paid matador in the history of the sport.

Elder, shrub and small tree found worldwide in temperate and subtropical areas. They have divided leaves and clusters of tiny white flowers. Their small berries are important to wildlife and used in making wine, jellies, and medicine. The common elderberry shrub *(Sambucus canadensis)* has coarse-toothed leaflets, white flower clusters, and purple berries; height: to 13ft (4m). There are 40 species. Family Caprifoliaceae. △450.

Eldjarn, Kristjarn (1916–), Icelandic statesman and archeologist. He was curator of the National Museum of Iceland (1947–68). He was elected president of Iceland in 1968 and again in 1972.

El Dorado, city in S Arkansas, 80mi (129km) ESE of Texarkana; seat of Union co. Oil discovered 1921; chief oil town in Arkansas. Settled 1843; inc. 1851. Pop. (1970) 25,283.

El Dorado, mythical city of fabulous wealth, located in the interior of South America, which spurred many expeditions particularly in the 16th century. Departing from Peru, Ecuador, Venezuela and Brazil, the conquistadores' searches through the Amazon valley extended geographical knowledge of the continent, but did not result in large-scale colonization, given the harsh climate and living conditions encountered. The first official expedition, led by Felipe de Hutten, left the Venezuelan coast in 1541.

Eleanor of Aquitaine (1122?–1204), queen consort of France, and later of England, and duchess of Aquitaine. She married Louis VII of France, accompanying him on the Second Crusade (1147–49). Divorcing in

Ilya Ehrenburg

Albert Einstein

Dwight D. Eisenhower

Eland

1152, she married Henry (later Henry II of England) and had three sons, Richard, Geoffrey, and John. Eleanor supported her sons' revolt against Henry (1173), helped collect Richard's ransom (1193), and supported John on his accession (1199).

Eleanor of Castile (1230?–1290), queen consort of England, married Edward I (1254), and gave him her father's claim to Gascony. She is chiefly remembered for the crosses her husband had made to mark her funeral procession from Lincoln to London and her fine tomb at Westminster Abbey.

Eleanor of Provence (1220?–1291), queen consort of England, married Henry III in 1236. Her French relatives and courtiers were unpopular at the English court. A loyal wife, she raised troops for her husband during the Barons Wars (1264–65).

Eleaticism, teachings of the Eleatic school of Greek philosophy. Founded in the 6th century BC by Parmenides and including Xeno among others, the school taught that absolute reality is immobile, immutable, and indivisible. Change in the world, which is perceived by the senses, is only apparent; reason alone knows the real essence. *See also* Parmenides.

Elecampane, large-leaved, Old World perennial plant naturalized as a weed in NE United States and E Canada. A hairy plant, it has yellow, daisylike flowers. Height: to 5ft (1.5m). Family Compositae; species *Inula helenium.*

Elections, selection of candidates for public office through voting. In modern times, the electoral process, with its choice of competing candidates, popular enfranchisement, and use of the secret ballot has become an integral part of democracy. The electoral tradition dates back to the Greek city-states of the 5th and 6th centuries BC. The US Constitution granted the right to hold elections, delegating to the states responsibility for establishing methods. Though the right to vote was originally a function of owning property, a requirement often accompanied by age, sex, and sometimes religious restrictions, enfranchisement has been gradually extended to the general populace through passage of constitutional amendments. Nondemocratic societies utilize elections as a rubber stamp for their policies without offering voters any true choice among alternative candidates. △902, 904, 1396.

Electoral College, method outlined by the US Constitution for the indirect selection of the president and vice-president. The Electoral College is composed of representatives from the states. Each state has the same number of electors as it has US representatives and senators, and each slate of electors is pledged to a presidential and vice presidential candidate. Voters in each state select the slate of electors that represents the candidate of their choice. Each state's chosen slate then votes for the president and vice president. In modern practice, the candidate with a plurality of votes in each state receives all that state's electoral votes. If one party's candidates have not received a majority of the elector's votes, the election is decided in the House of Representatives. △1398.

Electra (*c.* 418–414 BC), tragedy by Sophocles. The heroine, Electra, helps her brother Orestes avenge their father Agamemnon's death by plotting to kill their mother Clytemnestra and stepfather Aegisthus. There is controversy as to the accuracy and originality of this play. Euripides wrote a similar play with the same title in 413 BC.

Electra Complex. *See* Oedipus Complex.

Electrical Capacity. *See* Capacitance.

Electrical Circuit, the path provided for an electrical current, composed of conductors and conducting devices and including a source of electromotive force that drives the current around the circuit. Current flows according to several definite laws of which the most important is Ohm's Law. *See also* Ohm's Law. △1532, 1542, 1650.

Electrical Generators. △1542.

Electrical Outlet. △1650.

Electrical Panel Box. △1650.

Electrical Stimulation of the Brain, research technique in which a minute electrical current is applied to a small area of the brain via ultrafine electrodes which may be permanently implanted in an animal's skull. If stimulation of a portion of the brain causes a particular behavior, it is assumed that that portion helps control this behavior. △666.

Electrical Switch. △1532, 1650.

Electric Automobile, vehicle powered by electricity supplied by storage batteries. Displaced by automobiles with gasoline engines after the 1920s, it generated interest again during the fuel shortage of the 1970s. It is still considered impractical, however, owing to its relatively short traveling radius between recharges and its low speed. △1092, 1698.

Electric Current. *See* Current, Electric.

Electric Eel, freshwater tropical fish found in South America. Not a true eel, its ribbonlike body is dark brown to black and bordered by an anal fin extending along its underside. It breathes air at water surface. Electric organs make up 80% of its body and produce charges up to 650 volts. Length: 9.5ft (2.9m). Family Electrophoridae (also called Gymnotidae); species *Electrophorus electricus.* △514.

Electric Field, or electrostatic field, region surrounding an electric charge in which a force would be experienced by another charged particle. The force is attractive if the charges differ in polarity and repulsive if they are the same. The strength of the field *(E)* upon unit charge at a distance *r* from a charge *Q* is equal to $Q/4\pi r^2\mathbf{E}$, where **E** is the permittivity. △1544.

Electric Fish, freshwater tropical fish with electric organs for generating high voltages. The knifefish found in N South America are long, thin, and have a long rippling anal fin. Family: Gymnotidae; species include banded *Gymnotus carapo.* The electric catfish native to tropical Africa is pinkish with black spots. Length: to 4ft (1.2m); weight: 50lb (22.5kg). Family Malapteruridae; species *Malapterurus electricus. See also* Electric Eel. △514, 618.

Electric Flux, quantity of electricity displaced across an area in a dielectric medium, expressed as the product of the area and the component of the electric vector at right angles to the area.

Electric Furnace, enclosure heated by electric current. Electric furnaces are used for melting and producing metals, alloy steels, and refractory materials. Three main methods of heating are used: striking an arc between electrodes in the furnace; inducing eddy currents in the material to be melted by an alternating magnetic field; and by passing a high current through the material, heat being produced by the resistance. △1594.

Electricity, the form of energy associated with static or moving electric charges. No explanation can be given of the nature of an electric charge, the study of electricity being concerned with the properties of matter that is so charged. Charge exists in two forms, called for convenience positive and negative. The basic unit of negative electric charge is the electron; the proton and the positron are positively charged to an equal but opposite extent. The electron and the proton are the charged components of atoms, so that an atom containing equal numbers of electrons and protons is electrically neutral, whereas an excess of either will cause the atom concerned to be charged—negatively if the electrons are in excess and positively if the protons are in excess.

Electrostatics is concerned with the properties of charges at rest, largely with the forces that exist between charges. It is an observed fact, for which there is no explanation, that like charges repel each other, whereas there is a force of attraction between unlike charges. The region surrounding a charge, within which these forces act, is called an electric field. Electric charges are also acted upon by forces when they move in a magnetic field and a flow of charged particles creates its own magnetic field. Electricity and magnetism are, in fact, different aspects of the same phenomenon, known as electromagnetism.

Current electricity, the form of electricity that is supplied by power stations, consists of a flow of charged particles. In metal atoms the outer electrons are not tightly bound to the rest of the atom; they are therefore free to flow through a metal wire when acted upon by an electromotive force. A current of one ampere consists of a flow in one direction of some six million million million electrons in one second. △1486, 1530, 1536, 1540–46.

Electric Light Bulb. △1486.

Electric Meter. △1650, 1818.

Electric Motor, an electric rotating machine that converts electrical energy into mechanical energy by the interaction of a magnetic field with an electric field. Electric motors are convenient, economical, safe, free from smoke and odor, comparatively quiet, and have replaced most other motive power in industry, farms, and homes when there is a convenient source of electricity. Electric motors may be alternating current (induction, synchronous, and repulsion) or direct current (self-exciting, compound, shunt series, and universal). △1486, 1532, 1540, 1584.

Electric Organ, specialized organ in some fish that is composed of electroplaques and produces, stores, and emits electricity. *See also* Bioelectricity. △514.

Electric Process, or Arc Furnace Process, in steel production, a method for producing steel using electricity as the source of heat. This produces very high temperatures necessary for melting. Carbon electrodes produce electric arcs that strike into the metal bath. The use of three arcs to produce heat in three phases is in general use.

Electric Ray. *See* Torpedo Ray.

Electric Shock, in First Aid. △758.

Electrocardiogram (ECG), a graphic tracing of the electric current generated by the heart muscle during a heartbeat, used to determine abnormality. It is made by applying electrodes to various parts of the body to lead off the heart current to the recording instrument. After electrodes are in place, a millivolt from an outside source is introduced. Computerized electrocardiograms are now in use in most large hospitals.

Electrochemical Cells. *See* Cells, Electrochemical.

Electrochemical Equivalent, number of grams of a given element liberated or deposited from ions in electrolysis by passage of one coulomb of electricity.

Electrochemical Machinery (ECM). △1606.

Electrochemical Series. *See* Electromotive Series.

Electrochemistry, branch of physical chemistry concerned with electrolytes. It includes such topics as the ionization of acids and bases, the properties and reactions of ions in solution, the conductivity of electrolytes, and the study of the processes occurring in electrochemical cells and electrolysis. △1506, 1566.

Electroconvulsive Therapy (ECT), electrical stimulation of the brain leading to convulsions; used primarily in treating some emotional disturbances. When current is applied, the individual immediately loses consciousness, his body becomes rigid, and his breathing stops for a few seconds. Then a brief period of muscular convulsions occurs. After treatment, the individual has a temporary memory loss and may be confused. Three to eight treatments are often sufficient to break through a severe depression. △770.

Electrocurrents. △1566.

Electrode. △1484, 1554, 1566.

Electrodialysis. *See* Dialysis. △1562.

Electrodynamics, a branch of physics concerned with the motion of electrically charged particles and their effects upon each other.

Electroencephalography, study of the electrical activity of the brain by means of an electroencephalograph (EEG). This consists of a number of electrodes, which can be attached to the scalp to pick up the tiny oscillating currents produced by brain activity; a high-gain amplifier; and a means of recording the brain waves detected as a continuous trace on a paper strip. Interpretation of these waves, which have frequencies between about 8 and 25 hertz, requires great skill. The instrument is used in brain research and in the diagnosis of epilepsy and some other brain diseases. △820.

Electrolysis, chemical reaction caused by passing an electric current through a conducting liquid (electrolyte). The reaction is the result of transfer of electrons at the electrode surfaces. For instance, in electrolysis of dilute acids, hydrogen ions gain electrodes at the cathode: $H^+ + e \rightarrow H$; $2H \rightarrow H_2$. At the anode hydroxide ions lose electrons: $OH - e \rightarrow OH$; $2OH \rightarrow H_2O + O$; $2O - O_2$. The acid becomes more concentrated, the overall reaction being $2H_2O \rightarrow 2H_2 + O_2$. The type of electron-transfer reaction occurring depends on the electrode potentials of ions present, and the electrode material may play a part in the reaction. For example, in electrolysis of copper salts with a copper anode, atoms of the electrode ionize and enter into solution: $Cu \rightarrow Cu^{2+} + 2e$. Electrolysis is an important method of obtaining chemicals, particularly extracting reactive elements such as sodium, potassium, magnesium, aluminum, and chlorine. △1554, 1566.

Electrolyte, liquid that can conduct electricity. In electrolytes the current is carried by positive and negative ions rather than by electrons. These are present in fused ionic compounds, in solutions of ionic compounds, or in solutions of acids and bases, which dissociate into ions. △1566.

Electrolytic Solution, solution that is an electrolyte, that is, a conductor of electricity. Water itself is a relatively poor conductor but its conductivity is increased by adding ionic compounds. Thus, a solution of sodium chloride contains sodium ions (Na^+) and chloride ions (Cl^-), which transport the current. Covalent acids and bases also form electrolytic solutions in water by dissociating into ions: for example, $HCl \rightarrow H^+ + Cl^-$. △1566.

Electromagnet. *See* Magnetism.

Electromagnetic Clutch. △1538.

Electromagnetic Field. △1484.

Electromagnetic Induction. *See* Induction.

Electromagnetic Interaction of Molecules. △1484.

Electromagnetic Radiators. △1802, 1794.

Electromagnetic Spectrum, distribution of different types of electromagnetic waves with regard to frequency or wavelength, ranging from low-frequency (high-wavelength) radio waves, through infrared (heat) waves, light, ultraviolet waves, X rays, to very-high-frequency (very-low-wave-length) gamma rays. *See also* Electromagnetic Wave. △1526.

Electromagnetic Wave, wave of energy composed of electric and magnetic fields vibrating sinusoidally at right angles to each other and to the direction of motion; it is thus a transverse wave. The waves travel in free space at a constant speed of 186,282 mi (299,792.5 kilometers) per second (speed of light), which is reduced when traveling through a more dense medium, such as air or glass. The properties of the waves depend on their frequency, the electromagnetic spectrum extending from low-frequency radio waves, through infrared waves, light, ultraviolet waves, X rays, and high-frequency gamma rays. All these waves are produced, basically, by the acceleration of charged particles. The higher-frequency waves result from transitions between energy levels in the nucleus (gamma rays) or atom (X rays, ultraviolet, light, infrared). Radio waves are produced by the acceleration of free electrons. Electromagnetic waves can undergo reflection, refraction, interference, diffraction, and polarization. Other phenomena, such as the absorption or emission of light, can only be explained by assuming the radiation to be comprised of quanta of energy rather than waves. *See also* Quantum Theory. △1520.

Electrometallurgy, a branch of metallurgy dealing with the application of electric current for the extraction or refining of metals. The raw ore is subjected to an electric current that causes the metal to be deposited at the positive pole in a process known as electrowinning. Some ores require leaching with aqueous solution before being electrolyzed; others do not. Electroplating is a process in which metals are deposited on a base of less valuable metal, as in silver plating. The operation of the electric furnace in the manufacture of steel and the refining of other metals is also called electrometallurgy. △1540, 1566.

Electrometer. △1568.

Electromotive Force (e.m.f.), the sum of the potential differences in a circuit. It is equal to the energy liberated when unit charge passes completely around the circuit in the direction of the resultant e.m.f. △1532, 1536, 1542, 1548.

Electromotive Series, series of chemical elements arranged vertically in decreasing order of their electrode potential. The series illustrates the relative tendencies of metals to form positive ions in solution, the more electropositive metals being higher up the series. For example, metals higher than hydrogen displace hydrogen from acids by reactions of the type $Ca + 2H^+ \rightarrow Ca^{2+} + H_2$. The series is also called the electrochemical series, especially in the context of relative abilities of elements to form ions in chemical reactions. △1566.

Electron, stable lightest elementary particle (symbol e) with negative charge, mass 9×10^{-31} kg (1/1836 that of the proton), and spin ½. Discovered by J. J. Thomson (1897), electrons are constituents of matter, moving around the nucleus in complex orbits. Their total charge balances that of the protons in the nucleus of a neutral atom. Removal or addition of an atomic electron produces a charged ion. Chemical bonds are formed by the transfer or sharing of electrons between atoms. When not bound to an atom they are responsible for electrical conduction. Beams of electrons are used in several electronic devices, such as TV tubes. High-energy beams, from particle accelerators, are used in nuclear research. *See also* Beta Rays; Current, Electric; Electron Emission; Lepton. △1480, 1484, 1530, 1548.

Electron Beam Machining. △1606.

Electron Configuration. *See* Configuration, Electron.

Electron Emission, liberation of electrons from the surface of a substance. It can occur as a result of the effect on the substance of heat (thermionic emission), light (photoelectric emission), high electric field (field emission), bombardment by ions or other electrons (secondary emission), or it may result from radioactive decay. In all cases, the electrons must acquire energy from the outside source in excess of the work function of the substance. Most electron and cathode-ray tubes depend on thermionic emission, while photoelectric cells rely on photoelectric emission. Field emission is important in the field-emission microscope and secondary emission is the principle behind electron multipliers and storage tubes. *See also* Radioactivity. △1546–48.

Electronic Circuits, numbers of electronic components wired together to form a unit capable of performing some function, such as detection or amplification of a signal or acting as a gate in a logic circuit. The components commonly used in electronic circuits are resistors, capacitors, inductors, and transformers in conjunction with electron tubes or semiconductor devices. For most purposes semiconductor devices have replaced electron tubes and wiring between components is largely by printed circuits in which the components are soldered to a board on which connections are made by a copper conducting film; a photographic mask is used to coat the part of the film required for interconnections, the unprotected metal being removed by etching. Double-sided printed circuits are in common use, in which both sides of the board have a circuit printed on them. *See also* Integrated Circuits. △1546–48.

Electronic Computer. *See* Computer, Electronic.

Electronic Control Systems, a control system based on an electronic circuit. Complex control systems rely upon computers, the control functions are then carried out by logic circuits. These circuits consist of gates, which give a high output current when the input currents conform to a predetermined pattern. For example, an AND gate gives a high output when all the inputs are simultaneously high. *See also* Control Systems. △1670.

Electronic Data Processing (EDP), a method of selecting and sorting a wide range of information through the use of punched cards or an electronic digital computer. The computer is far faster than cards, but requires human instruction, called programming. △1674.

Electronic Music, music produced by electronic devices rather than by traditional instruments. Such music may simply reflect the fact that a musical performer is playing an instrument that uses electronic resonators to produce the sound (as in an electric organ), or may be an entire composition artificially produced on tape or by a computer. A number of new electronic instruments have been invented in the 20th century including the Ondes Martenot, the Theremin, and the Moog Synthesizer. Some composers who have composed new works entirely out of electronically-produced sounds include Karkheinz Stockhausen, Morton Subotnick, and Vladimir Ussachevsky. △1364.

Electronics, study and use of circuits based on the conduction of electricity through electron tubes and semiconducting devices. The science began with the discovery in 1887 by Heinrich Hertz (1857–94) of radio waves, but was unable to progress far until J. J. Thomson (1856–1940) discovered the electron in 1897. This enabled John Fleming (1849–1945) to invent the diode electron tube, which was modified into the triode by Lee De Forest (1873–1961) in 1907. These devices, with further modifications and improvements, provided the basic components for all the electronics of radio, TV, and radar until the end of World War II.

A major revolution occurred in 1948 when a team at Bell Telephone Laboratories, led by William Shock-

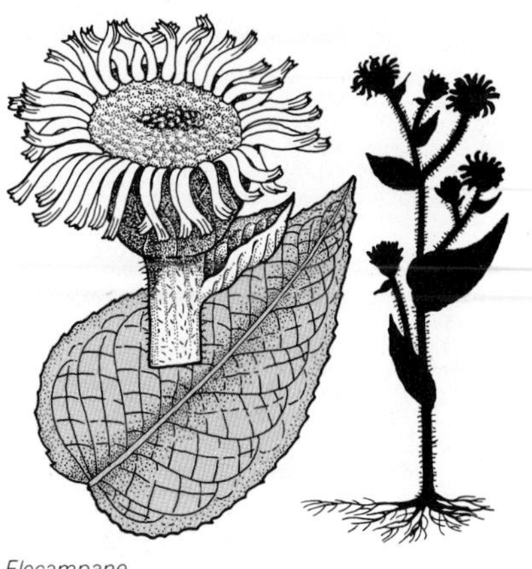

Elecampane

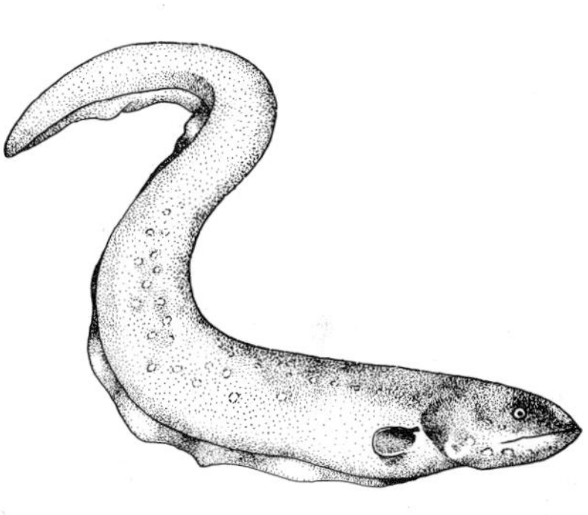

Electric eel

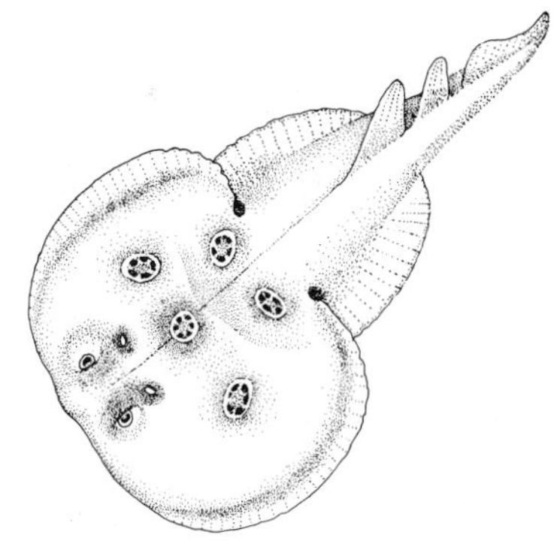

Electric fish

Electric furnace process

ley, produced the first semiconducting transistor. Semiconductor devices are much lighter, smaller, and reliable than vacuum tubes; moreover they do not require a high operating voltage and they lend themselves to microminiaturization in the form of integrated circuits. These characteristics have enabled electronic computers and automatic control devices to change the face of both industry and scientific research; they have also enabled man to walk on the moon.

The idea of a computer was first proposed by the 19th-century British mathematician, Charles Babbage (1792–1871). The first large electronic computer (ENIAC) was built at the University of Pennsylvania, during World War II, using 18,000 electron tubes. Modern computers contain up to 80,000 transistors and are considerably smaller than ENIAC. △1546–48, 1668.

Electronic Video Recording (EVR). △1800.

Electron Microscope, type of microscope that uses a beam of electrons instead of light to illuminate the object. The electron beam is produced by electron emission using an electron gun and is focused by a magnetic or electrostatic lens. It is directed onto the sample, the emerging electrons being focused by a second magnetic lens onto a fluorescent screen, which can be photographed. By accelerating the electrons to 100 keV a resolution of about half a millionth of a millimeter can be obtained. The transmission microscope produces a two-dimensional image and requires a very thin sample; the scanning microscope can produce a three-dimensional image. △1506.

Electron Tube, electronic device consisting of a system of electrodes arranged within an evacuated glass tube; for special purposes a gas at low pressure may be introduced into the tube. The diode, used for rectification, consists of a negative cathode, which emits electrons when heated (either directly or indirectly by a separate heater filament), and a positive anode or plate. The triode, used for amplification, has a perforated control grid situated between the cathode and the anode; a signal fed to the grid will provide an amplified signal at the anode. A tetrode has an extra electrode (screen grid) and a pentode has a fifth electrode (suppressor) between the grid and the anode. Electron tubes have been largely replaced by transistors and other semiconductor devices. △1548.

Electron Volt, unit of energy (symbol ev) equal to the energy acquired by an electron in falling freely through a potential difference of one volt. It is equal to 1.602×10^{-19} joule.

Electrophoresis, movement of electrically charged particles in a fluid under the influence of an applied electric field. Positive sols, such as metallic oxides or hydroxides, migrate to the cathode, and negative sols (metals, metallic sulfides) to the anode. Bacteria, viruses, and especially proteins may be separated, analyzed, and purified by electrophoresis.

Electroplating, deposition of a coating of one metal on another by making the object to be coated the cathode in an electrolytic cell. Positive ions in the electrolyte are discharged at the cathode and deposited as metal ($M^+ + e \rightarrow M$). Electroplating is used to produce a decorative or corrosion-resistant layer, as in silver-plated tableware, chromium-plated automobile parts, and nickel-plated steel. △1542, 1566.

Electroscope, instrument for detecting the presence of an electric charge. The commonest device is the gold-leaf electroscope in which two gold leaves hang from an insulating support. A charge applied to the support causes the leaves to separate. △1790.

Electrostatic Cleaner, or precipitator, an air-cleaning device that employs an ionization field that imparts a positive charge to particles in the air. The particles pass between charged metal plates and are precipitated onto them.

Electrostatic Field. *See* Electric Field.

Electrostatic Generator. *See* Van de Graaff Generator.

Electrostatic Induction. *See* Induction.

Elegiac Tradition, a literary form that originated in Greece in the 7th century BC. In classical literature, the term referred to poetry written in elegiac couplets and concerning themes such as war, friendship, and death. In modern usage, poems written in the elegiac tradition need not follow a prescribed metrical pattern, but generally deal with the subject of death.

Element, substance that cannot be split into simpler substances. All atoms of a given element have the same atomic number, and thus the same number of electrons—the factor determining chemical behavior. The atoms can have different mass numbers and, in general, a natural sample of an element is a mixture of isotopes. At present the known elements range from hydrogen (at. no. 1) to the highly unstable, element 106. They have a striking variation in distribution. Hydrogen and helium are the most common elements in the universe; oxygen and silicon are most common in the earth's crust. Technetium, astatine, promethium, and all elements of atomic number greater than 93 are not found in the earth's crust at all, being radioactive elements made artificially. *See also* Periodic Table. △1552, 1556.

Element 104, element with atomic number 104, first claimed in 1964 by a Soviet team at the Joint Institute for Nuclear Research at Dubna. They obtained the isotope of mass number 260 (half-life 1.5 seconds) by bombarding plutonium with neon ions. The element was named Kurchatorium after Igor Vasilevich Kurchatov, the former head of Soviet nuclear research. Later, in 1969, Albert Ghiorso and a team at Berkley, California, obtained the isotope with mass number 257 (half-life 4–5 seconds) by bombarding californium with carbon nuclei. They proposed the name Rutherfordium after the New Zealand physicist, Ernest Rutherford.

Element 105, element with mass number 105, first reported by a Soviet team at the Joint Institute for Nuclear Research at Dubna. They claimed the isotopes of mass numbers 260 and 261, as a result of bombarding americium with neon ions. In 1970 the team at Berkley, California, led by Albert Ghiorso, reported the isotope 260 (half-life 1.6 seconds) obtained by bombarding californium with nitrogen nuclei. The Soviet team has suggested the name Nielsbohrium, after Niels Bohr, and the Americans have suggested Hahnium, after Otto Hahn.

Elementary Particles and Antiparticles, bodies of matter that cannot be or have not been subdivided and are thus the basic constituents of matter. They are distinguished from each other by their mass (usually expressed in equivalent energy units) and a set of quantum numbers, including charge and spin. Except for the photon, they can be classified by their nuclear interactions into hadrons (mesons and baryons), which are subject to the strong interaction, and leptons, which are subject to the weak interaction. Charged particles also experience electromagnetic interaction. Each elementary particle has an associated antiparticle, which has the same mass and a charge, baryon number, and strangeness equal in magnitude but opposite in sign. Of the large number of particles known, most of which have been discovered in the last 25 years, only the proton, electron, neutrino, photon, neutron (when in a nucleus), and their antiparticles are stable. The others break up (decay) after a characteristic time (lifetime) to form stable particles. When an elementary particle collides with its own antiparticle, mutual annihilation occurs with the production of radiant energy and, at high energies, particle-antiparticle pairs. Particles are studied by their high-energy reactions produced in particle accelerators and by cosmic rays. *See also* Quark. △1484.

Elementary School, school that provides primary or basic education, starting with 1st grade. In many systems the elementary school runs through 8th grade, but students may move to a middle school in 5th or 6th grade or to a junior high school in 7th grade.

Elementary Subparticles. *See* Subparticles, Elementary.

Elephant, largest land animal, found in Africa and India. They are herbivorous mammals distinguished by their long tusks and trunk. The tusks are elongated upper incisors, sometimes over 11ft (3.4m) long. The flexible, grasping trunk is an elongated muscular nose and upper lip; at the tip are nostrils and one or two fingerlike extremities for picking up small objects. Elephants have poor vision and fair hearing, but their senses of smell, touch, and balance are acute. Intelligent animals with complex emotions and definite personalities, they are gregarious, show concern for fellow herd members, and are easily trained to perform complex tasks. Adults have no enemies besides man. Average lifespan in captivity is 60 years. The largest is the African bush elephant *(Loxodonta africana)*. The African forest *(L. cyclotis)* is the smallest and the Indian or Asian *(Elephas maximus* or *E. indicus)* is intermediate. Elephants are only living members of mammal order Proboscidea; extinct members are mammoths and mastodons. Height: to 13ft (4m) at shoulder; weight: over 6ton. △540, 548.

Elephant Bird, large, flightless bird of Madagascar that became extinct 1,000,000 years ago. Ostrich-like, it had large legs but small vestigial wings. Its eggs—the largest single cells known—measured up to 13×9.5in (33×24cm). Height: to 10ft (3m); weight: to 1,000lb (450kg). Family: Aepyornithidae.

Elephant Fish. *See* Chimaera.

Elephantiasis, disease caused by parasitic invasion of lymph channels, with swelling of legs, and external genitals, and thickening and fissuring of skin. △732.

Elephantine, island in S Egypt, in Nile River below Aswan Dam; site of many ancient ruins, most notable are the Elephantine papyri, describing a Jewish colony (*c.* 5th century BC), and the Nilometer, dating from Ptolemic era, used to measure depth of the Nile.

Elephant Seal, largest seal, breeds on S California coast and in sub Antarctic regions. Named for its large size and elephantlike trunk. N species *Mirounga angustirostris;* more numerous S species *Mirounga leonina.*

Elephant's-foot, or Hottentot's bread, tropical climbing vine native to S Africa. Its tuberous roots are edible. Length: 10ft (3m). Family Dioscoreaceae; species *Dioscorea elephantipes.*

Elephant Shrew, any of about 20 species of small insect-eating African mammals. They have long, pointy snouts, long tails, and powerful hind legs. Length: 3.5–12.5in (89–318mm). Family Macroscelididae. *See also* Insectivore.

Eleusinian Mysteries, religious rites performed at Eleusis, Attica, in ancient Greece to honor the myth of Demeter (goddess of harvest) and Persephone. Based on the cyclical changes of the seasons, hopes for fruitful harvest, and the promise of salvation, the lesser mysteries were held around February and the greater at the end of September or beginning of October to coincide with the sowing of the harvest—the symbolic reunion of the corn-mother (Demeter) and the corn-maiden (Persephone) after Persephone's stay in the underworld with Pluto (which coincided with the storage of the harvest underground). The ceremony concluded with the showing of an ear of corn. At first only citizens of Attica were allowed to be initiates, or "seers;" later all Greeks and Romans, except criminals, could participate. The mysteries were finally ended by Roman Emperor Theodosius in the 4th century AD.

Eleuthera Island, central Bahama Islands, E of New Providence Island; site of US missile tracking station. Industries: tomatoes, pineapples, dairy products. Colonized by British 1647. Area: 164sq mi (425sq km). Pop. 7,247.

Eleutheria, an ancient Greek festival commemorative of deliverance from the Persian armies. It was instituted after the Battle of Plataea (479 BC), in which the Greeks defeated the Persians under Mardonius.

Elevator, a car or platform used for vertical transportation of passengers or freight to different levels of a building. The car or platform travels in vertical guides in a shaft or hoistway. Powered mechanisms regulate hoisting and lowering. Modern elevators in large buildings utilize computers for scheduling and traffic problems, making operation completely automatic. Some elevators can travel 1800ft (550m) per minute. In 1853 Elisha G. Otis exhibited what is considered the first modern elevator in the Crystal Palace at the New York World's Fair. A mechanical elevator, it featured automatic braking in the event that the hoisting mechanism failed. The first successful electric elevator appeared in 1889.

Elevator, Grain. *See* Grain Elevator.

Elfbrandt v. Russel (1966), US Supreme Court case declaring a state statute requiring a loyalty oath of all public servants to be unconstitutional. The court held the state could not punish for mere membership in an unpopular group or organization.

Elf Owl, smallest owl, found only in the SW United States and Mexico. It and its slightly larger European counterpart, the little owl *(Athene noctua)*, feed mainly on insects. Length: about 6in (15cm). Species *Micrathene whitneyi. See also* Owl.

Elgar, Edward (1857–1934), English romantic composer. His *Pomp and Circumstance Marches* (1902–07) brought him fame. He composed a great deal of orchestral music, including two symphonies and the *Enigma Variations* (1899).

Elgin, city in NE Illinois, on the Fox River, 38mi (61km) WNW of Chicago. Elgin watches were first made here in the 19th century; site of Judson College and Elgin Community College (1949). Industries: tools, machinery, chemicals, dairy products. Founded 1835; inc. 1854. Pop. (1970) 55,961.

Elgin Marbles (5th century BC), group of classical Greek sculptures, including large portions of the friezes and the pediments of the Parthenon and one of the caryatids of the Erechtheum, both on the Acropolis in Athens. Collected by Lord Elgin, British ambassador to Turkey, they were sold to the British government in 1816 and are now on display in the British Museum, London. As the largest surviving group of classical Greek sculpture, they show the level of artistry of Greek sculptors and are essential to a stylistic understanding of the Parthenon.

El Giza (Al-Jizah) city in Egypt, on W bank of Nile; suburb of Cairo, close to pyramids and Sphinx. Industries: cotton, textiles, footwear, beer, motion pictures. Pop. 345,261.

Eli, biblical high priest at Shiloh who tutored young Samuel in service to God. The news of his sons' deaths and the capture of the Ark of the Covenant by the Philistines caused his death, passing the high priesthood back to the family of Eleazar.

Elijah, biblical Tishbite prophet and teacher of Elisha bent on destroying idolatry. He lived in poverty, performing miracles (eg raising the widow's son from the dead). He was fed by ravens in the wilderness and departed from earth in a whirlwind.

Eliot, Charles W(illiam) (1834–1926), US educator, b. Boston. As president of Harvard University (1869–1909), he encouraged the electives system and raised the standards for admission. He was also influential in the upgrading of secondary education in the United States. In 1909 he began editing the 50-volume Harvard Classics, an anthology of world literature.

Eliot, George (1819–80), English novelist whose real name was Marian Evans. Her romantic union with G.H. Lewes, whose wife was still living, created a major scandal. In 1851 she joined the editorial staff of the *Westminster Review*. Early and well known novels, all realistic works about the problems of middle class people, include *Adam Bede* (1859), *The Mill on the Floss* (1860), and *Silas Marner* (1861). *Middlemarch* (1872) is often considered her best work.

Eliot, John (1604–90), early American missionary, b. England. He came to Massachusetts (1631), the first Christian missionary to the American Indians of New England. He became known as the "Apostle of the Indians" for his evangelistic work, including the founding of a village of American Indian Christian converts near Boston (1651), the first of 14 such villages set up by 1674.

Eliot, T(homas) S(tearns) (1888–1965), British poet and critic, b. St. Louis, Mo. He moved to England in 1914 and became a British citizen in 1927, the same year he converted to Anglo-Catholicism. He found early encouragement for his poetry in fellow expatriate Ezra Pound. After the successful reception of his first published poem, *The Love Song of J. Alfred Prufrock* (1917), he devoted the rest of his life to literature as a poet, playwright, critic, and editor. *The Waste Land* (1922) created a literary sensation with its unique, complex language utilizing literary allusions and mythical and religious symbolism to descry the emptiness of contemporary life. Later poems, notably *Ash Wednesday* (1930) and the *Four Quartets* (1935–42) held out hope through religious faith. Of his five plays in verse, *Murder in the Cathedral* (1935), his first, was the most successful. His critical works, including *The Sacred Woods* (1920), *The Use of Poetry and the Use of Criticism* (1933), and *Elizabethan Essays* (1934), did much to revive interest in earlier poetry and to raise the scholarly standards of 20th century criticism. In 1948 he was awarded the Nobel Prize for literature. △1420.

Elisha, biblical prophet of Israel. A disciple of Elijah, he annointed Jehu king over Israel, fulfilling the curse on Ahab.

Elizabeth, in the New Testament, wife of Zacharias and mother of John the Baptist. She was related to Mary, mother of Jesus.

Elizabeth (1709–62), czarina of Russia (1741–62). She was the daughter of Peter the Great and was herself a great patron of the arts. The University of Moscow and the Academy of Fine Arts were founded in her reign and a number of baroque churches and palaces were built. She conducted a war against Sweden (1741–43) and annexed the southern portion of Finland (1743). She never married and was succeeded by her nephew, Peter III.

Elizabeth, in full, Elizabeth Amalie Eugenie (1837–98), Bavarian-born empress of Austria, also queen of Hungary from 1867. Married to the young emperor Francis Joseph I of Austria in 1854, she was very popular with her subjects but led an uneasy private life. She was stunned by her son's suicide in 1889 and was murdered in Genoa by an Italian anarchist nine years later.

Elizabeth I (1533–1603), queen of England (1558–1603), the daughter of Henry VIII and Anne Boleyn. On her accession she reestablished Protestantism by the Acts of Supremacy and Uniformity (1559); Despite their relatively tolerant administration, Roman Catholic discontent led to the Rising of the Northern Earls (1569–70), the Ridolfi Plot (1571), and to subsequent plots in favor of Mary, Queen of Scots, the Roman Catholic claimant to the succession. As a threat to Elizabeth, Mary was eventually executed (1587). Refusing to marry, Elizabeth directed her foreign policy towards weakening the main Roman Catholic powers, France and Spain, without provoking war. But in 1587 war with Spain broke out and despite the defeat of the Armada in 1588 continued throughout her reign. Her last years were marked by financial difficulties and by the rebellion of the Earl of Essex. In addition to her own shrewdness and strength of character, Elizabeth had competent counselors, such as William Cecil, Lord Burghley, and her reign saw the rise of England as a major European naval power. Commerce and industry grew, and colonization began. The arts also flourished, particularly the theater, poetry, and architecture. △1158.

Elizabeth (1900–), queen consort of George VI of Great Britain. She was Lady Elizabeth Bowes-Lyon until her marriage (1923). Her children were Elizabeth, Queen of England, and Margaret, Countess of Snowdon.

Elizabeth II (1926–), queen of Great Britain, Northern Ireland, and the Commonwealth (1952–), daughter of George VI. She married (1947) Philip Mountbatten, Duke of Edinburgh, and they had four children, Charles, Anne, Andrew, and Edward. In World War II, she was a skilled truck driver and mechanic. She was crowned in 1953. She traveled extensively, particularly in the Commonwealth countries, and remained popular in Great Britain despite criticism of the institution of monarchy.

Elizabeth, city in NE New Jersey, on Newark Bay, 5mi (8km) S of Newark; seat of Union co; scene of many Revolutionary War battles, including Battle of Elizabethtown (1780) in which much of city was burned; site of Nathaniel Bonnell House (1682), and the 18th-century Boudinot House and Belcher mansion. Industries: sewing machines, chemicals, swimming pool equipment, biscuits. Settled 1664 on land purchased from Delaware Indians. Inc. 1855. Pop. (1970) 112,654.

Elizabethan Style, art style prevalent during Elizabeth I's reign in England (1558–1603). During this golden age of English prosperity and colonial expansion, the art produced reflected fierce patriotic love of all things English. Influenced by Netherlandish art rather than Italian, the style was vigorous, highly colored, naive in expression, stiff, direct, and lacking in grace.

Elizabethan Theater, drama that took place in England during the reign of Elizabeth I (1558–1603). Most often associated with William Shakespeare, Elizabethan drama combines two movements in Western art and thought: classical and medieval. Also drawing from native forms of folk drama, Elizabethan drama is characterized by a spiritual vitality and a belief, sometimes wavering, that the universe is benevolent, harmonious, and hierarchically ordered. Masters of the period are William Shakespeare (1564–1616) and Ben Jonson (*c.*1572–1637). △1148.

Elizabeth Farnese (1692–1766), queen of Spain, second wife of Philip V. Highly ambitious, she became the virtual ruler of Spain, plunging it into several wars. She was forced into retirement when her stepson Ferdinand VI became king but lived to see her own son Charles III crowned.

Elizabeth of Valois (1545–68), Spanish queen, married at an early age to King Philip II, although originally considered for Philip's unstable son, Carlos. She gave birth to two daughters and later became a figure of legend, in which she and Carlos were involved in an improbable, ill-fated love.

Elephant bird

Elephant seal

Elizabeth I

Elizabeth II

Elizabethville. *See* Lubumbashi.

El Kasserine. *See* Kasserine Pass.

El Khalil. *See* Hebron.

Elkhart, city in N Indiana, at the confluence of Elkhart and St Joseph's rivers. Industries: musical instruments, electrical equipment, mobile homes. Settled 1824; inc. 1877. Pop. (1970) 43,152.

Elkins, Stephen Benton (1841–1911), US senator, public official and industrialist, b. near New Lexington, Ohio. A Republican, he was elected to represent New Mexico in the Congress (1872). He later was appointed secretary of war (1891–93). While in the senate (1895–1911), he was joint author of the Mann-Elkins Act (1910) for railroad rate regulation, and author of the Mann (white-slave-traffic) Act (1910).

Elkins v. United States (1960), US Supreme Court decision in which the court ruled that illegally seized evidence could not be used in a federal prosecution. This rule strengthened the interpretation of the Fourth Amendment's prohibition of unreasonable searches and was soon adopted by the individual state courts.

Ellery, William (1727–1820), American patriot and a signer of the Declaration of Independence, b. Newport, R. I. He attended the Continental Congress (1776–81; 1783–85) and later served as Rhode Island's chief justice in 1785.

Ellesmere Island, ice-capped island of Canada, in Arctic Ocean, W of NW Greenland; 2nd largest and northernmost island of the Arctic Archipelago. The island's vegetation supports herds of musk oxen; site of many geological, glaciological, and geographical expeditions; Eskimo settlements. First sighted 1616 by William Baffin; not explored until late 19th century. Area: 82,119sq mi (212,688sq km).

Ellice Islands, coral island group in S Pacific Ocean, including Funafuti (principal city, site of government offices), Nanumea, Nonumanga, Nui, Niutao, Vaitupu, Nukufetau, Nukulaelae, and Niulakita; part of British Gilbert and Ellice island colony since 1915. The United States claims sovereignity over Funafuti and the latter three islands. Inhabitants are mostly Polynesian farmers and fishermen. Discovered 1764 by British Capt. John Byron. Area: approx. 10sq mi (26sq km). Pop. 6,332.

Ellington, (Edward) Duke (1899–1974), US jazz bandleader, pianist, and composer, b. Edward Ellington in Washington, D.C. One of the great figures of jazz history, he organized his first band in 1918 and continued as a great jazz bandleader through the 1970s, with many other great jazz musicians playing in his bands. He toured the world, made many recordings, and appeared in films. His many compositions include piano suites, classic jazz band arrangements, and many songs such as "Mood Indigo" (1930), "Caravan" (1937), and "I Got It Bad" (1941). △1366.

Ellipse, conic formed by cutting a right circular cone with a plane inclined at such an angle that the plane does not intersect the base of the cone. When the intersecting plane is parallel to the base, the ellipse becomes a circle. An ellipse is a conic with an eccentricity less than 1. In rectangular Cartesian coordinates its standard equation is $x^2/a^2 + y^2/b^2 = 1$. Two lines of symmetry can be drawn through the ellipse: the longer one is the major axis (length $2a$); the shorter is the minor axis (length $2b$). The area of an ellipse is πab. The ellipse has two foci on the major axis and one of its properties is that the sum of the distances from a point on the ellipse to the two foci is constant. △1454.

Elliptical Galaxy, type of regular galaxy having either a globular or lenticular structure and characterized by the absence of spiral arms. Graded E0 to E7 according to increasing ellipticity, elliptical galaxies consists of old stars free of gas and dust. *See also* Galaxy; Spiral Galaxy. △122.

Ellis, (Henry) Havelock (1859–1939), English psychologist and author. His seven-volume *Studies in the Psychology of Sex* (1897–1928) promoted the scientific study of sex. He was also a pioneer in the study of dreams and hallucinogenic drugs.

Ellis Island, island in New York harbor that served as chief US immigration station (1892–1943). Officials recorded arrivals here, often Americanizing names or giving immigrants entirely new names. Abandoned in 1954, it was proclaimed a National Historic Site (1965).

Ellison, Ralph (1914–), U.S. author, b. Oklahoma City. A short story writer and essayist, he won a National Book Award (1953) for his first novel, *Invisible Man* (1952). The book deals with the question of black identity in the U.S.

Ellora, Shrines of, a series of 34 rock temples cut from a hill in Maharashtra state, India (5th–10th century). They represent three religions: Buddhist, Hindu, and Jain. The Hindu Kailasa temple, dedicated to the god Siva, is the most magnificent.

Ellsworth, Lincoln (1880–1951), US polar explorer, b. Chicago. He financed the Norwegian explorer Roald Amundsen, the first person to reach the South Pole (1911) and made a successful dirigible flight with Amundsen from Spitzbergen over the North Pole to Alaska (1926). He explored vast regions of the Arctic Ocean (1931) and made the first flight over Antarctica (1935).

Ellsworth, Oliver (1745–1807), chief justice of the US Supreme Court (1796–99), b. Windsor, Conn. He served as a delegate to the Continental Congress (1777–84), on the Connecticut Governor's Council (1780–84), and as superior court judge (1785–89). He was prominent at the Constitutional Convention (1787) where he and Roger Sherman introduced the Connecticut Compromise, settling the controversy between large and small states over representation. He was also responsible for the term "United States" being used in the Constitution. He served as senator from Connecticut (1789–96), chaired the committee forming the federal judiciary. After serving as chief justice, he became commissioner to France (1799–1800). He served on the Connecticut Governor's Council (1803) and died before taking office of first chief justice of the new state supreme court.

Elm, hardy, deciduous trees of north-temperate zones, popular as shade trees. Suitable varieties include the American elm *(Ulmus americana),* English elm *(U. procera),* and Scotch elm *(U. glabra).* All are susceptible to the deadly Dutch elm disease. Height: over 100ft (30m). The smaller Chinese elm *(U. parvifolia)* and Siberian elm *(U. pumila)* are resistant to the disease. Family Ulmaceae. *See also* Dutch Elm Disease. △594.

Elmhurst, city in NE Illinois, 17mi (27km) W of Chicago's center; site of Elmhurst College (1871), and a large industrial park housing about 100 light industries. Settled 1843; inc. 1910. Pop. (1970) 48,887.

Elmira, city in S central New York, on Chemung River; seat of Chemung co; scene of signing of Treaty of Painted Post (1791); site of Confederate prison camp 1864–65, Elmira College (1853); home and burial place of Mark Twain. Industries: fire engines, iron, steel, food. Settled 1788; inc. 1864. Pop. (1970) 39,945.

Elmont, city in SE New York, on Long Island just E of borough of Queens; residential community with some light industry. Belmont Racetrack is nearby. Pop. (1970) 29,363.

El Monte, city in S California, 12mi (19km) E of Los Angeles; founded in 1852 by Santa Fe Trail pioneers. Industries: aerospace, electronic equipment, plastics. Inc. 1912. Pop. (1970) 69,852.

El Morro National Monument, historic site in W New Mexico, containing ruins of ancient pueblos and sandstone with carved inscriptions of Spanish explorers. Area: 1,279acres (518hectares). Est. 1906.

Elmwood Park, town in NE Illinois, on W edge of Chicago. Inc. 1914. Pop. (1970) 26,160.

El Paso, city and port of entry in extreme W Texas, across Rio Grande River from Ciudad Juárez, Mexico; seat of El Paso co. First visited in 1536 by Cabeza de Vaca; permanent settlement built by Juan María Ponce de León; site of University of Texas at El Paso (1913), scene of annual Sunbowl football game featured during the Sun Carnival (est 1901), Fort Bliss (founded 1848) headquarters of Army Air Defense Center. Industries: tourism, meat packing, clothing, copper refining and smelting, oil refining, food processing. Settled 1827; inc. 1873. Pop. (1970) 322,-261.

El Salvador, Republic of, nation in Central America, on the Pacific Ocean and bordered by Guatemala (W) and Honduras (N and E). The people are mixed Indian and Caucasian and mostly Roman Catholic.

Land and Economy. Two mountain ranges running E-W traverse the country creating valuable fertile upland plains. The climate is tropical, but the heat is modified by the elevation. The economy is primarily agricultural, relying especially on the coffee and sugar cane grown on the mountain slope plantations. Industrialization is progressing rapidly with many cotton textiles produced for export.

People. About 85% of the population is of mixed Indian and Caucasian stock with the majority employed in agriculture. Education is free, and literacy about 50%.

Government. El Salvador is a republic, with a president, elected every five years and ineligible for immediate reelection; a unicameral legislature, the National Assembly of Deputies, elected for two-year terms by popular vote; and a Supreme Court and lesser courts. There is universal suffrage at 18 years of age.

History. Spain took the country from the Indians in 1524 and established the first permanent settlement. El Salvador won its independence from Spain in 1821. Under Mexican control until 1823, when it became a member of the United Provinces of Central America, El Salvador regained its autonomy in 1839. Since that time political instability has been the keynote with frequent coups and revolutions and a rapid succession of presidents. Attempts to reunite the Central American nations were unsuccessful, although cooperation improved through the Organization of Central American States (1951) and a Central American common market (1959).

PROFILE

Official name: Republic of El Salvador
Area: 8,260sq mi (21,393sq km)
Population: 3,900,000
Density: 472per sq mi (182per sq km)
Chief cities: San Salvador (capital); Santa Ana
Government: Republic
Religion: Roman Catholic
Language: Spanish (official)
Monetary unit: Colon
Gross national product: $1,070,000,000
Per capita income: $300
Industries (major products): cotton textiles and yarn, footwear, cement
Agriculture (major products): coffee, sugar cane
Trading partners (major): United States, West Germany, Guatemala

Ely Cathedral. △1104.

Elyria, city in N Ohio, 23mi (37km) W of Cleveland on the Black River; seat of Lorain co; site of first secondary school W of Allegheny Mts (1830); International Society for Crippled Children founded here 1915. Industries: fittings, electric motors, chemicals, aircraft parts. Founded 1817; inc. 1892. Pop. (1970) 53,427.

Emancipation, Edict of (1861), declaration by Czar Alexander II of Russia that the serfs in that country were free and that serfdom was abolished. Under the edict the serfs were granted land in return for redemption payments to be paid by them to the former landowners over the next 49 years. In many ways the emancipation was unsuccessful. Often the amount of land the serfs received was insufficient to support them. Also, the commune in which they lived maintained control over a major portion of their lives. △1286.

Emancipation Proclamation, (1863) declaration by President Lincoln. In the early days of the Civil War, President Lincoln was urged by abolitionists to issue a law ending slavery. Lincoln, more anxious to save the Union than end slavery, waited until Union forces repelled the Confederates at Antietam, Md., in September 1862 before issuing the Emancipation Proclamation. It stated that, after Jan. 1, 1863, all slaves in the rebel states would be free. △1276.

Embargo Act (1807), act passed under President Jefferson to force England and France to remove restrictions on US trade. It prohibited ships from leaving the United States bound for any foreign ports but was a failure.

Embassy, headquarters of a diplomatic mission in a foreign country. It is the site where diplomatic business is conducted and also serves as an information center and usually the ambassadorial residence. *See also* Diplomatic Service; Extraterritoriality.

Embioptera. △492.

Embolism, blocking of a blood vessel usually by a clot, but also by a foreign body, gas bubble, or fat globule. Symptoms include coldness, numbness, tingling, severe pain. Anticoagulants and surgery are treatments. *See also* arteriosclerosis. △716.

Embourgeoisement, social theory developed in the 1950s to account for the disintegration of the Western working class's unique characteristics and its gradual assimilation into the middle class, or bourgeoisie. The economic shift from manufacturing to service industries contributed to this trend.

Embroidery, art of ornamenting textiles, fabrics, and other materials with needlework. Embroidery is not woven into a fabric but is sewn on an already finished cloth. About 300 different embroidery stitches exist, occurring in four categories: flat, looped, chained, and knotted stitches. From the time when needles were invented, whether a sharp fish bone, a thorn, a pointed stick, or a metal wire, the natural instinct seems to have been for man to decorate his utilitarian garments. The Bayeux Tapestry (11th century) is one of the most famous embroideries executed. Today crewel work (wool embroidery), needlepoint, and bargello are popular forms of embroidery.

Embryo. △700–02.

Embryology, biological study of the origin, development, and activities of an embryo. This science, in tracing the progression of events leading from an egg to an adult, follows the zygote through cleavage, morula stage, blastula stage, and gastrula stage when two and then three germ layers, precursors of body organs, appear. △700–02.

Emerald, variety of beryl, varying in color from light to deep green; highly valued as gemstone. Color due to small amounts of aluminum; stone may lose color when heated. Mined in Upper Egypt in 1650 BC; now found mainly in Colombia. Used as charm by ancients. *See also* Beryl. △244.

Emerald Dove. △538.

Emergency Powers of the President, inherent authority of the US president to act in times of national emergency. The definition and declaration of a national emergency is left to the president's discretion, although periods of foreign danger and economic depression are understood to fall into this category.

Emerson, Ralph Waldo (1803–82), US essayist and poet, a key figure in American thought and literature, b. Boston. After graduating from Harvard University (1821), he taught school, attended Harvard Divinity School (1825–26), and was a Unitarian minister in Boston (1829–32). Rejecting the formal structure of the church, he resigned his pastorate and went to Europe. There he met Thomas Carlyle, Samuel Taylor Coleridge, and William Wordsworth and became acquainted with German Romanticism. On his return to the United States he began giving lectures; many of these were published or were incorporated into his essays.

In 1835 he settled in Concord, Mass., becoming friends with Henry David Thoreau, Bronson Alcott, Margaret Fuller, and others of the Transcendentalist movement. Emerson's book *Nature* (1836) expressed the fundamental principles of Transcendental thought. Subsequent works included two series of *Essays* (1841, 1844); *Poems* (1846); *Representative Men* (1850), biographical essays; *English Traits* (1856), lectures given in England in 1847. *The Conduct of Life* (1860); *May-Day and Other Pieces* (1867), poetry; and *Society and Solitude* (1870). In these works Emerson preached his philosophy: belief in the soul; the unity of God with man and nature; self-reliance; and hope. *See also* Transcendentalism. △1374.

Emery, impure form of the mineral corundum, aluminum oxide, that occurs as dark granules with magnetite in them. An unusually hard mineral, it is used as an abrasive.

Emigration, leaving one's homeland to settle elsewhere. The 19th and early 20th centuries saw a great emigration to the United States. Fears and prejudice resulting from this movement led to passage of a quota system (1921). This was followed by the National Origins Act (1924), excluding Asians. The act was not reversed until 1965. △940, 1280, 1314.

Emilia-Romagna, region in N central Italy, bordering on Adriatic Sea; capital is Bologna; named for the ancient Aemilian Way (187 BC); contains good hydroelectric and transportation systems. Products: cereals, rice, vegetables, dairying. Industries: processed foods, tourism, motor vehicles, refined petroleum, chemicals. Area: 8,542sq mi (22,124sq km). Pop. 3,851,254.

Eminent Domain the power of the state to acquire private property for public use, without the owner's consent. Damages and due compensation for the property must be paid.

EMI Scanner. △750.

Emission, Electron. *See* Electron Emission.

Emission Spectrum. *See* Spectrum.

Emmanuel. For monarchs so named, *see* Manuel.

Emmet, Robert (1778–1803), Irish nationalist leader. In July 1803 he led an attack upon Dublin Castle, which was intended as a prelude to a French invasion to help his movement. He hoped to destroy the Act of Union (1801), which placed Ireland under the British Parliament. His plot failed, and he was arrested, tried, and executed. His speech upon sentencing, with the words "Let no man write my epitaph," inspired later Irish nationalists.

Emollient, an agent that softens or soothes the skin.

Emotion, human feeling involving complex mental and physical reactions. Emotions are associated with predictable physiological changes such as increased heart and breathing rates, sweating, dryness of the mouth, and trembling. Physiological studies have implicated the reticular formation in the brain as important for emotional changes: greater emotional intensity involves greater nervous activity in that part of the brain. Basic expressions of emotions, such as facial patterns of crying and smiling, appear to be unlearned. Other expressions are acquired from one's culture; eg, Americans register surprise by raising eyebrows and widening their eyes, while the Chinese register surprise by sticking out their tongues. △784, 788.

Empedocles, (490–430 BC), Greek philosopher. He attempted to harmonize the Eleatic concept of permanent being with the Heraclitean teaching of constant flux. Teaching the doctrine of the four elements: earth, water, air, and fire, he introduced the theory of value to account for the good and evil in the world. *See also* Eleaticism; Heraclitus.

Emperor Penguin. *See* Penguin.

Emphysema, accumulation of air in tissues, most often occurring in the lungs (pulmonary emphysema). Causes are unknown but air pollution and heavy smoking exacerbate the symptoms which include wheezing, cough, and shortness of breath. Treatment can include antibiotics, relief of spasms and secretion with inhalators, and ventilation exercises. △714.

Empire State Building. △1612.

Empire Style, neoclassical style in furniture and interior decoration which started in Paris after the French Revolution and spread throughout Europe. In England it corresponds to the Regency Style. In women's fashion it signified a high-waisted dress, embellished with embroidery.

Empiricism, from the Greek *empeiria* "experience," philosophical doctrine that experience is the only source of knowledge. Epicurus (341–270 BC) was one of the first empiricists. *See also* British Empiricism. △856, 858.

Emporia, city in E central Kansas, between Neosho and Cottonwood rivers; seat of Lyon co; site of Emporia College (1882) and Kansas State Teachers' College (1863). Industries: grain elevators, stockyards, printing equipment. Founded 1857; inc. 1870. Pop. (1970) 23,327.

Empyema, infection of the pleural cavity yielding large amounts of pus, usually secondary to a lung infection. Treatment includes antibiotics and drainage of the cavity.

Ems Dispatch (1870), final cause of the Franco-Prussian War in 1870. Alarmed at the candidacy for the Spanish throne of Prince Leopold, a relative of King William of Prussia, the French requested assurance of the permanence of Leopold's refusal. William declined, informing his prime minister, Otto von Bismarck, of the conversation, who in turn published an insulting version of the telegram and inflamed the French to war.

Ems River, river in West Germany; rises in Teutoburger Wald, NW West Germany and flows NW into North Sea near Emden. It is connected with Ruhr region by the Dortmund-Ems canal system. Length: 208mi (335km).

Emu, large, dark-plumed, flightless Australian bird. A strong runner with powerful legs, it lives in groups and feeds mostly on plant matter. Large greenish eggs (8–10) are incubated by the male in a scraped-ground

Duke Ellington

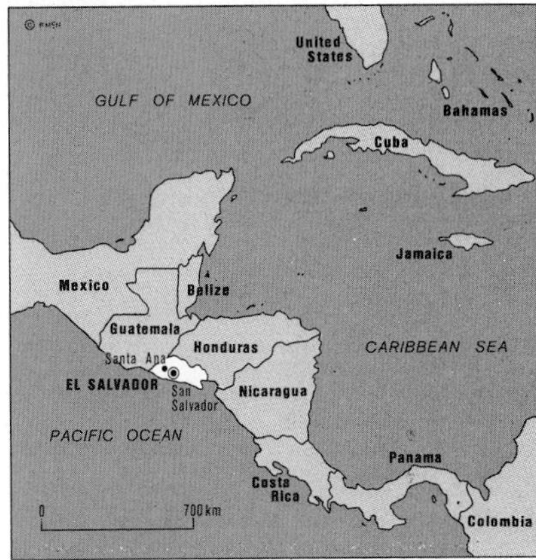
United States
GULF OF MEXICO
Bahamas
Cuba
Jamaica
Mexico
Belize
Guatemala
Santa Ana
Honduras
EL SALVADOR
San Salvador
Nicaragua
CARIBBEAN SEA
PACIFIC OCEAN
Panama
Costa Rica
Colombia
0
700km

El Salvador

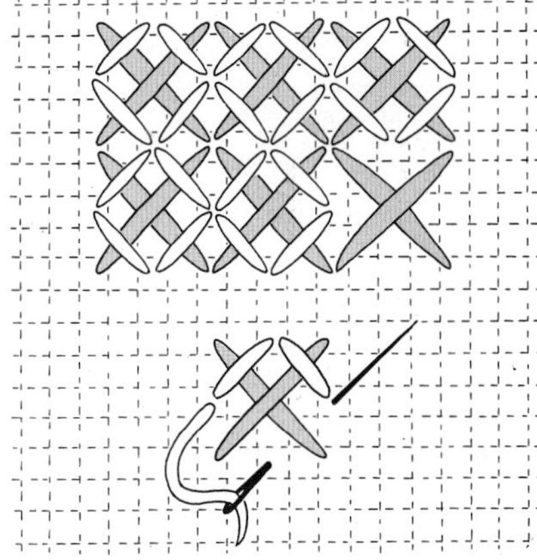

Embroidery

Ralph Waldo Emerson

nest. Height: 5ft (1.5m); weight: to 20lb (9kg). Species *Dromaius novaehollandiae.* △526, 590.

Emulsion, a mixture of liquids in which one is present in droplets of microscopic size. Emulsions may be formed spontaneously or by mechanical means if the liquids have no mutual solubility and they are stabilized by emulsifying agents. A familiar emulsion is milk (droplets of fat in an aqueous solution). △1504.

Enamel, paint that consists of zinc oxide and lithopone, brown linseed oil, and high-grade varnish. The finish is hard, glossy and highly durable. The term enamel paint is derived from its resemblance when dry to the finish found on glass-enamel products. It is not water soluble and must be thinned with turpentine or other spirit. △1812.

Enamel, Dental. △756.

Enamels, objects decorated with a vitreous glaze or combination of glazes, usually opaque, fused to a metallic, glass, or ceramic surface. The base of enamel is a clear, vitreous compound called flux, which is composed of silica, minium, and potash. The flux is colored by the addition of oxides of metals. The amount of acid in it regulates the density or opacity of the enamel. Pulverized enamel is carefully and evenly spread over those parts of the metal designed to receive it. The piece is then dried in front of a furnace, placed gently on a fireclay, and introduced carefully into the furnace. When the enamel shines all over it is withdrawn, a process that takes a few minutes. There are several different modes of enameling: champlevé, cloisonné, basse-taille, plique-à-jour, painted enamel, encrusted, and miniature-painted. These processes were used at different times in history. *See also* Cloisonné. △1608.

Encaustic Painting, painting technique in the ancient world and early Christian era, using pigments mixed with hot wax. The Mummy portraits from Fayoum (1st century BC to 3rd century AD) demonstrate the lively coloring, sculptural modeling, and excellent survival qualities of this art.

Enceladus, satellite of Saturn. △86.

Encephalitis, virus-caused disease of the brain and spinal cord usually epidemic, transferred from animal to man by insects. Similar to meningitis (bacterial infection), symptoms include fever, headache, vomiting, stiff neck and back, increasing to convulsions, hallucinations, and possible paralysis. Accurate diagnosis by analysis of spinal fluid is crucial to differentiate encephalitis from forms of meningitis treatable by antibiotics. Complete and spontaneous recovery is frequent; otherwise the symptoms are treated. *See also* Equine Encephalitis; Meningitis.

Encke, Johann Franz (1791–1865), German astronomer noted for his study and calculations of the movements of comets, including one which bears his name. Encke's comet has the smallest known orbit, passing close to the sun approximately every 3½ years. Encke was director of the Berlin observatory (1825–63).

Encke's Division. △84.

Enclosure, land policy, dating from the 12th century, involving subdivision and fencing of the common lands and large open fields of the medieval English agrarian economy. The practice led to problems in the 16th and 17th centuries when landlords expelled tenant farmers without adequate reason or compensation in order to enclose the land to serve their own interests. The practice peaked in the late 17th century, waning in the early 18th century. The process of enclosure began in places by private agreements but became chiefly associated with the policy of Parliamentary Enclosure Acts for individual parishes, mainly from 1750 onward. △1220.

Encomienda, feudal system that provided native labor for conquistadors in Spanish America in return for protection and Christian education. From "encomenda"-to entrust. Extensive abuses caused abolition of encomiendas after 1542. △1124.

Encyclical, letter sent to all churches of a particular area, originally by any bishop, but now by the Pope. It usually deals with doctrinal matters, but is not held to be infallible. Well-known encyclicals sent in modern times include Pope Paul's 1968 letter condemning birth control; Pius XI's 1931 letter against Italian Fascism and 1937 letter against the Nazis; and Pius X's letter condemning modernism in 1907. The term is also applied to letters issued by Anglican bishops at the conclusion of the Lambeth conferences.

Encyclopedia. △1780.

Encyclopedia, French (*L'Encyclopédie au Dictionnaire raisonné des sciences, des arts et des métiers,* 1751–80). Considered a literary monument of the entire 18th century and an embodiment of the spirit of Enlightenment, the French *Encyclopedia* was intended to be a complete guide to useful knowledge. Its principal director, Denis Diderot, and eminent contributors envisioned that the work would combat superstition and systematize knowledge. *See also* Enlightenment.

Encyclopedists, French philosophes who presented their rationalist, humanitarian, and deist views through the publication of the *Encyclopédie, ou Dictionnaire raisonné des sciences, des arts, et des métiers* in the latter half of the 18th century. Encountering severe opposition from the religious and political establishment, the primary editor, Denis Diderot and such prominent authors as Voltaire, Rousseau, and Montesquieu helped prepare the philosophical basis of the French Revolution.

Endecott, John (*c.*1589–1665), American colonist and first governor of Massachusetts Bay colony (1628–30), b. England. He and a small group settled Salem, Mass., (1628) and campaigned against the Pequot Indians in E Connecticut (1636). He arrested and deported Thomas Morton, a free-living trader who had established an Anglican settlement at Merry Mount, Mass. A strict Puritan, he also persecuted the Quakers.

Enders, John Franklin (1897–), US immunologist, b. West Hartford, Connecticut. He shared the 1954 Nobel Prize in physiology or medicine with Frederick C. Robbins and Thomas H. Weller "for their discovery of the ability of poliomyelitis viruses to grow in cultures of various types of tissue," work fundamental to the later development of the polio vaccine.

Endive, leafy Old World annual or biennial plant widely cultivated for its sharp-flavored leaves used cooked or in salads. It resembles leaf lettuce, but has more substantial leaves. There are two types: curly endive with slender, wavy-edged leaves and escarole with broad flat leaves. Family Compositae; species *Cichorium endivia. See also* Chicory. △334, 336.

Endocarditis, inflammation of the lining of the heart. Often bacteria-caused, it is also associated with rheumatic fever.

Endocrine System, body system made up of all the endocrine, or ductless, glands that secrete chemical substances known as hormones directly into the blood stream where they act to control body functions. The endocrine system, together with the nervous system, controls and regulates all body functions; the endocrine system is occasionally considered the chemical control or the "liquid nervous system." The endocrine system differs from other body systems in that its member parts—the ductless glands—are not structurally linked or connected to one another. The chief endocrine glands are (1) the pituitary gland, located at the base of the brain, often called the master gland. It secretes more than 15 hormones that act on other endocrine glands and in many areas of the body, regulating growth, development, and other body functions. (2) The thyroid gland, located in the throat, which secretes thyroxine to regulate growth and metabolism. (3) The parathyroid glands, also located in the throat, which regulate calcium metabolism. (4) The adrenal glands, situated atop the kidneys, which secrete adrenaline, the "stress" hormone, and various steroids that regulate salt and water balance in the body. (5) The islands of Langerhans in the pancreas, which secrete insulin for carbohydrate metabolism. (6) The sex glands, or gonads—in males, the testes, which secrete testosterone; in females, the ovaries, which secrete estrogens and progesterones. *See also* articles on specific endocrine glands. △690.

Endoderm, or entoderm, innermost cell layer of embryos of higher animals. It forms the liver, pancreas, digestive tract, and respiratory system. It also is the inner cell layer of a simple animal body.

Endodontics, dental specialty that deals with the treatment and prevention of diseases of the soft tissue in the center of the tooth called the dental pulp. Diseased pulp is removed but the tooth can be maintained in the jaw as long as the blood supply to the anchoring fibers is preserved or restored. This is often preferable to replacement with an artificial tooth.

Endogamy, set of institutionalized precepts that define the boundaries within which marriage is enjoined in a society. These vary from mere tendencies to strictly enforced laws deciding the group from which the spouse is taken. *See also* Exogamy. △876.

Endometrium, highly vascularized tissue lining the uterus. upon conception it forms part of the placenta to maintain the developing fetus during pregnancy. △700.

Endomorph. △814.

Endopterygote. △498.

Endoscope. △718.

Endosperm, tissue surrounding the developing embryo of a seed. It provides food for growth.

Endothermic Reaction, chemical reaction in which heat is absorbed, thus causing a fall in temperature. *See also* Chemical Reaction. △1572.

Energy, one of the great unifying concepts of physics. Energy has many forms: mechanical, atomic, heat, chemical, and others. It undergoes transformations: thermonuclear reactions in the sun release solar energy; photosynthesis in plants stores this energy in chemical form; ingestion of the plant by animals allows muscles to transform this energy yet again into physical action. The concept of energy came into being with Galileo, Newton, and Leibniz. Its conservation through all its transformations was established almost simultaneously by Joule, Rumford, and Kelvin in the mid-19th century. The relationship between energy, momentum, and mass of a particle was established in 1905 by Einstein, who recognized that energy and mass could be transformed into each other according to the relation $E = mc^2$. △1486.

Energy, Ionization. *See* Ionization.

Energy, Nuclear. *See* Nuclear Energy.

Energy Crisis. △1646.

Energy Level. See Atom.

Eneuresis, bed-wetting, or involuntary urination while sleeping, considered a disturbance only if it lingers long into childhood. It could indicate emotional difficulties or stress in the home. Behavior therapy may be an effective treatment.

Enfield, manufacturing town in N Connecticut, on the Massachusetts border. Settled as part of Massachusetts 1681; annexed to Connecticut 1749. Pop. (1970) 46,189.

Enforcement Acts, (1870–71), legislation passed to insure enforcement of the 14th and 15th Amendments to the Constitution. Three acts set heavy penalties for any form of coercion that prevented eligible voters from exercising their rights, provided for federal supervision of Congressional elections, and outlawed terrorist activities, giving the president special powers to deal with violence.

Engelbrektsson, Engelbrekt (1390–1436), Swedish national hero. He led a revolt against Eric of Pomerania, king of Denmark, Sweden, and Norway. A mine owner, Engelbrektsson in 1434 became leader of a peasants' and miners' uprising against the tyrannical king. The rebellion soon gained support from the clergy and the nobility. Engelbrekt seized castles throughout eastern and southern Sweden until the diet of 1435 accepted his demands and made him regent. He was murdered shortly thereafter.

Engels, Friedrich (1820–95), German political writer and Socialist. He was a disciple of Karl Marx, with whom he collaborated in formulating the theory of dialectical materialism. As agent in England of his father's textile business (1842–44) he took an interest in the workers' conditions and, under the influence of the Chartist movement, wrote *The Condition of the Working Classes in England* (1845). This brought him into touch with Marx, then an exile in England, and together they wrote the *Communist Manifesto* (1848). While Marx was doing research and writing in London, Engels supported him, and from 1870 until Marx's death (1883) he helped Marx with his writings. He completed *Das Kapital* (1894), which Marx left unfinished. △1326.

Engels, formerly Pokrovsk; port city in Russian SFSR, USSR, across Volga River from Saratov; served as capital of German Volga Autonomous SSR 1923–41; renamed 1932 to honor Friedrich Engels. Industries: bricks, food processing, chemicals, machinery. Settled 1747 by Ukrainians. Pop. 130,000.

Engel v. Vitale (1962), US Supreme Court case that extended the ban on prayers in schools to a nonsectarian reading. The court based its opinion on the First Amendment's establishment of religion clause.

Engineering Psychology, field related to industrial psychology and to human engineering. An engineering psychologist designs man-machine systems eg, the arrangement of a spacecraft command module. The emphasis is on designing complex equipment to fit human needs and capacities. *See also* Industrial Psychology.

England, largest part of Great Britain, bounded E by the North Sea, S by the English Channel, W by the Atlantic Ocean, Wales, and the Irish Sea, and N by Scotland.

Land and Economy. England is mainly lowland with low hills and downs in the SE, Cotswold hills in the NW, and a granite and sandstone plateau on the SW peninsula rising to over 2,000ft (610m) on Dartmoor. The Pennine range of hills extends S-N centrally, with moorland in the NE and SW and the Cumbrian Mts in the NW. The highest point is Scafell Pike, 3,210ft (979m). The principal islands are Isle of Man, off the Welsh coast, the Isle of Wight, off the S coast, and the Scilly Isles, off the SW coast. The principal lakes are situated in the Lake District and include Windermere (largest), Derwentwater, and Ullswater. The main rivers are the Thames, Ouse, Humber, Trent, Mersey, and Severn. Over 50% of the agricultural land is arable, and about 35% is permanent pasture; sheep are grazed on rough uplands. Main products are cereals, vegetables, beef, sheep, fruit in the S, dairy farming in the W. Fishing, especially herring and cod, is centered on the E coast. Mineral resources include coal (particularly in Northamptonshire, Derbyshire, Yorkshire, and Leicester), offshore petroleum (mainly in the North Sea), building stone, clay, and iron. Heavy industry, including iron and steel, shipbuilding, motor vehicles, textiles, railroad rolling stock, and engineering, is concentrated in the Midlands and N. Other industries include refining, pottery, aircraft, glass, electrical goods, agricultural machinery, and pharmaceuticals.

People. The people are of mixed ethnic origin, including Celt, Roman, Anglo-Saxon, and Norman. The main religious group is the Church of England.

History. Before the Roman invasion in AD 43, the Celts occupied England. The Romans remained until the 5th century but had been harassed by German tribes (Angles, Saxons, Jutes) from the 3rd century. Christianity arrived in the 6th century. By the 7th century Saxon kingdoms such as Sussex, Wessex, Kent, and Mercia were identifiable. The Danes and other Scandinavians invaded in the 9th century but their advance was halted by Alfred the Great (878). The struggles between the Danes and the English for control continued into the 11th century.

Edward the Confessor of Wessex took the throne in 1042, but when he died (1066) without heirs, William of Normandy invaded, conquered England, and became William I of England. William's dynasty was succeeded by the Plantagenets in 1154. Henry II, the first Plantagenet, was followed by less successful rulers, and in 1215 rebellious barons forced John to grant the Magna Carta. The barons' increased strength in the early 14th century led to the murder of Edward II (1327).

English rulers continued to press their claims to lands in France, which led to involvement in the Hundred Years War. In the mid-15th century, rival claims to the English throne triggered the Wars of the Roses, which ended with the victory of Henry VII and the establishment of the Tudor dynasty (1485). The Act of Union (1536) completed the unification of Wales and England. Under Henry VIII Protestantism became stronger as a result of Henry's struggles with the Roman Catholic Church. The Tudors continued on the throne through the reign of the childless Elizabeth I, who was succeeded in 1603 by James I (James VI of Scotland), the first Stuart monarch. For the subsequent history of England, *see* Great Britain.

PROFILE

Official name: England
Area: 50,333sq mi (130,362sq km)
Population: 45,870,062
Density: 911per sq mi (351per sq km)
Chief cities: London (capital); Birmingham; Liverpool

England, Church of, developed in Great Britain as a result of the conflict between the papal authority and that of monarchs. This tension reached its peak in the 16th century as religious dissatisfaction mounted. Henry VIII's divorce led to the break with Rome (1534), and the destruction of shrines. The Church of England's stand against Roman Catholics and Puritans eventually gave way to religious tolerance. *See also* Anglicanism.

Englewood, residential city in N central Colorado, 5mi (8km) S of Denver. Inc. 1903. Pop. (1970) 33,695.

Englewood, city in NE New Jersey; part of residential area is on slopes of Palisades along Hudson River; site of Actor's Fund Home for ill and retired actors. Founded before Revolutionary War by Dutch settlers; inc. as city 1899. Pop. (1970) 24,985.

English, the most universal of the world's languages, the mother tongue of about 300 million people in the United States, Canada, Great Britain, Ireland, Australia, New Zealand, most of the Caribbean islands, and as a second language by many millions more throughout the world. A Germanic language, it may be said to have come into existence with the arrival of the Anglo-Saxons in Great Britain in the 5th century AD.

English Channel, arm of the Atlantic Ocean, between France and Great Britain; connected with North Sea at E end by Strait of Dover. Train-ferry service between Dover, England and Dunkirk, France was started in 1936. Width: 20–150mi (32–242km). Length: 350mi (564km).

English Cocker Spaniel, small hunting dog (sporting group); one of the oldest land spaniels. A responsive and faithful dog, it has a well-developed head and square muzzle; low-set, lobular ears hang close to the head. A short, compact body is set on strong legs; the tail is short. The coat, which may be white and a color, roan, or black and tan, is short on the head and flat and longer on the body; chest, belly, and legs are feathered. Average size: 16–17in (40.5–43cm) high at shoulder; 28–34lb (12.5–15.5kg). *See also* Sporting Dog.

English Foxhound, hunting dog (hound group) used for riding to hounds; stouter than American foxhound. It has a large head with pronounced brow and long nose; low-set ears carried close to cheeks; a large-chested, muscular body; straight, strong legs with round feet; and tapering tail carried up. The short, dense, hard coat is black, white, and tan. Average size: 21–25in (53.5–63.5cm) high at shoulder; 60–70lb (27–32kg). *See also* Hound.

English Horn, woodwind musical instrument similar to the oboe, but 6in (15cm) longer and pitched one fifth lower, with curved double-reed mouthpiece and pear-shaped bell. It is used in solo passages in Franck's *D Minor Symphony* and Rossini's *William Tell*. *See also* Oboe. △1244.

English Renaissance Architecture, architecture of Elizabethan and Jacobean England (1558–1625), between the Perpendicular style of the late Gothic and the Palladian classicism of Inigo Jones. It was primarily secular architecture and achieved its fullest expression in great country houses such as Longleat, Burghley House, and Wollaton Hall. These houses, often of an E or H shape, looked outward through large windows and were typically set with towers, gables, and parapets. △1192.

English Setter, bird dog (sporting group) bred 400 years ago in England. An aristocratic outdoor dog, its long, lean head has a square muzzle and hanging lips; rounded ears hang close to the head. The medium-length body and legs are graceful, and a straight, feathered tail tapers to a point. The long, straight flat coat can be black; white and tan; black, lemon, orange, or liver with white; or solid white. Average size: 25in (63.5cm) high at shoulder; 60lb (27kg). *See also* Sporting Dog.

English Springer Spaniel, hunting dog (sporting group); specialist for finding game. It has a broad head and square, lean jaw; long, wide, hanging ears set at eye level; and a neat, compact body set on muscular legs. The docked tail is carried horizontally. A flat or wavy coat is feathered on ears, chest, legs and belly; colors are liver or black with white or tan markings; blue or liver roan; white with tan, black, or liver markings. Average size: 18–20in (46–51cm) high at shoulder; 45–55lb (21–25kg). *See also* Sporting Dog.

English Toy Spaniel, small dog (toy group) known in England since the 16th century; probably originated in Japan or China. It has a well-domed head; square, deep muzzle; and short nose turned up between large, dark eyes. Low-set ears hang almost to the ground. The body is small and compact; legs are short and stout; tail is docked and carried level with the back. The long, silky, wavy coat may be black and tan (King Charles variety), chestnut red (ruby), red and white (Blenheim), or white, black, and tan (Prince Charles). Average size: 10in (25cm) high at shoulder; 9–12lb (4–5.5kg). *See also* Toy Dog.

Engraving, intaglio (incised) printing process. Tools called burins are used to cut out lines drawn on a copper plate or on an end-grain block of wood. There

John Franklin Enders

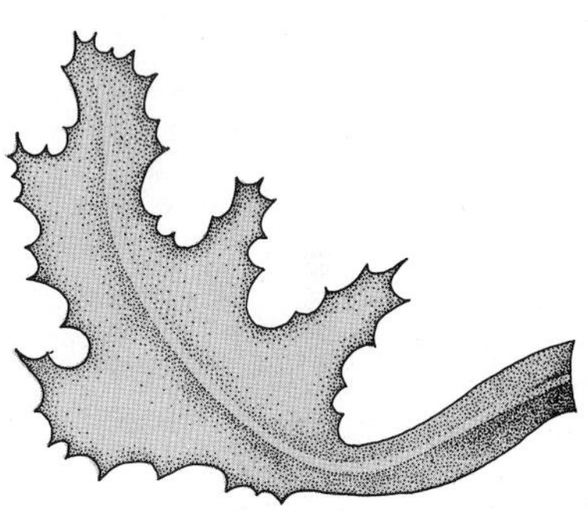

Endive

Buckingham Palace, London

English springer spaniel

are many different kinds of burins to cut different size lines. When magnified, the engraved line has a pointed end. After a proof of the print is made on an etching press, corrections may be made on the plate or woodblock with such tools as a scraper and burnisher. In modern engraving, different intaglio processes such as etching, aquatint, and engraving are frequently combined in a single plate.

Enid, city in N Oklahoma, 65mi (105km) NNW of Oklahoma City; seat of Garfield co; site of Phillips University (1907) and Vance Air Force Base. Industries: oil refining, grain elevators, meat packing. Founded 1893 on site of US land office in Cherokee Strip. Inc. 1894. Pop. (1970) 44,986.

Eniwetok, uninhabited coral atoll in W central Pacific Ocean; part of the Ralik Chain, Marshall Islands; approx 40 islands encircle a lagoon with a circumference of 50mi (81km); taken from Japan by United States during WWII; scene of US atomic and thermonuclear weapons tests (1950s).

Enki. *See* Ea.

Enlightened Despotism. *See* Despotism.

Enlightenment, or **Age of Reason,** vast revolution of western thought in the 18th century. It was based on an ultimate reliance in the perfectibility of man through reason in his relations with himself, his fellows, and the universe. Extending to all the branches of the western intellectual world, this school of thought included Rousseau, Hume, Voltaire, Mendelssohn, Addison, Kant, Montesquieu, Franklin, Jefferson, and many others, and made possible such dramatic events as the French and American revolutions. Supported by the rising bourgeoisie and opposed by church and nobility, the Enlightenment fostered a new humanism. It raised the individual to the position of ultimate importance, placed a new faith in the progress of man, with the state as its natural agent; and espoused a belief in natural religion (Deism), law, and universal order. Some vocal proponents were the Masons and the Encyclopedists. △1180, 1184.

Enlil, chief god of the Sumerian pantheon and later of Babylon and Assyria. He was guardian of the city of Nippur, the political and religious center of southern Mesopotamia. As the god of air Enlil shared his dominion with three supreme deities, Anu, god of heaven, Ea, god of water, and Ninhursag, goddess of Earth, but he alone was responsible for bringing the Me, or laws governing all existence.

Enna, town in Sicily, Italy, 64mi (103km) SE of Palermo; capital of Enna prov; scene of Sicilian slave revolt 134–32 BC; site of octagonal towers and castle of Frederick II; mythical birthplace of Ceres, and scene of rape of Proserpina by Pluto; agricultural center and summer resort area. Pop. 28,653.

Enneads, the writings of the Greek Neo-Platonic philosopher Plotinus, as collected and published by his disciple Porphyry *c.* 300AD. The *Enneads* dealt with such questions as the relationship between the One and Matter.

Ennius, Quintus (239–169 BC), early Latin poet, called the "father of Roman poetry." Speaking Oscan, Greek, and Latin, he was a teacher as well as an adaptor of Greek plays. The *Annales* was his principle work. △1028.

Enoch, several biblical figures, including Cain's eldest son whose name was given to the city built by Cain. Also, the son of Jared and father of Methuselah.

Enschede, city in E Netherlands, on Twente Canal; devastated by fire (1862); site of university (1961) and natural history museum; customs station. Industries: pharmaceuticals, textiles, paper, dairy products, beer. Founded 1118. Pop. 139,245.

Ensenada, Zenón de Somodevilla, Marqués de la (1702–81), Spanish statesman. In 1743 he became chief minister to Philip V and thereafter he and the queen, Elizabeth Farnese, were the virtual rulers of the country. He fell from power in 1754, when Ferdinand VI arrested him. *See also* Elizabeth Farnese.

Ensenada, seaport city in NW Mexico, on Pacific Ocean. Industries: fishing, fish processing, wine, agriculture, mining. Pop. 113,320.

Entebbe, town in S central Uganda, E Africa, on NW shore of Lake Victoria; capital of Uganda 1894–1962. International airport there was scene of Israeli raid to rescue passengers of hijacked plane (1976). Crops: coffee, cotton, fruits. Founded 1839. Pop. 10,900.

Entellus Langur. *See* Hanuman.

Entente, in World History. △1306, 1336.

Entente Cordiale. △1300.

Enteritis, chronic or acute inflammation of the lining of the intestine. Causes include emotional distress, allergy, or infectious disease. Mild to extreme diarrhea and abdominal pain are symptoms. Treatment usually includes a bland diet. *See also* Gastroenteritis.

Enterokinase, an enzyme released by the intestine during digestion. It activates the digestive enzyme trypsin. *See also* Trypsin.

Entoderm. *See* Endoderm.

Entomology, scientific study of insects. *See also* Insect. △492, 494.

Entropy, a quantity related to the number of accessible quantum states available to a system. If the number of such states is N, then the entropy S of the system is given by $S = k \ln N$, where k is the Stefan-Boltzmann constant. Since an isolated system will always tend to its most probable states (largest value of N) its entropy tends to increase. This is the Second Law of Thermodynamics. For example, in a system of 10 atoms that have two directions of spin, the number of different combinations of states N is 2^{10} for sufficiently high temperatures; thus the entropy of this system is $10\,k \ln 2$. But at low temperatures, all spins become aligned, the total number of possible states drops to one, and the entropy goes to zero. This is the Third Law of Thermodynamics. *See also* Statistical Mechanics; Thermodynamics. △1510.

Enugu, city in S Nigeria; capital of East-Central state; trade and coal mining center; site of technical college (1955). Pop. 160,567.

Enumerated Goods, colonial products listed by the English Parliament as being exportable only to England, to keep profits in the mother country. Products included tobacco, sugar, rice, furs, and naval stores.

Enumerated Powers. *See* Delegated or Enumerated Powers.

Environment, aggregate of conditions, substances, and other organisms affecting existence of an organism. Physical factors of the environment include water, temperature, and soil. △580.

Environmental Protection Agency (EPA), federal agency under the executive branch. It was created to reduce and control pollution by a variety of research, monitoring, and enforcement activities. The EPA coordinates and supports research and antipollution activities by state and local governments, private and public groups, individuals, and educational institutions. It was established in 1970.

Enzymes, group of proteins that function as catalysts in biological chemical reactions. As they are not used up in these reactions, they are effective in tiny quantities and as they are highly specific, enormous numbers of them occur in nature. Many enzymes require the presence of accessory substances (coenzymes) in order to function effectively. Enzymes are important in heredity; many genes function by producing specific enzymes. The names of most enzymes end in the letters *-ase* except for a few, such as pepsin, that retain older names. △1572–74.

Eocene, the second oldest of the five major epochs of the Tertiary period, extending from the end of the Paleocene to the beginning of the Oligocene. During the Eocene all the major orders of modern mammals and many modern bird orders appeared. △276.

Eogyrinus. △566.

Eohippus, or dawn horse, extinct progenitor of the horse that lived during Eocene epoch (58 million years ago) in swampy areas of North America. It had a small head with large eyes set mid-face, short neck, and arched back. Each forefoot had four toes, the hind feet three. Teeth were simple and suitable for browsing on soft vegetation. Height: 17.7–23.6in (45–60cm). △576.

Eolian (or Aeolian) Formation, one that was created by wind transported material. This may be a dune on a riverbank or ripple marks in sand on a beach or desert, or the growth phase of dune building. It also can be used to describe shapes carved in rock by the wearing away of softer materials. *See also* Butte; Desert; Dune. △266.

Eolithic Age, or "Dawn Stone" Age, name given to the period between approximately 2,500,000 and 500,000 years ago in which man, or near-man, used fractured stone tools. Eoliths are so primitive that the untrained eye cannot always distinguish them from naturally broken stones. *See also* Paleolithic Age. △648.

Eos, Greek mythological figure. Eos was the dawn-goddess, daughter of Hyperion and Thea, who drove through the sky in a chariot drawn by a pair of horses. Homer and other poets described her in colors evocative of the morning sky: "rosy-fingered" and "saffron-robed." Eos was often involved in romantic adventures.

Eosinophil, white blood cell with an affinity for the red dye eosin. It increases in number in certain diseases.

EPA. *See* Environmental Protection Agency.

Epaminondas (died 362 BC), Greek statesman and military leader. He was active in the restoration of Theban political power, and instrumental in the winning of independence for Messenia and Arcadia. Epaminondas developed new military strategies used successfully against Sparta (371–362 BC), and which led to the decline of Sparta's military supremacy.

Epeirogeny, in geology that form of diastrophism that results in the formation of large features of the earth's crust such as continents, and oceans and the creation of large areas within those features, such as plateaus and basins. This leaves the formation of mountains as the distinct preserve of orogeny. The movements that constitute epeirogeny are primarily vertical ones. In some processes that result in the formation (or deformation) of mountain topography, epeirogeny and orogeny interact and overlap, making distinctions difficult. *See also* Deformation; Orogeny; Tectonics. △252.

Ephedrine, a widely used drug, chemically similar to epinephrine (adrenalin), that stimulates the central nervous system and is used to counter the effects of depressants, to treat bronchial asthma by dilating bronchioles, to dilate pupils of the eyes, as a nasal decongestant, and to treat low blood pressure.

Ephemeris (pl. Ephemerides), list of tables providing the positions of a planet or comet for a given selection of dates, as derived from orbital data. The term also signifies an annual publication supplying such tables along with information concerning the Sun, eclipse and occultation data, data for certain stars, astronomical constants, etc. One of the most important of such publications is *The American Ephemeris and Nautical Almanac,* which, since 1960, has been merged with the (British) *Astronomical Ephemeris.*

Ephemeris, or the "Daily Round," poetic book written by 4th-century Roman rhetorician and poet Ausonius. The speaker in *Ephemeris* recounts the various activities of his day, each activity being described in a different meter.

Ephemeris Time (ET), system of time reckoning normally employed in the compilation of astronomical data for almanacs and Ephemerides. It takes no account of irregularities in the Earth's rotation and is calculated on the basis of the tropical year. It is slightly in advance of Universal Time.

Ephesians, New Testament epistle written by Paul during his first captivity in Rome. Addressed to the Christian church at Ephesus, it stresses unity for all through Christ.

Ephesus, ancient Ionian city of W Asia Minor, site of a noted temple of Artemis (Diana). Trade made it a rich seaport under the Greeks and Romans. Croesus, king of Lydia, captured it (*c.* 550 BC), Cyrus the Great (*c.* 546 BC), Alexander the Great (334 BC), and the Romans (133 BC) later held it. It was sacked by the Goths (AD 262). The important church Council of Ephesus was held there in 431.

Ephesus, Councils of, (1) Council of 431, also Third General Council (Roman Council) convoked by Roman Emperor Theodosius II, it condemned the doctrine of Nestorianism, the belief that there are two separate persons, one human and one divine, in the body of Christ. (2) Robber Council of 449, or Latrocinium, also convoked by Theodosius II. It acquitted Eutyches, the first of the Monophysites (doctrine of one nature in Christ), of heresy and reinstated him, while deposing Flavian, patriarch of Constantinople. *See also* Eutyches.

Ephomeroptera. △492.

Ephors, ancient Greek magistrates in several Dorian states including Sparta. Elected annually, they came to dominate Spartan politics and policy in the 5th century BC. △996.

Epic, long narrative poem in grandiose style in which heroes perform superhuman tasks of strength. The earliest known form of Greek literature, epics were originally used to transmit history orally. Using the literary device of repetition, they often involved gods, men, and legendary battles. Homer is the author of the two most famous epics, the *Iliad* and the *Odyssey*. Later examples include *Beowulf*, Vergil's *Aeneid*, John Milton's *Paradise Lost*, and Edmund Spenser's *Faerie Queene*.

Epicanthic Fold, or Mongolian eyefold, downward and inward fold of the upper eyelid over the inner corner of the eye, producing the so-called "slant" eye characteristic of numerous peoples of Asiatic origin, some American Indians, and the Khoisan groups of Southern Africa. △658.

Epicenter, the spot on Earth's surface directly above the focus of an earthquake. Depending on the character of the focus, the epicenter may be a small circle or a line. *See also* Focus, Earthquake. △174.

Epictetus (*c.* 50– *c.* 138), Greek Stoic philosopher. His teachings were recorded in *Discourses* and *Enchiridion* by his disciple, Arrian. An admirer of Socrates and Diogenes, he stressed the brotherhood of man, influencing Christian thought.

Epicureanism, school of Greek philosophy founded by Epicurus in the late 4th century BC. Opposing the idealistic and skeptical mood of the times, Epicurus wanted to provide security in an unsure world. He grounded his system on the uncontestability of sense experience; pleasure and pain are the ultimate good and evil. Intelligent choice is necessary for the good life. Under the Roman Empire, Epicureans chose to withdraw from view and the last known member of the school was Diogenes of Oenoanda (*fl.* 200 AD).

Epicurus (341–270 BC), Greek philosopher, founder of the Epicurean school. Although only fragments of his works remain, his loyal disciples passed on his doctrines of friendship, peace of mind, and spiritual enjoyment as goals of the good life. *See also* Epicureanism.

Epicycloid. △1454.

Epidamnus, important seaport in Illyria (modern Durazzo, Albania) settled by Greeks in the 6th century BC. Pirates, with the blessing of Queen Teuta, menaced both Greek and Roman shipping. It was seized by Rome in the 3rd century BC and its name was changed to Dyrrachium.

Epidemic, uncontained and rapid spread of a disease through a general population. The study of epidemics concerns itself with causes and patterns of contagion and methods of containing disease. Black plague, smallpox, and typhoid have been causes of historic epidemics; hepatitis, influenza, venereal disease are present concerns of epidemiologists. △734.

Epidermis, outer layer of skin that contains no blood vessels. It is made up of two cell layers, including the outer, horny *stratum corneum* that protects the delicate underlayers from injury and infection and the inner *stratum germinativum* containing cells to replace sloughed off outer cells and the pigments responsible for skin color. A boundary membrane separates the epidermis from the dermis. △686.

Epidural Anesthesia. △704.

Epiglottis. △680, 694.

Epigram, A Greek word meaning "inscription." In classical literature, the term refers to a brief Greek or Latin poem expressing, in a pointed or witty fashion, one single thought.

Epilepsy, cerebral disorder characterized by disturbances in consciousness, motor and sensory functions, often accompanied by convulsions. Causes of epilepsy are not clearly understood but are believed by some to be related to minute brain lesions. Seizures usually first manifest themselves in children between 3 and 15 years old, slightly more often in males. They are divided into several categories, the most familiar being grand mal, petit mal, and pyschomotor. Grand mal seizures, up to five minutes long, may anticipate their onset with so-called auras, and may involve calling out, loss of consciousness, loss of muscular control. Petit mal attacks are shorter, up to 30 seconds duration, and milder, although there may be an almost unnoticeable loss of consciousness. Psychomotor attacks last up to two minutes, with confusion of motor and sensory abilities evident. Treatment calls for minimizing brain trauma if possible, anti-convulsant drugs, and education of the patient to lead as normal a life as possible. *See also* Aura. △722.

Epinay, Louise Florence Pétronille de La Live d' (1726–83), French woman of letters. A prominent figure in 18th-century French literary circles, she wrote several novels and pedagogical works. She took a personal interest in the welfare of other writers, and conducted a popular salon at La Chevrette, near Montmorency. She formed close friendships with many Philosophes, including Denis Diderot, Baron Friedrich de Grimm, and Jean-Jacques Rousseau.

Epinephrine, or adrenaline, hormone produced by the medulla of the adrenal glands. It is chemically a catecholamine, $C_6H_3(OH_2)CHOHCH_2NHCH_3$ and is secreted under conditions of stress to prepare the body for "flight or fight" by stimulating the blood flow and increasing the blood sugar level. Synthetic ephinephine, made from pyrocatechol, and the extract obtained from the adrenal glands of sheep and cattle are used in medicine. △690.

Epiphany, Christian feast, celebrated on January 6th. It commemorates Christ's baptism, his presentation to the Magi, and his first miracle at the marriage feast at Cuna.

Epiphyses. △682.

Epiphyte, or air plant, plant that grows on another plant but is not a parasite. They usually have aerial roots and produce their own food by photosynthesis. Epiphytes are common in tropical forests. Examples are certain ferns, orchids, and Spanish moss. △452, 454.

Epirus (Epirusipeiros), province on mainland of NW Greece, bounded by Pindus Mts (E), Albania (N and W), Ionian Sea (S); Arta is the administrative center. This province occupies the S portion of a region known in ancient times as the home of the oracle of Dodona; united under Pyrrhus (3rd century BC); made a republic *c.* 200 BC and sided with Macedonia against Rome; plundered by Aemilius Paullus (AD 167) and subsequently occupied by Serbs, Albanians, Venetians, and Turks (1430); semi-independent state controlled by Ali Pasha of Albania (1788–1820); S Epirus passed to Greece 1881; N Epirus remains part of Albania. Industries: cattle, sheep, dairy products, olives, citrus fruit, rice. Pop. 352,604.

Episcia, genus of perennial plants native to South America, with trailing stems, hairy leaves and single flowers of red, purple, or white. There are about 30 species, many grown as houseplants. Family Gesneriaceae.

Epistemology, branch of philosophy that critically examines the nature, limits, and validity of knowledge or belief, at one time contrasted with metaphysics and logic. Beginning with the work of Descartes, in the 17th century it was recognized that many previously "philosophical" questions would be better studied scientifically, and what remained of metaphysics was absorbed into epistemology. *See also* Descartes; Logic; Metaphysics. △858.

Epistles, 21 writings forming a section of the New Testament; more than half are attributed to Paul. The Epistle to the Romans contains the single most complete formulation of Paul's teachings. Written in response to problems facing the first Christian congregations, some contained instructions to specific communities, others were directed to all Christians.

Epistolary Novel, novel in the form of a letter or series of letters. The genre was popular in the 18th century. Samuel Richardson established the English vogue for it with *Pamela* (1740), and Rousseau used the form in *La Nouvelle Heloise* (1761). Many Epistolary novels are sentimental because the letter form provides opportunity for the discussion of emotions. △1188.

Epithalamium, nuptial poem, usually lengthy and serious in tone, written to honor a bride and bridegroom and pray for their prosperity. The form was perfected by the classical poets Sappho, Anacreon, Pindar, Theocritus, and Catullus. The most famous examples in English literature are Edmund Spenser's "Epithalamion" and "Prothalamion."

Epithelium, the protective membrane that covers every surface of the body that might come into contact with foreign matter. Thus, epithelium covers not only the skin, but various internal organs and surfaces

Enna, Sicily

Oil spills: major concern for the Environmental Protection Agency

Ephesus, Turkey: temple of Adrian

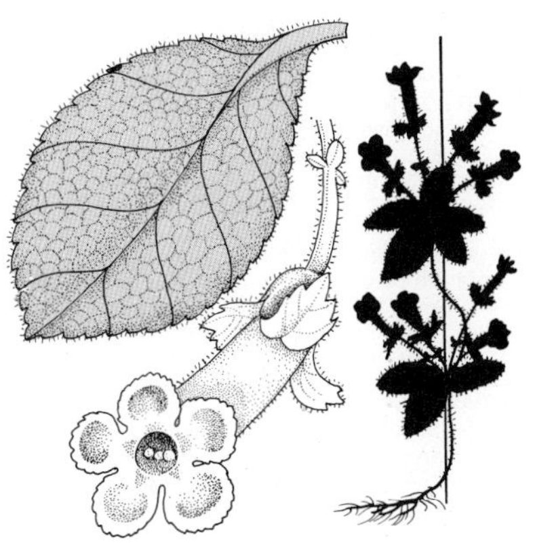

Episcia

such as the intestines, nasal passages, and mouth. There are various types of epithelial cells, including ciliated, columnar and squamous or flattened. Membranes may be one cell layer thick or many layers such as on the skin. Epithelial cells may also produce protective modifications such as hair and nails, or secrete substances such as fat. △476, 478.

Epoch. *See* Geologic Time.

Epode, form of lyric poetry in which a long line of poetry is followed by a shorter one. It is often preceded by stasima, a pair of elaborate stanzas. Its inspiration is attributed to Archilochus in 7th-century BC Greece.

Epodes, collection of 17 poems of varying length, written by the Roman poet Horace and appearing in 30 BC. Modeled to some extent on the poems of Archilochus, *Epodes* also reflects the influence of Catullus. These poems contain Horace's first attempts at impassioned political commentary.

Epoxy, any of a group of thermosetting polymers with outstanding mechanical and electrical properties, stability, heat and chemical resistance, and adhesive qualities. Used in casting and protective coatings. Popular epoxy glues are sold in two separate components, a viscous resin and an amine or anhydride hardener, which are mixed just before use. △1618.

Epsom Salts, hydrated forms of magnesium sulfate found in nature in the mineral epsomite and in mineral waters and used in medicine as a cathartic.

Epstein, (Sir) Jacob (1880–1959), English sculptor, b. New York City. After studying in Paris, he went to England where he became a citizen in 1907. His works include controversial monumental sculptures and bronze portraits. Among his famous works are "Rima" (1925; London, Hyde Park) and an alabaster "Adam" (1939; Blackpool).

Equal Time Provision, in broadcasting, right granted to candidates for the same political office to equal air time on local and network broadcasts. Legislation for equal air time was passed by the US Congress first in 1934 and frequently has been augmented since then.

Equation, mathematical statement that two expressions are identical. An equation of the form $x^2 = 8 - 2x$ is true only for certain values of x ($x = 2$ or $x = -4$). These values are the solutions of the equation. This type of equation is contrasted with an *identity,* such as $(x + 2)^2 = x^2 + 4x + 4$, which is true for all values of x. Equations are classified in various ways: the highest power of the variable (2 in the case above) is the degree of the equation. Equations are said to be linear, quadratic, cubic, quartic, etc. according to whether their degree is 1, 2, 3, 4, etc. *See also* Differential Equation; Simultaneous Equations. △1452, 1454.

Equation, Chemical. *See* Chemical Equation.

Equation, Differential. *See* Differential Equation.

Equation, Partial Differential. *See* Partial Differential Equation.

Equator, imaginary circle on the Earth's surface that lies midway between the North and South poles and is the zero line of terrestrial latitude. It divides the Earth into the Northern and Southern hemispheres.

Equatorial Bulge. △178.

Equatorial Currents, the parts of the North and South Atlantic and Pacific gyres that flow near the equator. As they move west, their waters warm and begin to deflect either north or south in a clockwise or counterclockwise direction. Nearer the equator is the Equatorial Countercurrent, which flows east between the North and South Equatorial Currents. △224.

Equatorial Guinea, Republic of, nation in W Africa. The people are Negroid and mostly Roman Catholic. As one of the emerging African nations, it is striving to stabilize its place in the world economic picture.

Land and Economy. The country consists of Macias Nguema Island (Ferdinand Po) in the Gulf of Guinea, Rio Muni prov. on the mainland facing the Gulf, and Pagalu Island (Annabon), less than 7sq mi (18sq km) in area and located 370mi (596km) SW in the Atlantic. The hot, humid climate supports an agricultural economy; the main products are coffee, cacao, and timber. Libreville on Macias Nguema Island and Port Gentil on the coast of Rio Muni are the major ports.

People. There are three principal ethnic groups: Bubis, who occupy Macias Nguema Island; Fangs, who occupy Rio Muni; and Nigerians, who live in both areas but primarily on Macias Nguema. Most of the people are Roman Catholic although a large number still practice animism. Spanish is the official language, but a large number of African languages are also spoken.

Government. Equatorial Guinea is a republic, with a 1973 constitution providing for a president, 2 Provincial Councils, and a 60-member Assembly, all elected by universal suffrage. The first president, Francisco Macias Nguema, who was elected in 1971, named himself president for life in 1972.

History. Originally a Spanish colony, the country began a movement toward independence in 1960 with local elections. Greater autonomy was achieved in 1964, followed by complete independence in 1968. In 1969 most of the Spanish left the area to avoid confrontation with the natives. Equatorial Guinea has taken its place among the emerging Third World nations and has become a member of the Organization of African Unity and the United Nations.

PROFILE

Official name: Republic of Equatorial Guinea
Area: 10,831sq mi (28,005sq km)
Population: 290,000
Density: 29.1per sq mi (11.2per sq km)
Chief city: Malabo (capital)
Government: Republic
Religion: Roman Catholic
Language: Spanish (official)
Monetary unit: Peseta
Gross national product: $60,000,000
Per capita income: $210
Industries (major products): negligible
Agriculture (major products): cacao, coffee, timber
Trading partners (major): Spain

Equidae, horse family including one genus, *Equus,* with five subgenera—true zebra, Grevy's zebra, Asiatic wild ass, African wild (and domestic) ass, and wild (and domestic) horse. Class Mammalia; order Perrissodactyla. *See also* Horse.

Equigravitational Point, the point between two celestial bodies, such as Earth and Moon, at which the sum of the two gravitational forces is zero. A space vehicle reaching this point will begin to be accelerated toward the body it is approaching.

Equilateral Triangle, triangle having all three of its sides equal in length; the three interior angles will also be equal and each of magnitude 60°. *See also* Triangle. △1462.

Equilibrium, in economics, position that it is natural to move toward and that, if all things remain equal, there is no tendency to move from. In economics, an equilibrium for the economy as a whole is a position at which the total demand for goods and services equals the total supply of those goods and services. At this position there tends to be neither inflationary pressures nor recessionary tendencies. An equilibrium of supply and demand is a position where market price is set such that the quantity that producers are willing to produce equals the quantity that consumers are willing to buy.

Equilibrium, Chemical. *See* Chemical Equilibrium.

Equilibrium Constant, constant characterizing the chemical equilibrium of a particular reversible reaction at a specified temperature. *See also* Chemical Equilibrium.

Equilibrium of the Firm, in the economics theory of the firm, position at which the firm maximizes its profit position. A business firm maximizes profit by equating marginal revenue and marginal cost. When the firm produces that output at which the addition to revenue for the last unit produced is equal to the addition to cost for the last unit produced, the firm is in an equilibrium position. The firm has no tendency to move from this equilibrium, and it will always expand output to reach this position or contract output to reach this position. *See also* Firm, Theory of.

Equilibrium Price. *See* Market Equilibrium.

Equilibrium Quantity. *See* Market Equilibrium.

Equilibrium Sense, or vestibular sense, human ability to remain upright in relation to gravity and to detect changes in position and momentum. The principal organs of equilibrium are contained in the inner ear —the utricle, which transmits orientation information, and the semicircular canals, which are concerned with acceleration and deceleration. These systems help humans locate their bodies in space. △676.

Equine Encephalitis, a virus-caused disease associated with a similar disease in horses, in the United States divided into Eastern and Western equine encephalitis. Both seem to attack the very young (under one year) more than other age groups, with the Eastern variety also affecting the very old. Symptoms include headache, drowsiness, vomiting, and, later, muscular twitching and convulsions. Treatment is usually symptomatic.

Equinox, one of the points at which the ecliptic intersects the equator, called the vernal equinox as the sun crosses the equator moving north (on or about March 21) and the autumnal equinox as the sun moves south (on or about September 21).

Equity, in economics, the value of an item less any amount owed on it. Equity normally refers to the difference between a firm's assets and its liabilities. As the asset value increases relative to liabilities, the equity is greater.

Equity, in law, a field of jurisdiction that involves the application of morals to the interpretation of the law. It is a sense of fairness and justness applied to the court's decision. △908.

Equivalence principle, principle that energy and mass are equivalent according to the equation $E = mc^2$ (c is the velocity of light). *See also* Relativity Theory. △1524.

Equivalent, Electrochemical. *See* Electrochemical Equivalent.

Era. *See* Geologic Time.

Era of Good Feeling (1817–23), period during the presidency of James Monroe. The Federalist party had declined and there were almost no open party rivalries.

Erasistratus (*c.*300–250 BC), Greek physician. He made important discoveries concerning the heart and brain, among which were his description of the heart valves, his idea of the heart as a pump, and his detailed studies of the brain and the linking of brain convolutions with increasing complexity in the brain.

Erasmus, Desiderius (*c.*1466–1536), Dutch scholar, considered the greatest of the Renaissance humanists. The illegitimate son of a priest named Gerard, he himself was ordained a Catholic priest (1492). He traveled much, including six visits to England, where he became a friend of Thomas More. The first edition of his *Adages* (1500) brought him fame. In 1501 he published his version of Cicero's *De officiis,* the first of many classical works he edited. His *Enchiridion militis (Manual of the Christian Knight)* (1503) emphasized simple piety as an ideal of Christianity and called for reform of the church. *The Praise of Folly* (1509) is a satire on human nature. Beginning in 1514 he worked with the publisher Johann Froben in Basel, publishing *Novum Instrumentum* (1516), his important Latin translation of the Greek New Testament, and a number of editions of the Christian Church Fathers, notably Jerome (1516). His *Colloquies,* satirizing church and society, appeared in 1518. His works had an early influence on Luther and other Protestant reformers, but he himself sought change from within the Catholic church and found the course of the Reformation at least as upsetting as the faults of the Catholic church that he had criticized. In *On Free Will* (1524) he openly clashed with Luther. *See also* Humanism. △1130, 1152.

Erastus, Thomas (1524–83), German-Swiss physician and professor who became involved in religious controversies. His real surname was Lieber. Influenced by Huldreich Zwingli, he supported the doctrine of the Eucharist that allowed only a symbolic presence of Christ's body in the bread. He opposed the presbyterian form of government that was established under Frederick III.

Eratosthenes. △40.

Erbium, metallic element (symbol Er) of the lanthanide group, first isolated in 1843 by C.G. Mosander. Chief ores are monazite (a phosphate) and bastnasite (fluorocarbonates). The element is used in some specialized alloys and erbium salts are used as pink colorants for glasses. Properties: at. no. 68; at. wt. 167.26; melt. pt. 2,772°F (1,522°C); sp gr 9.045 (25°C); boil. pt. 4,550°F (2,510°C); most common isotope Er^{166} (33.41%). *See also* Lanthanide Elements.

Erech (Uruk), ancient Sumerian city of S Mesopotamia, on the Euphrates; modern Warka, Iraq. It prospered in the 5th millennium BC, becoming the capital of Lower Babylonia. Gilgamesh, the hero of the epic and flood, was once its king. △956.

Erechtheum Carvings (421–05 BC), six female figures (caryatids) that support the porch roof and ornamental capitals of the columns of the Erechtheum, an Ionic temple on the Acropolis, Athens.

Erewhon (1872), satirical novel by Samuel Butler. Higgs, the narrator, discovers the country of Erewhon (an anagram of "nowhere"), whose inhabitants worship the goddess Ydgrun (Mrs. Grundy) and consider physical illness to be a crime. Butler exposes the hypocrisies of Victorian society by means of ingenious paradox.

Erfurt, city in East Germany, on Gera River; capital of Erfurt district. One of Germany's oldest cities, first mentioned by St Boniface in 8th century. Martin Luther lived here as Augustinian Monk 1505–1508; scene of Congress of Erfurt (1808); site of Krämerbrücke (Merchants' Bridge, 1325) across Gera River, 15th-century cathedral, Governor's palace. Industries: commercial flower growing, optical instruments, precision tools. Pop. 195,994.

Erg, the unit of energy in the metric centimeter-gram-second (cgs) system of units. One erg is the work done by a force of one dyne acting through a distance of one centimeter. One joule equals 10,000,000 ergs.

Ergonomics, the application of psychological principles to man-machine systems. Ergonomics involves the design of machines, tools, and work areas to better fit human physiological and psychological limitations.

Ergot, fungus *(Claviceps)* disease of rye plants and other small grasses. Part of the fungal body contains alkaloids that are generally poisonous to man but when purified and in appropriate doses can be used medicinally—ergotamine to treat migraine headaches, ergonovine to induce uterine contractions to eject the afterbirth.

Erhard, Ludwig (1897–), German statesman and economist, largely responsible for West German economic recovery after World War II. Succeeding Konrad Adenauer as chancellor (1963–66), he resigned because of economic and administrative troubles and was made honorary chairman of the Christian Democrats.

Eric Bloodyaxe (died 954), king of Denmark, Norway, and Sweden (930–34). Eric, the son of Harald I Fairhair, the unifier of Norway, was twice king of England during the mid-10th century. In 934 he was driven from Norway for his cruel and unjust use of power. Eric was given charge of Northumbria by Athelstan. He ruled at York until expelled and murdered by a rival.

Eric II, called **the Memorable** (died 1137), king of Denmark (1134–37), son of Eric I, the Evergood. After a civil war that resulted in his obtaining control of South Jutland, Eric II's efforts eventually led to the political consolidation of Denmark.

Eric V, or **VII,** called **Klipping,** (1249–86), king of Denmark (1259–86). In 1282, Eric was forced by the nobles to sign the country's first constitution, which defined his duties to the lords and limited his powers. He was assassinated in 1286 because he failed to comply with it.

Eric VI, or **VIII,** called **Menved** (1274–1319), king of Denmark (1286–1319). Son of Eric V, he banished his father's assassins to Norway. Supported by the Norwegians, they raided and plundered Denmark for years. Eric's attempts to regain previous conquests along the Baltic coast also weakened the country's finances and aroused opposition to his rule.

Eric IX Jedvarsson (died 1160), king of Sweden, patron saint of Sweden. He led a crusade against pagan Finland (1157). He was killed by a Danish prince while attending mass. His feast day is May 18.

Eric X Knutsson (died 1216), king of Sweden (1208–16). He was the first king of Sweden to be crowned by the Swedish archbishop, ending the long struggle between the Church and royalty.

Eric XI Ericsson, called **the Lisping and the Lame** (d.1250), king of Sweden (1222–50). His brother-in-law, Birger Magnusson, however, was the real ruler during this period. Following Eric's death, Birger established the Folkung dynasty (1250).

Eric XIV (1533–77), king of Sweden (1560–68), who expanded the power of his monarchy, b. Stockholm. His aggressive foreign policy led to war against Denmark (1563–70). Dethroned by his brothers, Eric died in prison.

Eric Magnusson, or **Eric II,** called **Priest-Hater** (1268–99), king of Norway (1280–99). He continued the war against Denmark (1280–95) begun by his father Magnus VI; he made peace with Hanseatic cities (1285) by giving them concessions in Norway. He married (1282) Margaret of Scotland; their daughter Margaret was called the "Maid of Norway." In 1293 he married Isabella Bruce, sister of Robert Bruce of Scotland.

Eric VII of Pomerania (1382–1459), king of Denmark, Sweden, and Norway (1389–1439). A great-nephew of Queen Margaret, who secured the throne for him but actually ruled herself until her death in 1412. In two costly wars (1416–22, 1426–35) he attempted to wrest Schleswig from Holstein. His favoritism of Denmark over Norway and Sweden led to Engelbrekt Engelbrektsson's revolt in 1434, which eventually led to Eric's deposition in Denmark and Sweden in 1439 and in Norway in 1442. Until 1449 he raided his former kingdoms from Gotland in an attempt to regain the thrones. He then retired to Pomerania.

Ericson, Leif (*fl.* 1000), Norse explorer, son of Eric the Red. According to Norse sagas, he discovered and wintered in Vinland on the North American continent (*c.*1000). He was on a voyage from Norway to bring Christianity to Greenland and was blown off course. The lack of archeological evidence casts doubt on Vinland's location, but a probable site is Newfoundland. *See also* Vinland. △1068.

Ericsson, John (1803–89), US inventor, b. Sweden. He came to the United States in 1839 to build ships for the navy. During the Civil War, he constructed a new type of ironclad ship, the *Monitor.* The battle between the *Monitor* and the Confederate ironclad ship *Merrimack* made him a Union hero.

Eric the Red (950?–1000?), Norse explorer and discoverer of Greenland. Exiled from Norway and Iceland for manslaughter, Eric, on voyage of discovery, found Greenland (982). After three years there, he was able to bring colonists from Iceland to establish permanent settlements (986). △1068.

Eridu, ancient Sumerian city and modern site of Abu Sharein, S Iraq. Iraqi excavations (1946–49) indicated that Eridu dates from 5000 BC, making it the oldest settlement in S Mesopotamia; site of temples ornately adorned in silver, and lapis lazuli and painted pottery dating from 3500 BC.

Erie, city in NW Pennsylvania, on Lake Erie; seat of Erie co. Site was first occupied by French in 1753 as Fort Presque Isle; occupied by British 1760; Commodore Perry launched fleet here for Battle of Lake Erie (1813); site of restoration of Perry's flagship *Niagara,* Mercyhurst College (1871), Presque Isle State Park. Pennsylvania's only port on Great Lakes. Exports: lumber, coal, iron ore, petroleum, grain, fish. Industries: meters, boilers, plastics, paper. Inc. 1851. Pop. (1970) 129,321.

Erie, Lake, one of the Great Lakes, bordered W by Ontario, Canada, E by New York, S by Ohio and Pennsylvania, SW by Michigan; part Great Lakes-St Lawrence Seaway system. It is the shallowest and second smallest of the Great Lakes. Industrial centers on its shores have seriously polluted the lake, but government regulation has stimulated its recovery somewhat. Discovered in 1669 by the French explorer Louis Jolliet; British and French fought for its possession and then British and US forces. In the battle of Lake Erie during War of 1812, Oliver Perry led a successful naval engagement against the British. Area: 9,910sq mi (25,667sq km). Depth (max.): 210ft (64m).

Erie Canal, historic waterway in New York state, now part of the New York State Barge Canal. It provides an inland water route from the Hudson River (at Albany) westward to Lake Erie (at Buffalo), following generally the Mohawk River Valley. The need for a water route connecting the eastern seaboard with the Great Lakes was recognized in the 18th century, and the Mohawk Valley was seen as a logical route. After efforts to get federal financing failed, the New York State legislature in 1817 agreed to finance the canal's building, and work was begun. De Witt Clinton, who became governor that year, was its chief promoter. A great engineering feat of its day, the canal made use of numerous locks and aqueducts in the course of its 363-mi (584-km) length. It was finally completed in 1825 and was an immediate success. The Erie Canal formed the chief route for the migration of settlers to the Middle West and was the route by which agricul-

Jacob Epstein's St Michael

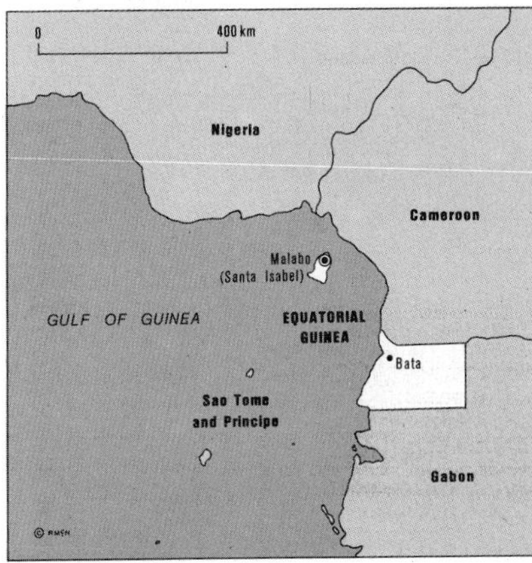

0
400 km
Nigeria
Cameroon
Malabo
(Santa Isabel)
GULF OF GUINEA
EQUATORIAL
GUINEA
Bata
Sao Tome
and Principe
Gabon

Equatorial Guinea

Lake Erie at Cleveland

Erie Canal

tural products were shipped E and manufactured products were shipped W. It was widened and deepened several times. The canal brought an economic boom to all of New York state, and its success caused a spate of canal building in other parts of the country. With the coming of the railroads around 1850, the importance of the Erie Canal lessened, and it fell into disrepair. In 1903, however, it was incorporated into the New York State Barge Canal system. It was repaired and modernized, and once again took its place as an important commercial route. △1400, 1762.

Erie Indians, also known as the Cat Nation, a sedentary tribe of Iroquoian-speaking North American Indians once occupying N Ohio, W New York, and NW Pennsylvania. Once numbering 15,000 persons, they were almost wiped out in a bloody war with the Iroquois in 1653–56; the few hundred survivors were incorporated into the Seneca tribe, mostly living in Oklahoma today.

Erigena, Johannes Scotus (*c.* 810–77), Irish philosopher and theologian. Little is known of his life. He translated works of Pseudo-Dionysius and Maximus the Confessor. His own major work, *De divisione naturae* (*c.* 865–70) discusses the doctrine of creation.

Erikson, Erik H(omburger) (1902–), US psychoanalyst, b. Germany. He extended Freudian theory into adolescence and adulthood, coining the term *identity crisis.* He emphasizes social relationships, however, rather than sexual needs, as the key to growing up. He also has done much to encourage the psychoanalytic study of historical personages in such works as *Young Man Luther* (1958) and *Gandhi's Truth* (1969, Pulitzer Prize 1970). △784, 814.

Erinyes, in Greek mythology, three demons of vengeance (Tisiphone, Megara, and Alecto). They ascended from Hades to pursue the wicked, especially sons who murdered their parents. The Erinyes were born of Earth and the blood of Uranus.

Eritrea, province in N Ethiopia, on Red Sea; capital is Asmara; chief ports are Assab and Massawa; under control of Ethiopia until taken by Ottoman Empire 16th century; during 19th century Ethiopia fought Egypt and Italy for control of Eritrea, but Italy claimed it after 1890, using it as base for capturing Ethiopia 1935. Since 1962 Eritrea has been part of Ethiopia. Eritrean separatists did not accept the union, and fighting between Eritrean nationalists and Ethiopian troops became particularly savage in the mid-1970s. Area: 48,000sq mi (124,320sq km). Pop. 1,836,800.

Erlander, Tage (1901–), Swedish politician and statesman. In 1933 he was elected to the Riksdag (Parliament), and served as minister for social affairs (1938–44) and minister without portfolio (1944–45). In 1946 Erlander became prime minister and chairman of the Social Democratic party. He remained at both positions until he retired in 1968. As head of government, Erlander concentrated on social welfare and educational reforms. In foreign policy he supported Sweden's neutrality, Scandinavian cooperation, and the United Nations.

Ermanaric (*fl.* 350–376 AD), Ostragothic king, formed a considerable empire in eastern Europe. Known by other names in various languages, he achieved a certain renown before his suicide during the invasion of the Huns, whereupon his empire crumbled. Reputed to have torn a woman to pieces with wild horses for her husband's treason, and endured the vengeance of her brothers, he is a recurring figure in European literature.

Ermetismo, the hermetic or "sealed in" movement in 20th-century Italian poetry. It was influenced by Stephane Mallarmé and Guillaume Apollinaire and was characterized by obscurity caused by complex, subjective imagery; typographical innovation; and unorthodox grammar and punctuation.

Ermine, small, slender-bodied mammal called a stoat in Eurasia and short-tailed weasel in North America. Ermines have short black-tipped tails and a brown coat that turns white in winter. The dense, silky winter coat has lost some of its commercial popularity. Length: 9 in (230mm); weight: to 10 oz (280g). Family Mustelidae; species *Mustela erminea. See also* Weasel.

Ernakulam, city in S India, on Malabar coast; site of numerous colleges, and Jewish community reputedly founded 2nd-3rd centuries. Industries: fishing, kerosene, lumber, perfume, soap. Pop. 213,811.

Ernst, Max (1891–1976), German painter and sculptor. Founder of a Dada group in Cologne (1919), he later became prominent in the surrealist movement. He used paintings and collages and developed the form known as frottage, in which rubbings are made on paper held over various textured surfaces, to express his often fantastic visions. His most outstanding sculptures are bronzes done since the early 1940s. △1318.

Eros, in Greek mythology, the god of love. A winged child, he was the youngest of the gods and the son of Aphrodite. He was known for the pranks he played on both men and the gods.

Eros, asteroid discovered in 1898 by C. G. Witt. It has an irregular shape. In 1931 and 1975 it approached to within 14,000,000 mi (23,000,000 km) of the Earth. Mean diameter 17mi (29km); mean distance from Sun 144,000,000mi (232,000,000km); mean sidereal period 1.76 yr. △78.

Erosion, in geology, the degradative alteration of landforms by the transportation of the debris of the earth via wind, water, glacial movement, gravity, and living organisms. Economically, erosion may have disastrous results as in the blowing away of topsoil or the weathering of man-made structures, or the alteration of water systems. *See also* Denudation; △258–60, 266.

Er Rif. *See* Rif Atlas.

Erskine Agreement (1809), assurances made by David Erskine, British minister to the United States, involving the British blockade, which prevented ships from entering ports in continental Europe. Although he had no authority to do so, Erskine informed Sec. of State Robert Smith that the blockade no longer applied to the United States. On this basis, Pres. James Madison legalized the resumption of trade with Britain. The British repudiated the agreement, and Erskine was recalled to England. Madision then revived the Non-Intercourse Act (1809).

Eruption, the appearance of volcanic materials on the earth's surface either on land or under sea. Any volcanic material constitutes an eruption, whether it is violent or simply leaking of laval material from volcanic fissures. Any constructive process resulting in the appearance of new material is also eruptive. △176, 250.

Ervin, Sam(uel James, Jr.) (1896–), US political figure, b. Morganton, N.C. He was a representative in the North Carolina General Assembly (1923, 1925, 1931), US congressman (1946–47), and associate judge of the North Carolina supreme court (1948–54), before becoming a US senator (1954–74). In the Senate, he was chairman of the Subcommittee on Constitutional Rights and the Senate Select Committee on Presidential Campaign Activities, the committee that in 1973 investigated the activities of the Committee to Reelect President Nixon.

Eryops. △566.

Erysipelas, contagious skin infection caused by a streptococcus organism. Symptoms include chills and fever, followed by well-delineated, elevated areas of the skin, which become red, shiny, and appear swollen.

Erythema, redness of skin caused by congestion of the capillaries, sometimes as a result of infection. Redness appears first on the face, usually lasts a week.

Erythrocyte, the yellowish, usually disk-shaped, nonnucleated vertebrate red blood cell containing the pigment hemoglobin that carries oxygen to the tissues and gives the blood its red color. Normal human blood contains about 5,000,000 such cells per cubic millimeter of blood on the average, but the number is somewhat higher in men and somewhat lower in women. △688.

Erythromycin, generic name of an antibiotic used to treat infections caused by streptococci, staphylococci, pneumococci and other gram-positive bacteria.

Erzgebirge (Krusnehory or **Ore Mountains),** range extending about 95mi (153km) along the Czechoslovakian-East German border. Uranium, lead, zinc, wolframite, tin, copper, bismuth, antimony, arsenic are the chief ores mined. Highest peak is Klínovec, 4,080ft (1,244m).

Erzurum, city in NE Turkey, near source of the Kara Su River, on Turkish-Russian rail line; capital of Erzurum prov.; site of strategic military station, First Nationalist Congress (July 1919), Atatürk University; trade and agricultural center. Founded 5th century as Theodosiopolis; captured 1071 by Seljuks, 1515 by Turks, and 1828, 1878, and 1916 by Russians. Industries: processed food, cement, metal works. Pop. 105,317.

Esarhaddon, King of Assyria (*c.* 681–669 BC), son of Sennacherib. He crushed revolts and defeated the Chaldaeans, who ruled Babylon. He conquered Egypt (675–669 BC) and overpowered Elam. His son Ashurbanipal succeeded him. △978, 980.

Esau, or **Edom,** son of Isaac and Rebecca, who sold his birthright to his twin brother Jacob. Isaac was then tricked into giving the blessing he meant for Esau to Jacob. Esau settled on Mt Seir and became the leader of the Edomites, a tribe in constant conflict with the Jews.

Escalante, Silvestre Vélez de (*fl.* 1768–79), Spanish explorer and Franciscan friar. In 1776–77, he took part in an expedition seeking a route to California. The expedition covered 2000mi (3220km) through areas now in Arizona, New Mexico and Colorado and is believed to mark the first time that white men penetrated what is now Utah. They also rediscovered the Grand Canyon.

Escalator, a moving staircase, electrically powered, driven by chain and sprocket, and held in the correct plane by two tracks. Usually inclined at 30° and limited to rise to 60ft(18m). As the tracks approach the landing, they pass through a protective comb device. It is used as transportation between floors in mass pedestrian areas such as department stores, office buildings, and subways. The Otis Elevator Company exhibited the first escalator in 1900 at the Paris Exhibition. △1662.

Escalator Clause, stipulation in a union-management work agreement that provides for an automatic upward adjustment in wages when the Consumer Price Index rises by a predetermined amount. Escalator clauses are designed to protect workers from the effects of inflation. *See also* Consumer Price Index.

Escapement. △1658.

Escape Velocity, Rocket, velocity required to free a rocket of the gravitational field of a celestial body or stellar system. Escape velocities for the Earth (7 miles per second); Moon (1.5mps); and solar system (25mps at the position of the Earth's orbit) can be calculated from the formula $v = (2GM/R)^{1/2}$, where G is the gravitational constant, M the mass of the planet or system, and R the distance of the rocket from the center of mass of the system. △144.

Escarpment, or scarp, steep slope of a continuous cliff face or a plateau. Loosening of less-resistant rock by wind or water produces spectacular cliff faces such as the Grand Canyon. Escarpments are produced by faulting and differential erosion. *See also* Faulting. △260.

Eschatology, branch of systematic theology, the study of final, last things. The term was first used in the 19th century with the critical analysis of the New Testament. It deals not only with the study of the kingdom of God, but also with the final destiny of mankind.

Esch-Cummins Act (1920), US legislation continuing federal railroad regulation. It authorized the Interstate Commerce Commission to control rates, supervise sales of securities and expenditures of profits, and consolidate existing lines. It also permitted railroads to pool traffic in the interest of economy.

Escobedo v. Illinois (1964), landmark US Supreme Court decision. It overturned the conviction of a man who had been denied assistance of his attorney during police interrogation and who subsequently confessed to murder. The court held that an accused must be permitted to consult with his attorney "when the process shifts from investigatory to accusatory." This case and *Miranda v. Arizona* (1966) were indicative of Chief Justice Warren's concern for police abuse and his faith in the adversary system of justice. *See also* Miranda v. Arizona (1966).

Escondido, city in S California, 28mi (45km) N of San Diego. Industries: avocado processing, textiles. Inc. 1888. Pop. (1970) 36,792.

Escorial, Museums of, Spanish art museums, 30mi (48.3km) NW of Madrid. The enormous San Lorenzo del Real monastery was begun in 1563 by Philip II as a church, monastery, and royal burial chamber and houses many works of Spanish art. Its church contains a huge high altar and 42 smaller altars as well as sculpture and paintings by Spanish and Italian artists of Philip's era. Decorations of later periods reflect the Mannerist and Baroque styles. The complex contains such items as manuscripts, enamels, goldwork, ivories, and tapestries.

Esdras, two books of the Bible, the first being the beginning of the Apocryphal books. Esdras I includes parts of Chronicles II, Ezra, and Nehemiah. Esdras II, also known as the Ezra Apocalypse, is the product of Jewish and Christian apocalyptic thought and uses the typical imagery of apocalyptic literature. *See also* Apocrypha.

Esfahān. *See* Isfahan.

Eshkol, Levi (1895–1969), prime minister of Israel (1963–69), b. as Levi Shkolnik in Ukraine. He went to Palestine as a Zionist and established one of the first kibbutzim (cooperative farms). After Israel's independence (1948) he became minister of finance (1952–53), succeeded David Ben-Gurion as prime minister, and created the Israel Labor party.

Esker, sand and gravel ridge of fairly gentle slope. It is the result of debris carried by streams that run under or through an old, almost stationary glacier or a retreating one. *See also* Erosion; Faulting. △262.

Eskimo, from Abnaki *Eskimantsic,* and Ojibwa *Askkimey,* meaning "eaters of raw flesh." Inhabitants of arctic and subarctic regions, these Mongoloid latecomers into North America are not regarded by anthropologists as actually American Indians, due to the cultural and linguistic differences they have developed. Their language is distinct from all other aboriginal Americans, and is related only to the Aleut. Today some 25,000 live in Alaska, 15,000 in Canada, and about 40,000 in Greenland. These people have adapted themselves particularly well to the harsh climate of the Far North, and are famous for their marine and mechanical skills. *See also* Aleut. △660, 878.

Eskisehir, city in NW central Turkey; capital of Eskisehir prov.; site of ancient Phrygian city of Dorylaeum. Industries: farm and railroad equipment, refined sugar, cement. Pop. 173,882.

Esophagus, a part of the digestive system, a muscular tube that connects the pharynx to the stomach. A series of involuntary muscular contractions (peristalsis) of the walls of the esophagus move food along from the pharynx to the stomach. Secretions of the mucous lining of the esophagus provide lubrication. △694.

ESP. *See* Extrasensory Perception.

Espalier, a tree or shrub trained to grow flat against a wall, fence, or other support. Espaliered trees are often grown in closely planted rows to form attractive symmetrical patterns. In North America, espaliers are grown chiefly for ornament, but in Europe it was long customary to espalier entire orchards for high yields per acre.

Esparto, or needlegrass, coarse grass with sharply pointed grains and long bristles, used in Mediterranean region for ropes, cord, and paper. Height: to 3ft (0.9m). There are about 150 species. Family Gramineae; genera *Stipa* and *Lygeum.*

Esperanto, artificial language devised in 1887 by the Polish linguist L.L. Zamenhof in the hope that it would eventually become the language of all of mankind. Its spelling and grammar are completely consistent, while its vocabulary is based mainly on that of Western European languages. △866.

Espionage, theft of state secrets considered crucial to national security. Espionage is understood to be internationally practiced, although spying is classified as high treason by most governments. Military data is of the highest value, but political information also is important. While earlier espionage activities were generally conducted by individuals or small groups, modern espionage usually involves large spy networks utilizing advanced technological methods.

Espionage Act (1917), US legislation that limited all activities obstructing the war effort. Given broad powers of censorship, postal surveillance, and deportation, the department of justice often acted indiscriminately against labor discontent and immigrants. The Act was amended in 1918 to limit offensive language and to authorize the postmaster general to prevent mail delivery to suspect groups and individuals. *See also* Sedition Act (1918).

Esquirol, Jean (Etienne Dominique) (1772–1840), French pioneer in the humane treatment of the mentally disturbed. He drafted the law (1838) that established humane treatment in France, founded the first instructional clinic in psychiatry (1817), and wrote the first modern work on clinical psychology, *Les Maladies Mentales* (1838).

Essay, short, prose nonfictional composition on a particular subject, written from a limited, personal point of view. The essay form originated with the French writer Montaigne in the 16th century. Famous English essayists include Abraham Cowley, Francis Bacon (17th century); Addison and Steele, Henry Fielding, Dr. Samuel Johnson, Oliver Goldsmith (18th century); Charles Lamb (19th century). Noted US essayists include Ralph Waldo Emerson, Henry David Thoreau, Oliver Wendell Holmes (19th century). Noted essayists of the 20th century include Clarence Day, James Thurber, George Santayana, Agnes Repplier, Christopher Morley, and E. B. White.

Essay on Population (1798). *See* Malthus, Thomas.

Essen, city in W West Germany, on the Ruhr River, 18mi (29km) NNE of Düsseldorf; grew up around a 9th-century Benedictine convent; from 13th-18th centuries it was a small, imperial state ruled by abbess of convent. Prussia annexed it 1802; site of 11th-century cathedral. Industries: steel, glass, textiles, chemicals. Founded 9th century; chartered as city 10th century. Pop. 698,102.

Essenes, Jewish religious sect, which existed in Palestine from the 2nd century BC to the end of the 1st century AD. The members of the sect lived in communal groups, isolated from the rest of society. Sharing all possessions in common, they stressed ritual purity and were stricter than the Pharisees in their observance. A secrecy developed about the sect, and they shunned public life as well as temple worship. The Dead Sea Scrolls were probably their work.

Essential oil, oil found in flowers, fruits, or plants. It is the source of their characteristic odor.

Essequibo, longest river in Guyana, South America; rises in Serra Uaçari on E Brazil-W Guyana boundary; flows N to Atlantic Ocean, N of Georgetown; navigable for most of 630mi (1,014km).

Essex, Robert Devereux, 2nd earl of (1566–1601), English courtier and soldier. A dashing figure, he reached his peak of favor with Elizabeth I in 1596 after a successful attack on Cadiz. He was made earl marshall (1597) and was sent to Ireland as lord lieutenant (1599). His signing of an unauthorized truce with the Irish rebels provoked the queen's anger and his fall from favor. Unable to regain her affection, he led a rebellion (1601), which failed, and he was subsequently executed.

Essex, one of the seven kingdoms (the Heptarchy) of Anglo-Saxon England. It included modern London, Middlesex, Essex, and much of Hertfordshire. In the 7th century it was merged with Mercia and came under Danelaw jurisdiction during the 8th and 9th centuries. *See also* Heptarchy.

Essex, county in SE England (reorganized 1974), bounded by North Sea and Thames; flat indented coastline with resorts, including Southend-on-Sea, and ports, including Harwich. Inland N is mainly agricultural, producing cereals and vegetables; some dairy farming in S. Towns in SW are part of Greater London. Other towns include Chelmsford and Colchester. Area: 1,528sq mi (3,958sq km). Pop. 1,408,103.

Essex, city in NE Maryland; suburb of Baltimore; site of Essex Community College (1957). Pop. (1970) 38,193.

Essex, USS, US 32-gun frigate. It captured or destroyed more than 40 merchant ships or whalers in an attempt to lessen British naval superiority during the War of 1812. The *Essex* was destroyed in 1814 by British ships while attempting to run a blockade in Chile.

Essex Decision (1805), British decision to halt search and seizure of US vessels attempting to circumvent the British blockade by carrying goods to a neutral port before reshipping them to a belligerent port. The "broken voyage" procedure took place during the Napoleonic Wars, in which the United States tried to remain neutral.

Essex Junto, group of New England businessmen and politicians, some of whom were from Essex County, Mass., who supported the Federalist policies of Alexander Hamilton. They were active at the Hartford Convention, which opposed the War of 1812.

Ermine

Max Ernst: sculpture

Sam Ervin

Essen, West Germany

Estado da India. △1122.

Estates General, national assembly composed of separate divisions, or "estates", each representing, historically, a different social class. In France, the assembly was divided into three estates—clergy, nobility, and commoners—representing the three major divisions of European society before the French Revolution. From its establishment in 1302, the upper classes in the French assembly traditionally allied against the Third Estate. In 1789, however, the three estates united in their refusal to dissolve the assembly at the command of Louis XIV, thus precipitating the French Revolution. The Dutch parliament still retains the name States (Estates)-General. *See also* French Revolution. △1224.

Estavenico (1500?–39), Moroccan scout and guide for explorers Panfilo de Nárvaez and Cabeza de Vaca. He was one of four survivors of the party that explored the Florida coast in 1528. In 1539 he guided Fray Marcos into the area of the present state of New Mexico, but died at Indian hands.

Este, Italian aristocratic family that ruled in Ferrara (13th–16th centuries) and in Modena and Reggio (15th–18th centuries). An important Guelf family in support of the papacy through the Middle Ages, the Este decisively established their rule over Ferrara in 1240. With the rule of Niccolo III came control over much of Emilia. **Ercole I** (reigned 1471–1505) and his son, **Cardinal Ippolito I** (died 1520), were both patrons of the poet Ludovico Ariosto, who dedicated his *Orlando Furioso* to the cardinal. **Alfonso II** (reigned 1559–97) was the patron of the poet Torquato Tasso.

Ester, any of a class of organic compounds formed, along with water, by reaction between an alcohol and an acid. The commonest type, those formed by carboxylic acids, have the general formula RCO.OR'. Simple esters are fragrant volatile compounds, used as flavorings. Fats are esters of glycerin and long-chain carboxylic acids. *See also* Fat.

Esterházy Family, Magyar clan whose many prominent members since the 16th century contributed greatly to the histories of Austria and Hungary. Instrumental in freeing Hungary from the Turks, the Esterházys were noted for their military and political ability, as well as their generous patronage of such artists as Joseph Haydn.

Esther, biblical book that describes measures taken by Esther to avert the mass killing of her people, the Jews. It was Haman the Agagite who advised the Persian King that Jews were a pernicious race and received permission to undertake their annihilation. The feast of Purim, a Jewish holiday, celebrates Haman's overthrow. This book is supposedly written by Mordecai, Esther's cousin and guardian.

Estivation, ability of certain organisms, including snails and some rodents, to spend the summer in a dormant state. It serves, in desert areas, as a survival mechanism during water and food shortages.

Estonia (Estonskaja), constituent republic of the USSR. It is a low plateau covered with glacial deposits and many lakes and has a mild climate. It is bordered W by the Baltic Sea, SW and N by Gulfs of Riga and Finland, S by Latvia, and E by the USSR. It extracts considerable amounts of shale oil and gas and has a productive fertilizer industry. Pig-raising, fishing, and dairy-farming are major occupations in an economy that has been collectivized and integrated into the USSR since the late 1940s.

People and History. Members of the Finno-Ugrian family of peoples, Estonians reached the area in the beginning of the Christian era from the Volga region and intermarried with German settlers. Their culture is influenced both by the Germans and the Finns. Over 55% of the population is urban and about 35% belongs to the Lutheran Church. The Russian minority is over 20%. Pagan Estonian tribes were conquered in the 13th century by Danes and Germans. Christianity was introduced, and Estonian peasants came under the economic subjugation by Hanseatic merchants (1561). By 1629, Sweden held all of Estonia, which was conquered by Russia in 1710. By the mid-19th century nationalist rebellions started, were repressed, and heavy emigration to the United States followed. Russia's defeat in WWI led to the formation of an independent republic in 1918, an independence recognized by the USSR in 1920. A dictatorship established in 1934 gave Estonia more political stability, but the Nazi-Soviet Pact of 1939 placed the Baltic countries under USSR rule. The country was occupied by the Germans in WWII and retaken by Soviet forces in 1944.

PROFILE

Official name: Estonia Soviet Socialist Republic
Area: 17,431sq mi (45,100sq km)
Population: 1,357,000
Chief cities: Tallinn (capital); Tartu
Government: Constituent republic of USSR
Religion: Lutheran (major)
Language: Estonian
Industries: paper, plywood, textiles, fertilizers, electrical and radio apparatus, glass, leather goods, concrete, bricks, processed fish
Agriculture: fishing, timber, dairy cattle, hogs, flax, potatoes, sugar beets
Minerals: shale oil, natural gas, peat, limestone, dolomite, marl, clay, phosphorite

Estrada Palma, Tomás (1835–1908), first President of Cuba (1902–06). Long active in the struggle against Spain, he continued the public works and other economic programs begun during the American occupation.

Estrées, Gabrielle d' (1573–99), mistress to Henry IV of France, who fell in love with her in 1590. Henry is said to have altered his political affairs for their relationship, and she was about to become his wife when she became ill and died. She gave him three children.

Estremadura (Extremadura), historic region in W central Spain, on the Portuguese border; crossed by Tagus and Guadiana rivers; includes provinces of Cáceres and Badajoz; battlefield during Spanish-Portuguese wars; birthplace of Francisco Pizarro and Hernán Cortéz. Industries: sheep and pig raising, lumber, silver, coal, copper, wine, oil, cereals. Pop. 1,145,376.

Estrene, steroid hormone (formula $C_{18}H_{22}O_2$) formed from estradiol and found in pregnancy urine. It is one of the three estrogens but has less activity than estradiol. It is used in the treatment of menopausal symptoms. *See also* Hormones; Steroid.

Estrogens, the female sex hormones. They control the menstrual cycle, prepare for fertilization and nourishment of the embryo, and determine the female secondary sex characteristics. Estrogens are produced in the ovaries, cortex of the adrenal glands, and testes and are also made synthetically. They are used in oral contraceptives and to treat the symptoms of menopause, threatened abortion, and many other conditions. Evidence suggests that long-term administration of estrogens may increase the risk of uterine cancer. △700,726.

Estrus cycle, physiological changes occurring during the female reproductive cycle of most placental mammals. Controlled by hormones, it is evident among mammals other than man. Cycles of different animals vary in frequency and length. Typically, ovulation is associated with the estrus (heat) period. △700.

Estuary, coastal region in which a river mouth opens into the ocean and greatly changes the salinity of the seawater. Estuaries are typified by the ratio of inflow to loss of fresh water or by shape. To some extent, an estuary is a drowned river mouth, or one whose access to open sea is partially blocked by offshore bars, spits, or sand islands. △226.

ET. *See* Ephemeris Time.

Eta, Japanese minority group, generally regarded as the lowest caste in traditional Japanese society. Thought to be descendants of groups such as butchers and tanners, associated with the taking of life, they are still shunned by many Japanese, despite the removal of their legal disabilities in the last century.

Eta Carinae. △114.

Eta Meson, uncharged elementary particle (symbol η) that is a meson with zero spin. *See also* Hadron.

Etching, method of intaglio (incised) printing used especially for reproducing black and white designs. In this process, acid, which bites into a metal plate, is used to eat away the outlines of the design. When magnified, the etched line has almost square ends. The etching process allows a more freely drawn figure than does the engraving process.

First, the artist covers the metal plate, usually copper, with an acid-proof ground made of a mixture containing asphaltum. Next, the design is drawn onto the grounded plate with an etching needle so that the lines penetrate the ground. The plate is then placed in an acid that eats away the exposed line. To create shading, the etcher places an acid resist over the desired areas and once again immerses the plate to allow the acid to wear away the still exposed lines. When the plate is finished, it is rolled with ink and placed in an etching press to be printed. Corrections and changes can be made by covering the plate with a new ground and reworking it.

Ethane. △1558.

Ethanol, or ethyl alcohol, colorless volatile liquid (C_2H_5OH) produced by the fermentation of molasses, grains, etc, or by the catalytic hydrogenation of ethylene. Its many uses include beverages, cleaning solutions, rocket fuels, cosmetics, and pharmaceuticals. Properties: sp gr 0.789; melt. pt. -179.1°F (-117.3°C); boil. pt. 173.3°F(78.5°C).

Ethelbald (died 757), king of Mercia (716–57). Although not noted as a great warrior, by 731 he controlled all of England south of the Humber River. He also encouraged the development of the church by making large grants of land and freeing ecclesiastical lands from most obligations to the king. He was killed by his own bodyguard.

Ethelbert (died 616), king of Kent, who came to power in 560. Although his attempt to extend his kingdom westward was thwarted in 568 by the West Saxons, by the late 6th century he was the strongest ruler in England south of the Humber River. The first Christian king in Anglo-Saxon England, he allowed Augustine and his monks to settle and preach in Canterbury and founded the see of Rochester.

Ethelbert (died 866), king of Kent and Wessex. An elder brother of Alfred the Great, he succeeded to the throne of Kent in 858 and to that of Wessex in 860, thus uniting the two kingdoms. During his reign the Danes sacked Winchester.

Ethelfleda (died 918), daughter of Alfred the Great, known as "Lady of the Mercians." She married Ethelred, Ealdorman of the Mercians, whom she succeeded (911). She joined her brother, Edward the Elder, to recover British territory from the Danes, capturing Derby (917) and Leicester (918).

Ethelfrith (died 616), king of Northumbria. Uniting the kingdoms of Bernicia and Deira, he inflicted defeats on the Scots (603) and the Welsh (613–16), and laid the foundations of Northumbrian political dominance in Britain. He was killed by supporters of his successor, Edwin of Deira.

Ethelred I (died 871), the fourth son of Ethelwulf of Wessex, he was king of Wessex and Kent (866–71). During his short reign he was besieged by the Danes, who occupied York (866) and attacked much of England. He was succeeded by his brother Alfred.

Ethelred II (968–1016), king of England (978–1016), called the Unready (fr. OE without *rede* or counsel). He ascended the throne on the murder of his half brother, Edward the Martyr (978), and was soon beseiged by Danish plunderers. In 994 he began to pay off the raiders with money raised by the Danegeld, but the Danes returned nonetheless in 997. A massacre of Danes in 1001 brought only severe retaliation from the Danish king Sweyn and his successor, Canute.

Ethelwulf (died 858), son and successor of Egbert, king of Wessex from 839 to 858. During most of his reign he successfully defended his realm against Danish attack, and in 852, to help Burgred of Mercia, he subdued the North Welsh. A religious man, in 855 he traveled to Rome with his fifth son Alfred (the Great). As he returned from that pilgrimage he married Judith, daughter of Charles II of France. Thereafter he allowed his son Ethelbald to rule Wessex, while he ruled only in Kent, where a third son, Ethelbert, succeeded him.

Ether, colorless volatile flammable liquid ($C_2H_5OC_2H_5$) prepared by the action of sulfuric acid on ethanol followed by distillation. It is used as an anesthetic, industrial solvent, fuel additive, and refrigerant. This compound (diethyl ether) is a typical member of the ethers with the general formula ROR. Properties: melt. pt. -177.2°F (-116.2°C), boil. pt. 94.1°F (34.5°C).

Ether, the hypothetical medium that was supposed to fill all space, even inside matter, and to offer no resistance to motion. Postulated as a medium to support the propagation of electromagnetic radiations, it is now regarded as an unnecessary assumption. △1522.

Ethical Culture, Society for, association founded in the United States by Felix Adler in 1876. Adler broke with Judaism and Christianity, and developed a moral system that does not have to rely on a religious basis, the essential ethical rule being to live so as to evoke the best in others, and therefore in oneself.

Ethics, the study of human conduct in the light of moral principles; also called moral philosophy. Moral principles may be postulated on religious, political, or individual criteria. They may be thought to be innate or to evolve from experiential discrimination. △858, 860.

Ethiopia (Yaitopya), independent nation in E Africa. Ruled by Haile Selassie for 44 years until a coup deposed him in 1974, it is on the coast of E central Africa. Coptic Christians make up the largest religious group. The first known coffee plant was grown here.

Land and Economy: An inland country until federation with Eritrea in 1952, it is bounded by the Red Sea, Afars and Issas, Kenya, and Sudan. A high central plateau, 8,000ft (3,200m) above sea level, is cut by the Blue Nile and Rift Valley, dropping off to lowlands of Sudan (W) and Somali plains (SE). The climate ranges from temperate to humid, with a June-September rainy season. With 90% of the population in farming, the country is self-sufficient in food. The major export is coffee. Development of potash reserves is expected, and copper mining is underway. Development programs have been financed by foreign countries and international agencies.

People: Ethiopians are descended from two African tribes, the Hamite (Cushite) and Semite, and from Negroes dating from the 8th century BC. The main religion is Coptic Christian. Amharic is the official language, but English is widely spoken. Literacy is estimated at 5%.

Government: Ruled since Haile Selassie's removal as a one-party socialist state; Ethiopia's 1955 constitution provides for a Chamber of Deputies elected by universal suffrage and an appointed senate. All political parties were barred by Selassie.

History: The Old Testament records a visit to Ethiopia by the Queen of Sheba. Its ruling house is said to have descended from King Solomon's son. Modern history dates back to Menelik (reigned 1889–1913), whose line of succession led to Emperor Haile Selassie, crowned in 1930. His reign was interrupted by the 1936 Italian invasion. British troops freed the country in 1941. Selassie was deposed by a military junta in 1974; the new socialist government vowed to abolish the feudal land system, nationalize financial institutions, abolish the monarchy, and offer religious freedom. From 1970 Arab- and Muslim-backed guerrillas in Ethiopia's province of Eritrea started a secession movement that was a severe economic drain on the government.

PROFILE

Official name: Ethiopia
Area: 471,777sq mi (1,221,902sq km)
Population: 27,240,000
Density: 57per sq mi (22per sq km)
Chief cities: Addis Ababa (capital); Asmara
Government: Military junta
Religion: Coptic Christian
Language: Amharic
Monetary unit: Ethiopian dollar
Gross national product: $2,240,000,000
Per capita income: $83
Industries: food processing, cement, shoes, textiles, brick
Agriculture: coffee, wheat, barley, millet, tobacco, sugar cane, cattle, sheep, civet
Minerals: platinum, gold, silver, manganese, tin, asbestos, potash, sulphur, salt, coal, iron
Trading partners: United States

Ethmoid Bone. △682.

Ethnocentrism, intense identification with one's own culture as the best. All human groups have a conscious and an unconscious tendency to assume the superiority of their own culture while devaluing other cultures and the unfamiliar. Ethnocentrism is an automatic, emotional response, not a rational one. *See also* Discrimination; Prejudice. △894.

Ethnography, study of the culture of a single tribe or society. Ethnographers gather anthropological data by direct observation during a period of residential fieldwork. Techniques used include participation in the group's economic and social life, linguistic fluency, and interviews with informants. *See also* Anthropology; Ethnology. △874.

Ethnolinguistics, the study of the interrelationship of language and culture in the present as well as the ancient past. Social organization and life styles of ancient peoples are deduced from studying their vocabularies. Edward Sapir suggested that people see the world as their language presents it to them. △866.

Ethnology, the comparative study of cultures. Using ethnographic material from two or more societies, ethnology can attempt to cover their whole cultural range or concentrate on a single cultural trait. Originally a term covering the whole of anthropology, toward the end of the 19th century historical ethnology was developed in an attempt to trace cultural diffusion. Now ethnologists concentrate on cross-cultural studies, using statistical methods of analysis. *See also* Anthropology, Cultural; Ethnography. △658–60, 874–82.

Ethology, study of animal behavior, first outlined in the 1920s by Konrad Lorenz of Austria and Niko Tinbergen of the Netherlands. Ethologists study natural processes that range across all animal groups, such as the release and inhibition of innate behavior patterns. Field, rather than laboratory, observation is emphasized, but experimental models are used. Evolutionary and neuroanatomical studies are included. △464, 536, 556, 558.

Ethyl Alcohol, *See* Ethanol.

Ethylene. △1556, 1558, 1564.

Etna, Mount (Mongibello), active volcano on E coast of Sicily, Italy; highest active volcano in Europe and highest mountain in Italy. Pindar and Aeschylus described the first known eruption (475 BC); major eruptions occurred in 1169, 1669, 1971; lower slopes are used for agriculture. Height: 10,958ft. (3,342m).

Eton, district in S England, in Berkshire, on Thames opposite Windsor; site of famous private school, Eton College, founded 1440–41 by Henry VI. Pop. 3,954.

Etruria, ancient region in Italy, bounded by the Tiber River, Apennines, and Tyrrhenian Sea. Inhabitants migrated from Asia Minor *c.* 900 BC and divided into several city-states; Etruscan civilization peaked *c.* 500 BC; it was gradually taken over by Rome. Site of kingdom created by Napoleon AD 1801; inc. by French Empire 1808; commercially and agriculturally prosperous; celebrated for its art. △1010.

Etruscan Language. △1010.

Etruscans, earliest inhabitants of Etruria NW of the Tiber (modern Tuscany) who came to prominence and dominated an extensive empire in central Italy by 500 BC, before the rise of Rome. The Etruscans formed a religious confederation of independent city-states with its center at Volsinii. Their origins remain obscure. They developed a vital culture, material artifacts of which show distinct characteristics that were derived from E Mediterranean and Greek sources. But much of their sophisticated metalwork, naturalistic sculpture (including the Capitoline wolf, bronze portrait busts, and painted terracotta sarcophagi), and funerary frescoes depicting everyday scenes and festivals reveal an energetic, individual style not directly based on any other tradition. Their language was entirely unlike those of the other early Italian peoples. Herodotus maintained that the Etruscans emigrated from Lydia in the 12th century BC. Modern scholarly opinion is divided as to their early development but it is certain that their civilization had attained cultural unity by the 7th century BC.

By 500 BC the Etruscans were at the zenith of their power, controlling Umbria, much of Latium, and colonies in the major islands of the Mediterranean and in coastal Spain. Rich in iron ore and clay, they exploited these materials to the fullest in their arts and carried on an extensive trade with the East. Their influence in the Mediterranean conflicted with Greek interests and diminished by the late 5th century BC. At the same time the Celts halted their northern expansion and the Samnites forced them from Campagna. The Romans, two of whose kings, Tarquinius Priscus and Tarquinius Superbus, were Etruscan, adopted many features of Etruscan art, religion, politics, and technology before they began in the 4th century to spread over Italy and vanquish Etruscan cities. Veii fell in *c.* 396 BC, and Etruscan independence ended entirely in 88 BC, when the last families allied with Roman general Sulla against Marius. △1010.

ETV. *See* Educational Television.

Etymologiae. △1780.

Etymology, the branch of philology dealing with the history and derivation of words. The term also refers to the derivation of a given word. The etymology of the word *telephone,* for example, is that it is a combination of the Greek *tele* ("distant") and *phone* ("sound"). The word *coach,* by contrast, is derived from the city of Kocs, in Hungary, where coaches were invented and first used. △424.

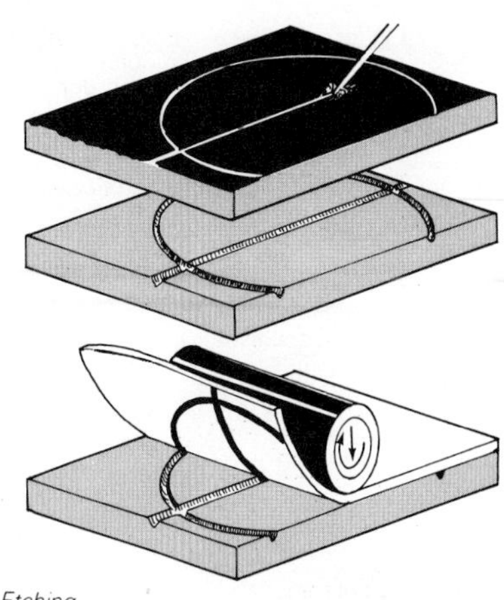

Etching

Ethanol: rectification

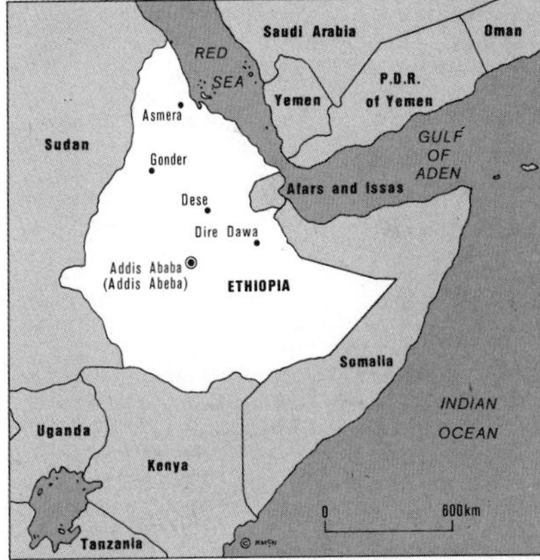
Saudi Arabia
Oman
RED SEA
P.D.R. of Yemen
Yemen
Asmera
Sudan
Gonder
GULF OF ADEN
Afars and Issas
Dese
Dire Dawa
Addis Ababa (Addis Abeba)
ETHIOPIA
Somalia
INDIAN OCEAN
Uganda
Kenya
0
600km
Tanzania

Ethiopia

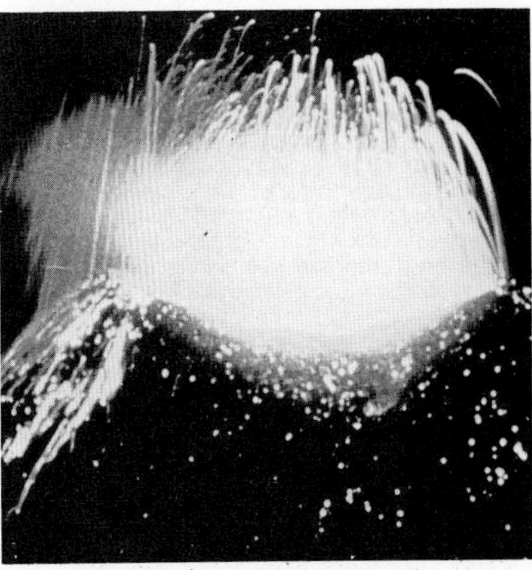

Mount Etna: night eruption

Etzioni, Amitai W(erner) (1929–), US sociologist, b. Cologne, Germany. Associated with Columbia University for most of his career, Etzioni has done research in social change, complex organizations, and political sociology. His works include *A Comparative Analysis of Complex Organizations* (1961) and *The Active Society: A Theory of Societal and Political Processes* (1968).

Euboea (Evvoia) mountainous island in SE central Greece, in Aegean Sea, separated from mainland by Euripos channel; 2nd-largest island in Greece, after Crete; Chalcis is the administrative center. Under Athenian domination 506–411 BC, taken by Philip II of Macedon 350–194 BC; after the fall of Rome, it was held successively by Byzantines, Venetians, and Turks (1470–1821); it was inc. into Greece after independence was declared (1830). Industries: livestock, grapes, timber, grains, marble quarries, lignite and magnesite mining. Area: 1,467sq mi (3,800sq km). Pop. 162,986.

Eucalyptus, group of trees native mainly to Australia and Tasmania and cultivated in warm and temperate regions. They are a valuable source of hardwood and oils. Generally, they have tall, slender trunks, sometimes covered with exuded gum; bluish or whitish leaves; petalless flowers with abundant nectar; and woody fruits. Height: to 300ft (91m). The 500 species include the Australian mountain ash *Eucalyptus dalryurpleana;* the Tasmanian blue gum *E. globulus;* and the coolabah tree *E. coolabah.* Family Myrtaceae. △448, 590.

Eucharist, Christian sacrament, the central rite of the mass or church service. It reenacts the Last Supper: Christ gave his disciples bread, saying, "This is my body," and wine, saying, "This is my blood." △ 1026.

Euchre, card game usually played by two sets of partners using a 32 card deck, from seven to ace in each suit. Each player receives five cards, and trump is then established by using a card from the deck or a trump nominated by a player. There are five tricks in each game, which count toward points. The team that establishes trump must win all five tricks to score two points. Scoring three or four tricks counts as 1 point. If they fail to make three tricks, their opponents receive two points. It takes five points to make a game.

Eucken, Rudolf Christoph (1846–1926), German philosopher. Winner of the 1908 Nobel Prize for literature and author of *The Meaning and Value of Life,* he considered himself a philosopher of life as man experiences it and as process and evolution. He believed that all conscious beings were bound together by independent spiritual life, also that there was a social need for new philosophies. Works include *Individual and Society* (1923) and *Socialism: An Analysis* (1921).

Euclid (330?–275 BC), Ancient Greek mathematician, about whom very little is known, except that he taught at Alexandria during the reign of Ptolemy. He is remembered for his text books on geometry, especially the *Elements,* which was first printed in 1482 in a Latin translation of the Arabic. Other works include *Data* (on geometry) and *Phaenomena* (on astronomy) and several books that have been lost. △1444, 1462.

Euclid, city in NE Ohio, on Lake Erie, adjacent to Cleveland; site of National American Shrine of Our Lady of Lourdes. Industries: multigraphing equipment, road machinery, airplane parts, castings. Settled 1798; inc. 1848. Pop. (1970) 71,552.

Euclidean Geometry, geometry based on similar assumptions to those used by Euclid (*c.* 300 BC) in his book *Elements.* Euclid's geometry is a prime example of an axiomatic system of reasoning, although his original postulates have since been extended. He used a number of simple "definitions" of point, line, etc, together with a set of axioms, which he called "common notions." These concerned basic ideas about equality, of the type "the whole is greater than the part." Finally, he proposed five postulates on geometrical properties, including the famous fifth postulate on parallel lines. On these foundations, he built a vast structure of theorems on the properties of plane and solid figures. Euclid's geometry is the geometry that fits normal measurements made on Earth. *See also* Axiomatic Method; Non-Euclidean Geometry. △ 1462.

Euclid of Megaro, (*c.* 450–368 BC), founder of the Megarian school of philosophy. The main influence on his school was Socrates. The influence of Eleaticism is also evident in his stress on the unity of goodness. *See also* Eleaticism; Megarians.

Eudes, or **Odo** (died 898), West Frankish king and count of Paris, son of Robert the Strong, came to rule (888) when the East Franks overthrew Charles III the Fat. Troubled by rebellion in Flanders and Aquitaine, and by constant battle with the Normans, he was forced to submit first to Arnulf, king of the East Franks, and later to king Charles III the Simple. He died in disgrace after a 10-year reign. He was an ancestor of the Capetians.

Eudocia Macrembolitissa (*c.* 1020–1096), wife of Byzantine emperor Constantine X; assumed rule as a widow in her 40s and was obliged to marry a general, Romanus IV, to help ward off the Turks. His military campaign failed, however, and the empress managed to secure the succession of her son, Michael.

Eudoxia (1669–1731), Russian tsarina, was married to the warlike Tsar Peter I the Great in 1689. The marriage was unsuccessful, and she was sent to a monastery in 1698, which she secretly left. She was imprisoned and her lover tortured to death in 1718, but regained her freedom in 1727 after her grandson became tsar as Peter II.

Eugene, city in W Oregon, on Willamette River, 62mi (100km) S of Salem; seat of Lane co; headquarters of Willamette National Forest; site of University of Oregon (1872). Industries: meat packing, timber, fruit and vegetable canning. Settled 1851; inc. 1864. Pop. (1970) 78,389.

Eugene of Savoy (1663–1736), French prince and general in the service of the Holy Roman Empire. He entered Austrian service in 1683 and won distinction fighting the Turks at Vienna (1683), Belgrade (1688), and Zenta (1697). In the War of the Spanish Succession (1701–14), his victories over the French included Blenheim (1704), Oudenarde (1708), and Malplaquet (1709), all won with the English Duke of Marlborough. In 1714, Eugene negotiated the Peace of Rastatt. He again defeated the Turks in the war of 1714–18.

Eugene Onegin (1823–31), Romantic novel in verse by Aleksandr Pushkin. Composed in 14-line stanzas, the poem develops the character of Onegin as a prime example of the "superfluous man"—detached, arrogant, and cynical. Alternately bored and disgusted by high society, he is nevertheless unable to escape its restrictions. △1240.

Eugenics, movement founded in the 19th century by Francis Galton that proposed controlled improvement of the human race through selective breeding, ie, encouraging people with the best qualities to mate with each other while preventing criminals, the retarded, and the insane from mating. Galton concluded that "geniuses" ran in families and were largely the products of superior heredity. Modern scientists, however, recognize that variations in environment are just as important in influencing differences as are variations in heredity. △416.

Eugénie (1826–1920), consort of Napoleon III and French empress. Born of a Spanish father and American mother, she became the wife of Louis Napoleon shortly after he declared the second empire in 1853. Regent in her husband's absences (1859,1865,-1870), her influence as a Catholic and conservative was often felt in French affairs. When the empire fell in 1870 she fled to England, where she became friends with Queen Victoria after her husband's death in 1873. Her only child, a son, was killed in 1879 in the Zulu War.

Eugénie Grandet (1833), novel by Honoré de Balzac. It involves the tragic fate of an heiress whose father banishes her penniless suitor and disinherits her. On his death, however, Eugénie does inherit, but her lover marries another. She marries hopelessly, is soon widowed, and resigns herself to philanthropy.

Euglena, flagellate protozoa found in fresh water. It has an elongated body that appears green because of the 15 or so chloroplasts in it; there is a characteristic "eyespot" and a single flagellum. It moves by beating the flagellum and by alternately elongating and contracting the body to produce a squirming motion. Length: 3/2500–4/250in (.03–.4mm). Most common is *Euglena gracilis.* Class Mastigophora. △406.

Eulachon, or candlefish, marine smelt of inshore temperate waters or cold seas of Northern Hemisphere. It has oily flesh and was used by Indians to make torches. Length: 12in (30.5cm). Family Osmeridae; species *Thaleichthyes pacificus.*

Eulalia, tall perennial grass native to SE Asia and widely cultivated for lawn or border ornamentals. It has white, plumelike flower clusters and striped leaves. Species *Miscanthus sinensis.* Or, perennial grass of Australia and SE Asia important as forage. Genus *Eulalia.* Family Gramineae.

Euler, Leonhard (1707–83), Swiss mathematician. After studying under Bernoulli in Basle he was appointed professor in St. Petersburg. In 1741 he went to Berlin as head of the Academy of Sciences, but returned to St. Petersburg in 1766. His mathematical expertise was very wide-ranging and in spite of failing eyesight he published over 800 papers on subjects including mechanics, algebra, optics, and astronomy. △1466, 1470.

Euler, Ulf Svante von (1905–), Swedish physiologist. He shared the 1970 Nobel Prize in physiology or medicine with Julius Axelrod and Bernard Katz for work on the chemistry of nerve transmission. Euler demonstrated that the nerve endings of sympathetic nerves release the chemical noradrenaline, which acts to transmit the nerve impulse from one cell to another.

Euler Diagram, simple diagram used in logic to illustrate syllogisms. Classes of objects are represented by circles so that, for example, a premise of the type "some *a* is *b*" can be represented by overlap of these circles. *See also* Venn Diagram. △1470.

Eumenides, in Greek mythology, earth and fertility goddesses. They also had moral and social functions.

Eunuchoidism, a deficiency of testicular function which, before puberty, retards development of genitals, and of secondary sex characteristics (facial hair, deepening voice). It can also occur after puberty with milder effect.

Euonymus, genus of deciduous or evergreen shrubs and woody vines found in North America, Central America, Europe, and Asia. They have square twigs, short, narrow leaves and inconspicuous flowers. The fruits are orange-red. Height: 2–12ft (0.6–3.7m) Among 120 species are strawberry bush *Euonymus americanus,* burning bush *E. atropurpureus,* European spindle tree *E. europaeus,* and evergreen, climbing *E. fortuneii.* Family Celastraceae.

Euphotic Zone. △626.

Euphrates (Firat, or **Al-Furat),** river formed by the confluence of the Murat Nehri (E) and the Kara Su (W), it flows from E Turkey across Syria into central Iraq where it joins the Tigris River. Mesopotamia, along the lower Euphrates, was the birthplace of the ancient civilizations of Babylonia and Assyria, and site of the ancient cities Sippar, Babylon, Erech, Larsa, Ur. Length: 2,235mi (3,598km).

Eureka, city in NW California, 83mi (134km) S of Oregon border; seat of Humboldt co. Industries: fishing, lumbering, tourism. Inc. 1856. Pop. (1970) 24,337.

Euripides, (*c.* 484–406 BC), Greek playwright. Considered one of three great writers of Greek tragedy, with Aeschylus and Sophocles, he was a close friend of Socrates, who may have influenced his writing. His plots were complicated; his ideas sometimes controversial and offensive; but his language was simple. His heroes, whether gods or mortals, are portrayed with sceptical candor. His contemporaries saw him as a morose misogynist. Only 18 of his 92 plays survive. His reputation grew after his death. △988.

Eurodollar. △1384.

Europa, in Greek mythology, wife of Asterius, mother by Zeus of King Minos of Crete. She was carried off to Crete by Zeus, who was disguised as a white bull.

Europa, satellite of Jupiter; one of the Galilean satellites. Diameter 1,800mi (2,900km); mean distance from planet 414,000mi (670,600km); mean sidereal period 3.55 days. △86.

Europe, western fifth of the Eurasian land mass, considered a separate continent. Of the continents only Australia is smaller.

Land. Mainland Europe is a roughly triangular peninsula of Eurasia, wide where the Ural Mts form much of the E boundary and growing narrow as it reaches W to the Iberian Peninsula. The Caucasus Mts also help separate the continent from Asia and provide its highest peak, Elbrus (18,481ft; 5,637m). Other major ranges are the Apennines of Italy, the Pyrenees between France and Spain, the Kjølens of Scandinavia, and the Alps of W central Europe. Plains reach from W France across N Germany and Poland and over much of the USSR. Major islands of Europe include the British Isles, Sicily, Sardinia, Corsica, and Iceland. The Caspian and Black seas help to separate

Europe from Asia. The Caspian is the world's largest lake, with an area of about 144,000sq mi (372,960sq km). Because of wide channels leading to the Mediterranean, the Black ranks as a sea rather than a lake. Europe's longest river, the Volga, drains into the Caspian Sea. Other important waterways are the Danube of central Europe and the Rhine and Rhône farther W.

Lying mostly in the N temperate zone and being nearly surrounded by seas, such as the Mediterranean, North, Baltic, Norwegian, and Barents, Europe has a mild climate. The far N, the E, and parts of Spain suffer from little rainfall; but about 75% of the land supports pine, cedar, oak, and other forests. The far N consists of tundra. Wolves and bears are now scarce, but rabbits remain plentiful and deer survive in many places. Important for furs are fox, mink, and weasel. Birds include finches, thrushes, and grouse, but storks are becoming scarce. Eggs of the Caspian Sea sturgeon are world-famous as caviar.

People. Southern Europeans are often short and dark; short, lighter people live in the central areas, and taller, fair ones occupy the N. People of the SE are often Greek Orthodox. Those of the S central and W, except for scattered examples, are Roman Catholic, and many of those N of France and Italy are Protestant. Major languages include Germanic tongues in the N, Slavic in the central and E, and Latin (Romance) in the W central and S.

Economy. Many European farms are relatively small, raising a variety of crops—from beets and potatoes to wheat and rice. Grapes, olives, and citrus fruits flourish in the S. Scandinavia and the Low Countries are noted for dairy products. A few countries, especially the USSR, have petroleum, and iron ore is fairly common. Lead, zinc, manganese, and nickel are also found. European industry is highly developed, although the Mediterranean nations are somewhat less diversified.

History. About 500 years before the Christian era, Greece had an advanced civilization, but by Christ's time the Romans flourished. After the fall of the Roman Empire in AD 476, warlike tribes fought for power. Crusades to take the Holy Land from the Muslims brought Europeans in contact with Arabic medicine and culture, and late in the 13th century Christians ceased mounting Crusades and gradually launched a new age of learning and artistic achievement, the Renaissance. The development of printing from movable type in the 1450s increased the spread of information, which continued as Christopher Columbus and Vasco da Gama explored the seas and Martin Luther questioned Roman Catholic practices. In E Europe the Ottoman Turks built an empire, German Catholics held central Europe in the Holy Roman Empire, and in the W the English gained power, especially after defeating the Spanish Armada in 1588. The French Revolution at the end of the 18th century caused monarchs to worry about holding their thrones, a concern that continued as Napoleon Bonaparte undertook the conquest of Europe. After his defeat in 1815, European nations concentrated on empire building around the globe. Germany's growing strength helped lead to World War I (1914–18), and during that period of turmoil Communist revolutionaries overthrew the Russian monarchy. Aggressive dictators came to power in Germany and Italy, leading to World War II (1939–45), which revealed the USSR as a major power and left Europe divided between Communist and non-Communist ideologies. The free nations of W and S Europe have sought closer economic and cultural links, through such organizations as the European Economic Community. The Communist countries have developed similar ties while contacts between the two blocs have become more frequent and closer. △190, 990, 1052, 1066, 1070–76, 1088–90, 1102, 1128, 1158, 1182, 1226, 1232, 1262, 1298, 1302–06, 1332–40, 1344, 1350, 1390.

PROFILE

Area: 3,700,000sq mi (9,583,000sq km)
Largest nations: USSR, European (1,940,000sq mi; 5,000,000sq km); France (211,207sq mi; 549,000sq km); Spain (194,897sq mi; 504,800sq km)
Population: 725,000,000
Density: 196per sq mi (75per sq km). Most populous nations: USSR, European, 250,000,000; Germany, West, 61,900,000; Italy, 55,000,000
Chief cities: Paris; Moscow; London
Manufacturing (major products): steel, automobiles, chemicals, airplanes, textiles
Agriculture (major products): wheat, oats, barley, sugar beets, grapes, dairy products
Minerals (major): petroleum, iron ore, lead, zinc, nickel, manganese, magnesium

European Atomic Energy Community (Euratom), since 1958 an organization of European countries to control and develop the nuclear energy capabilities of its member nations. Treating this energy as a resource of the entire European community, Euratom has facilitated international coordination of both manpower and materials. △1356.

European Common Market. *See* European Economic Community.

European Corn Borer, European moth caterpillar that has become the most destructive insect pest of corn in North America. It is flesh-colored with dark spots. Length: to 1in (25mm). Species *Ostrinia nubilalis.*

European Deer. *See* Fallow Deer.

European Economic Community (Common Market), multinational economic and political organization dedicated to European development. Its initial members were France, West Germany, Italy, Belgium, the Netherlands, and Luxembourg. Established in the Treaty of Rome (1957), its objectives are to abolish tariffs among member nations and to establish common tariffs against non-member nations. The general purpose of this association was to create an economic union of common policies in the areas of agriculture, trade, antitrust, labor supply, transportation, capital requirements, wage policies, and the establishment of new enterprises. △942, 1356.

European Flounder. *See* Plaice.

European Free Trade Association, multinational group established by agreement in 1959 in Stockholm. Comprised of Austria, Denmark, Norway, Portugal, Sweden, Switzerland, and the United Kingdom, it seeks to promote free trade among its members. A great deal of competition has existed between the group and the European Common Market, since both have essentially the same objectives, although the latter is more politically oriented. △1356.

European Mouflon. *See* Mouflon.

European Willow. △450.

Europium, metallic element (symbol Eu) of the lanthanide group, first isolated as the oxide 1901 by Eugène Demarçay. Chief ores are monazite (phosphate) and bastänite (fluorocarbonate). The metal is used in pyrophoric alloys and as a neutron absorber in reactors. Properties: at. no. 63; at. wt. 151.96; sp. gr. 5.25 (25°C); melt. pt. 1519°F (826°C); boil. pt. 2622°F (1439°C); most common isotope Eu^{153} (52.18%). *See also* Lanthanide Elements.

Europus. *See* Dura.

Eurydice, in Greek mythology, the wife of Orpheus. In fleeing from Aristaeus she was mortally bitten by a snake. Orpheus pursued her to the Underworld and persuaded Hades to release Eurydice. They made a bargain that Orpheus broke when he turned to look at his wife before emerging to earth. Eurydice was whisked back to Hades forever. △840.

Eurypterids. △564.

Eurythmics, a system of musical and dance training which has influenced ballet and acting. Developed by the Swiss Emile Jaques-Dalcroze in the early 20th century, it first involves a set of gymnastic exercises in response to music. This leads a student later to improvise an interpretation of an entire musical composition by means of gestures and body movements.

Eustachian Tube, a mucous-lined tube that connects the middle ear and the nasopharynx and functions to equalize internal and external pressure. It sometimes carries infection from the throat to the middle ear. △676.

Eutectic. *See* Alloy.

Euthanasia, the action of inducing the painless death of a person for reasons assumed to be merciful.

Eutrophication, the process by which a lake or stream becomes rich in inorganic nutrients by natural or artificial means. Compounds of nitrogen, phosphorus, iron, sulfur, and potassium are vital for plant growth, but in excess, the growth of algae and other aquatic weeds is overstimulated and the waterway becomes choked with algal growth or bloom. Since all living things need oxygen, the use of it by the aquatic weeds deprives other biota and results in a net decrease of oxygen affecting all the plant and animal life in that water. Turbulence aerates water, increasing oxygen content. △296.

Eutyches (*c.* 378–454), early church heretic and

Euboea, Greece

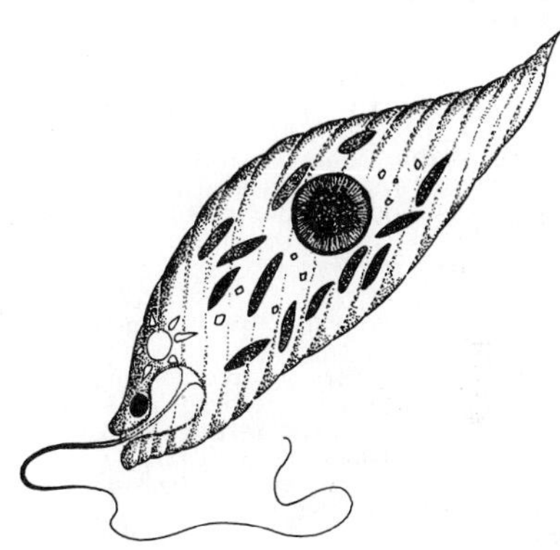

Euglena

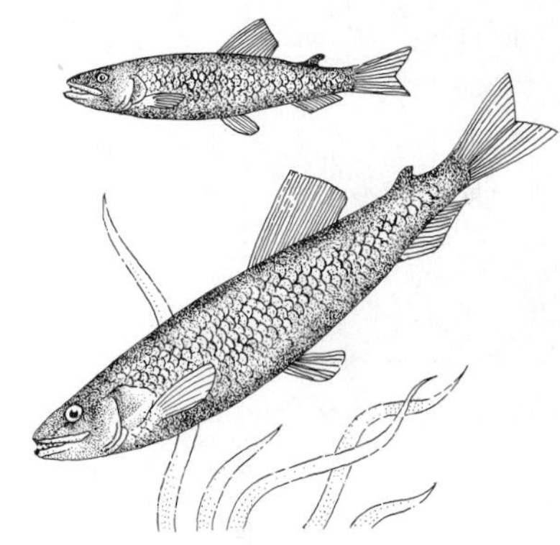

Eulachon

Euonymus

cleric. As superior of a large monastery at Constantinople, he was accused in 448 of the heresy of denying the human nature of Christ and recognizing only his divine nature. As the first real Monophysite, he was deposed by Flavian, patriarch of Constantinople; he was acquitted by the Robber Council at Ephesus (449), but was then attacked by the pope, and deposed and exiled at the council of Chalcedon (451).

Evagoras (d. 374 BC), ruler of Cyprus (410–374 BC). He brought Athenian culture to Cyprus. His fleet harried the Persian-controlled coastline of Greece. After Athens made peace with the Persians in 387 BC, he had to fight the Persians alone. In 381 BC his fleet was destroyed and he had to surrender to Artaxerxes II. He remained as nominal ruler of Cyprus.

Evangelicalism, popular movement within Protestantism, emphasizing the God-given directive to preach the Word. Scripture is central to faith and gives direction to men's lives. Evangelists stress the basic evil nature of man. Influenced by Martin Luther, they believe that justification is through faith alone.

Evangeline (1847), narrative poem by Henry Wadsworth Longfellow. Based on the expulsion of Acadian settlers from Canada during the French and Indian Wars, it is a story of two lovers, Evangeline and Gabriel, who are separated. They meet years later as Gabriel lies dying; Evangeline, now a nun, recognizes him and dies of shock.

Evans, (Sir) Arthur John (1851–1941), English archeologist who excavated the ruins of the city of Knossos in Crete, and found evidence of a Bronze Age civilization which he named the Minoan Age. He authored *The Palace of Minos* (4 vols., 1921–35).

Evans, Maurice (Herbert) (1901–), English actor. He joined the Old Vic company (1934) and played many Shakespearean roles before emigrating to the United States (1935) and becoming a US citizen (1941). He played many Shakespearean parts on Broadway and entertained the troops during World War II with his so-called G.I. version of *Hamlet*. He has also played many Shaw roles in New York, notably in *The Devil's Disciple* (1950) and *Heartbreak House* (1959). He appeared with Helen Hayes (1962–63) in a program of extracts from Shakespeare.

Evans, Walker (1903–75), US photographer, b. St. Louis. He is famed for his portrait images of the poverty-stricken rural South of the 1930s, many published in *Let Us Now Praise Famous Men* (coauthored by James Agee, 1941). His works also include stark studies of Victorian architecture and building interiors. *See also* Agee, James.

Evanston, city in NE Illinois, on Lake Michigan 15mi (24km) N of Chicago; site of Grosse Point Lighthouse (1860), Northwestern University (1851), National College of Education (1886), Kendall College (1934); national headquarters for Rotary, National Merit Scholarship Corporation, and National Women's Christian Temperance Union. Industries: textbooks, foodstuffs, hospital and dairy supplies. Settled 1826; inc. 1892. Pop. (1970) 79,808.

Evansville, port city in extreme SW Indiana, on the Ohio River; seat of Vandenburgh co; shipping and commercial center; site of University of Evansville (1854), Indian mound village state memorial. Industries: aluminum, refrigeration equipment, pharmaceuticals, fabricated plastics. Founded 1812; inc. 1819. Pop. (1970) 138,764.

Evaporation, in chemistry, removing liquid as vapor in order to concentrate solutions or to form crystals, usually performed at the solution's boiling point. The rate of evaporation is affected by heat input, liquid agitation, and speed of vapor passing over the liquid's surface. △1504, 1564, 1568.

Evarts, William Maxwell (1818–1901) US political leader, b. Boston. He was attorney general (1868–69), fighting for law reform and defending President Johnson at his impeachment. He smashed the "Tweed Ring" (1870), and defended Henry Ward Beecher (1875). Pres. Rutherford B. Hayes appointed him secretary of state (1877–81), and he later served in the Senate (1885–91).

Eve, in Genesis, first woman, created by God from Adam's rib to be his companion and wife. Tempted into eating the forbidden fruit, Eve made Adam eat it, causing God to drive them from the Garden of Eden. △810, 844.

Evening Primrose, any of various annual, biennial, and perennial plants of genus *Oenothera* native to the Western Hemisphere, with four-petalled yellow, pink, or white flowers that open in the evening. The North American common evening primrose *(O. biennis)* is now widely naturalized in Europe. Height: to 6ft (1.8m). Family Onagraceae.

Evening Star, not a star but a planet visible near the horizon in the early evening, appearing as a brightly shining object that does not twinkle. Although Mars, Jupiter, and Saturn occasionally appear as evening stars, the term most often refers to Venus, which shines so brightly as to be sometimes visible during daylight.

Everest, (Sir) George (1790–1866), a British surveyor-geographer for whom Mt. Everest is named. He went to India when he was only 16 and began his career of exploration and surveying in that country. The survey and boundaries of India today are in great part based on his work. His career also included surveys of the Himalayas. He returned to England in 1843.

Everest, Mount, highest mountain in the world, in central Himalayas between Tibet and Nepal, Asia. First successful attempt to reach the top was accomplished on May 29, 1953 by a British expedition led by Edmund Hillary and Tenzing Norkay of Nepal. Named after George Everest, the 1st surveyor-general of India; Tibetan name is Chomo-Lungma, or Mother Goddess of the World. Height: 29,028ft (8,854m).

Everett, Edward (1794–1865) US political leader, b. Dorchester, Mass. He was a member of the House of Representatives (1824–34), governor of Massachusetts (1835–39), US minister to England (1841–45), president of Harvard (1846–49), and senator (1853–54). Under Pres. Millard Fillmore, Everett served as secretary of state for about four months (1852). In 1863 at Gettysburg, Pa., he delivered the main address that took place before Lincoln gave his short Gettysburg address.

Everett, city and port in NE Massachusetts, on Mystic River. Industries: chemicals, foundries, oil storage. Founded 1643; divided from Malden 1870; inc. as city 1892. Pop. (1970) 42,485.

Everett, port city in NW Washington, on Puget Sound, 28mi (45km) N of Seattle; seat of Snohomish co. Capt. George Vancouver first landed in the area 1792. Industries: aircraft, lumber, paper products, tourism, fishing, salmon canning, agriculture, dairying. Settled 1862; inc. 1893. Pop. (1970) 53,622.

Everglades National Park, park in S Florida, the third largest national park. It reaches from Lake Okeechobee to Florida Bay. The park is noted for its vast swamps, saw grass, hammocks, and coastal mangrove forests. Protected species such as the alligator, crocodile, egret, and bald eagle are found here. Area: 1,400,533acres (567,216hectares). Est. 1947.

Evergreen, plants that retain their green foliage for a year or more. Deciduous plants lose their leaves every autumn. Evergreens are divided into two groups: narrow-leaved or conifers and broad-leaved. Conifers include fir, spruce, pine, hemlock, and juniper. Among the broad-leaved evergreens are English holly, southern magnolia, box, mountain laurel, heath, and rhododendrons. All conifers are not evergreen, such as the deciduous larches. Evergreens are used extensively in landscape architecture, especially in northern gardens. *See also* Conifer. △440;442.

Evergreen Park, town in NE Illinois; named for numerous pine trees in area. Inc. 1893. Pop. (1970) 25,487.

Everlasting, or **immortelle,** type of flower that keeps its color and shape when dried. Best known is the *Helichrysum,* with daisylike yellow, brown, purple, or white blooms. Other popular plants include globe amaranth *(gomphrena globosa), Statice, Lunaria,* and *Xeranthemum.* For drying, flowers are cut when just starting to open and hung upside down in bunches to dry in a well-ventilated room.

Evers, John Joseph (1881–1947), US baseball player, b. Troy, N.Y. He was the second baseman on the Chicago Cubs' famed "Tinker-to-Evers-to-Chance" double play combination. Evers was elected to the Baseball Hall of Fame in 1946. *See also* Chance, Frank Leroy; Tinker, Joseph Bert.

Evers, Medgar Wiley (1926–63), b. Decatur, Miss. US civil rights leader who was shot and killed on June 12, 1963, outside his home in Jackson, Miss. At that time he was field secretary of the Mississippi National Association for the Advancement of Colored People.

Everson v. Board of Education (1947), US Supreme Court case holding that providing tax-supported bus transportation to religious schools was not in violation of the Constitution's prohibition against the establishment of religion.

Evert, Christine Marie ("Chris") (1954–), US tennis player, b. Ft. Lauderdale. A leading woman player, she won in the US (1975), British (1974), and French (1974–75) singles championships. She turned professional in 1972.

Everyman (first printed *c.*1529), author unknown (Dutch origin), one of the oldest morality plays in the English language. Everyman, summoned by Death to appear before God for judgment, calls on his friends for help: Strength, Beauty, Knowledge, Good Deeds, and Fellowship. Only Good Deeds will accompany him to the judgment seat.

Évian-les-Bains, town in E France, on S shore of Lake of Geneva; fashionable health spa. Industries: liqueurs, precision instruments. Pop. 6,052.

Evidence, facts or proof provided by testimony during legal process. Lawyers produce evidence that is considered by the judge and jury in a trial. △912.

Evolution, theory that organisms originate from simpler forms of another organism and that a new species is the end of gradual development and change from the simpler forms. Early work with evolutionary theory was initiated by Jean Lamarck during the early 1800s, but it was not until Charles Darwin wrote *The Origin of Species* during the mid-1800s that the theory was considered worthy of argument.

Present-day evolutionary theory is derived from Darwin's work and maintains that in any population of a gene pool, there are random mutations in genetic forms and characteristics. Mutated forms are of no value to the survival of an organism. Most species reproduce in greater quantities than their environment can support, and so only those members best adapted to the environment survive. When mutated characteristics provide survival advantages, mutants survive to pass on these new characteristics. In this way a species effects gradual changes to adapt and survive in a competitive, and often changing, environment.

Evolution also occurs over a geographical area. A species tends to be widely distributed over a range of conditions and small groups of the population develop in specialized ways to better adapt to their particular conditions. The resulting subspecies do not differ greatly from their near neighbors, but there may be a complete species change from one end of the spectrum to the other. *See also* Darwinism; Natural Selection. △408–10, 418–20, 574–76.

Evolution, Stellar. △102.

Evolutionary Socialism is based on the assumption that movement from capitalism to socialism can be made through the ballot (i.e., the government can be an instrument of reform), and that revolution is not necessary. *See also* Socialism.

Evvoia. *See* Euboea.

Excalibur, in medieval legend, the name of King Arthur's sword. According to Sir Thomas Malory, who recounted the Arthurian legend in the 15th century, the name means "cut-steel." Malory described two versions of its origin. In the first, the boy Arthur miraculously pulled the sword out of a stone; in the second, he was given the sword by the Lady of the Lake.

Exceptional Children, Education of, programs for children who are below or above the average in health or ability. Some retarded or otherwise handicapped children are sent to special schools, but public schools try to serve as many as possible in regular classes, with teachers and counselors providing extra attention. Schools also try to provide accelerated programs for gifted students.

Exchange Network. △1792.

Exchange Rate, rate at which one country's currency can be converted to another country's currency. The exchange rate will vary according to the demand for and supply of the countries' goods and services. The overall state of the country's balance of payments determines whether the rate will change. *See also* Balance of Payments. △940.

Excise Tax, tax paid by the manufacturer of consumer goods, usually luxury goods such as jewelry, perfume, tobacco, and alcohol. The excise tax is normally a percentage of retail selling price.

Excited State, state of an atom, ion, molecule, when its energy level is higher than that of the ground state. An atom, for example, can be in an excited state as a result of absorption of a photon, causing one of the electrons to occupy an orbital of higher energy.

Exclusion Principle, Pauli, basic law of quantum mechanics, proposed by Wolfgang Pauli (1925), stating that no two electrons in an atom can possess the same energy and spin. More precisely, the set of four quantum numbers characterizing an elementary particle must be unique. In atoms, these numbers specify an electron's spin direction and the energy state in which it resides or would reside in a magnetic field.

Exclusive Powers, rights delegated by the US Constitution to the national and state governments. Certain powers are granted specifically to the federal government, others to the states. Still others are concurrent and may be exercised by both. The states may employ powers not explicitly granted to the federal government or denied to the states.

Excretory System. *See* Urogenital System. △694.

Executive Calendar, nonlegislative calendar of the US Senate on which presidential documents, such as foreign treaties and cabinet nominations, are listed.

Executive Order, special US presidential enactment affecting operations in federal agencies. Orders may deal with the creation of emergency offices or set down provisions for stabilizing the economy.

Executive Privilege, right invoked by the US President to justify withholding information from Congress or the courts. Presidents have cited the need for confidentiality, endangerment of national security, and the public interest to defend their actions. The precedent was established by President Washington in 1796 when he refused to supply Congress with certain documents. During the 1973 Watergate controversy, President Nixon claimed executive privilege when he refused to surrender the White House tapes.

Executive Session, closed hearing of a congressional committee for the purpose of examining and developing proposed legislation before it is sent to the floor.

Exercise. △698.

Exeter, city in SW England, on Exe River, 37mi (60km) NE of Plymouth; episcopal seat, famous for cathedral (1270–1369) and Guildhall (1160), probably the oldest municipal building in England; railroad, industrial, commercial, and tourist center for area. Industries: agricultural machinery, metal and leather products, pharmaceutical goods. Pop. 95,598. △1104.

Exeter Book, manuscript copied *c.* 975, containing the largest extant collection of Old English poetry. The manuscript, probably copied from an earlier book, was given to Exeter Cathedral by Bishop Leofric. It contains both religious and secular verse, as well as 95 riddles.

Exeter Compact (1639), agreement made by 35 settlers of Exeter, N.H., led by John Wheelwright, who had been banished from the Massachusetts Bay Colony. They agreed to "such government as should be to their best discerning agreeable to the Will of God."

Existentialism, philosophical movement arising in Germany shortly after World War I, later spreading to France and Italy, and discussed after World War II in the popular press. Not a philosophical "school" as such, few doctrines are shared by all its exponents. Developing the ideas in Sören Kierkegaard's writings on "existence," Karl Jaspers expounded the themes that have since been remolded by such writers as Martin Heidegger, Jean-Paul Sartre, Nikolai Berdyaev, and Albert Camus into a liberal philosophy with no hope for man's perfectability. △856.

Exobiology, study of environmental conditions and possible biochemical and evolutionary pathways to life beyond Earth. It is concerned with such experiments as creation of amino acids from electrical discharges in methane-ammonia atmosphere (eg primeval Earth or present Jupiter) or survival of bacteria or mosses under Martian conditions. The Viking lander (1976) is designed to test Martian soil for gaseous byproducts of metabolic activity.

Exodus, biblical book, second book of the Pentateuch, named by Greek translators for its account of the Israelites' flight from Egypt after God freed them from bondage. The narrative is divided into two sections, the first historical and the second legislative. △982.

Exogamy, set of rules defining the inner social circle in which marriage (or in some cases all sexual relations) is forbidden. An example is the nuclear family in Western society. *See also* Endogamy; Incest taboo. △876.

Exophthalmos, abnormal protrusion of the eyeball caused by edema, aneurysm, or endocrine disorder. Onset may be sudden or gradual depending on the cause.

Exopterygote. △496.

Exorcism, ritual expulsion of evil spirits from a person, place, or thing, usually performed by a religious leader, such as a priest, witch doctor, or sorcerer. Exorcism is a practice common to a great many religions. It is performed with verbal incantations, whippings, or sacrifices.

Exoskeleton. △484, 494.

Exothermic Reaction, chemical reaction in which heat is evolved, thus causing a rise in temperature. *See also* Chemical Reaction. △1572.

Expansion, phase of the business cycle that occurs as economic conditions improve and move toward prosperity. Expansion is normally associated with increases in employment and increases in purchasing power. *See also* Business Cycles.

Expansion, mathematical process of replacing an expression by a sum of individual terms or by an infinite series. Thus, the expression $(x + 1)(x + 3)$ can be expanded to $x^2 + 4x + 4$: the function $\sin x$ can be expanded into the converging series $x = x^3/3! + x^5/5! = \ldots$.

Expansion, Coefficient of, the number indicating the rate of change of volume of a given substance as the temperature or pressure on that substance changes. For a gas, the coefficient of expansion is usually large; for a solid, it is much smaller.

Expansion Chamber. *See* Cloud Chamber.

Ex Parte Garland (1867), US Supreme Court decision declaring unconstitutional a federal loyalty oath requirement (1865) for attorneys practicing in the federal courts. The plaintiff had taken a federal oath in 1860 and had later been pardoned for Confederate activities.

Ex Parte McCardle (1869), important US Supreme Court decision recognizing that the jurisdiction of the court to hear appeals is controlled by Congress. This decision raised the possibility of Congress entirely abolishing the appellate jurisdiction of the Supreme Court, leaving it a very limited role in the judicial system, but no efforts toward this end have ever been successful.

Ex Parte Milligan (1866), US Supreme Court decision overruling President Lincoln's Civil War proclamation subjecting civilians to trials for treason by military courts. The court declared such a practice unconstitutional and asserted that Lincoln had exceeded his authority.

Expatriation, voluntary renunciation of citizenship in favor of that of another state. An individual's right of expatriation was confirmed by the US Congress (1865). Grounds for expatriation include willingness to swear allegiance to a foreign state, serving in a foreign army without US government consent, or voting in a foreign election.

Experimental Psychology, use of scientific experimental design in psychological investigations. Close observation, careful recording, and other components of the scientific method are easiest to carry out in a laboratory, but psychologists also use them in clinics, schools, or the community at large.

Experimenter Bias. *See* Self-fulfilling Prophecy.

Exploration, Petroleum. *See* Petroleum. △178, 284.

Explosives, chemical compounds that, on ignition by heat, friction, impact, or detonation, undergo rapid decomposition or burning, producing large amounts of gas or heat and exerting tremendous pressure as they expand. △1560, 1810.

Exponent, superscript number placed to the right of a symbol indicating its power; for example, in a^4 (=

Mount Everest

Evergreen: cedar

Chris Evert

Exeter, England

$a \times a \times a \times a$), 4 is the exponent. Certain laws of exponents apply in mathematical operations. For example: $3^2 \times 3^3 = 3^{(3+2)} = 3^5$; $3^4 \div 3^3 = 3^{(4-3)} = 3^1$; $(3^2)^3 = 3^{(2\times 3)} = 3^6$; $3^{-5} = 1/3^5$. *See also* Power.

Exponential Function, in general a function of x of the form a^x, where a is a constant. More specifically, the exponential function is e^x, where e is the base of natural logarithms, 2·7182818. . . . It can be represented by a power series $1 + x + x^2/2! + \ldots$.

Export-Import Bank of the United States, an independent federal agency. Its purpose is to aid in financing and facilitating exports and imports and the exchange of commodities between the United States and any foreign country or agencies. Authorized 1934, revised by subsequent Congressional acts.

Ex Post Facto Law, a law of retrospective effect that punishes a person for an offense that was not punishable at the time it occured. It is illegal to do so in the United States.

Exposure Meter, Photographic. △1526.

Expressionism, movement in early 20th-century art that had two main outlets of creativity—Die Brücke, founded in Dresden in 1905, and the Blue Rider, a Munich group dating from 1911. Die Brücke reacted to the current academic style of painting and sought a more emotional and freer style of expression. Its main members were Ernst Kirchner, Karl Schmidt-Rottluff, and Erick Heckel. These artists painted in rapid brushstrokes, often using broken lines, rough textures, intense colors, and angular forms charged with emotion. They made woodcuts as well as paintings and were somewhat influenced by van Gogh, Ensor, and Munch. The Blue Rider group was especially influenced by cubism and was headed by Kandinsky, whose abstract expressionist style had great influence over later abstract painters. Among the active members of this group were Alex von Jawlensky, Paul Klee, Franz Marc, and August Macke. World War I brought an end to both of these groups. △1294.

Expressionist Theater, a theatrical style originating in Germany and popular in Europe and America throughout the 1920s. A reaction against theatrical realism, its beginnings are in August Strindberg's later works, especially *The Ghost Sonata* (1907). It attempted to present emotional rather than apparent reality and used symbols and bold psychological interpretations of people and events. Two important Expressionists are Frank Wedekind (German, 1864–1918), and Elmer Rice (American, 1892–1967).

Expropriation. *See* Eminent Domain.

Extension Education, programs designed to "take the college to the people," ie, people who cannot enroll in full-time courses. Government efforts to teach farmers new agricultural techniques encouraged the growth of extension education. Many universities offer extension courses in night or weekend classes and through correspondence, radio, and television.

Extinction, in experimental psychology, the pattern an organism follows when it stops performing a given behavior. Basically, a behavior will gradually extinguish (stop occurring) if it is not followed by any reward (reinforcement).

Extradition, the surrender of a person by one state or country to another where the person has been accused or convicted of a criminal offense.

Extrapolation, process of estimating the value of a function beyond the range of its known values. One method is simply to extend a curve on a graph beyond the region for which known values exist. Various mathematical approximation techniques also exist. *See also* Interpolation.

Extrasensory Perception (ESP or psi), a hypothesized ability to respond to events in the external world without using sensory information or any process of rational inference. ESP includes clairvoyance, precognition, and telepathy, and is one of the concerns of parapsychology. A typical ESP study might require subjects to try to guess stimuli (for example, playing cards) that are presented in a random order. When subjects can consistently name the cards at rates exceeding chance guessing, there is said to be evidence for ESP. Though parapsychologists such as J. B. Rhine have succeeded in objectifying and controlling the study of ESP phenomena to some extent, this area of psychology remains controversial in the eyes of many scientists. The chief difficulty for investigators of ESP phenomena is to find ESP effects that are consistent and reproducible—hallmarks of scientific objectivity. On the other hand, scientists will also be the first to admit that there are events and phenomena that are as yet unexplainable by modern science. *See also* Parapsychology. △672, 824.

Extraterritoriality, state of legal immunity granted to members of the diplomatic corps, their families, and the premises they occupy. Immunity takes the form of exemption from arrest or prosecution and from search or seizure.

Extrinsic Factor, or Vitamin B_{12}, provides cobalt, a trace element needed in erythrocyte formation; deficiency results in pernicious anemia. *See also* Intrinsic Factor.

Extrusion, in geology, the breaking out of igneous material onto the earth's surface. Any volcanic product reaching the surface becomes extrusive material whether it is ejected through a volcano's cone or through pipelike channels or fissures in the crust. Extrusive material varies in size and composition from light, volcanic ash to huge ejections of plutonic material from deep beneath crustal rock. *See also* Igneous Rock; Volcano. △176.

Extrusion, operation of forcing copper, aluminum, magnesium, their alloys, or plastics at the optimum temperature through a die to manufacture specific shapes such as rods, tubes, and various hollow or solid sections. Plastic extrusion can produce composite sheets, and coat film and wire.

Eye, the special sense organ of vision. It converts light energy to nerve impulses that are transmitted to the visual center of the brain. Each eye lies in a bony socket, called the orbital cavity, which also includes muscles and other tissues to hold and move the eye, and protective structures, such as the lacrimal apparatus that produces tears. The eyeball itself is spherical and composed of three layers: the sclera, the choroid, and the retina. The *sclera* is a tough fibrous membrane—seen as the white of the eye—that helps retain the eye shape; it contains a "window," the transparent *cornea* that protects the iris. The *choroid*, or middle layer, contains blood vessels to provide food and oxygen to the eye. It contains the *iris*, the pigmented part of the eye, in the center of which is a hole, the *pupil*, through which light passes to the *crystalline lens* where the light rays are bent to make an image on the *retina*. The retina, the innermost layer of the eye, contains the nerve cells—*rods and cones*—responsible for converting the image into a nerve impulse that in turn is transmitted along the *optic nerve* to visual centers of the brain. A watery fluid, the *aqueous humor*, is present between the cornea and iris; a jellylike substance, the *vitreous humor*, behind the lens; both help maintain shape of the eye. △674.

Eyebright, small annual and perennial plants widely distributed in northern and southern temperate and subarctic regions. They have terminal spikes of white, yellow, or purple tubular flowers. European eyebright *(Euphrasia officinalis)* was formerly used to treat eye diseases. Family Scrophulariaceae.

Eyeshadow. △1814.

Eyre, Lake, salt lake in Australia, in NE South Australia state; lowest point on continent, 39ft (12m) below sea level; largest lake in Australia. Area: 3,430sq mi (8,884sq km). Depth (max.): 4ft (1m).

Ezekiel, Book of, book of the Old Testament, third of the major prophet books. It is a record of the life of the priest and prophet Ezekiel, who preached to the Jews in Exile. It records his visions and prophecies of the destruction of Jerusalem (582 BC) and his judgment of Israel's eventual redemption and restoration.

Ezra, in the Bible, a continuation of Chronicles I and II. It records the priest Ezra's journey from Babylon to Jerusalem to spread the law of Moses. It also includes an account of the rebuilding of the Temple, part of the city's restoration after it was destroyed by Nebuchadnezzar, and a census of Ezra's companions on his trip to the Holy City.

F

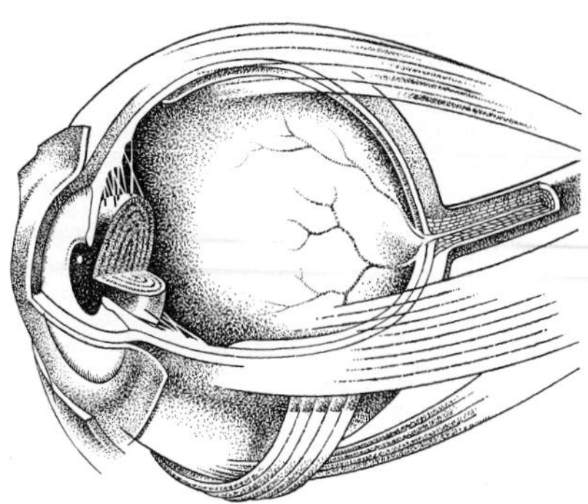

Eye

FAA. *See* Federal Aviation Administration.

Fabian, Saint, Roman Catholic pope (236–50). He reorganized the church, dividing Rome into seven areas, and provided for churches to be governed by presbyters and deacons under his review. He began a registry for the deeds of martyrs; he was martyred during the persecution of Christians by the Emperor Decius.

Fabian Society, a non-Marxist organization of British socialists who believed that socialism would be attained through gradual political change. Including George Bernard Shaw and Beatrice and Sidney Webb, the society gained widespread recognition and led to the formation of the Labour party (1900). △1326.

Fabius Maximus Verrucosus, Quintus (died 203 BC), called Cunctator (Lat. "delayer") (died 203 BC), Roman consul, dictator, and priest. A conservative military genius, he is famed for his strategy of avoiding pitched battle while conducting harassing raids during the Second Punic War, a tactic that wore Hannibal's forces to exhaustion. The Romans became bored with his methods, removed him from office, and were defeated at Cannae. Reinstated in 214, he served with honor until his death. The term *Fabian* came to mean a policy of delay.

Fable, a literary genre in the form of a short allegorical tale which is intended to convey a moral. The characters are often animals, whose words and deeds are used to satirize those of human beings. The oldest extant fables are the Greek tales of Aesop and the Indian stories of the *Panchatantra.* Other collections of fables were made by Jean de La Fontaine, John Gay, and Ivan Krylov.

Fabliau, a genre in French narrative poetry of the 12th and 13th centuries consisting of a short poem involving commonplace characters in humorous, but coarse situations. The *fabliaux* stem from the oral traditions of Europe and the Orient, but the first written *fabliau* was *Richeut,* about 1160. Later Boccaccio and Chaucer incorporated these popular stories in their larger works. *See also* Canterbury Tales; Decameron.

Factor Analysis, in statistics and psychometrics, a complex mathematical method for reducing a large number of measures or tests to a smaller number of "factors" that can completely account for the results obtained on all the tests, as well as for the correlations between them. *See also* Intelligence Testing.

Faculae, very bright areas seen on the Sun's surface just before the appearance of a sunspot or sunspot group in the same region, and persisting for some time after its decay. *See also* Sun. △96.

Faeroe Islands, group of 22 volcanic islands in N Atlantic Ocean between Iceland and Shetland Islands; possession of Denmark since 1380. Seventeen of the islands, which are high and rugged with little vegetation, are inhabited. Since 1947 the people have had home rule and send two representatives to Danish parliament. Industries: fishing, whaling, fowling, sheep raising, farming. Settled by Norsemen in 11th century. Area: 540sq mi (1,339sq km). Pop. 36,681.

Fafnir, in Teutonic mythology, a wicked giant who gained possession of a treasure by murdering his own father. He changed himself into a dragon to guard it and was eventually slain by the hero Sigurd.

Fahrenheit, Gabriel Daniel (1686–1736), German physicist and instrument maker. He invented the alcohol thermometer (1709), the first mercury thermometer (1714), and devised the temperature scale that bears his name. He also showed that atmospheric pressure causes variations in the boiling point of liquids, and that water, below its freezing point, can remain in a liquid state. *See also* Thermometer. △1508.

Faïence, earthenware covered with a decorative layer of white opaque glaze made of lead and tin. The clay used is of a fine quality so that it can be thinly shaped and can withstand being fired at a high temperature. Faïence is often called delftware because Delft was a center of production in the 17th century. Faïence was also produced in Rouen during this period. △964.

Fainting, or syncope, temporary impairment of consciousness accompanied by general weakness of muscles. An attack may be preceded by giddiness, sensory distortions, nausea, pallor, profuse cold sweat. Causes may include a deficient flow of blood to the brain, a change in the blood contents, or emotional disturbances. △758.

Fairbanks, Charles Warren (1852–1918), US political leader, b. Union co, Ohio. The last of the "log cabin statesmen," he was a Republican senator (1897–1905). He was vice president under Pres. Theodore Roosevelt (1905–09).

Fairbanks, Douglas (1883–1939), US silent film star, b. Douglas Ullman in Denver. He was a co-founder of United Artists Films (1919). His swashbuckling acrobatics and breezy charm enhanced many costume adventures, including *The Mark of Zorro* (1920), *The Three Musketeers* (1921), *Robin Hood* (1922), *The Black Pirate* (1926), and *The Private Life of Don Juan* (1934).

Fairbanks, city in central Alaska, on the Tanana and Chena rivers, 400mi (644km) N of Anchorage and 100mi (161km) S of the Arctic Circle. Severe temperatures range from −66°F (−54°C) to 96°F (36°C); snowfall averages 60 inches (1,524mm). University of Alaska was founded here 1922; Eielson Air Force Base and Fort Wainwright are nearby. Construction of Alaskan oil pipeline in 1970s accelerated growth. Industries: industrial chemicals, fur goods, gold, silver, and coal mining. Founded in 1902 when gold was discovered. Pop. (1970) 22,640.

Fairborn, city in SW Ohio; formed 1950 by merger of Fairfield (1799) and Osborn (1853). Nearby is Wright Patterson Air Force Base. Industries: cement, limestone quarrying. Pop. (1970) 32,267.

Fair Deal, Pres. Harry Truman's legislative program proposed in his 1949 inaugural address. The Fair Deal was an extension of Pres. Franklin D. Roosevelt's New Deal. Although a public housing bill passed, the program was largely rejected by a Republican-Southern Democrat coalition.

Fair Employment Practice Committee (FEPC), federal agency established (1941) to curb racial discrimination in war production and government employment. The FEPC was not entirely effective. The discrimination against southern blacks who had migrated to industrial areas in the North finally brought an executive order from Pres. Franklin D. Roosevelt (1943) requiring non-discrimination clauses in war contracts.

Fairfax, residential city in N Virginia, 16mi (26km) SW of Washington, D.C.; seat of Fairfax co; historic courthouse (1799) contains the wills of President and

Eyebright

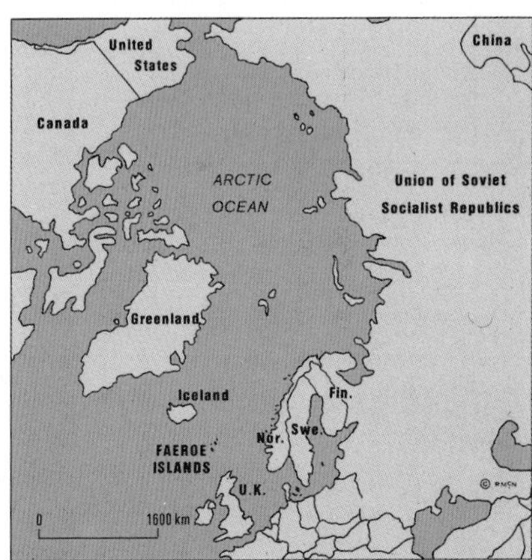

United States
China
Canada
ARCTIC OCEAN
Union of Soviet Socialist Republics
Greenland
Iceland
Fin.
Swe.
Nor.
FAEROE ISLANDS
U.K.
0
1600 km

Faeroe Islands

Douglas Fairbanks

Mrs. George Washington. Settled 1700; inc. 1892. Pop. (1970) 21,970.

Fairfax of Cameron, Thomas, 3rd Baron (1612–71), English soldier. He was commander in chief of the Parliamentary Army (1645–50) in the Civil War. A popular commander, he won a decisive victory at Naseby (1645) but played a limited role in politics.

Fairfield, city in SE Australia; W suburb of Sydney. Industries: tiles, terra cotta, wool. Pop. 101,226.

Fairfield, city in W California, 40mi (64km) SW of Sacramento. Industries: sleeping bags, aluminum cans. Founded 1859; inc. 1903. Pop. (1970) 44,146.

Fairfield, town in SW Connecticut, in Fairfield co, on Long Island Sound; summer resort. Settled 1639. Pop. (1970) 56,487.

Fair Labor Standards Act (1938), New Deal legislation, also known as the Wages and Hour Act, to regulate hours and wages for workers engaged in interstate commerce. It established minimum wages ($ .25 an hour), maximum working hours (44 per week), time and a half for overtime, and prohibited child labor. The law was upheld by the Supreme Court in *United States* v. *Darby Lumber Co.* (1941).

Fair Lawn, borough in NE New Jersey. Industries: textiles, cement products. Inc. 1924. Pop. (1970) 37,795.

Fairmont, city in N West Virginia, at convergence of West Fork and Tygart rivers; seat of Marion co; site of Fairmont State College (1867). Industries: coal mining, glass, steel and aluminum products. Settled 1793 around Prickett's Fort (1774) for protection against Indian raids; inc. 1843. Pop. (1970) 26,093.

Fair Oaks, town and railroad station east of Richmond, Va. It was the site of a Civil War battle in 1862. *See also* Seven Pines, Battle of.

Fair Trade Laws, in the United States, laws that allow manufacturers to fix the minimum resale price of their goods. Prior to the enactment of the laws dealers could sell below the price of the manufacturer if they wished. The California Fair Trade Act of 1931 was amended in 1933 to make the price set between the manufacturer and the contracting dealer binding upon all resellers. In following years most states enacted similar laws, but by the 1970s most of these laws had been repealed because they restrained free trade.

Fairy Ring, a circle or ring of mushrooms, usually *Marasmius oreades,* that appears seasonally in lawns or meadows. It is usually marked by richer, greener growth. In folklore the area enclosed was said to be the dancing ground of fairies.

Fairy Shrimp, branchiopod crustacean found in temporary pools and small ponds. It has an elongated trunk of 20 or more segments and anterior paddlelike limbs with gills for feeding and respiration. It has no carapace and its eyes are on stalks. Length: ⅜–5⅛in (1–13cm). Order Anostraca. *See also* Crustacean.

Fairy Tales and **Folktales** spring from an ancient world-wide oral tradition which, like language itself, obeys universal laws and structures. That there are many versions of the same tale in different parts of the world is not merely coincidence, but a function of a universal need for the same social utopia and the subsequent collective oral creation of a tale that satisfies a specific aspect of that need. Some tales, like those of Hans Christian Andersen, are largely of literary origin, while others, like those of Charles Perrault *(Mother Goose Tales),* are reworkings of older oral tales. *See also* Andersen, Hans Christian; Perrault, Charles. △832.

Faisal I (1885–1933), king of Syria (1920) and Iraq (1921–33). He became a member of the Turkish parliament in Constantinople (1913) and later directed the Arabs in a desert campaign under the British against the Turks until the capture of Damascus (1918). After the French ousted him as king of Syria (1920), he secured the throne of Iraq and formed the state of Iraq (1921). His son, Ghazi, and grandson, Faisal II, successively succeeded him.

Faisal Ibn al-Saud (1906–75), king of Saudi Arabia (1964–75); son of King Ibn Saud; brother of King Saud. He was viceroy of Hejaz (1926), became crown prince and foreign minister of Saudi Arabia (1953), and king after Saud was deposed (1964). He began educational and economic programs and joined other Arab states in the Six Day War against Israel (1967). He was assassinated by a nephew.

Faisal II (1935–58), third king of Iraq (1939–58), grandson of Faisal I. After the death of Ghazi, his father, he became king, with Abdul Illah as regent. Both were assassinated in a coup d'etat led by Abdul Karim Kassem; Iraq became a republic.

Faith Healing, the supplication to a divine being or power for cures. It can be traced to the miraculous works of Jesus Christ and his apostles as recorded in the New Testament. Such prayers and rituals may be traced throughout the history of man. Christian Science is structured around belief in faith healing. △748.

Fakir, Muslim or Hindu monk or wandering mendicant. Fakirs are thought to possess special powers, to be able to perform magic and incredible feats of endurance, such as walking on fire. △820.

Falaise, town in N France, 19mi (31km) SE of Caen; birthplace of William the Conqueror; important during the Normandy campaign of WWII; site of château (12th–13th century), and annual livestock and wool fair held since 11th century; agricultural market. Pop. 6,711.

Falange, Spanish political party. It was founded in 1933 by José António Primo de Rivera, son of the dictator. Closely fashioned after the Fascist party in Italy and the Nazi party in Germany, it became the sole legal political party after the forces of Francisco Franco triumphed in the Spanish Civil War. Its power declined in the 1960s and 1970s, although it remained the only legal political party. *See also* Civil War, Spanish. △1334.

Falashas, ethnic group in Ethiopia, probably descendants of early converts to Judaism. Once a large group, they now number about 30,000. Their form of Judaism relies solely on observance of the Old Testament. They speak local dialects, attend services led by priests, and celebrate only biblical feasts.

Falcon, widely distributed, bold, hawklike bird of prey, sometimes trained by man to hunt game. They have keen eyesight, short hooked bills, long pointed wings, streamlined bodies, strong legs with hooked claws, longish tails, and gray or brownish plumage with lighter markings. They hunt during the day, feeding on insects, birds on the wing, rodents, and other small animals on the ground. They lay brown-spotted white eggs (2–6) in a tree-hole nest. Length: 6–25in (15–64cm). Family Falconidae.

Falconry, sport in which birds and small animals are hunted, using falcons. The falcon, a bird of prey closely related to the hawk, is taken when young to be trained. The falconer wears a glove upon which the hooded falcon sits. When the hood is taken off, the falcon heads straight for the quarry, leaving the prey untouched after the kill. The falcon then returns to the falconer's wrist. Falconry attained its greatest popularity in late medieval and early modern Europe, and was one of the chief pastimes of royalty before declining after the 17th century. Although still used for hunting in certain parts of the world, it has never regained the favor it once enjoyed.

Falkenhayn, Erich Georg Anton. △1306.

Falkland Islands (Islas Malvinas), group of islands SE of Argentina in S Atlantic Ocean. A British crown colony, group includes 2 large islands, East and West Falkland, and 200 small islands; discovered by English navigator John Davis in 1592. Capital is Stanley; main industry is sheep farming. Exports: wool, skins, tallow, guano. Area: 4,618sq mi (11,961sq km). Pop. 2,045.

Fall, Albert Bacon (1861–1944), US political figure, b. Frankfurt, Ky. He was one of New Mexico's first US senators (1912–21). President Harding appointed him secretary of the interior in 1921. He resigned in 1923 under pressure of a senate investigation and was later (1931) convicted of having accepted bribes from oil interests in the Teapot Dome scandal. *See also* Teapot Dome Scandal.

Falla, Manuel de (1876–1946), Spanish composer who developed Spanish nationalism in music by using Spanish folk songs as the basis for many of his compositions. Among his popular works are the opera *La Vida Breve* (1905), *Nights in the Gardens of Spain* (1915) for piano and orchestra, and the music for the ballets *El Amor Brujo* (1915) and *The Three-Cornered Hat* (1919). △1364.

Fallen Timbers, Battle of (1794), two-hour engagement in which US Gen. Anthony Wayne defeated the Ohio Indians. The battle led to the 1795 treaty at Ft Greenville, which opened the Northwest Territory for US exploration.

Falling Bodies, Law of, theory propounded by Galileo, disproving Aristotle's contention that bodies of different weights fall at different speeds. Galileo's law proved that falling bodies obey the law of uniformly accelerated motion. He performed experiments showing that the gravity of the Earth produced constant downward acceleration and that this acceleration was independent of size, weight or composition of the falling bodies. *See also* Gravitation. △1486, 1490.

Falling Water, house built by Frank Lloyd Wright in Bear Run, Pa. (1936–37). Constructed of local stone over a waterfall, this house is less unconventional than his other work, incorporating features of the accepted International Style. *See also* International Style. △1322.

Fall Line, the imaginary line connecting falls or rapids created by streams or rivers crossing from harder rock formations to softer plains terrain. Specifically, the term refers to the boundary between the US coastal plain and the more mountainous Piedmont Region. There, from north to south, the Delaware, Potomac, James, Savannah and other rivers form falls or rapids as they cross that boundary.

Fallopian Tube, or oviduct, either of two narrow ducts leading from the upper part of the uterus into the pelvic cavity and ending near each ovary. After ovulation, the ovum enters and travels through the Fallopian tube where fertilization can occur. The fertilized ovum, or embryo, continues into the uterus where it becomes implanted. If the fertilized ovum remains in the tube, an ectopic (or tubal) pregnancy occurs. If fertilization does not occur, the ovum is shed along with uterine lining at menstruation. Conception can be prevented by removing or somehow closing the Fallopian tubes. △700.

Fallout, Atomic, radioactive contamination in the atmosphere following a leakage or accident at a nuclear reactor or a nuclear bomb explosion. Large wind-borne particles fall to Earth after a few hours, no more than 300mi (483km) from the source. Lighter particles entering the troposphere are detected after a longer period at about the same latitude as the source. Any particles entering the stratosphere eventually fall over the whole Earth's surface, often many years later. △1746.

Fallow Deer, European deer, introduced in the United States and commonly kept in parks. The Middle Eastern species may be extinct. It is fawn-colored with white spots. Antlers are flattened and palmate with numerous points. Length: to 4.5ft (1.4m); height: to 3ft (1m); weight: to 160 lb (72kg). Family Cervidae; species *Dama dama. See also* Deer.

Fall River, city and port in SE Massachusetts, on Mt Hope Bay, at mouth of Taunton River; seat of Bristol co; scene of Revolutionary War skirmish, and of trial of Lizzie Borden (1892). Battleship *Massachusetts* (WWII) is berthed here as war memorial. Industries: paper boxes, women's clothing, textile machinery, luggage. Settled 1656 as Freeman's Purchase; inc. 1803; chartered as city 1854. Pop. (1970) 96,898.

Falmouth, town in SW Massachusetts, on Cape Cod; site of Woods Hole Oceanographic Institution (1930), Marine Biological Laboratory, and US Fish and Wildlife Service Station; library has handwritten copy of Katherine Lee Bates' poem "America the Beautiful." Industries: tourism, cranberry culture, boating. Settled 1660; inc. 1686. Pop. (1970) 15,942.

False Decretals, also called **Pseudo-Isidorian Decretals,** collection of purported Church documents published in France about 847–52 and compiled by Isidore Mercator. They were identified with St. Isidore of Seville (died 636) and believed to be genuine until 1558. Included were false documents—58 papal decrees, 1 canon, and forged papal letters—intermixed with genuine documents—early papal letters, canons of 54 councils, and papal writings. They were assembled to support claims of papal supremacy and to support the bishops against secular interference. Throughout the Middle Ages the canons in the Decretals were one of the main sources of canon law; by the early 19th century the genuine parts had been distinguished from the forgeries.

False Pregnancy, signs of pregnancy, such as the absence of menstruation, without the presence of an embryo. It can be caused by psychological factors, by an endocrine disturbance, or by a tumor.

False Scorpion. △490.

False Teeth. *See* Denture.

Famagusta (Ammókhostos), port city on E coast of island of Cyprus, on Famagusta Bay. During 15th and 16th centuries it was seat of Venetian governors of Cyprus; site of medieval governor's palace and Cathedral of St Nicholas; British naval base during WWII. Nearby a Jewish internment center for illegal Palestinian immigrants was maintained 1946–48 by Britain. Before 1975 war, city's population was about 67% Greek, 33% Turkish. Chief industry is citrus fruits. Founded 3rd century BC. Pop. 42,500.

Familiar Spirit, supernatural spirit closely associated with a magician or religious leader. The familiar spirit is a widespread concept. He is usually the servant of a magician and can take the shape of an animal.

Family, institutionalized bio-social group made up of adults and children. It forms a unit that deals with both economic and affective needs and provides a socio-cultural context for the procreation, care, and socialization of offspring. It can consist of a nuclear or extended network. *See also* Kinship. △876–82.

Family Compact, a union of urban commercial interests that dominated the executive and legislative councils of Upper Canada from about 1790 to before the Rebellion of 1837. They were pro-British and reactionary and opposed to confederation. The term derived from 15th-century European monarchical consanguinity. In French Lower Canada a similarly powerful group was called the Chateau Clique.

Family Compact, agreements between the French and Spanish branches of the Bourbon dynasty. The first two, signed in 1733 and 1743, were general friendship treaties between France and Spain. The third, signed in 1761, made Spain an ally of France against England in the Seven Years War. It also committed the Spanish Kingdom of the Two Sicilies and the duchy of Parma to the war.

Family Planning. △706.

Fan, in geology, a spread of fine and coarse materials resulting from the rapid deposition of both dissolved and suspended materials carried downstream by a river. The alluvial deposits appear at river outlets on desert floors when the velocity of the river water drops very suddenly. △258.

Fanfani, Amintore (1908–), Italian politician and statesman. A leader of the Christian Democratic party from 1954, he served continuously as head of various Italian government ministries from 1947, including three times as premier (1954, 1958–59, 1960–63). Though in the early 1960s he represented his party's left, in the mid-1970s he was the spokesman for Christian Democratic anti-communist and pro-clerical positions.

Fang, a long pointed tooth, particularly a hollow grooved tooth used by a snake to inject its venom, or, loosely, a tooth that a carnivorous animal uses to seize and tear prey.

Fang-Bulu, a pair of Bantu languages of the Niger-Kordofanian family of African languages, found in Gabon and Cameroon. Together with Yaoundé they are understood by about 1,000,000 speakers.

Fan K'uan. △1044.

Fanny Hill (1748–49), novel by John Cleland, first issued in two volumes. It is an account, told in her own letters, of the seduction and subsequent career of a London courtesan. The original publication was suppressed.

Fan-si-pan, mountain peak in NW Vietnam, between Red and Black rivers. Highest point in the country, 10,306ft (3,143m).

Fan-tailed File Fish. △516.

Fanti, black African people of Ghana. An Akan people numbering about 250,000, they follow a matrilineal system of political succession and material inheritance and a patrilineal system of military succession. They traded between the African interior and Europe and became embroiled in conflicts with the Ashanti. They were first aided and later dominated by the British.

Fantin-Latour, Ignace Henri Jean Théodore (1836–1904), French painter. Noted for his realistic group portraits, including "Hommage à Eugène Delacroix" (1864; Paris, Louvre), he also did still lifes and lithographs illustrating the music of Wagner and others.

Fan-vaults. △1106.

FAO. *See* Food and Agricultural Organization.

Farad, unit of capacitance (symbol F) equal to the capacitance of a capacitor that acquires a charge of one coulomb when a potential difference of one volt is applied across the plates.

Faraday, Michael (1791–1867), English physicist, chemist, and experimentalist. He liquefied chlorine, discovered benzene and two chlorides of carbon, and enunciated the laws of electrolysis. Moving from chemistry to electricity, he discovered electromagnetic induction, made the first generator, built a primitive electric motor, and studied nonconducting materials (dielectrics). The unit of capacitance (the farad) is named after him. △128, 1484.

Faraday's Laws, (1) the mass of substance liberated from an electrolyte is proportional to the current passing and the time for which it passes; (2) when the magnetic flux through a circuit changes an electromotive force is induced in the circuit proportional to the rate of decrease of magnetic flux.

Farce, a type of comic drama characterized by its unrealistic characterizations, its improbable plot lines, and an emphasis on physical humor. Modern farce is a 19th-century invention and was developed by Arthur Wing Pinero in England and Eugène Marin Labiche and Georges Feydeau in France.

Fargo, William George (1818–81), US businessman, b. Pompey, N.Y. With Henry Wells he organized a shipping company with routes between Buffalo and the West (1844). Wells, Fargo & Company handled express service between New York and San Francisco, especially during the gold rush. Through mergers and reorganization, it became the American Express Company (1850). Fargo served as mayor of Buffalo (1862–66) and president of the American Express Company (1868–81).

Farinelli, Carlo Broschi (1705–82), Italian male soprano, one of the most notable of the 18th century "castrati"—Italian male singers who became sopranos as the result of childhood castration. He debuted in 1722, was a sensation in his day, and after 1737 was the official singer of the Spanish royal court. △1174.

Farm Bloc, bipartisan, pro-farmers group formed in Congress after World War I. It helped provide bank credit for farmers in the 1920s and favored price supports, parity, and cooperative marketing. *See also* Bloc.

Farm Buildings. △310.

Farm Cooperative. *See* Cooperative Farming.

Farm Credit Administration, agency established under the Farm Credit Act (1933). The administration replaced all existing farm loan agencies. It aids farmers and farmers' cooperatives by granting long and short term credit, for mortgages, production, and marketing. It oversees the entire Farm Credit System.

Farmer, James Leonard (1920–), US civil rights leader, b. Marshall, Texas. He helped to found the Congress of Racial Equality (CORE) in 1942 and served as its national director until 1966. He subsequently taught and was an assistant secretary of the Department of Health, Education, and Welfare.

Farmer-Labor Party, third party movement organized after World War I by trade union officials. Based on a semi-Socialist ideal of workers and farmers exercising controlling power, the party called for nationalization of all public utilities, basic industries, and banks. Most of its strength came from the states of Washington, South Dakota, and Montana. In 1923, as representatives of the Workers' Party of America (Communist) became dominant in the Farmer-Labor party, the original leaders withdrew from the movement.

Farmers Branch, city in NE Texas; N suburb of Dallas. Industries: food processing, insecticides, brooms, metal products. Settled 1841; inc. 1946. Pop. (1970) 27,492.

Farmers' Educational and Cooperative Union of America, US organization that represents farm families. It promotes farm interests and helps farmers to develop their own self-help institutions, such as cooperatives. Members, about 250,000. Founded 1902.

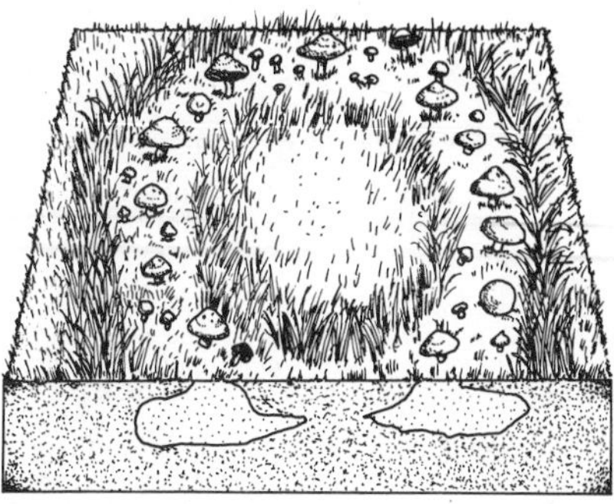

Fairy ring

Falling Water, designed by Frank Lloyd Wright

Henri Fantin-Latour: self-portrait

Michael Faraday

Farmers' Union, US farm organization that emerged in Louisiana during a period of falling agricultural prices in the 1880s. It later became part of the Southern Alliance.

Farming. △306–10, 320, 370–76.

Farming Corporation. △308.

Farm Machinery, equipment used for growing and harvesting crops. Implements have evolved from sticks to self-powered or tractor-drawn machines that, in some cases, have cut labor twentyfold. Soil preparation, planting, cultivating, and spraying can now be done in multi-foot swaths instead of single rows. Harvesters combine multiple farming operations into a single, self-powered machine. △304, 310.

Farnese, celebrated Italian family. Through the skill of **Ranuccio Farnese** (died *c.*1460), who militarily defended the Papal States and won the gratitude of Pope Eugenius IV (1431–47), the family began to increase its wealth and establish itself among the Roman aristocracy. Ranuccio's son Alessandro became **Pope Paul III** (1534–49), and his illegitimate son **Pier Luigi** (1503–47) was first duke of Parma and of Piacenza (from 1545). Pier Luigi's grandson **Alessandro** (1545–92), also duke of Parma and Piacenza, served Philip II of Spain as regent of the Netherlands (from 1577). The line ended with the death of **Antonio** in 1731.

Farnese, Alessandro (1468–1549). *See* Paul III, Roman Catholic pope.

Farnese Bull, large sculpture group originally done by Greek artists in Rhodes. A Roman copy of the group, depicting the punishment of Dirce by binding her to the horns of a bull, was found in the Caracalla baths and can now be seen in the National Archeological Museum, Naples.

Farnese Palace, a noted palace in Rome, designed by Antonio da Sangallo for Cardinal Alessandro Farnese in the 16th century. Michelangelo worked on it and it was completed by Giacomo della Porta. It is now the site of the French Embassy in Rome.

Farouk (1920–65), king of Egypt (1936–52), son and successor of King Fuad I. He opposed the Wafd party, failed to expel the British and was forced to abdicate after being overthrown by dissident military officers. Egypt then became a republic. He was noted for his extravagant life style.

Farquhar, George (1678–1707), English dramatist. His comedies were distinguished by humor combined with depth of character. *The Beaux Stratagem* (1707) opened at the Drury Lane Theatre shortly before he died.

Farquhar Islands, group of islands in Indian Ocean, NE of Malagasy Republic; British-owned and part of British Indian Ocean Territory. Area: 3sq mi (8sq km).

Farragut, David Glasgow (1801–70), US admiral and Union Civil War hero, b. Stony Point, Tenn. In the War of 1812, he served in the Pacific fleet. Operating on the Mississippi River during the Civil War, he won a victory at New Orleans in 1862. At Mobile Bay, Ala., in 1864, he ignored torpedoes to run his fleet through the Confederate blockade.

Farrell, James T(homas) (1904–), US author, b. Chicago. A novelist and short story writer, his most noted work is *Studs Lonigan* (1932–35), a trilogy of novels about the youth and young manhood of a tough Irish-American in Chicago. Other works in the same naturalistic genre include five novels about Danny O'Neill and a trilogy about Bernard Clare (or Carr). In addition to his numerous novels, he also wrote several collections of short stories and some significant literary criticism.

Farside, Lunar, side of the moon permanently turned away from the earth, owing to the satellite's captured rotation. Some 9% of the farside may be viewed from Earth because of lunar libration. Compared with the earthside, the farside has far fewer maria, but many craters. It was first photographed by the Russian probe Luna 3 in 1959. *See also* Libration; Mare. △54, 58.

Farsightedness, or hyperopia, correctible optical defect in which the rays of light entering the eye are focused behind the lens, causing distortion and making close vision difficult. Causes are a too-short eyeball or ineffective refraction. △674.

Fasces, emblem adopted by the Italian Fascist party in 1919. The fasces, depicting an ax surrounded by rods, was the symbol of state power in ancient Rome. *See also* Fascism. △1014.

Fascism, nationalist, anti-Communist movement founded in Italy by Benito Mussolini in 1919 as a reaction to the revolutionary movements that swept Europe after World War I. Glorification of the state and complete individual subordination to its authority were basic to Fascist dogma, as was preservation of a rigid class structure and law and order. The Fascist party was organized in military fashion with its black-shirted members using the ancient Roman salute. As the head of the party, Mussolini was seen as the embodiment of Italy's highest ideals and its salvation from the threats of anarchy and Communism. The Fascists ruled Italy from 1922 until the war's end in 1945. *See also* Fasces; Mussolini, Benito; World War II. △1334–36.

Fashoda Incident (1898), largely diplomatic struggle between France and Great Britain for control of Egypt's Upper Nile. Britain desired continuous territory from Egypt to South Africa, and France wanted a path from the Atlantic Ocean to the Red Sea. Their respective expeditions, led by Britain's Lord Kitchener and Maj. J.B. Marchand, met at Fashoda. France backed down after a British threat of war.

Fast, Howard Melvin (1914–), US author, b. New York City. A prolific writer; many of his novels are about the American Revolution and the quest for liberty. They include *Conceived in Liberty* (1939), *Citizen Tom Paine* (1943), *Freedom Road* (1944), and *April Morning* (1961). He also wrote under the pseudonyms E.V. Cunningham and Walter Erickson.

Fastolf, Sir John (1378?–1459), English soldier and administrator. He fought at Agincourt (1415) and again in France (1417–40). He was a counselor to Richard, Duke of York, and invested his large war profits in English estates. Shakespeare's Falstaff was modeled on Sir John.

Fat, substance used by animals to store energy and shield them from the cold. Fats are esters of glycerin with carboxlic acids such as palmitic, lauric, and stearic acid, which have 16 or 18 carbon atoms. Vegetable oils are similar to fats, but are viscous liquids rather than semisolids, and have double chemical bonds in the acid molecules, that is, they are unsaturated. △1560, 1570–72.

Fate of the Animals (Mare). △1294.

Fates, also called Parcae, corresponding to the Greek Moerae. There were three, the daughters of Night. Clotho, the spinner, personified the thread of life. Lachesis was chance, the element of luck that a man had a right to expect. Atropos was inescapable fate, against which there was no appeal.

Fathom, a unit used in measuring the depth of water. One fathom equals 6ft (1.83m). Originally it was the span of a man's arms.

Fatima (606–632), daughter of the prophet Mohammed, wife of Ali. Fatima and Ali felt deprived of their rightful inheritance by Abu Bakr, first Muslim Caliph after Mohammed's death. Their disappointed followers, the Shi'a sect of Islam, honor Ali as the rightful successor to Mohammed and offer devotion to Fatima, similar to that offered the Virgin Mary in Roman Catholicism. Her symbol, the "hand of Fatima," is often displayed in Shiite processions, and she is accorded a place of honor in heaven. *See also* Abu Bakr; Shi'a.

Fátima, village in W central Portugal; site of shrine of Our Lady of the Rosary of Fátima, Roman Catholic pilgrimage site, visited 1967 by Pope Paul VI.

Fatimid, or **Fatimite,** dynasty of North African caliphs (909–1171) claiming descent from Fatima, related to the Shiites (a Muslim sect). Exploiting social friction, Ubaydullah aroused the Berbers to become the first Fatimid caliph (in Tunisia). He captured the Abbassid holdings of Cyrenaica, Libya, and Alexandria (914). The third caliph, al-Mansur, seized Sicily (946). The fourth, al-Aziz, took Egypt (969), made Cairo the capital, and built the great mosque, Al-Azhar. The Fatimid realm eventually encompassed all of North Africa, Sicily, Egypt, Syria, and western Arabia, including Baghdad. The Normans, Turks, Venetians, and Crusaders took territory in the 11th through 13th centuries. The viziers and generals then took control, until Nureddin and Saladin of Syria liquidated the Fatimid caliphate in Egypt in 1171.

Fats and Oils, natural substances of animal or plant origin (or synthetic compounds). Usually fats are solid and oils liquid at room temperature; both are greasy in texture. Fats and oils are one of the principal foods. △696.

Fatty Acid. *See* Lipid. △1570, 1572.

Faulkner, Brian (1921–), politician of Northern Ireland. A member of the Unionist party, he became a member of the Northern Ireland Parliament in 1949 and was minister of home affairs (1959–63), commerce (1963–69), and development (1969–71). He was prime minister of Northern Ireland (1971–72) and continued as leader of his party until 1974. He was chief executive of the Northern Ireland administration (1974) and a member of the Constitutional Convention (1975). In these capacities he showed a willingness to accept power sharing with Roman Catholics.

Faulkner, William (1897–1962), US author, b. New Albany, Miss. He was raised in Oxford, Miss., where he later made his home. He joined the Royal Air Force in Canada in 1918, briefly attended the University of Mississippi after World War I, and lived for a short time in the early 1920s in New York City, New Orleans, and Europe. His first book was a collection of poems, *The Marble Faun* (1924). *Soldier's Pay*, a novel, appeared in 1926 and another novel, *Mosquitoes*, in 1927. With *Sartoris* (1929), his third novel, Faulkner created Yoknapatawpha County, the setting of most of his future works.

Drawing on his own background and on the people he knew best, he wrote a series of novels and stories that depict the South through the 19th and 20th centuries. The primary themes of the so-called Yoknapatawpha Saga include the relationship of the past to the present and the effects of the disintegration of traditional Southern society. An innovative stylist, he often used the stream-of-consciousness technique and complex time sequences. He was awarded the Nobel Prize in literature for 1949. His works include *The Sound and the Fury* (1929), *As I Lay Dying* (1930), *Sanctuary* (1931), *Light in August* (1932), *Absalom, Absalom!* (1936), *The Unvanquished* (1938), *The Hamlet* (1940), *Go Down, Moses and Other Stories* (1942), *Requiem for a Nun* (1951), *A Fable* (1954), *The Town* (1957), *The Mansion* (1959), and *The Reivers* (1962). He received Pulitzer Prizes for the latter two works. △1374.

Fault Block, in geology, crustal region bounded partly or completely by faults, which acts as a single unit during block faulting or any similar tectonic event. The Sierra Nevada mountains (California) are a prime example. *See also* Tectonics. △250.

Faulting, in geology, that process of fracture and displacement of materials that produces a fault. A fault is a distinct break in rock structures, and this break may extend for either a few centimeters or hundreds of miles. Faults are classified by the inclination of the fault surfaces and direction of the relative movement of the resulting fault blocks. △250, 252, 276.

Faunus, in Roman mythology, a fertility god. Mainly a woodland deity, his female counterpart was Fauna.

Faure, François Félix (1841–99), French merchant and politician, 6th president of the Republic after the resignation of Jean-Paul Casimir-Périer in 1895. In this position he helped bring about the Franco-Russian alliance and took an unfortunate conservative stance on the Dreyfus Affair. He died in office.

Fauré, Gabriel (1845–1924), French Romantic composer. His numerous works are characterized by a soft, refined, intimate quality and the prominence of melody. He composed chamber music, solo piano pieces, operas, many songs, and a highly regarded *Requiem* (1887). One of his most popular works is the *Elegie* for cello and orchestra (1883). *See also* Romanticism in Music. △1246.

Fauset, Jessie Redmon (1882–1961), US novelist, b. Philadelphia. Her novels, which relate the problems of middle-class blacks in Northern cities, include *There is Confusion* (1924), *Plum Bun* (1929), *The Chinaberry Tree* (1931), and *Comedy: American Style* (1933).

Faust (1808–1831), drama by Johann Wolfgang von Goethe based on the legend of Dr. Johann Faustus (1480–1540). There is also a drama by Christopher Marlowe and an opera by Gounod on this theme. The Goethe play is in two parts with a prologue. In the first part, Faust promises to forfeit his soul to Mephistopheles in exchange for one moment of perfect contentment. Mephistopheles tries various means to please Faust, which end in Faust's seduction of Margaret, an innocent young girl; this affair ends in tragedy as Margaret becomes insane and finally dies. In Part II Helen of Troy is recalled from Hades. She and

Faust have a child, Euphorion, representing the spirit of poetry. After Helen and Euphorion disappear into the air, Faust and Mephistopheles establish an abode for contented people. Realizing that contentment lies in helping others, Faust pronounces himself perfectly contented and dies. Although he has lost his wager, his soul is taken into heaven. △1222.

Fauvism, first major avant-garde movement in 20th-century painting. It was characterized by intense use of pure, brilliant color, often rapid brushwork, and somewhat flatly painted surfaces. The subject matter tended to be landscapes, still lifes, and figure compositions, sometimes portraits. The movement came about as a reaction to the academic style and was influenced by the work of Gauguin and Van Gogh. The group contained many artists who had studied under Gustave Moreau. Among its members were Henri Matisse, Albert Marquet, Georges Rouault, Maurice de Vlaminck, André Derain, A.C. Friesz, Georges Braque, Raoul Dufy, and Kees van Dongen. These artists exhibited together in the Salon d'Automne of 1905, at which they were dubbed "fauves," meaning "wild beasts," because of their use of brilliant color, and in the Salon des Indépendants of 1906. After this period, many of the artists evolved different styles, including Cubism, and their painting no longer shared the common traits of fauvism. △1294.

Fayetteville, city, NW Arkansas, 50mi (81km) N of Fort Smith; seat of Washington co; site of summer mountain resort and University of Arkansas (1871). Industries: electrical components, hardwood products. Settled 1828; inc. 1906. Pop. (1970) 30,729.

Fayetteville, city in S central North Carolina, on Cape Fear, 50mi (81km) S of Raleigh; seat of Cumberland co. A Tory center during American Revolution, town was renamed (1783) for Marquis de Lafayette; served as state capital (1789–93) and was scene of state convention that ratified US Constitution (1789). Industries: textiles, lumber, power tools. Inc. 1783. Pop. (1970) 53,510.

FBI. *See* Federal Bureau of Investigation.

FCC. *See* Federal Communications Commission.

FDA. *See* Food and Drug Administration.

FDIC. *See* Federal Deposit Insurance Corporation.

Fealty, in feudalism, the loyalty and obligations due to a king or lord by his vassal, or the specific oath of loyalty and consent taken by the vassal. In about the 9th century, fealty meant refraining from participation in any action that endangered the lord's life or property. By the 11th century, the positive duties of a vassal to his lord were established, including personal military service, financial obligations, and other forms of personal service. The oath of fealty was followed by an act of homage, and in the case where the granting of a fief was involved, by the rite of investiture. △1098.

Fear, intense emotional state aroused by anticipation of pain or injury from some event. Some capacity for fear is desirable and adaptive because it can lead to avoidance of or escape from harmful events. Abnormally strong or inappropriate fears, however, can become phobias. *See also* Phobia. △784.

Feather, growth comprising the skin covering of birds. It is composed of keratin, a fibrous protein. Body contour feathers grow in demarcated skin tracts separated by bare areas. Short, fluffy down feathers serve for insulation and long, quill-like contour feathers constitute wing and tail surfaces. Contour feathers have a central shaft with paired, interlocking branches. These are shed and replaced (molted) at least once a year. *See also* Bird. △528.

Featherbedding, union requirement that an employer hire or retain employees for services that are not performed or are not meant to be performed, or that obsolete work methods be maintained, or that limits be set on work an employee may perform. The Taft-Hartley Act forbids the practice, but the wording is so vague that few unions have been declared in violation.

Feather Star, crinoid echinoderm found in shallow marine waters clinging to underwater debris. Ten arms with feathery branches radiate from the tiny central disc. Reproduction is sexual. Class Crinoidea; species include rosy feather star *Antedon.* △504.

February, second month of the year. Its name is derived from the Roman god Februus. February has 28 days except in leap years, when it has 29. The birthstone is the amethyst.

February Revolution, insurrection of the French working class in 1848, causing the rapid downfall of the government of King Louis Philippe. The result of a poor economy and increasingly reactionary king, this revolution saw the creation of a troubled constitutional republic, with the election in December of Louis Napoleon (later Emperor Napoleon III) as its president. Paralleled by similar rebellions throughout Europe, the republican movement was largely unsuccessful.

Februus, in Roman mythology, the Etruscan god who corresponded to Dis Pater. The month of February was sacred to him; it was the month of the dead. In Etruria they also invoked a certain Mancus who must have been another Dis Pater.

Fechner, Gustav Theodore (1801–87), German physician and psychologist who helped found experimental psychology by using objective, precise methods to study psychophysics—the relationships of physical stimuli to sensation and perception. "Fechner's law" is that the relationship between the strength of a stimulus and the perceived intensity of a sensation is a constant.

Federal Aviation Administration (FAA), agency of the Department of Transportation (since 1967), formerly the Federal Aviation Agency. Its responsibilities include regulating air commerce to foster aviation safety, promoting civil aviation and a national system of airports, developing and operating a system of air traffic control for both civilian and military aircraft.

Federal Budget, US expenditure plan of the federal government, which includes agency budgets and detailed plans for the disbursement of funds by various budget categories. The Office of Management and Budget, an executive agency directly responsible to the president, prepares a budget proposal, which is reviewed in the executive branch. The president presents the final budget to Congress in an annual budget message. Congress, through the committee process, reviews the proposed budget and it may cut funds from various budget categories or increase funding in any area. The final budget is subject to presidential approval.

Federal Bureau of Investigation (FBI), agency of the Department of Justice. It is charged with investigating all violation of federal laws, with the exception of those assigned to other agencies. The FBI's wide range of responsibilities includes jurisdiction in criminal, civil, and security fields. Among these are subversive activities such as espionage and sabotage, interstate gambling and interstate transportation of stolen property, and assault on or killing of the president. The FBI achieved great prominence under its long-time director, J. Edgar Hoover. During the mid-1970s its activities came under critical public scrutiny and were investigated. Est. 1908.

Federal Child Labor Law. *See* Keating-Owen Act.

Federal Communications Commission (FCC), an independent US federal government agency created by the Communications Act of 1934 to regulate interstate and foreign wire and broadcast communications. Its seven members are appointed by the president. Proposed consolidations of telephone and telegraph companies, quality of their services, and their general administration are subject to FCC supervision. The FCC also licenses the operation and supervises the activities of all radio and television stations, and has the authority to investigate complaints of unfair practices, to hold hearings, and to award damages.

Federal Courts, US judicial system comprised of the US Supreme Court, the US courts of appeals and US district courts. There are also special courts, which include the Court of Claims, Customs Court, the Court of Customs and Patent Appeals, Territorial Courts, courts for the District of Columbia, Tax Court of the United States, and the Court of Military Appeals.

Federal Deposit Insurance Corporation (FDIC), US agency established by the Glass-Steagall Act (1933) to protect bank depositors. To prevent savers from being wiped out in bank failures, the corporation insured individual accounts up to $5,000, raised gradually to $40,000, in all Federal Reserve banks and qualified state banks. The corporation works to prevent the development of unwise banking practices and acts as receiver for national banks in receivership. It is administered by a 3-member board.

Federal Emergency Relief Act (FERA) (1933), early New Deal legislation to provide relief for unemployed workers. It created the Federal Emergency Re-

Fátima, Portugal

William Faulkner

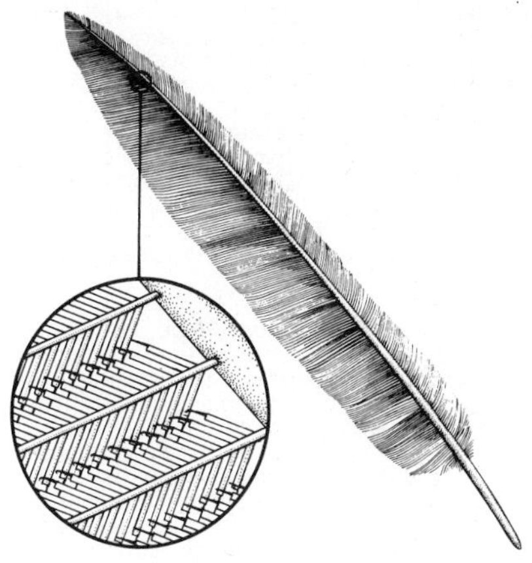

Feather

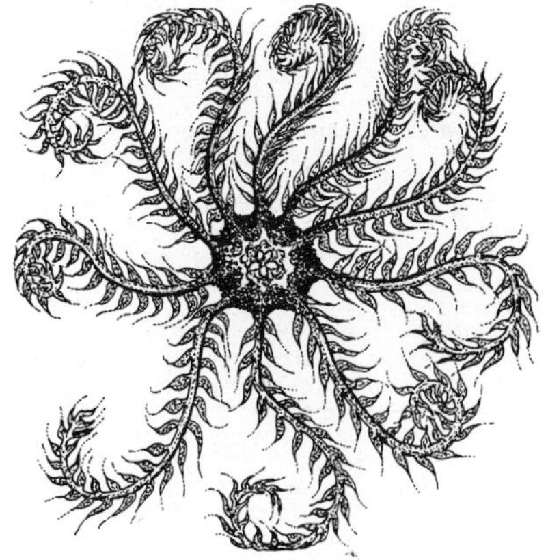

Feather star

lief Administration with Harry Hopkins as administrator; $500,000,000 was allocated, with half for direct aid to states and the rest to be distributed on a matching basis with state and local funds. Set up to provide work rather than handouts, the agency, which was replaced by the Works Progress Administration, put 4,000,000 people to work building roads, parks, schools, sewers, and other public works.

Federal Farm Loan Board, US agency established under Federal Farm Loan Act (1916) and authorized to charter federal land banks and national farm loan associations. Land banks provide funds to the loan associations, which grant loans at low interest rates to farmers on the security of farm mortgages.

Federal Housing Administration (FHA), US agency created by the National Housing Act (1934). The FHA assists homeowners and farmers by providing insurance for construction and improvement loans granted by banks and other lending agencies. The authority of the FHA was expanded in later legislation to include the administration of low-rent public and other housing. The FHA became a part of the Department of Housing and Urban Development (HUD) when it was created in 1965.

Federalism, division of political power between US federal and state governments. The powers of the federal government are delegated by the Constitution; other "residual" powers are reserved to the states, guaranteeing them a considerable degree of autonomy. The federal government has supreme authority; the states cannot nullify federal law nor can they withdraw from the union. An increasing centralization of power has been a feature of American federalism since the New Deal programs of the 1930s.

Federalist Papers, The, a series of 85 essays on political theory published from 1787–88. Written by Alexander Hamilton, James Madison, and John Jay, the Federalist papers strongly showed support for the Federalist Constitution. All but the last eight essays appeared in the New York papers, and were widely read as they were published. Although the essays were not significantly influential at the ratification convention, they are widely accepted as a classical work on political theory. They were published in a two-volume edition in 1788.

Federalists, US political party led by George Washington, Alexander Hamilton, John Adams, and John Jay. It was formed in 1787 to promote ratification of the Constitution. The Federalists represented mainly planters, merchants, bankers, and manufacturers. The Federalist Papers were essays written by Hamilton, James Madison (who later became an anti-Federalist), and Jay expressing the Federalists' support for sound money, government banking, and strong federal powers. The Federalists were opposed to the states' rights, agrarian philosophy of the Republicans led by Thomas Jefferson.

Federal Power Commission (FPC), independent US federal agency to regulate interstate aspects of the electric power and natural gas industries. The FPC's responsibilities include issuing permits and licenses for non-federal hydroelectric power projects and regulating rates of interstate wholesale transactions in electric power and natural gas. The FPC supervises environment requirements in the construction of new projects. The FPC was established in 1920; the statutes regulating its activities were amended and revised in 1935 and 1938 and by subsequent legislation and executive orders.

Federal Register, US government publication, issued daily, that prints presidential proclamations, reorganization plans, and executive orders, as well as regulations proposed by public agencies.

Federal Reserve System, central banking authority of the United States, established by the Federal Reserve Act of 1913 and strengthened by the Banking Acts of 1933 and 1935. Twelve regional banks are supervised by a Federal Reserve Board of Governors, with each of seven members appointed by the US president for 14 years. All national banks are members as are many state and commercial banks. More than three-fourths of all US commercial bank deposits are in member banks. Each member bank owns stocks in its district bank and must maintain reserves on deposit there. The purpose of the Federal Reserve System is to maintain sound monetary and credit conditions in the United States. It attempts to do so by regulating the flow of money through its Federal Reserve Notes, the US legal tender, and by regulating credit through varying its discount rate on loans to member banks and by varying the percentage of total deposits member banks must keep in reserve.

Federal Savings and Loan Insurance Corporation, independent US federal agency in the executive branch. Founded in 1934, it operates under the supervision of the Federal Home Loan Bank Board. It was established to insure the safety of savings in the thrift and home financing institutions and provides coverage of up to $20,000. It also works to prevent default of an insured institution.

Federal Style, US architectural style between *c.*1780 and *c.*1820, based on English neoclassicism and influenced by the designs of Robert and James Adam. Buildings in this style were usually made of brick with windows and doors that were often framed by shallow wall arches. Other elements of the style included slender proportions and delicate decoration. Outstanding architects using this style were New Englanders Charles Bulfinch and Samuel McIntire.

Federal Theater, an experiment (1935–39) in federal subsidy of the theater that grew out of the Works Progress Administration and sought to alleviate unemployment problems in the US theater. It flourished under the direction of Hallie Flannagan, bringing live theater to more than 20 states and staging important productions of *Murder in the Cathedral, Macbeth* (an all-black cast), *Doctor Faustus,* the experimental "living newspaper," and many more.

Federal Trade Commission (FTC), an independent US federal administrative agency. Established in 1915, its main objective is to maintain the free enterprise system and to maintain fair competition. The FTC functions in the area of interstate commerce to prevent unfair competition. It safeguards the public by preventing the dissemination of false or deceptive advertisements of consumer products. The five members are appointed by the president and approved by the Senate.

Federal Trade Commission v. Cement Institute (1948), The Supreme Court decided that the cement industry's trade association (the Cement Institute) was setting cement prices in a way that harmed competition. Specifically, the Cement Institute was using "an unfair method of competition" that violated the Federal Trade Commission Act. The Cement Institute was employing a delivered price arrangement, under which participants charged any customer the same (nonmarket) price.

Federal Trade Commission v. Colgate-Palmolive Co. (1965), US Supreme Court decision upholding a Federal Trade Commission order prohibiting deceptive television advertisements using undisclosed props or mock-ups.

Federal Truth in Lending Act, law passed by the US Congress in 1968 to protect consumers by providing that banks and other credit agencies inform borrowers of the cost of loans and other forms of credit.

Feedback, process of returning a part of the output energy of a device to the input. In negative feedback the output energy is arranged to cause a decrease in the input energy. A governor is a negative feedback device, the output being coupled to the input so that constant speed is obtained, irrespective of load. In positive feedback, the output energy reinforces the input energy. This occurs when a loudspeaker feeds into a microphone coupled to the same amplifier. In this case the amplifier will oscillate. △1548, 1670.

Feeds, term applied to the diet of farm animals provided by man. Feeds include such grains as wheat, corn, rye, soy beans, seeds, and some nonvegetative matter, such as fish meal. Many feeds are prepared commercially after extensive nutritional research.

Feiffer, Jules (1927–), US cartoonist and writer, b. New York City. He was a regular contributor of cartoons to the *Village Voice* in New York City (1953–56), to the *London Observer* (1958–1966; 1972–present), and to *Playboy* magazine from 1959. His cartoons have won numerous awards and his play *Little Murders* (1965) was voted best play of the year by London critics.

Feininger, Lyonel (1871–1956), US painter, b. New York City. On the faculty of the Bauhaus (1919–33), he worked mostly in watercolors and graphic media. His style was strongly influenced by the cubists. In 1937 he returned to the United States where his style reached its maturation in such watercolors as "Dawn" (1938; Museum of Modern Art, New York City).

Feira de Santana, city in E Brazil, 60mi (97km) NNW of Salvador; noted site of cattle fairs; railway, livestock, and shipping center. Exports: cotton, tobacco, beans. Pop. 136,000.

Feke, Robert (*c.*1706–50), US painter, b. Oyster Bay, N.Y. Little is known of him, except from 1741 to 1750. Considered to be the finest early American portrait painter, he primarily painted prominent citizens in several cities. His works include "Isaac Royall Family" (1741).

Feldspars, group of common aluminum silicate minerals; principal constituents of igneous rocks. Orthoclase and microcline are potassium feldspars of monoclinic and triclinic system, respectively. Members of the plagioclase series (sodium and calcium feldspars) have physical properties similar to microcline, but with crystals frequently twinned. Several are cut as gems: amazonite, a green form of microcline; moonstone, white with a bluish stain, is a plagioclase variety as is labradorite, an iridescent red, blue, or green, and sunstone, a spangled variety, frequently reddish. Hardness 6; sp gr 2.55. △242, 246, 1558.

Felidae, cat family containing 3 genera *(Felis, Pantheon, Acinouyx)* and 36 species of carnivores, ranging from the housecat to the tiger. Order Carnivora. *See also* Cat.

Feller, Robert William Andrew ("Bob") (1918–), US baseball player, b. Van Meter, Iowa. A fast right-hand pitcher, he played with the Cleveland Indians (1936–41; 1945–56) and recorded 266 wins and three no-hitters. He was elected to the Baseball Hall of Fame in 1962.

Fellini, Federico (1920–), Italian film director. He was famous for the realism and macabre satire of his works, which were often autobiographical. His major films include *La Strada* (1956), *La Dolce Vita* (1959), *8½* (1963), *Clowns* (1970), *Roma* (1972), and *Amarcord* (1974).

Feminism, women's movement to obtain equal opportunity in politics, education, and employment. In the 18th century, when Mary Wollstonecraft's *Vindication of the Rights of Women* (1792) appeared, law and theology had long treated women as inferior to men. Women in the French and American revolutions had pressed without success for the inclusion of women's emancipation in the new constitutions. Women could not control property, the disposal of their children, or their own persons. In 1848 at the Seneca Falls Convention in New York, feminists, referred to as suffragettes because of their emphasis on gaining the right to vote, issued a declaration of independence for women. The movement, led by Susan B. Anthony and Elizabeth Cady Stanton, spread through the United States and Europe. Emmeline Goulden Pankhurst used militant means and hunger strikes to attempt to win suffrage in Britain, founding the Women's Social and Political Union in 1903. After marching, demonstrating, and being jailed, women won further entrance into higher education, trades and professions, and property rights. In the United States the woman-suffrage advocate Susan B. Anthony had been dead for 14 years when women finally won the right to vote in 1920. Margaret Sanger pressed for legalized birth control, winning it in the 1930s; a UN Commission on the Status of Women was established in 1946; but the Women's Liberation Movement, as it came to be known, had an upsurge of strength in the 1960s. The National Organization for Women (NOW), formed in 1966, and other women's groups tried to remove remaining legal and social barriers to equality for women by encouraging legalized abortion, federally supported child-care centers, and equal pay for women. The Equal Rights Amendment, passed in 1972 by Congress after pressure from Bella Abzug, Shirley Chisholm, and others in the National Women's Political Caucus, met opposition as it was submitted for ratification by the states. *See also* Seneca Falls Convention; Woman Suffrage; Women's Liberation Movement.

Femoral Artery and Vein. △688.

Femur, upper leg bone, extending from the pelvis to the knee. It is the longest and strongest bone of the skeleton. Its rounded smooth head articulates with the pelvis at the acetabulum, or hip socket; its large flattened lower end—felt on both sides of the knee—articulates with the tibia, the larger of the lower leg bones. △682.

Fence Lizard, or spiny lizard, any of North and Central American lizards. Rough-scaled, its body is short and broad and grayish-brown, green, or blue. Most males have prominent blue patches on each side of belly. They are insectivorous. Length: 4–15in (10–38cm). There are 50 species; 15 are native to the United States. Family Iguanidae; genus *Sceloporus*. *See also* Lizard.

Fencing, the sport of dueling with foil, épée, and

saber. It is conducted among individuals and teams, on a strip 40ft (12.2m) long and 6ft (1.8m) wide, which is marked off by 2 parallel warning lines 10ft (3m) from each end, beyond which the fencers may not step. Fencers wear wire-mesh masks, heavy canvas jackets, and gloves. The tip of the weapon is blunted and points are scored by touching the opponent. In épée matches, the whole body is included in the target area; with foils, the torso is the target area. With both weapons, touches are made with the point. In saber matches, the target area is any part of the body above the waist. Winning touches are five in foil or saber, and three in épée. The scoring is done electrically. Fencing was first included in the Olympic Games in 1896. In the United States the sport is regulated by The Amateur Fencers League of America (formed 1891).

Fénelon, François de Salignac de (1651–1715), French churchman and philosopher. He was tutor to the Duke of Burgundy (1689), then Archbishop of Cambrai (1695), but lost favor owing to his espousal of "Quietism"—a variety of Catholic mysticism—and his *Telemachus* (1699), a work somewhat critical of the government of Louis XIV.

Feng Yü-hsiang (1882–1948), one of the colorful warlords of 20th-century China. He built up in N China a large, personally devoted army that remained a significant force in modern Chinese politics until 1930. Feng's conversion to Christianity earned him the title of Christian General. His wife, Li Tehch'uan, remained active in the government of the Chinese People's Republic.

Fenian Cycle (Finn Cycle), group of Irish sagas dealing with the semi-divine hero Finn and his sons Oisin and Diarmaid. Written in Gaelic *c.*1200, the stories have an older oral tradition and feature incidents of heroic prowess and magical intervention upon which some of the incidents in Arthurian literature are based. The longest story in the cycle is *The Old Men's Conversation,* which is actually a collection of Finn stories.

Fenian Movement, 19th-century Irish nationalist organization. Formed in 1858, the Fenians sought independence from Britain by revolution. Following the arrests of their leaders in 1866 and the lack of response to their activities in Ireland, Irish immigrants in the United States took up their cause. Under John O'Neill the American Fenians planned several invasions of Canada, which were thwarted by United States and Canadian authorities (1866–70). A Fenian campaign in England (1866) also failed. △1314.

Fennel, aromatic herb native to Europe and Asia Minor and widely cultivated for food flavoring. Its shoots are eaten as a vegetable. It has divided leaves, yellow flowers, and small, oblong seedlike fruits. Height: to 3ft (0.9m). Family Umbelliferae; species *Foeniculum vulgare.*

Fenollosa, Ernest Francisco (1853–1908), US Orientalist and poet. He became a champion of Japanese traditional art in Japan's turbulent period of modernization. While teaching in Tokyo (1878–86) he helped form Japanese policies of art preservation and education. He was curator of Oriental art at the Boston Museum of Fine Arts (1890–97) and professor at the Imperial Normal School, Tokyo (1897–1900). As his literary executor, the poet Ezra Pound used Fenollosa's notes to produce some of his most influential poetry (*Cathay,* 1915).

Fenugreek, annual plant native to S Europe and Asia. It has white flowers and long, beaked pods. It is used as forage and a potherb. Height: to 2ft (61cm). Family Leguminosae; species *Trigonella foenum-graecum.*

FEPC. *See* Fair Employment Practice Committee.

FERA. *See* Federal Emergency Relief Act.

Ferber, Edna (1887–1968), US author, b. Kalamazoo. She began her writing career as a newspaper reporter and then turned to fiction. Initially she wrote popular short stories about Emma McChesney, a business-woman. Many of these were collected in *Roast Beef, Medium* (1913), *Personality Plus* (1914), and other books. Her later novels are colorful and panoramic, dealing with a wide variety of Americans. These novels include *So Big* (1924), which won her a Pulitzer Prize in 1925; *Show Boat* (1926), which was made into a successful musical; *Cimarron* (1930); *Giant* (1952); and *Ice Palace* (1958). She also wrote several successful plays in collaboration with George S. Kaufman, including *Dinner at Eight* (1932) and *Stage Door* (1936). Many of her works were made into motion pictures.

Fer-de-lance, widely distributed Central and South American lance-headed pit viper that hunts rats. It has black-edged, light diamond markings on brown ground color. Terrestrial, its venomous bite is often fatal to human beings. Up to 70 live young are born at one time. Length: to 8ft (2.5m). Family Viperidae; genus *Bothrops. See also* Pit Viper; Snake.

Ferdinand I (1793–1875), emperor of Austria (1835–48), king of Hungary (1830–48). This weak sovereign let Prince Metternich govern for him. Faced with revolutions in Hungary, Italy, and Vienna, he was forced to abdicate and flee in 1848. His nephew Francis Joseph succeeded him as emperor of Austria in 1849.

Ferdinand I (1503–64), Holy Roman emperor (1556–64), king of Bohemia and of Hungary (1526–64). He succeeded to the thrones of Bohemia and Hungary on the death of his brother-in-law Louis II. He never really controlled Hungary; he had to pay tribute to Sultan Suleiman I to retain his title. He had a strong hold on Bohemia, where he suppressed the Protestants. His elder brother, Holy Roman Emperor Charles V, gave him considerable control over Germany. Ferdinand warred against the German Protestants with varying success, ending in the religious truce of the Treaty of Augsburg (1555). In 1558 Charles V abdicated in his favor. △1128.

Ferdinand II (1578–1637), Holy Roman Emperor (1619–37) and king of Bohemia (1617–37) and Hungary (1621–37). The Bohemian revolt against him in 1618 precipitated the Thirty Years War, which dominated his reign. *See also* Thirty Years War. △1154.

Ferdinand III (1608–57), Holy Roman emperor (1637–57). The son of Ferdinand II, he was nominal imperial commander in the Thirty Years War from 1634. In 1648 he accepted the Peace of Westphalia, ending the war. *See also* Thirty Years War.

Ferdinand (1861–1948), prince (1887–1908) and tsar of Bulgaria (1908–18). A prince of Saxe-Coburg, he was chosen to succeed Alexander as ruler of Bulgaria. Russia opposed his selection, so he was not recognized by the major powers until 1896. In 1908 he declared Bulgaria independent of the Ottoman Empire and himself the tsar. With Russian backing he allied Bulgaria with Serbia, Greece, and Montenegro in the first Balkan War (1912–13), which ended Turkish dominance in the Balkans. But in the second Balkan War (1913), Greece and Serbia joined with Romania and Turkey in defeating Bulgaria. Most of Macedonia was lost to Greece and Serbia. Bulgaria joined the Central Powers in World War I. After defeat in the war, Ferdinand abdicated in favor of his son Boris III.

Ferdinand I (Ferdinand the Great) (died 1065), Spanish king of Castile (1033–65) and León (1037–65). He succeeded his father, Sancho III of Navarre, in Castile, conquered León, and took parts of Navarre from his brother. He successfully fought the Moors, making vassals of the rulers of Seville, Toledo, Zaragoza, and Badajoz. His kingdoms were divided at his death among his sons.

Ferdinand I (1379?–1416), Spanish king of Aragón and Sicily and count of Barcelona (1412–16). A prince of Castile, he acted as regent for his nephew John II. In 1410 his uncle, Martin, died, leaving vacant the thrones of Aragon and Sicily and the county of Barcelona. After defeating his rivals, Ferdinand succeeded to his uncle's offices. He was succeeded by his son Alfonso V.

Ferdinand II (Ferdinand the Catholic) (1452–1516), Spanish king of Aragon (1479–1516), of Castile and León (as Ferdinand V, 1474–1504), of Sicily (1468–1516), and of Naples (1504–16). He became joint king of Castile and León after marrying Isabella I in 1469 and inherited Aragon from his father, John II, in 1479. After he and Isabella conquered the Moorish kingdom of Granada in 1492, they ruled over a united Spain. In 1492 they sponsored the voyage of Christopher Columbus to the New World, expelled the Jews from Spain, and initiated the Spanish Inquisition.

Under Ferdinand, Spain became involved in the Italian wars against France. The result was an almost united Italy under Spanish control. After Isabella's death in 1504, Ferdinand acted as regent in Castile for their insane daughter Joanna and later for her son Charles I (who succeeded Ferdinand and ruled most of Europe as Holy Roman Emperor Charles V). In 1506 Ferdinand married Germaine de Foix and used her rights in Navarre as pretext for conquering that kingdom.

Ferdinand III (1199–1252), Spanish king of Castile (1217–52) and León (1230–52). He was the son of

Fence lizard

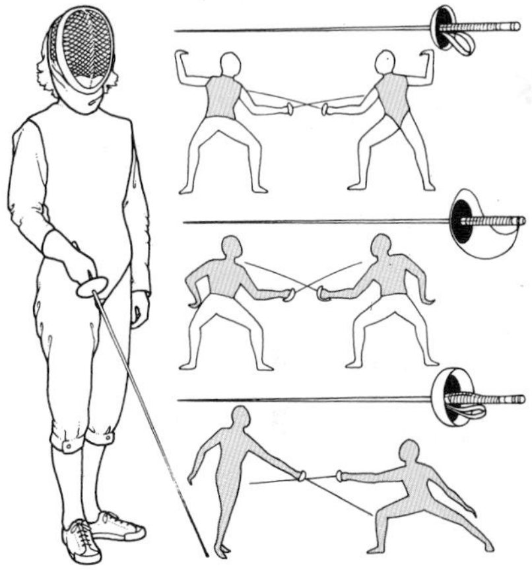

Fencing

Edna Ferber

Fer-de-lance

Alfonso IX of León and Barengaria of Castile. His mother renounced her rights to Castile in his favor in 1217, and when he inherited León from his father in 1230, he permanently united the two kingdoms. He spent most of his reign successfully fighting the Moors. He expelled them from Córdoba, Jaén, Seville, and Murcia. Thus, at his death all of Spain except for the kingdom of Granada had been Christianized. His son Alfonso X succeeded him. Ferdinand was canonized in 1671.

Ferdinand IV (1285–1312), Spanish king of Castile and León (1295–1312). He succeeded his father in 1295, and his mother, Maria de Molina, was regent during his minority and successfully protected his throne from numerous usurpers. He took Gibraltar from the Moors in 1309. His son Alfonso XI succeeded him.

Ferdinand VI (1712?–1759), king of Spain (1746–59), son and successor of Philip V. Upon becoming king, he forced into retirement his stepmother, Elizabeth Farnese, but kept José de Ensenada as a chief minister until 1754. Ferdinand kept Spain out of the Seven Years War during his lifetime. In 1758 his wife died, triggering in him a deep melancholy that verged on insanity. He was succeeded by his half brother, Charles III.

Ferdinand VII (1784–1833), king of Spain (1808–33), son of Charles IV and María Luisa. As crown prince he was involved in court intrigues, made overtures to Napoleon I, and was arrested (1807) by his father. An uprising in 1808 forced his father's abdication, but the French forced Ferdinand himself off the throne and installed Joseph Bonaparte. Ferdinand was imprisoned by the French during the Peninsular War but was restored in 1814. Thereafter his reign was increasingly reactionary. All mainland colonies in the Western Hemisphere were lost during his reign. He altered the Spanish constitution so his daughter Isabella II could succeed him, which set off the Carlist wars. *See also* Carlists.

Ferdinand I (1423–94), king of Naples (1458–94). Born in Valencia, Spain, he was the illegitimate son of Alfonso V of Aragon (also Alfonso I of Sicily and Naples from 1442). Pope Calixtus III refused to recognize his title to the kingdom of Naples; but after war with the Angevin pretender to the throne, he made peace with Calixtus' successor, Pius II. A 1485 nobles' rebellion (backed by Pope Innocent VIII) was suppressed.

Ferdinand II (1469–96), king of Naples (1495–96). His father, Alfonso II, abdicated when Charles VIII of France invaded in 1495, but Ferdinand, now king, defeated the occupation forces in 1496 with Spanish aid. His sudden death that same year allowed the Spanish to usurp the Neapolitan throne.

Ferdinand IV (1751–1825), king of Naples. *See* Ferdinand I, king of the Two Sicilies.

Ferdinand I (1345–83), king of Portugal (1367–83), son and successor of Peter I. His overwhelming ambition for the throne of Castile kept Portugal in almost continuous war with that country. Finally, in 1382 he married his daughter and heiress to King John I of Castile; upon Ferdinand's death, however, his illegitimate half brother, John I, was elected king.

Ferdinand II (1816–85), king consort of Portugal (1837–53). A prince of Saxe-Coburg-Gotha, in 1836 he married Maria II of Portugal and after her death in 1853 was regent to their son, Peter V, until he came of age. In later years, he was offered and refused the crowns of Greece and Spain.

Ferdinand I (1865–1927), king of Romania (1914–27). Named heir in 1889, he became king when his uncle Carol I died in 1914. Ferdinand kept Romania neutral in World War I until 1916 when Romanian armies invaded Transylvania. Although the Romanians were crushed by the armies of the Central Powers, Ferdinand had won the loyalty of his people and he returned in triumph in 1918. His coronation took place in 1922. By the terms of the peace treaties, Romania more than doubled its territory, although many of the settlements were disputed. Ferdinand's land reform efforts failed.

Ferdinand I (1751–1825), king of the Two Sicilies (1816–25) and of Naples (as Ferdinand IV). Son of Don Carlos de Bourbon (later Charles III of Spain), his reign in Naples from 1759–1825 was interrupted from 1806–1815 by the French occupation. His 1768 marriage to Marie Caroline, sister of French queen Marie Antoinette, marked the beginning of his reactionary policies. In 1816 he united his kingdoms of Naples and Sicily into the Kingdom of the Two Sicilies. The constitutionalist uprising of 1820 forced him to grant a constitution, but with the aid of Austria he regained his hold in 1821.

Ferdinand II (1810–59), king of the Two Sicilies (1830–59), son of Francis I. Originally considered a liberal, he came to be noted for his despotic rule; in 1849 he quelled a popular revolution begun in 1848, the first of many uprisings to sweep Europe that year. Ultimately, his authoritarian rule weakened the kingdom and led to its collapse and incorporation into a united Italy in 1860 after his death.

Ferdinand I de' Medici (1549–1609), grand duke of Tuscany. The younger son of Cosimo the Great, he resigned his cardinal's hat to succeed his brother Francesco (1541–87) as grand duke in 1587. By marrying Christine of Lorraine (granddaughter of Catherine de' Medici, herself a Florentine and then French queen) in 1589, he provided a French counterbalance to Spanish influence in Italy.

Ferdinand II de' Medici (1610–70), grand duke of Tuscany (from 1620). Son of Cosimo II (1590–1620) and father of Cosimo III (1642–1723), he was a pupil of Galileo. In 1657 he established the Academia del Cimento, said to be the first academic institution in Europe devoted to the natural sciences. His weak rule in the midst of Medici extravagence is held responsible for depletion of family fortunes.

Ferdinand III (1769–1824), grand duke of Tuscany and archduke of Austria. Succeeding as grand duke in 1790 when his father, Leopold II, became Holy Roman emperor, his reign was interrupted by the French occupation (1799–1814). Noted for his enlightened and liberal rule, he managed to avoid the reactionary violence typical of Italian restorations after Napoleon's defeat as well as overwhelming dependence on Austria.

Ferdinand Marie, Vicomte de Lesseps. *See* Lesseps, Ferdinand Marie, Vicomte de.

Fergana (Ferghana), formerly Skobelev, city in E Uzbek SSR, USSR; capital of Fergana oblast; site of teachers' college. Industries: cotton, silk, clothing. Founded 1876 by Russians as Novy Margelan. Pop. 111,000.

Ferguson, (Sir) Samuel (1810–86), Irish poet and antiquary, keeper of the records of Ireland. His poetry, including *Lays of the Western Gael* (1865), *Conary* (1880), and *Deirdre* (1880), based on Irish legends, anticipated the literary renaissance in his country. *See also* Irish Literary Renaissance.

Ferguson, city in E Missouri, 10mi (16km) NW of St Louis. Founded 1845 by William Ferguson. Inc. 1894. Pop. (1970) 28,759.

Fermentation, energy-yielding pathway by which sugar and starch molecules, catalyzed by enzymes or micro-organisms such as yeast, are broken down anaerobically. Old-established uses, where the major products are carbon dioxide and ethanol, include bread making, wine and beer brewing, cheese maturing, and drug manufacture. Fermentation is a major metabolic degrading pathway where the products may differ due to different enzymes directing the last stages. △350.

Fermi, Enrico (1901–54), Italian physicist who worked mainly in the fields of atomic behavior and structure, and the quantum theory. He showed that transmutations may be caused by neutron bombardment of elements, synthesized transuranium, and constructed the first atomic pile. He was honored with the 1938 Nobel Prize and by having the element fermium named after him. △1484, 1746.

Fermium, radioactive metallic element (symbol Fm) of the actinide group, first identified (1953) as a decay product of U^{235} produced in the first large hydrogen-bomb explosion (1952). Properties: at. no. 100; most stable isotope Fm^{257} (half-life 80 days). *See also* Transuranium Elements.

Fern, tracheophyte, or nonflowering plant, that produces spores rather than seeds. Some are vines, some trees, and some float on ponds. Many grow on trees. Most grow in warm, moist areas. The best known genus, *Pteridium* (bracken), grows in old fields. They are characterized by two perennial generations: the conspicuous sporophyte that possesses leafy fronds, stems, and roots, and reproduces by minute spores usually clustered on the leaves; and the inconspicuous gametophyte that resembles tiny moss and produces sperm and ova. Ferns usually have flat leaves on a stalk. Fronds unroll from curled fiddleheads and are divided into leaflets. Ferns were represented during Devonian times. Class Filicinae. △424, 438.

Fernández de Córdoba, Francisco (died c. 1518), Spanish conquistador, discovered Yucatán in 1517 while procuring slaves. He was killed by the Maya Indians about a year later.

Fernández de Córdoba, Gonzalo (1453–1515), Spanish general, known as the Great Captain. He negotiated the surrender of the Moors in Granada in 1492. He was commander of the troops of Ferdinand and Isabella in the Italian wars and was successful in removing French influence from Naples and Sicily. He became the first viceroy of Naples after the Spanish victory.

Fernández de Lizardi, José Joaquín (1776–1827), Mexican novelist and journalist. He is generally considered the first Spanish-American novelist. His best work is his first novel, *El periquillo sarniento* (1816), which criticizes Spanish government and education. He was an outspoken newspaper editor both before and after the 1821 independence.

Fernando Pó (Macías Nguema Biyogo), island in Bight of Biafra, off coast of W Africa; province of Equatorial Guinea; contains fertile volcanic farmland. Exports: cocoa, coffee, copra. Malabo is capital and country's largest city. Discovered 1472 by Fernão do Po, a Portuguese navigator; ceded to Spain 1778. Area: 779sq mi (2,018sq km). Pop. (island) 61,197.

Ferndale, city in SE Michigan; Woodward Avenue (city's main street) follows section of old Saginaw trail between Detroit and Saginaw. Industries: chemicals, steel. Inc. as village 1918, as city 1927. Pop. (1970) 30,850.

Fern Palm. *See* Sago Palm.

Ferrara, city in N Italy, 57mi (92km) SW of Venice; capital of Ferrara prov. An independent commune in 10th century, city was ruled by House of Este 1240; prosperity declined under papal rule 1598; ceded to France 1797; restored to pope 1815; birthplace of Girolamo Savonarola, reformer and martyr of the Roman Catholic church (1452); site of Este Castle (1385–1570), Cathedral of St Giórgio (1185), university (1391). Industries: agriculture, chemicals, sugar, alcohol, shoes. Pop. 156,644.

Ferrarese School, northern school of painting of the Italian Renaissance. Among the artists of this school in the 15th century were Cosimo Tura and Ercole de' Roberti. During the 16th century, this school was led by Dosso and his brother Battista del Dosso, and was influenced by Venetian and Roman artists of the period.

Ferré, Luis Alberto (1904–), governor of Puerto Rico (1969–73), a champion of statehood for the island. The founder-leader of the New Progressive party, he also was a member of the commission that studied the status of the commonwealth.

Ferret, small, carnivorous weasel-like animal. They are agile killers, with long necks, slender bodies, long tails, short legs, pink eyes, and yellow fur. The wild black-footed *Mustela nigripes* of North America is rare. The domesticated *Mustela putorius caro,* related to the European polecat, is used by hunters to kill rats and flush rabbits from their burrows. Length: 19in(48cm); weight: 1lb(.45kg). Family Mustelidae. *See also* Polecat; Weasel.

Ferric Compounds, those compounds in which the element iron has a higher valance (usually three) than in ferrous compounds.

Ferrites. △1608.

Ferrol (El Ferrol del Caudillo), port city in NW Spain; site of a major Spanish naval station; birthplace of Gen. Francisco Franco. Industries: shipbuilding, iron works. Founded 1726. Pop. 87,736.

Ferromagnetism, form of magnetism exhibited by substances, such as iron, cobalt, and nickel, with high magnetic permeabilities. *See also* Magnetism. △ 1534–36.

Ferry, Jules François Camille (1832–93), French republican statesman, opposed the empire of Napoleon III, holding several political offices after its fall. Twice premier (1880–81; 1883–85), he accomplished extensive educational reform, arousing clerical enmity, and oversaw the establishment of a French colonial empire in Africa and Indochina. He was assassinated. △1300.

Fertile Crescent, historic region in the Middle East. It curves across the N section of the Syrian desert, including parts of Jordan, Iraq, Israel, Syria, Lebanon; is watered by Tigris and Euphrates rivers; site of many violent invasions from the Arabian peninsula; location of man's earliest cultures; artifacts have been found dating from 8,000 BC.

Fertility Drug, a drug used to induce ovulation. Some drugs used are Clomiphene, a weak estrogen that is thought to stimulate pituitary gland gonadotropin secretion, and Perganol, which contains human pituitary gonadotropin. Both can induce ovulation, but both must be used carefully and often result in multiple pregnancy.

Fertilization, impregnation of an egg nucleus by a sperm nucleus to form a zygote. Stages of fertilization are: penetration—sperm clumps on egg surface; activation—completion of egg meiosis; and fusion of egg and sperm nuclei—restores diploid number of chromosomes. It is external (fish, amphibians) or internal (reptiles, birds, mammals). △462, 700.

Fertilizer, substance (natural or artificial) added to soil, containing chemicals to improve plant growth by increasing soil fertility. Manure and compost were the first fertilizers. Other natural substances, such as bonemeal, ashes, guano, and fish, have been used for centuries. Modern chemical fertilizers, composed of nitrogen, phosphorus, and potassium in powdered, liquid, or gaseous forms, are now widely used. Specialized fertilizers also contain essential trace elements. △302, 316, 320.

Fès (Fez), city in N central Morocco, approx. 150mi (242km) ENE of Casablanca; a sacred city of Islam containing over 100 mosques. Industries: agriculture, leather goods, metal works. Founded 790. Pop. 290,000.

Fescue, grass native to Northern Hemisphere and cultivated widely for pasture and fodder. Some species, such as red fescue *(Festuca rubra)*, are also used in lawn mixtures. The short, five-leaved sheep fescue *(F. ovina)* grows in dense tufts on mountains and forms turf in sandy soil. Blue fescue has smooth, silvery leaves in clumps and is cultivated for ornamental borders. There are about 100 species. Family Gramineae.

Fetch. △226.

Fetish, object possessing supernatural powers. The power of the fetish derives from a deity or consecration or is inherent. Claws or amulets may be fetishes. They are often carried around, especially by witch doctors, as sources of magical power. *See also* Amulet; Totem; Witch Doctor.

Fetishism, sexual dysfunction in which a particular object or body part becomes an essential aspect of sexual arousal and gratification. In religious fetishism, a particular object is imbued with inordinate religious importance that is not consistent with the usual norms of the culture.

Fetus. △702.

Feuchtwanger, Lion (1884–1958), German novelist and dramatist. A pacifist and left-wing Jewish intellectual, his novels included *Success* (1930), *The Jewish War* (1932), *The Oppermanns* (1933), *The Sons* (1935), and *The Day Will Come* (1942). He worked with Bertolt Brecht on several dramas.

Feudalism, the social system that prevailed in most of Western Europe during the 10th through the 13th centuries, consisting of a body of social institutions based on the contract of vassalage and the distribution of fiefs.

Geographical distribution. Feudalism dominated during this period in France, Germany, Burgundy-Arles, Italy, England, the Christian kingdoms of Spain, and some former Roman territories of the Near East. Occasionally the term is applied to other areas of the world during other periods, but these feudal-type societies are not part of the same political and social development.

Characteristics. Feudalism was characterized by decentralization of government, with many small kingdoms existing in each present-day nation. It was based upon the loyalties and obligations between individuals of different social classes, particularly between the lord and his vassals. The rights to real property were divided; the owner of the property retained certain rights to the land, while the vassal had others. Political powers normally assigned to the state were likewise apportioned, including defense, administration of justice, and taxation. The church participated in feudal relationships, churchmen being vassals of secular lords and in turn having secular vassals.

Development. Feudalism arose in the 7th century Frankish kingdom of the Merovingians in France. By the Carolingian period in the 8th century, it was well established there and spread to the rest of Western Europe, coming to England with the Norman Conquest (1066). During a period of political and social instability, it provided a means of mutual protection, of reclaiming war-ravaged land for agriculture, and of institutionalizing legal and moral obligations. △902, 1098.

Feuerbach, Anselm von (1829–80), German painter of the Romantic school who lived in Italy after 1855. His early works showed the influence of the Parisian Thomas Couture, but his principal works were executed in Italy where he came under the influence of the great Italian Renaissance masters. Renowned as a portrait painter, his best works are formal, static portraits and a few landscapes.

Fever, elevation of the body temperature above normal, caused by infection, numerous other disorders. Fever can be reduced medically or mechanically, but the cause should be determined first.

Fever Blister. *See* Cold Sore.

Feverfew, bushy Eurasian perennial plant widely naturalized in E North America. It has fine-lobed aromatic leaves and small, white flower heads borne in open clusters. Height: to 3ft (91cm). Family Compositae; species *Chrysanthemum parthenium.*

Fez. *See* Fès.

FHA. *See* Federal Housing Administration.

Fianna Fáil, "Warriors of Eyre," a political party formed in Ireland in 1926 to oppose the 1921 treaty that created the Irish Free State. The party controlled Irish politics almost continuously from the 1930s to 1973, and has taken a stance of absolute Irish independence, revitalization of the Gaelic language, and Irish economic improvement.

Fiat Money, money that has a value only because it is issued by a government and has the confidence of the population; ie, it cannot be redeemed for any commodity that is intrinsically valuable. The most common example is paper currency.

Fiber, Natural, naturally occurring fibrous material that can be made into yarn, textiles, carpets, rope, felt, etc. Natural fibers are made up of long narrow cells. Animal products are based on protein molecules; they include wool, silk, mohair, angora, and horsehair. Vegetable fibers are mainly cellulose; they include cotton, linen, flax, jute, sisal, and kapok. Asbestos is a natural inorganic fiber. A class of fibers, including rayon and acetate, is obtained from natural products modified chemically. △1620.

Fiber Optics, branch of optics employing the phenomenon that light entering a glass fiber is conducted by reflection from one end of the fiber to the other without loss of energy. Images may be magnified, distorted, or scrambled, depending on the configuration of the fiber bundles. Fiber optics is used in medicine to observe organs internally (endoscopy), and in photography, spectroscopy, and television for image intensification.

Fiber, Synthetic, fiber made from a synthetic resin by forcing it through a fine nozzle (spinneret). The resin is melted and extruded through the spinneret, or first dissolved in a solvent which is removed, either by hot air or by a liquid-coagulating bath. The result is a monofilament which can be woven into textiles, made into rope, etc. For many textiles, particularly in clothing, staple yarn is used, consisting of short fibers twisted together. Synthetic fibers are polymeric materials having long-chain molecules. Many types, with various properties, exist, including nylon and other polyamides, polyesters, and acrylics. △1560, 1618.

Fiberglass. △1620.

Fibonacci Ratios. △1444.

Fibrillation, small involuntary contraction of muscle, most often associated with heart disorders. Symptoms of the more common atrial fibrillation include fainting and nausea; ventricular fibrillation can be fatal.

Fibrils, in Anatomy. △684.

Fibrin, fibrous protein that polymerizes during the clotting process to form the basic meshwork of the blood clot. *See also* Blood Clotting. △740.

Fermentation of beer

Enrico Fermi

Ferret

Feverfew

Fibrinogen, precursor protein of fibrin, synthesized by the liver and released into the blood stream. It is converted to fibrin by thrombin during the clotting process. *See also* Blood Clotting. △740.

Fibroblasts. △740.

Fibro (Fibrous) Cartilage. △682.

Fibroma, tumor, usually benign although tending to ulcerate, composed mainly of fibrous or connective tissue. It can occur in the mouth, uterus, or gastrointestinal tract.

Fibrositis. △698.

Fibula, smaller of the two lower leg bones. It extends from the knee region to the ankle, ending in the projection that may be felt on the outer side of the ankle. *See also* Tibia. △682.

Fichte, Johann Gottlieb (1762–1814), German philosopher. He turned Kantian influence in the direction of subjective idealism in *System of Morality* (1800) and embraced romantic nationalism in his *Addresses to the German Nation* (1807–08). His philosophic system is pivoted on the so-called "ego," which becomes aware of its own freedom and its unity with the absolute.

Ficino, Marsilio (1433–99), Italian philosopher. A Greek scholar and head of the Florentine Academy, he promoted the study of Plato and philosophy generally. Although a humanist, he had inclinations toward mysticism. His *De Religione Christiana,* a synthesis of Greek mysticism and Christianity, was the standard Latin text on the subject for 100 years. *See also* Humanism. △1130.

Fiddler Crab, amphibious crab found worldwide that burrows in sandy beaches and drier parts of salt marshes. It is named for the male's huge claw that is used in courtship signaling and mating season battles. Width: under 1in (25mm). Family Ocypodidae; genus *Uca. See also* Crab. △622.

Fief, in feudalism, a unit of property granted by a lord to his vassal as a reward for past services or in exchange for future service, loyalty and mutual protection. The lord maintained the ultimate rights to the land, while the vassal had its use and most of the profits from it.

Field, Cyrus West (1819–92), US financier and promotor of the first trans-Atlantic telegraph cable, b. Stockbridge, Mass. Field conceived the idea after his retirement from business, and after two unsuccessful attempts the cable was laid by the steamship *The Great Eastern* in July 1866. Field also developed the Wabash Railroad with Jay Gould.

Field, Marshall (1834–1906), US businessman and philanthropist, b. Conway, Mass. At age 16 he became an errand boy in a dry goods store in Pittsfield, Mass. He quickly worked his way up to salesman. In 1856 he went to work for the Chicago store of Cooley, Wadsworth and Company, becoming a junior partner in 1862. In 1867 he and Levi Leiter bought Potter Palmer's department store. Field bought out Leiter in 1881 and renamed the firm Marshall Field and Company. He emphasized customer service: easy credit and return, single-pricing. He was a founder (1878) of the Art Institute of Chicago and the Columbian Museum (1893, later the Field Museum of Natural History), and a major contributor to the University of Chicago.

Field, Stephen Johnson (1816–99), US jurist and public official, b. Haddam, Conn. A California state representative (1849), state supreme court justice (1859–63), and associate justice of the US Supreme Court (1863–97), he championed due process of law and opposed judicial interference in governmental affairs.

Field Artillery, light and medium artillery pieces, either drawn by trucks or self-propelled and capable of deploying rapidly into field positions. *See also* Artillery; Howitzer. △1732–34.

Field Data Map. △274.

Field Emission. *See* Electron Emission.

Field Hockey, a sport that uses many of the elements found in ice hockey, soccer, and basketball. It is played by 2 teams of 11 persons each, 5 forwards, 3 halfbacks, 2 fullbacks, and a goal-keeper, on a field 100 yards long (91.5m) and 55–60 yards wide (50–55m). At each end of the field is a goal 7ft (2.1m) high and 12 feet wide (3.7m). In front of the goal is a 16-yard (14.6m) striking zone (15-yard, 13.7m for women). A goal, which may be scored from the striking zone, counts as one point. Each match consists of two 35-minute halves (30 for women). Players carry a stick approximately 36 inches in length (91.4cm) with a canelike curve to the striking edge. The plastic ball (about the size of a baseball) is advanced by throwing, catching, or striking. Penalties vary according to team and individual, technical and personal, whether they are made by the attacking team or defending team, and whether they are made inside or outside the striking circle. Field hockey was developed in England in mid-19th century.

Fielding, Henry (1707–54), English novelist. He wrote comedies, such as *Historical Register for the Year 1736,* and later took up political journalism. His novels include *Joseph Andrews* (1742) and *Tom Jones* (1749). △1854.

Field Mouse, any of the many small, mostly herbivorous, mostly nocturnal rodents that forage in the wild all over the world. They live on the ground in grassy nests and feed on seeds and grass. Genus *Microtus.*

Field of the Cloth of Gold (1520), conference between Henry VIII of England and Francis I of France held near Calais, France. Richly dressed, handsomely attended, and with lavish surroundings, the two kings failed to make the hoped-for alliance against the Holy Roman Emperor Charles V. △1128.

Fields, W.C. (1880–1946), US vaudeville and film comedian, b. William Claude Dukenfield in Philadelphia. He was famed for his portrayal of hard-drinking, misanthropic braggarts in such films as *Tillie's Punctured Romance* (1928), *My Little Chickadee* (1940), and *Never Give a Sucker an Even Break* (1941). He was also acclaimed for his serious portrayal of Mr. Micawber in *David Copperfield* (1935).

Field Spaniel, hunting dog (sporting group) introduced to US in 1880s; has good scenting powers and can retrieve. A beautiful dog, its well-developed head has a long, lean muzzle; long, wide ears hang in folds. The medium-length body has a straight or slightly arched back; legs are long; the tail is carried low. Colored black, liver, golden liver, mahogany, or roan, the flat coat is silky and abundantly feathered on chest, belly, and legs. Average size: 18in (45.5cm) high at shoulder; 35–50lb (16–22.5kg). *See also* Sporting Dog.

Field Trials, a competition for hunting dogs. Trials are divided into five categories: beagle trials, hound trials, pointing dog trials, retriever trials, and spaniel trials. In each of these categories, the animal, on land and/or in water, must perform one or more maneuvers in the sighting, retrieving, and returning of the game. Field trials originated in England in the 17th century, and the first public trials in the United States were conducted in 1874 near Memphis, Tenn. Over 7,000 field trials are held annually in the United States.

Fieschi, noble Genoese family of the Middle Ages. Their Guelf (pro-papal and anti-imperial) politics and alliances with Angevin kings of Sicily dated from mid-13th century, when Sinibaldo Fieschi became Pope Innocent IV, and were to shape the family destiny until Andrea Doria decisively put Genoa into imperial hands in 1528 and the line ended. Ottobono Fieschi also became pope, as Adrian V (1276), and Caterina Fieschi (1447–1510) was later canonized as St Catherine of Genoa.

Fiesole, town in central Italy, NE of Florence. A major Etruscan city, it was conquered by Romans 283 BC; acquired by Florence 1125; site of Etruscan and Roman ruins, cathedral (1028); health resort. Industries: straw plaiting, stone quarrying. Pop. 13,401.

Fife, county in E Scotland, between firths of Tay and Forth; capital is Cupar. Former Pictish kingdom, it officially became a region 1975; ecclesiastical capital of Scotland until the Reformation; one of Scotland's most prosperous counties with fertile soil and rich coal fields; site of St Andrews, Scotland's oldest university. Products: sugar beets, livestock, wheat, oats, barley, turnips. Industries: quarrying, coal mining, fisheries, shipbuilding, engineering works, weaving, brewing. Area: 505sq mi (1,308sq km). Pop. 326,989.

Fife, shrill-toned musical instrument similar to flute, but with a smaller barrel and six to eight finger holes, sometimes with keys like the piccolo's. It has been used with drums by infantry since the Crusades. *See also* Flute.

Fifth Column, saboteurs, spies, and other non-uniformed para-military elements operating behind the battle area, conducting guerrilla warfare or othe operations designed to confuse or disorient the op posing force. *See also* Guerrilla Warfare.

Fifty-Four, Forty or Fight, expression used by Americans in their struggle with England over owner ship of the Oregon territory. Settlers extended lanc rights to latitude 54° 40'N. It was a Democratic cam paign slogan in 1844.

Fig, mainly evergreen trees found in warm regions especially Polynesia, Indo-Malaysia, and Asia Minor Among the hundreds of species is the common or chard fig, *Ficus carica,* native to the Mediterranean Its tiny flowers have no petals and are found on the inside of fleshy receptacles that become the thick outer covering holding the seeds, the true fruit of the fig tree. Height: to 30ft (9.1m). Other fig species in clude banyan *(F. benghalensis),* sycamore *(F. sycomo rus),* and rubber tree *(F. elastica).* Family Moraceae △340, 450.

Fighting Fish, betta, or Siamese fighting fish, fresh water tropical fish of Indochina and Malay Peninsula Popular with home aquarists, this aggressive fish i short-finned and drab in its natural form. Selective breeding has produced brilliantly colored specimen with long, flowing fins. Males will fight until exhaustec or injured. Length: 2–3in (5.1–7.6cm). Family Ana bantidae; species *Betta splendens.*

Figure-Drawing Test, in psychology, a projective technique used to assess personality. The subject is asked to draw a person and then a person of the opposite sex. The technique has been useful in the diagnosis of mental disorders and reveals informatio about the subject's self-concept, spontaneity, sexua identity, and other personality dimensions. *See also* Projective Techniques.

Figure Painting. △1228.

Figure Skating, sport, created by Jackson Haines, US ballet master, in Austria in 1864 after the introduc tion of steel blades to skates in 1850 by E. W. Bush nell of Philadelphia. Although the first figure skating organization was founded in Canada in 1878, it wa not until Sonja Henie's performance in the 1936 win ter Olympic Games that the sport reached interna tional prominence.

Figures of Speech, figurative language; that is, lin guistic constructions in which words or thoughts are employed in unusual combinations to heighten effec or establish unusual connections or oppositions. The are sometimes divided into two types: the trope meaning "turn," in which the literal meaning of the words changes; and those figures in which not th words, but the thought expressed undergoes an in ventive twist. For example, puns and metaphors ar tropes, while apostrophes and antitheses are not. *See also* Metaphor; Pun.

Figwort, perennial Northern Hemisphere plants wit a strong smell and loose, terminal clusters of yellow greenish, or purple flowers. The figwort family (Scro phulariaceae) consists mostly of herbs and sma shrubs. Some members are saprophytes or parasites some lacking chlorophyll.

Fiji, independent nation in SW Pacific Ocean. It is a archipelago, consisting of the islands of Vitu Levu Vanua Levu and about 800 much smaller islets. Th main islands are of volcanic origin, Mt Tomaniivi rising to 4,341ft (1,323m) on Viti Levu, whereas the smalle islands are low-lying coral reefs. The climate is gene ally hot and wet. Main products are copra, sugar, rice bananas, hardwood, gold, and manganese. Industr apart from handcrafts is limited to sugar and copr processing. Indigenous Fijians are of Melanesia stock, with Polynesians, mainly Tongans, forming minority group. Both groups are outnumbered b Asian Indians, descendants of laborers taken there t work the sugar plantations. Government is base upon the British system, with representation propo tional to ethnic groups. Discovered in 1643 by Tas man; visited by Captain Cook in 1774; ceded to Bri ain in 1874 after tribal wars and exploitation b Europeans. Fiji retained some self-government, whic was expanded after WW II. In 1970 it became a independent nation with dominion status within th British Commonwealth.

PROFILE

Official name: Fiji.
Area: 7,053sq mi (18,272sq km).
Population: (1973 est.) 551,000.
Density: 78 per sq mi (30 per sq km).
Chief city: Suva (capital), 54,157.
Government: Prime Minister, Ratu Sir Kamises Mara.

eligions (major): Methodist and Hindu.
ross national product: $195,000,000.
rading partners (major): Great Britain, Australia, United States.

ilament, in electricity. △1486.

ilarete (Antonio Averlino) (*c.*1400–*c.*1465), Italn sculptor and architect. Best known as the sculptor the bronze doors of St. Peter's, Rome (completed 445), he also designed the Ospedale Maggiore in ilan and wrote *Il trattato d'architettura.*

ilariasis, group of disorders caused by infection ith a nematode worm, usually in the tropics. Lymph volvement is typical, with chills, headache, nausea, nd muscle pain preceding lymphatic inflammation. reatment with drugs reduces symptoms. *See also* ephantiasis. △732.

ilbert, trees and shrubs native to the Northern Hemphere. They have yellow male catkins and small redentered female flowers that bear edible brown nuts ometimes called hazelnuts. Height: 3–35ft (0.9– m). There are about 15 species. Family Betulaceae; enus *Corylus.*

ilibuster, unlimited speaking by members of the US enate to prevent a bill from coming to a vote. Conervative Southern senators have filibustered actively attempts to block civil rights legislation. Cloture losure) of debate can stop a filibuster but a twoirds vote of the Senate is needed and thus cloture used infrequently.

ilibusters, individuals who intervened in Latin merica in violation of US neutrality laws and set up, r attempted to set up, private protectorates. Filibustring occurred during the Wars of Independence, but as concentrated in the decade of the 1850s when he ports of Baltimore and New Orleans, in particular, erved as privateering bases.

illing, Dental, the sealer material used to fill a denl cavity. After the decayed parts of a tooth with aries have been thoroughly removed with a dental ill, the hole left is filled with various kinds of quicketting, long-wearing materials. △756.

illmore, Millard (1800–74), 13th president of the nited States, b. Locke, N.Y. He married twice: Abiail Powers in 1826 and Caroline Mcintosh in 1858. lawyer in New York state, he was an early leader in he Anti-Masonic party. After serving in the state legisture, he was elected to the US House of Representaves (1832). In 1835, he changed his affiliation to the ew Whig party and remained in the House until 843, rising to become Ways and Means Committee hairman. In 1848, he became comptroller of New ork and later that year, he was a successful viceresidential candidate, running with Zachary Taylor. s vice-president he presided over the Senate during he bitter slavery debates of 1850. When Taylor died n July 9, 1850, Fillmore became president. As presient he attempted to avoid a national crisis by mediatng between the proslavery, antislavery forces. He enouraged and signed the Compromise of 1850, which ncluded the Fugitive Slave Law. His enforcement of hat law embittered the Whig abolitionists and helped ring into being the new Republican party. He—and he Whig party itself—were victims of the great slavry dispute; he was not nominated in 1852.
Career: New York State Assembly, 1829–31; US louse of Representatives, 1833–43; comptroller, tate of New York, 1848–49; vice-president, 1849–0; president, 1850–53.

ilmer, (Sir) Robert (died 1653), English political hilosopher. He advocated the "divine right of kings" his *Patriarcha* (publ. 1680), which was attacked by ohn Locke for claiming that sovereignty descended o kings as an inviolable inheritance from God. *See lso* Divine Right of Kings.

iltration, process of removing solids from liquids by assage through a suitable medium such as filter aper, glass wool, or sand. △1562.

imbria. △700.

inancial Intermediaries, institutions that bridge he gap between savers and borrowers. They receive unds from the saver and in turn pay interest on these unds, then loan funds to the borrower and receive a ayment in return. Examples include commercial anks, savings banks, savings and loan associations, inance companies, insurance companies.

inback Whale, or common rorqual, one of the fastst and largest whales, it may swim 30mph (48kmph) when pursued. Length: to 79ft (24m); weight: over 50 tons. Species *Balaenoptera physalus. See also* Rorqual.

Finch, any of a family (Fringillidae) of small or medium-sized birds, including sparrows, cardinals, canaries, buntings, and grosbeaks, found over most of the world, except Australia, New Zealand, and the Pacific islands. Some are drab, a few brightly colored, and most have a cone-shaped bill and feed on seeds, with some eating berries, other fruit, and insects. Most finches lay 2 to 6 eggs in open cup-shaped nests.

Findlay, city in NW Ohio, on Blanchard River; seat of Hancock co; site of Findlay College (1884). Industries: tires, plastics, sugar refining. Inc. as city 1887. Pop. (1970) 35,800.

Finger Lakes, series of 11 long, narrow, glacial lakes in central New York, including Canandaigua, Cayuga, Keuka, Owasco, Seneca, and Skaneateles. Cayuga and Seneca are longest, approx. 35mi (56km). New York State's wine industry is here. City of Hammondsport at end of Keuka Lake is its commercial center; site of Wells College and Cornell University on Cayuga Lake; Keuka College on Keuka Lake. Skaneateles Lake supplies Syracuse with part of its water supply. Many resorts and tourist attractions are in the Finger Lakes region.

Fingerprint. △1478.

Finisterre, cape in NW Spain, on coast of Galicia in Atlantic Ocean; has an irregular coast with sandy beaches, inlets, and rocky headlands.

Fink, Mike (1770?–1823?), US frontiersman, b. Ft. Pitt (Pittsburgh). His own tall tales about himself contributed much to his becoming a semi-legendary folk hero. He fought against the Ohio Indians, then became a keelboatman on the Ohio and Mississippi rivers. In 1822 he accompanied the Ashley trapping expedition up the Missouri River and in the following year was killed in a shooting incident along the Yellowstone River.

Finland, Republic of, an independent country of N Europe. Historically, Finland has been dominated by Russia or Sweden. The Finns are a hardy, prosperous people who have excelled in commerce and the arts.
Land and economy. Geologically, Finland lies on the Fenno-Scandian shield, one of the most ancient portions of the earth's crust. It was covered with glaciers in the Ice Age; hence, its relative flatness, its low, rounded hills, and multitude of lakes, rivers, and bogs. The Finnish population lives primarily in the fertile coastal areas. The central plateau contains a wealth of forestlands. Farther N lies Lapland and the treeless tundra of the Arctic Circle. Finland's economy has traditionally centered on its vast timber resources. Since WWII, however, new industries, such as shipbuilding and metalworking, have developed. Helsinki, the capital, is the manufacturing center. Most business is in private hands, and the majority of Finland's farms are small. About 60% of the country's total export income is derived from forest products.
People. The origins of the Finns are uncertain. The Finnish language is related to Hungarian and Estonian and more remotely to Turkish. It is not an Indo-European tongue. The Finno-Ugrian peoples arrived in Europe prior to the Slavs. More than 90% of Finland's population speaks Finnish, while about 7% speaks Swedish. The state church of Finland is the Evangelical Lutheran Church, to which 90% of all Finns belong. The rapid industrialization of the postwar period caused an exodus from rural to urban areas.
Government. The constitution provides a parliamentary form of government. The chief executive is the president, elected to a six-year term; he appoints the prime minister and his cabinet, directs foreign policy, and serves as commander-in-chief of the armed forces. The Finnish parliament is a single chamber comprising 200 members elected to 4-year terms. The prime minister and his cabinet deal with daily functions of government. Finland has several political parties. Each of Finland's 12 provinces has its own elected officials.
History. The Finno-Ugrian peoples, who were nomadic hunters, reached the Baltic area more than 2,000 years ago. In the Middle Ages, Sweden conquered and Christianized the Finns. For more than 400 years, until 1809, Finland was an integral part of Sweden. Russia controlled Finland in the 19th century. A growing nationalism led to an independence movement; the country became a republic in 1919. After the outbreak of WWII, the Soviet Union invaded Finland (1939) and took control of strategic territories. The Finns later allied themselves with Germany, but signed an armistice with the Soviet Union and Great Britain in 1944. After the war Finland estab-

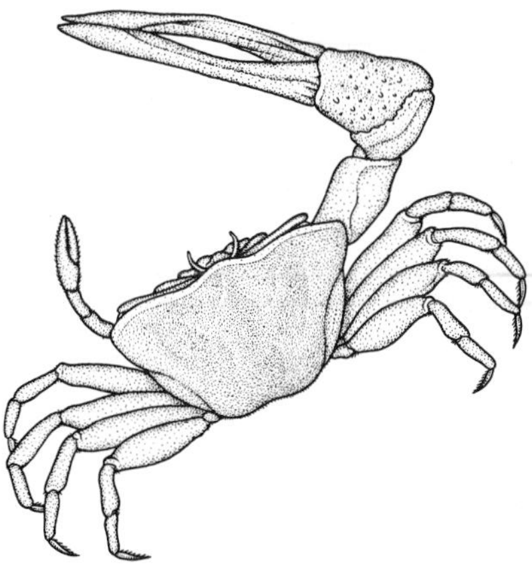
Fiddler crab

Cyrus W. Field

Millard Fillmore

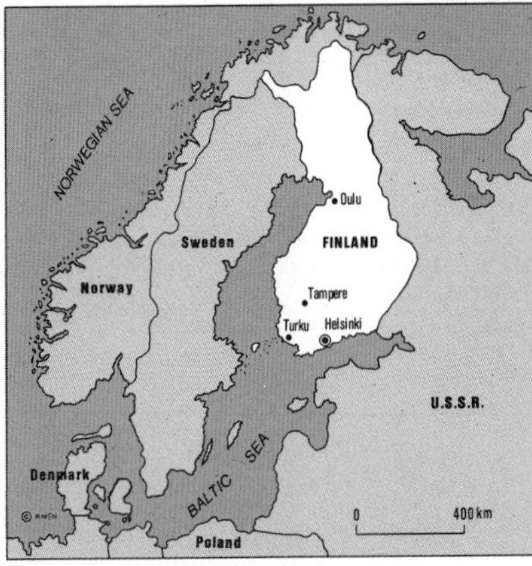
NORWEGIAN SEA
Oulu
Sweden
FINLAND
Norway
Tampere
Turku
Helsinki
U.S.S.R.
Denmark
BALTIC SEA
Poland
0
400km
Finland

lished sound economic relations with the Soviet Union and the nations of the West.

PROFILE

Official name: Finland, Republic of
Area: 130,120sq mi (337,009sq km)
Population: 4,700,000
Density: 36per sq mi (14per sq km)
Chief cities: Helsinki (capital); Tampere; Turku
Government: Democratic
Religion: Evangelical Lutheran Church (official)
Language: Finnish, Swedish (both official)
Monetary unit: Markka
Gross national product: $21,700,000,000
Per capita income: $3,700
Industries (major products): paper, machinery, metalworking, furniture, electrical products
Agriculture (major products): forest products, dairy products, wheat, sugar beets
Minerals (major): copper, zinc
Trading partners (major): Sweden, West Germany, Great Britain

Finland, Gulf of, E arm of Baltic Sea, between Finland and USSR; chief ports are Leningrad and Tallinn, USSR and Helsinki, Finland. Width: 10–75mi (16–121km). Length: 285mi (459km).

Finlay, Carlos Juan (1833–1915), Cuban physician who suggested in 1881 that yellow fever was spread by a mosquito. He presented his theory at an international conference in Washington, D.C., but it was not until 1900 that a US medical delegation headed by Walter Reed went to Cuba to help confirm the hypothesis. By destroying mosquitoes and isolating patients, the disease was virtually eradicated in Finlay's country and elsewhere.

Finlay River, river in N British Columbia, Canada; important tributary of the Peace River; rises in the Stikine Mts; flows 210mi (338km) SE to the Parsnip River at Finlay Forks. Length: 240mi (386km).

Finley, Charles O(scar) (1918–), US baseball executive, b. Ensley, Ala. As owner of the Oakland Athletics, he became one of the game's most controversial figures. His contract dispute with Catfish Hunter in 1974 was extensively covered in the press. He eventually lost his star pitcher to the New York Yankees.

Finn MacCool, in ancient Irish literature, the leader of the Fianna Eireann, a band of poets and hunters. He was the son of Cool (Cumhail).

Finno-Ugric Languages, group of languages spoken by about 20,000,000 people in parts of NE Europe and Siberia. The Finnic branch includes Finnish, Estonian, Lappish, and, in the Soviet Union, Mordvinian, Udmurt, Mari, and Komi. The Ugric branch consists of Hungarian plus two minor languages of Siberia: Khanty (Ostyak) and Mansi (Vogul). Together with the remote Samoyed languages the Finno-Ugric languages form the Uralic family.

Fins. △512.

Finsteraarhorn, mountain peak in S central Switzerland, on boundary of Valais and Bern cantons; first climbed 1812. Highest of Bernese Alps, 14,019ft (4,276m).

Fiord, or **fjord,** narrow, steep-walled bay with mountainous, glaciated coasts, or a very narrow drowned estuary. Fiords are almost always perpendicular to the coastline that they are part of and they appear to have been formed from narrow fingers of glacier. *See also* Glaciology. △262.

Fir, evergreen trees native to cooler, temperate regions of the world. They are pyramid-shaped and have flat needles and erect cones. Included are the silver and balsam firs. Height: 50–300ft (15–91m). Family Pinacea; genus *Abies.* △440–42.

Fire Ant, reddish black ant, 0.12 to 0.24in (3–6mm) long, native to South America and introduced into southern parts of the United States. It is a mound builder that feeds on young plants and seeds. It has a very painful sting. Family Formicidae, species *Solenopsis saevissima richteri. See also* Ant; Hymenoptera.

Firearms. △1728, 1730, 1732.

Fireball. *See* Bolide.

Fireball, Primordial. *See* Primordial Fireball.

Fire Blight, a highly infectious and destructive disease of apples, pears, and related fruit trees that causes a blackened, scorched appearance of leaves and twigs, as if seared by fire. Other symptoms of the disease, caused by the bacterium *Erwinia amylovora,* include cankers on stems and discolored flowers and fruit. Control of the disease is difficult. Some tree varieties are resistant to the disease.

Fire Bug. *See* Harlequin Bug.

Fireclay, clay that will withstand high temperatures without deforming. Fireclay is used for firebrick, crucibles, and many refractory shapes. Fireclay approaches kaolin in composition, better grades containing at least 35% alumina when fired.

Fire Extinguisher. △1510, 1816.

Firefly, light-emitting beetle found in moist places in temperate and tropical regions. Adults are soft-bodied and slender. Light-emitting organs on the abdomen underside give off flashes of light in a species-characteristic rhythm. The flashing is believed to be a sexual attractant. The luminous larvae and wingless females of some species are called glowworms. Length: to 0.5in (13mm). There are 2,000 species. Family Lampyridae.

Fire Island, long, narrow stretch of land off S central Long Island; separates Great South Bay from the Atlantic Ocean. Fire Island National Seashore occupies part of the island; includes beaches, wooded areas, and marshland. Popular summer resort area. Length: 32mi (52km).

Firenze. *See* Florence.

Fire Salamander. △518.

Fireside Chats, series of radio talks by Pres. Franklin D. Roosevelt. Beginning early in 1933, the president made these informal broadcasts at intervals to reassure the public by explaining the issues and his policies. This was the first effective use of radio made by a president. △1324.

Firestone, Harvey S(amuel) (1868–1938), US manufacturer, b. Columbiana co, Ohio. After selling buggies and rubber carriage tires, he founded the Firestone Co. in Akron in 1900. He was the first to manufacture the pneumatic tires used on the Ford Model T automobile and also produced nonskid tire treads, motor truck treads, and farm tractor tires. In 1926 he started vast rubber plantations in Liberia. His Firestone Tire and Rubber Company became one of the largest rubber companies in the United States.

Firethorn. *See* Pyracantha.

Fireworks. △1810.

Firing, in ceramics. △1608.

Firm, Theory of the, in economics, that part of price theory devoted to analysis of the individual business firm. The analysis includes the computation of total cost, average cost, and marginal cost, as well as total and marginal revenue. Theory of the firm concentrates on an analysis of the method of maximizing the firm's profit. Profit maximization differs depending upon whether the business firm is a monopoly, an oligopoly, an imperfectly competitive firm, or a purely competitive firm. *See also* Price Theory.

Firn, mountain snow that has been converted to granular ice in a mountain glacier and, with an accumulation of broken rock materials at its base, digs out round basins called cirques. △262.

First Aid. △758.

First Amendment, addition to the United States Constitution mandating the freedoms of speech, the press, religion, and peaceful assembly. It is included within the Bill of Rights, and has been increasingly enforced by the US Supreme Court. Chief Justice Earl Warren increased the assurance of the First Amendment in the *New York Times v. Sullivan* (1964), which concerned the protection of the press from libel, and in *NAACP v. Alabama* (1958), which protected any peaceful demonstration from harassment by a state agency.

First World War. *See* World War I.

Firth, William Powell. △1252.

Firtin, Thomas. △1242.

Fiscal Policy, government spending and tax policies, used to achieve a particular economic goal. Fiscal policy may be used to dampen inflationary pressures or to stimulate expansion within the economy. When the economy is suffering from inflation, th traditional fiscal policy is to decrease governmer spending and increase taxes, thus easing deman pressures by diminishing the money in consumer pocketbooks. The traditional fiscal policy during a re cession is to increase government spending and cu taxes, thus stimulating the economy by increasing de mand for goods and services.

Fischer, Robert James "Bobby" (1943–), contro versial US chess player, b. Chicago. He was the U (1958–60; 1962–63) and world champion (1972 75). He was named an international grand master i 1958. In 1975 he refused to defend his world's title

Fish, Hamilton (1808–93), US political leader, b New York City. A lawyer, he served in Congres (1843–45) as a Whig. He later served as lieutenar governor (1847–48) and as governor (1849–50) c New York. He was a US Senator (1851–57). As secre tary of state under Pres. Ulysses S. Grant (1869–77 Fish successfully handled the *Alabama* claims di pute. *See also* Alabama Claims.

Fish, aquatic vertebrate characterized by fins; resp ration through gills; streamlined fusiform body; scale bony plate, or scaleless body covering; and two-cham bered heart. Fish are the most ancient form of verte brate life, dating from Silurian period (450,000,00 years ago). Fish reproduce bisexually; fertilization i external or internal, and eggs develop in the water c inside the female, according to species. There ar 25,000 species, representing 40% of all living verte brates, divided into 34 orders and 48 families. Th classification of fish varies. Generally they are divide into two superclasses: Agnatha, jawless fish includin hagfish and lamprey, and Pisces. Pisces is divided int two main classes: Chondrichthyes (cartilaginous fish including subclasses Elasmobranchii (shark and ray and Holocephali (chimeras); Osteichthyes (bony fish including the lungfish and lobefin and the higher bon fish. Length: 0.5in–over 40ft (1.3cm–12m). △390 92, 510–16.

Fish Culture, or aquaculture, breeding and raisin fish under controlled conditions. The goal is high-leve production for food or for stocking lakes, ponds, an streams for sportsmen. The most widely bred fish i the world are carp, rainbow trout, and Mozambiqu cichlid. Fish culture for food supply is practiced on large scale only in Asia. △388.

Fisher, Dorothy Canfield (1879–1958), US autho b. Lawrence, Kan. A short story writer and novelis who lived mainly in rural Vermont, she wrote abou farmers and people of the academic world. Her novel include *The Bent Twig* (1915), *Rough Hewn* (1921 *The Deepening Stream* (1930), and *Seasoned Timbe* (1939).

Fisher, Geoffrey Francis (1887–1972), archbisho of Canterbury (1945–61). He was active in educatio for many years, at Marlborough College and at Repto School, where he was headmaster. His ecclesiastica career began with the bishopric of Chester, and h was bishop of London for six years. As archbishop c Canterbury he was active in the cause of church unity he visited the pope at Rome and served as presiden of the World Council of Churches.

Fisher, Saint John (*c.* 1459–1535), English Roma Catholic prelate. Fisher held several posts at Cam bridge, and preached moral austerity before opposin Henry VIII's proposed divorce (1529). Created card nal (1535), he was tried and executed for denying tha Henry was supreme head of the church under the Ac of Supremacy. He was canonized in 1935.

Fisher, large, long-tailed carnivorous marten of North America that has commercially valuable fur. The have brown to black fur with white-tipped outer hairs Females are smaller than males and their fur is more valuable. Good climbers, they are the only know predators of porcupines. Length: 3.5ft (1m); weight to 18lb (8kg). Family Mustelidae; species *Martes per nanti. See also* Marten; Sable.

Fishery, or **Commercial Fishing,** harvesting larg amounts of fish from the seas, large inland lakes, an rivers for food and other commercial uses. Fishin boats and fleets employ several methods for catchin fish, including pole and line, harpoon, purse seine and trawling. About 70% of the commercial fish catc is taken in the Northern Hemisphere; the greates catches are taken in the area between the Philippine and Japan. Other fishing areas include the North At lantic, the North Pacific, and the North Sea. The mos significant Southern Hemisphere areas are the Pacifi coast of Peru and the South African coast. Herrings sardines, and anchovies make up the largest percent age of the total catch. Others caught in large comme cial quantities are cod, haddock, hake, redfish, sea bream, mackerel, tuna, salmon, and flatfish. Major fishing nations include the United States, Soviet Union, Japan, Spain, Peru, Iceland, and the Scandinavian countries. △386.

Fishes, The. *See* Pisces.

Fishing, a water sport popular in both fresh and salt water. The two basic types of freshwater fishing include fly casting and bait casting, and the technique is to "play" the fish rather than reel it in by force. To this extent, the equipment used for fly rods and reels is light. The bait used is either live (worms, insects, and minnows) or artificial (flies and lures). Bait casting requires a sturdier rod and reel, and the bait can either be live or artificial. Some of the various techniques include trolling from a moving boat, bottom fishing, or casting and pulling in. Saltwater fishing generally requires heavier rods and reels, and includes trolling and casting from the surf, and trolling and bottom fishing at sea. Popular freshwater game fish include bass, pike, muskellunge, salmon, and trout. Ocean game fish include bonefish, marlin, sailfish, tarpon, and tuna. Numerous tournaments are held for the number and size of fish caught and for accuracy and distance in casting. △930.

Fish Louse, common parasitic crustacean found on the skin or in the gill cavity of freshwater or marine fish. It has a top-to-bottom flattened body, one pair of compound eyes, and a shieldlike carapace. Large claws on antennae and two suckers on the jaws are used for attachment to the host. Subclass Branchiura. *See also* Crustacean.

Fisk, James (1834–72), US financial speculator, b. Bennington, Vt. In 1866, he founded the brokerage house of Fisk and Belden. His unscrupulous stock market activities gained him a fortune. With Jay Gould, he attempted to corner the gold market in 1869, precipitating Black Friday. He escaped prosecution. *See also* Black Friday.

Fission, form of asexual reproduction. The parent cell divides into 2 or more daughter cells. Binary fission produces 2 equal daughter cells (bacteria, blue-green algae, protozoa). Multiple fission produces 4, 8, or 16 daughter cells, each developing into a new organism. △422, 466.

Fission, Nuclear, form of nuclear reaction in which a heavy atomic nucleus, such as uranium, splits into two parts at the same time emitting two or three neutrons and releasing a large quantity of energy—3×10^{-11} joules per fission or 7.5×10^{13} joules per kg (compared to 4×10^{7} joules per kg for coal). Every 100,000 atoms of natural uranium contains six atoms of the isotope U-234 and 720 atoms of U-235; the rest is U-238. U-235 is fissioned by neutrons traveling at all speeds, whereas U-238 absorbs all but the fast neutrons (traveling at over 17×10^{6} m/s), forming the fissile plutonium-239 isotope. As most neutrons released in the fission process are fast, a chain reaction cannot be sustained in natural uranium, as most neutron collisions will be with the plentiful U-238. In a thermal reactor, a moderator is used to slow down the neutrons released in the fission so that enough neutrons are released in the process to sustain a chain reaction. In a fast reactor, no moderator is used, but the natural uranium is enriched with U-235 or Pu-239. In the atom bomb, pure U-235 or Pu-239 is used and the chain reaction is uncontrolled. However, these isotopes can be safely stored in quantities below the critical mass, as so many neutrons escape from the surface that the chain reaction cannot be sustained. *See also* Binding Energy, Fission Reactor. △1482, 1638.

Fission Reactor, device for producing energy from nuclear fission. There are two main types: thermal and fast reactors. Thermal reactors use thin natural-uranium fuel rods embedded or immersed in a moderator so that neutrons escaping from one rod are slowed down before entering another. The heat of the reaction is collected by a coolant, which may be a gas or a liquid. In advanced gas-cooled reactors carbon dioxide is the coolant. In the boiling-water reactor the coolant water is allowed to boil in contact with the fuel elements. In the pressurized-water reactor boiling is prevented by increased pressure. In both cases the water acts as moderator. The heated coolant is used to raise steam in a heat exchanger in order to drive a turbine and generator, as in a conventional power station. In a fast reactor natural uranium enriched with U-235 or Pu-239 is used without a moderator. Owing to the high core temperature (7,500°C), liquid sodium is used as the coolant. In a breeder reactor the core of a fast reactor is surrounded with a blanket of natural uranium, some of the escaping neutrons being captured by U-238 to form more Pu-239 than is needed to enrich the core. *See also* Fission, Nuclear. △1482, 1638.

Fistula, abnormal opening between two internal organs such as lung and heart, or from an organ to the body surface.

Fitch, John (1743–98), US inventor, b. Windsor, Conn. With profits gained as supplier to the Continental Army during the Revolution, he bought Grand Ohio Company lands (1780). In 1787 he built what is believed to be the first US steamboat. He constructed and operated three steamboats on the Delaware River (1787–90), having secured exclusive rights to operate in New Jersey, Pennsylvania, New York, Delaware, and Virginia. After losing his financial backing, he committed suicide.

Fitchburg, city in N Massachusetts; seat of Worcester co; site of Fitchburg State College (1894). Industries: paper, plastics, textiles, clothing. Settled 1740; inc. 1872. Pop. (1970) 43,343.

Fitzgerald, (Lord) Edward (1763–98), Irish nationalist, served for a time in the British army in America during the Revolution and was severely wounded at Eutaw Springs (1781). He was discharged for his sympathies with the French Revolution. He later joined the revolutionary United Irishmen and helped form the uprising of 1798. He was betrayed and died of wounds received during his capture before the unsuccessful rebellion took place.

FitzGerald, Edward (1809–83), English author and translator. His most noted achievement was his free translation from the Persian of the *Rubáiyát of Omar Khayyám* (1859). He also translated Calderon (1853) and Aeschylus (1865). *See also* Rubáiyát of Omar Khayyám.

Fitzgerald, Ella (1918–), US jazz and popular singer, b. Newport News, Va. Her first big hit was "A-Tisket A-Tasket" in 1938. After 1942 she soloed in nightclubs, theaters, and concerts and established an international reputation, also appearing in films. In the 1950s and 60s she toured Europe, Canada, Japan, and Australia.

Fitzgerald, F(rancis) Scott (Key) (1896–1940), US author, b. St. Paul, Minn. He began his first novel, *This Side of Paradise* (1920), while in the army, which he entered in 1917. He drew on his own experiences, as he generally did, and the book, along with *The Beautiful and the Damned* (1921), established him as a chronicler of the "Jazz Age," the frenetic period after World War I. In 1920 Fitzgerald married Zelda Sayre, also a writer. To finance their expensive and hectic life, he wrote popular short stories for magazines.

During most of the 1920s he lived in Europe, mingling with wealthy and sophisticated expatriates. His masterpiece, *The Great Gatsby,* was published in 1925. Frequently in debt, Fitzgerald was also plagued by his wife's growing insanity and his own bouts of alcoholism and loss of popularity in the 1930s, during which time he became a scriptwriter in Hollywood. His last novels were *Tender Is the Night* (1934) and the unfinished *The Last Tycoon* (1941). △1374.

Fitzgerald, George Francis (1851–1901), Irish physicist who worked with electrolysis and electric waves and who is noted for his electromagnetic theory of radiation. As an explanation of the Michelson-Morley experiment, he suggested the theory that objects change shape (the Lorentz-Fitzgerald contraction) due to their movement through the ether. *See also* Michelson-Morley Experiment; Relativity Theory.

Fitzsimmons, Robert "Bob" (1862–1917), English boxer. He won the world heavyweight championship from James J. Corbett (1897) in Carson City, Nev., and lost it to James J. Jeffries (1899) in Coney Island, N. Y. Fitzsimmons was elected to the Boxing Hall of Fame in 1954.

Fitzwilliam, (Sir) William (1526–99), English political figure. Lord deputy of Ireland (1572–75, 1588–94), he suppressed Irish rebellions arising from the "plantation" scheme of settling Scots and English in Ireland. He was governor of Fotheringhay Castle when Mary, Queen of Scots, was executed there (1587).

Fiume. *See* Rijeka.

Five, The, or "The Russian Five," a group of five prominent Russian composers (Rimski-Korsakov, Borodin, Mussorgski, Balakirev, and César Cui) who banded together to promote Russian nationalism in music in the late 19th century.

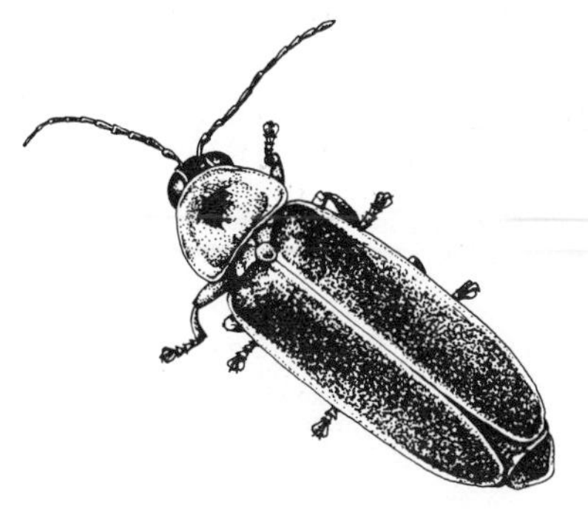

Firefly

Hamilton Fish

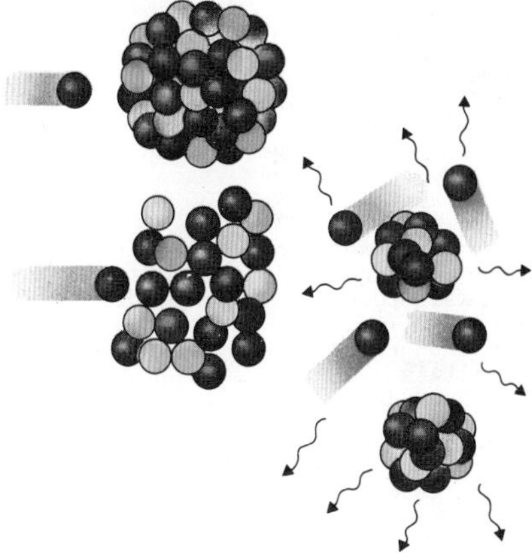

Fission

F. Scott Fitzgerald

Five Civilized Tribes, a term adopted by early writers to include those American Indians regarded as being more advanced, due to agricultural, political, and social successes. They included the Cherokee, Chickasaw, Choctaw, Creek, and Seminole tribes.

Five Dynasties Period (907–60), period of contention and division in China following the collapse of the great Tang era. It takes its name from the five abortive attempts to reestablish imperial unity and control until this was achieved by the Sung Dynasty. During this period nine classics were first printed from wood blocks. △1042.

Five Nations, a reference to the League of the Iroquois prior to 1722. This included the Cayuga, Mohawk, Oneida, Onondaga, and Seneca tribes. In 1722, the Tuscarora were allowed to join, making this the Six Nations, by which the League is best known in history.

Five-Year Plan, series of national economic plans for the Soviet Union. Introduced by Stalin in 1928 to develop the country as quickly as possible, an agriculturally and industrially self-sufficient nation was the ultimate goal. Certain quotas of manufactured goods and agricultural products were to be met, and bonuses were given when quotas were reached ahead of time. △1312.

Fizeau, Armand. △1522.

Fjord. *See* Fiord.

Flag. △2712–18.

Flag, North American flowering plant with sword-shaped leaves and a large asymmetrical flower. Included are sweet flag *(Acorus calamus)*—Family Araceae; cattail flag *(Typha latifolia)*—Family Typhaceae; and blue flag *(Iris versicolor)*—Family Iridaceae.

Flagellate, any of numerous protists (single-celled organisms) placed in the superclass Mastigophora. They all possess, at some point in their life cycles, one to several whiplike structures called flagella for locomotion and sensation. Most have a single nucleus and many are covered with a thin, firm outer covering (pellicle) or coated with a jellylike substance, cellulose, or chitin. Reproduction is by fission (asexual splitting) or sexual (involving the production of gametes). They are divided into two major groups: the phytoflagellates, resembling plants, and the zooflagellates, resembling animals. Phytoflagellates contain chlorophyll and produce their food photosynthetically (such as *Eglena* and all dinoflagellates). Zooflagellates are colorless and take in food independently or live as symbionts or parasites (such as *Trypanosoma*). Flagellates may be solitary or colonial (*Volvox,* for example). △466.

Flagg, James Montgomery (1877–1960), US painter and illustrator, b. Pelham Manor, N.Y. From 1892 he was a regular contributor to popular picture magazines and he enjoyed considerable fame and success during his lifetime. He is particularly remembered for his 45 World War I military posters, including the recruiting poster "I Want You," with Uncle Sam pointing at the viewer.

Flagler, Henry Morrison (1830–1913), US businessman and promoter, b. Hopewell, N.Y. He was a business associate of John D. Rockefeller, and a partner in Rockefeller, Andrews & Flagler, the firm that became the Standard Oil Company (1870). Based on his view of Florida as a resort area of great potential, he bought small railroads there and organized them into the Florida East Coast Railway (1886), greatly extending the rail lines. He also formed steamship lines, dredged Miami Harbor, erected large hotels to encourage tourism, and invested millions, through anonymous gifts, in the construction of schools, churches, and hospitals.

Flagstad, Kirsten (1895–1962), Norwegian soprano. She first performed in 1913 but was relatively unknown outside Scandinavia until her debut at the Metropolitan Opera in New York in 1935. She was one of the great 20th-century Wagnerian sopranos, singing leads in Wagner's operas at the Metropolitan and the Bayreuth Festivals. She was the first director of the Royal Norwegian Opera (1958–60).

Flagstaff, city in N Arizona, 63mi (101km) NE of Prescott; seat of Coconino co. Elevation: 6,907ft (2,107m) above sea level. Noted as a health resort; location of Northern Arizona University (1899). Industry: lumber. Settled 1876; inc. 1928. Pop. (1970) 26,117.

Flagstone, any hard, evenly stratified stone, such as shale or slate, that splits into flat pieces. Used for paving in outdoor paths, terrace floors, etc.

Flaherty, Robert (Joseph) (1884–1951), pioneer US director of documentary films, b. Iron Mountain, Mich. In Canada he made *Nanook of the North* (1922) about Eskimo life, followed by *Moana of the South Seas* (1925), an idyllic treatment of Samoa. His other major films are *Industrial Britain* (1932), *Man of Aran* (1934), and *Louisiana Story* (1948).

Flamboyant Style, final phase of French Gothic architecture (14th–16th century). The name comes from the flamelike forms of the elaborately ornate tracery used in cathedrals, as on the west facade of the Cathedral at Rouen (1370). △1106.

Flamen, in ancient Rome, a priest devoted to the worship of one deity. Flamens were chosen from the patrician class and offered daily sacrifices to the deity. They were identified by the apex (a conical cap).

Flamenco, dance and dance music of Spanish gypsies. It is characterized by stamping of the feet (zapateado), hand clapping (palmada), the skillful use of castanets, colorful costumes, and erotic movements. The dancing is often accompanied by florid, sad songs *(cante flamenco* or *cante hondo)* and guitar. Famous flamenco dancers have included Vincente Escudero and José Greco.

Flame Test, testing for the presence of metallic atoms, whose main spectral emission lines give characteristic colors in a Bunsen flame, performed on a platinum wire dipped in hydrochloric acid. Lithium and calcium produce a red color, sodium yellow, potassium lilac, strontium crimson, barium apple-green, copper blue-green, and lead, arsenic, antimony, and tin blue-gray.

Flamingo, long-necked, long-legged wading bird of tropical and subtropical lagoons and brackish lakes. They are pinkish or reddish and have large wings and webbed feet. They invert their specialized bills to filter small organisms from the water. They nest in huge colonies, laying a single chalky white egg in a cone-shaped mud nest. Height: to 5ft (1.5m). Family Phoenicopteridae.

Flamininus, Titus Quinctius (*c.* 230–174 BC) Roman statesman and military leader, instrumental in establishing the Roman protectorate over an autonomous Greece. His victory at Cynoscephalae (197) in Macedonia against Philip V marked the first meeting of Roman legions and Macedonian phalanxes.

Flanders (Vlaanderen, or Flandre), former county in W Belgium and France, encompassing modern boundaries of East and West Flanders provs., Belgium, and a portion of France's Nord dept. The area flourished in 13th and 14th centuries with Flemish cloth industry; part incorporated into Spanish Netherlands in 1584, after some of it was given to France; Louis XIV annexed portions in 1668; part of the region was ceded to France (1797), but was later awarded to the Netherlands.

Flanders Field, near Waregem, Belgium, a cemetery in which the US Army buried 368 casualties of World War I. The field was made famous in a poem, "In Flanders Fields," by the Canadian John McCrae, a medical officer later killed in the war.

Flannagan, John Bernard (1895–1942), US sculptor, b. Fargo, N.D. Trained as a painter, he turned to sculpture in 1925, working mainly in common fieldstone. He produced such noted works as "Jonah and the Whale" (1937), "Triumph of the Egg" (1937 and 1941), and "Beginning" (1941). He is regarded as one of the foremost "primitive" sculptors of the 20th century.

Flare, Solar, intense localized eruption of high-energy radiation occurring in the sun's chromosphere above an associated sunspot group on the photosphere. Flares are accompanied by ejection of high-energy particles that cause radio and magnetic disturbances on earth. *See also* Sunspot. △96.

Flare Star. △114.

Flash-distillation. △1766.

Flast v. Cohen (1968), US Supreme Court decision that allowed a taxpayer's suit attacking a federal spending bill on the ground that it violated the First Amendment prohibition against establishment of religion. The *Flast* decision was distinguished from *Frothingham v. Mellon* (1923) by the specificity of complaint. *See also* Frothingham v. Mellon (1923).

Flatbill. *See* Paddlefish.

Flat-Coated Retriever, powerful water dog (sporting dog group) developed in England from the Labrador retriever and the Newfoundland. Not particularly popular in the United States, this retriever has a long head, large nose, and long jaw capable of carrying hare or pheasant. Small ears are close to the head. The body has a short, square back, and the short, straight tail is carried up. A black or liver-colored coat is dense and flat. Average size: 23in (58cm) high at shoulder; 60–70lb (27–32kg). *See also* Newfoundland; Retriever; Sporting Dog.

Flatfish, bottom-dwelling, mainly marine fish found in all but coldest seas. Includes some of the world's most valuable food fishes—halibut, flounder, plaice, turbot, and sole. Flatfish have a flat body, both eyes on same side, and a white underside. Length: to 10ft (305cm); weight: to 700lb (315kg). Order Pleuronectiformes; 600 species.

Flathead, river in W Canada and N Montana, rises in SE British Columbia, flows S through Flathead Lake, Montana, to Clark Fork River near Paradise. Length: 245mi (394km).

Flathead Indians, term applied to many North American Indian tribes, from their custom of deforming heads of infants to develop an elongated skull as a socially-desirable shape. The usage applies most specifically to the Chinook. Ironically, the inhabitants of the Flathead Reservation in Montana never followed this practice; early travelers may have seen flat-headed slaves among the people.

Flatworms. *See* Platyhelminthes. △472.

Flaubert, Gustave (1821–80), French novelist. He spent most of his life in Rouen among the provincial bourgeoisie featured in many of his works. A Realist, his novels include *Madame Bovary* (1857), *Salammbô* (1862), *Sentimental Education* (1869), and *The Temptation of St Anthony* (1874).

Flax, slender and erect plant with dainty flowers that last only one day. Species include: blue, perennial *Linum perenne,* with small leaves, branching stems, and blue flowers; crimson *Linum grandiflorium,* a 1-ft (30-cm) annual; yellow *Linum virginianum,* native to America; and *Linum usitatissimum,* cultivated for linen fiber and linseed oil. Family Linaceae. *See also* Linseed Oil. △362.

Flea, wingless, flat jumping insect found worldwide. They feed on the blood of birds and mammals and live a year or more. They may carry bubonic plague, endemic typhus, and tapeworm. Length: 0.1in (2.5mm). Order Siphonaptera. △498.

Fleabane, small annual, biennial, and perennial plants found wild worldwide. Most have lance-shaped leaves and daisylike flowers with yellow disks and white, rose, or purplish rays. Hybrids are cultivated in gardens. Height: 4–40in (10–102cm). Family Compositae; genus *Erigeron.*

Fleahopper, green to shiny-black jumping leaf bug found worldwide. It sucks plant juices and may be a pest on cultivated plants. There are several generations a year. Length: to 0.08in (2mm). Family Miridae.

Fledermaus, Die (1874), 3-act opera by Johann Strauss II, German libretto by C. Haffner and Richard Genée; after the French comedy *Le Reveillon* by Henri Meilhac and Ludovic Halévy. Its world premiere was in Vienna. Baron von Eisenstein (tenor) is wanted by the police. When they go to his house they arrest Alfred (tenor), his wife Rosalinde's (soprano) lover, by mistake. Eisenstein and his friend Falke (baritone) make the most of the baron's freedom by attending a ball given by Prince Orlofsky (mezzo-soprano). Rosalinde and her maid Adele (soprano) are also at the ball, where much champagne and revelry lead to complications for all.

Fleming, (Sir) Alexander (1881–1955), Scottish bacteriologist. He shared the 1945 Nobel Prize in physiology or medicine for his part in the discovery of penicillin and its therapeutic effect. In 1928 Fleming noticed that a mold, identified as *Penicillium notatum,* liberated a substance that inhibited the growth of some bacteria. He named it penicillin. However, the importance of this discovery was not recognized until further work by Howard Florey and Ernst Chain. △746.

Fleming, Peggy Gale (1948–), US figure skater, b. San Jose, Calif. She was the US women's champion (1963–68) and the world's champion (1966–68). She won a gold medal at the Winter Olympics in 1968 and then became a professional ice-show and television performer.

Fleming's Rules, memory devices to relate the directions of the current, field, and mechanical rotation in electric motors and generators. In the *left hand rule* the forefinger represents flux, the second finger the electric motive force, and the thumb motion; when extended at right angles to each other the appropriate directions are indicated. The *right hand rule* applies the same principle to generators.

Flemish, one of the two official languages of Belgium, the other being French. It is spoken in the northern half of the country by about 5½ million people. Flemish is actually the same language as Dutch, but for historical and cultural reasons it is called Flemish in Belgium and Dutch in the Netherlands. △866.

Flemish Gothic Architecture, Belgian architectural style significant in Flanders in the 14th and 15th centuries when the wool trade made the cities of Ghent, Bruges, and Ypres prosperous. Secular architecture, like the Cloth Hall at Ypres, was particularly important. Cathedrals, like that at Antwerp, had very high and ornate towers. △1136.

Flemish Renaissance Architecture, Belgian architectural style of the 16th century centered in Antwerp. It was influenced by the Italian Renaissance through visiting architects and through the translations of Alberti and Serlio. The Town Hall of Antwerp (1561–66), designed by Cornelius Floris, is a characteristic structure, with its dominating gable, large windows, and free ornamentation. Strapwork decoration was common and influenced English Renaissance architecture. △1136.

Fletcher v. Peck (1810), first US Supreme Court case interpreting the contract clause of the Constitution. Chief Justice John Marshall expanded the meaning of the term "contract" to include land grants from states.

Fleurantia. △566.

Fleurs du Mal. △1240.

Fleury, André Hercule de (1653–1743), French cardinal, received his position and the powers of first minister through his tutelage (1715) of the young Louis, later King Louis XV of France. Named a cardinal and first minister in 1726, he set the financial affairs of France in order, compensating for the excesses of Louis XIV. Under his guidance France enjoyed a brief period of peace, but became involved in two successional wars in the decade before his death.

Flexner, Abraham (1866–1959), US educator. One of his major contributions was *Medical Education in the United States and Canada* (1910), which stimulated reform of the medical schools. Flexner also criticized secondary and higher education. He founded and was first director of the Institute for Advanced Study, Princeton, N.J.

Flicker, North American woodpecker with brownish to yellowish plumage and red, black, and white spots and bars. Unlike other woodpeckers, they do not drill into wood for food but use their slender, curved bills to hunt for ants on the ground. They do cut nest holes in trees. Genus *Colaptes. See also* Woodpecker.

Flight, Bird, propulsion through air by flat wing surfaces extended and moved by powerful muscles anchored to the breastbone. A bird's wing acts both as wing (providing lift) and propeller (providing thrust). The downstroke provides most of the power. Flight is partially controlled by the flight feathers being manipulated so air is always exerting the greatest pressure on the lower surface for maximum lift. The position of the wing feathers, especially near the tips, also determines altitude and speed. Tail feathers are important for balance and steering. A bird's hollow bones and streamlined trunk also aid in flight. Their legs are capable of exerting a powerful thrust for takeoff and absorbing the shock of landing. Though birds specialize in soaring, gliding, long-distance flight, or short bursts of speed, many can vary performance depending on need. *See also* Bird. △528.

Flight Dynamics, Aircraft. △1718.

Flightless Birds, large, non-flying birds often having weak or poorly developed wings but strong legs, webbed feet, or other adaptations for walking, running, or swimming. They include the ostrich, rhea, cassowary, emu, kiwi, and penguin. Others, such as the New Zealand wren and some rails, often live on islands and fly with great difficulty. △526, 614.

Flight Simulator, device for training pilots and crews that duplicates the instrument behavior and physical attitude of an aircraft in flight. A more sophisticated simulator, in addition to being an exact replica of a particular aircraft, may also have a visual display to contribute realism.

Flint, city in S Michigan, on Flint River, 58mi (93km) NNW of Detroit; seat of Genesee co; one of world's leading auto production centers; site of branch of University of Michigan, and junior college. Industries: paints, varnishes, airplane engines, automobiles, automobile accessories. Founded 1819 as fur trading post; chartered 1855. Pop. (1970) 193,317.

Flint Clay, a hard, flinty fireclay. Flint clay is a kaolinite, usually found at greater depths than most clays. It is used almost exclusively in the production of firebrick and crucibles.

Flintlock. △1728.

Flint Sickle. △1582.

Float, in finance, the amount of funds "in process," that is, tied up in checks that have been written but not yet collected.

Float Glass Process. △1608.

Floating Currencies. △1384.

Flocculi, or plages, cloudy markings on the solar disk, visible on spectroheliograms. They appear to be chromospheric phenomena—clouds of calcium or hydrogen associated with faculae. *See also* Faculae.

Flood, the rising of some water in a stream, lake, or behind a dam to such a level that regions normally never underwater are submerged. The height of the water between normal level and the crest of the flood is the flood wave. When a stream overflows its banks (the channel it has cut) it inundates the flat adjoining ground or floodplain. Rivers without deep channels in flat regions have well-established floodplains and floods occur in such areas whenever more than normal amounts of water enter the drainage system. *See also* Drainage System; Hydrology. △258, 1764.

Flood Control. △1764.

Floodplain, a flat portion of a river valley consisting of alluvium deposited by the river; normally found at the river's lower or middle course. The plain is nearly at the high water level of the river and is covered with water when the river overflows its banks at flood stage. *See also* Alluvium. △258.

Florence (Firenze), city in central Italy, on the Arno River; capital of Firenze prov. and Tuscany region; site of Roman military colony; 12th-century trade and industrial center; scene of Guelph-Ghibellines power struggle (13th century); under Medici rule 1434–1527, when it was restored to dukes of Florence. City was the cultural and artistic center of W Europe 14th–16th centuries; suffered major flood damage in 1966. Notable buildings include 13th-century Cathedral of Santa Maria del Fiore and Church of Santa Croce, the Campanile, Strozzi palace, the Medici-Riccardi palace, the Uffizi gallery. Industries: ornamental glass and pottery, furniture, tourism. Pop. 457,659. △1140.

Florence, industrial city in NW Alabama, on the Tennessee River; seat of Lauderdale co. Industries: cotton, minerals, textiles, steel fabrication. Settled 1818; inc. 1826. Pop. (1970) 34,031.

Florence, city in NE South Carolina; seat of Florence co; transportation and supply point during Civil War. Industries: railroad repair, foundries, bottling, clothing, electronic equipment. Founded 1855; inc. 1871. Pop. (1970) 25,997.

Florentine Academy. △1130.

Florey, (Sir) Howard Walter (1898–1968), British pathologist, b. Australia. He shared the 1945 Nobel Prize in physiology or medicine for his part in the discovery of penicillin. Florey isolated the antibacterial agent from the mold discovered by Alexander Fleming, work that made the large-scale preparation of penicillin possible. △746.

Florida, city in E central Cuba, 22mi (35km) WNW of Camagüey; railway and agricultural center. Crops: sugarcane, oranges, cattle. Pop. 73,640.

Florida, state in the extreme SE United States, which extends farther S than any continental state.

Land and Economy. Florida is a peninsula about 500mi (805km) long with an average width of 120mi

Flamingo

Flanders lace

Flicker

Florence, Italy

(193km) between the Atlantic Ocean and the Gulf of Mexico. At its S end the Florida Keys, a chain of small islands, stretch W. The land is mostly level, with thousands of lakes and vast swamplands, of which the Everglades in the S are most notable. The St Johns in the NE and the Apalachicola in the W are the largest of the many rivers. The subtropical climate favors two major elements in the economy—agriculture and tourism. Florida is a leader in the production of fruit and vegetables. It is a year-round resort area that offers varied facilities for recreation. The John F. Kennedy Space Center at Cape Canaveral is the nucleus of an electronics and research industry.

People. One of the fastest-growing states, Florida increased its population two and one half times between 1950 and 1970. The influx came mainly from states of the North and the Middle West and included many retired persons, who tended to settle in cities and towns. More than 80% of the people reside in urban areas. Jacksonville, which covers most of Duval County, is the largest US city in area. St Augustine, settled by the Spanish in 1565, is the oldest community of European origin in the United States.

Education. There are more than 60 institutions of higher education.

History. The Spanish explorer Ponce de Leon landed on the E coast in 1513 and claimed the land for Spain. The first permanent settlement at St Augustine became the center of East Florida. Pensacola, founded in 1698, was the center of West Florida. Both Floridas were ceded to Great Britain in 1763 after the Seven Years' War, but were returned to Spain in 1783 after the American Revolution. All Florida was purchased by the United States in 1819 for $5 million and became a territory in 1821. Between 1835 and 1842 most of the native Seminole Indians were exterminated in war. Florida seceded from the Union in January 1861 to join the Confederacy, but was little affected by the Civil War and the Reconstruction period. After 1880, building of railroads, clearing of forests, and draining of swamps signaled an era of growth. Space exploration from Cape Canaveral began in the 1950s, and it was the site of most of the US satellite launches, including the manned moon landing mission in 1969.

PROFILE

Admitted to Union: March 3, 1845; rank, 27th
US Congressmen: Senate, 2; House of Representatives, 15
Population: 6,789,443 (1970); rank, 9th
Capital: Tallahassee, 72,586 (1970)
Chief cities: Jacksonville, 528,865; Miami, 334,-859; Tampa, 277,767
State Legislature: Senate, 40; House of Representatives, 120
Area: 58,560sq mi (151,670sq km); rank, 22d
Elevation: Highest, 345ft (105m), in Walton co. near Alabama border. Lowest, sea level
Industries (major products): processed foods, chemicals, electrical equipment, transportation equipment, paper
Agriculture (major products): citrus fruits, vegetables, cotton, poultry, cattle
Minerals (major): phosphate rock, titanium
State nickname: Sunshine State
State motto: "In God We Trust"
State bird: Mockingbird
State flower: Orange blossom
State tree: Sabal Palm

Floridablanca, José Moñinoy Redondo, Conde de (1728–1808). Spanish statesman. As a minister for Charles III, he successfully suppressed the Jesuits. Becoming chief minister, he governed with efficiency, effecting numerous reforms. He allied Spain with France and the American colonies during the American Revolution. He continued to serve under Charles IV until 1792. During the upheavals of the Peninsular War, he headed the ruling junta briefly before his death.

Florida Keys, chain of small coral and limestone islands, extending in an arc off the S tip of Florida in a curve to the SW. The more significant islands are Key West, Key Largo, Long Key, Vaca Key, and Big Pine Key; resort area, with commercial fishing. Length: approx. 150mi (242km).

Florissant, city in E Missouri, on Missouri River, 13mi (21km) NW of St Louis; site of Old St Ferdinand's Shrine and Convent (1789; rebuilt 1820), historic French and Spanish houses; farming and orchard area. Founded by French fur traders and trappers 1769; inc. 1829. Pop. (1970) 65,908.

Flotation, separation process whereby certain particles are carried out of suspension by a foam, used in the concentration of copper, lead, and zinc ores. An aqueous suspension of powdered ores, dosed with chemicals to affect their surface tensions, is aerated and a specific mineralized froth skimmed off. △1504.

Flounder, or fluke, sanddab, turbot, and (incorrectly) sole, marine flatfish found in shallow and deep waters of Atlantic and Pacific. An important food fish, it is gray, brown, or green on the eye side. Length: to 46in (116.8cm); weight: to 26lb (11.7kg). Families: right-eye Pleuronectidae, left-eye Bethidae; species include summer *Paralichthys dentatus*. *See also* Flatfish. △516.

Flow Charts or **Diagrams,** used in scheduling programs. Various tasks or activities are listed within circles interconnected by directional time-sequence (flow) lines. A "critical path," commanding priority attention from management, can be determined as establishing minimum program time. Flow charts must be updated as variations in predictions occur. △1674.

Flower, reproductive structure of a flowering plant. Set on a shortened stem, it has four sets of organs arranged in whorls, or rings: sepals, leaf-like structures that protect the buds; petals, often brightly colored; stamens, stalks bearing anthers and pollen; and pistil, with ovary, style, and stigma. Reproduction occurs when pollen is transferred from the anthers to the stigma. A pollen tube grows down to the ovary where fertilization occurs and a seed is produced. The ovary bearing the seed ripens into a fruit and other flower parts wilt and fall. Flowers are bisexual, containing stamens and pistils, or unisexual, containing stamens or pistils. △424, 444.

Flower Animals. *See* Anthozoa.

Flowering Ash. *See* Manna.

Flowering Fern. *See* Royal Fern.

Floyd, William, (1734–1821), American legislator and a signer of the Declaration of Independence, b. Brookhaven, L.I. After serving as New York's delegate to the Continental Congress (1774–77; 1778–83), he was elected to the first US House of Representatives in 1789.

Flu. *See* Influenza.

Flugelhorn, brasswind musical instrument similar to the cornet, but with a wider bore and bell. It has a mellow tone like a French horn. *See also* Cornet.

Fluid Flow, the behavior of a moving fluid, determined by its velocity, pressure, and density. These three independent quantities are related by three basic equations: the equation of continuity, which relates the amount of fluid flowing into a volume with the amount flowing out of that volume; Euler's equation of motion, which shows how the velocity of the fluid changes with time at a given point in space; and the adiabatic equation, which describes the exchange of heat between different parts of the fluid. In incompressible fluid flow, which applies to most liquids, these equations take on a particularly simple form. Compressible flow equations are necessary for high-speed aerodynamic calculations. Often a fluid is treated as "ideal," meaning that no internal friction, or viscosity, is supposed. The equations for realistic fluids are so complicated that complete solutions to most problems do not exist; numerical solutions must be attempted by computer techniques. △1496.

Fluidization, powderization of a solid so that it can be handled like a fluid. Fluidization not only allows solids to be conveniently transported, but hastens gas-solid reactions when the gas is injected from below, thus maintaining a fluidized bed—an ideal condition for industrial drying or roasting operations.

Fluid Mechanics, the study of the behavior of liquids and gases. Fluid *statics* includes the study of pressure, density, and the principles of Pascal and Archimedes. Fluid *dynamics* includes the study of streamlines, Bernoulli's equation, and the propagation of waves. Engineers use fluid mechanics in designing bridges, dams, and ships. Physicists use fluid mechanics in studying the structure of the nucleus. Astronomers have used fluid mechanics to explain the spiral structure of the galaxies. △1496, 1504.

Fluke, or trematoda, a parasitic flatworm. Infection results from ingestion of uncooked fish containing encysted worms or by entry through the skin of larvae present in infected waters. The worms may then enter various tissues such as the liver, lungs, and intestines, causing edema and decreased organ function, or they may stay in the bloodstream. Once contracted, treatment is difficult. Prevalent in Asian countries, these flukes are not common in the more developed parts of the world. △472.

Fluke. *See* Flounder.

Fluorescence, emission of radiation, usually light, from a substance the atoms of which have acquired energy from a bombarding source of radiation, usually ultraviolet waves or electrons. When the source of energy is removed the fluorescence ceases. With phosphorescence, which is produced by a similar process, the emission persists for a short time. △1526, 1554.

Fluoridation, addition of inorganic fluorides, usually sodium fluoride, to the water supply to about one part per million, with the intention of reducing tooth decay.

Fluorine, gaseous nonmetallic element (symbol F) of the halogen group, isolated 1886 by Henri Moissan. Chief sources are fluorspar and cryolite. The element, obtained by electrolysis, is the most electronegative of all elements and attacks many compounds. It is used in making fluorocarbons and in extracting uranium. Properties: at. no. 9; at. wt. 18.9984; density 1.696 g dm^{-3}; melt. pt. −363.3°F (−219.62°C); boil. pt. −306.65°F (−188.14°C); most common isotope F^{19} (100%). *See also* Halogen Elements. △1554, 1566.

Fluorite, a halide mineral, calcium fluoride (CaF_2) found in sedimentary rocks and pegmatites. Cubic system crystals and granular and fibrous masses. Brittle, glassy, and colorless when pure. Hardness 4; sp gr 3.1. Chinese make carvings called "green quartz."

Fluorocarbon Plastics, plastics made from a class of chemically inert compounds, composed entirely of carbon and fluorine. The best known is the resin polytetrafluoroethylene, or Teflon. They are valued for their nonflammability, low chemical activity, and low toxicity.

Fluorocarbons, technically chlorofluoromethanes, used as propellants in aerosol spray cans and as refrigerants. These are highly volatile and inert gases, yet in the stratosphere they are broken down by sunlight to release chlorine atoms reacting with ozone to reduce the ozone layer that protects organisms from dangerous quantities of solar ultraviolet rays. △292.

Flute, woodwind musical instrument, now usually made of silver alloy. Air is blown across a mouth hole near the end of a straight tube held horizontally; holes covered by keys arranged in the Boehm system provide a range of 3 octaves, permitting rapid scales and trills. Tones are mellow in the lower register and brighter in the higher. △1244.

Fly, any of various large, stout-bodied, two-winged insects belonging to the order Diptera. Most have spherical heads, large compound eyes, and a pair of long, movable antennae on the head. All have mouths that take in food by suction. A second pair of wings is vestigal, forming knobs called halteres used for balance. The housefly *(Musca domestica)* comprises 90% of all flies occurring in human habitations. It is a hazard to public health wherever decomposing organic waste and garbage accumulate. Adult houseflies are gray with yellow areas on the abdomen. On their feet they carry millions of disease-causing microorganisms. Tiny glandular pads on the feet enable flies to walk on vertical planes or hang from ceilings. Their white larvae are called maggots. *See also* Diptera; Housefly. △492.

Fly Agaric or **Fly Amanita,** a species of poisonous but rarely fatal mushroom *(Amanita muscaria)* common to open woods and pastures. It has a broad yellow, orange-red, or scarlet cap with prominent white warts, a ring high on the stem and concentric rings above the bulb. Said to be hallucinogenic, it produces delirium, convulsions, and digestive upsets. △428.

Flycatcher, various small birds that catch insects in mid-flight. New World flycatchers, commonly known as tyrant flycatchers, include phoebes, peewees, and kingbirds, and inhabit most of the Western Hemisphere but are chiefly found in the tropics. Fierce defenders of their nesting territories, they lay white to olive, often spotted, eggs (2–4) in cup-shaped nests. Old World flycatchers live in Eurasia, Africa, parts of Asia, Australia and nearby regions. Some are brightly colored. They lay their eggs (2–6) in cup-shaped branch nests, holes in trees, or gravel pits. Family Muscicapidae.

Flying Dragon, gliding lizard native to SE Asia and Indonesia. It has a dewlap and wattles on the sides of its neck and 5–6 elongated ribs support extensible kin folds that are spread for gliding flight from branch o branch. Length: 8–12in (20–30cm). Family Agamiiae; genus *Draco*. *See also* Lizard.

lying Fish, marine fish found worldwide in tropical eas. Dark blue and silver, it uses its enlarged spineess pectoral and pelvic fins to glide above water surace for as long as 13 seconds. Length: to 18in (45.7 m). Family Exocoetidae; species 50, including *Exocoetus volitans* and Atlantic *Cypselurus heterurus*.

lying Fox, fruit-eating bat with a foxlike head, found n the tropics from Madagascar to the SW Pacific. lying foxes sometimes cause substantial damage to ruit crops. They are usually grayish brown or black. Vingspan: 5.5ft (1.7m), weight: to 2lb (0.9kg). Genus *Pteropus*. *See also* Fruit Bat. △600.

lying Gurnard. *See* Gurnard.

lying Lemur, or **Colugo,** nocturnal gliding mammal of SE Asia resembling a large flying squirrel. "Wingpans" to 3ft (91cm); weight: to 4lb (1.8kg). The two pecies (genus *Cynocephalus*) are the only members of the order Dermoptera. △540.

lying Snake. △520.

lying Squirrel, gliding rodent of the squirrel family hat lives in forested areas of Eurasia and North and South America. They glide by means of furry memranes on both sides of the body that stretch out flat nd taut when the legs are extended. Except for some ndian species that weigh over 4lb (1.8kg), most flying quirrels are small. △546.

M. *See* Frequency Modulation.

M Broadcasting. △1794.

ocal Length, distance from the midpoint of a mirror r the center of a thin lens to the focal point of the ystem. For a spherical surface it is half the radius of urvature. For converging systems it is given a positive value, for diverging systems, a negative value. △518.

och, Ferdinand (1851–1929), French marshal. He vas instructor and then director (1903–11) of the cole de Guerre. In World War I he was a commander n the battle of the Marne (1914), the first battle of pres (1915), and on the Somme (1916). In March 918, Foch became supreme allied commander, haping the final victory over the Germans. *See also* Vorld War I.

ocus, either of two points on the major axis of an llipse such that the distance from one focus to any oint on the ellipse and back to the other focus is onstant. When the distance between the foci is zero he figure is a circle. For an orbiting celestial body, uch as a planet, the center of gravitational attraction es at one focus, the primary focus, of an ellipse. The ther focus is the secondary focus.

ocus, Earthquake, region in earth from which a uake originates. Quakes are classified by the depth f occurrence. Most quakes are shallow-focus. Shalow-focus ranges from 37–186mi (60–300km). Deepocus is 186–435mi (300–700km) into earth's inteior. *See also* Earthquake.

oehn, a warm, dry wind on the lee or downwind side of mountains, tending to produce aridity. *See also* Vinds.

og, water vapor in the atmosphere condensed at or ear the ground, as opposed to water vapor conensed in the air in clouds. *See also* Precipitation. △16.

oggia, city in Italy, 162mi (261km) ESE of Rome, in enter of Great Apulian Plain; capital of Foggia provnce. Frederick II held parliament here 1240; heavily amaged during WWII; military airfields were capured by British 1943; remains include ruins of castle of Frederick II; agricultural region and wool market. ndustries: olives, grapes, tobacco, cellulose, paper. op. 141,667.

okine, Michel (1880–1942), Russian choreograher. He joined the Maryinsky Theatre (1889) in St etersburg and taught at the Imperial School of Balet. After choreographing *The Dying Swan* for Anna avlova (1905), he became chief choreographer for iaghilev's Ballets Russes in Paris in 1909. He first ame to the United States in 1919, settled in New ork City in 1923, and became a US citizen in 1932. le continued choreographing for major ballet compaies in Europe, South America, Australia, and the United States. His most noted works are *Les Sylphides, Firebird, Petrouchka,* and *Bluebeard.* △1368.

Fokker, Anton Herman Gerard (1890–1939), US aircraft pioneer, b. Java. Educated in the Netherlands, he founded the Fokker aircraft works in Germany (1912), which designed and built the Fokker biplanes and triplanes used by Germany in World War I. After the war he set up factories in Holland, and in 1922 emigrated to the United States, where he became a citizen and established the Fokker Aircraft Corporation of America in New Jersey.

Folding, in geology, pronounced bending in the layer of rock. Folds are defined according to the axes of the folds. Thus, an upfold, which is an arch, is an anticline; a downfold, a syncline. The fold system may be symmetrical (in neat waves), asymmetrical, overturned, or recumbent (the axis of the fold is parallel to the horizon). A single folding is known as a monocline. △250–52.

Folic Acid, yellow crystalline derivative of glutamic acid (formula $C_{19}H_{19}N_7O_6$) forming part of the vitamin B complex and used in the treatment of anemia. *See also* Vitamin.

Folies-Bergère, Parisian music hall specializing in extravagant revues with many beautiful, scantily clad women. Built in 1869, it has provided the sophisticated setting for many great French entertainers, including Maurice Chevalier and Fernandel.

Folk Art, term used to describe the art of folk cultures, especially those of isolated rural communities with traditions that have continued for generations. It also applies to the art of ethnic groups, such as Hassidic Jews and Pennsylvania Mennonites. Folk art usually involves the decoration of useful, everyday objects within a community, such as cradles, plows, ox yokes, weather vanes, and quilts. Much care is given to the decoration of objects to be used at special occasions, such as community festivals and marriages. Often, the same motifs, which are usually simple in design, are handed down from generation to generation to be used in surface decoration. △1416–18.

Folklore, the lore of the common people, or the traditions, customs, and beliefs of the people as expressed through nonliterary tales, songs, and sayings. In contrast to "art literature," which is transmitted through the printed page, "folk literature" has an oral source, and is transmitted primarily through memory and practice. The best-known study of folklore is Sir James Frazer's *The Golden Bough* (1890–1915).

Folk Music, music associated with communities, nationalities, and peoples rather than composed by individuals; often handed down orally from generation to generation. American folk music includes ballads, gospels, spirituals, and work songs among other forms.

Folk Tales. *See* Fairy Tales and Folktales.

Folk Theater, a type of drama or entertainment that uses folklore, traditional and regional material, and nonprofessional actors. It is generally performed by natives of rural areas and is often impromptu. Elements of folk drama—music, dance, or themes—are often incorporated into more professional pieces of drama. In some ways, medieval drama, which combined religion with superstitions and agricultural themes, was folk theater.

Folkways, shared patterns of behavior and beliefs common to a particular group of people. The term was first used by W.G. Sumner in 1906. Folkways are not the result of individual adjustment, but instead are learned directly from other members of the group. Unlike mores, they are usually not verbalized as law.

Follicle-stimulating Hormone (FSH), hormone produced by the anterior pituitary. It regulates ovulation by stimulating the ovary to secrete estrogens, thus promoting development of the egg. It stimulates spermatogenesis in the male.

Folsom, village in NE New Mexico; gives name to Folsom culture, a distinctive prehistoric hunting pattern; site of archeological excavation (1925) containing Stone Age artifacts dating Folsom man from 8000 BC. Pop. (1970) 75.

Folsom Culture, early North American culture characterized by the use of fluted stone spear points. The first "Folsom point" to be found was in 1926 at Folsom, N.M. Folsom people lived around 9000 to 7000 BC, hunted a now extinct form of bison on the Great Plains, and gathered food.

Florida: citrus groves

Flying dragon

Foggia, Italy

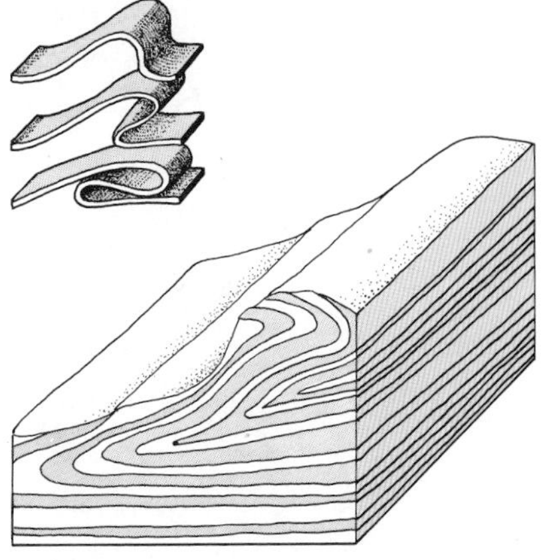

Folding (geological)

Fomalhaut, or **Alpha Piscis Austrini,** white main-sequence star in the constellation Piscis Austrinus. Characteristics: apparent mag. +1.16; absolute mag. +1.8; spectral type A3; distance 23 light-years.

Fon, Kwa-speaking people of S Benin (Dahomey) and Nigeria. Their polygynous, patrilineal society is based on subsistence agriculture, with a market system using cowrie shells as money. Hunters form a class with special social and religious status, while ancestor worship plays an important part in their religion.

Fond du Lac, city in E Wisconsin, at S end of Lake Winnebago; seat of Fond du Lac co; farming and manufacturing center; popular resort area. Industries: dairy products and equipment, tools, leather goods. Settled 1836; inc. 1852. Pop. (1970) 35,515.

Fong, Hiram Leong (1907–), US political leader, b. Honolulu. The son of Chinese immigrants, he served (1938–54) in the territorial legislature, with three terms as speaker. In 1950, he was vice president of the Territorial Constitutional Convention. In 1959 he became one of Hawaii's first US senators and was reelected in 1964 and 1970.

Fontaine, Jean de la (1621–95), French poet and fabulist. Elected to the Académie Française in 1683, he drifted from one patron to another. He was best known for his *Books of Fables* (1668–94), a delightful collection of animal tales based on Aesop's and other fables, in which he passed judgment on society. △1172.

Fontainebleau, town in N France, near W bank of the Seine, 37mi (60km) S of Paris; surrounded by forest of Fontainebleau; site of French Renaissance palace built by Francis I, now serves as the summer residence of France's president; US art school, military college, school of engineering. Industries: tourism, cabinetmaking, grape shipping. Pop. 18,094.

Fontainebleau, French palace built 1528–40 for King Francis I. Begun by the master mason Gilles Le Breton and completed by the Italian architects Primaticcio and Serlio, it is irregular in plan. The appeal of its exterior depends on lakes, formal gardens, and vistas. Its interiors, decorated by Primaticcio, Rosso, and others, are of more architectural interest. △1146, 1150.

Fontainebleau Conference. △1378.

Fontanel, soft space at the junction of the cranial bones of an infant. The fontanels close as the cranial bones grow toward each other, and do not exist in older children or adults.

Fontanne, Lynn (1887?–), US actress, b. England. She began her long stage career as a child in the Drury Lane Pantomime; her first US appearance was in *Mr. Preedy and the Countess* (1910). Married to actor Alfred Lunt (1922), she appeared with him in many plays, such as *The Taming of the Shrew* (1935), *O Mistress Mine* (1946), *Quadrille* (1952), and *The Visit* (1958). She produced as well as appeared in *Point Valaine* (1935), *Idiot's Delight* (1936), and *Amphitryon 38* (1937). She also played in films, such as *The Guardsman* (1931).

Fontenelle, Bernard Le Bovier, Sieur de (1657–1757), French philosopher. A member of the French Academy and of the Academy of Sciences (1697), he wrote a history of proceedings and eulogies for members. In *Plurality of Worlds* (1686) and *History of Oracles* (1687) he emerged as a gifted popularizer of science and anticipated the urbanity and sophistication of Enlightenment style. *See also* Enlightenment.

Fontenoy, town in SW Belgium, 5mi (8km) SE of Tournai; scene of 1745 battle during which French, under Marshal Saxe, defeated British and allies, led by Duke of Cumberland. Pop. 665.

Fonteyn, (Dame) Margot (1919–), English ballerina. Trained at the Sadler's Wells Ballet School, she became a member of the Royal Ballet (1939–59). She has been a guest artist with every major US and European ballet company. Late in her career she continued to dazzle audiences, especially in her appearances with Rudolf Nureyev. She has been acclaimed as one of the most exquisite classical dancers of this century. △1368.

Foochow (Fuzhou, or **Fu-chou),** formerly Minhow; port city in SE China, on Min River, 25mi (40km) from the coast of the East China Sea; capital of Fukien prov. Dates from the T'ang dynasty (618–906); visited by Marco Polo (13th century). One of the first treaty ports open to foreign trade (1842), it flourished as the major port in China (1850) and world's largest tea-exporter but declined (early 20th century) with the lessened demand for tea and silting of Min River. In 1949, after Communist takeover, port was blockaded by Nationalist Chinese. A large thoroughfare connects the old walled city to the riverside commercial section. Industries: chemicals, textiles, food processing, paper, bamboo, tea, plastics, machine shops. Pop. 900,000.

Food, material containing essential nutrients (proteins, fats, vitamins, minerals, carbohydrates) taken into an organism to maintain life and growth. Foods of plant origin are cereals, tubers, legumes, nuts, vegetables, fruits, oils, and sugars; those of animal origin are meat, eggs, fish, shellfish, milk, and fat. △302, 326–62, 372–98.

Food Additive, any of various substances added to food. They include flavors, flavor enhancers, antioxidants and other preservatives, coloring matter, sweeteners, and vitamins and essential mineral salts.

Food and Agricultural Organization (FAO), specialized agency of the United Nations. It serves as coordinator for worldwide food production, distribution, and consumption. Its member countries have no enforcement powers. It has field technicians and provides fellowships for studies of underdeveloped countries. Organized in 1943, it joined the United Nations in 1945. Its headquarters are in Rome. △942.

Food and Drug Administration (FDA), federal agency within the Department of Health, Education, and Welfare. Its purpose is protecting against impure and unsafe foods, drugs and cosmetics, and other potential hazards. The FDA is divided into several bureaus, including biologics, drugs, foods, radiological health, veterinary medicine, and medical devices and diagnostic products. It was established in 1906 with revisions in 1931.

Food Chain, transfer of food energy through a series of organisms with each organism eating the member below it. Its sequence is green plants (producers), herbivores (primary consumers), and carnivores (secondary consumers). Decomposers act at each stage and at the end of the chain. △580.

Food Poisoning, or ptomaine poisoning, can be caused by a number of organisms, most common being *Salmonella*. Such organisms are most frequently ingested from animals or animal products such as meat, most often fowl, and eggs. Symptoms include colicky abdominal pain, watery diarrhea, nausea, and fever. Vomiting may occur. Symptoms usually appear within 8–48 hours after infected food has been ingested and will usually subside within two to five days although the diarrhea may persist longer. In severe cases, dehydration is a complication. Treatment includes bed rest, fluids to prevent dehydration, no food until cramps and vomiting subside. △736.

Food Preservative, substance used to preserve food in an edible condition, by making it or its environment unfavorable to the growth of microorganisms, and to ensure that it retains its original quality. Traditional methods used to prevent spoilage are dehydration, exclusion of air, smoking, salting, pickling, and immersing in wine. Quality is preserved by the use of ascorbic acid to prevent discoloration, of sulfur dioxide and benzoic acid as firming and bleaching agents, and of glutamates to preserve the flavor of meat. △380, 396.

Food-production Revolution, worldwide development of advanced agricultural technology during the 20th century. Scientific improvements in new crop varieties, growing techniques, natural and artificial animal breeding, pest and disease control, electricity, and mechanization have resulted in greatly increased productivity. △398.

Foot, in poetry, unit of verse meter. Each foot is composed of a group of two or three syllables, one of which is stressed. Most commonly used feet are anapest, dactyl, iamb, trochee. *See also* Meter.

Foot-and-Mouth Disease, or hoof-and-mouth disease, aphthous fever, contagious viral disease of cattle, swine, sheep, goats, horses, and deer. Its symptoms are fever; blisters of the mouth and hoofs; drooling; weight loss; and death. Vaccine is available but its cost is prohibitive and it does not guarantee prevention. The disease rarely occurs in man. Effective inspections, quarantines, slaughter of diseased animals, and sanitation have kept the disease under control in the United States.

Football, contact sport played in the United States. It is second in popularity only to baseball. It is played by 2 teams of 11 persons each—a fullback, two halfbacks, a quarterback, a center, two guards, two tack les, and two ends—on a field 100 yards (91.5m) lon by 53 yards (48.5m) wide. The field is marked off b latitudinal stripes every 5 yards (4.6m) and is flanke on each end by an area (end zone) 10 yards (9.1m long. At each end of the end zone are H-shaped goa posts. An inflated leather, speroid ball is used, wit the object of moving the ball—by the ground or air— across the opponent's goal line. The defending tear must stop the ball carrier by pushing him out c bounds or by bringing him to the ground (tackling). game consists of two halves, each having two 15 minute quarters. At the end of each half, the team exchange goals. The scoring can occur in four ways a touchdown is six points (crossing the opponent' goal line), a conversion is one point (kicking the ba through the uprights of the goal post following touchdown), a field goal is three points (kicking th ball through the uprights of the goal posts), and safety is two points (downing the ball carrier behin his own goal line). In other than professional footbal the conversion can count as two points if the ball run or passed into the end zone following the touch down. Except for certain instances in professiona ball, games can end in a tie. Each half starts with kickoff, and after the receiving team has run back th ball, it must advance 10 yards in 4 attempts (downs or turn the ball over to the opponents. The ball i usually turned over by punting (kicking) on the las down or attempting a field goal. If a player fumble and loses possession of the ball during the series c downs, the opposing team takes over the ball. Subst tutions are freely allowed.

History. Football has its roots in England in th Middle Ages and has similarities to rugby and socce The US version of the game was adopted after 1875 College football began in 1869 and has since flou ished with a host of post-season contests, the mos prominent being the Rose Bowl, an annual ever since 1916. Professional football also began in th 19th century, and the National Football League (NFL first formed in 1920 as the American Professiona Football League, has enjoyed the greatest success The American Football League, formed in 196C merged with the NFL in 1969. △1408.

NFL CHAMPIONS

1933	Chicago Bears
1934	New York Giants
1935	Detroit Lions
1936	Green Bay Packers
1937	Washington Redskins
1938	New York Giants
1939	Green Bay Packers
1940	Chicago Bears
1941	Chicago Bears
1942	Washington Redskins
1943	Chicago Bears
1944	Green Bay Packers
1945	Cleveland Rams
1946	Chicago Bears
1947	Chicago Cardinals
1948	Philadelphia Eagles
1949	Philadelphia Eagles
1950	Cleveland Browns
1951	Los Angeles Rams
1952	Detroit Lions
1953	Detroit Lions
1954	Cleveland Browns
1955	Cleveland Browns
1956	New York Giants
1957	Detroit Lions
1958	Baltimore Colts
1959	Baltimore Colts
1960	Philadelphia Eagles
1961	Green Bay Packers
1962	Green Bay Packers
1963	Chicago Bears
1964	Cleveland Browns
1965	Green Bay Packers
1966	Green Bay Packers

SUPER BOWL WINNERS

1967	Green Bay Packers
1968	Green Bay Packers
1969	New York Jets
1970	Kansas City Chiefs
1971	Baltimore Colts
1972	Dallas Cowboys
1973	Miami Dolphins
1974	Miami Dolphins
1975	Pittsburgh Steelers
1976	Pittsburgh Steelers
1977	Oakland Raiders

Foot Binding, the practice of compressing girls' fee with tight bandages to prevent growth of the feet. I China this was common up to the 19th century amon the middle and upper classes. Foot binding rendere women's feet useless and suggested that their me were sufficiently prosperous to support them. △818

Foot-pound, the unit of energy in the English foot-slug-second system of units. One foot-pound is the work done by a force of one pound acting through a distance of one foot.

Foraminifera, marine, planktonic, ameboid protozoans characterized by multichambered lime shells. Accumulations form the white cliffs of Dover and chalk beds of Mississippi and Georgia. The size of a pinhead, shells may be spiral-shaped, straight, or clustered. Filaments of protoplasm extend from the perforations in the shell and form a covering web. Examples are *Globigerina, Polystomella, Nodosaria.* △506.

Forbidden City, a walled area in N Peking, China, in the Inner or Tatar City; site of Imperial Palace, T'ien an Men Square, Great Hall of the People, the Museum of History and Revolution, and the Temple of Heaven; so named because it was formerly closed to the public. Area: 0.3sq mi (0.8sq km).

Forbidden City, western name for Lhasa, capital of Tibet; name derives from its remoteness and the hostility of the Tibetan clergy toward foreign visitors. *See also* Lhasa. △1208.

Force, loosely speaking, a push or pull. A force acting on a body may (1) balance an equal but opposite force or combination of forces to maintain the body in equilibrium, (2) change the state of motion of the body (in magnitude or direction), or (3) change the shape or state of the body. There are four basic forces in nature. The most familiar, and the weakest, is the gravitational force, an attractive force which varies inversely as the square of the distance between any two masses. Much stronger is the electromagnetic force, which also follows the inverse-square law and may be attractive or repulsive. Two other forces are recognized, both operating only on the subatomic level. The weak nuclear force associated with the decay of particles is intermediate in strength between the gravitational and electromagnetic force, while the strong nuclear force associated with the "glue" holding nuclei together is the strongest force known in nature. △1488, 1490.

Force Acts, three laws passed to outlaw the Ku Klux Klan. The first act (May 31, 1870) set penalties for persons interfering with citizens' (blacks') rights to vote. The second act (Feb. 28, 1871) strengthened federal regulation of elections. The third act (April 20, 1871) declared Klan activities to be high crimes and permitted the president to suspend habeas corpus to suppress such "armed combinations." He did so in nine South Carolina counties. *See also* Ku Klux Klan.

Forceps. △752.

Forcing, in horticulture, speeding up the development of a plant or part of a plant, usually by providing heat and moisture. Forcing was formerly widely used in northern regions to produce leaf vegetables during winter. It is still often used to accelerate the blooming of bulbs and cut stems of flowering shrubs such as forsythia or dogwood.

Ford, Ford Madox (1873–1939), English novelist, poet, and critic; b. Ford Madox Hueffer. He is best known for his influence on such writers as Ezra Pound, Joseph Conrad, and D. H. Lawrence and for his editorship of *English Review,* a literary magazine. His chief work is the tetralogy *Parade's End* (1924–28).

Ford, Gerald Rudolph (1913–), 38th president of the United States (1974–77), b. Omaha, Nebraska. He was originally named Leslie King, Jr., but assumed his stepfather's name when his mother remarried. He graduated from the University of Michigan and the Yale University law school and was admitted to the Michigan bar in 1941. In 1948 he married Elizabeth Bloomer; they had four children. After service in the Navy in World War II, he was elected (1948) as a Republican to the US House of Representatives. A conservative and a loyal party supporter, he rose in Republican ranks, and in 1964 he was named House minority leader. In 1973, when Vice President Spiro T. Agnew was forced to resign, President Nixon nominated Ford to replace him. He became vice president on Dec. 6, 1973, the first to come into office under the 25th Amendment to the Constitution.

By the time Ford became vice president, the Nixon administration was deeply involved in the Watergate affair. Ford repeatedly expressed his confidence that Nixon was not involved in the scandals. Nixon was forced to resign, however, on Aug. 9, 1974, and Ford became president. Ford retained most of the Nixon cabinet and advisers, and, a month after he assumed office, pardoned Nixon for all crimes he might have committed while president. He was widely criticized for the pardon. Ford continued the Nixon policy of easing tensions with both the Soviet Union and China. In domestic affairs, he opposed Democratic programs aimed at countering the recession, maintaining that their great costs would add to inflation, and vetoed a number of such bills. In 1976, Ford announced his intention to run for a full term. He entered the Republican primaries, where he was opposed by Ronald Reagan, the former governor of California. Ford received the Republican nomination but was defeated by Democrat Jimmy Carter.

Career: US House of Representatives, 1949–73; vice president, 1973–74; president, 1974–77. △1358.

Ford, Henry (1863–1947), US automobile maker and industrialist, b. Dearborn, Mich. He developed a working gasoline automobile (1892), and later founded Ford Motors (1903). He brought out the economical Model T in 1908. He initiated the conveyor-belt assembly line (1913) and introduced the 8-hour day with a $5 minimum wage, while opposing unionization. Ford established a closely controlled organization whose industrial and transport holdings made Ford Motors materially self-reliant. He established the Ford Foundation (1936) which he and his son Edsel endowed and contributed over $40,000,000 to charitable causes (1908–47). △1692.

Ford, John (1895–1973), US film director, b. Sean O'Fearna in Cape Elizabeth, Me. He won Academy Awards for best director for *The Informer* (1935), *The Grapes of Wrath* (1940), *How Green Was My Valley* (1941), and *The Quiet Man* (1952). Other notable films include *The Horse Soldiers* (1959) and *Cheyenne Autumn* (1964).

Forecasting. △218.

Foreign Aid, money or credit extended to less developed nations to help them in their development programs. Technology may also be provided. Often the more developed nations set conditions for receiving aid, including adherence to certain policies; spending all or most of the aid money on goods or services of the granting nation; or using the grantor country's ships to transport goods. Foreign aid is a relatively recent phenomenon. △1342, 1386.

Foreign Legion, skilled professional military group of mixed national origin, created in 1831 to control French colonies around the world. After fighting in two world wars and later French colonial struggles, the Legion moved its headquarters from Algeria to S France.

Foreign Service, corps of agents who serve as their country's diplomatic representatives abroad. The Rogers Act (1924) combined the US diplomatic and consular services into one agency under the jurisdiction of the State Department. It also provided for promotion on the basis of merit, although ambassadors remain political appointees. Members of the foreign service are trained to staff embassies, legations, and consulates, and to conduct negotiations with representatives of their host nations.

Forensic Medicine, branch of science dealing with the relations and applications of medical facts to legal matters. Forensic medicine would, for example, concern itself with the definition of death or with the timing of death if foul play is suspected. △920.

Forester, C(ecil) S(cott) (1899–1966), English author best known for the writing of sea stories, b. Egypt. After giving up the study of medicine, Forester turned to the writing of fiction. His series of 12 novels concerning the saga of Horatio Hornblower of the English navy, beginning with *The Happy Return* (1937), was very popular, as was his adventure tale *The African Queen* (1935).

Forest Fires, burning of woodland vegetation, caused by natural means, such as lightning, or by accident or arson. Ground fires burn the humus layer of the forest floor; surface fires burn undergrowth and surface litter; stand fires burn tree trunks, but not foliage; crown fires burn all vegetation. Control of forest fires has three main aspects: prevention, spotting, and fire fighting. Prevention is largely a matter of public relations, as most fires are started by people rather than by nature. Spotting is a system of locating fires in their early stages, usually by lookouts in high towers or airplanes. Fire fighting varies with type of fire and degree of severity.

Forestry, the science of managing wooded areas with their associated waters and wastelands. The chief objective is usually the raising of timber, but conservation of soil, water, and wildlife is also a consideration. Systematic management had its beginnings in German states in the 16th century, where forests were divided into sections for timber felling and regenera-

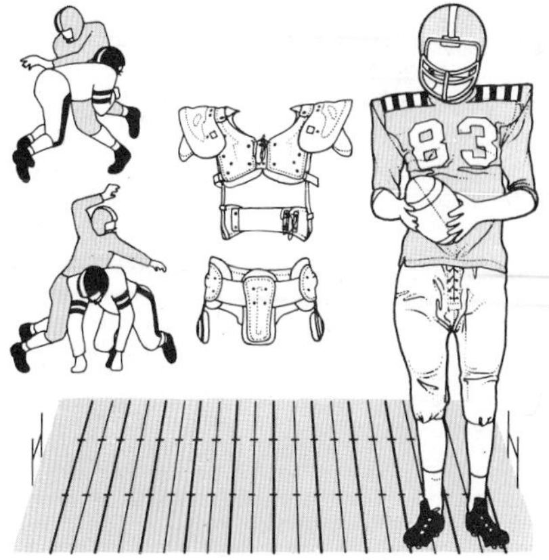
83
Football

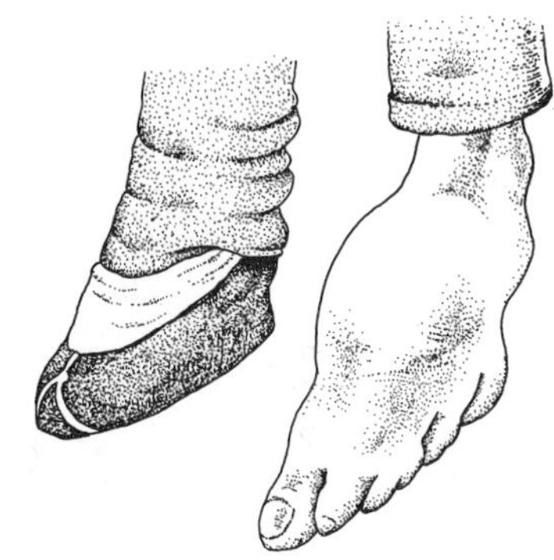
Foot-binding

Gerald R. Ford

GENTLEMEN
OUR
COUNTRY
Henry Ford

tion, to sustain annual yield. Education in technical forestry began in western Europe in the 19th century. Now many universities throughout the world offer forestry curricula. Modern forestry includes silviculture, dendrology, forest protection, engineering, utilization, and management. Many operations are included, with emphasis on cycles of cutting and replenishment, selection and breeding, insect control, and limitation of forest fires. △364, 1610.

Forests, Types of. There are a number of systems for classifying forest types. One system includes the following eight categories: (1) temperate region deciduous forests, made up of summer-green trees of North America, Europe, temperate Asia, and South America; (2) deciduous monsoon forests of Asia with heavy rainfall; (3) tropical deciduous forests blending with grasslands; (4) temperate coniferous forests dominated by pines and firs; (5) tropical rain forests, typified by those of central Africa and South America, with profuse, diverse growth; (6) coastal rain forests where warm ocean currents influence the climate; (7) temperate rain forests with broadleaved evergreen trees; (8) tropical scrub forests in dry areas. △592–603.

Forget-me-not, perennial plant native to Eurasia and North America that is one of the spring's first flowers. The pink, flaring, five-lobed flowers change to blue as they mature. They are a popular garden flower. Water forget-me-nots grow in marshlands and have shorter, weaker stems. There are 50 species. Family Boraginaceae; genus *Myosotis*.

Forgetting, inability to bring memories to consciousness. A traditional theory attributes forgetting to the decay of memory information with time, but modern psychology tends to regard interference from other memories as critical. Forgetting is viewed as an inability to retrieve stored information because other information "gets in the way." *See also* Memory. △670.

Forging, the shaping of metal articles by hammering or pressing metal blanks between pairs of forging dies. The upper die is attached to the ram of a forging hammer or press so that it can be raised and dropped (with or without additional pressure) against the rigidly supported lower die. Most metals are forged hot, but cold forging is an important technique. △1604.

Forlanini, Enrico. △1682.

Forlì, city in Italy, SE of Bologna; capital of Forli prov. Founded by Rome 2nd century, city was scene of struggle between Guelph and Ghibelline factions during 13th century; Caterina Sforza, widow of Gerolamo Riario, ruled city 1488–1500, when she surrendered to Cesare Borgia; city was part of Papal States 1504–1859; site of 12th-century Abbey of S. Mercuriale, 15th-century citadel, 14th-century Palazzo Communale. Industries: textiles, shoes, chemicals, appliances. Pop. 103,156.

Formaldehyde, colorless suffocating and poisonous gas (HCHO) prepared by the catalytic oxidation of methane or methanol. It is used in the manufacture of plastics, as a germicide, preservative, and reducing agent, and as a corrosion inhibiter. Properties: melt. pt. −133.6°F (−92°C); boil. pt. −6°F (−21°C).

Formalism, in Architecture. △1322.

Formica, a trademarked plastic material that forms a hard, smooth, heat- and stain-resistant surface for furniture and wallboards. Layers of resin-impregnated paper are bonded together under heat and pressure. The top sheet is patterned and colored, frequently with a wood grain.

Formic Acid, colorless fuming liquid (HCOOH) prepared by treating sodium formate with sulfuric acid and distilling or by acid hydrolysis of methyl formate. It is used in the manufacture of paper, textiles, insecticides, and refrigerants. Properties: sp gr 1.22; melt. pt. 46.9°F(8.3°C); boil. pt. 213.5°F(100.8°C).

Formosa. *See* Taiwan.

Formosa Strait, branch of the Pacific Ocean, between Fukien prov., China, and Taiwan; it links the East China and South China seas. Width: 115mi (185km).

Formosus (816?–96), Roman Catholic pope (891–96). Made a cardinal bishop in 864, he was excommunicated by Pope John VIII, but he was absolved by Marinus I in 883. After his death, Formosus' body was placed on trial for having received two bishoprics. Found guilty, the body was thrown into the Tiber River. His papal decrees were declared invalid but later reinstated.

Formstecher, Solomon (1808–89), German Jewish philosopher, a great force in the reform movement within Judaism, which he analyzed and justified in his literary works. As a rabbi, he stressed the dynamics of religion and the progressive nature of Judaism.

Formula, in mathematics, general rule or relationship expressed in mathematical symbols. Examples are the formula $V = 4/3\pi r^3$, for the volume of a sphere, and the cosine formula (or rule) $c^2 = a^2 + b^2 - 2ab \cos C$, for the sides of a triangle.

Fornix. △666.

Forrest, Edwin (1806–72), US actor, b. Philadelphia. He began his acting career in Philadelphia's Walnut Street Theatre (1820), then toured with several itinerant companies and a New Orleans company before his success as Othello in New York (1826). His rivalry with English actor William C. Macready climaxed in a riot in New York City (1849), resulting in 22 deaths, known as the Astor Place Riot. He continued his acting career until 1872, although he was more known for his colorful personal life than for his acting skill.

Forrest, Nathan Bedford (1821–77), Confederate general, b. Bedford co., Tenn. A plantation owner, he headed a group of cavalry raiders that made daring attacks on Union communications during the Civil War. After the war, he became involved in the Ku Klux Klan, serving as head (Grand Wizard) of the vigilante organization.

Forrestal, James Vincent (1892–1949), US banker and cabinet member, b. Beacon, N.Y. A naval aviator during World War I, he became an investment banker and president of Dillon, Read & Company (1938). President Roosevelt appointed him undersecretary of the navy (1940–44) and secretary (1944–47). When the departments of war and the navy were reorganized, he became the first secretary of defense (1947–49).

Forster, E(dward) M(organ) (1878–1970), English author. His novels deal with the individual's blind acceptance of social convention, denying the free and spontaneous in life. They include *Where Angels Fear to Tread* (1905), *The Longest Journey* (1907), *A Room with a View* (1908), *Howards End* (1910), and, his most famous work, *A Passage to India* (1924). His short stories were collected in *The Celestial Omnibus* (1911) and *The Eternal Moment* (1928). *The Art of the Novel* (1927) is an important collection of lectures in literary criticism. *Abinger Harvest* (1936) and *Two Cheers for Democracy* (1951) are collections of essays on literature, society, and politics. Forster also, with Eric Crozier, wrote the libretto for Benjamin Britten's opera version of Melville's *Billy Budd* (1951). Though Forster's novels are conventional in structure, the excellence of his style places him among the foremost fiction writers of his time.

Forsyte Saga, The (1922), trilogy of novels (*The Man of Property*, 1906; *In Chancery*, 1920; *To Let*, 1921) and two stories ("Indian Summer of a Forsyte," 1918; "Awakening," 1920) by John Galsworthy about the fortunes of an upper-middle-class family in Victorian and Edwardian times. The proprietary instinct of the Forsytes, concentrated in the figure of Soames, is their chief source of power. Soames's inability to retain possession of his wife, Irene, represents the Forsytes' failure in the area of human relationships. In two other trilogies—*A Modern Comedy* (1924–28) and *End of the Chapter* (1931–33)—Galsworthy continues the story of the Forsytes.

Forsythia, or golden bells, ornamental shrub that flowers in April with bright yellow, bell-shaped flowers; the leaves, which may have marginal teeth, appear afterward. Height: 4–8ft (1.2–2.4m). Species include the showy *Forsythia spectabilis*; *F. obovata*, grown in northern areas; and *F. suspensa*. Family Oleaceae.

Fort, a strong, armed place surrounded by protective works and garrisoned with armed troops. Throughout history different materials from earth and stone to timber and concrete have been used to construct the defensive works. Designs of forts have varied from simple rectangles and squares to more elaborate forms such as lunettes or star shapes. "Fort" can also refer to an unfortified place where troops are stationed. △1732.

Fort. For other sites, *see* second part of name.

Fortaleza (Ceará), port city in NE Brazil, 270mi (435km) NW of Natal; capital of Ceará state. Industries: sugar refining, textiles, soap, shipping. Founded 1609. Pop. 842,231.

Fortas, Abe (1910–), US jurist, lawyer, and public official, b. Memphis, Tenn. He was appointed by Pres. Lyndon Johnson to be an associate justice of the US Supreme Court in 1965. In 1968 he was nominated to be chief justice. When the nomination was blocked by a Senate filibuster, he asked that his name be withdrawn. In 1969 he resigned under pressure when his financial association with a former client convicted of stock manipulation was made public.

Fort Collins, residential and industrial city in W Colorado, 40mi (64km) NNE of Boulder; seat of Larimer co. Industries: plastics, timber, sugar, canned goods. Settled 1864; inc. 1879. Pop. (1970) 43,337.

Fort-de-France, port city and capital of Martinique, French West Indies, on Fort-de-France Bay; tourist resort; Napoleon's wife, Empress Josephine, was born nearby. Settled 1762 by French. Pop. 99,051.

Fort Dodge, city in central Iowa, on Des Moines River; seat of Webster co; site of Fort Dodge Historical Museum and Iowa Central Community College (1921). Industries: meat packing, animal feeds, fertilizers, gypsum mining. Founded 1850 as Fort Clarke; inc. 1869. Pop. (1970) 31,263.

Fort Donelson National Military Park and Cemetery, historic area in Dover, Tennessee, on Cumberland River; site of Confederate fort taken by Union forces under Gen. Ulysses S. Grant, Feb. 16, 1862, opening way for Union invasion of Nashville. Est. 1928.

Forten, James (1766–1842), US philanthropist and abolitionist, b. Philadelphia. A wealthy sailmaker, he refused to outfit slave ships, supported the work of William Lloyd Garrison, and organized blacks to protect Philadelphia during the War of 1812.

Forth, Firth of, sunken estuary of the Forth River, Scotland, running W to E between Alloa and the North Sea. Edinborough is on the S shore. Length: 51mi (82km).

Fort Lamy (N'Djamena), capital of Chad, N central Africa, on the Chari river; it is a transportation center and major regional market for livestock, salt, dates, grains. Pop. 135,502.

Fort Lauderdale, city, SE Florida, 25mi (40km) N of Miami; seat of Broward co. Est. by Maj. William Lauderdale as military post in 1838. Over 270mi (435km) of natural and artificial waterways within the city. Inc. 1911. Pop. (1970) 139,590.

Fort Lee, borough in NE New Jersey, on Hudson River; named for Revolutionary War fort built to defend Hudson River; early center of motion picture industry; W terminus of George Washington Bridge (1931). Chief industry is motion picture film processing. Settled 1700; inc. 1904 when it was separated from Ridgefield township. Pop. (1970) 30,631.

Fort McHenry National Monument and Historic Shrine, historic area containing fort in Baltimore, Maryland; scene of a British attack 1814; Francis Scott Key wrote "The Star-Spangled Banner" while watching the battle from a ship in the harbor. Area: 43acres (17hectares). Est. 1925.

Fort Macleod, town in Alberta, Canada, 100 mi (161km) S of Calgary. The fort began in 1874 as a post of the North West Mounted Police under the command of Col. James F. Macleod. The first incorporated town in Alberta (1892), Fort Macleod attracted eastern settlers and continues to be a center of ranching and grain farming. Pop. 2,725.

Fort Myers, coastal city, SW Florida, seat of Lee co. Settled 1835 as Fort Harvie in Seminole War; used as Union base in Civil War; site of Thomas Edison's winter estate. Inc. 1905. Pop. (1970) 27,351.

Fort Peck Dam, dam on Missouri River, NE Montana; largest earth-filled dam in the world. Built by US Bureau of Reclamation (1933–40) as a flood control and navigation improvement project, it is now used as a source of hydroelectric power and irrigation water. Lake formed by dam (Fort Peck Reservoir) is 189mi (304km) long. Dam is 250ft (76m) high and 21,026ft (6,412m) long.

Fort Pierce, residential city, E Florida, seat of St Lucie co. Settled 1838 as fort in Seminole War. Used for amphibious training base in World War II. Inc. 1901. Pop. (1970) 29,721.

Fort Pulaski National Monument, national monument containing brick fortification on Cockspur Island, SE Georgia, at the mouth of the Savannah River; built 1829–47 by the United States; Confederate troops seized it Jan. 1861; Union troops retook it April 1862. Area: 5,517acres (2,234hectares). Est. 1924.

Fort Smith, city, W Arkansas, on Oklahoma border; seat of Sebastian co. Industries: sheet metal, auto bodies, optical equipment, glass. Settled 1817; inc. 1842. Pop. (1970) 62,802.

Fort Sumter, in Charleston Harbor, S.C. In April 1861, the Civil War began here when Confederate cannon fired on the Union garrison commanded by Maj. Robert Anderson. Although 4,000 shells were fired, no one on either side was killed. After two days, Anderson surrendered to Confederate Gen. P.G.T. Beauregard. △1276.

Fortune Theater, London playhouse opened in 1600. Managed by Edward Alleyn and Philip Henslowe. Thomas Dekker, George Chapman, and Thomas Heywood all wrote plays for the Fortune in competition with Shakespeare and the Globe Theater. It was demolished in 1661.

Fort Wayne, city in NE Indiana, at confluence of St Joseph and St Marys rivers; seat of Allen co; 2nd-largest city in Indiana. French built trading post here *c.* 1680; it was captured by British during French and Indian War and held by Indians (1763) during Pontiac's Rebellion; the Miami Indians were subdued by Anthony Wayne (1794). Development was spurred by Wabash and Erie canals, and railroad in the mid-1800s. City contains burial place of John Chapman (Johnny Appleseed); site of Concordia Senior College (1839), St Francis College (1890), Indiana Institute of Technology (1930). Industries: heavy trucks, copper wire, stainless steel, mining machinery, pumps, tanks. Inc. 1840. Pop. (1970) 178,021.

Fort William. *See* Thunder Bay.

Fort Worth, city in N central Texas, 30mi (48km) W of Dallas; seat of Tarrant co. Developed mid-19th century by US cavalry as a fortress for westward-bound settlers, by 1870 the city was supply center for cattlemen on the Chisholm Trail. In early 20th century, Fort Worth was packinghouse and oil refining center; since WWII, industrial development has increased rapidly; site of Texas Christian University (1873), Texas Wesleyan College (1890), Amon Carter Museum of Western Art, annual Southwestern Exposition and Fat Stock show, Carswell Air Force Base. Industries: aviation, automobiles, food processing, brewing, machinery. Settled 1843; inc. 1873. Pop. (1970) 393,476.

Forty-niners, name given to California gold miners. After gold was discovered at Sutter's Mill in 1848, fortune hunters were attracted to California. So many came in 1849 that the emigrants were called forty-niners.

Forum, Roman, chief market and public gathering place of ancient Rome from the 6th century BC, when the swampy area it occupies was drained. Set in a valley from the Capitoline hill along the Quirinal, Oppian, and Palatine hills, it held many civic buildings including basilicas and temples, the curia (senate), treasury, rostra (speaker's platform), and the arches of Septimius Severus and Titus. The emperors built additional forums when it became inadequate for their needs. △1020.

Fosdick, Harry Emerson (1878–1969), US clergyman, b. Buffalo. Ordained a Baptist minister in 1903, he was a professor of practical theology at Union Theological Seminary, New York City (1915–46). Between 1930–46 he was pastor of the interdenominational Riverside Church in New York City. He spoke out critically against the fundamentalist resurgence in the 1920s.

Fossa, catlike carnivorous animal of the civet family native to Madagascar. They have short legs and red-brown fur. Nocturnal forest-dwellers, they eat small wild animals and are thought to be predators of farm animals. Length: body—28in (71cm); tail—28in (71cm). Family Viverridae; species *Cryptoprocta ferox.*

Fossil, any direct evidence of the existence of an organism more than 10,000 years old. Fossils mostly consist of original structures, such as bones or shells, or wood, often altered through mineralization or preserved as molds and casts. Imprints such as tracks and footprints are also fossils. Leaves are often preserved as a carbonized film outlining their form. Occasionally organisms are totally preserved in frozen soil (mammoths), peat bogs and asphalts lakes (woolly rhinoceroses), or trapped in hardened resin (insects in amber). Fossil excrement, called caprolites, frequently contains undigested and recognizable hard parts. Very few animals and plants that die become fossilized. Since fossils reveal evolutionary changes through time, they are essential clues for geologic dating. *See also* Geologic Time; Index Fossil. △270–276, 560–564.

Fossil, Index. *See* Index Fossil.

Fossil Fuels. △282–86.

Foster, Abigail Kelley (Abby) (1810–87), US reformer, b. Pelham, Mass. While a schoolmistress, she was inspired by the writings of William Lloyd Garrison, the abolitionist and, together with her husband Stephen Symonds Foster, she joined the anti-slavery cause. Her appointment to the executive committee of the American Anti-Slavery Society split the group, however, with many objecting to having a woman on the committee. After 1850, she turned her attention to women's rights.

Foster, Stephen C(ollins) (1826–64), US composer of songs, b. Lawrenceville, Pa. He gained knowledge of black spirituals by writing for ministrel shows. Though his songs were very popular, he had little business sense and died in poverty. Many of his songs are now American classics. They include *Oh! Susanna* (1848), *Camptown Races* (1850), *Old Folks at Home* (1851), *My Old Kentucky Home* (1853), *Jeanie with the Light Brown Hair* (1854), and *Old Black Joe* (1860).

Foster, Stephen Symonds (1809–81), US abolitionist, b. Canterbury, N.H. He and his wife, Abigail Kelley, denounced both slavery and organized religion, feeling it lacked reformist zeal. He wrote *The Brotherhood of Thieves* (1843), an attack on the clergy.

Foster, William Zebulon (1881–1961), US labor and political figure, b. Taunton, Mass. Early in his career he was affiliated with the Socialist party, the Industrial Workers of the World, and the American Federation of Labor. He led the four-month steel strike in 1919. In 1920 he joined the Communist party and was its presidential candidate in 1924, 1928, and 1932. He became national party chairman (1945), a post he held until his death. In 1948 he was accused of advocating the overthrow of the US government. Ill health prevented his coming to trial.

Foucault, Jean Bernard Léon (1819–68), French physician and physicist. In addition to proving that the Earth spins on its axis, he worked on a method to measure the absolute velocity of light, and by 1850 he showed that it is slower in water than in air. Also credited with pointing out the occurrence of eddy currents (Foucault currents) and devising an improved reflecting telescope mirror.

Fouché, Joseph, Duc d'Otrante (1763–1820), French master of political intrigue who retained power as minister of police (1799–1802, 1804–10; 1815) throughout the turbulent political times of Napoleon and the Revolution. Girondist and then Jacobin, he was an anti-Christian and proponent of regicide in the early 1790s, later changing in preparation for Napoleon, in whose governments he managed to secure a place of prominence. Exiled (1816), he died a very rich man.

Foundation, in architecture. △1582.

Foundry, a workshop in which metals are processed by melting and casting in molds. Modern foundries are highly automated both in mixing of the sand and clay used for molds and in the molding process itself. Pattern-making is a skilled operation. Sand or clay is packed over the pattern, which is then removed, forming a cavity in which the casting is made. The mold is made in halves, each enclosed in its own mold box. The halves are joined with pins and bushings before pouring. *See also* Mold, Metal. △1584.

Fountain Valley, city in S California, 28mi (45km) SE of Los Angeles; site of marine helicopter facility. Industries: mobile homes, aerospace, electronic parts. Inc. 1957. Pop. (1970) 31,886.

Fouquet (Foucquet), Jean (*c.*1420–c.1480), French painter. The most prominent French painter of the 15th century, he was court painter to Charles VII and Louis XI and protégé of Etienne Chevalier, for whom he illuminated a book of hours. Influenced by a trip to Italy and by the rich sculpture of French churches, he painted portraits and historical and religious scenes. △1146.

Fouquet, Nicolas (1615–80), member of the French

E. M. Forster

Forsythia

Fossil

Stephen Foster

moneyed aristocracy, held a number of financial offices, finally becoming minister of finance in 1653 under Louis XIV, with the aid of the diplomat Mazarin. Constant warfare and corruption made a chaos of government financial records, and when Mazarin died Louis XIV had Fouquet arrested in 1661 for embezzlement. He was banished after a four-year, illegal trial. The king changed his sentence to life imprisonment.

Fouquier-Tinville, Antoine Quentin (1746–1795), ruthless French Revolutionary, served as prosecutor for the Revolutionary Tribunal which accounted for the execution by guillotine of thousands during the Reign of Terror. After Robespierre's loss of power, Fouquier-Tinville was himself guillotined.

Four Corners Monument, monument commemorating the only point in United States common to four state boundaries: Colorado, New Mexico, Arizona, and Utah.

Four Freedoms, expression of post-World War II goals that was part of Pres. Franklin D. Roosevelt's State of the Union Address (January 1941). They were freedom of speech and expression; freedom of worship; freedom from want; and freedom from fear. Some of these sentiments were echoed in the Atlantic Charter (1941). △816.

Four Horsemen of the Apocalypse, allegorical figures described in the Biblical Book of Revelations (6:1–8) as one of the visions appearing when seals of the book are opened. The riders are: (1) on a white horse, rider with a bow and crown of conquest; (2) on a red horse, a rider with power and a sword to take peace from the earth; (3) on a black horse, a rider with a pair of balances; and (4) on a pale horse, Death as the rider. The four are given the power to kill with the sword, with hunger, with death, and with the beasts of the earth.

Fourier, François Marie Charles (1772–1837), French utopian socialist. He supported cooperativism and set forth detailed plans for the organization of the communities (called phalanxes). Unlike most socialist writers, Fourier suggested that capital for the enterprise come from the capitalist, and he provided for payment to capital in his division of output. *See also* Utopian Socialism.

Fourier Series, series of sine and cosine functions used to represent other periodic functions. Any single-valued periodic function can be analyzed as a sum of simple harmonic components, thus:

$$f(x)=\frac{a_0}{2}+(a_1 \cos x + b_1 \sin x)+ (a_2 \cos 2x + b_2 \sin 2x) + \dots .$$

In this series the *n*th coefficients a_n and b_n are given by

$$a_n=\frac{1}{\pi}\int_{-n}^{n} f(x) \cos nx\, dx.$$

$$b_n=\frac{1}{\pi}\int_{-n}^{n} f(x) \cos nx\, dx.$$

Fourier analysis, named after the French physicist Jean Baptiste Fourier, is an invaluable tool in handling complex periodically changing quantities in many branches of science.

Four-o'clock, bushy, tuberous plant with flowers that open in the late afternoon. Perennial in the tropics, it is treated as an annual in cold climates. The trumpet-shaped flowers are pink, red, lavender, yellow, or white, often on the same plant. Height: 1.5–3ft (46–91cm). Species include common *Mirabilis jalapa.* Family Nyctaginaceae. *See also* Bougainville.

Four-Party Politics, or **Burns' Thesis,** US system of national politics as described by historian James MacGregor Burns. Burns characterized the two major parties as having "congressional and presidential structures." A popular congressman, secure in his own district, will align with his party's policies; in a contested district, he will identify with the presidential party.

Fourteen Points (1918), Pres. Woodrow Wilson's unsuccessful plan to achieve a liberal peace after World War I. It called for an end to secret agreements; navigational and economic freedom; reduction of armaments; impartial adjustment of colonial claims; evacuation of Russian, Belgian, and French territories; readjustment of Italian frontiers; autonomy for the nationalities in Austria-Hungary; restoration of occupied Romanian, Serbian, Montenegran territories; autonomy for nations under Turkish rule; Polish independence; and the formation of an association of nations. Although not adopted as a group at the Versailles peace treaty, several points were included in the treaty, and Wilson's dream of a League of Nations was realized. *See also* League of Nations; Versailles, Treaty of. △1306.

Fourth Dimension, time considered as an additional dimension, together with the three dimensions of space, in a full description of the motion of a particle. *See also* Relativity Theory. △1524.

Fovea. *See* Blind Spot; Optic Nerve.

Fowl, various domestic or game birds raised or hunted for food. *See* Game Bird; Poultry.

Fowler, Henry Watson (1858–1933), English lexicographer. He is known for *A Dictionary of Modern English Usage* (1926; rev. ed. 1965 by Sir Ernest Gowers) and other writings on English usage and style.

Fox, George (1624–91), English religious leader, founder of the Society of Friends (Quakers). He embarked upon his evangelical calling in 1646 in response to an "inner light." He was imprisoned eight times between 1649–75. In 1671–72 he traveled to America to visit Quaker colonists there. His *Journal,* amended by William Penn, appeared in 1694.

Fox, William (1879–1952), US film tycoon, b. Hungary. Owner of a vast cinema chain, he founded the Fox Film Company in 1915 (later 20th-Century Fox) to produce and distribute films. Fox experimented with sound films but later lost his company and declared bankruptcy.

Fox, small, wild animal native to all continents except Australia and Antarctica. Foxes are generally sharp-muzzled, big-eared, and bushy-tailed. The typical North American red fox *(Vulpes fulva)* is about the size of a small dog. It is usually yellowish-red or reddish-brown above and white or grayish below. Other color phases may occur in the same litter. Omnivorous, its diet includes small mammals, insects, eggs, fruit, and grass. The Old World red fox *(Vulpes vulpes)* is similar but slightly larger. Height: 16in (41cm) at shoulder; length: 23in (58cm) without tail. Family Canidae; genera *Vulpes, Urocyon. See also* Canidae. △594, 606.

Foxe, John (1516–87), English Anglican clergyman and historian. He was a Protestant who went into exile to avoid Mary I's persecution, returning in Elizabeth I's reign to complete his monumental *Actes and Monuments of these latter and perilous Dayes,* commonly called *Foxe's Book of Martyrs* (1563). A graphic description of religious persecutions from John Wycliffe to Thomas Cranmer, the book aroused widespread bitter hostility in England to Roman Catholicism, yet Foxe was a tolerant man and opposed the execution of Jesuits in 1581.

Foxglove, any of a genus *(Digitalis)* of hardy Eurasian biennial and perennial plants with long, spiky clusters of two-lipped, tubular flowers. The common biennial foxglove *(D. purpurea),* source of the heart-stimulant digitalis, is widely grown for its showy white, rose, purple, or blue flowers. Family Scrophulariaceae.

Fox Indians, more accurately known as Mesquakie, from *Meshwakuhug,* "the Red Earth People"; the name comes from a French error in translation. An Algonquian-speaking tribe of North American Indians inhabiting Wisconsin. Always warlike, they allied themselves with the Sauk. Today most of the approximately 550 Mesquakie live in and around Tama, Iowa.

Fox River, river in SE central Wisconsin; rises in Columbia co, flows S near Wisconsin River (the two rivers are connected by a canal here); turns NE into Lake Winnebago, and drains from N end of lake, continuing to its mouth at the head of Green Bay; forms waterway between Wisconsin River and Lake Michigan. Length: approx. 175mi (282km).

Fox Terrier, a popular hunting dog (terrier group) recognized in two varieties since the 1880s—the smooth and the wire. The fox terrier has a narrow, tapered head; V-shaped, drooping ears; a short, straight-backed body; straight legs; and a high-set tail carried up. The predominately white coat is smooth, flat, and hard in the smooth variety and broken, hard, and wiry in the wire. Average size: 15.5in (39.5cm) high at shoulder; 15–19lb (7–8.5kg). *See also* Terrier.

FPC. *See* Federal Power commission.

Fraction, quotient of the form a/b; *a* is called the numerator and *b* the denominator. If *a* and *b* are whole numbers the quotient is a simple fraction. *See also* Fraction, Algebraic; Fraction, Complex. △1446.

Fraction, Algebraic, fraction in which the denominator or both numerator and denominator are algebraic expressions. For example, $\frac{x}{(x^2+2)}$ is an algebraic fraction.

Fraction, Complex, fraction in which both numerator and denominator are themselves fractions.

Fractional Distillation. *See* Distillation.

Fracture, break in a bone. The amount of stress that a bone can sustain without fracture apparently depends on both the size and the age of the bone. A compound fracture is one in which the bone has broken through the skin. △720, 758.

Fragonard, Jean Honoré (1732–1806), French painter. A student of Jean Chardin and François Boucher, he also studied the Italians and the northern landscape painters of the 17th century. Using many different styles during his career, he is best known for the lighthearted spontanaity of his amorous scenes, rustic landscapes, and decorative panels.

Fra Mauro. △52.

Frambesia. *See* Yaws.

Frame of Government, William Penn's outline of laws for colonial government in his proprietorship of Pennsylvania. His third frame of government, the Charter of Liberties (1701), was the basis of Pennsylvania's constitution until 1776. *See also* Charter of Liberties.

Frame of Reference, mathematical coordinate system for describing events in space and time with respect to a given observer. In the theory of relativity, this frame of reference is four-dimensional, and the description of events in other frames of reference depends on the relative speeds of those frames with respect to the frame of reference of the observer.

Framingham, town in E Massachusetts, on Sudbury River between Worcester and Boston; site of Framingham State College (1839). Industries: chemicals, automobiles, footwear. Settled 1650; inc. 1700. Pop. (1970) 64,048.

France, Anatole (1844–1924), pseud. of Jacques Anatole François Thibault, French author. After writing poems and short stories he achieved recognition with the novels *The Crime of Sylvester Bonnard* (1881) and *Thais* (1890). He supported Zola in the Dreyfus affair, and his writing became increasingly political as in the novels *Contemporary History* (1896–1901) and *Penguin Island* (1908). He was elected to the French Academy (1896) and awarded the Nobel Prize for literature (1921).

France, the largest nation in W Europe. For centuries, France has been at the center of Western culture, both as a major political power and as a leader in the arts and sciences. Its capital, Paris, is one of the world's most beautiful and finest cities.

Land and Economy. The geography of France may be divided into three principal regions; Alpine mountains, ancient uplands, and low-lying plains. The Pyrenees (SW) and the Alps (SE) are the tallest and most recent mountains geologically. The best farmlands are in the Paris Basin, which extends from the English Channel to the plateau region of the Massif Central, and in the Aquitane Basin in W and SW France. The major river systems are the Seine, Rhône, Loire, and Garonne. About three-fifths of the land area of the country is under cultivation. France is one of the world's leading producers of wheat, dairy products, and wine. French industry ranks fifth in the world. Iron and steel, aircraft, motor vehicles, chemicals, textiles, and foodstuffs are among France's most valuable manufactured products. The country's major import is oil.

People. France has been inhabited since prehistoric times. The chief ethnic strains are Celtic (Gauls), Germanic, and Latin. The French language is descended from the Latin tongue brought to Gaul by the conquering Romans. French is spoken in all parts of France and often serves internationally as a language of diplomacy. The majority of modern French people are urban dwellers. In religion, most are Roman Catholics. No country can boast greater achievements in the fine arts than those of the French. As in many countries, the traditional extended family is giving place to the nuclear family.

Government. The constitution of the Fifth French Republic was approved by the French people in 1958. This constitution, under the sponsorship of Charles de Gaulle, shifted much power from parliament to the president of the republic. The president is elected to a seven-year term, has the right to dissolve parliament and call new elections, and may present bills to popular referendum. Parliament consists of two houses, the National Assembly and Senate. France has many political parties, including Socialists, Gaullists, Radicals, Communists, and Independent Republicans.

History. The area of France was ruled by the Romans from 51 BC until the 5th century. The Merovingian dynasty established the Franks, and in the late 8th century Charlemagne came to power, firmly entrenching the Carolingian dynasty. Royal authority subsequently weakened and was not revived until the Capetians came to the throne in the late 10th century. During the Middle Ages the monarchs were able to increase their authority gradually at the expense of the nobility and to extend their dominions over what is now modern France. Struggles with England, as in the Hundred Years War, and the Holy Roman Empire were frequent.

France emerged from the Middle Ages as the leading nation-state of Europe. The boundaries of France have changed very little since the reign of Francis I (r.1515–47). French power and influence expanded under Cardinal Richelieu, minister to Louis XIII (r.1610–43). The reign of Louis XIV was the golden era in the history of the French monarchy. The French Revolution (1789) destroyed the monarchy; the First Republic was est. in 1792. Napoleon was crowned emperor in 1804, and France dominated European politics in the Napoleonic era. After Napoleon's defeat (1815), a restoration of the monarchy was followed by the Second Republic (1848–52) and then the Second Empire (1852–70). During the 19th century France contended with Great Britain in establishing a colonial empire, while contending with an awakening Germany for power on the continent. Germany's victory in the Franco-Prussian War (1870) was humiliating to France. In 1907 France allied herself with Russia and England in the Triple Entente. Although a victor in World War I, France suffered great human and economic loss. In World War II, France was unprepared for Germany's air and armored attacks. The country fell in June 1940, and political instability marked the post-war years. France was instrumental in forming the European Economic Community. Charles de Gaulle became premier in 1958, establishing the Fifth Republic. The Gaullist party controlled French politics until 1974, when Valéry Giscard d'Estaing, an Independent Republican, was elected president.

Following is a list of the rulers of France. △1096, 1170, 1224–26.

RULERS OF FRANCE

Pepin III (the Short)	751–68
Carloman	768–71
Charlemagne	768–81
Louis I (the Pious)	814–40
Charles II (the Bald)	840–77
Louis II	877–79
Louis III	879–82
Carloman	879–84
Charles the Fat	885–87
Odo (Eudes)	888–98
Charles III (the Simple)	893–923
Robert I	922–23
Rudolf	923–36
Louis IV	936–54
Lothair	954–86
Louis V	986–87
Hugh Capet	987–96
Robert II	996–1031
Henry I	1031–60
Philip I	1060–1108
Louis VI	1108–37
Louis VII	1137–80
Philip II Augustus	1180–1223
Louis VIII	1223–26
Louis IX (St Louis)	1226–70
Philip III	1270–85
Philip IV (the Fair)	1285–1314
Louis X	1314–16
John I	did not rule
Philip V	1316–22
Charles IV	1322–28
Philip VI	1328–50
John II (the Good)	1350–64
Charles V	1364–80
Charles VI	1380–1422
Charles VII	1422–61
Louis XI	1461–83
Charles VIII	1483–98
Louis XII	1498–1515
Francis I	1515–47
Henry II	1547–59
Francis II	1559–60
Charles IX	1560–74
Henry III	1574–89
Henry IV	1589–1610
Louis XIII	1610–43
Louis XIV	1643–1715
Louis XV	1715–74
Louis XVI	1774–92
Louis XVII	did not rule
National Convention	1792–95
Directory	1795–99
Consulate	1799–1804
Napoleon I	1804–14
Napoleon II	did not rule
Louis XVIII	1814–24
Charles X	1824–30
Louis Philippe	1830–48
Louis Napoléon	1848–52
Napoleon III	1852–70
Adolphe Thiers	1871–73
Marshal Patrice de MacMahon	1873–79
Jules Grévy	1879–87
Sadi Carnot	1887–94
Jean Casimir-Périer	1894–95
Félix Faure	1895–99
Émile Loubet	1899–1906
Armand Fallières	1906–13
Raymond Poincaré	1913–20
Paul Deschanel	1920
Alexandre Millerand	1920–24
Gaston Doumergue	1924–31
Paul Doumer	1931–32
Albert Lebrun	1932–40
Marshal Philippe Pétain	1940–44
Charles de Gaulle	1944–46
Félix Gouin	1946
Georges Bidault	1946
Léon Blum	1946
Vincent Auriol	1947–54
René Coty	1954–59
Charles de Gaulle	1959–69
Georges Pompidou	1969–74
Valéry Giscard d'Estaing	1974–

PROFILE

Official name: French Republic
Area: 211,207sq mi (547,026sq km)
Population: 53,100,000
Density: 251per sq mi (97per sq km)
Chief cities: Paris, the capital; Marseilles; Lyon; Toulouse
Government: Democratic
Religion (major): Roman Catholic
Language: French (official)
Monetary unit: Franc
Gross national product: $270,800,000,000
Per capita income: $3,020
Manufacturing (major products): automobiles, aircraft, electronics, steel, chemicals, aluminum, textiles, clothing, perfume
Agriculture (major products): livestock, wheat, potatoes, sugar beets, wines, fruits
Minerals (major): iron, coal, petroleum, bauxite, uranium, gypsum, potash
Trading partners (major): West Germany, Great Britain, United States, Italy

Franche-Comté, historic territory in E France. Peopled by the Celtic Sequani, this land came under the rule of the Romans in 52 BC and was then variously under Burgundian, Frankish, independent, German, Holy Roman, Austrian, Spanish, and French rule in the centuries that followed. Its final assumption into France came about in 1678, and it was broken up into *départements* after the Revolution.

Franchise Operations, business operations based upon an agreement between two parties that one will market the product of the other under specified conditions. They are common in the fast food area, where the company may furnish almost everything except human labor and some of the capital.

Francis (1554–84), duke of Alençon and Anjou, youngest son of Henry II of France and Catherine de Médicis. He opposed his mother, a Catholic extremist, and brother in the Catholic-Huguenot Wars and later led two invasions of the Spanish-controlled Netherlands. Although very homely, he was twice considered for marriage to Queen Elizabeth I.

Francis I (1708–65), Holy Roman emperor (1745–65), duke of Lorraine (1729–35) and Tuscany (1737–65). In 1736 he married the Hapsburg heiress Maria Theresa. Her accession (1740) precipitated the War of the Austrian Succession. In 1745 Francis succeeded Charles VIII as emperor, but the real ruler was his wife. *See also* Austrian Succession, War of the; Maria Theresa of Austria. △1128.

Francis II (1768–1835), Holy Roman emperor (1792–1806), emperor of Austria as Francis I (1804–35). Repeatedly defeated by France, in 1806 he was forced by Napoleon to dissolve the Holy Roman Empire but had already proclaimed himself Austrian emperor. In 1810 his daughter, Marie Louise, married Napoleon, but in 1813 Austria rejoined the anti-

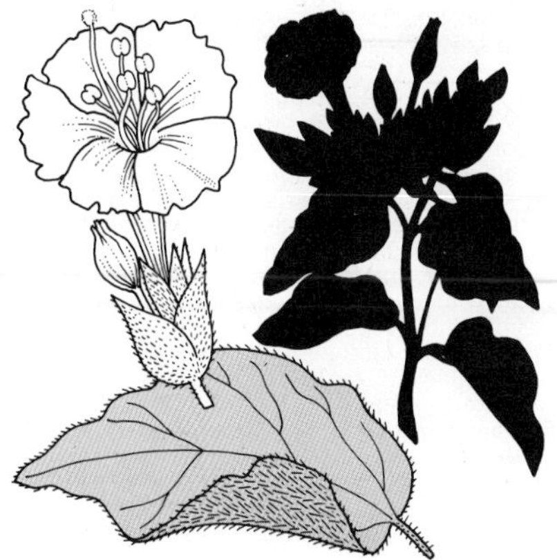
Four-o'clock

Fox terrier

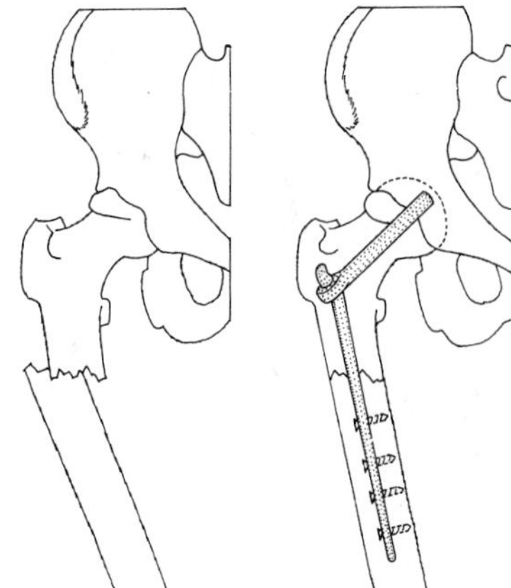
Fracture (left); *surgical repair* (right)

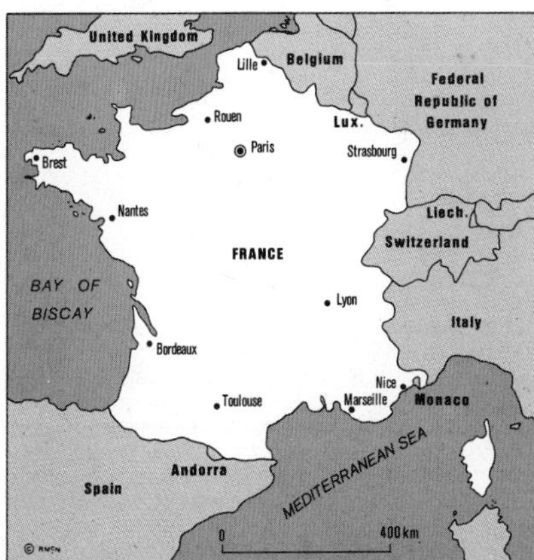
United Kingdom
Belgium
Lille
Federal Republic of Germany
Rouen
Lux.
Paris
Brest
Strasbourg
Nantes
Liech.
Switzerland
FRANCE
BAY OF BISCAY
Lyon
Italy
Bordeaux
Nice
Toulouse
Marseille
Monaco
Andorra
Spain
MEDITERRANEAN SEA
0
400km
France

French coalition. From 1809 Austrian affairs were run by Prince Metternich.

Francis I (1494–1547), king of France (1515–47). A leader of the Renaissance, he was best remembered for his contributions to the humanities, which include establishment of the *Lecteurs royaux* (a teaching group) and support of the arts. He was a man of valor and action unsuited for subtle political complexities. Repression of religious reform, centralization of monarchical power, and foolish financial policies earned the dissatisfaction of his people. Excluding the Marignano expedition to Italy of 1515, his foreign policy met with little success, embroiling him in a long and costly struggle with the Emperor Charles V over the imperial crown. After a severe defeat at Pavia in 1525, Francis was imprisoned and forced to give up Burgundy as a condition of the Treaty of Madrid (1526). An ensuing war with Charles (1527–29) led to the loss of Italy, but campaigns in the 1540s were more successful. He was succeeded by his son, Henry II.

Francis II (1544–60), eldest son of Henry II and Catherine de Médicis, grandson of Francis I. Although king of France for 17 months (1559–60), he seems never to have actually ruled in more than name. Young and poor of health, he was married to Mary Stuart at the age of 14, and his kingdom was controlled by two uncles—Charles, cardinal of Lorraine, and Francis, duke of Guise.

Francis I (1777–1830), king of the Two Sicilies, son of Ferdinand I and Marie Caroline (sister of Marie Antoinette). Early in his career, as regent for his father, he had liberal sympathies towards the Carbonari uprising of 1820 and opposed the reactionary Austrian troop intervention in Naples. However, after his accession to the throne in 1825, he became an extreme reactionary, requesting a greater Austrian presence.

Francis II (1836–94), king of the Two Sicilies (1859–60). The son of Ferdinand II and the last Bourbon king of Naples, he was driven from his throne by Giuseppe Garibaldi and deposed by the plebiscite of October 1861. His dominions were then annexed by Victor Emmanuel II in 1861.

Francis II (1435–88), duke of Brittany, sought independence through rebellion against King Louis XI. He invaded Normandy but made peace in 1468. He took part in another unsuccessful rebellion against Charles VIII. Charles acquired Brittany by marrying Francis' daughter Anne.

Franciscans, the Order of Friars Minor, religious order founded by St Francis of Assisi in 1209. The original Rule of St Francis, reformulated in 1223, stressed not only individual but corporate poverty. There have been many disputes over the question of poverty. The Capuchin order resulted from a 16th-century reform. △1086.

Francis de Sales, Saint (1567–1622), French religious leader, a Roman Catholic saint. A renowned preacher, he was a leader of the Counter-Reformation in France. He was instrumental in the conversion of Chablais from Calvinism. In 1602 he was appointed bishop (in exile) of Geneva. With Jeanne de Chantal he founded the Visitation Nuns. His *Introduction to the Devout Life* (1609) teaches the perfection of spiritual life. The patron of writers, his feast day is January 29.

Francis Ferdinand (1863–1914), archduke of Austria, heir apparent and nephew of Francis Joseph, emperor of Austria. He married Countess Sophie Chotek (1900) but publicly renounced all claims to the throne for their children because she was only from a minor Czech noble family. He and his wife were assassinated by the Serbian nationalist Gavrilo Princip in Sarajevo, Bosnia, on July 28, 1914. The ensuing Austrian ultimatum to Serbia precipitated World War I. △1304.

Francis Joseph (1830–1916), emperor of Austria (1848–1916), king of Hungary (1867–1916). He succeeded his uncle Ferdinand who abdicated amidst the turmoil of the revolution of 1848. He quickly brought the revolution under control, defeating the Hungarians under Kossuth and the Italians under Victor Emmanuel II of Sardinia, both in 1849. But in the Italian War of 1859 he lost Lombardy to Sardinia and in the Austro-Prussian War (1866) he lost Venetia to Italy and, more importantly, lost Austria's prestige among the German states. In 1867 he was forced to grant Hungary coequal status with Austria in the Dual Monarchy. His long reign was beset by nationalist strife, court intrigue, and personal tragedy. His brother Maximilian, Emperor of Mexico, was executed by Mexican nationalists (1867); his son, Crown Prince Rudolf, committed suicide (1889); his wife, Empress Elizabeth, was assassinated (1898) as was his nephew, the heir apparent Archduke Francis Ferdinand (1914). Francis Joseph died in the midst of World War I, two years before the complete collapse of his empire. △1232.

Francis of Assisi (1182?–1226), founder of the Franciscans, Roman Catholic saint, b. Giovanni de Bernardone. In 1205 he renounced his worldly life for one of poverty and prayer. In 1209 he received permission from Pope Innocent III to begin a monastic order. The Franciscans were vowed to humility, poverty, and devotion to aiding mankind. In 1212 he established an order for women, the Poor Clares, and in 1221, a lay fraternity. He traveled to France, Spain, and to the Holy Land in 1219–20. In 1221 he gave up leadership of his order to retire to his birthplace, Assisi, Italy. In 1224 he received the stigmata, the appearance of the crucifixion wounds on his own body. His feast day is October 4. △1086.

Francis Xavier, Saint. *See* Xavier, Saint Francis.

Francium, radioactive metallic element (symbol Fr), discovered (1839) by Marguerite Perey. It occurs naturally in uranium ores and is a decay product of actinium. Properties: at. no. 87; most stable isotope Fr^{223} (half-life 22 min). *See also* Alkali Elements.

Franck, César (1822–90), French Romantic composer, b. Belgium. His organ music is considered among the best after J.S. Bach. He also composed chamber music, *Symphonic Variations* for piano and orchestra (1885), and the popular *Symphony in D Minor* (1888). △1246.

Franck, James (1882–1964), US physicist, b. Germany. Franck studied and taught at German universities. With Gustav Hertz he experimented with electron bombardment of gases, providing support for Niels Bohr's theory of atomic structure and information for Max Planck's quantum theory. He and Hertz shared the 1925 Nobel Prize for physics. In 1935 he went to the United States, became a citizen and ultimately worked on the development of the atomic bomb.

Franco, Francisco (1892–1975), Spanish general and caudillo (dictator) of Spain (1939–75). A professional soldier, he was from early in his career associated with right-wing politics. He joined the 1936 military uprising that set off the Spanish Civil War and quickly became the Nationalist leader. He assumed leadership of the Falange party, and by 1939, with the aid of Nazi Germany and Fascist Italy, he successfully brought the war to an end and became Spain's dictator. Despite his association with Germany and Italy, he kept Spain neutral in World War II.

After World War II, Franco presided over Spain's impressive economic development and kept firm control over its politics. He declared Spain a monarchy in 1947 with himself as regent. In 1969 he designated Juan Carlos, grandson of the last king of Spain, as heir to the throne, and Juan Carlos became king upon Franco's death. *See also* Civil War, Spanish; Falange. △1326.

Franconia, historic region of Germany around the Main River. A duchy of the East Frankish kingdom, it was later divided among several ecclesiastical princes, of whom the bishop of Würzburg was the most powerful. Bavaria still has districts of Upper, Middle, and Lower Franconia.

Franco-Prussian War, also called the **Franco-German War,** 10-month conflict in 1870–71 between French emperor Napoleon III and the combined forces of Germany. Bismarck, wishing to bring the south German states into a national union, encouraged the growing rift between France and Prussia in the late 1860s. When the throne of Spain was offered to a prince from the ruling house of Prussia, the French protested vigorously, demanding assurance from King William I of Prussia that the offer would never be accepted. He refused to give it, and Bismarck inflamed the French to declare war by publishing the Ems Dispatch. As Bismarck had hoped the south German states, seeing France as the aggressor, joined the North German Confederation. They were led by General von Moltke, who after a successful series of battles began a siege of Paris that ended three months later with the city's collapse. This French disaster led to the unification of Prussia and southern Germany, their annexation of Alsace-Lorraine, dissolution of French controls on Russian agression, the indirect unification of Italy, the formation of the Paris Commune and a new French republican government, and a European tension that precipitated two world wars. *See also* Ems Dispatch. △1250, 1298.

Frangipani, shrubs and small trees native to Central America and the West Indies and now grown in other warm regions. They have fragrant white, yellow, pink, or red flowers and a milky sap. Family Apocynaceae; genus *Plumeria.*

Frank, Jacob (*c.*1726–1791), Polish mystic and leader of Frankite movement. Opposed to rabbinical Judaism and the Talmud, Frank believed himself to be the Messiah and was excommunicated by the rabbis in 1756. He then joined the Roman Catholic church in 1759, but was imprisoned as a heretic (1766–72). Frank conducted mystical ceremonies that sought redemption in impurity, and his followers regarded him as "Lord of Holiness." After his death, his daughter Eve assumed the role of godhead incarnate in the movement as the "Holy Mistress." Eventually the sect died out.

Frankenstein (1818), novel by Mary Wollstonecraft Shelley that deals with a monster created from inanimate matter. Unloved because of its revolting appearance, the monster takes revenge on its creator, Dr. Frankenstein. The 1931 film version, starring Boris Karloff and directed by James Whale, was a great success and spawned countless sequels and imitations.

Frankfort, Henri (1897–1954), US archeologist, b. Netherlands. He made important comparative studies of ancient Egypt and Mesopotamia. He directed expeditions in Egypt (1925–29) at Abydos, Tell el-Amarna, and Amat (1925–29) and in Iraq (1929–37) at Tell Asmar and Khorsabad. He was director of the Oriental Institute of the University of Chicago (1932–49) and of the Warburg Institute, University of London (1949–54). His books include *Ancient Egyptian Religion* (1948), *The Birth of Civilization in the Near East* (1951), and *Art and Architecture of the Ancient Orient* (1954, rev. ed. 1958).

Frankfort, capital city of Kentucky, on Kentucky River, 52mi (84km) E of Louisville; seat of Franklin co.; site of Kentucky State College (1886), "Liberty Hall" (1796) reportedly designed by Thomas Jefferson, the Old Capitol (1827–30), Frankfort Cemetery where Daniel and Rebecca Boone are buried. Industries: tobacco, whiskey-distilling, shoes, furniture. Settled 1779; named capital 1792. Pop. (1970) 21,902.

Frankfurt, Treaty of. △1248.

Frankfurter, Felix (1882–1965), US jurist and educator, b. Austria. An assistant US attorney (1906–11) and law officer in the War Department (1911–14), he helped found the American Civil Liberties Union (1920). He was a New Deal "brain trust" advisor to Pres. Franklin Roosevelt, who appointed him an associate justice of the US Supreme Court (1939–62). One of the most scholarly justices, he advocated judicial restraint and pursued a middle-of-the-road course on the area of civil liberties.

Frankfurt-on-Main (Frankfurt-am-Main), city and port in central West Germany, on the Main River, 17mi (27km) N of Darmstadt. In 8th century it became one of Charlemagne's royal residences; made a free imperial city 1372; annexed by Prussia 1871; site of 13th–15th-century Gothic church of St Bartholomew, house in which Goethe was born (1749), Städel Art Museum (1816), and university (1914). Industries: chemicals, clothing, machinery, electrical equipment. Founded 1st century AD by Romans. Pop. 661,816.

Frankfurt-on-Oder, city in E Germany, on Oder River, 50mi (81km) ESE of Berlin; capital of Frankfurt district. During Middle Ages city was river crossing on trade route from Germany to Poland. City was under siege during Thirty Years' War (1631), Seven Years' War (1759), Napoleonic Wars (1806–08, 1812–13), and in WWII when 70% of city was destroyed before Soviet capture March 18, 1945. Industries: machinery, textiles, shoes, soap. Chartered 1253. Pop. 62,011.

Frankfurt School. △1360.

Frankincense, or olibanum, gum resin extracted from bark of various trees *(Boswellia)* found in Africa and Asia. It is burned as incense and the spicy oil, extracted from the resin, is used in perfumes.

Franking Privilege, right to send official mail without charge. This right is extended to members of the US Congress, the president and vice president, cabinet officials, and others.

Franklin, Benjamin (1706–90), US inventor, diplomat, and statesman, b. Boston. As a young man, he worked in Philadelphia as a printer, where he published the witty *Poor Richard's Almanac* (1732–57). He made a number of inventions, such as the Franklin stove, and experimented with electricity. He also initiated a great many civil improvements in Philadelphia, including a library, a fire company, and a university. He represented Philadelphia at the Albany Congress (1754), where he proposed that the colonies unite under an elected council and a president with veto power. The idea was rejected at that time but was to come to fruition later on when the Constitution was written. He spent 16 years in England prior to the American Revolution (1757–62, 1766–75), attempting to reconcile the differences between Britain and the colonies. Returning to the colonies he was a delegate to the Second Continental Congress. There he helped draft and signed the Declaration of Independence and organized a postal system, serving as postmaster general (1775–76). Sent to France (1776–85), he helped bring that country into the Revolution on the colonists' side. He was one of the signers of the peace treaty in Paris (1783) that ended the Revolution. Franklin also attended the Constitutional Convention (1787).

Franklin, (Sir) John (1786–1847), English rear admiral and arctic explorer. He served England in the Battle of Copenhagen (1801) and the Battle of Trafalgar (1805). He later commanded two explorations of the North American coast (1819–22 and 1825–27), for which he was knighted. In 1845 he led an ill-fated arctic exploration in search of a northwest passage. When no word was heard from him, a series of expeditions was organized to learn his fate. Finally, in 1859, a search party sent by his wife found that he and all of his crew had been lost.

Franklin, John Hope (1915–), US historian and educator, b. Rentiesville, Okla. He taught at Brooklyn College and the University of Chicago. His books include *From Slavery to Freedom, A History of American Negroes* (1947), *Emancipation Proclamation* (1963), and *Color and Race* (1968).

Franklin, district and northernmost region in Canada; encompasses islands N of Canadian mainland (almost coextensive with Arctic Archipelago), and Boothia and Melville peninsulas; with districts of Mackenzie and Kewatin, it comprises Canada's Northwest Territories; inhabited by Eskimos; oil reserves. Founded 1895; boundaries est. 1920. Area: 549,253sq mi (1,422,565sq km).

Franks, Germanic people who settled along the Rhine in the 3rd century AD. Under Clovis (reigned 481–511) they overthrew Roman rule in Gaul and established the Merovingian empire. The empire was later divided into the kingdoms of Austrasia, Neustria, and Burgundy, but it was reunited by the Carolingian dynasty, notably Charlemagne. The partition of Charlemagne's empire produced the East and West Frankish kingdoms, which became respectively Germany and France. *See also* Austrasia; Burgundy; Carolingians; Merovingians; Neustria. △1054, 1066.

Franz Josef. *See* Francis Joseph.

Franz Josef Land (Zeml'a Franca-Iosifa), archipelago in the Arctic Ocean; part of Archangel'sk Oblast, USSR; a group of approx. 85 islands including Aleksandra Land, George Land, Wilczek Land, Graham Bell Island, Hooker Island, and Rudolf Island; generally ice-covered; most northerly land in E hemisphere; site of meteorological station (est. 1929 by USSR). Discovered 1873 by Australian expedition under Karl Weyprecht and Julius Von Payer; claimed 1926 as a Russian national territory. Area: 8,000sq mi (20,720sq km).

Frascati, town in central Italy, 12mi (19km) SE of Rome; site of villa of Cicero; nearby are ruins of ancient Tusculum; birthplace of Cato the Elder; summer resort area. Industries: wine, pasta, tourism. Pop. 18,023.

Frasch Process, named after German-born chemist Herman Frasch, a method for mining sulfur from the earth by pumping superheated water to the sulfur deposits, melting the mineral, and forcing it to the surface. The process was first put to practical use in Louisiana and by 1902 had made the United States independent of imported sulfur.

Fraser, Peter (1884–1950), prime minister of New Zealand (1940–49), b. Scotland. He emigrated to New Zealand in 1910. He helped organize the Social Democratic party (1913) and its successor, the Labour party (1916). He was elected to parliament in 1918, and he became minister of education, health, marine, and police in the Labour government in 1935. As prime minister, he led New Zealand during World War II. Afterward, he was one of the architects of the UN.

Fraser, Simon (1776–1862), Canadian explorer and fur trader. Fraser moved to Canada from the United States in 1784 and joined the Northwest Company in 1792. He extended their trade routes west to British Columbia (1805–08) and founded a string of trading posts. His exploration of the Fraser River and Red River did not prevent personal bankruptcy.

Fraser, river in S British Columbia, Canada; rises in the Rocky Mts and flows NW then S around the Cariboo Mts and into the Strait of Georgia. Discovered 1793 by Alexander Mackenzie and explored 1808 by Simon Fraser. Length: 850mi (1,369km).

Fraunhofer, Joseph von (1787–1826), German physicist and optical instrument maker. His studies of the dark lines (Fraunhofer lines) in the solar spectrum were instrumental in establishing spectroscopy. Although he mapped the positions of these lines, he was unable to explain them. He also invented a diffraction grating device. *See also* Diffraction. △1480.

Frazer, (Sir) James George (1854–1941), Scottish anthropologist, folklorist, and classical scholar. He gained recognition with the publication of *The Golden Bough: a Study in Magic and Religion* (1890) which held that the history of thought is a logical progression from the magical to the religious to the scientific. Although much of his theory has been discredited, he was influential in breaking ground in research of primitive customs. Other works include *Folk-Lore in the Old Testament* (1918).

Frazier, Joe (1944–), US boxer, b. Beaumont, S.C. An Olympic heavyweight champion (1964), he won a portion of the world's heavyweight title when he beat Buster Mathis (1968) in New York City and was undisputed champion after he beat Jimmy Ellis (1970) in Oakland, Calif. He lost the title to George Foreman (1973) in Kingston, Jamaica. His bouts with Muhammad Ali were his most notable.

Frazier, Walt ("Clyde") (1945–), US basketball player, b. Atlanta. Known as an outstanding defensive guard, he joined the New York Knicks in the National Basketball Association in 1967. He became the Knicks all-time scoring leader.

Fredegund (died 597), Frankish queen. She married Chilperic I of Neustria after inducing him to murder his wife, Galeswintha. War ensued with Austrasia, whose king Sigebert I, Chilperic's brother, was married to Galeswintha's sister, Brunhilde. After Chilperic's murder (584), she was regent for her son Clotaire II.

Frederick I (*c.* 1123–90), Holy Roman emperor (1152–90) and German king (1152–90), called Frederick Barbarossa. A Hohenstaufen, he succeeded his uncle, Conrad III. He planned to absorb Lombardy into a personal kingdom, but the Italian cities, encouraged by Pope Alexander III, formed the Lombard League against him. He set up an antipope, but after his defeat at Legnano (1176) he was reconciled with Alexander and made peace (1183) with the Lombards. He asserted his authority in Germany, at first conciliating but later (1180) overthrowing the Guelph, Henry the Lion. He drowned in Cilicia en route to join the Third Crusade. *See also* Hohenstaufen Dynasty; Lombard League. △1072, 1084.

Frederick II (1194–1250), Holy Roman emperor (1215–50), German king (1215–50), and king of Sicily (1198–1250), *b.* Italy. Son of Emperor Henry VI and Constance of Sicily, he devoted himself to Italian affairs. When elected German king at the instigation of Pope Innocent III, he promised to make his son, Henry, king of Sicily. Instead he gave Germany to Henry (1220), although he later deposed him (1235) and made another son, Conrad IV, German king. In Sicily, Frederick set up a centralized royal administration. Attempting to extend his rule to Lombardy, he was met by a revival of the Lombard League and papal opposition. He went on crusade and was crowned (1229) king of Jerusalem, but this failed to appease the pope. In 1245, Innocent IV deposed him, and civil war ensued in both Germany and Italy. *See also* Lombard League. △1072.

Frederick III (1415–93), Holy Roman emperor (1440–93) and German king (1440–93). He succeeded his cousin Albert II. After the death in 1458 of his ward Ladislas V of Bohemia and Hungary, he attempted to win those thrones. Instead he lost Austria, Carinthia, Carniola, and Styria to Matthias Corvinus of Hungary, only recovering them on Matthias' death in 1490. By marrying in 1477 his son

Francisco Franco

Felix Frankfurter

Fraser River, Canada

Joe Frazier

Maximilian to Mary, heiress of Burgundy, he acquired an enormous inheritance for the Hapsburgs.

Frederick III (1831–88), emperor of Germany (1888). The son of William I, he married (1858) Victoria, eldest daughter of British Queen Victoria. Liberal and popular, he died 90 days after his accession and was succeeded by his son, William II.

Frederick I (1471–1533), king of Denmark and Norway (1523–33). Frederick discouraged fighting with Sweden, kept Denmark's finances in order, and tolerated the spread of Lutheranism.

Frederick II (1534–88), king of Denmark and Norway (1559–88). During his reign, Denmark prospered. Frederick encouraged large-scale farming by nobles, aiding the expansion of agriculture. He built the Kronborg fortress at Helsingör.

Frederick III (1609–70), king of Denmark and Norway (1648–70), the son of Christian IV. From 1657–60 Frederick fought unsuccessful wars with Sweden. In 1660 he increased his power by becoming Denmark's absolute monarch.

Frederick III (c.1286–1330), antiking of Germany (1314–26), called the Fair. Son of Albert I of Germany, he was elected (1314) king by a minority of the electors in opposition to Louis IV. Civil war ensued until his defeat by Louis at Mühldorf (1322). He was imprisoned (1322–25), then acknowledged Louis as emperor and became joint ruler (1325–26).

Frederick I (1657–1713), first king of Prussia (1701–13). He succeeded his father, Frederick William, the "Great Elector," as Frederick III of Brandenburg. An ally of Emperor Leopold I, he gained the latter's approval of his assumption of the title "king in Prussia" in 1701. He promoted the cultural development of Brandenburg.

Frederick II (1712–86), king of Prussia (1740–86), called Frederick the Great. Succeeding his father, Frederick William I, he adopted an aggressive policy toward Austria and made Prussia a major European force. In the War of the Austrian Succession (1740–48) he won Silesia from Austria. During the Seven Years War (1756–63), Austro-Russian forces reached Berlin (1760), but Russia's withdrawal from the war enabled Frederick to recover and make a peace confirming the status quo. Later he gained Polish Prussia in the first partition of Poland (1772) and waged another war against Austria (the War of the Bavarian Succession, 1778–79). Frederick carried out some internal reforms, but his administration was autocratic and overcentralized. A patron of Voltaire, among others, he wrote extensively in French and was a gifted musician. *See also* Austrian Succession, War of the. △1180.

Frederick III (1272–1337), king of Sicily. Brother of James of Aragon, he strengthened the Aragonese hold on Naples and Sicily against Angevin claims. After he was crowned in 1296, he fought with Naples and the papacy. After 1310 he resumed the title "king of Sicily," which he had given up according to a 1303 peace agreement, and appointed his son Peter as his successor.

Frederick I (1372–1440), elector of Brandenburg (1417–40), b. Nuremberg. Burgrave of Nuremberg, he aided Sigismund's election (1409) as German king and in return was named margrave (1415) and elector (1417) of Brandenburg. He was the first Hohenzollern ruler of that territory. *See also* Hohenzollern Dynasty.

Frederick V (1596–1632), elector palantine (1610–23) and king of Bohemia (1619–20), called the Winter King. A Protestant, he married (1613) Elizabeth, daughter of James I of England. In 1619 the Bohemian nobles deposed their king, Emperor Ferdinand II, and elected Frederick in his place. Defeated (1620) in the Battle of the White Mountain, Frederick lost both Bohemia and the Palatinate.

Frederick I (1370–1428), elector of Saxony (1423–28), called the Warlike. As margrave of Meissen he founded (1409) the University of Leipzig. He fought against the Hussites and was rewarded by Emperor Sigismund with Saxony.

Frederick III (1463–1525), elector of Saxony (1486–1525), called the Wise. Although he remained a Roman Catholic, he protected Martin Luther, bringing the latter's case before the Diet of Worms (1521) and giving him refuge afterward at Wartburg. △1152.

Frederick, city in N Maryland; seat of Frederick co; home of Francis Scott Key; site of Hood College (1893) and Fort Detrick, US Army research center. Industries: glass, optical and electronic equipment, dairy products, textiles. Settled 1745; inc. 1817. Pop. (1970) 23,641.

Frederick Augustus I (1750–1827), elector (1768–1806) and king (1806–27) of Saxony. He entered the war against France, but after the Prussian defeat at Jena (1806), he made a separate peace with Napoleon, who approved the title king of Saxony and made him (1807) grand duke of Warsaw. He was captured by the Prussians in the Battle of Leipzig (1813) and lost much of his kingdom to Prussia at the Congress of Vienna (1815).

Frederick Augustus II (1797–1854), king of Saxony (1836–54). Coregent with his uncle King Anton from 1830, he instituted the 1831 constitution. As king he resisted further change. His refusal to accept the Frankfurt Parliament's plan for a united Germany in 1848 led to a revolt in 1849, which was repressed with Prussian aid.

Frederick Louis (1707–1751), prince of Wales, father of George III of England. The alienated eldest son of George II, he led opposition to his father's government after a bitter quarrel over Frederick's allowance. He managed to topple prime minister Robert Walpole and later settled the grievances with his father.

Frederick Henry (1584–1647), prince of Orange-Nassau. Son of William the Silent, he succeeded his brother Maurice in 1625 as stadtholder of the Dutch Republic. In 1631 the stadtholdership was granted to the House of Orange on a hereditary basis. Frederick Henry established an alliance (1635) with France and Sweden against the Hapsburgs in the Thirty Years War and successfully campaigned against Spanish outposts in the Netherlands. One year after his death the independence of the Netherlands was recognized by the Peace of Westphalia.

Fredericksburg, city in NE Virginia, 41mi (86km) SW of Alexandria, on Rappahannock River; site of many colonial landmarks including homes of George Washington's mother and sister, law office of James Monroe, the Rising Sun Tavern (1760), home of John Paul Jones; scene of Battle of Fredericksburg 1862; industrial and farm trading center. Industries: tourism, clothing, shoes, cement, cinder blocks. Settled 1671, it was named for King George III's father; laid out 1727; inc. 1781 as town, 1879 as city. Pop. (1970) 14,450.

Fredericksburg, Battle of (1862), one-sided victory for Confederate Gen. Robert E. Lee's Army of Northern Virginia over Maj. Gen. Ambrose Burnside's Army of the Potomac. Lee's men, positioned behind stone walls on top of Marye's Heights, stopped 14 attacks, killing or wounding nearly 13,000 of the 114,000 Union men. The Confederates lost about 5,300 of their 72,500 troops. △1276.

Frederick William (1620–88), elector of Brandenburg (1640–88), called the Great Elector. At the Peace of Westphalia (1648), which ended the Thirty Years War, he received Eastern Pomerania, and by intervention in the war (1655–60) between Poland and Sweden, he won recognition of his sovereignty over Prussia, formerly a Polish fief. In addition to these acquisitions, he built up the army, curtailed the privileges of the nobility, and fostered trade.

Frederick William I (1688–1740), king of Prussia (1713–40). Succeeding his father, Frederick I, he devoted himself to building up the strictly disciplined army and further centralizing the government. He intervened briefly in the Great Northern War and won part of Western Pomerania. He despised the arts and was brutal to his son, Frederick II.

Frederick William II (1744–97), king of Prussia (1786–97). He succeeded his uncle, Frederick II. He joined (1792) the alliance against France but made peace in 1795 in order to consolidate his acquisitions in the east as a result of the second (1793) and third (1795) partitions of Poland. He kept an extravagant court and left the country virtually bankrupt.

Frederick William III (1770–1840), king of Prussia (1797–1840). Son and successor of Frederick William II, he declared war on France in 1806 and suffered a disastrous defeat at Jena. After the Peace of Tilsit (1807), major reforms were carried out by his ministers, Barons Stein and Hardenberg. Later, allied with Russia, Prussia took part in the final defeat of Napoleon. After 1815 the king joined the Holy Alliance and refused to grant a promised constitution.

Frederick William IV (1795–1861), king of Prussia (1840–61). He succeeded his father, Frederick William III. He gave way at first to the 1848 revolution, calling a constituent assembly, but he later dissolved the assembly and issued a conservative constitution. When the Frankfurt Parliament offered him the German crown (1849) he refused it because it came from an elected body. His own plan for a German confederation excluding Austria was abandoned (1850) because of Austrian opposition. His brother William became regent in 1858 when Frederick William could no longer govern.

Fredericton, capital city of New Brunswick, Canada, at the head of St John River; seat of York co; location of the University of New Brunswick (1859); major trade and rail center; lumber is the major industry. Settled 1740 by French; made provincial capital 1785. Pop. 23,612.

Fredonia, village in SW New York; site of State University of New York at Fredonia (1866), and one of earliest chapters of Women's Christian Temperance Union (1873); noted Concord grape region. Industries: wineries, food processing. Settled 1805; inc. 1829. Pop. (1970) 10,326.

Free Association, psychoanalytic (Freudian) technique to recover repressed memories or discover unconscious associations. The patient is instructed to relax and let his thoughts run freely and then to give an uncensored report of his stream of consciousness. Unconscious material presumably reveals itself as it guides the "free" associations.

Free Church. *See* Congregational Church.

Free City, designation used during the Middle Ages for important European cities that were recognized as autonomous states, exempt from duties and taxes and under imperial protection. Hamburg, Bremen, and Lübeck held this status in Germany until 1937. Danzig (Poland) and Fiume (Yugoslavia) were, for a time, free cities under the League of Nations.

Freedman v. Maryland (1965), US Supreme Court case dealing with state movie censorship. The court held the state procedures unconstitutional in violation of free speech protections but did list a constitutional and acceptable censorship system.

Freedmen's Bureau, US government agency established in 1865 at the end of the Civil War to aid newly freed blacks. Administered by the War Department, the agency provided relief work and educational services, as well as legal protection for blacks in the South. The bureau also acted as a political machine, recruiting black voters for the Republican party.

Freedom of Information Act (1967), US law signed by President Johnson that superceded the Disclosure of Information Act (1966). The law's purpose was to give the public greater access to government records. The new act permitted government agencies to exercise full discretion about disclosure of information only in such areas as national defense, confidential financial information, and law enforcement. The effect of the 1967 act was weakened by agency reclassification of their information under permitted exemptions.

Freedom of the Seas, fundamental principle of international law affirming that no state has sovereignty over the seas beyond its territorial waters and guaranteeing the right to fish and sail on the high seas, to fly over them, and to lay cables and pipelines.

Freedom Rides, 1961 civil rights trips to the South sponsored by Congress of Racial Equality. They led to the desegregation of interstate terminals and subsequently to the Interstate Commerce Commission's ruling providing "non-racial" seating in buses.

Free Enterprise, system in which the market concept is supreme, that is, the market decides what goods will be produced and who will consume them. Individual firms may combine resources as they wish in the production process, and individual consumers may purchase whatever goods they wish, limited only by their means. Significant government control of the economic process is absent.

Free Fall, state of motion of an unsupported body in a gravitational field. *See* Gravity. △1724.

Free French, a group formed by Charles de Gaulle upon the creation of the Vichy government in 1940 for the continuance of the war against Germany. Operating outside France, these men were soon aligned with internal resistance groups, and though considered traitors by the Vichy administration, they managed to gain the increasing support of the French people. The Free French aided the Allies throughout the war, forming a provisional government after the D-Day invasion in 1944.

Freemasonry, secret fraternal order begun in England in the 17th century. Members are commonly called "Masons." The name stems from the fact the order uses secret rituals used by real stonemasons in the Middle Ages. Those craftsmen called themselves "free and accepted masons" when seeking work. The group's name was taken from that title.

Freeport, major town on SW coast of Grand Bahama Island, Bahama Islands, in West Indies. Tourism is main industry. Pop. 25,859.

Freeport, city in NW Illinois, on Pecatonica River; seat of Stephenson co; scene of second Lincoln-Douglas debate (1858). Industries: farm machinery, cosmetics, plastics. Settled 1835; inc. 1855. Pop. (1970) 27,736.

Freeport, village in SE New York, on S shore of Long Island, 25mi (40km) ESE of New York City. Jones Beach State Park is nearby. Industries: tourism, oystering, deep-sea fishing. Settled 1650; inc. 1892. Pop. (1970) 40,374.

Free Port, area in which goods may be landed and reshipped without customs intervention. Free ports aid in quicker movement of ships and goods. When the goods are moved to the consumer, they then become subject to customs duties. Free ports include Copenhagen, Singapore, Stockholm, and New York City.

Freeport Doctrine (1858), a statement made by Sen. Stephen Douglas during one of the Lincoln-Douglas debates held in Freeport, Ill. On the slavery question, Douglas said a territory could effectively exclude slavery by not passing the police regulations necessary to enforce it. Although Douglas won the Senate seat, his Freeport Doctrine caused the South to turn against him, which cost him the presidential nomination in 1860.

Free Radical. *See* Radical.

Free Recall Learning, in psychology, technique used to study verbal learning and memory. A person is allowed to study a list of items then must try to recall as many of the items as possible, in any order.

Freer Gallery, US art museum, Washington, D.C. This art collection was founded by Charles Land Freer and is one of the most extensive collections of Oriental works in the United States. In addition, it contains several paintings by US artists such as John Singer Sargent and Winslow Homer and numerous works by James Whistler, including the famous Peacock Room he designed for the London home of F. R. Leyland. The collection is housed in a Renaissance-style building dating from 1920.

Free Silver, in US history, coinage of silver at a ratio of 16 to 1 with gold. Proponents in the 1870–1890s included inflationists, who favored increasing the amount of money in circulation, and mine operators. With the repeal (1893) of the Sherman Silver Purchase Act (1890), free silver became a campaign issue in 1896.

Free Soil Party (1848–54), US coalition political party. It was opposed, for economic reasons, to the extension of slavery into the new territories. Charles Sumner and Salmon P. Chase were among the members. In 1848 they chose ex-Pres. Martin Van Buren as their presidential candidate. In 1854 the Free Soilers joined the Whigs and anti-slavery Democrats to form the Republican party.

Freetown, seaport and capital city of Sierra Leone, West Africa; capital of British West Africa 1808–74; site of Njala University (1963), Fourah Bay College (1827), University of Sierra Leone (1967), and a technical institute; excellent harbor. Exports: diamonds, iron ore. Industries: food, beverages, cigarettes, petroleum refining, shoes, beer. Area settled 1787; Freetown founded 1792 by freed slaves from England. Pop. 178,600.

Free Trade, economic policy favoring the elimination of tariffs or duties in international trade. Protectionists oppose free trade, advocating import duties and restrictive quotas to safeguard domestic industry from foreign competition. △940.

Free Verse, verse with no regular meter and no apparent form. The unsystematized rhythm is close to that of prose. Dylan Thomas was one of the many modern poets who employ free verse.

Freeway. △1750.

Free Will, in philosophy, is the power of an individual to determine his own behavior. The controversy between affirmation and denial of free will has been persistent in Western thought and has influenced philosophy, law, theology, ethics, and psychology. Theologists have struggled to make the concept of God's omnipotence and omniscience compatible with man's responsibility for his own salvation. Forensic law tries to define the point at which individuals become legally responsible for their behavior. Progress in the physical and biological sciences have narrowed the realm of free will to the point that most psychologists are determinists. This is problematical for those who see moral decisions and artistic creation diminished when viewed as merely a series of causally determined events. Advocates of free will have argued that the human will, unlike inanimate objects, can initiate its own action. Others, like Spinoza, have found freedom through determinism by identifying free will with the affirmation of a reality. Existentialists, like Sartre, believe men to be totally free and entirely responsible, a state which is the source of dread. Those arguing against free will use the concept of the unconscious to provide the unseen motive for apparently existential behavior. In common practice persons believe they determine their actions and hold each other accountable. The practical result of this is that members of a society behave more ethically. Thus the concept is useful, if misnamed, since individuals perhaps possess neither freedom nor unfettered will. △812, 858.

Freeze-drying, technique used in preserving foods by removing water from the frozen state at a low temperature in a high vacuum, avoiding the concentration effect that occurs when a solution is evaporated. Freeze-drying retains the palatability and nutritional value of food and is used commercially for meat, fish, and instant coffee. △396.

Freezing and Melting. △1504, 1568.

Freezing Point, the temperature at which a substance changes phase from liquid to solid. The freezing point for most substances increases somewhat as pressure increases. △1504.

Frege, Gottlob (1848–1925), German logician. He was a professor of mathematics at Jena (1879–1918), and, along with George Boole, one of the founders of symbolic logic and the creator of a logistic system in which the notion of a propositional calculus appears in modern dress. Frege attempted to derive arithmetic from a set of logical axioms in his *Foundations of Arithmetic* (1884).

Frei, Eduardo Montalva (1911–) Chilean statesman. He was a founder member, in 1934, of the National Falange, later the Chilean Christian Democratic party. He was a senator from 1949–1957. In 1957 the National Falange and the Social Christian Conservative party merged to form the Christian Democratic party in an attempt to get Frei elected as president. Although this move failed in 1958, it succeeded in 1964, when Frei was elected, serving 1964–70.

Freiburg im Breisgau (Freiburg), city in SW West Germany, at edge of Black Forest. Hapsburgs took possession of city 1368 and it was held by Austrians until 1805, except for two short periods of French possession; site of University (1457), and 13th-century Gothic cathedral. Industries: textiles, optical goods, paper, chemicals. Pop. 163,509.

Freight Cars. △1708.

Freighter, a ship designed to carry dry cargo or freight, as distinct from oil tankers and bulk carriers of ore or grain. Most modern of the cargo ships are the container ship, which carries prepacked, truck-delivered, steel containers, and the LASH (Lighter Aboard Ship) vessel, which carries steel lighters or barges, each about 60ft (18m) long and 30ft (9m) wide and carrying 500 tons of cargo. The superstructure of the LASH hull is dominated by a large traveling crane supported by legs from each side of the ship. Tracks for the crane extend well aft of the stern deck, so that barges may be lowered directly into the water or picked up from the water and placed in their storage position. △1680.

Freitas, Jos Pedro de. △748.

Frémont, John C(harles) (1813–90), US explorer and general, b. Savannah, Ga. He made a number of important expeditions but was best known for his exploration and mapping of the Oregon Trail (1842). Frémont was sent to serve the army in California during the Mexican War. He disobeyed Gen. Stephen Kearny, was court-martialed in 1848, and resigned his commission. He served as senator from California (1853–54) and was the first presidential candidate of

Frederick III, emperor of Germany

Frederick II of Prussia

Fredericksburg, Virginia

Freetown, Sierra Leone

the Republican party. Campaigning on an anti-slavery platform he lost to James Buchanan. After serving in the Civil War, he was territorial governor of Arizona (1878–83).

Fremont, city in W California, SSE of Oakland; site of a General Motors complex, and Mission San Jose de Guadalupe (1797), which is now restored as a museum. Inc. 1956. Pop. (1970) 100,869.

French, Daniel Chester (1850–1931), US sculptor, b. Exeter, N.H. In addition to "Minute Man" (1875; Concord, Mass.), which commemorates the American Revolution, he did the seated figure of Lincoln in the Lincoln Memorial (1919; Washington, D.C.).

French, major world language, spoken in France and parts of Belgium, Switzerland, Canada, Haiti, and a number of other countries. Descended from Latin, it is one of the Romance languages and is thus part of the Indo-European family. It was one of the two official languages of the League of Nations and is one of the six official languages of the United Nations.

French and Indian Wars (1754–63), a series of wars in colonial North America. A part of a larger conflict, the Seven Years War (1756–73), it pitted Britain and American colonists against French Canadian colonists and Indians. The fighting began (1754) when Virginia troops under George Washington attempted to evict French Canadians who had built Fort Duquesne on land Virginia claimed and were defeated. Initial British efforts to capture the French forts in the West and then cities on the Canadian rivers were unsuccessful. They were defeated badly at the Battle of the Wilderness (1755) by superior Indian and French land forces. By 1757, Prime Minister William Pitt had improved British resources as they took the fortresses at Louisburg, Duquesne (1758), but were repelled at Ticonderoga. Ticonderoga fell in 1759. On the plains of Abraham the British under Gen. James Wolfe decisively defeated the French under the Marquis de Montcalm (1759) and gained Quebec. Both leaders were killed. Montreal surrendered to Britain's Gen. Jeffrey Amhurst (1760). The Treaty of Paris (1763) gave almost all of French Canada to Britain, as well as French Louisiana east of the Mississippi River and part of Florida. The war ended French military and political power in North America. △1216.

French Bulldog, sweet-tempered dog (nonsporting group) bred from toy English bulldogs in France in 1860s. It has a large, square bulldog face with short nose; prominent lower jaw; and thick, hanging lips. Its broad-based, erect, bat-type ears distinguish it from the larger bulldog. The body is short; legs stout and muscular; and short tail straight or screw-shaped. Soft, loose skin is wrinkled on head and shoulders; a short coat is all brindle, fawn, or white; or brindle and white. Average size: 12in (30.5cm) at shoulder; 19–28lb (8.5–12.6kg).

French Canadians. The French founded the first settlements in Canada in 1604. Immigration declined after 1675, but today they represent 31% of the Canadian population. Dominated by the Jesuits and European commercial interests, the French settled into a paternalistic, authoritarian society unable to prevent British encroachment. After 1760 French Canadians followed a course of opposition to confederation, defending their language and culture with success. The Riel Rebellions (1869 and 1885), opposition to World War I, and urban industrialization after World War II further weakened their influence. Only in Quebec have they succeeded in preserving social autonomy.

French Community, association composed of France, her overseas territories, and her former African colonies, established in 1958 as the successor to the French Union. The constitutionally created Community handled the foreign policy and the military, cultural, judicial, and economic affairs of its member states. With the achievement of independence by the African nations by the end of 1960, Community was replaced by bilateral and multilateral agreements. △1350.

French Equatorial Africa, former French federation in W central Africa, consisting of Chad, Gabon, Middle Congo (now Congo) and Ubangi-Shari (now Central African Republic). Territories colonized by French in late 19th century; became autonomous republics 1958; gained independence 1960.

French Guiana (Guyane Française), Department of, a French overseas department on the NE coast of South America. It was the site of the infamous Devil's Island penal colony. A dense tropical forest covers about 90% of the land, rendering most of the area uninhabitable. The small population lives mostly along the coast, 75% in Cayenne and vicinity. The country's economy is dependent upon France, since agricultural output does not meet local demands, and the fishing industry provides the only real export surplus. However, huge undeveloped bauxite deposits appear promising. Aside from a few Indians and blacks, the population is composed mostly of Creoles and Europeans. The vast majority lives in urban areas along the coast. Most of the people are Roman Catholics. French Guiana operates as a regular department of France, electing one deputy each to the national assembly and senate in Paris. The country itself is administered by a perfect and an elected 16-member council-general. Explored by the Spanish about 1500, the country was settled by the French in 1604. The colony, controlled at various times by the Dutch, English, and Portuguese, came into permanent French possession in 1817. The people have had full French citizenship since 1848 and have sent deputies to Paris since 1870. French Guiana became a French Department in 1947.

PROFILE

Official name: Department of French Guiana
Area: 34,749sq mi (90,000sq km)
Population: 51,000
Density: 1.4per sq mi (0.5per sq km)
Chief city: Cayenne (capital)
Government: Overseas Department of France
Religion: no official
Language: French (official)
Monetary unit: franc
Gross national product: $40,000,000
Per capita income: $940
Industries: negligible
Agriculture (major products): timber, cocoa, bananas, shrimp
Minerals (major): bauxite
Trading partners (major): France, United States

French Horn, brass wind musical instrument. The principal symphony orchestra horn, it has a flared bell, long conical tube coiled in a circle, three valves, and funnel-shaped mouthpiece. Versatile, but difficult to play, its romantic mellow tones, blending with either brass or woodwinds, were favored by Wagner, Brahms, and Richard Strauss. △1244.

French Panama Canal Company, French company that obtained rights in 1878 to build a canal across Panama. Badly managed, and plagued by technical troubles and disease in Panama, the company went bankrupt in 1889. The rights were transferred to a new company and later sold to the United States.

French Renaissance Architecture. △1146.

French Revolution, popular uprising in France that began in 1789, resulting in the overthrow of the monarchy of Louis XVI and the establishment of a short-lived republic. The revolutionary era ended with the establishment of the empire in 1804. The revolution was begun by the meeting of the States General—a legislative body representing in three parts the clergy, the nobility, and the common people—in 1789, but the events which led to this meeting can be traced to the reign of Louis XIV. The "Sun King" had incurred an enormous debt in financing his long wars, and the debt was a part of the inheritance of Louis XVI. Since France did not levy realistic taxes on its nobility, which had become divorced from any real function, or the church, there were exceedingly heavy taxes on the working classes, who further experienced a bitter famine in the winter of 1788. In addition, the unwieldy government set up by Louis XIV had become outdated and had lost all semblance of effective popular representation. This paralleled the rise of a wealthy and well-educated bourgeoisie inflamed with the principles of the Enlightenment. Pressured from all sides, the French king was compelled to call the States General for the first time in 175 years.

Well-intentioned but vacillating, Louis allowed control of the new assembly to fall to the bourgeoisie by a series of reversed decisions that won him no allies. Meanwhile, Parisian rebels had armed themselves and gained munitions and concessions in storming (July 14, 1789) the Bastille, a nearly empty but symbolic prison. The power of the new National Assembly established, the representatives wrote the beginnings of the constitution of 1791, ensuring basic human rights; the demise of feudal monopoly, inequality, and privilege; and the restriction of royal power. The king, however, lacked ambition to form a coherent constitutional monarchy, and a worsening economic picture aroused urban workers. In an effort to survive financially, the assembly claimed the property and income of the French church, adding the papacy to its list of enemies. Attempting escape to royalist forces, King Louis was captured and, shortly before the Jacobin coup over the more moderate Girondists, was finally executed in 1793. During this time the Paris commune had forced several reforms, a republic had been created under the National Convention of 1792, and France had declared war on Austria and Britain. Internal rebellion met with mass executions, and the guillotine dealt with political enemies by the thousands. This period, called the Reign of Terror, was administered by the fanatic idealist Maximilien Robespierre, himself guillotined in the popular Thermidorian Reaction of 1794. His death lessened the power of the Paris commune, and of the Jacobins, who were slaughtered throughout France. After internal struggles had somewhat subsided, the National Convention was dissolved in favor of the Constitution of the year III, setting off a riot that was effectively suppressed by the cannon fire of the young Napoleon Bonaparte. The new constitution established the government of the Directory in 1795, which was composed of a distinct executive (the five directors), legislature, treasury, and judiciary. Its main fault was the lack of central organizing power in a wildly unstable France.

Meanwhile, France was at war with half of Europe. The enlistment by law of all men between the ages of 18 and 25 had given it an army that, separated from civilian politics and often commanded by men risen from the ranks, was efficient, dedicated, and increasingly resentful of civilian disloyalty and inadequate supplies. With this army, Napoleon performed magnificently in Italy and Austria. When threatened by a royalist resurgence in 1797, three of the directors used the power of this new hero to establish a dictatorship dependent for survival on the victories of French armies. Faced with a military crisis, strongly in need of some sort of stability, France was ripe for the establishment of Napoleon Bonaparte as first consul of a new government in 1779. Effectively ending the bloody and temporarily unsuccessful attempt for democracy, Napoleon's government soon became a military dictatorship. He was made emperor of the French in 1804 and was followed by a constitutional monarchy in 1814. *See also* Bastille; Directory; Girondists; Jacobins; Napoleon I; Reign of Terror. △1224.

French Somaliland. *See* Afars and Issas, French Territory of the.

French Territory of Afars and Issas, Africa. *See* Afars and Issas, French Territory of the.

French Theater, had its beginnings in the medieval church drama. Throughout the 18th century, France was the cultural center of Europe, and it has since been the starting point of many new artistic movements. △1172.

French Union, from 1946–58, interdependent network comprising metropolitan France and its overseas departments, territories, settlements, and UN trusteeships and protectorates. The union replaced the old French colonial system and was, in turn, replaced in 1958 by the French Community.

French West Africa, former federation of eight French overseas territories, including modern republics of Dahomey, Guinea, Ivory Coast, Mauritania, Niger, Mali, Upper Volta, Senegal; federation abolished 1959.

Freons, trade name for a group of fluorocarbons used as refrigerants, aerosol propellants, cleaning fluids, and solvents. They are all clear, stable, and inert liquids. Examples are Freon-11, CCl_3F; Freon-12, CCl_2F_2; and Freon-14, CF_4.

Frequency, Wave. *See* Wave Frequency.

Frequency Distribution, statistical method of grouping raw data into classes, to illustrate visually how often an event has occurred. A common example is a grade distribution for a group of students. △1474.

Frequency Modulation (FM), variation of the frequency of a transmitted radio carrier wave by the signal being broadcast. The technique gives radio reception fairly free from static interference. △1794.

Frere, John. △1292.

Fresco Painting, method of painting on freshly spread plaster while it is still wet. In true fresco, or *buon fresco,* the paint combines chemically with the moist plaster so that, when dry, the painted surface does not peel. Dry fresco, or *fresco secco,* involves the application of paint in a water and glue medium to a dry plaster wall. It does not last as well as true fresco. △1104, 1138, 1142.

Fresnel, Augustin Jean (1788–1827), French physicist whose pioneer work in optics helped to establish and to remove several objections to the wave theory of light. His work involved light-aberration studies, production of devices to create interference fringes, and obtaining circularly polarized light. *See also* Diffraction.

Fresnel Lens, a type of theatrical spotlight consisting of a piece of heat-resistant glass cast with concentric portions of lenses of different diameters and approximately the same focal length. The Fresnel lens is two or three times more efficient than a plano-convex lens.

Fresnillo De Gonzalez Echeverria, city in N central Mexico; site of mining school, airfield, and railroad junction. Industries: silver, gold and copper mining, cereals, livestock. Founded 1554 by Francisco de Ibarra. Pop. 101,316.

Fresno, city in S central California, 155mi (250km) SE of San Francisco; seat of Fresno co; site of oldest junior college in California, Fresno City College (1910), and California State University-Fresno (1911). Industries: agriculture, wines, prefabricated structures. Founded 1872; inc. 1885. Pop. (1970) 165,-972.

Freud, Anna (1895–), English psychoanalyst, b. Austria, youngest of Sigmund Freud's six children. She applied psychoanalysis to the development of children, was an early user of play therapy, and wrote a number of books including *Normality and Pathology in Childhood* (1965).

Freud, Sigmund (1856–1939), Austrian psychiatrist and founder of the psychoanalytic movement, b. Freiberg, Moravia. Working with Josef Breuer, Freud developed new methods for treating mental disorders—free association and dream interpretation (summarized in *The Interpretation of Dreams,* 1900). He developed theories of the neuroses involving childhood relationships to one's parents and stressed the importance of sexuality in both normal and abnormal development. These controversial aspects of his theories were not well-received by his contemporaries, but gradually his ideas became widely discussed and gained acceptance. Later Freud extended psychoanalysis to a wide variety of cultural and social-psychological phenomena.

The impact of Freud's writings (such as *The Psychopathology of Everyday Life,* 1904; *The Ego and the Id,* 1923; and *Civilization and Its Discontents,* 1930) on modern thought is incalculable. The influences on medicine, psychotherapy, and psychology are obvious, but they also are considerable for literature, religion, education, and child care. Freud brought sex out into the open as a topic fit for discussion. He caused psychologists to realize that human motivations could be unconscious and made them look very closely at child-parent relations as a source for both healthy and sick development. No individual has influenced the development of modern psychiatry and psychology more than Freud. △1282.

Frey, in Norse mythology, the son of the fertility god Njord, and himself ruler of peace, fertility, rain, and sunshine. He was one of the Aesir, and Gerd, daughter of the giant Gymir, was his wife. The boar was sacred to him.

Freycinet, Louis Claude de Saulces de (1779–1842), French explorer, sailed with Captain Baudin in exploration of the southern Australian coast (1800–1805). He made maps and wrote a report of this expedition, and in 1817 commanded another on the *Uranie,* gaining valuable additions to natural history, published in *Voyage Around the World* (13 vols., beginning 1824). He helped found the Paris Geographical Society in 1821.

Friar, title given to a brother or member of one of the mendicant orders established during the Middle Ages. Often distinguished by the color of their mantles, the four chief mendicant orders are the Dominicans, Franciscans, Carmelites, and Augustinians. △1086.

Friars, The, a theatrical club founded in 1904 as The Press Agents Association. Among the founders were Charles Emerson Cook and Channing Pollock. George M. Cohan was chief officer from 1912–42.

Fribourg, town in W Switzerland, 17mi (27km) SW of Bern on the Sarine River; capital of Fribourg canton; ruled by Kyburgs 1218, Hapsburgs 1277, Savoy 1452; became member of the Swiss Confederation 1481; site of a university (1889), and Cathedral of St Nicholas (13th century). Products: chocolate, cheese. Industries: food processing, metal working, chemicals. Founded 1178. Pop. 40,200.

Frick, Ford (Christopher) (1894–), US baseball executive, b. Wawaka, Ind. A one-time newspaper reporter, he served as head of publicity for the National League before being elected president of that league (1934–51). Ford served as baseball's commissioner (1951–65) and was elected to the Baseball Hall of Fame in 1970.

Frick, Henry Clay (1849–1919), US industrialist, art collector, and philanthropist, b. West Overton, Pa. He organized Frick and Co. and built 12,000 coke ovens to become the world's largest supplier of ovens. During the Homestead Steel Strike of 1892 he was attacked by an anarchist but recovered to become chairman of the board of Carnegie Steel Co. He endowed hospitals and educational and charitable institutions.

Friction, resistance encountered when surfaces in contact slide or roll against each other or when a fluid flows along a surface. Sliding friction is caused by the momentary interlocking of irregularities in the surfaces, rolling friction by deformation of the surface, and both are directly proportional to the force pressing the surfaces together and the surface roughness. Fluid-viscous friction is velocity dependent as well as material affected. △1488, 1492.

Friction, Coefficient of, a number associated with any two materials characterizing the force necessary to push one material along the surface of the other. If one body has a weight N and the coefficient of friction is $^a/_b$, then the force f necessary to move the body without acceleration along a level surface is $f = {^a/_b}\,N$. The coefficient of *static* friction determines the force necessary to *initiate* movement; the coefficient of *kinetic* friction determines the (lesser) force necessary to *maintain* movement. △1488, 1492.

Fridley, city in SE Minnesota, on Mississippi River; suburb of Minneapolis. Much of city was destroyed by tornadoes in 1965. Industries: pumps, machine tools, dies, cosmetics, linseed oil. Settled 1847; inc. 1957. Pop. (1970) 29,233.

Fried, Alfred Hermann (1864–1921), Austrian pacifist author and editor. He founded the German Peace Society in 1892 and tried to institute legislative means of maintaining peace in the world. After being awarded the Nobel Peace prize, with Tobias Asser, in 1911, Fried protested World War I from Switzerland and tried to prevent the treaty conditions that helped create World War II.

Friedan, Betty (1921–), US feminist leader, author, b. Peoria, Ill. Through her best-selling book, *The Feminine Mystique* (1963), she prompted women to examine their roles in society. She was a founder and the first president (1966–70) of NOW (National Organization for Women).

Friedman, Milton (1912–), US economist, b. Brooklyn, N.Y. An important member of the Chicago school of economics, he supports monetary policy as the best means of controlling the economy. Extremely influential, he has published extensively. His works include *A Monetary History of the United States 1867–1960* (1963), written with Anna Schwartz, a seminal book in monetary economics; *A Theory of the Consumption Function* (1957); *Essays in Positive Economics* (1953), which suggests economic decisions should not consider normative judgments; and *Capitalism and Freedom* (1962), which argues for a guaranteed income. He was awarded the 1976 Nobel Prize in economics.

Friedrich, Caspar David (1774–1840), German painter. One of the greatest German Romantic painters, he created eerie, symbolic landscapes, such as "Monk at the Seashore" (1808; Berlin) and "Men Observing the Moon" (1819; Dresden). △1242.

Friends, The Religious Society of, also known as Quakers. This religious movement was started in 1647 by George Fox in England. The Friends believe in the inward nature of religion and object to established churches and ministries. Coming to America in 1656, they established religious communities in Rhode Island, and in 1682 William Penn settled a religious colony in Pennsylvania. The Quakers are known for their simple style of living and pacifist ideals. Worldwide membership is about 200,000.

Freischutz. △1256.

Friesland, province in N Netherlands; includes part of West Frisian Islands in North Sea, and extends W to shore of Ijsselmeer; Frisians, a Germanic group, in the area, still speak a strong dialect, hardly recognizable as Dutch; association with the United Provinces was not formalized until 1748. Capital is Leeuwarden. Industries: dairy and cattle farming. Area: approx. 1,325sq mi (3,432sq km). Pop. 521,751.

John C. Fremont

French bulldog

Fresco painting: Cathedral of Saint Sofia, Kiev

Sigmund Freud

Frieze, in architecture, (1) the middle section of an entablature, between the architrave and the cornice; (2) the relief carving on such a middle section; or (3) the space between a picture-rail (or panel top) and the ceiling or cornice of a room.

Frigate, small warship of 1,000–3,000 tons providing antisubmarine protection to fleet and merchant ships. Frigates are normally slower, less well-armed and less costly than destroyers. In the 18th century the frigate was a three-masted sailing ship with 32 to 48 cannon, employed like a modern cruiser. *See also* Cruiser. △1738–40.

Frigatebird, rapidly flying, powerful seabird that soars over tropical oceans, stealing food from other birds. It has a small, dark body; short, fragile legs; scissorlike tail; and tremendous saillike wings. One chalky white egg is laid in a nest on a bush or rock on an oceanic island. Length: 3ft (91cm). Family Fregatidae. △530.

Frigg, in Norse mythology, the wife of Odin and the mother of Balder. She was known as Frija and Frea to Germanic people. The word Friday is derived from her name.

Frigidity, female inability to perform sexually, the result of organic or psychogenic factors. It may vary in severity from diminished sexual feeling to an inability to achieve sexual arousal in any form. Reality factors (such as fear of pregnancy or disease) are somewhat more important in explaining female frigidity than male impotence. *See also* Impotence.

Frilled Lizard, dull-colored, Australian lizard with a fold of skin that spreads into a ruff when the mouth is opened in aggressive display. The cartilaginous frill has serrated edges, red, blue, and brown spots and is 8in (20cm) wide. It is arboreal and frequently runs on its hind legs. Length: to 36in (91cm). Family Agamidae; species *Chlamydosaurus kingi. See also* Lizard.

Friml, Rudolf (1879–1972), US composer of popular operettas, b. Czechoslovakia. His first success came in 1912 with *The Firefly* followed by *Rose Marie* (1924), *The Vagabond King* (1925), and *The Three Musketeers* (1928). He later added the popular song "The Donkey Serenade" to *The Firefly* and also composed for films and Broadway.

Fringe Benefits, compensation in addition to wages that generally involves noncash payments. They may be required as part of a collective bargaining contract or freely provided by the employer. Fringes include insurance policies paid for by the employer, time off with pay, retirement programs, etc. Their value sometimes equals as much as 25% of money wages.

Frisch, Karl von (1887–), Austrian ethologist who shared the 1973 Nobel Prize in physiology and medicine for his pioneering work in the new field of ethology. He deciphered the "language of bees" by studying their "dance recruitment" in which one bee tells others in the hive the direction and distance of a food source.

Frisian Islands, chain of islands in North Sea, off the coast of W Europe; owned by Netherlands, West Germany, and Denmark. The Danish North Frisians are primarily resorts; the German North Frisians are mainly dunes and mud flats where cattle and sheep are raised; the German East Frisians also have resorts; the West Frisians (Netherlands) follow N coastline of country and are primarily sand flats and dunes, with some cattle grazing and small resorts.

Fritillary, strong-flying moth that usually feeds at night and prefers violet leaves. Most have brown or orange wings marked with black or silvery spots and zigzag lines. Family Nymphalidae. *See also* Moth.

Friuli, historic region of NE Italy, bordering N and E on Austria and Yugoslavia, S on the Adriatic Sea, and W on the Veneto region. The SE portion includes the former Free Territory of Trieste. From the 2nd century BC it was under Roman rule until it became a Lombard duchy in the 6th century AD. Later passing to the Franks and the Holy Roman Empire, it was acquired by Venice in 1420 and Austria in 1797. In 1866 and 1919 Italy received those portions of the territory it now holds.

Friuli-Venezia Giulia, autonomous district in NE Italy; Trieste is the capital: Founded after WWII, it encompasses Udine and Pardenone provinces; granted limited autonomy 1963. Industries: shipyards, dairying, textiles, ceramics. Area: 3,028sq mi (7,843sq km). Pop. 1,225,894.

Frobisher, (Sir) Martin (*c.*1535–94), English navigator. In 1576, searching for a northwest passage to India, he reached the Canadian inlet since named Frobisher Bay. His crew returned with samples of black earth, starting rumors of gold. He was sent to the same area in 1577 in a vain search for gold, and made a third trip for colonization in 1578. Frobisher later served under Sir Francis Drake (1585); was sent to Spain by Sir Walter Raleigh (1592); and was knighted for his part in destroying the Spanish Armada (1588).

Froebel, Friedrich Wilhelm August (1782–1852), German educator. His main interest was the education of preschool children, and in 1837 he opened a school that he later named the Kindergarten. He stressed that children should be allowed to develop through activities such as play. His ideas influenced later educational theorists.

Frog, tailless amphibian, found worldwide, characterized by long hind limbs, webbed feet, and external eardrums behind the eyes. Most frogs begin life as fishlike larvae (tadpoles) after hatching from gelatinous eggs usually laid in water. Some frogs remain aquatic, some are terrestrial, some live in trees, and some burrow underground. Most have teeth in the upper jaw and all have long sticky tongues, attached at mouth front, to capture live food. Male frogs frequently have vocal sacs in the throat region.

Frogs of the family Ranidae are found worldwide and are the only amphibians correctly called frogs. True frogs are streamlined and smooth-skinned with bullet-shaped bodies, pointed heads, large eardrums, and long, webbed toes. Toads have rough, bumpy skin and are toothless. Bullfrogs, leopard frogs, and green frogs are well-known US representatives. Length: 1–12in (2.5–30cm). Subclass Salientia (or Anura) is divided into 16 families. *See also* Amphibia; Toad. △518.

Frog-bit. △452.

Frog Hopper. *See* Spittle Bug.

Frogs, Greek comedy by Aristophanes (405 BC). A satire about the resurrection of the dead, the play takes its title from a chorus of frogs. Aeschylus and Euripides, both dead, compete when Dionysus travels to Hades to bring back to life the better writer.

Frohman, Charles (1860–1915), US theatrical manager and producer, b. Sandusky, Ohio. His successes began with his production of Bronson Howard's *Shenandoah* in 1889. He became known for developing many new talents such as the actresses Julia Marlowe, Maude Adams, and Ethel Barrymore, and for promoting the playwrights James Barrie and Edmund Rostand.

Fromm, Erich (1900–), psychoanalyst and author, b. Germany, moved to the United States in 1933. Fromm applied psychoanalysis to peoples and cultures, stressing the role of interpersonal relationships, loving, and productivity in an impersonal, industrialized society. His popular books include *Escape from Freedom* (1941) and *The Art of Loving* (1956).

Fronde, (1648–53), a number of civil reactions against the growing power of the French throne. The Fronde of the Parlement (1648–49) started when Anne of Austria, acting as regent for Louis XIV, proposed to cut the salaries of high court officials. The Parlement rejected this plan and, after a series of armed conflicts, was able to force some restrictions on royal authority. The Fronde of the Princes (1650–53) was a rebellion led by nobles desirous of greater political power. The Great Condé, a powerful military leader, inspired riots and war against the King but was defeated, losing his bourgeois and aristocratic support. The crown's victory established a monarchy whose authority was unchecked until 1789. △1170.

Frondizi, Arturo (1908–), president of Argentina (1958–62), leader of the Radical party whose candidacy was endorsed by Juan Perón. Unable to cope with the country's economic problems or soothe labor unrest, Frondizi was ousted by a military fearful of Peronist resurgence.

Front, Wave. *See* Wave Front.

Front, Weather, the interface or transition zone between two air masses of different density as well as different temperature, since this usually regulates density. Thus a polar front separates cold and warm air masses that have originated respectively in polar and tropical regions and often creates cyclonic disturbances that dominate the weather. Fronts of different kinds are often depicted on weather maps. With stationary fronts, air masses remain in the same areas and weather changes little. Cold fronts occur as a relatively cold and dense air mass moves under warmer air. With warm fronts, the warmer air is pushing over colder air and replacing it. An occluded front on the other hand, is a composite of two fronts. When a cold front overtakes a warm or a stationary front, occlusion occurs and a wave cyclone often develops, with cyclonic weather changes. *See also* Air mass; Cyclone. △214–16.

Frontal Lobe. △666.

Frontenac, Louis de Buade, compte de Palluau et de (1620–98), governor of New France (1672–82, 1689–98), Frontenac rose to brigadier in the French army (1639–89). He founded Fort Frontenac (1673), appeased the Iroquois, and favored fur traders over farmers. His autocratic rule led to recall in 1682. In his second term, Frontenac repulsed an English attack (1690) and briefly attempted an attack on New York. He encouraged LaSalle's explorations and extended French domain to Lake Winnipeg and the Gulf of Mexico.

Fronton Games, a variety of games played with a ball off of walled surfaces, either by hand or with rackets, a bat, or wicker baskets. Included in the various games are *Frontennis,* played with tennis-like rackets and a hard rubber ball; *Pelota de goma,* played with hardwood bats and a rubber ball; *Pelota de cuero,* played with a hardwood bat and a leather ball; *Fronton a mano,* played by hand with a hard leather ball; and *Jai Alai,* played with curved wicker baskets. In all games, of which *Jai Alai* is most popular, the general idea is to return the ball—after it has caromed off of one or more walls—before the second bounce. *See also* Jai Alai.

Frost, Robert (Lee) (1874–1963), US poet, b. San Francisco. After his father's death (1885), his Scottish-born mother brought her family to New England. Frost dropped out of Dartmouth College to work in a cotton mill and as a cobbler. He then attended Harvard for two years but dropped out because of ill health. He farmed (1899–1906) then taught school (1906–12). He wrote poetry, but few poems were published. In 1912 he took his family to England. His lyric poems *A Boy's Will* (1913) and narrative poems *North of Boston* (1914) were enthusiastically received in England, establishing his reputation as a poet. In 1915 he returned to the United States and purchased a farm in Franconia, N.H. From 1916 he taught in a number of universities and colleges including Amherst, Harvard, and the University of Michigan. He published many volumes of poetry and received the Pulitzer Prize for poetry in 1924, 1931, 1937, and 1943. In 1961 he recited his poem "The Gift Outright" at the inauguration of John F. Kennedy. He used simple forms and colloquial speech in his poems depicting the landscape and people of New England often to make profound statements about life and death. Among his many well known poems are "Birches," "The Death of the Hired Hand," "Mending Wall," "The Road Not Taken," and "Stopping by Woods on a Snowy Evening." △1420.

Frostbite, freezing of the body tissues, either superficially or penetrating beneath surface cells. Symptoms are hard, white areas of skin. First-aid treatment includes rapid rewarming of the affected area in water of about 100°F (38°C).

Frothingham v. Mellon (1923), US Supreme Court case in which a citizen was denied the right to challenge a congressional spending bill. The court held that her status as a taxpayer was not, by itself, sufficient indication of an interest or possible injury to sustain her as a proper party to sue the government. The decision was modified in *Flast v. Cohen* (1968). *See also* Flast v. Cohen.

Fructose, white crystalline sugar ($C_6H_{12}O_6$) that occurs in fruit and honey. It is made commercially by the hydrolysis of beet sugar and is used in foods and medicine. △1570.

Fruit, mature ovary of a flowering plant. It serves to reproduce and spread the plant and is important to humans and animals as food. Fruits are classified as simple, aggregate, or multiple. Simple fruits, dry or fleshy, are produced by one ripened ovary of one pistil and include legumes, nuts, apples, pears and citrus fruits. Aggregate fruits develop from several simple pistils; examples are raspberry and blackberry. Multiple fruits develop from a flower cluster; each flower produces a fruit with all merging into a single mass at maturity; examples are pineapple and fig. △338–40.

Fruit Bat, large Old World bat that feeds chiefly on fruit and flowers. Larger species are gregarious and roost in large groups. Family Pteropodidae. *See also* Flying Fox.

Fruit Fly, or pomace fly, yellowish fly, 0.12 to 0.16in (3–4mm) long, found worldwide. Primarily found around decaying fruit; a few are parasitic on insects. Several species in this group are used in heredity studies. Family Drosophilidae. *See also* Diptera.

Frunze, city and capital of Kirgiz SSR, USSR, on Chu River; birthplace of General Mikhail V. Frunze; site of university, medical and teachers' colleges, theater, museum, botanical gardens. Industries: textiles, food processing, machinery. Founded 1862 as Pishpek, a Russian fortress. Pop. 431,000.

Frustration, the prevention of the satisfaction of an aroused physiological, psychological, or social need. Frustration may be imposed from the outside or it may also originate from within an individual, as in setting goals beyond one's ability. Frustrations may lead to increased effort, to anger, and to aggressive behavior. *See also* Aggression.

Fry, Christopher (1907–), English dramatist, actor, and stage director, b. Christopher Harris. His plays are often set in ancient or medieval times and written in blank verse. He is noted for reviving the comic element in poetic drama, as in *A Phoenix Too Frequent* (1946), *The Lady's Not for Burning* (1949), and *Venus Observed* (1950).

Fry, Elizabeth (1780–1845), English social worker and prison reformer. The daughter of John Gurney, a rich Quaker banker, she married Joseph Fry (a London merchant) in 1820. She agitated for more humane treatment of women prisoners and of convicts sentenced to transportation to Australia and later became active in other fields of reform, notably improving standards for nurses and facilities for women's education. In 1838 she was requested by King Louis Philippe of France to inspect French prisons, which led to penal reforms in France.

Frye, Northrop (1912–), Canadian literary critic. His first book, *Fearful Symmetry* (1947), was a masterly study of William Blake's poetry. Frye has set forth his principles of criticism in *Anatomy of Criticism* (1957). He was affiliated with the University of Toronto from 1939 as both teacher and administrator.

FSH. *See* Follicle-stimulating Hormone.

FTC. *See* Federal Trade Commission.

Fuad I (1868–1936), sultan of Egypt (1917–22); first king of modern Egypt (1922–36); son of the deposed Khedive, Ismail Pasha. He founded the University of Cairo (1906); succeeded his brother, Hussein Kamil, as sultan; and opposed the Wafd party, which forbade him to rule without parliament. He suspended (1928) and restored (1935) the constitution. His son, Farouk I, succeeded him.

Fuchs, (Sir) Vivian Ernest (1908–), British geologist and explorer who made the first land crossing of the Antarctic. He led the Falkland Island Dependencies Survey in the Antarctic (1947–50). In 1957 he headed the British section of the Commonwealth Transarctic expedition and made the hazardous 2,250 mi (3,620km) journey across the Antarctic, which earned him knighthood.

Fuchsia, or lady's-eardrop, shrubby plant found mainly in temperate America and New Zealand. It has crisp, oval leaves, trailing stems, and trumpet-shaped, waxy flowers. The 80 species include the crimson-purple *Fuchsia procumbens* and cultivated *Fuchsia speciosa*. Family Onagraceae.

Fu Ch'un Mountains. △1044.

Fucus. △432.

Fuel Cell, electrochemical cell for direct conversion of the energy of oxidation of a fuel to electrical energy. Suitably designed electrodes are immersed in an electrolyte, and the fuel (eg, hydrogen) is supplied to one and the oxidizer (eg, oxygen) to the other. Electrode reactions occur, leading to oxidation of the fuel, with production of current. Fuel cells are used in space vehicles. △1566.

Fuel Conservation. △1646.

Fuel Enrichment, Nuclear. △1638.

Fuel Injection, method of introducing fuel into the cylinders of an internal combustion engine, utilizing a pump rather than piston-created suction. It distributes fuel more evenly for greater power with less tendency for engine knock or vapor lock. △1632.

Fugger, Jakob. △1126.

Fugitives, The, Southern writers who championed regionalism and agrarianism in the 1920s. They published (1922–25) *The Fugitive* magazine. They included John Crowe Ransom, Allen Tate, and Robert Penn Warren.

Fugitive Slave Laws, laws passed in 1793 and 1850 to ensure that escaped slaves were returned to their owners. When slavery was abolished in Northern states, the Underground Railroad and laws helped Southern slaves obtain freedom. The Compromise of 1850 had a tougher fugitive slave law than the 1793 statute, with heavy penalties. According to the 1850 laws, fugitive slaves were denied legal rights. Abolitionists fought against the new law.

Fugue, in music, a composition of several simultaneous parts or voices where one melody is used successively in each voice. In other words, the accompaniment for a melody in one voice is the same melody in other voices. Fugue writing was a popular form in music of the Baroque period and reached its peak in the music of J. S. Bach. Composers of the 20th century have also given it some attention. △766.

Fuji, city in S central Japan, 20mi (32km) NE of Shizuoka; commercial and market center. Paper milling is the main industry. Pop. 180,639.

Fujisawa, city in Japan, on Sagami Bay, 11mi (18km) SW of Yokohama; site of 14th-century Buddhist temple. Pop. 228,978.

Fujiwara, a strong and wealthy Japanese family since the 7th century, after whom the Fujiwara (late Heian) period of history (857–1160) was named. Influencing the imperial family through marriage of Fujiwara women to it, they exerted control of the government as "advisors" to the emperor. Although their power reached its zenith under Michinaga Fujiwara (966–1027), their influence continued to be felt into the 20th century. △1046.

Fujiyama (Fuji-san), highest and most sacred mountain in Japan, in Fuji-Hakone Izu National Park, 70mi (113km) WSW of Tokyo. A dormant volcano, it is noted for symmetrical cone; site of summer and winter sports, mountain climbing. Height: 12,389ft (3,779km).

Fukien (Fujian), province in SE China, on Formosa Strait opposite Taiwan. Foochow is the capital. The climate is warm and moist; inhabitants are of mixed Asian stock, speaking over 100 dialects. An important overseas port in T'ang dynasty (618–906), it flourished as a center of Chinese culture during Sung dynasty (960–1279). Because of its strategic location near Taiwan, Fukien has maintained a large military complex since 1950. Industries: fishing, shipbuilding, rice, tea, sweet potatoes, maize, sugar cane, fruit, lumber, sugar refining, paper, food processing. Area: 46,000sq mi (119,140sq km). Pop. 17,000,000.

Fukui, city in Honshu, Japan, 70mi (113km) NNW of Nagoya; capital of Fukui prefecture; former seat of a feudal daimyo landholder; site of heavy bombing 1945, 1948 earthquake, university (1949). Industries: rayon, habutai, paper, leather, woodworking, soy sauce, textiles. Pop. 200,509.

Fukuoka, city in N Kyushu, Japan, on SE shore of Hakata Bay and Naha River; capital of Fukuoka prefecture; one of three ancient Japanese ports; battle site of Mongol invasions led by Kublai Khan (1274 and 1281); foreign trade began in 1899; site of Kyushu Imperial University (1910), 16th-century Shinto Temple. Industries: Hakata (china) dolls, textiles, herbs, fish, rice pottery, chemicals. Pop. 853,270.

Fukushima, city in N central Japan, on Abukuma River, 150mi (242km) N of Tokyo; capital of Fukushima prefecture; site of feudal castle, railroad junction; seat of Fukushima University and Fukushima medical college. Industries: tea, silk, rice, tobacco, fishing, lumber, horse breeding. Pop. 227,451.

Fukuyama, city in SW Honshu, Japan, on Inland Sea; important commercial and industrial center. Industries: rice, soybeans, silk, electronic equipment. Pop. 255,086.

Fulani, Fulah, or **Fulbe,** African people of mixed Negro and Berber origins, living scattered through W Africa. Their language belongs to the West Atlantic group of the Niger-Congo family. Originally a pastoral people, they helped spread Islam throughout W Africa from the 16th century and were politically ascendant until defeated by the French and British in the 19th century.

Frilled lizard

Frog

Robert Frost

Fruit fly

Fulbright, James William (1905–), US Senator (Dem.) from Arkansas. b. Sumner, Mo. A member of the 78th Congress (1943–45) and US Senate (1945–75), he served as chairman of the Senate Foreign Relations Committee (1959–74). Considered one of the most articulate critics of administration foreign policies, especially with regard to Vietnam, which he strongly opposed, he was defeated by Arkansas Gov. Dale Bumpers in a primary bid (1974) for a sixth term.

Fulbright Scholarships, US government grants for international exchange study. Recipients receive financial support for a year of graduate work, research, or teaching in another country. The awards are named for US Sen. J. William Fulbright, sponsor of the Fulbright Act of 1946.

Fulcrum, the point about which a lever rotates. Its importance was recognized by Archimedes, who said: "Give me a lever long enough and a fulcrum strong enough and I will move the world." *See also* Lever. △1488, 1652.

Fu Literature, prose poems popular during China's Han dynasty (202 BC–AD 220). *Fu* were elaborately descriptive and about such subjects as the capital cities. They glorified the dynasty. Ssu-ma Hsiang-ju (179–117 BC) was the best practitioner.

Fuller, (Sarah) Margaret (1810–50), US author, b. Cambridgeport, Mass. A leader of the Transcendentalists, she edited (1840–42) their journal, *The Dial.* During 1839–44 she conducted a series of classes for women in Boston. These formed the basis for her feminist treatise, *Women in the Nineteenth Century* (1845). During 1844–46 she was literary critic for the New York *Tribune.* Subsequently, in Italy, she became involved in the Revolution of 1848 with her husband Marchese Giovanni Angelo Ossoli. She died in a shipwreck while returning to the United States. *See also* Transcendentalism.

Fuller, Melville Weston (1833–1910), chief justice of the US Supreme Court (1888–1910), b. Augusta, Me. He was appointed chief justice by President Cleveland. A strict constructionist, his most important cases included *Plessy* v. *Ferguson* (1896), which upheld "separate but equal" laws of segregation and *Lochner* v. *New York* (1905), a "due process" clause interpreted so the state could not set a 10-hour day for bakers. He was known as an authority on international law, helped to settle a boundary dispute between Venezuela and Great Britain (1899), and was a member af the Hague Tribunal (1900–10).

Fuller, R(ichard) Buckminster (1895–), US architect and engineer, b. Milton, Mass. Believing that only technological design can solve modern world problems, he invented several revolutionary designs. The best known is the geodesic dome, a spherical structure composed of light, strong, triangular parts. His largest dome, 384ft (117m) in diameter, is the Union Tank Car Co. maintenance shop in Baton Rouge, La. (1958). He is also the author of several unorthodox books, including *Operating Manual for Spaceship Earth* (1969) and *Earth Inc.* (1973). △1412.

Fullers' Earth, claylike substance that contains more than half silica. Originally used to remove oil and grease from wool, it is now used to decolor petroleum and vegetable oils. *See also* Silica.

Fullerton, city in S California, 17mi (27km) NE of Long Beach. Industries: aerospace, food processing, electronics. Founded 1887; inc. 1904. Pop. (1970) 85,987.

Full Faith and Credit Clause, Article 4 of the US Constitution, declaring that each state must accept the statutes, public acts, and judicial (noncriminal) proceedings of other states.

Fulmar, or shearwater, scavenging oceanic bird of Arctic and Antarctica. Heavily built with dull coloring, it has a large head; hooked bill; short neck; throat pouch; long, broad wings; and short tail. A single white egg is laid on bare rock. Length: 12–25in (30–63cm). Family Procellariidae. △534.

Fulton, Robert (1765–1815), US inventor and engineer, b. Little Britain, Pa. He began as a painter, but soon became involved in inventions and engineering projects. He obtained many patents in Britain and in the United States, including some for torpedoes and other tools of naval warfare. His main interest was in navigation and, as early as 1796, he was urging the United States to build canals. His great triumph was the steamboat *Clermont,* whose voyage between New York City and Albany pioneered the use of the steamboat for carrying passengers and freight. △1858.

Fulton, city in E central Missouri, 100mi (161km) W of St Louis; seat of Callaway co; site of Westminster College (1851) and William Woods College (1891). On Mar. 5, 1946, Winston Churchill made his "Iron Curtain" speech at Westminster College. College now houses Churchill Memorial and Library. Industries: firebrick, printing, farm equipment. Founded 1825; inc. as town 1859, as city 1903. Pop. (1970) 12,248.

Fumarole, a vent, usually volcanic, but without lava, ash, or other rock debris surrounding it, from which gases and vapors are emitted. The fumarole is sometimes described by the composition of its gases, such as a chlorine fumarole. The term is also applied to a spring or geyser that emits steam. △176.

Fumigant, substance used for killing bacteria, molds, vermin, and such, by exposure to vapors. Common fumigants are sulfur dioxide, produced by burning sulfur, and formaldehyde and hydrocyanic acid.

Fumitory, any of a genus *(Fumaria)* of annual or biennial plants with finely dissected leaves and clusters of small, single-spurred flowers, including *F. officinalis* once grown as an antiscurvy medicine. Family Fumariaceae.

Funabashi, city in Honshu, Japan, on Tokyo Bay. Industries: tobacco, rice, wheat, horsebreeding. Pop. 325,426.

Function, mathematical relationship or correspondence between two sets of numbers or other entities. For example, associated with a set of numbers x there is another set of numbers y such that each value of x has a corresponding value of y equal to x^3 ($x = 1$ corresponds to $y = 1$, $x = 2$ corresponds to $y = 8$, etc.). Here, y is said to be a function of x, expressed by $y = x^3$; x is called the independent variable and y the dependent variable. The set of values of x is the domain of the function and the set of values of y is the range.

A function is often referred to as a mapping; that is, a rule associating objects in one set with objects in another. It defines a relationship (functional relationship) between number, quantities, etc. For example, the area of a circle is a function of its radius ($A = \pi r^2$), the logarithm of a number is a function of the number (log x), etc. A general notation for a function of x is $f(x)$ or $F(x)$. *See also* Graph.

Functional Disorders, mental disorders that cannot be accounted for by an organic disturbance. They include schizophrenia, depression, manic depressive psychosis, and paranoia. Though their precise nature is unknown, functional disorders are presumably caused by psychological factors.

Functional Fixedness, inability to perceive or use objects in novel ways, which limits the ability to solve problems or use alternatives in thinking processes. Someone who walks back to the shed for a special tool to pick an out-of-reach apple, ignoring a fallen branch he could have used to knock it down, is suffering from functional fixedness.

Functionalism, important sociological theory devised by Emile Durkheim (1858–1917). Functionalism says that man's customs, collective sentiments, and institutions are not present in isolated individuals but rather emerge only as a result of human interaction. It also suggests that these aspects of society form a cohesive whole that is exterior to the individual and exerts control over his actions. This causal relationship—from society to man—marked the beginnings of the study of sociology. △1360.

Functional Psychology, early movement, founded by John Dewey, that stressed the usefulness—the functions—of activities such as perceiving, judging, and feeling in adapting to problems of everyday living. Functionalism was a forerunner of applied psychology.

Functional Relationship. *See* Function.

Functions, Trigonometric. *See* Trigonometric Functions.

Fundamentalism, movement within US Protestantism attempting to maintain what it believes to be traditional interpretations of the Christian faith. It emerged in reaction to liberal, or modernist, trends within Protestantism in the later 19th century. Conservatives began to establish schools and conferences emphasizing literal interpretations of the Bible. It took its name from *The Fundamentals* (1910–12), a series of widely distributed small books produced by conservative scholars. The doctrines most emphasized by fundamentalists are: the divinely inspired and infallible nature of the Bible; the Trinity; immediate creation by the command of God; Man's fall into depravit the necessity for salvation of being "born again" b faith in Christ; Christ's deity, virgin birth, miracle-work ing power, and substitutionary atonement for ma and his physical resurrection, ascension, and imm nent premillennial Second Coming; and the physic resurrection of man for Heaven or Hell. Fundamenta ism also stresses domestic and foreign evangelisr and strong opposition to evolution, Communism, an ecumenism. △850.

Fundamental Orders, basic laws of the Connecticu colony. In 1639 representatives from Hartforc Wethersfield, and Windsor met and developed a cod of laws similar to one enacted by the Massachusett colony. The principal authors were Roger Ludlov Thomas Hooker, and John Haynes. The documer established 11 basic laws to govern the inhabitant The document stressed the community's welfare ove the individual's. A governor and a legislature or Ger eral Court were to be elected and Congregationalisr was the established religion. It was replaced by th Connecticut charter of 1662.

Fundamental Particles. △1484.

Fundy, Bay of, inlet of the Atlantic Ocean separatin New Brunswick, Canada, and Nova Scotia, Canada Industries: shipping, fishing, tourism. Length: 170m (273km). Width: 58mi (93km).

Fungicide, in agriculture and gardening, a chemica that kills fungi, used to prevent or reduce crop losse from fungus diseases. The most important group c fungicides—including a majority of copper, sulfu and organic compounds—is used to protect health but susceptible plants from fungus infections. Th other main group of fungicides—including dinitr compounds, lime sulfur, and organic mercury com pounds—is used to eradicate fungus infections a ready established in plant tissues.

Fungus, any of a wide variety of plants that canno make their own food by photosynthesis, includin mushrooms, truffles, molds, smuts, and yeasts. Fung range in size from single-celled yeasts, visible onl under a microscope, to giant puffballs about 5f (1.5m) in diameter. They have relatively simple struc tures, with no roots, stems, or leaves. The main body or thallus, of a typical multicellular fungus consists o a usually inconspicuous network of very fine fila ments, called a mycelium. The mycelia occasionall develop spore-producing, often conspicuous, fruitin bodies, such as mushrooms and puffballs.

Fungi are divided into three ecological groups or the basis of their food sources. Fungal parasites de pend on living animals or plants; saprophytes utilize the materials of dead plants and animals; and sym bionts obtain food in exchange for a variety of "ser vices" performed for other plants. All three groups are of great importance to man. The parasites are respon sible for many destructive plant diseases and for a fev but sometimes serious diseases of man and other ani mals. The saprophytes are important in decay pro cesses that recycle dead organisms into materials fo living ones. The symbionts include a group of fung (mycorrhizae) that play key roles in the nourishmen of many higher plants and in the decomposition o rocks into soil. *See also* Mold; Mushroom. △424–28

Fungus infection, or mycosis, broad category of dis orders, which may or may not be contagious. Diseases caused by fungi range from superficial disorders, such as athlete's foot or other ringworms, to serious pulmo nary and central-nervous-system infections. Symp toms such as fever, loss of weight, and malaise may be mild and the disease may go undiagnosed since symp toms frequently resemble bacterial disease. Fungi cidal drugs are useful in the treatment.

Funk, Casimir (1884–1967), US biochemist, b. Po land. His idea that deficiency diseases such as beriberi, scurvy, and rickets were caused by the lack of a specific chemical substance established the "vita min hypothesis."

Funkia. *See* Hosta.

Fu Pao-shih. △1208.

Furnace. △1508.

Furnace, Electric. *See* Electric Furnace.

Furneaux Islands, group of islands off NE coast o Tasmania, Australia, at E end of Bass Strait, separated from Tasmania by the Banks Strait; includes Flinders Island (largest), Cape Barren Island, Clark Island, and many smaller islands. Discovered 1773 by British nav igator Tobias Furneaux. Industries: dairy products sheep, tin. Area: approx. 900 sq mi (2,331sq km). Pop. 1,240.

Fur Trade, Western, buying and selling in North America of pelts taken from fox, bear, otter, beaver, raccoon, seal, and other animals. The desire for furs opened the wilderness. Trading companies were formed in the 18th century and exploitation brought the animals near extinction. Protective laws were passed in the 19th century. *See also* American Fur Company; Hudson's Bay Company.

Furuncle, or boil, a staphylococcus-caused inflammation, which manifests as a painful pustule around a central core.

Furze, or gorse, prickly, evergreen shrub native to European wastelands. It has dark green spines and fragrant, yellow flowers. Height: to 4ft (1.2m). Family Leguminosae; species *Ulex europaeus.*

Fuse, in electrical engineering, a safety device protecting against overloading. Fuses are commonly a strip of easily fusible metal placed in an electrical circuit such that when overloaded, the fuse will melt, interrupting the circuit and preventing damage to the rest of the system. △1542, 1650.

Fuseli, Henry (Johann Heinrich Füssli) (1741–1825), Swiss-English painter, writer, and draftsman. Encouraged to paint by Sir Joshua Reynolds, he made many fantastic and grotesque drawings illustrating the works of Shakespeare, Milton, and others. △1228.

Fushun, city in NE China, on Hun River; site of one of the world's largest opencut coal mines. Industries: mining, oil refining, aluminum reduction, chemicals, heavy machinery. Developed by Russia as mining center 1902; under Japanese control from 1905 until after WWII, when it was regained by China. Pop. 1,700,000.

Fusin (Fuxinshi, or **Fou-hsin),** city in NE China, 25mi (40km) NE of Mukden. Developed by Russians as an agricultural and mining region about 1900; mines were controlled by Japan 1905–end of WWII, when they were restored to China. Industries: coal mining, synthetic fuel oil, carbon black, heavy machinery, chemicals, firebrick, aluminum. Pop. 350,000.

Fusion, Nuclear, or thermonuclear reaction, reaction between light atomic nuclei in which a heavier nucleus is formed with the release of energy. This process, which is the basis of the energy produced in the interior of stars, has only occurred on earth in hydrogen bomb explosions. In order for a thermonuclear reaction to occur, the electrostatic repulsive forces between the interacting nuclei have to be overcome; this involves temperatures in excess of 40×10^6 °C. In the case of the hydrogen bomb the heat is provided by an atom bomb surrounded by a layer of hydrogenous material. Controlled fusion reactions are the subject of much contemporary research. The problem is to contain a highly ionized gas (plasma) within a magnetic field long enough for a thermonuclear reaction to occur. The temperature above which this will occur is called the ignition temperature. *See also* Fusion Reactor. △1482, 1638.

Fusion Reactor, device in which nuclear physics fusion takes place. Contemporary research is concentrating on devising methods of containing a plasma (highly ionized gas) so that it yields more energy than is required to raise it to its ignition temperature (minimum temperature for a fusion reaction to occur). The Lawson criterion (worked out in 1957 by J. D. Lawson) shows that for the deuterium-tritium reaction at its ignition temperature, the product of the plasma density (particles per cm^3) and the containment time (seconds) must exceed 10^{14} for energy breakeven. The most promising devices consist of a toroidal (tire-shaped) vessel through which high current pulses are passed to create the plasma and raise its temperature. The current pulse also creates a strong magnetic field, which makes the charged particles travel along helical paths and thus contract away from the walls of the tube. This pinch effect helps toward solving the problem of containment, but unfortunately the plasma develops kinks due to plasma instabilities. Devices of this type include the U.S. Stellarators and the Russian Tokamaks. The latter are now regarded as the most promising and several are in operation outside the U.S.S.R. Other devices using linear magnetic bottles, stoppered at the ends by magnetic mirrors, and laser beams to raise the temperature of pellets of hydrogenous substances have been tried unsuccessfully. *See also* Fusion, Nuclear. △1482.

Future Shock, term coined by Alvin Toffler, who used it as the title of his 1971 bestseller, to describe the impact of rapid change on people and societies. Characterized by disorientation and anxiety, and generated by urbanization and rootlessness, future shock results from the sudden breakdown of old social systems and values.

Futurism, early modern movement in painting and sculpture; began in Italy in 1909. Its aim was to glorify the modern machine, such as the automobile and the locomotive, rather than to attempt to depict nature and figures realistically. Many futurists, such as Marcel Duchamp, showed the simultaneous movements of persons. Some were influenced by cubism. Leading futurists included the painters Carlo Carrà and Gino Severini and the sculptor Umberto Boccioni. △1294.

Fuxinshi. *See* Fusin.

Fuzhou. *See* Foochow.

Fyodor I (1557–98), tsar of Russia (1584–98). The son of Ivan the Terrible and Anastasia Romanova, he was the last of the Rurik dynasty. During his reign, the autonomy of the Russian Orthodox Church was established with the creation of the Patriarchate of Moscow in 1589. Russia's influence over Siberia and the Caucasus was extended. He was succeeded by his brother-in-law Boris Godunov, who had actually controlled the government.

Fyodor II (1589–1605), tsar of Russia in 1605 after his father, Boris Godunov, died. When Dmitri the Pretender invaded Moscow, he provoked the people to murder Fyodor.

Fyodor III (1656–82), tsar of Russia (1676–82). He was a weak ruler, and his government was run by Vasily Golytsin, who introduced military reforms and abolished the system whereby an officer's rank in service was based on the rank held by the noble family he came from. Fyodor died childless. He was succeeded by the joint reign of his brother Ivan V and half-brother Peter I (the Great). *See also* Golytsin, Vasily.

Sarah Margaret Fuller

Melville Weston Fuller

Fulmar

Robert Fulton

G

g, a unit of acceleration based on the acceleration of falling bodies near the earth's surface: one g = 32 ft/sec² (9.8m/sec²). *See also* Gravity. △178.

G, the universal constant of gravitation, equal to 6.67 × 10^{-11} newton-meter²/kg².

Gabbro, intrusive igneous rock, dark in color, granite-like in texture, and made up primarily of plagioclase feldspar and pyroxene. A very strong traprock, it is used for crushed stone. *See also* Igneous Rocks; Plagioclase. △246.

Gable, Clark (1901–60), US film actor, b. Cadiz, Ohio. His impudent, virile magnetism made him a screen idol for 30 years. His films included *Red Dust* (1932), *It Happened One Night* (1934), *Gone With the Wind* (1940), *The Tall Men* (1955), and *The Misfits* (1960).

Gabo, Naum (Naum Pevsner) (1890–), US sculptor and architect, b. Russia. He worked in several European cities. A founder of the Constructivist movement in sculpture, he published the *Realist Manifesto* (1920) with his brother Antoine Pevsner, a work explaining the principles of that style. His works include a huge public sculpture in Rotterdam (1957).

Gabon Republic, nation in W Africa, on the equator. The people are chiefly Bantus and Pygmies. Recent discoveries of mineral deposits have stimulated the country's economy.

Land and Economy. The tropical climate creates heavily forested areas throughout the country. Mountains and plateaus dominate the inland portion, falling away to coastal lowlands along the Atlantic. The economy is thriving; newly discovered deposits of manganese, uranium, and crude oil have added to the already immense timber profits. Export values far exceed import costs, and new rail lines should aid greater development.

People. The majority of the people are Bantu Negros with a considerable number of Fangs and Pygmies. English is the official language, but a large number of native languages and dialects are in common use. Although there is no official religion, the majority of the people is Muslim. Education is mandatory from 6 to 16 years of age.

Government. The republic consists of a president, a 47-member unicameral National Assembly, and an independent Supreme Court.

History. After discovery by the Portuguese in the 15th century, Gabon became an important slave-trade center. In 1839 the French incorporated the area into the French Congo and reestablished it as a separate colony in 1910. It became an overseas territory of the French Union in 1946 and an autonomous member of the French Commonwealth in 1958. Gabon proclaimed its independence in 1960 and joined the United Nations the same year. Omar Bongo, upon assuming the presidency in 1973, declared Gabon a one-party state.

PROFILE

Official name: Gabon Republic
Area: 103,346sq mi (267,666sq km)
Population: 500,000
Density: 4.8 per sq mi (1.8 per sq km)
Chief cities: Libreville (capital); Port Gentil
Government: Republic
Religion: Islam
Language: French (official)
Monetary unit: franc
Gross national product: $310,000,000
Per capita income: $630
Industries (major products): plywood
Agriculture (major products): timber
Minerals (major): petroleum, manganese, uranium
Trading partners (major): France, United States, West Germany

Gaboon Viper, nonaggressive viper native to Central African forests and closely related to the puff adder. The stocky body supports a head twice as wide as the neck. Its fangs are 1.5in (4cm) long and a brilliant geometric pattern of yellow, blue, pale purple, and brown serves as camouflage. It has enlarged, hornlike scales between its nostrils. Length: to 6ft (1.8m). Family Viperidae; species *Bitis gabonica*. *See also* Puff Adder; Viper. △598.

Gaborone, capital of Botswana, 150mi (240km) NW of Pretoria, South Africa; served as administrative headquarters of former Bechuanaland Protectorate (1965); remained capital after protectorate's independence as Botswana (1966). Pop. 14,467.

Gabriel, biblical archangel, who is also mentioned in the New Testament. He, with the archangels Michael, Raphael, and Uriel, stood next to God. He destroyed Sodom and interpreted prophetic visions. The word Gabriel is a Hebrew description of the angelic office, but religious tradition has made it a proper name.

Gadfly. *See* Deer Fly.

Gadolinium, metallic element (symbol Gd) of the lanthanide group, first isolated as the oxide in 1880. Chief ores are monazite (phosphate) and bastänite (fluorcarbonate). The element has some specialized uses including neutron absorption and the manufacture of certain ferrites. Properties: at. no. 64; at. wt. 157.25; sp gr 7.898 at 25°C; melt. pt. 2,394°F (1,312 °C); boil. pt. 5,432°F (3,000°C); most common isotope Gd^{158} (24.87%). *See also* Lanthanide Elements.

Gadsden, city in NE Alabama, on Coosa River; seat of Etowah co; site of a junior college. Industries: steel, textiles, tires, rubber products. Settled 1840; inc. 1871. Pop. (1970) 53,928.

Gadsden Purchase (1853–54), the acquisition of 45,000 square miles (116,550 sq km) of land in southern New Mexico and Arizona, south of the Rio Grande River, from Mexico. Following the Treaty of Guadalupe Hidalgo (1848), ending the Mexican War, the United States-Mexico border was only vaguely described, and Pres. Franklin Pierce wanted to purchase this strip that was considered the best route for a railroad to the Pacific. The sale was negotiated by James Gadsden, Minister to Mexico, for $10,000,000.

Gadwall, temperate N Hemisphere surface-feeding dabbling, or river, duck with a drab, broad body and flat bill; long neck; short legs; and webbed feet. After courtship rituals, the female lays cream-colored eggs (8–12) in a marsh depression. Length: 20in (50cm). Species *Anas strepera*. △534.

Gaea, in Greek mythology, the goddess of earth. She was the mother and wife of Uranus and the mother of Cyclopes and the Erinyes.

Gaelic, language spoken in scattered parts of Ireland and Scotland. The variety spoken in Ireland is also referred to as Irish and sometimes Erse. It is one of the official languages of Ireland and is taught in all schools but the number of speakers continues to diminish. In Scotland it has no official status and is gradually dying out. Gaelic is one of the Celtic languages. △866.

Gaelic Revival. △1222.

Gaeta, seaport in central Italy, on the Tyrrhenian Sea; site of 12th-century cathedral; a prosperous duchy from 9th-12th centuries. Pop. 22,799.

Gafsa, town in central Tunisia; phosphate mining and agricultural region; site of thermal springs, Roman ruins, large mosque; archeological study area of prehistoric Capsian culture. Industries: handicrafts, dates, olives, figs, fruits. Pop. 32,408.

Gagarin, Yuri Alekseyevich (1934–68), Russian cosmonaut and national hero, the first man to orbit the earth. His historic flight took place on April 12, 1961, in the 5-ton spacecraft Vostok ("East"). Attaining a height of 188mi (303km), Gagarin made his single orbit in 1 hr. 48 min. and landed safely in the Soviet Union. He died seven years later in a plane crash. △142.

Gage, Thomas (1721–87), English general in North America. He fought in the French and Indian War with Gen. Edward Braddock, taking part in the unsuccessful march on Fort Duquesne (1755). Later governor of Montreal (1760), he succeeded General Jeffrey Amherst as head of the British forces in North America (1763) and became governor of Massachusetts (1774). His soldiers fought the patriots at Lexington (April 1775), the battle that began the American Revolution. He resigned in October of the same year.

Gaillardia, or blanketflower, genus of showy annual and perennial plants mostly native to W North America. The garden perennial *G. aristata* has striking 4in (10cm) daisylike flowers with reddish disks and yellow or red rays. Height: 3ft (91cm). Family Compositae.

Gainesville, city in N central Florida, 65mi (104km) SW of Jacksonville, seat of Alachua co; home of University of Florida. Industries: wood products, electronic equipment. Founded 1854; inc. 1869. Pop. (1970) 64,510.

Gainsborough, Thomas (1727–88), English painter. In 1740 he became a pupil in London of the French engraver Hubert Gravelot. Throughout his life he preferred painting idyllic landscapes but turned to portraits to earn a living. In 1759 he settled in Bath, where he painted many of his friends in the theater, including David Garrick and Mrs. Siddons. His elegant, refined, and vividly colored portraits were influenced by Anthony Van Dyck. In 1768 he became an original member of the Royal Academy. He moved to London in 1774 and won the favor of George III, becoming the rival of Sir Joshua Reynolds. In his last years he painted "fancy pictures"—life-sized idealized portraits of rustics. Well-known works include *The Blue Boy, Perdita,* and *Lady Innes*. △1192.

Gaiseric or **Genseric** (*c.* 390–447), king of the Vandals and Alans (428–477). After invading Africa from Spain (429), he ruled Carthage (439), remaining independent from Rome by defeating Roman armies and maintaining a fleet in the Mediterranean. In 455 he occupied and plundered Rome. He died in control of N Africa and much of the Mediterranean. △1054.

Gaj, Ljudevit. △1232.

Gal (from Galileo), measure of acceleration equal to 1 centimeter per second per second.

Galactic Cluster. *See* Cluster, Stellar.

Galactosemia, a genetic inability to convert galactose (in milk) to usable glucose. Symptoms, appearing in infants within a few days of birth, include vomiting, possible edema, and feeding difficulty. It is controlled by eliminating milk and milk products from the diet.

Galahad, in Arthurian legend, son of Lancelot and Elaine. He qualified as the best knight by passing the test of the Perilous Seat and drawing a sword from a floating stone, so replacing Percival as the seeker of the Holy Grail. Galahad is successful in the quest because he is a pure knight.

Galápagos Islands, archipelago owned by Ecuador in Pacific Ocean, 650mi (1,047km) W of Ecuador, on the Equator. Group consists of 13 large and many smaller islands, mainly barren lava piles; there is vegetation on upper slopes of high, volcanic mountains. Islands are known for unusual range of wildlife; named for huge almost-extinct land tortoises; visited by Charles Darwin 1835. Discovered 1535 by Tomás de Bertanga, Spanish navigator; Ecuador claimed the archipelago in 1832. Area: 3,029sq mi (7,845sq km). Pop. 3,000.

Galápagos Tortoise, nearly extinct turtle found on the Galápagos Islands. Each island has at least one isolated population. They are strictly herbivorous. Height: to 67.5in (1.7m); weight: to 500lb (225kg). Family Testudinidae; species *Geochelone elephantopus*. △418, 522.

Galati, port city in Romania, on the Danube River; capital of Galati co; in ancient times an important Roman port; seat of International Danube Commission (1856–1945). Exports: grain, timber. Industries: iron, steel, shipbuilding, grain, chemicals, textiles. Pop. 179,189.

Galatia, region of Asia Minor near modern Ankara in Turkey. The Gauls held the area from the 3rd century BC but their expansion was halted by Attalus I in 230 BC. Galatia was conquered by the Romans in 189 BC and its name given to a large Roman province in 25 BC. △1020.

Galatians, New Testament collection of letters by Paul, written in indignation at the increase in false teachings, arguing against Judaizing teachers and stressing apostolic authority.

Galaxy, any of the innumerable vast collections of stars distributed throughout the enormous void of the universe, of which the Milky Way galaxy is a typical example. Formerly called extragalactic nebulae, galaxies are gravitationally bound rotating systems, each comprising billions of stars and having either irregular or, far more commonly, regular structures. Regular galaxies are differentiated into elliptical and spiral systems, the latter being further subdivided into normal and barred spirals. Although they tend to be grouped into clusters, galaxies are apparently retreating from each other at enormous speeds, as demonstrated by red shifts in their spectra. The more distant galaxies, which are observed at an earlier period in the life of the universe, seem to be retreating at greater velocities—evidence supporting big-bang theories of cosmology. *See also* Andromeda Galaxy. △118–122.

Galaxy, Double. *See* Double galaxy.

Galaxy, Radio. *See* Radio Galaxy.

Galaxy, Spiral. *See* Spiral Galaxy.

Galaxy Cluster, system of associated galaxies often comprised of hundreds or thousands of separate members all moving together through space. Several thousand clusters are known, one of the most notable being the Virgo-Coma cluster, a gigantic concentration of about 10,000 galaxies located near the north galactic pole. △120–22.

Galbraith, John Kenneth (1908–), US economist, b. Iowa Station, Ontario. His works have made him well known to the general public. Three of his best known books are *American Capitalism: The Concept of Countervailing Power* (1952); *The Affluent Society* (1958); and *The New Industrial State* (1967). In general, Galbraith takes the position that many accepted theories about consumption are outmoded. An early supporter and advisor to John F. Kennedy, he was ambassador to India (1961–63).

Galen (*c.* AD 130–200), Greek physician. His work and writings provided much of the foundation for the development of medicine. He tried to synthesize all that was known of medical practice and to develop a theoretical framework for an explanation of the body and its diseases. He made numerous anatomical and physiological discoveries, including ones concerning heart-muscle action, kidney secretion, respiration, and nervous-system function. He was among the first to study physiology through the use of detailed and ingenious animal experimentation. Galen's theories influenced medical practice for centuries. William Harvey's 17th-century discovery of the circulation of the blood was one of the first major steps away from Galenian medicine. △708, 814.

Galena, a sulfide mineral, lead sulfide (PbS). A major ore of lead in igneous and sedimentary rock. Cubic system, granular masses, cubic and octahedral crystals common, sometimes fibrous. Lead-gray, metallic, brittle. Hardness 2.5–2.7; sp gr 7.5. △242.

Galerius (died 311), Roman emperor (305–11), full name Gaius Galerius Valerius Maximianus. Diocletian appointed him caesar of the east in 293. He fought the Persians, losing in 296 but defeating them in 297. He became coemperor with Constantine in 305. Originally he had urged Diocletian's persecution of Christians, but on his deathbed he issued an edict of toleration.

Galesburg, city in NW Illinois, 45mi (74km) WNW of Peoria; seat of Knox co; founded by a group of pioneers from Mohawk Valley, New York, led by George Washington Gale; birthplace of Carl Sandburg (1878); site of a Lincoln-Douglas debate (1858). Industries: marine parts, lawn mowers, automotive and steel products. Inc. 1857. Pop. (1970) 36,290.

Galicia, region in SE Poland (Western Galicia) and W Ukraine (Eastern Galicia), bordered by Czechoslovakia (S) and Carpathian Mountains (N); part of Poland from 14th century until the partitions of Poland (1772, 1795, and 1815) when Austria took possession; in 1918 Poland took W Galicia and was awarded E Galicia in 1921. The 1939 partition of Poland gave E Galicia to Ukraine; agricultural area with some mineral wealth, especially oil. Products: rye, wheat, corn, potatoes, flax, tobacco, hops. Area: 32,332sq mi (83,740sq km).

Galicia, region in NW Spain; bounded by Atlantic Ocean (N and W), Portugal (S), Asturias and León provs. (E); includes provinces of Lugo, Orense, Pontevedra, La Coruña; scene of 19th-century literary and cultural revival; site of Shrine of Santiago de Compostela; pilgrimage center; naval base. Industries: fishing, livestock, mining, dairying, chemicals, textiles. Area: 11,256sq mi (29,153sq km). Pop. 2,583,674.

Galilean Satellites. △86.

Galilee, region in N Israel, bounded by Jordan River and Sea of Galilee (E) and Plain of Esdraelon (S); it was ruled from 8th century BC by Babylonia, Persia, Egypt, Syria; came under Roman dominance in 63 BC. It was the home and ministry of Jesus Christ; his disciples were area fishermen; center of Judaism and Talmudic studies after the fall of Jerusalem AD 70. Nazareth is a major urban center in the region. Industries: olives, grains, fishing.

Galilee, Sea of (Kinneret, Lake), fresh-water lake in N Israel, on W Syrian-E Israeli border; approx. 75% of its water is fed and drained by the Jordan River. Israel's major reservoir, it is industrially important as a fishing center and source of irrigation for the Negev Desert. In biblical times, it was site of nine prosperous fishing towns on its shores, including Magdala, Capernaum, Tabigha, and Tiberias (the only one still remaining); site of numerous archeological excavations. Area: 64sq mi (166sq km).

Galileo (1564–1642), Italian scientist, professor at Pisa, later moving to Padua and then to Florence. While studying medicine he deduced the formula for the swing of a pendulum from the oscillation of a hanging lamp in Pisa Cathedral. He later studied the laws of falling bodies, disproving Aristotle's view that the rate of fall is proportional to the weight. His work on the three laws of motion was important, although it was Newton who formulated them mathematically. He also discovered the parabolic flight path of projectiles. His work on astronomy followed his invention of the telescope, which enabled him to discover sunspots, lunar craters, Jupiter's satellites, and the phases of Mercury. In *Sidereus Nuncius* (1610) he announced his support for the Copernican view of the universe, with the earth moving around the sun. This was declared a heresy by Pope Pius V. In *Dialogo Sopra i Due Massimi Sistemi del Mondo* (1632) he defied the pope by making his views even more explicit; as a result he was brought before the Inquisition at the age of 70. While publicly recanting, he is said to have muttered: "Eppur si muove" (meaning "Even so the earth *does* move"). For his remaining years he was silenced by the Church. △1442.

Gall, Franz Joseph (1758–1828), German anatomist and physiologist who correctly identified the

Clark Gable

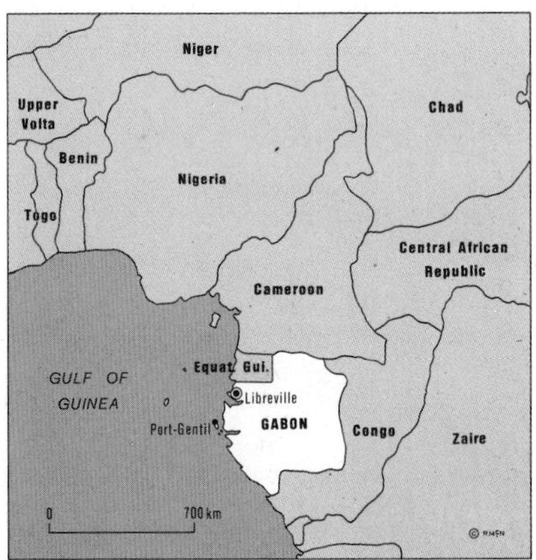
Niger
Upper Volta
Chad
Benin
Nigeria
Togo
Central African Republic
Cameroon
Equat. Gui.
GULF OF GUINEA
Libreville
Port-Gentil
GABON
Congo
Zaire
0
700 km

Gabon

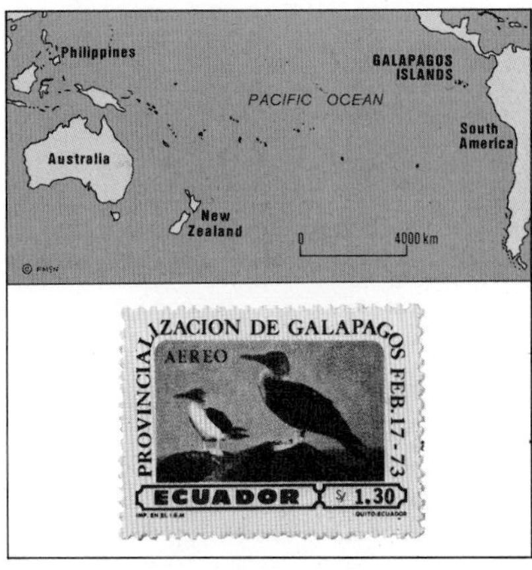
Philippines
GALAPAGOS ISLANDS
PACIFIC OCEAN
South America
Australia
New Zealand
0
4000 km
PROVINCIALIZACION DE GALAPAGOS FEB. 17-73
AEREO
ECUADOR
S/ 1.30

Galápagos Islands

Galileo

function of several areas of the brain and suggested that these areas controlled or were related to certain parts of the body. He extrapolated from this and founded phrenology, the study of the external structure of the skull to determine the character of an individual. △762.

Gall, an abnormal swelling or protuberance of plant tissue stimulated by an invasion of any of a wide variety of parasitic or symbiotic organisms, including bacteria, fungi, insects, and nematodes. Most gall organisms stunt but do not kill the affected plants.

Galla, Hamitic people who make up 40% of the population of Ethiopia, living mainly in the south. Characteristically tall and dark-skinned, they are predominantly nomadic pastoralists. In the 16th century they invaded their present homelands from the south and east. Their religions include Christianity, Islam, and paganism.

Galla Placidia (*c.* 388–450), West Roman empress, daughter of Theodosius I. Held hostage by the Visigoths (410–16), she was compelled to marry the chieftain Ataulf (414). After his death she was returned to the Romans and married Constantius who became coemperor. Their son was Valentinian III, for whom she ruled as regent. She commissioned much of the great mosaic work at Ravenna.

Gallatin, Albert (1761–1849) US statesman and financier, b. Abraham Alfonse Albert Gallatin in Switzerland. As secretary of treasury under Presidents Jefferson and Madison (1801–14) he aided in negotiating the Treaty of Ghent to end the War of 1812. A member of the US House of Representatives (1795–1801); his contribution to fiscal reform led to a standing committee on finance. He endorsed federal financial aid for roads and canals. He also served as minister to France (1816–23) and England (1826–27). He promoted the study of Indian linguistics and customs and founded the American Ethnological Society in 1842.

Gallatin River, river in Wyoming and Montana; rises in the Gallatin Range in NW Wyoming, NW corner of Yellowstone National Park, flows N to Montana, unites with Jefferson and Madison rivers to form the Missouri River. Length: 125mi (201km).

Gallaudet, Thomas Hopkins (1787–1851), US educator, b. Philadelphia. At Hartford, Conn., in 1817 he founded the first United States school for deaf-mutes, where he served as principal until 1830. He also worked for educational opportunities for blacks and women.

Gall Bladder, pear-shaped organ, located under the large right lobe of the liver, that stores bile secreted by the liver. When bile is needed for digestion the gall bladder is stimulated to contract, expelling the stored bile through the cystic duct, into the common bile duct, then into the small intestine. Gallstones sometimes form in the gall bladder, impairing its function. △694.

Galleon, general-purpose wooden sailing ship appearing in the 16th century, larger than the earlier carrack and caravel. The galleon featured a larger front and rear deck structure (forecastle and quarterdeck), and was rigged with a front spritsail, two main masts with several square sails each, and one or two lateen masts at the rear. *See also* Carrack. △1678, 1738.

Galley, oared Mediterranean ship, much larger and wider than the ancient trireme, and used by the Italian, French, and Turkish navies in the 15th and 16th centuries. More maneuverable than fully-rigged sailing ships, galleys were less effective in the more turbulent Atlantic due to their low freeboard. △1738.

Gallicanism, movement affirming the supreme ecclesiastical authority of the French bishops, councils, and crown at the expense of the papacy. Begun in the late 13th century, Gallicanism was reconfirmed in the Pragmatic Sanction of Bourges (1438) which reduced the pope's duties and authority in France. The Concordat of Bologna (1516) gave more power to the crown as opposed to the clergy. The controversy continued into the 20th century.

Galli-Curci, Amelita (1889–1963), US soprano, b. Italy. She studied in Italy and made her debut in 1909 as Gilda in Verdi's *Rigoletto*. She became a famous soprano in the Italian repertoire and subsequently appeared in Chicago (1916–24) and New York (1920–30).

Gallic Wars, the campaigns of 58–51 BC whereby Caesar conquered the Gauls. His intervention was requested against the Helvetii and the invading Germans. By 57 he had subdued SW and N Gaul and extended Roman influence to the Rhine and N France and Belgium. In 56 he conquered the Veneti, leaders of anti-Roman Confederacy, and in 55–54 marched into Germany and Britain. He put down occasional revolts in N Gaul and then faced a united Gallic force under Vercingetorix, defeating it with quick, bold strategy (51). His classic commentary *The Gallic Wars* describes the campaigns. △1018.

Gallienus (died 268), Roman emperor (253–68), full name Publius Licinius Valerianus Egnatius. He ruled with his father, Valerian (253–60), then alone. He ended his father's persecution of Christians. He barely succeeded in holding the empire together. He was murdered by his own soldiers. △1030.

Gallinaceous Bird, bird living and nesting on or near the ground. They include the peacock, partridge, quail, curassow, grouse, turkey, chicken, and other species found throughout most of the world. Their strong, usually spurred legs are well-adapted for walking and running and the feet, equipped with three toes in front and one behind, are used to scratch for seeds, grains, and fruit. These game birds often have soft, abundant plumage, brighter colored in the male. They usually nest in a simple ground depression. Order Galliformes.

Gallinule, weak-flying marsh bird that lives in and near temperate and tropical ponds and lakes. Narrow-bodied, they have bright forehead shields; short, bright beaks; long necks, legs, and toes; and short tails. Length: 1ft (30cm). Family Rallidae.

Gallipoli Peninsula, narrow cape of W Turkey, extends between Aegean Sea (W) and Dardanelles (E); site of Gelibolu port on NE coast; scene of 1915 WWI Gallipoli Campaign which was an Allied expedition to gain control of the Dardanelles and Bosporus straits and Constantinople, thus opening Black Sea supply route to Russia; although Australia, New Zealand, and France sent reinforcements, Allied troops withdrew by January 1916 without gaining hold, and suffering heavy losses. Length: approx. 50mi (81km). △1306.

Gallium, metallic element (symbol Ga) of group IIIA of the periodic table, predicted by Mendeleev (as ekaaluminum) and discovered spectroscopically in 1875 by Lecoq de Boisbaudran. Chief sources are as a by-product from bauxite and some zinc ores. The metal is used in high-temperature thermometers and in semiconductors. Properties: at. no. 31; at. wt. 69.72; sp gr 5.91 at 29.6°C; melt. pt. 85.6°F (29.78°C); boil. pt. 4,357°F (2,403°C); most common isotope Ga^{69} (60.4%).

Galloping Inflation. *See* Hyperinflation.

Galloway, Joseph (1731?–1803), US Tory and colonial legislator. He served in the Pennsylvania legislature (1756–75), the last 10 years as speaker. His proposal at First Continental Congress for an American legislature having equal veto rights with Parliament on colonial laws was rejected. He became the British civil administrator for Philadelphia during the Revolution and later lived in England.

Galloway, ancient breed of sturdy, black, hornless beef cattle, native to Galloway in SW Scotland. *See also* Beef Cattle; Cattle.

Gallstones, or cholelithiasis, stonelike formations, usually containing cholesterol, found in the gall bladder. Affecting three times as many women as men, gallstone cause is not known positively but may be related to liver dysfunction. Symptoms range from none to excruciating pain. △718.

Gallup, town in NW New Mexico, 20mi (32km) E of Arizona border; seat of McKinley co; provides entrance to region of many Indian reservations; site of annual Intertribal Indian Ceremonial; important trade center. Industries: uranium and coal mining, livestock, wool processing, tourism. Founded 1879; inc. 1891. Pop. (1970) 14,596.

Gallus, Gaius Cornelius, (*c.* 62–26 BC), Roman politician and poet. A general of Octavian's, Gallus took part in the defeat of Antony and Cleopatra, and was appointed first governor of Egypt. He pioneered the form of Latin love elegy perfected by Ovid.

Gall Wasp, small black wasp found worldwide. The female lays eggs in plant tissue and a gall develops as the larvae hatch and mature. They are usually found on oak trees and roses. Length: 0.16–0.32in (4–8mm). Family Cynipidae. △502, 594.

Galsworthy, John (1867–1933), English novelist and playwright. His novels deal with the English upper middle class. The most noted of his novels are those about the Forsyte family, grouped in three trilogies: *The Forsyte Saga* (1906–22), *A Modern Comedy* (1924–28), and *End of the Chapter* (1931–33). His plays, such as *Justice* (1910), deal with social issues and were quite popular. *See also* Forsyte Saga, The.

Galt, (Sir) Alexander Tilloch (1817–93), Canadian politician. Arriving in Canada from England in 1835, Galt joined the British American Land Company, becoming commissioner in 1844. He sat in the Legislative Assembly (1849–50, 1853–67) and promoted the Grand Trunk Railway. As minister of finance (1858), he urged confederation on the British and was an influential figure at the Quebec Conference as chief spokesman for the English of Lower Canada. A businessman and political pamphleteer, Galt developed business interests in the Northwest and became Canadian high commissioner (1880–83).

Galt, John (1779–1839), Scottish writer. Galt produced poems, dramas, and historical novels, but particularly remembered are his studies of life in Scotland: *The Ayrshire Legatees* (1821), *Annals of the Parish* (1821), and *The Entail* (1823).

Galt, town in SE Ontario, Canada, on the Grand River; agricultural region. Industries: mining equipment, textiles, plastics, foundries. Founded 1816. Pop. 38,134.

Galton, (Sir) Francis (1822–1911), English anthropologist, explorer, and eugenicist, who conducted important studies on human intelligence. He believed heredity to be more important than environment in human development, and was a proponent of selective parenthood. He was influential in the development of standard statistical techniques, such as curves of normal distribution, correlation of coefficients, and percentile grading. Works include the important *Natural Inheritance* (1889).

Galton Bell Curve. △1474.

Galvani, Luigi or **Aloisio** (1737–98), Italian physician and physicist who became professor of anatomy at Bologna and did pioneer studies in electrophysiology. His experiments with frogs' legs indicated a connection between muscular contraction and electricity, although the correct explanation was given by Volta. Nevertheless, Galvani's name is commemorated in the galvanometer, galvanic currents, and galvanized iron. △1186, 1530.

Galvanizing, the coating of iron or steel articles with zinc, either applied directly in a hot zinc bath or electrodeposited from cold sulfate solutions. Ash cans, nails, pails, and wire netting may be thus protected from atmospheric carbonic acid due to preferential attack on zinc rather than iron.

Galvanometer, instrument for detecting, comparing, or measuring electric currents, usually by the reaction between the magnetic field created by the current and a magnet. The main types are the moving-coil galvanometer and the moving-magnet instrument.

Galveston, city in E central Texas; port of entry on Galveston Island in Gulf of Mexico; seat of Galveston co. Originally part of Mexico and occupied by pirate Jean Laffite, it was annexed to Republic of Texas 1839; served as Confederate naval center during Civil War; first US city to adopt commission plan of municipal government. Industries: oil refining, shipbuilding, tourism. Exports: grain, cotton, flour, sulfur, chemicals, fertilizer. Settled 1830s; inc. 1839. Pop. (1970) 61,809.

Gama, Vasco da (*c.* 1469–1525), Portuguese navigator and discoverer of the sea route to India. In 1497 he led the historic expedition in search of a maritime route to the Indies. He reached South Africa, sailed around the Cape and across the Indian Ocean to Calicut, India. He thus established the route still used by ships today, opening up the resources of Asia to Western European powers. In 1524, he went to India as viceroy, becoming head of the first European enclave in Asia. He died there only months later. △1122.

Gambetta, Léon (1838–82), French politician. He opposed Napoleon III as a legislator, organized French resistance in the Franco-Prussian War (1870–71), and helped form the Third Republic. A champion of French unity, he was prime minister in 1881–82, when he tried unsuccessfully to reform French government, gaining recognition after his death.

Gambia, Republic of The, nation in W Africa. The people are Negroid and mostly Muslim. It is the smallest state in Africa, with an economy dependent upon one product—the peanut.

Land and Economy. The country includes the island of Banjul at the mouth of the Gambia River and an approximately 10-mi (16 km) wide strip of land on each side of the river for about 290mi (467km) inland. It is one of the poorest countries in Africa; rice and other foods are grown but only for local consumption. In recent years tourism has been promoted by the government in an attempt to boost the economy.

People. Five major tribes make up the country; the Mandinkas are the largest. English is the official language; however, a number of native languages and dialects are in use. There is no official religion but 85% of the people are Muslim; most of the rest practice animism. About 90% of the people farm.

Government. A republic, The Gambia has chosen to remain within the British Commonwealth. There is a president and a 32-member legislature with a speaker, all of whom are elected for 5-year terms.

History. Inhabited since ancient times, the country includes the famous Stone Circles, ironstone pillars in groups, which probably represent burial grounds, dating from about 400 BC. Early Portuguese settlements in the 1450s did not survive; the British arrived in 1588 and finally took control in 1765. It became a British Crown Colony in 1888. The Gambia achieved independence in 1965, but in a 1970 referendum chose to join the Commonwealth.

PROFILE

Official name: Republic of The Gambia
Area: 4,361mi (11,295sq km)
Population: 500,000
Density: 1150 per sq mi (44per sq km)
Chief cities: Banjul (capital); Georgetown
Government: Republic
Religion: Islam
Language: English (official)
Monetary unit: dalasi
Gross national product: $40,000,000
Per capita income: $120
Industries (major products): negligible
Agriculture (major products): peanuts, peanut oil
Trading partners (major): Great Britain, Japan, Netherlands

Gambia River, river and major trade artery in W Africa; rises in Fouta Djallon Mts, Guinea; flows NW through Senegal and W into Atlantic Ocean at Banjul. Lower 200mi (322km) of river, all in Republic of The Gambia, are navigable year-round. Length: 700mi (1127km).

Game Bird, any bird hunted by humans for food, especially members of the two major bird orders Galliforme and Anseriforme. Galliformes include the chicken, turkey, quail, pheasant, partridge, guan, and curassow. Typically, they are ground birds with strong legs adapted for walking and running and strong toes to scratch the ground for fruits and seeds. They often have abundant plumage and elevated tails and make simple ground-depression nests. Anseriformes, including the duck, goose, and swan, are waterfowl, with rounded, open nostrils, dense undercoats of down, and special glands to waterproof their plumage. △384.

Gamelan, traditional Indonesian orchestra, formed mostly of percussion instruments resembling Western gongs, chimes, glockenspiel, etc. All play the same melody with slight variations using a five-tone scale.

Gamete, haploid reproductive cell that joins with another cell to form a new organism. Female gametes (ova) are motionless; male gametes (sperm) are motile. △416, 462.

Game Theory, branch of mathematics concerned with the analysis of problems involving conflict. Game theory can be applied to "true" games such as poker and chess, but its application is much wider, including problems in business management, sociology, economics, and military strategy. They involve situations in which there is a conflict of interest, incomplete information, and an element of chance. Game theory is concerned with analyzing the basic features of these problems and devising methods of finding the best strategy, that is, the one with the highest probability of obtaining a successful result. It was first introduced by Emil Borel and developed by John von Neumann in 1928. △1476.

Gametophyte, generation of plants that bears the female and male gametes (sexual reproductive cells). In flowering plants these are the germinated pollen grains (male) and ovules containing the embryo sac (female). *See also* Alternation of Generations; Fern; Moss. △424, 438.

Gamma Globulin, one of the protein components of the blood serum. It contains approximately 85% of the circulating antibodies of the blood, and is thus the major serum immunoglobulin. *See also* Antibody.

Gamma Radiation. △1480, 1554.

Gamma-Ray Astronomy. *See* Astronomy, Gamma-Ray.

Gamma Rays, highly energetic electromagnetic radiation emitted spontaneously by certain radioactive substances when the nucleus makes a transition to a lower energy state. They usually accompany the emission of alpha or beta rays. Their energies are characteristic of the emitting isotope, the rays being very penetrating, and lie at the extreme end of the electromagnetic spectrum, beyond the X ray region, with a wavelength range of about 10^{-11} to 5×10^{-13} meters. *See also* Annihilation. △1480.

Gamow, George (1904–68), US nuclear physicist and cosmologist, b. Russia. Educated in Leningrad, he worked in various European universities before going to the United States in 1934. He was a proponent of the "big-bang" theory of the creation of the universe, and he contributed to the deciphering of the genetic code. He also proposed the quantum theory of radioactivity and the liquid-drop model of atomic nuclei. With Edward Teller, he established the Gamow-Teller theory of beta decay and the internal structure of red giant stars.

Gander, town in NE Newfoundland, Canada; site of important WWII airbase, now used for departure of transatlantic flights. Pop. 7,720.

Gandhara, historic area in modern NW Pakistan, on middle Indus River. Originally a Persian colony (6th century BC), it passed to Maurya empire of India 324–185 BC; under Asoka, Gandhara flourished as a cultural and Buddhist center; its greatest prosperity came with the leadership of Kanishka during the Kushan dynasty (AD 1st-3rd centuries), who developed the Gandhara School of art, noted for statues of Buddha and Buddhist reliefs: in 5th century, the entire area was besieged by the Huns.

Gandhi, Indira Nehru (1918–), Indian political figure, the first woman elected (1966) prime minister of India. The daughter of Jawaharlal Nehru, she served as president of the Indian National Congress party in 1959–60. In 1975, after nine years as prime minister, she was found guilty of using illegal practices in the election of 1971. She refused to resign, invoked emergency powers, and arrested many of her opponents.

Gandhi, Mohandas (Karamchand) (1869–1948), Indian leader. Known as the Mahatma ("Great Lord"), he is considered the father of India because of his leadership of the country's nationalist movement from 1919 to 1947, when independence was granted. His method, called *Satyagraha* ("soul force"), included all forms of non-violent resistance to British rule, such as strikes, refusal to pay taxes, refusal to respect courts. Gandhi's beliefs included: the importance of simple, moral lifestyles over other accomplishments; tolerance and respect for all men (in contrast to the prevalent system); the dignity of labor; a self-sufficient, self-governed India. His experiences in South Africa, where he spent 21 years trying to end oppression of the Indians and the massacre of a mob at Amritsar by the British in 1919 led him to believe that freedom could not be taken by force. In 1920 he instituted a hand-spinning and weaving program. In 1930 he led thousands on a dramatic 200-mile (322km) protest march to the sea. His methods succeeded, and he came to be considered an exemplar of the moral life. He was assassinated by a Hindu Brahmin who objected to his religious tolerance. △1330–32.

Gandolfi, family of, Italian artists in Bologna. **Gaetano** (1734–1802), influenced by Tiepolo, was a church painter and decorator; his brother **Ubalde** (1728–81) was a decorator and sculptor; and Gaetano's son **Mauro** (1764–1834) was an engraver and portrait painter.

Ganges, sacred river in India; rises in the Himalayan Mts, and is formed by the confluence of two headstreams, Bhagirathi and Alaknanda; it flows S then SE, receiving tributaries, and empties into the Bay of Bengal through the combined Brahmaputra-Ganges delta. In Hindu religion and legend, the Ganges is the earthly personification of the Goddess, Ganga; pilgrims travel to bathe in its waters for purification. Plains of Ganges are extremely fertile and support one of the world's most densely populated areas; dams divert water to the dry lands for irrigation; also

SHELTON'S
Gallup, New Mexico

Vasco da Gama

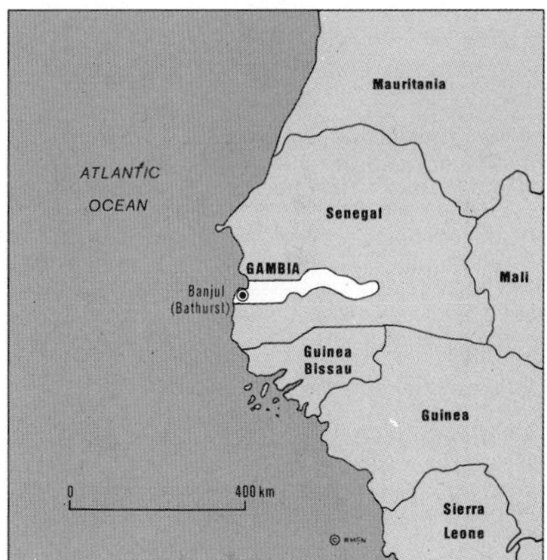
Mauritania
ATLANTIC
OCEAN
Senegal
GAMBIA
Banjul
(Bathurst)
Mali
Guinea
Bissau
Guinea
0
400 km
Sierra
Leone
Gambia

Indira Gandhi

used for hydroelectric power. Length: 1,560mi (2,496km).

Ganglion, any identifiable, relatively large concentration of neurons or cell bodies in the nervous system. Ganglia are found both inside and outside of the central nervous system, eg, the basal ganglia are located within the cerebral cortex. △664.

Gangrene, death of body tissues associated with loss of blood supply and bacterial infection; also seen as a result of diabetes or of an embolism or thrombosis. Symptoms include inflammation and ulceration of the organ or skin.

Gannet, fast-diving marine bird of cooler offshore waters, related to tropical boobies. Heavy-bodied with a tapered bill, long pointed wings, short legs, and webbed feet, it is white with a yellowish head and black wing tips. It feeds on fish and nests in huge colonies on rocky islands. One chick is reared although 1-3 bluish eggs are laid. Length: 25–35in (63–89cm). Family Sulidae. △534.

Gannett Peak, mountain in the Wind River Range in central Wyoming; highest point in the state, 13,785ft (4,204m).

Ganoid Fish, primitive bony fish with hard scales of bone overlaid with layers of enamellike substance. Although most are extinct, modern examples are bowfin, gar, paddlefin, and sturgeon. △510.

Gans, Herbert (1927–), US sociologist, b. Germany. Doing research in collective behavior and urban sociology, he urged that social planning be included in urban renewal programs. His books include *The Urban Villagers* (1962), *The Levittowners* (1967), and *Popular Culture and High Culture in America* (1974).

Ganymede, in Greek mythology, the son of Tros, king of Troy. Zeus, charmed by his unusual beauty, sent an eagle to carry Ganymede to Olympus. There he became the cup bearer of the gods.

Ganymede, largest of Jupiter's satellites; one of the Galilean satellites. Ganymede is larger than Mercury. Diameter approx. 3,100mi (5,000km); mean distance from planet 621,000mi (1,000,000km); mean sidereal period 7.15 days. △86, 152.

GAO. *See* General Accounting Office.

GAR. *See* Grand Army of the Republic.

Gar, primitive freshwater bony fish found in shallow weedy waters of North America, east of Rocky Mountains. Its long cylindrical body is covered with bony diamond-shaped flat plates. It has a long snout studded with teeth and vertebrae resembling those of reptiles. Length: to 10ft (305cm); Weight: to 302lb (136kg). Family Lepisosteidae; species 8, including alligator gar *Lepisosteus spatula* and longnose *Lepisosteus osseus.* △510.

Garbanzo. *See* Chick-pea.

Garbo, Greta (1905–), Swedish film actress, b. Greta Gustaffson. She is famous for her aura of mystery and legendary romantic beauty. Her silent films included *Torment* (1926) and *Flesh and the Devil* (1927), but her greatest successes were the sound films *Anna Christie* (1930), *Grand Hotel* (1932), *Queen Christina* (1933), *Anna Karenina* (1935), *Camille* (1936), and the comedy *Ninotchka* (1939). She retired in 1941. △1362.

García Lorca, Federico (1898–1936), Spanish poet and dramatist. Lorca's poetry, from *Book of Poems* (1921) to *Poet in New York* (1940), was internationally acclaimed. His plays include *The Shoemaker's Prodigious Wife* (1930) and *Blood Wedding* (1933), performed in the United States (1935) as *Bitter Oleander.* He was killed by Fascist soldiers at the outbreak of the Spanish Civil War.

García Márquez, Gabriel (1928–), Colombian novelist. His novel *One Hundred Years of Solitude* (1967) has become one of the most popular books ever in the Spanish-speaking world. It focuses on the remote town of Macondo, which was also the setting of his previous novels. The events are sometimes nonrealistic but the town's up-and-down history has been interpreted as symbolic of Latin America's. Macondo's feuding, eccentric citizens are both funny and tragic. *Withered Leaves* (1955) began the saga.

Garcilaso de la Vega (1539–1616), Peruvian historian. Calling himself "El Inca," he was one of the first accomplished writers in the New World. His best-known work is *The Royal Commentaries of Peru* (1609–17), a history of the Inca empire and its downfall. Slightly idealized, it is still an eloquent description of Inca civilization. *La Florida de Inca* (1605) retraced de Soto's expedition.

Garcilaso de la Vega (*c.*1503–36), Spanish poet, courtier, and soldier. He helped to introduce Italian metrical forms into Spain. His poems, including sonnets, an eclogue inspired by Virgil's tomb, *canciones,* and elegies, were published with those of Juan Boscán in 1543. He was killed in battle.

Garda, Lake (Lago di Garda), lake in N Italy; largest of Italian lakes; fed by the Sarca River; drained through Mincio River into the Po; resort area. Area: 143sq mi (370sq km).

Garden, Mary (1874–1967), US soprano, b. Scotland. She made her debut at the Paris Opéra-Comique in 1900 as Charpentier's *Louise* and premiered the role of Mélisande in Debussy's *Pelléas and Mélisande* in 1902. These roles propelled her to stardom and were subsequently identified with her. Later she appeared at the Manhattan (1907–10) and Chicago (1910–31) Operas.

Gardena, city in SW California; suburb of Los Angeles; site of Japanese cultural exhibit; population is 25% Oriental. Industries: aerospace, electronic components, textiles. Inc. 1930. Pop. (1970) 41,021.

Garden City, town in SE New York, on S shore of Long Island; site of Adelphi College (1896), Nassau Community College (1960). Industries: printing, publishing. Founded 1869; inc. 1919. Pop. (1970) 25,-373.

Garden City, city in SE Michigan, 15mi (24km) W of Detroit. Industries: wire cloth, aluminum extrusions, golf balls. Inc. as village 1927, city 1934. Pop. (1970) 41,864.

Garden Grove, city in S California, S of Anaheim; suburb of Los Angeles and Long Beach, where a majority of residents are employed in aerospace and defense industries. Founded 1877; inc. 1956. Pop. (1970) 121,371.

Gardenia, genus of evergreen shrubs and small trees native to tropical Asia and Africa; they have white or yellow fragrant, waxy flowers. Height: to 18ft (5.5m). Family Rubiaceae.

Garden of the Gods, park near Colorado Springs, Colorado; site of rock formations of red and white sandstone eroded into unusual shapes; contains natural amphitheater where annual Easter sunrise service is held. Area: 770acres (312hectares).

Garden Spider. △488.

Gardiner's Island, island in Gardiner's Bay, New York, W of Montauk Point. Settled by Lion Gardiner in 1639; first permanent English settlement of present-day N.Y. state. Held by Gardiner descendants for more than 300 years. Wildlife on island includes deer, pheasants, ospreys, and wild turkeys; now used as a hunting preserve. Area: 3,000acres (1,215hectares).

Gardner, John (1933–), US author, b. Batavia, N.Y. A teacher of English literature and creative writing, he wrote poems, short stories, and novels. These include *Nickel Mountain* (1973) and *October Light* (1977).

Garfield, James Abram (1831–81), 20th President of the United States, b. Orange, Ohio, attended Williams College. In 1858 he married Lucretia Rudolph; they had six children. A lay preacher in the Disciples of Christ church, he was admitted to the bar and elected to the Ohio senate in 1859. He served in the Civil War until 1863, when he was elected to the US House of Representatives. A loyal party man, he rose in power in the House and by 1876, was Republican leader there. He supported the Radical Republicans and was a hard-money advocate.

The 1880 Republican convention deadlocked and he was finally—on the 36th ballot—nominated as the compromise candidate. Chester Alan Arthur was chosen as his running mate.

His four-month administration was characterized by party squabbles for federal jobs and political patronage. On July 2, 1881, a disappointed job seeker, Charles J. Guiteau, shot and mortally wounded the president. He died on September 19 and was succeeded by Arthur.

Career: Ohio State Senate, 1860–61; US House of Representatives, 1863–80; president, 1881.

Garfield, city in NE New Jersey, at confluence of Passaic and Saddle rivers; named for President James Garfield. Industries: paper, embroideries, chemicals. Inc. as city 1917. Pop. (1970) 30,722.

Garfield Heights, city in NE Ohio, adjacent to Cleveland. Industries: iron, steel, chemicals, oil. Founded 1904 as South Newburgh; named changed 1919, inc. 1932. Pop. (1970) 41,417.

Garfish, or gar pike, billfish, silver gar, marine needlefish found in all tropical and temperate waters, also in bays and coastal rivers. Its long garlike body is green and silver with a dark-green back stripe; jaws are elongated with sharp teeth. Length: to 4ft (122cm). Family Belonidae; species 26 including Atlantic *Tylosaurus marinus* and *Belone bellone.* △510

Gargantua, La vie tres horrificque du grand (1534), satirical book by François Rabelais. Chronologically preceding *Pantagruel* (1532), the story focuses on the educational and martial adventures of Gargantua, Pantagruel's father. The author mocks educational and religious traditions and celebrates an ideal of self-disciplined freedom. △1172.

Garibaldi, Giuseppe (1807–82), guerrilla general in the mid-19th century movement for Italian independence and unification. A political exile, influenced by the liberal thought of Giuseppe Mazzini, in 1834 he went to Latin America, where he led Italian forces for Uruguay against Argentina. During 1848–49 his confrontation at Milan with the Austrians, symbol of European reactionary forces, and in central Italy with the French elevated him to the stature of a national hero symbolizing Italian unity. In 1860, Garibaldi successfully led his guerrilla army against Sicily and Naples, uniting Italy under King Victor Emmanuel II of Sardinia-Piedmont. He attacked Rome in 1862 and 1867 but was defeated. He commanded a French army in the Franco-Prussian War (1870–71) and sat in the Italian Parliament from 1874. △1250.

Garland, Hamlin (1860–1940), US author, b. West Salem, Wis. Garland's works are marked by strong social comment. His realistic short stories dealing with the hardships of farmers are collected in several volumes, the first of which was *Main-Travelled Roads* (1891). Feeling that something stronger was needed to carry his message, Garland wrote several propagandist works, including *Jason Edwards: An Average Man* (1892) and *A Spoil of Office* (1892). He also published an autobiography, *A Son of the Middle Border* (1917).

Garland, Judy (1922–69), US singer and film actress, b. Frances Gumm in Grand Rapids, Minn. Beginning her film career at 13, she gained popularity in the Andy Hardy films and *The Wizard of Oz* (1939). "Over the Rainbow" from *The Wizard of Oz* became her trademark song. Her other major films included *Meet Me in St. Louis* (1944), *Easter Parade* (1948), and *A Star is Born* (1954). Her later life was marked by great personal unhappiness, but she made a successful comeback on the international concert circuit, breaking box-office records in the 1960s.

Garland, city in NE Texas, 14mi (23km) NE of Dallas; agricultural area. Industries: electronic equipment, oil, aircraft, food products, varnish, clothing. Inc. 1891. Pop. (1970) 81,437.

Garlic, bulbous herb native to S Europe and central Asia. It has onionlike foliage and a strong-smelling bulb made up of sections called cloves that are used for flavoring. Family Liliaceae; species *Allium sativum.* *See also* Allium.

Garmisch-Partenkirchen, town in S West Germany, in the Bavarian Alps at foot of Zugspitze. Olympic games were held here 1936; international winter resort and commercial center. Towns of Garmisch and Partenkirchen were combined 1935. Pop. 27,367.

Garner, Erroll (Louis (1921–77), US jazz pianist and composer, b. Pittsburgh. Self-taught, he developed a unique "stride" piano style featuring full chords in the left hand. He was one of the most popular and highly regarded jazz pianists of the 1940s through the 1960s and during that period he appeared on television more than any other jazz musician. He wrote "Misty" (1959) and made many recordings.

Garner, John Nance (1868–1967), US political figure and Vice-president (1933–41), b. Blossom Prairie, Tex. He was a Texas legislator (1898–1902) and US Congressman (1903–33), serving as speaker of the House (1931–33). Vice-president under President Roosevelt, he helped obtain passage of New Deal legislation. He retired in 1941.

Garnet, Henry Highland (1815–82), US abolitionist and diplomat, b. New Market, Md. He escaped from slavery, graduated from Oneida Institute, and became a Presbyterian minister. His influence as an abolitionist was great until he exhorted slaves to revolt in an 1843 speech in Buffalo, N.Y. The more moderate Frederick Douglass then supplanted him. After taking various pastorates, he was appointed US minister to Liberia in 1881.

Garnet, two series of common orthosilicate minerals: the pyralspite series (pyrope, almandite, and spessartite); and the ugradite series (uvarovite, grossularite, and andradite). Found in metamorphic rocks and pegmatites. Cubic system dodecahedral and trapezohedral crystals and rounded grains and granular masses. Brittle, glassy, of many hues; hardness 6–7.5, sp gr 4. Some varieties important as gemstones. △244.

Garnier, Francis (1839–73), French naval officer and explorer, b. Marie Joseph François Garnier. He served (1860–62) in French campaigns against China and what is now Vietnam. He was named governor of French-ruled Saigon in 1862. In 1866 he left on a hazardous exploring expedition along the Mekong River and accurately mapped the region. After service in the Franco-Prussian War (1870–71) Garnier returned to Asia. In 1873 he was sent with a military force to Hanoi to arbitrate a local dispute. Garnier seized the city, and then, extensively using artillery, conquered most of the cities in northern Vietnam. He was, however, killed in battle, and the first French attempt to conquer northern Vietnam collapsed.

Garnierite. △278.

Garonne River, river in SW France; rises on slopes of Pyrenees, in Spain; flows NW to join the Dordogne River N of Bordeaux and form the Gironde Estuary, which empties into the Atlantic Ocean. Length: 357mi (575km).

Gar Pike. *See* Garfish.

Garrick, David (1717–79), English actor. He is credited with replacing the formal declamatory style of acting with easy, natural speech. His success in his formal acting debut as Richard III resulted in his being hired by the Drury Lane Theatre (1742), where he remained until his retirement in 1776, becoming its manager in 1747. He traveled on the Continent with his wife (1763–65), returning to play successfully until his final performance in *The Wonder, a Woman Keeps a Secret* (1776). The Garrick Club and the Garrick Theater, both in London, were named in his honor.

Garrison, William Lloyd (1805–79), US abolitionist, who exerted great influence on the anti-slavery movement, b. Newburyport, Mass. In 1831 he started the *Liberator* in Boston, which held considerable sway until Garrison closed it down in 1865, after it published the amendment to the Constitution abolishing slavery in the United States. In 1831 he founded the New England Anti-Slavery Society, influential until 1840. After the Civil War he concentrated on other reform programs, including temperance and women's suffrage. △1276.

Garrison Dam, dam on Missouri River, near Riverdale, W central North Dakota. One of world's largest earth-filled dams, it is 210ft (64m) high. Reservoir formed by dam is Lake Sakajawea, 178mi (287km) long and 14mi (23km) wide at some points. Built by US Army Corps of Engineers and completed in 1956, it was designed for flood control, irrigation, and power generation. Length: 11,300ft (3,400m).

Garrison v. Louisiana (1964), US Supreme Court case holding that the rule of *New York Times v. Sullivan* (1964) was applicable in criminal libel prosecutions. Therefore, criticism of public officials was not libelous unless knowingly false. *See also* New York Times v. Sullivan (1964).

Garter Snake, harmless snake, usually striped, ranging from S Canada through Central America. Twelve species live in the United States, including the slender ribbon snake and stouter true garter snake. Their ground color is usually olive-brown with yellow, orange, red, or blue stripes often checkered or spotted with black. They often live near water, are good swimmers, and feed on frogs, fish, and earthworms. Length: to 2ft (61cm). Family Colubridae; genus *Thamnophis*. *See also* Snake.

Garvey, Marcus (1887–1940), US black nationalist leader, b. Jamaica, British West Indies. While an editor in Jamaica, he organized the Universal Negro Improvement Association (UNIA), based on the theory that blacks and whites could not live together while blacks were a minority. Favoring a back-to-Africa movement, Garvey brought his plan to New York in 1916 where he attempted to find investors for his Black Star Line, a fleet of ships to carry blacks back to Africa. In 1922 the Black Star Line failed and the UNIA collapsed, and in 1923 Garvey was convicted of mail fraud. In 1927 he was pardoned by Pres. Calvin Coolidge.

Gary, Romain (1914–), original name Romain Kacev, French novelist. He emigrated to France from Russia in 1928 and after fighting in World War II entered the diplomatic service. His best known novel is *A European Education* (1945), about Polish wartime resistance. Other works include *The Roots of Heaven* (1956), *Promise at Dawn* (1960), *White Dog* (1970), and *The Gasp* (1973).

Gary, city in NW Indiana, on S tip of Lake Michigan, 35mi (56km) SE of Chicago; one of world's largest steel centers. Dunes National Lakeshore Park is nearby; serviced by Burn Harbor to the E. Industries: steel, hardware, springs, windshield wipers, clothing, bedding, steel bridges. Founded 1905 by US Steel Corp.; inc. 1906. Pop. (1970) 175,415.

Gas, state of matter in which a substance has no fixed shape or volume, flowing freely and expanding to fill any container. The interactions between the atoms or molecules are low compared with thermal energies and the particles have random motion. The viscosity of gases increases with temperature. *See also* Liquid; Solid. △1502–04, 1562, 1568.

Gas, Natural, a naturally occurring, combustible, gaseous mixture of hydrocarbons used as a fuel and in the production of plastics, drugs, antifreeze and dyes. Natural gas is the gaseous element of petroleum and is extracted as casehead gas from oil wells. Certain wells, however, yield only natural gas. Before natural gas may be used as a fuel, the heavier hydrocarbons of butane and propane are extracted and as liquids are forced into containers as bottled gas. The remaining gas, called "dry gas," is piped to consumers for use as fuel. Dry gas is composed of the light hydrocarbons methane and ethane. *See also* Petroleum. △284, 1642, 1646.

Gasca, Pedro de la (1485–1567), Spanish priest and special envoy of the Crown, sent to Peru in 1546 to reestablish royal authority following the uprising of Gonzalo Pizarro. Gasca successfully carried out his mission; Pizarro was executed and the audiencia of Lima reorganized. Gasca left Peru in 1550.

Gascony (Gascogne), historic region and province in SW France, bounded by Bay of Biscay (W), Pyrenees (S), and Garonne River (N and E). Settled 6th century by Basques; Franks established duchy of Gascony 632; captured and held mid-12th–15th centuries by English; became part of France 1453 at end of Hundred Years' War. The region was divided into three departments and made part of four others in 1790. △1096.

Gaseous Nebulae. △104.

Gases, Noble. *See* Noble Gases.

Gasoline, fuel used in internal-combustion engines. Gasoline is a colorless volatile highly flammable mixture of alkane hydrocarbons with 6–9 carbon atoms, obtained by distillation of petroleum. Commercial gasoline contains additives such as antioxidants and antiknock agents. Its quality is specified by its octane rating, obtained by comparison of performance with a standard mixture of hydrocarbons. △1632, 1644–46.

Gasometers. △1502.

Gaspee, HMS, British revenue cutter enforcing customs laws in Narragansett Bay, R.I. It was burned by colonists active in smuggling (1772). It was an important act of colonial defiance before the revolution.

Gaspé Peninsula, peninsula in SE Quebec, Canada, S of St Lawrence River, N of New Brunswick; contains several lakes and rivers, thick forests; good hunting and fishing. Length: approx. 150mi (242km).

Gassendi, Pierre (1592–1655), French philosopher, Catholic priest (1617), and scientist. In the *Syntagma philosophicum* (1649) he revived Epicurean atomism and defended the veracity of sense knowledge against Descartes in reply to that author's *Meditations*.

Gastonia, city in SW North Carolina; seat of Gaston co. Named for William Gaston, North Carolina Supreme Court judge; textile center. King's Mountain National Military Park is nearby. Inc. 1877. Pop. (1970) 47,142.

Greta Garbo

James Garfield

Judy Garland: with Gene Kelly

William Lloyd Garrison

Gastric Juice, a mixture of substances secreted into the stomach; they break down complex proteins and carbohydrates into simpler units during digestion. They include hydrochloric acid, the enzyme pepsin, and mucus. △694.

Gastritis, inflammation of the lining of the stomach, chronic or acute. It may be caused by chemicals, food, or disease.

Gastrocnemius. △684.

Gastroenteritis, inflammation of the lining of the stomach and intestine. It may be caused by viruses, bacteria, chemicals, or allergy. *See also* Gastritis.

Gastroenterology, branch of medicine that deals with the diagnosis and treatment of diseases and disorders of the gastrointestinal tract, including the stomach and small and large intestines. △718.

Gastrolith. △560.

Gastropod, mollusk usually identified by coiled shell and body, found in marine and fresh waters and on land. This univalve class includes snails, slugs, sea hares, limpets, whelks, and periwinkles. The body consists of a head with tentacles and a foot, both forming the base for movement, and asymmetrical vascera and mantle, which secrete the coiled shell. Land types (pulmonate gastropods) have modified mantle and mantle cavity used for breathing air. Sea hares and slugs are symmetrical and do not have a visible shell; limpets have a tent-shaped shell. Class Gastropoda. △476.

Gastrotricha, phylum of microscopic, many celled animals similar to rotifers. Structurally similar to simple worms, they have bristles covering the entire body. Reproduction is hermaphroditic and parthenogenetic (egg develops without fertilization).

Gas Turbine. *See* Turbine. △1632.

Gates, Horatio (1727–1806), US general, b. England. He served under Gen. Edward Braddock in the French and Indian War. In 1772 he returned to America and settled in Virginia. He soon joined the patriot's cause, and in 1776 he was appointed commander of the army in the north. Aided by Benedict Arnold and Daniel Morgan, he decisively defeated the British under Gen. Burgoyne at Saratoga, N.Y. (1777). But in 1780 he was defeated by Gen. Cornwallis at Camden, S.C., and relieved of his command.

Gates, (Sir) Thomas (died *c.*1621), member of the London Company, which organized the first settlement of Virginia. He was separated from the other colonists en route from England (1609) and, shipwrecked, was unable to rejoin them until late spring of 1610. Only a handful of the original 500 had survived, and he was dissuaded, with others, from a return to England only by the arrival of Governor De La Warr. After De La Warr left for England to bring aid to the colony, Gates was governor (1611–14). He left the colony in 1614 and died before he could return.

Gathas, collection of hymns, believed to be the work of Zoroaster, that are the basis of the Avesta or sacred book of Zoroastrianism. They contain the fundamental teachings of the prophet and are concerned with man's duty in the conquest of evil.

Gatling, Richard Jordan (1818–1903), US inventor, b. Winton, N.C. He invented and manufactured machines for sowing cottonseed, rice, and wheat before perfecting a revolving machine gun (1862). The Gatling gun, at first rejected by the Union army, was improved (1865) and adopted by the US government (1866). He invented a new gun metal of steel and aluminum in 1886. △1730.

GATT. *See* General Agreement on Tariffs and Trade.

Gatun, town in Panama Canal Zone, Central America; site of man-made Gatun Lake, formed by the Gatun Dam across the Chagres River, and the two sets of Gatun Locks, which raise and lower vessels from the lake. Area of lake: 166sq mi (430sq km).

Gaucho, colorful cowboy of Argentine history and legend, an important political force in the 18th and 19th centuries. At first free-wheeling nomads of the Argentine pampas, the mixed-blood gauchos became farmhands and horse soldiers as civilization advanced, and fenced their lands. They became the subject of a distinctive South American literature.

Gaudi, Antoni (1852–1926), Spanish architect. He created a modern style of architecture distinctively Mediterranean in character, combining Gothic elements with Art Nouveau. His designs, which combine sculptural and pictorial elements, include, in Barcelona, the Church of the Sagrada Family, Güell Park, and dwellings for factory workers.

Gauguin, (Eugène Henri) Paul (1848–1903), French painter. A leader of the anti-naturalist-symbolist movement in art, he gave up a career as a stockbroker to devote all his energies to painting. He exhibited in the first four postimpressionist shows (1879–86) and in 1891 left his family in France to go to Tahiti. In the South Seas he executed his most famous paintings—primitive, exotic, aggressive glorifications of the Noble Savage, using abstract patterns and flat, strong colors in depictions of native figures and landscapes. He also produced woodcuts and painted wood-reliefs in the same primitive style. Gauguin's life was dogged by illness, poverty, and harassment from the French colonial government for his protests against social injustice on the various South Seas islands where he lived for short periods. A friend of Vincent van Gogh, he had a large following in symbolist circles in Paris. △1292.

Gauhāti, city in NE India, on Brahmaputra River; capital of ancient kingdom of Kamarupa (1100); served as Muslim capital of upper Brahmaputra 1500–1824. Pop. 223,741.

Gauls, ancient Celtic peoples who settled Gaul, the area S and W of the Rhine, N of the Pyrenees, and W of the Alps, in the 4th and 3rd centuries BC. The Romans under Caesar conquered Gaul (58–51 BC) and thereafter the Gauls were thoroughly Romanized. The successful Gallo-Roman culture survived until the German invasions of the 5th and 6th centuries AD, which gradually created a number of independent kingdoms. *See also* Gallic Wars. △1018.

Gaunt, John of. *See* John of Gaunt.

Gaur, ancient ruined city in NE India, 8mi (13km) S of English Bazar; Hindu capital of Bengal, captured by Muslims, it served as center of Muslim government and culture (1200–late 16th century); site of Kadam Rasul Mosque (1530), Golden Mosque, Bara Sona Mosjid.

Gaur, or seladang, large wild ox formerly in hilly forests from India to Malay Peninsula, now much reduced in range. Black to brown with white stockings, it has a saddlelike hump on its back and flattened, curved horns. Height: to 7ft (2.1m) at shoulder; weight: 2000lb (900kg). Family Bovidae; species *Bos gaurus. See also* Ox. △582.

Gauss, Karl Friedrich (1777–1855), German mathematician. As a child prodigy from a poor family his education was sponsored by the duke of Brunswick. In 1807 he became director of Göttingen Observatory, where he remained until his death. He contributed to the study of electricity and magnetism and made significant advances in such branches of mathematics as number theory and the theory of series. The unit of magnetic flux density is named after him.

Gauss's Law, the total electric flux of a closed surface in an electric field is the magnitude of the charge within that surface divided by the electric constant. The law also applies to surfaces drawn in a magnetic field and similar statements can be made for a gravitation field.

Gautama. *See* Buddha.

Gautier, Theophile. △1240, 1862.

Gavelkind, system of inheritance common in Britain before the Norman Conquest. As compared with primogeniture, by which the firstborn son inherited his father's estate or tenement, the custom of gavelkind entitled all sons to share equally in the estate.

Gavial, crocodilian living in India and Burma. Characterized by a long, narrow, rodlike snout, it is harmless to man, feeding almost exclusively on fish. Length: to 21ft (6.4m). Family Gavialidae; species *Gavialis gangeticus. See also* Crocodile.

Gavle (Gefle), seaport city in E Sweden; seat of Gävleborg co; site of Viking burial ground, 16th-century castle, 17th-century church. Exports: iron ore, wood pulp. Industries: shipyards, lumber, textiles, chemicals. Chartered 1446. Pop. 72,987.

Gavotte, originally a peasant dance of the 14th century. It was popularized by Marie Antoinette and became a fashionable 18th-century court dance. Similar to, but livelier than, the minuet, it has a 4/4 rhythm.

Gay, John (1685–1732), English poet and dramatist. His best-known work is the ballad-opera *The Beggar's Opera* (1728), a political satire burlesquing Italian opera style. *The Threepenny Opera* (1928) by Bertolt Brecht and Kurt Weill is based on *The Beggar's Opera.*

Gaya, holy city in NE India, on Phalgu River; sacred pilgrimage center administered by Hindus and Buddhists; nearby, Lord Buddha received enlightenment and God Vishnu sacrificed demon of Gaya; seat of Magadha University (founded by Buddhists 1962). Pop. 169,464.

Gay-Lussac, Joseph Louis (1778–1850), French chemist and physicist who did pioneer research on the behavior of gases. He discovered the law of combining gas volumes (Gay-Lussac's law) and the law of gas expansion often also attributed to J.A.C. Charles (who discovered it earlier but did not publish his results). In the field of chemistry, he prepared (with Louis-Jacques Thenard) the elements potassium and boron; investigated fermentation and hydrocyanic acid; and invented a hydrometer.

Gay-Lussac's Law. *See* Charles' Law.

Gaza (Ghazzah), seaport city in W Israel, on Gaza Strip, on SE Mediterranean Sea coast. One of five city-kingdoms of Philistines, it was under frequent attack because of its strategic position between Palestine and Egypt; became a Muslim holy city after capture by Arabs AD 634; part of British Palestine mandate 1917–48; under Egyptian rule 1948–67, when it was occupied by Israel; largest city and administrative center of the Gaza Strip. Pop. 118,300. *See also* Gaza Strip.

Gaza Strip, small region in W Israel, on SE Mediterranean Sea; part of Britain's Palestine Mandate after WWI; by 1947 Britain intended to give up the area; the peace talks of Arab-Israeli War (1948–49) made it an Egyptian possession; it was occupied by Israel after 1967 war. Since WWII, it has served as a Palestine Arab refugee center. Area: 140sq mi (363sq km). Pop. 365,000.

Gazelle, dozen species of fast, graceful, small-to-medium antelopes native to Africa and Asia, frequently inhabiting plains and treeless areas. The lyre-shaped horns, common to both sexes in African species, are generally lacking in females of Asiatic species. All are light brown with white rump. Bedouins hunt gazelles with falcons and dogs.

Dorcas gazelle of N Africa is a typical small representative. Two Asiatic gazelles, Mongolian and Tibetan (genus *Procapra*), are somewhat goatlike in appearance and inhabit mountainous plateaus. The gerenuk *(Litocranius walleri)* and the dibatag or Clarke's gazelle *(Ammodorcas clarkei)* are sometimes considered gazelles. Length: 39–49in (1–1.2m); height: 20–25in (51–64cm) at shoulder. They can run 40mph (64kmph) for over 15 minutes. Family Bovidae; genus *Gazella. See also* Antelope. △606.

Gazetteer, a geographical index or dictionary containing, generally in alphabetical order, a list of names and descriptions of places. The first such gazetteer was edited in 1693 by the English historian Laurence Echard *(The Gazetteer's: or, Newsman's Interpreter: Being a Geographical Index).*

Gaziantep, formerly Aintab; city in SW Turkey, between the Taurus Mts and Euphrates River; capital of Gaziantep prov.; agricultural and trade center. Ancient Hittite city, it was taken by Saladin 1183; conquered by Ottomans 1516; resisted French occupation 1920–21; returned to Turkey 1921. Exports: pistachio nuts, grapes. Pop. 160,152.

G-Clamp. △1602.

Gdańsk (Danzig), seaport city in N Poland, on Gulf of Danzig; capital of Gdańsk prov.; settled by Slavs in 10th century; taken over by Poland 15th century; made part of Prussia 1793; Treaty of Versailles (1919) est. it as a free city, serving as port for Poland; inc. into Germany 1939; returned to Poland 1945. Industries: shipbuilding, metallurgy, machinery, chemicals, food processing, lumber. Pop. 364,300.

Gdynia, seaport city in N Poland, on Gulf of Danzig, Baltic Sea; major port and naval base. Industries: shipbuilding, metallurgy, machinery, food processing. Inc. 1926. Pop. 190,100.

Gear, a toothed wheel, usually attached to a rotating shaft. Operating in pairs, the teeth of one gear engage those of the other, to transmit and modify rotary motion and torque. The smaller member of a gear pair is called a pinion. If the pinion is on the driving shaft, speed is reduced and torque amplified; if the gear is on the shaft, speed is increased and torque reduced. A screw-type gear, called a worm, may have only one tooth; a pinion must have at least five. △1654.

Geb, in Egyptian mythology, the earth god, son of Shu and Tefnut, husband of Nut and father of Osiris. He is depicted as a goose, or as a man with a goose on his head. In the Egyptian myth of creation, the air separates Geb, the earth, from Nut, the sky. △834.

Geber, or **Jabir (Jabir ibn-Hayyan)** (*c.* 720–815), Arab alchemist whose works were studied by Roger Bacon. The identification of Geber with Jabir is uncertain, but Geber is known to have performed scientific experiments as well as attempting to convert mercury into gold. He felt that a transmutation of baser metals into nobler ones was possible. He prepared nitric acid and distilled vinegar.

Gecko, any of about 65 species of small to medium, mostly arboreal lizards wide-spread in warm areas worldwide. Their remarkable climbing ability is due to microscopic suction cups on their feet. They make chirping or barking calls. Length: 1–6in (3–15cm). Family Gekkonidae. *See also* Lizard.

Geddes, Norman Bel (1893–1958), US stage and industrial designer, b. Adrian, Mich. His stage designs, a major influence on the art after 1920, featured the use of steps, platforms, and imaginative lighting effects. His plan for staging Dante's *The Divine Comedy* (published 1921) is still considered brilliant. He was responsible for sets, costumes, and lighting for over 200 plays, operas, and musical comedies; among the most notable *Hamlet* (1931) and Werfel's *The Eternal Road* (1936). He also designed theaters and numerous industrial products.

Gefle. *See* Gavle.

Gegenschein, or counterglow, faint luminous patch visible at a point along the ecliptic, that is diametrically opposite to the sun. Best seen in tropical regions it is a phenomenon allied to the zodiacal light, and often appears as an extension of it.

Gehrig, Lou (1903–1941), US baseball player, b. Henry Louis Gehrig in New York City. Known as the "Iron Horse," he played for the New York Yankees (1925–39) and established a record by playing in 2,130 consecutive games. He had a lifetime batting average of .340 and hit 493 home runs. His career was ended by a terminal illness. He was elected to the Baseball Hall of Fame in 1939.

Gehrig's Disease. *See* Amyotrophic Lateral Sclerosis.

Geiger Counter, or **Geiger-Müller Counter,** type of ionization chamber in which a high voltage is applied across the electrodes. Radiation or particles entering the chamber ionize gas atoms and the resulting ions, gaining energy from the electric field between the electrodes, can produce many more ions. The resulting current quickly subsides so that a pulse of current is produced for each particle. Each pulse activates a counting circuit enabling several thousand particles per second to be counted. *See also* Ionization Chamber. △1480, 1554.

Geisel, Theodor Seuss. *See* Seuss, Dr.

Geissler Tubes. △1480.

Gel, coherent mass consisting of a liquid comprising minute particles dispersed or arranged in a fine network throughout the mass. Their appearance may be notably elastic or jellylike (as in gelatin or fruit jelly) or quite rigid and solid (as in silica gel, a material resembling coarse white sand used as a dehumidifier, and vulcanized rubber).

Gelatin, colorless or yellowish protein obtained from collagen in animal cartilages and bones by boiling in water. It is used in photographic film, sizing, capsules for medical drugs, explosives, and as a culture medium for bacteria.

Gelibolu Peninsula. *See* Gallipoli Peninsula.

Gellée, Claude. *See* Lorrain, Claude.

Geller, Uri. △824.

Gellius, Aulus (*fl.* 2nd century), Roman author. A lawyer, he spent some time in Athens. His *Attic Nights,* a miscellany, is valuable as a source of quotations from other authors whose works are otherwise lost.

Gelsenkirchen, city and port in W West Germany, on the Rhine-Herne Canal; site of 16th–18th-century moated castle. Industries: coal, glass, clothing, oil refining. Pop. 360,981.

Gem, any of about 100 minerals, either opaque, transparent, or translucent, valued for their beauty, rarity, and durability. The most highly valued stones are transparent ones, such as the diamond, ruby, emerald, and sapphire. Pearl, amber, and coral are gems of organic origin. Gemstones are cut to bring out their color and brilliance and are often set in jewelry. Gems with a design cut into the stone are intaglios; with a design in relief, cameos.

In ancient Babylon, intaglios were used for rings and amulets. Intaglios and cameos were used in Greek and Roman jewelry. Antique classical gems often carried engraved pictures of notable contemporary statues and paintings that have since been destroyed and are evidence of the existence of these lost works of art. During the Byzantine period, Constantinople became the center of gem-cutting. Especially during the Middle Ages, many gems were thought to have magical powers. During the Renaissance, northern Italy became the center of skillful gem engraving, using classical gems as models. The art of cutting and polishing gemstones was developed in the 15th century probably beginning in France and the Netherlands. *See also* Lapidary. △244.

Gem, Artificial, imitations of natural gemstones made of various substances. The first appeared in prehistoric times. Glass is frequently used; the best quality being made of material containing lead oxide and cut and polished. Plastics have replaced glass in some instances. Pearls are simulated by coating glass beads with pearl essence, a derivative of fish scales. Imitation diamonds are made of strontium titanate or rutile. Ruby and sapphire, emerald and spinel are also made synthetically. *See also* Gems. △244.

Gemeinschaft, in sociology, ideal-type concept formulated by Ferdinand Toennies in 1887, denoting social systems based on spontaneous, small-group, face-to-face relationships. The family and "primitive" societies are often called Gemeinschaft-like. *See also* Gesellschaft. △888.

Gemini, or the Twins, northern constellation, situated on the ecliptic between Taurus and Cancer and lying northeast of Orion; the third sign of the zodiac. It contains the star cluster M 35 (NGC 2168) and the planetary nebula NGC 2392. Brightest star: Beta Geminorum (Pollux). The astrological sign for the period May 21–June 21. △130, 826, 1724.

Gemini Space Program, the US manned-flight space program that followed Mercury, preceded Apollo. The Gemini was a two-person craft first manned by Maj. Virgil Grissom and Lt. Cmdr. John Young on March 23, 1965; they made three earth orbits. Subsequent flights and experiments through Gemini 12 (Nov. 11–15, 1966) demonstrated space walks, space docking maneuvers, and tests of longevity including a 14-day flight by Lt. Col. Frank Borman and Cmdr. James Lovell, Jr., in December 1965. All were preparatory to the moon landing. △1724.

Gemistus Pletho, Georgius (*c.* 1355–*c.* 1452), medieval Byzantine philosopher whose Neo-platonic theories advanced the Italian renaissance. He also worked to unite the Roman and Greek churches against the Turks, but his theological doctrines were received with considerable displeasure by the Byzantine establishment.

Gemsbok. *See* Oryx.

Gender, the classification of nouns and pronouns according to sex. Personal pronouns and some nouns have a different word for masculine, feminine, neuter, or common gender. "I" and "you" have assumed gender.

Genealogy, the study of family origins and history. The genealogist compiles lists of ancestors and then arranges them in pedigree charts. Genealogy began with early oral traditions and advanced to written pedigrees, and began to develop in its present form in the early 16th century.

General Accounting Office (GAO), an independent regulatory agency under the control and direction of the US comptroller general. It was created in 1921 and audits government expenditures. The GAO directly assists Congress by reporting on spending, suggesting more efficient use of funds and studying proposed legislation. The GAO also settles claims against the United States.

General Agreement on Tariffs and Trade (GATT), international trade agreements, based on

Paul Gauguin: self-portrait

Gazelle

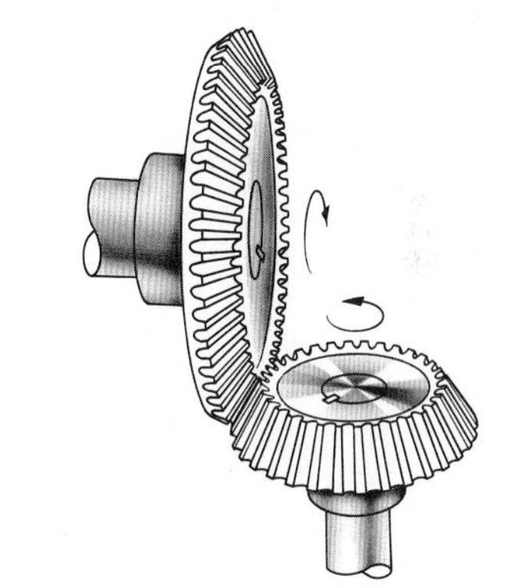

Gear

YORK

Lou Gehrig

the most-favored nation principle, that involve most noncommunist countries. Any tariff reduction one nation gives to another member of the group must be extended to all members. GATT is designed to prevent "tariff wars." The agreement has been periodically renegotiated since 1948. *See also* Most-Favored Nation Clause. △942.

General Amnesty Act (1872), US law pardoning all but the most prominent ex-Confederates (about 500 persons). The law allowed some 150,000 persons barred from holding public office under the 14th Amendment to do so, except if prohibited by a two-thirds vote of Congress.

General Council. *See* Council, Ecumenical.

General Equilibrium, in economics, an equilibrium in the production sector, in the consumption sector, and in the resources sector of the economy as a whole. This analysis attempts to account for interrelationships by showing the effect of a change in the price of one good or resource on all other sectors of the economy.

General Paresis, chronic brain disorder associated with a syphilitic infection of the central nervous system; also known as paresis and general paralysis. It involves general mental deterioration and paralysis and is ultimately fatal. This last or fourth stage of neurosyphilis is rarely seen today because of the effectiveness of antibiotic therapy. *See also* Syphilis. △762.

General Services Administration (GSA), US federal agency that is responsible for government property. It establishes policy and provides an economical and efficient system for the management of real and personal property. The business arm of the government, it also operates information centers, provides information on consumer products, and awards contracts. Established 1949.

General Theory of Relativity, part of Einstein's theory of relativity that applies to observers whose relative motion is not constant. *See also* Relativity Theory. △1524.

Generator, Electric, a device for producing electrical energy. Most frequently it refers to a device that converts the mechanical energy of a turbine or internal combustion engine into electrical energy by employing electromagnetic induction. The term is also used for other sources such as chemical batteries, fuel cells, and solar cells. △1532, 1536, 1540.

Genes, biochemical substances in the chromosomes that encode the hereditary information that determines an individual's characteristics. The building block of genes is DNA (deoxyribonucleic acid), a chemically complex substance that is the basis of genetic organization in both plants and animals. *See also* Chromosomes; Heredity. △416, 420.

Genesee River, river in N Pennsylvania; rises in the Allegheny Mts; flows through W New York, through Letchworth State Park (noted for its picturesque gorge and waterfalls), to Lake Ontario at Rochester; supplies hydroelectricity to Rochester. Length: 158mi (254km).

Genesis, first book of the Old Testament and Pentateuch. It is comprised of three sections. The first relates the history of the universe and God's relation to it; the second is an account of man before Abraham; and the third recounts Israelite history until the descent into Egypt.

Genessee Chief, The (1852), one of the earliest US Supreme Court cases, in which the court overturned one of its previous decisions. The court held that its admiralty jurisdiction extended to the Great Lakes and not just US tidal waters.

Genessee Road (1797), 100-mile (161km) road from Fort Schuyler to Geneva, N.Y. Built of logs and gravel, the road became a turnpike in 1800 and later part of the Mohawk Route.

Genêt, Edmond Charles (1763–1834), French diplomat known as Citizen Genêt to Americans who supported the French Revolution. Named French minister to the United States (1792), he began outfitting privateers to harass British commerce. President Washington ordered him to stop this activity but Genêt challenged Washington's authority. The President demanded his recall (1793), but Genêt decided to remain and became a US citizen (1804). He published *The Upward Force of Fluids* (1825), which was the first American book on aeronautics.

Genêt, Jean (1910–), French dramatist and novelist. The hardships of his childhood quickly led him into delinquency and crime. It is in his books such as *Our Lady of the Flowers* (1944) and *Thief's Journal* (1949) that he records his experiences of Europe's bars, brothels, and prisons. His plays, among the best known of which are *The Maids* (1947) and *The Balcony* (1956), are concerned with an equivocal world of illusions, masks, and mirrors.

Genet, catlike carnivore of the civet family native to W Europe and S and E Africa. Solitary and nocturnal, genets have long slender bodies, short legs, gray to brown fur with black or brown spots, and banded tails. Length: body—19in (48cm); tail—19in(48cm); weight to 4.5lb (2kg). Family Viverridae; genus *Genetta*. *See also* Civet Cat.

Genetic Code. △414, 420.

Genetics, biological science and study of heredity, mutation, and development in similar or related plants and animals. Geneticists study molecular structures involved in heredity and evolution and the genes involved in the structure or alteration of a population. They also study the effects of heredity or environment on character and how these two factors interact. Related areas of study involve various inherited diseases and defects. Heredity is also examined relative to behavior, learning ability, and physiology. The application of genetics has provided improved plant and animal stocks for human use. △414–16, 776.

Geneva (Genève), city in SW Switzerland, on Rhone River, at S end of Lake Geneva; capital of Geneva canton. Former seat of Burgundian kingdom, it was conquered by Franks in 6th century; passed to Holy Roman Empire in 12th century; accepted the Reformation 1536 and became center of Protestantism under John Calvin 1541; became part of Swiss Confederation 1815; scene of Geneva Convention 1864, an international agreement on the wartime treatment of soldiers; headquarters of the League of Nations 1920–46; European center for United Nations; site of University of Geneva, founded by Calvin 1559, 10th-12th-century Gothic cathedral. Industries: banking, watches, jewelry, enamelware, iron goods, tourism. Pop. 173,618.

Geneva Conventions, series of rules outlining the treatment of wounded soldiers and prisoners during war. The first Geneva Convention was in 1864. The rules are also known as the Red Cross treaties. △1288.

Geneva (Leman or Genève) Lake, crescent-shaped lake in SW Switzerland; S section extends into E France; it is crossed E to W by the Rhone River. Surrounded by mountains, it is noted for clear blue water and great beauty; site of several lakeside resorts. Length: 45mi (72km). Width: approx. 9mi (14km). Area: 224sq mi (580sq km).

Genghis Khan (1167?–1227), original name Timujin, conqueror and emperor of the Mongol empire stretching across central Asia from the Caspian Sea to the Sea of Japan. He united the Mongol tribes and demonstrated military genius and ruthlessness as he captured Peking (1227), took over Iran, and invaded Russia as far as Moscow. He established law codes, tolerated ethnic and religious minorities, and increased contact between East and West. His empire was divided and expanded by his sons and grandsons. △1112.

Genoa (Genova), seaport city in NW Italy, on the Gulf of Genoa; capital of Genoa prov. and region of Liguria. An important commercial center in the Middle Ages, its fortunes declined in the 15th century and it came under foreign control; occupied by Napoleon 1796; inc. by France 1805; passed to Sardinia 1815; birthplace of Christopher Columbus (*c.* 1451); site of Cathedral of San Lorenzo, Ducal palace, Church of San Donato, university (1471), Academy of Fine Arts (1751). Exports: rice, wine, olive oil, silk, coral, marble, macaroni. Industries: iron, steel, textiles, shipbuilding, chemicals. Pop. 842,764.

Genocide, deliberate governmental policy aimed at destroying a racial, religious, or ethnic group. The word has become synonymous with the Nazi extermination of Jews during World War II, although the practice existed for centuries. The UN General Assembly has defined genocide as an international crime, but no court with international criminal jurisdiction exists. △816.

Genotype, genetic or hereditary makeup of an individual that may or may not be manifested in observable traits or behaviors; contrasted with phenotype, the observable characteristics. *See also* Phenotype. △416.

Genova. *See* Genoa.

Genre Painting, art term usually referring to realistic portrayals of scenes of daily life. This type of painting was quite prevalent among Dutch and Flemish masters of the 17th century.

Genro, "elder statesmen" who indirectly ruled Japan from 1881–1901, a period of extreme modernization, and were influential for another three decades. They formed the Constitution of 1889 and made several other political changes whereby the government grew more responsive to the people.

Gens, in Roman history, a clan, or a group of families, claiming descent from a common ancestor and sharing a common name. Other requirements for membership in any particular gens included purity of blood, personal liberty, and descent from free-born parents. In anthropology, the term is used to identify a patrilineal descent group.

Gent. *See* Ghent.

Gentian, perennial plant in temperate regions; many species are alpine plants. It has heart-shaped leaves and usually blue, tubular flowers. Among 300 species are the dark blue *Gentiana clusii*, fringed *Gentiana crinita*, and yellow *Gentiana lutea*, whose bitter root is used as a gastrointestinal tonic. Family Gentianaceae.

Gentian Violet, a purple dye used in biology as a bacterial stain and in medicine as a bactericide to kill certain bacterial strains.

Gentile, Giovanni (1875–1944), Italian philosopher and educator. He founded the *Giornale critico della filosofia italiana*, a journal of philosophy and literary criticism, in 1920. In 1924 he and his friend, Benedetto Croce, parted over Gentile's support of fascism. Gentile's philosophy, "actual idealism," was an extreme continuation of the idealism of Hegel. He was minister for education (1922–24) under the Fascists and editor of the *Enciclopedia Italiana* (1925–43). He was killed by anti-Fascist partisans.

Gentileschi, Orazio (1563–1647), Italian painter. A follower of Caravaggio, he is known for his portraits and historical paintings. In 1626 he went to England as the court painter to King Charles I, where he introduced the style of Caravaggio.

Gentleman Jim. *See* Corbett, James John.

Gentlemen's Agreement (1907), series of diplomatic notes by which Japan voluntarily withheld passports from Japanese coming to the United States except those with prior domiciles, a parent, spouse, or child in the United States. An imperfect exclusionary scheme, it was later replaced by the Immigration Bill of 1924. *See also* Japanese Exclusion.

Genus, group of closely related plant or animal species with common characteristics. The genus name is usually a Latin or Greek noun. Example: genus *Quercus* denotes oak trees and *Felis* denotes all cats. A genus contains from one to several species. △408.

Geochemistry, study of the chemical composition of the earth and the changes that have resulted from chemical and physical processes. △1558.

Geode, small, hollow rock nodule with inner walls lined with crystals, generally quartz or calcite. Formed by gelatinous silica and mineral-bearing water within a cavity, the beautiful crystals are prized by collectors.

Geodesic Dome, in modern architecture, a dome or vault made of light, straight structural elements arranged to form a hemispheric surface. Originally designed by R. Buckminster Fuller, such a dome provides economy by means of lightness of materials and lack of supporting columns. At the same time structural stresses are spread out evenly over the entire dome rather than focused at one or a few points.

Geodesy, a branch of geophysics that includes determination of the size and shape of the earth, its gravitational field, and the location of fixed points. △180.

Geoffrey of Monmouth (*c.*1100–1154), English chronicler best known for his *Historia Regum Britanniae (History of the Kings of Britain)*. Based on Latin manuscripts, Welsh genealogies, and oral tradition, it is primarily a fictional account but was accepted as an historical document until the 16th century. During the

Middle Ages, the *Historia* was translated into French, Middle English, Welsh, Spanish, and Old Norse. Included were the tales of King Arthur and his court, which became the basis for medieval Arthurian romance.

Geography, science that studies the relationship between the earth and mankind. It includes the size and distribution of land masses, seas and resources, climatic zones, and plant and animal life. Because it seeks to relate all the earth's features to man's existence, geography differs from other earth sciences such as geology, meteorology, and oceanography, which study this planet's features as specific phenomena. △180–210, 300, 578–80.

Geoid, the theoretical surface of Earth. The roughly elliptical Earth is bulged out at the Equator and flattened at the poles. *See also* Geodesy. △178.

Geological Survey, United States, federal agency that makes maps and conducts geological research. This research involves US topography, geology, and mineral and water resources, plus the classification of land as to mineral character and water and power resources. It enforces department regulations regarding oil, gas, and other mining leases. Established 1879.

Geologic Time, the time scale of the history of the earth divided into periods ranging into millions of years. Until recently, only methods of relative dating were possible. These include the world-side study, a comparison and correlation of sequences of rock formations and the fossils they contain. The gathered data are used to distinguish earlier from later deposits, to estimate periods of passed time, and to reconstruct geologic and climatic events by assuming that geological processes in the past were the same as today. Measurement of the disintegration of certain radioactive elements in rocks (called absolute dating) has provided previously unattainable accuracy. The largest divisions of geologic time are called eras, each of which is broken down into periods. Periods, in turn, are subdivided into series or epochs. *See also* Historical Geology. △276.

Geology, study of the materials of the earth, their origin, arrangement, classification, change, and history. Geology is divided into several categories: geophysics, the study of physical properties of earth; geochemistry, the chemical makeup of earth; mineralogy, arrangements of minerals; petrology, rocks and their combination of minerals; stratigraphy, arrangement and succession of rocks in layers; paleontology, study of fossilized plant and animal remains; geomorphology, study of landforms; structural geology, classification of rock structures and the forces that produced them; hydrology, study of surface and subsurface waters; economic geology, study of materials of practical use to man; engineering geology, study of the land in terms of construction on it; environmental geology, geological study applied to the best use of the environment by man; oceanography, combination of several fields as they relate to the total study of oceans. *See also* Historical Geology. △270–76.

Geomagnetic Storm. *See* Magnetic Storm.

Geometric Art. △1000.

Geometric Isomer. *See* Isomer.

Geometric Mean, square root of the product of two numbers. For example, the geometric mean of 8 and 2 is $\sqrt{8\times 2} = 4$. The geometric mean of n numbers is the nth root of their product $\sqrt[n]{a\cdot b\cdot c\cdot \ldots}$. *See also* Arithmetic Mean.

Geometric Progression, sequence of numbers in which the ratio of each term to the preceding term is a constant (called the common ratio). It has the form $a, ar, ar^2, ar^3, \ldots$ The sum of these terms, $a + ar + ar^2 \ldots$, is a geometric series. If there are n terms the sum equals $a(1-r^n)/(1-r)$. Infinite geometric series converge to $a/(1-r)$ if r lies between -1 and $+1$. △1456.

Geometry, branch of mathematics concerned broadly with studies of shape and size. To most people geometry is the Euclidean geometry of simple plane and solid figures. Geometry is, however, a much wider and more abstract field with many subdivisions. Analytic geometry, introduced in 1637 by Descartes, applies algebra to geometry and allows the study of more complex curves than those of Euclidean geometry. Projective geometry is, in its simplest form, concerned with projection of shapes—operations of the type involved in drawing maps and in perspective painting—and with properties that are independent of such changes. It was introduced by Jean-Victor Poncelet in 1822. Even more abstraction occurred in the early 19th century with formulations of non-Euclidean geometry by Farkas Bolyai and N.I. Lobachevski. Differential geometry—based on the application of calculus and ideas such as the curvature and lengths of curves in space—was also developed during this period. Geometric reasoning was also applied to spaces with more than three dimensions. Topology is a very general form of geometry, concerned with properties that are independent of any continuous deformation of shape. *See also* Topology. △1462, 1466.

Geometry, Euclidean. *See* Euclidean Geometry.

Geometry, Non-Euclidean. *See* Non-Euclidean Geometry.

Geomorphology, a science dealing with the land and submarine relief features of the earth's surface and the physical, chemical, and biological processes that act upon them. It seeks to interpret these features through the use of the principles of physiography and of dynamic and structural geology. △182.

Geophone. △54.

Geophysics, earth science that deals with the physics of earth. The areas that are called geophysical are geodesy, geothermometry, seismology, tectometry, hydrology, oceanography, atmospheric and meteorologic studies, the related fields of geomagnetism and geoelectricity, geochronology and geocosmogony, and geophysical exploration and prospecting. △178.

Geopolitics, study of the relationship between geography and political life. Three basic environmental factors are believed to have an impact on the political development of nations: actual physical configurations; climatic variables; and wealth of natural resources. Geopolitics fell into disrepute because of its identification with Nazi propaganda of the 1920s.

George, Henry (1839–97), US economist and reformer, b. Philadelphia. A printer and then newspaperman in California, he proposed (1871) a tax by the government on the rent derived from land so that economic rent would benefit the populace rather than a few landowners. He expanded this theory in his famous book, *Progress and Poverty* (1879). In 1880, he moved to New York City where he ran unsuccessfully as liberal and labor candidate for mayor. He was again a candidate in 1897 when he died.

George, Saint, early Christian martyr who became patron saint of England. According to tradition he was born in Palestine and martyred at Nicomedia sometime before 323. Many stories grew up about St George, including the 12th-century tale of his killing a dragon to save a maiden. Scholars now class all these as legendary.

George I (1660–1727), king of Great Britain and Ireland (1714–27); elector of Hanover (1698–1727). A great-grandson of James I of England and a Protestant, he succeeded Queen Anne under the provisions of the Act of Settlement (1701), thus becoming the first Hanoverian king of England. He favored the Whigs over the Tories, suspecting the latter of Jacobite sympathies. In 1715 and 1719 he put down Jacobite uprisings. In 1718 he formed the Quadruple Alliance with Holland, France, and Germany that guaranteed Hanoverian succession. He was disliked in England because he did not speak English and spent much of his time in Hanover.

George II (1683–1760), king of Great Britain and Ireland (1727–1760); elector of Hanover (1727–1760). Influenced by Robert Walpole, he supported the Whigs. He brought Britain into the War of the Austrian Succession (1740–49) to protect Hanover, personally commanding victorious forces at Dettingen (1743). He suppressed the last Jacobite rebellion (1745–46). His reign also saw imperial acquisitions in Canada and India.

George III (1738–1820), king of Great Britain and Ireland (1760–1820); elector and then king of Hanover (1760–1820); grandson of George II. He initially sought an active role in government during the ministries of Bute, Grenville, Pitt, Grafton, and North (1760–82), influencing the disastrous colonial policy that led to American independence (1776) but effectively suppressing the anti-Catholic Gordon Riots (1780). He consolidated Tory power by calling the "Younger Pitt" to office (1783–1801, 1804–05), though opposing and defeating Pitt's plans for Catholic emancipation (1801). Suffering increasingly from bouts of insanity after 1765, he became blind (1805) and completely insane (1811). Under the Regency Act

Genet

Genoa, Italy

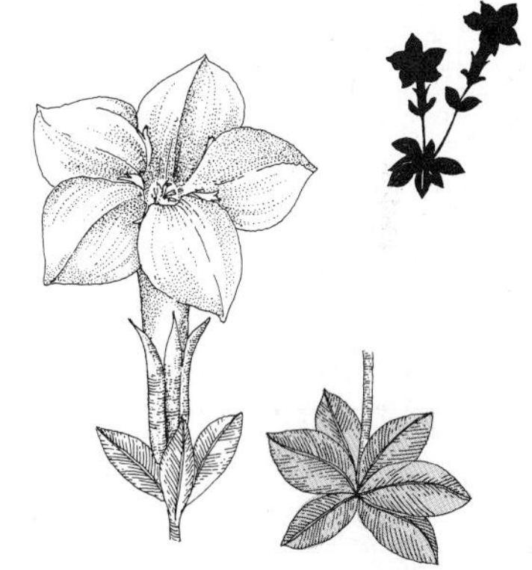

Gentian

Henry George

(1811) his son (later George IV) acted as regent (1811–20). △1218.

George IV (1762–1830), king of Great Britain and Ireland (1820–30). He served as regent during the periods of George III's madness (1788–89; 1811–20). In 1785 he secretly married Maria Fitzherbert, but she was Roman Catholic and the marriage was not recognized. In 1795 he married Caroline of Brunswick in order to obtain parliamentary settlement of his debts. They separated within a year. In 1812 he decided to retain his father's Tory advisers instead of replacing them with the Whigs, whom he had supported earlier. A patron of the arts, he was, however, disliked for his extravagances and dissolute habits. He was succeeded by his brother William IV.

George V (1865–1936), king of Great Britain and Northern Ireland and emperor of India (1910–36). He became heir apparent after his elder brother, Albert, Duke of Clarence, died (1892). He married Princess Victoria Mary of Teck (1893). Of the house of Saxe-Coburg-Gotha, he adopted the surname Windsor (1917). △1332.

George VI (1895–1952), king of Great Britain and Northern Ireland (1936–52) and emperor of India (1936–48). He was proclaimed king when his brother, Edward VIII, abdicated. George married Lady Elizabeth Bowes-Lyon (1923). He visited Canada and the United States (1939) and South Africa (1947). He was succeeded by Elizabeth II.

George I (1845–1913), king of the Hellenes (1863–1913). Made king by Great Britain, France, and Russia with approval of Greek national assembly. He favored a monarchial democracy and backed constitution of 1864 giving power to an elected parliament. He gained territory for Greece through the Balkan Wars. He was assassinated in 1913 and was succeeded by his son Constantine I.

George II (1890–1947), king of the Hellenes (1922–23; 1935–47). He was forced out by the military in 1923, and Greece was declared a republic. After much political upheaval dictator Joannes Metaxas brought George back in 1935. He dissolved parliament and suspended the constitution. George fled in 1941 when Germany invaded Greece but ruled again from 1946 until his death.

George, Lake, glacial lake in E New York, N of Albany; outlet N to Lake Champlain. Discovered by Isaac Jogues, a French Jesuit, in 1646; scene of many battles during French and Indian Wars and American Revolution. Center of a large tourist area and largest lake within Adirondack State Park. Area: 33mi (53km) long, 1–3mi (1.6–5km) wide.

Georgetown, largest city and capital of Guyana, South America, on mouth of Demerara River. During Dutch occupation (1784), it was called Stabroek, and was the capital of united colonies of Essequibo and Demerara; renamed Georgetown 1812. Principal port of country, it is site of outstanding tropical botanical gardens and a university (1963). Exports: sugar, rice, timber, bauxite, diamonds, gold. Industries: sawmills, shipbuilding, food processing, brewing, rum distilling, woodworking. Founded 1781. Pop. 66,070.

George Tupou I (died 1893), king of the S Pacific kingdom of Tonga. He assumed rule after considerable civil confusion, and established a constitutional monarchy in 1862.

George Washington Carver National Monument, historic site in SW Missouri, containing the Carver farm, his birthplace and childhood home. Area: 210acres (85hectares). Est. 1943.

Georgia, state in the SE United States, on the Atlantic Ocean N of Florida. In the Civil War, it was one of the six original states of the Confederacy.

Land and Economy. A coastal plain in the E and S occupies about half the state. To the N is the Piedmont, a region of rolling hills and farmland. In the extreme N, the Blue Ridge Mts run from E to W. Of the many rivers that flow SE, the Savannah, the Ogeechee, and the Altamaha are the largest. The products of Georgia's forests and farms, which formed its economic base from earliest times, are still important, but manufacturing development during WWII moved the main emphasis to industry. Manufacture of aircraft, automobile and truck bodies, and boats has become a major enterprise. Atlanta is the financial center of a multi-state region.

People. Almost all Georgia's people were born in the United States. Business expansion has attracted thousands of residents from the N states. Urban growth came late and slowly, but in 1970 more than 60% of the population lived in urban areas.

Education. There are more than 60 institutions of higher education.

History. In 1732, George II of Great Britain gave Gen. James E. Oglethorpe a large land grant in the area. Oglethorpe founded a settlement on the Savannah River the next year. At the Battle of Bloody Marsh in 1742, he defeated the Spaniards, who threatened the colony from Florida. Georgia became a royal province in 1754. Its delegates to the Continental Congress in 1776 supported national independence, and Georgia was among the earliest to ratify the US Constitution. In 1792, Eli Whitney of Savannah invented the cotton gin that simplified the processing of cotton, bringing prosperity to all Southern planters. The state was ravaged in 1864 by the Union armies of Gen. William T. Sherman. It was readmitted to the Union in 1870, but its economy and society were slow in recovering from the effects of the war.

PROFILE

Admitted to Union: Jan. 2, 1788, 4th of the 13 original states to ratify the US Constitution
US Congressmen: Senate, 2; House of Representatives 10
Population: 4,589,575 (1970); rank, 15th
Capital: Atlanta, 497, 421 (1970)
Chief cities: Atlanta, Columbus, 155,028; Macon, 122,423; Savannah, 118,349
State legislature: Senate, 56; House of Representatives, 180
Area: 58,876sq mi (152,489sq km); rank, 21st
Elevation: Highest, Brasstown Bald, 4,784ft (1,459m). Lowest, sea level
Industries (major products): textiles, paper, naval stores (turpentine, resin, gums), lumber, transportation equipment, processed foods, chemicals
Agriculture (major products): peanuts, nuts, poultry, hogs, peaches
Minerals (major): clays, marble, bauxite
State nicknames: Empire State of the South, Peach State
State motto: "Wisdom, Justice, and Moderation"
State bird: brown thrasher
State flower: cherokee rose
State tree: live oak

Georgian Architecture, style of English architecture that flourished between the accession of George I to the throne in 1714 and the death of George IV in 1830. Early Georgian architecture was strongly influenced by the Palladian revival, led by Colin Campbell and Lord Burlington. A more historical neoclassicism, developed by Robert Adam and John Soane, led to the later Greek revival phase. In the United States, the Royall House, Medford, Mass. (*c.* 1747), and Independence Hall, Philadelphia, are good examples of the Georgian style, while the White House, Washington, D.C., is a fine example of the neoclassical trend.

Georgian Bay, inlet of Lake Huron in SE Ontario, Canada; contains 30 islands, comprising Georgian Bay Islands National Park. Length: approx. 125mi (201km), width: 50mi (81km).

Georgian Poets, group of British poets during the early reign of George V (*c.* 1910–20) who, in reaction to what they felt to be the sterility of Victorian poetic conventions, attempted to reinvigorate poetry with freshness and honesty. Edward Marsh edited five volumes of *Georgian Poetry* (1912–1922), including such poets as Rupert Brooke, W.H. Davies, and Ralph Hodgson. Their reliance on conventional diction and their reluctance to experiment weakened their intended effects.

Georgian SSR (Socialist Republic Gruzinskaja), one of 15 union republics in USSR, bounded by Azerbaijan SSR (SE), Armenian SSR and Turkey (S), Black Sea (W), Caucasus Mts (N and NE); Tbilisi is the capital. Region was conquered by Pompey for Rome 65 BC; Christianized by St Nino *c.* 330; ravaged by Mongol invasions 13th century but rebuilt under rule of Erekle II (1744–98) who est. Russian protection by treaty with Catherine the Great. Tsar Alexander I annexed Georgia to Russia 1801, causing war with Persia (1804–13). Area regained independence after Russian Revolution (1917), but was inc. into USSR 1921 by Joseph Stalin; became constituent republic 1936. The Georgian language (dating from *c.* 325 BC) is the most important of the Caucasian languages and the only one to be used in ancient as well as modern literature. Industries: wine, brandy, tea, tobacco, fruit, grain, hydroelectricity, maganese mining, steel, pig iron, textiles, lumber, coke; oil and kerosene pipeline terminus. Area: 26,911sq mi (69,699sq km). Pop. 4,688,000.

Georgics, an instructive poem written over a period of seven years by 1st-century BC poet Vergil, portraying the joys of country life. Personifying nature, this work vividly depicts the hard struggles and great rewards of the farmer's life.

Geosyncline, a great basin or trough where deposits of sediment and volcanic rock, thousands of meters thick, have accumulated during slow subsidence through long geologic periods. The term was proposed by the 19th-century scientist James D. Dana to describe the formation basin of the Appalachian Mountains. The different kinds of marine fossils in the strata indicate that the Appalachians were formed from an uplifted shallow-water basin and the Alps from a deep-water one. *See also* Syncline. △252.

Geotropism, responses of plant growth to the stimulus of gravity. In general, plant stems are negatively geotropic and grow up; roots are positively geotropic and grow down. Growth curvature is caused by accumulation of auxin on the lower side of the stem, increasing growth and bending it up. Growth response may also be at right angles to gravitational force (horizontal rhizomes) or any other angle (branches of main roots). *See also* Auxin. △430.

Gera, city in S East Germany, capital of Gera district, 47mi (76km) ESE of Erfurt; rail and road junction. Industries: textiles, metals, tobacco products, food processing. Chartered early 13th century. Pop. 111,-099.

Geranium, house and garden plant native to S Africa. Shrubby or trailing, it is densely branched with hairy, fan- or ivy-shaped leaves that emit a spicy aroma. Red, pink, or white flower clusters are borne on stalks above the leaves. Care: full sun, soil (3 parts loam, 1 part peat moss, 2 parts sand) kept dry between waterings. Propagation is by stem cuttings. Height: 1–3ft (30–91cm). Family Geraniaceae; genus *Pelargonium*. △444.

Gerard, John. △742.

Gerbil, small rodent native to dry areas of Asia and Africa, often domesticated as a pet. It has big eyes and ears, long hind legs, and long tail. Its fur may be buff, gray, brown or red. Mostly nocturnal, plant-eating burrow-dwellers, gerbils often hoard food but require little water. Females bear litters of 1–8 young three weeks after breeding. Length: 3–5in (7–12cm). Family Cricetidae. △606.

Geriatric Psychology. △802–04.

Geriatrics, branch of medicine that deals with the diseases and other medical problems of the elderly, who are subject to degeneration and aging of certain tissues and other disorders not common in younger people. △802–04.

Géricault, (Jean Louis André) Théodore (1791–1824), French painter. A forerunner of the Romantic movement, he began as a painter of battle scenes and then became a copyist of the Italian masters. He later associated himself with the Romantic cry for revolution. His most famous painting, "Raft of the Medusa" (1819), took for its subject a shipwreck that was a political scandal. He wrote numerous pamphlets attacking government activities. On a visit to London he drew many sketches depicting poverty in the streets, as well as realistic sketches of horses and horse races. △1228.

German, language spoken by about 120,000,000 people in West and East Germany, Austria, Switzerland, and by German communities in many other countries. High German *(Hochdeutsch)*, of the south, is the standard dialect, but Low German *(Plattdeutsch)* is generally spoken in the north. Like the other Germanic languages, German belongs to the Indo-European family.

German Confederation (1815–66), loose federation of German states under Austrian presidency, created by the Congress of Vienna to replace the Holy Roman Empire. It collapsed with the 1848 revolutions, was restored in 1850, and was finally destroyed by the Prussian defeat of Austria in 1866. △1230, 1250.

German East Africa, German protectorate in East Africa from 1885 until World War I, when it became three League of Nations mandates under the British, Portuguese, and Belgians. The former colony is now included in the independent nations of Tanzania, Ruanda, and Burundi.

Germanic and Scandinavian Mythology. Qualities that are singularly Teutonic are difficult to isolate in the mythology of the north countries. What does make Germanic folklore somewhat unique, however, is the mass of recorded literature, written and colected by monks, antiquarians, and ethnologists. One of the collections is known as the *Elder Edda,* short poems composed in the 8th to 11th centuries in Norway, Iceland, and Greenland, including the story of Siegfried and the Nibelungenlied. The *Younger Edda* is a collection of the early 13th century; a 9th-century collection of myths and heroic stories is the *Old Norse Scaldic Verse.*

Germanic Languages, group of languages forming a subdivision of the Indo-European family. One branch includes English, German, Yiddish, Dutch, Flemish, Frisian, and Afrikaans; another includes Swedish, Danish, Norwegian, Icelandic, and Faroese. Gothic, the language of the ancient Goths but long extinct, constituted a third branch. △866.

Germanicus Caesar (15 BC–AD 19), Roman general, nephew of Tiberius and brother of Claudius I. He campaigned in Pannonia and Germany for Tiberius and commanded the Gallic and German provinces. After defeating Arminius (16) he was given command of the eastern provinces. A popular leader and a scholar, he quarrelled with Piso, governor of Syria, who is thought to have poisoned him. Germanicus' children included Agrippina II and Caligula.

Germanium, metalloid element (symbol Ge) of group IVA of the periodic table, predicted (as ekasilicon) by Mendeleev and discovered in 1886. Chief source is as a by-product from smelting zinc ores or from the combustion of certain coals. The element is important in transistors, rectifiers, and similar semiconductor devices. Properties: at. no. 32; at. wt. 72.59; sp gr 5.3 at 25°C; melt. pt. 1,719°F (937.4°C); boil. pt. 5,126°F (2,830°C); most common isotope Ge^{74} (36.54%). △1506, 1552, 1558.

German Measles, or rubella, a virus-caused contagious disease characterized by a light pink rash beginning on the face and spreading down. The disease is mild, requiring only symptomatic relief, usually of itching. Young children are frequently immunized against rubella to prevent contagion to women in child-bearing years since rubella can cause serious damage to a fetus. △724.

German Shepherd, dog used for sheepherding, police work, and guiding the blind; (working group) bred from old breeds of German herd and farm dogs. An aloof and self-confident dog, it has an arched forehead; long, strong muzzle; pointed, erect ears; a long, solid body; medium-length, straight, oval-boned legs; and bushy, curved tail. The medium-length double coat is straight and harsh; kennel clubs accept most colors except white. Average size: 24–26in (61–66cm) high at shoulder; 60–85lb (27–38kg). *See also* Working Dog.

German Shorthaired Pointer, breed of dog that is an all-purpose pointer, night trailer, and retriever (sporting group). This intelligent dog has a clean-cut head with broad skull, squarish muzzle, and large nose; the broad ears lie flat. The body is short-backed and powerful, legs well-muscled, feet webbed, and tail docked. Coat is short, thick, and hard, and colored solid liver or liver and white spotted. Average size: 23–25in (58–63.5cm) high at shoulder; 55–70lb (25–32kg). *See also* Sporting Dog.

German Wirehaired Pointer, all-purpose hunting dog (sporting group) bred in Germany and brought to United States in 1920. Popular in the Midwest, this dog has a long head and muzzle with beard and whiskers; rounded, hanging ears; brown eyes set under bushy eyebrows; muscular legs with webbed feet; and docked tail. The 2in (5cm) long water-resistant coat is straight and wiry; color is liver and white. Average size: 24–26in (61–66cm) high at shoulder; 60lb (27kg). *See also* Sporting Dog.

Germany, a nation in central Europe divided since 1945 into two independent countries, West Germany and East Germany. For centuries the German peoples have occupied the strategic central region of Europe. A unified German nation existed from 1871 to 1945. Twice in the 20th century this German nation initiated and was defeated in world wars. The history of Germany since 1945 is covered in the separate articles on East Germany and West Germany that follow this article.

The Germans enter recorded history in the time of Julius Caesar's Gallic campaigns. The Goths, Allemani, Teutons, and Franks were among the more notable early Germanic tribes. The history of the German nation begins with Charlemagne (AD 800) who extended Frankish power over much of W Europe. In the medieval period German power, which was paramount in Europe, was focused in the Holy Roman Empire and in the Hapsburg dynasty. The Reformation was begun in Germany (1517) by Martin Luther; the Protestant movement spread rapidly, but left the German states as disunited as before. The Thirty Years War (1618–48) ended with Germany reduced to hundreds of tiny states and petty kingdoms. Unification began with the rise of Prussia under the Hohenzollerns in the 17th century. Its center was Berlin, capital of the Brandenburg state. Prussia allied itself with Russia and Britain in defeating Napoleon (1815) and subsequently gained the Rhineland, part of Poland, Westphalia, and most of Saxony. German nationalism became apparent after 1830 in widespread revolts and calls for a national constitution and parliament. Under Chancellor Otto von Bismarck Prussia organized all German states N of the Main River; the S states joined Prussia in the Franco-Prussian War (1870–71), creating a unified German empire. Germany allied itself with Austria-Hungary (1879) and Italy (1882), and under Kaiser Wilhelm II sharply increased its military and naval strength. In World War I, Germany fought France, Great Britain, Russia, and the United States. Harsh terms were imposed on Germany by the victors. The world-wide economic collapse after 1929 led to severe political dislocations in Germany. Adolf Hitler and the National Socialist party gained power in 1933, and Hitler soon installed himself as dictator. The German economy recovered strongly. Germany rearmed; in 1936 alliances were made with Italy and Japan. Germany began the war with the invasion of Poland (1939). By 1941, Germany was at war with Great Britain, the Soviet Union, and the United States. Defeat came in 1945. *See also* Holy Roman Empire. △1072, 1248–50.

Following is a list of the rulers of Germany until 1945.

RULERS OF GERMANY

Frederick I	1701–13
Frederick William I	1713–40
Frederick II the Great	1740–86
Frederick William II	1786–97
Frederick William III	1797–1840
Frederick William IV	1840–61
William I	1861–88
Frederick III	1888
William II (Kaiser Wilhelm)	1888–1918
Friedrich Ebert	1919–25
Paul von Hindenburg	1925–34
Adolf Hitler	1934–45

Germany, East, officially the German Democratic Republic, a Communist nation in central Europe. After World War II, Germany was divided into four occupation zones. The Soviet zone became East Germany in 1949. Berlin, which lies in East Germany, is divided into E and W sectors. East Berlin is the capital of East Germany.

Land and Economy. East Germany lies on the North German Plain. It is bordered by the Baltic Sea (N), Poland (E), and by Czechoslovakia and West Germany (S) and (W). The country is drained by the Elbe River, a major commercial waterway. Except for extensive deposits of a soft, brown coal called lignite, the country is poor in mineral resources. The Communist government owns nearly all farmland, which has been organized into cooperative and state farms. Manufacturing is the fastest growing segment of the East German economy, led by the chemical and metallurgical industries. The economy ranks second only to the Soviet Union in total output of E European nations.

People. In East Germany the dominant ethnic type is Nordic, or Teutonic. There is also more Slavic influence apparent here than among other Germans, as in physical types, names, and style of settlement. Most East Germans are Protestants, although the Communist regime discourages religious practice. Between 1945 and 1960, more than 3,000,000 East Germans migrated to West Germany; to halt this outflow of workers, the Communist government built the Berlin Wall (1961). German is the official language throughout the country, but several dialects are spoken. Study of the Russian language is compulsory in all schools. About 75% of the population live in cities. The living standard in East Germany is below that of West Germany, but is the highest standard of any of the Communist-bloc countries of E Europe.

Government. The East German republic is governed by the Communist party, called the Socialist Unity Party. The constitution provides a bicameral legislature, parliamentary executive, council of ministers, and council of state. The constitution also specifies the country's formal alignment with the Soviet Union. The nation is divided into 15 administrative districts. The courts are controlled by the ministry of justice and the prosecutors. Nearly all judges belong to the Socialist Unity party. Political dissent is not permitted.

History. At the end of World War II the Soviet Union stripped its German occupation zone of much of its industrial capacity. During the Cold War, Berlin

George III

Savannah, Georgia

Geranium

0
400 km
NORTH SEA
Sweden
Denmark
BALTIC SEA
Rostock
GERMAN
DEMOCRATIC
REPUBLIC
Berlin
Magdeburg
Halle
Leipzig
Dresden
Karl-Marx-Stadt
Neth.
Belgium
Poland
Lux.
Federal
Republic of
Germany
Czechoslovakia
France
Austria
Switzerland
Liech.
Hungary

East Germany

became the focus of East-West tension. In 1948, the Communists blockaded West Berlin by shutting off all entry routes; for nearly a year all supplies from the West were airlifted to the city. The German Democratic Republic was established under Soviet auspices in 1949. A revolt by East German workers in 1953 was quelled by Soviet troops. The East German economy recovered strongly in the 1960s; the country became one of the world's ten leading industrial powers.

PROFILE

Official name: German Democratic Republic
Area: 41,768sq mi (108,179sq km)
Population: 17,170,000
Density: 411per sq mi (159per sq km)
Chief cities: East Berlin (capital); Leipzig; Dresden
Government: Communist
Religion (major): Protestantism
Language: German (official)
Monetary unit: Deutsche mark
Gross national product: $38,200,000,000
Per capita income: $2,350
Manufacturing (major products): chemicals, clothing, electrical equipment, iron and steel, heavy machinery, optical products, processed foods
Agriculture (major products): dairy products, potatoes, barley, oats, livestock, rye
Minerals (major): iron ore, copper, lignite, tin, potash
Trading partners (major): Soviet Union, Czechoslovakia, Poland, West Germany

Germany, West, officially the Federal Republic of Germany, a nation in central Europe. West Germany is the fourth-ranking industrial power in the world; it is also the most populous European nation outside the USSR. The area of West Germany is more than twice that of East Germany and has nearly four times the population. West Germany is closely allied with the nations of the West, both politically and economically. Its capital is Bonn.

Land and Economy. West Germany reaches from the Alps (S) to the North Sea. The Bavarian Alps, with many peaks reaching above 6,000ft (1,830m), are drained by the Danube. The South German Hills contain some of the country's most fertile farmlands and are drained by the Main and Neckar rivers. The major land region is the North German Plain, a broad lowlying area that is traversed by the Rhine, Ems, Weser, and Elbe rivers. West German agriculture provides about two-thirds of the nation's food requirements; food imports are substantial. The country is overwhelmingly industrial. The Ruhr Valley is the chief manufacturing region. The industrial establishment is especially notable for its vast steel works, automobile, electronics, chemical, and textile industries.

People. The West German population includes a variety of ethnic strains, but the two principal groups are the Nordic, or Teutonic, Germans of the N; and the Alpine type of the S. A wide variety of dialects are still in use throughout the country; the universal literary language is Middle High German. About half of all West Germans are Protestants, and nearly half are Roman Catholics. West Germans have one of the highest living standards in the world; over 80% of the population lives in urban communities.

Government. West Germany is a constitutional democracy. Parliament consists of two houses, the Bundestag (Federal Diet) and the Bundesrat (Federal Council). The Bundestag is the law-making body; its 496 members are elected by secret ballot to 4-year terms. This house also elects the chief executive of government, the chancellor. The Bundesrat, whose members are appointed by the 10 states, approves or rejects legislation passed by the Bundestag. The leading political parties in West Germany are the Christian Democratic Union, the Social Democratic party, and the Free Democratic party. West Germans 18 years old and older are entitled to vote.

History. Germany lay in ruins at the end of World War II, its cities devastated, its economic life brought to a halt. The invading Soviet, US, and British forces sought to eradicate Nazism; the country was divided into occupation zones, as was the city of Berlin. War criminals were tried at Nuremburg. The Cold War began with the Soviet blockade of Berlin (1948). The British, French, and US zones were united to form the West German nation (1949). For 10 years the economy had a 10% annual growth rate. West Germany rearmed and joined the North Atlantic Treaty Organization (NATO) in 1955. Konrad Adenauer was the country's first chancellor. Willy Brandt, who served as chancellor from 1969 to 1974, resigned over an espionage scandal. He was succeeded by Helmut Schmidt.

PROFILE

Official name: Federal Republic of Germany
Area: 95,790sq mi (248,096sq km)
Population: 61,900,000
Density: 646.2per sq mi (249.5per sq km)
Chief cities: Bonn (capital); West Berlin, Hamburg, Munich, Cologne
Government: constitutional democracy
Religion: Lutherans (over 50%); Roman Catholics (45%)
Language: German (official)
Monetary unit: Deutsche mark
Gross national product: $357,000,000,000
Per capita income: $2,950
Manufacturing (major products): iron and steel, chemicals, automobiles, electrical goods, tools, processed foods, cameras, scientific instruments
Agriculture (major products): livestock, grains, sugar beets, wines, fruits, vegetables
Minerals (major): coal, iron ore, potash
Trading partners (major): France, Italy, Great Britain, United States

Germicide, any substance for destroying disease-causing microorganisms. Germicides include antiseptics, disinfectants, and antibiotics.

Germinal. △1238.

Germination, growth of the plant embryo after the seed ripens and falls from parent. It may occur immediately or after a dormant period. To germinate, a seed or spore needs favorable temperatures and light conditions, moisture, and oxygen. The process begins with the rehydration of embryo protoplasm and production of amino acids and energy that produce embryo growth. Germination is completed when the root appears outside the seed coat.

Germiston, city in NE Republic of South Africa; site of world's largest gold refinery. Industries: chemicals, textiles, engineering. Pop. 197,020.

Gerona, city in NE Spain; capital of Gerona prov.; site of 14th-century Gothic cathedral, Romanesque cloister, 13th-century church. Industries: textiles, chemicals, electronic equipment, soap. Area: (prov.) 2,273sq mi (5,887sq km). Pop. (city) 50,338; (prov.) 414,397.

Geronimo (1829–1909), chief of the Chiricahua Apaches. He led his tribe in war against white settlers in Arizona for more than 10 years. The Apaches hid in the Sierra Madre Mountains between raids. In 1886 he surrendered his tribe to General Miles, and they were taken by way of Florida and Alabama to Ft. Sill, Okla., where they lived until 1913, when they were freed.

Gerontology. △802–05.

Gerouisa, a council of Spartans consisting of 28 aristocrats over 60 years of age and two kings. They had great political and judicial power.

Gerry, Elbridge (1744–1814), US political figure and vice president (1813–14), b. Marblehead, Mass. Elected to the Massachusetts General Court (1772), he obtained supplies during the American Revolution and signed the Declaration of Independence and the Articles of Confederation. He refused to sign the Constitution until the Bill of Rights was added. Special envoy to France during the XYZ Affair (1797–98), he was governor of Massachusetts (1810–11) but gerrymandering led to his defeat in 1812. Elected vice president under James Madison, he died in office.

Gerrymandering, US political practice that permits the majority party in a state legislature to rearrange electoral districts for its own political advantage. Strong party districts are combined with weaker ones in such a way as to ensure the party a permanent majority. This political maneuver was named after Elbridge Gerry by his political opponents in 1811. During his second term as governor of Massachusetts his party rearranged the election districts in its favor in order to retain control of the state.

Gershom, in the Bible, eldest son of Moses and Zipporah. While traveling to Egypt, Zipporah circumcised Gershom to avert God's threat on Moses' life.

Gershon, Levi ben, commonly known as Gersonides (1288–1344), Jewish philosopher. He produced commentaries on the Bible as well as on Aristotle and Averroës. His philosophical system argued the necessity of God's existence from the order in the universe. His major work is *The Book of the Wars of the Lord,* or *Milhamot.*

Gershwin, George (1898–1937), US composer, b. Brooklyn, N.Y. His popular songs and orchestral works contain elements of jazz and popular music. His best known orchestral works are *Rhapsody in Blue* (1923) for piano and orchestra, *An American in Paris* (1928), and *Piano Concerto in F* (1925). His masterpiece is the folk opera *Porgy and Bess* (1935). He also composed for films and Broadway shows. His *Of Thee Sing* (1931) was the first musical comedy to win a Pulitzer Prize. His brother Ira Gershwin (1896– won fame as his lyricist. △1256.

Gerson, Jean Charlier de (1363–1429), French theologian. He became chancellor of the University of Paris in 1395, but his greatest work was his effort to end the Great Western Schism (1378–1417) during which two, and later three, men claimed the title of pope. At the Council of Constance (1415) Gerson advocated the doctrine called *conciliarism:* the church in council has authority superior to the pope as an individual. The council arranged the end of the schism. *See also* Constance, Council of.

Gersonides. *See* Gershon, Levi ben.

Gesell, Arnold L(ucius) (1880–1961), US child psychologist, b. Alma, Wis. He pioneered the practical application of psychology to the education of children. He wrote a number of popular books (eg, *The Child from Five to Ten,* 1946, with Francis L. Ilg), developed widely used tests, and was for many years the foremost US authority on child development. He established and directed (1911–1948) the Yale University Clinic of Child Development and was research consultant for the Gesell Institute of Child Development from 1950 to his death.

Gesellschaft, in sociology, ideal-type concept formulated by Ferdinand Toennies in 1887, denoting social systems based on large groups and indirect, impersonal relationships. Modern industrial societies and bureaucracies are often called Gesellschaft-like. *See also* Gemeinschaft. △888.

Gesneria, mostly herbaceous, perennial plants of the family Gesneriaceae, native to tropical South America. Most species found today were first cultivated in greenhouses. These plants are tuberous and have ornamental, showy flowers that make them popular houseplants. Woody gesneriads also originated in South America and have showy flowers. *See also* African Violet; Episcia; Gloxinia.

Gestalt Psychology, viewpoint in psychology that stresses the importance of patterns or whole configurations in experience. Gestalt theory is most often applied to perception. People can "see" a complete picture even if certain fragments are missing. A melody has a total configuration to the human ear that is more than the sum of individual notes. Gestalt theory opposes studying behavior processes by analyzing their parts individually. △776.

Gestapo, secret state police of Nazi Germany. Originally founded (1933) by Hermann Goering in Prussia, it soon became a national organization. It was taken over by Heinrich Himmler (1936–45) and became in effect a unit of the SS. With virtually unlimited powers, the Gestapo ran the Nazi concentration and extermination camps. *See also* Himmler, Heinrich.

Gestation, period of carrying young in uterus between fertilization and birth. Gestation periods are specific to species and range from 12 days (Virginia opossum) to 22 months (Indian elephant).

Gethsemane, in the New Testament, the garden where Jesus met with his disciples on the eve of his crucifixion. It was here Jesus was betrayed by Judas and arrested by the Romans. The Gospel of Luke locates it at the foot of Mount Olivet, east of Jerusalem. The exact spot has not been determined.

Getty, Jean Paul (1892–1976), US businessman, b. Minneapolis. He inherited his father's oil business, George F. Getty, Inc., becoming its president in 1930. In 1956 he consolidated his holdings in the Getty Oil Company, becoming its director. In 1957 *Fortune* magazine concluded that he was probably the world's richest private citizen. After 1959 he lived almost exclusively at his English Sutton Place. The J. Paul Getty Museum, Malibu, Calif. (founded 1954, moved into a new building 1973) houses part of his extensive art collection.

Gettysburg, borough in S Pennsylvania; seat of Adams co; scene of historic Civil War battle, the Gettysburg Campaign (1863), where Robert E. Lee and his Confederate troops were defeated by Union Army under George Meade; site of Gettysburg Address made by President Lincoln (Nov. 19, 1863), Gettysburg National Cemetery for Civil War victims, Gettysburg National Military Park, and farm of President Dwight D. Eisenhower. Industries: tourism, electrical equipment, shoes. Settled *c.* 1780; inc. 1806. Pop. (1970) 7,275.

Gettysburg, Battle of (July 1–3, 1863), conflict that stopped Confederate Gen. Robert E. Lee's invasion of Pennsylvania. The three-day battle ended in a victory for Union Major Gen. George Meade. The climax came with the Union's repulse of "Pickett's Charge," a desperate attack against artillery and dug-in infantry by forces led by Confederate Gen. George Pickett. The battle pitted about 93,000 Union men against about 70,000 Confederates. Both sides lost about 20,000 men. △1276.

Gettysburg Address (Nov. 19, 1863), Pres. Abraham Lincoln's speech at the dedication of the national cemetery on the Civil War battlefield site at Gettysburg, Penn. One of the most quoted of modern speeches, it is famous for its eloquence and brevity. The final sentence contains a phrase that has become a definition of democracy: "government of the people, by the people, for the people."

Following is the text of the Gettysburg Address.

THE GETTYSBURG ADDRESS

Fourscore and seven years ago our fathers brought forth on this continent a new nation, conceived in liberty, and dedicated to the proposition that all men are created equal.

Now we are engaged in a great civil war, testing whether that nation, or any nation so conceived and so dedicated, can long endure. We are met on a great battlefield of that war. We have come to dedicate a portion of that field as a final resting place for those who here gave their lives that that nation might live. It is altogether fitting and proper that we should do this.

But, in a larger sense, we cannot dedicate—we cannot consecrate—we cannot hallow—this ground. The brave men, living and dead, who struggled here, have consecrated it far above our poor power to add or detract. The world will little note, nor long remember what we say here, but it can never forget what they did here. It is for us the living, rather, to be dedicated here to the unfinished work which they who fought here have thus far so nobly advanced. It is rather for us to be here dedicated to the great task remaining before us—that from these honored dead we take increased devotion to that cause for which they gave the last full measure of devotion—that we here highly resolve that these dead shall not have died in vain—that this nation, under God, shall have a new birth of freedom—and that government of the people, by the people, for the people, shall not perish from the earth.

Geum, genus of perennial plants grown in Europe, Asia, and North America. They have orange, yellow, or red semidouble or double roselike flowers and pinnately divided leaves. The leaflet at the leaf tip is larger than the others. Height: 1.5–2ft (46–61cm). Family Rosaceae.

Geyser, a hot spring that erupts intermittently, ejecting superheated water and steam; the water occupies a natural crooked tube reaching deep into the earth. When the water at the bottom boils, the resulting steam pushes up, causing the rest to boil vigorously and fountain into the air. Most geysers occur in Iceland, New Zealand, and Yellowstone National Park. △176.

Ghaghara (Gogra), navigable river, rises in Tibet, China, flows SE through Nepal meeting Ganges River in E India. Length: 570 mi (918km).

Ghana, West African empire from the 4th to 13th centuries. It conducted an extensive gold and salt trade and exacted tribute from surrounding states. Its decline began with the Muslim invasions in the 11th century.

Ghana, independent African nation, formerly the British Gold Coast colony. Ghana's 334-mi (538-km) coast was a 15th-century trading post for Europeans.

Land and economy. Ghana is located on the W coast of Africa just N of the equator, bounded on the N by Upper Volta, on the W by the Ivory Coast, on the E by Togo. Its lengthy coastline backs onto plains whose rivers and streams are passable only by canoe. Along the Ivory Coast frontier is a band of tropical forests (Ashanti) producing minerals and timber. Ghana's chief crop is cacao beans (70% of its exports). Industrial diamonds, bauxite, manganese are its chief minerals. With the completion of the mainly US-financed Akosombo hydroelectric project on the Volta River, Ghana has started its first heavy industry, an aluminum reduction plant.

People. Fifty languages still spoken today are derived from the tribes (Adansi, Akwamu, and Ga) who migrated down the Volta River in the 13th century. English is the official tongue. About 25% of the population is literate. Most of the Ghanians (45%) are animists, followed by Christians (43%), and Muslims (12%).

Government. Ghana's 1969 constitution provides for three branches of government and a president elected by universal suffrage. It also prescribes measures to prevent another Nkrumah-type regime.

History. Named for an ancient kingdom mentioned in folklore, Ghana's first contact with Europe came in 1482 when the Portuguese landed and built a trading base. An English trading company, formed about 1672, was taken over by the British government, which ruled until 1951, when a constitution was adopted, and Kwame Nkrumah was elected prime minister. In 1956, UN action ended Britain's trusteeship over Togoland. It merged with Ghana and on March 6, 1957, became a completely independent state within the commonwealth. Nkrumah was given dictatorial powers in 1964 and declared Ghana a socialist state with one legal party. In 1966 a coup ousted his regime, calling it corrupt and oppressive. Free elections were held in 1969; however, a 1972 bloodless coup put army Col. Ignatius K. Acheampong in power. He ousted Communist technicians and promised neutrality. △1116.

PROFILE

Official name: Republic of Ghana
Area: 92,099 sq mi (238,280sq km)
Population: 10,300,000
Density: 112 per sq mi (43 per sq km)
Chief cities: Accra (capital); Kumasi
Government: military socialist
Religion: animist (major), Christian, Muslim
Language: English (official)
Monetary unit: new cedi
Gross national product: $3,660,000,000
Per capita income: $287
Industries (major products): wood products, cement, rubber
Agriculture (major products): cacao, corn, cassava, nuts, sweet potatoes, wood
Minerals (major): bauxite, industrial diamonds, gold, manganese
Trading partners (major): United Kingdom, United States, Japan, European Common Market

Ghats, two mountain systems in S India; the Western Ghats extends from the Tapti River to Cape Comorin and forms the W edge of Deccan Plateau; the Eastern Ghats extends from the Mahanadi River to the Nilgiri Hills and forms the E edge of Deccan Plateau. Length: (Western) 1,000mi (1,610km); (Eastern) 900mi (1,450km). Height: (Western) 3,000–5,000ft (915–1525m); (Eastern) 2,000ft (610m). Highest peak is Anai Mundi: 8,841 ft (2,697m).

Ghazali, al- (1058–1111), Muslim scholar and mystic. He was a professor at the Nizamiya college at Baghdad, spent 11 years in an almost monastic life as a Sufi, and finally returned to teaching. He wrote on law, philosophy, theology, and mysticism. Because of his analysis of Islamic theology and his writings on inner devotion, he has been called the renewer of the religion of Islam. *See also* Sufism.

Ghent (Gent or Gand), city in NW central Belgium, 31mi (50km) NW of Brussels; capital of East Flanders prov.; major cloth center in 13th century; site of signing of treaties of Pacification of Ghent (1576) and, in 1814, to end War of 1812 and establish freedom of the seas; besieged and occupied by Germans in WWI and WWII. Industries: flower seeds, bulbs, metallurgy. Pop. 149,265.

Ghent, Treaty of (1814), treaty between the United States and Great Britain that ended the War of 1812. With neither side making major concessions, the Belgian document was essentially an agreement to end hostilities and to restore prewar boundaries.

Gheorghiu-Dej, Gheorghe (1901–65), Romanian statesman, chief of state (1961–65). After his rescue from a Nazi prison camp in 1944, he was elected secretary general of the Communist party and served in that capacity until his death, except for a brief period in 1954–55. A domestic Communist, he and his group were shunted aside by Soviet-trained Romanians until 1952. Under his leadership, a degree of independence from the USSR was achieved and industrialization advanced.

Ghetto, section of a city inhabited almost exclusively by one ethnic group. The term originated in Europe, designating a separate area of a city for Jews. The first compulsory ghettos were in Spain and Portugal in the late 14th century. Characterized by homogeneity, cultural cohesion, shared economic conditions, and exclusivity, ghettos are often founded in religious, racial, or cultural heritages. Ghettos also may generate alternate life styles that deviate from those of the larger society.

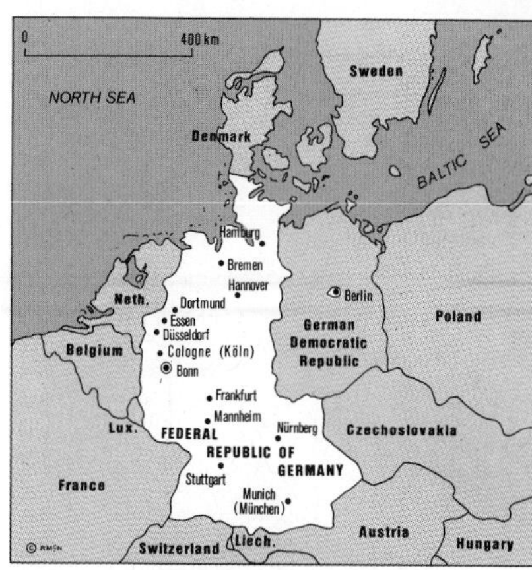
0
400 km
NORTH SEA
Sweden
Denmark
BALTIC SEA
Hamburg
Bremen
Hannover
Berlin
Neth.
Dortmund
Essen
Düsseldorf
Cologne (Köln)
Bonn
German Democratic Republic
Poland
Belgium
Frankfurt
Mannheim
Lux.
FEDERAL REPUBLIC OF GERMANY
Nürnberg
Czechoslovakia
France
Stuttgart
Munich (München)
Austria
Switzerland
Liech.
Hungary

West Germany

Geronimo

George Gershwin

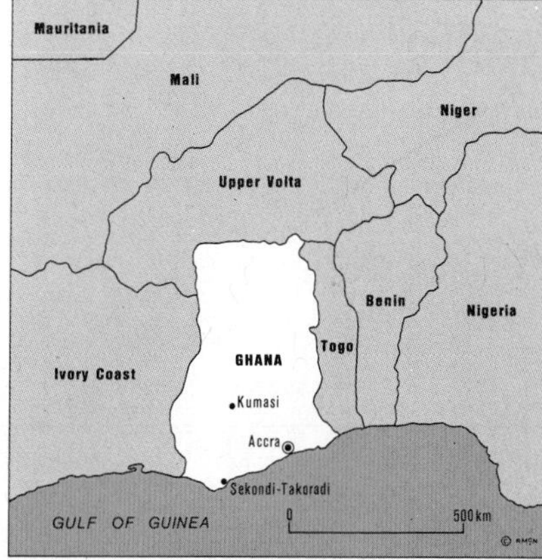
Mauritania
Mali
Niger
Upper Volta
Benin
Nigeria
Togo
GHANA
Ivory Coast
Kumasi
Accra
Sekondi-Takoradi
GULF OF GUINEA
0
500 km

Ghana

Ghibellines, pro-imperial political faction in Italy during the Middle Ages, opposed to the pro-papal Guelphs. The name Ghibelline derived from a castle, Waiblingen, belonging to the Holy Roman imperial family, the Hohenstaufens; but, during the struggles that occurred in north and central Italy between Emperor Frederick II and the popes (mid-13th century), the term came to designate those in the imperial camp.

Ghiberti, Lorenzo (1378–1455), Italian sculptor, goldsmith, architect, painter, and writer. He made two of the three huge, richly gilded bronze doors for the Baptistry in Florence, known as the Doors of Paradise. On the first (1403–24) he depicted 28 New Testament scenes. For the second (1425–47) he was allowed to use his own judgment and created his masterpiece; he chose 10 scenes from the Old Testament, each one appearing like a picture in a frame, with the plane of the background as the sky or ground. A major transitional figure between the late Gothic and Renaissance worlds, he also designed the stained-glass windows for the Duomo in Florence and wrote the first artist's autobiography. △1134.

Ghirlandaio, Domenico (1449–94), Italian painter. One of the most prolific Italian fresco painters in 15th-century Florence, he epitomized the trend toward realism of figures, settings, landscapes, and detail. He worked on the Sistine Chapel with Botticelli and others, his major contribution being the *Calling of the First Apostles*. Michelangelo was an apprentice in his large workshop.

Ghost Crab, or sand crab, amphibious crab found worldwide. They live on sandy beaches and mud flats and are relatively independent of water when mature. Their compact body is protectively colored and fast moving. Width: to 2in (5cm). Family Ocypodidae; genus *Ocypode*. *See also* Crab; Crustacean.

Ghost Dance Cult, millennial cult that flourished among Indians of W North America in the late 19th century. Prophets announced the imminent return of the dead, restoration of the Indians, and departure of the whites. This would be hastened by correct practices, including long dances.

Ghost Flower. *See* Indian Pipe.

Ghost Shark. *See* Chimaera.

Giacometti, Alberto (1901–66), Swiss sculptor and painter. During the 1930s he produced surrealist sculpture and during the 40s and 50s he produced his greatest works—emaciated, dreamlike figures, built of plaster of Paris on a wire foundation. His paintings and drawings are more representational, but their gray coloring and agitated brushwork give them the same visionary quality. *See also* Surrealism.

Gianbologna. △1150.

Giant Grouper. *See* Jewfish.

Giant Panda, large bearlike mammal of China, a member of the raccoon family. Covered with thick, woolly, white fur, it has a black nose, and brownish-black eyepatches, ears, legs, and shoulder band. Primarily vegetarians, they may eat fish or small rodents. A popular though rare zoo animal, it bears cubs in January but is hard to breed in captivity. Height: 4–5ft (1.2–1.5m) at shoulder; weight: 250lb (114kg). Family Procyonidae; species *Ailuropoda melanoleuca*. *See also* Panda.

Giant's Causeway, promontory in Northern Ireland, on N coast of Antrim; formed by columnar basalt. It consists of several thousand pillars, mainly hexagonal, of varying height.

Giant Schnauzer, cattle dog (working group) bred in Württemberg and Bavaria in Germany. A loyal, reliable dog used for police work in Germany, it has a rectangular, elongated head; high-set, V-shaped ears that can be cropped; a strong, compact body; long, muscular legs; and high-set, docked tail. The hard, wiry coat, which is either solid black or pepper and salt, features a coarse topknot, beard, and eyebrows. Average size: 21.5–25.5in (54.5–65cm) high at shoulder; 65–78lb (29–35kg). *See also* Working Dog.

Giant Star, star belonging to a luminosity class midway between main-sequence stars and supergiants. They lie directly above the main sequence on the Hertzsprung-Russell diagram and are characterized by large dimensions, high luminosity, and low density. Giants are found throughout the entire surface-temperature range. Those of spectral type G-M (the red giants) contrast with corresponding dwarfs of the main sequence. △100–02.

Giap, Vo Nguyen (1912–), Vietnamese general and minister of defense. A successful practitioner of modern guerrilla warfare, he led the Viet Minh forces that drove the Japanese out of Vietnam in 1945 and decisively defeated the French at Dien Bien Phu (1954). He later commanded North Vietnamese forces against the troops of South Vietnam and its ally, the United States, in the Vietnam War of the 1960s and 1970s, during which he organized the 1968 Tet offensive. Giap's position as deputy premier was reaffirmed by the North Vietnamese National Assembly on June 7, 1975.

Giauque, William Francis (1895–), US chemist, b. Canada. Giauque is noted for discovering isotopes of oxygen and hydrogen and for his studies of phenomena at extremely low temperatures. In 1926 he suggested a method for producing temperatures approaching absolute zero, until then believed impossible in practice. He received the 1949 Nobel Prize for chemistry.

Gibberellin, organic compound that stimulates stem elongation, fruit and flower formation, dormancy, and plant response to light and temperature. Originally isolated from the fungus *Gibberella fujikuroi*, it may interact with some auxins. △430.

Gibbon, Edward (1737–94), English historian. Author of one of the great classics of history, *The History of the Decline and Fall of the Roman Empire* (6 vols., 1776–88); he displayed such a sense of the sweep and continuity of history that his first volume achieved immediate success. The succeeding five volumes, adding to his acclaim, carried the history to its natural conclusion, the fall of Constantinople in 1453. Of independent means, Gibbon traveled widely during his lifetime. He decided to write his great history in 1764 while visiting the Forum in Rome.

Gibbon, small, slender, long-limbed arboreal ape living in SE Asian and East Indies forests. They have shaggy brown, black, or silvery gray coats. Most agile of all tree-living mammals, they travel by swinging from branch to branch with their arms. Height: to 3ft (91.5cm); weight: 11–28lb (5–13kg). Species include the siamang *Hylobates syndactalus*. △554.

Gibbons, Grinling. △1602.

Gibbons v. Ogden (1824), first US Supreme Court decision dealing with the commerce clause of the Constitution. The Court's broad definition of the word "commerce" is primarily responsible for the extensive power of the federal government to regulate interstate activity.

Gibbs, Josiah Willard (1839–1903), US theoretical physicist and chemist, b. New Haven, Conn. While a professor at Yale, he devoted himself to establishing the basics of physical chemistry. He applied thermodynamics to physical happenings, which led to statistical mechanics and eventually quantum mechanics. In addition to evolving the concept of free energy and chemical potential, he was responsible for the Phase Rule and for the creation of vector analysis, although he did not publish on the latter topic.

GI Bill, name applied to US federal legislation to help veterans of the armed forces. The first such law, the Servicemen's Readjustment Act of 1944, provided job placement services, grants to help pay for education, unemployment insurance, and guarantees for loans to buy homes, farms, or businesses. Later laws extended benefits first to Korean War veterans and then to all veterans.

Gibraltar, town at NW end of Rock of Gibraltar, between Mediterranean Sea and Atlantic Ocean; a British crown colony. One of the Pillars of Hercules, the colony is a free port and military fortress. Taken from Spain by British 1704, it was formally ceded to Britain by Treaty of Utrecht (1713); Spain has made many attempts to reclaim it; in a 1967 UN-supervised referendum, residents reaffirmed allegiance to Britain. During WWI and WWII it served as a key naval station; economy depends on military installations, port dues, and tourism. Area: 2.5sq mi (6.5sq km). Pop. 26,833.

Gibson, Althea (1927–), US tennis and golf player, b. Charleston, S.C. She was the first black to play at the Forest Hills (1950) and Wimbledon (1951) championships. The highlight of her career came when she won the US and English women's singles championships (1957–58). She later played professional golf.

Gibson, Charles Dana (1867–1944), US illustrator, b. Roxbury, Mass. Noted for his illustrations of the Gibson Girl. His books of illustration include *The Education of Mr. Pipp* (1899), *The Americans* (1900), *The Social Ladder* (1902), and *The Gibson Book* (1906).

Giddings, Joshua Reed (1795–1864), US abolitionist, b. Tioga Point, Pa. An Ohio congressman (1838–59), Giddings was such a militant opponent of slavery that he was censured and resigned and was then reelected. First a Whig, then a Free-Soiler and later as a Republican, he fought the "gag rule" and opposed the annexation of Texas and the Mexican War.

Gide, André (1869–1951), French novelist, playwright, and critic. He rejected his Protestant upbringing and was regarded as a disturbing influence on youth because of his controversial views. His works *The Immoralist* (1902) and *The Counterfeiters* (1926) show a parallel search for spiritual truth and liberation of the individual. *The Journals of André Gide* (4 vols., 1947–51) was an autobiographical work. He was an editor of the *Nouvelle Revue française* and was awarded the Nobel Prize for literature in 1947. △1376.

Gideon, biblical judge, Israelite hero, and father of Abimelech. Called by an angel of God, he destroyed the altar of Baal. After a victorious attack on the Midianite camp, with only 300 soldiers, he refused to be made king.

Gideon v. Wainwright (1963), landmark US Supreme Court decision overruling *Betts v. Brady* (1942). The court held that representation by an attorney is a constitutional necessity in all criminal trials. This decision led to the establishment of legal aid programs for indigents and formed the foundation for the Escobedo and Miranda decisions. *See also* Escobedo v. Illinois (1964).

Gierek, Edward (1913–), Polish Communist political leader. He organized the Polish resistance movement in Belgium during World War II. When riots over increased food prices and shortages broke out in Gdańsk and other port cities in 1970, Gierek succeeded Gomulka as party chief. Besides attempting to satisfy worker demands, Gierek took steps to improve relations with the Roman Catholic Church. △1344.

Gifford, Henri. △1676.

Gifted Children, children with very high intelligence and/or creativity, sometimes defined as those with IQs above 135 (where the average IQ is 100). *See also* Intelligence Quotient.

Gifu, city in Honshu, Japan, on Kiso River; capital of Gifu prefecture; former medieval castle town, taken in 1564 by Oda Nobunaga; center of civil struggles in 17th century; site of Institute of Nawa Entomology (1896). Industries: tourism, chemicals, automobiles, textiles, paper, sake, lead, woodworking, cutlery. Pop. 385,727.

Gigantism, or giantism, generalized over-growth of an individual, believed to be caused by pituitary disturbance or by pre-pubescent overproduction of the growth hormone. The body may remain in proportion or have distorted extremities and head. *See also* Acromegaly. △726.

Gigantopithecus. △646.

Gigli, Beniamino (1890–1957), Italian tenor. He studied in Rome, made his debut in 1914, and became a favorite in Italian opera houses until 1920. He succeeded Caruso at the Metropolitan Opera in New York City (1920–32; 1938–39). During World War II he sang in Europe, revisiting the United States for a series of farewell concerts in 1955.

Gijón, seaport city in N Spain, on the Bay of Biscay; of Roman origin, it was recaptured from Moors by Christians in early 8th century; refuge port for defeated Spanish Armanda (1588); site of ancient Roman baths, 15th-century church; summer resort. Industries: glass, food, tobacco, steel, iron, chemicals. Pop. 187,612.

Gila Monster, sluggish, poisonous lizard found in deserts, near water, of SW United States and N Mexico. It has a stout body, massive head, fat tail, and beadlike scales of orange-pink, yellow, and black. Nocturnal, it eats small mammals and eggs. Length: to 24in (61cm). Family Helodermatidae; species *Heloderma suspectum*. *See also* Lizard.

Gila River, river in W New Mexico; flows W across Arizona to the Colorado River at Yuma. Length: 630mi (1,014km).

Gilbert, (Sir) Humphrey (1539?–83), Canadian explorer. A brilliant navigator, Gilbert wrote a "Discourse" on the Northwest Passage (1576) and sailed to Canada from his native England in 1578 and 1583. He established the first British colony in North America at St. John's, Newfoundland (1583). Gilbert used his private means in searching for a passage to the Pacific.

Gilbert, William (1540–1603), English physicist and physician to Queen Elizabeth I. Considered the "father of electricity," his *De Magnete, Magneticisque Corporibus* (1600) laid the foundation for the scientific study of magnetism. He was the first to recognize terrestrial magnetism and concluded that a type of magnetism keeps the planets in their orbits. He coined the terms electricity, magnetic pole, electric attraction, and electric force. The C.G.S. unit of magnetomotive force is named the gilbert in his honor. △1534.

Gilbert, (Sir) William Schwenck (1836–1911), English librettist and playwright. He collaborated with Sir Arthur Sullivan on an immensely successful series of 14 comic operas frequently performed by D'Oyly Carte's company. His lyrics reveal an exuberant, often macabre humor and a talent for inventive rhymes. Gilbert and Sullivan works include *H.M.S. Pinafore* (1878), *The Pirates of Penzance* (1879), *The Mikado* (1885), and *The Yeomen of the Guard* (1888).

Gilbert Islands, British coral island group of W central Pacific Ocean, on the equator, N of Ellice Islands. Inhabitants are mainly Micronesians. Annexed to Britain 1915, its administrative seat is Tarawa. Area: 102sq mi (264sq km). Pop. 44,206.

Gilbert of Sempringham, Saint (*c.*1083–1189), English Roman Catholic priest who founded the Gilbertines, the only monastic order of exclusively English origin. He was born in Lincolnshire, the son of a Norman knight. He began the order for women only, but it grew to have double monasteries, with houses for monks and nuns.

Gil Blas (1715–35), picaresque novel in four volumes by Alain René Le Sage. Gil Blas, the innocent hero, seeks his fortune and is corrupted by the people and adventures he encounters. Finally, his good intentions triumph. The speed and wit of the narrative make it Le Sage's masterpiece.

Gilboa, Mount, mountain ridge in NE Israel, on Esdraelon plain; scene of battle in which King Saul was defeated by Philistines and killed himself. Length: 10mi (16km). Height: 1,630ft (497m).

Gilded Age, period after the Civil War when wealth and political power received increased public attention. The period also was characterized by a good deal of corruption and speculation. The term came from the novel *The Gilded Age* (1873) by Mark Twain and Charles Dudley Warner.

Gilded Age, The (1873), novel by Mark Twain and Charles Dudley Warner attacking political corruption. The novel is about Col. Beriah Sellers, who persuades his friend Squire Hawkins to speculate disastrously in land. The novel's title has become a popular term for the post-Civil War boom years.

Gilead, mountainous region in Jordan, on Jordan River, between Dead Sea and Sea of Galilee; traditional reconciliation place of Jacob and Laban, birthplace of the prophet Elijah, and place where Jephthah was made a judge of Israel.

Gilgamesh Epic, an anonymous Babylonian epic based on early Sumerian sources. It appeared in two versions: the first written *c.*1800 BC; the second, *c.* 1200 BC. The epic recounts the struggles of Gilgamesh, mythic king of Uruk, against his enemies. It deals with such themes as the transitory nature of human existence, the value of friendship, and the importance of heroes. △834, 956.

Gill, Irving John (1870–1936), US architect, b. Syracuse, New York. He developed a heavy cubic style, using concrete blocks in his California houses. He studied with Louis Sullivan, worked independently from 1896 in southern California and built Dodge House (1916) in Los Angeles. *See also* Sullivan, Louis.

Gillespie, Dizzy, (1917–), US jazz trumpeter and bandleader, b. John Birks Gillespie in Cheraw, S.C. He was one of the founders with Charlie Parker of the modern "bebop" (now called "bop") style in the 1940s. After 1950 he led his own combos and made many recordings with other jazz performers. In 1956 he was the first jazz musician sponsored on an overseas tour by the US State Department. His arrangements for the big bands of the 1940s widely influenced other jazz musicians.

Gill Netting. △386.

Gills, the breathing organs of aquatic animals through which the animals obtain oxygen from the water. Gills contain many small blood vessels called gill capillaries. As water flows over the gills, the oxygen diffuses into the capillaries and is carried to larger blood vessels. Waste products carried back to the gills by the blood diffuse out through the gills into the water. Gills are found in echinoderms, mollusks, aquatic arthropods, fishes, and larval forms of amphibians. △486, 512.

Gilman, Arthur (1837–1909), US educator and writer, b. Alton, Ill. He established the first classes for women at Harvard University (1879) and founded Radcliffe College (1893). He wrote on historical and literary subjects, including *The Story of Rome* (1886) and *The Making of the American Nation* (1887).

Gilman, Daniel Coit (1831–1908), US educator, b. Norwich, Conn. He helped establish Sheffield Scientific School at Yale University, where he taught until becoming president of the University of California (1872–75). He was the first president (1875–1901) of Johns Hopkins University, which he was instrumental in making one of the world's major universities. He was first president of the Carnegie Institution, Washington, D.C. (1901–04). He was also president of the National Civil Service Reform League (1901–07).

Gilpin, Charles Sidney (1878–1930), US actor, b. Richmond, Va. Beginning as a song and dance man in restaurants, variety theaters, and fairs, he became an actor on joining the Canadian Jubilee Singers (1903). He was with the Abyssinia company (1905–06) and the Pekin Stock company (1907), then toured again until 1914. In 1916 he became manager of the Lafayette Theatre Company in Harlem. His first Broadway appearance was in *Abraham Lincoln* (1919), followed by *Emperor Jones* (1920–24). He received a Drama League award (1921) for his contributions to the theater, and was given a Spingarn medal by the NAACP the same year.

Gilpin, Henry Dilworth (1801–60), US lawyer, b. England. In the office of US attorney general (1840–41), to which he was appointed by Pres. Martin Van Buren, he argued the Amistad case against John Quincy Adams. He also served as editor of James Madison's papers.

Gin. △352.

Ginger, herbaceous, perennial plant native to tropical E Asia and Indonesia and grown commercially in Florida. It has fat, tuberous roots and yellow-green flowers with purple edges spotted with yellow. The kitchen spice is made from the tubers of *Zingiber officinale.* Family Zingiberaceae. *See also* Cardamom.

Gingivitis, inflammatory disease of the gums that makes them tender and swollen and leads to their bleeding easily. In severe cases ulceration and fever may develop. It is believed that poor diet, bad tooth alignment, and faulty dentures predispose to infections.

Ginkgo, or gingko, maidenhair tree, oldest extant species of tree, native to temperate regions of China, Korea, and Japan. Dating from the Triassic Period most species were destroyed during the Ice Age. A good city tree, it was introduced in the United States in 1784. It has fan-shaped leaves and small, foul-smelling fruit with edible, nutlike seeds. Height: to 120ft (37m). Family Ginkgoaceae; species *Ginkgo biloba.* △440, 572.

Gin Rummy, two-handed card game with a standard deck. This game evolved from rummy and differs only in the scoring and the number of cards dealt each player (10). In knock rummy, a player may elect to go out if the unmatched cards in his hand total 10 points or less. Whichever player has the fewest number of points wins the hand. *See also* Rummy.

Ginsberg, Allen (1926–), US author, b. Newark. The major writer of the Beat Generation, his work is influenced by his interest in Zen Buddhism and meditation and by the use of drugs. His most famous poems are "Howl" (1956), a condemnation of American society, and "Kaddish for Naomi Ginsberg (1894–1956)" (1961), a lament for his mother, who became insane. *See also* Beat Generation.

Ginsburg v. United States (1966), US Supreme Court decision affirming the federal obscenity law

Ghost crab

Giant panda

André Gide

Ginseng

conviction of publisher Ralph Ginsburg. The court used a "context" test and stated that commercial exploitation of erotic material was the evil at which the law aimed.

Ginseng, two perennial plants from North America and E Asia. Both have yellow-green flowers and 5-ft (1.5-m) leaves. The dried tuberous roots are valued for use in Chinese traditional medicine. Height: to 18in (46cm). Family Araliaceae; species Chinese *Panax schinseng* and North American *Panax quinquefolius.*

Giolitti, Giovanni (1842–1928), Italian statesman and 5-time prime minister. From 1889–1890 he served as treasury minister in the Francesco Crispi government. He first served as prime minister from 1892–1893, supporting a program of financial reform and reorganization. His fourth term as prime minister (1911–14) ended because of his opposition to Italian entry into World War I. During his last term (1920–21) he was generally tolerant towards the Fascists, but withdrew his support in 1924. △1300.

Giorgione, Il (c.1475–1511), Italian painter, *b.* Giorgio Barbarelli. One of the major painters of the Venetian High Renaissance, he was a pupil of Bellini. He broke away from his teacher's style and evolved his own mysterious, romantic one creating a unity of figures and landscape. His "Tempest" (*c.*1507, Academy, Venice), puzzling to his contemporaries, is the first landscape of mood. Only a small number of the paintings attributed to him (among them the Castelfranco "Madonna" and "Laura") are universally accepted as his, and many of the works he undoubtedly began were finished by Titian and Sebastiano del Piombo, whom he influenced greatly. △1142, 1144.

Giotto (*c.*1266–1337), Italian painter. The father of all modern painting, he was the first artist to create visually and psychologically convincing human forms, and the first since the Greeks to represent three dimensional form and space. He revolutionized art completely, arranging his dramatic, individualized figures realistically in relation both to each other and to their setting. His knowledge of anatomy and perspective was inaccurate, but through the use of light and shadow he gave his figures depth that cut into the space around them. His greatest achievement was the fresco cycle in the Arena Chapel at Padua (*c.*1305), a serenely dramatic, simple rendering of 38 scenes from the life of Joachim and Anna, the Virgin Mary, and Christ. He was also the architect of the Campanile (belltower) of the Duomo in Florence; just begun at his death, its 26 bas-relief scenes begin with the creation of man and end with the depiction of his most advanced achievements. △1140.

Giovanni di Paolo (1403–83), Italian painter. He was one of the most influential and prolific Sienese painters of the 15th century. His style is distinctive for the languid grace of the figures, who often have wistful, even ugly faces; in his later work the forms are heavier and distorted, and the colors darker.

Giraffe, even-toed, hoofed, cud-chewing mammal inhabiting African savannas. The tallest existing mammal, it has a long neck, long legs and blotched coloring. Like other mammals, it has only seven neck vertebrae. The unique horns of both sexes are two to four bony knobs covered with skin; sometimes a fifth knob is present between the eyes. Though shy, they live in large herds. They mate in summer. The gestation period is 15 months and a single calf is born. Able to outrun a horse, its maximum speed is 28mph (45kmph). Height: to 18ft (5.5m); weight: to 1.5ton (1,350kg). Family Giraffidae; species *Giraffa camelopardalis. See also* Artiodactyla; Ruminant. △548, 586.

Girard, Stephen (1750–1831), US financier and philanthropist, b. France. Captain of a ship involved in US coastal trade with the West Indies, he settled in Philadelphia (1776) and developed a worldwide trading fleet, amassing a fortune. He supported the United States during the War of 1812 and founded the Bank of Stephen Girard (1816), and helped establish the second Bank of the United States. He left most of his money to social welfare institutions and endowed a Philadelphia school for male orphans, Girard College, which opened in 1848.

Giraud, Henri Honoré (1879–1949), French military commander, served in World War I and later in North Africa, and was captured by the Germans in 1940. He escaped two years later and commanded French forces in Africa. He briefly shared the presidency of the French Committee of National Liberation with de Gaulle in 1943 but retired shortly thereafter because of their differences.

Girder. △1604–06, 1610.

Girl Scouts, an organization for girls. Its purpose is to inspire girls to develop personal values and to share planned activities. There are a wide variety of projects in social action, environmental action, youth leadership, career exploration, and community service. It was founded in Savannah, Ga., by Juliette Gordon Low in 1912 and was modeled after the Boy Scouts and Britain's Girl Guides. Its publications include *American Girl, Brownie Reader,* and *Girl Scout Leader.* Membership: about 3,000,000.

Girondists, also **Girondins,** political organization of the French Revolution that began with legislators from Gironde. The bourgeois Girondists advocated a mild republicanism and tried to prevent the execution of Louis XVI. They managed to start a war with Austria, for the inspiration of national unity, but conflicted increasingly with the Jacobins and lost their leaders to the guillotine in a Parisian revolt in 1793.

Girouard v. United States (1946), US Supreme Court case that overruled earlier decisions and held that a man who would not bear arms but would serve as a noncombatant in the US Army could not be denied naturalization as a US citizen.

Girtin, Thomas Joseph. △1242.

Giscard, d'Estaing, Valéry (1926–), president of France, elected 1974. Giscard first entered the ministry of finance in 1949. In 1956 he was elected to parliament. He served as minister of finance in the cabinets of Debré and Pompidou (1962–66). His parliamentary group represented the right wing of the Gaullist majority. In the 1974 presidential elections, he narrowly defeated a coalition of the Communist and Socialist parties.

Giselle, romantic ballet by Vernoy de Saint Georges, Theo Gauitier, and Jean Coralli; music by Adolphe Adam. The first production was in Paris in 1841 with Carlotta Grisi in the title role. *Giselle* has been unsurpassed in a hundred years both in choreography and music. Famous interpreters of the title role include Alicia Markova, Nora Kaye, and Margot Fonteyn. △1368.

Gish, Lillian (1896–), US stage and film actress, b. Lillian de Guiche in Springfield, Ohio. She is famous for her portrayals of delicate heroines in the silent films of D. W. Griffith. Her films included *The Birth of a Nation* (1915), *Intolerance* (1916), *Broken Blossoms* (1918), *The Scarlet Letter* (1926), and the sound films *The Night of the Hunter* (1955) and *The Unforgiven* (1959). She returned to the stage in *Uncle Vanya* (1930) after a 17-year absence, and appeared in such plays as *Camille* (1932), *Crime and Punishment* (1947), *All the Way Home* (1960), and the musical *A Musical Jubilee* (1975).

Gist, Christopher (*c.*1706–59), American frontiersman, b. Maryland. He explored and surveyed the Ohio River Valley (1750–51) and accompanied George Washington on the expedition to order the French out of the Ohio Valley (1753–54). He served as a guide on Braddock's ill-fated march on Fort Dusquesne (1755). He died of smallpox while attempting to enlist the Cherokees against the French.

Gitlow v. New York (1925), US Supreme Court case in which the court, upholding a conviction for publication of a Communist pamphlet, held that the First Amendment's freedom of speech provisions were protected against incursions by the individual states.

Giza (Al-Jizah), city in N Egypt, on W bank of Nile River; suburb of Cairo; capital of Giza governorate; Great Sphinx and pyramid of Khufu (Cheops) are nearby; site of University of Cairo (1908). Industries: motion pictures, textiles, cigarettes, footwear, tourism. Pop. 345,261.

Glacial Groove. △262.

Glacial Polish. △262.

Glacier, a large mass of ice, consisting mainly of recrystallized snow, which moves slowly by creeping downslope or outward in all directions due to the stress of its own weight; it survives from year to year. Glaciers terminate where the rate of loss of ice by melting and ablation is equal to the forward advance of the glacier. There are three main types: mountain or valley glaciers, piedmont glaciers, and ice sheets and ice caps. △262–64.

Glacier National Park, park in NW Montana along the continental divide in the Rocky Mts; adjoins Waterton Lakes National Park in SW Alberta, Canada; together they form the Waterton-Glacier International Peace Park. Est. 1932. It is characterized by many glaciers, glacier-fed lakes, mountains, forests, and waterfalls. A variety of animal and plant life are found in this pristine wilderness. Area: 1,013,100acres (410,306hectares). Est. 1910. *See also* Waterton Lakes National Park.

Glaciology, study of glaciers. A glacier is a moving ice mass made up of snow and ice. They may be classified by climate into polar and temperate, both built up by snowfall and decreased by melting. The movement of the ice-river creates strains both within itself and on the terrain it moves over. Variation of glaciation at different historic periods is a subdivision of glaciology. *See also* Glacier; Historical Geology. △262–64.

Gladiators. Perhaps originally an Etrurian custom, gladiatorial combats were first recorded at Rome in 264 BC. Gladiators were generally prisoners of war, slaves, or condemned prisoners, who were trained to fight one another or wild beasts in public arenas. The gladiator who lost a battle was usually killed, though onlookers sometimes waved their handkerchiefs as a signal that they wished his life to be spared. Abolished by Constantine I in AD 325, the combats persisted into the 5th century.

Gladiolus, genus of 300 species of flowering plants native to Europe and Africa and widely cultivated. They grow from a corm that may be planted in early spring to a flowering spike of funnel-shaped flowers and tall, swordlike leaves. Cultivated hybrid species are various colors. Height: to 3ft (0.9m). Family Iridaceae. *See also* Iris.

Gladstone, William E(wart) (1809–98), English political figure. He entered Parliament as a Tory in 1832 and served as president of the Board of Trade in Sir Robert Peel's cabinet (1843–45). Thereafter he held several cabinet posts, serving most impressively as chancellor of the exchequer. He joined the Liberal party in 1859 and became its leader in 1867. He was prime minister four times (1868–74, 1880–85, 1886, 1892–94). A social reformer and Christian moralist, his programs included disestablishment of the Church of Ireland (1869) so that Irish Catholics would no longer have to support a church to which they did not belong, the Irish Land Act (1870), which gave the Irish tenant farmers some security, the Elementary Education Act (1870), introduction of the secret ballot, and reorganization of the judiciary. He denounced the Turkish atrocities in Bulgaria (1875) and achieved a third parliamentary Reform Act (1884). His attempts to reform Irish government included the Land Bill of 1881 and the advocacy of the Irish Home Rule Bill (defeated in 1886 and 1893), which led to his government's defeat in 1886 and 1894 and shattered the Liberal party.

Gland. *See* Endocrine System; Hormones.

Glanders, or equinia, farcy, contagious disease of horses, donkeys, and mules attacking the mucous membranes and lymphatic systems. The organism *Malleomyces mallei* enters the digestive tract, gets into the blood, traveling to the lungs and skin, resulting in sticky nasal emissions, fever, vomiting, and ulcers. It is cured by antibiotics. Infection to humans and premises can occur from exposure to broken skin of affected animals.

Glasgow, city in SW central Scotland; largest city in Scotland. Situated on both banks of the Clyde River, 20mi (32km) from its mouth, it is a major port accessible to ocean-going ships; site of University of Glasgow (1451), Royal College of Science and Technology (1796 as Anderson's Institution), Art Gallery and Museum (1901), cathedral (1197–1457), and Provand's Lordship, a museum that is oldest house in Glasgow (1470). Industries: shipbuilding, heavy engineering, flour milling, brewing, distilling, textiles, tobacco, chemicals, printing. Pop. 896,958.

Glass and Glassware, an amorphous substance made by melting together silica and smaller proportions of alkali with a base, such as lime or lead oxide, which hardens the mixture and lowers its temperature, resulting in its fusion without crystallization. Glass melts slowly and can be worked only while it remains warm and supple. It must be cooled gradually to prevent breakage. Fused silica is the simplest glass and is used when stability through changing temperatures is needed. Soda-lime glass is used in the manufacture of bottles and drinking glasses. Flint glass, which is heavy and refracts light well, is used in lenses and prisms.

Glass objects, especially jewelry and small containers, were found in Egypt as early as 2500 BC. Glass figurines and vessels were common in the Middle East during the 8th and 7th centuries BC and also in

Greece. Probably around the 1st century AD in Syria, the blowing pipe was discovered and revolutionized the glass-making industry by allowing glassware to be mass produced in a variety of thinness and size. The 12th through the 14th centuries saw a highly developed industry producing enamel Islamic mosque lamps in Syria and Egypt. During the 13th century Venice rose to prominence as a glassmaking center of delicate, thin, colored glass. Crystal glass, which was strong enough to be engraved, was produced in Bohemia. In the late 17th century heavy, lead glass was developed in England. During the 19th century, cut glass and pressed glass were fashionable in the United States. Scandinavia has been a leader in the glassmaking industry in the 20th century, both in industrial and decorative design. △1560, 1608.

Glass Blowing, handcraft. A hollow iron blowpipe, 4–5 feet (1.2–1.5 meters) long, is dipped into molten glass to form a bubble from which any variety of objects are formed by squeezing, stretching, twirling, reheating, or cutting. When the final design is achieved, it is broken from the pipe. The glass can also be blown into iron molds. In the commercial production of glass-blown products, a machine is used. △1608.

Glass Fish, formerly called ambassid, freshwater fish found in shallow waters of N India. A favorite aquarium fish, it has a translucent body. Length: to 2in (5.1cm). Family Centropomidae; species includes *Chanda ranga.*

Glass Harmonica, antique musical instrument improved by Benjamin Franklin (1763) and used by Mozart (1791) and Beethoven (1814). Delicate sounds are produced by fingertips touching glass saucers in graduated rank, revolving in water on a horizontal, pedal-operated spindle.

Glass Lizard. *See* Glass Snake.

Glass Snake, or glass lizard, legless lizard found in North America, Eurasia, and Africa. It is cylindrical with a groove along each side and is chiefly brown or green, though some are striped. It has moveable eyelids. Length: 24–48in (61–122cm). Family Anguinidae; genus *Ophisaurus. See also* Lizard.

Glasswort, fleshy plant found in salt marshes throughout temperate regions of the Northern Hemisphere. It has succulent stems, and inconspicuous leaves and flowers. Family Chenopodiaceae; genera *Salicornia* and *Salsola.*

Glastonbury, market town in SW England, on Brue River, 22mi (35km) SW of Bath. According to legend, it was site of first Christian church in England, founded by Joseph of Arimathea, and burial place of King Arthur. Industries: tanning, footwear. Pop. 6,571.

Glauber, Johann Rudolf (1604–68), German chemist and physician. He was the first to realize that an acid reacts with a base to form a salt. He prepared hydrochloric acid, sodium sulfate (known as Glauber's salt), and tartar emetic.

Glaucoma, group of eye diseases characterized by increasing pressure of fluid within the eye leading to progressive loss of vision. Causes are unknown although heredity seems to be a factor. It occurs most frequently in patients over 40 and is accompanied by need for frequent changes in corrective lenses, mild headache, and impaired ability to adapt to the dark.

Glaucus, the name of several figures in Greek mythology. Pontius Glaucus was a sea divinity. Once a fisherman, he was changed into a god and endowed with the gift of prophecy. Glaucus of Potniae was the son of the king of Thebes (Sisyphus) by Merope, and father of the Trojan war hero Bellerophon.

Glazer, Nathan (1923–), US sociologist, b. New York City. Early in his career Glazer coauthored *The Lonely Crowd* (1950) with David Riesman. Most of his research has been in urban sociology and ethnic and race relations. His other works include *American Judaism* (1957) and *Beyond the Melting Pot* (1963), coauthored with Daniel Patrick Moynihan.

Gleizes, Albert (Léon) (1881–1953), French painter and writer. Through his writings, he was the chief disseminator of cubist ideas. In 1911 he exhibited with the first cubist group. In 1912 he and Jean Metzinger published the influential *On Cubism.* By 1919 his paintings had become religious in tone, combining Catholic themes with cubist ideas. *See also* Cubism.

Glencoe, Massacre of, in Scotland the killing of the MacDonalds on Feb. 13, 1692, for a technical failure to declare allegiance to the new British king, William III. About 40 died in the surprise attack by Campbell soldiers under orders of Sir John Dalrymple, the king's secretary of state.

Glen Cove, city in SE New York, on N shore of Long Island, at entrance to Hempstead Harbor; site of Webb Institute of Naval Architecture. Industries: office supplies, hardware, radios. Settled 1668; inc. as city 1918. Pop. (1970) 25,770.

Glendale, town in SW central Arizona, 8mi (13km) NW of Phoenix. Industries: agriculture, lettuce, melons, truck crops. Founded 1892; inc. 1910. Pop. (1970) 36,228.

Glendale, city in S California, 6mi (10km) N of Los Angeles; first land grant from Spain in California (1784). Industries: defense and aerospace plants; motion pictures. Inc. 1906. Pop. (1970) 132,752.

Glendora, city in S California, 22mi (35km) ENE of Los Angeles. Industries: citrus fruit, sprinklers and pumps. Inc. 1911. Pop. (1970) 31,349.

Glendower, Owen. *See* Owen Glendower.

Glenn, John Herschel, Jr. (1921–), US astronaut b. Cambridge, Ohio. He piloted the first US orbiting spacecraft, Friendship 7, on Feb. 20, 1962 (3 orbits). He co-authored *We Seven* (1962) and wrote *P.S., I Listened to Your Heartbeat.* He was elected to the US Senate from Ohio (1972).

Glider, a winged aircraft with no power source of its own, which sustains flight through the controlled loss of altitude. A glider gains altitude only by descending in upward-moving air, such as thermal updrafts, that is, rising faster than the glider's rate of descent. It is capable of virtually all the maneuvers of a powered aircraft.

Glinka, Mikhail (1803–57), Russian composer, important as the founder of nationalism in Russian opera and the first Russian composer to receive acclaim outside his own country. His two operas, *A Life for the Tsar* (1836) and *Russlan and Ludmilla* (1842), inspired the composers who called themselves the "Russian Five." Late in his life he lived in Italy and Spain and wrote songs and orchestral music including the *Jota Aragonesa.* △1246.

Gliwice, city in SW Poland, 14mi (23km) W of Katowice. Chartered 1276, city became part of Prussia 1742, and part of Poland by Potsdam Conference 1945. Industries: coal mining, smelting, chemicals. Pop. 170,900.

Globeflower, perennial flowering plant native to colder parts of the Northern Hemisphere. The yellow sepals form large blossoms and buttercuplike leaves surround the stem. The European globeflower *(Trollius europaeus)* is cultivated in the United States and has yellow or orange globular blooms. There are about 15 species. Family Ranunculaceae.

Globe Theater, Elizabethan public theater most closely associated with Shakespeare's career. Built in 1598 and patterned after the 16th-century playhouses, it had polygonal walls with a roof over the stage and galleries. It was built by the Chamberlain Company of which Shakespeare was an original shareholder. Destroyed by fire in 1613, it was rebuilt in 1614 but was permanently closed down by the Puritans in 1644. △1148.

Globigerina, one-celled genus of marine protozoa whose empty shells are an important component of ocean floor ooze. Its shell is spiralled into a lumpy sphere with needlelike extensions. *See also* Foraminfera. △506.

Globular Cluster. *See* Cluster, Stellar.

Globulins, a complex mixture of globular proteins found in the blood serum, some of which serve as carriers of lipids, hormones, and inorganic ions. The immunoglobulins are included in this general category.

Glochidium, bivalve larva of freshwater clam. It develops from fertilized eggs in the gills of the female and is expelled into the water where it must become parasitic on fish to survive. When it develops into a young clam, it drops to the bottom and grows to adult size.

Glockenspiel, musical percussion instrument with set of steel bars on horizontal frame, tuned to chromatic scale, and played with two hammers. It is called a celeste when played from a keyboard, as in Mozart's

Giorgione: painting in oil

Lillian Gish

Glasgow, Scotland

Mikhail Glinka

The Magic Flute (1791). The bell-lyra is a portable glockenspiel for marching bands.

Glomar Challenger. △170.

Glomeruli. △694.

Glomerulonephritis, kidney disease apparently related to streptococcal infection. Chronic forms may be fatal.

Glorious Revolution (1688–89), events resulting in the deposition of James II of England (1685–88). The birth (1688) of a son to James, a Catholic convert, led to fears in England of a Catholic heir to the throne. Tories and Whigs united in inviting William of Orange, Dutch Protestant husband of Mary, daughter of James, to remove James. William landed (1688), and James fled to France. In 1689 Parliament invited William and Mary to rule England jointly. The Declaration of Rights and Bill of Rights (1689) barred Catholic succession to the throne and demonstrated Parliament's supremacy over the crown.

Glossolalia, speaking in tongues, vocalization of sounds, which are usually unintelligible, made by individuals in a state of religious ecstacy. Pentacostal sects cite the Bible (Acts 2) for authority and there are other references in the New Testament. *See also* Pentacostalism.

Glottis, aperture between the vocal cords at the lower end of the pharynx. It opens into the trachea.

Gloucester, Gilbert de Clare, 8th Earl of (1243–95), English noble. He joined Simon de Montfort (1263), then siding with Prince Edward, he defeated de Montfort at Gresham (1265). He fought the Welsh (1276–83), and married Edward I's daughter, Joan (1290).

Gloucester, Humphrey, Duke of (1391–1447), English noble and literary patron, youngest son of Henry IV. He fought at Agincourt (1415) and was regent of England (1420–21). He became protector (1422–29) under his brother Bedford during Henry VI's minority. His marriage (1422) to Jacqueline of Hainault was annulled (1428) and her lands lost to Burgundy. He quarreled with his uncle, Henry Beaufort, refusing to recognize him as papal legate and opposing his policy of peace with the French. Arrested for high treason (1447), he died in custody.

Gloucester, Richard de Clare, 7th Earl of (1222–62), English noble. He was sent as envoy to Scotland (1255) and Germany (1256). Defeated by the Welsh (1257), he joined Simon de Montfort, but quarreled with him (1259), and with Prince Edward (1261).

Gloucester, Robert, Earl of (died 1147), illegitimate son of Henry I of England. He joined his half-sister Matilda in invading England (1139) and captured Stephen of England (1141), but failed in his claims for the English throne.

Gloucester, Thomas of Woodstock, Duke of (1355–97), English noble, youngest son of Edward III, brother of John of Gaunt. After unsuccessful campaigns in Brittany and Essex (1380–81), he led the lords appellant against his nephew Richard II in 1386, but was arrested in 1397, and probably murdered.

Gloucester, city in England, on the Severn River; river port and market town; seat of Gloucestershire. Industries: timber, grain, matches, toys, aircraft components. Pop. 90,134.

Gloucester, city and port in NE Massachusetts, on Cape Ann. For three centuries it has been a major fishing port; Eastern Point Light is near harbor entrance. Industries: tourism, fishing, fish processing. Area explored 1605–06 by Samuel de Champlain; settled 1623; inc. 1642; received city charter 1873. Pop. 27,941.

Glowworm, luminous firefly larva or a wingless adult female firefly. *See also* Firefly.

Gloxinia, herbaceous plant with tuberous roots and short stems, native to South America. *Sinningia speciosa* (common gloxinia) has elongated, bell-shaped flowers ranging from purple to violet, sometimes with red or white variations. Family Gesneriaceae. *See also* Gesneria.

Glubb, (Sir) John Bagot (1897–), British commander of Jordan's Arab Legion, known as Glubb Pasha. After World War I he helped the British oversee Palestine and Trans-Jordan but resigned to join the Arab Legion, which kept order among the tribes. In 1948 he created a Palestinian force against Israel. Hussein I of Jordan dismissed him (1956) because of anti-British feeling in the Middle East. Among his books are *Story of the Arab Legion* (1948) and *Syria, Lebanon, and Jordan* (1967).

Glucagon, protein hormone secreted by the alpha cells of the endocrine pancreas. It helps regulate blood sugar by raising blood glucose levels. *See also* Insulin. △690.

Gluck, Christoph Willibald von (1714–87), German operatic composer who studied in Italy and Vienna. After composing his early operas in the Italian tradition, Gluck became dissatisfied with the pomp and mannerisms of older operas and set out to reform them, putting text and music into a more meaningful, coherent whole. Consequently, the art of opera was reformed, operas became more realistic and effective, and Gluck's ideas influenced Mozart, who composed several operas. Gluck's finest operas were *Orfeo ed Euridice* (1762), *Alceste* (1767), and *Iphigénie en Tauride* (1779). △1174.

Glucose, colorless crystalline sugar ($C_6H_{12}O_6$) that occurs in fruit and honey. Other carbohydrates in the bodies of animals are converted to glucose before being utilized as an energy source. It is prepared commercially by the hydrolysis of starch using hydrochloric acid and is used in confectionary, tanning, treating tobacco, and pharmaceuticals. △1570–74.

Glucoside, a carbohydrate-containing compound that yields a glucose and a nonsugar component when decomposed by the process of hydrolysis.

Glutamic Acid, colorless crystalline amino acid used in the form of its sodium salt (sodium glutamate) as a food flavoring. *See also* Amino Acid. △1570.

Gluteus Maximus. △684.

Glycerin, or glycerol, thick syrupy sweet liquid ($CH_2OH{\cdot}CHOH{\cdot}CH_2OH$) obtained by the saponification of fats and oils in the manufacture of soap or from propylene or acrolein. It is used in the manufacture of plastics, explosives, cosmetics, foods, antifreeze, paper coating, etc. Properties: sp gr 1.26; melt. pt. 64.4°F (18°C); boil. pt. 554°F (290°C). △1570–72.

Glycine, colorless soluble cystalline amino acid; the principal amino acid in sugarcane. *See also* Amino Acid. △1572.

Glycols, or diols, class of alcohols containing two hydroxyl groups. The simplest is ethylene glycol, or ethane diol, $C_2H_4(OH)_2$, a viscous liquid used in plastics and antifreeze.

Glycosuria, excretion of an abnormally large amount of sugar in urine. It is found with disease such as diabetes.

Gnat, a common name for many species of small, biting dipterous flies. In the United States, black flies, buffalo gnats, sand flies, midges, fungus gnats and fruit flies are all termed gnats. In Great Britain, mosquitoes are commonly called gnats. *See also* Diptera.

Gnatcatcher, warbler ranging from N United States to Argentina and named for its habit of searching crevices and leaves for insects. It is grayish with a slender, depressed bill. The blue-gray gnatcatcher *(Polioptila caerulea)* has a beautiful song and builds a lichen-covered nest high in a tree. Other species nest in low bushes. Pale bluish-speckled eggs (3–5) are laid. Length: 5in (12.5cm). Family Sylviidae; subfamily Polioptilinae.

Gneiss, general term that describes a coarse-grained rock laminated with minerals and largely recrystallized, but which lacks the breaking pattern of schist. They derive by metamorphic process from igneous or sedimentary rocks. *See also* Metamorphic Rocks. △248, 252.

GNMA. *See* Government National Mortgage Association.

Gnomonic Projection. △180.

Gnosticism, religious movement including numerous sects, widespread by the 2d century AD. All Gnostics promised salvation through a special knowledge of God revealed to them alone. These sects incorporated many tenets of Christianity, and Gnosticism was a serious competitor of early Christianity, which condemned it as heresy.

GNP. *See* Gross National Product.

GNP Deflator, type of price index that measures changes in price level of all final purchases of goods and services in the economy. It is used to adjust money GNP for the price level. If the level of GNP is $727.1 billion in current dollars and the GNP deflator is 109.3, real GNP would be found by 727.1 ÷ 109.3 = 6.652. Thus, real GNP is found by deflating money GNP by the GNP deflator. The GNP deflator will be similar to the consumer price index (CPI) and the index of industrial production (IIP).

Gnu, or wildebeest, large, oxlike antelope. The white-tailed gnu *(Connochaetes gnou)* is almost extinct, except for a few protected herds in S Africa. The brindled gnu *(Connochaetes taurinus)* lives in E and S Africa. They have a massive, buffalo-like head, horns, and slender body. Both sexes bear horns. The brindled gnu is silver with brownish bands and black neck, face, and shoulder mane. Its beard is black or white. The horselike tail is used to brush away flies. Length: to 78in (2m); height: to 51in (1.3m); weight: to 605lb (272kg). Family Bovidae. *See also* Ruminant.

Go, board game of Oriental origin for two players. On a board consisting of 361 intersections, black and white stones are alternately placed one at a time with the object of encircling the opponent's pieces and territory. The more skillful player generally uses the white stones.

Goa, city in S India, on Arabian Sea; made a Portuguese colony when captured 1510 from the sultan of Bijapur; in 1961, Goa was inc. with Daman and Diu to form a self-governing union territory. Industries: rice, cashews, spices, salt, oil, fishing, lumber, coir, coconuts, manganese mining. Pop. 626,978.

Goat, horned ruminants raised mainly for milk, meat, leather, and hair. Closely related to sheep, goats are brown or gray, have a bearded chin, pronounced odor in males, and bulging forehead in both sexes. The horns of males sweep up and backward. The male is a buck or billy, the female a doe or nanny, and the young a kid. Wild species are generally nomadic in rugged mountains. The gestation period is five months and usually two young are born. Five species include the ibex *(Capra ibex)*, markhor *(Capra falconeri)*, and wild goat or besang *(Capra hircus)*, which is thought to be a forerunner of many domestic breeds. Length: to 55in (1.4m); height: to 33in (85cm). Family Bovidae; genus *Capra*. *See also* Ruminant. △378.

Goatfish, or surmullet, marine fish found in tropical and temperate inshore and shallow waters. It is an elongated, brilliantly colored fish, with a forked tail and long fleshy whiskers. Length: to 24in (61cm). Family Mullidae; species, 55 including Atlantic spotted *Pseudopeneus maculatus*.

Goatsucker, large-mouthed, nocturnal bird widely distributed in warm areas, including the whippoorwill, nighthawk, and nightjar. Their plumage helps them blend with their surroundings. Some species have elongated, ornate tails and wing feathers. They fly with their mouth, surrounded by bristles, open to catch insects. They lay scrawled eggs (2) on bare ground or leaves. Length: 7–12in (17.5–30cm). Family Caprimulgidae.

Gobelins, site of a French workshop that produced famous large wall hangings during the 17th century. The Gobelins workshop of Flemish artists was organized by Charles Le Brun, painter to King Louis XIV.

Gobi (Mandarin Shamoh), desert in central Asia; one of the world's largest deserts; extends E and W from Kinghan Mts to Tien Shan; fierce sandstorms, harsh winters, hot summers and erratic cloudbursts make it uninhabitable; scattered, nomadic Mongolian sheep and goat herding tribes live along grassy periphery of desert. Elevation: 3,000–5,000ft (915–1,525m). Area: approx. 500,000sq mi (1,295,000sq km).

Gobineau, Joseph Arthur, comte de (1816–82), French writer and diplomat whose racist views had great following in Nazi Germany. Gobineau's *Essay on the Inequality of the Human Races* (1854; 1884) claims intellectual and moral superiority for the white race, especially Aryans.

Goby, marine tropical fish found inshore or around coral reefs. Popular with aquarists, it is brightly colored. Suction area, formed from fused pelvic fins, is on front of body and is used to hang onto underwater surfaces. Length: 0.5–4in (1.2–10.2cm). Family Gobiidae; species 400, including neon goby *Elactinus oceanops* and the tiny *Pandaka pygmaea*.

God, the name given in many religions to the creator and mover of the universe, in others to a variety of supernatural beings. Judaism, Christianity, and Islam are monotheistic, holding that there is one God. In Hinduism, Brahma is considered the soul of the world, but there are lesser gods. In polytheistic religions such as those of ancient Greece and Rome there is a heavenful of gods and goddesses. Skeptics deny the existence of any god (atheism). *See also* Agnosticism; Allah; Atheism; Brahma; Buddhism; Christianity; Deism; Greek Mythology; Hinduism; Islam; Jehovah; Judaism; Zeus. △856.

Godavari, river in central India rises in Western Ghats Mts; flows SE across Deccan Plateau to Bay of Bengal, NW of Rajahmundry; navigable in lower course; densely populated delta; source of the Rampadasagur hydroelectric-irrigation project. Sacred to the Hindus, there are many pilgrimage centers along its banks. Length: 900mi (1,450km).

Godfrey of Bouillon (*c.*1061–1100), first Latin ruler of Jerusalem (1099–1100). For service in his army, Holy Roman Emperor Henry IV rewarded Godfrey with the duchy of Lower Lorraine (*c.*1082). In 1096 he set out on the First Crusade. After the capture of Jerusalem (1099) he refused the title king, but became ruler as the defender of the Holy Sepulchre. His brother succeeded him as Baldwin I.

Godiva, Lady (died 1080), English benefactress, wife of Leofric, earl of Mercia. According to tradition she rode naked through the streets of Coventry (1040) to obtain the people's relief from taxation by her husband. She founded endowed monasteries at Coventry and Stow.

Godolphin, Sidney Godolphin, 1st Earl of (1645–1712), English political figure. Secretary of state (1684) under James II, he regained office under William III (1688–96) but maintained secret contact with James. A Tory, as lord treasurer under Anne (1702–10), he helped finance the military campaigns of his ally the duke of Marlborough.

Godoy, Manuel de (1767–1851), Spanish statesman. He became the lover of Queen María Luisa and rose rapidly in the court of King Charles IV. He became chief minister in 1792. He allied Spain with France against Great Britain during the Napoleonic upheavals, an alliance that resulted in the defeat of Trafalgar (1805). Opposition to him increased after France overran Spain in the Peninsular War. He was captured by a mob at Aranjuez but was rescued by the French. They gave him refuge, and he died in France.

Godthåb, capital of Greenland, on SW coast; location of scientific station, oil and liquid gas bunkers, fish processing industry. Oldest Danish settlement in Greenland, founded 1721. Pop. 6,104.

Godunov, Boris (1551–1605), tsar of Russia (1598–1605). When his brother-in-law Tsar Fyodor died, Boris was chosen tsar. His persecution of the boyars and his inability to deal with a famine made him unpopular. Therefore, when a pretender to the throne claiming to be Prince Dmitri (Fyodor's son), who had actually been killed as a child, invaded in 1604, he was able to gain popular support. Boris died suddenly, and his own son was overthrown as tsar by the pretender.

Godwin, Earl of Wessex (died 1053), English noble. He aided the accession of Edward the Confessor (1042). Edward later married Godwin's daughter, Edith. His opposition to the king's favorites led to his family's fall from royal favor. Outlawed (1051), he landed in England (1052), and the king was forced to restore him to power.

Godwin, William (1756–1836), English political philosopher, husband of Mary Wollstonecraft and father of Mary Shelley. A dissenting minister (1778–83), he became an atheist and anarchist. His belief in the power of man's reason is expressed in *Enquiry Concerning Political Justice* (1793) and in the novels *Caleb Williams* (1794) and *St Leon* (1799). *See also* Shelley, Mary; Wollstonecraft, Mary.

Godwin-Austen (Dapsang or K2), mountain in Pakistan in Karakoram Range, S central Asia; second highest peak in the world; discovered 1856 in survey of India and named for topographer Henry Godwin-Austen, surveyor of the region. The summit was first reached in 1954 by Ardito Desio. Height: 28,250ft (8,616m).

Godwit, seacoast-wintering sandpiper with long, upcurved bill. Nesting on grassland or tundra, it breeds noisily and lays 4 greenish eggs. Length: 1ft (30cm). Genus *Limosa.*

Goebbels, Joseph (1897–1945), German Nazi leader. He joined the Nazi party in 1924 and worked with Gregor Strasser, leader of the left wing of the party. Switching loyalty to Hitler in 1926, Goebbels founded the paper *Der Angriff* and became the leading Nazi propagandist. He was elected to the Reichstag in 1928, and when the Nazis came to power (1933), became minister of propaganda. As such he ruled much of Germany's cultural life. He was a brilliant orator and a masterful propagandist. He committed suicide with his entire family in April 1945.

Goering, Hermann Wilhelm (1893–1946), German Nazi leader. A World War I flying ace, he early joined the Nazi party and took part in the abortive Munich putsch in 1923. Elected to the Reichstag in 1928, he became its president in 1932. When the Nazis came to power in 1933, Goering became minister of air and prime minister of Prussia, where he founded the Gestapo. In 1936 he became director of the four-year economic plan. As virtual creator of the German air force, he enjoyed great prestige at the beginning of World War II, but defeat in the Battle of Britain and the Allied air raids on Germany discredited him. Sentenced to death at Nuremberg, he committed suicide. △1336.

Goes, Hugo van der (*c.*1440–82), Flemish painter. His Portinari Altarpiece in Florence, combining realism and monumentality, influenced many Italian painters. He created a popular art in which he introduced lower-class types and greater individuality of the figures. His later religious paintings, executed after he had gone mad, are dramatic and powerful.

Goethals, George Washington (1858–1928), US engineer and military officer, b. Brooklyn, N.Y. A graduate of West Point (1880) he worked on the Tennessee River dams and Muscle Shoals locks and fortified Narragansett Bay and New Bedford. Named chief engineer of the Isthmian Canal Commission by Pres. Theodore Roosevelt (1907), he completed the task despite yellow fever, labor troubles, and crumbling substrata. He was governor of the Canal Zone (1914–16). After retiring from the Army (1916) he was recalled to duty as acting quartermaster general (1917–19).

Goethe, Johann Wolfgang von (1749–1832), German poet. One of the greatest German writers and thinkers, his range is vast: from simple love poems to profound philosophical poems or scientific theories. In his long life he was lawyer, botanist, politician and civil servant, physicist, zoologist, painter, and theater manager. Johann Gottfried von Herder taught him to appreciate Shakespeare, and this influenced his *Götz von Berlichingen* (1773). His major works include *The Sorrows of Young Werther* (1774), a novel *Italian Journey* (1816), the classical drama *Iphigenie auf Tauris* (1787), *Torquato Tasso* (1789), *Egmont* (1788), *Wilhelm Meisters Lehrjahre* (1795–96), *Elective Affinities* (1809), and his most famous work, *Faust* (1808, 1832). *See also* Faust. △1222.

Gog and Magog, according to the Bible two hostile forces that will appear on earth before the end of the world. In Celtic mythology, Gogmagog was a chieftain in Western England who was slain by Corineus. In the Guildhall, London, they are two wooden statues representing a race of giants conquered by Trojan Brutus, legendary founder of Britain.

Gogol, Nikolai (1809–52), Russian novelist and dramatist whose work marks the transition from pure Romanticism to early realism. He made his reputation with folk tales, such as *Taras Bulba* (1835), the stories *Diary of a Madman* (1835) and *The Nose* (1836), and the drama *The Inspector General* (1836), which show the early development of his characteristically grotesque satirical style. Dismayed by reactionary criticism, he turned to religion for spiritual support and lived mostly in Rome from 1836 to 1848. Here he completed the first and only published part of his major work *Dead Souls* (1842) and the short story *The Overcoat* (1842). He spent the last ten years of his life working on the second part of *Dead Souls* but this was destroyed before publication.

Gogra. *See* Ghaghara.

Goiânia, city in SE central Brazil; capital of Goiás state; site of Catholic University (1959), and federal University (1964). Principal industry is livestock. Pop. 362,152.

Goiter, enlargement of the thyroid gland accompanied by swelling at the front of the neck. Caused most frequently by iodine deficiency, it is occasionally accompanied by hypothyroidism or, in areas where goiter is endemic, by cretinism in children. Usual treatment is to increase intake of iodides; hormone therapy or surgery is more rare. △696, 726.

Gnu

Goat

Johann Goethe

Nikolai Gogol

Golan Heights (Ha Golan, Ramot), disputed region in SW Syria. During the seven-day Arab-Israeli War (1967), Israel occupied the area and later colonized it; Syria subsequently rejected the UN peace plan (November 1967) and broke off diplomatic ties with Britain and United States. Conflicts continued between Syria and Israel. △1380.

Golconda, ruined town and fortress in SE India; a Bahmani kingdom 1364–1512, capital of a Muslim sultanate and famous for diamonds, 1512–1687; conquered by Aurangzeb 1687–88 and annexed to Delhi empire.

Gold, metallic element (symbol Au) of the third transition series, known from earliest times. The metal occurs native: some gold is also obtained as a by-product in the electrolytic refining of copper. It is used in jewelry and as a monetary standard. Gold leaf can be made as thin as 0.0001 mm. Colloidal gold is sometimes used in coloring glass. The radioisotope Au^{198} (half-life 2.7 days) is used in radiotherapy. The metal is unreactive, being unaffected by oxygen and common acids. It dissolves in aqua regia. Properties: at. no. 79, at. wt. 196.9665; sp gr 19.32; melt. pt. 1,945 °F (1,063°C); boil. pt. 4820°F (2,662°C); most common isotope Au^{197} (100%). *See also* Transition Elements. △242, 1554, 1596.

Goldberg, Arthur Joseph (1911–), US public official and jurist, b. Chicago. Appointed general counsel for the Congress of Industrial Organizations (CIO) and the United Steelworkers of America (1948), he was instrumental in both the AFL-CIO merger (1955) and the passage of the Ethical Practices Act (1957). Named US secretary of labor by President Kennedy (1961–62), he was later appointed an associate justice of the US Supreme Court (1962–65), where he defended civil rights, personal liberties, and due process. In 1965, he was appointed by Lyndon Johnson to be US ambassador to the United Nations.

Goldberg, Reuben Lucius ("Rube") (1883–1970), US cartoonist, b. San Francisco; known especially for his elaborate drawings of fantastically involved machinery performing ridiculously simple operations. He was a nationally syndicated cartoonist from 1921 and created several comic characters including "Lala Palooza" and "Boob McNutt." In 1948 his political cartoon *Peace Today* won a Pulitzer Prize.

Golden Algae, a group of mostly microscopic primarily freshwater plants (division Chysophyta). The best-known members of the group are the tiny single-celled diatoms, common among both salt- and freshwater plankton. Many single-celled golden algae form colonies. The multicelled types are usually threadlike in form. All members of the group contain characteristic yellow-brown pigments that in many cases mask the algae's green chlorophyll. △432.

Golden Ass, The, or **Metamorphoses** (2nd century AD), prose work by Lucius Apuleius. In 11 books it recounts the adventures of Lucius of Corinth, who in Book III is transformed into an ass by the magic of Pamphile and her maid Fotis. It is the only Roman novel to survive intact.

Golden Bells. *See* Forsythia.

Golden Bull (1222), Hungarian "Magna Carta" issued by Andrew II (1175–1235), under pressure from the lower nobility. This document extended certain rights to the nobility, including tax exemption, freedom to dispose of their property, prohibition of arbitrary imprisonment, and guarantee of annual assembly.

Golden Bull (1356), edict promulgated by Holy Roman Emperor Charles IV defining the procedures for electing the Holy Roman emperor. It provided for election by majority vote of seven princely electors. The procedures remained in effect until the dissolution of the empire in 1806.

Golden Eagle, Northern Hemisphere eagle with brown plumage and gold feathering on the head and neck. An excellent hunter, it flies over open country, preying on birds and small mammals. Sometimes small groups attack large animals. Species *Aquila chrysaetos. See also* Eagle.

Goldeneye, diving duck of cool temperate regions. It has yellow eyes, short black bill, rounded head, and black and white plumage. Species *Bucephala clangula. See also* Duck.

Golden Fleece, in Greek mythology, the magic fleece of a ram given by Hermes to Nephele, the wife of Athamas. When Athamas's second wife, Ino, out of jealousy planned death for Nephele's children, Phrixus and Helle, the ram carried them away. When Phrixus arrived at Colchis he sacrificed the ram and hung the fleece in a wood guarded by a dragon. The quest of Jason and the Argonauts was for the Golden Fleece, a task put on him by Aetes.

Golden Mole, blind burrowing mammals found in Africa south of the Sahara. They have two picklike claws on each front paw and a leathery padded snout for pushing through soil. They feed on worms and other small invertebrates. Length: 3–7in (8–18cm). Family Chrysochloridae.

Golden Plover, arctic-breeding, migratory, meadow-living shorebird that is black below and brown above with gold spots. Genus *Pluvialis. See also* Plover. △532.

Golden Retriever, hunting dog (sporting group) bred in Scotland in the 19th century for water and land bird retrieving. Ruggedly built, it has a broad head and rectangular muzzle; short, rounded ears hanging flat; shortish body; medium-length legs; and a curved tail. The flat coat can be straight or wavy with a ruff at the neck and feathering on the legs and tail; color is golden. Average size: 23–24in (58.5–60cm) high at shoulder; 65–75lb (29.5–34kg). *See also* Sporting Dog.

Goldenrod, North American perennial plant that grows almost everywhere. It has small yellow (sometimes white) flowers in one-sided clusters and blooms in late summer. Height: 1–8ft (0.3–2.4m). *Solidago luteus*, hybrid of goldenrod and aster, is cultivated in gardens. Family Compositae.

Golden Section, mathematical principle of proportions considered pleasing to the eye, used in antiquity and revived for architecture during the Italian Renaissance. It was based on the ratio 3:5, in which the smaller part of the building is to the size of the greater part approximately as the greater is to the whole. △1444.

Golden Wattle, shrub or small tree native to Australia. Its yellow flowers grow in clusters. Height: to 30ft (9m). Family Leguminosae; species *Acacia longifolia.*

Goldfinch, small (to 4.5in, or 11.4cm) seed-eating, sparrowlike bird that frequents woods and cultivated areas in North America and Europe. They often live in flocks and lay bluish-white eggs (3–6) in a cup-shaped nest. The yellow American goldfinch *(Spinus tristis)* has a black crown and tail and black and white wings. The red-faced European goldfinch *(Carduelis carduelis)* has a brownish body with yellow and black wings. Family Fringillidae.

Goldfish, freshwater carp originally found in China. Probably the most popular aquarium fish, it was domesticated by the Chinese about 1000 years ago. The wild form of this hardy, adaptable fish is plain and brownish. Selective breeding has produced gold and variegated red, yellow, white, and black forms with flowing fins, including the fantail, blackmoor, lionhead, comet, celestial, eggfish, and shubunkin. Family Cyprinidae; species *Carassius auratus.*

Golding, William (1911–), English novelist. His novels are concerned with the nature of humankind. They include *Lord of the Flies* (1954), *The Inheritors* (1955), *Pincher Martin* (1956), *Free Fall* (1959), *The Spire* (1964), and *The Scorpion God* (1971).

Goldoni, Carlo (1707–93), prolific Italian dramatist. He substituted written comedies for traditional commedia dell' arte improvisations. Called the Molière of Italy, Goldoni ridiculed the aristocracy and endowed women characters with spirited independence. His most famous play is *La Locandiera* (1753).

Gold Rush, California, frenzied search for gold. It was first discovered on John A. Sutter's ranch in the Sacramento Valley. Known as the 49'ers, the wild and unruly mob of miners and adventurers grew to 80,000 in one year and California was able to enter the Union with a 100,000 population in 1850. Few found gold, and Sutter lost everything when his land and cattle were looted. △1274.

Goldsboro, city in E central North Carolina; seat of Wayne co; site of branch of East Carolina University, and Seymour Johnson Air Force Base. Industries: furniture, textiles, shoes, tobacco. Inc. 1847. Pop. (1970) 26,810.

Goldsmith, Oliver (1728–74), Irish poet, novelist, essayist, and dramatist. His works include the essay *The Citizen of the World* (1762), the poems "The Traveller" (1764) and "The Deserted Village" (1770), a novel *The Vicar of Wakefield* (1766), and the play *She Stoops to Conquer* (1773). Goldsmith hated the literary pedantry of his day and sought to achieve a naturalness in his own work. △1188.

Gold Standard, monetary situation under which the amount of currency within an economy is tied to the quantity of gold backing within that economy. Under the gold standard the money supply cannot expand faster than the quantity of gold stock does. △1384.

Gold Standard Act. *See* Currency Act (1900).

Goldwater, Barry Morris (1909–), US Senator (Rep.) b. Phoenix, Ariz. He served in the Senate (1953–64), and then was an unsuccessful candidate for president (1964). He was reelected to the Senate (1968, 1974). The best-known and most outspoken conservative in the Republican party, he was labeled a "hawk" in his stand toward Vietnam. He opposed pursuit of a detente with the USSR. He wrote: *Arizona Portraits* (2 vols.; 1940); *The Conscience of a Conservative* (1960); *Where I Stand* (1964); and *The Conscience of the Majority.* (1970). During the 1970s he became a respected spokesman for the Republican party.

Goldwyn, Samuel (1882–1974), US film producer, b. Samuel Goldfish in Poland. He is noted for his tasteful, commercially successful films, including the first feature film, *The Squaw Man* (1913); *Wuthering Heights* (1939); *The Little Foxes* (1941); *The Best Years of Our Lives* (1947); *Guys and Dolls* (1955); and *Porgy and Bess* (1959). He formed Goldwyn Pictures in 1919 and later merged with Louis B. Mayer to form Metro-Goldwyn-Mayer (1924). △1362.

Golf, sport played with a small hard ball and a series of clubs over a course. The course is usually more than 6,000 yards (5,460m) long and is divided into 18 consecutive numbered holes varying in length from 100 to 650 yards (91m to 595m) from tee to green. Competition may be at 18, 36, 54, or 72 holes, and the winner may be decided by the lowest stroke total (medal play) or by the amount of holes won from an opponent (match play). Play begins off the tee with the object of getting the ball into the cup or hole on the green. The hole is 4.5in (11.4cm) in diameter and 4in (10.2cm) deep. The area between the tee and the green is the fairway, which may contain such hazards as water, sand traps, tall grass, and trees. Players use a set of golf clubs for the various drives, approach shots, and putting. For the long drives, there are four woods standardized with the numbers from 1 to 4. For shorter shots, irons, standardized 1 through 10, are used. Once on the green, a putter is used. Other specialized clubs are sometimes substituted for the standard clubs. Players either compete individually, or with partners, where one ball is used for each pair of partners, who play their ball on alternate shots.

Golf has its origins in Scotland in the 15th century. In 1754 the Royal and Ancient Golf Club of St Andrews, Scotland—where the basic rules of golf were established—was founded. The game is now enjoyed worldwide with international tournaments for amateurs (Walker and Americas Cups) and professionals (Curtis and Ryder Cups). Other famous tournaments include those in the United States (the Masters, Open, and the PGA), and Great Britain (Open). There is competition for both men and women and an annual professional tour in the United States (sanctioned by the Professional Golf Association), Europe, and Asia.

Golgi, Camillo (1844–1926), Italian histologist. He shared the 1906 Nobel Prize in physiology and medicine with Santiago Ramón y Cajal for their work on the structure of the nervous system. Golgi developed staining techniques for the study of cell parts and described detailed nerve structures.

Golgi Body. △412.

Golgotha, site outside Jerusalem, also called Calvary, where Jesus and two others were crucified under the rule of Roman procurator Pontius Pilate. Two places, the Church of the Holy Sepulchre and a hill near Damascus Gate, have each been proposed as the site.

Goliardic Songs, songs of the Middle Ages which resembled hymns and were sung in Latin, but which attacked religion rather than praised it. They were sung by wandering vagabond "scholars" through the 13th century, when they declined because the church began to take strong measures against them.

Goliath, biblical Philistine giant slain by David who accepted Goliath's challenge and felled him with a stone from a slingshot. This encouraged the Israelites, who had been held at bay by Goliath, to defeat the Philistines.

Gomel', city in Belorussian SSR, USSR, 140mi (225km) N of Kiev on Sozh River; capital of Gomel' oblast. City was acquired 1772 by Russia from Poland; Jews accounted for 40% of population until WWII when city was taken by Germans, and Jews were executed (1941–43). Industries: farm machinery, ship repair, fertilizer, tugboats, glass, plywood, paper; trades in wool, flax, lumber. Pop. 272,000.

Gómez, Juan Vicente (1857–1935), president of Venezuela (1908–15, 1922–29, 1931–35). A financial backer and adviser to President Cipriano Castro, Gómez took complete control of the government when Castro left on a trip to Europe. During his 27-year tenure, Venezuela became a major producer and exporter of petroleum; the revenues were used to cancel the country's debts and to initiate an impressive public works program.

Gómez Palacio, city in N Mexico 3 miles (4.8km) across the Nazas River from Torreón. Industries: textiles, tanning, iron, steel, explosives, chemicals, liquor, sugar, tobacco. Pop. 139,743.

Gomillion v. Lightfoot (1960), US Supreme Court civil rights decision. The court found that it had jurisdiction to hear a case involving statutory redistricting that eliminated almost all of the black voters from the electoral districts of Tuskegee, Ala. Declaring this law unconstitutional, the court weakened the non-intervention stance it had taken in *Colegrove v. Green.*

Gompers, Samuel (1850–1924), US labor leader, b. England. He emigrated with his parents to New York City in 1863 and went to work as a cigar maker, joining the local union in 1864. He served as its president (1877–81). In 1881 he helped to found the Federation of Organized Trades and Labor Unions. When it was reorganized as the American Federation of Labor in 1886 Gompers became its first president, serving until his death except for the year 1895. Gompers successfully competed with the older Knights of Labor and later with the more radical Industrial Workers of the World. He stressed basic issues—higher wages and shorter hours—not social upheaval. During World War I he organized and headed the War Commission on Labor and served on the Advisory Commission to the Council of National Defense.

Gomulka, Wladyslaw (1905–), Polish Communist political leader. Active in the defense of Warsaw in 1939, he had been imprisoned for anti-Fascism during the 1930s. A leader of the Polish Workers' party and a member of the National Council of Poland after World War II, he was dismissed in 1949 and imprisoned from 1951–54 for ideological impurity. Reinstated as a member of the central committee of the Communist party in 1956, he became first secretary and denounced the Russian terror tactics. He also pressed for and achieved greater freedom for Poland within the Marxist framework. Gomulka did, however, remain a supporter of the Soviets in their foreign policy (eg, 1968 invasion of Czechoslovakia). He was forced to resign during the food riots of 1970. △1346.

Gonadotropins, general name for the two pituitary hormones, follicle-stimulating hormone and luteinizing hormone; present in both males and females, where they stimulate development and function of the sex organs, the ovary and testis. △702.

Gonads, primary sex glands. In males they are the testes; in females, the ovaries. Gonads produce several hormones, including testosterone (males) and estrogen (females). Gonadal hormones are crucial in the development of physical sexual characteristics such as the enlargement of breasts and growth of pubic hair and may be related to sexual behavior. In humans, however, these hormones have more to do with the development of sexual behavior than with the precise form it takes. △690.

Gonçalves, Vasco dos Santos (1921–), Portuguese army officer and politician. He was a leading member of the armed forces movement that overthrew the government of Marcello Caetano in April 1974. Gonçalves, a leftist, became premier in July 1974; he continued as premier after Francisco da Costa Gomez became president in September 1974.

Goncourt, Edmond de (1822–96), French novelist and social historian. He wrote in collaboration with his brother Jules until his death (1870). Novels of which he was the sole author include *La Fille Élisa* (1877) and *Les Frères Zemganno* (1879). The Prix Goncourt, one of France's top literary awards, was provided for in his will.

Gondwanaland, the name given to the southern continent which began to break away from the single land mass Pangaea about 200,000,000 years ago. The name comes from Gondwana, a geological province in east central India that is a key to the theory that South America, Africa, and India were once a single continent. △170–72.

Gone With the Wind (1936), novel by Margaret Mitchell. It won a Pulitzer Prize (1937) and was made into a successful motion picture (1939). Set in Georgia during the Civil War and Reconstruction, it deals with Scarlett O'Hara, an indomitable, scheming woman, and her efforts to maintain and restore her plantation home, Tara. The story is complicated by Scarlett's unfulfilled love for Ashley Wilkes, an ineffectual idealist, and by her relationship with Rhett Butler, a cynical war profiteer who loves her. △1362.

Gongorism, literary term originally referring to 17th-century baroque poetry of Luis de Góngora. It is deliberately complex and is characterized by Latinized vocabulary, neologisms, obscure allusions, and unconventional syntax. As a literary phase it reflects the decadence of the late Golden Age in Spain.

Goniometer, instrument used mainly by mineral collectors to help in the identification of crystal forms by measuring the critical angles of related sets of crystal faces. These angles are characteristic for certain minerals. △1506.

Gonorrhea, most common venereal disease, caused by a gonococcus and transmitted usually through sexual activity. Sometimes carriers of the disease, particularly females, show no symptoms. In males, symptoms usually occur between two and eight days after exposure and include a profuse, purulent discharge from the urethra; homosexual men may also have anal or pharyngeal infections. Females may show increased or painful urination, vaginal discharge, or signs of rectal infection. Complications include systemic infection, endocarditis, meningitis. Infants of infected parents may be infected at birth. Treatment is a course of antibiotics. △728.

Gonzaga, Italian dynasty that ruled Mantua (1328–1708) and Montferrat (1536–1708). The family's power in Mantua was established by **Luigi Gonzaga** (1267–1360), a supporter of the Holy Roman Emperor. **Giovanni Francesco** (1395–1444), a general in imperial service, was a patron of the humanist Vittorino da Feltre. **Giovanni Francesco II** (1466–1519) was a leader of Italian defense against Charles VIII's French invasion (1494) and wed Isabella d'Este, a great Renaissance art patron. △1142.

González de Ávila, Gil (died 1543), Spanish conquistador. In 1522 he conquered Nicaragua, Honduras, and Costa Rica but was soon ousted by Francisco Fernández de Córdoba.

Gonzalez, Pancho (1928–), US tennis player, b. Richard Alonzo Gonzales in Los Angeles. He won the US lawn and clay court singles titles (1948–49) and was a member of the US team which won the Wimbledon and Davis Cup competitions (1949). He turned pro (1949) and was long the pro champion.

Good Hope, Cape of. *See* Cape Province.

Goodman, Benjamin David ("Benny") (1909–), US jazz clarinetist and bandleader, b. Chicago. He formed his own band in 1934 and became famous in 1939 as the "King of Swing" with his theme songs "Let's Dance" and "Goodbye." His Carnegie Hall appearance in 1938 was the first performance there by any jazz musician. After 1944 he continued to play with many other great jazz performers, made many best-selling recordings, appeared on television and in films, and toured worldwide. Widely acclaimed as a jazz clarinetist, he also played classical music.

Good Neighbor Policy, US policy of nonintervention in the affairs of Latin America. President Hoover in 1928 urged a new approach to offset hostility bred by previous US armed intervention in the Caribbean. President Roosevelt introduced the Good Neighbor Policy in his inaugural speech (1933) and declared his opposition to military interference. The Organization of American States, an extension of this policy, was founded (1945) to foster hemispheric solidarity. In 1961, President Kennedy introduced the Alliance for Progress, an updated version of Roosevelt's policy. △1354.

Goodnight, Charles (1836–1929), US cattle rancher, b. Illinois. He went to Texas in 1846, becoming a Texas Ranger and Indian fighter. A pioneer cattleman in New Mexico and Colorado, he established the Goodnight Trail (from Ft. Sumner, N.M. to Belknap, Tex.), and in 1866, with Oliver Loving, the Goodnight-Loving Trail (from Ft. Sumner to Wyo-

Samuel Goldwyn

Golf

Samuel Gompers

Benny Goodman

ming). In 1877, in partnership with John Adair, he set up the prosperous JA ranch in Texas. He sought to improve the herds through breeding and also produced the first cattalo, a cross between a bison and polled Angus cattle.

Good Samaritan, subject of a New Testament parable found in Luke's gospel. The compassion of the Samaritan towards a beaten man is contrasted with the negligence of Israel's leaders who are preoccupied with ceremonial law. △816.

Good Society. △1360.

Goodyear, Charles (1800–60), US industrial inventor, b. New Haven, Conn. Despite early business failures that sent him to debtor's prison, he patented an acid and metal coating (1837) and discovered and patented vulcanized rubber (1844). Financial difficulties forced him to sell his rights for a fraction of their worth and allowed others to reap profits from his work.

Goose, widely distributed waterfowl, related to ducks and swans, valued as game and raised commercially for their dark, protein-rich meat, feathers used in pillows, and the delicacy *pâté de foie gras.* Heavier than ducks, they have blunt bills, long necks, shortish legs, webbed feet, and, in the wild, a combination of gray, brown, black, and white dense plumage underlaid by down. They live near fresh or brackish water but spend time on land, grazing on meadow grasses. They fly with flocks in V-shaped formations making long, noisy migrations. Wild geese breed in colonies, mate for life, and build grass-and-twig, down-lined nests for 4–7 eggs. Weight: 3–16lb (1.3–7.2kg). Family Anatidae. △382–84, 612.

Gooseberry, very hardy shrub *(Ribes grossularia)* of the saxifrage family, native to cool or temperate regions of Europe and North America. Fruit may be red, white, amber, or green.

Goose Flesh. △678.

Goosefoot, or pigweed, many species of herbs and sub-shrubs, with mealy, often lobed, leaves that look like goose feet. The 550 widely distributed species, mostly weeds, also include spinach and beets. Family Chenopodiaceae.

Goose Star. △504.

Gopher, small, stout, burrowing rodent of North and Central America that has fur-lined, external cheek pouches and long incisor teeth outside the lips. Black to almost white, they live mostly underground, digging shallow tunnels to get roots and tubers and deep ones for shelter and food storage. Length: 5–17in (127–432mm). Family Geomyidae. *See also* Ground Squirrel.

Gopher Tortoise, true tortoise native to SE and SW United States and Mexico. Vegetarian, it has a brownish-tan, high-domed shell, stumpy legs, and powerful forelimbs for digging burrows. Length: 15in (38cm). Family Testudinae; genus *Gopherus. See also* Turtle.

Goral, shaggy, mountain-dwelling, goatlike ruminant found in Central Asia, China, Korea, and Burma. Its brownish fur blends with rocks. It has short, conical horns and lives in small family groups. Length: to 51in (1.3m). Family Bovidae; genus *Naemorhedus.*

Gordian Knot, a knot tied by king Gordius which bound the yoke of his chariot to a tree. The ends of the knot could not be seen. It was said it could only be untied by the conqueror of Asia. Alexander the Great cut the knot with his sword.

Gordon, Charles George (1833–85), English soldier and administrator, known as Chinese Gordon. He first distinguished himself in the Crimean War (1853–56). In 1860 he took part in the China expedition that captured Peking. He was personally responsible for the burning of the Summer Palace. He commanded the British-Chinese forces in the Taiping Rebellion (1863–64). In 1873 he was appointed governor of Equatoria (S Sudan) by the khedive of Egypt. Between 1877–79 he was governor of the Sudan, where he attempted to suppress the slave trade. In 1884 he returned to the Sudan and attempted to put down the Mahdi Rebellion. For 10 months in 1885 he was trapped and besieged at Khartoum. He was killed two days before a relief force from England arrived.

Gordon Setter, superior bird and gun dog (sporting group) dating from 1620 in Scotland. An eager worker, its finely chiseled head is heavy, with a long muzzle and broad nose. Low-set ears are folded close to the head; the strong body is deep-chested; legs are big-boned. The feathered tail is carried horizontally and flags constantly as the dog moves. The soft, straight or slightly waved coat is long on ears, chest, belly, and legs; colors are black with tan marks. Average size: 24–27in (61–68.6cm) high at shoulder; 55–80lb (25–36kg). *See also* Sporting Dog.

Goren, Charles Henry (1901–), US bridge expert, b. Philadelphia. A two-time world champion (1950, 1957), he also won 26 US titles (including two ties). He wrote many books on the game, as well as syndicated articles.

Gorenko, Anna Andreyeuna. *See* Akhmatova, Anna.

Gorgas, William Crawford (1854–1920), US surgeon whose successful mosquito-control program in Panama wiped out malaria and yellow fever there and made possible the building of the Panama Canal.

Gorges, (Sir) Ferdinando (1566?–1647), English colonizer. He was a founder of the Virginia Company of Plymouth (1606), which acquired charter rights to New England. Gorges transferred charter to Council for New England (1620), which granted patents to the Plymouth and Massachusetts Bay colonies. Gorges received full rights to Maine (1639). *See also* Pilgrim Patent.

Gorgias, dialogue of Plato, on the philosophy of rhetoric as it relates to ethics. Consisting of a discussion between Gorgias, Socrates, and Callicles, Socrates (presenting Plato's viewpoint) argues that the techniques of rhetoric should serve the ends of justice.

Gorgon, monster figures in Greek mythology. According to Hesiod, they were Stheno, Euryale, and Medusa, the daughters of Phorcus and Cero. △836.

Gorgonian. *See* Sea Fan.

Gorilla, gregarious great ape living in African rain forests. The largest primate, they are mostly brown or black and are powerfully built, with long arms and short legs. They walk on all fours and live mostly on the ground, searching for fruits and other vegetarian foods. Gorillas are generally shy and peaceful. Unless provoked, they rarely attack humans. Height: to 70in (178cm); weight: 600lb (270kg). Species *Gorilla gorilla. See also* Primates. △554.

Gorkha. *See* Gurkha.

Gorki (Gor'kij), formerly Nizhni Novgorod; city in Russian SFSR, USSR, 250mi (403km) NE of Moscow, at confluence of Volga and Oka rivers; capital of Gorki oblast. City united with Moscow state 1417; trade and cultural center 18th-19th centuries; renamed in 1932 for Russian writer; site of 14th-century kremlin, Archangel Cathedral (1631), state university (1918), convents, palace. Industries: automobiles, aircraft, plastics, textiles, clothing, shipyards, woodworking, food processing, oil refining, glass, chemicals. Founded 1221. Pop. 1,170,000.

Gorky, Maxim (1868–1936), Russian dramatist and writer, b. Aleksei Maksimovich Peshkov. Gorky championed the worker and peasant in *Sketches and Stories* (1898); in the play *The Lower Depths* (1902), produced by the Moscow Art Theatre with Anton Chekhov's support; and in the novel *Mother* (1907). He also wrote autobiographical volumes (1913–24) and other plays, including *Yegor Bulichev* (1932) and *The Enemies* (1935). He has been called the father of social realism.

Gorlovka, city in Ukranian SSR, USSR, in Donets Basin; industrial center; site of mining school. Industries: coal and mercury mining, coke, fertilizer, steel, chemicals, machinery. Founded 1867. Pop. 335,000.

Gorse. *See* Furze.

Goshawk, swift hawk with gray or brownish plumage and a long, rounded tail. It feeds on small mammals, including rabbits and squirrels, and birds. Length: 20in (51cm); wingspan: 4ft (122cm). Species *Accipiter gentilis. See also* Hawk. △538.

Gospel, four histories of the life of Christ in the New Testament: Matthew, Mark, Luke, and John. The name is from Middle English "godspel," meaning "good tale." △1026.

Gospel Songs, informal and emotional religious spirituals or hymns that developed from slave songs, Protestant hymns, and the call and response singing in slave churches. Gospel style usually involves choral singing with a lead singer or singers. Originally performed at revivals or religious celebrations during the early 20th century, it had a strong influence on black rock music beginning in the 1950s. *See also* Spirituals.

Gosplan, state planning committee of the Soviet Union, one of the more important units in the economic decision-making process. Responsible directly to the council of ministers, Gosplan creates and administers plans in all sectors of the economy.

Gossaert, Jan (Mabuse) (*c.*1478–1533), Flemish painter. He is largely responsible for introducing the Italian Renaissance style to the Low Countries. He traveled widely in Italy and absorbed diverse Italian influences into his many religious paintings and portraits.

Göta Canal, waterway in S Sweden; connects Göteborg (W) with Stockholm (E); consists of a series of rivers, lakes, coastal waterways, and canals. The canal was built 1810–32 by Baron Baltzar von Platen and Scottish engineer Thomas Telford, from the 16th-century plan of Bishop Hans Brask, and serves several industrial towns in S Sweden. Total length: 360mi (580km).

Göteborg (Gothenburg), city in SW Sweden, at confluence of Göta and Kattegat rivers; seat of Goteborgoch Bohus co, chief seaport and 2nd-largest city in Sweden. Settled by Dutch merchants, it became important port after mid-18th century as the center of British trade with Europe; its system of liquor regulation (1865) became basis of Swedish liquor laws; made a free port 1921; site of Dutch-style canals, several museums, university (1891), oceanographic institute, technical college (1829). Industries: shipyards, automobiles, food processing, textiles, ball bearings, timber, brewing, fishing. Founded 1619 by King Gustavas Adolphus. Pop. 446,875.

Gotha, city in SW East Germany. Since 1785 city has been center of geographical research and publishing; *Almanach de Gotha,* authoritative reference work on nobility and royalty, has been published here since 1836; site of 15th-century church of St Margaret, 17th-century castle. Industries: publishing, rubber products, precision instruments. Founded 1189. Pop. 57,328.

Gothenburg. *See* Göteborg.

Gothic Architecture, architecture of medieval Europe from the 12th to the 16th century. Characterized by the pointed arch and ribbed vault, Gothic architecture is religious in inspiration and ecclesiastical in nature. Its greatest and most characteristic expression is the cathedral, a structure of soaring spaces, lightness, and multiple articulation of forms. The introduction of a system of flying buttresses was a technical advance that made the light walls and large windows possible. An early prototype is the Abbey Church of St Denis (1140–44). Ever higher and lighter structures with increasingly intricate vaulting and tracery followed. The Gothic style was succeeded by the Renaissance style, which originated in Italy in the 15th century. △1092–1094, 1104–06.

Gothic Art, originally an architectural style that began in the middle of the 12th century in northcentral France and spread to other forms of art, especially sculpture and stained glass, and to England, Spain, Italy, Germany, and even as far as Sweden. From it evolved the International Gothic style and, in the 15th century, the Renaissance style. The Gothic style was first used in ecclesiastical architecture to solve technical problems created by the Romanesque style. In rebuilding the church of St Denis (1140–44), Abbot Suger used the first Gothic arches. Soon the rib vault and broad stained-glass windows became standard architectural practice.

The High Gothic phase is apparent at Chartres, where the cathedral was rebuilt after the fire of 1194. The building contains numerous large stained-glass windows and has flying buttresses for support, as well as rib vaults and pointed arches. Other High Gothic cathedrals include those of Bourges, Rheims, and Amiens. The next phase, the Rayonnant, involved refinements of the High Gothic style, such as in Sainte-Chapelle, built around 1240 for Louis IX. The outbreak of the Hundred Years War interrupted the further development of the Gothic style in France. However, by then it had spread to the rest of Europe. In England, Canterbury Cathedral is early Gothic, and Salisbury and Lincoln cathedrals are High Gothic. The Decorated style in England from 1290 to 1350 involved such elements as star vaults and the ogee arch.

Eventually the Gothic style spread beyond ecclesiastical architecture to that of private estates and municipal buildings. Gothic sculpture usually involved that done for the exterior doors of cathedrals, such as the Royal Portal at Chartres. The realism of the High Gothic style is exemplified by the west facade of Notre Dame in Paris. In the Late Gothic, sculptured figures were carved in affected poses with vacant expressions. In the 15th century the decline was checked and the figures became stronger, as in the "Entombment of Christ" at Solesmes, France. Gothic painting is known essentially from panel paintings for altarpieces and from illuminated manuscripts such as the 13th-century Psalter of Isabelle de France, with its jewel-like miniatures; the 14th-century Belleville Breviary by Jean Pucelle; and the *Book of Hours* made for Jean, duc de Berry, by the Limburg brothers in the 15th century. △1092–94, 1104–06.

Gothic Novel, type of novel particularly popular in 18th-century England and 19th-century England and the United States, containing strong elements of the supernatural. The emphasis is on setting and story rather than characterization. Mary Wollstonecraft Shelley's *Frankenstein* (1818) is an outstanding example. Gothic novels were important influences on the poetry of the Romantic period, the short stories of Poe, and later novels. *See also* Novel. △1188.

Gothic Revival, revival of Gothic decorative themes and architectural motifs. The movement began with Horace Walpole's Gothic-style English mansion "Strawberry Hill" (1770). Many landowners went so far as to place Gothic "ruins" on their estates. The style was used in private homes in 18th century England, the United States, and France and was extended to public buildings and churches in the 19th century. Trinity Church, New York City (1839–46), is a prime example. △1412.

Goths, Germanic people, who by the 3rd century AD lived N of the Black Sea. They split into two groups, the Ostrogoths and the Visigoths. Conquered (*c.* 370) by the Huns and later allies of the Eastern Roman Empire, the Ostrogoths conquered Italy (489) under Theodoric and ruled there until ousted by Emperor Justinian in the mid-6th century. The Visigoths settled in Lower Moesia at the end of 4th century. Under Alaric they sacked Rome in 410. Moving into Gaul and northern Spain, they reached the height of their power under Euric (reigned 466–84). They were expelled from Gaul by the Franks (507), but their Spanish kingdom survived until the Moorish conquest (711). The Goths were Arian Christians. *See also* Alaric; Theodoric the Great. △1054.

Gotland, island off SE coast of Sweden, in Baltic Sea; capital is Visby. Island belonged to Sweden 13th century; became part of Denmark 1570; was returned to Sweden by Treaty of Brömsebro 1645. Industries: sugar-beet processing, barley, rye, cement, fisheries, sheep, tourism. Area: 1,225sq mi (3,173sq km). Pop. 54,093.

Gottfried von Strassburg, (*fl.* 1200–1220), Middle High German romance poet. Little is known of his life, but he was apparently well educated in literature and theology. He was a rival of Wolfram von Eschenbach and an admirer of Walther von der Vogelweide. The subject matter of his Arthurian stories, such as *Tristan und Isolt,* is largely borrowed from French and British sources, but his treatment of characters is often more profound and perceptive than the originals. *See also* Arthurian Romance.

Göttingen, city in E West Germany, on the Leine River, 55mi (89km) SSW of Brunswick; site of 14th-century town hall and wall, University of Göttingen (1737). Industries: optical and precision instruments, textiles, aluminum. Founded 953. Pop. 113,963.

Gouache Painting, painting method using opaque watercolor. The paint is mixed to a thick consistency. Upon drying, the colors lighten and are similar to pastels in appearance.

Goujon, Jean (*c.* 1510–68), French Renaissance sculptor and architect known for his decorations in low relief for buildings. He was associated with Pierre Lescot, the architect of the Louvre, where a number of Goujon's works are found today. △1146.

Gould, Jay (1836–92), US speculator, b. Roxbury, N.Y. He joined (1867) the directorate of the Erie Railroad and participated in looting the line. In 1869, his attempt to corner the gold market resulted in financial panic. Avoiding prosecution, he later bought control of Union Pacific and other railroads, and eventually controlled half the railroad mileage in the US Southwest. *See also* Black Friday. △1278.

Gounod, Charles (1818–93), French composer. He composed church and choral music but is chiefly known for his operas, the most successful of which were *Faust* (1859), *Mireille* (1864), and *Roméo et Juliette* (1867). △1246, 1256.

Gourami, or kissing gourami, white tropical fish of Malay Peninsula, Thailand, and Sunda Islands. Popular with aquarists, it has a protrusible, suckerlike mouth; two fishes often join mouths for unknown reasons. Length: to 10in (25.4cm). Family Anabantidae; species include *Helestoma temmincki.*

Gourd, annual vine grown in North America for ornamental rather than eating purposes. Fruit shapes range from round to irregular. Its smooth or warty rind may be green, yellow, orange, white, or red. The 750 species are mainly from tropical and subtropical regions. Family Cucurbitaceae. *See also* Melon; Pumpkin. △446.

Gournia, ancient Cretan market town (1600–1400 BC), the only well-preserved late Minoan settlement on Crete.

Gours. △256.

Gout, possibly hereditary form of arthritis associated with an excess of uric acid. Adult males are primary victims. Symptoms usually effect one joint, often the big toe, with intense pain that may last several weeks.

Government. △906.

Government National Mortgage Association (GNMA), US federal agency under the Department of Housing and Urban Development. It is concerned with assisting in the production and financing of housing and in the conservation and rehabilitation of existing housing. It was established in 1968.

Government Printing Office (GPO), federal agency that provides printing services. It executes orders for printing and binding placed by Congress and the departments of the US government. The GPO operates mail-order sales and government bookstores. Selected publications are distributed to libraries throughout the United States. Established 1860.

Governors Island, fortified island in upper New York Bay; purchased by Dutch from Indians 1637 and used as home by colonial governors; site of Castle Williams (1807–11) and Fort Jay (early 19th century). During Civil War, Confederate soldiers were held in Castle Williams. Area: 173acres (70hectares).

Gowon, Yakubu (1934–), Nigerian political and military figure. A general, he took power through a coup in 1966. He fought successfully against the Biafran secessionists from 1967 to 1970 in a war he partly precipitated by massacres of Ibos and broken political promises. He was himself overthrown in 1975.

Goya, Francisco José de (1746–1828), Spanish painter. The leading artist of the neo-Baroque style, he sympathized with the Enlightenment and the French Revolution but was still esteemed at the Spanish Court, where he painted a portrait, "The Family of Charles IV," shocking in its almost grotesque revelation of the corrupt inner life of its subjects. Among Goya's most vivid, expressive works are his portraits and nude studies of his mistress, the Duchess of Alba. When Napoleon's occupation of Spain failed to bring reforms, Goya's bitter disillusionment was reflected in such brilliantly colored, dramatic works as "The 3rd of May, 1808," commemorating the execution of a group of Madrid citizens. Although continuing to paint vigorously in his old age, partly spent in self-chosen exile, his paintings and several series of etchings ("The Disasters of War" and "The Disparates") seem a powerful reflection of private despair. △1228.

Gozzi, Carlo (1720–1806), Italian writer. Gozzi was an opponent of the theatrical reforms of Carlo Goldoni, who wished to substitute prepared dialogue for the improvisation of the *commedia dell'arte.* Gozzi, in an attempt to revive the *commedia dell'arte* and to disprove Goldoni, wrote ten comedies for the stage.

Gozzoli, Benozzo (*c.* 1421–97), Italian painter, b. as Benozzo di Lese di Sandro. His numerous frescoes, such as that of the Medici Family as the Magi in the Chapel of the Medici Palace, Florence, faithfully depict 15th-century Italian life. He began as an assistant to Fra Angelico, but his work is entirely secular in mood and outlook.

GPO. *See* Government Printing Office.

Graben, an elongated, trenchlike, down-dropped segment of the Earth's crust enclosed by two or more similarly trending normal faults. The Basin and Range province in Utah and Nevada consists of grabens and

Charles Goodyear

Gordon setter

Maxim Gorky

Charles Gounod

horsts that form sedimentary basins and mountain ranges. *See also* Horst. △250.

Gracchus, Gaius Sempronius (153–121 BC), Roman statesman. He swore to avenge the murder of his brother Tiberius. As tribune (123–21) he organized the radical social reforms planned by his brother Tiberius (died 133 BC) and sought to check the power of the senate by uniting the plebeians and the equites and by reforming agrarian laws to benefit the poor. He granted seats in the judiciary (formerly controlled by the senate) to the equites. His visionary progressive measures were short-lived; he was defeated in the election of 121, his measures attacked, and he was killed during the riots that followed. △1012.

Gracchus, Tiberius Sempronius (163–133 BC), Roman statesman and reformer. An aristocrat appalled by the grossly unequal distribution of wealth, he declared his intention to reform agrarian law in favor of the poor. He was elected tribune in 133 and proposed the Sempronian Law to reapportion public lands. The law was passed but before it could be implemented another election was scheduled. The senate, wary of Tiberius' power, postponed the voting. Tiberius was murdered during a riot involving senators and their followers. His brother Gaius sought to avenge his death and carry out his reforms. △1012.

Grackle, New World blackbird with a long, creased, keel-shaped tail and jaw modifications to allow it to open nuts that, along with insects and eggs, are its favorite food. The common purple grackle *(Quiscalus quiscula)* of E North America is iridescent; length: 11in (28cm). The larger boat-tailed grackle or jackdaw *(Cassidix mexicanus)* of SW North America and SE United States marshlands builds a twig, stick, and mud nest for its blotched greenish, bluish, or brownish eggs (3–6). Family Icteridae.

Graebner, Fritz (1877–1934), German ethnologist who postulated the theory of the Kulterkreise (culture complex), which held that all primitive cultures derived from a single type. His theory founded the culture-historical school of ethnology in Europe.

Graft, Tissue, a portion of skin, bone, or other tissue removed from its original site and transferred elsewhere in the body to repair a defect. The tissue may be taken from the individual requiring the repair (autograft), from another individual of the same species (homograft or allograft), or from an individual of another species (heterograft).

Grafting, a method of plant propagation in which, typically, a twig of one variety (the scion) is forced to grow on the roots of another variety (the rootstock or stock). Most fruit trees are propagated by a grafting process called budding, in which the graft scion is a single bud. Grafting is an efficient way to produce new plants that are genetically identical with the parent plant from which the scions are cut. Grafting onto special rootstocks is widely used to produce dwarf fruit trees that have normal-size fruit. △324.

Grafton, Augustus Henry Fitzroy, duke of (1735–1811), English statesman. In 1765 he was secretary of state under Rockingham and became first lord of the state under Pitt (Lord Chatham). Due to Pitt's illness he became the effective prime minister. He was forced to resign in 1770, following the crisis in the American colonies and the Wilkes affair, but he later served as lord privy seal under North, Rockingham, and Shelburne.

Graham, "Billy" (William Franklin) (1918–) US evangelist, b. Charlotte; N. C. Although ordained as a Southern Baptist, he became the "first evangelist" (1944) of Youth for Christ. The Billy Graham Evangelistic Association serves as a base for worldwide crusades. He has a weekly syndicated column, delivers radio broadcasts, and founded the magazine, *Decision* (1960). *Peace With God* (1952), *World Aflame* (1965), and *Angels* (1975) were successful books, and he also has great facility with mass audiences and mass media. △850.

Graham, Martha (1894–), US modern dancer and choreographer, b. Pittsburgh. After studying with Ruth St Denis and Ted Shawn, she founded her own company and created a new dance technique, which is taught at her school in New York City. Her company is one of the longest-lived and most widely traveled of all modern dance groups. She believes dance should be realistically expressive, rather than romantic, and that it should portray universal, rather than personal, experience. △1368.

Graham, Thomas. △1502.

Graham's Law. △1502.

Graian Alps (Alpes Graies or Alpi Graie), mountain range of France and Italy; forms an arc from Cottian Alps (SE France) to Little St Bernard Pass (French-Italian border) to Dora Baltea Valley (NW Italy). Highest peak is Gran Paradiso, 13,323ft (4,064m).

Grail, Holy, object of quest of the knights of Arthurian romance. The cup supposedly was used by Christ at the Last Supper, and possibly by Joseph of Arimathea to catch the blood flowing from Christ's wounds. The quest of the grail became a search for mystical union with God.

Grain. △326.

Grain, Production and Trade. △302, 326.

Grain Elevator, machine used to load grain into a granary, or the granary itself. The machine is typically a trough-fed conveyor belt that carries grain to the top of tall cylindrical buildings for storage. Grain is removed from granaries through chutes or other means of gravity.

Gram, unit of mass (symbol g) defined as one thousandth of a kilogram. *See also* Physical Units.

Gram Atom, the quantity of an element whose mass in grams is equal to its atomic weight. It has been replaced by the SI unit, the mole. *See also* Mole.

Grammar, the branch of the science of linguistics that deals with a language's inflections, its phonetic system (phonology), and with the arrangement of words in sentences (syntax). The rules for the English language were developed on the basis of Latin grammar that is inflectional (use based on form), even though English was more of a syntactical language (use based on word order). New approaches are being advanced, and grammar is evolving as the language evolves. △864.

Grammar, Transformational, an approach to grammar described in 1957 by Noam Chomsky and Zellig Harris. It begins with a sentence and goes through all possible rules for the transformation of that sentence. The relationship between these transformed constructions is treated as a process or series of processes.

Gram Molecular Volume, the volume occupied by a mass of gas equal to its molecular weight in grams (2 grams of hydrogen, 32 grams of oxygen, etc.). At a given temperature and pressure it has approximately the same value for all gases. It is 22.415 liters for a perfect gas at 760 millimeters of mercury pressure and 0°C.

Grampus, or Risso's dolphin, beakless blunt-snouted dolphin found in all oceans. It is dark above and light below. Length: 13ft (4m). Species *Grampus griseus. See also* Dolphin.

Gram's Method, method of staining bacteria for classification. A bacterial smear is stained with gentian violet, washed with Gram's solution, and counterstained with safranine. The violet stain is retained by Gram-positive bacteria and lost by Gram-negative bacteria.

Granada, city in SW Nicaragua, on NW shore of Lake Nicaragua; capital of Granada dept. The oldest city in Nicaragua, it is a trade center in an agricultural region; historical residence of conservative Nicaraguan landholding aristocracy. Industries: sugar, coffee, animal skins. Founded 1523. Pop. 51,363.

Granada, city in S Spain, 80mi (129km) SE of Córdoba at junction of Darro and Genil rivers; capital of Granada prov. Important as Moorish fortress and stronghold 8th-15th centuries, its surrender in 1492 to the Christian armies of Ferdinand and Isabella marked the end of Moorish control in Spain. The city, renowned for its Moorish art and architecture, is site of Alhambra Palace (1248–1354), the 11th-century Alcazaba Moorish citadel, 16th-century cathedral containing tombs of Ferdinand and Isabella, Carthusian monastery of Cartuja (1516), University of Granada (1531). Industries: tourism, textiles, soap, liqueurs. Area: (prov.) 4,838sq mi (12,530sq km). Pop. (city) 190,429; (prov.) 733,375.

Gran Columbia. △1234.

Grand Alliance, War of the (1688–97), war between France and the Grand Alliance. Louis XIV of France invaded the Palatinate while the Holy Roman Emperor Leopold I was fighting the Turks. Leopold formed an alliance (the Grand Alliance) with the Netherlands, Spain, and England. There were notable French victories at Namur (1692, 1695) and an English naval victory at La Hogue (1692). Peace was concluded at the Treaty of Ryswick (1696).

Grand Army of the Republic (GAR), US Civil War veterans organization. It consisted of Union Army and Navy veterans and was founded in 1866 by Dr. Benjamin F. Stephenson. In the 1890s the group's more than 400,000 members succeeded in their efforts to have a day (Memorial Day) set aside to honor the memory of Civil War dead. They also lobbied for pension bills and other veterans' benefits. The last GAR encampment, the 83rd, took place at Indianapolis (1949) with 6 survivors present.

Grand Banks, underwater plateau in the Atlantic Ocean off the coast of Newfoundland. Growth of abundant marine life is encouraged by flow of Gulf Stream along its E edge; one of world's most important fishing grounds.

Grand Canal, inland waterway in NE China; extends from Peking (N) to Hangchow (S); one of the world's oldest and longest waterways. Construction began in 6th century BC and continued for 2,000 years; the major building (605–18) was done under Sui dynasty; it was reconstructed and lengthened (1265–89) to Peking under Yuan dynasty and Kublai Khan. Modern canal is mainly used for industrial purposes. Length: 1,000mi (1,610km). Width: 100–200ft (31–61m). Depth: 2–15ft (.6–5m).

Grand Canal, main waterway in Venice, Italy; crossed by three bridges, including the Rialto Bridge; with smaller canals it forms major Venetian transportation system. Length: approx. 2mi (3km). Width: 100–200ft (31–61m).

Grand Canyon. △270.

Grand Canyon National Park, park in NW Arizona. It spans the great gorge of the Colorado River, along the most spectacular parts. There is vast exposure of rocks representing eons of geological time. The canyon is 217mi (349km) long and 4–18mi (6–29km) wide. Area: 673,575acres (272,798hectares). Est. 1908.

Grand Cayman, largest island of Cayman Islands, British West Indies, in NW Caribbean Sea; capital is Georgetown. Exports: fruit, rope, hardwoods. Area: 76sq mi (198sq km). Pop. 7,323.

Grand Coulee Dam, the world's largest concrete dam, in N central Washington, on Columbia River. Constructed 1933–42 under auspices of Columbia Basin Project, it is used for irrigation, flood control, and navigation; and is largest US source of hydroelectricity; Franklin D. Roosevelt Lake, a leading US reservoir, was created by the dam and extends 151mi (243km) to the Canadian border. Height: 550ft (168m). Length: 4,173ft (1,273m).

Grandfather Clause, in US history, legal device used to prevent blacks from voting. It required eligible voters to be descended from blacks enfranchised in 1856. It was judged unconstitutional by the Supreme Court (1915).

Grandfather Clause, in business law, any provision in a law that protects the rights of firms that existed before the law was passed. For example, a law might be passed that requires new companies to install expensive pollution equipment, but exempts existing companies from this provision.

Grand Forks, city in E North Dakota, on Red River; seat of Grand Forks co; site of University of North Dakota (1883), and US Bureau of Mines research laboratory. Industries: meat packing, beet-sugar refining, flour milling. Settled 1871; inc. 1881. Pop. (1970) 39,008.

Grand Island, city in S Nebraska on the Wood River; seat of Hall co; site of Stuhr Museum of the Prairie Pioneer, designed by Edward Durell Stone. Industries: farm and irrigation equipment, beverages, concrete, house trailers. Founded 1857; inc. 1872. Pop. (1970) 31,269.

Grand Jury, a group of varying size, that is a part of a court and investigates in secret the acts of a crime within its jurisdiction. It also determines which person(s) should stand trial for the crimes under its investigation.

Grand Mal, type of epileptic attack characterized by loss of consciousness and muscle contractions, lasting up to five minutes. *See also* Epilepsy. △722.

Grand Ohio Company (1748–76), a land association. Its members were London and Virginia land speculators. A royal charter granted (1749) 200,000 acres (81,000 hectares) in the Ohio Valley west of the Alleghenies to the company. The company promised family settlements and forts on the upper Ohio River, but the French and Indian wars delayed implementation of the plans.

Grand Prairie, city in NE Texas, 13mi (21km) W of Dallas. Industries: aircraft, steel products, tanks, bottling. Pop. (1970) 50,904.

Grand Rapids, city in W Michigan, on Grand River, 61mi (98km) WNW of Lansing; seat of Kent co; site of an Indian village; site of Calvin College (1876), Aquinas College (1886), Grand Rapids Junior College (1914), Reformed Bible Institute (1940), and Grace Bible Institute (1946). Industries: furniture, business machinery, auto parts, chemicals. Founded 1826 as trading post; chartered as city 1850. Pop. (1970) 197,649.

Grand River, river in N South Dakota, formed by the confluence of North and South Forks; empties into the Missouri River near Mobridge. Shadehill Dam was built on river in 1951 for flood control and irrigation; part of Missouri River Basin project. Length: approx. 200mi (322km).

Grand Teton National Park, park in NW Wyoming. It has a series of peaks embracing the most spectacular part of the Teton Range. The area was a landmark of Indians and "Mountain Men." It includes part of Jackson Hole, winter feeding ground for elk. Area: 310,442acres (125,729hectares). Est. 1929.

Grange, National, created in 1867, the first important farm organization, now the second largest. The Grange has supported farm cooperatives and stock companies to process agricultural products. It now generally speaks for the smaller farmer, opposing the end of acreage limitation and seeking high support prices for farm products.

Grange, Red (1903–), US football player, b. Harold Edward Grange in Forkville, Pa. Also known as the "Galloping Ghost," he won fame at Illinois as a three-time All-American (1923–25). A popular player in the 1920s, he played for Chicago in the National Football League (1928–35) and for New York in the American Football League (1926–27), a circuit that his manager, C. C. Pyle, originated to showcase Grange's talent. He was elected to the Football Hall of Fame (1963).

Granger Cases (1876), group of US Supreme Court decisions upholding the Granger Laws. The court affirmed that individual states had the right to regulate businesses that were public by nature, such as railroads and grain warehouses. *See also* Granger Laws; Granger Movement; Munn v. Illinois.

Granger Laws, US state laws passed in the 1870s for the regulation of railroads and grain warehouses. Laws were passed by state legislatures in Illinois, Wisconsin, Iowa, Minnesota, and other Midwestern states. In general, they set maximum transportation and storage rates and established regulatory commissions. *See also* Granger Movement; Munn v. Illinois.

Granger Movement, US agrarian movement that began in the 1860s. Organized on a local basis, individual granges established cooperative grain elevators, mills, and stores. Together, grangers brought pressure on state legislatures to regulate railroads and grain elevator costs. *See also* Granger Cases. △1278.

Granite, igneous rock from deep within the earth, composed chiefly of potash, feldspar, and quartz, with some mica or hornblende. Its texture is grainy and even, and its color is usually light gray, though feldspar may redden it. Its durability makes it a valuable construction material. *See also* Igneous Rocks. △246.

Granite City, city in SW Illinois, on Mississippi River. Industries: sheet metal, tin plate, auto frames, lubricants. Inc. 1896. Pop. (1970) 40,440.

Grant, Cary (1904–), English film star, b. Archibald Leach. His many films include sophisticated comedies such as *Topper* (1937) and *Bringing Up Baby* (1938) and stylish thrillers such as *Notorious* (1946) and *North by Northwest* (1959).

Grant, Ulysses Simpson (1822–85), commander of the Union forces in the Civil War and 18th president of the United States (1869–77), b. Point Pleasant, Ohio (original Christian name: Hiram Ulysses), graduate, West Point, 1843. In 1848 he married Julia Dent; they had four children. Grant served with distinction in the Mexican War but in 1854 he was forced out of the army for alcoholism. He remained in private life until the Civil War began; in 1861 the governor of Illinois named him commander of a volunteer regiment.

Grant rose swiftly in rank and assignments and won the first major Union victory at Fort Donelson (Feb. 16, 1862). He barely escaped defeat at the battle of Shiloh but the Vicksburg Campaign (1862–63) was one of his greatest triumphs. In October 1863 he became commander of the West. In March 1864, President Lincoln, after a long search, named him commander in chief of the Union forces. Grant personally took command of the forces in the Wilderness campaign (May-June, 1864), which was supposed to destroy the Confederate forces of General Robert E. Lee. It was the bloodiest campaign of the war but failed to defeat Lee. Grant next confronted Lee at the siege of Petersburg (June 1864–April 1865); its fall, on April 3, resulted in Lee's surrender to Grant and the end of the war.

Still in charge of the army after the war, Grant was responsible for administering the Reconstruction policies of the government toward the South. At first a moderate, he tended to side with President Andrew Johnson against the Radical Republicans. In 1867, Johnson named Grant as secretary of war. The incumbent secretary, Edwin M. Stanton, with the backing of other Radicals, refused to vacate the office, and instituted impeachment proceedings against Johnson. Grant eventually became secretary, but by that time he had joined the Radicals, and his relations with Johnson had deteriorated.

Grant's popularity as a war hero made him attractive as a political figure. In 1868 the Republican party, under the control of the Radicals, nominated Grant unanimously for president. He was easily elected over his Democratic rival, Horatio Seymour.

Grant was almost totally lacking in political ability and judgment; from the beginning, his administration was a failure. With the exception of Secretary of State Hamilton Fish, his cabinet and staff consisted of old friends, political hacks, and wealthy contributors to the party. Graft and corruption, none of which immediately touched the president, were rife. Grant, with the backing of the Radicals, entered on a punitive Reconstruction policy toward the South.

Grant was easily renominated and reelected in 1872. His second four years were no better than the first; numerous members of his administration were involved in the scandals. He retired from office totally discredited as a politician. He retained his renown as a great general, however, and enjoyed the esteem of the public.

Career: US Army, 1843–54, 1861–68; secretary of war, 1867–68; president, 1869–77. *See also* Civil War, American; Reconstruction.

Grant's Gazelle, a heavily built gazelle of the East African plains, noted for its long, graceful, diverging, ringed horns. Height to 35in (89cm); weight to 175 lbs (79kg); body fawn with inconspicuous lateral band; reddish and white markings on head; white patch on rump. Family Bovidae; species *Gazella granti. See also* Gazelle.

Granule, in astronomy. △94.

Granuloma, growth or nodule of connective tissue and capillaries usually associated with a disease such as tuberculosis, syphilis, or a nonorganic foreign body.

Granuloma Inguinale, mildly contagious venereal disease characterized by granuloma, then by ulcerations of the skin in the genital-anal area. Antibiotics are effective.

Granville, John Carteret, 1st Earl of (1690–1763), English statesman. Secretary of state (1721–24) in Walpole's administration, he used his position to gain influence with the king and intrigue against Walpole. He was lord-lieutenant of Ireland (1724–30), and lord president of the council (1751–63). An expert in foreign affairs he never succeeded, however, in forming his own administration.

Granville-Barker, Harley Granville (1877–1946), English dramatist-producer who co-managed the Court Theatre (1904–07) and was one of the theatrical forces of his day. Instrumental in producing the works of young playwrights, he is also known for his *Prefaces to Shakespeare* (6 vols.; 1934).

Grape, deciduous vine found in mild to temperate regions of North America, Europe, and China. Grapes have long been cultivated for making wine and eating. Both cultivated and wild species have small, greenish flowers and small, purple, red, or green clustered fruits. Cultivated grapes are also dried to make raisins. Family Vitaceae; genus *Vitis.* The grape family includes 600 species of vines and shrubs. △344–48.

Granada, Spain

Grand Canal, Venice, Italy

Grand Teton National Park, Wyoming

Ulysses S. Grant

Grapefruit, important citrus fruit *(Citrus paridisi)* of the rue family, similar to the shaddock, a West Indies fruit, from which it was developed. Grown in Florida, Texas, and California, it is a subtropical evergreen tree yielding a sour fruit with a thick yellow rind, and a yellow juicy pulp. Many seedless or pink-fleshed varieties have been developed.

Grape Hyacinth, perennial, bulbous plant native to the Mediterranean region. They have long, narrow leaves and bell-shaped flower clusters that are blue, white, or pink. Family Liliaceae; genus *Muscari.*

Grape Ivy, climbing, evergreen house plant with rambling stems and glossy, toothed leaves, native to N South America. Care: bright indirect light, soil (equal parts loam, peat moss, sand) kept slightly dry between waterings. Propagation is by stem cuttings. Family Vitaceae; species *Cissus rhombifolia. See also* Houseplant.

Grapes of Wrath, The (1939), a realistic, brutal novel by John Steinbeck about American farmers during the Depression. It deals with the Joad family (Tom, Pa, Ma, Rose of Sharon, Grandma, Grandpa), who leave their drought-ridden Oklahoma farm for California. Economic conditions are no better there, and hardship continues to plague them. The novel received a Pulitzer Prize and was made into a film (both 1940).

Graph, diagram representing a functional relationship between numbers or quantities using Cartesian coordinates. Two scales (axes) are drawn at right angles. The point of intersection (origin) has the value zero and the scales have positive values to the right and above the origin and negative values to the left and below the origin. Distances along the horizontal axis (abscissa) represent values of the independent variable (x); those along the vertical axis (ordinate) give values of the dependent variable (y). Thus a point on the graph represents a pair of numbers and a curve represents all possible pairs of numbers belonging to the function. Graphs are used for representing experimental results, by plotting a number of points and drawing a smooth curve through them, showing the relationship between the variables. △1452, 1470.

Graphite, gray and soft crystalline allotrope of carbon that occurs naturally in deposits of varying purity and is made synthetically by heating petroleum coke. It is used in pencil leads, lubricants, electrodes, electrical brushes, rocket nozzles, and as a moderator in nuclear reactors. Properties: sp gr 2.0-2.25.

Graphite-moderated Reactor. △1638.

Graph Theory. △1470.

Graptolite, any of an extinct group of colonial invertebrate animals of doubtful relationships; sometimes considered a separate phylum but also thought to be related to the chordates. They are found most frequently as flattened fibers of carbon resembling pencil marks in black shales of Ordovician and Silurian age. Uncompressed graptolite skeletons etched out of limestone show that they were composed of many small tubes regularly arranged along branches, which are presumed to have been attached to a common bladder-like float. The skeletal covering of the tubes is made of a chitin-like material. They are valuable as index fossils. △564.

Grass, Günter (1927–), German novelist, poet, and playwright. His prose narrative combines evocative description with historical documentation in the Mannerist style. Powerful techniques were employed to effect grotesque comedy in *Cat and Mouse* (1961) and *The Tin Drum* (1959) and to satirize the Nazi era, the war, and its aftermath, as in *Dog Years* (1963). Other works include *From the Diary of a Snail* (1972) and *Inmarypraise* (1974).

Grass, nonwoody plants found worldwide. Long, narrow leaves sheathe the hollow, jointed stems. Stems may be upright or bent and may lie on the ground or grow underground. The small flowers, lacking petals and sepals, are arranged in spikelets between two bracts. Since grass grows from the base, removal of the tips does not inhibit growth, making it suitable for lawns and pastures. Kentucky bluegrass is favored for lawns in cool areas; buffalo grass and Bermuda grass in warm areas. Branched fibrous roots prevent soil erosion.

The seedlike fruits of grass store oil and protein and are called grains. Economically, the grasses are the most important plant family. Cereal grasses such as rice, millet, corn, and wheat are cultivated for seed. Others are grown as forage for domestic grazing animals and for erosion control and ornamentation. Furniture is made of some grasses, such as bamboo. Height: 1in–100ft (2.5cm–30m). There are 5,000–10,000 species. Family Gramineae. *See also* Monocotyledon. △452–54, 584–86.

Grasse, town in SE France, 17mi (27km) W of Nice. In 12th century it was an independent republic; became part of countship of Provence 1227. Chief industry is manufacture of perfumes. Pop. 30,907.

Grasshopper, plant-eating insect found worldwide. They have hind legs enlarged for jumping. The forewings are leatherlike and hind wings are membranous and fan-shaped. When at rest, the wings are folded over the back. Length: 0.5–4in (12.7–102mm). Order Orthoptera; families Acrididae and Tettigoniidae. *See also* Locust; Mormon Cricket; Orthoptera. △494.

Grasslands. △584–91.

Grasso, Ella (Tambussi) (1919–), US political leader. b. Windsor Locks, Conn. A Democrat, she served in the Connecticut general assembly (1953–55) and as Connecticut secretary of state (1958–70). She was a US congresswoman (1971–74). In 1974 she was elected governor of Connecticut, the first woman to win that office in the United States on her own merits (not as a replacement for her husband).

Grass of Parnassus, about 30 species of perennial herb *Parnassia* of the saxifrage family, growing to 18in (46cm) and native to damp, cold to temperate or mountainous regions of North America and Eurasia. They have a graceful, showy appearance.

Grass Pink, or swamp pink, orchid found in wet areas in NE and SE United States. Each plant has a cluster of 2 to 10 pink flowers with purple, cream, or rust-red hairs covering the large lower petal. Leaves are narrow and pointed. Family Orchidaceae; species *Calopogon pulchellus.*

Grass Snake, or ringed snake, a single species of egg-laying Old World snake *(Natrix natrix)* belonging to the same genus as American water snakes. Variable in color, it is usually brown with a yellow collar. Length: to 6ft (1.8m). Family Colubridae. △522.

Gratian(us), Flavius (359–83), Western Roman emperor (375–83). Coemperor first with his father, Valentinian I, he later ruled with his brother Valentinian II. Advised by St Ambrose, he tried to stamp out paganism in the empire. He was assassinated by supporters of Maximus.

Grattan, Henry (1746–1820), Irish statesman. Trained as a lawyer, he entered the Irish parliament (1775) and through his oratory quickly became a leader of the party supporting Ireland's independence from the British parliament, a goal achieved in 1782. Always a supporter of parliamentary reform, he spent his later years striving for Roman Catholic emancipation.

Grau, Shirley Ann (1929–), US author, b. New Orleans. Her novels and short stories about the South include *The Black Prince and Other Stories* (1955) and *The Keepers of the House* (1964). She won a Pulitzer Prize (1965) for the latter.

Grave Creek Indian Burial Ground. *See* Mammoth Mound.

Gravenhage. *See* Hague, The.

Graves, Robert (1895–), British poet, novelist, and critic. After publishing his autobiography, *Goodbye to All That* (1929), he emigrated to Spain. Other works include *I, Claudius* (1934), *Claudius the God* (1934), *The White Goddess* (1947), and *The Crowning Privilege* (1955).

Graveyard School of Literature. △1222.

Gravimeter. △54, 178.

Gravireceptors, nerve endings and organs located in skeletal muscles, joints, and inner ear that are sensitive to bodily equilibrium and gravitational field direction and strength. They have been found to be temporarily affected by prolonged weightlessness.

Gravitation, one of the four forces known (the others being electromagnetism and the weak and strong nuclear forces). Immensely weak compared to the other forces, gravitation is nonetheless obvious to man because of the great mass of the earth. The gravitational force F between two masses m_1 and m_2 a distance r apart was found by Isaac Newton to be $F = Gm_1m_2/r^2$, where G is a constant of proportionality called the universal constant of gravitation. A more powerful treatment of gravitation was developed by Albert Einstein, who showed in his general theory of relativity how to understand gravitation as a manifestation of the underlying structure of space-time. Only recently have attempts been made to detect the *gravitational waves* predicted in Einstein's theory. △1486, 1490.

Gravitational Field. △1484.

Gravitational Interactions of Molecules. △1484, 1550.

Gravitational Waves, waves of energy, similar to electromagnetic waves, postulated by Einstein's general theory of relativity as being emitted from a massive accelerating body, such as an exploding or collapsing star, and as traveling at the speed of light. Experimental results put forward as evidence for such waves have not yet been generally accepted.

Graviton, hypothetical elementary particle of zero mass thought to be continuously exchanged between bodies of mass and thus to be the carrier of the gravitational force. △1484.

Gravity, the gravitational force field of a planet or other celestial body at its surface. The earth's gravity produces an acceleration of 32ft/sec^2 (9.8m/sec^2) for any unsupported body. If the mass M and radius R of a planet are known, the acceleration due to gravity (g) at its surface can be determined from $g = GM/R^2$, where G is the universal constant of gravitation. △178, 1490–92, 1550.

Gravity, Artificial, a force mimicking that of gravity but produced kinematically (ie, by acceleration or rotation). It could be maintained on space stations or on long space voyages to provide more nearly earthlike environment. △144.

Gravity, Center Of. *See* Center of Gravity.

Gravity Anomaly, deviation in gravity from the expected value. Gravity measurements over deep ocean trenches are lower than average, those in mountainous regions are higher than average. △178.

Gray, Asa (1810–88), US botanist, b. Oneida Co., N.Y. He made many contributions to plant taxonomy, and his donation of a valuable collection of books and plants to Harvard University in 1865 led to the establishment of that school's department of botany. His *Manual of Botany for the Northern United States* (1848) is considered a classic.

Gray, Elisha (1835–1901), US inventor, b. Barnesville, Ohio. He received his first patent for a self-adjusting telegraph relay (1867). He also invented and patented the telegraphic switch, telephonic repeater, type-printing telephone, and telautograph. He claimed priority in inventing the speaking telephone, but Alexander Graham Bell's patent rights were upheld by the US Supreme Court. △1792.

Gray, Robert (1755–1806), US sea captain and explorer. *b.* Tiverton, R.I. In 1787–89, on an expedition to the Pacific Northwest, he sailed on to Canton where he traded with the Chinese. He returned to Boston in 1790, his ship, *The Columbia,* being the first US vessel to circumnavigate the globe. In his later explorations of the Northwest he discovered and named the Columbia River (1792).

Gray, Thomas (1716–71), English poet. His "Elegy Written in a Country Churchyard" (1751) brought him fame. Other poems include "Ode on the Death of a Favourite Cat Drowned in a Tub of Gold Fishes" (1747) and "The Descent of Odin" (1768). His letters are important for their witty observations of contemporary life.

Graylag, common gray wild goose of Europe thought to be the ancestor of the domestic goose. Species *Anser anser. See also* Goose.

Grayling, fresh water food and sport fish found in N North America and Eurasia, characterized by a long, flaglike dorsal fin and small mouth. Length: 12–16in (30.5–40.6cm). Family Salmonidae; species includes *Thymallus arcticus.* △390, 510.

Gray Mullet. *See* Mullet.

Graywocke, any of a variety of sandstones that consist of a heterogeneous mixture of rock fragments, feldspar, and quartz of sand size strongly bonded together in a mud matrix. Graywockes are thought to have originated in deep sea water through the action of currents. *See also* Sandstone.

Graz, formerly Gratz; city in Austria, on Mur River,

87mi (140km) SSW of Vienna, in Styrean Alps; home of astronomer, Johannes Kepler (1594–1600); site of 17th-century arsenal, university (1585), and technical university (1811). Industries: steel, machinery, paper, glass, leather, textiles. Pop. 249,211.

Great Awakening, series of loosely related 18th-century religious revivals in the American colonies. The revivals started with the preachings of Jonathan Edwards in New England (1734), William Tennent in New Jersey, Samuel Davies in Virginia, and were united by the forceful tour of George Whitefield (1739–41). Baptist revivals occurred in 1760 and Methodism evolved in the pre-Revolutionary period. The revivalism, although initially fostering intolerance, eventually led to the formation of many churches, and a general spirit of religious freedom. Colleges and universities such as Princeton, Brown, Rutgers, Dartmouth, and Pennsylvania started as seminaries during the Great Awakening.

Great Barrier Reef, coral reef off NE coast of Queensland, Australia; tourist area; contains the largest deposit of coral in the world. Length: 1,250mi (2,013km). Area: more than 80,000sq mi (207,200sq km).

Great Basin, desert area in W United States; comprises most of Nevada, parts of Utah, Idaho, California, Wyoming, and Oregon; area of interior drainage to Great Salt Lake; includes Mojave Desert, Death Valley, and Carson Sink; complex topographical basin.

Great Bear Lake, lake in NW Territories, Canada; drains into the Mackenzie River; the lake is icebound eight months a year; explored 1825 by John Franklin. In 1929 radium ore was discovered on the E shore. Length: 192mi (309km). Depth: 1,356ft (414m).

Great Bear, The. *See* Ursa Major.

Great Britain, kingdom in NW Europe, officially called United Kingdom of Great Britain and Northern Ireland. It consists of England, Wales, Scotland, Northern Ireland (Ulster), the Channel Islands, and the Isle of Man. For a description of the land, economy, and people of the constituent parts of Great Britain, see separate articles on England, Northern Ireland, Scotland, and Wales.

Great Britain is a constitutional monarchy. The Parliament, the supreme legislative power, has two houses: the House of Lords, with about 1,000 members drawn from the hereditary peerage, life peers, and the episcopate, and the House of Commons, with 635 members elected for a maximum of 5 years. Wales was united to England in 1536, and Scotland in 1707; both send representatives to Parliament, but plans for devolution envisage a greater degree of autonomy for both countries. Northern Ireland, represented in the House of Commons by 12 members, also had its own parliament at Stormont (Belfast) from 1921 to 1972, when all powers were assumed by Parliament because of sectarian violence in Ulster. The Channel Islands and the Isle of Man are crown dependencies with their own legislatures. The Channel Islands, as part of the old Duchy of Normandy, came under the control of the English crown in 1066. The Isle of Man became subject to England in 1346.

History. The history of Great Britain prior to the accession of James I in 1603 is described in the England article. The kingdoms of Great Britain, England, and Scotland were under one rule from 1603, when James VI of Scotland ascended the English throne as James I. Although the realms were not formally united until 1707, the history of Great Britain begins with James' accession. For the history of England prior to 1603, *see* England.

The relations of James I and his son Charles I with Parliament were stormy, as Parliament's control of taxation thwarted many of the crown's plans. The struggle led to the first Civil War (1642–46) and then the second Civil War (1648), which was followed by the execution of Charles I and the proclamation of the Commonwealth (1649), headed by Oliver Cromwell. The Restoration in 1660 brought Charles II to the throne. His brother James II acceded in 1685 and was opposed for his Roman Catholicism, particularly after the birth of a male heir. William of Orange, husband of James' Protestant daughter Mary, invaded in 1688 in the Glorious Revolution, and as William III, he and Mary ascended the throne in 1689. After William's death, their daughter Anne took the crown, and by the Act of Settlement, the crown passed to the house of Hanover in 1714.

The early years of the Hanoverians were devoted to consolidation domestically, while Britain was becoming a great colonial and maritime power abroad. The loss of the American colonies in the Revolutionary War was balanced by gains in India. Demands for political reform were stimulated by the American and French revolutions but the governing class resisted attempts at reform. Rebellion in Ireland in 1798 was followed in 1800 by the union of Ireland and Britain. Political changes received new impetus with the extension of the franchise in the Reform Act of 1832.

The 19th century was a time of development for Britain as the nation continued its rapid industrialization and became the world's foremost power, with a huge overseas empire. Politically, the long reign of Queen Victoria was marked by the emergence of national political parties. The Liberal party was long headed by William Gladstone, while the Conservatives were led by Benjamin Disraeli and Randolph Churchill. Further extensions of the franchise, the growth of trade unions, and reforms in Ireland were major domestic issues. In the early 20th century, the Liberals' influence declined and the new Labour party increased its power in Parliament.

The great events of the 20th century all had major effects on Britain. The nation was slow to recover from World Wars I and II and was severely hit by the Depression of the 1930s. After World War II, its colonies achieved independence, and Britain's position as a world power eroded. Domestically, the country was split by Ireland's demands for independence and was shocked by the abdication of Edward VIII in 1936. Although the monarchy remained popular, Elizabeth II had no real power. Neither Conservative nor Labour governments were able to solve Britain's economic problems, although hopes were raised by its entry into the European Economic Community in 1973. △ 1156, 1330.

Following are lists of the rulers and prime ministers of England and Great Britain.

RULERS OF ENGLAND AND GREAT BRITAIN

Egbert (Ecgberht)	829–39
Ethelwulf	839–58
Ethelbald	858–60
Ethelbert	860–66
Ethelred I	866–71
Alfred the Great	871–99
Edward the Elder	899–924
Athelstan	924–40
Edmund I	940–46
Edred	946–55
Edwy	955–59
Edgar	959–75
Edward the Martyr	975–78
Aethelred II (the Unready)	978–1016
Edmund II (Ironside)	1016
Canute (Cnut)	1016–35
Harold I (Harefoot)	1035–40
Hardecanute	1040–42
Edward the Confessor	1042–66
Harold II	1066
William I (the Conqueror)	1066–87
William II (Rufus)	1087–1100
Henry I (Beauclerc)	1100–35
Stephen	1135–54
Henry II	1154–89
Richard I (Coeur de Lion)	1189–99
John (Lackland)	1199–1216
Henry III	1216–72
Edward I (Longshanks)	1272–1307
Edward II	1307–27
Edward III	1327–77
Richard II	1377–99
Henry IV	1399–1413
Henry V	1413–22
Henry VI	1422–61
Edward IV	1461–83
Edward V	1483
Richard III	1483–85
Henry VII	1485–1509
Henry VIII	1509–47
Edward VI	1547–53
Mary I	1553–58
Elizabeth I	1558–1603
James I	1603–25
Charles I	1625–49
Commonwealth	1649–60
Charles II	1660–85
James II	1685–88
William III and Mary II	1689–94
William III	1694–1702
Anne	1702–14
George I	1714–27
George II	1727–60
George III	1760–1820
George IV	1820–30
William IV	1830–37
Victoria	1837–1901
Edward VII	1901–10
George V	1910–36
Edward VIII	1936
George VI	1936–52
Elizabeth II	1952–

PRIME MINISTERS

Sir Robert Walpole	1721–42
Earl of Wilmington	1742–43

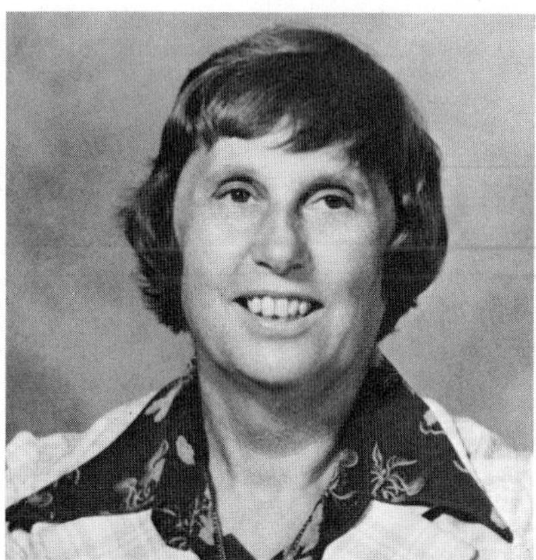

Ella Grasso

Thomas Gray

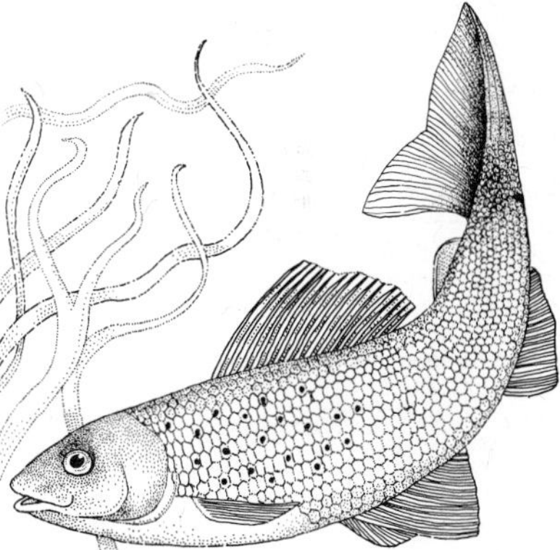

Grayling

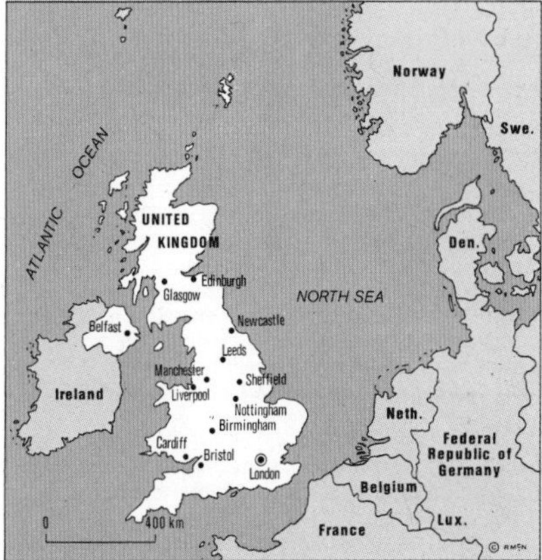
Norway
Swe.
ATLANTIC
OCEAN
UNITED KINGDOM
Edinburgh
Glasgow
NORTH SEA
Newcastle
Belfast
Den.
Leeds
Manchester
Sheffield
Liverpool
Ireland
Nottingham
Birmingham
Neth.
Federal Republic of Germany
Cardiff
Bristol
London
Belgium
0
400 km
France
Lux.

Great Britain

Henry Pelham	1743–54
Duke of Newcastle	1754–56
Duke of Devonshire	1756–57
Duke of Newcastle	1757–62
Earl of Bute	1762–63
George Grenville	1763–65
Marquess of Rockingham	1765–66
William Pitt the Elder (Earl of Chatham)	1766–68
Duke of Grafton	1768–70
Frederick North (Lord North)	1770–82
Marquess of Rockingham	1782
Earl of Shelburne	1782–83
Duke of Portland	1783
William Pitt the Younger	1783–1801
Henry Addington	1801–04
William Pitt the Younger	1804–06
William Wyndham Grenville, Baron Grenville	1806–07
Duke of Portland	1807–09
Spencer Perceval	1809–12
Earl of Liverpool	1812–27
George Canning	1827
Viscount Goderich	1827–28
Duke of Wellington	1828–30
Earl Grey	1830–34
Viscount Melbourne	1834
Sir Robert Peel	1834–35
Viscount Melbourne	1835–41
Sir Robert Peel	1841–46
Lord John Russell (later Earl)	1846–52
Earl of Derby	1852
Earl of Aberdeen	1852–55
Viscount Palmerston	1855–58
Earl of Derby	1858–59
Viscount Palmerston	1859–65
Earl Russell	1865–66
Earl of Derby	1866–68
Benjamin Disraeli	1868
William E. Gladstone	1868–74
Benjamin Disraeli	1874–80
William E. Gladstone	1880–85
Marquess of Salisbury	1885–86
William E. Gladstone	1886
Marquess of Salisbury	1886–92
William E. Gladstone	1892–94
Earl of Rosebery	1894–95
Marquess of Salisbury	1895–1902
Arthur J. Balfour	1902–05
Sir Henry Campbell-Bannerman	1905–08
Herbert H. Asquith	1908–15
Herbert H. Asquith	1915–16
David Lloyd George	1916–22
Andrew Bonar Law	1922–23
Stanley Baldwin	1923–24
James Ramsay MacDonald	1924
Stanley Baldwin	1924–29
James Ramsay MacDonald	1929–31
James Ramsay MacDonald	1931–35
Stanley Baldwin	1935–37
Neville Chamberlain	1937–40
Winston Churchill	1940–45
Winston Churchill	1945
Clement Attlee	1945–51
Sir Winston Churchill	1951–55
Sir Anthony Eden	1955–57
Harold Macmillan	1957–63
Sir Alex Douglas-Home	1963–64
Harold Wilson	1964–70
Edward Heath	1970–74
Harold Wilson	1974–76
James Callaghan	1976–

PROFILE

Official name: United Kingdom of Great Britain and Northern Ireland
Area: 94,226sq mi (244,045sq km)
Population: 56,400,000
Density: 599per sq mi (231per sq km)
Chief cities: London (capital); Birmingham; Glasgow
Government: monarchy and parliament
Religion: Anglicanism (England), Presbyterianism (Scotland)
Languages: English
Monetary unit: pound sterling
Gross national product: £92,841,000,000
Per capita income: $3,380
Industries (major products): motor vehicles, machinery, textiles, iron, steel
Agriculture (major products): cereals, potatoes, sheep, cattle
Minerals (major): coal, iron ore, petroleum
Trading partners (major): United States, West Germany, Netherlands, France

Great Circle, circle on a spherical surface whose center is coincident with the center of the sphere. Thus lines of longitude lie on great circles; lines of latitude, with the exception of the equator, do not.

Great Dane, giant hunting and fighting dog (working group) bred in Germany over 400 years ago for bear hunting. Also called German mastiff, it has a narrow, long head with large, blunted muzzle; high-set, medium-length ears that droop forward, or if cropped are erect; broad, deep chest; short back; long, strong legs; and straight, slender tail. The short, smooth coat is brindle, fawn, blue, black, or harlequin. Average size: 30in (76cm) minimum height at shoulder; to 150lb (68kg). *See also* Working Dogs.

Great Depression. *See* Depression, Great.

Greater Antilles, largest of three major island groups of West Indies, between Atlantic Ocean (NE) and Caribbean Sea (S and SW), and Gulf of Mexico (NW). Group includes Cuba, Haiti, Dominican Republic, Jamaica, Puerto Rico; Puerto Rico is a commonwealth associated with United States; remaining four islands are independent.

Greater Reed-mace or Bulrush. △454.

Greater Sunda Islands, larger of 2 island groups comprising Sunda Isles, Indonesia; located in W Malay Archipelago, between South China Sea and Indian Ocean; includes Java, Sumatra, Borneo, Celebes, and adjacent small islands. Pop. 112,138,626.

Greater Weaver. △516.

Great Falls, city in central Montana, on Missouri River; seat of Cascade co. Nearby is Giant Springs; site of College of Great Falls (1932), and log cabin of cowboy artist Charles Russell. Industries: oil and copper refining, flour. Inc. 1888. Pop. (1970) 60,091.

Great Lakes, chain of five freshwater lakes in central North America, between Canada and the United States; includes lakes Superior, Michigan, Huron, Erie, Ontario; they are connected by straits, small rivers, and canals. Formed at the end of the Ice Age, they are drained by the St Lawrence River. First of lakes to be discovered was Huron, visited by Samuel de Champlain in 1615; French traders and explorers continued developing and exploring the land for France until 1763 when Canada was ceded to Great Britain. War of 1812 saw conflict between US and Britain over lakes Ontario and Erie. Opening of New York state's Erie Canal 1825 connected this area with Hudson River and Atlantic (now accomplished by Barge Canal). Deepening of St Lawrence for seaway opening in 1959 connected Great Lakes with world shipping; Illinois Waterway connects it with Mississippi River; steel, iron ore, coal, petroleum, and grains are shipped from April until December. Industrialization and population increases have created pollution problems especially in lakes Erie, Ontario, and Michigan. Major cities on the lakes include Chicago, Detroit, Buffalo, Cleveland, Milwaukee. Combined surface area of lakes is 95,000sq mi (246,050sq km). *See also* articles on each lake. △206.

Great Leap Forward, government policy inaugurated by Mao Tse-tung in China in 1958 to try to catch up with and surpass Western powers in economy in record time. Peasants were organized into communes, and tens of millions were mobilized to smelt iron in primitive handmade furnaces. The resulting chaos and decline in agrarian and industrial production led to its abandonment by 1960–61. △1348.

Great Miami River. *See* Miami River.

Great Plains, high, grassy slope of central North American continent, reaching from central Canada down the central plains states to Texas; W border is the Rocky Mts. Somewhat sparse in population, the principal economic activities are farming, cattle, and sheep raising; wheat is dominant crop.

Great Pond Snail. △482.

Great Pyrenees, bearlike guard and mountain dog (working group) that originated in Asia and appeared in Europe 1800–1000BC. A favorite of royalty and peasant alike, it has a wedge-shaped head with rounded crown; medium-sized, V-shaped ears carried close to the head; a straight, broad body; shortish, sturdy legs; and a long tail curled over the back. The white double coat is long, flat, and thick. Average size: 25–32in (63.5–81.3cm) high at shoulder; 90–125lb (40–56kg). *See also* Working Dog.

Great Red Spot. *See* Jupiter. △80.

Great Saint Bernard Pass, Alpine pass on the Italian-Swiss border that links Valais canton, Switzerland, and Valle d'Aosta, Italy. Altitude: 8,110ft (2,474m).

Great Salt Lake, large, shallow lake of salt water in NW Utah; fed by the Bear, Weber, and Jordan rivers, it is a descendant of prehistoric Lake Bonneville that covered much of the Great Basin. Area: approx. 2,000sq mi (5,180sq km). Depth: 35ft (11m).

Great Sand Dunes National Park, high shifting dunes of San Luis Park in S central Colorado. Est. 1932. Area: 36,740acres (14,880hectares).

Great Schism (1378–1417), rift between the Roman popes and the king of France. It began when Pope Gregory XI died in 1378 and was succeeded by an Italian, Urban VI. The French cardinals dissented, declared the election invalid, and elected an anti-pope, Clement VII (and his successor Benedict XIII), who stayed at Avignon. The Roman pope was supported by the Holy Roman Empire, England, Hungary, Poland, and other northern European countries, the anti-pope was backed by France, Scotland, Spain, Portugal, and some German princes. Reconciliation took place at the Council of Constance.

Great Slave Lake, lake in Northwest Territories, Canada; the 5th-largest lake in North America. Discovered 1771. Length: 298mi (480km). Depth: 2,015 ft (615m).

Great Smoky Mountains, part of the Appalachian Mt system, on the North Carolina-Tennessee border. One of the oldest ranges on earth, it is rich in hardwood and holds the largest virgin forest of red spruce. Named for the smoky haze that envelops them, they were first settled in early 19th century in lower valleys. Artifacts of these early pioneers have been preserved by the National Park Service. Log cabins, barns, farm implements, and a great mill powered by a water wheel are on display. Highest point is Clingmans Dome, 6,643ft (2,026m). In 1926 it was set aside as Great Smoky Mts National Park. Area: 516,626acres (209,079hectares).

Great Train Robbery, The (1903), US film. This western was the longest narrative film of its time (302 feet, which ran 11 minutes). In a series of short, interdependent scenes, the director, Edwin S. Porter, made a number of editing innovations, including parallel and overlapping action sequences. △1316.

Great Trek, migration of Boer farmers and pastoralists from the Cape Colony (South Africa) in the late 1830s and 1840s to escape British domination. Defeating the Xhosa peoples in their new lands, these "Voortrekkers" formed the Transvaal and the Orange Free State and maintained independence for most of the time preceeding the Boer War (1899–1902).

Great Wall, fortified wall in N China, extending from Shanhaikuan to Chiayükuan; originally built as a series of many walls, it was unified under the Ch'un dynasty (204 BC). The Ming dynasty (1368–1644) is responsible for the modern form of the wall; constructed of stone, earth, and brick, its purpose was to ward off northern invaders; guard stations and watch towers are spaced at regular intervals. Length: 1,500mi (2,415km). Width: 15–30ft (5–9m) at the base, 12ft (4m) at the top. Height: 20–50ft (6–15m). △886, 1038.

Great White Fleet, popular name for the US battle fleet that President Theodore Roosevelt sent on a world cruise in 1907–08, primarily as a show of force against Japan. The core of the fleet consisted of 16 new battleships whose hulls were painted bright white in keeping with existing US naval tradition.

Great White Shark. *See* White Shark.

Grebe, brownish, grayish, or blackish freshwater diving bird found worldwide that flies laboriously, with legs set so far back it cannot walk on land. White, bluish, or greenish chalky eggs (2–8) are laid in a soggy aquatic weed nest after special courtship rituals. Length: 9–14in (23–36cm). Family Podicipedidae. △526.

Greco, El (1541?–1614?), Spanish painter, b. Domenikos Theotokopoulos in Crete. He was trained by Greek monks as an icon painter. In 1577 he settled in Toledo and tried to win favor at the Spanish Court but never really succeeded. The intensely personal vision reflected in his works is ecstatically mystical and passionate, with elongated, distorted figures; disturbing color schemes; eerie, supernatural lighting; and a disregard for normal rules of perspective. His early style was influenced by Michelangelo and other Italian masters, his later style by Byzantine art, but through all phases of his career his art remained uniquely individual. His first major commission in Spain was the enormous Altar of San Domingo el Antiguo in Toledo; some of his later paintings, such as "Burial of Count Orgasz," "Agony in the Garden," and "Resurrection" depict an increasingly rapturous vision of suffering. In his final years he painted many portraits and one famous landscape, "View of Toledo."

Greece, a small nation on the Balkan Peninsula in the E Mediterranean Sea. A magnificent civilization flourished there in the 1st millennium BC, and splendid ruins stand throughout Greece, attesting to that golden age. Modern Greece is a small, underdeveloped country, which has undergone considerable political turmoil in the 20th century.

Land and Economy. Greece has a diverse geography. The mainland territory is very mountainous, and is enclosed by the sea on three sides. The soil is generally poor, except in the scattered plains of central and N Greece. Nearly half of all Greeks are farmers; important crops include fruits and vegetables, tobacco, olives, and wheat. Tobacco is the country's major export product. Greece is historically a maritime country; nearly one-fifth of its territory consists of 437 islands, and shipping is of special economic importance. The Greek merchant fleet is the seventh largest in the world. Greek manufacturing has only begun developing large-scale enterprises since about 1960. Tourism provides a major contribution to the national income.

People. The Greeks call themselves "Hellenes." The Greek language is spoken by nearly all Greeks, making Greece one of the most homogeneous of all nations. Modern Greek differs sharply from the Greek tongue of ancient times. The official religion of Greece is the Greek Orthodox Church, with 97% of all Greeks as members. Since World War II, the population has been moving steadily from the poorest farming villages to the cities. The family is the dominant social unit; a Greek's primary loyalty is to his kinsmen. The living-standard has been rising steadily.

Government. Greece became a democratic republic in 1973, replacing the constitutional monarchy. The 1952 constitution was restored the following year, and Greece became, by referendum, an "uncrowned democracy." Most political power lies with the president. The legislative body is the Chamber of Deputies, elected every five years. The country is divided into 52 administrative districts, each directed by a governor. Cities and towns are governed by elected officials.

History. Greece was ruled by the Ottoman Turks for more than 500 years, until the 1820s when France, England, and Russia recognized Greek independence. The constitutional monarchy was est. in 1844. For many decades Greece sought to acquire foreign territories inhabited by Greeks. By the end of World War I, Greece had added Thrace, Crete, a portion of Macedonia, S Epirus, and many islands. In World War II, Greece repelled an assault by Italy (1940), and was attacked and occupied by German forces (1941). The Greek army seized power in 1967, and King Constantine fled the country. Col. George Papadopoulos became prime minister. This military government resigned in 1974, and was replaced by a civilian government led by Constantine Karamanlis. *See also* Greece, Ancient. △992–1006.

PROFILE

Official name: Hellenic Republic
Area: 50,944sq mi (131,944sq km)
Population: 8,980,000
Density: 176per sq mi (68per sq km)
Chief cities: Athens (capital); Salonika; Piraeus
Government: republic
Religion: Eastern Orthodox
Language: Greek (official)
Monetary unit: drachma
Gross national product: $18,600,000,000
Per capita income: $860
Manufacturing (major products): textiles, clothing, cigarettes, shoes, processed foods, chemicals
Agriculture (major products): wheat, olives, tobacco, citrus fruits
Minerals (major): iron, lignite, bauxite, magnesite, chromite
Trading partners (major): West Germany, Great Britain, France, Japan, Italy

Greece, Ancient, civilization that flourished on the Greek peninsula, in Asia Minor (modern Turkey), on the N coast of Africa, and in the western Mediterranean from about 3000 BC until 146 BC, when the weakened Greek cities fell before the power of the Roman Empire. The civilization of the ancient Greeks has had a profound influence on the modern Western world; in virtually every field of the arts, sciences, and philosophy the ancient Greeks laid the groundwork for the modern discipline. Democracy was introduced by the Greeks and was practiced in its purest form in the Greek city-states. The philosophies of Socrates, Plato, and Aristotle continue to influence Western thought.

In the 3rd millennium BC, a culture known today as the Aegean civilization developed centered on the island of Crete (the Minoan civilization) and in the Peloponnesus on the mainland (the Mycenaean civilization). The Minoans made primitive use of bronze and developed a pictograph script (known to modern archaeologists as Linear A). They built great palaces and developed the rudiments of a maritime trade. The culture of the Mycenaeans roughly paralleled that of the Minoans (their pictograph writing is known as Linear B) and is believed to have been largely borrowed from the Minoans. This Bronze Age of Greek history is the period celebrated in the epic poems of Homer. By about 1400 the Minoan civilization on Crete had deteriorated, but the Mycenaeans on the mainland continued to prosper until the 12th century. About that time they were conquered by the Dorians, who invaded from the north. Beginning about 1400, various Greek-speaking peoples had begun migrating into southern Greece, including, in addition to the Dorians, the Achaeans, Aeolians, and Ionians. As they settled into agricultural communities, they developed the self-contained political, economic, and social unit known as the city-state. As populations grew and agricultural land became scarce, colonies were planted on the Greek islands, in Asia Minor, in North Africa, and in Italy, France, and Spain. Eventually, these colonies became themselves city-states, virtually independent of the sponsoring cities. Thus was the groundwork laid for a great Greek empire.

The Greek city-states developed separately and were often at war with each other. Nevertheless, they shared certain common traits. They all spoke Greek, and they shared similar religious traditions. Politically, they typically evolved from a monarchy to an aristocracy to a tyranny and, finally, either to a democracy or an oligarchy or military dictatorship. Except for cooperating in such religious ventures as the Olympic Games and in maintaining such shrines as the Delphic Oracle, the Greek city-states were basically independent of each other until the beginning of the Persian Wars in 512 BC. That long conflict began when the Greek colonies in Asia Minor revolted against their Persian overlords and were given aid by Athens, the largest and richest of the Greek cities. Persia retaliated by attacking the Greek mainland. In order to counter the great Persian army, Athens organized the Delian League in 478. All the important Greek cities, including Sparta, were members. The great Greek victories at Marathon (490), Salamis (480), and Plataea (479) ended the Persian threat to Greece, but the Delian League continued to fight the war until its successful conclusion in 449. The success of the Delian League in the war encouraged Athens to continue it afterwards, and it became, in effect, the instrument of the Athenian empire. At its height it comprised almost 150 Greek cities. Athens, under the leadership of Pericles, now entered into its Golden Age. Art, architecture, literature, and philosophy flourished. Pericles successfully put down (448) an attempt by Euboea to break away from the Delian League. In 445, Athens and Sparta signed a truce that gave each of the great Greek cities 15 years of peace. In 431, however, the increasing rivalry of the two cities erupted into the Peloponnesian War. In time the strength of the Athenian navy was overwhelmed by the great Spartan army, and Athens was destroyed as a power. Sparta was the most powerful Greek city for the next 30 years.

Continuing rivalries weakened the Greek cities, however, and they were unable to defend themselves against the growing power of Macedon, a country in northeastern Greece. Under Philip II, who ruled from 359–336, Macedon conquered Upper Macedon, Thrace, and Chalcidice. More important, Philip created the greatest army the world had seen. His son, Alexander the Great, who ruled from 336–323, used that army to conquer the entire Greek world and place it under his Macedonian Empire. Under Alexander, Greek civilization was spread throughout the known Western world and as far east as India. His empire did not survive his death, however, and was divided among his generals. As Macedonian influence declined, the Greek cities revived their rivalries. Alliances were formed, such as the Aetolian and Achaean leagues, to forge some kind of unity, but they were mostly unsuccessful. Warfare was almost incessant. In the meantime, Rome was growing in power. In 146 what was left of the Greek cities fell under Roman control, and the ancient Greek world came to an end. Hellenism, as Greek culture had come to be called, retained its strength, however, and became the basis for the civilization of the Roman Empire. *See also* Alexander the Great; Delian League; Peloponnesian War; Persian Wars; Sparta. △992–1006.

Greed (1923), US film, adapted from Frank Norris's *McTeague*, a harsh, naturalistic novel set in San Francisco and Death Valley. Rated as director Erich von Stroheim's greatest work. But because of his extravagance in its filming, it was also the cause of his downfall as a director. The film originally ran 10 hours but was cut to two despite von Stroheim's protests. It

Great Dane

Great Smoky Mountains

Austria
Hungary
U.S.S.R.
Romania
Yugoslavia
ADRIATIC SEA
BLACK SEA
Bulgaria
Italy
Albania
Salonika (Thessaloniki)
Lárisa
IONIAN SEA
GREECE
Athens (Athínai)
Pátrai
Turkey
MEDITERRANEAN SEA
0
400km
Iráklion

Greece

Athens, Greece: Acropolis

starred Zasu Pitts, Gibson Gowland, and Jean Hersholt. △1370.

Greek, one of the two great classical languagès of antiquity. Its descendant, Modern Greek, is spoken by about 10,000,000 people in Greece and 500,000 more on Cyprus. Greek has profoundly influenced the vocabulary of many languages. The word *photograph,* for example, is a combination of the Greek words for *light* and *write.* Like English, Greek is an Indo-European language.

Greek Architecture, the Hellenic architecture of the Dorians, who succeeded the Myceneans in Greece. The major works were produced between 700 and 146 BC and followed a definite system of construction based on rules of form and proportion. The greatest structures are temples of post-and-lintel construction. These vary from the simplicity of the Doric order to the greater elegance and decoration of the Ionic and Corinthian orders. The best example of the Doric is the Parthenon. The Ionic was more common on the coast of Asia Minor, as in the temples of Miletus, and the Corinthian was only used extensively after the masterpieces of the Athenian empire had been built. △1000–02.

Greek Art. △1000–02.

Greek Mythology. The Greek imagination was anthropomorphic, creating the Olympian pantheon in man's image, with all his faults and virtues. In the myths, the gods are capable of great pettiness or vindictiveness, revenge and favoritism. Even the creation of the universe takes place without magic as a series of procreations. The Greek myths were generally explanatory, offering answers to questions of human nature and the universe, clarifying abstract ideas, or explaining religious matters in a more or less rational manner bordering on the scientific. Because of this rationalism the myths never gained importance in the religion of the people. △832.

Greek Revival Architecture, architectural style of the late 18th and early 19th centuries occasioned by the discovery of Greek architecture. Its first example was James Stuart's garden temple at Hagley, England, but the style became even more influential in US public buildings. Benjamin Latrobe's Bank of Pennsylvania, Philadelphia (1799), the first example of Greek revival in the United States, is an imitation of a Greek Ionic temple. △1198.

Greek War of Independence (1821–29), the rebellion of Greece against Turkish rule that led to the independence of modern Greece. In 1820 Prince Ypsilanti led a premature raid against the Turks. He was defeated but other groups staged isolated raids all over Greece, and the Turks made brutal reprisals. From 1822–24 there were two civil wars in Greece between the various factions. In 1824, Mehemet Ali of Egypt joined the Turks; Athens fell in 1826. Britain, France, and Russia intervened in 1827, the year the Turkish fleet was crushed at Navarino. By the Treaty of Adrianople (1829), Greek autonomy was established, followed in 1832 by independence. *See also* Greece. △1230.

Greeley, Horace (1811–72), US journalist whose editorial policies helped to rouse northern popular opinion against slavery, b. near Amherst, N.H. His liberal views gained him the editorship of the *Jeffersonian* (1838) and the *Log Cabin* in the presidential campaign (1840). In 1841, he founded and edited the New York *Tribune,* where his progressive ideals of socio-economic reform and his powerful antislavery editorials were highly influential. His homilies included "Go West Young Man." He helped to organize the Republican party in the 1850s and supported Abraham Lincoln in his presidential campaign (1860). Greeley fruitlessly sought office, broke with the Republican party and finally became the unsuccessful presidential candidate for the dissenting Liberal Republicans in 1872.

Greeley, city in N Colorado, seat of Weld co, approx. 38mi (61km) NE of Denver. Main industry is food processing; site of Colorado State College (1889). Settled 1870; inc. 1885. Pop. (1970) 38,902.

Greely, Adolphus Washington (1844–1935), US general and arctic explorer, b. Newburyport, Mass. He led an expedition to northern Greenland (1881) and was one of six survivors at Cape Sabine (1884), recounting his experiences in *Three Years of Arctic Service* (1885). He became chief of the US Signal Corps (1887) and built 21,000 miles of telegraph lines in the United States, Puerto Rico, Cuba, the Philippines, China, and Alaska. Promoted to major general, he directed relief after the San Francisco earthquake and fire (1906).

Green, Duff (1791–1875), US journalist and statesman, b. Woodford co, Ky. He was editor of the St Louis *Enquirer* and later bought the *United States Telegraph* in Washington, D.C. (1825). He managed Andrew Jackson's campaign for president (1828), became a member of his "kitchen cabinet." He later broke with Jackson to back John Calhoun, his son-in-law, on nullification (1830). President Tyler sent him on diplomatic missions to England (1843) and Texas and Mexico (1844–45). In 1844 he founded the New York *Republic,* a newspaper sympathetic to the South. He had obtained a charter and funds for a Southern Pacific railroad when the Civil War broke out. He operated ironworks for the Confederacy during the war.

Green, Thomas Hill (1836–82), English philosopher. A representative of English neo-Hegelianism, or idealism, he reacted against empiricism and evolutionist materialism. He contended that they led to meaninglessness and moral nihilism. His most important work is *Prolegomena to Ethics* (1883).

Green, William (1873–1952), US labor leader, b. Coshocton, Ohio. He served as secretary-treasurer of the United Mine Workers (1912–24) and as president of the American Federation of Labor (1924–52). As president of the AFL, he built up the craft unions and membership. The federation split when John L. Lewis formed the Congress of Industrial Organizations (CIO) in 1935. Green wrote *Labor and Democracy* (1939).

Green Algae, a large group of marine and freshwater algae (division Chlorophyta). Green algae range in size from microscopic single-cell types to large complex plants. Some of the single-cell types form colonies. Others live in a symbiotic relationship with fungi, forming the plant known as a lichen; and others live in symbiotic associations with certain marine invertebrates. The larger types take a variety of forms, including tubes, threads, and leaflike sheets such as sea lettuce. The chlorophyll in these green algae is not obscured by other pigments. *See also* Lichen. △432.

Greenaway, Kate (1846–1901), English author and illustrator of books for children. Her illustrations of a joyous world of children are executed with charm and delicacy, but without sentimentality. Her first major success was *Under the Window* (1879). Other titles include *Marigold Garden* (1885) and *A Apple Pie* (1886). The Kate Greenaway Medal is the English counterpart of the Caldecott Medal in the United States.

Greenback Party (Independent Party, National Greenback Party), minor US political party, organized in 1875 to elect Peter Cooper as president. It was supported by western farmers and debtors determined to persuade Congress to issue additional "greenbacks" to stimulate a general price increase. Party members also favored the eight-hour day for labor, a graduated income tax, and an interstate commerce law. They opposed railroad land grants. The party declined after the 1880 election and, in 1884, it merged with the Anti-Monopoly party. *See also* Anti-Monopoly Party.

Greenbacks, legal tender notes not backed by specie, issued by the US government in 1862 during the Civil War. Those remaining in circulation after 1878 became part of the nation's currency.

Green Bay, city and port of entry in E Wisconsin, 112mi (180km) N of Milwaukee, on S end of Green Bay and at mouth of Fox River; seat of Brown co; home of Green Bay Packers professional football team; site of Tank Cottage (1776), and National Railroad Museum. Industries: cheese processing, fisheries, shipyards, paper, iron, steel. Trading post est. by Jean Nicolet 1634; settled 1701; inc. 1854. Pop. (1970) 87,809.

Greenberg, Henry Benjamin ("Hank") (1911–), US baseball player, b. New York City. A power hitter, he hit 331 home runs while playing for the Detroit Tigers (1930–41; 1945–46) and the Pittsburgh Pirates (1947). He was elected to the Baseball Hall of Fame in 1956.

Greenbrier, or cat brier, climbing, woody vine native to North America, Europe, Asia, and Bolivia. It has prickly stems, small flowers that are green, yellow, or white, and black berries. The extract sarsaparilla is obtained from the dried roots of some species. Family Liliaceae; genus *Smilax.*

Greene, (Henry) Graham (1904–), English novelist and dramatist. His novels, written from a Roman Catholic viewpoint, include *Brighton Rock* (1938), *The Power and the Glory* (1940), *The Quiet American* (1955), *Our Man in Havana* (1958), *Travels with My Aunt* (1969), and *The Honorary Consul* (1973). His plays include *The Living Room* (1953) and *The Potting Shed* (1957). △1376.

Greene, Nathanael (1742–86), American Revolutionary general, b. Potowomut, R.I. In 1776 he skillfully led the left wing of the American forces at the battles of Trenton, Princeton, and Brandywine. He was appointed Commander of the Army of the South in October 1780. He led a strategic retreat in 1781, then in 1782 he turned and routed the British, sending them back to three coastal bases in Georgia and the Carolinas.

Green Flash, the greenish or bluish hue of the upper rim of the Sun just as it is about to disappear with setting or appears with rising, due to atmospheric effects on the sun's light.

Greenhouse, or hothouse, glass- or plastic-paned structure with a wood or metal frame. Temperature and humidity can be controlled for growing plants out of season. Earliest greenhouses date from ancient Rome; Pliny described mica-glazed pits used to grow plants and vegetables for Tiberius Caesar. Greenhouses range in size from small lean-tos and window greenhouses for the home to huge public and commercial greenhouses. △366.

Greenhouse Effect, the heating effect on the earth caused by the absorption by the atmosphere of long-wave (infrared) radiation emitted from the earth's surface and its counter radiation back to the surface, as opposed to short-wave (ultraviolet) radiation transmitted rather freely from earth through atmosphere to space. *See also* Radiation. △292.

Greenland, Danish island-territory in the NW Atlantic. The people are predominately Eskimo and mostly Lutheran. The largest island in the world, 1,660mi (2,673km) long and 800mi (1,288km) wide at its widest, over 85% of Greenland is ice-capped and uninhabitable. The economy is based almost entirely upon fish. The population, almost entirely Eskimo with the exception of a few Danish officials, generally lives along the SW coast. Greenlanders have Danish nationality and send two representatives to the Danish parliament. Eric the Red, who discovered the island in 982, purposely misnamed it to attract colonists. By the 12th century there was a colony of about 10,000, but by 1400 the settlements had disappeared. Colonization was re-instituted in 1721 under Hans Egede of Norway, "the Apostle of Greenland," and Godthåb was founded in 1727. The island has been under direct Danish control since 1729.

PROFILE

Official name: Greenland
Area: 840,000sq mi (2,175,600sq km)
Population: 46,331
Chief cities: Godthåb, (capital); Holsteinsborg; Sukkertoppen
Government: part of Denmark
Gross national product: $80,000,000
Per capita income: $1,730
Agriculture (major products): fish and fish products
Minerals (major): quartz, mica, feldspar, cryolite, chiolite.

Green Mountain Boys, militia formed in 1764 to uphold the settlers' rights to the New Hampshire grants (now Vermont). Ethan Allen assumed command of the Green Mountain Boys in 1770 and they helped take Fort Ticonderoga from the British, May 10, 1775.

Green Mountains, northern branch of Appalachian Mts, extends S to N from W Massachusetts, through Vermont and into SE Canada; heavily wooded and scenic area; range is famous for its granite quarries, especially in Barre, Vermont area. Highest peak is Mt Mansfield, 4,393ft (1,340m).

Green River, longest tributary of the Colorado; flows from W Wyoming S to SE Utah. Length: 730mi (1,175km).

Greensboro, city in N North Carolina, 26mi (42km) E of Winston-Salem; seat of Guilford co; birthplace of O. Henry; site of Greensboro College (1838), Guilford College (1834), Bennett College (1873), University of North Carolina at Greensboro (1891), North Carolina Agricultural and Technical State University (1891). Nearby is national military park commemorating Revolutionary War battle of Guilford Courthouse. Industries: cellophane products, chemicals, textiles. Settled 1749; inc. 1829. Pop. (1970) 144,076.

Green Snake, or grass snake, slender North American and Asian snake. The rough green snake *(Opheodrys aestivus)* of North America has keeled scales; the smaller, smooth green snake *(O. vernalis)* is unkeeled. Both are solid green with pale bellies. Length: to 30in (76cm). Family Colubridae. *See also* Colubrid; Reptile; Snake.

Green Turtle, edible marine turtle found in tropical waters of Atlantic and Pacific. In danger of extinction, with a head too large to fit inside the shell. Its forelegs are powerful flippers. Length: to 4ft (1.2m); weight: to 500lb (225kg). Family Cheloniidae; species *Chelonia mydas. See also* Turtle. △522.

Greenville, port city in W Mississippi, on Lake Ferguson where it joins Mississippi River; seat of Washington co; trade and processing center of fertile Mississippi-Yazoo delta area. Industries: saws, metal products, automobile parts. Inc. 1886. Pop. (1970) 39,648.

Greenville, city in E North Carolina, on Tar River; seat of Pitt co; site of East Carolina University (1907). Founded 1786 and named for patriot Gen. Nathanael Greene of American Revolution. Pop. (1970) 29,063.

Greenville, city in NW South Carolina, on Reedy River; seat of Greenville co; site of Furman University (1825), Bob Jones University (1927). Industries: textiles, clothing, chemicals, machinery, electronic equipment. Settled 1797; inc. 1907. Pop. (1970) 61,436.

Greenville, Treaty of Fort (1795), agreement signed by Indians of Ohio and Indiana after their defeat by US Gen. Anthony Wayne in the Battle of Fallen Timbers. The Indians ceded most of their lands giving the United States full control of the Northwest Territory. The agreement restored peace between the United States and the Indians and broke the British-Indian alliance.

Greenwich, borough of Greater London, SE England, on S bank of the Thames River; site of the Royal Observatory (1675–1958), royal palace (1433) housing the Royal Naval College, and Greenwich Hospital. The Greenwich meridian serves as basis for standard time and nautical calculation throughout the world, accepted by Washington Meridian Conference (1884). Pop. 235,549.

Greenwich, residential town in SW Connecticut, on Long Island Sound, on New York border. Industries: publishing, printing. Settled as part of New York 1640; annexed by Connecticut 1656. Pop. (1970) 59,775.

Greenwich Time, Greenwich Mean Time (GMT), or **Greenwich Civil Time (GCT),** system of time reckoning based on mean solar time as measured on the Greenwich (0°) meridian. Calculated from 0 hours to 24 hours, it is equivalent to Universal Time.

Gregoras, Nicephorus (*c.*1295–*c.*1360), Byzantine scholar and theologian, best known for his voluminous historical writings on the 150 years before his death. A Platonist, he served as a diplomat for the Greek Orthodox church but, becoming involved in a controversial theological dispute, was forced to retire to a monastery.

Gregorian Chant, religious music of the Roman Catholic Church, named for Pope Gregory I (590–604) but believed to have originated after Gregory. The music is sung by choir and soloists, with simple melodies and no accompaniment, steady rhythms, and religious text. △1100.

Gregory, (Lady) Augusta (Persse) (1859–1932), Irish playwright. She recorded the folklore, humor, and dialect of the peasants of western Ireland in such one-act plays as *Spreading of the News* (1904) and *The Rising of the Moon* (1907). With W.B.Yeats she organized the Abbey Theatre of Dublin and toured the United States with it in 1911. *See also* Abbey Theatre.

Gregory I, Roman Catholic pope (590–604) and saint. A Benedictine monk, he was concerned for the poor. When consecrated, he maintained his belief in monasticism as a new life for the church. He removed lay officials from the Vatican, warned against fanaticism, and initiated the conversion of Anglo-Saxons through the Benedictine order, earning the title "The Great." △1052.

Gregory VII, Roman Catholic pope (1073–85) and saint, b. Hildebrand. His pontificate was filled with conflict and an unsuccessful plot was made on his life because of his relation with King Henry IV, who was later excommunicated. A reformer, he opposed simony, increased the papacy's temporal power, and tried to free the clergy from family and civil ties. △1072, 1086.

Gregory IX, Roman Catholic pope (1227–41), b. Ugolino di Segni (*c.*1143). Made cardinal deacon by his uncle, Pope Innocent III, he served as a papal legate to Germany. He ordered the 1233 Inquisition and placed the Dominicans in charge of it. In 1234, he formed the Decretals, a code of canon law still used in the 20th century.

Gregory XI, Roman Catholic pope (1370–78), b. Pierre Roger de Beaufort (1331) in France. The last of the Avignon popes, he was advised by Catherine of Sienna to move back to Rome in 1377. His concern for recovering lands of the papal states led to war. He issued the first condemnation of John Wycliffe's teachings.

Gregory XII, Roman Catholic pope (1406–15) b. Angelo Corrario (*c.*1327). In 1390, he was appointed the Latin patriarch of Constantinople and later served as secretary to Pope Innocent VII. Because he failed to end the Great Schism, cardinals demanded his resignation and elected a new pope. He was a cardinal bishop when he died.

Gregory XIII, Roman Catholic pope (1572–85), b. Ugo Buoncompagni (1502). He served as a papal legate to France and Belgium. Concerned with education, he supported schools, training the clergy, and missionary work, giving special support to the work of the Jesuits. He restored the Catholic Church in Poland.

Gregory of Nazianzus, Saint (*c.*330–*c.*390), Roman Catholic bishop, theologian, and Doctor of the Church. He was born in Cappadocia (now in Turkey) and became a friend of St Basil the Great, who made him a bishop. For a time Gregory was patriarch of Constantinople, upholding the Nicene Creed against the Arian heresy, but retired to lead a monastic life and write. During his career he produced more than 680 poems, letters, and orations. His most important contribution was his exposition of the Trinity: God the Father, God the Son, and God the Holy Spirit.

Gregory of Tours, Saint (*c.*538–593), bishop and historian of Gaul. After he became bishop of Tours in 573 he used his influence to end political feuds. He is most important, however, for his writings. His *History of the Franks* consists of two books on current affairs which are major sources on his times. He also wrote on miracles, martyrs, and church fathers.

Grenada, State of, island republic in SE Caribbean Sea 90mi (145km) N of Venezuela. The country consists of Grenada, the southernmost of the Windward Islands, and the smaller islands of Carriacou and Petit Martinique. The main island, covered with forested, volcanic mountains, is 21mi (34km) long and 12mi (19km) wide. The economy is almost entirely agricultural. Over 50% of the population is of African descent and another 40% is mixed African and East Indian. There are a few Carib Indians (the original inhabitants) and a few whites. Christianity predominates. About 93% of the people are literate. An independent nation within the British Commonwealth, Grenada is ruled by a governor general, appointed on recommendation of the prime minister. There is also a House of Representatives and a Senate. Discovered by Christopher Columbus in 1498, the island was colonized by the French in 1650. Ceded to the British in 1763, it remained a British colony until 1974 when it became an independent nation. It has been a member of the United Nations since 1974.

PROFILE

Official name: State of Grenada
Area: 120sq mi (310sq km)
Population: 87,300
Density: 728per sq mi (281.7per sq km)
Chief city: Saint George's (capital)
Government: associated state of Great Britain
Language: English (official)
Monetary unit: East Caribbean dollar
Gross national product: $30,000,000
Per capita income: $300
Agriculture (major products): bananas, coconut, nutmeg
Trading partners (major): Great Britain

Grenade. △1810.

Grenadine Islands, archipelago in S Windward Islands, at E end of Caribbean Sea; extends over 60mi (97km) between Grenada and Saint Vincent in West Indies; includes approx. 600 small islands; S Grenadines are included in independent state of Grenada. Industries: cotton, limes, livestock, tourism. Pop. 13,247.

Horace Greeley

Nathanael Greene

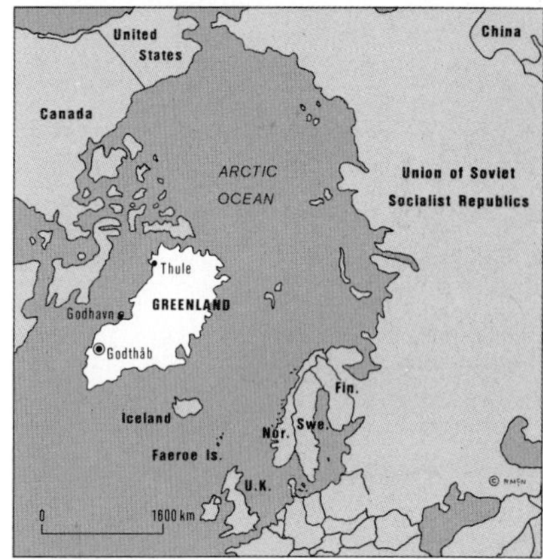
United States
China
Canada
ARCTIC OCEAN
Union of Soviet Socialist Republics
Thule
GREENLAND
Godhavn
Godthåb
Iceland
Fin.
Nor.
Swe.
Faeroe Is.
U.K.
0
1600 km

Greenland

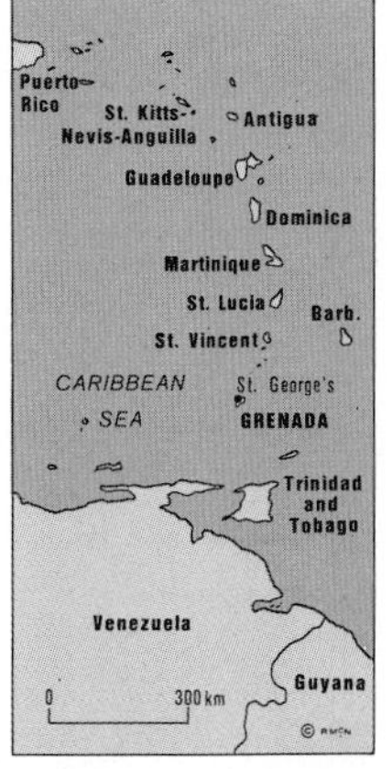
Puerto Rico
St. Kitts
Nevis-Anguilla
Antigua
Guadeloupe
Dominica
Martinique
St. Lucia
Barb.
St. Vincent
CARIBBEAN SEA
St. George's
GRENADA
Trinidad and Tobago
Venezuela
Guyana
0
300 km

Grenada

Grendel, half-human monster, adversary of Beowulf in the great Old English epic of about the 8th century. Grendel was one of Cain's descendants and the personification of evil. He threatened and murdered the Danes of Hrothgar's Hall until the hero, Beowulf, a young warrior of the Geats, destroyed him by tearing off his arm.

Grenoble, city in SE France, on Isère River; surrounded by French Alps; capital of Isère dept.; capital of Dauphiné until 1349 when lands passed to the crown; site of University of Grenoble (1339), nuclear research center (1959), 13th-century cathedral, winter Olympics (1968). Industries: chemicals, plastics, kid gloves, sports equipment. Pop. 161,616.

Grenville, George (1712–70), English statesman; member of Parliament from 1741; navy treasurer (1756–62), first lord of the admiralty (1762–63), and prime minister (1763–65). He was responsible for the Stamp Act, which provoked violent reactions in the colonies and eventually caused the downfall of his ministry. *See also* Stamp Act.

Grenville, William Wyndham, Baron (1759–1834), English prime minister. A longtime friend of the younger William Pitt and a supporter of Roman Catholic emancipation, he formed the "ministry of all the talents" (1806–07) after Pitt's death. *See also* Pitt, William.

Gresham's Law, or "bad money drives out good money." Specifically, the law means that if two kinds of money, say gold and silver coins, are in circulation, and if gold is overvalued at the US mint while silver is simultaneously undervalued, then people will spend gold coins and hoard silver ones.

Grey, Charles, Second Earl (1764–1845), British prime minister. During his administration (1830–34), the First Reform Bill was passed (1832). Grey supported limited parliamentary reform, although he himself was in the Whig party's right wing.

Grey, Lady Jane (1537–54), Queen of England. A cousin of Edward VI, she was married to Guilford Dudley, son of the duke of Northumberland, as part of the duke's scheme to oust the Tudor dynasty. On Edward VI's death in 1553, she was proclaimed queen, but Princess Mary's claim quickly was established and Lady Jane was executed in February 1554. *See also* Mary I.

Grey, Zane (1875–1939), US novelist, b. Zanesville, Ohio. One of the best-known writers in the western genre, his most popular novel was *Riders of the Purple Sage* (1912). His cowboy stories present brawny heroes, loyal to the ethics of the frontier, who overcome callous villains. He was also a noted writer on fishing.

Greyhound, a coursing dog (hound group) known 2700 BC in ancient Egypt and favored by royalty over the centuries. Traditionally used to hunt hare, it is also used for racing. A graceful dog, it has a long, tapered head and muzzle; small ears thrown back and folded; dark, bright eyes; broad, muscular back; well-arched loin; long legs; and a long, fine, tapered tail. The short, smooth coat can be any color. Average size: 26in (66cm) high at shoulder; 65lb (29kg). *See also* Hounds.

Gribble. △486.

Grieg, Edvard (1843–1907), Norwegian composer. Called the "Chopin of the North," he used Norwegian folk themes in his music, much of which is for the piano or voice. Among his best-known works are the song "I Love Thee," the two *Peer Gynt* suites for orchestra, and the immensely popular *Piano Concerto in A minor.* △1246.

Griffenfeld, Peder Schumacher, Count (1635–99), Danish statesman. Well-educated son of a wine merchant, he became secretary to Frederick III in 1665, and was made a count in 1673. His draft of the King's Law establishing absolute monarchy was delivered to Christian V. His efforts to establish peace with Sweden resulted in war (1675). In 1676 he was unjustly charged with treason. Pardoned on the scaffold, he spent his remaining years in prison.

Griffith, Arthur (1872–1922), politician and a founder of the Irish Free State. He edited "The United Irishman" (1899–1906), which proclaimed the Sinn Fein policy of national self-reliance. He was president of the Sinn Fein party (1910) and of Dail Eireann (1922). △1314.

Griffith, Clark (Calvin) (1869–1955), US baseball player and executive, b. Stringtown, Mo. A major league pitcher who won 236 games, mostly in the 1890s, he was also owner of the Washington Senators (now Minnesota Twins). He was elected to the Baseball Hall of Fame in 1946.

Griffith, D(avid) W(ark) (1875–1948), US filmmaker, b. La Grange, Ky. He directed the first of his 500 short films for the Biograph Company in 1908. For these films he greatly advanced the expressive range of cinematic techniques. His feeling for realistic narrative and characterization and his sense of varied composition, lighting, and dramatic editing (montage) established the art of film in the United States. His principal feature films include *Enoch Arden* (1911); *The Birth of a Nation* (1915); *Intolerance,* a complex masterpiece that failed commercially (1916); *Broken Blossoms* (1918); *Way Down East* (1920); *Orphans of the Storm* (1922); and *Isn't Life Wonderful* (1924). *See also* Birth of a Nation, The; Montage. △1316.

Griffon, or griffon vulture, carrion-eating bird of prey of Eurasia and N Africa. It has gold or sandy-brown plumage. Gregarious, large flocks nest in caves or on cliffs. A single white, often flecked, egg is laid. Length: 40in (102cm). Species *Gyps fulvus.*

Grijalva, Juan de (*c.* 1489–1527), Spanish conquistador. He led an expedition along the Mexican coast from Yucatán to modern Veracruz, where he received gifts of gold sent by Montezuma.

Grimaldi, Genoese Guelph (pro-papal) family of Middle Ages, and lords of Monaco from 15th century. With the Fieschi, the Grimaldi were leaders in Genoa's mid-13th-century pro-Angevin struggle against Emperor Frederick II, which began a long period of ties to the house of Anjou. In 1419 a branch of the family took possession of Monaco and in 1659 assumed the title of prince, now held by Prince Rainier III (reigned 1949–).

Grimké, Sarah (1792–1873) and **Angelina** (1805–79), US abolitionists and feminists, b. Charleston, S.C. Sisters in a wealthy Southern family, the two women went North and joined the Society of Friends. They soon became involved in the antislavery movement, writing abolitionist appeals to Southerners (1836). Opposition to their speaking against slavery in public places led to their demand for women's rights.

Grimm, Jacob Ludwig Karl (1785–1863) and **Wilhelm Karl** (1786–1859), eminent German philologists. They are best remembered for their collections of folklore. Jacob collected the tales from German peasants, and Wilhelm arranged them. The first volume of the tales was published in 1812, the second in 1815, and a volume of historical notes in 1822. Some of the best-known tales are "Snow-White," "Rumplestiltskin," "Tom Thumb," "The Golden Goose," "Hansel and Gretel," and "Rapunzel."

Grimm's Law. A landmark in the history of the scientific study of language, the law of consonantal mutations was first developed in Jacob Grimm's *Deutsche Grammatik* (1822). Grimm discovered significant correlations among German and other Indo-European languages, demonstrating that sound changes are not random, but a regular process. The importance of the finding lay in its successful application of the genetic method to philology, and in its rejection of the speculative approach to the history of language.

Grimsby, seaport in E central England, near mouth of Humber River estuary, Humberside; one of world's leading fishing ports; trades in fish, grain, coal, timber. Industries: frozen and processed foods, chemicals. Pop. 95,685.

Grinding Machine, or grinder. △1606.

Gris, Juan (1887–1927), Spanish painter and writer. He settled in Paris in 1906 and, with Picasso and Braque, became a leading cubist artist. His later works included collages, architectonic paintings, richly colored still lifes, and stage sets and costumes for Diaghilev. *See also* Cubism. △1296.

Grisaille, a painting executed entirely in shades of gray. It may be the first stage of an oil painting, the model for an engraver to work from, or a work in its own right.

Grissom, Virgil (1926–67), US astronaut, b. Mitchell, Ind. He was a member of the first US space team (Mercury program) and was the second American in space (1961). He was killed in a flash fire while training for a moon flight.

Grist Mill. △350.

Griswold v. Connecticut (1965), landmark US Supreme Court decision in which Justice William O. Douglas developed the "penumbra theory" of the right to privacy as protected by the First Amendment. The Court invalidated a state anti-contraceptive law.

Grivas, George (1898–1974), a Greek general who led the Greeks of Cyprus in rebellion against Great Britain from 1955–1959. He formed the EOKA force to fight for *enosis* (union with Greece) but clashed with Archbishop Makarios and retired. He returned in 1964 but could not achieve his goal.

Grizzly Bear, large omnivorous brown bear once widespread in W North America, now rare except in W Canada, Alaska, and Yellowstone and Glacier parks. Length: to 8ft (2.4m); weight: 790lb (356kg). Species *Ursus horribilis.*

Grodno, city in Belorussian SSR, USSR; 150mi (242km) W of Minsk, on Neman River, near Poland and Lithuanian boundaries; capital of Grodno oblast. City was taken by Lithuanian forces 14th century; part of 1569 Polish-Lithuanian union; annexed to Russia with partition of Poland 1795; occupied by Germany in WWI and WWII; became part of the Soviet Union July 16, 1944; site of 12th-century ruins of Borisoglebsk Church, castle built by King Stephen of Poland (1586), 16th–17th-century baroque churches. Industries: wool, leather, tobacco, furniture, glass, electrical equipment, automobile parts, bicycles, appliances, chemicals. Pop. 132,000.

Groin, an artificial dam of rocks or wooden pilings that juts out from a beach face, causing sand to accumulate against the updrift side. Groins are now considered a less effective and more expensive way of maintaining beaches than a beach-nourishment program. △268.

Gromyko, Andrei (1909–), Soviet diplomat. In 1943 he was appointed ambassador to the United States and took part in the Yalta and Potsdam Conferences. In 1946 he became Soviet representative to the United Nations and in 1952 ambassador to Britain. After being appointed to the Communist party Central Committee in 1956, he was made foreign minister in 1957.

Groningen, city in NE Netherlands; capital of Groningen prov.; fine medieval buildings; trade center for regional agricultural products. Industries: textiles, machinery, printing. Pop. 168,843.

Grooming, behavior pattern of self-care, usually stereotyped, practiced by many animals. Mutual grooming, such as fur grooming among monkeys and apes, serves to cement pair-bonding and social bonds in groups.

Gropius, Walter (1883–1969), German-born architect and director of Bauhaus (1919–28). He pioneered the functional design that became known as the International Style. Its principles are embodied in his Fagus Factory at Alfeld (1911) and in the US embassy at Athens (1957–61). He joined the Harvard University architecture school in 1937. *See also* Bauhaus; International Style. △1298.

Gros, (Baron) Antoine-Jean. △1228.

Grosbeak, finches with large, seed-cracking beaks that frequent wooded areas throughout much of the world, feeding on seeds, grain, fruits, and tree buds. The males are bright red, yellow, or blue; the females are duller, often brownish. Brown-spotted, blue or greenish eggs (2–5) are laid in cup-shaped, rootlet-lined nests built in trees or bushes. Length: 6–10in (15–25cm). Family Fringillidae.

Grossglockner, peak in S Austria, in the Hohe Tauern range in the Tirol Alps. Highest point in Austria, 12,460ft (3,800m).

Gross National Product (GNP), total market value of all final goods and services produced in the economy in one year. GNP is equal to consumption plus investment plus government expenditures plus net exports. It is also equal to the payments to the factors of production such as wages and salaries, rental income, interest, incorporated and unincorporated income and capital consumption allowance, and indirect business taxes. Since the price level changes over time, current GNP is adjusted for such changes and real GNP is obtained for some base period "normal" price level. △1386.

Grosvenor, Gilbert Hovey (1875–1966), US geographer, writer, and conservationist, b. Turkey. In 1899 he became president of the National Geographic Society, and in 1903 he became editor of the *National Geographic Magazine.* Under his administration, the society increased its membership and undertook numerous geographical explorations. He wrote several books, including *Young Russia* (1914) and *Discovery and Exploration* (1924).

Gros Ventres, an Algonquian-speaking tribe of North American Indians occupying the Milk and Missouri rivers, Montana, and nearby Saskatchewan. They are a division of the Arapaho who separated in early days and formed a distinct group. They number approximately 1,000 persons today, living on the Fort Belknap Reservation in Montana. *See also* Hidatsa.

Grosz, George (1893–1959), German illustrator and painter. He savagely satirized corruption in Germany in books of pen drawings and caricatures, such as *Ecce Homo* (1920). He had to flee Germany and came to the United States in 1932, where he continued to satirize bourgeois materialism. His paintings, however, are lyrical and romantic.

Grotefend, Georg Friedrich (1775–1853) German classical scholar. He pioneered the decipherment of the cuneiform (wedge-shaped) script, first copied at Persepolis in Iran in 1802, deducing correctly that the inscriptions were in three languages.

Grotius, or **De Groot, Hugo** (1583–1645), Dutch jurist and statesman. He is considered a founder of international law. He held the chief political office of Rotterdam from 1613 until 1618, when he was ousted by political foes. He was sentenced to life imprisonment but escaped in 1621 and lived in Paris. His most famous work was *De Jure Belli et Pacis* (The Law of War and Peace, 1625).

Groton, town in SE Connecticut, 45mi (72km) E of New Haven, on Long Island Sound and Thames River opposite New London. Town is site of Fort Griswold, taken September 1781 by British force headed by Benedict Arnold; US Navy submarine base, site of 1954 launching of the *Nautilus*, the first nuclear-powered submarine. Industries: shipbuilding, agriculture, fishing. Settled 1650; inc. 1705. Pop. (1970) 38,244.

Ground Beetle, predatory beetle found worldwide and often seen running on the ground or hiding under rocks or logs. Length: 1/8–3 1/3in (3–85mm). Family Carabidae. △500.

Groundhog. *See* Woodchuck.

Ground Pine, any of several club mosses with creeping stems and erect branches whose foliage somewhat resembles pine needles. *See* Club Moss.

Groundsel, large worldwide genus of herbaceous annual and perennial plants and woody shrubs and small trees. Perennial golden groundsel or ragwort *(Senecio aureus)* of E North America has flat-topped clusters of yellow, daisy-like flowers. Height: 2ft (61cm). Family Compositae. *See also* Ragwort.

Ground squirrel, small, terrestrial squirrel of Eurasia, Africa, and North America. Active by day, they find shelter in burrows or crevices and eat plants, seeds, insects, and sometimes eggs and small animals. Most have grayish-red to brown fur; some are striped or spotted. Length, excluding tail: 4.5–13.5in. (11.4–34cm.); weight: 0.25–1.75lbs. (113–793g). Genus *Citellus*.

Ground State, lowest possible energy level of an atom, ion, molecule. *See also* Excited State.

Ground Water, water that lies in a zone beneath the surface of the earth. The water comes chiefly from the atmosphere, although some is of volcanic or sedimentary origin. Ground water moves through rocks and soil and can be tapped by wells. △254.

Group Dynamics, area of social psychology concerned with the ways members of groups interact with each other and come to decisions or otherwise achieve the group's purpose. The term was originated by Kurt Lewin in the 1930s. Studies of group dynamics are concerned with such matters as how individual group members influence each other, how problems can be solved collectively, how individuals are affected by group (conformity) pressures, and how effective the group finds different styles of leadership. Findings from such studies have many practical implications—constructing groups for maximum effectiveness, developing management techniques, etc.

Grouper, tropical marine fish found from Florida to South America and in Indo-Pacific oceans. It has a large mouth, sharp teeth, mottled pattern, and ability to change color. Length: to 12ft (3.6m); weight: 50–1,000lbs. (23–450kg). Family Serranidae; species giant, *Epinephelus itajara* and Queensland, *Epinephelus lanceolatus*.

Group Insurance, any insurance plan under which a number of persons and their dependents are insured under a single policy. This policy is issued to their employer or to the institution with which they are affiliated (for example, a union). Individual certificates are given to each insured person.

Group Theatre (1929–41), an offspring of the Theatre Guild of New York, which provided American theater with innovation and excitement during the 1930s. In 1931 theater luminaries Lee Strasberg, Cheryl Crawford, and Harold Clurman were in charge. The group produced several American classics: Sidney Kingsley's Pulitzer Prize-winning *Men in White* (1933), William Saroyan's *My Heart's in the Highlands* (1939), and many of Clifford Odets' best works, including *Awake and Sing* and *Waiting for Lefty*. It also developed an ensemble of fine actors including John Garfield, Frances Farmer, Sylvia Sidney, Morris Carnovsky, Elia Kazan, and Lee J. Cobb.

Group Theory, branch of abstract algebra applicable to symmetry properties. A group is a collection of entities, with associated operations, obeying a specific set of rules (associative law, existence of an inverse, etc). The theory is concerned with the properties of such groups. It was developed mainly by the French mathematician Evariste Galois during the early 19th century in his study of the solutions of equations and has many applications in mathematics and physical science. The symmetry elements of an object, for example—operations, such as rotations, that bring an object back to its original position—form a group. Group theory is particularly useful in quantum mechanics, spectroscopy, and theories of elementary particles. △1458, 1468.

Group Therapy, psychotherapy practiced in a group situation, in which the group itself usually becomes an integral part of the treatment. Though the amount of time the therapist spends with any individual patient in group therapy is minimal, this form of therapy offers several distinct advantages. Group influence is a very powerful aid to therapeutic suggestion, and the group generates an atmosphere of mutual helping, support, and constructive criticism, which in turn builds these interpersonal skills in the group members. In family therapy the group members are members of the same family. Groups are frequently organized on the basis of problems that the members have in common, eg, smoking, obesity, sexual difficulties, aging. △774.

Grouse, plump game bird of N Northern Hemisphere. Hen-to-turkey-sized, they are fowllike but have feathered tarsi and toes enabling them to walk on snow, feathered nostrils, and often distensible, brightly-colored air sacs on their neck. Some species, such as the ptarmigan, are seasonally monogamous, with males helping rear the young; others, including the sage grouse, are polygamous and the males do not help with the young. Family Tetraonidae. *See also* Capercaillie; Prairie Chicken; Ptarmigan; Sage Grouse.

Grove, Lefty (1900–), US baseball player, b. Robert Moses Grove in Lonaconing, Md. A left-hand pitcher, he played for the Philadelphia Athletics (1925–33) and the Boston Red Sox (1934–41), won 300 games, and struck out over 2,200 batters. He was elected to the Baseball Hall of Fame in 1947.

Grove Snail. △482.

Growth, irreversible process in an organism that increases its size, weight, or protein content. This process involves cell division or enlargement, or the addition of outside material. △788.

Growth Curve, graphic plotting of growth measurements as they vary with time. Growth results from cell division or enlargement and is evident by an increase in size, weight, or amount of outside materials absorbed. As time progresses, the resulting curve may be linear, S-shaped, or irregular.

Growth Factor, substance required by an organism for its growth but which it is unable to synthesize and must therefore obtain from its diet. *See also* Vitamin.

Growth Hormone, or **Somatotropin,** protein hormone produced by the anterior pituitary; it effects general growth of the body. Over-secretion results in acromegaly in the adult, and giantism in the young; under-secretion results in "pituitary dwarfism." △690.

Growth Ring. *See* Annual Ring.

Grenoble, France

Greyhound

Angelina Grimké

Sarah Grimké

Grozny (Groznyj), city in Russian SFSR, USSR, in Caucasus Mts; capital of Checheno-Ingush ASSR. An oil-producing center since 1893, city has pipeline terminus to Black Sea and Donets Basin. Industries: oil, petrochemicals, food processing, machinery, sawmills, wood products. Founded 1818 as a fort on Russian frontier. Pop. 341,000.

Grünewald, Matthias (*c.*1475–1528), German painter, b. Mathis Gothart Neithart. Although a contemporary of Dürer, he was almost untouched by the Renaissance, except in his use of perspective and his feeling for light and color. He used Renaissance techniques only to heighten the emotional impact of his late Gothic imagery. His greatest work was the folding altarpiece for Isenheim Monastery in Alsace (1513–15), a majestic sequence of religious scenes with great variations in mood and level of intensity; the facial expressions are exalted and passionate. △1144.

Grunion, also smelt, marine silverfish found in shallow tropical and temperate waters, particularly along Baja and S California coast. It spawns en masse high on the beach at the highest tide; eggs hatch at the next high tide. Family Atherinidae; species *Leuresthes tennis.*

Grunt, marine fish found in shallow tropical waters of W Atlantic and Pacific. A deep-bodied fish with large mouth, it produces sounds by grinding pharyngeal teeth. Family Pomadasyidae; species includes bluestripe *Haemulon sciurus.*

GSA. *See* General Services Administration.

Guacharo. *See* Oilbird.

Guadalajara, city in SW Mexico, near Santiago River; capital of Jalisco state; site of 16th–17th-century cathedral, governor's palace (1643), university, theater, state museum, baroque churches, direct railroad line to United States; noted for scenic beauty and mild climate. Industries: wheat, corn, peanuts, fruit, textiles, brewing, metal goods, tourism. Founded 1531; est. 1542. Pop. 1,196,218.

Guadalajara, town in central Spain, 34mi (55km) NE of Madrid; capital of Guadalajara prov.; ruled by Moors 8th-11th centuries; captured by Christians 1085; site of the Infantado Palace (1461), Roman bridge. Crops: cereals, vegetables, olives, grapes, fruit. Industries: woolens, leather, soap. Area: (prov.) 4,707sq mi (12,191sq km). Pop. (city) 31,917; (prov.) 147,732.

Guadalcanal, tropical island in W central Pacific Ocean, approx. 600mi (966km) E of New Guinea; largest island of British Solomon Island Protectorate. Inhabitants are mostly Melanesians. Port of Honiara is government center, and site of an international airport; scene of heavy fighting between Japanese and US forces in WWII. Crops: coconuts and lumber. Discovered 1788 by English. Area: 2,510sq mi (6,501sq km). Pop. 23,922. △1338.

Guadalquivir, river in S Spain; rises in the Sierra de Cazorla; flows W and SW, empties into Gulf of Cadiz; serves as source of irrigation for near Sierra Morena; site of several hydroelectric plants. Length: 408mi (657km).

Guadalupe-Hidalgo, Treaty of (1848), signed by the United States and Mexico to end the Mexican War. Long negotiations between Nicholas Trist and Santa Anna were stalled until Mexico City finally fell. The United States acquired the present states of Texas, California, Nevada, Utah, New Mexico, and Arizona plus parts of Wyoming and Colorado. The United States agreed to pay $15,000,000 and to pay Mexican debts owed to Americans.

Guadalupe Mountains National Park, park in W Texas. The mountains rise from the desert and contain portions of the world's most extensive Permian limestone fossil reef. The park also features a tremendous earth fault, lofty peaks, and unusual flora and fauna. Area: 81,077acres (32,836hectares). Est. 1966.

Guadeloupe, overseas French department in E West Indies, in Leeward Islands; comprised of islands of Basse-Terre (Guadeloupe proper) (W), Grande Terre (E), and several lesser dependencies. Basse Terre (city) is capital and Pointe-à-Pitre is chief port and trade center. Discovered 1493 by Christopher Columbus; settled 1635 by French; dept. est. 1946. Exports: rum, pineapples, sugar, bananas, coffee. Tourism is main industry. Area: 683sq mi (1,769sq km). Pop. 327,000.

Guadiana, river in S central Spain; rises in La Mancha Plateau; flows W then S to form part of the Spanish-Portuguese border; empties into the Gulf of Cádiz; used for irrigation in the Merida region of Spain; source of hydroelectric power and transportation. Length: 510mi (821km).

Guam, southernmost and largest of the Mariana Islands, in W Pacific Ocean; an unincorporated US territory. Approx. half the inhabitants are Chamorros, a Micronesian people; site of US Navy base and large carved stones that may have been erected by an ancient culture previous to the immigration of the Chamorro. Guam was the first US territory to be occupied by Japan during WWII (1941). Discovered 1521 by Ferdinand Magellan. Area: approx. 209sq mi (541sq km). Pop. 86,926.

Guan, medium-sized game bird found in Central and South American tropical forests, feeding mainly on fruit. They are greenish, brownish, or grayish with brownish-red or coppery markings. Family Cracidae.

Guanaco. *See* Llama.

Guanay, white-breasted Peruvian cormorant; a bird that feeds on anchovies in the Humboldt Current area. It is the main source of the fertilizer guano. Length: 20–40in (51–102cm). Species *Phalacrocorax bougainvilli.*

Guangzhou. *See* Canton.

Guano, dried excrement of sea birds and bats. It contains phosphorous, nitrogen, and potassium and is a natural fertilizer. It is found mainly on certain coastal islands off South America and Africa. △624.

Guantánamo, city in E Cuba, 10mi (16km) N of Guantánamo Bay; trade and agricultural center; served by port of Caimanera on Guantánamo Bay; site of US naval station and airport. Pop. 130,061.

Guaraní Indians, concentrated in S Brazil and in Paraguay. The Guaraní who remained independent and not collected in Jesuit missions are distinguished from the Christianized Guaraní by the name "Cainguá." The Guaraní language still is spoken by mestizos and acculturated Indians of the area; it is the second official language of Paraguay.

Guaranteed Annual Income, any of several proposed programs in which a family is guaranteed a certain base income by the government. The income the family earns is therefore supplemented by the amount necessary to raise them to the base level. The major criticism of guaranteed annual income programs is that they provide no incentive to earn income. *See also* Negative Income Tax.

Guaranteed Annual Wage, employer's assurance to his employees that they will have some minimum level of wages or work over the year. Although the idea began in the late 19th century, the movement has never really attracted many supporters; although a variation, the supplemental unemployment benefit, is one goal of workers in some industries.

Guarnieri, a family of violin makers who worked in Cremona, Italy, beginning with **Andrea Guarnieri** (*c.* 1626–1698). His grandnephew **Giuseppi Antonio Guarnieri** (1683–1745) was the greatest craftsman of the family.

Guasave, city in W Mexico, on Sinaloa River. Industries: fishing, livestock, wheat, cotton. Founded 1595 by Spanish as a Guasave Indian mission. Pop. 148,-475.

Guatemala, Republic of, nation in Central America, on the Atlantic (NE), Pacific (S) oceans and bordered by Mexico (W and N), Belize (E), Honduras (E), and El Salvador (E). The country is one of the world's leading coffee producers.

Land and Economy. The Sierra Madre Mts, many of volcanic origin, parallel the Pacific Ocean in the S, branching off into four principal ranges in the N. A mountain plain approx. 30mi (48km) wide extends along the Pacific side for approx. 200mi (322km) from Mexico to El Salvador. The climate is tropical but moderated by the elevation. Although the economy is basically agricultural (coffee and bananas are the chief exports), mining has become increasingly significant. The principal ports, Puerto Barrios on the Atlantic and San Jose on the Pacific, are connected with the capital of Guatemala City by a transcontinental railroad.

People. Over 50% of the people are of Indian origin; the remainder are mostly Ladinos (mixed Spanish and Indian). The majority of the people are Roman Catholic and Spanish speaking. Elementary education is free and compulsory.

Government. A republic, the government is invested in three departments: executive, with a president elected for 6 years and ineligible for reelection for another 12 years; legislative, with a unicameral National Congress, elected every 4 years; judicial, with a Supreme Court and lesser courts. There is universal suffrage at 18 years of age.

History. The home of the Mayan Empire for 1000 years, Guatemala was occupied by the Spanish from 1524–1821. Under Mexican control until 1823, when it became a member of the United Provinces of Central America, it re-established its independence in 1839. Throughout its history, Guatemala has been characterized by political upheaval and revolution. Justo Rufino Barrios attempted to form a regional union in the late 19th century and although he failed became the national hero. Communists and anti-Communists battled for control after World War II, and the United Fruit Company, a US firm, played a major role in domestic affairs. In the 1970s, Guatemala pressed its claims to Belize, a British colony, and nearly went to war in 1975. In 1976 the nation was rocked by a severe earthquake that left about 25,000 dead and almost 20% of the population homeless.

PROFILE

Official name: Republic of Guatemala
Area: 42,042sq mi (108,889sq km)
Population: 5,690,000
Density: 135.3per sq mi (52.3per sq km)
Chief cities: Guatemala City (capital); San Pedro Carcha
Government: republic
Religion: Roman Catholic
Language: Spanish (official)
Monetary unit: quetzal
Gross national product: $1,860,000,000
Per capita income: $360
Industries (major products): food, beverages, tobacco
Agriculture (major products): coffee, cotton, bananas
Minerals (major): zinc, lead
Trading partners (major): United States, El Salvador, West Germany

Guatemala City, capital city of Guatemala, 50mi (81km) N of the Pacific Ocean, on a plateau in the Sierra Madre; largest city in Central America. Est. 1776 as capital to replace Antigua (which had been destroyed by earthquakes) as the colonial capital of Spanish Central America, city became the capital of the Central American Federation 1823–38; destroyed by earthquakes 1917–18, 1976; political, cultural, commercial, transportation, and educational center; site of the national and presidential palaces, a cathedral (1782–1815), San Carlos University (1676). Exports: coffee, minerals, gold, copper, silver, lead. Industries: mining, furniture, textiles, clothing, food processing, handcrafts. Founded 1527. Pop. (municipal) 730,991.

Guava, trees and shrubs native to tropical America and the West Indies and the source of fruits of the same name. The large white flowers produce a 4in(10cm) berry-like fruit, usually yellow with white, pink, or yellow flesh. The 140 species include the common *Psidium guajava* and the strawberry guava *(P. cattleyanum),* with purplish-red fruits. Family Myrtaceae.

Guayaquil, city and port in W Ecuador, on the Guayas River, 40mi (64km) inland from Pacific coast; capital of Guayas prov. it is largest city of Ecuador. In 17th and 18th centuries city was frequently attacked and burned by buccaneers. Industries: textiles, leather goods, soap, alcohol. Founded 1535 by Sebastián de Benalcázar of Spain. Pop. 794,300.

Guaymas, port city in NW Mexico, on Gulf of California, near Yaqui River; noted for excellent fishing; resort area. Exports: gold and silver ores, cotton, pearls, tobacco. Industries: shipping, lumber, shark liver oil extracting, tourism. Est. in early 18th century by Jesuit missionaries. Pop. 60,981.

Guayule, shrub native to desert regions of N Mexico and Texas. The latex extracted from it is a commercial source of rubber. Height: 2–3ft (61–91cm). Family Compositae; species *Parthenium argentatum.*

Gubbio, town in central Italy, 23mi (37km) E of Perugia; site of 13th-century church of St Francis and well-preserved Roman theater from 1st century BC; known for its ceramics. Pop. 31,085.

Guchkov, Aleksandr (1862–1936), Russian political figure. He was the founder of the Octobrist party (1905), supporting a constitutional monarchy. In World War I he was head of the Russian Red Cross and chairman of the Central War Industries Committee. He was president of the third Duma and was sent to receive the abdication of Czar Nicholas II. From

March to May 1917 he was minister of war in the provisional government but resigned. He left Russia after the Bolshevik Revolution (November 1917).

Gudgeon, freshwater carp found in rivers from England to Central China. It has a small mouth, fleshy whiskers on the upper lip, elongated body, and variable color. Length: to 15.7in (40cm). Family Cyprinidae; species includes common *Gobio gobio.*

Gudrun, a heroine in old Norse legends, the wife of Sigurd and the sister of Gunnar. She is depicted in several poems as a suffering wife and sister.

Guelph, city in SE Ontario, Canada, 15mi (24km) ENE of Kitchener on the Speed River; site of Ontario Reformatory and University of Guelph (1964). Industries: tobacco warehouses, textiles, electrical appliances, rubber, iron, steel. Founded by novelist John Galt 1827. Pop. 58,364.

Guelphs, Italian pro-papal political faction of Middle Ages, opposed to pro-imperial Ghibellines. "Guelph" derives from "Welf," the name of the German family contending with the Hohenstaufens for the imperial crown in the 12th and 13th centuries, but came to cover the Italian opponents of Hohenstaufen Emperor Frederick II. As each Italian city-state took sides and the Hohenstaufen line died out in 1268, Guelphism came to designate pro-Angevin, pro-papal sympathy into the 15th century.

Guenon, long-tailed, slender, medium-sized monkey of sub-Saharan Africa. They are day-active tree dwellers living in small troops dominated by an old male. Their omnivorous diet consists mainly of fruit, leaves, and roots. They make good pets while young but often turn savage as they grow older. Genus Cercopithecus. *See also* Monkey.

Guereza, Ethiopian name applied to any of several African monkeys of the genus *Colobus* (especially *C. guereza*) that have long white hair along the sides of the body and tail contrasting sharply with the black or reddish ground color. *See also* Colobus.

Guernica, town in N Spain; center of Basque nationalism; site of old oak tree under which medieval Vizcaya parliament met. The severe bombing by Germans during Spanish Civil War (1937) was protested in Pablo Picasso's "Guernica." Industries: food processing, furniture, metallurgy. Pop. 14,678.

Guernsey, second-largest of Channel Islands of United Kingdom, NW of Jersey; constitutes a bailiwick with several smaller islands, including Alderney and Sark. Guernsey breed of dairy cattle was developed here. Capital is St Peter Port. Industries: farming, dairying, tourism, horticulture. Area: 24sq mi (62sq km). Pop. 46,182.

Guernsey, common breed of dairy cattle originally from English Channel Isle of Guernsey. Well-known in the United States, it gives rich, yellow milk, second only to the Jersey breed in butterfat content, but greater in overall volume. Larger than Jerseys, Guernseys are brown and white. Weight: 1,700 lb (765kg). *See also* Dairy Cattle.

Guerrero, Vicente (1782–1831), leader in the struggle for independence and president of Mexico (1829). After the defeat of Morelos, Guerrero carried on the revolution from his base in the south. He supported Iturbide's empire and then the administration of Guadalupe Victoria. A rebellion gave him the presidency, but he was ousted less than nine months later by his vice president and political rival, Anastasio Bustamante.

Guerrilla Warfare, small-scale ground combat operations designed to harass rather than destroy an opponent. Such tactics are often employed by insurgents or irregular soldiers lacking powerful weapons. By conducting limited forays against supply lines and small installations, they are often able to avoid open engagements with conventional military units and tie down a disproportionate share of their adversaries' military strength. Although practiced effectively by such diverse groups as the American revolutionaries of the 18th century and the Viet Cong troops in Southeast Asia, guerrilla warfare is normally not decisive by itself and is generally complemented by conventional combat.

Guevara, Ernesto "Che" (1928–67), revolutionary leader and theorist, a key-figure in Fidel Castro's Cuba. A physician born in Argentina, Guevara became associated with Castro in Mexico and returned with him to Cuba in 1956 to carry out the guerrilla activities directed against the regime of Fulgencio Batista. When Castro came to power, Guevara was placed in charge of economic planning. Guevara disappeared in 1965; two years later he was captured and killed in Bolivia.

Guggenheim, US family of industrialists and philanthropists. **Meyer Guggenheim** (1828–1905), b. Switzerland. Immigrated to Philadelphia in 1847 and prospered in the lace import business. He bought rich silver and lead mines in Colorado and financed smelters. He retired about 1895, leaving control of his enterprises to his 7 living sons. Of these, **Daniel** (1856–1930) took the leading role in expanding the family businesses, becoming president of the resulting firm, the American Smelting & Refining Co., which by 1910 controlled 80% of the world's silver and lead output. A prominent philanthropist, he established the Daniel and Florence Guggenheim Foundation. **Solomon R.** (1861–1949), endowed a foundation to foster nonobjective art. Its museum, designed by Frank Lloyd Wright, opened in New York City in 1959. **Simon** (1867–1941) was a US senator from Colorado and chairman of American Smelting & Refining. In memory of his son, he established the John Simon Guggenheim Memorial Foundation, which provides fellowships for study and research. Meyer's other sons were **Isaac** (1854–1922); **Murray** (1858–1939); **Benjamin** (1865–1912), lost on the *Titanic;* and **William** (1868–1941).

Harry Frank Guggenheim (1890–1971), son of Daniel, promoted the family's interests in Chile and was US ambassador to Cuba (1929–33). **Peggy Guggenheim** (1898–), daughter of Benjamin, was a patron and collector of modern art.

Guggenheim Museum. △1322.

Guiana, Dutch. *See* Surinam.

Guiana Highlands (Guiana Massif), mountainous tableland in N South America, extends from Venezuela to French Guiana; includes forested plateau, mountains of crystalline rocks, sandstone, lava caps, and waterfalls, notably Angel Falls, the world's highest waterfall, 3,212ft (979m). Products: cedar, mahogany, vanilla, rubber, medicinal plants, gold, diamonds. Length: approx 1,200mi (1,932km). Width: 200–600mi (322–966km).

Guidance System, Spacecraft, system of gyroscopes, detectors, radar antennae, receivers, computers, vernier engines, and other elements necessary to stabilize, correct, and control a space vehicle path. Gyroscopes define the coordinate axes of the body, and detectors measure differences between these directions and the planned ones. Servomechanisms operate vernier engines or swing gimbaled nozzles to correct errors. Tracking radar dishes follow the craft. Balloons or aircraft give meteorological data to central computers, which determine adjustments necessary to correct for atmospheric conditions.

Guided Missile, missile capable of being controlled during the major part of its flight, either by ground crew or by onboard systems reacting to perceived conditions. Initial guidance is concerned with flight stability on lift-off and is usually handled from the ground. Midcourse guidance places the missile roughly on target. Final guidance makes fine adjustments to the flight path, possibly using information obtained from the target itself. △1734.

Guide Fossil. *See* Index Fossil.

Guild, one of many organizations formed by special interest or skilled groups during the Middle Ages, from about the 10th to the 15th centuries. In the period of feudalism, guilds were formed for self-protection, social life, and profit by those outside the rural manorial system. In 10th-century England, the London peace-guild was formed to protect city land owners. In the 12th and 13th centuries, craftsmen in towns throughout Europe organized guilds to maintain price and quality levels of goods, to protect their interests, and to supervise the training of apprentices. By the 14th and 15th centuries, there were also religious guilds, burial guilds, merchant and moneylender guilds. At first self-governing, guilds in the later Middle Ages were subject to municipalities and became politically influential. The longest-lasting guilds were those made up of teachers and students; these were primarily responsible for the forming of the university system. △1090.

Guildford, city in Surrey, SE England, on Wey River 26mi (42km) SW of London. A market center and seat of University of Surrey (1966), it has many historic buildings. Industries: engineering, plastics, knitwear. Pop. 56,887.

Guild Socialism, type of British socialism that advocated government control of the means of produc-

Puerto Rico
St. Kitts
Antigua
Nevis-Anguilla
GUADELOUPE
Basse-Terre
Dominica
Martinique
St. Lucia
St. Vincent
Barb.
CARIBBEAN SEA
Grenada
Trinidad and Tobago
Venezuela
0
300 km
Guyana
Guadeloupe

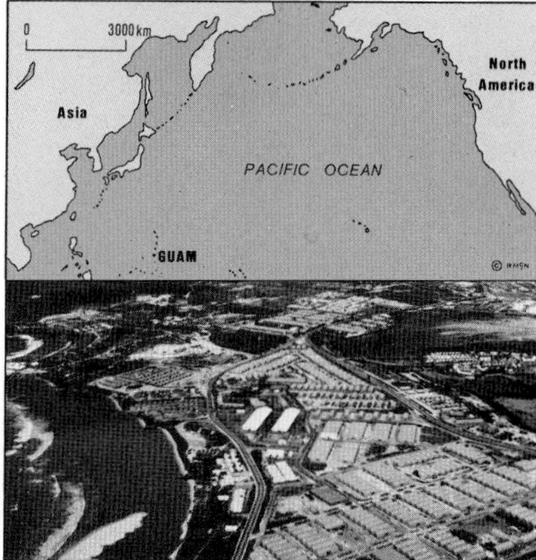
0
3000 km
Asia
North America
PACIFIC OCEAN
GUAM
Guam

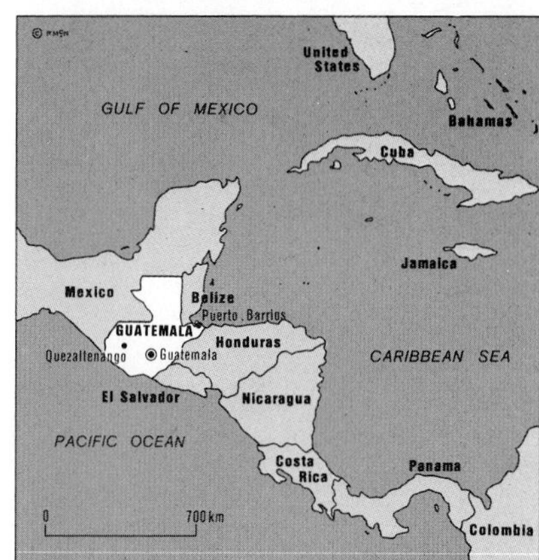
United States
GULF OF MEXICO
Bahamas
Cuba
Jamaica
Mexico
Belize
Puerto Barrios
GUATEMALA
Honduras
Quezaltenango
Guatemala
CARIBBEAN SEA
El Salvador
Nicaragua
PACIFIC OCEAN
Costa Rica
Panama
0
700 km
Colombia
Guatemala

Guatemala: village market

tion and the contracting of workers through national guilds. Based more on the control of industry than direct political involvement, the Guild Socialist movement was prominent from 1906–25, when disorganization and financial troubles caused its effective demise.

Guilford, town in S Connecticut, in SE New Haven co, on Long Island Sound; contains central green surrounded by some of Connecticut's oldest houses; Rev. Henry Whitfield led English settlers here and built stone house (1639–40) which is now a museum. Town named for Guildford, Surrey, England. Industries: publishing, fruit orchards, light manufacturing. Settled 1639. Pop. (1970) 12,033.

Guilford Courthouse, Battle of (March 15, 1781), American Revolutionary conflict near Greensboro, N.C. A force led by British Gen. Charles Cornwallis was confronted by the American troops under Gen. Nathanael Greene and Gen. Daniel Morgan. After the initial engagement, Greene retreated, saving the bulk of his army but inflicting heavy losses on the enemy. Cornwallis was forced to retreat to Wilmington, N.C., for reinforcements.

Guillaume de Lorris (*c.* 1210–37), French romance writer. He began the *Roman de la Rose* (*c.* 1230), an allegory in which a courtly lover becomes enamored of a rosebud whose reflection he sees during a dream. Before the poem was completed, Guillaume died, and Jean de Meung composed the second half. *See also* Jean de Meung; Roman de la Rose.

Guillemot, small, usually black and white seabird of cold Northern Hemisphere coastlines. They dive for ocean-bottom food. Nesting in colonies, they lay oval eggs (2) on rocky coasts. Length: 13in (33cm). Genera *Cepphus* and *Uria*.

Guilt. △786.

Guimarães Rosa, João (1908–67), Brazilian novelist and short-story writer. Noted for his linguistic experimentation and his depiction of life in Brazil's interior backlands, he is his nation's most acclaimed mid-20th-century fiction writer. The intimacy with which he writes about people's problems in the remote backlands derives largely from his experiences there as a doctor. He burst into prominence with the short-story collection *Sagarana* (1946). The epic novel *The Devil to Pay in the Backlands* (1956) is considered his finest work.

Guinea (Guinée), Republic of, nation of W Africa on the Atlantic coast. The country is traditionally divided into four regions: Lower Guinea, the narrow coastal area; Foutah Djallon, a highland area rising sharply from the coast; Upper Guinea, with plains sloping NE to the Sahara; and the Forest Region, an isolated hill area in the SE. The Niger, Senegal, and Gambia rivers all have their source in the Foutah Djallon. The agricultural economy relies heavily on coffee and banana crops. The mineral wealth—huge reserves of high-grade bauxite, large deposits of iron ore, gold, and diamonds—holds great potential for the future.

People. There are three main ethnic groups: the Foulahs (or Peuls), the Malinkes, and the Soussou. French is the official language, but seven other languages are in common use. The majority of the people are Muslim. The literacy rate is about 10%, which impedes economic progress.

Government. A republic, the country is governed by a president elected every seven years, and a National Assembly of 75 members, elected every five years. There is universal suffrage.

History. Visited by the Portuguese in the early 1500s, Guinea, through the slave trade, became a center of European interest during the next 300 years. The French gained control in the early 1800s, establishing the colony of French Guinea in 1891. It became a territory in 1946, and chose independence through a referendum vote in 1958. Under Pres. Sekou Touré, Guinea has been supportive of Communist-bloc countries but accepts large grants from both Communist and non-Communist nations to aid its economic progress.

PROFILE

Official name: Republic of Guinea
Area: 94,926sq mi (245,858sq km)
Population: 4,400,000
Density: 46.3per sq mi (17.9per sq km)
Chief city: Conakry (capital)
Government: republic
Language: French (official)
Monetary unit: syli
Gross national product: $575,000,000
Per capita income: $137
Agriculture (major products): coffee, bananas
Minerals (major): aluminum, bauxite, diamonds
Trading partners (major): France, Norway, United States

Guinea-Bissau, Republic of, nation of W Africa, on the Atlantic coast. Formerly known as Portuguese Guinea, the nation gained its independence in 1974.

Land, Economy, and People. The heavily forested coastal area, hot, humid and swampy, rises gradually to inland grassy plains. The many rivers are the main source of transportation as the country has no railroads and few paved roads. The government is striving to diversify the economy, which is based almost entirely on the peanut. More than 30 tribes and subtribes make up the almost entirely black population. Although Roman Catholicism is the official religion, the majority practice animism, and there is a large majority of Muslims.

Government and History. A republic, the country is governed by the National Popular Assembly, made up of 120 deputies elected to three-year terms. Fifteen members are chosen to form the State Council, whose leader serves as the nation's president. Explored by the Portuguese in the 15th century, the area became an important slave trade center in the 17th and 18th centuries. Colonization began in the 19th century. In the 1960s local patriots conducted guerrilla warfare until the Portuguese granted independence in 1974.

PROFILE

Official name: Republic of Guinea-Bissau
Area: 13,948sq mi (36,125sq km)
Population: 520,000
Density: 35.8per sq mi (13.8per sq km)
Chief city: Bissau (capital)
Government: republic
Religion: Roman Catholic (official)
Language: Portuguese (official)
Monetary unit: Portuguese Escudo
Gross national product: $158,000,000
Per capita income: $275
Agriculture (major products): peanuts, rice, millet, coconuts, palm oil
Trading partners (major): Portugal

Guinea, Gulf of, inlet of the Atlantic Ocean, off W Africa, formed by great curve in coastline extending from the Ivory Coast to the Gabon estuary; E section includes Bight of Biafra.

Guinea Fowl, pheasantlike African and Madagascan game bird typified by the common domestic guinea hen *(Numida meleagris)*. It is bluish, grayish, or blackish with white spots and an ornamental crest. Other species have spurs; some have feather tufts on the head; and one has a long, ornamental tail. They travel in large flocks, often running, in open forest or brushland, feeding on vegetable matter and small invertebrates. They lay pitted, buff eggs (6–15) in a shallow grass-lined ground nest. Length: 20in (51cm). Family Numididae.

Guinea Pig, domesticated form of South American rodent, now a laboratory animal and pet. Large-headed and short-legged, guinea pigs have no tails and come in many colors and textures. Bred as food by the Incas, guinea pigs grow rapidly and produce up to 5 litters yearly. Vegetarians, they make good pets, being clean, healthy, and gentle. Length: to 10in (254mm); Weight: to 2lb (907g). Species *Cavia porcellus*. *See also* Cavy.

Guinevere, in Arthurian legend, Arthur's queen and Lancelot's love. In Thomas Malory's *Le Morte d'Arthur* she betrayed the king and was sentenced to die at the stake, was rescued by Lancelot and later restored to Arthur. Toward her life's end she took the veil and then was buried with her king.

Guinne. *See* Guyenne.

Guinn v. United States (1915), US Supreme Court case in which the court declared unconstitutional a state law imposing a literacy-test requirement for voter registration on certain citizens.

Guiscard, Robert (*c.*1015–85), Norman soldier who drove the Byzantines out of southern Italy and established Norman power in Sicily. Guiscard allied himself with the papacy and delivered Pope Gregory VII from the siege of Emperor Henry IV. He had hoped to conquer the Byzantine Empire but died in Cephalonia during a campaign.

Guise, House of, ducal house of Lorraine, most influential family in 16th-century France. **Claude, duke of Lorraine** (1496–1550) founded the house. His son **François** (1519–63) supervised the massacre of a congregation of Huguenots at Vassy in 1562, which precipitated the Wars of Religion. His brother **Charles** (1524–74), cardinal of Guise, played an important role at the Council of Trent. François' son Henri fought in the 3rd and 4th religious wars and helped organize the St. Bartholomew's Day Massacre in 1572. He led the Holy League, which opposed any toleration of Protestantism. The Guise family's power declined when the Huguenot Henry IV converted to Catholicism in 1593. △1154.

Guitar, stringed musical instrument with fretted neck and flat body, played by plucking or strumming its four to seven strings, sometimes 12, tuned in pairs. Of Oriental origin, it was brought to Spain in the 12th century and replaced the lute in 17th-century Europe in accompanying folk songs. Spanish concert virtuosos, especially Andrés Segovia, developed music for classical guitar. Jazz and rock instrumentalists use an electrically amplified modification. △1500.

Guitar Fish, elasmobranch found worldwide in tropical and temperate marine waters. A bottom-feeding ray that travels in schools, its elongated body is flattened along the side of the head and trunk. It is usually brown with spots, and its young are born alive. Length: 5–6ft (1.5–1.8m). There are nine genera and 45 species including *Rhinobatos productus*. Family Rhinebatidae.

Guizot, François (1787–1874), French leader of the conservative constitutional monarchists, and a historian. Guizot held several ministry posts during the July Monarchy (1830–48). The Guizot Law promised all citizens secular, primary education. Although he had success in foreign affairs, his conservative domestic policies and some scandals brought about his dismissal in 1848. △1288.

Gujarat, state in W India, on Arabian Sea; capital is Ahmedabad. Est. 1960 when former state of Bombay was separated into Marathi- and Gujarati-speaking areas; archaeological finds link this region to the Indus Valley civilization (3000–1500 BC) and the Mauryan Empire (320–185 BC); center of Jainism under the Anhilvada kingdom (755–1233); became independent sultanate 1401; under British domination (19th century); became state of Bombay 1947; home of Mahatma Gandhi and site of his religious retreats (1915–35). Industries: agriculture, dairy products, mining, textiles, oil refining, machine tools. Area: 72,000sq mi (186,480sq km). Pop. 26,660,-929.

Gujranwala, city in Punjab, NE Pakistan; capital of Gujranwala district; market center for cotton and grains. Industries: iron safes, brassware, textiles, pottery, ivory bangles. Pop. 289,300.

Gula, in Babylonian mythology, the goddess of healing, daughter of Anu, associated with Shamash. She is depicted as a healer and destroyer, able to control disease and death. Her festival was held in late April.

Gulag Archipelago (1973–74) prose work in two volumes (1958–68) by Soviet author Aleksandr Solzhenitsyn. It is a detailed factual account of life in Soviet prison camps between 1918 and 1956, derived from the author's own experience and correspondence with over 200 other survivors of the camps.

Gulfport, city in SE Mississippi, on Gulf of Mexico; seat of Harrison co; severely damaged by Hurricane Camille 1969. Industries: tourism, shipping and processing of timber and agricultural products, seafood packaging. Founded 1891 as seaport of Gulf and Ship Island Railroad. Inc. as town 1898, as city 1904. Pop. (1970) 40,791.

Gulf Stream, the relatively swift-moving western boundary current of the North Atlantic gyre which flows from the equator north along the North American east coast. Though long considered to be one huge wide mass of water, research indicates it is many interacting thin streams which cause the local variations in water temperature. Its warm waters affect the coastal climate. △224.

Gulfweed, any of a group of large brown seaweeds of the genus *Sargassum*. The best known gulfweed, *S. bacciferum*, floats by means of berry-shaped air bladders and is common in tropical American seas. *See also* Brown Algae.

Gull, or sea gull, graceful seabird found soaring and gliding along most coastlines. Gregarious, particularly during feeding, they eat carrion, rubbish, fish, shellfish, eggs, and young birds. Generally gray and white with black markings, they have hooked bills, pointed wings, rounded tails, and webbed feet. They lay smudged brownish eggs (2–3) in a seaweed-and-grass ground nest. Length: 11–32in (28–81cm). Family Laridae. △530.

Gulliver's Travels (1726), satirical fable in four parts by Jonathan Swift. The author uses Gulliver as a vehicle to satirize man. Lemuel Gulliver, a surgeon, visits Lilliput, Brobdingnag, Laputa, and the land of the Houyhnhnms and Yahoos. The inhabitants of the first are tiny and of the second are immense; the wise men in the third land engage in ridiculous enterprises; in Houyhnhnm land horses have reason and beasts take the form of men. △1188.

Gum Arabic, or acacia gum, soluble yellowish gum obtained from certain species of acacia trees and consisting of a complex carbohydrate polymer. It is used in foods, cosmetics, pharmaceuticals, and adhesives.

Gumbo. *See* Okra.

Gums, secretions of plants that swell or are soluble in water. Gums are chemically complex, consisting mainly of various saccharides bound to organic acids by glycoside linkages. Common examples are gum arabic, agar, and tragacarth. *See also* Resin.

Gums (anatomy). △756.

Gun Camera. △1788.

Gun Control Act (1968), US law passed to supplement the Omnibus Crime Control and Safe Streets Acts (1968) in strengthening and extending restrictions on the sale of firearms. These two measures were the first pieces of gun-control legislation enacted since 1938. In October 1970, the Supreme Court declared unconstitutional the section of the law that required vendors of certain dangerous devices to register all purchasers. The court held that this could force purchasers to give information that could incriminate them.

Gunnery, Naval. △1738–40.

Gunpowder, mixture of saltpeter (potassium nitrate), charcoal, and sulfur. When ignited in a confined space, it expands rapidly and produces a propellant force. Used extensively in firearms to about 1900, it was replaced by other chemicals. △1810.

Gunpowder Plot (1605), Roman Catholic conspiracy to blow up England's James I and the houses of Parliament and to establish Roman Catholicism in Britain. The plotters, led by Robert Catesby, took gunpowder into the cellars beneath Parliament and a man named Guy Fawkes was to ignite it. The authorities, however, were alerted and Fawkes was arrested and executed along with his fellow conspirators. The plot increased antagonism between Roman Catholics and Protestants.

Gunther, John (1901–70), US author, b. Chicago. A foreign correspondent for the Chicago *Daily News* (1924–36), he gained intimate knowledge of Europe and wrote *Inside Europe* (1936). This was the first in a series of lively, journalistic works surveying political and social life abroad. Over the years, he traveled widely, interviewing political figures and observing life for subsequent studies. These include *Inside Asia* (1939), *Inside Latin America* (1941), *Inside USA* (1947), *Inside Africa* (1955), *Inside Russia Today* (1957), *Inside Europe Today* (1961), and *Inside South America* (1967). He also wrote novels and *Death Be Not Proud* (1949), a moving memorial to his son who died of cancer at the age of 17.

Guntur, city in SE India, 220mi (354km) N of Madras; ceded to Great Britain 1823; important market for textiles and tobacco. Pop. 273,385.

Guppy, or millions fish, live-bearing topminnow found in fresh waters of West Indies, Venezuela, Guianas, and N Brazil. The wild guppy is gray with bright-colored spots; selective breeding has produced lyretail, swordtail, and veiltail varieties. A popular aquarium fish. Length: to 2.5in (6.4cm). Family Poecilidae; species *Poecilia* or *Lebistes reticulatis.*

Gupta (*fl.c.* AD 320–480), ruling dynasty of the Maurya Empire covering most of northern India. Their state was the prototype of Indian empires to follow. The Guptas conquered territory and collected tribute from defeated rulers but allowed them to remain on their thrones and continue to rule. The Guptas were considered benevolent, and art and literature flourished under their rule. △1034.

Gurkha, or Gorkha, Hindu ruling caste of Nepal since 1768. They speak a Sanskritic language. Their racial characteristics are a mixture of Mongoloid and Caucasoid. The name often denotes a Nepalese soldier in the British or Indian army.

Gurnard, also flying gurnard, tropical marine bottom-dwelling fish. It has a large bony head and enlarged pectoral fins used to glide above the water surface. Length: to 18in (45.7cm). Order Dactylopteriformes; species include *Dactylopterus volitans.*

Guru, a Sanskrit term for a teacher and spiritual master. In traditional Hindu education, boys lived in the home of a guru, who was their guide in studying the sacred books (Vedas) and saw to their physical health and ethical training. In many Hindu sects the guru is responsible for initiating novices. In Sikhism the guru was the leader of the community until the guruship was terminated in 1708.

Gustavus I Vasa (?1496–1560), king of Sweden, son of Erik Johansson who supported the Sture party. He led a victorious rebellion against the invading Danes in 1520. In 1523 he was elected king and the Kalmar Union was destroyed. During his reign Sweden became independent of Denmark, the Protestant church was established, and the Bible was translated into Swedish. Founder of the Vasa dynasty, he established hereditary monarchy in 1544.

Gustavus II Adolphus (1594–1632), king of Sweden, succeeded his father Charles IX (1611) during a constitutional crisis. Aided by Chancellor Axel Oxenstierna, Gustav's reign was distinguished by sweeping legal, administrative, and educational reforms. He established secondary schools, reformed the Riksdag, 1617, and established uniform judicial procedures. He ended war with Denmark (1613) and Russia (1617). Hoping to increase Sweden's control of the Baltic and to support Protestantism, he entered the Thirty Years' War in Germany and died in battle. His daughter Christina succeeded him. △1154.

Gustavus III (1746–92), king of Sweden, succeeded his father Adolf Frederik in 1771 during a period of civil strife. His new constitution strengthened sovereign power. During his reign, known as Gustavian Enlightenment, he instituted financial reforms, religious toleration, a free press, and a strong navy. A gifted writer and patron of the arts, he founded the Swedish Academy. An aristocratic conspiracy led J. Anckarström to assassinate him.

Gustavus VI (1882–1973), king of Sweden, succeeded Gustavus V in 1950, the last Swedish king to hold political power. He was a fine athlete, archeologist, and an authority on Chinese ceramics. His grandson Carl Gustavus succeeded him.

Gutenberg, Johann (1400?–?68), German goldsmith and printer. He is credited with the invention of printing from movable type. Gutenberg was experimenting with printing in the 1430s, and the process he developed was based on techniques used for making playing cards and mass-produced woodblock prints. He went into a partnership with Johann Fust, and when the association was dissolved, Gutenberg gave up claims to his invention. He printed the first Bible, known as the Gutenberg Bible (*c.*1455).

Gutenberg Discontinuity. △166.

Guthrie, (Sir William) Tyrone (1900–71), English director and playwright who directed the Scottish National Players (1926–28), the Festival Theatre of Cambridge (1929–30), and the Old Vic-Sadler's Wells Company. He also worked in other countries and directed the theater named for him (1961) in Minneapolis. He was known for his productions of Shakespeare.

Guthrie, Woodrow Wilson ("Woody") (1912–67), US folk singer, guitarist, and songwriter, b. Okemah, Okla. After many personal tragedies in childhood he ran away from home, traveled around the United States, and performed on radio stations in Los Angeles and Tijuana, Mexico. He wrote many notable folk-style songs including "This Land Is Your Land," "Hard Traveling," and "So Long, It's Been Good to Know You." He was the father of singer Arlo Guthrie. △1366.

Gutta-percha, or palaquium, evergreen tree found in Malaya, Sumatra, and Borneo. It is the source of gutta-percha, a rubberlike gum used in electric insulation, golf balls, and dentistry. This flat-topped tree has long, oval leaves that are green above and copper with silky hairs below. Height: to 100ft (30.5m). Family Sapotaceae; species *Palaquium gutta.*

Gutters and Downspouts. △1610.

Guyana, Republic of, nation in NE South America, on the Atlantic Ocean. Once known as British Guiana, Guyana proclaimed its independence in 1970 after 152 years as a British colony.

Land, Economy, and People. A flat coastal area roughly 50mi (81km) in width contains about 90% of

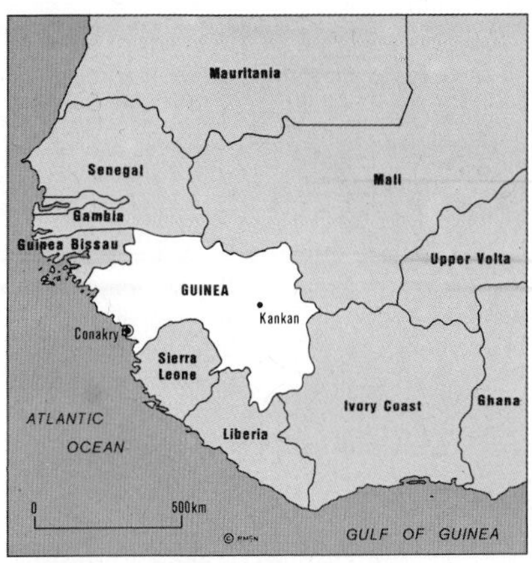
Mauritania
Senegal
Mali
Gambia
Guinea Bissau
Upper Volta
GUINEA
Kankan
Conakry
Sierra Leone
Ivory Coast
Ghana
ATLANTIC OCEAN
Liberia
0
500km
GULF OF GUINEA

Guinea

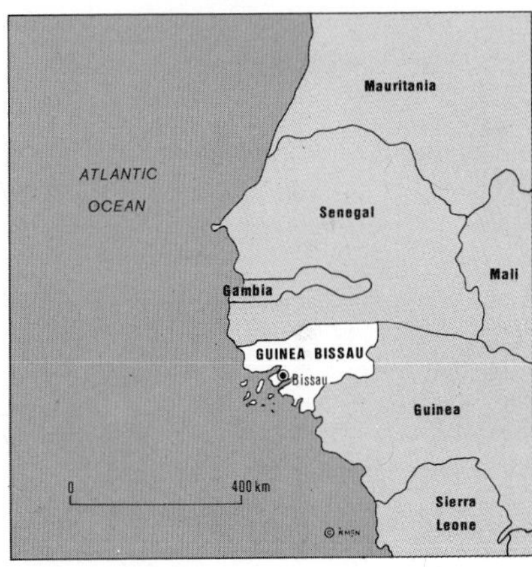
Mauritania
ATLANTIC OCEAN
Senegal
Mali
Gambia
GUINEA BISSAU
Bissau
Guinea
0
400km
Sierra Leone

Guinea-Bissau

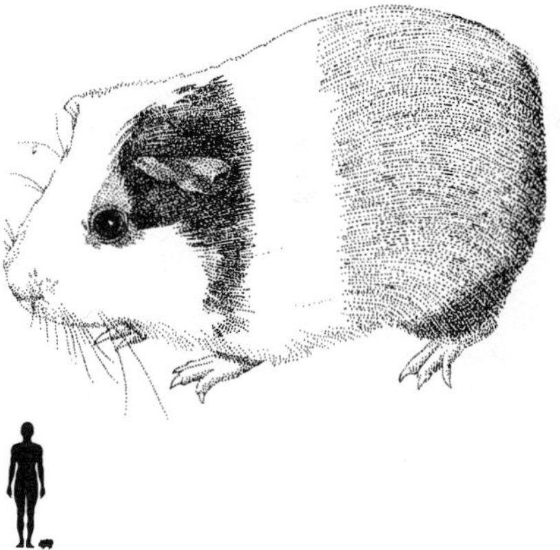

Guinea pig

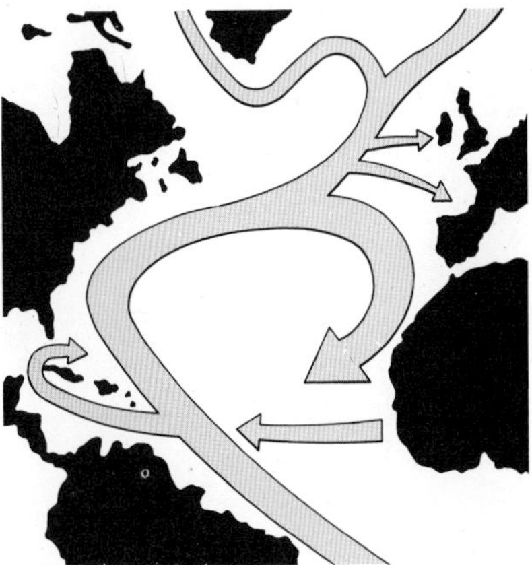

Gulf Stream

the population. Most of the rest of the country is covered by dense tropical forest, making access to the rich inland bauxite difficult. The economy, improving through the exploitation of mineral resources, remains heavily agricultural, relying principally upon sugar and rice. About half the people are of East Indian descent, having been imported by the British as laborers. About 33% are of African descent; most of the rest are American Indian or of mixed lineage. The principle religious groups are Christian, Hindu, and Muslim.

Government and History. The constitution provides for a unicameral 53-member national assembly. Members are elected for five years under a system of proportional representation. The major political forces are the People's National Congress and the People's Progressive party.

Explored by the Spanish in 1499, the area was settled by the Dutch in 1620, who ceded it to the British in 1814. The British brought in African slaves and large numbers of indentured East Indians to work the plantations. Guyana achieved self-government as a British Commonwealth nation in 1966 and gained full independence in 1970. In a step to bolster the economy the aluminum industry was nationalized in 1974.

PROFILE

Official name: Republic of Guyana
Area: 83,000sq mi (214,970sq km)
Population: 800,000
Density: 9.6per sq mi (3.7per sq km)
Chief city: Georgetown (capital)
Government: republic
Language: English (official)
Monetary unit: Guyana dollar
Gross national product: $340,000,000
Per capita income: $380
Industries (major products): rum
Agriculture (major products): sugar cane, coconuts, rice, corn
Minerals (major): bauxite
Trading partners (major): United States, Great Britain, Canada, Trinidad and Tobago

Guyenne, also Guienne, province of SW France, part of Aquitaine. Guyenne passed to the English in the 12th century. After the Treaty of Paris in 1259, Henry III of England held the province as a vassal of France's Louis IX. By the close of the Hundred Years' War, France had reconquered Guyenne. Many bitter struggles of the 16th century Wars of Religion and the Fronde in the 17th century were fought in Guyenne. △1096.

Guy of Lusignan. △1084.

Guyot, a flat-topped seamount whose top is thousands of meters below sea level. It is thought that the flat top was caused by wave action at sea level, thus their present depth is important proof for the lowering of the ocean floor. △228.

Guzmán Blanco, Antonio (1829–99), the central figure in Venezuelan political life from 1870 to 1889, four times elected president (1873, 1880, 1882, 1886). Guzmán suppressed the Conservatives and transferred much of the Church's authority to the state. He successfully attracted foreign capital and allowed private groups to manage the country's revenues.

Gwalior, city in N central India, 65mi (105km) SSE of Agra, S of Chambal River; overlooked by the Gwalior fort, a Hindu stronghold on the Rock of Gwalior, which houses elaborate shrines, temples, and palace of Man Singh; 15th-century Jain figures are sculpted out of the cliffs of the hill; was the capital of the former princely state of Gwalior (dissolved 1956). Industries: cotton, flour, oilseed processing, textiles, porcelain, plastics. Pop. 369,121.

Gwinnett, Button (1735?–77), American patriot and a signer of the Declaration of Independence, b. England. He represented Georgia at the Continental Congress in 1776 and 1777. He was later killed in a duel with Gen. Lachlan McIntosh after a Georgian expedition failed in a campaign against the British.

Gwyn, or **Gwynne, Nell** (1650–87), English actress. She made her first stage appearance at 15 in *The Indian Emperor*. Much in demand as a speaker of prologues and epilogues, she attracted the attention of King Charles II while reciting the epilogue to Dryden's *Tyrannic Love* (1669), later becoming his mistress and bearing him two sons. Her last stage role was in *Conquest of Granada* (1670).

Gyges of Sardis, king of Lydia (*c.* 687–657 BC), founder of the Mermnad dynasty, he increased Lydian holdings, coined money, and sent offerings to Delphi. His tomb was excavated in 1964.

Gymnastics, sport that involves the performance of various athletic feats on a horizontal bar, long and side horse, flying rings, parallel bar, and balance beam, in addition to rope climbing, club swinging, trampolining, and tumbling. Except for rope climbing, which is scored on speed, events are scored on the basis of form, difficulty of optional exercises, and execution. Men and women compete separately in individual and team competition. The all-around individual champions are determined by excellence in six or more events; team competitions are scored on the basis of total points for all events. Gymnastics was brought to the United States in the 1800s and became part of the modern Olympic Games in 1896. Although ancient Greece used gymnastics as a method of training for the Olympics, it was Frederick Jahn, a German, who introduced the side bar with pommels, the horizontal and parallel bars, the balance beam, and jumping standards in the late 1700s.

Gymnosperm, seed plants having seeds borne on open scales, usually in cones. Most trees commonly referred to as evergreens are gymnosperms. All living seed-bearing plants are divided into two main groups: gymnosperms and angiosperms, that have seeds enclosed in an ovary. Gymnosperms are abundant in nature and widely cultivated. They include cycads, ginkgo, pines, spruces, cedars, and ephedras. *See also* Angiosperm; Conifers. △424, 440, 562.

Gynecology, branch of medicine that deals with diseases and disorders of the female reproductive tract. Most gynecologists are also obstetricians. *See also* Obstetrics. △728, 754.

Györ, port city in NW Hungary, at the confluence of the Rába and Danube rivers; seat of Györ-Sopron co; 12th-century cathedral. Industries: steel, textiles, flour milling, distilling. Settled by Romans. Pop. 100,065.

Gypsies, nomadic people, probably originating from N India, now inhabiting Europe, Asia, Siberia, America, Africa, and Australia. Speaking the distinctive Romany language and traditionally living in decorated horse-drawn carriages, gypsies have been distrusted and persecuted in Europe since their first appearance in the 13th century. They were originally believed to have come from Egypt, hence their name. They are known for their resourcefulness in leading a nomadic life in urban societies.

Gypsophila, genus of the pink family containing annual or perennial plants commonly known as baby's breath, native to Europe, Asia, and North Africa. Growing 6in to 3ft (15–91cm), they have narrow leaves and pink or white flowers in single or double blossoms. They are grown in gardens or for cut flowers.

Gypsum, the commonest sulfate mineral and source of plaster of Paris. Hydrous calcium sulfate ($CaSO_4 \cdot 2H_2O$). Huge beds in sedimentary rocks. Monoclinic system prismatic or bladed crystals. Varieties are alabaster, massive; selenite, transparent and foliated; satinspar, silky and fibrous. Clear, white, and tinted. Hardness 2; sp gr 2.3. △278, 1554.

Gypsum Cement. *See* Plaster of Paris.

Gypsy Moth, small tussock moth whose caterpillar feeds on the leaves of more than 500 species of shrubs and trees. The caterpillar is covered with tufts of stiff hairs. When young, the larva is pale brown. As an adult, it has five pairs of blue and six pairs of red tufted spots on its back. Length: 2in (5cm). Species *Porthetria dispar*. *See also* Tussock Moth.

Gyre, a large circular flow of ocean water with a calm center region called an eddy. There are three gyres in both the Atlantic and Pacific and one in the Indian Ocean. They are narrowest and swiftest on their western sides. △224.

Gyrfalcon, bird of prey found in Arctic tundra and nearby mountains. It has a hooked beak, long pointed wings, and long tail. It is gray-brown or a mixture of dark and whitish coloring. It feeds on birds and mammals and lays spotted buff-colored eggs in a stick nest on a cliff. Length: 20–25in (51–63.5cm). Species *Falco rusticolus*.

Gyrocompass, a compass that consists of a continuously driven gyroscope, used where a magnetic compass would be unreliable owing to large masses of iron or steel nearby. The heavy base of the gyroscope confines the spinning axis to a horizontal plane so that the rotation of the earth causes it to assume a position parallel to the axis of the earth. Thus, it always points to true north.

Gyropilot, an automatic pilot consisting of devices for detecting and correcting changes in the attitude of an airplane. The gyropilot makes the correction by moving the appropriate control (rudder for azimuth and sudden change in heading, aileron for roll, and elevator for pitch).

Gyroscope, a symmetrical but nonspherical body, usually mounted in gimbals allowing unrestricted motion. If the body is set spinning, a change in the orientation of the outer gimbals will not change the orientation of the spinning body; thus one can determine changes in direction aboard a vessel without external references. A torque applied to a fast-spinning gyroscope, such as can be applied by leaning it out of the vertical, will result in a phenomenon known as precession: the gyroscope will not fall but will rotate about its fixed point, with the axis of spin describing a cone around the vertical. △1656.

Gyrus. △666.

H

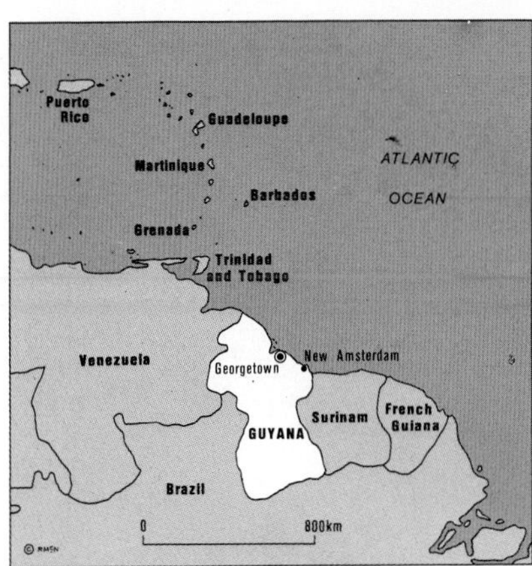
Puerto Rico
Guadeloupe
Martinique
ATLANTIC OCEAN
Barbados
Grenada
Trinidad and Tobago
New Amsterdam
Venezuela
Georgetown
French Guiana
Surinam
GUYANA
Brazil
0
800km
Guyana

Haakon VII (1872–1957), king of Norway. Formerly Prince Charles, son of Denmark's King Frederick VIII, he was offered the crown in 1905 when Norway separated from Sweden. During Nazi occupation he established a government in exile in England.

Haarlem, city in W Netherlands, near North Sea, on Spaarne River; capital of North Holland prov.; center of 16th–17th-century Dutch painting. City has many fine museums and monuments. Industries: flowers, tulip bulbs, ships, textiles, electronic equipment. Chartered 1245. Pop. 172,235.

Habakkuk, biblical author and eighth of the 12 minor prophets. His short book bemoans the condition of Judah and the success of God's enemies.

Habasesti. △656, 1586.

Habeas Corpus, legal term from Latin for "You have the body." The most common legal form (habeas corpus ad subjectiendum) is a writ issued to a person detaining another. In it he is ordered to appear with reasons for detention before a judge or court. Consideration and decisions are then arrived at as to whether the prisoner is justly detained.

Haber, Fritz (1868–1934), German physical chemist whose early work involved electrochemistry and thermodynamic gas reactions. With Karl Bosch (1908–09), he invented the process (Haber process) for converting atmospheric nitrogen into ammonia. He was awarded the 1918 Nobel Prize for this work. He also devised the means of manufacturing large amounts of ammonia for use in nitrogen fertilizers.

Habsburg. *See* Hapsburg.

Hachinohe, port city in N Honshu, Japan, on the Oirase River; Industries: fisheries, cement, textiles, food processing, chemicals. Pop. 208,801.

Hachioji, city in SE central Honshu, Japan, 27mi (43km) W of Tokyo. Industries: weaving, silk, poultry, wood. Pop. 253,527.

Hackberry, any of about 80 species of shrubs and trees, making up the genus *Celtis* of the elm family. The common hackberry *(C. occidentalis)* of E North America usually grows to 40–60ft (12–18m) and has an edible, cherrylike fruit.

Hackensack, city of NE New Jersey, on Hackensack River; Revolutionary War camping ground for both sides; site of Von Steuben House (1739). Industries: chemicals, metal goods, machinery. Est. 1647 as Dutch trading post; inc. 1868; chartered as city 1921. Pop. (1970) 35,911.

Hackney, light horse breed for heavy harness and carriage use. An English breed developed during the early 18th century from the Norfolk Trotter and Thoroughbred, it has short legs and robust build. Colors are chestnut, bay, or brown, with white marks. Its tail is docked and its mane pulled for show. Small Hackneys qualify as ponies. Height: 48–56in (122–142cm) at shoulder; weight: 800–1,200lb (360–540kg).

Hadar. *See* Beta Centauri.

Hadassah, the Women's Zionist Organization of America, founded in 1912 by Henrietta Szold. The largest Jewish women's organization in the United States, it was founded in efforts to improve health conditions in Israel. It developed welfare centers and hospitals for care and training purposes, such as the Hadassah Medical School in 1949. There are about 1,500 chapters and groups, with 350,000 members.

Haddock, marine food and commercial fish found in cold and temperate waters, primarily in Northern Hemisphere. Dark gray and silver, it has a large, dark blotch near the pectoral fins. Length: to 44in (111.8cm); weight: to 36lb (16.3kg). Family Gadidae; species *Melanogrammus aeglefinus.* △392, 516.

Hades, in Greek mythology, the son of Cronus and Rhea and brother of Zeus and Poseidon. Hades ruled as master of the Underworld, or Hades. He was also known as Pluto. △838–40.

Hadhramaut (Hadhramawt), region in E Yemen, along S coast of Arabian Peninsula; site of a pre-Islamic civilization, comprised of the British-protected Quaiti and Kathiri sultanates from 19th century until 1967, when both sultans were overthrown by National Liberation Front, and the People's Republic of Yemen was formed. Main towns are Seiyun, Tarin, Shibam, and Mukalla. Inhabitants are mostly Muslim peasants of Arab descent. Crops: dates, tobacco, cereals, coconuts, coffee. Area: approx. 58,000sq mi (150,220sq km). Pop. 240,000.

Hadley Cell, an atmospheric circulation cell, named for British scientist George Hadley, who proposed it (1735) to explain the trade winds, in which winds rise and flow poleward from the equator and then descend and flow equatorward, transferring heat convectively. *See also* Easterlies.

Hadrian, Publius Aelius (76–138), Roman emperor (117–138). He was adopted by Emperor Trajan who named him his successor. As emperor, Hadrian pacified Moesia (118), withdrew the Eastern army to the Euphrates, and suppressed Bar Cocheba's revolt in Jerusalem (132). He continued to persecute the Jews, destroying the Temple of Jerusalem and building a Roman temple in its place. He traveled extensively throughout the empire and had defensive walls built in Germany and in Britain. He promoted major building programs, including the Arch of Hadrian in Athens, the Pantheon in Rome, and his villa at Tibur. After the drowning of his male lover Antinoüs, he encouraged his deification. He enlarged and reformed the civil service and provided alms and circuses for the poor of Rome. △1020.

Hadrian's Villa, seaside country palace built for the Emperor Hadrian *c.*135 AD at Tivoli, Italy. Because it covered 7sq mi (18.13sq km), it cannot be considered a typical Roman villa. Instead, it was a royal city, which contained many extravagant and sophisticated buildings. △1024.

Hadrian's Wall, northern boundary wall of Roman Britain erected by Emperor Hadrian 122–126 AD and extending 73.5mi (118km) from Wallsend-on-Tyne to Bowness-on-Solway. About 7.5ft (2.3m) thick and 6–15ft (1.8–4.6m) high, it supported many stone forts along its length. The Romans held it until 400. An extensive ruin survives.

Hadron, member of a class of elementary particles that are subject to strong interaction. The group can be divided into baryons, such as the neutron and proton, and mesons, such as the pion, kaon, and eta meson. Over 150 hadrons have been discovered, mostly since about 1950, and with the exception of the proton and antiproton they are all unstable. Unlike leptons, they have a measurable size; experiment indicates a substructure postulated to consist of quarks. *See also* Lepton; Multiplet; Quark; Strange Particles. △1484.

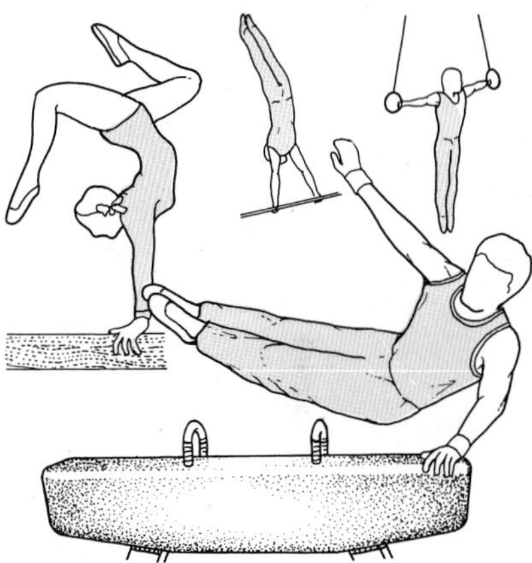
Gymnastics

Gypsy moth

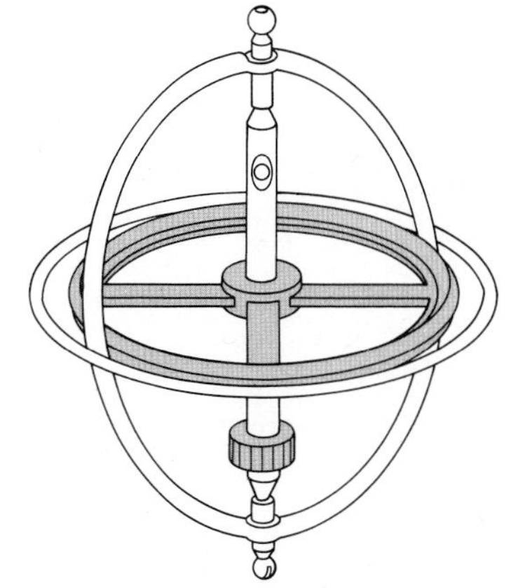
Gyroscope

Haeckel, Ernst (1834–1919), German biologist and philosopher. An eminent naturalist, he wrote monographs on invertebrates before espousing Darwin's evolutionary theory. In his *Riddle of the Universe* (1899) he embraced materialism, offering a religion of the universe.

Haerbin. *See* Harbin.

Hafnium, metallic element (symbol Hf) of the third transition series, first discovered in 1923. Chief source is as a by-product in obtaining zirconium. It is used as a neutron absorber in reactor control rods. Properties: at. no 72; at. wt. 178.49; sp gr 13.31; melt. pt. 4041°F (2229°C); boil pt. 8316°F (4606°C); most common isotope Hf^{180} (35.24%). *See also* Transition Elements. △1554.

Hagen, city in W West Germany, on the Ennepe River. Industries: iron, steel, chemicals, machinery, paper. Chartered 1746. Pop. 201,512.

Hagerstown, city in NW Maryland, on Antietam Creek; seat of Washington co; nearby are Antietam National Battlefield site and cemetery, and Fort Frederick (1756). Industries: dairy equipment, clothing, shoes, publishing. Settled 1740; inc. 1791. Pop. (1970) 35,862.

Hagfish, or slime eel, eellike, jawless fish found in temperate-to-cold marine waters. It has underdeveloped eyes, slightly rounded tail and 4–6 fleshy whiskers around its suctorial mouth. Feeding by drilling into fish and eating interior parts, it secretes a slimy mucous from pores along its sides. Length: under 30in (76cm). Family Myxinidae; species, 21 including the common North Atlantic *Myxine glutinosa*. *See also* Cyclostome. △508.

Haggadah, Passover, the story of the Exodus and the redemption of the people of Israel by God, read during Passover services. Developed over a period of centuries, it includes excerpts from the Bible, rabbinical writings, psalms, stories, and prayers.

Haggai, biblical author and 10th of the 12 minor prophets. After the Captivity, he encouraged the people in rebuilding the Temple in Jerusalem. △1104.

Haggard, Henry Rider (1856–1925), English novelist. He was in the colonial service in the Transvaal 1875–79, and Africa provides the background for his romantic adventure novels, including *King Solomon's Mines* (1885), *She* (1887), and *Allan Quatermain* (1887).

Hagia Sophia (532–37), a masterpiece of Byzantine architecture designed by Anthemius of Tralles and Isidorus of Miletus for Emperor Justinian. Originally a Christian church, it was converted to a mosque (1453) and then in the 20th century restored as a museum. The central dome, flanked by half domes and semidomes, is supported on pendentives. The interior is lavishly decorated with colored marble and gold-touched mosaic. △1056.

Hagiographa, third and final part of the Jewish Scripture (Christian Old Testament). It contains poetic and historical sacred writings, consisting of Psalms, Proverbs, Job, Song of Songs, Ruth, Lamentations, Ecclesiastes, Esther, Daniel, Ezra, Nehemiah, and Chronicles I and II.

Hague, The ('s Gravenhage or **Den Haag),** capital of the Netherlands, in W Netherlands on shore of North Sea; capital of South Holland prov.'s Gravenhage translates as "the count's wood," referring to the 13th-century hunting lodge of the counts of Holland around which the city grew; city became an important European intellectual and political center by 17th century. Many medieval structures remain, including the Binnenhof, the Hall of Knights, and the Mauritshuis, which contains works by Rembrandt and Vermeer; site of International Court of Justice. Much of The Hague's economy depends upon diplomatic and administrative activities. Industries: textiles, metals, chemicals, processed foods. Pop. 550,613.

Hague Peace Conferences, meetings hailed because they inaugurated arms arbitration and enabled neutrals to arbitrate between warring nations. They also allowed any party to call for an impartial investigation and arranged for an international court at The Hague (1899). The second conference (1907) developed rules for "civilized warfare" that later were disregarded.

Hahn, Otto (1879–1968), German chemist. He became director of the Kaiser-Wilhelm Institute in 1928. With Lise Meitner he discovered protoactinium and several nuclear isomers; he was later a co-discoverer of nuclear fission, for which he won a Nobel Prize in 1944. During World War II he remained in Germany but was in disfavor. After the war he was appointed president of the Max Planck Institute.

Hahnium. *See* Element 105.

Haida, tribe of North American Indians speaking the Skidegattan branch of the Na-Dené language; closely related to the Tlingit and the Tsimshian. They inhabit the Queen Charlotte Islands in British Columbia; a small group that moved to Alaska in the 19th century is now known as the Kaigani. The Haida are regarded as the typical totem pole Indians, and are famed for their wood sculpture. Today approximately 1,500 occupy the area.

Haifa (Hefa), principal seaport city in N Israel, on Mediterranean Sea; 2nd-largest city in Israel; urban, transportation, and industrial center; site of Haifa University (1963) and technical institute (1924); world center of Bahaism. Industries: shipping, oil refining, chemicals, textiles, automobiles, cement, fishing, shipbuilding and repair. Pop. 217,400.

Haiku, a Japanese poetry form consisting of 17 syllables in a five-seven-five pattern, it came into prominence through its mastery by Matsuo Bashō (1644–94), still regarded as the finest practitioner. He was adept at both cheerful and sad *haiku*. The form remains extremely popular in Japan. Despite its brevity, its best authors have adapted it to modern conditions.

Hail, pellets of concentric ice layers, like an onion, formed in clouds and falling to earth's surface. *See also* Precipitation.

Haile Selassie (1891–1975), emperor of Ethiopia (1930–74) b. as Lij Tafari Makonnen. Through his relative Emperor Menelik II, he rose rapidly to a position of power. By 1916 he gained control of Ethiopia as imperial regent. After Empress Zauditu, Menelik's daughter, died (1930), Tafari became Emperor Haile Selassie ("Might of the Trinity"). After Italy invaded Ethiopia in 1935, he was forced into exile (1936) although he appealed to the League of Nations to support his cause. He and the British drove out the Italians in 1941. He consolidated his rule after his return and subsequently became a leader among independent African nations, helping to found the Organization of African Unity in 1963. Unrest at lack of reforms increased in the late 1960s and early 1970s, and he was deposed by the military in 1974.

Hainan, island off SE China, in South China Sea, separated from mainland by Hainan Strait; second-largest Chinese island; under Chinese control since AD 1st century and long a place of political exile. Occupied by Japanese during WWII; taken 1950 by Chinese Communists. Industries: rubber, coffee, rice, sugar cane, fruit, lumber; tin, copper, maganese, lead, silver, coal, graphite, and antimony mining. Area: 13,000sq mi (34,000sq km). Pop. 2,800,000.

Hainault Scythe. △1582.

Hainaut, medieval county in Low Countries, now divided between Belgium (Hainaut province) and France (Nord department). The Belgium province is a dairying, mining, and textile center. Hainaut was united by marriage with the county of Flanders (1191). Later, as part of Holland, it passed through the hands of the Bavarian Wittelsbach house in the 14th century; Burgundy and the Hapsburgs in the 15th century. In the 16th century, it engaged in the revolt against Spain.

Haiphong (Hai-phong), seaport city in N Vietnam, 10mi (16km) from Gulf of Tonkin on narrow connecting channel on branch of Red River Delta; manufacture, trade, and food processing center. Developed by French, city became chief naval base of French Indochina; occupied during WWII by Japanese; bombed by French 1946 in French-Indochina war; included in new state of N Vietnam 1954; heavily bombed by United States in Vietnam War (1965–68 and 1972). Industries: cement, glass, chemicals, cotton. Est. 1874. Pop. 182,496.

Hair, an appendage of the skin that has protective and sensory functions. Hair is made up of three layers: outer flat scalelike cuticle layer, middle keratinized cortex layer that contains the pigment, and inner medulla layer. Hair grows in a follicle, a tubular structure extending down through the epidermis to the upper dermis. The hair follicle ends in a papilla, a highly vascularized point that supplies nourishment for hair growth. △686,1574.

Hair Worm. *See* Horsehair Worm.

Haiti, Republic of, independent nation occupying W third of Caribbean island of Hispaniola. The people are descended from slaves and French settlers; it is the world's oldest black republic. The economy depends on the export of coffee and bauxite.

Land and Economy. Two-thirds of the country is rough, mountainous terrain unsuitable for cultivation; 2,200,000acres (891,000hectares) are arable. The temperature in the main population areas ranges from 70° to 90°F (21°–32.2°C) with humidity high along the coast. Coffee is its chief export product; bauxite and copper its main minerals. Haiti is one of the most densely populated countries in the world; 90% of the people live on farms too small for family subsistence.

People. About 90% of the people are of African descent, the rest of European or Levantine stock or mulattoes. The official language is French, but the majority speaks creole, a dialect derived from Norman, French, Spanish, African, and Arawak Indian words. Roman Catholicism is the state religion; voodoo is widely practiced. Haiti's literacy rate is 10%, the lowest in Latin America.

Government. The current law is the 1964 constitution with a lifetime term for the president. No political parties are recognized.

History: Discovered by Christopher Columbus in 1492, Hispaniola was divided in 1672 when Spain ceded a portion to France. Slaves, brought from Africa to work the plantations, gained independence in 1804 and renamed the area Haiti. In 1822 Haiti conquered the Spanish-speaking part of the island (Dominican Republic), which broke away in 1844. From 1843 to 1915 Haiti had 22 dictatorships. Dr. Francis (Papa Doc) Duvalier was elected president in 1957; a 1964 constitution awarded him a lifetime term. Following his death in 1971, he was succeeded by his son, Jean Claude Duvalier.

PROFILE

Official name: Republic of Haiti
Area: 10,714sq mi (27,749sq km)
Population: 4,969,113
Density: 463.8per sq mi (179per sq km)
Chief cities: Port-au-Prince (capital); Cap Haitien
Government: president, Jean Claude Duvalier
Religion: Roman Catholic (state religion)
Language: French (official)
Monetary unit: gourde
Gross national product: $694,000,000
Annual per capita income: $148
Industries: cigars, molasses, rum
Agriculture: coffee, sugar cane, bananas, tobacco, rice
Minerals: bauxite, copper
Trading partners: United States (60% of total exports)

Hake, marine food and commercial fish found in cold and temperate waters. Its elongated, streamlined body is silvery with brown. Length: to 4ft (121.9cm); weight: to 40lb (18.1kg). Family Gadidae or Merlucidae; species include Atlantic silver *Merluccius bilinearis* and Pacific *Merluccius productus*. △516.

Hakodate, major port city on SW Hokkaido Island, N Japan, on the Tsugaru-Kaikyo (strait); formerly capital of Hokkaido prefecture; opened to US ships 1854. Industries: shipbuilding and repair, iron works, fishing. Pop. 241,663.

Halakah, the legal aspects of Judaism. It consists of practices, rites, and the very conduct of Jews, and is contrasted with Haggadah, or nonlegal materials. It is traced to Moses on Mt Sinai, but has been developed throughout time.

Halcyon, Greek mythological figure. The daughter of Aeolus, best known as the beloved wife of Ceyx, king of Thessaly. When Ceyx was drowned in a shipwreck, Halcyon ran to the seashore to find his body. The gods, feeling sorry for the couple, changed them into kingfishers. There are seven days each winter when the sea is calm ("halcyon weather"), for then Ceyx and Halcyon make their nest on the water and care for their children.

Hale, Edward Everett (1822–1909), US author, b. Boston. Best known for his short story "The Man Without a Country" (1863).

Hale, George Ellery (1868–1938), US astronomer, b. Chicago. Hale organized Chicago's Kenwood observatory in 1888, the Yerkes (Wis.) observatory in 1895, the Mt Wilson, Calif., observatory in 1904 and initiated work on the Mt Palomar, Calif., observatory, whose 200-inch (508-cm) telescope bears his name. He invented an instrument, the spectroheliograph, for photographing the Sun and later developed the spectrohelioscope for observation of the Sun. He was widely honored for his work in solar studies, paricularly the discovery of the Sun's magnetic field. △44.

Hale, Nathan (1755–76), American Revolutionary War captain and hero. He was hanged by the British as a spy. A Yale graduate, he taught school before joining the Continental Army in 1775. Having volunteered to go behind British lines on Long Island to gain military secrets, he was captured on Sept. 21, 1776, and hanged the next day. His last words are said to be, "I regret that I have but one life to lose for my country."

Haleakala National Park, park in Hawaii, on Maui Island. It features 10,023ft (3,057m) dormant Haleakala volcano, whose large and colorful crater provides a species of the rare silversword plant. Many native and migratory birds are found here. Area: 27,282acres (11,049hectares). Est. 1961.

Hale Observatories, two astronomical observatories in California: on Mt Wilson (Wilson Observatory) near Pasadena, and Mt Palomar (Palomar Observatory), NE of San Diego; jointly managed by California Institute of Technology and Carnegie Institution of Washington, D.C. △44.

Hale Reflector. △42.

Haley, Bill △1366

Halfbeak, marine and freshwater fish of E Pacific and Atlantic. Silver with a crimson jaw, it has a long, needlelike lower jaw and uses its short pectoral fins in attempts to glide like flying fish. Length: 12–18in (30.5–45.7cm). Family Exocoetidae; species, 60, including *Hyphorhamphus unifasciatus.*

Half Breeds, US Republican party faction in the late 1870s that favored civil service reform and a liberal policy toward the South. Their opponents were known as "stalwarts."

Half-Cell. △1566.

Half-life, the time taken for one-half of the atoms present in a given amount of radioactive isotope to undergo one disintegration. *See also* Radioactivity. △276.

Haliburton, Thomas Chandler (1796–1865), pseud. Sam Slick, Canadian judge and humorist. A judge of the Nova Scotia supreme court (1842–56), Haliburton wrote several books on law and history. He used the adventures of Sam Slick, a fictional rude Yankee peddler, to chide the laziness of Canadians as opposed to US industriousness. The Slick stories include *Sam Slick in England* (1843–44) and *Sam Slick's Wise Saws and Modern Instances* (1853).

Halibut, flatfish found in deep cold to temperate seas worldwide. An important commercial fish, it is brownish on the eye side; white below. Prolific, producing 2,000,000 eggs at one spawning, they live up to 40 years. Length: to 9ft (274.3cm); weight: to 700lb (315kg). Family Pleuronectidae; species Atlantic *Hippoglossus hippoglossus* and giant Pacific *Hippoglossus stenolepsis.* △392, 516.

Halide, salt of a halogen, or an organic compound containing a halogen. The halide salts, fluorides, chlorides, bromides, and iodides, contain negative ions. The alkyl halides are organic compounds such as methyl chloride (CH_3Cl), containing an alkane radical bound to a halogen atom.

Halifax, Charles Montagu, Earl of (1661–1715), English statesman whose political success was a result of his great financial skills. He became lord of the treasury and in 1692 established the borrowing system of the national debt. He founded the Bank of England and was chancellor of the exchequer in 1694; he became first lord of the treasury in 1697 and was prime minister (1714–15). Twice impeached (1701, 1703) but never convicted, he was also a successful minor poet.

Halifax, port city and capital of Nova Scotia, Canada, on Atlantic Ocean; seat of Halifax co; important embarkation port during WWII; site of naval base since 1910, Saint Mary's University, Dalhousie University, Nova Scotia Technical College. Industries: oil refining, breweries, iron, fishing. Founded 1749. Pop. 122,-035.

Halifax, city in N England, in West Yorkshire. Industries: wool, textiles. Pop. 91,171.

Halite, the most abundant halide mineral of the halite group, sodium chloride (NaCl). Found in sedimentary rocks, salt domes, and dried lakes. Cubic system interlocking cubic crystals; also granular and massive. Colorless, white, or gray with glassy luster. Hardness 2.0; sp gr 2.2. Important as table salt and source of chlorine. △240–42, 1506.

Hall, Asaph (1829–1907), US astronomer, b. Goshen, Conn. He was professor of mathematics at the US Naval Observatory, Washington D.C. (1862–91) and professor of astronomy at Harvard (1896–1901). In 1877 he discovered Phobos and Deimos, the two moons of Mars.

Hall, Charles Francis (1821–71), US arctic explorer, b. Rochester, N.H. His first expedition (1860–62), along the SE coast of Baffin Island, discovered traces of the Eskimos' attack on Martin Frobisher who was searching for the Northwest Passage (1576–78). Hall's second expedition (1864–69) found remnants of John Franklin's expedition lost in 1845. He died while leading a government party to the North Pole (1871).

Hall, G(ranville) Stanley (1846–1924), seminal figure in US psychology, b. Ashfield, Mass. He is credited with many firsts; eg, founding one of the first US psychology laboratories, the first US psychology journal (1887), and the American Psychological Association (1892). His books *The Contents of Children's Minds* (1883) and *Adolescence* (1904) contributed powerfully to the development of the child-study movement. In 1909 he brought Freud and Jung to Clark University, of which he was president (1889–1920), thus introducing psychoanalysis to the United States. His many successful students included John Dewey and James M. Cattell.

Hall, Lyman (1724–90), American patriot and a signer of the Declaration of Independence, b. Wallingford, Conn. A physician in Georgia, he was sent by that state to the Continental Congress (1775–80). He later served for one year (1783) as the governor of Georgia.

Hallé, (Sir) Charles (1819–95), English conductor, b. Germany. At first a pianist, he formed a symphony orchestra in Manchester, England, in 1857, which subsequently became known as the Hallé Orchestra. In 1893 he established the Royal Manchester College of Music.

Halle, city in S central East Germany, on Saale River; capital of Halle district; site of University of Halle (1694) which combined with University of Wittenberg (1817), medieval town hall, 15th-century tower; birthplace of George Handel (1685). Industries: coal mining, food processing, machinery. Founded 9th century. Pop. 257,337.

Halleck, Fitz-Greene (1790–1867), US poet, b. Guilford, Conn. An influential member of the Knickerbocker school, he coauthored with Joseph R. Drake the *Croaker Papers* (1819), satirical poems on contemporary affairs. His poetry was collected in *Poetical Works* (1847). For many years he was secretary to John Jacob Astor. *See also* Knickerbocker School.

Haller, Albrecht von (1708–77), Swiss biologist, physician, and poet. Well known as a botanist for his descriptions of alpine flora and as a poet for his glorification of the mountains (*Die Alpen,* 1729), he was appointed professor of anatomy, medicine, and botany at the University of Göttingen in 1736. There he did research on the contractility of muscle tissue, and his resulting treatise (1752) laid the foundations of modern neurology. He returned to his native Bern in 1753, maintaining a private medical practice. His anatomy summary, *Elementa physiologiae corporis humani* (8 vols., 1757–66), became the first standard physiology text.

Halley, Edmund (1656–1742), British scientist who accurately predicted the return in 1758 of the comet bearing his name, and who first published a map of the winds (1686). △1160.

Halley's Comet. △90.

Halloween, in medieval times a holy evening. It took place on Oct. 31, the eve of All Saints' Day. The souls of the dead were to visit their former homes on this day.

Hallstatt, town in W Austria, on Hallstätter Lake; archeological excavations (1846–99) unearthed cultural relics dating from *c.* 900 BC, known as the Hallstatt era of the Iron Age. Industries: tourism, salt mines, wood carving. Pop. 1,340. △990.

Hallucination, perceptual experience without appropriate sensory (receptor) stimulation, which can be viewed as a falsification of reality. Though they may

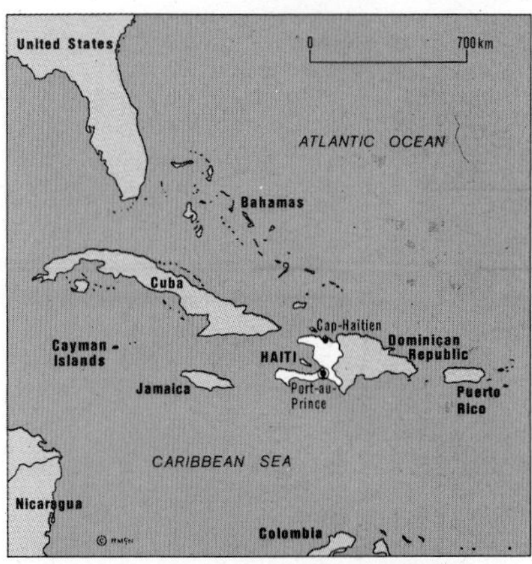
United States
0
700km
ATLANTIC OCEAN
Bahamas
Cuba
Cayman Islands
Cap-Haïtien
Dominican Republic
HAITI
Port-au-Prince
Jamaica
Puerto Rico
CARIBBEAN SEA
Nicaragua
Colombia
Haiti

George Hale

Nathan Hale

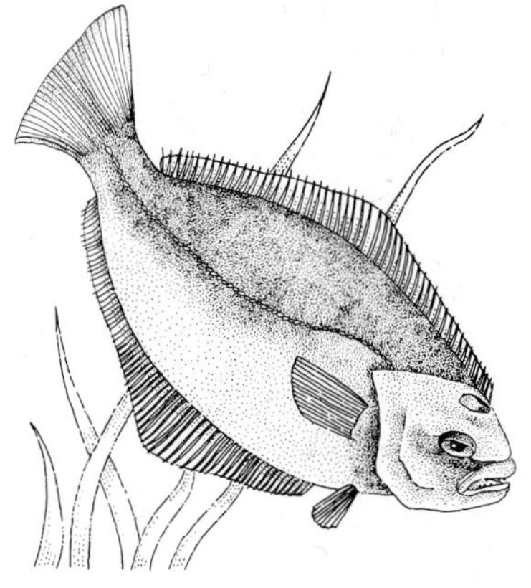
Halibut

occur in any sense (hearing, sight, touch, taste, or smell), auditory hallucinations appear to be the most common. Though usually symptomatic of psychotic disorders, hallucinations may also occur during altered states of consciousness. △760, 764.

Hallucinogen, drug that causes hallucinations, that is, unusual perceptions without external cause. Hallucinogenic drugs, such as marijuana, mescaline, and lysergic acid diethylamide (LSD), have been used in primitive religous ceremony and have an extensive illicit use. Some are employed in experimental investigation and treatment of mental illness. △1560.

Halo Effect, tendency of an evaluator to bias his judgments of a person in the direction of his first impression of that person. For example, physically attractive people may be evaluated as having more pleasant personalities than less attractive people. *See also* Attitudes.

Halogen Elements, elements fluorine, chlorine, bromine, iodine, and astatine belonging to group VII of the periodic table. They react with most other elements and with organic compounds; reactivity decreases down the group. The halogens are strongly electronegative and produce crystalline salts containing negative ions of the type F^-, Cl^-, etc. The name halogen means "salt-producer." △1554, 1568.

Halophytes. △620.

Hals, Frans (1580–1666), Dutch painter. He was unique in his ability to capture fleeting expressions in his paintings of robust, vital figures, such as the *Laughing Cavalier.* He also created many group portraits of drinkers, governors of charitable institutions, and children and musicians. His later works, more subdued in color and mood, have a dignity and strength approaching his contemporary, Rembrandt. △1168.

Halsey, William Frederick, Jr. (1882–1959), US admiral, b. Elizabeth, N.J. He graduated from the US Naval Academy (1904). A destroyer commander in World War I, "Bull" Halsey led carrier raids against the Japanese-held Marshall and Gilbert islands early in World War II. He was fleet commander in campaigns against the Solomons and the Philippines and the terms of Japanese surrender were signed aboard his ship, the *Missouri.*

Hälsingborg, port city in SW Sweden, on the Øresund opposite Helsingør, Denmark; site of 13th-century church, 12th-century castle. Industries: shipbuilding, sugar refining, copper, clay, brewing, rubber, coal. Pop. 82,137.

Halsted, William Stewart (1852–1922), US physician, b. New York City. Halsted became the first professor of surgery at Johns Hopkins University in Baltimore. He pioneered the use of cocaine as a "block" anesthetic and expanded on the then-new techniques of antisepsis in surgery by introducing rubber gloves. He experimented intensively (on animals) to refine and improve operating procedures, including vascular surgery.

Haltom City, formerly Bird's Fort, later Birdville; city in NE Texas; N suburb of Fort Worth; scene of meeting between Sam Houston and Indians that determined boundaries of white and Indian territories in Texas (1843). Settled 1842; inc. 1944. Pop. (1970) 28,127.

Ham, in Genesis, second of Noah's three sons. After the Flood, his irreverence resulted in a curse by Noah, who predicted that Ham's descendants would be subservient to those of his brothers, Shem and Japheth.

Ham. △380.

Hamadan, city in W Iran, at foot of Mt Alvand; capital of Hamadan governorate. Ancient city of Ecbatana, it was capital of Media 6th century BC; passed to Arabs AD 645; chief trade center of W Iran. Industries: agriculture, rugs, leather, wood products. Pop. 124,167.

Hamadryas, or sacred baboon, small baboon living in the plains and rocky hills of NE Africa and Arabia. Adults and males have a rufflike mane around the neck. It was sacred to ancient Egyptians. Weight: to 40lb (18kg). Species *Comopithecus hamadryas. See also* Baboon.

Hamamatsu, city on S central Honshu, Japan, near the Pacific coast approx. 55mi (89km) SE of Nagoya; site of daimyo castle; suffered Allied bombings May-June 1945. Industries: textiles, tea, musical instruments. Pop. 432,221.

Haman, biblical prime minister of Ahasuerus, king of Persia. An enemy of the Jews, he was hanged on gallows erected for Mordecai, cousin to Ahasuerus' wife Esther, who was to die for refusing to bow before Haman.

Hamburg, city that is also a constituent state of West Germany, on the Elbe River near its mouth on the North Sea; capital of the state. A successful medieval trading port, by 1510 it was an imperial free city. Present urban area was created 1937 by incorporating towns of Harburg, Wandsbek, and Altona into city structure; site of 19th-century Renaissance town hall, 18th-century Renaissance-style church, University of Hamburg (1919); birthplace of Johannes Brahms and Felix Mendelssohn. Industries: food products, chemicals, metal goods, fishing, publishing. Founded AD 808 by Charlemagne. Pop. 1,814,100.

Hamden, town in S Connecticut; N residential suburb of New Haven; site of Quinnipiac College (1929), Mount Sacred Heart College (1954), South Central Community College (1967), and many pre-Revolutionary War and Civil War houses. Industries: firearms, machinery, electronics, rolled steel, aircraft, handbags. Settled 1638; inc. 1786. Pop. (1970) 49,357.

Hamilcar Barca (died 228 BC), military commander of Carthage, father of Hannibal and Hasdrubal. He fought with distinction in Sicily and during the First Punic War and withdrew without surrender. After quelling a revolt of mercenaries led by Spendius and Matho (241–38), he conquered S and E Spain. He was drowned at Helice during a siege.

Hamilton, prominent Scottish family, descendants of Sir James Hamilton of Cadzow (died 1479) and his wife Mary, sister of James III of Scotland. Their son, James, was made first earl of Arran. The second earl (died 1575) attempted unsuccessfully to secure a royal marriage for his son. The son's suit to Mary, Queen of Scots, failed and he died insane, his estates passing to his younger brother, the Marquess of Hamilton, whose grandson, the first duke of Hamilton (1606–49), played a disastrous role in the royalist cause in the English civil war. The fourth duke (1658–1712) was killed in a duel with Lord Mohun.

Hamilton, Alexander (1755–1804), US political figure, b. Nevis, West Indies. During the first years of the republic he was the leading proponent of a strong national government. He came to the North American mainland in 1772 and studied at King's College (now Columbia) in New York City in 1773–74. He joined the Continental Army in 1776 as a captain, and in 1777 General Washington appointed him his aide-de-camp and secretary. In 1780 he married into the influential Schuyler family of New York. After the war he became a lawyer in New York and a member of the Continental Congress. At the Annapolis Convention (1786), he proposed the Philadelphia Constitutional Convention of 1787. Hamilton served as a delegate to the Constitutional Convention. He was the principal contributor to *The Federalist Papers,* advocating the new constitution, and led the fight in New York State for ratification. As the first secretary of the treasury (1789–95) he established the national currency and the Bank of the United States (1791) and proposed the assumption of all state war debts by the national government, numerous excise taxes and import tariffs, and the encouragement of manufacturing and industry. Although he resigned from the cabinet in 1795, he remained politically active. A leading spokesman for the Federalists, he opposed Thomas Jefferson and his Democratic-Republicans. He advocated strong measures against revolutionary France and strong ties with England, the country's leading trading power. He alienated many of his fellow Federalists by first working against President John Adams, then by throwing his support to Thomas Jefferson rather than to his own Federalist rival in New York, Aaron Burr, when the 1800 election resulted in an electoral tie. In 1804 he thwarted Burr's campaign for governor of New York. Burr challenged him to a duel and killed him.

Hamilton, Emma, Lady (1761?–1815), wife of ambassador and archeologist Sir William Hamilton and, from 1798, mistress to Lord Horatio Nelson, by whom she had a daughter, Horatia (*b.*1801). *See also* Nelson, Horatio.

Hamilton, Richard. △1372.

Hamilton, capital and chief seaport of Bermuda Island, at the head of Great Sound. Founded 1790 and settled by English; inc. 1793; made capital 1815; made a free port 1956. Tourism is the major industry. Pop. 2,127.

Hamilton, city in SE Ontario, Canada, approx. 40mi (64km) SW of Toronto on Lake Ontario; seat of Wentworth co; site of Royal Botanical Gardens, airport, harbor, railroad. Industries: textiles, iron, steel. Settled 1813. Pop. 307,473.

Hamilton, city in New Zealand, on central North Island, on Waikato River; commercial center of dairy farming and sheep raising region; site of University of Waikato (1964). Founded 1864. Pop. 71,600.

Hamilton, city in SW Ohio, on Great Miami River 27mi (43km) N of Cincinnati; seat of Butler co; site of branch of University of Miami (1968). Industries: automobile bodies, safes, pumps, motors. Founded in early 19th century on site of abandoned Fort Hamilton; inc. 1857. Pop. (1970) 67,865.

Hamilton River. *See* Churchill River.

Hamite Subrace, former subdivision of the Caucasoid race. Designation of the pale-skinned pastoralists of black Africa (such as Berbers) as Hamites has been discredited by linguistic investigations showing their languages to be of diverse origins. △658–60.

Hamlet (*c.*1601), 5-act tragedy by William Shakespeare. Written in blank verse, it was probably based on the *Ur-Hamlet* (original *Hamlet*) by Thomas Kyd. At its first performance (*c.*1601) the part of Hamlet was doubtless played by Richard Burbage, the star of Shakespeare's company. Tradition credits Shakespeare himself with originating the part of the Ghost. Hamlet, prince of Denmark, is told by his father's ghost that Claudius, the late king's brother and new husband of the widowed queen Gertrude, poisoned the late king. Hamlet promises the Ghost to avenge his father's death. Weeks pass, and still Hamlet delays. He writes passionate letters to Ophelia, daughter of Claudius' counsellor Polonius. A company of players arrives at the castle and Hamlet arranges for them to act out a tragedy similar to the alleged murder of his father. As the player poisons his victim Hamlet watches his uncle and sees signs of guilt, but fails to act on an opportunity to kill Claudius while the king is at prayer. He denounces his mother and accidentally stabs Polonius. Convinced he is mad the king and queen have Hamlet banished to England. When he returns, Ophelia has gone mad and drowned. Hamlet and Ophelia's brother Laertes fight over the right to be her chief mourner. The king takes advantage of their antagonism to urge them to fight a duel with a poisoned sword, and also poisons a cup of wine intended for Hamlet. The Queen drinks the poisoned wine and dies; Hamlet and Laertes wound each other with the poisoned sword and Laertes dies asking Hamlet's forgiveness. Hamlet stabs the king then dies himself, saying "The rest is silence."

Hamlin, Hannibal (1809–91), US political leader, b. Paris Hill, Maine. He was a lawyer, and served in the House of Representatives (1843–47), Senate (1848–57), and as Republican governor of Maine (1857). Opposed to slavery, he became vice president under President Abraham Lincoln (1861–65) and was his close advisor. He returned to the Senate for two terms (1869–81).

Hammarskjöld, Dag (1905–61), Swedish diplomat, succeeded Trygve Lie as secretary general of the United Nations (1953). His "quiet diplomacy" secured release in 1955 of 11 US airmen held prisoner in China. In 1956 he helped resolve the Suez Canal crisis. In 1960 he sent a UN force to keep peace in the Congo. En route to Katanga for peace talks his plane crashed. He was awarded a posthumous Nobel Prize in 1961. His book *Markings* (1964) is a spiritual diary. △1382.

Hammer. △1602.

Hammerhead Shark, aggressive, man-eating fish found in all tropical marine waters and warmer temperate zones. Recognized by its unusual head that is extended laterally in two hammerlike lobes with an eye and nostril located at the tip of each lobe. It is grayish above and whitish below. Length: to 15ft (4.6m); width: 36in (0.9m); weight: to 1,500lb (675kg). Species, several including the common *Sphyrna zygaena.* Family Sphrynidae; *See also* Chondrichthyes; Sharks. △618.

Hammerstein, Oscar, II, (1895–1960), US lyricist and librettist, b. New York City, who collaborated with Jerome Kern (*Show Boat,* 1927); and Richard Rodgers (*Oklahoma,* 1943; Pulitzer Prize), (*Carousel,* 1945), (*South Pacific,* 1949; Pulitzer Prize), (*The King and I,* 1951). Rodgers and Hammerstein gave the US musical a new direction and substance. His lyrics also won two Academy Awards: "The Last Time I Saw Paris" (1941) and "It Might As Well Be Spring" (1945). △1428.

Hammer v. Dagenhart (1918), US Supreme Court decision that declared unconstitutional a federal law prohibiting the interstate shipment of goods produced in factories employing children under age 14 or long hours. This case represents the old restrictive view of the powers of the federal government and was overruled in *United States v. Darby* (1941).

Hammett, Dashiell (1894–1961), US author, b. St Mary's co, Md. Considered the originator of hard-boiled, realistic, seamy detective novels, he created Sam Spade, a tough but honest private eye, and Nick Charles, a sophisticated detective. His works include *Red Harvest* (1929), *The Maltese Falcon* (1930), *The Glass Key* (1931), and *The Thin Man* (1932). *See also* Detective Story.

Hammond, city in NW Indiana, on Illinois border; connected to Calumet Harbor on Lake Michigan, Ill. and Indiana Harbor, Ind. by a ship canal; named for George Hammond, founder of meat packing plant (1868); site of the Calumet branch of Purdue University. Industries: books, soap, margarine, steel forgings. Settled 1851; inc. 1884. Pop. (1970) 107,790.

Hammond Organ, electrophonic keyboard instrument producing amplified music with discs rotating in an electromagnetic field. Invented by Laurens Hammond in 1934 to replace pipe organs in small churches, it was later used in jazz and popular music.

Hammurabi (*fl.* 1792–50 BC), king of Babylonia in the first dynasty. He extended his rule over Mesopotamia, organized the empire, built canals and wheat granaries, and classified the law (the Code of Hammurabi). △954, 958.

Hammurabi, Code of, ancient code of law compiled under Hammurabi, king of Babylonia (*fl.* 1792–50 BC). Found carved on a diorite column by J. de Morgan in Sousa in 1901, it is now in the Louvre. Composed of 3,600 lines of cuneiform, it illustrates Babylonian social structure, economic conditions, industries, law, and family life. △908, 958.

Hamnam (Hamhung, Hungnam), port city in North Korea, on the Sea of Japan; formed by merger of Hamhung and Hungnam; birthplace of Gen. Yi Song-gye, founder of Yi dynasty that ruled Korea 1392–1910. Hungnam was annexed to Korea 1910. Industries: pig iron, carbonates, bricks, cement, acid, calcium. Pop. 143,600.

Hampton, Wade (*c.* 1752–1835), US military figure, politician, and planter, b. Halifax co, Va. He served as a colonel in the American Revolution and as a major-general in the War of 1812 but resigned from military service after a dispute with his commanding officer, Gen. James Wilkinson, over an unsuccessful campaign against Montreal (1813). One of the wealthiest planters in the United States, he also served as a member of the House of Representatives (1795–97, 1803–05).

Hampton, Wade (1818–1902), US political and military figure, b. Charleston, S.C., the grandson of Wade Hampton (*c.* 1752–1835). He opposed secession, but joined the Confederate army, raised a force called Hampton's Legion, and led a brigade in the cavalry of General James "Jeb" Stuart, whose death (1864) made him commander of the cavalry corps. Elected governor of South Carolina (1876–79), he restored home rule. He served in the US Senate (1879–91) and as commissioner of Pacific railroads (1893–99).

Hampton, seaport city in SE Virginia, on James River, 7mi (11km) N of Newport News; site of many US government installations; oldest continuous English settlement in America. Industries: defense, tourism, seafood packing, fertilizer, building materials. Founded 1610; inc. 1908; consolidated with Elizabeth City co 1952. Pop. (1970) 120,779.

Hampton Roads, a partly-sheltered harbor in SE Virginia, through which the James, Nansemond, and Elizabeth rivers flow to the Chesapeake Bay; since colonial times, it has been an important harbor and one of the busiest US ports, serving Newport News and Hampton (N shore), Norfolk and Portsmouth (S shore); site of Civil War naval battle between the *Monitor* and *Merrimack*. Length: 4mi (6km). Depth: 40ft (12m).

Hampton Roads Conference (February 1865), unsuccessful Civil War peace efforts at Hampton Roads, Va. Confederate Vice Pres. Alexander H. Stephens and two other southern leaders met with Pres. Abraham Lincoln and Sec. of State William H. Seward of the Union to discuss peace terms. President Lincoln insisted on restoring the Union, and the Confederate delegates were adamant about the recognition of the independence of the southern states, so no agreement was reached.

Hamster, small, nocturnal, burrowing rodent native to Eurasia and Africa with internal cheek pouches for carrying food. Golden hamsters, popular pets and lab animals, are descendants of one nest discovered in Syria in 1930. Smaller and lighter than wild species, golden hamsters reproduce frequently with up to 15 per litter, offering a useful supply for research. Disease-resistant and almost odorless, golden hamsters are—unlike wild ones—easy to handle. They eat fruit, greens, seeds, nuts, and meat. Length: to 6in (15cm). Family Cricetidae; Species *Mesocricetus auratus.*

Hamtramck, city in SE Michigan, entirely within city of Detroit. Named for Col. John Francis Hamtramck, commander of Fort Detroit. Industries: automobiles, paint, plastics, sausages. Settled by French late 18th century; inc. as city 1922. Pop. (1970) 27,245.

Han, either of two rivers in China. In E central China, rises in Nancheng, flows SE to Yangtze River at Hankow. Length: 750mi (1,208km). In SE China, rises on border of Fukien-Kiangsi provs., flows S to South China Sea at Swatow. Length: 100mi (161km).

Hanau, city in central West Germany, on Main River 10mi (16km) E of Frankfurt. Old town, chartered 1303, grew around medieval castle of counts of Hanau; new town was founded in early 17th century by Protestant Dutch refugees; they were united 1833; site of St Mary's church (14th century), Philippsruhe and Wilhelmsruhe palaces (18th century), Dutch-Walloon church (1600–08); much of old town's notable buildings were destroyed during WWII bombings; birthplace of Brothers Grimm. Industries: metal and mineral processing, engineering, rubber goods, chemicals, jewelry. Pop. 54,868.

Han Chinese, or **Han-Jen,** Mongoloid people constituting about 94% of the Chinese population and inhabiting the densely populated eastern half of China. They consist of various groups sharing the same culture, traditions, and written language, although within the Han Chinese language there are several mutually unintelligible dialects. Their ancient hierarchical society, based on Taoist, Confucian, and Buddhist tenets, has been reorganized under communism and the traditional agricultural economy is being modernized.

Hancock, John (1737–93), US statesman and revolutionary, b. Braintree, Mass. He was chosen to represent Massachusetts at the Continental Congress (1775–80, 1785, 1786), serving as president (1775–77). His was the first signature on the Declaration of Independence (1776). He helped to draw up the constitution of Massachusetts (1780) and became that state's first governor (1780–85). He was reelected governor in 1789 and served until his death.

Hancock, Winfield Scott (1824–86), US military leader, b. Montgomery Square, Pa. A veteran of the Mexican War, he was appointed brigadier general (1861) and fought in the Peninsular and Antietam campaigns, and at Fredericksburg, Chancellorsville, and Gettysburg, where he repulsed Pickett's charge (1863) and was badly wounded. After the war, he was chief of the military department of Texas and Louisiana. In 1880, he was the unsuccessful Democratic candidate for president.

Hand, Learned (1872–1961), US jurist, b. Albany, N.Y. He was a judge with the US District Court of New York (1909–24) and the US 2nd District Court of Appeals (1924–51), becoming chief judge (1939). He is also known for his eloquent addresses, including the "Spirit of Liberty," which he delivered in 1944. Some of his lectures were published in *The Bill of Rights* (1958).

Handball, a ball game played between two or three individuals or between two two-player teams with a black hard rubber ball. It is most popular in the United States. It is played on a court, indoors or out, of one wall (20 × 34 ft; 6 × 10m), or three or four walls (20 × 40ft; 6 × 12m). In the single-wall game, the wall is 16 feet (4.9m) high. In the three- and four-wall game, three walls are 20 feet high (6.1m), and the back wall is 12 feet high (3.7m). In all games, the object is to keep the ball out of the opponent's reach, and points are scored when the non-server cannot return the ball. The first player or team to score 21 points wins. The serve changes hands when the server cannot return the ball. Play begins by bouncing the ball once and hitting it off one or more of the walls; the ball must then be returned before a second bounce. In order to protect the hands, special gloves are used. Handball—the four-wall variation—was played in Ireland in the Middle Ages. One-wall hand-

Alexander Hamilton

Dag Hammarskjöld

Oscar Hammerstein

John Hancock

ball was introduced in Brooklyn, N.Y., in the 1880s. Intercollegiate and national championships are held annually.

Handel, George Frideric (1685–1759), German composer who lived in England after 1712, b. Georg Friedrich Handel in Halle. With J. S. Bach, Handel is regarded as the greatest composer of the Baroque period. He composed a great many operas (eg, *Atalanta, Serse, Berenice*), oratorios (eg, *Samson, Esther, Judas Maccabeus*), organ music, chamber concertos, sonatas, and songs. Among his most popular works are the *Water Music* (1715–17) and the *Royal Fireworks Music* (1749), both composed for outings and holidays promoted by the English royal court. Handel's best known work is the oratorio *The Messiah* (1741), famous for its "Hallelujah Chorus." Handel was greatly honored in his own day, especially in England. He is buried in Westminster Abbey. *See also* Baroque Music. △1196.

Handy, W(illiam) C(hristopher), (1873–1958), US composer and musician known as the "father of the blues," b. Florence, Ala. He led his own band in 1903 and was particularly popular after composing several hits including "Memphis Blues" (1912), and "St. Louis Blues" (1914). After 1923 he devoted his time exclusively to composing and publishing many other classic blues songs. △1366.

Han Dynasty (202 BC–AD 220), Chinese dynasty. It was founded by Kuang Wu-ti and was ruled by his family for more than four centuries. It is considered by the Chinese to be one of their greatest periods of rule. Han rulers laid the administrative and ideological basis for more than 2,000 years of stability and greatness for the Chinese empire. Under the Han the Confucian state cult was formalized through the examination system, bureaucratic patterns for rule were fashioned, literary and art traditions established, and imperial expansion spread Chinese influence throughout E Asia. △1038.

Hangchow (Hangzhou), port city in E China, on Hangchow Bay; capital of Chekiang prov.; S terminus of the Grand Canal; capital of Wu-Yüeh kings (907–960) and Southern Sung dynasty (1132–1276); visited and written about by Marco Polo (13th century); sacked by Taiping forces (1861); fell under Communist control (1949); site of monasteries and shrines dating from 10th century; seat of Chekiang and Hangchow universities. Industries: silk, pig iron, steel, chemicals, food processing, tools, electronic equipment, rubber, cement, paper. Pop. 1,100,000.

Hang Gliding, sport that consists of flying with only the aid of a wing, popular in the United States. The pilot is suspended beneath the wing and supported by a harness device around his waist. He also uses a triangular trapezelike bar to support himself. The various types of gliders fall into two categories—the sailwing and the rigid wing—and weigh as much as 100 lb (45kg). The lift-off is made from a cliff or surface with an incline steep enough for the pilot to achieve flight. Once in the air, the pilot uses his body to control the craft's center of gravity. The sport, which is dangerous, recorded six deaths in the United States in 1973. Hang gliding has its origins in the late 19th century. The sport is now governed by the US Hang Gliding Association, first formed in 1971 as the Southern California Hang Gliding Association.

Hangzhou. *See* Hangchow.

Han-Jen. *See* Han Chinese.

Hankow. *See* Wuhan.

Hanna, Marcus Alonzo (1837–1904), US politician, b. New Lisbon, Ohio. A wealthy businessman and a power in the Ohio Republican party, he was the chief backer of William McKinley, helping him to become Ohio governor (1891–93) and engineering his nomination for president in 1896. Hanna ran the 1896 campaign and was a close adviser to President McKinley. From 1897–1904, he was a US senator.

Hannibal (247–183 BC), Carthaginian general, one of the foremost military commanders in history, son of Hamilcar Barca and brother of Hasdrubal. He took command of Carthaginian forces in Spain (221 BC), conquered much of the land, and besieged and broke Saguntum, an ally of Rome. With 35,000 select troops and elephants he crossed the Alps into Italy and with forces reduced by the difficult march won brilliant victories at Ticinus and Trebia (218). He then crossed the Apennines, pillaged Etruria, destroyed two Roman legions, and, unable to draw Fabius Cunctator into battle, halted at Apulia for the winter. At Cannae in 216 he wiped out Roman forces in his greatest triumph, but, deprived of support from Carthage, was unable to take Rome. He was gradually forced south, his gains fading from want of reinforcements. In 203 he was ordered to Carthage and, after 16 years of battle in Roman territory, was finally defeated at Zama in 202 by Scipio Africanus Major. He governed Carthage and sought constitutional reforms until his enemies forced him to flee to Syria where he was defeated in a naval battle against the Rhodian fleet. He went to Bithynia where he committed suicide to thwart extradition to Rome. *See also* Punic Wars. △1012.

Hannibal, city and riverport in NE Missouri, on Mississippi River. Famous as boyhood home of Samuel Clemens (Mark Twain); it is site of his home, a museum, and statue that memorialize him. Industries: printing, cement, lumber, candy, metal products. Settled 1818; inc. 1845. Pop. (1970) 18,698.

Hanoi (Ha-noi), city in NE Vietnam, on Red River, approx. 50mi (81km) from its port at Haiphong; capital of Vietnam 1954–1976; transportation, manufacture, and trade center. City was 7th-century seat of Chinese rule; taken by French 1883, it became capital of Tonkin; 1887–1945 capital of Indochina; liberated 1945 by the Viet Minh (the Communist-dominated Vietnam Independence League), it was recaptured by French 1946–1954; bombed by United States during Vietnam War; site of university (1956), Institute of Oriental Medicine, polytechnical college, Pagoda of Great Buddha. Industries: rice milling, textiles. Pop. 414,620.

Hanover (German, **Hannover**), former kingdom and province of Germany. Most of the area was part of the duchy of Brunswick-Lüneburg held by the Guelph family. In 1692, Duke Ernest Augustus was created elector of Hanover, and his lands were known thereafter as Hanover. His son George succeeded to the British throne in 1714; the personal union with Britain lasted until 1837, when, on the accession of Victoria in Britain, Hanover went to her uncle Ernest Augustus. Divided during the Napoleonic era, Hanover was reconstituted as a kingdom in 1815. It allied itself with Austria in the Austro-Prussian War of 1866 and, after Austria's defeat, was annexed by Prussia. After World War II it was incorporated into the state of Lower Saxony.

Hanover (Hannover), city in N West Germany, on Leine River, 35mi (56km) WNW of Brunswick; capital of Lower Saxony. In 1636 city became residence of dukes of Calenberg-Göttingen (predecessors of House of Hanover who ruled Britain 1714–1901); site of 15th-century Gothic city hall, 14th-century Marktkirche (market church), Leineschloss (17th-century chateau) that houses parliament of Lower Saxony, university (1880), and medical school (1963). Industries: steel, rubber, machinery textiles, chemicals. Founded 12th century; chartered 1241. Pop. 523,941.

Hanover, House of, royal family of Great Britain from 1714 to 1901. In 1692, Augustus of Hanover married Sophia, of the Palatinate, granddaughter of James I of England. By the terms of the English Act of Settlement (1701) their son succeeded in England as George I (1714). His successors were George II, George III, George IV, William IV, and Victoria. Salic law forbade Victoria's accession in Hanover, so her uncle Ernest Augustus, Duke of Cumberland, became king there in 1837. Victoria was succeeded (1901) by her son Edward VII, who took his father's family name, Saxe-Coburg.

Hansberry, Lorraine (1930–65), US playwright, b. Chicago, Ill. She won the New York Drama Critics Circle Award for *A Raisin in the Sun* (1959), later a film and a Broadway musical. Her other major play was *The Sign in Sidney Brustein's Window* (1964); *To Be Young, Gifted and Black* (1969) is a dramatic work adapted by Robert Nemiroff from her writings.

Hanseatic League, German commercial union of the Middle Ages which grew from smaller local unions, or Hansas. Containing several German cities, the League functioned as protector of the merchants of its member towns and worked to establish favorable trade conditions in foreign lands. Pressured by the Dutch and English, and by increasing German political organization, the League had lost its effectiveness by the mid-17th century. △1092.

Hansen's Disease. *See* Leprosy.

Hanson, John (1721–83), US political figure, first president of the United States under the Articles of Confederation (1781–82), b. Charles co, Md. He was a member of the Maryland colonial legislature, Congress of Confederation, and the Continental Congress (1780–82). His one-year term as president before the Constitution was adopted made him strictly a presi ing officer under the Articles.

Hanukkah, or **Chanukah,** meaning "consecration or "dedication," an 8-day festival celebrated in Jud ism. it is also known as the Feast of Lights. It is a maj ceremony, involving services at home and in syn gogue, which commemorates the rededication of th Temple in 165 BC and the miracle of a one-day suppl of oil lasting for eight days. Gifts are given and game played.

Hanuman, or entellus langur, leaf-eating monkey o S Asia that has bristly hairs on top and sides of it head. Species *Presbytis entellus. See also* Langur.

Hapsburg, name of a royal Austrian family, one o the principal houses of Europe in the 15th throug 20th centuries. The name derives from Habichtsbur (hawk's nest), the family castle in Switzerland.

Beginning with Otto, the first count of Hapsburg, i the 11th century, there was a direct male line unt 1740 when the Pragmatic Sanction allowed a daugh ter, Maria Theresa, to succeed, an event that change the name of the house to Hapsburg-Lorraine.

Frederick V, the Hapsburg king of Germany, wa crowned Holy Roman Emperor in 1452, and the titl remained in the family until the empire was dissolve in 1806. His son Maximilian married (1477) Mary daughter of Charles the Bold of Burgundy, which a lowed the family to acquire the Netherlands, Luxem bourg, and Burgundy. Maximilian's descendant gained control of Spain, Naples, Sicily, and Sardinia The peak of Hapsburg power was reached unde Charles I, king of Spain (HRE Charles V) in the 16th century. His vast realm proved too unwieldy, how ever, and the family split into two branches, the Span ish Hapsburgs and the Austrian Hapsburgs. The Span ish Hapsburgs died out in 1700. The last rulinc Austrian Hapsburg, Charles I, abdicated in 1918.

Well-known Hapsburgs include Marie Antoinette queen of France, Marie Louise, second wife of Napo leon I, Maximilian, emperor of Mexico, and Empero Francis Joseph of Austria-Hungary. △1128, 1154 1182, 1248.

Hara-kiri, or more properly, "seppuku," Japanese form of ritualized suicide by disembowelment. Sep puku originated with samurai in the middle ages. Al though it was generally voluntarily performed to avoic becoming an enemy prisoner, to prove loyalty, or tc protest the actions of a superior, leaders often or dered subordinates to commit seppuku following ar insubordination. It is still practiced today, most often as a form of protest.

Harappa Civilization. △962.

Harbin (Haerbin), port city in Manchuria, China, or Sungari River; capital of Heilungkiang prov. A Russian concession 1896–1924, it was under Japanese rule 1932–45; fell to Communist control 1950. Industries: oil, coal, machinery, aircraft, sugar refining, tractors, meat packing, food processing, railroad shops. Pop. 2,750,000.

Harbor. △1760.

Harbor Seal, also called common seal or spotted seal *(Phoca vitulina),* North American seal usually found in coastal waters of Canada and Alaska. Adults have a spotted grey or black coat, pups are born white or gray. They feed on fish and crustaceans, come ashore frequently, and congregate in herds when they are on land. Size is about 5ft (1.5m), 150lbs (68kg), but they can grow larger. Although they are not hunted commercially, they are useful to man for clothing and food.

Hardecanute (*c.*1019–42), king of Denmark (1035–42), king of England (1040–42). Son of Canute of England and Emma of Normandy. His claim to the English throne after Canute's death was opposed by his half brother Harold Harefoot, who was elected king in 1037. Hardecanute attacked England in 1040. Harold died in 1040, and Hardecanute became king. Cruel and oppressive, he avoided dynastic struggle by indicating Edward the Confessor, Emma's son by Aethelred, as his successor.

Hardhead. *See* Croaker.

Harding, Warren Gamaliel (1865–1923), 29th president of the United States (1921–23), b. Blooming Grove (now Corsica), Ohio, attended Ohio Central College. In 1891 he married a wealthy widow, Florence Kling De Wolfe, who urged him into a political career. He bought and published a newspaper in Marion, Ohio. He served in the Ohio state senate as a Republican and in 1904 he served a term as lieutenant governor. He unsuccessfully ran for governor in

1910, and in 1914 he was elected to the US Senate.

After the 1920 Republican convention deadlocked, Harding was chosen as presidential candidate by a clique of party leaders in a "smoke-filled room." He ran on a platform of returning the country to "normalcy," a word of his own coinage. He easily defeated his Democratic rival, James M. Cox.

An unambitious, easygoing man, Harding displayed almost no talent or taste for the presidency. He left control of the administration to his advisors, who became known as the "Ohio gang." Soon reports of large-scale corruption and graft circulated—the most important example was the Teapot Dome scandal—and congressional investigations were begun. Harding became ill and died before most of the scandals, among the worst in US history, were uncovered. He was succeeded by Vice President Calvin Coolidge. Among Harding's staff who were prosecuted after his death were Albert B. Fall, his secretary of the interior, and Harry M. Daughtery, his attorney general.

Career: Ohio State Senate, 1899–1903; Ohio lieutenant governor, 1904–05; US Senate, 1915–21; president, 1921–23. *See also* Teapot Dome Scandal.

Hardness Scale, a scale used to furnish a rough estimate of a mineral's resistance to scratching by testing it against a predetermined series of minerals (or test objects) graded from 1 through 10. A flat surface of the mineral to be tested is scratched by a sharp edge of the test object. Anything scratchable by talc is valued at 1, by diamond at 10.

Hardwar, city in N India, on Ganges River; considered one of the seven most sacred pilgrimage centers in the country; site of Gangadwara temple and bathing ghat; scene of the Kumbh-Mela, large bathing festival held every 12th year. Pop. 58,500.

Hardwick Hall. △1144.

Hardy, Thomas (1840–1928), English novelist and poet. His novels, most of them tragic works set in the region of Wessex, include *Far From the Madding Crowd* (1874), *The Return of the Native* (1878), *The Mayor of Casterbridge* (1886), *Tess of the d'Urbervilles* (1891), and *Jude the Obscure* (1895). Hardy later concentrated on poetry, in volumes such as *Wessex Poems* (1898). Noted poems by him include "The Darkling Thrush" (1900), "Channel Firing" (1914), and "The Convergence of the Twain" (1914). Between 1903 and 1908 he published *The Dynasts*, an epic-drama. △1240.

Hare, large member of the herbivorous rabbit family (Leoporidae) widely distributed around the world, with long ears and large hind feet. In contrast to rabbits, true hares (genus *Lepus*) move by leaping as well as running and their young are born with open eyes and a full coat of fur. Length 15–30in (38–76cm); weight: 3–15lb (1.3–7kg). Hares include jackrabbits, snowshoe rabbits, and European hares. *See also* Rabbit. △546.

Harebell, or Scottish bluebell, slender-stemmed perennial bellflower native to Eurasia and North America. It bears nodding blue, bell-like flowers. Many North American wildflowers are also called harebells. Height: to 2ft (61cm). Family Campanulaceae; genus *Campanusla rotundifolia*. *See also* Bellflower.

Harelip, congenital cleft in the upper lip caused by the failure of the two parts of the palate to unite. Heredity may be a factor, as may metabolic disorders or diseases of mother or infant. Corrective surgery usually is postponed until an affected child is 18 months old.

Harem, a man's wives, concubines, and female servants. It is especially associated with Islam, which requires the strict segregation of women. The most famous harem was that of the Turkish sultans, which often had several hundred women, guarded by eunuchs, before its abolition in 1909. *See also* Concubinage.

Hare Plan. See Proportional Representation.

Hargeysa, town in N Somali Democratic Republic, E Africa; capital of former British Somaliland 1884–1960, livestock center. Pop. 40,255.

Harlan, John Marshall. (1833–1911), US jurist and lawyer, b. Boyle co, Ky. A county judge (1858), and Kentucky state attorney general (1863), he was appointed an associate justice of the US Supreme Court (1877–1911) where he was noted for his advocacy of civil rights, best revealed in his eloquent dissent in *Plessy v. Ferguson* (1896), the case that established the "separate but equal" racial segregation doctrine, which stood as law until 1954.

Harlan, John Marshall (1899–1971), US jurist and lawyer, b. Chicago, the grandson of Supreme Court Justice Harlan (1833–1911). He received the Legion of Merit Award in World War II and later served as chief counsel for the New York State Crime Commission (1951–53). Appointed to the US court of appeals in February 1954, he was made an associate justice of the US Supreme Court in November 1954. An advocate of judicial restraint in matters concerning social and economic legislation, he defended the expansion of civil rights and liberties.

Harlem, community of Manhattan borough, New York City. A fashionable 19th-century community, an influx of blacks *c.* 1905–1920 made it one of the largest black settlements in the United States and a political and cultural center for blacks. Founded 1658 by Dutch; annexed to New York City 1731.

Harlem Renaissance, period of creativity, particularly in literature, among US blacks in the 1920s. Centered in Harlem, the black ghetto in New York City (not all the writers were New Yorkers, however), the Renaissance produced such writers as Countee Cullen, Langston Hughes, and Claude McKay. *See also* Harlem. △1420.

Harlequin Bug, or fire bug, calico bug, collard bug, orange and black bug that is a vegetable garden pest in S United States. They suck juices from plants. Length: .35in (8.9mm). Family Pentatomidae; species *Murgantia histrionica. See also* Stink Bug.

Harlequin Duck, small sea duck with a short bill and distinctively patterned plumage. Species *Histrionicus histrionicus. See also* Duck.

Harley, Robert, 1st Earl of Oxford (1661–1724), English statesman. He gradually assumed leadership of the Tory party, supplanting both Marlborough and Godolphin in Queen Anne's confidence. As chancellor of the exchequer (1710), he promoted peace with France and the formation of the South Sea Company. He survived impeachment in 1715 for conduct relating to the treaty of Utrecht (1713) and for his Jacobite leanings.

Harlingen, barge port and city in SE Texas, 18mi (29km) N of Mexican border, connected with Gulf Intercoastal Waterway to Rio Grande River. Industries: canneries, shrimp processing, cotton, packing plants. Founded 1904; inc. 1910. Pop. (1970) 33,503.

Harlow, Harry F. (1905–), US psychologist, b. Fairfield, Iowa. He did important work with monkeys in the areas of learning, motivation, and social development. He showed that peer and play experiences during early infancy are essential for normal development. Harlow's research has significant implications for human child development. △784.

Harlow, Jean (1911–37), US movie actress, b. Harlean Carpenter in Kansas City, Mo., known as the "blonde bombshell," an almost legendary figure of the Hollywood 1930s. Her first major role was in *Hell's Angels* (1930). She was also talented in sophisticated comedies.

Harmodius and Aristogiton (died 514 BC), the "tyrannicides," two Greeks of noble families who attempted to kill the Athenian tyrant Hippias and his brother Hipparchus. The plot failed, only Hipparchus was killed, and Harmodius and Aristogiton were executed. When the tyranny was overthrown three years later, the people hailed them as the liberators of Athens. According to Thucydides, the plot developed from Aristogiton's anger at Hippias' advances toward his young friend.

Harmonic, oscillation of a periodic quantity, such as a musical note, whose frequency is a whole-number multiple of the fundamental frequency. *See also* Timbre. △1500.

Harmonica, or mouth organ, simplest reed instrument. It is a box in various sizes holding free metal reeds in diatonic scale, which are vibrated when the player blows or inhales through openings while moving the harmonica across his lips. Of European origin (*c.*1820), it is considered an amateur or novelty instrument, except when played in bands or by expert soloists.

Harmonic Motion, repeated motion as of a pendulum, atomic vibrations, or an oscillating electrical circuit. Simple harmonic motion is governed by a restoring force proportional to the displacement of the particle: $F = Kx$, where K, called the spring constant, determines the strength of the restoring force. The above equation pervades all branches of physics.

George F. Handel

W.C. Handy

Warren G. Harding

Harlequin duck

Harmonic Progression, sequence of the form 1/*a*, 1/*b*, 1/*c*, ... , where *a*, *b*, *c*, etc., form an arithmetic progression. The simplest is formed by the reciprocals of the positive integers: 1, 1/2, 1/3, 1/4, ... Strings with lengths proportional to these terms (and with identical diameter and tension) vibrate with harmonic musical tones.

Harmonium, keyboard instrument producing music when air propelled by a pedal-operated bellows vibrates metal reeds. It is equipped with stops to vary tone colors. Developed in France (*c.*1840), it became popular in the United States in modified form as a small parlor organ.

Harmony, town in Pennsylvania where, in 1805, the Harmony Society first settled. The society was a religious group of Germans who held communal property and practiced austerity and also celibacy.

Harmony in Red (Matisse). △1294.

Harmsworth, Alfred Charles William. *See* Northcliffe, Viscount.

Harness Racing, sport popular in the United States, Australia, and New Zealand. It consists of racing over an oval circuit with horse-drawn sulkies. The sulky, a two-wheeled carriage, holds the driver. The horses are classified according to gaits—trotters (diagonally gaited), and pacers (laterally gaited). The distance raced is usually 1 mile (1.6km), and the horses race from a running start. There are several classes of races, with a parimutuel betting system that pays off on first, second, and third place finishes and various combinations. Harness racing began in the 1830s in the United States but was impeded by the cumbersome four-wheeled sulky. The high, two-wheeled sulky was developed in the 1840s, and in 1891 the modern low-wheeled sulky was introduced. The most famous races include the Hambletonian and the Roosevelt International Trot. The US Trotting Association, formed in 1938, governs the sport in the United States.

Harold I Harefoot (died 1040), English king of Danish origins, succeeded his father Canute in 1035. Despite Hardecanute's rival claim, he became ruler of all England (1037). *See also* Canute.

Harold II (1022?–1066), king of England (1066). Second son of Godwin, earl of Wessex, as a young man he was appointed to the earldom of East Anglia. His succession in 1053 to the earldom of Wessex thus made him the most influential figure in England except the king. Upon the death of Edward the Confessor, the council, following the dying king's request, named Harold king. William of Normandy at once gathered an army of 15,000 men to enforce his rival claim. Tostig, Harold's disenfranchised brother, joined forces with Harold III of Norway to attack from the north. Harold soundly defeated this force at Stamford Bridge (Sept. 25, 1066), but had to march south immediately to meet William's army at Hastings. In this battle Harold was defeated and killed. △1076.

Harold III (1015–66), called "Hard-Ruler," king of Norway, son of Sigurd Sow. A great warrior, he served the Byzantines. Shared throne with Magnus I until Magnus's death in 1047. From 1047 to 1064 he tried to conquer Denmark, and he died while helping Earl Tostig in the effort to conquer England in 1066.

Harold Bluetooth (*c.* 910–c.985), king of Denmark beginning *c.*935. On a runic stone at Jelling he wrote that he "had united all Denmark and Norway under himself and made the Danes Christians." Unable to maintain his hold on Norway, he was killed by the forces of his son Sweyn.

Haroun al-Raschid (*c.*764–809), fifth Abbasid caliph (786–809); son of al-Mahdi; successor of his brother, al-Hadi. He successfully invaded Asia Minor, reaching the Bosporus in 782; concluded a treaty with the Byzantine empress Irene; and subdued northern part of Africa. He had diplomatic relations with Charlemagne and China; killed or imprisoned the Barmecides, a rich, generous Persian family in 798; crushed uprisings; patronized the arts; and encouraged canals, mosques, and public works. He captured Heraclea (S Italy) and Tyana (S Turkey) in 806 and imposed a tax on the Byzantine emperor Nicephorus I. Al-Amin succeeded him. △1062.

Harp, ancient musical instrument with strings plucked by hand. Used in symphony orchestras, it came from Egypt (*c.*3000 BC) and later Ireland (*c.* 800). A large triangular frame supported vertically carries 46 strings tuned diatonically, C strings colored red and F strings blue; seven pedals raise the pitch by halftones. The double-pedal harp was invented by Sebastian Erard in Paris (1810). △1244.

Harper's Ferry National Historic Park, historic area in NE West Virginia; site of John Brown's raid on US arsenal Oct. 16, 1859; captured by Confederate troops 1862. Area: 1,530acres (620hectares). Est. 1955.

Harper v. Virginia Board of Elections (1966), US Supreme Court decision declaring a state poll tax unconstitutional as an invidious discrimination and denial of equal protection.

Harpies, in Greek mythology, wind spirits. They were associated with the underworld.

Harpoon, a weapon, usually a barbed spear, used in hunting fish and whales. It has a flat triangular, sharpened head, detachable from the shaft and attached to a strong line. The harpoon may be thrown by hand or shot from a gun. The head of a modern whaling harpoon carries an explosive charge.

Harp Seal, North American seal *(Pagophilus groenlandicus)* that ranges widely over the Arctic seas, with the largest herds found off the W coast of Greenland and the E Arctic Ocean. To whelp, they migrate to Labrador and the Gulf of St Lawrence. Adults are silver with black harp-shaped marks on their backs; pups are pure white. Large scale commercial hunting of the seals, desirable for their pelts, blubber, and meat, has decreased the population despite quotas set by the Canadian government.

Harp Shell. △482.

Harpsichord, sensitive keyboard musical instrument resembling a small, often ornately decorated grand piano. Its metal strings are mechanically plucked by quills (not struck by hammers), producing thin, tinkling tones blending well with the flute and violin. Traditionally associated with Baroque music (16th–18th centuries), it was later replaced by the piano. It was revived in this century by Wanda Landowska and Rosalyn Tureck.

Harpy Eagle, broad-winged, long-tailed eagle of tropical rain forests in New Guinea, the Philippines, and South America. Included are the monkey-eating eagle *(Pithecophaga jefferyi)* of the Philippines and the harpy *(Harpia harpyja)* of South America that feeds on Capuchin monkeys. There are four species. *See also* Eagle.

Harrier, diurnal bird of prey with owllike face that frequents pastures and grasslands where it pounces on small animals. They have small bills, long wings, legs, and tails, and may be gray, black, or brown with a white rump. Bluish-white eggs (3–8) are laid in a ground nest. Length: 15–20in (38–51cm). Genus *Circus.*

Harrier, pack hunting dog (hound group); first English pack dates from 1260. Used for hare hunting and can be followed on foot. A smaller version of the foxhound, it has a medium-sized head with a pronounced forehead; flat, thin, ears carried close to the head; a level, muscular body; straight, well-boned legs; and a long, high-set tail. The short coat is black, tan, and white. Standard size: 19–21in (48.26–53.5cm) high at shoulder; 40–50lb (18–22.5kg). *See also* Hound.

Harriman, (William) Averell (1891–), US political leader and diplomat, b. New York City. After a financial career, he went into public service (1934) as an administrator for the National Recovery Administration and worked under presidents from F.D. Roosevelt to Lyndon Johnson. He was ambassador to Russia and to England. He also was secretary of commerce (1946–48), Mutual Security Agency director (1951–53), governor of New York (1954–58), and an unsuccessful candidate for the presidential nomination (1956). As President Johnson's ambassador-at-large (1965–69), he was chief negotiator at the Paris peace talks to end the Vietnam War (1968–69).

Harriman, Edward Henry (1848–1909), US railroad magnate and financier, b. Hempstead, N.Y. In 1870 he bought seat on the New York Stock Exchange and started his railroad career with Illinois Central, moving in 1898 to buy the Union Pacific. His contest in 1901 with James Hill for control of Northern Pacific led to a serious Wall Street financial crisis. △1278.

Harris, Benjamin (1673?–1716), English journalist and publisher of the first newspaper printed in America. He worked as a journalist in London until 1686 and then emigrated to America, where he opened a bookshop in Boston and became the leading publisher in the colonies. In 1690 he issued *Publick Occurrences Both Forreign and Domestick.* He returned to London in 1695 and published the newspaper *London Post* (1699–1706).

Harris, Joel Chandler (1848–1908), US author, b. Eatonton, Ga. Harris is famous for his Uncle Remus stories, retellings of black folk literature. His first collection was *Uncle Remus: His Songs and His Sayings* (1880). Other volumes include *Nights with Uncle Remus* (1883) and *Mr. Remus and His Friends* (1892). He was on the staff of the *Atlanta Constitution* newspaper for 24 years.

Harris, Townsend (1804–78), US statesman, b. Sandy Hill, N.Y. A New York City merchant, he was a Democratic member of the city's board of education and helped charter the College of the City of New York (1847). President Buchanan sent him to Japan in 1855 as the first American consul general after Commodore Perry opened Shimoda and Hakodate ports to US trade. He negotiated the first formal US-Japanese commercial treaty (1858) and served as the first US ambassador to Japan (1859–61).

Harrisburg, capital city in SE Pennsylvania, 100mi (161km) W of Philadelphia, on Susquehanna River; seat of Dauphin co. John Harris built a trading post and ferry here 1718; by 1785 the town of Harris' Ferry was appointed co seat and known as Harrisburg; scene of Harrisburg Conventions of 1788 and 1828 which proposed 12 amendments to the federal constitution; became state capital 1812. It is site of the capitol (1906), John Harris Mansion (1766), Rockville Bridge (1899), Sunken Gardens, Harrisburg Area Community College (1965). Industries: steel, food processing, textiles, clothing, metal products, aircraft parts. Settled 1717; inc. 1860. Pop. (1970) 68,061.

Harrison, Benjamin (1833–1901), 23rd president of the United States (1889–93), b. North Bend, Ohio; graduate, Miami University (Ohio), 1852. He was the grandson of William Henry Harrison. In 1853 he married Caroline Scott; they had two children. In 1896, after his wife's death, he married her niece, Mary Dimmick; they had one child. A highly successful corporation lawyer in Indiana, Harrison became a leader in the new Republican party. He served with distinction in the Union army during the Civil War. After the war, he returned to his law practice in Indiana and increased his involvement in Republican politics.

In 1881 he was sent to the US Senate. He was defeated for reelection in 1887, but the following year the Republicans nominated Harrison to run for the presidency against the incumbent, Grover Cleveland. After a notably corrupt campaign, Harrison won the election with a majority of the electoral votes, although President Cleveland polled the most popular votes. As President, Harrison signed into law the Sherman Antitrust Act, the Sherman Silver Purchase Act, and the McKinley Tariff Act. He ran for re-election in 1892 but was defeated by Cleveland.

Career: US Army, 1862–65; US Senate, 1881–87; president, 1889–93.

Harrison, William Henry (1773–1841), soldier and 9th president of the United States (March 4–April 4, 1841), b. Charles City co, Va. He attended Hampden-Sydney College and the University of Pennsylvania medical school. He was the son of Benjamin Harrison, a signer of the Declaration of Independence.

Harrison was a professional soldier who won fame in the Northwest Territory as an Indian fighter in the battles of Fallen Timbers (1794) and Tippecanoe (1811). He was governor of the Indiana Territory (1800–13), and during the War of 1812 he commanded US troops in the Indiana and Illinois country.

In 1814, Harrison settled in North Bend, Ohio. His fame as a soldier made him an attractive political figure to the Ohio Whigs. He served in both the US House of Representatives and Senate and was briefly (1829) US minister to Colombia. In 1836 he was nominated by one faction of Whigs for the presidency but was defeated.

The Whigs nominated Harrison for president in 1839 and chose John Tyler as his running mate. Thus was born the campaign slogan "Tippecanoe—and Tyler, Too." Despite Harrison's aristocratic Virginia background, he was pictured as a plain western farmer living in a log cabin. It was the most spectacular campaign in US history, and the old soldier won by a landslide. Harrison was inaugurated and began assembling his cabinet. He contracted pneumonia, however, and died only a month after taking office.

Career: US Army, 1791–98, 1812–14; US House of Representatives, 1816–19; US Senate, 1825–28; US minister to Colombia, 1829; president, 1841.

Harrow, borough of NW Greater London, England: mainly residential; some light industry; site of Harrow chool (1571), whose graduates include Byron, Galsorthy, Peel, Palmerston, and Churchill; St Mary's hurch (11th century). Pop. 219,484.

Harrow, agricultural implement used to smooth and ulverize plowed land, to cover seeds and fertilizers,) cut up crop residues before plowing, and to root ut weeds after sowing.

Hart, John, (1711–79), American legislator and a gner of the Declaration of Independence, b. Stonngton, Conn. After serving as a delegate from New ersey to the Continental Congress (1776), he beame chairman of the New Jersey council of safety 777–78).

Hart, Lorenz Milton (1895–1943), American lyriist, b. New York City. He combined his talents with omposer Richard Rodgers to produce such hit musials as *Dearest Enemy* (1925), *A Connecticut Yankee* 1927), *The Boys from Syracuse* (1938), *Pal Joey* 1940), and *By Jupiter* (1942).

Hart, Moss (1904–1961), US dramatist, b. New York City. He collaborated with George S. Kaufman on nany comedies including *Once in a Lifetime* (1930), *Merrily We Roll Along* (1934), Pulitzer Prize winner *You Can't Take It With You* (1936) and *The Man Who Came to Dinner* (1939). His most successful musical was *Lady in the Dark* (1941) written with Kurt Weill nd Ira Gershwin. In 1956 he directed *My Fair Lady.* He wrote a well received autobiography, *Act One* 1959).

Hart, William S(urrey) (1872–1946), US star and writer-director of silent Western films, b. Newburgh, N.Y. His major films included *Wagon Tracks* (1919?), *The Toll Gate* (1920), *White Oak* (1922?), *Three Word Brand* (1921), *Pinto Ben* (1924), and *Tumbleweeds* (1926).

Harte, (Francis) Bret(t) (1836–1902), US author, b. Albany, N.Y. In 1865 he published *Outcroppings,* an anthology of local California verse, and in 1867 *The Lost Galleon,* a collection of his own poems, and *Condensed Novels and Other Papers,* a collection of parodies of famous authors. In 1868 he became editor of *Overland Monthly* and published *The Luck of Roaring Camp and Other Sketches,* a collection of stories that brought him national recognition and led to a contract for 12 articles for *The Atlantic Monthly.* The articles were mediocre, and thereafter Harte's popularity declined. His magazine articles are collected in many volumes, including *Mrs. Skagg's Husbands* (1873) and *Tales of the Argonauts* (1875). *See also* Local Color.

Hartebeest, large antelope native to African grasslands south of Sahara Desert. Light to dark brown, both sexes have lyre-shaped horns united at the base and rising sharply from the forehead. Its shoulders are higher than the rump, causing a clumsy gait, but it can run 40mph (64kmph). Lichtenstein's hartebeest *(Alcelaphus lichtensteini)* is a common game animal. Length: to 78in (2m); height: to 59in (1.5m); weight: to 400lb (180kg). Family Bovidae. *See also* Ruminant.

Hartford, capital city and port of entry in central Connecticut, on the Connecticut River; largest city of Connecticut. First settlers came from New Town, Mass. (1635–36), led by Thomas Hooker and Samuel Stone; they formed Connecticut Colony (1639) and adopted Fundamental Orders. Hartford was joint capital with New Haven (1701–1875), when it was appointed sole capital; scene of Hartford Convention (1814). Known as the insurance capital of the world, it has approx. 35 insurance company headquarters; site of old State House (1796), Wadsworth Atheneum (1842), Harriet Beecher Stowe House (1871), Mark Twain Memorial (1873), capitol (1878), Trinity College (1823), University of Hartford (1957), American School for the Deaf (1817); birthplace of Noah Webster, John Fiske, J.P. Morgan. Industries: typewriters, precision instruments, computers, electrical equipment, tobacco processing. Inc. 1784. Pop. (1970) 158,017.

Hartford Convention (1814–15), secret meeting called by leaders of five New England states opposed to the War of 1812, which they said hampered commerce. Convention resolutions sought to strengthen states' rights over conscription and taxation, and some delegates favored withdrawal from the Union. However, news of Jackson's victory at New Orleans and the end of the war also ended the Hartford Convention.

Hartford Fern. *See* Climbing Fern.

Hartford Wits. *See* Connecticut Wits.

Hartshorne, H. △786.

Harun-ar-Rashid. △1062.

Harunobu, Suzuki (1718–70), Japanese ukiyo-e (color) printmaker. His elegant, poetic prints usually depicted genteel young ladies in houses or gardens, often with bands of clouds above or streams flowing in the background. He perfected a technique of printing in more than 10 colors.

Haruspication, divination, especially by examination of the entrails or liver of specially slaughtered animals. Haruspication was important in ancient Rome and still is practiced in Borneo and South America. *See also* Divination.

Harvard University, oldest US university, located mainly at Cambridge, Mass. Academic colleges include faculties for divinity, art, sciences, education, law, engineering, public administration, public health, and medicine. Founded in 1636 by a grant from the General Court of Massachusetts Bay Colony. In 1638 it was named for its first benefactor, John Harvard. △1216, 1406.

Harvestman, or daddy-longlegs, spiderlike animal, found worldwide, with legs that may be several times the body length. The head and abdomen are broadly joined. It feeds on living or dead insects and plant juices. Body length: 0.1–0.5in (2.5–12.7mm). Order Phalangida.

Harvest Mite. *See* Chigger.

Harvey, William (1578–1657), English physician and anatomist. In 1628 he discovered the circulation of the blood. This finding, a landmark in medical history, marked the beginning of modern physiology. Harvey, a careful experimenter, was one of the first to use quantitative methods in biological research, and his view of the heart as a pump helped establish a mechanistic way of thinking that subsequently pervaded much of science. His findings on blood circulation, published in *De Motu Cordis et Sanguinis (On the Motions of the Heart and Blood),* were ridiculed at first and only later were generally accepted. Harvey also made important studies in embryology. △688.

Harvey, city in NE Illinois, on Little Calumet River; site of oil research center. Industries: railroad and building equipment, diesel engines. Founded 1890; inc. 1895. Pop. (1970) 34,636.

Harz Mountain, mountain range on border of East and West Germany, extending about 60mi (97km) between Elbe and Leine rivers; resort and mining area. Highest peak is Brocken, 3,747ft (1,143m).

Hasa, Al, oasis region in E Saudi Arabia, on W coast of Persian Gulf; controlled by Turks 1875 to 1914 when captured by Ibn Saud. The largest oasis in Saudi Arabia, it is fed by numerous artesian springs. Industries: oil, dates, wheat, rice. Area: 41,200sq mi (106,708sq km). Pop. 500,000.

Hasan (*c.* 625–69), fifth Orthodox caliph (661–69), eldest son of Ali and Fatima (daughter of Muhammad). He succeeded Ali; led a sensual life; abdicated in favor of Muawiya (the first Omayyad caliph); and retired to Medina. His brother, Husein, upheld the family's claim.

Hasdrubal, name of two Carthaginian generals. The elder (died 221 BC) was the son-in-law of Hamilcar Barca and succeeded his command in Spain where he expanded Carthaginian power and founded Cartagena. The younger (died 207 BC) was Hamilcar Barca's son and the brother of Hannibal. He took command in Spain when Hannibal marched into Italy. Defeated by Publius Cornelius Scipio (215), he crossed the Alps to join Hannibal but was forced to withdraw to the Metaurus valley (207) where his army was defeated and his head sent to Hannibal's camp. *See also* Punic Wars. △1012.

Hashemite, a branch of Koreish, including Mohammed the Prophet, and a modern Arab dynasty of his descendents founded by Husayn ibn-Ali, king of the Hejaz (1916–24). His first son, Ali, succeeded him for a year. His second son, Abdullah, became king of Trans-Jordan (1921–51), succeeded by his grandson, Husein ibn-Jalal. And his third son, Faisal, became king of Iraq (1921–33). Faisal's branch of the Hashemite dynasty was destroyed in the 1958 revolution in Iraq.

Hasidism, a popular pietist movement within Judaism founded by Israel Baal Shem Tov (1699–1761). It taught the ability of all men to reach God, and followers became known for tolerance and glorification of

Harp

Benjamin Harrison

William Harrison

Harrow

the founder. The movement, centered in E Europe until World War II, strongly supported Orthodox Judaism. Main centers are now in Israel and the United States. △844.

Hassam, (Frederick) Childe (1859–1935), US painter and illustrator, b. Boston, Mass. His use of brushstroke and color shows the influence of Impressionism. Many of his early paintings were of street scenes and women; later he did landscapes, especially of the shore.

Hassan II (1929–), king of Morocco (1961–), son and successor of Mohammed V. He dissolved the National Assembly in 1965, assumed all executive and legislative powers, and in 1970 provided a new constitution by referendum. He survived attempted coups (1971, 1972), eliminated foreign ownership of business (1973), and seized much of the Spanish Sahara (1976) after organizing a march of hundreds of thousands of his subjects across the border of that colony (1975).

Hastings, Warren (1732–1818), British colonial administrator, the first governor general of India (1772–84). He fought at the battle of Plassey with Clive (1757), served on the Calcutta Council, and was governor of Fort William. He reorganized the revenue collection system and closed the British East India Company stores. Pitt's India Act of 1784 brought Hastings home for impeachment proceedings for corruption in his Indian administration. He was impeached (1788), but in 1795 he was acquitted.

Hastings, seaside resort in S England, in East Sussex; famous for Battle of Hastings (1066) and as chief of Cinque Ports. Pop. 72,169.

Hastings, Battle of (1066), battle fought near Hastings, Sussex, England, between King Harold of England and a rival claimant to his throne, William, duke of Normandy. Harold's defeat and death in battle led to the establishment of the Norman dynasty by William the Conqueror. *See also* William I.

Hastings Hours. △1106.

Hat Act (1732), law passed by Parliament to protect English hatting industry by banning hat exports from the American colonies and limiting the number of hatter apprentices.

Hatch Act (1887), US federal law passed to promote agriculture by granting government subsidies to agricultural experiment stations. The act was sponsored by US Representative William H. Hatch of Missouri.

Hatch Act (1939), US legislation to prevent federal civil service employees from engaging in political campaigns, soliciting contributions, or influencing voters. The act was passed in the wake of abuses in certain state elections in 1938.

Hatchet Fish, marine fish found in deep temperate and tropical seas. Only fish that flies by moving its pectoral fins, it is silvery and has light organs along the underside of its deep, muscular abdomen. Length: to 3.5 in (8.9cm). Family Sternoptychidae (or Characidae); species: 21, including *Carnegiella marthae.* △626.

Hathor, ancient Egyptian goddess of love and happiness, music, and dance, depicted with the horns of a cow or as a cow. She was thought to appear at the bedside of a newborn child to determine his fate. △834.

Hatshepsut (died *c.*1469 BC), queen of Egypt (*c.* 1490–1469 BC), daughter of Thutmose I. She married her half brother, Thutmose III, ruled as "king" with him, revived mining in the Sinai, and built obelisks at Karnak. △972.

Hatta, Muhammad (1902–), Indonesian political figure. He was arrested and exiled by the Dutch in 1935 for revolutionary activities. In World War II he collaborated with the Japanese. In 1948 he became premier and defense minister of the revolutionary government of Indonesia. As such he suppressed communist activities. In 1949 he was a delegate to the Hague Convention at which the Netherlands granted Indonesia independence. He served again as prime minister (1949–50) before becoming vice president until 1956, when he resigned in objection to President Sukarno's policy of "guided democracy." After Sukarno's overthrow (1966), Hatta served as an adviser to the new government.

Hatteras, Cape, SE part of Hatteras Island off the E coast of North Carolina; notable for its beaches, migratory wildlife, fishing, and violent storms. Area: 28,500acres (11,543hectares).

Hattiesburg, city in SE Mississippi, on Leaf River; seat of Forrest co; site of University of Southern Mississippi (1911); trade center for agricultural region. Industries: lumber products, explosives, chemicals. Founded 1881; inc. 1884. Pop. (1970) 38,277.

Hauptmann, Bruno (Richard) (1889–1936), US carpenter convicted of and executed for kidnapping and murdering the son of Anne Morrow and Charles A. Lindbergh; b. Germany. The boy was abducted from the Lindbergh home in Hopewell, N.J., (March 1, 1932) and found dead nearby (May 12, 1932), despite a $50,000 ransom paid for his release. Hauptmann, when arrested, had part of the ransom money, but maintained his innocence to the end.

Hausa, Negroid people of Islamic culture, inhabiting N Nigeria and S Niger. Hausa society is feudal and based on patrilineal descent. Their language is a member of the Chad group of Afro-Asiatic languages; it is the official language of N Nigeria and a major trade language of W Africa. Hausa crafts, especially weaving, leatherwork, and silver, are the basis of an extensive trade.

Hausa States, the loosely connected predominantly Hausa communities of N Nigeria. Frequently conquered by neighbors, they came under British administration in the early 20th century and became a part of Nigeria. They were converted to Islam in the 14th–16th centuries. △1116.

Haustoria. △444.

Havana (La Habana), capital city of Cuba, on NW coast, 90mi (145km) SSW of Key West, Florida; excellent harbor; site of El Morro Castle (1597), cathedral (1704), University of Havana (1728), international airport; center of Cuban politics and commerce. City was a major Spanish naval station in New World; taken by English 1762; restored to Spain 1763; scene of sinking of US battleship *Maine,* Feb. 15, 1898, which precipitated the Spanish-American War. Industries: textiles, chemicals. Exports: sugar, tobacco, coffee. Founded 1519; capital of Cuba since 1898. Pop. 1,-700,300.

Havana Brown Cat, domestic short-haired cat breed developed from black Shorthair and chocolate-point Siamese breeds. It has a long head, large ears, oval chartreuse eyes, and medium-sized body. The tobacco brown coat is smooth and of medium length.

Havasupai, also known as Supai, Yuman-speaking tribe of North American Indians related to the Yávapai and Huálapai. They separated from the parent Yuman peoples about AD 1000–1200, and fled into the Grand Canyon, where they occupy the Cataract Canyon area of the Colorado River, Arizona. Never a large tribe, today about 500 survive as the most isolated single group of Indians in the United States.

Haverhill, city in NE Massachusetts, on Merrimack River; home of John Greenleaf Whittier, site of Bradford Junior College (1803), and Northern Essex Community College (1960). Industries: shoes, chemicals, paints. Settled 1640 as Pentucket; inc. 1641 as town, 1870 as city. Pop. (1970) 46,120.

Haversian Canal. △662.

Hawaii, state of the United States, situated in the Pacific Ocean about 2,400mi (3,864km) SW of California.

Land and Economy. Hawaii is an archipelago of 8 large and 124 small islands, many of them uninhabited, stretching over 2,000mi (3,220km) SE to NW. Of volcanic origin, the islands are mountainous; volcanic activity occurs at intervals. Valleys support rich agriculture. Federal government operations, particularly defense establishments, and an extensive tourist business are major aspects of the economy. Hawaii's geographic isolation conditions its economic life in many ways.

People. The population displays a mixture of origins, reflecting the 19th- and 20th-century immigrations from Asia, the United States, and Europe. Intermarriage has complicated the pattern, and no racial strain is in the majority. The 1970 census showed about 40% of Caucasian blood, 26% Japanese, with smaller elements of Chinese, Hawaiians (descendants of the original Polynesian settlers), Koreans, Filipinos, and others. More than 80% of the people reside in urban areas, mostly in and around Honolulu on the island of Oahu.

Education. There are 13 institutions of higher education. The state-supported University of Hawaii, centered in Honolulu, has several other campuses.

History. Voyagers from Polynesian islands to the S reached the Hawaiian Islands as early as AD 800 and over the next five centuries created a society. The first white visitor was Britain's Capt. James Cook in 1778. The islands became a supply center for merchant ships, and in 1820 US missionaries arrived, followed by businessmen who started the sugar industry. US influence grew, and in 1893 a group of US citizens deposed Queen Liliuokalani, last in the line of monarchs who had ruled Hawaii, and set up a republic with Sanford Dole as president. In August 1898, the United States formally annexed the islands, and they became a territory in 1900. Their development as a defense bastion proceeded; the base at Pearl Harbor on Oahu was the site of the Japanese attack in December 1941 that took the United States into WWII.

PROFILE

Admitted to Union: Aug. 21, 1959; rank, 50th
US Congressmen: Senate, 2; House of Representatives, 2
Population: 769,913 (1970); rank, 40th
Capital: Honolulu, 324,871 (1970)
Chief cities: Honolulu; Kailua, 33,783; Kaneohe, 29,903; Hilo, 26,353
State Legislature: Senate, 25; House of Representatives, 52
Area: 6,450sq mi (16,706sq km); rank, 47th
Elevation: Highest, Mauna Kea (on island of Hawaii) 13,796ft (4,208m). Lowest, sea level
Industries (major products): processed foods, concrete, electronic components
Agriculture (major products): sugar, pineapples, vegetables, cattle
Minerals (major): sand, gravel
State nickname: Aloha State
State motto: *Ua mau ke ea o ka aina i ka pono* ("The life of the land is perpetuated in righteousness")
State bird: Nene (Hawaiian goose)
State flower: Hibiscus
State tree: Kukui (candlenut tree)

Hawaiian Honeycreeper, medium-sized, brightly colored songbirds found in the Hawaiian Islands. Their beak shapes and sizes vary but most have tubular, brush-tipped tongues and feed on nectar. The green honeycreepers, or parrotbills, have dense, fluffy plumage. Thick-skinned honeycreepers have leathery skin and bright plumage. Most build cup-shaped nests for their spotted eggs (2–3). Family Drepanididae.

Hawaii Volcanoes National Park, park in Hawaii on Hawaii island. This park is the scene of impressive active volcanism. It is characterized by luxuriant vegetation at the lower levels, and rare plants and animals. Area: 229,615acres (92,994hectares). Est. 1916.

Hawk, temperate and tropical diurnal birds of prey with short, hooked bills for tearing meat and strong claws for killing and carrying their prey. Females are larger than males. They have red, brown, gray, or white plumage with streaks and bars on the wings. They lay eggs (3–5) in a sturdy twig-and-stick nest high in a tree. The downy young, or hawklets, are blind and helpless and fed by the parents for six weeks. Length: 1–2ft (30.5–61cm). Order Falconiformes; genera *Accipiter* and *Buteo.*

Hawkins, or **Hawkyns, (Sir) John** (1532–95), English naval commander. With Queen Elizabeth I's support, he led two lucrative expeditions to Africa and the West Indies (1562–63, 1564–65). On his third expedition (1567–69) the Spaniards destroyed most of his ships. He was prominent in plans to improve the navy and in the battle against the Spanish Armada (1588).

Hawk Moth, or **Sphinx Moth, Hummingbird Moth,** medium-to-large moth characterized by narrow wings, spindle-shaped body, and long sucking tube coiled beneath its head. Strong fliers, they usually feed at dusk, hovering over flowers like hummingbirds and sucking nectar through the extended tube. The large, smooth-skinned caterpillar is called a hornworm because of a hornlike protrusion on its posterior segment. Family Sphingidae. *See also* Moth. △502.

Hawksbill, or tortoise-shell turtle, carnivorous marine turtle found in tropical seas. Characterized by a middorsal keel on its carapace, it is prized for its brown and yellow horny plates. Length: to 33in (84cm). Family Cheloniidae; species *Eretmochelys imbricata. See also* Turtle. △524.

Hawley-Smoot Tariff (1930), legislation designed to protect US goods from foreign competition. The tariff was the highest in US history, raising rates 38%–49% on agricultural goods and 31%–34% on other commodities. Other countries reacted by passing high tariffs against US goods, causing a decline in foreign trade, and contributing to the Depression.

Hawthorn, or haw, thorn, thorn apple, shrub or small tree grown in North America and Europe. They have white, pink, or red flowers in spring, bone-hard thorns, nd small red fruit eaten by some birds and used for elly or jam. Height: to 30ft (9.1m). Family Rosaceae; enus *Crataegus*. △450.

Hawthorne, Nathaniel (1804–64), US novelist and hort-story writer, b. Salem, Mass. After graduating rom Bowdoin College (1825), he returned to Salem, where he began to write tales and historical sketches. Like Edgar Allan Poe, he was a leader in the development of the short story as a particularly American ictional form. His *Twice-Told Tales* appeared in 1837. Unable to make a living as a writer, however, he worked as a clerk in the Boston Customs House during 1839–41. While living in Concord, Mass., he wrote *Mosses from an Old Manse* (1846). Subsequently, he worked at the Salem Customs House 1846–49) and wrote his first novel, *The Scarlet Letter* 1850). The following year *The House of Seven Gables*, a novel, and *The Snow Image and Other Twice-Told Tales* were published.
In 1853 he was appointed US consul in Liverpool, England. He lived in England until 1858 and then in Italy (1858–59). Other works include the novels *The Blithedale Romance* (1852) and *The Marble Faun* (1860). *See also* individual works.

Hawthorne, city in S California, 12mi (19km) SW of Los Angeles. Industries: toys, cash registers, defense products. Inc. 1922. Pop. (1970) 53,304.

Hawthorne Effect. *See* Hawthorne Studies.

Hawthorne Studies, sociological investigations made (1924–32) at the Hawthorne Plant of the General Electric Company in Chicago. The major conclusion was that human relations had more effect on worker satisfaction and productivity than such factors as temperature, lighting, and rest breaks. Another finding has been called the *Hawthorne effect:* the interest the researchers showed for the workers caused a temporary increase in worker productivity. △924–28.

Hay, John Milton (1838–1905), US political leader, b. Salem, Ind. He was a writer and Lincoln's personal adviser. From 1865–70 he was secretary of US legations in Paris, Vienna, and Madrid. He was assistant secretary of state (1878–81). In 1897 he became ambassador to England. He served as secretary of state under Pres. William McKinley and Pres. Theodore Roosevelt (1898–1905). His Open Door Policy prevented the partition of China and he negotiated for the Panama Canal.

Hay-Bunau-Varilla Convention (1903), US agreement with Panama in which the United States was given sovereignty over a 10-mile (16-km) wide strip of land across Panama, to be used for a transoceanic canal, in return for a guarantee of Panamanian independence, and an immediate payment of $10,000,000 and $250,000 annually in perpetuity. The agreement was reached after the United States had helped Panama achieve its independence from Colombia.

Hayden, Melissa (1928–), Canadian ballerina, noted for her dazzling technique and great dramatic ability. She joined the American Ballet Theatre in 1945 and became a soloist within one year, and was with the New York City Ballet from 1950, except for a period (1953–55) when she returned to the Ballet Theatre.

Haydn, Franz Joseph (1732–1809), Austrian composer, b. Rohrau. One of the greatest composers of the Classical period, from 1761 to 1790 he served as musical director for the wealthy Esterházy family and composed many of his best works. Later he made two trips to England, composing the last 12 of his 104 symphonies for concerts there. Haydn brought the sonata form to masterful fruition in these symphonies, many of which have popular names, including "Military," "Clock," and "London"—all composed in the early 1790s.
His works influenced his friend Mozart, who in turn influenced him. One of the most prolific of all composers, Haydn also composed many songs, string quartets, masses, chamber music pieces, concertos, and two oratorios late in his life, *The Creation* (1798) and *The Seasons* (1801). *See also* Classical Music; Oratorio. △1196.

Hayes, Helen (1900–), US actress, b. Washington, D.C. She made her professional debut at the age of five in Washington, beginning a long and distinguished stage career. She appeared in dozens of productions, notably *Dear Brutus* (1918), *Victoria Regina* (1935–39), *The Glass Menagerie* (London, 1948), and *The Skin of Our Teeth* (Paris, 1955). Her film career included *The Sin of Madelon Claudet* (1931), for which she won an Academy Award (1932); *What Every Woman Knows* (1934); *Anastasia* (1956); and *Airport* (1969), which also won her an Academy Award. She also made many radio appearances, such as "This is Helen Hayes" (1945) and "Weekday" (1956), and acted in TV productions of *Dear Brutus* and other plays. A New York theater was renamed in her honor in recognition of her 50 years on the stage (1955). Her autobiography, *A Gift of Joy* (with L. Funke), appeared in 1965.

Hayes, Roland (1887–), US tenor, b. Curryville, Ga. After studying at Fisk University, Hayes became the first black to achieve international fame for his interpretations of German lieder, French songs, and spirituals.

Hayes, Rutherford Birchard (1822–93), 19th president of the United States (1877–81), b. Delaware, Ohio, graduate, Kenyon College (1843), Harvard law school (1845). In 1852 he married Lucy Webb; they had eight children. Originally a Whig, Hayes was an early supporter of the new Republican party. He served in the US House of Representatives (1865–67), where he supported the Radical Reconstruction program. He was elected governor of Ohio three times (1867, 1869, 1875). In 1876 he won the Republican nomination for president. His Democratic opponent was Gov. Samuel J. Tilden of New York.
The Hayes-Tilden election was extremely close, with electoral votes of four states in dispute. An electoral commission, in an openly political decision, awarded all disputed votes to Hayes, who thus won by one electoral vote, even though Tilden had polled more popular votes.
Despite the cloud under which he came into office, Hayes, once president, was a courageous and honest administrator. He ended the era of Reconstruction by removing federal troops from the last two southern states (Louisiana and South Carolina). He made important reforms in the civil service, which were unpopular with important segments of the Republican party, and he was not renominated in 1880.
Career: US Army, 1861–65; US House of Representatives, 1865–67; Ohio governor, 1868–72, 1876–77; president, 1877–81.

Hayes, river in E Manitoba, Canada; rises in series of lakes NE of Lake Winnipeg; flows NE to Hudson Bay near York Factory; extensively used as travel route for Hudson's Bay Co. Length: 300mi (483km).

Hay Fever, seasonal allergy induced by pollens, which may vary from season to season. Symptoms include itching of the nose, pharynx, and eyes, which can develop abruptly, followed by tearing, sneezing, clear nasal discharge. Headache, depression, and insomnia may also accompany attacks. Control of symptoms with medication is possible; desensitization is often effective. △714.

Hay-Herrán Treaty (1903), agreement that would have allowed the United States to use a 6-mile (9.6km) zone across Panama to construct an interoceanic canal. Colombia was to receive an initial payment of $10,000,000. The US Senate approved the treaty, but Colombia rejected it.

Haymarket Massacre (May 4, 1886), riot in Haymarket Square, Chicago. In the incident seven policemen were killed and scores injured by a bomb explosion that occurred during a protest meeting being held by anarchists. Although the bomb thrower was never found, eight anarchists were arrested, tried, and convicted. Seven were sentenced to death and one to life imprisonment. Four of the condemned men were actually executed. One committed suicide, and the three others were pardoned in 1893 by Gov. John Altgeld. The incident turned public opinion against the labor movement, and membership in organizations such as the Knights of Labor declined.

Hay-Pauncefote Treaty (1901), promised equal rates through the Panama Canal to all nations and the opening of the canal without discrimination to all vessels, commercial or military. It was negotiated by US Secretary of State John Hay, and Lord Pauncefote, British ambassador to the United States.

Hays, Arthur Garfield (1881–1954), US civil rights lawyer, b. Rochester, N.Y. He practiced international law in London (1914–15). With Clarence S. Darrow, he was a defense lawyer in two important cases, the Scopes trial (1925) and the Sweet segregation case (1926). He appeared for the defense in the Sacco-Vanzetti case (1927), and the trial of the "Scottsboro boys," nine Alabama blacks accused of murder in 1931. He was general consul and later national director of the American Civil Liberties Union (from 1912) and wrote *Let Freedom Ring* (1928), *Trial by Prejudice* (1933), and *Democracy Works* (1939).

Havana, Cuba

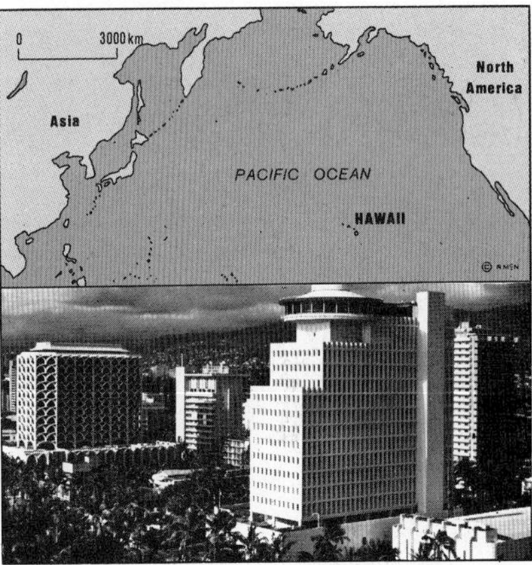
0
3000km
Asia
North
America
PACIFIC OCEAN
HAWAII

Hawaii

Nathaniel Hawthorne

Rutherford B. Hayes

Hayward, city in W California, on San Francisco Bay; site of California State College at Hayward (1957), Chabot Community College (1961). Industries: steel, food processing, school buses, carnations and roses, chemicals, building materials. Settled 1854; inc. 1876. Pop. (1970) 93,058.

Haywood, William Dudley (1869–1928), American labor leader, b. Salt Lake City. In 1905 he helped organize the Industrial Workers of the World (IWW). A militant leader, he advocated violence by workers. He was tried and acquitted on taking part in the assassination of Frank R. Steunenberg, former governor of Idaho. At the entrance of the US into World War I he was arrested and convicted of sedition. During his release on bail in 1921, he fled to the Soviet Union, where he lived the rest of his life.

Hazelnut. *See* Filbert.

Hazelton, city in E Pennsylvania, 20mi (32km) S of Wilkes-Barre. Industries: shoes, furniture, paper products, foam rubber, coal, iron, steel. Settled 1826; inc. 1892. Pop. (1970) 30,426.

Hazlitt, William (1778–1830), English essayist and critic. Hazlitt abandoned his education for the ministry, met Charles Lamb in London, and wrote for various periodicals from 1812 onward. His miscellaneous essays include the famous *Characters of Shakespeare's Plays* (1817–18) and *The Spirit of the Age* (1825).

Headache, one of the most frequent discomforts suffered by humans. It may be caused by or accompany disease, and may also be caused by emotional disorder or distress, pressure on cranial nerves, or by the dilation or contraction of certain blood vessels. The most frequent causes of minor short-lived headaches are daily tensions and fatigue. Chronic long-lasting headaches with no apparent medical basis are classified as cluster, tension, or migraine headaches, the last often accompanied by a family history. Diagnosis of the cause of chronic headaches may often be lengthy. Mild pain may be relieved by analgesics; other treatment depends on diagnosis. *See also* Migraine.

Head Deformation, changing the shape of the head in infancy. Boards or bandages are bound tightly to the infant's soft head; thus the forehead or back of the head is flattened or the crown lengthened. The practice existed in the Pacific Northwest, Borneo, the New Hebrides, and elsewhere. △818.

Headhunting, taking and sometimes preserving the heads of enemies. Once a widespread custom, it is still found in New Guinea and was reported in Europe after 1900. Captured heads are believed to give victors their victims' powers, to prove courage, or to be necessary for fertility.

Health. △696–9, 734–9.

Health, Education, and Welfare, Department of (HEW), federal cabinet-level department within the executive branch. Created in 1953, its primary focus is on human concerns. HEW is charged with vast responsibilities that include the social security program, improving the quality of US education, and making public health services more widely available. Its most important agencies include the Public Health Service (1798), the Office of Education (1867), the Social Security Administration (1946), and the Social and Rehabilitation Service (1967). It is directed by the secretary of Health, Education, and Welfare. △1358.

Health Insurance, classification of insurance that insures against the financial consequences of an individual's loss of health. Medical expense insurance is health insurance that indemnifies the insured for hospital and surgical related expenses. Disability income insurance is health insurance that promises to pay a stipulated monthly income to the insured should he become disabled.

Hearing, or audition, process by which sound waves are transformed into the experience of hearing. Sound waves are systematic compressions and decompressions of the air. The physical mechanism of hearing begins when sound waves strike the outer ear (the auricle); they next strike the eardrum, and the vibration continues along three small bones, the ossicles, which are attached to the cochlea, the organ of audition. Within the cochlea are receptors called hair cells, which transmit via the auditory nerve to the brain. Many of the distinctions humans make among sounds are psychological; for example, the difference between noise and music is learned in part, although physical factors do play a role. △676.

Hearing Aid, electronic sound-reproducing device to increase the sound intensity at the ear. Modern aids use a small crystal microphone, a microminiaturized battery-powered amplifier, and an earpiece often shaped to fit into the auditory canal. The device consists either of two parts connected by a thin wire (the battery and amplifier being hidden in the clothing) or of one tiny unit placed behind the ear or housed in eyeglass frames.

Hearn, Lafcadio (1850–1904), US author, b. Greece. After failing at a journalism career in the United States, he became a Japanese citizen. He wrote a number of books and essays on Japanese life, including *Out of the East* (1895) and *Shadowings* (1900).

Hearne, Samuel (1745–92), Canadian fur trader and explorer, b. England. Hearne navigated for the Hudson's Bay Company (1768–70). In 1770 he made the first overland voyage to the Arctic Ocean. He founded Cumberland House in 1774, the first inland trading post of the Hudson's Bay Company. Captured by the French (1782) when Fort Prince of Wales was taken, he commanded Fort Churchill (1783–87). Hearne was an early advocate of western expansion.

Hearst, George (1820–91), US mining magnate and political leader, b. Franklin co, Mo. A prospector and geologist in California, he made successful investments in mines in Montana, South Dakota, and Nevada. He acquired the San Francisco *Examiner* (1880), later published by his son William Randolph Hearst. With his wife Phoebe Apperson Hearst (1842–1919) George engaged in philanthropy, donating part of his fortune to the American University, the University of California and establishing free libraries. He was an unsuccessful candidate for the governorship of California (1882) and served as a US senator (1886–91).

Hearst, William Randolph (1863–1951), US publisher, b. San Francisco. He built a publishing empire that included 18 newspapers, nine magazines, a syndicated weekly supplement, news services, and radio stations. Along with his rival, Joseph Pulitzer, he practiced sensational journalism and prompted war fever for Spanish-American War (1898). He served as a congressman from New York (1903–07).

Heart, a chambered muscular organ that contracts rhythmically due to its unique cardiac muscle tissue. Through its contraction it pumps blood throughout the body. In man, the heart is located behind the sternum (breastbone) between the lower parts of the lungs. It lies in a double-walled sac, the pericardium, the outer fibrous layer of which is separated from the inner serous layer by pericardial fluid that serves to protect the heart. The heart itself is divided into halves by a muscular wall, the septum. The right side contains only deoxygenated blood; the left side, only oxygenated blood. Each side is divided into two chambers: an upper thin-walled atrium, or auricle, and a lower thick-walled ventricle. The opening between atrial and ventricular chambers is guarded by atrioventricular valves—the tricuspid on the right side, the mitral, or bicuspid, on the left side.

The heart contracts rhythmically; the average heart beat for an adult is 70 to 72 beats per minute. The beat is controlled mainly by the heart's own "pacemaker," the sinoatrial node, a bundle of muscle cells, blood vessels, and nerves located where the superior vena cava opens into the right auricle. An electrical impulse originates in the sinoatrial node and travels through the two atria to the ventricles, causing contraction. The rhythmic series of contractions pumps blood through the body. △688.

Heart Attack, or myocardial infarction, the diminishing or failure of blood supply to the heart, generally though not always the result of coronary occlusion or thrombosis. The pain of a heart attack is typically persistent, described as constricting or oppressive; shortness of breath is common. Vomiting, nausea, and pale, cold, moist skin may occur. If the victim survives, immediate hospitalization is necessary. Treatment in specialized coronary care units makes the prognosis good. *See also* Angina Pectoris. △688, 716.

Heartburn, or pyrosis, burning sensation along the esophagus occurring soon after eating, especially overeating. It is caused by gastric contents spreading back to esophagus and throat. It may be relieved by standing, drinking fluids, or by antacids.

Heart Defects, Congenital, anomalies of the circulatory system caused during embryonic development. Most common is a hole in the membrane separating the two ventricles of the heart. Symptoms may include murmurs and pulmonary artery hypertension. Surgery is common but not always necessary, or in the cases of infants may be postponed. *See also* Heart Murmur.

Heart Failure, disorder in which an abnormality in the circulatory system prevents the heart from pumping blood at the rate necessary to supply body tissues. Symptoms include respiratory distress, in later stages even in bed, edema, fatigue. Treatment is with bed rest, avoidance of stress, and medication.

Heart-lung Machine, a device that supplies and distributes oxygen to the body when the natural circulation is interrupted during open-heart surgery. It consists of an oxygenator, which substitutes for the lungs and a pump, which performs the circulatory functions of the heart.

Heart Murmur, sounds heard because of vibrations in the torso and turbulence in the heart and the blood vessels around the heart. Intensity, pattern, and location of sound classify the murmurs, most frequently associated with rheumatic fever and congenital anomalies, although not all murmurs indicate disease or disorder.

Heart of Atlanta Motel v. United States (1964), US Supreme Court civil rights decision. The court decided to uphold the ban on racial discrimination in public accommodations of the Civil Rights Act of 1964 as a valid Congressional exercise of the commerce power.

Hearts, card game played by two to eight players using a standard 52–card deck. After all the cards have been distributed, the player to the left of the dealer leads. Suits must be followed if possible. The object is to avoid taking tricks that contain hearts, or to capture all the cards in the heart suit. In a variation of the game, called Black Lady, the queen of spades counts as 13 "hearts." All other hearts count as one point each.

Heart Transplant. *See* Organ Transplant.

Heat, a form of energy related to atomic and molecular energy states. Historically, heat was felt to be a material substance (called caloric) that was contained in bodies and could flow from one to another. (Indeed, an earlier version of this theory postulated *two* fluids, caloric and frigoric, that carried heat or cold between substances.) Under this theory, boring a cannon produced heat because the cannon material was broken up and released some of its (finite) store of caloric. But if that were so, continued boring would at last produce no further heat. Count Rumford of Bavaria (Benjamin Thompson) showed that he could produce unlimited amounts of heat by boring cannon with a blunt tool, and postulated that heat might be related to motion. James Joule then determined the mechanical energy needed to produce a given amount of heat energy (by rotating paddles in water and measuring the temperature increase). Thus the caloric theory was supplanted by the kinetic theory of heat. △1486, 1508.

Heat Balance, or heat budget, the equilibrium between the solar radiation received by the Earth and its atmosphere, and the radiation that they, in turn, emit. About one-third of the solar radiation is reflected, mostly from clouds, and scattered back into space, whereas the rest is absorbed by clouds, atmosphere, and Earth. The heat absorbed powers the circulation of the atmosphere, oceans, and water cycle. Eventually the heat is reradiated into space, maintaining the Earth's heat equilibrium. *See also* Circulation, Atmospheric.

Heat Content. *See* Heat of Reaction. △1564.

Heath, Edward Richard George (1916–), British politician. After a term in civil service and in merchant banking, he became a Conservative member of Parliament (1950). Subsequent parliamentary appointments include government chief whip (1955–59); minister of labor (1959–60); lord privy seal with foreign office responsibilities (1960–63); leader of the opposition (1965–70); and prime minister (1970–74). He successfully concluded negotiations for Britain's entry into the European Economic Community (1973), but was defeated by Harold Wilson's Labour party (1974) and lost the leadership of the Conservatives to Margaret Thatcher. △1356.

Heath, genus *(Erica)* of evergreen shrubs and trees native to Africa, the Mediterranean region, and Britain. They have small, thick or needlelike leaves and small bell-like flowers. The fruit is usually a small berry. The heath family (Ericaceae) includes 500 species of herbs, shrubs, and small trees.

Heather, small, evergreen shrub native to Europe

and Asia Minor. It has scalelike leaves and small bell-shaped flowers of pink, lavender, or white. It is common on the moors of Great Britain. Family Ericaceae; species *Calluna vulgaris*.

Heath Hen, grouse that once lived in E United States, becoming extinct during the early 1900s. Species *Tympanuchus cupido cupido. See also* Prairie Chicken.

Heat of Formation. *See* Heat of Reaction.

Heat of Fusion, the amount of heat energy absorbed by a liquid at its freezing point in changing to a solid. Heats of fusion vary from about one calorie per gram (helium) to 80 cal/g (water). These quantities of heat are also released by the substances as they melt. △1504.

Heat of Neutralization, heat evolved by the complete neutralization of one mole of an acid or base. For all strong acids or bases its value is approximately 13,700 calories per mole (57,500 joules per mole).

Heat of Reaction, heat released or absorbed when substances react together. Usually it is measured for complete reaction between stoichiometric numbers of moles at constant pressure, in which case it is the change in heat content (or enthalpy). Conventionally, it is taken to be negative for exothermic reactions and positive for endothermic ones. The heat of formation of a compound is the heat of reaction to form one mole of the compound from its elements (in their standard states). △1504, 1564, 1572.

Heat of Sublimation, the heat to supply to a substance at constant temperature necessary to transform it directly from solid to vapor, without passing through the liquid phase.

Heat of Vaporization, the heat absorbed by a liquid at its boiling point as it changes to a gas. Values range from 5 cal/gram (helium) to 1,211 cal/gram (copper). △1504.

Heat Pump, year-round air conditioning system based on the principle of refrigeration. Cooling is obtained by placing the evaporator in the conditioned air space. Heating is done by having the condenser in the conditioned space. As in normal refrigeration systems, a source of external power, such as electricity, is required in the condensing portion of the cycle.

Heatstroke, or sunstroke, occurs in conditions of high heat and humidity to persons predisposed. Symptoms are cessation of sweating and loss of consciousness.

Heat Transfer, the passage of heat—the total quantity of energy in a given quantity of matter—to other things, moving from warmer heat sources to cooler heat sinks. The heat may be conceived as the energy of the random motions of the molecules or atoms of which matter is composed, transferred to other things by means of one or more of the processes of conduction, convection, or radiation. Conduction involves the direct transfer of energy by means of the elastic impact of the internal particles or molecules of a substance, like the passage of heat from a hot cup to the hand holding it. Convection involves transfer by fluid motion, like heating of a hand in the air from a car heater. Radiation involves the transfer by electromagnetic waves, like heating of a hand in the sun by its long infrared rays. All three transfer processes are intimately intermingled in the heating and cooling of the land, sea, and air of the earth. △212, 216.

Heat Treatment, the subjecting of a metal or alloy to a cycle of heating and cooling to alter its physical properties. In a process called annealing, metal is heated to a predetermined temperature, held for a time, then cooled to room temperature. This improves ductility and reduces brittleness. Annealing is intermittently carried out during the working of a piece of metal, when ductility is lost through hammering. Annealing temperatures vary, but must not be in a range that allows crystal growth. △1592–94, 1604.

Heaven. △840.

Heavy Water, or **Deuterium Oxide,** water in which the hydrogen atoms are replaced by deuterium atoms; used as a moderator in some nuclear reactors. Molecular weight 20. *See* Deuterium. △1482.

Hebe, in Greek mythology, goddess of youth, daughter of Zeus and Hera. She performed domestic duties on Olympus and served as cupbearer to the gods.

Hébert, Jacques René (1757–94), French Revolutionary journalist. He gained political power through his newspaper by arousing the Parisian working class. This popular influence helped cause the Reign of Terror and the deposition of the Girondists in 1793, and later pressure by the Jacobins resulted in plans for a popular rebellion. Hébert was seized and guillotined in 1794.

Hebrew, the language of the Jews and Judaism, a Semitic language. As a result of the influence of the Babylonians, it was submerged by Aramaic. After the destruction of the 2nd Temple in AD 70, its use almost totally ceased. With the use of Hebrew by poets, and rabbinic usage, it became a literary and even holy language used in synagogue services. In the 18th century, Hebrew was revived and became used in secular circles. In 1948, when the state of Israel was founded, Hebrew was declared the official national language. △982.

Hebrews, New Testament epistle. The authorship is uncertain and it has been attributed to Paul, Luke, Barnabas, and Apollos. A discussion of Christianity's superiority over Judaism, it stresses that Christ is more worthy than Moses.

Hebrides (Western Isles), islands off the W coast of Scotland in the Atlantic; divided into the Inner Hebrides (principal islands: Skye, Rhum, Eigg, Islay, and Mull) and Outer (principal islands: Lewis with Harris, North and South Uist). Occupations are fishing, farming. Pop. 60,000.

Hebron (Al Khalil), town in W Jordan; traditionally one of the oldest cities in the world; taken by Judas Maccabeus in 2nd century BC, by the Edomites 586 BC, by Arabs AD 636, by crusaders 1099; 16th-century Hebron became part of Ottoman Empire; part of League of Nations mandate 1922–48; joined Jordan in 1948. Town is the traditional burial place of Sarah and Abraham; site of 12th-century crusader church and wall built by Herod. Industries: tanning, manufacturing of blue hand-blown glass. Pop. 38,300.

Hecate, Greek goddess who presided over magic and spells. Daughter of Perses and Asteria, she had power over heaven, earth, and the sea. She bestowed wealth and all the blessings of daily life. Hecate was represented clad in a long robe and holding burning torches.

Hecatoncheires, in Greek mythology, 100-armed, 50-headed sons of the deities Uranus and Gaea. The most famous was Briareus. He and his brothers successfully aided Zeus against the attack by the Titans. They may have represented the forces of nature that appeared in earthquakes and tidal waves.

Hecht, Ben (1894–1964), US dramatist and journalist, b. New York City. He collaborated with Charles MacArthur, Gene Fowler, and others on such Broadway comedies as *Front Page* (1928) and *The Great Magoo* (1932). *Twentieth Century* (1933) was also made into a film starring John Barrymore. Hecht's many screenplays include *The Scoundrel* (1935), which won an Academy Award.

Hector, in Greek mythology, the son of Priam and Hecuba, the husband of Andromache. He was killed by Achilles in the Trojan War.

Hecuba, in Greek mythology, the wife of Priam, king of Troy, mother of Hector. She was taken prisoner when Troy was captured by the Greeks.

Hedgehog, spiny nocturnal Eurasian mammals of the family Erinaceidae. The European hedgehog *(Erinaceus europaeus)* is about 9in (23cm) long, brownish above and lighter below, and has a pointed snout. It feeds on insects and other small animals and defends itself by rolling into a prickly ball. △546.

Hedgehog Cactus, cactus native to North America that forms clumps with unbranched, cylindrical stems, and bright pink flowers. Its fleshy fruit is edible. Height: to 1.5ft (46cm). Family Cactaceae; genus *Echinocereus. See also* Cactus.

Hedonism, from the Greek *hedone* or "pleasure," may be of three types: pleasure of the moment, as taught by Aristippus; careful discrimination of pleasure sought, as taught by Epicureans; or emphasis on complete and lasting happiness as found in eudemonism. Basically, hedonism springs from the premise that man seeks pleasure in all he does. △858.

Heemskerck, Maarten van. △1144.

Hefa. *See* Haifa.

Hefei. *See* Hofei.

William Randolph Hearst

Edward Heath

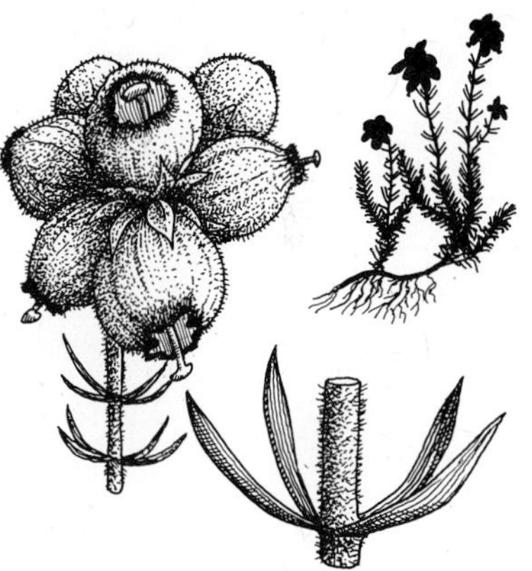

Heath

Heather

Hegel, Georg Wilhelm Friedrich (1770–1831), German philosopher. He studied at Tübingen (1788–93) and taught at Jena (1805). He was director of the gymnasium (high school) at Nürnberg until 1816, and professor of philosophy at Heidelberg, then Berlin, where he became famous for a romantic, metaphysical system that traced the self-realization of spirit by so-called dialectical "moments" to perfection. First in the *Phenomenology of Spirit* (1807) and then, in *Science of Logic* (1812–16), Hegel claimed to express the course of universal reason with his metaphysical dynamism. His lectures on the history of philosophy, aesthetics, and philosophy of history were published posthumously. *See also* Dialectical Logic. △858, 1290.

Hegira, the emigration of Mohammed from Mecca to Medina in 622. Islamic dating begins with this year, as indicated by the letters A.H. (Anno Hegirae). Thus AD 622 is 1 AH. *See also* Mohammed. △1058, 1062.

Heidegger, Martin (1889–1976), German philosopher. Influenced by Edmund Husserl, he has had a major influence on 20th-century existentialism. Publishing his principle work, *Being and Time,* in 1927, he sought the "meaning of being" in terms of the individual human situation. *See also* Existentialism. △858.

Heidelberg, city in SW West Germany, on Neckar River; University of Heidelberg (1386) became one of 19th century's leading universities; site of city hall (1701–03); Philosophenweg (Philosophers' Way), path overlooking city. Industries: printing presses, precision instruments, textiles, leather goods. Founded 12th century. Pop. 122,097.

Heidelberg Man, species of man contemporary with Pithecanthropus, known from a jawbone discovered near Heidelberg, Germany, in 1907. The massive teeth are human in arrangement, but the chin is undeveloped. *See also* Pithecanthropus. △650.

Heifetz, Jascha (1901–), US violinist, b. Russia. Perhaps the greatest violinist of the 20th century, he made his debut at age 7 and first performed in the United States at 16. He became a US citizen in 1925 and toured the world as a concert soloist, establishing a reputation for technical virtuosity. In 1936 he helped found the American Guild of Musical Artists. In 1941 he played trios with Artur Rubinstein and Emanuel Feuermann. He commissioned a number of new violin works including William Walton's *Violin Concerto.* He made many recordings and taught at the University of Southern California.

Heilungkiang, province in NE China, bordered by USSR; capital is Harbin; present-day boundaries were fixed in 1949; mining, lumber, and agricultural center. Area: 272,000sq mi (704,480sq km). Pop. 21,000,000.

Heine, Heinrich (1797–1856), German poet and prose writer. Heine felt himself an outsider, as seen in the early *Book of Songs* (1827). In 1826 he published his satirical, descriptive *Pictures of Travel,* and in 1831 he settled in Paris, writing on German life and letters. The pain and terror suffered in the last eight years of his life from a paralytic illness are recorded in *Poems 1853 & 1854* and *Romanzero* (1851). Most of his memoirs were destroyed by relatives.

Heinlein, Robert Anson (1907–), US science-fiction, TV, and film writer, b. Butler, Mo. He developed many of the common themes of modern science fiction in such well-known works as *The Green Hills of Earth* (1951), *The Puppet Masters* (1951), and *I Will Fear No Evil* (1970).

Heisenberg, Werner Karl (1901–76), German physicist and philosopher. He became professor at Leipzig and later in Berlin. He is best known for his discovery of the uncertainty, or indeterminancy, principle (1927), which holds that it is impossible to precisely measure both the velocity and position of an object at the same time. He was awarded the 1932 Nobel Prize for his work on quantum mechanics. *See also* Quantum Theory; Uncertainty Principle. △1480.

Heisenberg Uncertainty Principle. *See* Uncertainty Principle.

Heisman, John William (1869–1936), US football player and coach, b. Cleveland, Ohio. A college football star (1887–91), he began his coaching career in 1892. He was coach at Georgia Tech (1914–18), where he had an outstanding record. The Heisman Trophy, instituted (1935) in his honor, is granted annually to the outstanding US college football player.

Hejaz (Al-Hijaz) province in Saudi Arabia, along Red Sea coast. Center of Islam, it contains the Muslim holy cities of Mecca (birthplace of Mohammed) and Medina (first Islamic capital). A former independent kingdom under Hussein Ibn Ali (1916), it was taken by Ibn Saud in 1924 and has been part of Saudi Arabia since 1932. Products: dates, wheat, millet, livestock. Area: 150,000sq mi (388,500sq km). Pop. 2,000,000.

Helderberg War, first part of the Antirent War that swept New York State (1839–46). The farmers rebelled against the system of perpetual leases when the heirs of Stephen Van Rensselaer tried to collect $400,000 in back rents. Governor William H. Seward used militia to end the riots.

Helen, in Greek mythology, the immortal daughter of Leda and Zeus, sister of Pollux, and half-sister of Castor. She married Menelaus, king of Sparta, but after three years she was carried off by a prince of Troy. Since all of her many suitors had pledged to aid the man she would marry, her abduction provided the immediate cause of the Trojan War.

Helena, Saint (*c.* 255–330), mother of Roman Emperor Constantine I (Constantine the Great). She was the concubine of Constantius Chlorus. He married another woman when he became emperor as Constantius I, but Helena's son was named emperor in 306, and she became a Christian. Early church historians relate that Helena inspired the building of the Church of the Nativity in Bethlehem. Later tradition says that she found the true cross on which Christ died.

Helena, capital city of Montana, in W central part of state; seat of Lewis and Clark co. City was first settled by prospectors in 1864 as Last Chance Gulch; by 1868 population was 7,500 and $16 million worth of gold had been mined. In 1875 it was named capital of Montana territory, remaining as such when state was formed 1889; site of Carroll College (1910). Industries: mineral smelting, bakery equipment, ceramics, paints. Chartered as city 1881. Pop. (1970) 22,730.

Helgoland (Heligoland), island of West Germany, in North Sea. Under German control since 1890 (except for 1945–52); it played a strategic role in WWI and WWII with installation of German fortifications; now a resort and fishing area. Area: 150acres (61hectares). Pop. 3,200.

Helicopter, aircraft whose support is derived from lift provided by power-driven propellers or rotors revolving around a vertical axis. It is capable of vertical take-off and landing; hovering; and forward, backward, and lateral flight. Military applications include rescue, reconnaissance, and combat. In civil aviation short-haul transport, crop dusting, power and pipeline patrol are common uses. △1676, 1720.

Heliopolis (Misr al-Jadidah), ruined ancient holy city in N Lower Egypt, in the Nile delta, 6mi (10km) N of Cairo; noted center of sun worship for god Ra, from *c.* 1580–1090 BC. Formerly seat of viceroy of N Egypt, it was site of Cleopatra's Needles (obelisks, assembled here, now displayed in London and New York City) and temple containing historical records.

Heliostat. △94.

Heliotrope, herbaceous plant found worldwide. It has fragrant, five-lobed flowers in curled sprays. Seaside heliotrope *(Heliotropium curassavicum)* grows on beaches and swamps in the United States. Garden heliotrope *(H. arborescens)* is shrublike with purple or white flowers. There are 250 species. Family Boraginaceae.

Heliotropism. *See* Phototropism.

Heliozoa, or **sun animal,** order of freshwater, ameboid protozoa characterized by a spherical body surrounded by needlelike extensions of protoplasm. Many secrete a gelatinous capsule or a perforated silica skeleton. Length: 1/625–0.04in (1/25–1mm). Common examples are *Actinophrys sol* and *Actinosphaerium.*

Helium, gaseous nonmetallic element (symbol He) of the noble-gas group, discovered in 1868 by Pierre Janssen, who noticed its lines in the Sun's spectrum. It is the second most common element in the universe. The element was first obtained in 1895 from the mineral clevite. The chief source is from natural gas. Helium is also found in some radioactive minerals and in the earth's atmosphere (0.0005% by volume). It is used in balloons, in divers' air supplies to protect against the "bends," and in welding, semiconductor preparation, metallurgy, and other applications requiring an inert atmosphere. It has the lowest melting point of any element and is extensively used in low temperature research. The element forms no chemical compounds. Properties: at. no. 2; at. wt. 4.0026; sp gr 0.1785 g dm^{-3}; melt. pt. −457.96°F (−272.4°C) (26 atm); boil. pt. −452.07°F (−269.14°C); most common isotope He^4 (100%). *See also* Noble Gases. △1480, 1552–54.

Helix, a curve generated when a point moves over the surface of a cylinder in such a way that the curve is inclined at a constant angle to the axis of the cylinder, as in the thread of a bolt. △1454, 1574.

Hell. △840–42.

Hellas. △992.

Hellbender, large aquatic salamander of E and Central United States. Because metamorphosis is not complete, adults lose gills but lack eyelids and retain larval teeth. It has gray or brown loose, wrinkled skin. Length: to 30in (76cm). Family Cryptobranchidae; species *Cryptobranchus alleganiensis. See also* Salamander.

Hellebore, or bear's foot, winter-blooming herbaceous plant native to Eurasia. Most familiar is the Christmas rose *(Helleborus niger)* that bears large white flowers in midwinter to early spring. There are about 20 species. Family Ranunculaceae. *See also* Buttercup.

Hellen, the eponymous ancestor of the Hellenes, or the Greek people. According to an early ethnological theory (which was cast in the traditional mythological form of a genealogy), the Dorian, Ionian, and Aeolian tribes were descended from a common ancestor. He was identified as Hellen, son or brother of Deucalion, and father of Dorus, Xuthus, and Aeolus. The name Hellenes was generally acknowledged as that of the Greek people by the 7th century BC.

Hellenica, Xenophon's history of the Greeks from the close of Thucydides' account of the Peloponnesian Wars (411 BC) to the battle of Mantinea (362). Its style is erratic, and its contents often sketchy.

Hellenism, the culture of classical Greece, most particularly that of Athens during the 5th century BC. Art and architecture saw the expansion and embellishment of the Acropolis, most outstandingly the building of the Parthenon. Tragedy was perfected in the plays of Aeschylus, Sophocles, and Euripides, and comedy in those of Aristophanes. Herodotus and Thucydides excelled in the writing of history and Socrates, then Plato, established standards for philosophy.

Hellenistic Age, era from 323 to *c.* 30 BC in E Mediterranean and Near East between the death of Alexander and the ascension of Augustus. Greek dynasties (the Ptolemies and Seleucids) were established in Egypt, Syria, and Persia. Alexandria and Pergamum became major cultural and trading centers, adding unique elements to, while also preserving, much of Greek culture. Major literary figures were the poets Callimachus and Theocritus and the prose writer Lucian. Numerous Stoic and Epicurean philosophers flourished. Important works of art included the sculptures the "Venus de Milo" and the "Dying Gaul." Hellenistic city planning influenced the Romans, who eventually dominated and overshadowed Hellenistic culture. △1002.

Heller, Joseph (1931–), US author, b. New York City. His first novel, *Catch-22,* appeared in 1961. Subsequent works include *We Bombed in New Haven* (1968), a play, and *Something Happened* (1974), a novel. *See also* Catch-22.

Heller, Walter (1915–), US economist. Chairman of the Council of Economic Advisors (1961–64) and a consultant to President Johnson (1964–69), he is noted for his work on revenue sharing among different levels of government.

Hellespont. *See* Dardanelles.

Hellgrammite, or **Dobson,** aquatic larva of the dobsonfly found worldwide. These larvae have chewing mouthparts and are an important fish food. The adult has sickle-shaped jaws and clear, 2in (51mm) wings. Length: 1in (25mm). Order Megaloptera; Family Corydalidae.

Hellinger, Mark (1903–48), US theatrical producer, b. New York City. First active in journalism, he wrote the first column devoted to Broadway—"About Town." In 1930 he began writing for Florenz Ziegfeld and others. He later became a film producer.

Hellman, Lillian (1905–), US playwright and auıor, b. New Orleans. Her plays deal with psychologi-al weakness and contemporary social issues. In *The 'hildren's Hour* (1934) a child accuses two teachers f an abnormal relationship, ruining their lives. *The ittle Foxes* (1939) shows the violent passions within Southern family. *Watch on the Rhine* (1941) deals ith the difficult decision of a gentle man to act gainst a Nazi. Some of her later works are *The Au-umn Garden* (1951), *Toys in the Attic* (1960), and an daptation of the Burt Blechman novel *My Mother, Ay Father, and Me* (1963). Her nontheatrical writ-ıg includes three autobiographical volumes, *An Infinished Woman* (1969), *Pentimento* (1973), and *'coundrel Time* (1976).

Iells Canyon, canyon on the Oregon border of W entral Idaho; also called the Grand Canyon of the nake River. Length: about 40mi (64km). Height: ,032ft (2,450m).

Ielmet. △1098.

Ielmet Shell. △482.

Ielmholtz, Hermann-Ludwig Ferdinand von 1821–94), German anatomist, physicist, and physi-logist. He made great contributions in acoustics and ptics, expanding Thomas Young's three-color theory f vision and inventing an ophthalmoscope and an phthalmometer. His experiments on the speed of erve impulses led to a study of animal heat, which in urn led to work on the principle of conservation of nergy and the introduction of the concept of free nergy.

Ielots, class of probably indigenous Greeks between ree men and slaves. In Sparta they outnumbered Spartans. Often used in agriculture and as domestics, hey were owned by the state, which used them as oldiers after the Persian Wars. They were freed in 369 BC. △996.

Ielpmann, Robert (1909–), English dancer and horeographer, b. Australia. His name is associated vith the early history of the Sadler's Wells Ballet, vhich he joined in 1933. His most important creation vas *Master of Tregennis* (1934). He performed in the ilms *The Red Shoes* (1948) and *Tales of Hoffmann* 1950). △1368.

Helsingør, town and port in E Denmark, on the Øresund: site of 16th-century Kronborg castle, setting n Shakespeare's *Hamlet*. Industries: fishing, textiles, ourism, brewing. Founded 13th century; chartered as ity 1426. Pop. 30,211.

Helsinki (Helsingfors), seaport city in Finland, on Gulf of Finland; capital of Finland and of Uusimaa prov.; site of University of Helsinki (1640), national art gallery, sports stadium; scene of 1952 Olympic games and the initial US–USSR Strategic Arms Limitation Talks (SALT) (1969). Founded 1550 by Gustavus I of Sweden; rebuilt after fire of 1808; became capital 1812. Industries: food processing, textiles, china, chemicals. Pop. 517,000.

Helvetii, ancient Celtic people that inhabited S Ger-many and migrated in the 2nd century BC to the west-ern part of modern Switzerland. In 58 BC they invaded SW Gaul and were defeated by Caesar. They lived thereafter in Belgian Gaul and upper Germany under Roman control until AD 260 when they were attacked and later subjugated by the Alamanni. △1008.

Helvétius, Claude Adrien (1715–71), French materialist philosopher and Encyclopedist. His *On the Spirit* (1758) and *On Man* (1772) influenced Ben-tham's utilitarianism. Helvétius advocated an ethical hedonism that equated pleasure and the good.

Hematite, an oxide mineral, ferric oxide (Fe_2O_3). A common substance of altered sedimentary deposits. Rhombohedral system tabular crystals, flat scales, ra-diating masses (sometimes kidney-shaped). Earthy or metallic, red or black; hardness 5–6; sp gr 5.3. Most im-portant iron ore. Sometimes polished as gem. △242.

Hematoma, localized mass of usually clotted blood collected in an organ or tissue because of a break in a blood vessel. Treatment depends on location and size.

Hemichordata, a subphylum of the phylum Chor-data, which includes two orders of primitive marine animals, the Enteropneusta or Balanoglossida and the Pterobranchia. Most of the animals do not have com-mon names. Characteristics include a short noto-chord, or backbone; a partially or completely solid dorsal nerve chord, which is close to the surface; and optional gill slits. The most commonly observed is Balanoglossus, a wormlike organism living in mud or sand on the ocean floor. △508.

Hemingway, Ernest (Miller) (1899–1961), US au-thor, b. Oak Park, Ill. After graduating from high school in 1917 he worked as a newspaper reporter. In World War I he served as an ambulance driver in France, then joined the Italian infantry and was wounded. After the war he became a correspondent in Paris for the Toronto *Star*. He met Gertrude Stein, who strongly influenced his direct, terse prose. He published *Three Stories and Ten Poems* (1923), the short stories *In Our Time* (1924), and the novel *The Torrents of Spring* (1926), but it was with the novel *The Sun Also Rises* (1926) that he established his reputation as a writer. This novel about expatriates also established Hemingway as the spokesman for the Lost Generation. He maintained his reputation with *A Farewell to Arms* (1929) and such short stories as "The Killers" and "The Snows of Kilimanjaro." *To Have and Have Not* (1937) was not as well received as his two previous novels, but *For Whom the Bell Tolls* (1940), which drew on his experience as a corre-spondent in the Spanish Civil War, was a critical and popular success. Hemingway's nonfiction as much as his fiction concerned itself with people leading dan-gerous or especially virile lives and facing the conse-quences with stoic courage. *Death in the Afternoon* (1932) is about bullfighting; *Green Hills of Africa* (1935), about big-game hunting. The novel *The Old Man and the Sea* appeared in 1952. Hemingway re-ceived the Nobel Prize for literature in 1954. He com-mitted suicide in 1961. Several works were published after his death: *A Moveable Feast* (1964), memoirs of Paris in the 1920s; *Islands in the Stream* (1970), a novel; *The Nick Adams Stories* (1972). △1374.

Hemiplegia, paralysis of one side of the body. It can be caused by brain injury, and may be accompanied by spasticity.

Hemiptera, or Heteroptera, order of insects, includ-ing lice and water bugs, found worldwide. They may be winged or wingless and have three life stages: egg, nymph, and adult. The piercing and sucking mouth-parts are on the front of the head and extend along the underbody. Length: 0.25–4in (5.6–102mm). *See also* Assassin Bug; Bedbug. △492.

Hemlock, evergreen trees native to North America and Asia. The needles are linear and flat, with two white bands beneath. The small cones are pendulous and the branches droop. They are sensitive to dust, smoke, and wind. Height: 50–250ft (15–76m). Family Pinaceae; genus *Tsuga*.

Hemlock, poisonous herb found worldwide as a weed. Resembling the wild carrot, it has a taproot, lacy foliage, and umbels of white flowers. Its leaf stalks have conspicuous purple spots. Family Umbelliferae; species *Conium maculatum*.

Hemoglobin, iron-containing protein of red blood cells. It can bind oxygen or carbon dioxide, thus en-dowing the red cell with the ability to carry oxygen from the lungs to body tissues and exchange it for carbon dioxide.

Hemolysis, the destruction or breakdown of red blood cells at an abnormally high level, usually caused by hereditary defects, toxins, chemicals or by Rh in-compatibility in infants, the last called *Erythroblasto-sis fetalis*.

Hemolytic Anemia. *See* Anemia.

Hemolytic Streptococci, types of streptococcal bacteria that release an enzyme that destroys red blood cells and liberates hemoglobin, causing disease in men and animals. Best known is *Streptococcus py-ongens*, which causes scarlet fever.

Hemophilia, or bleeder's disease, hereditary disease characterized by failure of the blood to coagulate. Transmitted genetically as a sex-linked recessive trait, males only are affected. Spontaneous subcutaneous and intramuscular hemorrhaging occurs, as does hemorrhaging at slight injury. Replacement with nor-mal blood is the usual treatment, although coagula-tion factors have been isolated and are available on a limited basis. △716.

Hemorrhage, Cerebral. *See* Cerebral Hemorrhage.

Hemorrhaging, or bleeding, loss of blood from a broken blood vessel, usually caused by injury. Mas-sive hemorrhaging may cause faintness, sweating, rapid pulse and breathing. It may be internal or exter-nal. Treatment calls for stopping bleeding; replacing blood. △758.

Helicopter

Heliotrope

Helsingor, Denmark

Ernest Hemingway

Hemorrhoids, or piles, varicosities of the veins underlying the mucous lining of the anus and rectum. Extremely common, they manifest externally as small rounded lumps, which may enlarge under strain. Internally, the lumps are softer, more thinly covered, and bleed more easily. The most common complaint is itching. In extreme cases surgery may be indicated; usually heat and a topical or systemic analgesic are recommended. △716.

Hemp, annual herb native to Asia and cultivated throughout Eurasia, North America, and parts of South America. It has compound palmate leaves. Small, spikelike clusters of seed-producing flowers grow on female plants; male plants have branching clusters of pollen-producing flowers. The slender stems are hollow with fibrous inner bark, also called hemp and used widely for ropes and cloth. Its seeds are fed to birds and oil from the seeds is used in soap and paint. The flowers, leaves, and resinous juice are used to produce marihuana and hashish. Height: to 16ft (5m). Family Cannabinaceae; species *Cannabis sativa*.

Hempstead, town in SE New York, on W Long Island; site of Hofstra University (1935). Industries: electronic equipment, tools, chemicals, furniture. Settled 1643 by colonists from Connecticut; inc. 1853. Pop. (1970) 39,441.

Henbane, annual or biennial plant native to the Mediterranean. The entire plant is fatally toxic. Leaves are coarsely toothed, stems hairy, and the plant has a bad odor. Bell-shaped yellow flowers with purple veins produce black seeds which are the source of the alkaloid hyoscyamine. Height: 1–2.5ft (30.5–76.2cm). The 12 to 15 species include black henbane *Hyoscyamus niger*, white henbane *H. albus*, and Egyptian henbane *H. muticus*. Family Solanaceae. △742.

Henderson, Richard (1735–85), American colonizer and explorer, b. Hanover co, Va. He was a lawyer, deputy sheriff, and judge. He resigned from the bench (1773) after his farm burned. He organized the Transylvania Company, which bought much of Tennessee and Kentucky from the Cherokee Indians. With Daniel Boone he built Boonesborough, one of the first settlements in Kentucky (1775). He served on the North Carolina-Virginia boundary commission (1780) and helped plan the settlement at Nashville.

Hendricks, Thomas Andrews (1819–85), US political figure, b. Zanesville, Ohio. He was US senator from Indiana (1863–69) and governor of Indiana (1873–77). Samuel Tilden and he, Democratic nominees for president and vice president, respectively (1876), won the popular vote but a controversy over 19 electoral votes resulted in a Congressional commission favoring Republican Rutherford B. Hayes. Hendricks was elected vice president with President Cleveland (1884) but died shortly after taking office.

Hen Harrier. *See* Marsh Hawk.

Henley, William Ernest (1849–1903), English poet and editor. His most famous poems are "Invictus" (1875), which ends with the line "I am the master of my fate, I am the captain of my soul," and "England, My England" (1892). As an editor he introduced the works of Kipling, H.G. Wells, and Yeats to a wider audience.

Henna, or Egyptian privet, Jamaica mignonette, small shrub found in Middle East and N Africa and cultivated in Egypt. Since ancient times, a red dye has been extracted from the leaves and used as a hair color and cosmetic. Family Lythraceae; species *Lawsonia inermis*.

Hennepin, Louis (*c.*1640–*c.*1701) Belgian explorer and Franciscan missionary. He voyaged to Canada (1675) on a ship with Cavalier de la Salle. After doing missionary work among the Iroquois, he went on La Salle's expedition west. Reaching Peoria in 1680, Hennepin was directed to explore the upper Mississippi. He was captured by Sioux Indians but rescued by D. G. Duluth and then returned to France. In an account of his trips, he claimed to have explored the Mississippi to its mouth. The false claim discredited him.

Henrietta Maria (1609–69), queen consort of Charles I of England. After the Duke of Buckingham's death (1628), her influence over the king's foreign policy was paramount. Her subjects distrusted her because of her Roman Catholicism.

Henry II (973–1024), Holy Roman emperor (1002–24) and German king (1002–24). He succeeded his cousin Otto III. He maintained order in Germany, went to Italy three times (1004, 1013–14, and 1021–22) to subdue the Lombards, and fought constantly with the Poles. He was canonized in 1146. △1074.

Henry III (1017–56), Holy Roman emperor (1039–56) and German king (1039–56). He succeeded his father, Conrad II. Imperial power reached its zenith in Henry's reign. He made the duke of Bohemia and, for a time, the king of Hungary vassals of the empire and contained revolts in Germany. Supporting the Cluniac reform movement, in 1046 he deposed two rival popes and effected the election of Clement II. He later appointed three more popes in succession.

Henry IV (1050–1106), Holy Roman emperor (1056–1106) and German king (1056–1106). Embroiled in controversy with the popes over the lay investiture of clerics, he deposed Pope Gregory VII and was in turn deposed by the pope (1076). Rebellion in Germany made Henry seek papal absolution at Canossa (1077), but thereafter he continued the struggle, setting up the antipope Clement III. In 1104 his son Henry joined the German rebellion and deposed him. *See also* Gregory VII. △1072, 1086.

Henry V (1081–1125), Holy Roman emperor (1106–25) and German king (1106–25). Having deposed his father, Henry IV, he inherited the quarrel with the papacy over investiture. After a prolonged and violent struggle, he reached a compromise with Pope Calixtus II in the Concordat of Worms of 1122. *See also* Worms, Concordat of.

Henry VI (1165–97), Holy Roman emperor (1190–97) and German king (1190–97). The son of Frederick I, he married (1186) Constance, heiress of Sicily, and much of his reign was devoted to securing that inheritance; he was finally crowned king of Sicily in 1194. A rebellion in Germany was quelled when the rebels' ally Richard I of England came into his custody. He failed to get the consent of the German princes to make the empire hereditary in the Hohenstaufen family, although he was succeeded by his son Frederick II. △1072.

Henry VII (*c.*1275–1313), Holy Roman emperor (1308–13) and German king (1308–13). A Luxembourg, he succeeded the Hapsburg Albert I. He acquired Bohemia for his family by marrying his son to Elizabeth of Bohemia (1310). Henry revived imperial ambitions in Italy but, although crowned king of the Lombards (1311), could not maintain authority there.

Henry I (1068–1135), king of England, younger son of William I. On William II's death, he was crowned king (1100). His elder brother Robert, duke of Normandy, claimed his throne, but Henry defeated him and captured all his lands at Tinchebrai (1106). Henry married an Englishwoman and reformed the judicial and fiscal administration, but his reign was troubled by unruly barons, wars with the French and Welsh, and the death (1120) of his heir, William.

Henry II (1133–89), king of England, son of Geoffrey Plantagenet and Matilda, daughter of Henry I. He inherited the Angevin lands, obtained Aquitaine by marrying Eleanor (1152), and succeeded to the throne (1154). He reformed the judicial, monetary, and military systems, but his attempt to bring church courts under secular control through the Constitutions of Clarendon (1164) failed. By the Treaty of Montmirail (1169), Henry secured France's sanction for his sons' succession to his territories and Prince Henry was crowned heir (1170). After the murder of Thomas à Becket (1170), Henry's life was beset by trouble with the Roman Catholic Church, revolts in Ireland and Normandy, and strife with his own sons. △1076.

Henry III (1207–72), king of England, son of John, whom he succeeded when a minor in 1216. He married Eleanor of Provence (1236). His favoritism to foreigners led to resentment among his barons, who revolted against him and refused to finance his overseas campaigns. Forced to make substantial constitutional concessions by the so-called "Mad Parliament" (1258), he enlisted French and papal aid but the barons, under Simon de Montfort, defeated him at Lewes (1264). His son Edward's victory at Evesham (1265) enabled him to retain executive power while granting many reforms.

Henry IV (1367–1413) king of England, son of John of Gaunt and cousin of Richard II. Banished by Richard (1398), he returned to claim his father's estates (1399) and, finding Richard deserted by his supporters, induced him to resign his crown. Henry's reign was disturbed by Welsh and Scottish wars, assassination attempts, and rebellions, chiefly fomented by the Percy family.

Henry V (1387–1422), king of England, eldest son of Henry IV. After fighting on his father's behalf at Shrewsbury (1403), in Wales, and in Scotland, he succeeded him (1413) and immediately demanded the restoration of territories formerly ceded to France. Invading France, he captured Harfleur and won a great victory at Agincourt (1415). Further military and diplomatic success led to his adoption as the French king's heir by the Treaty of Troyes (1420).

Henry VI (1421–71), king of England, succeeded his father, Henry V, in 1422. After he came of age (1442) his reign was characterized by military and diplomatic disasters in France. At home, his feebleness permitted the Yorkist and Lancastrian factions to instigate the Wars of the Roses. Deposed by the Yorkists (1461), he was temporarily restored (1470) but was again deposed and murdered.

Henry VII (1457–1509), king of England, founder of the Tudor dynasty. Having killed Richard III at Bosworth (1485), Henry united the warring factions by marrying the Yorkist heiress, Elizabeth. His financial acumen restored England's fortunes after the devastations of civil war. He concluded various advantageous foreign treaties, such as the treaty of Etaples (1492) and took effective action against pretenders to his throne. △1128.

Henry VIII (1491–1547), king of England, succeeded his father, Henry VII, in 1509. In 1513, victories over the Scots (at Flodden) and French reestablished England as a European power, a position maintained by Cardinal Wolsey's diplomacy. Henry's decision to divorce Catherine of Aragon, who could not bear a male heir, in favor of Anne Boleyn, led to a confrontation with the papacy. Dismissing Wolsey (1529), he appointed Thomas Cranmer his advisor. He compelled the clergy to acknowledge him supreme head of the church, and he was excommunicated (1533–35). Under Thomas Cromwell's direction, he initiated other anti-ecclesiastical moves in the 1530s, including transferring church revenues to the crown, appropriating monastic property, and executing those who, like Sir Thomas More, objected. This reorganization of church government broke papal power in England. Successful campaigns against the Scots, and heresy and treason trials at home occupied his later years. From his controversial six marriages (Catherine of Aragon, Anne Boleyn, Jane Seymour, Anne of Cleves, Catherine Howard, Catherine Parr), he had only one son and two daughters. △1128.

Henry I (1008–60), king of France (1031–60). His reign was characterized by struggles with rebellious vassals. Although Henry was crowned by his father, Robert II, his younger brother Robert claimed the throne and was supported by their mother, Constance of Provence. In the ensuing civil war, Henry was forced to cede Burgundy to Robert. Henry at first supported (1035–47) and then fought unsuccessfully against (1054, 1058) William, duke of Normandy. He was succeeded by his son Philip I.

Henry II (1519–59), king of France (1547–59). The second son of Francis I, Henry and his older brother were held hostage in Spain from 1526 until the Peace of Cambrai (1530). Upon his brother's death, Henry became heir to the throne. He married Catherine de Médicis. As king, Henry continued his father's policies of strengthening the monarchy and effecting administrative reform. The struggles with Emperor Charles V also continued. A militant Catholic, he initiated harsh, systematic repression of Protestants. Defeated in Italy and faced with national bankruptcy, Henry signed the Peace of Cateau-Cambrésis (1559) with the Hapsburgs, giving up France's claims in Italy. He died after he was accidentally wounded in a tournament.

Henry III (1551–89), king of France (1574–89), last of the Valois dynasty. As duke of Anjou he defeated the Huguenots (1569) in the Wars of Religion. With his mother, Catherine de Médicis, he instigated the Massacre of Saint Bartholomew's Day (1572). Elected king of Poland in 1573, he returned to France to assume the throne on the death of his brother Charles IX (1574). He made peace with the Huguenots (1576), but when his younger brother Francis died in 1584 and the Protestant Henry of Navarre became heir to the throne, he renewed the wars. His troops were defeated at Coutras (1587). Henry de Guise, leader of the Catholic League, seized Paris and expelled Henry (1588). The king felt compelled to ally himself with Henry of Navarre. He was assassinated by a Catholic fanatic, Jacques Clément, during the siege of Paris.

Henry II (1503–55), king of Navarre (1517–55). Upon the death of his mother (Catherine de Foix) he claimed the throne of Navarre, which was disputed by Emperor Charles V. Henry invaded Navarre and was defeated. Although he never gained control of his ngdom, his grandson became Henry IV of France. 1154.

enry IV or **Henry of Navarre** (1553–1610), king Navarre (as Henry III, 1572–1610), first Bourbon ng of France (1589–1610). Raised as a Protestant, e nevertheless married (1572) Margaret of Valois, ster of the French king Charles IX. Henry escaped e Massacre of Saint Bartholomew's Day (1572) by nouncing his Protestantism. He was kept as a virtual risoner at the French court until his escape in 1576 hen he joined the Protestants. He became heir to e French throne in 1584 on the death of the ounger brother of King Henry III. King Henry was ersuaded by Henry de Guise, leader of the Catholic eague, to deny Henry of Navarre his right. The War f the Three Henrys resulted. Henry defeated the ing's forces in 1587 and was reconciled with him fter the Catholic League expelled the king from Paris 588). Henry III was assassinated in 1589, but Henry f Navarre did not gain Paris until after he renounced is Protestantism in 1594. With the Edict of Nantes 598) he gave the Huguenots political rights and eligious freedom. He encouraged economic growth nd Canadian exploration after more than three ecades of chaotic religious war. He was assassinated y a religious fanatic. His second wife was Marie de Medici, mother of the future Louis XIII.

Henry I (876?–936), king of Germany (919–36), called Henry the Fowler. Duke of Saxony, he was elected to succeed Conrad I as king. He asserted his authority over the German princes and reconquered Lotharingia (Lorraine, 925). He bought off (926) the Magyar raiders but in 933 defeated them on the Unstrut River. He was succeeded by his son, Otto I, first Holy Roman emperor. △1074.

Henry II (1335?–1379), Spanish king of Castile and León (1369–79). He was the illegitimate son of Alfonso XI and revolted against the rule of his half brother, Peter the Cruel. Henry defeated Peter in 1366, but Peter, with the aid of England in the person of Edward the Black Prince, maintained the throne. In 1369, however, after the departure of the English, Henry again defeated Peter and killed him in a duel. He was succeeded by his son, John I.

Henry III (1379–1406), Spanish king of Castile and León (1390–1406), son and successor of John I. His marriage to Catherine of Castile ended a long dynastic struggle; her father, John of Gaunt, renounced his claims to Castile in her favor. Henry was succeeded by his son, John II.

Henry IV (1425–74), Spanish king of Castile and León (1454–74), son and successor of John II. He was a weak ruler, and the nobles refused to accept as heiress to the throne his daughter, Juana La Beltraneja. He finally accepted his half sister Isabella but reneged after her marriage in 1469 to Ferdinand of Aragón. Upon Henry's death, civil war erupted between the forces of Isabella and those of Juana. Isabella won and succeeded to the throne.

Henry of Burgundy (died 1112), count of Portugal. He was a French noble in the service of Alfonso VI of León in the war to rid Spain of the Moors. He married Alfonso's illegitimate daughter and was granted Oporto and Coimbra. He assumed the style of count of Portugal. After his death, his son, Alfonso I, declared Portugal independent (1139) and became its first king.

Henry of Flanders (1174?–1216), Latin emperor of Constantinople (*r.* 1205–16). An effective ruler, he restored Latin control over Thrace and pursued a conciliatory policy towards the conquered Byzantines.

Henry of Navarre. *See* Henry IV (1553–1610).

Henry the Cardinal (1512–80), king of Portugal (1578–80), son of Manuel I and successor of Sebastian. He was created a cardinal in 1545 and acted (1562–68) as regent to his nephew, Sebastian. After Sebastian was killed in battle in North Africa, Henry assumed the crown. Henry's death marked the end of the Aviz dynasty, and, after Philip II of Spain asserted his rights in Portugal, the beginning of 60 years of Spanish rule.

Henry the Lion (1129–95), duke of Saxony (1142–80) and Bavaria (1156–80). The son of Henry the Proud, he only gradually recovered his father's lands. Both he and Emperor Frederick I sought to end the feud between their families, the Guelphs and Hohenstaufens. But Henry's power in Saxony, which he extended by conquest of the Wends, finally alienated Frederick, who confiscated his lands (1180), and forced him to flee to England. He was reconciled with Emperor Henry VI, Frederick's son, in 1195. △1072.

Henry the Navigator (1394–1460), Portuguese prince and patron of explorers. He was the third son of John I, the brother of Duarte, and the uncle of Alfonso V. In 1416 he established at Sagres (near Lagos) an observatory and a school for the study of geography and navigation. Although he made no journeys himself, he sponsored numerous Portuguese navigators who, in turn, made many important discoveries. They formed the basis for the great Portuguese empire of the 16th century. Among their discoveries were the Madeira Islands, and they explored the West African coast as far south as Sierra Leone. △1122.

Henry the Proud (1108?–39), duke of Saxony (1137–38) and Bavaria (1126–38). A Guelph, he inherited Bavaria from his father and was made duke of Saxony by Emperor Lothair II, whose daughter he married. Lothair designated him heir to the throne, but he was defeated in the election by the Hohenstaufen Conrad III, who deprived him of his duchies.

Henry, Andrew (1775?–1833), US miner and trapper, b. York co, Pa. He was one of the organizers of the St Louis Fur Company with William Clark and Manuel Lisa. He built Henry's Fork (1810) near the mouth of the Snake River in Washington. In 1822 he and William Ashley formed a partnership and built another fort at the mouth of the Yellowstone River.

Henry, Joseph (1797–1878), US physicist, b. Albany, N.Y. His improvements in electromagnetics were essential for the development of the commercial telegraph. His work with the induced current principle led to the development of the transformer. He introduced (1850) a system of using the telegraph for sending weather reports, making possible the US Weather Bureau. He became (1846) the first secretary of the Smithsonian Institution and was an organizer of the American Association for the Advancement of Science and its first president (1849).

Henry, O. (1862–1910), pseud. of William Sydney Porter, popular US short-story writer, b. Greensboro, N.C. His typical surprise ending gave rise to the term the "O. Henry ending." After editing and publishing the humor magazine *The Rolling Stone,* Henry served three years in prison on a charge of embezzlement. While in prison he published the first of his short stories signed "O. Henry" ("Whistling Dick's Christmas Stocking," 1899).

After his release, Henry moved to New York City, the scene of much of his fiction. Henry's first book, *Cabbages and Kings* (1904), was a collection of stories of revolution and adventure in Latin America. This work was followed by many more collections, including *The Four Million* (1906), *Heart of the West* (1907), *The Gentle Grafter* (1908), *Roads of Destiny* (1909), and *Strictly Business* (1910). In 1918 the O. Henry Memorial Awards, given to the best stories published each year in American magazines, were established.

Henry, Patrick (1736–99), US patriot, orator, and lawyer, b. Hanover co, Va. Elected to the Virginia House of Burgesses (1765–75), he denounced the Stamp Act. He was a member of the Continental Congress (1774–76), and became convinced that war with Britain was inevitable. It was then he delivered his "Give me liberty or give me death" speech and made his reputation as a gifted orator. He helped draw up the Virginia Convention and from 1776–79 and from 1784–86 he was governor of Virginia. He opposed Virginia's ratification of the Constitution as adverse to state's rights although he was a leader in the movement for the Bill of Rights.

Henry, unit of inductance equal to the inductance of a closed loop that gives rise to a magnetic flux of one weber for each ampere of current that flows.

Henry, Fort, confederate fort S of the Kentucky-Tennessee border, on the Tennessee River; scene of first important Union victory of the Civil War, when General Grant captured the fort (Feb. 6, 1862).

Henry IV, parts I (1598) and II (1600), 5-act historical dramas by William Shakespeare, based on Raphael Holinshed's *Chronicles* and an epic by Samuel Daniel. Part I takes up English history at exactly the point where Shakespeare ended his *Richard II.* King Henry believes that the wild behavior of his son Prince Hal is heaven's vengeance for Henry's sin in having deposed Richard II. Hal promises at his father's deathbed to reform, and upon becoming king he professes not to know his old tavern companion Falstaff and has his former cronies hustled off to prison.

Henry V (*c.* 1600), 5-act historical drama by William Shakespeare, based on Raphael Holinshed's *Chronicles,* a history by Edward Halle, and Robert Fabyan's *New Chronicles.* A nationalistic play, it dramatizes the

Henna

Queen Henrietta

King Henry V of England

Patrick Henry

enthusiasm of the people of Great Britain for fighting a foreign war. King Henry V's patriotism often becomes chauvinism. The wild Prince Hal protrayed in *Henry IV* has totally reformed, becoming a "mirror of all Christian kings." He leads his troops to victory over the French at Agincourt and woos the French king's daughter Katharine. The play was made into a film (1945), in which Laurence Olivier's performance as Henry won him the New York Film Critics Circle Award (1946).

Henry VI, Parts I, II, III (*c.*1590–92), historical dramas by William Shakespeare, based on Raphael Holinshed's *Chronicles* and material by Edward Halle. Shakespeare altered the chronology to suit his dramatic purpose, however, keeping Joan of Arc alive to take part in a battle that actually occurred 20 years after her death. The death of Henry V while his son is still a boy sets off rivalry and dissension among nobles contending for power. England loses its French possessions despite the valiant leadership of Lord Talbot. *Henry VI*, parts I, II, and III, are part of a tetralogy, with *Richard III*, dramatizing the Wars of the Roses.

Henry VIII (1613), historical play by William Shakespeare, probably in collaboration with John Fletcher, based on Raphael Holinshed's *Chronicles* and material by Edward Halle. It begins with a description of the splendor of the "Field of the Cloth of Gold" (1520) and ends with the christening of Princess Elizabeth (1533). During the first performance of the play a cannon used for a royal salute in Act I set fire to the Globe theater and it burned to the ground.

Henry's Law, principle in physical chemistry which states that the weight of a gas dissolved in a fixed quantity of a liquid is directly proportional to the pressure of the gas on the liquid, at constant temperature. Thus, the more a gas is compressed, the more will be absorbed in a liquid.

Hens and Chicks, also houseleek, sempervivum; a succulent perennial plant native to dry sunny regions of Europe, popular in rock gardens. The grayish, or bluish, tongue-shaped leaves grow in basal rosettes and are marked with red. The pink or rose daisylike flowers grow in clusters. Species include *Sempervivum tectorum*, with leaf rosettes 3–4in (7.6–10.2cm) in diameter, and *S. arachnoideum*, the cobweb houseleek, in which the 1in (2.5cm) leaf rosettes are covered with cobwebby, white fibers. Family Crassulaceae.

Henson, Matthew Alexander (1866–1955), US explorer. He accompanied Robert Peary in his discovery of the North Pole (1909). He recounted these experiences in *A Negro Explorer at the North Pole* (1912).

Heparin, a polysaccharide sulfuric acid ester occurring in the liver and lungs of animals that prolongs the clotting time of blood by preventing the formation of fibrin. It is used in vascular surgery and in treatment of postoperative thrombosis and embolism.

Hepatica, or liverleaf, genus of 10 species of small, herbaceous perennial plants native to wooded regions of North America and Eurasia. The three-lobed leaves stay green during winter and the flowers are blue, pink, or white. Family Ranunculaceae.

Hepatic Artery and Vein. △694.

Hepatitis, inflammation of the liver, in its most common form caused by two viruses differentiated as infectious hepatitis or serum hepatitis. Infectious hepatitis is usually spread through fecal contamination, serum hepatitis by blood transfusion or poorly sterilized injections. Symptoms include lethargy, nausea, fever, perhaps jaundice. Recovery is usually spontaneous although hospitalizing is usual to forestall complications and to provide symptomatic relief. △718.

Hepburn, Katharine (1909–), US stage and film actress, b. Hartford, Conn. She is famed for her intelligence, wit, and patrician looks. Among her sophisticated film comedies are *Holiday* (1938) and *The Philadelphia Story* (1940); she made nine films with Spencer Tracy, including *Adam's Rib* (1949) and *Pat and Mike* (1952). Her dramatic films include *Morning Glory* (1933), *Alice Adams* (1935), *The African Queen*, (1951), *Long Day's Journey into Night* (1962), *Guess Who's Coming to Dinner* (1967), *The Lion in Winter* (1968), and *A Delicate Balance* (1973). She scored a personal triumph in the 1969 stage musical *Coco*.

Hepburn Act (1906), US legislation that amended the Interstate Commerce Act (1887). It prohibited a railroad from transporting commodities in which it had a proprietary interest. It also prohibited free passes and rebates and authorized the Interstate Commerce Commission to impose maximum railroad rates.

Hephaestus, ancient Greek god of fire and crafts. Son of Zeus and Hera, he is equivalent to the Roman Vulcan. Blacksmith and armorer to the Olympian gods, with a forge under Etna (or Stromboli), he is depicted as crippled and uncouth but clever and able enough to create Pandora, the first woman, and to wed Aphrodite.

Hepplewhite, George (?–1786), English furniture designer and cabinetmaker. Light in scale, usually with tapered legs, his furniture combined pale woods with mahogany. There was often inlay or painted decoration present. Hepplewhite was best known for his shield-back chairs.

Heptaméron (1558), collection of 72 tales by Marguerite de Navarre, modeled on Boccaccio's *Decameron*. The stories, related by 10 travelers, provided scope for the author's moral and religious opinions on love and contemporary customs.

Heptarchy, generally recognized term for the seven Anglo-Saxon kingdoms from the 5th century to the Danish invasions in the 9th. Including Mercia, Northumbria, Sussex, Kent, East Anglia, Essex, and Wessex, the heptarchy represents a simplified historical version of the complex political makeup of England at that time.

Hera, in Greek mythology, the daughter of Cornus and Rhea, queen of the Olympian gods, sister and wife of Zeus. Depicted with crown and scepter, she was worshiped as patron of Argos and Samos. In myths she appears as a jealous scold who persecuted her rivals but aided heroes of her choice such as Jason and Achilles.

Heraclitus (536–470 BC), important pre-Socratic philosopher. He held that all things are constantly changing, even the universe as a whole. Since only change is real, the orderliness of successive changes, or the world's destiny, is all that remains the same. △858.

Heraclius (575?–641), Byzantine emperor (*r.* 610–41). One of Byzantine's greatest rulers, Heraclius came to power in difficult times. The government of the empire had come to a standstill; recurrent financial crises had eroded its economic, political, and military might. Byzantium's enemies had overrun vast territories: Slavs and Avars were settling in the Balkans, and the Persians were invading Asia Minor. Under Heraclius, far-reaching reforms in the army and administration led to an improvement in the internal situation. From 622 to 628, Heraclius fought and defeated the Persians. The Perso-Byzantine war is sometimes considered the first medieval crusade, since it restored the Holy Land and the Holy Cross to the empire.

Heraldry, historic system in which personal and inherited symbols are granted for the practice of bearing and displaying armorial ensigns. During the Middle Ages heraldic symbols were displayed on the shield and helm. The herald, frequently a tournament official, became an expert at identifying men and families by their insignia; his function evolved into one of designing and granting armorial bearings. Although heraldry is almost as old as civilization, its immediate origin dates to 12-century Germany; the practice soon spread to France, Spain, and Italy, and was brought to England by the Normans. Today, in England, the Court of Chivalry, officiated by the earl marshal and kings-of-arms, still awards arms to individuals and corporations, as well as honorary arms to approved American citizens of British descent.

Herat, city and provincial capital in NW Afghanistan, on Hari Rud. Originally the ancient city of Aria, Herat served as Tamerlane's capital in 15th century; site of palaces, tombs, mosques. Industries: handcrafts, textiles, carpets. Pop. 101,579.

Herb, seed plant with a soft rather than woody stem that withers away after one growing season. Most herbaceous plants are flowering plants, or angiosperms. Also, any plant used as a flavoring, seasoning, or medicine, such as thyme, sage, and mint. △358, 446.

Herbert, Edward, Lord Herbert of Cherbury (1583–1648), English philosopher. Called "the father of deism," he is remembered for *On the Truth* (Lat. *De Veritate*, 1624) and for his *Autobiography* (publ. 1764). *See also* Deism.

Herbert, Henry Howard Molyneux, 4th Earl of Carnarvon (1831–90), English statesman. A Cc servative, he put forth several liberal plans as und secretary for the colonies (1858–59) and colonial se retary (1866–67, 1874–78); he submitted the b (1867) for federation of the Canadian provinces, lea ing to Canadian independence; a bill to abolish Go Coast slavery (1874); and a plan for federation South Africa (1877). After resigning in protest ov the British entry into the Russo-Turkish conflict, h served as lord lieutenant of Ireland (1885–86), whe he opposed Gladstone's policy of home rule.

Herbert, Victor (1859–1924), US conductor ar composer of operettas, b. Ireland. He conducted th Pittsburgh Symphony Orchestra (1898–1904) ar composed such operettas as *Babes in Toylar* (1903), *Mlle Modiste* (1905), *The Red Mill* (1906 *Naughty Marietta* (1910), and *Sweethearts* (1913).

Herbicide, chemical preparation used for killing ve etation, usually weeds. Some are selective, and k only certain species of plants. Others kill all plant lif.

Herbivores. △548.

Herculaneum (Erolano) ancient city in Italy, on si of modern Resina and Portici at foot of Mt Vesuviu devastated AD 63 by earthquake; buried AD 79 wi Pompeii by eruption of Mt Vesuvius; archeologic excavations begun 1709 have unearthed Villa of th Papyri, a basilica, and theater.

Hercules, legendary Greek hero of great strengt and courage, generally depicted with a club and wea ing a lion skin. His 12 labors justify his fame. Hercule killed the lion of Nemea and the nine-headed Hydr captured the Erymanthean boar and golden-antlere Cerynean stag. He destroyed the Stymphalian bird then cleaned the Augean stables by diverting tw rivers through them. Hercules captured the Creta bull and the man-eating horses of Thrace, stole th Amazon Queen's girdle, the cattle of Eurstheus, an the golden apples of the Hesperides, and finall brought Cerberus out of Hades. △834.

Hercules, in Astronomy. △110.

Hercules Beetle, tropical American scarab beetle The male has two horns—a long one on the head an a shorter one on the thorax. Length: to 7.5in (19cm including horn. Species *Dynastes hercules*. △500.

Herder, Johann Gottfried (1744–1803), Prussia philosopher and cultural historian. Herder understoo human society to be an organic and secular totalit that developed as the result of an historical process His claim that the nation and its language defined a essential cultural unity anticipated "nationalist" sent ment. Herder was also a founder of German Romant cism and an opponent of Immanuel Kant. He wrot *Ideas and the Philosophy of History of Humanit* (1784–91), which applies the concept of history to a areas of human culture. △1222, 1290.

Heredity, transmission of physical and other charac teristics from parent to offspring by means of genes ir the chromosomes. Study of heredity began with the work of Gregor Mendel in the 19th century. Though physical traits are often determined directly by the laws of heredity (eg, eye and hair color), comple traits such as intelligence are influenced by environ mental factors. △416.

Hereford, widespread breed of beef cattle. Originally from Herefordshire, England, there are numerous herds in the United States and Argentina. They gain weight quickly on minimal feed and adapt to semiarid conditions. Red with white faces, they are usually horned. *See also* Beef Cattle. △372.

Herero, Negroid people of Namibia (South-West Africa). By tradition, the Herero are nomadic pastoralists, practicing ancestor worship, although European influence and Christianity are now evident. Both matrilineal and patrilineal descent exist in a society governed by localized autonomous political units. Large numbers of the Herero died during a revolt against German rule (1903–07).

Heresy, a persistent deviation from dogma, considered dangerous by orthodox members of a faith. The early Christian Church struggled over beliefs such as Arianism. In later times such outstanding rebels as Joan of Arc and Jan Hus were condemned as heretics. In modern times heresy charges are rare. *See also* Arianism; Gnosticism; Inquisition; Nestorianism. △1086.

Herkimer, Nicholas (1728–77), American general in the Revolutionary War, b. Herkimer, N.Y. Leading 800 men to aid Ft. Schuyler in New York, he was ambushed (Aug. 6, 1777) at Oriskany by the British and their Indian allies and was mortally wounded.

Herman, Woodrow Charles ("Woody") (1913–), US jazz bandleader, singer, clarinetist, and saxophonist, b. Milwaukee. He formed his first band in 1936 and was a top jazz bandleader for three decades. His theme song was "Blue Flame" (1939) and his many hits included "Caledonia" (1945), "Woodchopper's Ball" (1936 with Joe Bishop), "Bijou" (1944), and "Apple Honey" (1944).

Hermaphrodite, organism with both male and female sexual organs. Most are invertebrates (planarian, earthworm, snail), sessile, or slow moving. They reproduce by two individuals mating and exchanging sperm or one individual's ovum and sperm uniting. Hermaphroditic plants are termed monoecious. △462, 474.

Hermes, Greek god equivalent to the Roman Mercury, represented with winged hat and sandals and carrying a wand twined with snakes. Hermes was the messenger of the gods and patron of travelers, gamblers, thieves, and commerce. He conducted the souls of the dead to Hades. Arcadia, Athens, Sparta, Argos, and Boeotia were centers of his worship. △832.

Hermes Carrying the Infant Dionysus. △1002.

Hermitage, Russian art museum, Leningrad. The largest public art collection in the Soviet Union was first housed in Rastrelli's Winter Palace. When this building was damaged by fire, the collection was moved to the New Hermitage museum, built by a Munich architect (1840–49). Catherine the Great was responsible for the size and quality of the collection. She was able to acquire several important private collections that came onto the world art market while she was empress. The Hermitage has excellent examples of European painting, expecially of the French Impressionist school. It also has numerous examples of Russian art throughout history.

Hermit Crab, small, common crablike crustacean found in tidal pools and shallow water worldwide. It uses sea snail shells for protection of its soft abdomen, using larger shells as it grows to adult size. Some forms are terrestrial and do not use shells as adults. Family Paguridae. *See also* Crustacean. △490.

Hermit Thrush, North American songbird that is brownish with a spotted breast and reddish-brown tail. A fine singer, it grows to 7in (18cm). Family Turdidae; species *Hylocichla guttata.*

Hermon, Mount (Jabal ash-Shaykh), snow-capped mountain on Syria-Lebanon border, in Anti-Lebanon mountain range, 28mi (45km) WSW of Damascus; a sacred mountain of ancient Palestine; traditional scene of the Transfiguration. Height: 9,232ft (2,816m).

Hermopolis, ancient Egyptian center of worship of Thoth, the god of learning, and also of the Heliopolitan Ennead. Located 160mi (258km) S of Cairo, the modern site is called El Ashmunen. The Greeks associated the god Hermes with Thoth and renamed the site for him.

Hernández Colón, Rafael (1936–), governor of Puerto Rico (1973–), leader of the Popular Democratic party (PDP); defeated the incumbent governor Luis Ferré by an absolute majority.

Herndon v. Lowry (1937), US Supreme Court case in which the court overturned the conviction of an admitted Communist party member. The court said that the freedom of association protected by the First Amendment prohibited punishment for mere membership.

Herne, city and port in W West Germany, on Rhine-Herne Canal; site of Renaissance castle with Gothic chapel. Industries: textiles, radios, television sets. Chartered as city 1897. Pop. 101,514.

Hernia, protrusion of an organ, or part of an organ, through its enclosing wall or through connective tissue. Common types of hernias are protrusion of an intestinal loop through the umbilicus (umbilical hernia) or inguinal canal of the groin (inguinal hernia), or protrusion of part of the stomach or esophagus into the chest cavity through the opening (hiatus) of the esophagus into the diaphragm (hiatus hernia). △720.

Herniated Disc. *See* Slipped Disc.

Hero and Leander, fictional lovers of classical antiquity. Each night Leander swam the Hellespont from Abydos to Sestos to court Hero until he drowned one stormy night. Hero drowned herself in sorrow. Christopher Marlowe's poem recounting the tale is the best known celebration of their love.

Herod Antipas (21 BC–AD 39), tetrarch of Galilee and Petraea (4 BC–AD 39), son of Herod the Great. He had John the Baptist beheaded at the instigation of his wife Herodias and his step-daughter Salome. He refused to intervene in the trial of Jesus, leaving his fate up to the Roman procurator Pontius Pilate. The emperor Caligula banished him to Gaul in AD 39.

Herodotus (*c.* 484–425 BC), Greek historian and geographer. Little is known of him. He made lengthy journeys through the ancient world (Asia Minor, Mesopotamia, Babylon, and perhaps Egypt), spent long periods in Athens, and helped colonize Thurii in S Italy. He is most known for his lengthy, vivid, frequently anecdotal history of the Persian Wars. Considered the beginning of Western history writing, his work contains diverse information and is rich in anecdotes. *See also* Thucydides. △998.

Hero Figure △832–40.

Heroic Couplet, two consecutive lines of iambic pentameter rhyming verse used in epic or "heroic" poetry. It was mastered by John Dryden and perfected by Alexander Pope. In modern poetry the heroic couplet is associated with light verse or satire.

Heroin, synthetic derivative of morphine, requiring a smaller dose to produce similar but faster effects, including reduction of pain, euphoria, and depressed respiration. Nausea and vomiting are side effects. It produces dependence or addiction. Illegal in the United States, its abuse has been widely publicized. △730, 744.

Heron, wading bird with long, daggerlike bill found in lakes, streams, and swamps. White, bluish, grayish, or brownish, they have long thin necks, long broad wings, thin legs, and short tails. They crumble their well-developed powder down feathers to absorb body slime. Feeding mainly on fish, they nest in groups and lay 3–6 light-colored eggs. Height: 1–6ft (0.3–1.8m). Family Ardeidae. △618.

Herophilus (*fl.* 300 BC), Greek anatomist who practiced at Alexandria and was one of the first to experiment with post-mortem examinations. He identified various parts of the head and brain including the retina and also studied various glands and internal organs.

Herpes Simplex, acute herpes virus disease of the skin or mucous membrane in which clusters of fluid-containing blisters are seen, particularly on the lip borders, nostrils, or genitals. When accompanying a cold or fever, they are called cold sores or fever blisters.

Herpes Zoster. *See* Shingles.

Herpetology, zoological study of amphibians and reptiles. Areas of study include taxonomy (classification), life history, and geographical distribution. *See also* Zoology. △518–524.

Herrara, José Joaquín (1792–1854), Mexican military and political leader. He served as second-in-command under General Santa Anna in the war with the United States (1846–47) and succeeded him as president (1848–51). As president, he attempted to reorganize the government along federalist lines and established the country's international credit, but military and political disorders impeded any progress.

Herring, marine schooling fish found worldwide. One of the most important food fish, it is canned as sardine and sold as fresh or pickled herring. It has laterally compressed body, deeply forked tail fin, and large mouth. Length: 3–18in (7.6–45.7cm). Family Clupeidae; species 190, including *Clupea harengus.* △392, 516.

Herschel, Sir William (1738–1822), English astronomer. Born in Hanover, Germany, he fled to Britain during the Seven Years War. A renowned maker of telescopes, he made many discoveries, including the planet Uranus (1781), and mapped numerous galactic nebulae.

Hersey, John Richard (1914–), US author, b. Tientsin, China. A war correspondent, his early books were about World War II. Among them are *A Bell for Adano* (1944), a Pulitzer prize-winning novel about an American major in Sicily during the Allied occupation; *Hiroshima* (1946), a nonfiction work based on interviews with survivors of the atomic bombing; and *The Wall* (1950), about the Jewish resistance of the Nazis

Katharine Hepburn

Johann Herder

Woody Herman

Hermitage, Leningrad.

in Warsaw. Later works include *Under the Eye of the Storm* (1967) and *The Conspiracy* (1972).

Herskovits, Melville J(ean) (1895–1963), US anthropologist, b. Bellefontaine, Ohio. He made important studies of cultural change, economic anthropology, and African cultures. At Northwestern University he founded the first US program for African studies. His works include *The Myth of the Negro Past* (1941) and *Man and His Works* (1949).

Hertz, Heinrich Rudolph (1857–94), German physicist who became assistant to Hermann Helmholtz and held professorships at Karlsruhe and later at Bonn. He discovered, broadcasted, and received the radio waves predicted by James Maxwell. He also demonstrated the phenomenon of electromagnetic or electric waves ("hertzian waves"), and showed that their velocity and length could be measured and that heat and light are electromagnetic waves. The establishment of wireless telegraphy was dependent on his discoveries.

Hertz, SI unit of frequency (symbol H_Z) equal to the frequency of a periodic phenomenon that has a period of one second. This unit replaces the cycle per second. △1544.

Hertzsprung-Russell Diagram, or H-R diagram, graph of the relationship between a star's luminosity (usually indicated by increasing absolute magnitude on the Y axis) and its surface temperature (shown by spectral types or color indexes in descending order on the X axis). The graph, independently devised by Ejnar Hertzsprung and Henry Norris Russell, illustrates the fact that stars fall into very well defined classes, and indicates patterns of stellar evolution. △100–02.

Herzl, Theodor (1860–1904), Jewish leader and the founder of political Zionism. He was born in Austria-Hungary and worked as a lawyer and a journalist. He decided that the only solution to discrimination against Jews was to found a Jewish state. In 1897 he became president of the Zionist Organization, which worked throughout Europe to establish a Jewish national home in Palestine. Herzl wrote of himself as the founder of the Jewish state, and in 1949 his body was reburied in the newly established state of Israel. *See also* Zionism. △1380.

Herzliyya, town in W central Israel, on Mediterranean Sea; named in honor of Theodor Herzl, father of modern Zionism. Industries: tourism, flour, citrus fruits. Founded 1924. Pop. 38,500.

Hesiod (8th century BC), Greek poet. The first major poet after Homer, he was the first to reveal his personality through his poetry. Troubles with his brother about their inheritances moved him to compose his best known work *Works and Days*. In *Theogony* he traced the mythological history of the gods. He was considered a great classical poet, but his writings were not as acclaimed as Homer's. △998.

Hesperides, Greek mythological characters who figured in the "Twelve Labors of Hercules." The Hesperides were the daughters of Atlas and Hesperis. They had been entrusted by Juno with the guardianship of her precious golden apples, and were assisted in this task by a watchful dragon. As the last and most difficult of his labors, Hercules was told to steal the golden apples from the Hesperides. He sought the help of their father Atlas. Atlas, who had been condemned to bear the weight of the sky upon his shoulders, agreed to fetch the apples if Hercules would take his place in the meanwhile. But when Atlas returned with the prize, he was unwilling to resume his burden. Hercules tricked him, and carried off the apples of the Hesperides.

Hess, (Dame) Myra (1890–1965), English pianist. She made her debut in London in 1907 and first performed in the United States in 1922. She was especially known as an interpreter of the Baroque composers Scarlatti and J.S. Bach and of the concertos of Mozart.

Hess, Rudolf (1894–), German Nazi leader. He joined the Nazis in 1921 and took part in the abortive Munich putsch (1923). Although Adolf Hitler's deputy from 1933, he lacked influence. In 1941, he flew alone to Scotland, hoping to make peace with the British. Imprisoned for the rest of the war, he was afterward sentenced to life imprisonment in Spandau Prison, Berlin.

Hess, Victor Francis (1883–), US physicist, b. Austria. As a result of his investigations of the ionization of air, he suggested that a radiation similar to X rays came from space; these were later named cosmic rays. He shared the 1936 Nobel Prize for physics with Carl David Anderson. Soon after receiving the prize, Hess emigrated to the United States; he became a citizen after World War II.

Hesse, Hermann (1877–1962), German novelist and poet. He ran away from a theological school in Maulbronn and spent much of his life studying Indian mysticism and Jungian psychology, as expressed in the novels *Demian* (1919), *Siddhartha* (1922), *Steppenwolf* (1927), *Narziss und Goldmund* (1930), and *The Glass Bead Game* (1943). He received the 1946 Nobel Prize for literature.

Hesse (Hessen), state in central West Germany, bounded by Baden-Württemburg and Bavaria (S), Rhineland-Palatinate (W), North Rhine-Westphalia and Lower Saxony (N) and East Germany (E); capital is Wiesbaden. Hilly, agricultural area with some heavy forests, it contains some of Germany's oldest cities (Frankfurt, Mainz, Worms). Industries: wine making, chemicals, machinery, mining. Area: 8,150sq mi (21,109sq km). Pop. 5,441,300.

Hessian Fly, brown to black, 0.16 to 0.24in (4–6mm) long fly found north of the Tropic of Cancer and in New Zealand. It is a serious pest of wheat and other grains. Family Cecidomyiidae, species *Mayetiola destructor. See also* Diptera.

Hestia, Greek goddess of the burning hearth. In the myths, she is the unmarried daughter of Cronus and Rhea who scorned the attentions of Apollo and Poseidon and who was installed in Olympus by Zeus. She was revered as the oldest of the Olympian gods. In Greece a flame burned continuously at her state shrine. In Rome, six virgins tended the fire at her temple, where she was worshiped as Vesta. *See also* Vestal Virgins.

Heteroptera. *See* Hemiptera.

Heterozygote, an organism possessing a different characteristic on each allele of a chromosome pair. *See also* Homozygote. △416.

Heuchera, or alum root, herbaceous perennials of the saxifrage family. Growing to 28in (71cm), they are native to cool to temperate regions of North America, mostly near the Rockies. Their flowers may be white, greenish, red, or purple.

Hevelius, Johannes (1611–87), astronomer born in Danzig, where he used his home observatory to chart the lunar surface, catalog more than 1,500 stars, and discover four comets. His lunar atlas *Selenographia* charted features of the moon, many of which today bear the names he gave them.

Hevesy, Georg von (1885–1966), Hungarian chemist, winner of the 1943 Nobel Prize for chemistry. Codiscoverer of the element hafnium (1922), Havesy was also an early researcher into the uses of radioactive isotopes, including their use as "tracers" in living tissue. He fled Germany, where he had been teaching, in the early 1940s, to live in Sweden. He also worked with Niels Bohr in Copenhagen and Ernest Rutherford in England.

HEW. *See* Health, Education, and Welfare, Department of.

Hewes, Joseph (1730–79), American patriot and one of the signers of the Declaration of Independence, b. Kingston, N.J. A prosperous businessman and shipowner, he was a member of the Continental Congress (1774–77; 1779).

Hewins, Caroline (1846–1926), US pioneer in children's library work, b. Roxbury, Mass. She was head librarian for 50 years in Hartford, Conn., where she established one of the country's first children's libraries. She was the author of *A Mid-Century Child and Her Books* (1926).

Hexachlorophene, a germicide used as a local antiseptic on the skin.

Hexagon, six-sided plane figure. Its interior angles add up to 720°. For a regular hexagon, one whose sides and interior angles are all equal, each interior angle will be 120°. △1462.

Hexameter, verse line of six metrical feet. Dactylic hexameter, the oldest form of Greek verse, characterizes the epic poetry of Homer. Examples of English-language hexameter poems are Henry Wadsworth Longfellow's *Evangeline* and Arthur Hugh Clough's *Bothie. See also* Meter.

Hexapla, Old Testament edition compiled in six columns by the Alexandrian Origen (*c.*185–*c.*254) about 231–245. Each page has six versions of text: Hebrew Greek translation of the Hebrew, and the four Greek versions—Aquila, Symmachus, Septuagint, and Theodotion. Some sections have three additional Greek versions, or a total of nine columns. Manuscript copies of several parts of this work have survived.

Hextoses. △1570.

Heydrich, Reinhard (1904–42), Nazi official, deputy chief of the Gestapo. A protégé of Heinrich Himmler he participated in the Röhm purge in 1933 and in 1935 was appointed second-in-command to Himmler. After ruthless action against resistance in Norway and the Netherlands, Heydrich was made Deputy-Protector of Bohemia and Moravia in 1941. He was assassinated by Czech patriots in Prague in 1942, in reprisal for which the village of Lidice was razed to the ground and all its inhabitants murdered or deported.

Heyerdahl, Thor (1914–), Norwegian ethnologist whose "drift voyages" in primitive craft showed how ancient peoples may have crossed the oceans. With five companions, Heyerdahl drifted on the single sailed balsa raft, *Kon Tiki*, 4,300mi (6,923km) across the Pacific from Peru to Polynesia (1947) in an attempt to prove that the Polynesians came from South America and not from SE Asia. Pursuing his theory Heyerdahl led archeological expeditions to the Galápagos Islands (1953) and to Bolivia, Peru, and Colombia (1954). In 1970, Heyerdahl sailed from Africa to America in the papyrus boat *Ra II*. He wrote numerous books about his activities.

Heyward, (Edwin) DuBose (1885–1940), US author, b. Charleston, S.C. He began writing poetry and then turned to novels. His subject was generally South Carolina blacks. His works include *Porgy* (1925), later made into an opera by George Gershwin (1935), *Angel* (1926), *Mamba's Daughters* (1929), and *Star-Spangled Virgin* (1939).

Heyward, Thomas, Jr. (1746–1809), American patriot and a signer of the Declaration of Independence, b. St. Luke's Parish, S.C. A circuit judge in South Carolina (1779–89), he was that state's delegate to the Second Continental Congress (1776–78) and later served in the Revolutionary War.

Hialeah, industrial city, SE Florida, 5mi (8km) NW of Miami, Dade co. Settled 1921 on banks of Miami Canal. Site of Hialeah Park race track. Industries: aluminum, chemicals, electronic products. Inc. 1925; pop. (1970) 102,452.

Hiawatha, The Song of (1855), long narrative poem by Henry Wadsworth Longfellow based on American Indian folklore. It recounts the often fantastic adventures of Hiawatha, an Ojibwa Indian who becomes the leader of his people. The idea of the poem is derived from the Finnish epic *Kalevala*, and the meter is the same.

Hibernation, dormant condition adopted by certain mammals to spend the winter in a confined area. The mammal's adaptive mechanisms to avoid lack of food, desiccation, and extreme temperatures, include decreased blood pressure, heartbeat, respiration rate, and endocrine gland activity. △610.

Hibiscus, or mallow, rose mallow, genus of plants, shrubs, and small trees native to tropical and temperate regions of the Eastern and Western hemispheres. Most species have large white, yellow, or red flowers with darker or variegated centers. Valued as ornamentals, the hibiscus is also used in making perfume. Some species are considered weeds. Family Malvaceae.

Hickok, James Butler ("Wild Bill") (1837–76), US law enforcement officer, b. Troy Grove, Ill. He was a teamster, stagecoach driver, and marksman. He served in the Union Army during the Civil War as a guerrilla fighter and was a scout for George Custer in his wars against the Indians. He served as US marshal in Kansas (1869–71). In 1872–73 he toured the country with Buffalo Bill as a sharpshooter and trick rider. He was shot to death in a saloon in Deadwood, S.D., while playing poker.

Hickory, deciduous tree native to E North America. They are grown for ornament, timber, and nut production. Height: 130ft (40m). Family Juglandaceae; genus *Carya. See also* Pecan.

Hickory Pine. △440.

Hicks, Elias (1748–1830), US Quaker preacher and abolitionist, b. Hempstead, N.Y. A farmer, he made preaching tours through the United States and Canada. His strong unitarian beliefs caused a schism of e Society of Friends, resulting in two divisions, the .cksite and the Orthodox friends. His antislavery ews were published in *Observations on Slavery* 811).

icks, Granville (1901–), US author and editor, b. xeter, N.H. A Communist until 1939, he was editor *The New Masses* (1934–39). His literary criticism cludes *The Great Tradition* (1933), a Marxist inter-retation of US literature since the Civil War, and *igures of Transition* (1939), a study on late 19th-entury British literature. He remained an active riter after breaking with the Communists. His *Part of he Truth: An Autobiography* appeared in 1965.

icksville, city in SE New York, on W Long Island, E of Mineola. Industries: electronic devices, photo-raphic equipment, paper products. Settled 1648. op. (1970) 48,075.

idalgo y Costilla, Miguel (1753–1811), Mexican riest and revolutionary, the leader of the indepen-ence movement in its earliest phase. The Hidalgo evolt (1810–11) mushroomed quickly; within a few nonths, he had an "army" of 80,000 Indians and nestizos. Guanajuato and Valladolid were taken, but Hidalgo did not attack Mexico City. Defeated by the oyalists at Calderón bridge, Hidalgo took flight, but oon was captured, tried, shot, and decapitated.

idatsa, a sedentary, Siouan-speaking Indian tribe ccupying the Milk, Heart, and upper Missouri River rea in Montana. In late prehistoric times, the Hidatsa eparated from the Crow tribe to form a unit of their wn. Almost entirely wiped out by a smallpox epi-emic in 1837, they moved in with the Mandan, tak-ng on many of the traits of that people. Today, ap-proximately 1,000 Hidatsa live on Fort Berthold Reservation in North Dakota.

Hideyoshi. △1048, 1210.

Hierapolis, name of two ancient cities; it means Holy City in Greek. The city in Phrygia in W Asia Minor was ocated 7mi (11.3km) N of Laodicea. It was devoted to he worship of Leto. The Romans enlarged it, building baths around the hot springs that still exist. It was an early center of Christianity. The city in Syria, originally called Mabbog, was located 50mi (80.5km) NE of Allepo. A center of worship of the nature goddess Atargatis, it was a chief stop on the road between Antioch and Seleucia-on-Tigris.

Hierarchy, in sociology, a ranked system in which the comparative position of an individual or a group is determined according to his or its social proximity to power. The terms "upper class" and "lower class" come from those groups' positions on a hierarchical scale. △882, 890.

Hieratic. △870.

Hieroglyphics, form of writing with picture charac-ters. The Egyptians used hieroglyphs as an integral part of their designs in painting, sculpture, and carv-ing. The pharaoh's name, written in symbols and sur-rounded by an oval line (called a cartouche), appeared frequently in Egyptian art. In painting, hieroglyphs were painstakingly drawn and painted with brilliant colors. Beginning with the Ptolemaic period in Egypt, knowledge of hieroglyphs became limited to mem-bers of the priesthood. Around the 4th century AD, Christianity marked the end of the use of hieroglyphs in Egypt. It was not until the discovery of the Rosetta Stone in 1799 that the Egyptian hieroglyphs could be deciphered. △870, 970.

Hierro, island, formerly known as Ferro, westernmost of Canary Islands, Santa Cruz de Tenerife prov., Spain. Volcanic soil is unfertile. Industries: wine, brandies, figs. Area: 107sq mi (277sq km). Pop. 5,503.

Higashiosaka (Fuse), city in Honshu, Japan; formed by the union of Kasaka and Kusume, 1937. Industries: engineering works, chemicals, pottery, rubber. Pop. 500,173.

Higginson, Thomas Wentworth Storrow (1823–1911), US soldier and social reformer, b. Cambridge, Mass. A minister in several Massachusetts Unitarian churches, he devoted himself to abolitionism. He en-tered the Civil War and became a colonel of the first black regiment. When wounded (1864), he retired to write and aid liberal causes, such as women's suffrage. Among his many books are *Army Life in a Black Regi-ment* (1870), *Francis Higginson* (1891), *Cheerful Yes-terdays* (1898), and *Henry Wadsworth Longfellow* (1902).

High, in meteorology, an area of high pressure, often shown on weather maps, associated in the Northern Hemisphere with clockwise, outward, anticyclonic at-mospheric circulation. *See also* Low; Weather Maps. △214, 218.

High Blood Pressure, elevation of maximal (systolic) or minimal (diastolic) arterial blood pressure above normal levels, generally considered to be 140 milli-meters of mercury (mm Hg) for systolic pressure and 90 mm Hg for diastolic pressure. Persistence of high blood pressure, called hypertension, may be of un-known cause (essential, or primary, hypertension) or may be secondary to a variety of conditions, including kidney, cardiovascular, or central nervous system dis-ease, adrenal gland tumors, and toxemia of preg-nancy. Treatment of high blood pressure is by weight reduction, salt restriction, and antihypertensive drugs. Hypertension shortens life and, if untreated, leads ultimately to damage of vital organs. △768.

Higher Education. *See* College; Extension Educa-tion; Junior College; Land-Grant College.

High-fidelity Sound, sound that has been repro-duced without distortion. In hi-fi phonographs, the pick-up and amplifier must give a combined response that falls with increasing frequency to compensate for the pre-emphasis of high frequencies introduced dur-ing recording to reduce high-frequency noise. Hi-fi systems should be capable of reproducing all audible frequencies, the ratio of the loudest to the quietest sounds being up to 55 decibels. Frequencies up to at least 12,000 hertz should be distortion-free. △1668, 1798.

Highland Park, city in NE Illinois, on Lake Michigan; summer home of Chicago Symphony Orchestra; Fort Sheridan is nearby. Inc. 1867. Pop. (1970) 32,263.

Highland Park, city in SE Michigan, entirely within city of Detroit. Henry Ford est. factory here 1909; site of junior college. Industries: tractors, auto parts, food products. Inc. 1918. Pop. (1970) 35,444.

High Point, city in N North Carolina, 14mi (23km) SW of Greensboro. In 1850 railroad survey's highest point of new N-S route intersected with E-W highway on which town was established, hence name High Point. Southern Furniture Market is held four times a year here at exhibit complex; site of High Point Col-lege (1924). Industries: furniture, hosiery. Founded 18th century by Quakers; inc. 1859. Pop. (1970) 63,-204.

High Renaissance. △1140.

High School, secondary level of education, tradition-ally grades 9 through 12. However, in some systems, senior high schools only include 10th through 12th grades, while junior high schools include 7th through 9th. High school seeks to prepare students for a field of work or for college entrance.

High-temperature Physics, production and analy-sis of the effects of temperatures above 4,000°C. At such temperatures, atoms begin to be stripped of their electrons, and a fourth state of matter, called a plasma, is achieved. Normal stars are plasmas; so is the region around an exploding hydrogen bomb. To make controlled thermonuclear fusion a reality, physi-cists must find a way to confine a plasma at tempera-tures of over a million degrees.

Highways. △1704, 1748–50.

Hill, Ambrose Powell (1825–65), US military figure, b. Culpepper, Va. He fought in the Mexican and Civil wars, serving under General Johnston at the first battle of Bull Run (1861). He engaged in the Seven Days' Battles (June 26–July 2, 1862) and was repulsed at Mechanicsville, but aided Jackson, Long-street, and Hill in breaking the Union forces at the battle of Gaine's Mill. He also fought at Fredericks-burg and Gettysburg and was killed at Petersburg.

Hill, (Norman) Graham (1929–75), British automo-bile racer. He twice won the World Grand Prix For-mula 1 Championship (1962, 1968). He died in a plane crash in England.

Hill, James Jerome (1838–1916), US railroad mag-nate and financier, b. Canada. Starting out in the steamboat business on the Mississippi River, he saw the importance of transportation to the West. Hill put together the Great Northern Railroad Co. and gained control of the Northern Pacific. Hill was president of the Northern Securities Co., which in 1904 was de-clared to be in conflict with the Sherman Antitrust Act.

Hillary, (Sir) Edmund Percival (1919–), New Zea-land explorer and mountain climber who was first to

Heinrich Hertz

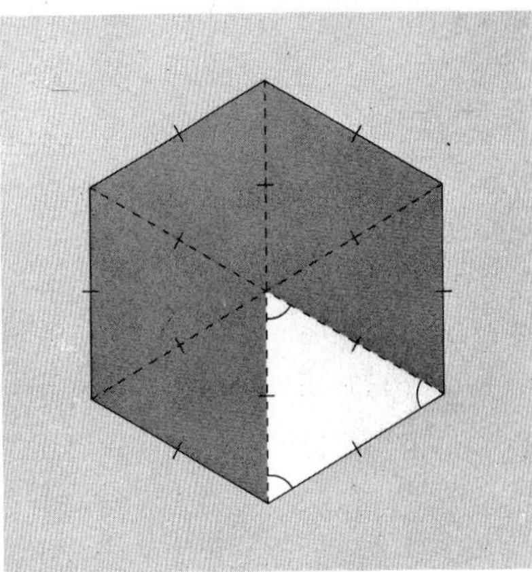

Hexagon

Hibiscus

Wild Bill Hickok

climb Mt Everest. He participated in the New Zealand and British expeditions to the Himalayas (1951 and 1952). In 1953, he and his Sherpa guide, Tenzing Norkay, reached the summit of Mt Everest, the world's highest mountain. In 1955, he led the New Zealand section of the Commonwealth Transantarctic expedition.

Hill-Burton Act (1946), legislation designed to assure better national health care. With federal funding and regulation the law resulted from concern over health in rural areas, and provided for the construction of small community health facilities to meet postwar needs. The US Public Health Service, under the Department of Health, Education, and Welfare, administers the funding, which has been greatly expanded since 1946.

Hilliard, Nicholas. △1144, 1192.

Hillman, Sidney (1887–1946), US labor leader, b. Lithuania. After leading a successful strike against Hart, Schaffner & Marx, a clothing firm in Chicago (1910), he rose in union ranks to become first president of the Amalgamated Clothing Workers (1915). He quit the American Federation of Labor to help found the Congress of Industrial Organizations (1935), headed the CIO's Political Action Committee (1943–46), and rallied labor support for President Roosevelt's New Deal. He established the American Labor party and helped form the World Federation of Trade Unions (1945).

Hilo, city on E coast of Hawaii on Hilo Bay; seat of Hawaii co; 2nd-largest city of Hawaii; tourist center; port of entry; site of Hilo College, Lyman House Museum, Hawaii Volcanoes National Park; severely damaged by tidal waves 1949 and 1960. Industries: sugar, rice, coffee, papaya, orchids. Settled 1820 by New England missionaries. Inc. 1911. Pop. (1970) 26,353.

Himalayan Cat, longhaired domestic cat breed developed recently from Persian and Siamese breeds. It has a Persianlike body, round head, small ears, short tail, and long thick coat. The eyes are Siamese blue and coat color is cream or white with seal, lilac, blue, or chocolate points.

Himalayas, great system of mountains in S Asia, extending N-S approx. 1,500mi (2,415km) in a long arc between Tibet and India-Pakistan and between the Indus River (E) and the Brahmaputra River (W); divided into 3 ranges: the Greater Himalayas (N), which include Mt Everest; the Lesser Himilayas, running parallel to the Greater; and the Outer Himalayas (S). The range marks the beginning of the high Tibetan plateau; its geological formation took place during the Tertiary Period. △198.

Himmler, Heinrich (1900–45), German Nazi leader. He took part in the abortive Munich putsch (1923) and in 1929 became head of the SS. After the Nazis came to power (1933), he assumed control of the entire German police system. A fanatic racist, he controlled the Jewish extermination program. He became minister of interior (1943) and head of the army's home organization (1944). In April 1945 he tried secretly to negotiate peace with the Allies and was expelled from the party. Captured by the British, he killed himself.

Hims. *See* Homs.

Hinayana Buddhism, "Small Vehicle," pejorative name for the older, more conservative schools of Buddhism; Hinayana claims to stand in direct succession from Buddha; its center is the brotherhood of Buddhist monks. Homage is paid to Buddha, but he is not worshiped. Each person must seek his own salvation, unaided by the meritorious Bodhistas. The goal of Hinayana is that of all Buddhism—the attainment of Nirvana. Also known as Theravada, "Way of the Elders," this is the Buddhism of Ceylon and SE Asia. *See also* Nirvana. △988.

Hincks, (Sir) Francis (1807–85), joint premier of Canada with Augustin Morin (1851–54), b. Ireland. Hincks established the Bank of the People (1835) and edited the *Examiner* (1839–55). He was a moving force in political reform, helped build Canadian railways, and agitated for free trade with the United States.

Hindemith, Paul (1895–1963), German composer who emigrated to the United States in 1933, then returned to his native Germany late in his life. A major 20th-century composer, Hindemith experimented with dissonance and atonality early in his career, but eventually his works became more melodic and tonal in character. He was a master of counterpoint in music, and many of his compositions are Neoclassic and contrapuntal in style. He composed prolifically in all forms. Among his works are the song cycle *Das Marienleben* (1924); symphonies; concertos, such as the viola concerto *Der Schwanendreher* (1935); ballets; chamber music; operas; and sonatas for every instrument. His best-known work is the symphony he derived from his opera *Mathis der Maler* (1934). *See also* Neoclassic Music. △1364.

Hindenburg, Paul von (1847–1934), German general and president (1925–32). Commanding the army on the eastern front in World War I, he defeated the Russians in the Battle of Tannenberg (August 1914). In 1916 he became supreme commander and, with his chief of staff, Erich Ludendorff, directed the entire war effort, civilians as well as military, until the end of the war. Elected president in 1925, he presided over the collapse of the Weimar Republic. △1334.

Hindi, the most widespread language in India, spoken principally in the north-central part of the country by about 180,000,000 people. It shares with English the title of official language. Like the other languages of northern India, Hindi is descended from Sanskrit and thus belongs to the Indo-European family. △866.

Hinduism, religion recognizing the *Veda* as authoritative. From 500 BC to AD 500 many conditions shaped the emerging faith; the result is a complex mixture of beliefs within a common social structure. Preeminent among the many popular Hindu gods is the Trimurti, or Trinity, consisting of Brahma, the Creator; Shiva, the Destroyer; and Vishnu, the Preserver. These gods compose the threefold manifestation of "Absolute Reality," or Brahman. The chief end of life in Hinduism is Moksa, liberation from suffering and rebirth. Three other goals: duty (dharma), material success (artha), and love (karma) were also formulated as part of the Hindu teaching. The four goals may be sought by following one or more of the three ways, or "yogas." These ways are the paths of personal devotion, works, and knowledge. Having about 470,000,000 followers worldwide, more than 85% of India's population is Hindu. △846, 1034–36.

Hindu Kush, principal Asian mountain range; extends WSW 500–600mi (805–966km) from NE Afghanistan; site of Baroghil Pass; sparsely populated. Highest peak is Tirich Mir in N Pakistan, approx. 25,260ft (7,704m).

Hindu Sacred Literature. The sacred oral traditions and written texts of Hinduism are the basis of Indian society. They are divided into *Sruti,* the primary revelation, and *Smrti,* which is everything else. The Vedas, hymns extolling the gods and containing the liturgy for ritual sacrifices, are the most sacred texts. The great epic poems contain important sacred material. The *Bhagavadgita,* part of the epic *Mahābhārata,* is the most influential Hindu text. It emphasizes devotion. The spells and rituals of the *Tantras* typify Hinduism on a popular level. *See also* Brahmanas; Mahābhārata; Ramayana; Sanskrit Literature.

Hipparchus (*fl.*150 BC), Greek astronomer who worked on the island of Rhodes. He estimated the distance of the moon from the earth, drew the first accurate star map with more than 1,000 stars, divided stars into orders of magnitude based on their brightness (a system fundamentally in use today), and developed an organization of the universe which, while it still had the earth at the center, provided for accurate prediction of the positions of the planets.

Hippias (5th century BC), Greek Sophist. Since none of his own writings survive, we know him only through the writings of Plato. Because of Hippias' claim to have mastered all the fields of learning of his time, Plato regarded him, and all Sophists, as superficial. *See also* Sophists.

Hippocampus. △666.

Hippocrates (*c.*460–377 BC), Greek physician often called "the father of medicine." Little is known about Hippocrates, and the writings known as the Hippocratic Collection probably represent the works of several people. Nonetheless, Hippocrates exerted a tremendous influence on medicine, freeing it from superstition, emphasizing bedside or clinical observation, and providing guidelines for surgery and for the treatment of fevers. Most importantly he is credited with providing an ideal of ethics and professional conduct for physicians through the Hippocratic Oath, the most famous Hippocratic document. △708.

Hippocratic Oath, an oath taken by physicians. It is based on the ideals and principles of the ancient Greek physician Hippocrates. Various abridged versions of the original oath are administered today.

Hipponax (6th century BC), Greek lyric poet. He i vented the scazon, or halting iambic form, but or fragments of his work remain. His poems were coar and satirical, concerned with love and quarrels b tween his friends. His bitter verses are said to ha driven two sculptors to suicide.

Hippopotamus, large, water-loving, plant-eati mammal related to the pig, native to Africa. *Hippopo amus amphibius* has a massive gray or brown bo with a big head, short legs, and short tail. Males weig up to 5tons; females are slightly smaller than male These hippos usually live in groups, spending mu time in water. They can close their nostrils underwat but usually rise to breathe at frequent intervals. Pigm hippopotamuses, *Choeropsis liberiensis,* are mu smaller, solitary, and spend more time on land. Th weigh about 400lb (180kg). Both are hunted as foo and for their hides and teeth. Family Hippopotamida △548.

Hirabayashi v. United States (1943), US Suprem Court decision unanimously upholding curfew an registration requirements placed on all persons Japanese ancestry early in World War II. The cou called it a justified temporary emergency war mea ure.

Hirohito (1901–), emperor of Japan (1926–). H visit to Europe in 1921 made him the first crow prince to travel abroad. Although he has general exercised little political power during his reign, he d persuade the Japanese government to surrender t the Allies in 1945, announcing that surrender himse on the radio on August 15. Under the constitutio drawn up by the occupation forces he lost much of h power, becoming mostly an imperial figurehead. He a recognized authority on marine biology. △1326.

Hirosaki, city in N Honshu, Japan, 21mi (34km) SW of Aomori; site of 17th-century Buddhist temple, ruir of feudal castle, university (1949); center for silk cu ture and fruit growing. Industries: textiles, soybean brewing, sake. Pop. 157,603.

Hiroshige, Ando (1797–1858), Japanese ukiyo- (color) printmaker. He first did portraits of women an actors and then turned to poetic landscapes. Th most famous are 53 wood-block prints depicting h trip from Edo to Kyoto by the Tokaido Highway.

Hiroshima, city in SW Honshu, Japan, at W end c Inland Sea; capital of Hiroshima prefecture; consist of 6 islands connected by 81 bridges; site of militar headquarters for Sino-Japanese war 1894–95, Russo Japanese war 1904–05, and regional headquarters i WWII. First atomic bomb was dropped here Aug. 6 1945, killing approx. 130,000 people, and destroy ing 90% of the city. Designated as "Peace City" b the Japanese government, memorials include Peac Park, Peace Tower, and a hospital specializing i treating survivors suffering from the effects of radia tion exposure; site of annual conference on atomi bombs, Hiroshima University (1949). Industries: sake canneries, paper, machinery, automobiles. Founde 1594. Pop. 541,998. △1338.

Hirsch, Samuel (1815–89), a rabbi and philosophe of Judaism, born in Prussia, best known for his wor for the Reform movement in Judaism in both Ger many and the United States. He served in Philadel phia as rabbi of a reform congregation. In 1869 h was appointed president of the first Conference o American Reform Rabbis. His philosophical system was based on the understanding of religion as dy namic rather than static.

Hispaniola, second-largest island in West Indies, be tween Cuba (E) and Puerto Rico (W), in N centra Caribbean Sea. Haiti occupies W third of island an Dominican Republic remaining (E) portion; mountain ous, agricultural region with subtropical climate. Dis covered 1492 by Christopher Columbus who est. Es pañola, first Spanish colony in New World; par became French colony of Santo Domingo; island de clared independent Republic of Haiti 1804, late formed Dominican Republic (1844). Industries: baux ite mining, coffee, cocoa, sugar cane. Area: 29,530sc mi (76,483sq km). Pop. (combined) 8,600,000. *See also* Dominican Republic; Greater Antilles; Haiti.

Hispano Suiza. △1694.

Hiss-Chambers Case (1949–50), legal case involv ing Alger Hiss, a former State Department employee who was accused of passing secret documents to Whittaker Chambers, a Communist agent. Hiss was convicted of perjury (1950) for denying that he passed the documents to Chambers, who testified against him. Hiss served a prison sentence.

Histamine, a substance derived from the amino acid histidine, occurring naturally in many plants and in animal tissues. Its several functions in the body include dilation of the capillaries. It is implicated in allergic reactions.

Histidine, colorless soluble crystalline amino acid, which is the precursor of histamine. *See also* Amino Acid.

Histoplasmosis, infection of the lymph nodes or reticuloendothelial system by the fungus *Histoplasma capsulatum*, usually by inhalation. Especially common in the US midwest, the infection itself is generally asymptomatic but causes severe symptoms such as pneumonia, anemia, and liver and spleen enlargement in a few cases.

Historia Augusta or **Augustan History,** important collection of biographies of the Roman emperors from Hadrian to Numerian, of unknown author and date. The original title of the manuscript is uncertain and the work itself has become garbled, with its original ordering uncertain. Nevertheless, it is an important document on Roman history.

Historia Naturalis. △1780.

Historical Geology, study of sedimentary rocks, which record in stone series of events in the history of the earth. The different layers contain plant and animal remains that give clues to the living systems and to water and temperature conditions that prevailed when a particular stratum was deposited. The injection of igneous material into a sedimentary layer is a record of the volcanic activity of a particular time and region. The composition of the rocks and the fossils in them give a record of the time and evolution of plants and animals. △274–76.

Historical Materialism. △902.

Historical Novel, type of novel in which the main characters, plot, setting are based on historical persons, events, places. Walter Scott's *Ivanhoe* (1820) and Charles Dickens' *A Tale of Two Cities* (1859) are major examples. James Fenimore Cooper, Alexander Dumas, Victor Hugo, William Makepeace Thackeray, and Leo Tolstoy all wrote historical novels.

Historicism, the view that an adequate account of any subject capable of description in time must be historical. All things must be explained in terms of their origins and comprehended in their development from inception to maturity, for example, the chicken from the egg. The term has been associated with the philosophy of F. Hegel and Karl Marx. Historicism often connotes deterministic expectation. *See also* Determinism.

Hitachi, port city on Pacific coast of Honshu, Japan, 83mi (133km) NE of Tokyo; most important mining and manufacturing center of Joban-Hitachi industrial district. Pop. 193,210.

Hitchcock, Alfred (1899–), English film director, in Hollywood since 1940. He created droll, sophisticated, and suspenseful thrillers, including *The Thirty-nine Steps* (1935), *Suspicion* (1941), *Notorious* (1946), *Dial M for Murder* (1954), *Rear Window* (1954), *Vertigo* (1958), *Psycho* (1960), and *Frenzy* (1972).

Hitler, Adolf (1889–1945), Nazi dictator of Germany, b. Austria. Brought up in Austria, he did not graduate from high school and for a time made his living painting postcards in Vienna. Moving to Munich in 1913, he served in the German army in World War I, became a corporal, and was decorated for bravery. After the war he returned to Munich and soon became leader (1921) of the small National Socialist German Workers' or Nazi party. Already an impressive demagogue, in November 1923 he attempted to seize the Bavarian government, but his Beer Hall Putsch was a fiasco. Imprisoned for nine months, he set out his extreme racist and nationalist views in *Mein Kampf*. After his release, Hitler worked to revive the Nazi party, which gathered strength dramatically with economic depression in 1929. As parliamentary government floundered and street violence (largely fomented by the Nazis) grew, President Hindenburg appointed Hitler chancellor in a coalition on Jan. 30, 1933. Within a month the Reichstag Fire gave him the excuse for establishing a one-party régime; and the process was completed by a purge (June 30, 1934) in which he liquidated possible rivals in both the party and the state. On Hindenburg's death (Aug. 2, 1934), Hitler proclaimed himself head of state. In the following years he consolidated his dictatorship and rearmed Germany for expansion. The remilitarization of the Rhineland (1936) was followed by the occupation of Austria (March 1938) and Czechoslovakia (October 1938 and March 1939) and the attack on Poland (September 1939). The last precipitated World War II. Initially successful in the west, the German armies began to meet setbacks after the invasion of Russia in 1941 and the entry of the United States into the war. An assassination attempt against Hitler (July 1944) led to further tightening of the brutal dictatorship at home; systematic extermination of the Jews was carried out throughout the war. As the war ended, Hitler married his mistress Eva Braun and committed suicide in Berlin (April 30, 1945). △1308, 1334–36.

Hittite Art. △976.

Hittites, ancient people who built a powerful empire in Asia Minor and N Syria (*c.* 2000–1200 BC). Primarily of Indo-European stock, they invaded Babylonia (*c.* 2000 BC), seized Cappadocia, and conquered Syria and Palestine. Ramses II of Egypt checked them near Kanesh on the Orontes River (*c.* 1290) and made a treaty. Boghazkeui and Carchemish were their great cities. After 1200 BC the Thracians, Phrygians, and Assyrians invaded the Hittite lands, and their loose empire broke up. △976.

Hives, popular term for the transient, itchy, reddish or pale raised skin patches of urticaria. Hives may be caused by allergy to certain foods or drugs, by irritants such as sunlight or animal danders, or by emotional stress. △724.

Hoarhound. *See* Horehound.

Hoatzin, shaggy crested, awkward-flying bird of N South American river valleys. It has a large crop for storing vegetable matter. The hatchlings have claws on their wings and are able to climb trees. Resembling a long slender crow, the brownish adult has rounded wings and a long tail. The female lays 2 to 5 oval spotted white eggs in a tree nest near a river. Species *Opisthocomus hoazin*.

Hoban, James (*c.* 1762–1831), US architect, b. Ireland. He designed the State Capitol in Columbia, S.C., in 1791 and the White House in Washington, D.C., in 1792.

Hobart, city in Tasmania, SE Australia, on the Derwent River; site of the University of Tasmania (1890); excellent deepwater port. Exports: wool, newsprint, food products, meat. Industries: cement, leather, metal ore, tourism. Founded 1804; inc. 1842. Pop. 52,900.

Hoba West Meteorite. △92.

Hobbes, Thomas (1588–1679), English philosopher. After serving as a tutor, Hobbes traveled extensively in Europe. Fleeing England (1642), he remained a royalist in exile until the restoration of Charles II (1660). In *De Corpore* (On Bodies), *De Homine* (On Man), and *De Cive* (On the State), he presented his view that matter and its motion comprise the valid subject matter of philosophy. Organic and inorganic matter obey similar laws of self-assertion and collision respectively. Nature, including the human, is a theater of necessary causes and determined effects. Hobbes' materialism is projected on the political plane in *Leviathan* (1651). *See also* Leviathan; Materialism. △874.

Hobbit, The (1937), introductory book of J.R.R. Tolkien's epic trilogy *The Lord of the Rings*. Bilbo Baggins, the comfort-loving hobbit of Shire, leaves home in the company of Gandalf the wizard and 13 elves on a quest for treasure-hoard. They bring back the One Ring of Power.

Hobbs, city in SE New Mexico, 18mi (29km) N of Eunice; site of New Mexico Junior College (1965); prospered after discovery of oil (1927). Industries: oil well supplies, thoroughbred horses, cotton, livestock, vegetables, dairying. Founded 1907; inc. 1929. Pop. (1970) 26,025.

Hobby, Oveta Culp (1905–), US newspaper publisher and first US secretary of health, education, and welfare (1953–55), b. Killeen, Tex. She rose from editorial positions to president and publisher of the *Houston Post* (1931–56). She was appointed director of the Woman's Army Corps (1942–45) and Federal Security Administrator (1953). After Congress created HEW, President Eisenhower appointed her secretary.

Hoboken, city in NE New Jersey, on Hudson River opposite Manhattan. John Stevens, builder of first steamboat and steam locomotive in United States, bought land for $90,000 from Dutch settlers in 1784

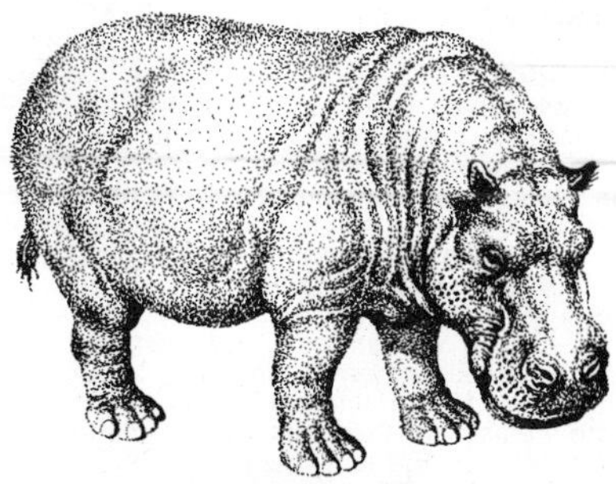

Hippopotamus

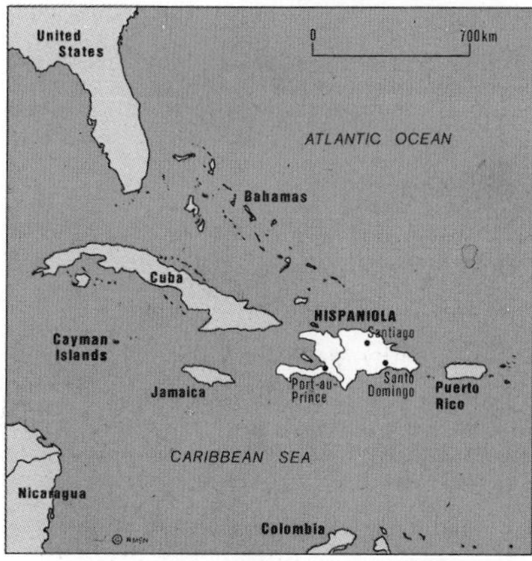
United States
0
700km
ATLANTIC OCEAN
Bahamas
Cuba
HISPANIOLA
Santiago
Cayman Islands
Jamaica
Port-au-Prince
Santo Domingo
Puerto Rico
CARIBBEAN SEA
Nicaragua
Colombia

Hispaniola

Alfred Hitchcock

Adolf Hitler

and laid township out 1804; he established his home on Castle Point; it is now site of Stevens Institute of Technology (1870). Industries: paper products, precision instruments, chemicals. Settled 1640 by Dutch; inc. as town 1849, as city 1855. Pop. (1970) 45,380.

Ho Chi Minh (1890–1969), Vietnamese political figure, b. as Nguyen That Thanh. In 1911 he left Vietnam as a seaman on a freighter. For part of World War I he lived in the United States. Between 1917–23 he lived in France. In 1919 he unsuccessfully petitioned the Versailles Peace Conference to recognize the right of self-determination of the Vietnamese people. In 1920 he joined the French Communist party. Returning to Vietnam after 1927, he presided over the founding of the Vietnamese Communist party in 1930. Threatened with arrest, he fled to Moscow in 1932, then moved to China in 1938. In 1941 he returned to Vietnam and founded the Viet Minh to fight the Japanese. With the Japanese driven out, in 1945 he declared Vietnam an independent nation and was himself appointed president. The French returned and contested Ho's authority until their defeat in 1954. The 1954 Geneva Conference recognized Ho as president of the Democratic Republic of Vietnam (North Vietnam). When the government of the South backed by the United States refused to hold elections in 1956 as had been agreed upon, Ho organized the National Liberation Front (Viet Cong) to attempt to gain control of the South. Vietnam was still divided at his death. △1378.

Ho Chi Minh City. *See* Saigon.

Hodeida (Al-Hudaydah), major seaport city in W Yemen Arab Republic, on the Red Sea; developed mid-19th century by Turks; main port of entry for Yemen. Exports: coffee, hides, dates. Pop. 40,000.

Hodgkin, Dorothy Mary Crowfoot (1910–), English chemist. After teaching at both Oxford and Cambridge she spent some time at the University of Ghana before becoming professor at Oxford. In 1964 she was awarded the Nobel Prize for her determination of the structure of vitamin B_{12} by X-ray crystallography. She also determined the structure of penicillin and several other macromolecules by the same process.

Hodgkin's Disease, condition characterized by painless enlargement of the lymph glands, lymphatic tissue, and spleen, with spread to other areas. Fever is a common symptom, and weight loss, anemia, loss of appetite, and night sweats may occur. The condition is twice as common in males as in females. Treatment varies with the stage of the disease but in general consists of radiotherapy, combinations of drugs, or both. Cure or long-term survival is achieved in most cases but depends on the extent of involvement at diagnosis.

Hoe, Richard March (1812–86), US inventor of the rotary printing press (1846), b. New York City. His press printed at far higher speeds than the traditional "flat-bed" press. Later developments by William Bullock and Hoe further increased the pace by printing on a roll or "web" of paper, rather than on single sheets. The rotary press and the web feed are the foundations of the newspaper industry.

Hofei (Hefei or Ho-fei), formerly Luchow; city in E China; capital of Anhwei prov. Industries: textiles, chemicals, food processing. Founded during Han dynasty (202 BC–AD 220). Pop. 400,000.

Hoff, Jacobus Hendricus van't (1852–1911), Dutch physical chemist, professor at Amsterdam, Leipzig, and Berlin. His research involved advanced investigations of the carbon atom; the theory that gas laws are also applicable to dissolved substances; and the chemical application of thermodynamics. He was awarded the first chemistry Nobel Prize in 1901 for his studies on chemical equilibrium, reaction rates, and osmotic pressure.

Hoffa, James Riddle (1913–75?), US labor leader, b. Brazil, Ind. Hoffa worked his way up in the International Brotherhood of Teamsters beginning in 1932. He served as Teamsters' vice president (1952–57) under Dave Beck, succeeding Beck as president (1957–71). Hoffa organized the Teamsters into a powerful union with a membership of 1,600,000 in 1967, when he began an 8-yr. jail term for jury tampering, with 5 yrs. added for mail fraud and mishandling of union funds. His sentence was commuted in 1971 by Pres. Richard Nixon. Hoffa was reported missing, apparently abducted, in 1975 and is presumed dead.

Hoffmann, E(rnst) T(heodor) A(madeus) (1776–1822), German novelist and composer. His works include an unfinished novel, studies of Beethoven and Mozart, and an opera, but he is famous for his Romantic tales, *The Golden Pot* (1813), *The Legacy* (1817), and *Mlle de Scudéry* (1818).

Hofmann, Melchior (1495–1543), German Anabaptist leader. He was a mystic, believed that Christ would soon return to earth for the judgment day, and urged his followers to be saintly. He spread Anabaptist beliefs in Holland, where his followers were called Melchiorites. Later he was imprisoned in Strasbourg and died after 10 years in prison.

Hofmannsthal, Hugo von (1874–1929), Austrian dramatist, poet, and essayist. He wrote *The Play of Everyman* (1911), a verse drama regularly staged at the Salzburg Festival, of which Hofmannsthal was a founder. He was one of Richard Strauss's librettists and collaborated with him on *Der Rosenkavalier* (1911) and other operas. The importance of language to Hofmannsthal is clearly expressed in the *Chandos Letters* (1902).

Hofuf (Al-Hufuf), city in E Saudi Arabia, in the Hasa oasis, on caravan route from Riyadh to United Arab Emirate; important market center for dates, fruit, and wheat. Industries: brass and copper wires, textiles. Pop. 100,000.

Hog, medium-sized mammal native to the Old World, including various domesticated pigs, wild boars, and wart hogs. They have long pointed heads, stocky bodies, short legs with cloven hoofs, and small tails. Usually they have short bristly hair. In the wild, groups live in wooded areas, digging with their snouts for plant or animal food. Rapid runners and good swimmers, they wallow in mud to protect their light skin from sunburn. They are clean, intelligent animals that do not overeat. Wild hogs are hunted for sport or food. Most domestic pigs are derived from the wild hog, *Sus scrofa*. Length: 2–6ft (61–183cm); weight: to 600lb (270kg). Family Suidae. △376–80.

Hogan, William Benjamin (Ben) (1912–) US golfer, b. Dublin, Tex. He won four US Opens (1948; 1950–51; 1953), two Professional Golfers' Association (PGA) titles (1946, 1948), two Masters Tournaments (1951, 1953), and the British Open (1953). In 1949, he was involved in an automobile accident that almost took his life, but he recovered to make a comeback.

Hogan, traditional Navaho dwelling. The hogan is a conical, hexagonal, or octagonal building with a domed roof. Traditionally built of logs and sticks covered with mud, sod, or adobe, it presented a very earthlike appearance. More modern hogans are of stone construction.

Hogarth, David George (1862–1927), English archeologist, writer, and diplomat. Between 1887–1907 he participated in several important excavations including those at Knossos, Crete, and Carchemish, Syria. From 1909 until his death he was director of the Ashmolean Museum at Oxford. In 1915 he was sent by the British government to Egypt to organize an Arab revolt against Turkey. In this endeavor he worked with Lawrence of Arabia. He was British commissioner on the Middle East Commission of the Paris Peace Conference (1919). His *A Wandering Scholar in the Levant* (1896) is a fascinating travel book. Important scholarly works include *The Ancient East* (1914), *The Archaic Artemis of Ephesus* (1909), and *Kings of the Hittites* (1926).

Hogarth, William (1697–1764), English painter, engraver, and printmaker. His early works were portraits. He did some historical painting but is most famous for his narrative prints, executed in a decorative Rococo style. In a series of engravings including "A Harlot's Progress," "The Rake's Progress," and "Marriage à la Mode," he satirized British social institutions. △1192.

Hog Cholera, or hog plague, a virus-caused communicable disease of swine. Symptoms include fever, loss of weight, diarrhea, sores on the under portion of the body.

Hogg, James (1770–1835), Scottish poet known as "The Ettrick Shepherd." He combined farming and literary work after publishing *The Mountain Bard* in 1807 on Walter Scott's recommendation, but made his reputation by *The Queen's Wake* (1813).

Hognose Snake, harmless North American snake ranging throughout the United States. It is stocky with an upturned snout. Variable in color, it is mostly spotted brown, gray, yellow, or orange. When alarmed it will hiss, spread its neck, then play dead. Length: to 33in (84cm). Family Colubridae; genus *Heterodon*. *See also* Puff Adder; Snake.

Hohenstaufen Dynasty, German princely family, several of whose members were Holy Roman emperors and German kings. Frederick married (1079) the daughter of Emperor Henry IV and was created duke of Swabia. His son was elected German king as Conrad III in 1138. Conrad was followed by Frederick I, Henry VI, Philip of Swabia, Frederick II, and Conrad IV. The family's power in Germany was challenged by the Guelphs, and in Italy they were in constant conflict with the Lombard cities and the papacy. Frederick II shifted the family's main interests to Italy, and the rapid decline of the family began with his death (1250). △1072.

Hohenzollern Dynasty, German princely family that ruled Brandenburg, Prussia, and Germany. Burgraves of Nuremberg from 1191, the Franconian line of the family received Brandenburg in 1415 (*see* Frederick I, elector of Brandenburg). Prussia, acquired by a junior branch of the family, was added to Brandenburg in 1618. Frederick William the Great Elector further expanded and consolidated their territories, and his son Frederick I adopted the title "king in Prussia." Frederick William I built up the famous Prussian army, and Frederick II used it to great effect against the Hapsburgs. Finally Germany was united in 1871 under the Hohenzollern emperor, William I. His grandson William II abdicated at the end of World War I (1918). △1250, 1300.

Hohokam Culture, farming culture of the southern Arizona desert, arising in the last centuries BC and surviving until about AD 1400. Sophisticated irrigation systems were the basis of Hohokam prosperity, and sizable settlements were founded; other remains include engraved and sculptured shells, pottery, and temple mounds, all showing Mexican influence.

Hōjō, Japanese family. Installing themselves as advisors to the young Kamakura Shoguns (military leaders), the Hōjō family effectively controlled the government of Japan 1200–1333. △1210.

Hokkaido, formerly Yezo; second-largest of the four main islands of Japan, and largest prefecture in Japan; capital is Sapporo; site of several national parks, major winter resort area, 1972 Winter Olympics. Crops: rice, corn, potatoes, barley, wheat. Industries: dairying, fishing, lumber, coal, paper, brewing, tourism. Became part of Japan 1604. Area: 30,313sq mi (78,511sq km). Pop. 5,184,287.

Hokusai, Katsushika (1760–1849), Japanese ukiyo-e (color) printmaker. His early work included portraits of women and actors. He also did illustrations of flowers, birds, and city scenes, but his landscape art was his greatest work. Known for his use of design and color, he showed man's relationship to nature, often portraying nature as the dominant force. △1048.

Holbein, Hans, the Younger (1497–1543), German painter, decorative artist, and woodcutter. In the field of decorative arts, he designed bookbindings, armor, silverware, and the like. His best-known woodcuts were his 51 prints of the "Dance of Death." The Italian influence is evident in his use of ornament and rich color in his portraits. In Basel, he painted portraits of the wealthy and became a close friend of Erasmus. Eventually he settled in London, where he did his greatest portraits of German merchants residing there and of the royal British court of Henry VIII. His carefully drawn portraits of Henry and his third wife Jane Seymour are famous examples of his realistic and decorative style. He died in London of the plague. △1144.

Holder, Geoffrey (1930–), US modern dancer, choreographer, director, and actor, b. Port-of-Spain, Trinidad. He has taught at the Katherine Dunham School, appeared on Broadway, and has his own dance company. His choreography is often based on the native dances of the West Indies. *The Prodigal Prince* (1968) is exemplary. In 1975 he directed the all-black Broadway musical *The Wiz*.

Holding Company, form of business organization. A corporation that owns sufficient stock in another corporation to exert control over it is called a holding company. This form of consolidation became legal first in New Jersey (1889). A prime example was the US Steel Corporation (1901) established by Elbert H. Gary and J. P. Morgan. Attempts to curb such combination led to the dissolution of several of the larger holding companies. New Deal legislation (1935) restricted them further.

Holes, Electron. △1546.

Holguín, city in SE Cuba, 19mi (31km) SW of Gibara, its port on the Atlantic Ocean. Located in fertile plateau area, known as "Cuba's granary," it is site of nationalist insurgency during Ten Years' War (1868–78), and Spanish Revolution (1895–98). Exports: tobacco, cattle products. Industries: tobacco, sugar cane, livestock, coffee, lumber, food processing, furniture. Founded *c.* 1720, and named for Garcia Holguín, Mexican conquistador of 16th century. Pop. 131,508.

Holiday, Billie (1915–59), US blues and popular singer, b. Eleanora Fagan in Baltimore. She sang in nightclubs in the 1930s and after that with the bands of Count Basie, Artie Shaw, Benny Carter, and Paul Whiteman. Her renditions of torch songs such as "My Man" and "Mean to Me" influenced other singers and have acquired a legendary status in the history of US popular and jazz music. △1366.

Holland, name popularly given to the entire Netherlands, properly refers only to one of the country's provinces. A medieval county in the Holy Roman empire in the 10th century after it gained independence from Lorraine, it was seized by the county of Hainaut in 1299 and passed to Burgundy (1433) and Austria (1482). In 1490 Maximilian of Austria put down a Dutch rebellion. In the next 200 years Holland became a sea power and led the United Netherlands in its long battle for independence from Spain.

Holland, city in W Michigan, on Lake Macatawa; site of Hope College (1851), annual tulip festival. Industries: furnaces, chemicals, glass. Founded 1847 by Dutch settlers; inc. 1867. Pop. (1970) 26,337.

Hollerith Code, a computer code consisting of 12 levels, or bits per character, which defines the relation between an alpha-numeric character and the punched holes in an 80-column computer data card.

Holley, Robert W(illiam) (1922–), US biochemist, b. Urbana, Ill. He shared the 1968 Nobel Prize in physiology or medicine for his part in discoveries of how genes determine the function of cells. Holley described the first full sequence of subunits in nucleic acid, the genetic material of a cell. This was an important step to understanding gene action.

Holly, any of 300 species of shrubs and trees found worldwide. They have alternate, simple leaves and small flowers. Male and female flowers are usually on separate plants. There is no nectar-secreting disk in the flowers. The one-seeded fruit is usually red. The English holly tree *(Ilex aquifolium)* has spiny evergreen leaves. Height: to 50ft (15m). American holly *(I. opaca)* has duller, smoother leaves and is taller. Both are widely cultivated as ornamentals. Family Aquifoliaceae. △450.

Hollyhock, biennial plant native to temperate Europe and China and now naturalized in the United States. They have leafy stems and showy flowers of red, white, rose, yellow, or orange. Height: 3–9ft (0.9–2.7m). Family Malvaceae; species *Althea rosea.*

Hollywood, city in SE Florida, 18mi (29km) N of Miami. Originally Hollywood-by-the-Sea; settled as port and resort. Industries: electronic equipment, building products, cement. Inc. 1925: Pop. (1970) 106,873. △1362.

Holm, Hanya (1898–), US modern dancer and choreographer, b. Johanna Eckert in Germany. She taught at the Mary Wigman school in Dresden, Germany, before opening a US branch in New York City in 1931. In 1936 her dance school became the Hanya Holm Studio. Her first major US creation was *Trend* (1937). *Metropolitan Daily* (1938) was the first televised modern dance. She choreographed many Broadway musicals, including *Kiss Me, Kate* (1948), *My Fair Lady* (1956), and *Camelot* (1960).

Holmes, Oliver Wendell (1809–94), US author and physician, b. Cambridge, Mass. A graduate of Harvard University, he studied medicine in Boston and Paris, receiving his medical degree in 1836. Meanwhile, he began to write poetry, gaining fame with "Old Ironsides" (1830). After practicing medicine for several years, he became professor of anatomy and physiology at Dartmouth College (1838–40) and later at Harvard (1847–82). He wrote a controversial study of childbed fever that emphasized its transmission through lack of personal hygiene by doctors. Combining literature with medicine, he wrote three novels dealing with abnormal psychology—*Elsie Venner* (1861), *The Guardian Angel* (1867), and *A Mortal Antipathy* (1885).

A noted wit, he began writing the "breakfast-table" series in 1857. In these conversations around a breakfast table, Holmes discusses a variety of topics. The series includes *The Autocrat of the Breakfast Table* (1858), *The Professor at the Breakfast Table* (1860), *The Poet at the Breakfast Table* (1872), and *Over the Teacups* (1891). His son, Oliver Wendell Holmes, Jr., was a Supreme Court justice.

Holmes, Oliver Wendell, Jr. (1841–1935), US jurist and legal scholar, b. Boston. He was the son of the physician and author, Oliver Wendell Holmes (1809–94). After serving in the Civil War, he then practiced law (1867–82). He co-edited the *American Law Review* (1870–73), *Kent's Commentaries* (1873), and wrote *The Common Law* (1881). He was a justice of the Massachusetts Supreme Court (1882–99), and served as its chief justice (1899–1902). He then became (1902) an associate justice of the US Supreme Court, serving until 1932. Known as "The Great Dissenter," he wrote eloquent dissents that showed his support of laws protecting child labor and in favor of wages and hours acts. Generally a champion of civil liberties, he expressed the "clear and present danger" standard in *Schenck* v. *United States* (1919) to prevent abuses of these liberties.

Holmes, William Henry (1846–1933), US artist, archeologist, and museum director, b. Harrison co, Ohio. From 1889–98 he worked for the US Geological Survey, preparing the Grand Canyon atlas and detailed reports on Yellowstone Park. In 1883 he published *Art in Shell of the American Indian,* in 1886 *Pottery of the Ancient Pueblo,* and many other important essays on Indian textiles and ceramics. Between 1894–97 he led an expedition to the Yucatán, publishing the superbly illustrated *Archaeological Studies Among Cities of Mexico* (1895–97). In 1897 he began a long career in museum work in Washington, D.C.: curator of anthropology, Smithsonian Institution, 1897–1902, 1910–20; chief of the Smithsonian's Bureau of American Anthropology, 1902–09; director of the National Gallery of Art, 1920–32.

Holmium, metallic element (symbol Ho) of the lanthanide group, first identified spectroscopically in 1878. Chief ore is monazite (phosphate). The element has few commercial uses. Properties: at. no. 67; at. wt. 164.9304; sp gr 8.795 (25°C); melt. pt. 2685°F (1474°C); boil. pt. 4883°F (2695°C); most common isotope Ho^{165} (100%). *See also* Lanthanide Elements. △1552–54.

Holocene Epoch. *See* Quaternary Period.

Holofernes, biblical Assyrian general enlisted by King Nebuchadnezzar to subdue Judea. He was slain by Judith, a Jewish widow, as he slept.

Holography, so-called three-dimensional photography in which laser light is used to store light wave patterns on a photographic plate. When light from a similar source is reflected against the plate, the three-dimensional image appears. Although the concept of holography was appreciated in the 1940s, experiments could not proceed until the development of a sufficiently coherent light source—the laser. △1528.

Holon, city in W central Israel, in Tel Aviv–Jaffa metropolitan area. Industries: textiles, metal products, food processing, glassware. Became a city 1941. Pop. 88,500.

Holoptychius. △566.

Holstein, S part of the West German state of Schleswig-Holstein. Part of the German duchy of Saxony *c.* 800; Holstein passed to Denmark in the 15th century, to Austria in 1864, and to Schleswig-Holstein in 1866. *See also* Schleswig-Holstein.

Holstein, or Holstein-Friesian, widespread breed of dairy cattle, originally developed in Holland, constituting the major proportion of milk producers in the United States. Their milk is low in butterfat, only 3-5%. Originally black and white, red and white strains have been developed. In 1951 one Holstein gave a record 21,402 quarts of milk. Weight: 1,500lb (675kg). *See also* Dairy Cattle. △372.

Holt, Harold (1908–67), prime minister of Australia (1966–67). He was the deputy leader of the Liberal party from 1956 until becoming prime minister on the retirement of Sir Robert Menzies. Holt drowned while swimming.

Holt, Joseph (1807–94), lawyer and public official, b. Breckinridge co, Ky. After serving as postmaster general (1859) and secretary of war (1861), he was appointed by President Lincoln as the first Army judge advocate (1862) to increase control of political prisoners. After Lincoln's assassination, he prosecuted the civilians accused of conspiring with John Wilkes Booth, winning convictions and the death penalty for Mary Surratt and Henry Wirz. In 1866, he was accused of suppressing evidence in the conspiracy trial. He resigned in 1875.

E.T.A. Hoffmann

Holly

Hanya Holm

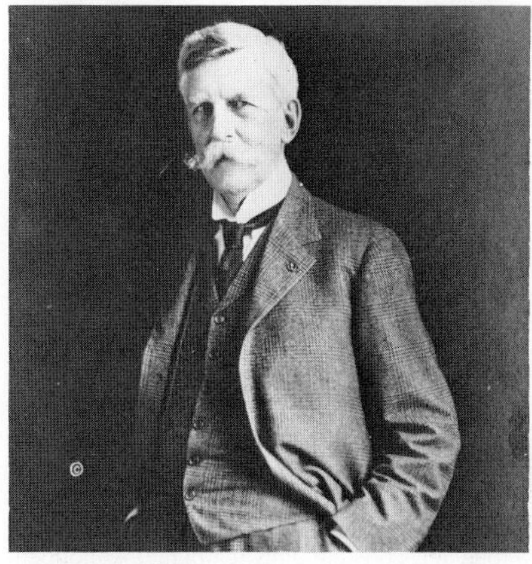

Oliver Wendell Holmes, Jr.

Holtzman Inkblot Technique, in psychology, a projective technique used to assess personality characteristics and to aid in the diagnosis of mental disorders. The individual must interpret a series of 90 ambiguous inkblots. Responses are interpreted in relation to those responses commonly given by disturbed and normal people. *See also* Projective Techniques.

Holy Alliance. In 1815 Czar Alexander I of Russia organized an alliance of the rulers of Russia, Prussia, and Austria at the Congress of Vienna. The members were supposed to live according to Christian principles and promote peace, but many regarded the alliance as useless and ineffective. Alexander was under the influence of mystical trends in Russia at the time, and the alliance was one of the results of this influence. △1230.

Holy League, name for a number of European alliances in the 15th to 17th centuries. The various purposes of these varying leagues included papal checks on French power, Spanish checks on Holy Roman imperial power, French Catholic assertions against French protestants, and European reactions to invasions by the Turks.

Holyoke, city in W Massachusetts, on Connecticut River. Named for Elizur Holyoke, pioneer settler, it was part of West Springfield until 1850. Mt Tom ski area and Mt Holyoke College are nearby. Industries: textiles, paper, metals. Chartered 1873. Pop. (1970) 50,112.

Holy Orders, in the Roman Catholic, Eastern Orthodox, and Anglican churches, the sacrament by which a person becomes a minister of the Gospel, a priest distinguished from the lay members of the church. The orders of bishop, priest, and deacon were instituted by Christ. The authority of bishops extends in succession from the Apostles. Only bishops can ordain new ministers. Other churches ordain ministers but do not believe in the Apostolic Succession. △1086.

Holy Roman Empire, a European empire founded in 962, when the German king Otto I was crowned in Rome, and surviving until 1806. Some historians date it to Charlemagne's coronation in 800. The emperors claimed to be the temporal sovereigns of Christendom, ruling in cooperation with the spiritual sovereign, the pope. However, the empire never encompassed even all of western Christendom (its basic areas were Germany, Austria, Bohemia and Moravia, northern Italy, and the Low Countries), and its relationship with the papacy was extremely stormy. The emperorship was based on the German kingship. Once elected by the German princes, the German king sought papal election as emperor. He did not always receive it; and from Maximilian I (reigned 1493–1519) the title emperor was assumed without papal coronation. By that time, although the office remained technically elective, the emperorship had become hereditary in house of Hapsburg, which held the office from 1438. Earlier dynasties who held the title included the Salians and Hohenstaufens. Under these rulers in the 11th, 12th, and 13th centuries the empire was at the height of its power. Under the Hapsburgs it became an increasingly nominal entity, its rulers concentrating on their dynastic interests in Austria while the other German princes pursued their own ends. The fiction was finally dissolved by Napoleon I, who forced the abdication of Emperor Francis II in 1806. △1072.

Holy See, centralized jurisdiction of the Roman Catholic Church. It includes the pope, with his authoritative powers as the visible head of the church. It is the seat of church government in Rome with powers over churches throughout the world. *See also* Papacy.

Homage, in feudalism. △1098.

Homeopathy, method of medical treatment based on the idea that "like cures like," or, in other words, that a disease should be treated by using drugs and other agents that produce the symptoms of the disease in a healthy person. Homeopathy was popularized by the 18th-century German physician C.F.S. Hahnemann and is now mainly of historical interest.

Homeostasis, tendency of a physical or biological system to try to maintain a balance or constancy. The term is most often applied to the way the human nervous system regulates such things as body temperature, water balance, and blood pressure.

Homeothermic Animal, warm-blooded organism with a relatively constant body temperature, independent of environmental temperature.

Homer (*c.* 9th century BC), Greek epic poet. No definite facts are known about him: by tradition he was blind; by tradition, he wrote the *Iliad* and the *Odyssey*. Seven cities claim to be his birthplace. His style was serious, realistic, and descriptive. Aristotle admired his beautiful writing; Vergil imitated it. His epics were used as texts by schoolchildren, and the Greeks regarded him as a genius. Other works have been ascribed to him, although it is unlikely that he wrote them. Later scholars have even questioned his existence. *See also* Homeric Hymns; Iliad; Odyssey. △998.

Homer, Winslow (1836–1910), US painter, b. Boston. He began as an illustrator for *Harper's Weekly* and usually drew naturalistic outdoor scenes. He painted several realistic oils of Civil War subjects in 1862. His best-known works are his paintings of the Maine coast, showing the moods of the sea and man pitted against them. Above all, Homer's careful handling of color and light and shadow in both oil and watercolor contributed to the realism of his work. △1416, 1422.

Homeric Hymns, a collection of hymns that were sung as invocations to the gods. Authorship is unknown, although some have been wrongly attributed to Homer. Of the surviving hymns, the most famous are Hymn to the Delian Apollo and Hymn to the Pythian Apollo.

Home Rule, in the United States, right of self-government granted to towns and municipalities. The states have given the local units the authority to deal with areas not preempted by the state legislature, while, at the same time, encouraging intergovernmental cooperation.

Home Rule, movement to secure autonomy for Ireland within the British Empire. Isaac Butt's Home Government Association (founded 1870) was succeeded by the more militant Home Rule Association, led by Charles Parnell. William Gladstone introduced two Home Rule bills (1886, 1893), but both were defeated. Moderate reforms (1898–1903) failed to pacify the demands for self-government. The Third Home Rule Bill was passed in 1912, but its implementation was delayed by the outbreak of World War I. It failed to satisfy either the growing Irish republican feeling or the Ulster Unionists. △1314.

Homestead Act (1862), US legislation enacted during the Civil War to encourage Westward expansion. The government granted 160 acres (65 hectares) of government land to anyone who would live on it and improve it for 5 years. Along with the Morrill Act for education, and with subsidies for the railroads, the Homestead Act opened the West to widespread settlement. △1274.

Homestead Massacre (July 6, 1892), violent labor incident. Striking workers at the Carnegie Steel Plant in Homestead, Penn., fired at 300 Pinkerton detectives hired by a company official, Henry C. Frick, who sought to break the union. During the battle 10 persons were killed and many others injured. The state militia was sent in on July 9, remaining for three months, and strike breakers worked in the plant, weakening the power of the steelworkers union.

Homo Erectus. △648.

Homogeneous Mixtures. △1562.

Homogenization, a process that reduces a substance contained in a fluid to very small particles and redistributes the particles evenly through the fluid. For example, the fat in milk is broken down so thoroughly that particles do not recombine and cream will not rise.

Homo Habilis. △648, 650.

Homology, similarity in form, function, or evolution of living things based on a common genetic heritage. For example, a man's arm and a seal's flipper are homologues, having developed from a common ancestor; the wing of a bird and of a bat are not because they evolved independently. *See also* Evolution.

Homophony, music characterized by a single melodic line accompanied by chords and other subordinate musical material, as opposed to monophony (melody without accompaniment) and polyphony (music with several simultaneous melodies). Of these three general styles, homophonic style is the one most familiar to modern listeners and is generally characteristic of most music since the time of Haydn. *See also* Polyphony.

Homoptera, order of insects, including scales and lantern flies, found worldwide. Most are terrestial plant feeders with sucking mouthparts on the back of the head; some adults lack mouthparts. They may be winged or wingless and have three life stages: egg, nymph, and adult. Length: to 6in (152mm). *See also* Aphid; Cicada; Leafhopper; Scale. △492.

Homo Sapiens. △658.

Homozygote, an organism possessing identical alleles on a chromosome pair. This is a purebred organism and will always produce the same kind of gamete. *See also* Heterozygote. △416.

Homs (Hims), city in Syria, on Orentes River; capital of Hims governorate; site of Arab mosque (1908). Industries: refined petroleum, processed foods, flour, cotton, silk. Pop. 216,000.

Homunculus, according to some 16th- and 17th-century biologists, was a completely formed miniature human being, found in the sperm head. Part of the preformation theory, specifically the belief held by a group of preformationists, called spermists.

Honan (Henan), province in NE China; capital is Chengchou. An ancient center of Chinese civilization (from 2000 BC), remains have been found of two capital cities of the Shang dynasty (1523–1027 BC); site of San Men Dam (1960s) and People's Victory Canal. Products: wheat, tobacco, sesame, cotton, peanuts, soybeans. Industries: coal and iron mining, aluminum, textiles. Area: 65,000sq mi (168,350sq km). Pop. 50,000,000.

Honduras, British. *See* Belize.

Honduras, Republic of, independent nation in Central America, bounded by Nicaragua, Guatemala, El Salvador, the Caribbean, and the Pacific; its agricultural economy is largely dependent on bananas and US investment to develop that crop.

Land and economy. Two major mountain ranges bisect the country, with tropical lowlands along the coasts and fertile valleys between the mountain branches. The dry season, from November-May, seriously affects the growing season. The economy is agricultural, based on bananas, forestry, and fishing. Beef exports have increased in the 1970s. Timber is an important resource, along with mineral deposits and offshore oil.

People. About 90% of the population is a mixture of Caucasian and Indian (mestizo) with small minorities of Indians and blacks. Education is secular and free from ages 7–15. The literacy rate is 50%. Most Hondurans are Roman Catholic, and freedom for all creeds is guaranteed by the constitution. The annual population growth is estimated at 3.4%. Spanish is the official language, although English is spoken in the N coastal banana-growing areas.

Government. The government has had 15 constitutions. The 1965 constitution provided for an elected president and congress. Two political parties are recognized.

History. W Honduras was the site of the Mayan Empire for centuries. It was claimed for Spain by Christopher Columbus in 1502, joined the Central American Federation in 1821, and gained independence in 1838. Frequent revolutions have marked its history; the latest was an army coup in 1972 over charges that the United Fruit Co. had bribed Honduran officials.

PROFILE

Official name: Republic of Honduras
Area: 43,277sq mi (112,088sq km)
Population: 2,582,000
Density: 59.7per sq mi (23per sq km)
Chief cities: Tegucigalpa (capital); San Pedro Sula
Government: Constitutional Republic
Religion: Roman Catholic
Language: Spanish
Monetary unit: Lempira
Gross national product: $869,000,000
Per capita income: $291
Industries (major): textiles, chemicals, food products
Agriculture (major): bananas, beef, coffee, corn, timber
Minerals (major): gold, silver, copper, zinc
Trading partners: United States, El Salvador

H I and H II Regions, interstellar regions made up of neutral (H I) or ionized (H II) hydrogen. H I regions produce characteristic emissions of radio waves at the frequency of 21cm. H II regions, having been excited by nearby hot stars, shine optically as emission nebulae. △104.

Honecker, Erich (1912–), East German political leader. He was imprisoned by the Nazis as a Communist. After World War II he rose in the East German Communist hierarchy and in 1971 succeeded Walter Ulbricht as party leader.

Honey, a thick sweet liquid, comprised primarily of the sugars levulose and dextrose, plus minerals and about 17% water. It is manufactured by honeybees, which collect nectar and partially digest it. It is then deposited in the hive cells, where the water is evaporated. It is an excellent food. *See also* Honeybee. △342.

Honey Ant, any of several genera of ants, found worldwide, in which "repletes" are found in the caste system. The replete ant serves as a storage vessel for plant nectar and honeydew, which it later feeds back to the workers. *See also* Ant; Hymenoptera.

Honey Badger. *See* Ratel.

Honeybee, the most common honeybee is *Apis mellifera,* which has been domesticated for the production of honey. It is found worldwide and is yellow and black in color and about 0.5in (12.5mm) long. It constructs its brood and honey storage cells from wax. Family Apidae, tribe Apini. *See also* Bee; Honey. △494, 498.

Honeydew Melon. *See* Gourd; Melon.

Honey Fungus. △426.

Honeyguide, small, drab bird of Africa and S Asia that leads humans and animals to bees' nests and shares in eating the honey, a food it otherwise would not be able to obtain because of its small beak. They also obtain nourishment from beeswax. Nest parasites, the female lays her egg in the nest of another species. The young, equipped with a sharp beak tip, kills his nest mates and then eats the food provided by the foster parents. The beak tip falls off and the young honeyguide develops the typical gray to green to yellowish-green adult plumage with brown and white on its tail. Length: 8in (20cm). Family Indicatoridae.

Honey Mesquite. *See* Mesquite.

Honeysuckle, woody shrubs and vines found in temperate areas worldwide. It has opposite leaves, bell-shaped, fragrant flowers, and berries eaten by birds. The North American trumpet honeysuckle *(Lonicera sempervirens)* is a woodland vine with long, tubular flowers, red outside and yellow inside. There are 200 species. Family Caprifoliaceae.

Hong Kong, British colony in S China, 90mi (145km) SE of Canton; capital is Victoria; comprised of Hong Kong Island, Kowloon Peninsula, the New Territories on the mainland, and approx. 235 islets in the South China Sea. Ceded to Britain after Chinese defeat during Opium War by terms of Treaty of Nanking (1842); peninsula was acquired 1860 and New Territories 1898. Since the est. of Communist regime in China (1950), over 3,000,000 people have immigrated to Hong Kong and live within a 40sq mi (104sq km) area. It is a major center of world commerce in the Far East due to the good harbor, administration, and absence of custom duties. Industries: agriculture, fishing, mining, tourism, textiles, plastics, electrical equipment, shipping, rope, paint, shipbuilding, tobacco, engineering, printing, publishing. Area: (total colony) 398sq mi (1,031sq km). Pop. 3,950,000.

Honolulu, capital city of Hawaii, on SE Oahu Island; seat of Honolulu co. Center of Hawaiian royalty and foreign consuls, it became the permanent capital of the kingdom of Hawaii 1845; remained capital after 1898 annexation of islands by the United States and after 1959 declaration of Hawaii as 50th state. On Dec. 7, 1941, the US naval base at Pearl Harbor was bombed by Japanese, precipitating US entry into WWII; during the war it served as strategic base and staging point for US Pacific forces. Paramount in Honolulu's development has been the rise in tourism, peacetime defense activity, expansion of harbor, diversification of industry, and construction of international airport; site of University of Hawaii (1907), Jackson College (1949), Kawaiahao Church (1841), Iolani Palace, Waikiki Beach, Punchbowl volcano, and Diamond Head crater. Industries: sugar processing, pineapple canning, tourism, defense. Pop. (1970) 324,871.

Honorius I, Roman Catholic pope (625–38). A disciple of Pope Gregory I, he continued his missionary work in England, established St Peter's Treasury, and restored many buildings in Rome. His concessions to the Byzantine Empire aligned him with the Monotheletes in the belief that Christ has only one will, as well as one nature. He was condemned a heretic, posthumously, causing controversy over the doctrine of infallibility.

Honshu, largest of four main islands in Japan, between Sea of Japan and the Pacific Ocean. Considered mainland of Japan, it produces 90% of Japan's industrial output; location of six of Japan's largest cities, including Tokyo. Industries: textiles, oil refining, rice, tea, machinery, electronics, chemicals, metals, shipbuilding, printing, publishing. Area: 89,000sq mi (230,510sq km). Pop. 82,569,581.

Hood, John Bell (1831–79), US military figure, b. Owingsville, Ky. He resigned from the US Army in April 1861 and joined the army of the Confederacy. He fought in the battle of Bull Run, after which he was promoted to general. He distinguished himself at Antietam, Fredericksburg, Gettysburg, and Chickamauga, where he lost a leg. He replaced Joseph Johnston as commander of the army resisting General Sherman's march through Georgia. Unable to stem Sherman, his troops fought their way to Nashville where they were badly defeated (1864). Hood resigned shortly thereafter and surrendered at Natchez, Miss., in May 1865.

Hood, Raymond (1881–1934), US architect, b. Pawtucket, R.I. He first achieved recognition for his neo-Gothic design for the Chicago Tribune Building (1922), which he worked on with John Mead Howells. With J. Andrew Fouilhoux he designed the Daily News Building (1930) and the McGraw-Hill Building (1930–31), which foreshadowed their work on Rockefeller Center (1931–39), a multibuilding complex in New York City in which two other architectural firms collaborated.

Hood, Fort, US army post in central Texas, near Killeen; site of former Fort Gates; named for Confederate Gen. John Hood; base specializes in armor training. Area: 209,000acres (84,645hectares). Est. 1942.

Hood, Mount, inactive volcano in the Cascade Range of NW Oregon; mountain climbing and skiing area; highest point in state, 11,235ft (3,427m).

Hoof-and-Mouth Disease. See Foot-and-Mouth Disease. △370.

Hooghly, tributary of the Ganges River, in NE India; formed at the confluence of the Bhagirathi, Jalangi, and Matabhanga rivers; flows S to Bay of Bengal near Sagar Island; commercially important trade route, almost entirely navigable. Length: 160mi (258km).

Hooke, Robert (1635–1703), English philosopher and experimental physicist. Active in astronomy, he determined the center of gravity of the moon and earth; implied that Jupiter rotated; indicated the 5th star in Orion; and built a Gregorian telescope. In other fields he described the nature of combustion, was the first to use the word "cell," made a compound microscope, and utilized balance springs in watches. His law of elasticity bears his name. △1506.

Hooker, Joseph (1814–79), Union Civil War general, b. Hadley, Mass. He led troops in the Eastern Campaigns of 1862. As commander of the Army of the Potomac, he was beaten by Robert E. Lee and Stonewall Jackson at Chancellorsville (May 1863). Later, in the West, he won the Battle of Lookout Mountain, Tenn.

Hooker, Richard (1554?–1600), English theologian. He was educated at Oxford, served as rector of a parish, and then was appointed to the Temple, one of the legal societies known as the Inns of Court. There he wrote much of his *Laws of Ecclesiastical Polity,* a strong and learned defense of the Church of England against Puritan attacks.

Hooker, Thomas (1586–1647), English colonist and Puritan clergyman. He left England for Holland and then New England (1633), seeking religious freedom. Pastor of first church of Cambridge, Mass., he was discontented with conditions there and led colonists to found and settle Hartford, Conn. (1636). He helped cause the adoption of the "Fundamental Orders of Connecticut" (1639), considered to be the first constitution in America. He also was an organizer of the New England Confederation. *See also* New England Confederation.

Hooke's Law, the proportionality between the force F applied to a spring and the distance x that it stretches: $F = kx$, where k is a constant describing the strength of the spring. *See also* Elasticity. △1506–08.

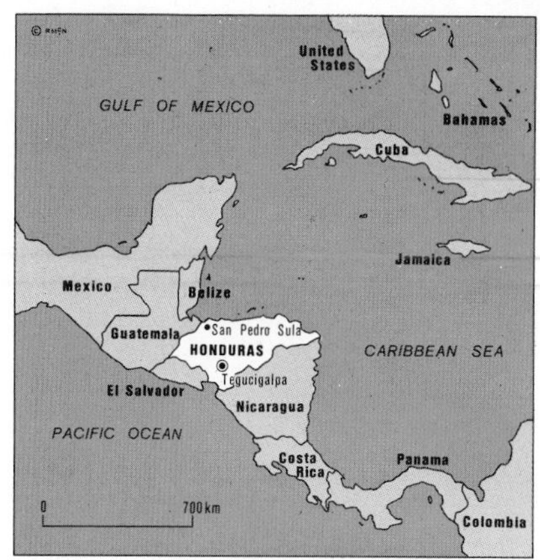
United States
GULF OF MEXICO
Bahamas
Cuba
Jamaica
Mexico
Belize
Guatemala
San Pedro Sula
HONDURAS
CARIBBEAN SEA
Tegucigalpa
El Salvador
Nicaragua
PACIFIC OCEAN
Costa Rica
Panama
0
700km
Colombia

Honduras

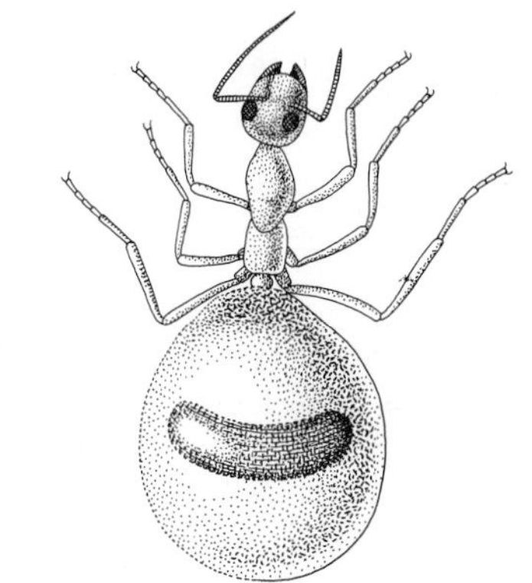

Honey ant

Honeybee

Hong Kong

Hookworm, roundworm common in warmer areas of the world, parasitic in man. Usually contracted when the larva penetrates the host's skin, it then migrates to the intestine where it causes anemia, laziness, and lack of physical and mental energy. Phylum Nematoda; species *Necator americanus* (tropical) and *Ancylostoma duodenale* (Europe and Asia). △474, 732.

Hooper, William (1742–90), American patriot and a signer of the Declaration of Independence, b. Boston, Mass. He was a member of the North Carolina state assembly (1773) and later served in the Continental Congress (1774–77).

Hoopoe, zebra-striped, fawn-colored bird that lives in open areas, city parks, and lawns throughout Old World warmer areas. It has a fanlike crest and long, curved bill. It utters a "hoo-hoo-hoo" call and feeds on small invertebrates. Nesting in a tree cavity or under a stone, the female defends herself and her brood—pale blue or whitish eggs (4–8)—by emitting a foul-smelling, blackish-brown liquid from a tail gland. Length: 1ft (30cm). Family Upupidae; species *Upupa epops.*

Hoop Snake. *See* Mud Snake.

Hooton, Earnest A(lbert) (1887–1954), US physical anthropologist, b. Clemansville, Wisc. Teaching at Harvard University (1914–54), he helped to establish it as a center of physical anthropology. His studies examined human evolution, racial differentiation, and the relationship between physical type and personality. His works include *Up from the Ape* (1931) and *Crime and the Man* (1939).

Hoover, Herbert Clark (1874–1964), 31st president of the United States, b. West Branch, Iowa; graduate, Stanford University, 1895. In 1899 he married Lou Henry; they had two sons. Hoover was a highly successful mining engineer and operated as an international mining consultant in many parts of the world. During World War I and in the postwar period, he was widely acclaimed for his humanitarian work in relief for war refugees. He headed numerous relief organizations and was US Food Administrator.

Hoover served as secretary of commerce in the administrations of both Presidents Harding and Coolidge. He won the Republican nomination for president in 1928 and easily defeated Democrat Alfred E. Smith.

Hoover's presidency began only months before the Great Depression, which was triggered by the stock market crash of October 1929. As a conservative who believed the economy to be in basic good health, he opposed massive government intervention, although he did establish the Reconstruction Finance Corporation. As the economy worsened, Hoover's popularity decreased.

In 1932 about 15,000 veterans, known as the Bonus Marchers, converged in protest against Washington, and Hoover used federal troops to disperse them. He ran for reelection in 1932 but was soundly defeated by Franklin Delano Roosevelt.

Career: chairman, Commission for Relief in Belgium, 1915–19; US Food Administrator, 1917–18; American Relief Administrator, 1919–23; secretary of commerce, 1921–29; president, 1929–33. △1324.

Hoover, J(ohn) Edgar (1895–1972), director of the Federal Bureau of Investigation (1924–72), b. Washington, D.C. He worked as a file reviewer for the Department of Justice (1917) and became assistant director of the Bureau of Investigation in 1921. He reorganized the bureau, compiling a vast fingerprint file and building a crime laboratory and training academy. Capture of notorious criminals in the 1930s brought fame and glamour to Hoover's FBI. After the bureau became the Federal Bureau of Investigation (1935), he concentrated on fighting Communism and investigating threats to internal security. He continued in office, by special presidential dispensation, beyond retirement age. He wrote *Masters of Deceit* (1958) and *J. Edgar Hoover on Communism* (1962).

Hoover Commission, US commissions, headed by former Pres. Herbert Hoover, to study the executive branch of the government. The first commission (1947–49) called for the establishment of the Department of Health, Education, and Welfare. The second (1953–55) made organization and policy recommendations.

Hoover Dam, one of the world's largest dams, on the Colorado River between Arizona and Nevada. Built by US Bureau of Reclamation, it opened in 1936; irrigates 650,000acres (263,250hectares) in S California and Arizona. Height: 726ft (221m). Length: 1,244ft (379m).

Hop, rough, twining vine native to North America, South America, and Eurasia. It has rough stems, heart-shaped leaves, and small male and female flowers borne on separate plants. The female catkins are covered with lupulin, a yellow powder used as a sedative. The dried female flowers of *Humulus lupulus* are used for flavoring beer. Family Moraceae. △350.

Hope, (Hawkins), (Sir) Anthony (1863–1933), English novelist. The most famous of his romantic novels is *The Prisoner of Zenda* (1894).

Hopeh (Hopei, or Hebei), province in NE China, on the Gulf of Chihli in Yellow Sea; capital is Shih-chia-chuang; remains of Peking man found here indicate Hopeh has been inhabited for at least 500,000 years. After the 14th century there was much agricultural development, due to the introduction of cotton cultivation and extended irrigation works; industrial development was aided after WWI by British and Japanese funding. In 1928 the Chinese Nationalists added parts of Chahar and Jehol provs. to Hopeh. Crops: cotton, wheat, soybeans, corn, millet, sweet potatoes, fruits, nuts, rice, oilseeds. Industries: chemicals, steel, machines, textiles. Area: 75,000sq mi (194,250sq km). Pop. 47,000,000.

Hopewell Culture, culture centered in Ohio and Illinois, and reaching its peak in the last centuries BC and the first four centuries AD. Hopewell people were efficient farmers, built complex earthworks, such as the serpent mounds of Ohio, for ceremonial and business purposes, and traded extensively. *See also* Cahokia Mounds.

Hoplite. △994, 996.

Hop Hornbeam, slow-growing, ornamental tree native to North America and Eurasia. It has scaly bark, translucent leaves, and green hoplike cones. The American hop hornbeam *(Ostrya virginiana)* is also called ironwood, because of its hard, heavy wood used for fence posts. Height: to 70ft (21m). There are seven species. Family Betulaceae.

Hopi, from Hópitu, meaning "the peaceful people," a Shoshonean-speaking tribe of North American Indians, the only such group to take on a Pueblo culture. They are famous for having retained the purest form of pre-Columbian life to survive in the United States today. About 6,000 Hopi people inhabit 11 villages in Coconino co, Arizona, on three mesas north of Winslow. △1392.

Hopkins, Gerard Manley (1844–89), English poet. He became a Roman Catholic (1866) and was later ordained a Jesuit priest (1877). The sinking in 1875 of a German ship carrying five nuns inspired the writing of his long poem *The Wreck of the Deutschland* (1875), which contains technical innovations and a dramatic intensity also found in shorter poems such as "God's Grandeur" (1877), "The Windhover" (1877), and "Pied Beauty" (1878). He contributed the principle of sprung rhythm to English poetry. His small body of verse was not published until 1918. △1240.

Hopkins, Harry Lloyd (1890–1946), US political adviser and administrator, b. Sioux City, Iowa. A close friend and adviser of Pres. Franklin D. Roosevelt, he worked both in official posts and behind the scenes to implement the New Deal and foreign policies. He headed the Federal Emergency Relief Administration (1933), the Civil Works Administration (1933–34) and the Works Project Administration (1935–38), served as secretary of commerce (1938–40), and went on special missions to Europe for the president.

Hopkins, Stephen (1707–85), American legislator and a signer of the Declaration of Independence, b. Providence, R.I. Governor of Rhode Island (1755–67), he later took part in the formation of the Navy and attended the general congress in Philadelphia (1774–76).

Hopkinson, Francis (1737–91), US political figure, poet, musician, and signer of the Declaration of Independence, b. Philadelphia. He composed the first secular song by a native Amerian, "My Days Have Been So Wondrous Free" (1759), and his satirical poem, "The Battle of the Kegs" (1778), was popular during the American Revolution. He represented New Jersey in the Continental Congress (1776), was judge of the admiralty in Pennsylvania (1779–89) and US district court judge (1789–91), and urged adoption of the Constitution. One of his final musical scores was *Seven Songs for the Harpsichord* (1788).

Hopper, Edward (1882–1967), US painter, b. Nyack, N.Y. A pupil of Robert Henri and greatly influenced by the Ashcan School, he was a realistic painter of the American scene. Hopper often placed lonely figures in his carefully drawn settings. Many scenes were of New York City and New England. *See also* Ashcan School. △1416.

Horace (65–8 BC), Roman poet, b. as Quintus Horatius Flaccus. Although he fought at Philippi (42 BC) with Brutus, he won favor in Augustan Rome. His friend Vergil introduced him to Maecenas, who as his patron provided him with an income and a farm. Horace's first *Satires* appeared in 35 BC, followed by *Epodes* (30 BC), *Odes* (*c.* 24 BC), *Epistles* (*c.* 20 BC), and *Ars Poetica* (*c.* 13 BC). His simple, direct Latin lyrics provided a vivid picture of the Augustan age. △1028.

Horehound, or hoarhound, common name for *Marrubium vulgare,* an aromatic herb of the mint family found in Eurasia and as a roadside weed in North America. Its woolly white leaves are used for flavoring cough lozenges and candies.

Horemheb. △972.

Horizon, in geology, a term used in two ways; first, a continuous horizontal surface or time-plane between two strata that has no thickness, and second, a horizontal layer from a few inches to a foot in thickness that is characterized either by a distinct fossilized flora or fauna or by a particular mineral.

Horizon, Celestial, great circle on the celestial sphere, the plane of which contains the line through an observer's position at right angles to the vertical. It lies midway between the observer's zenith and nadir and cuts the observer's meridian at the north and south points. △138.

Horizon, Soil. *See* Soil Profile.

Hormones, chemical substances, secreted by the endocrine, or ductless, glands of the body directly into the bloodstream. Hormones exercise chemical control of body functions, regulating virtually all body functions—growth, development, sexual maturity and functioning, metabolism, emotional balance (in part), and so on. Hormones circulate in the body in very small amounts and often exert their effects (on target organs, for example) at great distances from their point of secretion. They are somewhat slow to take effect, exert widespread action, and are also somewhat slow to disappear from the system. The secretion and activity of the various hormones are closely interdependent, with one stimulating or inhibiting secretion of another, with two or more acting together to produce a certain effect—in general maintaining an extremely delicate equilibrium that is important to health and well being. Too much or too little of any particular hormone, caused by disease or malfunction of the secreting endocrine gland, usually produces body abnormality or disease. In many cases this can be treated by administration of hormone or by correcting the endocrine gland disorder. There are numerous hormones. Some of the best known are thyroxin, adrenalin, insulin, estrogen, progesterone, testosterone. *See also* Endocrine System and separate articles on the various endocrine glands; on specific hormones; on hormonal diseases. △690, 726.

Hormuz (Ormuz), Strait of, strait between N end of Oman, SE Arabian Peninsula and S coast of Iran; connects the Persian Gulf with the Gulf of Oman.

Horn, a defensive or offensive structure—generally elongated and pointed—growing from the head region of some mammals. Considered a skin appendage, a typical horn is made up of a central bony core that is covered by a sheath of the skin protein keratin; in the rhinoceros, the entire horn is made of keratin. Horns typically grow during the entire life of the animal. *See also* Antler.

Hornbeam, small, hardy tree found throughout the Northern Hemisphere. It has smooth bark, a short trunk, spreading branches, and clusters of green nuts. The American hornbeam *(Carpinus caroliniana)* is sometimes known as blue beech. Family Betulaceae.

Hornbill, tropical African and Australasian brownish and black-and-white bird, named for its swollen, brightly-colored bill, often having folds and a horny hood. They also have long eyelashes. The female lays eggs (1–4) in a high tree trunk cavity and then uses droppings, mud, and regurgitated food to erect a barricade, imprisoning herself and her eggs for 6–16 weeks. The male feeds her through a tiny slit in the barricade wall. Length: 15–60in (38–152cm). Family Bucerotidae. △530, 534.

Hornbook, children's primer of the late 16th to late 18th centuries. The hornbook consisted of a sheet of paper mounted on a wooden frame shaped like a paddle and held by a handle. The paper contained the alphabet in small and large letters and, often, the vowels and consonants, the Lord's Prayer, and Roman numerals.

Horne, Lena (1917–), US singer, b. Brooklyn, N.Y. She starred in the film *Stormy Weather* (1943), and appeared on Broadway in *Jamaica* (1957). She was the first black woman to be given a long-term Hollywood contract.

Horned Owl, owl with hornlike feather tufts on its head, yellow eyes, and a frightening call. Fierce and strong, they feed on rodents, hares, and other small mammals. The eagle owl *(Bubo bubo)* is the largest European owl; the great horned owl *(Bubo virginianus)* is a typical North American species. Length: over 2ft (61cm). *See also* Owl.

Horned Rattlesnake. *See* Sidewinder.

Horned Ray. *See* Devilfish.

Horned Toad, or horned lizard, insect-eating lizard found in dry, open areas in W North America. It is sand-colored and has spines on head and body and a stumpy tail. Despite its formidable appearance it is harmless and makes a good pet. Length: 3–5in (7.6–12.8cm). There are 14 species. Family Iguanidae; genus *Phrynosoma*. *See also* Lizard.

Horned Viper, or horned asp, poisonous snake native to deserts of N Africa and Arabia. It is stocky, brown with black markings, and has a sharp, pointed scale over each eye. It sinks vertically into the sand. Length: to 2ft (61cm). Family Viperidae; species *Cerastes cerastes*. *See also* Viper.

Hornet. *See* Wasp.

Horney, Karen (1885–1952), US psychoanalyst, b. Germany. She extended classical Freudian theory to dwell more on the individual's current (rather than childhood) problems and to include environmental as well as intrapsychic factors. Her books include *Our Inner Conflicts* (1945) and *Neurosis and Human Growth* (1950).

Hornfels. △248.

Horns, family of wind musical instruments of ancient, universal origin, first used for signaling and ceremonies. Once made from animal horns and later from tractable metals, they have usually been made of brass since the Renaissance. They appeared in the opera orchestras of 17th-century Europe. The horn is the ancestor of the trumpet, trombone, tuba, baritone horn, which are instruments developed in the early 19th century by Adolphe Sax of Brussels. Sax added pistons and slides for playing chromatics to the traditional tubes with flaring bells and cupped or funnel-shaped mouthpieces. △1244.

Hornwort. △436.

Horoscope. △826.

Horowitz, Vladimir (1904–), US pianist, b. Russia. He first performed in public in 1921 and in the United States in 1928. He married Arturo Toscanini's daughter and became a widely renowned concert artist, famed for his technical virtuosity. In 1953 he retired from the concert stage but continued to make recordings. In 1965 he returned to the concert stage in a series of triumphant recitals at Carnegie Hall and in 1968 in Boston and Chicago. One of the world's great piano virtuosos, he has made a number of award-winning recordings, mainly in the Romantic repertoire.

Horse, hoofed mammal that evolved in North America but became extinct during late Pleistocene Epoch. Early horse forms crossed the Bering land bridge, radiated throughout Asia, Europe, and Africa and produced the modern horse family. The only surviving true wild horse is Przewalski's wild horse. Hunted by Paleolithic man for food, the horse was first domesticated about 5,000 years ago in Central Asia. Horses returned to the New World with the Spanish conquistadors in the 1500s.

Horses are characterized by one large functional toe and two side toes reduced to splints, molars with crowns joined by ridges for grazing, elogated skull, and simple stomach. Fast runners, they usually live in herds and walk, canter, trot, or gallop. Gestation is 11–12 months; one colt is born and it can walk at birth. Modern horse breeds are divided into two groups: *light* horse, for riding, racing, and driving, and *draft* horse, massive work animal. All species in the family can interbreed. The true horse is distinguished from other equines (zebras and asses) by its short ears, small head, and chestnuts (horny, wartlike growths on the inside hind legs), large hooves, and hair-covered tail. Family Equidae; species *Equus caballus*. △548, 576.

Horse Chestnut, or buckeye, tree native to temperate and tropical regions. The 15 deciduous *Aesculus* species include the common horse chestnut *Aesculus hippocastanum* that has large, palmate leaves, long, showy flower spikes, and large, spiny nuts containing two inedible kernels. They tolerate urban pollution and salt spray of seaside areas. Height: to 100ft (30.5m). The two *Billia* species are evergreen and native from S Mexico to Colombia. Family Hippocastanaceae.

Horsefly, black fly, 0.8 to 1.2in (20 to 30mm) long, a pest of man and other animals; found worldwide. The female has bladelike mouthparts and gives a painful bite. Family Tabanidae, species *Tabanus spp*. *See also* Deer Fly.

Horsehair Worm, hair worm or thread worm, long, thin worms with featureless body, usually black or brown. The young are parasitic in insects and the adults are free-living in soil or fresh water. Length: to 31.5in (800mm). Phylum Nematomorpha.

Horsehead Nebula, dark nebula forming part of the Orion Nebula (M42) and obscuring some of its light. The dark matter strikingly resembles a horse's head. △104.

Horse Mackerel, commercial marine food fish found in the Atlantic from the North Sea to Africa. Blue-green and silver with a white belly, it travels in schools. Family Carangidae (jack, scad, and pompano); species *Trachurus trachurus*. See also Osteichthyes.

Horsepower, a unit indicating the rate at which work is done, adapted by James Watt in the 18th century. He defined it as the weight (550lb) a horse could raise 1ft in 1 second, or 550ft-lb per second. At the output shaft of an engine or motor, it is termed "brake horsepower," or "shaft horsepower." In large reciprocating engines, it is termed "indicating horsepower" and is determined from pressure in the cylinders. The electrical equivalent of one horsepower is 746 watts.

Horse Racing, sport that consists of speed trials between two or more horses over an oval circuit. Most popular is thoroughbred racing, where the rider sits in a saddle atop the horse. The types of races include flat racing (on dirt), turf racing (on grass), and steeplechase racing (over an obstacled course with hurdles and water holes). Distances vary from three furlongs (for two-year-olds) and upward, and include a variety of races, by either age, sex, or weight (handicap). In the United States the horses start from a closed chute. Wagering is allowed via a parimutuel betting system, which pays off on first- second- and third-place finishers, as well as in other combinations of play (picking the first, second finishers, etc).

History. Horse racing began in Egypt around 1500 BC. Organized racing was popular in England among royalty in the 12th century. The oldest race is the Epsom Derby, which originated in England in 1780, and the most famous race is the Grand National Steeplechase, held annually at Liverpool, England, since 1939. In the United States, most popular is the Triple Crown for three-year-olds, which includes the Kentucky Derby, Preakness, and Belmont Stakes. *See also* Harness Racing. △930.

Horseradish, plant native to Europe and cultivated for its pungent, fleshy root used as a seasoning. It has escaped cultivation and is widespread as a weed. A coarse plant with lance-shaped, toothed leaves, it has white flower clusters at the plant top and egg-shaped seedpods. Height: to 3ft (91cm). Family Cruciferae; species *Armoracia lapathifolia*.

Horseshoe Crab, marine arthropod found on Atlantic and Gulf of Mexico coasts of United States and Asian coasts from Japan to Philippine Islands. Its horseshoe-shaped carapace is jointed to a spiny abdomen and ends in a long, stout spine. It has five pairs of walking legs and can swim upside down. Length: to 24in (61cm). Class Merostomata, genus *Limulus*. *See also* Arthropod. △490.

Horseshoe Pitching, a game played by two or more persons using horseshoes on an outdoor court. The court is usually 50ft (15.2m) long and 10ft (3m) wide. The actual pitching distance is 40 feet (12.2m) for men and 30 feet (9.1m) for women. The object is to encircle an iron peg 1ft (0.3m) high that is set into the ground at either end of the court. A game consists of 50 points. Encircling the peg (ringer) is three points, leaning against the peg is two points, and each horseshoe closer to the peg (within 6in; 15.2cm) than

Herbert Hoover

J. Edgar Hoover

Hop

Hornbill

that of an opponent's is one point. The game originated with Greek and Roman soldiers. The National Horseshoe Pitchers of the United States (formed 1914) oversees the professional aspect of the sport. Amateur competition is governed by the Amateur Athletic Union. *See also* Quoits.

Horseshoes. △1582.

Horsetail, or scouring rush, any of about 25 species of small, flowerless, rushlike plants (genus *Equisetum*) that occur on all continents except Australia. The hollow, round-jointed stems have a whorl of tiny leaves at each joint. Because of their high silica content, horsetails are very abrasive and were formerly used for polishing wood and scouring pots. Horsetails have existed for more than 300,000,000 years, and their fossils are found in coal from the Carboniferous period. △438.

Horse-whip Snake. △524.

Horst, an elongated upthrust block bounded by parallel normal faults on its long sides. *See also* Graben. △250.

Horta, Victor (Baron) (1861–1947), Belgian architect. His Hôtel Tassel in Brussels (1892) was one of the earliest Art Nouveau buildings. His work featured bold use of exposed iron supports and metal and glass ornament. He was also noted for interior design, as in the Baron von Ectvelde house (1895) and the Maison du Peuple (1896–99) in Brussels. △1192.

Horthy, Miklós von Nagybánya (1868–1957), Hungarian admiral and statesman, commander of the Austro-Hungarian fleet in World War I, regent of Hungary, 1920–44. At the end of World War I Horthy returned to Hungary to organize a counterrevolution against Béla Kun's Bolshevik government. As regent and head of state, he suppressed all political opposition and resisted the return of Charles I, deposed Austro-Hungarian emperor. Through his efforts, Hungary joined the Axis Powers in 1941. When Hungary was occupied by German troops in 1944, Horthy was deposed.

Horticulture, the cultivation of garden, orchard, and nursery crops. It includes fruit growing (pomology), the production of vegetables (olericulture), production of flowers (floriculture), and ornamental horticulture (landscape gardening). Horticulture became a major industry in 17th-century Europe, when the growth of large urban areas made it impractical for individuals to produce necessary garden crops on their own land. △324.

Horus, falcon-headed god of ancient Egypt, son of Isis and Osiris. In the myths, he came to rule earth after avenging the murder of his father. Horus is closely identified with all the pharaohs of Egypt, who used his name as the first of their titles and were thought to rule as him on earth, and after death, as his father Osiris in the underworld.

Horyu-ji Temple. △1048.

Hosea, biblical author and first of the 12 minor prophets. He condemned Israel for worshiping false gods and promised mercy to the faithful.

Hospitalet, city in NE Spain; suburb of Barcelona; site of agricultural institute. Industries: steel, textiles, chemicals. Pop. 241,978.

Hospitallers. *See* Knights Hospitallers. △1084, 1098.

Hospital Survey and Construction Act. *See* Hill-Burton Act (1946).

Hosta, or plantain lily, funkia, perennial plant native to E Asia and Japan. They have veined leaves and lilylike flowers ranging from white to blue to lilac. Family Liliaceae; genus *Hosta*.

Hot Bed, or hot frame, heated, wood or concrete, outdoor ground frame covered with glass or plastic doors used by gardeners to extend the growing season. Heat is supplied by an underground heating cable, steam, hot water, or fermenting manure covered with fine soil. Temperature can be as high as 90°F (32°C) in this structure and seedlings can be grown throughout the year.

Hothouse. *See* Greenhouse.

Hot Springs, city in W central Arkansas, 47mi (76km) WSW of Little Rock; seat of Garland co., in Ouachita Mts; site of health resort with 47 thermal springs; national park, 1921. Settled 1807; inc. 1851. Pop. (1970) 35,631.

Hot Springs National Park, park in central Arkansas. It features 47 hot mineral water springs used in the treatment of certain ailments; over 1,000,000gallons (3,790,000liters) of water a day, with an average temperature of 143°F (62°C) flow from the springs. Area: 3,535acres (1,432hectares). Est. 1921.

Hottentot, or Khoikhoi, Khoisan-speaking people of southern Africa, now almost extinct; characteristically of short stature, with a dark yellowish skin, probably of mixed Bushman and Negro origin. Traditionally they were nomadic pastoralists. Many of them were displaced or exterminated by the early Dutch settlers; their surviving descendants have mostly been absorbed into the Cape colored population.

Hottentot Bread. *See* Elephant's Foot.

Hottentot Fig, succulent vine found on deserts and seashores in warm regions and cultivated as a ground cover. Not a true fig, it has woody stems with succulent leaves and large, daisylike, yellow or rose-purple flowers. The fig-shaped fruits are edible but not tasty. Family Aizoaceae; species *Carpobrotus edulis*.

Houdini (1874–1926), US magician, b. Erich Weiss in Appleton, Wisc. No packing case or set of handcuffs could contain this escape artist, who also specialized in exposing fraudulent mediums in print. Author of *The Unmasking of Robert-Houdin* (1908), he had an extensive library on magic now in the Library of Congress.

Houdon, Jean-Antoine (1741–1828), French sculptor. He was a leading portrait sculptor, best known for his busts, including many of American Revolutionary leaders. They were executed in a classical style and reflected an individualistic treatment of character.

Houma, city in SE Louisiana, 49mi (79km) WSW of New Orleans, on intracoastal waterway; seat of Terrebonne parish; site of fine antebellum buildings. Industries: boats, seafood packaging, fisheries, sugar. Founded 1834; inc. 1848. Pop. (1970) 30,922.

Hounds, dogs that hunt by sight or by ground scent. Sight-hunters are coursing hounds; they chase quarry at great speed and overtake and kill or capture it. Probably man's oldest hunting companions, they are tall, have long legs, deep chests, and long heads. Large enough to take down elk and deer, they include the Saluki, Afghan, Irish wolfhound, and greyhound. Ground-scenters, or tailing hounds, follow game by ground scent and flush it. They have large noses, long ears, shorter legs, and are usually black, tan, red, and white. Examples are the bloodhound, beagle, and basenji.

Houphouët-Boigny, Félix (1905–), president of the Republic of the Ivory Coast from 1960. He served in the government of French West Africa and then led his country to independence in 1958, afterward maintaining good relations with France.

Hour Angle, angle measured westward along the celestial equator from the observer's meridian to the line passing through a celestial body and the celestial poles (hour circle of the body). It is given in hours, minutes, and seconds and ranges from 0 to 24 hours.

Housatonic, river in W Massachusetts; rises near Pittsfield in the Berkshire Mts; flows S through W Connecticut to Long Island Sound at Stratford. Length: 130mi (209km).

House, Edward M(andell) (1858–1938), US political figure and diplomat, b. Houston, Tex. He was known as Colonel House. Active in Texas Democratic politics, he helped Woodrow Wilson obtain the 1912 Democratic presidential nomination. He became Wilson's closest adviser. He was sent to Europe by Wilson in an attempt to prevent World War I (1914) and later to arrange a peace conference (1915). He was a member of the US peace commission and helped to draft the Treaty of Versailles and the Covenant of the League of Nations. He broke with the president in 1919 over Wilson's uncompromising idealism.

Housefly, black and gray fly, 0.24 to 0.28in (6–7mm) long, that breeds in animal waste and decaying vegetable matter. This species, with several closely related species, is found worldwide. Because of their breeding habits, and because they also feed on human food, they transmit several diseases, including typhoid, yaws, tuberculosis, and various intestinal protozoa. Family Muscidae, species *Musca domestica*. *See also* Blowfly; Diptera. △492.

Household Equilibrium, or consumer equilibrium, in economics, condition that occurs when the consumer allocates his income between the purchase of various goods and services in such a way that he obtains the highest level of satisfaction (utility). While he may choose between alternative goods, substituting one for another, the consumer's total bundle of goods is limited by his total income or budget, ie, the budget constraint.

Houseleek. *See* Hens and Chicks.

Housemaid's Knee. △720.

House of Commons, lower house of the bicameral British parliament and the repository of virtually all legislative authority. The power of the House of Commons is rooted in its control of financial matters. The Commons has 635 members—516 from England, 36 from Wales, 71 from Scotland, and 12 from Northern Ireland. Members are elected either at large or as representatives of specific districts and serve terms of no more than five years. A general election may be called before that time if the prime minister (the leader of the majority party in the Commons) cannot secure a majority on important issues. Although the Commons originated in the 13th century, it did not achieve complete legislative supremacy until the Parliamentary Act of 1911 removed from the House of Lords its veto power over money bills. *See also* House of Lords; Parliament, British. △904.

House of Lords, upper house of the British parliament, having both legislative and judicial functions. In its legislative capacity the Lords have been completely subordinate to the House of Commons since the Parliament acts of 1911 and 1949 checked virtually all its power except the right to delay passage of a bill for a year. It has no absolute veto over Commons legislation. All bills except for appropriation may be initiated by the Lords. Life peers, whose titles may not be inherited, and hereditary peers sit in the House. Hereditary peers may resign their titles to run for election to the Commons. There are special "law lords" who act as judges when the house acts as Great Britain's highest court. *See also* House of Commons; Parliament, British.

House of Representatives, one of the two chambers of the US Congress and part of the legislative branch of the federal government. The House was intended to represent the popular will and its members are directly elected. Total membership is fixed at 435, with representatives serving two-year terms. A representative must be at least 25, a US citizen for 5 years, and a resident of the state from which he or she is elected. Certain exclusive powers are delegated to the House by the Constitution. The primary ones are the authority to originate revenue bills, the right to initiate impeachment proceedings, and the power to elect the president in case of a tie or lack of majority in the electoral college. The presiding speaker is a leader of the majority party. Each party has a floor leader who manages party programs. The committee system is a dominant feature of the House and has the power to control proposed bills. Bills passed by the House are sent to the Senate for consideration. *See also* Congress of the United States; Senate of the United States. △902, 906, 1218.

Houseplants, plants suitable for indoor gardening. Most houseplants originated in tropical areas of Central and South America at elevations with fluctuating temperatures. Commercial sources now produce them under artificial conditions. Preferred temperatures for houseplants are 60–70°F (15.6–21°C) during the day and 55°F (12.8°C) at night. It is important for houseplants to have proper amounts of water and light.

Shady houseplants include schefflera *(Brassaia)*, Boston fern *(Nephrolepis)*, and dumbcane *(Dieffenbachia)*; semi-shady types include Norfolk Island pine *(Araucaria)* and English ivy *(Hedera helix)*; semi-sunny types include wandering Jew *(Tradescantia)*, rubber-plant *(Ficus)*, coleus, and African violet *(Saintpaulia)*; sunny types are *Citrus*, wax begonia, and geranium *(Pelargonium)*.

Houseplants need watering, fertilizing, and repotting according to species. In summer they benefit from being put outdoors in shady areas. They should be brought indoors before the first frost. Many houseplants have dormant periods: ferns and palms rest in the winter, cactus in the fall, and many plants after flowering.

House-Tree-Person Technique, in psychology, a projective technique devised by J.N. Buck and used to assess personality characteristics. The subject is asked to draw, in turn, pictures of a house, tree, and person. Interpretations of the drawings are assumed to reveal the subject's attitudes toward his home (house), his unconscious self (tree), and his ideal self (person). The technique is used in the diagnosis of mental disorders in both adults and children. *See also* Projective Techniques.

Housing and Urban Development, Department of (HUD), US federal cabinet-level department within the executive branch. It was created in 1965. The purpose of HUD is to assist in the growth and development of urban communities and metropolitan areas, so that they provide decent housing, a suitable living environment, and expanding economic opportunities. HUD's programs include Community Planning Development, Housing Production and Mortgage Credit, Federal Disaster Assistance, and Federal Insurance. It is directed by the secretary of Housing and Urban Development. △1358.

Housman, A(lfred) E(dward) (1859–1935), English poet and classical scholar. Although he devoted his life to scholarship, he is best known as the author of two small volumes of poetry, *A Shropshire Lad* (1896) and *Last Poems* (1922).

Houston, Samuel (1793–1863), US soldier and statesman, b. Lexington, Va. He lived with the Cherokee Indians for three years, and later took an Indian wife. In the War of 1812, he fought with Andrew Jackson against the Creeks. He was a congressman from Tennessee (1823–27) and governor (1827–29). Moving to Texas, he became commander-in-chief of the Texas army (1835). The successful battle at San Jacinto (1836) against Santa Anna's Mexican army assured his reputation. He was the first president of Texas, serving 1836–38 and 1841–44. When Texas became a state (1845) he was its first senator (1846–59). His pro-Union stance isolated him and when Texas voted to secede (1861), he was removed from office and retired.

Houston, industrial city and port of entry in SE Texas, 25mi (40km) NW of Galveston Bay, connected to the Gulf of Mexico by Houston Ship Canal; seat of Harris co. The largest city in Texas, it served as capital of Republic of Texas 1837–39, 1842–45; ship canal was completed 1914 and city developed as a deepwater port. Coastal oil fields, natural gas, sulfur, salt, limestone for chemical production, demand for shipbuilding in WWII, and est. of NASA's Manned Space Center led to Houston's tremendous growth. It is the site of World Trade Center (1962), Houston International Airport (1969), Manned Space Center (1961), Astrodome (1965), Rice University (1891), Texas Southern University (1927), University of Houston (1934), University of St Thomas (1947), Sam Houston Historical Park. Exports: petroleum products, cotton, rice, lumber. Industries: oil and oil refining, natural gas, synthetic rubber, meat packing, printing, publishing, sugar and rice processing, agriculture, chemicals, steel, electronic equipment, oil well machinery. Founded 1836 and named for Sam Houston; inc. and made co seat 1837. Pop. (1970) 1,232,802.

Hovercraft. △1682.

Hover Fly. △492.

Howard, prominent English family, particularly in the Tudor era; dukes of Norfolk and earls of Surrey. John Howard was named 1st duke of Norfolk by Richard III (1483). He was killed at Bosworth (1485). His son (1443–1524) and grandson (1473–1554), both called Thomas, conquered the Scots at Flodden (1513). Thomas II's son, Henry, Earl of Surrey, was executed on trumped-up treason charges (1542). The fourth duke (1536–72) also was executed for treason. Catherine Howard married Henry VIII.

Howard, Bronson Crocker (1842–1908), US playwright, b. Detroit. He founded the first professional association of playwrights. He was one of the earliest Americans to write dramas about life in the United States, and his play *Saratoga* (1870) was influential in making this theme fashionable. His numerous comedies and dramas included *Moorcroft* (1874), *The Banker's Daughter* (1878), *One of Our Girls* (1885), *Met by Chance* (1887), and *Aristocracy* (1892).

Howard, Catherine (1520?–42), fifth queen of Henry VIII, granddaughter of Thomas, 2nd duke of Norfolk. Henry married her in July 1540, but evidence of premarital unchastity was produced against her (November 1541). She was beheaded in February 1542.

Howard, Charles. *See* Carlisle, Charles Howard, earl of.

Howard, Charles, 1st Earl of Nottingham. *See* Nottingham, Charles Howard, 1st Earl of.

Howard, Frederick, 5th Earl of Carlisle (1748–1825), English politician and writer. One of the commissioners sent to America by Lord North in 1778, he tried to reconcile the Colonies with England. He was viceroy of Ireland (1780–82) and guardian of Lord Byron (1798). In addition to writing political tracts, he also was the author of a group of poems and two tragedies.

Howard, Oliver Otis (1830–1909), US military leader, b. Leeds, Maine. He fought in the battles of Bull Run, Fair Oaks (where he lost his right arm), Antietam, Fredericksburg, Chancellorsville (where he was defeated by Stonewall Jackson), and Gettysburg. As commander of the Army of the Tennessee, he accompanied Sherman's troops through Georgia. At the war's close, he headed the Freemen's Bureau during Reconstruction, that helped and protected Southern blacks. He was a founder and president (1869–73) of Howard University, superintendent of the US Military Academy at West Point (1881–82), and directed campaigns against the Indians.

Howard, Sidney Coe (1891–1939), US playwright, b. Oakland, Calif. A master of play construction and characterization, his first successful play, *They Knew What They Wanted* (1925), the story of an elderly husband and his young wife, won a Pulitzer Prize. Other plays include the Freudian drama *The Silver Cord* (1926); *Alien Corn* (1933), about an artist in a hostile community; *Yellow Jack* (1934), dramatizing the battle against yellow fever; an adaptation of Sinclair Lewis' novel *Dodsworth*, about the marital difficulties of a prosperous US businessman on a European tour; and *Paths of Glory* (1935). He also wrote the screenplay for the film *Gone with the Wind* (1939), a Civil War drama.

Howard University, federally aided university in Washington, D.C., administered by the Department of Health, Education, and Welfare. It was established in 1867, and offers instruction in 17 colleges and schools. It is jointly supported by congressional appropriations and private funds. The university admits students regardless of sex, race, creed, or color but has a special responsibility for the training of black students.

Howe, Elias (1819–67), US inventor, b. Spencer, Mass. Trained as a machinist, he invented the sewing machine. His first patent was in 1846, but it was 1854 before he cleared his titles legally and became wealthy from his invention. In the Civil War, he served as a private and used his own money to support the regiment.

Howe, Gordie (1928–), Canadian ice hockey player. He scored 786 goals while playing for the Detroit Red Wings (1946–71) in the National Hockey League. He came out of retirement (1973) to play for Houston of the World Hockey Association, along with his two sons, and was a standout in the new league.

Howe, Julia Ward (1819–1910), US author, lecturer, and suffragist, b. New York City. She is best known as author of the "Battle Hymn of the Republic," which first appeared in the *Atlantic Monthly* during the Civil War. In 1843 she married the Boston educator Samuel Gridley Howe. She was an active campaigner for women's rights, and also wrote books, stories, and poems.

Howe, Richard Howe, Earl (1726–99), British admiral. After notable service in the Rochefort expedition (1757) and at Quiberon Bay (1759), he commanded the British navy in North America early in the American Revolution, supporting his brother, Gen. William Howe. He won the famous First of June naval victory (1794) against the French and was appointed admiral of the fleet in 1796.

Howe, Samuel Gridley (1801–76), US educator of the blind, b. Boston. He first received blind students as pupils in his father's house on Pleasant Street in Boston. This was the beginning of the now famous Perkins School for the Blind, of which he was first director (1832–76). He also took an interest in the treatment of mentally defective children and campaigned for prison reform and abolition of slavery. His wife was Julia Ward Howe, author of "The Battle Hymn of the Republic" and active in the woman suffrage movement and in movements for international peace.

Howe, William Howe, Fifth Viscount (1729–1814), British general. Despite his disagreement with the British policy in North America, he was sent to Boston (1775) and fought in the Battle of Bunker Hill. From 1775 to 1778 he commanded British forces in North America, scoring some successes. Lack of sup-

Hottentot fig

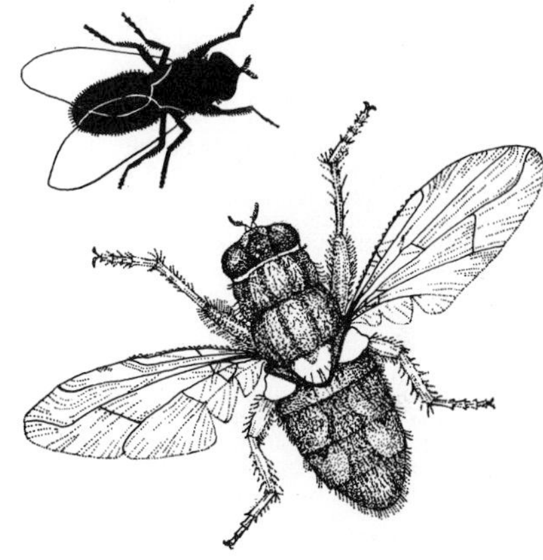

Housefly

Sam Houston

Julia Ward Howe

port from Britain led him to resign (May 1778). △1218.

Howells, William Dean (1837–1920), US novelist and critic, pioneer of American literary realism, b. Martins Ferry, Ohio. As assistant editor (1866–71) and editor (1871–81) of *The Atlantic Monthly*, Howells promoted the works of Henry James, Mark Twain, and others. *Their Wedding Journey* (1872) and *A Chance Acquaintance* (1873), two of the first realistic novels of ordinary middle-class life in the United States, brought little critical reaction, but *The Rise of Silas Lapham* (1885), his best known work, brought national recognition. In the "Editor's Study" (1886–91) and the "Easy Chair" (1900–20) of *Harper's* magazine, his essays and criticisms continued to promote European and American realist writers.

Some of Howells' novels that depict American life include *A Modern Instance* (1882), *Indian Summer* (1886), *A Hazard of New Fortunes* (1890), and *The Quality of Mercy* (1892). His socialist sympathies are reflected in the novels *A Traveler from Altruia* (1894) and *Through the Eye of the Needle* (1907). At the time of his departure from *The Atlantic Monthly* in 1881, Howells was one of the most influential figures in American literary life, but long before his death he was considered out of fashion, his realism genteel, and his optimism unjustified. *See also* Realism.

Howitzer, a projectile-firing artillery piece that, because of its low muzzle velocity, is capable of curved fire and hence may reach targets hidden to high-velocity guns. Howitzers were first used in the late 16th century. △1734.

Howland Island, island in W central Pacific Ocean, E of the Gilbert Islands and NW of Phoenix Islands; a US possession; site of airport, guano deposits. Area: 1sq mi (approx. 3sq km).

Howler Monkey, Central and South American monkey noted for the loud penetrating call of the male. The largest New World monkeys, they are gregarious tree dwellers and feed chiefly on leaves. Height: to 36in (91cm); weight: to 20lb (9kg). Genus *Alouatta*. *See also* Monkey. △602.

Howrah, city in E India, on Hooghly River opposite Calcutta; seat of Howrah district. Industries: iron, steel, food processing, textiles, jute. Pop. 599,740.

Hoxha, Enver (1908–), Albanian Communist leader. Educated in French schools, he taught French until his articles criticizing the Albanian government led to his dismissal from his post in 1934. Hoxha led the underground resistance movement to the 1939 Italian invasion and occupation and in 1941 established the National Liberation Front. In 1946, when Albania became a people's republic, he became premier. Hoxha resigned the premiership in 1954 to become first secretary of the central committee. In 1960 Hoxha quarreled with Russia and led his country into a close relationship with the People's Republic of China.

Hoyle, Edmond (1672–1769), English writer on card games. His works became widely accepted as the highest authority on the games. His *A Short Treatise on the Game of Whist* (1742) and his treatises on backgammon and chess are still used. His name in the expression "according to Hoyle" is also still used to convey a sense of authority.

Hoyle, (Sir) Fred (1915–), British astronomer and cosmologist. He worked with Thomas Gold and Hermann Bondi on the development of the steady-state theory at Cambridge, subsequently (1966) becoming director of the Institute of Theoretical Astronomy. He held academic posts in the United States and also wrote several books, including science-fiction novels. *See also* Steady-State Theory. △48.

Hoysala (*c.* 1100–1326), Indian dynasty that ruled the southern Deccan and Cauvery Valley. Vishnuvardhana won much territory, but his weak son Narasimha I lost it. His grandson Ballala II came to his aid. The dynasty's strength or weakness depended greatly upon the individual on the throne rather than a structure of rule. △1036.

Hradec Králové, city in N Czechoslovakia, 60mi (97km) E of Prague, on Elbe River; capital of Východočeský district. Prosperous area during Middle Ages, it suffered during the Hussite and Thirty Years wars; made a bishopric 1653; scene of the nearby Battle of Königgrätz (1866). It is the site of two medieval marketplaces, 14th-century town hall and cathedral, 17th-century palace, medical school (1946). Industries: photographic equipment, musical instruments, chemicals, machinery. Founded 10th century. Pop. 66,744.

H-R Diagram. *See* **Hertzsprung-Russell Diagram.**

Hrdlička, Aleš (1869–1943), US physical anthropologist, b. Bohemia. He made extensive studies of North American human antiquity and founded the *American Journal of Physical Anthropology* in 1918, which he edited until 1942.

Hsi (Si or West River), river in S China; rises in Yunnan prov. at confluence of the Hungshui and Yu (Siang) rivers; flows generally E through Kwangsi and Kwangtung provs. to South China Sea at Canton, forming a vast delta with the Chu (Pearl) River. The delta is a rich agricultural and densely populated area. River is navigable for most of its 1,250mi (2,013km).

Hsia Dynasty (2205?–1766? BC), the legendary earliest period of dynastic rule in China. △968.

Hsian (Xi'an), city in central China, 80mi (129km) N of the confluence of the Wei and Yellow rivers; capital of Shensi prov. Formerly called Hsien-yang, capital of China under Shih Hwang Ti (247–210 BC); it was called Changan under the Western Han dynasty (202 BC–AD 9), and Siking under the Tiang dynasty (618–906). It was the first seat of Buddhism, Judaism, Islam, and Nestorian Christianity in China; Empress Dowager and Emperor Kuang Hsü fled to Hsian after the Boxer Rebellion (1900–02). Chiang Kai-shek kidnapped here (1936), resulting in agreement for united front with the Communists. It is the site of Northwestern University (1937), Northwestern Institute of Technology (1960); within city walls (1368–1644), there are many notable palaces, temples, and historical ruins. Industries: textiles, iron, steel, thermoelectricity, cotton, chemicals, cement. Pop. 1,900,000.

Hsiang (Siang), navigable river in SE central China; rises in NE Kwangsi Chuang, flows N into Tung-t'ing Hu Lake; a N-S trade route; highly developed agricultural valley. Mineral resources include coal, antimony, and lead. Length: 715mi (1,151km).

Hsiangt'an (Xiangtan), port city in SE China, 20mi (32km) SSW of Ch'angsha, on Siang River; Mao Tse-tung was born nearby. Industries: tea processing, rice, cotton, herbs, coal mining. Pop. 300,000.

Hsinchu, city in NW Taiwan, Republic of China, 40mi (64km) SW of T'aipei; commercial center. Industries: oil refining, fertilizers, textiles, agriculture. Founded early 18th century by Chinese settlers from mainland. Pop. 201,678.

Hsining (Xining), city in W China, approx. 100mi (161km) NW of Lanchow on Hsining River; capital of Tsinghai prov. Industrial growth was spurred by completion of highway to rich Tsaidam basin, and by the completion of railroad system 1959; distribution center for agricultural produce. Industries: chemicals, machinery, flour milling, meat packing, textiles, coal mining. Pop. 250,000.

Hsüan Tsung (685–762), Chinese emperor (reigned 713–56) of the T'ang dynasty. Also known as Ming Huang ("The Enlightened Emperor"), he provided the empire with one of its most important periods of wealth, grandeur, and cultural brilliance. His rule is known as the golden age of Chinese poetry. He abdicated when confronted by revolts.

Hsüchou (Xuzchou), city in E central China, 175mi (282km) W of Yellow Sea; transportation center. Industries: iron and coal mining, steel, tools, food processing. Pop. 1,500,000.

Hsun-tzu (*fl.* 298–238 BC), Chinese philosopher. In reaction to Confucian idealization of the past, he held that mankind is essentially unchanged throughout time, and that human nature is basically evil. △1040.

Hsü Shên (AD 55?–149), author of the first Chinese dictionary. Although he employed a complicated system of character arrangement, he ended the chaos created by the absence of a dictionary. His work also helped Chinese writers to understand their language heritage.

HUAC. *See* Un-American Affairs Committee.

Huai (Hwai), river in E China; rises in the Tungpeh Mts; flows into the Yellow River; irrigates a rich agricultural region. Length: 350mi (564km).

Huainan, city in E China, approx. 110mi (177km) NW of Nanking; China's major coal mining center. Founded 1949. Pop. 350,000.

Hua Kuo-feng (*c.* 1918–), Chinese political leader; premier, chairman of the Military Commission, and chairman of the Communist party of the People's Republic of China (1976–). When Teng Hsia-ping was ousted as prime minister in early 1976, he was replaced by Hua, a party functionary then almost unknown in the West. After the death of Mao Tse-tung later that year, it became known that Hua had also been named chairman of the party, thereby making him, in effect, the successor to both Mao and Chou En-lai.

Huálapai, Yuman-speaking tribe of North American Indians living along the upper Colorado River east to Peach Springs, Ariz. They are closely related to the Yávapai and Havasupai. Never more than 1,000 persons, today they are mainly stock raisers, with a population of approximately 700 living on the Huálapai Reservation.

Huancayo, city in S central Peru, 125mi (201km) E of Lima; capital of Junín dept.; agricultural center; predominantly Indian population; site of church (1617) and many examples of colonial architecture. Industries: silver, copper, and coal mining; potatoes, wheat, maize, Indian textiles. Pop. 91,200.

Huangho. *See* Yellow River.

Huangshih, city in China, on Yangtze River. Industries: iron, steel, cement, building materials, textiles, food processing. Founded 1950. Pop. 200,000.

Huari, also Wari, an important prehistoric cultural period in Peru, named for a major archeological site in the Mantaro Basin. The Huari Empire lasted from about AD 600–1000, and exerted considerable influence throughout the Peruvian region.

Huáscar (*c.* 1495–1533), son of Huayna Capac, who became emperor at his father's death. He controlled northern Peru at the time of Pizarro's arrival but shared the empire with his younger half brother Atahualpa who rebelled against him and had him murdered.

Huayna Capac (died 1525), last of the great Inca rulers (1493–1525), restored order to an empire torn by civil war (1511–12). He died on the eve of the Spanish conquest; his realm was divided between his two sons, Atahualpa and Huáscar.

Hubble, Edwin Powell (1889–1953), US astronomer, b. Marshfield, Mo. Educated at Chicago and Oxford universities, he worked at Mount Wilson Observatory from 1919. The first to state formally that galactic nebulae were galaxies outside the Milky Way, he also detected and studied their recession. △46, 112, 122.

Hubble Constant, ratio of the velocity of recession of a galaxy to its distance. All galaxies beyond the Local Group are receding from us and from each other, as indicated by their red shifts, the velocity increasing with distance. The limit of the observable universe should thus occur when the recessional velocity equals the velocity of light. Assuming that the Hubble constant holds at very large distances this limit is about 10 billion (10^{10}) light-years. If the rate of expansion of the universe has always been constant the Hubble constant gives the age of the universe as about 10^{10} years. △112, 122.

Hubble's Variable Nebula. △46.

Hubertusburg, Peace of, treaty ending the Seven Years War between Prussia and Austria in 1763. Through this agreement, Prussia supported the succession of Joseph II to the imperial throne. In return, Prussia was awarded Silesia and gained considerable control over German politics.

Hubris, in Greek mythology and literature, the wanton arrogance or presumptuousness of spirit that led to insolent disregard of moral laws and restraints. The wrath of the gods, personified by Nemesis, would inevitably descend upon the guilty.

Huckleberry, shrub native to North America with oval leaves, bell-shaped flowers, and dark-blue berries. Family Ericaceae; genus *Gaylussacia*.

Huckleberry Finn, The Adventures of (1884), novel by Mark Twain, a more serious and accomplished sequel to *Tom Sawyer*, which combines adventure with social comment on pre-Civil War Mississippi Valley life and the moral problems that confront a young boy. The novel, considered to be Twain's most characteristic in character, plot, and style, and his finest, is regarded by some critics as the greatest American novel. The story is narrated by Huck Finn, who flees his drunken father and his confining life with Widow Douglas and Miss Watson.

Huck meets Miss Watson's runaway slave, Jim, and together they travel down the Mississippi River on a raft, encountering numerous adventures and giving shelter to two confidence men, one of whom sells Jim. Huck and Tom Sawyer attempt to rescue Jim, but it develops that Miss Watson has meanwhile died, freeing Jim in her will. Huck's father has also died, leaving intact his son's fortune, but Huck plans to leave again, lest Aunt Sally attempt to "sivilize" him. *See also* Tom Sawyer, The Adventures of. △1374.

HUD. *See* Housing and Urban Development, Department of.

Huddersfield, city in N central England, in West Yorkshire. Industries: wool, textiles. Pop. 130,964.

Hudibrastic Verse, couplet written in the same mock heroic meter and tone that was first employed by Samuel Butler in his satirical poem *Hudibras* (1663). *See also* Heroic Couplet; Mock Epic.

Hudson, Henry (died 1611), English navigator and explorer. During his last four years he led several expeditions in search of a passage to China. On his first trip he reached Newland (Spitsbergen), opening up fisheries there to England. On a third trip (1609) he reached the American coast, sailed up the river that bears his name, opening up the area for later trade. On a fourth trip, he passed through the strait which bears his name and entered the inland sea (Hudson Bay). In 1611 he was set adrift by an angry crew and never heard from again.

Hudson Bay, inland bay in E Northwest Territories, Canada; bound on E by Quebec, S by Ontario, SW by Manitoba. Part of Northwest Territories, the bay contains Southampton, Mansel, and Coats islands; many rivers drain into the bay, including Churchill and Nelson; navigable July–October. Explored by Henry Hudson in 1610. Length: 850mi (1,369km). Width: 650mi (1,047km).

Hudson River, river in E New York state; rises near Mt Marcy in the Adirondacks and flows S to New York Bay at New York City. Discovered 1524 by Giovanni da Verrazano and explored 1609 by Henry Hudson, it has become one of the most important waterways of the world. Ocean vessels can navigate to Albany. Divisions of the New York State Barge Canal connect the Hudson with Lake Champlain, the Great Lakes, and the St Lawrence River. The lower end of the river is flanked on the W by the Catskill Mts, passing such points of interest as West Point, Hyde Park, and Bear Mt. Length: approx. 315mi (507km).

Hudson River School, group of US landscape artists active between 1825 and 1875. They were so named because many painted romantic scenes of the Hudson River Valley. Among the most famous of this group were Thomas Cole, John Kensett, George Inness, and Asher Brown Durand.

Hudson's Bay Company, corporation chartered in 1670 by Charles II of England to promote trade and settlement in the Hudson Bay region of North America and to seek a northwest passage to the Orient. The company concentrated on the fur trade, establishing coastal forts, such as Fort Albany (1678) and Fort Churchill (1717), for this purpose. Intense French competition ended after Canada was awarded to Britain in 1763, but the new North West Company based in Montreal proved a formidable adversary. Both companies opposed the Earl of Selkirk's plan to settle the Red River area and were involved in the fighting in that area between 1812–16. The two companies were forced to merge in 1821 under the older name. Until 1856 the company monopolized western Canada. A government investigation of the company in 1857 led to its reorganization and refinancing in 1863. In 1869 it lost its right to govern territories and much of its land to the newly created government of Canada. The sale of land to settlers and the railroads allowed the company to expand into many diverse businesses and industries. In 1930 the huge conglomeration was forced to split up and divest. The fur company remained centered in London. The stores and other businesses still retained were incorporated in Canada. It remains one of the chief business firms in Canada. △1200.

Hudson Strait, strait in NE Canada, between S Baffin Island and N Quebec; connects Hudson Bay with Atlantic Ocean and Foxe Channel; passageway to the Arctic Ocean. Length: 450mi (724km).

Hué, city on E coast of Vietnam, on Hué River; former capital of Annam; market and rice trade center with rail connections; site of University of Hué (1957), airport, and nearby naval station. Founded *c.* 3rd century, the city was occupied by Chams and Annamese; it was a dynastic seat after 16th century. First Vietnamese king was crowned here 1802; city was taken by French 1883 and occupied WWII by Japanese; scene of postwar struggle for independence from French. Much of the city was destroyed during long and heavy fighting (esp. Tet offensive 1968) during Vietnam War, but is being reconstructed. Pop. 156,-537.

Huelva, city in SW Spain, 53mi (85km) WSW of Seville on the Odiel River; capital of Huelva prov.; site of Roman aqueduct, and monastery where Christopher Columbus lived before crossing the Atlantic (1492). Exports: cork, sulfur, copper. Industries: fishing, petrochemicals, tourism. Area: (prov.) 3,894sq mi (10,085sq km). Pop. (city) 96,689; (prov.) 397,683.

Huerta, Adolfo de la (*c.*1882–1955), Mexican politician and diplomat. A leader of the movement opposed to the re-election of Porfirio Díaz, Huerta became provisional president of Mexico in 1920. He led an unsuccessful revolt against Obregón and Calles (1923–24).

Huerta, Victoriano (1854–1916), Mexican general and president (1913–14). Instructed by President Francisco Madero to suppress the revolt led by Félix Díaz, Huerta instead joined forces with the rebels. Madero was arrested and killed; Huerta became president. Defeated by the Constitutionalists led by Carranza, Huerta fled to the United States.

Huggins, Charles Brenton (1901–), US physician, b. Halifax, Nova Scotia. He shared the 1966 Nobel Prize in physiology or medicine with F.P. Rous for his pioneering work in cancer chemotherapy and his development of ways of investigating and treating cancers through the use of hormones.

Hugh Capet (*c.*938–96), king of France (987–96), founder of the Capetian dynasty. Hugh inherited the title of duke of the Franks from his father Hugh the Great in 956. He allied himself (978–86) with the German emperors against the Carolingian king of France, Lothair. In 987 he was elected king of France on the death of Lothair's son Louis V, the last Carolingian king of France. Although his election was disputed by Charles I of Lower Lorraine, he was able to fix the succession on his son, who became Robert II.

Hughes, Charles Evans (1862–1948), US secretary of state and chief justice of the US Supreme Court (1930–41), b. Glen Falls, N.Y. He achieved national prominence as counsel for the state committees investigating abuses in New York gas utilities and insurance companies (1905–06). Twice governor of New York (1907–10), he was appointed by President Taft as associate justice of the Supreme Court (1910–16). He was the Republican presidential candidate (1916) but lost to Woodrow Wilson. He served as secretary of state under Presidents Harding and Coolidge (1921–25). He organized the Washington Conference on Armaments and negotiated over 50 treaties with foreign nations. He was a member of the Permanent Court of Arbitration (1926–30) and judge of the Permanent Court of International Justice (1928–30). Appointed chief justice by President Hoover, he was a moderate conservative. He upheld constitutional liberties and freedom of the press, but restrained judicial power over administrative agencies. His rulings against the National Recovery Administration and other New Deal agencies prompted President Roosevelt to try and increase the number of justices (1937).

Hughes, Howard Robard (1905–76), U.S. industrialist, aviator, and motion picture producer, b. Houston. He inherited (1925) an industrial corporation from his father who had invented a widely used cone-shaped oil drill. In 1935 he set the world speed record of 352 mph (566 kph) in an airplane of his own design. Subsequently he became one of the richest men in America, heading the Summa Corp. (formerly the Hughes Tool Co.), the Hughes Aircraft Co., and other companies. In the 1930s and 40s he occasionally produced motion pictures. The last 20 years of his life were lived in almost total seclusion.

Hughes, Langston (1902–67), US author, b. Joplin, Mo. He gained notice during the Harlem Renaissance, his first book of poems, *The Weary Blues,* appearing in 1926. A prolific poet, short-story writer, playwright, and novelist, his works deal with black life in America and combine racial pride and protest. In addition to 10 books of poetry, he is noted for the "Simple" stories, sketches concerning a black Everyman. *See also* Harlem Renaissance. △1420.

Hugh the Great (died 956), duke of the Franks, son of Robert, Count of Paris. Hugh held vast lands between the Seine and Loire rivers and was suzerain of Normandy and Burgundy. He helped to elect the

Howler monkey

Hudson River, New York

Howard Hughes

Langston Hughes

Carolingian Louis IV king, but fought him when Louis tried to assert his independence. He was the father of Hugh Capet, who became the first Capetian king of France.

Hugo, Victor (1802–85), French poet, dramatist, and novelist. He received a pension from Louis XVIII for his first collection of *Odes* (1822) and presented his manifesto of Romanticism in the *Préface de Cromwell* (1827). Later works include the plays *Hernani* (1830) and *Ruy Blas* (1838) and the novels *Notre Dame de Paris* (1831) and *Les Misérables* (1862). He led the Romantic and later the Humanitarian movement until the death of his daughter in 1843 caused a 10-year cessation of writing, and political convictions sent him to voluntary exile in the Channel Islands (1852–70). Returning to Paris on the fall of the Second Empire, he became a senator and received widespread recognition and respect. △1238–40.

Huguenots, French Protestants of the 16th–18th centuries. The Reformation began in France shortly after it did in Germany (1517). Persecution of Protestants then started, and many, including John Calvin, fled France. Although persecuted in France, Protestantism spread and gained supporters among the aristocracy. In 1560, Protestant nobles led by Louis I de Bourbon, prince de Condé, attempted to seize power, but many of the rebels were killed. In 1562 tension between the Roman Catholics and Protestants touched off the Wars of Religion, which lasted until 1598 and included the St Bartholomew's Day Massacre of Protestants (1572). When the Protestant Henry IV ascended to the throne (1589), he found that he could pacify his kingdom only by converting to Catholicism (1593) and promulgating the Edict of Nantes (1598). The edict recognized Catholicism as the official religion but gave Protestants considerable rights.

Under Louis XIII (*r.* 1610–43) Protestant rights were gradually reduced, and civil wars broke out again. Louis XIV (*r.* 1643–1715) reaffirmed the remaining Protestant rights in 1643 but later began to withdraw them, and persecution resumed. He revoked the Edict of Nantes in 1685. With their religion once more illegal, hundreds of thousands of Protestants, including many skilled artisans and members of the bourgeoisie, fled France. In the 18th century French public opinion began to turn against persecution of Protestants. In 1789 their full civil rights were restored, and religious equality was guaranteed by the Napoleonic Code of 1802. △1154, 1170.

Hu Han-min (1879–1936), modern Chinese revolutionary leader and close associate of Sun Yat-sen. An early top figure in the ruling Kuomintang, Hu was elected president of the Legislative Yuan in 1928. His arrest by Chiang Kai-shek in 1931 caused a major crisis in the Kuomintang, which led to his eventual release.

Huhehot (Huhehaote), city in N China; capital of Inner Mongolia Autonomous Region. Connected by rail to Peking, it is an important trade and distribution center for NW China. Industries: chemicals, textiles, farm machinery, flour milling, food processing. Pop. 700,000.

Hui Tsung (1082–1135), Chinese emperor (reigned 1101–25). The last emperor of the Northern Sung dynasty, he spent his last decade in captivity. He founded the first imperial Chinese academy of painting, established imperial porcelain kilns, and was an accomplished painter.

Huk (Hukbalahap), peasant revolutionary movement in the Philippines. Originally formed to resist the Japanese in World War II, they soon became Communist oriented. After the war they fought for reforms against the Philippine government. The guerrilla group won much popular support because of the repressive tactics used against them, but they were undermined and largely defeated by the reforms of President Ramón Magsaysay and the surrender and imprisonment of their leader, Luis Taruc, in 1954. The movement revived briefly in 1969–70.

Hulagu Khan. △1112.

Hull, Cordell (1871–1955), US secretary of state under Franklin D. Roosevelt (1933–44), b. Overton co, Tenn. A strong spokesman against totalitarianism, he advocated maximum aid to the Allies. Considered the "Father of the United Nations," he received the Nobel Peace prize (1945). He was member of House of Representatives (1907–21, 1923–31) and authored the first federal income tax law (1913).

Hull, Isaac (1773–1843), US naval officer, b. Derby, Conn. In the War of 1812 he commanded the frigate *Constitution* when it defeated the British warship *Guerrière* in a battle that lasted fewer than 30 minutes. It was the first US naval battle of the war and helped US morale.

Hull, Robert Marvin "Bobby" (1939–), Canadian ice hockey player. He played for the Chicago Black Hawks in the National Hockey League (1957–72) before jumping to Winnipeg in the World Hockey Association (1972) for a $2,750,000 contract package. While in the NHL, he scored 604 goals.

Hull, city in SW Quebec, Canada, on the Ottawa River; seat of Hull co; site of a hydroelectric station. Industries: lumber, iron, steel. Pop. 60,176.

Hull (Kingston-upon-Hull), city in NE England, in Humberside, at mouth of Hull River on Humber estuary; a major seaport and industrial town, among world's leading fishing ports; exports industrial products of Midlands and North; seat of University of Hull. Chartered 1299. Pop. 285,472.

Hull-Nomura Discussions, negotiations between US Sec. of State Cordell Hull and Japanese Ambassador Kichisaburo Nomura in Washington (1941) in an attempt to avoid war. Hull was waiting for Nomura's reply to one of his proposals when the attack on Pearl Harbor began (Dec. 7, 1941).

Human Anatomy. *See* Anatomy.

Human Development. △776.

Humanism, a philosophical viewpoint that stresses human reason as a source of authority and strives for human good in the present world. Humanist ideas can be found from ancient to modern times, but the flowering of humanism came during the Renaissance. Italian scholars of the 14th century began a fresh study of Greek and Latin authors, called the "new learning." Medieval scholars studied the classics to bolster Christian theology. Renaissance men like Petrarch and Vittorini da Feltre studied the classics for their own sake and saw them as means to educate people for their own improvement. The movement spread northward from Italy to include such scholars as Sir Thomas More, Michel de Montaigne, John Calvin, and Desiderius Erasmus. These men were typically skeptical of the authority of the Roman Catholic Church but did not abandon religion. Calvin broke with the Church, but Erasmus remained in it as a reformer. Since the Renaissance a wide variety of thinkers have called themselves humanists. In the 20th century, the New Humanist literary critics reacted against naturalism. Some Christian humanists reject traditional views of God and the church as getting in the way of the well-being of humankind. △1130.

Human Rights, powers, conditions of existence, and possessions to which an individual has a claim or title by virtue of being human. The concept of the inalienable rights of the human being has traditionally been linked to the idea of the higher or natural law. Important commentaries on that idea in earlier times appear in the works of several of the Greek dramatists, the Greek and Roman stoics, early Christian thinkers, Aquinas, medieval English legal scholars, Grotius, Milton, and Locke. The concept of human rights was most notably formulated, however, in the 18th century with the United States Declaration of Independence (1776) and Constitution (1789), with its Bill of Rights (1791), and in the French Declaration of the Rights of Man and of the Citizen (1789). These documents gave new expression and scope to rights proclaimed earlier in such compacts between monarchs and nobles as the English Magna Carta (1215), Petition of Right (1628), and Bill of Rights (1689). Important also in the development of the concept of human rights were the various international agreements during the 19th and 20th centuries aimed at abolishing slavery and the traffic in women and children, alleviating labor conditions, and establishing the laws of war. During its existence the League of Nations (1919–46) attempted to promote the fulfillment of such agreements. Reaction against the horrors of World War II led to such important developments in the field of human rights as the Atlantic Charter (1941), Declaration of the United Nations (1942), and the Charter of the United Nations (1945). The Commission of Human Rights of the UN Economic and Social Council proposed an International Bill of Rights of which the first part, the Universal Declaration of Human Rights, was proclaimed by the UN in 1948.

Human Sacrifice. △1118.

Humayun. △1202.

Humbert I and II, kings of Italy. *See* Umberto I; Umberto II.

Humboldt, (Baron) (Friedrich Heinrich) Alexander von (1769–1859), German scientist and explorer. He made scientific trips in Europe and Central and South America; established the use of isotherms; studied volcanoes, the origins of tropical storms, and the increase in magnetic intensity from the equator toward the poles. His *Cosmos* (5 vols., 1845–62) is a classic scientific work. △234–36, 1186.

Humboldt, (Baron) Wilhelm von (1767–1835), German statesman and writer. A civil servant, Humboldt reformed the Prussian educational system and was instrumental in the founding of the University of Berlin (1810). He was the author of important works on aesthetics and political theory. Humboldt is best remembered for his contributions to philology and linguistic philosophy. He was the brother of the naturalist Alexander von Humboldt.

Humboldt Current, a cold ocean current of the South Pacific that flows north along the northern coast of Chile and Peru to southern Ecuador with a width of 550 miles (885 km). It is slow and shallow, transporting 525,000,000 cu ft (14,857,000 cu meters) of water per second. There is rich plankton growth, making this among the world's greatest fishing grounds for anchovies and tuna.

Hume, David (1711–76), philosopher, historian, and man of letters, b. Edinburgh, Scotland. Hume left Scotland in 1734 and lived thereafter in London and Paris. His remarkably original *A Treatise of Human Nature* (1739–40) initially was a literary failure. More successful were his *History of England* (1754–62) and various essays and philosophical "inquiries." He also held a succession of minor official posts and traveled extensively. Widely known for his humanitarianism and skepticism, Hume held a form of empiricism that affirmed the contingency of all phenomenal events. The posthumous *Dialogues Concerning Natural Religion* (1779) indicates the extent of his atheism. △856–58.

Humectant, substance such as glycerol, which has an affinity for water, added to stabilize moisture content. Humectants are used in cosmetic moisturizing creams, and in products such as tobacco, in which a certain moisture content has to be maintained.

Humerus, upper arm bone, extending from the scapula, or shoulder blade, to the elbow. The rounded head of the humerus joins with the scapula at the glenoid cavity. A notch, or depression, called the olecranon cavity, on the posterior roughened lower end of the humerus provides the point of articulation for the ulna, one of the forearm bones. △682.

Humidity, or relative humidity, a measure of the water-vapor content of air, the ratio of the actual vapor pressure to the saturation vapor pressure, at which water normally condenses, usually expressed in percentage and measured by a hygrometer. *See also* Hygrometer. △212, 216.

Hummingbird, brightly colored New World birds that are the smallest of all birds. Mostly tropical, their almost invisible, rapid wing beats create a humming noise. They have narrow heads, short weak legs, long slender bills, and long, bushy-tipped protractile tongues with two tubes for sucking nectar from flowers. Unmatched by any bird in flying ability, they can fly slowly or quickly, up or down, back and forth, or hover. During courtship, males perform spectacular aerial displays. The female builds a delicate cup nest of plant down, moss, and saliva for her eggs (2). Length: 2.25in (6cm)–8.5in (21.6cm). Family Trochilidae. △526, 528, 530, 602.

Hummingbird Moth. *See* Hawk Moth.

Humpback Whale, whalebone whale worldwide in distribution. Long knobby flippers and rounded back characterize this humpback whale. Height: 40ft (12m); weight: 32tons. Genus *Megaptera*. △624.

Humperdinck, Engelbert (1854–1921), German music teacher and composer. He is chiefly remembered for his first opera, *Hansel and Gretel* (1893), based on Grimm's *Fairy Tales*, a phenomenal success in its day. His only other successful opera was *Die Königskinder*, which was introduced at the Metropolitan Opera in New York City in 1910. △1246.

Humphrey, Duke of Gloucester. *See* Gloucester, Humphrey, Duke of.

Humphrey, Hubert H(oratio) (1911–), US vice president and senator, b. Wallace, S.D. He served as mayor of Minneapolis, Minn. (1945–49). With Democrat and Farmer-Labor party support, he then entered the US Senate. He was elected vice president in 1964 on a ticket with President Lyndon B. Johnson. When Johnson decided not to run for reelection in 1968, he won the Democratic presidential nomination despite opposition from those who were upset by his participation in the escalation of the Vietnam War. He lost the election to Richard Nixon. In 1970, he was reelected to the Senate. He was an unsuccessful contender for the Democratic presidential nomination in 1972.

Humphrey's Executor v. United States (1935), US Supreme Court decision ruling that the president had no power to remove federal agency commissioners except for good cause shown. The court limited the holding of *Myers v. United States* (1926) and rejected its dictum.

Humus. △312.

Hunan, province in SE central China, S of Tung Ting Lake; capital is Changsha; birthplace of Mao Tse-tung. Industries: coal, tungsten, antimony and zinc mining; rice, tea, oilseed, wheat, beans, cement, electrical equipment, tools. Area: 80,000sq mi (207,200sq km). Pop. 38,000,000.

Hunchback of Notre Dame, The (1831), novel by Victor Hugo, published as *Notre Dame de Paris*. Esmerelda, a gypsy dancer, kidnapped for Archdeacon Frollo by Quasimodo, the hunchback bell-ringer, is ultimately hanged for Frollo's own crime, after which Quasimodo hurls Frollo from the cathedral.

Hundred Days (March 4–June 16, 1933), first days of the New Deal. During this period following his inauguration, Pres. Franklin D. Roosevelt proposed and Congress approved many of the New Deal bills designed to bring economic relief and recovery from the Depression. Banks and businesses were regulated, aid was given to farmers and homeowners, and programs were initiated to provide work for the unemployed. *See also* New Deal.

Hundred Schools, term referring to the classical period of Chinese philosophy (551–233 BC). The primary concern of the many philosophical schools of the late Chou period was ethics. Of the reputed "hundred schools," six were to prove historically significant, and of these, only Confucianism has had central importance in Chinese history. *See also* Confucianism.

Hundred Years War, hostilities between France and England pursued, with some interruptions, between 1337 (French seizure of English-held Guyenne) and 1453 (English defeat at Castillon). The refusal of Edward III of England to pay feudal homage for his French territories began the war, the first phase of which saw English successes at Crécy (1346) and Calais (1347). As ransom for the French king, captured in 1356, England forced considerable territorial concessions (1360). Richard II desired peace, but French determination to eject the English gradually won them back their ceded territories. Henry V temporarily arrested this trend at Agincourt (1415) and with the Treaty of Troyes (1420). Subsequent English failure at the siege of Orléans (1428–29) and the Battle of Patay (1429), through Joan of Arc's intervention, ensured their ultimate expulsion from French soil. △1096.

Hungary, independent nation of central Europe. It is a member of the Communist bloc but has historical ties to W European culture.

Land and Economy. Its landlocked frontiers were marked after WWI, and Hungary is bordered NE by the USSR, N by Czechoslovakia and the Danube River, E by Romania, W by Austria and Yugoslavia. Mostly a flat plain, the Alfold (Great Plain), the country is divided by a highland running NE to W. Hungary had a predominantly agricultural economy before WWII; it was subsequently heavily industrialized. The farm labor force has fallen from 50% in 1950 to 30%; the country is self-sufficient in agriculture. Hungary is dependent on imports for raw materials, mostly from the USSR. Major enterprises are either state-owned or cooperatives. Economic reforms produced greater freedom of production, pricing, wage increases, and financial rewards.

People. Ancestors of modern Hungarians came from the Russian steppes between the Volga and the Urals, displacing the Huns and Avar peoples. Culturally and physically Hungarians are a mixture of Magyar (major), Slovak, Ruthene, Romanian, Serb, Croat, and Turk. About 65% of the population is Roman Catholic with Protestant and Greek Orthodox minorities. The large Jewish population, once 6% of the total, was largely eliminated during the WWII German occupation. Literacy is estimated at 98%.

Government. A unicameral elected National Assembly elects the Presidential Council. Candidates for assembly seats and legislation originate in the Hungarian Socialist Workers (Communist) party.

History. The Magyars, founders of Hungary, came from the region between the Volga and the Urals. Driven N early in the Christian era, they lived as vassals in the 5th–9th centuries at the mouth of the Don River. Organized into tribes, they moved W to the mouth of the Danube, and adopted Christianity. With the exception of a short period after WWI, Hungary was a monarchy for 1,000 years. Its brief Communist dictatorship in 1919 was followed by a 25-year regency under Adm. Nicholas Horthy, a regime purged by German occupation in WWII. The Nazis were driven out by the Soviets, and the USSR supported a dictatorship by Communist leader Matyas Rakosi (1947). The violent Hungarian uprising of 1956 erupted against his repressive regime. Moderate Imre Nagy replaced Rakosi; however, Soviet forces crushed the national uprising, Nagy was executed by the Russians, and Janos Kadar became first secretary of the Hungarian Communist party. Some freedoms have been tolerated.

PROFILE

Official name: Hungarian People's Republic
Area: 35,919sq mi (93,030sq km)
Population: 10,500,000
Density: 292 per sq mi (113per sq km)
Chief cities: Budapest (capital), Györ, Miskolc, Debrecen
Government: Communist republic (people's)
Religion: Roman Catholic (major)
Language: Hungarian (official)
Monetary unit: Forint
Gross national product: $19,500,000,000
Per capita income: $1,900
Industries: iron, steel, machines, tools, chemicals, motor vehicles, communication equipment, milling, distilling, pharmaceuticals
Agriculture: corn, wheat, potatoes, grapes
Minerals: bauxite, coal, natural gas
Trading partners: USSR, E Europe

Hung-shui (Hongshui), river in S China. Rising in Kweichow-Yunnan border region, it joins Yü River at Kweihsien to form the West River. Length: 900mi (1,449km).

Hunkers, conservative urban democrats who favored ties between the state chartered banks and federal deposits. The Hunkers opposed Van Buren's Independent Treasury Bill of 1837. Their opposition delayed its becoming law until 1840. The separation of the Hunkers from the Democratic party in New York State was partly responsible for the Whig victory in the 1840 presidential election.

Huns, nomadic Mongol people, probably of Turkish, Tataric, or Ugrian stock, who spread from the Caspian steppes (present-day Soviet Union) to wage a series of wars on the Roman Empire. Lacking the cultural development attributed to more sedentary peoples, they were very skilled in the arts of war, particularly military horsemanship. During the first half of the 4th century, they conquered the Ostrogoths and the Visigoths, coming west to the Danube River. About 432, the Huns were collecting an annual tribute from Rome. Attila moved still further westward to Italy and Gaul, but after his death in 454, the power of the Huns was broken. Many took service in the Roman armies. The rest settled on the lower Danube. △1054.

Hunt, James Henry Leigh (1784–1859), English journalist and poet. His often imitative poetry includes "Abou ben Adhem." He edited the *Examiner* with his brother, John, from 1808–21. They were both imprisoned for two years for attacking the prince regent. He aided John Keats and Percy Shelley and was joint editor with Lord Byron of *The Liberal*. *Autobiography* (1850) contains some of his best writing.

Hunt, Richard Morris (1827–95), US architect, b. Brattleboro, Vt. Influenced by French Gothic and Italian Renaissance style, he is best known for the large town and country houses he built for the wealthy. Examples are "Biltmore" in North Carolina and "The Breakers" in Newport, R.I. He also built the Tribune Building in New York City and the U.S. National Observatory, Washington, D.C. His brother was the painter William Morris Hunt.

Hunt, William Holman. △1252.

Hunter, Catfish (1946–), US baseball player, b. James Augustus Hunter in Hertford, N.C. A right-hand pitcher, he made baseball history when he won his release in a contract dispute with Charles O. Finley, owner of the Oakland Athletics. He then signed a contract with the New York Yankees (1975) for more than $3,000,000.

Alexander Humboldt

Hummingbird

Hubert Humphrey

Denmark
BALTIC SEA
U.S.S.R.
German Democratic Republic
Poland
Federal Republic of Germany
Czechoslovakia
Miskolc
Debrecen
Liech.
Austria
Budapest
HUNGARY
Szeged
Pécs
Yugoslavia
Romania
Italy
0
400 km

Hungary

Hunting-gathering Societies, small-scale societies where the members subsist mainly by hunting and by collecting plants rather than by cultivation. There is a very low subsistence ratio of people to land so the groups are always small bands. Although their technology is extremely simple they have very sophisticated kinship and ritualistic systems. Hunting-gathering societies are most numerous in lowland South America and some parts of Africa. △878–80.

Huntington, Samuel (1731–96), American jurist and a signer of the Declaration of Independence, b. Windham, Conn. Before becoming governor of Connecticut (1786), he served as chief justice of the state's superior court (1784) and as president of the Continental Congress (1779–81).

Huntington, port and largest city in W West Virginia, 48mi (77km) W of Charleston, on Ohio River; seat of Cabell co; transportation, shipping, commercial center for tobacco and fruit. Industries: chemicals, coal, electrical products, handblown glassware. Founded 1871. Pop. (1970) 74,315.

Huntington Beach, city in S California, 14mi (23km) SE of Long Beach; noted for its beaches. Industries: oil refineries, communications, metallurgy, truck farming, food packing. Inc. 1909. Pop. (1970) 115,960.

Huntington Park, suburban city in S California, 4mi (6km) S of Los Angeles. Industries: chemicals, steel castings. Founded 1856; inc. 1906. Pop. (1970) 33,-744.

Huntington's Chorea. *See* Chorea.

Huntsville, city in N Alabama, 23mi (37km) NE of Decatur, seat of Madison co. First settlement in Alabama to receive charter (1811); temporary capital and site of Alabama constitutional convention (1819); burned by Union troops 1862. Industries: sheet metal goods, farm implements, natural gas wells. Settled 1805. Pop. (1970) 137,802.

Hunyàdi, János (1387–1456), Hungarian soldier and national hero. Voivode (governor) of Transylvania (1440); regent for Ladislas V (1446–52). This brilliant general took part in the Hussite Wars and defeated the Turks in several battles. Although many nobles had deserted his army, in 1456 he defeated the Turkish fleet on the Danube River and broke the siege of Belgrade, his greatest achievement.

Hupeh (Hupei, or Hubei), province in central China; capital is Wuhan. Industries: agriculture, iron, steel, silk, cattle, coal, paper. Area: 72,000sq mi (186,480sq km). Pop. 32,000,000.

Hurling, a game similar to field hockey, the national sport of Ireland. It is played outdoors by 2 teams of 15 people each on a field 80 by 140 yards (73 by 127m) with goal posts 16 feet (4.9m) high and 21 feet (6.4m) wide, with a crossbar 8 feet (2.4m) above the ground. Each player carries a 3-foot (0.9-m) field hockey–type stick; the ball used is rubber covered with horsehide, and about 10 inches (25.4cm) in circumference. The object is for the player to catch the ball on the stick, run with it and hurl it toward a teammate or toward the goal he is attacking. The ball may not be picked up or thrown by hand. Three points are scored by getting the ball into the net under the crossbar, one point by hitting it over the crossbar. The sport is governed by the Gaelic Athletic Association, formed in 1884. *See also* Field Hockey.

Hurok, Sol (1888–1974), US impresario, b. Russia, who rose from a peddler and a streetcar conductor (1906) to one of the foremost art forces of his time. During his long career he presented more than 4,000 artists including Marian Anderson, Anna Pavlova, the Comédie Française, the Old Vic Company, and Andrés Segovia.

Huron, small confederation of Iroquoian-speaking tribes of North American Indians who once occupied the St Lawrence Valley from Ontario to Georgian Bay. Almost completely annihilated in wars for control of the fur trade with the Iroquois (1650–56) when their population was reduced from 15,000 to about 500 persons, they wandered widely throughout the east, settling finally in Ohio, where they became known as the Wyandot. Others fled to the Great Lakes area, and eventually settled in Kansas. Today, some 1,250 live on reservations in those states and in Ontario, Canada.

Huron, Lake, second-largest of the Great Lakes; forms a boundary between the United States and Canada. Michigan borders its S and W shores; its many islands, attractive shoreline, and clean water make it a popular recreational area. Lake Huron drains Lake Superior and feeds Lake Erie; part of the Great Lakes–St Lawrence Seaway system, carries ocean-going vessels and is subject to violent storms. Étienne Brulé, French explorer, is believed to be the discoverer (1612) of Georgian Bay of Lake Huron; Samuel de Champlain visited Lake Huron in 1615. Area: 23,010sq mi (59,596sq km). Depth: max. 750ft (229m). △206.

Hurricane, an intense and devastating tropical cyclone with winds ranging from 75 to 136 mi (121 to 219 km) per hour and up, known also as a typhoon in the Pacific. Arising over oceans 10 to 20 degrees from the equator, hurricanes have a calm central hole, or eye, surrounded by inward spiraling winds and cumulonimbus clouds, with barometric pressure falling to 28.5 in (72.4 cm) or lower. Storm winds and waves of hurricanes take many lives and cause extensive shipping and coastal damage, but weather satellites usually provide adequate warning of their approach. *See also* Weather Modification. △214–16.

Hurst, Fannie (1889–1968), US author, b. Hamilton, Ohio. A short-story writer and novelist, her works are sentimental tales about women. Her novels include *Lummox* (1923), *Back Street* (1931), and *Imitation of Life* (1933).

Husayn. *See* Husein.

Husayn ibn-Ali (1856–1931), Arabian leader. After 1908 he reigned over Mecca and the Hejaz (a kingdom in NW Arabia), then controlled by Turkey. He revolted successfully against the Turks (1916) and made himself king of Arabia, but Ibn-Saud, ruler of Nejd, defeated him and forced him to abdicate in 1924. After exile in Cyprus (1924–30), he died in Amman, Jordan, the capital of his son, Abdullah. His other son, Faisal I, was king of Iraq. △1380.

Husein or **Husayn** (*c.* 626–80), Muslim leader. He was the second son of Ali and Fatima (Muhammed's daughter). When his older brother Hasan was forced to abdicate as the fifth caliph, Husein was unable to restore his family's claim. Husein and his followers were massacred on Oct. 10, 680, by the Umayyads. The day of his defeat is celebrated as a holy day by the Shiite sect of Muslims, who consider Husein to be a saint and the rightful heir of Muhammad.

Hu Shih (1891–1962), Chinese philosopher, educator, and diplomat. He studied at Columbia University under John Dewey and became an influential teacher at Peking University. From 1938 to 1942 he was ambassador to the United States and from 1946 to 1948 chancellor of Peking University. △1270.

Huss, or **Hus, Jan** (1369?–1415), Bohemian (Czech) religious reformer. A teacher and priest at Prague, he became leader of a reform movement and was influenced by the beliefs of the English reformer John Wycliffe. Huss got into conflict with the pope and other church authorities and was excommunicated. He was treacherously arrested at Constance in 1414 and burned as a heretic the next year.

Hussein I (1935–), king of Jordan (1953–). Educated in England, he succeeded his father who was declared insane. Pro-Western, he was attacked by other Arab leaders, especially President Nasser of Egypt. Political pressure kept Jordan out of the Central Treaty Organization (1955) and forced the dismissal (1956) of Gen. John Bagot Glubb, British commander of the Arab Legion (Jordanian Army). Hussein imposed martial law in 1957. In 1967 he led his country into the Arab-Israeli War and lost all of Jordan west of the Jordan River to Israel. In 1970 he defeated a Palestinian-led civil war, but at the 1974 Arab summit meeting he was forced to relinquish Jordan's claim to west bank Jordan to the Palestinian Liberation Organization.

Husserl, Edmund (1859–1938), German philosopher, known as the founder of the phenomenological movement. He studied man's consciousness as it related to objects and the structure of experience. His work influenced many later philosophers and sociologists. Among his important books are *Ideas: General Introduction to Pure Phenomenology* (1913) and *Cartesian Meditations* (1931).

Hussitism, religious reform and nationalist movement in Bohemia led by John Huss (1369?–1415). A disciple of the English theologian, John Wycliffe, Huss preached in Czech rather than in Latin and opposed the authority of the pope, which led to his excommunication in 1409. Emperor Sigismund urged Huss to attend the Council of Constance in Geneva in 1414 to attempt a conciliation. There he was tried for heresy and burned at the stake. A revolt followed in Bohemia, as much to oppose the prosperous German Catholics and the wealth of the Church as to further religious reform. These Hussite wars (1420–33) strengthened the country's nationalism.

Huston, John (1906–), US film director, writer, and actor, b. Nevada, Mo. He is the son of the actor Walter Huston. His screenplays include *Jezebel* (1939) and *Sergeant York* (1941). Among his directorial credits are *The Maltese Falcon* (1941), *The African Queen* (1951), and *The Misfits* (1960).

Huston, Walter (1884–1950), US actor, b. Walter Houghston in Canada. He began his career in Toronto in vaudeville, coming to New York and appearing in *Mr. Pitt* and *Desire Under the Elms* (both 1924). He played stage roles until 1929, then turned to films. He won the New York Film Critics' Circle Award for his performance in *Dodsworth* (1936). He appeared in most of the early films directed by his son John, winning an Academy Award for his role in *The Treasure of Sierra Madre* (1948).

Hutcheson, Francis (1694–1746), Scottish philosopher. In his best known book, *Inquiry into the Origin of Our Ideas of Beauty and Virtue*, Hutcheson referred to an innate "sense" or "feeling," which distinguished the beautiful and the good. The phrase "the greatest good for the greatest number" utilized by Jeremy Bentham was of his coinage. *See also* Utilitarianism.

Hutchinson, Anne Marbury (1591?–1643), English colonist and religious leader. After settling the Massachusetts Bay Colony (1634) with her family, her ideas of personal apprehension of God's grace conflicted with the Puritan "covenant of works" established by the church and state. Banished by Gov. John Winthrop after a sedition trial (1637), she settled Portsmouth, R.I., with her followers until her husband's death (1642). She then moved to Long Island and then to the Pelham area of New York City where she was killed by Indians.

Hutchinson, city in S central Kansas, on the Arkansas River; seat of Reno co; site of a planetarium, Kansas state fairgrounds, Hutchinson Community College (1928). Industries: grain, livestock, oil. Inc. 1872. Pop. (1970) 36,885.

Hutter, Jacob (d.1536), Austrian Anabaptist and founder of the Hutterites. When Anabaptists in the Tyrol were persecuted, Hutter led three groups into Moravia and established communal styles of living. He was charged with heresy for his beliefs and was burned at the stake at Innsbruck.

Hutterites, German-speaking Anabaptists practicing communal living. The sect originated in Moravia in the 16th century, moved to the Russian Ukraine, and in 1874 to the W United States. Some also live in western Canada. Communities are governed by bishops and preachers. All things are held in common ownership. Family life, simple ways, and pacifism are stressed.

Hutton, James (1726–97), Scottish geologist. At a time when the science of geology did not exist, he sought to formulate theories of the origin of the earth and of atmospheric changes. He concluded that the earth's history could be explained only by observing current forces at work within it and thus laid the foundations of modern geological science. His great work is *Theory of the Earth* (2 vols., 1785, 1795). △268-70.

Huxley, Aldous (Leonard) (1894–1963), English novelist. He abandoned his medical studies, became a journalist and began to satirize the hedonism of the 1920s in novels such as *Crome Yellow* (1921), *Antic Hay* (1923), and *Point Counter Point* (1928). *Brave New World* (1932) presents a nightmarish utopia of the future. Later novels include *Eyeless in Gaza* (1936), *The Devils of Loudun* (1952), and *Island* (1962). *Brave New World Revisited* (1958) is a collection of essays. *See also* Brave New World.

Huxley, Andrew Fielding (1917–), English physiologist. He made significant contributions to an understanding of how a nerve impulse is conducted along a fiber. He shared the 1963 Nobel Prize in physiology or medicine with John C. Eccles and Alan L. Hodgkin for this work.

Huxley, (Sir) Julian Sorell (1887–1975), English biologist, the son of Leonard and brother of Aldous Huxley. Julian's writings and lectures promoted modern evolutionary theory and helped to revive the study of evolution. He served as secretary of the Zoological Society of London (1935–42) and as the director general of UNESCO (1946–48). He is the author of *The Individual in the Animal Kingdom* (1911) and *Heredity, East and West* (1949).

Huxley, Thomas (Henry) (1825–95), English biologist and educator. He was the nineteenth century's leading proponent of Darwinism and agnosticism. Unable to afford a university education, he served in the Royal Medical Service (1846–50). As assistant surgeon on the exploratory ship *HMS Rattlesnake*, he conducted important studies of marine life. For these studies he was elected to the Royal Society in 1851, of which he was president 1883–85. In 1854 he became a lecturer at the Royal School of Mines, with which he would be affiliated until 1885, and was instrumental in its evolving into the Royal College of Science. In an 1860 debate at Oxford University he brilliantly defended Darwinism against an attack led by Bishop Samuel Wilberforce. In the 1870s he was instrumental in reforming the British educational system. His most famous work is *Evolution and Ethics* (1893). He was the grandfather of three noted Huxleys: Andrew (physiologist), Aldous (novelist), Julian (biologist).

Huygens, or **Huyghens, Christian,** name often Latinized as Hugenius (1629–95), Dutch physicist and astronomer. He made numerous contributions to science, notably the first statement of the wave theory of light, the recognition of Saturn's rings, and the use of the pendulum in clocks. △68.

Hyacinth, bulbous plant native to the Mediterranean region and Africa. It has long, thin leaves and spikes of flower clusters. The small flowers may be white, yellow, red, blue, or purple. Family Liliaceae; genus *Hyacinthus.*

Hyades, in Greek mythology, the daughters of Atlas, nymphs placed by Zeus among the stars as reward for the care given the infant Dionysus after the death of his mother Semele. Another story has them mourning for their dead brother Hyas until they are made a constellation. △116.

Hyaline Membrane Disease, disease of newborns, usually premature, in which a glassy membrane lines the alveoli (air cells), alveolar ducts, and bronchioles of the lungs.

Hyaluronidase, protein enzyme that participates in the breakdown of some complex muco-polysaccharides of connective tissue, such as hyaluronic acid. Present in most cells, it is also a constituent of some insect and snake venoms.

Hybrid, the offspring of two true-breeding parents of different gene composition; the cross result of the combination of homozygous parents. △420, 582.

Hybrid Vigor, the inordinate strength demonstrated in some hybrid offspring, not characteristic of the parents.

Hyde, Douglas (1860–1949), Irish nationalist leader and author. A major force in reviving Irish literature through the Gaelic League, of which he was first president (1893–1915), he was chosen first president of Eire (1938–45).

Hyderabad, city in S India, in Musi River valley; capital of Andhra Pradesh state; capital of former state of Hyderabad (1724–1948); site of ancient ruins, Char Minar (1591), and Old Bridge (1593); seat of Osmania University (1918). Industries: tobacco, textiles, machine tools, food processing, furniture. Founded 1589 as capital of Golconda kingdom. Pop. 1,316,-802.

Hyderabad, city in Sind, Pakistan, on Indus River; site of university (1947). Industries: gold and silver embroidery, jewelry, pottery, and textiles. Founded 1768 by Ghulam Shah Kalhora. Pop. 698,100.

Hydra (Idhra or Ydra), Greek island in the Aegean Sea, off E coast of Peloponnesus; mostly rocky terrain; played important role in Greek War of Independence (1812–29). Chief town is Hydra on N coast. Industries: sponge fishing, trading. Pop. (island) 2,766; (town) 2,546.

Hydra, freshwater coelenterate with cylindrical body and six tentacles around its mouth opening. Possessing thread cells that shoot poisonous thread capsules (nematocysts) at prey, they move by gliding or somersaulting. Length: 0.5in (13mm). Reproduction is either sexual or by asexual budding or regeneration. Class Hydrosoa; order Hydroida; species include *Hydra littoralis.* △468.

Hydra, or the Water Monster, extensive equatorial constellation, the largest star group in the sky, situated south of Cancer and Leo to the west and Virgo and Libra to the east. It contains the open cluster M48 (NGC 2548). Brightest star Alpha Hydrae (Alphard). △134.

Hydrangea, primarily deciduous woody shrubs and vines of the saxifrage family, native to the Western Hemisphere and Asia. They are grown for their showy clusters of flowers, which may be white, pink, or blue. Some will change color if iron or alum is fed to the roots.

Hydration, assimilation of water onto an ion, electron, or compound either by weak bonds, as in hydrate formation, or by chemical combination with an unsaturated compound. Gypsum is the hydrate of calcium sulfate, zeolite of feldspar. Ethylene can be hydrated industrially to produce ethanol.

Hydraulic Engineering, a branch of engineering concerned with the principles of fluid flow and their practical application. △1764.

Hydraulic Jack. △1612, 1664.

Hydraulic Mining, methods of surface mining that involve the breaking down of earth or rock by high-pressure jets of water delivered by large nozzles (called hydraulic giants). It is sometimes used in mining terrace placer deposits. Large quantities of water transport loosened materials to sluices where the valuable minerals are recovered in riffles. Also used for removing overburden from iron ore deposits and in alluvial tin mines.

Hydraulic Press. △1606.

Hydraulics, the physical science and technology of the behavior of fluids (usually water or oil) in both static and dynamic states. It deals with practical applications of fluid in motion, such as the flow through pipes, and the design of storage dams, pumps, and water turbines, and devices for utilization and control (nozzles, valves, jets, and flow meters). *See also* Fluid Mechanics; Hydrodynamics. △1496, 1504.

Hydrazine, fuming corrosive liquid ($H_2N{\cdot}NH_2$) obtained by the reaction of sodium hydroxide, chlorine, and ammonia or by the oxidation of urea. It is used as a jet and rocket fuel, in explosives, and as a corrosion inhibitor. Properties: sp gr 1.004, melt. pt. 35.6°F (2.0°C), boil. pt. 236.3°F (113.5°C).

Hydride, chemical compound of hydrogen with another element, especially a more electropositive element. The hydrides of the electropositive metals, such as lithium hydride (LiH), and sodium hydride (NaH), are saltlike ionic compounds containing the negative ion H^-. They are useful reagents for hydrogenation reactions.

Hydrocarbon, organic compound containing only carbon and hydrogen. Many thousands of different hydrocarbons exist; they fall into two main classes, aliphatic and aromatic hydrocarbons. The aliphatic hydrocarbons are mainly open-chain compounds, including such groups as the alkanes (paraffins), the alkenes (olefins), the alkynes (acetylenes), and terpenes. Aromatic hydrocarbons have properties similar to benzene; most contain benzene rings as in naphthalene and anthracene. △1562–64, 1570–72.

Hydrocephalus, accumulation of abnormal amounts of fluid in the cranium, usually because of obstruction or excess production, resulting in reduction of brain size and mental deterioration.

Hydrochloric Acid, or muriatic acid, solution of the pungent colorless gas hydrogen chloride (HCl) in water obtained by the action of sulfuric acid on salt, as a by-product of the chlorination of hydrocarbons, or by the electrolysis of brine. It is widely used in the chemical, food, and metallurgical industries. The concentrated commercial acid contains 38% HCl and has sp gr 1.19. △1566–68.

Hydrodynamics, a branch of fluid mechanics dealing with the motion of fluids and the forces acting on solid bodies immersed in fluids. Practical applications were introduced by Archimedes, but the basic theory was not understood until the 17th century. Later, Leonhard Euler, who recognized that dynamical laws for fluids can be expressed in simple form only if the fluid is assumed to be incompressible, derived the basic equations for a frictionless fluid. Principles are important in nozzle design, flow measurements, and predictions of wing lift in flight. Recent theories have made possible the development of modern aircraft wings, the design of gas turbines and compressors, and the development of rockets. △1496, 1504.

Hydroelectric Power Plant, a center in which the

Sir Julian Huxley

Hyacinth

Hyderabad, India

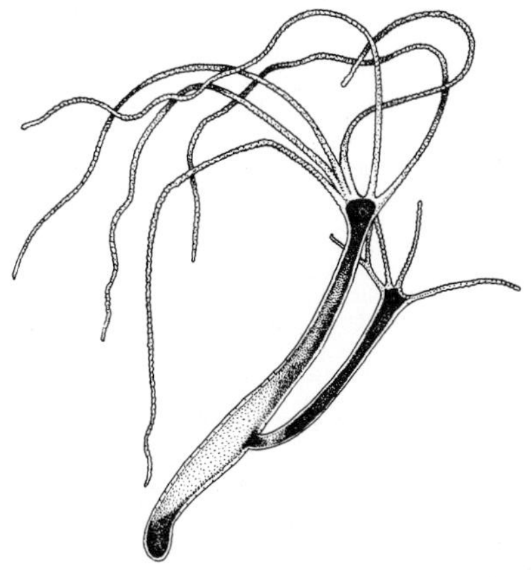

Hydra

mechanical energy of falling water is converted into electrical energy. The typical hydroelectric facility includes a dam, behind which is a reservoir; hydraulic turbines, through which controlled dam overflow falls; power generators situated directly above the turbines that drive them; and an electrical transmission system. △286, 1634.

Hydrofluoric Acid, colorless corrosive fuming liquid consisting of a solution of the gas hydrogen fluoride (HF) in water, prepared by distilling a mixture of sulfuric acid and fluorspar. It is used in frosting and etching glass, pickling metals, and cleaning stone and brick.

Hydrofoil, a flat or curved plane surface designed to obtain reaction from the water through which it moves. Also, an underwater fin, attached by struts to a seaplane or speedboat for lifting the hull as speed is increased. Hydrofoil ships are capable of speeds up to 80 knots. △1676, 1682.

Hydrogen, gaseous nonmetallic element (symbol H), first identified as a separate element by Henry Cavendish (1766). It is usually classified along with the alkali metals in group 1A of the periodic table. Hydrogen is the most abundant element in the universe (75% by mass) and the lightest of all. Properties: at. no. 1; at. wt. 1.0079; density 0.08988 g dm^{-3}; melt. pt. −434.45°F (−259.14°C); boil. pt. −421.91°F (−252.87°C); most common isotope H^1 (99.985%). *See also* Deuterium; Tritium. △1480, 1550, 1552, 1554, 1558.

Hydrogenation, chemical reaction between molecular hydrogen and an element or compound, sometimes under pressure, usually in the presence of a metal catalyst such as nickel, platinum, or palladium. An unsaturated compound, such as benzene, may accommodate the extra hydrogen, but a saturated species will break up (destructive hydrogenation).

Hydrogen Bomb. *See* Nuclear Weapon.

Hydrogen Bond, type of chemical bond formed between certain hydrogen-containing molecules. The hydrogen atom must be bound to an electronegative (electron-withdrawing) atom, the bond being formed between the positive charge on hydrogen and the negative charge on an atom in an adjacent molecule. Hydrogen-bonding occurs in water, and in many biological systems. △1554, 1574.

Hydrogen Peroxide, syrupy liquid (H_2O_2), usually sold in aqueous solution, prepared by electrolytic oxidation of sulfuric acid or discharge through a mixture of oxygen and hydrogen in the presence of water. It is used in bleaching, as a disinfectant, and as a rocket fuel oxidizer. Properties (anhydrous): sp gr 1.46; melt. pt. 28.4°F (−2°C); boil. pt. 317.4°F (158°C).

Hydrogen Sulfide, colorless poisonous gas with the smell of bad eggs (H_2S) prepared by the action of sulfuric acid on iron sulfide. It is used in chemical analysis. Properties: melt. pt. −118.8°F (−83.8°C); boil. pt. −76.3°F (−60.2°C).

Hydrographic Chart, or nautical chart, a map of the physical features of oceans and adjoining coastal areas. They also contain tide and current information. The most detailed ones exist for coastal areas because more information has been collected, but new sonar devices are enabling the mapping of deep-water parts of the ocean.

Hydrography, the science of charting the water-covered areas of the earth. Navigational charts have been made since the 13th century, but these were accurate only for seacoasts. Interest in the charting of oceanic areas away from seacoasts only developed in the 19th century. The US Coast Survey, established in 1807, produced its first official nautical charts in 1845. Now, detailed bathymetric surveys are available for geological studies. Hydrographic offices are run by governments of maritime nations to furnish their mariners with nautical charts. △236.

Hydrology, study of the earth's waters; their occurrence, circulation, distribution, chemical and physical composition. The hydrologic cycle describes the evaporation of water from various bodies, atmospheric water and its movement, and its return to land. The continental water systems, both surface and underground, are studied by hydrologists. *See also* Limnology; Oceanography. △254–58; 1766.

Hydrolysis, reversible chemical reaction of water with a substance, often assisted by catalysts. Hydrolysis proceeds by a double decomposition mechanism, exemplified by the reaction $AB+HOH \rightleftharpoons AH+BOH$, where A and B are different molecular entities. In digestion enzymes catalyze the hydrolysis of carbohydrates, proteins, and fats into forms that the body can assimilate.

Hydromechanics. △1496.

Hydrometer, instrument for measuring density or specific gravity of a liquid. It consists of a long-necked, sealed glass bulb that is weighted. The neck is calibrated to read specific gravity. When immersed in the liquid to be measured, its depth gives liquid density. Hydrometers are used to check concentrations of liquids in storage batteries, freezing points of radiator solutions, "proof" of alcohol. △1496.

Hydronephrosis, enlargement of certain kidney structures by distention with urine, resulting from obstruction of the urinary tract.

Hydrophobia. *See* Rabies.

Hydrophone, an electroacoustic device for receiving sound or seismic waves transmitted through water. *See also* Seismology.

Hydrophyte, or aquatic plant, plant growing only in water or damp places. The waterlily is considered the most important water garden plant. Among the oxygen-producing plants used in home aquariums are anacharis and cabomba. Others that float are azola, water fern, and water hyacinth.

Hydroponics, or soilless agriculture or tank farming, growing of plants in solution or a moist inert medium containing necessary nutrients instead of soil. This technique was developed during the 1850s. It requires special apparatus including tank, solution reservoir, pump, and timer installed in a greenhouse. Added nutrients include potassium nitrate, ammonium sulfate, calcium sulfate, and monocalcium phosphate. Although developed for use in areas where soil and growing conditions are inadequate, the technique is not used on a large scale. Crops that do well under hydroponic methods include tomatoes, lettuce, kale, spinach, and cucumbers. Houseplants may be grown hydroponically in ceramic or glass containers filled with water and feed biweekly with diluted plant food. Suitable plants include African violet, fuchsia, coleus, philodendron, and geranium. △ 312.

Hydrosphere, the aqueous vapor of the entire atmosphere and the envelope of the earth, including oceans, lakes, streams, and underground water. The water at the earth's surface measures 350,000,000 cu mi (1,465,000,000cu km), 99% of which is contained in the oceanic water layer.

Hydrostatics, a branch of fluid mechanics dealing with the charateristics of liquids at rest and with the pressure in a liquid, especially that exerted on an immersed body. Practical applications of laws have resulted in development of parabolic telescope mirrors and submarines. *See also* Fluid Mechanics; Hydrodynamics. △1496.

Hydrotherapy, the use of water within or on the surface of the body to treat disease.

Hydrotropism, plant growth in response to water stimulus. It is not a strong tropism and plant responses to higher oxygen and water content, such as the growth of willow roots through riverbanks, are often confused with it.

Hydroxide Ion, the ion OH^-, produced in solutions of bases. *See also* Base. △1566.

Hydrozoan. △470.

Hyena, predatory and scavenging carnivore native to Africa and S Asia. The spotted or laughing hyena *(Crocuta crocuta)* of the sub-Sahara is the largest and has sparse gray fur with dark round spots. The brown hyena *(Hyaena brunnea)* of S Africa is smaller and has dark brown bands around its legs and feet. The striped hyena *(Hyaena hyaena)* of N Africa, India, and the Near East is the smallest and has yellow-gray fur with black stripes. Weight: 75–175lb (34–79kg). Family Hyaenidae. △586.

Hygiene, Mental. *See* Mental Health (Hygiene) Movement.

Hyginus Rill. △60.

Hygrometer, instrument used to measure the water-vapor content, or humidity, of the atmosphere. One type, the psychrometer, compares the wet and dry bulb temperatures of the air, whereas other types measure absorption or condensation of moisture from the air or chemical or electrical changes caused by that moisture.

Hygroscopic, term designating a substance that, on standing, reacts with or absorbs water vapor from the air. Magnesium and calcium chlorides are typical examples. Some hygroscopic solids, said to be deliquescent, absorb sufficient water to dissolve, yielding a concentrated solution.

Hyksos, Semitic people who established a dynasty of Egyptian kings ruling from Memphis in Egypt. About 1685 BC they invaded Egypt from Canaan in the east using horsedrawn chariots; seized the kingship from the Pharaohs; and ruled a great empire on the lower Nile. In 1550 BC Amasis I, with the help of Nubian mercenaries, drove them out and set up the XVII dynasty. △960.

Hymenoptera, insect order of sawflies, ants, wasps hornets, and bees. All have a complete life cycle, with egg, larva, pupa, and adult. They have two pair of membranous wings, which move together in flight. They are found worldwide, living solitarily or in social groups. The larvae are grublike or caterpillarlike, and feed on plants or are parasitic or predaceous. △492.

Hyperbaric Chamber, a sealed chamber in which pressures higher than normal atmospheric pressure are employed in the treatment of diseases. Because of increased oxygen level, some bacteria (especially those causing tetanus and gangrene) are retarded. Babies born with heart defects receive more oxygen from the chamber during operations. Carbon-monoxide poisoning and pressure-related diseases such as decompression sickness are also successfully treated with hyperbaric chambers.

Hyperbola, plane curve traced out by a point that moves so that its distance from a fixed point, the focus, always bears a constant ratio (the eccentricity) greater than one to its distance from a fixed straight line (the directrix). The curve has two branches and is a conic section. Its standard equation in Cartesian coordinates is $x^2/a^2 - y^2/b^2 = 1$. △1454.

Hyperglycemia, abnormal amount of sugar in the blood, one of the symptoms of diabetes mellitus. *See also* Diabetes Mellitus.

Hyperides (389–322 BC), a leading Greek orator and public prosecutor. An early supporter of Demosthenes, he supported the Lamian war. After Athens was defeated, Hyperides was condemned to death.

Hyperinflation, or galloping inflation, or runaway inflation, condition in which inflation breeds more inflation because it affects the expectations of consumers. If consumers feel that prices are going to rise very rapidly and they therefore attempt to spend money before its purchasing power declines, hyperinflation results. Hyperinflation has generally been associated with wartime or postwar conditions.

Hyperinsulinism, overproduction of insulin, which may result from tumors in the pancreas or from other organic disturbances such as pituitary dysfunction, or from functional causes such as overexertion or poor nutrition. Hyperinsulinism produces symptoms of hypoglycemia, or low blood sugar, such as sweating, dizziness, headaches.

Hyperion, in Greek mythology, a Titan, son of Uranus and Gaea and the father of Helios, the Sun; Selene, the Moon; and Eos, the dawn. Hyperion drove his chariot across the sky each day and returned each night by the River Oceanus.

Hyperkinetic Children, children with a disorder marked by excessive and apparently pointless activity, difficulty in concentrating, and impulsiveness. The causes of this hyperactivity are unknown. Drug treatment has reduced the symptoms of many patients.

Hyperon, member of a class of elementary particles with an anomalously long lifetime. The group includes the lambda particle (symbol λ), sigma particles (Σ^+, Σ°, Σ^-), xi particles (Ξ°, Ξ^-), and omega particle (Ω^-). A lambda can replace a neutron in a nucleus to form a hypernucleus. *See also* Baryon; Strange Particles. △1484.

Hyperopia. *See* Farsightedness.

Hyperplasia, an increase in the normal number of cells in an organ or tissue, as opposed to an increase in the size of the cells (hypertrophy).

Hypersensitivity, a condition wherein an individual reacts to a stimulus such as light, Sun, or a chemical to an uncommon degree. Most hypersensitive reactions are treated as synonymous with allergies. Most common are hay fever, asthma, infantile eczema, and some food reactions. Some individuals become sensitized to drugs, such as penicillin, or to chemicals after initial contact. Sensitivity to light and sun increases as pigmentation in the skin decreases. *See also* Allergy. △112.

Hypertension. *See* High Blood Pressure.

Hyperthyroidism, excessive production of thyroid hormone, with enlargement of the thyroid gland (goiter). Enlargement may be diffuse and accompanied by protrusion of the eyeballs (exophthalmic goiter, or Graves' disease) or may be due to nodules or tumors, which are usually benign. Symptoms include rapid heart rate, high blood pressure, high metabolism, and weight loss. *See also* Goiter.

Hypertrophy, enlargement of an organ, such as the heart, caused in part by an increase in the size of its cells, as opposed to an increase in the number of cells (hyperplasia).

Hyperventilation, prolonged deep and rapid breathing, or any condition in which excessive amounts of air enter the alveoli (air cells) of the lungs, reducing carbon dioxide in the blood to undesirably low levels.

Hypnosis, state of heightened suggestibility that resembles sleep. Very little has been learned about hypnosis since it was first described two centuries ago. Since the time of F. A. Mesmer (1733–1815), it has provoked far more emotional and superstitious concern than serious research. It is, however, fairly well established that hypnosis is physiologically close to a state of relaxed wakefulness; there is increased suggestibility; there can be a slight improvement in recall; in some cases of deep hypnosis it is possible to produce hypnoanesthetic effects; and hypnosis can relieve symptoms in hysterical (conversion) reactions. △748.

Hypnotic, any drug that induces sleep. *See* Drug.

Hypochondria, exaggerated chronic concern with illness, infection, or pain, without appropriate justification. Hypochondriacs constantly complain of aches and pains, weakness, and fatigue and seek out doctor after doctor in hope of cure. They respond well to placebo treatment. *See also* Asthenic Reaction.

Hypodermic Injection, introduction of a fluid under the skin. *See also* Injection.

Hypoglycemia, abnormally low amount of sugar in the blood, which may result from fasting, excess insulin, and various metabolic and glandular diseases. Symptoms are dizziness, headache, cold sweats, and, in severe cases, odd behavior, hallucinations, and convulsions.

Hypomanic Personality, personality pattern disturbance showing a mixture of elevated mood state and restless agitation. It is distinguished from the *hypomanic reaction* in which there is a sudden appearance of manic-like behavior, which though not psychotic may represent the early stage of a true manic reaction.

Hypotension, abnormally low blood pressure, seen in severe hemorrhage or circulatory disturbances (circulatory shock). It may occur on change of position in persons with certain kidney or adrenal gland diseases (postural hypotension), or it may follow the administration of certain drugs.

Hypotenuse, side opposite the right angle in a right-angled triangle. It is the longest side of the triangle. *See also* Triangle. △1462.

Hypothalamus, principal forebrain structure, often described as the primary sensory sending structure. Along with other neural areas, it regulates several motivational stages, including the initiation of hunger, thirst, and sexual behavior. △666, 678.

Hypothesis, an assumption made to account for or relate known facts. The formulation of an hypothesis is basic in everyday experience as well as in scientific investigations, where it is stated as a formal proposition. Consequences inferred from an hypothesis are put to further inquiry, thus enabling the assumption to be tested in a particular situation. In science, hypotheses are held provisionally. Even the great unifying concepts of modern science are merely working hypotheses, open to modification or rejection in the face of new facts.

Hypothyroidism, deficiency of thyroid hormone, most common in women and resulting in low metabolism, fatigue, menstrual disorders, and, if severe, anemia and mental deterioration. If severe in children, mental retardation and short stature, a condition called cretinism results. *See also* Cretinism. △726.

Hyrachyus. △574.

Hyracotherium. △576.

Hyrax, gregarious plant-eating mammal native to Africa and SW Asia. Tree climbers, they resemble short-eared rabbits. Length: to 24in (61cm). They are the only members of the order Hyracoidea. Family Procaviidae. △540, 548.

Hyssop, common name for *Hyssopus officinalis,* an aromatic herb of the mint family. A hardy perennial native to Eurasia, it is used in seasoning food and in medicine. It is also cultivated as an ornamental subshrub.

Hysterectomy, an operation in which all or part of the uterus and its surrounding structures are removed. Hysterectomy may be subtotal, with removal of the body of the uterus only; total, with removal of the cervix; or radical, with removal of the entire uterus and its surrounding connective tissue.

Hysteresis, phenomenon occurring in the magnetic and elastic behavior of substances in which the strain for a given stress is greater when the stress is decreasing than when it is increasing. When the stress is removed a residual strain remains. The phenomenon is particularly important in ferromagnetic materials, in which the magnetization lags behind the magnetizing force.

Hysteria, psychoneurosis characterized by emotional instability, suggestibility, dissociation, and psychogenic functional disorders. Conversion hysteria has symptoms that are the same as organic diseases. Dissociative hysterias alter conscious awareness and are manifest as amnesia, sleepwalking. Leading researchers in hysteria have included J.M. Charcot, Pierre Janet, and Sigmund Freud. Freud believed hysteria was caused by frustrated sexual needs and could be relieved by a "catharsis reactivation" of the memory. △766.

Hysterical Personality, in psychology, personality characteristics of naivete and emotional immaturity with a defensive style of denial and repression. The term is now rare, because anxiety reaction, phobic reaction, and conversion reaction are felt to be more descriptive of the various manifestations. △ 766.

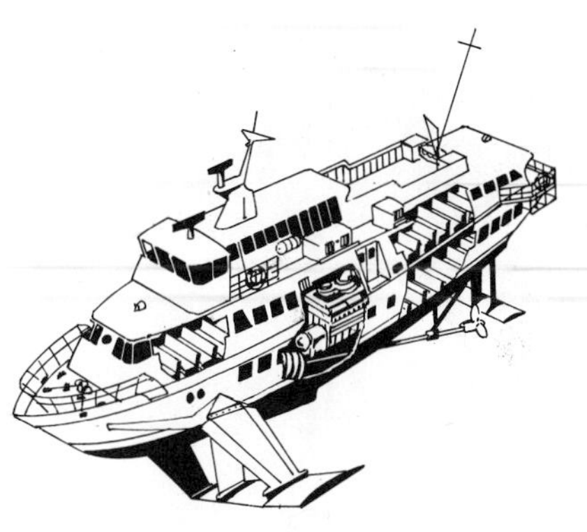

Hydrofoil

Hyena

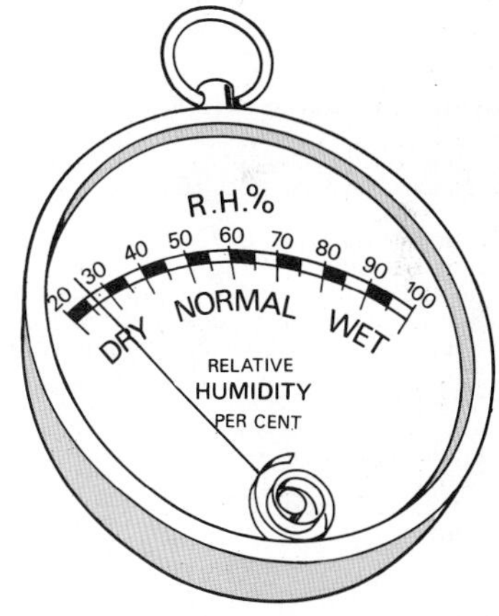
R.H.%
20
30
40
50
60
70
80
90
100
DRY
NORMAL
WET
RELATIVE
HUMIDITY
PER CENT

Hygrometer

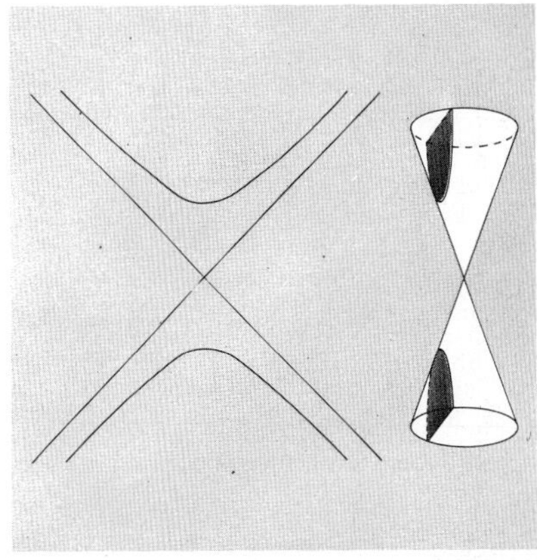

Hyperbola

I

Iamb, metrical foot consisting of an unstressed followed by a stressed syllable, or a short followed by a long, as in the word *amaze*. The meter is called iambic. Iambic trimeter is characteristic of Greek drama; iambic pentameter is predominant in English-language verse. *See also* Meter.

Iasi, city in NE Romania, 10mi (16km) from frontier between Romania and USSR; capital of Iasi co; capital of Romania until 1861 when it was moved to Bucharest; scene of signing of Treaty of Iasi (1792) ending Russo-Turkish War (1787–92); site of University of Iasi (1860), 15th–19th-century monasteries, 15th-century Church of St Nicholas. Industries: furniture, textiles, pharmaceuticals, chemicals. Pop. 183,776.

Ibadan, city of SW Nigeria, W Africa, approx. 90mi (145km) NNE of Lagos; capital of Western state; industrial and commercial center, handles regional cacao and cotton trade; site of University of Ibadan (1962). Industries: plastics, soap, chemicals, cigarettes, wood and metal products, processed foods. Founded 1830 as a military base in Yoruba civil war. Pop. 758,332.

Ibagué, city in W central Colombia, 60mi (97km) W of Bogotá, on the E slope of the Andes Mts; capital of Tolima dept. Industries: gold mining, coffee, rice, sugar cane. Founded 1550. Pop. 172,091.

Ibañéz del Campo, Carlos. △1354.

Ibaraki, city in S Honshu, Japan, 13mi (21km) NNE of Osaka; agricultural area. Pop. 163,903.

Ibarra, Francisco de (*c.*1539–75), Spanish conquistador, explored an area N of Zacatecas, Mexico, that became the audiencia of Nueva Vizcaya. Ibarra was named governor and captain-general of the area in 1562; the appointment was re-confirmed in 1573.

Iberia, ancient region S of Caucasus Mts, USSR; it approximates E part of Georgian SSR. Founded as independent kingdom between 6th–4th centuries BC, it became a vassal of the Roman Empire after defeat by Roman general Pompey (65 BC). Inc. 8th century as part of Georgia.

Iberian Peninsula, peninsula in SW Europe, occupied by Spain and Portugal, separated from Africa by Strait of Gibraltar and from the rest of Europe by Pyrenees Mts; bordered by Atlantic Ocean (N and W) and Mediterranean Sea (S and E). Area: 230,400sq mi (596,736sq km).

Iberians, the prehistoric people of S and E Spain in pre-Roman and early Roman times. Their culture was distinct from that of Celtic-dominated N and central Spain. The best known group of tribes was the Tartessians. Both Greek and Carthaginian influences can be detected in their alphabet and art forms. Their economy was based on agriculture, mining, and metalworking.

Iberville, Pierre Le Moyne, Sieur d' (1661–1706), Canadian naval officer and explorer. Scion of a great Canadian family, he engaged in diplomatic missions and in 1685 helped seize Rupert House, Albany, and Moose Factory from the Hudson's Bay Company. In 1688–89, he led an expedition to the Mississippi delta and established Fort Maurepas (now Biloxi), which was the first French settlement on the Gulf coast. Iberville fought the British on land and sea in the 1690s with great success. He was governor of Louisiana from 1703 until his death.

Ibex, several species of wild Old World goats. Long, backward curving horns measure up to 5ft (1.5m) on the male. All have great climbing ability and long, yellow-brown hair. Height: 3ft (0.9m) at shoulder; weight: 240lb (108kg). The Alpine ibex *(Capra ibex)*, once common, is now almost extinct. *See also* Goat. △608.

Ibis, tropical lagoon and marsh wading bird with long, down-curved bill, long neck, and lanky legs. Closely related to the spoonbill they may be black, whitish, or brightly colored. Feeding on small animals, they nest in colonies, laying 2–5 light colored eggs. Length: 2–3ft (61–91cm). Subfamily Threskiornthinae. △526.

Ibiza, island of Spain, 80mi (129km) off E coast, in W Mediterranean SW of Majorca; part of Balearic group. Noted for Roman, Carthaginian, and Phoenician artifacts, the mild climate and beautiful scenery have made Ibiza a major tourist center. Industries: tourism, fishing, salt works, almonds, figs, olives. Area: 221sq mi (572sq km). Pop. 45,075.

Ibizan Hound, coursing breed of dog. Believed to be the sacred dog of ancient Egypt. Brought to United States in 1956. This graceful dog has a long, slender head and muzzle; prick ears; long, arched neck; deep chest; straight back; and low-set, sickle-shaped tail. The short, solid color coat can be white, red, and lion; white and red; or white and lion. Average size: 22–28in (56–71cm) high at shoulder; 42–50lb (19–23kg).

Ibn Daud, Abraham Ben David Halevi (*c.*1110–1180), popularly known as Rabad I, a Spanish philosopher. Although Jewish, he was well-versed in the literature of Islam and Christianity. His theological works defend Judaism and stress the necessity of trust in God's protection of Israel. He appears in these treatises as philosopher, historian, and theologian. Also a talented physician, he was martyred in Castile.

Ibn Ezra, Abraham (1092–1167), prominent Jewish scholar of Spanish descent, well-versed in philosophy, theology, and literature, and a physician. Traveling almost constantly after 1140, he was known for his wisdom. His works are brief, including poems which employ visual effects. He produced commentaries on the Old Testament.

Ibn-Saud (*c.*1880–1953), founder and first king of Saudi Arabia (1932–53). He lived in exile with his family in Kuwait until 1900 when he captured Ar Riyadh, the chief city of his family, in Nejd (N central Arabia). By 1912 he had recaptured all of Nejd. In 1924–25 he defeated Husein Ibn Ali, his rival for control of Arabia, thus securing Hejaz (the region with Mecca and Medina). In 1932 he constituted his domain as Saudi Arabia with himself as king. He granted oil-drilling concessions to US companies in the 1930s. Although anti-Zionist, he played only a minor role in the Arab-Israeli War of 1948. He was succeeded by his oldest son, Prince Saud.

Ibn Taymiyah (1263–1328), Islamic theologian and jurist. Independent in his opinions, he was imprisoned several times on charges of questioning religious practices. Stressing the authority of the Koran and orthodox Islamic practices, he was the source for the later traditionalist movement called Wahhabism.

Ibn-Tufayl, or Abubacer (d.1185), Moorish Islamic philosopher. Little is known of the life of this scholar. A physician, astronomer, and poet, he is best known for his "philosophical novel" *Hayy ibn Yaqzan* (trans. as *Philosophus Autodidactus,* 1671), whose hero achieves continuous union with God.

Ibo, or **Igbo,** Kwa-speaking people of eastern Nigeria. Originally their patrilineal society consisted of politically and socially autonomous village units, but during the 20th century an ethnic unity developed in reaction to British colonial rule, and they now form the bulk of the Nigerian urban middle class.

Ibrahim Pasha (1789–1848), Egyptian general. The son of Muhammad Ali, governor of Egypt under the Ottoman Empire, in 1816–18 he campaigned against the Wahhabis of Arabia. Between 1824–27 he fought the Greek insurgents, sending many into slavery in Egypt. When his father turned against the Ottoman sultan, Ibrahim conquered Syria (1832–33) and became its governor. In 1841 Turkey, supported by Britain and Austria, forced him to withdraw to Egypt. He was named regent of Egypt in 1848 because of his father's senility.

IBRD. *See* International Bank for Reconstruction and Development.

Ibsen, Henrik (1828–1906), Norwegian playwright. He profoundly influenced world theater with tense, skillful dramas of complex individuals in conflict with bourgeois institutions. His widely translated works include *Brand* (1866), *Peer Gynt* (1867), *A Doll's House* (1879), *Ghosts* (1881), *An Enemy of the People* (1882), *The Wild Duck* (1884), *Hedda Gabler* (1890), *The Master Builder* (1892), and *When We Dead Awaken* (1899). △1240.

Içá. *See* Putumayo.

Icarian Sea. *See* Aegean Sea.

Icarus, in Astronomy. △78.

Icarus, mythological Greek character who was imprisoned with his father Daedalus by King Minos of Crete. Daedalus, architect of the Labyrinth, made wings of feathers and wax in order to escape Minos. Daedalus was successful, but Icarus, despite a warning, flew too near the sun, melted his wings, and fell into the sea. The Icarian Sea bears his name.

ICBM. *See* Intercontinental Ballistic Missile.

Ice, or **Snow, Crystals,** usually taking the form of six-sided crystals, platelets, or columns, made when water vapor condenses below the freezing point and composing high cirrus clouds but also often present in gray portions of other clouds. Clumps of numerous ice crystals form snowflakes. *See also* Cloud; Precipitation. △216.

Ice Ages. △264.

Iceberg, a large drifting piece of ice, broken off from a fresh-water glacier. In the Northern Hemisphere the main source of icebergs is the SW coast of Greenland. In the south, the glacial flow from Antarctica releases huge tabular icebergs, some over 60mi (97km) long. Icebergs can be dangerous to shipping, since only a small portion is visible above the water. *See also* Glacier. △264.

Ice Boating, a winter sport, also known as ice yachting. The boats are stiletto-shaped craft with three ski-like runners and a raked mast. The most popular craft used is the bow-steered Skeeter class, which is 22ft (6.7m) long, weighs about 300lb (135kg), and is limited to 75sq ft (7sq m) of sail. Competition crafts are classified according to sail area and can hold one or two persons. The sport originated in the 18th century in Scandinavia and became popular in the United States and Canada in the 1860s. The most prominent competition is the Ice Yacht Challenge Pennant of America, begun in 1881.

Icebreaker, a ship with a heavy bow and armored sides, designed to make a passage through ice. Powerful engines enable the ship to plow through the ice. For breaking thick ice, the bow is designed to climb partly up on the ice, permitting the ship to break the ice with its weight. Propellers forward and aft allow great maneuverability. Iceboats are used regularly to clear channels in the Great Lakes and in the Baltic Sea, and they have also been used in Arctic and Antarctic explorations.

Ice Cave. △264.

Ice Cream. △374.

Icefish. △514.

Ice Hockey, a fast-action sport, most popular in the United States and Canada. It is played by two teams of six persons each on a rink usually 200 feet long and 85 feet wide (61m by 25.9m), surrounded by walls 3.5 to 4 feet (1.1–1.2m) high. Ten feet (3m) from each end of the rink is a goal net 4 feet (1.2m) high and 6 feet (1.8m) wide. The rink is evenly divided by colored lines into three zones—attacking, neutral, and defending—each 60 feet (18.3m) long. A vulcanized rubber puck 1 inch (2.5cm) thick and 3 inches (7.6cm) in circumference is used. Each player wears ice skates, carries a wooden stick that is angled at one end, and wears protective equipment; the goalie has leather leg guards and usually wears a face mask. Besides the goalie, the other five players are made up of two defensemen, two forwards, and a center. Play begins at center ice; the object is to advance the puck into the opponent's goal. Each goal counts as one point and regulation games (three 20-minute periods) may end in a tie, or in sudden-death following the end of regulation time. Substitutions are freely allowed, and the game is officiated by two linesmen and a referee. Only the referee may call penalties, which are for such violations as high-sticking, roughing, or tripping. A penalty results in one or more players leaving the ice and going to the penalty box for two or more minutes. Depending upon the penalties, teams may play short-handed.

History. Ice hockey originated in Canada in the 1870s and later came to the United States. Amateur hockey has been an event in the winter Olympic Games since 1920. There are two professional major leagues, the National Hockey League (formed 1917) and the World Hockey Association (formed 1972). The NHL has 18 teams divided into 4 divisions and plays an 80-game schedule. The WHA has 14 teams divided into 3 divisions and plays a 78-game schedule. Following the end of scheduled play in both leagues are playoffs. Most famous is the NHL playoff for the Stanley Cup, which is awarded to the winner in the NHL. In the WHA the playoff prize is the Avco Cup.

Iceland (Island), independent island nation in the North Atlantic Ocean. Its economy is dominated by fishing, which Iceland feels is threatened by foreign fishing trawlers.

Land and economy. Situated E of Greenland and just S of the Arctic Circle, Iceland is 75% volcanic in origin with a 6,590ft (2,010m) above sea level lava desert, glaciers, and lakes. The rest is either grazing land or under cultivation. Damp, cool summers characterize a climate tempered by the Gulf Stream. Winter temperatures average 30°F (−1°C) with high winds. Fishing is the economic mainstay, with 14% of the population dependent on it; 14% depends on agriculture, and 30% on manufacturing and construction. Fish products account for 70% of exports. Its per capita income is higher than the European average.

People. Icelanders are descended from Norwegian settlers and Celts from the British Isles; the Icelandic language has remained almost unchanged since the 12th century and remains closest to Old Norse. Literacy is rated at 99.9%, the highest in the world. Religious freedom is complete. About 97% of the population belongs to the Evangelical Lutheran Church, with other Protestant and Roman Catholic minorities.

Government. Iceland is a constitutional republic with elected president and parliament *(Althing)*.

History. Settled by Norwegians in the 9th and 10th centuries, ruling chiefs established a republic, the *Althing*, said to be the oldest parliament in the world. In 1262, Norway took control of the island, and it passed to Denmark in the 14th century. In the early 19th century the rise of nationalism brought demands for independence, and home rule and sovereignty were granted under the Danish crown. During WWII Iceland depended on the United States for defense, until a plebiscite in 1944 established it as an independent republic. A conservative coalition government allows a US-NATO presence on Iceland. In the mid-1970s the presence of foreign fishing fleets near Iceland led to clashes, particularly with British ships, that caused some dislocations in foreign relations.

PROFILE

Official name: Republic of Iceland
Area: 39,768sq mi (103,000sq km)
Population: 210,000
Chief city: Reykjavik (capital)
Government: Constitutional republic
Religion: Evangelical Lutheran
Language: Icelandic
Monetary unit: Krona
Gross national product: $700,000,000
Per capita income: $4,835
Industries: processed fish (canning and freezing), aluminum smelting, cement, ammonium nitrate, diatomite, clothing, shoes, chemicals, fertilizers, hydroelectric power
Agriculture: potatoes, turnips, hay, fish, cattle, sheep
Minerals: natural hot water, skeletal algae, perlite
Trading partners: United States, United Kingdom, West Germany

Icelandic Literature. Early Icelandic literature emerged in the 13th century from the oral tradition of Eadic and skaldic poetry, both of which were based on ancient Icelandic mythology. Other early writings (14th–16th centuries) include sagas of Norse monarchs, translations of foreign romances, and religious works. From the 14th–19th centuries the *rímur*, a narrative verse poem, was popular. The 19th century was probably the most important period in the development of Icelandic literature. Romantic lyric poets such as Bjarni Thorarensen and Jónas Hallgrímsson were influential in stimulating literary activity. Other figures were Jón Thóroddsen, who published the first novel in Icelandic, and Matthías Jochumsson, the founder of modern Icelandic drama. The late 19th century saw the development of Icelandic realism. Important 20th-century writers include Gunnar Gunnarsson and Halldor Laxness.

Iceland Moss, a flattened, branched, partially erect lichen that grows in arctic and high cold mountainous regions. Especially in Scandinavia, Iceland moss has been used as a medicine and as food for livestock and people.

Iceland Spar, a transparent form of calcite that has the property of bending light two ways so that an image seen through it appears double. It is used in polarizing prisms, in polarizing microscopes, and other optical instruments. *See also* Calcite.

Ice Skating, a winter sport, believed to have originated in Scandinavia in the 2nd century AD. The first completely iron skates were introduced in the 17th century. Previously, ice skates were made of bone and then wood. In the 1850s steel skates, with straps and clamps to fasten them to the shoes, were introduced. This was soon followed by the permanent skate, where the skate and the shoe formed a single unit. The first US skating club was organized in Philadelphia in 1849. In 1958 the first properly maintained rink was established on the lake in New York City's Central Park.

I-ch'ang (Yichang, or Ichang), city in E central China, on Yangtze River; terminus for ocean-going steamers from Shanghai; site of airport; opened to foreign trade 1876. Crops: rice, tea, beans. Pop. 160,000.

Ichikawa, city in central Honshu, Japan, 10mi (16km) E of Tokyo. Pop. 261,055.

I Ching, meaning "Book of Changes," a Chinese work that is one of Confucianism's Five Classics. Along with the Four Books, they make up the canon of Confucianism. *I Ching* contains material for divination, plus philosophical writings. According to legend the former were written in about the 11th century BC and the latter by Confucius around the 6th century BC. *I Ching* tries to explain human existence and natural occurrences. △822, 1114.

Ichinomiya, city in SE Honshu, Japan; site of 7th-century Shinto shrine; textile center. Pop. 219,274.

Ichneumon Wasp, parasitic wasp that attacks other insects and spiders. The female's ovipositor is as long as its body or longer. Found worldwide, the largest representative found in the United States is 1.5in (38.1mm) or more in length and its ovipositor is several times the length of its body. Family Ichneumonidae. *See also* Hymenoptera. △502.

Ichthyology, zoological study of fish. Although true fish are in the Class Osteichthyes, it also includes lam-

Ibis

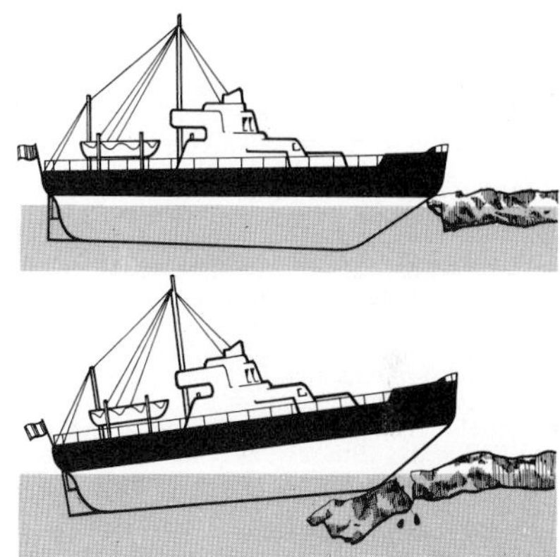

Icebreaker

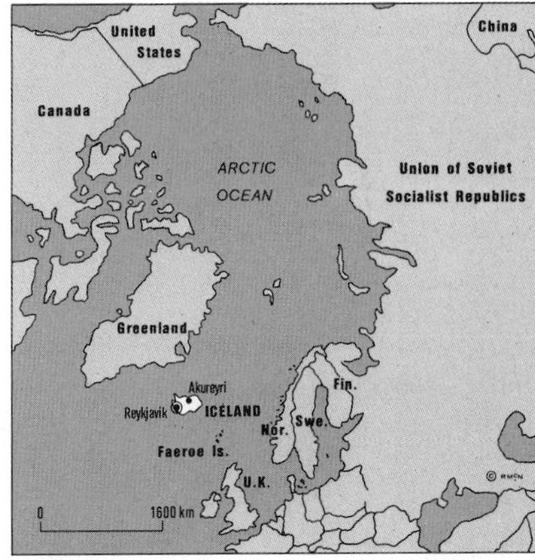
United States
China
Canada
ARCTIC
OCEAN
Union of Soviet
Socialist Republics
Greenland
Akureyri
Reykjavik
ICELAND
Fin.
Nor.
Swe.
Faeroe Is.
U.K.
0
1600 km

Iceland

Iceland

prey, shark, ray, and skate, and sometimes whale and porpoise (mammals). △510–516.

Ichthyornis, extinct ternlike North American bird of the Cretaceous period. Although it had a keeled breastbone and well-developed wings like modern birds, it had teeth in individual sockets, a characteristic of earlier birds.

Ichthyosaur, extinct fish-shaped, marine reptile of from 65–225,000,000 years ago. These fish eaters had limbs reduced to paddles, a fleshy back fin, and a fishlike tail. Fossils indicate they bore live young. Length: to 30ft (9m). △570, 572.

Icthyostega. △566.

Ichthyosis (fish-skin disease), characterized by harshness, dryness, and scaliness of the skin, caused by excessive growth of the horny layer. The disease is usually hereditary. △724.

ICJ. *See* International Court of Justice.

Iconoclastic Controversy, a dispute in the Byzantine Empire over devotion to sacred images. Between 726 and 843, six emperors ordered icons to be taken out of churches and persecuted orthodox Christians for venerating them. The Second Council of Nicaea decided that Christians could venerate, but not worship, images. This stand was reaffirmed by a synod in 843, and the controversy ended. △1056, 1060.

Iconography, in religion, symbolic and pictorial representation of religious concepts and personages, central in the worship of the Eastern churches. Early Christian art was basically symbolic, and grew mystical. *See also* Iconoclastic Controversy. △848.

Iconography, in art history, the study and interpretation of themes, symbols, and subject matter in the visual arts. Iconography began in the 16th century and was largely considered a part of archeology in the 18th century. In the 19th century it was chiefly concerned with symbolism in Christian art, but 20th-century iconographers also study secular art and that of religions other than Christianity. Leading 20th-century iconographers include Aby Warburg and Erwin Panofsky. △1060.

Ictinus (5th century BC), Greek architect. After designing the Parthenon with Callicrates (447–432 BC), he worked on rebuilding and enlarging the Temple of the Mysteries at Eleusis. He also designed the Temple of Apollo Epicurius at Bassae (*c.* 430 BC), most of whose columns still stand.

Id, in psychoanalytic theory, the deepest level of the personality, which includes primitive drives (eg, hunger, anger, sex) that demand instant gratification. Even after the ego and the superego develop and limit these instinctual impulses, the id is a source of energy and often of unconscious conflicts. *See also* Ego; Superego. △786, 812.

Ida, Mount (Kaz Dağı), mountain in Ida mountain range, NW Turkey, SE of site of ancient Troy. According to Homeric legend, mountain was dedicated to Cybele, goddess of fertility and mother goddess of Anatolia.

Idaho, state in the NW United States, bordered on the N by the province of British Columbia, Canada.

Land and Economy. Much of the state is mountainous and forested, with many lakes. The Snake River, along the W boundary, flows for 40mi (64km) through Hells Canyon, which is more than 1mi (2km) deep. Hydroelectric dams have been built in this part of the river. In the S, irrigation projects have created agricultural areas, especially along the upper valley of the Snake, where crop and livestock production and processing are centered. Year-round resorts and wilderness hunting and fishing have made tourism a major source of income.

People. Idaho is among the states lowest in population density. More than 66% of its people live in or near the Snake River valley in the S, and more than half inhabit areas classified as urban. About 98% were born in the United States, but only about 50% are native to the state. Immigration has been chiefly from other W and N states.

Education and Research. There are nine institutions of higher education. The National Reactor Testing Station in the E Snake River valley is an important nuclear research center.

History. In 1805, the US explorers Meriwether Lewis and William Clark traversed the region. In a few years fur trappers were active and trading posts were established; missionaries moved among the Indians. The Oregon Trail, leading to the new Pacific Coast settlements, crossed S Idaho. Discovery of gold in 1860 brought a rush of immigrants, and Idaho Territory was created in 1863. Intermittent war with the Indians ended in 1877 with the surrender of Chief Joseph of the Nez Perce tribe. After Idaho's admission to the Union, labor disputes marked by violence racked the state. By 1900 the steady development of the state's resources was under way.

PROFILE

Admitted to Union: July 3, 1890; rank, 43rd
US Congressmen: Senate, 2; House of Representatives, 2
Population: 713,008 (1970); rank, 42nd
Capital: Boise, 74,990 (1970)
Chief cities: Boise; Pocatello, 40,036; Idaho Falls, 35,776
State Legislature: Senate, 35; House of Representatives, 70
Area: 83,557sq mi (216,413sq km); rank, 13th
Elevation: Highest, Borah Peak, 12,662ft (3,862m); Lowest, Snake River, 710ft (217m)
Industries (major products): processed foods, lumber, paper, chemicals
Agriculture (major products): potatoes, sugar beets, wheat, sheep, cattle
Minerals (major): silver, lead, zinc, phosphate rock
State nickname: Gem State
State motto: Esto perpetua (Let It Be Forever)
State bird: Mountain bluebird
State flower: Syringa
State tree: Western white pine

Idaho Falls, city in SE Idaho, on Snake River; seat of Bonneville co; headquarters for Idaho's operations of US Atomic Energy Commission; site of Latter-Day Saints temple (1945) and annual sun dance performance by the Bannock Indians. Industries: sugar beets, potatoes, cement, steel products, camp-trailers. Settled 1860s; chartered 1891. Pop. (1970) 35,776.

Ideal Gas Law, the law relating pressure, temperature, and volume of a gas: $pV = NkT$, where N is the number of molecules of the gas and k is a constant of proportionality. From this law, one can see that at constant temperature, the product of pressure and volume (pV) is constant (Boyle's Law); and at constant pressure, the volume is proportional to the temperature (Charles' Law). *See also* Boyle's Law; Charles' Law. △1502.

Idealism, doctrine or view that asserts the ideal as fundamental. The doctrine gives preference to mind (spirit, soul) negatively, as opposed to materialism; that which pertains to "ideas" or "ideals," as alternatives to objects, entities, and "reals." Idealism stresses supra-spatial and temporal categories and content, rather than experiential or tactile entities. Idealism can be qualified in many ways, eg, subjective, epistemological, or aesthetic idealism, Platonic or Hegelian idealism. △858.

Ideograph, system of using pictures to represent ideas or emotions, such as a picture of the sun to present the idea of "day" or "warmth" or a picture of a man pointing to his mouth to show hunger. It is often found with pictographs. *See also* Pictography. △870.

Idomeneus, in Greek mythology, Cretan king. He led the Cretans at the siege of Troy. On his way home during a stormy sea voyage, he pledged to sacrifice to the gods the first living thing he met, if he returned home safely. Idomeneus' son greeted him and he offered the boy as a sacrifice. A plague ensued and the Cretans banished Idomeneus.

Idris I (1890–), king of Libya. Grandson of a Muslim leader, he used Italian and British aid to become chief of Cyrenaica, sided with the British in World War II, and was ruler of Libya when it became independent in 1950. He was deposed in 1969 by a military junta with socialist aims.

Idrisids, ruling Islamic family of what is now Morocco (788–974). Idris I (died 793), a descendant of the Prophet Mohammed, founded the state and its capital city, Fez, with support from the local Berber tribesmen. The dynasty later became less unified and suffered from attacks by Berbers. It fell in the 10th century to the Fatimids, a succeeding dynasty led by Ubaydulla.

Idylls of the King (1842–1885), series of poems by Alfred Tennyson based on the Arthurian legend. It includes *Morte d'Arthur* (1842), *Guinevere* (1859), *The Holy Grail* (1871), and *Balin and Balan* (1885). The works romanticize the legend with its story of the triumph of sin over virtue.

Ieyasu Tokugawa (1542–1616), Japanese shogun. Building on the work of Nobunaga and Hideyoshi, Ieyasu completed the unification of Japan and was made shogun, military ruler of the country, in 1603. Acting as regent for Hideyoshi's heir, Hideyori, Ieyasu defeated his last opponents at Sekigahara in 1600 but later turned against Hideyori in 1615, destroying his forces on trumped-up charges and becoming unchallenged supreme leader. He ensured his line's continuity by retiring early in favor of his son, who in turn did the same. The Tokugawa shogunate (1603–1867) remained in power through a tightly controlled coalition of daimyo (feudal lords) and strategic land and mine possessions until 1867. △1048, 1210.

Ife, city in SW Nigeria, W Africa, approx. 50mi (81km) ENE of Ibadan; trade center in agricultural region; oldest Yoruba town (*c.* 1300); site of many fine artworks dating from 12th century, Ife Museum, and University of Ife. Pop. 150,818.

Ife, Kingdom of, SW Nigeria from about the 11th century to its defeat by other tribes in the 1880s. Its capital, Ife, became the spiritual center of the Yoruba and now handles considerable agricultural trade. △1116.

Ifni, region of SW Morocco, on Atlantic Ocean; former Spanish overseas territory, controlled by Spain 1860–1969; ceded to Morocco 1969, after border fighting between Spanish and Moroccan forces. Area: 580sq mi (1,502sq km).

Igbo. *See* Ibo.

Iglesias, Miguel (1822–1901), military and political leader of Peru. In the War of the Pacific (1879–83) between Peru and Chile, he rose to a position of major command and was responsible for the peace treaty of Ancón (1883) whereby Chile gained territory and occupied parts of Peru for 10 years. When Chilean troops left, Iglesias was overthrown (1886) and spent the rest of his life in Spain.

Igloo, Eskimo dwelling, especially snow house of eastern Eskimos built of snow blocks stacked into a low dome and welded together by frozen water. Igloos are constructed as temporary dwellings in the winter and provide excellent defense against the cold.

Ignatius of Antioch, Saint, 1st-century bishop of Antioch and martyr. On his way to Rome under sentence of death, he wrote seven letters to Christian communities *(Epistles).* These letters are valuable sources on the early church. Ignatius was put to death in Rome during the reign of Trajan.

Ignatius of Constantinople, Saint, called Nicetas (799–878), patriarch of Constantinople. He was the son of Emperor Michael I of the Byzantine Empire. He became a monk, then an abbot, and finally was elected patriarch of Constantinople (846), the leading center of the church in the Eastern Empire. Ignatius became involved in disputes, was deposed (858) and replaced by Photius, but was restored (867) to his position.

Igneous Rocks, the broad class of rocks produced by the cooling and solidifying of the molten magmas deep within the earth. They may take intrusive or extrusive forms. Intrusive rocks, such as granite, are those formed beneath the earth's surface by the gradual cooling of molten material; extrusive rocks, such as basalt, are formed by the rapid cooling of molten material upon the earth's surface. △244–46.

Ignition, Engine, the process or means of igniting fuel in an engine. Air and gas vapor are mixed in the carburetor, then delivered to the cylinder, where the mixture is compressed. The heat of compression and the higher pressure favor ready ignition and quick combustion. The charge is then ignited by a spark produced by the spark plug. The main type of ignition in common use is the battery-and-coil system. *See also* Spark Plug, Engine. △1632.

Igor (died 945), duke of Kiev (912–45). According to the medieval Russian *Primary Chronicle,* he was the son of Rurik, the semilegendary founder of the first Russian dynasty. Igor unsuccessfully led (941) an expedition against Constantinople; he later signed a commercial treaty with the Byzantines. He died while attempting to collect tribute from Slavic tribesmen.

Igorot, several ethnic groups of northern Luzon in the Philippines. Medium-sized with brown skin and straight hair, they are believed to be a mixture of early Indonesian and later Malayan stocks. Two main subdivisions are the wet-rice, terrace-cultivating, highland Igorot and the dry-rice, seasonal-garden Igorot of the lower rain forests. All work brass and iron and do weaving.

Iguaçu (Iguassu) Falls, waterfalls in Brazil, on Iguaçu River, 14mi (23km) above its confluence with the Paraná River. Two main sections are composed of hundreds of waterfalls separated by rocky islands; drops approx. 210ft (64m) into a narrow gorge. Argentina and Brazil national parks are on either side; first mapped 1892.

Iguala, city in S Mexico, on the Cocula River; scene of proclamation of the Plan of Iguala (1821), which prescribed Roman Catholicism as Mexico's sole religion, independence from Spain, and the right of any person to hold office; communication, distribution, and processing center for surrounding agricultural region. Pop. 60,980.

Iguana, lizard found in the New World, and in Madagascar and the Fiji Islands. Its teeth are attached to the inner edges of the jaw. There are 400 terrestrial, arboreal, burrowing, semi-aquatic, and semi-marine species, or large iguana of tropical America. It is greenish with a serrated dewlap on throat and crest along back. Length: to 6ft (1.8m). Family Iguanidae; genus *Iguana*. *See also* Lizard. △524.

Iguanodon, primitive, bipedal ornithopod dinosaur living in Europe during late Jurassic and early Cretaceous times. It had a spiked thumb that may have served as a defense weapon. Its jaws and teeth, like those of later ornithischian dinosaurs, were specialized for grinding food plants. Length: 30ft (9m). *See also* Ornithopoda. △570.

IGY. *See* International Geophysical Year.

Iiwi. △538.

IJsselmeer, large freshwater lake in NW Netherlands, formed in 1932 by dike which divided the Zuider Zee into the saline Wadden Zee and the freshwater IJsselmeer. Large land areas have been reclaimed by control of water level in the shallow lake. Dike supports a roadway. Length of dike: 19mi (31km).

Il Cortegiano (1528), Platonic treatise by Baldassare Castiglione, written in the form of dialogues on the qualities and duties of an ideal courtier. Set at Urbino before the death of Guidobaldo da Montefeltro (1508), contemporary characters such as Aretino and Bembo discuss the preoccupations of their time. Valuable as a record of all aspects of court society, it asserts the Renaissance ideal and was widely popular all over Europe.

Île-de-France, historical region and province of N central France, bounded by Picardy (N), Champagne (E), Orléannis (S), and Normandy (W). Hugh Capet est. in 987 the first French crown lands that were to encompass this region, whose capital was Paris; site of many Gothic cathedrals and châteaus, including Fontainebleau and Versailles.

Île de la Cité, island in Seine River in Paris, France; site of Notre Dame Cathedral and Palais de Justice; original settlement of Paris. *See also* Paris.

Ile du Diable. *See* Devil's Island.

Ileitis, inflammation of the ileum, part of the small intestine. Symptoms of acute ileitis resemble those of acute appendicitis.

Ilesha, city in SW Nigeria, W Africa; shipping center for regional agricultural products. Crops: nuts, yams, cacao. Pop. 192,302.

Ilex. *See* Holly.

Ilhéus (Ilhéos), city in E Brazil, on the Atlantic, at mouth of Cachoeira River. Exports: cacao, coffee, sugar, tobacco, lumber. Settled 16th century; inc. into Bahia state 18th century. Pop. 100,687.

Ili (I-li), river in China and USSR; formed by union of K'ung-chi-ssu and T'e-k'o-ssu rivers in N ranges of the Tien Shan; flows through a fertile valley in W China; empties into Lake Balkhash in the USSR. Length: 800mi (1,288km).

Iliac Artery and Vein. △688.

Iliad, historic Greek epic poem of the late 8th century BC, attributed to Homer; with the *Odyssey*, a rich source for understanding of the religion and people of the period. The *Iliad* describes the activities of the gods and mortals in the last weeks of the 10-year siege of Troy, when after a quarrel with Agamemnon, Achilles refused to continue the battle. After Achilles' friend, Patroclus, was killed by Hector, prince of Troy, Achilles led the invasion and killed Hector, returning Hector's body to King Priam for a hero's funeral. △998.

Iliamna Lake, lake in SW Alaska, at base of Alaskan Peninsula; Alaska's largest lake. Area: 1,000sq mi (2,590sq km).

Ilium. *See* Troy.

Ilium (bone). △682.

Illinois, state in the N central United States, on the E bank of the Mississippi River; one of the richest states in production and trade.

Land and Economy. Except for rolling hills in the NW, the land is virtually level. The Illinois is the largest of many rivers flowing SW into the Mississippi. The black loam soil is enormously productive; Illinois is among the top producers in many types of agriculture. In their scope and diversity, the state's nearly 20,000 factories are rivaled by few states. Reserves of bituminous coal and oil are extensive; mining and drilling are mostly in the S. Illinois products are widely distributed through the country and overseas. Chicago is the focus of many railroads and highways. Its port on Lake Michigan handles domestic waterborne commerce through the Great Lakes and the Illinois Waterway leading to the Mississippi and, since the St Lawrence Seaway was opened in 1959, has received large oceangoing vessels.

People. Farmlands and factories have attracted immigrants from other states and from foreign nations since the early 19th century. Many residents are of German, Scandinavian, Russian, Irish, and Italian descent. About 35% of Chicago's population is black; more than 80% of the people reside in urban areas.

Education and Research. There are about 140 institutions of higher education. The state-supported University of Illinois at Urbana has many branches. Notable privately endowed institutions include the University of Chicago and Northwestern University. A large concentration of medical facilities is in Chicago. The Argonne National Laboratory and the University of Chicago carry on extensive research. A large atom-smasher is at Batavia.

History. Father Jacques Marquette and Louis Jolliet, French explorers, sailed up the Illinois River in 1673, and a few French settlements were made in the next century. In 1763 the land was ceded to Great Britain; it was occupied by American troops in the Revolution. Illinois Territory was organized in 1809; it became a state nine years later. Illinois became a power in national politics with the emergence of Abraham Lincoln as a voice of the pro-Union, antislavery policies that brought him election as president. In 1942 the atomic age was inaugurated at the University of Chicago when researchers set off the first self-sustaining atomic chain reaction.

PROFILE

Admitted to Union: Dec. 3, 1818; rank, 21st
US Congressmen: Senate, 2; House of Representatives, 24
Population: 11,113,976 (1970); rank, 5th
Capital: Springfield, 91,753 (1970)
Chief cities: Chicago, 3,369,359; Rockford, 147,370; Peoria, 126,963; Springfield
State Legislature: Senate, 59; House of Representatives, 177
Area: 56,400sq mi (146,076sq mi); rank, 24th
Elevation: Highest, Charles Mound (in extreme NW), 1,235ft (377m); Lowest, Mississippi River (in extreme SW), 279ft (85m)
Industries (major products): steel, farm and construction machinery, communications equipment, electronic components, appliances, transportation equipment, processed foods.
Agriculture (major products): corn, soybeans, hogs, cattle
Minerals (major): coal, petroleum, fluorspar, stone
State nickname: Prairie State
State motto: "State Sovereignty-National Union"
State bird: Eastern cardinal
State flower: Meadow violet
State tree: Oak

Illinois Indians, confederation of Algonquian-speaking North American Indians who occupied Illinois, Wisconsin, Iowa, and Missouri in prehistoric times. They built Cahokia Mound near St Louis, one of the largest man-made structures in North America. Following the murder of Pontiac in 1769, the Ottawa warred on the Illinois, reducing the population from 8,000 to 225. Today, about 500 of their descendants live in Oklahoma, with a few in Kansas and neighboring states.

Illinois River, river in NE Illinois, formed by confluence of Des Plaines and Kankakee rivers; flows SW across Illinois to Mississippi River at Grafton; forms

Iconography: representations of the Sun

Idaho: Sawtooth National Recreation Area

Iguacu Falls, Brazil

Chicago, Illinois

major part of Illinois Waterway, connecting Great Lakes and Mississippi. Length: 273mi (440km).

Illuminated Manuscripts, illustrations of the Gospels and other religious books, dating from about the 5th century on. Early medieval illuminations were made primarily by monks in monasteries. Later, illumination became a widespread style of illustration, and many different schools developed, such as the Hiberno-Saxon, the Carolingian, and the Winchester schools. During the Gothic period, illumination was used for both religious and secular book illustrations. Illumination was at its height during the 14th and 15th centuries, when the International Gothic style was in use by such French and Flemish artists as Jean Pucelle, the Limbourg brothers, and Jean Fouquet. △1050.

Illusion, lack of correspondence between the physical measurement of an object and the perception of that object. Best known are the so-called optical (geometric) illusions, eg, the Müller-Lyer illusion in which two lines of equal length appear unequal because of the diagonal lines that are attached to their ends in different ways. There is no single explanation of geometric illusions; their effect occurs primarily in the brain. Other visual illusions center on the perception of color, brightness, motion, and depth. Explanations of the way they operate vary. Analogous phenomena occur in the other senses; there are touch illusions that resemble geometric illusions and several auditory illusions as well. △672.

Illusory Movement. *See* Apparent Movement.

Illyria, ancient region on the N and E shores of the Adriatic inhabited by the Dalmatians and the Pannonians, fierce piratical tribes of Indo-European origin. They remained free of Greek and Macedonian domination but were defeated by the Romans in 168 BC and their land was annexed as Illyricum and about AD 9 was divided as the imperial provinces of Dalmatia and Pannonia. Modern Illyria is N of central Albania. △1302.

ILO. *See* International Labor Organization.

Iloilo, city in Philippines, on SE Panay Island, on Iloilo Strait; capital of Iloilo prov. Region first settled by Malay chiefs; became commercial center about 1688; declared foreign trade port 1855; site of three universities. Exports: sugar, rice, copra, hemp, canned fish, piña cloth. Pop. 213,000.

Ilorin, city of SW Nigeria, W Africa; marketing and processing center for large agricultural region. Industries: cattle, poultry, cigarettes, palm products, handcrafts, pottery, wood carving, metal working. Pop. 241,849.

Image, Optical, points to which light rays from an object converge (real image) or from which they appear to diverge (virtual image) after reflection or refraction. A real image of an object can be projected onto a screen and can form an image in a photographic emulsion; this is not the case for a virtual image, such as that produced by a plane mirror. *See also* Aberration; Lens; Mirror. △1518.

Image Intensifier. △1526.

Imaginary Number. *See* Number, Complex.

Imagism, movement in poetry in the period 1909–17 whose credo summed up briefly was: use the language of common speech, create new rhythms, allow absolute freedom in choice of subject, present an image, produce poetry that is hard and clear, use concentration—the very essence of poetry. Amy Lowell was the principal exponent of the movement and brought out three anthologies called *Some Imagist Poets* (1915, 1916, 1917). *See also* Lowell, Amy.

Imamis, or **Twelvers,** a subgroup of the Shi'a sect of Islam. Forming the main body of the Shi'as, the Imamis assert that the 12th imam, or head of the Shi'a party, is still on earth, although hidden, and will return at some future time. About 1500, Twelver Shi'ism became the official religion of Iran. *See also* Islam.

Imhotep, vizier to Pharaoh Zoser of Egypt in the 3rd dynasty of the Old Kingdom (2663–2645 BC), and architect of the first great stone pyramid at Sakkarah. He is also credited with being a physician and writer. Imhotep was deified as the patron of scribes and son of Ptah, the builder-god of Memphis, during the time of the New Kingdom (1554–1075 BC), an honor that came to few men of common birth.

Imitation, or **Modeling,** patterning one's behavior after that of another; a basic form of social learning. Most modern psychologists regard imitation as an inborn tendency in higher primates, including humans. It is often cited as an important process in acquiring social behaviors, language, skills, and aggression. △784, 790.

Immanuel. *See* Manuel.

Immigration (US), movement of people to the United States, involving more than 40,000,000 people. Before 1890 immigrants were primarily Anglo-Saxon Protestants from the British Isles, Germany, and Scandinavia. Immigration after 1890 involved mainly Roman Catholics and Jews from eastern and southern Europe, forced to leave because of famine, lack of social and economic opportunities, political notability, or religious persecution. Once a particular group of immigrants settled in an area, they urged others from their homeland to join them. The Homestead Act of 1862 encouraged potential emigrants; the steamship lines vied for their patronage; Northern Pacific Railroad agents touted land bargains; and young American industries sent out a call for workers. The rate of immigration corresponded to economic cycles in the United States; increasing when prosperity was high. Attitudes of native Americans toward immigrants ranged from eagerness to exploit them and fear that they would denigrate the quality of life in the United States, to pride in the strength the country had derived from its ethnic mix. Earlier settlers were often racially biased against those who followed. There were many who blamed immigrants for rising crime rates, labor unrest, and the deterioration of cities. Chinese immigration was restricted in 1882 and Japanese in 1908; mechanisms to control immigration included restrictions on naturalization and denial of elective office to foreign-born. Restrictive policies won out with the passage of the Johnson Act (1924), which established a national origins quota favoring northwestern Europeans. The quota system, reaffirmed (1952) in the Immigration and Nationality Act, was abolished in 1965. The polyglot of subcultures that immigration brought to the United States offers to the mainstream a variety of life styles and values, encouraging cultural borrowing. The strong ethnicity of some immigrants has resisted the melting pot. *See also* Chinese Exclusion. △1278–80, 1394.

Immigration and Nationality Act (1952). *See* McCarran-Walter Act.

Immigration and Naturalization Service, a division within the Department of Justice. Established in 1891, it is responsible for administering the immigration and naturalization laws relating to the admission, exclusion, deportation, and naturalization of aliens in the United States.

Immune Reaction. △712.

Immunity. △740.

Immunity Act (Compulsory Testimony Act) (1954), US law that compelled witnesses appearing in national security cases to testify, by granting them immunity from prosecution for self-incriminating testimony. Introduced during a period when Congress was investigating possibilities of Communist subversion in the US government, the Immunity Act was passed as a means of eliciting testimony from witnesses who refused to testify under the provisions of the Fifth Amendment.

Immunization, a process or procedure that confers immunity against a disease, usually by stimulating the production of antibodies that combat the disease. In a common type of immunization, weakened forms of infecting organisms are injected into the bloodstream, causing only a very mild form of the disease but sufficient to stimulate antibody production that will provide lasting immunity. △740.

Immunoglobulin. *See* Antibody.

Immunology, study of immunity, autoimmunity, and allergy. It is concerned with the provision of active immunity (vaccination, etc) as a means of preventing disease, passive immunity (injections of antitoxins) to treat infection, and diagnosis by a variety of laboratory animals. Autoimmunity is an abnormal injurious reaction as a result of an overactive immune response to the body's own tissues. Allergic reactions result from an overactive response to harmless foreign substances such as dust, rather than to infective organisms. △740.

Immunosuppressive Drug, any chemical used to prevent or weaken the body's immune response, that is, its ability to form antigens. Such drugs are used so that a beneficial antigen (such as a tissue graft) may be retained or an allergic reaction may be preventec *See also* Antibody.

Impact Crater. △92.

Impala, or **Pala,** long-legged, medium-sized Africa antelope. Having sleek, glossy brown fur with blac markings on its rump, it is gregarious. Long, lyrat horns are found only on males. It leaps up to 30f (9m). Length: to 5ft (1.5m); height: to 39in (1m) a shoulder. Family Bovidae; species *Aepyceros melam pus.* △586.

Impatiens, genus of more than 100 species of succu lent annual plants native to damp areas of Indonesia They have white, red, or yellow spurred flowers anc seedpods that, when ripe, pop and scatter their seeds giving the plants the name touch-me-not. Tropical Olc World species are frequently cultivated as house plants and bloom throughout the year. Family Bal saminaceae.

Impeachment, method of removing public officials from office. Nationally, the House of Representatives is constitutionally empowered to initiate impeach ment proceedings. The Senate is empowered to try the accused, with a two-thirds vote necessary for con viction. Conviction by the Senate can lead to a crimi nal trial on the same charges. Twelve impeachments have been brought by the House, including that o President Andrew Johnson, who was acquitted (1868). The presidential pardon does not extend to individuals who have been impeached.

Impedance. △1544.

Imperfect Competition, situation existing when there are several firms in an industry producing products that are differentiated and barriers to entry into the industry are few. *See also* Competition. △938.

Imperialism, domination of one people or country by another. Such domination can be economic, cultural, political, and religious as well as physical. The building of trading empires by major European powers in the 16th century marked the beginning of modern imperialism. Overseas colonies were established to serve as a source for raw materials and to provide a market for manufactured goods. Exploitation of native populations over the centuries led eventually to the national liberation movements of the 20th century. △898, 1262.

Imperial Moth, large, stout-bodied yellow moth of E North America. Wingspread: 4–6in (10–15cm). The hairy caterpillar is green, brown, or blackish, with yellow spines on its two front segments. It eats tree leaves. Length: 3–4in (7.5–10cm); species *Eacles imperialis. See also* Moth.

Imperial Valley, valley in SE California, extending S into NW Mexico; most of it is below sea level and was desert until irrigated by All-American Canal that brings water from Colorado River. Has a growing season of 300 days and supports 2 crops per year. Crops: winter fruits and vegetables, dates, grain, cotton. Brawley, Calexico, and El Centro are main cities of valley.

Impetigo, skin disease caused by streptococcal or staphylococcal infection and characterized by multiple, spreading lesions with yellowish-brown crusts appearing primarily on the face and extremities.

Implication, logical proposition of the type "if *P* then *Q*," connecting two simple propositions—*P* (the antecedent) and *Q* (the consequent). In the form used in mathematical logic the two simple propositions need not be connected. This is called *material implication*—an example is "if the earth is flat then gold is a metal." A material implication is false only when the antecedent is true and the consequent false, otherwise it is true (the example given is a true implication). In normal discourse *formal implication* is used, in which the simple propositions are related in meaning; for example "if I am not given more money then I will leave this job." An implication is written as $P \rightarrow Q$, read "*P* implies *Q*."

Implied Powers, broad mandate "to make all laws which shall be necessary and proper" conferred upon the Congress by the US Constitution. *See also* Elastic Clause.

Impotence, male inability to perform sexually, the result of organic or psychogenic factors. Impotence may be temporary (eg, when brought about by anxiety regarding performance with a new sexual partner) or a more or less permanent condition in which almost no form of sexual arousal is possible. The term is used loosely to describe various sorts of sexual failure, including lack of erection, loss of pleasure, and inability to reach orgasm. *See also* Frigidity.

Impressionism, French school of painting during the late 19th century. Its main concern was with the use of color, especially to reflect light and atmosphere. Rapid brushstrokes were often used to reduce form to areas of broken color. Much Impressionist painting was done out-of-doors, and typical scenes were landscapes. Much attention was given to painting a subject as it appeared in sunlight. Claude Monet was a key figure in the Impressionist school. Other major painters of this group were Renoir, Degas, Pissarro, Sisley, Morisot, Bazille, and Manet. The first Impressionist exhibition took place in the spring of 1874 in the studio of the Parisian photographer Nadar. △1254, 1364.

Impressionism in Music, a movement in the history of music, roughly 1890 to 1930. The movement is represented chiefly in the works of Claude Debussy who, against his Romantic contemporaries, composed music that is subtle, soft, atmospheric, and refined rather than overtly emotional, with an emphasis on tone color rather than form. Debussy's first full-blown Impressionistic piece was the *Prelude to the Afternoon of a Faun* (1892), called by some musicologists the beginning of 20th-century music. Many other modern composers were subsequently influenced by Debussy's style and methods, including Ravel, Roussel, Delius, Respighi, Falla, Griffes, Scriabin, and Stravinsky and Schoenberg in their early works. *See also* Romanticism in Music. △1364.

Imprinting, a special form of learning that occurs within a critical period in very young animals. The first object encountered becomes the one that is followed thereafter. In nature, this is usually a parent; in experiments, humans, other animals, and even inanimate objects may become substitutes. Imprinting has been studied seriously only in birds, especially ducklings, but it also seems to occur in the young of some mammals and fish. △536, 784.

Inadequate Personality, personality pattern disturbance marked by continued failure in the face of intellectual, emotional, social, or physical demands. Such persons are not actually deficient in these areas but seem unable to perform, particularly under any form of stress. △766.

Inbreeding, breeding of two related offspring, either by mating brother and sister or by self-pollination. This technique results in the refining or strengthening of certain characteristics, and is used to produce uniform strains. △416.

Inca, Indian group that migrated from the Peruvian highlands into the Cuzco area about AD1250. Expansion and consolidation occurred at a slow but steady rate until the reigns of Pachacuti (*c.*1438) and his son, Topa Inca (died 1493), when Inca influence dramatically increased to include the area between Ecuador in the north and Chile to the south. The Inca empire was bureaucratic and militaristic: local administrators and leaders were moved to other areas and co-opted into Inca society; roads facilitated communication and the collection of tribute. The last of the emperors of a united realm, Huayna Capac, was dead only a short time when civil war broke out between his two sons. Pizarro used the internal conflict to advantage, completing the downfall of an already weakened empire. △1118, 1120, 1124.

Incandescent Lamp. △1532.

Incense Cedar, widely distributed genus *(Libocedrus)* of evergreen trees native to Chile, North America, New Zealand, and China. They may be pyramid-shaped or spreading and have flat, scalelike leaves. The cones are oblong. The aromatic wood is used for interior work and furniture, especially cedar chests. Height: 50–100ft (15–30m). Family Taxodiaceae.

Incest Taboo, taboo (prohibition accompanied by intense horror) on sexual relations within an exogamous kin group, which may be biological, classificatory, or affinal. It defines both impossible and possible sexual relations. *See also* Endogamy; Exogamy. △876.

Inchon (Inch'ŏn), port city in NW South Korea, on Yellow Sea; port opened for foreign trade 1883; site of arrival of UN forces in Korean War, 1950. Exports: rice, dried fish, soy beans. Industries: steel, iron, textiles, matches, flour, chemicals, lumber. Pop. 646,013.

Inchworm. *See* Measuring Worm.

Incisor, one of the front teeth in mammals, generally used for cutting, holding, or plucking. There are many variations: rodents have curved, continuously growing incisors for gnawing and carnivores have small points that help hold prey. The tusks of elephants are enlarged upper incisors. Man has two incisors in each half of each jaw, eight in all.

Inclination, Magnetic, or dip, the angle made by a free-floating magnet with the magnetic lines of force. At the north magnetic pole the inclination is zero; at the magnetic equator it is 90°. *See also* Declination, Magnetic. △168.

Inclined Plane, plane inclined to a horizontal reference plane. The angle of the plane is the angle between two lines, one in each plane, both at right angles to their line of intersection. △1652.

Income Tax, tax levied against the income of individuals or businesses. In the United States, the income tax is a progressive tax, ie, higher-income groups pay a higher percentage of their income in taxes. Although it is thus presumably based on the ability-to-pay principle, individuals in middle-income groups actually bear the major part of the burden. Corporations may be able to shift part of their income-tax burden to the consumer in the form of higher prices. The US government derives most of its revenue from the income tax.

Income Tax Amendment (1913), the 16th Amendment, allowing Congress to levy and collect taxes. During World War I, heavy taxes were placed on luxuries, high incomes, and excessive profits on war earnings. In the 1920s, Andrew Mellon helped engineer tax reductions for the wealthy, shifting a substantial part of the tax burden to middle-income groups and enabling the wealthy to feed the stock market speculation that led to the crash of 1929.

Incunabula, term meaning those books printed from the time of the invention of typography (in the 1450s) to the end of the 15th century. The known number of such works totals about 35,000. Georg Wolfgang Panzer produced the first catalog of those editions in 5 volumes 1793–97.

Indépendants, Salon des, society of artists founded in Paris in 1884 by Seurat, Signac, and others, which allowed any artist who so wished to display his works in its exhibitions. The artist was asked to pay a fee but was not required to have his work judged by a selection committee. Many artists whose works were considered avant-garde exhibited with this group.

Independence, city in W Missouri, 9mi (14km) E of Kansas City; seat of Jackson co; site of Mormon Colony 1831–33; world headquarters of Reorganized Church of Jesus Christ of Latter-Day Saints; home of Harry S. Truman and site of Harry S. Truman Library (1957). Industries: printing, publishing, oil refining, chemicals. Founded 1827; inc. 1849. Pop. (1970) 111,662.

Independence Hall, focal point of Independence National Historic Park, Philadelphia. It was built in 1732 as Pennsylvania's colonial statehouse and served as the meeting place of the Continental Congress and the Constitutional Convention. The Declaration of Independence (1776), Articles of Confederation (1781), and US Constitution (1787) were all adopted there.

Independent Variable. *See* Variable.

Index, in the Roman Catholic Church, the official list of books that members may not read or even own. The last edition was published in 1948, and since 1966 its prohibitions are not considered to be Church law.

Index Fossil, any fossil of limited time distribution that clearly marks certain beds or strata of rocks. Its occurrence in rocks located miles apart proves that these deposits were formed at the same time. These fossils are important in mapping rock formations and in locating valuable resources. *See also* Fossil. △276, 564.

Index of Refraction. *See* Refraction.

India, an independent nation on the Asian subcontinent. India has produced two major philosophies—Buddhism and Mahatma Gandhi's nonviolent resistance. It has 14% of the world's population, and population growth and a weak economy are persistent problems.

Land and economy. This subcontinent between Africa and Australia is bordered by the Bay of Bengal, Bangladesh, and Burma (E), the People's Republic of China, Nepal, Bhutan and Sikkim (N), Pakistan and the

Impala

Impatiens

Incense cedar

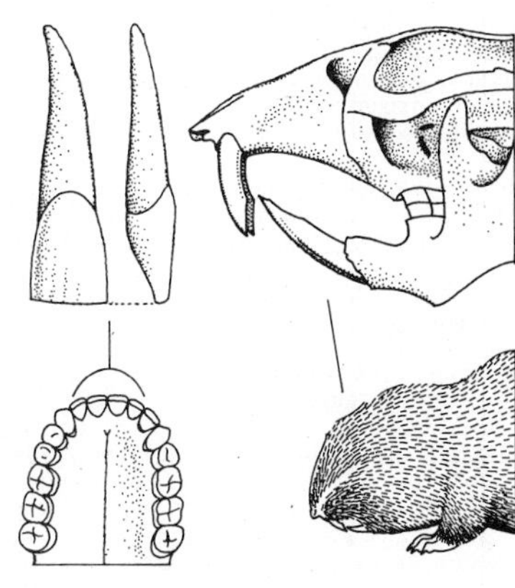

Incisor

Arabian Sea (W), and the island nation of Sri Lanka on the (S). A land with three seasons—cool, hot and dry, and rainy—it is divided into three regions. The N mountains (Himalayas) are the least populated. S of this is the flat, broad river plain (Gangetic plain) including the Ganges River—this is the most populous and prosperous portion. Below this is the hilly, dry plateau (Deccan plateau). Starting from primitive farming, India has made forward strides in agriculture since 1947; 70% of the population raises crops. Industry has been dominated by jute and cotton with steel and chemicals in recent production. Oil is being explored in the Bay of Bengal. In 1965, India undertook a plan to achieve self-sufficiency in food; however a soaring birth rate (12,000,000 Indians are born annually), makes it necessary to continue grain imports.

People. Ethnically, Indians are divided into two main groups, Aryans (N) and Dravidians (S). Eighty percent of the population is Hindu and practices a religion based on reincarnation and the caste system, a strict division of people into 4 major social classes with a total of 1,000 subdivisions. Outlawed now by the constitution, the caste system is breaking down. India has about 60,000,000 Muslims and minorities of Sikhs, Jains, Buddhists, and Parsis. Freedom of religion is guaranteed. Languages number 14, although 50% speak Hindi, the official language since 1965. Free, compulsory education through age 14 is assured.

Government. India is a democratic republic; power resides in the prime minister, who represents the majority party of the bicameral parliament. The prime minister heads the Council of Ministers (Cabinet) which is responsible to the lower house of parliament.

History. Indus Valley ruins reveal an Indian civilization dating from 2500 BC. In 1500 BC migrating shepherds (Aryans) from central Asia came down through the Himalayan passes, pushing the merchant Dravidians S. They perfected Sanskrit and initiated the caste system. Buddhism's founder, Siddhartha Gautama, lived from 563–483. The Golden Age of India under the Gupta dynasty (AD 320–500) was followed by Hun, Muslim, Tartar, and Mogul invasions. Vasco da Gama established Portuguese trading posts after 1498. By 1600 the British East India Company, with Mogul permission to trade in spices and textiles, controlled much of India. It was not until after the 1919 Amritsar Massacre of Indians that Mohandas Gandhi (1869–1948) emerged as a prominent nationalist leader. Under the banner of the mainly Hindu Indian National Congress he led the people against colonial rule with a mass movement based on nonviolent disobedience. In 1934, Muslims demanded that a separate state of Pakistan be carved out of India. After 40 years of India's struggle for freedom, Britain withdrew in 1947, and India attained self-government within the British Commonwealth. The same year partition gave Pakistan to the Muslims, and Kashmir became an Indian state. A 1950 constitution made India a democratic republic. Gandhi was assassinated in 1948. Jawaharlal Nehru was India's first prime minister. His daughter, Indira Gandhi, now holds that post. In 1975, citing threats to order in India, Gandhi imposed autocratic rule, destroying the effectiveness of political opposition and curtailing freedom of the press. △962, 986, 1034, 1202, 1266, 1330.

PROFILE

Official name: Republic of India
Area: 1,266,598sq mi (3,280,488sq km)
Population: 613,200,000
Density: 484per sq mi (186.8per sq km)
Chief cities: New Delhi (capital); Bombay; Calcutta; Madras; Poona
Government: Republic (with parliament)
Religion: Hindu (83%)
Language: Hindi (official)
Monetary unit: Rupee
Gross national product: $86,700,000,000
Per capita income: $117
Industries: cotton fabrics, iron, steel products, machinery, chemicals, processed foods, fertilizer, wool and silk, tanned hides, sewing machines, typewriters
Agriculture: tea, sugar, rice, wheat, nuts, barley, corn, rubber, cotton, tobacco
Minerals: coal, mica, manganese, salt, iron ore, bauxite, gypsum
Trading partners: United States, United Kingdom, Japan, USSR

Indiana, state in the N central United States, in the country's richest farming region.

Land and Economy. The land slopes gradually to the W and S, and many rivers, of which the Wabash is the largest, flow in this direction. There are numerous lakes, especially in the N. The original forest was cleared by the first settlers for farming, which remains a major sector of the economy; the state ranks high in agricultural production. Development of varied manufacturing, particularly in heavy industry complexes in the NW along Lake Michigan, has placed Indiana among the nation's leaders in this category. Access to the lake and to the Ohio River in the S, with an extensive highway and railroad system, ensures efficient distribution of Indiana's farm and manufactured products.

People. Early settlement was made largely by people from states to the E and SE; their descendants form the bulk of the population. About 95% were born in the United States and about 75% in Indiana. About 65% reside in areas classified as urban, mostly in many small communities.

Education. There are nearly 50 institutions of higher education. Indiana University, a state-supported institution at Bloomington, has several branch campuses. The University of Notre Dame, a Roman Catholic institution near South Bend, is nationally known.

History. The French explored the land and in the early 18th century founded several forts to protect their fur trade. France ceded it to Great Britain in 1763. During the American Revolution, US troops occupied the territory; it passed to the United States at the war's end. Indiana Territory was created in 1800. Severe fighting that lasted at least until 1811 was needed to subdue the Indians. After achieving statehood in 1816, Indiana remained a rural area until late in the 19th century, when the pace of industrialization quickened.

PROFILE

Admitted to Union: Dec. 11, 1816; rank, 19th
US Congressmen: Senate, 2; House of Representatives, 11
Population: 5,193,669 (1970); rank, 11th
Capital: Indianapolis; 745,739 (1970)
Chief cities: Indianapolis; Fort Wayne, 178,021; Gary, 175,415; Evansville, 138,764
State Legislature: Senate, 50; House of Representatives, 100
Area: 36,291sq mi (93,994sq km); rank, 38th
Elevation: Highest, 1,257ft (383m), NE corner, Wayne County, near E boundary. Lowest, Ohio River, 320ft (98m)
Industries (major products): steel, electrical machinery, aircraft, automobile parts, farm machinery, processed foods
Agriculture (major products): hogs, corn, soybeans, cattle
Minerals (major): coal, petroleum, limestone
State nickname: Hoosier State
State motto: "The Crossroads of America"
State bird: Cardinal
State flower: Peony
State tree: Tulip Tree

Indiana Company, group of Indian traders and colonial speculators that claimed land in the upper Ohio Valley. Organizers sought confirmation of title, but their claim was absorbed into the Grand Ohio Company.

Indiana Dunes National Lakeshore, scenic area in NW Indiana, along 3mi (5km) S frontage of Lake Michigan; site of 200ft (60m) sand dunes; beaches and marshes. Area: 8,721acres (3,532hectares). Est. 1966.

Indian Affairs, Bureau of (BIA), division within the US Department of the Interior. Originally established in 1824, the BIA's major responsibilities are the Indian and Alaskan peoples who live on reservations. The bureau works to train native peoples to manage their own affairs under a trust relationship with the federal government and to develop their resources. The BIA became an object of protest for Indian rights organizations, beginning in the late 1960s; the organizations charged the BIA with insensitivity toward Indians.

Indianapolis, capital and largest city of Indiana, in central Indiana, 150mi (242km) SE of Chicago at confluence of Falls Creek and White River; seat of Marion co. Selected as site of capital 1820, Indianapolis was made capital 1825; development was spurred in 19th century by the coming of National Road, introduction of Madison Railroad (1847), discovery of natural gas, development of trolley system, and beginning automobile industry. The annual 500-mi (805km) auto race at Indianapolis Motor Speedway is held in nearby suburb; site of War Memorial (1901), state capitol (1878), Butler University (1850), Indiana Central College (1902), Marian College (1937). Industries: chemicals, electrical machinery, transportation equipment, flour, meat packing, pharmaceuticals. Settled 1820; inc. 1847. Pop. (1970) 745,739.

Indian Architecture falls into three phases. Buddhist, Hindu, and Jain architecture, from the 2nd century BC, consists of religious structures—stupas, rock-cut cave temples, and the elaborately carved chaitya temples. Following the Mogul conquest in the 16th century a modified Islamic architecture was introduced: mosques, with minarets and elaborate grillwork, palaces surrounded by pools and gardens, and grandiose tombs, like the famous Taj Mahal. After the British conquest in the 18th century a variety of European classical styles were used in churches, administration buildings, and town houses. △970, 986, 1036–38.

Indian Claims Commission, federal agency created (1946) to hear and determine claims against the United States on behalf of any American Indian group.

Indian Languages, North American. There are more than 100 North American Indian languages, falling into many different families: Algonkian, Athapascan, Siouan, Iroquoian, Muskogean, among others, in the United States and Canada; Uto-Aztecan, in the United States and Mexico; Oto-Manguean, in Mexico; and Mayan, in Mexico and Guatemala. Nahuatl, the language of the Aztecs, is the most widely spoken of these languages; Navajo ranks first among those spoken in the United States.

Indian Languages, South American. There are more than 1,000 South American Indian languages, with approximately 10–12,000,000 speakers. Among the more important families are Chibchan, Arawakan, and Tupian. Widely spoken languages are Quechua (the language of the Incas) and Aymara, of both Peru and Bolivia, and constituting the Quechuamaran family. Another important language is Guarani, of Paraguay, belonging to the Tupian family. Most of the rest are spoken by only a few hundred or a few thousand people.

Indian Mutiny or **Sepoy Mutiny** (1857–58), uprising of the native soldiers in the British forces in India. The revolt occurred when Governor General Canning continued policies of Westernization in India, disregarding traditions of Hindus and Muslims alike. The immediate cause of the mutiny was the use of a mixture of pigs' and cows' lard in the cartridges that sepoys (the native soldiers) had to bite in order to use in their rifles. Hindus and Muslims were offended by the substance. Those who complied with orders to use the cartridges were shunned by their compatriots, and those who refused were imprisoned by the British. The rebels gained a focus when they took Delhi, and the Mogul Emperor Bahadur Shah II reluctantly took their side. Canning ordered British troops to retake Delhi. Sir Henry Lawrence held the loyalty of the sepoys in the Punjab, and Colin Campbell did the same in the Deccan. It was these forces that retook Delhi and Lucknow and gave the British the victory. After the suppression of the revolt, the British government took away the right of the British East India Company to rule India. △1266.

Indian Mythology, The characters of the Indian myths inhabit a wondrous land where the real and the miraculous are inseparable. The favorite stories deal with fairies and ogres and genii, objects that change their size and animals or people that change their shape. The earliest records of Indian mythology are in the Vedas and the explanatory texts appended to them, the Brahmanas, dating from the first and second centuries BC. The best loved tales are found in the Bhagavadgita and the Ramayana, or tales of Rama, of the late 16th century. *See also* Brahmana; Rig Veda. △1034.

Indian Ocean, world's 3rd-largest ocean, bounded approx. by S Asia (N), Antarctica (S), E Africa (W), SE Australia (E); chief arms are Arabian Sea, Bay of Bengal, Andaman Sea; seasonal monsoons control most of the currents. The first ocean to be extensively navigated, it was crossed by Vasco da Gama on the first voyage from Europe to India (1497), and traversed E-W by Juan Sebastián del Cano, first to circumnavigate the globe (1521); scene of large-scale oceanographic exploration during 19th and 20th centuries. Area (including numerous branches): 28,920,000sq mi (74,902,800sq km). △234.

Indian Pipe, or ghost flower, parasitic plant found in forests of Northern Hemisphere. It feeds on decaying organic matter. This plant has a translucent, white or pinkish, waxy stem with a nodding flower and no leaves. Height: 4–10in (10–25cm). Family Pyrolaceae; species *Monotropa uniflora*.

Indian Removal, Policy of, US program restricting eastern Indians to certain areas. This forcible removal action, originated by Sec. of War John C. Calhoun in 1823 and continuing until the policy of "reserving land" began in 1853, fixed a permanent Indian frontier and thereby encouraged white settlement. The Indians were removed to parts of Arkansas, Missouri,

Nebraska, Kansas, and Oklahoma. It was designed to remove the danger of hostile Indians in sections settled by whites. △1274.

Indian Reorganization Act (1934), also known as the Wheeler-Howard Act, a US resolution that attempted to increase Indian self-determination. It authorized funds for a credit program to encourage land purchase and education, and promoted tribal organization with officers, councils, and written constitutions. The bill was vigorously supported until the outbreak of WWII, and since then much Indian opposition to the bill's purpose has emerged.

Indian Reservations, tracts of land set aside by the US government for Indian use and occupancy. In the 1890s the long wars between the various Indian tribes and US settlers and Army came to an end. In the peace treaties lands were set aside for specific tribes in numerous states and territories. *See also* Dawes Act. △1274.

Indians, North American, the aboriginal people of North America, believed to be of generalized Mongoloid stock and to have crossed from Asia via the Bering Strait or the Aleutian Islands about 20,000 BC or earlier. These people spread throughout North, Central, and South America and developed into many distinct regional varieties with hundreds of different languages. The Indians of the United States, Canada, and Mexico may be divided into eight distinct cultural and geographic groups: the Arctic area (Aleut, Eskimo); the Northeastern-Mackenzie area (mainly Eastern Woodland tribes); the Northwest Coast area (Tlingit, Haida, Kwakiutl); the Southwestern area (Five Civilized Tribes, Tuscarora, Powhatan Confederacy); the Plains area (Blackfoot, Crow, Comanche, Dakota); the California-Intermountain area (Paiute, Shoshoni, Nez Percé); the Southwestern area (Pueblos, Navaho, Apache); and the Mesoamerican area (Maya, Toltec, Aztec). △1392.

Indians, South American, the aboriginal populations of South America, derived from North American groups that had migrated southward. Three main culture groups inhabiting distinct geographic areas are recognized. (1) Indians of the Andean area developed the highest cultures of the continent. After AD 1300 the Quechua culture dominated almost the entire region. The Incas encountered by the Spaniards were a Quechua branch. (2) The Indians of the Amazon Basin are mainly isolated primitive agricultural communities of many localized tribes. Some were cannibalistic. The use of blowgun and poisoned arrows is widespread. (3) The Indians of the pampas, including warlike nomadic tribes and the southern Araucanians. They successfully resisted Inca and Spaniard alike. In the southernmost portion of the continent live the Tierra del Fuegans who hunt and fish and have only rude temporary shelters. △1118–20.

Indian Territory, area set aside for Indians by the US government. The Indian Removal Act of 1830 gave the president authority to designate specific Western lands for settlement by Indians removed from their native lands. In 1834 the Indian Intercourse Act set aside Kansas, Nebraska, and Oklahoma N and E of the Red River as the Indian Territory. In 1854 Kansas and Nebraska were redesignated territories open to white settlement. W Oklahoma was opened to white settlement in 1889. In 1907 the last of the Indian Territory was dissolved when Oklahoma became a state.

Indian Web Spinners. △492.

India-Pakistan Wars, series of conflicts between India and Pakistan. War first broke out in 1947, when the two countries became independent of Britain. There were serious conflicts in 1947–48, 1965, and 1971. The genesis of the hostilities lay in the antipathy between Hindus and Muslims. Early in the 20th century the two groups worked together in the Indian National Congress to oppose Britain, but the Muslims gravitated to the Muslim League. During World War II, Muslim support made Britain more sympathetic to Muslim demands for a separate state. After independence (1947) religious rioting led to casualties of perhaps 1,000,000. Hindus (*c.*10,000,000) left Pakistan for India, and Muslims (over 7,000,000) fled from India to Pakistan. In Kashmir, in NW India, the Hindu ruler wanted his state to become part of India, while his Muslim subjects were oriented toward Pakistan. There were also disputes in Bengal and the Punjab. India consolidated its position in these areas, while Pakistan opposed India. The war in Kashmir continued until 1949, when the United Nations arranged a truce. India-Pakistan negotiations continued to 1954 without resolution of problems in Kashmir. In 1965 fighting erupted on India's frontier with W Pakistan in the desolate Rann of Kutch region. Fighting soon became widespread, with each nation launching troop and air assaults. With international intervention threatened, Pakistan and India agreed to another truce. An agreement on negotiations and a cease-fire was signed in 1966. An era of peace began to fall apart in early 1971 after civil war erupted between W and E Pakistan. India sided with the E, which called itself Bangladesh. The war climaxed with India's invasion of Bangladesh in December 1971. Fighting also started with Pakistan in the W. Pakistan was soon defeated; it lost E Pakistan, had about 100,000 troops captured; and suffered hardship. The force of world opinion led to a cease-fire in December. An accord signed in 1972 lessened tension, further reduced by Pakistan's recognition of Bangladesh in 1974. Mujibur Rahman, Bangladesh's leader in the fight for independence, led the new country until his overthrow and death in 1975. Relations continued to improve following Rahman's death.

Indicator, in chemistry, substance applied in minute quantities which, by a change of color, fluorescence, or by precipitate formation, allows the course of a chemical reaction to be followed. Indicators can detect end-points in reactions involving a change of pH or an oxidation-reduction reaction. Universal indicator is a liquid that undergoes a spectral range of color changes from pH 1 to 13. △1568.

Indic Languages, subdivision of the Indo-European family. Spoken mainly in the N two-thirds of India, but also in Pakistan, Sri Lanka, and Nepal, the major Indic languages are Sanskrit (the progenitor of all the others), Hindi, Urdu, Bengali, Punjabi, Marathi, Gujarati, Oriya, Assamese, Sinhalese, Sindhi, and Nepali. Romany, the language of the gypsies, is also an Indic language. △866.

Indifference Curve, or iso-utility curve, graphical representation of various combinations of two goods that would hold the consumer at a particular utility level. △936.

Indigestion, incomplete digestion or lack of digestion by the stomach or intestine, causing abdominal distress. It may result from excessive secretion of acid by the stomach, inability to absorb fats, or from an underlying disease such as gallstones or appendicitis. It is sometimes a manifestation of emotional stress. △718.

Indigo Bunting, small finch of North and South America. The male has deep blue plumage; the female is brown. Length: 5–6in (12.7–15.2cm). Family Fringillidae; species *Passerina cyanea*.

Indigo Snake, harmless, dark blue snake ranging from SE United States to Argentina. It hisses and vibrates its tail when disturbed. Length: to 110in (2.8m). Family Colubridae; species *Drymarchon corais*. *See also* Snake.

Indium, metallic element (symbol In) of group IIIA of the periodic table. Chief source is as a by-product from zinc ores. The element is used in certain low-melting alloys and in semiconductors. Properties: at. no. 49; at. wt. 114.82; sp gr 7.31; melt. pt. 313.9°F (156.61°C); boil. pt. 3776°F (2080°C); most common isotope is In^{115} (95.72%). △1552–54.

Indochina, SE peninsula of Asia, including Burma, Thailand, Cambodia, Vietnam, West Malaysia, Laos. Name refers to former federation of states of Vietnam, Laos, and Cambodia associated with France within the French Union (1945–54). European penetration of the area began in 16th century; by the 19th century France controlled Cochin China, Cambodia, Annam, and Tonkin, which formed into a union of Indochina 1887; Laos was added 1893. By the end of WWII France had announced plans for a federation within the French Union, allowing more self-government for the states. Cambodia and Laos accepted the federation, but fighting broke out between French troops and Annamese nationalists, who wanted independence for Annam, Tonkin, and Cochin China as Vietnam. The war resulted in a breakup of French control of the area, officially by the Geneva convention of 1954. The region again became a battleground in the 1960s and 1970s. *See also* Vietnam War. △1114, 1378.

Indo-European Languages, the world's largest language family, extending over all of Europe, the Western Hemisphere, and a part of Asia. It includes the Germanic, Romance, Celtic, Slavic, Baltic, Iranian, and Indic subgroups, thus embracing such disparate languages as English, Spanish, Russian, Greek, Icelandic, Welsh, Albanian, Lithuanian, Armenian, Persian, Sanskrit, and Hindi. About half the world's population

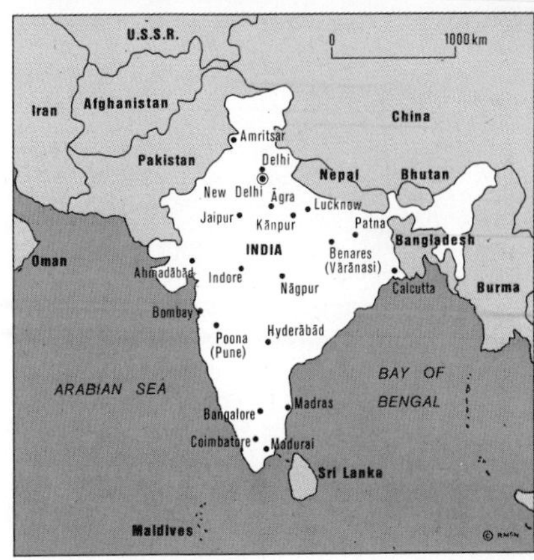
U.S.S.R.
0
1000km
Iran
Afghanistan
China
Amritsar
Pakistan
Delhi
Nepal
Bhutan
New Delhi
Āgra
Lucknow
Jaipur
Kānpur
Patna
INDIA
Bangladesh
Oman
Benares
(Vārānasi)
Ahmadābād
Indore
Calcutta
Burma
Nāgpur
Bombay
Poona
(Pune)
Hyderābād
ARABIAN SEA
BAY OF
BENGAL
Bangalore
Madras
Coimbatore
Madurai
Sri Lanka
Maldives
India

Ganges River, India

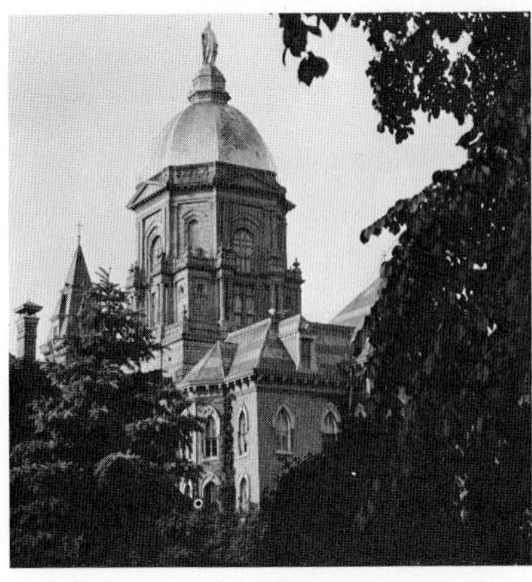
South Bend, Indiana: Notre Dame University chapel

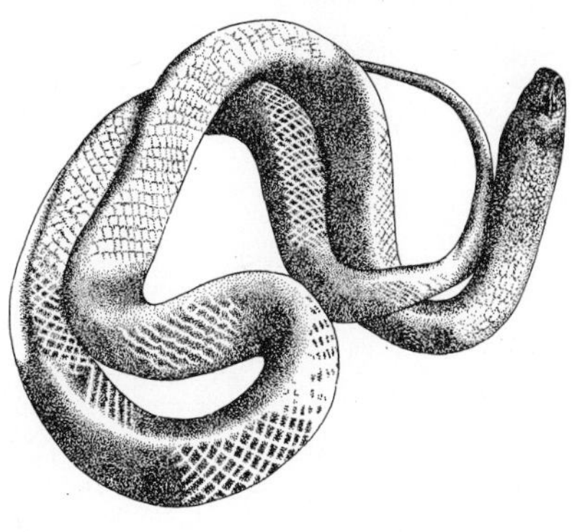
Indigo snake

speaks one or another Indo-European language. △864, 866.

Indonesia, independent nation between W Pacific Ocean and NE India Ocean. The site of ancient cultures and the unreached goal of Columbus in 1492. It has moved from communism to a republic and is primarily Muslim. A SW Asian archipelago of more than 13,500 islands, tropical Indonesia extends 3,000mi (4,800km) across the equator between Asia and Australia, forming a natural barrier between the Indian and Pacific oceans. Formerly the Netherlands East Indies, its major islands are Sumatra, Java, Sulawesi, and S Kalimantan (Borneo). Malaysia is to the N and W, the Philippines to the N, and Australia to the SE. Divided between shallow seas and volcanic mountains, Indonesia has frequent earthquakes and more than 20 typhoons each year. Average temperature is 80°F (27°C) and annual rainfall averages 80in (203cm). In spite of excellent volcanic soil and superior natural resources, Indonesia's development has been stymied by a lack of education and training. In 1966, the government undertook a foreign-aid plan to improve food and industrial production. Oil, rubber, and timber are its major exports.

People. Indonesians are primarily of Malay descent, probably coming from China's Yunnan prov. (2500 BC). A later influx of Indian traders who intermarried and spread the Buddhist-Hindu religion still influences the distinctive island of Bali. About 90% of Indonesians are Muslim. Freedom of religion is guaranteed by the constitution, and the literacy rate is 60%. Indonesian is the spoken and written language.

Government. A 1945 constitution provides for a centralized state and a Consultative Assembly divided between elected and appointed members who in turn elect the president.

History. Indonesia's Spice Islands were the destination of Columbus in 1492. By then Java and Sumatra had achieved two major empires of high civilization (12th and 14th centuries); some temples and examples of ancient art remain from this period. Western infiltration began in 16th century with the Portuguese, followed by the Dutch, who came in 1602 and ruled the rich colonial possession for 300 years. Movement for independence started between the two world wars. In August 1945, Sukarno, leader of a freedom crusade, declared a republic. Many short-lived administrations followed. In 1960, Sukarno imposed an authoritarian regime allied to Asian Communist states and the Indonesian Communist party (PKI). Murders of opposition army leaders and their families outraged the country. Sukarno's power was transferred to politically moderate General Suharto, who was elected president in 1973. In 1976 Indonesia forcibly integrated Portuguese Timor into Indonesia.

PROFILE

Official name: Republic of Indonesia
Area: 735,269sq mi (1,904,347sq km)
Population: 136,000,000
Density: 184.9per mi (71.3per sq km)
Chief cities: Djakarta (capital); Bandung
Government: Republic
Religion: Islam
Language: Bahasa Indonesian
Monetary unit: Rupiah
Gross national product: $15,000,000,000
Per capita income: $115
Industries: petroleum products, processed foods, cotton, textiles, tires, cement
Agriculture: timber, rubber, rice, sweet potatoes, tobacco, coffee, peanuts, soybeans, tea, spices, palm oil
Minerals: oil, tin, coal, bauxite, manganese, copper, nickel, gold, silver
Trading partners: Australia, France, Japan, United States, United Kingdom

Indore, city in W central India, on the Saraswati and Khan rivers; capital of former Indore state; site of the maharajas of Indore palace, Glass Temple, and monuments of the Holkar dynasty (1733–1818). Industries: textiles, iron, steel, chemicals. Pop. 494,664.

Indra, in Vedic mythology, ruler of heaven, great god of storms, thunder and lightening, worshiped as rainmaker and bringer of fertility to the fields. In the creation myth he slew the Vritra, dragon of drought, to give water, the Sun, and dawn to the Earth.

Induction, process by which an electromagnetic force (emf) is generated in a circuit when the magnetic flux through the circuit changes. The direction of the induced current is such that its magnetic field tends to keep constant the number of lines linked with the circuit. The magnitude of the current is proportional to the rate of change of flux. In a transformer the changing magnetic field created by the alternating current in the primary coil induces a current in the secondary coil. A generator consists of a constant magnetic field created by a permanent magnet or a current-carrying coil within which a conducting coil is rotated. This coil is thus subjected to a changing magnetic field and consequently an emf is generated within it. △1536, 1540.

Induction, Magnetic, or magnetic flux density, the magnetic flux passing through a unit area of a magnetic field in a direction at right angles to the magnetic force. It is measured in teslas. △1536–38.

Inductive Logic, method of reasoning by which a general proposition is supported through consideration of particular cases that fall under it; often contrasted to deductive logic. Aristotle referred to induction as "a passage from individuals to universals." *See also* Deductive Logic; Logic. △854.

Indulgence. △1152.

Indus River, river of India and Pakistan; rises in Kailas mountain range of Tibet, China; flows WNW through Jammu and Kashmir regions of India, then SW through Pakistan and into the Arabian Sea. Semi-navigable along shallow lower part, the river is used chiefly for irrigation and hydroelectric power. A 1960 treaty gave joint rights of use to India and Pakistan. The Indus Valley is the most densely populated and chief agricultural region of Pakistan; scene of prehistoric Indus civilization. Length: approx. 1,900mi (3,059km).

Industrial Chemistry. △1554, 1560.

Industrial Engineering, as defined by the American Institute of Industrial Engineers, "is concerned with the design, improvement, and installation of integrated systems of men, material, and equipment. It draws upon the specialized knowledge and skill in mathematical, physical, and social sciences together with the principles and methods of engineering analysis and design to specify product and evaluate the results to be obtained from such systems." An industrial engineer will find himself in the midst of industrial planning, management organization, and technical training programs.

Industrial Health, branch of medicine concerned with the health problems associated with a person's occupation and in particular with diseases that may result from occupational exposure to health hazards, e.g., the black lung disease of coal miners.

Industrialization. △1284.

Industrial Production Index, monthly measurement of the actual physical output of the economy, published by the Federal Reserve Board of Governors. This index expresses output as a percentage of annual production during 1957–59 and is therefore a real measure of the economy's productivity.

Industrial Psychology, application of psychology to increase efficiency in industry, business, and government. Industrial psychologists study work patterns, equipment design, selection and training of workers and managers, morale, consumer attitudes toward products and companies, advertising and selling techniques, and other topics. *See also* Engineering Psychology. △924–28.

Industrial Revolution, term traditionally applied to the widespread economic changes that took place in Great Britain, Western Europe, and the United States in the 18th and 19th centuries. It describes the process by which the economies of the countries were so transformed that the societies were changed from those in which most of the population made livings as farmers, merchants, and craftsmen to those based on modern industrialized economies. The term is also used more generally to describe a similar process in other parts of the world. Japan, for example, went through its industrial revolution in the first half of the 20th century, and in much of the Third World the industrial revolution was just beginning to develop in the last quarter of the 20th century. The conditions needed to bring about an industrial revolution include adequate supplies of labor, raw materials, and fuel; an efficient transportation system; enough capital, or wealth, to finance the building of the mills and factories in which the goods are produced; and a market in which to sell the goods. All these conditions were met in England in the 18th century. It was the first country to go through such an upheaval and its transformation is generally considered the classic example of an industrial revolution.

The population of Great Britain had doubled during the 17th century, creating more people than the agricultural, artisan, mercantile society could effectively use. The Bank of England, founded in 1694, was an instrument capable of providing the capital necessary for industrialization. Britain's expanding colonial empire offered both a source of raw materials (eg. cotton from the American colonies) and a market for its manufactured goods. Finally, Britain had large deposits of coal and iron ore. Textile making, a cottage industry in the 18th century, was the first to feel the effects of the revolution. The fly shuttle was invented in 1733, the spinning jenny in 1770, and the power loom in 1783. Large factories employing hundreds of persons were built. An international trade was established and great fortunes made.

In 1709 a process had been perfected for the production of pig iron by the use of coal. It allowed the making of the heavy machinery needed to convert Britain to an industrial economy. The revolution in metallurgy was climaxed in 1855 by the invention of the Bessemer process for making steel. The single most important invention, however, was the steam engine. James Watt, a Scot, patented an improved steam engine in 1769, and it was quickly adapted to many uses. Important among them were the steam railroad and the steamship, which together revolutionized transportation.

Along with the great wealth it produced, the industrial revolution brought serious social upheavals. The mechanization of agriculture (eg. the reaper) threw thousands out of work. Most of the displaced workers gravitated to the industrial cities, where mills and factories needed vast numbers of unskilled workers. Wages and living conditions were abominable; salaries were so low that women and children were forced into the labor market to augment family income. Vast amounts of coal were needed to fuel industry and transportation, and nowhere were the working conditions so bad as in the coal mines. There were virtually no social welfare programs in the laissez-faire atmosphere of the newly industrialized society. The sick, the injured, and the elderly could look only to woefully inadequate private charity for help.

In the United States, the industrial revolution was later than in England and developed along regional lines. The NE became industrialized quite early; the mill towns of New England developed only a generation or so after their English counterparts. Some of the newly settled western lands—notably Ohio and the coal-bearing areas of W Pennsylvania—were industrialized in the first half of the 19th century. The South, on the other hand, remained primarily agricultural until after the Civil War. Except for pockets of industry such as Birmingham, Ala., the South did not experience its industrial revolution until well into the 20th century. △1220, 1238, 1278, 1592.

Industrial Sociology, also called the sociology of work, sociological study of industry—the behavior of people involved in the making, distribution, and selling of goods; the nature of relationships common to work-centered situations; and the complex relationships between industry and society as a whole. △924–28.

Industrial Unions accept employees in the industry as members, regardless of skill level or occupation. Unlike the craft unions, the basic unit of organization is the employer, not the job. △1326.

Industrial Workers of the World (IWW), labor union; also known as the "Wobblies." This group was formed (1905) in Chicago by Daniel DeLeon, Eugene V. Debs, and William D. Haywood. It was designed to combine both skilled and unskilled labor in one organization. It was effective among lumbermen, migratory workers, and miners in the Northwest. The group, which advocated a socialistic society and employed militant tactics, supported strikes by textile workers (1912) and silk weavers (1919) in the East. The IWW split up after World War I. △1326.

Industry Equilibrium, in economics, condition in which there is no tendency for more firms to enter a particular industry nor is there a tendency for existing firms to leave it. This equilibrium position is expected to exist when normal profits are being earned by firms within the industry and may be disturbed if cost conditions change or if the industry is subjected to outside interference.

Indus Valley Civilization (*fl.c.*2500–*c.*1500 BC), ancient civilization of the Indus River Valley of present-day Pakistan. First rediscovered by British archaeologist John Marshall in 1921, it is the earliest known urban culture of the Indian subcontinent. Three major cities—Mohenjo-daro, Harappo, and Chanhu-daro—have been extensively excavated. All followed the same plan: a grid plan city with wide streets laid out before a hill citadel. Each city contained large granaries and an elaborate community bath. Agriculture was highly organized and trade was carried on with Mesopotamia. The pictographic script was deciphered in 1969 and found to be related to

Dravidian. It is believed that the cities were overrun by Aryan invaders. △962.

Ine or **Ini** (died 726?), king of the West Saxons, succeeding his kinsman Caedwalla, until 726, when he resigned and went to Rome. He fought both East and South Saxons. In 715 he fought against the Mercians at Adam's Grave, Wiltshire. His code of laws, the first for West Saxons, is an appendix to King Alfred's laws.

Inequality, mathematical statement that one expression is less, or greater, than another. The symbols >, for "is greater than," and <, for "is less than," are used: for example, $2x + 4 > 12$, which is equivalent to $12 < 2x + 4$. Inequalities of this type may be handled in a somewhat similar way to equations: thus, in the case above, $x > 4$. The symbols $\geq$ and $\leq$ are also used, for "greater than or equal to" or "less than or equal to," respectively.

Inert Gases. *See* Noble Gases.

Inertia, the quality possessed by bodies that requires force to be applied to change their states of motion. Newton's First Law of Motion is sometimes called the Law of Inertia. Frames of reference in which Newton's First Law holds are called inertial frames; Einstein's Special Theory of Relativity applies to all such frames. △1490.

Inertial Guidance, system of controlling missiles or spacecraft whose orbits are largely above the earth's atmosphere. Main components include gyroscopes for stability, sensors for detecting changes in orientation, motors or jets for correcting differences between planned and actual flight path, and accelerometers for determining velocity and position. It can be supplemented by radar observations and control to correct gyro drift. *See also* Guidance System, Spacecraft.

Infantile Autism. *See* Autism, Infantile.

Infantile Paralysis. *See* Polio.

Infantry, foot soldiers carrying portable firearms and equipment. Infantry forces are organized into platoons, companies, and battalions, and are equipped with rifles, machine guns, mortars, grenades, rocket-launchers, and other lightweight weapons, as well as supplies for several days of operations. Using voice and hand commands, radios, and flares, these units maneuver on the battlefield and cooperate with supporting arms. In defense, infantry units rely on earthworks such as foxholes to strengthen their combat power. △1736.

Infarction, localized cell damage caused by interruption of the blood supply, usually by a clot. A clot in one of the coronary arteries supplying the heart muscle (myocardium) is a cause of heart attacks (myocardial infarction). *See also* Coronary Thrombosis.

Infection, invasion of the body by microorganisms that multiply in the tissues and cause damage to cells, or the disease state caused by the invasion.

Infectious Mononucleosis, an infectious disease occurring primarily in adolescence and the twenties and thought to be associated with a herpes virus. Among its symptoms are enlargement of the spleen and lymph glands, liver dysfunction, fever, sore throat, and abnormal white blood cells. Although it is a benign disease, with low mortality, it poses the risk of rupture of the spleen.

Inferiority Complex, personality pattern marked by chronic feelings of unworthiness and a tendency toward setting excessively high standards and making unrealistic comparisons with others. △766.

Inferior Vena Cava. △688.

Infertility. △700.

Infinite, in Mathematics. △1448.

Infinite Set, mathematical set of objects, as of all the whole numbers, that contains an unlimited infinite number of members. A finite set, as of the letters of the Roman alphabet, contains a specific finite number of members. *See also* Sets. △1458.

Infinitesimal Calculus. *See* Calculus.

Inflammation, protective reaction of body tissue to destruction or injury, with resulting pain, heat, swelling, redness, distention of small blood vessels, and migration of white blood cells into the affected area.

Inflation, continual upward movement of prices. Though normally associated with periods of prosperity, inflation may also occur during recessions. Inflation usually occurs when there is relatively full employment. Under *cost-push inflation,* prices rise because the producers' costs increase. Under *demand-pull inflation,* prices increase because there is excess consumer demand for goods.

Many economists feel that money supply is a major factor in determining the rate of inflation. They contend that the rate of increase of the money supply ultimately controls the consumers' ability to demand goods. If the money supply is increased, then consumers' demands for goods increase relative to productive capabilities of the economy, which leads to increases in prices and to rationing the scarce goods. Therefore, the government often uses fiscal and monetary policy to control inflation. △938.

Inflection, in linguistics, a change in word form which distinguishes tense, person, number, gender, voice, or case. In English, this is usually achieved by adding endings to the word stem ("house, houses"; "jump, jumped"). Another type of inflection sees the word stem change ("bring, brought"). Although the system is relatively simple for some languages, it is far more complex for languages such as Latin, German, and French.

Inflorescence, flower or flower cluster. Inflorescences are classified according to branching characteristics. Racemose inflorescence has a main axis and lateral flowering branches, with flowers opening from the bottom up or from the outer edge in. Types include panicle, raceme, spike, and umbel. Cymose inflorescence has a composite axis with the main stem ending in a flower and lateral branches bearing additional later-flowering branches. △444.

Influenza, a highly contagious respiratory infection of viral origin and of varying severity. There are three general types of influenza viruses, with each type having many variations. Symptoms include headache, inflammation of the nose and throat, and muscle pain, often generalized. Influenza may occur in isolated cases, may affect many persons in a city, state, or region (epidemic), or may be worldwide, as in 1917 (pandemic). Mortality has been reduced by the availability of influenza vaccines and by the advent of antibiotics, giving protection against pneumonia, influenza's most serious complication. △714.

Information Theory, mathematical analysis of the laws controlling systems designed to communicate or manipulate information. Largely originated by Claude E. Shannon in 1948, the theory sets out to quantify both information itself and the ability of various systems to transmit, store, and process it. One of the basic postulates of information theory is that information can be treated like a measurable physical quantity, such as density or mass. The theory has been widely applied by communication engineers and some of its concepts have found application in psychology and linguistics. △1782.

Infrared Astronomy. *See* Astronomy, Infrared.

Infrared Radiation, long-wave, thermal radiation in the electromagnetic spectrum, between light and microwaves in frequency. *See also* Radiation. △212, 1516, 1520.

Inge, William (1913–73), US playwright, b. Independence, Kans. His plays show the deep feelings—hope, fear, desire—that lie below the surface of the lives of ordinary small-town people. *Come Back, Little Sheba* (1950), his first Broadway play, examines the lives of an alcoholic chiropractor and his wife. *Picnic* (1953) deals with the effect of a handsome wanderer on the repressed romantic feelings of several women. This play won a Pulitzer Prize. He also wrote *Bus Stop* (1955), about a group of people in a highway diner; *The Dark at the Top of the Stairs* (1957), about a family whose members cannot communicate with each other; *A Loss of Roses* (1959), dealing with a mother's too-strong attachment to her son; and two later plays, *Natural Affection* (1963) and *Where's Daddy?* (1966).

Inglewood, city in S California, 8mi (13km) SW of Los Angeles; location of Hollywood Park Racetrack and Northrop Institute of Technology (1942). Industries: electronics, aerospace, truck farming, machinery. Founded 1873; inc. 1908. Pop. (1970) 89,985.

Ingolstadt, city in S West Germany, on the Danube River. City was besieged in 1632 by Gustavus II of Sweden in Thirty Years' War, and destroyed by French in 1800. University built here in 1472 was stronghold of Catholic Reformation; site of Gothic Liebfrauen-münster (15th–16th century), and ruins of Jesuit college (1555). Industries: oil refining, textiles, automobiles. Founded AD 806. Pop. 70,841.

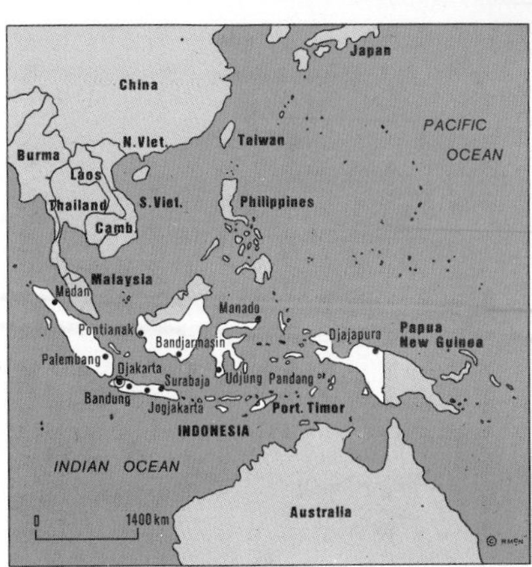
Japan
China
PACIFIC
OCEAN
N.Viet.
Taiwan
Burma
Laos
Thailand
S.Viet.
Philippines
Camb.
Malaysia
Medan
Manado
Pontianak
Bandjarmasin
Djajapura
Papua
New Guinea
Palembang
Djakarta
Surabaja
Udjung Pandang
Bandung
Jogjakarta
Port. Timor
INDONESIA
INDIAN OCEAN
Australia
0
1400 km

Indonesia

Indonesian children

Indus River

William Inge

Ingres, Jean Auguste Dominique (1780–1867), French painter. Painting in a classical style with emphasis on the careful drawing of figures, he was best known for his portraits, including one of the comtesse di Haussonville now in the Frick Museum, New York City, and his sensual pictures of bathers, including "Bather of Valpinçon" in the Louvre. He also executed large ceiling paintings. △1198.

Inherent Powers, powers that a nation uses to defend its sovereignty. Such powers are exclusive and not shared with the states.

Inhibitor, any compound that stops or substantially reduces the rate of a chemical reaction. Inhibitors are as specific in their action as catalysts and are widely used to prevent corrosion, oxidation, or polymerization. *See also* Antioxidant.

Ini. *See* Ine.

Initiative and Referendum, two methods of direct legislation. *Initiative* involves putting a proposition on a ballot for voter approval by securing the required number of voters' signatures. *Referendum* involves allowing the voters to approve a law previously approved by the legislature. If the law is defeated by the voters, it becomes null and void.

Injection, introduction of a fluid or gas into body tissues through a needle or catheter to treat, diagnose, or prevent disease. Injections are usually either intravenous (into a vein), intramuscular (into a muscle), or intrathecal (into the spinal cord).

Injunction, a legal writ issued by a court, ordering either the performance or the restriction of a certain act.

Ink, colored fluid or viscous solid used for writing, drawing, or printing. Color may be imparted by a suspended pigment or a soluble dye. Soluble dyes, often based on aniline, are suitable for ball-point pens. Printing inks usually contain finely divided carbon black suspended in a drying oil, often with added synthetic resins. Some inks dry by evaporation of a volatile solvent rather than by hardening of a drying oil.

Inkster, city in SE Michigan, on Rouge River; suburb of Dearborn. Settled in 1825 as Moulin Rouge; renamed 1863; inc. 1964. Pop. (1970) 38,595.

Inky Cap, any of the common terrestrial mushrooms (genus *Coprinus*) that have conical caps on thin stems and gills that dissolve into a fluid at maturity. *C. comatus* (shaggy mane or lawyer's wig) is considered choice. *C. atramentarius* contains an Antabuse-like substance and should not be eaten with alcohol.

Inland Sea (Seto-naikai), arm of the Pacific Ocean between Japanese islands of Honshu (N), and Shikoku and Kyushu (S); connected to Pacific by Straits of Akashi (NE), Naruto (SE), Bungo (SW), and Shimonoseki (W); divided into Iyo Sea (SW), Sue Sea (W), Harima Sea (E), Hiuchi Sea (central); includes numerous islands and islets; site of Inland Sea National Park, est. 1934. Area: approx. 3,670sq mi (9,505sq km).

Inn (En), river in central Europe; rises in SE Switzerland, flows NE through Engadine Valley, through W Austria, to SE West Germany and into Danube River at Passau; source of more than 20 hydroelectric plants. Length: 317mi (510km).

Innate Ideas, Platonic theory revived by the Rationalists, that certain "ideas," such as number, contradiction, and identity, are present in the mind at birth rather than being produced by subsequent experience. *See also* Rationalism.

Inner Hebrides. *See* Hebrides.

Inner Mongolia (Neimenggu, or Neimengku), autonomous region in N China, on N and NE rim of China bordering Outer Mongolia and USSR; capital is Huhehot. Separated from Outer Mongolia after 1911 revolution, it was made autonomous region in 1947. The terrain is mostly high plateau although the W is dominated by the Gobi Desert. Industries: agriculture, coal, iron, steel mills, grazing. Area: 454,633sq mi (1,177,500sq km). Pop. 13,000,000.

Inness, George (1825–94), US landscape painter, b. near Newburgh, N.Y. His early works showed the influence of the Barbizon School. His later landscapes became more delicate in color and detail, and he did some painting of the human figure. *See also* Barbizon School.

Innocent I, Roman Catholic pope (401–17) and saint. He developed the role of the papacy in religious controversies and condemned Pelagianism by excommunicating Pelagius in 417. He could not prevent the sacking of Rome by the Visigoths in 410, but stolen church treasures were returned. *See also* Pelagianism.

Innocent II, Roman Catholic pope (1130–43), b. Gregorio Papareschi. In 1122, he helped draft the Concordat of Worms and served as a papal legate to France. Antipope Anacletus II, elected in opposition to Innocent, led Rome until his death in 1138. Bernard of Clairvaux, supporting Innocent, helped end the schism. *See also* Worms, Concordat of.

Innocent III, Roman Catholic pope (1198–1216), b. Lotario di Segni (*c.*1161). He stressed moderation; increased papal control over civil matters; and established the courts of Inquisition in his quest to be political, as well as religious, ruler of Western Europe. During his papacy, the term "transubstantiation" became part of Communion dogma. He allowed the Franciscan and Dominican orders to form and backed the fourth and fifth crusades. *See also* Inquisition; Transubstantiation. △1084, 1086.

Innocent V, Roman Catholic pope (1276), b. Peter of Tarentaise (*c.* 1224) in France. The first Dominican elected to the papacy, he continued the crusade effort. In 1898, he was beatified.

Innocent XI, Roman Catholic pope (1676–89), b. Benedetto Odescalchi (1611). Educated by the Jesuits, he was known as "Father of the Poor" for his charitable works. He united Christian leaders against the Turks and was beatified in 1956 by Pope Pius XII.

Innsbruck, resort city in W Austria, on Inn River, 85mi (137km) SW of Salzburg; former residence of collateral line of Hapsburgs; capital of the Tirol since 1420; site of Winter Olympics 1964, 1976. Industries: chemicals, boats, metalworking, textiles. Pop. 115,293.

Inns of Court, four legal societies in London (Lincoln's Inn, Inner Temple, Middle Temple, Gray's Inn), dating from the 14th century, that have the exclusive right to admit persons to practice as barristers (lawyers) in England. The three grades of membership are benchers (senior members), barristers, and students.

Inn Yard Theater. In the latter half of the 16th century in England, the courtyards of inns were converted for the performance of plays. A trestle stage was set up at one end of the yard. People of rank sat in the roofed galleries on the walls of the inn, common people stood or sat in the open courtyard. Traveling companies, most notably the Queen's Men, performed at such noted inns as The Boar's Head in Aldgate and the Red Lion in Stepney.

İnönü, İsmet (1884–1973), Turkish army officer and statesman, closely associated with Mustafa Kemal (later called Atatürk) in the formation of the Turkish republic, and succeeding him as president (1938–50). He maintained Turkish neutrality in World War II. İnönü was premier 1923–37, 1961–65.

Inorganic Chemistry, one of the main branches of chemistry. It is concerned with the study of the atomic structure and properties of the elements, the relationships and reactions between them, and the preparation and properties of their compounds. It includes the study of elemental carbon, its oxides, metal carbonates, and sulfides, but all other carbon compounds belong to the study of organic chemistry. *See also* Organic Chemistry. △1568.

Input Device. △1672–74.

Input-Output Model, a matrix illustrating the flow of intermediate as well as final goods between the various sectors of the economy. The columns of the matrix may represent the input into each of the sectors and the rows may be used to represent the output of the sectors. An individual cell in the input-output matrix thus represents the input from one sector that results in output of another sector. The total of any one column thus represents the total of the input that is used and the total of any one row represents the total of the output that is produced. *See also* Models, Econometric.

Inquisition, a court set up by the Roman Catholic Church in the Middle Ages to seek out and punish heresy. The inquisitor held power direct from the pope to take testimony, question witnesses and those accused of heresy, and decide guilt or innocence. The accused had none of the rights expected in a democratic system of law and sometimes were questioned under torture. Punishments for the guilty ranged from penances and fines to banishment, imprisonment, and death by fire. Kings and nobles supported what amounted to organized persecution of Jews, Protestants, and others considered enemies of church and state, including those charged with witchcraft. The medieval Inquisition was active in Europe (except England and the Scandinavian countries) from the 12th to 15th centuries. A later tribunal, the Spanish Inquisition, was instituted in 1480 at the request of the rulers of Spain and was not finally and formally abolished until 1834. The Roman and Universal Inquisition, or Holy Office, was active in Europe in the 16th and 17th centuries. *See also* Spanish Inquisition. △1086.

In re Gault (1967), landmark US Supreme Court decision that extended various due process rights including the right to counsel and to remain silent to proceedings in a juvenile court.

In re Neagle (1890), US Supreme Court case in which the court broadly interpreted the power of the executive branch to act pursuant to constitutional duties and obligations regardless of a lack of prior Congressional action.

Insect, small invertebrate animals, including beetles, bugs, butterflies, ants, and bees. There are nearly 1,000,000 known species of insects—more than all other animal and plant species combined. They are common everywhere except seas and polar regions. Adult insects have three pairs of jointed legs, usually two pairs of wings, and a segmented body with a horny outer covering, or exoskeleton. The head has three pairs of mouthparts, a pair of compound eyes, three pairs of simple eyes, and a pair of antennae.

Most insects are plant eaters, many being serious farm and garden pests. Some prey on small animals, especially other insects, and a few are scavengers. Reproduction is usually sexual. Most insects have two active life stages, the *larva* (caterpillars and grubs) and the *adult* (butterflies and beetles). The larva is transformed into the adult by complete metamorphosis during the pupal stage. Young grasshoppers and some other insects, called nymphs, resemble wingless miniatures of adult insects. The nymphs develop during a series of molts, incomplete metamorphosis, and become adults with functional wings at the last molt. Silverfish and a few other primitive wingless insects do not undergo metamorphosis. The newly hatched silverfish is a tiny, sexually immature replica of the adult. Phylum Arthropoda; class Insecta. *See also* Arthropod. △492–502.

Insect Collecting, creation of a permanent collection of mounted insects, involving catching techniques, special killing methods, correct preparation, proper mounting, labeling, and attractive display. Usually only certain kinds are selected, especially butterflies, moths, and beetles. Capture often requires netting and digging. Night insects can be attracted by light or sugar solutions. Poison jars are used for killing and then the insects are relaxed on moist paper for proper pinning. Labeled collections are often displayed in mothproofed, glass-covered boxes. *See also* Insect.

Insect Control, any of various methods employed to reduce the population of insects harmful to man as disease carriers or as destroyers of valuable crops. The most common method has been the use of chemical sprays, mostly hydrocarbon derivatives. Since many of these have been found to be harmful to other organisms, however, biological controls such as introduced predators and sterilization techniques are considered more desirable. Engineering techniques used to combat disease-carrying insects include swamp drainage and spraying oil on bodies of water containing larvae. △634, 1558.

Insecticides, substances used to destroy or control insect pests. They may be stomach poisons, such as lead arsenate or sodium fluoride; contact poisons, such as DDT and organophosphates; and systemic poisons, such as octamethylpyrophosphoramide, which are more toxic to insects after absorption into the plant leaves on which they feed. Organophosphates are preferred to chlorinated hydrocarbons (such as DDT) because they break down into nontoxic substances and cause less ecological damage. △1558.

Insectivore, small order of nocturnal mammals (Insectivora), many of which eat insects. Nearly worldwide in distribution, some species live underground, some on the ground, and some in streams and ponds. Most insectivores have narrow snouts, long skulls, and five-clawed feet. Length: mostly smaller than 18in (46cm); weight: mostly less than 1lb (0.5kg). Only three families are always placed in the order: Erinaceidae (moon rats, gymnures, hedgehogs), Talpidae (moles, shrew moles, desmans), and Soricidae (shrews). However, five other families—including tree hrews, tenrecs, and solenodons—are often included the order. △546.

nsectivorous Plant, or carnivorous plant, plants ith mechanisms for trapping insects. The insects are gested with protease and other enzymes outside he plant body. These plants have poorly developed oot systems and are often found in nitrogen-deficient andy or boggy soils. The 500 species are classified 6 unrelated families and range in size from microcopic fungi to the pitcher fungus of Borneo that conains 7pt (3.31liters) of insect-trapping liquid. Some lants are active insect trappers, such as the Venus ytrap *(Dionaea muscipula)* with hinged leaves that lose on the insect; sundew *(Drosera intermedia)*, that aps insects with a sticky substance and then enloses them in leaves; and bladderwort *(Utricularia)* hat sucks insects into its underwater bladders. Other lants have pitcher-shaped leaves, such as the pitcher lant *(Sarracena flava)* and tropical liana *(Nepenthes)*. △444, 618.

nsolation, a contraction of "incoming solar radiaon" reaching the earth, measured in the solar contant and consisting of a broad range of electromagetic radiation from infrared to X- and gamma rays, ncluding visible light. *See also* Solar Constant. △212.

nstinct, traditional concept in the biological and soial sciences referring to behaviors that are unlearned nd innately determined, as opposed to behaviors hat are learned from experience. In the 19th century nstincts were often cited to explain behavior, but the erm fell into disrepute with the advent of behaviorsm. The term has recently been revived in the work f ethologists such as Konrad Lorenz. The behavior of nany lower organisms, such as courting behaviors of irds and aggressive patterns in fish, is, beyond doubt, nstinctive. However, it is much more difficult to apply he term accurately to the behavior of higher animals nd humans. △464, 812.

nstitutionalism, school of 20th-century American conomists, founded by Thorstein Veblen, who disareed with the traditional orthodox approach to ecoomics, which relied mainly on abstract reasoning. nstitutionalists believe that a more descriptive approach should be employed, with the focus on institutions and their roles. Each economic entity is examned in the context of the institutions that conditioned ts development.

nstitutionalization, process by which individuals nternalize value patterns and norms that are considered important by any social system of which they are part. Conformity to these values and norms is satisfying to individuals because it elicits positive reactions rom others in the group. Often these values and orms are related to important social concerns or "institutions," such as marriage or education, and entail pecific types of social interaction. *See also* Norms, Social. △1360.

nstrumental Conditioning. *See* Operant Conditioning.

nstrument Landing System, Aircraft, a combination of three radio systems that guide the pilot to a anding when visibility is poor. A glide slope beam sent from the runway indicates the proper angle of descent, as the localizer beam indicates its direction. The outer marker beam, set about 5mi (8km) from the runway, and the middle marker, at about 0.5mi (0.8km), show distance. △1752.

Instruments, Aircraft, measuring devices used to control the profile and direction of the flight path and gauges that indicate the condition of aircraft systems. Instruments associated with the flight profile or altitude are the altimeter, air speed indicator, and vertical speed indicator. Direction is observed with the directional gyro and the turn-and-bank indicator. The artificial horizon displays both kinds of information. Systems instrumentation may include engine condition gauges, radio navigation instruments, fuel-flow meters, and cabin pressurization and oxygen gauges along with displays for radar and electrical systems.

Insulation, Electrical, material of high resistance used to confine electricity within conductors. The type of material used varies with many parameters such as voltage, frequency, strength, flexibility, ease of removal, water resistance, temperature range, and chemical environment. Common materials include polyethelene, mylar, PVC, teflon, rubber compounds, paper, asbestos, mica, glass, porcelain. △1650.

Insulation, Heat, materials used for retarding the flow of heat, classified into reflective and bulk materials. Aluminum foil is the most common reflective material, although there is some industrial use of coated steel and refractory materials. Typical bulk materials include fiberglass wool, mineral wool, vegetable fibers and organic papers, foamed plastics, and fire brick.

Insulin, a hormone secreted by the pancreas and responsible for regulation of amino acid, lipid, and carbohydrate metabolism. Sugar unmetabolized because of lack of insulin accumulates in excess amounts in blood and urine, resulting in diabetes mellitus, in which protein and lipid metabolism is also affected. *See also* Diabetes Mellitus. △690, 726, 1574.

Insurance, formal social device wherein one party (the insured) transfers the financial consequences of risk of loss to another (the insurer) for a consideration (the premium). Insurance is practical because of the loss-sharing principle and the law of large numbers. Each insured contributes to a common fund, and the losses of the unfortunate few are reimbursed from this fund.

Intaglio Printing, type of printmaking in which a design is cut into a plate by such techniques as engraving, etching, soft ground, or aquatint. *See also* Printmaking.

Intarsia, the art of decorating furniture by use of inlay, with pieces of wood, ivory, mother of pearl, or tortoise shell. Used in antiquity and during the Renaissance, intarsia reached its peak during the 17th century. The rococo phase of intarsia that followed was called marquetry.

Integer, any of the numbers . . . −3, −2, −1, 0, 1, 2, 3, . . ., of which there is a limitless (infinite) number. The positive integers are the natural numbers. The negative integers and zero allow any two numbers to be subtracted. The theory of numbers is concerned with the properties of integers. △1448.

Integral, mathematical function used in calculus. For a graph of a function of a variable x, the integral is the area enclosed between the curve and the x axis. It is written in the form $\int f(x)dx$.

The symbol for an integral is an elongated "S," standing for "sum": the operation of finding an integral (integration of the function) is equivalent to dividing the area into a number of small rectangles parallel to the y axis, and taking the limit of the sum of their area as the number increases (and each elementary rectangle becomes thinner). A definite integral is the area between given values of x; if these are unspecified the integral is indefinite. The derivative of the indefinite integral of a function is the original function: thus, integration is the inverse of differentiation. △1460.

Integral Calculus. *See* Calculus.

Integrated Circuit (IC), complete electronic circuit incorporating semiconductor devices manufactured in one tiny unit. Hybrid integrated circuits have separate components attached to a ceramic base with interconnections by wire bonds or a conducting film. Monolithic integrated circuits have all the components manufactured into or on top of a single chip of silicon, interconnections between components being by conducting film. *See* Electronic Circuit. △1546.

Integration, in social science, drawing together groups to make a whole. The term is often applied to efforts to create harmony between blacks and whites in the United States. Desegregation—ending laws and customs that kept the groups separate—is easier than full integration. *See also* Assimilation.

Integumentary System, the covering of the body—in man, the skin. *See* Skin. △686.

Intelligence, general ability to learn and to deal with problems, new situations, and abstract concepts. No one definition suffices since intelligence can be manifested in so many different ways (eg, adaptability, memory, reasoning, cleverness). Psychologists operationally define intelligence as a score on a test that samples some of the important components of intelligence, especially those related to performance in school. *See also* Intelligence Testing. △672.

Intelligence Quotient (IQ), number summarizing an individual's relative standing in general intelligence as measured by a test. For the most common tests, the average score is defined as 100, with about 95% of all people falling between 70 and 130. *See also* Intelligence Testing. △768.

Intelligence Testing, began with the work of Alfred Binet, who in 1905 devised the first successful test, the Binet-Simon Scale, to aid in identifying mentally deficient pupils in Parisian schools. Subsequent de-

George Inness: June 1882

Innsbruck, Austria

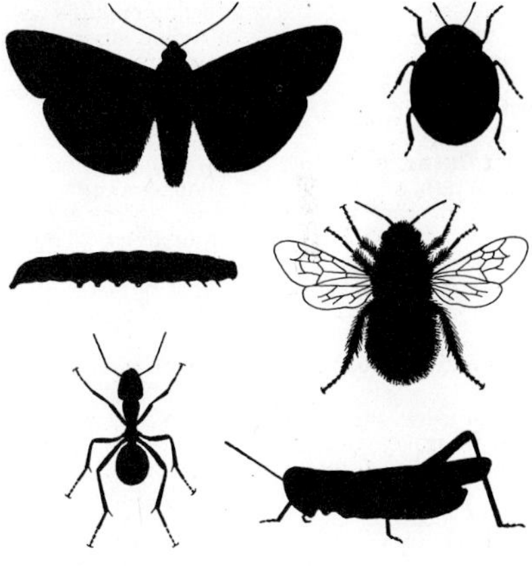

Insect

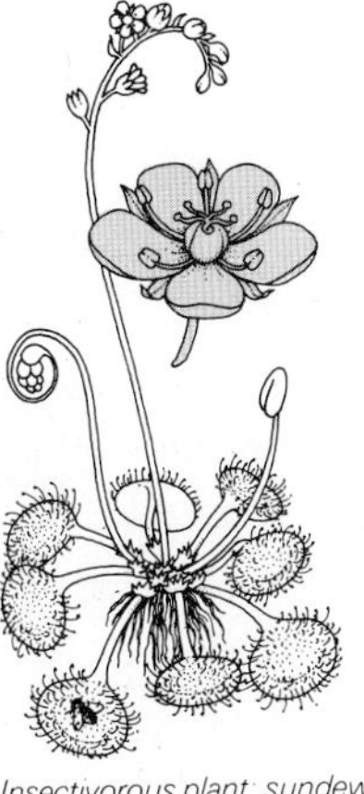

Insectivorous plant: sundew

velopments included the intelligence quotient (IQ), group tests first used to screen army recruits in World War I, and sophisticated tests such as the Wechsler Intelligence Scales. Modern tests are used for many purposes including predicting success in school, counseling job applicants, identifying exceptional children, and diagnosing the mentally disturbed. *See also* Intelligence; Intelligence Quotient; Stanford-Binet Scales. △768, 778.

Intendant, agent of the French king in the provinces. Primarily tax collectors in the 16th century, their power was greatly increased by Louis XIV, who made them his representatives at the local level, dealing with administrative, judicial, financial, and police matters. Their power was increasingly contested and the office was abolished during the French Revolution. △ 1170.

Intensity, Earthquake, effect of an earthquake on man and his works or on Earth's visible surface. Thus, intensity of an undersea quake is zero, that of a minor quake on a poorly constructed town is great. Earthquake intensity can be reduced by sound construction and proper location of cities. The modified Mercalli scale measures intensity from I (not felt except by a few people in special spots) to XII (extensive damage). *See also* Earthquake; Seismology. △174.

Intensity of Sound. *See* Sound.

Intensive Care Unit. △754.

Interaction, Nuclear, interaction in which elementary particles can take part and by which they may be classified. Hadrons (protons, neutrons, etc.) are subject to the strong interaction. This involves the strong force, which acts over a tiny range (10^{-13} cm, proton diameter). Two hadrons inside this range interact, in about 10^{-23} second, by producing other particles or being deflected. Leptons (electrons, etc.) are subject not to the strong but to the weak interaction, involving a much weaker force and a much lower probability of interaction. *See also* Elementary Particles. △1484.

Intercontinental Ballistic Missile (ICBM), long-range (5,000 miles plus) missile for military purposes. Installed in scattered well-protected underground sites (silos), they can deliver thermonuclear warheads across oceans in 30 minutes to a one-mile-wide error ellipse. Guided by self-contained inertial systems to eliminate jamming, capable of directing multiple warheads to targets hundreds of miles apart, and equipped with decoys, they are considered to have no effective counterweapon. *See also* Ballistic Missile; Inertial Guidance. △1734.

Interest Rates, price paid for the privilege of using money, a rate of return for the lender. The *prime interest rate* is the rate lenders charge their best customers, for example, blue-chip corporations. All other interest rates are adjusted in terms of the prime rate. Interest rates differ for different types of loans. Typically, riskier loans have higher rates of interest.

Interference, Wave. *See* Wave Interference.

Interferometer, instrument in which a wave, especially a light wave, is split into component waves that travel an unequal distance so that on recombination they form interference patterns. The patterns are used for accurate measurement of wavelength, length, index of refraction, etc, for testing the quality of lenses and prisms, and other purposes. The Michelson interferometer was used in ether-measurement experiments from which Einstein's special theory of relativity developed. The stellar interferometer is used to measure the diameters of giant stars. △1522.

Interferon, an antiviral agent produced by most cells of the body when infected with certain viruses. It has prospects for therapeutic use, but is still experimental.

Interglacial Age, the interval between ice ages; the period of glacial retreat. △264, 648.

Interior, United States Department of, federal cabinet-level department under the executive branch; directed by the secretary of the Interior. The department's responsibilities include the administration of approximately 500,000,000acres (202,500,000hectares) of federal land and 50,000,000acres (20,250,000hectares) of trust land, mostly the conservation of mineral and water resources, fish, and wildlife, the preservation of scenic and historical areas, and the promotion of mine safety. The department is also charged with the social and economic development of the US territories, and it administers service programs to Indians and Alaska native people. It was established in 1849 as the Home Department.

Interlocking Directorates, situation in which an executive of a company in a given industry also sits on the board of directors of other companies in the same industry. This practice is held to be "anticompetitive" and is generally outlawed by the Clayton Anti-trust Act of 1914. *See also* Clayton Anti-trust Act.

Intermediate Range Ballistic Missile (IRBM), missile capable of traveling distances between several hundred and 1,500 miles. Military advantages include extremely short warning time (about 5 minutes) and compatibility with mobile launchers (nuclear submarines). *See also* Ballistic Missile.

Intermolecular Forces. △1502.

Internal Combustion Engine, an engine in which fuel is burned within the engine rather than in a separate chamber. Piston and rotary-type gasoline and diesel engines are all internal combustion types. △1626, 1632.

Internalization, in social science, the process of taking into oneself society's attitudes, values, and ways of behaving. From parents, teachers, and others children learn roles and absorb normative standards. Taking in these norms is a major factor in the development of personality. Observing some standards for roles is necessary for social control of behavior. *See also* Role; Socialization. △888.

Internal Medicine, branch of medicine that deals with the diagnosis and treatment of diseases and disorders of adults that may be treated by medical means rather than by surgical or other techniques.

Internal Revenue Service (IRS), division of the US Treasury Department. The main purpose of the IRS is to administer and enforce the internal revenue laws. Individual income tax, social insurance, retirement taxes, corporation income, excise, estate and gift taxes are the main revenues collected by the IRS. It was established in 1862.

Internal Security Act (1950), US legislation, also known as the McCarren Act, designed to curb subversive activities. The act requires Communist and Communist front organizations to register with the government. Members of such groups are barred from employment in national defense work. Communists can be interned during times of national emergency, and aliens who are members of totalitarian groups are denied entry into the United States. Passed over President Truman's veto, it established a five-member subversive Activities Control Board to administer the provision.

International, Communist. △1326.

International Bank for Reconstruction and Development (World Bank) (IBRD), organization established in 1944 under an agreement drawn at the Bretton Woods Conference. Its role is to make loans to member governments to enable them to pursue developmental projects. Loans have been granted in such areas as agriculture, education, electric power, engineering, postwar reconstruction, telecommunications, and transportation. The major part of the bank's resources is derived from the world's capital markets. *See also* Bretton Woods Conference. △940–42.

International Boundary Commission, United States–Canada, commission created by a series of treaties between the United States and Great Britain in 1906, 1908, and 1925. It defines, marks, and maintains boundary lines between the United States and Canada.

International Centennial Exposition, the first "world's fair" held in the United States (May–November 1876), officially commemorating the 100th anniversary of the issuance of the Declaration of Independence. The exposition, covering 450 acres (182hectares) in suburban Philadelphia, cost $11,-000,000 to build. The US exhibits emphasized mining and manufacturing technology.

International Court of Justice, The (ICJ), United Nations judicial organ. Its predecessor was the Permanent Court of International Justice (PCIJ), in the League of Nations. The court consists of 15 judges from various areas of the world. Disputes between nations are heard and judgments are rendered. Its headquarters is in The Hague Peace Palace, the Netherlands. △912.

International Date Line, an imaginary line extending between the North Pole and the South Pole (approximately corresponding along most of its length t the 180th meridian of longitude) that arbitrarily mark off one calendar day from the next. This line is a co sequence of the various time zones that exist as o moves eastward or westward so that noon approx mately corresponds to the time at which the su crosses the local meridian.

International Geophysical Year (IGY) (July 1957 Dec. 1958), vast program to study the earth and i cosmic environment by scientists of 66 nation Achievements included launching of space satellite which led to discovery of the Van Allen radiation belt evidence of seismically active rifts in a chain of sul marine mountains; and approximate measurement c continental area of Antarctica. As one result of IG Antarctica was declared a nonmilitary area to be use only for scientific study.

International Gothic Style, painting style know for its decorative quality, especially in the use of gol its linear and stylized figures and landscapes; and it flatness of surface. It was dominant in Europe from th last half of the 14th century through the first part c the 15th century. Among its famous painters wer Italy's Gentile da Fabriano, France's Limbourg brot ers, and Germany's Master Francke. △1104–06 1136, 1146.

International Labor Organization (ILO), specia ized branch of the United Nations, consisting of abou 120 nations, established in 1919 as an associat agency of the League of Nations. It seeks, internatior ally, the improvement of working conditions, the rai ing of labor standards, and the promotion of ec nomic and social stability. ILO Headquarters is i Geneva, Switzerland. The ILO was awarded the Nob Peace Prize in 1969.

International Law, formerly called Law of Nation deals with the body of rules deemed legally bindin resulting from treaties, agreement, and customs b tween national states. Its sources are also interna tional statute laws enacted by agencies, conference or commissions of international organizations, such a the League of Nations or United Nations; by decision of international tribunals, and as the arbitration tribu nals of the World Court under the League of Nation and the UN; by instructions and manuals to diplomati agents; and by decisions of international law by na tional courts, such as prize courts; and are influence by the opinions of expert jurists and publicists. Sanc tions for failure to comply with these rules includ force of public opinion, self-help, intervention by thir parties, confirmation by such international organiz tions as the UN, and finally retaliation or war. △910

International Monetary Fund (IMF), agency seek ing to stabilize the currencies of over 100 participa ing nations. It promotes consultations on currency related problems, stimulates international trade, an promotes the establishment of stable currency ex change rates among members. Organized at the Bre ton Woods Conference (1944) and founded in 1945 its headquarters are in Washington, D.C. △942 1384.

International Monetary System, structure o world monetary relationships. When countries ex change goods and services with other countries, it i not uncommon for exports to exceed imports or im ports to exceed exports, thus creating a balance o payments deficit or surplus. When a deficit exists, country must pay the other country the difference This payment may involve exchange of gold or some mutually acceptable monetary unit (usually a so-calle hard currency, eg, the dollar). △1384.

International Phonetic Alphabet, a series of sym bols compiled to represent all of the sounds in al languages. In English it uses a different symbol for th "th" in "with" and the one in "them." The phoneti symbols are especially useful for distinguishing th different vowel sounds.

International Refugee Organization (IRO), tem porary United Nations agency established 1946 t assist refugees in Europe and Asia who could not o would not return to their home countries after Worl War II. The agency supplied care in refugee camps vocational training, orientation for resettlement, an a tracing service for lost relatives. The agency wa replaced (1952) by the Office of the United Nation High Commissioner for Refugees.

International Relations. △940–42.

International Style, US name for the architectura style developed in Europe in the 1920s that stresse function and abhors ornament in design. It feature stark, asymmetrical cubic shapes with windows ac centing horizontal lines. Frank Lloyd Wright and Walter Gropius were early proponents. △1322.

International Telecommunications Union (ITU), UN agency that controls the use of telegraph, telephone, and radio services internationally. It prepares scientific and technical studies for improving communication. Its headquarters are in Geneva, Switzerland.

International Trade. △940–42.

International Whaling Commission, commission organized in 1946, by 16 countries. It promotes conservation of whale stocks, enabling the whaling industry to develop in an orderly fashion and to maintain a strong commercial enterprise. Its headquarters are in London.

Interoceptive Sense, or deep sense, conveys information about stimuli occurring within the internal organs and tissues of the body. The receptors are so-called free nerve endings within the organs, and they convey information about the deformation of the organs, such as the expansion of the lungs. The same receptors also probably convey information about internally caused pain, eg, heart attack.

Interpol (International Criminal Police Organization), organization composed of police forces from more than 100 countries, including most of the countries of the western world and Yugoslavia (the only Communist member), established in 1923. Its headquarters are in Paris. Interpol's principal functions are to provide member nations with information concerning international criminals and to assist in their apprehension.

Interpolation, mathematical procedure for finding intermediate unknown values of a function lying between two known values. A common method is to assume that the three values lie on a straight line. *See also* Extrapolation.

Interposition, doctrine espousing the right of states to block enforcement of federal law. It was invoked in the South during the Civil War and, more recently, after the Supreme Court's desegregation rulings.

Interrupted Fern, large North American fern of rocky, dry areas with tall, erect fronds having small, fertile pinnae midway. When ripe, the pinnae drop off, leaving gaps in the frond. Its fiddleheads are woolly. It is a popular greenhouse plant. Height: to 4ft (122cm). Family Osmundaceae; species *Osmunda claytoniana*.

Intersection, point, or locus of points, common to two or more geometrical figures. Two nonparallel lines meet in a point; two nonparallel planes meet in a line. △1462, 1458.

Interstate Commerce Act (1887), established the Interstate Commerce Commission (ICC), thus placing the nation's railroads under federal government supervision. Subsequently, the act has been broadened to include carrier industries (e.g., pipelines, trucking) that compete with railroads. The main function of the ICC is to regulate rates and control entry into the transportation industries over which it has jurisdiction.

Interstellar Matter, gas molecules and dust grains distributed at very low densities throughout the space between the stars of the galaxy. The matter consists mainly of cold neutral hydrogen, although small amounts of other elements such as carbon and helium have been found, as well as minimal quantities of simple compounds such as water, ammonia, cyanogen. The dust grains are mainly ice or perhaps ice-covered graphite particles. *See also* H I and H II Regions; Nebula. △104.

Intertropical Convergence Zone (ITC). △220.

Intestinal Obstruction, impediment to passage of the feces through the intestine. Obstruction may occur when the intestine fails to contract, most commonly because of inflammation of the membrane covering the abdominal organs (peritonitis). It may also result from adhesions, hernias, tumors, foreign bodies such as gallstones, or other mechanical causes, or from constant contraction of the intestine. The symptoms are colicky pain and, depending on the site of the obstruction, nausea and vomiting or abdominal distention or both.

Intestine, part of the digestive system, either the small intestine or the large intestine, or colon. *See also* Colon; Small Intestine. △694.

Intolerable Acts (1774), British legislation designed to punish the colonists after the Boston Tea Party. Also known as the Coercive Acts, they closed the Boston port and moved the customs house to Salem. (Boston Port Bill). British officials who were accused of capital offenses would be tried in England (Administration of Justice Act); another law (the Massachusetts Government Act) had the effect of annulling the Massachusetts Charter, giving the governor power to control and limit town meetings and making the council and judiciary appointive instead of elective. The colonists' opposition to the acts resulted in the calling of the First Continental Congress. △1218.

Intoxication. *See* Alcoholism.

Intracoastal Waterway, water passage, partly natural, partly man-made; extends from Boston down the Atlantic coast to Miami, then up the W coast of Florida across the Gulf of Mexico to Brownsville, Tex.; provides partly sheltered route for commercial and pleasure craft.

Intrauterine Device (IUD), a device inserted into the uterus to prevent pregnancy. IUDs are made of metal or plastic and are of various shapes, including a loop, coil, T, and triangle. △706.

Intrauterine Environment. △768, 776.

Intrinsic Factor, a mucoprotein present in gastric juice, involved in absorption of vitamin B_{12} by the intestine. *See also* Extrinsic Factor.

Introversion-Extroversion, in psychology, a basic dimension of personality, first described by Carl Jung. An "introvert" is a person who is self-centered, shy, and more rigid in thinking and behavior. An "extrovert" is oriented toward other people and more gregarious. Each basic type represents an endpoint on a dimension of personality where most people lie somewhere in the middle. *See also* Personality. △814.

Intrusion, an emplacement of rock material that either was forced or flowed into spaces among other rocks. An igneous intrusion, called a pluton, consists of magma that never reached the earth's surface but filled cracks and faults, then cooled and hardened. A sedimentary intrusion consists of clay, chalk, salt, or other plastic sediment forced upward under pressure. *See also* Dike. △252, 270.

Invar. △1508.

Inventory Control, the process of organizing and minimizing the amount of raw material and/or final product held in storage for manufacturing and distribution. In recent times, linear programming has been employed to reduce storage time, warehouse space, and distribution costs while meeting customer delivery schedules and maintaining sufficient stock. Computers are quite often used to monitor parts inventories and reorder times and to keep overall records. *See also* Linear Programming. △1674.

Inverse Square Law. △1490.

Inversion, an atmospheric condition in which a property of the air, like moisture or temperature, increases with altitude. In a temperature inversion, the air temperature rises with altitude and a cap of hot air encloses the cooler air below. With little wind or turbulence to break up the condition, pollution builds up in the enclosed air, often to dangerous degrees.

Invertebrate, animal with no spinal column, or backbone. Included are 20 phyla, the two largest being Arthropoda and Mollusca. *See also* Animal. △466, 506.

Investiture, the installation into an office by a superior authority. The right to invest bishops and abbots in their positions became a matter of intense struggle between medieval popes and emperors. Gregory VII forbade lay investiture and Holy Roman Emperor Henry IV then sought to overthrow the pope. A compromise—secular selection and spiritual investiture—was reached in the Concordat of Worms (1122). △1072, 1086.

Invisible Hand, as described by Adam Smith, theory that individuals, acting in their own self-interest, will do what they should do for the good of the entire society, as if led by an invisible hand. It is another expression of the doctrine of laissez faire. *See also* Laissez Faire. △1290.

Involutional Psychotic Reactions, symptoms of mental disturbance that occur during the physiological decline of middle age. They are characterized by severe depression and sometimes paranoid thinking

Intercontinental ballistic missile: launching

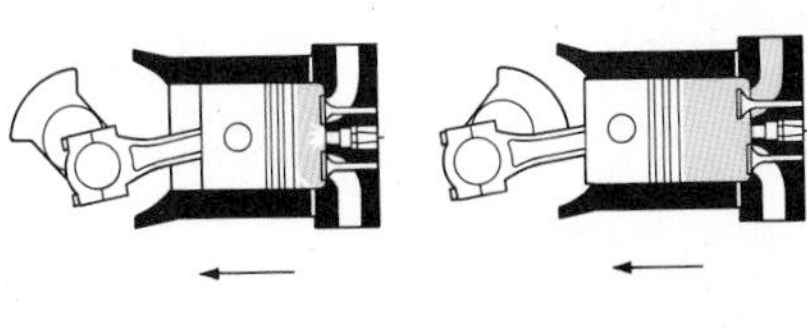

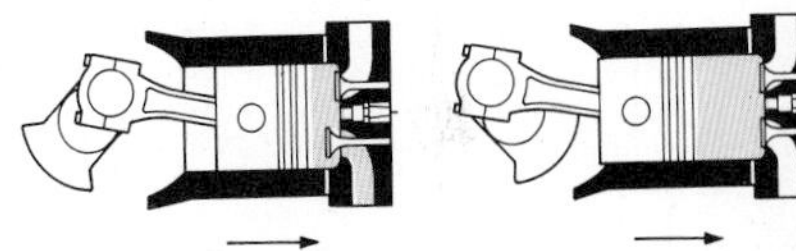

Internal combustion engine: 4-stroke

Intracoastal waterway: Miami, Florida

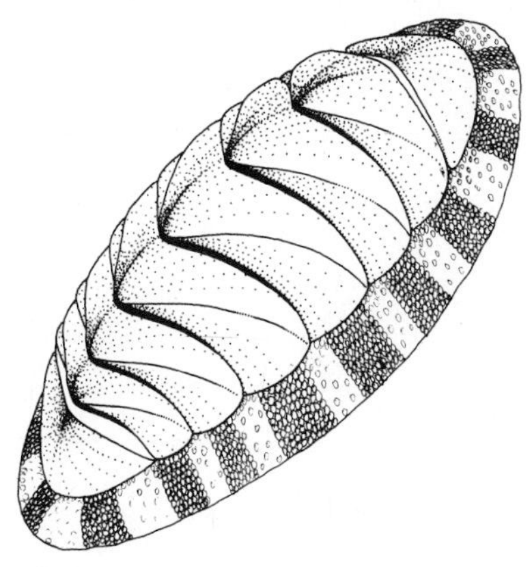

Invertebrate: mollusk

and are often accompanied by agitation and suicidal tendencies.

Io, in Greek mythology, a mistress of Zeus, whom he turned into a heifer in order to prevent her discovery by his wife, Hera. Suspicious Hera had the hundred-eyed Argus guard Io. With the aid of Hermes, who put Argus to sleep, Io escaped, swam the Ionian Sea, and was restored by Zeus. △86, 152.

Io, satellite of Jupiter; one of the Galilean satellites. Recent research has confirmed that Io has an atmosphere. Diameter 2,272mi (3,658km); mean distance from planet 262,000mi (421,820km); mean sidereal period 1.77 days. △86, 152.

Iodine, nonmetallic element (symbol I) of the halogen group, discovered (1811) by Bernard Courtois. Iodides are found in sea water. The black volatile solid gives a violet vapor. Chemically it resembles chlorine, but is less reactive. It is used as a medical antiseptic and potassium iodide is used in photography. The isotope I^{131} (half-life 8 days) is used in treatment of thyroid-gland disorders. Properties: at. no. 53; at. wt. 126.-9045; sp gr 4.93; melt. pt. 236°F (113.5°C); boil. pt. 363.83°F (184.35°C); most stable isotope I^{127} (100%). *See also* Halogen Elements. △1562, 1568.

Io Moth, large yellowish, stout-bodied moth of North America with large eyespots on its hind wings. The caterpillar is green with a white-bordered, reddish stripe on each side of its body. Its venomous spines can sting tender skin. Length: 2in (5cm). Species *Automeris io. See also* Moth.

Ion, particle of atomic size with a positive or negative charge. Simple ions can be formed by atoms gaining or losing electrons. More complex ions are charged groups of atoms held together by covalent bonds. Positive ions are called cations (they are drawn to a cathode): negative ions are called anions (drawn to an anode). Many crystalline solids are composed of arrays of ions of opposite charge. Ions are also responsible for the conduction of electricity by liquids and gases. *See also* Ion, Complex; Ionic Bond; Ionization. △1506, 1554, 1556, 1562.

Ion, Complex, in general, any ion consisting of a group of atoms held together by covalent bonds.

Iona, island off W Scotland, in Inner Hebrides, separated from the Isle of Mull by the Sound of Iona; landing place (AD 563) of St Colomba. Area: 2,264acres (917hectares).

Ionian Islands (Iónio Nísoi), island group off SW Greece, in Ionian Sea; consists of seven main islands, Corfu, Paxos, Leukas, Ithaca, Cephalonia, Zante, and Cerigo, and several smaller ones. Unified as a province under Byzantine Empire AD 890, it was captured by Venetians 1500–1797; ceded to France under Treaty of Campo Formio (1797); made a British protectorate 1815 called "United States of the Ionian Islands"; ceded to Greece 1864. Industries: shipping, timber, fruit, livestock, fishing, soap, shipbuilding, wine, grains. Area: 890sq mi (2,305sq km). Pop. 183,633.

Ionians, original Greek peoples. They were largely responsible for Classical Greek culture including Homeric epic, elegy, iambic poetry, architecture and sculpture, and the rational thought that dominated the 6th century BC.

Ionian Sea, branch of the Mediterranean Sea, between W Greece and SW Italian Peninsula and E Sicily; connected to the Adriatic Sea by Strait of Otranto, and to the Tyrrhenian Sea by Strait of Messina; forms the gulfs of Squillace and Taranto. Ionian Islands lie in the E waters; chief ports are Catania and Syracuse (Sicily), Corfu and Patras (Greece), Taranto (Italy). Depth: 10,000ft (3,050m).

Ionic Bond, or electrovalent bond, type of chemical bond in which ions of opposite charge are held together by electrostatic attraction. *See also* Chemical Bonds. △1506, 1554, 1556, 1558.

Ionic Equilibrium, equilibrium state existing in solutions of electrolytes. Strong acids and bases are completely dissociated into ions when in aqueous solution, but weak acids or bases are only partly dissociated. Electrolyte, AB, when placed in solution, may partly dissociate into A^+ and B^-. $[A^+][B^-]/[AB]$, where [] indicates activities, is a constant, termed the equilibrium constant.

Ionic Order, one of the five orders of classical architecture. It developed in the Greek colonies of Asia Minor in the 6th century BC and became known in Greece in the 5th century BC. It is characterized by slender columns with 24 flutes and prominent volutes, or spiral scrolls, on the capitals. The best example of the Ionic order is the Erechtheum on the Acropolis. △1002.

Ionic Radius. △1558.

Ionic Transport. *See* Transport.

Ionization, process in which neutral atoms or molecules are converted into ions. Positive ions can be formed by supplying energy to detach electrons from the atom, as by the action of X rays, ultraviolet radiation, or high-energy particles. The minimum energy to form an ion is the ionization energy (or potential). The opposite process—electron capture by a neutral species to yield a negative ion—is much less probable. Both types of ion can also be produced by breaking bonds, which can be induced by photons, particles, etc, or may occur spontaneously, as in the ionization of acids when dissolved in water. △1552.

Ionization Chamber, instrument for measuring the intensity of ionizing particles or radiation, such as X-rays. The gas-filled chamber contains two electrodes across which a voltage is applied. Passage of radiation through the chamber ionizes the gas and the ions formed move towards the charged electrodes. The current thus produced in an associated circuit is proportional to the radiation intensity. *See also* Geiger Counter. △1480, 1554.

Ionization Energy or Potential. *See* Ionization.

Ionosphere, the deep region of ions or charged particles in the atmosphere. *See* Atmosphere.

Ion Propulsion, method of propelling rockets by heating metals such as cesium to produce ions and electrons. The ions are accelerated through a potential difference to provide power. Presently in development, ion propulsion offers advantages of longer acceleration periods, high mass efficiency, and increased lifetimes for satellite control systems.

Iowa, also Ioway, Siouan-speaking tribe, closely related to the Oto and Missouri, who lived in various areas of Iowa for centuries. They apparently separated from the Winnebago in early times to form a separate tribe. Never a large group (1000–1200 people), they now number 250, occupying their own land in Iowa and Oklahoma.

Iowa, state in the N central United States, on the W bank of the Mississippi River.

Land and Economy. Level or slightly rolling, the land rises gradually to the W and N. Iowa was originally prairie, covered with high grass that was plowed to create farmland. Timber is found primarily along the rivers. The state is bounded on the E by the Mississippi and on most of the W by the Missouri; the principal river in the state is the Des Moines. As an income source, agriculture maintains a fair balance with industry, which has grown steadily. Farm-related manufacturing is important, but the state's industrial production is broadly diversified.

People. The first settlers came in the 1830s from the E and S states. Later, farmers from Europe, notably Germans, Scandinavians, Scots, Irish, and Dutch, came to work the soil. About 80% of Iowa's people were born in the state, and fewer than 60% live in urban areas.

Education and Research. There are nearly 60 institutions of higher education. The University of Iowa and Iowa State University are both state-supported. Agricultural research at these and other institutions has contributed largely to the state's development and use of the land.

History. As part of the Mississippi valley, Iowa was included in the Sieur de la Salle's claim to the region for France in 1682. French hunters and trappers explored the region until it was sold to the United States in the Louisiana Purchase of 1803. Indians still occupied the land, and it was not legally opened for settlement until after the Black Hawk War in 1832. In 1838 Congress created the Territory of Iowa. After admission to the Union in 1846, Iowa grew rapidly as a farming area. Industrial development was intensive after WWII.

PROFILE

Admitted to Union: Dec. 29, 1846; rank, 29th
US Congressmen: Senate, 2; House of Representatives, 6
Population: 2,825,041 (1970); rank 25th
Capital: Des Moines, 201,404 (1970)
Chief cities: Des Moines, Cedar Rapids, 110,642; Davenport, 98,469
State Legislature: Senate, 50; House of Representatives, 100
Area: 56,290sq mi (145,791sq km); rank, 25th
Elevation: Highest, 1,675ft (510m), in Osceola co, NW part of state. Lowest, 480ft (146m), Mississippi River
Industries (major products): processed foods, farm and construction machinery, electrical machinery
Agriculture (major products): hogs, cattle, corn, soybeans, alfalfa
Minerals (major): cement components, limestone, sand, gravel
State nickname: Hawkeye State
State motto: "Our liberties we prize and our rights we will maintain"
State bird: Goldfinch
State flower: Wild rose
State tree: Oak

Iowa, river in SE Iowa; rises in N Iowa; flows SE to Mississippi River near Muscatine. Length: approx. 329mi (530km).

Iowa City, city in E Iowa, on Iowa River; seat of Johnson co; seat of University of Iowa (1847). Industries: sheet metal, pharmaceuticals, creameries, hatcheries. Founded 1839; inc. 1853. Pop. (1970) 46,850.

Iphigenia, in Greek literature, daughter of Agamemnon and Clytemnestra, sister of Electra, Chrysothemis, and Orestes. Iphigenia was demanded in sacrifice to Artemis after her father killed a hind sacred to the goddess. Relenting at the last moment, Artemis carried her off to install Iphigenia as priestess of her temple at Aulis. The dramatist Euripides told her story in *Iphigenia at Aulis*. △998.

I-pin, formerly Suchow; city in S central China, at junction of Min and Yangtze rivers. Pop. 275,000.

Ipoh, city in Malaysia, on Kinta River; capital of Perak state; captured by Japanese 1941; site of Chinese rock temples; commercial center for Kinta valley region. Industries: tin mining, rubber. Pop. 247,689.

Ipswich, city in Suffolk, E England, on Orwell estuary; manufactures agricultural machinery. Pop. 122,814.

IQ. *See* Intelligence Quotient.

Iqbal, Muhammad (1876–1938), Indian Muslim poet, philosopher, and political leader. In 1930 he became president of the Muslim League. He advocated the establishment of an independent Muslim state on the Indian subcontinent. For this he is considered to be the father of Pakistan. He wrote poetry and philosophical essays in both Urdu and Persian. His most significant book of poetry is *The Secrets of the Self* (1915).

Iráklion (Candia), largest city and seaport on island of Crete, S Greece, in Sea of Crete; capital of Crete governorate and Iráklion prefecture. Founded AD 832 by Muslim Saracens, it was conquered by Byzantines (961), Venetians (1204), Turks (1669); became part of Greece 1913; site of ancient ruins of Cnossus. Exports: wine, olive oil, raisins, almonds. Pop. 77,783.

Iran, independent nation in the Middle East. Known as Persia until 1935, it is a mountainous W Asian monarchy, pulled toward modernization by the discovery of petroleum and the subsequent economic and social revolution.

Land and economy. The world's 4th-largest oil producer, Iran is bordered on the N by the USSR and the Caspian Sea, S by the Persian Gulf and the Gulf of Oman, W by Turkey and Iraq, and E by Afghanistan and Pakistan. It is enclosed by rugged mountains guarding the entrance from Turkey and the USSR. Zagros (NW) is an area of volcanic cones and intense degrees of heat and cold. Fertile valleys mark its central portion with oil in the foothills. The N highlands (Elburz range), forming an arc around the Caspian Sea's S shore, have heavy rains and a volcano (Demavend). Rice, cotton, silk, and tea are grown in the plains. The E uplands are barren and largely uninhabited. Annual rainfall ranges from about 40in (102cm) along the Caspian to 8in (20cm) inland. Revenue from Iran's oil sales is being invested in heavy industry, nuclear energy, petrochemical plants, water resources, steel mills, a gas pipeline to the USSR, and in industries in foreign countries. Traditional exports include Persian carpets and caviar.

People. A varied blend of Indo-Europeans who came down the Asian steppes *c.* 2000 BC, plus Turks, Baluchis, Kurds, Armenians, Assyrians, Arabs, Georgians, Dravidian Brahuis, and Afghan Hussars, they are distinguishable by the dialect spoken; 75% also speak Persian. Literacy is estimated at 30%. Over 90% of Iranians belong to the Shiite sect of Islam.

Government. Iran is a constitutional monarchy headed by the shah. The bicameral parliament is divided into two houses. The Majlis (consultative assembly) has 200 members elected for 5 years. The Senate has 60 members; half elected by popular vote, half nominated by the shah.

History. According to Babylonian inscriptions, a Persian state was in existence in 1500 BC. During the next 1,500 years succeeding waves of Indo-Europeans swept across the land. In 480 BC, the Persians were defeated by the Greeks; in 331 BC Alexander the Great added Persia to his empire. By AD 641, conversion to Islam was complete. From 1500–1700, Persia was ruled by a dynasty of Iranian rulers (Safawids) before Ottoman Turks deposed them. A 1906 revolt by the masses hastened approval of a constitution with parliamentary provisions under a shah. In 1926 Riza Khan Pahlavi instituted a new dynasty. He resigned in 1941 and was succeeded by his son, Mohammed Riza Pahlavi. After WWII the Teheran conference guaranteed Iran's independence. △984.

PROFILE

Official name: Empire of Iran
Area: 636,294sq mi (1,648,001sq km)
Population: 32,900,000
Density: 51.7per sq mi (20per sq km)
Chief cities: Teheran (capital); Isfahan; Meshed; Tabriz
Government: Constitutional monarchy
Religion: Islam (Shi'a sect)
Language: Persian (Farsi)
Monetary unit: Rial
Gross national product: $35,600,000
Per capita income: $762
Industries: petroleum products, iron, steel, textiles, carpets, wool, food products
Agriculture: wheat, rice, barley, cotton, tobacco, fish (caviar), silk, sheep, nuts, fruit
Minerals: oil, iron, copper, lead, chromite, zinc, coal, emeralds, turquoise, sulfur, coal, manganese
Trading partners: United States, West Germany, United Kingdom, Japan

Iranian Languages, subdivision of the Indo-European family. The major Iranian languages are Persian, Pashto, Kurdish, Mazanderani, Gilaki (of Iran), Baluchi (of Iran and Pakistan), and Tadzhik and Ossetian, spoken in the Soviet Union.

Irapuato, city in central Mexico. Industries: farming, mining. Pop. 175,966.

Iraq (Al-'Iraq), independent nation in the Middle East. Once the ancient land of Mesopotamia, it was formed after WWI. Petroleum is its economic base in a one-party political system based on Arab nationalism.

Land and economy. Land of the Tigris and Euphrates rivers, it is bordered by Turkey (N), Kuwait (S), Iran (E), Syria (NW), Jordan (W), Saudi Arabia (SW), and the Persian Gulf (SE). The land drops from 10,000ft (3,000m) above sea level, along the Turkey and Iran boundary, to the Persian Gulf marshes; 68% is desert, waste, or urban; 18% agriculture; 10% grazing lands; and 4% forests. Temperatures can reach 120°F (49°C) in July with an average annual rainfall of 4–7in (102–178mm). More than 60% of revenue is derived from the nationalized petroleum industry. Iraq is the world's 8th-largest oil producer. It leads the world in date production. Exports include hides, skins, wool, and cement. Imports are wheat, rice, machinery, tea, and sugar. Basra is the only port.

People. Iraqis are mainly of Arab descent. Muslims compose 95% of the population and include Arabs, Kurds (15%–20%), Turks, Persians, and Indians. Non-Muslims include Assyrians, Yezidis, Sabians, Chaldeans, Armenians, and Jews. The mountain-dwelling Kurds are the most distinctive group in language, customs, and militant desire for regional autonomy. Literacy is estimated at 20%–40%. Arabic is the official language.

Government. A 1970 constitution provides for a 14-member Revolutionary Command Council (RCC) as the governing body. The chief of state is elected by the RCC. Legislation is enacted by decree. Although the judicial system is modeled on the French, secret spy trials and executions in 1968–69 led to foreign condemnation.

History. Home of the Babylonians, Parthians, and Sumerians and a center of arts and learning before the 7th-century Muslim conquest, Iraq became an outpost of the Ottoman empire in the 19th and early 20th centuries. Misrule and neglect fired Arab nationalism. Although hampered by isolation, lack of education, and religious antagonisms, an Arab movement gained momentum before WWI. The three Turkish provinces of Basra, Baghdad, and Mosul were formed into a British-mandated territory after WWI and in 1932 became a sovereign state under pro-Western Hashemite rule. An army revolution in 1958 led to a pro-communist regime, and in 1968 the Ba'ath party, now the only legal party, took power.

PROFILE

Official name: Republic of Iraq
Area: 167,924sq mi (434,924sq km)
Population: 11,100,000 (1975)
Density: 66.1per sq mi (25.5per sq km)
Chief cities: Baghdad (capital); Basra; Mosul
Government: Socialist military government by Ba'ath party
Religion: Islam
Language: Arabic (official)
Monetary unit: Dinar
Gross national product: $5,600,000,000
Per capita income: $645
Industries: petroleum products, processed foods, textiles, cigarettes, cement, skins
Agriculture: wheat, barley, rice, dates, millet, cotton, tobacco, sheep
Minerals: oil
Trading partners: USSR, United States, France, Italy, United Kingdom, Netherlands, Spain

Irbid, city in N Jordan, 42mi (68km) N of Amman; agricultural and marketing center; garrison town in conflicts between Israel and Jordan. Pop. 120,000.

Irbil (Erbil), city in NE Iraq, between Great and Little Zab rivers; capital of Irbil prov.; site of ancient city of Urbillum (Arbela), an important shipping center to Baghdad; modern transportation and commercial center. Industries: grain, tobacco. Pop. 90,320.

IRBM. *See* Intermediate Range Ballistic Missile.

Ireland (Eire), Republic of, country in NW Europe in the British Isles between the Atlantic and the Irish Sea, occupying the NW and S parts of the island of Ireland.

Land and Economy. The Irish Republic consists of a central fertile plain, with scattered glacial deposits (including the extensive Bog of Allen), surrounded by broken upland masses including the Donegal Mts (NW), Wicklow Mts (SE), and Kerry Mts (SW). Carrantuohill is the highest point, 3,414ft (1,041m). It has numerous lakes, including the famous Lakes of Killarney in the SW, extensive sea inlets, bays, and many small islands, especially along the rugged W coast. Shannon is the major river, and is the longest in the British Isles. Settlement is very dispersed and agriculture, especially livestock raising, is the main industry; others are mainly agriculture-based. There are also textile, brewing, and engineering industries. Most of Ireland's trade is with the United Kingdom.

People. The people are predominantly Roman Catholic (over 95%). Irish (Irish Gaelic) is the first official language and is taught in schools and widely understood. English is the second official language.

Government. Ireland is a republic having parliamentary democracy with a written constitution. The president is elected every seven years. There are two houses of the Irish legislature—the Dail (House of Representatives) and the Seanad (Senate). Bills passed by the Dail may be amended or delayed by the Seanad. The country is partitioned into 26 counties, grouped in 4 provinces (Ulster, Munster, Leinster, and Connaught).

History. The early inhabitants of Ireland were relatively free from the invasions of the rest of the British Isles until the 8th-century incursions of Norsemen. At that time the people were organized in tribes under provincial kings of Ulster, Munster, Leinster, Connaught, and Meath. Brian Boru became king of all Ireland in 1002 and finally defeated the Norsemen in 1014, freeing the country from foreign interference. The country was conquered by the English under Henry II in 1171, thus initiating the strife with England that continued to modern times. Up to 1782 the Irish parliament (introduced 13th century) was not independent of Britain: even with the repeal of Poyning's Law, Roman Catholics could not hold political office. William Pitt achieved legislative union in 1800 and Catholic Emancipation in 1829. The country suffered from the Great Potato Famine 1845–49, which killed hundreds of thousands, and from emigration, especially to the United States. An act to grant Home Rule was passed in 1914, but it was suspended during WWI. Independence from Great Britain was achieved in 1922 (after civil war), when the Irish Free State was formed. It was renamed Eire in 1937 and Republic of Ireland in 1949. *See also* Ireland, Northern. △1314.

PROFILE

Official name: Republic of Ireland
Area: 27,136sq mi (70,282sq km)
Population: 3,100,000
Density: 114per sq mi (44per sq km)
Chief cities: Dublin (capital); Cork; Limerick
Government: Head of State, president
Religion: Roman Catholicism
Languages: Irish, English
Monetary unit: Irish pound

Iowa countryside

U.S.S.R.
CASPIAN SEA
Union of Soviet Socialist Republics
Turkey
Tabrīz
Syria
Tehrān
Mashhad
Iraq
Kermānshāh
Esfahān
Afghanistan
IRAN
Ābādān
Neutral Zone
Kuwait
Shīrāz
Pakistan
Saudi Arabia
Qatar
United Arab Emirates
Oman
ARABIAN SEA
0
700 km

Iran

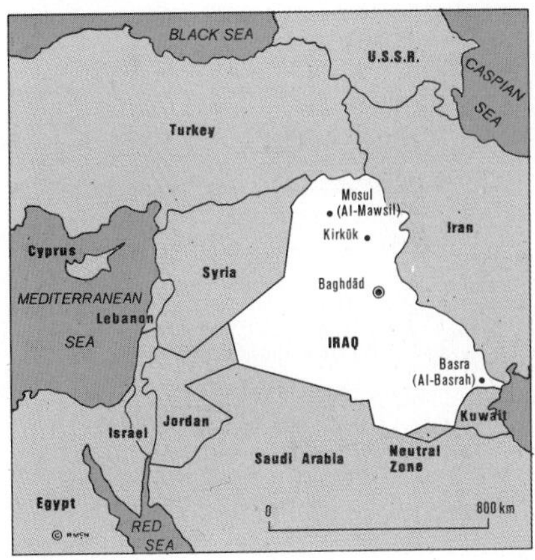
BLACK SEA
U.S.S.R.
CASPIAN SEA
Turkey
Mosul (Al-Mawsil)
Kirkūk
Iran
Cyprus
Syria
Baghdād
MEDITERRANEAN SEA
Lebanon
IRAQ
Basra (Al-Basrah)
Israel
Jordan
Kuwait
Saudi Arabia
Neutral Zone
Egypt
RED SEA
0
800 km

Iraq

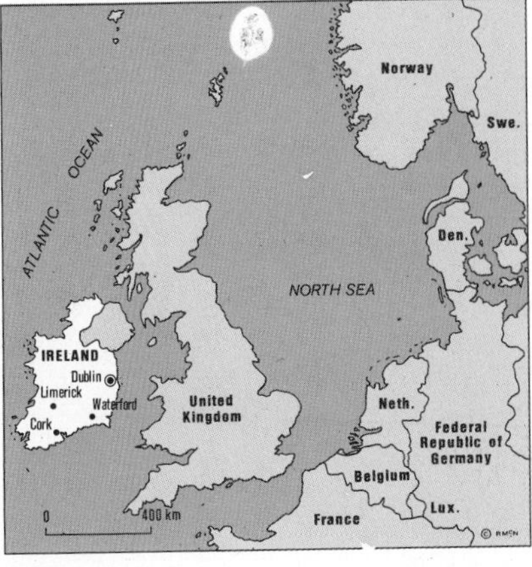
Norway
ATLANTIC OCEAN
Swe.
Den.
NORTH SEA
IRELAND
Dublin
Limerick
Waterford
Cork
United Kingdom
Neth.
Federal Republic of Germany
Belgium
Lux.
France
0
400 km

Ireland

Gross national product: \$6,300,000,000
Per capita income: \$2,165
Industries (major products): processed food, tobacco, beer, machinery
Agriculture (major products): meat, dairy produce, corn, root crops
Trading partners (major): Great Britain, United States, West Germany, France

Ireland, Northern, part of the United Kingdom of Great Britain and Northern Ireland, occupying the NE of Ireland, bounded S and W by the Republic of Ireland and N and E by the Irish Sea. The region is divided into six counties.

Land and economy. Northern Ireland is a mainly volcanic plateau with the Sperrin Mountains rising to 2,241ft (684m) in the W and the Mourne Mountains rising to 2,795ft (852m) in SE from lowlands of Armagh and Down. It has many lakes, mainly in Fermanagh, with largest lake in the United Kingdom, Lough Neagh. The principal rivers are the Foyle, Lagan, and the Upper and Lower Bann. It is primarily an agricultural region; industry is centered in Belfast and Londonderry and includes textiles (especially linen), textile machinery, shipbuilding, and engineering.

Government. Formerly, Northern Ireland had its own parliament (Stormont) in addition to representatives at Westminster. From 1974 it was under the direct rule of the British Parliament.

History. The political problems of Northern Ireland date from extensive settlement of Scottish and English Protestants in the reign of James I. In 1690, at the Battle of the Boyne, Irish Roman Catholics supported James II, whereas the Protestants followed William III. Ireland was partitioned in 1921 into the Irish Free State (a dominion of the British Empire), with six counties of Ulster remaining in Great Britain. Thus the political problems of the province arise from religious conflict between the Protestant majority and the Catholic minority. Parallel with this is the conflict between the Republicans, who want Northern Ireland to be reunited with the Irish Republic, and those who want to remain part of Great Britain.

In the 1960s civil strife developed as a result of protests by the Catholic minority against discrimination. Troops were sent in 1969 to restore order. However acts of terrorism continued as a result of the activities of the Provisional Irish Republican Army and the extreme Protestant Ulster Defence Association. In 1972 the Ulster Parliament at Stormont was suspended and direct rule assumed from London. In 1973 a new assembly was introduced, with proportional representation. Government was by an executive formed 1974 from representatives of the major political parties. This attempt at "power sharing" collapsed in May 1974, when the Protestant Ulster Workers Association called a successful general strike. Direct rule from Britain was resumed. △1314.

PROFILE

Official name: Northern Ireland
Area: 5,452sq mi (14,121sq km)
Population: 1,525,187
Density: 279.7per sq mi (107.9per sq km)
Chief cities: Belfast (capital); Londonderry

Irene, Byzantine empress (*r.* 797–802). At the death of her husband Leo IV, Irene was left regent and co-ruler with her young son Constantine VI. Mother and son disagreed on the issue of iconoclasm, and the period of their joint rule was a stormy one. In 797 Irene dethroned Constantine, and became the first woman to control the empire as an independent ruler in her own right. Unlike her predecessors, Irene believed in the veneration of icons. In 787, under her encouragement, the Second Council of Nicaea restored the orthodox use of icons. *See also* Iconoclastic Controversy.

Irian Barat (West Irian), formerly Dutch New Guinea; Indonesian prov. comprised of W half of island of New Guinea and surrounding islands. Formerly under Dutch control, it became independent 1962; part of Indonesia 1963; capital is Djajapura. Area: 162,000sq mi (419,580sq km). Pop. 957,000.

Iridium, metallic element (symbol Ir) of the third transition series, discovered (1803) by Smithson Tennant. It occurs associated with platinum; chief source is as a by-product from smelting nickel. The element is used alloyed with platinium in pen tips, electrical contacts, and similar applications. Properties: at. no. 77; at. wt. 192.22; sp gr 22.42 (17°C); melt. pt. 4370°F (2410°C); boil. pt. 7466°F (4130°C); most common isotope Ir^{193} (62.6%). *See also* Transition Elements. △1552–54.

Iris, the colored part of the eye. It controls the amount of light that enters the pupil in the center of the eye by increasing or decreasing the size of the pupil. The iris is part of the choroid, the middle layer of the wall of the eye. △674.

Iris, genus of about 300 species of flowering plants widely distributed, mostly in temperate areas. They may be bulbous or rhizomatous. The showy flowers have three erect inner pétals, called standards, three drooping outer sepals, called falls, and flat, swordlike leaves. Bearded garden irises are rhizomatous hybrids; height: to 3ft (90cm). The fragrant orrisroot comes from the dried rhizomes of fleur-de-lis *(Iris florentina). See also* Crocus; Gladiolus.

Iris, in Greek mythology, a minor deity representing the rainbow. She is a messenger of the gods and is depicted as swift-footed, golden-winged, and robed in many colors. She appears in the *Iliad* and, in her role as messenger, is prominent in the myth of Ceyx and Halcyone.

Irish Free State. *See* Ireland, Republic of.

Irish Land Question, problems arising from unjust and inefficient land management in 19th-century Ireland. Absentee landlords, extortionate rents, and multiplication of uneconomic small holdings reduced the Irish peasantry to a subsistence level. William Gladstone's first Irish Land Act (1870) recognized the principle of secure tenure. In 1881 rent tribunals were established. Michael Davitt's Land League (founded 1879) agitated for further reforms. The Land Purchase Act (1909) enabled occupying tenants to buy land on easy terms. △1314.

Irish Literary Renaissance, period of exceptional literary creativity in Ireland in the late 19th and early 20th centuries. An outgrowth of the movement for self-government, it emphasized the revival of an Irish literature. Under the leadership of the Irish National Theatre Society, which founded the Abbey Theatre Company, Irish drama was fostered. Among those involved in the movement were William B. Yeats, Lady Augusta Gregory, AE, J. M. Synge, and Sean O'Casey.

Irish Moss, or carrageen, a small dark purple seaweed *(Chondrus crispus)* with tufted fronds, common on North Atlantic coasts. Commercial Irish moss, which consists of dried carrageen or another similar purple seaweed *(Gigartina mamillosa),* is used as an agent for thickening or emulsifying foods and drugs. *See also* Red Algae.

Irish Rebellion of 1798, uprising against British rule by the United Irishmen, that attempted to establish a republic with French support. Wolfe Tone headed the expeditionary force sent from France. The leaders were arrested, and the revolt in the north was crushed at Ballinahinch. An uprising by Wexford's Catholic peasantry was defeated at Vinegar Hill (1798). △1314.

Irish Republican Army (IRA), semi-military, primarily Roman Catholic organization dedicated to establishing a united Irish republic. Formed in 1919, the IRA waged guerrilla warfare against British rule. Some members ("Irregulars") rejected the Anglo-Irish settlement (1921), fighting a civil war until 1923. Periodically active since that time, in 1969 the "provisional" wing ("Provos"), committed to armed struggle, split from the "official" IRA, which emphasized political activities. Thereafter, the Provos became prominent in the violence among Roman Catholics, Protestants, and British troops in Northern Ireland. △1314.

Irish Sea, arm of Atlantic Ocean, between Ireland and Great Britain; connected with Atlantic by North Channel (N) and by St George's Channel (S). Scotland, Wales, and England are on its E shore and Ireland on W. Chief ports are Dublin, Liverpool, Barrow-in-Furness. Isle of Man, Anglesey, and Holyhead are largest islands. Area: 40,000sq mi (103,600sq km).

Irish Setter, bird and gun dog (sporting group) bred in Ireland as red and white dog from early 18th century and as the popular solid red from 19th. A beautiful dog, it has a long, lean head with deep muzzle and low-set, hanging ears. The body and neck are long and the legs sturdy. A tapered tail is carried straight. The fine, flat mahogany or chestnut red coat is longer on ears, legs, chest, belly, and tail. Average size: 26–27in (66–69cm) high at shoulder; 50–70lb (23–32kg).

Irish Terrier, an all-round working dog (terrier group) bred in Ireland for vermin control and brought to US about 1873. Lithe, yet animated, it has a long, flat head, squared off by chin whiskers. The small, V-shaped ears droop forward. Legs and body are moderately long. The tail, docked to ¾ length, is set high. Its dense, wiry coat is whole-colored in bright red, red wheaten, or golden red. Average size: 18in (45.5cm) high at shoulder; 27lb (12kg). *See also* Terrier.

Irish Theater, plays written in English or Gaelic on Irish subjects by Irish playwrights and performed by Irish actors. Although undistinguished until the 1900s due to the lure of London for Irish talent, much progress was subsequently made. *See also* Irish Literary Renaissance; Abbey Theatre.

Irish Water Spaniel, water dog (sporting group) developed in Ireland of ancient lineage. Its large, domed head with square muzzle has a curly topknot and long, lobular ears. The medium-long body is higher at hindquarters. Legs are medium-long with large feet. A long, characteristic "rat tail" tapers to a fine point. A solid liver coat is in tight ringlets on the body and longer and wavy on the legs and belly. Average size: 22–24in (56–61cm) high at shoulder; 45–65lb (20–29kg). *See also* Sporting Dog.

Irish Wolfhound, large Celtic hunting dog (hound group) dating from 273 BC and used by royalty to hunt Irish wolf and elk. A commanding dog, it has a long head with long, pointed muzzle; small, thrown-back ears; deep and wide-chested body with long back and drawn-up belly; long, straight legs; and long, slightly curved tail. The coat is rough on body, legs, and head; wiry and long over eyes and under chin. Colors are gray, brindle, red, black, white, and fawn. Average size: 34in (86cm) high at shoulder; 140lb (63kg). *See also* Hound.

Iritis, inflammation of the iris, the colored part of the eye, which forms the contractile pupil. Usually the disease also involves the muscular ciliary body at the base of the iris. Pain, redness, and mistiness of vision are the symptoms, caused by trauma, infection, or systemic disease.

Irkutsk, city in Russian SFSR, USSR, 45mi (72km) from Lake Baikal, on Angara River; capital of Irkutsk oblast; largest city in E Siberia; growth spurred from trade with China and Amur Valley, Lena goldfields; cultural and educational center. Industries: lumber, machine tools, electrical equipment, mica processing, hydroelectricity. Founded 1652. Pop. 451,000.

IRO. *See* International Refugee Organization.

Iron, common metallic element (symbol Fe) of the first transition series, known from earliest times. Chief ores are hematite (Fe_2O_3), magnetite (Fe_3O_4), and iron pyrites (FeS_2). It is obtained in a blast furnace by reducing the oxide with coke (carbon), using limestone to form a slag. The pure metal—a reactive soft element—is rare: most iron is used alloyed with carbon and other elements in the various forms of steel. The element has four allotropic forms, one of which is ferromagnetic. Properties: at. no. 26; at. wt. 55.84; sp gr 7.874; melt. pt. 2795°F (1535°C); boil. pt. 4982°F (2750°C); most common isotope Fe^{56} (91.66%). *See also* Steel Transition Elements. △1220, 1554, 1584, 1592.

Iron, Steam. △1818.

Iron Act (1750), law passed by Parliament to protect the English iron industry by eliminating duties on iron exported to the American colonies and limiting colonial manufacture of certain iron products.

Iron Age, period succeeding the Bronze Age in which man learned to smelt iron. The Hittites probably developed the first important iron industry in Armenia soon after 2000 BC. Iron's superior strength and the widespread availability of its ore caused it gradually to supersede bronze. *See also* Bronze Age. △1592.

Iron Curtain, term coined in 1946 by Winston Churchill in a speech at Westminster, Mo., to describe the division between Communist Eastern Europe and the West. Soviet policy restricts travel, communications, and exchange of ideas across this boundary.

Iron-deficiency Anemia. *See* Anemia.

Iron Guard, extreme right-wing, anti-Semitic, Romanian Fascist group, also called the Legion of the Archangel Michael. It flourished during the 1920s and 1930s. King Carol II, in order to establish a dictatorship, in 1938 outlawed all political parties and reportedly ordered the killing of 14 Guard leaders and the arrest and imprisonment of hundreds more. The Guard again became powerful under the dictatorship of Ion Antonescu in World War II.

Iron Law of Oligarchy, social theory devised by Robert Michels that suggests that a certain amount of oligarchy—government by the few—is inevitable when control is needed as a result of conflict in society. Even in a democracy, Michels said, elitism follows from leadership.

on Lung, a term popularly used for the Drinker spirator, which is a device that provides long-term tificial respiration. It consists of a metal tank in hich the patient's body is enclosed but with his head utside. By alternating negative and positive pressure the tank, breathing is maintained.

on Meteorite. △92.

on Ore. △1592.

ony, figure of speech in which what is said is the pposite or different from what is meant. Irony can so refer to a situation or event, as when, intending ood, evil is done. Often found in epigrams, it hides eep passion under a cloak of indifference, eg, Oscar Vilde's "A thing is not necessarily true because a man ies for it." *See also* Epigram.

roquois Confederacy or **Iroquois League,** North merican Indian confederation of five (later six) tribes ving in upper New York State. The confederacy, inuding the Mohawk, Oneida, Onondaga, Cayuga, and eneca tribes, joined with the Tuscarora tribe in 722, to become known as the Six Nations. The conederacy was marked by good organization and effecve leadership. Voting in the federated council was onducted by tribe, and war could be waged only after unanimous decision, although some intertribal conict occurred.

roquois War (1642–53), territorial expansion war arried out by the Iroquois confederation of Mohawk, Oneida, Onondaga, Cayuga, and Seneca Indians. The oquois, or Five Nations, enlarged their New York erritory to the north, west, and south by dispersing he Hurons (1649), the Tabacco Indians, Neutral Naons (1650), the Eries (1656), Conestogas (1675), nd Illinois (1684).

rrational Number. *See* Number, Irrational.

rrawaddy (Irawadi), river in central Burma, formed y union of Mali and Nmai rivers; flows S, traversing ength of Burma, and serves as economic and comnunications route for Myitkyina, Bhamo, Mandalay, Pakokku, Pye, Henzada; forms a vast delta extending 180mi (290km) to Andaman Sea; beginning in S Burma, between Bassein River (W) and the Irrawaddy River, it is one of world's greatest rice-producing regions. With the Chindwin River, its chief tributary, the rrawaddy is one of the major rivers of Asia. River ength: approx. 1,000mi (1,610km).

rredentists, Italian party of late 19th and early 20th centuries that sought annexation of nearby territories, such as Trentino and Trieste, containing large numbers of Italians. After Italy's unification (1860–70), they aimed to gain Italian-inhabited areas controlled by Austria and worked to keep Italy out of the Triple Alliance, which included Austria. They also influenced taly's decision to enter World War I with the Allies again against Austria).

rregular Galaxy. △122.

rrigation, artificial watering of land to supply necessary moisture for growing crops. It occurs worldwide n regions with inadequate precipitation and dates to 2000 BC in Egypt. Primitive forms, such as buckets and water wheels, are still used in remote areas. Surface water in streams, rivers, and lakes or subsurface water from wells is used, depending on locality. Dikes, sprinklers, surface gravity, or underground pipes transport the water to desired locations. Suitable drainage systems are imperative when irrigating because concentrations of dissolved salts are injurious to plants and salt-saturated soil is agriculturally worthless. △314, 1614, 1762–64.

IRS. *See* Internal Revenue Service.

Irtysh (Irtyš), river in NE Kazakh SSR and W Siberia, USSR, and central Asia; rises in W Mongolian Altai Mts, China; flows W into Lake Zaisan, then NW in Kazakh and Siberia to join Ob River near Khanty-Mansiysk; largest tributary of the Ob River; navigable for complete length of 2,760mi (4,444km).

Irving, (Sir) Henry (1838–1905), English actor-manager, b. John Henry Brodribb. With his partner Ellen Terry he dominated the London stage for 30 years. He made his first professional appearance in 1856 and first played with Terry in *Katherine and Petrucchio* (1867). He began his long association with the Lyceum Theatre in an adaptation of *The Pickwick Papers* (1871). He inaugurated his management of the Lyceum with *Hamlet* (1878), and continued to produce many other Shakespeare plays as well as those of other authors. He made his last appearance at the Lyceum in *The Merchant of Venice* (1902), after which he made occasional appearances at other London theaters and on tour. △1240.

Irving, Washington (1783–1859), US author, b. New York City. The first American to achieve international fame as a writer, he began his career writing satirical pieces for newspapers and was a participant in the *Salmagundi Papers* (1807–8). Under the name Diedrich Knickerbocker, he wrote *A History of New York* (1809), a social satire that gained him acclaim. In 1815 he went to England, where he lived for many years. While there, *The Sketch Book of Geoffrey Crayon, Gent.* (1820) appeared. Many of the stories in *The Sketch Book* drew on scenes and legends from his childhood in New York State. The most famous stories are "The Legend of Sleepy Hollow" and "Rip Van Winkle."

In 1826 he went to Madrid, where he did research for his four books about Spanish life and history. These included *A Chronicle of the Conquest of Granada* (1829), *The Legends of the Alhambra* (1832), and two books on Columbus (1828, 1831). After returning to the United States in 1832, he traveled briefly in the West, which provided the background for *Astoria* (1836) and *The Adventures of Captain Bonneville, U.S.A.* (1837). Except for an interlude (1842–46) as US minister to Spain, he spent the rest of his life at his home in Tarrytown, N.Y. △1374.

Irving, city in NE Texas; NW suburb of Dallas; site of Texas Stadium (home of Dallas Cowboys, professional football team), Dallas–Fort Worth Airport (1974), site of the University of Texas at Irving. Industries: building supplies, insecticides, cleaning materials, electronic equipment, tools, food processing, oil distribution. Inc. 1914. Pop. (1970) 97,260.

Irvington, town in NE New Jersey, adjoining Newark. Founded 1692 as Camptown, it was renamed 1852 for Washington Irving. Industries: model electric trains (since 1900), cutlery, metal castings. Inc. 1898. Pop. (1970) 59,743.

Irwin, James. △146.

Isaac, in the Bible, only son of Abraham and Sarah, born when Abraham was 100 and Sarah in her 90s. God, who commanded Abraham to sacrifice Isaac in an act of faith, rescinded the order just before the killing. Isaac married Rebecca and they had two sons, Jacob and Esau.

Isaac I Comnenus (died 1061), Byzantine emperor (*r.* 1057–59) and first ruler of the Comnenian dynasty. A former general, Isaac was known chiefly for military victories against the Seljuk and Patzinak Turks.

Isaac II Angelus (*d.* 1204), Byzantine emperor (*r.* 1185–95, 1203–04). Under Isaac, government corruption was rampant; it was said by contemporaries that the emperor himself sold government posts like vegetables in a market.

Isabel of Bavaria (1371–1435), daughter of the duke of Bavaria and queen consort of Charles VI of France. The insanity of her husband occasioned her meddling in state affairs, most conspicuously the treaty of Troyes (1420) in which she disinherited her son, the future Charles VII, in favor of Henry V of England.

Isabella (1292–1358), queen of England (1308–27), wife of Edward II, daughter of Philip IV of France. Neglected by her husband, she formed a liaison with Roger de Mortimer. They raised armies, deposed Edward II, and proclaimed her eldest son, Edward III, king (1327). She virtually ruled England until 1330 when Edward III had Mortimer executed. *See also* Mortimer, Roger de.

Isabella I, or **Isabella the Catholic** (1451–1504), Spanish queen of Castile and León (1474–1504). She was the daughter of John II. When her half brother Henry IV died, Isabella contested the right of Henry's daughter, Juana of Portugal, to succeed. A long struggle resulted, but Isabella won and was crowned in 1479. She married Ferdinand II of Aragon, and they ruled their two kingdoms jointly, thereby forming the basis for a unified Spain. The reign of Isabella and Ferdinand was one of the most important in Spanish history. The last Moorish stronghold on the peninsula, the kingdom of Granada, was rechristianized under the rule of the Catholic kings, as Ferdinand and Isabella were known. Christopher Columbus, under their sponsorship, discovered the New World, thereby opening the way for the great Spanish empire of the 16th century. The Jews were expelled from Spain, the Spanish Inquisition was inaugurated, and a policy of forcible conversion of the Moors was begun. All these took place in the momentous year of 1492. Upon

Irish setter

Irish terrier

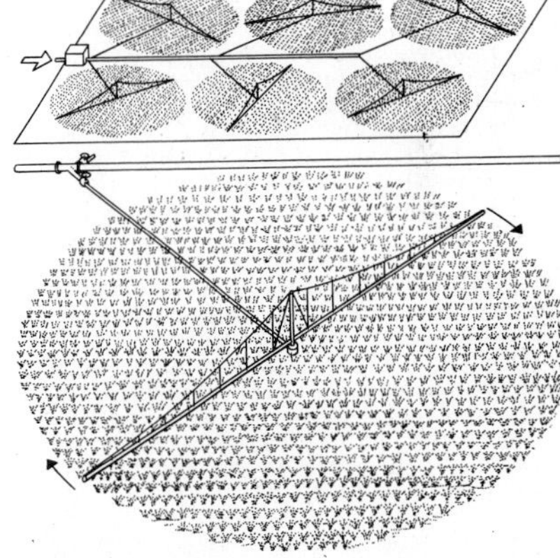

Irrigation

Washington Irving

Isabella's death, she was succeeded in Castile by her daughter Joanna. *See also* Spanish Inquisition.

Isabella II (1830–1904), queen of Spain (1833–68). She was the daughter of Ferdinand VII and Maria Christina. Her father changed Spanish law so that she could succeed. Her uncle, Don Carlos, contested her right to the crown, and the first of the Carlist wars began. Until she came of age, Isabella's reign was under the regency first of her mother and then Baldomero Espartero. Her reign was beset by constant conflict and in 1868 she abdicated. In 1870 she renounced her claims in favor of her son, Alfonso XII. *See also* Carlists.

Isaiah, biblical prophet during the reigns of Judah's kings, Uzziah, Jotham, Ahaz, and Hezekiah. The Book of Isaiah, thought to be written by several persons over a long span of years, describes Messianic blessings and announces the birth of Immanuel as a sign that Judah will not perish. △982.

Ischemia. △678.

Ischia, island off S Italy in the Tyrrhenian Sea, between Gulf of Gaeta and Bay of Naples. Known as Emerald Isle, it is a health resort and tourist center; suffered last volcanic eruptions 1301; earthquakes are common. Chief town is Ischia, containing remains from 5th-century BC Greek construction. Area: 18sq mi (47sq km). Settled in 8th century BC. Pop. 14,139.

Isfahan (Eṣfahān), city in central Iran, on Zayandeh River; capital of Eṣfahān prov. The ancient city of Aspadana, it was Arab capital 7th century. Seljuk Turks (1051) and Shah Abbas I (1598) adorned the city with beautiful and ornate buildings, including the Shaykh Lutfullah Mosque, Masjid-i-Shah (imperial mosque), and the Ali Qapu (gateway to the royal palace). The city was besieged by Afghans 1723, and most of the population was massacred. Considerable restoration has been done; site of University of Eṣfahan (1966). Industries: steel, textiles, carpets, metalwork, handcrafts. Pop. 444,000.

Isherwood, Christopher William Bradshaw (1904–), English writer who collaborated with W.H. Auden on experimental verse dramas: *The Dog Beneath the Skin* (1935) and *The Ascent of F6* (1936). Isherwood wrote novels on international politics. *All the Conspirators* (1928) was his first; he then went to Germany for 4 years and developed material for *The Last of Mr. Norris* (1935) and *Goodbye to Berlin* (1939). These formed the basis for John Van Druten's play *I am a Camera* (1951) and the musical *Cabaret* (1966). He emigrated to the United States in 1939. Later he withdrew into Hindu mysticism.

Ishihara Test, a method of detecting the presence of color blindness by showing the subject plates that contain dots of various sizes and colors. *See also* Color Blindness.

Ishii, Kikujiro (1866–1945), Japanese diplomat. In 1907–08 he negotiated the Gentleman's Agreement with the United States that excluded the immigration of Japanese laborers into the United States. He was ambassador to France (1912–14), foreign minister (1915–16), and ambassador to the United States (1918–19). In 1917 he negotiated the Lansing-Ishii Agreement with the United States that recognized Japanese interests in China.

Ishikari, second-longest river in Japan, in W Hokkaido; rises in mountainous interior, flows SW to Ishikari Bay near Otaru; irrigates the Ishikari lowland, rich rice-producing area. Length: 225mi (362km).

Ishmael, several biblical figures, most notably Abraham's son by Hagar and half brother to Isaac. He married an Egyptian and fathered 12 sons and one daughter, who married Esau, Isaac's son.

Ishtar, principal goddess of the Assyro-Babylonian pantheon. In ancient mythology she is the daughter of Anu, the sky god, and Sin, the moon god. Through the centuries, as she absorbed local deities and her power grew, she came to exhibit diverse attributes, those of a compassionate mother goddess and of a lustful goddess of sex and war. Ishtar is identified with the Sumerian Inanna, Phoenician Astarte, and the biblical Ashtoreth. Because of her confusion with other gods her name became synonymous with goddess. △978.

Isidore of Seville (*c.* 560–636), Spanish scholar, chronicler, and Archbishop of Seville. His most important work is *Etymologiae*, an encyclopedia of knowledge that became a standard source during the Middle Ages. He is perhaps best known for the "False Decretals," a collection of documents dealing with papal supremacy and the rights of bishops. Although attributed to Isadore, they were actually for the most part forged in France in the mid-9th century. △1780.

Isidorus of Miletus (6th century), Greek architect. With Amthemius of Tralles he built the Hagia Sophia in Constantinople (532–37). A younger namesake rebuilt the church's great tower. *See also* Hagia Sophia.

Isis, in Egyptian mythology, the wife of Osiris and mother of Horus, worshiped as the protector of children. After the murder of Osiris by his brother Seth, Isis searched for and retrieved the dismembered parts of Osiris' body and magically revived him. The epitome of faithfulness and maternal devotion, her fame was spread throughout the ancient world by the Ptolemies and the Romans. △834.

Iskenderun, formerly Alexandretta; port city in S Turkey, 60mi (97km) SE of Adana, on Gulf of Iskenderun. City was taken by Arabs 7th century; occupied by Turkey 1515; became part of French-mandated Syria after WWI; regained by Turkey 1939. By mid-20th century it was the main Turkish port on the Mediterranean. Exports: cotton, grain, fruit, wool, hides. Founded after 333 BC by Alexander the Great to commemorate his victory over the Persians at Issus. Pop. 69,382.

Islam, monotheistic religion founded by Mohammed in Arabia in the 7th century. Members of this faith are called Muslims. The Koran (sacred book) and the Hadiths (oral reports of Mohammed's words, or comments on his words) are the primary Muslim sources. The central themes of Islamic doctrine are belief in the unity of God or Allah, in Mohammed's prophetic mission, and in the universal Judgment Day to come. Islam is strictly monotheistic, hence *shirk* or idolatry is an unforgivable sin. Allah's mercy is shown by the fact that he sent 28 prophets to mankind, including Moses and Jesus, the last being Mohammed. Muslims are expected to observe the Sharia, the law defining the path in which God wants them to walk. A Muslim's duty is further set by the Five Pillars of Islam: confession of faith, customarily through reciting the *shahada*, "There is no God but Allah, and Mohammed is his prophet"; prayer five times daily; fasting during the sacred month of Ramadan; almsgiving; and making at least one pilgrimage to the shrine at Mecca.

During Mohammed's lifetime, his followers were all in Arabia. After his death in 632, Muslim armies quickly conquered an empire three times the size of Rome's and stretching from Spain to the Indus valley. The great Islamic empires were broken up, but there are currently over 400,000,000 Muslims spread over the world. There are heavy concentrations in the Middle East, North Africa, Afghanistan, Pakistan, and Indonesia and smaller but still substantial numbers in central and southern Africa, India, China, SE Asia, the Philippines, and parts of the USSR. There are 800,000 Muslims in the Western world. *See also* Koran; Mohammed; Shi'a; Sunnis. △846, 1058, 1062.

Islamabad, city in NE Pakistan, 9mi (14km) NE of Rawalpindi; capital of Pakistan. Construction of the city began in 1960, to replace Karachi as capital; site of National University (1965), Grand National Mosque; nearby are ruins of Taxila. The economy of Islamabad is based mainly on government activity. Pop. 235,000.

Islamic Architecture, architectural style developed by the followers of Mohammed. Because the earliest (7th century) Muslims were nomadic, their first mosques were captured Christian churches whose spires served as minarets. Later, liturgical needs dictated architectural form: minarets from which the faithful could be summoned; a courtyard with a central fountain for ritual washing, surrounded by colonnaded walks for protection from the sun; a praying chamber surmounted by a dome and horseshoe arches to lend magnificence; and rich surface decorations of mosaic, carved stone, and paint. A notable early example is the Mosque of Damascus (715). Later mosques that exemplify the style are those at Tabriz, Persia (1204), Cairo (1384), and Isfahan, Persia (1585). △1064.

Islamic Art, the arts produced by peoples who, beginning with the 7th century, adopted the Islamic faith. During Mohammed's time, the Arabs had little art of their own; they adopted the art of countries they conquered, such as Syria, Egypt, Mesopotamia, and Persia. The mosque, with its *mihrab*, or prayer niche, and *mimbar*, or prayer pulpit, was highly decorated, as was the Koran, the sacred book of the Muslims. Calligraphy and illumination were major forms of decoration. Religious art was highly geometric, often using the arabesque, because the Muslim religion forbade use of human or animal forms in religious decoration. Humans and animals appear frequently in secular paintings, such as in frescoes and mosaics. Islamic art included highly ornamented metalwork often inlaid with red copper. The most famous cente of metalwork was 13th-century Mosul, in N Mesopo tamia. Islamic art also included highly developed po tery and ceramics, with excellent glazes and decora tion, such as those produced during the 12th and 13t centuries in Persia and during the 13th and 14th cer turies in the city of Kashan. The Islamic *minai*, c enamel, technique reached its zenith in the 16th cer tury in Isfahan, where entire walls were decorated i faience. Perhaps the best known art of the Islami world is the highly developed one of rug making Some of the finest carpets in the world date from th 16th and 17th centuries and were made from woc and silk under the rule of the Safavids. △1064, 1204

Islamic Law, or **Sharia,** practical ordinances of th Islamic religion. Found in the Koran, it is believed t be the revelations by God to Mohammed, the trad tional sayings of Mohammed, the consensus of th community in the past, and analogical reasoning. Th Sharia is divided into two sections of equal impor tance: Ibadet, duties owed to God by way of worship and Muamalet, practical duties toward men and soci ety. There are four schools of law, often called Fou Rites of Muslim Law, in the different areas of the Mus lim world, differing only slightly in interpretation. Mus lims once were expected to submit totally to the law of one of the schools, but modern Muslim states have adopted legal codes limiting the dominance of the Sharia, and attempts are being made to adapt it tc modern times.

Island Arc, the chain of volcanoes that occur alonc one side of a deep ocean trench. They rest on the plate of lithosphere that is not moving down into the deep earth. Their andesitic lavas may be formed from the partially melted material of the descending plate Northern Japan and the Aleutian Islands are examples of island arcs.

Isle Royale National Park, park in NW Michigan, largest island in Lake Superior. It is distinguished for its wilderness character with heavy forestation, wolves, moose, and pre-Columbian copper mines. Area: 539,341acres (218,433hectares). Est. 1940.

Isle of Wight, island off the S coast of England; separated from the mainland by the Solént and Spithead; independent administrative county. The island's mild climate and attractive scenery have made it a popular tourist resort. Area: 147sq mi (382sq km).

Isleta, or Tuei, Tanoan-speaking tribe of Pueblo Indians living along the Rio Grande Valley in New Mexico. The largest Southwestern pueblo in size, it has a population of approximately 2,500.

Islets of Langerhans. △690.

Ismail (1486–1524), shah of Persia (1502–24), founder of the Safavid dynasty. He reestablished Persian independence after centuries of Arab control and established Shiite Islam as the state religion of Persia. He warred successfully against the Uzbek Turks (1510) but was defeated by the Ottoman sultan Selim I (1514).

Ismailia (Al-Isma'iliyah), city in NE Egypt, on Lake Timsah; capital of Ismailia governorate; seat of Suez Canal administration; rail and commercial center. Founded 1863 by Ferdinand de Lesseps as base of operations for construction of Suez Canal. Pop. 167,500.

Isma'ilis, or **Seveners,** the smaller of two subgroups of the Shia sect of Islam. All the Shiites believe in the authority of a succession of imams, spiritual guides, going back to Mohammed's son-in-law, Ali. A dispute arose about the successor to the sixth imam. Those who chose Isma'il, and on his death his son Mohammad, are called Isma'ilis. They are also called Seveners, because they believe that Mohammad was the seventh and last imam. They look for his return on Judgment Day. *See also* Imamis; Shi'a. △1112.

Ismail Pasha (1830–95), ruler of Egypt (1863–79). In 1867 he received the title khedive. The high price received for Egyptian cotton because of the US Civil War and its aftermath swelled the treasury. Ismail built schools, palaces, irrigation projects, and the Suez Canal. But much of the money was squandered and in 1875 Egypt was forced to sell its interests in the canal to Britain. In 1876, Egypt's finances were put in the control of a Franco-British debt commission. The Ottoman sultan replaced Ismail Pasha with his son Tewfik Pasha in 1879.

Isobar, a line of equal and constant pressure at the earth's surface or at a constant height above it on a weather or other map. The patterns of isobars depict ow the atmospheric pressure varies, showing highs" and "lows" across the area of the map. *See lso* High; Low. △218.

socrates (436–338 BC), Athenian rhetorician. He vrote speeches for others, as well as numerous tracts n politics and education, but was himself shy of pubc speaking. He founded a school in Athens and was n influential teacher and prose stylist *(Panegyricus)*.

sogamy, in biology, the fusion of reproductive cells hat act like sex cells but that are similar in size and tructure. It is found in algae, some protozoans, and rimitive plants and is unlike anisogamy, where male nd female sex cells differ in appearance.

solates. △866.

solation. △420, 582.

solationism, US policy advocating noninvolvement n European foreign wars and alliances. It was first enunciated by President Washington and, with the xception of the War of 1812, followed by all presidential administrations to the beginning of the 20th century. After World War I, its spirit was reaffirmed by he Senate's refusal to join the League of Nations. A series of neutrality acts in the 1930s were designed o keep the United States out of the impending European war. After World War II, a new internationalist spirit was evident, but the aftermath of the Vietnam War rekindled a degree of isolationism. △1308.

Isomers, two or more chemical compounds having the same molecular formula but different properties as a result of having a different arrangement of atoms within the molecule. Structural isomers have different structural formulae, for example, urea ($CO[NH_2]_2$) and ammonium cynate (NH_4CNO) have the same molecular formula (CH_4N_2O). Geometric isomers differ in their symmetry about a double bond; the cis- form of a compound has certain atoms or groups on the same side of a plane, whereas the trans- form has them on opposite sides. For example, maleic acid is the cis-form of fumaric acid. Optical isomers are mirror images of each other and differ only in the direction they rotate the plane of polarized light and the angle of their crystal form. △1558, 1570.

Isometrics. △698.

Isomorphism. △242, 1458.

Isoniazid, a drug used to treat tuberculosis.

Isopod, any of about 4,000 species of crustaceans, including seven aquatic and one terrestrial suborder, characterized by flattened, oval bodies with all the hard-plated segments more or less alike. The land forms are the familiar sow bugs and pill bugs. Marine species include wood-borers (gribbles) and specialized fish parasites. △484.

Isoptera. △492.

Isostasy, the maintenance of an equilibrium in the earth's crust and its crustal movement. There exists a balance between the land masses and the continental plates on which they float so that the plates rise and sink on the surface of Earth's mantle in such a fashion that the relative constancy of the system as a whole is maintained. The spread of the continental plates by the upwelling of material from deep within Earth's crust is balanced by the subduction or submergence of the opposite edges of the plates. *See also* Continental Drift; Tectonics. △170.

Isotherm, a line of equal and constant temperature on a weather or other map. The patterns of isotherms depict how the temperature changes across the area of the map. △1502.

Isotonic Solution, solution in which cells can be immersed without taking up water, or with the same osmotic pressure as another solution with which it is compared.

Isotope, any of the atoms of an element with the same number of electrons or protons (same atomic number) but a different number of neutrons in the nucleus, so that both mass number and mass of the nucleus vary between isotopes. The atomic weight of an element is an average of the isotope masses. The isotopes of an element all have similar chemical properties, since these depend on the number of electrons orbiting the atom; physical properties, however, do vary. Most elements have two or more naturally occurring isotopes, some of which are radioactive (radioisotopes). Many radioisotopes can be produced artificially by bombarding elements with high-energy particles, such as alpha particles. Radioisotopes are used in medicine, research, and industry. *See also* Dating, Radioactive; Radioactivity. △1480.

Iso-utility Curve. *See* Indifference Curve.

Israel, an independent nation in the Middle East. Predominantly a Jewish state, Israel is on the edge of the Mediterranean. Its main problems are peace with its Arab neighbors and an economy drained by efforts to maintain its sovereignty.

Land and economy. At the E end of the Mediterranean Sea, Israel is bordered by Lebanon (N), Syria and Jordan (E), Egypt (SW), and the Mediterranean (W). It is divided into four regions: the coastal plain along the sea, the Jordan Rift Valley (including the Jordan River, Sea of Galilee, and the Dead Sea), the central mountains, and the Negev Desert, which constitutes half of the total area. Highest point is Mt Meron, 3,963ft (1,209m) above sea level. The Dead Sea, 1,302ft (397m) below sea level, is the lowest point on the earth's continental surface. Present area includes all land assigned under the 1947 UN partition resolution, plus the land occupied after the 1967 Israel-Arab war (the Sinai Peninsula, W bank of Jordan, and a small area of Syria). Parts of the Sinai were returned in 1974–75. Principal privately owned export products are citrus fruits, polished diamonds, machinery, plastics, chemicals, pharmaceuticals, and clothing. Government-owned enterprises include mining, chemicals, petroleum refining, and railways. Israel produces 80% of its own food needs; 20% of the land is under cultivation; out of 1,058,000acres (428,490hectares), 448,000acres (181,440hectares) are irrigated. Its three seaports are Haifa, Ashdod, and Elat. The international airport is at Lod.

People. Since independence, immigration has quadrupled Israel's Jewish population (the majority coming from Arab countries); non-Jewish minorities include Muslims, Christians, and Druses. An estimated 45% of the Jewish population was born in Israel, 28% in Europe or the Western Hemisphere, 27% in Asia or Africa. Hebrew and Arabic are official languages. The school system provides ten years of free, compulsory classes. The country has 7 universities; literacy is estimated at 88% of Israeli Jews and 48% of Israeli Arabs. Military service is compulsory for men and unmarried women.

Government. Israel is a republic with power in the hands of the prime minister. Legislative power lies in the Knesset, a unicameral body elected by direct secret ballot.

History. Once the land of Canaan, then Israel, then Palestine, the modern state of Israel was born on May 14, 1948, after 2,000 years of Jewish statelessness and half a century of efforts by Zionists. In 1917, Britain's Balfour Declaration supported the idea of a Jewish state and assumed a Palestine mandate. Nazi persecution increased immigration in the 1930s and 1940s, and in 1947 a UN partition plan divided Palestine into two states, one Arab and one Jewish, with Jerusalem an international city. Neither side agreed, and civil war broke out; when Britain gave up the mandate in 1948, Israel was declared a state. Arab armies crossed the frontier and were defeated. A 1949 armistice brought no peace; terrorism continued on both sides. Proclaiming an imminent Arab attack, Israel invaded the Sinai in 1956. A UN cease-fire ended the hostilities. In 1967 Egyptian armies recaptured the Gaza Strip and closed the Gulf of Aqaba. In the Six-Day War that followed, Israel occupied more territory, including Old Jerusalem and the entrance to the Suez Canal. In 1973, Egypt and Syria, aided by the USSR, launched another war which was settled by a UN cease-fire and disengagement agreement. One of the major problems between Israel and the Arab states is the future of Palestinians (Arabs) who once lived in the country. Israel contends that its differences can be settled by direct negotiation. It has not favored US efforts to draw up a settlement. Prominent political leaders since independence have included David Ben-Gurion, Levi Eshkol, and Golda Meir. △1380.

PROFILE

Official name: State of Israel
Area: 7,993sq mi (20,702sq km)
Population: 3,400,000
Density: 425per sq mi (164per sq km)
Chief cities: Tel Aviv-Jaffa; Jerusalem (capital); Haifa
Government: Republic
Religion: Hebrew
Languages: Hebrew and Arabic
Monetary unit: Israeli pound
Gross national product: $11,700,000,000
Per capita income: $2,732
Industries: polished diamonds, processed food, chemicals, tires, petroleum products, aircraft, electronics, textiles, clothing, plastics, pharmaceuticals
Agriculture: citrus fruits, vegetables, cotton, durra, wheat, barley, olives, bananas, melons, figs
Minerals: gypsum, limestone, copper, iron, phos-

Isfahan, Iran

Islamic art

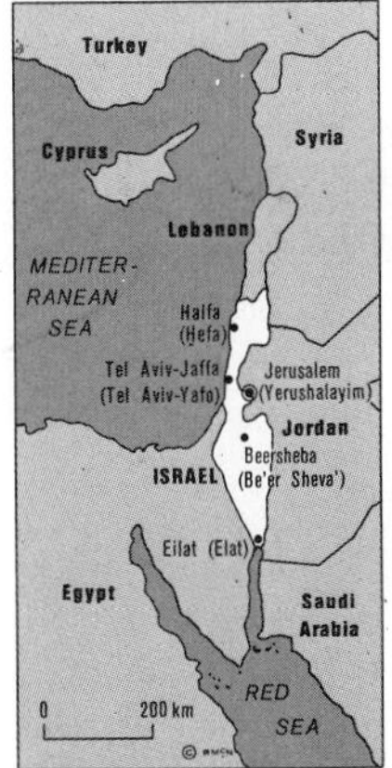
Turkey
Cyprus
Syria
Lebanon
MEDITER-RANEAN SEA
Haifa (Hefa)
Tel Aviv-Jaffa (Tel Aviv-Yafo)
Jerusalem (Yerushalayim)
Jordan
ISRAEL
Beersheba (Be'er Sheva')
Eilat (Elat)
Egypt
Saudi Arabia
RED SEA
0
200 km
Israel

Haifa, Israel

phates, magnesium, manganese, clay, rock salt, sulphur, potash
Trading partners: United States, European Common Market

Israel, name with many biblical connotations, including the people dwelling in Palestine; the name given the North Kingdom; the name given Jacob after he wrestled with the angel; and the name taken by the returning exiles after the Babylonian captivity.

Istanbul, city and seaport in NW Turkey, on both sides of Bosporus at entrance to Sea of Marmara; capital of Istanbul prov. Known as Byzantium until Constantine chose it as site for new capital of his Eastern Roman or Byzantine empire (AD 330), renamed Constantinople. It was patterned after Rome, set out on seven hills; some of the ancient moats and walls remain. The Hagia Sophia (built AD 360, converted from a church to a mosque and later to a museum) survives and is one of world's great architectural creations. Captured by Ottoman Turks 1453 the city was the capital until 1922; with the establishment of the new Turkish Republic after WWI the capital was moved to Ankara; site of Istanbul University (1453), a technical university (1944). Mosques of Beyazid II, Sulayyman I, and Ahmed I have been built since 1508, when an earthquake destroyed much of city. Industries: shipbuilding, cement, textiles, glass, shoes, pottery, tourism. Founded 660 BC by Greeks. Name was changed 1930. Pop. 2,312,751.

Istanbul Boğazi. *See* Bosporus.

Isthmian Festival, ancient Greek athletic and musical contest held at the sanctuary of the sea god Poseidon on the Isthmus of Corinth. It was particularly popular with Athenians.

Italian Art. Roman art was modeled after Greek art. By the 6th century, trade with the Byzantine empire had brought a Byzantine influence to Italian art, which lasted through the 11th century. The chief centers of the Italo-Byzantine style were Venice, Tuscany, Rome, and the deep south. Mosaics and stylized, geometric forms became standard. Icon panels were the main type of paintings during the 11th through the 13th centuries, with major schools in Siena, Lucca, and Pisa. Many painted crucifixes and altarpieces date from this period, with Giotto and Duccio as outstanding masters. By the time of the Renaissance, the emphasis was on balance and harmony, with such masters as Ghiberti, Donatello, Botticelli, and Michelangelo. △1134, 1138–42.

Italian East Africa, a group of Italian colonies federated from 1936–41, including Ethiopia and the older Italian possessions of Eritrea and Italian Somaliland. Italian rule was generally unpopular, and the British invasion of 1941–42 was well received. These lands are now included by Ethiopia and Somalia.

Italian Greyhound, delicate breed of dog (toy group) 2,000 years old. A favorite in ancient Pompeii; brought to England in early 17th century. This elegant dog has a long, narrow head; small, thrown-back, and folded ears; long, slender neck and body with curved back; long, straight legs; and a slender, curved tail carried low. The short, glossy coat may be any color. Average size: 6–10in (15–25.5cm) high at shoulder; 7–10lb (3–4.5kg). *See also* Toy Dog.

Italian Literature. Italian vernacular literature emerged in the 13th century with the work of the Sicilian poets at the court of Frederick II; they developed the sonnet, a form that spread throughout Europe. Religious poetry also flourished. Major figures of the 14th century were Dante (early 14th century), whose *Divine Comedy* ranks as a masterpiece of world literature, Petrarch, and Boccaccio. Their writings established Tuscan as the vernacular literary language, although the humanists in the 15th century wrote in Latin. The Renaissance produced outstanding poetry and philosophy, especially in the work of Tasso, Ariosto, and Machiavelli. The 19th-century political movement for Italian unification and independence inspired a literary flowering. The major figure to emerge was Gabriele d'Annunzio. Important 20th-century writers include Alberto Moravia, Cesare Pavese, Eugenio Montale, and Umberto Saba, among others. △1100.

Italo-Ethiopian War (1935–36), conflict between Italy and Ethiopia. The war had its roots in the Italian defeat by the Ethiopians at Aduwa in 1896, which preserved Ethiopian independence. Partly in revenge and partly to create a larger empire, the Italian dictator Benito Mussolini followed a small conflict with full-scale war in 1935. The modernized Italian army won easily over the poorly-equipped Ethiopians, and Ethiopian Emperor Haile Selassie was forced into exile. Ethiopia then became part of Italian East Africa until Haile Selassie was reinstated in 1941 by South African, Free French, and British forces.

Italy (Italia), independent nation in S Europe. A land of widely divergent customs, dialects, and character, it has been a democracy since the end of WWII.

Land and economy. A 700-mi (1,127-km) long peninsula shaped like a boot, Italy extends into the Mediterranean and includes the islands of Sardinia, Sicily, Pantelleria, and the Lipari group. It is bordered N by Austria, Switzerland, and France, and W by Yugoslavia. Except for the fertile Po valley in the heel of the boot and small coastal areas, the terrain is mainly rugged and mountainous. In 1976 the extreme NE region was rocked by a major earthquake. The climate is generally Mediterranean and mild except in the Alps and Dolomite ranges. High levels of industrial investment brought impressive growth in the 1954–1963 period. Following a brief recession, growth gathered momentum again until slowed by strikes, higher labor costs, and recessions in the 1970s. Essentially a private enterprise system, the government controls some major industries and commercial enterprises, electricity, transportation, radio, and television. Mountains and unfavorable climate make it largely unsuited for agriculture and there are few mineral deposits, with the exception of natural gas. Until recently, living standards and productivity in the S, with high density and lower population, were much below the N. About 40% of the gross national product comes from industry and construction; agriculture accounts for 10% and services for 49%. Tourism is a major economic factor.

People. Italy is marked by a great divergence among its people. In the industrial N and the central portion, habits and culture are close to W European countries. The poverty-stricken and often primitive S is closer to North Africa and still shows signs of Moorish and Spanish occupation, particularly in regard to the closely circumscribed position of women. Minority units are small, the largest being German-speaking people of Bolzano prov. and the Slovenes near Trieste. There are also ancient communities of Albanian, Greek, Ladino, and French peoples. About 99% of the population is Roman Catholic, the state religion. Literacy is estimated at 93%. Education is compulsory between the ages of 6 and 14. In 1974, Italians voted to retain a law permitting divorce, a statute opposed by the church.

Government. A 1948 constitution established Italy as a highly centralized democratic republic with a bicameral elected parliament. The president is elected by parliament. After the ruling Christian Democrats, the Italian Communists comprise the 2nd-largest party in Italy.

History. The unification of Italy as a constitutional monarchy under King Victor Emmanuel in 1870 marked the start of modern Italy. Before that it had been divided and torn apart since the fall of the Roman Empire. A monarchy with an elected parliament, Italy joined the Allies in WWI. In 1922, Benito Mussolini came to power; he eliminated political parties, reduced personal liberties, and installed a fascist dictatorship. In WWII, Italy joined with Germany until 1943, when Sicily was invaded by the Allies. A strong Italian resistance movement drove out the Germans in 1945. Under the 1947 peace treaty, some border adjustments were made with France and Yugoslavia, and Italy gave up its overseas possessions. Italy's position with the Roman Catholic Church has been governed by a series of accords, the most recent being the Lateran Pact of 1929, which recognized the sovereignty of Vatican City. *See also* Rome, Ancient; Sardinia. △1010–1030, 1250.

PROFILE

Official name: Italy
Area: 116,303sq mi (301,225sq km)
Population: 55,000,000
Density: 473per sq mi (182.6per sq km)
Chief cities: Rome (capital); Milan; Naples; Turin; Genoa
Government: Democratic republic
Religion: Roman Catholic
Language: Italian
Monetary unit: Lira
Gross national product: $128,400,000,000
Per capita income: $2,520
Industries: industrial and electrical machinery, motor vehicles, steel products, typewriters, shoes, textiles, machine tools, synthetic fabrics, chemicals, oil refining, processed foods
Agriculture: grapes, olives, tobacco, cattle, sheep, fish, citrus fruits, wheat, rye, rice, tomatoes, nuts
Minerals: coal, zinc, lead, copper, marble, natural gas
Trading partners: Federal Republic of Germany, France, United States

Itching. △724.

Ithaca (Itháki), island of Ionian archipelago, SW central Greece, at entrance of Gulf of Corinth; legendary home of Homer's Odysseus. Industries: olives, vineyards, currants. Area: 37sq mi (96sq mi). Pop. 4,156.

Ithaca, city in S central New York, at S end of Cayuga Lake; seat of Tompkins co. In the Finger Lakes region, it is the site of Cornell University (1865), Ithaca College (1892), US plant and soil laboratory. Industries: adding machines, shotguns, salt, research instruments. Settled 1789; inc. as city 1888. Pop. (1970) 26,226.

Ito, Prince Hirobumi (1841–1909), Japanese statesman. Ito became a major promotor of westernization following study in England (1863). He played a major part in the Meiji Restoration and served as interpreter for the emperor (1868) and governor of Hyogo. Part of the Iwakura Mission to the United States and England, he was the chief architect of the constitution (1889) and was foreign minister, president of the house of peers, president of the privy council, negotiator of the treaty of Shimonoseki (1895), and four times prime minister. He was assassinated by a Korean patriot.

Iturbide, Agustín de (1783–1824), helped Mexico achieve independence (1821) and was named emperor (1822–23). Iturbide joined forces with Vicente Guerrero and issued the Plan of Iguala (1821), a call for the union of colonists under an independent monarchy. Iturbide himself was crowned, but his reign was a short one. Dissent crystallized when Santa Anna and Guadalupe Victoria issued the Plan of Casa Mata, calling for the end of the empire and the creation of a republic. Iturbide abdicated and was exiled. Early in 1824, he returned to Mexico, was arrested and shot.

Itzá, Toltec Indian group that migrated to northeastern Yucatán (Mexico) between AD 975 and 1200. The ceremonial center of Chichén was transformed into a city by the Itzá; the Itzá themselves were absorbed into Maya society. △1118.

IUD. *See* Intrauterine Device.

Ivan III (1440–1505), grand duke of Russia, known as Ivan the Great. He brought Yaroslav, Rostov, and Novgorod under Moscow's control and in 1480 freed Russia from the Mongols. He began the long struggle with Poland for control of Belorussia, the Ukraine, and Lithuania. His marriage to Zoë, niece of the last Byzantine emperor, led to his claim that Moscow was a "third Rome," the direct heir of Byzantium. Important buildings in the Kremlin were constructed during his reign. △1176.

Ivan IV, or **Ivan the Terrible** (1530–84), tsar of Russia (1533–84). He won control of the Volga by taking over Kazan and Astrakhan and expanded control over Siberia. His conflict with the boyars led to his formation of the *Oprichnina,* a group of soldiers who killed and took away the land of the boyars. In 1547 he was crowned first tsar of all Russia. He attempted to gain free access to the Baltic in wars with Poland and Sweden (1558–82) but failed. He was known for his cruelty; in a fit of rage, he killed his eldest son. He had seven wives. △1176.

Ivan V (1666–96), tsar of Russia (1682–96). He was feeble in mind and body, and although he reigned with his half brother Peter the Great, he had little influence or control. His daughter Anna became tsarina in 1730.

Ivan VI (1740–64), tsar of Russia (1740–41). Grandnephew of Tsarina Anna, she proclaimed him her heir. However, Elizabeth, Peter the Great's daughter, led a revolt in 1741, became tsarina, and put Ivan in prison. He was killed in an attempted escape.

Ivanhoe (1819), novel by Sir Walter Scott, based on the enmity Scott supposed to have existed between Saxon and Norman in England under Richard I. Wilfred of Ivanhoe returns from Richard's crusade and after various adventures, including a tournament and captivity in a Norman castle, is reunited with the lady Rowena.

Ivanovo, formerly Ivanovo Vozinesensk, city in Russian SFSR, USSR; capital of Ivanovo oblast. Industries: textiles, textile machinery, leather, dyes. Founded 1871 by inc. of two villages. Pop. 419,000.

Ives, Charles (1874–1954), US composer, b. Danbury, Conn. A successful insurance executive, he is recognized as a pioneer in 20th-century music, predating many other composers in his use of dissonance and unusual effects. His works often contain American folk music as a thematic basis, such as the *Variations on "America"* for organ (1891) and the *Symphony*

No. 2 (1902). He composed songs, symphonies, and chamber and piano music. His *Symphony No. 3,* though composed in 1904, won a Pulitzer Prize in 1947. △1364.

Ivory, hard, yellowish-white dentine, comprising the bulk of an elephant's tusk, or a similar substance obtained from tusks or teeth of other mammals.

Ivory Carving, carving, or sometimes an engraving, done on an extremely durable form of dentin or tooth, usually the tusks of large animals. Ivory has been used for decoration and sculpture since prehistoric times; ivory figures and furniture date as early as predynastic Egypt. The Greeks carved large ivory statues, none of which survive. Byzantine ivory altarpieces date from the 9th to 11th centuries. Much ivory carving was done throughout Europe during the 11th and 12th centuries. During the 14th century, the Embriachi family was known for their carvings of ivory caskets and altarpieces in Italy. During the 15th century, France was a center for the production of large-scale Gothic ivories, often of religious subjects. Ivory carving of such items as tankards in a Baroque style was prevalent throughout Germany and Flanders during the 17th and 18th centuries. △1204, 1590.

Ivory Coast (Côte d'Ivoire), Republic of, nation in W Africa, on the Atlantic coast. The country is one of the world's leading producers of tropical wood, coffee, and cocoa.

Land and economy. A mountainous plateau rising gradually from a coastal plain, the Ivory Coast is heavily forested with valuable tropical hardwoods. Mountainous regions dominate the W and NW areas. The climate is tropical with heavy rainfall in the inland forest regions. The economy is agricultural, relying heavily on the coffee, cocoa, and timber industries. The Ivory Coast is first in Africa and second in the world in the production of tropical hardwood; however, coffee is its most valuable export. Rubber plantations were introduced in the 1960s.

People. There are more than 60 tribes within the country. Tribal villages abound, with many local chiefs. Abidjan presents a strong contrast to the rest of the country for it is highly Europeanized. Animistic religions dominate, but about 25% of the people are Muslim.

Government. A republic, the government consists of a president elected every 5 years; a unicameral legislature (national assembly) with 100 members elected every 5 years; and a judicial branch with all judges appointed by the president.

History. The French began ivory trade in the area in the 15th century and obtained rights to the territory in 1842, but did not actually occupy the area until 1882. It was the French Territory of West Africa from 1904 until granted its independence in 1960. It signed an agreement with France in 1961 retaining their close ties. From 1960 the nation was led by Pres. Felix Houphouët-Boigny.

PROFILE

Official name: Republic of Ivory Coast
Area: 124,503sq mi (322,463sq km)
Population: 4,900,000
Density: 39.4per sq mi (14.9per sq km)
Chief city: Abidjan (capital)
Government: Republic
Language: French (official)
Monetary unit: CFA Franc
Gross national product: $2,393,000,000
Per capita income: $511
Agriculture (major products): coffee, cocoa, timber
Minerals (major): diamonds
Trading partners (major): France, United States, West Germany

Ivry-sur-Seine, city in N France, on Seine River; suburb of Paris. Industries: chemicals, tiles, chocolate, paint, rubber. Pop. 60,455.

Ivy, woody, evergreen vine native to Europe and Asia. Its long, climbing stems cling to upright surfaces by aerial roots. The leaves are leathery. The common English ivy (*Hedera helix*) is propagated by cuttings and grows outdoors in moist shady or sunny areas. It is an outdoor ornamental in all but the coldest areas of the United States. Family Araliaceae.

Ivy Arum, a single species of climbing plant *(Scindapsus aureas)* of the arum family, native to the Solomon Islands, with large leathery leaves, spotted and lined with yellow. It climbs by aerial rootlets arising from nodes. Commonly kept as a houseplant, it needs warmth, moisture, and considerable light.

Iwaki (Taira), city in NE Honshu, Japan, on Iwaki River; transportation center. Industries: coal mining, chemicals, machinery. Pop. 327,164.

Iwakura, Tomomi. △1272.

Iwo, city in SW Nigeria, W Africa; regional trade center for cacao, farm products; coffee milling. Pop. 183,-907.

Iwo Jima, formerly Sulphur Island; largest of the Japanese Volcano Islands in W Pacific Ocean; scene of successful US campaign to take island from Japanese 1945; it was returned to Japan 1968. Industries: sugar refining, sulfur mining. Area: 8sq mi (21sq km).

Iwo Jima, Battle of (February–March 1945), US assault during World War II on a Japanese-held island. US Marines suffered 20,000 casualties in this desperate battle. The flag-raising on Mt Suribachi at the end of the battle is remembered as a symbol of courage.

IWW. *See* Industrial Workers of the World.

Ixtacalco, city in S central Mexico, adjacent to Mexico City; site of Floating Gardens; industrial area. Pop. 474,700.

Ixtacihuatl (Iztaccíhuatl), dormant snow-capped volcano in central Mexico, on Puebla-Mexico state border, 35mi (56km) SE of Mexico City; named by the Aztecs, means "white woman"; contains three summits; last erupted 1868. Height: 17,342ft (5,289m).

Ixtapalapa, city in S central Mexico, 5mi (8km) SE of Mexico City; on site of pre-Columbian Indian village. Pop. 533,569.

Izanagi and Izanami, in Japanese mythology, celestial mates who emerged out of chaos to magically create the islands and their gods from a drop of sea water. The offspring, Amaterasu Omikami, the Sun goddess, and her brother Susano-O-No-Mikoto, the storm god, were the progenitors of the next generation of gods. △834, 840.

Izhevsk (Izevsk), city in Russian SFSR, USSR, on Iz River, in Ural Mts; capital of Udmurt ASSR; major Russian arms manufacturing center (19th century); forms industrial complex with Votkinsk, 30mi (48km) NE; railway, industrial, and cultural center. Industries: armaments, steel, tools, furniture, construction machinery, paper milling equipment, sawmills, breweries, motor vehicles. Founded 1760 around an old ironworks in the Urals. Pop. 422,000.

İzmir, formerly Smyrna; port city in Turkey, on Gulf of İzmir; capital of İzmir prov. City was ruled by Ottoman Empire 1424–1919, when it was tentatively assigned to Greece; it passed to Turkey by terms of Treaty of Lausanne, Oct. 11, 1922. City has been seat of SE headquarters of NATO since 1952; 2nd-largest port in Turkey. Exports: fruit, tobacco, cereal, silk, carpets, cotton. Settled by Aeolians and Ionians in 11th century BC. Pop. 753,443.

Istanbul, Turkey: Blue Mosque

Fed. Rep. of Ger.
Czech.
Liech.
Austria
Switzerland
Hungary
France
Milan
Venice (Venezia)
Trieste
Turin (Torino)
Genoa (Genova)
Bologna
San Marino
Yugoslavia
Florence (Firenze)
ITALY
Rome (Roma)
Naples (Napoli)
Bari
Albania
Cagliari
MEDITERRANEAN SEA
Palermo
Catania
Algeria
Tunisia
300 km

Italy

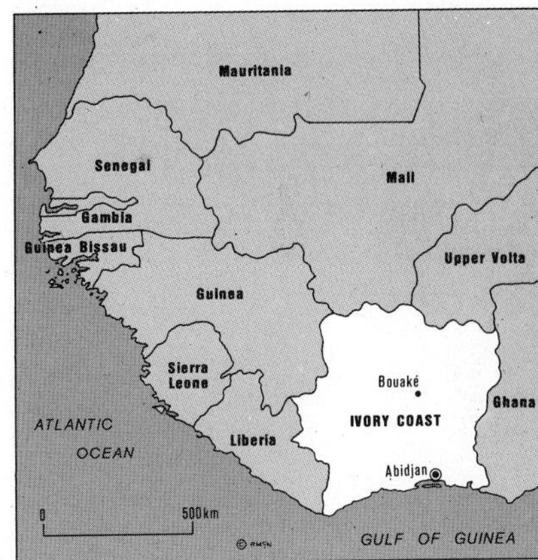
Mauritania
Senegal
Mali
Gambia
Guinea Bissau
Upper Volta
Guinea
Sierra Leone
Bouaké
Ghana
ATLANTIC OCEAN
IVORY COAST
Liberia
Abidjan
500km
GULF OF GUINEA

Ivory Coast

Ixtaccihuatl, Mexico

J

Jabalpur, city in central India, 150mi (242km) NNE of Nagpur; capital of Jabalpur district; site of Jabalpur University (1957) and military post; transportation and distribution center. Industries: cement, pottery, cloth, weapons, ammunitions, brassworks, cigarettes. Pop. 426,224.

Jabir. *See* Geber.

Jabiru, largest stork of Western Hemisphere, found from Mexico to Argentina. It is black and white with reddish-orange lower neck. It typically nests in top of palm trees. Height: to 55in (140cm). Species *Jabiru mycteria. See also* Stork.

Jacana, long-toed water bird of tropical lakes with a slender body, narrow bill, wrist spurs, and tapered claws. It is black or reddish-brown, sometimes with a bright frontal shield. Known as "lily-trotter," it runs over floating vegetation, feeding on aquatic plants and small animals. Buff or brown, black-splotched, waxy eggs (4) are laid in a floating nest after noisy breeding. Length: 10–13in (25–33cm). Family Jacanidae. △618.

Jacaranda, tree native to tropical America and cultivated in greenhouses worldwide. The ornamental *Jacarunda mimosifolia* and *J. cuspidifolia* have showy blue flowers. There are 50 species. Family Bignoniacea.

Jack, or crevalle jack, bony food and game fish found in warm waters of the American Pacific and Atlantic coasts. It has a high body profile with massive head and snub nose. Colors are green and silver with yellow blotches. Length: 2.5ft (76.2cm); weight: 20lb (9.1kg). Family Carangidae; species *Caranx bartho.*

Jackal, big-eared, Old World wild dog that resembles a coyote in habits, size, and general appearance. They prey on small animals, ranging from newborn antelopes to insects, and eat carrion, fruit, and seeds. The golden or Asiatic jackal *(Canis aureus)* ranges from Turkistan in Asia to Tanzania in Africa. The black-backed and side-striped jackals *(Canis mesomelas* and *Canis adustus)* inhabit savannas of E and S Africa. Length: 2ft (0.6m); weight: 20lb (9kg). Family Canidae. *See also* Canidae. △550.

Jackdaw, gregarious black bird of Eurasia and N Africa. It is smaller than a crow and has a gray neck and whitish eyes. Colonies breed in holes in buildings with both parents building the nest and feeding the young. The female incubates the eggs (2–8). Species *Corvus monedula. See also* Crow.

Jackfruit. △340.

Jack-in-the-pulpit, North American perennial, woodland plant with a green or brown hoodlike covering over the flower spike. Male and female flowers are often on separate plants. The one or two long, stalked leaves have three ovate leaflets. Its fruit is a cluster of red berries. Sometimes called Indian turnip, its tuberous roots were used by Indians as food. Height: to 3ft (0.9m). Family Araceae; genus *Arisaema triphyllum.*

Jackrabbit, big, slender, long-eared hare of W North America. Jackrabbits rely on their great speed, powerful leaps, and evasive moves to escape coyotes and other predators. Most are gray with white underparts, but the common northern white-tailed jackrabbit has a lighter winter coat. *See also* Hare. △546.

Jackson, Andrew (1767–1845), 7th president of the United States (1829–37). He was born in the Waxhaw settlement on the border between North and South Carolina. His long military career began in the American Revolution, when he was captured by the British at the age of 13. Orphaned about that time, he wandered to western North Carolina (now Tennessee), where he was admitted to the bar. He settled (1788) in Nashville, where he married Rachel Donelson Robards. He was a delegate to the Tennessee constitutional convention in 1796 and served briefly as US representative and senator from the new state. He was also a judge in the Tennessee superior court.

In the War of 1812, Jackson defeated the Creek at the Battle of Horseshoe Bend (1814). His brilliant generalship against the British in the Battle of New Orleans (1815) made him the great hero of the war. In 1818 he was sent to fight the Seminoles on the Georgia border. He pursued them into Spanish Florida, where he caught and executed two British subjects and captured Pensacola. His actions enraged both the Spanish and the British, but it only made him a greater hero in the eyes of the US public. He served briefly as territorial governor of Florida.

Jackson soon emerged as the leader of one faction of the old Jeffersonian Republican party. To many, particularly westerners, he became the symbol of a new democratic, eqalitarian society. Jackson ran for president in 1824 against John Quincy Adams, Henry Clay, and William H. Crawford. Jackson won the most votes, but the election was decided by the House of Representatives. In what the Jacksonians called a "corrupt bargain," Clay threw his support to Adams, who was elected.

Jackson won the 1828 election easily. His presidency shifted the balance of power from the landed gentry and urban commercial interests of the East to the farmers and small businessmen of the West and the working classes of the East. He greatly increased the power of his party—now known as the Democratic party—by the introduction of the spoils system. He defended the Union against the rising states rights and nullification tendencies of the South.

Jackson won a landslide victory in 1832. In his second term, Jackson's fight with eastern commercial interests was centered on his long, ultimately successful, opposition to the Second Bank of the United States.

Career: US House of Representatives, 1796–97; US Senate, 1798; US Army, 1812–18; governor, Florida territory, 1821; president, 1829–37. *See also* Democratic Party; War of 1812.

Jackson, Helen Hunt (1830–85), US author who wrote poems, stories, novels, and travel sketches, b. Amherst, Mass. *Verses* (1870) brought some critical acclaim. A historical account of the government's injustice to the American Indian, *A Century of Dishonor,* was published in 1881, after which she served as government investigator of conditions among the Mission Indians of California. Neglect of her report prompted her to write the famous novel *Ramona* (1884), concerning the Indian problem.

Jackson, Jesse (1941–), US civil rights leader, b. Greenville, N.C. Ordained a Baptist minister in 1968, he worked with Martin Luther King, Jr., running Operation Breadbasket, the economic organ of the Southern Christian Leadership Conference. He broke with SCLC in 1971, forming the Chicago-based Operation PUSH, a black economic organization.

Jackson, Robert Houghwout (1892–1954), US jurist and lawyer, b. Spring Creek, Pa. An assistant US attorney general (1936), US solicitor general (1938), and US attorney general (1940), he was appointed an associate justice of the US Supreme Court (1941–54). His opinion in *Youngstown v. Sawyer* (1952) declared Pres. Truman's steel mill seizures unconstitutional. From 1945 to 1946 he was chief US prosecutor at the Nuremburg war crimes trials.

Jackson, Thomas ("Stonewall") (1824–63), Confederate Civil War general, b. Clarksburg, Va. His stand at the First Battle of Bull Run (1861) gained him his nickname, "Stonewall," and he pushed his troops so hard that they were called "Jackson's Foot Cavalry." Known as Robert E. Lee's best general, he won victories in the Shenandoah Valley (1862) and at Chancellorsville, where he was killed in May 1863.

Jackson, city in S Michigan, on Grand River; seat of Jackson co; named for Andrew Jackson, 7th US president; site of Jackson Community College (1928). Industries: automotive parts and accessories, machine tools, plastics, surgical bandages. Founded 1829; inc. as village 1843, as city 1857. Pop. (1970) 45,484.

Jackson, city in SW central Mississippi, on Pearl River; capital and largest city of Mississippi; seat of Hinds co. Originally a trading post est. 1700s and known as Le Fleur's Bluff, it was chosen as site of state capital 1821; scene of race riots in 1960s and again in 1970 at Jackson State College. It is site of Millsaps College (1890), Belhaven College (1894), old capitol (1839), governor's mansion (1839). Industries: textiles, glass, electrical equipment, meat products, lumber, oil, natural gas. Inc. 1833. Pop. (1970) 153,968.

Jackson, city in W Tennessee, 85mi (137km) ENE of Memphis, on Forked Deer River; named for Pres. Andrew Jackson. Home of John "Casey" Jones is preserved as museum; site of Union University (1834), Lane College (1882), Lambuth College (1924), Jackson State Community College (1965). Industries: textiles, lumber, furniture, livestock, tile, power tools, store fixtures, aluminum foil. Settled 1819; inc. 1823 as town, 1845 as city. Pop. (1970) 39,996.

Jackson Hole, valley in NW Wyoming, E of Teton Range; N section is in Grand Teton National Park; remainder is in Teton National Forest and Jackson Hole Wildlife Park. The region was first visited by trapper David Jackson (1828–29). Area: approx. 384sq mi (995sq km).

Jacksonville, seaport city in NE Florida, on St John's River; seat of Duval co and largest city in Florida; served as Confederate base during Civil War; developed into a deepwater port during 19th century; devastated by fire 1901; site of Confederate Monument (1898), Fort Caroline National Monument, Edward Waters College (1866), Jones College (1918), Jacksonville University (1934), Gator Bowl. Industries: cigars, fertilizers, concrete, food processing, tourism, lumber, phosphate, paper, chemicals. Settled 1816 by Lewis Hogan; inc. 1832. Pop. (1970) 528,865.

Jack the Ripper (*fl.* 1888), murderer of at least seven prostitutes in the East End of London in late 1888. The name given the murderer came from his mutilation of his victims. Despite public outcry at police inefficiency, he has never been definitely identified.

Jacob, in the Bible, son of Isaac and Rebekah and younger twin brother of Esau. While fleeing after tricking Esau out of Isaac's blessing, he wrestled with an angel to obtain God's blessing. He married Leah and Rachel; the descendants of his son Joseph became the 12 tribes of Israel.

Jacob, François (1920–), French biologist. With Jacques Monod he discovered that a substance that they named *messenger RNA* carried hereditary information from the cell nucleus to the sites for protein synthesis and that certain genes, called operator genes, control the activity of other genes. They shared the 1965 Nobel Prize in physiology or medicine with another French biologist, André Lwoff. △414.

Jacobins, French political radicals belonging to a club that played an important role during the French Revolution. The club met in a former Dominican monastery in the Rue St Jacques. Begun in 1789 by some deputies to protect the revolution from a reaction by the aristocrats, the club split in 1791 when the moderates left it. Thereafter more democratic and more popular in orientation, the Jacobin movement developed a network of clubs throughout France where leaders conferred and public discussions were held. In 1793–94, the club was an instrument of Maximilien Robespierre and, as the greatest power in the country, became part of the government's administrative machinery. It ceased to exist after Robespierre's downfall in 1794. Political radicals or sympathizers with the French Revolution are also called Jacobins. △1224.

Jacobites, name given to supporters of James II and his Stuart descendants, who attempted to regain the English throne after the Glorious Revolution of 1688 deposed James II. With unofficial French encouragement, Jacobites were found among Scots (the homeland of the Stuarts), Irish (James II was Catholic), and disgruntled Tories (Whigs dominated the government). In 1715 the "Old Pretender," called James III by his supporters, attempted insurrection and failed; in 1745 the "Young Pretender," called Charles III, did the same. By the late 18th century, the claims of the "king over the water," as the Jacobite pretenders were termed, had only occasional sentimental appeal.

Jacobs, Helen Hull (1908–), US tennis champion, b. Globe, Ariz. She set a record by winning the singles title at Forest Hills, N.Y., 4 years in a row (1932–35). She also won several US outdoor doubles (1932, 1934, 1935), as well as the US mixed doubles (1934). She won the singles title at Wimbledon, England (1936) and was elected to the Tennis Hall of Fame (1962).

Jacob's Ladder, or Greek valerian, charity, perennial plant native to Europe. It has feathery leaves and small, cup-shaped, blue flowers in clusters. Height: to 3ft (91cm). Family Polemoniaceae; species *Polemonium caeruleum.*

Jacquerie, violent insurrection of the lower classes against the nobility in NE France in 1358 during the Hundred Years' War. Enraged by the increased war taxes and the pillaging of the English invaders and the French nobility, the peasants and some townspeople revolted. They destroyed numerous castles and killed the inhabitants. The revolt, which spread throughout the region, was defeated by the nobles, who executed the leader Guillaume Carle and massacred thousands of peasants. △1102.

Jacques-Cartier, city in S Quebec, Canada, 12mi (19km) SW of Montreal. Industries: aircraft engines, tools, truck bodies. Pop. 52,527.

Jade, a semiprecious mineral of two major types—jadeite, which is often translucent, and nephrite, which has a waxy quality. Both types are extremely hard and durable. Jade is found mainly in Burma and Turkestan and comes in many colors, most commonly green and white. Jade carving is usually done with diamond drills and lapidary wheels. The earliest Oriental jade carving was done in China in the late Neolithic period, when ceremonial objects and items of personal adornment were made. By the Chou dynasty (*c.* 1027–256 BC), jade carving was a highly developed art. During the Ming dynasty (1368–1644), the dragon motif was introduced into jade carving. During the Ch'ing dynasty (1644–1912), jade carving reached its peak in such creations as enormous jade "mountains" and screens. Jade was also used extensively for decorative objects and tools in Central America and Mexico, especially in the Mayan culture of Yucatán. △1204.

Jade Plant, succulent, treelike houseplant native to S Africa and Asia. It has smooth, fleshy, rounded leaves, thick stems, and small white flowers. Care: bright light, soil (equal parts loam, peat moss, sand) kept dry between waterings. Propagation is by stem and leaf cuttings. Height: to 30in (76cm). Family Crassulaceae; species *Crassula argentea.*

Jadwiga (1370–99), queen of Poland (1384–99), daughter of Louis the Great of Hungary and Poland, granddaughter of Casimir III. At the age of 11 she succeeded her father and was recognized as "king" by the Sejm. In 1386 Poland was saved from its enemies by Jadwiga's marriage to Jagello, the grand duke of Lithuania, a powerful neighbor to the east.

Jaeger, gull-like predatory, fast-flying seabird that breeds in the Arctic and winters in the subtropics. It has a dark, stocky body with pointed wings and long tail feathers. It feeds on small land animals and seabirds. Olive brown, black-spotted eggs (2–3) are laid in a shallow depression of tundra moss. Length: 13–20in (33–51cm). Genus: *Stercorarius.*

Jaén, city in S Spain, 178mi (287km) S of Madrid; capital of Jaen prov.; site of Moorish citadel and 16th-century church. Industries: linen, olive oil, alcohol. Area: (prov.) 5,212sq mi (13,499sq km). Pop. (city) 78,156; (prov.) 661,146.

Jagatai, or **Chagatai** (d.1242), Mongol ruler. A son of Genghis Khan, he led armies in his father's conquests. Upon his father's death (1227) he was awarded Turkistan and Afghanistan as his khanite. In the early 14th century his descendants, the Jagatids, divided the khanite, with Samarkand the capital of the west and Kashgar the capital of the east. Tamerlane reunited the khanite *c.* 1369. The Jagatid dynasty was swept away by the conquering Uzbek Mongols *c.* 1500.

Jagatid Dynasty. *See* Jagatai.

Jagellon, name of 2nd and last dynasty of Polish kings, beginning with the marriage of Jagello of Lithuania to Queen Jadwiga of Poland (1386) and ending with the death of Sigismund II (1572). Intervening rulers included **Ladislas III** or **VI** (1434–44); **Casimir IV** (1447–92); **John Albert** (1492–1501); and **Sigismund I** (1506–48).

Jagganath. △1034.

Jagow, Gottlieb von. △1302.

Jaguar, spotted big cat found in woody and grassy areas from S Texas and New Mexico to Argentina. It has a chunky body, rounded ears, and yellowish coat with black rosettes. This fierce cat eats large mammals, turtles, and fish. The gestation period is 99–105 days and 2–4 young are born. Length: body, 44–84in (112–213cm); tail, 21–26in (53–66cm); weight: 150–225lb (68–101kg). Family Felidae; species *Panthera onca. See also* Cat. △602.

Jaguarundi, small, ground-dwelling cat found in Central and South America. Weasellike, it has a long, slender body, short legs, long tail, small head, and is black, brown, gray, or fox red with no spots. Types, according to color, include colcollo, jaguarundi, and eyra. Length: 36–52in (91–132cm); weight: 10–20lb (4.5–9kg). Family Felidae; species *Felis vagouaroundi.*

Jahangir (1569–1627), Mogul emperor of India (1605–27). Although he revolted against him in 1599, his father Akbar still named him his successor. He continued the expansion of the empire, conquering Mewar in 1614 and Ahmadnagar in 1616. He granted trading privileges to the Portuguese and the British East India Company. An indolent, pleasure-loving man, he allowed himself to be dominated by his Persian wife and her family. He was succeeded by his son Jahan.

Jai Alai, a fast-action game, the most popular of the fronton games. It is played on a court about 176 feet (53.6m) long and 95 feet (29m) wide, bounded on the front, back, and one side by walls 44 feet (13.4m) high. The fourth wall has a wire netting, behind which the audience sits. Each player has a curved wicker basket (a *cesta*) attached to his arm. A hard-rubber ball is used. The object is to hurl the ball so that after it bounces off one of the side walls it cannot be returned to the front wall. Depending upon the number of players (two, four, six), 6 to 40 points are needed to win. Jai alai originated about the 17th century in the Spanish Basque regions and is now also popular in Latin America and the United States, where pari-mutuel betting is allowed. *See also* Fronton Games.

Jainism, ancient monastic religion of India. Its roots are traced back through a series of teachers, the last being Parshva in the 8th century BC and Mahavira in the 6th century BC. Jains do not accept Hindu scriptures, rituals, or priesthood, but they do believe that people go through cycles of rebirth. Monks can attain release from the cycle by ascetic living and meditation. Jains are extremely careful to observe the rule of not injuring any living creature *(ahimsa).* There are about 2,000,000 Jains today.

Jaipur, city in NW India, 140mi (225km) W of Agra;

Andrew Jackson

François Jacob

Jaguar

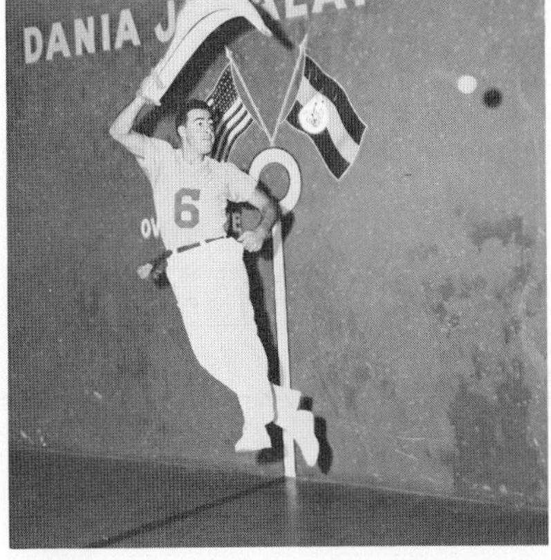
DANIA J
6

Jai alai

capital of Rajasthan state and former Jaipur state; site of Rajasthan University (1947), maharajah's palace, and 20-ft (6-m) crenellated wall that surrounds the city; transportation and commercial center. Industries: banking, jewelry, enamels, muslins, glass, ivory, marble carvings. Founded 1727 by Marharajah Jai Singh II. Pop. 615,258.

Jakarta. *See* Djakarta.

Jalapa Enriquez, city in E central Mexico, on the slopes of the Sierra Madre Oriental; conquered by Hernán Cortes 1519; served as military base *c.* 18th century; site of Mt Orisaba, Indian villages, local museum containing archaeological collection, university. Industries: coffee, tobacco, tourism. Pop. 122,377.

Jalisco, state in W central Mexico, bordered by the Pacific Ocean (W); conquered 1529 by Nuno de Guzman; occupied by French during the wars of intervention; retaken 1866. Terrain is mountainous (S), with tropical plains along the coast; site of two universities, technological institute. Products: wheat, maize, rice, grains, lumber, cinnabar, iron, tin, silver, gold, livestock. Industries: processed foods, textiles. Area: 30,941sq mi (80,137sq km). Pop. 3,322,750.

Jama. *See* Zama.

Jamaica, island in the Caribbean, 90mi (145km) S of Cuba; economy depends on agriculture, bauxite, mining, and tourism. The majority of population is of African descent. It is an independent member of the British Commonwealth.

Land and economy: Mountains cover 80% of the land, which has a tropical maritime climate in the path of the tradewinds. The economy depends on tourism, mining, light manufacturing, construction, and agriculture; bauxite and alumina are chief export products. Principal crops are sugar cane for rum and molasses, bananas, and citrus fruits. Some 150 US concerns manufacture tires, chemicals, cement, and food products. Tourism attracts 400,000 visitors a year. Unskilled rural migrants moving to the cities have raised the unemployment rate to 25%.

People: More than 90% of the inhabitants are of African origin, together with large groups of Asians, Indians, and Chinese. English is the official language, but many speak a Jamaican Creole. Primary education is free, and literacy is estimated at 85%. The Anglican Church is predominant.

Government: The Jamaica Constitution, signed in 1962, set up a British-style parliamentary system of government. The British crown appoints governor-general, but executive power resides in the cabinet, led by an elected prime minister, an elected House of Representatives, and appointed Senate. Local parish government is headed by elected council members.

History. Jamaica was discovered by Christopher Columbus in 1494 and was held by the Spanish until 1655 when British forces occupied the island. Sugar and slavery made it an important possession. After a long period of colonial rule, Jamaica started on the road to independence in the 1930s. In 1945 the Jamaica Labor party formed the first government under adult suffrage.

PROFILE

Official name: Jamaica
Area: 4,411sq mi (11,424sq km)
Population: 1,861,300
Density: 422per sq mi (163per sq km)
Chief city: Kingston (capital)
Government: Parliamentary system in British Commonwealth
Religion (major): Anglican
Language (major): English
Monetary unit: Jamaican dollar
Gross national product: $1.2 billion
Per capita income: $616
Industries (major products): tires, chemicals, clothing, food products
Minerals: bauxite, alumina
Trading partners: Great Britain, United States, and Canada

James I (1208–76), king of Aragon, called "the Conqueror." He founded a Barcelona-based Aragonese empire in the Mediterranean after inheriting the powerful NE Spanish state in 1213. He enlarged it by conquering the Balearic Islands (1229–35) and Valencia (1238).

James II (1260?–1327), king of Aragon (1291–1327) by virtue of his brother's death. He gave up his claim to Sicily, which had been left him by his father, and received Sardinia and Corsica as compensation. He was, however, only able to make good his claim to Sardinia (1324).

James I (1566–1625), king of England, son of Mary, Queen of Scots. Crowned James VI of Scotland on his mother's abdication (1567), James passed his minority mainly under the control of the Presbyterians, who wished to protect him against Roman Catholic influence. Forced to choose between France and England as allies for Scotland, James opted for Protestant England (1586). On Elizabeth I's death, he became king of England (1603). He concluded peace with Spain (1604), but at home his failure to conciliate either the Puritans or the Catholics caused discontent. His reliance upon favorites and his troubled relationship with the House of Commons weakened his effectiveness as a ruler.

James II (1633–1701), king of England, Scotland, and Ireland, second son of Charles I. After the Restoration (1660), James, then duke of York, was prominent in national affairs and won a naval victory over the Dutch at Southwold Bay (1672). As a Roman Catholic, he was forced to resign the admiralty by the Test Act (1673). Despite the rival claim of the duke of Monmouth, James succeeded his brother Charles II (1685), but his support of Roman Catholicism alienated his subjects. Compelled to flee (1689), he lived his last 12 years in exile.

James I (1394–1437), king of Scotland (1406–37). His father, Robert III, decided to send him to France to keep him safe from the duke of Albany, next in line to the throne. On his way to France he was captured (1406) and detained by the English. Though he technically succeeded to the throne on his father's death (1406), neither the regent Albany nor Albany's son, who succeeded him as regent (1420–24), ransomed James until pressured by the nobles to do so in 1424. Upon his return James became an energetic and decisive monarch, taking measures to break the power of the nobles and Highland lords, restore law and order, and improve commerce and the army. He had many of his enemies arrested or slain and confiscated their estates. He acted against corruption and brought the chief financial officers of the kingdom under his personal supervision. His attempts to retain church revenues embroiled him with the papacy. He improved the system of justice for common people and sought to have the Scottish parliament meet annually and to include burghers as members. He was assassinated by a group of conspirators led by the earl of Atholl. James is generally believed to be the author of *The Kingis Quair* (*c.*1423), a long love-dream allegory in vernacular Scots about his captivity and romance with his future wife Joan. This work, in the tradition of Chaucer, marks the beginning of the golden age of Scottish literature.

James II (1430–60), king of Scotland (1437–60). Only six years old when his father, James I, was assassinated, for years he was under the domination of vying clans, particularly the Douglases. In 1452 he killed the current earl of Douglas and destroyed the clan's power by 1455. He improved the courts and regulated the coinage. He was killed while in England aiding the Lancastrians in the Wars of the Roses.

James III (1451–88), king of Scotland, son of James II, whom he succeeded in 1460. Unable to control his nobles, James was challenged by his brother Albany, whom Edward IV of England recognized as king in 1482. Peace was arranged with Albany, but a fresh rebellion resulted in James' defeat at Sauchieburn and his subsequent murder.

James IV (1473–1513), king of Scotland, nominal leader of the rebels who killed his father, James III, in 1488. A strong and energetic monarch, James maintained his authority throughout Scotland. Peace with England (concluded 1497) was promoted by his marriage to Henry VII's daughter, Margaret (1503), but in 1513 he led an invasion of England and was killed at Flodden.

James V (1512–42), king of Scotland, succeeded his father, James IV (1513). Efforts to retain control of his nobles and independence from his uncle, Henry VIII of England, occupied most of James' reign. His death followed the English rout of his forces at Solway Moss. He was succeeded to the throne by his infant daughter Mary.

James, three persons in the New Testament: **James the Greater** (died *c.* 43), one of the Twelve Disciples of Jesus, brother of the disciple John. He was beheaded on orders of Herod Agrippa I. **James the Less,** also one of the twelve Disciples, son of Alphaeus and one of the three Marys at the cross and tomb. **James the Brother of Jesus** (died *c.* 62), a witness to the Resurrection and a leader, perhaps first bishop, of the church in Jerusalem. He was either stoned to death or thrown from a tower. He is usually identified as the writer of the epistle of that name. The Roman Catholic Church claims he is a cousin, not a brother, of Jesus and that he is the same person as James the Less.

James, Henry, Jr. (1843–1916), US novelist, short-story writer, and critic, b. New York City. The son of Henry James, Sr., and brother of William James, he received his early education abroad but went to Harvard Law School for a law degree. Encouraged by William Dean Howells, he entered upon a literary career and published his first novel *Watch and Ward* in 1871. In 1876 he established residence in England, and in 1915 became a British subject.

James, the master of a complex prose style, had a keen insight into values of character. He felt strongly that a writer should "never allow anything to enter a novel which was not represented as a perception or experience of one of the characters." Usually the central figure in his works was an American involved in one of the arts, either wealthy himself or moving in wealthy or influential circles. In many of these novels the principal theme lies in the contrast of American and European traits. Among his many works are the novels *Roderick Hudson* (1876), *Daisy Miller* (1879), *The Portrait of a Lady* (1881), *The Bostonians* (1886), *The Wings of the Dove* (1902), and *The Ambassadors* (1903). △1238, 1374.

James, Jesse (Woodson) (1847–82), US outlaw, b. Clay co, Mo. He and his brother Frank fought for the Confederacy during the Civil War. In 1866 they formed an outlaw band and terrorized the frontier, robbing banks and trains in Missouri and nearby states. In 1882, while living under the assumed name Tom Howard in St Joseph, Mo., he was shot by Robert Ford, one of the members of his own gang, for a large reward. △1276.

James, William (1842–1910), US philosopher and psychologist, b. New York City. Regarded by many as the greatest of American psychologists and an outstanding philosopher, he pioneered research in many areas, including emotions, consciousness, attention, and the laboratory study of human functions. A precursor of the functionalist school, he also did much to establish psychology as relevant to practical problems. His masterpiece, *Principles of Psychology* (1890), is one of the great achievements in psychology. Other noted works include *The Varieties of Religious Experience* (1902) and *Pragmatism* (1907). *See also* James-Lange Theory; Pragmatism. △772, 858.

James-Lange Theory, an early theory of emotion developed independently by William James in 1884 and Carl Lange in 1885. It identified emotion as the awareness of the bodily state (visceral and muscular reactions) activated by an emotional stimulus. The theory is now regarded as overly simple and incomplete. *See also* Emotion.

James River, river in Virginia, formed by the confluence of the Jackson and Cowpasture rivers in central Virginia; flows E into Chesapeake Bay at Hampton Roads. First permanent English settlement in North America was made on lower river at Jamestown (1607). Union forces used river in their unsuccessful attempts to take Richmond. River is navigable to Richmond for about 100mi (161km) of its 340mi (548km).

Jamestown, city in W New York, at S end of Chautauqua Lake; site of Jamestown Community College (1934). Industries: furniture making, tools, airplane and automobile parts, textiles. Settled 1810; chartered as city 1886. Pop. (1970) 39,975.

Jamestown Settlement, first successful English colony in America (1607). Despite able leadership of John Smith, the Virginia Company colony nearly failed because of malaria, hunger, and Indian attacks. New settlers and supplies (1610), marriage of John Rolfe to Pocahontas, and commercial development of tobacco by Rolfe (1614) enabled the colony to grow. The House of Burgesses first met and slavery was initiated in 1619. Jamestown was placed under direct royal rule in 1624. *See also* Pocahontas; Powhatan; Rolfe, John; Smith, John. △1216.

Jami, real name Nur ud-din Abd ur-rahman ibn Ahmad (1414–92), Persian poet who was the leading figure in Middle Eastern literature in the 15th century. The last of the classical Persian poets, he treated both romantic and philosophical themes. His influence spread throughout the Middle East and as far as the Muslim parts of India.

Jammu and Kashmir, once the largest princely state of India, possession of its 54,000sq mi (139,860sq km) and legendary Vale of Kashmir is now divided between India and Pakistan. Bordered by India and Pakistan, the Himalayas stand above heavily populated valleys of the Indus and Jhelum rivers.

sic economy includes rice cultivation, animal husndry, a few silk factories, rice and flour mills, and urism. The population of the Indian State is 4,615,-'6, and the capital is Srinagar. Muslims constitute e largest religious group, with some Buddhists, Doas, and Sikhs; Kashmeri is the language; several onasteries are served by lamas; education is free. ter early Buddhist and Hindu rule, it became part of e Mogul empire in 1587 and came under British omination in 1846. When India was partitioned in 947, the battle for Kashmir started. After years of ghting, the UN decision of 1972 set cease fire lines.

amnitzer. △1150.

amshedpur, city in NE India, at junction of Subarareka and Karkhai rivers. It was founded early 20th entury as a steel mill area of the Tata Iron and Steel orks; first mill opened 1911. Industries: blast furaces, coke ovens, chemicals, wire, agricultural quipment, iron, steel. Pop. 414,330.

ane Austen. △1238.

ane Eyre (1847), novel by Charlotte Brontë. It is markable for the characters of Jane, a penniless overness of great spirit and wit, and her sardonic but assionate employer, Mr. Rochester. Their marriage prevented by the dramatic revelation that he has a natic wife still living. Jane flees, and only after ochester is injured and blinded in a fire set by his ife, who is killed in it, are they reunited. △1238.

anesville, city in S central Wisconsin, 32mi (52km) E of Madison on Rock River; seat of Rock co; site of allman House and Underground Railroad station; ade center in dairying, grain, and tobacco region. dustries: fountain pens, electrical equipment, auomobiles. Founded 1835; inc. 1853. Pop. (1970) 6,426.

anet, Pierre Marie Felix. △762.

anissaries, elite, disciplined soldiers of the Ottoman army. Established in the 14th century by the sulan Orkhan, they were originally recruited from Chrisan youths and other war captives who had been onverted to Islam. They eventually made and unade sultans, became ungovernable, and were masacred in their barracks by the sultan Mahmud II 826). △1108.

anov, Arthur. △774.

ansen, Cornelis (1585–1638), Dutch theologian. t the University of Louvain he studied problems aised for Catholics by Lutheran and Calvinist docrine. He also became involved in a conflict between he university and the Jesuits over teaching theology. n his writings he argued for a return to St Augustine's iews on grace and salvation. Jansen was bishop of pres at the time of his death. His *Augustinus,* which was the basis for the doctrine called Jansenism, was eclared heretical after his death. *See also* Jansenism.

ansenism, a reform movement in the Roman Catholic Church in the 17th and 18th centuries. The name omes from the Dutch theologian Cornelis Jansen 1585–1638), but the movement grew strongest in rance, led by Antoine Arnauld (1612–94) and others nd centered at the abbey of Port-Royal. Some Janenist ideas, such as doctrines of predestination, esembled Protestant beliefs, but the Jansenists adocated reforming rather than leaving the church. Still, their ideas were condemned in four papal bulls. Controversy between Jansenists and the church auhorities who opposed them flared up at intervals until he movement was virtually broken up during the eign of Louis XIV.

Jansky, Karl. △46.

January, first month of the year. It was named after the god Janus and has 31 days. The birthstone is the garnet.

Janus, in Roman mythology, god of all doorways. He was also the god of all beginnings and presided over daybreak. The month of January is named after him. △842.

Janus, satellite of Saturn. △86.

Japan (Nihon), independent nation in E Asia. Since WWII, its economic development has made it one of the world's financial powers.

Land and economy. The Japanese archipelago, off the E coast of Asia, is made up of four main mountainous islands—Hokkaido, Honshu, Shikoku, and Kyushu—and some 3,000 smaller islands. About 80% of the country is hills and mountains with active and nonactive volcanoes and frequent earthquakes. The climate ranges from subtropical on S Honshu to cold on Hokkaido. Tropical storms in the early fall carry torrential rain and typhoons. Although only 19% of the land is arable, persistence and skill result in high per-acre yields; farms produce 80% of the food needed, including rice. Fish is a major source of food and income, and Japan has been a world leader in its total catch. Natural resources are few, and hydroelectric power provides less than half the supply needed; thermal power has also been developed. Japan must import many minerals needed for heavy industry. It ranks second to the United States in motor vehicle production. Japan leads the world in large ship building, and its merchant fleet is among the world's largest. Exports earn about 10% of the gross national product.

People. The Japanese are a Mongoloid people originally from mainland Asia. There has been little mixture for the past 1,000 years. Buddhism, the dominant religion, influences philosophy, institutions, and the arts. Shintoism, a belief based on myths and legends, was the state religion in the 19th century and was used by the government to support the Emperor's divinity. After WWII, its official status was removed. Christians number about 750,000. Schooling is free through junior high school. Very competitive exams regulate the entrance to higher education. Literacy is almost 100%.

Government. Japan is a constitutional monarchy, with the Emperor as symbol of state. The bicameral Diet, main body of power, is elected by universal adult suffrage. Executive power rests in the cabinet and the prime minister (a Diet member). Conservative pro-Western governments have ruled since WWII.

History. According to tradition, Japan was founded 660 BC by the Emperor Jimmu, descendant of the Sun Goddess and ancestor of the present royal family. Two changes in AD 405 brought a social revolution: the use of Chinese script and the introduction of Buddhism; these innovations started the adoption of Chinese culture. First contact with the West came in 1552 when a Portuguese navigator was blown off his course and landed; traders and missionaries followed. Fearing eventual conquest, Japan expelled all foreigners in 1638. Japan was isolated until 1854, when US Commodore Matthew Perry opened it up to trade. Japan won Taiwan (Formosa) from China in 1894; Korea was annexed in 1910; the German Pacific islands became Japan's mandate after WWI, and Manchuria fell to Japan in 1931. In 1933, Japan resigned from the League of Nations. The military's influence on government increased, and Japan attacked China in 1937 and bombed the US base at Pearl Harbor, Hawaii, on Dec. 7, 1941. After almost four years of war, Japan was defeated, losing all its non-Japanese possessions; government was placed under Allied control. Reforms gradually introduced a self-governing democracy. Japan's remarkable postwar economic recovery was matched by increased participation in international affairs and agencies. △1046–48, 1210, 1272.

PROFILE

Official name: Japan
Area: 143,689sq mi (372,155sq km)
Population: 111,100,000
Density: 773per sq mi (298per sq km)
Chief cities: Tokyo (capital); Osaka; Yokohama; Kyoto; Nagoya
Government: Constitutional monarchy
Religion: Buddhism
Language: Japanese
Monetary unit: Yen
Gross national product: $457,000,000,000
Per capita income: $3,812
Industries: motor vehicles, ships, electronics, precision instruments, iron, steel, chemicals, fertilizer, textiles, ceramics, wood products, food products, optics, television, toys
Agriculture: rice, wheat, barley, tobacco, potatoes, tea, beans, fruits, fish, forests
Minerals: coal, gold, silver, copper, lead, zinc, salt, petroleum
Trading partner: (major) United States

Japan, Sea of, branch of W Pacific Ocean, lying between Japan (E), the Korean peninsula (SE), and the coast of the USSR (W). Area: 389,100sq mi (1,007,769sq km).

Japan Current. *See* Kuroshiro Current.

Japanese, the national language of Japan, spoken by virtually all of the country's 111,000,000 people. It belongs to no linguistic family, though in grammatical structure it resembles Korean and may actually be related to it. Written Japanese uses both Chinese ideographs, known as *kanji,* and syllabic characters, known as *kana.* The latter, of which there are two

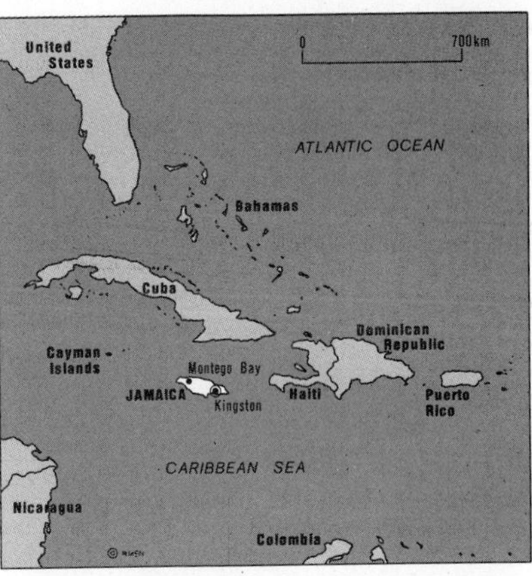
United States
0
700km
ATLANTIC OCEAN
Bahamas
Cuba
Dominican Republic
Cayman Islands
Montego Bay
JAMAICA
Kingston
Haiti
Puerto Rico
CARIBBEAN SEA
Nicaragua
Colombia
Jamaica

Henry James

Jesse James

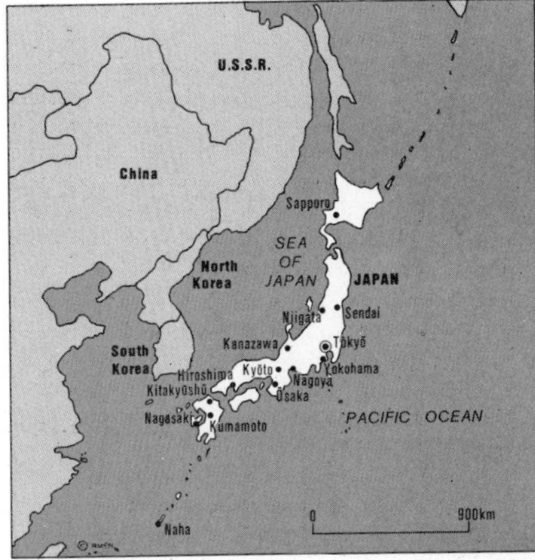
U.S.S.R.
China
Sapporo
SEA OF JAPAN
North Korea
JAPAN
Niigata
Sendai
South Korea
Kanazawa
Tōkyō
Hiroshima
Kyōto
Yokohama
Kitakyūshū
Nagoya
Ōsaka
Nagasaki
Kumamoto
PACIFIC OCEAN
0
900km
Naha
Japan

types—*hiragana* and *katakana*—each consisting of 50 characters can in theory represent any word in the language. But because of the large number of homonyms in Japanese there would be too many ambiguities and thus most Japanese words are spelled with a combination of the ideographs and syllabic characters.

Japanese Architecture, architectural style derived from Chinese religious structures in the 6th century. The Buddhist temple is constructed of gracefully curved wooden columns supporting the wide overhanging roof and thin exterior walls of woodwork and plaster. The gateway, drum tower, and pagoda are also built of wood, and the group is usually set on a picturesque wooded hillside. One-story domestic structures are traditionally built according to modules whose basic unit is a mat, 6 feet by 3 feet. Interior wooden posts support the roof. The outer walls are movable panels of wood or rice paper that slide in grooves. The interior is flexibly subdivided by screens and decorated with simplicity and delicacy. △1048.

Japanese Art. Originally was strongly influenced by China. From the **Asuka period** (593–710) come primitive tomb and wall paintings as well as Buddhist scrolls. During the **Nara period** (710–784), figures in painting became less angular and more lifelike and robust. The **Heian period** (780–1180) saw Japanese painting come into its own, in screens, hand scrolls, book illustrations, and landscapes. During the **Kamakura period** (1185–1338), many scroll paintings were produced. There was a trend toward realism in both scrolls and portraits, and the new ink brushstroke technique was introduced. During the **Muromachi period** (1338–1573), cultural activity centered around the Zen monasteries. Masanobu (*c.* 1453–1540) and his son Motonobu (*c.*1476–1559) founded the Kanō school. The following **Momoyama period** produced large numbers of wall paintings such as decorative frescoes for the castles of warriors. During the **Edo period** (1615–1867), the Nanga painting school reacted to the academicism of the Kanō school. Outstanding printmakers made *ukiyo-e* prints of Kabuki actors, women, and landscapes. After the fall of the Tokugawa shogunate (1868), many Japanese artists attempted to assimilate Western painting styles, while others clung to the traditional Japanese style. △1048.

Japanese Beetle, beetle native to E Asia and accidentally introduced in North America about 1916. Adults are greenish-bronze and coppery brown and feed on fruits and leaves of many plants. The cream-colored to brown, 1in (25mm) larvae feed primarily on grass roots and soil humus. Length: 0.5in (13mm). Species *Popillia japonica.*

Japanese Chin. *See* Japanese Spaniel.

Japanese Exclusion, attempt to deny immigration rights to Asians. Between 1891–1910, about 25,000 Japanese had immigrated to the United States, particularly to the Western states. Since many of these immigrants were laborers, US workers felt threatened. The Gentlemen's Agreement (1907) between Japan and President Theodore Roosevelt sought to limit Japanese entry. Some states passed legislation that restricted the rights of Japanese in America. The Immigration Bill (1924) excluded Japanese as aliens ineligible for US citizenship. *See also* Gentlemen's Agreement.

Japanese Literature, the body of creative writing of Japan. Japanese literature is one of the oldest and richest in the world. The earliest extant works are the *Kojiki* (712) and the *Nihongi* (720), both histories written in Chinese characters used phonetically. The earliest recorded Japanese poetry is in the *Manyoshu* (760), which contains poems dating to the 4th century.

Heian Period: 794–1185. The invention of the Kana syllabaries (*c.* 800) encouraged writing. The *Kokinshu* (905), an anthology of poetry commissioned by the emperor, provided a pattern for *tanka* (short poems). Classical prose developed during this period. *Taketori Monogatari (Tale of the Bamboo Cutter)* is the oldest surviving work. Diaries and accounts of court life also flourished, such as Sei Shonagon's *Makura no Soshi* (*Pillow Book, c.*1000). By far the most significant work was Murasaki Shikibu's *Genji Monogatari* (*The Tale of Genji, c.*1010), the first true novel and one of the world's classics.

Middle Ages: 1185–1603. The *Shinkokinshu* (1206) was an influential collection of poems that are dark in tone and are similar to the *renga* (linked verse) that developed during this period. The No theater was refined by Kanami Kiyotsugu (1333–84) and his son Zeami Motokiyo (1363–1443). Although the "war tales" genre appeared in this period, typified by *Heike Monogatari (Tale of the Heike),* Buddhism colored much of the prose. Notable works are: *Hojoki* (*Account of My Hut, c.*1212) and *Tsurezuregusa* (*Essays in Idleness, c.*1333).

Tokugawa Period: 1603–1868. During this period literature, once the preserve of the aristocracy, became the field of the commoners. Although *tanka* were still written, *haiku* became popular, and Matsuo Basho (1644–94) was the greatest poet of this form. There were developments in the puppet theater and Kabuki, which benefited from the work of the great dramatist Chikamatsu Monzaemon (1653–1725). Perhaps the most famous prose writer of the period was Saikaku Ihara (1642–93).

Modern Period: With the increase in foreign contacts, Western literature had a major influence. Poetry flourished, and major figures such as Yosano Akiko (1878–1942), Ishikawa Takuboku (1885–1912), and Hagiwara Sakutaro (1886–1942) found new means of expression through contact with Western poetry. Writers of modern fiction have earned a reputation abroad as well as at home. They include such figures as Natsume Soseki, Tanizaki Junichiro, Mishima Yukio, Abe Kobo, and Nobel Prize-winner Kawabata Yasunari.

Japanese Music. The music of Japan owes its heritage to Chinese music. Japanese sacred music is divided into *gagaku,* which is orchestral music first introduced into Japan from China around AD 600, and *kangura,* which originated in the 13th century and is used in modern worship. The latter centers around a few notes and is played on the koto (zither) and flutes. Japanese music also includes traditional, ceremonial Nogaku, or No, drama, involving singers accompanied by flutes and drums. Secular music includes vocal music, such as opera, and especially chamber music. In general, the scale most frequently used in Japanese music is the semitonic penta-scale. Rhythm is usually double time. Japanese music tends to be monophonic rather than polyphonic.

Japanese Mythology. The oldest recorded myths of the Japanese appear in the *Kojiki,* a Shinto text of AD 712. In it is described the creation of the world when the gods Izanagi and Izanami made Earth out of muddy water. When Buddhism was introduced from Korea in the 5th and 6th centuries it brought countless new figures to the country's mythology, and the old gods were declared to be reincarnations of Buddhist deities. △834, 840.

Japanese Spaniel, Asian dog (toy group) also called Japanese Chin. Probably originated in ancient China; brought to West by Comm. Perry in 1850. It has a large, rounded head with short muzzle and wide nose between the prominent dark eyes; square, compact body; small, slender legs; and tail twisted over the back. The profuse, long, straight coat is black and white or red and white. Average size: 9in (23cm) high at shoulder; 7lb (3kg). *See also* Toy Dog.

Japanese Theater, descended from ritual dances, assumed three major forms: No, puppet theater, and Kabuki. In addition to the traditional forms, newer styles of drama, influenced by the West, have developed out of the desire to portray modern events and ideas realistically. *See also* Kabuki Theater.

Japanning, the use of colored varnish to produce a hard, brilliant coating imitative of Japanese lacquer.

Japheth, in Genesis, Noah's son who, with his brothers Shem and Ham, survived the Flood aboard the ark.

Japurá, river in NW South America; rises at the confluence of the Caquetá and Apaporis rivers, SW Colombia; flows SE to unite with the Amazon River near Tefé, Brazil. Length: approx. 1,750mi (2,818km).

Jaques-Dalcroze, Émile (1865–1950), Swiss composer and musical educator. From 1892, he was a professor at the Geneva Conservatory. He is best known for his system of "eurhythmics," which attempts "to make feeling for rhythm a physical experience." To teach this system, he founded the Institut Jaques-Dalcroze at Geneva (1915), with branches throughout Europe and the United States.

Jarring, Gunnar (1907–), Swedish diplomat and scholar. As professor of Turkish languages at Lund University, he wrote on dialects and tribes of central Asia. He served as Swedish minister to India, ambassador to the United States (1958–64) and to the USSR (1964–73). He was prominent in the United Nations and served as special envoy to the Middle East during Arab-Israeli conflicts.

Jasmine, climbing shrub known in the Mediterranean since ancient times and grown as an ornamental. It produces fragrant yellow, red, or white flowers, and the oil is used in perfumes. Species include *Jasminum sambac* and the white *J. officinale,* which is hardy in temperate zones. Height: 15–20ft (4.6–6m); fam Oleaceae.

Jason, hero of Greek mythology. Sent on a quest f the Golden Fleece by his uncle King Pelias to preve him from claiming his throne. Jason sailed aboard th *Argo* with heroes including Heracles, Theseus, C pheus, Castor, and Pollux and had adventures wi Harpies and Amazons. He found the fleece in Colch and fled with the sorceress Medea, daughter of th king. Later, tragedies left him a wanderer who die under the prow of the old *Argo. See also* Medea.

Jasper National Park, Canada's 2nd-largest n tional park, in the Canadian Rocky Mts, W Canad named for fur trading agent Jasper Hawes; a gam reserve; fishing and mountain climbing. Are 4,200sq mi (10,878sq km).

Jaspers, Karl (1883–1969), German philosophe His existentialist works show the influence of his stu ies in psychopathology, as well as his study of Kierk gaard and Nietzsche. The main themes of his philos phy appear in *Philosophy* (1932). Other works i clude *Truth and Symbol* (1947), *The Way to Wisdo* (1950), and *Philosophical Faith and Revelatio* (1962). *See also* Existentialism.

Jasperware, unglazed stoneware first made in En land by Josiah Wedgwood in 1775. White in its nat ral state, jasperware is then stained, most common pale blue, but also dark blue, lilac, green, black, an yellow. White decorations in the neoclassical style ar molded separately and then applied to the piece jasperware. Jasperware objects include vase plaques, cameos, tableware, and portrait medallion

Jaundice, yellowing of the skin and other tissue prominently the whites of the eyes, by an excess bile pigment in the blood, with subsequent accumula tion in the tissues. It may occur in the newborn as result of faulty metabolism of bile pigment or second ary to other causes; if severe in the premature infan it may produce widespread destruction in the brain. I adults, jaundice may occur when the flow of bile fror liver to intestine is blocked by an obstruction such a a gallstone, or in diseases of the liver such as cirrhos or hepatitis. In addition to the yellowing of tissues, th symptoms of jaundice include itching, dark urine, an pale stools. *See also* Cirrhosis; Hepatitis. △718.

Jaurès, Jean (Léon) (1859–1914), French politica leader. He entered the chamber of deputies in 1885 in 1893 he became a Socialist. He founded (1904 and edited the socialist journal *L'Humanité* and i 1905 helped form the unified French Socialist party His socialism was more idealistic and democratic tha Marxism. In 1914 he was assassinated by a fanatica nationalist for advocating arbitration rather than wa with Germany. △1326.

Java (Djawa), island in Indonesia; member of th Greater Sunda Islands, bounded by Sumatra (SE) Malay Peninsula (E), and lying between the Java Se and Indian Ocean; Djakarta is the capital. It is th 4th-largest island of Indonesia, constituting thre provinces, two autonomous districts, and more tha 65% of the country's total population, making Jav one of the most densely populated areas of the world 2,200 people per sq mi (850 per sq km). A mountain ous area, it is crossed by numerous volcanic forma tions, some of which are still active; the climate is warm and humid, with moderate rainfall; extensive irrigation systems make it a fertile agricultural area Long before recorded history, Java was a center o civilization, as indicated by the 1891 discovery of the Java man and other fossilized human remains. From the 4th–15th centuries it served as the seat of a highly developed Hindu-Buddhist civilization, whose cente was the powerful Majapahit state; its rule over much of Indonesia and the Malay Peninsula was haltec 1518 by Muslim conquest; European settlement began 1596 and continued with est. of Dutch Eas India Co. post at Batavia 1619. Island was occupied 1811–16 by Britain under Thomas S. Raffles; retaken and held by Dutch until Japanese occupation of WWII; scene of Dutch-Indonesian conflicts 1945–46 ending in Linggadjati Agreement and independent Indonesia (1947); site of Bandung Technical Institute (1959), University of Indonesia (1950), National University (1949), University of Padjadjaran (1957), Air langga University (1954), Diponegoro University (1960), Gadjah Mada University (1949); cultural, political, economic center. Crops: sugar, kapok, rubber, tea, coffee, tobacco, cacao, cassava, peanuts, maize cinchona, rice, sweet potatoes, bananas, fruit trees soybeans. Industries: teak wood, textiles, agriculture, fishing, handcrafts. Area: 48,842sq mi (126,501sq km). Pop. 78,201,000.

Java Man, or *Pithecanthropus erectus,* extinct race of hominid whose skeletal remains were found at Trinil, Java, in 1891. His skull was apelike, but his limb structure was akin to modern man's. *See also* Pithecanthropus. △650.

Java Sea (Djawa, Laut), shallow extension of the Pacific Ocean in SE Asia; bordered by Java (S), Borneo (N), Flores Sea and Makassar Strait (E), Sumatra (W); scene of WWII Allied defeat by Japanese naval forces (1942), leaving Java vulnerable to Japanese invasion. Depth (max.): 300ft (92m). Area: 120,000sq mi (310,800sq km).

Javelin, in field events, wooden or metallic spear with a metal tip weighing a minimum of 1lb, 12.218oz (800g). It has an overall length that varies from 8ft, 6.362in to 8ft, 10.299in (260–270cm). △1726.

Jaw. △756.

Jawara, (Sir) Dauda Kairaba (1924–), Gambian political figure. He served as minister of education and prime minister (1960–70) of Gambia when it was a British colony and became its president when it became a republic in 1970.

Jay, John (1745–1829), first chief justice of the US Supreme Court (1789–95), b. New York City. He was an influential member of the Whig party, and during the American Revolution he served as a delegate to the Continental Congress (1774–77, 1778–79), becoming its president during the second period. He was chairman of the committee that drafted the first state constitution of New York (1777) and was appointed the first chief justice of New York (1777–89). He also served as minister to Spain (1779–82) and then went to join Benjamin Franklin in Paris to negotiate a peace with Great Britain. He was secretary for foreign affairs under the Articles of Confederation (1784–89). Together with Alexander Hamilton and James Madison he wrote the *Federalist Papers* (1787–88), explaining and urging ratification of the US Constitution. As a member of the New York Constitutional Convention, he helped secure ratification (1787) by that state. While US chief justice, he ruled on *Chisholm* v. *Georgia* (1793) which was reversed with the adoption of the 11th Amendment, stipulating that a state could not be sued by an individual (1795). In 1794 he was sent to Britain as a peace negotiator and concluded the controversial Jay's Treaty. When he returned, he was governor of New York (1795–1801). *See also* Federalist Papers, The; Jay's Treaty.

Jay, any of several harsh-voiced, often brightly colored, birds related to magpies and crows (family Corvidae). About 1ft (30cm) long, they have strong, cone-shaped bills, eating almost anything in their open forest and brushland homes. They usually lay 3 to 7 pale green or white spotted eggs in an open nest in a tree. *See also* Blue Jay.

Jayavarman VII. △1114.

Jay's Treaty (1794), agreement between the United States (represented by John Jay) and Britain (represented by Lord Grenville) principally to settle points of dispute outstanding between them since the Revolutionary War. Its provisions regarding trade helped establish American commerce. The United States agreed not to aid privateers hostile to Britain, and Britain withdrew from the Northwest Territory.

Jazz, musical style that evolved in the United States in the late 19th century out of African and European folk music, popular songs, and American vaudeville. Jazz is characterized by a steady rhythm, usually four beats to the bar, with accents on the second and fourth beats; prominence of melody, often with elements derived from the blues; and improvisation and spontaneous creation by the performer. Early jazz was developed in New Orleans in the form of blues, Dixieland, and ragtime music. In the 1920s jazz spread to Chicago and New York City and became known across the world as a unique musical style indigenous to America. Subsequent developments included the big "swing" bands in the 1930s and the "bebop" (now called "bop") style of the 1940s. Jazz elements influenced serious composers such as Maurice Ravel and Darius Milhaud and also became a part of other popular musical styles such as rock-and-roll. Among the greatest of jazz musicians were Louis Armstrong, Duke Ellington, W. C. Handy, Scott Joplin, Benny Goodman, and Art Tatum. △1366.

JCS. *See* Joint Chiefs of Staff.

J-Curve, diagrammatic representation of the theory of rising expectations. When plotted on a graph, the process of rapid social, political, and economic improvements followed by a revolution creates an inverted "J." *See also* Rising Expectations. △1360.

JD. *See* Julian Day.

Jean (1921–), grand duke of Luxemburg (1964–). He succeeded his mother, Grand Duchess Charlotte, on her abdication.

Jean de Meun or **Meung,** real name Jean Clopinel (*c.*1250–*c.*1305), French poet and scholar. He continued the *Romance of the Rose* by Guillaume de Lorris. Under Jean de Meun, the work, originally a romantic allegory, became a satire on women, royalty, and the church. Meun also translated the *Life and Letters of Abélard and Héloïse.*

Jeanneret, Charles Edouard. *See* Le Corbusier.

Jeans, (Sir) James Hopwood (1877–1946), English scientist, author, and professor of astronomy at the Royal Institution, London. He investigated stellar dynamics and proposed the tidal, or catastrophic, theory of planetary origin. He also presented his continuous-creation theory, studied gas kinetic theory, and was a scientific popularizer. △48.

Jeep. △1702.

Jeffers, (John) Robinson (1887–1962), US poet, b. Pittsburgh. His work reflects his pessimistic view of civilization and even humanity itself. Although the setting for his work is modern, the source is often the Bible or classical literature. Noted works include *Tamar, and Other Poems* (1924) and *Medea* (1947).

Jefferson, Thomas (1743–1826), 3rd president of the United States (1801–09), b. Goochland (now in Albermarle) co, Va., graduate, William and Mary College. In 1772 he married Martha Wayles Skelton; they had six children.

Jefferson received the education and upbringing of an 18th-century landed aristocrat. He was a talented architect and musician, an inventor, and a respected amateur botanist. His political writings, based on John Locke and Jean Jacques Rousseau, made him the foremost advocate of democracy of his day. He was admitted to the Virginia bar in 1767.

In the Virginia House of Burgesses, Jefferson led the patriot faction, and his writings spread his influence throughout the colonies. He was a delegate (1775) to the First Virginia Convention. At the Second Continental Congress in 1775–76, he was asked to draft the Declaration of Independence, his most famous work. He became governor of Virginia in 1779, but he was not an effective administrator. He served in the Second Continental Congress, which sent him (1785) as minister to France. While there, he witnessed the early stages of the French Revolution and sympathized with the revolutionary movement.

In 1790, President Washington named Jefferson secretary of state. A factional rivalry soon developed in the cabinet between Alexander Hamilton and Jefferson. Hamilton's faction represented the urban, commercial interest and favored alliance with Britain, while the Jeffersonians were agrarians and favored France. The factions gradually formed into political parties: the Hamiltonians became Federalists and the Jeffersonians became Republicans (later Democrats).

In 1796, Jefferson ran against John Adams, and when Adams won, Jefferson became vice president. Jefferson was elected president in 1801 after a deadlock in the House of Representatives. He set about ridding the presidency of its royalist trappings and sought to reduce the overall influence of the federal government. He pushed through the Louisiana Purchase and sent the Lewis and Clark Expedition to explore the West. In his second term, he sponsored the ill-fated Embargo Act of 1807. After his retirement, he founded the University of Virginia.

Career: member, Virginia House of Burgesses, 1769–75; delegate, Second Continental Congress, 1775–76; governor of Virginia, 1779–81; minister to France, 1785–89; secretary of state, 1790–93; vice president, 1797–1801; president, 1801–09. *See also* Declaration of Independence; Louisiana Purchase.

Jefferson, Territory of, region roughly encompassing the present state of Colorado. Organized by settlers (1859) out of part of Kansas Territory, it was never recognized by Congress, which instead created the Territory of Colorado in 1861.

Jefferson City, capital city of Missouri, located in central part of state on Missouri River; seat of Cole co; occupied by Union troops during Civil War June 1861; site of 1917 Italian Renaissance capitol of Carthage marble, housing paintings by Thomas Hart Benton and N. C. Wyeth; Missouri state museum; and Lincoln University (1866). Industries: shoes, clothes, electrical appliances, bookbinding. Chosen as state

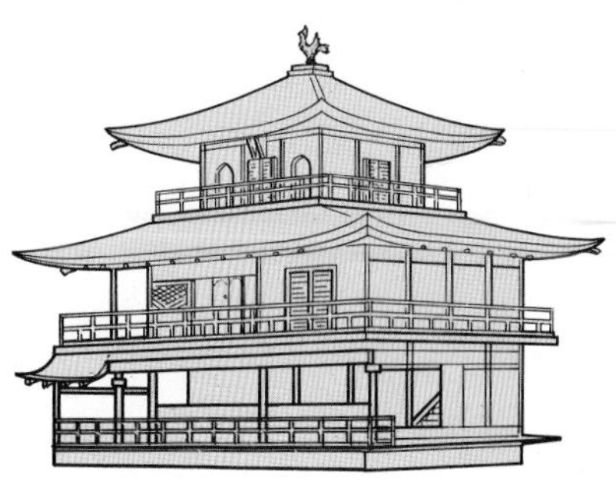

Japanese architecture

Jasmine

John Jay

Thomas Jefferson

capital 1821; legislature moved there 1826. Inc. as town 1825, as city 1839. Pop. (1970) 32,407.

Jeffreys, (Sir) Harold (1891–), English astronomer and geophysicist. He ascertained that the four outer planets are very cold, constructed models of them, and investigated the origin of the solar system. Studying the thermal history of the Earth, he was the first to hypothesize that its core is liquid. He co-authored the standard tables of earthquake-wave travel times and explained the origin and function of monsoons, sea breezes, and cyclones.

Jeffries, James Jackson (1875–1953), U.S. boxer, b. Carroll, Ohio. He beat Bob Fitzsimmons (1899) for the world's heavyweight championship in Coney Island, N.Y. He retired (1905) for lack of opposition, but returned to fight for the title (1910) and lost to Jack Johnson in Reno, Nev. He was elected to the Boxing Hall of Fame in 1954.

Jehad. *See* Jihad.

Jehoshaphat, in the Bible, son of Asa and king of Judah. He and Ahab, king of Israel, signed an alliance, the first between the two countries.

Jehovah, a variant form of the name of the God of Judaism. It developed from YHWH (or JHVH, YHVH; a Hebrew tribal name for God) and the vowel symbols of the word *Adonai* ("My Lord") during the Middle Ages. It came to be used synonymously for the ineffable name *Yahweh.* Christians quickly assumed this transliterated form. In the 19th and 20th centuries, scholars began the return to *Yahweh.*

Jehovah's Witnesses, Christian group taking its name from a passage in the Old Testament: "Ye are my witnesses, saith Jehovah" (Isaiah 43:10). They are active in preaching and door-to-door missionary work and distribute millions of Bibles and tracts. Centered in the United States, they have also held international conferences. The Watch Tower Bible and Tract Society, incorporated in 1884, acts as the legal agency for the witnesses.

Jehu. △982.

Jelacic, Josip, Count. △1232, 1248.

Jelecote Pine. △442.

Jellyfish, marine coelenterate found in coastal waters and characterized by tentacles with stinging cells. The adult form is the medusa. It has a bell-shaped body with a thick layer of jellylike substance between two body cell layers, many tentacles, and four mouth lobes surrounding the gut opening. The common *Aurelia* is transparent with four violet circles near its center. Diameter: 3in–12in (76.2–304.8mm). Class Scyphozoa. △470, 626.

Jena, city in S East Germany, on the Saale River; scene of 1806 Prussian defeat by Napoleon; site of University of Jena (1557–58). Industries: glass, optical and precision instruments, pharmaceuticals. Founded 9th century; chartered 13th century. Pop. 88,346.

Jenkins, William Fitzgerald. *See* Leinster, Murray.

Jenkins' Ear, War of (1739–41), war between England and Spain arising out of long-term mercantile and maritime grievances, most notorious of which was the boarding of Robert Jenkins' ship at Havana in 1731 by a Spanish official who cut off one of the English captain's ears.

Jenner, Edward (1749–1823), English physician. He developed vaccination as a means of preventing smallpox. Aware that a cowpox infection seemed to protect people from a subsequent smallpox infection, Jenner inoculated a healthy boy with cowpox. The boy developed that mild disease but months later when inoculated with smallpox did not develop that dreaded disease; he had been vaccinated against it. This finding established the principle of vaccination as an invaluable tool in medicine. △1186.

Jerboa, jumping, burrowing rodent of Eurasian and African deserts with hindlegs four times longer than front legs. Nocturnal, it has a satiny, sand-colored body and an extremely long tail. Herbivorous, it does not drink water. Length: 2–8in (51–203mm). Family Dipodidae. △606.

Jeremiah (*c.* 650–585 BC), Hebrew prophet whose life and teachings are recorded in the Old Testament Book of Jeremiah, the 24th book of the Bible. He fearlessly denounced social injustice and false worship in the Kingdom of Judah. When Babylonia invaded Judah, captured Jerusalem, and took many Jews into exile, Jeremiah saw this as a punishment from God. He urged the people to make peace and to believe in God, teaching that they could preserve their worship even in disaster and exile. His ideas were influential in later Old Testament writings and in the New Testament.

Jerez de la Frontera, city in SW Spain, 13mi (21km) NE of Cadiz, N of Guadalete River. An ancient Roman colony, it was taken by Moors 711, reconquered 1264 by Alfonso X. Site of 15th-century church of Santiago; Gothic church of San Miguel (1462); Carthusian Monastery (1477), now a national museum. Industries: lumber, citrus fruits, livestock, vegetables, cork, olives, grain, bottles, barrels, sherry. Pop. 149,867.

Jericho, ancient city of Palestine, in Jordan valley, N of Dead Sea; modern Ariha is near ancient city. Captured by Joshua from Canaanites (1,400 BC), city was later destroyed by Herod (1st century BC) and rebuilt S of old site; destroyed several times after this. In 1950 excavations revealed a Hellenic fortress from the 2nd century and site of Herod's city.

Jerome, Saint (*c.* 347–420), Bible scholar and father of the Roman Catholic Church. His original name was Eusebius Hieronymus. After a thorough literary education he spent four years of intense study in a monastic type of community in the Syrian desert. Later he went to Rome and became secretary to Pope Damasus I. The pope commissioned Jerome to prepare a standard text of the Gospels for use by Latin-speaking Christians. Jerome revised the Gospels from the Old Latin and later made a new translation of the Psalms and the Old Testament from Greek and Hebrew sources. His work was the basis for what later became known as the Vulgate, or authorized Latin text of the Bible.

Jersey, largest island in Channel Islands of United Kingdom; constitutes a bailiwick; capital is St Helier. Official language is French, although English is spoken everywhere. Main occupations: farming, horticulture, tourism. Area: 45sq mi (117sq km). Pop. 72,629.

Jersey, widespread breed of small dairy cattle of French descent, developed on the Isle of Jersey. The butterfat content of their milk, 5.3%, is the richest of all dairy cattle, but relatively low in volume. Usually fawn or brown, some American varieties have white markings. *See also* Dairy Cattle. △372.

Jersey City, port city in NE New Jersey, on Hudson River and Upper New York Bay, across from New York City; seat of Hudson co; 2nd-largest city in state. Originally a Dutch settlement, it came under British control in 1664; in 1779 "Light-Horse Harry" Lee, under George Washington, captured it; site of St Peter's College (1872), Jersey City State College (1929), New Jersey College of Dentistry and Medicine (1955). Industries: oil refining, chemicals, paper products, locomotives, clothing. Founded 1630; inc. 1838 as Jersey City. Pop. (1970) 260,545.

Jerusalem (Yerushalayim, or **Al-Quds),** city on Israeli-Jordanian border, 35mi (56km) SE of Tel Aviv; capital of Israel and Jerusalem district; sacred city of the Christian, Jewish, and Muslim religions. Originally a Jebusite stronghold (2000–1500 BC), city was captured by King David after 1000 BC and known as "city of David"; it developed into religious center of country. Destroyed by Nebuchadnezzar of Babylon *c.* 586 BC, it was rebuilt by Herod *c.* 35 BC, but again destroyed by Titus AD 70. The Roman colony of Aelia Capitolina was established, and Jews were forbidden within city limits (135–mid-5th century). Christian control was granted by Persians *c.* 614. City was conquered 1077 by Muslim Seljuks, whose mistreatment of Christians precipitated the Crusades, as a result of which was formed the kingdom of Jerusalem 1094–1187. It was held by Turks from 1244–1917, when it became the British mandated territory of Palestine; it was divided in 1949 between Jordan and Israel, in 1950 it was designated capital of the new state of Israel; it was reunited after the 1967 Six-Day War. City contains many educational institutions, including Hebrew University (1925), and many churches, synagogues, and shrines. Industries: tourism, diamond processing, plastics, shoes, construction. Pop. 304,-500.

Jerusalem, Latin Kingdom of, feudal state created in Palestine and Syria by the Crusaders. After Jerusalem fell in the First Crusade (1099), Godfrey of Bouillon ruled it. He refused to be king, but his brother, Baldwin I, took the title, as did many successors, such as Baldwin II, the Angevins Fulk and Baldwin V, Guy of Lusignan, Amalric II, and Emperor Frederick II. The kings, who were elected, ostensibly oversaw the Latin counties of Antioch, Edessa, Tripoli, and Jerusalem but the feudal lords fought among themselves. The kingdom warred with the Mamelukes of Egypt, the Seljuk Turks, and the Byzantine emperors. The royal authority was undermined by the military orders (eg the Knights Templars), and the Seljuks seized Edessa (1144). Saladin captured Jerusalem in 1187, and the kingdom essentially ended when the Christians were defeated at Gaza (1244). Acre, the capital after Jerusalem fell, was captured in 1291.

Jerusalem Artichoke, North American perennial sunflower with edible (potatolike) tubers used as food for man and livestock. It is not a true artichoke. Height: to 12ft (3.6m). Family Compositae; species *Helianthus tuberosus.*

Jesuit Martyrs (1648–49). The Jesuits began missionary work in Canada in 1609. Under the leadership of Isaac Jogues and Jean de Brebeuf, they worked to convert the Hurons and Iroquois to Roman Catholicism. Brebeuf, Antoine Daniel, Gabriel Lalemant, Charles Garnier, and Noël Chabanel were killed by the Iroquois after a series of epidemics in 1648. Their bravery in the face of British and Indian opposition was legendary, leading to canonization in 1930. *See also* Brebeuf, Jean de. △1154, 1164.

Jesuits, officially the Society of Jesus, a Roman Catholic order of religious men founded by Ignatius Loyola in 1540. The order played a significant role in the Counter-Reformation. They often were the first Christian missionaries in the New World, Asian, and African areas. Because they gave allegiance only to their general in Rome and the pope, they came to antagonize many European rulers. In 1773 Pope Clement XIV, pressured by the kings of France, Spain, and Portugal, abolished the order. They continued to exist in Prussia and Russia. The order was reestablished in 1814. The largest male order, today there are over 33,000 members. It takes as long as 15 years to gain full membership in the order. Jesuits have distinguished themselves in education, scholarship, and missionary work. △1154.

Jesus, Society of. *See* Jesuits.

Jesus Christ (*c.* 4 BC–*c.* AD 30), the founder of Christianity. His name combines a well known Hebrew name, Jesus (originally Joshua, "God is salvation"), with Christ, which comes from a Greek translation of a Hebrew word for messiah, anointed one, a long-expected king and deliverer of Israel. What is known of Jesus' life comes from study of the Gospels of Matthew, Mark, Luke, and John, the first books of the New Testament. He was born about 4 BC, near the end of the reign of Herod the Great. (A 6th-century error put the first year of the Christian calendar several years after Christ's birth date.) Jesus' mother, Mary, and her husband, Joseph, lived in Nazareth in Galilee, but they had to journey to Bethlehem in Judea for a census and Jesus was born there in a stable. He probably grew up in Galilee. About AD 26 or 27, John the son of Zachariah began a preaching and baptizing ministry in Galilee, and Jesus was one of the many who went to John and were baptized in the Jordan River. Thereafter, Jesus began his own ministry, preaching to growing numbers and gathering 12 disciples around him. He told people to love God and to love their neighbor—who is anyone, even a foreigner or an enemy. He taught that salvation depends on true devotion to God's will rather than on following the letter of the religious law.

In about 29 or 30 Jesus and his disciples went to Jerusalem just before the Jewish feast of the Passover. The city gave him a triumphal welcome, but he knew that the end of his earthly ministry was near. A small group in the priestly hierarchy in the Temple in Jerusalem feared Jesus was a source of trouble. A few days after the entry into Jerusalem, Jesus gathered his disciples for a Last Supper, at which he instituted the sacrament of Holy Communion. That same night he was arrested by agents of the priests and denounced before Pontius Pilate, the Roman governor, on the charge that he claimed to be king of the Jews. Roman soldiers crucified Jesus on a hill outside the city wall; he died after suffering for three hours and was buried. On the third day his tomb was found empty. On 9 occasions he appeared to his disciples, and 40 days after his Resurrection he ascended into heaven. His followers then began their own ministry to take his word to all people.

Christians worship Christ as the Son of God, who lived as a man to bring God's message to the world. They also believe he is one with God; he is at once truly human and truly divine. By his preaching and the sacrifice of his death and his Resurrection, he showed humankind how to live rightly and how to find eternal life. *See also* Apostle. △1026.

Jet, a dense variety of lignite coal formed from driftwood buried on the sea floor; often polished as jewelry. △244.

Jet Engine, Aircraft. *See* Turbojet Engine.

Jet Lag, phenomenon experienced after lengthy jet travel in which the individual's biological and psychological rhythms are disrupted and the mind literally has to catch up with the body. Symptoms include confusion, mood alterations, irritability, sleep disturbance, and other signs of stress. △760.

Jet Propulsion, the movement of a body by way of thrust provided by the rearward discharge of a jet of gas (or fluid), as in jet engines or rockets. In jet engines the ejected gas consists of a mixture of air taken from outside and gases resulting from internal combustion. *See also* Rocket. △1718, 1744.

Jet Stream, a narrow, swiftly moving wind between slower currents at altitudes of 6 to 10mi (10 to 16km) in the upper troposphere or lower stratosphere, principally in the zone of prevailing westerlies. High-flying aircraft may be helped or hindered by the jet stream and the rapid wind variations around it. *See also* Circulation, Atmospheric.

Jetty, an engineered structure designed to direct and confine a current or tide. They are often built in pairs on either side of a harbor entrance or at the mouth of a river. Groins, breakwaters, seawalls, and small piers are examples of jetties.

Jewelry. △1554.

Jewelweed, North American succulent plant found in marshes, swamps, and damp woods. Pale jewelweed, or touch-me-not *(Impatiens pallida),* has pendant, pale yellow blossoms; height: to 5ft (1.5m). The spotted jewelweed *(Impatiens biflora)* has orange flowers with purple spots. When crushed, the stems and leaves exude a juice that is a remedy for the itching caused by poison ivy. Family Balsaminaceae.

Jewfish, also giant grouper, marine fish found in tropical and temperate waters of the Atlantic and Pacific. It is spotted and mottled. Length: to 8ft (2.5m); weight: to 750lbs (340kg). Family Serranidae; species include *Epinephelus itajara* and *Premicrops lanceolata.*

Jews, a people who have maintained an identity over thousands of years in spite of dispersion and persecution. The Jews originated in the ancient Middle East, and for centuries they lived in kingdoms in Palestine. Then they were dispersed over the world, sometimes living as ghetto minorities, sometimes as citizens. In the 20th century Jews established the national state of Israel. Millions more live in other countries—6,000,000, for example, are US citizens. Jews differ among themselves in physical appearance, language, and to some extent in customs, so there is no simple definition of Jewishness. The sense of identity is found in religious beliefs and traditions going back through the Hebrew prophets to the time of Moses and Abraham. *See also* Judaism. △844, 982.

Jew's Harp, primitive musical instrument. Probably first called "Jaw's Harp," it is an iron frame held in the player's teeth, with a flexible metal strip vibrated by his finger. The player changes tone and pitch by shaping his mouth.

Jex-Blake, Sophia Louisa (1840–1912), English physician who fought vigorously and successfully to obtain legislation so that women could receive the M.D. degree and a license to practice medicine and surgery. She founded a medical school for women in London in 1874 and another in Edinburgh in 1886.

Jezebel, in the Bible, Phoenician wife of Ahab, king of Israel. She supported worship of Baal and, clashing with Elijah, drove him out of Israel. Her death was caused by Jehu, usurper of her son Jeram's throne. Ahaziah, her daughter, was queen of Judah.

Jhansi, walled city in N central India; capital of Jhansi district of Uttar Pradesh state; served as capital of Maratha principality 1770–1853; scene of European massacre (1857) during India Mutiny; its fortress, built by Bundela Rajputs, dates from 1613. Industries: railroad workshops, rolling mills, brassware, rugs, silk. Founded 1732. Pop. 173,292.

Jibuti. *See* Djibouiti.

Jicarilla. *See* Apache.

Jidda (Juddah), port city in Saudi Arabia, on the Red Sea 46mi (74km) W of Mecca; under Turkish rule until 1916, when it joined independent Hejaz; taken 1925 by Ibn Saud; site of several government ministries, traditional tomb of Eve; serves Mecca as port for pilgrims. Pop. 194,000.

Jig, a dance, originating in England, that reached its popularity during the 16th century. Jigs were frequently named for the clown characters who danced them in English comedy, and "Nobody's Jig" was among the most popular. In the United States, jigs were the forerunners of dances in minstrel shows. Most jigs are couple dances in 6/8 time. The Irish jig and English Morris jig are complicated solo dances.

Jihad, or **Jehad,** religious war of Muslims against nonbelievers. Established in the Koran as a divine institution, such warfare is a sacred religious duty undertaken especially for the purpose of advancing Islam and protecting Muslims from evil. There are four ways in which Muslims may fulfill their Jihad duty: by the heart, by the tongue, by the hand, and by the sword.

Jilin. *See* Kirin.

Jim Crow Laws, measures enacted in the US South from 1877 to the 1950s to legalize racial segregation in public facilities, including theaters, schools, parks, and restaurants. The term "Jim Crow" was derived from the name of a minstrel act and came to mean segregation. The laws began to be challenged after the 1954 Supreme Court ruling *(Brown* v. *Board oi Education of Topeka, Kansas)* which stated that segregated schools were unlawful.

Jimson Weed, also thorn apple; poisonous bad-smelling weed originally native to Asia. All parts of the plant are toxic and can cause death. Leaves are wavy-toothed, and the trumpet-shaped flowers, to 4in (10.2cm), are white or purplish. Alkaloids present are atropine, hyoscyamine, and scopolamine. Height: 4ft (1.2m); family Solanaceae; species *Datura stramonium.* △742.

Jingoism, term used to describe a posture of chauvinism or aggressive nationalism. It originated in the Russo-Turkish War (1877–78) when British supporters of the war came to be called jingos, after a line of a popular song of the day: "We don't want to fight, yet by jingo, if we do/We've got the ships, we've got the men/And got the money, too!" △1262.

Jinnah, Muhammad Ali (1876–1948), founder of Pakistan. He obtained his law degree in England and returned to practice in India. In 1906 he joined the Indian National Congress where he became an advocate of Hindu-Muslem unity. Between 1910–19 he was a member of the legislative council of the viceroy. In 1913 he joined the Muslim League and became its president in 1916. In 1920 he resigned from the Indian National Congress although he still hoped Hindus and Muslims could work together. But in 1940 he called for a completely separate Muslim nation on the Indian subcontinent. With the creation of Pakistan in 1947, Jinnah became governor general and president of the constituent assembly. △1330.

Jinzhou (Chinchou), city in NE China, on main line of Peking-Mukden railroad; noted transportation center. Industries: textiles, paper, oil refining, chemicals. Pop. 400,000.

Jívaro, or **Shuara,** a tribe of Indians of the E Andean region of Ecuador and Peru, famed for their manufacture and use of the *tsantsa,* the shrunken heads of their victims. They once numbered over 30,000 people; today, 20,000 inhabit the lowland Andean Montaña region.

Joab, in the Bible, David's nephew and general of David's army. Failing to reconcile David and his son Absalom, Joab killed Absalom. Backing Adonijah's claim to the throne, Joab was killed by Solomon.

Joan I (1273–1305), queen of Navarre (1274–1305), queen of France (1285–1305). Daughter of Henry I of Navarre, she married Philip the Fair of France in 1284. She was the mother of three French kings: Louis X, Philip V, Charles IV.

Joanna or **Joanna the Mad** (1479–1555), Spanish queen of Castile and León (1504–55). She was the daughter of Ferdinand II and Isabella I and inherited Castile and León at her mother's death. Her father acted as regent for her until she married Philip I, son of the Holy Roman emperor. Always mentally unstable, she became insane after the death of Philip in 1506 and Ferdinand again acted as her regent. Her son Charles I (later Holy Roman Emperor Charles V) was joint ruler after Ferdinand died in 1516. Another son, Ferdinand, succeeded Charles as emperor.

Edward Jenner

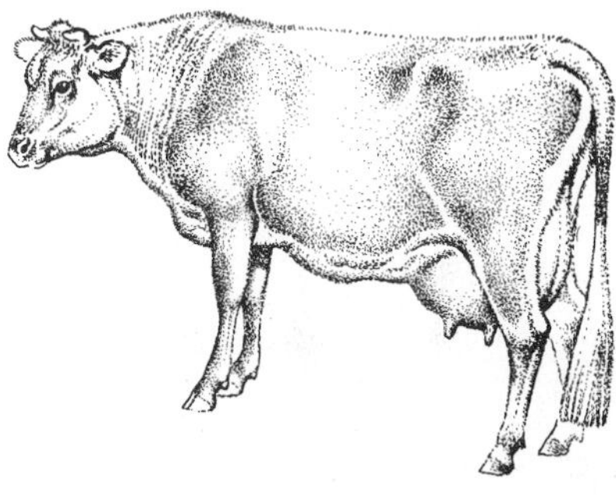

Jersey cattle

Jerusalem, Israel

Jewelweed

Joan of Arc (Fr. Jeanne d'Arc) (1412–31), the national heroine of France and a Roman Catholic saint; also known as Joan of Lorraine and the Maid of Orléans; b. Domremy-la-Purcelle. A deeply religious peasant girl, she claimed to hear heavenly voices and see visions of saints urging her to save France, which was then in the midst of the Hundred Years War (1337–1453), ravaged by the English and their Burgundian allies, while the dauphin Charles VII remained uncrowned because Reims, the traditional place of investiture, was held by his enemies. In early 1429, wearing men's clothes, Joan went to the dauphin, recognizing him immediately though he had hidden himself among his courtiers, and persuaded him to give her troops. She then went to Orléans and, inspiring the French forces, broke the long English siege of that city. She next drove the English from the Loire towns and defeated them at Patay. After this victory she persuaded the indecisive dauphin to proceed to Reims and be crowned with herself standing near him. She then attempted to liberate Paris but was unsuccessful.

In early 1430 she was captured by the Burgundians and turned over to Bishop Pierre Cauchon, who had taken the English side, to be tried at Rouen for witchcraft and heresy. The proceedings against her occupied the winter and spring of 1431. Under great pressure she resolutely maintained her innocence, except for a few days during which she signed an abjuration of heresy. After being sentenced to imprisonment, she withdrew her abjuration and reaffirmed her innocence, was turned over to secular authorities, and burned at the stake. In 1456, after the English had been driven out of France, new proceedings annulled the 1431 trial and verdict. In 1920 she was canonized a saint and the French government declared an annual national holiday in her honor for her role in awakening national consciousness in France. △1096.

Job, biblical patriarch and book that describes Job's life and raises the question: Is Job's goodness, wealth, and rank a form of selfishness? Satan asks if Job fears God for naught and, if the blessings were removed, would he curse God to his face? Receiving permission, the Devil destroys Job's property and his children and inflicts him with a terrible disease, causing his wife's breakdown. Job's reply to all this suffering, "Shall we not receive good at the hand of the Lord, and shall we not receive evil?" answers Satan's question. Later, Job curses the day he was born when three men of wisdom come to console him. Jehovah appears and eloquently reproves Job, rebukes his opponents, and vindicates the patriarch's integrity.

Job Corps, agency within the US Department of Labor. The purpose of Job Corps is to administer programs that provide disadvantaged youths with education, vocational training, and work experience. It was authorized by the Economic Opportunity Act of 1964.

Job Satisfaction. △924–26.

Jodhpur (Marwar), walled city in NW India; site of old fortress housing gem collection of the maharaja; riding breeches named after city. Industries: textiles, ivory carvings, lacquerware, bicycles. Founded 1459 by Rao Jodha. Pop. 317,612.

Joel, biblical author and second of the 12 minor prophets. The first prophet to Judah, he reflects on the country's ruin and despair, later detailed by other prophets.

Joe-Pye Weed, perennial plant of E North America. It has leaves in whorls and terminal clusters of pink or purple flower heads. Height: 3–12ft (0.9–3.6m). Family Compositae; genus *Eupatorium*.

Joffre, Joseph Jacques Césaire (1852–1931), French military figure. He began his military career as an engineer in the colonies. In 1911 he was appointed commander in chief of the French army. Underestimating German strength at the outbreak of World War I, he at least led an orderly retreat and made a successful counterattack at the Battle of the Marne (1914). After the Germans nearly captured Verdun (1916), he was relieved of his command and served as chief military adviser to the government, then as chairman of the Allied War Council.

Jogjakarta, city in S Java, Indonesia, 175mi (282km) WSW of Surabaja, at foot of Mt Merapi; capital of Jogjakarta autonomous district; served as capital of Dutch-controlled sultanate 1755; scene of native uprising led by Prince Dipo Negoro protesting Dutch forced-labor practices and exploitation (1825–30); Javanese stronghold during Indonesian independence movement (1940s); temporary capital of Indonesia 1945–49; site of palace of Jogjakarta sultans (1757), housing Gadjah Mada University (1949), Java University (1921), Sono Budojo Museum, and 11th-century Hindu temples. Industries: cigars and cigarettes, railroad shops, sugar, silvercraft, wood carving, leather goods, batik cloth. Founded 1749 by Sultan Hamengku Buwono I. Pop. 342,267.

Johannesburg, city in NE Republic of South Africa; became a municipality in 1896; occupied by British forces 1900; in 1903 an elected council assumed local government. Johannesburg is the country's largest and leading industrial city, producing 20% of South Africa's annual output and containing the world's richest gold deposits; site of University of Witwatersrand (1922), Rand Afrikaans University (1966), Union Observatory (1903), art gallery, theaters, zoo. Industries: gold mining, chemicals, leather products, textiles, engineering. Founded 1886 as gold mining camp; chartered 1928. Pop. 654,682.

John VIII, Roman Catholic pope (872–82). He served in the Curia for 40 years. As pope, he built fortifications to protect Rome, founded the papal navy, and asked Christians to protect Europe. Conspiracies developed within Rome and he was poisoned by a relative.

John XXIII (?1370–1419). *See* Cossa, Baldassare.

John XXIII, Roman Catholic pope (1958–63), b. Angelo Guiseppe Roncalli (1881). Before his election, he served as director of the Society for Propagation of the Faith, a diplomat in Bulgaria, and papal nuncio in France. He convened the Second Vatican Council to deal with renewal of the church and unity of all Christians in 1962. In his concern for the care of souls, he made many ecumenical advances. △1388.

John I Tzimisces (925–76), Byzantine emperor (*r.* 969–76). A former general, John proved himself a successful statesman as well. As emperor, he defeated an alliance of Bulgarians and Russians in the Balkans, thereby bringing the Balkans under imperial control; consolidated the Byzantine position in the Near East; and conducted skillful diplomatic negotiations with the medieval German Empire.

John II Comnenus (1088–1143), Byzantine emperor (*r.* 1118–43). Known to his contemporaries as Calojohn ("John the Good," or "John the Handsome"), he was the greatest ruler of the Comnenian dynasty. John gained important military successes in the Balkans and in Asia Minor.

John III Dukas Vatatzes (1193–1254), Byzantine emperor (*r.* 1222–54). Under John's leadership, the Empire of Nicaea emerged as the most powerful of the Greek states during the period of Latin rule in Constantinople. *See also* Constantinople, Latin Empire of.

John V Palaeologus (1332–91), Byzantine emperor (*r.* 1341–47, 1355–76, 1379–91). During the first part of his reign, the boy emperor was pushed into the background by the rebellion of John Cantacuzenue. After the fall of his rival, John V Palaeologus converted to Roman Catholicism, hoping to bring about a union of Eastern and Western Christendom.

John VI Cantacuzenue (*c.* 1292–1383), Byzantine emperor (*r.* 1347–55) and historian. After a stormy rule as rival emperor to the legitimate monarch John V Palaeologus, Cantacuzenue retired to a monastery and wrote a four-volume history of the years 1320–56.

John (1167?–1216), king of England, youngest son of Henry II. In Richard I's absence, he had himself declared heir (1191) and succeeded Richard in 1199. His probable murder of his nephew Arthur (1203), territorial losses in France (1204–05), and aggressive acts against the church made him extremely unpopular. Excommunicated in 1212, he was forced to submit and enlist the pope's support against his enemies (1213). At Runnymede (1215) he was compelled to accede to his barons' demands in the Magna Carta. Thereupon John attacked his opponents. Civil war ensued, during which John died, possibly poisoned. *See also* Magna Carta. △1076.

John I (1316), king of France, posthumous son of Louis X. He lived only five days. His uncle Philip V usurped the throne at the expense of John's sister.

John II, called the Good (1319–64), king of France (1350–64). He succeeded his father Philip VI. He appointed dishonest, unpopular advisers. He was forced to debase the coinage and impose harsh taxes in order to pursue the Hundred Years War. In 1356 he was captured by the British at the Battle of Poitiers. While he was in captivity in England his son (later Charles V) put down the Jacquerie rebellion. With the signing of the Treaty of Brétigny (1360), John was released in exchange for a huge ransom and other hostages. When one of the hostages escaped, John returned to England, where he died. △1096.

John I (1487–1540), or **John Zápolya,** governor of Transylvania (1511–26) and king of Hungary (1526–40). He was elected king by the Hungarian nobles as a rival to the Hapsburg claimant, Holy Roman Emperor Ferdinand I. The ensuing civil war, in which Turkey favored John, ended when John agreed that Ferdinand would succeed him. Instead, John I was succeeded by his infant son, John II.

John II (1540–71), or **John Sigismund Zápolya,** king of Hungary (1540–71). Holy Roman Emperors Ferdinand I and Maximilian II opposed his claim, which was supported by the Turks.

John Albert, or **John I** (1459–1501), king of Poland (1492–1501), son of Casimir IV. During his reign the nobility and the gentry acquired extensive privileges at the expense of the peasants and burghers, according to the terms of the 1496 Statute of Piotrkow (the Polish Magna Carta). John Albert unsuccessfully invaded Moldavia, which occasioned a counterattack by the Turks.

John II Casimir (1609–72), king of Poland (1648–68), son of Sigismund III. A Jesuit and cardinal, John was released by the pope from his vows upon accepting the throne. Succeeding his brother Ladislas IV, he was faced with an invasion by the Cossacks and Tatars in 1649. Wars with Russia and Sweden occupied him from 1654–67, during which time the Swedes occupied much of Poland and John at one time was forced to flee to Silesia. After abdicating in 1668, he returned to France and was known as the abbé de Saint-Germaine.

John III Sobieski (1624–96), king of Poland (1674–96), commander of the Polish army (1665). Plotted against Poland (1669–72). He allied himself with Charles of Lorraine and successfully relieved the Turks' siege of Vienna in 1683. By decisively defeating the Turkish armies, three times the size of his own, he saved Europe from Muslim conquest and was acclaimed the hero of Christendom. He was a patron of the arts and letters but the remaining years of his rule were marked by a decline in his prestige as a result of the country's political stagnation. His death marked the virtual end of Polish independence; thereafter, foreigners occupied the Polish throne for 70 years.

John I or **John the Great** (1357–1433), king of Portugal (1385–1433). He was the illegitimate son of Peter I and grand master of the powerful Knights of Aviz. After the death of his half brother Ferdinand I, he resisted the plan for a regency for Ferdinand's daughter, Beatrice, and her husband, the king of Castile. After an ill-fated invasion from Castile, John was elected king in 1385 and ushered in one of the great periods of Portuguese history. He was succeeded by his son Duarte. Another son was Henry the Navigator.

John II (1455–95), king of Portugal (1481–95). He was the son and successor of Alfonso V. He was a great patron of navigators and explorers (although he turned down Christopher Columbus), and Portugal's great empire had its beginnings in his reign. He was succeeded by a cousin, Manuel I, who was also his brother-in-law.

John III (1502–57), king of Portugal (1521–57), son and successor of Manuel I. The Portuguese empire reached its height during his reign but had already begun to decline by its end. Brazil was colonized during his reign. He introduced the Inquisition into the country in 1536 and generally favored clerical, particularly Jesuit, interests. He was succeeded by his grandson, Sebastian.

John IV (1605–56), king of Portugal (1640–56). As duke of Braganza he freed Portugal from the Spanish rule of Philip IV. He became king in 1640, thereby founding the Braganza dynasty, and increased the power of Portugal during his reign. He was succeeded by his son, Alfonso VI; his daughter, Catherine of Braganza, married Charles I of England.

John V (1689–1750), king of Portugal (1706–50). The son of Peter II, he came to the throne during the War of the Spanish Succession and kept Portugal's part in that conflict small. He generally allied himself with England. Rich from gold from Brazil, he beautified Lisbon and kept a luxurious court. He favored clerical interests and reduced the power of the Cortes. He was succeeded by his son Joseph.

John VI (1769–1826), king of Portugal (1816–26). The son of Maria I and Peter III, he took over when his mother became insane in 1792 and was named regent in 1799. During the upheavals of the Napoleonic Wars, he was forced to flee (1807) to Brazil. He was named king at his mother's death in 1816 and returned to Portugal in 1821. Attempting to rule constitutionally, he put down a revolt led by his wife, Queen Carlotta, and his son, Dom Miguel. His son, Dom Pedro I, left behind in Brazil as regent, declared Brazil independent in 1822 and became its first emperor. At his death, John VI was briefly succeeded by Dom Pedro (as Peter IV) and then by his granddaughter, Maria II.

John, called **the Fearless** (1371–1419), duke of Burgundy (1404–19). He fought the Turks at Nikopol (1396) and was imprisoned for a year. In 1408 he put down an insurrection in Liège. He fought his cousin Louis, duc d'Orléans, for control of the mad French king Charles VI. In 1407 he had Louis assassinated and was forced to flee Paris. He returned later in the year and gained control of the government. Open civil war broke out in 1411 between the Burgundians and the Armagnacs, supporters of Charles, the young duc d'Orléans. John was forced to flee Paris again in 1413. In the midst of the Hundred Years War he returned to Paris, seized the king, and massacred the Armagnacs. He was assassinated in 1419.

John, one of the Twelve Disciples of Jesus. The brother of the disciple James the Greater, together they were called Boanerges ("Sons of Thunder") by Jesus for their militant devotion. John is the author of the fourth Gospel, three epistles, and the Revelation. He witnessed the Transfiguration and accompanied Jesus to Gethsemane. Jesus left the care of his mother to John. He is reputed to have once visited Rome and miraculously escaped martyrdom and to have died at an old age at Ephesus. △1026.

John, Augustus (Edwin) (1878–1961), British portrait and landscape painter and etcher. His portraits depict mainly gypsies, beggars, and tramps. His works include "Lyric Phantasy" (1911) and "Galway" (1916). Also noted for portraits of famous people, including "George Bernard Shaw" (1914).

John, First, Second, and Third Epistles, part of the New Testament, the first letter was authored by the Apostle John. The second and third are often attributed to him but there is evidence they were written by another John. These epistles tell of faith through Jesus Christ, warn against false teachers, and call for unity.

John, Gospel of, one of the New Testament's four gospels, it was written by the Apostle John and supplements the first three gospels that were devoted to Jesus' life in Galilee. It differs noticeably from the other gospels, because it uses no parables, stresses the kingly nature of Christ, and puts a unique emphasis on the Holy Spirit.

John Birch Society, conservative anticommunist organization. It was founded in 1958 in Belmont, Mass., with the aim "less government, more responsibility, and a better world." It is opposed to the United Nations, North Atlantic Treaty Organization, foreign aid, and cultural or other exchanges with the Soviet Union. Members: about 90,000.

John Dory, also **Dory,** marine food fish found along E Atlantic coast of Europe. Its disk-shaped body is yellow to olive. Length: to 27.6in (70cm); weight: to 44lb (20kg). Family Zeidae; species include *Zeus faber.* △392.

John Henry, hero of American folk ballad celebrating the black railroad worker who outdrove a steam drill with his hammer while working on the Big Bend tunnel of the Chesapeake and Ohio Railroad. The story originated during the actual drilling in the West Virginia hills in 1873. John Henry's legend traveled through America's work camps gathering details until he became as famous as Paul Bunyan and Pecos Bill.

Johnnycarp. *See* Goldfish.

John of Austria, called **Don John** (1547–78), Spanish military leader and statesman. He was the illegitimate son of Holy Roman Emperor Charles V and half brother of Philip II of Spain. He suppressed the Morisco rebels in Granada (1569). In 1571 as admiral of the Holy League formed by Pope Pius V, Spain, and Venice he defeated the Turks in the naval Battle of Lepanto. He took Tunis from the Turks in 1573. Appointed governor general of the Netherlands (1576), he had to contend with William the Silent's rebellion.

John of Austria, the younger, called **Don John** (1629–79), Spanish general and statesman. The illegitimate son of Philip IV, he suppressed Masaniello's revolt in Naples (1647) and the rebels in Catalonia (1651–52). He was viceroy of Sicily (1648–51). During the war between Spain and France, he was sent to the Netherlands as governor general (1656). After defeat by the French and English under Turenne in the Battle of the Dunes (1658), he was recalled to Spain. He failed (1661–64) to reconquer Portugal. With other nobles, he gained control of the government of the young king Charles II (1677) and exercised power until his death in 1679.

John of Brienne (*c.*1148–1237), king of Jerusalem (1210–25), emperor of Constantinople (1228–37). A minor French noble, he married Mary of Montferrat, queen of Jerusalem (1210). He became regent for their daughter Yolande in 1212. He captured Damietta in Egypt (1219) during the Fifth Crusade. In 1225 he married his daughter to Holy Roman Emperor Frederick II, who then claimed the title king of Jerusalem. In 1228 John was elected regent of Constantinople, then ruled as coemperor with Baldwin II after 1231. In 1236 he successfully defended Constantinople against Bulgaria and Nicaea.

John of Gaunt, Duke of Lancaster (1340–99), fourth son of Edward III and brother of Edward, the Black Prince. English nobleman and statesman, he was a dominant administrator and peace-maker between factions during Edward III's senility and the minority of his nephew Richard II. His first marriage made him duke of Lancaster (his oldest son, Henry Bolingbroke, became Henry IV); his second gave him claims to Castile, which he failed to make good; his third marriage legitimatized four children, henceforth known as the Beauforts.

John of Leiden (1509–36), Dutch religious leader. He headed the Anabaptists, who believed in polygamy and communal property. In 1535 his city of Münster was taken by the Roman Catholic bishop, and John was tortured to death.

John of Salisbury (*c.*1115–80), English churchman. He studied theology in France (1136) but returned to England (1150) to become secretary to the archbishop of Canterbury. The *Policraticus* (1159) and the *Metalogicus* (1159) reveal the urbanity and humanism of the author, who supported Thomas à Becket in his controversies with King Henry II. After Becket's murder, John became bishop of Chartres (1176).

John O'Groats, point in Scotland, at NE tip of mainland, on Pentland Firth. Dutchman John de Groot settled here in 16th century; it is supposedly the northernmost point of Scotland; however, that distinction actually belongs to Dunnet Head, several miles away. Expression from "Land's End to John O'Groats" is used to denote longest land distance in Britain, 876mi (1,410km).

Johns, Jasper (1930–), US painter, b. Augusta, Ga. His early work was in the abstract expressionist style, which he abandoned to begin painting canvases covered with images (flags, targets, and numbers). Examples of works of this period are "Three Flags" (1858) and "Target with Four Faces" (1955). After 1961 he began to attach real objects to the canvas. Common objects found in the street or studio appeared against painted fields ("False Start," 1959). He also executed numerous lithographs and drawings that show the influence of collage and imprint technique. △1372.

Johnson, Andrew (1808–75), 17th president of the United States (1865–69), b. Raleigh, N.C. In 1827 he married Eliza McCardle; they had five children. Johnson came from an extremely poor family who apprenticed him as a young boy to a tailor. He had no formal education; his wife taught him to write.

Johnson was an early supporter of Andrew Jackson and between 1828 and 1843 he served in a variety of local and state offices. In 1843 he entered the US House of Representatives; he served there until 1853, when he became governor of Tennessee. In 1857 he went to the US Senate. By that time, Johnson had won a wide reputation as a Jacksonian Democrat. He was a strong advocate of homestead laws, and his views on slavery, while basically southern, were mild. He was a Unionist and refused to leave the Senate when Tennessee seceded from the Union. He became a leader of the War Democrats, and in 1862 President Lincoln named him military governor of Tennessee. Johnson's status as a southerner and a War Democrat caused him to be chosen—on a National Union ticket—as Lincoln's running mate in the 1864 election. Johnson assumed the presidency when Lincoln was assassinated only a month after inauguration.

Johnson assumed office immediately after the end of the Civil War. He favored a moderate Reconstruction policy toward the South; the Radical Republicans,

Johannesburg, South Africa

Pope John XXIII

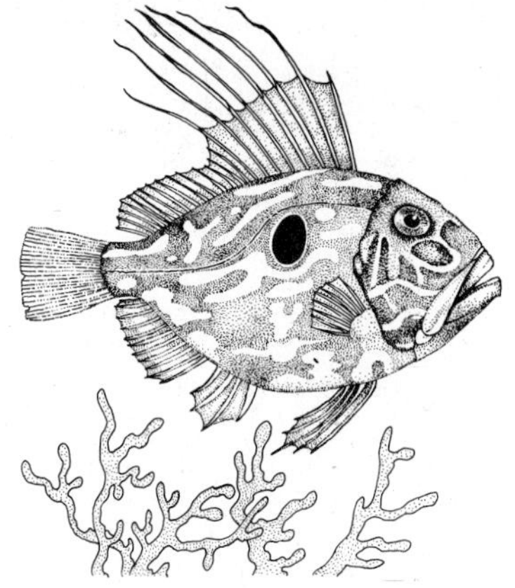

John Dory

Andrew Johnson

who controlled Congress, advocated a harsher policy. The result was unprecedented dissension between the executive and legislative branches of government. Congress passed the constitutionally questionable Tenure of Office Act, the president deliberately defied it, and the House of Representatives impeached him—Johnson was the first president to be impeached. The Senate, by a small margin, refused to remove him from office. Johnson's political effectiveness was at an end, however, and he did not run for reelection 1868. He went to the Senate again in 1875 but died shortly after taking office.

Career: alderman, Greeneville, Tenn., 1828–30; mayor, Greenville 1830–33; state representative 1835–37, 1839–41; Tennessee state senator, 1841–43; US House of Representatives, 1843–53; governor of Tennessee, 1853–57; US Senate, 1857–62; military governor of Tennessee, 1863–64; vice president, 1865; president, 1865–69; US Senate, 1875. *See also* Impeachment; Reconstruction; Tenure of Office Act.

Johnson, James Weldon (1871–1938), US author and black leader, b. Jacksonville, Fla. He wrote successful songs and light operas with his brother, John Rosamond Johnson (1873–1954), but is best known for his poetry—especially *God's Trombones* (1927), seven sermons in verse—and the novel *The Autobiography of an Ex-Coloured Man* (1912). He served as US consul in Venezuela and Nicaragua and helped found the NAACP.

Johnson, John Arthur ("Jack") (1878–1946), US boxer, b. Galveston. Johnson won the world's heavyweight title from Tommy Burns (1908) in Sydney, Australia, and lost it to Jess Willard (1915) in Havana, Cuba. The controversy caused by his marriage to a white woman and a charge of violating the Mann Act caused him to leave the United States in 1912; he returned in 1920 and served a one-year prison term. He was the first black heavyweight champion and was elected to the Hall of Fame in 1954.

Johnson, Lyndon Baines (1908–73), 36th president of the United States (1963–69), b. Stonewall, Tex., graduate South West Texas Teachers College, 1930. In 1934 he married Claudia Alta (Lady Bird) Taylor; they had two daughters. In 1935, Johnson became state director for the National Youth Administration, a New Deal agency. He was elected to the US House of Representatives in 1937 as a New Deal Democrat. He served there (except for a brief period in the Navy in World War II) until elected to the Senate in 1948.

Johnson rose quickly in the Senate hierarchy, and in 1954 he became majority leader. He proved to be one of the most effective leaders in Senate history. He suffered a heart attack in 1955 but recovered and was back to work within a year.

After losing the presidential nomination to John F. Kennedy in 1960, Johnson became Kennedy's running mate. Kennedy gave Johnson extensive duties as vice president; in particular, Johnson was placed in charge of the space program. After Kennedy was assassinated on Nov. 22, 1963, Johnson was sworn in as president within minutes.

Johnson immediately embarked upon the most ambitious legislative program since the New Deal. Within the next few years, Congress passed into law a medical program for the elderly (Medicare); a series of strong civil rights acts; various antipoverty and urban renewal projects; and federal aid to education, science, medicine, and the arts. Johnson was elected by a landslide in 1964 and continued his domestic programs, which he named the Great Society.

Johnson's successful domestic record was not matched in foreign affairs. He greatly expanded the Vietnam War after securing the approval of the Senate in the Gulf of Tonkin Resolution. The war became costlier, both in manpower and in money; it grew increasingly unpopular, and a strong antiwar faction arose. Senators Eugene McCarthy and Robert F. Kennedy entered primary contests to oppose Johnson for the 1968 nomination. In March 1968, however, Johnson announced that he would retire. At the same time he announced a partial halt to the bombing in Vietnam, with the view toward opening peace talks. *See also* Vietnam War.

Career: US House of Representatives, 1937–48; US Senate, 1949–61; vice president, 1961–63; president, 1963–69. △1358.

Johnson, Philip Cortelyou (1906–), US architect, b. Cleveland, Ohio. He worked basically in Mies van der Rohe's style, but departed from its austerity. He is noted for his glass-walled New Canaan house (1949), the New York State Theater (1962–64), and the Amon Carter Museum in Fort Worth.

Johnson, Richard Mentor (1780–1850), U.S. political leader, b. Beargrass, Ky. A lawyer, he served as a Democrat in the US House of Representatives from 1807, interrupting his legislative career for service in the War of 1812, and in the Senate (1819–29). He then returned to the House, supporting Andrew Jackson. He was elected vice president under Pres. Martin Van Buren by the Senate because the general election failed to produce a majority, and served from 1837–41.

Johnson, Samuel (1709–84), English lexicographer, poet, and critic. He settled in London in 1735 and began writing pieces for *Gentleman's Magazine*. A prolific writer, Johnson's works include the satire *The Vanity of Human Wishes* (1749), *Rasselas* (1759), the 10-volume *Lives of the Poets* (1779–81), the periodical *The Rambler* (1750–52), the *Dictionary of the English Language* (1755), which established his reputation, and the essays comprising *The Idler* (1758–60). He was a founder (1764) of The Club, later known as The Literary Club, which included David Garrick, James Boswell, Edmund Burke, and Oliver Goldsmith. Boswell wrote a noted biography of Johnson. △1188.

Johnson, Walter Perry (1887–1946), US baseball player. One of the greatest pitchers of all time, he won 416 games, 110 of them shutouts, and struck out 3,508 batters in his career with the Washington Senators (1907–27). He was elected to the Baseball Hall of Fame in 1936.

Johnson, (Sir) William (1715–74), Irish-born American colonial administrator. Johnson emigrated to the colonies, settling in the Mohawk Valley about 1738. He served as superintendent of Indian affairs (1755–74). He was instrumental in gaining the support of the Iroquois confederacy in the wars with the French, whom he defeated in the Battle of Lake George (1755). He was created a baronet that year.

Johnson City, city in NE Tennessee, 106mi (171km) N of Knoxville; site of East Tennessee State University (1909). Industries: hardwood floors, iron foundries, farming, lumber, textiles, furniture, tobacco, electrical components, tourism. Settled 1777; inc. 1869. Pop. (1970) 33,770.

John the Baptist, in the New Testament, Nazarite prophet and son of Zacharias and Elisabeth. He was born in Judah six months before the birth of Jesus. He spent 30 years in the desert preparing for his priestly duties and later preaching the word of God. He baptized Jesus at Betharba. He was executed by Herod Antipas, whose wife Herodias demanded John's head after his disapproval of her marriage. △1026.

Johnston, Joseph (1807–91), Confederate Civil War general, b. Cherry Grove, Va. He commanded the Confederate troops at the First Battle of Bull Run and in the Peninsular Campaign. When he was wounded at Fair Oaks, Va. (June 1862), Robert E. Lee took command of the Confederate army.

Johnstown, city in SW Pennsylvania, on Conemaugh River 60mi (97km) E of Pittsburgh; river was channeled (1943) for flood prevention. Industries: mining equipment, stoves, fertilizers, iron, steel, coal. Settled 1770; inc. as village 1800, as borough 1831, as city 1889. Pop. (1970) 42,476.

Joint Chiefs of Staff (JCS), the principal military advisors to the president, the National Security Council, and the secretary of defense. Its responsibilities include planning the strategic direction of the armed forces. The JCS consists of a chairman and the chiefs of staff of the Army, Air Force, and Navy. The commandant of the Marine Corps participates equally when matters under discussion involve the Marine Corps.

Joint Committee, a Congressional committee composed of members from both the House of Representatives and the Senate. Upon referral of a bill, the committee decides favorably or unfavorably, recommends amendments, or allows proposed legislation to die in committee without action. Joint committees may be either permanent or temporary, and the composition is controlled by the political party in power.

Joints, in Anatomy. △682.

Joints and Joining, Wood. △1612.

Joinville, Jean de (1224–1317), French chronicler. A hereditary royal steward, he was a friend of King Louis IX, whom he accompanied on his first Crusade (1248–52) and in captivity. He wrote *Histoire de Saint Louis,* a vivid, detailed narrative of the first Crusade and of the pious Louis IX. The work was begun *c.* 1280 and was completed in 1309.

Joist, a support used in ceilings and floors, usually small timbers or metal beams placed parallel to each other from wall to wall. △1610.

Joliet, city in NE Illinois, on Des Plaines River 30mi (48km) SW of Chicago; seat of Will co; named for Louis Joliet, French explorer who first visited area with Jacques Marquette in 1673; site of St Francis College (1874), Joliet Junior College (1902), Pilcher Park Arboretum, and Bird Haven (sanctuary for hundreds of bird species). Industries: chemicals, wire, earth-moving equipment, wallpaper. Settled 1831; inc. as city 1852. Pop. (1970) 78,887.

Joliot-Curie, Irène (1897–1956) **and Frédéric** (1900–58), French physicists. Irène, the daughter of Pierre and Marie Curie, met Frédéric Joliot when they were both working as assistants to the Curies. She worked on the physical, and he the chemical aspects of radioactivity. Their discovery of artificial radioisotopes was rewarded by a Nobel Prize in 1935. Active in the resistance during World War II, they became Communists. Although Frédéric was responsible for France's first nuclear reactor he was removed from his official position for political reasons.

Jolliet, Louis (1646–1700), French-Canadian explorer who, with Jacques Marquette, was the first white man to travel the Mississippi River from its confluence with the Wisconsin River to the mouth of the Arkansas River. His expedition was commissioned in 1672 by the governor of New France, who hoped to prove that the Mississippi emptied into the Pacific Ocean.

Jolson, Al (1888–1950), US comedian and singer, b. Asa Yoelson in Russia, raised in Washington, D.C. Sentimentally singing "Swanee" and "Mammy" in blackface, often on his knees, this vaudeville and Broadway stage performer later produced and starred in *The Jazz Singer* (1927), the first talking picture, which was based on his life. Other successful films and stage musicals followed.

Jonah, fifth of the 12 minor prophets and subject of the Book of Jonah in the Old Testament. After the fall of Jerusalem, he was sent to Nineveh as a prophet but, feeling it hostile, attempted an escape during which he was swallowed by a fish. Miraculously saved he went to Nineveh and was instrumental in saving it from God's threatened judgment. △840.

Jonathan, several biblical figures, including Saul's son and David's loyal friend who was killed in the battle of Mt Gilboa. Also, a priest descended from Gershom and Moses; the son of the priest Abiathar and an uncle and a brother of David.

Jonathan, Joseph Leabua (1914–), prime minister of Lesotho (1965–). He founded the Basutoland National party and was a leader in the movement for independence from South Africa. When elections in 1970 were unfavorable to him, he seized power, arrested opponents, and exiled the king.

Jones, Casey (1864–1900), US railroad engineer, b. John Luther Jones in Cayce, Ky. He became an engineer on the Illinois Central Railroad (1890). In 1900 his train the "Cannonball Express" struck the rear of two freight trains at Vaughan, Miss. Rather than jump to safety, he stayed on the train to hold the brake in place. He was killed but immortalized in the "Ballad of Casey Jones."

Jones, (Alfred) Ernest (1879–1958), British psychiatrist. He introduced psychoanalysis into Britain (1910) and founded the London Clinic for Psychoanalysis (1925). He helped to bring Sigmund Freud to safety in England after the Nazi invasion of Austria. His best known writing is *The Life and Work of Sigmund Freud* in three volumes (1953–57).

Jones, Inigo (1573–1652), English architect. He designed elaborate machinery and settings for court masques and in 1615 became the king's surveyor of the works. As a result of his architectural studies in Italy he imported the style of Palladio to England. He designed the Palladian Queen's House, Greenwich, and the Royal Banqueting Hall in Whitehall, London. The latter, with its solidity and perfect proportions, is generally considered his masterpiece. He continued designing through the Civil War period and influenced the Palladian revival of the 18th century. △1148, 1192.

Jones, James (1921–), US author, b. Robinson, Ill. His best known novels, *From Here to Eternity* (1951) and *The Thin Red Line* (1962), deal with army life. Other works include *Go to the Widow Maker* (1967).

Jones, John Paul (1747–92), American Revolution

ary War naval officer, b. John Paul in Scotland. He joined the Continental navy in 1775, and proved successful at capturing supplies and enemy vessels. With his flagship *Bonhomme Richard* he engaged the British ship *Serapis* in an epic battle off the coast of England (1779). He boarded and captured the *Serapis* while his ship burned and then sank. He was awarded a Congressional gold medal (1787). Jones served in the Russian navy (1788–89). △1218.

Jones, Robert Tyre, Jr. ("Bobby") (1902–71), US golfer, b. Atlanta. Although never turning pro, he won four US Opens (1923, 1926, 1929, 1930), three British Opens (1926, 1927, 1930), and crowned his reputation in 1930 by winning golf's amateur "grand slam," which included the US and British opens and the US and British amateurs. He also helped to conceive and design (1934) the Augusta National Golf Course, home of the Masters Tournament.

Jones Act (1916), legislation reinforcing the US commitment to Philippine independence. The United States promised to withdraw from the island when a stable government was formed. The act also provided for a governor to be appointed by the US president, granted the governor veto power (with presidential approval) and appointive authority (with confirmation by the Philippine Senate). The Senate was to be elected by male suffrage. Free trade between the United States and the Philippines was also included.

Jonesboro, town in NE Arkansas, 67mi (108km) NNW of Memphis, Tenn.; seat of Craighead co; trading center. Industries: cotton gins, lumber. Founded 1859; inc. 1883; pop. (1970) 27,050.

Jones v. Mayer (1968), U.S. Supreme Court civil rights decision. The court upheld the constitutionality of the Anti-Discrimination Act, saying that the 13th Amendment gave Congress the power to bar all racial discrimination, private as well as public.

Jongleur, in the Middle Ages, a strolling entertainer; juggler, acrobat, singer, and musician of popular material, unlike the troubador, whose style was courtly. Jongleurs were largely responsible for the transmission and distribution of folklore throughout Europe. △1100.

Jönköping, city in Sweden, on S end of Lake Vättern; border treaty was signed here 1809 between Sweden and Denmark. Industries: airplanes, machinery, paper, matches. Chartered 1284. Pop. 55,372.

Jonson, Ben (1572–1637), English dramatist, lyric poet, and actor. A friend of Shakespeare, he was popular and influential in Elizabethan and Stuart drama. His comedies include *Everyman in His Humour* (1598), *Everyman Out of His Humour* (1599), *Volpone* (1607), *Epicoene* (1609), *The Alchemist* (1610), and *Bartholomew Fair* (1614). He also wrote the neoclassic tragedies *Sejanus* and *Catiline* and several court masques. His poems include the famous "Drink to me only with thine eyes." △1148.

Joplin, Scott (1868–1917), US composer b. Texarkana, Tex. He wrote ragtime piano music, such as "Maple Leaf Rag" (1899) and "The Entertainer" (1902), and one opera, *Treemonisha* (1911). His music underwent a revival of popularity in the 1970s. △1366.

Joplin, city in SW Missouri, 72mi (116km) W of Springfield; site of Missouri Southern College (1937), Ozark Bible College (1942), and a mineral museum; important lead and zinc area. Industries: alcohol, leather goods, fertilizers, missiles. Founded 1839; inc. 1874. Pop. (1970) 39,256.

Jordaens, Jacob (1593–1678), Flemish painter. He is known for his religious, mythological, and realistic works and for his portraits. He was considered to be Flanders' main painter after the death of Rubens. His works include "The Ferry at Antwerp" and "The King Drinks!"

Jordan (Al-Urdunn), independent nation in the Middle East. A constitutional monarchy, its economy was damaged by Middle East wars, but has recovered with financial aid from foreign countries.

Land and economy. An arid rocky desert with few natural resources, Jordan is bordered by Israel (W), Saudi Arabia (S), Syria (N), and Iraq (E). It is landlocked except for a 16-mi (26-km) strip along the Gulf of Aqaba that provides access to the Red Sea. A N-S geological depression forming the Jordan River, Lake Tiberias, and the Dead Sea is its outstanding topographical feature and divides Jordan into the East Bank and the West Bank. The rainy season extends from November to March; the rest of the year is dry. US aid improved the economy, which had been hindered by low agricultural production, lack of tourists, and a large refugee population, after the loss of the West Bank in the 1967 war with Israel. Irrigation of the Jordan Valley added vegetables, wheat, olives, and barley to crops grown by small landowners. Phosphate is its chief export (30%), along with tobacco, distilling, flour milling, soap, and textiles.

People. Dating back to nomadic tribes in the Bronze Age, Jordan's population today is of Arab stock with small groups of Circassians, Chechens, Turkomans, Armenians, and Druzes. 50% are rural dwellers, 44% urban, and 6% nomads. One third of its people live on the West Bank (occupied by Israel). On the East Bank are about 750,000 Palestinian Arabs and 500,000 refugees. Sunni Islam is the principal religion (97%) with the remainder Christian. Literacy is 35%–40%.

Government. Jordan is a constitutional monarchy with power vested in the king, who signs all laws and holds veto power over both houses of the National Assembly.

History. A part of the Ottoman Empire from the 16th century to WWI, the present countries of Israel and Jordan were given to Great Britain as the mandate for Palestine and Transjordan. In 1922, Britain divided the mandate into the Emirate of Transjordan, with the Hashemite Prince Abdullah as ruler; it continued the Palestine mandate. In 1946 the Transjordan mandate came to an end, and the area became the independent Hashemite Kingdom of Transjordan. Jordan's W boundary was changed in a 1949 agreement. Jordan, fighting with the Arab states in the 1967 Six-Day War with Israel, lost W lands as far as the Jordan River and old Jerusalem.

PROFILE

Official name: Hashemite Kingdom of Jordan
Area: 37,738sq mi (97,741sq km)
Population: 2,700,000
Density: 72per sq mi (28per sq km)
Chief cities: Amman (capital); Zarqa
Government: Constitutional monarchy
Religion: Islam
Language: Arabic
Monetary unit: Dinar
Gross national product: $1,000,000,000
Per capita income: $286
Industries: tobacco products, flour milling, distilling, building materials, olive oil, textiles, mother of pearl, plastic, cement, steel, leather goods
Agriculture: vegetables, wheat, barley, olives, fruits
Minerals: potash, phosphate
Trading partners: United Kingdom, Federal Republic of Germany, Syria, Kuwait, Lebanon, Japan, Yugoslovia

Jordan (Nahr Al-Urdunn, or **HaYarden),** river in the Middle East; rises in the Anti-Lebanon Mts at the confluence of the Hisban, Dan, and Banias rivers; flows S through Jordan, Israel, and the Sea of Galilee and empties into the Dead Sea. Frequently mentioned in the Bible, it is the traditional site of Christ's baptism. Length: 200mi (322km).

Joseph I (1678–1711), king of Hungary (1687–1711) and Germany (1690–1711) and Holy Roman emperor (1705–11). He was involved through most of his reign with the War of the Spanish Succession, allied with England and Holland against France, attempting to gain the throne of Spain for his brother, the future Emperor Charles VI.

Joseph II (1741–90), king of Germany (1764–90) and Holy Roman emperor (1765–90). He was dominated by his mother and co-ruler Maria Theresa until her death (1780), but then initiated radical social reforms in place of her policy of slow progress. His beliefs were formed by reading Voltaire and the French *encyclopédistes*, but his instrument was an all-powerful state for which he was the sole spokesman. His measures to allow religious toleration, end the nobility's stranglehold on local government, and to promote unity by compulsory use of the German language were not popular. The clergy and nobles opposed them, and even the peasants rebelled in many of his states. The schemes typical of Joseph's "enlightened despotism" were largely reversed by his brother Leopold II, who succeeded him. △1180.

Joseph, in Genesis, eldest son of Jacob and Rachel. After receiving a coat of many colors from Jacob, he was sold into slavery by his jealous brothers. In Egypt, he lived with Potiphar. During the great famine, his stores from the seven good years fed all of Egypt and his father and brothers. In the New Testament, Joseph is the name of several men including the husband of Mary, mother of Jesus. He was of the house of David, and settled as a carpenter in Nazareth. To escape Herod, he fled with his family to safety in Egypt. He died before Jesus was crucified.

Lyndon B. Johnson

Joseph Johnston

John Paul Jones

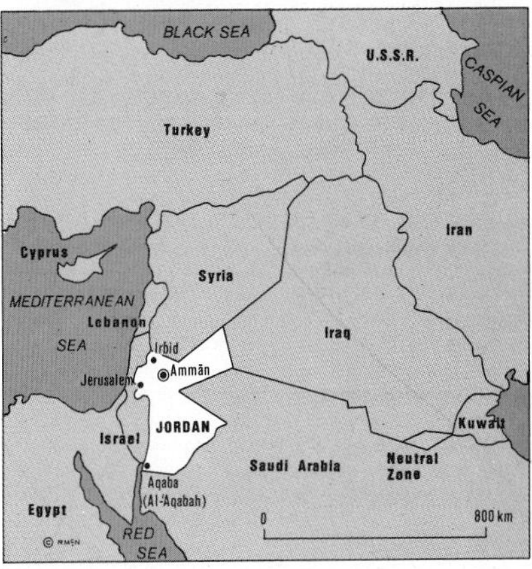
BLACK SEA
U.S.S.R.
CASPIAN SEA
Turkey
Iran
Cyprus
Syria
MEDITERRANEAN SEA
Lebanon
Irbid
Iraq
Jerusalem
Ammān
Israel
JORDAN
Kuwait
Saudi Arabia
Neutral Zone
Aqaba (Al-Aqabah)
Egypt
RED SEA
0
800 km

Jordan

Joseph, Chief (1840?–1904), American Indian, b. Oregon. He was chief of the Nez Percé tribe of the Wallowa Valley, succeeding his father (1873). He is best known for his brilliant tactics during his attempt (1877) to lead 800 of his people through Idaho, Washington, and Montana to Canada while fighting off the US Army. He was finally forced to surrender to Colonel Miles, 40mi (64km) from the Canadian border after a five-day battle.

Joseph, Father (1577–1638), French religious and political figure, b. François Le Clerc du Tremblay. His zeal for religious reform brought him to the attention of Cardinal Richelieu, whom he served as an unofficial foreign minister. Unpopular and known as Richelieu's "gray eminence," he wholeheartedly supported the Thirty Years War.

Josephine (1763–1814), consort of Napoleon I and empress of the French. She was born Marie Joséphine Tascher de la Pagerie, and her first marriage, to Vicomte Alexandre de Beauharnais, ended with his death (1794) in the Reign of Terror. She married Napoleon (1796) as the young officer rose to spectacular military fame. He forgave her indiscretions and infidelity, and she was coronated with Napoleon in 1804. Her inability to bear him a son caused him to seek and obtain annulment of their marriage (1809). He remained, however, generous and devoted to her.

Joseph of Arimathea, in the New Testament, a prosperous Israelite and member of the Sanhedrim who was converted to Christianity by Jesus. He begged for and received Jesus' body from Pilate for burial.

Josephus, Flavius (*c.* 37–*c.* 100), Jewish leader and historian, b. Joseph ben Matthias in Jerusalem. A member of the Pharisees, who sought cooperation with the Romans, he was sent to Rome in 64 to obtain the release of Jewish prisoners. Returning to Jerusalem, he was reluctantly drawn into the revolt against Rome (66–70). Appointed military governor of Galilee, he defended the city as best he could, then fled (67) to a cave with 40 diehards. All but Josephus and one other died rather than surrender. Josephus ingratiated himself to the Roman commander, Vespasian. When Vespasian became emperor in 69, Josephus took his family name, Flavius, as his own. In 70 Josephus went to Rome where he obtained citizenship and remained for the rest of his life. Between 75–79 he wrote his *History of the Jewish War,* the only detailed account of the revolt. In *The Antiquities of the Jews* he traced their history from the Creation up to the outbreak of the revolt. His *Against Apion* is a defense of Judaism.

Joshua, biblical book named for Joshua, the son of Nun, who became leader of the Israelites after Moses' death. The book, divided into three sections, deals with the conquest of Canaan, its apportionment, and the farewell and death of Joshua, emphasizing that divine action was responsible for Israel's conquest of Canaan.

Joshua Tree, grotesque desert tree found in the United States from California to Utah. It has dagger-shaped, spine-tipped leaves and greenish-white flowers in long clusters. Height: to 40ft (12m). Family Agavaceae; species *Yucca brevifolia.*

Josiah, in the Bible, son and successor of Amon as king of Judah, he ascended to the throne at the age of eight after his father was murdered. During his reign a copy of the Deuteronomic Code was discovered and, guided by its precepts, he vowed to remove all forms of idolatry.

Joule, James Prescott (1818–89), English physicist. He established a reliable value for the mechanical equivalent of heat, laying the foundation for the law of conservation of energy. Joule's law (1840) states how to measure the rate of heat production in a part of an electric circuit. The joule, a unit of work, is named in his honor. △1492.

Joule, the unit of energy in the metric meter-kilogram-second (mks) system of units. One joule is the work done by a force of one newton acting through a distance of one meter. One joule is about ¾ of a foot-pound. *See also* Erg. △1508.

Joule-Thomson Effect. △1502.

Jourdan, Jean Baptiste (1762–1833), French general under Napoleon. He served chiefly in the north until 1799 and then saw service in Italy, becoming general in chief of the army there in 1802. Napoleon named him a marshal in 1804. Jourdan remained in the army after the Bourbon restoration and was given a title by Louis XVIII in 1816.

Journalism. △1422, 1776.

Journal of the Plague Year, A (1721), novel by Daniel Defoe, supposedly the narrative of a Londoner who observed the Great Plague of 1664–65. There are vivid descriptions of the symptoms of the plague, its effects, and the measures taken to contain it.

Joust, in the Middle Ages in Western Europe, one of the main attractions at a tournament of knights. In the 11th century, the joust was single combat on horseback with lance and sword, ending in the death or injury of one of the knights. The church continually condemned jousts, and by the 15th century they were reduced simply to the unhorsing of the heavily armed adversary.

Joyce, James (1882–1941), Irish novelist. He was educated by Jesuits but renounced Catholicism and left Ireland in 1904 to live and work in Europe. Joyce revolutionized the form and structure of the novel. In his novels action and thought are abandoned because they can be located in time, which ceases to be a positive factor, and consciousness itself is presented. The stream-of-consciousness technique is increasingly apparent in Joyce's work, which includes *Dubliners* (1914), *A Portrait of the Artist as a Young Man* (1916), *Ulysses* (1922), and *Finnegans Wake* (1939), all set in Dublin. *See also* Stream-of-Consciousness Novel. △1376.

Joyce, William (1906–46), anti-British propagandist, b. Brooklyn, N.Y. He grew up in Britain, and before World War II he was a member of Sir Oswald Mosley's British Union of Fascists. In 1939, Joyce left England for Germany and throughout the war broadcast Nazi propaganda in English to Britain, which called him "Lord Haw-haw" because of his affected speech. He was captured in 1945, tried and found guilty of treason, and hanged.

J Particles. *See* Quark.

Juana la Beltraneja (1462–1530), Spanish princess, known as La Beltraneja. Her mother was Juana of Portugal, queen consort to Henry IV of Castile; her father was generally believed to be Beltrán de la Cueva, a courtier. The Cortes recognized Juana as Henry's heir, but he first recognized his half sister Isabella before switching later to Juana. When he died, Isabella seized the throne and civil war erupted. Despite help from the Portuguese, Juana lost to Isabella in 1476, and retired to a convent.

Juan Carlos I (1938–), king of Spain (1975–). The grandson of Alfonso XIII, he was designated as heir to the throne by Francisco Franco in 1969. He became king when Franco died in 1975.

Juan de Fuca Strait, strait between S Vancouver Island, SW Canada, and the N shore of W Washington; N arm of strait is called Haros Strait. Discovered 1592 by Spaniard Juan de Fuca. Length: approx. 100mi (161km); width: 10–20mi (16–32km).

Juan Fernández Islands, volcanic island group in S Pacific Ocean, approx. 400mi (644km) off the coast of Chile. The three main islands comprising the group (Más a Tierra, Más Afuera, and Santa Clara) are under jurisdiction of Chile. Alexander Selkirk, the model for Daniel Defoe's *Robinson Crusoe,* spent five years on Más a Tierra in the early 1700s. Area: 70sq mi (181sq km).

Juárez, Benito (1806–72), president of Mexico (1858–72). With the triumph of the liberal Juan Alvarez, Juárez was appointed minister of justice and wrote the law limiting church and military prerogatives that bore his name. Elected chief justice of the supreme court (1857) he automatically became chief of state in 1858 in accordance with the constitution of 1857. From 1858 until 1867, Juárez presided over a government in flight: in Veracruz hiding from the rival Comonfort administration; in the north during the period of Maximilian's empire. From 1867 until his death, Juárez governed from Mexico City.

Juárez. *See* Ciudad Juárez.

Juba I (85?–46 BC), king of Numidia, now roughly Algeria. In wars between Caesar and Pompey, he took Pompey's side, defeating forces of Caesar under Gaius Scribonius Curio in 49 BC. After the defeat of Pompey's forces at the Battle of Thapsus (46 BC), he committed suicide.

Juba, river in E Africa; rises in the mountains of S Ethiopia at the confluence of the Dava and Ganale rivers; flows S and empties into the Indian Ocean near Kismayu, Somali; used for irrigation. Length: 1,000mi (1,610km).

Judaea, ancient name for S end of Palestine when it was under Persian, Greek, and Roman rule, before it became kingdom of Judah; bounded by Samaria (N), Jordon and Dead Sea (E), Sinai Peninsula (S), Mediterranean Sea (W).

Judah, in the Bible, fourth son of Jacob and Leah and forefather of one of the most important tribes of ancient Israel. Also, the southern kingdom when, after Solomon's death, only the tribes of Judah and Benjamin followed the house of David. There were wars between the kings of Judah and Israel for 60 years. △982.

Judah Ben Samuel (*c.* 1150–1217), a teacher in the Ashkenaz movement in Judaism. He was a scholar who wrote on ethics and theology. Because he did not sign his works, it is difficult to identify his writings. He was a mystic, and legends attribute to him miraculous powers he used to save Jews from persecution.

Judaism, often defined as the religion and civilization of Jews, involves all aspects of life. Difficult to define, it is primarily an historical religion, which concentrates on the works of God throughout the past, present and future. It is a monotheistic religion stressing man's relationship with God. The foundations are the Old Testament and the Talmud which show religion as part of everyday living. They cover civil laws as well as religious ones. The religion and the community are interwoven. Through faith, good living and conduct, salvation may be attained. Modern Judaism is split into three large groups—Orthodox, Conservative, and Reform Judaism. They mainly differ in the practice of ritual observances and the use of Hebrew in services. Some beliefs are formulated differently in each group. Judaism as a religion today continues to encompass an awareness of a common historical development, a rich literature, and the sense of national identity. *See also* Talmud; Torah. △844, 982.

Judas Iscariot, in the New Testament, the son of Simon and one of the 12 apostles, always enumerated last. He betrayed Jesus to the Romans with a kiss, usual greeting of the disciples, for 30 pieces of silver. His name connotes treachery and evil.

Judas Maccabeus (died 161 BC), Jewish warrior who led a revolt against Syria, starting in 167 BC. When edicts of King Antiochus IV threatened to end Jewish religious practices, a revolt broke out, and Judas took command. Using guerrilla tactics, he defeated Syrian armies and later recaptured the Temple in Jerusalem. The festival of Hanukkah celebrates his retaking of the Temple. Judas was killed in battle, but his brothers continued the fight and made Judea independent.

Judas Tree, or redbud, small tree native to S Europe and W Asia. It has round leaves and purplish-rose flowers in clusters. Height: to 40ft (12m). Family Leguminosae; species *Cercis siliquastrum.*

Juddah. *See* Jidda.

Jude, Epistle of, a book of the New Testament of the Bible, a letter in one chapter. The letter exhorts all Christians to keep the faith and live righteously. The author calls himself the brother of James, probably the one mentioned in Mark 6:3. The letter may have been written about AD 70–80, but some authorities argue for another author and a date in the 2nd century.

Judge. △912.

Judgement of Paris (Rubens). △1162.

Judges, biblical book that originally contained the Book of Ruth. It is an account of events from Joshua to Samson and is considered a valuable early history of the Israelites in Palestine.

Judicature, Supreme Court of, system resulting from the reorganization of the Higher Courts of Great Britain by act of Parliament (1971). The Supreme Court of Judicature is made up of the Appeal Court, which hears civil and criminal appeals from High Court of Justice and the Crown Court; the High Court of Justice, having civil jurisdiction; and the Crown Court, which deals with higher levels of criminal work than are handled by magistrate courts and with important and difficult criminal and civil cases. The Appeal Court, in cases of major legal importance, can submit a case for final appeal to the judges of the House of Lords.

Judiciary Acts, a series of legislation that established the structure of the US judicial system. The first (1789) set up the Supreme Court, with a chief justice and 5 associates, 13 district courts, and 3 circuit courts and created the office of attorney general. The second act (1801), reducing the number of justices to 5, creating 16 circuit courts and adding marshals, clerks, and attorneys, was repealed in 1802. Later that year, a new act restored the number of Supreme Court justices to six and established six circuit courts.

Judith, book included in the Roman Catholic Bible but considered apocryphal by Protestants and Jews. It recounts the story of Judith, a Jewish widow, who delivered the city of Bethulia from the Assyrian siege. She advised the Assyrian general Holofernes to expect victory and then beheaded him as he slept.

Judo, a form of jujitsu and one of the most popular of the Japanese martial arts. It is a system of weaponless self-defense that was developed in 1882 by Jigoro Kano, a Japanese jujitsu expert. Kano modified many of the holds he considered too dangerous to be used in sport, and also developed the system of belts —a ranking method used to determine the proficiency of judo practitioners. A white belt indicates a novice and a black an expert. There is a wide range of colors in between as well as other colors beyond the black belt awarded to those who are considered "masters." Kano's methods, which placed more of an emphasis on physical fitness and mental discipline than on self-defense, depend greatly upon the skill of using an opponent's weight and strength against him. Such a technique makes it possible for a physically inferior individual to overcome a physically superior one. Judo matches begin with a ceremonial bow, after which each contestant grabs the other by the collar and sleeve of his jacket. The techniques used include holds, trips, strangles, and falls, with the end of the match signaled by one of the contestants slapping the mat two times to acknowledge defeat. A point system is also employed. International competition is held every two years.

Jugular Vein. △688.

Jugurtha (*c.* 156–104 BC), king of Numidia (108–106 BC). On the death of his father (118 BC) he had one of his brothers murdered. With Rome's approval, he divided Numidia with another brother. In 112 BC he attacked and seized Cirta, his brother's capital; a number of Romans were killed. In retaliation Rome invaded Numidia (111 BC), beginning the Jugurthine War. Jugurtha quickly made peace and was ordered to Rome to explain his actions. While in Rome, he had a potential rival murdered. War broke out again. Jugurtha defeated a Roman force in 110 BC with the aid of his father-in-law Bocchus of Mauretania, but in 106 BC Bocchus turned Jugurtha over to the Romans. He died in a Roman prison. △1018.

Jujitsu, a weaponless system of self-defense, used in hand-to-hand combat; involves such techniques as striking, kneeing, holding, throwing, choking, and joint locking. The methods used in jujitsu are varied and include as many as 50 different systems, including judo, karate, and aikido, that have been developed over a period of 2,000 years by Buddhist monks in Japan, China, and Tibet. The origins of jujitsu can be traced to 16th-century Japan, where Japanese warriors devised a secondary combat system to complement the tactics of their swordsmen. By the early 19th century—when the samurai were forbidden to carry weapons—jujitsu became a highly specialized form of self-defense. *See also* Judo.

Jukebox. △1798.

Jukes Family, a family with an unusually extensive background of crime and mental retardation, as reported in 1875 by R.L. Dugdale and A.H. Estabrook. The record of the Jukes family was interpreted as proof that heredity determines development, but modern scientists regard such evidence as inconclusive because environmental influences were not taken into account.

Juliana (1909–), queen of the Netherlands (1948–). She succeeded to the throne upon the abdication of her mother, Queen Wilhelmina. Married in 1937 to the German prince, Bernhard, she retained the loyalty of the Dutch during World War II. Of her four daughters, Beatrix, the eldest, is heiress-apparent to the throne.

Julian Alps, forested mountain range of NE Italy and NW Yugoslavia, between Carnic Alps and Dinaric Alps. Highest peak is Triglav, 9,396ft (2,866m).

Julian Day or **Julian Date (JD),** day specified according to a dating system introduced by Joseph Scaliger (1582) and named for his father Julius Caesar Scaliger. Julian days, which commence at noon (1200 hrs), are calculated from Jan. 1, 4713 BC, independent of months and years. Julian dating is used in astronomy principally in studying long-period phenomena, such as variable stars.

Julianus, Flavius Claudius, or Julian the Apostate (331–63), Roman emperor (360–63). Leader of an attempt to revive classical paganism, he opposed Christianity. His efforts on behalf of the pagan cults were futile, however, because Christianity had already become firmly established throughout the Roman Empire.

Julius I, Roman Catholic pope (337–52) and saint. He played a major role in increasing Roman and papal authority and in condemning Eastern Arianism. His attempt to unite the West in opposing Arian heresy failed. *See also* Arianism.

Julius II, Roman Catholic pope (1503–13), b. Guiliano della Rovere (1443). The nephew of Pope Sixtus IV, he tried to recover papal lands and, in 1506, established the Swiss Guard to protect the pope and Rome. He built up the treasury through the sale of benefices and began St Peter's basilica. △1140.

Julius Caesar (*c.*1598), 5-act tragedy by William Shakespeare, based on Plutarch's lives of Caesar, Antony, and Brutus. Presented countless times worldwide, it was filmed eight times, notably in the 1952 US production. Brutus, a noble Roman patriot, reluctantly conspires with Cassius to assassinate Caesar. In turn the conspirators are outwitted and defeated at the hands of the triumvirate Octavius, Antony, and Lepidus.

July, seventh month of the year. It was named after Julius Caesar and has 31 days. The birthstone is the ruby or onyx.

July Monarchy (1830–48), conservative regime of the wealthy bourgeoisie, set up after the July Revolution with Louis Philippe as king. Although the franchise was extended somewhat, the institutions of the July Monarchy differed little from those of the Restoration. Social problems were ignored. The left opposition was harshly repressed. Economic depression and demands for parliamentary reform brought down the regime.

July Revolution (1830), insurrection in France against the reactionary government of King Charles X. The immediate cause was the July Ordinances that dissolved the newly elected chamber of deputies, reduced the electorate, and imposed rigid press censorship. Street fighting broke out in Paris. Charles was forced to flee. He abdicated and named his grandson Henri his heir, but he was rejected in favor of the duc d'Orléans who was proclaimed King Louis Philippe. It was a triumph of the upper middle class over both the reactionaries and the more revolutionary forces favoring a republic.

Jumping Hare, or springhaas or springhare, a nocturnal burrowing rodent native to dry areas of Africa. It has short front legs for digging and long hind legs and tail for jumping. Gray to brown in color, it eats plants and roots. Length: 14–16in (35–40cm.); weight: 9lb (4kg). Species *Pedetes capensis.*

Jumping Mouse, mouse-size nocturnal rodent of North America, N Europe, and Asia having long hind legs and a tail that is longer than its body. Plant-eaters, they travel by leaping or jumping, and they hibernate underground. Family Zapodidae. △546.

Jumping Spider, worldwide spider that leaps on its prey trailing a strand of silk so it can climb back. Most are brightly colored and active during the day. Length: to 0.7in (18mm). Family Salticidae. *See also* Spider. △488.

Junco, or snowbird, hardy North American finch frequently observed when the first snow falls. The typical eastern junco *(Junco hyemalis)* is slate-colored with a white belly and outer tail feathers. Females and other species are reddish-brown. They lay their eggs (4–5) in a ground nest. Length: 6in (15cm). Family Fringillidae.

June, sixth month of the year. It was named for the goddess Juno and has 30 days. The birthstone is the pearl or moonstone.

Juneau, Solomon Laurent (1793–1856), US fur trader and political figure, b. Canada. He settled on the shore of Lake Michigan as an agent of the American Fur Co. and then, with his partner Morgan Martin, he established the settlement that was to become Milwaukee (1835). He was that city's first mayor (1846).

Juneau, seaport city and capital of Alaska, on Gas-

James Joule

James Joyce

Benito Juárez

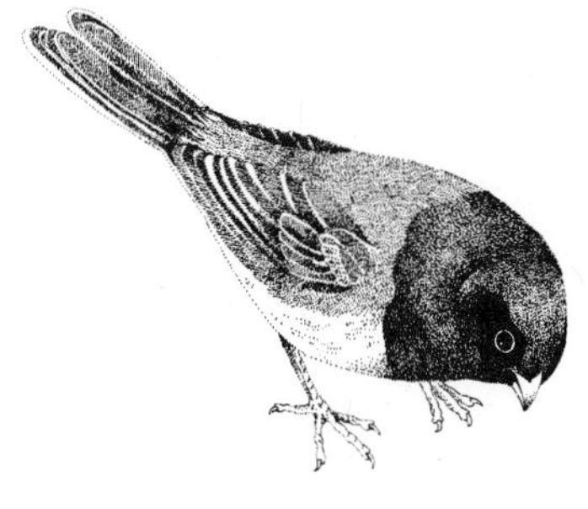
Junco

tineau Channel, 90mi (144km) NE of Sitka, bordering British Columbia; transportation center connecting with Seattle, Wash., and Vancouver, B.C. Industries: mining, lumbering, salmon canning. Founded 1880, administration seat transferred from Sitka 1906; made state capital 1959; pop. (1970) 13,556.

June Beetle, large green beetle that is a serious farm and garden pest. Adults eat leaves and fruit of many plants. The stout, dirty-white larvae injure roots of grasses, garden vegetables, and ornamentals. Species *Cotinus nitida.*

June Bug. *See* May Beetle.

June Days (June 23–26, 1848), insurrection of French radical workers. The conservative government forces, frightened by and determined to destroy a strong workers' movement, dissolved the national workshops, which employed one-third of the Parisian adult males. In a bloody weekend of fighting, 9,000 workers were killed. In the repression that followed, 3,000 prisoners were shot and 4,000 were deported.

Jung, Carl Gustav (1875–1961), Swiss psychiatrist. After working with Sigmund Freud (1906–1914), Jung broke with him to found his own school, analytic psychology. For many years Jung investigated and wrote extensively about the human personality, especially its spiritual and unconscious aspects, including the archetypes of the collective unconscious. He identified introversion and extroversion as basic personality types and stressed the importance of personal transformations and self-discovery for the development of a healthy personality. Though his writings are sometimes regarded as obscure, Jung's insights and scholarship rank him among the foremost theorists in psychology. Among his noted works are *Wandlungen und Symbole der Libido* (1912, tr. as *Psychology of the Unconscious;* 1952 rev. ed., tr. as *Symbols of Transformation*) and *Modern Man in Search of a Soul* (1933). △774, 814.

Jungfrau, mountain peak in S central Switzerland, in Bernese Alps; site of Jungfraujoch pass and alpine research station. First climbed in 1811. Height: 13,642ft (4,161m).

Jungle. △596–603.

Jungle Cat. *See* Chaus.

Jungle Fowl, often known as red jungle fowl *(Gallus gallus),* the ancestor of all domestic poultry, long domesticated by man and bred into many varieties. The jungle fowl is native to Southeast Asia where noisy flocks frequent deep woods and forest edges. Chickenlike, they have high arched tails, double-wattled throats and combs. *See also* Chicken.

Junior College, or community college, institution giving two years of education beyond high school. Some students start their higher education here and transfer to a four-year college. Others take two-year courses of vocational or technical training. Two-year colleges also offer part-time adult education programs. More than 90% of US two-year college students are enrolled in public institutions.

Juniper, genus of evergreen shrubs and trees native to temperate regions of the Northern Hemisphere. They have needlelike or scalelike leaves and may be tall and upright or low and spreading. These shapes make them popular as ornamentals. The aromatic timber is used for making pencils, and the berrylike cones for flavoring gin. Family Taxodiaceae. △440–42.

Junkers, in German history, the landed aristocracy of Prussia. They formed the officer class of the Prussian, later German, army and dominated the civil service. Otto von Bismarck was a Junker.

Junkus, Hugo. △1714.

Juno, in Roman mythology, chief goddess, the sister and wife of Jupiter. She was the goddess of childbirth and therefore was worshipped mainly by women. She later became the female deity of the state.

Juno, asteroid discovered (1804) by Karl Ludwig Harding. Diameter 150mi (240km); mean distance from Sun 247,000,000mi (398,700,000km); mean sidereal period 4.36yr. △78.

Jupiter, in Roman mythology, the supreme deity. He presided over the sky. He was depicted holding a sceptre, a symbol of his authority. Juno was his wife.

Jupiter, largest of the planets and fifth from the Sun. Jupiter has 13 satellites, the four largest having diameters greater than 1,900mi (3,060km). It has a gaseous surface with outer clouds of frozen ammonia crystals. The temperature under the clouds is estimated to between 0°F (−18°C) and 100°F (38°C). Mean distance from the Sun, 483,000,000mi (778,000,000km); mass and volume, 318 and 1300 times that of Earth, respectively; equatorial diameter, 88,700mi (143,000km); polar diameter, 84,000mi (135,000km); rotation period, 9hr 50–56min; period of sidereal revolution, 11.86 years; composition, mainly hydrogen, which may be squeezed into a metallic state near the core where pressures and temperatures are high. *See also* Solar System. △80–82, 86, 152.

Jura Mountains, mountain range in E France and NW Switzerland; extends from Rhine River at Basel, to Rhône River, SW of Geneva. Region contains pine forests, good pasture lands, rivers producing hydroelectric power. Highest peak is Crêt de la Niege in France, 5,652ft (1,724m).

Jurassic Period, the middle division of the Mesozoic Era. It lasted from 195,000,000 to 135,000,000 years ago. There were large saurischian dinosaurs such as *Atlantosaurus* and *Allosaurus* and ornithischian dinosaurs such as *Camptosaurus* and *Stegosaurus.* Plesiosaurs and pterosaurs appeared. The first known bird, *Archaeopteryx,* dates from this period. Cycads were dominant plants. Primitive mammals were present, among them the group ancestral to the later marsupials and placentals. *See also* Geologic time; Mesozoic Era. △276.

Jury. △912.

Justice, Department of, federal cabinet level department within executive branch. It is responsible for the enforcement of federal laws, furnishing legal counsel in federal cases, and construing the laws under which other departments act. It conducts all suits in which the United States is concerned in the Supreme Court, supervises federal penal institutions, and upon request gives legal advice and opinions to the president and other heads of the executive departments. It is directed by the attorney general, who also supervises and directs the activities of the US attorneys and marshals in the various judicial districts. The Justice Department was established in 1870, but the office of attorney general existed from 1789.

Justinian I (the Great) (*c.* 482–565), Byzantine Emperor (*r.* 527–565). Born the son of a Balkan peasant, Justinian became one of the most cultured men of his time, and one of the greatest rulers of the Byzantine Empire. Under Justinian, the generals Belisarius and Narses reconquered for Byzantium large parts of the old Roman Empire in North Africa, Italy, and Spain. Together with his forceful wife Theodora, he embarked upon vast building programs; the Church of St Sophia in Constantinople was erected during his reign. Justinian's most lasting achievement was his legislative work, in particular his revision of Roman law. △908, 1052, 1054, 1056, 1060.

Justinian Code, monument of Byzantine law, and the greatest contribution of the Emperor Justinian to posterity, the Code was prepared in the 6th century by a commission headed by the legal scholar Tribonian. To the revision of Roman law, Justinian added other legislative works, now known collectively as the "Corpus of Civil Law." △908.

Jute, natural fiber obtained from *Corchorus capsularis* and *Corchorus olitorius,* both native to India. Grown as a crop in India and Bangladesh, the plants mature in three months from seed and grow to 15ft (4.6m). The fiber is obtained from the bark by soaking and thrashing. Jute is used to make burlap, twine, and rope. △362.

Jutes, one of the three Germanic-speaking tribes that invaded England in the 5th century after the decline of Roman rule. They settled around Kent and the Isle of Wight. Bede called them *Iutae,* and some believed they came from the western fiords of Jutland. But their social system was Frankish in character, differing from the other two tribes, the Saxons and Angles. Modern scholars believe the Jutes may have come from the Rhine delta region.

Jutland (Jylland), peninsula in N Europe, containing Denmark and N Schleswig-Holstein state of West Germany. It is bounded by Skagerrak (N), North Sea (W), Kattegat and Little Belt (E), and Eider River (S). Largest naval battle of WWI took place between British and German fleets off W coast of Jutland. Land along E coast is fertile, supporting dairying and livestock; W coast is sandy and marshy. There are many lakes on peninsula. Highest point is Denmark's Yding Skovhøj, 568ft (173m). Iron, marble, and limestone are mined. Politically, Jutland refers only to Danish part of peninsula; its area (including offshore islands) is 11,441sq mi (29,632sq km) and pop. is 2,109,370.

Jutland, Battle of (1916), naval battle between the British Grand Fleet, under Admiral Jellicoe, and the German High Seas Fleet, under Admiral Scheer. Although inconclusive, the battle damaged many German ships and significantly lowered German morale. △1304.

Juvenal(is), Decimus Junius (*c.* 55–*c.* 140), Roman poet. His harsh, bitter, and direct satires denounced the affectations and immorality of the empire. △1028.

Juvenile Delinquency. *See* Delinquency, Juvenile.

K

Battle of Jutland

Ka. △840.

Kaaba, or **Ka'ba,** central shrine of Islam, in the Great Mosque in Mecca. A cube of stone and marble, in one corner sits the Black Stone, by tradition given to Adam on his fall. The object of pilgrimage, each Muslim circles it seven times, touching the Black Stone for forgiveness. △1058.

Kabbala. *See* Cabala.

Kabinda. *See* Cabinda.

Kabuki Theater, a stylish mixture of dance and music, mime and naturalism, a major form of entertainment in Japan since the late 16th century. In contrast to the No theater, which had its origins with the nobility, Kabuki was the theater of the common people. It has always emphasized visual delights and acting skills, but it also draws morals by presenting tragic conflicts. Character traits are accentuated by symbolic makeup colors and costume changes. Steeped in Kabuki tradition, one family often performs for many generations. The color and grace of Kabuki have been a strong influence on many Japanese and Western film makers.

Kābul, city and capital of Afghanistan and Kābul prov.; easternmost city on Kābul River; largest city in Afghanistan. Included in Muslim empire of Delhi 1526–1738; occupied by British 1842 (First Afghan War) and 1879; modernized by the emir Abd-er-Rahman Khan. Old streets and bazaars mingle with modern business center; site of university (1931), tomb of Timur Shah, Kābul Museum. Industries: food processing, textiles, leather goods. Pop. 498,800.

Kachina. *See* Katchina.

Kádár, János (1912–), Hungarian politician, premier 1956–58, 1961–65. Active in the Communist party beginning in his youth, he fought in the resistance movement during World War II. In 1949 he served as head of the secret police. He was deputy premier in Imre Nagy's government during the 1956 Hungarian revolution. He replaced Nagy as premier Nov. 4, 1956, and pursued a policy of accommodation with the Soviets. He again served as premier 1961–65. △1344.

Kaesong, city in S North Korea, 35mi (56km) NW of Seoul, on the North-South Korean boundary; because of its strategic position during Korean War (1950–53), it was passed between communist and UN possession many times; scene of war's first peace conference in 1951; remained in North Korean territory by Panmunjom armistice in 1953; trade center. Pop. 140,000.

Kaffir Cat, or African wild cat, Caffre cat, Egyptian cat, small buff and dark-striped cat found throughout Africa and Syria. Worshipped by ancient Egyptians, it is thought to be an ancestor of the domestic cat. Length: body—24 in (61cm); tail—12in (30.5cm). Family Felidae; species *Felis lybica*. *See also* Abyssinian Cat; Cat.

Kafirs, or **Nuristanis,** people speaking a Dardic language and living in the Hindu Kush mountains of Nuristan in Afghanistan, and near Chitral in W Pakistan. Kafir women cultivate grain; men herd cattle and goats, and hunt. Despite fierce opposition, Islam has been introduced into their traditionally polytheistic society.

Kafka, Franz (1883–1924), Austrian novelist, b. Prague. Son of a successful Jewish businessman, Kafka suffered under his father's dominance. Little known in his lifetime, he became famous in 1945 with the English translation of his novels, such as *The Trial* (1925), *The Castle* (1926), *America* (1927), and *Metamorphosis* (1915). His work recorded modern man's fate of having been caught in an incomprehensible nightmare world. The heroes persisted in hope, but their endeavors were absurd. His collections of autobiographically oriented short stories foreshadowed his novels.

Kabul, Afghanistan

Kaganovich, Lazar. △1310.

Kagoshima, prefecture and city, its capital, on S Kyushu, S Japan. City is a port lying on Kagoshima Bay; originally the seat of the Satsuma daimyo; St Francis Xavier landed here 1549; besieged by British 1863; suffered destruction from fire 1877 and volcano (Ontake) 1914; bombed by Allies June–August 1945. Industries: lumber, mining, Satsuma ware, shipbuilding. Pop. (city) 403,340.

Kagu, nearly extinct, almost flightless, heron-sized New Caledonian bird. It has a large head with back-pointing crest, large black-and-white barred wings, and orange-red legs. It feeds on insects and worms and emits sharp calls, chiefly at night. Aggressive males help build a twig-and-leaf nest for a single brown-splotched, rust-colored egg. Length: 22in (56cm). Species *Rhinochetus jubatus*.

Kahn, Louis (1901–74), US architect, b. Estonia. His design for the Yale University Art Gallery, New Haven, Conn. (1953), which included a space-frame ceiling, was considered a dramatic break with the International style. One of his most important works was the Richards Medical Building at the University of Pennsylvania (1960), famous for its separation of functional (elevators, pipes, stairwells) and formal (living and working areas) spaces. He also designed the Salk Institute for Biological Studies, La Jolla, Calif. (1959–65), and the Kimbell Art Museum, Fort Worth, Tex., which opened after his death.

Kaffir cat

K'ai-feng, historic city in E central China; served as capital of China during the Five Dynasty period (907–60) and under Northern Sung dynasty (960–1127) as Pienching; site of a Jewish settlement that flourished from 1163 until lost under Muslim influences (15th century). Industries: silk, flour. Pop. 299,100.

Kailua, city in Hawaii, on SE coast of Oahu Island, on Kailua Bay, 13mi (21km) NE of Honolulu; site of agricultural experiment station. Pop. 33,783.

Kaiserslautern, city in W West Germany, on Lauter River; devastated during Thirty Years War (1635) and French Revolution (1793); seat of provincial government 1889; site of University of Trier and Kaiserslautern (1970) and remains of Charlemagne's 9th-century castle. Industries: ironworks, textiles, furniture, machinery, beer. Chartered 1276. Pop. 101,158.

Kala-azar, an insect-borne disease carrying a high mortality and caused by infection with the parasite *Leishmania donovani,* apparently transmitted by the sandfly. The liver and spleen are particularly affected and become enlarged. Additional symptoms include fever, anemia, fluid retention, and wasting. The disease occurs worldwide but primarily along the Mediterranean coast, in southern Russia and Asia, and in South and Central America and Mexico. △732.

Kalahari, desert in Namibia, Botswana, and South Africa; between Orange and Zambezi rivers; inhabited by San and Khoikhoi, nomadic hunters and farmers. Area: 100,000sq mi (259,000sq km).

Kagu

Kalamazoo, city in SW Michigan, 47mi (76km) S of Grand Rapids, on Kalamazoo River; seat of Kalamazoo co; site of Kalamazoo College (1833), Western Michigan University (1903), Nazareth College (1897), and Kalamazoo Valley Community College (1966). Industries: paper, drugs, musical instruments, gas heaters, machine tools. First settled 1829; inc. as city 1884. Pop. (1970) 85,555.

Kalanchoe, genus of succulent, perennial plants native to Old World tropics. It has oval, waxy leaves and scarlet flower clusters. Often grown as a houseplant, varieties include *K. pinnata* with feathery leaves and the cigarette plant *(K. verticilata)* with cylindrical leaves and clusters of plantlets growing at the leaf tips. Height: 7in (17.8cm). Family Crassulaceae.

Kale, cabbage-related plant grown as a cool weather crop. A short-stemmed, loose plant, it has large, bluish-green, curly-edged leaves that are eaten as a vegetable. It matures in 60–65 days. Height: 12–16in (30.5–40.6cm); width: 24–36in (61–91cm). Family Cruciferae; species *Brassica oleraceae acephala.*

Kaleidoscope, optical toy invented by Sir David Brewster (*c.* 1816). It consists of a cylinder with mirrors on one end that reflect fragments of colored glass or beads in a symmetrical design, seen through a viewer on the other end. By rotating part of the tube, one can produce a nearly infinite number of designs. Later kaleidoscopes employed lenses that reflected images of distant objects rather than glass chips.

Kalf, Willem. △1168.

Kali, a goddess in Hindu mythology. Often destructive, she also protects humanity from disease. She is usually depicted as black, with blood on her hands and parts of her face. As a destroyer she is adorned with a skull or skulls, which show her predilection for blood sacrifices, and frequently with snakes. When she acts charitably she is often called "Blessed Dark One." In India she has many shrines. △838.

Kalinin, Mikhail Ivanovich (1875–1946), Soviet political figure, first president of the Soviet Union (1923–46). Popular with the peasants, he was elected to the Communist party Central Committee in 1919 and to the Politburo in 1925.

Kalinin, city in Russian SFSR, USSR, 100mi (161km) NW of Moscow on Volga River; capital of Kalinin oblast. A rival of Moscow, it was annexed to Moscow by Ivan III 1485; site of 14th-century monastery and castle. Industries: iron products, textiles, railroad cars, rubber. Founded 1180 as a fort. Pop. 367,000.

Kaliningrad (Königsberg), city and seaport in W European USSR, on the Pregolya River; capital of Kaliningrad oblast. A member of the Hanseatic League in 1340, it became residence of dukes of Prussia in 1525; made coronation city of kings of Prussia in 1701; occupied by Russia 1945 after a long siege; site of University of Königsberg (1544), 14th-century Gothic cathedral and 17th-century citadel; birthplace of Immanuel Kant (1724) who taught at the university. Industries: shipbuilding, food processing, automobile parts, textiles. Founded 1255 as Königsberg; name changed in 1946 when Potsdam Conference awarded it to USSR. Pop. 315,000.

Kallikak Family, a family in which mental retardation occurred with unusual frequency, reported by Henry Goddard in 1912. Goddard regarded his study as proof that mental retardation is caused by hereditary factors, but modern scientists regard such evidence as inconclusive because environmental influences were ignored. Goddard's work nevertheless is important as an early effort to find the causes of retardation. △914.

Kalmar Union (1397–1523), union of Denmark, Norway, and Sweden. It began with the crowning of Eric of Pomerania, grand-nephew of Queen Margaret of Norway and Denmark, which was held in the city of Kalmar (1397). Queen Margaret had appointed Eric heir after her son Olav IV's death. The constitution she presented for the union is regarded as a draft since it was written on paper, not parchment, and the seals are damaged. The union established a common defense system but did little to disturb the countries' domestic systems. It lasted until the coronation of Gustav I (1523).

Kalmia, evergreen shrub native to North America with long leaves and bell-shaped flowers of pink, purple, or white. Height: 2–10ft (0.6–3m). Family Ericaceae; genus *Kalmia.*

Kamairu. △874.

Kamakura, city in Honshu, Japan, on Sagami Sea near mouth of Toyko Bay; site of bronze statue of Buddha, Museum of Modern Art, and Museum of National Treasures. An important ancient city of Japan, it was seat of Yoritomo shogunate 1192–1333, and Ashicaga shogunate 1333–1573; suffered earthquake 1923; now mainly a residential and resort area; fishing industry. Pop. 139,249.

Kamchatka Peninsula, peninsula in NE Russia SFSR, USSR; separates the Sea of Okhotsk (W) from Bering Sea and Pacific Ocean (E); terminates (S) at Cape Lopatka. A fishing, timbering, and fur trapping area with some farming and cattle raising in S, it was first visited by Russians 1696; they completed conquest in 1732. Area: 104,200sq mi (269,878sq km). Pop. 275,000.

Kamehameha, five kings of Hawaii. **Kamehameha I** (*c.* 1758–1819) united all of the Hawaiian Islands under the Kamehameha dynasty by 1810. He instituted harsh laws and punishment for transgression, but modernized his kingdom by doing away with human sacrifice and by offering the peasants protection from landlords. **Kamehameha II** or **Liholiho** (1797–1824) was responsible for admitting the first US missionaries. **Kamehameha III** or **Kauikeaouli** (1813–1854) was the brother of Kamehameha II. He came to the throne so young that Kaahumanu, Kamehameha I's favorite queen, acted as regent until 1832. Kamehameha III was a liberal ruler who adopted constitutions in 1840 and 1852 and secured his country's independent recognition. **Kamehameha IV** or **Alexander Liholiho** (1834–63) made social and economic reforms, and opposed annexation to the United States. His brother, **Kamehameha V** (1830–1872), the last in the dynasty, was less democratic.

Kamenev, Lev B(orisovich). △1310.

Kamikaze ("Divine Wind"), suicide tactic employed by Japanese pilots in late World War II entailed crashing explosive-laden planes onto US ships. First employed in late 1944, this tactic inflicted serious losses on the US Navy at Okinawa. △1210.

Kampala, capital and largest city of Uganda, in E Africa, 21mi (34km) NNE of Entebbe. A well-planned modern city, it has mosques, Hindu temples, Anglican and Roman Catholic cathedrals; site of Makerere University College (1963); a commercial center and livestock and agricultural market. Industries: textiles, food processing. Made capital 1962. Pop. 331,889.

Kampen, Karl van. *See* Campbell, John Wood, Jr.

Kananga, formerly Luluabourg; city in S central Zaire, on the Lulua River; capital of Kasai-Occidental prov. In 1895 troops of Independent State of Congo revolted; they were not defeated until 1901; since 1960, when Zaire became independent, there have been many clashes between rival tribes. Industries: cotton, food processing. Founded 1884. Pop. 483,438.

Kanazawa, city on central Honshu, Japan, on the Sea of Japan; capital of Ishikawa prefecture; prominent as the seat of the Maeda daimyo (16th–19th centuries); site of Kenokuran Park, with a famous No theater. Industries: textiles, machinery. Pop. 361,379.

Kanchenjunga (Kinchinjunga or **Kangchenjunga),** mountain in E Himalayas, between Nepal and Sikkim; the central peak of the Himalayan range; third-highest mountain in the world; has 5 peaks, the tallest of which is 28,168ft (8,591m).

Kandahar, city and provincial capital in S Afghanistan, approx. 285mi (459km) SW of Kabul. Leading trade center; 2nd-largest city in Afghanistan. Wall encircles old section of city; sacked by Genghis Khan 1222; captured by Mongul empire 16th century and by Persians 1625; revolted for independence 1706–08; became first Afghan capital 1709; site of tomb of Ahmed Shah Durani. Industries: textiles, fruit, sheep. Pop. 130,212.

Kandinsky, Wassily (1866–1944), Russian painter, theorist, and writer on art. His discoveries and experimentation with abstract painting resulted in truly innovative and revolutionary contributions. His early academic style evolved into a semi-abstract method in 1908 ("The Street in Murrau"). His first completely abstract work was "Composition I" (1910). Among his noted works of this period are "Small Pleasures" and "Black Lines" (1913). After 1921 his works became more geometric in form ("Black Relation," 1924). △1318, 1372.

Kandy, city in Sri Lanka, on the Kandy Plateau; former capital of ancient kings of Ceylon (1592); occupied by Portuguese 16th century, Dutch 18th century, captured by the British 1815; site of Dalada Maligawa noted Buddist temple, which contains what is traditionally believed to be one of Buddha's teeth, brought to Ceylon (Sri Lanka) in 4th century; a palace, an museum, oriental library, University of Sri Lanka (1942); market center for region producing tea, rice, rubber, cocao. Chief industry is tourism. Pop. 78,000.

Kaneohe, residential city in Hawaii, on E coast of Oahu Island, on Kaneohe Bay; site of ancient fish ponds, coral gardens, missile tracking station. Pop. (1970) 29,903.

Kangaroo, any of about 47 species of herbivorous leaping marsupial mammals of the family Macropodidae, native to Australia, Tasmania, New Guinea, and adjacent islands. Size ranges from 9in (23cm) to 8ft (2.4 m). All have long, powerful hind legs and long tails used for balancing. Short forelimbs function as arms, but the digits of the hand bear sharp claws and the thumb is not opposable. The head is small, the ears large and rounded, the coat soft and woolly. Young kangaroos, called joeys, are only partially developed at birth and attach themselves to the mother's teats within a pouch for months. *See also* Marsupial. △544.

Kangaroo Rat, tiny, desert-dwelling rodent that carries seeds in its cheek pouches. They have long hind legs and tail and they are hoppers. They dry and store seeds and seldom drink water. Family Heteromyidae genus *Dipodomys.*

K'ang-hsi (1654–1722), Chinese emperor (as Shêng tsu, 1662–1722). He campaigned deep in Mongolia added three provinces in the north (1662–1705) made a treaty with Russia on the northern border (1689), conquered Yunnan and Formosa (1681–83) and won control of Tibet (1705–21). While he ruled as a conqueror, keeping the peace with strategically placed garrisons, he adopted Chinese culture, encouraging the arts and sponsoring collections of Chinese literary classics and major works of reference notably a 5,000-volume encyclopedia. He tolerated the Christians and for a time actively encouraged the Jesuit scholar-missionaries, but in 1717 he issued an anti-Christian decree.

Kankakee, city in E Illinois, on Kankakee River, 54mi (87km) SW of Chicago; seat of Kankakee co; site of Olivet Nazarene College (1907). Industries: ranges water heaters, furniture, pharmaceuticals, limestone quarrying. Inc. 1855. Pop. (1970) 30,944.

Kano, city in N central Nigeria; capital of state of Kano; commercial center for agricultural region producing nuts, cotton, cattle. City dates from before the 10th century, when it was part of the Hausa empire it was a Muslim posession 16th century; conquered by the Fulani in early 19th century; taken by British 1903. Industries: textiles. Pop. 357,000.

Kano School, school of Japanese painting originating in the 15th century. The style, based on Chinese ink painting, was usually simple and restrained, but occasionally elaborate, as in decorative screen painting. Masanobu (*c.* 1453–1540) founded the school The official painter to the shogun, he received important commissions from many lords and government officials. His son Motonobu (*c.* 1476–1559) continued this tradition. Other artists of the Kano School included Eitoku, Sanraku, Tanyu, Naonobu, Sansetsu and Tsunenobu, all of whom painted during the 17th and 18th centuries. During the 17th century part of the school moved to Edo and was henceforth called the Edo Kano. Kano artists remaining in Kyoto became known as the Kyoto Kano. △1048.

Kanpur, city in India; major industrial center and railroad junction; site of Indian Institute of Technology since 1960. Industries: leather, textiles, sugar. Pop 1,154,388.

Kansas, state in the central United States. The geographical center of the 48 coterminous states is in Smith co near the N boundary.

Land and economy. The land rises gradually from E to W, marked by some level areas and hill ranges The highest portions are a high plateau. Important rivers are the Kansas and the Arkansas. The only lakes are man-made. In much of the state the soil is especially suitable for wheat-growing, and in all sections pasturage is plentiful for raising beef and dairy cattle Manufacturing is centered in the cities of the E and S Oil is drilled and refined in the SE, and large natural gas deposits occur in the SE and SW.

People. Pioneers from the E and S states flocked to Kansas when settlement began in 1854. They were followed by German, Swedish, Czech, and Russian farmers. Only about 2% of the present population is foreign-born. About 65% live in urban areas.

Education. There are more than 50 institutions of higher education.

History. The Spanish explorer Coronado traversed the region in 1541 and French hunters and traders were present through the 18th century, but when the land passed from France to the United States in the Louisiana Purchase of 1803, it was still Indian country. The tribes were moved to other lands, and in 1854 the Territory of Kansas was created and opened for settlement. Immigrants came from the then slave states of the South and the anti-slavery states of the East. Violence between the factions marked the struggle for Kansas' future. It was admitted to the Union as a free state in 1861, just before the Civil War began. After the war, Kansas was an assembly and supply area for thousands of immigrants bound for the Far West. The state's own population grew from 364,000 in 1870 to over 1,400,000 in 1890 as its agricultural potential was realized.

PROFILE

Admitted to Union: Jan. 29, 1861; rank, 34th
US Congressmen: Senate, 2; House of Representatives, 5
Population: 2,249,071 (1970); rank, 28th
Capital: Topeka, 125,011 (1970)
Chief cities: Wichita, 276,554; Kansas City, 168,213; Topeka
State legislature: Senate, 40; House of Representatives, 125
Area: 82,264sq mi (213,064sq km); rank, 14th
Elevation: Highest, 4,135ft (1,261m), Wallace co, extreme NW. Lowest, 700ft (214m), Verdigris River, SE corner
Industries (major products): aircraft, other transportation equipment, processed foods, machinery, chemicals
Agriculture (major products): wheat, cattle, sorghum
Minerals (major): petroleum, natural gas, coal
State nickname: Sunflower State
State motto: Ad Astra per aspera ("To the Stars Through Difficulties")
State bird: western meadowlark
State flower: sunflower
State tree: cottonwood

Kansas City, city in NE Kansas, at confluence of Kansas and Missouri rivers, across Missouri-Kansas border from its sister city, Kansas City, Mo.; seat of Wyandotte co; 2nd-largest city in Kansas. Part of an Indian reservation 1818, it was acquired by Wyandotte Indians 1843, who called it Wyandotte City; sold to federal government 1855. Modern city was formed 1886 with inc. of many adjoining communities. It is site of Kansas City Kansas Community College (1923), Donnelley College (1949). Industries: livestock, packing houses, grain storage, soap, flour, automobiles, paper products, chemicals. Pop. (1970) 168,213.

Kansas City, city in W Missouri, on Missouri River, across Missouri-Kansas line from its sister city, Kansas City, Kan. The 2nd-largest city in Missouri, it was est. 1821 as trading post by François Chouteau; industrial development started *c.* 1865–80 with introduction of railroad and expansion into cattle trade center. It is the site of Avila College (1866), Rockhurst College (1910), University of Missouri at Kansas City (1929). Industries: food processing, aerospace equipment, chemicals, petroleum products, livestock, packing houses, hay, grain. Inc. 1846 as Town of Kansas, 1853 as City of Kansas, 1889 as Kansas City. Pop. (1970) 507,330.

Kansas-Nebraska Act (May 30, 1854), US Congressional measure, sponsored by Sen. Stephen A. Douglas, which allowed US territories to decide for themselves such domestic matters as whether to allow slavery. The act did away with the earlier policy of congressional mandate for the territories. The act was written to solve the growing slavery controversy, but actually caused the problem to become worse since neither pro- nor anti-slavery forces were satisfied with the measure.

Kant, Immanuel (1724–1804), German philosopher. From 1740–46 he studied at Königsberg, then supported himself as a private tutor. In 1755 he returned to the university and was made a professor in 1770. The order, regularity, and modesty of his life was undisturbed by the notoriety caused by the publication of his "critical philosophy;" particularly *The Critique of Pure Reason* (1781), *Critique of Practical Reason* (1788), and *Critic of Judgment* (1790). In addition to his technical treatises, Kant produced several topical essays in support of religious liberalism and enlightenment. *See also* Enlightenment. △854, 858–60.

Kaohsiung (Kachsiung), port city in S Taiwan; site of naval base. Industries: fertilizer, shipbuilding, paper products, wood, cement, aluminum, textiles, fisheries, petrochemicals. Pop. 806,300.

Kaoliang, several grain sorghums native to China and Manchuria. They have slender, dry, pithy stalks; open, erect panicles; and small, white or brown seeds. They are used for human food, alcoholic liquor, thatching, and fuel. *See also* Sorghum.

Kaolin. *See* China Clay.

Kaon, or **K meson,** elementary particle that is a positively charged or neutral meson with zero spin. *See also* Hadron. △1484.

Kapital, Das (3 vols., 1867, 1885, 1895), major work of economic analysis by Karl Marx in which he presents his theory of capitalism. Marx believed that capitalism was dependent upon the exploitation of labor. Volumes 2 and 3, edited by Friedrich Engels, were published after the death of Marx. △902, 1288–90, 1360.

Kapok, tropical tree grown commercially in Java, Sri Lanka, the Philippines, and Africa. A horizontally branching tree, it has palmate leaves and white or pink flowers. Its pods burst to release silky fibers, the commercial kapok used for flotation devices. Height: to 120ft (37m). Family Bombacaceae; species *Ceiba pentandra. See also* Balsa; Baobab. △362.

Karachi, largest city in Pakistan, on the Arabian Sea, NW of the Indus River delta, in SE Pakistan. Former capital of Pakistan (1947–59); early Hindu settlement; passed to British 1843, and developed into a major port. It now serves as chief trade center for inland agricultural products, as well as Pakistan military headquarters; site of major airport. Industries: shipping, automobile assembly, oil refining, steel, food processing, textiles, chemicals. Pop. 3,442,000.

Karaganda, city in Kazakh SSR, USSR, 135mi (217km) SSE of Tselinograd; capital of Karaganda oblast; central core of approx. 50 mining settlements that surround it. Industries: coal mining, iron and steel foundries, flour milling, cement mining equipment, footwear. Founded 1857 as a copper mining settlement; old city was est. early 1930s, new city developed after WWII. Pop. 541,000.

Karageorge (Karadjordje), or **George Petrovic,** (1762–1817), Serbian national hero. He led an insurrection against the Turks, enjoying victories at Ivankovac, Misar, and Belgrade, and freeing the whole province of Belgrade from Ottoman rule by 1806. He began to lay the foundations for administrative and government institutions, making an internationally recognized alliance with Russia in 1812, but Turkey reneged on her agreements, and Karageorge was forced to flee to Austria in 1813. △1232.

Karajan, Herbert von (1908–), German conductor. He conducted the Berlin State Opera (1938–45). From 1945 to 1955 he had a number of conducting assignments. In 1955 he became permanent conductor of the Berlin Philharmonic Orchestra. In 1957 he also became a director of the Salzburg Festivals, and from 1956 to 1964 he was also director of the Vienna State Opera.

Karakoram Range, mountain range in India and Pakistan; includes Godwin Austen, 28,250ft (8,616m), which is the second highest peak in the world.

Kara-Kul (Karakul'), lake in E Tadzik republic, USSR, near Chinese border on Palmir plateau. Depth: 780ft (238m).

Karakul, breed of sheep from central Asia with curled, glossy fur on adults and wiry, coarse hair on young. Tightly curled, black or gray pelts derived from young lambs are called "Persian lamb." "Broadtail" pelts are obtained from still- or new-born lambs. This short, uncurled, glistening hair forms a pattern called moiré. *See also* Sheep. △376.

Kara-Kum (Kara Kumy) Desert, desert area in S Central Asia USSR; extends from the Caspian Sea (W) to the Amudarja River (E) including most of Turkmen republic. The Kara Kum canal carries irrigation water 500mi (805km) from Kelif to Ashkhabad. Desert extends 600mi (966km) E to W, and 250mi (403km) N to S. Area: 115,000sq mi (297,850sq km).

Karate, martial art considered one of the most lethal methods of unarmed combat in the world. The technique, which involves a formal method of physical and mental training, includes a variety of blows using the hands, legs, elbows, and head. As a competitive sport,

Kamakura, Japan

Kangaroo

Hutchinson, Kansas

Karakul

contestants are only allowed to use a few of the techniques so as to avoid serious injuries and all punches, blows, strikes, or kicks are minimized.

Karelian Autonomous Soviet Socialist Republic (ASSR) (Karelia), autonomous region in NW European USSR, bounded by Murmansk oblast (N), White Sea and Arkhangelsk oblast (E), Vologda and Leningrad oblasts, and Finland (W); capital is Petrozavodsk. First est. 1923 as an autonomous republic, it absorbed 14,000sq mi (36,260sq km) of Finnish land after 1939–40 war between USSR and Finland, and was raised to a constituent republic in 1940 (Karelo-Finnish SSR), but returned to present status in 1956. Agriculture is carried on in S; fishing and lumbering are chief industries; area contains valuable mineral deposits. Area: 66,540sq mi (172,339sq km). Pop. 714,000.

Kariye Camii. △1060.

Karl-Marx-Stadt, formerly Chemnitz; city in S East Germany, 40mi (64km) SW of Dresden, on Chemnitz River; capital of Karl-Marx-Stadt district. Devastated during Thirty Years War (1618–1648), it recovered at end of 17th century with introduction of cotton industry; site of 15th-century church of St Jacob, 12th-century palace church, and early 12th-century palace that was formerly a Benedictine abbey founded by Emperor Lothair. Industries: carpets, hosiery, machinery, machine tools. Founded 1143 and awarded a linen-weaving monopoly. Pop. 299,312.

Karloff, Boris (1887–1969), b. William Pratt, English character actor noted for horror films after his appearance in *Frankenstein* (1931). He portrayed monsters with compassion in such films as *Scarface* (1932), *The Ghoul* (1933), and *Bedlam* (1946). In his last film, *Targets* (1968), he played a horror-film actor.

Karlovy Vary (Carlsbad), town in Czechoslovakia, on the Ohre River about 70mi (113km) W of Prague; noted health resort with sulphur springs. Carlsbad Decrees of 1819, which provided for press censorship and supervision of universities, were formalized here. Pop. 45,310.

Karlsruhe, city in SW West Germany, on Rhine river, 37mi (60km) S of Mannheim; capital of duchy (1771) and of former state of Baden 1919; severely damaged in WWII; site of university (1865), technical college (1825), school of fine arts, and school of music; center for atomic research since 1956. Industries: textiles, jewelry, chemicals, brewing, pharmaceuticals, oil refining. Founded 1715 by margrave of Baden-Durlach. Pop. 258,409.

Karma, Vedic concept related to belief in reincarnation. According to Karmic law, the acts in past incarnations explain present circumstances, just as acts in this life can affect future lives. Salvation involves canceling the effects of past evil deeds by virtuous actions in this life. *See also* Hinduism; Reincarnation; Veda. △846.

Karnak, village in central Egypt, on the Nile River, 1mi (1.6km) E of Luxor, with which it shares site of ancient city of Thebes. Many ruins of the pharaohs' architecture remain, including Great Temple of Amon from XVIII dynasty (1570–*c.*1342 BC); its half is a court and hypostyle (structure resting on pillars) hall, 388ft × 170ft (118m × 52m), containing 134 pillars in 16 rows; E half contains many halls and shrines.

Karnische, Alpen. *See* Carnic Alps.

Karst Topography, a limestone plateau characterized by irregular protuberant rocks, sinkholes, caves, disappearing streams, and underground drainage. Such topography is named after its most typical site in the Karst region of Yugoslavia. △256.

Kasai (Cassai), river in SW Africa; rises in central Angola, flows E, then N and NW through W Zaire to the Congo River; forms part of Angola-Zaire boundary. Navigable for 475mi (765km) of its 1,338mi (2,154km) length.

Kashmir. *See* Jammu and Kashmir.

Kashmir, or **Cashmere, Goat,** small wool goat native to the Himalaya Mountains of India and Tibet. It has a thick white coat with long guard hairs and silky underwool used in textiles. △608.

Kaskaskia, village in SW Illinois, at the confluence of the Kaskasia and Mississippi rivers; oldest town in the West, dating from 1700 as a French Jesuit mission. French held it until 1765 when it was taken by British; on July 4, 1770, George Rogers Clark captured it for United States. It began to decline in 1819 and, as the Mississippi encroached on it, disappeared almost entirely. Pop. (1970) 79.

Kassel, city in West Germany, on the Fulda River, 71mi (114km) WNW of Erfurt; transportation and manufacturing center; site of 14th-century church. Pop. 215,039.

Kasserine Pass, road and rail passage in W Tunisia, approx. 5mi (8km) NW of town of El Kasserine. Djebel Chambi Mt forms SW flank of pass; scene of Allied victory over German attack in decisive WWII battle in February 1943. Width: 2mi (3.2km).

Kassites or **Cassites,** an ancient people, possibly of Persian origin, who penetrated Mesopotamia in the 3rd millennium BC. By the middle of the 18th century BC they had conquered Babylonia. They introduced the horse and had a system of government dominated by a small feudal aristocracy. In the 1st millennium BC the Elamites forced the Kassites to withdraw to the Zagros Mountains in Iran, where they were known until about the beginning of the Christian era. △958.

Katchina, or **Kachina,** spirit-god among the Pueblo Indians, or a dancer masked to resemble one. Katchinas were believed to be ancestral spirits who brought rain and corn. Elaborate rituals surrounded them. △418.

Katmandu, capital of Nepal, in central Nepal at N foot of Mahābhārat mountain range, S Himalaya Mts; Political, commercial, and educational hub of Nepal; site of university (1958). Founded in AD 723; made capital 1768. Pop. 153,405.

Katowice, city in S Poland, 45mi (72km) WNW of Krakow; occupied by Germans 1939–1945; important railroad, educational, and cultural center. Industries: coal mining, metal working, iron, zinc. Founded 16th century. Pop. 306,000.

Kattegat, arm of North Sea, between Sweden (E) and Jutland Peninsula, Denmark (W).

Katydid, green to brown leaflike insect found worldwide. Its wings are arched over its back and it has long antennae. Most species produce a call sounding like "katy-did." Tropical species are the largest. Length: over 5in (127mm). Family Tettigoniidae. *See also* Orthoptera. △494.

Katzenbach v. McClung (1964), US Supreme Court case. The court ruled, as it did in *Heart of Atlanta Motel* v. *United States,* that the Constitution's commerce clause alone granted Congress the power to pass the anti-discrimination Civil Rights Act of 1964 and that the act was therefore constitutional. *See also* Heart of Atlanta Motel v. United States (1964).

Katzenbach v. Morgan (1966), US Supreme Court case that upheld a provision of the Voting Rights Act of 1965 that prohibited a state from imposing a requirement of literacy in the English language as a qualification for voting.

Katz v. United States (1967), US Supreme Court decision reversing a conviction based on evidence obtained by a wiretapped public telephone. The court rejected its earlier narrow position in *Olmstead* v. *United States* and said that the protective mantle of the Fourth Amendment did extend to telephone calls and therefore warrants and judicial approval were required. *See also* Olmstead v. United States (1928).

Kauai Island, one of the Hawaiian Islands; geologically the oldest, containing extinct volcanoes. Extremely wet, it receives an annual rainfall of 450in (1,143cm). Industries: sugar cane, pineapples, rice, tourism. Area: 549sq mi (1,422sq km).

Kaufman, George Simon (1889–1961), US playwright, b. Pittsburgh, Pa. He collaborated on comedies: *Beggar on Horseback* (1924) with Marc Connelly; *Dinner at Eight* (1932) and *Stage Door* (1936) with Edna Ferber; *You Can't Take It With You* (1936) and *The Man Who Came to Dinner* (1939) with Moss Hart. Kaufman contributed to George Gershwin's *Of Thee I Sing* (1932), *Guys and Dolls* (1950), and *Silk Stockings* (1955).

Kaunas, city and port in W European USSR, in Lithuania on Neman River; became part of Russia 1795 during the third partition of Poland; taken by Germans WWI; became capital of Lithuania 1918–1940; again taken by Germans in WWII; site of Lithuanian Gothic church of Vytautas (15th century), university (1922), polytechnic institute (1950), and a medical institute (1951). Industries: iron, steel, chemicals, plastics, textiles. Founded late 10th century. Pop. 322,000.

Kaunda, Kenneth (1924–), president of Zambia from 1964. He became involved in nationalist politics in 1949, and by 1960 was the leader of the United National Independence party. He served as a legislator and became president upon Zambia's independence from Britain. He nationalized copper mines and in 1972 outlawed all but his own political party.

Kauri Pine, evergreen tree native to New Zealand. It has flaky bark, bronze-green leaves, and round cones. It is valued for its strong timber and kauri resin used in varnishes and adhesives. Height: to 100ft (30m). Family Pinaceae; species *Agathis australis.*

Kavafis, Konstatínos Pétrou. *See* Cavafy, Constantine.

Kawabata, Yasunari (1899–1972), Japanese novelist. Influenced by French writing of the 1920s and Japanese linked verse, Kawabata was perhaps best known for his understanding of women. *Snow Country* (1947), *Thousand Cranes* (1949), and *The Sound of the Mountain* (1954) are his best known works. He received the Nobel prize for literature in 1968.

Kawaguchi, city in central Honshu, Japan, on Ajikawa and Kizagawa rivers; NW suburb of Tokyo; industrial area. Pop. 305,886.

Kawasaki, industrial city on central Honshu, Japan, on Tokyo Bay between Tokyo and Yokohama; suffered extensive damage from Allied bombings WWII; site of 12th-century temple. Industries: machines, automobiles, petrochemicals, ships. Pop. 973,486.

Kayak, canoe of Eskimo origin, traditionally built of sealskins stretched on a wooden framework. It is decked, apart from the cockpit, and propelled by a single double-bladed oar. Silent and maneuverable, it is still favored for hunting. *See also* Canoe. △1676.

Kayseri, city in central Turkey, at foot of Mt Erciyas; capital of Kayseri prov. City became part of Ottoman Empire 1515 after being captured by Crusaders 1097, the Mongols 1243, and Mamelukes of Egypt 1419; site of many historical remains. Industries: textiles, sugar, cement. Pop. 167,700.

Kazakh, Turkic-speaking people who inhabit the Kazakh Soviet Socialist Republic and the adjacent Sinkiang area of China. Traditionally nomadic pastoralists, herding horses and sheep, they have undergone stabilization in this century within the Soviet collective farm system.

Kazakh (Kazachskaja) Soviet Socialist Republic, constituent republic of S USSR, bordered by Siberia (N), China (E), Kirghiz, Uzbek, and Turkmen republics (S), and Caspian Sea (W); capital is Alma-Ata. Gradually taken by Russia 1730–1856, it became an autonomous republic 1920 and a constituent republic 1936. Central part of region is steppe with desert; mountains are in S and E, and lowlands in N and W; much of the USSR wheat and cattle are raised here; region contains large iron ore deposits and coal mines as well as copper, lead, zinc, nickel, chromium, silver. Industries: synthetic rubber, textiles, medicine, fertilizers. Area: 1,050,00sq mi (2,719,500sq km). Pop. 12,850,000.

Kazan, Elia (1909–), US stage and film director and author, b. Istanbul, Turkey. He won the New York Drama Critics Circle Award for his direction of Thornton Wilder's *The Skin of Our Teeth* (1942). His career included directing Arthur Miller's and Tennessee Williams' plays on Broadway. In 1958 he won a Tony Award for his direction of Archibald MacLeish's *JB.* He also directed films, including *A Tree Grows in Brooklyn* (1944), his Academy Award-winning *Gentleman's Agreement* (1947) and *On the Waterfront* (1954). He wrote two best sellers, *America, America* (1963), which he also made into a movie, and *The Arrangement* (1967). He was one of the founders of the Actors' Studio.

Kazan, port and city in E European USSR, on the Volga River, 200mi (322km) E of Gorkij; capital of Tatar ASSR. An 18th-century outpost of Russian colonization, in 1773 city was burned by Emelian Pugachev, peasant leader; rebuilt by Catherine II; site of University of Kazan (1804) where Lenin and Tolstoy studied. Industries: electrical equipment, building materials, food products, chemicals, explosives, furs. Founded 1437. Pop. 904,000.

Kaz Daği. *See* Ida, Mount.

Kea, New Zealand parrot that is olive-colored with red and yellow wings and a brush-tipped tongue for feeding on nectar. During winter it frequents sheep-raising areas, feeding on carcasses and sometimes killing sheep. Species *Nestor notabilis.* △538

Kearny, Stephen Watts (1794–1848), US general b. Newark, N.J. He participated in the War of 1812 and in numerous Indian wars on the Western frontier. Commanding the army in the West in 1846, he took possession of New Mexico and promised full citizenship to the natives. He also led a successful march to California, taking San Diego (1846) and San Gabriel and Los Angeles (1847). In a clash with Commodore Robert Stockton over who was authorized to set up government in California, Kearny was supported by the federal government.

Kearny, town in NE New Jersey, between Passaic and Hackensack rivers at head of Newark Bay, 2mi (3km) N of Newark. Industries: bricks, tiles, plastics, chemicals, textiles. Inc. 1899. Pop. (1970) 37,585.

Keating-Owen Act (1916), US legislation banning interstate transportation of goods produced by child labor. Also known as the Federal Child Labor Law, it was declared unconstitutional (1918) in *Hammer* v. *Dagenhart.* The Child Labor Act of 1919 was also declared unconstitutional (1922). The states failed to ratify a proposed constitutional amendment submitted in 1924 that would have given Congress jurisdiction over child labor.

Keaton, Buster (1895–1966), US film comedian, b. Joseph Francis Keaton in Piqua, Kans. His sophisticated acrobatic slapstick style evolved in shorts made from 1919 to 1929 for several directors. In *Our Hospitality* (1923), *Sherlock Junior* and *The Navigator* (1924), *Go West* (1925), *The General* (1926), *College* (1927), and *The Cameraman* (1928), his sad-faced hero survived impossible catastrophes triumphantly. After more than 30 years in eclipse, Keaton's career resumed shortly before his death.

Keats, John (1795–1821), English romantic poet, b. London. He gave up medical studies to devote himself to writing poetry. Becoming a member of the Leigh Hunt circle, he wrote his first important poem, "On First Looking into Chapman's Homer," in 1816. Other poems include "Endymion" (1817), "The Eve of St Agnes" (1819), "Lamia" (1820), "The Fall of Hyperion" (1818–19), "To a Nightingale" (1819), and "Ode on a Grecian Urn" (1819). Keats had an unhappy love affair with Fanny Brawne and died of tuberculosis in Rome. △1240.

Keble, John (1792–1866), English clergyman and poet. At Oriel College, Oxford, Keble's sermon "National Apostasy" (1833) launched the Oxford, or Tractarian, Movement, which began as a High Church endeavor to revive the independence and power of the Anglican Establishment. The *Christian Year* (1827) and *Lyra Innocentium* (1846) were examples of his considerable poetical gifts. *See also* Oxford Movement.

Keel, The. *See* Carina.

Keeshond, Dutch dog of Arctic origin (nonsporting group); national dog of Holland during late 18th-century civil strife. It has a foxlike face, characteristic spectacles markings; small, triangular, erect ears; compact body; straight legs; and high-set, curved tail. A mixture of gray and black with gray or cream undercoat, the long, harsh coat stands out, except on legs and head, where it is short and smooth. Standard size: 18in (46cm) high at shoulder; 32–40lb (14–18kg). See also Nonsporting Dog.

Kefauver, (Carey) Estes (1903–63), US political leader, b. Madisonville, Tenn. He served in the US House of Representatives (1939–48), moving to the Senate (1949–63) after defeating the local machine candidate. As chairman of the Senate crime-investigating committee, he earned a national reputation for honesty when the hearings were televised. He was the Democratic vice-presidential candidate in 1956.

Keflavík, town on SW coast of Iceland, about 22mi (36km) WSW of capital city Reykjavík, on SW shore of Faxa Bay; site of Keflavík Field (international airport); noted for fisheries. Pop. 5,663.

Keitel, Wilhelm (1882–1946), German general. His appointment (1938) as chief of new army high command marked Adolf Hitler's assertion of total control over the German army. Hitler's closest military adviser throughout the war, Keitel was tried and executed as a war criminal.

Kekkonen, Urho (1900–), president of Finland (1956–). A lawyer, writer, sportsman, and life-long public servant, he maintained good relations with the USSR. Called the "builder of neutrality," he concluded the Finnish-Soviet Treaty in 1948, extended in 1970, which guarantees that Finnish territory cannot be used to launch an attack on the USSR.

Keller, Helen Adams (1880–1968), US author and social worker, b. near Tuscumbia, Ala. She overcame the loss of sight, hearing, and speech, yet achieved distinction as a lecturer and scholar. Illness rendered her blind and deaf at the age of nineteen months, and later she became dumb. Her teacher, Anne Sullivan, helped her to speak at the age of seven and remained with her 1887–1936. Keller obtained a degree cum laude from Radcliffe College in 1904 and mastered several languages. She lectured throughout the world and worked extensively for the relief of the handicapped. Her books include *The Story of My Life* (1902), *The World I Live In* (1908), and *The Open Door* (1957).

Kellogg, Frank Billings (1856–1937), US diplomat and political leader, b. Potsdam, N.Y. A lawyer, he was prosecutor of the Standard Oil trust case (1911). He was a Republican senator from Minnesota (1917–23) and was a delegate to the Pan American Conference in Chile (1923). He was ambassador to Great Britain (1924–25). As Pres. Calvin Coolidge's secretary of state (1925–29), he is best known for his part in negotiating the Kellogg-Briand Peace Pact (1928). After receiving the Nobel Peace Prize (1929), he became a judge on the Court of International Justice.

Kellogg-Briand Pact (ratified 1929), originally between the United States and France and later ratified by the European powers, it renounced war as a solution to controversies. It marked the beginning of US acceptance of international cooperation. Contemporary discussion centered around interpretation, especially of self-defense, and the pact's practicality.

Kells, Book of (8th century), a finely illuminated copy of the Gospels in Latin, containing local records. It was discovered in what is now Meath County, Ireland, and is now at Trinity College, Dublin.

Kelp, any of various large brown seaweeds common on Atlantic and Pacific coasts. Kelps typically consist mainly of rootlike holdfasts, stemlike stipes, and leaflike blades. Giant kelp *(Macrocystis)* exceeds 150ft (46m) in length. Formerly a principal source of iodine and potassium compounds, kelp is now used chiefly as a fertilizer. *See also* Brown Algae.

Kelvin, William Thomson, 1st Baron (1824–1907), Irish physicist and mathematician who developed James Joule's convertibility ideas of heat and work. He devised the absolute, or Kelvin, scale of temperature and provided theoretical knowledge for the laying of the first transatlantic cable. Among his inventions are the galvanometer, electrometer, and tide predictor. His work laid the foundation for thermodynamics and for the theory of electric oscillation. △1512.

Kelvin, the temperature scale developed by Lord Kelvin with a zero point at absolute zero and a degree the same size as the degree Celsius. The freezing point of water occurs at 273 °K (or kelvins) and the boiling point at 373 kelvins. *See also* Temperature Scales. △1508.

Kemerovo, city in central Siberian USSR, on the Tom River, 125 mi (201km) E of Novosibirsk; capital of Kemerovo oblast; major coal mining center of Kuznetsk Basin. Industries: coke, chemicals, fertilizers, mining machinery, plastics. Founded 1720 as Shcheglova; name changed 1863. Pop. 404,000.

Kendo, martial art, the traditional Japanese form of stick fighting. The two contestants wear protective armor and fight with sticks, usually made of bamboo. The footwork is vital, with short, fast, gliding steps the preferred technique to overcome an opponent.

Kenitra, port city in NW Morocco, 10mi (16km) from the Atlantic Ocean, on the Sebou River; US forces landed November 1942. Exports: mineral ores, agricultural products. Industries: food processing, oil refining, fertilizer, spinning. Pop. 139,206.

Kennan, George F(rost) (1904–), US diplomat, b. Milwaukee, Wis. He joined the Foreign Service in 1925, and served in the Soviet Union (1933–37), Czechoslovakia (1938–39), and Germany (1939–41). He was head of the State Department's policy planning staff (1947) and advisor to the secretary of state (1949). He became ambassador to the USSR (1952), but was recalled at the demand of the Soviet government. He became a permanent professor (1956) at the Institute for Advanced Study in Princeton, N.J., and later served as US ambassador to Yugoslavia (1961–63). Kennan, who helped formulate President

Boris Karloff

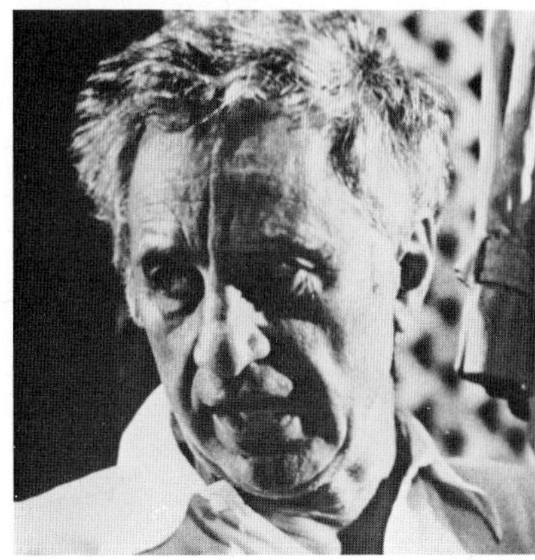

Elia Kazan

John Keats

Helen Keller

Truman's foreign policy of "containment" of the USSR, was the author of several notable international relations works, including *American Diplomacy 1900–1950* (1951), *Realities of American Foreign Policy* (1954), and *Democracy and the Student Left* (1968). His *Memoirs 1925–50* (1967) won a Pulitzer Prize.

Kennebec River, river in Maine; rises in Moosehead Lake, central Maine; flows S to the Atlantic Ocean. Length: approx. 150mi (242km).

Kennedy, Edward Moore (1932–), US Senator, b. Brookline, Mass. Youngest of three brothers who were US senators, he was elected to finish his brother John's term as senator from Massachusetts (1962). He was assistant Democratic whip (1969–71) and worked for liberal legislation, particularly in health and welfare. After his brothers John and Robert were assassinated, he was frequently mentioned as a presidential candidate.

Kennedy, John Fitzgerald (1917–63), 35th president of the United States (1961–63), b. Brookline, Mass.; graduate, Harvard, 1940. In 1953 he married Jacqueline Bouvier; two children survive. He was the son of Joseph P. Kennedy and the brother of Edward M. Kennedy and Robert F. Kennedy. After distinguished service in the Navy in World War II, Kennedy was elected to the House of Representatives as a Democrat in 1946. He served there until he entered the Senate in 1953.

In 1956, Kennedy made an unsuccessful bid for the vice-presidential nomination and then immediately began preparations for the 1960 presidential nomination. He won seven primaries in 1960 and was nominated on the first ballot. He chose Lyndon B. Johnson as his running mate.

Kennedy, who defeated Richard M. Nixon by a small margin, was the first Roman Catholic president and, at 43, the second youngest president. Kennedy's domestic program, named the New Frontier, called for increased federal involvement in civil rights, education, medicine, urban renewal, and medical insurance.

It was foreign affairs, however, that occupied most of Kennedy's attention. The ill-fated Bay of Pigs invasion of Cuba took place shortly after his inauguration. In June 1961 he met in Vienna with Nikita Khrushchev of the Soviet Union; the meeting was not productive and Kennedy stepped up the US involvement in Vietnam partly as a result of the failure of that meeting. Kennedy established the Peace Corps and a new Latin American policy, known as the Alliance for Progress. His most spectacular success in foreign affairs occurred in October 1962, when, during the Cuban Missile Crisis, he forced the Soviet Union to remove its missiles from Cuba.

In November 1963, Kennedy embarked on a political trip through Texas. While riding through the streets of Dallas in a motorcade on November 22nd, he was shot and killed. The Warren Commission later decided that he had been assassinated by Lee Harvey Oswald.

Career: US House of Representatives, 1947–53; US Senate, 1953–61; president, 1961–63. *See also* Cuban Missile Crisis; Peace Corps; Vietnam War; Warren Commission. △1358, 1390.

Kennedy, Joseph Patrick (1888–1969), US businessman and public official, b. Boston. He worked his way up in the business world and made a fortune in the stock market of the 1920s and in motion pictures. He was appointed chairman of the Securities and Exchange Commission (1934–35) and later ambassador to Great Britain (1937–40). After resigning that post he again became involved in business and many philanthropic endeavors, especially the Joseph P. Kennedy Memorial Foundation, founded for his son killed in World War II. He was father of John F. Kennedy, Robert F. Kennedy, and Edward M. Kennedy.

Kennedy, Robert Francis (1925–68), US lawyer and political leader, b. Brookline, Mass. He served as counsel to the Senate Permanent Subcommittee on Investigations, presided over by Sen. Joseph McCarthy. After managing the successful 1960 presidential campaign of his brother John, he became US attorney general (1961–64), a post in which he vigorously enforced civil rights laws and investigated corruption in organized labor. After his brother's assassination, he left the cabinet and was elected (1964) senator from New York. While a candidate for the Democratic presidential nomination, he was assassinated after a speech in Los Angeles in June 1968.

Kennelly, Arthur Edwin (1861–1939), US electrical engineer, b. England. In 1902, after Guglielmo Marconi's experiments with radio waves, Kennelly noticed that the waves could reach beyond the Earth's horizon. He suggested that they did this by bouncing off a layer of ions high in the atmosphere. Physicist Oliver Heaviside made a similar proposition, and the layers are called Kennelly-Heaviside layers.

Kenner, city in SE Louisiana, on Mississippi River; site of New Orleans International Airport. Industries: lumbering, woodworking, sheet metal. Founded 1855; inc. 1952. Pop. (1970) 29,858.

Kenny, (Sister) Elizabeth (1886–1952), Australian nurse. She became famous for her then unorthodox method of stimulating and reeducating muscles affected by infantile paralysis (polio), a method at first disapproved of by most physicians, but by the 1940s largely accepted, with nurses and physiotherapists being trained in her methods.

Kenosha, city and port of entry in SE Wisconsin, 35mi (56km) S of Milwaukee, on Lake Michigan; seat of Kenosha co; site of Wisconsin's first public school (1849), Carthage College (1846), and University of Wisconsin extension center. Industries: automobiles, clothing, brass and copper products, truck farming, electronic equipment, tourism. Settled 1835; inc. 1850. Pop. (1970) 78,805.

Kent, county in extreme SE England, S of the Thames estuary and NW of the Straits of Dover; capital is Maidstone. Romans landed here 1st century BC; it was the first kingdom of Anglo-Saxon Heptarchy; converted to Roman Christianity by Augustine, Archbishop of Canterbury, 597; remained a subkingdom until 9th century. The Medway and Stour rivers drain Kent; apart from the North Downs, the county is low-lying, with Romney Marsh (renowned for sheep) in the SE; site of numerous castles, notably the 15th-century Dover castle, 11th–15th-century Canterbury Cathedral, 11th-century Rochester Cathedral, chapel (*c.* AD 350, reputedly the earliest place of Christian worship in England), 7th-century King's School. Crops: hops, fruits, vegetables, cereals. Industries: paper, pottery, iron, shipbuilding, brewing. Area: 1,443sq mi (3,737sq km).

Kent, city in NE Ohio, on Cuyahoga River, 8mi (13km) ENE of Akron; site of Kent State University (1910). Industries: mail trucks, furniture, air compressors. Settled 1805 as Franklin Mills; inc. as village of Kent 1867, as city 1920. Pop. (1970) 28,183.

Kent, Kingdom of, SE division of Anglo-Saxon Britain, settled by the Jutes under Hengist (*c.* 450). Culturally distinct from its Saxon and Mercian neighbors, Kent remained a separate kingdom until the West Saxon conquest (825).

Kentucky, state in the E central United States. A border State between North and South, Kentucky remained neutral in the Civil War.

Land and Economy. The land is generally rolling except in the SE, where the Pine and Cumberland mts dominate a rugged plateau. The Ohio River forms the N boundary and the Mississippi the W. The Kentucky and Tennessee rivers are the largest in the state. About 40% of the land is forested. The rich agricultural region is mostly in the center. Grasslands provide pasturage for cattle and for horses, for which Kentucky is famous. Manufacturing, expanding since WWII, is in the larger towns. Mining and oil drilling are concentrated in the SE.

People. Kentucky was first settled by English, Scots, Irish, and German immigrants from Virginia, North and South Carolina, and Pennsylvania; as large plantations developed, slaves were brought in. All these elements are present in the population, which has retained a rural character to a large degree. Slightly more than 50% reside in urban areas.

Education. There are about 40 institutions of higher education.

History. The region was the first W of the Allegheny Mts to be colonized. In the 1770s, the frontiersman Daniel Boone blazed the Wilderness Road from Virginia and North Carolina through Cumberland Gap in the SE corner of Kentucky. Thousands of settlers followed this route, while others came down the Ohio River. After a period of war with the Indians and dispute over land rights, Kentucky was admitted to the Union in 1792. At the outbreak of the Civil War, the state's loyalties were divided. Kentuckians fought in both Union and Confederate armies, and the state was invaded by both. After the war, Kentucky prospered; industry gradually became important in its economy.

PROFILE

Admitted to Union: June 1, 1792; rank, 15th
US Congressmen: Senate, 2; House of Representatives, 7
Population: 3,219,311 (1970); rank, 23d
Capital: Frankfort, 21,902 (1970)
Chief cities: Louisville, 361,706; Lexington, 108,137; Covington, 52,535
State legislature: Senate, 38; House of Representatives, 100
Area: 40,395sq mi (104,623sq km); rank, 37th
Elevation: Highest, 4,150ft (1,266m), Big Black Mt, Harlan Co. Lowest, 540ft (165m), Ohio River
Industries (major products): processed foods; tobacco products, machinery, chemicals
Agriculture (major products): tobacco, corn, soybeans, dairy cattle, hogs, fruit
Minerals (major): coal, petroleum, natural gas, fluorspar, stone, sand, gravel
State nickname: Blue Grass State
State motto: "United We Stand, Divided We Fall"
State bird: Kentucky cardinal
State flower: goldenrod
State tree: tulip tree

Kentucky and Virginia Resolutions (1798 and 1799), first important declarations of states' rights. Written by Thomas Jefferson (Kentucky Resolutions) and James Madison (Virginia Resolutions), they expressed opposition to the Alien and Sedition Acts. These resolutions stated that the federal government had no right to exercise powers not granted it by the Constitution and that states had the right to judge the constitutionality of any federal acts.

Kentucky River, river in Kentucky; formed in N central Kentucky by joining of North and Middle forks, flows NW to Ohio River at Carrollton; navigable by use of locks. During pioneering days was main means of entry into region. Boonesboro on the river is built on site of fort built by Daniel Boone (1775). Frankfort, state capital, is also on river. Length: 259mi (417km).

Kenya, independent nation in E Africa. The largest tea producer in Africa, it includes the city of Nairobi, the E African commercial center.

Land and economy. Located on the E coast of Africa, Kenya is bordered by Ethiopia and Sudan (N), Tanzania (S), Uganda and Lake Victoria (W), and Somalia and the Indian Ocean (E). The N 60% of the country is arid. The Great Rift Valley, 30–40mi (48–64km) wide, includes Mt Kenya, 17,040ft (5,197m), and the high plateaus, 3,000–10,000ft (915–3,050m) above sea level, containing some of Africa's most fertile land. About 85% of the population lives in the S 40% of Kenya. A program of resettlement has been moving subsistence African farmers from tribal reserves onto lands purchased from Europeans. The largest producer of tea in Africa, 90% of its exports is agricultural. Nairobi is the commercial center for East Africa. Tourism (safaris) is important to the economy.

People. Kenya's ethnic origins are divided between Kikuyu (20%), Luo (14%), Baluhya (13%), Kamba (11%), Kisli (6%), and Meru (5%). Among non-Africans 31% are Asians, Europeans, and Arabs. Religious estimates include Protestants (37%), Roman Catholics (22%), Muslims (3%). Africans are mainly subsistence farmers, Asians are in commerce, and the Europeans are large farmers, businessmen, and professionals. Overall literacy is estimated at 25%.

Government. An elected National Assembly elects the president, who is chief of state and commander of the armed forces in a strong central government.

History. Movements from the coast inland brought groups of African, Cushite, Bantu, and Nilotic-speaking people into what is now Kenya. Britain and Germany divided its trade and territory until 1920, when it became a protectorate of the United Kingdom. The first African participation in government came in 1957 with a restricted direct vote. From 1952–59 terrorist Mau Mau rebellions against Britain wracked the country. Independence within the Commonwealth of Nations came on Dec. 12, 1963, when the Kenya African National Union party formed a government headed by Jomo Kenyatta. Protests against Kenyatta's increasingly autocratic rule were repressed in the mid-1970s.

PROFILE

Official name: Republic of Kenya
Area: 224,960sq mi (582,646sq km)
Population: 13,300,000
Density: 59per sq mi (23per sq km)
Chief cities: Nairobi (capital); Mombasa, 255,400
Government: Elected National Assembly elects chief of state
Religion: Animist, Christian
Language: English (official), Swahili (national)
Monetary unit: Kenya shilling
Gross national product: $2,500,000,000
Per capita income: $172
Industries: bark extracts, hides, dairy products, construction materials, petroleum products
Agriculture: coffee, tea, cereals, cotton, sisal, cattle, forests, corn, fruits

Kenyatta, Jomo (1893?–), president of Kenya. He entered politics in defense of his own Kikuyu tribe and of black African rights. He was imprisoned (1953) for Mau Mau terrorism and exiled but was then elected president of the Kenya African National Union (1960). He helped gain Kenya's independence from Britain in 1963, and became president in 1964. He suppressed opposition and outlawed opposition political parties (1969).

Kenzo Tange. △1320.

Kepler, Johannes (1571–1630), German astronomer. He became Tycho Brahe's assistant (1600) and, after Tycho's death, used his master's extremely accurate observational data to deduce three laws of planetary motion, especially the statement that planets move in elliptical orbits around the sun. Kepler's work was a vindication of Copernicus and a foundation for Isaac Newton's work. △38,1160.

Keratin, a fibrous protein present in large amounts in the superficial cells of the skin where it serves as a protective layer; also in hair, wool, and horns. △686.

Keratomalacia. △696.

Kerensky, Aleksandr F(eodorovich) (1881–1970), Russian political figure, head of the provisional government (July–November 1917). Elected to the Duma (legislature) as a moderate socialist in 1912, he became prime minister in July 1917, shortly after the overthrow of the tsar (March 1917). He suppressed Kornilov's uprising but had to flee after the Bolshevik Revolution (November 1917). He wrote several accounts of this period. △1306, 1310.

Kérkira. *See* Corfu.

Kern, Jerome (David) (1885–1945), US composer of musical comedies, b. New York City. *Sally* (1920) contained the song "Look for the Silver Lining" and *Roberta* (1933), with Otto Harbach, introduced "Smoke Gets in your Eyes." His greatest musical play is considered to be *Showboat* (1927), in collaboration with Oscar Hammerstein. △1428.

Kerosene, a distilled petroleum product heavier than gasoline and lighter than diesel fuel. Kerosene, known historically as an illuminant, is now used in camping stoves, tractor fuels, and turbine fuels for jet and turboprop aircraft.

Kerouac, Jack (1922–69), US author, b. Lowell, Mass. A poet and novelist, his novel *On the Road* (1957) is considered a preeminent work of the Beat Generation. He also wrote *Dharma Bums* (1958). *See also* Beat Generation.

Kerr-Mills Act (1960), amendment to the Social Security Act that was a forerunner of the 1965 Medicaid program. The 1960 act provided for supplementary aid to the elderly poor who were not qualified for aid under the Social Security public assistance program. The bill arranged for increased payments to be made through the existing program and through a new program (Medical Assistance to the Aged), funded mainly by the federal government with some state participation.

Kerry Blue Terrier, all-round working dog (terrier group) bred in Co. Kerry, Ireland, as Irish blue terrier. A long-lived breed, the Kerry blue has a long head with face whiskers; V-shaped, folded ears; a short, straight back; powerful, long legs; and a long tail. The soft, dense coat is wavy and trimmed for show; color is any shade of blue-gray or gray-blue. Standard size: 17–19.5in (43–50cm) high at shoulder; 30–40lb (13.5–18kg). *See also* Terrier.

Kesey, Ken (1935–), US author, b. La Junta, Colo. A novelist, he wrote *One Flew Over the Cuckoo's Nest* (1962) about inmates of an insane asylum. It was made into a successful play and film. Another novel by Kesey is *Sometimes a Great Notion* (1964).

Kesselring, Albert (1887–1960), German general. Air chief of staff from 1936, he commanded air operations in the early years of World War II. He became supreme commander in Italy (1943) and of the western front (1945). Convicted as a war criminal, he served only five years of a life sentence before release.

Kestrel, or windhover, small falcon of Europe, Asia, North America, and Africa that hovers over its prey—usually rodents, insects, or small birds—before attacking. Length: 12in (30cm). Species *Falco tinnunculus.*

Ketchikan, town in SE Alaska, on SW coast of Revillagigedo Island; center of salmon and halibut fishing. Industries: pulp, fishing, tourism, timber, fur, uranium mining. Pop. (1970) 6,994.

Ketone, group of organic substances containing a carbonyl group (C:O) and having the general formula R'.C:O.R", where R' and R" are univalent hydrocarbon radicals. The simplest member of the group is acetone, dimethyl ketone (CH_3COCH_3).

Ketone Bodies, the three chemical compounds acetoacetic acid, hydroxybutyric acid, and acetone. When present in the blood in high concentrations, they lead to lowered pH. Occurs in starvation, diabetes mellitus, and low-carbohydrate, high-fat diet.

Kettering, city in SW Ohio, S of Dayton; site of Kettering College of Medical Arts (1967). Industries: electric motors, precision tools, building materials. Founded 1796. Inc. as Van Buren township 1841; inc. as village and renamed 1952; inc. as city 1955. Pop. (1970) 71,864.

Kettledrums. *See* Timpani.

Key, Francis Scott (1779–1843), US poet, b. Carrol co, Md. He wrote the US national anthem, "The Star Spangled Banner," while watching the shelling of Ft McHenry (1814) as a prisoner on a British ship in Chesapeake Bay. The anthem first appeared anonymously as a poem, "In Defense of Fort M'Henry." It was adopted as the national anthem by Congress in 1931. △1428.

Keyishian v. Board of Regents (1967), US Supreme Court case overruling *Adler* v. *Board of Education* and striking down a series of state laws allowing removal of public employees on grounds of disloyalty. The court found such laws vague and overly broad in scope.

Keynes, John Maynard (1883–1946), English economist. He first came to prominence with *Economic Consequences of the Peace* (1919), which criticized the inequitable, unworkable economic provisions of the Versailles Treaty. *Treatise on Money* (1930) presented the theory of return on capital and the theory of the demand for money and analyzed the relationship between saving and investment. *The General Theory of Employment, Interest, and Money* (1936) was profoundly influenced by the Great Depression. In it, Keynes established the foundation of modern macroeconomics. He advocated governmental economic planning and the active intervention of government in the economy to stimulate employment and prosperity. △938, 1324.

Key West, southernmost city of the continental United States, in SW corner of Florida, on Key West Island, seat of Monroe co. Less than 4mi (6km) long and 2mi (3km) wide; site of US Navy station. Industries: commercial fishing, cigar making. Est. 1822; inc. 1828. Pop. (1970) 29,312.

KGB, committee of state security of the USSR; regulates both the secret and regular police force and the detention (labor) camps in the Soviet Union. Although the KGB and its antecedents (NKVD, NKGB) had a history of almost autonomous control through systematic terrorism over the state security apparatus, the KGB has, since the late 1950s, been subordinate to Communist party control and concerns itself mainly with internal intelligence.

Khabarovsk (Chabarovsk), city in southeastern USSR, on Amur River; capital of Khabarovsk Kraj, served as capital of Soviet Far East 1926–38. Industries: oil refining, shipbuilding, trucks, aircraft, machine tools. Founded 1858 as a tsarist fortress. Pop. 462,000.

Khalid ibn Abd al-Aziz al-Saud (1912–), king of Saudi Arabia (1975–). In 1962 he was appointed first deputy prime minister and was crown prince (1965–75). On March 25, 1975, a few hours after his half brother King Faisal's assassination, he was chosen king of Saudi Arabia. Although king, he retained his duties as prime minister. Extremely popular with the people, he continued most of Faisal's policies.

Khatchaturian, Aram (1903–), Soviet composer whose works often contain elements of Armenian folk music. His works include several concertos and three popular ballets, *Gayane* (1942), *Masquerade* (1944), and *Spartacus* (1953). *Gayane* contains the well-known "Saber Dance." △1364.

Khalkas, people who constitute 75% of the population of the Mongolian Peoples Republic. Traditionally nomadic pastoralists, they have to some extent been

John Kennedy

Kentucky: Kentucky Derby

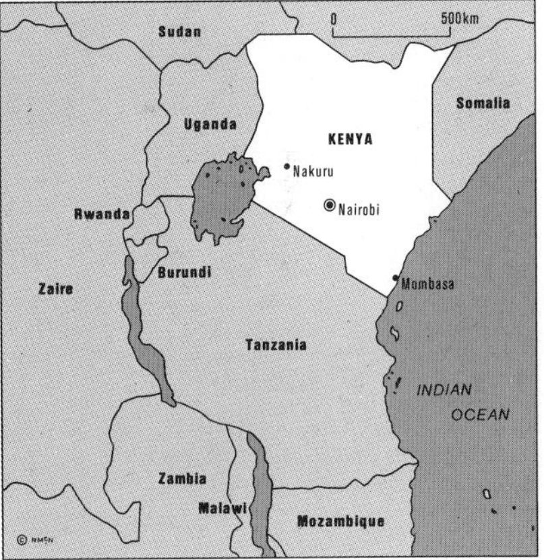
Sudan
0
500km
Somalia
Uganda
KENYA
Nakuru
Nairobi
Rwanda
Zaire
Burundi
Mombasa
Tanzania
INDIAN
OCEAN
Zambia
Malawi
Mozambique

Kenya

Francis Scott Key

settled by the Soviet attempts to develop collective farms.

Khalkidhikí. *See* Chalcidice.

Khalkis. *See* Chalcis.

Khania (Canea), port town in NW Crete, Greece, on Gulf of Khania; taken by Ottoman Empire 1646; served as capital of Crete from 1841 to mid-20th century; heavily damaged during German invasion 1941. Exports: wines, citrus fruits, olives. Pop. 40,564.

Kharkov (Char 'Kov), city in Ukrainian republic, USSR, 400mi (644km) SW of Moscow, at the confluence of the Kharkov, Lopan, and Udy rivers; capital of Kharkov oblast. In 17th century city served as stronghold of Ukrainian Cossacks in defending Russia's S border; served as capital of Ukraine 1921–34; site of Cathedral of Protectoress (1686), Cathedral of the Assumption (1771), and a university (1805). Industries: food and tobacco processing, chemicals, printing. Founded 1656. Pop. 1,223,000.

Khartoum (Al-Khurtum), capital of Sudan, at junction of the Blue Nile and White Nile rivers; capital of Khartoum prov.; commercial and transportation center. City was founded 1820s by Mohammed Ali; besieged by Mahdists in 1885; occupied and rebuilt by British Gen. Horatio Kitchener 1898; named seat of government in 1956 when Sudan became independent; site of governor-general's palace, several churches and cathedrals, Kitchener School of Medicine (1924), University of Khartoum (1956), Gordon Memorial College (1903). Industries: cement, gum arabic, chemicals, cotton textiles. Pop. 261,840.

Khazars, Turkic people who first appeared in the lower Volga River region around the 2nd century AD. They allied themselves with the Byzantine Empire in fighting the Persians (610–41). Between the 8th and 10th centuries their empire extended from north of the Black Sea to the Urals and from west of the Caspian Sea to the Dnieper River. From 737 their capital was Itil. They conquered the Volga Bulgars, taxed the eastern Slavs, and fought against the Arabs, Persians, and Armenians. In the 8th century, their ruling class was converted to Judaism by exiles from Constantinople. In 965 their empire was destroyed by the army of Sviatoslav, duke of Kiev. Some scholars believe that they are the progenitors of many Eastern European Jews.

Khepri, or **Khepera.** △838.

Kherson (Cherson), seaport city in Ukrainian SSR, USSR, on Dnieper River near its mouth on Black Sea; capital of Kherson oblast. Founded 1778 by Grigori Potemkin as a naval station, shipbuilding center, and fortress (still standing), it is site of 18th-century cathedral containing Potemkin's tomb. Industries: cotton textiles, shipbuilding, food processing. Pop. 261,000.

Khios. *See* Chios.

Khirbat Qumran (Qumran), ancient village in NW Jordan, on NW shore of the Dead Sea. In 1947 Dead Sea Scrolls (writings of a Jewish sect that lived here *c.* 100 BC–AD 68) were found in nearby caves. Romans destroyed village AD 68 and est. a fortress. Land was taken by Israelis in 1967 Arab-Israeli War.

Khmer Empire. *See* Cambodia. △1114.

Khmer Rouge, name given to the Communist National United Front, the ruling power of Cambodia since April 1975. After the overthrow in 1970 of the neutralist Sihanouk government, in which the Communist's had participated, the Khmer Rouge turned to armed conflict in its ultimately successful bid for power. In April 1976 Khieu Samphan was named chief of state and Tol Saut premier. △1378.

Khmers, or Cambodians, people of mixed Mongoloid/Australoid racial background who constitute 90% of the population of Cambodia; they also live in Thailand and the Mekong delta region of Vietnam. Traditionally agriculturalists cultivating rice and practicing weaving and metalwork, the Khmers are mainly Theravada Buddhists.

Khoikhoi. *See* Hottentot.

Khoisan, a group of Afro-African languages of South Africa. Hottentots (Khoi, in their tongue) and Bushmen (San) are the two largest groups of native speakers. Sandawe and Hatsa of Tanzania are also Khoisan. All are characteristically click-languages.

Khorana, Gobind (*c.* 1922–), US biochemist, b. India. He shared the 1968 Nobel Prize in physiology or medicine for his part in discoveries about how genes determine cell function. Khorana established how the genetic code should be read—in nonoverlapping triplets in sequence with no gaps.

Khrushchev, Nikita Sergeevich (1894–1971), Soviet political figure, first secretary of the Communist party (1953–64) and head of the Soviet government (1958–64). He joined the party in 1918 and was elected to the central committee in 1934. Noted for economic success and ruthless suppression of opposition in the Ukraine, where he was secretary of the Communist party, he was elected to the Politburo in 1939. He denounced Stalin (died 1953) in a spectacular speech to the Twentieth Party Congress, expelled his staunchest backers from the central committee, and became premier in 1958. Favoring détente with the West, he yielded to US President Kennedy in the Cuban missile crisis (1962). This development, economic setbacks, and trouble with China led to his ouster by Brezhnev and Kosygin in 1964. He was noted for his folksy and irascible qualities. △1312, 1344.

Khufu or **Cheops,** ancient Egyptian king (*c.* 2900–2877 BC), founder of the IV dynasty. He built temples and the Great Pyramid of Khufu at Giza near Cairo.

Khyber Pass, major pass from central Asia to Pakistan, through Safed Koh mountain range; used for centuries by invaders, merchants, migrating peoples; connects the Kabul River Valley in Afghanistan (W) with Peshawar, Pakistan (E). A modern strategic military road, it was scene of intense fighting during Afghan Wars 1839–42 and 1878–80; site of two former British outposts, Ali Masjid and Landi Kotal. Elevation: 3,500ft (1,068m). Length: approx. 30mi (49km).

Kiang, wild Asian ass found in mountains of Tibet and Sikkim up to 18,000ft (5490m). The most numerous wild ass, it is red and white in summer and dun colored in winter. Height: 59in (150cm) at shoulder. Family Equidae; species *Equus hemionus kiang. See also* Ass. △608.

Kiangsi (Jiangxi), province in SE China; capital is Nan-ch'ang; mostly mountainous terrain; fertile regions are drained by the Kan River. Originally known as Kan, under Chou dynasty (772–481 BC), ruled by dynasties of Western Chin, Southern Sung, and T'ang, until passed to Manchu rule 1650. Products: rice, wheat, beans, sweet potatoes, citrus fruits, tobacco, sugarcane, cotton, peanuts. Industries: lumbering, fishing, porcelain, silk, mining of tungsten, coal, uranium. Exports: bamboo, varnish, turpentine, fish. Area: approx. 66,000sq mi (170,940sq km). Pop. 22,000,000.

Kiangsu, province in E China; capital is Nanking; one of China's smallest and densely populated regions; an extremely fertile region, it contains the Yangtze River delta and is also highly industrialized; site of Shanghai, chief manufacturing city of China. Under Ming dynasty (1368–1644) became a separate province 1667; taken by Japan 1937; freed by Chinese Nationalists 1945; and taken by Communists 1949. Products: rice, cotton, wheat, barley, soybean, peanuts, tea, sugar cane. Industries: silk, fertilizer, textiles, food processing, cement. Area: approx. 41,000sq mi (106,190sq km). Pop. 47,000,000.

Kibbutz. △1360.

Kickapoo, major tribe of North American Indians of Algonquian linguistic stock, originally occupying south-central Wisconsin. They are closely related to Fox and Sauk. In 1852 part of the tribe went to Texas, and on into Mexico, where many of their descendants still inhabit a reservation area in Chihuahua. Eventually most of the Kickapoo moved to Oklahoma, where some 1,500 now live.

Kid, Thomas. *See* Kyd, Thomas.

Kidd, William (*c.*1645–1701), pirate, also known as "Captain Kidd." A sea captain, he began his career as a privateer for the British against the French and pirates in the West Indies. Sailing to London, he was commissioned in 1695 to continue these actions in the Madagascar area. However, when he reached Madagascar he turned pirate himself, prompted in part by the lack of French booty. He eventually abandoned ship and went to New England to exonerate himself. He was sent to England, tried for murder and piracy, and hanged.

Kidney, either of a pair of excretory organs that extract water and waste from the blood, producing the secretion urine that is discharged from the body. Lying in the small of the back, the kidneys are fist-sized and bean-shaped. Each kidney is made up of about 1,000,000 highly specialized tubules, known as nephrons. The upper end of each nephron is saclike (Bowman's capsule) and contains numerous specialized capillaries, the glomeruli, that filter the blood entering through tiny branches of the renal artery. The filtered fluid passes through other portions of the convoluted and straight tubule, where further action takes place. Eventually the "cleaned" blood reenters the circulatory system through the renal vein. The waste-containing fluid, urine, is passed into the ureter, which carries it to the bladder. The amount of fluid passing through the glomerulus filter daily is some 190 quarts (180 liters), but much of the fluid is reabsorbed before urine is formed. △694.

Kidney, Artificial, a device used therapeutically to remove waste products from the blood in cases of kidney malfunction. The blood is shunted through this mechanism, which, by way of a series of semipermeable membranes, substitutes for the normal kidney in filtering the blood. The process is called artificial dialysis. *See also* Dialysis; Kidney. △728.

Kidney Stones (renal calculi), small, hard, pebblelike masses composed largely of mineral salts and formed in the kidney. Passage of a stone through the tube leading from the kidney to the bladder causes excruciating pain. △728.

Kidney Transplant. *See* Organ Transplant.

Kidron, valley in Jordan, occupied by Israel, from 1967; source of Kidron Brook, which flows E to separate Jerusalem from the Mount of Olives and empties into the Dead Sea; the biblical reference to the valley of Jehoshaphat, traditionally located in the N section of Kidron Valley, is said to have been a place of judgement (Joel: 3).

Kiel, seaport city in West Germany, 40mi (64km) NW of Lubeck on Kiel Bay; capital of Schleswig-Holstein state; joined Hanseatic League 1284; ceded to Denmark 1773, to Prussia 1866; scene of sailors' mutiny that began German revolution (1918); site of university (1665), dairying research institute, 13th-century castle where Tsar Peter III was born. Industries: shipyards, textiles, processed food, printed materials. Chartered 1242. Pop. 271,719.

Kiel, Treaty of (Jan. 14, 1814), dissolved the union of Norway and Denmark that had begun in 1380. After Napoleon's defeat at Leipzig, Swedish Crown Prince Charles (Bernadotte) invaded Denmark. As a result, in the Treaty of Kiel, Frederick VI ceded Norway to Sweden. Sweden gave up Western Pomerania and Rügen to Denmark.

Kiel Canal (Nord-Ostsee Kanal), man-made waterway in N West Germany, connecting North Sea with Baltic Sea. Built to facilitate movement of German Fleet 1887–95, in 1905–14 it was widened and deepened for use by ocean-going vessels; declared an international waterway by Treaty of Versailles (1919), an act that was repudiated by Adolf Hitler; it was restored for international traffic following WWII. Length: 61mi (98km).

Kierkegaard, Sören (1813–55), Danish philosopher. His writings fall into three periods, the aesthetic, the ethical, and the religious. The founder of Christian existentialism, he believed that his God is known only by a "leap of faith," which also is a leap into the eternal and the irrational. Only the immediacy of personal experience confers reality. His fierce independence and defiance of authority made his life painful and lonely. His main works are *Either/Or* (1843), *Fear and Trembling* (1843), *Stages on Life's Way* (1845), and *Concluding Unscientific Postscript* (1846). *See also* Existentialism. △856.

Kiev, city and port in Ukrainian SSR, USSR, on E bank of Dnieper River, 470mi (757km) SW of Moscow; capital of Ukrainian SSR and Kiev oblast; 3rd-largest city of USSR. City was part of Lithuania 14th century, Poland 16th century, taken by Russia 1686; served as capital of independent Ukrainian Republic 1918–19; taken by Bolsheviks 1920. In 1934 capital of Ukrainian SSR was moved from Kharkov to Kiev; site of cathedral of St Sophia (1037, USSR's oldest), monastery of St Michael (1108), Church of St Andrew (1753), university (1834). Industries: beet sugar, flour, footwear, furniture, shipbuilding, machine tools. Founded before 5th century. Pop. 1,764,000. △1176.

Kigali, city in Rwanda, E of Lake Kivu; capital of Rwanda since 1962, when Rwanda gained its independence; the government began intensive economic expansion with hopes of attracting private industry; chief administrative and economic center; site of international airport, technical school. Industries: iron, tin, cotton, textiles. Pop. 60,000.

Kiklådhes. *See* Cyclades.

Kikuyu, Negroid people forming the dominant group in Kenya. Traditionally, they live by intensive cultivation; crops include millet and sorghum, with coffee and corn as cash crops. Their patrilineal, egalitarian society is based around the village community, organized into age groups with initiation ceremonies as each individual qualifies for a new group. The Mau Mau rebellion against British rule in 1952–56 was organized by the Kikuyu.

Kilimanjaro, Mount, mountain in NE Tanzania; highest mountain in Africa, near the Kenya border; site of peaks Kibo, 19,340ft (5,899m) and Mawenzi 16,896ft (5,153m), joined by a broad saddle. Well-developed S slope produces coffee and sisal. Kibo was first climbed in 1889, Mawenzi in 1912.

Killdeer, noisy, ploverlike shore bird of North American meadows known for its *kill-dee* alarm call and distraction displays. It is white with a double black breast ring and chestnut rump and tail. It lays marked eggs (4) in a scrape nest. Species *Charadrius vociferus.*

Killeen, city in central Texas, 60mi (97km) N of Austin; site of Central Texas College (1967), Fort Hood, and Gray Air Base. Industries: concrete products, cotton, corn, livestock. Settled 1882; inc. 1908. Pop. (1970) 35,507.

Killer Whale, toothed whale inhabiting all oceans, especially those in colder regions. A fierce predator of large animals, it is black above and white below and distinguished by a white patch above each eye and a long erect dorsal fin. Length: 30ft (9m). Species *Orcinus orca.* △552.

Killifish, or **Killie,** freshwater fish also found in brackish coastal marshes of America. A hardy topminnow popular with aquarists, it is used to control mosquitoes. Length: 1.5–6in (3.8–15.2cm). Family Cyprinodontidae; species: 300, including common *Fundulus heteroclitus.*

Kilmer, (Alfred) Joyce (1886–1918), US poet and critic, remembered chiefly for one poem, "Trees" (1913), b. New Brunswick, N.J. At the time of his death in World War I, his poetry was beginning to show greater quality.

Kiln, in ceramics, an oven for firing ware. Early kilns were holes in the ground into which the ware was placed. A wood pyre was built over it. Later, special wood and coal oven-type kilns were built. Today, most kilns are electrically or gas fueled. Commercial kilns are continuous, the most successful being tunnel kilns. Here, ware is conveyed slowly from a comparatively cool region at the entrance to the full heat in the center. As it nears the exit, it cools gradually.

Kilogram, unit of mass (symbol kg) defined as the mass of the international prototype cylinder of platinum-iridium kept in Paris. 1 kilogram is equal to 2.20462 pounds. *See also* Physical Units.

Kilowatt Hour, unit of electrical energy equal to the energy used when a power of one kilowatt (1000 watts) is expended for one hour. It is the unit for which domestic and industrial users of electricity are charged. △1650.

Kimberley, city in Republic of South Africa, 60mi (97km) ENE of Nelson; Cecil Rhodes took control of Kimberley diamond fields 1888; it was besieged for four months during Boer War 1899. The world's diamond center, the land is marked by deep pits, the result of extensive diamond mining. Industries: diamond mining, cutting, polishing; processing of lime, gypsum, iron, manganese, asbestos. Pop. 105,000.

Kimberlite. △244.

Kim Il Sung (1912–), chief of state of the Democratic People's Republic of Korea (North Korea) and chairman of its Korean Workers' party from 1948, b. Kim Sung Chu. He joined the Korean Communist party in 1931. He led guerrilla fighting against the occupying Japanese in the 1930s and a Korean unit in the Soviet army in World War II. In 1950 he led a North Korean invasion of South Korea that precipitated the Korean War (1950–53).

Kinesthetic Sense, or proprioception, internal sense that conveys information from the muscles and tendons of the body. Specialized receptors connect to a nervous system tract that provides information about the contraction and expansion of muscles. This sense is also called the position sense because it allows humans to know the position of their limbs without reference to vision, giving them a sense of "feeling."

Kinetic Art, term used to describe art, especially sculpture, in which an element of motion is present. Early kinetic art included mobile sculpture by Duchamp, Calder, and Gabo, as well as Moholy-Nagy's light machine of 1930. Sometimes kinetic sculpture is designed so that the parts can be completely rearranged, as in Kobashi's art. Ultvedt's sculptures are driven by electric motors with gears, cranks, and levers, and Tinguely's sculptures are often driven by water. Kinetic painting includes op art. △1372.

Kinetic Energy, energy of motion. A body of mass m and speed v has a kinetic energy of $\frac{1}{2}mv^2$. *See also* Energy; Potential Energy. △1986.

Kinetics, Chemical. *See* Chemical Kinetics.

Kinetic Theory. In the kinetic theory, temperature is a measure of the number of energy states available to the atoms of a system. Heat is a measure of the amount of energy that the system gains or loses as a result of a temperature change. Two materials at the same temperature may be very different potential sources of heat; this difference is measured by a characteristic called heat capacity, or specific heat. *See also* Thermodynamics. △1486, 1508.

Kinetoscope. △1788.

King, Billie Jean Moffit (1943–), US tennis player, b. Long Beach, Calif. She won in the US (1967; 1971–72; 1974), British (1966–68; 1972–73; 1975), Australian (1968), and French (1972) singles championships. An outspoken advocate of sports equality for women, she heightened interest in women's tennis with her 1973 victory over male star Bobby Riggs.

King, Martin Luther, Jr. (1929–68), US clergyman and civil rights leader, b. Atlanta, Ga. Pastor of a Baptist church in Montgomery, Ala., in 1955 he led the black boycott of Montgomery's segregated transport system; when it was successful, he and the passive resistance tactics he advocated attracted national attention. Thereafter he founded and worked through the Southern Christian Leadership Conference to further desegregation nationally. He organized the massive March on Washington in 1963, opposed the Vietnam War, and had begun a national campaign against poverty when he was assassinated in Memphis, Tenn., April 4, 1968. In 1964 he was awarded the Nobel Peace Prize. △1358.

King, Rufus (1755–1827), US statesman, b. Scarborough, Maine. As a member of the Continental Congress (1784–87), he introduced legislation calling for a constitution and prohibiting slavery in the Northwest Territory. He then helped to draft and pass the federal Constitution. He moved to New York in 1788. He served as a US Senator (1789–96; 1813–25) and as ambassador to Great Britain (1796–1803; 1825–26). He was an unsuccessful presidential candidate (1816).

King, William Lyon Mackenzie (1874–1950), prime minister of Canada (1921–30; 1935–48). A lawyer and social worker, King was a successful labor mediator before entering politics. His career was marked by the drive for national unity, concessions to the Progressives, and support of French-Canadian rights. Trained by Sir Wilfred Laurier, King led the Liberals (1919–48). He was more interested in foreign policy than social legislation and a firm supporter of free enterprise.

Kingbird, or tyrant flycatcher, aggressive New World flycatcher, centered in tropical America, that dives at intruders and snaps up insects. The eastern kingbird *(Tyrannus tyrannus)* is black with a white belly, white-tipped tail, and red crest. It lays brown-flecked, white eggs (4–5) in a cup-shaped nest. It grows to 6.8in (17cm).

King Cobra. *See* Cobra.

Kingfish, or whiting, marine food fish found in Atlantic, it is metallic silver with dark bar markings. Length: to 17in (43.1cm); weight: 2–3lb (0.9–1.4kg). Family Sciaenidae; species include Atlantic Northern *Menticirrhus saxatilis.* △516.

Kingfisher, compact, highly colored birds that have straight sharp bills and dive for fish along the rivers, streams, and lakes where they live. They swallow the fish head first when back on their perch. They nest in a deep, horizontal hole in a soil bank, laying white eggs in a filthy nest. The young form a circle and rotate to receive food brought by the parent. Wood kingfishers have flattened, hook-tipped bills and live

Mount Kilimanjaro

Billie Jean King

Martin Luther King

Kingfisher

in forests feeding on land animals, large invertebrates, small frogs, and snakes. They drill a nest in a tree or soil bank. Length: 5–18in (13–46cm). Family Alcedinidae.

King George's War (1744–48), inconclusive struggle between France and Britain for control over North America. Both sides enlisted Indian aid in fighting over disputed boundaries in Nova Scotia, New England, and the Ohio Valley. By the Peace of Aix-la-Chapelle (1748) conquered territory was restored by mutual agreement.

King James Bible, the translation of the Bible ordered by King James I of England in 1604 and completed in 1611, also called the Authorized Version. Whether or not it was specifically authorized by the king for use in churches, the King James Version became the standard Bible in Anglican communion. Considered a masterpiece of translation, this Bible has had great influence on English literature. Several revisions of the King James text have been published, the Revised Version in the late 19th century and the Revised Standard Version (1946–57). *See also* Bible. △1148, 1152.

King John (*c.*1596), 5-act tragedy by William Shakespeare, based on an older drama from Raphael Holinshed's *Chronicles*. John, having seized the throne from Prince Arthur, prepares to defend himself against France and Austria, supporters of Arthur, but the marriage of his niece and the French dauphin brings a peaceful settlement. Excommunicated by the pope for disobedience, John is suspected of murdering Prince Arthur. His lords turn against him and join the dauphin and John is poisoned by monks. The dauphin and his army return to France and peace is restored.

King Lear (*c.*1605), 5-act tragedy by William Shakespeare based on an older anonymous play *King Leir* and Raphael Holinshed's *Chronicles*. Lear, king of Britain, divides his realm between his flattering daughters Goneril and Regan, leaving his youngest daughter Cordelia, who loves him, with nothing. When his older daughters turn him out, Cordelia joins him in exile. When Cordelia is killed, Lear dies of grief. Goneril poisons Regan and kills herself; her husband, the duke of Albany, succeeds to the throne.

Kinglet, fearless, active songbird that breeds in cool areas of North America and Eurasia. They have a small crest that reveals a brightly colored spot when expanded; short, straight bill; and downlike plumage. They feed on insects. Both parents build a bulky, hanging nest for small white or buff spotted eggs (5–10) laid in tiny chambers. The female incubates the eggs and both parents feed the young. Length: 3–4in (7.6–10cm). Genus *Regulus*.

King Philip's War (1675–76), Indian war in New England. The Indian chief Philip (Metacomet) of the Wampanoags, who was friendly to the Plymouth Colony, believed increased colonization meant the destruction of the Indians. The war started over the murder of an Indian; 12 towns in central Massachusetts were destroyed in the conflict. The war ended when troops of the New England Confederation defeated the Narragansett Indians (1675) and the Nipmucks (1676) and killed Philip in Rhode Island (1676). *See also* New England Confederation.

Kings Canyon National Park, mountain wilderness in S central California, approx. 55mi (88km) E of Fresno; contains some of the highest peaks of the Sierra Nevada, thousands of giant sequoias and Kings River; named for surveyor Clarence King. Area: 708sq mi (1,834sq km).

King Snake, harmless, shiny snake found from central and S United States to Central America. Its color varies, being mostly black with white or yellow markings. It feeds on other snakes, including poisonous species. Length: to 50in (1.3m). Family Colubridae, genus *Lampropeltis*. *See also* Snake.

Kings I and II, biblical books, called Third and Fourth Kingdoms in the Greek Septuagint. These books recount the histories of Judah and Israel from the beginning of Solomon's reign (970 BC) through the fall of Judah and destruction of Jerusalem (586 BC). Having reference to previous historical accounts, the unknown author presents this material to suit his purpose, as a revelation of God's presence in the history of Israel.

Kingsport, city in NE Tennessee, 22mi (35km) NW of Johnson City, on Holston River. Industries: printing, paper, chemicals, plastic, glass, cement, flour milling, dairy products, bottling, sheet metal, leather. Settled 1761; inc. 1915. Pop. (1970) 31,938.

Kingston, city in Ontario, Canada, on Lake Ontario; Canada's capital 1841–44; site of Fort Frontenac and Fort Henry, built during War of 1812, Queen's University, Royal Military College, Roman Catholic bishoprics, cathedrals. Industries: textiles, aluminum products, synthetic yarns, ceramics, locomotive manufacture. Founded 1783 by United Empire Loyalists. Pop. 61,870.

Kingston, seaport city on SE coast of Jamaica, West Indies, in the Caribbean Sea; capital and commercial center of Jamaica with excellent harbor; site of University College of West Indies (1946), Royal Botanical Gardens, handcrafts market, Institute of Jamaica and museum. Founded 1692 after earthquake destroyed Port Royal, it became permanent capital 1872; was severely damaged in 1907 earthquake. Industries: tourism, food processing, oil refining, clothes, shoes. Exports: sugar, rum, molassas, bananas. Pop. 550,-100.

Kingston, city in SE New York, on Hudson River; seat of Ulster co; served briefly as capital of New York in 1777; burned by British October, 1777. Industries: clothing, marine and engineering equipment. Founded 1615 by Dutch as trading post; settled 1652; chartered as village of Wiltwyck 1658; taken by English 1667 and renamed; chartered as city 1872. Pop. (1970) 25,544.

Kingston-upon-Hull. *See* Hull.

Kingstown, capital and seaport in St Vincent, Windward Islands, in the West Indies, on SW coast at head of Kingstown Bay; site of botanical garden (1763); port of entry and tourist center. Exports: cotton, sugar cane, molasses, cacao, fruit. Pop. 17,258.

Kingsville, city in S Texas, 34mi (35km) SW of Corpus Christi; seat of Kleberg co; site of Texas Arts and Industries University (1917), and headquarters of 2,000-sq mi (5,180-sq km) King Ranch. Industries: cottonseed oil, butter, brooms. Exports: cattle, cotton, winter vegetables. Settled 1902; inc. as town 1911, as city 1916. Pop. (1970) 28,915.

Kingwana. *See* Swahili.

King William's War (1689–97), North American part of the war between England and France. Frontenac, French governor of Canada, sent expeditions against the New York, New Hampshire, and Maine frontiers. The English, under Sir William Phipps (of Massachusetts), sailed up the St Lawrence River to take Quebec, but failed (1690). Bloody border conflicts with the Indians also occurred. Port Royal, Nova Scotia, was captured and then lost by the English (1690–91).

Kinkajou, nocturnal foraging mammal of the raccoon family found in forests of Central and South America. Slender-bodied, it has a small round head and long tongue. Primarily a fruit and insect eater, it lives almost entirely in trees, aided by a long prehensile tail. The soft woolly fur is tawny-yellow to brown. Length: to 22.5in (572mm); weight: to 5.5lb (2.5kg). Family Procyonidae; species *Potos flavus*.

Kinsey, Alfred C. (1894–1956), US zoologist, b. Hoboken, N.J., noted for his studies on human sexual behavior. He was a professor of zoology and later director of the Institute for Sex Research, Indiana State University. He is best known for his publications *Sexual Behavior in the Human Male* (1948) and *Sexual Behavior in the Human Female* (1953) based on thousands of personal interviews.

Kinshasa, formerly **Léopoldville,** capital and largest city of Zaire, on border of Zaire and Republic of Congo; port on Stanley Pool of Congo River; transportation hub. In 1926 it replaced Boma as the capital of the Belgian Congo; when Zaire gained its independence (1960), it continued as the capital of the new country; in 1966 name was changed from Leopoldville. Industries: food processing, brewing, tanning, chemicals, textiles. Founded 1881 by Henry Stanley and named Leopoldville for his sponsor, Belgian King Leopold II. Pop. 1,323,039.

Kinship, system standing for a complex of rules in a society governing descent, succession, inheritance, marriage, residence, and sexual relations. Kinship terms do not stand for blood relations but are culture-specific: two people are kinsmen if they are consanguinally related, although kinship is often extended to cover relations of affinity as well. *See also* Clan; Endogamy; Exogamy; Family; Incest Taboo; Nuclear Family. △876, 880–82.

Kiowa, major tribe of Tanoan-speaking North American Indians who moved from their earlier Yellowstone–Missouri River homeland into the southern Plains region, where they eventually allied with the Comanche and Arapaho. With these tribes they became one of the widest-ranging peoples of the western United States, raiding as far south as northern Mexico. Today about 330 Kiowa live in the Anadarko area of Oklahoma.

Kiowa Apache, North American Indian tribe that split from the parent Apache group several centuries ago, migrating south onto the Plains from the British Columbia-Montana region. They integrated thoroughly with the Kiowa and only their Athapascan language distinguishes them from that tribe. About 450 survive today in Oklahoma, living intermixed with the host group.

Kipling, (Joseph) Rudyard (1865–1936), British author, b. India. He achieved recognition with his stories about India, including *Plain Tales from the Hills* (1887), and with his novel *The Light That Failed* (1891). *His Barrack Room Ballads and Other Verses* (1892), including the poem "If," underlined his imperialist views. He wrote many children's adventures and animal stories, including *The Jungle Book* (1894), *Captain's Courageous* (1897), and *Kim* (1901), and the schoolboy stories *Stalky and Co.* (1899). His post–World War I stories, such as *Debits and Credits* (1926), show a more profound artistry.

Kirchhoff, Gustav Robert (1824–87), German physicist, professor at Heidelberg and later in Berlin. He worked with Robert Bunsen, and developed the spectroscope and used it to discover the elements cesium and rubidium (1860). He also examined the solar spectrum, worked on black-body radiation, and enunciated several laws (Kirchhoff's laws) relating to electric circuits. *See also* Blackbody.

Kirchhoff's Laws, two rules about multiple-loop electric circuits that are based on the laws of the conservation of charge and energy. Essentially they state that (1) charge does not accumulate at one point and thin out at another, and (2) around each loop the sum of the electromotive forces equals the sum of the potential voltage across each of the resistances.

Kirchner, Ernst Ludwig (1880–1938), German painter and printmaker. He was a leader of the expressionist artists known as Die Brücke. His most famous works are two versions of *Street, Berlin* (1907, 1913). *See also* Brücke, Die.

Kirghiz (Kirgizskaja) Soviet Socialist Republic, constituent republic of Central Asian USSR; borders on China (SE) and Kazakh republic (N), Uzbek (W), and Tadzhik republics (SW) SSRs; capital is Frunze. Russia annexed this region between 1865–76 when it conquered central Asia. The people fought Bolshevik control 1917–21. In 1924 it became an antonomous oblast within Russian republic and a constituent republic in 1936. Region is mostly mountainous; highest peak is Pobedy Peak, 24,409ft (7,445m), on Chinese border. Industries: irrigated farming, livestock, farm machinery, textiles, sugar refining, building materials. Area: 76,600sq mi (198,394sq km). Pop. 2,933,000.

Kirghiz, central Asiatic, Turko-Mongolian people, who inhabit the Kirghiz Soviet Socialist Republic. A Muslim people, whose language with its rich oral tradition belongs to the Turkic group, they are nomadic pastoralists who were colonized by Russia in the 19th century. The process of settlement and industrialization has recently accelerated.

Kirin (Jilin, or Chi-lin), city in NE China, on the Sungari River; capital of Kirin prov. 1750–1954. Early junk-building and lumber center (17–18th centuries), a seat of military government 1750–1911; industrial growth came with introduction of the railroad in 1912. Industries: chemicals, lumber, paper, matches, food processing, tobacco, plastics. Founded 1673. Pop. 1,200,000.

Kirkuk, city in NE Iraq; headquarters of Iraq Petroleum Co.; oil pipeline terminus to ports on Mediterranean Sea. Industries: oil, textiles, cotton, grains, sheep. Pop. 207,900.

Kirkwood, city in E Missouri, 13mi (21km) W of St Louis. Industries: lime, cement, lumber products. Founded 1852; inc. 1865. Pop. (1970) 31,769.

Kirov, city and riverport in Russian SFSR, USSR, on W bank of Vyatka River; capital of Kirov oblast. It became capital of an independent republic that was annexed by Ivan III in 1489; site of 17th-century cathedral. Industries: metal products, meat processing, lumber, leather, furs. Founded 1181. Pop. 349,000.

Kirovabad, city in W Azerbaijan SSR, USSR, S of Kura River, 110mi (178km) SE of Tbilisi; under Persian control from 17th century until it was taken by Russia in 1804; birthplace of Persian poet Nizami Gandzhevi (1141); site of 17th-century mosque. Industries: building materials, carpets, wine, cotton textiles, agricultural implements. Founded AD 1139 after earthquake had destroyed original city (6th century) 4mi (6km) E. Pop. 195,000.

Kirovograd, city in Ukrainian SSR, USSR, on E bank of Ingul River, 155mi (250km) SE of Kiev; capital of Kirovograd oblast. Between 1881 and 1919 it was scene of several pogroms. Industries: agricultural machinery, food processing, building materials. Founded as fortress 1754 and named for Empress Elizabeth (Elisavetgrad); name changed to Kirovograd 1935. Pop. 189,000.

Kisangani, formerly Stanleyville; city and port in N central Zaire, on the Congo River; a transportation center of NE Zaire. In the 1950s it was a stronghold of Patrice Lumumba until his assassination in 1961; site of university (1963). Industries: metal goods, beer, textiles. Founded 1883 by Henry M. Stanley as Stanleyville. Pop. 149,900.

Kish, ancient city of Mesopotamia. It was located in the Euphrates River Valley east of Babylon. In the 4th millennium BC it was a rich, strong Sumerian city. Excavations since 1922 have revealed that Sargon, king of Akkad, built a palace (*c.* 2800 BC) and Nebuchadnezzar and Nabonidus, kings of Babylon, erected temples (6th cent. BC.) △956.

Kishinev (Kišsin'ov), city in Moldavian SSR, USSR, 90mi (145km) NW of Odessa on the Byk River; capital of Moldavian SSR. Town was captured by Turks in 16th century, and by Russians 1812; Romania held city 1918–40; Axis powers controlled it 1941–44, and USSR seized it Aug. 24, 1944; site of university (1945). Industries: building materials, food processing, plastics, rubber, textiles. Founded early 15th century. Pop. 357,000.

Kissing Bug, or conenose, brown to black bug found in South and Central America, Mexico, and Texas. It bites humans and rodents, usually about the mouth, and is a carrier of Chagas' disease. Length: 1–11/3in (25–33mm). Family Reduviidae; genera *Triatoma* and *Rhodinus*. *See also* Assassin Bug.

Kissinger, Henry Alfred (1923–), US political scientist and secretary of state, b. Germany. While a professor at Harvard, he wrote several books on political science and served as advisor to various government agencies. He became Pres. Richard Nixon's assistant for national security (1969) and became the chief advisor on foreign policy. Nixon named him secretary of state (1973) and he continued in that post under Pres. Gerald Ford. In 1973 he shared the Nobel Peace Prize with Le Duc Tho for arranging a cease-fire in the Vietnam War, even though actual fighting continued to 1975. He arranged summit meetings for Nixon in China and Russia for détente. He also mediated the Middle East problems. △1352, 1390.

Kissing Gourami. *See* Gourami.

Kitakyushu, port city in N Kyushu, Japan, on Shimonoseki Strait, site of technical institute (1921); important commercial center. Industries: shipbuilding, fishing, iron, steel, textiles, chemicals, machinery, glass, cement. Formed 1963 with inc. of Kokura, Moji, Tobata, Wakamatsu, Yawata. Pop. 1,042,321.

Kitasato, Shibasaburo (1852–1931), Japanese bacteriologist famous for the isolation of the bacilli that cause tetanus, anthrax (1889), and dysentery (1898). In 1890 he prepared a diphtheria antitoxin. He also discovered the infectious organism that causes bubonic plague. He studied under Robert Koch in Germany.

Kitchen Cabinet, Pres. Andrew Jackson's unofficial group of advisors. From 1829–31, Jackson suspended Cabinet meetings and relied on the Kitchen Cabinet. The members included Isaac Hill, Amos Kendall, Duff Green, Francis P. Blair, and Sec. of State Martin Van Buren.

Kitchener, Horatio Herbert (Earl), (1850–1916), English military leader and colonial administrator. He crushed the Mahdi's revolt at Omdurman (1898) and subsequently blocked French expansionism in the Sudan. He was British commander in chief (1900–02) in the Boer War and then in India (1902–09), where his quarrel with Lord Curzon, the viceroy, caused the latter's resignation. Proconsul of Egypt (1911–14), he then became secretary of state for war, brilliantly but autocratically organizing the British army at the start of World War I. He was drowned when his ship was sunk by German submarines while on a mission to Russia.

Kitchener, formerly Berlin, city in SE Ontario, Canada, in the Grand River Valley; site of Woodside National Park; renamed in 1916 in honor of Lord Kitchener. Industries: rubber products, metal products, packaged meats. Settled by Mennonites from Pennsylvania 1806. Pop. 224,390.

Kitchen Midden, or **Shell Mound,** prehistoric refuse heaps composed chiefly of the discarded remains of edible shellfish mixed with evidence of human artifacts. Most of these middens were established in Europe and North Africa (from about 4,000 to 2,000 BC) after the disappearance of the large game animals hunted by early man during the Ice Age. Middens are also known from North, Central and South America.

Kite, diurnal bird of prey found in tropical and subtropical areas worldwide. They have hooked bills, narrow wings, long, sometimes forked tails, and long, curved claws. Hawklike, they circle, soar, and glide. Most European and Asian species are scavengers; American species generally feed on small live animals. They lay their eggs (2–5) in a bulky tree nest. Length: 18–24in (46–61cm). Family Accipitridae.

Kithara, ancient stringed musical instrument, traditionally associated with the Greek god Apollo. It is played by plucking five to seven strings on a U-shaped frame with a sounding board. *See also* Lyre.

Kittiwake, whitish arctic gull with a greenish-yellow bill, black wing tips, and short dark legs that flies low over open seas. To 14in (36cm) long, with a wingspan of 3ft (.91m), it lays spotted pale eggs (1–3) in a cup-shaped nest in sea cliffs. Family Laridae; species *Rissa tridactyla*.

Kitwe, city in N central Zambia, S Central Africa, 180mi (288km) N of Lusaka; site of Zambia Institute of Technology. Industries: copper mining, food processing, clothing, plastics. Founded 1936. Pop. 160,000.

Kiva, underground ceremonial chamber of Pueblo Indians. Each religious society has its own kiva, and many of its rites are performed here. Kivas are rectangular or circular and are highly decorated.

Kiwi, chicken-sized, flightless, fast-running, forest and scrub land bird of New Zealand. It has hairlike feathers and a long, flexible bill used to probe for food along the ground, usually at night. Large white or greenish eggs (1–2) are laid in a leaf-lined scrape or burrow. The male incubates the eggs. Species *Apteryx australis*. △538.

Klamath, tribe of about 1,000 Shapwailutan-speaking North American Indians, closely related to the Modoc, who inhabit the Klamath Lake area in Oregon.

Klee, Paul (1879–1940), Swiss painter. He was an influential genius of the abstract art movement. Influenced by cubism and fascinated by hieroglyphics, primitive art, and children's drawings, he developed his own pictorial language. His great technical skill in various media allowed him to combine subtle coloring with this new language, resulting in witty, inspiring works that convey great meaning through simple compositions. He studied art in Munich (1900), traveled in Italy and France (1905), and earned a meager living doing exhibitions and illustrations after returning to Munich (1906). By the end of World War I, Klee had established himself as a master. He taught painting at the Bauhaus until his final return to Switzerland in 1933 after his art was confiscated by the Nazis for being "degenerate." His most famous work is *Twittering Machine* (1922). △1294.

Kleitman, Nathaniel (1895–), US physiologist, b. Russia. A pioneer in the study of sleep, in 1952, with his colleague Eugene Aserinsky, he discovered that rapid eye movements occur when a person is asleep and dreaming, a discovery important for subsequent researchers into the stages of sleep.

Klemperer, Otto (1885–1973), German conductor. He was encouraged by Gustav Mahler and spent the early part of his career in German opera houses. He premiered in the United States in 1926, and in 1933 he left Germany and became conductor for the Los Angeles Philharmonic. In 1939 illness led him into semi-retirement, but he returned as director of the Budapest Opera (1947–50). In 1951 illness nearly stopped his career. Nevertheless, he returned to the podium with performances of operas and the symphonic works of such composers as Beethoven and Bruckner.

Kinglet

Henry Kissinger

Kittiwake

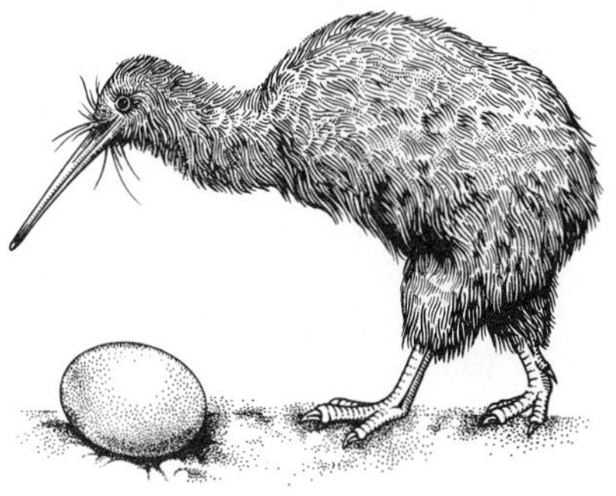
Kiwi

Kline, Franz (Joseph) (1910–62), US painter, a leading artist of the post–World War II abstract expressionist movement. △1320.

Klipspringer, small antelope, native to rocky areas of Africa below the Sahara Desert. Short, spiked horns are usually only on the male. It has a thick coat of grizzled, bristly hair and tiny, cylindrical hooves that permit leaps onto small footholds. Height: to 23in (0.6m) at shoulder; weight: to 35lb (16kg). Family Bovidae; species *Oreotragus oreotragus*. *See also* Antelope.

Klondike Gold Rush (1896–1904). The discovery of gold by George Carmack at Bonanza Creek (1896) in the Klondike region of the Yukon territory of Canada began an onrush of prospectors sailing up the Lynn Canal to Dyea and Skagway. By 1899 most claims had been staked, and the population of Dawson had grown to 25,000. Access to the Yukon caused the Alaska Boundary dispute, and $100,000,000 of gold was mined before the lodes were exhausted in 1904.

Kluckhohn, Clyde Kay Maben (1905–1960), US anthropologist who made valuable contributions to ethnographic studies of the Navaho Indians. He also conducted important work in the study of value systems and cultural patterns. Works include the popular *Mirror for Man* (1949) and the classic *Navaho Witchcraft* (1944).

Klystron, an electron tube that is velocity modulated and makes use of the controlled speed of a stream of electrons. They are used in ultra-high frequency circuits, where they can produce oscillations up to 400,000 megacycles per second.

K-Meson. *See* Kaon.

Knee. △682.

Knickerbocker School, name given to a group of writers associated with New York City in the first half of the 19th century. Besides individual publication, their work appeared in New York newspapers and in *Knickerbocker* magazine. Among the writers were William Cullen Bryant, Lydia M. Child, James Fenimore Cooper, Joseph R. Drake, Fitz-Greene Halleck, Washington Irving, Clement Moore, George P. Morris, James K. Paulding, Nathaniel Willis, and Samuel Woodworth.

Knife Fish. △516.

Knight, in the Middle Ages in Western Europe, a fully equipped mounted warrior, provided with a helmet and chain mail before the 14th century and with a complete suit of steel armor by the 15th century. Under the feudal system, a knight was one of the armed retainers of a lord or king, and was bound to the lord as a vassal. Knight service, or the equivalent in monetary donations, was due the lord by most vassals. Originally, the knight was a practical warrior, but by the 12th century he was a romantic figure and idealized as the symbol of manhood and virtue. Less and less often associated with actual warfare, some knights made their living entirely by the ransoms earned in tournaments. △1098, 1592, 1726.

Knights Hospitallers or **Knights of Saint John of Jerusalem,** military religious order established early in the 11th century. They cared for Christian pilgrims who fell ill in Jerusalem, where they had a hospital and hostel. During the Crusades the Hospitallers policed routes to Jerusalem, together with their bitter rivals, the Knights Templars. After the fall of Jerusalem they sought to protect the Mediterranean from the Turks. Today there remain a Catholic charitable order and an Anglican one, which still maintains a hospital in Jerusalem.

Knights of Labor, workers' group formed in Philadelphia (1869). It was organized by Urish S. Stephens, a tailor, and became a national organization in 1878. Skilled and unskilled workers, regardless of race, sex, or color, were eligible to join the local assemblies, which together formed one union. It reached peak membership of over 700,000 in 1886. The union declined after the Haymarket Square incident in May 1886, and several strike failures. The organization was dissolved in 1913. *See also* Haymarket Massacre.

Knights of Saint Crispin, Order of the, US secret shoemakers union formed by Newell Daniels in Wisconsin (1867). By the time of its first International Grand Lodge Meeting in New York (1868), it had about 600 chapters. Its aim was the improvement of conditions for all shoemakers by combating the growing industrialization of the industry. Union corruption and employer opposition led to its demise by 1875, with many of its members joining the Knights of Labor.

Knights of the White Camellia, 19th-century US vigilante organization dedicated to the reestablishment of white supremacy. It was founded in New Orleans (1867) and was similar to the Ku Klux Klan.

Knights Templars, military religious order established in 1118 with its headquarters in the supposed Temple of Solomon in Jerusalem. With the Knights Hospitallers the Templars protected routes to Jerusalem for Christians during the Crusades and amassed a great fortune for their order. Fighting between the two orders contributed to the failure of the Crusades. The possessions of the Templars in France attracted King Philip IV, who urged Pope Clement V to abolish the order in 1312. Their property was confiscated and many were tortured and executed. △1084.

Knopf, Alfred A(braham) (1892–), US publisher, b. New York City. He began his career with Doubleday (1912–14) and by 1915 had started his own business (Alfred A. Knopf, Inc.) in New York City. It flourished and in 1960 he sold the company to Random House, Inc. He was responsible for bringing translations of noted contemporary foreign authors to the American public. His company established a reputation for having a high standard in selection of books for publication.

Knossos (Cnossus), ancient city in Greece, on the N coast of Crete, 4mi (6km) SE of Candia. Occupied prior to 3000 BC, it was center of Bronze Age culture; early Minoan culture was destroyed 1500 BC; rebuilt and destroyed again *c.* 1400 BC ending Minoan civilization. Knossos prospered as a Greek city; it was traditional capital of King Minos; site of great palace *c.* 2000 BC, including a labyrinth, a chamber built, according to Greek myth, by Daedalus to house the Minotaur. △964.

Knot, sandpiper that nests in Siberia and winters in temperate coastal areas. It is generally chestnut and brown with black markings and feeds on small animals. Spotted greenish to buff eggs (4) are laid in a tundra scrape. Length: 10in (25cm). Species *Calidris canutus*.

Knot, a unit of measurement equal to one nautical mile per hour. Ship and airplane speed is measured in knots as is that of wind and currents.

Knotweed, or doorweed, wire grass, widespread flowering annual weed plant. It has small, lancelike leaves and brown flowers and grows prostrate with the wiry branches forming dense mats. Family Polygonaceae; genus *Polygonum*. △444.

Knowledge, Sociology of, study of the complex relationships between social and political structures on the one hand and intellectual life on the other. △1290.

Know-Nothing Party ("American Party," "Native American Party"), third-party political movement active in the 1850s. Party members, when asked about their motives, purposes, and program, would reply, "I know nothing." In fact, however, Know-Nothings were fanatically patriotic and strongly opposed to Roman Catholics, particularly Irish Catholics who immigrated to the United States in the 1850s. By 1856 the party was more a conservative Unionist movement than the nativist organization it had been earlier. After the 1856 presidential campaign, the party disintegrated.

Knox, (William) Frank(lin) (1874–1944), US publisher and political figure, b. Boston. A Rough Rider in the Spanish-American War, he also served in World War I. He started in the newspaper business as a reporter, became general manager (1928–31) of the Hearst papers, and owner of the *Chicago Daily News* (1931). In 1936 he was the unsuccessful Republican candidate for vice president on the Alfred M. Landon ticket. President Franklin Roosevelt appointed him secretary of the navy in 1940 as a gesture of bipartisanship in defense preparation. He died in office.

Knox, Henry (1750–1806), American Revolutionary War military officer, b. Boston. As commander of the Continental Army artillery he hauled the guns captured at Fort Ticonderoga to Boston. He took part in every major battle of the war and was close adviser to George Washington, becoming a brigadier general in 1776. He founded the Society of the Cincinnati (1783). He was the first secretary of war (1785–94).

Knox, John (*c.*1515–72), leader of the Protestant Reformation in Scotland. He was ordained a Roman Catholic priest but took up the cause of the Reformation. He was imprisoned in France and later lived fc a time in exile in England and after Mary I came to th throne (1553) went to Geneva, where he was in fluenced by John Calvin. Knox continued to promot the Protestant cause in Scotland. After a struggle wit Scotland's new Catholic ruler, Mary Queen of Scots from 1561 his side prevailed by the late 1560s. He i one of the great leaders of Presbyterianism. *See als* Presbyterianism.

Knoxville, city in E Tennessee, 105mi (169km) NE o Chattanooga on Tennessee River; seat of Knox co City was a supply center for westward-bound wago trains (1792); Tennessee's first capital 1697–1812 1817–19; headquarters of Confederate armies in Tennessee 1861; taken by Union troops at Battle o Fort Sanders 1863; site of Tennessee Valley Author ity, University of Tennessee (1794), Knoxville Colleg (1863). Industries: livestock, farming, tobacco, marbl quarrying, ore processing, textiles, furniture, cement steel products, glass, chemicals, plastics, railroa shops, tourism, lumber. Settled 1786; inc. 1815. Pop (1970) 174,587.

Koa, Hawaiian tree valued for its wood, used in cab netmaking. It has clustered flowers and 6-in (15-cm pods. Height: to 60ft (18m). Family Leguminosae species *Acacia koa*.

Kobe, port city on SW Honshu, Japan, on N shor of Osaka Bay; capital of Hyogo prefecture. In 187 Kobe absorbed Hyogo, an important fishing port sinc 9th century; since the late 1800s it has become a major port of Japan; cultural center; site of severa early Buddhist structures, Kobe University of Econom ics (1948), and Kobe University (1949); suffered Al lied bombings in WWII. Industries: shipping, ship building, rubber, steel, textiles, printing. Pop 1,288,937.

Koblenz. *See* Coblenz.

Kobo Daishi. *See* Kukai.

Koch, Robert (1843–1910), German bacteriologist He was awarded the 1905 Nobel Prize in physiolog or medicine for his discovery of the bacillus tha causes tuberculosis. This work laid the foundation fo methods of determining the causative agent of a disease.

Kochi, seaport on S coast of Shikoku, Japan, on Tosa Bay; capital of Kochi prefecture. Industries: agriculture, fishing, machinery, silk, paper. Pop. 786,882.

Kodály, Zoltán (1882–1967), Hungarian compose who, with Bartók, collected Hungarian folk tunes and used them in his compositions, which include the *Psalmus Hungaricus* (1923) and the *Peacock Variations* (1939) for orchestra, and a popular suite from his opera *Háry János* (1926). △1364.

Kodiak Bear. *See* Alaskan Brown Bear.

Kodiak Island, island in the Gulf of Alaska, SE of the Alaska Peninsula. Chief industry is fishing, especially salmon; Kodiak bear and Kodiak king crab are native Island was covered with ash 1912 when Mt Katma erupted on mainland; site of US Navy base. Area 5,363sq mi (13,890sq km).

Koestler, Arthur (1905–), Hungarian writer While working as a journalist during the Spanish Civil War, he was captured by Franco's forces and imprisoned until 1937. He then went to France to work and was interned in a concentration camp after the German invasion, escaping in 1940. He joined the British army and later settled in England. His novels include *Darkness at Noon* (1941), *Thieves in the Night* (1946), and *The Call Girls* (1972). His later philosophical works explore the nature of art, science, and man and include *The Sleepwalkers* (1959), *The Ghost in the Machine* (1967), *The Case of the Midwife Toad* (1971), and *The Thirteenth Tribe: The Khazar Empire and its Heritage* (1976).

Kohlberg, Lawrence. △786.

Köhler, Wolfgang (1887–1967), German psychologist, emigrated to the United States in the 1930s. With Kurt Koffka and Max Wertheimer, Köhler was a seminal figure in gestalt psychology. He did important work in animal learning and problem solving, summarized in *The Mentality of Apes* (1925). △672.

Kohlrabi, garden vegetable with lobed leaves borne on a bulblike, above-ground stem. The edible, turniplike bulb is greenish-white or purplish. It matures in 55–60 days. Family Cruciferae; species *Brassica oleracea gongylodes*.

Kohoutek's Comet. △90.

Kokomo, city in N central Indiana, N of Indianapolis; seat of Howard co; scene of Elwood Haynes' first successful automobile road test 1894. Industries: glass, radios, automobile parts, rubber goods. Founded 1842; inc. 1865. Pop. (1970) 44,042.

Kolar Gold Fields, city in S India, 145mi (233km) W of Madras. Center of India's gold mining industry, produces 95% of the country's gold; mines opened *c.* 1885. Pop. 167,610.

Köln. *See* Cologne.

Kolyma, river in Russian SFSR, USSR; rises in Kolyma Mts, flows N and E into Arctic Ocean. From June to October it is navigable for approx. 1,000mi (1,610km) of its 1,500mi (2,415km).

Kommunizma, Pik. *See* Communism Peak.

Komodo Dragon, giant monitor lizard found in SE Asian jungles. It is solid brown and feeds on carrion, also killing young deer and wild pigs. Its dwindling populations are strictly protected. Length: to 10ft (3m); weight: to 300lb (135kg). Family Varanidae; species *Varanus komodoensis. See also* Lizard; Monitor Lizard. △552.

Komsomolsk-on-Amur (Komsomolsk), city in Russian SFSR, USSR, on W bank of Amur River. Industries: steel, oil refining, wood products. Founded 1932 by Young Communist League. Pop. 218,000.

Kondratieff Cycles, long-term business cycles that last 50–60 years. Named for Russian economist N. D. Kondratieff, these cycles involve long movements of trade, output, and price changes and may be associated with major technological changes. *See also* Business Cycles.

Kongo, or **Bakongo,** Negroid people of the Atlantic coast of W Africa, living in the Congo Republic, Zaire, and Angola. Once they had a powerful empire, and their culture is still rich in sculpture and music. Their traditional livelihood is based on sedentary agriculture, staple crops including cassava and manioc, with coffee as a cash crop. Ancestor worship and fetish cults dominate their religion.

Kongo, Kingdom of the, African state from the 14th century to about 1700. In the area now included in Zaire and Angola, it was ruled by a king, or *manikongo.* The kingdom began trade with Portugal in 1482. The Portuguese brought Christianity, which Manikongo Afonso I tried to spread. Afonso was, however, hampered by the greed of the Portuguese, who carried on a brisk slave trade. Under continued depredations by the Portuguese and repeated attacks from interior tribes, the kingdom finally collapsed, and Portugal took control.

Konstanz (Constance), port city in S West Germany, on Lake Constance, 75mi (121km) S of Stuttgart; became a free imperial city in 1183; scene of Council of Constance (1414–18) which ended Great Schism by disposing of three popes and electing a new pope, Martin V. City passed to Austria 1548, to Baden 1805; site of 11th-century cathedral, Kaufhaus (1388 council meeting place), university (1966); birthplace of Count Graf von Zeppelin (1838), soldier and aviator. Industries: textiles, chemicals, electrical equipment. Founded as Roman fort AD 4th century. Pop. 60,821.

Konya, city in S central Turkey, 145mi (233km) S of Ankara. It was capital of Seljuk sultans of Rum, 1073–1472, when it became part of Ottoman Empire; served as religious center of whirling dervishes, founded here in 13th century; site of teacher training college (1962). Industries: sugar, flax, fruit, cotton goods, leather. Pop. 157,934.

Koo, Vi Kyuin Wellington (1887–), Chinese diplomat Ku Wei-chün. He served as Chinese representative at the Paris Peace Conference in 1919 and subsequently as Chinese ambassador to France (1936–41), Britain (1941–46), and the United States (1946–56). He represented China at the conference that established the United Nations (1945), and was a justice on the International Court (1957–67).

Kookaburra, or laughing jackass, large, heavy kingfisher of Australia and Tasmania known for its loud, fiendish screams. Groups often scream in unison at dawn, midday, and dusk. A wood kingfisher, it feeds on rodents, lizards, and other land animals. Species *Dacelo gigas. See also* Kingfisher.

Kootenay (Kootenai), river in Canada; rises in Rocky Mts, SE British Columbia; flows S through NW Montana and NW Idaho, then N through Kootenay Lake in Canada; unites with the Columbia River at Castlegar; explored by David Thompson 1807; used to generate hydroelectricity. Length: 407mi (655km).

Kopernik, Mikolaj. *See* Copernicus, Nicolaus.

Köppen, Wladimir Peter (1846–1940), German meteorologist who classified world climates on the basis of variations in temperature, rainfall, plant distribution, and seasonal changes. △220.

Koran, the sacred scriptures of Islam. The book was written in Arabic, and the Arabic title is Qur'an. According to Muslim belief, the Koran contains the actual word of God as revealed to the Prophet Mohammed in the 7th century. Its 114 chapters, or *suras,* are the source of Islamic belief and a guide for the whole life of the community, making known to men the correct way to live. The message of the Koran holds true eternally, and wherever the Muslim religion has spread the book has been dutifully studied. *See also* Islam; Mohammed. △1058.

Kore, term derived from the Greek word for "maiden," generally applied to the draped, standing female statues of the Greek Archaic period of art. A male statue from the same period is called a *kouros.* △1000.

Kore. in mythology. *See* Persephone.

Korea, Democratic People's Republic of, independent nation in NE Asia, known as North Korea. Established after WWII, its communist government operates N of the 38th parallel.

Land and economy. North Korea, a country where 16% of the land is arable and cultivated, is located in NE Asia with the Soviet Union (N) and South Korea (S) as its neighbors. Moderately high mountain ranges and hills separate the valleys and small plains. Warm in the summer, it is cold in the winter with some snow. Its mineral resources are highly developed and it ranks among the world leaders in yield of tungsten, graphite, and magnesite. It produces sufficient coal for its own needs. With assistance from the Soviet Union and China, Korea has developed its economy, especially nationalized heavy industry. Agriculture is collectivized, with rice and corn the main crops. Individuals are allowed to grow small plots for household use.

People. North Koreans' background is essentially the same as that of South Koreans. Racial origins are Tungusic (Mongol and Chinese). Between 1925 and 1940, many South Koreans worked in the industrial sections of the N. They returned S after 1945 when the peninsula was divided between US and Soviet spheres. Korean is the official language. There are two writing styles, one phonetic and the other based on Chinese characters. Confucianism was the dominant religion until 1945. Literacy is 90%.

Government. North Korea is controlled by the Communist Labor party (KLP) headed by a premier and a Supreme People's Assembly.

History. Korea was a semi-independent state with Chinese ties until conquered by Japan in 1910. After the defeat of Japan in WWII, Korea was separated along the 38th parallel into US and Soviet zones; the USSR occupation was N of the parallel. Numerous efforts to unite the countries failed, and observed elections to determine choice of government were allowed only in the S. On Aug. 15, 1948, the S portion became the Republic of Korea. The Soviets established the Democratic Republic of Korea in the N. In 1950 North Korean forces invaded South Korea. The United States aided the Republic, while Communist countries assisted the N. The war ended in a stalemate in July 1953. From 1953, North Korea continued, under Premier Kim Il Sung, its criticism and harassment of South Korea while developing its economy and taking a gradually fuller role in world affairs.

PROFILE

Official name: Democratic People's Republic of Korea
Area: 46,540 sq mi (120,539 sq km)
Population: 23,800,000
Density: 511 per sq mi (197 per sq km)
Chief cities: Pyong Yang (capital); Hamhung
Government: Communist People's Assembly
Religion: none
Language: Korean
Monetary unit: Won
Gross national product: $3,500,000,000
Industries: cement, coke, iron, ferro alloys, textiles
Agriculture: rice, barley, wheat, soybeans, cattle, fish, sweet potatoes, yams
Minerals: tungsten, magnesite, lead, zinc, pyrite, cement, iron ore, copper, gold, phosphate, salt, coal
Trading partners: USSR, People's Republic of China

Knossos, Crete

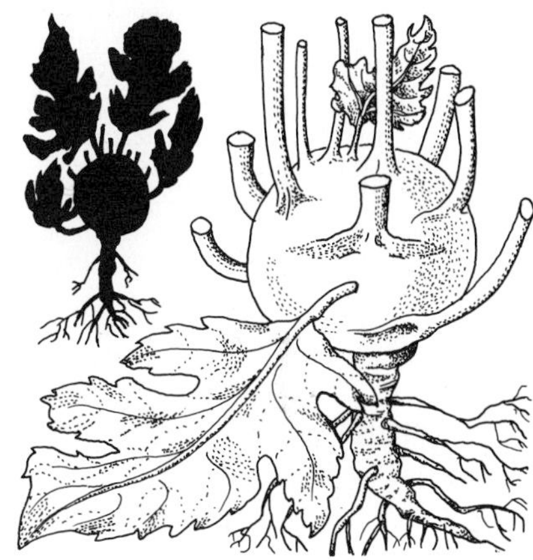
Kohlrabi

Kookaburra

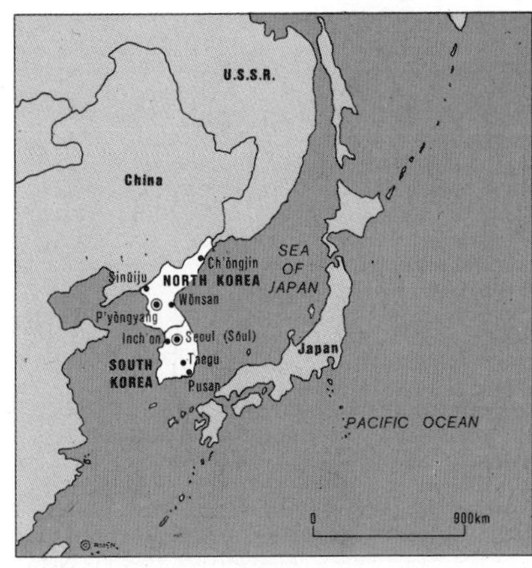
U.S.S.R.
China
SEA OF JAPAN
Ch'ŏngjin
Sinŭiju
NORTH KOREA
Wŏnsan
P'yŏngyang
Inch'ŏn
Seoul (Sŏul)
Taegu
SOUTH KOREA
Pusan
Japan
PACIFIC OCEAN
0
900km
Korea

Korea, Republic of, independent nation in NE Asia, known as South Korea. It occupies the S portion of the Korean peninsula. It is a racially mixed society; its main crop is rice.

Land and economy. Located on the peninsula projecting SE from China, South Korea is a 600-mi (966-km) long by 135-mi (217-km) wide mountainous area below the 38th parallel, with harbors on its W and S coast. Seoul, the Republic of Korea's capital, sits in the NW central part of the country. The climate is hot and humid in the summer, dry in the winter. Poor in natural resources, lacking skilled workers, and densely populated, Korea still suffers from the aftereffects of the Korean War. Economic growth was impeded by 1974–75 oil price increases, which caused inflation. About 25% of the gross national product comes from agriculture, fishing, and forestry; another 25% from manufacturing. About 20% of the land is arable, and 80% is devoted to grain, especially rice. Coal provides Korea's fuel requirements and is also exported. About 25% of South Korea's budget is allocated to defense expenditures. The United States has supported Korea with military and civilian aid.

People. High in population density, Korea is a racially mixed society. Descended from the Tungasics (Mongols with Chinese mixture), the people are concentrated in the fertile valleys of the S and the urban Seoul section. More than 600,000 Koreans live in Japan. Korean is the national language, with English developing as the 2nd tongue. Literacy is rated at 85%. About 16% of the population practices Buddhism and Shamanism; Confucianism is a cultural influence. There are about 2,000,000 Christians.

Government. Authority is vested in the president, who is elected by direct secret ballot. The constitution provides for an elected unicameral National Assembly.

History. Legend has it that Korea's founder was of divine origin; Korea's calendar starts with the founding date of 2333 BC. When it was unified in AD 7th century, it had been a semi-independent state much influenced by China. In 1910, Japan annexed Korea. After WWII, the 1945 Potsdam Conference divided Korea into Soviet and US occupation zones. Unification efforts failed, and on June 25, 1950, North Korean forces invaded the South. The United States helped South Korea, and Chinese Communists aided the North. The war ended in a stalemate on July 27, 1953. Syngman Rhee was Korea's first president (1948–60); riots caused by allegations of election irregularities deposed him. In a 1961 military coup, Maj. Gen. Park Chung Hee took power. Since then, he has consolidated his power and has been elected to three terms as president.

PROFILE

Official name: Republic of Korea
Area: 38,031sq mi (98,500sq km)
Population: 33,460,000
Density: 880 per sq mi (340 per sq km)
Chief cities: Seoul (capital); Pusan; Inchon
Government: Democracy
Religion: Buddhism, Shamanism, Christianity
Language: Korean
Monetary unit: Won
Gross national product: $12,380,000,000
Industries: rubber products, glass products, electronics, petrochemicals, clothing, plywood, processed food, furniture, ships, fertilizers
Agriculture: rice, barley, wheat, tobacco, soybeans, fish, forests, yams
Minerals: tungsten, coal, iron ore, bismuth, graphite, cement
Trading partners: United States, Japan

Korean War (1950–53), conflict primarily between the United States and the Republic of Korea (South Korea) on one side and the Democratic People's Republic of Korea (North Korea) and the People's Republic of China on the other side. When Japanese occupation of Korea ended at the close of World War II, the country was divided along the 38th parallel. The north came under the influence of the Soviet Union and the south under the influence of the United States. On June 25, 1950, troops from North Korea invaded the south. President Harry S. Truman reacted swiftly by committing US ground, sea, and air power to the defense of South Korea. The United Nations also condemned North Korea's action and placed token forces of 15 other nations under US command. President Truman named General Douglas MacArthur as supreme commander.

After initial victories by the North Korean forces, the UN forces counterattacked, staged an amphibious landing at Inchon, and drove the Communist forces from the south. The UN forces pursued the Communists into the north, captured Pyongyang, the capital, on October 19, and by the middle of November had driven the forces almost to the Yalu River, which separates Korea and China. That incursion into North Korean territory had been made with the intention of unifying the two Koreas, despite a warning from China that it would not countenance such a move. In November 1950 a Communist counteroffensive was launched, this time with hundreds of thousands of Chinese troops, who streamed across the border. In the bloodiest fighting of the war, the tide again changed, and the UN forces were driven back into the south and Seoul, the South Korean capital, was retaken by the Communists. After months of fierce fighting, the battle lines were drawn more or less along the 38th parallel, where they remained until the end of the war.

General MacArthur was opposed to Truman's policy of containing the war so as to avoid a major land war in China. After MacArthur made public statements in favor of carrying the war into China, Truman fired him for insubordination on April 10, 1951, and replaced him with Gen. Matthew B. Ridgway. On July 10, 1951, General Ridgway began truce talks with North Korea. By now the goal of unifying Korea had been discarded, and the United States aimed at keeping the 38th parallel as the border. The talks dragged on, with sporadic fighting alternating with cease-fires, until July 27, 1953, when an armistice was finally signed. The two Koreas remained independent of each other with a 2.5mi (4km) demilitarized zone carved out between them. Casualties in the war were high. The United States suffered 54,000 men killed and 100,000 wounded. The losses of the two Koreas and China were several times that figure. △1382.

Korematsu v. United States (1944), US Supreme Court decision that upheld the constitutionality of the Japanese evacuation and encampment program ordered by Pres. Franklin Roosevelt early in World War II to combat a "potentially grave danger to public safety." The court justified the incarceration of US citizens without the rudiments of due process protections as "an emergency war measure," but many commentators have criticized the court for succumbing to mass hysteria generated by the war.

Körfezi. *See* Iskenderun.

Korinthos. *See* Corinth.

Koriyama, city in N central Honshu, Japan, on Abukuma River. Scene of heavy damage during WWII. Industries: machinery, textiles, chemicals. Pop. 241,673.

Kornberg, Arthur (1918–), US biochemist, b. Brooklyn, N.Y. He shared the 1959 Nobel Prize in physiology or medicine for his work on the synthesis of deoxyribonucleic acid (DNA), the hereditary material of most cells, and ribonucleic acid (RNA), the hereditary material of some viruses.

Kornilov, Lavr Georgievich (1870–1918), Russian general. Appointed supreme military commander by Kerensky (August 1917), he rebelled unsuccessfully against the provisional government a month later. After the Bolshevik Revolution (November 1917), he led White forces in the Civil War and was killed while attacking Krasnodar. △1310.

Korolenko, Vladimir. △1240.

Kortrijk. *See* Courtrai.

Koryaks, Paleo-asiatic people who inhabit the Koryak National Okrug in the Soviet Far East. Linguistically related to the Chukchi, the Koryaks are nomadic fishermen and reindeer herders who have undergone some Soviet collectivization.

Kosciusko, Thaddeus (1746–1817), Polish patriot and soldier. Championing the ideals of French liberal philosophy, he came to America in 1776 to fight with the Revolutionary army. He became an aide to Gen. Washington and was granted American citizenship. Returning to Poland in 1784, he was a major general in the army (1789). After the second partition of Poland in 1793, he led a revolutionary movement to regain Polish independence. Initially successful (he became the dictator of Poland), the invading armies of Russia and Prussia proved too strong. Kosciusko was imprisoned (1794–96) and exiled. He believed in the equality of men and liberated his serfs. He contributed the property granted him by the US Congress for the education of black Americans. Kosciusko worked for Polish independence from his various places of exile until his death.

Kosciusko, Mount, peak in Australian Alps; winter sport resort. Highest peak in Australia, 7,316ft (2,231m).

Kosice, city in E Czechoslovakia, on Hernád River, 135mi (217km) NE of Budapest; formerly part of Hungary, it became part of Czechoslovakia 1920 by Treaty of Trianon; site of 14th–15th-century Gothic Cathedral of St Elizabeth, and 14th-century Franciscan monastery. Industries: iron, steel, petroleum refining. Chartered 1241. Pop. 136,397.

Kosinski, Jerzy (1933–), US novelist, b. Poland. His works include *The Painted Bird* (1965) and *Steps* (1968; National Book Award 1969), both books involving a series of incidents of grotesque violence, and *Cockpit* (1975).

Kossuth, Lajos (1802–94), Hungarian leader. He entered the National Diet in 1830 and quickly made a name for himself as a fiery, eloquent advocate of autonomy for Hungary, within or independent from the Austrian Empire. He was imprisoned for his political activities between 1837–40. After a successful campaign for a separate constitution for Hungary, he was named finance minister in 1848 in the new government. He led the insurrection of July 1848 and was appointed virtual dictator of Hungary. In 1849 he was named president of an independent Hungary, but his army was crushed by the Austrians with Russian help. He was forced to flee to Turkey. He traveled to the United States where he was hailed as a liberator. He lived in England and Italy, refusing amnesty as late as 1890. After his death his body was returned to Budapest and buried in state. △1248.

Kostroma, city in Russian SFSR, USSR, on W bank of Volga River at the mouth of the Kostroma River; annexed by Moscow 1364; scene of election of Michael Romanov as tsar in 1613; site of 16th-century Ipatyev Monastery and the Uspenky Cathedral (1250). Industries: linen, metallurgy, ship repairing, plywood, footwear. Founded 1152. Pop. 223,000.

Kosygin, Aleksei N(ikoloevich) (1904–), Soviet political figure, premier since 1964. Elected to the Communist party Central Committee (1939) and Politburo (1948), he was removed in 1953 but regained his seat in 1960. After Khrushchev's fall (1964), he became premier and second in command to Leonid Brezhnev. He is considered mainly an economic administrator. △1344.

Koufax, Sanford ("Sandy") (1935–), US baseball player, b. Brooklyn, N.Y. Koufax played for the Dodgers (1955–1966), won five consecutive earned run average titles (1962–66), struck out a National League record of 382 batters in 1965, and retired early because of an arthritic elbow. He was elected to the Baseball Hall of Fame in 1972.

Kraepelin, Emil (1856–1926), German psychiatrist, pioneer in the classification of mental disorders. By studying the symptoms from many case histories he distinguished two broad classes of psychoses, dementia praecox (now called schizophrenia) and manic-depressive psychosis. △762.

Krafft-Ebing, Richard von (1840–1902), German psychiatarist. His *Psychopathia Sexualis* (1886) described sexual pathologies and did much to bring discussions of the sex drive into the open. He also was one of the first physicians to conclude that general paresis was caused by syphilis.

Kraft, Adam. △1106.

Krait, SE Asian snake of the cobra family, with potent venom. The blue krait and black-and-yellow banded krait are common. Length: to 4ft (1.2m). Family Elapidae; genus *Bungarus*. *See also* Cobra.

Krakatoa (Rakata), small volcanic island in center of Sunda Strait, Indonesia, between Java and Sumatra. Violent eruption, and ensuing 50ft (15m) tidal wave, killed 36,000 people in 1883 and produced atmospheric effects experienced around the world for months afterward. During 1960s it was again active.

Krakow (Crakow), city in S Poland, on the Vistula River; capital of Krakow prov. City was made a bishopric *c.* 1000; Polish royal residency 1300–1600; taken by Sweden in 1655 and by Austria in 1795; made independent state in 1815; retaken by Austria in 1846; made part of independent Poland after WWI; site of Polish Academy of Sciences, University of Krakow (1364), Jagiellonian University, several museums and galleries containing Rennaissance art. Industries: steel mills, metals, chemicals, electrical equipment, rail equipment. Founded *c.* 700. Pop. 583,000.

Kramář, Karel (1860–1937), a leader in the Czech struggle for independence from Austria-Hungary. A proponent of pan-Slavism, he saw in Russia a source of support, even suggesting a Russian grand duke as king of the Czechs. Tomáš Masaryk, on the other hand, gained support from western European nations. After 1918, Masaryk dominated the new republic, Kramar serving as prime minister (1918–19).

Kranach, Lucas. *See* Cranach, Lucas.

Krasnodar, city and port in Russian SFSR, USSR, on E bank of Kuban River, 160mi (258km) S of Rostov-na-Donu; capital of Krasnodar Krai; site of Worker's Scientific Institute. Industries: food processing, oil refining, machine tools, textiles, metalworking. Founded 1794 by Catherine II. Pop. 465,000.

Krasnoyarsk (Krasnojarsk), city and riverport in S Central USSR, on W bank of upper Yenisei River; capital of Krasnoyarsk Krai. Founded 1628 by the Cossacks as a fort, it was frequently attacked in later 17th century by Tartars and other tribes; became capital of Yeniseisk government 1822; site of Siberian Institute of Forestry. Industries: shipbuilding, heavy machinery, cement, lumber, flour milling. Pop. 576,000.

Krebs, Hans Adolf (1900–), British biochemist, b. Germany. He shared with F. A. Lipmann the 1953 Nobel Prize in physiology and medicine for his discovery of the citric acid cycle, the process that results in the production of energy in living organisms.

Krebs' Cycle, or **Citric Acid Cycle,** final stage in the oxidation of food to produce energy, occurring in the mitochondria of living cells. Acetyl coenzyme A is converted to hydrogen atoms and carbon dioxide by a cyclic sequence of enzyme-catalyzed reactions. The hydrogen atoms undergo further oxidation in the electron transport (respiratory) chain, during which energy in the form of ATP is produced and water is formed. △1572.

Krefeld, city in W West Germany, on Rhine River, 19mi (31km) WSW of Essen. An important linen-weaving center until it passed to Prussia in 1702, it developed into center of silk industry when given monopoly by Frederick II. Industries: textiles, steel, dyes, machinery. Chartered 1373; inc. neighboring Verdingen 1929. Pop. 226,795.

Kreisler, Fritz (1875–1962), US violinist and composer, b. Austria. He studied at the Vienna and Paris conservatories and made his debut in the United States in 1888. He was a world-famous violin virtuoso and also composed numerous short violin pieces and an operetta, *Apple Blossoms* (1919).

Kremlin, The, the historic nucleus of Moscow; a 90-acre (36.5-hectare) site bounded by the Moscow River and Kremlin Quay (S), Red Square and Lenin's tomb (E), Moscow Historical Museum and St Basil's Cathedral (W), and old Alexander Gardens (S). The term "kremlin" is a medieval expression meaning the walled central section of any town; several other old cities retain theirs, but Moscow's is the most famous. Its walls were completed between 1485–95 and are adorned with 20 different towers. Within the walls several cathedrals face onto a central square. Along the walls are palaces and museums. The largest building, the Great Kremlin Palace (1838–49), was the tsar's Moscow residence. It now houses the Supreme Soviet (parliament) of USSR and Communist party conventions. In 1955 the Kremlin was opened to the public.

Kretschmer, Ernst. △814.

Krill. △624.

Krishna, river in S India; rises in the Western Ghat Mts near Mahabaleshwar; flows SE to Bay of Bengal, S of Maghilipatnam. Named for the god Krishna, it is sacred to the Hindu religion. Length: 800mi (1,288km).

Krishna, most celebrated hero of Hindu mythology, who in his youth performed labors similar to those of Heracles. He slew the king of the Hayas and demons of Putana and Dhenuka, carried off a princess and conquered Saubha, with trickery and deceit typical of folk heroes. He is generally depicted in a bejeweled sari and conical crown carrying a flute. △1034.

Krishna Menon, Vengalil Krishnan (1897–1974), Indian diplomat and political figure. He lived in England between 1924–47 where he joined the Labour party and served as secretary of the Indian League (1929–47), which advocated independence. Between 1947–52 he was high commissioner for India in Great Britain. He served as India's UN delegate (1952–62) and was sharply critical of the United States. He served in the national legislature (1953–67, 1969–74). He served as minister of defense (1957–62), but was dismissed after India's poor showing in its border war with China.

Kristiansand, seaport in S Norway, on the Skagerrat, approx. 160mi (258km) SW of Oslo; chief port of S Norway. Founded 1641 by Christian IV, it was made an Episcopal see 1682, when Gothic cathedral was built; occupied by Germans 1940–44. Exports: fish, lumber. Industries: shipbuilding, food processing and canning, textiles, brewing. Pop. 56,152.

Krivoy Rog (Krivoj Rog), city in SE central Ukrainian republic USSR, 80mi (129km) SW of Dnepropetrovsk on the Ingulec and Saksagan rivers; rich iron producing region. Burial mounds (8th–4th century BC) indicate Scythians inhabited area and made use of iron ore. Germans occupied area 1941–44 and destroyed most of mining installations. Industries: foundries, coal mining, steel, chemicals, cement, coke. Founded 17th century. Pop. 573,000.

Kroeber, Alfred Louis (1876–1960), US cultural anthropologist, one of the most important anthropologists of the first half of the 20th century. He helped to advance the study of American Indian ethnology, linguistics and folklore, and social structure. His numerous works include the text *Anthropology* (1923).

Kronshstadt (Kronštadt), town in NW European USSR, on Kotlin Island in Gulf of Finland, 25mi (40km) W of Leningrad. Island was taken from Sweden by Peter the Great 1703 and fortified; in 1712–16 a naval base was added. Town now serves as chief naval base for Soviet Baltic fleet. Sailors stationed here greatly aided Bolsheviks in the Russian Revolution of 1917. Industries: lumber, clothing, footwear, shipyards. Pop. 40,000.

Kropotkin, Pëtr A(lekseevich) (Prince) (1842–1921), Russian anarchist. Jailed for seditious propaganda in St Petersburg in 1874, he escaped into exile in 1876. Again jailed in France in 1883–86 for anarchist activities, he lived in London after 1886, returning to Russia after the March 1917 revolution. Supporting Kerensky and the war against Germany, he denounced Bolshevik centralism and forcible suppression of opposition. A prolific author, he wrote *Memoirs of a Revolutionist* (1899).

Kruger, (Stephanus Johannes) Paulus (1825–1904), Boer political figure also known as Oom Paul. He helped settle the Transvaal, and after its annexation by the British (1877), he worked for independence and served as president (1883–1900). He organized continuing resistance to British rule and defeated the Jameson Raid of 1895, designed to capture Transvaal. During the Boer War (1899–1902) he represented the Boers in Europe, where he died.

Krugersdorp, city in NE Republic of South Africa, 20mi (32km) W of Johannesburg; site of Pardekraal monument (1838), an annual pilgrimage center, technical college, Sterkfontein Caves; important gold mining center for Witwatersrand. Named in honor of Stephanus Johannes Paulus Kruger. Industries: gold, uranium, manganese, asbestos, lime. Founded 1887. Pop. 100,500.

Krum (*r.* 802–14), one of the greatest Bulgarian rulers, or khans. Krum successfully engaged Byzantium in warfare (808–13), nearly capturing Constantinople in 813. After killing the Byzantine Emperor Nicephorus, he made his skull into a drinking cup. During his short reign progress was made toward establishing the absolute power of the khan and the encouragement of Slavic elements to the detriment of the Bulgar aristocracy.

Krupp Family, German industrial family, particularly prominent in steel and arms manufacturing. **Alfred Krupp** (1812–87) expanded his father's small iron foundry into a giant industry. He was the first steelmaker to install the Bessemer process and was one of the leaders in the industrial development of the Ruhr valley. His son **Friedrich Alfred Krupp** (1854–1902) expanded into shipbuilding and the manufacture of chrome and nickel steel alloys and armor plate. Krupp had the monopoly of German arms manufacture during World War I. Among its products was Big Bertha, a monstrous but inaccurate train-borne gun that shelled the Paris area from a distance of 70 mi (113km). Under Friedrich's son-in-law, **Gustav von Bohlen und Halbach** (1870–1950), who assumed the Krupp name, the Krupp works were a mainstay of the Nazi war effort. His son **Alfried Krupp** (1907–67) was imprisoned for his war activities and required to sell a portion of his Krupp interests. Alfried's son Arndt decided not to enter the business, and it passed from family control.

Krutch, Joseph Wood (1893–1970), US author, educator, and naturalist, b. Knoxville. He taught English at Columbia University (1937–52) and was drama

Seoul, South Korea

Kraków, Poland: Wawel Castle

Fritz Kreisler

Fritz Kreisler

Kremlin, Moscow

critic for the *Nation* (1924–32, 1937–52). His literary criticism includes *Five Masters: A Study in the Mutations of the Novel* (1930) and studies of Edgar Allan Poe (1926) and Samuel Johnson (1944). In 1950 he moved to Arizona and began writing a series of nature books foreshadowing the ecological concerns of the 1960s and 1970s.

Krypton, gaseous nonmetallic element (symbol Kr) of the noble-gas group, first discovered 1898. Krypton is present in the Earth's atmosphere (0.00015% by volume) and is obtained by the fractionation of liquid air. It is used in fluorescent lamps. The meter is defined by the wavelength of an emission line in the krypton spectrum. Chemically it is extremely inert but it does have a well-defined difluoride. Properties: at. no. 36; at. wt. 83.8; density 3.733 g dm^{-3}; melt. pt. −249.88°F (−156.6°C); boil. pt. −242.14°F (−152.3°C); most common isotope Kr^{84} (56.9%). *See also* Noble Gases. △1552, 1558.

K2. *See* Godwin-Austen.

Kuala Lumpur, city in S Malay Peninsula, Malaysia, 200mi (322km) NW of Singapore; capital of Malaysia, Selangor state, and largest city of the Malay Peninsula. Made capital of the Federated Malay States (British protectorate 1895), Federation of Malaya 1948, and Federation of Malaysia 1963, it is site of University of Malaya (1949) and 4,000-acre (1,628-hectare) industrial estate. Industries: tin, rubber. Founded 1857 as a tin mining camp. Pop. 451,728.

Kuang Hsü (1871–1908), Chinese emperor (1875–1908). The ninth Manchu Emperor, his personal name was Tsai-t'ien. Kuang Hsü was raised and controlled by the infamous Empress Dowager except for the brief period of the Hundred Days Reform in 1898, after which she imprisoned him until his death. △ 1270.

Kubitschek, Juscelino (1902–76), president of Brazil (1956–61), a physician whose political career began in the 1930s. As chief executive, he initiated the same kind of developmental projects that made him an outstanding provincial governor.

Kublai Khan (1216–1294), Mogul emperor (1260–94). Grandson of Genghis Khan, in 1279 he completed the conquest of China, deposing the Sung dynasty and founding the Yuan dynasty that would rule until 1368. His attempt to conquer Japan failed (1281) when his fleet was destroyed by a typhoon. He respected and encouraged Chinese scholarship and art. He brought economic prosperity through vast public works projects and the encouragement of trade. Marco Polo visited his court at Peking. △1112.

Kudu, Nyala, Sitatunga, and **Bushbuck,** several species of striped antelopes native to Africa south of the Sahara. All females are hornless. Greater kudu, the largest, stands 51in (130cm) at shoulders, with wide, spiraling horns and long fringe of hair from chest to neck. Lesser kudu is smaller without a neck fringe. There are two species of nyala—one in SE Africa, one in the Ethiopian mountains. The former has a conspicuous black belly fringe. The secretive bushbuck is smaller, with short horns and habits similar to the North American white-tailed deer. Sitatunga is a large swamp-dweller, feeding on aquatic vegetation. Family Bovidae; genus *Tragelaphus. See also* Antelope. △586.

Kuei-yang (Kweiyang, Guiyang), city in SW China, 220mi (354km) S of Chungking; capital of Kweichow prov. Rail center; site of Kweichow University. Industries: cement, paper, textiles, chemicals, petroleum products. Pop. 1,500,000.

Kuhlman, Kathryn. △748.

Kuhn, Richard (1900–67), Austrian-German chemist. He became professor at Heidelberg and was awarded a Nobel prize in 1938 for his work on the synthesis of vitamins A and B_2. He was forced by the Nazis to decline the prize and had to await the end of the war to receive the honor.

Kuibyshev (Kuybyshev, or Kujbyšev), city and river port in SE Russian SFSR, USSR, on left bank of Volga River at mouth of Samara River; capital of Kuibyshev oblast; scene of Pugachev's rebellion against Catherine II (1773–74); seat of anti-Bolshevik provincial government and Russian constituent assembly; during WWII, when Moscow was threatened by German army, Kuibyshev became temporary capital; site of university (1919). Industries: automobiles, aircraft, ballbearings, flour milling, oil refining. Founded 1586. Pop. 1,047,000.

Kuiper, Gerard Peter (1905–73), Dutch-born US astronomer, b. Harenkarspel, Netherlands. He emigrated in 1933. One of the most influential authorities on the solar system, he has made important discoveries about the outer planets and advanced the condensation theory of planetary genesis.

Kukai (774–835), real name Kobo Daishi, founder of the Shingon school of Japanese Buddhism. He renounced Confucianism, studied in China, and in the *Ten Stages of Consciousness* (830) showed a systematic grasp of major Oriental religions. His monastery at Mt Koya is the base for Shingon sects with followers numbering about 8,000,000.

Ku Klux Klan, secret white supremacy organization. First founded (1866) in Pulaski, Tenn., after the Civil War, it used intimidation and terror in an attempt to establish white supremacy in the South and to prevent newly enfranchised blacks from voting. Its trademark was the white hood and robe that its members wore. The chief executive of the Klan is the Grand Wizard (Nathan Bedford Forrest is believed to have been the first). It was formally disbanded (1869) and in 1870–71 the Ku Klux Klan Acts were passed to aid enforcement of the 14th and 15th Amendments. The Klan was revived in Georgia (1915) by William J. Simmons. It was anti-immigrant, anti-Catholic, and anti-Jewish, as well as white supremacist. It was prominent in the 1920s when membership reached 5,000,000. After a series of newspaper exposés, membership declined until it was about 9,000 in 1930. After World War II, Samuel Green again revived the Klan. The Klan continued operations in the 1970s but had no national importance. *See also* Force Acts. △1278.

Kulturkampf, name given to Otto von Bismarck's attempt to subordinate the Roman Catholic Church to the German state (1871–87). The restrictive laws passed were openly resisted, and the Catholic Center party grew steadily. From 1878 the laws were gradually repealed. △1300.

Kumamoto, city in W central Kyushu, Japan, approx. 75mi (121km) S of Kitakyushu; capital of Kumamoto prefecture. An important castle town under Hosokawa daimyo 1632–1868, it became trade center for agricultural products; site of Buddhist temple, Kumamoto Medical University. Industries: food processing, marketing, textiles, chemicals. Pop. 440,020.

Kumasi, city in central Ghana, approx. 115mi (186km) NW of Accra; capital of Ashanti Region; 2nd-largest city in Ghana. Flourished as capital of Ashanti kingdom from 18th century; besieged by British 1874, 1896, and 1900; annexed by Britain 1901, after violent native uprising; industrial development spurred by construction of railroad *c.*1901 to major ports on Gulf of Guinea; seat of Kumasi College of Technology (1951). Industries: cacao, handcrafts, lumbering. Pop. 234,274.

Kumquat, hardy evergreen tree or shrub *(Fortunella)* of the rue family. Growing to 15ft (4.6m), they yield a small citrus fruit, orange when ripe. The shrubs are often grown for ornament and the fruit is used to make jelly or marmalade.

Kun, Béla (1885–1937), Hungarian Communist political leader. An associate of Lenin and a Bolshevik from his youth, he received training in Moscow after his release from a Siberian prisoner-of-war camp. In 1919, after replacing Mihály Károlyi as premier, he changed the newly formed republic into the Hungarian Soviet Republic, introducing radical changes in the government. Defeated with the help of the Romanians, he fled to Vienna and later to the Soviet Union in 1920.

Kung Fu, a martial art, a generic term referring to the many styles of Chinese infighting. Although it was developed in Canton, China, as *gung fu,* its acceptance as an Oriental concept of self-defense is questionable.

Kunlun, central Asian mountain system lying between the Himalaya and the Tien Shan ranges; forms natural boundary between N Tibet and Torim basin of Sinkiang; sparsely settled by nomads. Highest peak is 25,348ft (7,731m). Length: 1,000mi (1,610km).

Kunming (K'un-ming), city in S China, 380mi (612km) SW of Chungking, on N shore of Lake Tien, on Burma Road; capital of Yunnan prov.; on railroad line to Hanoi and N Vietnam. A strategic area during WWII, it was used as US air base, and Chinese military headquarters; seat of university (1934). Exports: fur, tea, precious stones, tin. Industries: iron, copper smelting, textiles, chemicals, machinery, electrical equipment, food processing. Pop. approx. 1,700,000.

Kuomintang or **Nationalist Party,** the ruling political force in China from 1928 until 1949 and subsequently in Taiwan. Initially a secret revolutionary alliance against Manchu rule in China, it became an open political party in 1912 and was reorganized with Leninist structure and discipline by Sun Yat-sen in 1924 with the aid of Soviet advisers. Sun provided the Kuomintang with the program and doctrine that remain the basic program of the Nationalists in Taiwan. Sun was later succeeded by Chiang Kai-shek as head (1938–75) and by Chiang Ching-Kuo (1976–). △ 1270, 1328.

Kurchatovium, *See* Element 104.

Kurdistan region of SW Asia, including parts of E Turkey, NE Iraq, NW Iran, and small sections of NE Syria and Soviet Armenia. It extends N to S from the Aras River and Turkish border with Armenian republic, SSR, USSR, to Diyala Tributary of Tigris River in Iraq, and E to W from mountains of Iran W of Hamadân to Tigris River. In the 7th century the Kurds were converted to Islam by the conquering Arabs. They were under the control of Seljuk Turks in 11th century, Mongols from 13th–15th centuries, and then became part of the Ottoman Empire. When this empire was liquidated by Treaty of Sèvres in 1920, Kurdistan was to become autonomous, but Kurdish demands were not met. The people are nomadic herders, with some farming in the valleys of the high mountains. Area: 74,000sq mi (191,668sq km). Pop. 2,750,000.

Kurds, people who inhabit Kurdistan, a geographical region consisting of the adjacent mountain areas of Turkey, Iraq, and Iran. They are seminomadic pastoralists as well as sedentary farmers cultivating wheat and cotton. Although the latter have lost many tribal characteristics, Kurdish national feeling remains strong.

Kurgan, city in Russian SFSR, USSR, on Tobol River, 140mi (225km) E of Chelyabinsk; capital of Kurgan oblast; site of Neolithic burial mounds (*c.* 6,000 BC); trading center for farm products. Industries: agricultural machinery, electrical equipment, machine tools, food processing. Founded 17th century. Pop. 244,000.

Kuril (Kuril'skije) or **Kurile Islands,** chain of 30 large and many smaller islands extending 750mi (1,208km) from S Kamchatka Peninsula to NE Hokkaido, Japan, separating Sea of Okhotsk from Pacific Ocean. Of volcanic origin, the islands have active volcanoes and many earthquakes. Islands were discovered 1634 by Martin de Vries, Dutch navigator; Russian fishermen occupied N islands; Japanese fishermen occupied S islands. In 1875, Russia withdrew from islands in exchange for Japan's surrender of Sakhalin. Since end of WWII, dispute over ownership of islands has been major reason for failure of Japan and USSR to sign peace treaty. Industries: whaling, vegetables. Highest peak is Atlasova volcano, 7,674ft (2,341m) on Atlasova Island. Area: 6,020sq mi (15,592sq km). Pop. 15,000.

Kurosawa, Akira (1910–), Japanese film director. In *Rashomon* (1950), he introduced the savage, bloodthirsty world of the Samurai warriors to Western audiences. The popularity of his genre was confirmed with *Seven Samurai* (1954), later remade by John Sturges as *The Magnificent Seven.* He also made films in a modern idiom, notably *Living* (1952). △1370.

Kuroshio Current, also called the Japan current. It is the western boundary current of the North Pacific gyre and flows along the east coast of the Japanese islands. It is comparable to the Gulf Stream along the east coast of North America.

Kursk, city in Russian SFSR, USSR, at confluence of Tuskoc and Seim rivers. An old city, it was destroyed by Mongols 1240 and rebuilt as a frontier post 1586. Important WWII victory for USSR occurred nearby (1943). Industries: chemicals, synthetic fibers, shoes, electrical equipment. Founded 1095. Pop. 284,000.

Kush or **Cush, Kingdom of,** former state in Nubia. Lasting roughly 1100 BC to AD 350, it conquered Egypt in the 7th–8th centuries BC. It was thereafter defeated by the Assyrians and moved its capital to Meroë in the Sudan. After Roman and Arab attacks in the north, Meroë was captured by the Axumites around AD 350, and the Kushites are thought to have fled west, possibly to the Lake Chad area. △974, 1116.

Kushan Dynasty. △986.

Kutch, Rann of, large salt marsh, W India; site of battles between India and Pakistan in 1965 and 1971.

Kutuzov, Mikhail I(larionovich) (1745–1813), Russian general. Supreme commander against Napoleon, he met and withstood the enemy at Borodino (1812). Then, after abandoning Moscow, he forced the French to retreat in winter through desolate territory, harrying them by guerrilla warfare. A brilliant leader, he became a field marshal in 1812.

Kuvasz, guard and herding dog (working group) brought to eastern Europe from Tibet in the 15th century. It has an elongated head with straight muzzle; V-shaped ears held close to the head; medium-length body, quite broad across the back; medium-length legs; and long tail carried low. The white, medium-length double coat covers slate gray or black skin. There is a mane on the neck and chest; feathering on legs; and short smooth hair on head, ears, and paws. Average size: 28–30in (71–76cm) high at shoulder; 100–115lb (45–52kg). *See also* Working Dogs.

Kuwait (Al-Kuwait), State of, independent Arab state in NE corner of the Arabian peninsula on the Persian Gulf. A leading oil producer, it is one of the world's wealthiest countries.

Land and economy. Except for Al-Jahrah Oasis and a few fertile sections in the SE and coastal areas, the country is almost entirely desert. The vast majority of the population is concentrated in the cities. Kuwait has about 15% of the world's petroleum reserves, and oil dominates the economy. The sharp increases in oil prices in 1974 sent the country's economy skyrocketing. The government has utilized its huge financial resources to create a welfare state with no taxes and free medical care, education, and social security.

People. The people are predominantly Arab, and Arabic is the official language. Islam is the official religion. More than half of the people are literate and with expanded free educational facilities, the literacy rate is rapidly increasing. Almost half of the people are not Kuwaitis and have no voice in the government.

Government and history. A constitutional monarchy, the country is governed by an emir and a 50-member National Assembly. Founded in 1756 by members of the al-Sabah dynasty, Kuwait is still ruled by the family today. In 1899 a treaty was drawn up in which Great Britain administered foreign relations and protected the territorial rights. Kuwait became independent in 1961, and shortly thereafter Iraq lay claim to the country. Through a protection agreement with the United Kingdom, Kuwait requested and received British troops to forestall the Iraqis. Since then, relations between Kuwait and Iraq have improved. Kuwait joined the United Nations in 1963.

PROFILE

Official name: State of Kuwait
Area: 6,200sq mi (16,058sq km)
Population: 738,663
Density: 135.2 per sq mi (52.2 per sq km)
Chief city: Kuwait (capital)
Government: constitutional monarchy (emirate)
Religion: Islam (official)
Language: Arabic (official)
Monetary unit: Kuwaiti dinar
Gross national product: $7,165,000,000
Per capita income: $8,449
Industries (major products): light and heavy petroleum and petroleum products
Minerals (major): crude petroleum, natural gas
Trading partners (major): Japan, United States, Great Britain, West Germany, Saudi Arabia, Iran

Kuybyshev. *See* Kuibyshev.

Kuznets, Simon (1901–), US economist, b. Russia. He developed the national income accounting system in the 1930s. The Kuznets cycle, an intermediate business cycle of about 20 years duration, was discovered by and named after Kuznets. He received the 1971 Nobel Prize in economics for his research on the economic growth of nations.

Kuznetsov, Anatoly (1929–), Soviet novelist and short-story writer. His works include the novels *Sequel of a Legend* (1957) and *Babi Yar* (1966), several volumes of short stories, and film scenarios. Defecting because of oppressive surveillance and censorship, he settled in England in 1969 and took a new name, A. Anatoli, to dissociate himself from his past work.

Kuznetz (Kuzneck) Basin, basin of W Siberia, USSR, between Kuznetz Ala-Tau range and Salair Ridge, often called Kuzbas. Rich coal and iron ore deposits discovered 17th and 18th centuries have made it a major industrial region. Area: 10,000sq mi (25,900sq km).

Kwakiutl, major tribe of North American Indians speaking the Wakashan tongue, and closely related to the Bellabella. From a total population of 3,500 in 1600, they presently number some 2,500, occupying Queen Charlotte and northern Vancouver islands in British Columbia. They are the classic "potlatch" people, whose wooden sculpture and totem poles are world famous.

Kwangju, formerly Koshu; city in SW Korea; capital of South Cholla prov.; railroad and educational center. Industries: textiles, rice milling, rayon, beer. Pop. 502,753.

Kwangtung (Guangdong), southernmost prov. in China, on South China Sea; Canton is the capital. Prov. has an 800-mi (1,280-km) coastline with approx. 730 islands, Hainan being the largest. The British community of Hong Kong and Portuguese colony of Macao lie on the coastal Pearl River estuary. After 211 BC, Kwangtung came under Chinese suzerainty; it was an important center for China's early trade and foreign contacts, mainly through Canton, which had seen Arab, Hindu, and Parsi trade for centuries, and after *c.* 1650 European contacts through Portuguese traders. Prov. was scene of unrest during Chinese Revolution (1911); city was occupied by Japanese (1938–45) during Sino-Japanese War. Area: 89,344sq mi (231,401sq km). Pop. approx. 40,000,000.

Kwashiorkor, meaning "displaced child," is a disease of infants and young children occurring primarily in the tropics or subtropics and caused by a diet deficient in high-quality protein and calories. Children with the disease show retarded growth, mental apathy, anemia, fatty liver, digestive and skin disorders, and changes in skin pigment, with thick patches that may become pinkish and virtually raw. △696, 732.

Kweichow (Guizhou), prov. in S China, bounded by provinces of Szechwan (N), Hunan (E), Yunnan (W), and by Kwangsi Chuang autonomous region (S); capital is Kweiyang. In the rural area the population includes mostly Miao aboriginal tribesmen, who were cast out of other provinces because of their unwillingness to accept Chinese customs; they are noted for their embroideries. Kweichow came under Chinese suzerainty 10th century; during WWII it served as military base for Chinese and Allied forces. Area: approx. 67,181sq mi (173,999sq km). Pop. approx. 17,000,000.

Ky, Nguyen Cao (1930–), Vietnamese political figure. He fought with the French until their defeat in 1954. He then joined the South Vietnamese air force. After the overthrow of Diem in 1963 he became air commander. Following the coup led by Nguyen Van Thieu (1965), he was appointed premier, then was elected Thieu's vice president (1967–71). He fled to the United States in 1975.

Kyd (Kid), Thomas, 1558–94, English playwright, friend of Christopher Marlowe. His play *The Spanish Tragedy* (*c.* 1585) was the first "blood and revenge" drama, similar to Shakespeare's *Hamlet*. It was later revised by Ben Jonson. Kyd may have written a lost play suggesting *The Taming of the Shrew*.

Kyoga Lake, lake in S central Uganda, E Africa, N of Lake Victoria; formed by Victoria Nile in its middle course. Area: 1,710sq mi (4,349sq km).

Kyoto, city in W central Honshu, Japan, approx. 26mi (42km) NE of Osaka; capital of Kyoto prefecture; early center of silk industry; site of the imperial residence for over 1,000 years, containing palaces, shrines, and other early structures. Modern city is site of Kyoto University (1897), Doshisha University, Kyoto University of Industrial Arts and Textiles (1949). Industries: lacquerware, porcelain, embroidery, precision tools and machines, food processing, metals. Pop. 1,419,165.

Kyushu, island of S Japan, 3rd-largest and southernmost of four principal Japanese islands. Terrain is mountainous, with irregular coast forming many natural harbors; the Chikugo River, longest on Kyushu, irrigates the NW rice growing region. Most densely populated of the Japanese islands, its industrial cities include Kitakyushu, Kumamoto, Kurume, Fukuoka; chief port is Nagasaki, first to be opened to Western trade. Crops: rice, tea, tobacco, fruits, soybeans. Industries: mining, textiles (silk), porcelain, metals, machinery. Area: approx. 16,205sq mi (41,971sq km). Pop. 12,072,179.

Kyzyl (Kizil) Kum Desert, desert in Uzbek and Kazakh SSR, USSR, between Amu Darya and Syr Darya rivers. Irrigated agriculture is carried on in river valleys; semi-nomadic tribesmen raise caracul sheep in sparsely vegetated desert. Area: 115,000sq mi (297,858sq km).

Kudu

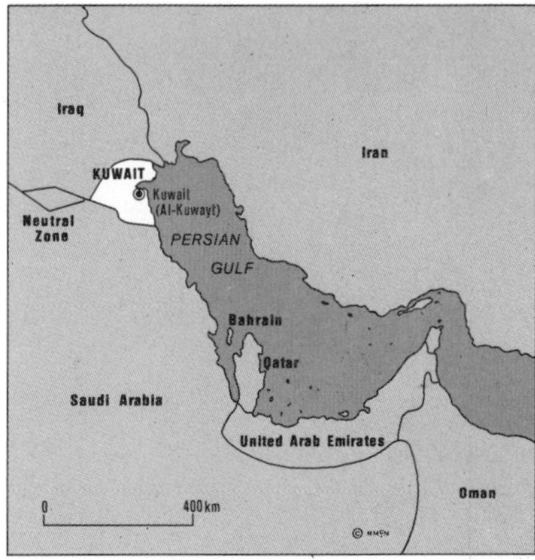
Iraq
Iran
KUWAIT
Kuwait (Al-Kuwayt)
Neutral Zone
PERSIAN GULF
Bahrain
Qatar
Saudi Arabia
United Arab Emirates
Oman
0
400km
Kuwait

Kwangtung Province, China

Kyoto, Japan: Silver Pavilion

L

Labor, in childbirth, the normal delivery of the fetus at the end of pregnancy. The first stage, lasting 2 to 10 hours, is measured from the onset of contractions that occur at 5-minute intervals lasting at least 30 seconds each. During this stage the cervix dilates up to 4in (10cm). Transition follows as the cervix is almost fully dilated, leading to the second stage when dilation is full. This stage may last from 30 minutes to 2 hours, at the end of which the infant is born. The third stage takes about 5–10 minutes, and is the period from birth to delivery of the placenta. △704.

Labor, Child. *See* Child Labor.

Labor, Department of, US federal cabinet level department within the executive branch. The Labor Department administers and enforces statutes benefiting wage earners, improving their working conditions, and providing opportunities for employment. The department is headed by the secretary of labor. It was established in 1884 as the Bureau of Labor in the Department of the Interior. In 1903 it was part of the Department of Commerce and Labor; in 1913 it became a separate department.

Labor Disputes Act. *See* Smith-Connally Anti-Strike Act.

Labor Force, all members of the population who are working, looking for work, or have a job (even if they are currently not at work because they are on vacation, sick, on strike, etc). In the United States, labor force statistics are gathered by the Department of Labor, Bureau of Labor Statistics.

The absolute size of the labor force varies with the time of the year and with economic conditions. Normally the labor force expands in the summer as schools close and contracts in the fall as schools open. In recessions, when employment opportunities are limited, many people leave the labor force (ie, they stop looking for work) and return to it when jobs are available. The size of the labor force is an important measure of the health of the economy.

Labor-Management Relations Act. *See* Taft-Hartley Act.

Labor Movement in the United States, historic attempt of working people to improve working conditions and their economic position. Unlike their European counterparts, which have often worked for a change in the governmental system to socialism or Communism, US labor unions and their members have generally accepted capitalism. Members of craft unions, organized on a trade or occupational basis in the late 18th century, could be fined or imprisoned when employers, using English common law, accused them of criminal conspiracy. The Supreme Court restricted use of this doctrine in 1842, and thereafter the legality of unions depended on the means they employed to gain better worker conditions. The National Labor Union, formed in 1866, and the Knights of Labor (1869) included trade unions, suffragettes, farmers' organizations, and other reform groups of diverse goals; each soon foundered. Samuel Gompers, learning from their mistakes, organized the American Federation of Labor (AFL) in 1886; membership was restricted to skilled laborers only and the AFL had the pragmatic goals of raising wages, improving work conditions, honoring contracts, and instigating collective bargaining.

The struggle between management and labor often erupted into violence, as when police and labor protestors were killed in the Haymarket Massacre (1886) in Chicago. The federal government did not remain neutral, and federal troops were used against strikers when violence broke out in response to the government's use of the Sherman Antitrust Act against the American Railway Union. Opposed by the federally backed employers on one side and the more radical Industrial Workers of the World (IWW) on the other, the AFL nonetheless grew to include 4,000,000 workers by 1920. Another 1,000,000 belonged to unaffiliated unions, including the railroad brotherhoods. The influence of the federal government over labor-management relationships enhanced labor's prestige during World War I, but during the prosperity of the 1920s union membership decreased. Under President Franklin D. Roosevelt's New Deal policies in the 1930s, a series of laws, including the National Labor Relations (Wagner) Act (1935), made organizing easier. The right to join a union and the duty of employers to bargain with workers were ensured. This stimulated organization on an industry-wide basis, including workers formerly excluded from the craft unions. When the automobile, steel, and other mass-production industrial unions were expelled from the AFL, they created the Congress of Industrial Organizations (CIO) in 1938.

Rivalry between the CIO and AFL and labor's increased power during World War II stimulated union growth until 14,000,000 workers were organized by 1945. George Meany, president of the AFL, and Walter Reuther, president of the CIO, negotiated a merger in 1955, and by then 17,500,000 workers were in unions. Because of apathy at the local union level, power often became concentrated in the hands of a few national leaders. Amid charges of corruption, union power was curbed by the Taft-Hartley Act of 1947 and the Landrum-Griffin Act of 1959. Membership in the AFL-CIO declined, partly due to the expulsion of allegedly corrupt unions such as the International Brotherhood of Teamsters, and partly due to the growing percentage of the white collar workers (traditionally difficult to organize) in the work force. Young workers in the 1960s saw the unions as unsympathetic to their concerns with civil rights, war, and pollution. Future growth will depend on organized labor's ability to adapt to the needs of white-collar, female, minority, and young workers. Labor has shown some success in these areas, and there has been increased unionization among teachers, government employees, and health and farm workers. △936.

Labour Party, British socialist political party with financial and institutional links with trade unionism. Established under this name in 1906, the Labour party rapidly gained strength, joining World War I coalition governments and subsequently becoming the official opposition, eclipsing the Liberal party. Ramsay MacDonald formed the first, short-lived Labour administration (1924). In power (1929–31) with Liberal support, and as part of Churchill's World War II administration (1940–45), Labour took office alone in 1945 under Clement Atlee with an extensive program of reconstruction, nationalization, and expanded social welfare services. Thirteen years in opposition (1951–64) adjusted Labour's policies to postwar affluence and gained support outside its traditional working-class base. The party returned to power under Harold Wilson (1964–70, 1974–76).

Labrador, region in Newfoundland, E Canada; bordered by NE Quebec (W and S) and Labrador Sea (E); the coastal region is indented with fjords, the mountains becoming increasingly higher toward N; the inland plateau is heavily forested, with innumerable lakes and rivers, notably the Churchill River, which drains into Lake Melville. The coast was known to the Norsemen *c.* 10th century, and was visited by John Cabot (1498) and Corte-Real (1500); came under Great Britain by Treaty of Paris 1763; boundaries between Newfoundland and Quebec under dispute 1809–1927 when matter was settled by British Privy Council; became part of Canada 1949. Industries: lumbering, fishing, mining. Area: 112,826sq mi (292,219sq km). *See also* Newfoundland.

Labrador Current (Arctic Current or Arctic Stream), current of N Atlantic Ocean, flows S from Baffin Bay along coast of Labrador, E Canada, to meet the Gulf Stream in the Grand Banks area of NW Atlantic Ocean; the meeting of the cold water and ice flow from Labrador current with the warm waters of the Gulf Stream causes dense fogs in this area.

Labrador Duck, extinct sea duck. Species *Camptorhynchus labradorius.*

Labrador Retriever, water dog (sporting group) developed in Newfoundland around 1822. Strongly built, it has a wide head; long, powerful jaws; a wide nose; low-set, hanging ears; short, wide body; and medium-length legs. The distinctive tail, thick at the base and tapered to a point, is carried up. The hard, dense coat is short; colors are black, yellow, or chocolate. Average size: 22.5–24.5in (57–62cm) high at shoulder; 60–75lb (27–34kg). *See also* Sporting Dog.

Lac, a secretion of the lac insect, *Laccifer lacca,* deposited on tree twigs. Sticky and resinous, it is harvested in Asia mainly for use in shellac and red lac dye. From 17,000 to 90,000 insects are needed to produce 1lb (454g) of shellac. Lac products have been used in India since 1200 BC.

Lacaille, Nicholas Louis de (1713–62), French astronomer noted for mapping the constellations visible from the Southern Hemisphere and naming many of them. In 1750 he led an expedition to the Cape of Good Hope. There, over a period of two years, he mapped the position of 10,000 stars, giving them all catalog numbers. His *Star Catalog of the Southern Sky,* still in use, was published in 1763.

Laccolith, an intrusive igneous rock body that forms a dome over the strata which it has penetrated. The base is typically horizontal while the upper surface is convex. Generally under 10mi (16km) in diameter with thicknesses of 100–3,000ft (30–915m), they contain more acidic than basic rocks. The Henry Mountains of Utah have a well-known laccolith. △176, 246.

Lace Bugs. △500.

Lacewing, or aphid lion, delicate green insect found worldwide. It is found on grass and weeds, feeding on aphids. Length: 0.5–1in (13–25mm). Order Neuroptera; family Chrysopidae. *See also* Neuroptera.

Lachine, city on Montreal Island in S Quebec, Canada, at E end of Lake St Louis, SW of Montreal. Scene of massacre of settlers by Iroquois Indians in 1689. Industries: iron, steel, tires. Pop. 44,345.

Lachrymal Gland. △674.

Lac Insect, scale insect found in tropical and subtropical areas. The Indian *Laccifer lacca* is found in SE Asia and India and is the major source of lac for the production of shellac and varnishes. The female scale lives in a resinlike cell and is capable of producing a layer of lac 0.5in (13mm) thick. Length: to ⅛in (3mm). Family Lacciferdae. *See also* Scale Insect.

Lackawanna, city in W New York, on Lake Erie, 5mi (8km) S of Buffalo. Industries: shipbuilding, steel, abrasives, refractories. Inc. 1909. Pop. (1970) 28,-657.

Laclède (Liquest), Pierre (1724?–78), French fur trader. He began a fur business in New Orleans (1755). After acquiring trading rights with the Indians in the Missouri River valley, he cleared land at the junction of the Missouri and Mississippi rivers (1764). The settlement established there became St Louis. He oversaw its growth into an active trading community.

La Coruña, seaport city in Spain, on Atlantic Ocean; capital of La Coruña prov. Captured 1370 by Portugal, it was launching point of Spanish Armada 1588; destroyed by Sir Francis Drake 1589; taken by French 1823, and by Carlists 1836. Industries: wine, linen, hams, sardines, leather. Area: (prov.) 3,041sq mi (7,876sq km). Pop. (city) 189,654; (prov.) 1,004,188.

Lacquer, paint that forms a film by loss of solvent by evaporation. The film is usually composed of a cellulose ester (such as nitrocellulose) in combination with an alkyd resin and the solvent may be a ketone (such as methylbutyl ketone), an alcohol, or some other cellulose solvent.

Lacquerware, objects such as furniture and utensils painted with lacquer, which is the painting medium derived from the resin of the *Rhus vernicifera*, a tree common in Japan and China. Lacquer is applied in several layers. When dry, the durable surface is hard and impervious to water.

Lacrimal Gland, protective accessory organ of the eye that produces tears. Located in the orbital cavity in a slight depression, the gland produces, under autonomic nervous control, slightly germicidal tears that flow through ducts to the surface of the eye to lubricate it. △674.

La Crosse, city in W Wisconsin, at confluence of Mississippi, Black, and La Crosse rivers; seat of La Crosse co; site of Wisconsin State University (1909), Viterbo College (1931), Western Wisconsin Technical Institute. Industries: dairying, farm equipment, air conditioning units, beer, rubber, truck trailers. Founded late 18th century as French fur trading post; inc. 1856. Pop. (1970) 51,153.

Lacrosse, a fast-action ball game, popular in the United States and in Canada, where it is the national game. It is played by two teams of 10 persons each on a field 110yd (100m) long and 60–70yd (55–64m) wide. In Canada there are 12 players on a side; in box lacrosse, 6 on a side. Each team defends a goal 6ft wide and high (1.8m) at one end of the field and scores points by putting the ball in the opponent's goal (1 point). A game consists of four 15-minute periods, plus two 5-minute overtime periods if a regulation game ends in a tie. Each player carries a stick, or crosse, with an adjustable meshwork head. The hard rubber ball, at least 7.75in (19.7cm) in circumference, is kept in play by being carried, passed, or hit with the stick, or rolled, or kicked. Only the goalkeeper may touch the ball with his hands. Besides the goalkeeper, each team has three attack players, near the opponent's goal; three midfielders, who play on both attack and defense; and three defensemen, near their own goal. Players wear protective pads and masks. Defensive play consists of impeding attacking players by body checking or taking the ball away. Rule infractions for various kinds of rough play result in personal fouls, for which the player must leave the game for 1–3 minutes, and expulsion fouls, for which the player is suspended for the game. Minor infractions are technical fouls, resulting in the ball's loss or the player's suspension for 30 seconds.

Lacrosse was developed by Canadian Indians as baggataway; each side sometimes had as many as 1,000 men. French Canadians adopted the sport, calling it *la crosse* for the netted stick's resemblance to a bishop's crosier. The game's modern rules were framed in the 1860s by William G. Beers, who promoted it vigorously. Long played primarily in eastern colleges, the game's US popularity grew rapidly in the 1960s and 1970s. *See also* Box Lacrosse.

Lactation, the act of secreting and producing milk to feed young. After hormonal-induced breast enlargement during pregnancy, a pituitary hormone (prolactin) stimulates breast cells to begin secreting milk. The milk "comes in" the breast's lactiferous ducts leading to the nipple in from 1 to 3 days after delivery and then is stimulated by suckling, which, in turn, triggers neural and hormonal changes that control and maintain lactation. *See also* Breast. △690.

Lactic Acid, colorless optically active syrupy liquid (formula $CH_3CHOHCOOH$) formed from lactose in milk by the action of bacteria: used in foods and beverages, in tanning, dyeing, and adhesive manufacture. Properties: sp gr 1.2; melt. pt. 64.4°F (18°C); boil. pt. 251.6°F (122°C). △686.

Lactogenic Hormone, or prolactin, polypeptide hormone produced by the pituitary gland. It stimulates secretion of milk by the mammary gland following delivery of the baby. △690.

Ladino, a dialect of Spanish spoken by the descendants of Jews who were exiled from Spain in 1492. Prior to World War II it was spoken by Jews in a number of countries in E and S Europe, the N coast of Africa, and the Western Hemisphere. Today most Ladino speakers live in either Turkey or Israel.

Ladislas I (1040?–95), king of Hungary (1077–95), son of Bela I. Heroic and beloved, he reestablished internal order after dealing with barbarian and German invasions and a recurrence of paganism. Known for his wise laws, he also subjugated Bosnia, Croatia, and part of Transylvania. He was canonized by the Roman Catholic Church in 1192.

Ladislas II (1456–1516), king of Bohemia (1471–1516) and of Hungary (1490–1516). Son of Casimir IV of Poland, he was the first ruler of the Jagellonian family and a weak king, totally unsuited to his position. His claim to the crown of Hungary was contested by Matthias Corvinus. The aristocracy increased its power during his reign.

Ladislas I (or IV) Lokietek (1260–1333), king of Poland (1320–33). He became duke of Poland as Ladislas IV in 1296 and worked to unite Poland. After wars lasting from 1305–12, he united Great and Little Poland. Crowned in 1320, he introduced legal reforms. As an ally of the Teutonic Knights, he saved Danzig from Brandenburg, but later warred with the Knights from 1327 to 1333.

Ladislas II (or V) Jagello (1350–1434), grand duke of Lithuania (1377–86) and king of Poland (1386–1434). As grand duke he opposed the Teutonic Order (1377–86) and then married Jadwiga, queen of Poland, which led to his election as king and his acceptance of Roman Catholicism. His lands stretched from the Baltic to the Black Sea and almost to Moscow. With Lithuanians, he defeated the Teutonic Knights at Tannenberg (1410). Poland became a great power during his reign.

Ladislas III (1424–44), king of Poland (1434–44) and king of Hungary as Ladislas I (1440–44). He led a successful Crusade against the Turks in 1443, but was defeated by them and killed at the Battle of Varna in the next year.

Ladislas IV (or VII) (1595–1648), king of Poland (1632–48), son of Sigismund III. After fighting with Russia, Sweden, and the Ottoman Empire, he won favorable settlements from each. However, he failed to solve internal problems with the Sejm and lost part of the Ukraine to Russia following the 1648 Cossack revolt.

Ladoga (Ladožskoje), lake in NW European USSR; largest lake in Europe. Formerly divided between Finland and USSR, since 1947 it has been entirely within USSR. It is drained by Neva River which empties into Gulf of Finland; canals along S part of lake connect Leningrad with Caspian Sea. During WWII, the lake's frozen surface was a lifeline for supplying Leningrad during winter months (1941–43). Island of Valaam (one of many) in lake is site of 12th-century Russian monastery. Area: 7,000sq mi (18,130sq km).

Ladybird Beetle, or ladybug, lady beetle, beetle that typically preys on aphids, scale insects, and other plant pests. They are about the size and shape of a small split pea, and are tan, red, or black with red, black, yellow, or white markings. Because they have big appetites and reproduce rapidly, they are a beneficial insect. Family Coccinellidae. △500.

Ladybug. *See* Ladybird Beetle.

Lady Fern, feathery fern found in temperate areas of the world in moist, shady places. The 30in (76cm) leaves are 10in (25cm) wide and grow in circular clusters. Height: to 36in (91cm). Family Aspliniaceae; species *Athyrium filix-femina*. *See also* Fern.

Lady with the Unicorn. △1106.

Laertes, in Greek mythology, king of Ithaca and father of Odysseus. It was on his funeral canopy that Penelope worked to delay her selection of a suitor in the *Odyssey*.

LaFarge, Oliver (1901–63), US writer and anthropologist, b. New York City. He used his archeolog-

Labrador retriever

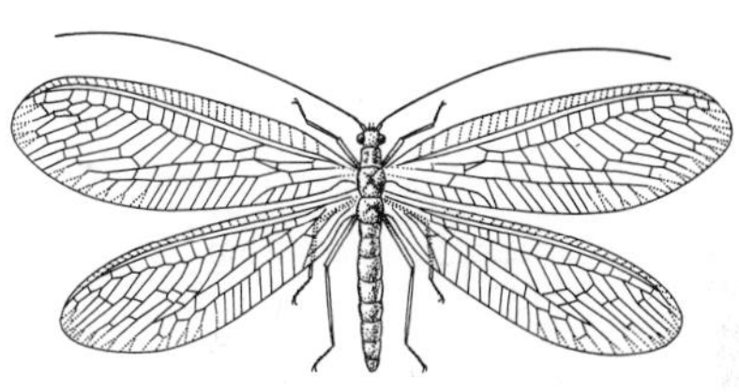

Lacewing

Lacquerware (18th-century Venetian)

Lacrosse

ical and ethnological expeditions to Arizona, Guatemala, and Mexico as the inspiration for his prize-winning stories and novels. Among his works are *Laughing Boy*, a perceptive study of Navaho life (1929, Pulitzer Prize), and *Sparks Fly Upward* (1931).

Lafayette, Marie Joseph Paul Yves Roch Gilbert du Motier, Marquis de (1757–1834), French officer, statesman, and hero of the American Revolution. Sympathetic to the American cause, he arrived in Philadelphia in 1777 and was commissioned a major general. He was wounded at Brandywine and wintered at Valley Forge (1777–78) with Washington. In 1778–80 he was in France negotiating for financial and military aid. In 1781 he distinguished himself in the Yorktown campaign that led to Cornwallis' surrender. He returned to France in 1781, but made a visit to the United States in 1784. In 1789 he first became a member of the States-General, then the National Assembly. After the fall of the Bastille in that year he was appointed commander of the militia. He lost his popular support when in 1791 he ordered his troops to fire on a crowd petitioning for the abolition of the monarchy. In 1792 he led an army in the Austrian campaign, but was relieved of his command after the overthrow of the monarchy. He fled France and was imprisoned by the Austrians until released on Napoleon's demand in 1797. He lived in retirement until the Restoration (1814) when he became a member of the Chamber of Deputies. He made a triumphant visit to the United States in 1824–25. In 1830 he played a major role in the July Revolution, supporting the moderates and favoring Louis Philippe's ascendancy. △1224.

Lafayette, city in W central Indiana, on Wabash River; seat of Tippecanoe co; scene of Battle of Tippecanoe (November 1811) between US Troops and Indians; now a state memorial; site of Purdue University (1865). Industries: meat packing, aluminum, rubber goods. Founded on site of 18th-century French fort. Pop. (1970) 44,955.

Lafayette, city in S Louisiana, 55mi (89km) WSW of Baton Rouge; seat of Lafayette parish; site of University of Southwestern Louisiana (1900) and Heyman Oil Center, headquarters for numerous oil companies. Industries: lumber, oil, natural gas, sashes, doors, concrete pipes, sugar refining, packing plants. Founded 1770s by Acadians fleeing Nova Scotia; inc. as town 1836, as city 1914. Pop. (1970) 68,908.

Lafitte, Jean (*c.* 1780–*c.* 1826), pirate. The leader of a large pirate band on the Gulf of Mexico, he disposed of stolen Spanish goods through the black market in New Orleans. He received a pardon from President Madison for leading his men against the British in the latter part of the War of 1812. After the war, he and his pirates lived on an island that today is Galveston, Tex. There, they resumed raids against Spanish ships. In 1821, following US complaints, he left the island and disappeared.

La Follette, Robert Marion (1855–1925), US political leader and Progressive party presidential candidate (1924), b. Primrose, Wis. A Republican congressman (1885–91), he helped draft McKinley Tariff Act (1890). He served as governor of Wisconsin (1900–06) and made the state's programs a model for other states. As a US senator (1906–25), he sponsored a resolution to investigate naval oil leases (Teapot Dome Scandal 1921). He was also a founder of the National Progressive Republican League (1911), and was that party's unsuccessful presidential candidate (1924). Domestically a liberal, he was an isolationist in foreign affairs.

LAFTA. *See* Latin American Free Trade Association.

Lagash. △956.

Lagerkvist, Pär Fabian (1891–1974), Swedish writer, his characteristic note was of radical pessimism at man's inhumanity to man. Major works include *Anguish* (1916), *The Eternal Smile* (1920), *The Hangman* (1933), and the plays *Man Without a Soul* (1936) and *Let Man Live* (1949). International recognition came with *The Dwarf* (1944), *Barabbas* (1951), *The Sibyl* (1956), and *Death of Ahasuerus* (1960). He was awarded the Nobel Prize for literature in 1951.

Lagerlöf, Selma (1858–1940), Swedish novelist, pacifist, and feminist. Her marvelous narrative power was at its best in *Gösta Berlings Saga* (1891), *Jerusalem* (1901–02), *The Ring of the Löwenskölds* (1931), in various collections of short stories and children's books, and in her memoirs of childhood. She was awarded the Nobel Prize for literature in 1909.

Lago di Como. *See* Como, Lake.

Lagoon, the shallow stretch of seawater protected from waves and tides of the ocean by energy-absorbing sand or coral barriers. Lagoons lie roughly parallel to the coast and are often stagnant. They receive sediment from both streams and the ocean which forms thick muddy deposits. Thus they support abundant plant and animal life. △268.

Lagos, capital city of Nigeria, in SW Nigeria, on Atlantic coast approx. 75mi (121km) SW of Ibadan, occupying Lagos Island and mainland areas; capital of Lagos state. City grew as Yoruba settlement 17th through 19th centuries, coming under British control 1861 after years of Portuguese exploitation through slave trade; became capital of independent Nigeria 1960. Modern city has undergone an industrial-commercial boom, attracting a young population and creating housing and sanitation problems; has an excellent harbor; site of international airport, National Museum. Industries: brewing, ship repair, food processing, textiles, rubber products. Pop. 901,000.

Lagrange, Joseph Louis (1736–1813), French mathematician. Educated at Turin, Lagrange became professor of mathematics there before his appointment as head of the Berlin Academy on Leonhard Euler's recommendation. Later appointments and honors were numerous. He created the calculus of variations, devised a mathematical analysis of perturbations in gravity, and made contributions in many other areas, including the mathematics of sound and mechanics.

Lagrangian Points, or positions, points in space where a small body, influenced by the gravitational attraction of two larger ones, will tend to remain at rest relative to them. In such a three-body system, the most stable of these positions, originally postulated (1772) by J. L. Lagrange, are the two points where the small body occupies one vertex of an equilateral triangle with the larger ones at the other two.

LaGuardia, Fiorello Henry (1882–1947), US lawyer and political leader, b. New York City. He entered New York state politics and was deputy attorney general (1915–17). He served as a Republican US representative (1917–19). After World War I, when he was in the air corps, he returned to the House (1923–33). As New York City mayor (1934–45), he fought corruption, strengthened the police and fire departments, and generally promoted public works projects. During World War II, he directed the Office of Civilian Defense (1941–42) and the Permanent Joint Board on Defense between the United States and Canada (1940–46). In 1946, he was named to head the UN Relief and Rehabilitation Administration.

La Habana. *See* Havana.

La Habra, city in S California, 19mi (31km) NE of Long Beach; site of large distribution complexes for surrounding farm areas, oil refineries. Founded in 1860 by Basque sheep farmers; inc. 1925. Pop. (1970) 41,350.

Lahore, city in E Pakistan, on the Ravi River near Indian border; capital of Punjab prov.; commercial and industrial center. Lahore was settled in ancient times; important city during Ghazni and Ghuri sultanates (11th–12th centuries); increased in importance as part of the Sikh kingdom (1767); passed to Britain 1849; site of the Shalamar Gardens, several impressive tombs and a mosque, University of Punjab (1882), and a military cantonment. Industries: iron, steel, textiles, rubber, gold and silver jewelry. Pop. 1,985,800.

Lahti, lakeport city in S central Finland, on the Päyänne lake system; site of 1912 city hall designed by Eliel Saarinen. Industries: beer, clothing, furniture. Chartered as city 1905. Pop. 89,360.

Laing, R(onald) D(avid) (1927–), Scottish psychiatrist. His unusual views about mental illness have gained him international attention as the "philosopher of madness." Laing holds that the mentally ill are not necessarily abnormal, that a psychosis may be a reasonable reaction to the stresses of the world. His books include *The Divided Self* (1965) and *Politics of the Family* (1971).

Laissez Faire, policy advocating governmental noninterference in the economic sphere. A reaction to the tight controls of mercantilism, laissez faire was described by Adam Smith in *Wealth of Nations* (1776). He envisioned a free enterprise system based on private ownership that, if guided by individual initiative and unhindered by bureaucracy, would develop a "natural" and beneficial economic order. Unprecedented industrial growth in the late 19th century led to a concentration of economic power and to demands that big business be subject to governmental regulation. *See also* Mercantilism. △1300.

Lake, an inland body of water, generally of considerable size and too deep to have rooted vegetation completely covering the surface. Lake water has a low concentration of dissolved materials and it freezes at 0° C rather than having the indefinite freezing properties of sea water. The expanded part of a river and a reservoir behind a dam are also termed lakes. △258, 296, 616.

Lake Charles, port of entry and city in SW Louisiana, on Lake Charles; connected with Gulf of Mexico by a 30mi (48km) channel; seat of Calcasieu parish; site of McNeese State College (1939) and Sowela Technical Institute; shipping center for oil, lumber, rice, cotton. Industries: oil refining, chemicals, rubber, concrete pipe. Settled 1852; inc. 1867; chartered as city 1886. Pop. (1970) 77,998.

Lake District, region of NW England, in Cumbria, containing the principal English lakes. Its spectacular mountain and lakeland scenery and its associations with William Wordsworth and Samuel Coleridge make it a major tourist attraction. Highest point is Scafell Pikes, 3,210ft (979m). Among its 15 lakes are Derwentwater, Grasmere, Hawes Water, Buttermere, Windermere. Interesting ruins in district are Druids Circle at Keswick, ancient castles and churches, remains of Roman occupation. Lake District National Park was est. 1951. Area: 80,000acres (32,370hectares). △1240.

Lake Dwellings, the remains of prehistoric settlements built on piles found within the margins of lakes in Germany, Switzerland, Italy, and France. A lacework of tree trunks across the piles formed the platform on which were erected huts with clay floors. Cattle and sheep were also raised on the platform. Archeologists have established a culture sequence (from the Neolithic into the Iron Age) for Central Europe based on sequences of lake dwellings one upon the other.

Lake Erie, Battle of (1813), War of 1812 battle in which the US fleet under Cmmdr. Oliver H. Perry defeated British Capt. Robert Barclay's fleet near Put-In-Bay, Ohio. The victory gave the United States control of Lake Erie cutting off supplies to British troops in the area. Perry's report, "We have met the enemy and they are ours," made him a national hero.

Lake George, village in E New York, at S tip of Lake George in foothills of Adirondacks; seat of Warren co; site of reproduction of 18th-century Fort William Henry (1755–57) built by William Johnson, and of ruins of Fort George, built 1759 by Jeffery Amherst to replace Fort William Henry; recreation and sports area. Inc. 1903. Pop. (1970) 1,046.

Lakeland, city in central Florida, 30mi (48km) E of Tampa. Contains nineteen lakes within city limits; headquarters of Florida Citrus Commission. Settled 1870s; inc. 1885. Pop. (1970) 41,550.

Lakeland Terrier, hunting dog (terrier group) bred in England's Lake District. The Lakeland's narrow build is suited to its purpose—squirming through rocky dens after game. The head is rectangular; ears V-shaped and folded; body narrow; legs long, to run with hounds; and docked tail carried straight up. The hard, wiry coat is fairly long with furnishings on muzzle and tail; colors include blue, black, liver, red grizzle, and wheaten. Average size: 14.5in (37cm) high at shoulder; 17lb (7.6kg). *See also* Terrier.

Lake of the Woods, lake in Canada, SE of Montreal, and W of Ontario; receives Rainy River, and is drained by the Winnipeg River. Length: 70mi (113km). Width: 60mi (97km).

Lake Poets, term first occurring in the *Edinburgh Review* of 1807, referring to English poets Samuel Taylor Coleridge, Robert Southey, and William Wordsworth. They spent much time together in the Lake District; however, only Wordsworth was deeply influenced by the locality, having been born there.

Lakewood, suburban city in S California, NE of Long Beach. Inc. 1954. Pop. (1970) 82,973.

Lakewood, residential town in N central Colorado, in Jefferson co; suburb of Denver. Pop. (1970) 92,787.

Lakewood, city in NE Ohio, 5mi (8km) W of Cleveland on Lake Erie. Industries: bolts, screws, conveying equipment. Settled as East Rockport; renamed in 1889; inc. as city 1911. Pop. (1970) 70,173.

Lakshmi, or Lakshmi-Sri or Padma, in Hindu mythology, the lotus goddess, wife of Vishnu, who existed at the beginning of creation floating on the rolling ocean, borne by a lotus leaf. Lakshmi was worshipped as a fertility goddess of the soil and the family. She is depicted sitting or standing on the lotus, holding a lotus, or symbolically as the lotus. △836, 1034.

Lama, a superior monk of Tibetan Buddhism. The two principal lamas are the Dalai Lama and the Panchen Lama. Since the 8th century, the monastic orders have been the center of Tibetan religion and society. Traditionally regarded as an honor, before the Communist invasions in 1950, 20% of Tibetan males were monks. *See also* Dalai Lama; Lamaism.

Lamaism, Western term for the religion of Tibet. It is a mixture of Mahayana Buddhism and Tibet's pre-Buddhist Bonism. King Srong-tsen Gampo (*c.* 620–50) sent to China and India for Buddhist teachers. The Bon priests opposed the new ways, but Buddhism was reintroduced into Tibet in the 8th century by the Indian scholar Padmasambhava. There are now two sects, Red Hat and Yellow Hat. The Dalai Lama, a member of the Yellow Hat, became revered as the "Living Buddha" and the spiritual and temporal ruler of Tibet. Each new Lama is considered a reincarnation of the one before him. In 1950 the Chinese occupied Tibet. In 1959 the Tibetans tried a revolt that failed, and the 14th Dalai Lama fled to India. △988.

Lamar, Lucius Quintus Cincinnatus (1825–93), US politician, b. Putnam co., Ga. A member of the US House of Representatives (1857–60), he drafted the Mississippi ordinance of succession and was active in the Confederacy. After the war he concentrated his efforts on restoring good relations between North and South. He returned to the House (1873–77), was a senator (1877–85), secretary of the interior (1885–88), and associate justice of the Supreme Court (1888–93).

Lamar, Mirabeau Buonaparte (1798–1859), US statesman, b. Warren co, Ga. He was president of the Texas Republic (1838–41), established the public school system, and secured foreign recognition for the republic. After mismanaging finances, he was replaced by Sam Houston. Lamar later favored annexation, fought in the Mexican War, and was the US minister to Nicaragua and Costa Rica (1858–59).

Lamarck, Jean Baptiste Pierre Antoine de Monet, Chevalier de (1744–1829), French biologist. He promoted theories of biological transformation, asserting that acquired characteristics are heritable. His theory, known as Lamarckism, influenced evolutionary thought throughout most of the 19th century. Proposed in 1809 in *Philosophie zoologique,* Lamarckism maintains that new biological needs of an organism promote a change in habits from which develop new structures that are then transmitted to offspring as permanent characteristics. The giraffe, for example, would develop a long neck in order to reach needed food in the form of leaves high on a tree. The theory caused much debate and was eventually rejected, although followers of Michurin and Lysenko in the Soviet Union held similar theories until recently. △418.

Lamartine, Alphonse-Marie Louis de (1790–1869), French Romantic poet. His *Méditations poétiques* (1820), containing psalms, odes, and moving elegies, won him fame and patronage in a diplomatic career. Later poems, collected in *Récueillements poétiques,* echoed his liberal political position, which culminated in his becoming a hero of the 1848 Revolution with his oratory and his *Histoire des Girondins.*

Lamb, Charles (1775–1834), English essayist and poet. He collaborated with his sister Mary Ann (1764–1847) in *Tales from Shakespeare* (1807). He contributed regularly to the *London Magazine* (1820–23), in which his *Essays of Elia* first appeared.

Lamb (meat). △370, 376, 378.

Lambda Particle. *See* Hyperon.

Lame Duck, term used to describe an officeholder between the time he is defeated for reelection and the time his successor takes over. Before ratification of the 20th Amendment (also known as the "Lame Duck Amendment") in 1933, Congress and the president held office until the March following a November election. Newly elected officials now assume office in January.

Lamentations, biblical book by the prophet Jeremiah discussing Israel's desperate situation and the beginning of the exile.

La Mesa, city in S California, 8mi (13km) NE of San Diego; trade center for surrounding farm areas. Inc. 1912. Pop. (1970) 39,178.

Laminar Flow, fluid flow without turbulence. In laminar flow, the fluid flows in layers in a predictable way. As the velocity increases, or as the viscosity of the fluid decreases, a point is reached at which laminar flow breaks up into turbulent flow, marked by the existence of eddies. For a given fluid this point occurs at a certain value of the Reynolds number.

La Mirada, city in S California, 17mi (27km) SE of Los Angeles; noted for beautiful scenery; name derived from Spanish for "the view." Inc. 1960. Pop. (1970) 30,808.

Lamont v. Postmaster General (1965), US Supreme Court case declaring unconstitutional a Congressional statute authorizing the detention of Communist political propaganda. The court said that requiring a written request for delivery abridged the First Amendment.

Lamp. △1542.

Lampedusa, Giuseppe Tomasi, Principe di (1896–1957), Italian novelist. A wealthy prince, he traveled widely. Though always interested in literature, he did not write his sole novel, *The Leopard* (published 1958), until 1955–56. *Racconti* (1961) is a collection of stories and memoirs.

Lamprey, also sea lamprey, lamprey eel, eel-like, jawless fish found in marine waters on both sides of the Atlantic and in the Great Lakes. Adults spawn in fresh water and are brown, green, red, or blue above and whitish below. Lampreys live in salt water and attach themselves by mouth to other fish, sucking their blood. Length: to 3ft (91cm); weight: to 2.25lb (1kg). There are 8 genera and 25 species including sea lamprey *Petromyzon marinus.* Family Petromyzondiae. *See also* Cyclestome. △508.

Lamp Shell. △506.

Lanai, island in central Hawaii, W of Maui; it was purchased in 1922 by a pineapple company and developed as a pineapple growing center. Highest point is Mt Lanaihale, 3,370ft (1,028m). Area: 141sq mi (365sq km).

Lancashire, county in NW England, bordered by Irish Sea (W), Cumbria (N), North and West Yorkshire (E), Greater Manchester and Merseyside (S); drained by the Lune and Ribble rivers. Lancaster is co seat; Blackpool and Blackburn are the major towns. It lost much of its area and the majority of its pop. with the co reorganization in 1974. Area: 1,175sq mi (3,043sq km). Pop. 1,341,000.

Lancaster, House of, English royal line. The dynasty was founded by Edmund "Crouchback," earl of Lancaster (1245–96), the second son of Henry III. On the death of Edmund's son Henry, 1st duke of Lancaster (1361), the Lancastrian titles and lands passed to his daughter, Blanche, and her husband, John of Gaunt. Their son, Henry Bolingbroke, became Henry IV (1399) on deposing Richard II. He was the first of England's three Lancastrian kings. Bolingbroke's son, Henry V, died (1422), leaving his heir, Henry VI, a child. Dissensions during the regency (1422–42) and Henry VI's feebleness as king weakened the Lancastrians, encouraging Yorkist claims to the throne and leading to the Wars of the Roses (1455–85).

Lancaster, John of, Duke of Bedford. *See* Bedford, John of Lancaster, Duke of.

Lancaster, city in S central Ohio, 27mi (43km) SE of Columbus on Hocking River; seat of Fairfield co; birthplace of Gen. William Tecumseh Sherman (1820). Industries: glass, shoes, machinery. Founded 1800; inc. 1831. Pop. (1970) 32,911.

Lancaster, city in SE Pennsylvania, on the Conestoga River; seat of Lancaster co. A rich agricultural area in Pennsylvania Dutch country, it served as state capital 1799–1812; site of Wheatland, home of Pres. James Buchanan (built 1828 and a national shrine since 1962), Franklin and Marshall College (1787), Lancaster School of the Bible (1933), Evangelical Lutheran Church of the Holy Trinity (*c.* 1760), and Old City Hall (1795). Industries: linoleum, watches, radio tubes, cigars, razors, tools. Settled by German Mennonites 1709; inc. as borough 1742, as city 1818. Pop. (1970) 57,690.

Lancelet. *See* Amphioxus.

Lan-chow (Lanzhou, or Lan-chou), city in NW China, on S Yellow River, near Great Wall; capital of

Marquis de Lafayette

Fiorello LaGuardia

Lake District, England

Jean Baptiste Lamarck

Kansu prov.; nearly destroyed by earthquake 1920, since rebuilt; under Chinese Communist control 1949. A major transportation center, it is beginning of Silk Road that leads to central Asia; served by many railroads; seat of university (1946), teachers' colleges. Industries: food processing, cement, textiles, leather goods, fruits, tobacco, livestock, dairy products, oil refineries, chemicals. Pop. approx. 1,500,000.

Landau, Lev Davidovitch (1908–68), Soviet physicist. His many contributions included the basic theories describing ferromagnetism and liquid helium. In the 1930s he calculated the way in which the atoms in small regions (called domains) of a substance like iron line up in a magnetic field, creating the strong effect known as ferromagnetism. In the 1940s and 1950s he created the theory that underlies the superfluid behavior of liquid helium. He received the Nobel Prize in physics in 1962.

Land Crab, crab found in tropical America, W Africa, and Indo-Pacific with gills placed in carapace cavities to breathe air. A forest floor scavenger, it migrates to water to breed. Size: to 12in (30cm) across back. Family Gecarcinidae. *See also* Crab. △490.

Land Dyak, or Dayak, indigenous people of SW and C Borneo. Based on subsistence agriculture, hunting, and fishing, their society is remarkably classless, with both matrilineal and patrilineal descent. The inhabitants of whole villages live in a single communal long house. A complex, animistic, polytheistic religion is practiced and Western influence so far has been slight.

Land-Grant College, one of many US institutions that were financed by the Morrill Act of 1862 or later federal laws. The 1862 act allowed states to sell federal land to fund colleges that were to teach "agriculture and the mechanic arts." Later acts provided more federal aid. The land-grant colleges pioneered in providing low-cost higher education and in establishing research and public service as functions of colleges. Many developed into major state universities.

Land-Grant Railroads, railroads financed and built by sale of public lands to encourage railroad construction. Beginning with the first grant made in 1850, over 155,000,000 acres (63,000,000 hectares) were granted. In return, the railroads agreed to transport US property and troops without charge. This was later adjusted to a 50% reduction of commercial rates and discontinued in 1946.

Landis, Kenesaw Mountain (1866–1944), US jurist and baseball executive, b. Millville, Ohio. Baseball's first commissioner (1920–44), he was a US district judge before taking over baseball's reins following the 1919 "Black Sox" scandal. He restored the game's integrity through his strong disciplinarian leadership. He was elected to the Baseball Hall of Fame in 1944.

Landon, Alfred Mossman (1887–), US political leader, b. West Middlesex, Pa. After receiving a law degree, he made a fortune as an independent oil operator. He was elected governor of Kansas in 1932 and nominated as the presidential candidate in 1936, carrying only two states in Franklin D. Roosevelt's landslide victory. A progressive Republican, Landon was a successful reform governor and fought the Ku Klux Klan and oil and utility monopolies. He vigorously opposed US entry into World War II and after the war urged liberalized world trade and recognition of Communist China.

Landrum-Griffin Act (1959), US act, officially the Labor-Management Reporting and Disclosure Act; represents an attempt to protect the worker from the labor union, whether or not he desires such protection. The law sets up a financial reporting system, voting procedures, a bill of rights for union members, and financial safeguards. It is designed to enhance internal union democracy and prevent Communist party members and convicted felons from holding office.

Landscape Painting, the artistic painting of natural outdoor scenes. In the West it began in approximately the 14th century with the frescoes at the pope's palace in Avignon (*c.* 1343). In the East landscape art had been perfected by the 8th century. Landscapes held a major place in Flemish and Italian art of the Renaissance, culminating in the works of Rembrandt and Leonardo da Vinci. The 19th century also saw great English landscape painters such as Turner and Constable, the Impressionists in France, and the Hudson River School in the United States. In the 20th century general interest in landscape painting has declined, although a number of artists have continued to make it their main concern (eg, the American John Marin). △1242.

Land's End, extreme W point of England in SW Cornwall; the Longships lighthouse is just offshore. The peninsula's scenery is a tourist attraction.

Landslide or **Landslip,** noticeable slip or fall of a mass of earth or rock. The phenomena are classed according to the angle of the slide and the type of material that is descending and whether or not it is wet. Landslides are frequently the indirect result of man's activities such as road or dam construction, both of which undercut rock formations and their support structures. *See also* Avalanche.

Land Snail. △476.

Landsteiner, Karl (1868–1943), US pathologist, b. Austria. He distinguished four different blood types, later labeled A, B, AB, and O, and paved the way for scientific blood transfusion. He showed that blood of some groups is incompatible with that of others and that if incompatible bloods are mixed they will form clotlike lumps. His findings explained why some transfusions of blood in the past had been beneficial, while others had been fatal. He won the Nobel Prize in physiology or medicine (1930) and later helped to identify the RH factor.

Lanfranc (*c.* 1005–89), archbishop of Canterbury. A Benedictine in 1041, he became head of the celebrated monastery school of Bec, France, in 1045. He was a trusted counsellor of William the Conqueror and *c.* 1063 became abbot of St Stephen's, Caen. After his consecration at Canterbury (1070), he made his diocese dominant over the others and replaced Saxon prelates with Normans, bringing the English Church closer to the reforms of Pope Gregory VII.

Langdon, John (1741–1819), US political leader, b. Portsmouth, N.H. A wealthy merchant, he was active in anti-British activities before the Revolutionary War and made an unsuccessful attempt to acquire Canadian support for the colonies. A delegate (1775, 1776, 1783) to the Continental Congress, he also financed the New Hampshire militia in the Saratoga campaign. He served as New Hampshire's governor (1788, 1805–09, 1810–11) and US senator (1789–1801).

Lange, Christian Louis (1869–1938), Norwegian peace maker. He worked for the Nobel Committee (1900–09) and the International Parliamentary Union (1909–33) and represented Norway in the League of Nations. An advocate of disarmament, he received the Nobel Peace Prize in 1921 (with Karl Branting).

Lange, Dorothea (1895–1965), US photographer, b. Hoboken. Her portraits and studies of the hardships of the Depression years among the urban poor and migrant laborers of California and her devastating images of rural America, made for the Farm Security Administration (1935–42), have an eloquence, strength, and spareness that make them classics of documentary work. Her photographs had nationwide political impact.

Langley, Samuel Pierpont (1834–1906), US astronomer and pioneer in the design and construction of airplanes, b. Roxbury, Mass. He was director of the Allegheny Observatory and professor at the University of Pittsburgh before he became secretary of the Smithsonian Institution. He did research on solar radiation and invented the bolometer for recording variations in heat radiation. He is noted for successfully flying the first mechanically propelled heavier-than-air machines (1896), but failed in his launching of a manned plane in 1903 shortly before the successful flight of the Wright brothers.

Langmuir, Irving (1881–1957), US chemist, b. Brooklyn, N.Y. With the General Electric Company, he pioneered the development of gas-filled tungsten light bulbs, invented the atomic blowtorch, and made extensive studies in surface chemistry. He was awarded a Nobel Prize in 1932, being the first US chemist to be so honored.

Langrenus. △52.

Langston, John Mercer (1829–97), the first black to win US elective office (city council, Brownhelm, Ohio, 1855), b. Louisa, Va. He later became (1868) inspector general of the Freedmen's Bureau, lecturer and dean at Howard University (1869–76), minister to Haiti (1877–85), and US congressman (1890–91).

Language, the sum total of sounds and signs (written alphabet, hieroglyphs, ideographs) by which human beings communicate facts, ideas, feelings. All human languages consist of words and rules for their use and combination. Linguistics studies the structure and history of languages and has distinguished from 2,500 to 5,000 different languages. A language, in this sense, is the particular form that verbal communication has among a geographically and culturally distinct people. △780, 864–66, 870–72.

Langur, or leaf monkey, 15 species of medium to large monkeys of S Asia and East Indies that feed mainly on leaves. They are slender and have long hands and tails. Gregarious, day-active tree dwellers, they are found from sea level to snowy Himalayan slopes at an elevation of 13,000ft (4,000m). Length: 16–31in (41–79cm). Family Cercopithecidae; genus *Presbytis*. *See also* Monkey. △554, 620.

Lanier, Sidney (1842–81), US musician and poet, b. Macon, Ga., whose verse reflects Southern social change and the rhythms and thematic development of music. In 1867 Lanier published his first novel, *Tiger-Lilies*. Publication in 1875 of "Corn" and "Symphony," poems dealing with agricultural conditions in the South and industrial conditions in the North, respectively, brought him national recognition. Subsequent important poems include "The Song of the Chattahoochee" (1877), "The Marshes of Glyn" (1878), and "The Revenge of Hamish" (1878). Series of lectures were later published as *The Science of English Verse* (1880), *The English Novel* (1883), and *Shakespeare and His Forerunners* (1902). He was a flutist in Baltimore's Peabody Orchestra and a teacher of English literature at Johns Hopkins University. △1420.

Lanolin, a purified fatlike substance derived from sheep's wool and used with water as a base for ointments and cosmetics.

Lansing, town in NE Illinois; S suburb of Chicago. Industries: bottling, farming. Inc. 1893. Pop. (1970) 25,805.

Lansing, capital city of Michigan, 50mi (81km) WSW of Flint on Grand River; site of original Michigan State University (1850), now in East Lansing, Lansing Community College (1957). Industries: automotive parts, trucks, tractors, tents, awnings. Settled by 1840 by New Yorkers; made state capital 1847; inc. 1859. Pop. (1970) 131,546.

Lantern Fish, marine fish found in Atlantic and Mediterranean. Identified by light organs along sides, it is found in deep water during the day and near the surface at night. Length: 1–6in (2.5–15.2cm). Family Myctophidae; species 150, including *Myctophum punctatum*. △626.

Lantern Fly, tropical and subtropical plant hopper with a wingspread often exceeding 6in (152mm). Its long head has a hollow part, formerly thought to emit light. Family Fulgoridae. *See also* Homoptera. △500.

Lanthanide Elements, or **Rare Earths,** series of rare metallic elements with atomic numbers between 57 and 71. They are: lanthanum, cerium, praseodymium, neodymium, promethium, samarium, europium, gadolinium, terbium, dysprosium, holmium, erbium, thulium, ytterbium, and lutetium. Their properties are similar and resemble those of lanthanum from which the series takes its name. They occur in monazite and other rare minerals and are placed in group IIIb of the periodic table. All form trivalent compounds (some also form divalent and quadrivalent compounds). *See also* Periodic Table. △1522, 1554.

Lanthanum, metallic element (symbol La) of the Lanthanide group, first identified in 1839. Chief ores are monazite (phosphate) and bastnasite (fluorocarbonate). The metal is used in lighter flints. Properties: at.no. 57; at. wt. 138.9055; sp gr 6.15 (25°C); melt. pt. 1688°F (920°C); boil. pt. (6,249°F) (3,454°C); most common isotope La^{139} (99.91%). *See also* Lanthanide Elements. △1554.

Lanugo, soft woolly hair that covers the human fetus and that of other mammals during development. It is shed and virtually disappears at birth.

Lanús, city in E Argentina, 6mi (10km) S of Buenos Aires; administrative center; site of technical school. Industries: textiles, paper, chemicals, rubber products, tanneries. Pop. 375,428.

Lanzhou. *See* Lan-chow.

Laocoön (*c.* 2nd century BC), marble sculpture group. It illustrates the myth of the Trojan priest who objected to his people's bringing the wooden horse within the city walls and so angered the gods who sent two large serpents to kill him and his two sons. The sculpture was discovered on the Esquiline hill in ome in 1506 and is now in the Vatican Museum. △ 002.

aos (Lao), independent nation in SE Asia. Its devel- pment has been hampered by geography and a low- vel economy. For six centuries a monarchy, it fell to ıe Pathet Lao Communist forces in 1975.

Land and economy. Located in the very center of ıe SE Asian peninsula, Laos borders on five nations: hina (N), Vietnam (E), Cambodia (S), Thailand (S and V), including 500mi (805km) along the Mekong iver, and Burma (NW). Covered with jungles and ıountains, Laos has no access to the sea. Its three- eason climate is monsoonal. With natural resources ırgely unexplored, 85% of the population is en- aged in subsistence farming. Exports are primarily n, timber, and coffee. Almost all manufactured prod- cts are imported.

People. Laos' sparse population is concentrated long the Mekong River valley. The Lao majority is escended from a SW Chinese people, the Tai, who ıigrated in the 13th century. Mountain tribes without common language or tradition inhabit the central nd S regions. Theravada Buddhism is the principal eligion, while the mountain tribes are animist. Lao is ıe dominant language. French is the language used ı schools, and many tribes speak dialects never re- orded. Literacy is about 25%.

Government. Laos has been ruled as a Communist eople's republic since 1975. The king and other old egime leaders remained as advisors.

History. United in the 14th century under King Fa Igum, Laos was the object of centuries-long inva- ions by neighboring countries. Siam ruled in the 19th entury, France in 1883, Japan in WWII, and France gain in 1946, when Laos gained independence vithin the French Union. Conflicts among the conser- atives, Communists (Pathet Lao), and neutrals kept he country in turmoil. In 1962 a coalition govern- nent named neutralist Prince Souvanna Phouma pre- nier. In 1964 the Communist forces, with aid from Communist North Vietnamese troops, seized Laotian erritory, and in 1971 the United States bombed their upply line through Laos (Ho Chi Minh Trail). In 1973 coalition government with Pathet Lao was formed. ı 1975 the coalition was dismantled and the King- om of a Million Elephants was succeeded by the Communist Pathet Lao regime. △1378.

PROFILE

)fficial name: People's Democratic Republic of Laos
\rea: 91,428sq mi (236,799sq km)
'opulation: (1973 est.) 3,181,000
Density: 35 per sq mi (13 per sq km)
:hief city: Vientiane (capital)
Government: Communist people's republic
Religion: Theravada Buddhism
.anguage: Lao (dominant), French
Monetary unit: Kip
Gross national product: $202,000,000
'er capita income: $100
ndustries: opium, cigarettes, textiles
Agriculture: coffee, rice, maize, tobacco, cotton, poppies, citrus fruits, teak, cardamon
Minerals: tin
Trading partners: Malaysia, Singapore, Thailand, Japan

.ao Tzu (*c.* 604–*c.* 531 BC), Chinese philosopher. Ac- cording to Chinese legend he founded Taoism, a reli- ion which became a mystical reaction to the moral- political concerns of Confucianism (Buddhism now embraces both). Although there is uncertainty about ıis identity, he is believed to have been the author of *Tao Te Ching*, Taoism's main scriptural book. *Tao* is he "Way"; *te* is its "virtue." Its emphasis on persever- ınce, nature, and the cyclical has greatly influenced Chinese culture. △1040.

.a Paz, largest city and administrative capital of Bolivia in W Bolivia; former location of Inca village; one of the centers of revolt during war of indepen- dence; scene of revolutions and civil disorders inter- nittently into the 1960s. Industries: tanning, flour nilling, brewing, distilling, manufacturing clothing, urniture, metal products. Altitude: 12,000ft 3,660m). Pop. 850,000.

Lapidary, the art of cutting and polishing gemstones. Originally all gems were cut *en cabochon* (smooth, polished surface, convex) or in flat plates. Tiny cuts, producing facets, were then added. Soft gemstones are sometimes tumbled to polish; most are shaped by grinding on abrasive wheels. Numerous facets with three or four sides bring out light and color. Most common faceted forms are brilliant cut, rose cut, and drop cut. *See also* Gems. △244.

Lapis Lazuli, or **Lazurite,** a semiprecious gemstone, silicate mineral, found in metamorphosed limestones. Cubic system rare dodecahedral crystals, more often granular masses. Glassy, deep blue; hardness 5–5.5; sp gr 2.4. △244

Laplace, Pierre Simon, Marquis de (1749–1827), French astronomer and mathematician. Of obscure origins, Laplace rose to high positions through his political adaptability and great scientific talents. He is noted for his contributions to gravitational theory, which were expounded in *Traité de Mécanique Céleste* (1799–1825), to mathematical physics, and to probability theory.

Lapland, vast region in N Europe, almost entirely within the Arctic Circle, contains N and NE part of Norway, northernmost parts of Finland and Sweden, and the Kola Peninsula of Russia. Land is mountainous in Norwegian and Swedish sections; tundra predominates over the NE, and the Norwegian coast offers excellent hunting and fishing. Lapland is rich in high grade mineral deposits, and supports large reindeer herds. There is a great variety in temperatures; the extreme cold of winter is moderated on the W fringes of Norway where the harbors are open all year. The midnight sun in the summer months causes rapid growth of vegetation. Area: 150,000sq mi (388,500sq km). Pop. 36,500.

La Plata, city in E Argentina, 35mi (56km) ESE of Buenos Aires; capital of Buenos Aires prov.; well-planned city laid out in 3mi (5km) square centered on Plaza Moreno, site of cathedral. Parks surrounding it contain gardens, museums, and observatories. Industries: meat packing, oil refining, electrical equipment. Founded 1882. Pop. 337,060.

Lapps, people inhabiting N Scandinavia and the Kola Peninsula of the Soviet Union. The mountain Lapps are nomadic herders of reindeer, while those of the forest and coast are seminomadic and live by hunting, trapping, and fishing. Their racial origins are uncertain, although they are linguistically related to the Finno-Ugrian people.

La Puente, suburban city in S California, NNE of Long Beach. Settled 1841; inc. 1956. Pop. (1970) 31,092.

Lapwing, slow-flying, crested plover found in the Eastern Hemisphere and South America. It is usually black, white, and sand-colored. Pear-shaped, blotched eggs (4) are laid near water. Family Charadriidae; species *Vanellus vanellus*.

Laramie, city in SE Wyoming, 50mi (81km) WNW of Cheyenne, on Laramie River; seat of Albany co. Area developed rapidly with growth of cattle and mining industries in 19th and 20th centuries; site of Wyoming University (1886), Medicine Bow National Forest, Fort Sanders (1866), army fortress built to protect the Overland Trail and employees of Union Pacific Railroad; trading, distribution, and processing center. Industries: tourism; gold, silver, coal, iron, petroleum processing; livestock. Founded 1868; inc. 1874. Pop. (1970) 23,143.

Larch, genus *(Larix)* of deciduous trees native to cold and mountainous regions of the Northern Hemisphere. They have cones and needlelike leaves that are shed annually. The wood is valued for its toughness. Family Pinaceae. △440.

Lardner, Ring(gold) W(ilmer) (1885–1933), US short-story writer and humorist, b. Niles, Mich. He spent 15 years as a reporter for Chicago newspapers and served for a time as editor of a baseball weekly. In 1915 he published *You Know Me, Al*, a collection of short stories about baseball players. His great talent lay in re-creating the language of the common people and delineating their lives satirically. Among his best known stories are "Haircut," "Champion," and "The Love Nest."

Laredo, city in S Texas, across Rio Grande from Nuevo Laredo, Mexico; seat of Webb co. Occupied by Texas Rangers 1846 and Texas Volunteers 1847; port of entry handling imports and exports between United States and Mexico. Industries: agriculture, coal, natural gas, oil refining, railroad shops, tiles, brooms, clothing, tourism. Founded 1755 by Spanish settlers; inc. 1852. Pop. (1970) 69,024.

Lares, in Roman mythology, gods of the cultivated fields. The Latins, Sabines, and Etruscans worshipped the Lares at the point where two fields came together. The household Lar was invoked for important family occasions (marriages, funerals).

Large Intestine. *See* Colon.

Lark, small, inconspicuous Old World birds found in open areas, chiefly in Africa. Known for their beautiful

Irving Langmuir

Sidney Lanier

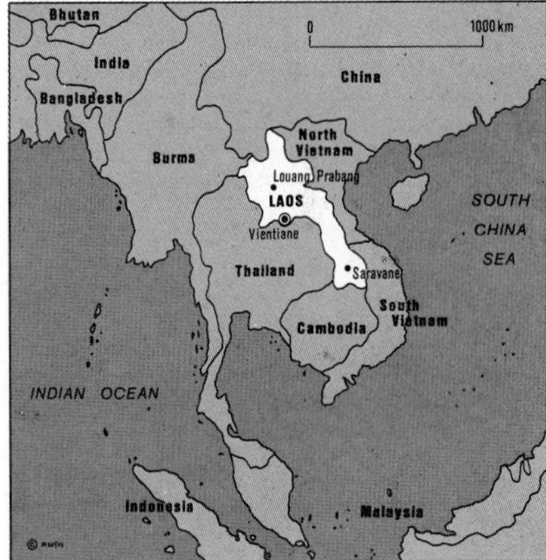
Bhutan
0
1000km
India
China
Bangladesh
North Vietnam
Burma
Louang Prabang
LAOS
Vientiane
SOUTH CHINA SEA
Thailand
Saravane
South Vietnam
Cambodia
INDIAN OCEAN
Indonesia
Malaysia

Laos

Lapland: traditional costume

songs, they grow to about 6in (15cm), have crested heads; cone-shaped bills; long, pointed wings; and a straight claw on their rear toes. They feed on insects, larvae, crustaceans, and berries. Buff or whitish eggs (2–7) are laid in a grass cup-shaped nest on the ground. The male defends the nest, often using the broken-wing ruse. Family Alaudidae.

Larkspur. *See* Delphinium.

La Rochefoucauld, François, duc de (1613–80), French classical writer and moralist. His *Maxims* (1665) reflect the wave of pessimism at that time and his belief that self-interest is at the root of all human behavior.

La Rochelle, port city in W France, on Bay of Biscay 75mi (121km) SSE of Nantes; capital of Charente Maritime dept. A Huguenot stronghold during the 16th century the city fell to Cardinal Richelieu 1627–28, site of Renaissance town hall and old fishing port. Industries: chemicals, tourism, fishing, naval and aircraft construction, automobiles. Chartered 12th century. Pop. 73,347.

Larousse, Pierre (1817–75), French lexicographer. He founded the publishing firm Larousse, which produced *The Great Universal Dictionary of the 19th Century* (1866–76) as the first of the famous Larousse series of dictionaries and encyclopedias. They are invaluable sources of information on French history, literature, art, and customs. △1780.

Larva, a developmental stage in many animals, occuring between birth and maturity, in which the immature animal is structurally different from its parents. The larva has a well-developed alimentary system and stores food so that transformation to the adult stage can occur. Time of larval stage varies with species. Some larvae are: the planula (cnidaria); the pilidium (ribbonworm); the trochophore (annelid); the nauplius (crustacean); caterpillars, grubs, maggots, and nymphs (insects); the tadpole (frog). △494, 498.

Laryngitis, inflammation of the larynx (organ of speech) usually occurring during a respiratory-tract infection and accompanied by dryness, soreness, and hoarseness.

Larynx, or voice box, triangular-shaped box located between the trachea and the root of the tongue. Folds in the lining of the larynx form the vocal cords, thin bands of elastic tissue that vibrate when outgoing air passes over them, setting up sound waves that are changed into sound by the action of throat muscles and the tongue. △692.

La Salle, René Robert Cavelier, Sieur de (1643–87), French explorer in North America. In 1668 he sailed for Canada to make his fortune in the fur trade. He explored the Great Lakes area and was commandant of Fort Frontenac on Lake Ontario (1674). His greatest achievement was exploring the Mississippi River to its mouth (1682) and claiming it for the king of France. He named the adjacent lands Louisiana after Louis XIV. His later efforts to colonize the area were unsuccessful.

LaSalle, city in S Quebec, Canada, on the St Lawrence River; suburb of Montreal on S shore of Montreal Island. Inc. 1912. Pop. 72,912.

Lascaux, Cave Paintings of, prehistoric paintings in a cave in the Department of Dordogne, southwestern France. Discovered in 1940, the caves consist of the Great Hall, with a ceiling covered with Paleolithic animal paintings, including four huge bulls; the Painted Gallery, with red and black bovine animals and horses; the Lateral Passage, with damaged paintings; and the Chamber of Engravings, with engraved figures and animals. The Main Gallery has friezes of animals, the Chamber of Felines is decorated with cats, and the Shaft of the Dead Man contains a painting of a man between a rhinoceros and a bison. △950.

Las Cruces, city in SW New Mexico, on the Rio Grande, approx. 42mi (68km) NNW of El Paso, Texas; seat of Dona Ana co; agricultural region and trade center; site of White Sands Missile Range, NASA testing site; forts Fillmore and Seldon; University of New Mexico (1888). Industries: food processing, canning, textiles, livestock. Pop. (1970) 37,857.

Laser, a device that provides light amplification by stimulated emission of radiation. A natural development of the maser, it operates by the same principle of "pumping" atoms up to high-energy states and then passing radiation of a certain frequency through them to stimulate them to emit similar radiation. The intense coherent beam of light emitted by lasers has been used to measure the distance from the Earth to the Moon, "weld" retinas to chosen points in an eye, and measure amounts of pollution in the atmosphere. *See also* Maser. △1528.

Laser Machining. △1606.

Lashkar, city in N central India, adjoining city of Gwalior (S). It served as capital of former Gwalior state, abolished in 1956 and inc. as part of Madhya Pradesh state; site of Victoria College and the palace of the maharaja of Gwalior; trade and commercial center. Founded *c.* 1800, just S of Gwailor. Pop. (met. Gwalior-Lashkar) 406,160.

LASH Ship (Lighter Aboard Ship), large commercial freighter developed in the United States with giant elevators at the rear, enabling the ship itself to lift cargo barges, or lighters, aboard and thus reducing the need for deepwater ports and extensive docking facilities.

Laski, Harold Joseph (1893–1950), English political scientist, educator and socialist. He was chairman of the Labour party (1945–46). Through teachings, writings, and lectures, he advocated socialism in England and the United States. He wrote *Democracy in Crisis* (1933), *The American Presidency* (1940), and *Reflections on the Revolution of Our Time* (1943).

Las Palmas (Las Palmas de Gran Canaria), seaport city in Spain, on NE Grand Canary Island; capital of Las Palmas prov.; chief port and largest city of Canary Islands; site of governor's palace, 18th-century cathedral. Exports: sugar, tomatoes, almonds, bananas. Industries: fishing, tourism. Founded 1478. Area: (prov.) 1,569sq mi (4,064sq km). Pop. (prov.) 579,-710; (city) 287,038.

La Spezia, city in Italy, on Gulf of Spezia; capital of La Spezia prov.; site of medieval Castel Saint Giorgio, and rebuilt 15th-century cathedral; major naval base of Italy since 1861. Industries: shipbuilding, iron foundries, oil refining. Pop. 129,219.

Lassa Fever, a little-understood, mysterious viral infection, first recognized as a disease in Africa in 1969. The infection can produce wide-ranging symptoms, including very high fever, mouth ulcers, heart damage, muscle aches, and kidney failure, and affect almost every part of the body. The disease occurs sporadically and is often fatal.

Lassen Volcanic National Park, park in N California. Lassen Peak is the only recently active volcano in the United States exclusive of Alaska and Hawaii. It erupted in 1914 and was active until 1921. The park features impressive volcanic phenomena. Area: 106,933acres (43,308hectares). Est. 1916.

Last of the Mohicans, The (1826), novel by James Fenimore Cooper about the efforts of Natty Bumppo and his Mohican Indian friends to rescue two girls captured by the Iroquois during the French and Indian wars. The book is one of the Leather-Stocking Tales. *See also* Leather-Stocking Tales, The. △1374.

L'Astrée. △1172.

Last Supper, or **Lord's Supper,** in the New Testament, St Paul's designation for the sacred meal instituted by Jesus on the eve of his crucifixion. The 12 disciples were present to eat the Passover meal and take communion. △1026.

Las Vegas, city in S Nevada, 25mi (40km) WNW of Hoover Dam; seat of Clark co, largest city in Nevada. It was settled by Mormons 1855, in an unsuccessful attempt at lead mining; abandoned 1857. Growth was spurred 1905 with completion of railroad; area experienced a rapid population growth in 1950s and 1960s. It is famous for numerous nightclubs, casinos, and hotels; site of University of Nevada at Las Vegas (1957). Industries: tourism, ranching, mining, dairy products. Inc. 1911. Pop. (1970) 125,787.

La Sylphide. △1368.

Latakia (Al-Ladiqiyah), city in W Syria, on the Mediterranean Sea; capital of Latakia governorate. Originally the ancient Phoenician city of Ramitha, it was captured by Saladin 1188; part of the Ottoman Empire from 16th century to WWI. While Syria was a French League of Nations mandate, Latakia served as capital 1920–42 of Alawites territory; became part of Syria 1946; in 1959 a deepwater port was completed. Exports: asphalt, cotton, fruit, bitumen, cereals. Industries: tobacco, sponge fishing, cotton ginning, vegetable oil milling. Pop. 67,799.

La Tène. △1008, 1050.

Latent Heat, the heat absorbed by a substance as changes its phase, that is, goes from solid to liquid c liquid to gas. When ice melts, its temperature remain the same until it has been completely transforme into water; the heat necessary to do this is called th heat of fusion. Similarly the heat necessary to tran form water into steam at constant temperature called the heat of vaporization. △1504.

Lateran Councils, five general councils of th Roman Catholic Church, named for the Basilica of S John Lateran in Rome, where they were held. The firs council was held in 1123. Available sources show tha it condemned simony and confirmed the Concordat c Worms. The second, in 1139, produced 30 decree dealing with such matters as simony and marriage c clerics. The third, in 1179, decreed that the pope wa to be elected by the College of Cardinals alone. Th fourth council, in 1215, showed the power of Pop Innocent III. Of 70 decrees, some of the most impo tant were those condemning the Albigensians an Waldensians and proclaiming a new Crusade. Th fifth, in 1512–17, condemned what were considere false opinions and established many regulations fc the conduct of the Church. The work of this counc was carried further by the Council of Trent. *See als* Worms, Concordat of.

Lateran Treaty (Feb. 11, 1929), concordat betwee Italy and the state of Vatican City. By its term (confirmed by the Italian constitution of 1948), Ital recognized the Vatican as an independent and sover eign state with the pope as its temporal head. Roma Catholicism was affirmed as Italy's official state rel gion, and the Vatican recognized Italy's claims to th papal states and Rome as well as the Italian stat itself.

Laterite, a reddish soil found in humid tropical re gions. It is produced by the sub-aerial decay of rocks It contains aluminum and/or iron hydroxides and ma be used as an ore of either metal if concentrations ar sufficiently high.

Latex, milky fluid produced by certain plants, th most important being that produced by rubber trees which contains about 60% water, 35% rubber, an 5% proteins, carbohydrates, and lipids. It is used i paints, special papers, and adhesives and to mak sponge rubbers. Synthetic rubber latexes are also pro duced.

Latex Paint, a synthetic latex; vinyl resined water based paint. Such polymer emulsions have come int widespread use since the late 1940s due to their ex cellent flexibility, toughness, adhesion, color reten tion, chemical resistance, and ease of use due to thei solubility in water. △1812.

Lathe, a machine tool that performs turning opera tions that remove unwanted material from a work piece (either wood or metal), which is rotated agains a cutting tool. Several types of lathes are used: th speed lathe has a cutting tool supported on a rest an is hand-manipulated; an engine lathe's cutting tool i clamped onto a power-driven slide; screw-cuttin lathes have a lead screw that drives the carriage or which the cutting tool is mounted; a turret lathe ha a pivoted holder for cutting tools. △1606.

Latimer, Hugh (*c.*1485–1555), English clergyma and Protestant martyr. He lived in a time of struggl between Roman Catholic and Protestant forces i church and state, and he passed in and out of favor During the reign of Edward VI he was free to preach and his plain-spoken sermons helped establish Prot estant ideas in England. When Mary Tudor, a Catho lic, became queen, Latimer was charged with heres and burned at the stake with Bishop Nicholas Ridley Latimer's last words were: "We shall this day ligh such a candle, by God's grace, in England as I trus shall never be put out."

Latimeria. *See* Coelacanth.

Latin, one of the two classical languages of antiquity, the language of the Roman Empire, the official language of the Roman Catholic Church, and the forerunner of the modern Romance languages. In the Middle Ages Latin was the language of science and philosophy in all Western countries and a knowledge of Latin was essential to any liberal education until well into this century. The Latin (or Roman) alphabet is used to write more than 100 languages (including English) today. And Latin words form a large part of the vocabulary of all, but especially Western, languages. △ 866, 870.

Latin America. *See* Central America; South America. △1118–20, 1234, 1354.

Latin American Conferences, series of meetings in the 1930s to revise and improve US policy in Latin America. It marked the beginning of Pres. Franklin D. Roosevelt's Good Neighbor Policy. The Montevideo Conference (1933), attended by Sec. of State Cordell Hull, denied any state the right to intervene in the affairs of any other state. In 1936, at the Buenos Aires Conference, which President Roosevelt himself attended, the Western Hemisphere states agreed to consultation when war was threatened. At the Lima Conference (1938), attended by Hull, the Declaration of Lima was adopted. This document reaffirmed the sovereignty of American states as well as a policy of resistance to intervention by foreign powers. *See also* Good Neighbor Policy.

Latin American Free Trade Association (LAFTA), grouping of 11 area states desirous of attaining economic integration. The member states—Argentina, Brazil, Chile, Mexico, Paraguay, Peru, Uruguay, Bolivia, Colombia, Ecuador, and Venezuela—pledged themselves (1960) to eliminate tariffs and other restrictions on imports. The goal of achieving a free-trade zone was extended into the 1980s. △942.

Latin League, name of several confederations of the Latins (Latini) first formed for religious and later for political purposes. The league of Ferentina was the political hub of Latium from the 6th to the 4th centuries BC. Representatives of individual states met at the shrine of Diana to choose officers and determine policy. The only documented league was that led by the ancient city of Alba Longa, which was destroyed by the Romans *c.* 600 BC. Rome and the league signed a defensive pact in 493 BC against invading tribes. By 338 BC Rome had absorbed or colonized the separate Latin states and subsequently drew from them manpower and wealth. △1012.

Latin Rite, organization and liturgical practices of the churches belonging to Western Catholicism, or the Roman Catholic Church, as distinguished from the Eastern Rite. *See also* Eastern Rite.

Latins (Latini), ancient inhabitants of Latium in W Italy, nomadic invaders of diverse stock of whom the S Villanovans are thought to have introduced the Latin tongue. These tribes drew together to form communities *(populi)* and later larger political states that began in the 4th century BC to be dominated by Rome. The Latins evolved a political structure of equal representation of states that was retained even after their colonization by Rome. Loyal to Rome, they were granted Roman citizenship in the 1st century BC. *See also* Latin League. △1780.

Latissimus Dorsi. △684.

Latitude. △180.

Latium (Lazio), autonomous region in central Italy; comprised of provs. of Roma, Frosinone, Latina, Rieti, and Viterbo; bordered by the Tyrrhenian Sea (W), Apennines (E), Tuscany (N), and Campania (S). Capital is Rome; Civitavecchia is the major port. Products: wheat, vegetables, fruit, meat, olives, grapes. Industries: fashion, motion pictures (Rome), chemicals, pharmaceuticals, food, fishing, tourism. Est. 1948; received autonomy 1970. Area: 6,642sq mi (17,203sq km). Pop. 4,565,448.

La Tortuga. *See* Tortuga.

Latosols. *See* Pedalfer.

La Tour, Georges de (1593–1652), French painter, known for his religious and genre scenes. His early style was Manneristic, but his mature style was naturalistic, after the Baroque manner of Caravaggio. His early works include "The Cheat" and "St. Jerome." His mature works include "Christ and St Joseph in the Carpenter's Shop" (*c.*1645).

Latrobe, Benjamin Henry (1764–1820), US architect, b. England. His numerous monumental public buildings include some of the earliest examples of Greek revival and Gothic revival in the United States, including the Bank of Pennsylvania, Philadelphia (1798) and the Philadelphia water works (1799). He also worked on the Capitol in Washington, D.C., and rebuilt it (1815–17) after it was destroyed by the British.

Latter Day Saints, Church of Jesus Christ of. *See* Mormons.

Latter Day Saints, Reorganized Church of Jesus Christ of, a Mormon group that rejected Brigham Young's leadership after the death of the first leader, Joseph Smith. There are more than 150,000 members, with headquarters in Independence, Mo. *See also* Mormons.

Lattice, Crystal. *See* Crystal Lattice.

Latvia (Latvijskaja Sovetskaja Socialisticeskaja Republika), constituent republic of the USSR. It is a large fertile lowland located in NE Europe, bordered by Estonian (N) and Lithuanian (S) republics, Baltic Sea (W), and Russian republic (SE). One-fifth of the country is less than 130ft (40m) above sea level; it has 2,980 lakes. Forests cover 26% of the country. The climate is damp, and the largest waterway is the Western Dvina River. Collectivization of agriculture has reduced the number of private farms to about 1,500. Nationalized industrial production has increased, with machinery, metals and textiles the leading products.

People and history. The majority of the people are Letts and Latgolians, Baltic groups akin to the Slavs. About 25% are Russians, with minorities of Belorussians, Lithuanians, Poles, and Jews. Lutherans and Roman Catholics were the dominant religious groups before the USSR discouraged organized religion. Conquered and Christianized in the 13th century by Germans, the Letts subsequently came under Polish, then Swedish rule. Through the Russian victories over the Swedes and the 18th-century partitions of Poland, Latvia passed to Russia. German merchants and landowners continued their domination, making serfs of the Letts until the mid-19th century. After the collapse of Russia in WWI, a democratic republic was declared in 1918. By 1936 political weakness permitted a dictatorship. The USSR was granted military bases in 1939 and in 1940 occupied the country. Latvia was occupied by Germany in WWII from 1941–44, when it was retaken by the USSR.

PROFILE

Official name: Latvia Soviet Socialist Republic
Area: 24,595sq mi (63,701sq km)
Population: 2,365,000
Chief city: Riga (capital)
Government: Constituent republic of USSR
Religion: Lutheran and Roman Catholic
Language: Latvian
Industries: textiles, machinery, electrical equipment, shipbuilding, distilling, food and dairy processing
Agriculture: stock raising, dairy farming, forests

Laud, William (1573–1645), English clergyman. He became predominant in the Anglican church after Charles I's accession (1625), supporting the king against Parliament. Appointed chancellor of Oxford University (1629) and archbishop of Canterbury (1633), he tried, with disastrous results, to insist on uniformity of action and observance within the national church. Parliament impeached him for high treason (1640), and he was tried (1644) and cleared by the House of Lords but was executed under a bill of attainder.

Laudanum, alcoholic tincture of opium, prepared from granulated opium and formerly used medicinally to treat diarrhea. In the early 19th century, opium addicts frequently used laudanum. The name was originally given by Paracelsus in the 16th century to a preparation made of gold and pearls mixed with opium.

Laughing Gas, or nitrous oxide, colorless nonflammable gas (formula N_2O) obtained by the decomposition of ammonium nitrate or from nitrites and used as an anesthetic. Properties: melt. pt. −131.4°F (−90.8°C); boil pt. −127.3°F (−88.5°C).

Laughing Jackass. *See* Kookaburra.

Launcelot, Sir, legendary knight of King Arthur's Round Table, the subject of numerous medieval and later romances. As the lover of Queen Guinevere, he caused dissension among Arthur's knights that resulted in the breakup of their fellowship.

Launching, Ship. △1680.

Laurasia, the name for the northern continent containing North America and Eurasia that formed when a northern rift, the Tethyan trench, split apart Pangaea from east to west along a line slightly north of the equator. The name is a combination of Laurentian, a geologic period in North America, and Eurasia. *See also* Continental Drift. △172.

Laurel, evergreen shrubs and trees native to S Europe and cultivated in United States. Included is the noble or bay laurel *(Laurus nobilis)* with stiff, leathery, oval leaves, tiny yellowish flowers, and purple berries; height: 60–70ft (18–21m). The foliage was used by ancient Greeks to crown their victors. Family Lauraceae.

Laurel and Hardy, comedy team that starred in more than 70 films. **Stan Laurel** (1890–1965) (Ar-

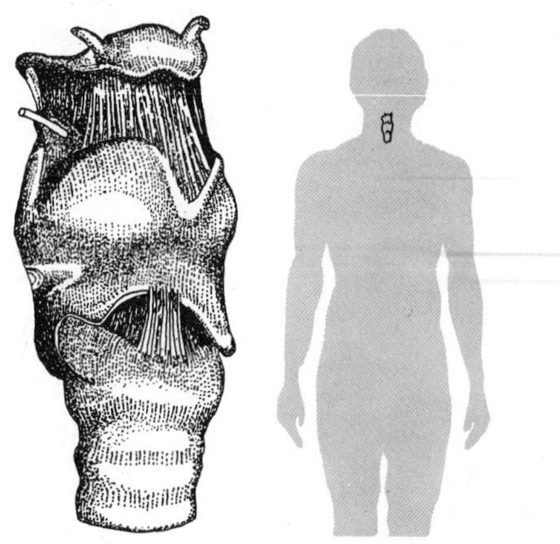

Larynx

LUCKY
PORTAL
PANCAKE HOUSE

Las Vegas, Nevada

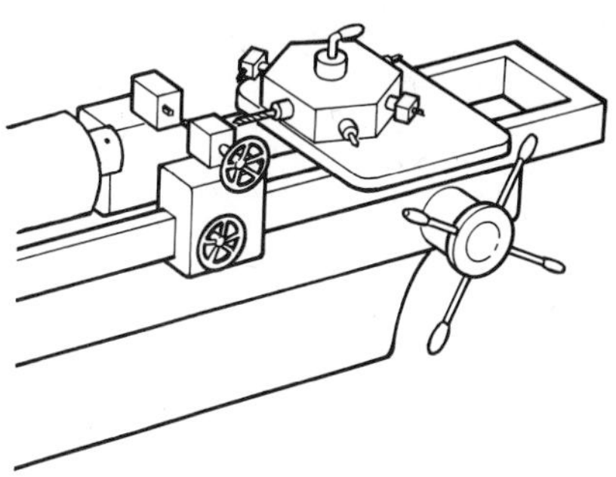

Lathe

Laurel and Hardy (left *and* center)

thur Stanley Jefferson), British-born gag inventor and director, was the thin, bumbling oaf, and the American **Oliver Hardy** (1892–1957) was the fat, pompous lady-chaser. Their best films, made before 1941, include *From Soup to Nuts* (1929) and *The Music Box* (1932).

Laurelwood. *See* Madroño.

Laurens, Henry (1724–92), US Revolutionary War leader, b. Charleston, S.C. An opponent of British policy in America before the Revolution, he served in the Continental Congress (1777–79) and was its president (1777–78). While on a diplomatic mission to the Netherlands in 1780 he was captured by the British. He was exchanged for Lord Cornwallis in 1782.

Laurens, John (1754–82), US Revolutionary War soldier, b. Charleston, S.C. He drew up the terms of Lord Cornwallis' surrender (1781), negotiated his father's release from the Tower of London, and served as George Washington's aide-de-camp. He also secured money, arms, and supplies from the French in 1781. He died in battle.

Laurentian Highlands. *See* Canadian Shield.

Laurier, (Sir) Wilfrid (1841–1919), prime minister of Canada (1896–1911). A lawyer, Laurier was the first French Canadian to lead a federal party (Liberals, 1888–1919). Throughout his career, Laurier propounded religious reconciliation and national unity. Entering commons in 1874, he was pro-tariff and opposed to clerical politics. He opposed the Riel Rebellions and African War (1899) and supported Canada's entry into World War I, despite opposing the draft.

Lausanne, city in W Switzerland, on Lake Geneva, on S slope of Mt Jorat. Originally a Celtic settlement, it was destroyed *c.* 379; episcopal see since 6th century; adopted Reformation 1536; became capital of Vaud canton 1803; scene of Lausanne Conference 1922; site of Gothic cathedral (1275), 13th-century bishop's palace, 13th-century castle, university (1890). Industries: radios, leather, clothes, beer, chemicals, wine, woodworking. Pop. 137,883.

Lausanne, Treaty of (1923), agreement signed at Lausanne, Switzerland, that abrogated the harsh Treaty of Sèvres (1920) imposed after World War I on the collapsing Ottoman Empire and ended the war between Greece and Turkey. Turkey obtained full sovereignty over mainland Turkey and renounced claims to Greek islands in the Aegean. Britain obtained Cyprus, and Italy received Rhodes and the Dodecanese Islands.

Lava, molten rock or magma that reaches the earth's surface and flows out through a volcanic vent in streams or sheets. There are three main types of lavas: vesicular, like pumice; glassy, like obsidian; and even-grained. Chemically lavas range from acidic to ultrabasic, though 90% of all lavas are basic. Basic lavas have a low viscosity and flow easily covering large areas. Acid lavas are highly viscous and rarely spread far. △176.

Laval, Pierre (1883–1945), French political figure. He began politics as a Socialist but left that party in 1920. In 1923 he reentered parliament and moved steadily to the right as he progressed through the senate and ministerial appointments to become premier (1931–32, 1935–36). In 1940 he entered the government of Marshal Pétain at Vichy and became its head in 1942. His capitulation to German demands earned him bitter hostility from the resistance in France and execution for treason when the war ended.

Laval-des-Rapides (Laval), city in S Canada, NW of Montréal on Ile Jésus in the St Lawrence River. Formed by merger of island communities in 1965; 2nd-largest city in Quebec. Industries: chemicals, paper, iron. Pop. 228,010.

Lavender, common name for aromatic herbs or shrubs of the genus *Lavandula* of the mint family. *L. spica,* erroneously known as *L. vera* or *L. officinalis,* is a Mediterranean woody perennial ornamental subshrub. Its fragrant flowers when dried are used for sachets and to perfume linens and clothing. Oil from the leaves is used in perfume and both flowers and leaves are used in making lavender water and aromatic vinegar. △446.

Laver, any of various edible purple gelatinous seaweeds of the genus *Porphyra.* In Japan, laver (called *amanori* or *nori*) is pressed and dried for use in cooking. In Europe, red laver (chiefly *P. laciniata* and *P. vulgaris*) is stewed or pickled. *See also* Red Algae.

Laveran, Charles Louis Alphonse (1845–1922), French physician. He contributed greatly to tropical medicine and parasitology, winning the 1907 Nobel Prize in physiology and medicine for his work on the role played by protozoa in causing diseases. Laveran discovered the parasite responsible for malaria and studied trypanosomiasis and leishmaniasis.

Lavoisier, Antoine Laurent (1743–94), French chemist. The father of modern chemistry, he was an advocate and practitioner of accurate measurement. His careful experiments enabled him to demolish the phlogiston theory by demonstrating the function of oxygen in combustion. He named both oxygen and hydrogen and showed how they combined to form water. In collaboration with Berthollet and others he published *Methods of Chemical Nomenclature* (1787), which laid down the modern method of naming substances. His *Elementary Treatise on Chemistry* (1789) was the first textbook of chemistry. He was guillotined after the Revolution, having been arrested for his former activities as a tax-farmer (a tax collector empowered to make a personal profit, which Lavoisier used to finance his research). △1552.

Lavrov, Peter. △1286.

Law, (Andrew) Bonar (1858–1923), British statesman, b. Canada. A member of Parliament from 1900, he led the Unionists in the British Parliament (1911–21), was chancellor of the exchequer (1916–18), and prime minister (1922–23).

Law, John (1671–1729), Scottish economist. The regent of France allowed him to execute his plan for a paper currency in that country. He inaugurated the "Mississippi Scheme" for American colonization. His bank (founded 1716) became the Banque Royale (1718), and he became controller-general of finance (1720). Speculation in the shares of his Mississippi Company (Compagnie d'Occident) (1719–20), however, brought about his ruin.

Law, system of rules governing human conduct imposed by politically organized society and enforced by threat of punishment. Custom is probably the prime source of law. Religious and ethical systems usually developed a legal order, as exemplified by the early law codes of Hammurabi (Babylonia), the law of Manu (India), Islamic law (Arabia), and Mosaic law (Palestine). Ancient Greek laws, together with the law of twelve tables, formed Roman Law, which was codified in the *Corpus Juris Civilis* of Justinian, and greatly affected the growth of Western law. German law temporarily replaced Roman law after the collapse of the Roman Empire. This later blended with Roman law and during the Renaissance and the revival of trade it spread through the world as modern civil law. The law of nature, a simplified restatement of Roman law, especially incorporating those laws of contract and property, prepared the way for the codifications of continental Europe, most famous of which is the Napoleonic Code. In England, common law developed as the outgrowth of Germanic customary law and was based on judicial precedents. US law, founded on English common law, has the unique feature of the coexistance of federal and state law. Modern law reflects the complexity of modern society, with an ever-widening range to regulate many different branches of human conduct. △908–12, 918.

Law Enforcement. △918.

Lawn Bowling, an outdoor game, most popular in England and Canada, is played on a smooth grass plot about 120 feet square (36.6m square), which is divided into 6 alleys 120 feet long and 20 feet (6.1m) wide. After one of the players throws a small white ball (jack) at some spot not less than 75 feet (22.9m) down the alley, each player in turn rolls a ball toward the jack. A point is given for each ball nearer the jack than that of an opponent's ball. Usually, 21 wins. In a singles match, each player rolls four balls. In a team match, each player rolls two balls. Lawn bowling originated in Great Britain about the 13th century.

Lawn Mower. △1820.

Law of Supply and Demand. *See* Supply and Demand, Law of.

Lawrence, D(avid) H(erbert) (1885–1930), English author. The son of a coal miner, he became a schoolteacher. In 1909 he had some poems published in the *English Review* and in 1911 his first novel *The White Peacock* appeared. In 1912 he went to Europe with Frieda von Richthofen, whom he married in 1914. During World War I, because of his pacifism and her being German, many people suspected them of being spies. In 1919 they left England to travel and live in Europe, Ceylon, Australia, New Mexico, and Mexico. Lawrence believed that modern Western society was dehumanizing, that people were losing contact with their basic physical and sexual selves. The semiautobiographical novel *Sons and Lovers* had appeared in 1913. *The Rainbow* (1915) and *Women in Love* (1921) traced a family's history through several generations, concentrating on two women of the last generation. In the 1920s Lawrence wrote novels such as *The Plumed Serpent* (1926) with Nietzschean heroes. *Lady Chatterley's Lover* (1928) was long banned in England and the United States because of its explicit description and discussion of sex. Among his best known short stories are "The Prussian Officer" and "The Rocking-Horse Winner." *Etruscan Places* (1932) is his most important travel book. *Studies in Classic American Literature* (1916) is a provocative work of criticism. Lawrence died of tuberculosis at age 45.

Lawrence, Ernest Orlando (1901–58), US physicist, b. Canton, S.D. He became professor at the University of California where he built the first cyclotron, a subatomic particle accelerator. His invention earned him the 1939 Nobel Prize. With the cyclotron he researched atomic structure, produced radioactive phosphorus, iodine, and other medicinal isotopes, and caused various elements to exhibit transmutation. In his honor, the element lawrencium was named. △1484.

Lawrence, T(homas) E(dward) (1888–1935), British author and soldier, known popularly as Lawrence of Arabia. He worked in the Middle East as an archaeologist. In World War I he worked for British intelligence, organizing a revolt of Arab tribesmen against the Turks and acquiring a legendary reputation. His *The Seven Pillars of Wisdom* (1926) is an account of this campaign. Discontented with British policy in the Middle East, he sought obscurity in the Royal Air Force, joining under the name "Ross." He died in a motorcycle accident.

Lawrence, city in NE Kansas, on Kansas River 28mi (45km) E of Topeka; seat of Douglas co; center of free state abolitionists; scene of attack Aug. 21, 1863 by William Quantrill's pro-slavery group in which 150 people were killed; site of University of Kansas (1863) and Haskell Institute (1884), largest Indian school in country. Industries: farm chemicals, corrugated boxes, greeting cards, food processing. Founded 1854 by members of New England Emigrant Aid Society and named for society's treasurer, Amos A. Lawrence; inc. 1858. Pop. (1970) 45,698.

Lawrence, city in NE Massachusetts, on Merrimack River; seat of Essex co. Industries: textiles, textile machinery, leather goods, clothes. Founded 1655 as part of Methuen and Andover, to 1847; inc. as city 1853. Pop. (1970) 66,915.

Lawrencium, radioactive metallic element (symbol Lr) of the actinide group, first made (1961) by bombarding californium with boron nuclei. The element has been made only in trace amounts and has not been identified chemically. Properties: at. no. 103; most stable isotope Lr^{256} (half-life 8s). *See also* Transuranium Elements.

Laws of Motion, three laws proposed by Sir Isaac Newton in his *Principia* (1687) that form the basis of the classical study of motion and force. According to the First Law, a body resists changes in its state of motion—a body at rest tends to remain at rest unless acted on by an external force, and a body in motion tends to remain in motion at the same speed and in the same direction unless acted on by an external force. According to the Second Law, the change in motion of a body as a result of a force is directly proportional to the force and inversely proportional to the mass of the body; that is, if the change in motion, or acceleration, is a, the force is F, and the mass is m, then $a = F/m$. According to the Third Law, to every action there is an equal and opposite reaction. This law may be expressed mathematically in the relation between the impetus acting on a body, Ft (force multiplied by time) and the change in momentum, mv (mass multiplied by velocity); according to the Third Law, $Ft = mv$. *See also* Acceleration; Force; Momentum. △1488, 1492.

Laws of Thermodynamics. *See* Thermodynamics.

Lawton, city in SW Oklahoma, 80mi (129km) SW of Oklahoma City; seat of Comanche co; site of Cameron College (1907) and Fort Sill, US field artillery center. Industries: mobile homes, cotton, cement products, bedding. Inc. 1901. Pop. (1970) 74,470.

Layering, a method of plant propagation that induces root formation on a stem or branch while it is still attached to the parent plant. In simple stem layering the stem or branch is fastened down and covered with soil until a root system develops, when the stem or branch is cut from its parent and grown as a separate individual. In air layering a ball of moistened rooting-soil mixture is placed on the branch or stem to be layered, held in place by a plastic wrap, and left until a root system develops. Root formation is accelerated by slashing the bark in the layering region. △324.

Laysan Finch. △614.

Lazarus, the name of two men in the New Testament. In chapters 11–12 of the Gospel of John, Lazarus is the brother of Mary and Martha of Bethany. He died and four days later Jesus miraculously restored him to life. In Luke 16:19–31 Lazarus is the poor man in Christ's parable about a beggar and a rich man.

Lazurite. *See* Lapis Lazuli.

LDCs. *See* Less Developed Countries.

Leaching, removal of a soluble mineral or other material by dissolution and carrying away by ground water. If calcium carbonate is removed, the result is a cavern. △312.

Leacock, Stephen (1869–1944), Canadian humorist, b. England. He came to Ontario as a child. He later taught political science but gained popularity for his irreverent sketches, which appeared in newspapers and magazines.

Lead, city in W South Dakota, in Black Hills, 33mi (53km) WNW of Rapid City; site of Homestake Mine, one of largest gold mines in US, in operation since 1877. Industries: gold mining, tourism. Founded 1876 after discovery of gold. Inc. 1890. Pop. (1970) 5,420.

Lead, metallic element (symbol Pb) of group IVA of the periodic series, known from ancient times. Chief ore is galena (sulfide), from which it is obtained by roasting. It is used in pipes, batteries, cable sheaths, and alloys such as solder and type metal. The element is also used in making the gasoline additive tetraethyl lead. It is also used as a shield for X rays and other radiation. Chemically, it is unreactive and resists corrosion. Properties: at. no. 82; at. wt. 207.19; sp gr 11.3; melt. pt. 617.5°F (325.3°C); boil. pt. (3,182°F) (1,750°C); most common isotope Pb^{208} (52.3%). △1552–54.

Lead Chamber Process. △1582.

Lead Poisoning, condition caused by absorption of lead from the digestive tract, lungs, or skin. It occurs among children who eat chips of lead-containing paint in deteriorating buildings and among workers in lead-using industries. Its first symptoms, such as mild diarrhea, anemia, and irritability often go unnoticed until serious effects such as convulsions occur. If untreated it can be fatal.

Lead Processing. △1596.

Leadville, mining town in central Colorado; seat of Lake co; gold discovered 1860, silver in 1877; city had declined by 1893 but revived in late 1890s gold rush; site of Tabor Home and Matchless Mine Museum. Tourism is major industry. Inc. 1878. Pop. (1970) 4,314.

Leaf, thin and flat plant organ that is involved with photosynthesis and transpiration. Leaves are simple or compound (divided into leaflets), have parallel or netlike veins for transporting water and nutrients and small openings (stomata) for exchanging gases. Growing laterally from the stem or twig, a leaf consists of a blade and a stalk, or petiole, attaching it to the branch or stem. It has limited growth, maturing for one or more seasons and then dropping off. Modified leaves include: succulent leaves with thick, fleshy water storage tissue; tendrils that coil around supports; and spines that become hard, slender, and conical (thorns are modified branches). △430, 448, 562.

Leaf Beetle, small, oval beetle that feeds on leaves. Many, including the Colorado potato beetle and striped cucumber beetle, are yellow with black markings. Family Chrysomelidae.

Leaf Butterfly. *See* Dead Leaf Butterfly.

Leaf-cutting Ant, or parasol ant, large ant that cuts and transports bits of leaves to its nest. These beds of macerated leaves are used to grow the fungi that leaf-cutters eat. They live in large colonies in sometimes enormous underground nests. Genus *Atta.* △602.

Leafhopper, brightly colored insect found worldwide. These insects suck juices from trees and plants, some sucking enough juice to remove the chlorophyll. Others carry plant diseases. Length: to 0.5in (13mm). Family Cicadellidae. *See also* Homoptera.

Leaf Insect, leaf-mimicking insect found in the tropics. They are related to walking sticks but have broad bodies, wings, and legs. Length: 3–6in (76–152mm). Family Phasmatidae. *See also* Orthoptera; Walking Stick. △492.

Leaf Mold, compost or humus composed chiefly of rotted vegetable matter, such as fallen leaves. *See* Compost.

Leaf Monkey. *See* Langur.

Leaf-nosed Bat, any of a large variety of small insect-eating bats living in the tropics and subtropics worldwide. They have fleshy leaflike organs on the end of their snouts that probably aid them in detecting echoes. Families Hipposideridae and Phyllostomatidae.

Leaf Roller, insect larva that nests in a rolled leaf. Leaf rollers include some moth caterpillars of the Tortricidae family and some skippers—bean skipper *Urbanus proteus* and canna skipper *Calpodes ethlius.*

Leafy Sea Dragon. *See* Sea Dragon.

League of Nations, international organization (1919–46), forerunner of the United Nations. Created as part of the Treaty of Versailles ending World War I, it required that members respect the territorial independence of all members, excluding acts of aggression. The refusal of the United States to participate impaired the league's efficiency and, although some achievements were accomplished, it could not prevent World War II. Dissolved in 1946, it did provide the groundwork for establishing the United Nations. △1306–08, 1336.

League of Women Voters, a national organization of women eligible to vote. It was founded "to promote political responsibility through informed and active participation of citizens in government." The nonpartisan organization is comprised of women citizens 18 years and older who distribute information on issues and candidates, and campaign to encourage registration and voting. It publishes studies, books, and pamphlets on national issues. Founded 1920. Members, about 160,000.

Leah, in the Bible, daughter of Laban and sister of Rachel. She was made the bride of Jacob after he worked seven years to win Rachel's hand, because their father felt the eldest should marry first. Leah was the mother of Reuben, Simeon, Levi, Judah, Issachar, Zebulun, and Dinah.

Leakey, Louis S. Bazett (1903–72), English archeologist and anthropologist who discovered fossils in East Africa that proved man to be older than had been thought. In 1931 he began to research Olduvai Gorge in Tanzania. He found there animal fossils and tools. In 1959 his wife Mary found a hominid fossil now regarded as an Australopithecine, and thought to be 1,750,000 years old. Leakey authored numerous books, including *Adam's Ancestors* (1934) and *Stone-Age Africa* (1936). △648.

Lear, Edward (1812–88), English artist and writer, traveled in Europe and Asia. His nonsense verse, including *The Book of Nonsense* (1846) and *Laughable Lyrics* (1876), portrays a world of fantasy, often tinged with melancholy. A popularizer of the limerick, he illustrated his books with line drawings. *See also* Limerick.

Learning Curve, in psychology, graph of learner's improvement in performing some task; ie, proficiency of performance plotted against time or trials of practice. On most tasks, performance tends to improve fastest early in learning, and much more slowly as the learner has more practice.

Learning Theory, in psychology, a comprehensive theory of how learning takes place and what factors affect learning, remembering, and forgetting. Important early theorists were John B. Watson, Ivan Pavlov, Clark L. Hull, and E.L. Thorndike. More recent contributors include behaviorist B. F. Skinner and the cognitive psychologists. Modern researchers tend to investigate particular problems rather than formulate universal theories. *See also* Cognitive Psychology. △778.

Lease, Mary Elizabeth (1853–1933), US lawyer, reformer, and temperance advocate, b. Ridgeway, Pa.

Lausanne, Switzerland

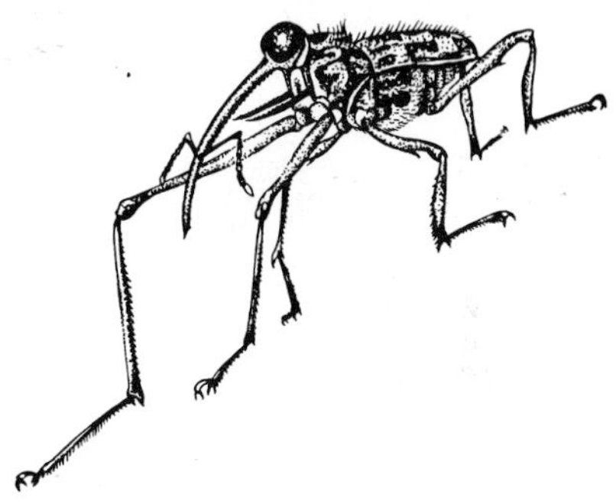
Leaf beetle

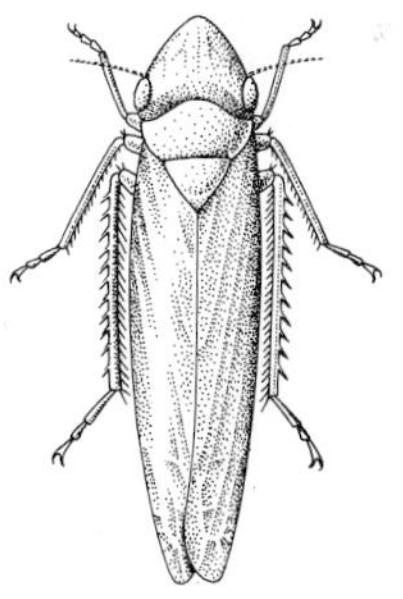
Leaf hopper

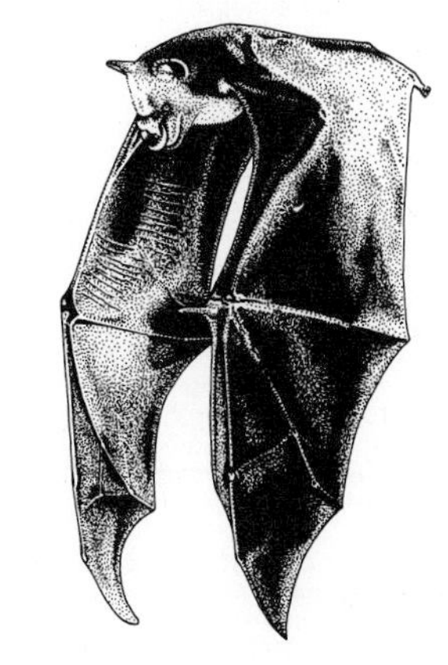
Leaf-nosed bat

Known for her fiery oratorical style, she was active in populist politics in Kansas, supporting the popular election of senators, the government control of railroads, women's suffrage, and prohibition.

Least Bittern, small bird of temperate and tropical Americas. It is secretive, lives on swamp floors, and lays bluish or greenish white eggs (3–6) in a canopied grass nest on the ground. Length: 1–1.5ft. (30–46cm). Species *Ixobrychus exilis*. *See also* Bittern.

Leather, animal hides cured by tanning to prevent decay and increase flexibility; often finished by glazing, enameling, or lacquering and colored by staining or dyeing. Suede is produced by raising a nap on the flesh side by buffing with emery. Artificial leathers were formerly a strong fabric coated with pyroxylin but are now usually vinyl polymers. *See also* Tanning.

Leatherback Turtle, sea turtle found in all tropical oceans. The largest of all turtles, it has a smooth, black, leathery skin with seven ridges running lengthwise, and no external plates. Its forelegs are enormous flippers. It feeds on jellyfish. Length: to 7ft (2.1m); weight: 1,200lb (540kg). Family Dermochelyidae; species *Dermochelys coriacea*. *See also* Turtle. △522.

Leather-Stocking Tales, The, five novels by James Fenimore Cooper about Natty Bumppo, an American frontier scout. The title is derived from Natty's nickname, Leather-Stocking, which refers to his deerskin leggings. The novels are *The Pioneers* (1823), *The Last of the Mohicans* (1826), *The Prairie* (1827), *The Pathfinder* (1840), and *The Deerslayer* (1841). The narrative of Natty's life follows a different sequence, however: *Deerslayer, Mohicans, Pathfinder, Pioneers, Prairie*. The novels trace the adventures of Natty and his Indian friend, Chingachgook, during the French and Indian wars and in the post-revolutionary United States.

Leatherwork. △1590.

Leavenworth, city in NE Kansas, on W bank of Missouri River; seat of Leavenworth co; oldest city in Kansas. Democratic party of Kansas was founded here 1858; site of Fort Leavenworth (1827) and federal penitentiary. Industries: flour milling, steel, furniture. Founded 1854 by pro-slavery settlers from Missouri; inc. 1855. Pop. (1970) 25,147.

Leaves of Grass (1855), collection of poems by Walt Whitman, revised and augmented until 1892. The first edition contained 12 poems, the first and longest of which was later titled "Song of Myself." Scholars agree that the crucial edition is the third (1860), which contains many new poems, including the famous "Out of the Cradle Endlessly Rocking," and regroupings of previous ones.

Lebanon (Al-Lubnan), independent nation in the Middle East. The historic home of the Phoenicians, it was engulfed by civil war between its religious divisions in the mid-1970s.

Land and economy. Situated on the E end of the Mediterranean Sea with a coast of 120mi (193km), it is bordered by Syria (N and E) and Israel (S). Topographically, it is dominated by a narrow coastal plain. Behind this plain are the Lebanese Mts, the fertile Beqaa Valley, and the Anti-Lebanon range leading to Syria. About 65% of the land is desert, waste, or urban; 27% agricultural, and 8% forests. The main rivers are the Litani and the Orontes. The climate is Mediterranean. Lebanon's revenue derives from trade, which accounts for two-thirds of the national income; agriculture, which employs half of the workers; terminals of oil pipelines from Iraq and Saudi Arabia; and banking, which has generated Arab capital. Until fighting in the mid-1970s, tourism was important. The basis of the economy is strict private enterprise with very few government controls. Beirut is the Middle East's foreign exchange center.

People. With its population almost evenly divided between Arabs and Christians (Maronites), Lebanon also includes Armenians and Greek Orthodox. Muslims are divided into three sects—Sunni, Shiite, and Druse. The official language is Arabic. Agriculture provides a living for the majority, and the cities of Beirut and Tripoli are commercial centers. Lebanon has the highest percentage of skilled workers in the Middle East. Literacy is 86%, highest in the Arab world.

Government. A parliamentary republic provides for division of public positions among all religions. A unicameral legislature and president are both elected.

History. Driven by orthodox Byzantine persecution, Lebanon was colonized in the 6th century by the Monothelites (now Maronites) and was often a refuge for heretics. It was then fragmented politically and ruled by various factions for centuries. Lebanon was governed by a Christian military governor, assisted by a council representing all other sects, from 1864 until the end of WWI, when it became a French mandate. By 1943 the country was independent. Turmoil marked its presidential administrations and, in 1958, the United States sent Marines to quell a revolt. Lebanon has been the seat of Palestinian commando raids into Israel, bringing Israeli raids in reprisal. Demands by Muslims for a greater voice in government escalated in the 1970s. In 1975 civil war erupted between Muslims and Maronite Christians. After savage battles that ultimately wrecked the economy and left thousands dead, Pres. Suleiman Franjieh, a Christian, was forced to resign in 1976, and Syrian troops moved in to restore order. Elias Sarkis was inaugurated as the new president September 1976.

PROFILE

Official name: Republic of Lebanon
Area: 4,015sq mi (10,632sq km)
Population: 2,900,000
Density: 706.5 per sq mi (272.8 per sq km)
Chief cities: Beirut (capital); Tripoli
Government: Parliamentary republic
Religion: Christian (Maronites) and Islam
Language: Arabic (official)
Monetary unit: Lebanese pound
Gross national product: $3,700,000,000
Per capita income: $874
Industries: food products, textiles, leather goods, cement, publishing
Agriculture: apples, citrus fruits, olives, tobacco, grapes, cereals, wheat
Minerals: oil
Trading partners: France, Middle East countries

Lebanon, city in SE Pennsylvania, 80mi (129km) NW of Philadelphia; seat of Lebanon co. Industries: steel, steel fabricating, textiles, chemicals, clothing. Founded 1753; inc. as city 1868. Pop. (1970) 28,572.

Lebedev, Pyotr Nikolayevich (1866–1911), Russian physicist noted for demonstrating that light exerts minute pressure on solid bodies. He was a professor at the University of Moscow and also worked on the origin of the Earth's magnetism. A physical research institute in Moscow was named in his honor.

Le Bel, Joseph Achille (1847–1930), French chemist who proposed that the chemical bonds from a carbon atom are arranged in space as if they pointed towards the corners of a regular tetrahedron. This theory allowed chemists to work out the molecular structures of organic compounds. He is regarded as the cofounder of stereochemistry, in collaboration with J. H. van't Hoff.

Lebensraum. △1334.

Le Breton, Gilles. △1146.

Le Brun, Charles (1619–90), French painter. He painted religious, mythological, and historical subjects, as well as portraits. He was also a draftsman and decorator. He achieved great prestige in his time and helped Paris succeed Rome as the new capital of the arts. His notable works include *Portrait of Jabach and His Family* and *Chancellor Séguier*. △1166.

Le Carré, John (1931–), pseud. of David Cornwell, English novelist. He writes well-crafted thrillers. His best known book is *The Spy Who Came in from the Cold* (1963), a realistic treatment of spies and their world that draws on his own experience in British Intelligence. Later novels include *The Looking-Glass War* (1965), *A Small Town in Germany* (1968), and *Tinker, Tailor, Soldier, Spy* (1974).

Le Châtelier's Principle, a principle announced by the French chemist Henry-Louis Le Châtelier (1850–1936) in 1888. It states that if a system (usually of chemically interacting substances) in a state of equilibrium is disturbed (by heat, for example) the system will tend to neutralize the disturbance and restore equilibrium. This applies not only to reversible chemical reactions but also to reversible physical processes such as the evaporation or crystallization of a liquid.

Lecithin, substances containing fatty acids and choline and found in many animal tissues, especially in nerves, semen, and the liver.

Léclanché Cell. △1532.

Lecompton Constitution (1857), a pro-slavery constitution that was drafted in Lecompton, the capital of Kansas Territory. The constitution's article on slavery, which gave a choice of limited or unlimited slavery, was submitted to a popular election and passed because Free-Soilers refused to vote. Congress then declined to admit Kansas as a slave state. The constitution was defeated in another election (1858) and Kansas became a free state.

Le Corbusier (1887–1969), French architect, b. Charles Édouard Jeanneret in Switzerland. He promoted the International modern style but eventually developed his own style. His prolific ideas and experiments with modern construction methods resulted in unique designs for both individual houses and entire cities. Often inspired by industrial designs he used strong cubist forms, usually of white concrete, and often placed his buildings on pillars. After 1940 he developed a complex modular system of harmonious but differing proportions, represented in his chapel at Ronchamp near Belfort (1954). He also designed the main glass wall and windowless end walls of the UN Secretariat, New York City (1947) and the Visual Arts Center, Harvard University (Cambridge, Mass., 1961–62). △1322.

Ledbetter, Huddie ("Leadbelly") (1888–1949), US composer and blues singer, b. Mooringsport, La. Imprisoned for murder, he was pardoned but was sent back for attempted murder. Folklorist John A. Lomax discovered him in prison and used his songs for a book *Negro Folk Songs as Sung by Lead Belly* (1936). He is best known as the composer of many classic blues songs including "Goodnight Irene," "The Midnight Special," and "Rock Island Line." Many of his songs were adaptations of traditional folk music.

Ledum, small, evergreen, bog shrub found in damp, acid soils of cold northern climates. It has small, white flowers. Family Ericaceae; genus *Ledum*.

Ledyard, John (1751–89), US explorer, b. Groton, Conn. He went to sea and joined the British marines. He sailed with Capt. James Cook around the Cape of Good Hope (1776–79) and published *Journal of Capt. Cook's Last Voyage to the Pacific* about his experience (1783). Punished for refusing to fight against the Americans during the Revolution, he finally deserted the British (1782). With the backing of Thomas Jefferson, he planned an expedition from Russia to Virginia by way of Siberia and the Bering Strait, but Catherine the Great had him arrested. He died in Africa readying an expedition to its interior. His dreams of establishing fur trade with China were unrealized.

Lee, Ann (1736–84), English mystic. Known as the founder of the United Society of Believers in Christ's Second Appearing, popularly called the Shakers, she was imprisoned many times in England for her beliefs before emigrating to America in 1774. She founded a colony at Niskeyuna (near Albany, N.Y.) in 1776 and gained many converts. She was followed as the anointed successor of Christ, and her beliefs in community of goods, withdrawal from the world and its sins, and celibacy were the basis of Shaker communities. She did not escape persecution in America, and the frequent beatings and jailings she suffered probably contributed to her early death.

Lee, Francis Lightfoot (1734–97), American patriot and a signer of the Declaration of Independence, b. Stratford, Va. After serving in the Continental Congress (1775–79) and helping prepare the Articles of Confederation, he briefly served in the Virginia senate. *See also* Declaration of Independence.

Lee, Gypsy Rose (1914–70), US performer, b. Rose Louise Hovick, Seattle, Wash. As a child she performed with her sister June. She first appeared as Gypsy Rose in the 1936 Ziegfield Follies. The 1961 play *Gypsy* is based on her memoirs.

Lee, Henry ("Light-Horse Harry") (1756–1818), US Revolutionary soldier and father of Robert E. Lee, b. Prince William co, Va. His excellent service during the Revolution earned him the nickname Light-Horse Harry Lee. He served as governor of Virginia (1792–95) and as a Federalist congressman (1799–1801). On the occasion of George Washington's death (1799), Lee described him as being "first in war, first in peace, and first in the hearts of his countrymen."

Lee, Richard Henry (1732–94), US political leader in the Revolution, b. Westmoreland co, Va. A spokesman for liberty, he opposed slavery, and during the Second Continental Congress (1776) he introduced a resolution calling for a "declaration of independence." He backed Washington as commander of the army and while in the Senate he was an advocate of the Bill of Rights.

Lee, Robert Edward (1807–70), commander of Confederate forces in the Civil War, b. Stratford, Va. Son of a hero of the Revolution and the governor of Virginia, he was a graduate of the US Military Academy at West Point (1829). Although Lee regarded slavery as evil and saw advantages of the Union, he believed even more in state's rights. His loyalty to his native Virginia was paramount. Declining Lincoln's offer to head Union troops, he became advisor to Jefferson Davis, the Confederate president (1861). After Gen. J. E. Johnston was wounded, Lee became commander of the Confederate forces (1862). In 1862 he led the successful defense of Richmond and won at the Second Battle of Bull Run. He lost the 1862 battle at Antietam but gave the Union its worst defeats at Fredericksburg (1862) and Chancellorsville (1863). His attempt to penetrate the North ended in the defeat at Gettysburg in July 1863. He surrendered to Ulysses S. Grant at Appomattox Court House on April 9, 1865. Lee's skill in analyzing military situations and use of field defenses are still studied. After the war Lee attempted to ameliorate the war wounds. He became president of what is now Washington and Lee University (1865). △1276.

Lee, Tsung-dao (1926–), US physicist, b. China. He showed that among sub-atomic particles, the law of conservation of parity (that nature, in effect, makes no distinction between right- and left-handedness) does not always hold. Working with Chen Ning Yang, Lee suggested that in certain types of sub-atomic reactions, parity is not conserved, and this was subsequently verified by experiment. He was awarded the 1957 Nobel Prize in physics.

Leech, freshwater, marine, and terrestrial annelid found worldwide in tropical and temperate regions. Its tapered, ringed body is equipped with a sucking disc at each end. Most leeches are found in ponds where they live on the blood of invertebrates, fish, amphibians, and turtles. Length: 0.5–2in (13–51mm). There are over 300 species. Class Hirudinea. *See also* Annelida. △474.

Leeds, city in N England; university and cultural center; important agricultural markets. Headingley cricket ground and large residential estates lie N of the modern city center. Industries: woolens, clothing, engineering, paper, textiles, printing. Pop. 494,971.

Leek, onionlike biennial garden vegetable originating in Europe and Asia. It has white or pinkish flowers and a small bulb that is cooked along with the broad, flat, folded leaves. Height: 2–3ft (61–92cm). Family Amaryllidaceae; species *Allium porrum.*

Leeuwenhoek, Anton van (1632–1723), Dutch maker of microscopes and naturalist. He ground lenses and built microscopes that magnified up to 270 times. The first to describe protozoa (1674) and bacteria (1676), Leeuwenhoek was elected to the Royal Society of England in 1680 for his contributions to science. He discovered red blood cells in a classic study of capillary circulation. His wide-ranging microscopic examinations included studies in anatomy, histology, physiology, embryology, botany, chemistry, and physics and helped to refute the then widespread belief that living things could evolve from lifeless matter.

Leeward Islands, N group of Lesser Antilles in E West Indies, extending SE from Puerto Rico to Windward Islands, between Atlantic Ocean (E) and Caribbean Sea (W). The islands are primarily of volcanic origin; now an agricultural and winter resort center; group includes the US Virgin Islands, Guadeloupe and dependencies (French), St Eustatius and Saba (Dutch), St Martin (jointly Dutch-French owned), British Leewards (Antigua, St Kitts-Nevis, Montserrat), and British Virgin Islands. Settlement was begun by British in the 17th century; conflict ensued shortly after with French settlements; possession was further contested by Spanish, who were later forced out. Islands were Anglo-French pawns for nearly two centuries, until end of Napoleonic Wars (1815). Dominica was part of Leewards 1833–1940; a severe earthquake shook Leewards Oct. 8, 1975. Industries: limes, coconuts, tobacco, vegetables, dairy products, tourism. Pop. 599,300.

Lefebvre, François, Duc de Danzig (1755–1820), French general. During the French Revolution he rose from sergeant to general, commanding the Army of the Rhine at the Battle of Fleurus (1794). While governor of Paris, he supported the coup d'etat (1799) whereby Napoleon became first consul. Named marshal in 1807, he led the capture of Danzig (1807). He voted for Napoleon's abdication, earning the right to remain in France under the restoration of the Bourbons. He rejoined Napoleon during the Hundred Days and therefore lost his title when the Bourbons returned to power in 1815.

Le Gallienne, Eva (1899–), US actress, director, and translator, b. England, the daughter of Richard Le Gallienne. She made her London acting debut in 1915, in New York 1916. She became famous for her starring role in Ferenc Molnar's *Liliom* (1921). She translated and acted in many of Ibsen's plays. In 1926 she founded and directed the Civic Repertory Theatre in New York, the first such company in the United States. In 1946 she cofounded the American Repertory Theatre with Margaret Webster. She directed her own translation of Chekhov's *The Cherry Orchard* on Broadway in 1968. She gave outstanding performances in *Camille* (1931) and *Royal Family* (1975), among many others.

Legal Tender Cases, name for several post-Civil War lawsuits brought before the US Supreme Court. They concerned the constitutionality of the Legal Tender Act (1862), which had been passed to meet Civil War currency needs. The notes issued under this act were without any reserve or specie basis and quickly depreciated in gold terms, becoming controversial because early debts could be paid with the cheaper currency. After several separate lawsuits, the court finally found the act valid in *Knox* v. *Lee* and *Parker* v. *Davis* (1871).

Legaspi, López de. △1260.

Legendre, Adrien Marie (1752–1833), French mathematician. His work on number theory and elliptic integrals was not properly appreciated until the end of his life. In his study of quadratic residues, Legendre discovered the law of reciprocity much praised and used by C. F. Gauss. He introduced the method of least squares, to calculate the paths of comets. His most influential work was *Elements of Geometry* (1794).

Léger, Alexis. *See* Perse, Saint-John.

Léger, Fernand (1881–1955), French painter. His work was important to the development of the cubist style. His works include *The Mechanic* (1920) and *Three Women* (1921). He also designed sets and costumes for ballets and operas. △1294.

Leghorn (Livorno), industrial town in Italy, on the Tyrrhenian Sea; capital of Livorno prov. Fortified in the 14th century by the Pisans, it prospered under Medici rule; it was the first free port on the Mediterranean (1590); site of 16th-century cathedral, remains of 17th-century city walls; seat of Italian naval academy. Exports: wine, marble, textiles, olive oil. Industries: shipbuilding, oil refining, iron, steel, distilling, chemicals. Pop. 172,794.

Leghorn, chicken breed, the most important variety being the White Leghorn. *See also* White Leghorn.

Legislature, representative assembly whose primary function is the enactment of laws. In the United States it is a bicameral body, composed of two chambers, the Senate and the House of Representatives, all of whose members are popularly elected. The legislature is empowered to levy taxes and appropriate public funds and to provide a check on the executive branch. It is also designed to reflect the interests and desires of its various constituents and to act as a forum for debate. △902, 910.

Legislative Processes, procedures followed by the legislature in enacting laws. Bills are introduced by a sponsoring legislator, often in response to pressure from constituents or private interest groups. In the United States, they are then sent for study and amendment to committee, where the majority of bills are shelved. If passed out of committee, a bill then goes to the floor for a vote. The procedure takes place in both the House and Senate before the bill is sent to the president for his signature. △910.

Legislative Reorganization Acts (1946, 1970), laws passed in an attempt to improve the efficiency of US Congress. Congressional standing committees were reduced by the 1946 act, salaries were raised, certain private bills were banned, and lobbyists were required to register officially. As a result of the 1970 act, records of the House of Representatives' activities were made more accessible to the public; a Senate veteran affairs committee was set up; and permission was given for an August recess in non-election years.

Legnica, city in SW Poland, on the Kaczawa River approx. 38mi (61km) WNW of Wroclaw; commercial and industrial center in farming region. Town was officially est. 1252 and contains medieval structures; scene of Battle of Legnica (1241), in which Poles stopped Tartar invasion; passed to Bohemia 14th century, and Prussia 1742; returned to Poland by Potsdam Conference 1945. Industries: textiles, food processing and marketing, metals. Pop. 75,800.

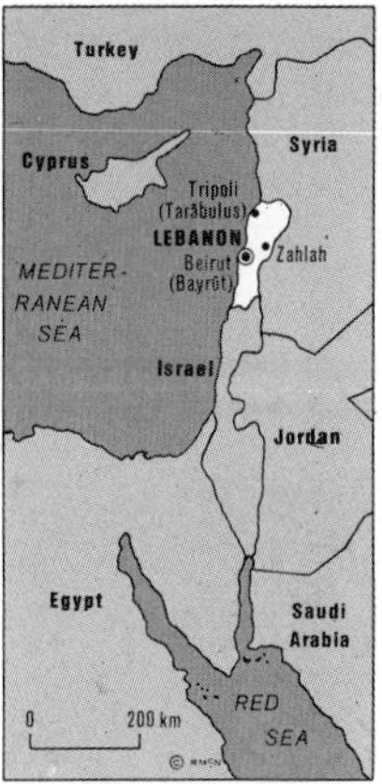
Turkey
Cyprus
Syria
Tripoli
(Tarābulus)
LEBANON
Beirut
(Bayrūt)
Zahlah
MEDITER-
RANEAN
SEA
Israel
Jordan
Egypt
Saudi
Arabia
RED
SEA
0
200 km
Lebanon

Robert E. Lee

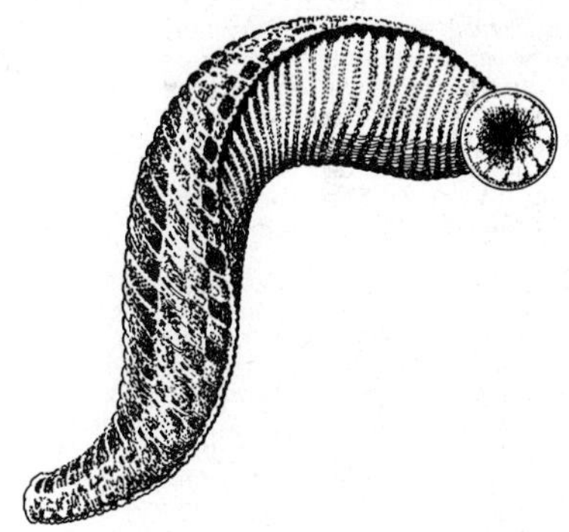
Leech

Leghorn, Italy

Legume (Leguminosae), family of many plants, shrubs, and trees including beans, clover, and acacia. Many have nitrogen-fixing roots and are planted for forage and cover crops. A legume can be the fruit, a seed-bearing pod, or the entire plant. △330.

Le Havre, commercial seaport city in N France, at mouth of Seine River on English Channel. Primarily a fishing and naval port until 1815, the city is now the principal export center for Paris and a transatlantic passenger port; site of a major Allied base during WWI; severely damaged during WWII; site of St Joseph church, a memorial to war victims, and Romanesque Church of St Honorine. Industries: chemicals, fertilizers, lumber, food processing, oil refining, shipbuilding. Founded 1516 as Le Havre-de-Grâce. Pop. 199,509.

Lehmann, Lotte (1888–1976), German soprano. She studied at the Berlin State Conservatory and made her debut in Hamburg in 1909. She sang successfully for many years with the Vienna State Opera (1914–38), the Metropolitan Opera in New York City (1934–45), and as a guest artist. She premiered many of the leading roles in Richard Strauss' operas.

Lehua, a showy hardwood tree common to many Pacific islands with bright red flowers borne in flat-topped clusters. The blossoms are used for decorative purposes. Species *Metrosideros villosa.*

Leibniz, Gottfried Wilhelm (1646–1716), German philosopher. He was educated at Leipzig, Jena, and Altdorf, studied jurisprudence (1667), and formulated ideas of a universal "characteristic" or logic. He went to Paris (1672) on a diplomatic mission and studied mathematics under Christian Huygens. He shared with Isaac Newton discovery of the calculus (1684). He contributed to the science of dynamics and forged a remarkable metaphysical system, based on the universality of centers of force and consciousness, known as "monads." Historiographer for the House of Hanover, courtier, and inventor, he was a truly encyclopedic genius, but published few complete works: *New Essays* (pub. 1765), *Theodicy* (1710), and many essays. *See also* Monad; Pre-established Harmony. △856–58.

Leicester, Robert Dudley, Earl of (1532–88), English nobleman, favorite of Queen Elizabeth I. The mysterious death (1560) of his wife apparently cleared the way for Leicester to marry Elizabeth. The queen, however, soon realized the impracticability of the match. Though the marriage never took place, Leicester remained influential despite his feud with William Cecil, his remarriage (1578), and support for the Puritans. As governor of the United Provinces (the Netherlands) (1586), he involved England in Protestant Europe's struggle against Spain.

Leicester, Simon de Montfort, Earl of. *See* Montfort, Simon de, Earl of Leicester.

Leicester, city in central England, 90mi (145km) NW of London; country seat of Leicestershire. In 9th century it was one of five boroughs of region conquered by Danes. During the War of the Roses, Richard III stayed in Leicester the night before he was killed; his body was brought back here for burial, Aug. 22, 1485; site of 14th-century church of St Martin, 15th-century Guild Hall, and University of Leicester (1957). Knitting frame was first installed here in 1680, and hosiery has been an important industry ever since. Industries: boots, shoes, textiles, textile and woodworking machinery. Founded by Romans as Ratae Coritanorum; there are many remains of Roman origin. Pop. 283,549.

Leiden, city in W Netherlands, on the Oude Rijn River; site of University of Leiden (1575); birthplace of artists Rembrandt, Lucas van Leyden, and others whose works are displayed in the municipal museum. Industries: metal working, printing, rugs and blankets, food processing. Pop. 101,221.

Leipzig, city in S central East Germany, at the confluence of the Pleisse, White Elster, and Parthe rivers. Founded as a Slavic settlement in 11th century, it became commercial center at intersection of important trade routes; scene of 1813 Battle of Nations, which ended Napoleon's power in Germany. Printing industry, founded 1480, is still important; site of Karl Marx University (founded 1409 as University of Leipzig), 16th-century church of St Thomas, 13th-century Pauline Church, old stock exchange (1682); birthplace of Richard Wagner is preserved. Industries: textiles, machinery, toys, chemicals. Chartered end of 12th century. Pop. 584,365.

Leipzig, Battle of, or **Battle of the Nations** (Oct. 16–19, 1813). The Prussians, Austrians, Russians, and Swedes inflicted a crushing defeat on Napoleon's outnumbered *grande armée,* which resulted in the final retreat of the French from Germany.

Leishmania, animallike, flagellate protozoan that is parasitic in the human liver and spleen. A small, ovate cell with no flagellum when in a human, it is carried by a sand flea in which it is elongate and has a flagellum. It causes the diseases leishmania and kala azar. Class Mastigophora; species *Leishmania donovani.* △732.

Leisler's Rebellion (1689–91), popular insurrection in colonial New York, led by Jacob Leisler, a Protestant champion of King William III. The rebellion ended with Leisler's hanging, although he was later pardoned by Parliament (1695).

Leisure, Sociology of, study of both the "leisure class" and leisure as a social by-product of technology and modernization. This branch of sociology seeks to understand and explain the interaction between the gaining of more leisure time by more people (a fairly recent phenomenon) and modern social systems and structures. △930–32.

Lemaître, Georges Édouard, (1894–1966), Belgian astronomer and cosmologist responsible for the "big bang" theory of the origin of the universe. In this theory the universe is thought to have begun suddenly and cataclysmically with the explosion of a primeval superatom. He studied at Cambridge and at the Massachusetts Institute of Technology. In 1927 he became professor of astrophysics at the University of Louvain where he proposed his theory, which explained the recession of the galaxies in terms of Albert Einstein's theory of general relativity.

Leman, Lake. *See* Geneva, Lake.

Le Mans, city in NW France, on Sarthe River 117mi. (188km) from Paris; capital of Sarthe dept.; besieged during Hundred Years' War (1337–1453); devastated by Huguenots 1562; scene of French defeat by Prussia 1870–71; birthplace of Henry II of England and John II of France; site of annual auto races, and Cathedral of St Julien du Mans (11th–13th centuries). Industries: food processing, textiles, machinery, automobile components. Founded by Romans 3rd century. Pop. 143,246.

Lemesos. *See* Limassol.

Lemming, plump mouse-size rodent living near the Arctic. It has long, soft, brownish fur, small ears, and a tiny tail. Prolific plant-eaters, lemmings often emigrate in search of food. Emigrating hordes of Norway lemming, famous for population explosions, sometimes drown attempting to cross wide bodies of water. Family Cricetidae. △584, 612.

Lemnos (Limnos), volcanic island of Greece, in N Aegean Sea, off Turkey; mountainous terrain, soil is fertile; capital is Kastron; sacred to ancient Greece, became colony of Athens *c.* 500 BC; passed to Venice 1464, taken by Ottoman Turks 1479 and ceded to Greece 1913; source of Lemnian earth (a medicinal soil). Industries: fruit, wine, silk, fish. Area: 186sq mi (482sq km). Pop. 17,367.

Lemon, an evergreen tree *(Citrus limonia)* of the rue family growing to 12ft (3.7m), probably native to subtropical Asia. It yields the familiar sour yellow citrus fruit. It is grown primarily in California in the United States, and is cultivated in subtropical regions elsewhere. △338.

Lemonwood, or wild coffee, tropical evergreen shrub native to South Africa and grown in S Florida. It has small, fragrant yellow flowers and shiny black fruit. Family Rubiaceae; species *Psycotria capensis.*

Le Moyne, family of Canada. Charles le Moyne (1626–85) fathered 11 sons when he was Sieur de Longueuil and Chateauguay, near Montreal. His sons included Charles Longueuil (governor of Montreal, 1724–29); Paul Joseph le Moyne (governor of Trois Rivières, 1757–60); Pierre le Moyne Iberville and Jacques le Moyne (soldiers and explorers); Jean Baptiste le Moyne Bienville (governor of Louisiana, 1717–25; 1732–43); and Paul le Moyne Maricourt (soldier). The le Moynes dominated political and military life in Quebec for much of the 18th century.

Lemur, primitive, mostly arboreal and nocturnal primate found in wooded areas of Madagascar and the Comoro Islands. They look like big-eyed squirrels with grasping, monkeylike hands and feet. Some are herbivorous, some feed mainly on insects, and others are omnivorous. Lemurs have changed little in 50,000,000 years and are believed to closely resemble the early ancestors of man and other primates. Length: 8in–4ft (20–122cm). Family Lemuridae. *See also* Primates. △554, 558.

Lena, river in E central Russian SFSR, USSR; rises on W slopes of Baikal Mts, W of Lake Baikal, flows NE and N along E side of central Siberian uplands into Laptev Sea through a delta 250mi (403km) wide; its tributaries number about 1,000. Yakutsk is only town on its course. River was first reached by Russians 1630. Navigable for 2,135mi (3,437km) of its 2,670mi (4,300km).

Lend-Lease, US program authorized by Congress in 1941 to give war aid to Great Britain. Aid was given on terms "the President deems satisfactory" and was soon extended to the USSR and China. Eventually nearly all US war allies were recipients. When the program ended in 1945, over $50,000,000,000 had been expended. △1340.

L'Enfant, Pierre Charles (1754–1825), US architect and engineer, b. France. He went to America (1777) and served in the Continental army. At George Washington's invitation he planned the national capital (1791), but the high cost of construction caused his dismissal. More than a century later the development of Washington, D.C., was pursued according to his plans.

Lenin, Vladimir Ilyich (1870–1924), sometimes N. Lenin, founder and leader of the Russian Communist party and the Soviet state, b. as Vladimir Ilyich Ulyanov. After his brother's execution for an anti-tsarist plot (1887), he joined Plekhanov's Marxists and became a professional revolutionary. Arrested in 1895 he was exiled to Siberia (1897–1900). In 1900 he started the revolutionary newspaper *Iskra (The Spark)* abroad, and in 1903 formed the Bolshevik party. He was in Russia for the 1905 uprising but abroad again 1907–17, consolidating a tight, loyal group. Entering Russia after the March 1917 revolution, with the help of the Germans, who permitted him to cross Germany by train, he and Leon Trotsky organized the Bolshevik Revolution (November 1917). As premier, he was responsible for the creation of the Cheka (secret police), the dissolution of the Constituent Assembly, the Treaty of Brest-Litovsk, nationalization of industry and the New Economic Policy. From 1918–21 he led the fight against anti-Bolshevik forces in Russia. Ascetic, disciplined, energetic, and totally political, he founded a utilitarian kind of Marxism based on the implementation of theory in action adapted to circumstances. His vast output includes *What Is To Be Done* (1902), *Imperialism: The Highest Stage of Capitalism* (1917), and *State and Revolution* (1917). *See also* Russian Revolution. △1310–12.

Leninabad, town in NW Tadzhik SSR, USSR, on the Syr Darya River, 90mi (145km) S of Tashkent; capital of former Leninabad oblast. City was captured 329 BC by Alexander the Great; fell to the Russians 1866; called Khodzhent until 1936. It has a teachers' college and theater. Industries: textiles, clothing, shoes, food canning, automobile repair. Pop. 103,000.

Leninakan, city in NW Armenian SSR, USSR, on a tributary of the Araks River, 55mi (89km) NW of Yerevan, near the Turkish border. Originating as a fortress, Aleksandropol, on the site of the old village of Gumri, it was renamed 1924 and destroyed by an earthquake in 1926. Industries: cotton and knitwear, lumber, bicycles, meat processing, penicillin. Exports: silk, cloth, rugs. Est. 1837. Pop. 164,000.

Leningrad (Leningrado), second-largest city of the USSR; major Baltic seaport at the E end of the Gulf of Finland, built on the Neva delta; capital of Leningrad oblast. Founded as St Petersburg (1703) by Peter the Great, it was capital of Russia 1712–1918; scene of the 1825 Decembrist revolt and the Red Sunday incident in the 1905 revolution; the original center of the Russian revolution of 1917; renamed Petrograd in 1914 and Leningrad in 1924; suffered extensive damage in WWII; rebuilt since 1945; major cultural center; site of A. A. Zhdanov University (1819), the Saltykov-Shchedrin public library, numerous other libraries and educational institutions, Academy of Sciences, Winter Palace (1754–62), Palace of Art, St Isaac's cathedral (1819–58). Industries: shipbuilding, heavy engineering, brewing, publishing, printing, food processing, textiles, electronics, chemicals. Est. 1703. Pop. 3,950,000.

Leningrad, Siege of (August 1941–January 1944), military struggle of World War II. Invading Germans surrounded and besieged the Soviet city for 900 days, causing widespread famine and the death of almost 1,000,000 of its 3,000,000 inhabitants. Supply lines across the ice of Lake Ladoga enabled the ity to survive until an army was marshaled strong enough to break the siege.

Lenin Peak, formerly Kaufmann Peak; mountain in Trans Alai Range between Kirgiz SSR and the Gorno Badakhshan Autonomous oblast, NE Tadzhik SSR, USSR; 2nd-highest peak in USSR. Height: 23,405ft (7,139m).

Lenni-Lenape, or Delaware Indians, a major Algonquian-speaking tribe of Eastern Woodlands Indians occupying New Jersey, E Pennsylvania, N Delaware, and Staten Island, Manhattan Island, and Long Island, New York. They are divided into three groups: the Unami, Unalachtigo, and Munsee. Some 10,000 originally occupied the eastern region, but were removed following the Revolution; today, about 1,000 of their descendants live in Oklahoma, and about 300 are in Ontario. Initially hostile to whites, they later served as excellent scouts, interpreters, and warriors during the American Revolution.

Lens, piece of transparent glass, plastic, quartz, etc. bounded by two surfaces, usually both spherical, that changes the direction of a light beam by refraction and hence can produce an image. A converging lens is convex in form (bulging at the center) and bends light rays toward the lens axis. A diverging lens is concave (thinnest at the center) and bends rays away from the axis. The image may be right-way-up or inverted, real or virtual depending on the relative positions of object and focal point of the lens; it may also be magnified or reduced in size. Lens images suffer from various aberrations so that they may be blurred and have false colors. An achromatic lens—a concave-convex lens combination of different indices of refraction—reduces chromatic aberration. *See also* Aberration; Image, Optical; Refraction; Wave Dispersion. △1518.

Lens, in Anatomy. △674.

Lens, Magnetic. *See* Electron Microscope.

Lent, in the Christian year, a period of 40 days beginning with Ash Wednesday and ending with Easter. It is a period in which fasting and penitence have long been observed in preparation for the remembrance of the crucifixion and resurrection of Jesus Christ.

Lentil, annual plant long grown in the Mediterranean region, SW Asia, and N Africa. It has featherlike leaves and is cultivated for its nutritious seeds, used as food, forage, and a source of flour. Height: to 18 in (46cm). Family Leguminosae; species *Lens culinaris.*

Lenz's Law, an electromagnetic law deduced in 1834 by Russian physicist Heinrich F. E. Lenz. It states that an induced electric current always flows in the direction that will oppose the charge that produced the current. For example, this law will indicate the direction of the current induced by a permanent bar magnet pushed and withdrawn through a coil of wire.

Leo, or the Lion, equatorial constellation situated on the ecliptic between Cancer and Virgo; the fifth sign of the zodiac. Four galaxies lie in this constellation: M 65 (NGC 3623), M66 (NGC 3627), M95 (NGC 3358), and M96 (NGC 3358). Brightest star: Alpha Leonis (Regulus). The astrological sign for the period July 23–Aug. 22. △130, 138, 826.

Leo I, Saint (*c.* 390–461), also called Leo the Great, pope (440–61). As a leader of the early Christian Church, he consolidated the authority of the Roman see, producing a central church government for the Western church. He also claimed Rome's jurisdiction over Spain, Gaul, and Africa. His support for doctrinal matters was considered important to the Eastern Church; he read the Dogmatic Letter, accepted as the "Voice of Peter" at the Council of Chalcedon.

Leo III, Roman Catholic pope (795–816) and saint. Unrest in Rome resulted in a brutal, physical attack on him during a harvest procession in 799. He sought Charlemagne's assistance and, in 800, crowned Charlemagne emperor. During his papacy, Latin became the empire's official language. △1066.

Leo IX, Roman Catholic pope (1049–54) and saint, b. Bruno of Toul in Alsace. Elected in the court of Emperor Henry III in Worms rather than Rome, he insisted on approval by the clergy and people of Rome. He developed a source of funds for preserving St Peter's and reformed the College of Cardinals by developing a papal cabinet that became the Curia. He traveled extensively, seeking out corruption. △1052.

Leo X, Roman Catholic pope (1513–21), b. Giovanni de'Medici (1475). He was made a cardinal deacon at age 13. Under his rule, Rome became the center of the Renaissance and Martin Luther posted his theses, beginning the Protestant Reformation. △1140, 1152.

Leo III (680?–741), Byzantine emperor (*r.* 717–741). Born of peasant parents in North Syria, Leo began his rise to power in the service of Justinian II. Anastasius II appointed Leo military leader of one of Byzantium's largest provinces. He became emperor after a revolt against Theodosius III, and thereupon established the Syrian dynasty. In 717–718, he successfully defended Constantinople against an Arab siege, and later expelled the Muslims from Asia Minor. Leo also developed a new system of provincial administration. The *Ecloga,* a legal manual published by Leo in 740, marked an important legislative advance. Leo opposed the veneration of icons, and thereby initiated a crisis in the Greek state that would last for over a century. *See also* Iconoclastic Controversy.

Leo I (400?–474), Eastern Roman emperor (457–74). He came to power during a period when there was conflict in the Roman army between Roman soldiers and barbarian mercenaries. In order to prevent the Vandal leader Aspar from taking control, Leo enlisted the help of the Isaurians, an Anatolian mountain tribe. Together they defeated Aspar and prevented barbarian domination of the army.

León, city in central Mexico, 32mi (512km) WNW of Guanajuato; site of railroad connecting El Paso, Tex., with Mexico City. Industries: iron goods, knives, shoes, silver, lead, copper, tin. Founded 1576; inc. 1836. Pop. 453,976.

León, city in W Nicaragua, near Pacific coast NW of Managua; capital of León dept.; 2nd-largest city in Nicaragua. Founded 1524 near Lake Managua by Fernández de Córdoba, city was moved to present site after earthquake 1609; historically a center of liberals rivaling Granada, the conservative center. Industries: cigars, cotton gins, leather goods. Pop. 90,897.

León, city in NW Spain, 82mi (132km) NW of Valladolid; capital of León prov. Occupied by Moors in 8th century, it was recaptured 882 by Alfonso III of Asturias; capital of medieval León kingdom until 1230 when Castile and León united; site of Romanesque church of San Isidoro (1149), 16th-century palace (now city hall), 13th–15th-century Gothic cathedral containing fine collection of Gothic stained glass, Renaissance-style monastery of San Marcos (1533–1541). Industries: leather, cotton, textiles, cigars, tourism. Area: (prov.) 5,972sq mi (15,467sq km). Pop. (city) 105,235, (prov.) 648,721. △1078.

Leonardo da Vinci (1452–1519), Florentine painter, sculptor, architect, engineer, and scientist. Apprenticed to Andrea del Verrocchio (1466–72), he remained at Verrocchio's studio probably until 1476. He was the founder of the Classic style of painting of the High Renaissance and was among the first to use the chiaroscuro technique. His early works include the unfinished "St. Jerome" (*c.* 1480) and a portrait of Ginevia de' Benci. He moved to Milan (1482) to act as civil and military engineer to Duke Lodovico Sforza, where he executed "Madonna of the Rocks," "Portrait of a Musician," and numerous other works, including the "Last Supper" (1495–98). He made many architectural plans and designed and directed court festivals. Here he also began his scientific work and wrote his *Treatise on Painting.* Returning to Florence (1500), he executed the "Mona Lisa" and began "St Anne with the Madonna and Child." One of his last known paintings is "St John the Baptist." In 1517 he became chief painter, architect, and engineer to Francis I at Amboise, France, where he died. *See also* Chiaroscuro; Renaissance Art. △1140–42.

León Cathedral. △1094.

Leonidas (died 480 BC), heroic king of Sparta (490?–480 BC) during the Persian king Xerxes' invasion of Greece. Stationed at the strategic pass of Thermopylae, Leonidas was either deserted by the majority of his outnumbered Greek forces, or commanded their retreat, and was left with only a few hundred Spartans and Thespians against the overwhelming Persian army. Not a man retreated in their two-day battle to the death.

Leonid Meteor. △92.

Leonine Rhyme, rhyme occurring within the verse line; usually the rhyming of the last syllable of the line with the middle one, which precedes the caesura. It was named after the 12th-century cleric, Leo of St Victor, who used it in his Latin verses. *See also* Caesura.

Leontief, Wassily (1906–), US economist, b. Russia. He developed the input-output table, which

Leicester, England

Le Mans, France

Lemming

Leningrad, USSR

relates the empirical data of general equilibrium. An input-output table clearly illustrates the inter-industry relationships of an economy or a subcomponent of the economy, the sources of the input, and the destinations of the output. The table is an essential tool in the development of rational government economic planning. For this work, he received the Nobel Prize in economics in 1973.

Leopard, athletic, spotted big cat found throughout Africa and S Asia. A round-headed cat with a short nose and long, thin tail, its dark-spotted coat is yellow. A good tree climber and swimmer, it feeds on birds, monkeys, antelope, and cattle. The gestation period is three months and 2–3 young are born. Length: body—37.4–59in (95–150cm); tail—23.6–37in (60–94cm); weight: to 200lb (90.7kg). There are 24 subspecies. Family Felidae; species *Panthera pardus*. *See also* Cat. △550.

Leopard Frog, true frog native to United States, found in meadows or near ponds. Most are metallic bronze or green with dark, oval spots on their slender bodies and powerful legs. The southern leopard frog is considered a separate species, *Rana spenocephala*. Length: 5in (13cm). Family Ranidae; Species *Rana pipiens*. See also Frog. △518.

Leopard Shark. △626.

Leopold I (1640–1705), Holy Roman emperor (1658–1705), king of Hungary (1655–1705), king of Bohemia (1656–1705). His reign saw almost constant warfare with either the Ottoman Turks or the French under Louis XIV. In 1664 the Turks gained control of Transylvania. In 1683 they besieged Vienna before being repulsed. In 1697 the Turks were defeated at Zenta, and Leopold gained most of Hungary. His armies fought against France in the Third Dutch War (1672–78). In 1686 Leopold formed the League of Augsburg against France. In 1688 France invaded the Palatinate, beginning the War of the Grand Alliance (1688–97). In 1701 the War of the Spanish Succession broke out. Leopold died before it ended.

Leopold I (1790–1865), first king of independent Belgium (1831–65). Son of the duke of Saxe-Coburg-Saalfield, he rose to corps command in the Russian army, serving 1805–14. In 1816 he married Princess Charlotte, daughter of the English prince who later became George IV. He refused the throne of Greece in 1830, but in 1831 was elected king of Belgium when it separated from Holland. His powers were limited under the new constitution, but he ably maintained the independence and unity of the nation and introduced important political and financial reforms.

Leopold II (1835–1909), king of Belgium (1865–1909). Succeeding his father, Leopold I, he initiated a period of colonial and commercial expansion. After financing Henry Stanley's Congo explorations (1879–84), Leopold persuaded the powers at the Berlin Conference (1884–85) to give him personal control over the Congo Free State. International protest, however, forced him to relinquish control to the Belgian government in 1908.

Leopold III (1901–), king of Belgium (1934–51), succeeded his father, Albert I. When the Germans invaded Belgium in 1940, Leopold led a hopeless defense, but was forced to surrender. The king's decision to become a German captive led some to oppose his reinstatement after the war. A national referendum (1950) showed a majority favored his return from exile, but he abdicated in 1951.

Léopoldville. *See* Kinshasa.

Lepanto, Battle of (1571), naval clash between forces of the Ottoman Empire and various Christian powers. When the Ottoman Turks attempted to take Cyprus from Venice in 1571, Greece, Austria, Spain, and Venice stopped them in this battle. Pope Pius V and King Philip II of Spain had assembled their forces with those of the Venetians at Messina, Sicily. The Turkish navy lay in the Gulf of Patras off the coast of Lepanto, Greece. Two hundred ships under Don John of Austria formed four squadrons and attacked them. The allied Christians then defeated the Turks. △1108.

Lepidodendron, a genus of extinct treelike club mosses of the order Lepidodendrales (class Lycopsida). Common during the Upper Carboniferous, it reached 100ft (30m) in height.

Lepidoptera, order of insects, including moths, butterflies, and skippers, widely distributed on every continent except Antarctica. They are characterized by four membranous wings covered with overlapping scales. Lepidoptera undergo complete metamorphosis. The larvae (caterpillars) have 5–8 pairs of legs and chewing mouthparts for feeding on plant tissues. Adults have sucking mouthparts for feeding on nectar and plant juices. Larvae of many species are farm and garden pests, but many adults are valuable plant pollinators. All species serve as food for many other small animals. There are about 17 superfamilies of Lepidoptera, including one of butterflies and one of skippers. They range in size from tiny moths only ⅛in (3.2mm) long to giant forms with wingspreads up to 11in (28cm). *See also* Insect. △502.

Lepidus, distinguished Roman family. **Marcus Aemilius Lepidus** (died 152 BC) was censor, curile aedile, praetor in Sicily, consul, and triumvir. An able senator, he is known for his extensive building programs. His descendant **M.A. Lepidus** (died 77 BC) was a tribune and as consul led an army against the senate leader Catulus, who defeated him. His younger son, **M.A. Lepidus** (died 13 BC), served as consul with Caesar, then as triumvir with Antony and Octavian, and again as consul, governing Rome and Italy during the Philippi campaign. He then governed Africa and fought in Sicily until Octavian forced him to retire.

Leprosy (Hansen's disease), a communicable disease caused by the microorganism *Mycobacterium leprae* in which granular nodules develop on the skin, mucous membranes, and peripheral nerves. The spread and enlargement of the skin nodules produce the leonine appearance of the face and the other well-known and dreaded deformities of the disease. In tuberculoid leprosy, one of the two main types, damage to the nerves occurs early in the disease, so that the skin nodules (leprids) may not be felt. In this form, the nodules contain very few microorganisms. In lepromatous leprosy, the nodules (lepromas) contain many *Mycobacterium leprae* organisms and thus are a source of spread of the infection to others. The disease can be arrested by drug administration, but nerve damage is irreversible. △732.

Lepsius, Karl Richard (1810–84), German archeologist who put Egyptology on a scientific basis. Spurning the tomb-robber methods of predecessors such as Giovanni Belzoni, Lepsius made extensive drawings and plans of his discoveries on his major expedition (1842–45) and published his findings in the 12-volume *Monuments of Egypt and Ethiopia* (1849–59).

Lepton, member of a class of elementary particles that are not subject to the strong interaction. The group consists of the electron, muon, and the two neutrinos together with their antiparticles. The neutrinos react solely through the weak interaction; the electron and muon, being charged, are also subject to the electromagnetic force. Leptons, which all have half-integral spin, are thought to have no quark substructure but to be truly elementary. *See also* Hadron. △1484.

Leptospirosis, or Weil's Disease, infection with the spirochete *Leptospira*. It is passed to many by contact with infected rats. Symptoms include fever, jaundice, hemorrhagic tendencies, and muscle pain.

Lérida, city in NE Spain, on the Segre River; capital of Lérida prov. Scene of Julius Caesar's victory over Pompey's generals, 49 BC; captured 1149 by Raymond Berenguer IV; site of medieval university. Industries: wine, leather, livestock, arms, chemicals, fruit. Area: (prov.) 4,644sq mi (12,028sq km). Pop. (city) 90,884; (prov.) 347,015.

Lerma, Francisco Gómez de Sandoval y Rojas, Duque de (1552–1625), Spanish statesman. As chief minister to Philip III, he was virtual ruler of Spain from 1598. Intent on stopping Spain's costly wars, he eased relations with James I of England and signed a truce with the Netherlands. He drove the Moriscos from Spain in 1609. He became a cardinal in 1618; that same year he was driven from office by his son.

Lerma. *See* Santiago.

Lermontov, Mikhail (1814–41), Russian poet and novelist. His poem "On the Death of the Poet" (1837) criticized the court for failing to prevent the duel in which Pushkin was mortally wounded. Exiled to the Caucasus for his outspokenness, he wrote the poem "The Demon" (1840) and the novel *A Hero of Our Time* (1840). He was himself killed in a duel.

Lesbos (Lesvos), island in E Greece, off NW Turkey in Aegean Sea; with Lemnos and Hagios Evstrátios forms department of Greece; Mytilene is the capital. An important cultural center 7th–6th centuries BC; home of Sappho, Alcaeus, Aristotle, and Epicurus; held by Macedonia, Rome, Byzantinum, and finally Ottoman Turks, who occupied the island 1462–1913, when it passed to Greece. Exports: olives. Industries: fishing, livestock, wine, wheat, citrus fruits, marble, soap. Settled *c.*1000 BC by Aeolians. Area: approx. 630sq mi (1,632sq km). Pop. 117,371.

Lesotho, formerly Basutoland; small kingdom in S Africa, completely surrounded by the Republic of South Africa. It is ruled by King Moshoeshoe II, head of state, and Prime Minister Leabua Jonathan, head of government.

Lesotho is dominated in E by Drakensburg Mts; the remainder is hilly tableland with a generally dry climate. Subsistence farming is carried on in W; main crops are maize, sorghum, and wheat. South Africa is a major factor in Lesotho's economic survival, as Sothos work in its mines, providing an important source of income. Lesotho is developing light industries, livestock grazing, and diamond exploitation. Over 97% of the population is of Basotho heritage, and a majority is Christian. Lesotho has one of the highest literacy rates in Africa (70%); the University of Botswana, Lesotho, and Swaziland is located in Roma.

Between the 16th–19th centuries, a Basotho tribal group emerged as a result of an influx of various displaced refugees from tribal wars. Chief Moshoeshoe I, ruling 1820–70, created the homogeneous and united tribe needed for defense against repeated Boer and Zulu attacks. He placed Basutoland under British protection 1868; when the protectorate was annexed to Cape Colony 1871 without Sotho approval, civil strife ensued until it was placed under direct control of Britain 1884–1959. It was governed by a British high commissioner in South Africa who worked through a resident commissioner of Maseru until Oct. 4, 1966, when Basutoland became the independent Kingdom of Lesotho.

PROFILE

Official name: Kingdom of Lesotho
Area: 11,720sq mi (30,355 sq km)
Population: 1,100,000
Density: 93.8 per sq mi (36.2 per sq km)
Chief city: Maseru (capital)
Religion: Christianity
Language: English, Sesotho
Monetary unit: South African rand

Less Developed Countries (LDCs), those nations found primarily in Africa, Asia, and Latin America, that are unable to produce an adequate income to provide for the needs of their population, with resulting widespread poverty. These nations generally exhibit high rates of population growth, low rates of saving and investment, and low rates of economic growth. △942, 1386.

Lesseps, Ferdinand Marie, Vicomte de (1805–94), French diplomat and promoter of the Suez Canal. He first had the idea of a canal to link the Red Sea and the Mediterranean in 1832, but he did not gain the initial concession until 1854. Digging began in 1859, using 30,000 Egyptian laborers, who were withdrawn in 1863. The work was finished with mechanical equipment from Europe. The canal was opened by the Empress Eugénie in November 1869. In 1879, de Lesseps headed a French company that began work on the Panama Canal, which he had to abandon nine years later, owing to political and financial troubles.

Lesser Antilles, one of three major island groups in West Indies archipelago, between Atlantic Ocean (E) and Caribbean Sea, stretching in an arc from Puerto Rico (N) to N coast of Venezuela, South America. The group includes Virgin Islands, Leeward Islands, Windward Islands, Barbados, Trinidad and Tobago, Netherland Antilles, and Venezuelan islands off NE Venezuela coast. Pop. 2,749,000.

Lessing, Gotthold Ephraim (1729–81), German philosopher and man of letters. He founded a literary journal (1759–65) with Christoph Nicolai and Moses Mendelssohn. He was responsible for the creation of a so-called native German drama, inspired by Shakespeare rather than classical French forms. In *Minna von Barnhelm* (1763), *Hamburg Dramaturgy*, (1767–69), and *Emilia Galotti* (1772) he worked out and illustrated his dramatic theories. *Nathan the Wise* (1779) portrayed his liberal humanitarianism and commitment to the German Enlightenment. *See also* Enlightenment. △1222.

Lesvos. *See* Lesbos.

Lethbridge, city in S Alberta, Canada, on the Oldman River; site of University of Lethbridge, federal agricultural research center. Industries: electronical equipment, brewing, sugar refining. Founded 1885. Pop. 40,706.

Letterpress Printing. △1770.

Lettre de cachet, before the French Revolution a

document sent by the king that could order one's imprisonment (or worse) without trial, or compliance to stated demands. These letters were rumored to have been occasionally given without a name to lesser rulers, who could then use them as a means of local control. A symbol of despotism, the *lettres* placed their objects beyond conventional justice and were outlawed in 1790.

Lettuce, annual salad plant widely cultivated. Varieties of *Lactuca sativa* are cool weather crops; hot weather causes them to bolt, or go to seed prematurely. The large leaves form a compact head or loose rosette. They mature in 45–90 days. Wild species include the compass plant *(Silphium laciniatum),* a prickly lettucelike plant believed to be the ancestor of cultivated forms. It has thin deeply lobed leaves and yellow flower heads; height: 3–5ft (0.9–1.5m). Blue lettuce *(L. floridana)* has lyre-shaped leaves and blue flowers; height: 3–6ft (0.9–1.8m). Family Compositae. △336.

Leucine, white soluble essential amino acid found in proteins. *See* Amino Acid.

Leucippus (5th century BC), Greek philosopher. He is believed to have been a native of Miletus in Asia Minor. He first stated the atomic theory of matter, which was developed by Democritus. *See also* Democritus. △1480.

Leucocyte. △*See* Leukocyte.

Leucotomy. *See* Lobotomy.

Leukemia, an acute or chronic malignant disease characterized by abnormal numbers or types of white blood cells (leukocytes) in blood, bone marrow, and other tissues. Besides its division into acute and chronic forms, leukemia is also classified by the type of leukocyte involved (lymphocytes, lymphoblasts, and others). The acute lymphoblastic form is the most common malignant disease of childhood; present treatment produces five-year survival in about half of affected children. In chronic leukemia, a more slowly progressing form, survival as long as 10 to 15 years has occurred in some cases. Treatment of leukemia is mainly by irradiation and drugs. The cause has not been determined. △716.

Leukocyte (white blood cell), a colorless, amebalike structure containing a nucleus and cytoplasm and found in the blood. Leukocytes are either granular (granulocytes) or nongranular (agranulocytes), depending on the presence or absence of granules in the cytoplasm. Granulocytes are subdivided into neutrophils, eosinophils, and basophils; agranulocytes are either lymphocytes or monocytes. Normal blood contains 5,000 to 10,000 leukocytes per cubic millimeter of blood. Excessive numbers of leukocytes, or immature forms, are seen in such diseases as leukemia. Leukocytes have a phagocytic action (destroy harmful cells) and multiply when infection is present in the body. △688.

Leukocytosis, an increase in the number of white blood cells above the normal maximum. Infection and inflammation are among the causes.

Leukopenia, reduction of number of white blood cells to below a normal level.

Leukoplakia, whitish patches on the gums, tongue, vulva, or mucous membrane of the cheeks, often seen in smokers and sometimes becoming malignant.

Levant, collective term for lands lining the E coast of the Mediterranean Sea, extending from Egypt to Turkey; still used when referring to Syria and Lebanon, known as the Levant States at the time of the French mandates.

Levator Scapulae. △684.

Le Vau, Louis (1612–70), French architect. His work was in the Baroque style. △1166.

Levee, broad low ridges of fine sediment deposited along the sides of rivers during floods. A levee may also be built artificially along the bank of a river or an arm of the sea to protect the land from flooding. △258.

Levelers (*fl.* 1645–49), Puritan political and religious movement in England. The name alludes derisively to their demands for equality. Their leader was John Lilburne, and their program, which found extensive support in Cromwell's army, demanded complete constitutional reform, with abolition of the monarchy, proportional representation, and one supreme representative legislature elected by universal adult male suffrage. Cromwell opposed and finally crushed the movement. △1156.

Lever, a simple machine used to multiply the force or velocity applied to a body. A lever consists of a rod and a fulcrum, or point about which the rod rotates. In a lever of the first kind (a crowbar, for example), the applied force and the body to be moved are on opposite sides of the fulcrum, with the point of application farther from it. This lever multiplies the force applied by the ratio of the two distances. In a lever of the second kind, (as in a catapult) these relative distances are reversed, and the result is a multiplication of the speed. △1488, 1652.

Leverrier, Urbain Jean Joseph (1811–77), French astronomer, joint discoverer (with John Couch Adams) of the planet Neptune. Like Adams, he realized that anomalies in the orbit of Uranus could be due only to the gravitational influence of a hitherto undiscovered planet, but he was luckier than Adams in that notice was taken of his theory, which was proved correct by the Berlin Observatory in 1846.

Levi, in Genesis, third son of Leah and Jacob. He and his brother Simeon avenged Shechem's rape of their sister, Dinah, by killing all the males in Shechem's city. For this deed, Jacob prophesied the scattering of the two brothers' people over Israel.

Levi, Carlo (1902–75), Italian writer and painter. He was exiled (1935–36) in Lucania, the setting of his novel *Christ Stopped at Eboli* (1945), for anti-fascist political activities. His later novels include *Words Are Stones* (1955) and *The Linden Trees* (1959). He served in Italy's Senate 1963–72.

Leviathan (1651), philosophical work by Thomas Hobbes. △898.

Lévi-Strauss, Claude (1908–), French anthropologist, b. Belgium. Between 1934–39 he taught and did research in Brazil. Between 1942–45 he taught at the New School for Social Research, New York City. He was French cultural attaché in the United States (1946–47) before serving as a professor at the University of Paris (1948–59). He was appointed to the chair of social anthropology at the Collège de France in 1960. He is the leading proponent of structural anthropology, which analyzes cultural systems in terms of their essential, formal structural relations. Influenced by structural linguistics, he views each culture as a system of communication. His works include *The Elementary Structures of Kinship* (1949), *Structural Anthropology* (1958), and the four-volume *Mythologiques* (1964–71).

Levitation. △822.

Levites, in Judaism, the assistants to the Temple priests as assigned by the Bible to the tribe of Levi. From the age of 20–50, they served in the sanctuary as musicians, gatekeepers, teachers, scribes, and caretakers. The Levite tradition is still handed down from generation to generation, and a Levite is called up to read the Torah after a kohen (priest) in the synagogue service.

Leviticus, biblical book, third book of the Pentateuch, dealing with the indescribable holiness of God. Primarily a manual to instruct priests on ritual technicalities, it also exhorts reverent use of the proper rituals in worshipping God. Many of the laws in Leviticus, traditionally ascribed to Moses, are repeated in Deuteronomy in less detailed form.

Lévy-Bruhl, Lucien (1857–1939), French philosopher. He described the psychology of primitive societies and propounded his view that primitive thought was "pre-logical," differing in nature from that of civilized societies. From Emile Durkheim, he took the concept of group ideas, which led him to stress the formative influence of tradition and the psychology of the society rather than the individual. His works include *How Natives Think* (1910), *Primitive Mentality* (1922), and *Primitives and the Supernatural* (1931).

Lewin, Kurt (1890–1947), US psychologist, b. Germany. He pioneered research in the areas of human motivation and group dynamics. His work, which greatly influenced other psychologists, became the seed for the sensitivity training movement, and demonstrated that social psychology could be applied to practical problems.

Lewis, C(live) S(taples) (1898–1963), British scholar, critic, and author. He was best known for his novels on religious and moral themes, including *The Screwtape Letters* (1942). He also wrote children's books and critical works, and was professor of medie-

Leopard

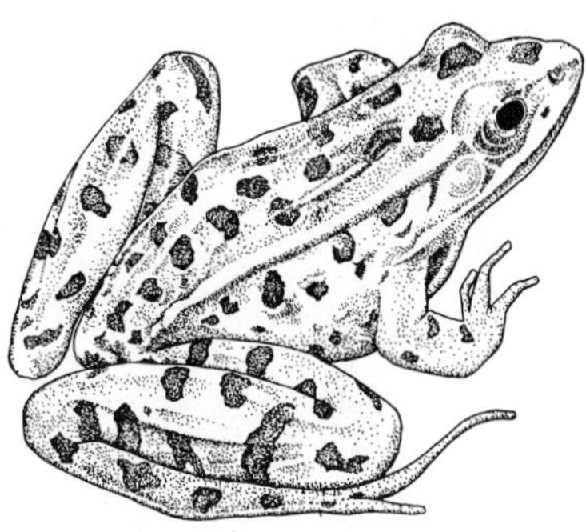

Leopard frog

Lepidoptera

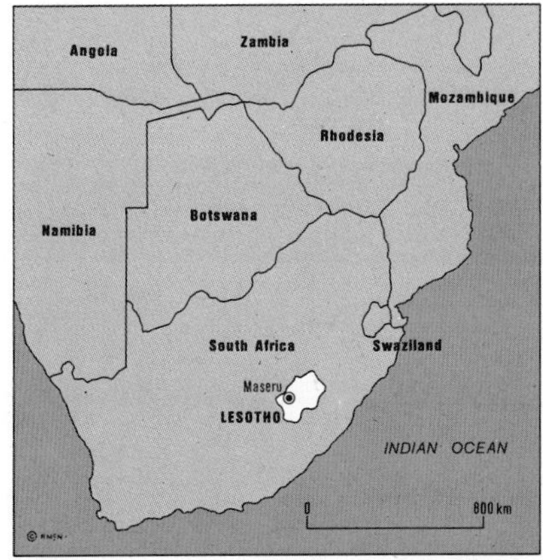
Angola
Zambia
Mozambique
Rhodesia
Namibia
Botswana
South Africa
Swaziland
Maseru
LESOTHO
INDIAN OCEAN
0
800 km

Lesotho

val and Renaissance English at Cambridge University (1954–63).

Lewis, Francis, (1713–1802), American patriot and a signer of the Declaration of Independence, b. Wales. A successful merchant, he was a delegate from New York to the Stamp Act Congress (1765) and attended the Continental Congress (1774–79).

Lewis, John L(lewellyn) (1880–1969), US labor leader, b. Lucas co, Iowa. A coal miner, he became active in union affairs and was elected president of the United Mine Workers Union (UMWU) (1920–60). After splitting with President William Green over unionization of mass-production industries, Lewis formed the Congress of Industrial Organization (CIO) and was its president (1935–40). He withdrew the UMWU from the CIO (1942). Lewis' strike actions during World War II led to the restrictive labor legislation of the Smith-Connally Act (1943) and Taft-Hartley Act (1947).

Lewis, Meriwether (1774–1809), US explorer. He was private secretary to President Jefferson (1801–03). In 1804, he and William Clark led an expedition from St Louis to the Pacific, the first exploration of the American northwest. They returned in 1806. Lewis was governor of the Louisiana Territory (1807–09). *See also* Lewis and Clark Expedition.

Lewis, (Harry) Sinclair (1885–1951), US author, b. Sauk Centre, Minn. The son of a country doctor, he attended Yale University, becoming involved in socialist activities. After graduation (1908), he held a variety of newspaper and editorial jobs. He began writing short stories, and his first novel appeared in 1914. It was not until the publication of the novel *Main Street* in 1920, however, that he gained acclaim. A satirist, he poked fun at American middle-class life. Among his targets were conformity and hypocrisy in business, medicine, and religion.

Lewis' early work, specifically *Babbitt* (1922) and *Arrowsmith* (1925), is generally considered his best. Other novels include *Elmer Gantry* (1927), *Dodsworth* (1929), *Ann Vickers* (1933), *It Can't Happen Here* (1935), and *Cass Timberlane* (1945). Awarded the Nobel Prize for literature in 1930, he was the first American to receive that honor.

Lewis, (Percy) Wyndham (1884–1957), English novelist, painter, and critic; founder of the Vorticist movement. The clarity of style displayed in his paintings is sustained in his fiction, such as *Tarr* (1918), *The Apes of God* (1930), and *Self-Condemned* (1954), which deals uncompromisingly with the weaknesses of human nature.

Lewis and Clark Expedition (1804–06), exploration of the Louisiana Purchase and the country beyond as far as the Pacific by two army officers, Meriwether Lewis and William Clark. The purpose of the successful expedition, backed by President Jefferson and Congress in 1803, was to find a land route to the Pacific, strengthen US claims to Oregon Territory, and to gather information about the Indians.

Lewiston, city in W Idaho, at confluence of Clearwater and Snake rivers; seat of Nez Perce co. In 1805 area was visited by Lewis and Clark; first capital of Idaho Territory (1863–64); site of Lewis-Clark Normal School (1955). Industries: paper, pulp mills, canning. Founded 1861. Pop. (1970) 26,068.

Lewiston, city in SW Maine, on Androscoggin River; 2nd-largest city in state; site of Bates College (1864). Industries: textiles, poultry, printing. First settled 1770 by Paul Hildreth of Massachusetts; inc. as town 1795, as city 1861. Pop. (1970) 41,779.

Lexicon Technicum. △1780.

Lexington, city in NE central Kentucky, 75mi (121km) E of Louisville, in bluegrass region; seat of Fayette co. A famous breeding center of thoroughbred horses, the city's first race track was constructed 1795; named by a group of hunters after the Revolutionary War battle of Lexington (1775). It contains homes of Henry Clay, John Hunt Morgan, and Mary Todd Lincoln; site of University of Kentucky (1865), Transylvania College (1780). Exports: oil, coal, farm and quarry products. Industries: tobacco, horses, automobile parts, electrical machinery, distilling, bluegrass seed, typewriters, paper products. Founded 1779; inc. 1832. Pop. (1970) 108,137.

Lexington, town in W central Virginia, 30mi (48km) NW of Lynchburg; seat of Rockbridge co; site of Washington and Lee University (1749) and Virginia Military Institute (1839); burial place of Stonewall Jackson and Robert E. Lee. Industries: fruit, lime, tourism. Founded 1777; inc. 1841 and 1874. Pop. (1970) 7,597.

Lexington and Concord, Battle of (April 19, 1775), first major battle of the Revolutionary War. Warned by Paul Revere and William Dawes that 700 British troops under Lt. Col. Francis Smith were marching from Boston to Concord to seize militia stores, 70 Minutemen under Capt. John Parker met them at the Lexington Green. A skirmish followed that left 8 Americans dead. The British reached Concord and destroyed the supplies, but were attacked by a larger force of American militia at Concord's North Bridge. The colonists harassed Smith's men all the way back to Boston, beginning a siege there that was to last nearly a year. △1218.

Leyden, Lucas van (*c.* 1494–1533), real name Lucas Hugensz, Dutch painter and engraver. "The Raising of Lazarus" (1508) is one of his best early works. A year later he executed a famous series of nine prints, "The Circular Passion." "Milkmaid" is one of the earliest genre engravings. His largest work is "Ecce Homo," influenced by Albrecht Dürer.

Leyden Jar, the earliest and simplest device for storing static electricity and the prototype electrical condenser, developed in 1745. It consists of a foil-lined glass jar partially filled with water and closed with a cork through which protrudes a knobbed brass rod that is wired to the foil. To charge the jar, friction is applied to the tip of the rod. A charge can be demonstrated by touching the rod and receiving a mild shock. The Leyden jar is used for classroom demonstrations. △1566.

Leyte, island in E central Philippines, SW of Samar Island and separated from it by the narrow San Juanico Strait. Island is irregularly shaped and mountainous, with many natural harbors; population is centered around Tacloban, a major oil port to the NE. Discovered 1521 by Ferdinand Magellan, it was governed by Spain until home rule was established by the United States 1901. Leyte Gulf (on E shore) was the scene of decisive US victory over Japanese air and naval forces Oct. 1944. Products: copper, asphalt, manganese, iron, sugar, corn, cotton, hemp. Area: 2,785sq mi (7,213sq km). Pop. (Leyte and Southern Leyte provs.) 1,340,000.

Lhasa (Lasa, or La-sa), city in SW China, on the Lasa River; capital of Tibet autonomous region; site of the great palace of the Dalai Lama, as well as many temples, monasteries, and convents. Many monastic institutions were closed or destroyed after Tibetan revolt from Chinese rule 1959. Called "Forbidden City" because of historical hostility of lamas to foreigners, it was first visited by Europeans in 1904. Pop. 175,000.

Lhasa Apso, Tibetan dog (nonsporting group) used to guard lamaseries. It has a narrow head with medium-long muzzle, large nose, and hanging ears. The long body is set on shortish legs; the tail is carried in a screw-shape over the back. Kennel clubs' preferred color for heavy, long, straight coat is golden. Average size: 11in (28cm) high at shoulder; 13–15lb (6–7kg).

Liang K'ai. △1044.

Libby, Willard Frank (1908–), US chemist, b. Grand Valley, Colo. He became a professor at Chicago and later at the University of California. During 1941–45 he worked on the separation of isotopes for the atom bomb. This led to an interest in nuclear physics and to the invention of carbon-14 dating of archeological objects, for which he was awarded a Nobel prize in 1960.

Liberalism, political and social philosophy that stresses protection of individual liberties and civil rights. The liberal doctrines, which evolved in the late 18th century, were an outgrowth of John Locke's theories, reflecting his faith in man's rational nature and urging limits upon governmental power. By contrast, contemporary liberals favor greater governmental control, believing that social and economic reforms can best be accomplished through legislation. △898, 902, 1288.

Liberal Party, British political party developed from the former Whigs after the 1832 Reform Bill. Its program of free trade, religious liberty, anti-imperialism, and low budgets appealed to the newly enfranchised industrial middle class, and the Liberals were in office almost continually for nearly thirty years (1846–74). After a Third Reform Bill (1884) Liberal prime minister Gladstone promoted Irish home rule, a course that weakened and split the party. With increased reliance upon minority groups, the Liberals were victorious in the elections of 1892, 1906, and 1908, but since World War I have lost much of their vote to the Labour party. Although nearly 20% of the British electorate voted Liberal in recent elections (which motivated the party's campaign for proportional representation), the party has managed to retain few parliamentary seats.

Liberal Party, Canadian political party. In 1854 more radical elements of the Reformers united to form the Liberal party. Their first administration (1873–78) under Alexander Mackenzie was anti-railway and advocated free trade. Under the leadership of Wilfrid Laurier (1896–1911) the Liberals supported ethnic conciliation, independence, and immigration. The party opposed conscription in World War II, finding support among the French and the western Progressives. Lester Pearson (1963–68) and Pierre Trudeau (1968–) have led their most recent governments.

Liberal Republican Party, political party organized in the late 1860s by Republican leaders to protest the conservative policies and scandals of U.S. Grant's first administration. Liberal Republicans favored leniency to the South, civil service reform, and a lower tariff. Leaders of the party included Carl Schurz, Charles Francis Adams, and Horace Greeley. Greeley, the party's presidential candidate in the 1872 campaign, was defeated, and the reform movement died out with Grant's reelection.

Liberator, The (1831–65), militant abolitionist newspaper founded by William Lloyd Garrison, an outspoken foe of slavery.

Libergier, Hugues. △1094.

Liberia, an independent republic in W Africa, bordered by Guinea (N), Ivory Coast (E), Atlantic Ocean (S), and Sierra Leone (NW). Liberia can be viewed as two geographical regions: a coastal plain extending approx. 50mi (81km) inland and a plateau region covered by a thick tropical rain forest, and broken by the Bomi Hills, Bong, and other mountains.

Economy. The economy is based on agriculture, mining, and industry. Liberia's most valuable cash crop is rubber; cacao, palm kernels, coffee, citrus fruits, kola nuts, and rice are also grown. The discovery of high-grade iron ore in the Bomi Hills has contributed greatly to Liberia's economic growth and provides its number one export. Other industries include rubber processing, oil refining, fish canning, and brewing. The economy relies heavily on US technical assistance, investments, and exports. Liberia's lenient tax and inspection policies encourage world trade.

People and government. Most of the people of Liberia belong to the more than 20 tribes, and speak numerous dialects, although English is the official language. The descendants of black US settlers, known as Americo-Liberians, provide most of the political and social leadership. Most of the tribal people inhabit small villages in the rain forest, while the Americo-Liberians live along the coast, mainly in Monrovia. The differences between the groups is lessening through intermarriage and education, although Liberia still has one of the lowest literacy rates in Africa.

Governmental power is divided among a president, Senate, House of Representatives, and Supreme Court. The presidency has power over all appointed officials, government revenues, and is leader of the True Whig party, which has been in power since 1877.

History. The coast of Liberia was inhabited by various seafaring tribes when Portuguese traders arrived in 15th century; the Portuguese monopolized trade until the 16th century, when Dutch, English, French, and German competitors established themselves. In 1817 the American Colonization Society began a project for resettlement of freed black slaves. The first settlement was at Cape Masurado (now Monrovia) in 1822. In 1847 the Independent Republic of Liberia was created, but suffered much from internal disorder and went bankrupt in the early 1900s. The US government assisted Liberia, who sided with the Allies in both world wars. Liberia is now a member of the United Nations and the Organization of African Unity.

PROFILE

Official name: Republic of Liberia
Area: 43,000sq mi (11,370sq km)
Population: 1,700,000
Chief cities: Monrovia (capital); Harper; Buchanan
Religion: Protestantism, Roman Catholicism, animism, Islam
Language: English
Monetary unit: Liberian dollar

Liberty Bell, historic US symbol and relic housed in Independence Hall, Philadelphia. It was first hung in 1753 with the Biblical inscription, "Proclaim Liberty throughout all the Land unto all the Inhabitants Thereof" (Lev. 25:10). It was rung in July 1776, commemorating the signing of the Declaration of Independence. While the British occupied Philadelphia (1777–78), the bell was removed to Allentown and returned in 1781. It was cracked in 1835 and again in 1846.

Liberty Island (formerly Bedloe's), island in SE New York, in New York Bay, SW of Manhattan Island; part of Statue of Liberty National Monument; connected to Manhattan by ferry. In 18th century island served as a quarantine station; in 1841 Fort Wood was built and the Statue of Liberty was placed on it in 1885. Although island is in New Jersey waters, it was agreed in 1834 to keep it part of New York geographically. Name changed from Bedloe's Island to Liberty Island 1956. Area: 10acres (4hectares).

Liberty Party (1840–48), first political party united by the anti-slavery issue. Made up of moderate abolitionists, it was organized in Warsaw, N.Y., in 1839 and in 1840 nominated James G. Birney (Ky.) for president. In 1844, the Liberty party helped to split the anti-slavery factions and contributed to the election of James K. Polk, a slaveholder. The Free Soil party replaced it.

Libra, or the Scales, southern constellation situated on the ecliptic between Virgo and Scorpius. As the seventh sign of the Zodiac, it formerly contained the First Point of Libra, the intersection of the ecliptic and the equator marking the autumnal equinox. Owing to precession this point has shifted westward into Virgo. Brightest star Beta Librae. The astrological sign for the period Sept. 23–Oct. 23. △156, 826.

Library, Public, tax-supported institution open to all citizens in the community where it is located. The services a public library offers vary in proportion to the size of the community served. The first free public tax-supported local library in the United States was probably at Peterborough, N.H. (1833); the first in a city was at Boston (1854). The movement accelerated with the notable efforts of philanthropist Andrew Carnegie, who, between 1897 and 1917 endowed more than 1,400 public libraries.

Library Classification. *See* Classification, Library.

Library of Congress, US national library located in Washington, D.C. It is supported mainly by congressional appropriations. The library was originally established (1800) to serve as a research facility for members of Congress. Since its founding its responsibilities have been expanded to include copyrighting, inter-library loans, and the publication of cumulative catalogs. Its collection includes over 60,000,000 items. The library is directed by a librarian appointed by the president and confirmed by Congress.

Library of Congress Classification System, means of classifying books first published in 1904. The system comprises 41 major subjects that are subdivided. Many academic libraries favor this system because of its pertinent subject headings and expansibility.

Libration, slight oscillatory motion of the Moon through which small portions of its far side become temporarily visible on Earth. It results from a combination of factors: namely, irregularities in the Moon's rotation caused by the effect of Earth's gravity; lack of uniformity in the Moon's orbital velocity compared with its axial rotation; and the inclination of the Moon's axis to its orbital plane, which produces a seasonlike latitudinal motion. △52, 58.

Libreville, capital city of Gabon, W Africa, at mouth of Gabon River on the Gulf of Guinea; administrative and educational center; formerly the leading port, trade has been dispersed to other harbors of Gabon; lumber is chief industry and export. Founded 1843 by French traders, and named Libreville ("Freetown") 1848. Pop. 105,080.

Librium, trade name for chlordiazepoxide hydrochloride, an agent used as a tranquilizer. △770.

Libya (Libiya), independent nation in N Africa. An invasion route for centuries, it gained independence through UN action. Oil is its chief commodity, and its government is a military dictatorship.

Land and economy. A country of 95% desert or semidesert, Libya, located on the N central coast of Africa, is bounded by 1,100mi (1,771km) of the Mediterranean Sea (N), Egypt (E), Sudan (SE), Tunisia and Algeria (W), and Niger and Chad (S). The highest point is 10,335ft (3,152m) in the S mountain area. Cultivation is possible only along the narrow coast, the slopes of two N hill areas, and a few oases. Libya has no permanent rivers; only 2% of the land is arable; 4% is used for grazing. The "ghibli," a hot, dust-filled wind from the S, occurs in the spring. Oil is Libya's main product and represents 99% of exports. Limited by meager rainfall, Libya is not self-sufficient in foodstuffs, although subterranean sources of water are being tapped. Lack of skilled workers has limited industrial expansion.

People. Libya's topographical features result in 90% of the people living on less than 10% of the land, primarily the coastal regions; 20% live in the largest cities, Tripoli and Benghazi. The population is a mixture of Arab and Berber; nomadic or semi-nomadic tribes, Tebou and Touareg, live in the S. Most of the nearly 200,000 foreigners in Libya are Egyptian. Islam is the dominant religion (Sunni Muslim). Arabic is the official language. Literacy is 30%–35%.

Government. Under a provisional constitution, the government is operated by a 12-man Revolutionary Command Council (RCC). The chairman of the RCC is the chief of state.

History. Occupied in ancient times by the Phoenicians, Carthaginians, Greeks, Romans, Vandals, and Byzantines, Libya spent centuries under foreign rule. It was an Italian colony from 1911 until WWII. In 1947, King Idris I combined with the Allies and liberated the country. On Nov. 21, 1949, a UN General Assembly resolution approved Libyan independence, making it the first country to achieve independence through UN action. On Dec. 24, 1951, it declared itself a constitutional monarchy under King Idris. A military coup overthrew his regime in 1969 and the new leader, Col. Muammar el-Qaddafi abolished the monarchy and announced the Libyan Arab Republic. Its goal of confederation with other Arab states has not been realized.

PROFILE

Official name: Libyan Arab Republic
Area: 679,216sq mi (1,759,540sq km)
Population: 2,350,000
Density: 3.5 per sq mi (1.3 per sq km)
Chief cities: Tripoli (capital); Benghazi
Government: Military dictatorship
Religion: Islam
Language: Arabic
Monetary unit: Libyan dinar
Gross national product: $5,900,000,000
Per capita income: $2,984
Industries: petroleum products, processed foods, leather goods, embroidered fabrics
Agriculture: wheat, barley, fruits, dates, olives, peanuts, tobacco
Minerals: oil
Trading partners: West Germany, Italy, United States, United Kingdom

Libyan Desert (As-Sahra' al-Libiyah), desert region in NE Africa, extending over SW Egypt, E Libya, NW Sudan; region consists of sand dunes, rocky plateaus; few inhabitants.

Lichee. *See* Litchi.

Lichen, a composite plant consisting of a fungus in which microscopic, usually single-cell, algae are embedded. The fungus and its algae form a symbiotic association in which the fungus contributes support, water, and minerals, while the algae contribute food produced by photosynthesis. Lichens can grow on almost any surface—rock, tree trunk, or soil—exposed to light. They are extremely slow-growing, often long-lived plants that are typically small, less than 1ft (30cm) in diameter. More than 15,000 species occur in most terrestrial habitats from the Arctic and Antarctic to the tropics. △434.

Li Ch'ing-chao (1081–after 1141), Chinese poet. She is regarded as one of China's greatest poets. A writer of *tz'u*, poems of irregular length most popular in the Sung dynasty (960–1279), her eloquence made the commonplace seem special. She often used objects from nature to symbolize a sense of loneliness and loss. Also a poetry critic, her comments on her contemporaries were perceptive.

Lichtenstein, Roy (1923–), US painter, b. New York City; a major exponent of the pop art movement. His works are typically large comic-strip sequences, complete with all the photo-reproduction techniques in evidence. The copies, which include the balloon with words, demonstrate the uniformity and rigidity of comic-strip art. △1372.

Licinius, Valerius Licinianus (?270–325), Roman emperor (311–23). In 313 Licinius, together with Constantine the Great, issued the "Edict of Milan," legislation that favored the Christians in the empire. A few years later, however, Licinius reversed his position and resumed attacks on the Christians.

Lick Observatory, astronomical observatory on Mt Hamilton in W central California, near San Jose; di-

John L. Lewis

Sinclair Lewis

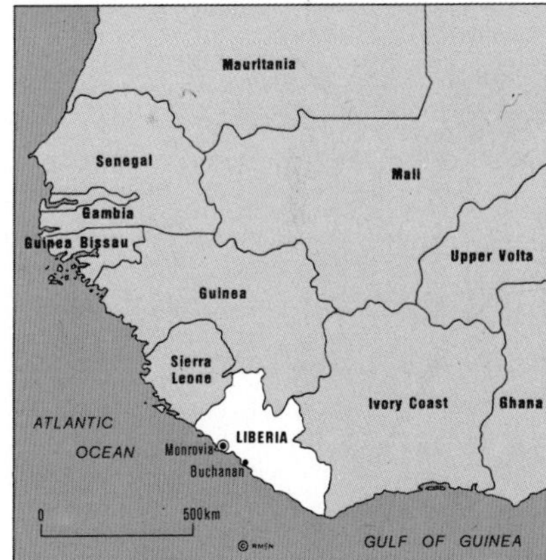
Mauritania
Senegal
Mali
Gambia
Guinea Bissau
Upper Volta
Guinea
Sierra Leone
Ivory Coast
Ghana
ATLANTIC OCEAN
LIBERIA
Monrovia
Buchanan
0
500km
GULF OF GUINEA

Liberia

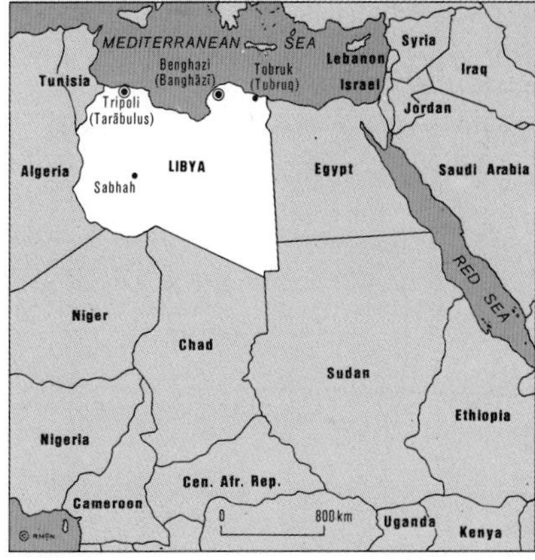
MEDITERRANEAN SEA
Syria
Lebanon
Iraq
Tunisia
Benghazi (Banghāzī)
Tobruk (Tubruq)
Israel
Tripoli (Tarābulus)
Jordan
Algeria
LIBYA
Egypt
Saudi Arabia
Sabhah
RED SEA
Niger
Chad
Sudan
Ethiopia
Nigeria
Cen. Afr. Rep.
Cameroon
0
800km
Uganda
Kenya

Libya

rected by University of California since 1888; location of the world's 2nd-largest refracting telescope. Est. 1874–75 through gifts of James Lick.

Licorice, perennial plant native to the Mediterranean region and grown in California. It has spikes of blue flowers. The dried roots are used to make candy, tobacco, beverages, and cough medicine. Height: to 3ft (91cm). Family Leguminosae; species *Glycyrrhiza glabra.*

Lictors. △1014.

Lidice, village in Czechoslovakia, 11mi (18km) NW of Prague; totally destroyed on June 10, 1942, by Nazis in retaliation for Czech assassination of Reinhard Heydrich. All men over 16 were killed and women were deported; now a national park and memorial.

Lie, Trygve (1896–1968), Norwegian diplomat, first secretary-general of the United Nations (1946–53). A lawyer and Labor party leader, he held ministerial posts beginning in 1935; he was foreign minister (1941–46). He headed Norway's delegation to the 1945 San Francisco conference that created the United Nations. In the Korean War, he supported UN action. Soviet hostility to his actions caused him to resign. △1382.

Liebig, Justus, Baron von (1803–73), German chemist. After training as an apothecary, he studied in Paris under Joseph Gay-Lussac and later became professor at Giessen and then at Munich. He was the first to realize that animals derive their energy from the combustion of food and to divide foods into carbohydrates, fats, and proteins. He introduced synthetic fertilizers into agriculture and showed that plants derive their minerals from the soil. He showed that fermentation was a chemical process and invented the chemical condenser that bears his name. He was made a baron in 1845.

Liebknecht, Karl (1871–1919), German lawyer and anti-war Socialist, son of Wilhelm Liebknecht. Imprisoned for treason, he was elected a legislator (1908). His resistance to German entry into World War I earned him another jail term. With Rosa Luxemburg, he was a leader of the extreme left, or Spartacist group, of Socialists, who favored a communist regime. Liebknecht and Luxemburg were both killed while under arrest (Jan. 15, 1919) during the Spartacist revolt in Berlin. △1324.

Liebknecht, Wilhelm (1826–1900), German revolutionary, journalist, and companion of Karl Marx, formed the short-lived revolutionary republic of Baden (in Germany) in 1848. After an association with Marx in London, he returned to Germany in 1864 to organize labor according to Marxian principles. He served as a legislator and was imprisoned for opposition to the Franco-Prussian War.

Liechtenstein, independent principality on the E shore of the Rhine River between NE Switzerland and W Austria. Liechtenstein is an alpine country with terraced slopes, suited for fruit trees, vines, and dairy farming; the fertile Rhine plain yields corn and vegetables. Prior to WWII, the economy depended primarily on agriculture; it now prospers with modern industries including machinery, textiles, processed foods, furniture, pottery, pharmaceuticals, wine, tourism, and postage stamps.

The native inhabitants of Liechtenstein are descendants of the Alamanni, a German tribe. By the early 1970s, due to increased economic development and the need for labor, 33% of the population consisted of foreigners. The state religion is Roman Catholicism, and German is the national language.

Liechenstein is a constitutional monarchy with a democratic and parliamentary base. The constitution (1921, amended in 1972), requires a parliament made up of 21 members, elected by male suffrage; parliament-approved proposals granting women suffrage have been defeated, making Liechtenstein the only W European country to deny women the right to vote. Switzerland maintains the country's postal, telephone, and telegraph services, and handles diplomatic relations with other states. Social legislation is modeled after that of Switzerland, and education is required through the secondary school level. Liechtenstein has no army; Swiss frontier guards are stationed at the border in accordance with customs treaty.

History. Liechtenstein was part of the Roman province of Rhaetia, which passed in mid-5th century to a Germanic tribe. In 1396 the county of Vadus was placed under the suzerainty of the Holy Roman emperor; in 1699 the lordship was sold to Austrian Prince Johann Adam von Liechtenstein, and in 1719 the territories were given the title Imperial Principality of Liechtenstein. Liechtenstein was a member of Napoleon's Confederation 1806–14, and the German Confederation 1815–66, until it achieved independence. Liechtenstein was closely aligned with Austria and then Switzerland; the customs treaty was signed between Switzerland and Liechtenstein in 1923.

PROFILE

Official name: Principality of Liechtenstein
Area: 62sq mi (161sq km)
Population: 21,350
Chief cities: Vaduz (capital); Schaan; Balzers
Religion: Roman Catholic
Language: German
Monetary unit: Swiss franc

Lie Detector, or polygraph, an electronic device that may be capable of detecting lies when used by a trained examiner. The polygraph monitors such things as heart rate, breathing rate, and perspiration, all of which may change when a person lies. Though neither foolproof nor acceptable in a court of law, lie detectors are often used by police when interviewing suspects.

Liège, city in E Belgium, 58mi (93km) ESE of Brussels; capital of Liège prov.; famous educational center during Middle Ages; won for France by Napoleon (1794–1815); Congress of Vienna (1815) gave the area to the Netherlands. Industries: foundries, firearms, machinery. Settled 558; est. as bishopric 8th century. Pop. 147,277.

Liepaja (Lepaya), second-largest city of the Latvian Republic, USSR, on the Baltic Sea, 120mi (193km) WSW of Riga. Founded by Teutonic Knights, it came under the rule of Lithuania 1418, Prussia 1560, Sweden 1701, and Russia 1795. It was a German naval base in both world wars. This ice-free port is a noted health resort known for its baths; site of city theater. Industries: steel, agricultural machinery, explosives, paints, wire, linoleum, cork and leather goods, shipbuilding, food processing, fish canning, timber. Exports: timber, steel products, linoleum, matches. Est. 1263. Pop. 88,000.

Life. △406–08, 424, 458.

Life Expectancy, potential length of individual human life based on the average for any given group. Life expectancy is affected by such things as the state of the economy, modernization, health standards, and infant mortality rates. △734, 802.

Life Insurance. A life insurance policy is a contract whereby the insurer agrees to pay to the beneficiary a predetermined amount on the death of the insured. The insured usually designates and retains the right to change the beneficiary. Life insurance may be classified as permanent or temporary. Permanent life insurance (whole life insurance) does not expire but remains in effect until the insured dies. Temporary life insurance remains in effect until a predetermined future point, then either matures (endowment insurance) or expires (term insurance).

Life-Support System, in aerospace technology, system supplying food, water, and oxygen to astronauts. Eleven pounds of water and two pounds of oxygen must be recycled per person each day. Food cannot yet be recycled and must be stored in dehydrated form. Liquid body wastes, used wash water, and water vapor in the cabin can be drawn through wicks, evaporated, and condensed again as pure water. Carbon dioxide can be vented or absorbed by plants.

Ligament, band of tough stringy connective tissue that joins bone to bone and reinforces joints. In the wrist and ankle joints, for example, they surround the bones like firm elastic bandages. Ligaments, which contain a gluelike organic substance known as collagen, form part of the supporting tissues of the body. △682.

Light, type of electromagnetic wave that on striking the retina of the eye causes a visual sensation. The wavelength range is very narrow being approximately 750–400 nanometers (10^{-9}m), different wavelengths producing different color sensations. Sources of light include incandescent (strongly heated), flourescent, and phosphorescent substances. Incandescent sources can be heated by an electric current, as in a light bulb, by combustion, as in a match, by nuclear fusion reactions, as in the Sun, or by other means. Many properties of light, such as reflection, refraction, interference, diffraction, and polarization, can be explained in terms of waves. Other phenomena, including the photoelectric effect and the emission and absorption of light, necessitate the assumption that light consists of a stream of photons. Both waves and photons travel in free space at the speed of light, about 186,000mi (300,000km) per second. *See also* Color; Fluorescence. △1516–22, 1526, 1550, 1554.

Light, Speed of, universal constant giving the speed of propagation of electromagnetic waves, including light, in free space and equal to 186,281.7mi (299,-792.5 km) per second. Symbol: *c. See also* Light. △1522.

Light Adaptation, shift in functional dominance from rod cells to cone cells within the retina as overall illumination increases. Unlike dark adaptation, this process is nearly instantaneous. Thus humans can discern color and form soon after emerging from prolonged darkness.

Light Clock. △1524.

Lighter. *See* Barge.

Lighter Aboard Ship. *See* LASH Ship.

Light Meter. △1526.

Lightning, the visible flash of light accompanying an electrical discharge between clouds or between Earth and clouds, produced by a thunderstorm. A typical discharge consists of several lightning strokes, initiated by leaders that follow an irregular path of least resistance, the lightning channel. Intense heating by the discharge expands the channel very rapidly to a diameter of 5 to 10in (13 to 25cm), creating the sound waves of thunder. △1530.

Light Particles (Photons). △1484.

Light Spectrum. △1480, 1554.

Light-Year, unit of astronomical distance equal to the distance traveled in free space by light in one year. One light-year is equal to 5.88×10^{12}mi (9.46×10^{12}km) or to 0.307 parsec. △1478.

Lignin, celluloselike organic compound that adds stiffness to plant cell walls. It fills spaces between cellulose fibers in wood and certain plants. Wood is 25–30% lignin. It is used to manufacture synthetic rubber and pigments. △448.

Lignite. *See* Coal.

Lignum Vitae, tropical, New World evergreen tree. It is the source of a hard, dense wood used in bearings, pulleys, etc. A short-trunked tree, its flowers are blue or purple. Height: to 30ft (9.1m). Family Zygophyllaceae; species *Guaiacum officinale.*

Liguria, region in NW Italy, on the Ligurian Sea between France and Tuscany; comprised of Genoa, Imperia, La Spezia, and Savona provs.; Genoa is the capital. Region is geographically divided into narrow coastal strip, the Italian Riviera (world-famous winter resort area), and mountainous inland region. It was conquered by Romans 2nd century BC, ruled by Genoa 16th century–1815, when it was annexed to Sardinia; it was active in movement for Italian independence. Products: vegetables, flowers, olives, fruits, wine grapes. Industries: shipbuilding, tourism, chemicals, lumber, textiles, fishing. Area: 2,098sq mi (5,434sq km). Pop. 1,866,186.

Li Hung-chang. △1270.

Lilac, ornamental shrub brought to America before the 18th century. It blooms in early May, bearing panicles (pointed clusters) of tiny white to purple flowers. Height: to 8ft (2.4m) with French hybrids to 15 ft (4.6m). Species include the common *Syringa vulgaris,* Persian *S. persica,* and the 3–4ft (0.9–1.2m) dwarf Korean *S. velutina.* Family Oleaceae.

Lilburne, John (?1614–57), English political figure, leader of the Levelers. After imprisonment (1638–40) for anti-episcopal writings, he fought for the Parliamentarians (1642–45) and resigned from army. His pamphleteering against the army leaders led to his arrest (1649) for treason. Freed and acquitted, he nonetheless continued under suspicion. *See also* Levelers. △1156.

Lilienthal, David Eli (1899–), US public administrator, b. Morton, Ill. He was appointed one of three directors of the Tennessee Valley Authority (TVA), a public corporation, in 1933. From 1941–46, he was TVA chairman. From 1946–50, he was an atomic energy commissioner. *See also* Tennessee Valley Authority.

Lilith. △958.

Liliuokalani, Lydia Kamekeha (1838–1917), last monarch of Hawaii (1891–93), b. Honolulu. A dedicated Hawaiian nationalist, Liliuokalani denounced American dominance and tried to restore lost power o the crown by changing the constitution. The plan alarmed resident Americans, who staged a rebellion aided by US troops (1893). The queen formally abdicated in 1895. The islands were annexed by the United States in 1898.

Lille, city in N France, 130mi (224km) NNE of Paris; capital of Nord dept. During 16th century dukes of Burgundy had official residence here; after 1668 it served as capital of French Flanders; birthplace of Charles de Gaulle (1890); site of 17th-century Flemish Vielle Bourse (old stock exchange), 17th-century gateways, and elaborate citadel (1667–1673). University of Douai moved here in 1808 (now University of Lille). Industries: textiles, machinery. Pop. 190,546.

Lilly, John. △668.

Lily, genus *(Lilium)* of perennial, bulbous plants grown in warm Northern Hemisphere regions. They are native to temperate and tropical regions worldwide. They have erect stems and various leaf shapes. The showy flowers are solitary or clustered in combinations of colors including white, red, orange, yellow, green, purple, and pink. Most lilies prefer well-drained, moist soil and a sunny location. Exact cultivation requirements vary according to species. Height: 3–9ft (0.9–2.7m). Family Liliaceae. The lily family includes over 2,000 species.

Lily of the Valley, perennial plant native to Europe, Asia, and E United States. It has broad, elongated leaves and tiny, white, bell-shaped fragrant flowers on a stalk. Family Liliaceae; species *Convallaria majalis.*

Lima, capital city of Peru, on central Pacific coast, just SE of port of Callao; capital of Lima dept.; commercial, administrative, and cultural center of Peru. Founded 1535 by Francisco Pizarro, and called the "City of Kings," it was seat of Spanish viceroyalty; occupied by Chilean forces 1881–83 (War of the Pacific); site of University of San Marcos (1551), cathedral (16th century), National Library (1821); suffered earthquakes 1687 and 1746. Products: cotton, vegetables, grain, sugar, fruit. Industries: textiles, leather goods, oil refining, furniture, food processing, foundries, cement, pharmaceuticals. Pop. 2,541,300.

Lima, city in NW Ohio, 68mi (109km) SSW of Toledo; seat of Allen co. Industries: aircraft parts, machine tools, building machinery, diversified agriculture. Founded 1831; inc. 1842. Pop. (1970) 53,734.

Lima Bean, perennial plant native to tropical America. Cultivated as an annual, it is a climber with oval leaves and yellowish-white flowers. Its broad, flat seeds are a popular vegetable. Family Leguminosae; species *Phaseolus limensis.*

Limassol (Lemosos), port city in S Cyprus, on Akrotiri Bay; capital of Limassol district; site of 15th-century castle. Industries: tourism, chrome, asbestos. Exports: wine. Pop. 51,500.

Limbic System, the brain's cortical and subcortical structures and their interconnections, all of which are involved in motivation and emotion. Destruction of limbic tissue usually results in deterioration in patterns of behavior. △666.

Limbur, Paul (Pol), Hermann, and **John (Jehanequin),** brothers (*fl.* before 1399–1439), Franco-Flemish illuminators. The most noted illuminators of their time, they worked mainly for Jean, duc de Berry, a patron of the arts. Their major work was *Très riches heures du Duc de Berry,* begun in 1413, a typical medieval illumination, with what is considered the first true genre painting in the North. *See also* Illuminated Manuscripts.

Lime, small tropical tree *(Citrus aurantifolia)* of the rue family, probably native to Asia. The trees grow to 8–15ft (2.4–4.6m) and yield the familiar small green acid fruit used for flavoring and juice. △338.

Lime, calcium oxide (quicklime) or calcium hydroxide (slaked lime). Calcium oxide, CaO, consists of whitish lumps obtained by roasting limestone (calcium carbonate) until all the carbon dioxide has been driven off. It is used as a refractory, a flux, and in glass making, water treatment, food processing, and as a cheap alkali. Calcium hydroxide, $Ca(OH)_2$, is a white crystalline powder obtained by the action of water on calcium oxide. It is used in mortar, plaster, cements, and in agriculture.

Limerick, short humorous verse, usually taking the form of five anapestic lines with the rhyme scheme *a a b b a.* First recorded in 1820, the form was popularized by Edward Lear in his *The Book of Nonsense* (1846). Subsequently it was employed to express a variety of subjects or thoughts in an epigrammatic manner. *See also* Lear, Edward.

Limestone, sedimentary rock composed primarily of calcium carbonate. Generally formed from deposits of the skeletons of marine invertebrates, it is used to make cement, as a source of commercial lime, and as a building material. *See also* Sedimentary Rocks. △248, 254–56.

Liming, practice of using lime to neutralize acid soil caused by the leaching of calcium and magnesium. Calcium carbonate, obtained from ground limestone, reduces acidity and restores necessary elements to the soil. Other liming substances are slag, marl, chalk, and oyster shells. Powdered lime is spread on the soil surface and plowed or harrowed under, or hydrated forms are sprinkled on the soil.

Limit, value approached by a mathematical function as the independent variable approaches some specified value. For example, the function $1/(x^2 + 1)$ has values $\frac{1}{2}, \frac{1}{5}, \frac{1}{10}, \frac{1}{17}$, etc., as x takes values of 1, 2, 3, 4, etc. As x increases indefinitely the functional value approaches zero: one says that the function tends to zero as x approaches infinity. The limit of a sequence is the value approached by the terms as the number of terms increases. Similarly, the limit of a series is the value approached by the sum as more and more terms are included. The concept of limits is fundamental to differential and integral calculus. *See also* Calculus; Series.

Limnology, science of freshwater lakes, ponds, and streams. These bodies of water are explored in terms of chemistry, physics, and biology. The plants, animals, and environment are quantitatively examined in light of food cycles, chains, habitat, and zonation of organisms. Freshwater bodies are subject to greater extremes of temperature and are therefore more fragile ecosystems and more specialized than those in marine environments. *See also* Hydrology. △296.

Limnos. *See* Lemnos.

Limoges, city in W central France, on Vienne River; capital of Haute-Vienne dept. Porcelain industry began 1771 (producing world-famous Limoges china); makes use of kaolin found in abundance nearby; site of cathedral (13th-16th centuries), ceramics museum, and museum containing many paintings by Renoir (born here 1841). Industries: china, shoes, textiles, clothing. Pop. 132,935.

Limon, José (1908–72), US modern dancer and choreographer, b. Mexico. After dancing with the Doris Humphrey-Charles Weidman Company (1930–40) he formed his own company (1945). One of the most prominent modern dance companies in the world, it toured South America, Europe, Canada, and the United States. From 1964 he was artistic director of the American Dance Theatre.

Limpet, simple gastropod mollusk found clinging to rocks along marine shores. It has a caplike, rather than coiled, shell and large muscular foot. Length: to 5in (127mm). Families Acmaeidae and Fissurellidae; species include keyhole limpet *Megathura.*

Limpkin, long-legged wading bird found from SE United States to South America and famous for its wailful cry. Related to crane and rail, it is brownish with whitish streaks. It uses its long bill for digging snails and lays brown-spotted pale eggs (6–7) in a large grass-and-rush platform nest over water. Length: 27in (69cm). Species *Aramus guarauna.*

Limpopo (Crocodile), river in SE Africa; its headstreams rise in the high country of central Republic of South Africa; it flows NE and E along N border of Transvaal prov. and turns SE as it enters Mozambique, continuing SE to Indian Ocean. Length: approx. 1,100 mi (1,771km).

Lincoln, Abraham (1809–65), 16th president of the United States (1861–65), b. Hardin co (now Larue co), Ky. In 1842 he married Mary Todd; Robert Todd Lincoln was their son. Lincoln was born into a very poor frontier family, and had little formal education. The family moved to Indiana in 1816 and to Illinois in 1830. In 1831, he settled in New Salem, Ill., where he worked in a store, ran a mill, and began reading law. He became a Whig and in 1834 was elected to the Illinois legislature. In 1836 he was admitted to the bar and began to practice in Springfield, and in 1846 he was elected to the US House of Representatives for one term.

Lincoln's opposition to slavery was slow in developing; it was the Kansas-Nebraska Act (1854)—considered pro-slavery—that finally crystallized his views. The author of that bill was Sen. Stephen A. Douglas

Belgium
Ger. Dem. Rep.
Poland
Lux.
Federal
Republic of
Germany
Czechoslovakia
France
Austria
LIECHTENSTEIN
Switzerland
Hungary
Italy
Yugoslavia
ADRIATIC
SEA
0
200km
Liechtenstein

Lilac

Queen Liliuokalani

Abraham Lincoln

of Illinois. In 1858, Lincoln, by now a Republican, was chosen to run for the Senate against Douglas. The race was the occasion for the Lincoln-Douglas debates on the Kansas-Nebraska Act and on slavery itself. Douglas won the election, but Lincoln won national fame. As a result, he became a leading candidate for the 1860 Republican presidential nomination, which he won on the third ballot. He went on to win the election over the badly divided Democrats.

Lincoln was inaugurated on March 4, 1861, after the southern states had seceded; on April 12, Fort Sumter was fired on and the Civil War began. After a somewhat slow start, Lincoln conducted the war with vigor and efficiency. He called up the militia, blockaded southern ports, and increased executive powers. He had early difficulties with his military commanders but after he chose Gen. Ulysses S. Grant his commander in chief, the war went well.

On Sept. 22, 1862, Lincoln issued the Emancipation Proclamation, which freed the slaves (but only in rebellious areas), and on Nov. 19, 1863, he delivered the Gettysburg Address. Lincoln won reelection in 1864, this time running on the National Union ticket with Andrew Johnson. He saw the war brought to a successful close but died before the South could be readmitted to the Union. On Apr. 14, 1865, while attending Ford's Theater, he was shot by John Wilkes Booth, a disaffected southerner. He died the next day.

Career: Illinois State Legislature, 1834–41; US House of Representatives, 1847–49; president, 1861–65. *See also* Civil War, American; Emancipation Proclamation; Gettysburg Address; Kansas-Nebraska Act. △1276.

Lincoln, Mary Todd (1818–82), wife of Abraham Lincoln, b. Lexington, Ky. She met and wed Lincoln in 1842 while living with her sister, the daughter-in-law of Illinois governor Ninian Edwards. She bore 4 sons: Robert Todd, Edward Baker, William Wallace, and Thomas, or Tad. Only Robert lived to adulthood. Lincoln's assassination and Tad's death (1871) pushed her into mental disorder; she was found insane in 1875, but in 1876 the decision was reversed.

Lincoln, Robert Todd (1843–1926), US lawyer, businessman, and eldest son of Abraham Lincoln, b. Springfield, Ill. A prominent attorney in Chicago, he was appointed secretary of war (1881–85) by President Garfield. He was the special legal counsel to the Pullman Company and later its president (1897–1911).

Lincoln, market town in E England; county seat of Lincolnshire; site of Lincoln Cathedral (built 1075–1501, restored 1922–32) and Lincoln castle (built by William the Conqueror, 1068). Industries: agricultural and metal products, machinery. Pop. 74,207. △1094.

Lincoln, capital city of Nebraska, located in SE part of state, 52mi (84km) SW of Omaha; seat of Lancaster co; site of University of Nebraska (1867), Nebraska Wesleyan University (1887), Union College (1891), and modern city hall with 400-ft (122-m) tower designed by Bertram Goodhue with sculptures by Lee Lawrie; home of William Jennings Bryan is preserved. Industries: rubber products, meat processing, railroad cars, flour milling. Founded 1864 as Lancaster; when Nebraska was admitted to Union 1867, name was changed in honor of Abraham Lincoln, and city was made capital; inc. as town 1869, as city 1887. Pop. (1970) 149,518.

Lincoln-Douglas Debates, series of seven 1858 debates between Sen. Stephen Douglas and Abraham Lincoln. Douglas was the incumbent Democrat running for the US Senate seat from Illinois. Lincoln was the Republican candidate. The issue was slavery and its political, legal, and moral implications. Lincoln was eloquent in his defense of the Union and democratic ideals. Although Lincoln lost the election, his view of slavery as a "moral, social, and political wrong" enhanced his standing as a national figure. Douglas' stance on slavery, expressed in his Freeport speech, evaded the moral issue. *See also* Freeport Doctrine.

Lincoln Park, residential city in SE Michigan, on the Ecorse River SW of Detroit; site of Council Point, where Indians conferred prior to start of Pontiac's War (1763). Inc. as village 1921, as city 1925. Pop. (1970) 52,984.

Lind, James (1716–94), Scottish physician famed for eradicating scurvy from the British navy with his recommendation to include fresh citrus fruit and lemon juice in the daily diet of seamen. Prior to his intervention, more British sailors died from scurvy than from combat wounds. He also made recommendations for combating typhus, for distillation of seawater for drinking, and for creating hospital ships.

Lind, Johanna Maria (Jenny) (1820–87), Swedish soprano. Known as the "Swedish Nightingale," she made her debut in 1838 and gave many triumphant operatic performances in Europe and recitals in the United States which were managed by P.T. Barnum. She was Sweden's most famous singer and one of the most glamorous and celebrated coloratura sopranos of the 19th century.

Lindbergh, Anne Morrow (1907–), US author, b. Englewood, N.J. Married (1929) to the aviator Charles Lindbergh, she accompanied him on many flights and wrote *North to the Orient* (1935) and *Listen! The Wind* (1938) recording her experiences. Other works include *Gift from the Sea* (1955), essays on the problems of women; *The Unicorn* (1956), poems; and *Dearly Beloved* (1962), a novel. Several volumes of her diaries and letters have also been published.

Lindbergh, Charles Augustus (1902–74), US aviator, known as "Lucky Lindy" and "The Lone Eagle," b. Detroit, Mich. He became an international hero when he landed his plane *The Spirit of St Louis* outside Paris on May 21, 1927, completing first nonstop transatlantic solo flight. He married Anne Morrow (1929), and their two-year old son was kidnapped and murdered in 1932. The resulting publicity forced the Lindberghs to live in England (1935–39). An isolationist, he was active in the America First Committee and was accused of pro-Nazi sentiments. He resigned his Air Corps Reserve commission but accompanied combat missions during World War II as consultant to aircraft manufacturers. In 1954 he was made brigadier general in the Air Force Reserve. He was awarded the Pulitzer Prize for his book, *The Spirit of St Louis* (1953).

Linden, city in NE New Jersey, 4mi (6km) SSW of Elizabeth. Industries: chemicals, paints, automobiles, petroleum products. Settled early 18th century; inc. as city 1924. Pop. (1970) 41,409.

Linden, or basswood, tree found in tropical to temperate zones. A common shade or honey tree and source of commercial lumber, it has heart-shaped, finely toothed leaves and white or yellow, nectar-filled flowers. Height: to 120ft (37m). Among 80 species is American *Tilia americana.* Family Tiliaceae.

Lindenhurst, village in SE New York, on Long Island on Great South Bay. Industries: lumber, paper, chemicals, electrical equipment. Settled 1869; inc. 1923. Pop. (1970) 28,338.

Lindisfarne Gospels, manuscript of the late 7th or 8th century. It combines Irish, classical and Byzantine elements of manuscript illumination.

Lindsay, Howard (1889–1968), US actor, producer, and playwright, b. Waterford, N.Y. He wrote comedies and musicals, mostly with Russel Crouse, including *Anything Goes* (1934), *Arsenic and Old Lace* (1941), and *State of the Union* (1945), a Pulitzer Prize winner. Their dramatization of *Life with Father* (1939), opening with Lindsay playing the lead, ran for seven years.

Lindsay, (Nicholas) Vachel (1879–1931), US author who styled himself the vagabond poet, b. Springfield, Ill. He traveled throughout the United States holding poetic revival meetings and attempting to stimulate a popular taste for poetry through what he called the higher vaudeville. *The Congo and Other Poems* (1914) and *General William Booth Enters into Heaven* (1913) contain much of his best work.

Line, set of points extending in two directions without end. The term can be synonymous with curve, or can be taken to mean a straight line—the shortest distance between two points. In a rectangular Cartesian coordinate system a straight line has the equation $y = mx + c$, where m is the gradient and c the intercept on the y-axis.

Lineage. △876, 882.

Linear A, script written on tablets found on Crete and the Greek mainland. It is a syllabic form of writing, but it is still not deciphered. It has been dated from 1450 to 1200 BC. △964.

Linear Accelerator, or linac, particle accelerator in which electrons or other charged particles travel through a straight vacuum chamber. Electrostatic accelerators are simple linear accelerators. In other types energy is gained in regions of high-frequency electric field, produced between cylindrical electrodes. Higher energies can be achieved by carrying the particles along a waveguide with a microwave field. Final energies depend on the length of the chamber, and can reach several GeV. △1484.

Linear B, Mycenaean Greek writing deciphere (1952) by Michael Ventris on tablets dating fro 1500–1200 BC. It used a syllabic form of writing wi the consonants simplified. The discovery showed th Mycenaeans on the Greek mainland were using Greek language. △872, 966.

Linear Function, mathematical function the value which is given by a polynomial involving no powers its variables, as in $f(x) = 7x + 3$. The graph of simple linear function is a straight line.

Linear Motor. △1540.

Linear Programming, mathematical procedure which a multi-variable linear function is analyzed t find maximum and minimum values. It is useful business planning and industrial engineering to pr duce optimal control conditions, as in inventory co trol, where costs must be minimized in terms of sto age time, warehouse space, customer delive schedules, reorder times, and transportation e penses. *See also* Inventory Control. △1672–74.

Line Islands, island group in central Pacific, S Hawaiian islands, extending across the equator fro Kingman Reef to Flint Island. US territories are Kin man Reef, Jarvis, and Palmyra islands; British territ ries are Washington, Fannin, and Christmas island Area S of the equator is claimed by both Britain an United States. Area: 158sq mi (409sq km). Po 1,180.

Line Spectrum. *See* Spectrum.

Ling, also red hake, squirrel hake, commercial foo fish found in Atlantic from Newfoundland to Virgini Brown and silver, it has long dorsal and ventral fin Length: 2.5ft (76.2cm); weight: 8lb (3.6kg). Famil Gadidae; species include *Urophycis chuss* and *Molv molva.* △516.

Lingua Franca, a language that serves as a means communication between people who normally do n speak the same language. A lingua franca may be hybrid language such as Pidgin English, used amon the hundreds of tribes in E New Guinea, or it may b a full-fledged language such as Swahili, which spoken mainly as a second language by millions people in East Africa. △866.

Linguistic Analysis, or philosophical linguistics, the philosophy of language. Of concern to philoso phers of language are such matters as a priori and posteriori sentences. Kant divided the category of priori sentences into analytic and synthetic, but th subdivision remains open to question. Issues of synta and linguistic usage are important areas of interest t present-day philosophers. The works of Rudolph Ca nap and Ludwig Wittgenstein of the Vienna Circle logical positivists are fundamental texts. *See also* Log ical Positivism.

Linguistic Geography. △866.

Linguistics, the science of a language system. Syn chronic (structural) linguistics is the study of the lan guage as it is actually spoken and the rules that go ern its structure. Diachronic (comparative) linguistic is the study of the history and formation of the lan guage or group of languages. It includes comparin languages, etymology, and the study of the culture o the people. *See also* Grammar; Phonetics; Syntax. △ 864–66.

Linkage Groups, a group of inherited characteristic or genes that occur on the same chromosome an that remain connected in such a way that they asso and are inherited together through successive gener ations. △416.

Linköping, city in SE Sweden, near Lake Roxen; cap tal of Österjötland co. Prospered in the Middle Age as a religious and intellectual center; site of 13th century castle, library, university, 12th-century Ro manesque cathedral, containing 344-ft (105-m) spire an episcopal see since 1120. Industries: motor vehi cles, airplanes, processed food, electrical appliances Pop. 80,767.

Linnaea, or twinflower, perennial trailing evergree vine found in cool, moist areas worldwide. It has glossy leaves and fragrant, pink, bell-shaped flower growing in pairs. Family Caprifoliaceae; species *Lin naea borealis.*

Linnaeus, Carolus (1707–78), Swedish botanist an explorer. He was the first scientist to outline the prin ciples for defining the genera and species of organ isms. He formalized binomial nomenclature, givin Latin names for the genus and the species to eac organism, making consistent use of specific names, and including all known organisms in a single classification. This approach was the foundation of the modern science of taxonomy. Linnaeus published his first nomenclatorial system, *Systema naturae*, in 1735, followed by *Genera plantarum* (1737) and *Species plantarum* (1753). *See also* Taxonomy. △418, 1186.

Linnet, small Old World songbird with brownish plumage that feeds on flax seed. Family Fringillidae; species *Carduelis cannabina*.

Linotype Composing Machine. △1770.

Lin Piao (1908–71), Chinese Communist military leader. He won fame as commander of the Fourth Field Army, which helped insure victory over Nationalist forces in 1949 and entered Korean War against United Nations forces in 1950. Lin was designated Mao Tse-tung's heir apparent while helping to lead the 1965–69 Cultural Revolution in China. He was later accused of plotting revolt and was said to have perished in a plane accident.

Linseed Oil, oil pressed from seeds of cultivated flax *(Linum usitatissimum)*. Because of its drying qualities, it is an important ingredient of oil paints and printing inks. See also Flax. △362.

Lin Yutang (1895–1976), Chinese writer. After studying philology at Harvard (1919–21) and Leipzig (1922–23), he was a professor at Peking University (1923–26). He edited a number of periodicals, the most notable of which were *Lunyü* (Analects fortnightly), which he founded in 1932, and *Jenchienshih* (This human world), a literary journal. In 1936 he emigrated to the United States. He subsequently wrote books on China, including *My Country and My People* (1935) and *Moment in Peking* (1939).

Linz, city in Austria, 95mi (153km) W of Vienna on the Danube River. Railroad junction and river port. Industries: steel, nitrate, machinery, electrical equipment, tobacco products; site of Roman camp (Lentia) AD 1st century. Pop. 204,600.

Lion, tawny, large cat, found in prides on African savannahs south of the Sahara and in SW Asia. It is yellow to buff with light spots under the eyes. The male has a long neck mane that darkens with age. A night hunter, it feeds on antelope, zebra, and bush pigs. The gestation period is three months and 2–6 young are born. Length: 8–11ft (2.4–3.3m); weight: 400–600lb (180–270.2kg). Varieties include Senegal, Masai, Somali, and Indian. Family Felidae; species *Panthera leo*. *See also* Cat. △550, 586.

Lion, The. *See* Leo.

Lionfish, or zebra, turkey, dragon, cobra fish, marine tropical fish found in shallow waters of Indian and W Pacific. A rust-red and white striped fish with numerous long spines and rays, it carries 13 venomous spines in its dorsal fin that can inflict painful and, in rare cases, even fatal wounds. Length: 2in (5cm). Family Scorpaenidae; species *Pterios volitans*.

Lions, Gulf of, arm of Mediterranean Sea, extending from Hyères, France (E), to Cape Creus, Spain (W). Chief port is Marseilles.

Lion-tailed Macaque. *See* Wanderoo.

Lipari Islands (Isole Eolie), volcanic group of small islands off the N coast of Sicily, Italy, in the Tyrrhenian Sea; includes islands of Stromboli, Vulcano, Salina, and Lipari. Exports: wine, raisins, fish, pumice. Industries: agriculture, livestock, fishing, lobstering. Area: 44sq mi (114sq km). Settled late 6th century BC. Pop. 13,774.

Lipase. △694.

Lipchitz, Jacques (1891–1973), sculptor, b. Lithuania. He was one of the finest of the early cubist sculptors. His early works include "Bather" and "Man with a Guitar" (1916). His later work was of a larger scale and included his most important "Figure" (1926–30). Subsequent works stressed sensuality and volume: "Benediction" (1942) and "Harpist."

Lipetsk (Lipeck), city in Russian SFSR, USSR, 65mi (105km) N of Voronezh, on Voronezh River; capital of Lipetsk oblast; founded as an iron milling center by Peter the Great. Industries: iron pipe and castings, tractors, chemicals, cement, food processing. Est. 1707. Pop. 290,000.

Lipid, one of a large group of organic compounds in living organisms that are insoluble in water but soluble in alcohol and ether. Lipids are a major food source for animals. They form an important food store and energy source of plant and animal cells and a structural component of cell membranes. The class includes animal fats, vegetable oils, and natural waxes; the basic components are fatty acids. Storage fat is composed chiefly of triglycerides, which consist of three molecules of fatty acids linked to the alcohol glycerol. △1570.

Lipmann, Fritz Albert (1899–), US biochemist, b. Germany. He was awarded the 1953 Nobel Prize in physiology or medicine "for his discovery of coenzyme A and its importance for intermediary metabolism." Coenzyme A plays an essential intermediary role in the body's metabolism of carbohydrates, fats, and proteins and thus in the transfer of energy in the body.

Li Po (*c.* 701–62), Chinese poet. He and Tu Fu are considered the two greatest poets of the T'ang dynasty (618–906), China's golden age of literature. He was known for his wandering and drinking, and his verse is said to have an airy, intoxicating quality. Unlike many of his contemporaries, he was not concerned with such matters as patriotism and heroism but rather with physical pleasure. "The Song of Wine" is one of his most famous poems.

Lipoma. △712.

Lippi, Filippino (1457?–1504), Italian painter. The son of Filippo, he followed the style of Botticelli in his early work; his mature style influenced the Florentine Mannerists in the 16th century. "Apparition of the Virgin to St Bernard" (c. 1488) is in his mature style. A later work, "Adoration of the Magi" (1496), precurses the Florentine Mannerists. *See also* Mannerism.

Lippi, Fra Filippo (1406?–69), Italian painter. One of the major forces in Florentine painting, he was influenced by Masaccio and Fra Angelico and in turn influenced Botticelli and others. His works include the Barbadori altarpiece (*c.* 1437), "Coronation of the Virgin" (c. 1441–47), "Annunciation" (*c.* 1438), and "Adoration of the Child" (*c.* 1459). △1134.

Lippizaners, a breed of horse that is of small stature, having a long back, thick neck, and powerful conformation. They have the ability to perform the intricate and delicate movements of *haute école*, often seen in the circus.

Lipset, Seymour Martin (1922–), US sociologist. His work has been concerned with political sociology, social stratification, and, more recently, student protest and universities. His books include *Union Democracy* (1953), *Political Man* (1960), and *Rebellion and the University* (1972).

Lipstick. △1814.

Liquefaction of Gases. △1502.

Liquefied Petroleum Gas. *See* LPG.

Liqueur, a flavored distilled liquor, with an alcohol content from 48 to 120 proof (24–60%); made by combining fruits or herbs with a base and spirit and sweetening with sugar syrup. Fruit, when used, is steeped in the spirit; herb liqueurs may be produced by distillation or percolation. Liqueurs were first produced by monks and alchemists and have been called balms, cremes, elixirs, and oils. They are popular after-dinner drinks and are also used as flavorings in desserts.

Liquid, state of matter, intermediate between a gas and a solid, in which a substance has a relatively fixed volume but flows to take the shape of its container. Liquids have higher viscosity than gases, and their viscosity decreases with temperature. *See also* Gas; Solid. △1502–04, 1562.

Liquid Crystal, any substance that flows like a liquid yet has the kind of ordered molecular structure characteristic of crystals. There are many organic crystalline substances that can be brought to a liquid crystal state when heated. They are classified according to the kind of molecular arrangement that obtains. Liquid crystals have unique properties that have been applied to optical displays and temperature-variation detection systems.

Liquid Oxygen, oxygen in the liquid state (at one atmosphere pressure, oxygen liquefies at −183°C.) It is widely used in rocket engines as an oxidizer reacting with various liquid fuels to produce high-velocity gases.

Lisbon (Lisboa), port city and capital of Portugal, on

Jenny Lind

Charles Lindbergh

Ling

Carolus Linnaeus

SW coast of Portugal, at the mouth of the Tagus River on Atlantic Ocean. An ancient settlement, the city was occupied by Phoenicians and Carthaginians before Moorish occupation 716; taken by Portuguese 1147, under King Alfonso I; after 14th century it became a leading European port, until Spanish occupation 1580–1640. With its fine harbor, it has again become a major port and handles most of Portugal's international trade; site of Moorish mosque, aqueduct, many medieval buildings, University of Lisbon (1911), Technical University of Lisbon (1930). Pop. 782,266.

Lister, Joseph, Lord (1827–1912), English surgeon. His acceptance of the germ theory and consequent introduction of antisepsis to surgical practice ushered in the era of modern surgery. Lister used phenol to kill germs and succeeded in lowering dramatically the rate of post-surgical infection.

Liszt, Franz (1811–86), Hungarian composer and pianist. He invented the solo recital and startled his contemporaries with his piano virtuosity and showmanship. He was patron and friend to many of the great artists of his day, such as Chopin and Grieg, and his music influenced subsequent composers, including Wagner, Richard Strauss, and Ravel. He composed two popular piano concertos, 19 Hungarian rhapsodies, études, numerous piano pieces, and many transcriptions for piano of other composers' music. His symphonic poems (eg, *Les Préludes*) were among the first successful efforts in this form. △1246.

Li Ta-chao (1889–1927), Chinese revolutionary. One of the original founders of the Chinese Communist party in 1921, he was an intellectual who strongly influenced the youth movement in China and became a key Communist organizer in north China until executed by the warlord Chang Tso-lin.

Litchi, or lichee, evergreen tree native to China and the Philippines. It has dense foliage of glossy, leathery leaves. The red, globular fruit, litchi nut, is edible dried or preserved. Height: to 40ft(12m). Family Sapindaceae; species *Litchi chinensis.* △340.

Liter, in the metric system, a unit of capacity equal to the volume occupied by one kilogram of water at 4° C and at standard atmospheric pressure. It is equivalent to one cubic decimeter. One liter equals 1.057 liquid quarts. *See also* Weights and Measures.

Literacy Acts, US legislation requiring literacy tests for new immigrants. From the mid-19th century, native American workers, influenced by economic conditions and prejudice, wanted immigration curbs such as literacy tests. Supported by interests anxious to use cheap immigrant labor, Congress defeated literacy tests in 1896, 1898, 1902, 1906. Laws passed in 1897, 1913, and 1915 were vetoed by the presidents. In 1917, Congress overrode President Wilson's veto to pass the first literacy act, which required aliens over 16 years old to read 30–80 English words.

Literature. △1028, 1100, 1148, 1172, 1188, 1238–40, 1374–76, 1420–22.

Literature, Children's. *See* Children's Literature.

Lithification. △246–48, 270–72.

Lithium, common metallic element (symbol Li) of the alkali-metal group, first isolated in 1817. Ores include lepidolite and spodumene. The element, which is the lightest of all metals, is used in alloys and as a heat-transfer medium. Chemically it is similar to sodium, although it does have some resemblance to the alkaline-earth metals. Properties at. no 3; at. wt. 6.941; sp gr 0.534; melt. pt. 354.2°F (179.0°C); boil. pt. 2,402°F (1,317°C); most stable isotope Li^7 (92.58%). *See also* Alkali Elements. △1552–54.

Lithium Salts. △770.

Lithography, in art, planographic (surface) method of graphic reproduction developed in the late 18th century and based on the inability of grease to mix with water. First, a design is made on a stone or metal plate. Usually, blue-gray Bavarian limestone is used. The design is drawn with a greasy substance such as lithographic crayons or pencils, rubbing ink, or asphaltum. The drawing is then etched with a syrupy solution of gum arabic and nitric acid. Next, the stone is washed with water. Eventually, lithographic ink is rolled onto the stone, and it is run through a press.

Lithosphere, that part of the Earth that is rock as opposed to hydrosphere, biosphere, and atmosphere. *See also* Earth. △166, 170.

Lithuania (Litovskeja Sovetskaja Socialisticeskaja Respublika), a constituent republic of the USSR. It is bounded W by Baltic Sea, N by Latvia, E by Belorussian republic, S by Poland, and SW by Kaliningrad oblast. Covered with glacial deposits, it is low and flat, is drained by the Neman River, and has nearly 2,000 lakes. Almost 50% of the land is arable; forests cover 17% of the area, and meadows and pastures 25%. The economy is largely agricultural (dairy farming and stock raising), but industry has been developed since 1940. There are no major mineral resources.

People and History. A predominantly Roman Catholic agricultural people, the Lithuanians work on some 1,800 collective farms. The population was depleted by huge emigration before WWI (mainly to the United States and Canada) and by the extermination of the Jewish minority during WWII. About 80% of the population is Lithuanian, with increasing minorities of Russians and Belorussians, and Letts. Settled by pagan Liths along the Neman River about 1500 BC, Lithuania was conquered by the Teutonic Knights in the 13th century and later emerged as a powerful duchy, one of the most extensive medieval states. Grand Duke Jagiello married the Polish queen Jadiwiga in 1386. The two states were allied until 1569 when they were formally joined. Through the 18th-century partitions of Poland, Lithuania passed to Russia. The collapse of Russia in WWI permitted Lithuanian nationalists to assert themselves, and an independent republic was proclaimed in 1918. Instability brought dictatorships, a fascist constitution in 1938, and Soviet occupation in 1940. During WWII Germany held the country from 1941 until it was regained by the Soviets in 1944.

PROFILE

Official name: Lithuanian Soviet Socialist Republic
Area: 25,174sq mi (65,201sq km)
Population: 3,129,000
Chief city: Vilnius (capital)
Government: Constituent republic of USSR
Religion: Roman Catholic
Language: Lithuanian
Industries: food processing, shipbuilding, textiles, machinery, metal products, chemicals, electrical equipment
Agriculture: dairy farming, hogs, flax, sugar beets, potatoes

Litmus, in chemistry, natural coloring matter used as an indicator. It is red in the acidic state, but changes to blue at pH 6.8. *See also* Indicator.

Little America, region in Antarctica, S of Bay of Whales, on outer edge of Ross Ice Shelf. Explored 1928–30 by Adm. R. E. Byrd's expedition; used as a headquarters for his 2nd expedition (1933–35), the US Antarctic Service Expedition (1939–1941), and the US Naval Operation High Jump expedition (1946–47).

Little Belt (Lille Baelt), strait between Fyn Island and the mainland of Denmark, connecting the Kattegat with the Baltic Sea.

Little Bighorn, Battle of the (June 25, 1876), engagement between Indians, under Sioux chiefs Sitting Bull, Crazy Horse, and Gall, and the 7th US cavalry detachment led by Col. George Custer. Custer's attempted surprise attack on the much larger Indian force was unsuccessful. The 2,500 Indians wiped out Custer's 266 officers and men near the Little Bighorn River in the Montana Territory.

Little Entente, an alliance between Romania, Yugoslavia, and Czechoslovakia after World War I to maintain post-war boundaries. Through political and economic unity, and the support of France and Poland, the alliance managed to prevent *Anschluss* (the uniting of Germany and Austria) and departure from the treaties of World War I until the rise of Hitler in the late 1930s.

Little Rock, Arkansas city and state capital, seat of Pulaski co. Made territorial capital 1821; state capital 1836; occupied by Union forces in Civil War, Sept. 1863. School desegregation began 1957. Industries: lumber, furniture, paper products, electrical equipment, plastic, bauxite and marble mining, cotton and grain farming, cottonseed products. Founded 1819; inc. 1835. Pop. (1970) 132,483.

Little Theater Movement, US early 20th-century theater movement. It was started by noncommercial organizations to create smaller, experimental types of theaters. More interested in artistic merit than financial success, the movement stressed freedom of expression and innovative techniques.

Littleton, town in NE central Colorado, 8mi (13km) S of Denver; seat of Arapaho co. Industries: explosives, precision instruments. Laid out in 1812; inc 1890. Pop. (1970) 26,466.

Little Turtle (*c.* 1752–1812), chief of the Miami Indians, b. near modern Fort Wayne, Ind. Known for his rhetorical skills, intelligence, and military talent, he and his army defeated Gen. Josiah Harmar in 1790 and Gen. Arthur St Clair in 1791. After several defeats however, he signed the Treaty of Greenville (Ohio) in 1795 and lost much land to the whites. A peacemaker later in his life, he refused to join Tecumseh's anti-white forces and encouraged many of his people to turn to agriculture.

Littoral Zone, strictly used, the beach area between high and low tides. However, the term also refers to the benthic zone between high tide and a depth of 656ft. (200m). The larger zone is divided into the eulittoral—from high tide to a 164ft (50m) depth and the sublittoral—from 164–656ft (50m to 200m). The lower edge of the eulittoral is the lowest limit at which abundant attached plants can grow. △622, 626

Litvinov, Maksim Maksimovich (1876–1951), Soviet diplomat. Involved in Russian revolutionary activity from 1898, he became Soviet ambassador to Britain after the Bolshevik Revolution (1917). As Soviet representative to the League of Nations, he was an eloquent advocate of disarmament and cooperation with the United States where he later served as ambassador (1941–43).

Li Tzu-ch'eng. △1206.

Liu Pang, Chinese emperor (reigned 206–194 BC) Known as Han Kao Tsu or the "High Progenitor," he was the first emperor of the Han Dynasty in China and a hero in Chinese history. A rough and ready general he united the country for one of its most famous periods of rule. △1038.

Liu Shao-ch'i (1900–74?) a leader of the Chinese Communist movement. Trained in Moscow 1920–22 he became one of the chief theorists of the Chinese Communist party and second in rank from 1954 until purged by Mao Tse-tung during the Cultural Revolution of 1965–69. He lived in disgrace until his death

Liutprand, or **Luitprand** (died 744), Lombard king (712–44). He unified and expanded Lombardy and brought it to the height of its power. His conquest of Roman lands was halted only by personal appeals to his Catholic conscience by popes Gregory II and Zacharias. He instituted several reforms of the Lombard penal code.

Live-forever, or stonecrop, succulent perennial plant native to Europe. It has smooth, thick, oval, grey-green leaves and clusters of tiny reddish-purple flowers. Height: to 2ft (61cm); family Crassulaceae; species *Sedum telephium.*

Live Oak, North American red oak trees. The spreading evergreen oak *(Quercus virginiana)* grows in SE United States. Its leathery leaves have rolled, unlobed edges. It is a valuable timber tree. In poor soil, it may be shrubby. Height: to 50ft (15m). Family Fagaceae. *See also* Oak.

Liver, the largest gland in the body, a soft, reddish-brown organ lying mostly in the upper right quadrant of the abdominal region. It has many functions, including formation of bile, carbohydrate storage, regulation in part of carbohydrate metabolism, breakdown of hormones, detoxification of drugs and other substances, destruction of worn-out red blood cells, and an important role in fat metabolism. It produces and secretes bile, which empties from hepatic ducts into the cystic duct leading to the gall bladder, where the bile is stored until needed. The bile empties into the common bile duct and then into the small intestine, where it functions in metabolism, primarily fat metabolism, acting to emulsify fats, make them water-soluble, and to activate other digestive enzymes. △694 740.

Liverleaf. *See* Hepatica.

Livermore, city in W central California, 23mi (37km) E of San Francisco Bay; site of University of California Livermore Radiation Center. Industries: wine, steel. Inc. 1876. Pop. (1970) 37,703.

Liverpool, city in NW England, in Merseyside, on Mersey estuary; a leading port since mid-18th century, it is country's 2nd-largest seaport; site of University of Liverpool (1903), 1754 town hall, Bluecoat Chambers of 1716–17, an art gallery; birthplace of William Gladstone (1809). Industries: food processing, electrical equipment, chemicals, rubber. Settled late 8th century by Norsemen; chartered 1207 by King John. Pop. 606,834.

Liverwort, any of about 10,000 species of tiny, simple, nonflowering green plants, which, like the related mosses, lack specialized tissues for transporting water, food, and minerals within the plant body. Liverworts are found in almost all nondesert land habitats, especially in the damp tropics; a few species even occur in Antarctica. Liverworts make up two classes (Hepaticae and Anthocerotae) of the plant division Bryophyta. *See also* Bryophyte. △436.

Livingston, family of US statesmen and lawyers. **Robert Livingston** (1654–1728) acquired lands and wealth in New York and controlled the provincial assembly. His grandson **Robert R. Livingston** (1718–75) was an influential Whig politician in New York. His son **Robert R. Livingston** (1746–1813) was a distinguished lawyer who negotiated the Louisiana Purchase while minister to France. Robert's brother **Edward Livingston** (1764–1836) was secretary of state (1831–33) under Andrew Jackson. Another grandson of the first Robert Livingston was **Peter Van Brugh Livingston** (1710–92), a Whig supporter prior to the American Revolution and president of the first provincial congress (1775). His brother **Philip** (1716–78) signed the Declaration of Independence. Another brother **William** (1723–90) was the first governor of New Jersey. William's son **Henry Brockholst Livingston** (1757–1823) was a justice of the US Supreme Court (1806–23).

Livingston, Robert R. (1746–1813), US Revolutionary war patriot and diplomat, b. New York City. He served in the Continental Congress (1775–76, 1779–81, 1784–85) and helped draw up the Declaration of Independence, although he thought the decision to separate from England was unnecessary. Under Pres. Thomas Jefferson, he and James Monroe went to France and successfully negotiated the Louisiana Purchase (1803) for $15 million. He also financed the first US steamship, Robert Fulton's *Clermont* (1807).

Livingston, William (1723–90), American patriot, b. Albany, N.Y. He served as New Jersey's representative in the Continental Congress (1774–76) and was elected the first governor of New Jersey (1776–90). A delegate to the Constitutional Convention (1787), he engineered New Jersey's unanimous ratification of the Constitution. Known as a clever satirical writer, his works include *Philosophic Solitude* (1741).

Livingstone, David (1813–73), Scottish clergyman and explorer in Africa. He first entered Africa as missionary in 1841. He discovered the Zambezi River (1851) and attempted to end the slave trade by introducing Christian ways. After crossing from the east to west African coasts, he was commissioned to explore the Zambezi (discovering Victoria Falls in 1855) and later the upper Nile (1866). Following considerable speculation on his well-being, Henry M. Stanley was sent to find him. The two met in 1871 on Lake Tanganyika. Livingstone could not be persuaded to leave and died in Africa, having published various accounts of his travels. His remains were buried in Westminster Abbey. △1268.

Livius Andronicus, Lucius (*c.* 284–204 BC), the originator of Roman epic poetry and drama. A Greek born in Tarentum, he was taken as a slave by a member of the Livian family when Tarentum surrendered. A teacher of Greek and Latin, his principal work, the *Odusia*, a translation of Homer's *Odyssey*, may have been intended as a schoolbook. He produced the first dramatic presentation ever given in Rome. Of his comedies and tragedies based on Greek works, only fragments remain. △1028.

Livonia, city in SE Michigan, W of Detroit; site of Madonna College (1937) and Schoolcraft College (1961). Industries: automobile parts, tools and dies, paints. Founded 1835; inc. 1950. Pop. (1970) 110,-109.

Livonian Brothers of the Sword, a group of knights who brought what is now Latvia and Estonia to Christianity by violent conquest. Founded with the pope's sanction in the early 13th century, the knights carried out several brutal campaigns and were finally crushed themselves by Lithuanian forces in 1236. The church then reorganized the band, which ruled for another three centuries.

Livorno. *See* Leghorn.

Livy (59 BC–AD 17), Roman historian, b. Titus Livius. With Tacitus and Sallust he is regarded as one of the three greatest Roman historians. He began his *History of Rome* around 29 BC. It covers Roman history from Aeneas' arrival in Italy, 753 BC to 9 BC. Livy used the best sources available at the time. His descriptions are vivid and he frequently draws moral conclusions. Thirty-five of the original 142 books are intact and fragments of all but two of the remaining books exist. △1028.

Lizard, reptile found on every continent. They have scales, paired copulatory organs, and flexible skulls. Typical lizards have cylindrical bodies with four legs, long tails, and movable eyelids. The majority are 12in (30.5cm) long. Chiefly terrestrial, many live in deserts. There are also semiaquatic and tree-dwelling forms, including the flying dragon. Burrowing species frequently have reduced limbs or are legless. There are two venomous species. Length: 2in–10ft (5cm–3m). There are 20 families of 3,000 species. Order Squamata; suborder Sauria. △520–22.

Lizard Fish, reptilelike fish (genus *Synodus*) found in shallow waters of the Atlantic and Pacific. A cylindrical fish with silver and olive-brown coloration, it uses its pectoral fins to prop itself up on the sandy bottom. Length: 12in (30.5cm). There are 36 species. Family Synodontidae.

Ljubljana, city in NW Yugoslavia, on the Ljubljanica River, 75mi (120km) NW of Zagreb; capital of republic of Slovenia; transportation, commercial, and industrial center. Location of the ancient Roman city of Emona (founded 1st century BC); destroyed by Huns AD 5th century; restored by Slavs, made part of Carinthia 12th century, under the Hapsburgs 1277; seat of Illyrian Provinces 1809–93; scene of Congress of Laibach 1821; under Austrian control until it was made part of Yugoslavia 1918. It is the site of medieval fortress, Tivoli Park, museum, art gallery, university (1595). Industries: textiles, paper, machinery, leather, tobacco, chemicals. Pop. 173,530.

Llama, or guanaco, alpaca, South American even-toed, ruminant mammal related to the camel. The guanaco is found in the wild; the llama and the alpaca are known only in domesticated form. They have been used as beasts of burden by the Indians for over 1,000 years. They have long, woolly coats and slender limbs and neck. The llama is structurally similar to the guanaco. The smaller alpaca is bred for its superb wool. Family Camelidae; genus *Lama*. △636.

Llanos, vast plains in N South America, in SW Venezuela and E Colombia; drained by the Orinoco River; sparsely populated; some cattle raising. Area: (Venezuela) approx. 125,000sq mi (323,750sq km); (Colombia) approx. 100,000sq mi (259,000sq km).

Llewellyn, Richard (1907–), pen name of Richard Llewellyn Lloyd, Welsh author. He gained popular success with *How Green Was My Valley* (1939), a novel about a Welsh mining family in the late 19th century. It was made into a film. His other works include *None But the Lonely Heart* (1943), *Chez Pavan* (1959), and *Up, Into the Singing Mountain* (1961).

Llewelyn ab Gruffydd (died 1282), Welsh prince. Despite paying homage to Henry III of England (1247), he rebelled successfully (1256–63) but was later compelled to acknowledge Wales subject to England (1267). Refusing homage to Edward I, Henry's successor (1272), he again rebelled but was forced to submit at Conway (1277).

Llewelyn ab Iorwerth or **Llewelyn the Great** (died 1240), Welsh prince. Master of most of Wales by 1202, Llewelyn exploited King John of England's political weakness to liberate Wales from English rule (1212–15). Between 1218 and 1238 Llewelyn consolidated his power by dynastic alliances.

Lloyd, Harold (1893–1971), US silent film comedian, b. Burchard, Kan. Star of hundreds of comedies, he was famed as a self-improving, daredevil, bespectacled boy in such films as *Safety Last* (1923), *The Freshman* (1925), *The Kid Brother* (1927), *Feet First* (1930), and *The Catspaw* (1934).

Lloyd George, David (1863–1945), Welsh political figure. A member of Parliament (1890–1944), he was the leading Liberal politician in the Britain of his time. Appointed chancellor of the exchequer (1908), he introduced the "People's Budget" (1909), financing social welfare through higher taxation of the wealthy, and the National Insurance Act (1911). An effective minister of munitions (1915) but critical of the conduct of the war, he became prime minister (1916) and was influential at the Versailles peace conference (1919). His handling of the Irish situation (1921) and party finance caused criticism, and he resigned (1922). Although still widely respected, he never again wielded power. △1300, 1308.

Lloyd's, London association of insurance underwrit-

Franz Liszt

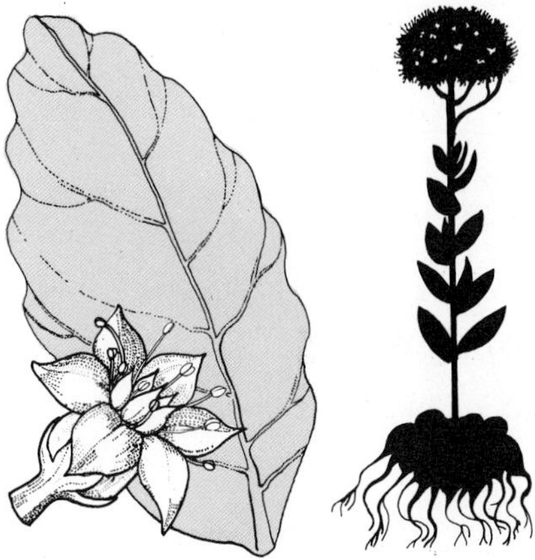

Live-forever

Liverpool, England

Robert Livingston

ers. It originated in the 17th century as a group of merchants meeting in Edward Lloyd's coffeehouse. Incorporated 1871, it specializes in international marine insurance, although most other forms of insurance are also undertaken. The corporation does not itself underwrite insurance business, which is transacted by individual syndicates.

Lobachevski, Nikolai Ivanovich, (1793–1856), Russian mathematician. Educated at Kazan University he was appointed professor there in 1814. His outstanding achievement was the creation of one of the first comprehensive non-Euclidean systems of geometry, which denies Euclid's axiom of parallels. △1462.

Lobby, group or individual representing special interests and attempting to influence legislation and government decisions. Lobbyists exert pressure through public relations, campaign contributions, personal contacts with public officials, and congressional testimony. Lobbyists are required to register annually with the House and Senate and to submit quarterly reports of their activities. △904.

Lobelia, trailing or bedding plant found worldwide. Many are grown as ornamentals. Flowers are red, white, or blue and irregularly shaped. Leaves are simple. Species include the blue-flowered, annual *Lobelia erinus;* the red, perennial *Lobelia cardinalis,* native to E North America; and the poisonous Indian tobacco *Lobelia inflata.* Family Lobeliaceae.

Lobengula (1833–94), Matabele king from 1870 in what is now part of Rhodesia. The initial instability of his rule caused him to invite British support in return for certain land and mineral concessions. This unfortunate policy allowed the formation of Cecil Rhodes' British South Africa Company (1889) and in 1893 the British destroyed the Matabele government and assumed effective rule.

Lobito, port city in W central Angola, on Lobito Bay, 240mi (386km) S of Luanda; an important W African port and trade link with interior; agricultural exports. Founded 1843. Pop. 97,758.

Lobotomy, or **Leucotomy,** a form of brain surgery consisting of cutting into the skull and severing nerve fibers that connect the thalamus with the frontal lobes of the brain. It was used for treating certain mental disorders, but modern tranquilizing drugs have replaced this operation except in rare instances. △770.

Lobster, large, long-tailed marine decapod crustacean, important commercially in North America and Europe. The true lobster possesses an enlarged, bulbous pair of pincers. The American lobster *(Homarus americanus)* reaches an average length of 10in (25cm) and weight of 3.5lb (1.6kg). The record is 45lb (20.3kg). The spiny lobster, lacking claws, wards off enemies with whiplike motions of stiffened antennae. *See also* Decapod, Crustacean. △458, 486, 490.

Local Color, literary form emphasizing customs, dialect, and other characteristics that have escaped standardizing cultural influences. The American form, influenced by English and French traditions, was popular in the late 19th century and had its greatest impact on the short story. Bret Harte's "The Luck of Roaring Camp" (1868) is often considered the first American example. Other local colorists include George Washington Cable, Mary E. Wilkins Freeman, Joel Chandler Harris, E. W. Howe, Sarah Orne Jewett, and Joaquin Miller.

Local Group of Galaxies, small galaxy cluster to which the Milky Way Galaxy belongs. The Local Group contains about 18 or 20 galaxies, including the Andromeda Galaxy (M 31) and its satellites. The system is about 2,000,000 light years across, with the Milky Way Galaxy at one end. *See also* Galaxy Cluster. △120.

Locarno, town in SE central Switzerland, on the N shore of Lake Maggiore, 11mi (18km) W of Bellinzona; scene of 1925 Locarno conference; site of 15th-century church, museum. Industries: printing, woodworking, pastry, flour, chemicals, beer, jewelry, beer, tourism. Pop. 14,143.

Locarno Pact, agreement made between Belgium, Italy, Great Britain, Poland, France, Czechoslovakia, and Germany in 1925 that demonstrated a resumption of normal European international relations and strengthened the member nations' commitment to the Treaty of Versailles. Gaining Germany's admission to the League of Nations, the pact was directed toward an age of peace, but was quickly abandoned by Hitler in 1936.

Locke, John (1632–1704), English philosopher. He studied at Oxford and served as physician to the Earl of Shaftesbury (until 1682). He went into exile in Holland (1683), but returned after the Glorious Revolution, when his *Essay Concerning Human Understanding* (1690), the first great work of British Empiricism, appeared. At the same time, his *Essays on Civil Government* (1690), establishing his version of the contract of government, was published. Locke advocated a concept of limited sovereignty, implying a right to restore liberty where threatened. In religion, he was a rationalist. △854, 858, 1184.

Lockjaw. *See* Tetanus.

Lockport, city in W New York, on Barge Canal 20mi (32km) ENE of Niagara Falls, seat of Niagara co. Industries: fruit, automobile parts, flour, pulp and paper, textiles, glass. Settled 1816; inc. 1865. Pop. (1970) 25,399.

Locks, Canal, gated basins or enclosures within which water levels may be varied to raise and lower boats. The first such gate, angled into the water's downward force, may have been invented by Leonardo da Vinci. *See also* Canal. △1762.

Lockyer, (Sir) Joseph Norman (1836–1920), British astronomer who discovered the element helium. He was a pioneer of the study of the Sun's spectrum. In 1868 he developed a technique for examining prominences at the edge of the Sun and attributed a portion of the spectrum to a new element which he named helium, 40 years before helium was discovered on Earth.

Locofoco Party, faction of Jacksonian Democrats that, during the period from 1835 to 1860, advocated suppression of paper money, curtailment of banking privileges, and protection of labor unions. Party members were named Locofocos when, on Oct. 29, 1835, they took control of a meeting in Tammany Hall by producing candles, lighting them with friction matches called "locofocos" and continuing the meeting after their opponents had turned off the gas.

Locomotive, any separate unit of a railroad that generates the power needed to pull freight and passenger cars. There are three main sources of power in use today—steam, oil, and electricity. Steam locomotives were in general use until the 1940s, when they were superseded by diesel and electric types. Electric locomotives are dependent on overhead trolley wires, a third (electrified) rail, or turbine-powered generators. △1676, 1706–10.

Locomotor Ataxia. *See* Tabes Dorsalis.

Locoweed, perennial plant native to the North American plains. It has clustered rosy or bluish-purple flowers and is poisonous to sheep, cattle, and horses. Height: to 18in (46cm). Family Leguminosae; species *Oxytropis lambertii.*

Locus, in geometry, the path traced by a specified point when it moves to satisfy certain conditions. For example, a circle is the locus of a point in a plane moving in such a way that its distance from a fixed point (the center) is constant.

Locust, any grasshopper that migrates en masse is considered a migratory locust. They are found where bodies of water or large humid areas meet arid areas. When a large population develops, the nymphs constantly irritate each other and finally they move en masse on foot. As they feed and develop, they emerge as adults and take to the air. The plant consumption of a swarm equals the daily food consumption of 1,500,000 people. Length: 0.5–4in (12.7–102mm). Order Orthoptera. *See also* Cicada; Grasshopper; Orthoptera. △496.

Locust Tree, deciduous trees and shrubs native to United States, Mexico, and Central America. The featherlike leaves are oblong and fragrant, flower clusters are white, pink, or purple. Family Leguminosae; genus *Robinia.*

Lod (Lydda), town in central Israel, 11mi (18km) SE of Tel Aviv. An ancient site, it was occupied by Samarians 4th century BC; devastated by fire AD 66 by Celestius Gallus during Jewish-Roman War, and AD 68 by Vespasian; later rebuilt by Hadrian; served as temporary seat of Jewish teachers after destruction of the Second Temple (70); made an episcopal see 5th century; destroyed by Saladin 1191, later rebuilt by Richard I of England; mentioned in Bible as site of Peter's healing of the paralytic; railway and airport center. Industries: telephone equipment, chemicals, oil products, cigarettes. Pop. 29,300.

Lode, an ore formation consisting of a closely spaced series of veins, usually in stratified layers. The veins are in tabular deposits in fissures and cracks of a body of rock from which they differ in composition. They are the result of the gradual precipitation of minerals carried by underground water or gases after the formation of the embedding rock (country rock). *See also* Ore. △278.

Lodge, Henry Cabot (1850–1924), US political leader, Senator (1893–1924), b. Boston. Prior to his political career he edited (1873–76) the *North American Review* and was (1876–79) a lecturer on US history at Harvard. He was a member of the House (1887–93) before entering the Senate (1893–1924). A friend of Theodore Roosevelt and a conservative Republican, he supported the acquisition of the Philippines and the establishment of a powerful army and navy. He successfully opposed US entry into the League of Nations and later criticized joining the World Court.

Lodi, industrial town in N Italy, on the Adda River approx. 20mi (32km) SE of Milan; built 1158, near ruins of ancient city (sacked by Milanese in 1111); site of Romanesque cathedral and Renaissance church; scene of Napoleon's victory over Austrians May 10, 1796. Industries: machinery, electrical equipment, dairying, ceramics, wrought iron. Pop. 42,757.

Lodi, city in central California, 12mi (19km) N of Stockton; settled by German farmers from the Midwest. Industries: citrus fruit, foundries, cannery, wine. Founded 1869; inc. 1906. Pop. (1970) 28,691.

Lodi, borough of NE New Jersey, 5mi (8km) SE of Paterson; site of Immaculate Conception Junior College (1923). Industries: chemicals, dyes, plastics. Inc. 1894. Pop. (1970) 25,213.

Lodis Dynasty. △1202.

Łódź, second-largest city in Poland, approx. 75mi (121km) SW of Warsaw; capital of Łódź prov. Before 19th century, town was a small regional market center; growth began when it came under Russian rule 1815, attracting many textile manufacturers; became part of Poland 1918, after which privately owned textile companies were taken over by government; site of university and technical university (1945). Pop. 762,000.

Loess, buff-colored deposit of fine silt or clay, generally unstratified and sometimes exposed in bluffs. The loess in the Mississippi Valley is believed to be of glacial origin, while that in the Mongolian desert seems to have been formed by the wind.

Loewe v. Lawlor. *See* Danbury Hatters' Case.

Lofoten Islands, Norwegian island group off NW coast of Norway, in Norwegian Sea; extends ESE from coast; SW of sister group, the Vesterålen. Chief islands are Moskenesoya, Aust Vagoya, and Vest Vagoya. Main industry is fishing. Area: approx. 475sq mi (1,230sq km).

Logan, Joshua (1908–), US stage and film director, b. Texarkana, Tex. His co-writing and stage production of *South Pacific* in 1949 won him a Pulitzer Prize. His successful films have included *Picnic* (1955), *Bus Stop* (1956), *Sayonara* (1957), *South Pacific* (1958), *Fanny* (1960), and *Camelot* (1967).

Logan, city in N Utah, 36mi (58km) N of Ogden, on Logan River; seat of Cache co; site of Mormon Tabernacle and Temple and Utah State University (1888). Industries: farming, livestock, food processing, farm machinery, plastics, pianos. Settled 1855 by Mormons; inc. 1859. Pop. (1970) 22,333.

Logan, Mount, peak in SW Yukon, Canada, in St Elias Mts. Highest peak in Canada, 2nd highest in North America; 1st ascent 1925. Height: 19,850ft (6,054m).

Loganberry, or **Logan Blackberry,** biennial bramble hybrid developed by Judge J. H. Logan in his California garden in 1881. A blackberry-red raspberry cross, it is disease prone and grown only on the Pacific coast. The canes produce large, red berries eaten fresh or preserved. Family Rosaceae; species *Rubus ursinus loganobaccus. See also* Blackberry. △360.

Logarithmic Function, mathematical function the value of which depends on the logarithm, to a particular base, b, of the independent variable, x, and is thus given by $f(x) = \log_b x$. For natural logarithms, where the base is exponential e, the logarithmic function is the inverse of the exponential function. △1456.

Logarithms, computation aid, devised by John Napier (1614) and developed by the English mathematician Henry Briggs (1556–1630). Numbers are converted to their logarithms, found from tables, and their multiplication, division, square root, cube root, etc, are determined by addition, subtraction, and division, respectively, of the logarithms involved. The resulting number is then checked in tables for its antilogarithm, that is, the inverse function of the logarithm, which gives the answer. A number's logarithm is the number, *x*, indicating the power to which a fixed number, *b*, must be raised to yield the specified number, *n*; that is, if $b^x = n$, then $\log_b n = x$. The number *b* is the logarithmic base: common logarithms have base 10; natural logarithms have base e (2.71828 . . .). A logarithm is written as the sum of an integer (the characteristic) and a decimal fraction (the mantissa). The characteristic indicates the location of the decimal point in the number, being positive for numbers greater than one and negative for those less than one. The mantissa is the logarithm of the digits in the number, regardless of decimal place. △1456.

Loggerhead Turtle, carnivorous sea turtle found in warm waters of the Atlantic and Pacific. Characterized by a large head, it has oarlike flippers and is red-brown. Length; 3ft (91cm); weight: 300lb (135kg). Family Cheloniidae; species *Caretta caretta*. *See also* Turtle. △520.

Logic, branch of philosophy dealing with the systematic study of the structure of propositions and the criteria of valid inference. In abstracting from the content of propositions in order to examine their logical form, logic evaluates soundness or validity rather than truth *per se*. The history of logic begins with Aristotle, proceeding through Arabian and European logic in the Middle Ages and various post-Renaissance scholars, and resulting in the mathematical elaborations of the 19th and 20th centuries. *See also* Symbolic Logic. △854, 858, 1444.

Logical Empiricism, synonymous expression for logical positivism. *See also* Logical Positivism.

Logical Positivism, also called scientific empiricism and logical empiricism, school of philosophy that evolved out of the Vienna Circle of the 1920s and 1930s. Beginning as a continuation of 19th-century Viennese empiricism, it resulted in a philosophical attitude based on logic. It rejected metaphysics as logically meaningless and advocated a thorough analysis of philosophical and scientific terminology.

Logos, in philosophy, means intellect or reason, or in a larger sense the rational principle that orders the universe. The Stoics thought of this principle as the soul of the world. In theology, there have been debates about the meaning of the Greek word *logos* as used in the Gospel of John. The term was translated as *Word*: "In the beginning was the Word and the Word was with God, and the Word was God. The same was in the beginning with God." *Word* can be taken to mean God or something else such as wisdom.

Logwood, or bloodwood, spiny evergreen tree native to Central America, West Indies, and Colombia. The small, fragrant flowers are yellow. Its dark red heartwood yields a dye used in biological stains. Height: to 40ft (12m). Family Leguminosae; species *Haematoxylon campechianum*.

Lohengrin, in Teutonic mythology, a knight, son of Parcival, associated with legends of the Holy Grail. In one story, Lohengrin arrives in Antwerp asleep in a boat drawn by a swan. He awakens to save a princess from an annoying suitor, then marries her. When the princess asks him his name, defying his wish, the swan boat appears and Lohengrin departs.

Loire River, longest river in France; rises in Cévennes Mts in SE France, flows N through central and W France to Atlantic Ocean at Saint-Nazaire. It is connected by canals to Rhône and Seine river systems. Length: 630mi (1,014km).

Loki, in Norse mythology, a mischievous demon. Although friends with Odin and Thor, he was known for his pranks. He was regarded as an enemy of the gods.

Lollards, followers of the 14th-century English religious reformer John Wycliffe. They challenged both doctrines and practices of the church, including transubstantiation and the need for confession. They rejected the sole authority of the pope, and they denounced the wealth of the church and church involvement in civil affairs. Lollards went out as "poor preachers," teaching that the Bible was the source of belief. They won support from some nobles as well as many common people, but after they were declared heretics the movement lost force. However, Lollard ideas helped prepare the way for the Protestant Reformation. *See also* Wycliffe, John.

Lomas de Zamora, city in E Argentina, 9 mi (14km) SSW of Buenos Aires. Industries: chemicals, electrical equipment, cement. Pop. 272,116.

Lombard, Peter (*c.* 1100–60) Italian theologian. He is best known for his *Sentences*, a series of four books on the Trinity, Creation and Sin, the Incarnation and Virtues, and the Sacraments and Four Last Things. This work became the source of Catholic theology until replaced by Aquinas' *Summa Theologica*.

Lombard, residential town in NE Illinois, 20mi (32km) W of Chicago; site of Lilacia Park, former private estate containing over 300 varieties of lilacs. Inc. 1869. Pop. (1970) 35,977.

Lombardi, Vince(nt T.) (1913–70), US football coach, b. Brooklyn, N.Y. He was considered the premier coach in the National Football League. While at Green Bay (1958–68) and Washington (1969), he compiled a 141–39–4 record and won the first two Super Bowls (1967, 1968). He was Coach of the Year in 1961 and elected to the Football Hall of Fame in 1971.

Lombard League, 12th- and 13th-century alliance of cities of Lombardy in northern Italy (including Milan, Venice, Brescia, Bergamo, Mantua, Verona). Founded in 1167 to resist the Holy Roman Emperor Frederick Barbarossa, by the Peace of Constance (1183) the league acknowledged fealty to Frederick, but the cities were granted local liberties and jurisdiction. The league was formed again in 1226 against Frederick II and ended with his death in 1250.

Lombards, Germanic people thought to have migrated from Gotland. They inhabited the area east of the lower Elbe until driven west by the Romans in AD 9. They were allied with Arminius in 175 and invaded N Italy in 568 under Alboin. They conquered much of Italy from their center Pavia and later adopted Catholicism and Latin customs. Their kingdom attained its zenith under Liutprand (died 744). They were defeated by the Franks under Charlemagne (774) and declined thereafter. △1066.

Lombardy (Lombardia), industrial region in N Italy; comprised of provinces of Bergamo, Brescia, Como, Cremona, Mantua, Milano, Pavia, Sondrio, and Varese; Milan is capital city. Geographically the region is marked by mountains, glaciers, and numerous lakes; it was center of powerful Lombard kingdom 569–774; defeated by Charlemagne 774. Products: cereals, sugar beets, vegetables, fruits, olives, livestock. Industries: automobiles, steel, chemicals, textiles. Area: 9,200sq mi (23,830sq km). Pop. 8,231,-667.

Lomé, seaport city and capital of Republic of Togo, W Africa, on Gulf of Guinea. An administrative, commercial, and industrial center, it is site of University of Benin (1970), rail line, airport. Industries: coffee, cocoa, palm nuts, copra. Pop. 83,845.

Lomonosov, Mikhail Vasilievich (1711–65), Russian scientist and poet. He helped found the University of Moscow (1755) and was one of the first Russian scientists to suggest the law of conservation of mass, atomic theory, and a kinetic theory of heat. He formulated Russian classical literary theory in his *Letter on the Rules of Russian Versification*. His poetry includes the odes *Evening Meditations* (1748) and *Morning Meditations* (1751).

Lomonosov Ridge, a submarine ridge that stretches from the Asian continental shelf, past the North Pole to the edge of the North American continental shelf near Ellesmere Island. Discovered in 1948–49 by Soviet polar explorers, it has aided in determining ocean water circulation, the pattern of ice drift, and major life provinces in the Arctic.

Lompoc, city in S California, 45mi (72km) WNW of Santa Barbara; site of La Purisima Mission (1791), an historic monument. Industries: flower seed, earth mines, oil refineries, food processing, truck farms. Inc. 1888. Pop. (1970) 25,284.

London, Jack (1876–1916), pseud. of John Griffith, US novelist and short-story writer, b. San Francisco. His works concentrate on the brute-in-man concept. His early years were spent along the San Francisco waterfront, which he describes in his autobiographical novels *Martin Eden* (1909) and *John Barleycorn* (1913). He spent three years as a sailor and traveled widely. During 1899–1903 he wrote essays, poems, over 100 short stories, and eight novels. *Call of the Wild* (1903), his most popular work, was written dur-

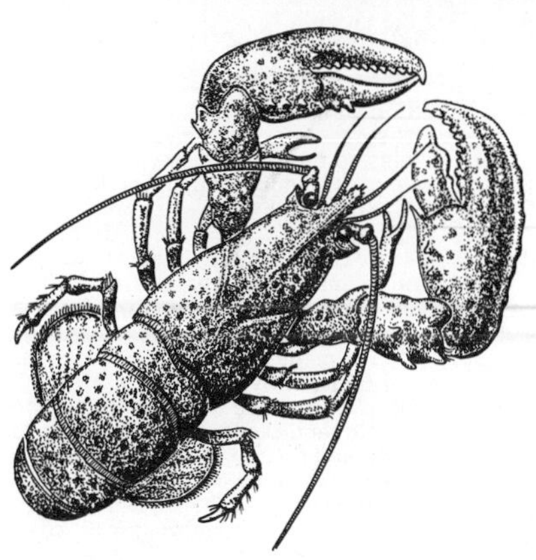

Lobster

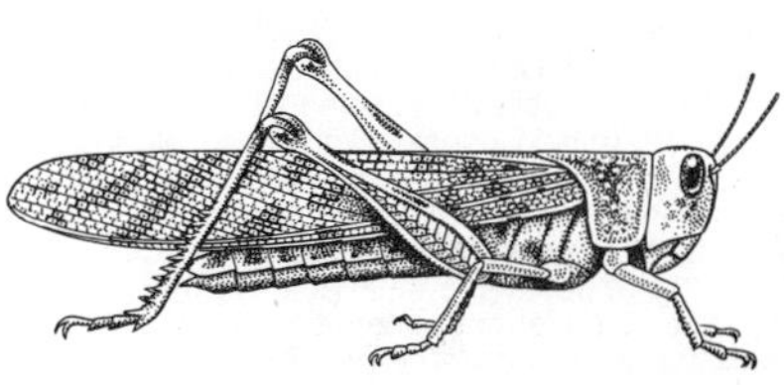

Locust

Henry Cabot Lodge

Loggerhead turtle

ing this period. He espoused socialism and was influenced by Marx and Nietzsche.

London, city in SE Ontario, Canada, on the Thames River; location of six colleges and universities. Industries: paper, textiles, refrigerators, diesel locomotives. Founded 1826; inc. as village 1840, town 1848, city 1855. Pop. 221,430.

London, capital city of the United Kingdom, located on both sides of Thames River, about 40mi (64km) from its mouth in SE England. A Roman town from AD 43–409, it was attacked by Danes 851; Alfred the Great freed London from their control in 886; city was political capital of England by 14th century. In 16th century Elizabeth I introduced social reforms and added to city's wealth and power. Almost destroyed by a plague in 1665 and fire in 1666, city went on to become a world leader in trade, culture, and politics by time Queen Victoria reigned (1837–1901).

In 19th century people began moving from city's center to outer rings of boroughs; the Industrial Revolution brought about working-class suburbs. WWI caused little damage to city, but WWII bombing killed 30,000 residents and destroyed 100,000 houses; site of Westminster Abbey (with a few remnants from original 1065 building), St Paul's Cathedral (rebuilt by Sir Christopher Wren 1668), Houses of Parliament (1840–60), Tower of London (1078), National Gallery (1838), Buckingham Palace (1705), Westminister Hall (1099), University of London (1836); Kensington, Hyde, Green, and St James parks.

International trade, although declining, is still one of London's major economic activities. Heathrow Airport (W of city), Gatwick Airport (S), and Foulnes (E) have greatly increased air freight shipments, while shipping from its docks has lessened. Famous London fogs have decreased considerably since passage of Clean Air Act of 1956; tourism continues to be an important industry. Industries: brewing, tanning, clothing, furniture, paper, printing, engineering. City is also center of banking and investment business. Its many theaters, museums, galleries, opera and concert halls also make it a cultural center. The City of London and its 32 boroughs make up Greater London. Pop. 8,196,807.

Londonderry (Derry), borough in Northern Ireland, at the mouth of the Foyle River on Lough Foyle; capital of Londonderry co; hilly farming and cattle-raising region. It grew around abbey founded by St Columba (546); destroyed by the Danes in 812; name changed from Derry to Londonderry when town passed to corporations of the City of London (1613); besieged by James II for 105 days (1689); site of many early structures including Roman Catholic and Protestant cathedrals, and a triumphal arch commemorating the 1689 siege; the modern city is important as a maritime center, with a naval base. Industries: shipping and shipbuilding, linens, fishing, tanning, brewing, and marketing of regional agricultural products. Area of borough; 814sq mi (2,108sq km). Pop. (city) 51,617; (borough) 182,173.

London Economic Conference (1933), international financial meeting, also known as World Monetary and Economic Conference. The United States met with the League of Nations members in London to work for international economic stability in the midst of the Depression. The meeting ended without accomplishment after the United States rejected the plan of returning to the gold standard.

London Naval Conference (1930), meeting of five nations in an effort to limit naval strength. The United States, Great Britain, and Japan agreed to limit submarine warfare and to institute a five-year moratorium on ship construction, but France and Italy refused to sign the treaty.

Long, Crawford Williamson (1815–78), US physician, b. Danielsville, Ga. In 1842 he began using ether as an anesthesia for surgery but did not publish or publicize his work until years later, after William Morton and others had been given credit. *See also* Morton, William.

Long, Earl Kemp (1895–1960), US political leader, b. Winnfield, La. The brother of Huey Long, Earl entered politics when he was appointed to state office by his brother. After a falling-out with his brother he ran unsuccessfully for lieutenant governor in 1931. They reconciled, and he became lieutenant governor (1936–38) after Huey's death. He was governor (1939–40) and operated the powerful machine that dominated Louisiana politics until 1960.

Long, Huey Pierce (1893–1935), US political leader, b. near Winnfield, La. Elected governor of Louisiana in 1928 by appealing to rural voters on a tax-the-rich program, he was impeached for bribery and misconduct in 1929 but was not convicted and served until 1931. He then built a powerful machine that controlled Louisiana politics for decades. He served in the US Senate (1931–35). He began (1933) the "Share Our Wealth" movement and proposed legislation against the wealthy, gaining wide popularity. He was feared by President Roosevelt and liberals as a potential dictator. His presidential bid, however, ended with his assassination.

Long Beach, city in S California, 20mi (32km) S of Los Angeles; oil discovered in 1921; site of four man-made oil islands in its harbor; the Queen Mary has been berthed here since 1967 and used as a tourist center, museum, and hotel. Industries: oil, automobile parts, canning, chemicals. Inc. 1888. Pop. (1970) 358,633.

Long Beach, residential city in SE New York, on an island in Atlantic Ocean off S shore of Long Island; resort area. Industries: clothing, umbrellas, labels. Inc. 1922. Pop. (1970) 33,127.

Long Branch, city in E central New Jersey, on Atlantic coast, 21mi (34km) SE of Perth Amboy; summer residence of presidents Grant, Hayes, Garfield, and Arthur. Industries: electronics, clothing, boats, summer resorts. Settled 1740; inc. 1904. Pop. (1970) 31,774.

Longevity. △802.

Longfellow, Henry Wadsworth (1807–82), US poet, b. Portland, Me. After graduating from Bowdoin College (1825), he studied modern languages in Europe and then taught at Bowdoin (1829–35) and Harvard University (1835–54), until he resigned to devote himself solely to writing. His first book of poetry, *Voices of the Night,* appeared in 1839. In 1841 *Ballads and Other Poems* was published. It contained two of his most popular shorter poems, "The Wreck of the Hesperus" and "The Village Blacksmith." Perhaps Longfellow is best-remembered for his narrative poems dramatizing American history and legend. These include *Evangeline* (1847), *The Song of Hiawatha* (1855), *The Courtship of Miles Standish* (1858), and *Paul Revere's Ride* (1861). In them, Longfellow combines the epic form and some of the techniques of European literature with his own simple and sentimental style.

Longhorn, almost extinct breed of beef cattle, originally from Mexico, descended from European cattle introduced by Spanish conquistadors. Once the mainstay of Western herds, they are now used only as rodeo and show animals. *See also* Beef Cattle; Cattle.

Long-horned Beetle, or long-horned borer, wood-boring beetle found worldwide. It has long antennae, long legs, and cylindrical white or yellow body. Length: 0.12–6in (2–152mm). Family Carambycidae. △500.

Long Island, fourth-largest island in the United States, in SE New York, separated from Manhattan by the East River; W end of island contains New York City boroughs of Queens and Brooklyn; E end counties of Nassau and Suffolk. Long Island Sound separates it from Connecticut (N); Atlantic Ocean is on its S. Originally inhabited by Algonquin Indians; Massachusetts Bay Colony and Dutch West India Company claimed it in 17th century. Treaty of Hartford (1650) divided it between them. Farming, fishing, and whaling were carried on in 18th and 19th centuries; many farms still on island. Easy access to New York City has caused rapid growth of industry and population. Glacial deposits provide sand, gravel; there are many wooded areas, beaches, bays, and inlets. Commercial and sport fishing are on S and E coasts. Limited natural water supply forces strict conservation measures. Tourism and recreation are supported on the E and S parts of the island. Length: 118mi (190km). Width: 12–20mi (19–32km).

Long Island, Battle of (Aug. 27, 1776), Revolutionary War battle. George Washington's army, divided by the East River, was defeated on Long Island by British Gen. William Howe. Driven back to Brooklyn, the American army retreated to Manhattan under the cover of night and fog, thus avoiding capture.

Longitude, a measurement of location, east or west of the prime meridian (the imaginary north-south line passing through both poles and Greenwich, England). Longitude is measured in degrees, minutes, and seconds and is 180° both east and west of the prime meridian. △180.

Longitudinal Wave, type of wave, such as a sound wave, in which the particles of the transmitting medium are displaced along the direction of energy propagation, that is, in the direction of wave motion. *See also* Wave.

Long March, a remarkable feat by Chinese Communist forces. They broke out of Nationalist encirclement in 1934 and for more than a year traveled 6,000 miles (9,600km) under the leadership of Chu Teh and Mao Tse-tung from Kiangsi Province through western China to Shensi Province. There, new Communist headquarters were established at Yenan. △1328.

Long Parliament (1640–1660), English Parliament summoned by Charles I and not formally dissolved until 1660. It impeached Charles' ministers and censured him in the Grand Remonstrance (1641). Its refusal to cooperate with Charles or be dissolved was a major victory for representative government over the crown. The Parliament was reduced by Pride's Purge (1648) and the remaining legislators, known as the Rump Parliament, condemned Charles I (1649). The Long Parliament thereafter had little authority and was dissolved at the Restoration (1660). *See also* Pride's Purge. △1156.

Longshore Drift. △268.

Longstreet, James (1821–1904), Confederate Civil War general, b. Edgefield District, S.C. Serving as a corps commander in both the Eastern and Western campaigns, he served prominently at the First Battle of Bull Run, Antietam, Fredericksburg, Gettysburg, Chickamauga, the Wilderness, and Richmond.

Longview, city in E Texas, 120mi (193km) E of Dallas; seat of Gregg co; site of Le Tourneau College (1946). Industries: petrochemicals, aircraft parts, steel, chemicals, plastic, paper, lumber, machinery. Inc. 1872. Pop. (1970) 45,547.

Longview, city and port of entry in SW Washington, at confluence of Columbia and Cowlitz rivers; transportation hub. Industries: pulp, paper, wood products, aluminum, metal. Founded 1922 as lumbering community; inc. 1924. Pop. (1970) 28,373.

Lookout Mountain, Battle of (Nov. 23–25, 1863). This battle in Tennessee was part of the Union's campaign to relieve the siege of Chattanooga. It was climaxed by Union Gen. Joseph Hooker's charge and capture of the strategically important mountain.

Loon, diving bird of Northern Hemisphere known for harsh and eerie, often nocturnal, call. It has black, white, and gray plumage. An excellent swimmer, it often stays submerged while fishing. It runs on water and flaps its wings to take flight; it splashes down on its chest later. It lays olive eggs (2) in a grass-and-reed nest near water. Length: 30in (76cm). Family Gaviidae. △526, 612.

Looper. *See* Measuring Worm.

Lope de Vega Carpio, Félix (1562–1635), Spanish dramatic poet, contemporary of Cervantes. He wrote nearly 2,000 plays of which 431 texts survive, dominating the Spanish theater for 50 years. He invented the "comedia" form, freeing drama from classical and medieval restraints. His *Fuente Ovejuna,* portraying peasants united against injustice, is considered the first major drama of class conflict.

López de Legaspi, Miguel (d. 1572), Spanish explorer. While in government service in Mexico, he was sent (1564) to claim the Philippines for Spain. He founded the first Spanish settlement in 1565 and then secured the Philippines militarily from the Portuguese and the natives, thus establishing Spanish rule over the Philippines.

Loquat, evergreen shrub or small tree native to China and Japan and naturalized in subtropical climates worldwide. Used for shade and hedges, they have white flowers and yellow, plumlike fruit prized as a dessert or flavoring. Height: to 20ft (6.1m). Family Rosaceae; species *Eriobotrya japonica.* △340.

Lorain, city and lakeport in N Ohio, on Lake Erie at mouth of Black River, 25mi (40km) W of Cleveland; important ore shipping port. Industries: shipbuilding, iron, steel, automobile assembling. Founded 1807; inc. 1834 as Charleston; renamed 1876. Pop. (1970) 78,185.

LORAN, navigational aid used to guide ships and airplanes to their destinations. The name LORAN stands for LOng-RAnge Navigation. It consists of two ground stations that emit electronic pulses, which the ships and planes can use to guide their course. The stations have a day range of 800mi (1,288km) and a night range of 1,600mi. (2,576km) and are accurate to within 1mi (1.6km) of their location.

Lord Dunmore's War (1774), dispute involving colonial settlers and Indians in a conflict over land. Virginia's royal governor, John Murray, Earl of Dunmore, took control of western Pennsylvania. Then settlers began moving into Kentucky. These two infringements into lands that the Indians considered theirs provoked the Shawnee and Ottawa tribes into war. Col. Andrew Lewis led his troops to victory over Chief Cornstalk at the Battle of Point Pleasant. The war ended with the Treaty of Camp Charlotte, by which the Indians relinquished hunting rights in Kentucky.

Lordosis, forward (concave) curvature of the spine, applied alike to normal curvature and to abnormalities such as swayback.

Lorentz, Hendrik Anton (1853–1928), Dutch physicist and professor at Leyden. His early work was concerned with James Maxwell's theory of electromagnetic radiation. This led him to the Lorentz transformation and the prediction of the Lorentz-Fitzgerald contraction, both of which were essential steps in the discovery of special relativity. He was responsible for the idea of local time. Some of his work was concerned with thermodynamics and the Zeeman effect, for which he was awarded a Nobel Prize in 1902 (jointly with Pieter Zeeman). *See also* Lorentz-Fitzgerald Length Contraction; Lorentz Transformation.

Lorentz-Fitzgerald Length Contraction, theory, put forward independently by H. A. Lorentz (1895) and George Fitzgerald (1893) to explain the result of the Michelson-Morley experiment, that a body moving with high velocity through the ether experiences a contraction in length in the direction of the motion. *See also* Relativity Theory.

Lorentz Transformations, relations (for H.A. Lorentz) connecting the space and time coordinates of an event as observed from two frames of reference, especially at relativistic velocities. Shown by Einstein (1905) to be a consequence of the theory of special relativity. *See also* Relativity Theory.

Lorenz, Konrad (1903–), pioneer Austrian ethologist. Lorenz did classic studies of imprinting in birds and aggression in other animals. He wrote the controversial *On Aggression* (1966) in which he argued that human aggression is instinctual. He received a Nobel Prize in 1973. △536, 784, 823.

Lorenzo the Magnificent. *See* Medici, Lorenzo de.

Lorestan. *See* Luristan.

Lorimer, George Horace (1867–1937), US editor, b. Louisville, Ky. A newspaper reporter, he became editor of the *Saturday Evening Post* in 1899, and raised the magazine to one of the most popular in the nation. He published fiction by such writers as Theodore Dreiser, Sinclair Lewis, Stephen Crane, and F. Scott Fitzgerald. He wrote several books, including *Letters from a Self-Made Merchant to His Son* (1902) and *Old Gorgon Graham* (1904). He retired in 1936.

Loris, primitive tailless, tree-dwelling nocturnal primate of S Asian and East Indies forests. They have soft, thick fur and big eyes, and feed mainly on insects. Length: 8–16in (20–41cm). Species slender *Loris tardigradus*, slow *Nycticebus coucang* and *N. pygmaeus*. *See also* Primates. △554.

Lorrain, Claude (1600–82), professional name of Claude Gellée, French landscape painter, draftsman, and etcher. With Nicolas Poussin, he was the finest artist of the classical Baroque style. His mature works include "Embarkation of St Ursula" (1641) and "Ermini and the Shepherds" (1666). His later works anticipated in many ways the Impressionists and Romantics ("Perseus and Medusa"). △1166.

Lorraine, historic region and former province in NE France, now comprised of Moselle, Meurthe-et-Moselle, Meuse, and Vosges depts.; part of medieval Austrasia, and kingdom of Lotharingia 9th century; passed to house of Lorraine 1048–1738; united as an official province of France 1766; E part was ceded to Germany 1871, passed back to France after WWI, again annexed to Germany during WWII, after which the region was returned to France. Chief cities are Nancy, Metz, Thionville, and Verdun-sur-Meuse. Products: hops, grapes, wine, beer, iron ore, coal, coke, dairy products.

Lory, brightly colored parrot, native to Australia, with a brush-tipped tongue for feeding on nectar and fruit. The typical Papuan lory *(Charmosyna papou)* of New Guinea is crimson with black cap and pants; green wings, back, and tail; and glossy blue nape. The smaller lorikeet *(Trichoglossus)* is also found, often in large groups, in Malaya.

Los Angeles, city in SW California, near shore of Pacific Ocean; the largest city in California, and 3rd-largest in the United States. Originally a cattle farming center known as El Pueblo de Nuestra Señora La Reina de los Angeles, it was taken from Mexico by the United States 1846; city grew as railroads arrived (Southern Pacific, 1876, and Santa Fe, 1885). The discovery of oil deposits (1894), improvements of harbor facilities (1912), and the developing motion picture industry at Hollywood (early 20th century) attracted settlers; as the city expanded, it attracted more diverse industries, and was chosen as host of the Summer Olympic Games 1932. Major problems of the city's growth have been its water shortage (a 300-mi/483-km pipe from the Colorado River supplies the city with most of its water) and air pollution. The metropolitan area of Los Angeles comprises approx. 34,000sq mi (88,060sq km), enveloping the separate cities of Beverly Hills, Santa Monica, and San Fernando. It is the site of Los Angeles County Museum of Art, Los Angeles County Museum of Natural History, Southwest Museum, Municipal Art Gallery; institutes of higher education include the University of California at Los Angeles (1881), University of Southern California (1879), California Institute of Technology, Loyola University of Los Angeles (1865); tourist attractions include Griffith Park, the Hollywood Bowl, the Plaza district of the old city, and the many Pacific seaside resorts; it is also the home of several professional sports teams, including Los Angeles Dodgers and California Angels (baseball), Los Angeles Rams (football), and Los Angeles Lakers (basketball). Industries: aircraft, heavy machinery, wood products, textiles, tires, chemicals, oil refining, food processing and canning, printing, publishing, plastics, clay, furniture, fine instruments, shipping, electronic equipment, entertainment, tourism. Founded 1781; inc. 1850. Pop. (1970) 2,809,596.

Lost Generation, designation for disillusioned American intellectuals, writers, and artists after World War I. The term is attributed to a remark made by Gertrude Stein, the author and art patron, to Ernest Hemingway. Her words, "You are all of a lost generation," appear in the preface of Hemingway's book, *The Sun Also Rises* (1926), a novel about a fun-seeking group of American and English expatriates. Other writers of the Lost Generation also expressed their loss of idealism, which had resulted from the war, in their work. Like Hemingway, many of the Lost Generation were expatriates in Paris. Other Lost Generation writers include F. Scott Fitzgerald, Ezra Pound, and John Dos Passos.

Lot, in the Bible, son of Haran and nephew of Abraham. He accompanied Abraham to Canaan, choosing to settle the fertile Jordan valley. When God destroyed Sodom and Gomorrah, Lot, his wife, and two daughters were allowed to escape, but his wife, disobeying God's orders, looked back and became a pillar of salt.

Lothair (941–86), Carolingian king of the Franks (954–86). He experienced a confused and limited reign and was never quite able to free himself of political domination. His continued efforts to obtain Lorraine brought the dangerous enmity of Holy Roman Emperor Otto II and strengthened the political position of Lothair's rival Hugh Capet. He was succeeded by Louis V, his son.

Lothair I (795?–855), Holy Roman emperor of the West with his father, Louis I, from 817. In the same year Louis made him heir over his younger brothers, Louis the Pious, Pepin, and later Charles the Bald, who were to rule separate kingdoms in his domain. However, when Louis I died (840), the two remaining brothers (Pepin had died in 838) defeated Lothair at Fontenoy (841) and divided the empire three ways.

Lothair II (or **III**), called "the Saxon" (1070?–1137), king of Germany and Holy Roman emperor (1125–37). He secured the throne and defeated the rival Hohenstaufens (1128–35), the family of the former Holy Roman emperor, Henry V. He fought in support of Pope Innocent II and expanded German rule. Invaded Italy (1136–37).

Lothair II (died 950), king of Italy during post-Carolingian period of chaos. From 931 he ruled as co-king with his father Hugh of Arles; but when Berengar II drove Hugh from Italy in 947, Lothair remained as the figurehead king of Italy while Berengar held the real power. Lothair was ultimately poisoned by Berengar.

Lothair II (826?–69), king of Lotharingia, now Lorraine (855–69), a central section of Charlemagne's

London, England: Tower Bridge

Henry Wadsworth Longfellow

Longhorn

Los Angeles

empire. Pope Nicholas I refused all his attempts to divorce his childless wife and marry Waldrada, his mistress, who had borne him children. △1066.

Lotharingia, the part of Charlemagne's empire inherited by his descendant Lothair II (855–69) for whom it is named. The Treaty of Verdun (843) divided the Carolingian empire among Charlemagne's three grandsons, the middle part going to Lothair I. Another split in 855 gave the northern part of Lothair's kingdom to his son Lothair II. Roughly, Lotharingia included modern Lorraine (the name is a later form of Lotharingia), Alsace, NW Germany, all of Luxembourg, Belgium, and The Netherlands.

Lotto, Lorenzo (*c.* 1480–*c.* 1556), Venetian painter. He was one of the finest artists of the High Renaissance. "The Assumption" is an early work. His mature work, marked by softer tones, includes "Christ Taking Leave of His Mother" and "Bridal Couple with Cupid." *See also* Renaissance Art.

Lotus, water lily native to Africa and Asia. Flowers are blue, white, or pink. The white lotus *(Nymphaea lotus)* was once considered sacred. Family Nymphaeaceae.

Loudness, magnitude of the sensation produced when the human ear responds to a sound. There is no simple relationship between loudness and the intensity of the sound; the response of the ear also depends to a certain extent on the frequency. △1498–1500.

Loudspeaker, device for converting oscillating electric currents into sound. The most common type has a moving coil attached to a stiff paper cone (often elliptical) suspended in a strong magnetic field. The oscillating currents in the speech coil cause the cone to vibrate at the frequency of the currents, thus creating sound waves. A modern loudspeaker gives uniform response between 80 and 10,000 hertz. For higher efficiency a small diaphragm is used at the apex of an exponential horn. △1486.

Louis I (1786–1868), king of Bavaria (1825–48), member of Wittelsbach family, succeeded his father, Maximilian I. He was best known for his generous patronage of the arts, which made Munich a vibrant cultural center. He quickly changed from liberal to conservative and became so unpopular that he had to abdicate at the time of the 1848 revolution in favor of his son Maximilian II. Louis' affair with Lola Montez caused a national scandal.

Louis II (1845–1886), king of Bavaria (1864–86), succeeded his father, Maximilian II. Generally disliked for his mental oddities. Supported Austria against Prussia; fought on side of Prussia in Franco-Prussian War; brought Bavaria into German Empire (1871). Patron of arts; he incurred massive national debts. He drowned himself after his ministers declared him insane.

Louis III (1845–1921), last of the Bavarian kings, assumed rule on behalf of the unstable King Otto I in 1912–13, and concentrated on internal development despite a raging world war. In 1918 he surrendered his powers after a socialist revolution and left the country.

Louis I, called **the Pious** (778–840), king of France and of Germany (814–840), emperor of the West, succeeded his father, Charlemagne (814–40). Sincerely religious, he was troubled by rebellious sons and their territorial squabbles, which they pursued to the neglect of all else and hastened the end of the Carolingian Empire. He divided his empire among his sons (817) to take effect after his death, but the final disposition took place only after his sons made war on each other. His son Lothair I succeeded him as emperor.

Louis III (863?–882), king of France (879–82). He and his brother Carloman divided their father's West Frankish kingdom and warded off rival claims by Louis the Younger, who based his opposition on their father's divorce of their mother. During Louis' reign Scandinavian maurauders, the Normans, posed a serious threat. In 881 Louis won a decisive victory that temporarily stopped the Norman invasions in northern France.

Louis IV or **Louis d'Outremer** (?921–954), king of France (936–954). Called d'Outremer (from overseas) because he was raised in England. He attempted to reestablish his father's claim to Lorraine (938) but was subverted by his vassal, Hugh the Great, working in collusion with Otto I of Germany. Louis allied himself with Otto, had Hugh excommunicated (948), and forced Hugh to make peace (951).

Louis V or **Louis le Fainéant** (967?–87), king of France. The last Carolingian ruler, he was crowned in 979 while his father, Lothair, was still ruling. He became sole king in 986 but was overshadowed by Hugh Capet, Duke of the Franks, who succeeded Louis to the throne. His nickname Fainéant means "do nothing."

Louis VI or **Louis the Fat** (1081–1137), king of France (1108–37). Working to build the power of the crown over independent local nobles, he notably increased the importance of the royal courts. With Abbot Suger of St Denis as his advisor, he worked closely with the church. He began a war (1104) against King Henry I of England, duke of Normandy, a struggle that was to continue intermittently for centuries. Before his death he arranged the marriage of his son, Louis VII, and Eleanor, daughter of the duke of Aquitaine.

Louis VII or **Louis the Young** (1120?–80), king of France (1137–80). His marriage to Eleanor of Aquitaine extended the French crown's lands to the Pyrenees Mountains. As king he consolidated royal power by cultivating the church and the emerging towns. In 1147 he went on the Second Crusade. On his return he claimed that his wife had been unfaithful and had their marriage annulled (1152). She then married his archrival, Henry II of England, whose holdings thereby became greater than those of Louis. A long war between France and England ensued.

Louis VIII (1187–1226), king of France (1223–26). He invaded England (1216) at the invitation of barons opposing King John but was defeated at Lincoln (1217) and returned to France. He then successfully launched a crusade against the Albigensians and broke their power in Avignon. *See also* Albigenses. △1096.

Louis IX or **Saint Louis** (1214–70), king of France (1226–70), canonized in 1297. Louis was guided throughout much of his career by his mother, Blanche of Castile, who served as his regent during his youth (1226–36) and during his first absence from France (1248–52). Recovery from a serious illness prompted Louis to go on the Sixth Crusade in 1248–54. Unsuccessful, captured, and ransomed, he returned after six years' absence. In 1270 he undertook another crusade and died of fever at Tunis.

Throughout his reign Louis worked for peace among Christian nations. In the Treaty of Paris (1259) he improved relations with England when he recognized Henry III as duke of Aquitaine. An exemplary medieval Christian, pious and chivalric, he supported the pope and arbitrated international disputes. Early in his reign he successfully defended his throne from usurpations of power by feudal lords. In order to discourage private warfare among his nobles, he reformed the administration of justice. The court of judicial officers met as a separate body, the Parliament of Paris, to consider feudal and royal rights and obligations. Subjects were allowed to appeal decisions of their lords to this royal body. △1084, 1096.

Louis X or **Louis the Stubborn** (1289–1316), king of France (1314–16). Son of Philip IV and Joan of Navarre, he dismissed his father's unpopular financial advisors and tried to raise money for a proposed campaign in Flanders by selling charters of privileges to clergy and dissident nobles. In 1315–16 he held the first representative assemblies in France, summoning them to approve royal taxes.

Louis XI (1423–83), king of France (1461–83), noted for enlarging its borders. He was involved in a nobles' plot to overthrow his father, Charles VII; confined (1447–56) to Dauphiné in southern France; and exiled to The Netherlands in 1456. In 1461 he took the throne and vigorously suppressed, as had his father, the rebellions of the nobles. He devoted most of his reign to struggles against Charles the Bold of Burgundy. These struggles were complicated by his nobles' frequent coöperation with Charles. Louis pursued a flexible policy aimed at peace with England, war with Burgundy, and the consolidation of his power at home. In 1482 he defeated Charles the Bold's daughter Mary of Burgundy, and the Treaty of Arras gave Burgundy to France. During his reign southern provinces also were added to France. He thus left his nation larger and more powerful. △1096.

Louis XII (1462–1515), king of France (1498–1515). He was a popular but inept ruler. During the reign of his cousin Charles VIII (1483–98), Louis led an unsuccessful noblemen's revolt. He was imprisoned but later restored to favor and fought for Charles in Italy (1494). He had his first marriage annulled so as to marry (1499) Anne of Britanny (Charles' widow) and thereby keep Britanny a part of France. His foreign wars were unsuccessful. Only briefly did he make good his claim to the duchy of Milan. Successful in dividing Naples with Ferdinand of Aragon, he lost it in a subsequent war (1503) with him. His subjects approved his administration of justice, low taxes, and support of the lower classes. His third wife (1514) was Mary Tudor, sister of Henry VIII of England.

Louis XIII (1601–43), king of France (1601–43), son of Henry IV and Marie de Médicis. He forcibly ended his mother's regency, had her Italian lover murdered, and exiled her to Blois. Increasingly however, he came to rely on her advisor, Cardinal de Richelieu. Both Louis and Richelieu favored strong royal authority, opposition to the Spanish and Austrian Hapsburgs, and strategic alliance with Protestant opponents of the Spanish, both in and out of France.

When Marie de Médicis attempted to oust Richelieu, Louis refused and exiled his mother. In 1635 he declared war on Spain and showed great courage in defending Paris against attack. His wife, Anne of Austria, whom he disdained, unexpectedly bore his child, the future Louis XIV, in 1638 after 20 years of childless marriage.

Louis XIV (1638–1715), king of France, (1643–1715) known as the "Sun King" and celebrated as an absolute monarch. So unexpected was his birth, his parents having been childless for 20 years, that he was called "the gift of God." His father, Louis XIII, died when he was four. During his minority Cardinal Jules Mazarin was minister of state, dealing with such matters as the revolt of the Fronde (1648–53). In 1661 Louis assumed the throne, determined to rule and overcome any weaknesses in French central authority. He entrusted finances and the elaboration of mercantile economic policy to Jean Colbert. More to his personal interest was the army, which François Michel Le Tellier had all but created afresh for Louis' purposes.

In 1667 and 1672 Louis warred in The Netherlands for added territory; during 1683–84 he was laying new claims in The Netherlands, Alsace, and Genoa. The War of the League of Augsburg (1688–97) created German enmity and little gain. His enemies—England, The Netherlands, the Holy Roman Empire—in the War of the Spanish Succession (1701–14) forced him to separate the crowns of France and Spain for his future heirs. △1164, 1170.

Louis XV (1710–74), king of France (1715–74). He became king at the age of five, succeeding his great-grandfather, Louis XIV. Cardinal Fleury served as his educator and advisor for almost 20 years and Guillaume Dubois was France's administrator during Louis' minority (1715–23). When Fleury died (1743), Louis XV took personal charge, with unfortunate consequences. Bored by the court life he inherited from Louis XIV, he was equally bored by the daily details of government administration. Court intrigues, unpopular and offensive to the clergy, usually involved his many mistresses, notably the duchess of Chateauroux, Mme. de Pompadour, and Mme. du Barry.

The Seven Years War (1756–63) brought France the loss of much of her colonial empire and virtual bankruptcy. Louis attempted to reform the parlements (1771) in order to tax the aristocracy. The new Maupeou parlements, named for his chancellor, represented his attempt to diminish aristocratic privilege, but Louis XVI restored the old parlements. In general, his reign was marked by disasters—financial, military, and political.

Louis XVI (1754–93), king of France (1774–92). He inherited a crown already unpopular with major elements of France and urgently in need of money. A series of ministers, Turgot, Jacques Necker, Charles de Calonne, unsuccessfully attempted to force the aristocracy to pay its share of taxes. The need for money became acute after French participation in the American Revolution (1778–1783).

When Louis summoned the Estates General (1789), he reverted to a method of raising taxes used infrequently since Louis X, and one that admitted others besides the king to share his power. The aristocrats quickly lost control to the Third Estate, middle-class members who constituted themselves as the National Assembly. Louis increasingly isolated himself from their reforming spirit, especially as events became more violent. After the fall of the Bastille (July 1789), a Paris mob brought Louis back to Paris from Versailles (October 1789). In 1791 he attempted to flee France with his wife, Marie Antoinette, and family. Brought back by the army, he agreed to support the Constitution of 1791 but intrigued with aristocrats, émigrés, and Austria against the new government. War fever and suspicion of his treason led to his imprisonment, abolition of the monarchy and establishment of a republic (1792). He was guillotined in 1793. *See also* Estates General; French Revolution.

Louis XVII (1785–95), second son of King Louis XVI of France and Marie Antoinette. Upon the guillotining of his father (1793), Young Louis was considered by royalist émigrés the next king of France. (His elder brother had died in 1789). He was first confined with his family but was later separated from them, and, according to accounts, put into solitary confinement and harshly treated. He died in prison.

Louis XVIII (1755–1824), Bourbon king of France (1814–24) restored to the throne after the end of Napoleon's empire. The younger brother of Louis XVI, he spent the years 1791–1814 in exile wherever the fortunes of Napoleonic wars allowed him: England, Verona, Sweden, Belgium. Restored to the throne by the Charter of 1814, he reluctantly accepted constitutional limitations of his power. He was deeply conservative and supported government censorship and clerical control of education. △1230.

Louis II, called **the German** (804?–876), king of Germany (843–876); one of the rebellious sons of Emperor Louis I. His brother Lothair became emperor (an empty title), and Louis and another brother, Charles, forced him to divide the empire three ways. Louis received the lands extending from the Rhine to the eastern frontier of the empire, essentially those that later formed Germany. Regarded as the founder of the German kingdom.

Louis III, called **the Child** (893–911), last Carolingian king of the Germans, ruled from 899 during the invasion of the Hungarians. Guided by the Archbishop Hatto, he died before he could become emperor.

Louis IV (1287?–1347), called "the Bavarian," of the Wittelsbach family, duke of Bavaria (1294–1347); king of Germany and Holy Roman emperor (1314–47; crowned 1328). Denied confirmation of his kingship by the papacy, Louis was excommunicated but electoral princes made him emperor nonetheless, which seriously weakened papal power in imperial elections. He was deposed by Pope Clement VI in 1346 but fought against his successor, Charles.

Louis I (1326–82), king of Hungary (1342–82) and Poland (1370–82), called "the Great." The son of Charles I, Louis was appointed king of Poland by Casimir III. Though the union of the two countries was not a success (Louis ruled Poland through regents), Louis, after a successful struggle with Venice for the Adriatic coast, had control of one of the largest realms in Europe, and Hungarian might was acknowledged throughout the Balkans. He encouraged commerce, industry, and science. In Hungary, he introduced administrative reforms that curbed the power of the nobility, but in Poland he granted the nobles a charter that gave them extensive privileges.

Louis II (1506–26), king of Hungary (1516–26), son and dissolute successor of Ladislas II. In 1521 the Turks captured Belgrade; in 1526 they crushed the Hungarians at the Battle of Mohács in which Louis and 20,000 perished. The Protestant Reformation expanded significantly during his reign.

Louis II (822?–875), king of Italy (844); emperor of the West (855–875); king of Lorraine (872–875); succeeded his father, Emperor Lothair I. He defended his kingdom from the Arabs and enlarged his possessions considerably at the expense of his two brothers, Lothair II and Charles of Provence. He had no male heirs.

Louis I (1838–89), king of Portugal (1861–89). He was the son of Maria II and Ferdinand II and succeeded upon the death of his brother Pedro V. Although his years in office were beset by political conflict, including strong republican pressures, his was generally a progressive reign. He freed the slaves in the colonies. His son Charles I succeeded him.

Louis II, de Bourbon, Prince de Condé (1621–1686), French nobleman and general. An opponent of Jules Mazarin, he led the Fronde revolt (1651–52). When it collapsed, he defected to Spain but was later restored to his French rights and titles. *See also* Fronde.

Louis, Joe (1914–), US boxer, b. Joseph Louis Barrow, Lafayette, Ala. He won the world's heavyweight title from James J. Braddock (1937) in Chicago, Ill, and retired undefeated (1949). He attempted to regain his title in 1950 but lost to Ezzard Charles in New York City. Louis held the title longer than any other heavyweight.

Louis (Bernstein), Morris (1912–62), US painter, b. Baltimore, Md. A painter of abstract and cubist works, he developed his own style through a technique of staining the canvas with thinned paint, aiming for a free expression of color, of which "Tet" (1958) is typical. △1372.

Louisbourg, town in Nova Scotia, Canada, 18mi (29km) SE of Sydney. Fortified 1720–40 by the French to maintain control of entrance to Gulf of St Lawrence; site of fort and its remains are preserved as a national historic park (Fortress of Louisbourg). Founded 1713. Pop. 1,578.

Louisiana, state in the S central United States, on the Gulf of Mexico at the mouth of the Mississippi River.

Land and economy. The state is a level coastal plain. The Mississippi River bisects its S half; the Red and Ouachita rivers are other major rivers. Vast marshes lie along the S coast. Agricultural production is widespread. Commercial fishing in the Gulf of Mexico is important. Major manufacturing is in the S, associated with the extraction of mineral resources. Much of Louisiana's oil is obtained from offshore wells. Water transportation has aided commerce; the Mississippi has long been a route for products of states to the N. New Orleans is one of the nation's leading ports.

People. Louisiana displays a broader range of national influences than most states. The French began settling about 1700, and were followed by Germans. A number of Acadian French deported by the British from Nova Scotia arrived in the 1750s, and Spanish joined the colony a few years later. Americans from other S and E states settled in the N. Slaves were imported for cotton and sugar plantations. French and Spanish influences are strongest in the S. New Orleans is notably cosmopolitan. About 65% of the population lives in urban areas.

Education. There are nearly 30 institutions of higher education. Louisiana State University is supported by the state, which also administers 10 other institutions. Tulane University is the best known of the privately endowed institutions.

History. The Sieur de La Salle claimed the area for France in 1682. By secret treaty, in 1762, France ceded it to Spain, which ceded it back in 1800. France sold it to the United States in the Louisiana Purchase in 1803. The next year the Territory of Orleans, comprising the present state, was organized. On its admission to the Union, it was renamed Louisiana. The Battle of New Orleans, last engagement of the War of 1812, was won by the Americans on Jan. 8, 1815. The state joined the Confederacy in January 1861, and Union troops took New Orleans in 1862 and controlled the Mississippi a year later. Louisiana's economy was wrecked by the Civil War, and postwar reconstruction proceeded more slowly than in much of the South. Industrial growth did not come until the 20th century.

PROFILE

Admitted to Union: April 30, 1812; rank, 18th
US Congressmen: Senate, 2; House of Representatives, 8
Population: 3,643,180 (1970); rank, 20th
Capital: Baton Rouge, 165,963 (1970)
Chief cities: New Orleans, 593,471; Shreveport, 182,064; Baton Rouge
State legislature: Senate, 39; House of Representatives, 105
Area: 48,523sq mi (125,675sq km); rank, 31st
Elevation: Highest, Driskill Mountain, 535ft (163m). Lowest, 5ft (2m) below sea level, at New Orleans
Industries (major products): chemicals, processed foods, petroleum products, paper products, wood products
Agriculture (major products): rice, sugarcane, cattle, sweet potatoes, soybeans, cotton
Minerals (major): petroleum, natural gas, sulfur, salt
State nickname: Pelican State
State motto: "Union, Justice, Confidence"
State bird: brown pelican
State flower: magnolia blossom
State tree: bald cypress

Louisiana Purchase (1803), a transaction involving a large area of land purchased from France by the United States. The 825,000sq mi (2,100,000sq km) of territory, from the Mississippi River to the Rocky Mountains, was bought for $15,000,000. With national security and the control of the Mississippi in mind, President Thomas Jefferson sent James Monroe to France to join Robert Livingston, US minister. The two men negotiated the purchase from Napoleon, who had lost interest in a colonial empire in the New World. The Louisiana Purchase doubled the area of the United States, and 13 states were admitted from the territory.

Louis Napoleon. *See* Napoleon III.

Louis of Nassau (1538–74), count of Nassau-Dietz, Netherlands leader. He was the brother of William the Silent and led the revolt against Spanish rule. When

Lorenzo Lotto: Adoration of the Shepherds (detail)

Lotus

Louis XIV

PLACE D'ARMES
New Orleans, Louisiana: French quarter

the duke of Alva arrived in 1564, Louis and William left the Netherlands to raise a fighting force. Defeated in several battles with the Spaniards, Louis was killed at Mookerheide.

Louis Philippe (1773–1850), king of France (1830–48). The revolution that brought him to power in 1830 was a bourgeois reaction to the aristocratic restoration of the Bourbons, Louis XVIII and Charles X. The revolution that ended his reign in 1848 was a proletarian and middle-class reaction to his own conservatism. He had, for example, refused to extend the right to vote to members of the lower classes. For much of his reign, however, he was a liberal, supporting constitutional restraint on the monarchy and becoming known as the "Citizen King." His chosen title, "Louis Philippe, King of the French," rather than "Philippe VII, King of France," was meant to convey the idea of a limited monarchy. △1248.

Louis XV Style, high period of French Rococo style in furniture and interior design. Rooms had walls set with mirrors in panels, replacing the large painted canvases and murals of the previous century. Decorative motifs included garlands and clusters of flowers and shells, often decorated with gold and silver. Furniture became twisted and ornate. Frequently, Chinese designs were used. △1224.

Louis XVI Style, final period of the French Rococo style, from about 1760 to the Revolution. Reacting to the elaborate Louis XV style, it emphasized the antique classic style. In furniture and interior design, straight lines replaced curved ones. The favorite color scheme was white and gold. In architecture, the return to classicism was marked by a preference for Doric columns. △1224.

Louisville, industrial city and port of entry in NW Kentucky, on the Ohio River; seat of Jefferson co; largest city in Kentucky; est. as military base 1778 by George Rogers Clark, the Virginia legislature officially chartered it 1780 and named it for Louis XVI of France; city developed into an important shipping center by mid-19th century; first major southern city to adopt ordinance against racial housing discrimination (1967). It is host to the famous Kentucky Derby, horse race held annually since 1875 at Churchill Downs; site of Locust Grove Mansion (1790), University of Louisville (1798), Spalding College (1829), Bellarmine College (1950). Industries: whiskey, appliances, synthetic rubber, cigarettes, trucks, trailers, paint. Inc. 1780. Pop. (1970) 361,958.

Lourdes, town in SW France, at foot of Pyrenees on Gave de Pau River; site of Roman Catholic shrine commemorating the appearances of Our Lady of Lourdes to St Bernadette in 1858; pilgrimage center. Pop. 17,939.

Lourenço Marques (Maputo), capital city of the state of Lourenço Marques and of Mozambique, SE Africa; first visited by Antonio do Campo (1502); explored by Portuguese trader Lourenço Marques; linked by rail to South Africa, Swaziland, and Rhodesia; site of University of Mozambique. Industries: coal, footwear, rubber. Inc. 1887. Pop. 383,-775.

Louse, Chewing, louse, ranging from white to reddish-brown to black, found worldwide. It has chewing mouthparts and feeds on feathers, hair, scales, and fatty matter. They do not attack humans. Length: 0.02–0.4in. (0.5–10mm). Order Mallophaga.

Louse, Sucking, flat, white to brown louse found worldwide. It sucks blood from mammals, including humans. Head lice *(Pediculus humanus capitis)* and body lice *(Pediculus humanus corporis)* carry epidemic typhus and transmit skin diseases. Length: 0.08–0.2in (2–5mm). Order Anoplura.

Lousewort. *See* Wood Betony.

Louvre, French art museum, Paris. France's enormous national collection contains art from most ages and countries and is housed in the Louvre Palace, which was built as a 16th-century chateau for Francis I. Francis I began the Louvre collection by commissioning the Italian artists Primaticcio and Andrea del Sarto to make bronze reproductions of famous statues of antiquity. Under Louis XIV, several important art collections, especially of Italian works, were acquired. During this period, French artists were given royal patronage and so produced many paintings for the Louvre collection. In 1848 the collection became the property of the state.

Lovebird, small parrot of the Old World, mainly Africa and Madagascar. Often kept in cages, the mates maintain a close relationship. The rosy-faced lovebird *(Agapornis rosericollis)* of S Africa inserts grass under his rump feathers and carries it to the nest.

Lovejoy, Elijah Parish (1802–37), US editor, preacher, and abolitionist, b. Albion, Me. After serving as editor of the St Louis *Times* (1827–32), he studied for the ministry, and edited the Presbyterian weekly, the St Louis *Observer* (1833–36). In 1836 he started an antislavery paper, the *Observer*, in Alton, Ill. Proslavery extremists tarred and feathered him, threw his presses into the Mississippi River, and in 1837 shot and killed him. Lovejoy became a hero of the antislavery cause.

Lovelace, Richard (1618–58), English cavalier poet, best known for his lyrics to "Lucasta." A handsome and courageous man, he supported King Charles I in Parliament (1642); was imprisoned, fled to France, and fought as a mercenary (1643–46); returned home and was again imprisoned (1648–49); and died in poverty.

Lovell, Bernard. △46.

Love's Labour's Lost (*c.* 1588), 5-act comedy by William Shakespeare. One of his earliest plays, it is a satire on literary affectations. Ferdinand, king of Navarre, and his 3 attendants decide to form a monastic academy of study. When the princess of France and her 3 ladies arrive he will not let them in the palace but has pavilions placed for them in the park. At a masque, the ladies exchange tokens and costumes so the lords woo the wrong ladies. When the lords ask for the ladies in marriage, the ladies impose a year's penance on them, after which the marriages can take place. The gentlemen grudgingly agree—for the present "love's labour's lost." The first recorded performance was at Queen Elizabeth's court in 1597.

Low, or depression, an area of low pressure, often shown on weather maps, associated in the Northern Hemisphere with counterclockwise, inward, cyclonic atmospheric circulation. *See also* High; Weather Maps. △214, 218.

Low Countries. △1158, 1168.

Lowell, Amy (1874–1925), US poet and critic, b. Brookline, Mass. A member of the prominent Lowell family, which included several poets, she decided at the age of 28 to become a poet herself and spent the next eight years studying form and technique. She originated polyphonic prose, a prose form that makes use of poetic technique. She assumed leadership of the Imagist movement in the 1910s. Her ability to recreate physical perception in her poems was probably her outstanding quality. Her volumes of poetry include *Men, Women, and Ghosts* (1916) and *What's O'Clock?* (1925; Pulitzer Prize 1926). *See also* Imagism.

Lowell, Francis Cabot (1775–1817), US textile pioneer, b. Newburyport, Mass. After studying the textile factories in England, Lowell returned to the United States and set up in Waltham, Mass., the first complete cotton spinning and weaving mill in the United States (1812–14). A group of investors known as the Boston Associates were associated with his venture, which was very successful during the War of 1812. The Waltham System influenced the development of US factories. When cheaper British textiles became available again, Lowell lobbied for protection of his industry, and the tariff of 1816 was passed. Lowell, Mass., a textile city, was named for him.

Lowell, James Russell (1819–91), US poet, author, and editor, b. Cambridge, Mass. Under the influence of his first wife, Maria White, he wrote some of his best poetry, and also became involved in the abolitionist movement. He gained acclaim for *Poems* (1844), *A Fable for Critics* (1848), the first series of *Biglow Papers* (1848), and *The Vision of Sir Launfal* (1848). In 1855 he succeeded Henry Wadsworth Longfellow as professor of modern languages at Harvard, where he taught until 1876. Much of his later work was literary criticism. He was the first editor of *Atlantic Monthly* (1857–61) and from 1864–72 was editor of *North American Review*. During 1877–80 he served as US minister to Spain and during 1880–85 was minister to England.

Lowell, Percival (1855–1916), US astronomer, b. Boston, famous for his prediction of the existence of the planet Pluto and his initiation of the search that ended in its discovery 14 years after his death. He founded Lowell Observatory at Flagstaff, Ariz., with his own money to study the "canals" of Mars, which he thought to be the traces of a once flourishing civilization. In 1905 he organized a systematic search for Planet X, an unseen planet beyond Neptune, now called Pluto. His astronomical works include *Mars and Its Canals* (1906), *The Evolution of Worlds* (1909), and *The Genesis of the Planets* (1916). △44, 68.

Lowell, Robert (1917–), US poet, b. Boston. A member of the prominent Lowell family, his works are very personal. Among his volumes are *Land of Unlikeness* (1944), *Lord Weary's Castle* (1946; Pulitzer Prize, 1947), *The Mills of the Kavanaughs* (1951), *For the Union Dead* (1964), and *Notebook 1967–68* (1969). *Life Studies* (1959), which won a National Book Award, includes both prose and poetry about his family life. A conscientious objector in World War II, he was jailed for his beliefs.

Lowell, city in NE Massachusetts, at confluence of Merrimack and Concord rivers, 28mi (45km) NW of Boston; seat of Middlesex co; site of huge textile mills (built 1820 at Pawtucket Falls) to utilize power loom designed by Francis Cabot Lowell, and Lowell Technological Institute (1895); birthplace of artist James Whistler (1834), whose home is a museum. Industries: plastics, chemicals, rubber products, electronic equipment. Founded 1653 as part of Chelmsford; inc. as city 1836. Pop. (1970) 94,239.

Lower California. *See* Baja California.

Lower Canada, former name of Quebec province (1791–1841). The name was changed to Canada East in 1841 and to Quebec in 1867.

Low Temperature Physics. *See* Cryogenics.

Loyalists, colonists remaining loyal to England during the Revolutionary War, also called Tories. They were mostly landholders, clergy (Anglicans), and office holders under British authority. The largest concentration of loyalists were in New York, Pennsylvania, the Carolinas, and Georgia. Many were eventually forced from the United States and returned to England or settled in Canada.

Loyalists, in the Spanish Civil War, the faction that supported the Second Republic; they were also known as republicans. They were opposed—and eventually defeated—by the Nationalists, or insurgents.

Loyang (Luoyang, or Lo-yang), city in E central China, on Lo River; temporary capital of China in 1932; nearby are the Lungmen Caves, containing Buddhist sculpture from T'ang period (618–906). Industries: tractors, mining machinery, coal mining, food processing, textiles. Pop. 500,000.

Loyola, Saint Ignatius of (1491–1556), Spanish religious leader who founded the Jesuits. An aristocrat, he was a warrior in his youth. While recovering from war wounds, he determined to be a knight in the service of God. His *Spiritual Exercises* (1522) gave ways to train body and soul for spiritual combat. After seven years study at the University of Paris, Ignatius and six companions went to Rome and asked permission from Pope Paul III to found an order to carry on spiritual and charitable works. The pope approved this plan, and in 1541 Ignatius became head of the Society of Jesus, or Jesuits. *See also* Jesuits. △1154, 1164.

LPG (Liquefied Petroleum Gas), a liquefied gas of light hydrocarbons, principally propane and butane, produced in the distillation of crude oil and the refining of natural gas. It is used as a fuel and raw material in chemical industries and as bottled gas for home heating and cooking.

LP Records. △1800.

LSD (lysergic acid diethylamide, or lysergide), a very potent synthetic hallucinogenic drug derived from lysergic acid. It has had limited use in the study and treatment of psychiatric disorders. Besides producing hallucinations and bizarre behavior, it has been reported to cause psychosis and chromosomal damage. △730, 1560.

Luanda (São Paulo de Luanda), seaport city in NW Angola, on Baja do Bengo; capital of Angola, and Luanda district. Economy of city was historically based on slave trade with the New World, under which it prospered until the abolition of slavery in the 19th century. Luanda became an important modern manufacturing and trade center. Industries: textiles, building materials, machinery, oil products, agricultural products. Founded 1576 by Portuguese. Pop. 475,-328.

Luang Prabang (Louang Prabang), port town in N Laos, on the Mekong River; capital of Luang Prabang prov.; historic royal capital; site of pagoda, residence of king of Laos; distribution center for teak, fish, and rubber. Pop. 25,000.

Lubbock, city in NW Texas, 250mi (403km) W of Fort Worth; seat of Lubbock co; site of Texas Technological College (1923), and Lubbock Christian University (1957); major cotton market. Industries: farm equipment, mobile homes, pumps, cottonseed oil. Founded 1891; inc. as city 1907. Pop. (1970) 149,-101.

Lübeck, seaport city in NE West Germany, on Trave River near its mouth on Baltic Sea. A free imperial city 1226, it was captured by French 1806; autonomy restored 1815 when it joined the North German Confederation; made part of Schleswig-Holstein 1937; site of 13th–15th-century city hall, 14th-century churches of St Jacob and St Catherine, Hospital and Church of Holy Ghost (13th century); all restored after suffering heavy damage in WWII. Industries: foundries, textiles, machine shops, shipyards. Founded 12th century; burned in 1138; reest. 1143. Pop. 242,-855.

Lublin, city in SE Poland, approx. 95mi (153km) SE of Warsaw; capital of Lublin prov.; city grew around a 12th-century fortification built for protection against Tartar invaders, and developed as a trade center along SE route to Ukraine; site of German WWII concentration camp, Majdanek; state university, Roman Catholic university. Industries: heavy machinery, food processing, tobacco products. Pop. 236,000.

Lubricant, oil, grease, graphite, or other substances introduced between moving parts to reduce friction and dissipate heat. Vegetable oils and animal fats and oils have been used from ancient times but most lubricants are now derived from petroleum. Solid lubricants are usually graphite or molybdenum disulfide and synthetic silicones are used where high temperatures are involved. △1572.

Lubumbashi, formerly Elisabethville, city in SE Zaïre, near Zambia border; capital of Shaba prov.; 2nd-largest city in Zaïre; capital of independent state of Katanga (now Shaba) 1960–63; site of a university (1955). Industries: copper smelting, textiles, food products, beverages, bricks. Founded 1910. Pop. 334,-857.

Lucan(us), Marcus Annaeus (39–65), Roman poet. A nephew of the younger Seneca, he was born in Spain. His *Bellum Civile* or *Pharsalia* is an epic on the civil war between Caesar and Pompey. It is admired more for its rhetoric than for its poetry. He was forced to kill himself after being implicated in a plot against Nero. △1028.

Lucca, city in N central Italy, 10mi (16km) NE of Pisa; capital of Lucca prov. Ancient town was settled prior 180 BC; it was a major Tuscan town when it was sold to Florence 1341; made independent republic 15th century until 1805, when it was given to Napoleon; made part of Tuscany 1847, and Italy 1860; site of cathedral of San Martino (11th–14th centuries), church of San Frediano (begun 6th century), Roman remains. Industries: textiles, paper, food products. Pop. 91,401.

Luce, Clare Boothe (1903–), US author, b. New York City. She was an editor of *Vanity Fair* magazine (1930–34), a journalist, and foreign correspondent. In 1935 she married publisher Henry Luce. She wrote the plays *The Women* (1937) and *Kiss the Boys Goodbye* (1938), and her books include *Stuffed Shirts* (1933). She served as a Republican from Connecticut in the House (1943–47), and was ambassador to Italy (1953–57). There was a bitter fight in the Senate following her appointment (1959) by Pres. Dwight D. Eisenhower as ambassador to Brazil, and she resigned immediately after her confirmation.

Luce, Henry Robinson (1898–1967), US publisher, b. China. From 1921–22 he was a reporter for the Chicago *Daily News.* In 1923 along with Briton Hadden he founded *Time,* a weekly news magazine. He also founded *Life* magazine in 1936, *Fortune* in 1930, and *Sports Illustrated* in 1954. An influential publisher, he and his wife Clare Boothe Luce were considered a force in US politics.

Lucerne. *See* Alfalfa.

Lucerne (Luzern), city in central Switzerland, 25mi (40km) SSW of Zurich on Lake of Lucerne; capital of Lucerne canton; joined Swiss Confederation 1332; site of several covered bridges decorated with paintings, monument for Lion of Lucerne, Glacier Garden, 15th-century town hall, 17th-century historical museum, 17th-century Baroque Jesuit church, 8th-century monastery. Industries: sewing machines, electrical apparatus, beer, metal products, aluminumware, elevators, printing. Pop. 69,879.

Lucerne (Luzern), lake in central Switzerland, bordering on Lucerne, Uri, Schwyz, Unterwalden cantons. The lake is surrounded by mountains crossed by Reuss River. Depth: 702ft (214m). Length: 23mi (37km). Width: .5–2mi (.8–3km).

Lucian (*c.* AD 120–180), Greek satirist, born in Samosata on the Upper Euphrates. Lucian is best known as the contributor of the satiric dialogue to Greek literature. He made use of this unique form of dialogue in some 80 works. His writing was witty, and drew attention to the foibles of contemporary life and manners. Religion and philosophy were among Lucian's favorite targets.

Lucilius, Gaius (*c.* 180–101 BC), earliest Latin satirist. Of good family and education, he was the friend of scholarly Greeks and knew Scipio well. Living mostly in Rome, his works were posthumously collected in an edition of 30 books. Only fragments survive. *See also* Satire, Roman. △1028.

Lucite, a trademarked vinyl plastic, also called plexiglass, made from an acrylic resin that consists of polymerized methyl-methacrylate. Clear and hard, it is used for costume jewelry, dentures, aquariums, containers, and novelties.

Lucknow, city in N India, on the Gomati River; capital of Uttar Pradesh state. It served as the capital of kingdom of Oudh 1775–1856, then of Oudh prov. 1856–77, and the United Provinces 1877; during one of the Sepoy Mutiny conflicts, the British were forced to abandon their fortress after a long siege (June-November 1857); it was retaken by British 1858; served as a center for the independent Pakistan movement (1942–47); site of many ancient buildings, notably the Pearl Palace, Imambara mausoleum, unfinished mosque and mausoleum of Mohammed Ali Shah; university (1921). Industries: railroad shops, paper, metal, distilling, printing, handcrafts. Pop. 783,718.

Lucretius, or Titus Lucretius Carus, (early half of 1st century BC), Latin poet and philosopher. According to Jerome, Lucretius was born in 94 BC, was sometimes mad and when lucid wrote books that were later corrected by Cicero, and killed himself in 51 or 50 BC. Little else is known of him apart from his one poem, *De Rerum Natura,* or *On the Nature of Things,* a rendering of the atomic theory of Lucretius' master, Epicurus. △1028, 1184.

Lucullus, Lucius Licinius (*c.* 115–56 BC), Roman military commander, served in various campaigns under Sulla before he became consul in 74. He then gained control of Roman lands in Asia, where he defeated Mithridates (74–71) and took Armenia (69). For his skillful economic reforms in his territories, which curtailed certain Romans' profits, he earned powerful enemies, and he was replaced by Pompey in 66.

Lüda. *See* Lu-ta.

Luddites, English textile workers who resisted mechanization of their industry (1811–16). Taking their name from a probably mythical Ned Ludd, they systematically wrecked machinery, to which they attributed low wages and unemployment. They were severely repressed.

Ludlow, Roger (1590–1664?), one of the founders of Connecticut, b. England. He was an Oxford lawyer and assistant of the Massachusetts Bay Company. He helped found Dorchester, Mass., and served (1634) as deputy governor of Massachusetts. He presided (1636) at Windsor over the first Connecticut court and also finished the state's first codification of laws, known as Ludlow's Code or the Code of 1650. He returned to England in 1654.

Ludovisi Throne. △1000.

Luftwaffe, German air force. Built up during the 1930s by the Hitler government, it was the most powerful air force in Europe at the beginning of World War II. It inflicted heavy damage on England during the Battle of Britain (1940–41).

Lugano, town in SE central Switzerland, on N shore of Lake Lugano, at mouth of Cassarate River. Town was taken from duke of Milan by Swiss Confederation 1512; site of 19th-century town hall, museum, 13th-century church of San Lorenzo, 15th-century church of Santa Maria; health resort, episcopal see. Industries: banking, chocolate, leather, metal, printing, flour, tourism. Pop. 22,280.

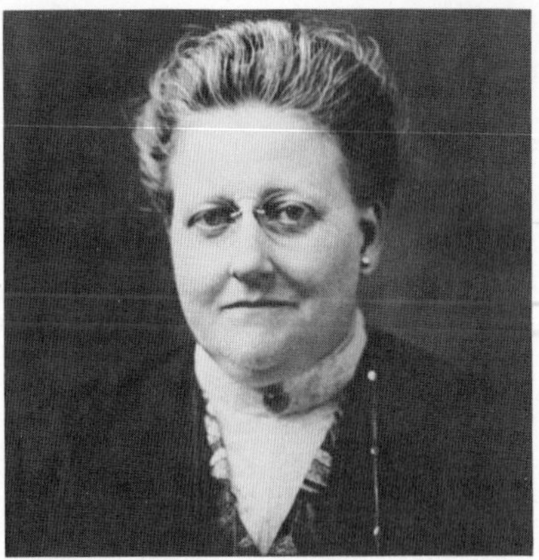

Amy Lowell

Robert Lowell

Luang Prabang, Laos

Lucerne, Switzerland

Lugano, Lake of, lake in S Switzerland and N Italy, between lakes Maggiore and Como; narrow irregular shape; drained by Tresa River. Area: 19sq mi (49sq km). Depth: 945ft (288m).

Lugansk (Voroshilovgrad), city in the Ukrainian republic, USSR, in the Donets Basin, on Lugan River, 420mi (676km) ESE of Kiev; capital of Voroshilovgrad oblast; occupied by Germans in WWII; site of agricultural and teachers' colleges and a metalworking school. Industries: steel-pipe rolling, coal mining machinery, enameling, meat packing, food, textiles. Est. *c.* 1795. Pop. 382,000.

Luitprand. *See* Liutprand.

Luke, apostle of Jesus. He was the author of one of the four gospels and the *Acts of the Apostles* of the New Testament. Luke, a physician and companion of the apostle Paul, wrote as an eyewitness of the life of Jesus and, when necessary, drew on other references then current. His gospel stresses the human and divine natures of Jesus and the concept of Christianity as a universal brotherhood.

Lully, Jean Baptiste (1632–87), French composer and court conductor for Louis XIV, b. Italy. His music is mainly ballets and operas. His operas, the style of which dominated French opera until the late 18th century, include *Alceste* (1674), *Amadis de Gaule* (1684), and *Armide et Renaud* (1686). △1174, 1196, 1244.

Lulu. △1256.

Luluabourg. *See* Kananga.

Lumbago, pain in the lower back (lumbar region). △720.

Lumber, timber or logs after being prepared for market. Logs are transported from the forest, stored in water or a storage yard. Each log then enters the sawmill on a chain conveyor and is brought to a head saw (a bank saw, gang saw, or circular saw). Logs are then broken down (turned into boards of various thicknesses); resawed (cut into thinner boards); ripped (the bark removed from edges of the boards); and crosscut (the ends squared and defects removed). After production, lumber may be dipped into a chemical preservative, measured and graded, and piled to dry in open air or in kilns. Lumber of large dimension, suitable for heavy construction, is called timber. △1610.

Lumen, unit of luminous flux in the SI system of units, defined as the amount of light emitted per second in a solid angle of one steradian from a small source of intensity equal to one candela.

Luminosity, in astronomy, the amount of radiation emitted by a star or other celestial body. Magnitude is the measure of luminosity. The brighter the object the lower the magnitude number assigned. In modern usage one magnitude is defined as a difference in brightness of 2.512 times. Thus, a difference of five magnitudes corresponds to a ratio of 100 to 1. The sun's apparent magnitude is -26.7; the faintest stars visible through the largest telescopes are of apparent magnitude 20. △112.

Luminous Prawn. △490.

Lumpfish, bony cold water marine fish found on Atlantic coasts. A bottom-dwelling fish, it has a globose body and a modified sucking disk formed by pelvic fins under and behind the head. Length: 2ft (61cm); weight: 20lb (9.lkg). Family Cyclopteridae; species *Cyclopterus lumpus*. *See also* Osteichthyes.

Lumumba, Patrice Emergy (1925–61), Congolese statesman. He created and led the Congolese National Movement and helped form an independent Republic of the Congo (now Zaïre) in 1960. He served as minister of defense and prime minister and was imprisoned in a power struggle with President Kasavubu and Colonel Mobutu. His execution shortly thereafter led to international protests.

Luna Moth, large North American moth of the giant silkworm family. Its 4in (10cm) wings are bright green with a purplish-brown band on the leading edge of the front wings and a large dark spot near the center of each hind wing. Species *Actias luna*. *See also* Moth.

Lunar Apennines. △52.

Lunar Base. △146.

Lunar Eclipse. *See* Eclipse, Lunar.

Lunar Mare. △56–60.

Lunar Module. △54, 1724.

Lunar Phases. △52.

Lunar Roving Vehicle (LRV). △54, 1724.

Lund, city in SW Sweden; became Roman Catholic archepiscopal see for Scandinavia 1103–04; site of University of Lund (1668), museum of folk customs, Romanesque cathedral. Industries: clothing, paper, printing, packaging materials, textiles. Pop. 54,410.

Lunda, a central African Bantu people who developed two powerful kingdoms through trade and conquest in the centuries before European domination. They follow complex and varying systems of inheritance and political structure.

Lungfish, or dipnoi, long, eellike bony fish found in shallow freshwater in Africa, South America, and Australia. A living fossil of a group dominant 300,000,000 years ago, it has air bladders and gulps air at the water surface. During the dry season, it curls up in mud cocoon and breathes air (except for Australian species). Family Lepidesirendiae; Family Ceratodontidae; Australian *Neoçeratodus forsteri;* species African *Protopterus aethipicus,* South American *Lepidosiren paradoxa*. *See also* Choanichthyes; Osteichthyes. △510, 566.

Lungs, organs of the respiratory system in which the exchange of gases between air and blood takes place. The lungs are located on either side of the heart and are covered by a double-layer sheet of connective tissue called pleura. Between the layers is the fluid-containing pleural cavity that cushions the lungs and prevents friction. The lungs themselves are filled with air sacs from the walls of which protrude alveoli. Alveoli are one cell thick and contain networks of fine capillaries. Gaseous exchange takes place between the blood-containing capillaries and the oxygen-containing alveoli walls. The freshly oxygenated blood then carries oxygen to all parts of the body. *See also* Respiratory System. △692.

Lungwort. △434.

Lunik. △54, 142.

Luoyang. *See* Loyang.

Lupercalia, ancient Roman festival. It was celebrated by the Luperci (priests) on February 15.

Lupine, annual and perennial plants and subshrubs native to the Mediterranean region, North America, and South America. They have oblong leaves, showy flowers of white, rose, yellow, or blue, and pods containing beanlike seeds. Height: to 8ft (2.4m). Family Leguminosae; genus *Lupinus*.

Lupus Erythematosus, an inflammatory disease of unknown cause involving the skin or generalized to the connective tissue of the body (systemic form). The skin lesions are red patches covered with scales, often on the cheeks and nose and forming a butterfly pattern. The systemic form varies in severity, is four times more common in women than in men, and may involve one or more organs in addition to the skin. Symptoms depend on the organ involved, but arthritis, weight loss, fatigue, fever, and anemia are common. Remissions and flareups are characteristic.

Lupus Vulgaris, tuberculosis of the skin, in which brownish nodules and ulcers are formed, and scarring is severe.

Luria, Alexander. △670.

Luria, Salvador E(dward) (1912–), US molecular biologist, b. Italy. He shared the 1969 Nobel Prize in physiology or medicine for contributing to the knowledge of the growth, replication, and mutation of bacterial viruses.

Luristan (Lorestan), governorate in W Iran, in region of Zagros Mts; capital is Khorramabad; mountainous petroleum-producing region; noted for the Luristan bronzes, metal works found in 1930s, thought to have been made by Scythian, Cimerian, or Median craftsmen as early as 8th century BC. Products: oil, wool, cattle. Area: 12,116sq mi (31,380sq km). Pop. 686,307.

Lusaka, capital city of Zambia, S central Africa; site of the University of Zambia (1965) and Hodgson Technical College. Industries: foodstuffs, beverages, clothing, cement. Founded by Europeans 1905. Pop. 176,000.

Lusitania, Roman province on the Iberian peninsula, comprising modern Portugal and parts of western Spain. It took its name from the Lusitani, a warlike tribe that bitterly fought Roman conquest of their lands. Their great leader was Viriatus, who showed great military and diplomatic talents in opposing the Romans until he was assassinated, probably with Roman collusion, in 139 BC. Traditionally, the Portuguese have looked upon themselves as descendents of the Lusitani. △1304.

Lusitania Sinking (May 7, 1915), attack by a German submarine in World War I on the British passenger ship *Lusitania*. It cost 128 American lives and followed the torpedoing of the tanker *Gulflight* and British liner *Falaba*. The United States protested the sinking of the British liner and Germany pledged to sink passenger ships only after warning.

Lu-ta (Lüda), municipality in China comprising Port Arthur (Lüshun) and Dairen (Talien), on Liaotung peninsula; site of many naval facilities, including Port Arthur Naval Base District; commercial, industrial and shipping center. Pop. 4,000,000.

Lute, stringed musical instrument with fretted fingerboard, pear-shaped back, and head with pegs for tuning. It was popular in 16th-century Europe for solos and ensembles. Early lute compositions survive today in Baroque revival, also in some by Bach and Handel. △1132.

Luteotropic Hormone. *See* Prolactin.

Lutetium or **Lutecium,** metallic element (symbol Lu) of the Lanthanide group, first isolated in 1907 from element ytterbium. Chief ore is monazite (phosphate). The element has no commercial uses. Properties: at. no. 71; at. wt. 174.97; sp gr 9.835 (25°C); melt. pt. 3,013°F (1656°C); boil. pt. 5999°F (3315°C); most common isotope Lu^{175} (97.41%). *See also* Lanthanide Elements.

Luther, Martin (1483–1546), German leader of the Protestant Reformation and founder of Lutheranism. He left the study of law in 1505 to become an Augustinian monk and later became a priest and a professor of theology. He agonized over the problem of salvation, finally deciding that it was won not by good works but was a free gift of God's grace. Luther's beliefs made him object to the sale of indulgences (which remitted penalties for sin) by the Roman Catholic Church, and in 1517 he posted his 95 Theses in Wittenberg. This started a quarrel between Luther and church leaders, including the pope. Luther decided that the Bible was the true source of authority and renounced obedience to Rome. He maintained his stand in debates with Johann Eck and at the Diet of Worms (1521). For this he was excommunicated, but strong German princes supported him, and he gained followers among churchmen and the people. Thus the Protestant Reformation began in Germany. Luther wrote hymns, catechisms, and numerous theological treatises and translated the New Testament into German. He married a former nun, Katharina von Bora, in 1525 and had six children. *See also* Lutheranism. △1152.

Lutheranism, the doctrines and the church that grew out of the teaching of Martin Luther. Luther hoped to reform the church rather than start a new one, but his doctrines led him to a complete break with the Roman Catholic Church. He believed that the Bible was the sole authority in religion and rejected the supremacy of the pope and the powers of the hierarchy of bishops. He held that grace cannot be conferred by the church but is the free gift of God's love. He objected to the Catholic doctrine of transsubstantiation—that, in the Eucharist, the bread and wine are actually transformed into the body and blood of Christ. Instead, Luther believed in the real presence of Christ "in, with, and under" the bread and wine. These and other essentials of Lutheran doctrine were set down in the Augsburg Confessions drawn up by Philipp Melanchthon in 1530. The confessions have ever since been basic documents of the Lutherans. From its start in Germany, Lutheranism spread to Scandinavia and other parts of Europe and around the world. Today the Lutheran Church is the largest Protestant denomination, enrolling about one third of all Protestants. There are large numbers of Lutherans in Germany, the United States, and Scandinavia. The church has no central governing body, and churches in each country have developed their own traditions. In 1947 the Lutheran World Council was formed as a coordinating body. *See also* Luther, Martin. △1152–54.

Luthuli, Albert John Mvumbi (1898–1967), South African civil rights leader. He moved from teaching to politics in response to South African racism. A Zulu chief, he was president (1952–60) of the African National Congress and was repeatedly harassed by the government for his nonviolent protest. He received the Nobel Peace prize in 1960. Although forced underground that same year, he continued to lead nonviolent resistance until his death. He wrote *Let My People Go* (1962).

Luxembourg, independent grand duchy in W Europe, bordered by West Germany (E), France (S), Belgium (N and W). It is ruled by a hereditary sovereign as the head of state and a premier as head of government who is responsible to a unicameral legislature (Chamber of Deputies).

Luxembourg is divided into two topographical sections, the heavily forested and elevated Ardennes plateau (N), and the fertile Bon Pays (S). The SW is part of the rich Luxembourg-Lorraine iron mining area, which makes Luxembourg a major iron and steel producer. The people, strongly Roman Catholic, enjoy one of the highest per capita incomes and one of lowest inflation rates in the world. Along with iron and steel production, the country's industries include chemicals, cement, tanning, textiles, agriculture, wine, slate, tourism, and banking.

Jean, ascending as grand duke in 1964, is the hereditary sovereign and chief of state: Gaston Thorn took office in 1974 as premier. The government runs as a democratic parliament; the Council of Government headed by the premier is responsible to the Chamber of Deputies. All laws and decrees are brought before a 21-member Council of State, advisors appointed by the grand duke for life.

Founded 963 as a fief of the Holy Roman Empire, it was made a duchy by John of Luxembourg, king of Bohemia, in 1354. After occupation by France (1684–97), Spain (1714), and Austria (1714), it was formally ceded to France by the Treaty of Campo Formio (1797). It was made a grand duchy (1815), and at the same time it joined the German Confederation (with its fortress garrisoned by Prussians). Luxembourg's neutrality was confirmed by London Conference 1867; during WWI and WWII, its neutrality was violated by German occupation forcing Grand Duchess Charlotte to establish a government-in-exile in London in WWII. When liberated by Allied troops, its policy of neutrality was abolished, and military service was initiated (abolished 1967). Luxembourg became a member of the United Nations (1946) and NATO (1948). Luxembourg signed a treaty with Belgium and Netherlands for full economic union, and the Benelux Economic Union became effective 1960.

PROFILE

Official name: Grand Duchy of Luxembourg
Area: 999sq mi (2,587sq km)
Population: 300,000
Chief cities: Luxembourg (capital); Esch-sur-Alzette; Dudelange
Religion: Roman Catholic
Language: Letzeburgisch, French, German
Monetary unit: Luxembourg franc
Gross national product: $1,900,000,000

Luxembourg, city in S Luxembourg, 25mi (40km) NE of Esch-sur-Alzette at the confluence of the Alzette and Pétrusse rivers; capital of the Grand Duchy of Luxembourg. The walled town developed around a 10th-century castle and grew to be one of Europe's strongest fortifications; the town was demilitarized and the fort dismantled by the Treaty of London (1867); held by Germany during both world wars. It is the site of Cathedral of Notre Dame (16th century), town hall (19th century), ducal palace (16th century); commercial, administrative, and cultural center. Industries: iron and steel, furniture, leather products, machinery, textiles, beer, tourism, food processing. Founded 10th century as Lützelburg. Pop. 77,500.

Luxemburg, Rosa (1870–1919), German socialist leader, b. Poland. She became a German citizen through marriage and after 1898 was a leader of the Social Democratic party. With Karl Liebknecht she founded the Spartacus (later Communist) party during World War I. She was arrested for her part in the Spartacist uprising in Berlin (January 1919) and was murdered while being taken to prison. △1326.

Luxor (Al Uqsor), city in Egypt, on E bank of Nile River: Partially occupies site of the ancient city of Thebes; site of Temple of Luxor, built by Amenhotep III, Temple of Karnak, and royal cemeteries. A major winter resort area, tourism is main industry. Pop. 84,-600.

Luzern. *See* Lucerne.

Luzon, largest island of the Philippines, occupying the N part of the group. Island is irregularly shaped with many natural harbors, and the principal land mass to N has three mountain ranges, all running N to S: Sierra Madre (E), Cordillera Central, and the Zambales Mts (W). Manila, largest city of the Philippines, Quezon City, the capital, and Malabon are grouped together on Manila Bay, just NW of the Philippines' largest lake, Laguna de Bay. The Cagayan is Luzon's longest river, flowing 200mi (322km) N from central Luzon to the Philippine Sea. As well as the most populous of the islands, it is the chief producer of agricultural and industrial products, including rice, coconuts, sugar, coffee, tobacco, abacá, fish, ships, lumber, textiles, chemicals, gold, copper, and chromite. Area: 40,420sq mi (104,688sq km). Highest peak is Mt Pulog, 9,606ft (2,930m). Pop. 16,669,724.

Luzon Bleeding Heart. △538.

Lvov, (Prince) Georgi Yevgenievich (1861–1925), Russian political figure, premier of the provisional government (March-July 1917). A Constitutional Democrat, he was authorized by the Duma to form a new government upon Tsar Nicholas II's abdication. After concessions to the left, he lost support and resigned as premier in favor of Kerensky. He settled in Paris.

Lvov (L'vov), commercial city of Ukrainian SSR, USSR, 115mi (184km) SW of Lutsk, between the Raztoche and Gologary Mts. on a tributary of the Bug River; capital of Lvov oblast. Founded 1250 by Galician prince Lev, it was ceded to Poland and chartered 1340; included in Austrian province of Galicia 1772; scene of WWI battles; became capital of the independent Ukrainian Republic 1918; reverted to Poland 1919; ceded to the USSR 1945. A cultural center, Lvov is the site of a university (1661), 14th-century Roman and Armenian Catholic cathedrals, 16th-century palace, 18th-century cathedral and many old churches and monuments. Industries: metalworking, leather, textiles, radio and telegraph equipment, glass, chemicals, woodworking, food processing, petroleum refining, automobile assembling, paint, agricultural machinery. Pop. 553,000.

Lyallpur, city in E Pakistan, approx. 75mi (121km) W of Lahore, in the Punjab region; important textile center, also a marketing and processing place for regional agricultural products. Founded 1892. Pop. 853,700.

Lycia, region in SW Asia Minor inhabited in ancient times by the Lycians who are thought to have migrated from Crete via Miletus. They fought with Priam at Troy and are mentioned in the *Iliad.* Defeated by the Persians (546 BC) and then by Alexander, the area was held by the Ptolemies until granted to Rhodes by the Romans (189 BC). It was freed from Rhodian rule in 169 BC.

Lydda. *See* Lod.

Lydgate, John (*c.* 1370–1450), English poet. He was a Benedictine monk at Bury St Edmunds. His vast output of poetry (over 145,000 lines) ranged from long didactic works, such as *The Falle of Princis,* to brief lyrics. Although a competent craftsman himself, Lydgate was heavily influenced by Geoffrey Chaucer. *See also* Chaucer, Geoffrey.

Lydia, a territory in west Asia Minor. Under the Mermnad dynasty (*c.* 700–550 BC), it was a powerful kingdom until it fell to the Persians and became their stronghold in the West. It was later taken by Alexander. It was the first realm to coin money and was famous for its musical innovations.

Lye. *See* Sodium Hydroxide.

Lyell, (Sir) Charles (1797–1875), Scottish geologist. Immensely influential in shaping 19th-century ideas about science, he wrote *Principles of Geology* (3 vols., 1830–33), which went into 12 editions in his lifetime. His geological ideas are based on uniformism. His other works include *Elements of Geology* (1838) and *The Geological Evidences of the Antiquity of Man* (1863). Lyell also first divided the Tertiary period into Eocene, Miocene, and Pliocene epochs. △1186.

Lymph, a clear, slightly yellowish, fluid derived from the blood. It contains white blood cells that function in immunity and in combating infection. Lymph flows through a series of vessels that make up the lymphatic system.

Lymphatic System, system of connecting vessels and organs that transport lymph through the body. Lymph flows into tiny and delicate lymph capillaries and from them into lymph vessels, or lymphatics. These extend throughout the body and join to form larger vessels that join at lymph nodes that collect

Luna moth

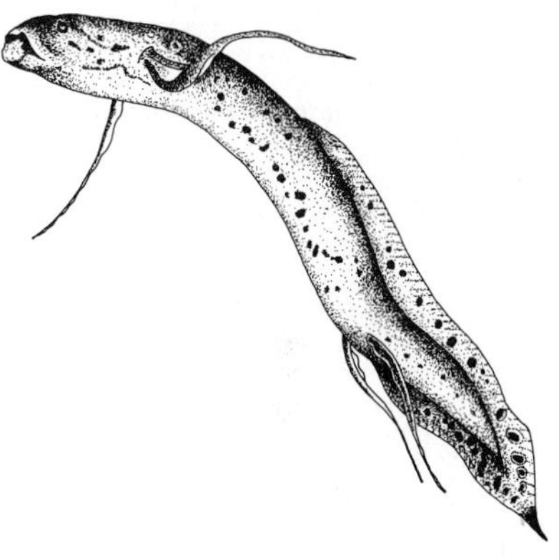

Lungfish

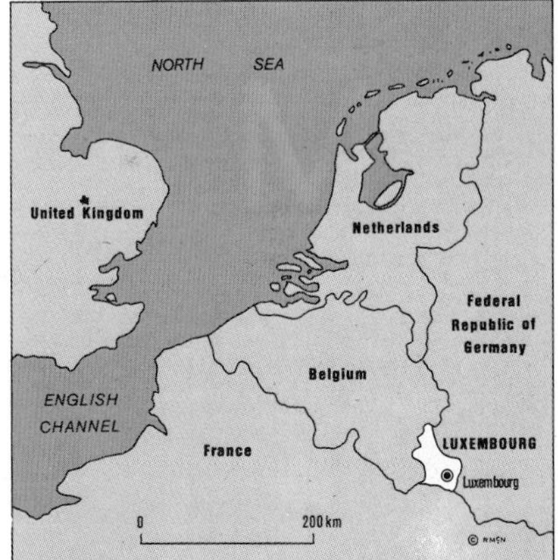

NORTH SEA
United Kingdom
Netherlands
Federal Republic of Germany
Belgium
ENGLISH CHANNEL
France
LUXEMBOURG
Luxembourg
0
200km

Luxembourg

Luxor, Egypt: Colossus of Memnon

lymph, storing some of the white blood cells. Lymph nodes empty into large vessels that link up into lymph ducts that empty back into the circulatory system. △688.

Lymph Node, a cavity of the lymphatic system into which lymph vessels empty. The nodes contain numerous lymph-carried white blood cells that act to destroy bacteria and other foreign invaders of the body. Lymph nodes are located throughout the body and often become swollen in presence of infection. *See also* Lymphatic System. △740.

Lymphocytes. △740.

Lymphogranuloma Venereum, a venereal disease resulting from infection by a parasitic microorganism of the genus *Chlamydia* in which ulcers appear on the genitals with subsequent enlargement of lymph nodes in certain regions.

Lynchburg, city in S central Virginia, 48mi (77km) ENE of Roanoke; served as Confederate supply base during Civil War; site of Virginia Seminary and College (1888), Randolph-Macon Women's College (1891), Lynchburg College (1903), Lynchburg Baptist College, Central Virginia Community College. Industries: tobacco, textiles, footwear, steel, medical supplies, electronic equipment. Founded 1757 by Quakers; inc. 1852. Pop. (1970) 54,083.

Lyndhurst, John Singleton Copley, Baron (1772–1863), English jurist, the son of American painter John Singleton Copley. Originally famed as a defender of radicals, he conducted the prosecution of Queen Caroline (1820). He was three times lord chancellor (1827–30, 1834–35, 1841–46).

Lynn, city in NE Massachusetts, on Massachusetts Bay, 11mi (18km) NE of Boston; site of first colonial ironworks (1643), first Christian Science Church (1875) and home of founder Mary Baker Eddy, and first turbojet engine (designed and built 1942). Industries: electrical equipment, jet engines, marine turbines. Founded 1629 as Saugus; inc. 1631; name changed 1637; inc. as city 1850. Pop. (1970) 90,294.

Lynwood, suburban city in S California, 8mi (13km) S of Los Angeles. Founded 1896; inc. 1921. Pop. (1970) 43,353.

Lynx, small cat found in forests of C and N Europe, along the French-Spanish border, and in North America. Ranging in color from yellow-gray to reddish-brown, it can be spotted or unspotted and its underparts are white. It has long legs, large feet, tufted ears, and beardlike hair on its cheeks. The gestation period is 67–74 days and 2–4 young are born. Length: body—33.5–43.4in (85–110cm); tail—4.7–6.7in (12–17cm). There are two species: *Lynx lynx* with several subspecies and *Lynx rufus*. Family Felidae. *See also* Bobcat; Canada Lynx. △592, 628.

Lyons (Lyon), city in E central France, at confluence of Rhône and Saône rivers; capital of Rhône dept. City became part of French crown lands 1307; developed as trading center on important route to Italy by 16th century; devastated 1793 by French Revolutionary troops; center of French resistance movement in WWII; site of oldest stock exchange in France (1506), university (1808), 12th–14th-century Cathedral of St John, annual international trade fairs; noted gastronomical center. Industries: silk, rayon, chemicals, clothing, metal. Founded 43 BC as Roman colony. Pop. 527,890.

Lyra, a small constellation (the Lyre) in the Northern Hemisphere between Hercules and Cygnus. It contains Vega, a star of the first magnitude, and two stars of the third magnitude. △132.

Lyra Ring Nebula. △106.

Lyre (Lyra), stringed musical instrument resembling a small kithara played with a plectrum. Its sound box is sometimes made of turtle shell. Used solo or to accompany singers, it originated in prehistoric Asia Minor and was used by Hebrews, Greeks, and Romans. *See also* Kithara. △998.

Lyrebird, two Australian songbirds: superb lyrebird *(Menura novaehollandiae)* and Albert's lyrebird *(M. alberti)*. These large, perching birds have lyre-shaped tails displayed during elaborate courtship performances. The female builds a large, dome-shaped nest with a side entrance for the single grayish-purple egg.

Lyric Poetry. △998.

Lysander (died 395 BC), Spartan general and statesman who restored the Peloponnesian fleet, winning great victories at Notium and Aegospotami, which were instrumental in Athens' eventual defeat. △994.

Lysenko, Trofim Denisovich (1898–1976), Russian agronomist and geneticist. He expanded Lamarckism, the theory of the inheritability of acquired characteristics, to include his own ideas of plant genetics. Lysenko, who promised the Soviet Union vast increases in crop yield and type through the application of his theories, enjoyed official sanction under Stalin, but in the 1950s his influence waned. △418.

Lysergic Acid Diethylamide. *See* LSD.

Lysine, crystalline soluble essential amino acid found in proteins. *See* Amino Acid.

Lysippos (*fl.* 2nd half of the 4th century BC), Greek sculptor. His work was influential and innovative in proportion, composition, and detail. His style directed much of later Hellenistic sculpture. One of his best-known works is "Apoxyomenos" ("Youth Scraping Himself"), of which a Roman copy is in the Vatican Museum, Rome. △1002.

Lysistrata, Greek comedy by Aristophanes (411 BC). The Athenian Lysistrata encourages the other women to entice and then ignore their husbands until the men end the war with Sparta. Its high-spirited broad humor and its treatment of the battle between the sexes have made it a classic.

M

Ma'adim Valley System. △74.

Maas. *See* Meuse.

Maastricht, city in S Netherlands, near Belgian border, approx. 15mi (24km) N of Liège, Belgium, on Meuse River; capital of Limburg prov. Built on site of Roman settlement, it contains 6th- and 12th-century churches. Town was frequently besieged by Spaniards 14th-18th centuries; occupied by Germans during WWII. Industries: steel, glass, cement, grain, dairy products. Pop. 98,927.

Mabbog. *See* Hierapolis.

Macadamia, two species of trees of the family Proteaceae, native to Australia. Both have stiff, oblong, lancelike leaves, but the leaves of *Macadamia ternifolia* have serrated margins and those of *M. integrifolia* have smooth margins. Macadamia trees may reach 60ft (18m) in height. The edible seeds of the tree are round, hard-shelled nuts, covered by thick husks that split when ripe.

McAdoo, William Gibbs (1863–1941), US political leader, b. near Marietta, Ga. A railroad president, he constructed the first tunnel under the Hudson River, connecting New York and New Jersey (1904–08). He was Pres. Woodrow Wilson's secretary of treasury (1913–18), serving as first chairman of the Federal Reserve Board and was director general of railroads (1917–19). An unsuccessful candidate for the Democratic presidential nomination (1924), he was a senator from California (1932–38).

McAllen, city in S Texas, 50mi (81km) WNW of Brownsville; transportation center and port of entry from Mexico. Industries: agriculture, food processing, oil refining, chemicals. Settled 1905; inc. 1911. Pop. (1970) 37,636.

Macao (Macau), Portuguese overseas province in SE China, on South China Sea, 40mi (64km) W of Hong Kong. Colony consists of Macao Peninsula and two islands, Taipa and Colôane. The city of Macao, approx. coextensive with the peninsula, was settled 1557 by Portuguese; it enjoyed great prosperity in 18th and 19th centuries as one of two Chinese ports (with Canton) open to foreign trade; declared a free port and independent by Portugal 1849; not recognized by China as Portuguese territory until 1887; Portuguese administration faced opposition from Communist Chinese. Industries: fishing, textiles, tourism. Area: approx. 6sq mi (16sq km). Pop. 314,000.

Macapagal, Diosdado (1911–), Filipino political figure. He served as vice president (1957–61) under Carlos Garcia and was elected president himself in 1961 through a coalition of the Liberal and Progressive parties. His attempted reforms concerning corruption and the economy were thwarted, and he was defeated in 1965 by Ferdinand Marcos.

Macaque, diverse group of omnivorous medium-to-large monkeys found from NW Africa to Japan and Korea. Most are yellowish-brown forest dwellers—agile on ground and in trees—and are good swimmers. Weight: to 29lb (13kg). Genus *Macaca*. *See also* Monkey. △554.

MacArthur, Douglas (1880–1964), US general, b. Little Rock, Ark. Son of Lt. Gen. Arthur MacArthur, he spent his entire life in military service. He led a brigade in World War I, and participated in all the important US offensives. He was made superintendent of West Point (1919–22) and later, US Army chief of staff (1930–35). He retired from the army (1937) to work in the Philippines, where he was when World War II began. He was recalled to active duty (1941). Escaping the Japanese invasion, he mounted the island-hopping assault that led to the Japanese defeat. He received the Japanese surrender and directed the occupation there after the war. He took command of the UN troops when the North Koreans attacked South Korea. President Truman relieved him of command following a policy disagreement (1951). *See also* Korean War.

Macau. *See* Macao.

Macaulay, Thomas Babington (1800–59), English historian, poet, and statesman. After serving two terms in Parliament as a Liberal, he was appointed a member of the supreme council of India, where he drew up a penal code used well into the 20th century.

He returned to Parliament (1839–47) and in 1847 began to write *History of England from the Accession of James the Second* (5 vols., 1848–61).

Macaw, tropical American harsh-voiced parrot often seen in zoos. They have partially bare faces, sword-shaped tails, and large powerful bills to eat nutmeats. Some smaller species have protective green plumage, but larger species are brightly colored, such as the scarlet macaw *(Ara macao)* that has a red tail and yellow wings with bright blue on its back and wings. △528–30, 536.

Macbeth (died 1057), king of Scotland, hero of Shakespeare's tragedy named after him. He killed Duncan I, whose armies he commanded, seizing the kingdom (1040). Macbeth survived Siward of Northumbria's attempt to dethrone him (1046) but was later defeated by him (1054) and then killed by Malcolm III.

Macbeth (*c.*1606), 5-act tragedy by William Shakespeare, based on Raphael Holinshed's *Chronicles.* Moved by his own ambition and that of his unscrupulous wife, Macbeth murders Duncan, king of Scotland, and takes the crown, fulfilling a witches' prophecy. One murder leads to another, Lady Macbeth goes mad and dies, and the rest of the witches' prophecy comes true when Macduff leads an army from ambush and Macbeth is killed. △1148.

MacBride, Sean (1904–), Irish political figure, the son of Irish patriots Maud Gonne and John MacBride. Sean served in the Irish Republican Army and then founded the Clann na Poblachta (1946) political party and was in the Irish parliament (1947–58), and represented Ireland at the Council of Europe (1954–63). Active in international peace causes, he was made UN commissioner for Namibia (1974), the year he also won the Nobel Peace prize.

Maccabees, prominent Jewish family that ruled Judea from 164–63 BC. In 168 BC the Seleucid ruler Antiochus IV invaded Jerusalem and in the following year rededicated the Temple to Zeus and outlawed Jewish religious practices. Mattathias, a high priest, and his five sons fled to the mountains and organized a guerrilla army. After Mattathias' death in 166 BC his son Judas Maccabaeus took command and recaptured Jerusalem in 164 BC. This event is celebrated as Hanukkah, the Festival of Lights. Judas Maccabaeus was succeeded as ruler of Judea by his brother Jonathan (*r.*160–143). The family maintained control of Judea until 63 BC when Pompey conquered the nation for Rome. Further attempts by members of the Maccabee family to regain control failed.

Maccabees, Books of, four historical books bearing a common title; I and II are part of the Apocrypha of the Old Testament. I Maccabees discusses the Maccabean leaders; II Maccabees glorifies the temple. Book III is a Greek document lauding the Jews saved from the elephants of Ptolemy IV. Book IV, also in Greek, deals with martyrdom.

McCarran-Walter Act, or **Immigration and Nationality Act** (1952), legislation that codified US immigration laws. It retained most of the provisions of the 1924 Johnson Act, which had established quotas for immigration based on the number of former nationals of each country in the United States. Subversives and some groups considered politically unreliable were declared ineligible. The act was amended in 1965.

McCarthy, Eugene Joseph (1916–), US political leader, b. Watkins, Minn. He was in military intelligence during World War II, taught (1946–49) at the College of St Thomas in St Paul, was a Democrat in the US House of Representatives (1949–59) and the Senate (1959–71). From 1967 he campaigned for the Democratic presidential nomination, opposing Pres. Lyndon B. Johnson's Vietnam policies. He lost the nomination, however, to Hubert Humphrey. In 1976, McCarthy ran unsuccessfully for the presidency as an independent. He was the author of *The Limits of Power* (1967) and *The Year of the People* (1969).

McCarthy, Joseph Raymond (1908–57), U.S. Senator, b. Grand Chute, Wis. A circuit judge before beginning his career in the Senate (1947–57), he achieved national attention by claiming, in a 1950 speech, that the State Department had been infiltrated by Communists. He continued to make accusations against organizations and public officials, exploiting the public's concern over the spread of Communism in Asia and Europe. He was appointed chairman of the Senate's Permanent Subcommittee on Investigations (1953), conducting controversial inquiries, including the nationally televised Army-McCarthy hearings (1954). His charges were not substantiated, and he was charged with using improper means. The Senate censured him (1954) and his popularity declined.

McCarthy, Joseph Vincent "Joe" (1887–), US baseball manager, b. Philadelphia. He began his career in 1926 when he guided the Chicago Cubs to a National League pennant. Later, with the New York Yankees (1931–46), he won eight American League pennants. He managed the Boston Red Sox (1948–50). He was elected to the Baseball Hall of Fame in 1957.

McCarthy, Mary Therese (1912–), US author, b. Seattle. A drama critic for many years, she also wrote several novels including *A Charmed Life* (1955) and *The Group* (1963). The latter, her most popular novel, traces the lives of eight Vassar alumnae after graduation. Among her nonfiction is *Venice Observed* (1956) and *Memories of a Catholic Girlhood* (1957).

McClellan, George Brinton (1826–85), US general and political leader, b. Philadelphia. He graduated from the US Military Academy (1846) and served in the Mexican War. In the Civil War he was Union commander (1861–62), but his conservative tactics led President Lincoln to remove him twice during that time. He ran unsuccessfully as the Democratic candidate for president against Lincoln in 1864 and was governor of New Jersey (1878–81).

McCormack, John William (1891–), US congressman, b. Boston, Mass. A loyal Democrat and New Deal supporter, he served in the House (1928–70), often as majority leader (from 1940), and became speaker in 1961. He retired from his post and his seat in 1970.

McCormick, Cyrus Hall (1809–84), US inventor, b. Rockbridge co, Va. He invented the reaper in 1831. A large scale manufacturing operation and widespread advertising, with his inventions of the twine binder and side-rake, brought him financial success and revolutionized harvesting.

McCullers, Carson (1917–67), US author, b. Columbus, Ga. Her first novel, *The Heart Is a Lonely Hunter,* appeared in 1940 and is about a deaf mute in a Southern town. Like her subsequent novels, it is a compassionate and sensitive work. Perhaps her most popular book is *The Member of the Wedding* (1946), which deals with a lonely twelve-year-old girl. The book was successfully dramatized in 1950. Other works include *Reflections in a Golden Eye* (1941) and *The Ballad of the Sad Cafe* (1951; dramatized 1963).

McCulloch v. Maryland (1819), landmark US Supreme Court case in which the court reinforced the federal government's supremacy over the states by denying a state the right to tax a US Bank.

Macdonald, (Sir) John Alexander (1815–91), first prime minister of the Dominion of Canada (1867–73; and again 1878–91). Macdonald became a lawyer in 1836 and then a power in Conservative politics after 1844. He supported responsible government after 1849 and served as prime minister of Upper Canada (1857–62). Macdonald encouraged western settlement, took over the Hudson's Bay Company lands (1869), and furthered railway interests before being implicated in the Pacific Scandal of 1873. He supported trade with England and favored high tariffs as part of his protectionist national policy.

MacDonald, (James) Ramsay (1866–1937), British political figure. Surmounting the problems of his illegitimate birth and poverty, he became a leader of the Independent Labour party (later the Labour party), and its treasurer (1912–24). A member of Parliament (1906–18) his opposition to Britain's role in World War I aroused furious opposition, and he was defeated in the 1918 elections. Returned to Parliament (1922–29), he became Britain's first Labour prime minister (1924). Prime minister again (1929–35), he was forced to seek Liberal and Conservative support for his financial policies (1931) and became increasingly distrusted by Labour. He lost power in 1935. △1324.

Macdonald, Ross (1915–), US author, b. Kenneth Millar in Los Gatos, Calif. The author of detective novels, he created Lew Archer, a tough, moral private investigator who operates in southern California. Macdonald's books include *The Galton Case* (1959), *The Goodbye Look* (1969), *Sleeping Beauty* (1973), and *The Blue Hammer* (1976).

McDonald Observatory, astronomical observatory on Mt. Locke, near Fort Davis, Tex.; sponsored by University of Texas in cooperation with University of

Lyons, France

Lyrebird

Douglas MacArthur

Eugene McCarthy

Chicago; studies bodies within solar system for future space exploration; has the third largest telescope (107-in reflector) in world, built in 1968 under contract with NASA. Founded 1932.

MacDowell, Edward (Alexander) (1861–1908), US composer, b. New York City. He studied with Franz Liszt. He is chiefly known for his piano music, which includes three sonatas, two concertos, and numerous suites and short pieces, eg, the *Woodland Sketches* (1896). △1246.

McDowell, Irvin (1818–85), Union Civil War general, b. Columbus, Ohio. He commanded the Union troops at the First Battle of Bull Run and later commanded a corps in the Army of the Potomac. Blamed for the defeat at the Second Battle of Bull Run, he was removed from command but later reinstated.

Mace, in Botany. △356.

Mace (weapon). △1592.

Macedonia, region in SE Europe, on Balkan Peninsula; its boundaries are included in NE Greece, SE Yugoslavia, and SW Bulgaria. Ancient Macedonian Empire (338–168 BC) was made a Roman province 148 BC; it was included in Bulgarian and Serbian empires when they fell in the 14th century to Ottoman Turks, who held it until 1912. Its independence from Turkey, and claims of Greece, Yugoslavia, and Bulgaria to the region, precipitated the Balkan Wars 1912–13. Territorial boundaries, with Bulgarian exclusion, were determined 1919; Bulgarian claim came after Greek-Bulgarian conflicts and settlement by League of Nations 1926. Industries: tobacco, grains, cotton, livestock, iron, copper, lead, chromite mining. Area: approx. 25,700sq mi (66,563sq km). △1004; 1300.

Macedonian Wars. Under Philip V, Macedon began to wage war with Rome. In the First Macedonian War (215–205 BC), Philip was victorious but he was defeated and humiliated and forced to relinquish his navy and pay heavy tribute to Rome as a result of the Second Macedonian War (200–197). His indemnity was decreased when he cooperated with Rome. His powerful son Perseus consolidated Macedon, extended its influence, and threatened Pergamum, thus bringing about the Third Macedonian War (171–168). Perseus lost his entire kingdom to Rome. Macedon was divided into four republics and later annexed as the first of the Roman provinces (146), thereafter declining. *See also* Philip V.

McGillivray, Alexander (1759?–93), American Indian leader, b. Creek co, Ala., who became a British agent and helped maintain Creek loyalty to England during the American Revolution. The son of a Scots trader and a Creek woman, he had a classical education in Charleston, S.C., before returning to his mother's people. After the war he signed conflicting treaties with both the Spanish and the Americans and led Indian attacks on US settlements.

McGinley, Phyllis (1905–), US author, b. Ontario, Ore. A poet, her verse is witty and satirical. Her books include *On the Contrary* (1934), *Pocketful of Wry* (1940), and *Times Three: Selected Verses from Three Decades* (1960; Pulitzer Prize in poetry, 1961). She is also the author of children's books.

McGovern, George Stanley (1922–), US senator and presidential candidate, b. Avon, S.D. A Democrat, he was a US representative from South Dakota (1957–61). He was elected to the US Senate in 1962 and reelected in 1968. An outspoken opponent of the Vietnam War, he ran for president against the Republican incumbent, Richard Nixon in 1972 but carried only the state of Massachusetts. He then returned to the Senate and was reelected in 1974.

McGraw, John J(oseph) (1875–1934), US baseball player and manager, b. Truxton, N.Y. He was one of the National League's great managers. McGraw played for five teams (1891–1906), but is best known for managing the New York Giants (1902–32), whom he guided to 10 pennants and three World Series victories. He was elected to the Baseball Hall of Fame in 1937.

McGuffey, William Holmes (1800–73), US educator, b. Washington co, Pa. Professor of languages at several universities and president of Cincinnati College (1836–39) and Ohio University (1839–43), he was the creator and author of the McGuffey readers, spellers, and primers, which taught grade school students good English and moral lessons. A major influence on the minds of 19th-century Americans, the McGuffey series sold 122,000,000 copies from 1836–1920.

Mach, Ernst (1838–1916), Austrian physicist and philosopher. He was interested in the physiology and psychology of the senses and in problems of epistemology. In physics, his name is associated with the Mach number. He believed that physical phenomena should only be explained by data perceived by the senses and he developed the main principles of scientific positivism. △1496.

McHenry, James (1753–1816), US patriot, signer of the Constitution, and surgeon, b. Ireland. After emigrating to Philadelphia (1771) he joined the Continental army as a surgeon (1775). He was George Washington's private secretary (1778–80) and served in the Maryland senate, the Continental Congress and as a delegate to the Constitutional convention (1787). He later was secretary of war (1796–1800).

Machiavelli, Niccolò (1469–1527), Florentine statesman and political theorist, an outstanding figure of the Italian Renaissance. He served from 1498 to 1512 as an official and diplomat of Piero Soderini's republican government of Florence. Machiavelli lost his post when the Medici returned to power; he devoted the remainder of his life to writing a number of important literary, political, and historical works. His *Discourses on the First Ten Books of Livy* (1513–17) argued that the experience of the past could provide solutions for the present. A pamphlet, *The Prince*, written in 1513, made Machiavelli famous. Advocating the need of the ruler to preserve and enhance his own power and that of the state by whatever means necessary, *The Prince* became a guidebook to power politics and made Machiavelli's name synonymous with cunning, ruthlessness, and political immorality. △1128.

Machine. △1582–84, 1662, 1816–22.

Machine Gun, a weapon that fires automatically and is capable of sustained rapid fire. The firing mechanism is operated by recoil or by gas from fired ammunition. The gun may be water- or air-cooled, and is often fired from a tripod. The ammunition is of .60 caliber or 15.24mm or under. The first widely used machine gun was invented by the American Hiram Maxim in 1883. The Maxim gun was first employed by the British in 1893 against tribal warriors in the Transvaal. △1730.

Machine Tools, stationary, power-driven machines for shaping or forming metal parts. Shaping is accomplished in several ways: by shearing, squeezing, or applying electricity or corrosive chemicals, and by cutting away excess in chips, as with lathes, shapers, planers, drilling machines, milling machines, grinders, and power saws. Cold-forming of such items as cooking utensils and automobile bodies is performed on punch presses. Hot-forming is done on forging presses. All cutting tools have work-holding and tool-holding devices and some means of controlling the depth of cut. △1594, 1606.

Mach Number, ratio of the speed of a moving body to the speed of sound in air, expressed as a decimal equivalent, 0.8 being subsonic and 1.2 supersonic. It takes its name from the Austrian investigator of supersonic speeds and shock waves, Ernst Mach (1838–1916). △1496.

Machu Picchu, ancient Inca city in S central Peru, in the Andes Mts approx. 50mi (81km) NW of Cuzco. The ruins sit on a high rock between two mountain peaks, and terraced gardens and stonework leading to a citadel extend over about 5sq mi (13sq km). Discovered 1911 by Hiram Bingham. △886.

MacInnes, Helen (1907–), US novelist, b. Scotland. Her first spy novel, *Above Suspicion*, appeared in 1941. Subsequently she repeated the espionage-suspense formula in other novels, including *The Venetian Affair* (1963) and *Message from Malaga* (1971).

McIntosh, William (1775?–1825), American Indian chief, b. Georgia. He sided with the Americans and led the lower Creeks against the British in the War of 1812. He was made a brigadier general and fought (1817–18) with Andrew Jackson against the Seminole tribes. In 1825 he signed a treaty giving Creek lands east of the Chattahoochee River to Georgia and was killed by the upper Creeks who opposed cession.

Mack, Connie (1862–1956), US baseball executive and manager, b. Cornelius McGillicuddy in Brookfield, Mass. As a manager, he had the highest win record in baseball history (3776). Mack owned the Philadelphia Athletics and managed the team (1901–50). He was also a player (1886–96) and a manager (1894–96) of the Washington Senators in the National League. He was elected to the Baseball Hall of Fame in 1937.

McKay, Donald (1810–80), US ship designer and builder, b. Nova Scotia. His Boston shipyard built the largest and fastest clipper ships. Long-voyage speed records were set by his *Flying Cloud* from Boston to San Francisco (1851), *Lightning* on the England to Australia route, and *Glory of the Seas* from New York to San Francisco (1869). Improved steam and iron vessels led to the shipyard's closing in 1873.

McKean, Thomas (1734–1817), American jurist and a signer of the Declaration of Independence, b. in Chester co, Pa. After representing Delaware as a delegate to the Continental Congress (1774–83), he later served as governor of Pennsylvania (1799–1808).

McKeesport, city in SW Pennsylvania, at the confluence of the Monongahela and Youghiogheny rivers; center of Whisky Rebellion (1794). Industries: steel tubes, boilers, barges, steel castings. Settled 1755 by David McKee; inc. as borough 1842; chartered as city 1890. Pop. (1970) 37,997.

Mackenzie, (Sir) Alexander (1764–1820), Canadian fur trader and explorer. Mackenzie moved to Montreal in 1778 from Scotland and joined a consortium of fur traders. In 1787 he became a partner in the North West Company after extensive trading in Detroit and the Great Lakes. In 1789, he journeyed from Fort Chipewyan along the Slave and Mackenzie rivers to the Arctic Ocean. In 1793, his journey to the Pacific via the Peace and Fraser rivers proved the impossibility of a sea passage to the west. It was the first crossing of North America north of Mexico. He quit the North West Company in 1799, published descriptions of his journeys, *Voyages. . . to the Frozen and Pacific Oceans* (1801), and sat in the Legislative Assembly (1805–08).

Mackenzie, Alexander (1822–92), prime minister of Canada (1873–78). Mackenzie edited the Reform newspaper *Lambton Shield* (1852–54) while working as a building contractor in Ontario. He presided over the first Liberal administration of Canada on a platform of trade with the United States and opposition to railroad interests.

Mackenzie, William Lyon (1795–1861), Canadian political leader and rebel. A shopkeeper in York (1820), he attacked the Family Compacts in the *Colonial Advocate* (1824). Between 1828 and 1836 he was six times elected and ejected from the Legislative Assembly for his espousal of independence. With Louis Papineau, he led the Rebellion of 1837 and was in exile in the United States until 1849. He fought against business interests and banks and encouraged free education and universal suffrage. His writings and speeches advanced the cause of confederation. *See also* Rebellion of 1837.

Mackenzie, river in W Mackenzie district, Northwest Territories, Canada; rises in the Great Slave Lake and flows NW into the Arctic Ocean. The entire system, including all of the headstreams, forms the largest river in Canada. It is of great economic importance for goods shipped N. Old fur-trading posts still remain along the river. Discovered 1789 by Alexander Mackenzie. Navigable for most of its 2,635mi (4,242km).

Mackenzie Mountains, mountain range in Northwest Territories, Canada, extending from E Yukon Territory through W Mackenzie district; forms watershed of the tributaries of the Mackenzie and Yukon rivers. Highest point is Keele Peak, 9,750ft (2,974m).

Mackerel, marine schooling fish of the N Atlantic. An important commercial fish closely related to the tunas, it is silvery blue with dark side bars. Length: 12in–5ft (30.5–152.5cm); weight: 1–100lb (0.5–45kg). Family Scombridae. Species of mackerel include the Atlantic *Scomber scombrus*, the king mackerel *Scomberomorus cavalla*, and the Spanish mackerel *Scomberomorus maculatus*. △392.

Mackerel Shark. △626.

McKim, Charles Follen (1847–1909), US architect, b. Chester co, Penn. In 1879 he founded the architectural firm of McKim, Mead, and White with William Rutherford Mead (1846–1928) and Stanford White (1853–1906). This firm became the best known of such organizations of its day, provided several notable designs for the Chicago World's Columbian Exposition of 1893, and introduced the extremely formal Italianate style into US public buildings, as in the Boston Public Library (1892). △1412.

Mackinac Island, island and state park in SE Michigan, in Straits of Mackinac in Lake Huron, 255mi

(411km) NW of Detroit; coextensive with Mackinac Island City; site of Mackinac College (1965); resort area. Pop. (1970) 517.

McKinley, William (1843–1901), 25th president of the United States (1897–1901), b. Niles, Ohio. He attended Allegheny College and in 1871 he married Ida Saxton. After serving in the Union Army, McKinley was admitted to the bar and practiced in Canton. In 1876 he was elected as a Republican to the US House of Representatives, and in 1889 he became chairman of the Ways and Means Committee. He wrote the protectionist McKinley Tariff Act (1890), which was unpopular with the public but highly regarded by Ohio industrialists, one of whom, Marcus A. Hanna, became McKinley's political manager.

McKinley was elected governor of Ohio in 1891 and reelected in 1893. In 1895, Hanna began a successful campaign to win the 1896 presidential nomination for McKinley. McKinley won the election over William Jennings Bryan, who ran on a platform of free trade and free silver coinage.

As president, McKinley fulfilled his conservative Republican platform. He became involved somewhat reluctantly in the Spanish-American War but saw it quickly ended. He was easily reelected in 1900, this time with war hero Theodore Roosevelt as his running mate. On Sept. 6, 1901, while in Buffalo, N.Y., McKinley was shot by Leon Czolgosz, an anarchist. He died on September 14 and was succeeded by Roosevelt.

Career: US House of Representatives, 1876–82, 1884–91; governor of Ohio, 1892–96; president, 1897–1901.

McKinley, Mount, peak in S central Alaska, in the Alaska Range; highest peak in North America. Permanent snowfields cover more than half of the mountain; wildlife is abundant, especially caribou and white Alaska mountain sheep. First scaled 1913 by Hudson Stuck, it was named for President McKinley; included in Mount McKinley National Park (1917). Height: 20,320ft (6,198m).

McLean, John (1785–1861), US jurist and lawyer, b. Morris co, N.J. A US congressman (1813–16), he served on the Ohio supreme court (1816–22) and was US postmaster general (1823–29). Appointed an associate justice of the US Supreme Court in 1829, he served for 31 years.

MacLeish, Archibald (1892–), US author, b. Glencoe, Ill. A poet and playwright, his works include *Conquistador* (1932; Pulitzer Prize 1933), an epic poem; *Collected Poems 1917–1952* (1952; Pulitzer Prize 1953); and *J.B.* (1958; Pulitzer Prize 1959), a play. Noted short poems by him include "Ars Poetica," "The End of the World," "You, Andrew Marvell," and "Immortal Autumn."

Macleod, John James Rickard (1876–1935), Scottish physiologist. He shared the 1923 Nobel Prize in physiology or medicine with Frederick Grant Banting for the discovery of insulin. The actual discovery was made by Banting and Charles Best working in Macleod's University of Toronto laboratory.

McLuhan, (Herbert) Marshall (1911–), Canadian author and educator. Gradually introducing the study of electronic mass communications into his English literature courses at the University of Toronto, McLuhan virtually established a new academic field with his theories about the impact of the media on our methods of perceiving. His works include *The Gutenberg Galaxy* (1962), *Understanding Media* (1964), and *The Medium Is the Massage* (1967).

MacMahon, Marie Edmé Patrice de (1808–93), French military and political figure. He gained fame in the Crimean War for his assault on the Malakoff Tower, which led to the fall of Sevastopol (1855). In the war against Austria (1859) he won an important victory at Magenta, for which he was made a marshal of France and duke of Magenta. Governor-general of Algeria 1864–70, he was called to serve in the Franco-Prussian War but was overwhelmed at the Battle of Worth. He put down the Paris Commune in 1871. In 1873 he was elected president of the Third Republic. A monarchist, he objected to but accepted the republican constitution of 1875. In 1877 he forced the resignation of the republican premier, dissolved the chamber of deputies, and called for new elections. But the new chamber was even more republican and MacMahon was forced to accept a republican ministry. He resigned in 1879 before his seven year term was up.

McMillan, Edwin Mattison (1907–), US chemist and physicist, b. Redondo Beach, Calif. He became professor of physics at the University of California and was awarded the Nobel Prize for chemistry in 1951 for his discovery of several transuranic elements. While working with E. O. Lawrence on the cyclotron he developed the synchrocyclotron for which he was awarded a share in the 1963 Atoms for Peace prize.

Macmillan, (Maurice) Harold (1894–), English political figure. As a member of Parliament (1924–29, 1931–64), he held a number of cabinet posts, including minister of housing and local government (1951–54) and chancellor of the exchequer (1955–57). He succeeded Anthony Eden as Conservative prime minister (1957–63), improving Anglo-American relations after the Suez crisis and trying unsuccessfully to obtain Britain's entry into the European Economic Community. △1330.

McMurdo Sound, Antarctica, SW inlet of Ross Sea between Ross Island and coast of Victoria Land; site of major US research and exploration base.

MacMurrough, Dermot (died 1171), Irish king. King of Leinster, it was his request for help that brought the Anglo-Normans to Ireland. He succeeded his brother in 1126 and secured his claim by 1141 after blinding or killing 17 rivals. He abducted the wife of another Irish king and was driven from the country in 1166. He was responsible for compiling the *Book of Leinster*, a collection of Gaelic traditions.

McNamara, Robert Strange (1916–), US businessman and public official, b. San Francisco. An executive of the Ford Motor Company from 1946, he rose to the presidency in 1960. He resigned in 1961 to become US secretary of defense, serving until 1968. In 1968 he became president of the World Bank.

McNary, Charles Linza (1874–1944), US political leader, b. near Salem, Ore. He served on the Oregon supreme court (1913–15) before becoming a US senator (1917–44). A prominent Republican, he sponsored Senate reform measures and supported New Deal social and political legislation. He was Wendell Willkie's vice-presidential running mate in the 1940 presidential election.

McNary-Haugen Bill, a series of similar bills designed to provide agricultural relief. A McNary-Haugen bill passed Congress twice (1927, 1928) but was vetoed both times by Pres. Calvin Coolidge. Provisions included the establishment of a federal board to buy surplus commodities, which would then be sold when domestic prices rose or would be exported for sale abroad. If the difference between domestic and international commodity prices was great enough that the government would suffer a loss, the producers would pay the difference.

MacNeice, Louis (1907–63), British poet, b. Belfast, N. Ireland. An important poet of the 1930s, he was less overtly political than his friends W.H. Auden and Stephen Spender. His poems include *Autumn Journal* (1939), *Autumn Sequel* (1954), *Visitations* (1954), and *Solstices* (1961). He worked for the British Broadcasting Corporation, for which he wrote several radio plays. *See also* Auden, W.H.; Spender, Stephen.

Mâcon, town in E France, capital of Saône-et-Loire dept.; Huguenot possession in 16th century; railroad center. Industries: wine, printing, copper founding. Pop. 33,445.

Macon, city in central Georgia, 78mi (126km) SE of Atlanta, seat of Bibb co; agricultural region and distributing center for grain, cotton, fruit, nuts, drugs; site of natural clay and limestone deposits, Mercer University (1833), Wesleyan College (1836), Macon Junior College (1968), Robins Air Force Base. Settled 1821; chartered 1832. Pop. (1970) 122,423.

Macon's Bill No. 2 (1810). Bill that repealed the Non-Intercourse Act against England and France. The United States, in the War of 1812, agreed to restore it against one of the warring countries if the other repealed its trade restrictions against US ships.

McPherson, Aimee Semple (1890–1944), US evangelist. In 1927 she founded the International Church of the Foursquare Gospel. Claiming to be guided by God, she professed faith healing and the gift of tongues. Her flamboyant methods won many followers, despite the scandal of a reported kidnapping in 1926.

Macpherson, James (1736–96), Scottish poet and historian. A sometime schoolmaster, Macpherson translated and composed several Gaelic and Scottish ballads and stories, including *The Works of Ossian* (2 vols., 1765). △1222.

Macroeconomics, study of the economic system as a unit, rather than its individual components as in microeconomics, including the fundamental decisions that an economic system must make, the deter-

Macedonia, Greece

Machu Picchu, Peru

Mackerel

William McKinley

mination of national aggregates (GNP, national income, personal income), the study of the monetary sector of the economy (the banking system), and the economic relationships among countries (international trade). Keynesian economics is typically closely identified with macroeconomics. *See also* Microeconomics. △938.

Macrophage Cells. △740.

Macy, Anne Sullivan (1866–1936), US educator, b. Feeding Hills, Mass. Helen Keller's teacher, she herself was partially blind and educated at the Perkins Institute for the Blind. In 1887 she began teaching Miss Keller with her pioneering methods of touch teaching. She aided her at Perkins and later at Radcliffe College, and although married, she remained Miss Keller's companion. She became totally blind in 1935.

Madagascar, island that constitutes the Malagasy Republic, in the Indian Ocean off SE coast of Africa; 4th-largest island in the world; mountainous with high plateaus, swampy plains; primarily agricultural economy. Chief city and capital is Tananarive. Discovered 1500 by Portuguese. Area: approx. 226,657sq mi (587,042sq km). *See also* Malagasy Republic.

Madame Bovary (1857), naturalistic novel by Gustave Flaubert, who was prosecuted for the novel's alleged immorality. Set in provincial Normandy, it relates the story of Emma Bovary, whose dreams of romance are not realized by her husband, a country doctor, or her lovers. She falls into debt and eventually commits suicide.

Madame Butterfly (1904), 3-act opera by Giacomo Puccini, Italian libretto by Giuseppe Giacosa and Luigi Illica, after David Belasco's play. First performed at La Scala, Milan, it was a fiasco, but was successfully revised three months later at Brescia under Arturo Toscanini. Pinkerton (tenor), a US Navy officer visiting Nagasaki, "marries" Madame Butterfly, Cio-Cio-San (soprano); when he returns three years later with an American wife, Butterfly kills herself. Other roles are Suzuki (mezzo-soprano) and Sharpless (baritone). △1256.

Madder, perennial vine native to S Europe and Asia with whorled leaves and greenish-yellow flower clusters. A red dye is produced from the roots. Height: to 4ft (1.2m). Family Rubiaceae; species *Rubia tinctorum.* The madder family includes primarily tropical plants, shrubs, and trees, such as the coffee and gardenia.

Madeira, river in W Brazil, formed by union of the Mamoré and Beni at the Brazil-Bolivia border; most important tributary of the Amazon. Length: 2,100mi (3,381km).

Madeira Islands, group of islands in Atlantic Ocean off coast of Morocco, N of Canary Islands; coextensive with Funchal district of Portugal. The group consists of two inhabited islands, Madeira and Porto Santo, and two uninhabited groups, Desertas and the Selvagens. Capital is Funchal on Madeira Island. Islands were discovered mid-14th century; year-round resort area. Industries: sugar cane, Madeira wine, embroidering, reed furniture. Area: 308sq mi (798sq km). Pop. 268,700.

Madhya Pradesh, state in central India; Bhopal is the capital. Previously ruled by the Gonds and Mahrattas, it was taken by the British 1820; Berar was inc. into its boundaries 1903 and its name was changed to the Central Provinces and Berar; in 1956, it inc. the former states of Madhya Bharat, Vindhya Pradesh, Bhopal, and part of Rajasthan; site of numerous colleges and universities. Industries: rice, wheat, corn, sugar cane, cotton, manganese, iron ore, coal, bauxite, spinning, weaving, steel. Area: 171,210sq mi (443,434sq km). Pop. 41,449,729.

Madison, Dolley (1768–1849), wife of President James Madison, b. Guilford co, N.C. Born Dolley Payne, the daughter of a Quaker family, she married in 1790 John Todd, who died three years later. In 1794 she left the Quakers to marry James Madison. During her time as first lady (1809–17) and as hostess for President Thomas Jefferson, a widower, she became known for her charm, grace, and talent for entertaining.

Madison, James (1751–1836), 4th president of the United States (1809–17), b. Port Conway, Va. He graduated from the College of New Jersey (now Princeton University) in 1771, and in 1794 he married Dolley Payne Todd.

Madison's first experience at statecraft was at the convention (1776) that drafted the Virginia constitution. He has been called the "father of the US Constitution"; he served at both the Annapolis Convention and at the Federal Constitutional Convention (1787). At the latter meeting, he played a major role in the final forming of the US Constitution. Along with John Jay and Alexander Hamilton he wrote the Federalist Papers in support of ratifying of the Constitution.

Madison served in the House of Representatives from 1789 to 1797. It was a period when the political party system was solidifying, and Madison quickly became a leader of the Jeffersonian faction. When Thomas Jefferson became President, he chose Madison as secretary of state, an office Madison held throughout Jefferson's two terms. He was Jefferson's personal choice to succeed him as president.

Madison's two terms as president were marked by deteriorating relations with Great Britain, culminating in the War of 1812. Highly unpopular, particularly in New England, it became known to his Federalist opponents as "Mr. Madison's War." The war went badly, and in 1814–15, the Hartford Convention was called by New England Federalists. It considered seceding from the Union, but the Treaty of Ghent, which ended the war in a stalemate, was signed before the convention could achieve any of its aims. Madison retired to "Montpelier," his plantation in Virginia.

Career: member, Continental Congress, 1780–83, 1787; delegate, Annapolis Convention, 1786; delegate, Federal Constitutional Convention, 1787; US House of Representatives, 1789–97; secretary of state, 1801–09; president, 1809–17. *See also* Annapolis Convention; Federalist Papers, The; War of 1812.

Madison, capital city of Wisconsin, on isthmus between Lake Mendota (N) and Lake Monona (S), 83mi (134km) W of Milwaukee; seat of Dane co; named for President James Madison; site of University of Wisconsin (1836), Edgewood College of the Sacred Heart (1927), Madison College, St Raphael's church (1854), Grace Episcopal church (1858), a Unitarian church designed by Frank Lloyd Wright; trading and manufacturing center. Industries: meat and dairy products, medical equipment, automobile parts. Est. as capital of Territory of Wisconsin 1836; inc. 1846 as village, 1856 as city. Pop. (1970) 172,007.

Madison, river, rises in Yellowstone National Park, NW Wyoming, flows W then N through SW Montana, joins the Jefferson and Gallatin rivers NE of Three Forks, Montana, to form the Missouri River. Water used for irrigation and hydroelectric power. Length: 183mi (295km).

Madison Heights, city in SE Michigan; N suburb of Detroit. Industries: steel, automobile and aircraft parts, tools and dies. Inc. 1955. Pop. (1970) 38,599.

Madonna of the Long Neck (Parmigianino). △1150.

Madonnas at Siena. △1104.

Madras, seaport city in SE India, on the Bay of Bengal; capital of Tamil Nadu state. The city grew around Fort St George, a British post (1640), and developed as a trading center; it was besieged and occupied by French 1746, but returned to British by the Treaty of Aix-la-Chapelle (1748); harbor was constructed 1862–1901; site of Madras University (1857); nearby is Mt St Thomas, legendary site of the martyrdom of Thomas the Apostle (AD 68); he is supposedly buried in Madras. Exports: hides, skins, oilseeds, cotton, chrome, magnesite. Industries: textiles, railroad stock, bicycles, printing, automobiles, motorcycles, motion pictures. Founded 1639. Pop. 2,086,036.

Madrid, capital city of Spain, and Madrid prov., on Manzanares River, 34mi (55km) WSW of Guadalajara. Taken from Moors 932 by Ramiro II of León again taken from Moors by Alfonso VI of Castile 1083; in 1561, Philip II made Madrid his official residence and capital of Spain. It was beautified in 18th century during Bourbon rule; occupied by French during Peninsular War (1808–14); the city developed tremendously during Isabella's reign (1833–68). Madrid remained loyal to the Republican government until entrance of Francisco Franco in 1939, during the Spanish Civil War; site of the Royal Palace (1737–64), now a museum, Ministerio de Hacienda national library, University of Madrid (1499), technical school, numerous museums (notably the Museo del Prado), several parks and plazas. Industries: plastics, wine, beer, publishing, motion pictures, optical instruments, electrical appliances, radio and telephone equipment, jewelry, leather goods. Area: (prov.) 3,087sq mi (7,995 sq km). Pop. (city) 3,146,071; (prov.) 3,792,561.

Madrigal, form of vocal music originating in Italy in the 14th century. Early madrigals feature two or three vocal parts and a highly ornamented upper voice Later forms in the 16th century featured love lyrics, nc set form, and four or five voices. The "classical" period of the madrigal (*c.* 1540–80) was dominated by Italian (Gabrieli, Palestrina) and Flemish composers (Lasso, Rore, Willaert). The "late" period (*c.* 1580–1620) featured the Italians (Marenzio, Gesualdo, Monteverdi) and English composers (Byrd, Morley, Weelkes, and Wilbye). △1174.

Madroño, or laurelwood, broad-leafed, evergreen tree native to British Columbia and N United States west of the Rocky Mountains. It has small, white flowers and orange-red fruit. Height: 50–100ft (15–31m). Family Ericaceae; species *Arbutus menziesii.*

Madurai, city in S India, 270mi (435km) SSW of Madras, on the Vaigai River; served as capital of Pandya dynasty (5th century BC–AD 11th century), and Nayak kingdom (*c.* 1550–1736); passed to British 1801 by the Carnatic Nawabs. Famous as the "city of festivals and temples," it contains the massive Meenakshi temple adorned with colonnades and gate towers enclosing the "Tank of the Golden Lilies" quadrangle; university (1966). Industries: weaving, dyeing of silk and muslin, brassware, wood carving, tourism. Pop. 493,842.

Maenad, from Gr. *mainomai* "to rage," female follower of Dionysus, the Greek god of wine and revelry. She is depicted carrying a staff entwined with ivy and surmounted by a pine cone while dancing orgiastic revels.

Maeterlinck, Maurice (1862–1949), Belgian playwright, essayist, poet, and mystic philosopher who wrote in French. A symbolist despite the realism of his time, his most popular plays are *Pelléas and Mélisande* (1892), a favorite of Sarah Bernhardt, made into an opera by Claude Debussy (1902), and *The Blue Bird* (1909), an allegorical fable. He won the Nobel Prize for literature 1911.

Magallanes, Estrecho de. *See* Magellan, Strait of.

Magazines. △1776.

Magdala, village in central Ethiopia; historically important as operational base for Emperor Theodore II (mid-19th century); made his capital (1867); destroyed 1868 by English; since rebuilt. △1268.

Magdeburg, port city in W East Germany, on Elbe River, 82mi (132km) WSW of Berlin; capital of Magdeburg district. In the 13th century city was granted a charter by archbishop of Magdeburg (prince of Holy Roman Empire) that served as model for hundreds of medieval towns in Germany. During Thirty Years' War (1618–1648) the city was burned and 85% of population perished; site of 11th-century Romanesque church and 13th-century cathedral; birthplace of physicist Otto von Guericke and Baron von Steuben. Industries: steel, paper, textiles, chemicals, machines. Founded 805. Pop. 270,692.

Magellan, Ferdinand (*c.*1480–1521), Portuguese and Spanish explorer. He commanded the first expedition to circumnavigate the globe. Twice wounded while exploring the East Indies for Portugal, he found vast trade potential in the Spice Islands. After fighting against the Moors, he fell out of favor with the Portuguese King Manuel and, renouncing his citizenship, went to Spain. There, he organized an expedition to reach the Spice Islands by sailing west. Leaving Spain with five ships in 1519, he reached Brazil and sailed south, seeking a westward passage. In November 1520 he sailed through the strait later named for him and reached the Philippines in March 1521. Although he was killed by natives in the Philippines, one of his ships did return to Spain, establishing a new route between Europe and Asia. △1122, 1260.

Magellan, Strait of, strait in S South America, between S Chile and the Tierra del Fuego island group; connects the Atlantic and Pacific oceans; especially important in colonial times for ships rounding South America. Discovered by Ferdinand Magellan 1520. Length: 350mi (564km).

Magellanic Clouds, two small satellite galaxies of the Milky Way Galaxy, visible in south circumpolar skies as misty stellar concentrations. The Small Cloud (Nubecula Minor), located in the constellation Tucana, is irregular; the Large Cloud (Nubecula Major), mostly in Dorado, is vaguely spiral. Distance about 150,000 light years. *See also* Galaxy. △110, 120, 126.

Maggiore, Lake, lake in N Italy and S Switzerland; 2nd-largest in Italy; crossed N to S by Ticino River and ed by the Maggia, Toce, and Tresa rivers; Borromean slands are off the W shore; bordered by the Swiss Alps; resort area. Area: 82sq mi (212sq km).

Maggot, the name given to many legless Diptera arvae. It is primarily used to describe those larvae that infest food and waste material. *See also* Diptera.

Magi. △822.

Magic, Black, practices of witch doctors, witches, magicians, or others designed to manipulate supernatural events so as to produce evil. This is often done by reversing normal religious practices, for example, reciting the "Lord's Prayer" backwards or making the sign of the cross on the floor. *See also* Sorcery; Witch Doctor.

Magic, Primitive, manipulation of supposed supernatural powers to achieve a desired effect. Delineation of the boundary between magic and primitive religion is generally impossible, but magic tends to be used for some limited practical end either benign or malevolent, while religion has a more philosophical role. In primitive societies, the dangerous force of magic is usually mediated by a particular person with special powers to control it. *See also* Magic, Black; Religion, Primitive; Sorcery. △742.

Magic Square, any square matrix divided into cells and filled with numbers or letters in ways once thought to have special magical significance. The most familiar lettered square is the SATOR square, composed of the words SATOR, AREPO, TENET, OPERA, and ROTAS. Arranged both vertically and horizontally the words read the same and form a cross through the middle that reads TENET. In arithmetical magical squares the numbers are generally arranged so that each column, every row, and the two main diagonals produce the same constant sum.

Maginot Line, series of fortifications constructed by France on its northeastern border with Germany. The purpose of the line was to prevent a quick German attack on France's vital frontier industries, but the defensive works also fostered a false sense of security. It was named after André Maginot, French minister of war (1929–32), who directed its construction and was still not complete at the outbreak of World War II (1939). The line was flanked by the Germans, and France fell in 1940.

Magistrate. △1014.

Magma, molten material that produces all igneous rocks. The term refers to this material while it is still under the earth's crust. In addition to its complex silicate solution, magma contains gases and water vapor. It is believed to exist in separate chambers beneath the surface of the earth. △166, 176, 278.

Magna Carta (1215), "great charter" of English civil liberties. It was issued by King John, under compulsion from his barons, at Runnymede, on June 15, 1215. John's financial exactions had united clergy and laity in demands for guarantees of civil rights. The 63 clauses into which Magna Carta is traditionally divided protected the rights of the church, the feudal lords, the lords' subtenants, and the merchants and regulated royal privileges, the administration of justice, and the behavior of royal officials. For subsequent generations Magna Carta became the basis and epitome of the subject's rights, protecting him against his sovereign's impositions. △1076.

Magna Graecia, area of southern Italy heavily colonized by Greece starting about the 8th century BC and continuing until the 2nd century BC. Of the colonial cities, Cumae was the most important. Others were Neapolis, Paestum, Elea, Croton, Sybaris, Heraclea, and Locri. Internecine struggles and the Punic Wars led to Roman dominance of the colonies.

Magnesium, common metallic element (symbol Mg) of the alkaline-earth group, first isolated (1808) by Sir Humphry Davy. Chief sources are magnesite, dolomite, and other minerals. Magnesium burns in air with an intense white flame and is used in flashbulbs, pyrotechnics, and incendiaries. Magnesium alloys are used in aircraft for their lightness. Chemically, the element is similar to calcium. Properties: at. no. 12; at. wt. 24.305; sp gr 1.738; melt. pt. 1199.8°F (648.8°C); boil. pt. 1994°F (1090°C); most common isotope Mg^{24} (78.7%). *See also* Alkaline-Earth Metals. △1552–54, 1572.

Magnet. *See* Magnetism.

Magnetic Anomaly, small variations in the Earth's magnetic field caused by iron objects or deposits. *See also* Anomaly. △170.

Magnetic Bottle, configuration of magnetic fields used to contain the plasma in a fusion reactor or experimental device, especially a linear configuration in which the ends are stoppered with magnetic mirrors. *See also* Fusion Reactor.

Magnetic Disc. △1800.

Magnetic Field, region surrounding a magnetic pole, or a conductor through which a current is flowing, in which there is a magnetic flux. A magnetic field can be represented by a set of lines of force emanating from the poles of a permanent magnet or running around a current-carrying conductor. These lines of force can be seen if iron filings are sprinkled onto a sheet of paper below which a permanent magnet is placed. The filings align themselves with the lines of force, the density of the lines being greatest where the field is strongest. △1490, 1534–38.

Magnetic Field, Earth, the composite of all the lines of force surrounding the dipole magnet that is the Earth. If the line between the magnetic poles (magnetic axis) is thought of as a bar magnet, the magnetic lines of force represent the paths of alignment of tiny magnets if they were free to move in space. △168, 1534, 1490.

Magnetic Field Reversal, the reversing of polarity whereby the north pole becomes the south and vice versa. Analyses of the magnetic direction of land and ocean basaltic lavas and sea-floor sediments have shown that the earth's main magnetic field has undergone frequent and rapid reversals. The field has changed 9 times in the last 4 million years. *See also* Sea-floor Spreading.

Magnetic Flux, measure of the size of a magnetic field expressed as the component of the magnetic field strength at right angles to a given area multiplied by the area. It is measured in maxwells (cgs units) or webers (SI units). △1534–36.

Magnetic Levitation Train. △1710.

Magnetic Mines. △1538.

Magnetic Poles, two regions in which the magnetism of a magnet appears to be concentrated. If a bar magnet is suspended to swing freely in the horizontal plane one pole will point north; this is called the north-seeking or north pole. The other pole, the south-seeking or south pole, will point south. Unlike poles attract each other, like poles repel each other. △1490, 1534.

Magnetic Poles, Earth, the ends of the bar magnet that is Earth. The north magnetic pole is at about 76°N latitude and 102°W longitude. The south magnetic pole is at about 68°S latitude and 145°E longitude. The magnetic axis does not pass through Earth's center. *See also* Magnetic Field, Earth; Polar Wander. △168.

Magnetic Recording, formation of a record of sounds on a wire or tape by means of a pattern of magnetization. In a tape recorder, plastic tape impregnated with iron oxide is fed past an electromagnet, which is energized by the amplified currents produced by a microphone. The variations in magnetization retained by the particles of iron oxide on the tape represent the oscillating current produced by the sound. For playing back, the tape is fed past a similar electromagnet, which feeds an amplifier and loudspeaker. △1474, 1798, 1800.

Magnetic Resonance, the phenomenon of absorption of radio and microwave frequencies by atoms placed in a magnetic field. Devices called electron-spin resonance (ESR) spectrometers use microwaves for the investigation of atoms and molecules. Nuclear-magnetic resonance (NMR) spectrometers use radio frequencies for research in nuclear physics.

Magnetic Storm, or geomagnetic storm, a disturbance in Earth's magnetic field. Since it encompasses all of Earth, the effects of such a storm are global. Auroras are seen, both in areas where such displays are normal and in others as well. Radio signals are disturbed. There is a regularly reappearing cycle of such magnetic storms as well as irregular ones. *See also* Aurora; Magnetosphere.

Magnetic Tape. △1798, 1800.

Magnetism, properties of matter and of electric currents associated with a field of force (magnetic field) and with a north-south polarity (magnetic poles). All substances possess these properties to some degree as orbiting electrons in their atoms produce a magnetic field in the same way as an electric current pro-

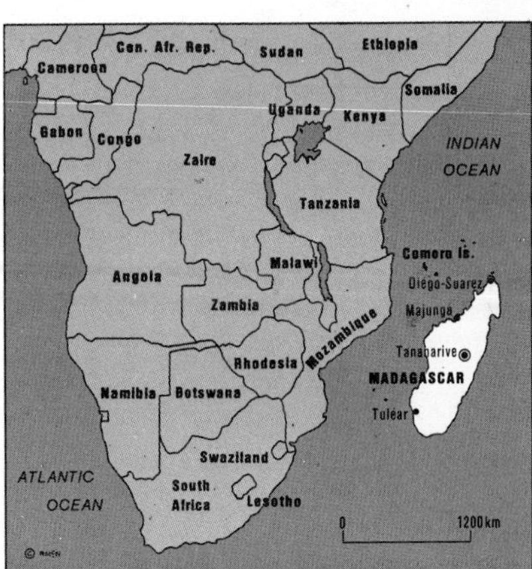
Cen. Afr. Rep.
Sudan
Ethiopia
Cameroon
Somalia
Uganda
Kenya
Gabon
Congo
Zaire
INDIAN
OCEAN
Tanzania
Comoro Is.
Diégo-Suarez
Angola
Malawi
Majunga
Zambia
Mozambique
Rhodesia
Tananarive
MADAGASCAR
Namibia
Botswana
Tuléar
Swaziland
ATLANTIC
OCEAN
South
Africa
Lesotho
0
1200km

Madagascar

James Madison

Madras, India

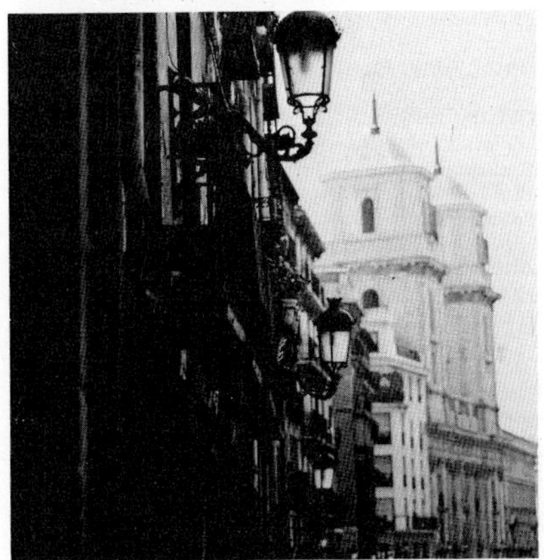

Madrid, Spain

duces a magnetic field; similarly, an external magnetic field will affect the electron orbits. All substances possess weak magnetic (diamagnetic) properties and will tend to align themselves with the field but in some cases this weak magnetism is masked by the stronger forms of magnetism: paramagnetism and ferromagnetism.

Paramagnetism is caused by electron spin and occurs in substances having unpaired electrons in their atoms or molecules. The most important form of magnetism, ferromagnetism, occurs in substances such as iron and nickel, which are capable of being magnetized by even a weak field due to the formation of tiny regions, called domains, that behave like miniature magnets and align themselves with an external field. These domains are formed as a result of strong interatomic forces caused by the spin of electrons in unfilled inner electron shells of the atoms. Permanent magnets, which retain their magnetization after the magnetizing field has been removed, are ferromagnetic. Electromagnets have a ferromagnetic core around which a coil is wound. The passage of a current through the coil magnetizes the core. △1490, 1534–38.

Magnetism, Terrestrial, magnetic field associated with the Earth. It is similar to that which would be produced by a powerful bar magnet, pointing north-south, situated at its center. The present positions of the Earth's magnetic poles are: N = 76°N lat, 102°W long; S = 68°S lat, 145°E long. The magnetic field at any point on the Earth's surface is defined by three magnetic quantities: the horizontal component of the magnetic flux density; the angle of dip (or inclination), that is, the angle through which a magnetic needle will dip from the horizontal when suspended in a vertical plane; and the angle of declination (or magnetic variation), that is, the angle between the geographic and magnetic meridians. The cause of the Earth's magnetism is not known. △168, 1534.

Magnetite, an oxide mineral, ferrous and ferric iron oxide ($FeFe_2O_4$). Most magnetic mineral, valuable iron ore. Found in igneous and metamorphic rocks. Cubic system octahedral and dodecahedral crystals, granular masses common. Black, metallic, and brittle. Hardness 6; sp gr 5.2. Permanently magnetized deposits are called lodestone.

Magnetochemistry, branch of chemistry concerned with investigating the magnetic properties of compounds. In particular, magnetic measurements made on transition-metal complexes, which are often paramagnetic due to unpaired electrons, give information on their structure and electron configuration. *See also* Magnetism. △1484.

Magnetohydrodynamics (MHD), study of conducting fluids under the influence of magnetic fields. A MHD generator is a source of electrical power consisting of a flame or plasma flowing between the poles of a strong magnet. The free electrons in the flame or plasma constitute a current when they flow, under the influence of the magnetic field, between electrodes inserted into the flame or plasma. The concentration of free electrons in a flame can be increased by adding to it elements, such as sodium and potassium, of low ionization potential.

Magnetometer, instrument for comparing magnetic field strengths or magnetic moments. It usually consists of a short bar magnet with a long nonmagnetic pointer attached to its center so that it is at right angles to the axis of the magnet. The magnet is pivoted, like a compass needle, at its center and the pointer travels over a calibrated scale. Field strengths of magnets are compared by measuring the deflections of the pointer.

Magnetopause, Earth. △108.

Magnetosphere, that region in space around the Earth in which the magnetic field of Earth has an important part in controlling the physical activity observed. The magnetosphere is a two-part region; the lobe closer to the Sun is larger and blunt, the other lobe, an elongated tail extending several hundred times the radius of Earth into space. The shape of the magnetosphere is determined by the stress exerted on the magnetopause (outermost edge) by the solar wind. △168.

Magnetron, a vacuum tube containing an anode and a heated cathode. The flow of electrons from cathode to anode is controlled by an externally applied magnetic field. When attached to a resonant line, it can act as an oscillator. It is capable of generating high frequencies and high power in short bursts and is used in radar systems and microwave ovens.

Magnificent Riflebird. △538.

Magnitogorsk, city in Russian SFSR, USSR, on the SW slope of Magnitnaya Mt, on the dammed upper Ural River, 160mi (258km) SSW of Chelyabinsk. An old village, in the early 18th century it was named Magnitnaya when magnetized iron was discovered in two nearby mountains; in 1930 the Soviet government began to develop the area; by 1933 it was a large city with US-built plants; it is now the leading USSR metallurgical center; site of teachers' and metallurgical colleges. Industries: military equipment, machinery, nitrate fertilizers, cement, clothing, shoes, foodstuffs, glass. Pop. 364,000.

Magnitude, in astronomy, numerical value expressing the brightness of a celestial object on a logarithmic scale. Apparent magnitude is the magnitude as seen from Earth, determined by eye, photographically, or photometrically, and ranges from positive through zero to negative values, the brightness increasing rapidly as the magnitude decreases. A difference of over 2.5, first magnitude being exactly 100 times brighter than sixth magnitude (just visible to the naked eye). Absolute magnitude indicates intrinsic luminosity and is defined as the apparent magnitude of an object at a distance of 10 parsecs. △40.

Magnitude, Earthquake, a measure based on the movement of the ground as recorded by seismographs. It is a logarithmic expression and the jump from one number to the next represents a factor of 30. On the Richter scale of earthquake magnitude, a small quake may be less than zero, a major (very infrequent) quake might register 7 or 8. *See also* Seismic Waves. △174.

Magnolia, trees and shrubs native to North America, Central America, Asia, and the Himalayas. Valued for their showy flowers of white, yellow, purple, and pink, they are mostly deciduous; some are evergreen and can stand cooler temperatures. Height: to 100ft (31m). Family Magnoliaceae. The magnolia family includes 10 genera of shrubs, trees, and vines native to North America and Asia. △450.

Magnus VII Eriksson (1316–74), king of Sweden and Norway (1319–65). Crowned at age three, he united Sweden and Norway because he was heir to both thrones. He ruled under a regent (1319–32) and lived most of his life in Sweden. The Black Death swept the kingdom during his rule. In 1365 he was defeated by his nephew, Albert of Mecklenburg, who then became king of Sweden, while Magnus retired to Norway.

Magpie, widely distributed chattering birds closely related to jays. The typical Northern Hemisphere black-billed magpie *(Pica pica)* is blackish with a long greenish-black tail, and white on its shoulders, wing linings, and belly. Both parents build a domed, stick and mud nest, lined with hair and feathers, for pale spotted eggs (6–9) incubated by the female. The male helps feed the young. Length: 20in (51cm). Family Corvidae. △528–30.

Magritte, René (1898–1967), Belgian painter. A leading surrealist, he was at first influenced by cubism and futurism; later, he evolved a realistic style. His early works include "La Statue volante" (1927) and "La Belle captive" (1931). His mature works, marked by brighter color and juxtaposition of objects, include "The Liberator" and "L'Empire des Lumières" (1954). △1318.

Magsaysay, Ramón (1907–57), president of the Philippines (1953–57). In 1950 he was appointed secretary of defense in order to crush the Hukbalahap rebellion. He accomplished this goal through army reform and land reform. In 1953 he opposed President Elpidio Quirino and won the presidency, but a conservative congress thwarted his measures for further reform.

Magyars, the people associated with the state of Hungary, descendants of Finno-Ugric and Turkish tribes who mingled with Avars and Slavs in the 9th century. Although incorporated into the Austro-Hungarian Empire, the fiercely independent Magyars demanded special minority rights to preserve their language and culture, finally achieving first the Dual Monarchy in 1867 and independence in 1918. △1074.

Mahabharata, meaning "Great Epic of the Bharata Dynasty," poem consisting of almost 100,000 couplets. It is considered one of India's two major epics, along with the *Ramayana.* The verse is important both as literature and Hindu religious instruction. The plot revolves around a power struggle between two related families. It was written *c.* 400 BC–*c.* AD 200 and compiled into its present form by *c.* AD 400.

Mahadevi. *See* Devi.

Mahan, Alfred Thayer (1840–1914), US naval officer and historian, b. West Point, N.Y. After graduation from Naval Academy (1859), he served in the Civil and Spanish-American wars. He lectured on naval history at the Naval War College in Newport, became its president, and published the celebrated *Influence of Sea Power upon History* (1890) and *Influence of Sea Power upon the French Revolution* (1892); his ideas on sea power strongly influenced Theodore Roosevelt. He was a delegate to the first Hague Peace Conference.

Mahayana Buddhism, one of the main schools of Buddhism. Emerging in India somewhere between the 1st century BC and the 1st century AD, the Mahayana school stressed compassion as well as wisdom as necessary for salvation, and claimed to be more universal in its appeal than the older, more conservative Hinayana school. The Bodhista, or "being destined for enlightenment," is seen as the ideal of human life. Various schools sprang from the Mahayana sect and spread to Tibet, China, Korea, and Japan. *See also* Buddhism. △988.

Mahican. *See* Mohican.

Mahisha. △1036.

Mah Jongg, a widely played game, believed to have originated in China. The equipment consists of 144 decorative rectangular tiles, made of wood, ivory, or plastic. There are 108 suit tiles, 28 honor tiles, and 8 flower or season tiles. The three suits are bamboo or sticks, circles or dots, and character or cracks. The game itself is complicated, but the basic object is to accumulate sets.

Mahler, Gustav (1860–1911), Austrian composer and conductor. Famous in his own lifetime as a conductor, Mahler was relatively ignored until the 1960s when his nine symphonies became recognized as important achievements of the Romantic period and bridges to 20th-century music. Many of his works combine orchestral with vocal and choral parts, require massive orchestras, and contain novel instrumental effects. *See also* Romanticism in Music. △1246.

Mahogany, tropical deciduous tree with wood valued for furniture making. It has leaves composed of smaller leaflets, large clusters of flowers, and winged seeds. Among 1,400 species is the familiar New World Honduran *Swietenia macrophylla* found from S Mexico to N South America; height to 60ft(18m). *Swietenia mahogonii* has a short, swollen trunk and is native to the West Indies and S Florida. Family Meliaceae. △364.

Mahrattas, or **Marathas.** △1202.

Maidan. △680, 1064.

Maidenhair Fern, dainty North American fern found in limestone areas. The wedge-shaped leaves are borne on slender, shiny black, erect stalks. Leaves of most unfold pink, then turn pea green. Height: 10–20in (25–51cm). Family Adiantaceae; species *Adiantum capillus-veneris. See also* Fern.

Maidenhair Tree. △440.

Maidstone, county town of Kent, SE England, on Medway River, 30mi (48km) SE of London. Industries: paper, brewing. Pop. 70,918.

Maidu, a Penutian-speaking tribe of North American Indians occupying the Feather River and American River area of N California. From a population of 9,000 their numbers were decimated by Gold Rush miners to approximately 1,100 today. They are excellent basket makers.

Mailer, Norman (1923–), US author, b. Long Branch, N.J. After serving with the US army in the Pacific in World War II, he wrote his first novel, *The Naked and the Dead* (1948). Since then he has written numerous articles and books, was a cofounder of *The Village Voice,* a New York City weekly newspaper, and ran unsuccessfully as an independent candidate for mayor of New York City (1969). In 1969 he won both a Pulitzer Prize and a National Book Award for his nonfiction work, *The Armies of the Night* (1968), a personal chronicle about the antiwar march on the Pentagon in Washington, D.C., in October 1967. Other works include *The Deer Park* (1955) and *An American Dream* (1965), both novels, and *Miami and the Siege of Chicago* (1969), nonfiction. *See also* Naked and the Dead, The △1374.

Maillol, Aristide (1861–1944), French sculptor, tapestry designer, painter, and draftsman. In 1893 he exhibited a tapestry at the National Society Salon; from 1894–98 he worked on woodcuts. His major works of sculpture include "Mediterranean," and "Action in Chains and Desire" (1905). His work, marked by subtlety and clear surface, brought him international fame.

Maimonides, or **Moses ben Maimon** (1135–1204), Jewish physician and philosopher. He was born in Spain but left to avoid persecution after a Muslim invasion and settled in Cairo. There he became doctor to the court of Sultan Saladin and also created hundreds of private patients. He became even more noted for his scholarly works on Judaic law and on philosophy. He tried to reconcile Aristotle's thinking with Hebrew theology. Maimonides' works influenced such thinkers as Thomas Aquinas. △858.

Maine, state in the extreme NE United States, on the Atlantic Ocean and bordered on the W, N, and E by the provinces of Quebec and New Brunswick, Canada.

Land and Economy. The coastline is broken by bays and inlets; hundreds of islands lie offshore. The land is generally rolling; the highest mountains are in the central part. Principal rivers are the Penobscot, Kennebec, and Androscoggin, which flow into the Atlantic. Thousands of lakes are in the interior. More than 75% of the state is forested. Maine's natural resources are the foundation of the economy. Coastal fisheries, chiefly lobsters, clams, and herring, and the great supply of timber are major income producers. Potatoes are a major crop. Recreational opportunities draw visitors all year, and tourism is an important source of revenue.

People. The population has grown slowly. Most of the residents are descended from English, Scots, Irish, and French settlers. Only about 50% resides in areas classified as urban.

Education. There are about 25 institutions of higher education.

History. Scattered English settlements were made along the coast soon after 1600, when the name "Maine" was applied to the mainland as distinct from the islands. The province was organized on a charter from Charles I of England in 1639. Its capital, Gorgeana (1642), later reincorporated as the town of York, was the first incorporated city in the American colonies. Under a new charter in 1691, the land became part of the colony of Massachusetts Bay. It remained part of the state of Massachusetts until admitted to the Union in its own right in 1820. Industrial development was gradual in the 19th century. WWII, which spurred shipbuilding and brought military and naval establishments to the state, was an economic stimulus.

PROFILE

Admitted to Union: March 15, 1820; rank, 23d
US Congressmen: Senate, 2; House of Representatives, 2
Population: 993,663 (1970); rank, 38th
Capital: Augusta, 21,945 (1970)
Chief cities: Portland, 65,116; Lewiston, 41,799; Bangor, 33,168
State legislature: Senate, 33; House of Representatives, 151
Area: 33,215sq mi (86,027sq km); rank, 39th
Elevation: Highest, 5,268ft (1,607m), Mt Katahdin; lowest, sea level
Industries (major products): wood products, lumber, paper, textiles, processed foods, shoes
Agriculture (major products): poultry, potatoes, blueberries, apples, vegetables
Minerals (major): granite, cement, feldspar
State nickname: Pine Tree State
State motto: Dirigo ("I Direct")
State bird: chickadee
State flower: pine cone and tassel
State tree: eastern white pine

Maine, USS, US battleship mysteriously blown up and sunk in the harbor of Havana, Cuba, in February 1898. The *Maine* disaster became an important precipitating event in the Spanish-American War. With Cubans revolting against Spain, the ship had been sent to protect US citizens, and the bombing was attributed to foreign enemies. The cry "Remember the *Maine*," incited war fever and in April the Spanish-American war began. △1278.

Maine Coon Cat, American semi-longhaired domestic cat breed found in Maine and Massachusetts. Derived from mongrel stock, it is a massive cat with distinctive long fur, pointed head, bushy tail, and coarse coat of any color. It can withstand severe weather.

Main River, river in E West Germany, formed by confluence of Roter Main and Weisser Main at Kulmbach; flows W through West Germany to Rhine River at Mainz; connected to Danube River by canal; navigable for about 240mi (386km). Length: 310mi (499km).

Main Sequence Stars, stars found along or near a diagonal distribution line on the Hertzsprung-Russell diagram. This line, known as the main sequence, runs from top left (hot bright blue stars) to bottom right (cool dim red stars) and represents the distribution class to which 90 percent of all the known stars, including the sun, belong. It also serves to trace the evolutionary pattern that most stars seem to follow for part of their existence, the stages at which they join or leave the main sequence being governed by their mass and energy output. △100–02.

Mainz, city in W central West Germany, on W bank of Rhine River, 20mi (32km) WSW of Frankfurt am Main; capital of Rhineland-Palatinate state; seat of first German archbishop (St Boniface, 746); became a free city 1118; archbishop made an imperial elector 1356. City passed to France 1797; made a fortress of German Confederation by Congress of Vienna (1815); birthplace of Johann Gutenberg, who made Mainz first printing center of Europe in 15th century; site of six-towered Romanesque cathedral (1009), 18th-century church of St Peter, Johann Gutenberg University, (founded as University of Mainz 1477, closed 1816, reinstituted 1946). Industries: wine, chemicals, motor vehicles, cement, optical instruments, machinery. Founded 1st century BC as Roman camp. Pop. 172,195.

Maithuna. △1036.

Maitland, William (?1528–73), Scottish nobleman, known as "Secretary Lethington." Made Mary Queen of Scots' secretary of state (1561), he resisted church domination of government affairs and tried to unite Scotland and England by ensuring Mary's right of succession to Elizabeth I. He died in prison after holding Edinburgh Castle (1571–73) against James VI's supporters.

Majolica (Maiolica), tin-glazed earthenware painted in blue, green, manganese purple, yellow, or orange and made in Italy from the 14th to the 18th century. The term originally referred to luster painted ceramics from Majorca that were shipped to Italy.

Majorca (Mallorca), island of Spain, largest of the Balearic Islands, in W Mediterranean, approx. 115mi (185km) from the Spanish coast; capital is Palma. Held at different times by the Romans, Vandals, and Byzantines, it was taken 797 by the Moors, captured and made kingdom of Majorca 1276 by James I, king of Aragon; scene of peasant uprising 1521–23, and romance between composer Frederic Chopin and author George Sand; served as Italian base opposing Loyalists during Spanish Civil War (1936–39); scene of annual dance festivals celebrating the harvest; site of Caves of the Dragon containing underground lakes, and 13th-century Franciscan school. The island offers beautiful scenery and mild climate. Industries: tourism, fishing, lead, iron and coal mining, wine, jewelry, handicrafts, limestone and marble quarrying, olives, figs, oranges, lemons, almonds. Area: 1,405sq mi (3,639sq km). Pop. 460,030.

Majority and Plurality. △902.

Makarios III (1913–), Cypriot clergyman and political figure, b. as Mikhail Khristodoulou Mouskos. Archbishop of the Orthodox Church of Cyprus and leader of the *enosis* (union of Cyprus with Greece) movement, he was elected president of Cyprus (1959), when it became independent of Britain. He later abandoned *enosis* because it inflamed Turkish Cypriots. In 1974 he was forced to leave the country for several months as Greece and Turkey interfered with the nation's internal affairs.

Mako, also called mackerel shark, found worldwide in tropical marine waters. Deep cobalt to blue-gray above and pure white below, it is a strong swimmer and known to attack man. Length: to 13ft (3.9m); weight: 1,000lb (450kg). Family Isuridae (also called Lamnidae); species long fin *Isurus paucus,* short fin *Isurus xyrhinchus. See also* Chondrichthyes; Shark. △516.

Malabar Coast, SW coast of India, between the Western Ghats (E) and Arabian Sea (W); Cochin and Calicut are the chief ports; traditional site where the Apostle Thomas started his missionary work (AD 52); Portuguese-based trading posts were est. here 1498–1503; area experienced an influx of Dutch 1656, French 1720s; by late 18th century, British had occupied the area. Industries: fishing, coconuts, rice, spices, rubber. Length: 550mi (886km).

Magpie

Norman Mailer

Maine: Portland lighthouse

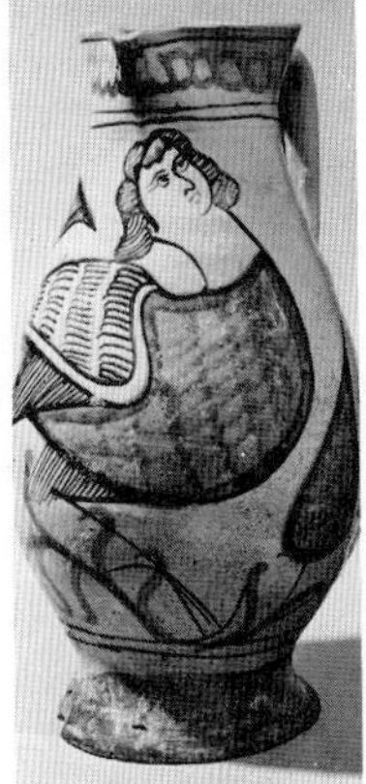

Majolica pitcher

Malabo, seaport town and capital of Equatorial Guinea, on Fernando Po Island in Gulf of Guinea. Industries: fish processing, cacao, coffee. Founded 1827 as British base to suppress slave trade. Pop. 20,000.

Malabsorption Syndromes, a group of diseases in which the common feature is either failure to digest certain nutrients or disruption of the process whereby the compounds produced by digestion are carried through the intestinal wall and into the blood for distribution to the tissues. Malabsorption has a variety of causes, among which are lesions of the small intestine, as in celiac disease or tropical sprue, abnormal bacterial growth in the intestine, disease of the intestinal lymph glands, or intolerance to certain substances such as sucrose. Ability to absorb fats, proteins, carbohydrates, vitamins, iron, calcium, sodium, potassium, and magnesium may be impaired, with the symptoms depending on the substance involved. Emaciation is a common manifestation. Treatment is mainly regulation of diet and replacement of deficiencies. △718.

Malachi, biblical author and last of the 12 minor prophets. His book of prophecies closes the Old Testament with the promise of Elijah's return to help Israel.

Malachite, a carbonate mineral, basic copper carbonate (CU_2CO_3 $(OH)_2$), found in weathered copper ore deposits. Monoclinic system, silky green; hardness 3.5–4; sp gr 4. Sometimes used as a gem. △242.

Málaga, seaport city in S Spain, on the Mediterranean Sea; capital of Málaga prov. Taken from Visigoths by Moors 711 it remained under Moorish rule until 1487, when it was captured by Ferdinand and Isabella. During the Spanish Civil War (1936–39), city was taken from loyalists by Francisco Franco; site of 8th-century fortress, 14th-century Moorish citadel, and several scenic parks. Industries: wine, olive oil, shoes, candy, flour, tourism. Founded *c.* 1100 BC by Phoenicians. Area: (prov.) 2,809sq mi (7,275sq km). Pop. (city) 374,452; (prov.) 867,330.

Malagasy Republic (Malgache), formerly Madagascar; nation in Indian Ocean about 250mi (400km) E of Africa. The people, a mixture of Asian and African descent, rely almost entirely on agriculture as the basis of their economy.

Land and Economy. Madagascar, the 4th-largest island in the world, stretches about 980mi (1,578km) N to S with a maximum width of 360mi (580km). Dominated by a central mountainous area that slopes gently to a coastal plain on the W but drops abruptly to the Indian Ocean on the E, the island provides fertile, usable land except for a small semi-arid section in the S. Eighty percent of the population is farmers owning cattle, sheep, pigs, and goats. Rice is the chief food crop and coffee the most valuable export. Malagasy is the world's largest producer of vanilla and is also one of the leading producers of graphite. The principal seaports are Tamatave and Majunga.

People. Physically the people of Malagasy resemble Africans, but their language is akin to Indonesian. Indonesians settled Madagascar over 2,000 years ago, but the influx of African peoples caused an amalgamation of races. Although 33% of the people is Christian, the majority practices ancient religious rites. About 50% of the people is literate.

Government. The president, who also serves as prime minister, is head of state and head of government. He is elected by the people for a seven-year term. Parliament is made up of a 107-member National Assembly, each member elected for a 5-year term, and a 54-member Senate, 36 members elected and 18 appointed by the government, each for a 6-year term. There is universal suffrage at age 21.

History. Although there was some Arab contact from 900, and Portuguese discovery in 1500, the island was finally settled by the French in the mid-1600s. In the 1780s the Merinas, a central highlands people, brought about unification. In 1885, France was granted protectorate rights by the British for ceding certain territorial rights to them. In 1958, Malagasy became an autonomous republic, and in 1960 gained full independence, with Philibert Tsiranana elected the first president. In 1972 a successful coup by General Ramanantsoa overthrew Tsiranana, but Ramanantsoa was assassinated, and Didier Ratsiraka took control.

PROFILE

Official name: Malagasy Republic
Area: 226,657sq mi (587,042sq km)
Population: 8,000,000
Density: 35.3 per sq mi (13.6 per sq km)
Chief cities: Tananarive (capital); Tamatave.
Government: Republic
Religion: Traditional beliefs, Christianity
Language: Malagasy (official), French
Monetary unit: Malagasy franc
Gross national product: $1,020,000,000
Per capita income: $130
Industries: cigarettes, sugar
Agriculture (major products): rice, sugar cane, cassava, coffee, vanilla
Minerals (major): graphite, salt, chromium ore
Trading partners (major): France, United States, West Germany

Malamud, Bernard (1914–), US author, b. New York City. A short story writer and novelist, his works generally deal with Jewish characters. His books include *The Assistant* (1957), *A New Life* (1961), and *The Fixer* (1966), a novel about a Jew accused of ritual murder. In 1967 Malamud won both a Pulitzer Prize and a National Book Award for *The Fixer.*

Malaria, an insect-borne, often chronic disease resulting from infection with one of four species of the parasitic microorganism *Plasmodium,* acquired through the bite of the *Anopheles* mosquito and affecting the red blood corpuscles. *Plasmodium falciparum* malaria is the most serious form, with severe complications that may lead to death. Attacks of fever, chills, and sweating typify the disease and occur as new generations of parasites develop in the blood, with the frequency of attacks related to the species involved. The disease is treated with antimalarial drugs. △732.

Malawi, independent republic in E central Africa; bounded by Tanzania (N and NE), Zambia (W), Mozambique (E, S, and SW). The president is the head of state and government and is answerable to a unicameral National Assembly. More than 20% of the land is covered by Lake Malawi, drained (S) by Shire River, its only outlet; much of the remaining area is plateau. The economy is overwhelmingly agricultural, with 25% of the land being arable. Chief crops are tea, tobacco, sugar cane, grain, and potatoes. Malawi's economy heavily depends on almost 30% of the populace working in industries in Rhodesia, South Africa, and Zambia. From 1950, Malawi began to develop its own light industries. Almost 99% of the population is Bantu-speaking black African, the majority being Christian or Muslim. Housing, education, health, and economic standards are relatively poor.

History. From 15th-18th centuries, Malawi grew with immigration of Bantu-speaking tribes from N and W. Visited by David Livingstone in 1859, who focused on the need for European intervention against slave trading. The British Central African Protectorate (Nyasaland) was est. 1891 and slave trade was ended. Against strong opposition from black Africans fearing white-oriented policies, the Federation of Rhodesia and Nyasaland was formed 1953. It survived until 1963; Nyasaland became independent as Malawi on July 6, 1964. In the same year, Malawi joined the United Nations; it became a republic 1966.

PROFILE

Official name: Republic of Malawi
Area: 45,193sq mi (117,050sq km)
Population: 4,552,000
Density: 100per sq mi (39per sq km)
Chief cities: Lilongwe (capital); Blantyre; Zomba
Religion: Christianity, Islam
Language: English, Cinyanja, Citumbuka (all official)
Monetary unit: Kwacha

Malay, the official language of Malaysia, spoken by about half the country's population, or some 6,000,-000 people. It is also one of the official languages of Singapore. Malay is for all practical purposes the same language as Indonesian, both belonging to the Austronesian family.

Malayalam, language spoken on the W coast of extreme S India, principally in the state of Kerala. It belongs to the Dravidian family of languages. There are about 20 million speakers. It is one of the 15 constitutional languages of India.

Malay Archipelago, island group in SE Asia, between the Indian Ocean and the E central Pacific Ocean, N of Australia. The world's largest archipelago, it includes major islands of Luzon, Mindanao, New Guinea, Celebes, Java, Sumatra, and Borneo. Malay Archipelago is a purely geographic label, as the islands have been claimed and reclaimed in various groups by different foreign powers since 1st century BC. Since WWII they have divided into three main autonomous groups: The Philippines (1946), Indonesia (1949), and Federation of Malaya (1957, now Malaysia). W half of New Guinea Island (Irian Barat) is Indonesian territory; E half is Papua New Guinea.

Malayo-Polynesian Languages, another name for the Austronesian languages. *See* Austronesian Languages.

Malay Peninsula, promontory in SE Asia, between Strait of Malacca and South China Sea; comprises SW Thailand and West Malaysia. A mountain range, culminating in Mt Gunong Tahan, 7,186ft (2,192m), extends along its entire length; it is one of world's richest tin and rubber areas. Length: 700mi (1,127km). Area: 70,000sq mi (181,300sq km).

Malaysia, Federation of, nation in SE Asia. Lying in the extreme SE tip of Asia, it occupies the S half of the Malay Peninsula and most of N Borneo. The people are principally Malay and Chinese. Malaysia is the world's leading producer of tin and contributes about 35% of the world's rubber supply.

Land and Economy. The country divides into two distinct sections: W Malaysia or Malaya, which consists of 11 states lying on the S half of the Malay Peninsula, and E Malaysia, which consists of two states, Sabah and Sarawak, 400mi (644km) across the South China Sea on the N shores of Borneo. A mountain range runs N–S through the heart of Malaya, sloping off to a coastal lowland plain to the W where the majority of the people live. Both Sabah and Sarawak have swampy, alluvial coastal plains with tropical rain forests dominating most of the land. The hot and humid climate of Malaysia is ideal for the rubber industry, the country's main source of income. Malaysia is the world's leading producer of tin, and the largest producer of iron ore in the Far East. Although most natives are farmers, industry has developed rapidly, and Malaysia now processes many of its own resources. The country has good highway and rail services, plus excellent coastal shipping facilities.

People. About 85% of the population lives in Malaya; more than 35% is of Malay origin, with almost as many Chinese. Malay is the official language, but English and Chinese are widely spoken.

Government. A federal constitutional monarchy provides for a House of Representatives including 144 members elected by the people, and a Senate composed of 48 members, two from each of the 13 states and 22 appointed by the central government. From the nine states governed by hereditary rulers, a supreme head of state is chosen each five years to represent the country at ceremonial functions. Each of the 13 states has its own executive and legislature.

History: Although the country contained settled communities 2,000 years ago, the first real kingdom was est. by Buddhists from Sumatra about 800. During the 13th century Singapore was settled, and Arab traders brought Islam to the area. The Portuguese, the first Europeans to arrive (1509), had been expelled by the Dutch by 1641. In the late 18th century, the British made their appearance and by 1826 had formed the Straits Settlement, a colony made up of Panang, Malacca, and Singapore. The opening of the Suez Canal in 1869 and the introduction of rubber trees from Brazil in 1877 made the area even more prosperous. When the Japanese withdrew after WWII, everything was left in a state of disrepair. The Communists attempted a take-over, but by declaring a state of emergency that lasted until 1960, the government was successful in allaying the threat. Accusing the British of neo-colonialism, Indonesia sent guerrilla fighters into Malaysia in 1963, but the problem was resolved by a 1966 treaty. Malaya achieved independence in 1957, and the federation was formed in 1963. Singapore, originally a member, withdrew in 1965 because of internal problems. A separatist movement in Sabah and Communist guerrillas remained as problems in the mid 1970s.

PROFILE

Official name: Federation of Malaysia
Area: 127,316sq mi (329,748sq km)
Population: 12,100,000
Density: 95.0per sq mi (36.7per sq km)
Chief cities: Kuala Lumpur (capital); Pinang; Ipoh
Government: Federal constitutional monarchy
Religion: Islam
Language: Malay
Monetary unit: Malaysian dollar
Gross national product: $6,400,000,000
Per capita income: $529
Industries (major products): petroleum products, refined sugar, rubber goods, steel, lumber
Agriculture (major products): rubber, rice, palm oil, tea, pepper, coconuts, spices
Minerals (major): tin, iron
Trading partners (major): Japan, United States, European Economic Community

Malcolm II Mackenneth (died 1034), king of Scotland (1005–34) who in 1018 defeated the Northumbrians at Carham and secured the Anglo-Saxon district of Lothian permanently for Scotland. In the same year he gained control over Strathclyde, and thus completed the political unification of northern Britain.

In 1031 he paid nominal homage to Canute, although the Danish ruler never interfered with his rule.

Malcolm III, or **Malcolm Canmore** (1031?–93), king of Scotland (1059–93). He succeeded his father, Duncan I, by slaying the usurper, Macbeth. Despite paying homage to William I (1072), he repeatedly raided England.

Malcolm X (1925–65), US militant black leader, b. Omaha, Nebr. While serving a prison sentence, he joined the Black Muslims, a black separatist group. He then became a Black Muslim minister on his release in 1952. He later came into conflict with the group's leader Elijah Muhammad and formed a rival group, the Muslim Mosque, in 1963. In 1964 he converted to Islam. He was assassinated in February 1965.

Malden, city in E Massachusetts, on Malden River. Industries: processed foods, aluminum products, tools. Founded 1640; chartered 1881. Pop. (1970) 56,127.

Maldives, Republic of, independent island nation in the Indian Ocean 400mi (644km) SW of Sri Lanka. The country consists of some 2,000 coral islands in 12 distinct clusters. The islands, lying in a hot, humid climate, are covered with coconut palms. The economy is based almost entirely on the fishing industry with bonita the main export. In a move to bolster the economy, the government has encouraged tourism. The people are mostly of Arab and Aryan descent living at subsistence level in a one-crop economy. Virtually the entire population is Muslim. Divehi, a dialect of Sinhalese, is the principal language; Arabic is also spoken. Most of the people are illiterate.

Government and History. A republic, the government consists of a president, elected every four years; the Majlis (House of Representatives), consisting of 54 members elected every five years; and a Supreme Court and lesser courts. The entire system directly reflects Islamic influence.

The Portuguese, the first Europeans to arrive, controlled the area from 1558–73. The Dutch gained control in the 17th century, only to be ousted by the British, who controlled the island from 1887 until 1965. Independence was achieved in 1965, and the republic was declared in 1968.

PROFILE

Official name: Republic of Maldives
Area: 115sq mi (298sq km)
Population: 114,469
Density: 995per sq mi (384per sq km)
Chief city: Male (capital)
Government: Republic
Religion: Muslim (official)
Language: Divehi (official)
Monetary unit: Rupee
Per capita income: est. less than $100
Industries (major products): lace products
Agriculture (major products): fish
Trading partners (major): Sri Lanka

Malebranche, Nicolas de (1638–1715), French philosopher and theologian. A priest and a student of Cartesian philosophy and science, Malebranche was involved in many theological debates. His principal work, *Search for the Truth* (1674–75) introduced his revision of Cartesian metaphysics and physical science. He was the author also of *Treatise on Nature and Grace* (1680), *Morals* (1684), and *Christian Meditations* (1683). *See also* Occasionalism.

Male Midlife Crisis, problem of middle-aged men resembling the emotional stress associated with the menopause in women. If he is not sufficiently well adjusted, decling physical powers and the approach of retirement may cause depression in a middle-aged man. △800.

Malenkov, Georgi M(aximilianovich) (1902–), Soviet political figure. Instrumental in organizing Stalin's purges (1934–39), he was elected to the Communist party Central Committee in 1939 and to the Politburo in 1946. After Stalin's death (1953) he became premier but was unseated (1955) as Khrushchev's authority increased. In 1957 he was expelled from the Central Committee. While in power he advocated "coexistence" and development of consumer goods production. △1344.

Malevich, Kazimir (1878–1935), Russian painter. He founded suprematism, a form of geometric abstractionism, in 1913. Malevich's manifesto, published in 1915, stated that the combination of geometric figures expressed "pure emotion." The epitome of the style is his *Suprematist Composition: White on White* (1919). △1318, 1372.

Malherbe, François de (1555–1628), French poet and critic, dictator of early 17th-century French literary style. He became a court writer in 1610 and severely criticized the emotional, decorative style of his contemporaries while pursuing simplicity and rationality in his own work. △1172.

Mali, independent republic in W Africa, surrounded by Algeria (N and NE), Upper Volta and Ivory Coast (S), Niger (E and SE), and Guinea, Senegal, and Mauritania (W). The flat lowlands of Mali are bisected W and E by the Niger River, dividing the Sahara Desert (N) from fertile agricultural region (S). The area produces sorghum, rice, millet, cotton, peanuts. Mali has various light industries including canning, cotton ginning, peanut oil extraction, bricks, textiles, and cigarettes; large mineral resources are largely unexploited. More than 83% of the population are black tribesmen; 65% of these are Muslim with an extremely low literacy rate.

Mali is governed by a president with unicameral legislature. Moussa Traoré was installed as president 1968 after a bloodless, military coup overthrowing a socialist regime. The constitution calls for the president to be invested by a majority of the legislative assembly.

Mali's importance peaked in the 14th century under the Mandingo Empire, which was a center for Muslim learning. By the early 15th century, the area was engulfed by civil strife that continued into the 18th century and was complicated by repeated invasions. French advancement began in the late 19th century and by 1898 Mali was almost totally occupied by the French and became French Sudan. The country voted in 1958 to join the French Community as the autonomous Sudanese Republic; it became the independent Republic of Mali in 1960. A devastating drought incapacitated the country in the early 1970s causing famine, disease, poverty, and a mass exodus by many tribes.

PROFILE

Official name: Republic of Mali
Area: 478,764sq mi (1,240,000sq km)
Population: 5,700,000
Chief cities: Bamako (capital); Mopti; Ségou; Kayes
Religion: Islam
Language: French, tribal languages
Monetary unit: Franc

Mali, a powerful West African trading empire of the Middle Ages (*c.*1000–*c.*1500), noted for its exports of gold. A Muslim state, it developed major cultural centers and reached its peak under Mansa Musa in the 14th century. △1116.

Malinowski, Bronislaw (1884–1942) Polish-English anthropologist, considered the founder of social anthropology. His work with the peoples of New Guinea and the Trobriand Islands helped him to formulate his functional theory, which held that every aspect or norm of a society is a function vital to its existence. He taught at the University of London and Yale. △874.

Mallard, river duck that is the ancestor of most domestic ducks. Males have a green head and neck and engage in complex courtship displays to attract females. It dabbles, or feeds from the surface. Species *Anas platyrhynchos. See also* Duck.

Mallarmé, Stéphane (1842–98), French poet. A leader of the symbolist movement, he was influenced by Baudelaire and Verlaine. Through his poetry he sought to evoke an intuitive ideal world. His works include *Hérodiade* (1869), *L'Après-midi d'un faune* (1876), and *Un Coup de dés jamais n'abolira le hasard* (1897). His style is complex. △1240.

Mallorca. *See* Majorca.

Mallow, annual and perennial plants native to temperate regions of North America, S Europe, and Asia. The flowers are pink and white. Many are considered weeds. Family Malvaceae; genus *Malva.* The mallow family includes over 900 species of plants native to temperate and tropical regions. Some are valued for their showy flowers and others for food or fiber.

Malloy v. Hogan (1964), landmark US Supreme Court decision overruling *Adamson* v. *California.* The court held that the Fifth Amendment's privilege against self-incrimination was applicable in state courts.

Malmédy, town in E Belgium; site of "Malmédy Massacre" in which 70 US war prisoners were killed by Germans, Dec. 17, 1944. Pop. 6,559.

Malmö, seaport city in SW Sweden, on the Øresund; major trade and shipping center during Hanseatic period; mostly ruled by the Danish, passed to Sweden 1658; now a naval and commercial port; site of Malm-

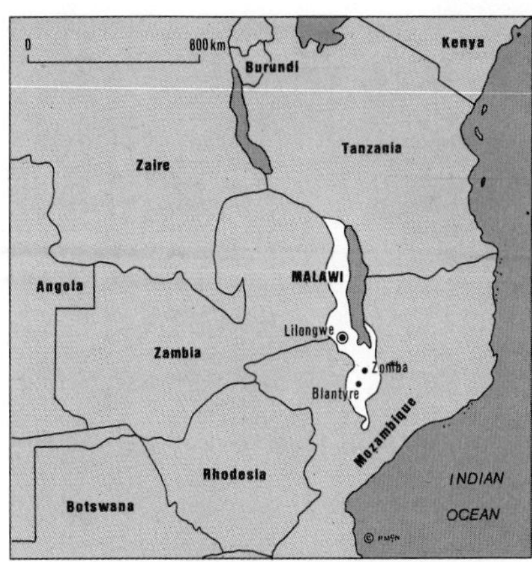
0
800km
Burundi
Kenya
Zaire
Tanzania
Angola
MALAWI
Lilongwe
Zambia
Zomba
Blantyre
Mozambique
Rhodesia
Botswana
INDIAN
OCEAN
Malawi

Burma
Thailand
Laos
Cambodia
Vietnam
Philippines
SOUTH
CHINA SEA
Kota Kinabalu
(Jesselton)
Penang
(Pinang)
Ipoh
MALAYSIA
Brunei
Kuala Lumpur
Johore Bahru
Kuching
Singapore
INDIAN
OCEAN
Indonesia
0
800km
Malaysia

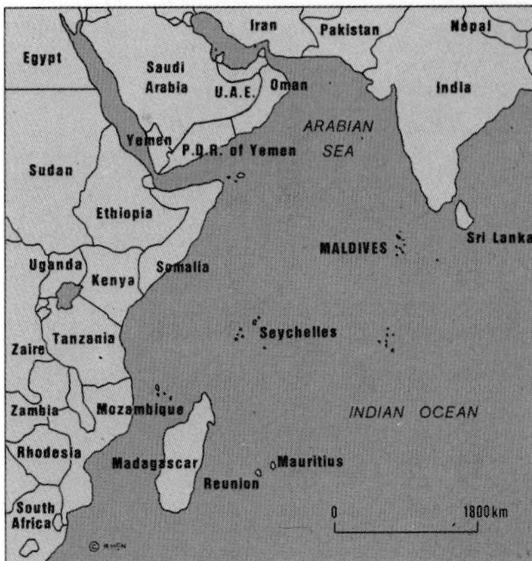
Egypt
Iran
Pakistan
Nepal
Saudi
Arabia
U.A.E.
Oman
India
ARABIAN
SEA
Yemen
P.D.R. of Yemen
Sudan
Ethiopia
MALDIVES
Sri Lanka
Uganda
Kenya
Somalia
Tanzania
Zaire
Seychelles
Zambia
Mozambique
INDIAN OCEAN
Rhodesia
Madagascar
Mauritius
Reunion
South
Africa
0
1800km
Maldives

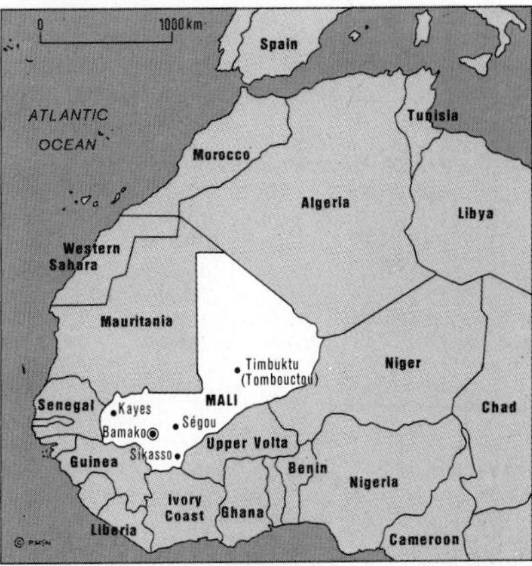
0
1000km
Spain
ATLANTIC
OCEAN
Tunisia
Morocco
Algeria
Libya
Western
Sahara
Mauritania
Timbuktu
(Tombouctou)
Niger
MALI
Senegal
Kayes
Ségou
Chad
Bamako
Upper Volta
Guinea
Sikasso
Benin
Nigeria
Ivory
Coast
Ghana
Liberia
Cameroon
Mali

öhus castle (1434), city hall (1546), 14th-century St Peter's Church. Exports: grain, sugar, clay, cement. Industries: shipping, processed foods, cement, textiles, clothing, metal goods, shipbuilding, railway cars. Pop. 258,311.

Malnutrition, inadequate dietary intake, which does not allow for optimum health. Common causes are economic deprivation, in which inadequate quantities of protein or calories are consumed; unavailability of foods containing necessary vitamins and minerals; poor eating habits; or metabolic defects involving the digestive tract, liver, kidneys, and red blood cells. △ 696, 732.

Malocclusion, the misalignment of the row of teeth in the upper jaw with those in the lower jaw, resulting in improper contact between the biting surfaces of the teeth. If untreated, it can lead to deformities of the jaws or difficulties in chewing. Malocclusion may be hereditary in origin or due to early loss of teeth due to decay. *See also* Orthodontics. △756.

Malory, (Sir) Thomas (*fl.* 1469), English prose writer, author of *Le Morte d'Arthur.* His identity is obscure, but he was probably the Thomas Malory from Warwickshire who fought in the Wars of the Roses, became a member of parliament in 1456, and served several prison sentences between 1450 and 1470. △1100.

Malpighi, Marcello (1628–94), Italian physiologist. He was the founder of microscopic anatomy, demonstrating how blood reaches the tissues through tiny vessels (capillaries) that are too small to be seen with the naked eye. Harvey had inferred that there must be capillaries, but had never seen them; Malpighi used the microscope to study the fine structure of plant and animal tissues and was able to pinpoint and explain the network of tiny veins he could see on the lung surface. He extended the use of the microscope into many fields, including the study of gland cells and of the brain, and also ventured into the field of embryology.

Malraux, André (1901–76), French novelist and politician. An archeologist who became involved in revolutionary activities in China, his early novels examine the heroism of individuals who, engaged in social revolution, are seen to transcend the human condition—*The Conquerors* (1928), *Man's Fate* (1933), and *Man's Hope* (1937). *The Psychology of Art* (1947–1950) examines art as a search for transcendental achievement. In 1959 he was appointed minister of cultural affairs by Charles de Gaulle.

Malt, grain product, usually derived from barley, used in beverages and foods. The grain is softened in water, allowed to germinate, and kiln-dried. This activates enzymes that convert the starch to malt sugar. Most malt is used in the manufacture of beer. *See also* Barley. △350.

Malta, an independent island country in the Mediterranean Sea, approx. 60mi (96km) S of Sicily; comprises Malta, Gozo, and Comino islands. The topography is flat, with a limestone top layer; the climate is temperate and hot in the summers. There are no rivers in Malta, and rainfall is barely sufficient for growing vegetables; terracing is practiced on a large scale. Agriculture supports approx. 25% of the population; crops are potatoes, wheat, onions, beans, oranges, cotton, grapes, and cumin seeds; livestock is also important. Malta's location is favorable for shipping routes, and it is noted for good harbors. Industries include manufacture of lace, buttons, gloves, hosiery, textiles, and skilled ship and dock repairing; the economy is also highly dependent on tourism. The population consists of elements of all the peoples who have inhabited the islands, including the Phoenicians. The islands are overpopulated, with severe unemployment; majority of the people is Roman Catholic.

In 1964 a new constitution was formed, with a 50-member legislature elected by proportional representation; defense and foreign affairs were controlled by the British governor and a high commissioner. Malta became a fully independent country in 1964. A republic was proclaimed in 1974 but Malta remained within the Commonwealth of Nations. Formerly a Carthaginian and Phoenician colony, it was taken by Romans 218 BC; in 1530 it was given to the Knights of St John by Emperor Charles V. It was held by Napoleon 1798–1800, when it was taken by the British. In the 19th century, Malta prospered as powerful British naval base, but in the 1970s it experienced a great economic decline as a result of Britain's withdrawal from naval facilities.

PROFILE

Official name: Republic of Malta
Area: 122sq mi (316sq km)
Population: 330,000
Chief cities: Valletta (capital); Sliema; Mdina; Victoria
Government: Republic
Religion: Roman Catholic
Language: Maltese, English, Italian

Maltese, aristocratic breed of spaniel dog (toy group) that has existed for 2,800 years as a pet of royalty and the wealthy. It has a medium-length head and fine, tapered muzzle; low-set drop ears; dark, round eyes, compact body; fine-boned legs; and long tail curved over the back. The long, flat, silky coat flows almost to the ground and is pure white. Average size: 5in (13cm) high at shoulder; 2–7lb (1–3kg). *See also* Spaniel; Toy Dog.

Malthus, Thomas (1766–1834), English economist and minister famous for his *Essay on the Principle of Population* (1798). According to Malthus, population increases geometrically, that is, in the order of 2, 4, 8, 16, 32, and so on. However, the food supply can only be increased arithmetically, that is, in the order of 1, 2, 3, 4, 5, and so on. Accordingly, population would eventually outdistance a nation's food supply, with famine, war, and disease as the inevitable consequences. △942.

Mamba, poisonous African tree snake of the cobra family. It has long venom fangs in its upper jaw and large front teeth in its lower jaw. The black mamba is largest. Others are green or green and black. Length: to 14ft (4.3m). Family Elapidae; genus *Dendroaspis. See also* Cobra.

Mamelukes, ruling dynasty of Egypt (1250–1811). Originally they were Turkish and Circassian prisoners of Genghis Khan who were sold as slaves to the sultan of Egypt, who trained them as soldiers. They fought for Egypt but then seized power. In 1250, Bahri founded the first Mameluke dynasty. It was a time of great cultural advancement with monuments and military conquests but internal political chaos. Ottoman sultan Selim I took control for a time, but the Mamelukes did not really lose power until Mohammed Ali Pasha ordered them all killed in 1811, leaving only the province of Baghdad under Mameluke control. △ 1084, 1110.

Mammal, class (Mammalia) of vertebrate animals numerous on all major land masses and in oceans. Characterized by full, partial, or vestigial hair covering and —in the female—by mammary glands. Mammals have an effective temperature-regulating system and a four-chambered heart, with circulation to the lungs separate from that to the rest of the body. The air-pumping ability of mammal lungs is increased by action of the muscular abdominal diaphragm. As a group, mammals are active, alert, and intelligent. They range in size from shrews weighing a fraction of an ounce to the largest of all animals, the up-to-150-ton blue whale. Mammals generally bear fewer young and give them better care than do most other animals.

Mammals include 17 orders of placentals, one marsupial order—all live-bearing—and an order of egg-laying monotremes. Mammals probably evolved about 180,000,000 years ago from a group of warm-blooded reptiles. They became the dominant land animals after the extinction of the dinosaurs about 70,000,000 years ago. *See also* Chordate; Marsupial; Monotreme; Placental Mammals; Vertebrate. △540, 542, 574.

Mammary Glands, glands that secrete milk to feed the young, a characteristic mammalian feature. *See* Breast; Lactation. △686.

Mammography, examination of breast tissue by X ray, often to detect the presence of a malignant tumor in an early stage of development. △738.

Mammoth, extinct, Pleistocene elephant. Its tusks were downwardly directed and often greatly curved. The most prominent types were the southern mammoth of Europe and Asia, the imperial mammoth of North America, and the woolly mammoth of N Eurasia and North America. The latter is known from frozen complete cadavers as well as bones. Many cave paintings by early man exist. Genus *Mammuthus.* △574–76.

Mammoth Cave National Park, park in central Kentucky. The caves are a series of underground passages featuring beautiful limestone, gypsum, and cave onyx formations. There are deep pits, high domes, and a river 360ft (110m) below the surface. Area: 51,354acres (20,798hectares). Est. 1936. △ 256.

Mammoth Mound (Grave Creek Indian Burial Ground), world's tallest prehistoric Indian burial ground of its kind, 69ft (21m) high, at Moundsville, W. Va.; 1,000–2,000 years old; many smaller earthworks are nearby. Excavations by tunneling (1838) revealed two burial chambers and numerous relics.

Man, Isle of, island off the NW coast of England, in the Irish Sea. Occupied by Vikings *c.* 600, it was a dependency of Norway until 1266; belonged to earls of Derby 14th century until 1735; part of the British crown since 1765. Tourism and agriculture are important; sheep and cattle thrive on the hills. Products: grain, root crops, fruit, flowers, vegetables. Industries: dairying, fishing, quarrying. Man has its own government. Capital is Douglas. Area: 221sq mi (572sq km). Pop. 56,248.

Man, Prehistoric, any of the evolutionary stages of early man preceding recorded history. Included are all the members of the family Hominidae beginning with the australopithecines, followed by the pithecanthropines and, ultimately, *Homo sapiens,* our own species. The australopithecines may have been derived from *Ramapithecus* of 13,000,000 years ago. *Australopithecus* itself existed from about 3,000,000 to 1,000,000 years ago and includes fossils formerly called *Zinjanthropus* and *Paranthropus.* The material is mostly from E and S Africa. The pithecanthropines of one to one-half million years ago are all grouped into *Homo erectus* and include Java Man and Peking Man as well as European and African representatives. The earliest *Homo sapiens* material is dated to about 100,000 years ago and believed to have diverged in two directions, one leading to Neanderthal Man and similar types in Asia and Africa, and the other to the modern races of man represented in Europe by Cro-Magnon Man of 30,000 years ago. △650–52.

Mana, usable spiritual power. For a long time anthropologists defined mana as a nonindividual supernatural force inherent in certain objects, a concept to be found in Melanesia and elsewhere. Modern anthropologists tend to limit mana to certain Melanesian cultures, where it is used to explain personal status and unusual powers. In this sense mana is the individual spiritual power that makes important people important. *See also* Manitou.

Management, Business. △928.

Management and Budget, Office of (OMB), federal agency within the executive branch. The OMB is charged with the development, supervision, and control of the annual US budget and the development of improved methods of administrative management. It also keeps the President informed of the work of many other government agencies. The OMB was established in 1970.

Managua, capital city of Nicaragua, in W central Nicaragua on S shore of Lake Managua; economic, industrial, and commercial hub of Nicaragua; suffered damage from earthquake 1931, after which much of the city was rebuilt, and another Dec. 23, 1972, that killed over 10,000 people and necessitated further reconstruction. City was made capital 1855, being neutral ground between bitterly opposed political factions in León and Granada. Pop. 374,178.

Manama (Al-Manamah), city in N Bahrain, SW Asia, in the Persian Gulf; capital, principal port, and commercial center of Bahrain. It was made a free port 1958; deepwater harbor was built 1962. Industries: oil refining, pearl fishing, boatbuilding, cloth. Pop. 89,728.

Manassas, town in NE Virginia, 25mi (40km) W of Alexandria; seat of Prince William co. Battles of Bull Run were fought nearby on July 21, 1861, and Aug. 29–30, 1862. Farm area. Inc. 1873; rechartered 1938. Pop. (1970) 9,164.

Manatee, large plant-eating aquatic mammal found in shallow coastal waters and large rivers of subtropical and tropical North and South America and W Africa. Length: 7–12ft (2.1–3.6m); weight: 500lb (225kg). Family Trichechidae; genus *Trichechus. See also* Sirenia. △548.

Manchester, city in NW England, in Greater Manchester; a major British city and commercial hub; in England's densest metropolitan region. Manchester Ship Canal (1887–94) made it a major port; center of liberalism and of Anti-Corn Law League in 19th century; home of University of Manchester and Hallé Orchestra. Industries: textiles, printing, publishing. Pop. 541,468.

Manchester, manufacturing town in N Connecticut, in E Hartford co. Industries: textiles, machinery, paper products. Settled 1672; inc. 1823. Pop. (1970) 47,994.

Manchester, city in S New Hampshire, on Merrimack River; state's largest city; one of seats of Hillsborough co; many textile mills moved S (1935) and city's economy suffered; site of St Anselm's College (1889), New Hampshire College of Accounting and Commerce (1932), Notre Dame College (1950), John Stark home, and Stark Park, a memorial to Gen. John Stark, hero of French and Indian and Revolutionary wars. Industries: textiles, rubber, automobile accessories. Settled 1722; inc. 1751 as Derryfield; renamed 1810; chartered as city 1846. Pop. (1970) 87,754.

Manchester Terrier, sport dog (terrier group) also known as black and tan terrier, bred in the Manchester area of England, and now registered in toy and standard varieties. Originally used for rat killing and rabbit coursing, this sleek dog has a long head. Ears are pointed and erect in the toy and erect or folded in the standard. The moderately short body is slightly arched; legs are long; and the tail is short and pointed. The smooth, short coat has well-defined zones of jet black and mahogany tan. Standard size: toy—5–12lb (2–5.4kg), 7in (18cm); standard—16lb (7kg), 14–16in (36–41cm). *See also* Terrier.

Manchu, a Tungusic tribal people related to the Jurchens who had ruled China as the Chin dynasty. The Manchu people grew in power and numbers in the 16th century and finally under their great leader Nurhachi created the military structure by which they were able to defeat Ming dynasty China and establish their own rule under the name Ch'ing Dynasty. △1206.

Manchukuo, former country in E Asia; founded 1932 by Japanese from conquered Manchuria and Jehol prov., China; Changchun served as the capital, later renamed Hsinking; ruled by Henry Pu Yi as a Japanese puppet state and developed industrially as a war base; dissolved 1945 at the close of WWII. △1328.

Manchuria, industrial region in NE China, bordered by Soviet Union (N and NE), Korea (SE), Yellow Sea (S), Inner Mongolia (W); Mukden is the chief city. The N, E, and W borders are lined with Khingan highlands and Ch'angpai Shan Mts; its central area is the alluvial Liao-Sungari lowland; the population is 90% Chinese. Ruled by lesser Chinese dynasties until *c.* 1125, region was ruled by the Nu-chen (later known as Manchus) 1125–1234, when they were dispersed by the Mongols; the Manchus reunited and conquered all of China 1606, ruling until 1912. Russian influence was dominant 1898–1904; Japan defeated Russian forces during Russo-Japanese War (1904–05). S Manchuria and Port Arthur developed rapidly with the introduction of the South Manchurian Railroad. Jehol prov. was annexed 1928; by 1931–32, Japanese troops had occupied Manchuria and Jehol prov. and created the puppet state of Manchukuo (1932–45); Russian takeover of Manchuria and China (1945–46) caused the dismantling and removal of more than 50% of the industrial plants; Nationalist regime was overthrown by Communists 1949. In 1954, Manchuria was divided into three provinces: Liaoning, Kirin, Heilungkiang; all are under control of Peking. Industries: iron, steel, mining, agriculture, chemicals, oil refining, textiles, ceramics, ships, lumber, livestock, food processing, aluminum, aircraft, locomotives. Area: 600,000sq mi (1,554,000sq km). △1328.

Manchurian Incident. On Sept. 18, 1931, Japanese forces seized Mukden and quickly extended their control over all of Northeast China, known as Manchuria. The Chinese regard this as the real start of World War II and their war with Japan. The United States and the League of Nations denounced Japanese actions. Japanese military leaders in Manchuria claimed they moved to maintain internal peace and security for Manchuria. △1328.

Manco Capac, legendary ancestor of the Incas, one of eight beings who emerged from Andean caves to found the city of Cuzco. In the official myth-history created by the Incas, Manco Capac is considered to be the first emperor, *c.* AD 1200.

Mandalay, city in central Burma, on Irrawaddy River; capital of Mandalay division and district; largest city and trade center of Upper Burma. City contains Fort Dufferin, a moated citadel; the Seven Hundred and Thirty Pagodas (Kuthodaw), Arakan Pagoda, many bazaars, a university (1958), palace of King Thebaw. Founded 1857 by King Mindon, Mandalay was last capital (1860–85) of Burmese Kingdom. It was occupied by Japanese 1942–45 and 85% destroyed. Industries: textiles, jade. Pop. 393,000.

Mandan, the Dakota name for a Siouan tribe of North American Indians inhabiting the upper Missouri River area between the Heart River and the Missouri River, in W North Dakota. From an early population of 3,600, disease epidemics introduced by white travelers decimated the tribe; today, about 350 live on the Fort Berthold Reservation in North Dakota.

Mandarin, the major dialect of Chinese, spoken by about three-fourths of the population of China, or some 600,000,000 people. It was the language of the imperial court and Peking and is spoken in all but the western and extreme southern provinces and the populous southeastern coastal strip.

Mandarin, Asian perching duck that typically lives in forest trees and nests in holes well above ground. Species *Aix galericulata. See also* Duck. △866.

Mandarin Orange. *See* Tangerine.

Mandible. △494, 682.

Mandolin, soprano stringed musical instrument of the lute family. Four to six pairs of wire strings tuned in fifths are played in sustained tremolo by a vibrating plectrum. A serenading instrument in 18th-century Italy, it was later a fad in America (1920s) and was used for novel effects in operas and symphonies. *See also* Lute.

Mandrake, herb native to the Mediterranean and used since ancient times as a medicine. The plant has narcotic properties and contains the alkaloids hyoscyamine, scopolamine, and mandragorine. Leaves are borne at the plant base, and the spindle-shaped and branched root is often thought to represent the human figure. Large greenish-yellow or purple flowers produce a many-seeded berry. Height: 1ft (30.5cm); family Solanaceae; species *Mandragora officinarum.*

Mandrill, colorful baboon living in dense rain forests of Central W Africa. They live in small troops and forage for their omnivorous diet on the forest floor. The bright colored male has a red-tipped, pale blue nose, yellow-bearded cheeks, and a naked reddish rump. Weight: to 120lb (54kg). Species *Mandrillus sphinx. See also* Baboon; Drill; Monkey. △558.

Man-eater Shark. *See* White Shark.

Manet, Édouard (1832–83), French painter. Associated with the Impressionist movement, his later work approaches abstraction in its emphasis on pattern. Manet's first work submitted to the Paris Salon of 1859, "Absinthe Drinker," was rejected; his "Spanish Guitar Player" received an honorable mention in 1861. "La Déjeuner sur l'herbe" was rejected by the 1863 Salon and prompted public and critical outcry when shown at the Salon des Refusés. "Olympia," shown two years later, elicited a similar response. Manet's erotic subject matter, harsh colors, and detached, impersonal style rendered these works controversial. In 1867 he exhibited at the Paris World's Fair and helped with the first Impressionist exhibition in 1874. Although he did not exhibit then, his work was closely aligned with that group. His colors had lightened, and his subject matter was more conventional, involving landscapes, beach scenes, and the like. A work of this period, "Bar at the Folies-Bergere," was well received by the public and the critics alike. *See also* Impressionism. △1252–54.

Manfred (1232–66), king of Sicily from 1258 and illegitimate son of Holy Roman Emperor Frederick II. Excommunicated, Manfred defeated the Guelphs (papal partisans) in 1260, but he was defeated and slain at Benevento by Charles of Anjou, to whom Pope Urban VI had offered the Sicilian throne.

Mangabey, large, silky gray monkeys that live in dense central African forests. Mangabeys associate in small troops and feed chiefly on fruit. Tree dwellers, they are generally silent and apparently communicate by expressive grimaces. Length: 15–35in (38–89cm); weight: to 13lb (6kg). Family Cercopithecidae; genus *Cercocebus. See also* Monkey. △598.

Manganese, metallic element (symbol Mn) of the first transition series, first isolated in 1774. Chief ores are pyrolusite (dioxide) and rhodochrosite (carbonate). The metal is used in alloy steels and certain ferromagnetic alloys. Properties: at. no. 25; at. wt. 54.938; sp gr 7.21–7.44; melt. pt. 2271°F (1244°C); boil. pt. 3807°F (2097°C); most common isotope Mn^{55} (100%). *See also* Transition Elements. △1554.

Manganese Nodules. △228.

Mange, animal skin disease caused by parasitic mites imbedded in the skin that lay eggs and die. The new generation matures and spreads the itchy lesions, causing loss of hair or fur. Secondary bacterial infections of the inflamed skin can be fatal.

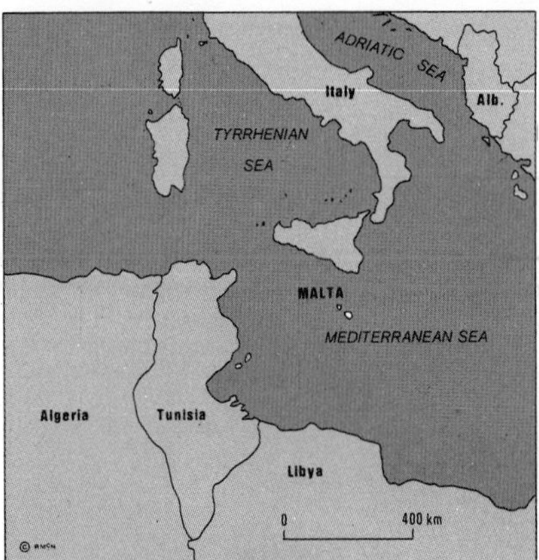
ADRIATIC SEA
Italy
Alb.
TYRRHENIAN SEA
MALTA
MEDITERRANEAN SEA
Algeria
Tunisia
Libya
0
400 km
Malta

Mamba

Mammoth

Mandalay, Burma (1892 engraving)

Mango, evergreen tree native to SE Asia and grown widely in the tropics for its fruit. It has oblong leaves, pinkish-white clustered flowers, and yellow-red fruit that is eaten ripe or preserved when green. Height: to 90ft (27m). Family Anacardiaceae; species *Mangifera indica.*

Mangosteen. △340.

Mangrove, tropical, evergreen tree and shrub found in swampy areas. Its stiltlike aerial roots cause thick undergrowth, making this tree important in building new land along tropical coasts. Seeds germinate while still on the tree. Among 120 species are the red *Rhizophora mangle* found from S Florida to South America and in W Africa; height: to 100ft (30m). *Rhizophora mucronata* grows in E Africa and tropical Asia. Family Rhizophoraceae. △620.

Mangrove Snake. △524.

Manhattan, city in NE Kansas, on Kansas River near confluence of Big Blue River; seat of Riley co; site of Kansas State University (1863); birthplace of Damon Runyon (1884). Industries: dress patterns, bottling, paint. Founded 1854 as Boston; renamed 1855; inc. 1857. Pop. (1970) 27,575.

Manhattan, borough of New York City in SE New York; coextensive with New York co; bounded by Hudson River (W), New York Bay (S), East River (E), and Harlem River (E and N). In 1626, Manhattan Indians sold the island to Peter Minuit of Dutch West India Co. for about $24 worth of trinkets. Town of New Amsterdam was built at tip of island; it served as capital of New Netherlands during Dutch control; English captured colony 1664 and renamed it New York. In 1898, Manhattan became one of five boroughs est. by Greater New York charter. A cultural, commercial, and financial center, it is site of Columbia University (1754), New York University (1831), City University of New York (1848), Manhattan College (1853), Barnard College (1889), Cooper Union (1859), Juilliard School of Music (1926), Metropolitan Museum of Art, Museum of Modern Art, Museum of the City of New York, Rockefeller Center, Lincoln Center for the Performing Arts, St Patrick's Cathedral, United Nations. Industries: electrical, chemical, fabricated metal products, publishing, broadcasting, stock exchange, port facilities, entertainment, tourism. Pop. (1970) 1,524,-541.

Manhattan Beach, city in S California, 13mi (21km) SW of Los Angeles. Industries: oil refineries, aerospace, electronic equipment. Inc. 1912. Pop. (1970) 35,352.

Manhattan Project, code name given to the US atomic bomb project during World War II. Work on the bomb, suggested by Albert Einstein and other scientists, was carried on in great secrecy under Gen. Leslie Groves at several locations in the United States. The first test was at Alamogordo, N.M., in 1945.

Manic-Depressive Psychosis, an affective psychotic reaction marked by severe mood swings ranging from exaggerated feelings of elation and optimism to deep depression. Manic and depressive symptoms may alternate in a cyclical pattern, be mixed, or be separated by periods of remission. Although disturbances of thought and judgment may be present, they are considered secondary to the disturbances of mood. *See also* Depression. △760, 764.

Manichaeism, heretic belief founded by the Persian sage Mani (*c.* 215–77) and based on asceticism and the battle between light and darkness. Mani preached that he, along with Jesus, Buddha, and the prophets, was sent to this world to release the particles of light stolen by Satan and trapped in the brains of men. The Manichaean sect spread to Egypt by the end of the 3rd century and to Rome and Africa in the 4th century; it survived until the 13th century in Chinese Turkestan. *See also* Zoroastrianism.

Manifest Destiny, slogan to justify the US westward and southward expansion movement in the 19th century. Coined by a Democratic editor, John L. O'Sullivan (1845), it was exploited by Pres. James K. Polk when the United States annexed Texas and won lands from Mexico. Later the theory of manifest destiny contributed to the acquisition of Alaska, Hawaii, and territory taken in the Spanish-American War.

Manihiki Islands. *See* Cook Islands.

Manila, largest city of the Republic of the Philippines, on Manila Bay, W Luzon island; capital of Republic of Philippines until Quezon City replaced it in 1948. The chief industrial, financial, and cultural center of the Philippines, the city has long been an important port, hosting Spanish galleons from the 16th century. Spanish traders built the old walled city (Intramuros) on the site of a Muslim settlement. Following the Spanish-American War (1898), development expanded beyond the old city, much of which was destroyed in WWII. The port receives the vast majority of imports to the Philippines, and is the site of the University of Manila, the University of Santo Tomás, the University of the Philippines, Far Eastern University, and Manila Central University, as well as the National Museum and Malacañan Palace. Industries: shipbuilding, textiles, tobacco, chemicals, lumber, food processing, shipping. Pop. 1,330,788.

Manila Bay, Battle of (1898), battle in the Spanish-American War in which US Admiral George Dewey defeated the Spanish fleet on May 1 in a seven-hour battle. Spanish losses were heavy, with 381 men killed and all the Spanish craft destroyed. US casualties included eight wounded; no ships were damaged.

Manila Hemp, or abaca, plant native to the Philippines and introduced into SE Asia and Central America. The fibers obtained from leafstalks of the mature plant are used for cloth, matting, and cordage. Fiber length: to 15ft (4.6m) Family Musaceae; species *Musa textilis.*

Manioc. *See* Cassava.

Manitoba, province in S central Canada, in the plains region. On the S it is bordered by the states of North Dakota and Minnesota. Its NE quarter touches Hudson Bay.

Land and Economy. In the S the land is chiefly prairie; rolling country and low hills lie to the N. Three great lakes—Winnipeg, Winnipegosis, and Manitoba—lie in the central portion. The Red River of the North, the Saskatchewan, Nelson, Winnipeg, and Assiniboine are the major rivers. More than one third of the land is forested, but the rich farmlands of the S and center support the agriculture that has been a mainstay of the economy.

People. Most of the population is of British origin, but there are strong elements of French, Ukrainians, Germans, and Scandinavians. The S is the most heavily populated area.

Education. The University of Manitoba, the University of Winnipeg, and Brandon University are the institutions of higher education.

History. French and English fur traders entered the region in the 1600s, and in 1670, Charles II of England granted the land to the Hudson's Bay Co., a fur enterprise. The first settlers were Scots in 1811. The Canadian government bought the rights of the Hudson's Bay Co. in 1870, and Manitoba joined the Confederation. Railroad building in the 1880s accelerated the development of the economy.

PROFILE

Admitted to Confederation: July 15, 1870; rank, 5th
National Parliament representatives: Senate, 6; House of Commons, 13
Population: 981,000 (1971); rank, 5th
Capital: Winnipeg
Chief cities: Winnipeg; St James-Assiniboia, St Boniface
Provincial legislature: Legislative Assembly; 57 members
Area: 251,000sq mi (650,090sq km); rank, 6th
Elevation: Highest: 2,800ft (854m), Duck and Riding mts; lowest, 400ft (122m)
Industries (major products): meat, apparel, railroad equipment
Agriculture (major products): wheat, barley, oats, cattle, dairy products, poultry
Minerals (major): copper, gold, zinc, silver
Floral emblem: pasqueflower

Manitou, a North American Indian (Algonquin) term for the spiritual power common to all things in nature. It was also used for any of numerous personified nature deities at whose head stood the Great Manitou or Kitchi-Manitou.

Manizales, city in Colombia, 110mi (177km) NW of Bogotá; capital of Caldas dept. Founded 1847 by gold prospectors, it was destroyed by earthquake (1878) and fire (1925); 45mi (72km) aerial tramway connects it with Mariquita; major coffee center. Industries: gold, silver, mercury mining. Pop. 219,496.

Mankato, city in S Minnesota, on Minnesota River; seat of Blue Earth co; city's name is Sioux word for blue earth (found here); site of Mankato State College (1866) and Bethany Lutheran College (1911). Industries: flour, brewing, oil refining, farm machinery. Inc. 1865. Pop. (1970) 30,895.

Manlius, Roman family name of the 3rd and 4th centuries BC, renowned for the political and military endeavors of its bearers. The consul Titus Manlius Imperiosus Torquatus was forced to kill his own son (340 BC) for disobeying orders against individual combat on the field of battle. The severity of this judgment strengthened the discipline of the Roman army.

Man-made Elements. △1552.

Mann, Horace (1796–1859), US educator, b. Franklin, Mass. He was elected to both the Massachusetts House and Senate (1827–37), where he worked for passage of a new state education bill. While secretary of the Massachusetts board of education (1837–48), he established teacher-training schools, increased teachers' salaries, and improved teaching practices. In 1848 he went to Congress as an anti-slavery Whig and in 1853 he became the first president of Antioch College.

Mann, Thomas (1875–1955), German novelist and essayist. He modeled his concepts of the "burger" from his wealthy merchant father and of the exotic artistic temperament from his mother. These two elements he later represented as the polarity inherent in human life. His most powerful works, in which he apologized for the conservative traditions in Germany, came from WWI. His opposition to fascism grew from WWII. His novels include *Buddenbrooks* (1901), *Tonio Kröger* (1903), *Death in Venice* (1912), *The Magic Mountain* (1924), *Joseph and His Brothers* (1933–43), *Doctor Faustus* (1947), and *Confessions of Felix Krull, Confidence Man* (1954). Leaving Germany in 1933, he took US citizenship in 1944 and settled in Zurich in 1952. He was awarded the Nobel Prize in literature in 1929 and the Goethe Prize in 1949.

Manna, or flowering ash, tree native to S Europe and Asia Minor. Its leaves, composed of 7 leaflets each, have rust-colored hairs underneath. Flowers are white and showy with large petals. Size to 60ft (18.3m). A sugary exudate, manna, is collected from cuts in the bark and used medicinally. Height: to 60ft (18m). Family Oleaceae; species *Fraxinus ornus.*

Mann Act (1910), prohibited interstate transportation of women for immoral purposes and extended federal control over social welfare. It originated with women pressing for the regulation of recruitment and forced entry into prostitution.

Mann-Elkins Act (1910), US legislation regulating interstate commerce. It required carriers to give advance justification of higher rates for shorter hauls than for longer hauls and established an unfinanced commerce court. It also authorized the Interstate Commerce Commission to suspend new rates for 120 days.

Mannerheim, Carl Gustaf Emil von (1867–1951), president of Finland. A baron, he served in the Russian army, rising to major general in World War I, before withdrawing at the Bolshevik Revolution (1917). He returned to Finland and was regent 1918–19. In 1920 he founded the Mannerheim League for Child Welfare. He was head of the defense council from 1931, was made a field marshal (1933), and commanded the Finnish forces 1939–44. He planned the Mannerheim Line for defense against Russia. He was president of Finland, 1944–46.

Mannerism, Italian style of painting, sculpture, and architecture that developed *c.* 1520–80 in opposition to the classicism of the High Renaissance. Characteristics of this style were distortions of the proportions of human figures and other forms; canvases were often crowded. In architecture, decorative motifs that often had no structural function were incorporated into designs. Active Mannerist artists were Pontormo and Rosso Fiorentino in Florence and Parmigianino in Rome. △1150.

Mannheim, Karl (1893–1947), sociologist. He was born in Hungary but lived in England after 1933. He is best known for his work on the sociology of knowledge. He tried to answer this question: If knowledge is affected by the social condition of those who are thinking about it, how is objective knowledge possible? His books include *Ideology and Utopia* (1929).

Mannheim, city in central West Germany, on E bank of Rhine River at mouth of Neckar River, across from Lüdwigshafen; major port of upper Rhine River. Originally a fishing village, it was fortified in 1606 and destroyed during Thirty Years' War (1622). Rebuilt in 1699, it was seat of Rhine Palatinate 1719–77; passed to Baden 1803; site of 18th-century palace, university (1967). Industries: automobiles, chemicals, cellulose, tobacco, paper, textiles, steel. Founded 766; chartered 1607. Pop. 327,992.

Man-of-War. △1738.

Man-of-War Bird. *See* Frigatebird.

Manometer, a device for measuring pressure. It consists of a U-shaped tube containing a liquid, one end open to the atmosphere and the other end attached to the vessel whose pressure is to be measured. If the pressure in the vessel is greater than atmospheric, it will force the liquid down on one side and up on the other. The difference in height of the liquid is used to determine the difference in pressure. △1496.

Manorial System, agriculture and land distribution system existing in the corn-raising areas of England, Northern France, Germany, and Denmark during the period of feudalism. Typical of the system were the English manor and the German *mark,* villages surrounded by arable fields and wasteland. A lord presided over the manor, which he held either outright or in fief from a greater lord or king. The villagers, or *villeins,* worked the land in common, with each villein family being directly responsible for one *virgate* or strip, which rotated from year to year. In exchange for the use of the land, the villein owed labor services in the lord's fields, payment of chickens, livestock, and an irregularly demanded money levy called *tallage.* Thus the labor of the villagers supported the lord, the knightly and clerical classes, and one another. The custom, or law, of the manor fixed the duties and payments of the villein, who might be considered a serf or a freeman. Justice was meted out and custom determined in the manorial court, often presided over by the lord and attended by the villagers as nominal and sometimes actual advisers. *See also* Feudalism. △1070.

Mansa Musa (d. 1337), Muslim emperor of Mali (1312–37). He brought his domain to the peak of its power and renown. He led an impressive pilgrimage to Mecca (1324–25) and gained international recognition by giving away vast quantities of gold. △1116.

Mansfield, Michael Joseph (1903–), US senator (1953–77), b. New York City, who had the longest tenure of any Senate majority leader. A mining engineer who taught (1933–42) history at Montana State University, he served as a Democrat in the US House of Representatives (1943–53). He entered the Senate in 1953 and succeeded Lyndon Baines Johnson as Senate majority leader in 1961. In that position he exerted influence in winning passage of major liberal reform policies and civil rights legislation before his retirement in 1977.

Mansfield, city in N central Ohio, 54mi (87km) WSW of Akron; seat of Richland co; site of reconstructed blockhouse from War of 1812, French provincial mansion (pre-Civil War), and writer Louis Bromfield's house, now an ecological center and experimental farm. Industries: rubber products, electrical industries, sheet steel, plumbing fixtures. Settled 1808; inc. as village 1828, as city 1857. Pop. (1970) 55,047.

Mansfield, Mount, peak in N Vermont; highest point in the Green Mts; large ski area. Height: 4,393ft (1,340m).

Manta. *See* Devilfish.

Mante. *See* Ciudad Mante.

Mantegna, Andrea (1431–1506), Italian painter. His work influenced northern Italian painting for 50 years. One of his early fine works is the altarpiece in S. Zeno, Verona (1456–59). In 1459 he went to Mantua as a court painter to the Gonzaga family. He remained there for the rest of his life. His works include the innovative "St Sebastian" and "Dead Christ," which modernized formal compositions, and "Madonna of Victory" (1495). △1138.

Mantinea, city in ancient S Greece, near Argolis border in E Peloponnesus; scene of Peloponnesian War battle during which Agis defeated the Argives and Mantineans (418 BC); Theban victory over Sparta resulting in death of Epaminondas (362 BC).

Mantis, or praying mantis, insect found worldwide. It has powerful front legs used to catch its insect prey. Colors range from brown and green to bright pinks, enabling each species to blend with the foliage or flowers it hides on. Length: 1–6in (25–152mm). Family Mantidae. △492, 598.

Mantissa. *See* Logarithms.

Mantle, Mickey Charles (1931–), US baseball player, b. Spavinaw, Okla. A home run hitter (536), he played only with the New York Yankees (1951–68) and helped lead them to 12 American League pennants. He was elected to the Baseball Hall of Fame in 1974.

Mantle, layer of Earth between core and crust. This is a solid layer since it transmits both P and S seismic waves. The mantle itself is not homogeneous, becoming denser with increasing depth. The shadow zones, or areas of deflected P and S waves, are part of the mantle, which is otherwise a good conductor of seismic waves since it is dense rock (usually olivine) in its lower layers. *See also* Moho. △166, 170.

Mantle Plume. △176.

Mantua (Mantova), city in N Italy, on Mincio River, 22mi (35km) SSW of Verona; capital of Mantova prov. An ancient Etruscan settlement, it became independent 1115; prospered politically and culturally under the Gonzagas 14th-18th centuries; passed to Austria 1708; taken by Napoleon 1796–97; ceded to Italy 1805, to Austria 1814, returned to Italy 1866; site of church of San Andrea (begun 1472), cathedral (rebuilt 16th century), Vergilian Academy of Sciences and Fine Arts. Industries: shipping, machinery, furniture, tourism. Pop. 66,089.

Manuel I or **Emmanuel I** (1469–1521), king of Portugal (1495–1521). He was the cousin of John II, whom he succeeded. He was king during what is known as Portugal's Golden Age. Portuguese explorers and navigators covered the globe, and Portugal's great empire in the East was developed. Enormous wealth poured into the country from that empire. In 1497, Manuel expelled the Jews and Moors from Portugal. His son, John III, succeeded him.

Manul. *See* Pallas' Cat.

Manumission, the legal granting of freedom to slaves. US slave owners sometimes freed their slaves in their wills, and many opponents of slavery hoped such manumission would bring a gradual end to the system. The Emancipation Proclamation (1862) and finally the 13th Amendment (1865) ended slavery.

Manure. △316, 320.

Manuscript. △872.

Manx, language formerly spoken on the Isle of Man. Closely related to Scottish Gaelic, it was spoken by all the native inhabitants of the island until about 1700, when English began to be introduced. By 1900 there were only a few thousand speakers left and the last of these were gone by 1950.

Manx Cat, tailless, short-haired domestic cat bred on Isle of Man in Irish Sea. An intelligent and devoted pet, it has a round head, prominent ears, short back, and hindquarters higher than the shoulders. The luxurious double coat can be any color. Because of frequent back deformity, Manx have a tendency to hop. They are difficult to breed.

Manzanita, or bearberry, shrub with broad, oval leaves, white or pink flower clusters, and reddish-brown fruit. Height: 8–12ft (2.4–3.7m). Family Rubiaceae; species *Arctostaphylos manzanita.*

Maori, or **Maui,** Polynesian people who have inhabited New Zealand for at least 600 years. Noted for artistic skills such as woodcarving and singing, the Maoris experienced a loss of cultural identity following their uprising against and subsequent defeat by British colonists in 1860. They are fully integrated into Western-oriented New Zealand society, and most Maoris have adopted Christianity. △82, 1260.

Mao Tse-tung (1893–1976), Chinese Communist leader. One of the original founders of the Chinese Communist party in 1921, Mao eliminated competitors for leadership and became chairman in 1935 and one of the foremost leaders in the world Communist movement. A leading theoretician on guerrilla warfare, Mao held that the path to power in China lay through the mobilization of the peasantry. He helped in the founding of the Kiangsi Soviet Republic in China in 1931, led the famous Long March (1934–36), and built his reputation as a theorist and military leader in Yenan from 1936 until the end of World War II when he launched his successful drive for rule over all China. In 1949, Mao created the Chinese People's Republic and remained its chief decision maker through remaining decades during which he eliminated competitors and sought to transform China's traditional culture into a revolutionary Communist society. △1270, 1348.

Map, any graphic representation of various geographical, geologic, political, ecological, physio-

Manhattan, New York City

Manitoba, Canada

Thomas Mann

Mao Tse-tung

graphic, or meteorological variables on the earth's surface. There are many different techniques for plotting and showing the distribution of these features. Maps can be flat, or three dimensional, or plotted on a spherical surface called a globe. *See also* Map Projection. △180.

Maple, deciduous trees native to temperate and cool regions of Europe, Asia, and North America. They have unisexual, yellowish or greenish flowers and winglike seeds. They are grown for ornament, shade, or timber depending on species, while the sugar maple is also tapped for its sap. Most species have brilliant foliage in autumn. Height: 15–120ft (4.6–37m). Family Aceraceae; genus *Acer.*

Maple Heights, city in N Ohio, 10mi (16km) SE of Cleveland. Inc. as village 1915. Pop. (1970) 34,093.

Maplewood, village in E Minnesota; residential suburb of St Paul. Inc. 1957. Pop. (1970) 25,222.

Mapping, in Mathematics. △1472.

Map Projection, any systematic method of drawing the earth's meridians and parallels on a flat surface. Only on a globe can areas and shapes be represented with any fidelity. On flat maps of large areas distortions are inevitable. Projections are either geometrical derivations (cylindrical, conical, or azimuthal) or networks and grids derived mathematically in the transposition from globe to flat surface. △180.

Mapp v. Ohio (1961), landmark US Supreme Court case overruling previous decisions and strengthening the interpretation of the Fourth Amendment's ban on illegal searches. The court declared that evidence obtained in such a search was inadmissible in subsequent criminal prosecutions.

Map Turtle, or sawback, lake and river turtle of N and central United States. Flat-shelled, many have ridged dorsal keels. Their limbs, head, and shell are marked with numerous whorls and lines. Females are often larger than males. They eat mollusks. Length: to 11in(28cm). Family Emydidae; genus *Graptemys. See also* Turtle.

Maquis, name given to the French underground resistance movement against the Germans in World War II. Originating in 1943 from Corsica where resisters hid in dense thickets *(maquis),* they fought mainly in the mountains bordering Italy and Switzerland.

Marabou. *See* Adjutant Stork.

Maracaibo, port city in NW Venezuela, between Lake Maracaibo and Gulf of Venezuela; capital of Zulia state; Venezuela's 2nd-largest city; site of cathedral, colonial edifices, university (1891). Founded 1571 by a German adventurer-explorer, it was seized 1669 by Henry Morgan; expanded after discovery of oil 1917. Industries: coffee, cacao, sugar, dairy products, beer, lumber. Pop. 665,578.

Maracaibo, Lake, Lake in NW Venezuela, S arm of Gulf of Venezuela; major transport route; fed by Catatumbo River (SW); rich oil field region. Discovered 1499 by Alonso de Ojeda. Area: 5,217sq mi (13,512sq km).

Maracay, city in N Venezuela, on Pan American Highway, 50mi (81km) WSW of Caracas; capital of Aragua state; capital of Venezuela 1908–35; site of agricultural school, national airport, military aviation school. Industries: textiles, coffee, cacao, sugar, tobacco, timber, cattle, paper, soap. Pop. 192,863.

Maracock. *See* Passionflower.

Marat, Jean Paul (1743–93), French political figure, b. Switzerland. A noted physician in London and Paris, his *Philosophical Essay on Man* (1773) was attacked by Voltaire for its extreme materialism. At the outbreak of the French Revolution (1789) he founded the inflamatory journal *L'Ami du Peuple.* He was forced to flee to London (1790, 91) and to hide in the Paris sewers. Backed by Robespierre and Danton, he came out of hiding and was elected to the National Convention where he worked for the Jacobins. He was stabbed to death in his bath by Charlotte Corday, a Girondist sympathizer.

Marat Dead (Rousseau). △1228.

Marathi, language spoken in W India, principally in the state of Maharashtra. It is one of the Indic languages and thus part of the Indo-European family. Speakers of Marathi number about 45,000,000. It is one of the 15 constitutional languages of India. △1202.

Marathon, a plain on the E coast of Greece connected to Athens by a main road, and the scene of the Persian invasion Sept. 490 BC. Here an Athenian force under Miltiades defeated a numerically superior army led by Datis and Artaphernes and freed Attica from the threat of Persian invasion. *See also* Persian Wars. △992.

Marathon Racing, one of the most demanding of track and field events. The standard marathon race is 26 miles, 385 yards (42.2km). The race duplicates the length run by Pheidippides to announce the Greek victory at Marathon in 490 BC. Usually, the race starts and ends on a stadium track, with the bulk of the race run through a marked course in city streets. Marathon racing was first included in the modern Olympic Games of 1896. The most famous distance race is the Boston Marathon, held annually in Boston since 1897.

Marble, Alice (1913–), US tennis player, b. Plumas co, Calif. A strong player with a powerful forehand and twisting service, she won the Wimbledon singles in 1939, doubles in 1938–39, mixed doubles 1937–38, 1939; also US outdoor singles in 1936, 1938–40, mixed doubles 1936, 1938–40. She turned professional in 1940. She wrote *The Road to Wimbledon* (1946).

Marble, metamorphic rock composed largely of recrystallized limestones and dolomites. The term is more loosely used to refer to any crystalline calcium carbonate rock that has good pattern and color when cut and polished. The color is normally white, but when tinted by serpentine, iron oxide, or carbon, can vary to shades of yellow, green, brown, or black. *See also* Metamorphic Rocks. △248.

Marblehead, town in NE Massachusetts, 15mi (24km) NE of Boston, on a rocky promontory jutting into Massachusetts Bay. Important in early history of US Navy, it was site of Fort Sewall (1742), used until end of Spanish American War (1899), St Michael's church (1714), Abbott Hall, Jeremiah Lee mansion (1768). Industries: boatbuilding, fishing, tourism, yachting. Founded 1629; separated from Salem and inc. 1649. Pop. (1970) 21,295.

Marbury v. Madison (1803), US Supreme Court case that established the supremacy of the Constitution over congressional legislation and the court's role as interpreter of the Constitution. It also established the court's power to overturn unconstitutional legislation.

Marceau, Marcel (1923–), French actor, the greatest mime of his time. In 1947 he founded a company to reawaken interest in the art of mime. Since that time his character, "Bip," became widely known and imitated. He and his mime company have toured extensively and appeared on television numerous times.

March, third month of the year. It was named for the Roman god Mars and has 31 days. The birthstone is the aquamarine or bloodstone.

Marchand, Jean Baptiste (1863–1934), French soldier and explorer of Africa. He led an expedition in 1898 to lay claim to a part of Sudan. Confronted there by the British in what is known as the Fashoda Incident, he withdrew. He later fought in the Boxer Rebellion and in World War I, when he commanded a division. *See also* Fashoda Incident.

Marches, autonomous region in E central Italy, on the Adriatic Sea; comprised of the provinces of Ancona, Ascoli Piceno, Macerata, and Pesaro e Urbino; capital city is Ancona. Region has mountains and hills with many rivers; part of the Papal States 16th century–1860, when it was united with Italy. Industries: agriculture, textiles, chemicals, fertilizer, fishing, refined petroleum. Area: 3,742sq mi (9,692sq km). Est. 1948; received autonomy 1970. Pop. 1,358,-089.

Marciano, Rocky (1924–1969), US boxer, b. Rocco Francis Marchegiano, in Brockton, Mass. He won the world's heavyweight championship from Jersey Joe Walcott (1952) in Philadelphia. He retired as undefeated champion (1956) and was elected to the Hall of Fame in 1959.

Marcion (died *c.*160), heretic sect leader. A wealthy shipowner native to Sinope, he was excommunicated in 140 and 144 for immorality. He then organized a sect that believed in a Christian gospel of love (as exemplified by Jesus in the New Testament), rejecting the Old Testament as a gospel of the God of Law. Marcion believed that only St Paul understood this distinction, and he wrote prologues to the Pauline epistles. The Marcionites were absorbed by the Manichaeists at the end of the 3rd century.

Marcomanni, ancient west German tribe first mentioned by Caesar. Driven from Saxony and Thuringia by the Teutones and Cimbri, they migrated to the upper Main, then to Gaul and Bohemia (*c.* 8 BC). A strong people, they fought against Roman campaigns led by Domitian, Nerva, and Marcus Aurelius. After AD 500 they moved from Bohemia to Bavaria.

Marconi, (Marchese) Guglielmo (1874–1937), Italian electrical engineer and inventor. He began experimenting with wireless telegraphy in 1894, forming the Marconi Wireless Telegraph Co., Ltd., in England in 1897 to encourage commercial applications. He improved inventions of others and originated a magnetic detector (1902), a directional aerial (1905), and a continuous wave generating system (1912), steadily increasing transmission distance. He attracted worldwide attention by making transatlantic contact between Poldhu, England, and St John's, Newfoundland, in 1901. Marconi and Karl F. Braun shared the 1909 Nobel Prize for physics for work in wireless telegraphy. A US court upheld the basic Marconi patents in 1914, bringing him fame as the creator of the wireless. After World War I he worked on short waves, then microwaves, living to see the advent of commercial radio. △1794.

Marcos, Ferdinand Edralin (1917–), Filipino political figure, president of the Philippines from 1965. After serving as a congressman from 1949 with the Liberal party, he moved to the Nationalist party in 1964. Elected president in 1965, he was reelected in 1969, becoming the first president of the Philippines to serve a second term. His presidency was marked by student unrest and guerrilla activity. In 1971 and 1972 he declared martial law and in 1973 he established a new and authoritarian constitution.

Marcus Aurelius (Antoninus) (121–180), Roman emperor (161–180) and philosopher, b. as Marcus Annius Verus. With his stepbrother Lucius Verus as co-emperor, he succeeded his adoptive father Antoninus Pius as emperor in 161. After the death of Lucius Verus in 169, he reigned as sole emperor. His reign was troubled by numerous revolts and invasions. In 161 he repelled a Parthian invasion of Syria. In 167–68, he drove the Marcomanni, a Germanic tribe, out of Italy. There were also revolts in Egypt, Spain, and Britain. He lowered the taxes of the poor and was lenient to political prisoners, but persecuted Christians. His *Meditations* is an important work of Stoic philosophy. △1020.

Marcuse, Herbert (1898–), US social philosopher. Born in Germany, he moved to the United States in 1934. In *Eros and Civilization* (1954) he attempted to fuse Marxist and Freudian theories. *One Dimensional Man* (1964), in which he argued that Americans were oppressed and beginning to accept oppression, made him a hero of the New Left radicals and provided a rationale for student revolts in the 1960s. △1360.

Marcy, Mount, peak in the Adirondack Mts, NE New York. Lake on S slope is source of the Hudson River. State's highest peak. Height: 5,344ft (1,630m).

Marduk, the supreme deity in the Babylonian pantheon of gods. Originally an earth deity who personified water's fertilizing quality, he acquired the attributes of local deities as the power of Babylon grew. Marduk became not only the grain producer, but the bringer of light and justice and the creator of all things. His attributes are the spade and the sword.

Mare (plural, maria), any of the dark expanses on the moon's surface. Originally thought to be seas (hence the Latin term), they are in fact huge circular or irregular plains, much smoother than the surrounding areas, perhaps of a basaltic material. △56, 60.

Marengo, Battle of. △1232.

Margaret I (1353–1412), queen of Denmark, Norway, and Sweden. She was the daughter of Waldemar IV of Denmark and the wife of Haakon VI of Norway. In 1376 her son Olaf, age 5, became Danish king under his parents' regency. At Haakon's death in 1380, Olaf became King Olaf V of Norway. After Olaf's death in 1387 Margaret ruled Denmark and Norway. She defeated Sweden's King Albert of Mecklenburg in 1389. In 1397 her nephew Eric of Pomerania was crowned king of Denmark, Norway, and Sweden.

Margaret of Austria (Savoy) (1480–1530), daughter of Hapsburg emperor Maximilian I, regent of Netherlands (1507–30) for her nephew Charles (later emperor Charles V). Born at Brussels, Belgium, in 1497 she wed the Spanish infante John and in 1501, Philibert II of Savoy. In 1529, with Louise of Savoy (mother of Francis I of France) she negotiated the Peace of Cambrai, sometimes called La Paix des Dames.

Margaret of Austria (Parma) (1522–86), illegitimate daughter of Hapsburg emperor Charles V (Charles I of Spain), Duchess of Parma. Married to the duke of Florence, Alessandro de' Medici, from 1531 until his death in 1537, in 1538 she wed Ottavio Farnese, duke of Parma (from 1547) and was regent of the Netherlands (1559–67) for Philip II of Spain, her half-brother. At first sympathetic to Netherlandish nationalists, then repressive, finally she resigned as regent when the harsh duke of Alva was brought in.

Margaret of Valois (1553–1615), wife of Henry of Navarre, later Henry IV of France. She was the daughter of Henry II of France and Catherine de Médicis, and her marriage was an abortive attempt to unify opposing religious factions. It was dissolved after Henry's accession to the throne in 1599. Noted for her beauty, elegance, and licentiousness, her Paris home became a center of fashion and culture. She left her *Memoirs,* a revealing picture of France in her day.

Margaret Rose (1930–), princess of Great Britain; the daughter of King George VI, and sister of Queen Elizabeth II. From 1960 the wife of Antony Armstrong-Jones, earl of Snowdon, she had two children, David, Viscount Linley (*b.* 1961), and Sarah Frances Elizabeth (*b.* 1964).

Margaret Tudor (1489–1541), queen of Scotland, daughter of Henry VII of England. She married Scotland's James IV (1503) and at his death (1513) became regent for their son, James V. Ousted from power (1515), she manipulated both the pro-French and pro-English factions, thereby maintaining considerable influence. She was able to end regency of James V (1524) and became his chief adviser (1528–34).

Margarine, a food made from vegetable fats with aqueous milk products, salt, flavoring, food coloring, emulsifier, and vitamins A and D blended in. Used for cooking and as a spread. Corn or safflower oil is the most popular modern fat ingredient due to interest in polyunsaturated fats in relation to health.

Margay, small cat found in forests from Mexico to S Brazil. A cat with a good disposition, it is sometimes kept as an unusual pet. Its coat is cream yellow with black spots. Length: body—17.7–27.6in (45–70cm); tail—13.8–19.7in (35–50cm). Family Felidae; species *Felis wiedii.*

Marginal Analysis, significant concept in economics that refers to basing decisions on the final units under consideration, a much more meaningful tool of analysis than comparison of totals. A primary application of marginal analysis is to the theory of the firm. The firm assumed to be interested in maximizing profits. It has been shown that it can maximize profits through equating the additional cost per unit of output to the additional revenue per unit of output. Marginal analysis is also useful in analyzing consumer decisions.

Marginalism, economic analysis simultaneously introduced in 1878 by economists William Jevons and Léon Walras. Marginal analysis involved the concept of the extra utility, eg the additional satisfaction someone gets from receiving an extra unit of some commodity. Previously, economists had difficulty explaining why water, which is so important to life, sold for a much lower price than such a seemingly superfluous good as diamonds. Marginalism made it clear that the last or extra unit of abundant water contains less satisfaction than the last or extra unit of relatively scarce diamonds.

Marginal Utility, in economics, the addition to total utility that occurs from obtaining one more unit of a good. For most goods, the marginal utility would be expected to be positive, implying that the consumer receives an addition to his total utility by obtaining increasing amounts of the good.

Margin Requirement, legal limit on the amount of cash that the buyer must put up as part of the purchase price of stocks and bonds; he may borrow the rest. For example, a 70% margin requirement means the buyer may obtain a loan for not more than 30% of the purchase price. The Federal Reserve Board sets margin requirements to discourage speculation and to prevent too much money from entering the stock market when money is tight.

Margrethe II (1940–), queen of Denmark, daughter of Frederik IX. In 1972, she became the first queen regent since the Middle Ages and the first democratically appointed sovereign in Denmark's history. Married in 1967 to the French Count Henri Laborde Monpezat, he became Prince Henrik of Denmark on their wedding day. They have two sons. The queen is well-educated, artistic, and speaks several languages.

Marguerite, or Paris daisy, perennial plant native to the Canary Islands. It has mounded foliage and white or lemon-yellow flower heads about 2in (5cm) across. Height: to 3ft (91cm). Family Compositae; species *Chrysanthemum frutescens.*

Mari. △956.

Maria I (1734–1816), queen of Portugal (1777–1816). She was the daughter of Joseph, and in 1760 she was married to his younger brother who (as Peter III) ruled jointly with her. Maria and Peter, under the control of her mother, Queen Marianna Victoria, banished from power the Marquês de Pombal. He had been Joseph's chief minister and the virtual ruler of Portugal for many years. Maria's mind, never strong, gave way after the death of her husband (1786). Her son, John VI, ruled in her stead from 1792. In 1807 she fled with the rest of the royal family to Brazil, where she died.

Maria II (1819–53), queen of Portugal (1826–53). She was the daughter of Peter I, who abdicated in her favor when he became emperor of Brazil (as Pedro I). She was betrothed to her uncle, Dom Miguel, but he attempted to usurp the crown, thereby setting off the Miguelist Wars. Maria's forces, led by her father and supported by English sea power, defeated Miguel in 1834. Her reign, however, was marked by continual political unrest. She was succeeded by her son, Peter V.

Maria Christina (1806–78), queen of Spain, consort of Ferdinand VII. At her behest Ferdinand named their daughter Isabella II as heir. She was regent to Isabella after Ferdinand's death and marshalled Isabella's forces against the Carlists, the supporters of Don Carlos, the late king's brother and pretender to the throne. Forced from the regency in 1840, she returned in 1843 and thereafter played a major role in the political intrigues and dissensions that marked Isabella's reign. *See also* Carlists.

Maria Luisa (1751–1819), queen of Spain, consort of Charles IV. She and her lover, Manuel de Godoy, were the actual rulers of Spain. When her husband was forced out by Napoleon I, she went into exile with him. She was Goya's patroness, and he did numerous paintings of her.

Mariana Islands, volcanic island chain in W Pacific Ocean, approx. 1,500mi (2,415km) E of the Philippines and N of the Caroline Islands; extends N to S approx. 500mi (800km) along the Marianas Ridge. Group includes Guam, Saipan, Tinian, Rota, Pagan, and ten other islands; most are mountainous volcanic formations. Discovered by Ferdinand Magellan 1521, and named Islas de los Ladrones (Islands of Thieves) the islands were named Marianas Islands in 1668. Spain sold islands to Germany 1899, and Japan received a mandate for them following WWI. The islands were taken by US forces 1944 and made a US Trust Territory; a US naval base was est. on Guam. The inhabitants of the island, excluding US personnel, are Micronesians, Chamorros, and Japanese. Agaña, Guam, Garapan, and Saipan are chief centers; site of ancient stone structures, notably on Guam, which have attracted archeological interest. Main occupation is subsistence farming. Exports: sugar cane, coconuts, coffee. Area: approx. 400sq mi (1,036sq km). Pop. 98,000 (concentrated in Guam).

Marianao, city in NW Cuba; suburb of Havana; city developed rapidly in late 19th century during sugar boom. Industries: chemicals, textiles, beer. Founded 1719. Pop. 350,260.

Maria Theresa of Austria (1717–80), empress of the Holy Roman Empire, archduchess of Austria, queen of Hungary and Bohemia. Daughter of Emperor Charles VI, her disputed succession to the Hapsburg lands led to the War of the Austrian Succession (1740–48). She married (1736) Francis Stephen of Lorraine, who became Emperor Francis I (1745). She made politically advantageous marriages for many of her children, including Marie Antoinette. *See also* Austrian Succession, War of the. △1180.

Marie Antoinette (1755–93), queen of France, daughter of Francis I and Maria Theresa of Austria. Married (1770) to the French dauphin, later Louis XVI, her extravagant and frivolous conduct caused her great unpopularity at court and made her hated by the populace. At the outbreak of the French Revolution

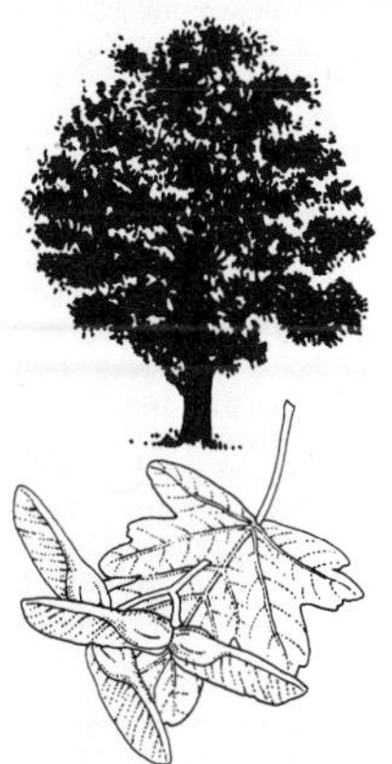

Maple

Marathon plain, Greece

Guglielmo Marconi

Marcus Aurelius: statue in Rome

(1789), a mob attacked the palace at Versailles. The removal of the royal family to Paris soon followed. Foiled at Varennes in an attempt to escape (1791), Louis and Marie were afterward viewed as traitors. They were guillotined two years later.

Marie de Médicis (1573–1642), queen of France. Daughter of the grand duke of Tuscany, she was married in 1600 to Henry IV of France, with whom she frequently quarrelled. He was assassinated the day after he crowned her queen in 1610. She was then regent for seven years, favoring Spain and the Catholic Church. Her ambitious and stubborn nature, however, led to disagreement with her son, Louis XIII. Cardinal Richelieu healed the breach, but Marie showed little gratitude and plotted against him. Despite her denunciation of Richelieu, Louis remained loyal to him. Marie was forced in 1631 to flee to Brussels, never again to see France.

Marie Louise of Austria (1791–1847), empress of France. After his victory at Wagram in 1809, Napoleon Bonaparte married her, the daughter of Emperor Francis I of Austria, in an attempt to unite himself with the old royal families of Europe.

Marietta, residential city in NW Georgia, 20mi (32km) NW of Atlanta; seat of Cobb co; site of aircraft industry, national cemetery. Inc. 1834. Pop. (1970) 27,216.

Marietta, city in SE Ohio, at the confluence of the Muskingum and Ohio rivers; seat of Washington co; named for Marie Antoinette; site of Marietta College (1797), and Gen. Rupert Putnam's home, now a museum. Industries: electrometallurgical products and chemicals. The oldest settlement in Ohio, it was founded 1788 by Manasseh Cutler and Gen. Putnam; inc. 1800. Pop. (1970) 16,861.

Marigold, scented mostly annual plants native from New Mexico to Argentina. Those most commonly cultivated are the French marigold *(Tagetes patula)*, height: to 1.5ft (45cm) and the African or Aztec marigold *(Tagetes erecta)*, height: to 3ft (91cm). They have showy yellow, orange, or red flower heads. Organic gardeners often plant marigolds to repel insects and nematode worms. Family Compositae.

Marihuana, a hallucinogenic drug prepared from the dried flowering spikes of the hemp plant *Cannabis sativa* and smoked in cigarettes. Of the two types, Indian and American, the former is the more potent. Marihuana produces feelings of elation, intensifies experiences, particularly sensations (possibly excepting touch), and distorts the time sense; large doses produce intoxication. The heightening of unpleasant experiences appears to have caused psychological disturbances in some unstable persons. △730.

Marimba, percussion instrument with tuned wooden bars ranging 5 to 6 octaves, set in a frame over resonators and struck with mallets. Brought from Malaysia via African Bantus to Guatemala, it is now used in marimba bands throughout Latin America. Darius Milhaud and Paul Creston wrote modern concertos for the marimba.

Marine Biology, science and study of life in the sea, including organisms that live in the water and along shores. Marine biologists explore how these organisms fit into the human environment as well as their own. △624–26.

Marine Corps, United States, branch of the armed forces that is a service within the department of the Navy. It consists of approximately 196,000 personnel, and it conducts the land operations connected with naval operations. The commandant of the Marine Corps is a member of the Joint Chiefs of Staff and participates on an equal basis when Marine Corps matters are under consideration. He is also responsible for Marine training and doctrine and for providing troops and equipment to the Fleet Marine Forces. The operational forces consist of three divisions, three aircraft wings, and supporting troops, and are organized into task forces to conduct amphibious operations. The US Marines officially began in 1798 as part of the Navy, although there had been a continental Marine Corps during the Revolutionary War. The Marine Corps has been involved in US military operations from the War of 1812 through the Vietnam conflict. *See also* Joint Chiefs of Staff; Navy, United States.

Marine Engineering, branch of engineering that deals with the construction, maintenance, and operation of the power plant and other mechanical equipment of seagoing vessels, docks, and harbor installations. △1760.

Mariner. △64, 70, 142.

Marini, Marino (1901–), Italian sculptor. A creator of paintings, portrait busts, and group statues, he is best known for his statues of horses and horsemen. They reveal oriental and classical influence, yet are vigorously modern. His work is represented in many European and US museums.

Marion, Francis (1732–95), American Revolutionary War officer, known as the "Swamp Fox," b. Berkley co, S.C. He commanded the South Carolina militia in guerrilla-type raids on the British. He participated in the defense of Charleston.

Marion, city in E central Indiana, NW of Muncie; seat of Grant co; site of Marion College (1920). Industries: automobile parts, glass, television and radio tubes, dairy products. Settled 1826; inc. 1889. Pop. (1970) 39,607.

Marion, city in central Ohio, approx. 45mi (72km) N of Columbus; seat of Marion co; preserves home of President Warren G. Harding. Industries: rubber products, flour, limestone, home appliances. Settled 1821; inc. as village 1830, as city 1890. Pop. (1970) 38,646.

Maris, Roger (Eugene) (1934–), US baseball player, b. Hibling, Minn. He set an all-time season home run record (61) in 1961, eclipsing Babe Ruth's 1927 mark (60), although Ruth had scored his hit total in a shorter season. Maris' career ran from 1957 through 1968.

Maritime Alps, S division of W Alps along French-Italian border; extends 120mi (193km) from Ligurian Apennines (Cadibono Pass) ESE to Cottian Alps (Maddalena Pass) WNW. Highest peak is Punta Argentera, 10,817ft (3,299m).

Maritime Law, or admiralty law, deals with laws relating to commerce and navigation, thus to all marine matters including questions of contracts, torts, injuries, piracy, and of prize. A branch of commercial law controlled by national courts and influenced by municipal law, it is composed of national laws and rules of their admiralty courts and international treaties and conventions. Its bases are customs and usages dating from ancient times—those of 8th or 9th-century Rhodes are the earliest known—and influenced by Roman civil law; they were codified during the Middle Ages. In England maritime law was once under the jurisdiction of separate courts of admiralty, but these cases are now assigned to the high court of justice. The US Constitution grants authority over maritime law to federal courts.

Marius, Gaius (*c.*157–86 BC), Roman general. Of equestrian family rank, he served in Numantia and later as proconsul in Spain. He married the patrician Julia (later Caesar's aunt) and served as Metellus' legate in Numidia, where he distinguished himself in the Jugurthine War. He was elected consul seven times and became the bitter enemy of Sulla. Marius created a new army of the proletariat with improved organization and training. When Sulla took command of the Roman forces in the East, Marius fled. He allied himself with Cinna, seized Rome, and slaughtered his enemies. Granted the eastern command, he died before assuming it. Sulla was victorious in the ensuing civil war. △1018.

Marjoram, or sweet marjoram, common name for *Majorana hortensis*, an herb of the mint family with aromatic leaves used for flavoring meats and dressings. It is not to be confused with pot marjoram *(Origanum vulgare)*.

Mark, apostle of Jesus. He was the author, with Peter's assistance, of one of the four gospels of the New Testament, written about 30 years after Jesus' death. This gospel was written for Gentiles, stressing Jesus's activities and nature as the Son of God, and does not refer to the Old Testament. △1026.

Market Equilibrium, market position from which there is no tendency to move; the position at which both buyer and seller are satisfied. This equilibrium occurs when the quantity supplied equals the quantity demanded at a particular market price, called the *equilibrium price.* The quantity is called the *equilibrium quantity.* Market equilibrium occurs when the supply and demand curves are equal and the market exactly clears at this market price.

Marketing, that portion of the production-distribution-consumption continuum dealing with the transfer of goods and services from one owner to another. The marketing function can occur at all levels, and one can examine the marketing practices at the wholesale or retail enterprise. Recent estimates suggest that approximately 50% of the consumers' expenditures pay for marketing activities, broadly defined, and that almost one third of the US labor force is engaged in commodity distribution. Marketing activities are expanding, and now include some responsibility for product development, design, packaging, pricing, and advertising. △936.

Market Mechanism, in economics, the interaction of supply and demand that determines a market price and market output level. The market mechanism is based on the demand schedule, which is a schedule of prices and the quantities that would be demanded by consumers at these prices, as well as the supply schedule, which is a schedule of prices and the quantities that would be supplied by producers at these prices. As prices increase, consumers will demand less and producers will be willing to produce more. As prices decline, consumers will demand more and producers will be willing to produce less. Through the interaction of the two forces, an equilibrium price is reached. △936.

Market Structure. A market economy may include many different market structures, ranging from purely competitive (many firms producing a homogeneous product, with free entry) to monopolistic (only one seller). Generally, as the market becomes less and less competitive, prices of goods tend to be higher and the output levels of the industry tend to be lower. As the degree of monopoly power increases, the market mechanism is less and less able to operate because more market control is placed in the hands of fewer firms.

Market System, the system of decision-making within a free enterprise, price-oriented economy. It determines, through response to consumer demands, what goods will be produced; through the individual firm's decision-making process, how these goods will be produced; and through the interaction of supply and demand, how these goods will be allocated. The market system basically involves the interaction of supply provided by the firms and demand provided by consumers in determining the quantity of the good. △936–38.

Markhor, largest wild goat; it inhabits mountains of Afghanistan and W Himalaya Mountains. Males have long, corkscrew horns, and shaggy beards. Height: 40in (102cm) at shoulder; weight: 200lb (90kg). Family Bovidae; species *Capra falconeri. See also* Goat.

Markievicz, Constance Georgine, Countess de (1876–1927), Irish Republican politician and patriot. Sentenced to death after the Easter Rebellion (1916) but released (1917), she served in the Sinn Fein Parliament (1918–22) and the Dáil (1923–27).

Marlborough, John Churchill, 1st Duke of (1650–1722), English general and political figure. He was a supporter of William of Orange in the Glorious Revolution (1688). Queen Anne created him duke of Marlborough (1702), and he led the English and allied armies against Louis XIV in the War of the Spanish Succession, gaining great victories at Blenheim (1704), Ramillies (1706), Oudenaarde (1708), and Malplaquet (1709). On the ascendancy of his political enemies, he was dismissed from all his offices (1711). He was restored to military command in 1714.

Marlborough, Sarah Jennings Churchill, Duchess of (1660–1744), favorite of England's Queen Anne. She married John Churchill, later duke of Marlborough (1678), and her influence with the future queen assisted his career. Through her Whig sympathies, she lost favor after 1707. She supervised the building of Blenheim Palace.

Marlborough, city in E Massachusetts, 15mi (24km) ENE of Worcester. Founded on site of Indian village (1657); it was severely damaged by Indians in King Philip's War (1676). Industries: shoes, miner's lamps. Inc. as city 1890. Pop. (1970) 27,936.

Marlin, popular marine sport billfish found in the warm waters of the Atlantic and Pacific. Not abundant in any area, it is dark blue with a coppery tint and violet-blue side bars. The long bill is rounded in cross-section. Length: to 26ft (7.9m); weight: 1,400lb (635kg). Species include the blue marlin *Makaira nigricans* and the Pacific striped *Tetrapturus audax.* Family Istiophoridae. △626.

Marlowe, Christopher (1564–93), English poet and playwright. From *Tamburlaine the Great* (1587) until his death six years later, he wrote six tragedies (one unfinished) and the heroic poem *Hero and Leander.* Noted for his supreme mastery of language, he used blank verse in his dramas and began the development of heroic tragedy by restoring to it the grandeur of the early Greek tragedians. His plays, which were the first ever written for the public theater, are *The Tragical History of Doctor Faustus* (1589), *The Jew of Malta* (1589), *Edward II* (*c.*1590), *The Massacre of Paris* (1590), and *Dido, Queen of Carthage* (completed by Thomas Nash). △1148.

Marmara, Sea of, sea in NW Turkey, between Europe (N) and Asia (S). It is connected with Black Sea (E) by the Bosporus, and with the Aegean Sea through the Dardanelles. Its largest island is Marmara, famous for alabaster and marble quarries. Istanbul is located at entrance of Bosporus on Sea of Marmara. Sea is easily navigable due to lack of strong currents and negligible tidal range. Area: 4,430sq mi (11,474sq km).

Marmoset, tiny day-active, tree-dwelling monkey of tropical America. The size of small squirrels, they have soft dense fur varying in color. Marmosets of certain genera are often called tamarins. Family Callithricidae; genera *Saguinus, Leontideus. See also* Monkey. △554.

Marmot, stocky, ground-living rodent of the squirrel family native to North America and Eurasia. Most have brown to gray fur; short, powerful legs; and furred tails. Plant-eaters by day, they find shelter and hibernate in grass-lined burrows. They mate in spring and have 2–8 young in early summer. Length, excluding tail: 15–28in (38–71cm); weight: 7–17lbs (3–8kg). Family Sciuridae. △584.

Marne-Champagne Operation (July 15–18, 1918), German World War I offensive to correct faulty supply lines in the Marne area and to draw off reserves from the planned Flanders attack. It was halted by 4th French Army with support of three US divisions. △ 1306.

Marne River, river in NE France; rises in Langres plateau, flows NW to Seine River near Paris. Marne Rhine Canal and Marne-Saône Canal connect it with Aisne, Meuse, Moselle, and Saône rivers. In 1914 and 1918 bitter battles were fought on its banks; US forces reached river August 1944. Navigable for 220mi (354km) of its 325mi (523km).

Maronites, Christian sect founded, according to claims, by St Maro in the 5th century and based on Monotheletic beliefs (only the divine will present in Christ). Probably dating from 7th century Syria, with present colonies also in Lebanon, Israel, Cyprus, and the United States, the sect was excommunicated in 680 at the Council of Constantinople. It was taken back into the Church in 1181, and in 1584 Pope Gregory XIII founded the Maronite College at Rome. The Maronites are a uniat body—an eastern church in union with Rome—and retain their own language (Syriac), canon law, and ceremonies.

Marot, Clément (1496–1544), French poet, one of the first to write sonnets. He held various positions at court but, because of his Lutheran sympathies, was twice forced to flee France. He wrote witty court poems and an important translation of the Psalms. △ 1172.

Marquand, J(ohn) P(hillips) (1893–1960), US author, b. Wilmington, Del. A novelist, he is noted for his books about wealthy New Englanders. Among these are *The Late George Apley* (1937; Pulitzer Prize 1938), *Wickford Point* (1939), and *H. M. Pulham, Esq.* (1941). He also wrote a number of detective stories and novels about a Japanese detective, Mr. Moto.

Marquesas Islands, volcanic island group, part of French Polynesia, in E central Pacific Ocean, S of the equator and N of Tuamotu; the group of twelve includes Fatu Hiva, Hiva Oa, and Nuku Hiva. Capital is Hakapehi on Nuku Hiva. French took possession and settled islands in 1842, bringing with them European diseases that decimated the native Polynesians. Islands are mountainous, with fertile valleys and several good harbors; scene of Herman Melville's *Typee.* Exports: tobacco, vanilla, copra, cotton. Discovered 1595 by Alvaro de Medaña, Spanish navigator. Area: 480sq mi (1,243 sq km). Pop. 5,184.

Marquette, Father Jacques (1637–75), French Jesuit missionary and explorer in America. In 1666, Marquette arrived in Quebec as a missionary priest. After two years, he moved deeper into the wilderness to preach among Indians around the Great Lakes. Chosen (1672) by the Canadian government to explore, he, Louis Jolliet, and five others discovered the Mississippi River. He was the first white man to live on the site of Chicago. △1122–24, 1216.

Marrakesh (Marrakech), city in W central Morocco, at NW foot of Atlas Mts; one of the cities of Islam and site of many medieval structures, notably the Koutoubya mosque; seat of Université Ben Youssef. Industries: tourism, leather goods. Founded 1062 by Yusuf ibn Tashfin. Pop. 305,000.

Marriage, state in which two individuals are joined together by a number of bonds, which include the economic, the religious, and the sexual. One major reason for marriage is the procreation and upbringing of children. Marriage is distinguishable from a sexual union accompanied by co-residence in that it involves rites that establish it officially in a society. *See also* Courtship; Polyandry; Polygamy. △794.

Marriage of Figaro, The (1786), 4-act opera by Wolfgang Amadeus Mozart, Italian libretto by Lorenzo Da Ponte, after Pierre Beaumarchais' comedy. Its Vienna premiere was conducted by Mozart. Although one of the oldest operas performed continuously in Western repertoires, it is musically and politically revolutionary. The story is of servants mocking aristocratic masters, challenging the feudal practice of "droit du seigneur." Principal roles are Figaro and the Count (baritones), Susanna and the Countess (sopranos), Cherubino (mezzo-soprano). △1174.

Marrow, soft tissue, containing blood vessels, found in the hollow cavities of bones. The marrow found in many bones, including the long bones, is somewhat yellowish and functions for fat deposition. The marrow in the flattish bones, including the ribs, sternum, cranial bones, parts of the pelvis, and the ends of the long bones, is reddish and contains reticular cells that give rise to myeloblasts. The myeloblasts give rise eventually to the red blood cells as well as to most of the white blood cells and the platelets. △662, 682.

Mars, fourth planet from Sun, with 2 satellites (Phobos and Deimos) and the only planet other than Earth that might support life. Its thin atmosphere is mainly carbon dioxide with traces of water vapor; Temperature, −100°F (−73°C) to over 60°F (16°C); mean distance from Sun, 141,320,000mi (227,940,000km); mass, 0.11 of Earth; diameter, 4,210mi (6,762km); rotation period, 24hr 37min; period of sidereal revolution, 687 days. *See also* Solar System. △68–76, 148.

Mars, in Roman mythology, god of war. Although second in importance only to Jupiter, there is little known of his early character. He was the father of Romulus and Remus.

Marsala, ancient Lilybaeum, seaport city in W Sicily, Italy, approx. 18mi (29km) S of Trapani on Cape Boeo; site of 16th-century cathedral and city walls; Garibaldi's forces landed here 1860 in conquest of Sicily. Exports: wines (famous white Marsala), salt, grain. Pop. 82,724.

Marseilles, seaport city in SE France, on Gulf of Lions; capital of Bouches-du-Rhône dept. Second-largest and oldest city in France, it is connected with Rhône River by an underground canal; during Crusades (11th-14th century) it was commercial center and shipping port for Holy Land. The 19th-century conquest of Algeria by France and opening of Suez Canal brought prosperity to the city. In the harbor is Chateau D'If, a prison built 1524 on small rocky isle; site of 13th–14th-century St Victor's Abbey Church, 17th-century city hall, and Chapelle de la Charité. Industries: flour, soap, vegetable oil, cement, sugar. Founded 600 BC by Phocaean Greeks from Asia Minor. Pop. 889,028.

Marsh, shallow lake whose waters are stagnant or feebly flowing and which is filled with vegetation, rushes, reeds, and types of trees whose roots like the muddy soil. A marsh may also be a piece of low land that at times dries enough to be tilled. Marsh areas may occur high in mountains or adjacent to the sea. △618–20.

Marshall, Alfred (1842–1924), English Neoclassical economist, one of the greatest modern economists. His *Principles of Economics* (1890) was a landmark work. Prior to its publication, economists had argued about whether demand or supply played a more important role in determining a product's price. Marshall, however, showed that supply and demand were like the blades of a pair of scissors. Both blades are equally needed if the scissors are to work properly. Many of Marshall's other concepts—elasticity; the short run, with variable and fixed cost; and the long run—were also important contributions to economics, and his microeconomic theory provided part of the foundation of modern economics.

Francis Marion

Roger Maris

Markhor

Marseilles, France

Marshall, George Catlett (1880–1959), US army officer and public official, b. Uniontown, Pa. As army chief of staff during World War II, he helped formulate Allied strategy. After the war, he was secretary of state (1947–49) and of defense (1950–51). He won the 1953 Nobel Peace prize for the European Recovery Program (Marshall Plan), which provided economic aid to postwar Europe. *See also* Marshall Plan. △ 1342, 1356.

Marshall, John (1755–1835), chief justice of the US Supreme Court (1801–35), b. Fauquier co, Va. He served as an officer in the Continental Army throughout the Revolutionary War. His only formal education was the study of law for several months under George Wythe at the College of William and Mary. He was a member of the Virginia House of Burgesses 1782–88. He gained national prominence as a member of the Virginia constitutional ratification convention (1788), when he argued successfully for the Constitution against Patrick Henry; and for his defense of Jay's Treaty during the ratification controversy. He accepted a post (1797) offered by President John Adams as minister to France and returned to the United States in great favor after negotiations with Charles Maurice de Talleyrand in the XYZ Affair. He refused the post as associate justice and became a Federalist member of the House of Representatives from Virginia (1799–1800). He served as secretary of state (1800–01) until his appointment as chief justice. Marshall raised the Supreme Court to great prestige and established basic precepts for constitutional interpretation. Important cases he presided over include *Marbury* v. *Madison* (1803), which set a doctrine of judicial review; *Fletcher* v. *Peck* (1810) and *Dartmouth College* v. *Woodward* (1819), establishing doctrines of sanctity of contracts; *McCulloch* v. *Maryland* (1819), which expanded congressional power through implied power; *Gibbons* v. *Ogden* (1824), which designated national power over commerce; and *Cohens* v. *Virginia* (1821), which established the supremacy of the Supreme Court over state legislatures. He also wrote *Life of George Washington* (5 vols., 1804–07).

Marshall, Thurgood (1908–), US jurist and lawyer, b. Baltimore, Md. A civil rights advocate opposed to civil disobedience, he was the special counsel and later chief counsel for the NAACP (1938–62). He played a key role in obtaining US Supreme Court desegregation decisions, including *Brown* v. *Board of Education of Topeka* (1954, 1955). A US Appeals Court judge (1961–65), he was appointed solicitor general in 1965. In 1967 he became the first black to be appointed an associate justice of the US Supreme Court. On the court, he consistently championed civil rights and civil liberties.

Marshall Islands, group of atolls and reefs in W Pacific Ocean, E of the Caroline Islands. Administered as a US Trust Territory of the Pacific Islands, it is comprised of two great chains, Ralik (W) and Ratak (E), which run almost parallel NW to SE, covering an ocean area of 4,500sq mi (11,655sq km). Native inhabitants are Micronesian; Kwajalein in Ralik Chain, and Majoru in Ratak Chain are government centers. Annexed to Germany 1885, the group was taken by Japan 1914; Japan received a mandate for islands from the League of Nations 1920; taken by US forces in WWII (1944). Exports: copra, sugar, coffee. Industries: coconuts, fishing, subsistence farming. Total land area: approx. 70sq mi (181sq km). Pop. 20,206.

Marshall Plan, a program of economic aid to Europe proposed by Sec. of State George C. Marshall in 1947. The European Recovery Act (1948) authorized the plan. The United States spent about $14,000,000,000 in 5 years to help the European nations recover from the destruction of World War II. The plan was considered a great economic, social, and political success. △1342, 1356, 1947.

Marshalltown, city in central Iowa, on the Iowa River, 48mi (77km) NE of Des Moines; seat of Marshall co; site of Marshalltown Community College (1927). Industries: grain, livestock, furnaces, valves, canned goods. Settled 1851; inc. 1863. Pop. (1970) 26,219.

Marsh Birds, birds with toes adapted for walking on marshy vegetation. Some, such as the coot, are aquatic. Many, including crane, limpkin, and seriema, are long-legged; others, including some rails, are tiny and live secretively on the forest floor. Order Gruiformes. △620.

Marsh Deer, or **Swamp Deer,** deer of E South American wetlands. It is reddish-brown with black legs and doubly forked antlers. Height: to 3ft (.91m); weight: to 200lb (91kg). Family Cervidae; species *Blastocerus dichotomus.*

Marsh Gas. *See* Methane.

Marsh Hawk, or hen harrier, Northern Hemisphere hawk with gray or brownish plumage, sometimes with white spots. Length: 20in (51cm). Species *Circus cyaneus.*

Marsh Mallow, perennial plant native to E Europe and naturalized in salt marshes of the E United States. It has pink flowers. Height: 3–4ft (0.9–1.2m). Family Malvaceae; species *Althea officinalis.*

Marsh Marigold, or cowslip, perennial herbaceous plant native to cold and temperate swamps of the Northern Hemisphere. It has hollow stems, kidney-shaped leaves, and large pink, white, or yellow flowers. There are about 20 species. Family Ranunculaceae; genus *Caltha.*

Marsic War. *See* Social War.

Marsilius of Padua (*c.*1275–1342), Italian political theorist, also known as Marsiglio dei Mainardini. He studied medicine in Paris (1311–20) and wrote the *Defensor Pacis* (1324), an antipapist landmark in political philosophy. This work refuted the pope's claims to "plenitude of power" even over secular matters, and instead said that the church should be subordinate to the state. He described the state as the great unifying power of society, with its power derived from the people through a popularly elected government. In 1326 he fled to Emperor Louis of Bavaria, where he spent the rest of his life.

Marston Moor, battle site 7 mi (11km) west of York, England. It was the scene of the decisive defeat of royalist forces under Prince Rupert by the Parliamentarians under Fairfax (July 2, 1644) in the English Civil War.

Marsupial, any mammal of the order Marsupialia, which consists of the kangaroos, wombats, bandicoots, opossums, and others, native to the New World and Australia. Most develop no placenta; females have a pouch (marsupium) on the abdomen containing the teats and serving to carry the young. Marsupials usually have numerous teeth; some over 44. Young are almost embryonic at birth. △544.

Marsupial Frog, South American tree frog. Females carry fertilized eggs in a pouch on their backs. The young may hatch as tadpoles or remain in the pouch until metamorphosed, depending on species. *Gastrotheca marsupiata* is green with dark spots on its back and has striped legs; length: to 3in (7.6cm). *See also* Tree Frog. △518.

Marsupial Mouse. △544.

Marten, carnivorous mammal of the weasel family found in forested areas in Eurasia and North and South America. Long-bodied and short-legged, they are hunted for their fur. The dark brown skins of the Siberian *Martes zibellina* are the most valuable but the skins of the lighter stone or beech *Martes foina* are also prized. Family Mustelidae. △458, 464.

Martha's Vineyard, island in Atlantic Ocean off SW coast of Cape Cod, SE Massachusetts; named by explorer Bartholomew Gosnold for his daughter and the grapevines he found when he visited the island in 1602; site of Duke's County Historical Society museum housed in 1765 home. Connected to mainland by ferry, it is a summer tourist center. First settled by English 1642. Area: 108sq mi (280sq km).

Martí, José (1853–95), Cuban poet and essayist. Known as the "apostle" of Cuban independence, he was idealistic and visionary. His verse reflected his belief that poetry and politics were inseparable. He was forced into exile and lived in New York before returning to Cuba, where he died fighting the Spanish. Latin Americans have been strongly influenced by his works and career. *Ismaelillo* (1882), *Versos libres* (published posthumously), and *Versos sencillos* (1891) contain his best poems. *The America of José Martí* (1953) is a collection of essays.

Martial(is), Marcus Valerius (*c.*40–*c.*104), Roman poet. He lived in Rome from about AD 64 enjoying the patronage of the emperors Domitian and Titus and the friendship of Juvenal and Quintilian. He wrote witty epigrammatic poems in new meters and forms. These were collected in 15 books. In AD 98 he retired to his native Spain.

Martial Law, the suspension of internal civil judicial procedures, and their replacement by direct military rule by the executive branch of government. In the United States, martial law has been used only infrequently, such as in the border states during the Civil War and in San Francisco following the 1906 earthquake.

Martin, Saint (died *c.* 397), often called St Martin of Tours. He was born in what is now Hungary but moved to Italy and then France. In 371 the people of Tours chose him their bishop. He preached to spread the faith and to combat the Arian heresy. One of many tales about this popular French saint is that he divided his cloak with a beggar.

Martin I, Roman Catholic pope (649–55) and saint. He stressed papal authority over all and refused to obey the emperor's edict forbidding religious discussions. He was arrested, publicly degraded, and exiled. He died shortly thereafter, being the last pope to be martyred.

Martin V, Roman Catholic pope (1417–31), b. Oddone Colonna (1368). After 39 years of schism, he tried to restore papal prestige and church unity through political means. He reorganized the Curia and, despite frequent correspondence with Constantinople, he failed in negotiations with the Eastern church.

Martin, John ("Mad"). △1242.

Martin, Joseph William, Jr. (1884–1968), speaker of the US House of Representatives, 1947–49 and 1953–55, b. North Attleboro, Mass. A prominent Republican, he spent 42 years in the House, (1925–67), also serving as minority leader for 20 years.

Martin. *See* Purple Martin; Swallow.

Martin du Gard, Roger (1881–1958), French novelist. His major works, *Jean Barois* (1913) and the eight-novel series *Les Thibaults* (1922–40), show an objective approach to the moral and intellectual preoccupations of his generation. He was awarded the Nobel Prize for literature in 1937.

Martinique, island in Windward Islands, West Indies; an overseas French dept.; volcanic island is largest of Lesser Antilles. Fort de France is capital and chief trade center; Mt Pelée volcano (N) is highest peak, 4,429ft (1,351m). Island has rain forests (N), which slope to plains and coastal valleys where agriculture is centered. French is the official language; site of technical colleges, Institut Henri Vizioz; birthplace of Empress Josephine. Discovered 1502 by Christopher Columbus, it was inhabited by Caribs until displaced by French settlers from 1635; attacked 17th century by Dutch and British, it was officially French after Napoleonic Wars; became overseas dept. 1946. Exports: sugar, rum, fruits, cocoa, tobacco, vanilla, vegetables. Agriculture and tourism are major industries: Area: 425sq mi (1,101sq km). Pop. 292,062.

Martinson, Harry Edmund (1904–), Swedish writer. From age seven he lived as a hobo and later as a seaman; these experiences influenced the underlying mood in both his poetry and his novels. His space fantasy *Aniara* (1956) became a successful opera. He shared the 1974 Nobel Prize for literature with Eyvind Johnson.

Martin v. Hunter's Lessee (1816), landmark US Supreme Court case in which Chief Justice Marshall upheld the court's right to reverse state court decisions that conflicted with rights granted under the Constitution.

Martynia, or unicorn plant, rank-growing, annual wild flower of S and central United States. Leaves and stems are covered with sticky hairs. Flowers are white, yellow, or violet and seed pods resemble unicorn's horn. Height: to 18in (46cm). Family Martyniaceae; species *Martynia proboscidea.*

Martyr. △1052.

Martyrium Style, in architecture. △1080.

Marvell, Andrew (1621–78), English poet and satirist. Though a Puritan and a friend of Milton, he genuinely admired both Cromwell and Charles I and was member of parliament for Hull during the Commonwealth and the Restoration. His poetry, combining intellectual wit and passion, includes "The Garden" (*c.*1653), "Bermudas" (*c.*1653), and "To His Coy Mistress" (published 1681).

Marwar, *see* Jodhpur.

Marx, Karl (1818–83), German social philosopher and political activist, founder (with Friedrich Engels) of the world Communist movement. He studied history, philosophy, and law and received a doctorate from the University of Jena in 1841. He rejected the philosophical idealism of G.W.F. Hegel but accepted his dialectical method and combined it with the philosophical materialism of Ludwig Feuerbach and Moses Hess to produce his own approach of dialectical materialism. In Paris after 1843 he met Friedrich Engels, with whom he was to share a lifelong collaboration. His association with such French radicals as P.J. Proudhon, Louis Blanc, and the followers of Saint-Simon and Fourier deepened his socialist commitments.

In Paris he wrote *Toward the Critique of the Hegelian Philosophy of Right* (1844), which proclaimed that "religion was the opium of the people." He also wrote, with Engels, *The German Ideology* (1845–46), describing inevitable laws of history. Expelled from France, he went to Brussels, published a newspaper, and joined the Communist League, an international workers' society, for which he and Engels wrote their epochal *Communist Manifesto* (1848). From 1848, Marx was to devote his life to scholarly and political activity aimed at analyzing and overthrowing capitalism. Expelled from Belgium (1848), he participated in the revolutionary movements in France and Germany. Expelled from both those countries, he finally went to London (1849), where he was to live until his death.

Although Engels assisted him financially, Marx's London years were largely spent under conditions of poverty, illness, and family tragedy as he toiled on research in the British Museum and produced a stream of writings, including *The Class Struggles in France, 1848–1850* (1950) and *Das Kapital* (3 vols., 1867, 1885, 1894), whose last two volumes were edited by Engels. The monumental *Kapital*, systematically criticizing what Marx saw as capitalism's exploitative and self-destructive tendencies, became the "bible of the working class." In 1864 he became one of the founders of the International Workingmen's Association (the "First International"), an association of labor, reform, and radical movements. His defense of the Paris Commune (1871) in speeches and *The Civil War in France* (1871) gave him an international reputation, and he became the leading spirit of the International. He denounced both the nonrevolutionary reformism of British labor leaders and the anarchism advocated by Mikhail Bakunin. Split into factions, the International dissolved in 1874. Marx, however, continued to be consulted by many as a kind of socialist prophet. During this period he generally, as in *Critique of the Gotha Programme* (1875), advocated a hard line and less collaboration with bourgeois elements. Since his death the ideas of Marx have continued to have immense influence. *See also* Communist Manifesto. △898,1288.

Marx Brothers, US vaudeville and film comedians. They were **Chico (Leonard)** (1891–1961), piano player with a broad Italian accent; **Harpo (Arthur)** (1893–1964), mute harp player; **Groucho (Julius)** (1895–), moustached wisecracker; and **Gummo (Milton)** (1897–) and **Zeppo (Herbert)** (1901–), who both left the team early. Their films included *Animal Crackers* (1930), *Duck Soup* (1933), and *A Night at the Opera* (1935). In 1947, Groucho became the host of "You Bet Your Life," one of TV's first quiz shows.

Marxism, school of socialism that arose in 19th-century Europe as a response to the growth of industrial capitalism, named for Karl Marx. Marx articulated an economic interpretation of history; all changes in social structure were determined by changes in productive activity. Increased productivity created more complex and oppressive forms of social organization and an increase in the numbers of the proletariat. The misery necessarily induced by capitalism would also produce an inevitable working-class revolution that would destroy capitalist society. Marxism, both a general theory and a scientific method of investigating the nature of economic systems, became a party ideology in the 1860s. △898.

Mary, Saint, the mother of Jesus Christ, often called the Blessed Virgin Mary. The Gospels tell of events in her life. The angel Gabriel appeared to her (the Annunciation) to tell her that she would conceive a child, by the power of the Holy Spirit, who would be called the Son of God. Thus she was a virgin at the time of the birth. The Gospels also tell of the birth of Jesus and of his mother's presence at his Crucifixion. Over the centuries beliefs developed about Mary in the Roman Catholic Church. The doctrine of the Assumption holds that Mary "at the conclusion of her life on earth was assumed body and soul into heavenly glory." The dogma of the Immaculate Conception holds that Mary from her conception was free of original sin. The Virgin Mary (Madonna) has been a favorite subject of painters and sculptors.

Mary, Queen of Scots (1542–87), daughter of James V of Scotland, whom she succeeded (1542). She married Francis II of France (1558), but after his death (1560) she returned to Scotland, determined to restore Roman Catholicism there. Her marriage to Henry, Lord Darnley (1565), strengthened her claim to the English throne. Darnley's implication in the murder of David Rizzio, her favorite (1566), occasioned her connivance at Darnley's death (1567). She then married the earl of Bothwell, her nobles revolted, and she abdicated (1567). Escaping from Lochleven (1568), she fled to England, where Elizabeth I imprisoned her. Her repeated intrigues in the Ridolfi Plot (1572) and the Babington Plot (1586) led Elizabeth to consent reluctantly to her execution.

Mary I, or **Mary Tudor** (1516–58), queen of England. The daughter of Henry VIII and Catherine of Aragon, she was known as "Bloody Mary." Her courageous backing of Catherine (1532–33) caused Henry's severe displeasure, but she was later reconciled with him and declared capable of inheriting the crown. On Edward VI's death she overcame Lady Jane Grey's challenge for the throne and became queen (1553). Her determination to reintroduce Roman Catholicism in England occasioned the major errors of her reign: her marriage to Philip of Spain (1554) and persecution of her Protestant subjects. News of the loss of Calais to the French (1558) hastened her death.

Mary II (1662–94), Queen of England, Scotland, and Ireland, wife of William III. Although her father, James II, was a Roman Catholic, Mary was a Protestant. She married the Dutch noble William of Orange in 1677, and her support enabled them to become joint sovereigns in 1689 following the Glorious Revolution that deposed James. She died from smallpox, and William then ruled alone.

Maryland, state in the E United States, on the Atlantic Ocean, just N of Virginia.

Land and Economy. Maryland is divided nearly in half by Chesapeake Bay, a 200-mile (320-km)-long arm of the Atlantic. E of the bay lies a coastal plain, a center of agriculture. To the W the land is rolling; the Blue Ridge Mts cross the W tip of the state. The Potomac River forms the irregular W boundary of most of Maryland. Baltimore, on the W shore of Chesapeake Bay, is the heart of the state's industry and one of the nation's leading ports. Shellfishing in Chesapeake Bay is important.

People. Maryland's first settlers were largely English, and their descendants predominated in the E. The industrialized Baltimore area drew immigrants of varied stock, but about 80% of the people were born in the United States. Nearly that percentage resides in urban areas. Baltimore is only about 30mi (48km) NE of Washington, D.C., and their metropolitan areas virtually merge to form a continuous community.

Education and Research. There are about 50 institutions of higher education. The University of Maryland is state-controlled. Best-known of the private institutions is Johns Hopkins University in Baltimore; its medical school is world-famous; the US Naval Academy is at Annapolis. Many scientific establishments doing research for the armed services and other agencies of the US government are in Maryland, close to Washington.

History. A charter for a large territory that included the present Maryland was granted by Charles I of England to Cecilius Calvert, 2nd Lord Baltimore, in 1632. His brother Leonard led the expedition that made the first settlements in 1634. Other communities sprang up in the late 17th century, and black slaves were imported to work tobacco plantations. Despite loyalist sentiment in some rural counties, Maryland was active in the drive for US independence. In the Revolution its troops were ranked among the best in the Continental army. In 1791, Maryland ceded a section of land on the Potomac River to create the District of Columbia, site of the national capital of Washington, D.C. In the Civil War, Maryland was one of the border states that did not secede from the Union, but its citizens served in both armies. The Battle of Antietam, one of the war's fiercest, was fought in W Maryland on Sept. 17, 1862. After the war, industry developed rapidly around Baltimore. In both world wars, the city was a major center of war matériel production.

PROFILE

Admitted to Union: April 28, 1788; 7th of the 13 original states to ratify the US Constitution
US Congressmen: Senate, 2; House of Representatives, 8
Population: 3,922,399 (1970); rank, 18th
Capital: Annapolis, 29,592 (1970)
Chief cities: Baltimore, 905,759; Dundalk, 85,577; Towson, 77,809
State legislature: Senate, 43; House of Delegates, 142

John Marshall

Thurgood Marshall

Marx Brothers

Mt. Vernon Place, Baltimore, Maryland

Area: 10,577sq mi (27,394sq km); rank, 42d
Elevation: Highest, 3,360ft (1,024m), Backbone Mt; lowest, sea level
Industries (major products): steel, copper, metal products, aircraft, ships and boats, processed foods, chemicals, apparel
Agriculture (major products): tobacco, corn, soybeans, apples, poultry
Minerals (major): stone, cement
State nickname: Old Line State, Free State
State motto: fatti maschii, parole femine ("Manly Deeds, Womanly Words")
State bird: Baltimore oriole
State flower: black-eyed Susan
State tree: white oak

Mary Magdalene, an early follower of Jesus Christ, from the village of Magdala on the W bank of the Sea of Galilee. According to the Gospels, Christ freed her of seven demons; she accompanied Christ on his preaching in Galilee, witnessed the Crucifixion and burial, and was the first person to see Christ resurrected. She has been confused with Mary of Bethany (sister of Lazarus) and a repentant prostitute who anointed Christ's feet. A Roman Catholic saint, her feast day is July 22.

Mary of Burgundy (1457–82), daughter and heiress of Charles the Bold. When Charles died in 1477, Mary attempted to save her inheritance (the Low Countries and part of France) from the French king by granting the people political privileges and marrying the Hapsburg archduke Maximilian. Her death left the land in the hands of the Hapsburgs.

Mary of France (1496–1533), queen of France, daughter of Henry VII of England. She married first Louis XII of France (1514), who died in 1515. Then, to the annoyance of her brother Henry VIII, she secretly married Charles Brandon, duke of Suffolk (1515).

Mary of Guise, or **Mary of Lorraine** (1515–60), regent of Scotland. She married James V of Scotland as her second husband (1538). He died (1542), leaving their infant daughter, Mary, queen of Scots. As regent (1554), Mary of Guise persecuted the Protestant faction and provoked a rebellion (1559), which, with English help, deposed her.

Masaccio, real name Tommaso Cassai or Tommaso di Ser Giovanni di Mone (1401–28), Italian painter. He worked in Florence. His classically balanced compositions show careful modeling of figures through use of light and shadow. He was influenced by Brunelleschi in his use of space and perspective, as shown in his fresco "The Trinity with Donors." With Masolino, he worked on the "Madonna with St. Anne" frescoes. Other famous works include the altarpieces for San Maria del Carmine in Pisa and the frescoes in the Brancacci Chapel in Florence. △1134.

Masai, Nilotic African people of Kenya and Tanzania, consisting of several subgroups. They are characteristically tall and slender. Their patrilineal, egalitarian society is based on nomadic pastoralism, cattle being equated with wealth. The traditional Masai kraal is a group of mud houses surrounded by a thorn fence. They have a system of age groups whereby individuals move together through a hierarchy consisting of junior and senior warriors followed by junior and senior elders. △1590.

Masaryk, Jan (1886–1948), Czechoslovak diplomat, son of Tomáš. Foreign minister under Eduard Beneš, he assumed the same role in the government-in-exile in London. He was also vice-premier. After the Allied victory, he returned to head the foreign ministry once again, attempting to resist increasing Communist domination. His fatal fall from his office window in 1948 was ruled a suicide by the government.

Masaryk, Tomáš (1850–1937), Czechoslovak statesman, first president of Czechoslovakia (1918–35). This noted writer devoted his life to gaining independence for Czechoslovakia. His Czechoslovak National Council was recognized by the Allies in 1918 as the provisional government of the future state. In 1918, Masaryk was elected president by acclamation. Minority problems and the fragmentation of political life were the two major problems during his tenure.

Mascarene Islands, group of islands in Indian Ocean, E of Madagascar. Discovered 16th century by Portuguese, comprised of islands of Mauritius and Rodriguez (part of the island country of Mauritius), and Réunion (belongs to France).

Mascon, any of several high-density regions of the moon's surface that produce stronger gravitational effects than the surrounding areas, causing noticeable perturbations in the orbits of spacecraft. The word is derived from the term "mass concentration" and the phenomenon seems to indicate that the lunar interior is not uniform.

Masefield, John (1878–1967), English poet and novelist. A writer of inventive and rhythmical verse, he was Poet Laureate from 1930 until his death. His long narrative poems include *The Everlasting Mercy* (1911), innovative in its use of colloquialism, and *Reynard the Fox* (1919). His most famous poem is "Sea Fever." He also wrote verse dramas and adventure novels.

Maser, a device using "inverted" populations of atoms (that is, atoms artificially kept in states of higher energy than normal) to provide amplification of radio signals. The term is an acronym for "microwave amplification by stimulated emission of radiation." The principle of the maser was first discovered by Charles Townes of Columbia University, who later received the Nobel Prize for his work. The first maser used electrostatic plates to separate high-energy ammonium atoms from low-energy ones. Radiation of a certain frequency would then stimulate the high-energy ammonium atoms to emit similar radiation and strengthen the signal. The very narrow frequency emitted made the ammonium maser one of the most accurate "atomic clocks" known. *See also* Laser.

Maseru, town in W Lesotho, S Africa, on the Caledon River; since 1966, it has served as the capital of the independent kingdom of Lesotho. Originally an obscure trading town, it flourished when made capital of British Basutoland protectorate 1869–71, 1884–1966; trade, transportation, and administrative center. Industries: candles, retreaded tires, carpets. Pop. 16,000.

Mashhad, city in NE Iran; capital of Khorasan prov. City served as capital of Persia under Nadir Shah (18th century); strategically important in 19th and 20th centuries because of proximity to Russian and Afghan borders. Name (meaning "shrine") is derived from Shiite shrine located here; it has tombs of Caliph Harun and Imam Reza, two ancient Shiite holy people; site of university (1947); important trade center and junction on caravan route. Industries: carpets, textiles, pharmaceuticals, food processing. Pop. 425,000.

Masinissa (*c.* 238–149 BC), Numidian king, fought against the Romans in Spain in the second Punic War, but changed sides in 206 and helped bring about the downfall of Carthage. He was supported in his North African kingdom by the Romans and gradually annexed Carthaginian lands. His reign greatly organized and settled the Numidian people. △1012.

Masochism, taking pleasure in being hurt or abused physically or psychologically. Masochism is often, though not always, linked with sexual arousal and gratification, and may take the form of a desire to be dominated or mistreated in one's relations with others.

Mason, George (1725–92), US Revolutionary patriot, b. Fairfax co, Va. He was elected to the Virginia House of Burgesses (1759). A strong defender of liberty and a constitutional philosopher, he wrote the Fairfax Resolves (1774), describing the colonial position in relation to the crown, and the Virginia Bill of Rights (1776), which Thomas Jefferson used as a model to the preamble of the Declaration of Independence. Mason served in the Virginia House of Delegates (1776–88). He was a delegate to the 1787 Constitutional Convention, but objected to the centralization of powers concept and refused to sign the document.

Mason, James Murray (1798–1871), Confederate official, b. Georgetown, D.C. He was a US senator from Virginia (1847–61) until the Civil War, when he became the Confederate diplomatic commissioner to England. En route to England he was seized (Nov. 8, 1861) by Northern officials while aboard the British steamer *Trent.* The incident caused a crisis in US-British relations. Released (Jan. 2, 1862), he went to England but failed to gain British recognition for the Confederate government.

Mason, John (1586–1635), founder of New Hampshire, b. England. He received a patent for a 60-mile (97-km) deep tract of land between the Merrimack and Piscataqua rivers, which he named New Hampshire. His heirs tried to make good on his claim and were involved in extensive litigation. In 1746 one of his descendants sold the rights to a dozen Portsmouth men (the Masonian Proprietors), who issued settlement permits and land titles in the undeveloped areas of Mason's grants.

Mason City, city in N central Iowa, 62mi (100km) NW of Waterloo; seat of Cerro Gordo co; site of Northern Iowa Community College (1918). Industries: brick, tile, beet sugar, portland cement, dairy products. Founded 1853 by members of Masonic order, for which city is named. Chartered 1870, as city 1881. Pop. (1970) 30,491.

Mason-Dixon Line, boundary between Pennsylvania and Maryland, surveyed by Charles Mason and Jeremiah Dixon (1763–67). It is the traditional line between the North and South.

Masonry. △1582,1612.

Masoretes, a group of Biblical scholars and scribes who wrote in Aramaic and were responsible for the Masorah, or elaborate marginal notes on the Hebrew Bible, written between the 6th and 12th centuries. These notes were intended as guides to understanding the Bible.

Masque, allegorical dramatic presentations given in England during the late 16th and early 17th century. They consisted of verse, comedy with plot, and, as an essential feature, an entrance for a group of masked dancers. Noted for their decor, famous masques include *The Masque of Blackness* (1605) and *The Masque of Beauty* (1608).

Masque of the Augurs. △1148.

Mass, central act of worship in the Roman Catholic Church. It involves a number of prayers, rituals, and the Eucharistic service. In the Church of England, high churchmen celebrate the Eucharist, or the Mass. *See also* Eucharist.

Mass, measure of the quantity of matter in a body. Mass may be defined in two ways. The gravitational mass of a body is determined by its mutual attraction to another, reference body, such as the Earth, as expressed in Newton's law of gravitation. Spring scales and platform balances provide a measure of gravitational mass. The inertial mass of a body is determined by its resistance to a change in its state of motion, as expressed in the second law of motion. Inertia balances provide a measure of inertial mass. According to Einstein's principle of equivalence, upon which his general theory of relativity is based, the inertial mass and the gravitational mass of a given body are equivalent. △830,1552.

Massachusetts, state in the NE United States, on the Atlantic Ocean, in the New England region.

Land and Economy. The coastline is indented by bays and inlets, creating many small harbors. Fish hook-shaped Cape Cod in the SE is a distinctive feature. To the W the land is rolling. The broad valley of the Connecticut River traverses the state from N to S. The Berkshire Hills are in the W. Besides the Connecticut, the principal rivers are the Housatonic (W) and the Merrimack (NE). Many smaller streams supply abundant water power to generate electricity. The Connecticut Valley is a notable farming area.

People. The state is the third most densely populated in the nation. The 1970 census showed 727 persons per sq mi (280.6per sq km), with about 85% residing in urban areas, principally in the E and the Connecticut Valley. Many are descended from the first English settlers, but in the 19th century many overseas immigrants, largely Irish, Poles, and Italians were drawn to employment in the factories. About 85% of the population was born in the United States.

Education. A pioneer in public education, Massachusetts has many universities and colleges. Harvard University at Cambridge (1636) is the oldest US university. The Massachusetts Institute of Technology also at Cambridge, is a major center of scientific training and research. The University of Massachusetts with its central campus at Amherst, is the state university.

History. The first settlement was made in 1620 at Plymouth on Massachusetts Bay by the Pilgrims, a group of English settlers seeking religious freedom. Boston was founded by English Puritans in 1630 and became the center of the colony of Massachusetts Bay. Through the years several wars were waged against Indians who ravaged frontier towns. Massachusetts strongly resisted the policies of the British crown that led to the Revolution. The first fight of the war was at Lexington on April 19, 1775; Bunker Hill (June 17, 1775) was the last battle in the colony. After achieving statehood, Massachusetts prospered. Its fishing and whaling fleets were famous, and large vessels from Massachusetts carried on a lucrative world wide trade. Manufacturing flourished, especially in textiles and shoes. The 19th century was a time of intellectual ferment, marked by the work of writers such as Ralph Waldo Emerson, Henry David Thoreau and Nathaniel Hawthorne; educators like Horace Mann; and abolitionists. In the Civil War, Massachusetts was a foremost supporter of the Union with men, money, and supplies. In later years, some industries declined but the state succeeded in maintaining its economic strength by accepting change and diversifying.

PROFILE

Admitted to Union: Feb. 6, 1788; 6th of 13 original states to ratify the US Constitution
US Congressmen: Senate, 2; House of Representatives, 12
Population: 5,689,170 (1970); rank, 10th
Capital: Boston, 641,071 (1970)
Chief cities: Boston, Worcester, 176,572; Springfield, 163,905; New Bedford, 101,777
State legislature: Senate, 40; House of Representatives, 240
Area: 8,257sq mi (21,386sq km); rank, 45th
Elevation: Highest, 3,491ft (1,065m), Mt Greylock; lowest, sea level
Industries (major products): electrical machinery, metal products, communications equipment, shoes, apparel, processed foods
Agriculture (major products): cranberries, dairy products, poultry, cigar-wrapper tobacco
Minerals (major): stone, sand, gravel
State nickname: Bay State
State motto: Ense petit placidam sub libertate quietem ("By the sword she seeks quiet peace under liberty")
State bird: chickadee
State flower: mayflower
State tree: American elm

Massachusetts Bay Colony, one of the earliest settlements in North America. It was founded as a trading company at Salem (1629). The charter brought to the colony by Puritan Governor John Winthrop (1630) encouraged a large migration of Puritans seeking religious and economic opportunities. This colony was not administered from England, since all the officers lived in the colony. There was an assembly, called a General Court, with representatives from the town meeting. The colony spread to Boston, Charlestown, and parts of Connecticut. Religious dissidents Roger Smith and Anne Hutchinson were expelled from the colony and settled in Rhode Island. The British crown sought to end self-government for the colony, the charter was cancelled (1684), and the area was put under direct English rule. It merged with Plymouth and Maine in 1691. *See also* Puritanism.

Massachusetts Emigrant Aid Society, US anti-slavery group organized in 1854 by Eli Thayer. Prompted by the Kansas-Nebraska Act, it founded Lawrence, Kan., and other free communities, bringing in 2,000 anti-slavery settlers. The ultimate goal was to make Kansas a free state. In 1855 the society became the New England Emigrant Aid Co.

Massachusetts Government Act (1774), one of Britain's Intolerable Acts. Britain virtually annulled the Massachusetts charter by appointing officials who had formerly been elected, limiting public meetings, and naming judges. In reaction, the colony adopted the Suffolk Resolves, and except for Boston, which was under the crown, acted as an independent state. *See also* Intolerable Acts;

Mass Action, Law of, principle that a chemical reaction rate is proportional to the product of the concentrations of each reactant. △1404.

Massapequa, residential community in SE New York, on S shore of Long Island, 10mi (16km) SE of Mineola; resort area. Pop. (1970) 26,951.

Massasauga, North American rattlesnake found in central and SW United States. It has large black blotches down its back and spots along sides. Length: to 30in (76cm). Family Viperidae; species *Sistrurus catenatus. See also* Rattlesnake.

Massasoit (1580?–1661), American Indian. He was chief of the Wampanoag tribe of Massachusetts and in Rhode Island. In 1621 he made a treaty with John Carver of Plymouth Colony that the Indians would not harm the Pilgrims if the Pilgrims respected the lands and rights of the Indians. He and his braves shared the first Thanksgiving with the Pilgrims. There were no wars between whites and Wampanoags as long as Massasoit was alive, and the Indians helped the Pilgrims to survive in their new country.

Mass Defect, the difference in mass between the total rest mass of protons and neutrons from which a particular nucleus is formed and the slightly lower mass of the nucleus itself. The mass defect is converted into energy so that the particles can be bound tightly together to form the nucleus. *See also* Binding Energy.

Massenet, Jules (1842–1912), French composer who dominated French lyric opera of the late 19th century. He composed many operas including *Le Cid* (1885), *Werther* (1892), and *Thérèse.* His two masterpieces are considered to be *Manon* (1894) and *Thaïs* (1894). △1246.

Massey (Charles) Vincent (1887–1967), governor-general of Canada (1952–59). An historian and professor, he was minister to the United States (1926–30) and the first native Canadian high commissioner in London (1935–46).

Massif Central, extensive mountainous plateau region in S central France; core is Auvergne Mts, which extend to Cévennes (SE) and Causses (SW). Hydroelectric power is produced along W edge, agriculture is carried on in valleys, grazing on mountain slopes; large deposits of coal and kaolin (for china) are mined. Highest peak is Puy de Sancy, 6,187ft (1,887m). Area: 33,000sq mi (85,470sq km), about 16% of France's area.

Massillon, city in NE Ohio, 8mi (13km) W of Canton. Industries: alloys, stainless steel, housewares, aluminum, printing. Founded 1826; inc. 1838. Pop. (1970) 32,539.

Massine, Léonide (1896–), Russian choreographer. He was principal dancer and choreographer for Diaghilev's Ballets Russes (1914–20) and later joined Ballet Theatre in New York City (1941–44). He created works for the International Ballet, Royal Danish Ballet, and Royal (British) Ballet, the last of which he joined in 1969 as a teacher and director. △1368.

Massive, Mount, mountain in Sawatch Range of the Rocky Mts, in central Colorado. It is 2nd-highest of US Rockies, 14,421ft (4,398m).

Mass Production, manufacture of goods in large quantities by standardizing and assembly-line methods. In the United States, it began in the cotton mills after Eli Whitney's revolutionary invention of the cotton gin (1793). The factory system, using unskilled labor (often women and children) to tend large machines, replaced the skilled worker using hand tools and helped to create industrial cities. Many of the methods were brought from England, but US inventors like Samuel Colt used interchangeable parts and precision measurements in the firearms industry. The proving ground for the assembly line, with parts on a conveyor belt moving past stationary workers, was Henry Ford's Highland Park plant (1913). Later, machines took over more and more of the repetitious labor. More recent developments include automated controlling devices, computers, and electronic sensors. △1660.

Mass Spectrograph, instrument for separating ions according to their mass (or more precisely, according to their charge-to-mass ratio). In the simplest types, the ions are first accelerated by an electric field and then deflected by a strong magnetic field; the lighter the ions the greater the deflection. By varying the field, ions of different mass can be focused in sequence onto a photographic plate and a record of charge-to-mass ratios obtained. In a mass spectrometer the ions are detected electrically. The apparatus is used to measure atomic and molecular mass, identify isotopes, determine chemical structure. △1482.

Mass Spectrometer. *See* Mass Spectrograph.

Mass Transportation, a system of transportation designed to convey large numbers of people over relatively short distances in the least possible space of time. Buses, subways, and railroads are vehicles used for mass transportation. △1700, 1708.

Massys, Quentin (*c.* 1465–1530), Flemish painter. He used elements of Italian Renaissance style in his paintings. His precisely drawn works included religious subjects and altarpieces with emphasis on decorative pattern. He was also a successful portrait painter. △1126, 1144.

Mastai-Ferretti, Giovanni. *See* Pius IX.

Mastectomy, removal of the breast by surgical operation, usually because of the presence of a malignant tumor. In a radical mastectomy, adjacent tissue, chest muscle, and underarm and chest-wall lymph nodes are also removed.

Masters, Edgar Lee (1869–1950), US author, b. Garnett, Kan. As a child, he lived near the Spoon River in Illinois. From this experience came his most notable work, *Spoon River Anthology* (1915), a series of

Boston, Massachusetts

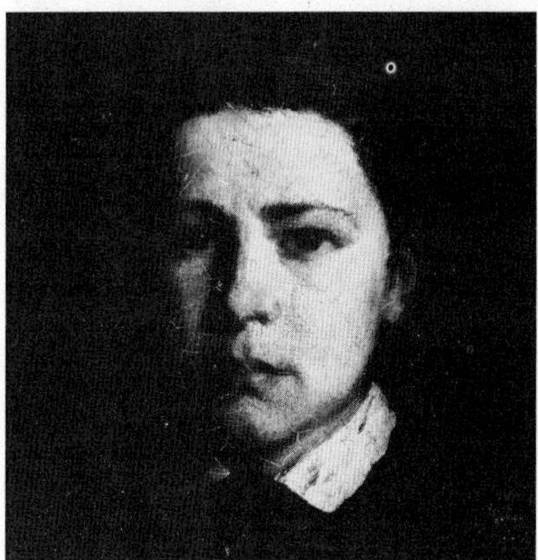

Jules Massenet

Leonide Massine (right)

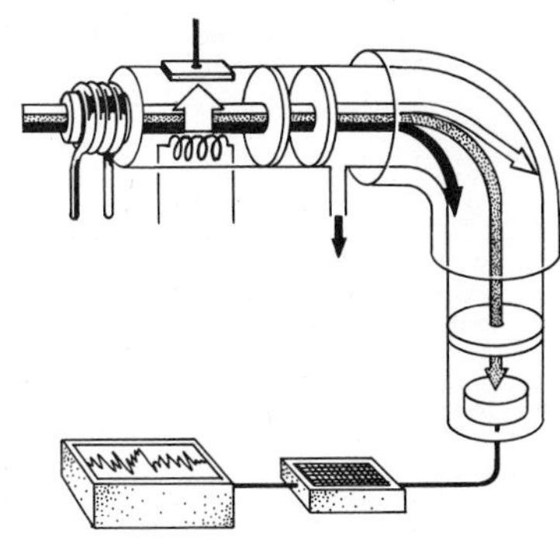

Mass spectrograph

free-verse epitaphs in the form of monologues. Never so successful in poetry again as in that work, he spent many of his later years writing biographies.

Masters, William Howell (1915–), US physician, b. Cleveland, Ohio. With his colleague (and later, wife) Virginia E. Johnson, he performed pioneer physiological studies of human sexual function published in *Human Sexual Response* (1966). Masters and Johnson later applied their knowledge and conclusions to the treatment of sexually dysfunctional couples and published *Human Sexual Inadequacy* (1970).

Masterson, William Barclay ("Bat") (1853–1921), US law enforcement officer and editor, b. Iroquois co, Ill. He was a buffalo hunter, Indian fighter, and Army scout, and at 23 he became deputy marshall of Dodge City, Kan. He became known for his efforts to bring law and order to Kansas. He was sports editor of the *New York Morning Telegraph* (1902–21).

Mastiff, massive watch and fighting dog (working group) bred in England over 2000 years ago. Properly called Old English mastiff, it has a broad, rounded head with dark-colored, blunt, square muzzle; small, V-shaped ears lying close to the cheeks; a deep-chested body; wide-set legs with large feet; and a high-set, long tail. The short, coarse, double coat is apricot, silver fawn, dark fawn, or brindle—all with dark muzzle, ears, and nose. Average size: 27–33in (69–84cm) high at shoulder; 165–185lb (74–83kg). *See also* Working Dog.

Mastigophora. *See* Flagellate.

Mastodon, extinct Mastodontidae, family of proboscideans existing from Oligocene through Pleistocene times. Differing from elephants in construction and placement of teeth, they had lower as well as upper tusks. The rusty-haired American mastodon was hunted by early man. Height: 9ft (2.7m). △576.

Mastoiditis, inflammation of the cavity of the mastoid process (bone lying behind the ear) or of its cells.

Masurian Lakes, low-lying area in NE Poland, covered by over 2,700 lakes; scene of heavy fighting early in WWI; assigned to Poland at Potsdam Conference, 1945.

Matabele, also called Ndebele, Bantu people of southern Africa, formed from Nguni (a Bantu subdivision) outcasts of South Africa in the 1820s and 1830s. Under the Zulu general Mzilikazi, they increased their numbers and migrated north, where they later conflicted with British settlers. Defeated in 1896, they settled into an agricultural and pastoral existence.

Mata Hari (1876–1917), Dutch courtesan and double agent, b. Gertrud Margarete Zelle. She was the wife of a Dutch colonial officer, with whom she lived in Java until 1901. She deserted him and traveled to Europe, calling herself Mata Hari and claiming to be a former temple dancer of Javanese birth. She became well known in Paris, and was in the pay of both French and German intelligence services. She was executed by the French as a spy during World War I.

Matamata, side-necked turtle found in South America. It is a mass of bumps, warts, and fringes of skin. The large head is flat and triangular with a long proboscis. Length: to 16in (41cm). Family Chelidae; species *Chelys fimbriata*. *See also* Turtle. △618.

Matamoros, city in NE Mexico, near the Rio Grande estuary, opposite Brownsville, Tex.; formerly called San Juan de los Esteros, it was renamed 1851 in honor of Mexican independence leader Marino Matamoros; fell 1846 to Zachary Taylor's forces during the Mexican War; site of highway linking Mexico with the United States. Industries: trade, fishing. Pop. 182,887.

Matchlock. △1728.

Maté, or yerba maté, South American evergreen shrub or tree. In the wild, it is a tree; cultivated, it is a small shrub. The dried leaves are used to make a stimulating beverage called Paraguay tea. Height: to 20ft (6m). Family Aquifoliaceae; species *Ilex paraguayensis*.

Materials Control or Handling. △1674.

Materialism, the philosophical contention that only matter, or physical entities, are real or existent. Everything real is explicable in terms of material constituents and their motions, interactions, and relationships. Materialism may or may not involve specific claims about the nature of history as it did with Karl Marx, or about values, as it did with the Epicureans. Many scientists are also materialists. *See also* Marx, Karl. △858.

Maternal Drive, a motive on the part of females to care for and protect their offspring. Such behavior in animals depends on hormonal changes and environmental cues (eg, the appearance of the young animal). Human maternal drive depends less on physiological factors and more on psychological and cultural conditions. *See also* Drive.

Mathematical Model, any set of formulae or equations that describe the behavior of a physical system in purely mathematical terms. Model theory, in mathematics, is concerned with the study of axiomatic systems in terms of objects, called models of the systems, that are constructed on the assumption that all the axioms in the system are true to them.

Mathematical Symbols. △1444.

Mathematics, study concerned originally with the properties of numbers and space; now more generally concerned with deductions made from assumptions about abstract entities. Mathematics is often divided into applied mathematics, which involves the use of mathematical reasoning in engineering, physics, chemistry, economics, etc, and pure mathematics, which is purely abstract reasoning based on axioms. However, the two fields are not totally independent—the subjects of pure mathematics are often chosen for their application to specific problems and the abstract results of pure mathematics, such as group theory and differential geometry, often find practical uses. The main divisions of pure mathematics are into geometry and algebra. Often analysis, reasoning using the concept of limits, is distinguished from algebra; it includes the differential and integral calculus. *See also* Algebra; Arithmetic; Calculus; Geometry; Set theory; Trigonometry. △1444–74.

Mathematics, Applied. *See* Applied Mathematics.

Mather, Cotton (1663–1728), American Puritan minister, b. Boston. The son of Increase Mather, he had a great influence on Massachusetts religious and political life. He wrote a manifesto (1689) in defense of the colonial imprisonment of royal Gov. Edmund Andros and, during the Salem witchcraft trials (1629–93), he supported the belief in demoniac possession as demonstrated in his *Wonders of the Invisible World* (1693). Works published during his life numbered over 400, including *The Ecclesiastical History of New England* (1702). He was one of the founders of Yale University, and was elected to the British Royal Society (1713).

Mather, Increase (1639–1723), American Puritan minister, b. Dorchester, Mass. He was minister of Boston's Second (North) Church (1664–1723). From the pulpit Mather and his son Cotton influenced both political and religious life in the colonies. During the revolts of 1688–89, when Massachusetts lost its charter, he represented the colony's interests in England and obtained a new colonial charter (1691). His writings include *Cases of Conscience* (1693), which helped to end the Salem witchcraft trials. He served as president of Harvard College (1685–1701).

Mathewson, Christopher ("Christy") (1880–1925), US baseball player, b. Factoryville, Pa. A right-hand pitcher, he played for the New York Giants (1900–16) and the Cincinnati Reds (1916), whom he also managed (1916–18). He won 373 games, recorded 77 shutouts, and was elected to the Baseball Hall of Fame in 1936.

Mathias, Robert Bruce ("Bob") (1930–), US athlete and congressman, b. Tulare, Calif. He won the Olympic decathlon when he was 17 (1948). He again won the event at the 1952 Olympics. He served as a Republican representative from California (1967–73).

Matilda, or **Maude,** (1102–1167), empress of Germany, daughter of Henry I of England, mother of Henry II. She married Henry V of Germany (1114). Although she was recognized as Henry I's successor, Stephen became king (1135). Landing in England (1139), Matilda gained general acceptance (1141), but Stephen besieged her in Oxford (1142) and forced her to leave England.

Matisse, Henri (Émile) (1869–1954), French painter and sculptor. His early painting included naturalistic compositions in neutral tones. He was greatly influenced by Paul Cézanne's cubism and by fauvism, and he developed a style of painting that was highly colored, with well-defined subject matter. Throughout his work, there is an emphasis on design and pattern, as in his large movement painting "The Dance." He made numerous collages using bright colors and designs cut from construction paper, as well as many church decorations in stained glass. As a sculptor, he worked briefly in terra cotta and bronze and treated his figures in a simple and rhythmic manner. △1294.

Matriarchy, hypothetical form of society that is not only matrilineal (transmission of group membership by the female line) but in which women are household heads and govern the group. *See also* Patriarchy.

Matrilineal Descent. △876.

Matrix (pl. matrices), array of numbers in rows and columns. The number of rows need not equal the number of columns. Matrices do not have single quantitative values in the same way that determinants do. They are more general mathematical entities that can be combined (added and multiplied) according to certain rules. They are useful in the study of transformations of coordinate systems and in solving sets of simultaneous equations. △1506.

Matsu (Ma tsu), island off SE China, 100mi (161km) NW of Taiwan, in East China Sea. After Communist takeover of China's mainland 1949, Matsu remained a Nationalist-held outpost and has since been the target of propaganda and artillery from the mainland.

Matsuyama, city in NW Shikoku, Japan, on the Inland Sea; capital of Ehime prefecture; site of daimyo castle, museum. Industries: textiles, paper, chemicals, machinery, mining, cattle. Pop. 322,902.

Matter, the substance of the universe. Ordinary matter is made up of electrons, protons, and neutrons. (The neutron is an unstable particle that splits into an electron and proton within about 1,000 seconds if left to itself.) These three particles are combined into elements, an ordered series of atoms having between one and about 106 protons in their nuclei. (Many other subatomic particles can be produced at high energies and live for short periods of time.) The elements other than hydrogen and helium were built up by thermonuclear reactions in stars; we are literally made up of stardust. Four forces are known to be associated with matter. At large distances, all unchanged matter exerts an attractive force; this is called gravitation. Changed particles exert an attractive or repulsive electromagnetic force. This force accounts for nearly all everyday phenomena—the sense of touch, for example, is dependent on the repulsion of molecules at close range. Two other forces hold the protons in the nucleus together; these are called the weak and strong nuclear forces. △1480, 1502–06.

Matter, States of, a classification of matter according to its structural characteristics. Four states of matter are generally recognized: solid, liquid, gas, and plasma. Any one element or compound may exist sequentially or simultaneously in two or more of these states: for example, water, ice, and water vapor can all exist at one temperature and pressure. Solids may be crystalline (have a regularly repeated molecular structure), as in salt or steel; or amorphous, as in tar or glass. Liquids have molecules that can flow past one another but which remain almost as close as in a solid. In a gas, molecules are so far from one another that they travel in relatively straight lines until they collide. In a plasma, such as a star, temperatures are so high that atoms are torn apart into electrons and nuclei. △1502–06.

Matterhorn, mountain peak in Switzerland, in the Pennine Alps, on Swiss-Italo border 6mi (10km) SE of Zermatt; noted for sheer cliffs, which have challenged climbers; first climbed 1865 by Edward Whymper. Height: 14,700ft (4,484m).

Matthew, apostle of Jesus. He was the author of the first of the four gospels in the New Testament. Matthew wrote for Jewish converts to Christianity, assuring them that Jesus of Nazareth is the Messiah expected in the Old Testament.

Matthias (1557–1619), Holy Roman emperor (1612–19), king of Bohemia (1611–17), king of Hungary (1608–18). He was the son of Holy Roman Emperor Maximilian II. As emperor, Matthias attempted to establish peace between Catholics and Protestants. He was deposed in Bohemia and Hungary by his brother, Archduke Maximilian, who established Ferdinand II in his place. △1154.

Matthias Corvinus (1440–90), king of Hungary (1458–90), the son of János Hunyadi. This enlightened despot was a patron of arts and letters. While protecting the peasants, he reformed the administration, strengthened the army, promoted commerce, and founded a new university at Buda and a famous library, the Bibliotheca Corvina. A brilliant soldier, he nearly fulfilled his dream of uniting central Europe under his rule. He took Bohemia from the Turks (proclaimed king of Bohemia, 1469) as well as Styria, Austria, and Corinthia. When Matthias died, Hungary was the most powerful state in central Europe.

Mattock. △304.

Maturity, as applied to personality, the ideal of facing life realistically and actively, changing what can be improved, accepting what cannot be changed, and enjoying decent pleasures. The mature person respects what is good in himself or herself and others and can relate warmly to others. Psychologists note that maturity in this sense is not always achieved when an individual reaches adulthood. △798.

Maude. *See* Matilda.

Maugham, W(illiam) Somerset (1874–1965), English novelist, short-story writer, and essayist; influenced by Maupassant. He traveled widely in Asia and the United States. His novels, including *Of Human Bondage* (1915), *The Moon and Sixpence* (1919), and *The Razor's Edge* (1944), deal with the unpredictable and passionate aspects of human nature.

Maui. *See* Maori.

Maui Island, island of S central state of Hawaii; 2nd-largest of the Hawaiian islands. Highest point is Haleakala Volcano in Haleakala National Park, 10,023ft (3,057m). Main commerce is sugar cane and pineapples. Chief town is Wailuku. Area: 728sq mi (1,886sq km). Pop. (1970) 38,691.

Mau Mau, primarily Kikuyu terrorists of the 1950s dedicated to the removal of whites from Kenya. There was considerable bloodshed on both sides of the conflict until the British victory in 1956. Many Kikuyu were gathered into camps, but the tribe was instrumental in the drive for Kenya's independence.

Mauna Loa, volcanic mountain on the S central island of Hawaii, in Hawaii Volcanoes National Park; contains Kilauea and Mokuaweoweo, two of the world's largest active craters; lava flows from its eruptions (1881, 1942, 1949) have reached the sea in recent years. Height: 13,680ft (4,172m).

Maupassant, Guy de (1850–93), French short-story writer and novelist. He was encouraged to write by Gustave Flaubert and, influenced by the Naturalists, produced the short story *Boule-de-suif* for their collection *Les Soirées de Médan* (1880). His other short stories include *La Maison Tellier* (1881), *Contes de la Bécasse* (1883), and *L'Inutile Beauté* (1890). *Pierre et Jean* (1888) is his finest novel; others include *Bel-Ami* (1885).

Maupertuis, Pierre Louis Moreau de (1698–1759), French astronomer, mathematician, and philosopher. Responsible for the first precise measurements of the meridian in Lapland (1737) and the "principle of least action" in physics. Maupertuis was also a pioneer in genetics and an early evolutionist, as well as a director (1740) of the Berlin Academy of Science.

Mauriac, François (1885–1970), French novelist and playwright. Mauriac was preoccupied with sin and salvation, and his novels, *A Kiss for the Leper* (1922), *Genitrix* (1923), and *The Desert of Love* (1925), portray the futility of pursuing fulfillment in materialism and secular love. His three-volume *Mémoires* (1959–67) stress his reactions to contemporary moral values. He also wrote a study of Charles de Gaulle (1964). He was awarded the Nobel Prize for literature in 1952.

Maurice, known as **Maurice of Nassau** (1567–1625), prince of Orange, stadholder of Netherlands (1587–1625). He was chosen stadholder by northern provinces on the death of his father, William the Silent. An excellent general, he was made commander in chief in 1585. By the time he was 30, he had driven out the Spanish occupation army. He agreed to truce with Spain (1609); reopened the conflict in 1621.

Maurice (1521–53), duke (1541–53) and elector (1547–53) of Saxony. Although a Protestant, he aided (1546) Holy Roman Emperor Charles V against the Protestant Schmalkaldic League, in return for which he was made elector. He later fought against Charles to free his father-in-law, Philip of Hesse. He died protecting his lands against the margrave of Brandenburg. *See also* Schmalkaldic League.

Mauritania (Mauritanie), an independent republic in W Africa, bordered by Spanish Sahara (N and NW), Algeria (N), Mali (E and S), Senegal (SW), the Atlantic Ocean (W). Along the S Senegal River, rich alluvial soil is irrigated by river flooding and rainfall, providing pasture for cattle and sheep; two-thirds of the country is covered by the Sahara desert region. In the mountainous regions, occasional rainfall is stored for the cultivation of large palm groves. The economy is traditionally based on agriculture; in the 1960s mining began adding to the nation's progress. Iron ore mining (begun 1963) was Mauritania's first heavy industry; its production brought an improved harbor and railroad. Some agriculture still exists in the Senegal valley where rice, wheat, peanuts, dates, and potatoes are grown, and sheep, goats, cattle, and camels are raised. The economy was severely affected by drought in the mid-1970s. About 80% of the inhabitants are Moors of Arab-Berber origin and are mostly nomadic and semi-nomadic herdsmen; approx. 20% are black African villagers. Islam is the state religion; the majority of Mauritanians speak Arabic, which is the official language, with French. Formal education, although increasing, is difficult to adapt to nomadic life style; some traveling schools have been established.

Mauritania's constitution provides for an elected president as head of state and government, in addition to a 40-member national assembly elected for a 5-year term by universal suffrage. Islamic law applies for civil and commercial disorders, while French criminal law is used for the judicial system.

Mauritania was settled by the Moors; by the 15th century, Portuguese, Dutch, and French traders had visited the area. In 1817 a treaty signed on the banks of the Senegal River confirmed French influence; Mauritania became a French protectorate in 1903, a French colony in 1920, and a territory in 1946. In 1958 a new capital at Nouakchott was created, and Mauritania was granted internal autonomy; complete independence was attained and a new republic formed in November 1960.

PROFILE

Official name: Islamic Republic of Mauritania
Area: approx. 419,230sq mi (1,085,806sq km)
Population: 1,160,000
Chief cities: Nouakchott (capital), Atar, Kaedi
Religion: Islam
Language: French, Arabic
Monetary unit: CFA (African Financial Community) franc

Mauritius, independent island nation, member of the Commonwealth of Nations, in the Indian Ocean approx. 500mi (805km) E of Madagascar. Sugar, the principal commodity, accounts for about 90% of the export trade.

Land, Economy, and People. The country consists of the main island, 38mi (61km) long and 29mi (47km) wide; Rodrigues Island, 334mi (554km) E; St Brandon Rocks, 250mi (403km) NE; and the Agalega Islands, 580mi (934km) N. Mauritius is a volcanic island fringed by coral reefs. The climate is maritime sub-tropical. The economy is dominated by the sugar industry; tea is a secondary crop. Favorably located in the Indian Ocean, it is a natural link for air and sea transport. Tourism is a growing factor in the economy. There are three important ethnic groups: Indian, European and Malagasy, and Chinese. Hindus and Muslims predominate, with a fairly large group of Christians. Literacy is nearly 100%.

Government and History. Queen Elizabeth II, the head of the Commonwealth, is represented by a governor-general. There is a Legislative Assembly consisting of a speaker, 62 elected members, 8 additional appointed members to assure balanced representation, and an attorney-general. Elections are held every five years; there is universal adult suffrage. Visited by the Portuguese in 1510 and abortively settled twice by the Dutch, the island was permanently settled by the French in 1721. The British captured the island in 1810 and controlled it until 1968, when it gained its independence.

PROFILE

Official name: Mauritius
Area: 720sq mi (1,865sq km)
Population: 830,700
Density: 1153.8per sq mi (445.4per sq km)
Chief city: Port Louis (capital)
Government: constitutional monarchy
Language: English (official)
Monetary unit: Mauritius rupee
Gross national product: $200,000,000
Per capita income: $240
Industries (major products): sugar, molasses
Agriculture (major products): sugar cane
Trading partners (major): Great Britain, Canada, Thailand

Maurois, André (1885–1967), French biographer, historian, and novelist. He wrote popular histories of England, France, and the United States, wartime reminiscences (*The Silence of Colonel Bramble,* 1918),

Cotton Mather

François Mauriac

0
1000 km
Spain
ATLANTIC
OCEAN
Morocco
Tunisia
Algeria
Libya
Western
Sahara
Nouadhibou
Atar
MAURITANIA
Nouakchott
Mali
Niger
Senegal
Chad
Upper Volta
Guinea
Benin
Nigeria
Ivory
Coast
Ghana
Liberia
Cameroon

Mauritania

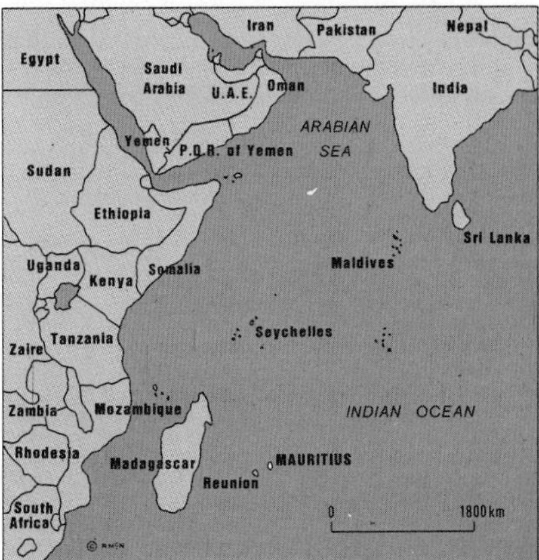
Iran
Pakistan
Nepal
Egypt
Saudi
Arabia
U.A.E.
Oman
India
ARABIAN
SEA
Yemen
P.D.R. of Yemen
Sudan
Ethiopia
Sri Lanka
Uganda
Kenya
Somalia
Maldives
Tanzania
Zaire
Seychelles
Zambia
Mozambique
INDIAN OCEAN
Rhodesia
Madagascar
MAURITIUS
Reunion
South
Africa
0
1800 km

Mauritius

and novels, such as *Atmosphere of Love* (1928). But he remains best known for his numerous biographies, including those of Percy Shelley (1923), Benjamin Disraeli (1927), Marcel Proust (1949), and Victor Hugo (1954). He was elected to the Académie Française in 1938.

Maury, Matthew Fontaine (1806–73), US naval officer and one of the founders of oceanography, b. near Fredericksburg, Va. He was superintendent of the US Naval Observatory and Hydrographic Office (1842–61) and produced charts showing winds and currents for the Atlantic, Pacific, and Indian oceans. By mapping a profile of the sea bed, he showed that a transatlantic cable would be feasible. In 1868 he became professor of meteorology at Virginia Military Institute. His text *The Physical Geography of the Sea* (1855) introduced modern oceanography. △234, 236.

Mausoleum. △1002.

Mawrya, Indian dynasty. *See* Gupta.

Maxentius, Marcus Aurelius Valerius (died 312), Roman emperor from 306, whose father, Emperor Maximian, abdicated in 305. He managed to gain the imperial throne with his father's help but was plagued by the rivalries of Lucius Domitius Alexander in Africa and Constantine in Spain. Constantine finally killed him in the Battle of Milvian Bridge.

Maxilla. △682.

Maximian (Marcus Aurelius Valerius Maximianus) (died 310), Roman emperor (286–305, 306–08). Named by Diocletian first as caesar, then as augustus, he was responsible for governing Italy and the West. He abdicated with Diocletian (305); was recalled to aid his son Maxentius, now emperor; and was again emperor (306–08) until deposed by Maxentius. △1030.

Maximilian I (1459–1519), Holy Roman emperor (1493–1519) and German king (1486–1519). Son and successor of Holy Roman Emperor Frederick III, he inherited the Low Countries by his marriage to Mary of Burgundy (1477). He was almost constantly at war with France, first to secure Mary's lands, and then to protect his possessions in Italy.

Maximilian II (1527–76), Holy Roman emperor (1564–76), king of Bohemia (1562–76), and king of Hungary (1563–76). He was the son and successor of Holy Roman Emperor Ferdinand I. A Protestant sympathizer, he was tolerant to Protestants in his domain. He ended a war with the Ottoman Turks (1568) by a truce with Sultan Selim II in which he agreed to continue paying tribute for his lands in Hungary.

Maximilian (1832–67), emperor of Mexico (1864–67), archduke and younger brother of Emperor Franz Josef of Austria. Maximilian courted the liberals and alienated the conservative supporters of the French-dominated regime; he refused to return Church properties confiscated during the preceding administrations. When Napoleon III withdrew from the Mexican venture, Maximilian was easily defeated by forces led by Porfirio Díaz and Juan Álvarez.

Maximilian I (1756–1825), king (1806–25) and elector (1799–1806) of Bavaria. He was made king by the peace of Pressburg (1805) after allying himself with Napoleon I. He later joined (1813) the anti-Napoleon coalition. At the Congress of Vienna (1815) he strongly opposed the consolidation of Germany, protecting Bavarian independence. He granted a liberal constitution to Bavaria in 1818.

Maximilian II (1811–64), king of Bavaria (1848–64). He was the son of King Louis I. At his accession he attempted unsuccessfully to form a coalition of small German states against the large powers, Prussia and Austria. He later supported Austria in order to stem Prussian power. He was a great patron of art and literature.

Maximilian I (1573–1651), duke (1597–1651) and elector (1623–51) of Bavaria. Head of the Catholic League, he fought against the Protestants in the Thirty Years War. After his army defeated (1620) Elector Frederick V of the Palatinate at White Mountain, Holy Roman Emperor Ferdinand II awarded Maximilian Frederick's electoral vote. This award was confirmed by the Treaty of Westphalia (1648).

Maximizing, in economics, the tendency to attempt to obtain the best for oneself, subject to certain constraints. The producer attempts to maximize his profit through getting the greatest rate of return (output) for a given set of inputs. The consumer attempts to maximize his welfare by making the optimal purchase of goods and services. △936.

Maximus, Saint (1) (*c.* 380–479), bishop of Turin whose discourses record northern Italian liturgy and the survival of paganism. (2) (*c.* 480–662), also called the Confessor, Greek theologian. An ascetic who opposed Monotheletism (belief in only the divine will in Jesus), he believed man brought evil into the world because of his desire for pleasure and that Christ was sent to restore the balance of reason over sense and so redeem the world.

Maxwell, James Clerk (1831–79), Scottish mathematician and physicist. He became professor at Aberdeen, then Kings College (London), and finally Cambridge, where he organized the Cavendish Laboratory. He mathematically showed that Saturn's rings must consist of small solid particles. He also investigated the motion of molecules in gases, developing with Ludwig Boltzmann the equations for the kinetic theory of gases. His greatest achievements were in the fields of electricity and magnetism and were published in his *Treatise on Electricity and Magnetism* (1873). He provided the equation underlying the electromagnetic theory and demonstrated that light and electricity exhibit similar properties and that light is an electromagnetic wave. △1484,1490.

Maxwell's Equations, a series of classical equations, proposed by James Clerk Maxwell (1831–79) in 1864, which linked light with electromagnetic waves. The equations connect the magnetic field strength, the electric displacement, the current density, the magnetic flux density, and the electric field strength. From these equations, which were a breakthrough in electromagnetic theory, Maxwell showed that each vector obeys a wave equation and it was this realization that led him to understand that light is propagated as electromagnetic waves.

May, fifth month of the year. The origin of the name May is unknown, although some believe it was derived from the Greek goddess Maia. It has 31 days. The birthstone is the emerald or agate.

May, Cape, S tip of New Jersey, at the entrance to Delaware Bay; a canal (built 1942–43) bisects the cape, providing a safer route for vessels following the Intracoastal Waterway.

Maya, one of the most important tribes of Central American Indians. They occupied Yucatán, Chiapas, and Tabasco in Mexico; all of British Honduras and Guatemala, and a part of Honduras. Speaking the Maya-Quiché language, in prehistoric times they were famous for their magnificent architecture, as well as their astronomical and mathematical knowledge, and sheer aesthetic excellence. △1118.

Mayagüez, seaport city in W Puerto Rico, on Mona Passage; severely damaged by 1918 earthquake and tidal wave; site of airport, college of the University of Puerto Rico (1763), US government agricultural research station. Products: sugar cane, coffee, tobacco, tropical fruits. Industries: shipping, needlework, beverages, canned foods, electronic components. Pop. (1970) 69,485.

Mayakovski, Vladimir (1893–1930), Soviet poet and dramatist. Leader of the futurist movement, he was founder (1923) and editor of the journal *Left Arts Front*. His work developed from the intensely personal to the socially conscious and propagandistic and includes the poems *The Cloud in Trousers* (1915) and *150 Million* (1920) and the plays *Mystery Bouffe* (1918), *The Bedbug* (1928), and *The Bathhouse* (1929). The major poet of the Soviet revolution, he died a suicide.

Mayan, family of languages spoken on the Yucatán Peninsula of Mexico and in Guatemala by the Maya Indians, whose ancestors built the great Maya Empire of a thousand years ago. There are several dozen of these languages, the most important being Yucatec, of Mexico, and Quiché, Cakchiquel, Mam, and Kekchi, of Guatemala. The ancient Mayas had a hieroglyphic writing system, which has still not been fully deciphered. △870.

Mayan Architecture, architecture of the Mayan people, in Central America and later in the Yucatán peninsula. The classic Maya period is AD 300–900. The greatest monuments are palaces and temples, the latter built on pyramidal platforms, with rich stone carving as ornament. △1118.

May Apple, also mandrake, perennial wildflower found in woodlands of E North America and E Asia. Each plant has two umbrella-shaped leaves and a waxy, ill-scented, white, nodding flower. The lemon-like fruit is edible; the poisonous root was used as a medicinal cathartic. Height: 12–18in (31–46cm). Family Berberidaceae; species *Podophyllum peltatum*.

May Beetle, or June bug, medium-sized, stout, brownish scarab beetle that feeds on tree foliage. The white grubs that eat roots of various crops are one of the most destructive soil pests. Genus *Phyllophaga*.

Mayer, Julius Robert von (1814–78), German physicist and physician who turned to physics as a result of his experiments on animal heat. This led to a determination of the mechanical equivalent of heat (for which J.P. Joule received credit), and a statement of the law of conservation of energy (credited to Hermann Helmholtz). He also stated that the ultimate source of living and nonliving energy was solar energy. Disappointed by lack of recognition he attempted suicide and was committed to an asylum.

Mayflower, or trailing arbutus, evergreen wildflower found in temperate woodlands. It has clusters of white or pink, spicy-smelling flowers and oval, leathery leaves. Family Ericaceae; species *Epigaea repens*.

Mayflower, ship that brought the Pilgrims from England to New England in 1620. Under Capt. Christopher Jones, the *Mayflower* set sail on September 16, and on November 19 the passengers sighted land. Before the Pilgrims disembarked on December 26 at Plymouth, Mass., they composed the famous Mayflower Compact, an agreement for the temporary government of the colony based on the will of the majority. The original *Mayflower* is lost, but a replica sailed by a British crew from England to Massachusetts in 1957 is on permanent exhibit at Plymouth, Mass.

Mayflower Compact, agreement to establish a preliminary government for the Pilgrims. It was signed by the 41 adult, male passengers of the *Mayflower* on Nov. 21, 1620, at sea off the New England coast. The compact bound signers to majority-rule government in the Pilgrim colony, pending receipt of a royal charter. The compact is significant as a first step in the development of democracy in America. *See also* Pilgrims; Plymouth Colony.

Mayfly, soft-bodies insect found worldwide. The adult lives only a few days and the aquatic larvae may live several years. Adults have fanlike front wings and vestigial mouthparts and often emerge from streams and rivers in swarms. Nymphs are brown with leaflike gills; length: 0.4–1in (10–25mm). Order Ephemeroptera.

May Fourth Movement. △1326.

Mayo Clinic, a voluntary nonprofit association of private physicians who practice medicine as a coordinated group in Rochester, Minn. The clinic was founded by Charles H. Mayo and William J. Mayo. In 1915 they donated $2,000,000 to establish the Mayo Foundation for Medical Education and Research as an adjunct to the clinic and in affiliation with the University of Minnesota.

Maypops. *See* Passionflower.

Mays, Willie (Howard, Jr.) (1931–), US baseball player, b. Fairfield, Ala. A right-hand power hitter with a total of 660 lifetime home runs, he had a career that included periods with the New York and San Francisco Giants (1951–52; 1954–72) and the New York Mets (1972–73). In addition to his hitting, he was noted as an outstanding center fielder.

Maywood, residential town in NE Illinois; suburb of Chicago on Des Plaines River; site of Chicago Lutheran Theological Seminary. Industries: tin cans, tubing, surgical equipment. Inc. 1881. Pop. (1970) 30,036.

Mazarin, Jules (1602–61), Italian papal nuncio who became cardinal and statesman in France. Chosen by Cardinal Richelieu to be his successor (1642), Mazarin derived great support from the young Louis XIV's regent, his mother, Anne of Austria. This situation made his power impregnable until his death, except for the period of the Fronde uprising (1648–53), when he controlled state matters in secret from abroad. His negotiations and treaties established a peace in Europe that favored France. The Peace of Westphalia in 1648 and the Peace of the Pyrenees in 1659 gained much new territory for France and the marriage contract with the Spanish infanta gave France's Louis XIV claims on Spain's inheritance. △1170.

Mazarin Bible or **Gutenberg Bible,** first Bible to be printed and first large book to be printed from movable metal type. It was probably printed about 1455 at Mainz by Johann Gutenberg, by whose name it is also known. It has 42 lines per page and is sometimes described as the 42-line Bible. The name Mazarin Bible is derived from the Mazarin Library in Paris, where a copy of the Bible was found in the late 18th century.

Mazatlán, seaport city in W Mexico, on the Pacific coast; major industrial and commercial center in W Mexico; terminus of railway connecting United States with Mexico City; resort. Exports: tobacco, metal ores, istle, shrimp, hides, oregano, fish, woods. Industries: trade, tourism. Pop. 171,835.

Mazzini, Giuseppe (1805–72), Italian patriot and political thinker of the Risorgimento (Italian unification movement). A member of the *Carbonari*, the Italian republican underground from 1830, in 1831 he founded the "Young Italy" movement, dedicated to republican unification of Italy. He fought in the Italian revolutionary movement of 1848, ruled in Rome in 1849 upon ouster of the pope, but then was exiled. Although he was active in revolutionary activities during the 1850s, he played a minor role toward the 1861 establishment of a unified Italian kingdom; having favored a unified republican state, he refused allegiance to the monarchy. △1238, 1248–50.

Mazzola, Girolamo Francesco Maria. *See* Parmigianino, Il.

M'Ba, Léon (1902–67), statesman of Gabon, became first prime minister of his semi-independent country in 1959 and first president after independence in 1961. Except for a temporary fall from power in 1964, when he was reinstated by French soldiers, he remained in office until his death. His chosen successor was Albert Bongo.

Mbabane, town in NW Swaziland, SE Africa, in the Mdimba Mts; capital and administrative center of the country; commercial center for surrounding agricultural region; tin and iron are mined nearby. Pop. 13,-803.

Mboya, Thomas Joseph (1930–69), Kenyan statesman. He served in the territorial government during the Mau Mau conflicts of the 1950s and led the All-African People's Conference and the Kenyan Independence Movement. After Kenya gained its independence in 1963, he held several ministries under Jomo Kenyatta, including labor (1963) and economic planning and development (1964–69). His assassination caused widespread internal unrest.

Mbuji-Mayi, formerly Bakwanga; city in S central Zaire, Equatorial Africa; capital of Kasai-Oriental region; commercial center on Sankura River; site of trade schools, hospital. City grew rapidly after Zaire's independence (1960); noted for diamond mining. Pop. 305,818.

Mbundu, or Ovimbundu, a Bantu people of western Angola once noted for extensive trade. They were defeated by the Portuguese in the 17th century. The Mbundu followed a mixed system of inheritance and were organized into several chiefdoms. This agricultural people numbers over 1,000,000.

Mead, George Herbert (1863–1931), US philosopher and social psychologist, b. Hadley, Mass. He taught at the University of Chicago (1894–1931). Influenced by John Dewey, Mead studied the mind, the self, and society. His theories have been used by scholars studying role theory and symbolic interactions. Compilations of his lectures were published posthumously and include *The Philosophy of the Present* (1932) and *The Philosophy of the Act* (1938). △892.

Mead, Margaret (1901–), US anthropologist, b. Philadelphia. She did classic field work in the cultures of the Pacific islands, New Guinea, and Samoa, summarized in such books as *Coming of Age in Samoa* (1928) and *Growing Up in New Guinea* (1930). She helped develop the national-character approach to studying complex societies, showing how the development of the individual is affected by the culture he lives in. More recently she has been concerned with modern societies and sex roles. Among her more recent works are *Male and Female* (1949), *Childhood in Contemporary Societies* (1955).

Mead, Lake, reservoir on the Nevada-Arizona border, in Lake Mead National Recreational Area; formed from impounding the Colorado River by the Hoover Dam. One of the largest reservoirs in the world; 247sq mi (640sq km). Depth: 589ft (180m).

Meade, George Gordon (1825–72), Union Civil War general, b. Cadiz, Spain, where his father was US naval agent. Originally an engineer, he led infantry in the war and rose to command the Army of the Potomac. In that post, his first and most successful battle was Gettysburg (July 1–3, 1863), where he defeated Robert E. Lee.

Meadowlark, either of two species—the eastern meadowlark *(Sturnella magna)* and the western meadowlark *(S. neglecta)*—of blackbird-related birds of North America, sometimes considered game birds. They are mottled brown with yellow breast and black bib. They feed on the ground and lay 4 to 6 bluish or greenish tinted spotted eggs.

Mealybug, fluffy, waxy scale insect found worldwide. It sucks sap from trees and other plants. Length: 0.2in (5mm). Family Pseudococcidae.

Mean, or arithmetic mean, the average; found by adding a group of numbers and dividing by the number of items in the group. The mean is the most common measure of central tendency and also usually the most meaningful, because it includes every number in the data set in its computation.

Meander, a naturally occurring looplike bend of a river or stream channel. They form on a flood plain where there is little resistance in the alluvium. They lengthen the river, thus reducing its gradient and velocity. Meanders migrate slowly downstream, depositing sediment on one bank while eroding the opposite. Sometimes meanders make complete loops, which when cut off form oxbow lakes. *See also* Oxbow. △ 258–60.

Mean Sea Level, average height of the sea calculated from readings taken hourly and over a 19-year cycle at certain points on the open coast. Used as a standard or fixed geodetic point. *See also* Geodesy.

Meany, George (1894–), labor union leader, b. New York City. A former plumber, Meany began his union career as business agent of a New York City local (1922–34). He was president of New York State Federation of Labor, secretary-treasurer of the American Federation of Labor (AFL) (1940–52) and a member of the War Labor Board during World War II. In 1952, Meany was elected president of the AFL and led the AFL–CIO since the two merged in 1955. He was delegate to the United Nations (1957–59). He was known for his efforts to end corrupt practices within organized labor and worked for legislation that would benefit the worker and society in general.

Measles (rubeola), an extremely contagious virus disease of the respiratory tract and reticuloendothelial system. Symptoms appear about two weeks after exposure and include cough, conjunctivitis, and typical spots on the oral mucous membranes. Three or four days later, a rash erupts behind the ears or on the face, then spreads over the body. Intolerance of light is characteristic. Complications such as pneumonia and encephalitis may occur, and middle-ear infection is a hazard of the disease. Death may result from complications or from severe disease. Vaccination or one attack usually produces immunity to measles. △ 724.

Measure for Measure (1604), 5-act comedy by William Shakespeare, based on George Whetstone's play taken from a story by Giovanni Battista Giraldi (called Cynthio). Different in method and spirit from Shakespeare's other plays, its moods are partly satire and partly religious exaltation. In the absence of Vincentio, duke of Vienna, his deputy Angelo imprisons Claudio, but offers to release him if Claudio's sister Isabella will keep a rendezvous with him. She agrees but sends Mariana. Angelo tells Isabella he has executed her brother; at this point the duke returns and sentences Angelo to death, but releases him when Isabella pleads for mercy. Claudio is produced unharmed and Angelo is betrothed to Mariana.

Measurement. *See* Weights and Measures. △ 1450, 1656.

Measuring Worm, or inchworm, looper, spanworm, moth caterpillar that crawls with characteristic looping movements, suggestive of measurement. Family Geometridae.

Meat. △378–80.

Mecca (Makkah), city in W Saudi Arabia; capital of Hejaz prov.; birthplace of Mohammed; holiest city of the Islamic faith; site of the Great Mosque (the Haram), which encloses Kaaba, holding the sacred black stone, and Zamzam, the holy well. City was an ancient caravan station and market center and an Arab shrine before the time of Mohammed; the flight (hegira) of Mohammed from Mecca 622 began Muslim era. Egypt controlled city during 13th century; Ottoman Turks held it 1517–1916, when Husein ibn-

Vladimir Mayakovski

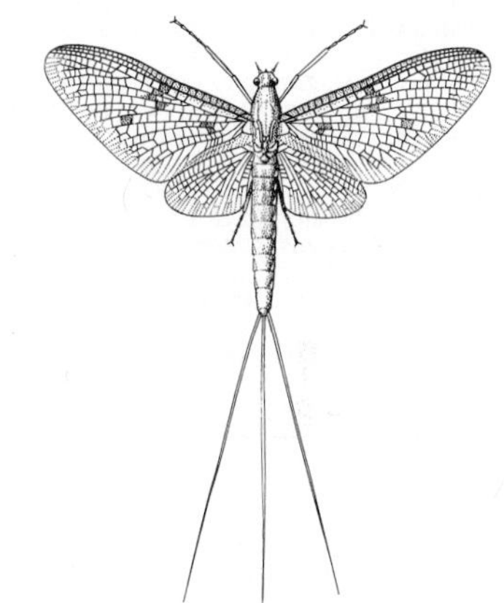

Mayfly

Willie Mays

George Meany

Ali secured Arabian independence. Mecca fell in 1924 to Ibn-Saud, who later founded Saudi Arabian kingdom. Much of Mecca's commerce depends on the pilgrims; oil revenues began to add income after WWII. Pop. 185,000. △846, 1058.

Mechanical Advantage. △1654.

Mechanical Engineering, field of engineering concerned with the economical design, construction, and operation of power plants, engines, and machinery, and with research and testing in search of new developments. Technical areas involving the mechanical engineer are mechanisms and kinematics, materials and materials testing, thermodynamics, heat production and distribution, manufacturing processes, drafting, fluid control. Some fields of specialization in mechanical engineering are power generation, heating and refrigeration, transportation.

Mechanics, branch of physics concerned with the behavior of matter under the influence of forces. It may be divided into statics—the study of matter at rest—and dynamics—the study of matter in motion, and into solid mechanics and fluid mechanics. Dynamics may be further divided into kinematics—the description of motion without regard to cause—and kinetics—the study of motion and force. In statics, the forces on a body are balanced and the body is said to be in equilibrium; static equilibrium may be stable, unstable, or neutral. Classical dynamics rests primarily on the three laws of motion formulated by Sir Isaac Newton in his *Principia* (1687). Modern physics has shown these laws to be special cases approximating more general laws. Relativistic mechanics deals with the behavior of matter at very high speeds, approaching that of light, while quantum mechanics deals with the behavior of matter at the level of atoms and molecules. *See also* Laws of Motion; Quantum Theory; Relativity. △1488.

Mechanics, Celestial. *See* Celestial Mechanics.

Mecoptera. △492.

Medan, city in NE Sumatra island, Indonesia, on Deli River; capital of North Sumatra prov.; largest city on the island; site of Islamic University of North Sumatra (1952), University of North Sumatra (1957); shipping and commercial center. Exports: rubber, tobacco, coffee, sisal. Industries: machinery, tile, automobiles, tourism. Pop. 479,098.

Medawar, (Sir) Peter Brian (1915–), English biologist. He shared the 1960 Nobel Prize for physiology and medicine with Frank Macfarlane Burnet for the discovery of acquired immune tolerance. Medawar confirmed Burnet's theory that an organism can acquire the ability to recognize foreign tissue during embryonic development, and if that tissue is introduced in the embryonic stage it may then be reintroduced later without inducing an immune reaction.

Medea, in classical mythology and literature, the daughter of Aestes, king of Colchis, granddaughter of Asteria, the starry heavens, and wife of the hero Jason. In some descriptions she is the daughter of Hecate. She helped Jason steal the Golden Fleece and escape. When he remarried, Medea killed Jason's bride and her own children and fled in a chariot drawn by dragons.

Medellín, city in NW central Colombia, approx. 150mi (242km) NW of Bogotá; capital of Antioquia dept. and 2nd-largest city of Colombia; in wealthy coffee-producing area; site of several 17th-century churches, gold mint. Industries: steelworks, sugar refineries, chemicals. Founded 1675. Pop. 1,039,-800.

Medford, city in E Massachusetts, on Mystic River; site of Craddock House (1634), Tufts University (1852), and examples of pre-Revolutionary War architecture. Industries: waxes, chemicals, publishing, printing. Settled 1630; inc. as city 1892. Pop. (1970) 64,397.

Medford, city in SW Oregon; seat of Jackson co; site of headquarters of Crater Lake National Park and Rogue River National Forest; summer resort area. Industries: lumber, canned fruit, farming. Inc. 1884. Pop. (1970) 28,454.

Median, in statistics, a measure of central tendency found by ranking the data from smallest to largest and locating the middle item, which is then called the median. If there is an even number of items, the average of the two middle items is taken as the median. The median is a "better" measure of central tendency than the mean when the distribution of the data is skewed.

Medicaid, a US program of medical care for the needy. A federal-state program, Medicaid is usually operated by the state welfare or health departments. Guidelines are set by the Welfare Administration of the US Department of Health, Education, and Welfare. Medicaid furnishes inpatient and outpatient hospital care, physician's services, nursing home services, and laboratory and X-ray services.

Medicare, a US program of medical care for the aged. Since going into effect in 1966, Medicare, which is federal health insurance, has been administered by the Social Security Administration. Benefits include a basic health-insurance plan, which covers hospital care, outpatient diagnosis, home health services; and a voluntary medical insurance program that covers physicians' fees. Costs are met by a special Social Security contribution; participants in the voluntary program also pay a small monthly premium.

Medici, Italian family that ruled Florence and, later, Tuscany from the 15th to 18th centuries, produced three popes, married into royal families throughout Europe, and provided magnificent patronage to the arts. A banking fortune provided the financial basis for the unofficial, Republican rule (from 1434) of **Cosimo the Elder** (1389–1464). His grandson **Lorenzo** ruled Florence and was an arts patron. In 1531, **Alessandro** became first duke of Florence. In 1569, **Cosimo** was named grand duke of Tuscany by the pope, and his successor **Francesco I** had the title confirmed by the Holy Roman emperor in 1575. Medici popes were **Giovanni** (Leo X, 1513–21), **Giulio** (Clement VII, 1523–34), and **Alessandro** (Leo XI, 1605). The line ended at Gastone de' Medici's death in 1737. *See also* individual biographies. △1126.

Medici, Alessandro de' (1510–37), first duke of Florence, illegitimate son of Lorenzo de' Medici (1492–1519). Appointed (1523) by his uncle, Pope Clement VII, to rule Republican Florence with his cousin Ippolito, he was expelled by a popular revolt (1527). He was restored (1531) as the first hereditary duke of Florence by his father-in-law, Emperor Charles V.

Medici, Cosimo de', the Elder (1389–1464), de facto ruler of Florence from 1434, patron of literature. With the Medici banking fortune he led the oligarchy that was expelled from Florence in 1433 but returned to rule permanently the next year. He was an early Renaissance patron of Greek scholars exiled by the fall of Constantinople in 1453 and of the artists Brunelleschi, Michelozzo, Lorenzo Ghiberti, Donatello, Andrea del Castagno, Fra Angelico, and Benozzo Gozzoli.

Medici, Cosimo I de' (1519–74), grand duke of Tuscany. Son of Giovanni de' Medici (1498–1526), he came from secondary branch of the Medici (descended from Lorenzo, 1395–1440) and became duke of Florence when the primary branch ended with death of Duke Alessandro (1537). Having conquered Siena and unified Tuscany, he was given title of grand duke of Tuscany in 1569 by Pope Pius V. He was patron of artists Ammanati, Vasari, Pontormo, and Bronzino.

Medici, Giovanni de' (1475–1521), original name of Pope Leo X (1513–21). *See* Leo X.

Medici, Lorenzo de' (1449–92), called Lorenzo the Magnificent, Florentine merchant prince, grandson of Cosimo the Elder, and successor to his father Piero (died 1469) as virtual ruler of Florence. Having survived attempted assassination in the Pazzi conspiracy (1478), like his predecessors he governed the Florentine Republic not with any official title, but by an elaborate system of political patronage. Himself a notable poet, he was a great Renaissance patron, having assembled the Florentine Platonic Academy and supported Marsilio Ficino, Pico della Mirandola, Politian (Angelo Poliziano), Guiliano da Sangallo, Botticelli, Verrocchio, Leonardo da Vinci, and Michelangelo.

Medicinal Leech. △474.

Medicinal Plants. △744.

Medicine, the science concerned with the cure and prevention of disease and the preservation of health. To judge from ancient pictographs showing medical procedures and from ancient skulls and skeletons, the practice of medicine goes back to prehistoric man. Egyptian medicine included magico-religious elements along with empirical therapies for many ailments. Hebrew medicine placed a marked emphasis on hygiene. Greek medicine had become thoroughly secular by the 6th century BC and there existed several medical schools. The Romans and then the Arabs carried on and developed further the Greek medical tradition. During the Renaissance this knowledge was brought back to Europe. The dawn of modern medicine coincided with accurate anatomical and physiological observations first made in the 17th century. By the 19th century practical diagnostic procedures for many diseases had been developed; bacteria had been discovered and immunizing serums were developed. The great developments of the 20th century include chemotherapy, or the treatment of various diseases with specific chemical agents, new surgical procedures, and sophisticated diagnostic devices such as radioactive tracers. △708–74.

Medicine Hat, town in SE Alberta, Canada, on the South Saskatchewan River; important railroad junction and river port. Industries: foundries, coal mining, lumber, grain elevators. Founded 1883. Pop. 26,-058.

Medicine Man. *See* Shaman.

Medieval Art, art dating from the collapse of the Roman civilization in the 5th century to the end of the 15th century. △1080, 1082, 1092, 1094, 1104, 1106.

Medieval Literature and Theater. △1100.

Medieval Music, music produced in Europe during the Middle Ages, roughly 1100 to 1400. Music during this period was dominated by Christian liturgical vocal choruses called chants, which were sung in polyphonic style, i.e., several different parts were sung simultaneously by different sections of the chorus. Perhaps the most significant composer of the period was the Frenchman Guillaume de Machaut (1300–77) who developed the form of the motet that other composers used for several hundred years. Secular songs were transmitted orally by traveling Saxon, French, and German troubadors. In the 14th and 15th centuries, guilds of professional musicians were formed, and musical notation began to become more sophisticated, enabling composers to transmit whole works to later generations. *See also* Gregorian Chant; Motet; Musical Notation; Polyphony.

Medina (Al-Madinah), city in Saudi Arabia, 210mi (338km) N of Mecca, 120mi (193km) from Red Sea coast. Originally called Yathrib, the city was renamed Medinat an Nabi, "the Prophet's city," after Mohammed fled there 622, making it his capital; in 661 the caliphs moved their capital to Damascus. Medina was under Turkish rule 1517–1916, when the independent Arab kingdom of Hejaz was formed; in 1932 it was inc. into Saudi Arabia; site of Great Mosque containing tomb of Mohammed (a Muslim pilgrimage site), Islamic University (1962), 12th-century wall, radio station. Lying in a prosperous oasis, the city is a noted pottery center. Crops: fruits, vegetables, grains. Pop. 100,000 △1058.

Medina-Sidonia, Alonso Pérez de Guzmán, Duque de (1550–1615), commander in chief of the ill-fated Spanish Armada of 1588. He accepted this post through loyalty to the king, although his lack of naval experience and the difficulty of his assignment caused him considerable doubt. His defeat by the English and by the Irish Sea, therefore, did not halt his career and he was retained by the Spanish king as "admiral of the ocean." In 1596 he lost Cádiz to the English and his squadron was defeated at Gibraltar (1606).

Meditation. △820.

Mediterranean Fruit Fly, yellow, spotted-winged fly, 0.16 to 0.2in (4–5mm) long, a serious pest in most fruit-growing areas of the world. An exhaustive effort is being made to keep it out of US citrus-growing areas. Family Tephritidae, species *Ceratitis capitata*. *See also* Diptera.

Mediterranean Sea, largest inland sea in the world; an arm of the Atlantic Ocean, between Africa and Europe; extends from the Strait of Gibraltar to the SW Asia coast; receives several tributaries, including the Nile, Rhône, Ebro, Tiber, Po, and Vardar rivers. In ancient times the Mediterranean was dominated by Roman and Byzantine maritime power; it was controlled by Venice and Genoa in the Middle Ages. In 1500 the discovery of the route around Cape of Good Hope to India gave trade power to the French, English, and Spanish ports. In 1869 the opening of the Suez Canal resulted in the Mediterranean becoming one of the world's busiest shipping waters. The salinity of the Mediterranean is approx. 10% as a consequence of rapid evaporation rate; the fish life is less impressive than in other oceans; however, the sea is a source of tuna, sponge, coral, sardines, and anchovies. Area: approx. 965,000sq mi (2,499,350sq km). △190.

Mediterranean Subrace, subdivision of the Caucasoid race, characterized by rather swarthy skin, dark often curly hair, brown eyes, short slender stature. Their habitat is Europe and the Mediterranean littoral, extending east to Arabia. △658–60.

Medulla Oblongata, principal hindbrain structure, the portion of the brain that joins the spinal cord. Medulla functions are necessary to maintain life, for example, they control respiration and heartbeat. The medulla also contains part of the reticular formation, an anatomically distinct tract of neurons that plays a role in arousal states: consciousness, wakefulness, and attention. General anesthetics, such as ether, probably work by depressing medulla activity. △666.

Medusa, monster figure of Greek mythology. She was one of the Gorgons, three monstrous sisters. According to mythology, Athena turned her hair to serpents and her face turned the viewer to stone. She was slain by Perseus, who used her head to destroy his enemies. △468, 832, 836.

Meer, van der, family of Dutch painters. Jan van der Meer II (Jan Vermeer II, 1628–91) was a landscape painter and the father of Jan van der Meer III (Jan Vermeer III, 1656–1705), who painted landscapes and animal subjects, and still-life painter Barent van der Meer (Barend Vermeer, 1659–1702). *See also* Vermeer, Jan.

Meerschaum or **Sepiolite,** a clay silicate mineral, hydrated magnesium silicate, found mainly in Asia Minor. Opaque white, fibrous; hardness 2–2.5; sp gr 2. Used chiefly for tobacco pipes.

Meerut, city in N India, 40mi (64km) NE of Delhi; capital of Meerut district. City dates to 3rd century BC; taken by Muslims 1191, Tamerlane 1398; ceded to British 1803 who est. military fort; first outbreak of Sepoy Mutiny began here May 10, 1857. Industries: textiles, chemicals, paint, sugar, steel smelting and refining, hosiery, soap. Pop. 250,126.

Megalithic Monuments, large structures generally built of undressed stone during the Neolithic and early Bronze Age. Megalithic building ranges N through Spain, up the coast of W Europe and into Scandinavia. The most ancient types were stone tombs, of which the basic unit was the dolmen, made of several upright supports and flat roofing slabs. Another type were the menhirs, simple uprights usually unconnected with any grave sites and often decorated with magical symbols. They were frequently arranged in parallel rows (as at Carnac, France) or in circles, half-circles, and ellipses (as at Stonehenge and Avebury, England).

Megaloptera. △492.

Megapode, or mound bird, Australian game bird with short, rounded wings, strong legs, and clawed feet. One group, typified by the hen-sized, crested scrub fowl *(Megapodius),* rakes debris into a large compost pile. In this mound, the female excavates a deep hole for each large oval egg (5–8). There is a long incubation period. Other megapodes, such as the turkey-sized, blackish maleo, often migrate to special areas to build their incubators in black sand warmed by the sun or in areas heated by underground volcanic action. Family Megapodiidae.

Mégara, seaport town in E central Greece, on Saronic Gulf. In ancient Greece it served as the capital of Mégaris; flourished under the Dorians as a center of maritime trade, and est. colonies of Chalcedon and Byzantium; economic ruin came with the Peloponnesian War; birthplace of Euclid, mathematician who founded the Megarian school of philosophy and logic. Industries: wine, flour, olive oil. Pop. 15,450.

Megarians, school of Greek philosophy from the late 5th to the early 3rd century BC. Influenced by both Eleatic ontology and Socratic ethics, it in turn influenced Stoicism. Founded by Socrates' disciple, Euclid of Megara, the school held that "evil" is only a semblance and cannot exist; that "good" is indivisible and immutable. *See also* Eleaticism; Socrates.

Megatherium, a genus of extinct ground sloth, about 20ft (6.1m) long and very massive. During Pleistocene times, it ranged from South America into S United States. The front feet bore huge claws, and it had plant-grinding teeth along the sides of its jaws. △408.

Megazostrodon. △574.

Mehun-sur-Yèvre. △1106.

Meiji Restoration (1868), shift of power in Japan from the Tokugawa shogunate (1603–1867) to the emperor and his supporters. Spurred by foreign contact (such as Admiral Perry's visit in 1853) and a weakened central government, a group of young samurai allied against the Tokugawa shogunate, forcing an "imperial restoration" of power to Emperor Meiji, age 14 at the time. The samurai leaders engineered an abrupt change in the government, trading feudal isolationism for foreign trade, advanced technology, a more democratic government, and overall modernization of the Japanese state and society. *See also* Tokugawa. △1210, 1272.

Mein Kampf (My Struggle) (1924–26), two volume work by Adolf Hitler, considered the "bible" of the Nazi movement. Hitler dictated the first volume, basically an autobiography, when he was imprisoned in Bavaria after the unsuccessful Munich putsch of 1923. The second volume was devoted to the policies of National Socialism and the propaganda methods Hitler was to use later in his rise to power.

Meiosis, process of two consecutive nuclear divisions to form germ cells, reducing the chromosome number from diploid to haploid. Mature gametes are produced by the first meiotic division that reduces the chromosome number to half; the second division forms four haploid reproductive cells. Spermatogenesis yields four functional sperm and oogenesis yields one mature ovum, and three polar bodies that will degenerate. △412.

Meir, Golda (1898–), Israeli political figure, b. as Goldie Mabovitch in the Ukraine. In 1906 she emigrated to Milwaukee, Wis., with her family. She became a schoolteacher and active in the Zionist movement. She and her husband Morris Meyerson (hebraized to Meir in 1956) moved to Palestine in 1921 to live on a kibbutz. She became active in the Palestine labor movement, serving as the executive secretary of the Women's Labor Council (1928–32) and as its spokesperson in the United States (1932–36). In 1936 she was named head of the political department of Histadrut (General Federation of Jewish Labor). Between 1946–48 she often acted as de facto leader of the Jews in Palestine seeking an independent state because so many of the other leaders were imprisoned. After independence she served at the same time as ambassador to Russia and as minister of labor (1949–56). Between 1956–66 she served as foreign minister. She became secretary-general of the Mapai (later Labor) party in 1966. In 1969 she became prime minister. She resigned in 1974 after criticism over lack of preparedness at the outbreak of the 1973 Arab-Israeli War.

Meistersingers, German lyric poets of the 14th–16th centuries who were moralistic and followed a strict religious code, often forming private lodges in the south German towns. Strict rules, derived from the 12 old masters, such as Walther von der Vogelweide, were followed. The first meistersinger is thought to have been Heinrich von Meissen; Hans Sachs, the writer of over 4000 songs, is the best known.

Meitner, Lise (1878–1968), Austrian physicist. Together with Otto Hahn, she discovered protactinium and the fission of uranium, and investigated beta decay and nuclear isomerism. She worked with Fritz Strassmann on the products resulting from neutron bombardment of uranium. She is also noted for her research on disintegration products of actinium, thorium, and radium.

Meknès, city in N central Morocco, approx. 35mi (56km) WSW of Fès; prospered under Sultan Ismail who built an extravagant palace here 1672, part of which still exists. Industries: textiles, cement, metals, oil distilling, food processing and canning. Founded 10th century. Pop. 195,000.

Mekong (Lan-ts'ang Chiang), river in SE Asia; rises (as the Dza Chu) in Tibet, China; rushes S through Yunnan prov., forms Burma-Laos border, and part of Laos-Thailand border; flows S through Cambodia and South Vietnam into South China Sea, creating a vast river delta that is one of the foremost rice-producing regions in Asia. Length: approx. 2,600mi (4,186km).

Melancholia, in psychiatry, an emotional state marked by sadness and depression; often accompanied by agitation. The concept of melancholia has had two important uses in the history of psychiatry. Emil Kraepelin described involutional melancholia, a depressive disorder that included no prior history of the mood swings that characterized manic depressive disorders. It was also connected with aging; in women, it was often associated with menopause. Sigmund Freud made a classic distinction between the more normal state of mourning that followed a personal loss and melancholia, in which the depression

Medea

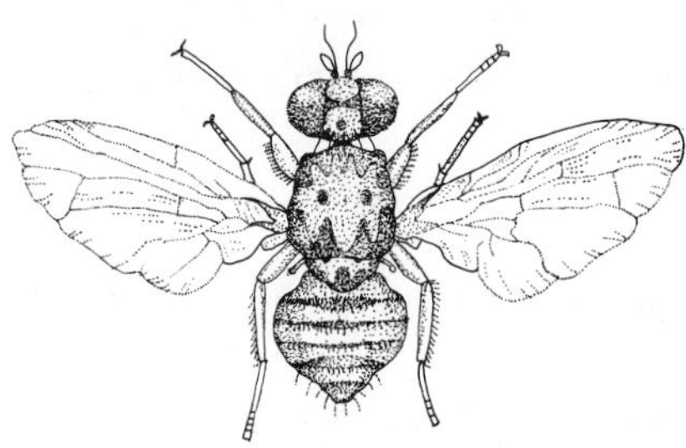

Mediterranean fruit fly

Golda Meir

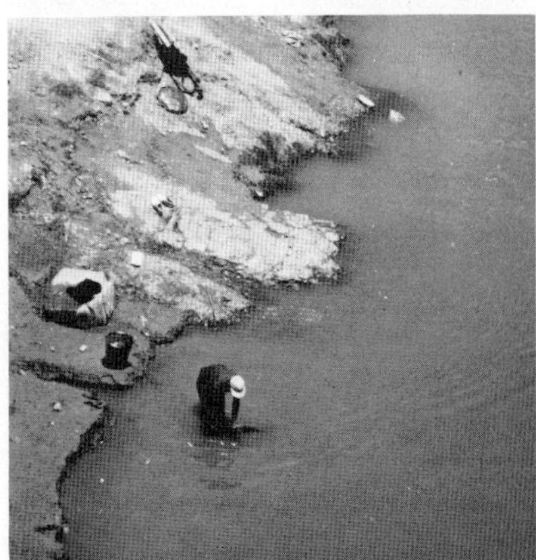

Mekong River, Laos

does not subside and takes the form of ambivalence, guilt, and self-punishment. *See also* Depression.

Melanchthon, Philipp (1497–1560), German educator, theologian, and leader of the Reformation. A humanist scholar, he wrote textbooks for study of Greek and Latin, and he helped found and reform universities in Germany. At Wittenberg he became a friend of Martin Luther and a leader in Luther's reform movement. In 1530, Melanchthon drafted the Augsburg Confession, which became a basic statement of Lutheranism. *See also* Lutheranism.

Melanesian People, inhabitants of the central Pacific, N and E of Australia and New Guinea. Most Melanesians live by fishing and subsistence agriculture, and there is considerable cultural diversity. Religious beliefs include totemism, animism, ancestor worship, and cargo cults.

Melanin, a dark pigment found in the skin, hair, and parts of the eye. Melanin, carotene, and hemoglobin are mainly responsible for skin color. △660, 686.

Melanocyte Stimulating Hormone (MSH), produced by the pituitary gland; stimulates certain cells in the skin to synthesize melanin, a brown skin pigment. *See also* Melanin.

Melba, (Dame) Nellie (1861–1931), Australian coloratura soprano. She made her debut in Paris in 1887 and subsequently appeared in Brussels (1887), London (1888), Paris (1889–91), and New York (1893–96; 1907–20). She became director of the Melbourne Conservatory in 1927.

Melbourne, William Lamb, 2nd Viscount (1779–1848), British statesman. He became a Whig member of Parliament (1806), but lost his seat (1812) for supporting Roman Catholic emancipation. Returned to Parliament (1816), he later became Irish secretary (1827) and home secretary (1830–34). As prime minister (1835–41) he was the young Queen Victoria's political mentor, encouraging moderate reforms but resisting further parliamentary liberalization.

Melbourne, capital city of Victoria state, Australia, on the Yarra River at the N end of Port Phillip Bay, major center of finance, commerce, and transportation; site of the University of Melbourne (1853), Conservatorium of Music (1910), and Royal Melbourne Technical College (1887). Exports: wool, flour, meat, fruit, dairy products. Industries: automotive, aircraft, textiles, agricultural machines, chemicals, tobacco. Founded 1835 by Tasmania settlers; inc. 1842; became capital 1851. Pop. 76,900.

Melbourne, city on Indian River, E Florida, Brevard co, 58mi (93km) SE of Orlando, site of Florida Institute of Technology. Industries: electronic and computer equipment. Inc. 1888. Pop. (1970) 40,236.

Melchites, originally the Christians of Egypt and Syria who accepted the decrees of the 451 Council of Chalcedon and remained in communion with Constantinople, calling themselves "Emperor's men." Today the term is applied to Eastern Orthodox Christians and Orthodox Christians of Egypt and Syria that have reunited with Rome. Led by the patriarch of Antioch, they follow a Byzantine rite in Arabic.

Meleager, in Greek mythology, a prince of Calydon and member of the *Argo* expedition. The Fates decreed at his birth that his life was linked to the life of a certain firebrand upon the hearth. When Meleager killed his uncles in an argument after the successful hunt of the Calydonian boar, his mother Althaea, in her grief and anger, took the brand that she had carefully preserved and threw it on the fire. Meleager burned and died.

Meletius, Saint (died 381), bishop of Antioch (360–81). Banished from his see by the emperor in 360, he was one faction in the Meletian Schism of Antioch (362–81). The supporters of Eustathius, bishop of Antioch (324–30), had Paulinius consecrated in 362 because they found Meletius' theology suspect. Although banished (365–66 and 371–78), Meletius was restored in 378 and presided at the Council of Constantinople (381). His feast day is February 12.

Mellon, Andrew W(illiam) (1855–1937), US financier, b. Pittsburgh. A banker and astute investor, he helped found Alcoa, Gulf Oil, Union Steel, Pittsburgh Coal, and Union Trust companies. As treasury secretary (1921–32) under Presidents Harding and Coolidge, he persuaded Congress to reduce taxes on the wealthy and reduced the national debt. His popularity declined during the Depression when his conservative policies were attacked. Appointed ambassador to Great Britain (1932–33) he resigned when Franklin Roosevelt became president. He donated an extensive art collection to the government and endowed the National Gallery of Art.

Melodrama, form of drama, originally French, relying on exaggerated acting style and strongly emotional situations rather than character development. Music is often provided to heighten the emotional effect. Melodramatic playwrights include Jean Jacques Rousseau (Pygmalion, 1770), Victor Hugo, Joseph Bouchardy, and Thomas Holcroft.

Melon, annual vine. The cantaloupe, or muskmelon, *(Cucumis melo reticulatus)* is from S Asia and Central America. It has a musky odor and netlike veins on its surface. The winter or casaba melon *(Cimelo inodorus)* is from S Asia and is grown in S United States. It has a ridged or smooth rind, like the honeydew, and is without a musky smell. Family Cucurbitaceae. *See also* Cantaloupe; Gourd. △338.

Melos (Milos), island in SE Greece, belonging to Cyclades Islands. Melos is the major town; 1820 excavations unearthed the famous statue of Venus de Milo. Industries: grain, cotton, olive oil, fruits, mining. Area: 58sq mi (150sq km). Pop. 4,910.

Melrose, city in E Massachusetts, 7mi (11km) N of Boston; birthplace of Geraldine Farrar (1882), Metropolitan Opera star. Industries: furniture, laboratory equipment, textile supplies. Founded by Puritans 1629, inc. 1850. Pop. (1970) 33,180.

Melting Point, the temperature at which a substance changes phase from solid to liquid.

Melville, George Wallace (1841–1912), US naval engineer and explorer, b. New York City. He made several voyages to the Arctic, and on his second trip with George DeLong (1879), the ship was frozen in for two winters before it sank near Siberia. Melville commanded one of two lifeboats that made it to Siberia. He then led the survivors on a 500-mi (805-km) hike along the coast to recover DeLong's body and the ship's records. *In the Lena Delta* (1884) is his account of that voyage. In 1887 he became chief of the Navy's Bureau of Steam Engineering. There he designed the ships' machinery, increasing their efficiency, and streamlined administrative work.

Melville, Herman (1819–91), US author, b. New York City. After his bankrupt father's death in 1832, Melville worked at various jobs until 1839 when he signed aboard a trading ship bound for England. In 1841 he signed on the whaler *Acushnet*. He jumped ship in the Marquesas Islands, where he spent a month among the natives of the Typee Valley. This experience became the subject of his first book, the novel *Typee* (1846). Shortly after publication of his second novel, *Omoo* (1847), he married Elizabeth Shaw, daughter of the chief justice of Massachusetts. The novels *Mardi* and *Redburn* followed in 1849.

After a visit to Europe in 1849, the Melvilles moved to a farm in western Massachusetts, where he wrote his greatest work, *Moby-Dick* (1851), several other novels *(White-Jacket, Pierre, Israel, Potter, The Confidence Man),* and some distinguished short fiction (collected in *The Piazza Tales*). He moved to New York in 1863 and worked as a customs inspector (1866–85).

After his death, the manuscript of *Billy Budd* was discovered along with a number of previously unpublished poems. A relatively neglected writer during his own lifetime, Melville is generally regarded today as one of America's greatest writers, not only as a symbolist, but also as a philosopher and social critic. △1374.

Membrane, Semipermeable. *See* Semipermeable Membrane.

Memling, Hans (*c.*1435–1494), Flemish painter, b. Germany. He probably studied in Brussels under Rogier van der Weyden. He was the head of a prolific workshop and painted chiefly religious works. His balanced compositions gave realistic attention to details, such as the color and texture of a fabric. △1136.

Memory, capacity to learn and remember information and experience. Modern psychologists often divide memory into two phases, short-term (STM) and long-term (LTM). An item in STM (eg, a phone number dialed once) lasts for several seconds after an experience, but fades unless it is rehearsed (practiced). An item enters LTM (relatively permanent storage) if it stays in STM long enough (depending on other factors such as its meaningfulness and importance). Many psychologists believe that items in LTM are never really lost. They view forgetting as an inability to get the items out of storage and into consciousness; eg, a person may often easily identify information that he or she cannot recall directly. △670.

Memory, Computer, part of a computer that stores information in words or bytes, each of which has an identification number (address) assigned to it for immediate use by the central processing unit. It may consist of magnetic cores or it may be a solid-state memory in which bits of information are stored as one of two states in bistable multivibrators. The latter form is smaller and faster than core memory but the stored information is lost if the supply voltage is cut. △1672–74.

Memory Drum, mechanical device for presenting items to be learned and remembered in psychological studies. Items such as words or syllables are presented one at a time, and the subject's recall for these items is tested later.

Memory Improvement. *See* Mnemonic Device.

Memphis, ancient city of Egypt, 14mi (23km) S of Cairo, part of which is now occupied by village of Mit Ra-hina. Huge statues of Ramses II, temples of Ptah, Ra, and Isis have been unearthed. City was important from its founding 3110 BC (by Menes, Egypt's first king), until 4th century BC when Alexandria began to develop. In the 7th century AD much of its ruins were used by Arabs in building Cairo.

Memphis, commercial city and river port in SW Tennessee, on Chickasaw Bluff above Mississippi River; seat of Shelby co; largest city in Tennessee. Location of French (1698), Spanish (1794), and US (1797) forts; first permanent settlement est. (1819) by Andrew Jackson, Marcus Winchester, and John Overton. Plagued with epidemics of yellow fever late 19th century. It is site of Memphis State University (1909), Southwestern University (1848), Riverside and deSoto parks, Liberty Bowl, and many antebellum houses. Industries: lumber, automobiles, food products, pharmaceuticals, paints, toiletries. Inc. 1826 as town; 1849 as city. Pop. (1970) 623,530.

Menander (342–292 BC), Greek comic playwright. Composer of 108 comedies in 30 years, he was a quiet, dedicated artist. His favorite theme was unhappy love; his style was amusing and perceptive rather than broadly humorous. With Philemon, he was one of the leaders of New Comedy. Mostly fragments remain, but an entire play, *The Peevish Man,* was discovered in 1957. △998.

Menarche, the first menstrual period at puberty. Age of onset varies from 10 to 15 years in the human female. *See also* Menstrual Cycle. △800.

Mencius, or **Meng-ko** (371–289 BC), "Second Sage" of Confucianism. A disciple of Confucius' grandson, Mencius spent most of his life searching for a feudal lord who would put his teachings into practice. He failed to win this support for his doctrines and, like Confucius, achieved his greatest success as a teacher. He actively refuted the rival doctrines of Mo Tzu and Yang Chu. His sayings are recorded in the *Book of Mencius. See also* Confucianism. △860, 1040.

Mencken, H(enry) L(ouis) (1880–1956), US journalist, critic, and editor, b. Baltimore, Md. He began his career on the Baltimore *Morning Herald* (1899) before joining the *Sun* (1906–56). From 1908 to 1923 he was affiliated with *The Smart Set.* Then he cofounded and edited (1924–33) the *American Mercury.* An iconoclast, he surveyed the American scene in his writing. His caustic commentary is collected in *Prejudices* (Six Series; 1919–27). He also wrote an extensive study of the American language.

Mende, Negroid people of Liberia and SE Sierra Leone. Their traditional livelihood is by shifting agriculture, rice being the staple crop with cocoa and ginger as cash crops. Their patrilineal society is noted for the *poro,* a secret society that holds ritual power over educational, moral, and military issues as well as religious beliefs.

Mendel, Gregor Johann (1822–84), Austrian naturalist. He discovered the laws of heredity and in so doing laid the foundation for the modern science of genetics. Mendel joined the monastery at Brno in 1824 and was ordained in 1847; his plant experiments began in 1856 in the monastery gardens. His experimental breeding of the garden pea led him to formulate three laws: the principle of segregation, the purity of gametes, and the mathematical ratio of possible combinations. His discoveries published in "Experiments with Plant Hybrids" (1866), were virtually ignored until 1900, when his work was rediscovered and recognized. △416, 1262, 1282.

Mendeleev, or **Mendeleyev, Dimitri Ivanovich** (1834–1907), Russian chemist. He studied at St Petersburg, where he later became professor. Having heard lectures of the Italian chemist Stanislao Cannizzaro he developed an interest in the relationship between the 63 elements then known, devising the periodic law and the modern form of the periodic table at about the same time as the German Lothar Meyer. His table enabled him to predict the existence of several elements, including gallium and scandium. His work, published in Russian in 1869, was quickly translated into German and brought him worldwide acclaim. His textbook *Principles of Chemistry* (1869, trans. 1905) became a standard. △1552.

Mendelevium, radioactive metallic element (symbol Md) of the actinide group, first made in 1955 by alpha-particle bombardment of Es^{253}. Properties: at. no. 101; most stable isotope Md^{258} (half-life 2 months). *See also* Actinide Elements. △1552–54.

Mendelssohn, Felix (1809–47), in full Jakob Ludwig Felix Mendelssohn-Bartholdy, German composer and conductor. A child prodigy, he composed the famous suite for *A Midsummer Night's Dream* at the age of 17. His *Violin Concerto* (1844) is a standard in the repertory. Among his other significant works are five symphonies (including the "Scotch" and "Italian" symphonies), many piano pieces called *Songs Without Words* (1830–45), and chamber music. His two oratorios, *St Paul* (1836) and *Elijah* (1846), are probably the greatest oratorios of the 19th century. Mendelssohn was also recognized as the foremost conductor of his day. *See also* Oratorio. △1246.

Mendelssohn, Moses (1729–86), Jewish philosopher. For his *Phaedo*, modeled on the Platonic original, Mendelssohn became known as the "German Plato." A translator of the Bible, he was also dedicated to Jewish emancipation. Jews learned German from Mendelssohn's Bible (1783) and the idea of toleration from his *Jerusalem* (1783). The state, he argued, could survive a plurality of religious beliefs.

Menelaus, in Homer's classic epic, the *Illiad,* the king of Sparta, husband of Helen and brother of the commander of the Greek forces at the siege of Troy, Agamemnon. The rulers of Greece came to the aid of Menelaus after Helen's abduction by the Trojan prince, Paris. During the war Menelaus met Paris in a duel, but Paris escaped. Helen and Menelaus were reunited after the success of the Greek siege.

Menelik II (1844–1913), emperor of Ethiopia (1889–1913). He became emperor with Italian support, succeeding John IV. He defeated an Italian invasion in 1896, effectively securing Ethiopian independence. Having proved himself an able and aggressive king, he greatly expanded and modernized his empire, establishing a capital at Addis Ababa, increasing imperial power, and constructing a railroad. △1268.

Mene, mene, tekel, upharsin, from the Aramaic, "numbered, numbered, weighed, divided," the handwriting on the wall that appeared before Belshazzar, king of the Chaldeans, at a feast (Book of Daniel 5:25). Daniel was called to read and interpret it and he predicted that God had weighed Belshazzar and his kingdom and found them wanting because Belshazzar did not follow the ways of God; the kingdom would be divided and given to the Medes and Persians. That night Belshazzar was killed and the Mede, Darius, took his kingdom.

Menes (*fl.* 3150 BC), Egyptian king credited with unification of upper and lower Egypt. He may have also used the names Aha, Narmer, and Scorpion. He is possibly the first Egyptian king of historical mention and is said to have founded his capital at Memphis.

Menger, Karl (1840–1912), German economist, member of the Austrian School. He is best known for his capital theory and for his theory of imputation. He pointed out that capital was a scarce productive resource, and consequently entitled to remuneration, just like labor. According to Menger's imputation theory, value is "imputed" to goods; they do not have any "intrinsic" value.

Menhaden, schooling, herringlike, marine fish found in the temperate Atlantic. An important industrial fish used for meal and oil, it is green or blue and silver. Length: to 20in (50.8cm). Family Clupeidae; species *Brevoortia tyrannus.*

Menhir. *See* Megalithic Monuments.

Menière's Disease, a disease of the labyrinth of the inner ear in which the symptoms are deafness, vertigo, and ringing in the ears.

Meninges, three membranes that cover the brain and spinal cord. The outermost membrane, the dura mater, is a tough protective covering. Within it is the second membrane, the arachnoid, whose blood vessels supply the nervous system with nourishment. The inner membrane, the pia mater, is a delicate layer on the surface of the brain and spinal cord. Between the arachnoid and the pia mater is the subarachnoid space, which contains cerebrospinal fluid. △664.

Meningitis, inflammation of the membranes (meninges) covering the brain and spinal cord, resulting from infection with meningococci or other microorganisms. △722.

Meniscus, curved upper surface of a liquid in a container, due to surface tension. The surface of water in an air-water-glass system is concave, whereas in an air-mercury-glass system the mercury surface is convex. △1504.

Menkaure, or **Mycerinius.** △960.

Menlo Park, city in W California, 23mi (37km) SE of San Francisco; site of Stanford University research center, aerospace industry. Settled 1861; inc. 1930. Pop. (1970) 26,906.

Menlo Park, community in central New Jersey, approx. 6mi (10km) SE of Plainfield; site of Edison National Historic Site preserving the buildings and equipment used by Thomas A. Edison; first incandescent light bulb was made here. Area: 20acres (8hectares). Est. 1962.

Menninger, Karl Augustus (1893–), US psychiatrist, b. Topeka, Kans. Founder, with his father and brother, of the Menninger Clinic and Foundation, Topeka, in 1920, he served on the staff there and as professor at the University of Kansas from 1946. Particularly interested in finding a common ground for psychiatry and sociology, he held posts with the bureau of prisons and with social rehabilitation groups. Works include *Man Against Himself* (1938), *The Human Mind* (1930), and *The Crime of Punishment* (1968).

Mennonites, Christian denomination named after Menno Simons (1496–1561). It is a development from the 16th-century Anabaptists. Strict discipline, separation from the world, and conformity to Scripture are essential. The churches are congregational in structure, with a lay clergy. *See also* Anabaptists.

Menominee, river in NE Wisconsin; rises at confluence of Michigamme and Brule rivers; flows SE forming a natural Wisconsin-Michigan border, empties into Green Bay near Menominee; used for hydroelectricity. Length: 125mi (201km).

Menominee, or **Menomini,** an Algonquian-speaking tribe of North American Indians once occupying the Menominee River, Wis., to the area around Michilimackinac. In 1975 the population was approximately 3,500, inhabiting the Menomini Reservation in NE Wisconsin.

Menopause, in humans, the time at which the menses or menstrual cycles disappear; this generally occurs between the ages of 45 and 55 years. △800.

Menorca (Minorca), island of Spain; 2nd-largest of the Balearic Islands, in the Mediterranean Sea, approx. 25mi (40km) NE of Majorca; capital is Mahon; S coast is known as its Riviera. Occupied at different times by Carthaginians, Romans, Vandals, Moors, in 13th century it was conquered by James I of Aragon; captured by British 1709; taken by France 1756; returned to Spain by treaty 1783; site of 14th-century cathedral, fine churches and palaces, air and naval base. Industries: shoes, cheese, textiles, soap, wine, tourism, marble, slate, lime, hemp, flax, fishing, citrus fruits, potatoes, olives, cereal, grapes. Area: 264sq mi (684sq km). Pop. 50,217.

Menotti, Gian-Carlo (1911–), US composer, b. Italy, known chiefly for his many operas. *The Medium* (1946) and *The Saint of Bleecker Street* (1954) both won Pulitzer Prizes. His *Amahl and the Night Visitors* (1951) was the first opera composed expressly for television.

Mensheviks, moderate faction of the Russian Social Democratic Labor party that broke with Lenin's Bolsheviks at the 1903 party congress because of his insistence on a centralized party of professional revolutionaries. After the Bolshevik seizure of power in November 1917, many Mensheviks capitulated to the Bolsheviks. The Mensheviks were suppressed in 1922. △1310.

Menshikov, Aleksandr Danilovich (1672–1729), Russian statesman. Raised from stableboy to second

Nellie Melba

Andrew W. Mellon

Herman Melville

Felix Mendelssohn

in command of the Russian Empire by Peter the Great, he became field marshal in 1708, fighting valiantly at the battle of Poltava (1709). He virtually ruled Russia under Catherine II, but was exiled to Siberia by her successor, Peter II, in 1727.

Menstrual Cycle, in humans and primates, the period during which the ovum matures and is released, and the endometrium (uterine lining) proliferates. The average cycle is 28 days divided into four phases: menstrual, starting at the onset of menses, lasting 3–5 days; proliferative, during which the ovum matures and the endometrium is replaced; ovulation, time when the egg is released, ready for fertilization, occurring at mid-cycle (day 14–15); and progestational, during which the endometrium is maintained ready for implantation should fertilization take place. During the latter phase, the site from which the egg is released becomes the corpus luteum and secretes progesterone. In the absence of fertilization, the corpus luteum degenerates, progesterone secretion drops, and menses begins, initiating a new cycle. In the event of conception, the corpus luteum remains, and maintains the endometrium with progesterone until the placenta is formed, which then starts to secret progesterone. The menstrual cycle normally begins at puberty (10–15 years) and ceases with menopause (45–55 years). △690.

Mental Health, absence of disease or the normal state, an application of the medical (disease) model to the psychological (mental) sphere. Although this extension has only limited usefulness in practice, "mental health" has come to represent, rather vaguely, all aspects of psychological disturbance, treatment, control, prediction, prevention, and causes. △760–62.

Mental Health (Hygiene) Movement, a social movement supporting humane treatment for the mentally ill, begun in the mid-1800s by Massachusetts schoolteacher Dorothea Dix. The movement called for the establishment of specialized hospitals for the mentally ill. △760.

Mental Retardation, intellectual deficiency, defined as subaverage general intellectual functioning originating in the developmental period (to age 16). Mental retardation can be described as mild, moderate, or severe. Mild (IQ 70–85) impairment permits a limited but more or less independent existence; moderate impairment (IQ 50–70) seriously limits the individual although special training may allow him to function minimally; severe impairment (IQ below 50) requires nearly total care and these individuals benefit very little from training. △768.

Mentha. *See* Mint.

Mentor, city in NE Ohio, on Lake Erie 22mi (35km) NE of Cleveland; farming region; site of preserved home of James Garfield, Lakeland Community College (1967). Founded 1799; inc. 1855. Pop. (1970) 36,912.

Menuhin, Yehudi (1916–), US violinist and conductor, b. New York City. A child prodigy, he gave his first concert at age seven and studied with Adolf Busch and Georges Enesco. He went on world tours playing standard repertoire and also many rare and unfamiliar works. In Europe he organized festivals at Bath and Gstaad and conducted the Bath Festival Orchestra (1958–68), which became the Menuhin Festival Orchestra. Regarded as one of the United States' foremost musicians, he has recorded extensively as violinist and as conductor.

Menzies, (Sir) Robert Gordon (1894–), Australian prime minister (1939–41, 1949–66). He served as attorney general (1934–39). As leader of the United Australia party, he was elected prime minister in 1939. Forced by the Labor party to resign in 1941, he was reelected in 1949. He supported ANZUS (1951) and SEATO (1954).

Meo. *See* Miao.

Meperidine. *See* Demerol.

Mercalli Scale. △174.

Mercantilism, 16th–18th-century trade policy advocating state intervention in economic affairs; basically, state regulation of the economy to maximize exports. Foreign trade was to be publicly controlled so as to produce the maximum possible surplus in the nation's trade balance, thus increasing the country's store of gold and silver, which constitute the "nation's wealth."

Mercator, Gerhardus (1512–94), Flemish geographer, cartographer. He developed the first modern type of map projection. He worked as cartographer to the Emperor Charles V and as cosmographer to the Duke of Jülich and Cleves (from 1559). In 1568 he produced the first nautical chart to use the Mercator projection (of which he was not the inventor). Mercator also popularized the name *atlas* for a bound collection of maps, by prefacing his collection (1595) with an illustration of the Titan Atlas supporting a globe. △180.

Mercedes. △1694.

Merchant Adventurers, English trading company, chartered in 1407. Its principal trade was exporting English woolen cloth to the Netherlands, but by 1550 its officers controlled almost three-quarters of England's overseas trade. Attacked as a monopoly in the 17th century, they lost many privileges, and their charter was abrogated (1689).

Merchant Banks. △934.

Merchant Marine Academy, United States, institution that trains officers for the US Merchant Marine. Founded in 1943, the academy offers courses in nautical science, ship management, and naval science. The school is located at Kings Point, Long Island, near New York harbor, which serves as a training ground. Graduates have a bachelor of science degree and are qualified for commission in the US Naval Reserve.

Merchant of Venice, The (*c.*1597), 5-act comedy by William Shakespeare. The "pound of flesh" plot comes from *Il Pecorone* by Giovanni Fiorentino (1558), and the casket story from Giovanni Boccaccio's *Decameron.* Antonio arranges a loan from Shylock to help his friend Bassanio win the hand of Portia. Bassanio's suit is successful but Antonio is unable to repay the money and Shylock claims a pound of flesh in forfeit. Portia, disguised as a lawyer, appears at the trial and saves Antonio's life by saying that Shylock may have the pound of flesh but not a drop of blood. Still in disguise, Portia tricks Bassanio, then reveals herself and chides him but eventually forgives him.

Mercia, kingdom of Anglo-Saxon England, covering at its greatest extent the area between Wales, the Thames and Humber rivers, and East Anglia. Settled by the Angles (*c.*500), Mercia pursued expansionist policies until Offa, king of Mercia (757–96), ruled over virtually all England. Its power declined with the late 9th-century Danish attacks and the ascendancy of Wessex.

Mercury, the smallest planet and the one closest to the Sun. It has a very thin atmosphere and is visible only after sunset or before sunrise. It has no satellites. Mean distance from the Sun, 36,000,000mi (58,000,000km); mass and volume, .055 and .037 times that of Earth, respectively; diameter, 3000mi (4800km); rotation period, 58.7 days; period of sidereal revolution, 88 days; temperature, daylight up to 800°F (426°C), nights down to 32°F (0°C). *See also* Solar System. △62, 150.

Mercury, liquid metallic element (symbol Hg) of group IIB of the periodic table, known from earliest times. Chief ore is cinnabar (sulfide), from which it is extracted by roasting. The element is a dangerous cumulative poison. It is extensively used in barometers, thermometers, and laboratory apparatus, and in mercury-vapor lamps and mercury cells. Properties: at. no. 80; at. wt. 200.59; sp gr 13.55; melt. pt. −37.97°F (−38.87°C); boil. pt. 673.84°F (356.58°C); most common isotope Hg^{202} (29.8%). △1504–06, 1566.

Mercury, in Roman mythology, god of merchants. His feast day was May 15. He was usually depicted holding a purse in his hand.

Mercury Poisoning, condition caused by ingestion, breathing, or absorption through the skin of mercury compounds. Mercury poisoning by inhalation has always been a problem in mercury-using industries but poisoning from ingestion of foods, chiefly fish and birds, containing mercury is a recent and serious problem. Mercury poisoning produces common symptoms, including uncoordination, loss of balance, sensory disturbances, and loss of peripheral vision, often causing a delay in proper treatment.

Mercury Switch. △1596.

Mercury Vapor. △1554.

Mer de Glace. △264.

Meredith, George (1828–1909), English novelist and poet. His novels and poems brought him little financial success, and he supplemented his income by journalism. His novels include *The Ordeal of Richard Feverel* (1859), *Beauchamp's Career* (1876), and *The Egoist* (1879), in which Meredith analyzes the movement of self-discovery with great psychological subtlety. His poetry, such as *Modern Love* (1862), is vigorous and inventive.

Meredith, James (1933–), US civil rights figure, b. Kosciusko, Miss. A student at Jackson State College (1960–62), he became the first black to attend the University of Mississippi, receiving his degree in August 1963. His entrance led to campus rioting and, for a time, he was escorted to classes by US marshals. △896.

Merganser, sea duck with slim, hooked bill that typically dives for fish. The American merganser *(Mergus merganser)* is also known as the goosander.

Mérida, city in SE Mexico; capital, major cultural, commercial, and communications center of Yucatán state; site of numerous examples of Spanish colonial architecture, notably 16th-century cathedral; university. Exports: hides, chicle, sisal, agricultural equipment. Industries: tourism, handicrafts, henequen. Founded 1542 by Francisco de Montejo. Pop. 253,-856.

Meriden, manufacturing city in S Connecticut, 17mi (27km) NE of New Haven, in New Haven co. Industries: hardware, plated ware, cut glass, cutlery. Settled 1661; inc. 1867. Pop. (1970) 55,959.

Meridian, city of E Mississippi; seat of Lauderdale co; served as capital of state in 1863; destroyed by Gen. William Sherman Feb. 16, 1864, during Civil War. Industries: hosiery, textiles, mattresses, shirts, wallboard. Settled 1831; inc. 1860. Pop. (1970) 45,083.

Mérimée, Prosper (1803–70), French novelist and short-story writer. He translated from the Russian and wrote historical novels and short stories, combining passion and objectivity. His works include the collections of short stories *Mosaïque* (1833) and *Colomba* (1840). He also wrote *Carmen* (1845), on which Georges Bizet based his 1875 opera.

Merino, important fine-wool sheep breed originated in Spain and introduced in the United States and Australia. Many local varieties have heavy white wool and soft, pliable under wool. They have short, woolly heads, folds of neck fat, and tightly spiralled horns on the male. *See also* Sheep; Wool. △376.

Merlin, small European falcon related to the American pigeon hawk. Length: 12in (30cm). Species *Falco columbarius.*

Merman, Ethel (1909–), US singer and actress, b. Astoria, N.Y. The song "I've Got Rhythm," in *Girl Crazy* (1930), began her stage career. Her loud, brassy voice was heard in musical comedies such as *Annie Get Your Gun* (1946–49) and *Gypsy* (1959), for which she won a N.Y. Drama Critics Award.

Meroe. △974.

Meron Mount, peak in N Israel; highest peak in the country, 3,692ft (1,126m).

Merovingians (*c.*448–751), dynasty of Frankish kings whose territory roughly coincided with modern France. Clovis I (*r.*481–511), the first of the line, established his authority by conquest and assassination. His conversion to Christianity solidified the bond between him and his subjects. The policy of equal inheritance rights for each son, however, led to the frequent division of the kingdom and savage battles for supremacy ensued. After the death of the last strong ruler, Dagobert I in 639, the separate regions were mainly ruled by powerful mayors of the palaces, who used the Merovingian kings as puppets. One of these mayors, Pepin the Short, ultimately deposed Childeric III in 751 to found the Carolingian dynasty.

Merrick, residential city in SE New York, on Long Island; light manufacturing. Pop. (1970) 25,904.

Merrill, Robert (1919–), US baritone, b. Brooklyn, N.Y. He studied in New York and made his debut at the Metropolitan Opera in 1945. He became a principal baritone at the Metropolitan, establishing himself as an outstanding operatic baritone, especially in the French and Italian operatic repertoires.

Merry Wives of Windsor, The (*c.*1597), 5-act comedy by William Shakespeare. According to tradition the play was written at the command of Queen Elizabeth, who after seeing *Henry IV* and being captivated by the character of Falstaff, wanted to see a play about

Sir John in love. The action concerns Falstaff's advances to Mistress Ford and Mistress Page and their ridicule of his efforts, using Mistress Quickly as a go-between. Ford's daughter Anne is wooed by Slender, Sir Hugh Evans, Dr. Caius, and Fenton, who eventually wins her.

Mersey River, river in England; formed by the junction of the Goyt and Etherow rivers, flows W through NW England, draining S Greater Manchester and N Cheshire; entering the Irish Sea through a wide estuary on which Liverpool stands. Length: 70mi (113km).

Merton, Robert King (1910–), US sociologist. Professor of sociology at Columbia University since 1941, he has been an influential sociological theorist in such areas as structural analysis and the sociology of science. Among his many books are *Social Theory and Social Structure* (1949) and *On the Shoulders of Giants* (1965). △914, 1360.

Merton, Thomas (1915–68), US poet and religious writer, b. France. While studying at Cambridge and Columbia universities he converted to Roman Catholicism, in 1941 became a Trappist monk, and was later ordained a priest. He is best known for his autobiography, *The Seven Storey Mountain* (1948) and wrote more than 15 volumes of poetry, meditation, and philosophy including *Figures for an Apocalypse* (1947).

Mesa, city in SW central Arizona, 15mi (24km) E of Phoenix, in Maricopa co. Shipping center for citrus fruits; winter resort. Industries: electronic components, aircraft parts. Founded by Mormons 1878; inc. 1883. Pop. (1970) 62,853.

Mesa, a large, broad, flat-topped hill or mountain of moderate height with steep clifflike sides. A mesa is capped with layers of resistant horizontal rocks, usually lavas. Buttes are smaller, more eroded mesas. Both occur commonly in arid areas of the Southwest. △260, 266.

Mesabi Range, hills in NE Minnesota that are rich in high-grade iron ore and talconite. Open-pit iron mines have been in operation since 1892.

Mesa Verde National Park, park in SW Colorado. It features the most notable and best-preserved pre-Columbian cliff dwellings and other works of early man in the United States. Area: 52,074acres (21,090hectares). Est. 1906.

Mescal. *See* Peyote.

Mescalero, a division of the Apache, once inhabiting the region between the Rio Grande and Pecos rivers in New Mexico. Approximately 2000 live on reservation lands in New Mexico today.

Mescaline, substance obtained from the dried tops of the Peyote cactus *Lophophora williamsii.* It produces visual hallucinations and other unusual psychological effects. △730.

Mesentery. △694.

Meshach, in the Bible, Daniel's companion who, with Shadrach and Abednego, was miraculously saved from the fiery furnace, punishment for eschewing idolatry.

Mesmer, Franz (or **Friedrich**) **Anton** (1734–1815), German physician. He developed the treatment of "animal magnetism" in Vienna and Paris. Animal magnetism was later called "mesmerism," now hypnosis. Though branded as a quack in his own lifetime, Mesmer's work was important because it aroused further interest in new therapies and the possible uses of hypnosis. *See also* Hypnosis. △762.

Mesoamerica. △1118.

Mesohippus, fossil horse descended from Eohippus. Existing during Oligocene epoch (38,000,000 years ago), it had longer legs and straighter back than Eohippus. Each foot had three toes, with the middle being longest. Teeth were low-crowned. Height: 24in (61cm). *See also* Eohippus.

Mesolithic Age, or Middle Stone Age, period in man's evolution following the Paleolithic, usually reckoned to begin about 10,000 BC in Europe. The first food-producing economies evolved, and boats and sleds were invented. Microliths, tiny flint scrapers for dressing skins, were a characteristic artifact. *See also* Paleolithic Age; Neolithic Age. △652,656,950.

Mesomorph. △814.

Meson, member of a subgroup of hadrons, all of which have zero or integral spin. They include the pions, kaons, and eta mesons. There is no restriction on the numbers of mesons produced or destroyed in a nuclear reaction or present in a particular energy state. *See also* Baryon; Hadron; Quark. △1484.

Mesophyte, plant that grows under average moisture conditions, thriving where there is a good balance of water and evaporation. These plants have well developed root and leaf systems. *See also* Hydrophyte; Xerophyte.

Mesopotamia, ancient region in SW Asia, between Tigris (E) and Euphrates (W) rivers, and extending between mountains of Armenia (N) and Persian Gulf (S); generally corresponds to modern central Iraq, NE Syria, and S Armenia. Historically, it was the site of one of the first permanent settlements (*c.* 5000 BC) as shown through excavations of Jarmo, which have also unearthed the earliest known pottery. Sumerians, occupying S, used stone as building material, developed written communication (*c.* 3000 BC), and a canal system. Semites initiated their dominance of the S *c.* 2350 BC. In N, Kingdom of Mitanni was dominant until 12th century BC, when Assyria reigned supreme. Assyria was superseded by Babylonia 612 BC; the area was under Persian control 539 BC–331 BC, when it fell to Alexander the Great and Seleucid Dynasty; it was successively ruled by Parthians (141 BC–AD22), Sassanians (226–628), Caliph at Mecca (641–750), Abbasid caliphate (750–1258), Mongols (1258–1410), Turks (1638–*c.* 1850s); occupied by Britain during WWI and became a British mandate 1920, and kingdom of Iraq 1921. △954–58.

Mesozoa, phylum of tiny, multicellular animals parasitic in invertebrates. Since they do not have well defined cell layers of ectoderm and endoderm, they are not included in the subkingdom Metazoa and may represent a separate line of evolution. Reproduction is complex and includes free swimming ciliated larva. A typical Mesozoan is composed of about 25 elongated cells. Length: 0.3in (7mm).

Mesozoic Era, the second of the three major divisions of geologic time. It is divided into three periods: the Triassic, Jurassic, and Cretaceous. Called the Age of Reptiles, dinosaurs dominated the land, ichthyosaurs and plesiosaurs the seas, and pterosaurs the skies. Mammals, birds, and flowering plants had their beginnings. For most of the era, the continents are believed to have been conjoined into one huge land mass (Pangea). *See also* Geologic Time. △276.

Mesquite, city in NE Texas; suburb of Dallas; site of a junior college. Industries: telephone equipment, pharmaceuticals, paint, rock quarrying. Inc. 1887. Pop. (1970) 55,131.

Mesquite, or **Honey Mesquite,** deciduous tree common in SW United States and Mexico. It has a 50-ft (15-m) taproot that allows it to grow in deserts, small leaflets, and 2-in (5-cm) spines. Bees make honey from the flower nectar and the pods are used as forage. Height: 9–20ft (2.7–6.1m). Family Leguminosae; species *Prosopis juliflora.*

Messerschmitt, Wilhelm (1898–), German aircraft designer and builder. He organized his own aircraft manufacturing company in 1923. His aircraft were the main support of the German Luftwaffe in World War II. In 1937 he became a member of Hitler's War Council. He produced the Me-262, a twin-jet, and a swept-wing jet fighter that the Russians used as a model for their MIG.

Messiah, a long-awaited king who, people hope, will bring an age of peace and righteousness. The term comes from a Hebrew word meaning anointed, that is, consecrated for office. In Old Testament times the Jews looked for a ruler to give them religious and political liberty. Jesus was falsely accused of claiming to be such a king. Early Christians sometimes called Christ the Messiah, and the name is still current in the titles of works such as Handel's oratorio, *Messiah.*

Messiah (1741), oratorio by George Frederick Handel. △1026.

Messier Catalog, a list of 109 star clusters, nebulae, and galaxies compiled by Charles Messier (1730–1817) in 1784. Messier's purpose was to make comet-hunting easier by listing all of the permanent celestial bodies. The catalog numbers are in common use. △104.

Messina, seaport city in Sicily, Italy, on the Strait of Messina; capital of Messina prov. A free city of Rome 241 BC, it was conquered by Saracens 9th century; prospered under Normans 1061; taken by Crusaders 1190; ruled by Spain 1282–1714; liberated by Gi-

Prosper Mérimée

Merlin

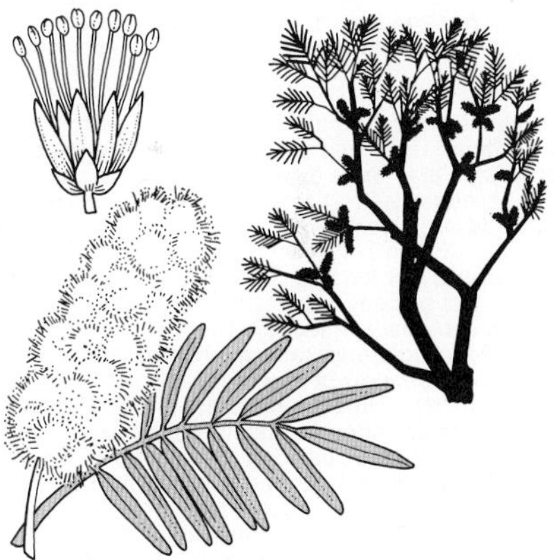

Mesquite

Messina, Italy

useppe Garibaldi 1860; severely damaged by earthquakes 1783, 1908; site of Norman-Romanesque cathedral (rebuilt 12th century), university (1548), biological marine institute (1806). Exports: wine, citrus fruit, olive oil, chemicals. Industries: chemicals, pharmaceuticals, processed foods. Founded *c.* 730 BC by Greeks. Pop. 270,246.

Meštrović, Ivan (1883–1962), Yugoslavian (Croatian) sculptor. Imprisoned for his political beliefs during World War II, he was released and eventually settled (1947) in the United States. His subject matter is chiefly religious. He carved numerous crucifixions, many of which are owned by churches.

Metabolism, chemical and physical processes and changes continuously occurring in a living organism. They involve the breakdown of organic matter, resulting in energy release, and the addition of organic components to store energy. These processes produce, maintain, and destroy protoplasm, releasing energy for vital functions. *See also* Anabolism. △406, 412.

Metabolite, any chemical substance that is involved in the metabolic processes of cells in organisms. These substances function in the various biological energy exchanges necessary for growth, maintenance, and reproduction. *See also* Metabolism.

Metal Detector. △1668.

Metal Fatigue, the progressive fracture of metals subjected to repeated cycles of stress. Metals will fail (break, tear, or otherwise deform permanently) under repeated or reversed loads at stress levels much lower than for a single loading. This phenomenon is of particular significance in the design of safe aircraft.

Metallic Elements. △1552–54.

Metalloid, element intermediate in properties between those of a metal and a nonmetal. In moving from left to right across the periodic table and moving down the groups, there is a transition from metallic to nonmetallic properties. Metalloid elements occur as borderline cases in groups III–VI; examples are germanium and arsenic. They are often semiconductors and have amphoteric hydroxides and oxides.

Metals, chemical elements that are typically lustrous solids, often malleable and ductile, that are good conductors of heat and electricity. The physical properties of metals can be modified by mixing with other metals or small amounts of a nonmetal, such as carbon, to form alloys. Chemically, metals are electropositive elements; that is, they lose electrons to form positive ions. Their oxides and hydroxides are bases and a metal, or its oxide, will react with an acid to form a metal salt. △1506, 1554, 1564, 1568, 1574, 1604–06.

Metamorphic Rocks, broad class of rocks that have been changed by heat or pressure from their original nature—sedimentary, igneous, or older metamorphic. The changes characteristically involve new crystalline structure, the creation of new minerals, or a radical change of texture. Thus the metamorphic slate made from sedimentary shale, the metamorphic gneiss from igneous granite. A special kind of metamorphism is the invasion of a rock by igneous material. △248.

Metamorphosis, change of form, structure, or substance during development of various animals, such as when a caterpillar changes into a moth. Sometimes this change is gradual (grasshopper) and is incomplete metamorphosis. Complete metamorphosis involves a change in habit or environment, as crawling maggots becoming flies capable of reproducing and flying. △494, 498.

Metaphor, figure of speech that draws a comparison. It differs from ordinary comparisons in its inventiveness and from a simile in the complexity of the idea expressed. "Fleece as white as snow," is a simile, whereas "His political life was a constant swimming against the tide," is a metaphor. *See also* Simile.

Metaphysical Poetry, 17th-century English literary form, characterized by complexity of thought, wit, elliptical syntax, and sometimes violent rhythms. The term, first applied by Dryden to Abraham Cowley, was popularized by Samuel Johnson. Contemporaries called such verse "strong-lined." Chief among the metaphysical poets was John Donne. Others include George Herbert, Richard Crashaw, Henry King, Andrew Marvell, and Henry Vaughan. △1148.

Metaphysics, the branch of philosophy that deals with the first principles of reality, with the nature of the universe. The term comes from the Greek *meta ta physika,* "after the things of natures." In Aristotle's works, the First Philosophy came after the Physics. Metaphysics is divided into ontology, the study of the essence of being, and cosmology, the study of the structure and laws of the universe. Great philosophers from Plato and Aristotle to Kant and Whitehead have written on metaphysics. Skeptics, however, have charged that speculation that cannot be verified by objective evidence is useless. △852, 858.

Metastasis, transfer of cells or microorganisms beyond their original sites, especially characteristic of malignant tumors and spreading infections such as tuberculosis.

Metatarsals. △682.

Metazoa, subkingdom of animals whose bodies originate from a single cell and are composed of numerous differentiated cells; from coelenterates through the mammals. It does not include sponges (subkingdom Parazoa) or protozoa (subkingdom Protozoa). △458.

Metchnikoff, Élie (1845–1916), Russian bacteriologist. He shared the 1908 Nobel Prize in physiology or medicine with Paul Ehrlich for work on the mechanism of immunity, which included the discovery that white blood cells were important in the body's resistance to infection and disease. He was also noted for his theories of longevity.

Metellus, distinguished Roman family, among the foremost of whom were: **Quintus Caecilius Metellus Macedonicus** (died 115 BC), general who led the pacification of Greece (146) and suppressed the Celtiberians in Spain. As censor he supported compulsory marriage to increase the birth rate. He was an active opponent of Tiberius and Gaius Gracchus. Three of his sons were consuls. His nephew **Q.C. Metellus Numidicus** (died *c.* 99 BC) commanded Roman forces in Numidia during the Jugurthine War. Opposed by his former legate Marius, he was elected consul (109) and was later exiled briefly. His son **Q.C. Metellus Pius** (died *c.* 64 BC), fought in the Social War. He took Sulla's side against Marius, was elected consul (80), and fought in Spain with Pompey.

Meteor, the luminescent phenomenon produced by small, stony or metallic bodies from interplanetary space entering the earth's atmosphere, as well as the solid body itself (more properly called a meteoroid). Brilliant meteors are called fireballs and consist of a large luminous head followed by a sparkling comet-like wake or train. Some, called bolides, explode with a sound like thunder. Most meteors disintegrate to dust before they reach the surface of the earth. *See also* Meteorite; Meteor Shower. △92.

Meteorite, a particle or body from space (meteoroid) that has survived passage through the atmosphere and come to rest on Earth. Meteorites generally have a pitted surface and fused charred crust. There are three main types: iron meteorites (siderites); stony meteorites (aerolites); and mixed iron and stone meteorites. Some are tiny particles; others weigh up to 60 tons. Meteorites have been dated to about the same time as the origin of the Earth—about 5000 million years ago. △92.

Meteorology, the study by scientists (meteorologists) of atmospheric and weather phenomena with the goals of the understanding, accurate prediction, and artificial control or modification of these phenomena, particularly as human and other life on Earth is affected. *See also* Climatology. △216–18.

Meteor Shower, the appearance of a swarm of hundreds of meteors occurring simultaneously and traveling in parallel paths although they appear to emanate from a single point, called the radiant. Radiant positions frequently rise together with various constellations and such commonly predictable showers are therefore named Leonid, Perseid, Geminid, etc. Other showers occur infrequently at varying intervals. It is thought that shower meteoroids are fragments of steadily disintegrating comets. △92.

Meter, pattern that occurs when the rhythm of a poem becomes regular enough to be measured. Meter imposes a regular recurrence of stresses that divides a line into equal units called metrical feet. Most commonly used feet are anapest, dactyl, iamb, trochee. The meter of a poem is described according to the kind and number of metrical feet per line. For example, iambic pentameter has five iambs per line.

Meter, unit of length (symbol m) defined as 1,650,-763.73 wavelengths of radiation corresponding to a line in the spectrum of krypton-86. 1 meter is equal to 39.3701 inches.

Methadone, a synthetic narcotic drug used to alleviate severe pain. Similar to morphine in effect, methadone has less serious side effects. Although it has addictive characteristics, withdrawal symptoms are mild, encouraging its use in easing withdrawal symptoms of other narcotics.

Methane, or marsh gas, colorless, odorless, flammable gas (formula CH_4), the first member of the alkane series of hydrocarbons. It is the chief constituent of natural gas, from which it is obtained; used in the form of natural gas as a fuel and in the pure form as a starting material for the manufacture of many chemicals. Properties: melt. pt. −296.5°F (−182.5°C); boil. pt. −263.2°F (−164°C). △1558.

Methanol, or methyl alcohol, colorless poisonous flammable liquid (formula CH_3OH) obtained synthetically from carbon monoxide and hydrogen, by the oxidation of natural gas, or by the destructive distillation of wood. It is used as a solvent, rocket fuel, denaturant for ethanol, and in chemical synthesis. Properties: melt. pt. −144°F (−97.8°C), boil. pt. 148.1°F (64.5°C). △1568.

Methodist Church, originally not planned as a new sect, started in England as a trend within Protestantism. With an emphasis on life rather than creed, Anglican theology was continued. John Wesley, an Anglican priest, founder of Methodism, stressed God's mercy. In 1784, the Methodist Episcopal Church in America was founded. The Bible is studied as a continuing form of inspired revelation. *See also* Wesley, John.

Methuselah, in the Bible, son of Enoch and sixth in line from Seth, son of Adam and Eve. He died at the age of 969 and is said to be the oldest person who ever lived. He was the father of many, including Lamech, the father of Noah.

Metric System, a decimal system of weights and measures based on the meter, which was originally defined in terms of the earth's circumference and is now defined in terms of a wavelength of light. Conversions between larger and smaller units are made by use of powers of ten. This system is used internationally by scientists and is in general usage in many countries. Used first in France (1799) its spread has been slow with a few countries still using other systems today. *See also* Weights and Measures. △1450.

Metronome, an instrument designed to indicate the exact rhythm of a musical composition, invented by J. N. Mälzel in 1816. It consists of a ticking pendulum that moves back and forth at a rate controlled by an adjustable weight sliding up and down the pendulum. Modern metronomes are often electric clocks. Metronomes help the musical performer to know the general pace of a work and the composer's intentions.

Metropolitan Museum of Art, US art museum, New York City. Founded in 1870, this museum has art from nearly every country and period. The original museum building, designed by Richard Morris Hunt, was completed in 1880 and is now part of the present building. Several wings designed by McKim, Mead, and White were added later. The section added in 1975, designed by Kevin Roche, houses the Lehman collection. The museum's collection includes numerous Egyptian, Greek, and Roman works. The medieval collection has art from the early Christian to the Gothic era, much of it housed in a separate building called The Cloisters. In addition to European sculpture, there are more than 4,600 European paintings ranging from the 15th century to the present, as well as some 1,300 US paintings and 350 US sculptures. The Altman collection of Chinese porcelains is part of the 30,000 pieces of Oriental art in the museum. The American Wing houses paintings, sculpture, furniture, and decorative arts.

Metternich, (Prince) Klemens Wenzel Nepomuk Lothar von (1773–1859), Austrian statesman. As a student in Strasburg during the French Revolution, he saw and came to loathe revolutionary excesses. In 1795 he married the granddaughter of the distinguished Austrian chancellor Wenzel von Kaunitz. He entered the Austrian foreign service in 1797. He was appointed ambassador to Saxony (1801), Prussia (1803), and France (1806) before becoming foreign minister (1809). Between 1809–13 he followed a policy of conciliation toward Napoleon, arranging the marriage of Archduchess Marie Louise of Austria to Napoleon in 1810. But in 1813 he formed the Quadruple Alliance with England, Prussia, and Russia to defeat Napoleon. He reached the zenith of his influence at the Congress of Vienna (1814–15), which, after the defeat of Napoleon, restored Europe to a grouping of stable, antidemocratic states. This period between 1815–48 has been called the Age of Metternich. He was finally driven from power by the Revolution of 1848. △1230, 1288.

Metz, city in NE France, on Moselle River; capital of Moselle dept. One of Roman Gaul's chief cities, it was burned by Vandals 406 and Huns 451. After 8th century, bishops of Metz ruled a vast empire; made a free imperial city in 12th century; taken by French 1552. In 1871, Germany took it in Franco-Prussian War; Treaty of Versailles (1919) restored it to France; site of Gallo-Roman ruins, Cathedral of St Étienne (1221–1516), Place Sainte Croix (13th–15th century). Industries: metals, machinery, tobacco, clothing. Pop. 107,537.

Meuse (Maas), river that flows into Netherlands from NE France, joins Waal River and enters the North Sea; forms border between Belgium and Holland; scene of heavy fighting during WWI, including the Battle of Verdun. Length: 560mi (902km).

Meuse-Argonne Offensive (September-November 1918), World War I campaign in which US troops cut the Sedan-Mezieres railroad, the main supply line for the sector's German forces. Coupled with British and French successes, this action helped end the war.

Mexicali, city in NW Mexico, bordering Calexico, Calif.; capital of Baja California state; seat of episcopal see. Products: cotton, cereal. Chief industry is tourism. Pop. 390,411.

Mexican Bean Beetle, brown or yellow ladybird beetle with 16 black spots on its wing covers. One of the few harmful ladybird beetles, it is a serious pest of beans. Species *Epilachna varivestis.*

Mexican Border Campaign (1916–17), punitive military expedition. Mexican revolutionary Pancho Villa's raids in New Mexico had resulted in the loss of US lives. In retaliation, a US force of 15,000 men under Gen. John J. Pershing entered Mexico on March 15, 1916. The expedition's forces grew and penetrated 300 miles (480km) into Mexico, arousing anti-American feeling there. US withdrawal (Jan. 27, 1917) averted war. Mexican Gen. Venustiano Carranza was soon able to establish a constitutional government.

Mexican Stone Pine. *See* Piñon.

Mexican War, (1846–48), conflict between Mexico and the United States. Mexican insistence on the Nueces River as the southwestern border of Texas clashed with the Texans' claim to the Rio Grande as the southern frontier. When US Gen. Zachary Taylor moved his troops into the disputed area, hostilities commenced. The US blockade of Mexican ports on the Gulf and Pacific coasts and the march inland from Veracruz to Mexico City and into northern and central Mexico from Texas forced Mexico to sue for peace. By the Treaty of Guadelupe Hidalgo, Mexico relinquished all claims to Texas above the Rio Grande and ceded New Mexico and California to the United States in return for $15,000,000. The final territorial adjustment was made with the Gadsden Purchase of 1853. △1274.

Mexico, a federal republic, located immediately S of the United States, that lifted itself into the modern world during the 20th century. Its people, descended from the Spanish and Indians, comprise the most populous Spanish-speaking nation in the world.

Land and Economy: Topographically, the country ranges from low desert plains and jungle coastal areas to high plateaus and mountains. Beginning in S Mexico, the Sierra Madres spreads into two arms, the Occidental running near the W coast, and the Oriental, a continuation of the Rockies, extending along the Gulf of Mexico as far S as Vera Cruz. Between the ranges lies the central plateau with temperate climate and vegetation. The coastal lowlands are tropical, becoming subtropical with altitude. Starting in 1950, the economic growth has been steady, with emphasis on production for export. Agrarian reform, started in the 1920s, is nearly completed. Dominance by foreign investors, except under special conditions, has been curtailed. Both oil and gas reserves were found in 1975, making Mexico self-sufficient in petroleum. Tourism attracts about 2,200,000 visitors and brings about $1,000,000,000 into the country.

People: About 65% of the Mexicans are mestizos of mixed Spanish and Indian blood, with the Indian predominant. Spanish is the official language, and about 77% of the people are literate. Education is secular, free, and compulsory until the age of 15, and vocational education is encouraged. Although most of the people are Roman Catholic, all church real estate is vested in the nation. Care of church buildings is the responsibility of the clergy. Programs for housing, health, and industry have increased life expectancy from 39 years in 1941 to 60 years.

Government: Under the constitution of 1917, Mexico is a federal republic of 31 states with power separated into the executive, legislative, and judicial branches. The president is elected by universal adult suffrage. Each state is headed by an elected governor with state powers limited.

History: The major Indian civilizations of the Olmec, Maya, Toltec, and Aztec existed in Mexico when Hernán Cortés crushed Mexico in 1519–21 and founded a Spanish colony that lasted 300 years. Father Miguel Hidalgo declared independence in 1810, and the republic was est. in 1822. Political leaders were Gen. Guadalupe Victoria, who became the first president of Mexico, and Gen. Antonio Lopez de Santa Ana who controlled politics from 1833–55. Santa Ana was the leader in 1836 when Texas declared itself independent of Mexico. Benito Juarez served from 1858–71. He deposed Austrian Archduke Maximilian (1864–67) who was supported as Mexican emperor by Napoleon III. Gen. Porfirio Diaz, president from 1877–80 and 1884–1911, became a dictator. Mexico's social and economic problems came to a head in 1910 when Pancho Villa and Emiliano Zapata led a revolt. Under various names, the revolutionary party continues to dominate Mexican politics. In 1976, inflation, balance-of-payment deficits, and other economic problems came to a head. The peso was sharply devalued, and the government instituted an austerity program. △1118, 1124.

PROFILE

Official name: Estados Unidos Mexicanos (United Mexican States)
Area: 761,602sq mi (1,972,549sq km).
Population: 59,200,000.
Chief cities: Mexico City (capital), Guadalajara
Government: Federal Republic
President: José López Portillo (took office Dec 1976)
Religion: Roman Catholic
Language: (official) Spanish
Monetary unit: Peso
Gross national product: $59,000,000,000
Per capita income: $870
Industries (major): petroleum products, iron, steel, chemicals, aluminum, pharmaceuticals, cement
Agriculture: cotton, coffee, sugar cane, cattle, fruits, corn, fish, wheat
Minerals: silver, gold, copper, zinc, coal, petroleum
Trading partners: United States (major)

Mexico, state in cental Mexico; terrain is mountainous (E), contains the Valley of Mexico (N), volcanic belt (S and W); chief river is Lerma; Toluca is capital. Area: 8,286sq mi (21,461sq km). Pop. 3,797,861.

Mexico, Gulf of, gulf on SE coast of the United States and E coast of Mexico; Cuba is at the Gulf's entrance; connects with Atlantic Ocean through straits of Florida, and with the Caribbean Sea through Strait of Yucatán. The Mississippi and Rio Grande rivers empty into the gulf; source of shrimp and petroleum. Depth (max.): 12,714ft (3,878m). Area: approx. 700,000sq mi (1,813,000sq km).

Mexico City, capital and largest city in Mexico, near the S edge of the great central plateau. The former capital of Aztec civilization, it was taken by Hernán Cortés 1521; seat of the viceroyalty of Spanish colonies 1521–1821; captured by Mexican revolutionaries 1821; taken 1847 in Mexican War; site of Summer Olympic Games 1968, canal (1900), National Palace, Palace of Fine Arts, University of Mexico (1551). Industries: chemicals, tourism, cement, tobacco, petroleum, textiles, glassware. Pop. 3,025,564.

Mezzotint, method of engraving by scraping a design into a copper plate with a rocker, a tool with a serrated edge. The roughened surface produced, called a burr, results in light and dark tones in the print.

MHD. *See* Magnetohydrodynamics.

Miami, resort city in SE Florida, 70mi (112km) SW of West Palm Beach on Biscayne Bay; seat of Dade co and 2nd-largest city in Florida. Originally a small Indian and agricultural community, it quickly developed (1895) when Henry M. Flagler extended Florida East Coast Railroad, dredged the harbor, and initiated the construction of recreational facilities; it experienced 1920s land boom; was devastated by hurricane 1926. It is site of Barry College (1940), Miami-Dade Junior College (1960), Orange Bowl and Miami stadiums, many sporting and recreational facilities, and luxury hotels. Industries: tourism, clothing, concrete, metal, meat products, fishing, printing, publishing. Inc. 1896. Pop. (1970) 334,859.

Prince Metternich

United States
Mexicali
Ciudad Juárez
Chihuahua
GULF OF MEXICO
Monterrey
MEXICO
San Luis Potosi
Tampico
Guadalajara
Mérida
Cuba
México City (Ciudad de México)
Veracruz
Puebla
Belize
CARIBBEAN SEA
Hond.
PACIFIC OCEAN
Guat.
El Sal.
Nic.
Costa Rica
Panama
Colombia
0
1600 km

Mexico

Mexico City: library, National University

Miami

Miami Beach, island city, in SE Florida, across Biscayne Bay from Miami on Atlantic Ocean. Dade co. Popular resort and tourist community; connected by four causeways to Miami; famous for hotels and palatial estates, winter entertainment. Inc. 1915. Pop. (1970) 87,072.

Miami River, formerly Great Miami; river in W Ohio; rises in Indian Lake, flows S into Ohio River at the Indiana line. Length: 160mi (258km).

Miao, or **Meo**, people inhabiting the mountains of China, Vietnam, Laos, and Thailand. Consisting of numerous groups, they are a predominantly agricultural people cultivating maize, rice, and the opium poppy. They traditionally practice spirit and ancestor worship.

Mica, a group of common rock-forming minerals of the sheet silicate (SiO_4) type. All contain aluminum, potassium, sodium, or calcium, and water in the form of OH ions. All have perfect basal cleavage. Common members are muscovite, biotite, phlogopite, and lepidolite. △242.

Micah, biblical author and sixth of the 12 minor prophets. A contemporary of Amos, Hosea, and Isaiah, he anticipated the destruction of Jerusalem, but incorporated elements of apocalyptic hope.

Michael, biblical archangel along with Gabriel, Raphael, and Uriel. A messenger of God, he appears as the defender of the Jewish people and is considered highest of the archangels. In the New Testament, he destroys the dragon (Satan).

Michael VIII Palaeologus (1234–82), Byzantine emperor (*r.*1259–82), and founder of the Palaeologan dynasty. A brilliant military commander and a consummate diplomat, Michael led the Greeks to a victory in their struggle against Latin rule. On June 25, 1261, his troops recaptured Constantinople, and Michael became the restorer of the Byzantine Empire.

Michael (1921–), king of Romania (1927–30, 1940–47), son of Carol II. From 1927 to 1930, power was actually in the hands of a council of regents. After Carol's final departure in 1940, the dictator Antonescu had effective control. On August 23, 1944, the young king had Antonescu arrested, cast Romania's lot with the Allies, and hastened the end of the war in Romania. The Communists forced him to abdicate in December 1947.

Michael (1596–1645), tsar of Russia (1613–45), founder of the Romanov dynasty. His election as czar ended the chaotic period known as the Times of Trouble that had existed since the death of Feodor I in 1598. Between 1619–33 he had to share his rule with his father, Feodor Nikitich Romanov, who was also patriarch of Russia. Michael made peace with Sweden (1617) and Poland (1618). During his reign some Western influences were introduced but the peasants were further reduced to serfdom. He was succeeded by his son Alexis.

Michelangelo Buonarroti (1475–1564), Italian sculptor, painter, and architect. Raised in Florence, he was apprenticed (1488) to the painter Domenico Ghirlandaio, and later became a student under the patronage of Lorenzo de' Medici. In 1496 he moved to Rome to begin work on the "Pietà." He spent all of his productive years in Florence and Rome, working on commissions. Noted for his temper and impatience, he was often in conflict with his patrons and associates. Despite these difficulties, patrons vied with one another for Michelangelo's favor. He considered himself primarily a sculptor and created realistic, three-dimensional heroic figures, endowed with an inner personality and pent-up energy, such as his "David." Among his early sculptures were his tender "Pietà" for St Peter's, his majestic "Moses," and his "Dying Slave" and "Rebellious Slave" for the tomb of Julius II.

Michelangelo's greatest painting achievement was his fresco work on the ceiling in the Sistine Chapel, which he completed in only four years. His figures have a sculptured roundness to their bodies. The enormous area is unified by theological themes such as the creation of the world and man, as in "The Creation of Adam," and the end of the world, as in "The Last Judgment." He used garland-bearing nude youths to link together the Genesis scenes, thereby unifying the whole.

As an architect, Michelangelo was commissioned by the Medici family to build the New Sacristy in Florence to house the tombs of members of the family. This project took 14 years to complete and included the allegorical figures of "Day" and "Night" in Giuliano's tomb. He also built the Laurentian Library for the Medicis, in which his recessed columns and other features differed from the current architectural practices. His most successful and influential building projects were his designs for the Campidoglio square civic center and for St Peter's interior. △1140, 1150.

Michelozzo (Michelozzi) (1396–1472), Italian sculptor and architect. He received many commissions in Florence from the Medici family. With Lorenzo Ghiberti, he worked on such projects as the north doors for the Baptistery in Florence. He worked with Donatello on many tombs. His most important work was the Medici-Riccardi Palace, Florence. △1134.

Michelson, Albert Abraham (1852–1931), US physicist, b. Germany. In 1887 he conducted an experiment with Edward Morley to determine the velocity of the Earth through the ether, using an interferometer of his own design. The negative result acted as the starting point for the development of the theory of relativity. He was able to determine quite accurately the speed of light, and was awarded a Nobel Prize in 1907. *See also* Relativity Theory. △1522.

Michelson Interferometer. *See* Interferometer.

Michelson-Morley Experiment, famous experiment performed in 1887 by US physicist A.A. Michelson and E.W. Morley to detect the velocity of the Earth with respect to a hypothetical medium in space called ether, which was supposed to carry light waves. The negative results seriously discredited the ether theory and led to Albert Einstein's proposal in 1905 that the speed of light is a universal constant. △1522.

Michener, James (1907–), US author, b. New York City. An editor, he turned to writing and won a Pulitzer Prize (1948) for his first collection of short stories, *Tales of the South Pacific* (1947). His novels include *The Bridges at Toko-ri* (1953), *Sayonara* (1954), *Hawaii* (1959), *The Source* (1965), and *Centennial* (1974). With *Hawaii*, Michener established a pattern of panoramic novels; the book spans generations of Hawaiians from the early Polynesians to later Americans, Chinese, and Japanese.

Michigan, state in the N central United States that borders on four of the five Great Lakes—Superior, Michigan, Huron, and Erie.

Land and Economy. Michigan comprises two peninsulas separated by the narrow Straits of Mackinac, which connect lakes Michigan and Huron. The Upper Peninsula to the N lies between lakes Superior and Michigan; to the S, the Lower Peninsula is between Lake Michigan and lakes Huron, St Clair, and Erie. The Lower Peninsula is level or rolling; it contains most of the population. The highest ground is in the Upper Peninsula. Manufacturing is largely concentrated in the cities in the S; the motor vehicle industry centers in Detroit and Flint. Mineral deposits and mining are located in the Upper Peninsula.

People. Michigan was settled by pioneers from the E states, but the economy attracted thousands of immigrants. Swedes, Norwegians, Finns, and Canadians came in the 19th century as lumbermen and miners. Before WWI, the motor industry was drawing numbers from Italy and E Europe. During WWII, an influx of blacks joined the labor force. Nearly 75% of Michigan's people lives in urban areas.

Education. There are nearly 90 institutions of higher education. The University of Michigan is the principal state-supported institution.

History. Beginning with a settlement at Sault-Ste-Marie between lakes Superior and Huron in 1641, the French built forts and settlements through the area, but lost its control to Great Britain by the 1763 treaty that ended the Seven Years' War. After the Revolution, the British did not evacuate the region until 1796, when they were compelled to by terms of the Jay Treaty (1794). Michigan became a US territory on July 1, 1805. In the War of 1812, the British captured Detroit, and their Indian allies terrorized the settlements. The opening of the Erie Canal in New York in 1825 aided Michigan's growth by linking it with the Atlantic through the lakes. After joining the Union, the state rapidly developed its timber and mining resources, which were superseded as the prime strength of the economy by the industrial boom, led by the motor vehicle sector, beginning about 1914.

PROFILE

Admitted to Union: Jan. 26, 1837; rank, 26th
US Congressmen: Senate, 2; House of Representatives, 19
Population: 8,875,083 (1970); rank, 7th
Capital: Lansing, 131,546 (1970)
Chief cities: Detroit, 1,512,893; Grand Rapids, 197,-649; Flint, 193,317
State legislature: Senate, 38; House of Representatives, 110
Area: 58,216sq mi (150,779sq km); rank, 23d
Elevation: Highest, 1,980ft (604m), Mt Curwood; lowest, 572ft (174m), Lake Erie
Industries (major products): motor vehicles and parts, machinery, machine tools, hardware, furniture
Agriculture (major products): dairy products, cherries, apples, pears, sugar beets
Minerals (major): iron ore, salt, gypsum, limestone
State nickname: Great Lake State, Wolverine State
State motto: Si quaeris peninsulam amoenam, circumspice ("If you seek a pleasant peninsula, look around you.")
State bird: robin
State flower: apple blossom
State tree: white pine

Michigan, Lake, 3rd largest of the Great Lakes, bounded by Michigan (N and E), Wisconson (W), and Illinois and Indiana (S); at the N end it is connected with Lake Huron by the Straits of Mackinac. Lake was discovered in 1634 by Jean Nicolet, French explorer. Passed to Britain 1763 and United States 1796. Area was relatively unsettled until 1830s due to transportation difficulties. The St Lawrence Seaway has opened lake to international trade. Indiana Dunes National Lakeshore is on S shore; many islands in N part of lake. Chicago is on its SW shore. Only one of the Great Lakes entirely within the United States. Area: 22,178sq mi (57,441sq km).

Michigan City, city in NW Indiana, on Lake Michigan; site of 100-acre (40.5-hectare) International Friendship Gardens, yacht basin and sand dune beaches. Industries: air compressors, plumbing products, metal, furniture. Founded 1832; inc. 1836. Pop. (1970) 39,369.

Michoacán, mountainous state in SW Mexico; extends NE to central plateau. Hydroelectric power plants aid development of Michoacán's coastal region; site of training center for Latin American rural teachers, sponsored by the Organization of American States. Products: sugar cane, tobacco, coffee, cereals, livestock, lumber. Industries: mining, tourism, oil. Area: 23,202sq mi (60,093sq km). Pop. 2,341,556.

Michurin, Ivan Vladimirovich (1855–1935), Russian plant breeder. His unorthodox theories of heredity (Michurinism), which included belief in the theory of acquired characteristics, were for a time accepted as the official science of genetics by the Soviet Union. Through grafting he managed to produce new strains of fruit, but his belief that grafting produces heritable changes has since been discredited.

Micmac, an Algonquian-speaking tribe of North American Indians once inhabiting Nova Scotia, Cape Breton Is., Prince Edward Is., and Newfoundland. They were probably the first Indians to meet the early white explorers from Europe, *c.* AD 100. About 4,000 still live in the northeastern area today.

Microbiology, biological study of microorganisms, their structure, function, and significance. Types of microorganisms include viruses, bacteria, protozoa, and microscopic unicellular algae and fungi. Aspects of this study involve disease organisms and useful organisms, such as bacteria to fight disease or yeasts to promote fermentation. Microbiology began during the 17th century with the invention of the microscope, enabling scholars to view microorganisms for the first time. Pioneers in the field include Robert Hooke, Anton Van Leeuwenhoek, and Louis Pasteur. △412, 422.

Microcephaly, the condition of having a very small head. It is usually accompanied by severe mental retardation and is thought to be caused by either genetic factors, infections during the mother's pregnancy, or radiation during pregnancy. *See also* Mental Retardation.

Microeconomics, one of the two major subdivisions of economics, the study of individual components of the economic system. Microeconomics involves the basic market process and the operation of supply and demand factors in determining market price and output as well as the study of the individual firm and how the firm makes decisions to maximize its profit situation. Microeconomics also typically involves analysis of the market conditions for the factors of production. *See also* Macroeconomics. △938.

Micrometer. △1656.

Micronesia, collective term for a large area of island groups in W Pacific Ocean, generally those S of Japan, W of the International Date Line, N of Melanesia and E of the Philippines; comprises a subdivision of Oceania, as do Polynesia and Melanesia; larger groups include Marianas Islands, Marshall Islands, Gilbert and Ellice Islands, Caroline Islands; native inhabitants are chiefly Polynesian and share related languages and cultures.

Microphone, device for converting sound into oscillating electric currents of the same frequency. Main types are: the carbon microphone, in which the sound pressure causes a variation in the electrical resistance of carbon granules held between a diaphragm and a carbon block; the crystal microphone, in which the sound impinges upon a crystal, creating an oscillating current by the piezoelectric effect; the moving coil microphone, in which a coil attached to a diaphragm oscillates in a stationary magnetic field. △1486, 1798.

Microscope, optical instrument for producing an enlarged image of a very small object. The compound microscope consists basically of two converging lens systems, the objective and the eyepiece, of short focal length. The object to be studied is placed close to the objective and is illuminated by a strong source of light. The light enters the objective, which produces a magnified image of the object. This image is further magnified by the eyepiece to produce the final image seen by the eye through the eyepiece. There are usually three objective lenses on a microscope giving a choice of low, medium, and high magnification. The highest magnification can be over 1,000 times so that details much smaller than one thousandth of a millimeter can be resolved. △1518.

Microscope, Electronic. *See* Electron Microscope.

Microwave, any electromagnetic radiation that has a wavelength that ranges between one millimeter and one meter. This range is between infrared and shortwave radio wavelengths. These waves, which travel in straight lines, are used in radar, in moderate distance communication, and for such specific applications as microwave ovens. △1792.

Midas, as described by the Roman, Ovid, a king rewarded by Bacchus for rendering a service to the god's teacher, Silenus. Midas asked that anything he touched should become gold. Bacchus agreed, with the result that Midas was unable to eat or drink because his food was immediately transmuted to the precious metal.

Mid-Atlantic Ridge. *See* Mid-Ocean Ridge. △228.

Middle Ages, period of European history between the Greco-Roman period and modern times. Dates used by historians to delineate the Middle Ages vary, but the period is generally considered to have begun with the sack of Rome by Alaric (410) or with the death of the last Roman emperor, Romulus Augustus, in 476. Dates for the close of the Middle Ages show even more discrepancy, as they depend less upon actual events and more upon the gradual transition to the period known as the Renaissance. In Italy, the Renaissance is said to have begun with the writing of Dante, Boccaccio, and Petrarch and the artistic works of Giotto and others in the late 12th and early 13th centuries. In England Chaucer (died 1400) is one of the primary literary landmarks for the close of the Middle Ages, and in Germany the printing of the Gutenberg Bible (*c.* 1455) may be considered a sign that the Renaissance was underway. Outside dates for the period are, therefore, the 5th to the 15th centuries.

Religion. The Middle Ages marked the rise of Christianity in the West, the emergence of a strong papacy, and the rise of monastic orders. It is the period of liturgical development, doctrinal disputes, church-state struggles, and the Crusades.

Society and Politics. The beginning of the Middle Ages in the West was characterized by barbarian invasions, the decentralization of power, and the rise of feudalism. In the East the cultural and political center was Constantinople, capital of the Byzantine Empire.

Art, Literature, and Learning. Although once considered a period void of learning and creativity, the Middle Ages produced an extension of literacy to greater numbers of people, the rise of vernacular literatures, the beginnings of universities, and its own unique form of art and architecture, such as the Romanesque and Gothic styles. Philosophy developed throughout the latter half of the period, reaching its peak in the 13th century. Much of our modern thought, music, and political structure has roots in this stormy and fascinating period. △1054–1106.

Middle East, term for the region comprising the lands of SW Asia and NE Africa; includes Turkey, Cyprus, Syria, Israel, Jordan, Iraq, Iran, Lebanon, Saudi Arabia, Yemen, P.D.R. Yemen, Oman, United Arab Emirates, Qatar, State of, Bahrain, Kuwait, Egypt, The Sudan, Libya. *See also* Individual countries.

Middlesbrough, city in NE England; port on Tees estuary. Industries: iron, steel, chemicals, engineering, shipbuilding. Pop. 393,960.

Middle Stone Age. *See* Mesolithic Age.

Middleton, Arthur (1742–87), American patriot and a signer of the Declaration of Independence, b. Charleston, S. C. A South Carolina delegate to the Continental Congress (1776–78; 1781–83), he was captured (1780) and later released by the British. He was elected to the state senate after the close of the Revolutionary War.

Middleton, municipal borough in NW England, 6mi (10km) NNE of Manchester on Irk River; site of 12th–16th century church of St Leonard. Industries: chemicals, engineering, soap, plastics. Pop. 53,419.

Middletown, city in S Connecticut, 14mi (23km) S of Hartford, on Connecticut River; site of Wesleyan University (1831). Industries: textiles, marine hardware. Settled 1650; inc. 1784. Pop. (1970) 36,244.

Middletown, city in SW Ohio, 11mi (18km) NE of Hamilton on Great Miami River; farming area. Industries: aircraft parts, paper, steel. Founded 1802; inc. as village 1866, as city 1883. Pop. (1970) 48,767.

Middle Years. △796–807.

Midge, punkie, or no-see-um, brown to black fly resembling the black fly; 0.025 to 0.2in (0.6–5.0mm) long. The female bites animals and other insects. Found worldwide, they breed in fresh, brackish, or salt water or moist earth. Family Ceratopogonidae. *See also* Diptera.

Midland, city in E central Michigan, on the Chippewa and Tittabawassee rivers; seat of Midland co. Industries: chemicals (important since 1890), metallurgy, pharmaceuticals, oil drilling, natural gas. Inc. as village 1869, as city 1887. Pop. (1970) 35,176.

Midland, city in W Texas, 20mi (32km) N of Odessa; seat of Midland co. Originally a small cow town, oil strike in 1921 brought economic and population boom. Industries: oil, cattle, chemicals, agriculture, natural gas. Founded 1884; inc. 1906. Pop. (1970) 59,463.

Mid-Ocean Ridge, the great median ridge of the sea bottom where new lithosphere is being formed. The ridges, consisting of two parallel crests with a deep valley between, are the spreading edges of the plates that cover the earth and are also known as the margins of tension. They form a world-encircling system that extends, with several side branches, along the Mid-Atlantic Ridge, up, around, and down through the Indian Ocean (the Mid-Indian Ridge), and across the Pacific (the Pacific-Antarctic Ridge). The system also extends into the continents in a few places, such as the Great Rift in Africa and along the Gulf of California. *See also* Sea-floor Spreading. △228.

Midrash, in Hebrew literature, rabbinical interpretation and exposition of the text of the Old Testament, written from about the 4th to 11th centuries. These writings are divided into *halakah,* which deals with legal sections of the Bible, and *haggadah,* which deals with biblical legends. A large part of the Talmud is Midrashic writing.

Midsummer Night's Dream, A (*c.* 1595), 5-act comedy by William Shakespeare. Since its first US performance in New York (1826) it has been revived many times, in New York, on tour, and at the Connecticut Stratford Festival. In early Athens, Lysander and Demetrius love Hermia, Helena loves Lysander. Puck, servant to the fairy king Oberon, gives Lysander a love potion, mistaking him for Demetrius. Oberon gives the same potion to his philandering Queen Titania, causing her to fall in love with Bottom, one of a traveling troup of players. By morning, all the spells wear off and all the lovers are reconciled.

Midway Islands, coral atoll in central Pacific Ocean, 1,300mi (2,080km) WNW of Honolulu; US territory comprised of two islands, Eastern and Sand, which are administered by the Department of the Interior. Islands were annexed to the United States 1867; received cable station 1903; came under authority of US Navy Department, and was made a civilian air base 1935; scene of Battle of Midway, an important WWII Allied victory over Japanese naval and air forces, June 3–6, 1942. Area: 2sq mi (5sq km). Pop. 2,220. △1338.

Midwest City, city in central Oklahoma; suburb of Oklahoma City; adjoins Tinker Air Force Base. Inc. 1942. Pop. (1970) 48,212.

Michelangelo's Pietà *(Florence, detail, showing figure modeled on Michelangelo)*

Albert Michelson

Lake Michigan

Microphone

Midwife Toad, European tailless amphibian that is brown with green and red spots. The mute male acts as caretaker of the eggs, keeping the strings wrapped around his legs until larvae hatch. Length: to 2in (5cm). Family Discoglossidae; species *Alytes obstetricans. See also* Frog. △518.

Mies Van Der Rohe, Ludwig (1886–1969), German-born architect who in the United States (1938–1969) perfected the elegant, unornamented skyscraper. He was a member and director (1930–33) of the Bauhaus. In 1938 he joined the Armour Institute (now Illinois Institute of Technology) and opened his own firm in Chicago. In all his works, such as Farnsworth House in Plano, Ill. (1950), Chicago's Lake Shore Drive Apartments (1951), the Seagram Building in New York (1958), his great concern with quality of materials and their handling is evident. *See also* Bauhaus; Skyscraper. △1322.

Mieszko I, of the Piast dynasty, first historical king of Poland (*c.* 960–92). In 963 he united several principalities so that his realm stretched from the Vistula to the Oder River, and in 966 he was converted to Christianity by Bohemian missionaries. Thus Poland was brought into the Western cultural sphere of influence. △1074.

Migdal, ancient fortified town in N Israel, approx. 30mi (48km) E of modern Haifa, on W shore of Sea of Galilee; thought to be the biblical Magdala, home of Mary Magdalene; site of many archeological excavations.

MIG Fighter. △1744.

Mignonette, plant native to N Africa. It has small flowers clustered in a terminal spike, thick stems, and coarse, lance-shaped leaves. Among 70 species is the annual *Reseda odorata* with strongly scented flowers; height: to 18in(46cm). Family Resedaceae.

Migraine, periodic attacks of headache, usually beginning on one side, in which constriction of the cranial blood vessels is a feature. Attacks are often accompanied by gastrointestinal and visual disturbances.

Migration, Animal, periodic movements of organisms, usually in groups, from one area to another, to find food, breeding areas or better climates. Thousands of lemmings die during migrations, improving the survival rate for those remaining by reducing competition for food. Birds usually migrate along established routes (flyways). Fish migrate between fresh and salt waters or from one part of the ocean to another. Mammals migrate, usually seasonally, in search of adequate food. Some invertebrates also migrate. △532.

Migration, Human, geographical movement of people either as individuals or as a group. Emigration is movement out of one nation to settle in another; immigration is movement into a country. Sociologists study migration for several reasons: to analyze the effects it has on pre-existing social structures; and to locate and predict migration trends.

Miguel (1802–66), Portuguese prince and pretender to the throne, younger brother of Peter IV. When Peter abdicated (1826) in favor of his infant daughter, Maria II, he made an agreement with Dom Miguel whereby Miguel would marry Maria and act as her regent in a constitutional monarchy. Miguel, however, with the aid of absolutists, tried to usurp the throne, thereby beginning the Miguelist Wars. In 1833, Maria's forces, under the leadership of her father, were finally able to defeat Miguel. He went into exile and renounced his claims to the throne, but his followers continued to make trouble during Maria's reign.

Mikado, ancient title of the emperor of Japan meaning "exalted gate." According to Shinto myth, the Mikado was directly descended from the nature gods.

Mikoyan, Anastas I(vanovich) (1895–), Soviet political leader. He joined the Communist party central committee (1923) and the Politburo (1934). After 1926 his specialty was trade, and he was commissar for foreign trade (1938). He was the first to denounce Joseph Stalin after his death (1953) and supported Nikita Khrushchev. He was first deputy premier (1955–57, 1958–64). He became Soviet president in 1964 but resigned the next year.

Milan (Milano), industrial city in N Italy, 76mi (122km) NE of Genoa; capital of Lombardy region and Milano prov. An important city of Western Roman Empire, it was a free commune by 12th century; powerful Italian state under Sforza family 1447–1535, when it was taken by Spanish; ceded to Austria 1713; ruled by Napoleon 1796–1814; made capital of Cisalpine 1804; part of Italy 1860. Milan is the site of white marble cathedral (1387–1858), Ambrosian library, Ospedale Maggiore (1456), La Scala theater, University of Milan (1924). Industries: machinery, textiles, chemicals, automotive. Pop. 1,713,539.

Milan, Edict of (313), legislation by which Constantine I (the Great) decreed religious tolerance throughout the Roman Empire. Thus the long and terrible persecution of the Christians by the emperors of Rome was ended, and the Christian church leaders were able to assume a powerful position in civil administration, wedding church to state.

Milan Decree (1807), statement of Napoleon's naval policy during Napoleonic Wars with Britain. It was in retaliation for Britain's prohibition of neutrals' trade with European ports that excluded British ships, unless the vessels first passed through a British port and paid duties there. The Milan Decree declared that any ship that complied with British regulations would be considered British property and could be seized. Napoleon's action further limited neutral trade.

Mildenhall Treasure. △1024.

Mildew, a name applied to various moldlike fungi, especially to two groups of serious plant pests: downy mildews and powdery mildews. The downy mildews (order Peronosporales) are parasites of higher plants that sometimes cause severe damage to crops. They form velvety gray patches of spores on leaves. One species, *Phytophthora infestans,* which causes late blight of potatoes, was responsible for the Irish famine of 1845–48. Powdery mildews (order Erysiphales) are a small but widespread group of plant parasites that form a characteristic powdery white coating on infected leaves. They are generally less destructive than downy mildews. △426.

Miles, Nelson Appleton (1839–1925), US Army officer, b. near Westminister, Mass. He distinguished himself first in the Civil War and later in the wars against the western Indians (1869–80). In 1877 he destroyed Chief Crazy Horse's village and defeated and captured Chief Joseph of the Nez Percé. In 1886 he accepted the surrender of the Apache army under Geronimo. He also led the occupying force in Puerto Rico during the Spanish-American War (1898) and became a lieutenant general before his retirement (1903).

Miletus, ancient, ruined Greek city in SW Turkey; one of the greatest cities in Asia Minor before 500 BC, it was known for its colonization, commercial, and cultural importance. It was taken by Persia late 6th century BC; conquered by Alexander 344 BC; experienced a brief revival under Romans. By AD 6th century all significance had diminished and site was abandoned.

Milford, city in S Connecticut, on Long Island Sound and Housatonic River. Industries: fishing, metal products, brass goods. Settled 1639; inc. 1959. Pop. (1970) 50,858.

Milgram, Stanley. △786.

Milhaud, Darius (1892–1974), a leading 20th-century French composer. He experimented with polytonality and included American jazz elements in works, such as *La Création du Monde* (1923) for orchestra. A prolific composer, he produced many operas, symphonies, concertos, chamber music pieces, ballets, and religious compositions.

Military Law, system of rules governing military personnel. Each nation's legislature usually sets its military code, including the establishing of tribunals and defining offenses and appropriate penalties. The US military law, based on the English code, is called the Uniform Code of Military Justice. The Constitution gives to the president, as commander in chief, and to Congress the ability to make military law. Civil law is superior to military law, but during war times it may be suspended and military laws extended to civil crime.

Military Reconstruction Act (1867), law passed by the US Congress, dividing the South (except Tennessee) into five military districts, each under the authority of a major general who controlled the government.

Milk. △372–74.

Milk, river in NW Montana, rises in Rocky Mts; flows NE across the Canadian border, turning E and SE into Montana, empties into Missouri River near Fort Peck Dam; used for irrigation and hydroelectricity. Length: 625mi (1,006km).

Milkfish, valuable food fish found in tropical waters of the Atlantic and Pacific. Cultivated on fish farms in the Philippines, this silvery fish has a deeply-forked tail. It spawns in brackish water. Length: to 5ft (152.5cm). Family Chanidae; species *Chanos chanos.*

Milk Snake, shiny patterned snake ranging from Canada to Ecuador. Closely related to the king snake, it is usually tricolored with brown (or red), black, and yellowish transverse rings or blotches. It feeds mostly on mice. Length: to 3ft (91.4cm). Family Colubridae; species *Lampropeltis doliata. See also* King Snake; Snake.

Milkweed, perennial plants with a milky sap native to North and South America. The seeds have silky plumes and flowers are greenish, orange, rose, or purple. Height: 2–5ft (0.6–1.5m). Family Asclepiadaceae; genus *Asclepias.* The milkweed family includes milky plants, shrubs, woody vines, and some succulent desert plants, mostly native to tropical Africa.

Milkweed Butterfly. *See* Monarch Butterfly.

Milky Way Galaxy, barred spiral galaxy containing the solar system. Often called the Galaxy or the Milky Way system, it is a lens-shaped structure 100,000 light years across with a dense nucleus and halo of stars surrounded by spiraling star and dust streams. The broad band of innumerable stars visible from Earth—the Milky Way proper—represents the Galaxy's outer edge; the central region, however, is optically obscured by dust and gas in the spiral arms. Our own Sun is situated on one of the spiral arms, about 32,000 light years from the center of the galaxy. *See also* Andromeda Galaxy; Galaxy. △104, 118.

Mill, James (1773–1836), British historian and economist. A divinity graduate from Edinburgh University, he proved too intellectual for his parishioners and thus he turned to a literary career. His monumental *History of India* (1818) gained him a position with India House in 1819. He published *Elements of Political Economics* (1821), the first English textbook on economics. He was the father of John Stuart Mill.

Mill, John Stuart (1806–73), English philosopher. He received an extraordinary education from his father, James Mill, recounted in his *Autobiography* (1873). He served in the East India Company, edited several periodicals, and was a member of Parliament (Westminster, 1865). He advocated a form of utilitarianism, in a book by that name (1861). *On Liberty* (1859) became famous for its defense of civil liberties. In *System of Logic* (1843) he attempted to provide a rigorous account of inductive reasoning. His epistemology was empiricist. *See also* Mill, James; Utilitarianism. △860, 898, 1288.

Millais, (Sir) John Everett (1829–96), English painter. He was a member of the Pre-Raphaelite Brotherhood. His carefully detailed landscape paintings are known for their accurate portrayal of nature. He also did portraits and historical works. *See also* Pre-Raphaelite Brotherhood. △1252.

Millay, Edna St. Vincent (1892–1950), US poet, b. Rockland, Me. A popular poet, her bohemian lifestyle personified the 1920s image of "flaming youth." She first attracted critical attention with her poem "Renascence" (1912) and later acquired a large following with such volumes as *A Few Figs from Thistles* (1920), *Second April* (1921), and *The Harp-Weaver and Other Poems* (1923), which won a Pulitzer Prize. She was also a political activist, supporting such causes as that of Sacco and Vanzetti.

Miller, Arthur (Asher) (1915–), US playwright, b. New York City. After his first play *The Man Who Had All the Luck* (1944), he wrote a novel *Focus* (1945), then a play *All My Sons* (1947), which won the Critics' Circle Award. *Death of a Salesman* (1949) won a Pulitzer Prize as well as the Critics' Circle Award. Other notable plays include *The Crucible* (1953), *A View from the Bridge* (1955), *After the Fall* (1963), and *The Price* (1968). He also wrote the screenplay for the film *The Misfits* (1961). △1374.

Miller, (Alton) Glenn (1904–44), US jazz trombonist and bandleader, b. Clarinda, Iowa. He played in the bands of Ben Pollack and Ray Noble before forming his own band in 1935. This band became the most popular dance band of all time, featuring a distinctive reedy sound and a popular theme song, "Moonlight Serenade" (1939), composed by Miller. Miller and his band appeared in early 1940s films. In 1942 Miller enlisted in the US Army air corps and eventually lost his life in an air crash.

Miller, Henry (1891–), US author, b. New York City. Most of his novels, which are fictionalized autobiography, were first published in Paris, where he lived during 1930–39. His work was banned in the United States until 1961 for its explicit treatment of sex. His books include *Tropic of Cancer* (1934) and *Tropic of Capricorn* (1938), novels, and *The Air-Conditioned Nightmare* (1945), nonfiction. △1374.

Miller's Thumb, freshwater fish found in fast-flowing streams of Europe. One of the sculpins, it has a large bony head and tapered body. Length: to 4in (10.2cm). Family Cottidae; species *Cottus gobio.*

Miller-Tydings Enabling Act (1937), legislation that amended the federal antitrust laws to give federal support to state "fair trade," or price-fixing, laws.

Millet, Jean François (1814–75), French painter. Somewhat influenced by the Barbizon school, he is best known for his landscapes showing groups of hard-working peasants, such as in "The Gleaners" (1857) and the "Angelus" (1859), both in the Louvre. △1252.

Millet, cereal grass that produces small, edible seeds, found worldwide. The stalks have flower spikes and the hulled seeds are white. In the Soviet Union, W Africa, and Asia it is an important food staple. In the United States and W Europe it is used mainly for pasture or hay. Pearl millet *(Pennisetum glaucum)* grows in poor soils and is used as food in India and Africa. Proso *(Panicum miliaceum)* is used as birdseed and livestock feed in the United States. Height: 1–10ft (30cm–3m). Family Gramineae. △326.

Millikan, Robert Andrews (1868–1953), US physicist, b. Morrison, Ill., professor at Chicago and later at the California Institute of Technology. His oil-drop experiment, in which he measured the charge on an electron, provided final proof that electricity exists in the form of particles. He also verified Einstein's photoelectric equation, did some preliminary cosmic-ray studies, and determined a value for Planck's constant. He was awarded a Nobel Prize in 1923 for his research on electronic charge and the photoelectric effect. △1490.

Millions Fish. *See* Guppy.

Millipede, or thousand-legger, invertebrate animal found worldwide. It has a flattened body, one pair of antennae, two pairs of legs per segment and is orange, brown, or black. They avoid light and feed on plant tissues. Some tropical species squirt a repellent or poisonous secretion from pores in body segments. Length: 0.2–11in (5–279mm). Class Diplopoda. *See also* Myriapoda. △484, 490.

Mills, C(harles) Wright (1916–62), US sociologist, b. Waco, Tex. A professor at Columbia University (1946–62), Mills was a controversial sociologist who attempted to expand on the theories of earlier thinkers, mainly Karl Marx and Max Weber. His research was in the areas of social psychology and political sociology. Among his many books are *From Max Weber* (1946), edited with Hans Gerth, *The Power Elite* (1956), *The Sociological Imagination* (1959), and *Listen Yankee* (1960). △890, 900, 1360.

Milne, A(lan) A(lexander) (1882–1956), English essayist, dramatist, and author of books for children. For his young son Christopher Robin he wrote the verses in *When We Were Very Young* (1924) and *Now We Are Six* (1927) and the stories in *Winnie-the-Pooh* (1926) and *The House at Pooh Corner* (1928).

Milo, or **Milon** (6th century BC), legendary Greek athlete, a spectacular wrestler who inspired numerous improbable legends. One of these states that he carried an ox on his shoulders through the Olympic stadium, killed it with one punch, and ate it that day. He was also known as a soldier and defender of his native Croton, a Greek colony in S Italy.

Miloš Obrenovich (1780–1860), Serbian ruler. It was largely due to his diplomatic skill that Serbia attained a measure of independence from the Turks in 1830, with himself recognized as hereditary prince. His autocratic methods brought such unpopularity that he had to abdicate in 1839, but he was reinstated in 1858.

Milpitas, city in W California, S of Palo Alto. Industries: automobiles, food distribution, citrus fruits, irrigation systems, paint. Inc. 1954. Pop. (1970) 27,149.

Miltiades (*c.* 550–489 BC), Athenian nobleman and father of Cimon, he is credited with the plan to meet the Persians in the field at Marathon (490 BC). He led an ineffective naval expedition at Paros (489 BC), where he was wounded.

Milton, John (1608–74), English poet and prose writer. Born in London, educated at Cambridge University, he traveled in Europe (1638–39), and served as Latin secretary to the Commonwealth government (1649–60). In 1652 he became blind. His work is characterized by Latinized language and grandeur of imagery. A Puritan, he nevertheless questioned Christian orthodoxy. His greatest works are *L'Allegro* and *Il Penseroso* (both 1632), *Comus* (1634), *Lycidas* (1637), *Areopagitica* (1644), *Paradise Lost* (1667), *Paradise Regained* (1671), and *Samson Agonistes* (1671). △1148, 1854.

Milton, town in E Massachusetts, 6mi (10km) S of Boston; site of St Columban's College and Seminary (1923), Curry College (1879), Capt. Robert Forbes house (1833), Harvard's meteorological observatory. Founded 1636; inc. 1662. Pop. (1970) 27,190.

Mi-lu. *See* Pere David's Deer.

Milwaukee, city and port of entry in SE Wisconsin, on W shore of Lake Michigan; seat of Milwaukee co. The North West Co. est. a fur trading post here 1795; by 1838, the village of Milwaukee was founded; great influx of German refugees 1848–1900 influenced and stimulated political, social, and economic growth; it was scene of racial disorder 1960s. It is site of Marquette University (1881), Alverno College (1857), University of Wisconsin at Milwaukee (1908). Industries: machinery, diesel and gas engines, construction and electrical equipment, beer. Inc. 1839 as village, 1846 as city. Pop. (1970) 717,372.

Mimas, satellite of Saturn. △86.

Mimicry, form of protection, including shape or coloration, developed by an organism to resemble its environment. For example, the viceroy butterfly mimics the coloration of the inedible monarch butterfly. *See also* Protective Coloration.

Mimosa, plants, shrubs, and small trees native to tropical North and South America. They have showy featherlike leaves and heads or spikes of white, pink, or yellow flowers. Family Leguminosae; genus *Mimosa.*

Minamoto. △1046, 1210.

Minaret. △1064, 1204.

Mind. △668–70.

Mindanao, second largest island of the Philippines, in S part of archipelago, NE of Borneo. The terrain is mostly mountainous, heavily indented with gulfs and bays. There is a large Muslim population as evidenced by several mosques. Products: corn, rice, coconuts, timber, coffee, abaca. Area: 36,537sq mi (94,631sq km). Pop. 7,292,691.

Mindoro, island in N central Philippines, S of Luzon and at N extreme of the Sulu Sea; with neighboring islands it constitutes the province of Mindoro. The island has several good harbors, and a mountain range divides it N-S; many streams and rivers drain the mountain region and irrigate fertile central plains (E and W). Farming and mining occupy most of the inhabitants, who are chiefly Visayan and Tagalog. Visited by Spaniards 1570 and besieged by Moros in the 17th and 18th centuries, the island was occupied in WWII by Japan until US forces attacked. Capital is Calapan on N coast. Highest peak is Mt. Halcon, 8,487ft (2,580m). Products: coal, sulfur, gold, coconuts, abaca, rice, fruits, corn. Area: 3,758sq mi (9,733sq km). Pop. 473,940.

Mindszenty, Jozsef Cardinal (1892–1975), Hungarian Roman Catholic prelate and cardinal. An outspoken opponent of totalitarianism, he spent much of his life in jail or self-imposed confinement: he was jailed in 1919 for opposition to Béla Kun's Bolshevik regime; in 1944, for opposing the German-controlled government. In 1948, after his celebrated trial, he was incarcerated by the Communist government. He was released briefly during the 1956 Hungarian revolution but with the return of the Communist power he sought asylum in the US legation in Budapest. In 1971, he left the legation for the first time in 15 years after agreeing to leave Hungary and live in Rome. He became a cardinal in 1946. △1346.

Mineralization, Fossil. △282.

Mineralogy, investigation of naturally occurring inorganic substances found on earth and elsewhere in the solar system. Major subdivisions are crystallography, composition and atomic arrangement in miner-

Milan, Italy

Darius Milhaud

Glenn Miller

John Milton

als; paragenetic mineralogy, associations and order of crystallization of minerals; descriptive mineralogy, physical properties used in identification of minerals; and taxonomic mineralogy, classification of minerals by chemical and crystal type. *See also* Geochemistry; Petrology. △242–44.

Minerals, natural, homogeneous and, with a few exceptions, solid and crystalline materials that form the Earth and make up its rocks. They have a definite chemical composition or range of compositions and are mostly formed through inorganic processes. More than 3,000 minerals have been identified. They are classified on the basis of chemical makeup, crystal structure (which is a reflection of the internal arrangement), and physical properties such as hardness, specific gravity, cleavage, color, and luster. Aggregates of minerals form rocks except in the few cases where a rock is composed of a single mineral. Minerals are economically important as ores (eg, those rich in valuable metals), as gems (eg, diamonds, rubies), as structural materials (eg, calcite and gypsum), in ceramics (feldspars), as chemicals, fertilizers, and as natural pigments. △242–44, 278–80, 1596.

Minerva, in Roman religion, the goddess of handicrafts, the professions, the arts, and, later, war. Commonly identified with the Greek Athena, Minerva was honored in association with Mars in the "Quinquatrus," which lasted five days during the spring. She was venerated throughout the empire. Particular homage was paid by corporations of artisans, flute players, and doctors.

Mines. △1810.

Minesweepers. △1736, 1740.

Ming Dynasty (1368–1644), the last of the great Chinese dynasties before the conquest of China by the Manchus. The Ming brought a period of cultural and philosophical advance during which China influenced many adjacent areas, including Japan. Great seagoing expeditions were launched to the S and W, reaching the E coast of Africa. Peking was laid out in its present form, and the traditional bureaucracy was reinforced. △1110, 1206.

Mingus, Charles (1922–), US jazz bass player, bandleader, and composer, b. Nogales, Ariz. He played in the bands of Red Norvo, Charlie Parker, Stan Getz, and others in the 1950s, then formed his own bands in New York City. He is well known for his highly original experiments and compositions attempting to bring other styles such as atonality and impressionism into jazz.

Miniature Bull Terrier, smaller version of the bull terrier; evolved from small bull terriers and the old toy bull terrier. Average size: up to 14in high (35.5cm) at shoulder; to 20lb (9kg). *See also* Bull Terrier.

Miniature Pinscher, small, deerlike dog (toy group) bred in Germany several centuries ago. It has a flat skull and tapering muzzle; erect ears cropped to a point; compact, wedge-shaped body; straight legs; and high-set, erect, docked tail. The smooth, hard, short coat may be red, black with tan and rust red, or solid brown with rust or yellow. Average size: 10–12in (25.5–30.5cm) high at shoulder; 8–10lb (3.5–4.5kg). *See also* Toy Dogs.

Miniature Schnauzer, German-bred dog classified in terrier group in US, but not in Germany or England. Breed dates from 1899 and was brought to US in 1923, where it has become one of the most popular of all breeds. Its rectangular head has abundant whiskers. Ears are either cropped with pointed tips or uncropped and folded. The short, deep body is set on strong legs. The docked tail is carried erect. Average size: 12–14in (30.5–35.5cm) high at shoulder; 15lb (7kg). *See also* Terrier.

Minimum Wage Law. *See* Fair Labor Standards Act.

Mining, the process of obtaining valuable metallic and nonmetallic materials from the Earth's crust. Included are underground, surface, and underwater methods. Mostly mining involves the physical removal of rock and earth. Petroleum, gas, and some sulfur are extracted by techniques not called mining. Any mining operation comprises four stages: prospecting, exploration, development, and exploitation. Once a valuable deposit has been found and delimited, decisions are made on modes of entry, subsidiary developments and removal techniques. In underground mining, shafts or cross-cut tunnels are dug. Surface mining involves both open-cut and open-pit methods. Underwater mining is accomplished by dredging. △278–82, 1640.

Mining, Coal. *See* Coal Mining.

Mining Bee. △502.

Mink, small semiaquatic mammal of the weasel family with soft, durable, water-repellent hair of high commercial value. Old World minks *(Mustela lutreola)* resemble American minks *(Mustela vison)* but do not have such valuable fur. They have long, slender bodies, short legs, and long, bushy tails. In the wild, mink have dark brown fur with long black outer hair. Ranch mink have been bred to produce skins of silver, pastels, and variations of natural shades. They eat fish, rodents, and birds. Length: 2ft. (61cm); weight: 21lb(1kg). Family Mustelidae.

Minkowski, Hermann (1864–1909), Russian-German mathematician, b. Alexota. Graduating from Königsberg, he held professorships successively there, at Zurich, and at Göttingen. He was deeply interested in the work on relativity of Einstein, a former pupil, and contributed to its mathematical foundations. It was he who first saw the necessity of treating time mathematically as a fourth dimension (Minkowski space-time).

Minneapolis, city and port of entry in SE Minnesota, just SE of St Paul, its twin city, at Falls of Saint Anthony; seat of Hennepin co; largest city in Minnesota. In 1683, Louis Hennepin, a French explorer, visited the falls; Fort Snelling military reservation was est. 1819; Minneapolis was settled 1847; St Anthony was annexed by Minneapolis 1872; the town developed into a lumber center and flour milling area. Minneapolis is the site of University of Minnesota (1851), Augsburg College (1869), Stevens House (1849), and Fort Snelling State Park; processing, distribution, trade, railroad, and grain market center. Industries: milling, farm machinery, food processing, electronic equipment, publishing, printing, fabricated metals, textiles. Inc. 1856. Pop. (1970) 434,400.

Minnesinger, name given to the poet-musicians of medieval Germany. Most of the poems, usually about chivalric love, were sung. Some minnesongs are preserved in medieval manuscripts, such as the Heidelberg collection. Among the best known of the Minnesinger were Walther von der Vogelweide (*c.* 1170–1230) and Oswald von Wolkenstein (*c.* 1377–1445). Minnesinger poems have been sources for many modern operas, novels, and plays.

Minnesota, state in the N central United States, bordered on the N by the provinces of Manitoba and Ontario, Canada.

Land and Economy. The land is level or rolling except in the rugged hills of the NE. Much of it is richly fertile. The N is forested. There are more than 10,000 lakes, some of which are sources of the central branch of the Mississippi River. In the NE, Minnesota borders on Lake Superior. Through the lake port of Duluth pass shipments of iron ore, which is found in the Mesabi Range N of the lake. Taconite, a rock containing low-grade iron, is mined as the higher-grade ores are depleted.

People. In the late 19th century, thousands of immigrants from Europe, chiefly Germans, Swedes, Norwegians, and Finns, came to work the state's forests, farms, and mines. Their descendants comprise a sizable element of the population. About 66% of the people resides in urban areas. The metropolitan area of Minneapolis-St Paul holds about half the population.

Education and Research. There are nearly 60 institutions of higher education. The state-supported University of Minnesota has several campuses. The Mayo Clinic at Rochester, one of the world's greatest medical centers, is a focus of research.

History. French fur traders entered the region in the 17th century and controlled it until 1763, when the part E of the Mississippi River passed to Great Britain by the Treaty ending the Seven Years' War. After the Revolution, this area was ceded to the United States, which acquired the lands W of the river from France by the Louisiana Purchase in 1803. Fort Anthony, now Fort Snelling, was built in 1820 at the junction of the Minnesota and Mississippi rivers; other tracts of land were bought from the Indians, and settlement began. Minnesota Territory was organized in 1849. Minnesota was the first state to respond to President Lincoln's call for troops in the Civil War. The state grew rapidly after the war; its population, which numbered 172,000 in 1860, was 1,310,000 in 1890.

PROFILE

Admitted to Union: May 11, 1858; rank, 32d
US Congressmen: Senate, 2; House of Representatives, 8
Population: 3,805,069 (1970); rank, 19th
Capital: St Paul, 309,828 (1970)
Chief cities: Minneapolis, 434,400; St Paul; Duluth, 100,578
State legislature: Senate, 67; House of Representatives, 134
Area: 84,068sq mi (217,736sq km); rank, 12th
Elevation: Highest, 2,301ft (702m), Eagle Mt; lowest, 602ft (184m), Lake Superior
Industries: (major products): processed foods, machinery, electrical equipment, chemicals, paper
Agriculture (major products): dairy products, oats, corn, soybeans, poultry
Minerals (major): iron ore, taconite, sand, gravel
State nickname: Gopher State, North Star State
State motto: L'Etoile du Nord (Star of the North)
State bird: loon
State flower: showy lady's-slipper
State tree: red (Norway) pine

Minnesota, river in S Minnesota; rises in Big Stone Lake on E South Dakota-W Minnesota line; flows SE then NE to Mississippi River at Mendota. Length: 332mi (535km).

Minnow, subfamily of freshwater fish found in temperate and tropical areas; includes shiners, dace, chubs, tench, and bream. More specifically, the term includes small fish of the genera *Phoxinus* and *Leuciscus.* Length: 1.5–18in (3.8–45.7cm). Family Cyprinidae.

Minoan Architecture, architectural style represented by the elaborate palaces at Knossos and Phaestos in Crete, built *c.* 2200 BC and rebuilt after an earthquake *c.* 1700 BC. The Palace of Minos at Knossos was composed of many small, brightly painted rooms and corridors that led to larger pillared halls, courtyards surrounded by colonnaded walks, and the grand throne room. △964.

Minoan Civilization (*fl. c.*3000–1200 BC), ancient culture of Crete, named for the legendary King Minos. Its capital was Knossus, an impressive city with large palaces. The Minoans traded throughout the Mediterranean region as evidenced by their distinctive "bull-motif" pottery found throughout the area. They were skilled metalworkers. Knossus was destroyed several times by earthquakes and rebuilt. Invasions by Mycenaean Greeks beginning around 1400 led to the gradual disintegration of the Minoan civilization. △964.

Minorca. *See* Menorca.

Minos, two characters in Greek mythology. One, son of Europa and Zeus, a famous law-giver, king of Crete and later consigned to Hades as a judge of human souls. The other, Minos II, his grandson, who exacted annual tribute from Greece in the form of human victims for the man-eating Minotaur that Minos kept in the labyrinth. *See also* Theseus.

Minot, city in NW central North Dakota, on Souris River; seat of Ward co; site of Minot State College (1913). Industries: farm machinery, building materials, meat packing. Settled 1885; inc. 1887. Pop. (1970) 32,290.

Minotaur. △832, 836.

Minsk, capital city of the Belorussian SSR; USSR, also a capital of the Minsk oblast, on Svislach River, 400mi (644km) WSW of Moscow. Known as early as 1067, it was ravaged by Tartars in 1505; annexed by Russia in 1793; partially destroyed by Napoleon 1812; occupied by Germans 1918 and Poles 1919; seized by Germans 1941; retaken by Soviet forces 1944; site of Belorussian State University (1921), Belorussian Academy of Sciences, polytechnic, lumber trade, medical, and teachers' colleges, swamp research institute, modern civic center, state museum, opera and ballet theaters, 17th-century cathedral. Industries: furniture, prefabricated houses, food processing, railroad shops, cement, automobiles, tractors, bicycles, lathes, instruments, machine tools, radios, phonographs, linen, cotton goods, shoes, mirrors, porcelain, leather goods. Pop. 916,000.

Minstrels and Troubadours. △1100.

Minstrel Show, type of US entertainment theater, consisting of songs, dances, and comedy performed by white actors playing caricatures of blacks. The first minstrel troupe, the Virginia Minstrels, appeared in 1843.

Mint, or *Mentha,* a widely distributed group of plants of the Labiatae family including such aromatic herbs as rosemary, lavender, sage and thyme, and such garden flowers as salvia. They are characterized by four-sided stems and opposite, aromatic leaves. The flowers, usually small and clustered at leaf joints or into spikes, always have an upper and lower lip. Mints are grown for ornament, for flavor and aroma, and for use in medicine. △358, 444.

Mint Act (1792), legislation providing for a US mint in Philadelphia, for a decimal system of coinage based on the dollar, and for the use of gold and silver for legal tender at 15-to-1 ratio. It also established the value of the US dollar at 24.75 grains of gold.

Minton, Sherman (1890–1965), US jurist and lawyer, b. Georgetown, Ind. Counselor of the Indiana Public Service Commission (1933–34) and a New Deal Democratic Senator from Indiana (1935–41), he sat on the US Circuit Court of Appeals (1941–49). As associate justice of the US Supreme Court (1949–56), appointed by Pres. Harry S. Truman, he often voted with the conservative bloc of the court.

Minuit, Peter (1580–1638), first governor of New Netherland, b. Netherlands. He bought Manhattan Island (1620) for Dutch West India Co. from Indians for $24 worth of trinkets. He was recalled as governor (1631). He returned (1638) as leader of New Sweden on the Delaware River, founding colonies at Trenton, N.J., and Wilmington, Del.

Minuteman Missiles. △1734.

Minuteman, term used to describe part of the militia formed (1774) by the Massachusetts Provincial Congress. The group was subject to call at a moment's notice, and fought at Lexington and Concord, April 19, 1775.

Miocene Epoch. *See* Tertiary Period.

Miohippus, fossil horse that lived during the Miocene Epoch (28,000,000 years ago). A slim, graceful animal the size of a Shetland Pony, it had three toes on each foot, but only the middle toe touched the ground. Teeth were low-crowned for browsing.

Mira, a variable star of the southern constellation Cetus. Mira is a binary, with a red giant primary, spectral type M6, and a faint B-type companion. Brightness varies over a cycle of about 330 days. △112.

Mirabeau, Honoré Gabriel Riqueti, Comte de (1749–91), French political figure. His extravagance and irresponsible romantic adventures led to several imprisonments, but by 1789 he was accepted as the leader of the Third Estate (bourgeoisie) because of his brilliant oratorical powers and bold defiance of the king. He tempered his opposition to the court after large royal gifts of money and was president of the National Assembly when he died.

Miranda, satellite of Uranus. △88.

Miranda v. Arizona (1966), landmark US Supreme Court decision illustrative of the liberal stance of the court regarding criminal matters during the term of Chief Justice Earl Warren. The court declared that detention by police was inherently coercive and that confessions obtained after police questioning were highly suspect. Expanding the doctrine of *Escobedo* v. *Illinois*, the court set out a stiff code of police conduct that required that an accused be fully informed of his rights and be allowed to contact counsel before questioning. *See also* Escobedo v. Illinois (1964).

Miriam, in the Bible, sister of Moses and Aaron. A prophet, she watched over the baby Moses until he was found in the bullrushes by the Pharaoh's daughter. For criticizing the marriage of Moses to a Cushite woman, she became leprous but was later healed.

Miró, Joan (1893–), Spanish painter and graphic artist. He also designed ceramics and stage sets. His early works were realistic landscapes and portraits that showed fauvist and cubist influences. Later his style became abstract and surrealistic. He is especially known for his imaginative use of highly colored freeforms. △1318.

Mirror, highly polished reflecting surface, usually glass, coated on back or front with silver or aluminum, that is usually plane, spherical, or paraboloid. Image production follows the laws of reflection. Plane mirrors produce a laterally inverted virtual unmagnified image. Spherical mirrors (portions of a spherical surface) are concave (caving inward) or convex (bulging out). A concave mirror converges a narrow beam of light; a convex mirror causes divergence. The image can be right-way-up or inverted, real or virtual depending on the relative position of object and focal point of the spherical mirror; it may also be magnified or reduced in size. A spherical mirror suffers spherical aberration, which is absent in the concave paraboloid mirror, such as used in reflecting telescopes. This shape thus produces a much sharper image. *See also* Aberration; Focal Length; Image, Optical; Reflection. △1518, 1522.

Mirror, Telescope. △42.

Mirror Plane. △1468.

Mishawaka, city in N Indiana, on St Joseph River, adjacent to South Bend; site of Bethel College (1947). Industries: guided missiles, rubber goods, plastics. Settled 1830, inc. 1899. Pop. (1970) 35,517.

Mishima, Yukio (1925–70), Japanese author, b. as Kimitake Hiraoka. His novels, short stories, plays, and essays reveal a conflict between his obsessions with beauty and violence. His early novel *Confessions of a Mask* (1949) is a partially autobiographical study of homosexuality. *The Temple of the Golden Pavilion* (1956) concerns a psychopathic monk who burns down his temple because of its beauty. *The Sailor Who Fell from Grace with the Sea* (1963) is a horror tale. His final work, the tetralogy *The Sea of Fertility* (1970), is an epic of modern Japan. In 1970, with members of Tatenokai ("The Shield Society"), his own army, he seized the commanding general's office of Tokyo's military headquarters and committed ritual suicide.

Mishna, collection of Jewish legal traditions and moral precepts that form the basis of the Talmud. The Mishna was compiled about AD 200 under Rabbi Judah I. It is divided into six parts: laws pertaining to agriculture; laws concerning sabbaths, fasts, and festivals; family laws; civil and criminal laws; laws regarding sacrifices; and laws concerning ceremonial regulations.

Miskolc, city in NE Hungary, on Sajó River; site of 13th-century Gothic church. Industries: iron, steel, vehicles, textiles, furniture, paper, wine, flour, lignite mining, shoes. Pop. 172,952.

Missile, self-propelled flying weapon, powered by rocket, ramjet, or turbojet. *Ballistic* missiles travel in the outer atmosphere and can only be powered by rockets. *Cruise* missiles travel in the lower atmosphere and can utilize jet engines. *Guided* missiles carry self-contained guidance systems or can be controlled by radio from the ground. *Unguided* missiles are freeflying with no control other than initial aim and amount of fuel. △1734, 1746.

Missionary Ridge, Battle of (Nov. 23–25, 1863). In the Chattanooga (Tenn.) Campaign, Union men under Gen. George Thomas attacked a Confederate line at the foot of this ridge and swept right up to the top. The Union victory gave the North control of Chattanooga for the rest of the war.

Mission Indians, a general term applied to those North American Indians who lived adjacent to the Spanish Catholic missions of coastal California about 1769–1823. Numbering about 40,000 persons, they were required to live in and around the missions and perform various labors. The term is unfortunate, since many unrelated peoples were involved; the major tribes included the Chumash, Costanoan, Diegueño, Fernandeño, Gabrielino, Juaneño, and Luiseño.

Mission Style, a style of architecture loosely associated with Spanish colonial missions built in North America from the 16th century. Typical buildings are the *presidio,* military stronghold; *hacendado,* large house of a wealthy landowner; and churches.

Mississauga, city in Ontario, Canada; on W side of Lake Ontario; SW suburb of Toronto. Pop. 156,070.

Mississippi, state in the S central United States, bordered on the S by the Gulf of Mexico and on the W by the Mississippi River. It was one of the six original states of the Confederacy in the Civil War.

Land and Economy. The land slopes from the hills in the NE. Much of it is suitable for agriculture. An E-W strip across the center, known as the Black Prairie, has exceptionally rich soil. Pine forests are widespread. The prinicpal rivers in the state are the Yazoo and its tributaries and the Peral. Mississippi's soils and its warm climate have made agriculture and forestry the mainstays of the economy. Commercial fisheries operate on the Gulf Coast. Since the mid-20th century, efforts to attract and encourage industry have been successful. The extraction and refining of petroleum, found chiefly in the S, is important.

People. The early settlers were English, Scots, and Irish from states along the Atlantic coast. Thousands of blacks were imported to work the cotton plantations; more than 35% of the population now is black. About 45% lives in urban areas.

Education. There are more than 40 institutions of

Mink

St. Paul, Minnesota: state capitol

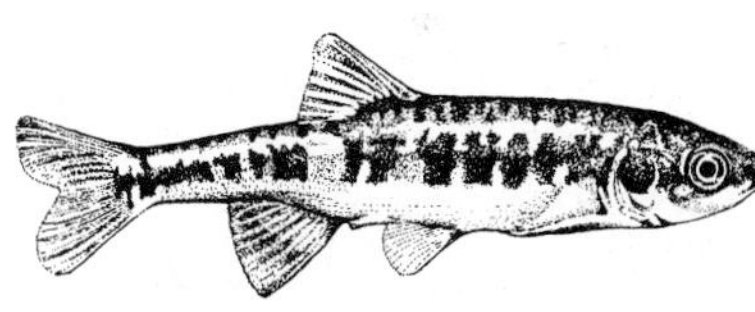
Minnow

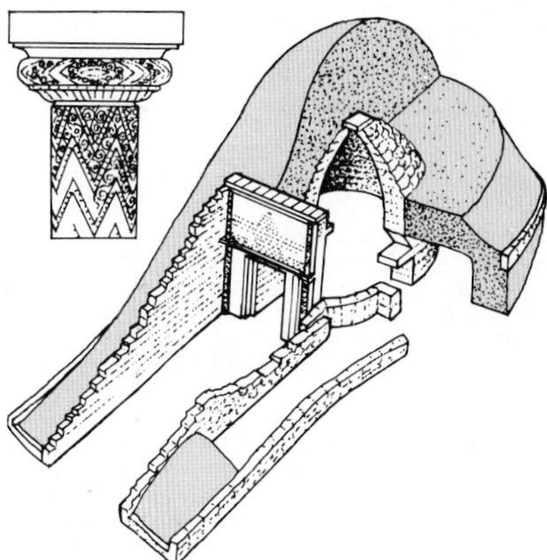
Minoan Architecture: Minoan arch and column

higher education. The University of Mississippi is the principal state-supported establishment.

History. The Sieur de la Salle, voyaging down the Mississippi River, claimed the region for France in 1682, and a French settlement was made on the Gulf coast in 1699. Great Britain received the area in 1763 by the treaty ending the Seven Years' War, but during the American Revolution the Spanish gained actual control and refused to recognize the transfer of the land to the United States by treaty after the war. Spain finally yielded in 1795 and the Territory of Mississippi was organized in 1798. Mississippi seceded from the Union on Jan. 9, 1861, and Jefferson Davis, a US senator from the state, became president of the Confederate States of America. The state was a battleground in the Civil War. Jackson and Meridian were burned by Union forces, and Vicksburg, on the Mississippi, fell on July 4, 1863, after a long siege. It took years to repair the ravages of war and the political turmoil of the Reconstruction era. William Faulkner, Nobel Prize-winning novelist, won his fame writing of life in his native state.

PROFILE

Admitted to Union: Dec. 10, 1817; rank, 20th
US Congressmen: Senate, 2; House of Representatives, 5
Population: 2,216,912 (1970); rank, 29th
Capital: Jackson, 153,968 (1970)
Chief cities: Jackson; Biloxi, 48,486; Meridian, 45,-083
State legislature: Senate, 52; House of Representatives, 122
Area: 47,716sq mi (123,584sq km); rank, 32d
Elevation: Highest, 806ft (246m), Woodall Mt; lowest, sea level
Industries (major products): lumber, wood products, paper, furniture, apparel, chemicals
Agriculture (major products): soybeans, cotton, dairy products, cattle, poultry
Minerals (major): petroleum, natural gas
State nickname: Magnolia State
State motto: Virtute et armis (By valor and arms)
State bird: mockingbird
State flower: magnolia
State tree: magnolia

Mississippi, river in central United States; rises in NW Minnesota, flows SE, forming many state borders, into the Mississippi river delta and the Gulf of Mexico; together with the Missouri River, it forms the longest river system in the world after the Nile and the Amazon. Chief tributaries are the Ohio, Missouri, Arkansas, Tennessee, Wabash, Cumberland, Platte, and Yellowstone. Major economic navigable waterway, it connects with the Great Lakes-St Lawrence Seaway (N) and the Intracoastal Waterway (S); discovered by Hernán DeSoto 1541; explored by Fathers Marquette and Joliet 1673. In 1803 the United States gained possession of river by terms of Louisiana Purchase; a major outlet for mid-continent development in 19th century; Union forces made use of it for many engagements, especially taking of New Orleans (1862) and Vicksburg (1863). Steamboats first traveled on river in 1811. Mark Twain, who served as a riverboat pilot, wrote *Life on the Mississippi* in 1883. By this time the railroads were giving river transportation strong competition. Since 1950s many improvements have been made to river's channels and traffic has increased, especially in moving bulkier freight (petroleum, limestone, chemicals). Springtime flooding as the tributaries bring melting snows and heavy rains to the Mississippi has had disastrous effects in some years. Despite dams on the upper river and floodways and levels at critical points, a year of especially heavy rains such as 1973 can still be ruinous. In the delta area sugar cane is raised, shrimp fisheries are maintained, and sulfur, natural gas, and oil are available in large quantities. Cotton growing is important in the lower valley and freshwater fish are plentiful upstream. From December to mid-March the upper course is frozen over; thick fogs also occur during warm spells of this period. Length: approx. 2,350mi (3,784km).

Mississippian Period. *See* Carboniferous Period.

Mississippi Bubble (October 1720), economic disaster in France caused by the collapse of the Compagnie des Indes (Mississippi Company). In 1717, the Scotsman John Law, backed by Philippe I, regent of France, gained a monopoly over commercial exploitation and colonization of Louisiana. Law claimed that Louisiana was rich in gold and silver; people rushed to invest. By 1719 Law controlled almost all French colonies and the royal bank. By 1720 doubts set in and the speculative bubble burst. Law fled France and his financial empire collapsed. France was left with an enormous national debt. In spite of the financial failure, the scheme had brought many settlers to Louisiana and had resulted in the founding of New Orleans in 1718.

Mississippi v. Johnson (1867), US Supreme Court decision refusing Mississippi a request for an injunction to stop President Andrew Johnson from enforcing the Reconstruction acts of 1867. The court held that executive functions are not subject to judicial restraint.

Missoula, city in W Montana, on Clark Fork of Columbia River; seat of Missoula co; site of Montana State University (1893), and headquarters of Lolo National Forest. Industries: lumbering, flour milling, sugar refining. First settled 1860; inc. 1889. Pop. (1970) 29,437.

Missouri, state in the central United States on the W bank of the Mississippi River.

Land and Economy. In the N and W the land is prairie and rolling hills. In the S, the low ridges of the Ozark Mts run NE-SW. The Missouri River flows W to E across the state to its junction with the Mississippi. The two great rivers have been major influences on the history of the state as lines of travel and transportation. Much of the farming lies N of the Missouri. A major portion of the industry is in the areas of St Louis on the Mississippi in the E and Kansas City on the Missouri in the W. The Ozark region is the center of most mining.

People. Missouri's early settlers came mostly from Kentucky, Tennessee, Virginia, and North Carolina. Germans, Irish, and English moved into the St Louis area in the mid-19th century. More than 90% of the present population was born in the United States. About 70% lives in urban areas.

Education. There are seven institutions of higher education. The first school of journalism in the United States was founded at the state-supported University of Missouri in 1908.

History. The first settlements were made by the French in the mid-18th century. The United States acquired the region from France in the Louisiana Purchase of 1803, and it became a territory in 1812. In the following decades Missouri was the main corridor of the westward migrations. St Louis became a supply center. Wagon trails to Oregon, California, and the Southwest began at St Joseph and Independence. Vivid pictures of these years in Missouri, a border state between the Northern and Southern cultures, appear in the writings of Mark Twain, a native of Hannibal. Missouri had been admitted to the Union without restrictions on slavery, but when the Civil War began sympathies were bitterly divided between the Union and the Confederacy. Guerrilla fighting and several pitched battles ensued before the state was kept in the Union. After the war and into the 20th century the state's development was steady. The two world wars, especially, stimulated growth of St Louis and Kansas City as industrial and distribution centers.

PROFILE

Admitted to Union: Aug. 10, 1821; rank, 24th
US Congressmen: Senate, 2; House of Representatives, 10
Population: 4,677,399 (1970); rank, 13th
Capital: Jefferson City, 32,407 (1970)
Chief cities: St Louis, 622,236; Kansas City, 507,-330; Springfield, 120,096
State legislature: Senate, 34; House of Representatives, 163
Area: 69,686sq mi (180,487sq km); rank, 19th
Elevation: Highest, 1,772ft (540m), Taum Sauk Mt; lowest, 230ft (70m), St Francis River, Dunklin county
Industries (major products): transportation equipment (space capsules, rocket engines, aircraft, automobiles), processed foods, chemicals
Agriculture (major products): hogs, cattle, poultry, soybeans, corn, winter wheat
Minerals (major): lead, barite, limestone
State nickname: "Show Me" State
State motto: Salus populi suprema lex esto ("The welfare of the people shall be the supreme law")
State bird: eastern bluebird
State flower: hawthorn
State tree: dogwood

Missouri, river in central and NW central United States, rises at the confluence of the Jefferson, Madison, and Gallatin rivers in S Montana, flows E to central North Dakota, S across South Dakota, E across Missouri and joins the Mississippi River just N of St Louis. Chief tributary of the Mississippi, and the longest river in the US, third longest in the world after the Nile and the Amazon. Fathers Marquette and Joliet first saw the river in 1683; Meriwether Lewis and William Clark explored parts of it 1804–06. Used by traders, gold seekers, and pioneers as a way to the Northwest. Known as the "Big Muddy" for its great erosion of farm lands along its banks. Flooding is also a serious problem, especially in the spring. Sioux City, Iowa, is head of navigation for river, due to dams upstream. Freezing of river December to March and resulting low water levels interrupt navigation; summer problem of low water is controlled by releasing water from Gavin Point Dam. Length: 2,565mi (4,130km).

Missouri Compromise (1820), US agreement to settle disputes between the states over slavery. With 11 free and 11 slave states, there was a balance in the Senate. When Missouri applied for admission as a slave state (1817), the balance was threatened. Heated disagreements over slavery broke out in Congress (1819). Henry Clay did much to ensure the passage of the agreement, which combined the admission of Maine as a free state with Missouri as a slave state and prohibited slavery in the Louisiana Purchase north of the 36° 30′ line.

Missouri Minnow. *See* Goldfish.

Mistletoe, tropical, evergreen plant semiparasitic on the branches of broad-leaved trees. It has small, thick, yellowish-green leaves. The small, yellowish flowers produce waxy, white, poisonous berries. Among 1,-000 species are *Viscum album* found throughout Europe and Asia and common mistletoe *Phoradendron flavescens* of E United States, usually found on oaks. Family Loranthaceae.

Mistral, Gabriela (1889–1957), Chilean poet. She received the Nobel Prize for literature in 1945. Her poetry exemplifies the trend to simplicity after the exoticism of *Modernismo*. Her main topics included love, her religious faith, and death. The man she loved committed suicide; some of her most moving lyrics were about her relationship with him. Her three main collections of verse were *Desolación* (1922), *Tala* (1938), and *Lagar* (1954).

Mitchel, John (1815–75), Irish revolutionary lawyer and journalist. He called for an Irish rebellion in his publication the *United Irishmen* and was shipped to Van Dieman's Land by the British. He escaped to America (1853), where he continued as a controversial journalist, active in the Irish nationalist movement. He returned to Ireland and was elected to the English parliament in 1875, but was declared ineligible.

Mitchell, Margaret (1900–49), US novelist, b. Atlanta. Her fame rests on an epic novel about the Civil War era, *Gone With the Wind* (1936; Pulitzer Prize 1937), one of the most popular books ever published in the United States. *See also* Gone With the Wind.

Mitchell, Maria (1818–89), US astronomer, educator, b. Nantucket Island, Mass. While conducting a special study of sunspots and nebula, she discovered a new comet in 1847. She was the first woman elected to American Academy of Arts and Sciences (1848) and was the first professor of astronomy at Vassar College (1865–88).

Mitchell, William ("Billy") (1879–1936), US military officer, b. France. He helped form the American Expeditionary Force aviation program in World War I and led air forces at the battles of St Mihiel and the Meuse-Argonne. He attacked the navy as vulnerable to air attack in *Our Air Force* (1921) and *Winged Defense* (1925). He was court-martialed in 1925 for his continued attacks.

Mitchell, Mount, peak in W North Carolina, in Black Mts; highest peak E of Mississippi River, 6,684ft (2,039m).

Mite, variously colored arthropod found worldwide as a parasite on plants and animals. The larva has three pairs of legs; the adult has four pairs and the head and abdomen are fused. Length: 0.02–0.1in (0.5–3mm). Class Arachnida; order Acarina. *See also* Chigger; Red Spider. △484.

Miter Shell. △482.

Mithra, or **Mitra,** god of India and Persia from ancient times, and the chief religious figure of Persia after the 6th century BC. A god of both rain and Sun, who had created life by spilling the blood of the sacred bull, Mithra came to represent all that was good in a cult that spread throughout Europe. Mithraism was gradually replaced by Christianity after the 3rd century AD. △838, 984.

Mithridates VI Eupator Dionysus (*c.*131–63 BC), last of the six kings of Pontus called Mithridates. As a youth he fled from his mother and seized Sinope. He imprisoned his mother, murdered his brother, wed his sister and extended his kingdom. A brave and clever leader, he occupied Lesser Armenia, Colchis, E Pontus, and much of Greece, engaging in the Mithradatic Wars against Rome. Finally defeated, he fled to Colchis and the Crimea, tried to raise another army and suffered a revolt led by his son Pharnaces. He ordered himself killed by a guard. △1018.

Mithridatic Wars, campaigns of expansion led by Mithridates VI, king of Pontus, against the Romans. The First Mithridatic War was brought on by Micomedes' attempts to invade Pontus (88–84 BC). As a result Mithridates took control of most of Asia Minor and much of Greece. Sulla defeated him in Greece and during the Second Mithridatic War (83–81) he repulsed Sulla's attempts to raid the Pontic coast. In the Third Mithridatic War (74–63), he was defeated by Lucullus, expelled from Pontus, and driven into the Crimea by Pompey.

Mitla, a Central American archeological site, probably 13th-century, near Oaxaca City, Mexico, famous for the unmatched mosaic work displayed on several buildings. Stone bands and panels of striking geometric patterns in high and low relief were precision-set into the rubble mass of the walls. Mitla succeeded Monte Albán as the Zapotec capital; by the time of the Spanish conquest, Mixtec influence predominated. The buildings were arranged in quadrangles. Tombs complemented the visible architecture.

Mitochondrion, small body found in the cytoplasm of most cells, containing enzymes and other agents necessary for metabolism. △412.

Mitosis, nuclear division of a cell resulting in two identical cells. This division includes five phases: interphase—DNA and chromosomes self-duplicate; prophase—chromosomes coil, centrioles start separating, and astral rays and spindles form; metaphase—doubled chromosomes are along cell's equatorial plate, centrioles move to opposite sides, and nuclear membrane disappears; anaphase—doubled chromosomes separate and move apart and cytoplasmic division starts; telophase—chromosomes uncoil, nuclear membrane forms, spindle and astral rays disappear, and cytoplasmic division is completed, resulting in two new cells identical to the original cell. △424.

Mixosaurus. △572.

Mixtec, Indian civilization centered in the province of Oaxaca, Mexico. At the time of the Spanish conquest, the Mixtec invasion and conquest of the Zapotec was underway. The Mixtec numbered 275,000 at the beginning of the 16th century; epidemics and forced migrations drastically reduced their number.

Mixture, in chemistry, any material that is made up of several components each of which retains its specific identity no matter in what proportion or how closely the components are mixed. *See also* Solution. △1568.

Mizar. △40.

MKS System, system of units based on the meter, the kilogram, and the second. *See* Weights and Measures.

Mnemonic Device, an aid to memory. Strategies designed to improve memory include rhymes, pegword systems, and visual imagery. For example, if a list of items is to be memorized, rhymed associations with the items will aid memory; eg, one is a bun, two is a shoe, three is a tree, etc. The numbers are peg words (previously memorized) that easily suggest the other words. A third set of items may be attached by visualizing an image of the first item in a bun, the second in a shoe, etc. *See also* Memory. △670.

Moa, extinct flightless ostrichlike bird of New Zealand thought to have been hunted out by the Maori tribe for food. They had small heads, variously colored downy feathers, and strong legs. Feeding on roots and shoots, they nested on ground. Height: to 12ft (3.6m). Order: Dinornithiformes.

Mobile, commercial and seaport city in SW Alabama, at the mouth of Mobile River, seat of Mobile co; site of US Air Force base; only seaport in state. Exports: cotton, coal, agricultural and forest products. Industries: textiles, paper, lumber, aluminum, shipbuilding. Settled 1711 by France, occupied 1813 by United States; inc. 1819. Pop. (1970) 190,026.

Mobile, a form of sculpture developed by Alexander Calder in the early 1930s and named by Marcel Duchamps. A mobile consists of a series of shapes (representational or abstract) cut from metal, wood, or plastic and connected by wires so that the parts and whole revolve freely when suspended in space. This form moves from the traditional ideas of sculpture as static toward objects in motion. △1418.

Möbius Strip. △1470.

Mobutu Sese Seko (1930–), president of Zaire and military commander, b. Joseph-Désiré Mobutu. He worked for Congolese (Zairean) independence with Patrice Lumumba, whom he later imprisoned and killed (1960–61) when he assumed control of the army. He became chief of state after toppling Joseph Kasavubu in 1965. His domestic policies included Africanization and economic development; in foreign affairs he sought to make Zaire a leader of black African nations.

Moby-Dick (1851), novel by Herman Melville. Now considered Melville's masterpiece, it was largely ignored until 70 years after its publication. Narrated by Ishmael, a wanderer, the plot line is deceptively simple. In the 1840s, Ahab, the one-legged captain of the whaling ship *Pequod,* sails from New Bedford across the Pacific to search out and destroy the white whale, Moby-Dick, which had maimed him. After cutting himself off from normal human contacts and establishing his power over the crew by various dramatic means, he finds Moby-Dick, but the whale destroys the *Pequod* with its captain and all the crew, except Ishmael, who survives floating on a coffin to be rescued by the *Rachel.* Melville's rich, ripe, rolling, rhetorical style, jammed with factual detail about whaling and sailing, and his complex development of symbolism, charges the massive novel with metaphysical and sociological overtones and undertones and gives it epic grandeur.

Mocambique. *See* Mozambique.

Mochica, a prehistoric cultural period of northern Peru, *c.*200 BC–AD 600, sometimes called "Early Chimú." Named for their home area in the Moche Valley, these people were famous for their magnificent pottery, large quantities of which have survived.

Mock Epic, or mock heroic, literary work that burlesques or satirizes the grand epic style. Famous examples are *The Rape of the Lock* (1714) by Alexander Pope, in which trivial events are described in highly exalted language; *Dunciad* (1728–43), also by Pope, a more serious satirical poem; and "Ode on the Death of a Favourite Cat" (1747) by Thomas Gray.

Mockingbird, any of a group of New World songbirds, known for their beautiful song. The common mockingbird *(Mimus polyglottos)* of the United States is typical of the group—about 10.5in (27cm) long, ashy above with brownish wings and tail marked with white. Perched high, it spreads its wings and tail and utters up to 20 songs. Males help build bulky, open, cup-shaped nests of grass and twigs for pale greenish-blue, brown-spotted eggs. An isolated group (genus *Nesomimus*) occurs on the Galapagos Islands.

Mock Sun. *See* Sun Dog.

Mode, in statistics, a measure of central tendency that is computed by determining the item that occurs most frequently in a data set. It is a quick measure of central tendency, but is not as commonly used as the median or mean.

Model, Mathematical. *See* Mathematical Model.

Models, Econometric, are composed of a number of mathematical equations (estimated, based on previous economic data), each representing a particular sector or subsector of the economy. Econometric models are used to simulate the operation of the economic system. Econometric models, unlike input-output models, are dynamic in nature. They allow time movements to occur and provide for interaction between the various sectors of the economy. *See also* Input-Output Model. △936.

Modena, city in N Italy, 207mi (333km) NNW of Rome; capital of Modena prov. A Roman colony 183 BC; it passed to House of Este 1288; made a duchy 1452; conquered by France 1796; joined kingdom of Italy 1860; site of 11th-century Romanesque cathedral, 17th-century ducal palace, 14th-century campanile, Palazzo dei Musei, university (1175). Industries: automobiles, machine tools, metalworking. Pop. 164,811.

Moderator. △1482, 1638.

Modern Architecture. △1298, 1322.

Modern Dance, dance style that began to develop in the early part of the 20th century as a protest against classical ballet and the overly personal interpretive dance of Isadora Duncan. In Europe and the United States, such innovators as Rudolph van Laban, Ruth St Denis, and Ted Shawn attempted to make dance a viable contemporary art form. Rather than merely to entertain, their aim was to communicate

Mississippi River: Baton Rouge, Louisiana

Jefferson City, Missouri: state capitol

Mistletoe

Billy Mitchell

with their audience and to heighten their viewers' awareness of life's experience. △1368.

Modernism, movement in the Roman Catholic church during the late 19th and early 20th centuries to adapt Catholic beliefs to developments in modern science, philosophy, and history. At first tolerated by Pope Leo XIII, the movement wanted the church to view the Bible more critically according to limitations of Biblical authors and to adopt a philosophy of action rather than doctrine. The modernists, however, who were centered at the Institut Catholique, Paris, were condemned by Pius X in 1907; all suspect clerics were required to take an anti-modernist oath.

Modesto, city in central California, 24mi (39km) SE of Stockton; seat of Stanislaus co; site of one of the world's largest wineries and canneries. Industries: food processing, paper products, fruit and nut orchards. Inc. 1884. Pop. (1970) 61,712.

Modigliani, Amedeo (1884–1920), Italian painter and sculptor. A few of his early works were landscapes, but the majority of his paintings deal with female portraits and nudes. Showing the influence of the Cubist style, his females usually have elongated limbs, small mouths, and eyes with overly large pupils. As a sculptor, he did numerous heads that show the influence of primitive African art in their vertically elongated style. *See also* Cubism.

Modoc, North American Indian tribe closely related to the Klamath. They inhabited N California. From an early population of 500, they declined to 334 members living on the Klamath Reservation in Oregon. They are noted for their defense against the US Army during the Lava Beds War of 1872–73.

Modulation, process of varying the characteristics of one wave system in accordance with the characteristics of another wave system. In amplitude modulation, the amplitude of a high-frequency (radio) carrier wave is varied in accordance with the frequency of a current generated by a sound wave. This enables the sound wave to be broadcast and, in fact, all forms of broadcasting rely on modulation. For static-free short-range broadcasting, frequency modulation is used. In this it is the frequency of the carrier wave that is modulated.

Moeritherium. △574.

Mogadisho, capital city and chief port of Somalia, E Africa, on the Indian Ocean, along Benadir coast. Taken 1871 by sultan of Zanzibar, it was leased (1892), then sold (1905) to Italy; occupied by the British 1941; commercial center connected to Gulf of Aden by road; site of 13th-century mosques, native fort restored 1933–34, museum, airfield. Industries: oilseed pressing, lumbering. Pop. 200,000.

Mogul, or **Mughal, Empire** (1526–1857), Indian domain founded by Babur, a Muslim descendant of both Tamerlane and Genghis Khan, in 1526 when he conquered Delhi and Agra. Under **Akbar** (*r.* 1556–1605), Babur's grandson, the empire was at its height, extending from Afghanistan to the Bay of Bengal, from Gujarat in the south to northern Deccan. Akbar's grandson **Shah Jahan** (*r.* 1629–58) built many splendid buildings, including the Taj Mahal. Under **Aurungzeb** (*r.* 1658–1707), a Muslim fanatic, there were many Hindu revolts that weakened the empire. The empire began to break up under **Muhammed Shah** (*r.* 1719–48). After 1803 the Mogul emperors were merely puppets of the British. In 1857 the last emperor, Bahadur Shah, was forced to abdicate because of his part in the Indian Mutiny. △1202–1204.

Mohair, a fiber similar to wool, obtained from the angora goat and used for knitting yarns. Produced only in Asia Minor for thousands of years, mohair became important in European textile manufacture in the 19th century. Angora goats are now raised in the United States and S Africa.

Mohammed (*c.* 570–632), Arab founder of Islam. Muslims believe him to have been the last and most perfect messenger of God, following Adam, Abraham, Moses, and Jesus. He was a wealthy merchant in Mecca. At the age of 40 he had a vision in a cave of Mt Hira near Mecca that commanded him to preach. His subsequent visions and teachings are recorded in the Koran, the holy scripture of Islam. His new religion alienated the leaders of Mecca. In 622 to escape an assassination attempt he fled to Yathrib (subsequently renamed Medina, "City of the Prophet"). Muslims date their years from this flight, the Hegira. Mohammed ruled Medina as a theocratic state. He defeated an attack from Mecca in 624 and conquered Mecca in 630. At the time of his death, his religion controlled Arabia and was making inroads in Syria and Iraq. *See also* Islam. △1058.

Mohammed II (1429–81), Ottoman sultan (1451–81), also known as Mohammed the Conqueror. In 1453 he captured Constantinople, ending the Byzantine Empire and firmly establishing the Ottoman Empire. He moved his capital from Adrianople to Constantinople and made it a cosmopolitan city by repopulating it with Muslims, Christians, and Jews from conquered territories. He conquered most of the Balkans (1456–58), but was stopped at Belgrade. △1056, 1108.

Mohammedanism, an archaic name for Islam, the religion founded by Mohammed in the 7th century. Muslims rejected the term Mohammedanism because it might suggest that Mohammed is deified. *See also* Islam. △846, 1058.

Mohammed Reza Pahlevi (1919–), shah of Iran (1941–). He succeeded his father, who was deposed by the British and Soviets because of his pro-German leanings. In 1953 he fled Iran after a clash with the then powerful premier Mohammed Mussadegh. He was quickly restored to power with US assistance. He remained under foreign domination until the early 1960s when steadily increasing oil revenues allowed him to plot an independent course. In 1963 he announced his "White Revolution" program of land redistribution, educational improvement, and female emancipation. He has in recent years attempted to build up Iran as the most important military power of the Near East, independent of US, Soviet, or Arab domination. The Iranian people have experienced considerable material improvement but the shah has allowed little political liberalization.

Mohave, or **Mojave,** a Yuman-speaking tribe of North American Indians once numbering about 3,000 persons living along both sides of the middle Colorado River. Today about 850 occupy the Colorado River Reservation in Arizona.

Mohawk, one of the major divisions of the League of the Iroquois. Most of the 1,500 Mohawk today live on the Grand River Reserve near the east end of Lake Ontario, Canada.

Mohegan, an important tribe of North American Indians of the Algonkin language family formerly occupying the Thames River area of Connecticut. They were the major tribe of the region following the end of King Philip's War; their most famous chief was Uncas. Once numbering 2,200, about 20 Mohegan people live with the Pequot near Norwich, Conn., today.

Mohenjo Daro, one of the main city centers of the Indus Valley civilization (about 2500 to 1500 BC). Its remains (in modern Pakistan) show that its inhabitants built large granaries, employed a system of writing, used standard weights and measures, traded extensively, constructed carts and boats, and were competent plumbers and metalworkers.

Mohican, or **Mahican,** an Algonkin-speaking tribe of North American Indians formerly inhabiting the upper Hudson River in New York, east to the Housatonic River in Connecticut. Once numbering about 3,000 persons, they joined the Stockbridge in 1736, and the surviving 525 today occupy the Stockbridge-Munsee reservation in Wisconsin. They have become well known from J.F. Cooper's *The Last of the Mohicans.*

Moho, the seismic discontinuity layer at the base of Earth's crust. The layer was discovered by Yugoslavian geophysicist Andrija in 1909 when the velocity of seismic waves was measured and found to be different in a number of sites at varying distances from an earthquake epicenter. The moho layer is about 6mi (10km) from the surface in ocean regions and 20mi (32km) from the surface under land masses. The moho is explained by a difference in density of rocks as they change from crust to mantle and therefore act as deflectors of seismic waves. *See also* Core, Earth; Seismology. △166.

Moh's Hardness Scale. *See* Hardness Scale.

Moiety. △882.

Moiseyev, Igor (1906–), Russian ballet dancer and choreographer. He danced with the Bolshoi Theater in the 1920s and 30s and in 1936 organized the Moiseyev Dance Company, which has toured the world. He received a Lenin Prize in 1967.

Moism, school of Chinese philosophy of Mo tzu and his followers (*fl.* 5th century BC). With representatives in all parts of China, the Moists were the only one of the "hundred schools" to have had group organization and regular meetings. Adhering to utilitarian doctrines, Moism advocated promotion of the general welfare and universal love. After the 1st century BC there are no longer any references in Chinese literature to Moism as an existent body of opinion. *See also* Hundred Schools; Mo tzu.

Mojave Desert, arid region with low, barren mountains in S California; surrounded by mountain ranges (N and W), borders the Colorado Desert (SE); formed by volcanic eruptions and deposits from the Colorado River; site of Death Valley National Monument; many mineral deposits and small streams. Area: approx 15,000sq mi (38,850sq km).

Moji. *See* Kitakyushu.

Molal Solution, solution containing one gram molecular weight of the desired species in one kilogram of solvent. When applied to electrolytes in solution, this measure refers to the concentration of undissociated substances, and has given rise to the concentration concept of molality.

Molar, one of the back teeth of mammals, adapted for grinding and chewing food. Several cusps—the points or ridges on the top surface—occlude with counterparts on the opposing molar. Herbivores have sharp cusps arranged in triangular shearing patterns for slicing. In man there are 3 permanent molars on each side of each jaw, a total of 12. *See also* Tooth.

Molarity, measure of concentration of a particular component in a solution, usually designated M. There are 6.02×10^{23} (Avogadro's number) molecules in a mole. Concentration may either be expressed as, for example, 1.2×10^{23} molecules per liter or, more conveniently, 0.2 moles per liter of solution. The concentration of such a solution is 0.2 M.

Molasses Act, or **Sugar Act** (1733), law passed by Parliament that charged a prohibitory duty on foreign molasses and sugar entering the English colonies. The act protected British West Indies sugar growers and was resented by American colonists.

Mold, any of a wide variety of tiny fungi that forms furry growths on food, leather, textiles, and other organic materials in moist environments. Some molds, including *Asperigillum* and *Penicillium,* are important in cheese-making or as sources of antibiotics and some organic chemicals. Like other fungi, molds cannot make their own food by photosynthesis. They are generally saprophytes that obtain their food by assisting in the decay of the organic materials on which they grow. The "body" of a mold, called the mycelium, consists of a network of fine filaments through which nutrients are absorbed. Molds reproduce by means of spores produced in sporecases or other reproductive structures that give molds their characteristic black, blue, green, orange, or red colors. Most familiar molds are members of the orders Mucorales and Eurotiales. △426.

Mold, Metal, mold for casting metal, usually made of sand or clay. This is packed over the face of the pattern that forms the cavity for the casting. The mold must be strong, resisting pressure of the hot, liquid metal, and permeable to allow gases to escape the cavity. It must also resist fusion with the metal that is poured in through special channels. *See also* Foundry. △1588.

Moldavia, historic region in E Romania, N of E Wallachia, E of Transylvania; included Bessarabia and Bukovina; conquered by Greeks, Romans, and Bulgars, under Mongol rule during 13th century; became a dominion of the Ottoman Empire 1504. A former Danubian principality founded 14th century, it merged with Wallachia 1861 to create Romania. At present the largest part is the Moldavian Soviet Socialist Republic, a constituent of USSR. Products: grain, livestock, grapes. Industries: lumbering, petroleum extraction. Area: approx. 14,690sq mi (38,047sq km).

Moldavia (Moldavian Soviet Socialist Republic or **Moldavskaja Sovetskaja Socialističeskaja Respublika),** constituent republic of the USSR, bounded N, E, and S by Ukrainian republic and W by Romania; occupies the central portion of former Bessarabia. After 1940 Soviet annexation of Bessarabia, the Moldavian autonomous republic, except for its predominantly Ukrainian districts, joined central Bessarabia to form Moldavian republic. It was held by Germans and Romanians 1941–44. The main cities are Kishinev (capital), Belicy, Bendery, Tiraspol. The main navigable river is the Dniester. Industries: canning (Tiraspol), wine, distilling, flour milling, sugar refining, tobacco processing. Exports: grapes, wine, fruit, nuts, hides, wheat, canned goods. Area: 13,012sq mi (33,701sq km). Pop. 3,752,000.

Mole, burrowing short-furred mammal of Eurasia and North America. About the size of a small rat, most moles have short tails and spadelike forefeet adapted for digging. Both the common European mole and the common eastern mole of North America live mostly underground and feed largely on earthworms and insects. Family Talpidae. △540.

Mole, unit of substance (symbol mol) defined as the amount of substance containing the same number of entities (atoms, ions, etc) as there are atoms in 0.012 kilogram of carbon-12. The mass of 1 mole of a compound is its gram molecular weight. *See also* Physical Units.

Mole Cricket, brown insect found worldwide. It has broad, spade-shaped front legs for burrowing in moist places. Although it spends most of its life underground, it is a strong flier. Length: over 1in (25mm). Family Gryllidae.

Molecular Biology, biological study of the chemical and physical makeup of molecules comprising living organisms. A major area of study is genes and their components and functions in heredity, evolution, and the makeup of living organisms, particularly humans. 412.

Molecular Model, a simple type of molecular model is made by joining small colored balls, representing atoms, by stiff metal springs, representing single bonds. The balls have holes, into which the springs fit, arranged to give possible spatial dispositions of bonds. More sophisticated models include different sizes of atom and allow scale models of molecules to be built. Molecular models are invaluable aids, not only in visualizing shapes of molecules but also in indicating "strain" in bonds and possible conformations that the molecule may adopt in reaction. △ 1562.

Molecular Weight, or relative molecular mass, sum of the atomic weights of all the atoms in a molecule. It is thus the average mass per molecule of a specified isotopic composition of a substance to 1/12 of the mass of an atom of carbon-12. The molecular weights of the reactants must be known in order to make quantitative calculations about a chemical reaction. △1484, 1568.

Molecule, smallest particle of a substance capable of independent existence and of exhibiting the characteristic properties of that substance. Molecules consist of two or more atoms held together by chemical bonds. For example, water molecules consist of two atoms of hydrogen bonded to one atom of oxygen (H_2O). △1484, 1502, 1556, 1558.

Molière (1622–73), pseud. of Jean Baptiste Poquelin, French playwright. Trained as a lawyer, he abandoned the law and joined an amateur dramatic group. His first important work was *L'Étourdi (The Blunderer),* performed at Lyons in 1655. An accurate observer of contemporary manners and types, he is remembered principally for his comedies of character, such as *The School for Wives* (1622), *Tartuffe* (1664), *The Misanthrope* (1666), and *The Imaginary Invalid* (1673). He wrote other kinds of plays as well: farce, as *The Imaginary Cuckold* (1660); comedy ballet, such as *The Bores* (1661); and spectacular "machine plays," eg, *Amphitryon* (1668) and *Psyche* (1671). Some of the plays are in verse, others in prose. He directed his own plays and often played the leading role himself. Although his plays ridiculed customs and character types, it was done without bitterness. △ 1172.

Molina, Luis de (1535–1600), Spanish theologian. After joining the Jesuits (1553), Molina taught at Evora, Portugal. His *Free Will as Gratuitous Gift* (1588) taught, in effect, that God bestows grace on those whose supplication is sincere. His notion that God is able to foresee just who will make good use of free will gave rise to the "Molinist Controversy."

Moline, city in NW Illinois, on Mississippi River; comprises Quad Cities region along with Rock Island and East Moline, Ill., and Davenport, Iowa; site of Black Hawk College (1946); headquarters of John Deere corporation since 1847. Industries: farm machinery, tools, ventilators. Settled 1847; inc. 1848. Pop. (1970) 46,237.

Mollet, Guy (1905–75), French political figure. A leader of the resistance during World War II, he was elected secretary-general of the Socialist party in 1946. As premier in 1956 he shared responsibility for the Suez Crisis. His failure to resolve the Algerian problem paved the way for Charles de Gaulle's return to power. He was de Gaulle's secretary of state (1958–59).

Mollusk, any of a large group of invertebrate animals of some 100,000 living species in the phylum Mollusca. Included are the familiar snails, clams, and squids, and a host of less well-known forms. Originally marine, the group now has representation in the oceans, fresh water, and on land. There are six classes: the primitive gastroverms, chitons, univalves (snails), bivalves (clams, etc), tusk shells, and cephalopods (squids, etc). The mollusk body is divided into three regions: the head, the foot, and the visceral mass. Associated with the body is a thin sheet of tissue called the mantle, which secretes the limy shell typical of most mollusks. The head is well developed only in snails and in the cephalopods, which have eyes, tentacles, and a well-formed mouth. The foot is used for crawling in univalves and for digging in bivalves. The visceral mass contains the internal organs of circulation (blood vessels and heart), respiration (gills), excretion (kidney), digestion (stomach and intestine), and reproduction (gonads). The sexes are usually separate but there are many hermaphroditic species. In most, the fertilized egg goes through several larval stages before attaining the adult form. △ 476–82.

Molly Maguires, a secret organization formed in 1862 by anthracite coal miners in Pennsylvania. Identified with the Ancient Order of Hibernians, an anti-landlord order in Ireland, they used terrorist tactics in the mines until 1876, when the group was infiltrated by a Pinkerton detective, and 24 members were arrested, tried, and convicted. Ten members were hanged for murder, the others jailed. The order was disbanded.

Molotov, Vyacheslav M(ikhailovich) (1890–), Soviet political figure. He changed his name from Skriabin to Molotov ("hammer") to escape the tsarist police. A Bolshevik since 1906, he joined the Communist party Central Committee in 1926 and the Politburo in 1949. A loyal ally and second in prestige to Stalin as chairman of the Council of the People's Commissars (1930–41), he was active in the purges of the 1930s. He served as foreign minister (1939–49, 1953–56), generally taking a hard line against the West. In 1957 he was expelled from the Central Committee and sent as ambassador to the Mongolian People's Republic as a result of Khrushchev's rise to power. In 1960–61 he represented the USSR at the International Atomic Energy Agency in Vienna. In 1964 he was expelled from the Communist party. △ 1310, 1342.

Molting, shedding and replacement of the outer covering, such as feathers, exoskeleton, skin, and hair. It occurs in birds, reptiles, and insects to replace old coverings or allow for growth. △522.

Moltke, Helmuth Joannes Ludwig, Graf von (1848–1916), German general. He was the nephew of Field Marshal von Moltke. He became chief of the German general staff in 1906 and planned Germany's World War I strategy, modifying the Schlieffen plan. In 1914 he was replaced by General von Falkenhayn. *See also* Schlieffen, Alfred.

Moltke, Helmuth Karl Bernhard, Graf von (1800–91), Prussian field marshal. He entered the Prussian army in 1822 and joined the general staff in 1833. From 1858 until he resigned in 1888, he was head of the general staff. He reorganized the army and was the strategist of Prussia's war against Denmark (1864), the Austro-Prussian War (1866), and the Franco-Prussian War (1870–71). △1250.

Moluccas (Spice Islands, Maluku), island group in E Indonesia; constitutes a province of Indonesia; Ambon is the capital; includes larger islands of Halmahera, Ceram, Buru; island groups of Sula, Batjan, Obi, Kai, Aru, Tanimbar, Banda, Babar, Leti; smaller islands of Ambon, Ternate, Tidore. Originally explored by Magellan (early 16th century), later settled by Portuguese; taken by Dutch *c.* 1605–21 to monopolize spice trade; occupied by British 1810–14 but returned to Dutch control. Industries: spices, copra, forest products, sago. Area: 32,307sq mi (83,675sq km). Pop. 995,000.

Molybdenite, a sulfide mineral, molybdenum sulfide (MoS_2). Major ore of molybdenum, found in pegmatites, igneous and metamorphic rocks. Hexagonal system tabular prisms, flakes, and fine granules. Lead-gray, metallic luster with layers flexible. Hardness 1–1.5; sp gr 4.7.

Molybdenum, metallic element (symbol Mo) of the second transition series, first identified and isolated in 1778. Chief ores are molybdenite (sulfide) and wulfenite (lead molybdate). It is used in alloy steels and molybdenum compounds are used as catalysts and

Amedeo Modigliani: portrait in oil

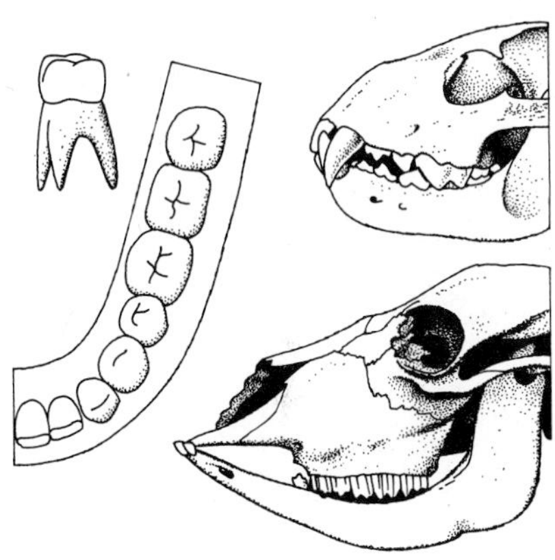

Molars

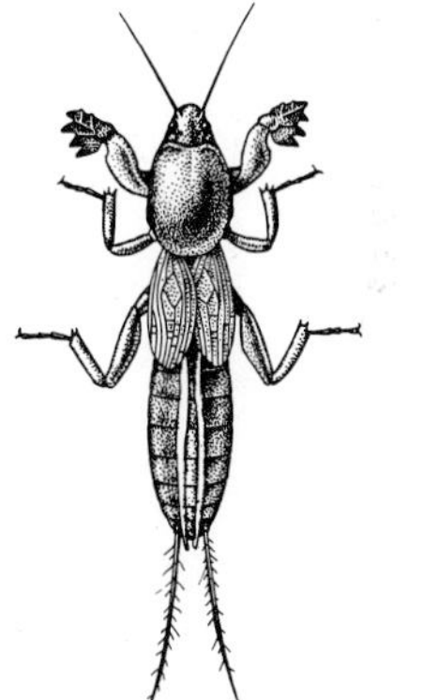

Mole cricket

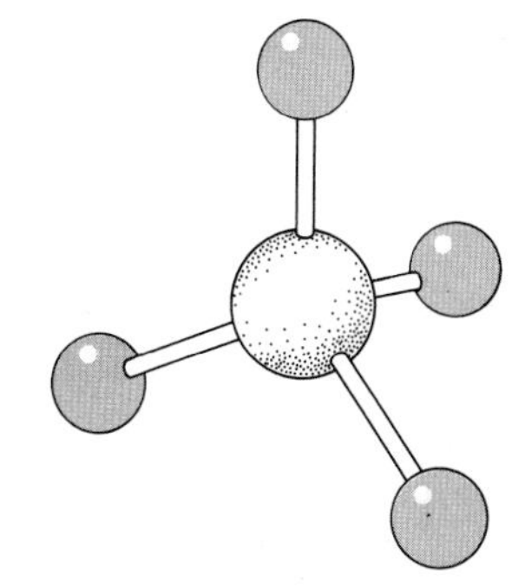

Molecule

lubricants. It is an essential trace element for plant growth. Properties: at. no. 42; at. wt. 95.94; sp gr 10.22; melt. pt. 4,730°F (2,610°C); boil pt. 10,040°F (5,560°C); most stable isotope Mo^{98} (23.78%). *See also* Transition Elements. △1552–54.

Mombasa, port and capital city of Mombasa Island in Kenya, in the Indian Ocean; includes portions of mainland, to which it is connected by a causeway; import, commercial, and industrial center. A center for Arab trade in slaves and ivory 8th–16th centuries, the city was burned several times by Portuguese; passed from Portuguese to Arabs 1698; taken by Zanzibar in the 19th century; passed 1887 to Great Britain; site of remains of Portuguese Fort Jesus (1593–94). Exports: coffee, fruit, grains. Industries: glass, processed foods, cement, soap, aluminum products, lime. Pop. 234,000.

Momentum, the product of the mass and velocity of a body. The principle that the total momentum of any system of bodies is conserved (remains constant) at all times, even during collisions, is one of the great fundamental laws of physics, holding an equivalent position to the law of the conservation of mass-energy. *See also* Angular Momentum. △1492.

Monaco, Lorenzo. △1134.

Monaco, sovereign principality in Europe, on the Mediterranean Sea (S), bounded on all other sides by France; near Italy. Major geographical regions are Monaco-Ville, the capital, a high rocky promontory that extends into the sea; La Condamine, the port area; and Monte Carlo, the residential and resort area, with its casino district. Gambling contributes directly only about 4% of the nation's income, but it attracts tourists whose spending amounts to 55%. Industry is responsible for 25%–30% of the nation's income. There are no personal or corporate income taxes; the government is supported by excise taxes, stamp sales, and taxes on alcohol and tobacco. There is a customs union with France. Native Monegasques are outnumbered eight to one by other nationalities, chiefly French, who comprise approx. 50% of the population. Originally settled by the Phoenicians, it later fell under Roman rule and was Christianized about AD 100. It passed through several rulers before coming under the Grimaldi family of Genoa in the 13th century. It is now ruled by descendants of a French branch of the family that assumed the name Grimaldi. France assumed protection of Monaco in 1860 and should the male Grimaldi line die out, Monaco would become an autonomous state under France. Monaco adopted a constitution in 1911 establishing a ruling princedom and an appointed council, which is now elected. The marriage of Prince Rainier to US movie actress Grace Kelly (1956) received worldwide attention.

PROFILE

Official name: Monaco
Area: approx. 370 acres (150 hectares)
Population: 23,614
Chief cities: Monaco-Ville (capital); Monte Carlo
Government: Hereditary monarch with elected National Assembly
Religion: Roman Catholic
Language: French
Monetary unit: Franc

Monad, in Greek usage, the number one; extended in philosophy to apply to any unit. The 17th-century German philosopher Gottfried Leibniz applied the term to autonomous centers of force that, he felt, comprise the fundamental metaphysical reality of which the universe is composed. These monads, or souls, do not interact, but are organized to correspond in a "pre-established harmony." They are also indestructible, indivisible, and eternal. *See also* Pre-established Harmony.

Monarch Butterfly, or milkweed butterfly, a large butterfly that has brownish-orange wings with black veins and borders. Its larva feeds on milkweed, giving it a taste disliked by birds. The viceroy butterfly mimics coloration of the monarch. Species *Danaus plexippus. See also* Viceroy. △502.

Monarchianism, 2nd–3rd century heretical movement in the Christian church. It safeguarded the Divine Unity (or monarchia) of the Godhead by not distinguishing the divine persons of the Trinity. In destroying the idea of the Trinity, monarchianism did not support the independent existence of Christ. This heresy is said to have originated with Noetus (*c.* AD 250) and was carried on by his disciples Epigonus and Cleomenes.

Monarchy, form of government in which one individual, whose power is usually hereditary, represents the state. Monarchs with absolute power are nearly extinct; those states that remain monarchies are generally constitutional, with the royalty performing ceremonial functions. △898, 1128, 1288.

Monastery. △848, 1052.

Monastic Architecture. △1080, 1092.

Monasticism, a religious way of life, typically an ascetic life apart from the rest of the world. Such a way of striving toward perfection has been found in Hinduism, Buddhism, Islam, and Christianity. St Anthony, in the 3rd and 4th centuries, is considered the founder of Christian monasticism. In the 5th century St Benedict set down rules for a monastery at Monte Cassino in Italy, and his laws were widely followed. The Benedictines, Cistercians, and other orders built great abbeys such as Clairvaux in France, and these often were centers of agriculture and of art and learning. Monks and nuns worked as well as devoting hours to prayer.

Monaural Tape Recorder. △1798.

Monck, or **Monk, George, 1st Duke of Albemarle** (1608–70), English soldier. In the English Civil War, he fought initially for Charles I (1643–44). Joining the Parliamentarians, he commanded unsuccessfully in Ireland (1647–49) and successfully in Scotland (1650, 1654) and defeated the Dutch at sea (1652). He engineered the Stuart Restoration (1660) and fought in the second Anglo-Dutch war (1666–67).

Monclova, city in NE Mexico; site of airport, railroad shops. Products: lead, zinc, silver, coffee. Pop. 80,-252.

Moncton, city in New Brunswick, Canada, on the Petitcodiac River; educational and cultural center for French Canadian sector of New Brunswick; site of three colleges, one seminary, and one university; major center of transportation. Founded 1763 as The Bend by German settlers; name changed in 1855 to honor the British General Robert Monckton. Pop. 47,-781.

Mondale, Walter Frederick (1928–), vice president of the United States (1977–), b. Ceylon, Minn. In 1955 he married Joan Adams; they had two sons and a daughter. As a young lawyer in Minnesota, he became active in the state Democratic-Farmer-Labor party. He served as state attorney general (1960–64), and when Hubert H. Humphrey became vice president (1965), Mondale was appointed to complete Humphrey's term in the US Senate. Mondale was elected to a full term in 1966 and again in 1972. He became identified with the more liberal wing of the Democratic party in the Senate; that fact was instrumental in his being chosen as the Democratic running mate of Jimmy Carter in 1976.

Mondrian, Piet (1872–1944), Dutch painter. His early works were naturalistic landscapes painted in neutral colors. He was later influenced by the fauvist and cubist styles. His fame rests on his balanced, geometric, abstract style, in which he used black lines in a gridlike pattern to outline rectangular shapes of white and primary colors. △1318.

Monera, a large biological grouping comprising the bacteria and blue-green algae. Sometimes considered distinct enough from other protists to be called a separate kingdom. The main difference is in the organization of the genetic materials. Monerans, also called procaryotes, do not have their genetic material packed into a distinct nucleus and lack mitochondria and chloroplasts. Those protists with a distinct nucleus containing several chromosomes are called eucaryotes.

Monet, Claude (1840–1926), French painter. Painting almost entirely out-of-doors, he included many seascapes and city scenes among his early works. In the 1870s, he began to use the loose, broken-color brushstroke of Impressionism to create in his works an atmosphere of pattern, light, and color. He painted numerous views of the Seine and many series of the same subject, such as his haystack and Rouen Cathedral facade series, showing the effects of sunlight on the subject at different hours of the day. He also painted enormous waterlily panels. △1254.

Money. △934, 1384.

Money Supply, in a general sense, that portion of the public's purchasing power that is readily available. Defined in the narrow economic sense, the money supply consists only of currency and demand deposits. A broader definition includes time deposits as well.

Moneywort, or creeping Jenny, creeping perennial plant native to Europe and naturalized in North America. It has pairs of penny-shaped, nearly evergreen leaves and yellow flowers and spreads rapidly by rooting runners to form a mat. Family Primulaceae; species *Lysymachia nummularia.*

Mongolia (Mongol Ard, Uls), landlocked nation in central Asia lying between China and the USSR. A vast plateau with extensive grasslands embraces the heartland of the country; part of the Gobi Desert occupies the S. An agricultural economy relies primarily on herd animals with more than 80% of the total land area devoted to pastureland. Herdsmen make up the majority of the labor force, all working for collective farms. More than 90% of the people are indigenous Mongolians; 75% Khalkha Mongols. The church was suppressed in the 1930s; at that time Tibetan Buddhist Lamaism was predominant. Only one active monastery remains.

Governmental power is vested in the People's Great Khural of Deputies, elected every three years by universal suffrage. From this body is chosen a nine-member Presidium to exercise state affairs. Under Genghis Khan in the 13th century, Mongolia conquered most of Asia and much of Europe. In the 14th century the empire collapsed and came under Chinese rule. During the 1911 Chinese Revolution, Mongolia, with Russian backing, declared its independence; a republic was formed in 1924. Officially recognized by China in 1946, Mongolia became a member of the United Nations in 1961. In 1966 a Mongolian-Soviet assistance pact reinforced their anti-Chinese position.

PROFILE

Official name: Mongolian People's Republic
Area: 604,247sq mi (1,565,000sq km)
Population: 1,290,000
Density: 2.13 per sq mi (0.8 per sq km)
Chief cities: Ulan Bator, capital; Darhan; Choybalsan
Government: People's Republic
Language: Khalkha Mongolian (official)
Monetary unit: Tugrik
Gross national product: $590,000,000
Per capita income: $460
Agriculture (major products): livestock
Minerals (major): coal, tungsten, copper, gold, tin, molybdenum
Trading partners (major): COMECON member countries

Mongolian Eyefold. *See* Epicanthic Fold.

Mongolian Wild Horse. *See* Przewalsky's Horse.

Mongolism (Down's syndrome), a condition that is usually caused by the presence of an extra chromosome 21 (three instead of the usual two), in which the typical features are mental retardation, flattened skull and nose bridge, shortened digits, and a vertical fold on the inner side of the eye, resulting in a slant-eyed appearance. △710, 768.

Mongoloid Race, one of the major human racial groupings. Mongoloid physical characteristics include: medium skin pigmentation; rather flat face; epicanthic fold; straight black hair; little facial or body hair. Mongoloids make up most of the population of Asia and the indigenous peoples of the Americas. △658.

Mongols, a nomadic people of Mongolia, Manchuria, and Siberia. They live in felt tents; eat meat and milk; and raise horses, sheep, and goats. Expert archers and horsemen, they were once savage conquerers and rulers of the largest territory in history. Under Genghis Khan (1167–1227) they built an empire that in part survived until the 16th century. They were poor administrators, however, and their empire was never really under their governmental control. △1112.

Mongoose, small, agile, carnivorous mammal of the civet family, native to Africa, S Europe, and Asia. They have slender, thickly furred bodies and long, bushy tails. Active hunters by day and night, they eat rodents, insects, eggs, birds, and snakes. The Indian mongoose *(Herpestes edwardsi)* is famous for killing cobras. Some species may be domesticated but their destructiveness is so great that they are not allowed in the United States, even in zoos. Length: 1.5–4ft (46–122cm). Family Viverridae.

Monism. △858.

Monitor and Merrimack, Civil War naval battle off Hampton Roads, Va., March 9, 1862. The *Merrimack,* a scuttled vessel, was raised and made into an ironclad by the Confederates. It was used to sink wooden Union ships. The *Monitor,* a new flat-top ironclad, battled the *Merrimack* and heavily damaged it, helping to maintain the Union blockade. △1276.

Monitor Lizard, powerful lizard native to Africa, S Asia, Indonesia, and Australia. It has a long, forked, snakelike tongue and a powerful tail. The majority are dull-colored with yellow markings. Many are semi-aquatic. Length: 8in–10ft (20cm–2m). There are 30 species. Family Varanidae; genus *Varanus*. *See also* Komodo Dragon. △614.

Monk, Thelonious (Sphere) (1920–), US jazz pianist, b. Rocky Mount, N.C. He helped develop the "bebop" (now called "bop") jazz style in the 1940s and displayed an inventive, unique piano style featuring dissonances and distinctive chord structures. He has composed many melodies and has appeared in major concert halls of the world.

Monkey, wide variety of mostly tree-dwelling, day-active, omnivorous primates inhabiting the tropics and subtropics. Most monkeys have high intelligence, flat manlike faces, grasping hands, and other characteristics of advanced, anthropoid primates. They fall into two broad groups—Old World monkeys (superfamily Cercopithecoidea) and New World monkeys (superfamily Ceboidea). The 60 Old World species, sometimes called true monkeys, include macaques, baboons, barbary apes, langurs, and colobuses. Some, such as baboons, are primarily ground dwellers, but all are excellent climbers. Most have short or long but always nongrasping tails. They range from Japan and N China through S Asia and nondesert Africa. The 70 species of New World monkeys include howlers, capuchins, spider monkeys, and marmosets. They are all tree dwellers, and most have grasping tails. Most have no thumbs, and the nostrils are usually separated more widely than in Old World monkeys. They live in tropical Central and South America. *See also* Primates. △554, 598.

Monkey-eating Eagle. △630.

Monkey Puzzle Tree, evergreen tree native to mountainous regions of Chile and Brazil. It has tangled branches, sharp, flat leaves, and edible nuts. It is grown mainly as an ornamental, but its timber is sometimes used in carpentry. Height: to 100ft (30m). Family Pinacae; species *Araucaria araucana*.

Monmouth, James Scott, Duke of (1649–85), English soldier, illegitimate son of Charles II, b. The Hague. He became a successful general and the hope of the Protestants opposing the succession of the Catholic duke of York. Exiled (1679), he plotted his father's murder (1683). In 1685 he returned to England and was proclaimed king. Following his defeat at Sedgemoor, he was executed.

Monmouth, Battle of (June 28, 1778), last important northern battle of the American Revolution. It was a long and hard battle fought to a draw near Monmouth Court House in New Jersey. The Battle of Monmouth led to the court martial of American Gen. Charles Lee, who was convicted of ordering an "unnecessary, disorderly, and shameful" retreat before the end of the conflict.

Monnet, Jean (1888–), French economist. Active in government since World War I, he served as a member of the British Supply Council, helping organize the Allied War effort. His Monnet Plan (1947) instituted the modernization of French industry and the 48-hour work week. He presided (1952–55) over the European Coal and Steel Community, which he established. It was an initial step toward European economic and political unity, and laid the groundwork for the European Economic Community. △1356.

Monoceros, or the Unicorn, faint equatorial constellation situated south of Gemini and east of Orion. The Milky Way passes through this group, which also contains several bright and dark nebulae, including the Rosette Nebula (NGC 2237), and some star clusters, such as NGC 2244.

Monocotyledon, subclass of flowering plants, angiosperms, characterized by one seed leaf (cotyledon) in the seed embryo. Plant leaves are usually parallel-veined and flower in threes. Lilies, orchids, palms and grasses are monocotyledons. The larger subclass is dicotyledon. This system of angiosperm classification has been used since the last half of the 17th century. *See also* Angiosperms; Dicotyledons. △452–54.

Monod, Jacques (1910–76), French biologist who, with François Jacob, developed the idea that messenger RNA carries hereditary information from the cell nucleus to the cellular sites of protein synthesis and also the concept of the operator gene controlling the activity of other genes. He and Jacob, together with André Lwoff, were awarded the 1965 Nobel Prize in physiology or medicine.

Monogamy. △794.

Monomer, chemical compound composed of single molecules as opposed to a polymer, which consists of molecules built up from repeated monomer units. For example, propylene is the monomer from which polypropylene is made, similarly methyl methacrylate is the monomer for polymethyl menthacrylate, which is sold as Lucite, Plexiglas, and Perspex. △1506.

Monomotapa, former SE African empire, also known as Mwanamutapa, of the Shona, a Bantu people, from the 15th century. Noted for its remarkable stone architecture and rich gold mines, the empire crumbled under pressure by the Portuguese by the 17th century. △1116, 1212.

Mononucleosis. *See* Infectious Mononucleosis.

Monophysitism, a theological view of the two natures of Christ which emphasized the divine nature at the expense of the human. Declared heretical in the 5th century, it nevertheless found followers throughout the Byzantine Empire and had major political consequences. △1056.

Monopoly, an industry containing a single firm, a situation of imperfect competition. The demand for the product class is the demand curve the monopoly firm faces. A monopoly has complete market power and may therefore determine either its level of output or its price. Normally, a monopolistic industry will charge higher prices and produce smaller output than more competitive industries. For this reason, antitrust laws attempt to prevent monopoly power. In a situation where the existence of a monopoly is deemed necessary, the government attempts to regulate its price structure to allow only a "fair" rate of return.

Monorail Train, a passenger train, gyroscopically stabilized and propelled by electric motors, that runs on a single rail. △1710.

Monosaccharide, a sweet-tasting carbohydrate that cannot be broken down by hydrolysis; a simple sugar. △1574.

Monosodium Glutamate (MSG), white crystalline powder with a meat-like taste obtained by alkaline hydrolysis of wheat gluten or of the waste liquor from sugar refining. It is used as a flavor enhancer for meat products.

Monotheism, belief in the existence of a single God in the universe. This God is envisioned as the creator of all and is both personal and transcendent. Judaism, Christianity, and Islam are the three major monotheistic religions.

Monotheletism, or **Monothelitism,** 7th-century heresy in the Christian church asserting the existence of only one will (divine) in Jesus rather than the orthodox belief in the existence of human and divine wills. This position, which was politically motivated to gain the support of Monophysites and so stave off the Persian and Muslim invasions, was drawn up in the Ecthesis of 638 and in the Typos of 648. The heresy was condemned at the Lateran Council of 649 and the Council of Constantinople in 680.

Monotreme, any of the egg-laying mammals of the order Monotremata, native to Australia and New Guinea. The platypus and the echidna are the only living representatives. *See also* Echidna. △544.

Monotype Machine. △1772.

Monreale Cathedral. △1060.

Monroe, James (1758–1831), 5th president of the United States (1817–25), *b.* Westmoreland co, Va. He attended William and Mary College and studied law (1780–83) under Thomas Jefferson, whose lifelong friend and political supporter he became. In 1786 he married Elizabeth Kortright; they had three children.

Monroe was wounded in the American Revolution, during which he achieved the rank of lieutenant colonel. He served in Congress under the Articles of Confederation and opposed the adoption of the US Constitution. He served as a diplomat, as governor of Virginia, and in the US Senate.

When Jefferson became president (1801) he sent Monroe on various special missions to Europe. Monroe and Robert Livingston negotiated the Louisiana Purchase (1803). He was secretary of state under President Madison and also served briefly as secretary of war. Chosen by the Jeffersonians to succeed Madison, he was easily elected.

Mombasa, Kenya

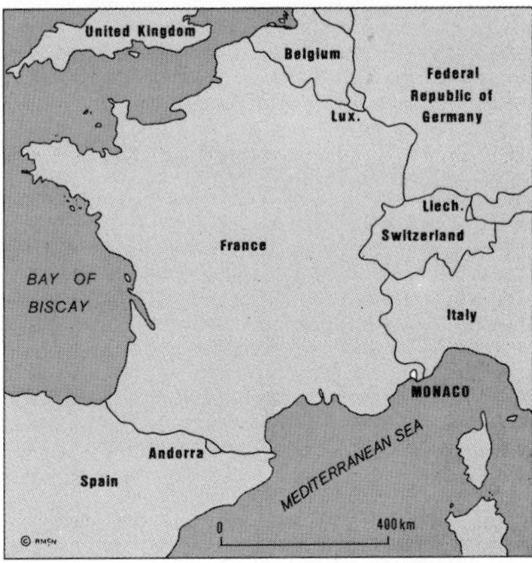
United Kingdom
Belgium
Federal Republic of Germany
Lux.
Liech.
Switzerland
France
BAY OF BISCAY
Italy
MONACO
MEDITERRANEAN SEA
Andorra
Spain
0
400km

Monaco

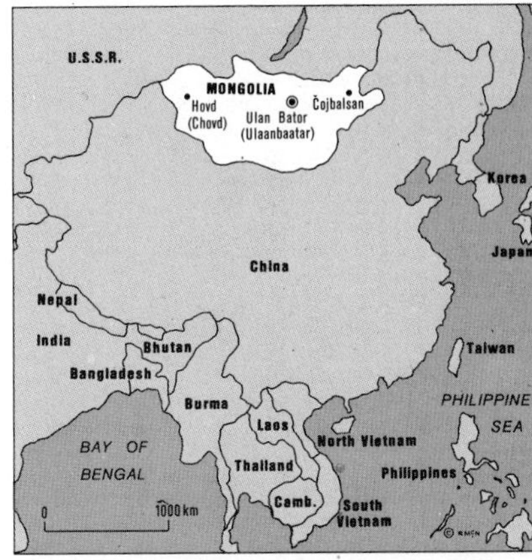
U.S.S.R.
MONGOLIA
Hovd (Chovd)
Ulan Bator (Ulaanbaatar)
Čojbalsan
Korea
Japan
China
Nepal
India
Bhutan
Bangladesh
Taiwan
Burma
PHILIPPINE SEA
Laos
North Vietnam
BAY OF BENGAL
Thailand
Philippines
Camb.
South Vietnam
0
1000km

Mongolia

James Monroe

Monroe's administration is remembered as the "era of good feelings." Relations improved with Britain, France, Spain, and Canada. His most impressive achievement was the Monroe Doctrine. The Missouri Compromise (1820) settled the slavery issue for three decades. Monroe encouraged the settling of Liberia, whose capital, Monrovia, was named after him.

Career: delegate, Continental Congress, 1783–86; US Senate, 1790–94; minister to France, 1794–96; governor of Virginia, 1799–1802, 1811; special envoy to France, Great Britain, and Spain, 1803–07; secretary of state, 1811–17; secretary of war, 1814–15; president, 1817–25. *See also* Louisiana Purchase; Missouri Compromise; Monroe Doctrine.

Monroe, Marilyn (1926–62), US film star, b. Norma Jean Baker in Los Angeles. A talented comedienne, known as a sex goddess, her personal life was tragic. She remains a subject of continuing fascination and analysis. Her films included *Gentlemen Prefer Blondes* (1953), The Seven-Year Itch (1955), *Bus Stop* (1956), *Some Like It Hot* (1959), and *The Misfits* (1960). △1362.

Monroe, city in NE Louisiana, on Ouachita River; seat of Ouachita parish; site of one of the largest natural gas fields in United States (1916), Northeast Louisiana State College (1931), and antebellum houses. Industries: carbon black, chemicals, paper, paper bags. Founded 1785 as Miro; renamed 1819. Inc. 1900. Pop. (1970), 56,374.

Monroe Doctrine (1823), US foreign policy statement formulated by John Quincy Adams and presented to Congress on Dec. 2, 1823, by Pres. James Monroe. The doctrine attempted to prevent European intervention in Latin America's new republics by asserting flatly that the Americas were no longer open to European colonization. The United States promised not to interfere in European affairs and discouraged European attempts to force colonial status on new Latin American nations. The doctrine was viewed with suspicion by some Latin Americans who saw it as justification for US intervention. △1234, 1274.

Monroe-Pinkney Treaty (1806), US agreement with Great Britain negotiated by James Monroe and William Pinkney to settle disputes over contraband, blockading, and the impressment of US seamen. Pres. Thomas Jefferson considered the terms of the treaty a defeat for US diplomacy and it was never ratified.

Monroeville, borough in SW Pennsylvania; suburb of Pittsburgh. Industries: steel, coal, nuclear industrial research. Settled 1810; inc. 1952. Pop. (1970) 29,-011.

Monrovia, seaport city and capital of Liberia, at the estuary of the St. Paul River; largest city in Liberia; seat of Monserrado co; site of University of Liberia (1862), several church missions, modern airport, government hospital, submarine base, modern harbor. Exports: iron ores (from the Bomi Hills), forest products, rubber, gold, palm oil and kernels, cassava. Industries: paint, fish processing, cement, bricks, oil refining, pharmaceuticals. Settled 1822 by freed US slaves on site chosen by the American Colonization Society; named in honor of US President James Monroe. Pop. 100,000.

Monrovia, city in S California, 14mi (23km) ENE of Los Angeles. Industries: dairy products, electronic equipment, chemicals, plastics, machinery. Inc. 1886. Pop. (1970) 28,324.

Mons, town in SW Belgium, 32mi (52km) SW of Brussels; Charlemagne declared it capital of Hainaut prov. in the 9th century; 14th-century center of the lace and cloth trade; scene of the British Expeditionary Force's first battle (1914); site of a technical college (1837) and State University Center (1965). Industries: mining, textiles, sugar. Pop. 28,727.

Mons Meg. △1732.

Monsoon, a seasonal wind produced by variations in air temperatures and pressures between continents and oceans. *See also* Winds. △212, 220.

Monstera, climbing plant of tropical America with deeply incised leaves. It bears edible fruits. The *Monstera deliciosa* is a popular house plant. It is commonly and incorrectly called a split-leaved philodendron. It rarely blooms indoors. The erect stem needs support for the leathery leaves that can grow 4ft (1.2m) long. Family Araceae.

Montagnards (The Mountain), far left members of the French Revolutionary government. They rose to power over the Girondists in 1793 and began the infamous Reign of Terror, when thousands were guillotined for often slight political differences. Allied with the Parisian Jacobins under Robespierre, the Montagnards gradually lost public support and were effectively ousted by the Thermidorean Reaction (1794).

Montagu, Charles, Earl of Halifax. *See* Halifax, Charles Montagu, Earl of.

Montaigne, Michel Eyquem, (Seigneur de) (1553–92), French essayist. Originally a magistrate, he retired from public life to his private lands in 1571 to compose his *Essais* (1580). Written in a style that alternated between high eloquence and racy colloquialism, the *Essais* constituted an intellectual autobiography that moved from stoicism through skepticism to a mature acceptance of all that life offered. A new edition of the *Essais,* with additions, was published in 1588, and he continued to work on them until his death. △1172.

Montale, Eugenio (1896–), Italian poet and critic. He worked as a librarian in Florence and as literary editor of *Corriere della Sera.* A hermetic poet, his work is influenced by T.S. Eliot, and includes *Ossi di seppia* (1925), *Le occassioni* (1940), and *Xenia Poems* (translated 1970). He was awarded the 1975 Nobel Prize for literature.

Montana, state in the NW United States bordered on the N by the Canadian provinces of British Columbia, Alberta, and Saskatchewan.

Land and Economy. The W 40% is mountainous. The Rocky Mts run from S to N, with many subsidiary ranges. The remainder of the state is largely high plains, where grazing and farming produce a major part of the state's income. The Missouri River flows from W to E across the state and is dammed to create the huge Fort Peck storage reservoir. Falls on the river generate electric power. Other large rivers are the Milk and the Yellowstone. Forests and mines, which are economically important, are situated in the mountains. Tourism is an important source of revenue.

People. Montana is one of the most sparsely populated states, with a density of only 4.8 persons per square mile (12.4 per sq km). A little more than half resides in urban areas. Almost all inhabitants are natives of the United States.

Education. There are 12 institutions of higher education.

History. French and Spanish fur traders and prospectors were active before 1800, but when the United States acquired the region from France by the Louisiana Purchase in 1803, it was little known. Reports by the Lewis and Clark expedition of 1804–06 led to the development of the fur trade and the establishment of settlements, army posts, and missions. Discovery of gold brought a rush of immigrants after 1852, and Montana Territory was organized in 1864. Military action over many years subdued hostile Indians. The opening of the Northern Pacific Railroad in 1883 was an enormous stimulus to the state's growth, especially in farming and mining.

PROFILE

Admitted to Union: Nov. 8, 1889; rank, 41st
US Congressmen: Senate, 2; House of Representatives, 2
Population: 694,409 (1970); rank, 43rd
Capital: Helena, 22,730 (1970)
Chief cities: Billings, 61,581; Great Falls, 60,091; Missoula, 29,497
State legislature: Senate, 50; House of Representatives, 100
Area: 147,138sq mi (381,087sq km); rank, 4th
Elevation: Highest, 12,799ft (3,904m), Granite Peak; lowest, 1,800ft (549m), Kootenai River
Industry (major products): lumber, wood products, processed primary metals, processed foods
Agriculture (major products): wheat, barley, potatoes, sheep, cattle
Minerals (major): copper, zinc, phosphate rock, petroleum, natural gas, coal
State nickname: Treasure State
State motto: Oro y plata (gold and silver)
State bird: western meadowlark
State flower: bitterroot
State tree: ponderosa pine

Montane. △580, 608.

Montcalm, Louis Joseph de, Marquis de Saint-Véran (1712–59), French general in North America. Commander-in-chief of French army in Canada (1756–59), he won several victories in the colonial wars against the British, including Fort Ontario (1756), Fort William Henry (1757), Fort Carillon (Ticonderoga, 1758), and Montmorency (1759). Lacking support from France, he was defeated by Gen. James Wolfe at Montreal, where he was mortally wounded.

Montclair, town in NE New Jersey, 6mi (10km) NNW of Newark; suburb of Newark and New York City; site of Washington's headquarters 1780, Montclair College (1908), and museum with several paintings by George Inness, who resided here. Industries: chemicals, paints, metalware. Settled 1666 as part of Newark; separated 1812; inc. 1868. Pop. (1970) 44,-043.

Monte Albán (*c.* 400 BC–*c.* AD 900), ancient Zapotec religious center located southwest of Oaxaca, Mexico. Monte Albán was built on a level hilltop and along the adjacent valleys; stepped platforms supported the religious monuments. △970.

Montebello, suburban city in S California, 8mi (13km) ESE of Los Angeles. Industries: rubber products, oil, television sets. Inc. 1920. Pop. (1970) 42,-807.

Monte Carlo, town in N Monaco, on the French Riviera and Mediterranean Sea; famous resort, tourist center with world's oldest casino; noted for scenery, mild climate, luxurious hotels, and annual car rally and Monaco Grand Prix. Founded 1856 by Prince Charles III of Monaco in agreement with a joint stock company that wished to build and operate the casino. Pop. 9,516.

Monte Carlo Method, method of solving certain types of physical problems by statistical experiments based on the application of mathematical operations to random numbers. It is based on the work of William Sealy Gossett (pseudonym Student) and takes its name from the famous casino in Monaco. △1476.

Montego Bay, seaport city in NW Jamaica, West Indies; commercial center with good harbor and rail connections; site of St James church, dome tower airport, remains of Arawak Indian settlement (visited by Christopher Columbus 1494) before European development. Industries: tourism, sugar cane, bananas, coffee, ginger, rum, fruit export. Pop. 42,800.

Montenegrins. △1232.

Montenegro (Crna Gora), constituent republic in SW Yugoslavia, at S end of Dinaric Alps, bordered by Albania (SE), Adriatic Sea (SW); Titograd is capital, and Kotor is major port. Region is mountainous and isolated; divided into Brda region and Montenegro proper (W) by Zeta River; population is largely Serbian. Region was independent principality of Zeta within Serbian Empire until 14th century, when defeated by Turks; formal recognition of independence occurred 1878 at Congress of Berlin; became one of six Yugoslavian autonomous republics 1946. Industries: sheep and goats, mining, corn, wheat, tobacco, iron, steel. Area: 5,332sq mi (13,810sq km). Pop. 530,361.

Monterey, city in W California, at S end of Monterey Bay; capital of Spanish prov. of California 1774–1822; site of California's first theater (1844) and first newspaper (1846). Founded 1770 by Franciscans; inc. 1859. Pop. (1970) 26,302.

Monterey Park, city in S California, 8mi (13km) E of Los Angeles; site of 2 Industrial parks. Inc. 1916. Pop. (1970) 49,166.

Monterey Pine, evergreen tree native to S California. It has heavy, irregular branches and bright green 6 in (15cm) needles. It is grown as an ornamental. Height: to 100ft (30m). Family Pinaceae; species *Pinus radiata.*

Monterrey, city in NE Mexico, 150mi (242km) S of Laredo, Texas; capital of Nuevo León state. Captured 1846 by US forces under Zachary Taylor; site of university (1937), Obispado chapel, 18th-century cathedral, Topo Chico hot springs. Industries: mining, petroleum, glass, textiles, furniture, processed foods, plastics, beverages, electrical equipment, flour, paper. Founded 1579. Pop. 830,336.

Montesquieu, Charles-Louis de Secondat, Baron de (1689–1755), French social philosopher, magistrate in Bordeaux. He launched his criticism of contemporary society in the *Persian Letters* (1721). His *Spirit of Laws* (1748) attempted to explain the evolution of societies in terms of environmental features: climate, geography, demography. Judicial laws, he held, had their seat in nature as surely as those of physical science. His method, however, was not entirely empirical, nor was his infant "sociology" free of abstraction. △1184

Montessori, Maria (1870–1952), Italian educator. After receiving a medical degree, she became interested in the education of retarded children. She then applied her methods, which emphasized free expression, to schooling normal children. Schools for young children, using her methods, have been started in many countries.

Monteverdi, Claudio (1567–1643), Italian composer, the first great opera composer and a pioneer in modern orchestration. He advanced violin technique by trying out new effects in orchestral playing. His many operas include *L'Orfeo* (1606), *Il Ballo delle Ingrate* (1608), and *L'Incoronazione di Poppea* (1642). He also composed religious music and many madrigals. △1174, 1196

Montevideo, capital city and port of Uruguay, in S part of country on the Rio de La Plata, 135mi (217km) E of Buenos Aires, Argentina; largest city in Uruguay and one of South America's major ports. Originally a Portuguese fort (1717), captured by Spanish 1724; became capital of Uruguay 1828; suffered from civil wars 1843–1851; site of University of the Republic (1849), the Prado (a park), with botanical gardens and a promenade, and the legislative palace. Industries: textiles, dairy products, wines, packaged meats, tourism. Pop. 1,280,000.

Montez, Lola (1818?–1861), born Maria Dolores Eliza Rosanna Gilbert. Irish-American adventuress, styled herself as a Spanish dancer but became famous rather for her great beauty and extravagant social life. She became the mistress of King Louis I of Bohemia in 1846, but her involvement in politics caused her exile and Louis' abdication two years later. She moved to America, married a San Francisco journalist, and toured Australia as a dancer.

Montezuma, name of two Aztec emperors. **Montezuma I** (*c.* 1390–1464) increased the geographical scope of the empire through a series of wars. **Montezuma II** (1480–1520) allowed the Spaniards under Cortés to enter central Mexico unhindered. Montezuma II was imprisoned by the Spaniards, and killed by his own subjects when they rose up against the intruders.

Montfort, Simon de, Earl of Leicester (1208–65), English baron. He married Henry III's sister (1238) and became adviser to the king. Complaints about his ruthless enforcement of English authority in Gascony (1248–52) caused his recall. Quarreling with Henry, he joined the barons at Oxford (1258). Henry's repudiation of his agreements occasioned the Barons' War (1263–65). De Montfort defeated him at Lewes (1264) and as virtual ruler of England under the Provisions of Oxford summoned a parliament, but was killed in renewed fighting at Evesham. *See also* Barons' War.

Montgolfier, Joseph Michael (1740–1810) and **Jacques Étienne** (1745–99), French pioneer balloonists. In 1783 they carried out their initial experiments with a model hot air balloon and gave their first public demonstration of manned balloon flight in June 1783. △1712.

Montgomery, Bernard Law, 1st Viscount Montgomery of Alamein (1887–1976), British general. As commander of the British Eighth Army, he stopped the German offensive in North Africa at Alamein (1942) and led the invasion of Sicily and Italy (1943). He helped plan the Normandy landings (1944), leading his troops into Germany, and commanding the British occupation forces there (1945–46). Made field marshal (1944) and viscount (1946), he was deputy supreme allied commander, Europe (1951–58). His abrasive personality caused conflict with other Allied commanders, notably General Eisenhower, but his total commitment to victory won universal admiration. △1336.

Montgomery, commercial city in SE central Alabama, 85mi (137km) SSE of Birmingham, seat of Montgomery co. Location of US Air Force Special Staff School; state capital in 1847; first capital of the Confederacy in 1861. Industries: livestock, cotton, lumber, meat-packing, fertilizer. Settled 1818; inc. 1837. Pop. (1970) 133,386.

Montgomery Convention, convention held in the capital of Alabama in February 1861, at which six Southern states voted to secede from the Union and to establish the Confederate States of America. Jefferson Davis was inaugurated as president.

Monticello, estate in central Virginia, 2.5mi (4km) from Charlottesville. The home of Thomas Jefferson for 56 years, it was built 1770–72 on lands he inherited from his father; it is owned by the Thomas Jefferson Memorial Foundation. It is an early example of American classic revival; designed by Jefferson, it contains many examples of Jefferson's inventiveness; set on a little mountain, or *monticello* (Ital.), it commands a spectacular view of surrounding countryside. Jefferson is buried here.

Montmorency, Ann, Duc de (1493–1567), French military commander. He was a distinguished leader in the wars of Francis I but fell from grace in 1541 for advocating appeasement of Holy Roman Emperor Charles V. He waged more campaigns under the next king, Henry II, until captured by the Spaniards in 1557. After his release he was not restored to command until Catherine de Médicis decided to use his prowess against the Huguenots and the English. He died in battle at St Denis.

Montmorency, Henry I, Duc de (1534–1614), French official and governor of Languedoc, son of Ann de Montmorency. At first an ardent Catholic, he later sided with the rebellious Huguenots (1575–77). After efforts to reunite the two factions, he supported the controversial succession of King Henry IV and was made constable in 1595.

Montmorillonite, a general name for a group of clay minerals, hydrous calcium-sodium aluminum-magnesium-iron silicate. Moisture sensitive clays weathered out of igneous rocks. Common constituent of soil. Used in paper industry for "carbon-less" paper. White, yellowish, or gray. Hardness 1–2; sp gr 2.5.

Montpelier, capital city of Vermont in N central Vermont, 37mi (60km) SW of Burlington at confluence of Winooski and North Branch rivers; seat of Washington co; location of land grant 1780; settled 1787; made state capital 1805. It is the site of Vermont College (1834), Wood Art Gallery (1899), Dewey House; birthplace of Adm. George Dewey. Industries: tourism, sawmill and granite machinery, granite, clothespins, maple sugar and syrup, plastics. Inc. 1855. Pop. (1970) 8,609.

Montpellier, city in S France, 6mi (10km) N of Mediterranean Sea; capital of Hérault dept. City was center of fief under counts of Toulouse until 13th century when it passed to kings of Majorca; in 1349 it was purchased by Philip VI of France; site of University (1289), botanical garden (1593); birthplace of philosopher August Comte (1798). Industries: cottons, candles, soaps, chemicals. Founded 8th century. Pop. 161,910.

Montreal, city on Montreal Island, Quebec, Canada, on N bank of St Lawrence River. The largest city in Canada, it is also the world's largest inland seaport. City was under French control until 1760 when British took over; occupied by Americans November 1775–June 1776; British and French clashed in Montréal 1837–38; served as seat of Canadian government 1844–49. Population is mostly Roman Catholic of French extraction. A major cultural and educational center, it is the site of many churches and cathedrals, museums, parks and recreational facilities; home of baseball's National League Montreal Expos, National Hockey League's Montreal Canadiens; location of the 1976 Summer Olympics, McGill University (1829), and the University of Montréal (1876); focal point of transportation, finance and industry in E Canada. Major industries: aircraft, electrical equipment, railroad rolling stock, textiles, metal wares, food processing, chemicals. Originally the Indian village of Hochelaga; visited 1535 by Jacques Cartier; settled 1642 by French. Pop. 1,197,753.

Mont-Saint-Michel, rocky isle 1mi (1.6km) off NW France, in Gulf of Saint-Mâlo (arm of English Channel); site of Benedictine abbey built 708 by St Aubert, destroyed 1203 and rebuilt. Base of the island is circled with ramparts, towers, and bastions rising three storeys to support the abbey and church. The church spire holds a statue of St Michael, 456ft (138m) above the bay. Nave of the church is 12th-century Romanesque style; the choir is 14th-century Gothic; the facade was added in 18th century.

Montserrat, island in Leeward Islands, British West Indies, between Atlantic Ocean (E) and Caribbean Sea (W). Plymouth is capital and chief port. The island is mountainous, volcanic, intensively cultivated; Soufrière is highest peak, 3,000ft (914m); site of severe earthquake Oct. 8, 1975. Discovered 1493 by Christopher Columbus, it was colonized 1632 by English; held briefly by French; returned to Great Britain 1783; member of former Leeward Islands colony and former member of Federation of West Indies; currently part of Caribbean Common Market; rejected self-government 1966. Shipping of agricultural produce, especially cotton, is main industry. Area: 38sq mi (98sq km). Pop. 12,302.

Eugenio Montale

Glacier National Park, Montana

Montevideo, Uruguay

Montreal, Canada

Montserrat, volcanic mountain in NE Spain; terrain is jagged and eroded; site of 9th-century Benedictine monastery, containing 13 hermitages, carving of Virgin Mary; here Ignatius Loyola conceived the idea of founding the Society of Jesus (Jesuits); traditional site of castle of Holy Grail. Approx. height: 4,054ft (1,236m).

Monza, city of N Italy, 10mi (16km) NE of Milan; scene of assassination of King Umberto I of Italy 1900; site of 6th-century cathedral (founded by Lombard queen Theodelinda), 13th-century town hall. Industries: felt hats, carpets, textiles. Pop. 105,356.

Moody, Helen Wills (1906–), US tennis player, b. Alameda co., Calif. Considered the greatest female player of her time, she won seven US (1923–25; 1927–29; 1931) and eight British women's singles titles (1927–30; 1932–33; 1935; 1938).

Moog Synthesizer, computer tool for composing music by translating ideas into synthetic sounds, electronically produced. Wave forms generated by programmed or random-manipulated circuitry and modified by altering intensity, frequency, duration, etc, are combined to create complex signal patterns. Output is obtained from selected mixtures preserved on magnetic tape. △1364, 1500.

Moon, natural satellite of the planet Earth and about the same age (4.5–5 billion years). The Moon has no light of its own and reflects less than 10% of the light that falls on it. The different phases of the Moon occur as it revolves around the earth and are determined by its position in relation to both the Earth and the Sun. When the shadow of the Moon covers part of the Earth's surface a solar eclipse occurs. When the Earth's shadow falls onto the Moon a lunar eclipse occurs. The tides of the Earth's oceans are a result of the gravitational influence of the Moon. With an escape velocity of 1.5mi (2.4km) per second there is no atmosphere as such. Mean distance from the Earth, 239,000mi (384,790km); mass and volume, .012 and .02 times that of the earth, respectively; diameter, 2,160mi (3,478km); rotation period and period of sidereal revolution, 27.32 days; surface temperature, from below −247°F (−155°C) to above 212°F (100°C). △52–60, 146.

Moonfish, or **Opah,** marine fish found in all seas and important as a food fish in Japan. Its oval-shaped body is laterally compressed; colors are blue and rose with white spots. Length: to 6ft (182.9cm); weight: to 600lb (270kg). Family Lampridae; species *Lamprius regius.*

Moonflower, twining herb similar to morning glory; it produces large, pure white flowers in early evening. A perennial in warm areas, it grows to 15ft (4.6m). Family Convolvulaceae; genus *Calonyction.*

Moon Illusion, illusion in which the Moon on the horizon appears larger than the Moon in the overhead (zenith) position. It is best attributed to misperception of distance, ie, the horizon sky appears farther away than the zenith sky. △672.

Moonquakes. △54, 56.

Moore, Clement (1799–1863), US scholar and author, b. New York City. Although he taught Oriental and Greek literature for many years, he is best-known for his poem "'Twas the Night Before Christmas" (1822).

Moore, George Edward (1873–1958), British ethical theorist, epistemologist, and metaphysician. While studying at Cambridge University, he published *Principia Ethica* (1903). This work, along with some papers, was a major factor in the declining influence of Hegelianism and Kantianism in British philosophy. He also published *Ethics* (1912), *Philosophical Studies* (1922), and *Some Main Problems of Philosophy* (1953) during his lifetime. *Philosophical Papers* (1959) and *Commonplace Book* (1962) were published posthumously. He held that "good in itself" could not be analyzed as a concept.

Moore, Henry (1898–), English sculptor and painter. As a draftsman, he is best known for his drawings of people seeking shelter in the London Underground during World War II. His artistic fame, however, has resulted chiefly from his sculpture. In the 1920s Moore did many sculptures of reclining women. During the next decade his figures became increasingly abstract, with holes used to help define space and form. His later works often include family groups. △1320.

Moore, Marianne (1887–1972), US poet, b. St Louis. Her verse covers a wide range of topics and is stylistically complex while emphasizing precise observation. Her works include *Observations* (1924) and *Collected Poems* (1951; Pulitzer Prize 1952).

Moorhead, city in W Minnesota, on Red River; seat of Clay co; site of Moorhead State College (1885) and Concordia College (1891). Industries: glass, sheet metal, dairy products. Founded 1871; inc. 1881. Pop. (1970) 29,687.

Moors, nomadic people of North Africa of Berber and Arabic stock. Early converts to Islam, the Moors crossed over to Spain and Portugal in 711 and very quickly conquered most of the peninsula. Abd ar-Rahman I, the last survivor of the Umayyad dynasty from Damascus, established the emirate (later caliphate) of Córdoba in 756. That city and Toledo, Seville, and Granada became the great centers of Moorish commerce and culture. Generally hospitable to Jews and Christians, the Moorish rulers were great patrons of art and architecture, science, and philosophy. Throughout their rule, the Moors were systematically opposed by the Christian rulers of northern Spain, who gradually extended their power south. At the same time, dissension grew within the Moorish ranks. The puritanical Almoravids came across from North Africa in 1086 and conquered the more worldly Spanish Moors. They in turn were replaced by the even more puritanical Almohads.

By that time Christian power was striking at the very heart of Moorish power. Toledo fell to the Christians in 1085, Córdoba in 1236, and Seville in 1248. By 1250 all of Portugal had been taken from the Moors. Only the kingdom of Granada remained Moorish; it survived until 1492, when it fell to Ferdinand and Isabella. As Spain and Portugal became re-Christianized, most of the Moors were expelled; a few converted to Christianity, but they generally suffered from the Spanish Inquisition. Today, the populations of Algeria, Mauretania, Morocco, and Tunisia are of basically Moorish stock. See also Almohads; Almoravids; Granada; Spanish Inquisition; Umayyads. △1078.

Moose, largest species of deer, found in Alaska, Canada, NW United States, Norway, Sweden, Siberia, Manchuria, and Mongolia in moist, wooded areas. It is dark brown with a broad muzzle, heavy mane, and large dewlap. The massive antlers grow to 78in (198cm). Once heavily hunted, moose are now protected. It is called an elk in Europe. Length: to 9ft (3m); height: to 5.5ft (1.7m) at shoulder; weight: to 1,800lb (810kg). Family Cervidae; species *Alces alces. See also* Deer. △592.

Moose Jaw, town in S Saskatchewan, Canada; site of Aldersgate College (1940). Industries: flour, grain, meat processing, oil refining. Founded 1882. Pop. 31,284.

Moraine, a general term indicating a mound, ridge, or other visible accumulation of unsorted glacial drift, predominantly till. End, or terminal, moraines are formed when a glacier is neither advancing nor retreating and the rock material is dumped at the glacier's edge. Ground, or frontal, moraines are sheets of debris left after a steady retreat of the glacier. *See also* Till. △262.

Moral Development. △786–88, 808.

Moravia, Alberto (1907–), pseud. of Alberto Pincherle, Italian novelist. His early novels, including *The Time of Indifference* (1929) and *The Fancy Dress Party* (1941), were increasingly critical of Fascism, and Moravia was forced into hiding until 1944. Later works, examining hypocrisy and alienation, include *The Woman of Rome* (1947), *The Conformist* (1951), and *Two Women* (1957). An essay collection, *Man as an End,* appeared in 1966.

Moravia, fertile region and former province of Czechoslovakia; bordered by Bohemia (W), White and Carpathian Mts (E), and Sudetes Mts (N); European textile center; horse breeding region. Made part of new Czechoslovakia 1918; occupied by Germans in WWII. Split into 19 administrative regions after Communist takeover in 1948. △1182.

Moravian Gate (Gap), strategic N-S mountain pass and ancient trade route of central Europe between SE Sudetes and W Carpathian Mts, where Silesia (formerly in Germany), Poland and Czechoslovakia meet.

Moray Eel, vicious marine fish found in rocks and reefs of tropical and temperate waters. It is eaten in parts of the world, but some species are poisonous. Its long, serpentine body is without pectoral fins. Colors are blue, brown, and slate, sometimes in a banded or spotted pattern. Length: 4–5ft (121.9–152.4cm). Among the 80 species are the Atlantic *Gymnothorax funebris* and the spotted *Gymnothorax moringa.* Family Muraenidae. *See also* Eel. △510.

Mordecai, biblical cousin and foster father of Esther. With Esther, he thwarted Haman's efforts to destroy the Jews.

Mordovinian (Mordovskaja) Autonomous Soviet Socialist Republic, autonomous republic in W central USSR; capital is Saransk. Annexed by Russia 13th century; made an autonomous oblast 1930, and an ASSR 1934. Products: rye, wheat, oats, beans, potatoes, corn, tobacco, livestock. Industries: beekeeping, lumber, automotive, food processing. Area: approx. 10,000sq mi (25,900sq km). Pop. 1,030,000.

More, Henry (1614–87), English philosopher. Attracted by Neoplatonism while at Cambridge (1635), he developed this into a basis for Christian mysticism, which nevertheless celebrated the value of reason and moderation in theology. He was the author of *Poems* (1647), *Divine Dialogues* (1688), and several metaphysical treatises. *See also* Cambridge Platonists; Neoplatonism.

More, (Sir) Thomas (*c.* 1478–1535), English statesman and author, a Roman Catholic saint. A leading humanist, he was a friend of Erasmus. His *Utopia* (1516) imagined an ideal state founded on reason. Shakespeare's play *Richard III* is based on More's history. During the 1520s he wrote several important treatises against Lutheranism.

In 1518 he entered in the service of Henry VIII. He was knighted in 1521 and became Henry's trusted friend and adviser and succeeded Cardinal Wolsey as lord chancellor (1529), although he had disapproved of Henry's divorce from Catherine of Aragon. He resigned in 1532 claiming poor health but probably as much over his growing disagreements with the king. In 1533 he enraged Henry by refusing to attend Anne Boleyn's crowning. Henry had him arrested and placed in the Tower of London (1534). More refused to subscribe to the Act of Supremacy that made Henry the head of the Church of England. He was beheaded on a charge of treason for this insubordination. *See also* Utopia. △924, 1130, 1148, 1152.

Moreau, Jean Victor (1763–1813), French military officer. During the French Revolution he rose to head of the Army of the Rhine and Moselle (1796) and proved himself a master strategist. After helping Napoleon in his rise to power, Moreau continued to fight the Austrians and won a decisive victory at Hohenlinden (1800). He was exiled for plotting against Napoleon and lived in the United States (1805–13). He then joined forces with France's opponents and was mortally wounded at the Battle of Dresden.

Morehouse's Comet. △90.

Morel, any of a genus of terrestrial mushrooms *(Morchella)* that have conic caps resembling pine cones and hollow stems, especially M. esculenta, one of the most prized edible fungi. Growing only in the wild, it can be found only in spring. Some "false morels" that resemble true ones are toxic.

Morelia, city in SW Mexico; capital of Michoacán state; site of Colegeo de San Nicolas (1540), the oldest institution of higher learning in Mexico, 17th-century baroque cathedral, 18th-century aqueduct. Founded 1541 as Valladohid, name was changed 1828 in honor of revolutionary hero Morelos y Pavón. Industries: lumber, handicrafts, agriculture. Pop. 209,507.

Morelos, state in S central Mexico; named in honor of Morelos y Pavón who led historic defense against Spain 1812; terrain is mountainous with semi-arid valleys. Products: sugar cane, tropical fruits, cereals, vegetables, rum, sugar. Area: 1,917sq mi (4,965sq km). Pop. 620,392.

Moreno, Jacob Levy (1892–), US psychiatrist, b. Romania. He pioneered the development of a number of therapeutic methods including psychodrama and group psychotherapy. He founded and directed the Moreno Institute and the Theatre of Psychodrama in Beacon, New York. His works include *Sociometry and the Science of Man* (1956) and *First Book on Group Psychotherapy* (1957). *See also* Psychodrama. △774.

Morgan, (Sir) Henry (*c.*1635–88), Welsh pirate. He became the leader of a band of buccaneers and served under the governor of Jamaica, Sir Thomas Modyford, against the Spanish (1666–70). Among his conquests were Santa Catalina island, Puerto Príncipe, Porto Bello, and Panamá. He was knighted and made lieutenant governor of Jamaica after the war.

Morgan, John Hunt (1825–64), Confederate general in the Civil War, noted for his cavalry raids behind enemy lines, b. Huntsville, Ala. In 1862 he and his men took a Union garrison in Huntsville, and he was made a brigadier general. That summer he was captured while on a raid behind Union lines in Kentucky, Ohio, and Indiana. He escaped, was assigned to a command in SW Virginia, and was killed in Greenville, Tenn., by Union troops.

Morgan, John Pierpont (1837–1913), US financier, b. Hartford, Conn. Beginning as a member of his father's banking firm, he played an important role in the consolidation of eastern railroads and the organization of US Steel Co. He established J. P. Morgan and Co., a finance house that engaged in gold speculation during the Civil War. Morgan was also a leading US art collector. △1278.

Morgan, Thomas Hunt (1866–1945), US geneticist, b. Lexington, Ky. He was one of the most important founders of the science of genetics. In 1907 Morgan made an important advance—the use of the Mediterranean fruit fly *Drosophila* as a tool for genetic research. He then went on to discover that chromosomes were the carriers of hereditary material. He was awarded the 1933 Nobel Prize in physiology and medicine.

Morgan, light horse breed developed in New England by Justin Morgan from a versatile horse of same name foaled in 1789. A superior saddle, driving, racing, and farm horse with stamina and docility, it has a high-held head, round and deep short-backed body, and wide-set thin legs. Height: 58–64in (147–163cm) at shoulder; weight: 800–1,200lb (360–540kg).

Morgan Le Fay, a fairy enchantress of Arthurian legend and romance linked with various personages in Celtic mythology. She was skilled in the arts of healing and of changing shape. She was once described as Arthur's sister, and on another occasion accused of stirring up trouble between Arthur and Guinevere, but finally emerged as a beneficent figure, carrying Arthur to Avalon, her marvelous island.

Morgantown, city in N West Virginia, 15mi (24km) NE of Fairmont, on Monongahela River; seat of Monongalia co; site of West Virginia University. Industries: coal mining and shipping, glass, coke, concrete blocks, chemicals, textiles. Settled 1776; inc. 1785. Pop. (1970) 29,341.

Morgenthau, Henry (1856–1946), US financier, diplomat and philanthropist, b. Germany. He emigrated to the United States as a boy, became a lawyer, and soon built a fortune in real estate. A Woodrow Wilson supporter, he was chairman of the Democratic National Committee (1912, 1916). He was ambassador to Turkey during World War I, representing the United States, England, France, Italy, and Russia. He was appointed chairman of the League of Nations Greek Refugee Settlement Commission (1923) and was incorporator of the US Red Cross. He wrote *All in a Lifetime* (1922) and *I Was Sent to Athens* (1929).

Morgenthau, Henry, Jr. (1891–1967), US public official. As publisher of the *American Agriculturalist* (1922–32), he first came to public service as a farm expert. Pres. Franklin D. Roosevelt named him secretary of the treasury (1934–45). He played an important role in wartime aid to Europe, including War Bond sales and Lend-Lease, but he is best known for the Morgenthau Plan to subdivide Germany into agricultural states and for his role in the Bretton Woods Conference (1944), at which the World Bank and the International Monetary Fund were established.

Moriscos, Christianized Moors of Spain. As Moorish Spain was reconquered by Christian rulers from the north, they generally established a policy of voluntary conversion of the Moors; later it was decreed that all Moors either convert or be expelled from Spain. Many Moors ostensibly became Christians but were secretly still Muslims, or were suspected of being. The Spanish kings regarded them as a threat, and they were persecuted by the Spanish Inquisition. In 1568 they revolted and were put down three years later. In 1609, Philip III ordered all Moriscos expelled.

Morison, Samuel Eliot (1887–1976), US historian, b. Boston. Educated at Harvard, he was a member of the faculty there during most of his long teaching career. He was named official US navy historian for World War II (1942), and retired from the navy as a rear admiral (1951). He directed the Harvard Columbus Expedition, which traced Columbus' routes across the Atlantic, and the ensuing *Admiral of the Ocean Sea* (2 vols., 1942) won him the Pulitzer Prize. He won a second Pulitzer Prize for *John Paul Jones* (1959). Among his other works are *The Growth of the American Republic* (with Henry Steele Commager, 1930), *The Oxford History of the American People* (1965), and *The European Discovery of America* (2 vols., 1971–74).

Morley, Edward William (1838–1923), US chemist, b. Newark, N.J. He worked with A.A. Michelson on the famous experiment (1887) that demonstrated the absence in the universe of a stationary hypothetical substance called ether that was supposed to carry light waves. *See also* Michelson-Morley Experiment. △1522–24.

Mormon, The Book of, one of the scriptures of The Church of Jesus Christ of Latter-day Saints, or Mormons. Joseph Smith, founder of the Mormon Church, told that in 1827 he was led by a heavenly messenger, Moroni, to discover a set of inscribed gold plates. These plates held the record, as told by a prophet named Mormon, of a migration from Jerusalem to the Americas beginning in 600 BC. *See also* Mormons.

Mormon Cricket, wingless grasshopper found in W United States. It feeds on range grasses, wheat, and alfalfa. When weather conditions are favorable for a number of years, they multiply rapidly, migrate, and do serious crop damage. Length: 1–2in (25–51mm). Family Tettigoniidae; species *Anabrus simplex*. *See also* Grasshopper.

Mormons, members of the Mormon Church. The full title is The Church of Jesus Christ of Latter-day Saints. The church was established in upstate New York in 1830 by Joseph Smith. He reported that an angel directed him to discover *The Book of Mormon*, the source of Mormon doctrine. Believing that they were to found Zion, or a New Jerusalem, Smith and his followers moved west. They tried to settle in Ohio, Missouri, and Illinois but were driven out. Other settlers resented and attacked Mormons for a number of reasons, one being the Mormon belief that a man could take several wives. Joseph Smith was lynched in Illinois in 1844. Brigham Young then rose to leadership and took the Mormons to Utah Territory (1847) where they established Salt Lake City. Opposition to the Mormons continued, but they prospered through hard work. The Mormon president renounced polygamy in 1890, and Utah became a state in 1896.

The Mormon Church has more than 2,000,000 members. Headquarters remains in Salt Lake City, but the church has spread to other states and abroad. Many young members undertake missionary trips. All "worthy" males are considered members of the priesthood. The church is governed by a hierarchy headed by the president and a council of 120. *See also* Mormon, The Book of; Smith, Joseph. △1274.

Morning Glory, family of twining and trailing vines native to tropical South America. Blue, purple, pink, or white flowers are funnel-shaped with 5 shallow lobes or a flaring disk; they bloom in summer and early autumn. Species of morning glory include the small-flowering *Ipomoea lacunosa*; *I. purpurea*, with heart-shaped leaves; and *I. pandurata*, or man-of-the-earth, which has a white flower with purple center and large underground tubers. Family Convolvulaceae.

Morning Sickness. △702.

Moro, Muslim peoples of the S Philippines, comprising nine separate groups speaking distinct languages. From the first Spanish settlements in the area in 1571 to their suppression by US forces under General John J. Pershing in 1913, the Moro lived by piracy and raiding their Christian neighbors to the north, as well as by fishing and trading.

Morocco (Al-Magreb), independent nation in N Africa. It is a constitutional monarchy with both modern and traditional elements.

Land and Economy. Situated on the NW corner of Africa with 1,200mi (1,932km) of coastline on the Atlantic Ocean and Mediterranean Sea, Morocco is bordered by Spanish Sahara and Algeria (S and E). The Atlas Mts run inland, parallel to the Atlantic, with ranges rising 13,600ft (4,080m) above sea level. Climate on the Atlantic side of the Atlas is semi-tropical; on the Mediterranean coast the climate is mild. The rugged Rif Mts face Gilbraltar. In the W and central portions of the country are rich plains and cultivated plateaus. About 70% of the Moroccans derive their income from agriculture. Morocco ranks first in world phosphate exports. Foreign-owned farm lands were nationalized in 1973. Tourism attracts over 1,000,000 people yearly to Morocco's ruins, oases, and legendary cities.

People. Moroccan population is made up of three main divisions: the indigenous Berbers and descend-

Alberto Moravia

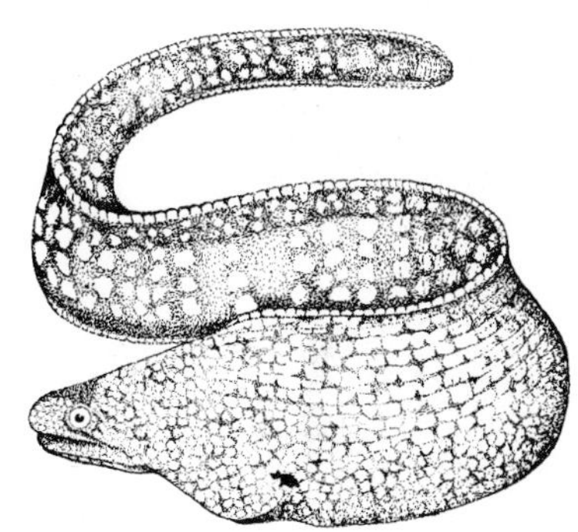

Moray eel

J. Pierpont Morgan

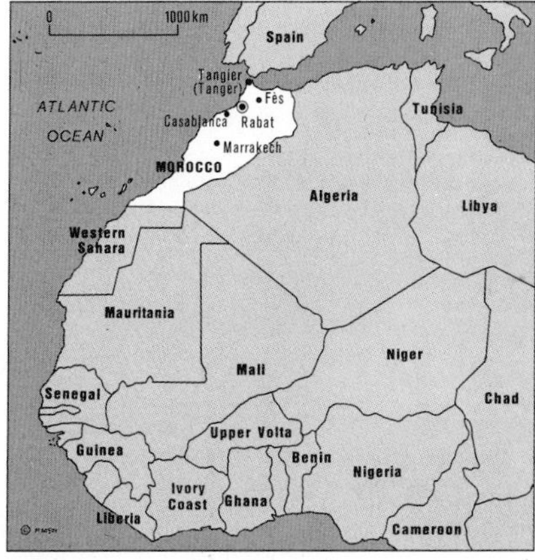

0
1000km
Spain
Tangier
(Tanger)
Fès
ATLANTIC
OCEAN
Casablanca
Rabat
Marrakech
MOROCCO
Tunisia
Algeria
Libya
Western
Sahara
Mauritania
Niger
Mali
Senegal
Chad
Upper Volta
Guinea
Benin
Nigeria
Ivory
Coast
Ghana
Liberia
Cameroon

Morocco

ants of 8th- and 11th-century Arab invaders. The slave trade brought many Sudanese to the S section. Foreign residents are mostly French and Spanish. Languages include Arabic, French, and Spanish. Berber is spoken in the rural areas. Islam is the established state religion. Literacy is estimated at 15%.

Government. Final civil and religious authority rests with the king. The unicameral parliament is elected by universal adult suffrage. The king may dissolve parliament and in emergency conditions may rule by decree.

History. The earliest records about this area were in Hanno's *Periplus*, which mentions Carthaginian coastal colonies. Islamic Arabs invaded in the 8th century, and the present Alaouite dynasty, rulers of Morocco since 1649, claims to be descended from the prophet Mohammed. European powers vied for Moroccan resources, and in 1912 it became a protectorate of France by terms of the Treaty of Fez. Nationalist uprisings continued for two decades, and nationalists organized for independence in 1944 under the Istiqlal Party. Political independence from France came on March 2, 1956. Later agreements with Spain restored Spanish zones of influence to Morocco. Mohammed V, sultan since 1927, was succeeded by his son, King Hassan II, and Morocco became a constitutional monarchy in 1962. Army revolts and several attempts to assassinate the King failed. Hassan dramatically asserted Moroccan claims to the Spanish Sahara in 1975 by leading a march into the area.

PROFILE

Official name: Kingdom of Morocco
Area: 172,413sq mi (446,550sq km)
Population: 17,500,000
Density: 102per sq mi (39per sq km)
Chief cities: Rabat (capital), Casablanca, Marrakech, Tangier
Government: Monarchy
Religion: Islam (state)
Language: Arabic
Monetary unit: Dirham
Gross national product: $4,844,000,000
Per capita income: $286
Industries: carpets, leather goods, clothing, textiles, processed food, wine, chemicals, pharmaceuticals
Agriculture: cereals, barley, wheat, corn, citrus fruits, sugar beets, sheep, dates, grapes, almonds
Minerals: phosphate, cobalt, antimony, lead, manganese, zinc, oil, coal
Trading partners: France, United States, West Germany, USSR

Moropus. △576.

Morosini, Venetian noble family dating from the 10th century. They gave four doges and many military leaders to the Republic of Venice and two cardinals to the Roman Catholic Church. **Andrea Morosini** (1558–1618) was official historian of the Republic and wrote *Historia Veneta ab anno 1521 ad annum 1615*. **Francesco** (1618–94) was an illustrious general and naval commander who was elected doge in 1688.

Morpheme, the smallest meaningful unit of speech. It may be an entire word—"work"—or a part of one—"re" in "rework". An inflectional (paradigmatic) morpheme is the added "s, es, ed, ing." A derivational morpheme is the "hood" in "motherhood." The root of the word is a separate morpheme. △864.

Morpheus, in Greek mythology, the god of dreams, supposedly expert in imitating the forms of men. He was the son of Hypnos, the god of sleep.

Morphine, the principal alkaloid of opium, used to dull sensation and relieve pain. *See* Opium.

Morpho Butterfly, large, tropical American butterfly noted for brilliant blue metallic luster of upper surfaces of its wings. Family Morphoidae.

Morphology, in biology. △572.

Morphology, Social. △876–82, 888–90.

Morrill Land Grant Act (1862), US legislation granting 30,000 acres (12,140 hectares) in each state per congressman to endow agricultural and technical colleges. The bill was first introduced in 1857 by Rep. Justin Morrill; 13,000,000 acres have been distributed, and some 70 colleges founded under the act.

Morris, family of US statesmen and landowners. **Richard Morris** (died 1672) bought land from the Dutch in what is now New York. His son, **Lewis Morris** (1671–1746), was the first governor of New Jersey (1738–46). His brother, **Robert Hunter Morris** (*c.* 1700–64), was chief justice of New Jersey (1738–56) and governor of Pennsylvania (1754–56). **Gouverneur Morris** was a grandson of Lewis and a half-brother of **Richard Morris** (1730–1810), who was appointed chief justice of the New York supreme court (1779). Richard Morris' son **Lewis Richard Morris** (1760–1825) was assistant to the secretary of foreign affairs (1781–83). From his manor in Springfield, Vt., Lewis participated in Vermont politics, and served in the US House of Representatives (1797–1803). *See also* Morris, Gouverneur.

Morris, Gouverneur (1752–1816), US statesman and diplomat, b. Morrisania, N.Y. Morris served his state in both legislative and executive capacities during the American Revolution. As a delegate to the Continental Congress (1777–78) and to the Constitutional Convention of 1787, Morris took an active part in establishing the bases for the new government. He later served as minister to France and England (1789–94) and in the US Senate (1800–03).

Morris, Robert (1734–1806), American banker, financier of the Revolution and a signer of the Declaration of Independence, b. England. Arriving in Maryland in 1774, he soon became vice-president of the Pennsylvania Committee of Safety (1775–76) and was a member of the Continental Congress (1776–78). US superintendent of finance (1781–84), he established the first US commercial bank and chartered the Bank of North America (1781).

Morris, William (1834–96), English poet and craftsman. With his friends Burne-Jones and Dante Gabriel Rossetti, he started a firm of decorators known as Morris and Company, which designed wallpaper, furniture, and tapestries. Also a poet, his most notable works are *The Defence of Guenevere and Other Poems* (1858), and *The Life and Death of Jason* (1867), and *The Earthly Paradise* (3 vol. 1868–70). One of his most important ventures was the Kelmscott Press, established in 1890. There he designed the type, page borders, and bindings of fine books.

Morrison Formation. △572.

Morristown, town in N New Jersey, on Whippany River; seat of Morris co; served as winter headquarters for George Washington during American Revolution (1776–77, 1779–80); site of Morristown National Historic Park (est. 1933), Villa Walsh College (1928). Industries: clothing, quarries, metal products, umbrellas. Settled 1709–10; inc. 1865. Pop. (1970) 17,662.

Morse, Samuel F(inley) B(reese) (1791–1872), US inventor and artist, b. Charlestown, Mass. As a portrait painter, Morse helped to found the National Academy of Design in 1826. Beginning in 1832, Morse experimented for 12 years on a practical system of using electricity to send messages by telegraphy. He developed the Morse Code to simplify the system. In 1844 he sent the message "What hath God wrought?" from Washington to Baltimore. He collaborated with Cyrus Field (1857–58) in laying the first transatlantic cable. Morse was also one of the founders of Vassar College (1861). △1790.

Morse, Wayne Lyman (1900–74), US political leader, b. Madison, Wis. He began his political career as a US senator (1945–69) with the Republican party, but grew critical of what he termed reactionary elements in the party and refused to support Dwight Eisenhower (1952). He declared himself a Democrat (1955) and was subsequently reelected to the Senate (1956–62). He ardently opposed the Vietnam War and voted against the Gulf of Tonkin resolution (1964). He lost his bids for reelection in 1968 and 1972, but won the Democratic primary for the Senate in 1974. He died before the election.

Morse Code, the code used for radiotelegraphy. It consists of dots and dashes created by the interrupting of a continuous radio wave. The dashes are three times the length of the dots. Characters vary in length from a single dot or dash to five dots or dashes or a combination thereof. △868, 1790, 1794.

Mortality Rates. △734, 802.

Mortar. △1614, 1734.

Morte D'Arthur, Le (*c.* 1469), Arthurian prose romance by Thomas Malory. Its 21 books deal principally with the quest for the Holy Grail, the death of King Arthur, and the disintegration of the fellowship of the Round Table. Malory borrowed much of his material from earlier French romances, but skillfully recast these diffuse originals into a continuous and dramatic narrative. His austere prose style further underlines the tragedy implicit in the downfall of Arthur. *See also* Arthurian Romance. △1100.

Mortimer, Roger de, 8th Baron Wigmore, 1st Earl of March (1287–1330), English nobleman. Having secured his position in Ireland against the Lacy family, he opposed the Despensers in Wales and was imprisoned (1322). Escaping to France, he returned to England (1326) as the paramour of Queen Isabella, and, after Edward II's deposition and death, virtually ruled England until executed by Edward III.

Mortmain, a term meaning the ownership of land by a perpetual corporation. Originally referring to tenure by a religious organization, it now includes ownership by charitable and business corporations. A French word meaning "dead hand," mortmain had a troubled history throughout the Middle Ages when the Roman Catholic Church acquired large properties that were exempt from taxation. In many countries tax-exempt church properties are now restricted to essential buildings and properties.

Morton, James Douglas, 4th Earl of (*c.* 1516–81), Scottish statesman. As Mary Stuart's lord chancellor (appointed 1563), he supported unenthusiastically her marriage to Lord Darnley, and subsequently approved Darnley's murder (1567), opposing Mary thereafter. Succeeding as regent (1572), he administered Scotland efficiently but was criticized for his pro-English policy. French influence at court finally caused his downfall and execution for complicity in Darnley's death.

Morton, Jelly Roll (1885–1941), US jazz pianist, bandleader, and composer, b. Ferdinand Joseph LaMenthe Morton in Gulfport, La. He played at first in New Orleans and began recording extensively in 1923 using small groups of top jazz musicians. He toured America with various bands and combos and is regarded as the first great composer and orchestrator of jazz.

Morton, John (1420?–1500), English statesman and prelate. After taking a degree in law at Oxford he practiced in the ecclesiastical courts of London and received substantial ecclesiastical preferment from the Lancastrians. Following their defeat in 1461 he lived in exile, returning only in 1470. In the tumultuous times that followed, Morton made himself useful as prelate and statesman to Edward II. When Richard III ascended Morton worked in the interests of the earl of Richmond, who, when he became Henry VII in 1485, appointed Morton archbishop of Canterbury (1486), lord chancellor (1487) and cardinal (1493).

Morton, William Thomas Green (1819–68), US dentist who pioneered in the use of ether as an anesthesia in 1846, b. Charlton, Mass. He publicized his work and generally received credit for the discovery, although ether had been used earlier by Crawford W. Long. *See also* Anesthesia. △752.

Morton Grove, town in NE Illinois, 15mi (24km) N of Chicago; forest preserves supply natural recreational facilities. Industries: pumps, electrical equipment, cosmetics. Inc. 1895. Pop. (1970) 26,369.

Mosaic, type of surface decoration using designs made of small pieces of material, such as stone, tile, or glass, closely set together in some adhesive material, such as wet mortar. Mosaics were often used in floor and wall decorations as early as the 4th millennium BC in Mesopotamia. In the Near East, mosaics were made of natural pebbles, and by the 5th century BC, the technique in Greece had developed to the degree where delicate designs with much detail were common. By the 3rd century BC, pebbles were replaced by cut marble cubes, or tesserae, in Hellenistic mosaics. During Roman times, floor mosaics, usually featuring a center design surrounded by a decorative, geometric border, were made. In the early Christian era, the floor mosaic was replaced by the wall mosaic, which was used to decorate church interiors. The marble cubes were replaced by brightly colored glass cubes, sometimes of golden color, especially during the Byzantine era. Mosaic art reached its height in the 6th century in such buildings as San Vitale in Ravenna, and again in the 11th and 12th centuries in Hagia Sophia in Istanbul. △1024, 1060.

Mosaic, any of several virus diseases that results in mottling of leaves with light green or yellow blotches. Some mosaics also cause curling and puckering of leaves and stunting of plants. They are serious diseases of many crops, including apples, peaches, beans, cucumbers, and tobacco.

Mosasaur, extinct marine lizard of Cretaceous times. Their powerful, crocodilelike bodies were propelled by paddlelike limbs and a flattened, sculling tail. They ate fish and mollusks. Mosasaurs are distantly related to modern land-living monitor lizards. *Tylosaurus* was a common North American genus. Length: to 30ft (9m). △570.

Mosby, John Singleton (1833–1916), Confederate partisan leader in the Civil War, b. Edgemont, Vt. He is known as the leader of "Mosby's Confederacy," a group of 200 men who attacked Union cavalry, destroyed communications, and appropriated supplies. After the war, Mosby joined the Republican party, held several minor political posts, and wrote his memoirs: *Mosby's War Reminiscences and Stuart's War Campaigns* (1887).

Moscow (Moskva), capital and largest city of USSR, and of Moscow oblast, in Russian SFSR, on the Moskva River E of its junction with the Moscow Canal, 400mi (640km) SE of Leningrad. Archeological remains indicate site has been inhabited since Neolithic times; Russian documents do not mention it until 1147 (as a village). It became a separate principality by end of 13th century and in 1367 the first stone walls of Kremlin were built. In 1341 it took principality of Vladimir and from 1462–1505 Grand Duke Ivan III (first to take the title of tsar) led successful campaign to annex principality of Novgorod; he defeated Tartars and invaded Lithuania. Polish troops occupied Moscow in 1610, but were driven out in 1612. Moscow was capital of grand duchy of Russia 1547–1712, when it was moved to St Petersburg (now Leningrad). In 1812 the city, which was built almost entirely of wood, burned to the ground; Napoleon and French troops were occupying city and fire forced them out. In 1918 it became capital of USSR. German siege of Moscow during WWII was broken by Russians, giving Germany its first major defeat of the war. The Kremlin is the center of the city, and the administrative center of the USSR; it includes palaces, churches, and government buildings within its 40-ft (12-m) walls. Adjoining it are Red Square, Lenin Mausoleum, the 16th-century cathedral of Basil the Beatified (now an anti-religious museum). City is also site of University of Moscow (1755), Tretyakov Gallery (1880), Bolshoi Theater, about 90 other institutes of higher education, and 450 scientific institutes. Industries: metalworking, oil refining, automobiles, film making, precision instruments, chemicals, wood and paper products, tourism. Pop. 7,061,000.

Moscow (or **Muscovy**), **Grand Duchy of,** 15th–18th century state. **Ivan I** (1301–40) began a consolidation of territories much increased by **Ivan III** (1440–1505), who absorbed Novgorod in 1478. **Ivan the Terrible** (1530–84) gathered together all the Russian lands under his rule and in 1547 became Tsar of all Russia. This consolidation was followed by a period of anarchy known as the Time of Troubles (1598–1613) that lasted until the Romanov dynasty was established. Conquests in Siberia and the Ukraine, despite Polish rivalry, further strengthened Moscow. Under **Peter the Great** (1672–1725) the kingdom of Russia became an empire. The cradle of Russian culture, Moscow was an autocracy ruled by a boyars' Duma and a national assembly. △1176.

Moscow (Moskva) river in W central USSR; rises W of Uvarovka in Smolensk-Moscow Upland, flows NW, then E past Moajsk and Zvenigorod, and SE past Moscow and Bronnicy to the Oka River below Kolomna. It receives the Severka and Pachra rivers from the right and the Ruza and Istra from the left. Below the mouth of the Moscow Canal, the river has a lock system and forms the Pererva Reservoir at L'ublino. It is navigable below the Moscow Canal April-November. Length: 315mi (507km).

Moseley, Henry Gwyn-Jeffreys (1887–1915), English physicist. His initial studies involved radioactivity; later he discovered a relationship between the X-ray spectra of the elements and their atomic numbers. His investigations showed that the atomic number of an element and not its atomic weight determines its major properties.

Moselle (Mosel), river in France and Germany; rises in Vosges Mts, NE France, flows NW past Remiremont, Épinal, and Toul; turns N to flow past Metz and Thionville, and NE to leave France and form Luxembourg-German boundary; flows through Germany to empty into Rhine at Koblenz; connected to Rhine, Meuse, and Seine rivers by canals. Along its steep slopes between Trier and Koblenz Riesling grapes are grown from which Moselle wines are made. Length: 320mi (515km).

Moses (*c.* 13th century BC), in the Bible, prophet and leader of the Jewish people. A Levite born in Egypt, he was found as a baby by the pharaoh's daughter and raised at court. Answering God's call, he led the Hebrew tribes from Egypt to Canaan and gave them the Ten Commandments. He did not enter the Promised Land but God allowed him to see it from Mt Pisgah just before he died. △982.

Moses, Grandma (1860–1961), b. Anna Mary Robertson in Greenwich, N.Y. At age 76 she gave up embroidery because of arthritis and began to paint. Having lived on farms her entire life, she painted landscapes in a primitive style, showing people involved in various farm activities.

Moskva. *See* Moscow.

Mosque, the Muslim place of worship. Usually decorated with abstract and geometric designs, the building's parts include the *mihrab,* or prayer niche, which shows the direction of Mecca; the *minaret,* or tower, from which the meuzzin calls prayers; the *courtyard* for washing before prayer; and the *madrasa,* or school. The first domed mosque, the Dome of the Rock, Jerusalem, was built in 691. Other famous mosques include the Mosque of the Prophet, Medina, containing Mohammed's tomb; the Mosque at Mecca, containing the Kaaba; and the 3-domed Pearl Mosque, Agra. △1064.

Mosquito, fragile, tan to black insect, 0.12 to 0.36in (3–9mm) long, of great economic importance; found worldwide. The adult female sucks blood from warm-blooded animals, including man. It transmits several diseases of man including malaria, yellow fever, dengue fever, viral encephalitis, and filariasis. The larvae are aquatic and are found in lakes, rivers, and salt marshes, and in other areas that retain water. Family Culicidae. *See also* Diptera. △492.

Mosquito Fish, freshwater fish of the SE United States known for its ability to eat large amounts of mosquito larvae. Colors are brown and gray with bluish shimmer. Length: 2.25in (5.7cm). Family Poecilidae; species *Gambusia affinis.*

Moss, any of about 15,000 species of small simple nonflowering green plants that typically grow in colonies, often forming dense carpets. Mosses are primitive plants that do not have specialized tissues for transporting water, food, and minerals, although they do have parts resembling stems, leaves, and roots of the higher (flowering) plants. They grow on soil, rocks, and tree trunks in a wide variety of land habitats, from the tropics to circumpolar regions. They favor shady damp places and some species live in freshwater lakes and streams. Because carpets of moss can absorb large amounts of water, they help reduce soil erosion. The peat mosses, which are especially water-absorbent, are widely used as a substitute for natural humus to improve soil quality. *See also* Bryophyte. △436.

Mössbauer, Rudolph Ludwig (1929–), German physicist. He is credited with discovering the Mössbauer effect (also called the recoil-free gamma-ray resonance absorption), which states that in certain cases gamma-ray energy may be emitted or absorbed by some excited nuclei without the nucleus exhibiting a recoil. This effect has been used to verify the theory of relativity and to study solid material properties. For his work he shared with R. Hofstadter the Nobel Prize in physics in 1961. *See also* Relativity Theory.

Mossi, Negroid people inhabiting Upper Volta and found in small numbers elsewhere in West Africa. Their traditional livelihood is a form of sedentary agriculture, staple crops including millet and sorghum. The Mossi feudal kingdom traditionally worshiped ancestors and practiced an earth cult; Christianity and Islam now prevail.

Moss Pink, creeping, evergreen, perennial plant with crowded leaves on numerous stems that form a mat on the ground. The flowers are purple, pink, rose, white, or lavender, often with darker centers. Family Polemoniaceae; species *Phlox subulata.*

Most Favored Nation Clause, provision in trade treaties whereby nations grant to each other the most favorable commercial benefits, such as tariff reductions, which, individually, each nation may accord to a third nation.

Mosul (Al-Mawsil), city in N Iraq, 200mi (322km) NNW of Baghdad, on Tigris River; capital of Ninawa prov. An ancient city, it was taken by Muslims 636; major Mesopotamian center 8th–13th centuries; occupied by Ottomans 1534–1918; under British occupation and mandate 1918–32; awarded to Iraq by League of Nations 1926 after a dispute for its possession between Iraq and Turkey. Nearby are ruins of ancient Nineveh; seat of Mosul University (1967). Industries: oil, cement, sugar, livestock, agricultural produce. Pop. 243,311.

Motet, musical form important in the development of

Samuel F. B. Morse

Wayne Morse

Moscow

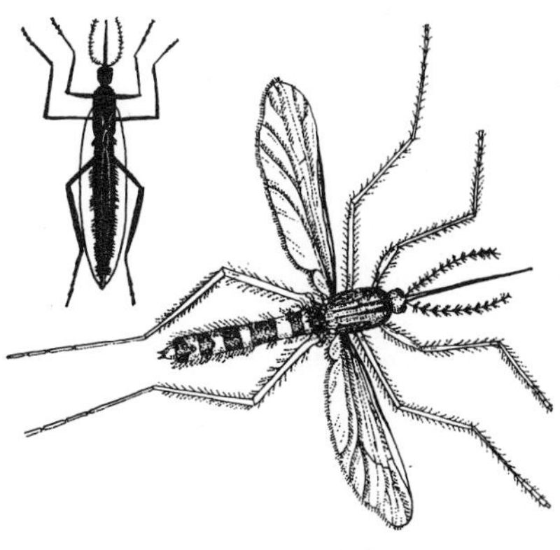

Mosquito

polyphonic music from about AD 1200 to 1600. The Medieval motet (13th and 14th centuries) consisted of three voice parts sung in Latin. The Flemish or Renaissance motet (15th and 16th centuries) consisted of four or five voice parts sung by chorus. Around 1600 the motet began to develop new features, such as instrumental accompaniment, solo singers, and use of languages other than Latin. These features developed mainly in Germany, as in the six motets of J. S. Bach. *See also* Polyphony.

Moth, chiefly nocturnal insects distinguished from butterflies and skippers by stout bodies and threadlike or featherlike antennae. At rest, a moth's wings are spread horizontally, held rooflike over its body, or wrapped around its body. Order Lepidoptera. *See also* Lepidoptera. △502.

Mother Carey's Chicken. *See* Storm Petrel.

Mother Goose, traditionally in France a figure who told folktales. The phrase *Les Contes de Ma Mère l'Oye* (Tales of Mother Goose) appeared on Charles Perrault's 1697 collection of tales. The name first appeared in England on a collection of 50 traditional folk rhymes and 16 songs from Shakespeare compiled by John Newbery in 1760. He called the collection *Mother Goose's Melody or Sonnets for the Cradle.*

Mother-of-Pearl, shiny substance lining many mollusk shells. It is composed of calcium carbonate deposited in layers interspersed with some organic material. Diffraction of light causes iridescent play of colors. It is used in making buttons and jewelry. *See also* Mollusk.

Motherwell, Robert (1915–), US painter, b. Aberdeen, Wash. Associated with the school of action painters, he is best known for his abstract expressionistic works.

Mothproofing Agent. △1560.

Motion. *See* Laws of Motion. △1494.

Motion, Stellar, change in position of a star due to both proper motion and to radial motion along the line of sight. △126.

Motion Pictures, series of sequential photographic images of a moving subject photographed with a motion picture camera and enlarged onto a screen by a motion picture projector to produce the effect of movement. Also, the art, industry, production techniques, distribution, and projection of films. △1316, 1362, 1370, 1788.

Motmot, Mexican and Central and South American bird that has a green body, turquoise head, and serrated bill for crushing insects. The ornamental, graduated tail often has a central naked rectrix decorated with a racket-shaped tip. They drill a tunnel into an earthen bank and excavate a cavity for the dull white eggs (3–4) that both parents incubate. Length: 7–18in (18–46cm). Family Motmotidae.

Motor, Electric. *See* Electric Motor.

Motorcycle, a two-wheeled automotive vehicle, that combines the principles of a bicycle and the internal combustion engine. First designed in 1884 by Gottlieb Daimler, it did not become popular until about 1910. Most have four-stroke engines. Transmission is through chain or gearing between engine and gearbox. Usually controls on handbars govern the throttle, clutch, and front brake. △1690.

Motor Neurons. *See* Effectors.

Mott, Lucretia Coffin (1793–1880), US social reformer, b. Nantucket, Mass. A Quaker, she championed intellectual freedom and was an outspoken opponent of slavery. She became a Quaker minister (1821) and traveled lecturing on social reform and religion. One of the founders of the American Anti-Slavery Society (1833), she also helped establish the Philadelphia Female Anti-Slavery Society. Because she was refused a seat as delegate to the World's Anti-Slavery Convention in London (1840), she turned some of her attention to feminism. With Elizabeth Cady Stanton, she organized the first women's rights convention at Seneca Falls, N.Y. (1848).

Mo tzu, or **Mo ti** or **Micius** (470–391 BC), founder of the Moist school of Chinese philosophy. Both a high government official and the founder of a school for government service, his belief in universal love clashed with the prevailing Confucian views. *See also* Confucianism.

Mouflon, or European mouflon, wild sheep of Sardinia and Corsica, introduced widely in Europe at various times. Smaller than argali and bighorn sheep, they bear woolly underfur and are considered an ancestor of domestic sheep. Family Bovidae; species *Ovis musimon. See also* Sheep. △548.

Moulmein (Maulmain), port city in S Burma, at mouth of Salween River, on E shore of Gulf of Martaban; division and district seat; communications center with railroad and airport. Exports: rice, teak. Pop. 322,000.

Moulton Bicycle. △1688.

Mound Bird. *See* Megapode.

Mound Builders, name given to the North American Indians responsible for groups of earthen mounds found in the Ohio and Mississippi river valleys. The mounds, sometimes with a hut-like structure inside, are either sacrificial or mortuary. They contain skeletons or ashes with buried ceremonial objects.

Mountain, a part of the earth's surface that rises conspicuously higher, at least 1,000 ft (305m), than the surrounding area. Mountains have a restricted summit area, comparatively steep sides, and considerable bare rock surface. They are identified geologically by their most characteristic feature, for example, fold, volcanic, or fault-block mountains. Mountains occur as single isolated masses, as ranges, and in systems or chains. △252, 608.

Mountain, The. *See* Montagnards.

Mountain Ash, small tree or shrub grown in Europe and the United States. The rowan tree *(Sorbus aucuparia)* of Europe is grown as an ornamental in the United States; height: to 50ft (15.2m). The North American *S. americana* grows to 30ft (9.1m) and *S. scopulina* has larger fruit. Family Rosaceae. △448.

Mountain Beaver. *See* Sewellel.

Mountain Goat, ruminant native to Rocky Mountains from Alaska to Montana and introduced in Black Hills of South Dakota. Classified as a goat-antelope, rather than a goat, its thick, shaggy fur is white to yellow and its shoulders are humped. It is a sure-footed climber and jumper although less graceful than the bighorn sheep. It is probably monogamous. Length: to 62in (1.6m); weight: to 200lb (90kg). Family Bovidae; species *Oreamnos americanus.*

Mountain Laurel, broad-leaved evergreen shrub native to E North America. It has pink or white flowers. The leaves are poisonous. Height: 4–25ft (1.2–7.6m). Family Ericaceae; species *Kalmia latifolia.*

Mountain Lion. *See* Puma.

Mountain View, city in W California, 11mi (18km) NW of San Jose; site of Moffet Naval Air Station and Ames Laboratory of the National Aeronautics and Space Administration. Industries: shipping, publishing, printing, research. Settled 1852; inc. 1902. Pop. (1970) 54,206.

Mountbatten of Burma, Louis Francis Albert Victor Nicholas Mountbatten, 1st Earl (1900–), British naval commander and statesman. A grandson of Queen Victoria, he saw distinguished naval service during World War II, ousting the Japanese from Burma. In 1947 he became India's last viceroy and was later first sea lord (1955–59).

Mount Desert, island off SE coast of Maine, partly in Acadia National Park; Bar Harbor is the chief city; resort area. Settled 1762. Area: 100sq mi (259sq km).

Mount McKinley National Park, park in central Alaska, the second largest national park. Mt McKinley, 20,320ft (6,198m), is the highest peak in North America. There are large glaciers, caribou, Dall sheep, timber wolves, grizzly bears, and other wildlife. Area: 1,939,493acres (785,495hectares). Est. 1917.

Mount Prospect, residential town in NE Illinois, 21mi (34km) NW of Chicago. Inc. 1917. Pop. (1970) 34,995.

Mount Rainier National Park, park in W central Washington. It is the greatest single-peak glacial system in the United States. Glaciers radiate from the summit and slopes of this ancient volcano. There are dense forests and subalpine flowered meadows. Area: 241,781acres (97,921hectares). Est. 1899.

Mount Rushmore National Memorial, memorial in SW South Dakota, in Black Hills, containing huge sculptured busts of US presidents George Washington, Thomas Jefferson, Abraham Lincoln, and Theodore Roosevelt carved out of granite into face of Mt Rushmore; designed by Gutzon Borglum, the work took 14 years to complete; visible for a distance of 60mi (97km). Area: 1,278acres (518hectares). Est. 1925; dedicated 1927; completed 1941.

Mount Vernon, city in SE New York, on Bronx River adjacent to New York City; site of Old St Paul's Church seized by Hessian soldiers during Revolutionary War; scene of journalist John Peter Zenger's arrest (1734) in classic freedom of press case. Industries: truck bodies, cosmetics, electronic components. First settled 1664 as Hutchinson's; inc. 1851 by Home Industrial Association of New York, as community of homes for New York City workers; chartered as city 1892. Pop. (1970) 72,778.

Mount Vernon, estate in Virginia, on Potomac River 15mi (24km) S of Washington D.C.; home and burial place of George Washington. The estate was part of the Washington family holdings 1674–1858, when the Mt Vernon Ladies' Association acquired the mansion, and eventually a total of 500acres (202hectares) of the 8,000acres (3,240hectares). The furnishings in the first story of the 2½ story mansion and Washington's bedroom are original. Museum in the estate was built 1928.

Mount Wilson Observatory. *See* Hale Observatories.

Mourning Athena. △1000.

Mourning Cloak Butterfly, common, medium-sized butterfly with purple-brown wings bordered with yellow. Its larvae feed on leaves or willows, elms, poplars, and hackberries. Species *Nymphalis antiopa.*

Mourning Dove, small, grayish dove common in North America, known for its plaintive, mournful cry. Species *Zenaidura macroura. See also* Dove.

Mouse, name for small rodents with pointed snouts and long tails, mostly members of the families Muridae and Cricetidae. The big-eared and short-legged gray or brown house mouse *(Mus musculus)* is probably best known. Prolific nest-builders, house mice may live in human habitations or in the wild. They are omnivorous and often destructive, and may carry human diseases. Domesticated as laboratory mice or pets, they are often albino or multicolored. Length: about 3in (76mm), excluding tails; weight: to 1oz (30g). △546.

Mousebird, or coly, small, crested, long-tailed, fruit-eating bird found in warm parts of Africa south of the Sahara. It is sometimes considered a pest. Mouselike, they are grayish with bright markings and scamper along branches. White or creamy eggs (2–6) are laid in a cup-shaped nest in a tree or bush. Family Coliidae.

Mouth Organ. *See* Harmonica.

Mouton, sheared sheepskin, processed in fur industry to resemble beaver or, occasionally, seal.

Moynihan, Daniel Patrick (1927–), US social scientist and public official, b. Tulsa, Okla. Moynihan has done social research, taught, and held several government positions, including assistant to the president for urban affairs (1969–73), ambassador to India (1973–75), ambassador to the United Nations (1975–76), and US Senator from New York (1977–). His best known books include *Beyond the Melting Pot* (1963), which described the emerging sense of independence among US minorities, and *The Negro Family: The Case for National Action* (1965), which focuses on the black family in the United States.

Mozambique (Moçambique), independent nation in E Africa, formerly called Portuguese East Africa. It gained its independence in 1975. Its chief export crop is cashew nuts.

Land and Economy. Seated on the SE coast of Africa with neighbors Tanzania (N), Malawi, Zambia, and Rhodesia (W), the Republic of South Africa and Swaziland (S), and the Indian Ocean (E), it is divided into lowlands (44% of country) and uplands, with mountains along the W border. The Zambezi River bisects the country. Droughts and floods are common in the S section. Although subsistence farming engages most of the population, Mozambique has been developing cash crops and is the world's leading exporter of cashew nuts. A portion of foreign earnings comes from migrant laborers working in South African and Rhodesian gold mines. Inexpensive power, irrigation, and commercial fishing are expected benefits from the new Cabora Bassa dam on the Zambezi River.

People. With Portuguese as the unifying language, Mozambique consists of numerous tribal groups: Tsonga and Changones in the S, Sena and Manica in the center, Nianja in the NW, Macuas in the N, and Makondes in the NE. Isolated N tribes are mainly animists or fetishists with some Islam practiced. S tribes have been affected by Catholic and Protestant missionaries.

Government. The revolutionary Communist coalition, Frelimo, has power to govern.

History. Portuguese rule of Mozambique started with Vasco da Gama's exploration in 1498. Traders, missionaries, and prospectors followed. Mozambique was given to Portugal at the Berlin West Africa Congress (1884–85), and in 1952 it was designated as an overseas province of Portugal. The 1974 revolution in Portugal paved the way for some reforms. After 10 years of anti-colonial agitation, an independence movement (Front for the Liberation of Mozambique) took power in September 1974 with promises of collective farms and education reforms. Most of the 185,-000 whites left the country.

PROFILE

Official name: People's Republic of Mozambique
Area: 302,328sq mi (783,030sq km)
Population: 9,200,000
Density: 30.4per sq mi (11.7per sq km)
Chief cities: Lourenço Marques (capital); Nampula
Government: people's republic
Religion: Tribal, Islam, Catholic
Language: Portuguese
Gross national product: $2,000,000,000
Per capita income: $334
Industries: cement, alcohol, textiles, food products
Agriculture: cashews, cotton, sugar, copra, tea
Minerals: coal, tantalite, copper, iron, bauxite, gold
Trading partners: USSR, People's Republic of China, Republic of South Africa

Mozart, Wolfgang Amadeus (1756–91), Austrian composer and musical genius, b. Salzburg. Playing and composing from early childhood, Mozart completed a total of 626 works before dying in poverty at the age of 35. Composing in the dominant Classical-Rococo styles of his time, he brought these forms to perfection. His operas *The Marriage of Figaro* (1786), *Don Giovanni* (1787), and *The Magic Flute* (1791) are ranked among the finest ever written. His 27 piano concertos set the form for concertos for decades to come. His 40 symphonies, piano sonatas, chamber music, sets of variations, vocal music, masses and other religious compositions all contain supreme achievements of the Classical period. *See also* Classical Music. △1174, 1196.

MS. *See* Multiple Sclerosis.

MSG. *See* Monosodium Glutamate.

MSH. *See* Melanocyte Stimulating Hormone.

Muawija. △1062.

Much Ado about Nothing (c.1598), 5-act comedy by William Shakespeare. The main plot, augmented by several characters of Shakespeare's own creation, is based on a work by Matteo Bandello. Claudio, persuaded by Don John that his fiancée Hero has been unfaithful to him with Borachio, denounces her as they are about to be married. Claudio has really seen Margaret, whom he mistakes for Hero, talking to Borachio. Hero faints and has it given out that she is dead. When Don John's villainy is revealed Claudio agrees to marry Hero's cousin to atone for Hero's death. At the altar the "cousin" is revealed to be Hero.

Muckrakers, name given by Pres. Theodore Roosevelt in 1906 to writers and critics in such magazines as *Collier's* and *McClure's,* who were exposing corrupt politicians and business practices. Roosevelt agreed that they were often right but deplored their sensational attacks. Leading muckrakers Ida Tarbell, Upton Sinclair, Lincoln Steffens, and Ray S. Baker worked hard to substantiate the charges and aroused public sentiment that led to many reforms in politics and business.

Mucopolysaccharide, any of the complex carbohydrates that are the chief constituents of the ground substance filling the spaces between cells and fibers of connective tissues. There exists a whole range of inherited disorders (mucopolysaccharidoses) that are marked by abnormal production, storage, and excretion of any of these substances. Symptoms include skeletal deformities, mental deficiency, heart defects, and deafness.

Mucous Membrane, membrane lining all body channels that communicate with the air, such as the respiratory tract, the digestive tract, and the glands secreting mucus. △686.

Mucus, a slippery, viscous fluid containing mucin produced by mucous linings of the body. It serves for lubrication and protection: nasal mucus traps airborne particles; mucus of the stomach protects the lining from irritation by secreted hydrochloric acid during digestion. △740.

Mud Dauber Wasp, black wasp with yellow markings, 0.75 to 1in (19–25mm) in length; found worldwide. It constructs its nests in the form of 1in (25mm) long mud tubes attached to building walls and ceilings. Its larva feed on spiders. Family Sphecidae, genera *Sceliphron* and *Chalybion. See also* Hymenoptera; Wasp. △502.

Mud Houses. △1616.

Mudpuppy, aquatic salamander of streams and rivers in S Canada and United States. It has dark red gills at the sides of the neck and brown-spotted skin. Fertilization is internal. Length: to 15in(38cm). Family Necturidae; species *Necturus maculosus. See also* Salamander.

Mudskipper, amphibianlike fish of Africa, Asia, and Australia. It gulps air and carries water in its gill cavities to survive out of water when the tide recedes. It hops on mud with its large pectoral fins. Length: 8in (20cm). Family Periophthalmidae, Species include *Periophthalmus barbarus.* △620.

Mud Snake, or hoop snake, snake found in swamps and lowlands of SE United States. A shiny, iridescent black with red sides, it has a stiffened, blunt tail tip. Eats aquatic salamanders. Length: 5ft (1.5m). Family Colubridae; species *Farancia abacura.*

Mudstone. △272.

Mud Turtle, freshwater, bottom-crawling turtle ranging from New England to Argentina. It has a short tail, fleshy chin barbels, and hinges across its undershell. There are 12 species. Length: 6in(15cm). Family Kinosternidae; genus *Kinosternon. See also* Musk Turtle; Turtle.

Muezzin. △848.

Mughal Empire. *See* Mogul Empire.

Mugwumps, US political faction in the 1880s composed of independent, or liberal, Republicans. In the 1884 presidential election, they deserted the Republican candidate, James G. Blaine, whom they considered corrupt, and supported the Democratic candidate, Grover Cleveland, whom they helped elect.

Muhammad, Elijah (1897–1975), leader of the Black Muslims (1934–75), b. Elijah Poole in Sandersville, Ga. He succeeded Wali Fard, the founder of the movement, as Black Muslim leader after Fard's disappearance in 1934. Under Muhammad, the Muslim doctrines were codified and the movement expanded and gained national attention. On his death, Elijah Muhammad was succeeded by his son Wallace. *See also* Black Muslims. △1062.

Muhammad Tughlu. △1202.

Muir, John (1838–1914), US naturalist, b. Scotland. An advocate of forest preservation, he was influential in the establishment of many national parks. Muir traveled the United States extensively, studying the glaciers and forests of the Sierra Nevadas, and exploring Alaska, where he discovered Glacier Bay and Muir Glacier. By 1867 he was urging the federal government to endorse a policy of forest conservation, and his writings and lobbying influenced conservation programs of both Presidents Grover Cleveland and Theodore Roosevelt.

Muisca. *See* Chibcha.

Mujibur Rahman (1920–75), Bangladesh political leader known as Sheikh Mujib, he worked towards the independence of Pakistan in 1947. He began in the 1960s the East Pakistani separatist movement, which culminated in the civil war of 1971. Mujib became prime minister of the newly formed Bangladesh in 1972, and president in 1975. He was killed in a coup d'état that overthrew his government.

Mukden (Shenyang, or Shen-yang), city in Manchuria, NE China, on Hun River, 100mi (161km) N of Yellow Sea; capital of Liaoning prov. City consists of three major divisions: old Chinese walled area containing former imperial palace and arsenal district; new Japanese-built city with administrative offices;

Lucretia Mott

Daniel Moynihan

Cen. Afr. Rep.
Sudan
Ethiopia
Cameroon
Somalia
Gabon
Congo
Uganda
Kenya
Zaire
INDIAN OCEAN
Tanzania
Malawi
Comoro Is.
Angola
Porto Amélia
Zambia
Moçambique
MOZAMBIQUE
Rhodesia
Madagascar
Beira
Namibia
Botswana
Inhambane
Swaziland
Maputo (Lourenço Marques)
ATLANTIC OCEAN
South Africa
Lesotho
0
1200km
Mozambique

Mudpuppy

Teihsi district, housing vast industrial complexes and residential areas. An early center for Chinese colonization in S Manchuria, city was captured by Manchus 16th century who made it their capital (1625) and gave it the present name. Mukden was made center of railroad system *c.* 1900; scene of important Japanese victory during Russo-Japanese War (1905), as a result of which Mukden and S Manchuria fell under Japanese control; seat of Chang Tso-lin and other Manchurian warlords; fell to Communist control November 1948; site of Manchurian Polytechnic Institute, Chinese Medical Institute, and Manchurian branch of Chinese Academy of Sciences; industrial and cultural center. Industries: coal, oil-shale, steel, machinery, chemicals, electrical equipment, agriculture, wire and cable. Pop. 3,750,000.

Mulberry, family *(Moraceae)* of trees and shrubs found in temperate regions and containing a milky latex. The family also includes two herbaceous plants, the hop and hemp plants. Other characteristics are simple leaves, unisexual flowers, and the production of fibers or edible fruits. Among the 1,400 varieties are 10 species of *Morus*, deciduous trees with fleshy, edible fruits, including the white mulberry *M. albas*, to 45ft (13.7m), of China, and the red mulberry *M. rubra*, to 70ft (21.3m), of E and central United States.

Mulch, layer of loose material placed over soil and around growing plants. Mulches, including leaves, straw, pine needles, woodchips, stones, newspaper, and synthetics (fiberglass, plastic) are used to stabilize soil temperature, keep weeds down, nourish plants, and conserve moisture. During winter, mulches also protect herbaceous perennials, produce humus, prevent soil heaving, and keep roots from freezing. Nature's mulches include fallen leaves, grasses, and snow.

Mule, hybrid cross between horse and ass. Known since ancient times and popularized in the United States by George Washington, it is compact and muscular with long ears. Almost always sterile, types include draft, sugar, farm, cotton, pack, and mining. Height: 48–70in (122–178cm) at shoulder; weight: 600–1,600lb (271–720kg).

Mule Deer, long-eared deer found from W Canada to N Mexico. A solitary animal, its antlers branch into two equal parts and it has a black tail. It is a popular game animal. Height: to 3.5ft (1.1m) at shoulder. Family Cervidae; species *Odocoileus Hemionus. See also* Deer.

Mulhouse, city in E France, on Ill River and Rhône-Rhine canal, 18mi (29km) NW of Basel, Switzerland. A free imperial city of 13th century, it joined a Swiss confederation in 1515. In 1586 it became a neutral republic until 1798 when it voted to unite with France; Germany held it 1871–1918; site of 16th-century town hall. Industries: cotton, wool, chemicals, automobile parts. Founded 717. Pop. 116,336.

Mullein, hardy biennial plant *(Verbascum)*, including common mullein *(V. thapsus)* that has 1-ft (30-m) leaves and long, dense, yellow flower spikes; height: to 6ft (1.8m). Family Scrophulariaceae.

Muller, Hermann Joseph (1890–1967), US geneticist, b. New York City. He was awarded the 1946 Nobel Prize in physiology or medicine for his discovery of the production of mutations by means of X-ray irradiation. Muller worked with geneticist Thomas Hunt Morgan, studied the rate and nature of mutations, and determined that X-rays could produce mutations. He warned against needless X-ray use and of the dangers of radioactive fallout.

Muller, Paul (1899–1965), Swiss chemist. He received the 1948 Nobel Prize in physiology and medicine for his discovery of the effectiveness of DDT as a contact poison against several insects, a discovery that at that time led to the control of many fly-borne diseases and to greater agricultural output.

Mullet, also called gray mullet, a schooling marine fish found worldwide in shallow tropical and temperate waters. Caught commercially, its torpedo-shaped body is green or blue and silver. Length: to 3ft (91.4cm); weight: to 15lb (6.8kg). Among the 100 species is the widely distributed striped *Mugil cephalus.* Family Mugilidae. △392.

Mulliken, Robert Sanderson (1896–), US chemist, b. Newburyport, Mass. After studying at M.I.T. he moved to Chicago, where he became professor. In 1966 he was awarded a Nobel Prize for his fundamental work on chemical bonds and molecular orbitals.

Mullions. △250.

Multan, city in E central Pakistan, in the Chenab River valley approx. 200mi (322km). SW of Lahore; industrial and commercial center. Ancient settlement was taken by Mahmud of Ghazni 1006 and by Tamerlane 1398; held by British 1848–1947; site of ancient Muslim tombs and Hindu temple. Industries: textiles, foundries, glassware, food processing, pottery, crafts. Pop. 596,000.

Multi-Channel Telephone Cable. △1792.

Multi-Party System, prevailing political system in most democratic societies where voting is on the basis of proportional representation. This entitles smaller parties to representation in the legislature along with major parties, which are often unable to muster majorities. The parties then ally to form temporary coalitions that support a leader and a program. Such alliances are tenuous and can lead to instability in government and frequent shifts in political rule.

Multiple Birth. △702.

Multiple Myeloma, malignant tumor of the bone marrow. It occurs mostly in middle age. Mild cases may be cured by surgery or irradiation.

Multiple Personality, relatively rare and extreme form of personality dissociation in which two or more distinct and often contradictory personality patterns coexist. These personalities may alternate and through amnesia be unknown to one another (eg. Dr. Jekyll and Mr. Hyde). Multiple personality should not be confused with the splitting of personality from reality in schizophrenia. *See also* Schizophrenia.

Multiple Sclerosis (MS), a disease of the nervous system, usually of the white matter (which conducts nerve impulses), in which there is degeneration of the sheath covering the nerve fibers (myelin sheath), resulting in weakness, lack of coordination, and speech and visual disturbances. Affected persons typically have relapses and remissions over many years. Its cause is unknown, but evidence suggests a possible viral origin. △722.

Multiple Stars, stellar systems consisting of three or more stars orbiting around a common center of gravity. One typical example is the Mizar-Alcor system in Ursa Major. The main star Mizar is triple while the fainter Alcor is a spectroscopic binary. *See also* Binary Star. △110.

Multiplet, group of elementary particles, all hadrons, with about the same mass, identical in all other properties except electric charge, and having up to four members. The nucleons and pions form multiplets. In strong interactions, members of a multiplet are all equivalent. A supermultiplet is a larger, more sophisticated and symmetrical grouping of hadrons involving eight quantum numbers, all members having identical spin.

Multiplication, arithmetical operation signified by $\times$, interpreted as repeated addition. Thus $a \times b$ is $a + a + \ldots + a$, in which b terms are added. In $a \times b$ ("a multiplied by b"), a is the multiplicant, b the multiplier, and the result is the product. *See also* Arithmetical Operations. △1446.

Mummy, a body treated for burial with preservatives. Mummification was most commonly practiced in ancient Egypt, where the internal organs were first removed, the body soaked in resin and other substances and then wrapped in linen bandage. The Incas of South America, the original inhabitants of the Canary Islands, and several other peoples also practiced mummification. Naturally preserved mummies have been discovered in Scandinavian peat bogs.

Mumps, a contagious disease, most common in children and caused by a myxovirus (one of a large group of viruses that includes the influenza virus). It has an incubation period of 18 to 22 days, after which fever and painful inflammation of the salivary glands begin, with marked swelling, especially in the parotid glands below and in front of the ears. Meningitis develops in about 10% of cases, and the infection may involve other organs such as the pancreas. In males past puberty, inflammation of the testes with subsequent sterility in some cases may occur. An attack of mumps results in persistent immunity.

Munch, Edvard (1863–1944), Norwegian painter and printmaker. As a printmaker, he made lithographs and woodcuts, often using many colors. He painted portraits and murals, but his best-known works are his highly expressionistic paintings that show basic human emotions, such as fear. For example, in "The Cry," the background is distorted to echo the circular shape of the cry from the figure's mouth. *See also* Expressionism. △1294.

Munchausen Syndrome. △766.

Münchhausen, Karl, Baron von (1720–97), German adventurer. He served in the Russian army against the Turks and later gained a reputation as a raconteur because of the amusingly extravagant stories he told of his adventures. An account of his exploits was written by R. E. Raspe and published in England in 1785.

Muncie, city in E Indiana, on White River, 50m (81km) ENE of Indianapolis; seat of Delaware co; site of Ball State University (1918). City is subject of studies by sociologists Robert and Helen Lynd, "Middle town" and "Middletown in Transition." Industries machine tools, wire, metal goods, glass. Settled 1818 inc. as town 1854, as city 1865. Pop. (1970) 69,080

Munich (München), city in S West Germany, on Isar River near Bavarian Alps; capital of Bavaria; major cultural and trade center. In 1255 city was chosen as site of residence for Wittelsbach family, and became capital of dukedom 1506; made capital of kingdom of Bavaria 1806; scene of "Beer Hall Putsch" (Nov. 8–9, 1923), Hitler's unsuccessful revolt against Bavarian government; site of University of Munich (founded 1472, transferred here 1826); Church of Our Lady (1468–88), Renaissance-style St Michael's Church (1583–97), Propyläen (1846–62), a monumental neoclassic gate; scene of world-famous annual beer festival, Oktoberfest. City hosted 1972 summer Olympics in which Palestinian guerrillas attacked Israeli living quarters. Industries: chemicals, brewing, pharmaceuticals, automobiles, processed food, tobacco, optical instruments, tourism. Founded 1158 by Henry the Lion, Duke of Saxony. Pop. 1,293,590.

Munich Agreement (1938), pact signed by representatives of Britain, France, Germany, and Italy. In it Neville Chamberlain for England and Edouard Daladier for France acceded to Adolf Hitler's demands for German occupation of the Sudeten area of Czechoslovakia. Although the agreement averted war temporarily and was hailed by many in Britain and France, it became a symbol of the Western nations' policy of appeasement toward Hitler. *See also* Sudetenland.

Munich Putsch, abortive coup led by Adolf Hitler and his Nazi party in Munich, November 8, 1923, against the Bavarian government. It is known as the "beer hall putsch" because it began in a Munich beer hall. *See also* Hitler, Adolf. △1334.

Municipal Court, lowest level of state court having original jurisdiction. Its territorial authority is restricted to the city or community where the court is located. It is associated with criminal and civil cases where the crime is normally a misdemeanor and civil claim is small. It is sometimes known as magistrate court, police court, county court, or justice of the peace court.

Munn v. Illinois (1876), US Supreme Court ruling that upheld the right of a state to regulate intrastate commerce. Affirming the conviction of a firm found guilty of violating an Illinois law that set maximum rates for grain storage, the court declared that states could regulate businesses operating in the public sphere. *See also* Granger Cases.

Muñoz Marín, Luis (1898–), the first elected governor of Puerto Rico, convinced the US Congress in 1952 to accept the island's status as that of a commonwealth, ending formal colonial ties and temporizing the question of statehood. Muñoz served four terms as governor until 1964. Out of office, he continued in his leadership position within the Popular Democratic party.

Munro, Hector Hugh (1870–1916), English author, pseud. Saki. A journalist, he wrote short stories that combine fantasy and wit. Among his works are *Not So Stories* (1902), *Reginald* (1904), *Reginald in Russia* (1910), and *Beasts and Super-Beasts* (1914). He was killed in France during World War I.

Munsell Color Tree. △1516.

Münster, port city in W West Germany, on Dortmund-Ems Canal. Founded as Carolingian episcopal see *c.* AD 800, its bishops ruled much of Westphalia as princes of Holy Roman Empire from 12th century to 1803; became part of Prussia in 1816 and capital of province; site of 13th-century cathedral, 14th–15th-century Lambertikirche (Church of St Lambert), 14th-century Gothic city hall, university (1902), and Westphalian state museum. Industries: textiles, beer, metal products. Pop. 203,324.

Munsterberg, Hugo (1863–1916), US psychologist, b. Germany. He is often described as the founder of applied psychology because of his pioneering efforts to bring psychology into education, law, and business. His publications include *Psychology and Industrial Efficiencies* (1913) and *Psychology and Social Sanity* (1914).

Muntjac, or **Barking Deer,** small S Asian deer. It is brown with cream markings and has tusklike canine teeth and short, two-tined antlers. It is generally found in pairs, and barks when agitated. Height: to 23in(580mm) at shoulder; weight: to 40lb(18kg). Family Cervidae; genus *Muntiacus*. *See also* Deer. △600.

Muntz Metal. △1596..

Muon, negatively charged elementary particle (symbol), originally thought to be a meson but now classified as a lepton. It has spin ½, a mass about 212 times that of the electron, and decays rapidly into an electron, neutrino, and antineutrino. *See also* Lepton; Neutrino. △1484.

Murasaki Shikibu (978?–1026?), Japanese diarist and novelist. As a lady at the court of the Empress Akiko, she kept a diary from 1007–1010, showing glimpses of court life in the capital. She is better known for her immense novel, *The Tale of Genji* (1001–1005), which is considered to be the oldest full novel in the world. Despite the lack of powerful action, her character delineation of Prince Genji and his lovers is superb.

Murat, Joachim (1767–1815), French military figure and king of Naples (1808–15). He helped bring Napoleon to power (1799) and was rewarded with the hand of Napoleon's sister Caroline (1800). His brilliance as a leader of the cavalry ensured many major victories, including Marengo (1800), Austerlitz (1805), and Jena (1806). He succeeded Joseph Napoleon to the crown of Naples in 1808. A popular and constructive monarch, he attempted to retain his crown after the French defeat at Leipzig (1813) by first negotiating with Austria. He then rejoined Napoleon during the Hundred Days. After defeat by the Austrians, he tried once more to regain his crown, but was captured and executed.

Murcia (Morcia), city in SE Spain, on Segura River 47mi (76km) SW of Alicante; capital of Murcia prov.; suffered destruction during Spanish Civil War (1936–39); site of 14th-century Gothic-Romanesque cathedral, with a 310-ft (95-m) tower, university (1915) 18th-century episcopal palace. Industries: vegetable canning, textiles, citrus fruits, gunpowder, aluminum. Settled by Romans; traditionally founded 825 by Moorish emperor Abder-Rahman II. Area: (prov.) 4,369sq mi (11,316sq km). Pop. (city) 243,759; (prov.) 832,313.

Murex. △482.

Murfreesboro, city in central Tennessee, 33mi (53km) SE of Nashville, on West Fork of Stones River; seat of Rutherford co; served as state capital 1819–25. Site of Civil War Battle of Stones River (December 1862–January 1863) is preserved in Stones River National Military Park (est. 1927). Industries: dairy products, hospital equipment, wood products. Founded 1766; inc. 1817. Pop. (1970) 26,360.

Muriatic Acid. *See* Hydrochloric Acid.

Murillo, Bartolome Esteban (1617–82), Spanish painter. He painted in Seville and was especially known for his religious pictures and for his sympathetic paintings of poor people, particularly of beggar boys. His later work included many paintings for the Cathedral of Seville and other public buildings. His careful draftsmanship and brushwork and his naturalistic style showed the influence of the Italian and Flemish masters.

Murmansk, city in Russian SFSR, USSR; capital of Murmansk oblast; ice-free port on the E shore of the Kola Gulf of Barents Sea, on NW Kola Peninsula, 625mi (1,006km) N of Leningrad; largest city in the world N of the Arctic Circle. Founded 1916 as a supply port, it was occupied by US, British, and French forces 1918; it was a major WWII port for Anglo-American convoys; site of a polar research station. Industries: fishing, shipbuilding, fish canning, metal and woodworking, nets, barrels. Exports: fish, lumber, apatite. Pop. 309,000.

Muromachi. *See* Ashikaga.

Murphy, Frank (1890–1949), US jurist and statesman, b. Harbor Beach, Mich. He was assistant US attorney (1919–20) and mayor of Detroit (1930–33). He served as governor general and later US high commissioner of the Philippines (1933–36). He was attorney general (1939–40) in Pres. Franklin D. Roosevelt's cabinet. In 1940, Roosevelt appointed him associate justice of the US Supreme Court and he served until his death. He was a champion of civil rights, dissenting, in *Korematsu* v. *United States* (1944), which concerned the internment of Japanese-Americans.

Murray Cod. △516.

Murray River, major river in Australia, in states of New South Wales, Victoria, and South Australia; flows W then S through Lake Alexandrina into Encounter Bay and empties into the Indian Ocean. Navigable for small vessels during the rainy season; used for irrigation. First explored 1824. Length: 1,609mi (2,590km).

Murre, two species of black and white sea birds, native to the Arctic Circle and northern oceans south to Portugal and Korea. Brünnich's murre *(Uria lomvia)* has a heavier beak and nests further north than the common murre *(U. aalge)*, which in some populations has a ring around the eye at breeding season. Length: to 16in (41cm). Family Alcidae. *See also* Auk.

Murrow, Edward Roscoe (1908–65), US journalist, b. Greensboro, N.C. He joined the Columbia Broadcasting System in 1935 and during World War II gained fame for his vivid descriptions of the Battle of Britain and the "Blitz" broadcast from London. After the war he became a CBS vice president and then news analyst. Murrow also produced many programs for television, including the popular *See It Now*, particularly noted for its stand against the activities of Sen. Joseph McCarthy, and *Person to Person*, interviews in people's homes. He was Director of the US Information Agency (1961–64). △1424.

Muscat (Masqat or Muskat), port town and capital of Oman on the SE Arabian Peninsula; fine harbor on the S coast of the Gulf of Oman makes it trade center for Oman. Exports: dried fish, dates, mother of pearl. Pop. 9,980.

Muscle, a type of tissue that has the ability to contract and can be excited to contract electrically, mechanically, or chemically. There are three basic types of muscle tissue: skeletal muscle, smooth muscle, and cardiac muscle. Skeletal muscle, or striated muscle, makes up the largest single tissue part of the human body, comprising about 40% of body weight. It is attached to the skeleton and is characterized by cross-markings, known as striations. It typically contains many nuclei per cell. Most skeletal muscles require conscious effort for contraction, and therefore are also known as voluntary muscles.

Smooth muscle lines the digestive tract, the blood vessels, and many other organs. Smooth muscle is not striated and typically has only one nucleus per cell. It is not under conscious control and is therefore also known as involuntary muscle. Cardiac muscle is found only in the heart and differs from the other types of muscle in that it beats rhythmically and does not need stimulation by a nerve impulse to contract. Cardiac muscle has some striations, but not so many as in skeletal muscle, is more regularly arranged, and has one nucleus per cell. △684.

Muscle Tone, or tonus, the continuous state of partial contraction of certain muscles of the body, which helps to maintain erect posture.

Muscovy, former principality in W central Russia. Founded *c.* 1280 by Alexander Nevski's son, Daniel, with the fortified village of Moscow at its center, it was united with the principality of Vladimir in the 15th century.

Muscovy Duck, tropical American perching duck with greenish black plumage and heavy red wattles. It has been domesticated worldwide and is raised for its succulent flesh. Species *Cairina moschata*.

Muscular Dystrophy, any of a group of disorders in which the characteristic feature is progressive painless degeneration and atrophy of the muscles with no nervous system involvement. Of the three main types, the most common is pseudohypertrophic muscular dystrophy, in which the symptoms of muscular degeneration begin in childhood and consist of increasing weakness, a peculiar swaying gait, and an initial apparent increase in muscle size (pseudohypertrophy), with subsequent atrophy. Those affected rarely reach maturity, since the heart and respiratory muscles become involved. This form of muscular dystrophy is sex-linked and affects males primarily.

Muscular System, the system of the body contain-

Hermann Muller

Munich, West Germany

Frank Murphy

Edward R. Murrow

ing the various types of muscle. *See* Muscle. △622, 684.

Muses, in classical mythology, nine daughters of the Titan Mnemosyne (memory) and Zeus. Each muse presided over a branch of literature, art, or science. Calliope was the muse of epic poetry, Clio of history, Erato of love poetry, Euterpe of lyric poetry, Polyhymnia of sacred poetry, Melpomene of tragedy, Terpsichore of choral dance and song, Thalia of comedy, and Urania of astronomy.

Museum of Modern Art, US art museum, New York City, founded in 1929 and moved in 1939 to its present quarters, designed by Philip Goodwin and Edward D. Stone and later expanded by Philip Johnson. The collection represents mostly European or US artists. Among the Impressionists and post-Impressionists represented are Monet, Cézanne, Gauguin, van Gogh, Toulouse-Lautrec, Redon, and Rousseau. There are numerous examples by Picasso. Other European artists include Matisse, Braque, Rouault, Duchamp, Kirchner, Klee, Chagall, Mondrian, and Dali. Some of the US painters represented are Hopper, Shahn, Wyeth, and Pollock. The large sculpture collection, some of which is displayed in a garden, includes such artists as Rodin, Maillol, and Moore.

Mushroom, any of a variety of relatively large fleshy fungi, many of which are gathered for food. The term is applied especially to stalked fungi with umbrella-shaped caps, such as the common edible meadow mushroom *(Agaricus campestris)* or the deadly amanita *(Amanita phalloides)*. Inedible mushrooms are sometimes called toadstools. Other fungi commonly called mushrooms include bracket fungi, puffballs, and morels. A typical mushroom fungus consists of two parts: an extensive underground cobwebby network of fine filaments—the mycelium—which is the main body of the fungus, and a short-lived fruiting body—the familiar visible mushroom—which may spring up overnight. Since many mushrooms are poisonous, wild mushrooms should be eaten only after they have been exactly identified as edible species. All simple tests of edibility, such as indications that a mushroom is eaten safely by insects, result every year in deaths or severe illness among mushroom gatherers. *See also* Fungus. △428.

Musial, Stan(ley Frank) (1920–), US baseball player, b. Donora, Pa. He played for the St Louis Cardinals (1941–44; 1946–63) and compiled 3630 hits and a .331 lifetime batting average. He was elected to the Baseball Hall of Fame in 1969.

Music, the production of sound in rhythmic, harmonic, and melodic patterns for the sake of artistic expression and the pleasure the sounds give the listener. Music is found in every culture, ancient and modern, but ancient music has survived only through oral traditions since notational systems for recording music are relatively recent inventions. *See also* Musical Notation. For articles on the history of music, *see* the names of individual composers, musicians, conductors, and orchestras; Medieval Music; Renaissance Music; Baroque Music; Classical Music; Romanticism in Music; Impressionism in Music; Neoclassical Music; Electronic Music.

For articles on music theory, *see* Musicology; Polyphony; Rhythm.

For articles on musical instruments, *see* Orchestra; Organ; Percussion Instruments; Piano; Stringed Musical Instruments; Woodwind Instruments.

For articles on the forms of musical composition, *see* Ballet; Concerto; Fugue; Jazz; Musical Comedy; Opera; Symphony. △1132, 1174, 1196, 1244–46, 1256, 1364–66, 1428, 1500.

Musical Comedy, originally musical theater characterized by song and dance routines interspersed with jokes; the music, songs, and dance became interwoven into the plot's usually weak structure. Later evolved out of comic opera, operetta, and vaudeville. Outstanding examples include *Oklahoma!* (1943), *South Pacific* (1949), *My Fair Lady* (1956), and *West Side Story* (1957).

Musical Instruments. △1244.

Musical Notation, systematic methods for transcribing musical sounds and compositions to a written form so that composers can transmit their musical ideas to other composers and performers. The system used today (5-line staffs, keynotes, bar lines, notes on and between the lines, etc) developed in the 1600s from an earlier system called "mensural" notation which was less precise and incapable of representing the complex musical patterns of music since the Baroque Period. *See also* Musicology.

Musicology, the study of music, including the historical and the theoretical analysis of musical performance and composition as well as the acoustic analysis of music as sound. One of the first great achievements of musicologists was the rediscovery and publication of the complete works of J. S. Bach in the 19th century. Because of this work Bach is now recognized as one of the greatest of all composers.

Musk, strong-smelling, semi-liquid substance obtained from pods under the belly skin of the male musk deer. It is used in the perfume industry because of its long-lasting and fixative qualities. Or, any penetrating, odoriferous substance secreted by many animals, such as civets, muskrats, and musk turtles. *See also* Musk Deer; △1814.

Musk Deer, small, timid forest and brushland deer of central and NE Asian highlands. They have long, thick, bristly, brown hair. The male has tusks instead of antlers and secretes musk, used in perfume and soap. Height: to 24in(610mm) at shoulder; weight: to 241lb(109kg). Family Cervidae; species *Moschus moschiferus.*

Muskegon, city and port in W Michigan, on Lake Michigan; seat of Muskegon co; site of Muskegon Business College (1885) and Muskegon County Community College (1926). Industries: office equipment, steel, brass, electric cranes. Founded 1810; inc. as village 1861, as city 1869. Pop. (1970) 44,631.

Muskellunge, freshwater fish found in the Great Lakes. A pike, it has a shovellike bill, sharp teeth, and elongated body. It eats fish, amphibians, birds, and small mammals. Length: to 5.5ft (167.6cm); weight: 110lb (49.9kg). Family Esocidae; species *Esox masquinongy.*

Musket. △1728.

Muskie, Edmund (1914–), US Senator, b. Rumford, Me. He was governor of Maine (1955–59) before entering the Senate. In 1968 he was a candidate for US vice president on the unsuccessful Democratic Party ticket with Hubert Humphrey. He was an unsuccessful contender for the Democratic presidential nomination in 1972.

Muskmelon. *See* Cantaloupe.

Muskogean, family of American Indian languages spoken originally in Florida, Georgia, Alabama, and Mississippi, but now mainly in Oklahoma. The major Muskogean languages are Choctaw, Chickasaw, Creek, and Seminole.

Muskogee, city in E Oklahoma, on the Arkansas River; seat of Muskogee co; site of Five Civilized Tribes Museum; nearby is restored Fort Gibson (1824). Industries: food processing, meat packing, seed mills, rare metals. Founded 1872; inc. 1898. Pop. (1970) 37,331.

Musk Ox, large, wild, shaggy ruminant, related to oxen and goats, native to N Canada and Greenland. In Europe and Siberia, it was exterminated in prehistoric times. Its deep brown fur reaches almost to the ground. Down-directed, recurved horns form a helmet over the forehead. Herd forms defensive circle for protection of calves. Length: to 7ft (2.1m); weight: to 902lb (410kg). Family Bovidae; species *Ovibos moschatus. See also* Ruminant. △612.

Muskrat, large, aquatic rodent native to North America. An expert swimmer having partially webbed hind feet and a long, scaly tail, its commercially valuable fur is glossy brown, durable, and waterproof. It lives in a tunnel or nests by a lake or stream. Length: to 14in (36cm); Weight: to 3lb (1.3kg). Family Cricetidae. △546.

Musk Turtle, small aquatic turtle native to United States. Abundant in sluggish streams, it has a high-domed carapace, and its reduced plastron is hinged. Musky secretion gives it nickname "stinkpot." Family Kinosternidae; genus *Sternotherus. See also* Turtle.

Muslim League, political organization of the Indian subcontinent, founded in 1906 by Aga Khan III to protect and promote the political rights of Muslims in India. At first it cooperated with the Indian National Congress, but fearing Hindu domination it turned to independent action. Under the leadership of Muhammed Ali Jinnah it called in 1940 for the establishment of a separate Muslim state. During World War II the League supported the British war effort in contrast to the Congress stance. It became the dominant part of independent Pakistan (1947), but by 1953 it had to contend with several competing parties. During the martial law imposed by Ayub Khan (1958–63) it was officially banned. In 1962 it split into two factions: the Convention Muslim League supporting Ayub Khan and the Council Muslim League in opposition to him. With Ayub's resignation (1969), the Convention faction fell apart. The Council faction fared poorly in 1970 elections and ceased to be a major political force in Pakistan.

Mussel, bivalve mollusk having thin, pear-shaped shells of equal size with iridescent interiors. Most marine species, found worldwide, occur in dense colonies on wharf pilings on rocky shores. A clump of threads called a byssus is used for attachment. Freshwater mussels, found in northern continents only, produce pearls and the shells are used for buttons. Families Mytilidae (marine), Unionidae (freshwater). *See also* Bivalve; Mollusk. △478.

Mussolini, Benito (1883–1945), Italian dictator, founder of Europe's first Fascist party, called Il Duce. An active socialist in his youth, amid post-war chaos he abandoned socialism and embraced ultra-nationalism and violent anti-leftism, organizing the Fascist party between 1919 and 1921. His Fascist militia's March on Rome (1922), unopposed by King Victor Emmanuel III, weakened liberal resistance and precipitated Mussolini's appointments as prime minister and head of government. Opposition was suppressed by assassination, the police, the Fascist militia, press control, and suspension of parliamentary government (1928). Possible conflict between the Roman Catholic Church and the state was obviated by the Lateran Treaty (1929). The 1930s saw Mussolini's imperialist attack on Ethiopia (1935) and close ties with Germany's Adolf Hitler (Rome-Berlin Axis). Il Duce waited until France fell before bringing Italy into World War II in 1940. Military failure caused his fall from power in 1943, but after his arrest he was freed by the Germans and set up in a puppet government until the German defeat (1945), when he was captured, tried, and executed by Italian Partisans. *See also* Lateran Treaty; World War II. △1334–36.

Mussorgsky or **Moussorgsky, Modest** (1839–81), Russian Romantic composer, one of the "Russian Five" who promoted nationalism in Russian music. He composed relatively few works, several of which are quite popular, including *Night on Bald Mountain* (1867) and *Pictures at an Exhibition* (1874), and the opera *Boris Godunov* (1874). △1246, 1256.

Mustang, feral horse of North American Great Plains descended from escaped Spanish horses. It has short ears, low-set tail, round leg bones and can be any horse color. During the 17th century there were 2–4,000,000 mustangs; today 20,000 survive in SW United States.

Mustard, annual and perennial plants, including radish, cabbage, turnip, alyssum, and stock, native to the north temperate zone. These plants have pungent flavored leaves, cross-shaped, four-petaled flowers, and pointed pods. There are 2,500 species, including black mustard *(Brassica nigra)* whose seeds are ground to produce the condiment mustard, and white mustard *(B. alba)* with seeds that produce a hotter mustard. Both have coarse leafy stems and loose clusters of yellow flowers; height: 6–10ft (1.8–3m). Family Cruciferae.

Mustard Gas, a poisonous gas first used in 1917 during World War I by the Germans. It is a blistering agent, one of the thioethers, compounded from carbon, hydrogen, sulfur, and chlorine. By 1918 both sides were using this gas. It inflicted many casualties but relatively few fatalities and was eventually banned.

Mutation, sudden variation in an inherited characteristic of an individual organism that makes it different from the parent organisms. This change, because it occurs in the genes, can be passed on to a mutant's offspring. Natural mutations are rare, occur randomly, and usually produce an organism unable to survive in its environment. Occasionally, the mutant is better adapted and, through natural selection, may become the next evolutional generation. The mutation rate can be increased by exposing genetic material to X rays, other ionizing radiation, or a mutagenic chemical substance, such as mustard gas. △420.

Mutual Fund, an investment company, financial group, or trust that has fluid capital stock and can sell its outstanding shares at net value. Mutual funds distribute earnings to shareholders who have the advantage of a wider range of investment opportunities than would otherwise be available to them individually.

Mutualism, relationship with mutual benefits for the two or more organisms involved. It is *obligative* if one species is incapable of surviving without the other and *facultative* if the organisms can survive independently. △434.

Mwanamutapa. *See* Monomotapa.

Myasthenia Gravis, disease that causes weakness of the muscles. Generally affecting the facial muscles first, it may spread to include muscles of the neck, trunk, and limbs. Its cause is unknown, but symptoms may be repressed with drugs.

Mycenae (Mikínai), ancient ruined city in NE Peloponnesus, Greece, approx. 7mi (11km) N of modern Árgos in Argolis dept. Founded 2900 BC, it grew to be a major center during the Bronze Age; its civilization became known as the Mycenaean era (*c.* 1600–1100 BC). Mycenae controlled the road from Peloponnesus to Corinth and a majority of the Aegean area. It declined *c.* 1100–470 BC with invasions of the Dorians and Argives; it fell to ruins *c.* 2nd century BC. Traditionally the residence and capital of King Agamemnon, it is the scene of dramatic tragedies portrayed by Aeschylus in the *Oresteia.* Famous archeological excavations by Heinrich Schliemann in 1874 and 1876 unearthed such notable ruins as the Treasury of Atreus, Lion Gate, beehive, and shaft grave tombs, an acropolis, palace, city walls, and numerous golden ornaments and weapons. △966.

Mycenean Architecture flourished 1400–1200 BC on Crete and the Greek mainland after the destruction of Knossos. The Myceneans adopted certain Cretan structures like the beehive tomb, as in the Treasury of Atreus at Mycenae, but also developed unique features, like the fortified acropolis at the center of a city and the monumental planning of buildings along a single axis. △966.

Mycorrhiza, or fungus root, symbiotic relationship between certain fungi and the root cells of some vascular plants. The soil fungus invades the roots, causing them to swell and then it grows a covering of threads around them. Water and minerals enter the roots through these threads. Sometimes the fungus digests organic material for the plant. Common hosts are orchid and pine tree roots. △448.

Mycosis. *See* Fungus Infection.

Myelin, protective sheath around peripheral nerve fibers; it insulates the fiber to prevent loss of electrical impulse during nerve conduction.

Myers v. United States (1926), landmark US Supreme Court case in which former President and then Chief Justice Taft established a presidential power of removal regarding any and all of his administrative subordinates without Congressional consent.

Mylar, trademarked polyester plastic made from xylene. It is used mainly as a film in capacitators and transducers and as a thin tape insulation for wire. Mylar is resistant to chemicals, impermeable to water and has high tensile strength. Mylar film is also used in meteorological balloons, as a base for metallic yarns, and in magnetic tape. Printer's films are stripped to a stable Mylar base prior to platemaking.

Myna, or mynah, tropical bird of SE Asia, related to the starling. They mimic other birds and are popular pets because they can sometimes be taught to talk. Wild mynas feed mainly on fruit but will eat almost anything. Bluish eggs (3–4) are laid in a tree cavity. Genera *Gracula* and *Acridotheres. See also* Starling.

Myocardial Infarction. *See* Heart Attack.

Myoglobin, a protein found in animals. In vertebrates it is the pigment responsible for the red color of muscle tissue. Like hemoglobin, myoglobin combines readily with oxygen for use in rapidly contracting muscles. Myoglobin has been used extensively in protein-structure research. In 1962 John C. Kendrew was awarded a Nobel Prize for his construction of a three-dimensional crystalline model of sperm whale myoglobin. △1574.

Myopia. *See* Nearsightedness.

Myosin, thick filimentous protein present in muscle cells; associated with actin in the contractile process. △684.

Myrdal, (Karl) Gunnar (1898–), Swedish economist. A professor of political and international economy at the University of Stockholm (1935–50, 1960–), Myrdal also served as executive secretary of the UN Economic Commission for Europe (1947–57). He is well known for *Political Element in the Development of Economic Theory* (1930) and for his massive study of US race relations, *An American Dilemma* (1944). In 1974 he was awarded the Nobel Prize for economics.

Myriapoda, class of arthropods with bodies made up of many similar segments. Each segment bears one or more pairs of legs. *See also* Centipede; Millipede. △490.

Myron (*fl. c.*480–450 BC), Greek sculptor. Often worked in bronze, his sculpture was in keeping with the classical tradition of idealized form and balanced, harmonious composition. Most of his works have been lost, but two that are identified through Roman copies are *Discobolus* and *Athena and the Satyr Marsyas.*

Myrrh, fragrant gum resin exuded from small trees and shrubs found in E Africa and Arabia. The brown resin is used in making incense and perfumes.

Myrtle, family (Myrtaceae) of trees and shrubs found in tropical and subtropical regions, especially in Australia and South America. Main characteristics are simple leaves, often marked with transparent dots; bisexual white, pink, or yellow flowers; and a berry fruit. The 100 genera and 3,000 species range in size from creepers to 300ft (91.4m) tall. The largest genus is *Eucalyptus.* The typical genus is *Myrtus,* trees and shrubs with glossy leaves and dark berries. △358.

Mysore, city in S India, 85mi (137km) SW of Bangalore; headquarters of Mysore division and Mysore district. City served as capital of Mysore dynasty 1799–1956, when princely states were disbanded; site of University of Mysore (1916), Chamundi Hill (housing a park and Hindu temple), maharaja's palace (1897), Jaganmohan and Lalitha Mahal palaces. Industries: textiles, rice, sandalwood oil, chemicals, leather goods, coffee, cigarettes. Pop. 263,131.

Mystery Play. *See* Church Theater.

Mythology, a body of myths, or traditional stories, dealing with gods and legendary heroes. The mythology of a people serves to present their world view, their explanations of natural phenomena, their religious and other beliefs. Mythological literature includes the Greek *Iliad* and *Odyssey,* the Scandinavian *Edda,* the Indian *Ramayana,* and the Babylonian *Gilgamesh,* among others. Various interpretations of mythology have been made by anthropologists such as Sir James Frazer and Claude Lévi-Strauss. In literature, myth has been used as the basis for poetry, stories, plays, and other writings. △832–840.

Myxedema, disease caused by insufficiency of thyroid hormone resulting in fatigue, a tendency toward weight gain, and poor tolerance to cold. Treatment involves administration of thyroid extracts. △726.

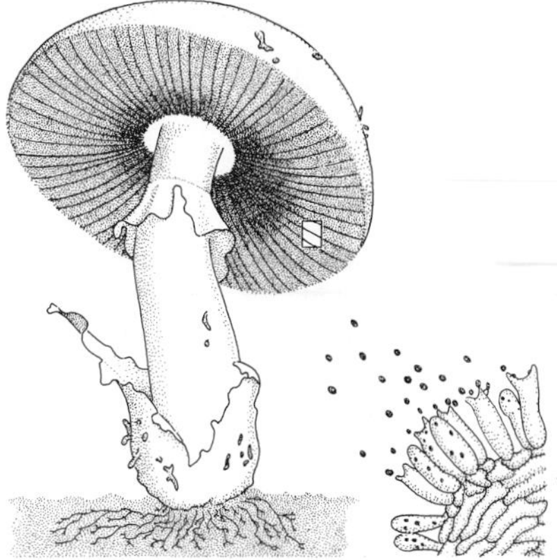

Mushroom

Mycenae, Greece

Myna

Mysore palace, India

N

NAACP. *See* National Association for the Advancement of Colored People.

Nabis, group of French painters organized by Paul Sérusier in 1892 and who patterned their works after Gauguin's colorful and decorative paintings. Associated with the group were Denis, Bonnard, Vuillard, Roussel, Vallotton, Toulouse-Lautrec, and Maillol. The Nabis exhibited together in 1892 and 1899, before dissolving as a group.

Nablus (Nabulus, or Shechem), town in W Jordan, 30mi (48km) N of Jerusalem. As ancient city of Shechem it was important in Biblical times; Samaritans made it their capital 9th century BC; there is still a small community of Samaritans here. Destroyed 129 BC,it was rebuilt and named Neapolis by Hadrian. After Arab-Israeli War of 1967 it was occupied by the Israelis. Industries: soap, olive oil, shepherd's coats. Pop. 44,223.

Nabokov, Vladimir (1899–), US author, b. Russia. He lived in Western Europe before going to the United States in 1940. Many of his novels were written in Russian and later translated into English. His works include *Laughter in the Dark* (1938), *Bend Sinister* (1947), *Lolita* (1955), and *Ada* (1969). He has also written short stories and poetry.

Nabonidus (Nabu-na'id). △954.

Nader, Ralph (1934–), US consumer affairs activist and lobbyist, b. Winsted, Conn. Nader's book *Unsafe at Any Speed* (1965), a call for improved automobile design, led to the enactment of the National Traffic and Motor Vehicle Safety Act of 1966. Nader subsequently expanded his range of interests: health hazards in mining; the use of nuclear power; meat processing methods; and investigations of the Internal Revenue Service, the Federal Trade Commission, and the US Congress. He heads a public interest law firm staffed with specialists in consumer affairs.

Naevius, Gnaeus. △1028.

Naga, people inhabiting the Naga Hills of Assam and the upper Chindwin river region of upper Burma. A farming people, cultivating rice, they were formerly notorious head-hunters. The Indian state of Nagaland was formed in 1961.

Nagano, city in Japan, on branch of Shinano River in central Honshu, 110mi (177km) NW of Tokyo; capital of Nagano prefecture; site of Buddhist Zenkoji Temple. Pop. 285,355.

Nagasaki, seaport in W Kyushu, Japan; capital of Nagasaki prefecture. It was the first Japanese port to receive Western ships (Portuguese and Spanish, mid-16th century); became a center of European and Christian influence in Japan; port was closed to foreigners 1641–1858, reopened 1859. The inner city was destroyed by second US atomic bomb dropped on Japan Aug. 9, 1945; it is now a shipbuilding, fishing, and silk center. Pop. 421,114.

Nagoya, port city in central Honshu, Japan, at head of Ise Bay (Pacific Ocean); capital of Aichi prefecture; grew around daimyo castle (1610); site of various Buddhist and shinto monuments, including a 2nd-century shrine; city suffered extensive bombing WWII; site of university (1939), technical institute (1949). Industries: automobiles, aircraft, machinery, textiles, chemicals, porcelain, lumber. Pop. 2,036,053.

Nagpur, city in W central India, 265mi (427km) N of Hyderabad; capital of Nagpur district and Nagpur division. City served as capital of kingdom of Nagpur (from 1743), Central Provinces (from 1861), Central Provinces and Berar (from 1903), Madhya Pradesh state (1947–56); site of Nagpur University (1923). Industries: cigarettes, textiles, pottery, glass, leather, pharmaceuticals, brassware, hand weaving. Founded 18th century by Gond prince. Pop. 903,826.

Nagy, Imre (1895–1958), Hungarian statesman, premier 1953–55 and 1956. Expelled from the Communist party in 1955 for alleged anti-Soviet nationalism, he was recalled to the premiership in 1956 in the wake of the anti-Soviet uprising of Oct. 24. He promised free elections, economic reforms, and abolition of the one-party dictatorship. He also demanded the withdrawal of Soviet troops and freed Cardinal Mindszenty from prison. Although the Soviets promised concessions, demonstrations continued and on Nov. 4, Soviet troops and tanks moved in to suppress the insurgents. Nagy and three of his associates were executed in 1958.

Naha (Nafa or Nawa), seaport city at S tip of Okinawa, Japan; capital of Okinawa prefecture. Industries: pottery, textiles, sugar, Panama hats, lacquerware. Pop. 276,380.

Nahr an-Nil. *See* Nile.

Nahua, the most important tribal group and language of central Mexico. The Aztec were the major division of the Náhuatl peoples. Today about 800,000 Indians still speak the language, primarily occupying the states of Mexico, Michoacán, Puebla, and Guerrero, with scattered remnants in Veracruz, and sections of Central America.

Nahum, biblical author and seventh of the 12 minor prophets. He predicted the eventual fall of Nineveh.

Nail, in anatomy. △686.

Nails, metallic fasteners, varying in size, pointed at one end and flattened to a head at the other; used for fastening wood. The main types are common wire nails, for rough work; box nails, similar to common but lighter in weight; finishing nails, including small brads, with narrow heads that can be set below the work surface; and casing nails, for moldings and trim. Nails of an inch or more in length are sold by the penny (d) size: 6d common nails, for example, are 2in (5.1cm) long and weigh about 175 to the pound; 6d finishing nails weigh 300 to the pound. Nails under an inch in length (brads or tacks) are specified by length. △1588, 1592, 1612.

Nairobi, capital and largest city of Kenya, in S central part of country; communications, administrative, and industrial center. It replaced Mombasa as capital of British East Africa Protectorate 1905; in the 1950s Nairobi was a Mau Mau rebellion center; scene of the first All Africa Trade Fair; site of airport, Nairobi National Park (1948), National University, several institutions of higher learning, Caryndon Memorial Museum, Sorsbie art gallery. Industries: beverages, cigarettes, textiles, chemicals, livestock, food processing, coffee, furniture, glass, building materials. Founded 1899 on site of Masai watering hole; made municipality 1919; inc. as city 1950. Pop. 478,000.

Naismith, James (1861–1939), US basketball pioneer, b. Almonte, Canada. While a physical education instructor at YMCA college in Springfield, Mass., he originated the game of basketball (1891), which still uses many of the rules he outlined. The early games used two peach baskets and a soccer ball.

Namath, Joe William ("Broadway Joe") (1943–), US football player, b. Beaver Falls, Pa. He won fame as a quarterback at the University of Alabama (1962–64) before joining New York in the American Football League (1965). Considered a top gate attraction, he was in part responsible for the American League's merger with the National Football League (1969). In 1967, he set a single season passing mark of 4007 yards (3666m). He also appeared in several films.

Namibia, also known as South West Africa, UN international territory in SW Africa; its principal export item is diamonds.

Land and Economy. In a region of sparse population, the international territory in SW Africa is bordered by Angola and Zambia (N), Botswana (E), Republic of South Africa (S), and the Atlantic Ocean (W). Most of the area is a high plateau with an uninhabited desert coastal strip. About 30% of the land is arable. Diamonds are the principal resource, accounting for 60% of all mineral exports. Exports bring $250 million into Namibia's treasury annually.

People. Namibia (88% non-white) is divided N and S by tribal and regional differences; the N section is the most westernized. Control of farming, mining, and industry is in the hands of the white minority (12%).

Government. The government consists of an assembly, elected by white voters, and administrators appointed by South Africa, which has final authority in all matters.

History. First settled by the Bushmen, it was a German protectorate from 1884, then under South African rule from 1915. A group of African states charged South Africa with instituting apartheid practices in the region, and in 1968 the UN named an 11-nation council to rule until self-government could be achieved. South Africa, however, refused to recognize the UN decision and continued to rule the area.

PROFILE

Official name: Namibia
Area: 317,887sq mi (823,327sq km)
Population: 746,328
Density: 2.3per sq mi (0.9per sq km)
Chief cities: Windhoek (capital); Tsumeb
Government: UN international territory; administered by South Africa; assembly
Religion: Animist and Christian
Language: Afrikaans and English (both official)
Monetary unit: Rand
Industries: diamonds, sheep pelts (major)
Agriculture: cattle, sheep
Minerals: diamonds, copper, lead, zinc, tin, vanadium, iron ore, silver, phosphate, manganese, cadmium, fluorspar
Trading partners: Republic of South Africa

Namur (Namen), town in S central Belgium, at confluence of Sambre and Meuse rivers; capital of Namur prov.; site of 18th-century cathedral of St Aubain, medieval citadel. It was the capital of the French department of Sambre-et-Meuse until 1814, when it passed to Belgium. Industries: glass, leather, soap, tourism. Pop. 32,507.

Nan-ch'ang, (Nan-ch'ang-hsien), city in SE China, on S Kan Kiang River; capital of Kiangsi prov. A walled city dating from 12th century, the fortifications were torn down for area reconstruction. Army Day, celebrated each year on August 1, commemorates Communist revolt against Nationalist forces under Chiang Kai-shek (1927). Industries: rice, tea, cotton, hemp, farm tools, paper, food processing. Pop. 900,000.

Nancy, city in NE France, on Meurthe River, 178mi (287km) E of Paris; capital of Meurthe-et-Moselle dept. City developed around castle of dukes of Lorraine; made duchy capital in 12th century; ruled by Stanislaus I, ex-king of Poland and duke of Lorraine, 1738–66; passed to French crown 1766. City contains outstanding examples of 18th-century architecture; site of Place Stanislas (1752–56), 15th-century Church of the Cordelien, Church of Notre Dame (1740), containing tomb of Stanislaus and his queen, and University of Nancy (1854). Industries: foundries, salt, glass, machine tools, textiles. Pop. 123,428.

Nanda Devi, mountain peak in the Himalayan system, N India; one of the highest in India; sacred to the Hindus who think Nanda, wife of the god Siva, lives there. Height: 25,645ft (7,822m).

Nanga Parbat, mountain peak in the Punjab Himalayan system, N India; the 7th-highest in the world; after six unsuccessful attempts, it was scaled in 1953 by an expedition led by Herman Buhl. Height: 26,660ft (8,131m).

Nanjing. *See* Nanking.

Nanking (Nanjing), city in E China, 150mi (274km) W of Shanghai, on Yangtze River; capital of Kiangsu prov.; served as capital of China until end of 14th century, then 1928–37 and 1946–49. Treaty of Nanking (1842) ended Opium War with Britain and opened five ports to foreign trade; Nanking was declared a treaty port 1858 but not opened until 1899; served as seat of Sun Yat-sen's provisional presidency (1912) during Chinese Revolution; capital of Kuomintang 1928; fell to Japan (December 1937) during Sino-Japanese War, causing mass destruction, called the "rape of Nanking." Nationalist capital, moved to Chungking 1937, returned to Nanking, 1946; under communist control April 1949. City is site of 26-mi (42-km) wall surrounding most of city and suburbs, tomb of Sun Yat-sen, Nanking University (1902), Ginling College (1915); it is the literary center of China; noted for porcelain and textiles, especially nankeen cloth. Pop. 2,000,000.

Nanking, Treaty of. △1270.

Nansei-shoto. *See* Ryukyu Islands.

Nansen, Fridtjof (1861–1930), Norwegian explorer, statesman, scientist, author, and humanitarian. A vigorous outdoorsman in his youth, he took up zoology and obtained his doctorate for tissue studies. He crossed the Greenland icecap on foot (1888), gaining material for two books, *Across Greenland* (1891) and *Eskimo Life* (1891). For his next expedition he constructed a ship, *Fram*, to be frozen in the Arctic ice, allowing him to drift to 84°N. Leaving the *Fram*, he and F.H. Johansen pushed to 86°14′N (1895), the farthest north man had gone. Nansen then settled to more formal scientific pursuits, and assumed an increasing role in government. As a Norwegian delegate to the League of Nations he repatriated half a million refugees and later worked to help the world's starving. He was awarded the Nobel Peace Prize in 1922. Other books include *Norway and the Union with Sweden* (1905), *Through Siberia* (1914), and *Armenia and the Near East* (1928).

Nansen Bottle, device, sometimes open-ended, used for the collection of subsurface water samples. △236.

Nanterre, city in N central France; WNW suburb of Paris. Industries: automobiles, perfume. Pop. 90,332.

Nantes, city in NW France, on Loire River, 107mi (172km) W of Tours; capital of Loire-Atlantique dept. An ancient Gallic capital prior to Roman conquest (58–51 BC), it was residence of dukes of Brittany late 10th century until 1525, when it became part of France; Henry IV issued Edict of Nantes here (1598) guaranteeing Protestants religious freedom; site of University of Nantes (1460), and ducal castle of 9th or 10th century. Industries: metals, dyes, clothing, biscuits, bicycles. Pop. 259,208.

Nantes, Edict of (1598), law granting considerable religious freedom to French Protestants, called Huguenots, promulgated by Henry IV at Nantes in Brittany. It guaranteed freedom of conscience, social and political equality, and established a special court, composed of both Catholics and Protestants, to hear disputes arising from the edict. Protestant worship was limited, however, to areas they already held (about 100 fortified towns) and was not permitted, in particular, within five leagues of Paris. Secret agreements promised the crown's financial support of the armies garrisoned in the 100 towns. Although it only recognized the status quo and disallowed Protestant expansion, Catholics (including Pope Clement VII) resented the edict. Louis XIII, acting on Richelieu's advice, withdrew the political and military provisions of the edict (1629). Louis XV revoked it entirely in 1685. △1154.

Nantucket, island in SE Massachusetts, 25mi (40km) S of Cape Cod in Atlantic Ocean; with Muskeget and Tuckernuck islands comprises Nantucket co, coextensive with town of Nantucket, the co seat. Formerly a large whaling port, now a tourist and artist center; annexed to Massachusetts from New York 1692; site of whaling museum, 18th-century windmill. Settled 1659. Area: 57sq mi (92sq km).

Napa, city in W California, 10mi (16km) N of San Pablo Bay; seat of Napa co; famous for its wine and vineyards. Industries: steel products, concrete, leather. Settled 1847; inc. 1872. Pop. (1970) 35,978.

Naphtha, any of several volatile liquid hydrocarbon mixtures. In the first century AD, "naptha" was mentioned by Pliny the Elder. Alchemists used the word for various liquids of low boiling point. Several types of products are now called naphtha (ie coal-tar naphtha, shale naphtha, petroleum naphtha). Petroleum naphtha contains aliphatic hydrocarbons, boils at higher temperatures than gasoline and lower temperatures than kerosene.

Naphthalene, an important hydrocarbon ($C_{10}H_8$) composed of two benzene rings sharing two adjacent carbon atoms. Naphthalene is soluble in ether and hot alcohol and is highly volatile. It is used in moth balls, dyes, and synthetic resins, in coal tar and in the high-temperature cracking process of petroleum. It crystallizes in white plates, melting at 176°F (80°C) and boiling at 424°F (218°C). △1560.

Napier, or **Neper, John** (1550–1617), Scottish mathematician. As the laird of Marchiston he treated mathematics as a hobby but nevertheless invented logarithms and the present form of the decimal notation. Napier's bones were calculating devices invented by him in an attempt to simplify logarithmic calculations. △1456.

Naples (Napoli), seaport and industrial city in Italy, 117mi (188km) SE of Rome, on Bay of Naples; capital of Campania and Naples provs. Founded on ancient Parthenope *c.* 600 BC, it was under Roman rule 4th century BC; under Byzantine rule AD 6th century; capital of kingdom of Naples 13th–19th centuries; ceded to Austria 1713; joined kingdom of Italy 1860. Notable buildings include church of Holy Apostles (founded by Constantine), church of St Paul (1817–31), university (1224), Virgil's tomb, 13th-century Gothic cathedral, medieval castles. Industries: textiles, steel, shipbuilding, tourism, aircraft, food processing. Pop. 1,278,051.

Napoleon I, full name Napoleon Bonaparte (1769–1821), famous general and emperor of France, military and organizational genius. Born in Corsica, he spoke French with an Italian accent and was an indifferent student at the military academy at Brienne. The hero of the French liberation of Toulon from the English (1793), he there made an important ally in Vicomte Paul de Barras. The fall of Maximilien Robespierre (1794) occasioned counter-revolutionary upheavals and monarchist plots. Increasingly the army became the key to control. Napoleon saved the National Convention at Barras's request; his reward was command of the Army of Italy. His victories there against Austria, he later said, "made me conceive the ambition of performing great things." His Egyptian campaign (1798) went badly, and during his absence the Coalition (England, Austria, Russia, and Turkey) regained most of Italy. In Paris, the government's control was deteriorating. Abbé Sieyès, one of the directors, believed only military dictatorship could prevent the return of the monarchists. Napoleon returned from Egypt and carried out the coup d'état of the 18th Brumaire. He thus became one of three consuls, with Sieyès another. By 1799 he was first consul. In 1800 he wrested victory at Marengo from the Austrians and made a precarious peace with England. He then turned to the establishment of order at home. He centralized the administration of local departments and the collection of taxes. He established the Bank of France and set the value of the franc. His Napoleonic Code established legal freedoms won in the Revolution, and the Concordat (1801) made peace with the Roman Catholic Church.

To end forever the threat from his monarchist rivals, Napoleon crowned himself emperor (1804), with Pope Pius VII presiding. European wars involved him thereafter, and he achieved his greatest victory at Austerlitz over Russia and Austria (1805). He was never able to overcome English superiority at sea, however, and his invasion of Russia (1812) was a di-

Nairobi, Kenya

Cen. Afr. Rep.
Sudan
Ethiopia
Cameroon
Somalia
Uganda
Kenya
Gabon
Congo
Zaire
INDIAN OCEAN
Tanzania
Comoro Is.
Malawi
Angola
Zambia
Mozambique
NAMIBIA (SOUTH WEST AFRICA)
Rhodesia
Madagascar
Botswana
Swakopmund
Windhoek
Keetmanshoop
Swaziland
ATLANTIC OCEAN
South Africa
Lesotho
0
1200km
Namibia

Namur, Belgium

Naples, Italy

saster. With his French subjects increasingly weary of war and his enemies closing in upon him, Napoleon was forced to abdicate (1814). Confined to the island of Elba, Napoleon escaped and, for 100 days, seemed triumphant. But his foreign enemies confronted him, and he was defeated conclusively at Waterloo (1815). He sought the protection of the English and was exiled once more, on St Helena, where he died, perhaps, as he claimed, of slow arsenic poisoning. In 1796 he married Josephine de Beauharnais, from whom he was divorced. He then married Marie Louise of Austria (1810), and they had one son, styled Napoleon II. △1224.

Napoleon II (1811–32), only son of Napoleon I and Marie-Louise. His full name was François Charles Joseph Bonaparte. His father's empire collapsed when he was three, and he was then taken by his mother to her father's court in Austria. In 1818 his grandfather, Francis I, created him duc de Reichstadt. Too ill to take advantage of the possibilities the 1830 revolution presented to Napoleon's direct heir, he died of tuberculosis in 1832.

Napoleon III (1808–73), also known as **Louis Napoleon,** emperor of France (1852–71). Nephew of Napoleon I and heir to the Napoleonic title and mystique when Napoleon II died (1832). Exiled because he was a Bonaparte, he twice attempted a military coup, then confidently awaited events to bring him to power. In 1848, under a new constitution providing popular election of the president, he won an overwhelming victory. He involved France in an unpopular war supporting Pope Pius IX against Italian republicans. Ensuing leftist uprisings caused parliament to disenfranchise 3,000,000 electors. He then dismissed the parliament, which was already wary of his lust for power, arrested his enemies, and became emperor (1852). Plebiscites gave his reign a semblance of legitimacy. Under Napoleon III, France enjoyed a period of economic vitality and a gradual relaxation of political authoritarianism. He tried to restore French importance by seeking peace. By supporting emerging nations—Poland, Italy, Germany, Romania, and Mexico—he cultivated new allies. He was unprepared for the rapid rise of Prussia, whose crushing defeat of France in the Franco-Prussian War (1870–71) ended his reign. Already in ill health, he died two years later. *See also* Franco-Prussian War; Second Empire. △1250.

Napoleonic Code. △908.

Napoleonic Wars. △1226.

Napoli. *See* Naples.

Nappe. △252.

Nara, city in S central Honshu, Japan, approx. 25mi (40km) E of Osaka; capital of Nara prefecture; resort, and cultural-historical center. It was the first capital of Japan, under Emperor Jimmu (710–84), site of first Buddhist temple, Horyuji (7th century), 8th-century bronze image of Buddha at the temple Todai-ji, Imperial Museum containing treasures from the 8th century, university (1949). Pop. 208,266.

Narayanganj (Narainganj), port city in Bangladesh, on Meghna River 12mi (19km) E of Dacca. Industries: jute, textiles, leather. Pop. 326,500.

Narbonne, town in S France, 31mi (50km) E of Carcassonne. Capital of Gallia Narbonensis *c.* AD 309, it was prosperous industrial town in 12th and 13th centuries; site of St Just Cathedral (13th–14th centuries), and 13th-century archepiscopal palace, now the town hall and museum. Industries: sulfur, copper, clothing. Founded 118 BC as Roman colony. Pop. 38,441.

Narcissus, numerous species of Old World bulb plants cultivated in gardens throughout the world. They bloom in early spring. The long, pointed leaves surround yellow, orange, or white trumpetlike flowers. Favorite species are the yellowish daffodil *(Narcissus pseudonarcissus)* and jonquil *(N. jonquilla).* Family Amaryllidaceae.

Narcissus, in Greek mythology, a beautiful youth who fell in love with his own reflection. According to legend, he rejected the love of the nymph Echo, and she induced him to fall in love with his own image. He pined away and was turned into a flower.

Narcotics, drugs used to reduce pain, diminish sensation, and induce sleep but which lead to profound stupor, coma, or convulsions when given in excessive doses. Morphine, codeine, and meperidine (Demerol) are among the narcotics commonly used in medicine. △730.

Nardone v. United States (1937, 1939), US Supreme Court cases affecting wiretap evidence. The court held that the provisions of the Communications Act of 1934 prohibiting unauthorized interception of communications rendered wiretap evidence or evidence derived from wiretap leads inadmissible.

Narragansett, a major Algonquian-speaking tribe of North American Indians related to the Niantic, who occupied Rhode Island, from Providence to the Pawtucket River, and western Narragansett Bay. Once the most powerful New England group, they were almost entirely wiped out during the tragic Pequot War of 1637, when their population of 5,000 declined radically.

Narthex. △1082.

Narváez, Pánfilo de (*c.* 1470–1528), Spanish conquistador. He was the chief lieutenant to Diego de Velázquez in the conquest of Cuba in 1514. In 1520, Velázquez sent him and a force of men to Mexico to arrest Hernán de Cortés. Instead he was defeated and imprisoned by Cortés. Released in 1521, he returned to Spain where Charles V commissioned him to conquer Florida. After a long, hazardous voyage he landed in Florida in 1528. He sent his ships on to Mexico and looked unsuccessfully for gold in the Tallahassee area, then sailed for Mexico in makeshift boats. He was lost at sea.

Narvik, seaport in N Norway, on Ofoten Fjord; ice-free harbor. Port site was chosen 1887; opened 1902; inc. 1907; scene of heavy fighting during WWII (1940). Exports: iron ore. Pop. 13,297.

Narwhal, small, toothed Arctic whale. The male has a twisted "horn"—half as long as its body—protruding horizontally through its upper lip. An overdeveloped tooth, the horn's function is unknown. Length: to 16ft (5m). Species *Monodon monoceros.* △552.

NASA. *See* National Aeronautics and Space Administration.

Nasca. *See* Nazca.

Nash, Ogden (1902–71), US poet, b. Rye, N.Y. His verse is humorous and satirical. Among his many volumes of poetry are *Free Wheeling* (1931), *The Face Is Familiar* (1940), and *You Can't Get There from Here* (1957). Collaborating with Kurt Weill, he wrote the lyrics for *One Touch of Venus* (1943), a musical comedy.

Nashua, city in S New Hampshire, on Merrimack River; one of seats of Hillsborough co; site of Rivier College (1933), Colonial House (1803), Marsh Tavern (1804, stagecoach stop), and New England Aeronautical Institute (1965). Industries: shoes, leather, paper, electronic equipment. Founded 1656 as fur trading post; inc. 1853 as city. Pop. (1970) 55,820.

Nashville, capital city of Tennessee and port of entry, in N central Tennessee, on the Cumberland River; seat of Davidson co. Settled 1779 as Fort Nashborough, it was made capital of Tennessee 1843; taken by Union troops 1862; scene of Battle of Nashville December 1864 in which Union Army overwhelmingly defeated Confederate troops. It is a noted country music and recording center; site of Vanderbilt University (1872), Fisk University (1867), Tennessee State University (1909), capitol (1855) containing tomb of President James Polk, country music hall of fame and museum, "Opryland U.S.A." Industries: railroad shops, automobile glass, clothing, footwear, food products, tires, chemicals, publishing. Inc. 1784 as town, 1806 as city. Pop. (1970) 447,877.

Nassau, port city on NE New Providence Island in the Bahamas, SE of Florida; capital and commercial center of Bahamas, with excellent harbor (sheltered by Hog Island); tourist resort; site of airport, cathedral, 18th-century forts, sea gardens. Founded 1660s by English as Charles Towne, it was renamed 1695; destroyed by French and Spanish 1703; rebuilt 1718 and later fortified; was 18th-century stronghold of Blackbeard and other pirates; free trade port after 1738. Exports: sponge, citrus fruit, tomatoes, sisal hemp. Pop. 101,503.

Nassau, House of, royal European family named for county on east bank of Rhine, founded by Walram I. The elder or German branch ruled Nassau until it was annexed by Prussia in 1866. Since 1890, Nassau has been the ruling house of the Duchy of Luxemburg. The younger (Dutch) branch, founded by Otto I (died 1292?), inherited Orange in 1544. Since William the Silent in 1579, members of this house have ruled the Netherlands almost continuously under the name of the House of Orange.

Nasser, Gamal Abdel (1918–70), Egyptian political figure, first president of the republic of Egypt (1956–70). A revolutionary since his youth, he was expelled from school in 1935 after being wounded while leading an anti-British demonstration. He graduated from the Royal Military Academy in 1938. In 1942 he founded the secret Society of Free Soldiers to combat corruption and foreign domination. He was wounded in action in the 1948 Arab-Israeli War. In 1952 he led the army coup that ousted King Farouk. As head of the Revolutionary Command Council he controlled Egypt, although Gen. Muhammad Naguib was nominal premier. In 1956 he was chosen president in an unopposed election. In 1956 he nationalized the Suez Canal, provoking the brief Anglo-French occupation. Between 1958–61 Syria was merged with Egypt as the United Arab Republic. In 1967 he brought on the third Arab-Israeli War by blocking the Israeli port of Elat. After Egypt's defeat he resigned but reconsidered after massive demonstrations in his support. He promoted land reform and economic and social development through a program he called Arab Socialism. The completion of the Aswan Dam (1970), built with Soviet assistance after the United States withdrew, was a high point in this program. Nasser sought to speak as a leader for all Arab people and pursued a neutralist policy encouraging Third World cooperation. △1352.

Nasser, Lake, lake in S Egypt and N Sudan; formed in 1960s by Aswan High Dam, in the process flooding many archeological sites, including Abu Simbel. Length: approx. 300mi (483km).

Nast, Thomas (1840–1902), US cartoonist, b. Germany. He was noted for his political cartoons that were instrumental in breaking up the corrupt Boss Tweed Ring in New York City. He is also credited with the creation of the political symbols of the Republican and Democratic parties.

Nasturtium, annual trailing plant native to Central and South America. Cultivated as a garden ornamental, it has round leaves and spurred, trumpet-shaped flowers of yellow, salmon, or scarlet. Among 50 species is the common nasturtium, or Indian cress, *Tropaeolum majus.* Family Tropaeolaceae.

Natal Province, province in E Republic of South Africa, bordered by Indian Ocean (E), Transvaal, Mozambique, and Swaziland (N), Orange Free State and Lesotho (W); capital is Pietermaritzburg. Visited by Boers on the Great Trek (1836–38), it became a British colony 1843; annexed to Cape Colony 1844; made separate colony 1856; granted internal self-government 1893; joined Union of South Africa 1910. The province is a narrow coastal belt, extending inland, bordered by Drakensberg Mts; highest point is Natal, approx. 11,200ft (3,410m); site of University of Natal, University of Durban, Natal National Park, railway. Industries: sugar, fruit, coal, cereals, textiles, cigarettes, furniture, gold, tin, livestock, rubber, oil refining, tanning, fertilizers, paper. Area: 33,578sq mi (86,967sq km). Pop. 3,418,942.

Nataraja. △1034.

Natchez, city in SW Mississippi, on bluffs overlooking Mississippi River; site of Fort Rosalie, built by French and burned by Indians 1729; area was taken by British from France 1763; seized by Spain 1779; passed to United States 1798; served as capital of Territory of Mississippi 1798–1802; state capital 1817–21; site of many antebellum homes, Natchez Junior College (1885). Industries: tires, wood, pulp, lumber, cotton, paper products. First visited by Robert La Salle 1662; inc. 1803. Pop. (1970) 19,704.

Natchez, an important tribe of Muskhogean-speaking North American Indians, once the largest and strongest tribe of the southern Mississippi region, although they never numbered more than 2,000 people. They are noted religious-political structure, in which the Sun played a major role. Today only a handful of Natchez people survive in Oklahoma.

Natchez Trace, road from Natchez, Mississippi to Nashville, Tennessee. Originally Indian trails, in 18th century it was used by French, English, and Spanish for commercial and military purposes; in early 19th century it was improved by the army and made into a post road; as steamboat transportation improved use of Trace declined; today it is generally the route of the Natchez Trace Parkway. Length: approx. 500mi (805km).

Nathan, George Jean (1882–1958), US drama critic, b. Fort Wayne, Ind. He reviewed 6,000 plays for such disparate publications as *The Bohemian, Puck, Smart Set,* and *The American Mercury.* In 1917 he was instrumental in gaining recognition for the work of Eugene O'Neill, and later did the same for Sean O'Casey, having their manuscripts published. He was a charter member of the New York Drama Critics Circle (1935). A prolific author, he published a *Theatre Book of the Year* from 1942–47, as well as many books, including *Encyclopedia of the Theatre* (1940).

Nathanael, in the New Testament, one of Christ's disciples. Almost nothing of him is related but his birthplace, Cana, and the genuineness of his calling. Some think he is identical with Bartholomew.

Natick, town in E Massachusetts, on Charles River, 18mi (29km) WSW of Boston. Founded in 1651 by John Eliot, "Apostle to the Indians," for Indian converts to Christianity, it was the first of his Praying Towns. Industries: shoes, electronic components, tools. Settled 1718; inc. 1781. Pop. (1970) 31,057.

Nation, Carry Amelia Moore (1846–1911), US social reformer, temperance leader, b. Garrard co, Ky. Her first husband, an alcoholic, turned her against liquor for life. Wielding a hatchet, which became her symbol, she began her anti-saloon campaign in Kansas in the 1890s where saloons were illegal. She carried her crusade into several states. She was arrested more than 30 times and was considered too fanatical by other temperance groups, which would not endorse her tactics.

National Academy of Sciences, US organization made up of elected members (based on original research in several fields of science). The academy acts as an official advisor to the federal government on science and technology matters. Its publications include *Proceedings of the National Academy of Sciences,* plus newsletters, books, monographs, and reports. Members, about 950. Founded 1863.

National Aeronautics and Space Administration (NASA), federal agency set up by Congress (1958) to supervise US space activities for peaceful purposes. NASA was responsible for all US space flights and all phases of space exploration—research, building and testing space vehicles, manned and unmanned spacecraft, and international cooperation and exchange.

National American Woman Suffrage Association (NAWSA), merger of the National and the American Woman Suffrage associations. A loose federation, NAWSA sought to enroll all women. With 2,000,000 members in 1917, it was one of the most active groups supporting women's political freedom. The group worked for women's suffrage both on federal and state levels. Prominent leaders of the association included Elizabeth Cady Stanton, who was president (1892–1900). Younger women broke away to organize the semi-militant Congressional Union for Woman Suffrage (1914). *See also* National Woman Suffrage Association; Woman Suffrage.

National Anthem. *See* Star-Spangled Banner.

National Association for the Advancement of Colored People (NAACP), civil rights organization. Its objectives are "to achieve through peaceful and lawful means, equal citizenship rights for all American citizens by eliminating segregation and discrimination in housing, employment, voting, schools, the courts, transportation, and recreation." Early leaders were W.E.B. Du Bois and Booker T. Washington. Whites were influential in the founding, but control of NAACP has been exercised by blacks. It set up the successful Legal Defense and Educational Fund to finance court battles over discriminatory practices, of which *Brown v. Board of Education of Topeka* (1954) was a major victory. It also cooperates with other minority protection groups. Its publications include *Crisis.* Members, about 500,000. Founded 1909.

National Bank Act of 1863, law passed to help finance the Civil War. It established a national banking system. National banks were required to have one third of their capital invested in US securities. They could issue national bank notes on 90% of these holdings. These notes became a uniform US currency.

National City, city in S California, 5mi (8km) S of San Diego; site of Pacific Reserve Fleet headquarters. Industries: food packing, defense, metal foundries. Inc. 1887. Pop. (1970) 43,184.

National Colored Farmers' Alliance and Co-operative Union, black farmers union organized in the 1880s after agrarian price declines. The crisis was precipitated by over-production and foreign competition. The farmers attacked the middlemen and the railroads.

National Convention, The, legislative body during the height of the French Revolution (1791–95). The National Assembly ordered the election of members to the Convention by universal suffrage. Within days the Convention made France a republic and condemned King Louis XVI to death. The Convention was dominated by the Mountain, a leftist group, and increasingly by Robespierre's faction. Excesses of the Reign of Terror led to a moderate reaction under the Thermidoreans. The constitution drawn up by the National Convention was implemented by its successor, the Directory.

National Debt, money owed by the government to purchasers of government securities, usually financial institutions and individuals within the country. When government spending exceeds tax revenues, the government must borrow money through deficit financing to make up the difference. While the US national debt has grown significantly over the past 25 years, its size relative to the level of the economy (measured by Gross National Product, GNP) has remained relatively constant. The major burden of the national debt is the interest that must be paid annually in order to maintain it. This interest has also remained a relatively constant percentage of the GNP. Deficit financing allows the use of discretionary policy, which, for the past several years, has always increased the national debt.

National Farmers' Union. *See* Farmers' Educational and Cooperative Union of America.

National Forest, woodland in the United States under the administration of the Forest Service. About 200,000,000 acres (81,000,000 hectares) in 44 states, Puerto Rico, and the Virgin Islands are national forests. Their boundaries are established by Congress and include about 20% private land being gradually acquired by the federal government. Timber is cut under supervision of government foresters; grazing in national forest range land is available under permit. Wildlife is protected and replenished.

National Grange, US fraternal organization of rural families. It promotes agriculture and the welfare of its members through legislation, education, community services, and credit union programs. Its publications include *View from the Hill* and *Grange Newsletter.* Members, about 600,000. Founded 1867.

National Greenback Party, US political party formed in the 1870s to promote the issuance of additional greenbacks. The party was supported by farm groups. In 1878 it became the Greenback Labor party. *See also* Greenbacks.

National Guard, volunteer citizen militia in the United States. Units of the National Guard are under state jurisdiction in peacetime and in times of national emergency may be activated for federal duty. Units are also activated during disasters and civil unrest. The 7th Regiment of the New York State Militia took the title "National Guards" (1824), and the term came into general use for state militias after the National Guard Association was formed in 1878. Units are located in all the states, and members are trained in the regular armed services. They thereafter attend regular meetings and field exercises.

National Industrial Recovery Act (NIRA), passed in 1933 to help business overcome the effects of the depression of the 1930s. NIRA permitted the firms in a given industry to cooperate rather than compete. Each industry was to draw up a code for its members to follow, including, among other things, prices to charge and outputs to produce. The act was to be administered by the National Recovery Agency (NRA), which was to enforce the industry codes. The NIRA was not successful, and, in 1935, the Supreme Court declared it to be unconstitutional. (*Schechter Poultry Corporation v. US*).

Nationalism, political and social force based on identification with the state. It has been instrumental in the emergence of the modern independent nation-state. Nationalist sentiment, drawing upon and extolling a common culture, language, and history emphasizes a sense of uniqueness and can be a powerful unifying agent. Conversely, it may exploit a distrust or hatred of other groups to condone aggressive action, as in Nazi Germany and Fascist Italy. Nationalism remains a significant political factor, especially among the underdeveloped "third world" nations. △1250, 1280, 1288.

Nationalist Party (China). *See* Kuomintang.

National Labor Relations Act. *See* Wagner Act.

National Labor Relations Board, independent federal agency. It has two principal functions: preventing

Narcissus

Narvik, Norway

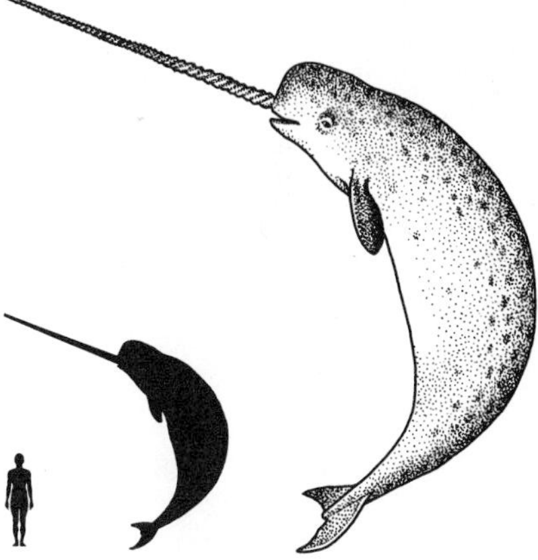

Narwhal

Ogden Nash

and remedying unfair labor practices by employers and labor organizations and conducting secret ballot elections among employees in appropriate collective-bargaining units to determine whether or not they desire to be represented by a labor organization. It was established in 1935.

National Labor Relations Board v. Jones and Laughlin Steel Corp (1937), landmark US Supreme Court case. It was decided during the famous "court-packing" attempts of Pres. Franklin D. Roosevelt to add enough members to the court to get his programs upheld. The court upheld the National Labor Relations Act allowing collective bargaining rights enforceable under the commerce clause and gave virtually limitless jurisdiction to the NLRB. This decision insured success for many New Deal economic programs.

National Organization for Women (NOW), US feminist group founded in 1966 by Betty Friedan and other feminists. A politically oriented organization, NOW aims to establish full equality for women and is a prime force behind the Equal Rights Amendment to the US Constitution.

National Park Service, federal agency within the Department of the Interior. This service administers and maintains an extensive system of national parks, monuments, historic sites, and recreation areas. The Park Service, established in 1916, is divided into four categories: natural, historic, cultural, and recreational. Natural areas are the national parks and monuments established for their scenic and scientific values. Historic areas mark sites of important movements, events, and US personalities. Recreational areas include parkways, reservoirs, seashores, and riverways. The cultural category is devoted to arts and crafts.

National Railroad Passenger Corporation, semi-public corporation to operate a rail system in the United States. Referred to as Amtrak, it was established by the Rail Passenger Service Act (1970) and began service in 1971. Governed by an 11-person board of directors, Amtrak is built on a for-profit basis, with investment capital and operating losses supported with federal financing in the initial stages of development. It is designed to provide a balanced transportation system by improving and developing intercity passenger rail service.

National Recovery Administration (NRA), bureau under Hugh S. Johnson established by the National Industrial Recovery Act (1933) to regulate industry for economic reform and recovery. The Supreme Court declared the act unconstitutional (1935) in *Schechter Poultry Corporation* v. *United States.*

National Republican Party, political party formed in 1828 following the election of Andrew Jackson as president. Staunchly opposed to Jackson, the National Republican party was strong in the Northeast. It supported the Bank of the United States, a protective tariff, and internal improvements. Daniel Webster and Henry Clay were dedicated leaders of the party. In 1832, Clay ran unsuccessfully for president against Jackson. The party expanded briefly to include more opponents to Jackson; by 1836, it had become the Whig party.

National Security Acts (1947, 1949), legislation to strengthen US military security. The 1947 act consolidated the army, air force, and navy into a single National Military Establishment. This was renamed and reorganized as the Defense Department in 1949, adding a non-voting chairman of the joint chiefs of staff. This 1947 act also established the National Security Council, which included the Central Intelligence Agency, responsible for intelligence activity relating to national security.

National Security Council (NSC), federal agency within the executive branch. The NSC, established in 1947, considers policies on matters concerning national security and makes recommendations to the president. The NSC is composed of the president, vice president, secretary of state, and secretary of defense.

National Socialism or **Nazism,** doctrine of the German National Socialist party under Adolf Hitler. Originating after World War I, national socialism was initially a leftist philosophy. Following the advent of Hitler as party leader (1921), the doctrine emphasized annulment of the Treaty of Versailles, Aryan supremacy, anti-Semitism, anti-Communism, German expansionism, and the cult of the führer. Nazi ideology was implemented during the Hitler regime in Germany (1933–45). *See also* Fascism. △1332.

National Urban League, a nonpartisan US organization. It consists of civic, professional, labor, and religious persons dedicated to the elimination of racial segregation and to aiding citizens with social and economic disadvantages. Its publications include *Urban League News* and *Urban League Housing News.* Members, about 50,000. Founded 1910.

National Woman Suffrage Association (NWSA) and **American Woman Suffrage Association (AWSA),** abolitionist and women's rights group that split (1869) in disagreement over supporting the 14th Amendment. NWSA opposed the Amendment for its exclusion of women; AWSA argued that at least black men should be given political freedom.

Nations, Battle of the. *See* Leipzig, Battle of.

Native American Party (1845–60), US political party based on the idea that immigrants were becoming too powerful and that only native Americans should hold political office. *See also* Know-Nothing Party.

Nativism, anti-Roman Catholic political movement in the United States in the 1840s. Fired by the influx of German and Irish immigrants, Native Americans, as they called themselves, feared the growing influence of the immigrants and the effects that their culture and beliefs might have on US society. The nativists formed organizations, often secretly, to keep immigrants from public office. Some of these groups were the Native American party, the Order of the Star Spangled Banner, the Know Nothing party, and the American Protective Association. A nativist convention in 1845 called for a change in the naturalization laws.

NATO. *See* North Atlantic Treaty Organization.

Natural Gas. *See* Gas, Natural.

Natural History, only surviving work of Roman writer Pliny the Elder. △1780.

Naturalistic Fallacy. △860.

Natural Monopoly, single-firm industry in which competition is not practical; a monopoly whose existence is deemed to be in the public interest, for example, the telephone industry or local utilities. *See also* Monopoly.

Natural Number. *See* Number, Natural.

Natural Philosophy, a term in common usage during the 17th and 18th centuries, roughly correlative in meaning with the contemporary phrase, natural science. Natural philosophy embraced both the physical and life sciences as well as mathematics. Isaac Newton entitled his great treatise in mathematical physics *Philosophiae Naturalis Principia Mathematica* (Mathematical Principles of Natural Philosophy, 1687).

Natural Selection, tendency for only the best adapted organisms to survive and reproduce in a particular environment. It is commonly referred to as survival of the fittest. *See also* Darwinism; Evolution. △408, 418.

Nat Turner Insurrection (1831), a slave uprising in Southampton co, Va. Seventy blacks, led by Nat Turner, killed 7 whites in their homes before the revolt was quelled by the militia. Turner was eventually caught after a manhunt that resulted in about 100 dead slaves. He and 19 others were hanged.

Naucalpan (Naucalpan de Juárez), city in central Mexico, 7mi (11km) NW of Mexico City; site of annual religious fiesta, held in September. Industries: textiles, agriculture. Pop. 373,605.

Nauplius Larva. △486.

Nauru, formerly Pleasant Island; island republic in W Pacific Ocean, S of the equator and W of the Gilbert Islands; discovered 1798 by John Hunter, British navigator, who named it Pleasant Island. Annexed by Germany 1888, it came under League of Nations Mandate and was administered by Australia after WWI; occupied by Japanese during WWII; made a trusteeship of United Nations 1947–68, after which it became an independent republic and member of the British Commonwealth of Nations. The native inhabitants are mostly Polynesian, of Micronesian and Melanesian descent. The economy is based on extensive phosphate mining, controlled by the Nauruans since 1970. Area: approx. 8sq mi (21sq km). Pop. 6,603.

Nautical Terms. △1680.

Nautilus, or chambered nautilus, cephalopod found in W Pacific and E Indian oceans at depths to 660ft (201m). Its large, coiled shell is divided into numerous, gas-filled chambers with the body located in the foremost chamber. Its head bears (60–90) retractible, thin, unsuckered tentacles, and it moves by squirting water from a funnel. The eyes have no lens and so function as pin-hole cameras. Shell size 4–8in (10–20cm). There are three surviving species of the formerly dominant suborder Nautiloid. Genus *Nautilus.* *See also* Cephalopod; Mollusk. △480.

Nautilus, in Military Science. △1684.

Navajo, Athapascan-speaking tribe, the largest Indian group in the United States. Their reservation lands in Arizona and New Mexico are the largest in the country. Famed for their fine weaving and silversmithing, they number over 125,000 persons. △1392.

Naval Stores Act (1705), legislation enacted by Parliament to encourage production of tar, turpentine, and ships' lumber in the colonies. The act reserved New England pine trees for export to England.

Navane, Kingdom of. △1078.

Navarino, Battle of (1827), naval battle in which the English, French, and Russian fleets, intervening in the Greek War of Independence, destroyed the Turkish-Egyptian fleet under Ibrahim Pasha. △1232.

Navarre (Navarra), province and former ancient kingdom in N Spain, on French border; capital is Pamplona. Originally inhabited by Vascones, it was conquered by Romans in 1st century BC; after the fall of Rome in 5th century, Navarre resisted invasions by the Visigoths, Arabs, and Franks for 400 years; it became an independent kingdom 10th century and was divided into three kingdoms 1035; ruled by French dynasties 1234–1512, when S part was conquered by Ferdinand II of Aragon and inc. into Castile 1515; N part passed to Henry IV, King of France, 1589. Industries: lumber, livestock, cereals, wine, grapes, sugar beets. Area: 4,024sq mi (10,422sq km). Pop. 464,-867.

Navigation, the science of determining the position of a craft and charting a course for guiding the craft from one point to another. Four main techniques are used: dead reckoning, piloting, celestial navigation, and electronic navigation. Position (the point of the earth's surface, established by latitude and longitude), direction (indicated as angular distance and measured in degrees of arc from true north), speed (rate of travel in nautical miles per hour), and distance must be plotted with special charts and instruments. *See also* Dead Reckoning.

Navigation Acts, corpus of laws imposing protectionist trade restrictions upon foreign commercial shipping. In Britain, the term specifically applies to the series of shipping laws passed in 1651, whereby British sea trade could only be carried on by ships flying the British flag, under the ownership and command of British subjects, and having partly British crews. These acts seriously hampered colonial and foreign trade, since no country could export goods to Britain in any ship that failed to meet the acts' conditions. They contributed to the unrest that led to the American Revolution and were not fully repealed until 1854.

Navigational Aids. △1752.

Navy, Department of the, federal agency within the Department of Defense. The primary mission of the Navy is to protect the United States by effective prosecution of war at sea. It also serves to support the forces of all US military departments and to maintain freedom of the seas. The US Marine Corps is part of the Navy Department. The Navy, established in 1775, is directed by the secretary of the Navy, who is appointed by the president. The secretary is responsible to the secretary of defense.

Navy, United States, the naval service of the US armed forces. It consists of over 500,000 personnel under the president, who is commander in chief of the armed forces, and the general supervision of the secretary of the Navy and his advisor, the chief of naval operations (CNO), who is the Navy's highest ranking officer. The CNO is a member of the joint chiefs of staff. The Department of the Navy provides the manpower, material, facilities, and services to support the naval operating forces. The CNO is responsible for the administration of these forces but not their military employment. Currently the Navy operates cruisers, destroyers and patrol ships, aircraft carriers, amphibious warfare ships, conventional and missile submarines, and aircraft. Major commands include the Sixth Fleet in the Mediterranean, the Second Fleet in the N Atlantic, the Third Fleet off the US Pacific coast, and the Seventh Fleet in the W Pacific. The Marines are under the Navy's authority. The Navy was established by Congress in 1798, although naval activities had begun during the Revolutionary War. In 1948 the Navy became a part of the Department of Defense. The Navy has taken an active part in US military operations from the Barbary coast wars to the Vietnam conflict. *See also* Defense, Department of; Joint Chiefs of Staff; Marine Corps, United States.

NAWSA. *See* National American Woman Suffrage Association.

Náxos, island in SE Greece in Aegean Sea; largest of the Cyclades Islands; ancient center of worship of Dionysus; member of Delian League but captured by Athens when it attempted to secede 470 BC; passed to Greece 1829. Industries: white wine, olive oil, fruit, white marble, granite, emery mining. Area: approx. 160sq mi (414sq km). Pop. 16,703.

Nayan. △608.

Nazarenes, group of 19th-century German painters, founded in Vienna in 1809 by Friedrich Overbeck and Franz Pforr, whose primary interest was in painting religious subjects in a primitive style. They were especially influenced by the simplicity of the painting style of the late Middle Ages and early Renaissance. Living in an abandoned monastery near Rome, the group attempted to revive the art of fresco painting of these earlier eras. △1228.

Nazareth (Nazerat), town in N Israel, 15mi (24km) SW of Sea of Galilee; capital of Northern District. In biblical times, it was the home of Mary, Joseph, and Jesus Christ; now a pilgrimage center and tourist resort; scene of Christian massacre by Baybar Muslims 1263; it was annexed to the Ottoman Empire 1517; during WWI, it was captured by Australian troops (1918); it came under British rule (1922–48) as part of the League of Nations Palestine mandate; captured by Israeli troops during Arab-Israeli war 1948 and inc. as part of Israel. Town is site of many religious monuments: Church of the Annunciation, containing Our Lady of American pilgrim house (built from donations by US Roman Catholics), Fountain of the Virgin, workshop of St Joseph, and the Table of Christ, traditional site of a meal shared by Christ and his disciples. Industries: food processing, cigarettes, pottery, mineral water bottling, textiles, leather goods. Pop. 34,000.

Nazca (Nasca), Indian civilization located in the southernmost coastal valleys of Peru, flourished 200 BC—AD 600. The Nazca, who developed without outside influence, were a relatively small group of farmers notable for their unique and highly stylized ceramics and textiles. △1120.

Nazism. *See* National Socialism.

Ndebele. *See* Matabele.

N'Djamena. *See* Fort Lamy.

Ndola, city in N central Zambia, S Central Africa, near Zaïre, 170mi (272km) N of Lusaka; site of Northern Technical College (1964); center of copper mining region. Industries: cement, footwear, soap. Pop. 114,000.

Ndongo, central African kingdom of the Bantu Mbunda people during the 16th–17th centuries. Subject to the depredations of slave traders from the Kongo, the kingdom was gradually conquered by the Portuguese.

Neanderthal Man, extinct race of Middle Paleolithic man, distinct from the ancestors of modern man, known from remains in Europe, N Africa and Asia. His thick clumsy bone structure had ape-like characteristics, but his brain capacity is comparable to modern man's. Neanderthal skeletons are everywhere found in association with so-called Mousterian stone implements, typical of which are large D-shaped scrapers for dressing skins and triangular spearpoints. *See also* Paleolithic Age. △652, 656.

Nearsightedness, or **myopia,** a condition in which visual images come to focus in front of the eye's retina, due to defects in refractive media or to abnormal length of the eyeball. It results in defective vision of distant objects and may be corrected by glasses that are concave on both surfaces. △674.

Nebraska, state in the W central United States, in the Great Plains region.

Land and Economy. Nebraska is a rolling prairie that rises steadily from E to W. Grasses are the principal native vegetation; trees appear mostly along rivers and streams. The Missouri River forms the E and part of the N boundary. The main rivers within the state are the Platte in the central area and the Niobrara in the N. Agricultural production is distributed throughout the state. Manufacturing industries, largely related to agriculture, are situated in the E cities. Petroleum drilling is in the SW area.

People. Early immigration came from E states. In the late 19th century, Germans, Swedes, and Danes arrived to work the farmlands. Most of the present population was born in the United States. About 60% lives in urban areas.

Education. There are nearly 30 institutions of higher education.

History. The region, part of the Louisiana Purchase from France in 1803, was little known until the Lewis and Clark expedition (1804–06) reported its findings. A few military posts were established in the SE. After 1830, the migration of pioneers bound for Oregon and California followed the Platte Valley westward. Nebraska Territory was created in 1854. After the Homestead Act was passed in 1862, thousands of settlers occupied the free lands that it offered. Building of the transcontinental railroads brought prosperity to the farms. Occasional instability of farm prices, as after the boom of WWI, led the state to develop industry to diversify and broaden the base of the economy.

PROFILE

Admitted to Union: March 1, 1867; rank, 37th
US Congressmen: Senate, 2; House of Representatives, 3
Population: 1,483,791 (1970); rank, 35th
Capital: Lincoln, 149,518 (1970)
Chief cities: Omaha, 346,929; Lincoln; Grand Island, 31,269
State legislature (unicameral): 49 members
Area: 77,227sq mi (200,018sq km); rank, 15th
Elevation: Highest, 5,426ft (1,655m), Johnson Township, SW Nebraska; lowest, 840ft (256m), SE Nebraska
Industries (major products): processed meat, grain, dairy products, farm equipment, electrical machinery, railroad equipment
Agriculture (major products): cattle, hogs, wheat, corn, rye, soybeans, sorghum
Minerals (major): petroleum, cement, sand, gravel
State nickname: Cornhusker state
State motto: Equality Before the Law
State bird: Western meadowlark
State flower: goldenrod
State tree: cottonwood

Nebuchadnezzar I. △954.

Nebuchadnezzar II or **Nebuchadrezzar** (died 562 BC), Chaldean King of Babylon (605–562 BC). During his reign of 43 years he defeated Necho II of Egypt in 605, captured Jerusalem and appointed Zedekiah king in 598, destroyed that city in 587 BC and for a second time carried Jews in exile to Babylon, conquered Tyre in 573, again overran Egypt in 568, and rebuilt the city of Babylon.

Nebula (plural nebulae), diffuse concentration of gas (chiefly hydrogen) or gas and dust particles in interstellar space. Formerly referred to as galactic nebulae, these objects, from which stars are thought to originate, are assigned to two main classes: bright nebulae (emission nebulae and reflection nebulae) and dark nebulae. Emission nebulae are largely gaseous and shine by the absorption and re-emission of energy from stars located within or near them. Reflection nebulae, containing much more dust, shine by reflecting light from nearby stars. Dark nebulae absorb energy but do not re-emit it as visible light and are only rendered visible when they happen to obscure light from star fields lying beyond them. △104–06.

Nebular Hypothesis. △48.

Necessary and Proper Clause, found in Article I, Section 8, Paragraph 18 of the Constitution, which deals with the powers of Congress. *See also* Elastic Clause; Implied Powers.

Neckar River, river in SW West Germany; rises in Black Forest; flows N past Stuttgart to Rhine River at Mannheim; connected to Danube by canal; navigable to Stuttgart; supports several hydroelectric plants. Length: 228mi (367km).

Necker, Jacques (1732–1804), financier, finance minister (1776–81) under Louis XVI of France, although a foreigner (Swiss) and a Protestant. He attempted financial reforms but was more attuned to politics than to economics. In his account of the king's finances (1781), he disguised a large deficit to encourage French participation in the American Revolution and revealed the large sums distributed to royal courtesans. Dismissed, but recalled in 1788, his sec-

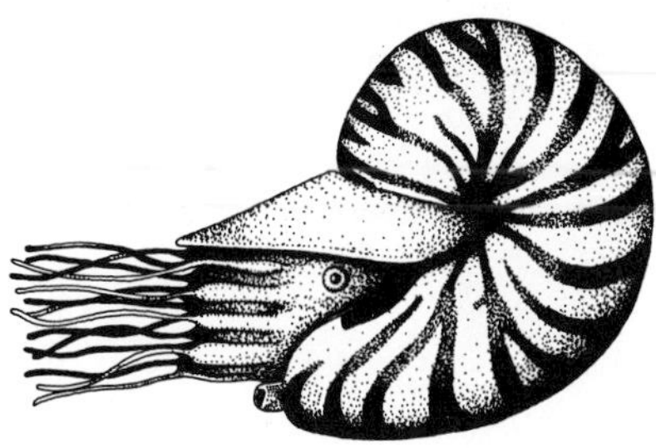

Nautilus

Navajo hogan

Nazareth, Israel

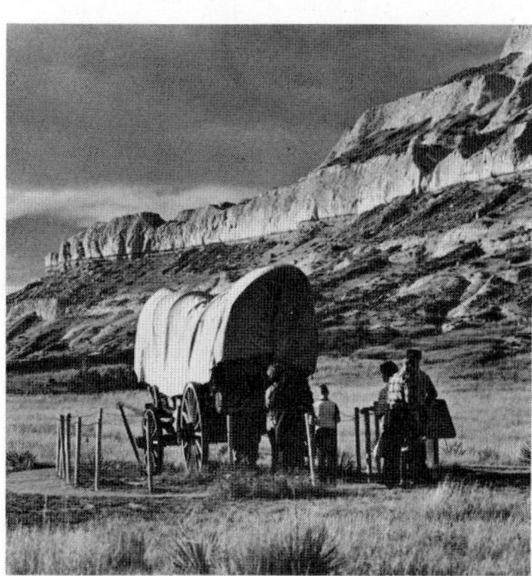

Scott's Bluff, Nebraska: replica of a conestoga wagon

ond dismissal was the immediate cause of the storming of the Bastille. He resigned (1790). △1224.

Nectarine, smooth-skinned peach grown in the E United States and California. Propagated from a peach seed or bud mutation, the tree shape and leaf characteristics are indistinguishable from those of a peach. The fruit, resembling a large plum, is cling or freestone. Family Rosaceae; species *Prunus persica nectarina. See also* Peach. △338.

Necturus. *See* Mudpuppy.

Needham, town in E Massachusetts, 10mi (16km) WSW of Boston. Industries: clothing, cans, electronics, paper products. Founded 1680; separated from Dedham and inc. 1711. Pop. (1970) 29,748.

Needlefish, primarily marine fish found in tropical and temperate waters and identified by its long jaw filled with fine, needle-sharp teeth and by its long, slender body. It is a ferocious fish capable of tremendous leaps; length to 4ft (121.9cm). Among the 60 species are the Indo-Pacific *Strongylura crocodilus*. Family Belonidae. *See also* Garfish.

Needlegrass. *See* Esparto.

Nefertiti or **Nefretete** (*fl.* 14th century BC), queen of ancient Egypt; wife of Ikhnaton; noted for her influence on her husband's religious ideas and for her exceptional beauty. △972.

Negative Income Tax, income-maintenance plan that provides a basic income to those who have none and a supplement to those with minimum income. A certain base income rate is determined and in order to achieve this income level, a family earning less than the base income is paid a "negative" tax by the government; those who are above the base level pay a positive income tax at some progressive tax rate.

Negative Ion. *See* Ion. △1554.

Negative Number. *See* Number, Natural.

Negev (Hanegev), desert region in S Israel; covers approx. 50% of Israel's total land area. In NW, Beersheba is the chief city and has fertile land irrigated by National Water Carrier Project; as it extends S, the area becomes more desolate. Region was scene of conflict between Egyptian and Israeli forces after Palestine mandate 1948; Egyptian blockage of Gulf of Aqaba (S Negev) was one of primary reasons for 1967 Arab-Israeli War. Mineral deposits include copper, phosphates, natural gas, gypsum, ceramic clay, feldspar, glass; oil, discovered 1955 and 1963, provides 8% of Israel's fuel needs. Area: 5,140sq mi (13,313sq km).

Negrillo Subrace, subdivision of the Negroid race, comprising the African pygmies, such as the Bambuti. Males average less than 59in (150cm) in height; other physical features are generally Negroid. *See also* Pygmy.

Negrito Subrace, subdivision of the Australoid race, comprising isolated Pacific and Indian Ocean pygmy peoples, such as the Malaysian Semang. Average male height is less than 60in (152cm); other physical features are generally Australoid. *See also* Pygmy.

Negritude, primarily a movement in poetry. It has developed into a philosophy in the works of its followers. Aimé Césaire used the term originally in his *Return to My Native Land* (1939) and defined it as "the simple recognition of the fact of being a Negro and the acceptance of this fact and of its cultural and historical consequences." The concept of Negritude was developed by Césaire, Léopold Senghor, and Léon Damas. *See also* Césaire, Aimé.

Negroid Race, one of the major human racial groupings, sometimes divided into Congoid and Capoid races, and including pygmy (Negrillo) populations. Negroid physical characteristics include heavy skin pigmentation; curly to spiral-tuft hair; thick lips; wide noses; high incidence of RO blood group. Negroids are indigenous to sub-Saharan Africa. △658.

Nehemiah, biblical author and book that is called Esdras II in the Douay Bible. This book recounts Nehemiah's efforts to rebuild the city of Jerusalem, including the reconstruction of the city's walls and sealing of the covenant. Several chapters are an apparently unaltered excerpt from Nehemiah's memoirs.

Nehru, Jawaharlal Pandit (1889–1964), Indian leader, the first prime minister of India (1947–64). The son of a leading Indian nationalist, Motilal Nehru, he was educated in England. He returned to India in 1912 and met Mohandas Gandhi in 1916. He actively joined the Indian independence movement in 1919. In 1929 he was elected president of the Indian National Congress. Between 1930–36 he spent much time in prison for his part in civil disobedience campaigns. He was imprisoned 1942–45 for failure to fully support the British war effort. With the founding of an independent India in 1947, he became the first prime minister and foreign minister of India. He led the new nation through its troubled beginning. He launched five-year plans to bring industrialization and socialization to India. In 1948 he seized the princely state of Hyderabad and went to war with Pakistan over Kashmir. In 1959 he dissolved the Communist government of Kerala state. He advocated neutralism and sought to lead the Afro-Asian bloc. In 1961 he seized Goa from the Portuguese and in 1962 had to contend with Communist Chinese incursions across the northern border. △1330, 1352.

Neisse River (Nysa Luzycka), river rising in NW Czechoslovakia; flows N to Oder River near Guben, East Germany; part of border between East Germany and Poland since 1945. Length: 140mi (225km).

Neithart, Mathis Gothart. *See* Grünewald, Mathias.

Nejd (Najd), region in central Saudi Arabia; vast plateau land; taken from Turkey by Wahabi leader Ibn Saud 1899–1912; after conquering Hejaz and Al Hasa, Nejd became part of Saudi Arabia 1932; site of oasis settlements; inhabited by Bedouins. Area: 447,000sq mi (1,157,730sq km).

Nekton, one of the large groups of the sea's population. It includes the large swimming migrating animals such as adult squid, fishes, and whales. *See also* Benthos; Pelagic Division; Plankton.

Nelson, Horatio Nelson, Viscount (1758–1805), English naval commander. Entering the navy in 1770, he first saw action in the Caribbean (1780). At the outbreak of war with France (1793), he served in the Mediterranean with distinction under Admiral Hood and his successors, losing his right eye and right arm. He rendered effective service at Cape St Vincent (1797) and won a crushing victory over the French at the Battle of the Nile (1798). Promoted to vice admiral, he fought the Battle of Copenhagen (1801) to disrupt the armed neutrality. Recalled to the Mediterranean (1803), he blockaded Toulon for two years until the French fleet finally eluded him. He was killed at the ensuing Battle of Trafalgar, in which the French fleet was destroyed. His long liaison with Emma, Lady Hamilton, was well publicized. *See also* Trafalgar, Battle of. △1226.

Nelson, Thomas, Jr. (1738–89), American patriot and a signer of the Declaration of Independence, b. Yorktown, Va. Virginia's delegate to the Continental Congress (1775–77, 1779), he succeeded Thomas Jefferson as governor of that state in 1781.

Nelson River, river in Manitoba, Canada; flows from Lake Winnipeg into the Hudson Bay. The mouth was discovered 1612; route for fur traders; site of first Hudson's Bay Co. trading post (1670). Length: 400mi (644km).

Neman (Nyeman), river in Belorussian SSR, USSR, and Lithuania; rises in Belorussia 30mi (48km) SSW of Minsk, flows W past Stolbtsy, Masty, Grodno, then N into Lithuania, past Alytus, and then W again past Kaunas, Jurbackas, Neman, Sovetsk, to Courland Lagoon, forming a small delta mouth. It receives the Viliya, Nevezys, and Dubysa rivers on the right and the Shchara and Sheshupe on the left. It is navigable for most of its 582mi (937km) and is used as timber route. The Lithuanian resorts of Druskininkai and Bristonas lie on its banks.

Nematocyst. △468.

Nematode, or roundworm, phylum of marine, freshwater, and parasitic worms identified by elongated, cylindrical body pointed at both ends, thick cuticle covering, and longitudinal muscles. Reproduction is sexual. Length: to 1ft (30.5cm). The 10,000 species include *Ascaris* (parasitic in intestine), hookworm, filaria (causes elephantiasis), and *Trichina*. △474.

Nemea, ancient city in S Greece; mythical site of slaying of Nemean lion by Hercules; site of temple of Zeus where and in whose honor the Nemean Games were played; games were est. 573 BC and held in the 2nd and 4th years of each Olympiad; 11 of Pindar's odes celebrated Nemean victories.

Nemertea, ribbon worm, proboscis worm, also called Nemertinea, marine phylum of flatworms similar to Platyhelminthes and identified by protrusile proboscis, anus, and circulatory system. Reproduction is sexual. Length: 1in (2.54cm) to several feet. The 550 species include the bootlace worm *Lineus* and *Eunemertes*. △506.

Nemours, town in N France, 12mi (19km) S of Fontainebleau, on Loing Canal. Made duchy 1404, it was part of House of Savoy 1528–1659; site of 12th-century castle from which Henry III issued edict revoking privileges of Huguenots (1585); 13th-century church, and bridge (1803). Industries: agriculture, brewing, glassmilling. Pop. 6,605.

Neoclassical Architecture, late 18th and early 19th century architectural style in the United States and Europe. The Napoleonic revival of the idea of the Roman Empire, as exemplified in the Louvre Colonnade (1667–70) by Claude Perrault, and the enthusiasm for archaeological knowledge stimulated by the excavations at Pompeii and Herculaneum, brought an international burst of imitation of classicism in architecture. The influence of monumental Roman temples was particularly dominant in the design of public buildings in the new United States, including Virginia's state capitol (1785) by Thomas Jefferson. James Stuart, co-author of the influential *Antiquities of Athens* (1762), designed the first example of Greek revival in Western Europe, a garden temple at Hagley, England (1758). The trend culminated with the Greek revival buildings of Karl Schinkel, such as the Royal Theater (1818–21) and Old Museum (1822–30) in Berlin. Neoclassicism emphasized a return to the pure forms of Greek and Roman architecture—solidity, severity, and rigid definition of masses. The classical orders were used for structure rather than ornamentation. This geometric clarity opposed the fluid, sculptural principles of Baroque architecture. △1198.

Neoclassical Music, music composed from roughly 1920 to 1950. The movement reacted against the emotionalism and subjectivity of Romanticism and sought to return to the ideals and some of the methods of music prior to the Romantic period, using as models the music of Bach, Handel, Mozart, and others. Thus, old forms were revived, such as the toccata, fugue, and concerto grosso, and the older ideal of objectivity with less emotion was stressed in musical composition. Some of the important composers who participated in the movement were Busoni, Prokofiev, Stravinsky, Hindemith, Bartok, Casella, and Piston. △1364.

Neo-colonialism. △1350.

Neodymium, metallic element (symbol Nd) of the Lanthanide group, first isolated in the form of its oxide in 1885. The pure metal was first obtained in 1925. Chief ores are monazite (phosphate) and bastnasite (fluorocarbonate). It has no important use. Properties: at. no. 60; at. wt. 144.24; sp gr 6.8–7.0, melt. pt. 1,875°F (1,024°C); boil. pt. 5,661°F (3,127°C); most common isotope Nd^{142} (27.11%). *See also* Lanthanide elements. △1552–54.

Neo-Impressionism, artistic style developed in the 1880s by French post-Impressionist painters Georges Seurat and Paul Signac and sometimes referred to as divisionism or pointillism. Painting in this precise style was done according to a scientific formula, in which tiny dots of color were used in varying proportions to delineate subjects and to create atmosphere and mood. △1254.

Neolithic Age, or New Stone Age, period in man's evolution following the Mesolithic, in which man first lived in settled villages, domesticated and bred animals, cultivated grain crops, and practiced pottery, weaving, and flint-mining. Stone axes were fitted with handles for the first time. *See also* Mesolithic Age. △652, 952.

Neomycin, an antibiotic or mixture of antibiotics active against a variety of bacteria. It is produced by a soil actinomycete.

Neon, gaseous nonmetallic element (symbol Ne) of the rare-gas group, first discovered (1898) by William Ramsay and M. W. Travers. Neon is present in the Earth's atmosphere (0.0018% by volume) and is obtained by the fractionation of liquid air. Its main use is in discharge tubes for advertising signs. The element forms no compounds. Properties: at. no. 10; at. wt. 20.179; density 0.8999 g dm^{-3}; melt. pt. −415.6°F (−248.67°C); boil. pt. −410.89°F (−246.05°C); most common isotope Ne^{20} (90.92%). *See also* Noble Gases. △1552–54, 1558.

Neo-Platonism, a school of philosophy that had its greatest importance between about 250 and 550. *Neo* means new, but this school was more than a new version of Platonic thought. It combined Pythagorean, Stoic, Platonic, and Aristotelian ideas with strains from Jewish, Oriental, and Christian religions. In their view of the basic problem of good and evil, Neo-Platonists tended to be mystical and poetic more than philosophical. Formative leaders of the movement were two 3rd century philosophers, Plotinus and Porphyry. One aim of these and other Neo-Platonists in Rome and Greece was to build a philosophy that could compete with the rising influence of Christianity. This effort failed, and the Emperor Justinian closed the Neo-Platonic academies in 529. Yet influences of Neo-Platonism persisted through medieval times. △852.

Neo-Pythagoreans, philosophical movement begun in the 1st century BC and continuing until diluted by the rise of Neo-Platonism in the 3rd century AD. Developing at the start of the Christian era, neo-Pythagoreanism combined Jewish and Hellenistic elements with the more religious and mystical aspects of Pythagorean thought and was an influence on Neo-Platonism. *See also* Neo-Platonism.

Neosho, river in SE Kansas and NE Oklahoma; rises in E central Kansas; flows generally S to Arkansas River near Muskogee; used for hydroelectricity. Length: 460mi (741km).

Neoteny, the persistence, in the adult animal, of larval characteristics, such as retention of gills, as in some salamanders. An entire order of tunicates, the Larvacea, is permanently larval, never reaching typical adult form. *See also* Mudpuppy; Salamander. △518.

Nepal, an independent kingdom between India (S) and China (N). One frontier cuts through Mt Everest, one of the world's tallest mountains. The nation consists of three regions: the Terai, S lowland region with arable land; a central mountain area, including the populated Katmandu Valley; and high mountains in the N, extending to the Himalayas. Two-thirds of the nation's income is from agriculture; less than 1% of the population works in industry. Literacy is estimated at 15%. The population is a mixture of Mongoloid and Indian backgrounds, resulting in many divergent languages. In the 18th century numerous small principalities were united under one rule. The expansion of the dominant Gurkhas was checked in 1792 by the Chinese, and in 1816 by a border clash with Britain, which was consolidating its Indian colony. In 1846 the Rana family assumed power, reigning by heredity until a revolution in 1950, and a constitution in 1959, followed by a return to Rana rule. In 1962 the king, Mahendra (reigned 1952–72), dissolved parliament and started a system of "basic democracy," which included an elected village council (panchayat), with zonal and district councils. These councils are responsible to the king, who is aided by an advisory state council and council of ministers. Upon the king's death (1972), his son, Crown Prince Birenda, took control.

PROFILE

Official name: Nepal
Area: 54,362sq mi (140,798sq km)
Population: 12,600,000
Chief cities: Katmandu (capital); Bhadgaon
Government: monarchy
Religion: Hinduism, Buddhism, Islam
Language: Nepali
Monetary unit: Nepali rupee

Neper, John. *See* Napier, John.

Nephritis, or glomerulonephritis or Bright's disease, an inflammatory disease of the kidney. Frequently caused by streptococcal infection, it may be chronic or acute. Acute nephritis is treated with bedrest; chronic cases may be helped with artificial kidneys or kidney transplants. △728.

Nephrosis, a syndrome characterized by the presence of edema, large amounts of albumin in the urine, and cholesterol in the blood.

Neptune, eighth planet from the Sun, observed in 1846 by J.C. Galle and H. d'Arrest. Neptune has two known satellites, Triton and Nereid. Mean distance from the Sun, 2,793,000,000mi (4,496,730,000km); mass, approx. 17 times that of Earth; equatorial diameter, 31,200mi (50,232km); rotation period, 15hr, 48min; period of sidereal revolution, 164.8 years. *See also* Solar System. △88,154.

Neptune, in Roman religion originally a god of fresh water. Eventually he became identified with the Greek Poseidon and became a deity of the sea. His female counterpart was Salacia. Neptune's festival took place in summer, when water was scarcest. Thus its purpose was probably the propitiation of the freshwater deity. In art his attributes are the trident and dolphin.

Neptunism, a discarded theory of the origin of Earth's forms. This idea proposed that all landforms were once deposited under water.

Neptunium, radioactive metallic element (symbol Np) of the actinide group, first made in 1940 by neutron bombardment of uranium. It is found in small amounts in uranium ores. Np^{237} is a by-product obtained in producing plutonium. Properties: at. no. 93; at. wt. 237.0482; sp gr 20.25; melt. pt. 1,184°F (640°C); boil. pt. 7056°F (3905°C); most stable isotope Np^{237} (2.14×10^6 yr). *See also* Transuranium Elements. △1552–54.

Nereis, or clamworm, polychaete worm that lives in sand or mud on the seashore. It is usually red or orange with numerous "paddles" on each side of its body. The forepart of its gut can be extended as a proboscis with a pair of jaws. Length: to 3ft (91cm). Family Nereidae. *See also* Annelida. △474.

Nernst, Walther Hermann (1864–1941), German chemist. He became professor at Gottingen and then in Berlin and was awarded the Nobel prize in chemistry in 1920 for his discovery of the third law of thermodynamics. His other important work was concerned with chain reactions in photochemistry. Although he served in World War I, he earned Nazi disfavor because two of his daughters married Jews.

Nero (Claudius Caesar) (37–68), Roman emperor (54–68), b. as Lucius Domitius Ahenobarbus. He was the son of Agrippina II, great-granddaughter of Augustus Caesar, and the stepson of Emperor Claudius I. He murdered his brother Britannicus (55), his mother (59), and his wife Octavia (62). He blamed the Christians for the burning of Rome (64) and began the first official persecution against them. After discovering a plot against him (65), he had many distinguished Romans, including Seneca, Lucan, and Thrasea Paetus, executed. But he was overpowered in a revolt in 68 and committed suicide. He was the last emperor of Julius Caesar's family.

Neruda, Pablo (1904–73), Chilean poet and winner of the Nobel Prize for literature in 1971. Neruda occupied a number of diplomatic posts and was active in politics; he was a Communist-party senator (1945–48) and supported the Marxist regime of Salvador Allende (1970–73). Neruda's poetry transcended politics and dealt with the question of the human condition in general. His best-known work is *Canto General* (1950). △1376.

Nerve, any collection of neurons (specifically axons), arranged like the wires of a cable, that travel between nervous system structures and other organs. *Afferent nerves*, or sensory nerves, transmit toward the central nervous system. *Efferent* nerves, or motor nerves, transmit from the central nervous system toward the periphery. Some nerves have both afferent and efferent fibers. For example, 12 cranial nerves (such as the optic nerve and the auditory nerve) originate in the brain and transmit to and away from sensory organs. *See also* Neuron. △664.

Nervi, Pier Luigi (1891–), Italian architect. He is noted for his innovative use of concrete in designs for large structures. His work includes the Florence Stadium (1932), famous for its cantilevered stairs and 70-ft (21.3-m) deep cantilevered roof. He used precast concrete trusses in the airplane hangars at the Orbetello air force base (1940). In the mid-1940s he invented *ferro cemento*, a strong, light, reinforced concrete that he used in the Turin Exhibition Hall (1948). He also designed the UNESCO Building, Paris (1953–57; with Marcel Breuer and Bernard Zehrfuss); the Pirelli skyscraper, Milan (1955), which has floors cantilevered from two tapering concrete pillars; and the Papal Audience Hall, Vatican (1971).

Nervous Breakdown, lay term for an emotional crisis or the sudden appearance of unusual or frightening behavior provoking psychiatric intervention. Sometimes viewed as synonymous with *neurotic breakdown* in which a period of acute anxiety follows the collapse of neurotic defenses.

Nervous System, one of the major organ systems of the body, with the overall function of relating an individual to his surroundings. It is made up of nervous tissue, that type of tissue that is irritable and conducts impulses, and its basic structural unit is the *neuron*, or nerve cell. In man the nervous system may be divided into three parts: the central nervous system, the peripheral nervous system, and the autonomic nervous system. The *central nervous system* consists of the brain and spinal cord. No function can be performed

Horatio Nelson

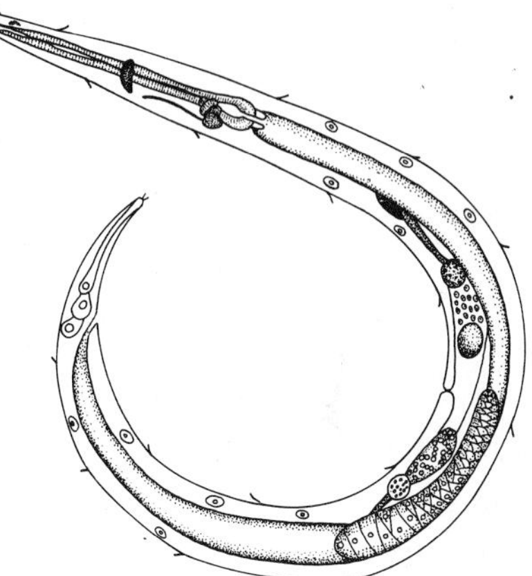
Nematode

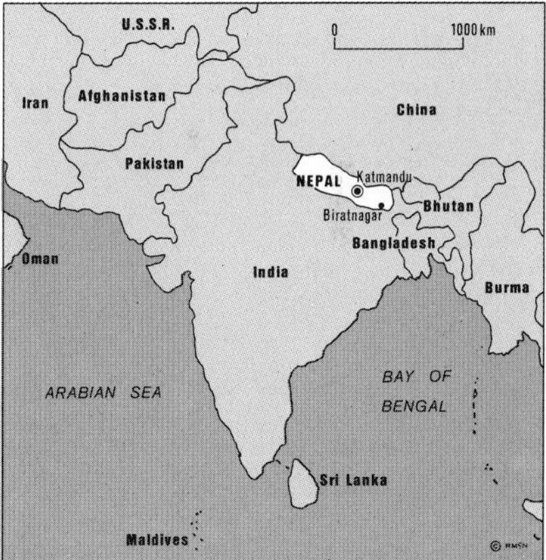
U.S.S.R.
0
1000km
Iran
Afghanistan
China
Pakistan
NEPAL
Katmandu
Biratnagar
Bhutan
Bangladesh
Oman
India
Burma
ARABIAN SEA
BAY OF BENGAL
Sri Lanka
Maldives
Nepal

Pablo Neruda

without some activity of the central nervous system, the major controlling mechanism of the body. The *peripheral nervous system* is a system of nerves and ganglia (nerve aggregations) that connect the peripheral parts of the body to the central nervous system. It has sensory nerves, carrying impulses from sense organs to the central nervous system; motor nerves, carrying motor impulses from the central nervous system to the muscles of the body; and some so-called mixed nerves, containing both sensory and motor nerve fibers. There are 12 cranial nerves originating from the brain, and 31 spinal nerves originating from the spinal cord.

The *autonomic nervous system*, sometimes considered a part of the peripheral nervous system, has an extensive network of nerves away from the brain and spinal cord that control the body's internal environment, regulating such activities as heart rate, peristaltic movements of the digestive tract, urinary bladder contraction, and such emotional reactions as blushing, sweaty palms, and pounding heart. The autonomic nervous system is itself divided into two parts: the *parasympathetic*, or craniosacral, part, which includes some facial-acting nerves and the pelvic nerve, controlling the lower colon and bladder; and the *sympathetic*, or thoracolumbar, part, which can accelerate heart rate, inhibit salivary secretion, stimulate adrenal secretion, among other functions. Functioning through its ganglionic fibers, the two branches of the autonomic nervous system are somewhat antagonistic, yet have independent functions as well. *See also* Brain; Nerve; Neuron; Spinal Cord. △662–64, 722.

Ness, Loch, freshwater lake in N Scotland, running SW to NE along the geological fault of Glen More; part of Caledonian Canal; legendary home of one or more aquatic monsters. Length: 23mi (37km). Depth: 754ft (230m).

Nest, construction built by an animal to house its eggs, young, or sometimes itself. It is made by some invertebrates, such as social insects, some fish, some amphibians, some reptiles, most birds, and many small mammals. Bird nests vary from the loose structures of owls and many seabirds to the elaborate retorts of weaverbirds. The majority are cup-or dome-shaped and made with twigs, leaves, and mud. Usually a solitary dwelling, some are shared, willingly with ostriches or unwillingly with Old World cuckoos and New World cowbirds. △530.

Nestorianism, a theological position which held that the human nature of Christ was independent from the divine nature. Declared heretical in 431, it nevertheless gained adherents in the Byzantine Empire. △1056.

Nestorius (died *c.* 451), patriarch of Constantinople. He was of Persian parents. As patriarch he became involved in a theological dispute on the persons of God. He was charged with believing in two distinct natures: a divine being, God, and a man, Jesus. It is true that Nestorius objected to the title *Theotokos* (Mother of God) for the Virgin Mary, preferring the title Mother of Christ. He distinguished divine and human natures in Christ, but he believed in some kind of moral union of the two natures. The Council of Ephesus (431) condemned the belief in two natures as a heresy, and Nestorius was deposed as patriarch. The Nestorian heresy was named for him, but some historians doubt he held these heretical beliefs. *See also* Nestorianism.

Netanya (Natanya), city in W Israel, 35mi (56km) SSW of Haifa on the Mediterranean Sea coast; site of Jewish Legion Museum; grave of Baron Edmond Rothschild and Wingate Institute for Physical Education are nearby. Industries: diamond processing, tourism, textiles, rubber products, citrus packing. Founded 1928 and named for Nathan Straus, US philanthropist who donated money to further Palestinian education and social services. Pop. 65,400.

Netherlands, independent nation in NW Europe. Low-lying and heavily populated, its economy and history have been shaped by its proximity to the sea.

Land and Economy. A low, flat land averaging 37ft (11m) above sea level, and with much land below sea level, it is bounded N and W by the North Sea, S by Belgium, E by West Germany. Dike systems have been used to reclaim land from the sea to add fertile lands to a densely populated country. Most of the land is used for pasture (43%) and farming (22%). About 80% of the arable land is in farms of less than 50acres (20hectares). Six percent of the work force is engaged in agriculture and fishing. Limited resources place unusual dependence on imports, both for industry and agriculture.

People. The Netherlands has one of the highest population densities in the world. Primarily of German stock (Frisians and Franks), the Dutch also include a Gallo-Celtic mixture. History and social and political attitudes have been largely shaped by their religion. Political parties are divided along ideological lines, and religion influences schools, trade unions, recreational societies, and the media. Freedom of religion is guaranteed: 40.4% is Roman Catholic; 28.3% Protestant Reformed; 9.3% Protestant Calvinist; and about 20% has no religious affiliation. Literacy is about 98%.

Government. The Netherlands is a hereditary constitutional monarchy; the 1954 constitution provided for a council of ministers, an elected parliament, and a president.

History. When Julius Caesar invaded the Netherlands, he found it inhabited by German tribes. In the 8th century, as part of Charlemagne's empire, it was passed to the house of Burgundy and the Hapsburgs, and in the 16th century Spain claimed it. Led by William of Orange, the Dutch revolted against the Spanish in 1568. In 1579 the seven N provinces became a republic—the United Netherlands, which became a great sea and colonial power. It came under French domination until Napoleon was defeated in 1813, when it joined with Belgium under a monarchy. Belgium withdrew in 1830, and the Dutch, led by William II, promulgated a liberal constitution in 1848. He was followed by Wilhelmina in 1898. Though neutral in WWI and II, the Netherlands was invaded by the Germans in 1940. The Queen and her daughter, Crown Princess Juliana, established a government-in-exile in London, and returned in 1945 when the Germans had capitulated. Queen Juliana succeeded to the throne in 1948. Some of the Netherlands' many overseas territories are still retained, but have increasing autonomy. Indonesia was given independence in 1949 and Surinam in 1975.

PROFILE

Official name: Kingdom of the Netherlands
Area: 15,770sq mi (40,844sq km)
Population: 13,597,616
Density: 862per sq mi (333per sq km)
Chief cities: Amsterdam (capital); Rotterdam; The Hague
Government: Constitutional monarchy
Religion: Roman Catholic and Protestant
Language: Dutch
Monetary unit: Guilder
Gross national product: $70,100,000,000
Per capita income: $4,440
Industries: metal, machinery, food processing, chemicals, textiles, oil refining, diamond cutting, pottery, electrical appliances, clothing, cheese
Agriculture: sugar beets, potatoes, cereals, flowers, cattle, fish, hogs, seeds, forests, wheat, barley, rye, oats, flax
Minerals: gas, oil, coal
Trading partners: Federal Republic of Germany, Belgium, France, United States

Netherlands Antilles, autonomous group of five main islands and part of a sixth in West Indies, Caribbean Sea, including Aruba, Bonaire, Curaçao (largest), Saba, St Eustatius, and S half of St Martin. Capital is Willemstad. Islands are associated with Netherlands; they were discovered 1490s by Christopher Columbus, Alonso de Ojeda, and Amerigo Vespucci; settled by Spanish 1527 at Curaçao; captured by Dutch 1634. Industries: oil refining (Curaçao and Aruba), seasalt, phosphates, tourism. Pop. 220,084.

Nettle, annual and perennial weed found worldwide. It has heart-shaped, toothed leaves, tiny, greenish flowers, and stinging hairs along the stem. Among 500 species is the stinging nettle *Urtica dioica*. Height: 2–4ft (61–121.9cm). Family Urticaceae. △444–46.

Nettle Rash. △724.

Net-vaults, in architecture. △1106.

Networks, mathematical. △1458, 1470.

Netzahualcóyotl, city in central Mexico; suburb of Mexico City. Pop. 571,035.

Neuchâtel, capital of Neuchâtel canton in Switzerland, on N shore of Lake Neuchâtel, at mouth of Seyon River. Governed 1648–1707 by counts under Holy Roman Empire, it passed to Prussian rule 1815; site of university (1838), museum, library, Romanesque cloisters, 12th–17th-century castle, observatory. Industries: chocolate, tobacco, watches, printing. Pop. 38,784.

Neumann, John von (1903–57), US mathematician, b. Budapest. After leaving Hungary in 1919 he studied at various European universities before finally settling at Princeton University in 1930, where he became professor in 1933. His early contribution to quantum theory was followed by work on the A-bomb at Los Alamos. He was also responsible for the development of game theory.

Neuralgia, pain along a nerve trunk or its branches. It may be the result of a virus infection of the nerve, alcoholic or lead poisoning, physical injury, or vitamin deficiency. It may also be purely psychological. Drugs are used for relief of neuralgic pain.

Neurasthenia. *See* Asthenic Reaction.

Neuritis, inflammation or degenerative lesion of the nerves accompanied by pain, paralysis, and impaired reflexes. Causes are many and treatment is directed toward the causative agent. △722.

Neurology, branch of medicine that involves the diagnosis and nonsurgical treatment of diseases of the nervous system. △722.

Neuron, or nerve cell, the basic structural unit of the nervous system. It is composed of a cell body and one or more dendrites and one axon. The dendrites and axon are nerve cell processes, extending beyond the cell body. Dendrites carry impulses to the cell body; they are often short and branched. An axon is usually a longer, unbranched process; it carries impulses away from the cell body. *See also* Axon; Dendrite. △664–66.

Neuroptera, order of carnivorous insects, including lacewings, ant lions, and owl flies, found worldwide. They have a complete life cycle: egg, larva, pupa, and adult. Wing span: 0.7–5.9in (18–150mm). *See also* Ant Lion; Hellgramite; Lacewing. △492.

Neurosis, personality disturbance involving persistent anxiety that is either directly experienced or controlled through the use of psychological defense mechanisms. *See also* Neurotic Personality; Psychoneurotic Disorders. △760, 766.

Neurotic Personality, personality style marked by neurotic patterns of anxiety and defense and the expression of such anxiety-reduction behaviors as obsessive-compulsive or hysterical patterns. *See also* Neurosis; Psychoneurotic Disorders.

Neustria, the W section of the Frankish empire (the E section being Austrasia). It was formed when the empire of Clovis I was divided among his four sons (511). In 687, Pepin of Austrasia overcame Neustria. In 912 part of it was ceded to the Scandinavian pirates and became Normandy. Although it was originally the area between the Meuse, the Loire, and the Atlantic Ocean, the name came to mean only Normandy and finally fell into disuse.

Neutrality, policy of noninvolvement in hostilities existing between other states. This status was recognized by international law as early as the 15th century. The rights and obligations of neutral powers have been codified by international treaties and conventions. A nation proclaiming its neutrality must be wholly impartial and refrain from helping or hindering any side. It must furthermore protect its own territory from encroachment by belligerents. △1352.

Neutrality Acts (1935–39), series of laws enacted before World War II. In 1935 an arms embargo was declared against any nations engaged in war, and civilian travel on belligerents' ships was forbidden. The act of 1936 extended the embargo and prohibited loans to belligerents. The 1937 act embargoed munitions to either side in the Spanish Civil War. The act of 1939 allowed "cash-and-carry" arms and munitions sales, and it was modified in 1941 to permit US merchant ships to be armed and to deliver cargo to belligerent countries.

Neutralization, chemical reaction conducted in an aqueous medium between equivalent weights of an acid and a base to produce water and a salt, which is neither acidic nor basic, but has a pH of approximately 7, often accompanied by the generation of heat.

Neutrino, uncharged massless elementary particle with spin ½ that has little reaction with matter and is difficult to detect. There are two sorts: the electron neutrino (symbol $_e$) is closely associated with the electron and is produced when protons and electrons react to form neutrons, as in the Sun. The more common antineutrino occurs when a neutron decays. The muon neutrino (symbol μ), associated with the muon, occurs in high-energy reactions. *See also* Lepton. △1484.

Neutron, uncharged elementary particle (symbol n) that occurs in the atomic nuclei of all chemical elements except the lightest isotope of hydrogen. It was first identified by James Chadwick (1932). In isolation it is unstable, decaying with a halflife of 11.7 minutes into a proton, electron, and antineutrino. Its neutrality allows it to penetrate and be absorbed in nuclei and thus to induce nuclear transmutations and fission. It is a baryon with spin ½ and a mass slightly greater than that of the proton. △1480, 1484.

Neutron Activation Analysis, highly sensitive method of identifying the chemical contents of something by bombarding it with high-energy neutrons that are absorbed by the atoms present in the sample. The resulting radioactive nuclei emit radiation of an energy and decay rate characteristic of the original atoms. The quantity present can also be found with extreme precision.

Neutron Star. *See* Pulsar. △108.

Neva, navigable river in Russian SFSR, USSR; issues from the SW corner of Lake Ladoga as Petrokrepost; flows W to the Gulf of Finland at Leningrad. It receives the Mga, Tosna, and Izhora rivers and is connected by the Mariinsk, Tikhvin, and Vyshnevolotsk canal systems with the Volga River, and by the White Sea-Baltic Canal with the White Sea. Length: 40mi (64.4km).

Nevada, state in the W United States, in the Great Basin region.

Land and Economy. At an average altitude of 5,500ft (1,676m), Nevada is a semi-desert region of nearly 100 basins separated by short mountain ranges running N to S. Its climate is dry; moisture-bearing winds are blocked by mountains in California to the W. There are few rivers within the state; the Humboldt, which is the longest, runs 290mi (467km) to disappear in the Humboldt Sink. Pyramid Lake is the only natural lake. Grazing and mining are important to the economy, but tourism is the state's major source of income. Visitors are drawn by the legalized gambling and the lenient divorce laws, which require only brief residence. The city of Las Vegas offers a wide range of entertainment. Resort areas such as Lake Tahoe, which is partly in California, and Lake Mead, formed by dams on the Colorado River on the S border, are year-round recreation centers.

People. Nevada is the third-least densely populated state, outranked only by Alaska and Wyoming. The 1970 census showed a density of 4.4 persons per square mile (1.7 per sq km). About 80% of the population resides in areas classified as urban.

Education. There are six institutions of higher education, including the state-supported University of Nevada.

History. Spaniards visited the area in 1776, but the first explorations were not begun until 1825 by British fur trappers who were followed by US "mountain men." In 1833 a party bound for California crossed the region along the Humboldt River. Their route became the Overland Trail, which took thousands westward after gold was discovered in California in 1848. In that year, the United States acquired Nevada by the treaty that ended the Mexican War. When the Comstock Lode, a rich deposit of silver and gold, was found in W Nevada in 1859, settlers flocked to the land. Nevada Territory was organized in 1861, only three years before it became a state. The mining rush created several boom towns and a number of personal fortunes, but changes in the prices of precious metals and depletion of the ores depressed activity; some boom towns became ghost towns and are now tourist attractions. The WWII quest for useful metals revived the mining industry, especially in copper.

PROFILE

Admitted to Union: Oct. 31, 1864; rank, 36th
US Congressmen: Senate, 2; House of Representatives, 1
Population: 488,738 (1970); rank, 47th
Capital: Carson City, 15,468
Chief cities: Las Vegas, 125,787; Reno, 72,863; North Las Vegas, 36,216
State legislature: Senate, 20; Assembly, 40
Area: 110,540sq mi (286,298sq km); rank, 7th
Elevation: Highest, 13,140ft (4,005m), Boundary Peak; lowest, 470ft (143m), Colorado River
Industries (major products): electronic devices, gaming devices, stone-clay-glass products
Agriculture (major products): cattle, other livestock
Minerals (major): copper, gold, mercury, lithium
State nickname: Sagebrush State, Silver State
State motto: All for Our Country
State bird: mountain bluebird
State flower: sagebrush
State tree: single-leaf piñon

Nevada Pupfish. △516.

Névé. △262.

Nevelson, Louise (1900–), US sculptor and painter, b. Russia. Her first sculpture show was in 1940 at the Nierendor Gallery in New York City. In the 1950s she began constructing her famous painted collection of boxes, wooden objects, and castoffs from old houses. Her "environmental sculptures" include "Sky Cathedral" and "Daun's Wedding Feast" (1959). Her later pieces are free-standing, including bins and barrels filled with long flexible poles. △1418.

Neville, Richard. *See* Warwick, Earl of.

Nevins, Allan (1890–1971), US historian, b. Camp Point, Ill. A former newspaper editor, he wrote *The Ordeal of the Union* (2 vols., 1947), and *The Emergence of Lincoln* (2 vols., 1950). He also won two Pulitzer Prizes for biographies of Hamilton Fish and Grover Cleveland.

New Albany, city in S Indiana, on Ohio River, opposite Louisville, Kentucky; seat of Floyd co. A shipbuilding center of 19th century, the riverboat *Robert E. Lee* was built here; home of William Vaughn Moody, poet and playwright. Industries: plywood, flour, glue, chemicals. Settled 1813; inc. as town 1819, as city 1839. Pop. (1970) 38,402.

Newark, city in W California, SE of San Francisco; site of Fremont-Newark Junior College (1966). Inc. 1955. Pop. (1970) 27,153.

Newark, city in NE New Jersey, on Passaic River and Newark Bay, W of lower Manhattan; seat of Essex co; largest city in New Jersey; connected to New York City by tunnel; site of George Washington's supply base as he retreated across state in 1776; scene of major 1967 race riot; site of Newark College of Engineering (1881), Essex County College (1968). Industries: electrical equipment, paints, chemicals, insurance. Settled 1666 by Puritans; inc. as town 1833, as city 1836. Pop. (1970) 382,417.

Newark, city in central Ohio, 30mi (48km) E of Columbus, on Licking River; seat of Licking co; site of Newark Works, a work area of prehistoric mound builders. Industries: glass, aluminum, petroleum products, paper containers. Founded 1802 and named for Newark, New Jersey; inc. 1826. Pop. (1970) 41,836.

New Bedford, city in Massachusetts, 50mi (81km) S of Boston on Buzzard's Bay; seat of Bristol co; Revolutionary War haven for American privateers, burned by British in 1778. City was a whaling capital until the late 1850s, when whaling declined; it was a textile center until 1920s; today it is an important fishing and scalloping port; site of Seamen's Bethel (1832, described in Herman Melville's *Moby Dick*), Bourne Whaling Museum, and a Whaleman Statue by Bela Pratt (1913). Industries: textiles, machinery, tools, copper, brass. Founded 1652; inc. as town 1787, as city 1847. Pop. (1970) 101,777.

New Berlin, city in SE Wisconsin; suburb of Milwaukee; mainly residential, with a few light industries. Founded 1840; inc. 1959. Pop. (1970) 26,910.

New Bern, port city in E North Carolina, at confluence of Neuse and Trent rivers; seat of Craven co. City served as meeting place of colonial assembly 1745–61, and provincial capital 1774; captured by Union forces 1862; site of Tryon Palace (1767), the colonial capital and governor's mansion, which was badly burned 1798 and restored in 1950s. Industries: lumber, boats, chemicals, tourism. Settled by Swiss and Germans 1710; inc. and made co. seat 1723. Pop. (1970) 14,660.

Newberry v. US (1921), important US Supreme Court decision declaring that the Constitution's control over elections extended only to the final choice of an officer. The court said that it did not apply to preliminary proceedings, thereby exempting primaries from any regulation.

Newbery, John (1713–67), English publisher and bookseller. He was the first publisher to produce children's books, establishing them as a branch of the publishing business. Although his books were published anonymously, Oliver Goldsmith and other distinguished writers were among his authors. In 1921, Frederic Melcher created the Newbery Medal in the United States for annual recognition of the best children's work written by an American.

New Britain, industrial city in N Connecticut, 9mi (14km) SW of Hartford. Industries: hardware, tools, household appliances, ball bearings. Settled 1687; inc. 1870. Pop. (1970) 83,441.

New Britain Island, largest island of the Bismarck Archipelago and part of Papua New Guinea, in SW

Nest

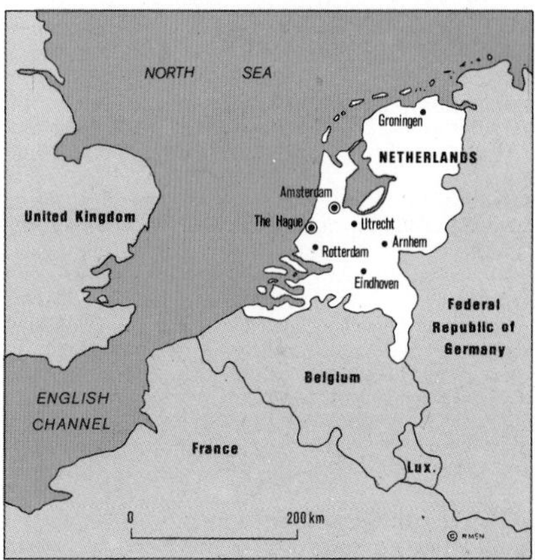
NORTH SEA
Groningen
NETHERLANDS
Amsterdam
United Kingdom
The Hague
Utrecht
Arnhem
Rotterdam
Eindhoven
Federal Republic of Germany
Belgium
ENGLISH CHANNEL
France
Lux.
0
200 km

Netherlands

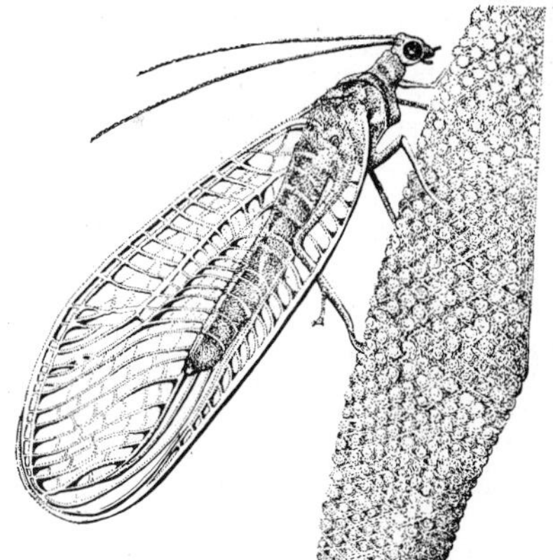

Neuroptera

GOLDEN NUGGET
1905
LUCKY
BINGO

Las Vegas, Nevada

Pacific Ocean, approx. 55mi (89km) E of New Guinea Island; chief town is Rabaul. Discovered 1606 by Dutchman Jacques Lemaire, it became German protectorate 1884; after WWI it was mandated to Australia, and reestablished as territory of Australia following Japanese occupation in WWII. Island has a mountainous terrain, with volcanoes exceeding 7,000ft (2,130m); noted for hot springs. Exports: copra, coconuts, cocoa. Industries: mining of gold, copper, iron, coal. Area: approx. 14,160sq mi (36,674sq km). Pop. 138,689.

New Brunswick, province in E Canada; one of the Maritime Provinces, bordered on the W by the state of Maine.

Land and Economy. The Gulf of St Lawrence, an arm of the Atlantic Ocean, is on the E, and the Bay of Fundy, which has the highest tides in the world, is on the S. The land rises gradually inland; the highest parts are in the NW. The St John is the principal river. More than 75% of the province is forest-covered, a valuable resource for the economy. Mineral deposits discovered in the N in the mid-20th century are important. Fisheries along the coasts are a source of income.

People. The original settlers were French, and a strong French element characterizes the population. The remainder are principally of English and Scots descent.

Education. Institutions of higher education are the University of New Brunswick, St Louis-Maillet, Le Collège de Bathurst, St Thomas University, and the University of Moncton.

History. The region was discovered by the French explorer Jacques Cartier in 1534. With Nova Scotia, it formed the French colony of Acadia. The colony was ceded to Great Britain by treaty in 1713, but British settlement was slow. More than 12,000 Loyalists from the American colonies fled into the area during the American Revolution, and this influx spurred the creation of the province in 1784. A boundary dispute with the United States was settled in 1842 and in 1867 New Brunswick joined Nova Scotia, Quebec, and Ontario to establish the Dominion of Canada.

PROFILE

Admitted to Confederation: July 1, 1867; one of the four provinces that were joined to form the Dominion of Canada
National Parliament Representatives: Senate, 10; House of Commons, 10
Population: 624,000; rank, 8th
Capital: Fredericton
Chief cities: Saint John; Moncton; Fredericton
Provincial legislature: Legislative Assembly: 58 members
Area: 28,354sq mi (73,437sq km); rank, 8th
Elevation: Highest: 2,690ft (820m), Mt Carleton; lowest, sea level
Industries (major products): pulp and paper
Agriculture (major products): potatoes, hay, fruit, dairy products
Minerals (major): copper, zinc, lead, silver
Floral emblem: purple violet

New Brunswick, city in central New Jersey, on Raritan River 9mi (14km) W of Perth Amboy; seat of Middlesex co. Occupied alternately by British and colonial troops during Revolution, it was scene of start of George Washington's march on Yorktown 1781; birthplace of Joyce Kilmer (1886); site of Rutgers University (1766). Industries: medical and surgical supplies, machinery, chemicals, leather. Settled 1681; inc. 1736. Pop. (1970) 41,885.

Newburgh, city in SE New York, on W bank of Hudson River; site of George Washington's headquarters 1782–83, Epiphany Apostolic College (1888), Our Lady of Hope Seminary (1900), Mount St Mary College (1930) Industries: clothing, leather goods, aluminum castings, radio parts. Settled 1708–09; inc. as village 1800, as city 1865. Pop. (1970) 26,219.

Newburyport, city in NE Massachusetts, at mouth of Merrimack River, 25mi (40km) ENE of Lowell; seat of Essex co. A former shipbuilding and whaling center, it was birthplace of William Lloyd Garrison (1805); site of Cushing House (1808) with furnishings of Federal period, Tristram Coffin House (1651). Industries: electronics, textiles, footwear, rum, silverware, fishing. Settled 1635; inc. 1764 when it was set off from Newbury. Pop. (1970) 15,807.

New Caledonia Island, largest island in French Overseas Territory of New Caledonia, in SW Pacific Ocean approx. 750mi (1208km) E of Australia; chief city and capital of territory is Nouméa. Discovered 1774 by Captain Cook, it was site of French Roman Catholic mission est. 1843; used as penal colony 1864–94; became part of official French Overseas Territory 1946. Inhabitants are mainly Melanesians, with some Europeans and Vietnamese; island has irregular climate and geography. Products: copra, coffee, cotton, nickel, iron, manganese, cobalt, chrome. Area: 6,531sq mi (16,915sq km). Pop. 84,000.

Newcastle, Thomas Pelham-Holles, Duke of (1693–1798), English political figure. A Whig, he supported Walpole and became secretary of state (1724–54). He succeeded his brother, Henry Pelham, as prime minister (1754) but resigned (1756). Though prime minister again (1757–62), his secretary of state, William Pitt, directed foreign policy.

Newcastle, William Cavendish, Duke of (1593–1676), English political figure and soldier. He was appointed governor to the prince of Wales (1638). General of forces in the northern counties during the English Civil War, he supplied financial and military aid to Charles I. After the Battle of Marston Moor (1644) he lived in exile until the Restoration (1660). He was created duke of Newcastle (1665).

Newcastle, formerly King's Town; city in SE Australia, 100mi (161km) NE of Sydney; site of University of Newcastle (1965). Industries: iron, steel, chemicals, textiles, shipbuilding, fertilizers. Founded 1804. Pop. 144,860.

New Castle, city in W Pennsylvania, at junction of Shenango and Neshannock rivers; seat of Lawrence co. Industries: bronze tools and parts, pottery, bricks, cement. Settled 1798 on site of Indian trading center; inc. as borough 1825, as city 1869. Pop. (1970) 38,559.

Newcastle Disease, a viral disease of birds, characterized by respiratory difficulty and nervousness. Adult birds may survive. Man can be infected when holding sick birds, usually developing conjunctivitis. No treatment exists, but preventive vaccines are available.

Newcastle-upon-Tyne, county town of Tyne and Wear, NE England; port on Tyne River; linked by tunnel and five bridges to Gateshead; home of University of Newcastle-upon-Tyne. Industries: shipbuilding, heavy engineering. Exports: coal, iron, steel. Pop. 222,153.

New City, residential village in SE New York; suburb of New York City; seat of Rockland co; farming area. Pop. (1970) 27,344.

Newcomen, Thomas (1663–1729), English inventor of the first economical atmospheric steam engine. In 1705 he built a model of the engine that consisted of a piston moved by atmospheric pressure within a cylinder in which a partial vacuum had been created by condensing steam. He shared the patent with Thomas Savery (1650–1715) who had invented (1698) an earlier but inferior steam engine. △1628.

New Criticism, type of literary criticism, primarily of poetry, that emphasizes close analysis of a work as an independent unit. It developed in the 1920s and 1930s in the United States through the influence of various critics and university professors, including John Crowe Ransom, Cleanth Brooks, René Wellek, and Allen Tate. It flourished particularly in the 1940s and 1950s. Although there is diversity among the New Critics, they agree that literary analysis should concentrate on the language and tone of a work rather than on its relation to a period, a tradition, or its author.

New Deal, in US history, the social and economic programs of the administration of Pres. Franklin D. Roosevelt. Elected in 1932 at the depths of the Great Depression, Roosevelt promised a "new deal" to the American people, hence the name that was given to all the domestic reforms of his administration. Although most historians do not credit the New Deal programs with ending the depression—only the defense spending of World War II did that—those programs were extremely important in restoring the confidence of the people during the 1930s and in relieving the worst effects of the Great Depression. Most of the New Deal programs have remained in effect and have been broadened by the policies of succeeding Democratic administrations, including the Fair Deal of Harry S. Truman, the New Frontier of John F. Kennedy, and the Great Society of Lyndon B. Johnson.

Promptly upon inauguration in 1933, Roosevelt embarked upon the most ambitious and revolutionary set of domestic reforms in the nation's history. Assisted by his group of advisors known as the Brain Trust, the President's first action was to declare a "bank holiday" in which the entire US banking system was reformed by the National Banking Act, and the nation in effect was taken off the gold standard. In the first months of the New Deal, the so-called Hundred Days, Roosevelt proposed, and Congress created such important federal agencies as the Agricultural Adjustment Administration, the National Recovery Administration, the Civilian Conservation Corps, the Public Works Agency, and the Tennessee Valley Authority. In 1934 he established the Securities and Exchange Commission and the Federal Communications Commission. In 1935 were founded the National Youth Administration, the Social Security system, the Works Progress (later, Projects) Administration, and the National Labor Relations Board. A minimum wages and hours law was passed, and the nation's tax system was overhauled.

Despite the cooperation of a Democratic Congress Roosevelt's New Deal programs were not without opposition. Republicans and conservative Democrats considered them socialistic threats to the free-enterprise system. The unprecedented power they gave to the federal government was a source of concern to states-rights advocates and to old-line liberals who looked with suspicion on all government activity. The most effective opposition, however, came from the Supreme Court. It struck down as unconstitutional several of the central agencies of the New Deal, including the National Recovery Administration and the Agricultural Adjustment Administration. Roosevelt's attempts to "pack" the court by naming additional pro-administration justices met with defeat, but eventually the court came to accept most of the New Deal.

Roosevelt—along with a Democratic Congress—was reelected in 1936, thereby giving him the voters endorsement to continue the New Deal. His second term, while less revolutionary than the first, nevertheless consolidated and expanded the programs of the first term. By the end of the second term, however, the approaching World War II was engaging more and more attention. The defense spending in preparation for that conflict finally ended the Great Depression, but the social and economic reforms of the New Deal had become permanent parts of American society. *See also* Agricultural Adjustment Act; Civilian Conservation Corps; Federal Communications Commission; National Labor Relations Board; National Recovery Administration; Public Works Administration; Securities and Exchange Commission; Social Security Act; Tennessee Valley Authority; Works Project Administration. △1324.

New Delhi, capital of India, in N India, on the Yamuna River in Delhi Union Territory. Planned by English architects Edwin Lutyens and Herbert Baker it was constructed 1920–30 to replace Calcutta as the capital of British India; where the old city of Delhi (SW) is primarily a commercial center, New Delhi's broad streets are lined with government buildings making it a busy administrative center; site of war memorial arch (1921), marble residence of the president of India, prayer ground where Mahatma Gandhi was assassinated (1948), and Balmiki and Lakshminarayan temples. Pop. 371,210.

New Democratic Party (NDP), Canadian political party founded in 1961 as an outgrowth of the Cooperative Commonwealth Federation. First headed by Thomas C. Douglas, the party advocates a moderate socialist program. While under the leadership of David Lewis (1971–74) it gained control of provincial governments in Manitoba, Saskatchewan, and British Columbia. In 1972 its 30 members in the House of Commons sided with the Liberal party in a coalition government that lasted until 1974 when the NDP lost 15 of its seats in a new election. Ed Broadbent then became party leader.

New Economic Policy (NEP) (1921–28), program of the Soviet government to restore the Russian economy and appease a hostile peasantry after the civil war. It replaced the seizure of grain from peasants with a fixed amount paid as a tax, allowed the surplus to be sold on the open market, loosened controls on trade and light industry, and stabilized the currency. A relatively liberal period, the NEP ended with forcible collectivization in 1928 under the first Five-Year Plan. △1310–12.

New England Confederation, formed (1643) by New England colonies of Plymouth, Connecticut, Massachusetts Bay, and New Haven for mutual safety and welfare. Rhode Island was refused admittance because of religious differences. The confederation was dissolved (1684) with direct English rule over Massachusetts Bay.

New England Restraining Act (1775), punitive measure sponsored by Britain's Lord North. The act restricted New England trade to Britain and the British West Indies and denied fishermen access to Newfoundland's fishing banks. The act was extended to include New Jersey, Pennsylvania, Maryland, Vir ginia, and South Carolina. The Battle of Concord occurred before the act arrived in the colonies, nullifying it.

Newfoundland, province in E Canada, on the Atlantic Ocean. It consists of the large island of Newfoundland, which was England's first New World colony, and of Labrador, a portion of the mainland to the N that extends inland about 400mi (640km) from the coast. The Strait of Belle Isle separates the parts.

Land and Economy. The surface of the island and of the mainland is generally rolling. The highest elevation on the island is Gros Morne, 2,666ft (813m). The highest in the province is in the far N of Labrador. The entire coastline is broken by deep bays and inlets with many islands. Thick forests cover much of the land, the exploitation of which is a major sector of the economy. Newfoundland's cod fisheries have been famous for nearly 500 years; in the late 20th century international competition and market uncertainties have affected them. Great reserves of mineral deposits, especially of iron in Labrador, remain to be developed. Agriculture is primarily subsistence farming.

People and Education. Almost all the population is in the island of Newfoundland; Labrador is sparsely settled. Most people live in small communities along the coasts. They are descended from the original settlers from the British Isles. Memorial University of Newfoundland at St John's is the only institution of higher education.

History. Norsemen are believed to have touched the coast of Labrador about AD 1000 and to have established a short-lived settlement on the N tip of Newfoundland. The recorded discoveries of the region were by the English navigator John Cabot, who found the island in 1497 and the Labrador coast in 1498. Sir Humphrey Gilbert formally claimed the island for England in 1583. It was a fishing station loosely administered from London, but as the population grew slowly it became a British colony by 1832. Labrador was under the jurisdiction of the governor of Newfoundland, and both remained apart from the Dominion of Canada until they joined the Confederation in 1949 as the province of Newfoundland.

PROFILE

Admitted to Confederation: March 31, 1949; rank, 10th
National Parliament Representatives: Senate, 6; House of Commons, 7
Population: 518,000 (1971); rank, 9th
Capital: St John's
Chief cities: St John's; Corner Brook
Provincial legislature: Legislative Assembly, 43 members
Area: 156,185sq mi (404,520sq km); rank, 7th
Elevation: Highest: 5,500ft (1,678m), Torngat Mts, Labrador; lowest, sea level
Industries (major products): pulp and paper, wood products, processed fish
Fisheries (major products): cod, lobster
Minerals (major): iron ore, lead, zinc, copper, fluorspar
Agriculture (major products): hay, potatoes, turnips, cabbage
Floral emblem: pitcher plant

Newfoundland, rescue and draft dog (working group) bred by Newfoundland fishermen. This dignified dog has a massive head with square, short muzzle; small, triangular ears close to the head; a full-chested, broad-backed body; shortish, strong legs with webbed feet; and broad, long tail. The long, full double coat is short on head, muzzle, and ears. Color is black, bronze, or white and black. Average size: 25–28in (63–71cm) high at shoulder; 110–150lb (50–68kg). *See also* Working Dog.

New France, French colony in North America corresponding roughly to Quebec, Ontario, and the Maritime provinces of Canada. Jacques Cartier claimed the region for France in 1534. The Company of New France was chartered to establish settlements and exploit the fur trade. In 1605 the first permanent white settlement was founded at Port Royal (now Annapolis Royal, Nova Scotia). Quebec was founded in 1608. By 1640 there were fewer than 300 colonists and subsequent wars with the Iroquois almost totally exterminated the population. The Company of New France was disbanded in 1663 and the colony was placed under a royal governor. In 1713 Acadia (Nova Scotia), Newfoundland, and the Hudson Bay area were lost to Britain. In 1763 France lost the complete colony to Britain. The approximately 65,000 colonists became British subjects.

New Frontier, President John F. Kennedy's name for his legislative program. The program included massive government aid for education, housing and slum clearance, mass transportation and highways, equal opportunity employment, medical care for the aged, tax reform, Peace Corps, trade negotiations, Alliance for Progress, and an extended space program. Kennedy first spoke of the "New Frontier" in his acceptance speech at the 1960 Democratic convention, and it expressed idealism and optimism. The program was only partly successful, due to a conservative coalition in Congress.

New Granada, an administrative area centered in present-day Bogotá, Colombia. The Kingdom of New Granada was founded in 1538. The *audiencia* (high court) of New Granada was installed in 1549. The captaincy-general of New Granada was created in 1564. The Spanish Crown established the viceroyalty of New Granada in 1717, disbanded it in 1723 and reestablished it in 1739. The term was used to describe present-day Colombia from 1830–61, when it was changed to the United States of Colombia.

New Guinea, island in the SW Pacific Ocean, N of Australia, in the E Malay Archipelago; second largest island in the world. It is administratively divided into two sections. Irian Barat (W), a province of Indonesia, and Papua New Guinea, a self-governing country since 1973. First sighted 1511 by Portuguese explorer Antonio d'Abreu; Dutch claimed the W side 1828, and British the SE side and nearby islands 1885. Australia gained control of the British section 1905, and the Netherlands transferred control of W section to Indonesia 1963. Area: 319,713 sq mi (828,057sq km). Pop. 2,968,000. *See also* Papua New Guinea.

New Hampshire, state in the NE United States, in the New England region, bordered on the N by the province of Quebec, Canada.

Land and Economy. In the SE, New Hampshire touches the Atlantic Ocean for 13mi (21km). Portsmouth is the only port. To the W and N the land is hilly, with occasional elevations of 3,000ft (915m). In the N are the rugged White Mts, where Mt Washington is the highest peak in the NE United States. The Connecticut River forms the W boundary; the Merrimack is the largest river in the state. There are more than 1,300 lakes, of which Winnipesaukee, Newfound, and Sunapee are the largest. About 85% of the state is forested. The scenic attractions and year-round recreational opportunities of the terrain have made tourism a mainstay of the economy. Industry is concentrated in the cities of the S and central portions and along the Connecticut and Merrimack rivers. The rigorous climate curtails the growing season for farming.

People. Most of the inhabitants, especially in rural sections and the smaller towns, are descended from the original settlers, but throughout the state there is a strong French-Canadian element that tends to concentrate in the larger cities. Urban areas contain about 60% of the population. The SE is the home of many who commute to jobs in Massachusetts.

Education. There are about 25 institutions of higher education. The state-supported University of New Hampshire has several campuses. Dartmouth College at Hanover is a notable privately endowed institution. The first free public library in the United States was est. at Dublin in 1822.

History. English explorers visited the coast as early as 1603, and the first settlement was made at the mouth of the Piscataqua River in 1623; New Hampshire became an English royal province in 1679. Indian raids harassed the frontier towns until 1759. In one of the first armed moves in the colonies against the British Crown, New Hampshire men captured Fort William and Mary at Portsmouth on Dec. 12, 1774. After joining the Union, the state had a population surge, but the growth rate declined as many left the farms in the westward migration. Expanding industry in the cities drew immigrants in the 20th century, and the growth rate exceeded that of the nation as a whole.

PROFILE

Admitted to Union: June 21, 1788; 9th of the 13 original states to ratify the US Constitution
US Congressmen: Senate, 2; House of Representatives, 2
Population: 737,681 (1970); rank, 41st
Capital: Concord, 30,022 (1970)
Chief cities: Manchester, 87,754; Nashua, 55,820; Concord
State legislature: Senate, 24; House of Representatives, 400
Area: 9,304sq mi (24,097sq km); rank, 44th
Elevation: Highest, 6,288ft (1,918m), Mt Washington; lowest, sea level
Industries (major products): shoes, textiles, electrical and electronics equipment, pulp, paper, lumber, wood products
Agriculture (major products): dairy and poultry products, maple syrup, apples
Minerals (major): sand, gravel, stone

Caraquet, New Brunswick

New Delhi, India: WWI memorial at the India Gate

Newfoundland: fishing village

Concord, New Hampshire: state capitol

State nickname: Granite State
State motto: Live Free or Die
State bird: purple finch
State flower: purple lilac
State tree: paper (white) birch

New Harmony, town in SW Indiana, on Wabash River. Originally settled by Harmony Society under George Rapp, it was sold to Robert Owen (1825), who founded a Utopian communistic colony attracting numerous educators, scientists, and other intellectuals; est. nation's first kindergarten, free public school, free library. It was dissolved in 1828 due to internal dissensions; 25 Rappite buildings remain. Founded 1814. Pop. (1970) 971.

New Haven, in S Connecticut, New Haven co, third largest city in the state, and the site of Yale University; located 70mi (110km) NE of New York City. The presence of Yale, one of the nation's oldest and most famous schools, has made the city a cultural center. Its elm-lined streets feature many old buildings as well as noted examples of modern architecture. Puritans founded New Haven in 1638. A bustling port in the 18th and 19th centuries, the city shared the role of Connecticut capital with Hartford 1701–1875. Noah Webster and Eli Whitney lived in the city.

Points of interest: Peabody Museum of Natural History, Yale University Art Gallery. Industries: firearms and ammunition, rubber products, locks, and tools. Inc. 1784; pop. (1970) 137,707.

New Haven Colony, colony in Connecticut founded in 1637–38 by Puritans under the leadership of Theophilus Eaton and John Davenport on land bartered from Indians. It was run as a strict theocracy with proper religious belief entitling citizenship. It was expanded (1643) to include Milford, Guilford, and Stamford. It joined the New England Confederation (1643) and later merged with the Connecticut Colony (1655) under a charter obtained by John Winthrop.

New Hebrides (Nouvelles Hébrides), volcanic island group in SW Pacific Ocean, E of Australia and NE of New Caledonia; comprised of approx. 80 islands forming a chain of about 450mi (725km). Chief islands include Espíritu Santo, Efate (site of Vila, the capital), Malekula, Pentecost, Malo, Tanna, Ambrim. Discovered 1606 by Pedro Fernandez de Queirós, and explored by Capt. James Cook 1774, the group was settled by English missionaries in the early 19th century; in 1887 joint British-French naval control of the islands was est.; the islands are still controlled by an Anglo-French condominium. Natives are Melanesian and Polynesian. Industries: fishing, copra, cattle, farming, mining. Area: 5,700sq mi (14,763sq km). Pop. 86,000.

New Humanism, movement in literary and social criticism in the early 1900s led by Irving Babbitt, a Harvard professor, and Paul Elmer More, an editor and writer. A later adherent to New Humanism was Norman Foerster, also a professor. Reacting against romanticism and naturalism in modern literature, they called for a return to classical standards and conservative moral values. New Humanist treatises include Babbitt's *Rousseau and Romanticism* (1919) and More's *Shelburne Essays* (1904–21; 1928–36).

New Iberia, city in S Louisiana; seat of Iberia parish; site of "Justine" (1822) and "Shadows on the Teche" (1834), excellent examples of Greek revival architecture; scene of annual sugar cane festival. Industries: paper and wood products, bricks. Founded *c.* 1765 by Acadians fleeing from Nova Scotia; inc. as Iberia 1836; name changed 1868. Pop. (1970) 30,147.

Ne Win, U (1911–), Burmese military and political figure, b. as Shu Maung. At the outbreak of World War II he cooperated with the Japanese in an effort to wrest Burma from Britain, but after 1943 his Burmese Independence Army also turned against the Japanese. He became defense minister upon Burma's independence (1948). In 1958 he deposed U Nu and had himself appointed prime minister. U Nu returned to office (1960–62), but Ne Win deposed him again and turned the country into an isolationist police state. He abolished private enterprise, introducing the "Burmese Way to Socialism." He ordered some 300,000 foreigners, primarily Chinese and Indian, out of Burma. Under a new constitution (1974), he became president. His government was confronted with economic setbacks, insurgencies by Communists and ethnic minorities, and demonstrations by workers and monks.

Newington, town in central Connecticut; suburb of Hartford. Industries: truck farming, tools, concrete. Founded 1670; inc. 1871. Pop. (1970) 26,037.

New Jersey, state in the E United States, on the Atlantic Ocean S of New York City. It is the most densely populated of the 50 states, and one of the most highly industrialized.

Land and Economy. The S 60% of the state is nearly level or gently sloping up to the W. In the N, hill ranges run SW to NE; the highest elevations are on Kittatinny Mt in the extreme NW. The Delaware River forms the W boundary and the Hudson, part of the E. The Hackensack, Passaic, and Raritan are the principal rivers in the state. The economy is greatly influenced by the cities of New York across the Hudson River and Philadelphia across the Delaware. Much of the state's industry is concentrated in the 90mi (145km) between these cities, which constitutes virtually a continuous metropolitan area. Each of the cities is one of the nation's leading ports, with huge docking facilities on the New Jersey side of the rivers. A network of highways and railroads, feeding from the cities, crosses the state. Thousands of New Jersey residents commute to jobs in New York and Philadelphia. Agriculture, centered in great truck farms, is principally in the center and the S. The Atlantic coast is a notable tourist area, especially the cities of Atlantic City and Asbury Park.

People. New Jersey has a population density of 915 persons per sq mi (353 per sq km). Nearly 90% of the people resides in urban areas. In the 19th century, immigrants from overseas settled in the industrial cities, and their descendants form a large segment of the population. About 10% of the residents are blacks; they account for more than half the population of Newark, the largest city.

Education. There are more than 60 institutions of higher education. Rutgers University, with its main campus at New Brunswick, is the state university; until 1956, it was a private institution. Princeton University, the 4th-oldest college in the United States, founded in 1746, is the leading privately endowed institution.

History. The Italian explorer Giovanni da Verrazano, in the service of France, explored the coast in 1524, but white settlement did not begin until the 1620s, when the Dutch founded the colony of New Netherland (later New York). Some of these pioneers settled in NE New Jersey. In 1664, the English seized New Netherland. The land between the Hudson and the Delaware was separated and renamed New Jersey. The colony supported the Revolution, and almost 100 engagements between American and British troops were fought on its soil. After achieving statehood, New Jersey began the development of its industry and transportation system. In the Civil War and both world wars, the state was a prime supplier of war material. The administration of Woodrow Wilson, governor 1910–13, when he resigned to become president of the United States, initiated many progressive measures of government.

PROFILE

Admitted to Union: Dec. 18, 1787, 3d of 13 original states to ratify US Constitution
US Congressmen: Senate, 2; House of Representatives, 15
Population: 7,168,164 (1970); rank, 8th
Capital: Trenton, 104,638 (1970)
Chief cities: Newark, 381,930; Jersey City, 260,545; Paterson, 144,824
State Legislature: Senate, 40; General Assembly, 80
Area: 7,836sq mi (20,295sq km); rank, 46th
Elevation: Highest, 1,803ft (550m), High Point; lowest, sea level
Industries (major products): chemical products, apparel, processed foods, electrical machinery, petroleum products
Agriculture (major products): tomatoes, corn, asparagus, apples, cranberries, poultry
Minerals (major): stone, sand, gravel
State nickname: Garden State
State motto: Liberty and Prosperity
State bird: eastern goldfinch
State flower: purple violet
State tree: red oak

New Jersey Plan (1787), plan for national government. It was introduced by William Paterson and offered by the small states at the Constitutional Convention in Philadelphia. An alternative to the Virginia plan, which favored the large states, it called for a single legislative body in which each state was represented equally, the delegates to be chosen by the state legislatures. It included a supremacy clause, which made the national government the authority over the states, which became a part of the Constitution. Elements of the plan were incorporated in the Connecticut Compromise. *See also* Connecticut Compromise.

Newlands, John Alexander Reina (1838–98), English chemist. In 1864 he announced his law of octaves, arranging the elements into eight columns according to increasing atomic weight. The law was ridiculed until Mendeleev announced his periodic law five years later.

New London, industrial city in SE Connecticut, 43mi (69km) E of New Haven, on Long Island Sound and mouth of Thames River; site of major US submarine base and surrounding naval support facility, US Coast Guard Academy (1876). Industries: pharmaceuticals, printing presses, shipbuilding. Founded 1646; burned by British 1781; inc. 1784. Pop. (1970) 31,630.

Newman, John Henry (1801–90), English theologian. Ordained in the Anglican Church (1824), he associated with Edward Pusey and John Keble, and became a leader of the Oxford Movement. In 1841 he wrote *Tract 90*, showing that the Thirty-Nine Articles of the Church of England were consistent with Roman Catholicism, and began to question his own Anglicanism. He became a Roman Catholic (1845), was ordained and received a doctorate of divinity in Rome (1846), and established a branch of the Oratorians in Birmingham (1847). As rector of the Catholic University of Dublin he delivered the lectures later published as *Idea of a University Defined* (1873). His *Apologia Pro Vita Sua* (1864), written in reply to accusations by Charles Kingsley, justifies his life as an Anglican. Newman was attacked by Cardinal Henry Manning and the Ultramontanes on the doctrine of papal infallibility, but was created cardinal by Leo XIII (1879).

New Mexico, state in the SW United States, bordered on the S by Mexico.

Land and Economy. The state occupies a plateau with a mean elevation of 5,700ft (1,739m). The Sangre de Cristo Mts, a S extension of the Rocky Mts, are in the N central part. Shorter ranges rise in other sections. The Rio Grande, flowing S through the center, is the principal river. Dams on the Rio Grande and other rivers have created artificial lakes for water storage and irrigation. Mineral production is the major sector of the economy. Nuclear and space research, directed by the US government, is important. The chief centers are Los Alamos, White Sands Proving Ground, and Hollaman and Kirtland Air Force bases. Tourism is a valuable source of income.

People and Education. Besides descendants of immigrants from other states, there are many residents of Spanish, Indian, or mixed ancestry. The blend of races is reflected in the state's culture. About 70% of the population lives in urban areas. There are 13 institutions of higher education.

History. Beginning in 1539, Spanish adventurers seeking gold traversed the region. In 1609 it became a province of the Spanish colony of Mexico; Santa Fe was founded and became the capital the next year. When Mexico won independence in 1821, the area remained a Mexican prov. In that year the Santa Fe Trail, a major trade route from Missouri, was opened. US troops occupied the province on the outbreak of the Mexican War in 1846, and the Territory of New Mexico was organized in 1850. In the Civil War, a Confederate invasion attempt was repulsed; fighting with hostile Indians continued until the 1880s. The New Mexican desert was the site of early research on nuclear weapons. The first atomic bomb was produced at Los Alamos and exploded at Alamogordo on July 16, 1945.

PROFILE

Admitted to Union: Jan. 6, 1912; rank, 47th
US Congressmen: Senate, 2; House of Representatives, 2
Population: 1,016,000 (1970); rank, 37th
Capital: Santa Fe, 41,167 (1970)
Chief cities: Albuquerque, 243,751; Santa Fe; Las Cruces, 37,857
State legislature: Senate, 42; House of Representatives, 70
Area: 121,666sq mi (315,115sq km); rank, 5th
Elevation: Highest, 13,161ft (4,014m), Wheeler Peak; lowest, 2,817ft (859m), Red Bluff Reservoir
Industries (major products): food products, chemicals, ordnance, lumber
Agriculture (major products): sheep, cotton, pecans, sorghum
Minerals (major): uranium, potash, petroleum, natural gas, copper, zinc, lead
State nickname: Land of Enchantment
State motto: Crescit eundo ("It Grows as It Goes")
State bird: roadrunner
State flower: yucca
State tree: piñon (nut pine)

New Netherland, Dutch colonial territory in North America, stretching from the Hudson to the Delaware River. The Dutch claim was based on the explorations of Henry Hudson. Under charter to the Dutch West India Co., settlers founded Ft Nassau (Albany) and New Amsterdam (New York City). The latter was settled by Peter Minuit (1626). The last and most able governor, Peter Stuyvesant, annexed New Sweden (1655). The area was taken over by England in 1664. *See also* Minuit, Peter; New Sweden; Stuyvesant, Peter.

New Orleans, city and port of entry in SE Louisiana, 75mi (121km) SE of Baton Rouge, between Lake Pontchartrain and Mississippi River; seat of Orleans parish and largest city in Louisiana. It remained under French rule until 1762 when it was secretly passed to Spain by Treaty of Fontainebleau; returned to France by Treaty of Ildefonso (1800); incorporated into the Louisiana Purchase (1803); served as capital of Louisiana 1812–49; scene of British defeat (1815) by Andrew Jackson in the War of 1812; fell to Union naval forces led by Adm. David G. Farragut in the Civil War. Additional commercial impetus came with improvement and expansion of harbor facilities (1930s), and installation of Saturn rocket booster plant (1960s). New Orleans is known nationwide as the home of jazz, with its many nightclubs located on Bourbon Street in the French Quarter; site of the annual Mardi Gras, French Market, St Louis Cathedral (1794), Southern Yacht Club (1849), Sugar Bowl, Louisiana Superdome, jazz museum, and many antebellum houses; among its many educational institutions are Tulane University (1834), Loyola University (1849), Dillard University (1869), Louisiana State at New Orleans (1958); transportation center. Imports: coffee, sugar, bananas. Exports: oil, petrochemicals, rice, cotton, lumber, sulfur. Industries: food processing, petroleum, natural gas, oil and sugar refining, shipbuilding and repair, tourism, aluminum, petrochemicals, paper products, furniture. Founded 1718 by the Sieur de Bienville; inc. 1805. Pop. (1970) 593,471.

New Orleans, Battle of, engagement fought on Jan. 8, 1815; the last battle in the War of 1812. It took place two weeks after the Treaty of Ghent was signed because news of the treaty had not reached New Orleans. The Americans under Gen. Andrew Jackson won the battle with only 71 killed, while the British suffered 2,500 casualties.

Newport, city in N Kentucky, at confluence of Ohio and Licking rivers; seat of Campbell co; served as station of Underground Railroad. Industries: steel rolling, clothing, brewing, stationery. Founded 1791; inc. as town 1795; chartered as city 1835. Pop. (1970) 25,988.

Newport, city and port in SE Rhode Island, on S Aquidneck Island in Narragansett Bay; seat of Newport co. It was founded 1639 by religious refugees from Massachusetts Bay led by William Coddington and John Clarke; united with Portsmouth 1640; joined Incorporation of Providence Plantations 1644; held by British during the American Revolution. Newport served as joint state capital with Providence until 1900. During 19th century, it developed into a fashionable resort area; its houses remain a popular tourist attraction; site of The Breakers (former summer residence of Cornelius Vanderbilt), Trinity Church (1726), Wanton-Lyman-Hazard House (1675), state house (1739), Touro Synagogue (1763), America's Cup races, National Tennis Hall of Fame, jazz and folk festivals, Salve Regina College (1934), US Naval War College (1885), US Naval Underwater Ordnance Station. Tourism is the chief industry. Inc. 1784. Pop. (1970) 34,562.

Newport Beach, city in S California, 18mi (29km) SE of Long Beach; tourist resort and yachting center. Industries: electronic equipment, boats, plastics. Inc. 1906. Pop. (1970) 49,422.

Newport News, city in SE Virginia, 11mi (18km) NNW of Norfolk, on James River; comprises Port of Hampton Roads, together with Norfolk and Portsmouth; scene of Civil War naval battle between *Monitor* and *Merrimac* (1862); embarkation point during both world wars; site of Mariners' Museum (1930); one of world's largest shipbuilding and repair centers. Exports: coal, oil, tobacco, grain. Industries: food processing, metal products, building materials, textiles, paper, oil refining. Settled 1620 by Irish colonists; inc. 1896. Pop. (1970) 138,177.

New Rochelle, city in SE New York, on Long Island Sound; site of College of New Rochelle (1904), Iona College (1940), preserved home of Thomas Paine. Settled by Huguenots 1688, and named for La Rochelle, France; inc. as village 1858, as city 1899. Pop. (1970) 73,385.

New South Wales, state in SE Australia, bordered by the Tasman Sea (E) which forms 680mi (1,095km) of coastline. The natural-surf beaches, Blue Mts, and snowfields in the Alps are popular tourist attractions. Sydney is the capital city, center of transportation and commerce, and has one of the world's finest harbors. Industries: iron, steel, textiles, agricultural machinery, cement, paper, petrochemicals, electrical equipment. Discovered by Captain Cook 1770; first settled at Botany Bay 1788; became part of the Commonwealth of Australia 1901. Area: 309,433sq mi (801,431sq km). Pop. 4,567,000.

New Spain, an administrative area within the Spanish colonial empire, centered in Mexico City. New Spain, the first permanent viceroyalty on the American mainland, was created in 1535. The viceroyalty covered a vast area: present-day Mexico; Central America; the SW United States; Florida; the West Indies; the Philippines.

Newspapers. △1776.

New Stone Age. *See* Neolithic Age.

New Sweden (1638–55), colony on the Delaware River, including parts of Delaware, New Jersey, and Pennsylvania. First settled by Peter Minuit for the New Sweden Co. (1638), the area was absorbed into New Netherland by Peter Stuyvesant in 1655.

Newt, tailed amphibian, often called salamander, of Europe, Asia, and North America. European newt is terrestrial except during the breeding season when it is aquatic and the male develops ornamental fins. Fertilization is internal. Family Salamandridae. *See also* Amphibia; Salamander. △518.

New Testament, 27 books of the Christian Bible consisting of the 4 Gospels, Acts of the Apostles, 21 Epistles, and Revelation. They were written in Greek during the early Christian era. They were approved in this order and form by 367. *See also* individual books.

Newton, (Sir) Isaac (1642–1727), English scientist. He became professor of mathematics at Cambridge in 1669, remaining there until 1696 when he was appointed warden of the mint. He was a member of Parliament for Cambridge and was knighted in 1705. Working at home during the 18-month closure (starting in 1664) of Cambridge University during the plague, he made his greatest discoveries: the law of gravitation, the laws of motion, the binomial theorem and the method of fluxions (the basis of calculus), and the combination of the colors of the spectrum to form white light (leading to the invention of the reflecting telescope). He invented infinitesimal calculus, of which the two divisions are differential and integral calculus, and derived the inverse square law.

Newton's major scientific discoveries were published in two works: *Philosophiae Naturalis Principia Mathematica* (1687) and *Opticks* (1704). The latter postulated a combination of the wave and corpuscular theories of light similar to the present view. He was a querulous man frequently in dispute with his contemporaries (notably Robert Hooke, who claimed he had stolen his ideas, and Gottfried Leibniz, who claimed to have invented the calculus). *See also* Calculus; Gravity; Spectrum. △1442, 1480, 1484, 1490, 1660.

Newton, city in NE Massachusetts, 7mi (11km) W of Boston, on Charles River; site of Newton College of Sacred Heart (1946), Andover Newton Theological Seminary (1825), Mount Alvernia College (1959), Mount Ida Junior College (1889), and homes of Samuel Francis Smith, Horace Mann, Nathaniel Hawthorne; birthplace of Roger Sherman (1721), signer of Declaration of Independence. Industries: paper, thread, yarn. Founded 1631. Pop. (1970) 91,066.

Newton, the unit of force in the metric meter-kilogram-second (mks) system of units. One newton is the force that gives a mass of one kilogram an acceleration of one meter per second per second. One pound is equivalent to 4.45 newtons. *See also* Dyne.

New Towns, planned urban communities, designed to relocate populations away from large cities and to create local employment. The British New Towns Act (1946) provided for public funds to be advanced for developing designated areas, such as Harlow (1946) near London and Cumbernauld (1955) near Glasgow.

New World Leopard. *See* Jaguar.

New York, state in the NE United States, on the Atlantic Ocean. New York City is in the extreme S.

Land and Economy. The seacoast is short, but New York harbor is one of the world's finest. The state's interior is mountainous in the E; the Catskills in the SE and the Adirondacks in the NE are the main systems. To the W stretches a gently rolling plateau. The Hudson River in the E empties into New York Bay. Its main tributary is the Mohawk River. Other important rivers are the Delaware and the Genesee. In the W, the state borders on two of the Great Lakes—

Atlantic City, New Jersey

Taos pueblo, New Mexico

Isaac Newton

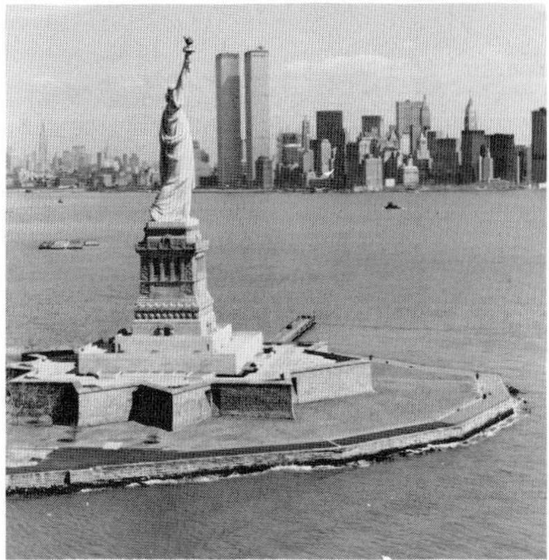

New York City

Ontario and Erie. It is the only state that touches the ocean and the Great Lakes. In the NE, Lake Champlain forms a border with Vermont. There are more than 2,000 other lakes. New York's economy is one of the nation's richest. Its manufacturing and agriculture are varied. The port of New York is among the world's leaders, and the city is a transportation and distribution center, the focus of highways, air and rail lines, and water routes. It is also the nation's financial capital and the site of many corporate headquarters.

People. From 1820–1964, when California surpassed it, New York was the most populous state in the Union. About 85% of its inhabitants live in urban areas. Traditionally, the population has been ethnically diverse. In the 19th century, New York was the port of entry for hundreds of thousands of immigrants from overseas, and many remained in the state to work in the factories or on transportation lines. Their descendants constitute a large segment of the population.

Education. There are more than 250 institutions of higher education. The State University of New York comprises about 25 university and college campuses. Columbia University and New York University in New York City are leading privately endowed institutions. The US Military Academy is at West Point.

History. Henry Hudson, an English navigator in the service of the Netherlands, discovered New York Bay and sailed up the river that bears his name in 1609, laying claim to the surrounding territory. Settlement began up the Hudson Valley, and the colony was named New Netherland. The English seized it in 1664 and renamed it New York. As a royal province, New York became a leader among the American colonies. It played a major part in the Revolution. Almost 100 engagements were fought in the colony, including the Battle of Freeman's Farm, or Second Battle of Saratoga, which was a turning point of the war. The opening of the Erie Canal in 1825, linking the Hudson with Lake Erie and creating a water route to the West through the Great Lakes, was an enormous stimulus to economic growth. New York sent about 500,000 men into the Union army in the Civil War. In later decades, its economic power, great population, and voting strength in national elections exerted tremendous influence in the nation's affairs.

PROFILE

Admitted to Union: July 26, 1788; 11th of the 13 original states to ratify the US Constitution
US Congressmen: Senate, 2; House of Representatives, 39
Population: 18,241,266 (1970); rank, 2d
Capital: Albany, 114,873 (1970)
Chief cities: New York, 7,895,563; Buffalo, 462,-768; Rochester, 296,233
State legislature: Senate, 60; Assembly, 150
Area: 49,576sq mi (128,402sq km); rank, 30th
Elevation: Highest, 5,344ft (1,630m), Mt Marcy; lowest, sea level
Industries (major products): apparel, publications, instruments, processed foods, paper and paper products, jewelry, sporting goods
Agriculture (major products): dairy products, apples, grapes, vegetables, poultry
Minerals (major): talc, titanium, garnet, salt, zinc
State nickname: Empire State
State motto: Excelsior (Higher)
State bird: bluebird
State flower: rose
State tree: sugar maple

New York City, largest city in population in the United States, in SE New York State at the mouth of the Hudson River; comprised of five boroughs: Manhattan, the Bronx, Brooklyn, Queens, and Richmond. The greater metropolitan area extends into SW Connecticut, SE New York state, and parts of NE New Jersey and W Long Island. New York is a great world trade center and financial hub.

Originally a trading post under Henry Hudson and Adriaen Block (*c.* 1610), Manhattan Island was bought 1626 from Indians by Peter Minuit of the Dutch West India Co., allegedly for $24 worth of beads and trinkets. New Amsterdam was the chief settlement, at the S end of Manhattan. In 1664 the British took the colony and renamed it New York, for the Duke of York; Dutch regained power for brief period (1673–74). A new charter was est. 1686 as citizens' dissent from British rule grew, culminating in an unsuccessful uprising 1689–91 led by Jacob Leisler; revolutionary sentiment increased with British imposition of the Stamp Act (1763), and solidified under the New York Sons of Liberty, who banished Governor Tryon and a British regiment from the city 1775; the city was unsuccessfully defended by George Washington 1776 and Britain held the city until 1781. New York served as the nation's capital 1789–90; Pres. George Washington was inaugurated at New York's Federal Hall.

The founding of the Bank of New York by Alexander Hamilton, and the opening of the Erie Canal (1825) made New York the principal US commercial and financial center. Following the Civil War, New York experienced a great influx of immigrants. The Greater New York Charter, unifying the five boroughs, was passed May 21, 1897. New York became the home of the United Nations 1945.

Noted areas of New York include Wall Street, Harlem, Fifth Avenue, Greenwich Village. Monuments and notable buildings include Grant's Tomb, Statue of Liberty, Fraunces Tavern (built 1719), St Patrick's Cathedral, the Cathedral of St John the Divine, Empire State Building, the World Trade Center, the United Nations Building, and the Pan Am Building. New York is the site of the Metropolitan Museum of Art, Museum of Modern Art, Museum of Natural History, Radio City Music Hall, Lincoln Center, and Carnegie Hall. The city hosts over 30 colleges and universities. Professional sports teams include New York Yankees and New York Mets (baseball), New York Jets (football), New York Rangers (hockey), New York Knickerbockers (basketball), and it is a boxing center. Area (with water surface): 365sq mi (945sq km). Pop. (1970) 7,895,563.

New York Times v. Sullivan (1964), landmark US Supreme Court decision reversing a libel conviction on the grounds that a state law did not afford enough protection for the freedoms of speech and the press. The court recognized that some falsehood was inevitable under a system of free debate and said only knowing lies regarding public officials could be considered actionable.

New Zealand, independent nation in S Pacific, a member of the Commonwealth of Nations. Populated mainly by descendants of English-speaking immigrants and indigenous Maoris, it has developed a high standard of living in an economy based on sheep-raising and dairy products.

Land and Economy. Located 1,200mi (1,932km) SE of Australia in the SW Pacific, New Zealand is composed of two islands, North Island and South Island, separated by the Cook Strait. With the exception of the flat Canterbury Plain, 3,000,000acres (1,215,000hectares) of rich grain-growing and sheep-raising land, much of South Island is formed by the Southern Alps, with peaks above 10,000ft (3,050m). Along the SW coast are fjords and mountains. The center of North Island is a volcanic plateau, and the base is the fertile plain of three rivers, constituting the major butter-producing area. The longest river in the country is the Waikato, 270mi (435km). Climate is delineated by regional contrasts, without extremes. Agriculture supports a high standard of living although 1971 inflation resulted in wage and price controls. Meat is the largest single export (35%), followed by wool and hides (22%) and dairy products (17.5%). Imports are principally manufactured products.

People. Of New Zealand's total population, about 250,000 are indigenous Maoris of Polynesian descent; the remainder are mostly British. Dominant religions are Anglican (33.7%), Presbyterian (21.8%), Roman Catholic (15.9%) and Methodist (7%). The official language is English; Maori is still spoken. The literacy rate is 90%. About half the population lives in the four main cities—Auckland, Wellington, Christchurch, and Dunedin. Education is free and compulsory. The social security system includes education, medical, and pension benefits.

Government. New Zealand has a parliamentary system as an independent member of the British Commonwealth. The leader of the political party winning the majority of seats in the elected unicameral body is prime minister.

History. The discovery of New Zealand in 1642 by the Dutch navigator Abel Janszoon Tasman was followed by Capt. James Cook's exploration for the British (1769–70). Sealing, whaling, and lumbering attracted white settlers, and in 1840, Great Britain annexed New Zealand and signed a treaty with Maori tribes, who nevertheless continued their struggle against colonization. Parliamentary government came in 1890, and full autonomy was granted in 1947 through the Statute of Westminster. The global recession in the 1970s that depressed New Zealand's economy was a major factor in a landslide victory for the National party over the Labour party in 1975 elections.

PROFILE

Official name: New Zealand
Area: 103,736sq mi (268,676sq km)
Population: 3,030,000
Density: 29 per sq mi (10 per sq km)
Chief cities: Wellington (capital); Auckland; Christchurch
Government: parliamentary, member of Commonwealth of Nations
Religion: Anglican and Presbyterian
Language: English
Monetary unit: New Zealand dollar
Gross national product: $11,700,000,000
Per capita income: $3,930
Industries: processed foods, meat products, wood products, cement, fertilizers, pulp, paper, steel, aluminum
Agriculture: wheat, sheep, beef cattle, forests, potatoes
Minerals: iron, natural gas
Trading partners: United Kingdom, United States, Australia

Ney, Michel, Duc d'Elchingen, Prince de La Moskova (1769–1815), French marshal, fought in Revolutionary and Napoleonic armies, called by Napoleon "the bravest of the brave" at Friedland (1807) and in the retreat from Russia. Urged Napoleon to abdicate and was sent by the Bourbons to stop Napoleon's return to Paris at the beginning of the Hundred Days (1815); instead he joined Napoleon and distinguished himself for bravery at Waterloo. Condemned for treason, he was executed by firing squad.

Nez Percé, from the French for "pierced nose," referring to their custom of wearing nose ornaments. A major Shahaptian-speaking tribe of North American Indians living in central Idaho, SW Washington, and NE Oregon. Famous for their skill as breeders of fine horses, about 1,750 reside on the Lapwai Reservation in Idaho.

Niagara Falls, city in SE Ontario, Canada, on the Niagara River; noted for view of falls from Queen Victoria Park. Industries: hydroelectric power, chemicals, fertilizers, silverware, sporting goods. Founded 1853; inc. 1904. Pop. 65,271.

Niagara Falls, city in W New York, 17mi (27km) NW of Buffalo, on the Niagara River above and below the falls of the river; site of Niagara Reservation State Park, Niagara Falls power plant (1890), Niagara University (1856), Niagara County Community College (1963); connected with Niagara Falls, Canada, by two bridges over Niagara River. Industries: electrochemicals, electrometallurgy, batteries, paper products, breakfast foods, tourism. Founded as two separate villages (Niagara Falls and Suspension Bridge) that combined and inc. as a city 1892. Pop. (1970) 85,-615.

Niagara Falls, great falls of Niagara River on boundary of United States (W New York) and Canada (SE Ontario). Divided by Goat Island into Horseshoe or Canadian Falls and American Falls, the falls were discovered by Father Louis Hennepin in 1678; power from falls was first used in 1882 to light streets of Niagara Falls. Falls drop 158ft (48m) on Canadian side and 167ft (51m) on American side. Face of Canadian Falls is 2,600ft (793m) and American is 1,000ft (305m). Cave of Winds, Whirlpool Rapids, Luna Falls are part of US Niagara Reservation State Park; Canadian government maintains Queen Victoria Park.

Niamey, capital of Niger, Africa, in SW Niger on the Niger River. Located at junction of two main highways, it has port facilities on river; largest city and economic, commercial, and cultural hub of country; became capital 1926. Industries: oil, bricks, food products (especially nuts). Pop. 78,991.

Nibbana. *See* Nirvana.

Nibelungenlied, a popular epic taken from Germanic sources and written in Middle High German *c.* 1203 by an unknown author. It resembles the Old Norse *Edda* poems and deals with some of the same characters (Siegfried, Kriemhild, Brünhilde, Gunther, Gudrun, and Hagen), but was written earlier than the *Edda.* The work features the Nibelung treasure, dragons, mermaids, and magic elements, but unlike the *Chanson de Roland* and other national epics, it deals primarily with the personal rivalries and adventures of the characters, not with events of national interest performed by idealized heroes. △1100.

Nicaea, one of the chief cities of ancient Bithynia, Asia Minor. The seat of two ecumenical councils (AD 325,787), it fell to the Seljuk Turks in 1078, then to the Crusaders in 1097. After 1333 the Turks held the city permanently.

Nicaea, Councils of. The First Council of Nicaea (AD 325) met at the order of Constantine I (the Great) of Rome. This first ecumenical council was attended by the major Eastern bishops, four Western bishops, and two papal legates. In conflict with Arianism, the council adopted a creed or test of faith that stated the divinity of Christ the Son and His position of equality within the Trinity. Arius and the two other bishops who refused to accept the creed were exiled to Illyricum. The council deliberated on other church matters and was the model for later church councils including the Second Council of Nicaea (787) convened by Irene, the Byzantine Empress. This was the seventh ecumenical council and the last to be recognized as such by both branches of the Catholic church. Its members ruled against the worship of images (iconoclasm). *See also* Arianism.

Nicaea, Empire of (1206–61), Greek empire founded by Theodore I (Lascaris) after the 4th Crusade overthrow of the Eastern Roman (Byzantine) Empire. Through conquest and alliance, the empire grew more powerful until, in 1261, Constantinople was finally recaptured from the Latins and the Byzantine Empire was restored.

Nicaragua, republic in Central America, bounded by the Caribbean Sea (E), Honduras (N), Costa Rica (S), and Pacific Ocean (W); the capital is Managua. The land area can be viewed as 3 main regions: a triangular area S inland from the Caribbean Sea, consisting of folded faulted structures; a low E coastal plain, Mosquito; and the most inhabited region, a lowland area extending from the Gulf of Fonseca NW to Costa Rican border. Approx. 50% of the land is forested, yielding products of fibers, medicines, balsams, resins, gum, and various woods. Agriculture, the chief economic activity, has been aided by the 1951 National Development Institute and the Nicaraguan Technical Agricultural Service (STAN) 1933, a joint project with US technical assistance. The United States proposed construction of a canal, by the Bryan-Chamorro Treaty 1916, to connect the Pacific Ocean and Caribbean Sea; however due to continuing political disputes, negotiations were terminated 1970. Chief crops are cotton, coffee, corn, beans, rice, sugar cane, cottonseed, cacao, citrus fruits, tobacco, sesame seeds, wheat. Industries include lumbering, refining sugar, cigars, matches, soap, cement, leather, textiles, clothing, soft drinks, beer, shoes. Chief minerals are gold, silver, salt, gypsum, marble. The majority of Nicaraguans are mestizos (85%), mulattoes (10%), and pure Indians (5%); about 90% are Roman Catholic.

Nicaragua's coast, inhabited by Indian tribes called Miskitos, was discovered by Columbus 1502; Fernandes Córdoba founded Granada and León in 1523. In mid-17th century the Mosquito coast in Nicaragua and Honduras became a British protectorate, but in 1786 Great Britain recognized Spanish title to Caribbean coast and in 1838 Nicaragua became independent; Managua was made capital 1855. William Walker, from Tennessee, seized Nicaragua and made himself president 1856; he was driven out of Nicaragua 1857, returned 1860 and was executed; his death helped unite Nicaragua's two political parties. The conservatives won power in 1863, and ruled stably for 30 years; in 1967 the son of former president Anastasio Somoza was elected president by universal adult suffrage.

PROFILE

Official name: Nicaragua
Area: 49,579sq mi (148,000sq km)
Population: 1,974,924
Chief cities: Managua, capital; León; Matagalpa
Religion: Roman Catholic
Language: Spanish
Monetary unit: Cordoba

Nicaragua, lake in SW Nicaragua; largest lake in Central America, receives waters of Lake Managua via Tipitapa River. Area was part of ocean until land rose around it; salt water fish such as sharks have adapted to the change from saline to fresh water. San Juan River drains the lake into the Caribbean Sea. Area: 3,089sq mi (8,001sq km).

Nicaragua Canal, an interoceanic route first proposed in the mid-19th century and still considered an alternative to the Panama Canal. The United States gained exclusive rights for the construction of a canal utilizing the San Juan River and Lake Nicaragua in 1913; the treaty was abrogated in 1970.

Nice, city in SE France, on Mediterranean Sea; capital of Alpes-Maritimes dept. Part of the House of Savoy in 13th and 14th centuries, it was held by France 1792–1814, when it was returned to Savoy until passed to France in 1860. The major French Riviera tourist center, it is scene of the Carnival of Nice held annually in January and February, ending on Shrove Tuesday; noted for villas and boulevards, of which Promenade des Anglais (1822) is the most outstanding; site of 17th-century cathedral, and the Croix de Marbre. Industries: tourism, olive oil, perfumes, electronics, cut flowers. Founded 5th century BC as Greek colony. Pop. 322,442.

Nicene Creed, a statement of Christian faith adopted at the Council of Nicaea in 325. The creed was formulated to uphold orthodox Christian doctrine against the Arian heresy. Followers of Arius held that Jesus was neither wholly God nor wholly man. The Nicene Creed affirms belief in". . .the only-begotten Son of God. . . Being of one substance with the Father." This creed is used by the Roman Catholic and Anglican churches and, with one difference in wording, by the Orthodox Eastern Church.

Nicholas I (800?–867), Roman Catholic pope (858–67) and saint, also known as Nicholas the Great. A stern ruler, he upheld apostolic succession and supported St Ignatius of Constantinople against Photius, who objected to the filioque clause in the Nicene Creed. This controversy led to the split between Eastern and Western Christianity.

Nicholas I (1796–1855), tsar of Russia (1825–55). Ascending the throne in 1825, he was immediately confronted with and crushed the Decembrist revolt that sought a constitutional monarchy (1825). He was successful in wars against Persia (1826–28) and Turkey (1828–29), gaining strategic territory for Russia. In 1830–31 he brutally suppressed a Polish revolt, abrogating Polish autonomy. Between 1832–33 Russian law was codified. Modest improvements were made in the position of serfs, but the secret police was expanded, censorship increased, and minorities and liberals suppressed. In 1849 Russia assisted Austria in suppressing the Hungarian revolt. Russian pressure on Turkey led to the Crimean War (1853–56).

Nicholas II (1868–1918), last tsar of Russia (1894–1917). During his reign, Russia occupied Port Arthur (1896) and Manchuria (1900), fought the disastrous Russo-Japanese War (1904–05), and saw the Revolution of 1905 that forced him to approve a legislative assembly *(Duma)*. In World War I he supervised the armed forces, leaving the government to his wife, who was under the influence of Rasputin. Ineffectual and reactionary, after the revolution of March 1917 he abdicated and was sent to Siberia. He and his family were executed in July 1918. △1286, 1308

Nicholas I (1841–1921), prince of Montenegro who conducted a brilliant campaign against the Turks (1876) and who doubled the size of his realm at the Congress of Berlin (1878). In 1910 he proclaimed himself king but, defeated by Austria-Hungary in World War I, he went into exile in 1916 and was formally deposed in 1918.

Nicholas of Cusa (1401–64), German philosopher and theologian, cardinal, and bishop. Writing on philosophy, theology, law, and science, he intellectually presaged the Renaissance. His principal work, *De Docta Ignorantia,* holds that truth is unknown to man.

Nicholas of Myra, Saint, the saint whose legends gave rise to the story of Santa Claus. Almost nothing is known about his life, but by tradition he was Bishop of Myra in the first half of the 4th century. He became a popular saint in the Middle Ages and is the patron saint of Greece and Russia. Many legends were told about him. In one, he restored to life three murdered boys; hence he is the patron of children. In another, he secretly gave gold to three poor girls as their dowry. From this came the custom of giving presents on the Eve of St Nicholas—a custom later transferred to Christmas Eve. The saint's name in Dutch, Sant Nikolaas, became Santa Claus.

Nicholson, Ben (1894–), English painter. He was a leading member of the abstract art movement in England. Influenced by the cubism of Georges Braque and the neoplasticism of Piet Mondrian, his work consisted mainly of semi-abstract still lifes in the 1920s. In the 1930s he began working on reliefs and in the 1940s on landscapes containing elements of still lifes. His later work took a geometrical form. △1318.

Nickel, metallic element of the first transition series, discovered in 1751 by A.F. Cronstedt. Chief ore is pentlandite. The main commercial use is in stainless steels and other special alloys. Nickel is also used in coinage and as a hydrogenation catalyst. The metal is ferromagnetic. Properties: at. no. 28; at. wt. 58.71; sp gr 8.902; melt. pt. 2,647°F (1,453°C); boil. pt. 4,950°F (2,732°C); most common isotope Ni^{58} (68.274%). *See also* Transition Elements. △1552–54.

Nicklaus, Jack (William) (1940–), US golfer, b. Columbus, Ohio. He won the Ohio Open in 1955 at 16, won the US Amateur title (1959, 1961), turned professional in 1961, and won five Masters Tournaments (1963, 1965, 1966, 1972, 1975). He also won three Professional Golf Association championships (1963, 1971, 1973), three US Opens (1962, 1967, 1972), and two British Opens (1966, 1970). Often acclaimed as the sport's greatest player, he has been professional golf's all-time money winner.

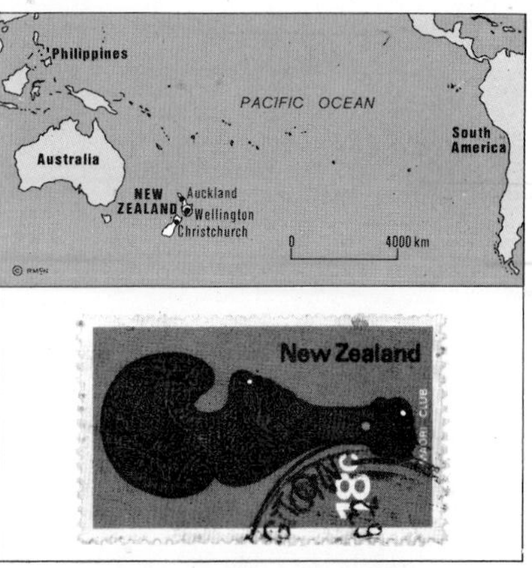
Philippines
PACIFIC OCEAN
Australia
South America
NEW ZEALAND
Auckland
Wellington
Christchurch
0
4000 km
New Zealand

New Zealand

Niagara Falls

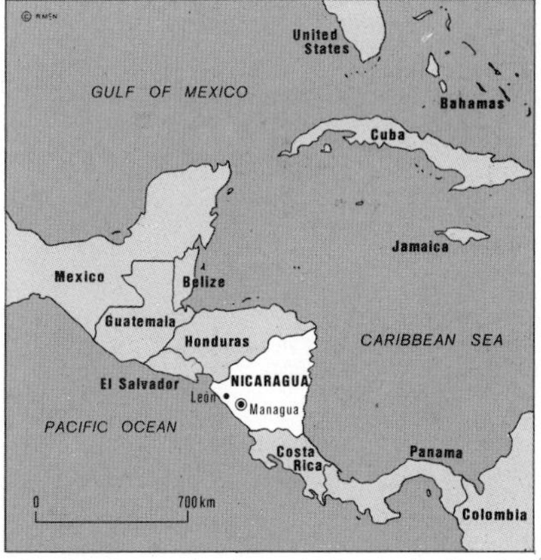
United States
GULF OF MEXICO
Bahamas
Cuba
Jamaica
Mexico
Belize
Guatemala
Honduras
CARIBBEAN SEA
El Salvador
NICARAGUA
León
Managua
PACIFIC OCEAN
Costa Rica
Panama
0
700 km
Colombia

Nicaragua

Nice, France

Nicobar Islands, island group in Bay of Bengal, India; includes 19 small islands. Population is mainly Mongoloid stock; held by Japanese during WWII; exports tropical fruit. Area: 707sq mi (1,831sq km). Pop. 14,563.

Nicola Pisano (*fl.* 1260–78), Italian sculptor. His innovative work helped lay the foundation of the classic Renaissance style. His works include the pulpit in the Pisa Baptistry, the pulpit in Siena Cathedral (1265–68), and the design for the Arca of St Dominico, Bologna (1267).

Nicolet, Jean (1598–1642), French explorer in North America. He traveled with Samuel de Champlain, and accounts of his journeys are found in *Jesuit Relations*. In 1634, searching for the Northwest Passage, he traveled up Lake Huron, passed through the Straits of Mackinac to Lake Michigan, and crossed Lake Michigan to Green Bay, becoming the first white man to visit the area.

Nicomachean Ethics, work by Aristotle setting forth part of his scientific and philosophical system based on a teleological view of the universe. In *Ethics*, Aristotle searches for the highest perfection of man, concluding finally that it is thought. Because virtuous action accords with reason, which seeks a mean between extremes, man should follow the contemplative life.

Nicosia (Levkosia), capital city of Cyprus, in the N central part of island; capital of Nicosia district. For 300 years descendants of France's Guy Lusignan ruled the island, and Nicosia was their capital. Their reign ended in 1489 when Venetians took the city; ruins of circular walls and fortifications survive from this period. Turks held city 1571–1878, when it passed to British. In 1960 Cyprus became an independent nation and Nicosia continued as capital; site of 13th-century church of St Sophia (now a mosque). Industries: cigarettes, pottery, leather, textiles. Pop. 115,000.

Nicotiana, genus of mainly New World herbs resembling henbane; it is the source of tobacco. There are about 60 species: 45 native to the Americas, 14 to Australia, and 1 to Pacific islands. *N. tabacum*, originally a tropical species, is the source of commercial tobacco, although *N. rustica*, a shrubby plant native to eastern North America, has a higher nicotine content and was used by the Indians. Other species include jasmine tobacco, *N. alata*, which has tubular flowers that open at dusk and emit a jasmine odor. Family Solanaceae. *See also* Tobacco.

Nicotinic Acid, vitamin of the B complex, lack of which causes the disease pellagra. *See* Vitamin.

Niebuhr, Reinhold (1892–1971), US Protestant theologian, b. Detroit. He became a professor of theology at Union Theological Seminary (1928) after having been a pastor in Detroit. An activist and controversialist, he participated in the formation of the National Council of Churches and Americans for Democratic Action and wrote 17 books, including *Moral Man and Immoral Society* (1932). Niebuhr became increasingly more conservative in later life, and critical of the socialism and pacifism he once espoused.

Niello, method of decorating silver or gold objects with incised designs filled with a black alloy. This method was used in Byzantine and Oriental art and became extremely popular in Italy in the 15th century.

Nielsbohrium. *See* Element 105.

Niemeyer, Oscar (1907–), Brazilian architect. An early advocate of modern architecture in Latin America, he is known for his nonfunctional and sculptural style. He worked on the design of the Ministry of Education and Health Building, Rio de Janeiro (1937–43), which was influenced by Le Corbusier, and the Brazilian Pavillion for the 1939 New York World's Fair, both in collaboration with Lúcio Costa. In 1959 he was commissioned to design the new capital city of Brasília but agreed to design only the government buildings. The Square of the Three Powers (Brasília) is considered his best work. △1322.

Niépce, Joseph (Nicéphore) (1765–1833), French chemist, inventor of the heliography process. Using camera and lens, he obtained unstable negatives in 1816 and permanent images by 1822. He worked with Louis Daguerre from 1829 until his death, after which Daguerre perfected their process, known as daguerreotypy.

Nietzsche, Friedrich (1844–1900), German philosopher. He studied classical philosophy at Bonn and taught at Basel (1869). He met and broke with Richard Wagner (1874). His *Birth of Tragedy* (1872) betrays the influence of Wagner's art. In 1879 he abandoned philology for philosophy, and celebrated his new notion of the "free spirit" in *Thus Spake Zarathustra* (1883–91). His aphoristic method was either misunderstood or ignored, and his later works, *Beyond Good & Evil* (1886), *On the Genealogy of Morals* (1887), *Ecce Homo* (1888) became increasingly shrill. △860.

Niger, republic in W Africa, bounded by Nigeria (S), Benin and Upper Volta (SW), Mali (W), Chad (E), Algeria and Libya (N). The country is land-locked and mostly arid, except along the Niger River in the SW and near the Nigerian border in S where there are strips of savanna land.

The economy is based on agriculture; about 90% of working inhabitants farms. Chief crops are corn, millet, groundnuts, rice, sorghum, cassava, sugar cane, dates; livestock including camels are raised. Industries are few, and include processed foods, bricks, cement, beverages, shoes, ginned cotton, construction materials, radios, and fishing. In the 1970s an ore plant was opened for production of high grade uranium found in the Air Mts, N central region. In 1974, Niger became a charter member of the West African Economic Community. During the dry season (September–May), approx. 100,000 farmers migrate to the Ivory Coast and Ghana for employment. The people are predominantly black Africans, 55% Hausa, 24% Djerma and Songhai tribes, 3% Tuareg; most live in the S, and are overwhelmingly Islamic.

History and Government. In the 14th century the Hausa people founded several city-states in S Niger; the 16th century brought Songhai empire rule to Niger; and by the 17th century, Djerma people had settled the SW. The Fulani tribe took control of S Niger in the early 19th century. The Conference of Berlin (1884–85) granted Niger territory to French, and it became a separate French colony 1922 with Zinder as capital, replaced by Niamey 1926. In 1946, Niger was granted an autonomous assembly, and in 1960 independence was granted; the leader of the Niger Progressive Party (PPN), Hamani Diori, became the republic's first president. Diori was reelected 1965 and 1970; in 1974 he was overthrown by a military group led by Lt. Col. Seyni Kountche.

PROFILE

Official name: Republic of the Niger
Area: 489,189sq mi (1,267,000sq km)
Population: 4,020,000
Chief cities: Niamey (capital); Maradi; Tahoua
Religion: Islam, Animism, Christianity
Language: French (official)
Monetary unit: Franc CFA

Niger, major river in W Africa; rises in the Fouta Djallon plateau in SW Republic of Guinea; flows NE through Guinea into Mali Republic where it forms an extensive inland delta, then flows in a great curve NE, E, and SE across border into Nigeria, then S into Gulf of Guinea through another vast delta. The river's course was determined by explorations by Mungo Park (1795–97) and Richard and John Lander (1830). The inland delta in Mali Republic has supported an irrigation project that has reclaimed 100,000acres (40,500hectares) since 1930; the delta at the Gulf of Guinea is a source of petroleum and palm oil; the river is also a major source of tigerfish and perch; at various points it has been dammed to create hydroelectric power. It is navigable (but not continuously due to rapids and bars) for over 1,000mi (1,610km) of its 2,600mi (4,186km) course.

Nigeria, independent nation in W Africa. Divided by tribal rivalries, it is ruled by the military. Petroleum is its economic mainstay.

Land and Economy. The most populous African country, Nigeria sits on the W coast of the continent bounded on the S by the Gulf of Guinea, with Cameroon (W), Chad (NW), Niger (N), and Benin (E) on its borders. Topographic regions, divided according to altitude and climate, are: hot, humid coast of mangrove swamps; a zone 50–100mi (81–161km) wide N of the swamps with tropical rain forest and palm oil bush; a relatively dry central plateau making up the largest N portion; and the semi-desert in the extreme N. Its navigable rivers—the Niger, the Benue, and the Cross—provide major transportation routes. Nigeria has two seasons, dry and wet. Annual rainfall varies from 150in (381cm) on the coast to 23in (58cm) in the N. About 60% of the country's income comes from agriculture, animal husbandry, and forests. By 1970, Nigeria's offshore and river petroleum deposits had made it one of the 10 largest oil-exporting lands in the world, accounting for 80% of exports. It is almost self-sufficient in food production.

People. A culturally heterogeneous land, Nigeria numbers about 250 tribal groups with varying customs and languages. Muslims compose the largest religious group (44%), with 34% Animist, and 22% Christian. Three major tribal tongues (Ibo, Hausa Fulani, and Yoruba) are spoken by 60% of the population. The N Islamic Hausa tribe speaks its own language. The W Yorubas are Muslim, and the Ibos, once the most influential in trade and the professions, compose the largest group and live in the E.

Government. Nigeria is governed by a 19-member Supreme Military Council which rules by decree, and a cabinet.

History. Europeans in search of trade brought colonial rule to Nigeria. By 1886, British interests had chartered the Royal Niger Co. The Crown, in an effort to consolidate the slave trade and to promote commercial interests, united the area in 1914 as a colony and protectorate. Africans were slowly added to the government structure, and in 1960, Nigeria was granted full independence as a federation under a parliamentary form of government. In 1963, Nigeria took another step and declared itself a federal republic. Tribal and racial tensions evoked a successful revolt in 1966 by army units under Maj. Gen. J.T.U. Aguiyi-Ironsi. He was killed in a second coup later in the year, and Lt. Col. Yakubu Gowon emerged as head of the Federal Military Government (FMG). Tribal unrest continued, and in 1967 the Ibos in the E announced secession from Nigeria and the formation of the Republic of Biafra. After a savage civil war, Biafra was conquered and reunited with Nigeria (1970). A lack of reprisals after the conflict helped to heal the wounds of war. Gowon ruled until 1975 when he was overthrown in a bloodless military coup.

PROFILE

Official name: Federal Republic of Nigeria
Area: 356,669sq mi (923,773sq km)
Population: 79,758,969
Density: 224per sq mi (86per sq km)
Chief cities: Lagos (capital); Ibadan; Ogbomosho; Kano
Government: military
Religion: Muslim, Christian, Animist
Language: tribal tongues and English
Monetary unit: Naira
Gross national product: $8,650,000,000
Per capita income: $250
Industries: processed food, cotton, textiles, cement, petroleum products, rubber goods, forest products
Agriculture: nuts, palm kernels, cacao, rubber trees, cotton, cattle, fish, tobacco, forests
Minerals: oil, coal, iron, limestone, natural gas, tin
Trading partners: European Economic Community, United Kingdom, United States, Japan

Night Blindness, an early symptom of vitamin A deficiency. The vitamin is necessary for the production of rhodopsin, a retinal substance vital to vision during times of low illumination.

Night-blooming Plant, plants with flowers that open at night and are usually sweet-scented and tubular-shaped. The night-blooming cereus, with pure white flowers, is the most popular. Other night-bloomers are certain honeysuckles, jasmines, tobacco, and evening primroses. Some night-blooming datura species, rarely cultivated, have poisonous leaves and seeds.

Nighthawk, North American goatsucker with buff to black mottled feathers. It lays its eggs on a gravel-covered roof that hides them. Species *Chordeiles minor*. *See also* Goatsucker.

Night Heron, thick-billed night-feeding bird with well-developed, ornamental head plumes, especially at breeding time. Length: 2ft (0.6m). Genera: *Nycticorax* and *Gorsachius*. *See also* Heron.

Nightingale, European thrush known for its beautiful nocturnal song. It has a brownish back and pale brown underparts with a reddish tail and rump, similar to the North American hermit thrush. Some tropical American thrushes (genus *Catharus*) are also called nightingales. Length: 6.5in (16cm). Species *Luscinia megarhynchos*. *See also* Thrush.

Nightmonkey. *See* Douroucouli.

Nightshade, family (Solanaceae) of herbs and shrubs characterized by alternate leaves; 5-petaled, bell-shaped flowers; a fleshy berry or dry capsule fruit; and the presence, in many, of toxic and fatal alkaloids. The 75 genera and 2,000 species include tobacco, petunia, potato, deadly nightshade, and henbane. The common black nightshade, *Solanum nigrum*, is a bushy, spreading plant, 2ft (61cm) tall; its berries are poisonous when green but harmless when ripe. △742.

Nihilism, historically, a 19th-century Russian political philosophy brought to public attention by Ivan Turgenev in the novel *Fathers and Sons* (1861). The nihilists believed that the existing social and economic order must be totally destroyed but had few constructive alternatives. They practiced terrorism and claimed responsibility for the assassination of Tsar Alexander II (1881). Because nihilist doctrines were so vague the movement eventually disintegrated. In the 20th century nihilism has come to signify a philosophical stance that denies an objective basis or intrinsic worth for moral or social values.

Nihon. *See* Nippon.

Niigata, port city on NW coast of Honshu, Japan, at mouth of Shinano River, opposite Sado Islands; capital of Niigata prefecture; opened to foreign trade 1869. Industries: textiles, fishing, machinery, paper, shipbuilding. Pop. 383,919.

Nijinska, Bronislava (1891–1972), Polish dancer and choreographer. She danced with the Maryinsky Company in St Petersburg, Russia, and Ballet Russe and founded the Théatre de Danse in Paris (1932). She choreographed for the Ballet Russe de Monte Carlo, Markova-Dolin Company, American Ballet Theatre, and others.

Nijinsky, Vaslav (1890–1950), Russian dancer. Although his career lasted only 12 years (1907–19), he was one of the greatest male ballet dancers. With the Ballet Russe, his most noted roles were in *Pétrouchka, Prince Igor, Les Sylphides,* and *Schéhérazade.* He toured South America, Europe, and the United States. Having become insane, he spent the rest of his life in retirement in England and Switzerland. △1368.

Nijmegen, city in E Netherlands, on Waal River, near West German border; site of 16th-century church and town hall; former member of Hanseatic League. Industries: machinery, electronic equipment, shoes, paper. Pop. 148,790.

Nike, in art. △1002.

Nikolayev (Nikolajer), seaport city in Ukrainian SSR, USSR, at confluence of Ingul and Bug rivers; taken by Germans 1941, recaptured by Russia 1944. Industries: shipbuilding, building materials, chemicals, cast iron works. Founded 1784. Pop. 331,000.

Nikon (1605–81), Russian priest and political leader, b. Nikita Minin. From a humble start he rose to be a priest and abbot. He so impressed Tsar Alexis that he was given a high church post, and in 1652 he became head of the Russian Church as patriarch of Moscow. For six years he virtually shared power with the tsar. Nikon also headed a movement to correct practices of the Russian Church that had deviated from those of the Greek Church. His harshness as a reformer made enemies, and he was deposed as patriarch in 1666. △1178.

Nile (Nahr an-Nil), river in NE Africa; longest river in the world; trunk is at Khartoum at convergence of White Nile and Blue Nile; flows N from E Africa draining basin covering 1,100,000sq mi (2,590,000sq km) or 10% of Africa; enters delta 12mi (19km) N of Cairo, to empty into Mediterranean; site of ancient Egyptian irrigation works dating from 4000 BC; Egypt, Sudan, and other African nations depend almost completely on the Nile as a source of hydroelectric power and irrigation by means of an advanced system of dams, including Aswan High Dam, Gebel Aulia, and Makwar. Length: 4,160mi (6,698km). △960.

Niles, residential town in NE Illinois; adjacent suburb of Chicago on Chicago River; site of Niles College of Loyola University, and copy of leaning tower of Pisa. Industries: duplicating machines, electronic equipment, tools, dies. Settled 1832; inc. 1899. Pop. (1970) 31,342.

Nilgai, or blue buck, large antelope native to the Indian peninsula, mostly in wooded areas. Only males have a throat tuft and small spiked horns. Gray-brown with white markings, its superficial resemblance to Brahman cattle makes it sacred to Hindus. Length: to 82in (2.1m); weight: 440lb (198kg). Family Bovidae; species *Boselaphus tragocamelus.*

Nilotes, large group of Negroid peoples of the upper Nile region of the Sudan and Uganda. They are characteristically tall and slender. Nilotic languages form a closely related group, classified as a branch of the Chari-Nile family. Nilotic peoples include the Luo of Kenya and Uganda, the Masai of Tanzania, and the Dinka and Nuer of the Sudan. There is a great variety of cultures, ranging from the concept of divine kingship among the Shilluk to the political egalitarianism of the Luo and Nuer.

Nimbus, a cloud from which rain is discharged. In meteorological cloud classification it is added to the names of clouds that typically produce rain or snow. Nimbostratus are the true rain clouds, dark and wet-looking with streaks of rain extending to the ground. Cumulonimbus are thunderhead clouds, with bases almost touching the ground and extending upward to 75,000ft (22,875m). These clouds can produce tornadoes. △214–16.

Nîmes, city in S France, 64mi (103km) NW of Marseilles; capital of Gard dept. A Roman colony 120 BC, it has been united with French crown since AD 1258; Huguenot stronghold; suffered after Revocation of Edict of Nantes (1685); site of impressive 1st-century Roman Arena (still in use), 2nd-century temple of Diana, 11th-century Cathedral of St Castor, Maison Carée (1st and 2nd centuries), museum of Roman antiquities. Industries: silk, coal, chemicals, metals. Pop. 123,942.

Nimitz, Chester William (1885–1966), US admiral, b. Fredericksburg, Tex. He served with the Atlantic Fleet's submarine division during World War I. When World War II broke out, he replaced Admiral Kimmel as commander in chief of the Pacific fleet, a command he held throughout the war. Nimitz led the landings on Midway (1942), the Solomon Islands (1942–43), the Gilberts (1943), Philippines (1944), and Iwo Jima and Okinawa (1945). After the war, he became chief of naval operations (1945–47). △1338.

Nimrod, in Genesis, son of Cush and grandson of Ham. A great hunter and conqueror of the Babylonians, he was the first biblical hero.

Nin, Anaïs (1903–77), US author, b. France. Her novels, all intense psychological studies, include *The House of Incest* (1936), *Winter of Artifice* (1939), and *A Spy in the House of Love* (1954). Extensive portions of her diaries and correspondence were published to critical acclaim in the 1960s and 1970s.

Ninety-Five Theses, document by Martin Luther "On the Power of Indulgences," posted in Wittenberg in 1517. Luther felt that the sale by the Roman Catholic Church of indulgences, which remitted some penalties for sin, interfered with proper penitence. He stated his theses to start a debate on this question. The controversy that followed led to Luther's break with the papacy. *See also* Luther, Martin; Reformation.

Ninety-Nine Articles. △1152.

Nineveh, ancient capital of Assyria. Existing as early as 1950 BC, its greatest development occurred during the reigns of Sennacherib (705–681 BC) and Assurbanipal. When Nineveh fell to Nabopolassar of Babylonia and his allies (612 BC), the Assyrian empire perished with it. △956, 980.

Ningpo (Ningbo or **Ning-po),** city in E China, 90mi (145km) ESE of Hangchow, on Yung River; site of Portuguese trading center 1533–45; port opened to foreign trade by Treaty of Nanking (1842); under communist control 1949; nearby is birthplace of Chiang Kai-shek. Industries: fishing, textiles, food processing, electrical equipment, furniture, lace. Exports: raw cotton, lumber, tea, fish. Pop. 350,000.

Niobe, in Greek mythology, queen of Thebes, daughter of Tantalus and wife of Amphion. She boasted of how many children she had borne (she had either six or seven of each sex), and said that Leto had only two children. Leto's offspring, Apollo and Artemis, killed all of Niobe's children. Distraught, Niobe fled Thebes. Zeus turned her to stone at Mt Sipylus.

Niobium, or **columbium,** metallic element (symbol Nb) of the second transition series, discovered (1801) by C. Hatchett. Chief ore is columbite-tantalite. The metal is used in alloy steels. Properties: at. no. 41; at. wt. 92.9064; sp gr 8.57; melt. pt. 4,474°F (2,470°C); boil. pt. 8,503°F (4,706°C); most common isotope Nb^{93} (100%). *See also* Transition Elements. △1552–54.

Niobrara, river in Wyoming and Nebraska; rises in High Plains in E Wyo.; flows E to Missouri River in NE Neb.; used for irrigation. Length: 430mi (692km).

Nippon, or **Nihon,** Japanese name for Japan. It is derived from the Chinese *Jeupenn,* literally "origin of the Sun," from which comes the name "Land of the Rising Sun" for Japan.

Nippur, ancient city of Babylonia. As the seat of the

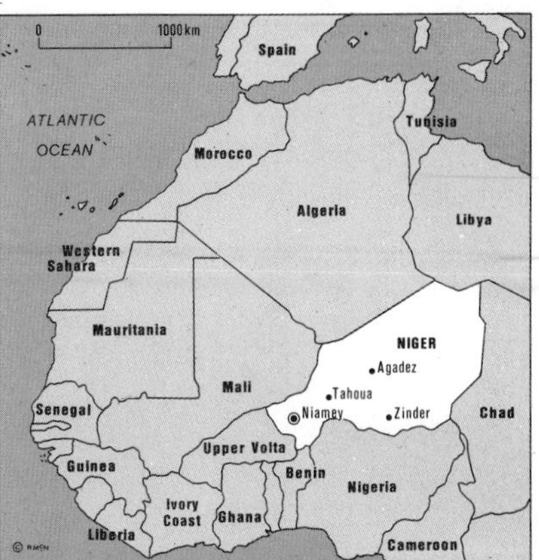
0 1000km
Spain
ATLANTIC OCEAN
Tunisia
Morocco
Algeria
Libya
Western Sahara
Mauritania
NIGER
Agadez
Tahoua
Mali
Senegal
Niamey
Zinder
Chad
Upper Volta
Guinea
Benin
Nigeria
Ivory Coast
Ghana
Liberia
Cameroon
Niger

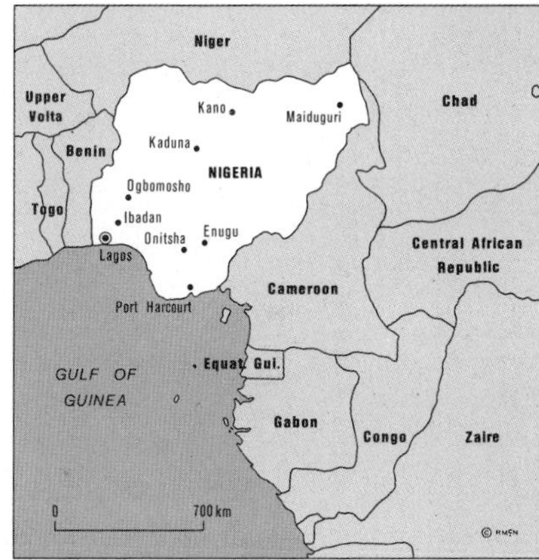
Niger
Upper Volta
Chad
Kano
Maiduguri
Benin
Kaduna
NIGERIA
Ogbomosho
Togo
Ibadan
Onitsha
Enugu
Lagos
Central African Republic
Cameroon
Port Harcourt
Equat. Gui.
GULF OF GUINEA
Gabon
Congo
Zaire
0 700km
Nigeria

Vaslav Nijinsky

Nile River

important cult of Enlil, it was the chief religious center of ancient Mesopotamia. It declined gradually after the 7th century BC.

Nirenberg, Marshall W(arren) (1927–), US biochemist, b. New York City. He was awarded part of the 1968 Nobel Prize in physiology or medicine for his part in discoveries about how genes determine cell function. Nirenberg found the key to the genetic code, deciphering the particular code triplet for the amino acid phenylalanine.

Nirvana, or **Nibbana,** the indescribable state attained by enlightened beings. Upon death, enlightenment is completed in the state of Parinirvana. In Buddhism, Nirvana is the extinction of craving; in Jainism, it is the place of liberated souls; and in Hinduism, it is the home of liberated souls united with the divine. *See also* Buddhism; Hinduism; Jainism. △988.

Niš (Nish), city in E Yugoslavia, on Nišava River; birthplace of Constantine the Great; site of university (1965). City was taken by Turks 1386; passed to Serbia 1878, and served as capital of Serbia until 1901; taken by Germans 1915 and 1941; by USSR 1944. Industries: tobacco, leather goods, machines. Pop. 127,178.

Nishinomiya, city in SW Honshu, Japan, on Osaka Bay; site of 7th and 8th century temples, Kobe Women's College. Industries: tourism, chemicals, textiles, sake. Pop. 377,043.

Niterói, city in SE Brazil on SE shore of Guanabara Bay opposite Rio de Janeiro; capital of Rio de Janeiro state; site of university (1960). Industries: shipbuilding, tobacco products, chemicals. Founded 1573; made city 1836. Pop. 324,367.

Nitrate, a name applied to any member of two classes of compounds derived from nitric acid. Nitric acid esters are covalent compounds with the structure R-O-NO_2 ("R" represents an organic combining group such as ethyl in ethyl nitrate). Nitric acid salts are ionic compounds that contain the nitrate ion and a positive ion, such as $(NH4)^+$ in ammonium nitrate.

Nitric Acid, colorless fuming corrosive liquid (formula HNO_3) obtained by the oxidation of ammonia in the presence of a platinum catalyst. It is used in the preparation of fertilizers, explosives, and a wide range of chemicals. Properties: sp gr 1.504, melt. pt. −46.9°F (−41.59°C).

Nitrocellulose, or cellulose nitrate, range of compounds prepared by treating cellulose (in the form of linters, cotton waste, cotton wool, or wood pulp) with a mixture of concentrated nitric and sulfuric acids. Nitrocellulose containing 12.5–13.5% nitrogen is used in explosives, such as dynamite and gun cotton, while material containing 10.5–12.2% nitrogen is used in plastics, such as celluloid.

Nitrogen, common gaseous nonmetallic element (symbol N) of group VA of the periodic table, discovered (1772) by Daniel Rutherford. It is the major component of the atmosphere (78% by volume), from which it is extracted by fractionation of liquid air. The main use is in the Haber process for producing ammonia for fertilizers—nitrogen is essential for plant growth. The element is chemically inert. Properties: at. no. 7; at. wt. 14.0067; density 1.2506 g dm^{-3}; melt. pt. −345.75°F (−209.86°C); boil pt. −320.4°F (−195.8°C); most common isotope N^{14} (99.63%). △1554, 1560, 1568.

Nitrogen Cycle, circulation of nitrogen through plants and animals in the biosphere. Plants obtain nitrogen compounds for producing essential proteins through assimilation. Nitrogen-fixing bacteria, in the soil or legume root nodules, take free nitrogen from the soil and air to form the nitrogen compounds used by plants to grow. The nitrogen is returned to the soil and air by decay or denitrification, accomplished by denitrifying bacteria. △312.

Nitroglycerin, an oily liquid used in the manufacture of explosives and in medicine to relieve chest pain in chronic heart disease.

Nitrous Oxide, a colorless gas with a pleasant odor, used as an anesthetic or analgesic during surgical or dental procedures. Also known as laughing gas since it initially produces exhilaration, sometimes accompanied by laughter.

Nixon, Richard Milhous (1913–), 37th president of the United States (1969–74), b. Yorba Linda, Calif. He was a graduate of Whittier College (1934) and Duke University Law School (1937). In 1940 he married Thelma Patricia Ryan; they had two daughters. In 1946, Nixon, a young lawyer practicing in Whittier, Calif., was chosen by a group of Republican businessmen to run for the US House of Representatives. He won and became a member of the House Un-American Activities Committee. He achieved national fame there by pursuing the Alger Hiss-Whittaker Chambers spy case. He emphasized his anti-Communism in 1950 when he was elected to the Senate against Helen Gahagan Douglas, whom he accused of being pro-Communist. In 1952, Dwight D. Eisenhower chose him as his vice-presidential running mate.

Nixon's eight years as vice president were unusually active, and in 1960 he was the Republican presidential candidate. He lost the election to John F. Kennedy in a close race. In 1962, Nixon ran unsuccessfully for governor of California; he then moved to New York to practice law. Nixon won the 1968 Republican nomination and the subsequent election.

Nixon was pledged to end the war in Vietnam and began the removal of US forces. He also increased the saturation bombing of North Vietnam and ordered the invasion of Cambodia (1970) and Laos (1971). He eased tensions with the Soviet Union and Communist China, visiting the mainland in 1972. Domestically, there was much unrest; antiwar activists created disturbances, and a severe recession accompanied by inflation caused Nixon to institute (1971) wage-and-price controls.

Nixon and his vice president, Spiro T. Agnew, were reelected in 1972 by a landslide. Almost immediately, however, Nixon was engulfed by revelations of unprecedented corruption in his administration, most of them lumped under the heading of the Watergate affair. There were widespread criticisms of public money spent on Nixon's private houses, and he was found to have greatly underpaid his federal income taxes. At the same time, Agnew was accused of taking bribes while governor of Maryland and while vice president. He was forced to resign, and Nixon appointed Gerald R. Ford to replace him.

In 1974 the Judiciary Committee of the House of Representatives voted a bill of impeachment against Nixon. Before the House could act on impeachment, however, the Supreme Court forced Nixon to release secret tapes that he had made of his private conversations. They revealed that Nixon had lied to the public about his involvement in the Watergate coverup. On Aug. 9, 1974, he resigned from office, the first president to do so. A month later his successor, Gerald R. Ford, issued a general pardon to Nixon. A number of his top aides, however, were convicted, fined, and imprisoned.

Career: US House of Representatives, 1947–51; US Senate, 1951–53; vice president, 1953–61; president, 1969–74. *See also* Vietnam War; Watergate Affair. △1358.

Niznij Tagil (Nizhniy Tagil), city in Russian SFSR, USSR, in the central Urals on the Tagil River, 80mi (129km) NNE of Sverdlovsk; site of teachers' college and museum. Industries: metallurgy, machine tools, agricultural machinery, building materials, chemicals, ceramics, woodworking, mining. Founded 1725; became city 1917. Pop. 378,000.

Njal Saga, an Icelandic family saga. It relates the story of the families of its two main heroes, Gunnar and Njal. It is considered the finest Icelandic work depicting life in the heroic age.

Nkrumah, Kwame (1909–72), African nationalist and statesman of Ghana. He was educated in Africa and the United States and after returning to Ghana (then the Gold Coast) he formed the Convention People's party in 1949. Building an increasing popular support, he was briefly imprisoned for preaching resistance to the British and led his country to independence in 1957, when he became prime minister. In 1960 he became president and worked steadily to increase his control of Ghanaian government. He alienated his following and was ousted by the military in 1966. △1332.

NLRB. *See* National Labor Relations Board.

NMR. *See* Nuclear Magnetic Resonance.

Noah, in the Bible, son of Lamech and 10th in descent from Adam. Chosen by God to survive the Flood, he built the Ark for himself, his family, and pairs of all animals. His sons, Ham, Shem, and Japheth, continued the human race after the flood. △838.

Nobel, Alfred Bernhard (1833–96), Swedish chemist, engineer, and industrialist. He invented dynamite and founded the Nobel Prizes. He received a patent for dynamite in Great Britain in 1866 and in the United States in 1867. In 1876 he patented a more powerful form of blasting gelatin, and in 1888 he produced ballistite, one of the first nitroglycerin smokeless powders. The immense fortune he acquired from the manufacture of explosives and from interests in the Baku oil fields in Russia was bequeathed to establish the prestigious international Nobel Prizes, first awarded in 1901.

Nobelium, radioactive metallic element (symbol No) of the actinide group, made in 1958 by bombarding Cm^{246} with C^{12} nuclei. The element has been made only in trace amounts and has not been identified chemically. Properties: at. no. 102; most stable isotope No.^{255} (half-life 3hrs). *See also* Transuranium elements. △1552–54.

Nobel Prizes, awards given each year to individuals or institutions for outstanding contributions in the fields of physics, chemistry, physiology and medicine, literature, peace, and economics. Established in 1901 by the will of Swedish scientist Alfred Bernhard Nobel, the prizes are awarded each December 10. The economics prize was first awarded in 1969. Four committees are designated to select the winning candidates: the Swedish Academy of Science for physics, chemistry, and economics; the Caroline Institute in Stockholm for physiology and medicine; the Swedish Academy in Stockholm for literature; and a committee of five, elected by the Norwegian parliament, for peace. The winner of the peace prize is chosen for outstanding work in promoting peace, international brotherhood, and disarmament. The peace prize is awarded in Oslo; all others are awarded in Stockholm.

NOBEL PRIZE WINNERS

Physics

Year	Winner
1901	Wilhelm C. Roentgen
1902	Hendrik A. Lorentz
	Pieter Zeeman
1903	Antoine H. Becquerel
	Marie S. Curie
	Pierre Curie
1904	John W. S. Rayleigh
1905	Philipp E. A. Lenard
1906	Joseph J. Thomson
1907	Albert A. Michelson
1908	Gabriel Lippmann
1909	Guglielmo Marconi
	Carl F. Braun
1910	Johannes D. van der Waals
1911	Wilhelm Wien
1912	Nils G. Dalén
1913	Heike Kamerlingh-Onnes
1914	Max von Laue
1915	William H. Bragg
	William Lawrence Bragg
1917	Charles G. Barkla
1918	Max K. E. L. Planck
1919	Johannes Stark
1920	Charles E. Guillaume
1921	Albert Einstein
1922	Niels H. D. Bohr
1923	Robert A. Millikan
1924	Karl M. G. Siegbahn
1925	James Franck
	Gustav Hertz
1926	Jean B. Perrin
1927	Arthur H. Compton
	Charles T. R. Wilson
1928	Owen W. Richardson
1929	Louis Victor de Broglie
1930	Chandrasekhara V. Raman
1932	Werner Heisenberg
1933	Paul A. M. Dirac
	Erwin Schrödinger
1935	James Chadwick
1936	Carl D. Anderson
	Victor F. Hess
1937	Clinton J. Davisson
	George P. Thomson
1938	Enrico Fermi
1939	Ernest O. Lawrence
1943	Otto Stern
1944	Isidor Isaac Rabi
1945	Wolfgang Pauli
1946	Percy Williams Bridgman
1947	Edward V. Appleton
1948	Patrick Blackett
1949	Hideki Yukawa
1950	Cecil F. Powell
1951	John D. Cockcroft
	Ernest T. S. Walton
1952	Felix Bloch
	Edward M. Purcell
1953	Frits Zernike
1954	Max Born
	Walther Bothe
1955	Willis E. Lamb, Jr
	Polykarp Kusch
1956	John Bardeen
	Walter H. Brattain
	William B. Shockley

1957	Tsung-Dao Lee
	Chen Ning Yang
1958	Pavel A. Cherenkov
	Ilya M. Frank
	Igor Y. Tamm
1959	Emilio G. Segrè
	Owen Chamberlain
1960	Donald A. Glaser
1961	Robert Hofstadter
	Rudolf L. Mössbauer
1962	Lev D. Landau
1963	J. Hans D. Jensen
	Maria Goeppert-Mayer
	Eugene P. Wigner
1964	Nikolai G. Basov
	Aleksander M. Prokhorov
	Charles H. Townes
1965	Richard P. Feynman
	Julian S. Schwinger
	Sin-itiro Tomonaga
1966	Alfred Kastler
1967	Hans A. Bethe
1968	Luis W. Alvarez
1969	Murray Gell-Mann
1970	Louis Néel
	Hannes Alfvén
1971	Dennis Gabor
1972	John Bardeen
	Leon Cooper
	John R. Schrieffer
1973	Leo Esaki
	Ivar Giaever
	Brian D. Josephson
1974	Antony Hewish
	Martin Ryle
1975	Aage N. Bohr
	Ben Mottelson
	James Rainwater
1976	Burton Richter
	Samuel C.C. Ting

Chemistry

Year	Winner
1901	Jacobus van't Hoff
1902	Emil H. Fischer
1903	Svante A. Arrhenius
1904	William Ramsay
1905	Adolf von Baeyer
1906	Henri Moissan
1907	Eduard Buchner
1908	Ernest Rutherford
1909	Wilhelm Ostwald
1910	Otto Wallach
1911	Marie S. Curie
1912	F. A. Victor Grignard
	Paul Sabatier
1913	Alfred Werner
1914	Theodore W. Richards
1915	Richard M. Willstätter
1918	Fritz Haber
1920	Walther H. Nernst
1921	Frederick Soddy
1922	Francis W. Aston
1923	Fritz Pregl
1925	Richard A. Zsigmondy
1926	Theodor Svedberg
1927	Henrich O. Wieland
1928	Adolf O. R. Windaus
1929	Arthur Harden
	Hans von Euler-Chelpin
1930	Hans Fischer
1931	Carl Bosch
	Friedrich Bergius
1932	Irving Langmuir
1934	Harold C. Urey
1935	Irène Joliot-Curie
	Frédéric Joliot
1936	Peter J. W. Debye
1937	Walter N. Haworth
	Paul Karrer
1938	Richard Kuhn
1939	Adolf F. J. Butenandt
	Leopold Ruzicka
1943	Georg von Hevesy
1944	Otto Hahn
1945	Artturi I. Virtanen
1946	John H. Northrop
	Wendell M. Stanley
	James B. Sumner
1947	Robert Robinson
1948	Arne W. K. Tiselius
1949	William F. Giauque
1950	Otto P. H. Diels
	Kurt Alder
1951	Edwin M. McMillan
	Glenn T. Seaborg
1952	Archer J. P. Martin
	Richard L. M. Synge
1953	Hermann Staudinger
1954	Linus C. Pauling
1955	Vincent du Vigneaud
1956	Cyril N. Hinshelwood
	Nikolai N. Semenov
1957	Alexander R. Todd
1958	Frederick Sanger
1959	Jaroslav Heyrovsky
1960	Willard F. Libby
1961	Melvin Calvin
1962	John C. Kendrew
	Max F. Perutz
1963	Giulio Natta
	Karl Ziegler
1964	Dorothy C. Hodgkin
1965	Robert B. Woodward
1966	Robert S. Mulliken
1967	Manfred Eigen
	Ronald G. W. Norrish
	George Porter
1968	Lars Onsager
1969	Odd Hassel
	Derek H. R. Barton
1970	Luis F. Leloir
1971	Gerhard Herzberg
1972	Christian Boehmer Anfinsen
	Stanford Moore
	William Howard Stein
1973	Ernst Otto Fisher
	Geoffrey Wilkinson
1974	Paul J. Flory
1975	John Cornforth
	Vladimir Prelog
1976	William N. Lipscomb, Jr.

Physiology and Medicine

Year	Winner
1901	Emil A. von Behring
1902	Ronald Ross
1903	Niels R. Finsen
1904	Ivan P. Pavlov
1905	Robert Koch
1906	Camillo Golgi
	Santiago Ramón y Cajal
1907	Charles L. A. Laveran
1908	Paul Ehrlich
	Élie Metchnikoff
1909	E. Theodor Kocher
1910	Albrecht Kossel
1911	Allvar Gullstrand
1912	Alexis Carrel
1913	Charles R. Richet
1914	Robert Bárány
1919	Jules J. P. V. Bordet
1920	S. August Krogh
1922	Archibald V. Hill
	Otto F. Meyerhof
1923	Frederick G. Banting
	John J. R. Macleod
1924	Willem Einthoven
1926	Johannes A. G. Fibiger
1927	Julius Wagner-Jauregg
1928	Charles J. H. Nicolle
1929	Frederick G. Hopkins
	Christiaan Eijkman
1930	Karl Landsteiner
1931	Otto H. Warburg
1932	Charles S. Sherrington
	Edgar D. Adrian
1933	Thomas H. Morgan
1934	George R. Minot
	William P. Murphy
	George H. Whipple
1935	Hans Spemann
1936	Henry H. Dale
	Otto Loewi
1937	Albert von Szent-Györgyi
1938	Corneille J. F. Heymans
1939	Gerhard Domagk
1943	Edward A. Doisy
	C. P. Henrik Dam
1944	E. Joseph Erlanger
	Herbert S. Gasser
1945	Alexander Fleming
	Howard W. Florey
	Ernst B. Chain
1946	Hermann Joseph Muller
1947	Carl F. Cori
	Gerty T. Cori
	Bernardo A. Houssay
1948	Paul H. Müller
1949	Walter R. Hess
	Antônio de Egas Moniz
1950	Philip S. Hench
	Edward C. Kendall
	Tadeus Reichstein
1951	Max Theiler
1952	Selman A. Waksman
1953	Fritz A. Lipmann
	Hans A. Krebs
1954	John F. Enders
	Frederick C. Robbins
	Thomas H. Weller
1955	A. Hugo T. Theorell

Marshall Nirenberg

Richard M. Nixon

Alfred Nobel

Nobelists George Seferis (left) and Par F. Lagerkvist

1956	André F. Cournand
	Werner Forssmann
	D. W. Richards
1957	Daniel Bovet
1958	George W. Beadle
	Edward L. Tatum
	Joshua Lederberg
1959	Arthur Kornberg
	Severo Ochoa
1960	F. Macfarlane Burnet
	Peter B. Medawar
1961	Georg von Békésy
1962	Francis H. C. Crick
	James D. Watson
	Maurice H. F. Wilkins
1963	Andrew F. Huxley
	John C. Eccles
	Alan L. Hodgkin
1964	Konrad E. Bloch
	Feodor Lynen
1965	François Jacob
	André M. Lwoff
	Jacques L. Monod
1966	Charles B. Huggins
	Francis P. Rous
1967	Ragnar A. Granit
	Haldan K. Hartline
	George Wald
1968	Robert W. Holley
	H. Gobind Khorana
	Marshall W. Nirenberg
1969	Max Delbruck
	Alfred D. Hershey
	Salvador E. Luria
1970	Bernard Katz
	Ulf von Euler
	Julius Axelrod
1971	Earl W. Sutherland
1972	Gerald M. Edelman
	Rodney R. Porter
1973	Karl von Frisch
	Konrad Lorenz
	Nikolaas Tinbergen
1974	Albert Claude
	Christian René de Duve
	George Emil Palade
1975	David Baltimore
	Renatto Dulbecco
	Howard Temin
1976	Baruch S. Blumberg
	Daniel C. Gajdusek

Literature

Year	Winner
1901	René F. A. Sully-Prudhomme
1902	Theodor Mommsen
1903	Björnstjerne Björnson
1904	Frédéric Mistral
	José Echegaray
1905	Henryk Sienkiewicz
1906	Giosué Carducci
1907	Rudyard Kipling
1908	Rudolf C. Eucken
1909	Selma O. L. Lagerlöf
1910	Paul J. L. Heyse
1911	Maurice Maeterlinck
1912	Gerhart Hauptmann
1913	Rabindranath Tagore
1915	Romain Rolland
1916	Verner von Heidenstam
1917	Karl A. Gjellerup
	Henrik Pontoppidan
1919	Carl F. G. Spitteler
1920	Knut Hamsun
1921	Anatole France
1922	Jacinto Benavente y Martínez
1923	William Butler Yeats
1924	Wladyslaw S. Reymont
1925	George Bernard Shaw
1926	Grazia Deledda
1927	Henri Bergson
1928	Sigrid Undset
1929	Thomas Mann
1930	Sinclair Lewis
1931	Erik A. Karlfeldt
1932	John Galsworthy
1933	Ivan A. Bunin
1934	Luigi Pirandello
1936	Eugene G. O'Neill
1937	Roger M. du Gard
1938	Pearl S. Buck
1939	Frans E. Sillanpaa
1944	Johannes V. Jensen
1945	Gabriela Mistral
1946	Hermann Hesse
1947	André Gide
1948	T. S. Eliot
1949	William Faulkner
1950	Bertrand A. W. Russell
1951	Pär F. Lagerkvist
1952	François Mauriac
1953	Winston Churchill
1954	Ernest Hemingway
1955	Halldór K. Laxness
1956	Juan Ramón Jiménez
1957	Albert Camus
1958	Boris L. Pasternak (declined)
1959	Salvatore Quasimodo
1960	Saint-John Perse
1961	Ivo Andric
1962	John Steinbeck
1963	George Seferis
1964	Jean Paul Sartre (declined)
1965	Mikhail A. Sholokov
1966	Samuel Y. Agnon
	Nelly Sachs
1967	Miguel Angel Asturias
1968	Yasunari Kawabata
1969	Samuel Beckett
1970	Aleksander Solzhenitsyn
1971	Pablo Neruda
1972	Heinrich Böll
1973	Patrick White
1974	Eyvind Johnson
	Harry Martinson
1975	Eugenio Montale
1976	Saul Bellow

Peace

Year	Winner
1901	Jean H. Dunant
	Frédéric Passy
1902	Elie Ducommun
	Charles A. Gobat
1903	William R. Cremer
1904	Institute of International Law
1905	Bertha von Suttner
1906	Theodore Roosevelt
1907	Ernesto T. Moneta
	Louis Renault
1908	Klas P. Arnoldson
	Fredrik Bajer
1909	Auguste M. F. Beernaert
	Paul H. Benjamin Estournelles de Constant
1910	International Peace Bureau
1911	Tobias M. C. Asser
	Alfred H. Fried
1912	Elihu Root
1913	Henri Lafontaine
1917	International Red Cross
1919	Woodrow Wilson
1920	Léon Bourgeois
1921	Hjalmar Branting
	Christian L. Lange
1922	Fridtjof Nansen
1925	J. Austen Chamberlain
	Charles G. Dawes
1926	Aristide Briand
	Gustav Stresemann
1927	Ferdinand E. Buisson
	Ludwig Quidde
1929	Frank B. Kellogg
1930	Nathan Söderblom
1931	Jane Addams
	Nicholas Murray Butler
1933	Norman Angell
1934	Arthur Henderson
1935	Carl von Ossietzky
1936	Carlos Saaredra Lamas
1937	E. A. R. Cecil
1938	Nansen International Office for Refugees
1944	International Red Cross
1945	Cordell Hull
1946	John R. Mott
	Emily Balch
1947	Friends' Service Council;
	American Friends' Service Committee
1949	John Boyd-Orr
1950	Ralph J. Bunche
1951	Léon Jouhaux
1952	Albert Schweitzer
1953	George C. Marshall
1954	Office of the UN High Commissioner for Refugees
1957	Lester B. Pearson
1958	Father George H. Pire
1959	Philip J. Noel-Baker
1960	Albert J. Luthuli
1961	Dag Hammarskjöld
1962	Linus C. Pauling
1963	International Red Cross;
	League of Red Cross Societies
1964	Martin Luther King, Jr.
1965	UNICEF (UN Children's Fund)
1968	René Cassin
1969	International Labor Organization
1970	Norman E. Borlaug
1971	Willy Brandt
1973	Henry A. Kissinger
	Le Duc Tho
1974	Sean MacBride
	Eisaku Sato
1975	Andrei D. Sakharov

Economics

Year	Winner
1969	Ragnar Frisch
	Jan Tinbergen
1970	Paul Anthony Samuelson
1971	Simon Kuznets
1972	Kenneth J. Arrow
	John R. Hicks
1973	Wassily Leontief
1974	Friedrich A. von Hayek
	Gunnar Myrdal
1975	Leonid Kantorovich
	Tjalling C. Koopmans
1976	Milton Friedman

Noble Gases, or **Inert Gases,** group of colorless, odorless, nonflammable gases forming group O of the periodic table. They are helium (atomic number 2), neon (10), argon (18), krypton (36), xenon (54), and radon (86). All have complete outer electron shells and were formerly thought not to form compounds. However, fluorides of krypton, xenon, and radon have now been produced. Argon occurs to the extent of 1% in the earth's atmosphere and helium and neon are produced commercially. *See also* Periodic Table. △1522, 1558.

Noble Savage. △874.

Nobunaga. △1048, 1210.

Noctiluca, genus of plantlike flagellate protozoa usually found floating near the surface of the sea. Phosphorescent dinoflagellate, it has a round body and one large and one small flagellum. Width: to .08in (2mm). Class Mastigophora.

Noctilucent Cloud, present in wave formations at heights of 45 to 55 mi (72 to 89 km), probably consisting of ice crystals formed on meteor dust, usually observed only at twilight.

Noctis Labyrinthus (the chandelier). △74.

Noddy, sooty-colored tern found along rocky tropical seacoasts. Famous for elaborate nodding displays, fearless males defend the colonies. A single blotched gray egg is incubated by both parents on a rocky shelf or stick-and-seaweed nest. Genus *Anous*. *See also* Tern.

Nodes of Ranvier. △664.

No Drama, the first significant Japanese dramatic form. It was created in the late 14th century by a father and son, Kannami and Zeami. Into the 19th century it was an entertainment for the aristocracy and the warrior class but it is broadly popular today. Formalized, dignified, and nonrealistic, No uses an all-male cast, which also sings and dances. The warriors, demons, and ghosts who often inhabit No frequently illustrate certain weaknesses. Performances traditionally lasted all day but have been shortened since 1945.

Nogales, city and port of entry in NW Mexico, on the Arizona border; occupied for a short time by Americans from Nogales, Ariz., during a border dispute (1918); site of railroad terminus, national highway. Industries: trade, livestock, minerals. Pop. 52,865.

Noguchi, Hideyo (1876–1928), Japanese bacteriologist known for isolating the causative agent of syphilis in the central nervous system. He improved the technique of the Wasserman reaction and devised the Wasserman skin test. Noguchi invented ways of cultivating microorganisms in the test tube, including the spirochetes that cause syphilis. △762.

Noguchi, Isamu (1904–), US sculptor, b. Los Angeles. Influenced by Giacometti and Alexander Calder, his abstract works are marked by great delicacy and employ all sorts of materials. He constructed many open-air sculptures, including the Garden of Peace for the Paris UNESCO Building.

Noise, any undesired sound. Common sources of objectionable noise are car and truck exhausts, aircraft jet engines, railroad trains, factory machinery. Experiments carried out to determine the effects of noise on work output tend to show that output is only seriously affected if the work is mental. Nevertheless, noise is often regarded as a form of acoustic pollution and many noise-abatement societies exist. Noise is usually measured on a decibel scale. △1496,1752.

Nomadism, way of life, usually accompanying pastoralism, in which a group or tribe has no fixed residence but moves around an area on a seasonal circuit. Many peoples are seminomadic, having settled abodes for part of the year. These societies are common in the Middle East where they live by camel or goat herding and follow the availability of fodder. *See also* Pastoralism. △878.

Nome, city in W Alaska, on the Bering Sea, 700mi (1,127km) W of Fairbanks. Port is open May to November; extensive oil fields nearby; center for Eskimo handicrafts; US Air Force base. City est. 1899 when gold was discovered. Pop. (1970) 2,488.

Nomenclature, Chemical. *See* Chemical Nomenclature.

Nominalism, theory of knowledge that denies reality to universal concepts. Here nominalists quarreled with the opposing philosophy of realism. Realists held there are universal concepts, forms, or ideas such as roundness. Nominalists said that the only things we can know are objects; roundness is no more than a name we give to circles and spheres. An epistemological possibility mentioned in Porphyry's *Eisagoge*, nominalism was formulated first by Roscellinus and later by Peter Abelard. Reformulated by Occam in the 14th century, nominalism more markedly separated faith from reason, contributing to the demise of scholasticism. △852.

Nomogram, a graphic representation of the relationships of numbers; a calculating chart with value scales of several mathematical variables. Nomograms are used in industry, engineering, and natural and physical science. Usually, it consists of three graduated parallel lines; known values on any two scales determine a transversal passing through the value on the third, which is the solution.

Nonakchott. *See* Nouakchott.

Nonalignment. △1352.

Nonconformists, term used to describe those whose religious beliefs diverged from established doctrine. More specifically, the nonconformists were Protestant dissenters who refused allegiance to the Church of England, as demanded by the Act of Uniformity (1662). Since 1880, non-Anglicans have had full religious and civil rights in England.

Non-Euclidean Geometry, self-consistent geometry that uses a different set of axioms from those of Euclid's geometry, in particular a set that does not include the parallel postulate. Euclid's fifth postulate is equivalent to the statement that if a point lies outside a line, then only one line can be drawn through that point that does not cut the first line. In the early 19th century Farkas Bolyai and, independently, N.I. Lobachevsky developed systems of geometry in which an infinite number of parallels could exist. This system, called a hyperbolic non-Euclidean geometry, was self-consistent; that is, it had no inherent contradiction in the results obtained from the postulates. Later G.F.B. Riemann introduced a form (elliptical geometry) in which no parallel can exist. Development of these systems cast light on the fundamental nature of geometry. Non-Euclidean geometry is also used in relativity theory. △1462.

Non-Importation Act (1806), US legislation banning the import of British items in an attempt to force British to stop impressing US seamen. Pres. Thomas Jefferson suspended the act in 1806. It was followed by the stronger Embargo Act in 1807.

Non-Intercourse Act (1809), US act replacing the unsuccessful Embargo Act. It reopened trade with all countries except France and England and authorized the president to resume trade with them if they ceased violation of neutral powers. *See also* Embargo Act.

Nonobjective Art, art that has no familiar forms, such as those of landscapes, inanimate objects, or human figures. Kandinsky was a forerunner in nonobjective painting, which began in 1910. Other early artists in this field were Dove, Doesburg, Malevich, Mondrian, and Delaunay. Nonobjective art has become part of the present international style. By extension, this term also applies to the early geometric style of Muslim art in the Near East and to the decorative art of similar cultures. △1318, 1372.

Non-Proliferation Treaty (1968), signed by the USSR, the United Kingdom, the United States, and over 80 non-nuclear weapon states. This treaty requires that each participating nation, under the auspices of the IAEA (International Atomic Energy Agency of the United Nations), agree that research and use of nuclear energy for peaceful purposes will not be redirected into military channels. The treaty pledges all signatory nations "to facilitate the fullest possible exchange of equipment, materials and scientific and technological information for . . . peaceful uses."

Non-sporting Dog, dog breeds that do not fit into other classification categories. Although many were once used as hunting and guard dogs, they are now pets. This catchall category varies widely in type. Dogs included are Bichon frise, Boston terrier, bulldog, chowchow, dalmatian, French bulldog, Keeshond, Lhasa Apso, poodle, schipperke, and Tibetan terrier.

Nootka, Wakashan-speaking tribe of North American Indians closely related to the Makah. Famous as whale hunters, their original population of 6,000 persons living along the coast of W Vancouver Island from Cape Cook to Cape Flattery now numbers approximately 2,250.

Noradrenaline. *See* Norepinephrine.

Nordenskjöld, Nils Adolf Erik, (Baron) (1832–1901), Scandinavian explorer and scientist. Born in Finland, he moved to Sweden in 1858 for political reasons. He made his first voyage in that year to Spitsbergen, a group of arctic islands north of Norway and Russia. A geologist, mineralogist, and mapmaker, he returned to Spitsbergen several times and in 1870 led an exploration of Greenland's inland ice. He later sailed the northeast passage, was made a baron by the Swedish king, and again visited Greenland. He published several accounts of his discoveries.

Nordic Subrace, subdivision of the Caucasoid race, characterized by tall stature, fair skin, blond hair, blue eyes, and long heads. This physical type predominates in Norway and Denmark and occurs throughout N Europe. △658–60.

Nord-Ostee Kanal. *See* Kiel Canal.

Norepinephrine, or **Noradrenaline,** a chemical substance which with adrenaline is secreted by the medulla of the adrenal gland. It is also liberated at the ends of sympathetic nerve fibers where it serves as a mediator in transmitting the nerve impulses to the effector organ. The release of norepinephrine may be inhibitory or excitatory depending on the organ involved and its state at that moment. *See also* Adrenal Gland. △770.

Norfolk, Thomas Howard, 2nd Duke of (1443–1524), English nobleman. Captured at the Battle of Bosworth Field (1485), he was imprisoned in the Tower of London (1485–89). Named lord treasurer (1501), he defeated the Scots at Flodden (1513), and his title of duke was restored (1514).

Norfolk, Thomas Howard, 3rd Duke of (1473–1554), English nobleman, brother-in-law to Henry VII. President of the royal council (1529), he suppressed the Pilgrimage of Grace (1536). Two of his nieces, Anne Boleyn and Catherine Howard, married Henry VIII. Condemned as an accessory to his son Henry, Earl of Surrey's treason (1546), Norfolk was imprisoned (1547–53) but released by Mary I.

Norfolk, city in SE Virginia, on Elizabeth River; comprises port of Hampton Roads, together with Newport News and Portsmouth; nearly destroyed by fire (1776) when attacked by Americans during American Revolution; occupied by Union army during Civil War. City is site of Norfolk State College (1935), Virginia Wesleyan College (1961); naval headquarters. Exports: coal, grain, tobacco, seafood, farm products. Industries: shipbuilding, automobiles, chemicals, textiles, agricultural machinery, peanut oil, food processing. Founded 1682; inc. 1845. Pop. (1970) 307,951.

Norfolk Island, island in SW Pacific Ocean, approx. 900mi (1,449km) E of Australia; territory of Australia. Discovered 1774 by Capt. James Cook, it was made British penal colony 1788–1855; came under New South Wales 1896, then Australia 1913; renowned for its beautiful pine forests. Industries: tourism, farming, livestock. Area: 13sq mi (34sq km). Pop. 1,380.

Norfolk Island Pine, stately evergreen pine widely grown as a pot plant 2–10ft (0.6–3m) high. In its native South Pacific it grows to 200ft (61m). Branches, with bright green needles to .5in. (1.3cm), grow in annual tiers of 4–7. Care and propagation: prefers cool temperatures, filtered sun, well-drained soil (equal parts loam, sand, peatmoss) allowed to dry between soakings, daily misting; propagation by seeds or cuttings of tip growth. Species *Araucaria excelsa*. *See also* Araucaria.

Nobelist Cordell Hull

Nobelist Paul Samuelson

Noddy

Norfolk Island pine

Normal, town in central Illinois, N of Bloomington; grew around Illinois State University (1857); farming area, especially of fruits and nursery stock; inc. 1865. Pop. (1970) 26,396.

Norman, city in central Oklahoma, 18mi (29km) S of Oklahoma City; seat of Cleveland co; site of University of Oklahoma (1892). Industries: air conditioners, packaged foods, petroleum. Founded 1889; chartered as city 1902. Pop. (1970) 52,117.

Norman Architecture. △1076,1082.

Norman Conquest, period following the invasion of England by William, duke of Normandy, who defeated King Harold at Hastings (1066) and was crowned king of England. Anglo-Saxon lords who had survived Hastings were killed or deprived of their lands in the wake of rebellions (1068–76). William strengthened his position by granting English lands to his Norman barons and establishing Norman feudalism. He brought the church into closer contact with the papacy, but chose his own archbishops. Norman influence encompassed architecture, literature, language, and the art of warfare. △1076.

Normandy (Normandie), region and former province in NW France, bounded historically by Picardy (NE), Ile-de-France (E), Maine (S), Brittany (SW), and English Channel (W and N); capital was Rouen; includes departments of Manche, Calvados, Eure, Seine-Maritime, and Orne. A Roman province, it was invaded by Northmen mid-9th century; became part of English kingdom 1066; conquered by France 1450; suffered economically when Edict of Nantes was revoked (1685), causing a mass migration of Huguenots; in 18th century prosperity returned; in 1790, France abolished provinces and new departments were devised; scene of Allied invasion (June 6, 1944) during WWII; Battle of Normandy, ended July 31, 1944 with the German retreat and Allied breakthrough. Forests, flat farmlands, and gently rolling hills characterize land. Industries: fishing, tourism, cattle. △1096.

Normandy Invasion. △1338.

Normans, Scandinavian pirates who, beginning in the 9th century, ravaged the coasts of Europe, going as far as Sicily, Greenland, and perhaps North America. Their longboats ascended the Loire; they plundered Paris, retreating only after payment of gold. In 912, Charles the Simple ceded them part of Neustria (afterwards called Normandy) and gave his daughter in marriage to their leader, Marching Rolf. Renamed Rollo, duke of Normandy, he became a vassal of Charles and adopted Christianity for himself and his followers. Meanwhile, England was enduring waves of attacks by Northmen. In 1066, William, duke of Normandy, conquered England and took its throne as William I. △1076.

Norms, Social. △888, 892.

Norris, Frank (1870–1902), US novelist, b. Chicago. Considered one of the most striking naturalistic writers, Norris first drew attention for *McTeague* (1899). He is also noted for his trilogy about wheat: *The Octopus* (1901), *The Pit* (1903), and *The Wolf* (unfinished).

Norris, George William (1861–1944), US lawyer and political leader, b. Sandusky co, Ohio. A Republican, he represented Nebraska first in the US House of Representatives (1903–13) and then in the Senate (1913–43). As a Senator, he voted against war with Germany (1917); sponsored the 20th ("lame duck") Amendment (1933); and helped set up the Tennessee Valley Authority (1933). He also helped establish Nebraska's unicameral legislature (1937).

Norris, John (1657–1711), English philosopher. Influenced by Nicolas Malebranche and the Cambridge Platonists, he is chiefly remembered as one of John Locke's earliest critics, in his *Cursory Reflections* (1691). He was the author of a systematic philosophical treatise *An Essay Towards the Theory of the Ideal or Intelligible World* (1701). *See also* Cambridge Platonists.

Norristown, borough in SE Pennsylvania, on the Schuylkill River; seat of Montgomery co. Gen. Winfield Scott Hancock, Civil War commander, was born here and is buried in Montgomery cemetery. Industries: clothing, woolen textiles, metal products, electrical machinery. Founded by Isaac Norris, a Quaker merchant; inc. as borough 1812. Pop. (1970) 38,169.

Norrkoping, port city in SE Sweden, at the head of Bråvikin; burned 1719 by Russians during Northern War; site of 17th-century Hedvig's Church. Industries: furniture, paper, processed food. Founded 14th century. Pop. 95,851.

Norsemen, Scandinavian vikings who invaded the coasts of Europe from *c.* 780–*c.* 1030. Navigators and explorers, they raided and settled in northwest Germany, France, Spain, the Low Countries, Britain, Ireland, and Scotland, in search of land, wealth, trade, and adventure. They left an art style and an iconography, but accounts of the pagan vikings, written by Christians, emphasize their barbarism. *Viking*, a Scandinavian word, means pirate or rover. △1068.

North, Frederick North, 8th Baron (1732–92), English political figure. Chancellor of the exchequer (1767–70) and prime minister (1770–82), he followed George III's policies, leading to losses in the American colonies. Resigning (1782), he served as secretary of state (1783) with Charles James Fox.

North Africa, area consisting of Morocco, Algeria, Tunisia, and Libya; bounded on the N by the Mediterranean, S by the Sahara, and E by Egypt, from which it is separated by 1,000mi (1,610km) of desert. Population and economic activity are concentrated along the coastline; has desert-type interior.

North African Campaign. △1338.

North America, continent in the Western hemisphere, and third largest continent of the world. Linked to the continent of South America at Panama's E border and only 55mi (89km) from Asia across the Bering Strait; it is bounded by the Arctic Ocean (N), Pacific Ocean and Bering Sea (W), and the Atlantic Ocean, Gulf of Mexico, and Caribbean Sea (E).

Land. The Appalachian Mts and Laurentian Highlands of E North America are old, worn down ranges, but the Rocky and other W mountains are young and rugged. The highest peak on the continent is Mt McKinley (20,320ft; 6,198m), in Alaska; the lowest point is Death Valley, California (282ft; 86m below sea level). In the central region vast plains provide good agricultural land; they give way to desert in the SW United States and N Mexico, and tundra in the far N. Mexico and Central America are generally mountainous but have valleys, plateaus, and coastal plains for farming. Northern Alaska and Canada and most of Greenland extend above the Arctic Circle, while southern Mexico, all of Central America, and most of the West Indies fall below the Tropic of Cancer. Greenland is the world's largest island (840,000sq mi; 2,175,600sq km).

Lakes and Rivers. Since Hudson Bay, the largest body of water in North America, is an inlet of the Atlantic Ocean, Lake Superior ranks as the largest lake of North America (31,820sq mi; 82,414sq km), and with Michigan, Huron, Erie, and Ontario it forms the Great Lakes. The St Lawrence River drains them and provides a navigable outlet to the Atlantic Ocean. The longest river is the combined Mississippi-Missouri system with a length of nearly 4,000mi (6,440km); other important rivers include the Yukon, Mackenzie, Colorado, Columbia, Delaware, Rio Grande.

Climate and Vegetation. Much of North America experiences hot summers and cold winters, but with extremes only in the Arctic, near the equator, in Death Valley, and in the high mountains; rain forests occur in Central America. Evergreens grow over much of the continent and form a belt across the N below the tundra region. Cypress thrive in the SE, oak and maple in the NE, and giant redwoods in the W; the plains support grasses and shrubs.

Animal Life. Bears, wolves, and pumas have grown scarce, but foxes remain widespread and lynxes occupy many forests. Coyotes range across the SW, and ocelots live S of the United States. These predators catch deer, rabbits, hares, and mice. Beaver and members of the weasel family are important for their fur. Birds include sparrows, robins, blackbirds, blue jays, wrens, doves, hawks, and owls. Snakes live nearly everywhere, with dangerous ones being rattlers and moccasins.

People. North America's first settlers probably arrived about 35,000 years ago from Asia by way of Alaska. Their descendants occupied the entire continent when Viking explorers came about AD 1000; Christopher Columbus called them Indians when he rediscovered the New World in 1492. Spaniards moved into the West Indies and other southern lands, while the English and French settled farther N; Swedes, Germans, and the Dutch also made early settlements. Europe's problems later drove numbers of Italians, Irish, and Jews to North America. Blacks came as slaves, while Japanese and Chinese arrived with less coercion to be laborers on the W coast. Descendants of the Spanish now dominate in Mexico, Central America, and some Caribbean islands, while French concentrations exist in Quebec province, Canada, and parts of the West Indies. Blacks outnumber whites in many Caribbean islands. Protestants are numerous N of Mexico, and Roman Catholics dominate in Spanish- and French-speaking areas.

Economy. The plains region produces grains and livestock, although industry has developed near major rivers and lakes. The S areas are also agricultural; major crops include cotton, tobacco, coffee, and sugar cane. The NE is heavily industrialized, the N and E produce forest products, and the W has mining, truck farming, and some manufacturing. Fishing is important along many of the coasts. The West Indies and other southern regions profit from tourist traffic.

History. About 500 years after the time of Christ, Mayan Indians of Central America developed a notable civilization, as did the Aztecs of Mexico later. Spanish conquerors in the 16th century destroyed their civilizations. In the same century the French started exploring what is now Canada. The English settled at Jamestown in 1607 and at Plymouth in 1620. English-French conflicts finally brought an English victory in 1763. Some colonies revolted against England's colonial practices in 1775 and declared their independence in 1776. After they won their struggle in 1783, they banded together as the United States, drawing up a constitution in 1787. Other colonies also grew restless; Haiti gained freedom from France in 1804, and Mexico and most of Central America threw off Spanish rule in 1821; Panama became part of Colombia, but British Honduras and most Caribbean islands remained under European domination. During the 19th century Canada and the United States expanded westward, even though the United States underwent a destructive Civil War in the first half of the 1860s. Canada gained dominion status in 1867 but did not become an independent part of the British Commonwealth for another 64 years. The Spanish-American War of 1898 ended Spain's hold in the New World and led to Cuba's independence in 1902 and to Puerto Rico's becoming associated with the United States. Panama, with US aid, broke from Colombia in 1903 and gave the US permission to build the Panama Canal. Since World War II, many islands of the Caribbean have become independent nations, and in the 1970s others press for freedom. △204, 1216.

PROFILE

Area: 9,400,000sq mi (24,346,000sq km). Largest nation: Canada, 3,851,809sq mi. (9,976,185sq km).
Population (1975 est): 320,787,000
Density: 34per sq mi (14 per sq km). Most populous nation: United States, 215,007,063
Chief cities: New York City; Mexico City; Chicago.
Manufacturing (major products): automobiles, iron and steel, petroleum products, pulp and paper, aircraft, drugs
Agriculture (major products): wheat, corn, oats, cotton, tobacco, cattle, hogs
Minerals (major): iron ore, coal, petroleum, gold, silver, nickel, uranium, copper

North America Nebula (NGC 7,000), bright emission nebula in the constellation Cygnus, situated east of Deneb. Its name derives from its shape, which resembles a map of North America. △118.

Northampton, city in England, on Nene River, 60mi (97km) NW of London; county town of Northamptonshire, site of one of four English round churches. Industries: footwear, leather goods, motor accessories. Pop. 126,608.

Northampton, city in W Massachusetts, on Connecticut River; seat of Hampshire co; home of Pres. Calvin Coolidge; his papers and memorabilia are in Forbes Library; site of Smith College (1871), Northampton Junior College (1896). Industries: cutlery, brushes, optical instruments. Founded 1654; inc. as town 1656, as city 1883. Pop. (1970) 29,664.

North Atlantic Treaty Organization (NATO), Western alliance providing for joint action in an attack against any member. It also promotes joint military aid and economic cooperation during peacetime. The original members were Belgium, Britain, Canada, Denmark, France, Iceland, Italy, Luxembourg, Netherlands, Norway, Portugal, and United States. Greece and Turkey joined in 1952 and West Germany in 1955. Its headquarters are in Brussels. The 1949 organizational treaty, known as the North Atlantic Pact, was signed in Washington, D.C. The policy body of the organization is the North Atlantic Council. Its military committee, from which France withdrew in 1966, is divided into three NATO military commands and a regional planning group that aids in the defense of Canada and the United States. △1342, 1356, 1390.

North Bay, town in SE Ontario, Canada, on Lake Nipissing; seat of Nipissing district; site of Nipissing

College (1967). Industries: mining equipment, lumber, dairy products, tourism. Pop. 49,063.

Northbrook, town in NE Illinois, NW of Evanston. Industries: insurance, truck bodies, oil burners. Settled 1836; inc. as Shermerville 1901, as Northbrook 1923. Pop. (1970) 27,297.

North Canadian, river in S United States; rises in plateau of NE New Mexico; flows E through Texas and Oklahoma to the Canadian River, near Eufaula, Okla. Length: 760mi (1,224km).

North Carolina, state in the E United States, on the Atlantic Ocean about midway on the E coastline.

Land and Economy. Along the coast stretches a chain of islands enclosing several large sounds. Beyond the broad coastal plain is the Piedmont plateau, a rolling, fertile region. In the extreme W are the Blue Ridge and Great Smoky Mts, some of which rise to over 6,000ft (1,830m). Mt Mitchell is the highest peak in the United States E of the Mississippi River. There are many small rivers. A mild climate and productive soil made agriculture the base of the economy through the 19th century, but abundant water power and natural resources encouraged the development of manufacturing. Much of the textile industry was attracted to the state from New England by lower labor costs.

People. The population is largely of English origin, with elements of Scots-Irish and Germans. Most of the early settlers came from other colonies. The state has a low percentage of foreign-born whites. Less than 50% of its population lives in urban areas.

Education. There are about 100 institutions of higher education. The University of North Carolina is one of the oldest state universities. Duke University is outstanding among the private institutions.

History. The first English colony in North America was established on Roanoke Island in 1585, but was abandoned the next year. Settlers began moving into the region from Virginia about 1660. A royal charter was granted to eight proprietors in 1663, and North Carolina became a royal province in 1729. It was the first colony to assert its will for independence from Great Britain, and in the Revolution contributed strongly to the Continental cause. The important battles of Kings Mountain and Guilford Courthouse were fought in North Carolina. The new state developed slowly. Before the Civil War, opinion was divided between Union and Confederacy, and North Carolina was the last state to secede, which it did on May 20, 1861, after hostilities had begun. On Dec. 17, 1903, Wilbur and Orville Wright made the first successful flight in a propelled heavier-than-air plane at Kitty Hawk on the coast. The industrial development of the state was spurred by both world wars; it was early known for its network of good roads.

PROFILE

Admitted to Union: Nov. 21, 1789; 12th of the 13 original states to ratify the US Constitution
US Congressmen: Senate, 2; House of Representatives, 11
Population: 5,082,059 (1970); rank, 12th
Capital: Raleigh, 123,793 (1970)
Chief cities: Charlotte, 241,178; Greensboro, 144,-076; Winston-Salem, 132,913
State legislature: Senate, 50; House of Representatives, 120
Area: 52,586sq mi (136,198sq km); rank, 28th
Elevation: Highest, 6,684ft (2,039m), Mt Mitchell; lowest, sea level
Industries (major products): textiles, tobacco products, furniture, bricks
Agriculture (major products): tobacco, sweet potatoes, peanuts, cotton, corn
Minerals (major): mica, lithium, feldspar
State nicknames: Tar Heel State, Old North State
State motto: Esse Quam Videri (To Be Rather Than to Seem)
State bird: cardinal
State flower: dogwood
State tree: pine

North Chicago, city in NE Illinois, S of Waukegan; scene of sit-down strike at steel plant (1937) that led to Supreme Court ruling (1939) outlawing such strikes. Industries: chemicals, pharmaceuticals, iron, steel, wood products. Inc. 1916. Pop. (1970) 47,275.

Northcliffe, Alfred Charles William Harmsworth, Viscount (1865–1922). British journalist and newspaper publisher, b. Ireland. He founded or revived periodicals and newspapers, such as the *Daily Mail* (1896) and *Daily Mirror* (1903) and gained control of *The Times* of London (1908). Created Viscount Northcliffe (1917), he used his publications to further his political ambitions.

North Dakota, state in the N central United States, bordered on the N by the provinces of Saskatchewan and Manitoba, Canada.

Land and Economy. The land rises from the fertile valley of the Red River on the E boundary; the highest point is in the SW. The Missouri River flows E and S through the center of the state. Garrison Reservoir, formed by a dam on the Missouri, is the largest of several artificial lakes that supply irrigation and power facilities. Devils Lake is the largest natural lake. Agriculture remains the principal sector of the economy, but petroleum has grown in importance since its discovery in the 1950s; petroleum products provide a major source of manufacturing income.

People. The first settlers came from other states, from Canada, and from Europe, chiefly Russia, Germany, Sweden, and the Netherlands. The state's population reached its peak in 1930. About 45% of the people lives in urban areas.

Education. There are 12 institutions of higher education.

History. French explorers visited the region as early as 1738, and in 1797 a British trading post was established in the NE. The United States acquired roughly the W half of the area from France in the Louisiana Purchase of 1803, and the remainder from Great Britain in 1818, when the boundary with Canada was fixed. Dakota Territory was created in March 1861; it was divided into North and South Dakota in 1889, and both were admitted to the Union on the same day. The Missouri River was a major route for pioneers and gold-seekers; after 1873 the railroads helped to expand farming. The International Peace Garden, a 2,200-acre (891-hectare) area that straddles the border with Manitoba, was dedicated in 1932 as a symbol of friendship between the United States and Canada.

PROFILE

Admitted to Union: Nov. 2, 1889, with South Dakota; rank, 39th or 40th
US Congressmen: Senate, 2; House of Representatives, 1
Population: 617,761 (1970); rank, 45th
Capital: Bismarck, 34,703 (1970)
Chief cities: Fargo, 53,365; Grand Forks, 39,008; Bismarck
State legislature: Senate, 51; House of Representatives, 102
Area: 70,665sq mi (183,022sq km); rank, 17th
Elevation: Highest, 3,506ft (1,069m), White Butte; lowest, 750ft (229m), Red River
Industries (major products): petroleum products, processed foods
Agriculture (major products): wheat, barley, flaxseed, rye, oats, cattle
Minerals (major): petroleum, natural gas, lignite coal, clay
State nicknames: Sioux State, Flickertail State
State motto: Liberty and Union, Now and Forever, One and Inseparable
State bird: meadowlark
State flower: wild prairie rose
State tree: American elm

Northern Cook Islands. *See* Cook Islands.

Northern Cross. *See* Cygnus.

Northern Crown. *See* Corona Borealis.

Northern Ireland. *See* **Ireland, Northern.**

Northern Porgy. *See* Scup.

Northern War (1700–21), war victoriously fought by Russia in alliance with Poland against Sweden. Charles II of Sweden forced Poland to capitulate in 1706, then moved against Peter the Great in 1708. Relying on inadequate support from Ivan Mazepa, the Swedish forces were destroyed at the Battle of Poltava on July 8, 1709. The Swedish navy was defeated by Russia in 1714. In 1719, Russian expeditions began invading Sweden until the Treaty of Nystadt was signed in 1721. As a result Russia gained the Baltic provinces, its "window into Europe," and suddenly emerged as a major European power.

North Glenn, residential suburban city in NE central Colorado, outside of Denver. Pop. (1970) 27,937.

North Highlands, town in N central California; residential suburb of Sacramento in Sacramento Valley. Pop. (1970) 31,854.

North Island, island of New Zealand, N of South Island, with which it comprises the principal land areas of New Zealand. The more populous of the two, its chief cities are Wellington (capital of New Zealand), Auckland, Hamilton, and New Plymouth; contains Lake Taupo, several mountain ranges, and fertile coastal areas; many natural bays and harbors. Indus-

Rouen, Normandy

Linville Gorge, North Carolina

Grizzly Creek Falls, North Dakota

North Island, New Zealand

tries: mining, food production and processing, dairying, timber. Area: 44,297sq mi (114,729sq km). Pop. 1,956,411.

North Kingstown, town in S central Rhode Island on Narragansett Bay; scene of Wickford Art Festival and Indian pow wow (annual); site of birthplace of Gilbert Stuart (1755), now a museum; Smith's Castle (1678), a museum with 18th- and 19th-century American furnishings; Old Narragansett Church (1707). Boating and fishing center. Industries: machine tools, fabricated metals, chemicals, plastics, textiles, tourism. Founded 1641 by Roger Williams. inc. as Kings Towne 1674; divided into North and South Kingstown 1723. Pop (1970) 29,793.

North Las Vegas, residential city in SE Nevada; N suburb of Las Vegas; tourist area. Pop. (1970) 36,216.

North Little Rock, industrial city in central Arkansas, across Arkansas River from Little Rock. Industries: chemicals, furniture, railroad shops and stockyard, cotton and soybean products. Settled 1856; inc. 1903. Pop. (1970) 60,040.

North Miami, city in SE Florida, suburb of Miami. Industries: boats, metal products. Inc. 1926. Pop. (1970) 34,767.

North Miami Beach, resort city in SE Florida, 3mi (5km) N of Miami Beach; site of Bal Harbour Shops, an exclusive shopping district. Inc. 1931: Pop. (1970) 30,723.

North Olmsted, city in N Ohio, 13mi (21km) WSW of Cleveland. Main industry is printing. Inc. 1951. Pop. (1970) 34,681.

North Pacific Current, warm, broad, slow, cyclical current in the N Pacific Ocean. It moves in a clockwise motion from the North Equatorial current, turns N by Japan and E in the N Pacific; forms the California current, which flows S to join the North Equatorial current.

North Platte, river in mid-West United States; rises at the confluence of many headstreams in the Park Mts, N Colorado; flows N into central Wyoming, E into Nebraska, where it unites with the South Platte River at North Platte, Nebr., to form the Platte River; used for irrigation and hydroelectricity. Length: 680mi (1,095km).

North Pole, northern end of the earth's axis, 90° latitude, 0° longitude; the Arctic Ocean encompasses the entire area. In 1607, explorer Henry Hudson tried to sail an eastern route across the North Pole; Robert E. Peary, US explorer, was the first person to achieve it (1909).

North Rhine-Westphalia (Nordrhein-Westfalen), state of W West Germany; capital is Düsseldorf; bounded by Belgium and Netherlands (W), Lower Saxony (N and E), Hesse (SE), and Rhineland Palatinate (S); highly industrialized area. State was formed in 1946 by uniting Westphalia (former Prussian prov.), N part of former Prussian Rhine prov., and former state of Lippe. Industries: iron, steel, chemicals, textiles, machinery, oil refining, coal mining. Area: 13,111sq mi (33,957sq km). Pop. 17,167,500.

North Saskatchewan, river in SW and S central Canada; flows E from Rocky Mts into Lake Winnipeg. Length: 760mi (1,124km).

North Sea, arm of the Atlantic Ocean, approx. 600mi (966km) long and 400mi (644km) wide, extending between European continent (S and E) and Great Britain (W). In the S it is connected to English Channel by Strait of Dover. In 1970 oil was discovered under sea floor; Britain is now tapping reserves in its territorial waters. Cod and herring fisheries are very important. Area: 222,000sq mi (574,980sq km).

North Sea Canal (Amsterdam Ship Canal), canal in Netherlands connecting Amsterdam to the North Sea. Built 1865–76, it renewed the importance of Amsterdam as commercial port. Length: 17mi (27km).

North Star. *See* Polaris.

North Tarrytown, town in SE New York, on E bank of Hudson River; site of Philipsburg Manor and Old Dutch Church, both built by Frederick Philipse in late 17th century, and Sleepy Hollow Cemetery, containing the graves of Washington Irving, Andrew Carnegie, William Rockefeller, and Whitelaw Reid; scene of capture of Maj. John André, which led to disclosure of treason of Benedict Arnold. Chief industry is automobile manufacturing. Inc. 1875. Pop. (1970) 8,334.

North Tonawanda, city in W New York, 10mi (16km) E of Niagara Falls. Industries: dies, castings, furniture, plastics, paints, chain hoists. Founded 1802. Inc. as village 1865, as city 1897. Pop. (1970) 36,012.

Northumberland, John Dudley, Duke of (?1502–53), English nobleman. He became lord high admiral (1543) and earl of Warwick (1546). He joined the regency council formed during Edward VI's minority and gained victories against the Scots (1547). Through his scheming with both Catholic and Protestant factions, he deposed the protector, Somerset (1549), and had him executed (1552). Gaining great power he proclaimed his daughter-in-law, Lady Jane Grey, queen, on Edward's death (1553), but Mary I had him executed.

Northumberland, county in N England, bounded by Scotland (N) and North Sea (E); includes Holy Isle and Farne Islands; hilly with Cheviot Hills (N) and Pennines (W); drained by Tyne, Blythe, and Tweed rivers. Chief towns are Newcastle-upon-Tyne (county town), Tynemouth, Berwick-on-Tweed; agricultural region, important for sheep and cattle, with industry centered around lower Tyne. Industries: shipbuilding, coal mining, iron works, chemicals, electrical machinery. Area: 2,018sq mi (5,227sq km). Pop. 794,975.

Northumbria, Kingdom of, Anglo-Saxon kingdom in northern England and Scotland. It was formed by the union of Bernicia and Deira under the Bernician King Aethelfrith (593–616), supreme English kingdom in the 7th century. Christianity was introduced under Edwin (616–32) and the arts flourished. With the invasions of the Danes and the rise of Mercia, Northumbria declined to an earldom after 944.

North Vancouver, town in S British Columbia, Canada, on the Burrard Inlet. Industries: sawmills, shipyards. Pop. 31,863.

North Vietnam. *See* Vietnam.

North West Company, Canadian fur trading company. An unchartered syndicate of eastern fur traders, the company coalesced between 1775 and 1779. In contrast to the Hudson's Bay Co., it sent explorers deep into the wilderness, assuming transportation costs of furs to Montreal along the St Lawrence. Peter Pond (1778) and Alexander Mackenzie (1793) extended its trading domain to the Pacific, establishing friendly relations with the Indians. Fort William (1805) and Astoria (1811) were threatened by the Red River Settlement (1812), leading to the Seven Oaks Massacre and outright battles with the Hudson's Bay Co. The advantages of the Hudson Bay route led to absorption of the North West Company by it in 1821.

North-West Frontier Province, province in NW Pakistan bounded by Afghanistan (N and W), located near Khyber Pass; capital is Peshawar; agricultural area; historically important during time of Alexander the Great; annexed to Pakistan 1947. Area: 41,000sq mi (106,200sq km). Pop. 10,937,000.

Northwest Ordinance (1787), US territorial legislation based on a proposal by Thomas Jefferson. Under the provisions of the ordinance, Congress would appoint a governor, a secretary, and three judges to govern the territory, and when the population numbered 5,000 adult, free males, a bicameral legislature would be added. Three to five states could be made from the territory, with 60,000 free inhabitants required for admission. The new states would be equal with the original states and have the same freedoms of worship, jury trial, and public education. It also banned involuntary servitude except as punishment for crimes. △1274.

Northwest Passage, sea route around northern Canada and Alaska between the Atlantic and Pacific oceans. Its crossing was first attempted by Martin Frobisher in 1576. An unsuccessful attempt by John Franklin (1845) was followed by McClure's crossing, partially by land, in 1854. Roald Amundsen made the first complete crossing (1903–06), across Lancaster Sound. A Royal Canadian Mounted Police schooner crossed in one season (1944), and in 1969 the *John A. Macdonald* was the first commercial vessel to make the journey. The route has never been commercially feasible and requires the use of icebreaking vessels.

Northwest Territories, a territory in N Canada, covering more than one-third of the country. It consists of the mainland N of 60° latitude W of Hudson Bay and of hundreds of islands in the Arctic Archipelago to the N, of which Baffin and Victoria are the largest. The territory extends beyond 80° N latitude. It is divided into three districts—Mackenzie, on the mainland to the NW; Keewatin, the mainland to the NE; and Frank lin, which includes the Arctic islands.

Land and Economy. Much of the vast wildernes area is rolling, or level and poorly drained; there ar hundreds of lakes, of which the most important ar Great Bear and Great Slave in Mackenzie district, an large areas of swamp. The Mackenzie, flowing into th Arctic Ocean, is the principal river. About 15% of th land is forested; beyond the tree line there is virtuall no vegetation of importance. Permafrost—perenn ally frozen ground—underlies most of the territory Fur-bearing animals are hunted by the native peoples Valuable mineral deposits are widespread, but trans portation problems make their exploitation difficult

People. Semi-nomadic Indians are scattered abou the area, and Eskimos live N of the tree line. Togethe they form a large segment of the population. Whit inhabitants are concentrated in and around Yellow knife on Great Slave Lake in S Mackenzie.

Education. Schools are few and dispersed and ca serve only a small part of the population. There are n institutions of higher education.

History. The Hudson's Bay Co., a fur trading enter prise, received from Charles II of England in 1670 charter to much of the huge lands W of Hudson Bay In 1870 the Canadian government bought the land from the company. The boundaries of the territor and of the interior districts were changed severa times before the present limits were defined.

PROFILE

Created territory: 1870
National Parliament Representatives: Senate, C House of Commons, 1
Population: 39,000 (1971)
Capital and chief city: Yellowknife
Territorial legislature: Territorial Council, 15 mem bers
Area: 1,304,903sq mi (3,379,699sq km); more tha one third of Canada
Elevation: Highest: 9,000ft (2,745m), Franklin an Mackenzie mts; lowest, sea level
Economy: furs; mineral resources: uranium, gold, pe troleum, nickel, copper, largely undeveloped
Floral emblem: mountain avens

Northwest Territory, region north of the Ohi River, east of the Mississippi River, and south an west of the Great Lakes. Also known as the Old North west, it became the first US territory in 1783 by th Treaty of Paris. It was organized by the Northwes Ordinance (1787). The states of Indiana, Ohio, Illinois Michigan, Wisconsin, and part of Minnesota wer created from this territory.

Norwalk, city in S California, SE of Los Angeles in Lo Angeles co; site of Cerritos College (1955). Founde 1850; inc. 1957. Pop. (1970) 91,827.

Norwalk, industrial city in SW Connecticut, on Lon Island Sound. Industries: electronics, textiles, appare Settled 1650; inc. 1893. Pop. (1970) 79,113.

Norway, an independent kingdom in Europe. It fjords and islands make it an international tourist a traction. Fishing and agriculture are the economi mainstays.

Land and Economy. Bounded E by Finland, Swe den, and the Soviet Union, Norway's coastline face (S to N) the Skagerrak, the North Sea, the Atlanti Ocean, and the Barents Sea of the Arctic Ocean. land of mountainous terrain and high plateaus, abou 25% of the country is forested and 3% arable, mainl in the high fertile valleys of the highlands and its man lakes. The Gulf Stream moderates the climate, espe cially along the coast; in the interior winters are harsh Average temperature in the spring-summer season i 70°F (20°C). Fishing, forestry, and agriculture com prise the economic base. Norway's merchant fleet i the world's 3rd-largest and is the largest foreign ex change earner. Exports, services, and shipping ac count for 40% of the gross national product. Inflatio is its most difficult economic problem.

People. Norwegians are mainly of Germanic de scent, mixed with the Finns and Lapps. About 25,00 Lapps continue to live in the N, following their trad tional reindeer culture. About 65% of the peopl lives in the S and along the coast. Over 95% belong to the Evangelical Lutheran Church, the state church Education is free through university level and is com pulsory to age 16. Literacy is almost 100%.

Government. Norway is a constitutional monarchy with the king functioning mainly as a figurehead an symbol of national unity, with some executive priv leges. Power is in the hands of the elected parliamen (Storting). Suffrage is universal.

History. The oldest inhabitants date back 8,000 10,000 years and were hunters and fishermen; begin ning in the early Christian era until the 9th centur Norway was divided into many small kingdoms com prised of immigrant Germanic tribes. In 1319, Norwa joined briefly with Denmark and then Sweden. In 1536 it was part of the Danish kingdom. After the 1814 Napoleonic Wars it joined with Sweden until Norwegian independence in 1905, when the Norwegian government asked Denmark's Prince Carl to take the throne. A plebiscite approved the monarch and Carl took the name of Haakon VII. His descendants still sit on the Norwegian throne. Neutral in WWI, Norway joined the Allies in WWII and was occupied by Germany. Its firm resistance to the German puppet, Vidkun Quisling, aided the liberation movement.

PROFILE

Official name: Kingdom of Norway
Area: 125,181sq mi (324,219sq km)
Population: 4,000,000
Density: 32per sq mi (12.3per sq km)
Chief cities: Oslo (capital); Bergen; Trondheim
Government: Constitutional monarchy
Religion: Evangelical Lutheran (state church)
Language: Norwegian
Monetary unit: Krone
Gross national product: $18,400,000,000
Per capita income: $4,735
Industries: paper and pulp, shipbuilding, fish processing, chemicals, metals
Agriculture: forests, fish, oats, rye, potatoes, cattle and dairy products, fruits
Minerals: copper, pyrites, nickel, iron, zinc, lead
Trading partners: Sweden, West Germany, United Kingdom, Denmark, United States

Norway Lobster. △486.

Norwegian, the official language of Norway, spoken by virtually all of the country's 4,000,000 people. The major dialect *bokmål,* spoken mainly in the cities, is very similar to Danish; *nynorsk* ("New Norse"), spoken in the countryside, more closely reflects the language as it was spoken in the Middle Ages.

Norwegian Current, ocean current formed by terminus of North Atlantic current; flows N along Norwegian coast into Barents Sea. The warmth of its waters going through the Norwegian Sea keeps that sea generally ice-free.

Norwegian Elkhound, ancient Nordic hunting dog (hound group) dating from 5000–4000BC and used on elk, lynx, and mountain lion. It has a wedge-shaped head; small, high-set, erect ears; square body; straight, medium-length legs; and high-set, tightly curled tail carried over the back. The dense, smooth, gray coat is short on head, ears, and front legs and longer on neck and under the tail. Average size: 20.5in (52cm) high at shoulder; 55lb (25kg). *See also* Hounds.

Norwich, city in E England; administrative center of Norfolk; ancient manufacturing and market town with cathedral and University of East Anglia. Pop. 121,-688.

Norwich, industrial city in SE Connecticut, in New London co. Industries: textiles, chemicals, paper, leather goods. Settled 1660; inc. 1784. Pop. (1970) 41,739.

Norwich Terrier, small hunting dog (terrier group) introduced in England in 1880 and brought to US after World War I. This rugged dog has a wide head; foxy muzzle; prick or drop ears; short, compact body; short, powerful legs; and medium docked tail. The Norwich's hard and wiry coat is all shades of red, wheaten, or black and tan grizzle. Average size: 10in (25.5cm) high at shoulder; 11–12lb (5–5.5kg). *See also* Terrier.

Norwood, city in SW corner of Ohio, 5mi (8km) NE of Cincinnati; site of the Athenaeum of Ohio (1829). Industries: automobiles, electric motors, printing, machine tools. Settled early 19th century; inc. 1888. Pop. (1970) 30,420.

Nose Cone, Rocket, that portion of a spacecraft that enters the atmosphere first. Nose cones must be designed to withstand head of reentry. Blunt shapes heat up less than narrow ones, since they form a bow shock wave that is detached from the ship and heats the atmosphere instead of the vehicle. Nose cones are often equipped with heat shields to dissipate heat by ablation. *See also* Ablation.

Nostradamus. △822.

Notharctus. △574.

Nothosaurus. △572.

Notochord, a flexible rod that is the primitive backbone present at some point in development in all chordates (a group that includes amphioxus and some not well-known animals as well as all vertebrates), and which distinguishes chordates from invertebrates. In vertebrates (except cyclostomes) the notochord is replaced by the vertebral column. △508.

Notornis, rare, flightless New Zealand bird related to rail and gallinule and once thought extinct. Turkey-sized, it has heavy curved bill, reddish shield on forehead, and bright blue-green plumage. Species *Notornis hochstetteri.*

Notre-Dame-la-Grande. △1082.

Nottingham, Charles Howard, 1st Earl of (1536–1624), English nobleman. Appointed lord high admiral by his cousin Elizabeth I and serving (1585–1619), he commanded the English fleet against the Spanish Armada (1588), led the Cadiz expedition with Essex (1596), and was created earl (1597).

Nottingham, city in N central England, on Trent River; formerly center of ancient Sherwood Forest, traditionally associated with Robin Hood. Industries: textiles, tobacco products, pharmaceuticals, lace, electrical equipment. Pop. 299,758.

Nouakchott (Nonakchott), capital city of Mauritania, W Africa, in SW part of country, approx. 4mi (6km) from the Atlantic Ocean. Originally a small fishing village, it was chosen as the capital of the republic 1957. In 1958 a program was started to build up the city; Nouakchott now has an international airport, is located on a major highway, and is site of modern storage facilities for petroleum, and a desalinization plant (opened 1969, the first in Africa). Industries: trade, handicrafts. Pop. 35,000.

Nouméa, seaport city in SW New Caledonia Island, S Pacific Ocean; capital of the French overseas territory of New Caledonia. A french penal colony 1864–97, it served as an Allied airbase during WWII; seat of South Pacific Commission (1947), est. to insure economic and social stability of the island. Pop. 57,-839.

Nova (plural novae), faint star that undergoes unpredictable increases in brightness by several magnitudes, and then slowly fades back to normal, the variations apparently being due to explosions in the outer regions. These phenomena, which are mainly hot young stars of Population I, are relatively common, and some—the recurrent novae—show comparatively frequent brightness variations. *See also* Variable Star. △114.

Novachord, electrophonic musical instrument, a simple electric organ, played on a single manual keyboard. Tones simulating the organ and other musical instruments are produced by a series of thermionic valves with discs rotating in magnetic fields.

Nova Lisboa, formerly Huambo; town in Angola, SW Africa; site of major railroad maintenance shops. Founded 1912. Pop. 49,832.

Nova Scotia, province in E Canada, one of the Maritime Provinces, on the Atlantic Ocean.

Land and Economy. Nova Scotia is virtually surrounded by salt water; a narrow isthmus links it to the province of New Brunswick on the W. Cape Breton Island, the NE tip of the province, is separated from the mainland by a narrow strait. The land is nearly level or gently rolling. There are many lakes but no rivers of importance. Natural resources of extensive forests and rich fishing grounds have been the traditional base of the economy. Sydney, with its steel mills, and the port city of Halifax are important manufacturing centers. The province has been a leader in Canadian coal production for many years.

People. The French were the first colonizers, but after the mid-18th century came a steady immigration from the British Isles, especially of Scots. The descendants of these immigrants form the bulk of the population, although there remains a sizable proportion of French.

Education. Dalhousie University at Halifax is the largest institution of higher education. Others include Acadia University, St Mary's University, St Francis Xavier University, Mount St Vincent University, and the University of King's College.

History. Nova Scotia's strategic position in the North Atlantic made it a prize in a struggle of empires. The first settlement was by the French at Port Royal in 1605, the first permanent white community in North America N of Florida. Other settlers came to the area, and the French named the land Acadia. In the 17th and 18th centuries until 1758, Nova Scotia was taken and retaken eight times by British and French. With the capture of Louisburg the British consolidated their hold. They deported more than 4,000

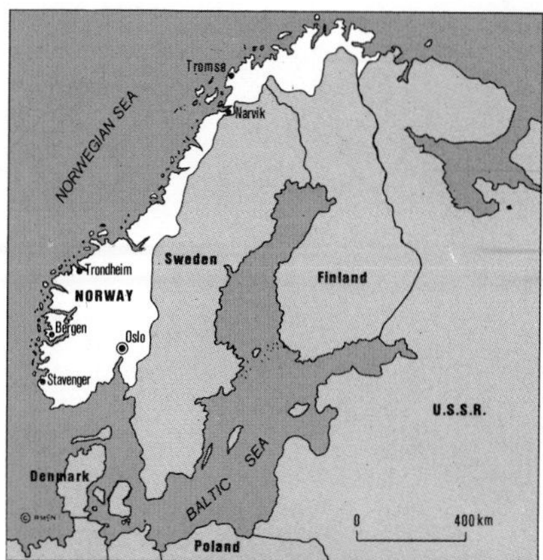
NORWEGIAN SEA
Narvik
Trondheim
NORWAY
Bergen
Oslo
Stavenger
Sweden
Finland
U.S.S.R.
Denmark
BALTIC SEA
Poland
0
400km
Norway

Norway: rural scene

Norwegian elkhound

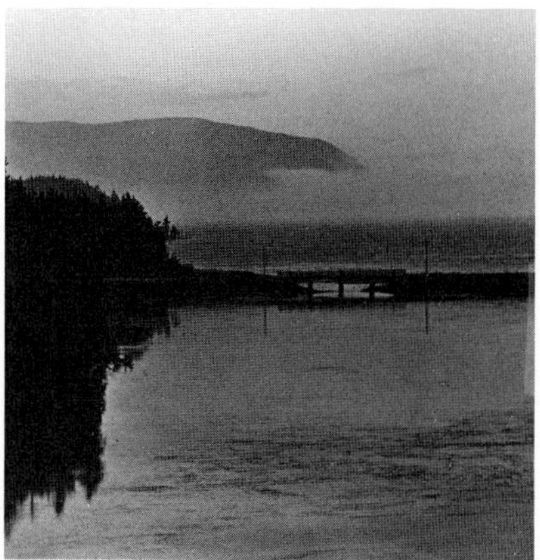
Nova Scotia

Acadians who refused to take a loyalty oath. During and immediately after the American Revolution, the province received thousands of immigrants from New England, many of them British Loyalists who had opposed revolution. Nova Scotia joined New Brunswick, Quebec, and Ontario in 1867 to establish the Dominion of Canada. In both world wars, Halifax was a center of naval operations and a principal port of embarkation for armies and supplies bound for Europe.

PROFILE

Admitted to Confederation: July 1, 1867; one of the four provinces that were joined to form the Dominion of Canada
National Parliament Representatives: Senate, 10; House of Commons, 11
Population: 766,000 (1971); rank, 7th
Capital: Halifax
Chief cities: Halifax; Dartmouth; Sydney
Provincial legislature: Legislative Assembly, 46 members
Area: 21,425sq mi (55,491sq km); rank, 9th
Elevation: Highest, 1,747ft (533m), North Barren; lowest, sea level
Industries (major products): iron and steel, pulp and paper, processed fish
Fisheries: lobster, cod, haddock, herring
Agriculture: dairy products, poultry, cattle, hogs, fruits
Minerals (major): coal, gypsum, salt, clay, sand and gravel, stone
Floral emblem: trailing arbutus

Novato, city in W California, N of San Francisco. Inc. 1960. Pop. (1970) 31,006.

Novaya Zemlya (Novaja Zeml'a), archipelago in the Arctic Ocean off NE coast of Russian SFSR, USSR; consists of two main islands and many smaller islands; N island is ice-covered year around, and the S main island has a sparse population that engages in reindeer herding and trapping. Discovered in 16th century. Area: 35,000sq mi (90,650sq km).

Novel, narrative prose fiction that is longer and more complex than a short story. A novel uses plot and characters imaginatively to create a picture of life in past or present time. The word is derived from the Latin *novus* (meaning "new"), through the Italian *novella* (short tales describing intrigues of everyday life). The novel was established as a literary genre in the 18th century. Daniel Defoe's *Moll Flanders* (1722) is generally considered the earliest example in English.

A novel can be classified as a romance, in which a hero lives through somewhat symbolic adventures (Cervantes's *Don Quixote*); a psychological novel, which develops the inner life of one or more characters (J.D. Salinger's *Catcher in the Rye*); a social novel, which portrays a large segment of society in action (Leo Tolstoy's *War and Peace*, John Steinbeck's *Grapes of Wrath*). *See also* Anti-novel; Gothic Novel; Historical Novel; Psychological Novel; Stream-of-Consciousness Novel. △1188.

Novella, type of prose narrative. The term is used to describe medieval and Renaissance tales, such as those by Boccaccio, which influenced the evolution of the novel. In modern times novella sometimes refers to a work of prose fiction that is longer than a short story but shorter than a novel.

November, eleventh month of the year. Its name comes from the Latin for ninth because it was the ninth month in the old ten-month calendar. The birthstone is the topaz.

Noverre, Jean Georges (1727–1810), French choreographer and ballet reformer. Noted for bringing ballet up to the art form it is today, he eliminated gestures and movements that hindered the grace and action of the dancers. His ideas and ideals were published as *Letters of the Dance and Ballet* (1760). △1194.

Novgorod, city in NW Russian SFSR, USSR, on the Volkhov River, 100mi (161km) SSE of Leningrad; capital of Novgorod oblast. One of Russia's oldest cities, it was originally a Varangian trading town; conquered by Rurik *c.* 862, and governed by Kiev until the 12th century, when it became capital of a vast territory and was called Novgorod the Great. Ruled by Prince Alexander Nevski 1238–63, the city fell to Moscow 1478; its downfall was completed by Ivan the Terrible in 1570 and the Swedes in 1616. During WWII it was held by the Germans (1941–44) and greatly damaged. Called the "museum city" due to its many architectural relics, the 12th-century kremlin contains the Cathedral of St Sophia (1045), the monument erected 1862 in commemoration of the 1,000th anniversary of the founding of Russia, historical museum, and the seat of the oblast government; site of several churches, cathedrals, and monasteries, and museum of revolution and old Russian art. Industries: distilling, meat packing, flour milling, clothing, shoes, lumber. Pop. 128,000. △1176.

Novi Sad, port city in NE Yugoslavia, on Danube River; capital of Vojvodina autonomous region; site of university (1960); held by Hungary (1941–45). Industries: electrochemical equipment, farm machinery, munitions, textiles. Pop. 141,712.

Novocain. *See* Procaine.

Novokuzneck (Novokuznetsk), city in Russian SFSR, USSR, at the head of the Tom River, 190mi (306km) SE of Novosibirsk; in 1932, Novokuzneck combined with Kuznetsk to form the city of Stalinsk. Industries: coal mining, iron, steel, aluminum, chemicals. Settled 1617. Pop. 499,000.

Novosibirsk, industrial city in Russian SFSR, USSR, on the Ob River, 1,750mi (2,818km) E of Moscow; capital of Novosibirsk oblast. It grew quickly, surpassing Omsk as Siberia's leading city *c.* 1930. During WWII it received complete industrial plants moved from war areas of the W USSR; site of an opera house, numerous higher technical institutes, agricultural, medical, and teachers' colleges, the W Siberian branch of the Academy of Sciences (1959), and a regional museum. Industries: diesel trucks, agricultural and mining machinery, hydraulic presses, heavy machine tools, cold-rolled steel, cotton, shipbuilding, lumber, bicycles, plastics, instruments, radios, leather goods. Founded 1896 after construction of Trans-Siberian Railroad. Pop. 1,161,000.

Novotný, Antonín (1904–75), Czechoslovak leader, first secretary of Communist party (1953–68), president (1957–68). Under Novotný's leadership, the country was a docile satellite, and the 1960 constitution solidified its bond to the Soviet system. In 1968, however, the party liberals reversed many oppressive measures and forced Novotný to resign both his positions.

NOW. *See* National Organization for Women.

Noyes, Alfred (1880–1958), English poet. Many of his poems were about the sea. His works include *Drake* (1906–08), *Tales of the Mermaid Tavern* (1912), *A Salute to the Fleet and Other Poems* (1915), and *The Torch Bearers* (1922–30). He is probably best-known for his poem "The Highwayman." Noyes also wrote criticism and fiction.

NRA. *See* National Recovery Administration.

Nu, U (1907–), Burmese political figure. In 1936 he was expelled from the University of Rangoon by the British for his nationalist activities. Early in World War II he was imprisoned by the British and not released until the Japanese takeover. He served as foreign minister in the Japanese-backed government, but at the same time he was organizing anti-Japanese guerrilla forces. He became Burma's first premier on independence (1948), serving until 1956. He returned briefly to power (1957–58) but was forced to resign by the military under Ne Win. He was reelected in 1960, but Ne Win again deposed him in 1962, this time imprisoning him until 1966. In 1969 he went into exile and led an opposition movement against Ne Win.

Nuba, collective name for a group of several unrelated peoples inhabiting the Kordofan region of S Sudan. Most Nuba peoples are agriculturalists and many tribes maintain cultivation terraces on the rugged granite hillsides of the region. Animal husbandry is also practiced. The Nuba peoples are in constant conflict with the Sudanese administration, whose authority many of them refuse to accept. Although Islam has made some converts, the predominant religious rituals are still closely linked to agricultural fertility rites, and in the more remote regions the men go naked and the women wear lip and nose ornaments piercing the skin.

Nubia, ancient state of NE Africa, dating from *c.* 20th century BC to *c.* AD 1400. At height of its power it extended from First Cataract of Nile (Aswan, Egypt) to Khartoum in Sudan between Red Sea and Libyan Desert. Remains have been found of ancient temples, palaces, tombs and towns. From 725–670 BC kings from this area ruled all of Egypt. △972–74.

Nubian Desert, uninhabited region in NE Republic of Sudan; W part of the Sahara Desert, between the Nile River and the Red Sea; consists of a large sandstone plateau, E of the Nile River. Area: approx. 157,000sq mi (406,630sq km).

Nuclear Energy, or **atomic energy,** energy released during a nuclear reaction as a result of the conversion of mass into energy according to Einstein's equation, $E = mc^2$. Nuclear energy is released in two ways: by fission and by fusion. Fission is the process responsible for the atom bomb and for the fission reactors now contributing to energy requirements throughout the world. Fusion provides the energy for the Sun and the stars and for the hydrogen (thermonuclear) bomb. It also offers the prospect of cheap energy once a method has been perfected for controlling fusion reactions.

Both methods of producing nuclear energy depend on the release of the binding energy of the nucleus. When fission occurs the nucleus of a heavy atom disintegrates into two smaller nuclei in which the binding energy per nucleon is higher than in the original nucleus; the difference in total binding energy is carried away by the two or three neutrons released in the fission. In a fusion reaction, two light nuclei combine to form a heavy nucleus, with the release of binding energy. *See also* Binding Energy; Fission, Nuclear; Fusion, Nuclear. △1482, 1638.

Nuclear Family, family consisting of two adults joined by conjugal link and their immediate offspring (joined by conjugal bond) only. *See also* Family; Kinship. △876, 1360.

Nuclear Fission. *See* Fission, Nuclear.

Nuclear Fission Reactor. *See* Fission Reactor.

Nuclear Fuel Breeding. *See* Breeder Reactor; Fission Reactor.

Nuclear Fuel Enrichment, separation of the fissionable isotope uranium-235 from the more abundant uranium-238 isotope. Gaseous uranium hexafluride undergoes diffusion separation utilizing cascades of barriers with microscopically small pores. The difference in mass between the two isotopes is minimal, but sufficient so that the heavier, slower-moving U-238 molecules are concentrated on one side. High-speed centrifugal-force separation methods are also used. *See also* Nuclear Fuels. △1638.

Nuclear Fuels, various chemical and physical forms of uranium used in nuclear reactors. Fluid fuels are required in homogeneous reactors. Heterogeneous reactors use many types of fuel—the pure metal, alloys of uranium, as well as its oxide or carbide. Thermal conductivity must be high, and the fuel must be resistant to radiation damage and easy to fabricate. *See also* Fission Reactor. △1638.

Nuclear Fusion. *See* Fusion, Nuclear.

Nuclear Magnetic Resonance (NMR), absorption of radio waves by certain nuclei in the presence of a strong magnetic field. In this field the nucleus, as a result of its spin, can have slightly different energy values. It can make transitions between these, acquiring the energy by absorbing radiofrequency radiation of the appropriate wavelength. △1568.

Nuclear Physics, the scientific discipline involved with the structure of the atomic nucleus. The constituent particles of the nucleus (smaller than the atom by a factor of about 10,000) attract one another so strongly that nuclear energies are about one million times larger than atomic energies. The principal tool for the explication of nuclear structure is the quantum theory. The fission and fusion of nuclear reactions are characterized by energy far exceeding that of chemical reactions, such as the bonding of atoms into molecules. The increasingly prominent role of nuclear physics in other branches of study has resulted in further emphasis on this specialty. △1482.

Nuclear Power Station. △1486.

Nuclear Radiation. *See* Radiation, Nuclear.

Nuclear Reactor. *See* Fission Reactor. △1638.

Nuclear Submarine. △1684, 1740.

Nuclear Test-Ban Treaty (1963), treaty signed in Moscow by the USSR, Great Britain, and the United States. It committed these three major powers to halt all nuclear tests in the atmosphere, under water, and in outer space and permitted only underground explosions. It was the first treaty pertaining to a major East-West issue that the United States had made with the USSR in almost 10 years.

Nuclear Weapon, or **atomic weapon,** devastating weapon whose enormous explosive force derives rom a nuclear fusion or fission reaction. The first atomic bombs, dropped by the United States on Hiroshima and Nagasaki in August 1945, consisted of two stable subcritical masses of uranium or plutonium. On being brought forcefully together the critical mass is exceeded, initiating an uncontrolled nuclear fission eaction. Huge amounts of energy and harmful radiaion are released: the explosive force can be equivalent to 200,000 tons of TNT. The much more powerul hydrogen bomb (or thermonuclear bomb), first ested in 1952, consists of a fission bomb that on exploding provides a high enough temperature to cause nuclear fusion in a surrounding solid layer, usually lithium deuteride. The explosive power can be that of several million tons (megatons) of TNT. Devastation from such bombs covers a wide area: at 12 mi 19km) from a 15 megaton bomb all flammable material bursts into flame. *See also* Fallout, Atomic; Manhattan Project. △1482, 1746.

Nuclease, an enzyme found in animal organs. It can split nucleic acids into nucleotides and into nucleosides or their components.

Nucleic Acid, complex organic acid forming the genetic material of living cells. There are two types, deoxyribonucleic acids (DNA) and ribonucleic acids RNA). The molecule consists of linked units called nucleotides, each containing a 5-carbon (pentose) sugar (ribose for RNA, deoxyribose for DNA), a purine or pyrimidine base (adenine, guanine, cytosine, thymine, or uracil), and phosphoric acid. Nucleotides may be partially hydrolyzed to form nucleosides (eg, adenosine), consisting of ribose or deoxyribose and a purine or pyrimidine base. △1570, 1574.

Nucleon, collective term for the nuclear constituents, the neutron and proton, the baryon members of a multiplet of two (doublet). As electric charge plays no part in strong interactions, they are considered as manifestations of a single state of matter. *See also* Baryon; Pion. △1484.

Nucleoside, sub-unit of nucleic acids consisting of a sugar and a nitrogenous base. *See also* Nucleic Acid.

Nucleosynthesis, the production of all the different kinds of chemical elements that exist in the universe from one or two simple atomic nuclei. This is believed to have occurred by way of large-scale nuclear reactions during cosmogenesis and to be in progress in the Sun and stars now. Starting with hydrogen and helium repeated nuclear fusion reactions can account for most of the elements up to iron. Elements heavier than iron can be explained by repeated neutron capture reactions.

Nucleotide, unit of nucleic acids; may also occur free in the cell acting as a coenzyme. *See also* Nucleic Acid. △1570, 1574.

Nucleus, Cell, central mass of protoplasm present in all plant or animal cells except bacteria and blue-green algae. △412.

Nudibranch, marine gastropod, usually found on seaweeds. The shell and mantle cavity have been lost and there are fingerlike respiratory organs along the sides of the body. Length: 0.4in (10mm) to several inches. Species include the sea lemon *Archidoris.* △476.

Nuevo Laredo, city in E Mexico, opposite Laredo, Texas, on the Rio Grande River. It was separated from Laredo during Mexican War (1848); site of chief US port of entry, Inter-American Highway, rail terminus, international trade center. Industries: trade (cotton and livestock), tourism. Founded 1755. Pop. 148,-867.

Nuevo León, state in NE Mexico; capital is Monterrey. Occupied by US troops during Mexican War, it became a state 1824. It has a mountainous terrain, with lowland plains and numerous rivers; enjoys one of the highest standards of living in Mexico; site of rail and road crossings. Products: maguey, sugar cane, cotton, grains. Industries: steel, iron, chemicals, textiles, beer, beverages, tourism. Settled late 16th century by Spain. Area: 25,136sq mi (65,102sq km). Pop. 1,653,808.

Nujiang. *See* Salween.

Nukualofa, capital town of independent kingdom of Tonga, in SW Pacific, on N coast of Tongatabu Island; site of royal palace and government buildings. Pop. 15,685.

Null, or **Empty, Set.** △1458.

Nullification, the theory that a state has the authority to overrule a federal law. The doctrine was expressed in the essay "South Carolina Exposition and Protest" (1828), which was written, but not signed, by John C. Calhoun. In 1832, the South Carolina legislature nullified the tariff laws of 1828 and 1832, which they considered oppressive. President Jackson responded by asking for, and receiving from Congress, the power to use military means to implement enforcement of revenue laws (Force Act, 1833). The nullification was rescinded.

Numantia, ancient town in Spain, on the Douro River north of the modern Soria, in Old Castile. The Celtiberian tribespeople of Numantia fiercely resisted Roman conquest from 195 BC until 133 BC against overwhelming odds. The Roman general Scipio Aemilianus finally entered the town after an eight-month blockade; he found the town in smoking ruins. The Numantians had set fire to their buildings and committed mass suicide. There are numerous archaeological sites in the area.

Numa Pompilius, second king of Rome (*c.* 715–673 BC). Although a legendary figure, he was probably based on a historical person. A number of reforms took place during his reign, including the extension of the calendar from 10 to 12 months, and the building of the regia, the seat of government. According to legend, he was aided in his activities by the counsel of the nymph, Egeria, who gave him knowledge.

Numbat. △544.

Number, Complex, number of the form $a + bi$, where a and b are real numbers and i is the imaginary unit, . Every number is a complex number with a real and an imaginary part, either of which may be zero. If b is zero it is a real number *(a)*; if b is not zero it is an imaginary number; if a is zero it is a pure imaginary number (*bi*). △1448.

Number, Irrational, number that cannot be expressed as a ratio of two integers, that is, any real number that is not a rational number. Examples include $\sqrt{2}$ and π (ratio of the circumference to the radius of a circle). △1448.

Number, Natural, or **whole number,** any of the numbers 1,2,3,4. . . . as used in counting, that are the simplest numbers, with no fractional, decimal, or imaginary part, and of which there is a limitless (infinite) number. They are all positive numbers, that is, greater than zero. Negative numbers are all less than zero. *See also* Integer. △1448.

Number, Prime, positive or negative integer, excluding one and zero, that has no factors other than itself or one. Examples are 2, 3, 5, 7, 11, 13, and 17. The integers 4, 6, 8, . . . are not prime numbers since they can be expressed as 2×2, 2×3, $2 \times 2 \times 2$, . . . , that is, as the product of two or more primes.

Number, Rational, number that can be expressed as a ratio of two integers. Thus ⅛, −0.75 (−¾), 3 (3/1), and 572/79 (7.240506 . . .) are rational numbers. △1448.

Number, Real, number that is either a rational or an irrational number. Numbers in the decimal system are real numbers. The position of any point on a scale, however long, can be represented by a real number. Real and imaginary numbers taken together are complex numbers. △1448.

Number, Whole. *See* Number, Natural.

Numbers, biblical book, fourth book of the Pentateuch. It includes two census lists of the Israelites; a history of events during their 40-year march to the Promised Land; the laws of God through Moses; and the announcement of Joshua as Moses' successor.

Number System, system for writing numerals to represent numbers and the rules for addition, subtraction, multiplication, division, etc, in that system. The decimal system, used almost worldwide today, and the binary system, used in computer science, are place-value systems. The relative positions of the digits in a written number indicate the value in terms of a sum of power multiples (squared, cubed, etc) of the number base. The decimal system has a base 10; the binary system, which uses the digits 0 and 1, has a base 2. Thus the decimal number 3718 is equal to $8 \times 1 + 1 \times 10 + 7 \times 100 + 3 \times 1000$ or $8 \times 10^0 + 1 \times 10^1 + 7 \times 10^2 + 3 \times 10^3$. △1448.

Numeral, symbol used alone or in a group to denote a number. The Arabic numerals are the 10 digits from zero to nine. The Roman numerals consist of seven letters or marks. The formation of numbers from nu-

Novaya Zemlya, USSR

Nubia, Egypt

Nuclear energy: National Accelerator Laboratory, Batavia, Illinois

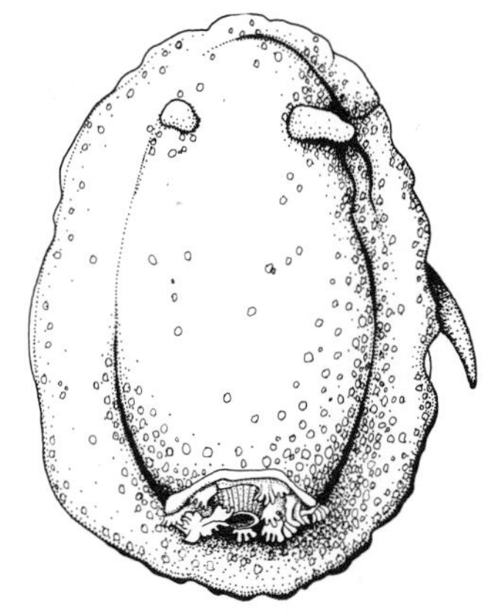

Nudibranch

merals depends on the system used. *See* Number System. △1448.

Numerator. *See* Fraction. △1446.

Numidia, ancient region of NW Africa (including much of modern Algeria) contained by the Carthaginian empire until the Punic Wars. The Numidian king Masinissa allied with Rome and the country prospered independently from 201 BC until the Jugurthine War. Subjugated by Rome, Numidia survived the Vandal invasion (5th century AD) but waned under the Arabs (8th century). △1020.

Numismatics, study or collection of coins, tokens, paper money, medals, and similar objects such as works of art. Besides having monetary value the collection also helps in the study of a culture's history.

Nur-ed-Din or **Nureddin** (1118?–74), ruler of Syria who defeated the armies of the 2nd Crusade before Damascus. After his armies led by his nephew Saladin had conquered Egypt, he was proclaimed Sultan of Syria and Egypt.

Nuremberg (Nürnberg), city in SE West Germany, 93mi (150km) NW of Munich on both sides of Pegnitz River. It became free imperial city in 1219; center of German Renaissance during 15th and 16th centuries; passed to Bavaria 1806; scene of annual congress of Adolf Hitler's National Socialist party; after WWII, site of Allied trials of Nazi war criminals (1945–46); birthplace of Albrecht Dürer, whose oil paintings decorate the walls of the town hall; 13th-century church of St Lorenz contains 60-ft (18-m) white stone tabernacle, sculpted by Adam Kraft (born here 1455); a national museum (1852) is housed in 14th-century Carthusian monastery. Industries: chemicals, textiles, precision instruments. Founded 1050; chartered 1219. Pop. 474,199.

Nuremberg Laws, German laws proclaimed on Sept. 15, 1935, by the National Socialist government of Adolf Hitler. They deprived Jews, including all persons who were one-quarter Jewish, of the rights of citizenship and prohibited marriage of Jews and non-Jews.

Nuremberg Trials (1945–46), war crimes trials of World War II German leaders held at Nuremberg, Germany, under the auspices of an international military tribunal established by Britain, France, the USSR, and the United States. Twenty-four leading National Socialists were tried for crimes against humanity. Twelve were sentenced to death, including Hermann Goering, Joachim von Ribbentrop, and Alfred Rosenberg, and others were imprisoned. Additional trials of Germans, including judges and other civilians, were held by a US military tribunal at Nuremberg.

Nureyev, Rudolf (1938–) Russian ballet dancer. He was a soloist with the Kirov Ballet (1958) until he defected from the USSR in 1961. He has danced with the Grand Ballet du Marquis de Cuevas (Paris), Chicago Opera Ballet, American Ballet Theatre, and is a permanent guest artist with England's Royal Ballet. He has often been a partner to Margot Fonteyn and Doreen Wells. △1368.

Nuristanis. *See* Kafirs.

Nurmi, Paavo Johannes (1897–1973), Finnish athlete. Between 1920 and 1932, he set 20 world track records. At the 1920 Olympics, he won two gold medals (10,000 meter run and cross country event). At the 1924 Olympics, he won three gold medals (1,500 and 5,000 meter runs and cross country), and, at the 1928 Olympics, he won his sixth gold medal (10,000 meter run).

Nursery School. △366.

Nurse Shark, carpet shark found in shallow tropical and subtropical waters of Atlantic and E Pacific, particularly inshore areas. This sluggish fish is yellow to gray-brown above and lighter below. It is recognized by thick, fleshy whiskers near its mouth. Its young are born alive. Length: 8.5ft (2.6m); weight: 330–370 lb (149–167kg). Family Orectolobidae; species *Ginglymostoma cirratum. See also* Chondrichthyes; Sharks.

Nut, dry, one-seeded fruit with a hard woody or stony wall. It develops from a flower that has petals attached above the ovary (inferior ovary). Nuts are often formed in association with modified leaves (bracts); the cup of an acorn is formed from fused bracts. A nut does not open at maturity. Examples are filbert, beech, chestnut, hickory, and walnut. △360.

Nut, in Egyptian mythology, the goddess of the sky, depicted touching the earth with her fingertips and toes while her star-studded belly forms the vault of the sky. She also appears in the form of a cow supported at each of her legs by a god and at her starry underside by Shu, the Egyptian Atlas. Nut serves also as protector of the dead and can be found painted on the lids of sarcophagi. △834.

Nutation, oscillating movement (period 18.6 years) superimposed on the steady precessional movement of the Earth's axis so that the precessional path of each celestial pole on the celestial sphere follows an irregular rather than a true circle. It results from the varying gravitational attraction of the Sun and Moon on the Earth, due to variations in their distances from Earth and in their relative directions.

Nutcracker, widely distributed, crowlike bird of evergreen forests of the Northern Hemisphere that stores nuts in autumn and eats them during winter. The European thick-billed nutcracker *(Nucifraga caryocatactes)* is a typical species. Length: 12in (30cm).

Nuthatch, bird found mainly in the Northern Hemisphere and occasionally in Africa and Australia. It walks in all directions on tree trunks and limbs where it wedges a nut into a crevice, opening it with its sharp bill. It also feeds on insects, spiders, and seeds, often visiting parks and gardens. Many nest in a tree or rock cavities; some erect mud barriers around the nest. Whitish eggs (5–8) are laid. Length: 3.5–7.5in (9–19cm). Family Sittidae.

Nutley, town in NE New Jersey, 6mi (10km) N of Newark; during post-Civil War times it was collecting spot for artists and writers. Industries: pharmaceuticals, woolen goods, paper. Settled 1680; inc. 1902. Pop. (1970) 32,099.

Nutmeg, evergreen tree native to tropical Asia, Africa, and America. Cultivated commercially, it has dark brown leaves, pale yellow flowers, and yellow apricotlike fruits. Among 300 species is *Myristica fragrans,* native to E India. Height: to 60ft (18.3m). First known to Europeans during the 12th century, its seeds yield the spice nutmeg and its seed covering the spice mace. Family Myristicaceae. △356.

Nutrition, the study of all the processes by which whole plants and animals take in and make use of food substances. It involves identifying the kinds and amounts of nutrients necessary for growth and health. Nutrients are generally divided into proteins, carbohydrates, fats, minerals, and vitamins. Human nutrition and diet is a special discipline and its study is undertaken by doctors, physiologists, biochemists, and agriculturalists. △696, 736.

Nyala. *See* Kudu, Nyala, Sitatunga, and Bushbuck.

Nyasa, Lake (Malawi, Lake), lake in SE Africa bounded by Malawi (S and W), Tanzania (N and NE), Mozambique (E); 3rd-largest lake in Africa; numerous rivers flow into it from E; however, the Shire River is its only outlet, flowing S into the Zambezi River. Discovered *c.* 1616 by Caspar Boccaro. Area: 11,430sq mi (29,604sq km). Depth (max.): 2,226ft (679m).

Nyasaland, former territory of S Africa, once part of the Bantu Malawi kingdom. It was a British protectorate from 1891 to 1964, when it achieved independence as Malawi. *See also* Malawi.

Nyerere, Julius Kambarage (1921–), president of Tanzania. He served as a legislator and chief minister in the Tanganyikan territorial government. An African nationalist leader, he became president of an independent Tanganyika in 1962 and in 1964 oversaw the merger of Tanganyika and Zanzibar as Tanzania.

Nyköping, port town in SE Sweden, on Baltic Sea; seat of Södermanland co.; site of Nyköpingshus castle (13th century), St Nicholas Church (13th-18th centuries), city hall (17th century). Industries: textiles, sawmills, furniture. Founded 13th century. Pop. 32,205.

Nylon, any of numerous synthetic materials consisting of polyamides formed into fibers, filaments, bristles, or sheets by extrusion through spinnarets and drawing. Nylon is characterized by elasticity and strength and is used chiefly in yarn, cordage, and molded products. Hard and tough or soft and rubbery nylon products can be made by varying the chemical balance. △1618–1620, 1644.

Nymegan, Treaties of. △1170.

Nymph, Insect. △494–96.

Nystagmus, involuntary eye movement, resulting from an early loss of central vision, dizziness, barbiturate intoxication, or inner ear or brain disease.

O

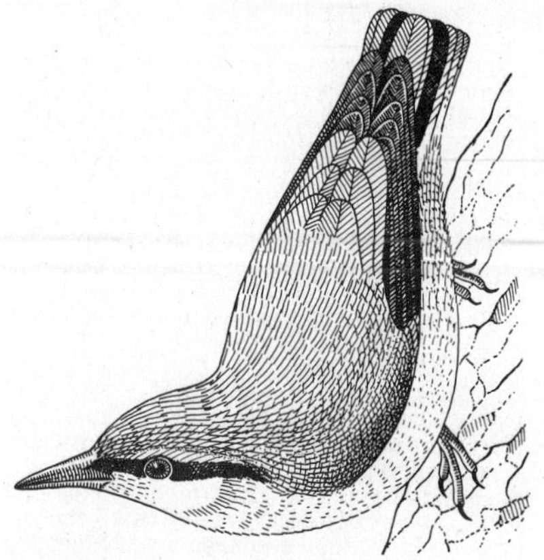
Nuthatch

Oahu, mountainous island in Hawaii, between Molokai and Kauai islands; 3rd-largest and economically most important of the Hawaiian Islands; Honolulu, the state capital, is on the S coast. It is the site of noted extinct volcanoes: Diamond Head, Punchbowl, and Koko Head; important military installations including Pearl Harbor. Industries: tourism, pineapples, sugar cane, fishing, dairy products. Area: 593sq mi (1,536sq km). Pop. (1970) 629,145.

Oak, hardwood trees and shrubs native to northern temperate regions and high elevations in the tropics. Most have a rounded and broadly spreading shape. The foliage turns red, yellow, or brown in the fall. The fruit, acorns, may take 1–2 years to mature and are relished by squirrels. These trees resist storm damage well and so are long-lived. Often too massive for small yards, they are excellent shade trees where space is available. They are also valuable timber trees. Family Fagaceae; genus *Quercus.* △448.

Oakland, city in W California, opposite Golden Gate Bridge; seat of Alameda co; site of San Francisco-Oakland Bay Bridge (1936); also center of the Bay Area Rapid Transit system (1972); site of Mills College (1852), Holy Name College (1868), and California College of Arts and Crafts (1907); home of baseball's Oakland A's. Industries: chemicals, food processing, shipping port, glass works. Founded 1820; inc. 1852. Pop. (1970) 361,561.

Oak Lawn, village in NE Illinois; SW suburb of Chicago. Industries: metal work, machine tools, musical instruments, kitchen cabinets. Inc. 1909. Pop. (1970) 60,305.

Oakley, Annie (1860–1926), US entertainer, b. as Phoebe Anne Oakley Mozee in Patterson Township, Ohio. After her father died when she was 9, she supported her family by shooting small game and became an expert marksman, performing astonishing feats. She married Frank E. Butler, who brought her into show business. She was the star of Buffalo Bill's Wild West Show for 17 years beginning in 1875. Irving Berlin's play *Annie Get Your Gun* and the film of it are based on her life.

Oak Park, city in NE Illinois; W suburb of Chicago; birthplace of Ernest Hemingway; residence of Frank Lloyd Wright, who designed many buildings here. Settled 1833; inc. 1901. Pop. (1970) 62,511.

Oak Park, city in SE Michigan, adjoining Detroit on N. Industries: automobile parts, tools and dies, wire, canvas products. Inc. as village 1927, as city 1945. Pop. (1970) 36,762.

Oak Ridge, city in E Tennessee, 17mi (27km) NW of Knoxville, on Clinch River; site of three Atomic Energy Commission installations: Oak Ridge National Laboratory (est. 1943), research and development; Oak Ridge Gaseous Diffusion Plant, uranium production; Oak Ridge Institute of Nuclear Studies (est. 1948), production of U-235; site was closed to public 1942–49 when it was producing uranium for atomic bomb. Inc. 1959. Pop. (1970) 28,319.

Oakville, city in Ontario, Canada, on Lake Ontario between Toronto and Hamilton. Industries: automobiles, electrical equipment, paint. Pop. 61,365.

Oak Wilt, a usually fatal fungus disease of oak trees whose symptoms include wilting and discoloration of leaves. Like its close relative the Dutch elm disease fungus, the oak wilt fungus kills trees by plugging water-conducting tissues in sapwood.

OAS. *See* Organization of American States.

Oasis. △254, 266.

Oat, cereal plant native to W Europe and introduced worldwide. It grows well even in poor soils. The flower is composed of numerous florets that produce one-seeded fruits. Mainly fed to livestock, oats are consumed by humans as breakfast foods. Family Gramineae; genus *Avena.* △454.

Oates, Joyce Carol (1938–   ), US novelist, short story writer, and poet, b. Lockport, N.Y. Her first book of short stories, *By the North Gate,* appeared in 1963. She has since published extensively. Oates' works are a grim assessment of modern American life; they are chronicles of violence and economic and emotional deprivation. In addition to *Them* (1969), the novel for which she won the 1970 National Book Award, her works include the novels *A Garden of Earthly Delights* (1967) and *The Assassins* (1975) and scores of poems and stories.

Oates, Titus (1649–1705), English conspirator. He and some accomplices invented the Popish Plot (1678), described as a Jesuit plan to assassinate Charles II and put James, duke of York, on the throne. Anti-Catholic hatred swept the land, and many Catholics were murdered. Oates was eventually found guilty of perjury (1685) and imprisoned; pardoned by William III (1689).

Oaxaca, city in S Mexico; capital of Oaxaca state. Taken by Spain 1521, it played a significant role in the Mexican revolution; site of gardens, university (1825), monastery of Santo Domingo, Inter-American Highway. Industries: tourism, pottery, silver filigree, sarapes. Founded 1486 as Aztec Huasyacac. Pop. 116,826.

Ob (Ob'), one of the largest rivers in W Siberia, Russian SFSR, USSR; formed by the union of the Biya and Katun rivers SW of Biysk; flows generally NW to the mouth of the Irtysh River, near Khanty-Mansisk, then N; it separates into many arms and flows to Ob Bay, an inlet of the Kara Sea, 75mi (121km) ENE of Salekhard; chief tributaries are the Tom, Chulym, Ket, Vokh, Kazym, Vasyugan, Intysh, Kanda, and N Sasva. Sometimes called the Oki, this major trade route freezes for 6 months; important source of hydroelectric power. Length: 2,287mi (3,682km).

Obadiah, biblical author and fourth of the 12 minor prophets. He condemned the Edomites, tribe of Esau, for their aid in the Babylonian invasion of Judah.

Obeah, or **obi,** system of religious beliefs and witchcraft found among blacks of the Caribbean and SE United States. In some of its magical practices it bears a strong resemblance to voodoo. Like voodoo, obeah is West African in origin. *See also* Voodoo.

Obelia, colonial branching coelenterate found in marine waters. Similar in appearance to delicate plants, the colony is formed of hydralike polyps. The medusa breaks off from the colony and undergoes sexual reproduction to produce new polyps. Order Hydroida. △468.

Obelisks. △978–80.

Oberammergau, town in Bavaria, S West Germany, 42mi (68km) SSW of Munich; famous for its Passion Play, presented by villagers every 10th year since 1634 in fulfillment of a vow for deliverance from the plague (1633). Industries: tourism, lumber, wood carving. Pop. 4,603.

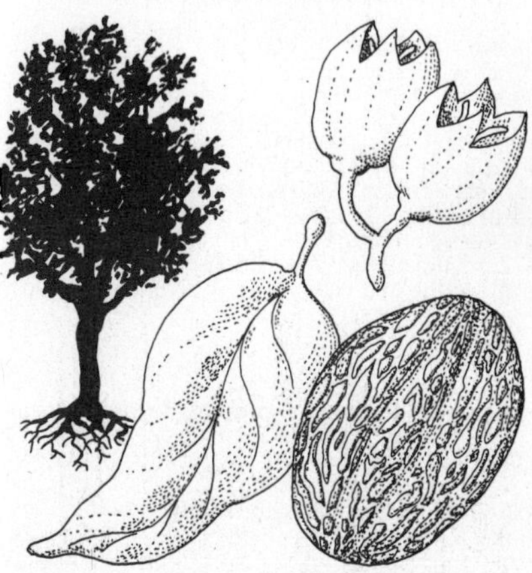
Nutmeg

Annie Oakley

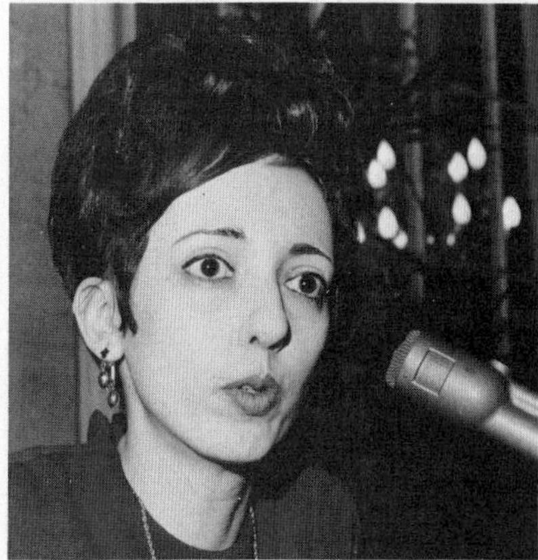
Joyce Carol Oates

Oberon, satellite of Uranus. △88.

Obesity, condition wherein excessive amounts of fat are stored beneath the skin and within organs. Medically, it is defined as an accumulation of body fat sufficient to impair health. People who are overweight by 30% or more risk diseases of the kidney, arteries, and heart and have a shorter life expectancy than those of normal weight. Obesity is usually caused by consumption of more calories than the body can use. Hormone imbalance, glandular defects, and genetic predisposition are also factors, although less common. Treatment is through reduction of caloric intake. △696, 726.

Obi. *See* Obeah.

Oboe, soprano woodwind musical instrument (from the French *hautbois*), ranging 2½ octaves, pitched a fifth above the alto version (English horn). The end-blown conical pipe has a double-reed mouthpiece like the bassoon. The oboe resembles the clarinet. Its mournful A-tone is traditionally sounded to tune symphony and chamber orchestras. The primitive oboe is traced to the Middle East (*c.*1800 BC) △1244.

Obregon. *See* Ciudad Obregon.

Obrenovic Dynasty, Serbian dynasty ruling 1817–42 and 1858–1903, established at the end of Turkish domination. The first in line, Milos, was forced to abdicate in 1839, a fate which befell many of his successors. His son Michael was reinstated and continued his father's policy of achieving complete Serbian liberation through clever diplomatic negotiation. Milan, on the other hand, attempted military conquests, but the line ended when Alexander, the most unpopular king, was assassinated. △1232.

Observatories. △44.

Obsessive-Compulsive Reaction, neurotic personality organization characterized by persistence of unwanted ideas (obsessions) and by performance of ritualistic behaviors (compulsions) that are felt to be unavoidable. Orderliness, intellectualization, and emotional control often characterize this reaction. Great attention to minutiae is associated with inability to make important decisions. △766.

Obsidian, a rare gray to black glassy volcanic rock. High in silica, it is the uncrystallized equivalent of rhyolite and granite. Hardness 5.5; sp gr 2.4. Polishes well and makes attractive, semiprecious stone. △246.

Obstetrics, branch of medicine that deals with pregnancy, labor, childbirth, and the care of the woman immediately following childbirth. It also treats any disorders and abnormalities of pregnancy. △702, 704.

O'Casey, Sean (1884–1964), Irish playwright. His first play, *The Shadow of a Gunman* (1923), made him famous overnight. *Juno and the Paycock* (1924), a tragedy of the Dublin slums, was followed by *The Plough and the Stars* (1926), a tragedy of the Easter Rebellion of 1916, and *The Silver Tassie* (1928), a realistic play about the horrors of the aftermath of war. His later works, in an expressionistic style, differ considerably from the realism of his early plays. In the 1930s and early 1940s he wrote plays calling for a radical transformation of society, such as *Purple Dust* (1940) and *Red Roses for Me* (1942). Late in his career he returned to Irish themes with such plays as *The Bishop's Bonfire* (1955) and *The Drums of Father Ned* (1958). His most important nondramatic work is a six-volume fictionalized autobiography *Mirror in My House* (1956).

Occam, or **Ockham, William of** (*c.*1285–1350), English theologian and philosopher. Writing against the pope and in favor of the Holy Roman emperor, he was excommunicated and expelled from the Franciscan order on charges of heresy. William was a leader of the nominalist school of philosophy. Contributing to the development of formal logic, he employed the principle of economy, known as "Occam's Razor." *See also* Nominalism; Occam's Razor. △858.

Occam's Razor, principle of economy of explanation named for philosopher William of Occam (*c.*1285–1350), also called Law of Parsimony. It holds that explanatory principles should not be needlessly multiplied; the simplest proof is usually the best.

Occasionalism, metaphysical position advocated especially by the 17th-century French philosopher Nicolas Malebranche to repair a deficiency in Cartesianism. Mind and matter only appear to interact or influence each other directly. Actually, God arranges that changes in mind correspond "on the occasion" of changes in matter. *See also* Cartesian; Malebranche, Nicolas.

Occipital Lobe. △666.

Occult. △822.

Occupational Sociology, the subdivision of sociology that studies working roles, which developed out of the older field of industrial sociology. △924.

Occupational Therapy, program to help disabled and handicapped persons develop skills to enable them to lead a productive life and have a vocation or occupation or to be able to seek employment.

Ocean, the continuous body of water that surrounds the continents and fills the Earth's great depressions. There are five main oceans, the Atlantic, Pacific, Indian, Arctic, and Antarctic. They cover 71% of the Earth's surface. The ocean floor is not flat but has a varied topography like land, with vast mountain chains, valleys, and plains. Ocean water consists of 3.5% dissolved minerals, hence its salty taste. It is constantly moving in currents and waves. △170, 222–28.

Oceania, collective name for the islands in central and S Pacific Ocean; includes Micronesia, Melanesia, Polynesia, and Australasia (Australia, New Zealand, and Malay Archipelago). *See also* individual islands. △1260.

Oceanography, ocean-going branch of geochemistry, geophysics, meteorology, biology, fluid mechanics, chemistry, and physics. This science studies oceans, past and present, the shorelines, sediments, rocks, muds, plants, animals, temperatures, tides, winds, currents, formation and erosion of abyssal depths and heights, and the effect of neighboring land masses. Since the Earth is largely ocean, the combined efforts of many specialists are necessary to determine a total picture of the effect of oceans on the Earth as a whole. △222–28, 236–38.

Ocean Perch. *See* Rosefish.

Oceanside, city in S California, 45mi (72km) N of San Diego; site of San Luis Rey Mission (1798); trading center. Industries: rubber products, flowers and bulbs, electronic equipment. Inc. 1888. Pop. (1970) 40,494.

Ocean Sunfish, huge, flat-bodied, marine bony fish found in open seas of temperate and tropical zones. Dark gray above and white below, it has huge dorsal and ventral fins, but no pelvic bones, pelvic fins, or tail. It swims on its side and drifts at surface. Length: to 11ft (3.4m); weight: to 2 tons. There are three species including common *Mola mola.* Family Molidae. *See also* Osteichthyes. △626.

Ocelot, or painted leopard, leopard cat, small, spotted New World cat found in scrub, rocky, and forest areas of S United States, Central and South America. A valuable fur animal, its yellowish or rust coat is marked with elongated dark spots. It feeds on small mammals and reptiles. Length: body—27–35in (69–89cm); tail—13–15in (33–38cm); weight: 20–40lb (9.1–18.1kg). Family Felidae; species *Felis pardalis. See also* Cat. △540.

Ocher, or **Ochre** (1) an earthy red or yellow iron ore frequently impure and used as a pigment; (2) several ferruginous clays; (3) various pigments, yellow to orange, prepared from natural ochers by washing, grinding, or calcining.

Ochoa, Severo (1905–), US biochemist b. Spain. He shared the 1959 Nobel Prize in physiology or medicine with Arthur Kornberg for work on the synthesis of ribonucleic acid (RNA), the hereditary material of some viruses and deoxyribonucleic acid (DNA), the hereditary material of most cells.

Ochs, Adolph (1858–1935), US newspaper publisher, b. Cincinnati, Ohio. He began his newspaper career as a printer's apprentice. In 1878 he bought the *Chattanooga Times.* He later purchased (1896) the *New York Times* and saved it from being driven out of business by the sensationalist press. He introduced the slogan "All the news that's fit to print," which appears on the paper's front page. Under his direction the *New York Times* became one of the most influential US newspapers.

O'Connell, Daniel (1775–1847), Irish political leader, known as the "Liberator." He formed the Catholic Association (1823) and entered the British Parliament (1828) supporting Roman Catholic emancipation, achieved in 1829. Advocating repeal of the union of Ireland with Britain, he formed the Repeal Association (1840). As lord mayor of Dublin (1841), he received support through the *Nation* newspaper. Countermanding a meeting arranged at Clontarf (1843), he was arrested for plotting sedition but subsequently pardoned. He broke with the more militant Young Irelanders (1845) and left Ireland (1847). △1314.

Ocotillo, or candlewood, desert shrub found in SW United States and Mexico. Its spiny stems have scarlet flowers at tips during the rainy season. Height: 6–25ft (1.8–7.6m). Family Fouquieriaceae, species *Fouquieria splendens.*

Octane Number, an indication of the antiknock properties of a liquid motor fuel. It represents the percentage by volume of isoctane in a reference fuel consisting of a mixture of isoctane and normal heptane that matches the knocking properties of the fuel being tested. The higher the number the less likely the possibility of the fuel detonating. △1644.

Octans, or **The Octant,** faint southern constellation in which the south celestial pole is located. Sigma Octantis, the star closest to the pole, is of the fifth magnitude. Brightest star Nu Octantis. △134–36.

Octave, in music, the interval between any given tone and another tone that is exactly twice (or half) the frequency of the first tone. In musical notation, such notes are given the same alphabetical designation; for example, a = 440 vibrations per second, a' = 880 vibrations per second.

October, tenth month of the year. Its name comes from the Latin for eighth because it was the eighth month in the old ten-month calendar. It has 31 days. The birthstone is the opal, beryl, or tourmaline.

October Revolution, Bolshevik overthrow of the Russian government on Oct. 25, 1917. *See* Russian Revolution. △1310.

Octopus, predaceous cephalopod mollusk with no external shell. Its saclike body has eight powerful suckered tentacles. It moves by jet propulsion and crawling and hides in crevices on the shallow sea bottom. Many of the 150 species are small but the common Pacific octopus *(Octopus vulgaris)* can attain a spread of 32ft (10m). *See also* Cephalopod; Mollusk. △480.

Odds, in Probability. △1476.

Ode, poetry form used by Greeks. Of moderate length, it usually expressed praise in a lofty, exalted manner. Choral odes had three parts: the first two had identical meter, the third part, a contrasting one. Pindar and Horace wrote odes. △998.

Odense, city and port in S central Denmark, 85mi (137km) WSW of Copenhagen on canal linking it with Odense Fjord; site of Hans Christian Andersen's home (now a museum), 13th-century cathedral of St Knud, 18th-century palace. Industries: metal goods, dairy products, motor vehicles, shipyards. Founded AD 1000. Pop. 102,698.

Oder (Odra), river in Czechoslovakia, East Germany, and Poland; rises in the mountains of NE Czechoslovakia; flows NW through SW Poland, past Wroclaw to junction with Neisse, from here turning N and forming Poland-East Germany border until it departs from the border a few miles from its mouth on the Oderhaft (bay), at Szczecin, NW Poland. River has been an important water route for N Europe since early times, serving a large area with many navigable tributaries, notably the Neisse and Warta rivers; Szczecin, a port on the river, was internationalized between WWI and WWII; lower course was made border between Poland and East Germany by Potsdam Conference 1945. Length: approx. 565mi (910km).

Oder-Neisse Line, boundary between East Germany and Poland formed by the Oder and Neisse rivers. It was est. in 1945 by agreement between Britain, the United States, and the USSR at the Potsdam Conference. By the agreement former German territory was transferred to Poland. The boundary was recognized by the East German government by a treaty with Poland in 1950, but the West German government did not confirm the Oder-Neisse Line until a 1971 treaty *See also* Potsdam Conference.

Odessa, city in Ukrainian SSR, USSR, 25mi (40km) NE of the mouth of the Dniester River on Odessa Bay capital of the Odessa oblast. It came under the Turks in 1764, and Russian control in 1791; made a naval base and port 1794; named Odessa in 1795; scene of the mutiny aboard the battleship *Potemkin* 1905; oc cupied by Axis forces during WWII. A cultural and educational center, it is site of state university (1865), polytechnical, agricultural, medical, and teachers' colleges, maritime academy, conservatory, base of the Soviet Antarctic whaling fleet and fishing fleet. Industries: agricultural machinery, construction equipment, fertilizer, leather goods, foodstuffs, shipbuilding and repairing, oil refining, linoleum. Founded 14th century. Pop. 892,000.

Odessa, city in W Texas, 56mi (90km) WSW of Big Spring; seat of Ector co; industrial and shipping center; site of Odessa College (1946). Industries: oil, livestock, chemicals, tile, oil-drilling equipment, limestone, salt, carbon black mining. Settled 1886 by Russian and German colonists; inc. 1927. Pop. (1970) 78,380.

Odets, Clifford (1906–63), US playwright. b. Philadelphia. Influenced by Sean O'Casey, Anton Chekhov, and the acting school of Stanislavsky, he helped found the Group Theatre (1931). Among Odets' plays of proletarian protest are *Awake and Sing* (1935), the expressionist one-act *Waiting for Lefty* (1935), and three plays later made into films: *Golden Boy* (1937), *The Big Knife* (1949), and *Country Girl* (1950). △1426.

Odin, one of the principal gods in Norse mythology. He was a war god and he appeared in heroic literature as the protector of heroes. Fallen warriors joined him in Valhalla. He carried a spear, rode an eight-legged horse, Sleipnir, and the wolf and raven were sacred to him. Odin was also associated with poets, musicians, and runes. △838.

Odo. *See* Eudes.

Odoacer, or **Odovacar** (*c.* 435–93), chief of the Germanic Heruli people and conqueror of the West Roman empire. The Heruli were Roman mercenaries until 476 when they declared Odoacer king. He deposed Romulus Augustulus and established his authority over Italy, proving himself a capable ruler. In 488 he was defeated by the Ostrogoth king Theodoric the Great. Odoacer ceded Ravenna and Theodoric invited him to a banquet where he was betrayed and murdered. △1054–56.

Odonata, order of primitive winged insects found worldwide. Those of the suborder Zygoptera (damselfly) have thin bodies with wings held vertically at rest. The long, slender, aquatic nymphs have three leaflike gills on the abdomen. Those of the suborder Anisoptera (dragonfly) have heavy bodies with wings held horizontally at rest. The stout nymphs have gills in the anal end. All prey on insects; none attacks man. Length: 0.75–5in (19–127mm). △496.

Odovacar. *See* Odoacer.

Odyssey, ancient Greek epic, generally ascribed to Homer. Written in 24 books, like its predecessor the *Iliad*, the story begins 10 years after the Trojan War. For seven of those years, Odysseus has been detained by the goddess Calypso. His efforts to return home to his loving family are delayed by visits to the land of forgetfulness and to the underworld, as well as encounters with the one-eyed cyclops, sea monsters, and sirens. When Odysseus finally returns to Ithaca, he discovers that his wife Penelope is being urged to remarry by various noblemen who want her fortune. Odysseus kills them all and is reunited with his family. *See also* Iliad. △988.

OECD. *See* Organization for Economic Cooperation and Development.

Oedipus, in Greek mythology and literature, son of Laius, king of Thebes, and Jocasta. Father of Antigone, Electra, Eteocles, and Polynices by his own mother. The 5th-century BC playwright Sophocles tells how Oedipus was saved from death as an infant and raised in Corinth, how he killed his father, solved the riddle of the Sphinx, and became king of Thebes, where he married Queen Jocasta, his own widowed mother.

Oedipus Complex, in psychoanalytic theory, incestuous fantasy in which a child desires the parent of the opposite sex. Sigmund Freud held that children pass through a stage (from about three to six) in which they develop a lively curiosity about sex. The son desires his mother and wants the father dead. The daughter wants sex with the father and hates her mother. ("Electra Complex" may be used to label the girl's feelings.) Freud believed that many adult neuroses originated in conflicts at the Oedipal stage.

Oersted, Hans Christian (1777–1851), Danish physicist and professor at Copenhagen. He took the first steps in elucidating the relationship between electricity and magnetism, thus founding the science of electromagnetism. The oersted unit of magnetic field strength is named after him. He was also the first scientist to isolate pure metallic aluminum. △1484.

Oersted, unit of magnetic field strength equal to the magnetic field that would cause a unit magnetic pole to experience a force of one dyne in a vacuum. △1534.

Offenbach, Jacques Levy (1819–80), French composer. He composed over 100 operettas, of which *Orpheus in the Underworld* (1858) is the most famous. He turned to serious opera only once with *The Tales of Hoffman* (1880), one of the masterpieces of the French repertory. △1246.

Office of Price Administration (OPA), US agency to control inflation by preventing abuses such as profiteering and hoarding, established (1941) by executive order of Pres. Franklin D. Roosevelt. Under Leon Henderson, the OPA planned wage and price controls in anticipation of an inflated economy during World War II.

Office of Strategic Services (OSS), US World War II agency. It was formed in 1942 to gather and interpret data on the enemy and to give support to anti-Axis resistance groups. It was headed by Maj. Gen. William ("Wild Bill") Donovan. Disbanded in 1945, many of its members later became associated with the Central Intelligence Agency.

Official Art. △1060.

Ogbomosho, city in SW Nigeria, approx. 50mi (81km) NNE of Ibadan; it was a Hausa stronghold against Fulani invasions early 19th century; processing and shipping center for region. Products: tobacco, cattle, fruits. Pop. 386,650.

Ogden, city in N Utah, 33mi (53km) N of Salt Lake City; seat of Weber co; site of two Mormon tabernacles, Hill Air Force Base, Weber State College (1889). Industries: dairy products, food processing, electronic equipment, brewing, tourism. Settled 1846 by Mormons and is oldest continuously settled area in state; inc. 1851. Pop. (1970) 69,478.

Oglethorpe, James Edward (1696–1785), English general and colonist. After military service against Turkey, he returned to England and became interested in social reform, particularly the problems of debtors. Taking a group to North America, he settled in Savannah and founded the colony of Georgia for imprisoned English debtors. It was chartered in 1732. Oglethorpe hoped to use the colony as a buffer between South Carolina and the Spanish possessions in Florida, but Georgia did not develop as he had planned.

Ogotai. △1112.

O'Hara, John (1905–70), US author, b. Pottsville, Pa. Originally a newspaper reporter, he turned to writing fiction. His short stories and novels are realistic narratives. Among his novels are *Appointment in Samarra* (1934); *Butterfield 8* (1935); *Pal Joey* (1940), which was a successful musical comedy; *Ten North Frederick* (1955), for which he won the 1956 National Book Award in fiction; *From the Terrace* (1958); *Ourselves to Know* (1960); and *The Big Laugh* (1962).

O'Higgins, Bernardo (1778–1842), Chilean independence leader, became commander of Chile's anti-royalist forces in 1813. O'Higgins issued Chile's declaration of independence in 1818 and was named supreme director by San Martín. In 1823, General Ramón Freire led an army revolt in southern Chile; O'Higgins was forced to resign and leave the country. △1234.

Ohio, state in the E central United States. Lake Erie marks most of its N boundary.

Land and economy. The land is a rolling plain with many rivers, including the Muskingum, the Scioto, the Miami, and the Maumee. Water transport on Lake Erie and the Ohio River, which forms the S boundary, is of great importance to the economy. Agriculture is profitable in most sections, and industry is widely distributed in cities and towns. Coal is found in the S and E.

People. Ohio was settled originally by pioneers from New England, Pennsylvania, and Virginia. Immigrants from overseas, principally Germans and Irish, flocked to the state in the early 19th century. For most of the 19th century, the state ranked 3d in the nation in population; its decline in rank reflects the growth of

Oboe

Ocelot

Hans Christian Oersted

John O'Hara

other states rather than a loss in Ohio. About 75% of the inhabitants lives in urban areas.

Education. There are more than 100 institutions of higher education, including five state-supported universities.

History. French and English traders operated in the region in the early 18th century. Great Britain acquired it in 1763 at the end of the French and Indian War. It became US soil after the American Revolution, and in 1787 Congress created the Northwest Territory, which included the present states of Ohio, Indiana, and Illinois, and lands to the N. The first settlement in Ohio was at Marietta in 1788. Ohio was separated from the Northwest Territory in 1800 and was accepted as a state three years later. Development of railroads and canals enhanced Ohio's geographical position midway between the Atlantic seaboard and the Mississippi Valley, and the state exerted great influence in national affairs. Seven presidents of the United States after 1868 were born in Ohio.

PROFILE

Admitted to Union: March 1, 1803; rank, 17th
US Congressmen: Senate, 2; House of Representatives, 23
Population: 10,652,017 (1970); rank, 6th
Capital: Columbus, 540,025 (1970)
Chief cities: Cleveland, 750,879; Columbus; Cincinnati, 452,524
State legislature: Senate, 33; House of Representatives, 99
Area: 41,222sq mi (106,765sq km); rank, 35th
Elevation: Highest, 1,550ft (473m), Campbell Hill; lowest, 433ft (132m), Ohio River
Industries (major products): automobiles, parts and accessories; tires, aircraft, boats, iron and steel, industrial machinery, household appliances, processed foods
Agriculture (major products): cattle, dairy products, hogs, sheep, corn, grapes, soybeans
Minerals (major): bituminous coal, lime, clay, salt, sand and gravel
State nickname: Buckeye State
State motto: With God, All Things Are Possible
State bird: cardinal
State flower: red carnation
State tree: Ohio buckeye

Ohio, navigable river in central United States; rises in Pittsburgh, Pennsylvania at the confluence of the Allegheny and Monongahela rivers; flows W and SW into the Mississippi River in S Illinois. Ohio River basin is populous and heavily industrialized; it has been subject to flood control and anti-pollution measures; used for hydroelectricity and industrial traffic. Discovered 1669 by LaSalle. Length: 981mi (1,579km).

Ohm, Georg Simon (1787–1854), German physicist. He was appointed professor at Munich in honor of his discovery of the law (Ohm's law) relating electrical current intensity, electromotive force, and circuit resistance. His name is also honored in the unit of electrical resistance. △1532.

Ohm, unit of electrical resistance equal to the resistance between two points on a conductor when a constant potential difference of one volt between the points produces a current of one ampere. △1532, 1544.

Ohm's Law, statement that the amount of steady current through a material is proportional to the voltage across the material, propounded by the German physicist Georg Simon Ohm. Ohm's Law is expressed mathematically as $V/I=R$ (V is the unit of volts; I is the amperes; R is the resistance, measured in units called ohms). △1532.

Oil. *See* Petroleum. △284, 1642.

Oilbird, or guacharo, South American bird equipped with batlike radar that can fly in total darkness. It is maroon-brown with white spots and has stiff bristles around its mouth, a yellowish, hooked bill, and weak legs. Groups feed on palm tree nuts and fruit at night, retreating deep into caves at dawn where they incessantly squeak and squawk. They glue organic matter to form a flattish, pedestal nest high on a ledge for whitish, brown-smudged eggs (2). Odorless oil, obtained from fat of the nestlings, supplied American Indians with oil for lighting and cooking. Length: 13in (33cm); wingspan: 3ft (92cm). Species *Steatornis caripensis.*

Oil-Drop Experiment, experimental method used (1916 onward) by R. A. Millikan to measure the electron's charge by subjecting charged oil drops to a variable electric field.

Oil Painting, painting medium using an oil base for paint pigments. Sometimes a diluting material is used with oil paints, and often a protective varnish is used to cover the paint on the canvas. Jan van Eyck was among the first painters to use an oil base containing resins. Other artists used oils as glazes to make their paintings appear yellow. With the 16th century came the use of canvas as a primary painting surface, and Venetians such as Titian and Tintoretto used oils successfully with little underpainting. In the 17th century Rubens used oils in the Flemish tradition, placing transparent colors over a white priming. Rembrandt used a dark ground and thin paint to make his shadows and heavier paint to make his light portions. Franz Hals and Velazquez also experimented with the use of oils. English painting between 1780 and 1850 has a dark appearance, due to the pigment bitumen. During the 19th century, the traditional use of layers of glazes over a ground was replaced by direct painting. Many 19th-century schools, such as Impressionism and Pointillism, developed different techniques of oil painting, and this experimentation continues today. △1136.

Oils, any of numerous plant, animal, mineral, or synthetic substances, usually liquid and greasy to the touch and soluble in organic solvents such as ether but not in water. When combustible, like petroleum, they are used as fuels. Many are used as lubricants and some are important foods. Fats and waxes are similar but solid or semisolid at standard temperatures. Essential oils are odiferous, volatile materials produced by various plant species. △362, 1504.

Ojibwa, or **Ojibway,** a variant of the name of the Chippewa tribe. It is more commonly used to refer to this Algonquian-speaking tribe in Canada.

Oka, either of two rivers in central Russian SFSR, USSR. One rises in N part of Kursk oblast; flows N and NE to the Volga River at Gorki; navigable for most of its length. Main tributaries are the Klyazma, Moksha, and Moskva; important for lumber and grain trade. Length: 919mi (1,480km). The other rises in the Sayan Mts, flows N to the Angara River. Length: 530mi (853km).

Okapi, even-toed, hoofed ruminant of African equatorial rain forests. It is purplish colored with striped legs and a tongue so long it reaches to the eyes for cleaning. Males have small, hair-covered horns. Although relatively common, it was unknown to science until 1900. Height: to 8ft (244cm) at shoulder. Family Giraffidae; species *Okapia johnstoni.* △598.

Okayama, city in SW Honshu, Japan, approx. 90mi (145km) W of Osaka; capital of Okayama prefecture; trade center for agricultural region; site of university (1949), 18th-century park and feudal castle. Products: rice, fruits. Industries: agricultural machinery, rubber, textiles. Pop. 375,106.

Okeechobee, lake in S central Florida, N of the Everglades; 3rd-largest freshwater lake in United States. Fed by Kissimmee River and drained by Caloosahatchee River; subject of flood control measures after destructive 1926 hurricane; part of Okeechobee (Cross-Florida) Waterway System. Area: 700sq mi (1,813sq km).

O'Keeffe, Georgia (1887–), US painter, b. Sun Prairie, Wis. Her microscopic paintings of flowers brought her popular attention. Her early works were stylized and associated with nonrepresentation ("Abstraction," 1926). Her later works, often involving a series of studies of particular objects, include "Black Iris, Lake George Barns" (1926) and "Stables" (1932). △1416.

Okefenokee Swamp, swampland in SE Georgia and NE Florida; drained by the Suwanee and St Mary's rivers; major part of the Okefenokee Wildlife Refuge (est. 1937). Area: 600sq mi (1,554sq km).

Okhotsk, Sea of (Ochotskoje More), NW arm of Pacific Ocean W of Kamčatka Peninsula and Kuril Islands; connected with Sea of Japan by Tatar and La Pérouse straits, and with Pacific Ocean by passages through Kuril Islands; icebound from November to June. Main ports are Magadan and Korsakov in Soviet Union; waters off W Kamčatka Peninsula are source of fish and crabs. Area: 590,000sq mi (1,528,100sq km).

Okinawa, largest member of the Okinawa Islands, Japan, in the Ryuku Islands chain, SSW of mainland Japan, in W Pacific Ocean. A volcanic-coral formation, densely vegetated, it was taken by US forces in WWII after a campaign lasting March-June 1945; it provided the United States with an air base close to mainland Japan; it was returned to Japan 1971. Area: 454sq mi (1,176sq km). Pop. 812,339.

Oklahoma, state in the S central United States in the Great Plains region.

Land and economy. From high plains in the NW, the land slopes to the SE, broken by hills and low mountains. Much of the state is grassland, with some forests in the E. The Arkansas River flows E through the center of the state; the Red River marks most of the S boundary. There are no large natural lakes, but many reservoirs have been created by dams. Oklahoma's grazing land and resources of petroleum and natural gas are widely distributed in the state. Manufacturing is largely involved with processing the products of natural resources.

People. White settlement of the region, which did not come until the 19th century, was principally by immigrants from other states. Oklahoma has one of the largest Indian populations in the United States. There are no reservations as in other states; the Indians mingle with other residents. About 68% of the total population resides in urban areas.

Education. There are about 40 institutions of higher education.

History. Most of the area was acquired by the United States from France in the Louisiana Purchase of 1803. It was successively part of several new larger territories. In 1834, Indian Territory was created as a home for the "Five Civilized Tribes" of Indians—Cherokees, Chickasaws, Creeks, Choctaws, and Seminoles —who had been moved by the federal government from states to the E. Part of the land that had been withdrawn from white settlement was opened in 1889 and was organized in 1890 as the Territory of Oklahoma. This was merged with Indian Territory to become one state.

PROFILE

Admitted to Union: Nov. 16, 1907; rank, 46th
US Congressmen: Senate, 2; House of Representatives, 6
Population: 2,559,253 (1970); rank, 27th
Capital: Oklahoma City, 368,856 (1970)
Chief cities: Oklahoma City; Tulsa, 330,350; Lawton, 74,470; Norman, 52,117
State legislature: Senate, 48; House of Representatives, 101
Area: 69,919sq mi (181,090sq km); rank, 18th
Elevation: Highest, 4,973ft (1,517m), Black Mesa; lowest, 287ft (88m), Little River
Industries (major products): petroleum products, machinery (construction and oil equipment); processed foods
Agriculture (major products): cattle, wheat, corn, sorghum, peanuts
Minerals (major): petroleum, natural gas, helium, gypsum, coal, zinc
State nickname: Sooner State
State motto: Labor Omnia Vincit (Labor Conquers All Things)
State bird: scissortailed flycatcher
State flower: mistletoe
State tree: redbud

Oklahoma City, largest city and capital of Oklahoma, in central Oklahoma, 88mi (142km) SW of Tulsa on North Canadian River; seat of Oklahoma co. Settled during the land rush, it was opened to homesteaders 1889; made state capital 1910; prospered with discovery of rich oil deposit (1928). It is site of Oklahoma City University (1911), Southwestern College (1946), Oklahoma Christian College (1950), National Cowboy Hall of Fame, Tinker Air Force Base. Industries: oil and oil refining, stockyards, meat packing, grains, cotton processing, steel products, aircraft. Inc. 1890. Pop. (1970) 368,856.

Okra, or gumbo, annual plant native to tropical regions of the Old World. It has yellow flowers with red centers. The sticky, green fruit pods are eaten as a vegetable. Height: 2–6ft (0.6–1.8m). Family Malvaceae; species *Hibiscus esculentus.*

Olaf V (1903–), king of Norway (1957–). He succeeded his father, Haakon VII. Olaf took part in the struggle for liberation during the German occupation in World War II, assuming supreme command of Norwegian forces in 1944.

Olbers, Heinrich Wilhelm Matthäus (1758–1840), German astronomer and physician known for his discovery of the asteroids Pallas (1802) and Vesta (1807), and five comets. He devised a new method of calculating the comets' orbits. Olbers also proposed his famous paradox: if stars are infinite in number and evenly distributed in space, the sky should be solidly bright with no darkness on the Earth. His explanation that interstellar dust obscures the light, was discarded in the 1970s in favor of the theory that expansion of the universe dims the light from distant objects. △1466.

Oldenburg, Claes (1929–), US painter and sculp

tor. One of the first abstract expressionists, he is noted for his wood, plastic, and plaster sculptures of household items, often grossly oversized. They became a standard pop art form. His works include *Dual Hamburger* (1962) and *Giant Light Switches* (1964).

Oldenburg, city in NW West Germany, on Hunte River, 80mi (129km) NW of Bremen; seat of counts of Oldenburg (*c.* 12th century–1667); annexed to Denmark 1667; residence of dukes of Oldenburg 1777–1918; site of two grand-ducal palaces (17th–18th century). Industries: tobacco products, linoleum, knit goods, musical instruments. Inc. 1345. Pop. 131,191.

Oldenburg Dynasty, dynasty that ruled in Denmark (1448–1863) and Norway (1450–1814). After the death of king Christopher III of Denmark, Norway, and Sweden, Denmark and Norway elected Christian, count of Oldenburg, as their monarch in 1450. Fourteen kings, alternately named Christian and Frederick, succeeded Christian I. Following the death of Frederick VII (1863), rule passed to the Glücksburg branch of the family (Christian IX).

Old English Sheepdog, drovers' dog (working group) bred in western England early in the 19th century. It has a square head and long, square jaws; medium-sized ears carried flat to the head; short, compact body; medium long, sturdy legs; and docked tail. The shaggy coat is hard-textured and profuse; colors are gray, grizzle, blue—all with or without white. Average size: 21–25in (53.5–63.5cm) high at shoulder; 55–65lb (25–29.5kg). *See* Working Dog.

Oldfield, Barney (1877–1946), US automobile racer, b. Berner Eli Oldfield in Waseon, Ohio. He was the first man to drive 60mph (96.6kph) on a circular track. In 1903, he was a winner of the US Automobile Club championship.

Oldham, town in NW England, 6mi (10km) NE of Manchester. Industries: cotton spinning, textile machinery, electrical equipment. Pop. 105,705.

Old Norse Literature, literature of the Scandinavian Norsemen from the 9th–12th centuries. It is mainly mythological poetry and sagas. The work was set down in stone and wood, but survived orally and was recorded in eddic and skaldic Icelandic verse.

Old Red Sandstone, a geologic term for freshwater deposits of Devonian age found in Great Britain, especially Scotland. The continental deposits embrace nearly the whole extent of the Devonian and are divided into Lower, Middle, and Upper portions. These strata are noted for their fish fossils among which are jawless fishes (ostracoderms), the first jawed fishes (placoderms), and by the Middle "Old Red," the first true bony fishes (osteichthyes) appear in abundance and variety. Deposits of equivalent age are found in Canada, Greenland, United States, Central Asia, Australia, and Antarctica.

Old Stone Age. *See* Paleolithic Age.

Old Testament, first portion of the Christian Bible or the Hebrew Bible. The number, order, and names of the books vary between Jews and Christians and between Catholics and Protestants. The earliest books of the Old Testament were first collected from older sources around 1000 BC. The Hebrew text, called the Masora, was adopted *c.* AD 100. Christian texts are based on a 3rd-century BC Greek text, the Septuagint. The books include the Pentateuch: Genesis, Exodus, Leviticus, Numbers, Deuteronomy; the prophets, including Joshua, Kings, Isaiah, Jeremiah, Ezekiel; and Hagiographa, including Psalms, Proverbs, Job, Song of Songs, Ruth, Lamentations, Esther, Daniel, Chronicles. *See also* individual books.

Olduvai Gorge, site in northern Tanzania famous for its Pleistocene fossil remains, particularly the sequence of Paleolithic cultures revealed there by the Leakey family. The site provides some of the earliest and most controversial evidence for the development of Australopithecines into *Homo erectus. See also* Australopithecus. △648.

Oleander, Eurasian evergreen shrubs with poisonous sap and loose clusters of fragrant red, pink, or white flowers, including *Nerium oleander*—height: to 20ft (6.1m); and sweet-scented oleander *(N. indicum)*—height: to 8ft (2.4m). Family Apocynaceae.

Oleaster, a small, deciduous tree *(Elaeagnus augustifolia)* of the family Elaeagnaceae, native to Eurasia. To 20ft (6m) high, with spines on branches. Narrow leaves are light green with hairy, silver undersides; silver-scaled flowers are small and fragrant. The yellow, olive-shaped fruit is edible. Commonly grown as an ornamental hedge.

Olfaction. *See* Smell.

Olfactory Bulb. △680.

Olibanum. *See* Frankincense.

Oligarchy, system of government in which power is concentrated in the hands of a privileged minority, which rules without popular support or any external check on their authority. △898, 904.

Oligocene Epoch. *See* Tertiary Period.

Oligopoly, a situation of imperfect competition, which exists in an industry that contains few firms producing similar products that are usually differentiated by either brand or type. The oligopolistic industry also has significant barriers to entry, either in terms of cost of entry or name recognition. In the automobile industry, for example, the cost of entry by a new firm is almost prohibitive and name recognition is extremely important. △938.

Olive, family (Oleaceae) of trees, shrubs, and vines found in warm regions. Main characteristics are one-seeded fruits and bad smelling wood. The 29 genera and 600 species include ash, lilac, ironwood, and marblewood. The common olive, *Olea europaea,* is native to the Mediterranean and cultivated in other warm regions. Its leathery leaves are lance-shaped; the trunk is gnarled and twisted; 30ft (9m) tall. It may live for 1,000 or more years. △360.

Olive Branch Petition (1775), final attempt at reconciliation with Britain by the Second Continental Congress. Written by John Dickinson, it was adopted on July 5, but ignored by King George.

Olive Oil, yellowish liquid oil, containing olein and palmitin, obtained by expressing olives. It is used for cooking, as a salad oil, in soap manufacture, and in medicine. Properties: sp gr 0.910–0.918. △1570.

Oliver, King (1885–1938), US jazz cornetist, composer, and pioneer jazz bandleader. △1366.

Olives, Mount of, historic ridge in W Jordan, separated from Jerusalem (E) by Kidron stream. The Mt of Olives and its four surrounding hills are associated with the preachings of Christ, his Ascension, David's flight from the city, and Zechariah's prophecy; the Garden of Gethsemane is on its W slope; site of many churches and part of Hebrew University (1925).

Olivier, Laurence, Baron Olivier of Brighton (1907–), English actor, producer, and director. He is often referred to as the greatest actor of the 20th century. His first stage appearance was at Stratford-on-Avon in 1922, and he worked with the Old Vic Company from 1937. He entered films after 1930, appearing in *Wuthering Heights* (1939), *Rebecca* (1940), *Othello* (1965), and *Three Sisters* (1970). His work in *Hamlet* (1948) won him an Academy Award. In 1962 he was appointed director of the National Theatre of England.

Olivine, a group of independent tetrahedral silicates $[(Mg,Fe)_2SiO_4]$. The group includes fosterite, tephorite, monticellite, fayalite, and peridote (gem quality). Orthorhombic system crystals, usually granular masses. Green, brown, gray; glassy and brittle. Hardness 6.5–7; sp gr 3.3. △244.

Olm. △518.

Olmec, one of the earliest known cultural periods of prehistoric New World chronology, covering about 1500–500 BC. The people of the Olmec culture produced some of the most remarkable aesthetic works in Mexican art. Their homeland seems to have been central Mexico, from the Pacific coast of Guerrero to Veracruz, but evidences of their culture have been found as far south as central Guatemala. △970.

Olmstead v. United States (1928), US Supreme Court decision declaring that Fourth Amendment protection against illegal searches did not extend to wiretapping phone conversations because there was no physical invasion involved. The Communications Act (1934) and the court's later decision in *Katz v. United States* effectively overruled the Olmstead doctrine. *See also* Katz v. United States (1967).

Olmsted, Frederick Law (1822–1903), US landscape artist, b. Hartford, Conn. He designed Central Park in New York City (1857–61) and the Capitol grounds in Washington, D.C. (1844–92), among other projects. He helped acquire the Yosemite Valley for a national park, serving as commissioner of Yosemite (1863–65). He also laid out the grounds at

Great Serpent Mound, Ohio

Oilbird

Oklahoma: buffalo ranchers

Old English sheepdog

the World's Fair in Chicago (1893) and worked on Biltmore, the Vanderbilt estate.

Olympia, area in ancient S Greece, near Alpheus River; center of worship of Zeus; scene of the Olympic Games (est. 776 BC), which were held in his honor; the temple of Zeus housed the elaborately adorned statue of Zeus by Phidias, one of the seven Wonders of the World; archeological excavations have unearthed great temples, a stadium, and celebrated statue of Hermes of Praxiteles.

Olympia, capital city and port of entry in SW Washington, on S tip of Puget Sound in Budd Inlet; seat of Thurston co. Settled *c.* 1845 as Smithfield by Edmund Sylvester and Levi Lathrop Smith, it was made first port of entry on Puget Sound by Congress 1851; name changed to Olympia, it was made capital of Washington Territory 1853; development was spurred with coming of railroad 1880s; during WWI and WWII its port was expanded. Olympia is site of capitol (1893), St Martin's College (1895), annual salmon run from Budd Inlet to Capitol Lake. Exports: forest and agricultural products. Industries: food canning, beer, oysters, lumber. Inc. 1859. Pop. (1970) 23,111.

Olympic Games, an athletic competition open to all nations, scheduled every four years, includes a winter and a summer meeting. The modern summer games began in Athens, Greece, in 1896. The winter games began in 1924 at Chamonix, France. The games were canceled during World War I (1916) and World War II (1940, 1944).

Summer events include archery, basketball, boxing, canoeing, cycling, diving, equestrian sports, fencing, field hockey, handball, judo, gymnastics, polo, rowing, soccer, shooting, swimming, track and field (includes decathlon and modern pentathlon), volleyball, water polo, weight lifting, wrestling, and yachting. Winter events include biathlon, bobsledding, ice hockey, luge, skating, and skiing. Additionally, the host country is allowed to name a sport of its choice. Although contestants represent countries, the events are officially won by individuals. A gold medal is awarded for first place, silver for second place, and bronze for the third place. In certain events, the competition is on a team basis. The winning country (unofficially) is the one to accumulate the most medals. Women first competed in 1912.

History. The Olympic Games began in 776 BC in Greece in honor of Olympian Zeus. They were held at Olympia once every four years until they were discontinued by Emperor Theodosius I of Rome at the end of the 4th century AD. Women were not allowed to compete or even watch the games. As a result, they formed their own four-year games (called Heraea) from around the 6th century BC until the 4th century when Greece was conquered by Rome. Although the modern Olympic Games were aimed at emphasizing individual excellence and the spirit of international goodwill, they often have been political in nature. In 1936, Adolf Hitler, who was hosting the games, refused to congratulate Jesse Owens, a black man, after he had won four gold medals. In 1972 the games in Munich were marred by the killing of 11 Israeli athletes by Arab terrorists, and the 1976 Montreal games suffered a boycott by African nations as well as the withdrawal of Taiwan. △996, 1408.

Olympic National Park, park in NW Washington. It is a mountain wilderness containing the finest remnant of Pacific Northwest rain forest. It features active glaciers and rare Roosevelt elk. The park extends to the seashore. Area: 896,600acres (362,880hectares). Est. 1938.

Olympus, Mount, highest mountain peak in Olympus Mts, N Greece. As the highest point in Greece, its summit is covered with clouds, and it was considered in ancient Greek mythology to be the home of the gods, closed to mortal eyes. Height: 9,570ft (2,920m).

Olympus Mons. △70.

Omaha, city and port of entry in E Nebraska, on Missouri River; seat of Douglas co; largest city in Nebraska. Area was ceded to US government 1854; it developed rapidly as a supply depot for westward travelers, and later as an industrial center (1869); capital of Nebraska Territory 1855–67. A leading livestock market and meat processing center, it is site of Creighton University (1878), University of Nebraska at Omaha (1908), College of St Mary (1923), Offutt Air Force Base, Fort Omaha (1868). Industries: packing plants, oil refining, food processing, farm machinery, fertilizers, computer components, telephone and railroad equipment, airplanes, chemicals. Inc. 1857. Pop. (1970) 346,929.

Omaha, a Siouan-speaking tribe of North American Indians that inhabited NW Nebraska, along the Missouri River. They are well known for their participation in a major political action against the US government concerning ownership of Indian lands in the 1880s. Today some surviving 2,000 Omaha people reside in Nebraska and Oklahoma.

Oman (Umān), formerly Muscat and Oman; an independent sultanate on SE Arabian Peninsula, bordered by Arabian Sea (SW), Gulf of Oman (NE), extends inland to Rub'al-Khali Desert. The Hajar Mts run parallel to the Gulf of Oman; the highest point is Jebel Sham approx. 9,777ft (2,980m); the interior is a gently sloping, broad plain. The economy is predominantly agricultural and subsistence; chief products are sugar cane, dates, wheat, barley, corn, millet, lime, olives. Industries include petroleum, which is partly limited by claims of the Iraq Petroleum Co., wine, fishing, oil refining. The people are mostly Arab, with minorities of Indians, Baluchis, and Negroes. Most of the inhabitants are religious adherents of Ibadism, an Islamic sect.

In 1508 the Portuguese settled the seaport of Muscat and held the area until it was taken by Turkey 1648; in 1741 Oman was recovered by Omans of Yemen, and Ahmad Ibn Said of Yemen founded the present royal line. In the early 19th century Oman was the most powerful of the Arabian states; but in 1856 most of the coasts of Iran, Baluchistan, and Zanzibar were lost, and Oman became politically and economically dependent on Britain. British influence was reaffirmed by a treaty 1939 and renewed 1951 between sultanate and Britain; rebellion against the sultanate 1954–57 was suppressed with British aid. In 1965 the United Nations demanded elimination of Britain's influence in Oman. The ruling sultan was removed 1970 by his son Qabus who promised to use oil revenues for development of Oman. In 1971 Oman joined the Arab League and the United Nations.

PROFILE

Official name: Oman
Area: 82,012sq mi (212,457sq km)
Population: 722,000
Chief cities: Muscat (capital); Matrah
Religion: Islam

Omayyads. *See* Umayyads.

OMB. *See* Management and Budget, Office of.

Ombudsman, official appointed to be an intermediary between the public and government. The office was created in Sweden in 1809 and has been adopted throughout Scandinavia and elsewhere. △906.

Omdurman (Umm Durman), city in NE central Sudan, on White Nile River, opposite Khartoum; largest city and chief commercial center of Sudan. City served as military headquarters of the Mahdi 1884; captured 1898 by British; site of Mahdi's tomb, Khalifa museum, university (1912). Industries: furniture, tanning, pottery, textiles, livestock, gum arabic. Pop. 232,200.

Omega Nebula (Horseshoe Nebula). △106.

Omega Particle. *See* Hyperon.

Omnibus Act (1868), law readmitting to the Union seven former Confederate states (Arkansas, Alabama, Florida, Georgia, Louisiana, North Carolina, South Carolina) that had complied with Reconstruction acts.

Omsk, city in Russian SFSR, USSR, on the Irtysh and Om rivers; capital of Omsk oblast; made administrative center of W Siberia 1824; seat of the counterrevolutionary Kolchak government 1918–19; site of medical, agricultural, and teachers' colleges and technical schools. Industries: agricultural machinery, textiles, footwear, flour, lumber, oil, petrochemicals. Founded 1716; chartered 1804. Pop. 821,000.

Ona, known as the "foot people," referring to their custom of walking instead of traveling by canoe. A member of the Tshon language family, this tribe of South American Indians was never populous; they were famed for their adaptation to the most rigorous climate in the Americas. About 25 still survive in the Tierra del Fuego region of Chile and Argentina.

Onager, wild ass found in semi-desert areas of Iran and India. It is a dun-colored animal with a triple, light-colored stripe on the back and shoulders. Height 48–51in (121.9–129.5cm) at shoulder. Family Equidae; species *Equus hemionus onager*. *See also* Ass. △628.

Onchocerciasis, infection with microfilarial worms that dwell in cysts in the skin, in the lymphatics, or in the eye, causing a local dermatitis. It is transmitted by bite of the blackfly.

Onega (Onezskoje), lake in S Karelian ASSR, Russian SFSR, USSR, between Lake Ladoga and the White Sea. The second largest lake in Europe, its outlet is the Svir, flowing from the SW corner to Lake Ladoga; main affluents are the Vodla, Vytegra, and Andoma rivers on the E; site of numerous inlets and islands along N shore, and supports fisheries and timber industries. Petrozavodsk is the only large town on its shores. Area: 3,710sq mi (9,609sq km).

Oneida, city in central New York, 5mi (8km) S of Oneida Lake; nearby is site of Oneida Community, utopian settlement (1848), reorganized 1880 as a business producing silverware. Mansion built by John Humphrey Noyes and his followers is still occupied by members of the Noyes family. Industries: silverware, paper, plaster, vegetable and fruit canning. Inc. 1846 as a village; 1901 as city. Pop. (1970) 11,677.

Oneida, the smallest, but most warlike, tribal member of the Six Nations of the Iroquois. Its homeland was around Lake Oneida in New York State. Most of the tribe was removed after the American Revolution to Wisconsin. Today 4,100 live on the Oneida Reservation in New York, and in northern and east-central Wisconsin.

O'Neill, Eugene (Gladstone) (1888–1953), US playwright, b. New York City. He wrote 45 plays, covering a wide range of subjects and dramatic styles. His plays reflect his pessimistic philosophy that man, robbed of his traditional faith by science, has nothing with which to replace it. He won the Nobel Prize for literature in 1936 for his dramas, and four Pulitzer prizes for *Beyond the Horizon* (1919), *Anna Christie* (1922), *Strange Interlude* (1928), and *Long Day's Journey into Night* (1967), produced after his death. His 11-act trilogy *Mourning Becomes Electra* (1931) transfers the Orestean story to New England. At the time of his death he was engaged on a cycle of plays about a long period in American life, including *The Iceman Cometh* (1946) and *A Moon for the Misbegotten* (1947). He is viewed as the United States' most important playwright. △1426.

Onion, hardy, bulbous, biennial plant native to central Asia. It has long been cultivated for its large, strong smelling, edible bulb. It has hollow leaves, white or lilac flowers, and prefers dryish, well drained soil and a sunny location. Height: to 18in (46cm). Family Liliaceae; species *Allium cepa*.

Onion Thrips. △492.

Onondaga, one of the members of the Six Nations of the Iroquois, and regarded as "Keepers of the Central Fire." This major group of North American Indians occupied the region around Onondaga co, New York, where some 1,400 still live.

Ontario, province in SE Canada, bordered on the S by four of the Great Lakes—Superior, Huron, Erie, and Ontario.

Land and economy. The country is rolling or level, of generally even elevation. Forests cover the land in the N toward Hudson Bay, while the center and S offer good farming land. Many rivers supply hydroelectric power for industry. The famous Niagara Falls are on the Niagara River on the SE border. The Great Lakes and the St Lawrence River provide excellent water transport; since the opening of the St Lawrence Seaway, oceangoing vessels can use Ontario's ports. Ontario is a leader in Canada in many economic aspects. As the most populous province and the site of the federal capital at Ottawa it exerts considerable influence in national affairs.

People. Most of the population traces its ancestry to the British Isles. There is an important French element, many of whom speak French. After WWII, Ontario received about 1,000,000 immigrants from war-torn countries in Europe. About 90% of the population is in the S part, which covers only about 15% of the total area. About 75% lives in urban areas.

Education. There are about 20 institutions of higher education. Among the most important are the University of Toronto, the University of Western Ontario, the University of Ottawa, Queen's University, McMaster University, and the University of St Michael's.

History. French explorers on the Great Lakes and up the rivers roamed through the region early in the 17th century and established a number of fur trading posts. The area became part of New France, the French colonies in North America, but was ceded to Great Britain by treaty at the end of the French and Indian War in 1763. The British ruled the region from Quebec. Its population expanded by the influx of thousands of British Loyalists fleeing the American colonies during and after the Revolution. For 50 years after 1791, Ontario was known as Upper Canada, separate from Quebec, but the two were reunited in 1841, and known as Canada until 1867, when the provinces of Ontario and Quebec were created and the Dominion was formed.

PROFILE

Entered Confederation: July 1, 1867; one of the four provinces that were joined to form the Dominion of Canada
National Parliament Representatives: Senate, 24; House of Commons, 88
Population: 7,637,000 (1971); rank, 1st
Capital: Toronto
Chief cities: Toronto; Hamilton; Ottawa (federal capital)
Provincial legislature: Legislative Assembly, 117 members
Area: 412,582sq mi (1,068,587sq km); rank, 2d
Elevation: Highest: 2,183ft (665m), Ogidaki Mt; lowest: sea level at Hudson and James bays
Industries (major products): motor vehicles and parts, aircraft and parts, iron and steel, metal products, copper products, agricultural and industrial machinery, pulp and paper, food products
Agriculture (major products): dairy products, beef cattle, hogs, poultry, oats, barley, winter wheat
Minerals (major): nickel, copper, uranium, gold
Floral emblem: white trillium

Ontario, city in SE California, 20mi (32km) W of San Bernardino; site of Chaffey College and Ontario Motor Speedway. Industries: citrus fruits, iron products, mobile homes, clothing. Founded 1882; inc. 1891. Pop. (1970) 64,118.

Ontario, Lake, smallest of the Great Lakes, bounded by New York (S and E) and Ontario prov., Canada (S, W, and N), fed by Lake Erie, the lake is drained to the NE by the St Lawrence River and carries oceangoing vessels via the St Lawrence Seaway; they bypass Niagara Falls by the Welland Canal to reach Lake Erie. Discovered in 1615 by Étienne Brulé. Pollution has decreased its supply of fish. Many resorts are on the lake. Chief Canadian cities are St Catherines, Toronto, Hamilton, Kingston; on the US side are Rochester and Oswego. Area: 7,540sq mi (19,529sq km).

Ontology, in philosophy, the branch of metaphysics that studies the basic nature of things, the essence of "being" itself. *See also* Metaphysics. △856.

Onychophora, a class of about 90 species of terrestrial invertebrates mainly tropical in distribution, lying between annelid worms and arthropods in evolutionary development. They are free-living and elongated and range in size from .6 to 6in (15–152mm) long, have up to 44 pairs of legs, and soft, velvety skin. The most common genus is *Peripatus*.

Onyx, a striped variety of chalcedony. Black and white onyx used in cameos. White and red called carnelian onyx; white and brown, sardonyx. Most found in India and South America.

Oogenesis, process of preparing ovum, or female reproductive cell, for fertilization. The diploid, primary egg cell develops into a haploid ovum through meiosis, yielding one mature egg and three polar bodies that will degenerate.

Ooze, a fine-grained pelagic deposit containing material of more than 30% organic origin, with the rest comprised of clay derived from colloidal matter. Oozes are divided into two main types according to their chief constituents. Calcareous ooze at depths of 2,000m to 3,900m (6,560–12,792ft) contains the skeletons of animals such as foraminiferans and pteropods. Siliceous ooze at depths of more than 3,900m contains skeletons of radiolarians and diatoms. △228.

OPA. *See* Office of Price Administration.

Opal, a noncrystalline variety of quartz, found in recent volcanoes, deposits from hot springs, and sediments. Usually colorless or white with rainbow play of color in gem forms, most valuable of quartz gems. Hardness 5.5–6.5; sp gr 2.1. △244.

Op Art, US art movement of the 1960s that rejects all signs of representation and insists on nonobjectivity. It often incorporates kinetic energy into designs of squares, lines, circles, and dots to create optical illusions. Often color is used in a powerful way to give a sense of depth to pictures. Also common are "invisible paintings," in which shapes emerge as the viewer's eye becomes accustomed to the colors of the canvas. △1372.

OPEC (Organization of Petroleum Exporting Countries). △1352, 1386.

Open, or **Galactic, Cluster.** *See* Cluster, Stellar.

Open Door Policy, arrangement allowing all nations equal commercial access to a particular country. Most often associated with China's early relations with the West, it was first formally espoused in 1899 by US Secretary of State John Hay. After the anti-foreign Boxer Rebellion (1900), the policy was modified, allegedly to protect China's territorial integrity but also, later on, to hinder Japanese encroachment. The policy ended during World War II with the recognition of China as a sovereign state.

Open Fuel System. △304.

Open-Hearth Process, in steel production, a method for producing steel in a regenerative, reverberatory furnace fueled by natural or coal gas. Lime and other slag-forming materials such as scrap iron are added to molten pig iron. The furnace is made of refractory materials containing lime and magnesia for removing impurities. △1594.

Open-Pit Mining, method of surface mining involving the terracing of level surfaces, called benches, into the ground. Utilized for coal, copper, iron ore, clay, gravel, and stone. Processes comprise drilling, blasting, loading, and hauling. Removal of water and flood control are often necessary. △282.

Open Shop, employment situation in which the worker may or may not join the union; membership in the union is not a condition of employment, either before or after hire. *See also* Closed Shop.

Open Society. △898.

Opera, stage drama where most or all of the dialogue is sung and accompanied by an orchestra. The first opera is reckoned to be *Dafne* by Jacopo Peri, introduced in Florence, Italy, in 1597. Important opera composers after Peri were Monteverdi, Lully, Rameau, Gluck, and Mozart through the 18th century. During the 19th century opera reached the heights of popularity with the Italian Romantic school (eg, Verdi, Puccini) and the great music dramas of Richard Wagner. Among the most notable opera companies of the 20th century are the Metropolitan Opera in New York City, the Paris Opera, Covent Garden in London, and La Scala in Milan, Italy. △1174, 1256.

Operant Conditioning, or **Instrumental Conditioning,** in psychology, a basic pattern of how learning takes place. Basically, behaviors that have pleasant consequences will tend to be repeated, while those followed by unpleasant consequences will tend not to occur again. Such consequences are called "reinforcements," and they can be used to acquire new behaviors, maintain old ones, or eliminate undesired behaviors. Many psychologists believe that much of human learning results from such conditioning. The procedure is also applied to changing the behavior of the mentally disturbed, in which case it is known as behavior modification. *See also* Behaviorism; Extinction; Learning Theory; Programmed Learning; Reinforcement; Shaping; Skinner Box. △772, 778.

Operation, Surgical. △752–54.

Operations Research (OR), the application of the scientific method to management problems that may be expressed in quantitative terms. It is employed in the direction of organizations pursuing specific objectives through integration of personnel, machines, money, materials, and information. A mathematical model is constructed and refined, normally using a computer. Particular problems are evaluated with this model, allowing the manager to arrive at decisions based on complex alternate strategies.

Operetta, music drama involving songs, dialogue, dancing, and a light, romantic story. Operettas developed largely as attempts by opera composers to reach wider audiences. Among the more significant operetta composers were Johann Strauss, Jr., Gilbert and Sullivan, and Victor Herbert.

Operon, region of a chromosome consisting of structural genes and an operator gene. This was a concept elucidated to explain control of gene activity. The structural genes direct the synthesis of enzymes involved in forming a cell constituent or the utilization of a nutrient. The operator gene responds to a molecule (called a repressor) and can exist open or closed. When the operator gene is open, the genes it controls are functional, producing proteins. When

Olympia, Greece

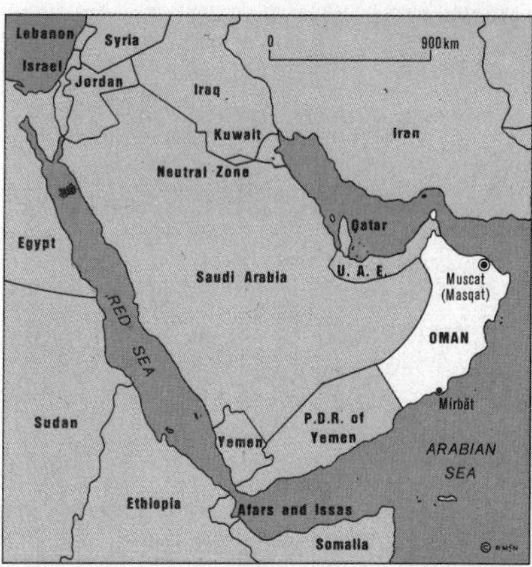

Lebanon
Syria
Israel
Jordan
Iraq
0
900km
Kuwait
Iran
Neutral Zone
Qatar
Egypt
Saudi Arabia
U. A. E.
Muscat
(Masqat)
OMAN
RED SEA
Sudan
P.D.R. of
Yemen
Yemen
Mirbāt
ARABIAN
SEA
Ethiopia
Afars and Issas
Somalia

Oman

Eugene O'Neill

Ontario: Sir Adam Beck—Niagara Power Development

interacting with the repressor, the operator gene is closed.

Ophthalmology, that branch of medicine that deals with the structure, function, and diseases of the eyes. It includes surgical and other treatment of eye disorders and the correction of defective vision. *See also* Optometry. △674.

Opium, drug derived from the juice of unripe seedpods of the opium poppy. Its components and derivatives have been used as narcotics and analgesics as long as history has been recorded. It produces drowsiness and euphoria, reduces pain, and has a noninhibitory effect. Morphine, codeine, and papaverine are common opium compounds. *See also* Heroin. △730, 744.

Opium War (1839–42), war fought by the British with China over issues of restrictions on trade by the Chinese and illegal opium smuggling by the Western traders, mainly British, into China. By the Treaty of Nanking in 1842 the Chinese were saddled with an indemnity for the cost of the war, forced to cede Hong Kong to the British, and required to open five ports for international trade. This marked the beginning of the so-called unequal treaties forced on China by the West. △1270.

Oppenheimer, J(ulius) Robert (1904–67), US physicist, b. New York City. He directed atomic energy research at the Los Alamos, N. Mex., project that produced the atom bomb in 1945. After the war, he was chairman of the Atomic Energy Commission's general advisory committee (1946–52) and worked for civilian and international control of atomic energy. Opposing development of the hydrogen bomb (1949), he was dropped from the AEC as a security risk (1953). He was director of the Institute for Advanced Study at Princeton University (1947–66). △1746.

Opposition, celestial configuration characterized by a difference of 180° in the longitude of the Sun and a superior planet, as viewed from the Earth. A planet is thus at opposition when it completes a straight line passing through Sun and Earth respectively. It is then usually at its closest to the Earth and is most clearly observable.

Optical Astronomy. *See* Astronomy, Optical.

Optical Glass. △1518.

Optical Illusion. *See* Illusion.

Optical Isomer. *See* Isomers. △1570.

Optical Rotation, angle through which a molar solution of a compound rotates the plane of polarization of a beam of light at a given temperature. Optical activity is associated with an asymmetrical assembly of groups about an atom. Many natural products show an ability to rotate polarized light counterclockwise; few rotate clockwise.

Optic Chiasma. △674.

Optic Nerve, second cranial nerve, which carries the visual stimuli from the retina of the eye to the visual center in the cortex of the brain. That part of the retina where the optic nerve enters the eye is known as the blind spot. *See also* Blind Spot. △674.

Optics, Crystal. *See* Crystal Optics.

Opto-electronics. △1668.

Optometry, science that deals with the examination of eyes and the prescribing of lenses and exercises to correct vision defects. It should not be confused with ophthalmology, the medical and surgical treatment of the eyes. △674.

Opuntia, cactus plants found from Canada to Argentina and characterized by small barbed bristles. Chollas have cylindrical joints and prickly pears have flattened joints. Others have rounded joints. Family Cactaceae; genus *Opuntia*. *See also* Cactus; Cholla; Prickly Pear.

OR. *See* Operations Research.

Oracles, intermediaries between gods and men in ancient Greece who answered questions about the will of the gods at their shrines. Consultations were highly ritualized; answers were often ambiguous. The oracle of Zeus at Dodona was the oldest; that at Delphi, the most famous.

Oral Character, in psychoanalytic theory, a personality influenced by what happened in the earliest, or oral, stage of development. At this stage, sucking, chewing, and swallowing are major concerns. Thus a baby who gets too much gratification at this stage may be overdependent as an adult, because he expects that someone will continue to "feed him."

Oral Contraceptive. *See* Birth Control Pill. △706.

Oral Surgery, the dental specialty that deals with the diagnosis and subsequent surgery necessary because of certain diseases, injuries, and defects of the jaws, gums, and teeth. Included are the removal of impacted and infected teeth, the treatment of tumors and lesions of the jaws, and the repair of jaw and facial injuries and of cleft palate and lip. △756.

Oran (Ouahran), leading port city and department capital in NW Algeria, on Gulf of Oran; an important trade center; scene of civil strife in 1950s involving many terrorist attacks, which led to exodus of European population. Industries: wine, wool, iron ore, wheat, tobacco, vegetables. Inhabited since prehistoric times, probably founded by Moorish Andalusians, 10th century. Pop. 325,481.

Orange, House of, royal house of the Netherlands. Orange, a principality (from 11th century) in southern France, was inherited by the Nassau house of western Germany. The prince of Orange, William the Silent, became stadtholder (1579) of the Netherlands. Except for brief intervals, the House of Orange has ruled the country ever since, usually with the strong support of the people. King William III of England was a prince of Orange. *See also* Nassau, House of.

Orange, city in S California, 22mi (35km) E of Long Beach; site of Chapman College (1861). Industries: fruit packing and processing, rubber products, industrial furnaces. Inc. 1888. Pop. (1970) 77,365.

Orange, city in NE New Jersey, NW of and adjoining Newark; known as the Oranges together with E Orange, W Orange, S Orange, and Maplewood. Industries: office machines, clothing, aircraft parts. Settled 1675; set off from Newark 1806 and from E, S, and W Orange 1861–63; inc. as city 1872. Pop. (1970) 32,566.

Orange (Oranje), principal river of S Africa; rises in Maluti Mts, N Lesotho; runs in an irregular E direction, forming boundary between Orange Free State and Cape prov., and part of that of Republic of South Africa and Namibia before reaching the Atlantic Ocean at Alexander Bay; supports many hydroelectric power plants and irrigation systems. Length: approx. 1,300mi (2,093km).

Orange, evergreen citrus fruit tree. There are two types. The sweet orange is native to Asia and widely grown in California and Florida. Fruit develops without flower pollination and is often seedless. There are many varieties of sweet oranges. The sour orange is widely grown in Spain as an ornamental and for marmalade production. It is grown in the United States for use as a rootstock for less hardy species. Height: to 30ft (9m). Family Rutaceae; genus *Citrus*. △338.

Orange Free State (Oranje-Vrystaat), province in E central Republic of South Africa; bounded E by Natal, N by Transvaal, SE by Lesotho, S and W by Cape prov.; capital is Bloemfontein. Annexed 1900 by Great Britain, it was called Orange River Colony until 1910, when it became a province of Union of South Africa; site of several technical and agricultural schools, University of Orange Free State (1855). Products: grains, fruit, livestock. Industries: gold, gypsum, coal, diamond mining, meat processing, matches, vinegar. Area: 49,866sq mi (129,153sq km). Pop. 1,661,756.

Orangemen, members of the Loyal Orange Institution. It was an Irish political and sectarian society founded in Ulster (1795) and named for Britain's Protestant William III, formerly prince of Orange. The society sought to maintain the Protestant succession, and eventually spread to Great Britain. The Orange society strengthened its position in Ireland and continued as bastion of Protestant Unionist opinion in the late 20th century.

Orangutan, stout-bodied, thick-necked great ape native to forests of Sumatra and Borneo. Orangutans have bulging bellies and a thin, shaggy, reddish-brown coat. In trees, they swing by their arms or walk on branches; on the ground, they walk on all fours. Their favorite food is the durian fruit. Height: 5ft (1.5m); weight: to 220lb (100kg); arm span: over 7ft (2.13m). Species *Pongo pygmaeus*. *See also* Primates. △554, 558.

Oratorio, form of musical composition on religious themes for solo voices, chorus, and orchestra. Usually performed in church or concert hall without acting, scenery, or costumes, the term came originally from 17th-century Italy, where liturgical plays set to music were presented in oratories (chapels). Emilio de Cavalieri and Giacomo Carissimi, the first oratorio composers, used Latin texts; Heinrich Schutz and his followers used their national languages. Some outstanding examples, still popular, include Bach's *Christmas Oratorio* (1734), Handel's *Messiah* (1742), Haydn's *Creation* (1797), Mendelssohn's *Elijah* (1846), Honegger's *King David* (1921), Kodaly's *Psalmus Hungaricus* (1923), and Stravinsky's *Oedipus Rex* (1927). △1196.

Oratory, the art of speaking in a manner that inspires listeners to intense emotion or action. It usually includes eloquent quotations and gestures and is used in politics, religion, and the law to gain support for a specific opinion. It conforms to a set of rules formed and revised since 460 BC. Pericles, Aristotle, and Cicero were teachers of the art. In the 20th century the trend has been toward a more informal style than oratory allows. △998.

Orbit, path, usually elliptical, followed by a celestial body moving around another body that acts as a center of gravitational attraction. Planetary orbits are described in terms of numerical quantities (elements), including the semimajor axis and eccentricity of the ellipse, the inclination of the orbital plane to that of the ecliptic, and the longitude of the ascending node and of the perihelion. The period of revolution and the mean orbital velocity can be derived from the values of these quantities. △50.

Orbitals, regions in space around the atomic nucleus in which electrons can move. In the simple "planetary" theory of the atom, the electrons are visualized as moving in circular or elliptical orbits. More advanced quantum mechanics replaces these localized, well defined paths by a probability distribution in space. The atomic orbitals are regions within which there is a high probability of finding the electron. Each orbital can accommodate two electrons and has a shape and energy characterized by the quantum numbers. Orbitals corresponding to *s* sub-shells of the atom are spherical, *p*-orbitals have 2 lobes, and *d* orbitals have 4 lobes. In molecules, the bonding electrons move in the combined electric field of all the nuclei. The atomic orbitals then become molecular orbitals—regions encompassing two nuclei, having a characteristic energy and containing two electrons. These molecular orbitals, which can be thought of as formed by overlap of atomic orbitals, constitute chemical bonds. *See also* Atom; Numbers. △1480, 1550–56.

Orchestra, group of musicians who perform together. The development of the modern symphony orchestra began in the 17th century, stimulated by the needs of composers to express themselves in new ways and by the development of new instruments and new ways of playing old instruments. Modern orchestras comprise about 80 to 120 musicians divided into sections playing strings (violin, viola, cello, bass, and harp), woodwinds (flute, piccolo, oboe, clarinet, and bassoon), brass (trumpet, trombone, French horn, and tuba), and percussion instruments (drum, cymbal, piano, etc). △1244.

Orchid, any member of the family Orchidaceae. Depending on the authority, there are from 15,000 to 35,000 species found worldwide in all regions, but especially common in the tropics. All are nonwoody perennials and grow in soil or as epiphytes (air plants) on other plants. All have a bilaterally symmetrical flower structure, with three sepals. Color and shape vary greatly, and flowers can be borne singly or in erect or pendant clusters. Flowers range in size from about 0.1in (2mm) to 15in (38cm) in diameter. One of the petals, called the lip, is often markedly different from the others. A club-shaped structure in the middle (columna) results from the fusion of male and female reproductive parts. Most, but not all, species are cross-fertilized by insects or birds. The only economically important orchid product is vanilla, obtained from several species of the genus *Vanilla*. △452.

Orchis, genus of orchids found on rich, wooded slopes of central United States. The upper petals are purple-rose; the large lower petal is white. The blooms are borne in clusters of 2 to 15 flowers; the 2 leaves are smooth and long. Height: to 1ft (30cm). Species include the showy *Orchis spectabilis*. Family Orchidaceae.

Orchitis, flamed and swollen testes, resulting from injury or infection. Symptoms are usually high fever, pain, nausea, and tenderness. Treatment may be antibiotics, bed rest, compresses, or drainage.

Orders of Architecture, types of classical columns, which fall into five orders: the Doric, Ionic, Corinthian, Tuscan, and Composite. Each order consists of a column with its base, shaft, and capital and an entablature above, and each has its own distinctive proportions and details. Of the five orders, the Doric, Ionic, and Corinthian are Greek; the Tuscan and Composite are Roman. *See also* individual orders. △1002.

Ordinance of 1784, territorial ordinance drafted by Thomas Jefferson after Virginia had ceded its western lands to the federal government. It provided for the artificial division of the lands into 16 districts, each eligible for statehood when its population reached 20,000.

Ordinance of 1787. *See* Northwest Ordinance.

Ordovician Period, the second oldest division of the Paleozoic Era, lasting from 500 to 430 million years ago. All life was still in the seas. Numerous invertebrates flourished, and included trilobites, brachiopods, corals, graptolites, mollusks, and echinoderms. Fragmentary remains of jawless fishes found in coastal deposits mark the first record of the vertebrates. *See also* Geologic Time; Paleozoic Era. △276, 568.

Ore, mineral or combination of minerals from which useful substances, especially metals, can be separated. Ores are divided into metallics (usually oxides and sulfides) and nonmetallics (such as sulfur and fluorite). Industrial rock deposits in beds (for example, gypsum and limestone) are not called ores. Occurrence is in veins, usually sharply angled tabular deposits; in beds or seams parallel to the enclosing rock; or in irregular masses. *See also* Lode. △278.

Oregano, the dried leaves and flowers of any of several perennial herbs of the mint family, native to hilly lands in Mediterranean countries and W Asia. Introduced into the Western Hemisphere for use as a food seasoning. The strong aroma and pungent taste make it popular in Italian and Mexican dishes.

Oregon, state in the NW United States, on the Pacific Ocean N of California.

Land and economy. The fertile Willamette Valley stretches N and S between the Coast Range (W) and the Cascade Range (E). About 65% of the state is a plateau E of the Cascades. The Columbia River on the N boundary is of great economic importance, supplying hydroelectric power to a wide region; its lower section is navigable by ocean vessels. Portland, on the Willamette River near its junction with the Columbia, is a major seaport. Dense forests of Douglas fir and ponderosa pine, especially in the mountains, support the lumber industry. Agriculture is largely centered in the Willamette Valley.

People. Most of the population is descended from the 19th-century settlers who came from other states. About 72% lives in urban areas.

Education. There are about 40 institutions of higher education.

History. Robert Gray, US sea captain, discovered the mouth of the Columbia River in 1792. The Lewis and Clark expedition, marching overland from the Middle West, reached this point in 1805 and a US trading post was est. there in 1811. This was sold to British interests, and the British regarded the region as their territory. The United States claimed it by right of prior discovery and settlement, and in 1846 the boundary with Canada was fixed at its current latitude 49°. US pioneers had been entering the area since the 1830s, and Oregon Territory was organized in 1848. It included the present state of Washington, which was separated in 1853. After Oregon became a state, settlement and development proceeded steadily in spite of occasional Indian uprisings.

PROFILE

Admitted to Union: Feb. 14, 1859; rank, 33rd
US Congressmen: Senate, 2; House of Representatives, 4
Population: 2,091,385 (1970); rank, 31st
Capital: Salem, 68,296 (1970)
Chief cities: Portland, 380,620; Eugene, 78,389; Salem
State legislature: Senate, 30; House of Representatives, 60
Area: 96,981sq mi (251,181sq km); rank, 10th
Elevation: Highest, 11,235ft (3,427m), Mt. Hood; lowest, sea level
Industries (major products): forest products, lumber, furniture, paper, processed foods, transportation equipment
Agriculture (major products): wheat, fruit, nuts, potatoes, oats, cattle, dairy products
Minerals (major): nickel, stone, sand and gravel
State nickname: Beaver State
State motto: The Union
State bird: western meadowlark
State flower: Oregon grape
State tree: Douglas fir

Oregon Trail, emigrant route to the Northwest, Oregon Country, extended approx. 2,000mi (3,200km) from Independence, Missouri, to the Columbia River region. The trail followed the Platte and North Platte rivers across Nebraska to Wyoming and through the Rocky Mts by the South Pass to the Colorado River basin, across Idaho following the Snake River to the Columbia River. It was originally used by fur traders and missionaries; the first wagon train over South Pass was led by Capt. Benjamin Bonneville (1832); by the 1840s the trail was well traveled by wagon trains. △1274.

Oregon Treaty (1846), compact with Great Britain that settled the Oregon boundary, established the 49th parallel as the line between the United States and Canada, and gave the United States undisputed claim to the Pacific Northwest. It also provided for British use of the Columbia River below the 49th parallel.

Orel (Or'ol), city in Russian SFSR, USSR, on the Oka River, 200mi (322km) SSW of Moscow; capital of Orel oblast; place of exile for Polish revolutionaries of the 1860s; held by Germans 1941–43; site of triumphal arch (1786), the Turgenev museum, museum of revolution and of natural history, and a teachers' college. Industries: weaving machines, glass, leather goods, construction equipment, clocks, beer, flour, grain, brewing, meat packing. Founded 1564 as S outpost of Moscow territory. Pop. 232,000.

Orem, city in N central Utah, 7mi (11km) NNW of Provo. Industries: steel, electronic equipment, skis, truck farming, fruit growing. Settled 1861; inc. 1919. Pop. (1970) 25,729.

Ore Mountains. *See* Erzgebirge.

Orenburg, formerly Chkalov; city in Russian SFSR, USSR, on the Ural River, just E of the Sakmara River mouth; capital of Orenburg oblast; scene of heavy fighting after the Revolution of 1917; capital of the Kirgiz Autonomous Republic 1920–24; renamed Chkalov after the Russian polar aviator; renamed Orenburg in 1957; site of medical, agricultural, and teachers' colleges, museums, cathedrals, churches, and a mosque. Industries: locomotive and car repair, flour, hides, meat processing, dairy products, grain, hops, animal feed, aircraft and tractor parts. Founded 1735. Pop. 345,000.

Oreopithecus, ancient primate of the Pliocene and Miocene epochs; a relative of the forerunners of both modern man and the Old World monkeys. In a genus by itself, fossil remains of the now extinct *Oreopithecus* have been found in southern Europe and East Africa from over 7,000,000 years ago. About 4ft (122cm) tall and semi-erect, *Oreopithecus* was apparently a vegetarian. △646.

Oresteia, a trilogy of tragedies by Aeschylus, produced in 458 BC and consisting of *Agamemnon, The Libation Bearers,* and *Eumenides.* The last and greatest work of Aeschylus, it is also the only surviving Greek trilogy. Each play is complete and stands alone; together they explore the themes of crime, revenge, and expiation.

Orestes, in Greek mythology, son of Agamemnon and Clytemnestra. With his sister Electra he killed Clytemnestra (his mother) and her lover Aegisthus to avenge the death of Agamemnon, whom Clytemnestra and Aegisthus had murdered. Orestes is a character in a number of Greek plays including Aeschylus' *Oresteia,* Sophocles' *Electra,* and Euripides' *Orestes.*

Øresund (The Sound), strait in Denmark, between Sjaelland Island and S Sweden; connects the Kattegat with the Baltic Sea. Length: 45 mi (72km).

Organ, largest, most complicated keyboard musical instrument. The player, at a console, regulates the flow of air, mechanically pressurized in the windchest, to ranks of pipes, producing diapason tones of solemn timbre, especially suitable for churches. Organs were built in Constantinople in the 7th century; large ones were constructed in England in the 10th century. Keyboards appeared *c.* 1300; reed pipes imitating other instruments *c.* 1500. Modern organs date from the Baroque period, when J.S. Bach wrote

J. Robert Oppenheimer

Orangutan

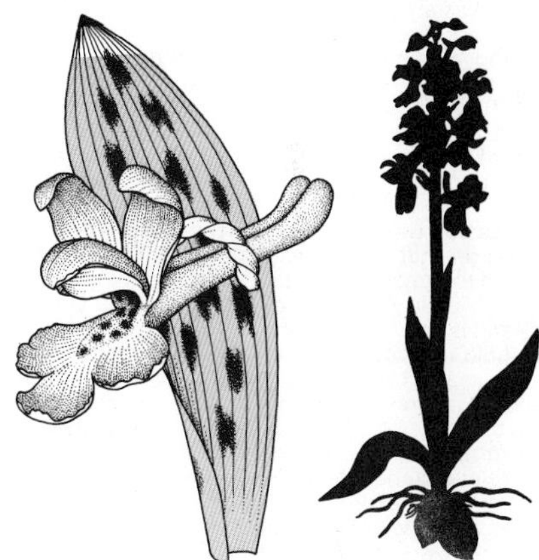

Orchis

Salem, Oregon

great compositions for them. Organs acquired crescendos and full orchestral effects in the 19th century. Electrification encouraged the building of elaborate machines in US film theaters (*c.* 1930) with the sound effects of horses, cannon, and airplanes. Purists such as Albert Schweitzer revived interest in Baroque organ music (*c.* 1900). △1196.

Organic Chemistry, one of the main branches of chemistry. Originally the study of substances produced by living organisms (hence its name), it has been broadened to include the study of all the compounds of carbon with the exclusion of the oxides, metal carbonates, and sulfides. *See also* Inorganic Chemistry. △1560, 1568–70.

Organic Functional Groups, groups of atoms that determine the chemical properties of organic compounds. For example, compounds containing the carboxyl group (-COOH) are fatty acids and behave accordingly. Similarly, compounds containing the hydroxyl group (OH) are alcohols, those containing a carbonyl group (CO) are ketones, and those with a -CHO group are aldehydes.

Organic Gardening, the cultivation of produce without the use of chemical fertilizers and insecticide sprays. Only natural fertilizers such as compost and mulch are used. Plants cultivated in this manner do not contain possibly harmful chemicals. △320.

Organismic Theory, in psychology, approach that views an individual as an integrated whole. Any behavior must be seen as an activity of the whole personality, not as an item for isolated study. Actions are said to be guided by the master drive for self-actualization.

Organization for Economic Cooperation and Development (OECD), organization of western European countries, the United States, and Canada. It offers assistance in economic growth to members attempting to decrease unemployment and provides help to underdeveloped countries. △942.

Organization for European Economic Cooperation (OEEC). △1342, 1356.

Organization of African Unity (OAU), association of over 40 African states for their mutual, coordinated development and unity in defense of African independence. It was an outgrowth of the Pan-African Movement. The organization has helped settle certain disputes and works towards a united African front in international affairs. Founded in 1963 at Addis Ababa (Ethiopia), the organization holds yearly summit conferences. The Republic of South Africa and Rhodesia are the only independent countries in Africa that are nonmembers.

Organization of American States (OAS), regional organization that seeks peaceful settlements of disputes and regional cooperation in self-defense. It consists of 20 Latin American countries and the United States and is an outgrowth of the 1948 Pan American Union held in Bogotá, Colombia. Its charter became effective in 1951. In 1962, it voted to exclude Cuba because of its Communist government and supported the US blockade of Cuba to prevent the installation of Soviet missiles. The OAS assisted in restoring diplomatic relations between Panama and the United States in 1964. Economic and diplomatic sanctions imposed on Cuba in 1964 were ended in 1975. The headquarters are in Washington, D.C. △1354.

Organization Man, term applied by W.H. Whyte in his book *The Organization Man* (1956) to the middle-class American whose greatest concern is with job security and benefits. △928.

Organometallic Compound, compound in which one or more organic groups of radicals are bonded to an atom of a metal. Metallic carbonates (such as sodium carbonate) and salts of common fatty acids (such as sodium acetate) are usually excluded from this classification. Typical examples are metallic alkyl compounds (such as tetraethyl lead and triethyl aluminum), Grignard reagents (such as ethylmagnesium iodide), and a number of compounds of transition metals.

Organ-pipe Cactus, cactus native to SW North and South America. It has long columns of stems; its night-blooming blossoms open in May, and the fruit is edible. Height: to 33ft (10m). Family Cactaceae; species *Lemairocereus thurberi. See also* Cactus.

Organ Transplant, the surgical implantation of an organ (such as a kidney or heart) from another individual to substitute for a malfunctioning or diseased organ in the patient. Careful pre-operative preparation and matching followed by post-surgical procedures are necessary to ensure that the tissue of the transplanted organ is not rejected by the immune system of the body into which it is placed. *See also* Immunology. △740.

Orgueil Meteorite. △92.

Original Sin, in Christian theology, the condition of every human being resulting from the fall of Adam and Eve. Due to this first sin, humanity lost the grace of God. The sin of Adam and Eve is endlessly transmitted to all human beings. △810, 844.

Origin of Species. △418.

Orinoco River, river in Venezuela; rises in Guiana Highlands; flows NW to Colombia, then N forming part of Venezuela-Colombia border, then E to Atlantic Ocean. Length and volume vary with season; navigable by small vessels; source of hydroelectric power. Sighted by Christopher Columbus 1498; navigated by Diego de Ordaz 1530–31. Length: approx. 1,500–1,700mi (2,415–2,737km).

Oriole, Old World songbird that is medium-sized, brightly colored, arboreal, and feeds on insects and builds cup-shaped nest for speckled white eggs (2–4). New World orioles, closely related to blackbirds, are frequently brightly colored and build hanging nests high in trees for speckled white eggs (2–6). Family Oriolidae. *See also* Baltimore Oriole.

Orion, spectacular equatorial constellation situated south of Taurus and Gemini. Four stars form a conspicuous quadrilateral containing a row of three other stars representing Orion's Belt. The five brightest stars of the first magnitude, include Beta (Rigel), Alpha (Betelgeuse), and Gamma (Bellatrix). This constellation contains the Orion Nebula and several binary stars. △110, 130, 134.

Orion Nebula (M42; NGC 1976), emission nebula in the constellation Orion, located in the Hunter's Sword. It is a mass of gas surrounding a quadrilateral grouping of four hot O-type stars (The Trapezium), from which it absorbs energy and re-emits it as visible light. △104, 106.

Orissa, state in E India, on the Bay of Bengal; Bhubaneswar is the capital. Ruled for centuries by Hindu dynasties, it was taken by Afghan marauders 1568, but soon afterwards came under Mogul domain; taken by the British 1803 and made a subdivision of Bengal until 1912 when Bihar and Orissa state was formed; made an autonomous state 1936; boundaries and population increased 1948–49 with inclusion of many princely states; made a constituent state of India 1950; site of Utkal University (1943) and many notable Hindu temples. Industries: fishing, rice, timber, sugar cane, tobacco, jute, iron ore, manganese, coal, mica mining. Area:. 60,162sq mi (155,820sq km). Pop. 21,934,827.

Orkneys, islands of United Kingdom in the North Sea, off the NE coast of Scotland, forming an insular administrative area (Orkney region). Pomona (Mainland) is the largest in the group of about 70 islands. Chief industry is dairy products. Area: 376sq mi (974sq km). Pop. 17,075.

Orlando, Vittorio Emanuele (1860–1952), Italian statesman and politician. Supporting Italian entrance into World War I (1915) and elected prime minister in 1917, he represented Italy at the Versailles Peace Conference (1919–20), but he withdrew from the conference in disagreement with Woodrow Wilson. Opposed to Fascism, Orlando retired from politics in 1925 but returned after Rome's World War II liberation (1943) and was elected to the 1948 constituent assembly. △1308.

Orlando, commercial and residential city in central Florida, 78mi (126km) NE of Tampa, seat of Orange co. Center of citrus region; site of Walt Disney World. Over 30 lakes within city limits. Industries: electronic and missile components, textiles, regional offices of major companies. Settled 1844; inc. 1875. Pop. (1970) 99,006.

Orléans, name of a royal family of France. The title was first created by Philip VI for his son, who died without heirs (1375). The 2d duke of Orléans was the younger son of Charles V (1391). In 1492 the duchy was united to the royal domain when its duke became Louis XII. Louis XIII gave the title to his brother, who also died without issue. In 1661, Louis XIV gave the title to his brother Philip, whose descendants have held it since. The only member of this line to become king was Louis-Philippe (*r.* 1830–48), although his father, Philippe-Egalité, and his heirs, the counts of Paris, have had their supporters, called Orléanists. Because of their close, but junior, position with the Bourbons, the house of Orléans was a real or threatened source of intrigue and opposition to the crown. Since the French Revolution the House of Orléans has been identified with constitutional monarchy and 19th-century liberalism.

Orléans, Gaston Jean Baptiste, Duc d' (1608–60), French prince, inveterate but unsuccessful intriguer against his brother, Louis XIII, and nephew, Louis XIV. He plotted to assassinate Richelieu; raised troops to support Marie de Medicis against her son, Louis XIII; and twice more rose against Louis and Richelieu. Drawn into the Fronde uprising (1652) and exiled, he was eventually reconciled with Louis XIV.

Orléans, Louis, Duc d' (1372–1407), French prince, younger brother of Charles VI. He became duc d'Orléans (1392). When the king became insane, he and Philip the Bold, duke of Burgundy, were bitter rivals for power. Philip's son John caused Louis's death, beginning a struggle between the two houses, the Armagnacs (Orléanists) and the Burgundians, that dominated French history in the 15th century.

Orléans, Louis-Philippe, Duc d', known as Philippe-Egalité (1747–93), French prince, supporter of democracy in the Revolution. In 1789 he was elected to the Estates-General by the nobility but chose to sit with the third estate. As a member of the National Convention, he supported the leftists (the Mountain), voted the guillotine for Louis XIV, and took for himself the new family name Egalité. His role during the Revolution was difficult and ambiguous, as many suspected him of personal ambition to be king. In 1792 his son, the future King Louis-Philippe, and friends fled France. Suspected of complicity, Philippe-Egalité was arrested and died on the guillotine.

Orléans, city in N central France, on Loire River, 70mi (113km) SW of Paris; capital of Loiret dept. The principal residence of French kings in 10th century, it was besieged by English 1428–29, and relieved by Joan of Arc. Briefly held by Huguenots during the 16th-century Wars of Religion, it was besieged by Roman Catholics in 1563 and held by them until Edict of Nantes in 1598; site of 17th–19th-century cathedral, 16th-century town hall, bronze statue of St Joan; scene of elaborate Feast of Joan of Arc, held each May. Industries: tobacco, textiles, chemicals. Founded *c.* 52 BC as Aurelianum by Romans. Pop. 95,828. △1096.

Ormolu, elaborate mounts applied to furniture and clocks during the reign of Louis XV and Louis XVI in 18th-century France. They were usually made of bronze or copper, which was gilded, and were known for their finely sculpted details of mythological subjects and floral designs.

Ornithischian Dinosaur, dinosaur with a birdlike pelvis. These herbivores appeared later in the fossil record than saurischian types. The earliest forms were bipedal, but later species became quadrupedal. The main divisions are Ornithopoda, Stegosauria, Ceratopsia, and Ankylosauria. △570–72.

Ornithology, scientific study of birds. Included are classification, structure, function, evolution, distribution, migration, reproduction, ecology, and behavior. In this science, nonprofessionals make substantial contributions in field research and observation. Museums and universities house collections of bird skins, skeletons, and preserved specimens. *See also* Bird; Bird Banding; Bird Migration. △526–538.

Ornithopoda, ornithischian dinosaurs, including all semi-bipedal herbivorous forms. Early representatives were Camptosaurus and Iguanodon. Later kinds were hadrosaurs or duck-billed dinosaurs. *See also* Trachodon. △570.

Orogeny, in its modern, narrowest usage, the process by which structures within mountainous areas are formed and deformed. Thus, all folding and faulting in upper layers and metamorphism in deeper ones result from orogenic activity. Each mountain region has its own very distinct features, but there are similarities of all processes of change that are common and part of the study of orogeny. *See also* Faulting; Folding. △276.

Or'ol. *See* Orel.

Orozco, José Clemente (1883–1949), Mexican painter. He is considered one of the finest Mexican masters. His realistic style, marked by social sympathy and commentary, has led him to be dubbed "the Mexican Goya." Three famous murals by Orozco are in the

United States at Pomona College, Claremont, Calif., The New School for Social Research, New York City, and Dartmouth College, Hanover, N.H. △1354.

Orpheus, in Greek mythology, the finest poet and musician, son of Calliope the muse of epic poetry, husband of Eurydice. After his wife died Orpheus descended into Hades to rescue her. He was successful but lost Eurydice when he disobeyed the command not to look back at her. Orpheus was killed by Maenads and rejoined his wife in Hades. Orpheus is usually depicted with the lyre he received as a gift from Apollo. △840.

Orphic Mysteries, mystic rites of Orphism, an ancient Greek religious movement popular in the 6th and 7th centuries BC. The mysteries take their name from Orpheus. Purification and initiation were important rites in the mysteries, which promised deliverance of the soul in the afterlife.

Orpine, any member of the stonecrop (or orpine) family, Crassulaceae, comprising 1,500 species of perennial herbs or low shrubs native to warm, dry parts of the world. Many are grown as pot plants or cultivated in rock gardens. All have thick leaves and red, yellow, or white flower clusters. Stonecrop *(Sedum)* and houseleek *(Sempervivum)* are well known representatives. △446.

Orr, Robert Gordon "Bobby" (1948–), Canadian ice hockey player. He joined the Boston Bruins in 1966 and the Toronto Maple Leafs in 1976. He was the most valuable player (1970–72) and was voted the best defenseman eight consecutive years (1968–75).

Orrery. △40.

Orsini, Roman princely family dating from the 10th century. The traditional rivalry between the Guelph (pro-papal) Orsinis and Ghibelline (pro-imperial) Colonna family often kept Rome in a state of civil war until the 16th century. Orsini popes were **Celestine III** (1191–98), **Nicholas III** (1277–80), and **Benedict XIII** (1724–30). The Orsinis were made princes of the Holy Roman Empire in 1629 and of Rome in 1718.

Ortega y Gasset, Jose (1883–1955), Spanish philosopher and humanist. Educated in the classic Jesuit tradition, he was early influenced by the Neo-Kantians at Marburg, but later rejected this school of thought in his *Adan en el paraiso* (1910). He saw man's present individual life as basic reality and believed that total chaos would occur if the masses were not guided by an intellectual minority. He founded the Institute of Humanities in Madrid (1948). His most famous work, *The Revolt of the Masses* (1929), advocated control by an elite. Other works include *The Mission of the University* (1944), *Man and People* (1957), and *Man and Crisis* (1958).

Orthodontics, dental specialty concerned with the prevention and correction of badly aligned, or maloccluded, teeth. Included are straightening crooked teeth, correction of chewing impairments, changing abnormal jaw relationships, and improving facial features around the mouth area. △756.

Orthopedics, branch of medicine that deals with the diagnosis and treatment of diseases, disorders, and injuries to bones, muscles, tendons, ligaments, and associated tissues. △720, 754.

Orthoptera, insect order found worldwide. It includes crickets, mantids, walking sticks, leaf insects, grasshoppers, cockroaches, and others. These insects may be winged or wingless and have chewing mouthparts. They have three life stages: egg, nymph, and adult. △492.

Ortolan, small European bunting often eaten as a delicacy and often trapped when flocks migrate to Africa. An insect and seed eater, it has an olive head and chest, yellow throat, brown-streaked black back, and pinkish underparts. The light-colored, spotted eggs (3–6) are laid in a cup-shaped nest amid plants. Length: 6in (15cm). Species *Emberiza hortulana.*

Orwell, George (1903–50), pseud. of Eric (Arthur) Blair; English journalist, critic, and novelist, b. India. Orwell fought with the Republicans in the Spanish Civil War. His books include the autobiographical *Down and Out in Paris and London* (1933) and *Homage to Catalonia* (1938); the antitotalitarian fable *Animal Farm* (1945); and *Nineteen Eighty-Four* (1949), a novel. △1778.

Ory, Kid (1886–1973), US jazz trombonist and bandleader, b. Edward Ory in La Place, La. His first band (1911–19) contained many of the famous figures of early jazz—Louis Armstrong, King Oliver, Jimmy Dodds, Sidney Bechet, and others. In 1921 he made the first jazz recordings by any black musician. He composed "Muskrat Ramble" (1926). △1366.

Oryx, or **Gemsbok,** four species of large, rapier-horned antelopes found in Africa. Both sexes carry long horns ringed at the base; female's are longer and slimmer. They are cream to brown with black markings on face and legs. Males have a tuft on the throat. Living in herds up to 60, they can kill lions. The Arabian *Oryx leucoryx,* the smallest, is almost extinct. The scimitar-horned *O. tao* of the Sahara, the only species with curved horns, domesticated in ancient Egypt, is also nearing extinction. *O. gazella beisa* lives in E Africa. Gemsbok *O. gazella gazella* of southern Africa survives mainly in Kalahari. Height: to 86in (2.2m); weight: to 462lb (208kg). Family Bovidae. △606.

Osage, river in W Missouri; rises at the confluence of the Marais des Cygnes and Little Osage rivers, flows NE to join the Missouri River near Jefferson City; used for hydroelectricity; its waters, impounded by Bagnell Dam, form the Lake of the Ozarks. Length: 360mi (580km).

Osage Indians, about 5,000 native Americans of Siouan linguistic stock who enjoy considerable prosperity on their oil-rich lands in Oklahoma. The Osage migrated steadily westward from the Atlantic coast and in the early 1800s sold their land in Missouri, moved to a reservation in Kansas, and later bought land in Oklahoma. Farmer-hunters of the Plains type, their society was divided between earth and sky people, or meat-eaters and vegetarians, and was known for its adherence to tradition.

Osage Orange, or bow wood, bodark (from Fr. *bois d'arc*), thorny tree native to the Red River Valley, Okla., and cultivated as an ornamental. Deciduous, it has dark orange bark, oblong leaves, and warty orangelike fruit. Family Moraceae; species *Maclura pomifera.*

Osaka, port city in S Honshu, Japan, at mouth of the Yodo River, head of Osaka Bay; capital of Osaka prefecture and 2nd-largest city and industrial center of Japan. It was capital of Japan 4th century (then called Naniwa); modern city grew around 16th-century castle of Hideyoshi; site of university (1931) and 1970 World's Fair. Industries: textiles, machinery, steel, chemicals, shipping and shipbuilding. Pop. 2,980,-487.

Osborne, Thomas, Earl of Danby. *See* Danby, Thomas Osborne, Earl of.

Osceola (1800?–38), US Indian chieftain, leader of the Seminole Indians in Florida in the Second Seminole War (1835–37). President Jackson ordered the Seminoles removed to the West, but Osceola took his people into the Everglades to continue the fight.

Oscillating Electric Fields. △1484.

Oscillating Theory of the Universe, cosmological theory postulating that the expansion of the universe will eventually slow down as it approaches a critical radius. Because a static universe is unstable it would then contract back to zero size, at which point expansion would recommence to produce an oscillating (expanding-contracting) system. The validity of the theory depends on the density of matter in the universe being less than 3×10^{-29} grams per cc. *See also* Big-Bang Theory of the Universe. △122, 126.

Oscillator, a device for producing alternating electric current. It employs tuned circuits and amplifying components. In radio broadcasting, where oscillators are used to generate high-frequency currents for carrier waves, they are stabilized by coupling the vibrations of a piezoelectric crystal with the electronic circuit.

Oscilloscope, an instrument in which the variations in a fluctuating electrical quantity, such as voltage, appear temporarily as a visible wave form on the fluorescent screen of a cathode ray tube.

Oshawa, city in Ontario, Canada, on Lake Ontario; prosperous farming area. Industries: automotive works, glass, textiles. Founded 1795 as Skaes Corner. Inc. 1924. Pop. 91,113.

Oshkosh, city in E Wisconsin, on Lake Winnebago, 80mi (129km) NW of Milwaukee; seat of Winnebago co; visited by French explorers in 18th century; trading post was est. early 19th century; destroyed by fire 1875. Industries: farming, dairying, tourism, lumber, beer. Founded 1827; inc. 1846. Pop. (1970) 53,221.

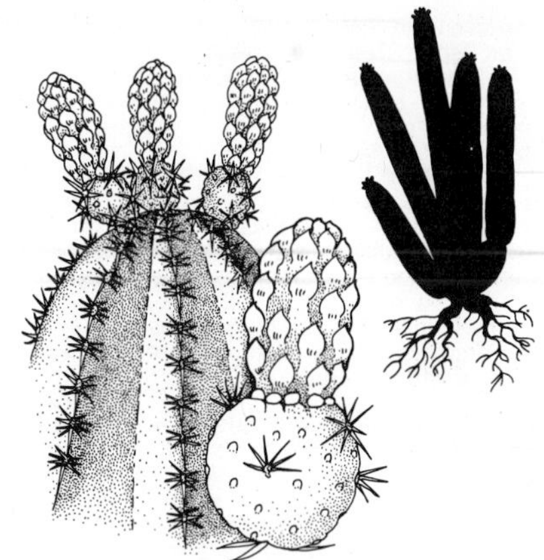

Organ pipe cactus

Oriole

Orléans, France

Orpine

Oshogbo, city in SW Nigeria, 50mi (81km) NE of Ibadan on Oshun River. Part of Ijesha, a Yoruban kingdom in 17th century, in 1839 it was scene of a battle in which Ibadan, a Yoruban city state, defeated Ilorin, a Fulani state. Industries: textiles, cigarettes, cotton ginning, trading. Pop. 242,336.

Osiris, in Egyptian mythology and religion, the god of the dead, son of Geb the earth and Nut the sky, husband and brother of Isis and father of Horus. He is generally depicted as a mummified man wearing a feathered crown and bearing the crook and flail of a king. In the myths Osiris was killed by his brother and dismembered; Isis retrieved the corpse and Horus avenged his death. △960.

Osler, (Sir) William (1849–1919), Canadian physician and educator. He taught at McGill University (Montreal) and at the University of Pennsylvania and Johns Hopkins. He was the first professor of medicine and chief physician at Johns Hopkins Hospital, Baltimore (1889–1904). An influential teacher, he wrote *Principles and Practice of Medicine* (1892) and *Science and Immortality* (1904).

Oslo, capital of Norway, in SE Norway at the head of Oslo Fjord, an inlet of the Skagerrak. Founded 1050 by King Harold III, city became capital 1299; suffered fire 1624, after which it was rebuilt by Christian IV who named it Christiania (renamed Oslo 1924). Largest city and chief industrial and commercial center of Norway, it contains many historic structures, including 17th-century church, national theater (1899), university (1811); site of 1952 Winter Olympics. Industries: metals, wood products, food processing, textiles, chemicals, shipping, tourism. Pop. 477,476.

Osman I or **Othman** (1259–1326), founder of the Ottoman Empire. He conquered NW Asia Minor and proclaimed his independence from the Seljuk Turks upon the collapse of their empire in 1299. △1108.

Osmium, metallic element (symbol Os) of the third transition series, discovered (1803) by Smithson Tennant. It occurs associated with platinum; chief source is as a by-product from smelting nickel. Like iridium, it is used in producing hard alloys. The tetraoxide (OsO_4) is a powerful oxidizing agent. Properties: at.no. 76; at. wt. 190.2; sp gr 22.57; melt. pt. 5,513°F (3,-045°C); boil. pt. 9,081°F (5,027°C); most common isotope Os^{192} (39.952%). *See also* Transition Elements.

Osmosis, diffusion of a solvent through a natural or artificial membrane, which blocks the passage of selected dissolved substances, into a more concentrated solution. Plant roots absorb water by osmosis; walls of living cells selectively allow passage of required substances. △412.

Osmotic Pressure, pressure exerted by a dissolved substance by virtue of the motion of its molecules. In dilute solutions, it varies with the concentration and temperature as if the solute were a gas occupying the same volume. It can be measured by the pressure which must be applied to counterbalance the process of osmosis into the solution. △1562, 1568.

Osprey, hawk of seacoasts, rivers, and lakes that dives for food, seizing fish with its talons. It has a short, hooked bill, broad, pointed wings, white head, and brownish-black plumage above, whitish below. Brown-blotched, white eggs (2–3) are laid in a large stick nest on or above ground. Length: 20–25in (51–63.5cm). Species *Pandion haliaetus.*

Ossa, Mount, mountain peak in NE Greece. In Greek mythology, the Aloadae, two giants who fought against the gods, piled Mt Ossa on top of Mt Olympus, and Mt Pelion on top of Mt Ossa, in attempt to reach heaven and overthrow the gods. Height: 6,490ft (1,980m).

Ossian, legendary Gaelic warrior and poet of the third century whose name was used by James MacPherson as the original author of his Ossianic poems (1763). Challenged by Dr. Samuel Johnson, MacPherson was forced to compose Gaelic poems purporting to be source material but later discovered to be faked. △1222.

Ossicles, Auditory. △676.

Ossification, the process of bone formation. In humans it begins at about the second month of embryonic development, continues through childhood and adolescence, and is completed by about age 25. Some bones, known as intramembranous bones, including the flat bones of the skull roof, develop from connective tissue cells. These cells become osteoblasts, or bone-forming cells, and secrete collagen fibers that combine with minerals and gradually lead to the formation of hard bone matrix. Other bones, known as endochondral bones, such as the long bones, develop from cartilage, with certain cartilage cells changing to osteoblasts. Epiphyseal plates, located typically at the ends of the long bones, are areas of continued bone growth. *See also* Bone. △682.

Ossory, ancient kingdom of Ireland, possibly within Kingdom of Leinster; founded 1st century AD, ruled in 9th century by Cerball. It probably disappeared by the 11th century, but its extent is indicated by the modern diocese of Ossory, centering on Kilkenny.

Osteichthyes, class of fish with bony skeletons, found in almost every water environment. It includes Actinopterygii (spiny-rayed fish) and Sarcopterygii (lungfish and lobefin). Characteristics include a single flap, or opercle, covering gill openings; an air bladder or primitive lung; and fins supported by bony rays. Most members of this class have scales. Fertilization is usually external, and the number of eggs laid at one time ranges from 100 to millions. Osteichthyes first appeared during Devonian period (350–400,000,-000 years ago). They were heavily armored and originally were adapted to fresh water. There are more than 20,000 living species. Superclass Pisces. △510.

Ostend Manifesto, document in American history, drawn up in Ostend, Belgium, in Oct. 1864, by Pierre Soulé, James Y. Mason, and James Buchanan. This document warned Spain that the United States would take Cuba by force if Spain refused to sell the island. Protests arose both in the United States and Europe and the manifesto was finally denounced by Secretary of State William Marcy.

Osteoarthritis, disease in which the cartilage of the joints is destroyed. It may be caused by aging or by postural or orthopedic abnormalities and may be relieved by physical therapy, analgesics, or cortisone. △712, 720.

Osteomalacia, loss of calcium and phosphorus from the bones in adults. It is caused by deficiency of calcium and vitamin D in the diet. Treatment involves a diet high in protein and calcium, supplemented with vitamin D concentrates.

Osteomyelitis, inflammation of the bone or bone marrow. It is usually caused by infection and accompanied by fever, swelling, and pain. Treatment is with antibiotics or surgery.

Osteopathy, an approach of medicine based on the theory that structural defects interfere with normal body functioning and cause disease and disorders. In the United States osteopaths may be licensed to practice osteopathic medicine, surgery, or other specialty. They use skeletal manipulations and other medical and surgical techniques to try to correct structural defects.

Ostia, ancient Italian city 16mi (26km) from Rome at the mouth of the Tiber; the naval base and important commercial harbor of Rome from the 4th century BC to the 3rd century AD. The town was deserted by the 9th century and became a builder's quarry and treasure trove until systematic excavations were begun in the 19th century.

Ostpolitik. △1390.

Ostracism, a procedure peculiar to Athens, instituted by Cleisthenes in 507 BC to prevent the growth of tyrants. If 6,000 citizens voted to do so, any individual aspiring to dictatorship was banished for 10 years. △996.

Ostracod, or seed shrimp, small crustacean common in seas and fresh water. It has a rounded or elliptical carapace, resembling two halves of a clam shell. Although some swim, others scurry along muddy bottoms. Length: 3/16–3/4in(5–19mm). There are a few terrestrial species. △490.

Ostrava, city in N central Czechoslovakia, near junction of Oder and Opava rivers; center of industrialized area and one of country's largest cities. Industries: coal, iron, steel, ship and bridge parts. Pop. 274,547.

Ostrich, largest living bird, found wild in central Africa where groups roam grasslands, feeding on plants and small animals, in company with grazing animals. It has a reddish or bluish, down-covered, small flat head and long neck. Its plump body is covered with soft black feathers and white wing and tail plumes. Flightless, it runs fast. Females scoop a hole in sand for large, shiny yellow eggs (12–16) incubated by the female by day and the male at night. Height: to 8ft (2.4m); weight: over 300lb (135kg). Species *Struthio camelus.* △526, 606.

Ostrogoths, or East Goths, ancient Germanic people. They were subjected to the Huns in the 4th century and settled in Pannonia (modern Hungary). Under King Theodoric (AD 471–526), the Ostrogoths conquered Italy (493) and set up a kingdom based at Ravenna. They were defeated by Byzantium in 552 and expelled from Italy. They were soon absorbed by other peoples. △1054.

Ostwald, Wilhelm (1853–1932), Russian-German chemist. He was a professor in Riga but later moved to Leipzig, remaining in Germany for the rest of his life. His interest in the work of Arrhenius on solutions led him to the dilution law that bears his name. His work on catalysis was of considerable industrial importance and was rewarded by the Nobel Prize for chemistry in 1909.

Oswald, Lee Harvey (1939–63), alleged assassin of Pres. John F. Kennedy, b. New Orleans. He went to the USSR in 1959 and renounced his US citizenship, but he returned in 1962 with his Russian-born wife, Marina. In Dallas (1963), he allegedly shot President Kennedy twice, fled and was captured. He was killed by Jack Ruby, a nightclub owner, while being held by Dallas police.

Othello (1604), 5-act tragedy by William Shakespeare, from Giovanni Battista Giraldi's (called Cynthio) *Il Moro de Venezia.* Its earliest recorded performance was at Whitehall Palace, London, in 1604. First performed in the United States in New York (1751), it has been revived countless times. In 1943 a Theatre Guild production ran for 295 performances, a record run for a Shakespeare play on Broadway. It was also the basis for an opera by Giuseppe Verdi (1887). Othello, a noble Moor in the service of Venice, marries Desdemona and sails to Cyprus, followed by Roderigo, who loves Desdemona. Iago, who hates Othello for appointing Cassio as his lieutenant instead of Iago, resolves to kindle Othello's suspicions by suggesting that Desdemona and Cassio are overly familiar. He also has his wife, Emilia, steal a handkerchief Othello gave Desdemona and put it in Cassio's room. When Othello sees Cassio with the handkerchief and is told by Iago that Cassio has confessed to having an affair with Desdemona, Othello resolves to kill the lovers. He gets Roderigo to kill Cassio, but he only wounds him; Iago then kills Roderigo. Othello smothers Desdemona in her bed. Emilia enters the room and Othello confesses and mentions the handkerchief. When Emilia declares she had given the handkerchief to Iago, Othello lunges at him. Iago kills Emilia and flees, is captured and brought back. Othello stabs him, then kills himself and dies upon the body of Desdemona. △1256.

Othman I. *See* Osman I.

Otosclerosis, disease of the bone surrounding the inner ear. The base of the stapes (one of the middle ear bones) is prevented from rocking against the oval window of the inner ear which impairs hearing. It can be treated with surgery.

Ott, Mel(vin Thomas) (1909–1958), US baseball player, b. Gretna, La. A home run hitter (511) with the New York Giants (1926–47), he also managed the team (1942–48). He was elected to the Baseball Hall of Fame in 1951.

Ottava Rima, eight-line stanza form with rhyme scheme ab ab ab cc. As originated in Renaissance Italy (and used by Ludovico Ariosto), each line has 11 syllables. In Elizabethan England this was adapted to a 5-syllable line. Later examples of this include Lord Byron's *Don Juan* (1819–24).

Ottawa, a group of native North Americans of the Algonkian linguistic family. They originally lived north of the Great Lakes with the Potawatami and Ojibway, but were famous traders and island-dwellers by the arrival of the French. Hunter-farmers of the Eastern Woodlands type, allied with the French and Hurons, they were broken into five groups by the Iroquois and Anglo-Americans and now live in the Great Lakes area, Kansas, and Oklahoma. Pontiac was a famous Ottawa.

Ottawa, capital of Canada, in SE Ontario on the Ottawa River and Rideau Canal; canal divides city into upper and lower towns. Queen Victoria chose it as capital of United Provinces of Canada in 1858, and in 1867 it became capital of Dominion of Canada; site of Ottawa University (1848), Grand Séminaire d'Ottawa (1847), Scholasticat St-Jean (1902), Petit Séminaire d'Ottawa (1925), Bruyère College (1925), St Patrick's College (1932), Carleton University (1942), 1200-

acre (486-hectare) Dominion experimental farm, Dominion Observatory, and National Art Gallery (1880). At Chaudière Falls in Ottawa River hydroelectric power is generated for municipal and domestic use. Industries: printing, publishing, logging, pulp, paper, food, beverages. Area was discovered 1613 by Samuel de Champlain; settled 1826 with building of Rideau Canal; inc. as city 1854. Pop. 298,087.

Otter, semi-aquatic carnivore found all over the world except in Australia. Otters have narrow, pointed heads with bristly whiskers, sleek, furred bodies, short legs with webbed feet, and long, tapering tails. The river otters *(Lutra)* of North and South America, Europe, Asia, and Africa are small to medium-sized, freshwater mammals that spend some time on land. The giant otters *(Pteronura brasiliensis)* may be 5ft (1.5m) long with a 2-ft (0.6-m) tail. They eat fish, frogs, reptiles, and birds. Their fur is valuable. Otters are sometimes tamed but may be difficult pets because they are playful and curious animals with great physical strength. Family Mustelidae.

Otter Hound, hunting dog (hound group) used for otter as early as 14th-century England. A boisterous dog with good scenting ability, it has a slightly domed, large but narrow head with long, square muzzle; low-set, long, hanging ears; level-backed body; heavy-boned legs with webbed feet; and a long, sickle-shaped tail. The rough coat, which may be any color, is 3–6in (7.5–15cm) long. Average size: 24–27in (61–68.5cm) high at shoulder; 75–115lb (34–52kg). *See also* Hounds.

Otter Trawl. △386.

Otto I or Otto the Great (912–73), Holy Roman emperor (962–73) and German king (936–73). He succeeded his father, King Henry I, in Germany. After subduing rebellious German nobles, he invaded (951) Italy to aid Queen Adelaide against Berengar II, who had succeeded her husband. Otto defeated Berengar, assumed the title king of the Lombards, and married Adelaide. In 955 he vanquished the Magyars at Lechfeld. He was crowned emperor in 962, reviving the Carolingian imperial title and founding the Holy Roman Empire. △1072, 1074.

Otto II (955–83), Holy Roman emperor (973–83). He was the son and successor of Otto I. After his accession he subdued a revolt by Henry, duke of Bavaria. In 978 Otto invaded France in retaliation against French efforts to obtain Lorraine. Shortly afterward he led an expedition to Italy to secure lands in S Italy that he claimed through his Byzantine wife. He was defeated by the Byzantines in 982.

Otto III (980–1002), Holy Roman emperor (983–1002). He was the son and successor of Otto II. Until he assumed the government in 996, a regency ruled for him, first under his mother Theophano, then under his grandmother, Adelaide. Shortly after taking over the government, he established his imperial seat at Rome. In 999 he raised his former tutor Gerbert of Aurillac to the papacy as Sylvester II. △1072.

Otto IV (1174–1218), Holy Roman emperor (1198–1215). He was elected German anti-king to Philip of Swabia in 1198. After Philip's death (1208), he was recognized as king and crowned emperor by Pope Innocent III. Otto's invasion of Italy led the pope to withdraw his support. In 1214, Otto was defeated at Bouvines by the French, who were allied with Frederick II, who had been elected by dissident nobles. The pope declared Otto deposed in 1215.

Otto, Nikolaus August. △1632.

Otto Cycle (Four-stroke Cycle). △1626.

Ottoman Empire, former state in Asia Minor, founded by Osman I in the 13th century. By the end of the 15th century, it had destroyed the Byzantine empire and conquered Egypt and Syria. At the height of its power under Suleiman the Magnificent (1520–66), the empire included much of SE Europe, W Asia, and N Africa. In the 17th and 18th centuries, a series of exhausting wars were fought against Poland, Austria, and Russia. The empire continued to decline until its dissolution after World War I, when the nationalist government convened at Ankara (1919) and finally proclaimed the republic of Turkey in 1923. △1108–10, 1232.

Ottumwa, city of SE Iowa, on Des Moines River, 75mi (121km) SE of Des Moines; seat of Wapello co; site of Ottumwa Heights College (1925). Industries: brass and iron goods, meat packing, farm machinery. Settled 1843; named Louisville 1844; inc. as Ottumwa 1851, as city 1857. Pop. (1970) 29,610.

Ouachita, river in Arkansas and Louisiana; rises in the Ouachita Mts, W Arkansas; flows E and SE into Louisiana to the Red River system near Monroe. Length: 600mi (966km).

Ouagadougou, largest city and capital of Upper Volta, in W Africa; trade and distribution center; served as capital of a Mossi Empire from 11th century until 1896 when French captured it. Industries: handcrafts, food processing, peanuts. Pop. 115,500.

Ouahran. *See* Oran.

Ouakari, or ukari, uakari, medium-sized, day-active monkey inhabiting treetops of the upper Amazon basin. The only short-tailed monkey of America, ouakaris have long shaggy coats and naked faces. They feed chiefly on fruit. Genus *Cacajao. See also* Monkey. △554.

Ouananiche, small, landlocked Canadian race of Atlantic salmon found only in the upper Saguenay and its tributaries and rivers flowing into the Gulf of St Lawrence. It is blue-green on its back and has cross-shaped black spots on its upper body. Weight: 3lb (1.4kg). Family Salmonidae; species *Salmo salarou-ananiche. See also* Salmon.

Oubangui (Ubangi), river in central Africa; originates at the confluence of the Bomu and Uele rivers; flows W and S forming part of boundary between Zaïre and Central African Republic; empties into the Congo River. Upper section is navigable only during wet season. Length: 660mi (1,063km).

Oudh, an ancient city of India in the district of Uttar Pradesh. It is one of the seven holy places of Hinduism and has many monuments and shrines, including the mosque of Rama's birthplace. It was the center of the Mogul Empire.

Ouija Board. △822.

Ounce. *See* Snow Leopard.

Outbreeding. *See* Crossbreeding.

Outer Hebrides. *See* Hebrides.

Ouzel, heavy-bodied, perching birds found in the mountains of Asia, Europe, and the Western Hemisphere. The ring ouzel has black plumage with a white chest collar and bright bill and facial markings. Family Cinclidae. *See also* Dipper.

Ovary, that part of a multicellular animal or a flowering plant that produces the egg cells, or female reproductive cells, and in vertebrates also produces the female sex hormones. In humans, an ovary—grayish-pink, about 1.5in by 1in (3.8cm by 2.5cm)—occurs on each side of the uterus. From puberty to menopause each month (except during pregnancy) one egg cell matures, ruptures from the ovary at ovulation, and passes into the Fallopian tube where it can be fertilized or will pass through into the uterus to be shed in menstruation. Under pituitary control, the ovary produces two female sex hormones: estrogen and progesterone, which control development and functioning of the female reproductive system. △700.

Ovenbird, perching bird found in varying habitats of South America and named for the oven-shaped nests built by some species. Included are the shaketail, spinetail, leafscraper, and other groups of woodcreeperlike birds. They are generally brownish or reddish-brown. Most feed on insects and some on seeds. Some species nest in cavities and others build globular mud-and-cow-dung or twig-and-leaf nests. A nest may have a side entrance, several chambers, and a tunnel approach. The eggs (2–9) are often white and usually incubated by both parents. Length: 5–9in (12.5–23cm). Family Furnariidae.

Overbeck, Johann (1789–1869), German painter. He was founder and leader of the Nazarene group of German religious painters. His importance is chiefly historical since the Nazarene movement was a critical transition from Classicism to Romanticism in German art. △1228.

Overland Park, city in NE Kansas; residential suburb of Kansas City (S). Inc. 1960. Pop. (1970) 76,623.

Overture, piece of orchestral music that opens an opera, oratorio, or stage play, or occasionally stands on its own, usually lively in character. Famous operatic overtures were composed by Mozart, Rossini (eg, *William Tell*), and Wagner. Noted concert overtures include the *1812 Overture* by Tchaikovsky.

Ovid (43 BC–AD 17), Roman poet, name in full Publius

Oslo, Norway

Wilhelm Ostwald

Ottawa, Canada: Parliament building

Otter

Ovidius Nasso. A popular, prolific poet, for no known reason he was exiled to a Black Sea outpost in AD 8. His works include *Amores,* 49 short love poems, many praising Corinna; *Ars Amatoria (The Art of Love),* a didactic work on how to get and keep a lover; and his masterpiece, the *Metamorphoses,* a collection of skillfully woven together mythological stories. *Tristia (Sorrows)* is an autobiographical work written while in exile. △1028.

Oviduct, tube that connects the ovaries and uterus, and through which egg cells are released from the ovary. In mammals it is known as the Fallopian tube. *See also* Fallopian Tube.

Oviedo, city in NW Spain, 230mi (370km) NW of Madrid; capital of Oviedo prov.; important industrial, mining, and agricultural center. City prospered in 9th century as the capital of Asturian kings; its importance declined in 10th century when capital was transferred to León; site of 8th-century Gothic cathedral, University of Oviedo (1604), meteorological observatory, courthouse, hospital, 14th-century cathedral, containing tombs of the Asturian kings. Industries: livestock, firearms, gunpowder, textiles. Founded *c.*760. Area: (prov.) 4,079sq mi (10,565sq km). Pop. (city) 154,-117; (prov.) 1,045,635.

Ovimbundu, or **Mbundu,** Negroid people of Angola. Their society is basically agricultural: crops include corn and beans, but hunting and animal husbandry are also practiced, and there is a trade in beeswax. Descent is matrilineal with regard to personal property and patrilineal with regard to land.

Ovulation, mature ovum released from the ovary, enabling fertilization to occur. In human females, one egg is released midway through the menstrual cycle. Occasionally two eggs are released simultaneously. Ovulation is stimulated by hormones from the pituitary gland: follicle-stimulating hormone (FSH) and luteinizing hormone (LH). △700, 706.

Ovum, egg or female gamete produced in the ovary and, after fertilization, capable of developing into a new individual. Oval or spherical, it is immobile and larger than a sperm. △700.

Owen, Robert (1771–1858), Welsh social reformer. He was the most famous of the early utopian socialist writers. His most important work was the three-volume *New View of Society* (1813–14). He felt people could be improved by bettering their environment and founded communities based on his concept of "villages of cooperation." In his model community in Scotland (New Lanark Mills) he paid high wages in the spinning mills, provided for better living generally for his employees, and made a profit. The New Harmony Venture he took over in Indiana in 1825 failed in 1829. △1236, 1324.

Owen Glendower (1359?–?1416), Welsh leader. Calling himself the Prince of Wales, he led a revolt against Henry IV (1399). As an outlaw he continually harassed the English. He captured and won over Edmund Mortimer (1402) and made an alliance with the Percies, thereby posing a serious threat to the English throne. Although defeated after Henry V's succession (1415), he remained a Welsh national hero.

Owens, Jesse (1913–), US athlete, b. John Cleveland Owens in Alabama. While a student at Ohio State, he broke several world records for jumping, hurdle racing, and flat racing (1935–36). At the 1936 Olympics (Berlin, Germany), he deflated Hitler's "Aryan" theory by winning the 100 meter race, the 200 meter race, the broad jump, and the 400 meter race. In the 200 meter race and the broad jump, he set world records that lasted over 20 years. △1408.

Owensboro, city in W Kentucky, on Ohio River; seat of Daviess co; site of Kentucky Wesleyan College (1866) and Brescia College (1874). Industries: chemicals, electrical equipment, steel, whiskey, tobacco. Settled 1800 as Yellow Banks; inc. 1817 as Rossborough; chartered as city 1866 and renamed for Col. Abraham Owen. Pop. (1970) 50,329.

Owens Valley Pupfish. △516.

Owl, nocturnal bird of prey found worldwide. Known for their forward-directed eyes and screams, hoots, and other sounds, the birds have come to be considered bad omens. Owls have rounded heads, hooked bills, rounded wings, short squarish tails, and long curved talons or claws. Their soft downy feathers are usually brown, black, or gray with white or lighter-colored markings. Using their keen eyesight and hearing, they feed at night on small mammals and birds, frogs, snakes, and sometimes fish. Most owls nest in hollow trees, rock niches, or on the ground. Round white eggs (1–11) are laid. The family Strigidae includes the horned, snowy, screech, and elf owls. Barn owls make up the family Tytonidae. Length: 5–27in (12.5–69cm). Order Strigiformes. △526.

Ox, (1) bovine member of a subdivision of the family Bovidae that includes true cattle and buffalo, water buffalo, and bison. (2) True cattle belonging only to the genus *Bos.* (3) Castrated male of domesticated cattle used as draft animal in various countries. *See also* Bison; Buffalo; Cattle; Water Buffalo.

Oxalic Acid, poisonous colorless crystalline fatty acid whose salts occur in some plants. It is prepared from carbon monoxide and sodium hydroxide and used for metal cleaning, textile cleaning, and in tanning. Properties: sp gr 1.653; melt. pt. 214.70°F (101.5°C).

Oxalis, or wood sorrel, creeping plants found in wooded areas. Common wood sorrel *(Oxalis acetosella)* is a stemless perennial native to temperate North America and Europe. Its flowers are white, veined with purple.

Oxbow, tightly looping stream meander with such an extreme curvature that only a neck of land is left between two parts of the stream, thus it resembles a U-shaped ox collar. Also called a horseshoe bend. *See also* Meander. △258.

Oxenstierna, Count Axel (1583–1654), Swedish statesman. Appointed chancellor (1612) under Gustav II, he was a skilled diplomat and a master military strategist. During Gustav's absence in 1614–16, he acted as vice regent. In 1629 he managed a truce with Poland and was given control of Swedish affairs in Germany. Gustav II died in 1632, and his daughter Christina, aged 6, came to the throne; during her minority, Oxenstierna was virtually ruler of Sweden until 1644. The presence of two of his relatives in the government increased his power. A reformer, he made significant social reforms. After Christina abdicated in 1654, Oxenstierna served her successor, Charles X, until his death.

Oxenstierna, Count Bengt Gabrielsson (1623–1702), Swedish diplomat. He served as governor of Poland and of Livonia, was a representative at the Congress of Nijmegen (1676), and in 1680–97 directed Sweden's foreign policy.

Oxford, city in England, at confluence of Thames (known locally as Isis) and Cherwell rivers; county town of Oxfordshire; seat of Oxford University (dating from 12th century); industrial center with major automobile works. Pop. 108,564.

Oxford, University of, English university, located in Oxford. The institution is a complex of several independent colleges with noted faculties in theology, modern languages, anthropology, humanities, physical sciences, music, and Oriental studies. Noted colleges include University (founded 1249), Balliol (1263), Merton (1264), Oriel (1326), Queen's (1340), New (1379), All Souls (1437), Magdalen (1458), Trinity (1554), and Jesus (1571). Women have been granted degrees from 1920 but it was not until 1959 that they were allowed full university status. Instruction is by lectures and a tutorial system.

Oxford and Asquith, Herbert Henry Asquith, 1st Earl of (1852–1928), English political figure. As a Liberal member of Parliament (1886–1918; 1920–24), he became home secretary (1892–95), chancellor of the exchequer (1905–08), and prime minister (1908–16). The Liberal party prospered in these years, and he is noted for his success, against heavy opposition, in abolishing the veto power of the House of Lords (1911) and promoting the Home Rule Bill. He retired from leadership of his party (1926). In the same year his book *Fifty Years of Parliament* appeared.

Oxford English Dictionary. △1780.

Oxford Movement (1833–43), efforts by the Church of England to restore the ideals of the earlier church, caused by a decline in religious interest and the development of liberal theology. Its main influence was in the ritual life of the church. John Newman, a leader, converted to the Roman Catholic Church. *See also* Newman, John Henry. △1148.

Oxidation Number. *See* Oxidation State.

Oxidation Reaction. △1566.

Oxidation-Reduction, or redox, chemical reaction involving simultaneous oxidation and reduction. In general, oxidation and reduction reactions occur together; thus in the reaction $Fe_2O_3 + 3C \rightarrow 2Fe + 3CO$, the iron oxide is reduced by the carbon, the carbon is oxidized by the iron oxide. Carbon is the reducing agent; iron oxide the oxidizing agent. The term "oxidation-reduction" is often used in a more restricted sense, to describe reversible reactions of this type. An example is reaction between iron and tin compounds: $2FeCl_2 + SnCl_4 \rightleftharpoons 2FeCl_3 + SnCl_2$. Another is the quinone-hydroquinone electrode reaction: $C_6H_4O_2 + 2H^+ + 2e \rightleftharpoons C_6H_4(OH)_2$. Oxidation-reduction reactions are important in many biochemical systems. △1554, 1564–66.

Oxidation State, measure of the extent to which an atom has lost electrons in a compound. It is stated as a number indicating the degree of ionization. Thus in sodium oxide, Na_2O, the sodium (Na^+) has an oxidation number of +1; the oxygen (O^{2-}) has an oxidation number of −2. In covalent and coordination compounds the oxidation number is the electric charge that the atoms would have if the compound were ionic. For example, in the ion $[CuCl_4]^{2-}$, regarded as formed from Cu^{2+} with 4 Cl^-, the copper has an oxidation number of +2. Oxidation numbers are often used in the names of chemical compounds, as in iron II chloride ($FeCl_2$) and iron III chloride ($FeCl_3$). △1566.

Oxide, chemical compound formed between oxygen and another element. Most elements form oxides, which fall into two main classes. Metallic oxides, such as CaO, TiO_2, etc, are mainly ionic compounds that are basic or, in some cases, amphoteric. Nonmetals have covalently bonded oxides, such as SO_2, CO_2, etc, that form acids in solution. Some, such as CO, are neutral. △1554, 1564.

Oxidizing Agent, chemical substance that causes oxidation reactions. Thus in the oxidation of carbon: $2C + O_2 \rightarrow 2CO$, oxygen is the oxidizing agent. Other common oxidizing agents include nitric acid, hydrogen peroxide, ozone, potassium dichromate, ferric compounds, and stannic compounds. △1564, 1568.

Oxnard, city in S California, 22mi (35km) E of Long Beach; originally founded 1868 as Richland, renamed 1875; departure point for tourists to the Santa Barbara Islands and Los Padres National Forest. Industries: electronic components, copper wire, agriculture, mining. Inc. 1903. Pop. (1970) 71,225.

Oxpecker, two species of African birds of the genus *Buphagus.* Both are brown with wide bills and stiff tails and reach 8in (20cm) in length. They cling to cattle and big game animals to remove ticks and maggots. Family Sturnidae.

Oxygen, common nommetallic gaseous element (symbol O), discovered (1774) by Joseph Priestley and independently (*c.*1772) by K.W. Scheele. It is the most abundant element in the Earth's crust (49.2% by weight), a constituent of water and many rocks. It is also present in the atmosphere (23.14% by weight), from which it is extracted by fractionation of liquid air. The element is used in steelmaking, in welding, in the manufacture of industrial chemicals, and in breathing and resuscitation apparatus. It is necessary for combustion and for the respiration of plants and animals. Chemically reactive, it forms compounds with nearly all other elements. Properties: at. no. 8; at. wt. 15.-9994; density 1.429 g dm^{-3}; melt. pt. −361.12°F (−218.4°C); boil. pt. −297.33°F (−182.962°C); most common isotope O^{16} (99.759%). *See also* Ozone. △1502, 1558–60, 1570.

Oxygen Cycle, release of oxygen into the atmosphere and water by plants during photosynthesis. This oxygen is utilized by plants and animals during respiration and in burning. The oxygen then combines with hydrogen to form water and carbon dioxide, again used in photosynthesis.

Oxygen Process, in steel production, a method of producing steel, using pure oxygen instead of air. A special pipe, called a lance, is employed through which a supersonic jet of oxygen is blown to a point above the pig-iron and scrap mixture. This method, superior to the Bessemer and open-hearth processes, is used widely in Japan, North America, and Europe. △1594.

Oxytocin, or **Pitocin,** peptide hormone secreted by the posterior pituitary. Its principal effect is on myoepithelial cells of the breast causing contraction of the ducts and ejection of milk. It also stimulates the contraction of the smooth muscle of the uterus, and it may play a part in the initiation of labor. It is used for the induction of labor.

Oyster, edible bivalve mollusk found worldwide in temperate and warm seas. Its porcelainlike shell, usually with unequal-sized valves, varies in shape according to environment. The eastern oyster *(Crassostrea virginica)* occurs along the Atlantic seaboard of the United States. Family Ostreidae. *See also* Bivalve; Pearl. △388, 478.

Oyster Catcher, warm area shorebird with a black and white stocky body and brightly colored, sharp-edged bill used to spear oysters and other seafood. After courtship, sand-colored eggs (2–4) are laid. Length: 21in (53cm). Family Haematopodidae.

Oyster Mushroom, a common arboreal fungus, *Pleurotus ostreatus*, that has a medium-size fleshy oyster- or fan-shaped cap and prominent gills. It usually has no stalk. It is edible. Oyster mushrooms are a favorite nesting ground for beetles.

Ozark Mountains (Ozark Plateau), mountainous upland region in S central United States, extends from SW Missouri across NW Arkansas into Oklahoma. The four main divisions include the Salem Plateau, Springfield Plateau, St Francis Mts, and Boston Mts, which contain the highest peaks exceeding 2,000 ft (610m). An eroded tableland, composed of limestone and dolomite rocks, the Ozarks are a source of lead and zinc. Noted for their scenery, forests, and numerous lakes, they are popular tourist region. Area: approx. 50,000 sq mi (129,500 sq km).

Ozone, unstable bluish gaseous allotrope of oxygen with characteristic odor (formula O_3) that decomposes into molecular oxygen. Ozone in the atmosphere is mainly present in the ozone layer 10–20 mi (16–32 km) above the Earth's surface, where it is responsible for absorbing a large portion of the Sun's dangerous ultraviolet radiation. Ozone is prepared commercially by irradiation of air and used as an oxidizing agent, in the purification of water, and for bleaching. △212.

Owl

Paasikivi, Juho Kusti (1870–1956), Finnish statesman. He was chairman of the Finnish delegation that signed a peace treaty with the USSR in 1920. He served as prime minister in 1918 and in 1944–46 and was president of Finland 1946–56.

Paca, William (1740–99), US political figure, b. near Abingdon, Md. A Maryland delegate to the Continental Congress (1774–79), he was a signer of the Declaration of Independence. He later served as Maryland's governor (1782–85) and as a US district judge (1789–99).

Paca, or spotted cavy, big-headed nocturnal rodent of Central and South America hunted for food by man and other animals. A plant-eating burrow-dweller, it has brown to black fur with rows of white spots. Length: to 30in (76cm); weight: over 20lb (9kg). Species *Cuniculus paca*. △602.

Pacemaker. △716.

Pachuca, city in central Mexico, surrounded by foothills of the Sierra Madre Oriental; capital of Hidalgo state; formerly inhabited by Aztecs; site of meteorological observatory, university (1869), mining and metallurgy school, 16th-century convent. Chief industry is silver mining. Founded 1534 on site of ancient Toltec city. Pop. 84,543.

Pacifica, suburban city in W California, S of San Francisco. Inc. 1957 as a conglomeration of small communities. Pop. (1970) 36,020.

Pacific, War of the (1879–83), conflict between Peru and Bolivia on one side, Chile on the other. The expropriation of Chilean holdings in the nitrate-rich province of Antofagasta induced Chile to declare war. Chile was victorious: Peru lost the provinces of Tarapacá and Arica; Bolivia became a land-locked nation.

Pacific Islands, Trust Territory of the, US trust territory in the Pacific Ocean, N of the Equator mostly in Micronesia; comprised of more than 2,000 islands, major ones include Caroline, Marshall, and Mariana (except Guam) islands; capital is Saipan. The Mariana Islands approved the Mariana Commonwealth Covenant (February 1976), a move toward a more permanent political relationship with the United States. The islands were seized by Japan 1914; occupied by US forces during WWII; they were approved as a US trusteeship by the United Nations 1947. Exports: fish, copra. Area: 700sq mi (1,813sq km). Pop. 102,250.

Pacific Ocean, the world's largest ocean, lying W of the North and South American continents, and E of Asia, Malaysia, and Australia, and extending N to S from the Arctic Circle to Antarctica. Its many arms include (N to S): Sea of Okhotsk, Sea of Japan, and the Philippine, South China, Coral, Tasman, Ross, Amundsen, Bering, and Bellingshausen seas.

With an area of approx. 69,000,000sq mi (178,700,000sq km), including its arms, the Pacific Ocean occupies about 33% of the surface area of the globe, and contains over 50% of the world's seawater, continually circulated by the two major Pacific Ocean currents, the North and South Equatorial currents. The E and N quarters of the Pacific Ocean floor comprise a great undersea plateau, occasionally pocked by deep troughs, and interrupted by long undersea mountain ranges. A series of long fracture zones runs E to W. The S, W, and central portions are characterized by an extensive volcano series, the Circum-Pacific Ring of Fire, which, with numerous coral formations, accounts for some 20,000 islands which dot this vast region.

The greatest known depth of the Pacific is 36,198ft (11,033m), in the Marianas Trench.

The continental shelves of the Pacific are a major commercial fishing ground, and, with advancements in undersea technology, the Pacific is becoming an increasingly important mineral resource.

The first settlers of the Pacific Islands were Asian migrants; their specific origins and settlement dates are unknown. European recognition of the Pacific as a separate ocean dates from the early 16th century when Vasco Nuñez de Balboa arrived at its E shore in 1513 and Ferdinand Magellan explored beyond the Philippines in 1520. Spain and Portugal dominated in early exploration of the Pacific; they were joined by the English and Dutch in the 17th century and France and Russia in the 18th, as the Pacific became important to European whalers. Although many islands had been charted prior to the 19th century, reliable undersea exploration did not begin until the 19th century led by expeditions of the US and British navies. △202, 232.

Pacific Scandal (1873), Canadian political controversy. L.S. Huntington, a Liberal, brought down the Conservative Macdonald administration, charging that building contracts for the Canadian Pacific Railway had been awarded to Hugh Allan in exchange for campaign contributions. The charges were never proved and the Conservatives regained office in 1878.

Pacifism, philosophy opposing war or violence as a means of settling disputes between nations. Elements can be found in ancient Hebrew and early Christian theology and in later Anabaptist and Quaker beliefs.

Oxalis

Oxford, England

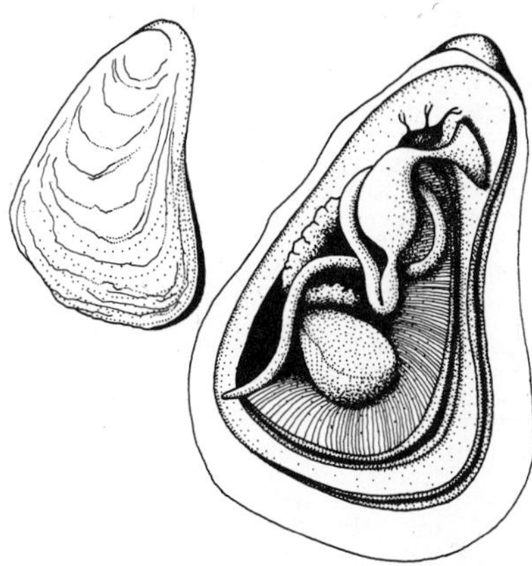

Oyster

International pacifist groups were organized during the 19th century, foremost among them the American Peace Society (1828), which later numbered Woodrow Wilson among its members. Eastern religions, the doctrines of Mohandas Gandhi, and the British Fellowship of Reconciliations were based on this philosophy.

Pack Rat, name for over 20 species of nocturnal rodents of North and South America that build large aboveground nests. In carrying nest material they often drop one object to pick up another; from this habit comes the name pack (= trade) rat. Length: 8in (203mm). Family Cricetidae. △604.

Paddlefish, flatbill, or spoonbill sturgeon, primitive bony fish closely related to sturgeon and found in the Mississippi and Yangtze river valleys. Bluish gray to olive brown, it has a long paddlelike nose extension, cartilaginous skeleton, and huge jaws. Length: 6ft (1.8m); weight: 30–50lb (13.5–22.5kg). Family Polyodontidae; species Chinese *Psephurus gladius,* American *Polyodon spathula. See also* Osteichthyes.

Paddle Tennis, a game similar to lawn tennis. It is played by 2 or 4 persons on an indoor or outdoor court 50 by 20 feet (15.3 by 6.1m), with a net 2 feet, 7 inches high (0.8m). A deadened tennis ball is used and each player has a short-handled wooden paddle. The scoring system is almost identical to the scoring system used in lawn tennis, where the first player to win six games wins the set. In championship play, a best-of-three series of sets determines the winner. Paddle tennis was invented in 1924 by Dr. Frank Peer Beal of New York City, originally as a game for children. In 1938, some alterations were made in the rules of play and the size of the court (now used in the adult version of the game). The sport is governed by the US Paddle Tennis Association. *See also* Tennis.

Paderewski, Ignace Jan (1860–1941), Polish pianist, composer, statesman. Shortly after his professional debut in 1887 in Vienna he established himself as the most popular concert pianist since Franz Liszt. Famous for his interpretation of another Pole, Frederic Chopin, as well as Schumann, Liszt, and Rubenstein. He was especially popular in the United States. Among his compositions is the well known *Minuet in G.* From 1910 to 1920, he devoted himself to the cause of Polish nationalism and raised funds to assist the victims of World War I on US concert tours. After the war he served as prime minister and foreign minister of Poland in a coalition ministry (1919). △1364.

Padua (Padova), industrial city in N Italy, 22mi (35km) W of Venice; capital of Padova prov. First mentioned 302 BC, it was a leading Italian commune 11th–13th centuries; it was ruled by Carrara family 1318–1405, when it passed to Venice; site of University (1222, 2nd-oldest in Italy; Galileo taught here), 13th-century cathedral, oldest European botanical garden (1545), 12th-century Palazzo della Ragione, and several medieval and Renaissance buildings. Industries: agricultural machinery, motorcycles, textiles, distilling, wine. Pop. 224,217.

Paducah, port city in SW Kentucky, on Ohio River; seat of McCracken co. Occupied by Gen. U. S. Grant in 1861, it was used as Union supply depot during Civil War; birthplace of Irvin S. Cobb; site of city hall (designed by Edward Durrell Stone); dark tobacco, livestock, and strawberry market. Industries: shipyards, shoes, railroad shops, machinery, concrete. Founded in 1821 as Pekin; inc. as village 1830, as city 1856. Pop. (1970) 31,627.

Paestum, ancient city in S Italy, on Bay of Salerno. Ancient Poseidonia was founded *c.* 600 BC by colonists from Sybaris; it was destroyed by Muslims AD 871 and deserted; ancient Greek ruins include classical wall paintings; site of village of Pesto.

Paganini, Niccolo (1782–1840), Italian violinist and composer. From 1805 on he made a series of triumphant appearances in the European capitals, mesmerizing audiences with his unequaled technical virtuosity. A charismatic showman, he did nothing to discourage rumors that he was in league with the devil. His style influenced many other Romantic musicians, notably Franz Liszt. He often played his own difficult, virtuosic compositions, which include six violin concertos and 24 caprices. △1246.

Paget, (Sir) James (1814–99), English surgeon known as a founder of the science of pathology. He discovered the parasitic worm *Trichina spiralis* that causes trichinosis, described the bone disease osteitis deformans (Paget's disease), and was also among the first to recommend surgical removal of bone-marrow tumors rather than amputation.

Pagoda, Eastern building in the form of a tower, which originated in India and spread with Buddhism to China and Japan. The form of the tower is polygonal. Its height is determined by the number of superimposed stories. Elaborately ornamented roofs often project from each story. △1036, 1048.

Pago Pago, town on Tutuila Island in SW Pacific Ocean, at shore of an inlet which forms an excellent harbor; site of US naval base; capital of American Samoa since 1899. Pop. 2,491.

Pahari Painting. △1204.

Pahoehoe, Hawaiian term for a lava flow that moves freely and cools with a smooth, ropelike surface. The term was first used geologically by C.E. Dutton in 1883. △176.

Paige, Satchel (1906–), US baseball player, b. Leroy Robert Paige in Mobile, Ala. A right-hand pitcher in the Negro Leagues, he did not get an opportunity to play major league ball until he was 42. He played in the major leagues for six years. He was elected to the Baseball Hall of Fame in 1971.

Pain, distinct, intense, and highly negative sensation, possibly the least understood of all the senses. Pain may arise from the skin or from the deeper tissues of the body, possibly through the overexcitation of free nerve endings in those tissues. Individual tolerance of pain varies, perhaps because of genetic differences but more likely because of cultural conditioning (for example, members of different ethnic groups have different average pain tolerances). △678.

Paine, Robert Treat (1731–1814), US political figure and jurist, b. Boston, Mass. A Massachusetts delegate to the Continental Congress (1774–78), he signed both the Olive Branch Petition (1775) and the Declaration of Independence (1776). He served as Massachusetts' attorney general (1777–90), helped draft the state's constitution, and was a state supreme court judge (1790–1804).

Paine, Thomas (1737–1809), American political writer and leader, b. England. He was an influential voice of colonial public opinion, and his pamphlet *Common Sense* (1776; published anonymously) became a rallying point for colonial patriots. His series of 16 papers, *The Crisis,* encouraged the patriots during the Revolutionary War. While in England he wrote (1791) *Rights of Man,* defending the French Revolution. For this he was indicted for treason and fled to France. He was jailed by the Jacobins (1793–94) when he advocated exile instead of death for King Louis XVI. Paine returned to the United States (1802), where he died in poverty. His main beliefs included the power of reason where there is freedom to debate, tolerance, equality of rights, and the dignity of man. △1218.

Paint, a coating applied to a surface for protective and decorative purposes. Paint—composed of pigment, or color, and a vehicle, a liquid that suspends the pigment—adheres to the intended surface and hardens when dry. Pigments are made of earth, oxides of metals, or synthetic materials. Vehicles may be oils, water mixed with a binding agent, organic compounds, or synthetic resins. Synthetic resins (alkyd or acrylate polymers) may be soluble in water or oil. Water-base paint is water-soluble; oil-based paint is soluble in turpentine or other oil-based solvents. △1812. 1560, 1562.

Painted Desert, badlands in N central Arizona, E of Colorado and Little Colorado rivers; erosion and heat have exposed colorful bands of red and yellow sediment and bentonite clay; includes Petrified Forest National Park (SE). Area: approx. 7,500sq mi (19,425sq km).

Painted Lady Butterfly, or thistle butterfly, insect whose larvae feed on thistles. Like the painted beauty *Vanessa virginiensis,* this butterfly's wing markings are brownish-black and orange-gold with small white spots near the front wing tips. Species *Vanessa cardui.*

Painted Leopard. *See* Ocelot.

Painted Turtle, freshwater turtle of the United States. It has bright orange or red markings around the periphery of its smooth, dark olive shell. Males have long front claws. Length: to 6in (15.2cm). Family Emydidae; species *Chrysemys picta. See also* Turtle.

Painting, the art of producing pictures on flat surfaces, one of the oldest of the arts. Such pictures are usually painted on canvas by using a brush and either oil or watercolor paints. Paintings produced on fresh wet plaster are called frescoes. For articles on the history of painting, *see* Abstract Art; Baroque Art; Cubism; Dadaism; Expressionism; Fauvism; Futurism; Impressionism; Mannerism; Neo-Impressionism; Op Art; Pop Art; Post-Impressionism; Realism; Romanticism; Rococo; Primitivism; Renaissance Art; and Surrealism. *See also* the names of individual painters. For different kinds of art, *see also* Genre Painting; Landscape Painting; Still-Life.

Paired-Associate Learning, in psychology, task used to study verbal learning and memory. Items such as words or syllables are presented for study in pairs, and the learners must try to give the second term of each pair when the first item is presented alone. *See also* Memory.

Paiute, a Shoshonean-speaking tribe of North American Indians divided into two major groups: the Southern Paiute (commonly called "Digger Indians" in the Gold Rush days), who occupied W Utah, N Arizona, SE Nevada, and California; and the so-called Northern Paiute (or "Snake Indians"), also known as the Mono-Paviotso, who inhabited W Nevada, S Oregon, and E California. About 4,000 live in both areas today.

Pakistan, nation in S Asia. The people, a mixture of races and nationalities, are overwhelmingly Muslim. The country was created in 1947 from W India.

Land and economy. The Indus River, flowing S through the heartland of Pakistan, causes fertile, alluvial plains the length of the country. The Hindu Kush Mts lie to the NW and the Himalayas to the NE. A plateau covers most of Baluchistan in the W and the Sind Desert occupies most of the SE. Annual rainfall varies from 5in (13cm) in the Sind to 30–40in (76-102cm) in the NW. The country's economy is based upon agriculture, employing 80% of the work force. Cotton is the most important crop, providing adequate amounts for the country's needs plus substantial surpluses for export. Wheat is the most important food crop. Little has been done in the way of mineral development, and fewer than 1% of the people are employed in industry. The government has been successfully introducing new industries to aid employment.

People. The cosmopolitan make-up of the population can be attributed to its location. Long the favorite invasion route of the Indian subcontinent, many of the invaders remained and settled among the local tribes. Five major languages and several dialects are spoken; however, Urdu and English are the official languages. Over 80% of the people are Muslim; most of the rest are Hindu. The people are 75% illiterate, but the government has instituted improved educational programs.

Government. A federal republic, the government is invested in a president, who serves as chief executive and head of state, and a unicameral National Assembly of 156 members. All are elected for five-year terms. The president may at any time dissolve the National Assembly and call for national elections; however, if he does, his own term expires automatically four months later. Each province has its own governor and legislature.

History. After a period of agitation in the 1930s, Muhammad Ali Jinnah led Pakistan to its independence in 1947. Fashioned from India, the original country was in two sections, East and West Pakistan, separated by 900mi (1,450km). A great migration followed, which disrupted the country's economy for many years: about 6,000,000 Hindus and Sikhs left Pakistan for India, and at the same time about 7,-000,000 Muslims left India for Pakistan. In 1971, East Pakistan, which had demanded more autonomy within Pakistan, revolted and war broke out. With India's help, East Pakistan became independent as Bangladesh. The W sector, under Prime Minister Zulfikar Ali Bhutto, initially had strained relations with Bangladesh, but diplomatic relations were resumed in 1971.

PROFILE

Official name: Islamic Republic of Pakistan
Area: 310,401sq mi (803,944sq km)
Population: 70,600,000
Density: 227.4per sq mi (87.8per sq km)
Chief cities: Islamabad (capital); Karachi; Lahore
Government: Republic
Religion: Islam
Language: Urdu, English
Monetary unit: Pakistan rupee
Gross national product: $7,600,000,000
Per capita income: $100
Industries (major products): textiles, processed foods, cement, petroleum products
Agriculture (major products): wheat, cotton, rice, sugar cane
Minerals (major): limestone, rock salt
Trading partners (major): United States, West Germany, Japan, United Kingdom

Pala. *See* Impala.

Palafox, José de (1775?–1847), Spanish general. His heroic defense of Saragossa in the Peninsular War (1808–14) made him a national hero. He supported Ferdinand VII in the uprisings of 1820–23 and later fought for Isabella II in the first Carlist Wars (1833–39).

Palaquium. *See* Gutta-percha.

Palate, the roof of the mouth, the bony front part known as the hard palate, the softer fleshy part in the back known as the soft palate. It separates the mouth and nasal cavities. △694.

Palatinate, two regions of West Germany. The Lower, or Rhenish, Palatinate is on the Rhine River. The Upper Palatinate is on the Danube River in Bavaria. The regions were often united historically and were important in the affairs of the Holy Roman Empire from 1356, when the count palatine of the Rhine became an imperial elector. Both regions were part of Bavaria during 1815–1946. In 1946 the Lower Palatinate became the state of Rhineland-Palatinate. The Upper Palatinate remained in Bavaria. *See also* Thirty Years War.

Palatine, town in NE Illinois, NW of Chicago; site of William Rainey Harper College (1965). Industries: safety equipment, machine tools. Inc. 1869. Pop. (1970) 25,904.

Palembang, port city in SE Sumatra, on both sides of Musi River; capital of South Sumatra prov. City served as capital of Hindu-Sumatran kingdom of Sri Vijaya (8th century); Dutch settled in city 1617 and est. a trading post and fortress 1659; scene of massacre of Dutch by sultanate 1811; sultanate was abolished 1825; occupied by Japanese during WWII; site of Sriwidjaja State University (1960). Exports: oil, rubber, coffee, coal. Industries: food processing, textiles, oil refining, rubber, fertilizer. Pop. 474,971.

Paleobotany, study of preserved remains of plants. Fossil plants occur as imprints of leaves, as spores and seeds, and as parts of branches and trunks. This division of paleontology has permitted the tracing of various evolutionary relationships among plants. *See also* Paleontology. △562.

Paleocene Epoch. *See* Tertiary Period.

Paleoclimatology, study of ancient climates. The main clues are the remains of plants and animals and the interpretation of various kinds of sediments. △272, 274.

Paleogeography, science that studies ancient geography. It seeks to determine what the physical and biological conditions of the Earth were during its various geological periods. The science also seeks to determine how conditions in one period led to conditions in the next and succeeding periods. Much of the data needed for good analysis is lacking, and most studies in this area are general.

Paleolithic Age, or Old Stone Age, period in man's evolution in which he used stone tools and weapons and had a hunting and food-gathering economy. Lower Paleolithic man (before about 220,000 BC) used chipped stone artifacts; Middle and Upper Paleolithic cultures also ground and polished stones. *See also* Eolithic Age. △650, 652.

Paleolithic Art, or "cave art," was practiced by early European man in caves, starting in around 30,000 BC. Beasts of chase such as bison and deer were represented naturalistically on the cave walls, probably as a part of some ritual. The first such cave was discovered in 1879 in the Spanish cavern of Altamira.

Paleologan Art. △1060.

Paleomagnetism, the study of both direction and intensity of Earth's magnetic field and the changes in it with geologic time. This is important in the investigation of the theory of continental drift. Since the "magnetic memory" of rocks is measurable, this determines their orientation in relation to magnetic north at the time of their solidification. Since neither the location nor intensity of the magnetic poles has changed very much, although the field of Earth has reversed at least once, the gross displacement of large rock formations as measured by their magnetic qualities can be explained by the continental drift theory. *See also* Continental Drift; Magnetic Field, Earth. △168, 172, 276.

Paleontology, geological study of animal and plant fossils. It is important in tracing the evolutionary history of existing and extinct organisms, as well as determining relative ages of geological deposits. The geological periods are: Precambrian, Cambrian, Ordovician, Silurian, Devonian, Carboniferous, Permian, Triassic, Jurassic, Cretaceous, Tertiary, and Quaternary. *See also* Evolution; Fossil; Geologic Time. △270, 410, 560–564.

Paleozoic Era, one of the major divisions of geologic time lasting from about 570 million to 225 million years ago. Its beginnings mark the earliest occurrence of a good fossil record. All the major animal phyla were present in the early seas of the era; later, some groups took to the land. The Paleozoic is subdivided into the Cambrian, Ordovician, Silurian, Devonian, Carboniferous and Permian periods. *See also* Geologic Time. △276, 568.

Palermo, seaport city in Italy, on Gulf of Palermo, 200mi (322km) SSW of Naples; capital of Sicily and province of Palermo. Founded by Phoenicians *c.* 8th century BC; it passed to Romans 254 BC; prospered under Saracens 9th–11th centuries; it was taken by Normans 1072 and became capital of kingdom of Sicily; seized by Giuseppe Garibaldi 1860; site of 12th–15th-century cathedral, 11th-and 12th-century churches, 12th-century Arab-Norman Palatine Chapel, academy of medical science, letters and arts (1621). Industries: shipbuilding, textiles, food products, chemicals. Pop. 653,533.

Palestine, region on the E shore of the Mediterranean. It has been the Holy Land for Jews, Christians, and Muslims. It was a country of herders and farmers from 4000 BC. Moses led the Jews out of Egypt and into Palestine (*c.* 2000 BC), where they became subjects of the Philistines until 1100 BC, when Saul, David, and Solomon established Hebrew kingdoms. Macedonia ruled 333–142 BC, when Pompey conquered the land for Rome. In succeeding centuries Christianity was dominant until Muslim Arabs seized power in 640. In 1099, Palestine fell to the Crusaders; in 1291 they were routed by the Ottoman Turks. Western influence filtered in through Russian Jews, immigrating after 1882, who embraced the Zionist movement. Arab nationalism was rising, and the British, with a League of Nations mandate over Palestine, attempted unsuccessfully to divide the country between Arabs and Jews. The Arabs feared economic and political results of immigration as WWII and Nazi persecution brought many Jews to Palestine. In 1947, Britain consigned the problem to the United Nations. Most of ancient Palestine became part of the new state of Israel. During the 1970s the Palestine Liberation Organization and other nationalist Arab groups demanded an independent Palestine for Arabs. *See also* Israel. △1380.

Palestine Liberation Organization (PLO), a council formed (1964) to coordinate the predominantly terrorist activities of the Arab guerrilla groups and refugee organizations of which it is composed. In Nov. 1974 Yasir Arafat, its chairman since 1968, appeared before the United Nations and received UN support for the establishment of an independent and secular Palestinian state. △1380.

Palestrina, Giovanni Pierluigi da (1526–1594), Italian composer of motets, masses, and other religious music. He is often regarded as the greatest composer of the Renaissance period, and his music was long taken as the standard of traditional Roman Catholic liturgical music. *See also* Renaissance Music. △1132.

Palladian Architecture, architectural style derived from the buildings and theories of the great Italian architect Andrea Palladio (1508–80), emphasizing symmetrical planning and musically based harmonic proportions. The style became popular in England in the Palladian revival of the early 18th century led by Colen Campbell and Lord Burlington. △1142.

Palladio, Andrea (1508–80), Italian Renaissance architect. He studied Roman architecture and published drawings of Roman ruins together with his own designs in *Four Books of Architecture*. In so doing, he revived symmetrical planning and harmonic proportions. His most notable buildings were villas and palazzos, typically with arch and column facades, such as the Villa Rotunda, Vicenza. △1140, 1142.

Palladium, precious metallic element (symbol Pd) of the second transition series, discovered 1803 by W.H. Wollaston. It is found associated with platinum in nickel ores. Chemically, it is similar to platinum, but more reactive. Properties: at. no. 46; at. wt. 106.4; sp. gr 12.02; melt. pt. 2,826°F (1,552°C); boil. pt. 6,021°F (3,329°C); most common isotope Pd^{106} (27.3%). *See also* Transition elements. △1552–54.

Pagoda

Thomas Paine

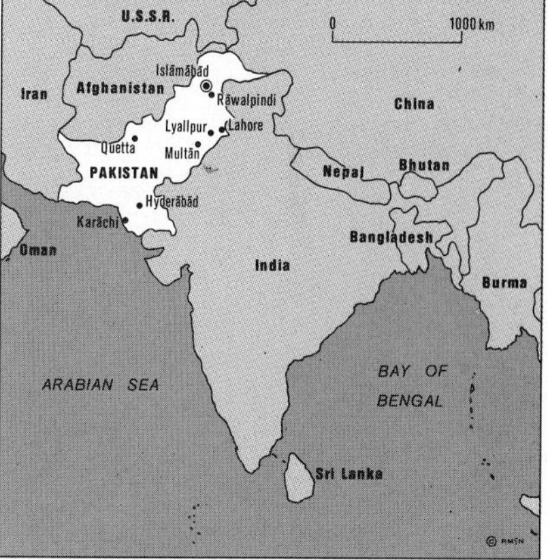
U.S.S.R.
0
1000 km
Iran
Afghanistan
Islāmābād
Rāwalpindi
Lyallpur
Lahore
Quetta
Multān
PAKISTAN
Hyderābād
Karāchi
China
Nepal
Bhutan
Bangladesh
Oman
India
Burma
ARABIAN SEA
BAY OF
BENGAL
Sri Lanka
Pakistan

Palermo, Sicily

Pallas, asteroid discovered (1802) by H. W. M. Olbers; the second largest asteroid. Diameter 280mi (450km); mean distance from Sun 257,000,000mi (414,000,000km); mean sidereal period 4.61 yr. △78.

Pallas' Cat, or manul, rare, small, longhaired cat found from the Caspian Sea to Tibet and north to Siberia, but always in the mountains. It has small rounded ears, circular pupils, short legs, and a compact body. Color is silvery to buff yellow with a pattern of dark spots and stripes. It has a fierce disposition. Length: body—20in (51cm); tail—10in (25cm). Family Felidae; species *Octolobus manul.* △606.

Pallava. △1034.

Palm, family of trees found in tropical and subtropical regions. Ancient flowering plants that date to the early Triassic (225,000,000 years ago), they have a woody, unbranched, columnar trunk with a crown of large, stiff leaves. The leaves may either be fanlike (palmate) or featherlike (pinnate). Rather than having a true bark covering, palm trunks are covered with fibers. Palm flowers are small, in large clusters, and green, yellow, or red in color. The fruits, which vary according to species, are berries, drupes, or nuts. An economically important family, palms are the source of wax, oil, fiber, sugar, and food; they are also ornamental plants. Family Palmaceae. △452.

Palma, seaport city in Spain, in Balearic Islands, on Bay of Palma; capital of Majorca Island and Baleares prov.; site of Gothic cathedral (1230–1601) containing tomb of King James II of Aragon, 13th-century church of San Francisco containing tomb of Raymond Lully, a Catalan philosopher, Moorish palace, 16th-century town hall. Industries: alcohol, pottery, leather, tourism, jewelry, wine, oil, livestock, flour, sugar, starch, silks. Area: (prov.) 1,936sq mi (5,014sq km). Pop. (city) 234,098; (prov.) 558,287.

Palm Beach, town in SE Florida, on N end of an island separating Lake Worth from Atlantic Ocean; resort. Settled 1870, it developed rapidly after 1893 when Henry Flagler realized resort potential of area and supervised and financed its planning. Inc. 1911. Pop. (1970) 9,086.

Palmer, Arnold (Daniel) (1929–), US golfer, b. Latrobe, Pa. He was responsible for raising golf to new levels of popularity and was named (1970) Athlete of the Decade by the Associated Press. He won the US Open (1960), two British Opens (1961, 1962), and four Masters (1958, 1960, 1962, 1964).

Palmer, Samuel (1805–81), English landscape painter and engraver. Influenced by William Blake, many of his works depict views of Shoreham, including "In a Shoreham Garden" (*c.* 1829). △1242.

Palmerston, Henry John Temple, 3rd Viscount (1784–1865), English political figure. Elected a Tory member of Parliament (1807), he served as secretary of war (1809–28). He left the Tories in support of George Canning (1828). Joining the Whigs, he became foreign secretary (1830) and prime minister (1855), playing a major role in European affairs. Except for a short period in 1858, he remained prime minister until his death. He is noted for effecting the independence of Belgium (1830–31), protecting Portugal and Spain from the threat of absolutism (1834), and annexing Hong Kong (1840–41). He maintained strict neutrality throughout the US Civil War.

Palmetto, fan-leaved palm native from S United States to Central America. The trunk is often covered with dead leaf bases. The 25 species include *Sabal palmetto,* the 90ft (27.4m) cabbage palm of SE United States; *S. bermudiana,* the 40ft (12m) Bermuda palmetto, with a crooked trunk; *S. umbraculifera* native to the West Indies with a massive trunk; and *S. texana,* the 50ft (15m) Texas palmetto, which has a bright red-brown trunk. Family Palmaceae.

Palmistry. △822.

Palm Springs, city in S California, 44mi (71km) SE of San Bernardino; named "Agua Caliente" by Spanish in 1774, because of numerous hot springs; noted tourist resort; site of Mt San Jacinto, Palm Canyon, and the Joshua Tree National Monument. Founded 1876; inc. 1938. Pop. (1970) 20,936.

Palm Sunday, in the Christian year, the Sunday before Easter and the beginning of Holy Week. Palm Sunday commemorates Christ's triumphal entry into Jerusalem, when the people spread palm branches before him.

Palmyra (Tudmur), ancient city in Syria. An important trade center as early as the 1st century BC, the city rose to prominence *c.* AD 130, during the reign of Hadrian and became a Roman colony *c.* 212. Odenathus built it into a strong autonomous state, and under Zenobia the kingdom became formally independent. It was destroyed by Aurelian in 273.

Palmyra Palm, fan-leaved palm tree native to India and Malaya. The sap is used to make a fermented drink; the seeds are edible. Height: to 100ft (30.5m); family Palmaceae; species *Borassus flabellifer.* △340.

Palo Alto, suburban city in W California, 17mi (27km) NW of San Jose; site of "El Palo Alto," a 1,000-year-old tree, and Stanford University (1885). Industries: electronic equipment, missile production. Founded 1891; inc. 1894. Pop. (1970) 56,181.

Palo Alto, Battle of (May 8, 1846), first battle of the Mexican War. Near Brownsville, Tex., US Gen. Zachary Taylor defeated a 6,000-man Mexican force under Gen. Mariano Arista. Nine US soldiers were killed, while the Mexicans lost 300–400 men.

Palolo Worm, polychaete annelid of the South Pacific that lives in holes among coral reefs. A nocturnal swimmer at breeding time, its posterior portion is filled with eggs or sperm. This portion develops an eyespot, separates from the body, and swims to the surface to mate. Family Eunicidae; species *Eunice viridis. See also* Annelida.

Palomar Observatory. *See* Hale Observatories.

Palomino, light horse developed from Spanish horses in the United States and Mexico. A riding horse, it is cream, golden, or light-chestnut, with white, silver, or ivory mane and tail. Height: 56–64in (142.2–162.6cm) at shoulder; weight: 900–1,300lb (405–585kg).

Palynology, originally the study of spores and pollen, now also investigates tiny fragments of animals and plants found in sediment. Neopalynology deals with living microorganisms and parts of plants. Paleopalynology explores fossils of plants and the ancient pollens and spores they produced. △560.

Pamela, or Virtue Rewarded (1740–41), novel in four volumes, by Samuel Richardson. △1188.

Pamir, mountainous region mostly in Tadzhik SSR, USSR, partly in Sinkiang, Uighur, China, Jammu and Kashmir, India, and along Afghanistan borders; the region forms a geologic structural knot from which the great Tien Shan, Karakorum, Kunlun, and Hindu Kush mountain ranges radiate. The climate is cold during winter and cool during summer; terrain includes grasslands and sparse trees; nomads herd sheep and coal is mined; site of several glaciers and of Terak Pass, used by Marco Polo enroute to China (1271). Highest peaks are Mt Communism, 24,590ft (7,500m) and Lenin Peak, 23,508ft (7,170m).

Pampas (Pampa), plain in S South America, mostly in E Argentina. Divided into two regions: the humid Pampas is very fertile, the heart of the economy of Argentina; the larger dry Pampas includes Buenos Aires, La Pampa, Santa Fe, and Córdoba prov. Area: 294,000sq mi (761,460sq km). △588.

Pampas Deer. △588.

Pampas Grass, species *(Cartaderia selloana)* of tall, reedlike grass of the family Poaccae, native to South America and widely cultivated in warm parts of the world as a lawn ornamental. Female plants bear flower clusters, 3ft (91cm) tall, which are silvery and plumelike. △454.

Pamplona, city in N Spain, 20mi (32km) from French border, on Arga River; capital of Navarra prov.; former capital of French kingdom. Taken 778 from Arabs by Charlemagne, it passed to Ferdinand of Aragón 1512; occupied by French during Peninsular War (1808–13); site of annual fiesta of San Fermín, including celebrated running of bulls; 1397 Gothic cathedral. Industries: sugar milling, brewing, canning, textiles, wine, candies, firearms, furniture, shoes, flour, musical instruments. Area: (prov.) 4,024sq mi (10,422sq km). Pop. (city) 147,168; (prov.) 464,867.

Pan, in Greek mythology, the son of Mercury and a dryad, god of woods and fields, the shepherd and his flock. He is depicted with the horns, legs, and hooves of a goat. A forest dweller, he pursued and loved the dryads and led their dances, while playing the syrinx, the pipes of his invention. △836.

Pan-African Movement, a loosely organized effort for the unification and independence of African nations and black people everywhere. The movement officially began at the Pan-African Congress of 1900 in London, organized by W.E.B. Du Bois and other Western blacks, and was followed by several other meetings in succeeding decades. The Pan-African Federation, created in 1944, was the first strong voice in the call for African rights, leading to considerable activity toward a unified Africa. Although still plagued by differences in structural concepts, the movement materialized in 1963 as the Organization of African Unity, which has enjoyed a limited success. *See also* Organization of African Unity.

Panama, independent Central American nation at the tip of the isthmus connecting North and South America. It is governed by a military junta. The economy is almost completely dependent on the Panama Canal Zone.

Land and economy: Panama is divided into 5 areas. The 60-mi (97-km) strip running E–W and including Colón produces most of the country's food, while the Pacific plains have fertile valleys with bananas, pasture land, and grains. Veraguas, a region of rugged, rainy, dense forests, produces coffee. The Caribbean plains, W of Canal Zone, produce cocoa and rubber, and the lowlands E of the Canal Zone have bananas and fishing. Two mountain systems, Sierra de Chiriquí and Cordillera de Veraguas, include volcanic peaks; the highest is Chiriquí, 11,401ft (3,475m). Half of the population are subsistence farmers in an economy dominated by trade and international commerce associated with the Panama Canal Zone.

People: Panamanians are largely Roman Catholic, and include descendants of Spanish colonials, immigrant West Indian blacks, and indigenous Indians. The literacy rate is 85%.

Government: Provisional junta government rules by decree. Parties were dissolved in 1968. Elections have been promised, and some liberties have been restored.

History: Spain's major explorers all had contact with Panama: Rodrigo de Bastidas explored it in 1501; Christopher Columbus sighted it the same year; Vasco de Balboa landed on his way to find the Pacific Ocean; and Francisco Pizarro stopped on his way to Peru in 1531. It remained under Spanish rule until 1821, when it joined the Confederation of Greater Colombia, and in 1903 it declared its independence. Pres. Arnulfo Arias was deposed in a 1968 military coup. After anti-U.S. riots, the United States and Panama agreed in 1974 to negotiate a new treaty giving Panama more revenue and eventual jurisdiction over the Panama Canal. *See also* Panama Canal Zone.

PROFILE

Official name: Republic of Panamá
Area: 29,209sq mi (75,651sq km)
Population: 1,700,000
Density: 58.2per sq mi (22.5per sq km)
Chief cities: Panamá City (capital); Colón
Government: Provisional junta
Religion: Roman Catholic
Language: Spanish (official)
Monetary unit: Balboa
Gross national product: $1,360,000,000
Per capita income: $904
Industries: petroleum products, textiles, wood products, processed foods
Agriculture: bananas, mahogany, pineapple, cocoa, coconut, sugar, shrimp
Minerals: clay, salt, traces of copper
Trading partners: United States, Canada, Mexico, South American countries

Panama, Isthmus of, narrow strip of land in S Central America, which connects South America with Central and North America. Sometimes used synonymously for entire Republic of Panama, it specifically refers to the narrowest part of the strip between Colón (N) and Balboa (S), which is the site of the Panama Canal.

Panama Canal, waterway built by the United States (1904–14) to connect the Atlantic and Pacific oceans, opening a shorter route for trade to the Far East. The Isthmus of Panama, owned by Colombia and also the narrowest point of Central America, was chosen as the location. After territorial disputes with Britain were settled in 1850 by the Clayton-Bulwer Treaty, the United States entered into the Hay-Herran Treaty with Colombia (1903), agreeing to pay $10 million and an annual rental of $250,000 in return for a 99-year lease over a 6-mile (9.7km) wide strip of land. When Panama gained independence, the US signed the Hay-Bunau-Varilla Treaty (1903) allowing US control of a canal zone 10 miles (16km) wide for all time with the same fees set in the Colombia treaty. Construction was carried on under US army engineer George W Goethals. Advances in treating malaria and yellow fever were made while treating victims working on the canal. In recent years Panama has sought to renegotiate the canal agreement. △1762.

Panama Canal Zone, an artificial, interocean, lock-operated waterway connecting the Atlantic and Pacific oceans through a 10-mi (16-km) wide Isthmus of Panama. The canal was built to eliminate the 8,000-mi (12,880-km) shipping route around South America. Started in 1881–89 by a French syndicate under Ferdinand de Lesseps, the project fell into bankruptcy, and the United States bought the strip for $10,000,000 in 1903 from newly independent Panama. The Panama Canal Act of 1912 gave the United States title to own, operate, and control the zone. The canal opened on Aug. 15, 1914. From 1974 there were negotiations to give Panama additional revenue and jurisdiction over the canal. Area: 553sq mi (1,432sq km). The population of 44,650 is administered by two US agencies, one to control the civil portion and the other the canal business.

Panama City, city in central Panama, capital of Panama since 1903 and Panama prov.; E of Balboa, at the head of the Gulf of Panama; administrative, commercial, and transportation hub; site of University of Panama (1935) and Santa Maria University (1965). Founded (old city) 1519. Pop. 418,013.

Panama City, resort city on Gulf of Mexico, NW Florida, seat of Bay co; site of US Navy Mine Defense Laboratory and Tyndall Air Force Base. Inc. 1909 by merging with adjoining villages. Pop. (1970) 32,096.

Pan-American Games, an athletic competition for all countries in the Western Hemisphere, similar to the Olympic Games. The various events included in this competition are modeled after the Olympics and have the same basic rules and regulations. The first games were held in 1951 in Buenos Aires, Argentina, and have since been held on a regular basis every four years.

Pan-American Union, existed as an independent, regional organization from 1910 until it was absorbed by the Organization of American States in 1948. The PAU was the name given to the secretariat of the OAS, 1948–70; after 1970, the name Pan-American Union no longer was used. △1234.

Pan-Arab Movement. After the Arabs gained independence from Ottoman and European controls, a sense of Arab unity developed because of a common language and culture. An Arab League was formed (1945), composed at first of seven states, but grew to 13 countries. It coordinated political, economic, and military activities through various treaties. An Arab Development Bank was created in 1959. Nasser of Egypt strengthened the movement, but his United Arab Republic (Syria and Egypt) lasted only until 1961. A union between Iraq and Jordan also dissolved in 1958. The unity intended in the movement was not helped by conflicts in the Ba'ath party, a socialist organization founded in 1940 that has branches in many Arab countries.

Pancreas, an elongated, somewhat triangular-shaped, soft gland lying behind the stomach to the left of the midline. It functions in digestion and as an endocrine organ. As a digestive organ, the pancreas secretes enzymes: trypsin that digests proteins, steapsin that acts on lipids, amylopsin that acts on carbohydrates, and other minor secretions. These pour into the pancreatic duct and then empty into the common bile duct, which opens into the small intestine. The pancreas also contains the islands of Langerhans that secrete the hormone insulin, which plays a major role in the body's metabolism of carbohydrates. *See also* Diabetes Mellitus; Insulin. △690, 694.

Pancreatitis, inflammation of the pancreas caused by alcohol intake or obstruction of the pancreatic ducts. It is characterized by severe pain, fever, and high blood pressure. Treatment involves diet, alcoholic abstinence, and administration of pancreatic extracts.

Panda, or wah, cat-sized mammal of the raccoon family native to Himalayan region. Mostly nocturnal vegetarians, pandas have long, soft red to brown fur, long bushy ringed tails, and dark eyepatches on their white faces. Length: 23in (584mm); weight: 8.5lb (3.9kg). Family Procyonidae; species *Ailurus fulgens*. *See also* Giant Panda.

Pandora, in Greek mythology, first woman. She was made at Zeus' orders for revenge against Prometheus, who had created man and stolen fire from heaven for man. Pandora was endowed with charm as well as with guile. She was sent to Prometheus' brother Epimetheus, and brought with her a box that she had been forbidden to open. When she opened it all the evils of the human race flew out. Hope remained at the bottom of the box. △834.

Panel Tracery. △1104.

Pangaea, the name for the single supercontinent that is hypothesized to have existed 200,000,000 years ago. Using calculations based on computer data, present land masses plus their continental shelves can be fitted together into this one continent. Pangaea was surrounded by Pantalassa, the ancestral Pacific. △172,410.

Pangolin, or scaly anteater, toothless scale-covered insect-eating mammal of Asia and Africa. When attacked it curls into a ball and raises its sharp scales. Length: 25–70in (64–178cm). They are the only members of the order Pholidota. △540,546.

Pankhurst, Emmeline Goulden (1858–1928), English political leader, leader of the women's suffrage movement, popularly known as Emily. With her husband, Richard Pankhurst, she worked to secure married women's property rights. When she set up the Women's Social and Political Union (1903), the movement for women's suffrage became militant (including arson, bombing, and hunger strikes), and she was imprisoned. During World War I she supported the cessation of women's suffrage militancy. *See also* Woman Suffrage.

Panmunjom Talks (1951–53), UN-North Korean truce discussions that ended the Korean War. It took two years to reach an agreement that gave South Korea slightly more territory than it had when the war began in 1950. A demilitarized zone was established between North and South Korea, and a repatriation committee was set up. A commission of five members representing each side was appointed to administer the truce.

Pannonia, province of ancient Rome SW of the Danube encompassing areas of modern Yugoslavia, Austria, and Hungary. The Romans fought the fierce Pannonians from 119 BC until completing their subjugation in AD 9. The province was split into Upper and Lower Pannonia *c.* AD 103 and subdivided again by Diocletian. Pannonia fell victim to the barbarian invasions of the 4th century and was abandoned by the Romans *c.* AD 405. △1020.

Pan Pipes (Syrinx), primitive musical wind instrument, probably from Asia. Several tubes of cane, reed, bamboo, or clay are joined like a raft; blown across one end, each pipe produces one note of a scale. Pan pipes are associated with the pastoral Greek god of fertility.

Pan-Slavic Movement, attempt to unite all Slavic peoples. Although proposed by the Croat Yuri Krizhanovich in 1659, the doctrine was first formulated by the Slovak Jan Herkel in 1826 under the influence of German romanticism and the study of folklore. Assimilated to Slavophilism in Russia, it was revived in World War II against the Nazis and to justify Soviet expansion after the war.

Pansy, common name for a cultivated hybrid violet *(Viola tricolor* var. *hortensis).* It is one of the oldest of European cultivated flowering plants. An annual or short-lived perennial, it grows to about 6 to 12in (15–30cm) tall. The velvety flowers, usually in combinations of blue, yellow, and white, have five petals. Heart-shaped or rounded leaves grow at the base and oval leaves grow from the stem. The wild pansy with mostly purple flowers has been introduced into North America. *See also* Violet.

Pantheism, religious system, contrasted with deism, that identifies God and the universe. All life is infused with divinity, as seen in Hinduism. No distinction is recognized between the Creator and creatures. Mysticism frequently shows a pantheistic language. John Toland first used the term *pantheist* in 1705.

Pantheon, in ancient times, temple for the worship of all the gods in a specific area; by extension, a building honoring illustrious public figures. The Pantheon in Rome was built by Agrippa (27 BC), destroyed, and rebuilt in the 2d century by Hadrian. Well preserved today, its dome, the largest built until modern times, is supported only by the walls of concrete it rests upon. The Panthéon in Paris was designed as a church by J.G. Soufflot and begun in 1764. During the French Revolution it was dedicated to the memory of great Frenchmen. Several times reconsecrated and secularized, it is today a public building. △1024.

Panther, or black panther, an all-black (melanistic) leopard or jaguar. In leopards, this form most fre-

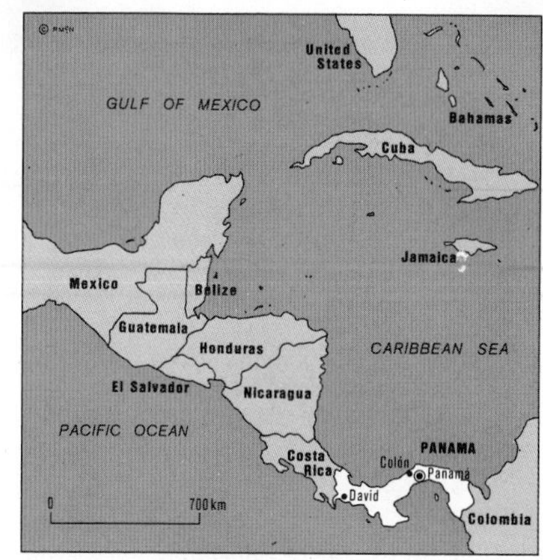
United States
GULF OF MEXICO
Bahamas
Cuba
Jamaica
Mexico
Belize
Guatemala
Honduras
CARIBBEAN SEA
El Salvador
Nicaragua
PACIFIC OCEAN
Costa Rica
PANAMA
Colón
Panama
David
Colombia
0
700km
Panama

Panama Canal

Pansy

Pantheon: Rome

quently occurs in the Bengal and Javan varieties. Panthers appear in the same litter as normally colored leopards or jaguars and spots in their black coat can be seen when viewed at a certain angle. Panther tigers have also been reported. *See also* Jaguar; Leopard.

Pantograph. △1462.

Pantomime, form of theater in which actors use symbolic movement, facial expression, and gesture without dialogue to convey meaning. This is sometimes accompanied by music. Its classical form was a group of dancers enacting a story sung by a chorus. One of the founders of modern pantomime was Jean-Louis Barrault *(Les Enfants du Paradis)*; among his students was Marcel Marceau *(The Over Coat* and *The Mask Maker)*.

Pantotheres. △574.

Paotow (Baotou, or **Pao-t'ou),** industrial city, N China, 90mi (145km) W of Huhehot on the Yellow River. Japanese occupied 1937–45. Industries: steel, textiles, automotive, fertilizer. Pop. 800,000.

Papacy, the pope and his authority as the head of the Roman Catholic Church. The doctrine of apostolic succession traces the authority of the pope, the bishop of Rome, from Christ through the apostles, particularly St Peter. The hierarchy developed in the early centuries and underwent many crises and changes throughout history. Basically, it is a system similar to that of the Roman Empire. *See also* Apostolic Succession. △1052, 1072, 1086.

Papago, a Piman-speaking tribe of North American Indians who inhabited the Gila and Santa Cruz river valleys of S Arizona, and N Sonora, Mexico. Less acculturated than their kinsmen the Pima, about 11,000 Papago people live south of Tucson, Ariz. today.

Papal States, central Italian temporal realm of the popes from 754 to 1870, generally including the modern Italian regions of Lazio, Umbria, Marche, and part of Emilia-Romagna. In 756, Pepin the Short, Frankish ruler, granted the exarchate of Ravenna (Donation of Pepin) to Stephen II, establishing the pope's temporal power. Because of rising power of communal governments, the "Babylonian Captivity" (1309–77), and the Great Schism (1377–1417), papal control was weakened in the Middle Ages, never to recover fully. Largely annexed by France between 1797 and 1809, they were restored in 1814, only to be annexed to Italy in 1860 and 1870.

Papantla, city in E central Mexico, approx. 70mi (113km) NNW of Jalapa; site of nearby ancient pyramid, contains hieroglyphics and small idols. Main industry is tourism. Pop. 94,623.

Papaw, or pawpaw, tree found in central and S United States. It has large, oval leaves, dull purple flowers, and sausage-shaped, yellowish, edible fruits that have a bananalike flavor. Height: to 40ft (12m). Family Annonaceae; species *Asimina triloba*.

Papaya, or tropical pawpaw, palmlike tree widely cultivated in its native American tropics for fleshy, melonlike, edible fruit. Height: to 20ft (6m). Family Caricaceae; species *Carica papaya*. △340.

Papeete, port town and capital of Tahiti and French Polynesia, on NW coast of Tahiti in Society Islands, S Pacific Ocean; trade center of the islands; site of an international airport. Exports: copra, mother of pearl, vanilla. Pop. 24,000.

Papen, Franz von (1879–1969), German political figure. A member of the Prussian parliament (1921–32), he was German chancellor in 1932. He lifted the ban on the Nazi militia and later helped Adolf Hitler become chancellor. He held various diplomatic posts in the Hitler regime. He was tried by the Nuremberg war crimes tribunal but was acquitted.

Paper, flat sheet of compacted cellulose fibers used for packaging, writing or painting upon, as a wall covering, etc. The word "paper" derives from papyrus, the plant that the Egyptians used at least 5,500 years ago to make sheets of writing material. The papyrus reed was soaked and slit into strips that were laid at right angles and pounded and pressed into a sheet. The modern process of manufacture originated about 2,000 years ago in China and consists of reducing wood fiber, straw, rags, and grasses to a pulp by the action of an alkali, such as caustic soda. The lignin and other noncellulose material is then extracted and the residue is bleached. After washing and the addition of a filler to provide a smooth and flat surface, the pulp is rolled into thin sheets and dried. Newsprint and other cheap papers are mechanical pulps made without chemical treatment and consist of finely divided wood without purification. The better quality papers are made from chemical pulps prepared as described. △1624.

Paper Nautilus. *See* Argonaut.

Papillae. △680.

Papillon, small dog (toy group) developed from 16th-century dwarf spaniel. A fine-boned dog, it has a small head and thin muzzle and distinctive erect, butterfly-type ears (drop, or Phalene-type, ears also occur). The straight-backed body is set on very slender legs, and the long, well arched tail is carried over the back. The long, silky coat is full on chest, ears, legs, and tail; it is white with patches of any color in a particular pattern. Average size: 8–11in (20–28cm) at shoulder; 5–11lb (2.3–5kg). *See also* Toy Dog.

Papineau, Louis Joseph (1786–1871), Canadian political figure. As a member of the House of Assembly of Lower Canada (Quebec) (1808–37) and its speaker (1815–37), he championed the French Canadians. He fled Canada during the Rebellion of 1837. In exile (1839–45) he became the inspiration for the nationalistic Parti Rouge. He served in the parliament of united Canada (1848–54).

Pap Smear, a sample of cells, often from the female genital tract, specially stained to detect malignant or premalignant disease. Named for its discoverer, George Papanicolaou. △738.

Papua New Guinea, independent nation of the W Pacific Ocean; consisting of the E half of New Guinea and the neighboring islands of the Bismarck Archipelago (including New Britain, New Ireland, Admiralty) and Bougainville. Most of the terrain is mountainous, and there are many volcanoes, especially in the Bismarck Archipelago. Lowland areas of size are restricted to New Guinea island N and S of the Central Highlands. Situated just S of the Equator, the climate is hot and wet throughout the year, giving rise to the natural vegetation of rain forest. Some of the most primitive people of the world live here and have cultures resembling stone age cultures; because of the difficult terrain isolated tribes are still being discovered. Agriculture is basically subsistence, with the main cash crops being coffee, cocoa, copra. The forests are exploited for hardwoods, and a large deposit of copper has been discovered on Bougainville. Although discovered by the Spanish in the 16th century, little was known about the region until German traders began operating there in the 1870s. Germany claimed New Guinea in 1884; Australia occupied it during WWI; and it became an Australian mandate in 1921. In 1974, Papua New Guinea became independent of Australia, joining the British Commonwealth. Government is by a house of assembly elected by citizens over 18.

PROFILE

Official name: Papua New Guinea.
Area: 178,221sq mi (461,691sq km).
Population: (1971) 2,489,936.
Density, 13 per sq mi (5 per sq km).
Chief cities: Port Moresby (capital), 66,244; Lae, 34,699; Rabaul, 24,778.
Religion: Animist, Christian.
Language: English.
Trading partners: (major) Australia, United States, Japan, Great Britain.

Papuan Hawk Owl. △538.

Papyrus, stout perennial plant that Egyptians used to make paperlike writing material. Native to S Europe and N Africa, it grows in shallow water. Height: to 10ft (3m). Family Cyperaceae; species *Cyperus papyrus*. △872.

Parabola, conic formed by cutting a right circular cone with a plane parallel to one of the cone's generators. A parabola is a conic with an eccentricity equal to 1. In rectangular Cartesian coordinates its standard equation is $y^2 = 4ax$, where a is a constant: the curve is symmetrical about the x-axis. A useful property of the parabola is that a line parallel to the x-axis is "reflected" at the curve through the focus, which lies on the x-axis (that is, a line from the focus to a point on the curve makes an angle with the normal at that point equal to the angle between the normal and a line from the point parallel to the x-axis). This property is used in parabolic reflectors in telescopes, searchlights, etc. △1454.

Paracelsus, Philippus Aureolus (1493–1541), Swiss physician and alchemist, b. Philippus von Hohenheim. He believed that alchemy should be devoted to the preparation of chemical remedies for disease rather than the discovery of methods for manufacturing gold. In addition to writing on mental disease problems, he was the first to describe zinc. △708.

Parachute, folding umbrellalike device of a light fabric such as nylon or dacron used to reduce the speed of a falling body. It consists of a canopy connected by shroud lines to a harness that holds the jumper or cargo. Prior to release all but the harness is packed in a small back, seat, or chest pack. The unit deploys at the pull of a ripcord. Parachutes are also used to shorten the landing roll of high-speed aircraft.

Parachute Jumping. *See* Sky Diving.

Paradise Lost (1667), epic poem by John Milton in blank verse. △1148.

Paradox, apparently contradictory statement intended to contain within it a germ of truth. It is often used in epigrams as in Shaw's "Youth is wasted on the young," meaning youth lacks wisdom and age lacks the energy to profit from its wisdom. *See also* Epigram.

Paraffin, or paraffin wax, white translucent waxy substance consisting of a mixture of solid alkanes (paraffins). It is obtained during petroleum distillation and used to make candles, waxed paper, polishes, and cosmetics. Properties: sp gr 0.88–0.915; melt. pt. 116–149°F (47–65°C). △1558.

Paraguay, independent nation in central South America. It is an entirely landlocked country whose capital, Asunción, was established in 1537. Its homogeneous population is Indian and Spanish in an agricultural economy.

Land and economy. Surrounded by Argentina, Brazil, and Bolivia, it reaches the Atlantic Ocean through a river system flowing through Argentina. The 1,584-mi (2,550-km) Paraguay River divides the country into two regions, the temperate E zone of rolling hills, forests, and grasslands, and the W (Chaco) portion of dense forests, unnavigable rivers, and little rainfall. With very few minerals and no petroleum, 90% of exports are meat, lumber, cotton, oils, coffee, tobacco. Cattle-raising is the backbone (35%) of the economy. Since 1968 a $33 million hydroelectric plant has provided most of its power needs.

People. With 90% of the people of mixed Indian (Guaraní) and Spanish descent, the country is culturally and socially homogeneous. Spanish is the official language; 90% understand Guaraní. Literacy is 30%. Roman Catholicism is the principal religion.

Government. Based on a 1967 constitution, the highly centralized government includes a five-year term for an elected president, bicameral congress with elected members. Power rests in the executive branch. Decrees are allowed when congress is not in session. Gen. Alfredo Stroessner has been president since 1954.

History. The Spaniard Alejo García was probably the first European to reach Paraguay. About 1520 he headed an expedition into the Inca Empire, and his reports inspired Sebastian Cabot's explorations (1526–29). Jesuits, who established agricultural colonies and tried to Christianize the Indians, were expelled in 1767. Paraguay gained independence from Spain in 1811 and in 1870 adopted a democratic constitution.

PROFILE

Official name: Republic of Paraguay
Area: 157,047sq mi (406,752km)
Population: 2,600,000
Density: 16.6per sq mi (6.4per sq km)
Chief cities: Asunción (capital); Villarrica
Government: Democracy
Religion: Roman Catholic
Language: Spanish (official), Guaraní (national)
Monetary unit: Guaraní
Gross national product: $798,000,000
Per capita income: $402
Industries: meat products, leather, wood products, tannin extract, vegetable oil
Agriculture: corn, wheat, beans, peanuts, tobacco, citrus fruits, beef cattle, timber
Minerals: ore
Trading partners: United States, Argentina

Paraguay, river in S central South America; rises in SW Brazil; flows S to form part of the Brazil-Paraguay and Paraguay-Argentina borders; empties into the Paraná River at SW corner of Paraguay; chief tributaries are Pilcomayo and Bermejo rivers; Asunción is the chief port. Length: 1,584mi (2,550km).

Parahippus. △576.

Parallax, apparent change in position of an object, seen against a remote background, when the viewpoint is changed. The parallax of a star (annual parallax) is the angle subtended at the star by the mean radius of the Earth's orbit (one astronomical unit); the smaller the angle, the more distant the star. *See also* Parsec. △40.

Parakeet, name given several different small, brightly colored parrots that are popular pets. Affectionate and clever, they are natural acrobats, climbing toy ladders and playing on swings in their cages. Some hobbyists breed parakeets. The eggs (5) hatch in less than 21 days. The most common pet parakeet is the Australian budgerigar *(Melopsittacus undulatus)* that can often be taught to mimic speech. The males have bluish nostrils, females brownish.

Paramagnetic Salt. △1512.

Paramecium, freshwater, ciliated protozoan characterized by streamlined "slipper" shape, front and rear ends, oral groove for feeding, food vacuoles for digestion, anal pore for elimination, and two nuclei. Its stiff outer covering is studded with small cilia. Reproduction is by asexual division and sexual conjugation, during which nuclear material is exchanged. Order Holotricha; species include *Paramecium bursaria* and *Paramecium aurelia*. △466.

Paramount, city in S California, SE of Los Angeles. Industries: oil refineries, metal products, plastics, furniture, automotive parts. Inc. 1957. Pop. (1970) 34,734.

Paramus, borough in NE New Jersey, 6mi (10km) NE of Paterson; site of Bergen Community College (1965). Industries: truck farming. Founded 1668; inc. 1922. Pop. (1970) 29,495.

Paraná, formerly Bajada de Santa Fe; city in E Argentina, 235mi (378km) NW of Buenos Aires; capital of Entre Ríos prov. Capital of the Argentine Confederation 1853–62. Industries: cement, dairy products, furniture; trade in beef and grain, fruit, poultry, fishing, lumber. Founded 1730. Pop. 107,551.

Paraná, river in SE central South America; important passage for inland communications; rises in SE Brazil, flows S into Argentina, forming SE and S border of Paraguay; joins the Uruguay River to form Río de la Plata. Length: 1,827mi (2,941km).

Paranoid Personality, personality pattern disturbance in which there is marked interpersonal sensitivity, suspiciousness, stubbornness, and tendency to refer unrelated events in everyday life to the self (self-reference). The break with reality that occurs in paranoid schizophrenia does not occur, however. △764,-766.

Paraplegia, paralysis of both lower limbs. It may be caused by injury to or disease of the spinal chord or by brain disorders.

Parapsychology, study of certain phenomena that have not yet been explained by known physical processes—for example, extrasensory perception, which includes telepathy and clairvoyance. Parapsychology developed from psychical research and includes investigations of the possibility of life after death. Such topics were formerly considered inappropriate for psychological study. *See also* Extrasensory Perception. △824.

Parasite, any organism that depends entirely upon another organism for its existence. The parasite usually lives in or on its host, nourishes itself at the expense of the host without rapidly destroying it, but often inflicting some degree of injury. Among the parasites that can infect man are single-celled animals such as *Plasmodium* (malaria) and ameba; several types of worms, insects, and arthropods. △426, 732.

Parasitism, relationship involving two different organisms. The parasite benefits, deriving nourishment from the host that is harmed but not usually killed. For example, a fungus (parasite) causes athlete's foot in humans (host). △472, 506.

Parasitology, branch of biology that deals with the study of parasites, organisms that live on other organisms. Some parasitologists concentrate on the study of those parasites responsible for diseases in humans or other animals. △422, 472.

Parasol Ant. *See* Leaf-Cutting Ant.

Parasol Mushroom, any of a family of common terrestrial mushrooms (Lepiotaceae) that have shaggy umbrella-shaped caps, especially *Lepiota procera,* which is considered one of the best edible species. Some parasols are toxic and many resemble amanitas.

Parasympathetic Nervous System. *See* Autonomic Nervous System.

Parathyroid Gland, any of the four pea-sized bodies, usually embedded in the back part of the thyroid gland, that secrete the hormone parathormone, which controls the amount of calcium and phosphorus in the blood. Abnormalities of this endocrine gland can usually be treated with parathyroid extract and regulation of calcium and phosphorus intake. △690.

Parazoa. *See* Porifera.

Parchment, the processed skins of animals such as sheep, goats, and calves, used as writing material; invented in the 2nd century BC. When made from calf or kid skin, parchment is called vellum. In modern usage, "parchment" and "vellum" refer to high-quality paper made from wood pulp and rags.

Parenchyma, soft tissue made up of nonspecialized, thin-walled cells. It is the chief substance of plant stems, leaves, and fruit pulp and stores nutrients and water. It also helps support plants along with woody cells (sclerenchyma).

Paresis, condition involving deterioration of personality, impaired judgment and disorientation, and paralysis caused by destruction of brain tissue in tertiary syphilis. Antibiotics are used in treatment. △762.

Pareto, Vilfredo (1848–1923), Italian economist and sociologist who emphasized a theoretical approach to economics. Pareto's main area of interest was the distribution of a country's income. He developed criteria for demonstrating the "optimum" (or best) social position and attempted to show empirically that the actual distribution of income in an economy followed an invariant law. His basic conclusion was that policies aimed at redistributing a country's income were ineffective. △890.

Pareto Optimum, named for Vilfredo Pareto, specific situation that exists in a society where society's welfare could not be improved through the exchange of commodities by individuals within the society or by any reallocation of resources within that society. The Pareto optimum implies that a maximum welfare position is being achieved. It implies also that the exchange of goods or services by individuals in the society would result in the decrease in utility to one of the individuals exceeding the increase in utility to the other.

Parhelion. *See* Sun Dog.

Parietal Lobe. △666.

Paris, capital city of France; located on Seine River 100mi (160km) from its mouth on the English Channel. The city proper consists of Paris department, and its suburbs lie in departments of Seine-St-Denis, Val-de-Marne, Hauts-de-Seine, Val-d'Oise, Yvelines, and Essonne. When the Romans took Paris in 52 BC, it was a small village on the river's Ile de la Cité. Under the Romans it grew in importance as an administrative center and bridging point of the Seine; Roman influence is still evident, especially in the catacombs of Montparnasse. The city became the capital of the Merovingian Franks in the 5th century; after raids by the Norse in the 9th century it was reestablished as the French capital by Capetian kings in the 10th century; this spurred growth on the right bank. During the 14th century, Paris rebelled against the crown and declared itself an independent commune, and it suffered from civil disorder during the Hundred Years War. In the reign of Louis XIII (1601–43), Cardinal Richelieu established Paris as the cultural center of Europe. The French Revolution began in Paris when mobs stormed the city prison (Bastille). Under the emperors Paris became a modern city, especially during the reign of Napoleon III (1852–70), when Baron Haussmann was commissioned to plan the boulevards and parks. Although occupied in the Franco-Prussian War (1870–71) and WWII the city was not badly damaged. Site of Cathedral of Notre Dame, Louvre, Les Invalides, Palais de Justice, Palais de Luxembourg, L'Opéra, Panthéon, Bibliothèque Nationale, Tribunal de Commerce, St-Chapelle, Palais de l'Élysée, La Madeleine, St-Germain-des-Prés, Bourse, Sorbonne, Hôtel-Dieu, and Eiffel Tower. Paris remains the hub of France despite recent attempts at decentralization and retains its importance as a cultural, commercial, and communication center of Europe. Industries: auto, marine, and railroad engineering, other mechanical and electrical engineering, chemicals, textiles, clothing, printing and publishing, luxury goods pro-

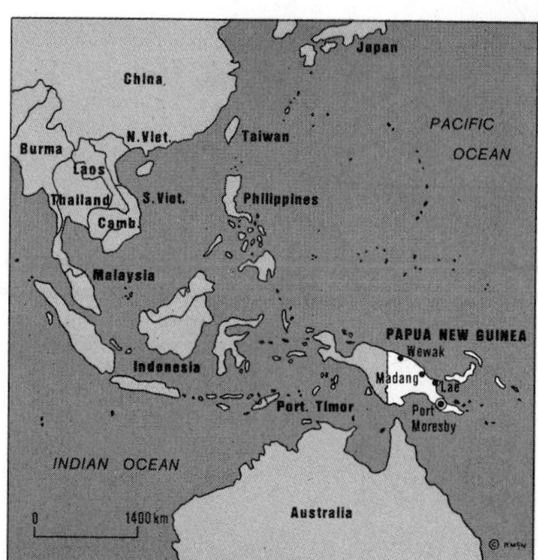

Japan
China
PACIFIC OCEAN
N.Viet
Taiwan
Burma
Laos
S.Viet.
Philippines
Thailand
Camb.
Malaysia
PAPUA NEW GUINEA
Wewak
Madang
Lae
Indonesia
Port. Timor
Port Moresby
INDIAN OCEAN
0
1400km
Australia

Papua, New Guinea

Peru
Bolivia
Brazil
PARAGUAY
Asunción
Encarnación
PACIFIC OCEAN
Uruguay
Argentina
Chile
ATLANTIC OCEAN
0
700km

Paraguay

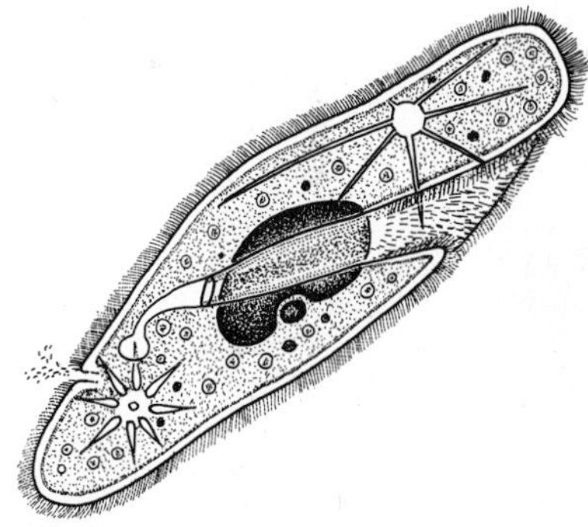
Paramecium

Paris: Eiffel Tower

duction. Pop. (city proper) 2,590,771; (metropolitan area) 8,196,746.

Paris, Congress of (1856), peace conference of the Crimean War in which England and France defended Turkey from Russian aggrandizement. It called for demilitarization of the Black Sea, liberty for Turkish Christians, and free navigation of the Danube River. △1814, 1815, 1230.

Paris, Peace of. △1308.

Paris, Treaty of (1763), diplomatic agreement signed by Britain, France and Spain ending the Seven Years War (1756–63). France ceded most of Canada to Britain in return for Guadeloupe and Martinique, and Spain ceded all its territories east of the Mississippi River to Britain. French settlers were allowed to leave the new British territories with their possessions.

Paris, University of, French university in Paris, also known as the Sorbonne. Major areas of academic study include Hispanic studies, geographical cartography, nuclear physics, and art. Founded 12th century.

Paris Daisy. *See* Marguerite.

Parity Prices, prices a farmer would need to receive for his products if he were to get as much for them now relative to prices of nonagricultural products as he did in agriculture's golden years (1910–14). The actual process of computing the exact price is somewhat more complicated. Since agriculture is now much more productive than in the early 20th century, Congress now sets the actual support price at some percentage of parity.

Parity Principle, principle of physics that there is no distinction to be made between the behavior of a system and that of its mirror image. The principle is usually formulated in terms of mathematical transformation between left- and right-handed coordinate systems. It holds for classical physics and for behavior involving strong interactions; parity is then said to be conserved. However, this symmetry does not apply to weak interactions, as in beta decay, in which the spin of the emitted electrons always has a preferred sense. *See also* Spin, Nuclear.

Park, Chung Hee (1917–), president of the Republic of Korea (South Korea). He seized power in a military coup in 1961, ruled for two years as a general, then resigned from the military. He was elected president in 1963, 1967, and 1971.

Park, Mungo. △1268.

Parker, Charles (Christopher) (1920–55), US jazz alto saxophonist, b. Kansas City, Kans. He recorded with Dizzy Gillespie in the 1940s and was one of the founders of the jazz style called "bebop" (now called "bop"). One of the most widely imitated of all jazz musicians of the 1940s and 1950s, he had enormous influence on other jazz saxophone players. △1366.

Parker, Dorothy (1893–1967), US author, b. West End, N.J. A drama and book critic, the first of her three collections of verse, *Enough Rope,* appeared in 1926. Her reputation now rests largely on her short stories, such as those collected in *Here Lies* (1939). She also collaborated in the writing of some 15 films and three plays.

Parker, Theodore (1810–60), US clergyman and social reformer, b. Lexington, Mass. He became a Unitarian minister in West Roxbury (1837), but he left that church (1845) because of his liberal religious philosophy and abolitionist sentiments. He then served as minister of the Congregationalist Society of Boston, eloquently advocating a variety of social reforms. Parker was one of the secret planners of John Brown's raid on Harpers Ferry.

Parkersburg, city in NW West Virginia, at junction of Ohio and Little Kanawha rivers; seat of Wood co; site of Ohio Valley College (1960); nearby is Blennerhasset Island, associated with conspiracy of Aaron Burr (1805). Industries: agriculture, lumber, coal mining, gas, oil, railroad shops, synthetic fibers, plastic, glass, paper products. Settled 1785; inc. 1820. Pop. (1970) 44,208.

Park Forest, town in NE Illinois, S of Chicago; a planned community with a few light industries. Inc. 1949. Pop. (1970) 30,638.

Parkinson's Disease, a chronic, progressive nervous disease occurring mostly in older males. Tremors, muscle weakness, and rigid facial expression are characteristic. Cause is not known, but influenza and hardening of the arteries are frequently associated with the disease. No cure exists, but physical therapy and a new drug, L-dopa, may relieve symptoms. △722.

Parkinson's Law. △926.

Parkman, Francis (1823–93), US historian, b. Boston. Of independent means, he set out to write a history of the conflict between the British and French in North America. In preparation, he made a series of trips, one of seven months over the Oregon and Santa Fe trails. As a result of that trip, he wrote *The Oregon Trail* (1849), his best known work. He published *France and England in North America* (8 vols., 1865–84), his masterpiece, in which he details the conflict from the earliest French settlement to the defeat of France at Quebec.

Park Ridge, city in NE Illinois, adjacent suburb NW of Chicago on Des Plaines River. Founded as Pennyville for George Penny, brickmaker who settled here in 1853. Main industry is insurance. Inc. 1873. Pop. (1970) 42,466.

Parks, Gordon, Sr. (1912–), US photojournalist and film director, b. Fort Scott, Kans. A cameraman for the Farm Security Administration (1942–43), he later became photojournalist for *Life* magazine (1948–72). His books include *The Learning Tree* (1963) and the autobiography *A Choice of Weapons* (1966). He directed the films *Shaft* (1971) and *Leadbelly* (1976).

Parkville, residential town in central Maryland; NE suburb of Baltimore. Pop. (1970) 33,897.

Parlements, highest judicial courts in France before the Revolution. The word is used particularly to mean the Paris parlement. The parlement evolved out of a medieval body with advisory functions, partly because the king wished to rationalize disputes between vassals, and partly because the vassals were eager to restrain royal power. Involved in the revolt of the Fronde (1651–53), the Paris parlement during the 18th century became a symbol of opposition to arbitrary royal rule. Louis XV's chancellor abolished the parlements (1771) to streamline the judicial system, but popular opposition to the move led Louis XVI to reinstate them (1774). They were abolished permanently by the 1790 constitution. △1170.

Parliament, British, bicameral legislative assembly at Westminster, England, having supreme political authority in Great Britain and Northern Ireland. In Henry III's reign (1216–72), Parliament emerged as a representative body of knights and burgesses. Gaining influence in the 14th century, it advised the king on domestic and foreign policy, dispatched justice, and passed legislation. Although summoned and dismissed on the king's initiative, its power lay in its right to control taxation, which is why monarchs tended to summon Parliament only when they wanted money. By 1400 a formal division had appeared between the "higher house" or "House of Lords" (evolved from the former *Curia Regis* or Great Council) and the "common house" or "House of Commons." As Parliament's power increased so did its clashes with the crown. The Long Parliament's victory over Charles I (1640) ensured Parliament's political ascendancy. The Hanoverian kings' withdrawal from governing facilitated the establishment of the authority of the prime minister, leaving the crown only a nominal supremacy. The 19th- and 20th-century evolution of universal adult suffrage made Parliament a democratically representative legislature, controlling administration and the nation's policies. △1156.

Parliamentary Law, rules governing procedures of deliberative bodies. The English Parliament, particularly the House of Commons, is the basis for most of the accepted rules, which have been adapted for use in other legislatures. A manual of parliamentary law formulated by Thomas Jefferson when he was presiding officer of the US Senate, is generally used by the US Congress. Robert's *Rules of Order* (1876), taken from the practices of Parliament and Congress, is a widely accepted authority on parliamentary law, but it is neither prescribed by statute nor by court decision and is not legally binding.

Parma, city in N Italy, 75mi (121km) SE of Milan; capital of Parma prov. Est. by Romans 183 BC, it was an important Roman road junction along the Via Aemilia; rebuilt during the Middle Ages; made a duchy by Pope Paul III; given to Marie Louise of Austria by Napoleon 1815; heavily damaged by Allied bombing WWII; site of cathedral (rebuilt 12th century), Palazzo della Pilotta (begun 1583), abbey of St Paolo (16th century); agricultural economy. Industries: cheese, machinery, pharmaceuticals, fertilizer. Pop. 170,267.

Parma, city in N Ohio, 8mi (13km) S of Cleveland. Industries: automobile parts, tools, dies, industrial research. Founded 1816; inc. as city 1932. Pop. (1970) 100,216.

Parmenides (*c.* 546–506 BC), founder of the Eleatic school of Greek philosophy. His main extant work is a poem, "On Truth." Developing the concept of "being" in contrast to the Heraclitean concept of "becoming," he taught that being is eternal, indivisible, immutable, and limited. *See also* Eleaticism; Heraclitus.

Parmigianino, or **Parmigiano, Il,** real name **Girolamo Francesco Maria Mazzuola** (1503–40), northern Italian artist. He was a master of the Mannerist style. One of the first Italian painters who was also an important etcher, he is famous for his drawings as well. His works include "Madonna with St Zachary," "Marriage of St Catherine," "Vision of St Jerome," and "Madonna of the Long Neck." △1150.

Parnassus (Parnassós), Mount, mountain peak in central Greece: In ancient times, it was considered sacred to Apollo, Dionysus, and the Muses; site of the sacred fountain of Castalia, just above Delphi, at the S foot of the mountain. The Corycian Cave, associated with the Bacchic festivals, lies on a plateau between Delphi and the summit. Height: 8,060ft (2,458m).

Parnell, Charles Stewart (1846–91), Irish nationalist. He entered the British Parliament (1875), vigorously supporting home rule for Ireland and rapidly taking over leadership of the Home Rule Bill. To gain concessions, he embarked upon a policy of parliamentary obstruction. He united all the Irish parties hostile to English rule, including the Fenians in Ireland and the United States. Supporting the Land League (1879), he was imprisoned (1881) for directing tenants to withold rent. Released under the Kilmainham treaty (1882), he found the Liberal government more tolerant than the Conservative. This trend was frustrated by the Phoenix Park assassinations (1882) and the subsequent defeat of William Gladstone's government. Reinstated, Gladstone introduced the Home Rule Bill (1886), marking the zenith of Parnell's power. The bill was defeated, however. Parnell's fall was assured by his suspected implication (1887; shown to be false 1890) in the Phoenix Park murders, and his proven adultery with the wife of one of his supporters (1890). *See also* Home Rule. △1314.

Parody, literary composition in which another author's language and style are imitated and exaggerated for comic effect. In ancient Greece, Aristophanes wrote parodies of Aeschylus and Euripides. In England, Henry Fielding's *Joseph Andrews* (1742) was a successful parody of Samuel Richardson's novel *Pamela, or Virtue Rewarded.* 20th-century writers who have made use of parody include Max Beerbohm, James Joyce, and Stephen B. Leacock.

Parotid Gland, largest of the salivary glands, located just in front of and a little below the opening of the ear. Along with the other salivary glands, it forms and secretes saliva. It is the gland that becomes swollen during mumps. *See also* Salivary Glands.

Parr, Catherine (1512–48), queen consort and sixth wife of Henry VIII. She was married four times, marrying her fourth husband, Thomas Seymour, after the king's death (1547). Because of her intercession, the princesses Elizabeth and Mary were reinstated at court. As queen, she tried to alleviate religious persecution.

Parrish, Maxfield (Frederick) (1870–1966), US illustrator and painter, b. Philadelphia. He was noted as a designer of illustrated books, magazine covers, posters, and murals.

Parrot, any of numerous tropical and subtropical birds that are popular as pets, including macaws, lories, lorikeets, parakeets, keas, kakas, and others. Brightly colored, they have thick, hooked bills. All nest in tree holes, rock cracks, or on the ground. Pet parrots should be kept in clean, warm, large cages and provided with fresh air, water, and proper food. Some can be taught to mimic speech. Length: 3in–3ft (7.6–92cm). Family Psittacidae.

Parrot Fever. *See* Psittacosis.

Parrotfish, marine fish of tropical Atlantic and Indo-Pacific identified by heavy, platelike teeth resembling a parrot's beak. A coral-eating fish that goes through many color changes, it builds a mucous cocoon for sleeping. Length: 4.5in–12ft (11.4–366cm). The 80 species include the rainbow *Scarus guacamaia*. Family Scaridae.

Parsec (symbol pc), astronomical unit of length equal to the distance at which the radius of the Earth's orbit subtends an angle of one second. It is thus the distance at which an object would have a parallax of one second, using the Earth-Sun distance as the baseline. One parsec is equal to 3.2616 light-years or 1.917 X 10^{13} mi. (3.086 X 10^{13}km).

Parsi, or Parsee, modern descendant of a small number of ancient Persian Zoroastrians who emigrated to Gujerat in India in the 8th century. The modern Parsis follow a mixture of Zoroastrianism and some Indian beliefs and practices. Concentrated today mostly in Bombay, the Parsis are a small but active Indian minority of about 125,000. *See also* Zoroastrianism. △846.

Parsley, smooth branching biennial herb, native to the Mediterranean region and widely cultivated for its tender, curled aromatic leaves used as flavoring and a garnish. It has greenish-yellow flowers and tiny, seedlike fruits. Height: to 3ft (0.9m). Family Umbelliferae; species *Petroselinum crispum*.

Parsnip, biennial plant native to Eurasia and widely cultivated for its edible white taproot. It has tall, ovate leaflets. Family Umbelliferae; species *Pastinaca sativa*.

Parson Bird, or tui, honey eater of New Zealand with greenish-blue plumage and white feathers under the throat. Once valued as a cage bird, it can be taught to whistle or repeat words. Length: 11in (28cm). Species *Prosthemadera novaeseelandiae*.

Parthenogenesis, form of asexual reproduction that produces a new individual by development of an unfertilized ovum. It can òccur in animals capable of sexual reproduction. An example of natural parthenogenesis is when a queen honeybee decides whether or not to fertilize her eggs. Artificial parthenogenesis may be induced by electric shock, mechanical stimulation, inorganic salts, organic acids, or temperature change. △486.

Parthenon, temple of the goddess Athena, erected (447–432 BC) by Pericles on the Acropolis in Athens. The architects, Ictinus and Callicrates, and the chief sculptor, Phidias, constructed a peripteral temple of the Doric order. The huge gold and ivory statue of Athena was destroyed in ancient times, and the inner chambers and porticos were ruined in the 17th century, but the surviving outer structure and sculptural pediments testify to the perfection of its design. △1002.

Parthia, ancient country in W Asia; originally a province in the Assyrian and Persian empires, the Macedonian empire of Alexander the Great, and the Syrian empire. Led by Arsaces, its first king, it freed itself from the rule of the Seleucidae (*c.* 2500 BC) and reached the height of its power under Mithridates I (1st century BC). The empire was overthrown *c.* AD 226 by Ardashir I, the first Sassanid ruler of Persia.

Partial Differential Equation, type of differential equation used when a function depends on two or more independent variables. For example, a wave in three dimensions has an amplitude *(U)* that depends on time and also on the three distance measurements *x, y,* and *z,* along mutually perpendicular axes. The differential equation representing the wave is

$$\frac{\partial^2 U}{\partial x^2} + \frac{\partial^2 U}{\partial y^2} + \frac{\partial^2 U}{\partial z^2} = \frac{1}{c^2}\frac{\partial^2 U}{\partial t^2}$$

Here *c* is the wave's velocity. The symbols

$$\frac{\partial^2 U}{\partial x^2},$$

etc., are called partial derivatives and express the rate of charge of *U* in the *x* direction, etc, only. Partial differential equations are extensively used in physical science. *See also* Differential Equation.

Partial Eclipse. *See* Eclipse.

Partial Pressure, pressure that a given component of a gas mixture would have if it alone were present. The pressure of an ideal-gas mixture is the sum of the partial pressures of its components (Dalton's Law of partial pressures). △1502.

Particle, Colloidal. *See* Colloidal Particle.

Particle Accelerators. *See* Accelerator, Particle.

Particles, Elementary. *See* Elementary Particles and Antiparticles.

Particle Wave Duality Theory. △1484.

Partridge, any of several Old World game birds, but in particular, the true partridge *(Perdix perdix)*, also known as the European gray partridge and as the Hungarian partridge, a highly valued game bird native to Eurasia and now established in the Americas. A medium-sized bird, it has gray plumage with transversely barred sides and a blackish, sometimes horseshoe-shaped, patch on the belly. It typically takes off fast and is very swift flying. Some partridges (genus *Alectoris*) have reddish breast and legs (chukar or rock partridge); some barring and collar; and some, mainly Asian, are brightly colored.

Partridgeberry, or twinberry, squawberry, evergreen trailing plant native to North America. A popular decorative plant, it prefers shady areas and has white flowers and red berries. Family Rubiaceae; species *Mitchella repens*.

Parturition. △704.

Parzival, late 12th-century romance epic (begun 1197 or 1198) composed in Middle High German by Wolfram von Eschenbach. Based largely on works by Chrétien de Troyes and Hartman von Aue, it deals with the legendary knights of King Arthur and the quest for the Holy Grail. Unique in the period and genre is its emphasis on married love, the lives of children, and inner development of the hero.

Pasadena, city in S California, 8mi (13km) NE of Los Angeles; site of California Institute of Technology (1891), the annual Tournament of Roses Parade (1890), and Rose Bowl football game. Industries: electronic equipment, ceramics, plastics, aircraft components, cosmetics. Founded 1874; inc. 1886. Pop. (1970) 112,981.

Pasadena, city in SE Texas, 10mi (16km) S of Houston, on Houston ship channel; trade and shipping center; site of San Jacinto College (1961); scene of Gen. Santa Anna's capture (1836). Industries: oil refining, synthetic rubber, chemicals, paper, agriculture, cattle. Settled 1892; inc. 1928. Pop. (1970) 89,277.

Pascagoula, city and port of entry in SE Mississippi; seat of Jackson co; site of "Old Spanish Fort" (1718). Industries: tourism, shipbuilding, oil refining, pet foods. Settled 1718. Pop. (1970) 27,264.

Pascal, Blaise (1623–62), French mathematician. A prodigy, he had written a book on conics by the age of 16 and later, with Pierre de Fermat, laid the foundations of the theory of probability. He also contributed to calculus and hydrodynamics before retiring from science in 1655 to devote himself to religious and philosophical writing, of which his *Pensées* are the best known example. △1172.

Pascal's Law, a concept, formulated by the French mathematician Blaise Pascal in 1647, which states that the pressure applied to an enclosed fluid is transmitted equally in all directions and to all parts of the enclosing vessel, if pressure changes due to the weight of the fluid can be neglected. This law has important applications in hydraulics.

Pashto or **Pushtu,** one of the two major languages of Afghanistan, spoken by about 10,000,000 people there, or about 60% of the population. It is also spoken in NW Pakistan by about 6,000,000 people. Pashto historically is the language of the Pathans, the indigenous inhabitants of this area. It is one of the Iranian languages and thus part of the Indo-European family.

Pashtuns. *See* Pathans.

Pasqueflower. *See* Anemone.

Passaic, city in NE New Jersey, on the Passaic River 4mi (6.4km) S of Paterson; scene of George Washington's crossing of the Passaic River on his retreat through New Jersey 1776. Industries: rubber, metal, pharmaceuticals, precision instruments. Founded by Dutch 1678 as Acquackanonk; name changed 1854; inc. as city 1873. Pop. (1970) 55,124.

Passenger Liner. △1680.

Passenger Pigeon, an extinct species *(Ectopistes migratorius)* of pigeon. Once extremely numerous in the United States, the passenger pigeon was slaughtered for meat and finally the wild birds disappeared; in 1914 the last captive representative died.

Passionflower, also maypops, maracock, climbing tropical plant found in America, Asia, Australia, and Polynesia. Flowers are red, yellow, green, or purple. The outer petals ring a fringed center. Leaves are lobed and some species produce small, egglike, edi-

Parrot

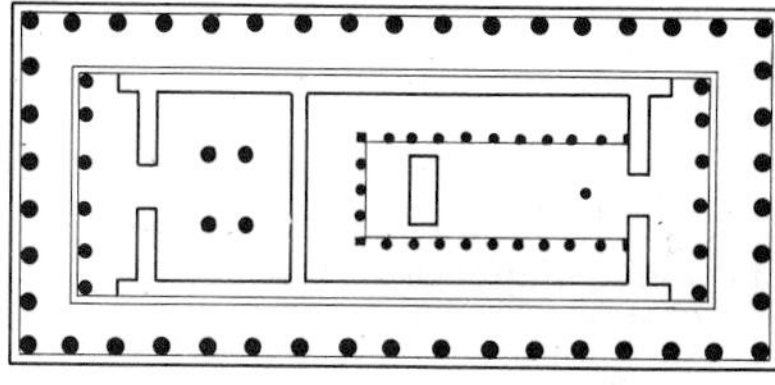

Parthenon

Partridge

Passionflower

ble fruits. 400 species *(Passiflora);* Family Passifloraceae. △340, 448.

Passion Music, a musical presentation of the New Testament story of Easter according to the gospels of St Matthew, St Mark, St Luke, and St John. This musical form grew out of the "passion plays" presented in the 12th century and developed into large choral works with orchestral accompaniment during the Renaissance and Baroque periods; for example, J. S. Bach's *St Matthew Passion.*

Passion Play, dramatization of Christ's passion, originally performed in medieval Europe. The most important survival is held every 10 years in Oberammergau, Germany, where the first performance of the present text was given in 1634 to fulfill a vow made by the villagers during a plague epidemic. The players are all townspeople.

Passover (Pesach), the Jewish festival of eight days that commemorates the Exodus from Egypt and the redemption of the Israelites. Also called the Feast of the Unleavened Bread. Symbolic dishes are prepared, including bitter herbs (maror) and matzo, or unleavened bread, which remind the Jew of his heritage and the haste with which the Jews fled Egypt. It is also a celebration of thanksgiving for freedom. The Seder, a ceremonial dinner, is a family celebration, in which the Haggadah is read.

Pasta. △328.

Pastel Painting, type of painting used especially for portraits, done with sticks of finely ground pigments usually used on paper. Because they are so soft, pastel colors smudge easily, and a fixative solution is therefore used. Pastels first came into use in the 16th century in northern Europe. They were used for portraits by such painters as Holbein and Clouet and later by the Impressionists, especially Renoir. During the 18th century, pastels were mixed with white to obtain the pale colors in vogue during the Rococo style, and since then the term "pastel" has also meant lightened color.

Pasternak, Boris (1890–1960), Soviet poet, translator, and novelist. The son of a painter and a concert pianist, he was early influenced by the family friends Leo Tolstoy and Aleksandr Scriabin. After studying music and philosophy, he turned to literature. His first book of poetry, *The Twin in the Clouds,* appeared in 1914. Another volume of poetry, *My Sister, Life,* published in 1922, established his reputation. At first he welcomed the Russian Revolution. His autobiographical *Safe Conduct* appeared in 1931 followed by the poems *Second Birth* (1932). By this time his individualistic works were being condemned by party regulars. He published no more original works during the next decade, turning instead to translation. Two books of simpler, more conforming poetry published during World War II were still criticized. After the death of Stalin, Pasternak began work on the novel *Dr. Zhivago.* Its hero, the poet-physician Yuri Zhivago, much like Pasternak, welcomes the Revolution but then finds his search for personal happiness barred by political circumstances. Denied publication in the Soviet Union, it first appeared in Italy in 1957. Pasternak was awarded the Nobel Prize for literature in 1958. Soviet authorities compelled him to retract his acceptance and expelled him from the Soviet Writers Union.

Pasteur, Louis (1822–95), French chemist and founder of microbiology. He made many important contributions to chemistry, bacteriology, and medicine. Among the most significant was his conclusive proof that spontaneous generation (life arising from nonliving matter) does not occur. In his best known work, Pasteur discovered that microorganisms can be destroyed by heat, a technique, now known as pasteurization, used to destroy harmful microorganisms in food. Pasteur also discovered that he could weaken certain disease-causing microorganisms—specifically the microorganisms causing cholera and anthrax in animals and rabies in man—and then use the weakened culture to vaccinate against the disease. △722, 736, 752, 1282.

Pasteurization, process of controlled heat treatment to kill bacteria, discovered by Louis Pasteur in 1862. Milk is pasteurized by heating to 161° F (72° C) and holding at that temperature for 15 seconds. Alternatively, it may be heated to 143°F (62°C) and held for 30 minutes. Sterilization uses higher temperatures, which would damage some foods. △736.

Pastoral, literary work portraying shepherds or rural life in an idealized manner in order to contrast their innocence with the corruption of the city or royal court. The pastoral in poetry, fiction, and drama has often been used as a vehicle for discussion of politics, religion, and other serious subjects. In classical times Theocritus and Vergil wrote notable pastoral poems, which were known as eclogues. Eclogues were revived during the Renaissance by Edmund Spenser and others. John Milton and Percy Shelley were noted for their pastoral elegies. Certain poets, such as William Wordsworth and Robert Frost, have sometimes been referred to as pastoral poets because of the pastoral or rural nature of their writing.

Pastoralism, mode of subsistence involving the herding of domesticated livestock. Pastoral societies are small scale due to the restrictively large amount of grazing land needed for each animal. In the Americas indigenous pastoralism is confined to the Andes but it is widespread in North Africa and central Asia. *See also* Nomadism. △878.

Patagonia, region in Argentina, E of the Andes Mts, extending to the Strait of Magellan. Magellan was first to visit the area 1520; colonized after wars with Tehuelche Indians 1880. Part of the region lies in S Chile but the name refers to the Argentinian part; the division was disputed between the two countries (1881) and the present boundaries were set 1902; sheep-raising region. Area: 311,000sq mi (805,490sq km).

Patas, large, reddish-gray monkey native to grassy woodlands and scrub forests of central Africa. It is day-active, ground-foraging, omnivorous, and lives in groups often led by a large male. Species *Erythrocebus patas. See also* Monkey.

Patch Test, a test for hypersensitivity to a substance in which patches of linen or paper containing it are placed on the skin and the reaction on removal is observed.

Patella, or kneecap, a large, flattened, roughly triangular bone just in front of the joint where the femur and tibia link. It is surrounded by bursae, sacs of fluid that cushion the joint. △682.

Patellar Bursae. △682.

Patent Law, legal system regarding issuance, infringements, and court jurisdiction of a patent, which is the exclusive protected rights of invention given to an inventor by a government for a fixed time (in the United States 17 years) after which it becomes public. The US patent system is designed to encourage maximum inventiveness. It is authorized by Art. I, Sec. 8 of the Constitution. The first patent bill was enacted in 1790; the US Patent Office was created in 1836 under the Department of Interior and transferred in 1925 to the Department of Commerce.

Paterson, William (1745–1806), US jurist, b. Ireland. As a New Jersey delegate to the Constitutional Convention (1787), he proposed the New Jersey Plan, giving more power to the states and less to the federal government. Paterson later served as a US senator (1789–90), resigning to become governor of New Jersey (1790–93). He was an associate justice on the US Supreme Court (1793–1806). Paterson, N.J., is named for him.

Paterson, city in NE New Jersey, at falls of Passaic River 14mi (23km) N of Newark; seat of Passaic co. Founded by Alexander Hamilton and the Society for Establishing Useful Manufacturers, it was formed as a planned community to promote industry. In 1792–94 cotton spinning mills were set up; by 1835 Samuel Colt began the manufacture of the Colt revolver; silk industry started shortly after. A national historic site was est. 1970 around falls in river; site of preserved cobblestone streets, Colt gun factory, mill owners' and workers' houses, spinning mills, waterworks and old bridges. Industries: clothing, chemicals, plastics, paper, food products. Founded 1791; inc. 1851. Pop. (1970) 144,824.

Pâtés. △380.

Pathans, or **Pashtuns.** Muslim tribes who constitute the major racial group in SE Afghanistan and NW Pakistan. They speak an eastern Iranian language, Pashto, and are composed of 60 tribes practicing both pastoralism and farming. Disputes among the warlike Pathans commonly result in fierce bloodfeuds.

Pathet Lao. △1378.

Pathology, branch of medicine that deals with the nature of disease and the changes it produces in the cells, tissues, and organs of the body. Pathologists usually do not treat patients but examine tissues to study pathologic, or abnormal, changes in the body.

Patna, city in NE India, 290mi (467km) NW of Calcutta on the Ganges River; capital of Bihar state and Patna division; served as the capital of ancient Mauryan empire 325–185 BC and Gupta empire AD 320–545; taken by British 1763; site of Asoka palace (*c.* 270–230 BC), and University of Patna (1917); railroad, commercial, and rice center. Pop. 459,731.

Paton, Alan Stewart (1903–), South African novelist and reformer. He gave up teaching in 1935 to take charge of a school for delinquent African boys. Strongly opposed to apartheid, he helped found and became president of the Liberal party (1953), a post he held until the party's dissolution by the government in 1968. *Cry the Beloved Country* (1948), his most famous and most popular novel, and *Too Late the Phalarope* (1953) both deal with racial exploitation. Other works include *The Long View* (1968) and *For You Departed* (1969).

Pátrai, seaport city in central Greece, on Gulf of Pátrai; capital of Akhaía dept. As member of Second Achaean League, city led battle against Macedonians 218 BC; served as Roman military colony (late 1st century BC) under Augustus who developed it into a prosperous seaport; held by Ottoman Turks 1458–1687, 1715–1828, when it passed to Greece; site of university (1966). Exports: currants, tobacco, wine, olive oil. Pop. 112,238.

Patriarchs. △1178.

Patriarchy, term that is employed to describe a social system in which property is inherited through the male line and in which the family group is ruled by the father or an elderly male. *See also* Matriarchy.

Patricians, privileged upper class or aristocracy of ancient Rome. The term may derive from *pater* ("senate member"). Patricians could hold political and religious office but could not marry plebeians. They wore distinctive clothing. As the lower classes sought and gained political equality, the significance of patrician birth diminished.

Patrick, Saint (*c.* 389–461), patron saint of and missionary bishop to Ireland, b. as Succat in Britain. The facts of his career are much interwoven with legend. Abducted by marauders at 16, he was carried to Ireland and sold to an Antrim chief. After six years he escaped to France, where he took holy orders. Returning to Ireland, he was ordained bishop (432). His missionary work was so successful that in his lifetime almost all the Irish were Christianized. He also introduced the Roman alphabet to Ireland. His grave at Downpatrick became a center of pilgrimage. △1052.

Patrilineal Descent. △876.

Patristic Literature, writings of the Fathers of the Christian Church. Written in Latin or Greek, the early works are apologetics, and the later ones deal with theological questions and explanations. Authors include St Clement I, St Justin Martyr, St Basil the Great, St Ambrose, St Augustine, and St Gregory of Tours.

Patronage, power that allows governmental officials to appoint persons, regardless of merit, to governmental or public jobs. Historically it has been used and abused by elected officials to broaden their own support. In the United States, patronage power was curtailed when the Pendleton Act of 1882 established the Civil Service Commission. High officeholders, however, still use the power, although they now give some regard to the appointee's qualifications.

Patroonships, colonization scheme used in New Netherland after 1629 in which land and manorial privileges were granted a "patroon" for settling a colony of 50 or more people on land purchased from the Indians. The first patroonships were Zwanendal on the Delaware River and Rensselaerwick on the Hudson River, the latter including all of Albany and Rensselaer counties.

Patterson, Floyd (1935–), US boxer, b. Waco, N. C. The first man ever to reclaim the world's heavyweight championship and the youngest (21) to hold the title. He was the Olympic middleweight champion (1952) and beat Archie Moore (1956) in Chicago, Ill., for the heavyweight title. He lost the title to Ingemar Johansson (1959) in New York City, regained it from Johansson (1960) in New York City, and lost it to Sonny Liston (1962) in Chicago.

Patti, Adelina (1843–1919), US coloratura soprano. △1256.

Patton, George Smith, Jr. (1885–1945), US military officer, b. San Gabriel, Calif. A graduate of the US Military Academy at West Point (1909), he was with the American Expeditionary Force (AEF) in France during World War I, where he became familiar with tanks. A controversial and highly successful officer, he commanded a tank corps in North Africa and the 7th Army in Sicily in World War II. After the D-Day invasion (1944), he commanded the Third Army in its dash across France and into Germany. His troops broke the German ring around Bastogne. He was known as "Old Blood and Guts."

Pau, city in SW France, 109mi (175km) S of Bordeaux on E bank of Gave de Pau; capital of Pyrenees-Atlantiques dept.; capital of former province of Bèarn (15th century); residence of kings of Navarre 1512; site of 12th-century castle in which Henry IV of France was born (1553); noted winter sports center. Industries: oil refining, wood, shoes, clothing. Founded 11th century. Pop. 74,005.

Paul, in the New Testament, the first Christian theologian and evangelist. He was born Saul in Tarsus of Jewish parents and became a Pharisee and well-educated Roman citizen. Enroute to Damascus to persecute Christians, he received a vision of Jesus. His conversion to Christianity after Christ's death made him a zealous disciple. He proclaimed that Jesus was the Messiah and was sacrificed to atone for the sins of man. His many epistles, recounting his travels and successful labors, were written to the Corinthians, Romans, Philippians, Hebrews, and others, and are a central part of the New Testament.

Paul III (1468–1549), Roman Catholic pope (1534–49), b. Alessandro Farnese, he was a flagrant nepotist, appointing his grandchildren cardinals. He condemned heretical books, leading to the development of the Index. He excommunicated Henry VIII in 1538 and convened the Council of Trent in 1545.

Paul VI (1897–), Roman Catholic Pope (1963–), b. Giovanni Battista Montini. Educated by Jesuits, he completed the Second Vatican Council begun by John XXIII. He has traveled extensively, fostering international peace and ecumenism. △1388.

Paul I (1754–1801), tsar of Russia (1796–1801). The son and despotic heir of Catherine II, he reestablished the principle of hereditary succession and instituted repressive measures to protect the autocracy from the influence of the French Revolution. Paul's hostility toward his son Alexander led to the murder of the unpopular sovereign by guard officers in March 1801. △1226.

Paul I (1901–1964), king of the Hellenes (1947–64). He succeeded George II and ruled during the insurrection of the Greek Communists. He received US aid to help Greece's economic recovery from World War II and was married to the popular Frederika of Brunswick.

Pauli, Wolfgang (1900–58), US physicist, b. Vienna. His work on quantum theory led him to his exclusion principle (the Pauli principle), which relates the quantum theory to properties of atoms. He received a Nobel Prize in 1945 for this work. In 1931 he postulated the existence of the neutrino and lived to see his prediction verified in 1956. *See also* Exclusion Principle; Quantum Theory. △1550.

Pauli Exclusion Principle. *See* Exclusion Principle; Pauli.

Pauling, Linus Carl (1901–), US biochemist, *b.* Portland, Ore. He studied in Europe and at the California Institute of Technology, where he later became professor. His early work on the application of wave mechanics to molecular structure, detailed in his book *The Nature of the Chemical Bond* (1939), was rewarded by the Nobel Prize in chemistry in 1954. He also worked on the structure of proteins. A keen protagonist of nuclear disarmament, he was awarded the 1962 Nobel Peace Prize. Later, he was an advocate of large doses of vitamin C as a treatment for the common cold.

Paulownia, genus of E Asian deciduous trees grown for their large, heart-shaped leaves and showy clusters of violet flowers. *P. tomentosa* has large clusters of fragrant flowers; height: 40ft (12m). Family Scrophulariaceae.

Pausanias. △994.

Pavia, city in N Italy; capital of Pavia province on the Ticino River; political center of 14th-century Italy under Visconti; scene of 1525 Spanish victory over Francis I of France; active in Risorgimento campaigns; liberated in 1859; site of 14th-century Carthusian monastery, church of 12th-century St Michael, 14th-century university; agricultural, industrial, and communications center. Industries: sewing machines, machinery, foundry products. Pop. 85,160.

Pavlov, Ivan P(etrovich) (1849–1936), Russian neurophysiologist. He made pioneer contributions to medicine, physiology, and psychology. His early work centered on the physiology and neurology of digestion, for which he received a Nobel Prize in 1904. However, he is best known for his work in describing the classical (Pavlovian) conditioning of behavior in animals. This work had a permanent effect on Russian psychology and a profound effect on behaviorism in the United States and on subsequent theories of how organisms learn. His major works (in English translation) are *Conditioned Reflexes* (1927); *Lectures on Conditioned Reflexes* (1928); and *Conditioned Reflexes and Psychiatry* (1941). *See also* Behaviorism;. Pavlovian Conditioning. △772, 778.

Pavlova, Anna (Matveyevna) (1885–1931), Russian ballerina. She was prima ballerina with the Maryinsky Theatre Company in St Petersburg, Russia, touring Europe and the United States. She left Russia in 1913 to tour with her own troupe, which introduced ballet to Japan, China, India, Egypt, and South Africa. She was known for her extraordinary grace and dramatic ability. △1368.

Pavlovian Conditioning or **Classical Conditioning,** in psychology, a basic pattern of how learning takes place, from the work of the Russian psychologist Ivan Pavlov. For example, an event (such as a bell sounding) is repeatedly paired with a stimulus (such as an electric shock) that always elicits a given response (such as leg withdrawal). Continued pairings of the bell and shock will eventually result in a "conditioned response"—the bell itself will elicit leg withdrawal. This pattern has had considerable impact on learning theories and has important applications in changing human behavior, such as that of the mentally ill. *See also* Behavior Modification; Extinction; Reinforcement. △772, 778.

Pawnee, a Caddoan-speaking tribe of North American Indians related to the Arikara, who occupied the Central Platte and Republican river areas in Nebraska. Today 1,200 inhabit a reservation set aside for their use in Oklahoma.

Pawpaw. *See* Papaw.

Pawtucket, city in N Rhode Island, 4mi (6km) NE of Providence, on Blackstone River; site of Slater Mill, first US textile mill, also first to use water power to spin cotton thread. Industries: textiles, yarn, hosiery, clothing, brass and iron foundries. Founded 1671; inc. 1885. Pop. (1970) 76,984.

Pax Romana, the 200-year period of peace in the Roman Empire that began in 31 BC with the rule of Augustus, following an era of violence and civil strife. It ended with the decline of the empire that began *c.* AD 180.

Payne-Aldrich Tariff Act (1910), protective legislation. It began as a reform measure reducing duty list goods, expanding the free list, and placing a progressive tax on inheritance. Supported by a strong manufacturers' lobby, the Senate eliminated the inheritance tax, generally changed the bill to return rates almost to those of the previous Dingley Act.

Pay Television, or pay TV. *See* Cable Television.

Paz, Octavio (1914–), Mexican poet. He is considered the outstanding Spanish American poet. His work has gone through many phases, from Marxism to surrealism to Oriental philosophies, but its dominant characteristics are a search for harmony, notably in erotic experience; an emphasis on objects; and, especially in his later work, a desire to make language more melodious. His writings on the theory of poetry have also been influential. The collection *Parole: Poetic Works* (1960) contains what he regards as his best poems. He added to it in 1968.

PCB. *See* Polychlorinated Biphenyl.

Pea, climbing annual plant *(Pisum sativum)*, probably native to W Asia. It has small, oval leaves and white flowers. The pods contain wrinkled or smooth seeds that are a popular vegetable. There are several varieties. The early dwarf pea (var. *humile*) is a low-growing plant and has small pods. The snow, or sugar, pea (var. *macrocarpum*) has soft, unlined edible pods. It grows to 6ft (1.8m). Family Leguminosae.

Peabody, city in NE Massachusetts, on the Danvers River; named for philanthropist George Peabody; site of the Peabody Institute, whose library contains his memorabilia. Industries: tanning (since early 18th

Louis Pasteur

George Patton

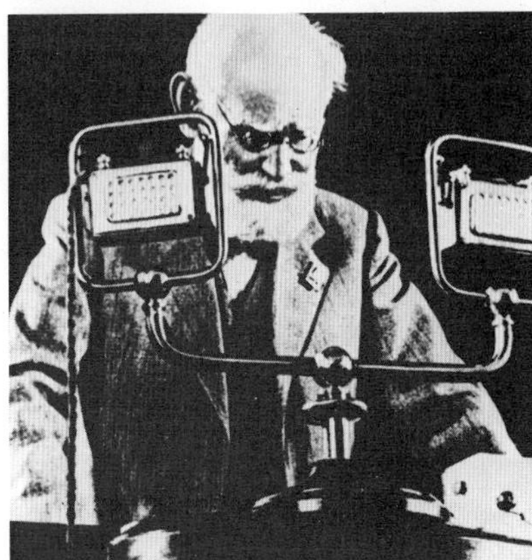

Ivan Pavlov

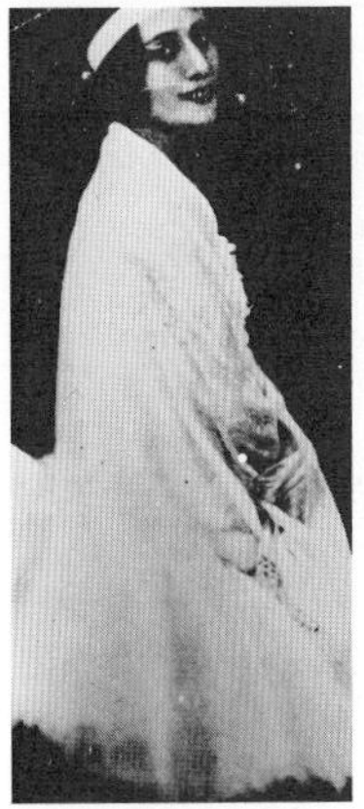

Anna Pavlova

century), chemicals, electronic equipment, machine tools. Settled 1633; inc. as town of South Danvers 1855; name changed 1868; inc. as city 1916. Pop. (1970) 48,080.

Peace Corps, a branch of ACTION (an independent US government agency). The purpose of the Peace Corps is to promote world peace and friendship by sending skilled US volunteers to countries overseas to provide trained manpower and to promote a better understanding between peoples. It was established in 1961 by Pres. John F. Kennedy.

Peace Mission Movement. *See* Divine, Father.

Peace River, river in Canada formed by merger of the Finlay and Parship rivers in N central British Columbia; joins the Slave River near Lake Athabaska; explored 1792–93 by Sir Alexander Mackenzie. Length: 945mi (1,521km).

Peach, small fruit tree native to China or Iran and grown throughout temperate areas. The oblong leaves appear after the pink flowers in spring. The fruit has a thin, downy skin, white or yellow flesh, and is freestone or cling. It is eaten fresh or preserved. Height: 20ft (6.1m). Family Rosacea; species *Prunus persica*. △338.

Peacock, technically the male peafowl, but the term is often used loosely for several species of peafowl (family Phasianidae) that are known for the male's brilliant ornamental tail feathers that he typically raises and spreads fanlike behind him during courtship display. Peacocks are native to Asia and Africa but are also widely kept in zoos. About 40–45in (102–114cm) long, with a train of that length, the typical peacock has a thin neck, small head with fan-shaped crest, blue neck and body, and metallic-green train covered with eyelike spots. They feed on the ground and in the wild lay 3 to 6 light-brown spotted eggs in a hidden ground nest.

Peacock Butterfly, any of several butterflies that have eyespots, resembling those of peacocks, on their wings. In Europe the name is often applied to *Vanessa io* and in E North America, to *Junonia coenia*.

Peale, family of US painters of portraits, miniatures, still lifes, historical scenes, and landscapes, active in the 18th and 19th centuries. The first and most noted member was Charles Wilson (1741–1827); his sons included Raphael, Rembrandt, Rubens, Franklin, and Titian. Charles' brother James was also an artist.

Peanut, spreading annual native to Brazil and grown widely in the United States. It has small leaflets and yellowflowers. Valued as a food crop, the subterranean seeds, or peanuts, are eaten in various forms. Height: 20 in (51cm). Family Leguminoseae; species *Arachis hypogaea*.

Peanut Worm. △506.

Pear, fruit native to N Asia and S Europe and grown worldwide in temperate regions. It has a pyramidal shape and clusters of white flowers appear among the glossy, green leaves. The greenish-yellow, brownish, or reddish fruit, picked unripe and allowed to mature in storage, is eaten fresh or preserved. Height: 50–75ft (15.3–22.9m). Family Rosaceae; species *Pyrus communis*. △338.

Pearl, river in Mississippi and Louisiana; rises in E central Mississippi; flows SW and S into the Gulf of Mexico; forms a natural border between Mississippi and Louisiana. Length: 485mi (781km).

Pearl, iridescent concretion produced by certain marine and freshwater bivalve mollusks. Composed almost entirely of nacre, or mother-of-pearl, the calcium carbonate compound forms the inner layer of mollusk shells. A pearl, the only gem of animal origin, results from an abnormal growth of nacre around minute particles of foreign matter, such as sand. The pearl oyster of the Persian Gulf produces the most valuable pearls. *See also* Bivalve; Mother-of-Pearl. △ 244, 478.

Pearl Harbor, inlet on the S coast of the island of Oahu, Hawaii, 6mi (10km) W of Honolulu, site of US naval base. By treaty of 1887, United States was permitted to use harbor for coaling and repairing station; Congress authorized construction of naval station 1908, drydocks completed 1919. On Dec. 7, 1941, the US Pacific fleet was largely destroyed by the Japanese attack on Pearl Harbor, signaling hostilities between those two countries in the Pacific theater of WWII. △1336.

Pearly Nautilus. *See* Nautilus.

Pearse, Patrick (or **Padraic**) **Henry** (1879–1916), Irish educator, author, and political figure. He headed the revival of interest in Gaelic culture, writing poems, short stories, and plays. Leader of the insurgents in the Easter Uprising against British rule (1916), he was court-martialed and shot.

Pearson, Lester Bowles (1897–1972), prime minister of Canada (1963–68). A combat pilot in World War I and professor of history (1924–28), he joined the department of external affairs (1935–41). He was US ambassador (1945–46), chairman of NATO (1951–52), and UN General Assembly president (1952–53). A Liberal member of Parliament and secretary of state from 1948, he assumed party leadership in 1958. He received the 1957 Nobel Prize for peace for his work in the Middle East. An energetic leader, he ruled as prime minister without a majority and retired in 1968 to become chancellor of Carleton University. He wrote several works on politics.

Peary, Robert Edwin (1856–1920), US arctic explorer. He made the first of several explorations of Greenland in 1886. Accompanied by his wife in 1891, he found evidence that Greenland was an island. In 1898, he announced plans for an expedition to the North Pole, and received financial aid from the Peary Arctic Club of New York. He reached his goal by sled in 1909, along with Matthew Henson, his black assistant, and four Eskimos, but Frederick A. Cook was said to have beaten him by a year. *See also* Cook, Frederick Albert.

Peary Land, region of Greenland; Morris Jesup, its N cape, is most northerly point of land in Arctic Region; explored by Robert Peary in 1892 and 1900. Highest point: 6,300ft (1,922m).

Peasantry. △886.

Peasants' War (1524–26). △1152.

Peat, dark brown, decayed organic material with a high carbon content built up in bogs. It is the first stage in coal development. Sphagnum mosses form most peat in the Northern Hemisphere; cord grass forms salt peat in salt marshes. Dried peat is used as fuel. △282.

Peat Moss, humus obtained from disintegrated sphagnum moss. The most widely obtainable source of humus, it is dug into soil to retain moisture and increase productiveness. It is also added to compost piles for aeration. △436.

Pecan, deciduous tree, native to S central United States, grown primarily as a nut crop. Its oblong nut has a sweet edible kernel. Height: 130ft (40m). Family Juglandaceae; species *Carya illinoensis*.

Peccary, omnivorous piglike mammal native to SW United States and Central and South America. It has thick fur and scent glands on its back. Collared peccaries, or javelinas *(Tayassu tajaçu)*, have dark gray fur with a whitish collar. White-lipped peccaries *(Tayassu pecari)* have brown fur. Weight: 50–66lb (23–30kg). Family Tayassuidae.

Pecking Order, hierarchical system of social organization based on dominance and submission operating on a descending scale. The leader has power over the entire community, the second in command has power over everyone but the leader, and so on. The term derives from the behavior of hens, which express their dominance by pecking their inferiors. *See also* Dominance Relationships. △464.

Pečora, river in N Russian SFSR, USSR, rising in Middle Ural Mts; flows N, W, and N again to Pečora Bay of the Barents Sea, forming a delta mouth at Naryan-Mar; it receives the Ilych, Shchugor, Usa, Kozhva, Izhma, and Tsilma rivers; supports fisheries, farming, and livestock raising along its course, and coal fields in its basin. Both the main river and tributaries are navigable for most of their 1,110mi (1,787km).

Pécs, city in S Hungary; capital of Baranya co; originally the Roman colony of Sopianae; site of Hungary's first university, founded by Louis the Great 1367. Industries: coal mining, wine, leather. Pop. 145,307.

Pectin, water-soluble sugar found in certain ripe fruits or vegetables. It is the removal of this substance that causes fruits and vegetables to soften when cooked. It also yields a gel that is the basis of jellies and jams. △1574.

Pectoralis Major. △684.

Pedalfer, acid soil, rich in iron and aluminum, formed in humid areas with high temperatures, especially tropical forests. *See also* Pedocal; Podzol; Soil. △312

Pedestal Rock. △266.

Pedocal, soil, rich in lime, that commonly forms in prairie regions with low rainfall, the lack of subsequent leaching, and low temperatures. *See also* Pedalfer; Podzol; Soil.

Pedology. △312.

Pedophilia, sexual deviation either heterosexual or homosexual in nature, in which a child becomes the object of sexual arousal, interest, or gratification. In its overt form it leads to child molesting. △766.

Pedro I (1798–1834), king of Portugal and emperor of Brazil. Pedro became regent of Brazil when his father, João VI, returned to Portugal in 1821. The Portuguese parliament asked Pedro to return to Europe in 1822; instead, Pedro declared Brazil independent and himself emperor. His preoccupation with affairs in Portugal and his inability to mediate political rivalries prompted his abdication in favor of his Brazilian-born son in 1831.

Pedro II (1825–91), emperor of Brazil (1831–89), ruled as regent until 1840 when he was declared old enough to be crowned. Despite internal revolts in the 1830s and 1840s and external threats from Argentina and Paraguay, Pedro II demonstrated greater skill than his father in governing. Slavery was abolished during his tenure (1888). He was forced to resign in 1889; Brazil became a republic.

Peel, (Sir) Robert (1788–1850), English prime minister. Entering Parliament as a Tory (1809), his offices included chief secretary for Ireland (1812–18), home secretary (1823–30), first lord of the treasury, chancellor of the exchequer, and prime minister (1834–35; 1841–45). As home secretary he founded the London police force (1829). In his later offices he lightened the burden of indirect taxation and by alleviating trade impositions enabled Britain to dominate world trade. He reorganized the Bank of England and launched a policy of reform in Ireland (1845). Losing support after repealing the Corn Laws (1846), he resigned. He is credited with the major role in the development of the Conservative party. △1236.

Pegasus, in Greek mythology, winged horse. Born out of the blood of Medusa, it carried the thunderbolt of Zeus. It was tamed by Bellerophon and helped him in his battles. According to legend, Pegasus threw Bellerophon when the latter attempted to fly to heaven. The Hippocrene, a sacred spring, was produced by a stamp of Pegasus' hoof.

Pegasus, or the Winged Horse, northern constellation situated southwest of Cygnus. Three of its brightest stars form a giant square with Alpha Andromedae. It contains no stars brighter than the second magnitude. △132.

Pei, I(eoh) M(ing) (1917–), US-Chinese architect noted for the integration of his structures with their environment. Important buildings include Mile High Center, Denver (1957), the National Airlines Terminal at Kennedy International Airport (1971), and the East Building to the National Gallery of Art, Washington, D.C. His work in large scale urban development is also distinguished.

Peirce, Charles Sanders (1839–1914), US philosopher, b. Cambridge, Mass. He was employed by the US Coast and Geodetic Survey until 1891 and lectured on logic (1879–84). He was a prolific author of essays and reviews, but their impact, like publication of his works, was mainly posthumous. His philosophy is best approached as an aspect of science, whose validity is contained in the sum of its practical consequences. He contributed to formal logic and practically to the theory of probability. He was the author, with William James, of "American pragmatism." *See also* Pragmatism. △858.

Peisistratus (6th century BC), Athenian tyrant. He first seized power in 561, but was ousted. After a second attempt, he withdrew to Thrace, amassing great wealth and using it to hire foreign mercenaries for a successful coup in 546. He was fair to the common people and increased Athens' trade. At his death (527), his sons, Hippias and Hipparchus, ruled until the last was deposed in 510.

Pekin, port city in Illinois, on Illinois River, S of Peoria; seat of Tazewell co. Industries: corn products, liquors, alcohol, yeast, malt, copper, iron. Settled 1824; inc. 1839. Pop. (1970) 31,375.

'eking (Beijing, or **Peiping),** capital of the People's epublic of China, on a vast plain between the Pei and un rivers, NE China. City served as China's capital 421–1911; after est. of Chinese Republic 1911–12, ne capital alternated between Peking, Canton, and an-k'ou; seat of government was transferred to Nan-ing 1928, and Peking, meaning "northern capital," vas known as Peiping. Occupied by Japanese 1937, was restored to China 1946; under Communist con-ol January 1949, who restored its name and made the capital of the People's Republic. The city is omprised of two walled sections: Inner or Tartar City, vhich houses the Forbidden City, and the Outer or hinese city; political, cultural, educational, financial, nd transportation center of China. Pop. 4,800,000.

'ekingese, breed of dog (toy group) considered sa-red in China in the past; dating from 8th century and ntroduced to West in 1860. It has a broad skull; hort, wrinkled muzzle; and broad, flat nose. Heart-haped ears have long drooping feathering; eyes are rominent. The medium-length body is heavy in front; ne legs are short and bowed. A high-set tail is carried ver the back. The long, thick, straight coat may be ny color. Average size: 6–9in (15.2–23cm); 6–14lb 2.7–6.3kg). *See also* Toy Dog.

'eking Man, or *Sinanthropus pekinensis,* extinct 'leistocene man known from remains first discovered n 1927 at Choukoutien, China. A hunter and user of tone tools and fire, *Sinanthropus* was more advanced han related Java Man. *See also* Java Man. △650, 52.

'elagianism, heretical Christian belief in the 5th entury. In opposition to St Augustine's belief that nan could only attain salvation through God's grace, he Pelagians saw man as a creature of inherent piritual grace and strong will and further denied origi-al sin and the need of the Church for salvation. 'elagius (360?–?420) and his followers were rigor-ously discouraged, but established an argument that hrives even now.

'elagic Division, the whole mass of ocean water. Its eritic zone extends from the low tide mark on shore out to a 200m (656ft) depth and represents an in-shore environment. The oceanic or open-sea zone has n upper lighted part and a lower dark one. The term elagic is also applied to all life that is not attached o the ocean floor. △624–26.

'elargonium, the garden geranium native to South Africa. The circular or lobed leaves of these perenni-als alternate on the stalk and are often aromatic. Five-petaled flowers are red, pink, purple, or white. Family Geraniaceae; Genus *Pelargonium. See also* Gera-nium.

Pelayo (died 737), Spanish king of Asturias (718–37). When the Moors conquered Spain from the Christians, beginning in 711, many of the local petty rulers retreated to the Asturian mountains. There they elected one of their members, Pelayo, as leader. His victory over the Moors at Covadonga (probably in 718) is traditionally regarded as the beginning of the long Christian reconquest of Spain.

Pelé, (1940–); Brazilian soccer player, b. Edson Arantes do Nascimento. The best player of his era, he led Brazil to three World Cup victories (1958, 1962, 1970) and was said to have been the highest paid athlete in the world during his career. He retired from international competition in 1971, but in 1975, he joined the New York Cosmos in the North American Soccer League.

Pelecypod, or bivalvia, marine mollusks including clams, oysters, mussels, and scallops. Class character-istics are two shells hinged together; laterally com-pressed foot; reduced head; huge mantle cavity; and complex, sheetlike gills. The two shells are fastened with an elastic horny ligament and closed by two large muscles. The shell's elevated knob near the ligament is the umbo, the oldest part of the shell. As the animal grows, its mantle produces calcareous layers along shell edges. Pelecypods feed by passing water through the body and straining out microscopic parti-cles of food. Class Lamellibranchiata. △478.

Pelée, Mount, volcanic peak in N Martinique, in Windwards, West Indies; it has erupted many times, most notably May 8, 1902, when it engulfed town of St Pierre killing approx. 40,000 people. Highest peak on the island, 4,429ft (1,351m).

Pelican, stout-bodied inland lake and marsh bird. Each has a pouch under its bill for scooping up fish driven into shallow areas. They are generally white or brown and have long hooked bills, long wings, short thick legs, and webbed feet. They lay white eggs (1–4) in a tree or ground nest. Length: 4–6ft (1.2–1.8m). Family Pelecanidae. △620.

Pelican Flower, or swan flower, perennial creeping vine of West Indies. Its 20-in, (51-cm) maroon and cream mottled tubelike flower has a repulsive odor that attracts flies. Family Aristolochiaceae; species *Aristolochia grandiflora.*

Pellagra, a disease characterized by dermatitis, in-flammation of mucous membrane, and gastrointesti-nal disorders caused by an inadequate intake of nia-cin, in protein-poor diets. Although common worldwide, it is especially prevalent in the Mediterra-nean region and Central America. Treatment involves administration of niacin and other B-complex vitamins and a well-balanced diet. △696.

Pelletier, Pierre-Joseph (1788–1842), French chemist known for his work in founding the chemistry of alkaloids. He first isolated chlorophyll, then the class of vegetable bases called alkaloids. With J.B. Caventou, he discovered such alkaloids as brucine, cinchonine, quinine, and strychnine.

Pellitory-of-the-wall. △446.

Pelly, river in Canada, in S central Yukon territory, rises in Mackenzie Mts; flows W to join Lewes River to form the Yukon River. Length: 330mi (531km).

Peloponnesian Wars (431–404 BC), conflicts be-tween Athens (Delian League) and Sparta (the Pelo-ponnesians). In the early years Athens maintained her position, but in 430 plague killed over one quarter of her people and in 429 Pericles died. Still, Sparta sued for peace which the demagogue Cleon refused. In 424 Sparta saved Megara from Athens and won other victories. A one year truce then prevailed, till Cleon marched on Thrace. The Peace of Nicias was con-cluded and was in effect a victory for Athens. The Athenian Alcibiades wrecked the peace with his los-ing Sicilian campaign (413). In the ensuing years grave internal troubles weakened Athens, which ca-pitulated in April 404. Thucydides called the conflict the worst disturbance in Greek history. △994, 998.

Peloponnesus (Pelopónnisos), peninsula in S Greece, connected to central Greece by the Isthmus of Corinth; site of ancient Sparta, Corinth, Argos, and Megalopolis. The entire peninsula was involved in the Persian Wars 500–449 BC; site of many battles be-tween Sparta and Athens for Grecian hegemony dur-ing Peloponnesian Wars (431–04 BC); dominated by Sparta, the peninsula fell to the Romans 146 BC who reduced it to a provincial state. It was awarded to the Villehardouin princes of France (1204) by leaders of the Fourth Crusade; held by Venetians 1687–1715; passed to Greece after its war of independence (1821–29). Industries: textiles, fishing, mining, tour-ism, fruit, olives, tobacco, wheat. Area: 8,300sq mi (21,500sq km). Pop. 986,912.

Pelvis, bowl-shaped structure that supports the soft internal organs of the lower abdomen. The pelvis is formed by the hip bone on each side, joined at the sacroiliac joint, with the sacrum in the back, and with the pubic bones in front. The pelvis is broader in females than in males. △682.

Pelycosaur. △568.

Pembroke Welsh Corgi, cattle dog (working group) brought to British Isles in 1107 by Flemish weavers; related to Keeshond and Pomeranian types. It has a fox-shaped head; medium-sized, erect ears tapering to a rounded point; long body; short, slightly turned-in legs; and a docked tail. The short, straight coat is slightly longer on neck, chest, and backs of legs; col-ors include red, sable, fawn, black and tan—all with or without white marks. Average size: 10–12in (25.5–30.5cm) high at shoulder; to 30lb (13.5kg). *See also* Keeshound; Pomeranian; Working Dog.

Pen. △1816.

Penates, in Roman mythology, gods of the house-hold. Initially gods of the storeroom, their protection eventually extended over the entire household.

Penda (577?–655), king of Mercia. He consolidated the Anglian tribes of midland England. A champion of heathenism, he killed the Northumbrian kings Edwin (633) and Oswald (642). Defeating Cenwealh of Wes-sex (645), he temporarily ruled England. He was slain by Oswy of Northumbria.

Pendleton, Edmund (1721–1803), US statesman and jurist, b. Caroline co, Va. As a delegate to the First Continental Congress (1774–75), he wrote the resolu-tion that called on that body to declare the colonies'

Peacock butterfly

Robert Peary

Sir Robert Peel

Pekingese

independence from England. Head of the Virginia Committee of Safety, he was governor of Virginia (1774–76), and he was president of the Supreme Court of Appeals of Virginia (1779–1803); he never had a decision overturned. He also helped revise and codify the statutes of Virginia.

Pendleton Act (1883), US civil service reform law. It established a civil service commission, provided for appointments of federal officeholders to be apportioned among the states, and prohibited the levying of campaign contributions on federal officeholders. *See also* Civil Service Commission.

Pendulous Sedge. △454.

Pendulum, any swinging body supported at a point. A simple pendulum consists of a small heavy mass attached to a string or light rigid rod. Small oscillations of such a pendulum have a frequency of $(L/g)^{1/2}$, where L is the length and g is the acceleration due to gravity. A compound pendulum has a supporting rod whose mass is not negligible, and its motion cannot be described as a simple relation. △1494, 1656, 1658.

Penelope, in Greek mythology, the wife of Odysseus, depicted as a woman of great beauty, fine character, and righteous conduct. As described in Homer's *Odyssey,* she had been married for only a year when her husband left for 10 years of war and 10 of wandering. She remained faithful, putting off her many suitors with the promise that she would choose one when her weaving was done. By day she worked, by night she undid her work.

Peneplain. △252, 260.

Penguin, stocky, black and white flightless aquatic bird of Antarctica and nearby coastlines and islands. It has a strong bill, short neck, flipperlike wings, short tail and legs, and webbed feet. It walks upright, bellyflops on the snow and swims well, even in rough seas. Feeding on fish and mollusks, penguins nest and court in colonies, sometimes forming long-lasting pairs. Fasting males incubate white eggs (1–2) in ground or hole nest. The king penguin holds eggs in an abdominal fold. Height: to 4ft (1.2m); weight: over 75lb (34kg). Order Sphenisciformes. △532, 534.

Penicillin, antibiotic agent considered the greatest discovery of 20th-century medical science. Developed by Sir Alexander Fleming in 1928, it is derived from molds and can also be produced synthetically. It is effective in combating many bacterial diseases. Allergic reactions range from itching to fatal shock. △744, 746.

Peninsular Campaign, series of Civil War battles (spring 1862) resulting from Union Gen. George McClellan's attack up the peninsula between the York and James rivers in Virginia. The Confederates, under generals Joseph Johnston and Robert E. Lee, prevented the 100,000-man Union army from reaching Richmond. Each side lost over 20,000 men.

Penki (Benxi, or Pen-ch'i), city in NE China, 30mi (48km) E of Liaoyang. Industries: steel, foundry, iron and coal mines. Pop. 750,000.

Penn, John (1741–88), US patriot and a signer of the Declaration of Independence, b. Caroline co, Va. A successful lawyer, he was a North Carolina delegate to the Continental Congress (1775–77, 1778–80).

Penn, William (1644–1718), founder of Pennsylvania, b. England. He joined the Quakers in 1666 and was imprisoned several times for his religious views (1666–70). He wrote *No Cross, No Crown,* explaining the Quaker-Puritan morality (1669), in prison. In 1681, to create a refuge for Quakers, he pressed King Charles II to honor loans made to Penn's father. He received a land grant, which he named Pennsylvania after his father. In organizing a government for the colony, he drew up a Frame of Government, the first constitution with an amendment clause. He also designed the city of Philadelphia. He first came to Pennsylvania in 1682. In an effort to settle the boundary dispute with Maryland, he left for England (1684), where he drafted the first plan for a union of the American colonies (1696). He was once again in Pennsylvania (1699–1701).

Pennacook, native Americans of the Algonquian linguistic family; originally lived as semi-sedentary hunters, farmers, and sea-fishermen in east-central New England. Although primarily peaceful, the 1,300 Pennacook (reduced from 2,000 by European disease) were so miserably treated by white settlers during King Philip's War (1675) that they fled to Quebec and New York State.

Pennsylvania, state in the E United States, in the Middle Atlantic region.

Land and Economy. Mountain ranges of medium height run roughly NE to SW across much of the state, interspersed with fertile valleys. In the SE lies a rich agricultural area. The Delaware River, forming the E boundary, enters Delaware Bay, an arm of the Atlantic Ocean. The Susquehanna, flowing N to S in the state's center, and the Allegheny in the W are important rivers. In the extreme NW the state borders Lake Erie. Pennsylvania's productive soil and abundant mineral deposits, especially of coal and iron, contributed to the growth of the manufacturing industries that have kept the economy in a prosperous balance. Manufacturing is centered in 12 metropolitan areas, notably Philadelphia, Pittsburgh, and Allentown-Bethlehem-Easton. Philadelphia, with access to the sea by the Delaware River, is one of the nation's major ports.

People. The original settlers were mostly from the British Isles. They were followed in the 18th century by Germans, erroneously called "Pennsylvania Dutch," who occupied farming lands in the E and SE. Mines and mills drew immigrants from Italy, Poland, Russia, Czechoslovakia, and Hungary. More than 70% of the population lives in urban areas.

Education. There are about 150 institutions of higher education. Pennsylvania State University is state-supported. The University of Pennsylvania is the leading private institution.

History. Swedish and Dutch settlements were made along the Delaware in the mid-17th century, but by 1674 the area was controlled by England. William Penn received a charter from Charles II of England in 1681 for what is now Pennsylvania. Philadelphia became the provincial capital and was the capital of the colonies during the American Revolution. The Declaration of Independence (1776) and the US Constitution (1787) were signed there. The city was the national capital 1790–1800. The Union victory at the Battle of Gettysburg (July 1863), which repulsed a Confederate invasion of the state, was a turning point of the Civil War. In both world wars, Pennsylvania was a major source of military supplies, shipbuilding being especially important.

PROFILE

Admitted to Union: Dec. 12, 1787; 2nd of the 13 original states to ratify the US Constitution
US Congressmen: Senate, 2; House of Representatives, 25
Population: 11,793,909 (1970); rank, 3d
Capital: Harrisburg, 68,061 (1970)
Chief cities: Philadelphia, 1,950,098; Pittsburgh, 520,117; Erie, 129,231
State legislature: Senate, 50; House of Representatives, 203
Area: 45,333sq mi (117,412sq km); rank, 33d
Elevation: Highest, 3,213ft (980m), Mt Davis; lowest, sea level, Delaware River
Industries (major products): steel, metal products, machinery and electrical machinery, chemicals and drugs, processed foods, apparel
Agriculture (major products): dairy products, poultry, grapes, peaches, apples, cherries
Minerals (major): anthracite and bituminous coal, cement, petroleum, zinc, clay
State nickname: Keystone State
State motto: Virtue, Liberty, and Independence
State bird: ruffed grouse
State flower: mountain laurel
State tree: eastern hemlock

Pennsylvanian Period. *See* Carboniferous Period.

Pennyroyal, common name for a number of plants, including the European *Mentha pulegium,* and the American *Hedeoma pulegioides,* sweet herbs of the mint family. They have purple flowers and leaves said to be offensive to mosquitoes.

Penobscot, native Americans of the Algonquian linguistic group. They were prominent members of the Abnaki Confederacy and active allies of the French until 1749. A seasonally nomadic Eastern Woodlands people, the 700 Penobscot lived in the Penobscot Bay and Penobscot River areas of Maine. They received a reservation at Old Town, Maine, after helping the colonists to independence. They are entitled to limited representation in the Maine legislature.

Penology, branch of criminology that studies and evaluates the programs, institutions, and organizations that treat criminal offenders. *See also* Criminology. △922.

Pensacola, city in extreme NW Florida on Gulf of Mexico, seat of Escambia co, 10mi (16km) NE of Alabama border. Used as base by both Union and Confederacy in Civil War; site of Navy air station. Industries: paper and cork products, chemicals. Settled 1559 by Spain; passed to United States 1821. Pop. (1970) 59,507.

Pentagon, five-sided plane figure. Its interior angles add up to 540°. For a regular pentagon, one whose sides and interior angles are all equal, each interior angle is 108°.

Pentagon Papers, documents pertaining to a secret military study of the US role in Vietnam. The study was carried out during the administration of Pres. Lyndon Johnson and made public by the New York *Times* and other newspapers (1971). The papers were passed on to the *Times* anonymously by Daniel Ellsberg, a former government researcher, to show how the military had been misleading the public about US involvement in Vietnam. The Nixon administration tried to stop publication of the study, which led to a court battle that the newspapers eventually won. Ellsberg was indicted (1971) for conspiracy, theft, and espionage but the charges were dismissed in 1973. The New York *Times* received a Pulitzer Prize for reporting the study (1972).

Pentameter, verse line of five metrical feet, introduced into English literature by Chaucer. Iambic pentameter is the most durable form of English poetry. William Shakespeare's *Sonnets,* Edmund Spenser's *The Faerie Queene,* and John Milton's *Paradise Lost* are outstanding examples.

Pentateuch, first five books of the Old Testament: Genesis, Exodus, Leviticus, Numbers, and Deuteronomy. It covers the period from the creation of the universe to the death of Moses.

Pentathlon, an athletic competition. It originated in ancient Greece, where it consisted of five events—foot racing, leaping, wrestling, discus throwing, and javelin throwing—all taking place on the same day. The modern pentathlon, held over a five day period, comprises a cross-country horse-back race, a swimming race, épée fencing, pistol shooting, and a 2.5 mile (4km) cross-country run. The competition has been an Olympic Games event since 1912.

Pentecost, in the Jewish calendar, a festival held seven weeks after the second day of Passover. It commemorates the giving of the law to Moses, but it is also a feast of harvest or Day of the First Fruits. In the Christian calendar Pentecost is a feast held 50 days after Easter to commemorate the descent of the Holy Spirit on the Apostles. After Christ's Ascension, the Holy Spirit gave special strength to his Apostles, as related in Acts 2:1—4. The day is called Pentecost in the Roman Catholic Church and Whitsunday in the Anglican churches.

Pentecostalism, dramatic religious movement of 20th century America, grew from the Fundamentalist and Holiness churches of the 19th century. Involving a number of churches, such as the Assemblies of God, with varying beliefs, Pentecostalism often entails speaking in tongues, faith healing, the baptism of the faithful, and a firm belief in the Second Coming of Christ.

Pentoses. △1570.

Pentothal, trademark of thiopental, short-acting barbiturate combined with sodium and used as an intravenous anesthetic. Side effects include restlessness, excitement, and delirium, particularly if pain is present. *See also* Barbiturates.

Pentstemon, or beardtongue, genus of North American perennial plants and shrubs with terminal clusters of tubular, white, pink, red, blue, or purple flowers. They have five stamens; one is sterile and bearded. Family Scrophulariaceae; genus *Pentstemon. See also* Figwort.

Penumbra. △1520.

Penza, city in Russian SFSR, USSR, on the Sura River, 350mi (564km) SE of Moscow; capital of the Penza oblast; site of industrial and teachers' colleges, and agricultural and regional museums. Industries: machine tools, calculators, washing machines, printing presses, agricultural implements, watches, bicycles, medical instruments. Founded 1663 as Moscow fortress; chartered 1682. Pop. 374,000.

Peony, perennial plant native to Eurasia and North America. They have glossy, divided leaves, large white, pink, or red flowers, and are frequently cultivated in gardens. Height: to 3ft (0.9m). Tree peonies grow only in hot, dry areas and have brilliant blossoms of many colors; height: to 6ft (1.8m). Family Ranunculaceae; genus *Paeonia.*

eople's Party. *See* Populist Party.

eoria, port city in central Illinois, on Lake Peoria and inois River; seat of Peoria co; transportation and ommercial center; site of Bradley University (1896) ıd marker commemorating Abraham Lincoln's Pe-ia address condemning slavery (1854). Area first sited by Père Marquette and Louis Jolliet 1673; Fort eve Coeur was built here 1680 by Robert La Salle. dustries: brewing, distilling, farm machinery, brick, e, stone. Settled 1819; inc. as town 1835, as city 345. Pop. (1970) 126,963.

eperomia, genus of succulent house plant native to opical America with waxy, ridged or smooth oval or ounded leaves of green, green and white, or copper-lack. Care: bright indirect light, soil (equal parts am, peat moss, sand) kept dry between waterings. ropagation is by stem cuttings. Height: to 10in 5cm).

epin II, or **Pepin of Herstal** (died 714), ruler of ustrasia (*c.* 679); mayor of palace and ruler of all the ranks (687–714). His defeat of the Neustrians at the attle of Tertry (687) marked the ascendance of the arolingians over the Merovingians.

epin the Short (714?–768), son of Charles Martel, ıler of Neustria and king of the Franks (751–768), ıe first Carolingian king. He deposed Childeric III 751), the last Merovingian ruler. He supported the xtension of papal control and was anointed by St oniface in a ceremony of symbolic importance. gain anointed by Pope Stephen II (754), he defeated ıe Lombards on the pope's behalf. The new papal nds thus acquired were known as the Donation of epin. The close relationship between the pope and ıe Carolingian kings tied papal development to the Vest rather than to Italy and the East. Pepin was the ather of Charlemagne.

epper, annual woody plant native to tropical Amer-ca. The fruit is a many-seeded, pungent berry with ize depending on species. Included are bell, red, ayenne, and chili peppers. Family Solanaceae; genus *apsicum.*

eppermint, common name for *Mentha piperita,* a erennial herb of the mint family widely cultivated for s essential oil, which is distilled and used as a medi-ine and for flavoring.

epper Tree, or Peruvian mastic tree, evergreen tree ative to tropical South America. Grown as an orna-nental, it has featherlike leaves, yellow flowers, and eddish berries. Height: to 50ft (15m). Family Anacar-iaceae; species *Schinus molle.*

epsin, enzyme secreted by glands of the vertebrate tomach as part of the gastric juice. In the presence f hydrochloric acid it catalyzes the splitting of whole roteins into smaller peptide fractions.

eptide, compound consisting of two or more amino cids linked by bonds between the amino group NH_2) of one and the carboxyl group (-COOH) of the ext. This type of linkage is called a peptide bond, and eptides containing three or more amino acids are alled polypeptides. Proteins consist of polypeptide hains, containing up to several hundred amino acids, ross-linked to each other in a variety of ways.

epys, Samuel (1633–1703), English diarist and aval administrator. He was secretary of the admiralty 1669–1688) except for a brief imprisonment for al-eged complicity in the Popish Plot. His *Diary* (1661–69) frankly describes his private life and English soci-ety during the Restoration. It includes a vivid account of the Restoration, the coronation ceremony (1661), he plague (1663), and the Great Fire of London 1666). Pepys' *Diary* was written in cipher (a system of shorthand) and was not deciphered until 1825 by Rev. John Smith.

Pequot, a major tribe of Algonquian-speaking North American Indians formerly inhabiting the New Lon-don-Thames River valley region of Connecticut and W Rhode Island. Their unfortunate participation in the Pequot War of 1636–37 reduced their original popu-lation of 2,500 to less than 1,200. Today no more than 100 to 175 persons claim any measurable amount of Pequot blood, most of whom live around the Mystic River in Connecticut.

Pequot War (1637), conflict between the Pequot Indians and the Connecticut colonists. Reacting to an attack that caused the death of 30 white settlers, the colonists destroyed the Pequot tribe. Capt. John Mason killed over 600 Indian men, women, and chil-dren in a battle on the Mystic River. A policy of exter-mination toward the Pequots continued, and survi-vors became slaves in the West Indies or to the Mohawk and Mohegan tribes.

Percentage, quantity or amount reckoned as a part of a whole, expressed in hundredths; the rate or pro-portion per hundred. A ratio is converted to a percent-age by multiplication by 100, thus, ¾ is equivalent to 75 percent (75%).

Percentile, in statistics and psychometrics, the per-centage of people who scored equal to or higher than a given score. For example, a percentile score of 85 indicates that whoever has this score was equal to or higher than the scores of 85% of those who were assessed. *See also* Statistics.

Perception, process by which the nervous system transforms energy into an impression of the world. The energy may be external (light, sound waves) or internal (stimulation of muscles and tendons). The end-product of the process is sometimes described as experience and sometimes as behavior. Perception is often called information processing. In this view, the central nervous system is analogous to a computer, the energy as input, and perception as the output of the process. △670.

Perch, freshwater fish found in lakes, ponds, and slow-moving streams of the United States east of the Rockies and in Europe. A food fish, it is brass or gold-colored with 6–9 black side bars. Eggs are laid in long sticky ribbons. Genera include the yellow perch *(Perca flavescens)* that grows to 15in (38.1cm); 1lb (0.5kg). The European perch *(Perca fluviatilis)* is found throughout most of Europe except Spain, Italy and N Scandinavia; it grows to 5–6lb (2.3–2.7kg). Family Percidae. △390, 516.

Percheron, draft horse breed developed in La Perche region of NW France from Flemish and Ara-bian breeds. Introduced in United States about 1840, it was the most popular draft breed, particularly for farm work. Color is black or gray. Height: 65–67in (165–170cm) at shoulder; weight: 1,900–2,100lb (855–945kg).

Perching Bird, largest bird order that includes over 5,000 or more than half the known species. Primarily land birds, many are migratory and found worldwide except in polar areas and a few isolated islands. Their habitats range from desert to tropical jungle to moun-tainous cliff. Some species are widespread, others are limited to small areas. Mostly songbirds, they evolved about 60,000,000 years ago and are today the most specialized of all birds.

All perching birds have grasping feet with the first toe placed backward; nine or ten flight feathers; and a symmetrical molting pattern. Species vary in size; beak formation—from birds of prey with strong, hooked beaks to nectar feeders with slender beaks and specialized tongues; coloring—drab to bright or multicolored; egg color; and nest formation. Length: 3–40in (7.6–102cm). Order Passeriformes. △526.

Percussion-cap Priming. △1728.

Percussion Instruments, instruments producing music by the striking together of solid objects. In drums a stick hits a membrane stretched across a frame. Some percussion instruments have indefinite pitch, for example, snare and bass drums, castanets, and gongs. Others are tuned: timpani, glockenspiels, chimes, and xylophones. Certain instruments nor-mally melodic, such as piano or guitar, may be used for percussion. In jazz, along with drums, they form the rhythm section, providing the basic beat and free-ing the band leader to play an instrument. △1244, 1500.

Percy, (Sir) Henry (1364–1403), English nobleman, known as Hotspur. The son of Henry, 1st earl of Nor-thumberland, he supported Henry IV's accession to the throne, defended the Scottish border, and de-feated Scottish invaders at Homildon Hill (1402). He revolted (1403) against the king when he was forbid-den to ransom his brother-in-law, Edward Mortimer. He was killed at Shrewsbury before joining the forces of his father and Owen Glendower.

Pere David's Deer, or mi-lu, deer extinct in its native Chinese marshlands but found in zoological parks throughout the world. It has long, three-tined antlers. Height: 45in (1,143mm) at shoulder. Family Cervidae; species *Elaphurus davidianus.*

Peregrine Falcon, or duck hawk, North American gray falcon found along coastal lowlands, nesting high on seacoast cliffs. A fast flyer, it dives at fantastic speeds. Species *Falco peregrinus. See also* Falcon.

William Penn

Pennsylvania: Independence Hall, Philadelphia

Peony

Samuel Pepys

Peregrinus, Peter (*fl.* 13th century), French military engineer and scientist. △1440.

Pereira, Nuno Alvares (1360–1431), Portuguese general and statesman. He was the chief supporter of John I in his successful campaign to rid Portugal of Castilian domination. Pereira became a national hero, known as the Great Constable, after defeating the Castilians at Aljubarrota in 1385, a defeat that assured Portuguese independence. After a long career as soldier and statesman, he became a Carmelite monk and retired to a monastery. He was beatified in 1918.

Pereira, city in W central Colombia, S of Manizales; capital of Risaralda dept.; site of technical university (1958); shipping center for livestock. Pop. 216,226.

Perennial, plant with a life cycle of three or more years. It is a common term for flowering herbaceous plants that die before winter and blossom the next season. Perennials are easy to grow and thrive with little attention. Used in all types of gardens and as borders, some popular perennials are lily, chrysanthemum, peony, daisy, iris, and delphinium. *See also* Annual; Biennial.

Perfume, aromatic substance that emits a pleasing fragrance. The scents of rose, citrus, lavender, sandalwood, etc, are provided by the essential oils of these plants. These are blended and combined with a fixative of animal origin, such as musk, ambergris, or civet. Fixatives add pungency and prevent the more volatile oils from evaporating too quickly. Liquid perfumes are usually alcoholic solutions containing 10–25% of the perfume concentrate; colognes and toilet waters contain 2–6% of the concentrate. △1814.

Pergamum, ancient city of NW Asia Minor in Mysia (Turkey). It became the capital of a Hellenistic kingdom under the Attalid dynasty (3rd century BC). Pergamum's grandeur and influence were enhanced by the Attalids. An agricultural, industrial, and mining center, it was also renowned for its arts, library, and cultural development. Bequeathed to Rome by Attalus III (133 BC), it declined under Roman rule.

Pergolesi, Giovanni (1710–36), Italian composer. △1196.

Periander, tyrant of Corinth (*c.* 625–585 BC). Son of Cypselus, he increased arts, trade, and industry; forbade luxury and idleness; was noted for a vivid character. The murder of his nephew who succeeded him ended the 73-year tyranny of the house of Cypselus.

Pericarditis, inflammation of the pericardium, a membranous sac enclosing the heart. It usually develops during rheumatic fever but also may be associated with other diseases. Treatment is directed toward underlying infection and in acute cases, surgical removal.

Pericardium, a double-walled sac that surrounds the heart, separating it from the rest of the chest cavity and protecting it from mechanical injury. Its lower margin is anchored to the diaphragm, its upper part to the base of large blood vessels entering and leaving the heart. The outer tough fibrous pericardial layer is separated from the inner thin serous layer by pericardial fluid.

Pericles (*c.* 495–429 BC), Athenian statesman who introduced many reforms including a daily allowance so that non-wealthy Athenians could serve in government. Although frequently criticized, he was reelected to high office every year from 443 on. Pericles worked to prepare Athens for war with Sparta and at the same time attempted to make Athens the cultural center of the world. He is responsible for constructing the Parthenon (447–432 BC) and other notable buildings. His character, wise policy, and rebuilding of the Acropolis caused later historians to christen his entire period the "Age of Pericles." △994, 996.

Pericles, Prince of Tyre (*c.* 1607), 5-act dramatic romance, partly attributed to William Shakespeare. Many scholars believe that Shakespeare had nothing to do with Acts I and II, but he is often considered to be the author of Acts III, IV, and V. The main source of the work was John Gower's *Confesio Amantis* (1385–93), although the legend of Pericles is Greek in origin.

Peridot, a gem variety of transparent green olivine, a silicate mineral. Large crystals found on St John's Island in Red Sea and in Burma; those of United States smaller. *See also* Olivine. △244.

Peridotite term derived from *peridot,* the French word for olivine. It is a heavy igneous rock of coarse texture composed of olivine and pyroxene with small flecks of mica or hornblende. It alters readily into serpentine. Rocks that consist essentially of olivine are called dunites. *See also* Igneous Rocks.

Perigee, point in the orbit about the Earth of the Moon or an artificial satellite, at which the body is nearest to the Earth. *See also* Apogee. △98.

Period. *See* Geologic Time.

Periodic Law, law first stated by D.I. Mendeleev (1834–1907) in 1869 asserting that the properties of the chemical elements are a periodic function of their atomic weights. The groupings of the elements based on this law formed the forerunner of the periodic table. From gaps in these groupings Mendeleev was able to predict the existence and properties of undiscovered elements. However, his table contained anomalies, which were not resolved until H.G.J. Moseley (1887–1915) discovered that periodicity was related to atomic number (rather than atomic weight) and the later discovery of isotopes. *See also* Periodic Table. △1552, 1554.

Periodic Table, arrangement of the chemical elements in order of their atomic numbers in accordance with the periodic law stated by D.I. Mendeleev and later modified by H.G.J. Moseley. In the modern form of the table, the elements are arranged into 18 vertical columns and seven horizontal periods. The vertical columns are numbered I to VIII, each of which is divided into two subgroups, the A subgroup forming the main group and the B subgroup containing the transition elements: in addition, the noble gases are collected into a ninth group, group O. The elements in each group have the same number of valence electrons and accordingly have similar properties. Elements in the same horizontal period have the same number of electron shells. The elements are arranged in the periods in order of increasing atomic number from left to right. △1552, 1560.

Periodontics, the dental specialty that deals with the prevention, control, and treatment of diseases of the tissues that surround and support teeth, especially the gums. Pyorrhea is the most common gum disease treated. △756.

Periodontitis. *See* Pyorrhea.

Peripatetic School (*fl.* late 4th–early 3rd centuries BC), Greek philosophers who followed the doctrines of Aristotle. The name derives from Aristotle's practice of walking (Greek: peripatein) while he taught.

Peripatus, or velvet worm, any of 65 living species of the subphylum Onychophora, intermediate in structure, between annelids and arthropods. It is confined to humid habitats in tropics and subtropics. The sluglike body has many pairs of legs ending in tiny claws. Length: to 6in (15cm).

Peripheral Nervous System (PNS), the portion of the nervous system not in the central nervous system; includes skin neurons and underlying organs. *See also* Nervous System.

Periscope. △1684.

Perissodactyla, order of mammals characterized by hoofs with an odd number of toes. The only living members of the order are horses, tapirs, and rhinoceroses. There are 152 extinct genera known from fossils. Perissodactyls bear their body weight on the central toes of their four feet. In horses only one toe is functional. △540.

Peristalsis, a series of involuntary muscular contractions that move food along the digestive tract: from the pharynx along the esophagus to the stomach; from the stomach through the small intestines; and, in what is known as mass peristalsis (occurring about once every 24 hours), through the large intestine, pushing feces to the rectum, where nervous impulses lead to the urge to defecate. Under certain conditions, peristalsis motions are reversed and vomiting occurs. △694.

Peritoneum, strong, colorless membrane that lines the abdominal wall and contains the abdominal organs. The greater omentum, a fold in the peritoneum, forms an apron over the intestines. Inflammation of the peritoneum is known as peritonitis.

Peritonitis, inflammation of the peritoneum, a membrane that lines the abdominal cavity and organs within. It may be general or local and is caused by infection or chemically irritating materials. Its principal symptom is severe abdominal pain with vomiting. Treatment is directed at the underlying cause.

Periwinkle, gastropod mollusk found in cluste along marine shores. Herbivorous, it nestles rath than clings in cracks of rocks. Its coiled shell has horny plate covering its opening. Length: 0.5–1i (1.3–2.5cm). Family Littorinidae; species include t common *Littorina littorea.*

Periwinkle, trailing or erect evergreen plants pop lar as ground covers and for hanging baskets. Th common creeping periwinkle *(Vinca minor)* has sma blue, white, or pink flowers. Some varieties have whi to purple or even variegated colors. Family Apocyn ceae.

Perkin, William. △1560.

Perkins, Frances (1882–1965), US social worke and political figure, b. Boston. She was executive d rector of the New York Council of Organization fo War Service (1917–19). She was a member of the Ne York Industrial Commission (1919–21, 1929–33), the New York Industrial Board (1923–33), serving a its chairman (1926–29). New York Governor Frankli D. Roosevelt (1929) named Perkins state industri commissioner. When he was elected presiden Roosevelt named her as the first woman to be a U cabinet member. She served as secretary of labo (1933–45), implementing New Deal labor legislatio She was a member of the Civil Service Commissio (1946–52).

Perm, formerly Molotov, city in Russian SFSR, USSR in the central part W of the Ural Mts, on the Kam River; capital of Perm oblast. In the early 18th centur the old village settlement was enlarged by Russia merchant princes, made a district town, and late named Perm (1781). Industries: lumber products leather, agricultural machinery, metallurgy, oil. Pop 850,000.

Permafrost. △612.

Permian Period, the most recent division of th Paleozoic Era lasting from 280 to 225,000,00 years ago. A time of widespread geologic uplift an mostly cool, dry climates with periods of glaciation i the southern continents. Reptiles diversified, espe cially the mammal-like reptiles. Some groups of am phibians continued to flourish. At the end of the pe riod, many ancient marine invertebrate group became greatly reduced or died out. The ancestra Alps, earliest Appalachians and Ural Mountains were formed. *See also* Geologic Time; Paleozoic Era. △ 276, 568.

Pernambuco. *See* Recife.

Pernicious Anemia, severe anemia involving pro gressive decrease in number of red blood cells, which grow larger in size. It is caused by deficiency of vita min B_{12}. Treatment is administration of B_{12} by injec tion.

Perón, Juan Domingo (1895–1974), president o Argentina (1946–55, 1973–74), one of the most im portant political figures of Latin America. When Ramón Castillo was overthrown in 1943, Perón, a ca reer military officer and leader of a politically active military club, became head of the labor department Through working-class and union support, Perón was elected president in 1946 and again in 1951. The Peronist program of economic nationalism and socia justice gave way to monetary inflation and politica violence; Perón was ousted by a military coup in 1955. Perón, in exile, continued to be a powerfu force in Argentine politics. He was re-elected in 1973 by a clear majority. △1354.

Perón, María Estela ("Isabel") Martínez de (1931–), Argentine political figure. The first woman chief of state in the Americas, she became president of Argentina when her husband, Juan Perón, died in office in 1974. She was overthrown on March 24 1976, in a coup led by the commanders of the armed forces.

Peroxide, a compound consisting of two oxygen atoms united to each other and yielding a solution of hydrogen peroxide when treated with acid.

Perpendicular Style, style of the last period of English Gothic architecture (*fl.* late 14th–mid-16th century). Named for the strong vertical lines of its window tracery and paneling, its characteristic fan vaulting can be seen in the Chapel of Henry VII, Westminster and King's College Chapel, Cambridge. △1104.

Perpetual Motion, the concept of a machine that would do work continually without any input of energy. Ingenious designs for such machines proposed over the course of many centuries have been doomed to failure by the laws of thermodynamics. △1512.

Perpignan, city in S France, 96mi (155km) SE of Toulouse on Têt River; capital of Pyrénées-Orientales dept. Capital of kingdom of Mallorca 13th century, it passed to France in 1659; site of Cathedral of St Jean (1324–1509), and 15th-century castle of kings of Majorca. Industries: tourism, distilleries, chocolate, clothing. Founded 10th century; chartered 1197. Pop. 102,191.

Perrault, Charles (1628–1703), French compiler of folktales. In 1697 he published *Tales of the Past, with Morals*. The eight tales included became classics: *Cinderella, The Sleeping Beauty, Red Riding Hood, Blue Beard, Diamonds and Toads, Riquet with the Tuft, Puss in Boots*, and *Hop o' My Thumb*. △1172.

Perry, Matthew Colbraith (1794–1858), US naval officer, b. Newport, R.I. The brother of Oliver Hazard Perry, he established the navy's apprentice system (1837) and organized the first navy engineer corps. In 1833 he supervised the construction of the first naval steamship and was called the father of the steam navy. He also was responsible for opening up Japan to the West (1852–54), negotiating a treaty that secured US trading rights there. △1272, 1278.

Perry, Oliver Hazard (1785–1819), US naval officer, b. South Kingston, R.I. After serving in the Tripoli campaign (1801–05), Perry began building warships. In the War of 1812 he built and manned a fleet in Lake Erie. In September 1813, near Put-In-Bay, Ohio, he met the British fleet. When his flagship, the *Lawrence*, began to sink, he moved to another ship and forced the British to surrender. This battle gave the United States control over the lake. His message following the battle, "We have met the enemy and they are ours," is often quoted. He died on a diplomatic mission to South America.

Perse, Saint-John (1887–), pseud. of Alexis Léger, French poet and diplomat. He served in the foreign service in Peking (1916–21), becoming an expert on East Asia. From 1933–40 he served as secretary general of the French Foreign Service. He was dismissed from his post for opposing appeasement and went into exile in the United States. His elaborately stylized verse epics include *Eloges* (1911), *Anabase* (1922), *Pluies* (1943), *Chronique* (1959), and *Oiseaux* (1962). *Evil* (1942) was inspired by World War II. He was awarded the Nobel Prize for literature in 1960.

Persephone, in Greek mythology, goddess of spring and queen of Hades. She was the daughter of the Earth goddess Demeter and Zeus. As goddess of death she sent the Furies on their errands. In her role as goddess of spring she is depicted as bearing a cornucopia overflowing with flowers, as she was before Hades stole her from earth. △838.

Persepolis, ancient ruined city in Persia, approx. 30mi (48km) NE of Shiraz, SW central Iran; served as capital of the Achaemenid empire 550–330 BC; site of palaces of Darius I and Xerxes; inscriptions of Shutruk-Nakhkhunte, a famous Elamite king (*c.* 1207–1171 BC); citadel containing a treasury looted by Alexander the Great (*c.* 300 BC); nearby Stakhr which served as the capital of the Sassanids *c.* AD 200; nearby archeological excavations have unearthed villages dating from 4000 BC. △984.

Perseus, in Greek mythology, son of Danae and the disguised Zeus, who came to Danae as a shower of gold. Perseus is a major hero in the myths. He severed the snake-haired head of the Gorgon Medusa, turned Atlas to stone, and rescued the princess Andromeda from sacrifice to a sea monster. △836.

Perseus, a constellation close to Cassiopeia and Auriga and typical of the autumn sky. It is roughly K-shaped with the downward arm of the K pointing toward the Pleiades and the upward arm ending in Algol, the "demon star" or "head of Medusa," which is actually an eclipsing binary. △110, 132.

Pershing, John Joseph (1860–1948), US military officer, b. Laclede, Mo. A graduate of the US Military Academy at West Point, he served in Indian campaigns, the Spanish-American War, and helped suppress the Philippine insurrection. In 1916 he led a punitive expedition against Pancho Villa into Mexico. He became a general (1917) and commanded the American Expeditionary Force (AEF) in World War I (1917–19). He insisted on the autonomy of his troops within the Allied Command and led the actions at Château Thierry and Belleau Woods. Returning as a hero in 1919 he became the first to hold the rank of general of the armies. He was army chief of staff (1921–24). His book, *My Experiences in the World War* (1931), won a Pulitzer Prize.

Persian, the principal language of Iran and one of the two official languages of Afghanistan. It is spoken by about 20 million of Iran's 32 million people, and by about 5 million more in Afghanistan. An Iranian language and thus part of the Indo-European family, it is one of the world's oldest languages and was a major language of ancient times. Since the 7th century it has been written in the Arabic script. △866.

Persian Architecture, Ancient (550–331 BC), architectural style combining influences from its Egyptian and Assyrian predecessors. △984.

Persian Cat, longhaired domestic cat breed that first appeared in Europe at the end of the 16th century. It has a wide head with small, well covered ears, wide-set eyes, short nose, full cheeks, and broad muzzle. The compact massive body is set on short, thick legs. The tail is short and full. Its coat is fine-textured and fluffy. Varieties are according to color and include Black, Blue, Red Tabby, Cream, Smoke, and White, all with copper eyes, and Blue-eyed White.

Persian Gulf, shallow extension of the Arabian Sea between Iran and Arabia, connected to the Gulf of Oman by the Strait of Hormuz; among its many islands, Bahrain is the largest. It was an ancient trade route; European conquests started in the 17th century with British capture of the Portuguese city of Hormuz 1622; the Perpetual Maritime Treaty (1853) between Britain and Arabs est. British supremacy of the gulf; this was supported by an international treaty 1907. The discovery of rich oil deposits in the 1930s increased the gulf's importance; after British withdrawal, the United States and USSR sought to gain some control in the 1960s. With Arab-Israeli conflicts, border clashes, and disputes over oil rights, the Persian Gulf has been the scene of much disturbance in the 1970s. Area: 90,000sq mi (233,100sq km). Length: 600mi (966km).

Persian Lamb. *See* Karakul.

Persian Literature. Pre-Islamic Persian literature (5th–7th centuries) was written in Avestan and Old Persian. The major work of the period is the *Avesta*, the sacred book of the Zoroastrians. Writings in modern Persian began to appear in the 9th century and for the next 500 years Persian writers produced a rich variety of verse. Among the most famous poets were Omar Khayyam (11th century), Rumi, Sa'di (13th century), and Hafiz (14th century). Persian literature declined in the 15th century, but there was a revival in the 19th–20th centuries with the introduction of modern literary forms and experimentation.

Persian Wars, conflicts during the first half of the 5th century BC, beginning when Athens aided revolting Ionians. In 492 10,000 Athenians encountered a far greater Persian army at Marathon and won. Ten years later Athens and Sparta were defeated at Thermopylae but had a great naval victory at Salamis. In the campaign of 479 the Greeks destroyed the remainder of the Persian fleet and supported further revolts. In 467 Cimon destroyed a Persian army. An agreement favorable to Greece was reached in 449. The wars resulted in increased Greek nationalism and sense of superiority to Orientals. △992–994.

Persicaria. △446.

Persimmon, tropical Asian tree of the genus *Diospyros* with reddish-orange fruit that is sour and astringent until it is dead ripe. Commercially sold persimmons come from the Japanese persimmon *(D. kaki)*. The common persimmon *(D. virginiana)* of E United States has delicious fruit but it is too small and pulpy to have commercial value. Family Ebenaceae.

Personality, global term referring to the totality of emotional, attitudinal, and intellectual characteristics of an individual. Psychologists use the term to refer to the more enduring, long-term characteristics of a person rather than short-lived traits or momentary emotional states. Personality traits are assessed in psychology by means of a variety of devices including personality inventories and projective techniques. Among the most influential theories of personality in psychology have been the Freudian approach (psychoanalysis) and theories of behaviorism. *See also* Personality Inventory; Projective Techniques. △814.

Personality and Society, the interaction of individuals with their culture. △876–82.

Personality Disorders, personality disturbances that are largely a function of character and that differ from neurotic disturbances in that they involve very

Periwinkle

Matthew Perry

Oliver Perry

John J. Pershing

little anxiety. The category includes: (1) *personality pattern disturbances,* long-standing and inflexible personality organizations that include *schizoid,* shy, and seclusive; *cyclothymic,* extraverted and moody; *paranoid,* suspicious and jealous; (2) *personality trait disturbances,* which show a single dominant characteristic such as passive-aggressiveness or compulsivity; and (3) *sociopathic personality disturbances,* marked primarily by antisocial or asocial behavior that lacks accompanying guilt feelings. Psychopathic behavior and drug and alcohol addiction are included in this grouping. △766.

Personality Inventory, in psychology, a test designed to assess personality characteristics. Such questionnaires typically give the subject a large number of questions to which he responds "yes" or "no" (for example, "Do you get along well with other people?"). Inventories do not have right or wrong answers, but rather describe the individual's personality makeup. One example is the Minnesota Multiphasic Personality Inventory.

Perspective, in art, way of showing three-dimensional objects and spatial relationships on a two-dimensional plane. The linear perspective system is based on the idea of parallel lines and planes converging in a vanishing point as they recede into the distance. Using this principle, the artist can give a sense of perceptual space and volume on his canvas. Instead of using central perspective, with a single vanishing point, the artist can also use angular, or oblique, perspective, with two vanishing points. Another kind of parallel perspective, with the viewpoint from above, is common in Chinese painting. Linear perspective was not used in painting until the late 15th century in Italy, when the architect Brunelleschi developed mathematical rules for perspective that involved a horizon line, or viewer's eye level, and a vanishing point. Masaccio used these principles in his painting. The use of linear perspective dominated in European painting until the end of the 19th century when Cézanne intentionally flattened his canvases and other artists used color and shading to create depth. In modern art, perspective is often used in a distorted way to change space, such as in the optical illusion paintings of op art. △1134, 1466.

Perspiration, a clear liquid secreted by the sweat glands as a way of regulating body temperature. Rate of perspiration increases in warm weather, after exercise, and for emotional reasons. *See also* Sweat Gland.

Perth, city in W Australia, on the Swan River; capital city of Western Australia state; site of the University of Western Australia (1911), and St George's and St Mary's cathedrals. The city grew rapidly after the discovery of the Coolgardie goldfields in 1890. Industries: automotives, cement, textiles, munitions, processed food. Founded 1829; inc. 1856. Pop. 97,000.

Perth Amboy, city and port of entry in central New Jersey, 17mi (27km) SSW of Newark on Raritan Bay. It served as capital of East Jersey 1684–1702 (when E and W Jersey merged), and as alternate capital with Burlington until 1790; site of mansion of Gov. William Franklin, used during Revolutionary War by Gen. William Howe. Industries: oil refining, printing, chemicals, smelting and refining of lead, copper, silver. Founded 1683; inc. as city 1718. Pop. (1970) 38,-798.

Pertinax Publius, Helvius (126–93), Roman emperor (193). The praetorian prefect Laetus, only three months after arranging the murder of Commodus to make Pertinax emperor, had Pertinax assassinated because of his attempts to curb the power of the Praetorian Guard. His short reign climaxed the strength of the Guard, which auctioned the empire between Sulpicianus and Didius Julianus.

Pertussis. *See* Whooping Cough.

Peru (Perú), the third-largest South American nation and home of the ancient Inca Empire. Its economy is based on rich mineral deposits. Fifty percent of the population is Indian. The country is ruled by a military junta.

Land and economy. Peru is bounded by Ecuador and Colombia (N), Chile (S), and Brazil and Bolivia (E). It has a 1,400-mi (2,254-km) Pacific coastline (W). Its immense mountain system, Cordillera de los Andes, divides the country into three regions. The coastal is a dry strip of desert that contains 40% of the population and produces 50% of the gross national product. The Sierra is a dry and cold mountain chain that limits transportation and communication. It contains rich mineral deposits and 50% of the country's population. Mt Huascarán, 22,205ft (8,882m), is in the Sierra. The third division, Montaña, is the hot, moist low country of tropical forests and largely unexplored jungles. Oil exploration takes place in the Montaña. Since the time of the Incas, Peru has been known for its abundant minerals—lead, copper, zinc, iron, silver, cadmium, tin, gold, coal, marble, limestone, and now oil. With half the population employed in agriculture, cotton, rice, coffee, and sugar are exported.

People. Descendants of the Incas make up 40% of Peru's population. Of the rest, 11% are Caucasian and 43% mestizo (mixed). Roman Catholicism is the state religion, practiced by 90% of the people. Spanish is the official language; many Indians speak Quechua and Aymara. Literacy is estimated at 60%. The forest Indians, still living a stone age existence, are said to be the most primitive tribe in the world today.

Government. Although Peru has had a constitution since 1933, the last free election took place in 1963. In 1968 a military junta ousted the president and undertook a program of agricultural reform, nationalization of essential industry, and restructuring of education.

History. When the Spanish landed in 1531, Peru was the center of the highly developed Inca civilization. Francisco Pizarro, in search of Inca treasure, conquered the country and by 1542 it had become a source of Spanish wealth and power. In 1820–24 José de San Martín and Simon Bolívar led a successful War of Independence and declared Peru independent. △1120.

PROFILE

Official name: Republic of Peru
Area: 496,223sq mi (1,285,218sq km)
Population: 15,300,000
Density: 30.8per sq mi (11.9per sq km)
Chief cities: Lima (capital); Cuzco; Callao; Arequipa
Government: Military junta
Religion: Roman Catholic
Language: Spanish
Monetary unit: Sol
Gross national product: $9,500,000,000
Per capita income: $617
Industries: fish meal, processed foods, textiles, chemicals, metal products, automobiles
Agriculture: beef cattle, cotton, sugar cane, rice, coffee, sheep, fish, corn, tobacco
Minerals: copper, iron ore, lead, petroleum
Trading partners: United States (major)

Perugia, city in central Italy; capital of Perugia prov. and Umbria region. One of major Etruscan cities, it passed to Rome 310 BC; became papal possession 1540; center of Umbrian school of painting that peaked 15th century; active in Risorgimento movement; site of 13th-century city walls and Maggiore fountain, Palazzo dei Priori (13th—16th centuries). Industries: chocolate, food, textiles, machines. Pop. 124,965.

Perugino, Il, real name **Pietro di Cristoforo Vannucci** (1446–1523), Italian painter. His works show a good sense of perspective and are executed with an ordered simplicity in the style of the Florentine school. His works include the fresco "St Sebastian" (1478). In 1481 he was commissioned with others, including Botticelli, to execute mural decorations of the Sistine Chapel in Rome.

Peruvian (Humboldt) Current, cold water current in the SE Pacific Ocean; runs N along the SW coast of South America, turning E by Peru. △224.

Pescadores (P'enghu Liehtao), group of several small islands of Nationalist China, in the Formosa Strait, between Taiwan and the Chinese mainland. Named by Portuguese in 16th century, the group was ceded to Japan by China 1895; retroceded 1946; part of Nationalist China since 1949. Main islands are P'enghu, Yuweng, Paisha. Products: sweet potatoes, peanuts, coral. Chief industry is fishing. Area: approx. 50sq mi (130sq km).

Pescara, seaport city in central Italy, 95mi (153km) ENE of Rome, on the Adriatic Sea; capital of Pescara prov. As Roman Aternum, it was nearly destroyed by barbarian attacks; heavily damaged WWII; seaside resort and tourist center. Industries: fishing, machinery, textiles, shipbuilding. Made provincial capital 1927. Pop. 113,520.

Peshawar, city in NW Pakistan, 10mi (16km) E of Khyber Pass; capital of North-West Frontier prov. City has been of historical strategic importance, and was repeatedly attacked from 1st century on by Afghan, Persian, and Mongol invaders; held by Sikhs 1823–49, when it was annexed to Britain; site of Buddhist relics, 2nd-century stupa, university (1950). Modern city is famous for handicrafts, carpets, leather goods. Industries: tobacco, textiles, firearms. Pop. 166,273.

Pesticides. △296, 318.

Petah Tiqwa, city in central Israel, 7mi (11km) NE of Tel Aviv-Jaffa; commercial center. Industries: asbestos, chemicals, textiles, farm equipment, food processing, rubber products, stone quarries. Founded 1878 as first modern Jewish agricultural colony in Palestine; inc. 1937. Pop. 83,200.

Pétain, Henri Philippe (1856–1951), French general and chief of state in the Vichy government during World War II. He distinguished himself by holding Verdun against the Germans (1916) and was appointed commander-in-chief under Marshal Foch (1917). Between the wars he served on the Higher Council of War (1920–30); commanded in Morocco (1925–26); served as war minister (1934) and ambassador to Spain (1939). He was recalled in 1940 to form the government that signed the armistice with Germany. Old, ill, perhaps senile, Pétain was chief of state and the symbol of French collaboration with Germany. His death sentence (1945) was commuted to life imprisonment by Charles de Gaulle. △1306.

Petal, organ that forms the corolla of a flower. Located inside the sepals, flower petals are usually conspicuous and brightly colored. Forms include: corolla tube; ray-formed (petunia); pair-formed—top petal enlarged, side petals smaller, and lower two fused (snapdragon, orchid); and reduced (grasses and some trees). △444

Petavius. △56.

Peter, Saint, chief of the 12 Apostles of Jesus Christ. Peter and his brother Andrew were fishermen, whom Jesus called to follow him (Mark 1:16). Peter's original name was Simon, and Jesus gave him his new name from the Greek *Petros* (rock): "thou art Peter, and upon this rock I will build my church" (Matthew 16:-18). There are many other references to Peter in the Gospels, and he is named first in lists of the Apostles. He failed his lord in one crisis. After Jesus was arrested, the night before his crucifixion, Peter three times denied he knew the master (John 18:15–27). But Peter was the first of the Apostles to see Christ after the Resurrection. The Acts of the Apostles show Peter as a leader of the Christians. It is believed that he founded a church in Rome and was martyred under Emperor Nero, around 64. As the first bishop of Rome, Peter is first in the list of popes. △1026.

Peter I, the Great (1672–1725), Russian tsar (1682–1725). Educated by foreigners, Peter ruled jointly with his half-brother Ivan (1682–89) and assumed the throne alone in 1689. After creating a disciplined army and a navy, he declared war on Turkey in 1696. He visited Europe 1696–97 and brought back technical specialists to aid Russia's development. In 1700, Peter allied Russia with Poland against Sweden, which was defeated at the Battle of Poltava in 1709. He married his mistress, the future Catherine I, in 1712, and again visited Europe 1716–17. In 1722 he successfully fought against Persia. An ambitious, tyrannical monarch, he fundamentally altered the character of Russia through westernization. He built a remarkable capital city at St Petersburg (Leningrad), checked the church's authority, reformed the central government, the military, and the civil service, and suddenly transformed Russia into a major European power. *See also* Northern War. △1178.

Peter II (1715–30), Russian tsar (1727–30). He succeeded Catherine I and was at first guided by Aleksandr Menshikov and later by his rival Vasili Dolgoruki. He died of smallpox.

Peter III (1728–62), Russian tsar (1762). Named in 1741 to succeed Elizabeth, Peter married the future Catherine II in 1745. On gaining the throne in 1762, he at once returned to Frederick II all conquered Prussian territory. He also issued an important edict releasing the gentry from conscription. He was murdered after a coup organized by guard officers, under his wife's direction, put her in power.

Peter I (1320–67), king of Portugal (1357–67), son and successor of Alfonso IV. As crown prince, he fell in love with his wife's lady in waiting, Inés de Castro. He refused to give her up, and the King connived to have her murdered (1335). In retaliation, Peter raised a revolution against his father, but peace was soon restored and Peter publicly forgave his lover's murderers. Nevertheless, after he became king, he enacted revenge against two of them; he had their hearts cut out. The tragic love affair is one of the favorites of Portuguese literature. Peter was succeeded by his son, Ferdinand I.

Peter IV, king of Portugal. *See* Pedro I, emperor of Brazil.

Peter, First and Second Epistles, New Testament

tters written by Simon Peter who was crucified for s devotion to Christ. Relying heavily on Paul's teachgs, he addressed his writings to converts to Christiity from Judaism and encouraged faith in the Secnd Coming of Christ. Warning against false teachers, e emphasizes the importance of apostolic witness.

eterborough, city in SE Ontario, Canada, on the tonabee River and Trent Canal, with one of the orld's largest hydraulic lift locks; site of Trent Univerty; center of a rich agricultural area. Exports: lumber, eas, leather, wool, cheese. Inc. 1905. Pop. 57,498.

eterborough, city in E central England, in ambridgeshire, on Nene River; site of 7th-century bbey; railroad and industrial center. Industries: machinery, bricks. Pop. 70,081.

eterloo Massacre (1819), killing by militia of sev-al people in a crowd assembled at St Peter's Fields, Manchester, England, to demand redress of grievnces and fair parliamentary representation. Magisates read the Riot Act to part of the crowd and called the militia almost immediately to scatter them. The eaths caused great public indignation.

Peter Pan (1904), 5-act fantasy by James M. Barrie, ublished in 1928. A favorite with children, it conerns Peter Pan, the boy who never grew up. He flies the nursery window, teaches Wendy and her two rothers to fly, and takes them to exciting adventures n Never-Never Land. They encounter Indians, Capain Hook and his pirate band, and a crocodile with a cking clock in his stomach.

Peter Principle. Lawrence Peter, in his 1969 book, *he Peter Principle,* suggested that in most large oranizations people are promoted until they reach the evel of their incompetence. △926.

Petersburg, port of entry and city in SE Virginia, 3mi (37km) S of Richmond, on S Appomattox River. ity was important for the Confederate Army during he Civil War as key supply station and railroad line to Richmond; site of Petersburg National Battlefield (est. 926). Industries: tobacco, luggage, optical goods, lothing, lumber, furniture, paint. Founded 1748; inc. 850. Pop. (1970) 36,103.

Petersburg, Battle of, US Civil War engagement. The siege of Petersburg, Va. ended on April 2, 1865, with a Confederate withdrawal. It led to Confederate Gen. Robert E. Lee's surrender to Union Gen. Ulysses S. Grant.

Peter the Cruel (1334–69), Spanish king of Castile and León (1350–69), son and successor of Alfonso XI. He was constantly at war with his illegitimate brother, Henry of Trastámara (later Henry II). Peter was generally backed by England in the person of Edward the Black Prince; Henry had the backing of Aragón and French troops under the command of Bertrand du Guesclin. Henry defeated Peter in 1366 and had himself crowned. The next year, however, Peter and Edward defeated Henry. In 1369, Henry won the decisive battle of Monteil and killed Peter in a duel.

Petipa, Marius (1822–1910), Russian ballet choreographer, b. France. After dancing with the Imperial Theater in St Petersburg and teaching at the Imperial School of Ballet, he was appointed choreographer of the Imperial Ballet in 1862. His "Don Quixote" (1869) and "Sleeping Beauty" (1890) helped him to become known as the "father of classic ballet." △1368.

Petit Mal, type of epilepsy in which brief episodes of unconsciousness, lasting less than 15 seconds, occur several times a day. It is found mainly in children. *See also* Epilepsy. △722.

Petra, ruined ancient city in SW Jordan. Held by Nabataeans (Arab Tribe) from 4th century BC until it was occupied by Rome AD 106, it was an early seat of Christianity; captured by Muslims 7th century and in 12th century by Crusaders; served as a center for caravan trade routes. Ruins were discovered 1812 by Johann Burckhardt; they include temples, palaces, homes, and theaters carved in varying shades of pink limestone. City is referred to as Sela in Bible and Wadi Musa by Egyptians.

Petrarch, Anglicized form of Francesco Petrarca (1304–74), Italian lyric poet and scholar. One of the most famous and widely imitated poets of the Middle Ages, he is considered, with Giovanni Boccaccio, one of the heralds of the Italian Renaissance. His works, including a collection known as *Rime spare* (scattered lyrics) and *Trionfi* (Triumphs), were read and imitated by Geoffrey Chaucer and other English and European poets through the 19th century. Most of his poems have as their subject "Laura," a woman whom Petrarch idealized in the style of earlier Italian lyric poets, but who was seen in a more realistic and human light.

Petrie, Flinders. △1292.

Petrified Forest National Park, park in E Arizona; an extensive natural exhibit of petrified wood, it also features Indian ruins and petroglyphs, as well as a portion of the Painted Desert. Area: 94,189acres (38,147hectares). Est. 1906.

Petrified Wood, the replacement of wood fibers with opal or chalcedony as a result of hot, silica-bearing waters, forming a fossil. *See also* Chalcedony; Opal.

Petrochemical, chemical substance derived from petroleum or natural gas. The refining of petroleum is undertaken on a very large scale not only for the fuels obtained (gasoline, kerosene, fuel oil, and natural gas) but also for the wide range of chemicals that can be obtained or derived from it. These chemicals include the common alkanes and alkenes, cyclohexone, benzene, toluene, and naphthalene. Ammonia is also regarded as a petrochemical as the hydrogen used in its manufacture is usually derived from petroleum. △1560, 1564.

Petroleum, a complex mixture of organically derived hydrocarbons, mostly liquids but including gases and solids. It is used as a fuel and raw material in chemical industries. An accepted theory of petroleum formation is that millions of years ago the fats and waxes of dead planktonic plants and animals accumulated on the bottom of seas and large lakes, where they were covered by sand and clay sediments. As pressure increased, the sand and clay were compacted, forcing the organic matter into more porous and permeable rock, such as sandstone or porous carbonates. The organic matter migrated until it became trapped, forcing the petroleum into pools. Oil shale is an organically derived rock, yielding petroleum after a difficult refining stage. △284–86, 1642–44.

Petroleum Refining, the process in which crude oil is separated into useful products. The primary method of separation is fractional distillation. Crude oil is heated to about 650°F (343°C), and is injected as a vapor into a fractioning column, a tower as high as 150ft (46m) containing 30 to 40 perforated trays. The vapor rises to the top of the column where it condenses and falls back through the trays, mixing with rising vapors. The process of evaporation and condensation continues until an equilibrium is reached, with lighter molecules at the top of the tower grading to heavier molecules at the bottom. The grades are siphoned off individually as a refined product. Less valuable products may be chemically changed. Lighter molecules may be made heavier through alkylation, isomerization, or catalytic reforming. Heavier molecules may be "cracked," or broken down into lighter ones by thermal or catalytic cracking. *See also* △1644.

Petrology, study of rocks, their origin, chemical composition, and occurrence. Formation of the three classes of rocks—igneous, of volcanic origin; sedimentary, deposited by water; and metamorphic, either of the other two, changed by temperature and pressure—are studied. Experimental petrology simulates in the laboratory those conditions necessary to produce the rocks and minerals found on earth and elsewhere in the solar system. *See also* Geochemistry; Mineralogy. △246–48.

Petronius, Gauis (died 66), Roman satirist. He was known as Petronius Arbiter because, according to Tacitus, he was the arbiter of elegance at Nero's court. He committed suicide after Nero had him arrested on the charges of a jealous rival. His *Satyricon,* a romance in prose and verse, remains in fragments. It uses both sophisticated Latin and colloquial language to mockingly portray the pretenses of the time. The best known extant episode describes the extravagant dinner party of Tremalchio, a parvenu. △1028.

Petunia, genus of herbs native to Argentina and grown as garden ornamentals. The tubular, 5-petaled flowers range in color from white to blue, yellow, pink, red, and purple. Species include *Petunia axillaris,* an erect plant with long white blooms lin (2.5cm) wide; the purple *P. integrifolia* and *P. violacea;* and *P. hybrida,* produced from natural species to provide blooms for cultivation. Family Solanaceae.

Pewee, small olive-brown North American woodland birds that have a *pee-a-wee* whistle. Genus *Contopus.*

Pewter, several alloys that consist mainly of tin and

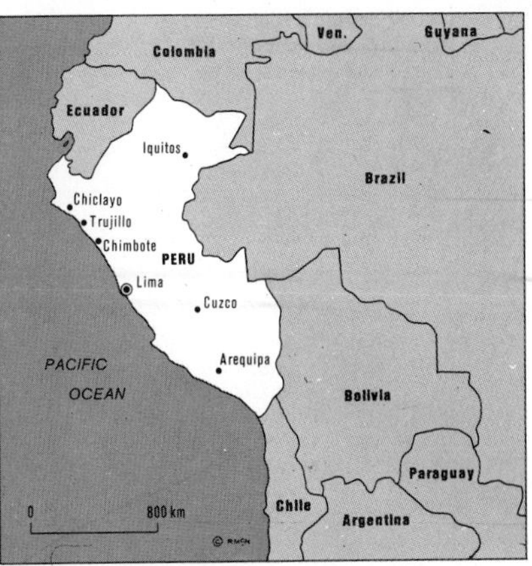
Colombia
Ven.
Guyana
Ecuador
Iquitos
Brazil
Chiclayo
Trujillo
Chimbote
PERU
Lima
Cuzco
PACIFIC
OCEAN
Arequipa
Bolivia
Paraguay
Chile
Argentina
0
800 km
Peru

Pescara, Italy

Petrarch

Petrified Forest National Park, Arizona

lead. The most common has four parts of tin to one of lead, combined with small amounts of antimony, copper, and bismuth. Pewter is soft, bluish-grey, and similar to tin in appearance. It was formerly used extensively for household objects but declined in popularity in the 19th century. Because of poisonous properties of lead and antimony, pewter has been replaced by other alloys in the making of domestic utensils, but is highly prized by antique collectors.

Peyote, two species of cactus of the genus *Laphophora* (family Cactaceae), native to North America and found in limestone soils of the Chihuahuan desert of Texas and northern Mexico. To 2in (5cm) tall and 3in (8cm) wide with a soft stem, *L. williamsii* has pink or white flowers in summer and a blue-green stem. *L. diffusa* has white or yellow flowers. Peyote contains many alkaloids, the principal one being mescaline, well known as a hallucinogenic. Its use is now prohibited by law in some places.

Pforr, Franz. △1228.

Phaestos, fertile plain on Crete where the Phaestos disk, a relic of pre- or early Hellenic language, was found. By 2000 BC there were palatial houses, destroyed *c.*1600 BC. △964.

Phaeton, in Greek mythology, son of Apollo, who drove his father's sun chariot across the sky but lost control of the horses causing the Earth to burn and Olympus to smoke. To save the world, Zeus struck him from the reins with a thunderbolt.

Phagocytosis, process by which cells can engulf extracellular particles to be later digested. For example, white blood cells phagocytose bacteria and kill them.

Phalanges. △682.

Phalanx. △1004.

Phalarope, small, long-necked, web-footed shorebird. The female woos the male, and builds a grass-and-moss nest and incubates the pear-shaped, light-colored, blotched eggs (3–4). Length: 8–10in (20–25cm). Family Phalaropodidae.

pH and pOH, measures of the concentrations of hydrogen ions (pH) and hydroxide ions (pOH) in solution. Since the hydrogen-ion concentration may be small, e.g. 10^{-5} gram molecules per liter, it is more conveniently expressed as the logarithm to the base 10 of its reciprocal, which is called its pH value, e.g. 5.0. A solution with a pH value less than 7 is acid; more than 7 basic; a neutral solution, such as NaCl in water, will have a pH of 7. pOH is a little-used unit defined as $-\log_{10} OH^-$, related to pH through the solubility product of water. The pH can be determined with a glass electrode or, less accurately, by colored indicators. *See also* Indicator. △1568.

Pharisees, a sect within Judaism, prominent in Israel in the 1st century AD, before the destruction of the 2nd temple in 70. The name of the sect means "separated," indicating their emphasis on purity and freedom from sin. Stressing oral tradition, they were concerned with the education of the people, and for this reason, are seen as the ancestors of the rabbis of today. They were unjustly condemned in the New Testament as hypocrites, while they strove for imitation of God.

Pharmaceutical, any substance, liquid, or drug used for medicinal purposes that appears in a standard pharmacopoeia. Apart from traditional remedies, modern drugs include a wide range of antibiotics and sulfa compounds that are effective against infections, corticosteroids used for inflammatory conditions, stimulants, depressants, analgesics, and narcotics that act on the nervous system, and specific compounds that are effective in various forms of heart disease. Together they provide the medical practitioner with an effective armory of chemotherapeutic agents.

Pharmacology, science that deals with the sources and properties of drugs, their use in treating disease, and their action on living organisms. It includes toxicology, the study of the poisonous effects of drugs. △744, 746, 748.

Pharmacopeia, a standard, authoritative, and usually official reference book containing selected lists of drugs, chemicals and medicinal preparations. Included are exact descriptions; tests for identity, purity, and strength and formulas for their preparation. △744.

Pharos, island off coast of N Egypt, in Mediterranean, connected to mainland by mole (stone structure) built by Alexander the Great *c.* 331 BC. Lighthouse completed by Ptolemy II (280 BC) and considered one of Seven Wonders of World was on Pharos; it was destroyed by an earthquake 1346. Pharos is part of city of Alexandria.

Pharynx, region at the back of the mouth that is the common passageway for food and air. It extends from the nasal cavities (from which it is separated by a flap of tissue called the uvula in the back of the mouth) to the glottis, the opening into the trachea, which is closed off by a "trap door," the epiglottis. The pharynx becomes continuous with the esophagus, which leads to the stomach. △692.

Phase Diagram, diagram showing the conditions under which different equilibrium phases of substances exist. For example, a curve of melting point against pressure of a pure solid divides the graph into two regions. Points in one represent temperatures and pressures at which the substance is solid; points in the other represent the liquid conditions. Systems of two or more components cannot be represented fully by a two-dimensional graph. Graphs of composition against temperature are used to show solubilities, ranges of stability of alloy phases, etc.

Phases, in astronomy, or figures, apparent changes in shape presented by the Moon in a manner corresponding to the amount by which its surface is illuminated by the Sun at various stages during each lunar orbit. The phases range from new, when the Moon lies between Earth and Sun and is totally invisible, to full, when the moon reaches opposition. Similar phases are seen from Earth for the inferior planets Mercury and Venus.

Pheasant, chickenlike game birds sometimes valued as ornamentals. The males are often brilliantly colored, especially on the wings and tail feathers. Females are smaller and brownish. In North America, the widely distributed ring-necked pheasant *(Phasianus colchicus)* has a dark green head, white neck ring, bronze breast, and coppery, black-spotted sides. It frequents fields and farmlands. After courtship rituals, the female lays olive-brown or pale bluish-green eggs (8–15) in a shallow grass nest. Length: 1.5–8ft (0.46–2.4m), including the long tail. Family Phasianidae.

Phenacetin or **Acetophenetidin,** a white crystalline compound ($C_{10}H_{13}NO_2$) derived from coal tar. A mild, nonaddicting drug used for reduction of fever and relief of pain. It is frequently combined with other substances, such as aspirin, in tablet form. Prolonged use of phenacetin may result in dizziness, kidney damage, and hemoglobin changes.

Phenix City, manufacturing city in E Alabama on Chattahoochee River; seat of Russell co. Industries: lumber and wood products. Inc. 1883. Pop. (1970) 25,281.

Phenobarbitol, trade names include Nembutal and Luminal, barbiturate that acts as a central nervous system depressant, frequently used to treat epilepsy and convulsions.

Phenol, any of a family of organic compounds that are known by the attachment of a minimum of one hydroxyl group to a carbon atom forming part of the benzene ring. "Phenol" is the specific name for monohydroxybenzene (C_6H_5OH) and the generic name for compounds containing one or more hydroxyl functions attached to an aromatic ring. Phenols are colorless liquids or white solids at room temperature with higher melting and boiling points than the parent hydrocarbons from which they are derived. Phenol is used by the chemical and pharmaceutical industries for conversion to such products as aspirin, dyes, fungicides, and bactericides, in addition to its application as a starting material for nylon and epoxy resins. △1560.

Phenolphthalein, a derivative of phenol. It is a chemical compound ($C_{20}H_{14}O_4$), prepared by a reaction between phenol and phthaleic anhydride in the presence of sulfuric acid. It is used as an indicator for alkalinity, in laxatives, and in dyes.

Phenomenalism, philosophical position that human knowledge is restricted to what appears either as physical objects or as the content of mental impressions. Phenomenalists either postulate an intrinsic reality behind experience or affirm the sufficiency of appearances alone for understanding reality. The position in the latter form is common among natural scientists. Both Kant and Hume held a variety of phenomenalism. *See also* Hume, David; Kant, Immanuel.

Phenomenology, in the 20th century, a philosophical movement concerned with direct investigation and description of immediately experienc phenomena. Arising with the works of Edmund Hu serl, phenomenology has undergone a series changes in the less transcendental approach of Mar Heidegger and the phenomenological existentialis of Maurice Merleau-Ponty and others. Phenom nology has had notable influence outside the field philosophy, in such areas of study as mathematics ar psychology.

Phenotype, observable characteristics of an indivi ual, often contrasted with genotype, the genet makeup. *See also* Genotype. △416, 420.

Phenylketonuria (PKU), or phenylpyruvic olig phrenia, condition in which proteins cannot be met bolized normally because the enzyme phenylalanin is absent. Infants with PKU excrete phenylpyruv acid in the urine. Special diets are used to treat th condition; untreated, it will usually produce seve mental deficiency.

Pheromone, or ectohormone, sociohormone, su stance secreted externally by certain animals to elic specific responses from members of the same sp cies. Common in mammals, insects, and fish, thes substances may be a component of body product such as urine, or secreted by specific glands. △46 464.

Phidias (Pheidias) (*fl.* 470–425 BC), Greek sculpto His direction of Pericles' program for the beautific tion of Athens allowed his thinking and work to dire the art of the Periclean age. Although all of his work are now lost, it is probable that he designed the Pa thenon sculptures. The sculptures display a style an form that were to become hallmarks of the class tradition. △1002.

Philadelphia, city and port of entry in SE Pennsy vania, bounded by Delaware River (E) and Schuylki River (W); seat of and coextensive with Philadelphi co. Known as "city of brotherly love," it was founde by William Penn 1681 as a haven of religious an racial freedom; by *c.* 1774 it was the commercia cultural, and industrial center of the American colc nies. Philadelphia was paramount in shaping the pol cies of the colonies; Carpenter's Hall and the Stat House were sites of the First and Second Continenta Congresses (Sept. 5, 1774 and May 10, 1775); a Independence Hall, the Declaration of Independenc was signed July 4, 1776; the Constitutional Conver tion met here and adopted the US Constitution Sep 17, 1787. Philadelphia served as capital of Pennsy vania 1683–1799, and of the United States 1790-1800; it was scene of first abolitionist movement i North America (1775), with American Anti-Slavery Sc ciety est. 1833; during WWI and II, Philadelphia wa prominent in production of war materials. Benjami Franklin est. the University of Pennsylvania (1740) Pennsylvania Hospital (1751), and first daily newspa per (1784); home of Betsy Ross, seamstress of the firs American flag. Its landmarks include Liberty Bell, In dependence National Historic Park (est. 1956), Chris Church (1727), Edgar Allan Poe's house, Rodin Mu seum, Academy of Fine Arts (1805), Philadelphia Zoo Philadelphia Museum of Art, Benjamin Franklin Me morial (1933), Drexel University (1891), Temple Uni versity (1884), Philadelphia College of Art (1876), US Mint. Professional sports teams include Phillies (base ball), Eagles (football), '76ers (basketball), and Flyers (ice hockey). Industries: shipbuilding, textiles, chemi cals, clothing, electrical equipment, metal products publishing, printing, oil refining, food products. Laic out 1682; chartered 1701. Pop. (1970) 1,950,098.

Philaret (1782–1867), Russian religious leader, b. as Vasili Drozdov. He was metropolitan of Moscow afte 1826 and wrote a catechism, published a collection of sermons, and began a translation into Russian o the New Testament. He played a leading role in the emancipation of the serfs.

Philemon, Christian to whom the apostle Paul ad dressed his New Testament epistle in behalf of Onesimus, a slave who fled from Philemon and converted to Christianity. In this letter, Paul teaches that freedom for all, slave or master, is attained through Jesus Christ.

Philip, Saint, one of the 12 Apostles of Jesus Christ The Gospel of John tells that Philip was from "Bethsaida, the city of Andrew and Peter" (John 1:44). Philip's name appears in all the lists of the disciples in the Gospels and Acts of the Apostles. He was present at the feeding of the five thousand (John 6:5–14).

Philip I (1052–1108), king of France. He enlarged his kingdom and fought repeatedly with the kings of England, William I and II, who as dukes of Normandy were technically his vassals. For his illegal marriage to ertrada de Montfort (both were already married), he as excommunicated by Pope Urban II, but restored n the understanding (openly disregarded) that he ave no further converse with her.

hilip II or **Philip Augustus** (1165–1223), king of rance. He doubled the area of his domain during a 3-year reign. He conducted many wars against lenry II of England and his sons, Richard and John. n 1202, Philip confiscated the French holdings of ohn, and at the Battle of Bouvines (1214) defeated he coalition John put together to support his claims, ncluding Holy Roman Emperor Otto IV and the ounts of Boulogne and Flanders. A strong ruler, hilip supported the Church and towns, improved the ortifications and streets of Paris, and sent out new dministrative officers to call up the army, to collect evenues, and to promulgate his laws.

hilip III (1245–1285), king of France. His striking ack of leadership and decision stimulated intrigues. His first adviser, Pierre de la Brosse, was hanged by supporters of the queen, Marie of Brabant. She in turn vied for power with the queen mother, Margaret. Marie and the king's uncle, Charles of Anjou, involved Philip in an unsuccessful war against Peter II of Aragon in Spain (1283–85).

Philip IV, called **the Fair** (1268–1314), king of France (1285–1314). Described by contemporaries as "the handsomest man in the world, but unable to do anything but stare fixedly at people without saying a word," later recognized as a skilled statesman, the first modern king. He recognized that wealth was the key to a monarch's power over church and rival lords. Claimed the right to tax the clergy for the defense of the realm, using as precedent the levies for the Crusades. Pope Boniface VIII opposed Philip, denouncing him by papal bull and threatening him with excommunication, but Philip refused to back down and convoked the first Estates-General (1302) of nobility, clergy, and commons to hear his justification. Philip secured the election of Pope Clement V and transferred him to Avignon (1309), beginning the "Babylonian captivity" of the papacy. Philip married Jeanne de Navarre (1284).

Philip V (1294–1322), called the Tall, king of France (1317–22). He succeeded John I, the infant son of his brother Louis X, bypassing his niece, thus establishing the precedent of denying the throne to females. He managed to assuage opposition and strengthen the throne.

Philip VI (1293–1350), king of France, grandson of Philip III, became king (1328) on the death of his cousin, Charles IV, managing to avert successionary wars. He then defeated the rebellious towns of Flanders, restoring their count, whose despotic rule caused further trouble at the outbreak of the Hundred Years' War in 1337. Losing control of Flanders after a severe naval defeat (1340), Philip violated the subsequent treaty, was crushed in Normandy (1346), and made a peace that survived him.

Philip II (382–336 BC), king of Macedon 359–336 BC. A superior statesman, diplomat, and general, he laid the foundations of Macedonia's greatness by uniting the country and promoting urbanization and trade and making an excellent professional army. His military genius enabled him to crush Athens and Thebes at Chaeronea in 338 BC. He was assassinated at the age of 46 and succeeded by his son Alexander the Great. △994.

Philip V (238–179 BC), king of Macedon (221–179), son of Demetrius II, adopted by Antigonus III whom he succeeded. He fought well in Greece against the Aetolian League and Sparta and tried to take Illyria from Rome. His pact with Hannibal precipitated the First Macedonian War (215–205), which he won. By attempting to expand his power in the Aegean he alarmed Pergamum and Rhodes and they convinced Rome to enter the Second Macedonian War (200–197) in which Philip was badly beaten. Thereafter he complied with Rome and strengthened Macedon internally. He was succeeded by his son Perseus. *See also* Macedonian Wars.

Philip I or **Philip the Handsome** (1478–1506), Spanish king of Castile. He was the son of Holy Roman Emperor Maximilian I and Mary of Burgundy. From his mother he inherited Burgundy and the Low Countries. He married Joanna, the daughter of Ferdinand II of Aragón and Isabella I of Castile. After the death of Isabella, Philip contested Ferdinand's right to act as regent for his wife and was declared co-ruler of Castile with her. He died the same year. He was the father of Holy Roman emperors Charles V and Ferdinand I.

Philip II (1527–98), king of Spain (1556–98), son of Holy Roman Emperor Charles V and Isabella of Portugal. His father gave him the duchy of Milan (1548), the kingdom of Naples and Sicily (1554), the Spanish Netherlands (1555), and upon his abdication, Spain (1556) along with its fabulously rich colonies in the New World. Thus, like his father, Philip ruled one of the great empires of history. A hardworking, pious ruler, Philip mostly allied himself with Roman Catholic interests on the continent, plunging Spain into the numerous religious wars of the time. He sent the Spanish Armada to England to topple the Protestant Elizabeth I from the throne. Its defeat marked the turning point in Spanish power. Of more general significance was the great drain on Spanish resources caused by Philip's expensive forays into European wars.

Philip married four times. His second wife was Mary I of England; he proposed marriage after her death to Elizabeth I but was refused. Philip built and held court at the Escorial, a somber but impressive combination palace, monastery, and fortress. He died there and was succeeded by Philip III, his son by his fourth wife. Another son, the legendary Don Carlos (1545–68), died early. John of Austria was his half-brother and Margaret of Parma his half-sister *See also* Spanish Inquisition. △1128, 1154.

Philip III (1578–1621), king of Spain, Naples, and Sicily (1598–1621), and king of Portugal (as Philip II, 1598–1621), son of Philip II. Most of the affairs of government were left to his chief minister, the duque de Lerma. His reign was generally peaceful although he did allow Spain to get involved (1620) in the Thirty Years War. He expelled the Moriscos, an action that accelerated Spain's economic decline. Philip was a great patron of the arts; Cervantes, El Greco, Zurbarán, and Lope de Vega all flourished in his reign. He was succeeded by his son Philip IV. *See also* Thirty Years War.

Philip IV (1605–65), king of Spain, Naples, and Sicily (1621–65) and king of Portugal (as Philip III, 1621–40), son of Philip III. Spain continued to decline during Philip's reign. The Conde de Olivares was in charge of the government until 1643. The Thirty Years War ended disastrously for Spain; most of the Netherlands was lost, as was Rousillon. Portugal rebelled and forced out the Spanish (1640). Velazquez was court painter during his reign, and Philip was patron to Rubens and Cano. He was succeeded by his son Charles II. *See also* Thirty Years War.

Philip V (1683–1746), king of Spain (1700–46), first Bourbon king of Spain. A grandson of Louis XIV of France, his designation as successor of Charles II precipitated the War of the Spanish Succession. That war's conclusion put Philip on the throne of a greatly weakened Spain; Gibraltar was lost to Britain during his reign. Philip was first under the influence of the princesse des Ursins, lady in waiting to his wife. After he remarried in 1714, the princesse's influence was replaced by that of the new queen, Elizabeth Farnese. Thereafter she and Cardinal Alberoni ran the government.

In 1724, Philip briefly abdicated in favor of his son, Louis I, but he resumed the throne after Louis' death. Spain under Philip was involved in the great European wars of the period: the War of the Polish Succession; the War of the Austrian succession; and the War of Jenkins' Ear, with Great Britain. He was succeeded by his son Ferdinand VI. *See also* Spanish Succession, War of the.

Philip the Good (1396–1467), duke of Burgundy (1419–67), most prominent of the Valois dukes, and perhaps the most powerful man in Europe during his reign. Maintaining a long alliance with England (in which Henry V was recognized as heir to the French throne), Philip nonetheless managed friendly relations with France, turning his attention to the enlargement and welfare of his own lands. A colorful patron of the arts, Philip loved pageantry and established the chivalrous Order of the Golden Fleece in honor of his marriage (1429) to Isabella of Portugal.

Philippi, ancient city of E Macedon renamed by Philip II (*c.* 356 BC). It was the site of two battles in which the armies of Cassius and Brutus were defeated by Antony and Octavian (42 BC). It became a colony for veterans and later received the first Christian missionaries.

Philippians, New Testament epistle written by Paul during his first imprisonment in Rome. In this letter to the church he established at Philippi in Macedonia, he stresses his joy in serving Christ, even when threatened with death.

Philippines (Filipinas), island-nation in SE Asia. The people are mostly farmers and predominantly Roman Catholic.

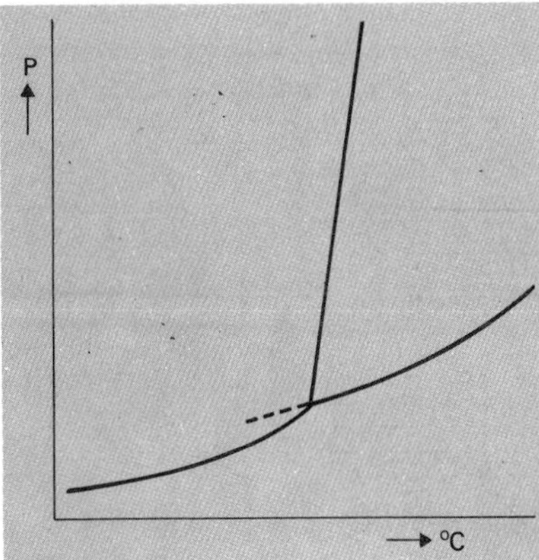
P
°C

Phase diagram

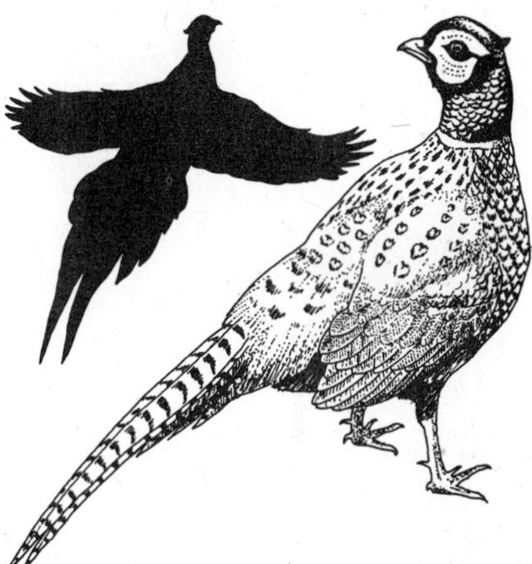

Pheasant

Philadelphia

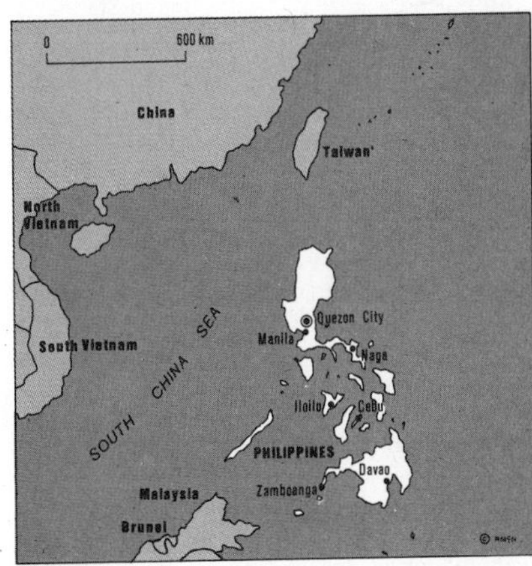
0
600 km
China
Taiwan
North Vietnam
South Vietnam
SOUTH CHINA SEA
Quezon City
Manila
Naga
Iloilo
Cebu
PHILIPPINES
Davao
Zamboanga
Malaysia
Brunei

Philippines

Land and economy. The country, an archipelago, approx. 500mi (805km) off the SE coast of Asia, consists of over 7,000 islands extending roughly 1,100mi (1,771km) N–S and 650mi (1,047km) E–W at its widest point. Two large islands, Luzon in the N and Mindanao in the S, are separated by a number of smaller islands known as the Visayan group. Most of the islands are mountainous, some volcanic, with the densest population concentrated in mountain plains. The climate is tropical and about 40% of the land area is covered with forest; timber is the principal export. The mountains are rich in mineral deposits, metallic and non-metallic, many still undeveloped. The country's economy is based on agriculture, with rice the principal food staple; however, the Philippines is the world's largest producer and principal exporter of coconuts and coconut products. The government has encouraged and furthered the development of industry.

People. Most of the Filipinos' ancestors came to the islands from SE Asia or Indonesia. The Aetas (Balugas), a short, black-complexioned people, are the only remaining aboriginals. Although a large number of languages and dialects is spoken throughout the islands, almost everyone speaks Filipino, a national language rooted in Tagalog, and English. The vast majority of the people is Roman Catholic.

Government. A republican form of government consists of an executive branch with a president, elected for a 4-year term; a legislative branch made up of a House of Representatives of not more than 120 members elected every 4 years, and a Senate of 24 members elected every 6 years; there is also a judicial branch headed by a Supreme Court. Local government is also elective.

History. Although Muslims arrived in the 15th century, the first mass contact with the outside world was in the 16th century with the arrival of the Spanish. Ferdinand Magellan, who was killed there, discovered the islands in 1521. The first permanent settlement was established on Cebu in 1565, and Manila was settled in 1571. Spanish soldiers methodically conquered the major islands, and the friars, who accompanied them, systematically converted the people to Roman Catholicism. Spain exploited the natural resources until the 19th century when, plagued by European troubles, their grip was relinquished. The opening of the Suez Canal in 1869, improving access to European markets, boosted the economy. In 1898, after the United States defeated Spain at the Battle of Manila Bay, the Philippines were ceded to the United States. Although promised independence, the Philippines were not established as a republic until 1946, the procrastination of the US government and the islands' involvement in WWII causing the delay. In the 1970s, under Pres. Ferdinand E. Marcos, the Philippines gradually decreased their close association with the United States.

PROFILE

Official name: Republic of the Philippines
Area: 115,830sq mi (300,000sq km)
Population: 44,400,000
Density: 383.3per sq mi (148per sq km)
Chief cities: Quezon City (capital); Manila; Cebu
Government: Head of State, President
Religion: Christian
Language: Filipino, English (official)
Monetary unit: Peso
Gross national product: $8,800,000,000
Per capita income: $210
Industries (major products): petroleum products, tobacco products, plywood, veneers, paper
Agriculture (major products): rice, corn, coconuts, sugar cane, lumber, sweet potatoes
Minerals (major): silver, gold, copper, zinc
Trading Partners (major): Japan, United States

Philippine Sea, arm of the W Pacific Ocean lying E of the Philippine Islands, S of Japan, W of Mariana Islands, and NW of New Guinea and the Caroline Islands. The Philippine Sea lies in the Philippine Trench following the line of the E coast of the archipelago; S arm of the sea was site of US defeat of Japanese fleet June 19–20, 1944. Depth: (max.) 34,578ft (10,546m).

Philistines, a non-Semitic people who probably came to Philistia from Crete in about the 12th century BC.

Phillips, Wendell (1811–84), US social reformer, b. Boston. He was a close associate of abolitionist William Lloyd Garrison and was one of the leaders in the Antislavery Society, serving as president (1865–70). He also spoke in favor of rights for Indians, and women, penal reforms, and labor organization and against the use of alcoholic beverages. He is most remembered for his impassioned anti-slavery speech in Boston (1837).

Phillips Curve, A.W. Phillips's theory that states that a definite statistical relationship exists between the level of unemployment and the rate of inflation. Phillips maintained that as unemployment decreases, the increasing demand for labor will cause rising prices. The rate at which prices increase is directly related to the productivity rate of the workers in the economy.

Philodendron, genus of trailing house plant native to tropical America with shiny, heart-shaped leaves, sometimes split. Large-leaved, climbing types need support. Care: bright indirect light, well-watered soil (equal parts loam, peat moss, sand). Propagation is by stem cuttings. Height: 4in–6ft (10cm–1.8m). Family Araceae; genus *Philodendron.*

Philo Judaeus, or **Philo of Alexandria** (*c.* 20 BC–*c.* AD 54), Jewish philosopher, b. Egypt. He belonged to a school of thinkers who tried to blend the theology of the Jewish scriptures with Greek philosophy. Philo believed that God should be worshipped, but he had a philosopher's view of the nature of God. He held that God is pure being, present everywhere by his power but nowhere as a substance.

Philology, an older name for linguistics. It is the study of both language and literature. Besides phonetics, grammar, and the structure of language, philology includes textual criticism, etymology, art, archaeology, religion, and any system related to ancient or classical languages. In the 1700s Englishmen discovered that Hindustani resembled Latin and Greek and began the "comparative philology movement" to find the common root.

Philosophes, French term designating a group of 18th-century thinkers with diverse special interests who nevertheless shared a strong commitment to the ideals of the Enlightenment. These ideals included rationalism, toleration, secularization, and the practical improvement of the conditions of life. Voltaire, Hume, and Lessing were eminent philosophes. *See also* Enlightenment. △1180, 1184.

Philosophical Linguistics. *See* Linguistic Analysis.

Philosophy, term derived from a Greek word meaning "love of wisdom." Those ancient Greeks called philosophers sought wisdom in all fields—the structure of matter, the nature of the good, the reality of God. In modern times scholars specialize—physicists conduct experiments to identify the particles of matter, theologians study about God, philosophers still ponder about questions such as "What is good?" The range of interests still pursued by philosophers can be shown by listing major fields: metaphysics, the study of the first principles of reality; epistemology, the theory of knowledge; logic, the principles of inductive and deductive reasoning; ethics, the study of right and wrong; aesthetics, the study of what is beautiful. *See also* Aesthetics; Epistemology; Ethics; Logic; Metaphysics. △852–60.

Phlebitis, inflammation of the wall of a vein, usually in the leg. It may be caused by infection, trauma, underlying disease, or by presence of varicose veins in the legs. Symptoms are pain, swelling, redness, and heat of the vein. Phlebitis may be long-lasting and complicated with blood clot. Treatment includes bed rest and anticoagulant therapy. △716.

Phloem, vascular tissue for distributing food materials in plants. It consists mainly of elongated sieve tubes and parenchyma, sometimes with companion cells. △430.

Phlogiston Theory, theory of combustion proposed in the 17th century by Johann Becher (1635–82) and popularized in the 18th century by Georg Stahl (1660–1734). It postulated that combustible materials contained an odorless, colorless, weightless material called phlogiston; combustion involved loss of this phlogiston and it thereby became dephlogisticated in turning to calx (ash). The theory was disproved by A.L. Lavoisier's (1743–94) discovery of the true nature of combustion.

Phlox, a genus of mostly perennial plants native to North America. The flowers are yellow, blue, purple, pink, red, or white. Height: to 5ft (1.5m). Family Polemoniaceae. The phlox family includes plants, shrubs, and small trees native to Eurasia and North America.

Phnom Penh, or **Phnum Penh,** capital city of Cambodia, in S Cambodia at junction of Mekong and Tonle Sab rivers. The city was the capital of the Khmers in 1434; its royal palace was erected 1813. It is now the site of an international airport and is an industrial center for regional products. The city was extensively damaged before Communist capture in 1975. The population was initially swelled by refugees and the drastically reduced as the new regime evacuated it inhabitants. Industries: rice milling, brewing, distilling textiles, lumber. Founded 1371. Pop. 468,900.

Phobia, irrational fear that tends to persist despite reassurance or contravening evidence. Psychoanalytic theory suggests that phobias such as fear of high places, closed spaces, infection, etc are actually symbolic displacements of more basic but repressed fears and impulses. △766.

Phobos, larger of Mars' two satellites. △76.

Phoebe, several American tyrant flycatchers, including the black phoebe *(Sayornis nigricans),* found from California to South America. It has a white belly and lives near water, hawking insects in flight and from water surfaces. It lays its eggs (3–6) in a mud-and foliage platform nest near a cave or bridge. Length: 6 in (15cm).

Phoenicia, ancient region of E Asia, along the E Mediterranean Sea coast; its great city-states included Tyre, Sidon, Tripoli, Byblos. It was founded *c.* 1600 BC; the Phoenicians were traders and colonizers by 1250 BC and by the 12th century BC, controlled the Mediterranean Sea trade; during the 6th century BC Persia began to absorb Phoenicia, completing the process by Roman times. The Phoenicians originated an alphabet that was later developed by the Greeks they were famous for their purple "Tyrian" dye and carved ivory. △978.

Phoenix, capital city in SW central Arizona, on Salt River; largest city of Arizona; seat of Maricopa co. Development began with diversion of Salt River for irrigation in the 1880s; it was made territorial capital 1889. Completion of Roosevelt Dam (1911) revitalized farming in the area; it was made state capital 1912. It is site of Phoenix College (1920), Grand Canyon College (1949), Heard, Arizona, and Pueblo Grande museums. Industries: data processing, electronic research and production, tourism, aircraft, fabricated metals, machinery, textiles, clothing, food products. Founded 1870; inc. 1881. Pop. (1970) 581,562.

Phoneme, minimum unit of distinctive sound (phone); a speech sound distinguishing meaning. The phoneme "p" distinguishes "tap" from "tab." A phoneme may include a phonetic variant, such as "th," as long as it is perceived as one sound. As long as there is no contrast in sound it is a single phoneme.

Phonetics, the science of speech sounds and the symbols by which they are shown in writing. It is based on a study of parts of the body and their position when making a particular sound. Speech sounds are classified by manner of articulation and point of articulation, the loudness or stress, and pitch or tone. △864.

Phonograph, a machine that reproduces sound that has been recorded on a disk. In 1877 Thomas A. Edison built the first phonograph. Modern phonographs use electric motors that rotate the record on the turntable at constant speed. The tone arm, with a stylus on the end, is placed in the spiral groove on the disk. Variations in the groove cause the stylus to vibrate. These vibrations are converted by the transducer to electrical signals, amplified, and converted into sound by the loudspeaker. △1798.

Phonology, the study of the nature, production, and reception of speech sounds (phonetics) and the functioning of speech sounds in their linguistic system. The sound patterns that occur in language and the changes that they undergo are studied, and changes in the phonemic system are recorded.

Phosphate, a name for numerous chemical compounds related to phosphoric acid (H_3PO_4). One group is composed of salts with the phosphate ion, the hydrogen phosphate ion, or the dihydrogen phosphate ion, and positively charged ions (eg those of sodium). Another group is composed of esters in which organic combining groups (eg ethyl) replace the hydrogen atoms.

Phospholipid. △1570.

Phosphor, substance that is capable of luminescence (storing energy and later releasing it as light). They are of two main types: the zinc sulfide phosphors, as used on cathode-ray tubes, and the oxygen type, as used on fluorescent light tubes. Zinc sulfide is often mixed with cadmium sulfide and a small quantity of metallic phosphates, silicates, borates, or tungstates.

Phosphorescence, a glow of light produced by

ome substances after having been illuminated or, in biology, production of light in an organism without noticeable heat. *See also* Bioluminescence. △1526.

Phosphoric Acid, group of acids the chief forms of which are orthophosphoric acid (H_3PO_4), metaphosphoric acid (HPO_3), and pyrophosphoric acid ($H_4P_2O_7$). Orthophosphoric acid is a colorless deliquescent substance obtained by the action of sulfuric acid on phosphate rock and used in fertilizers, soaps, and detergents. Metaphosphoric acid is obtained by heating orthophosphoric acid and is used as a dehydrating agent. Pyrophosphoric acid is formed from phosphorus pentoxide and water and is used as a catalyst and in metallurgy.

Phosphorus, common nonmetallic element (symbol P) of group V of the periodic table, discovered (1669) by the alchemist Hennig Brandt. It occurs, as phosphates, in many minerals; apatite is the chief source. The element is used in making phosphoric acid for detergents and fertilizers (phosphorus is an essential element for plant growth). Small amounts are used in rat poison and in matches. Phosphorus has several allotropes including the highly reactive white phosphorus and the more stable form, red phosphorus. Properties: at. no. 15; at. wt. 30.9738; sp gr 1.82 (white), 2.20 (red); melt. pt. 111.38°F (44.1°C) (white); boil. pt. 536°F (280°C) (white); most common isotope P^{31} (100%). △1554,1570.

Photocell. △1546.

Photochromic Glass, a form of glass, used in spectacle lenses and electronic devices, which darkens on exposure to ultraviolet light, then fades to its original clear state when the light is removed. Silver chloride or silver bromide crystals throughout the glass interact with light to cause this change.

Photocopying, the process of producing copies of drawings or written material by the use of light, heat, chemicals, or electrostatic charges. The devices used usually employ diffusion transfer or dye line processes. Diffusion transfer involves a master copy made by typing or drawing on translucent paper which is then placed on sensitized negative paper and exposed to light. Negatives are placed in contact with positive transfer and fed into the developer. When peeled apart the image is transferred to the positive paper. Dye line requires a translucent original and uses only one sheet of sensitized paper. △1774.

Photoelectric Cell, or photocell, type of electric cell whose operation depends upon the extent to which it is exposed to light. Formerly consisting of an electron tube with a photosensitive cathode, they are now almost exclusively made of light-sensitive semiconductors. They are used as switches (electric eyes), devices to measure light intensity (lightmeters), or as power sources. *See also* Solar Cell. △1550.

Photoelectric Effect, liberation of electrons from matter by light, ultraviolet radiation, X rays, or gamma rays falling on the surface. The effect can only be explained by the quantum theory. Photons in the incident radiation are absorbed by atoms in the substance and enable electrons to escape by transferring the requisite amount of energy to them. △1526.

Photoengraving, a process of preparing illustrations for letterpress printing in which their image is transferred by photography upon metal or plastic. It includes two steps: the preparation of a photographic negative copy of the material to be reproduced, and the making of a positive printing plate. The negatives are made on sensitized films with a copy camera which can produce an image of any size desired. Plates are made of zinc, copper, magnesium, or nylon coated with a photosensitive solution. The light passing through clear sections of the negative affects the coating and makes it insoluble in water. After exposure the plates are washed, leaving an image formed by the insoluble portions. The nonprinting surface is then etched with an acid. △1772.

Photogrammetry. △180.

Photographic Memory. See Eidetic Imagery.

Photography, process of obtaining a permanent record of an object, either in black-and-white or in color, on treated paper or film. In black-and-white photography a camera is used to expose a film to an image of the object to be photographed for a controlled time. The film is covered on one side with an emulsion containing silver bromide or chloride. The effect of the exposure is to make the silver compound easily reduced to metallic silver when treated with a developer. The action of the developer is to produce a black deposit of metallic silver particles on those parts of the film that were exposed to light, thus providing a "negative" image. After fixing (in "hypo") and washing, the negative can be printed by placing it over a piece of sensitized paper and exposing it to light so that the silver salts in the paper are affected in the same way as those in the original film. The dark portions of the negative let through the least light and the image on the paper is thus reversed back to a positive. Color photography works on a similar, but more complex, process. *See also* Camera. △1784–88.

Photography, Aerial. △1742.

Photon, quantum of electromagnetic radiation, which can be considered as streams of photons, the energy of the photons equaling the frequency of the radiation multiplied by the Planck constant. Absorption of photons by atoms and molecules of matter can cause excitation or ionization. A photon may be classified as a stable elementary particle of zero mass, zero charge, and spin 1 traveling at the velocity of light. It is its own antiparticle. Virtual photons are thought to be continuously exchanged between charged particles and thus to be the carrier of the electromagnetic force. △1484.

Photosphere, surface of the sun, which radiates the light and heat produced in the solar interior. Having a general temperature of 6,000K, it presents a granular appearance, often disturbed by sunspots, faculae, and associated transient phenomena. *See also* Sun. △94.

Photostatic Copying Machine. △1774.

Photosynthesis, chemical process occurring in green plants that manufactures food from water and carbon dioxide by using energy absorbed from sunlight. The reactions take place almost instantaneously in the chloroplasts—chlorophyll-containing bodies in the leaf cells. During the first part of the process, light is absorbed by the chlorophyll and splits water into hydrogen and oxygen. The hydrogen attaches to a carrier molecule and the oxygen is set free. The hydrogen and light energy build a supply of cellular chemical energy (adenosine triphosphate, ATP). Then the hydrogen and ATP convert the carbon dioxide into sugar (including glucose) and starch. Photosynthetic equation: $6CO_2 + 6H_2O$ + light energy$\rightarrow C_6H_{12}O_6 + 6O_2$. △430, 432.

Photo-telegraphy. △1790.

Phototropism, or **Heliotropism,** plant growth in response to a light stimulus that increases cell growth on the shaded side of plant. Leaves and stems respond positively to light and roots respond negatively or not at all. Examples include indoor plants leaning toward windows; leaves growing at right angles to light; and leaf positioning so overlapping occurs as little as possible. △430.

Phrenology, the general theory that an individual's personality and character traits can be determined by examining the shape and configuration of the skull. This theory was elaborated and popularized in the early 19th century by two Germans, Franz Josef Gall (1758–1828) and Johann Spurzheim (1776–1832). The basic ideas in phrenology have been debunked by 20th century psychology, which has found no evidence in support of the theory. △762.

Phrygia, ancient region in central Asia, generally corresponding to modern central Turkey. It was originally settled by Balkans *c.* 13th century BC; slaves were exported to Greece; art and culture peaked *c.* 600 BC; it was ruled by Lydia 7th century BC, and by Persia 546 BC; N Phrygia passed to Galatia 3rd century BC and the remainder came under Roman rule 133 BC; it was associated in legend with Midas and Gordius.

PHS. *See* Public Health Service.

Phthiraptera. △492.

Phylacteries, two leather boxes containing scriptural passages worn by adult Jewish males in Orthodox and Conservative services. These are ceremonially put on with leather straps for certain ritual prayers. Reform Judaism discarded their use.

Phylloxera, or **Grape Phylloxera,** a small yellowish insect of the order Homoptera that is a pest on grape plants in Europe and western United States. It attaches to the leaves and roots and sucks the plant's fluid, resulting in galls and nodules and leading to eventual rotting of the plant. The complex life cycle includes wingless stages that reproduce parthenogenetically. Females lay eggs that survive the

Philodendron

Phnom Penh, Cambodia

Phoebe

Phosphorus: processing

winter. Species *Phylloxera vitifoliae*. Family Phylloxeridae.

Phylum, major group within the animal kingdom or a subdivision in the plant kingdom. It is comprised of a diverse group of organisms with a fundamental characteristic in common. For example, fish and humans are in the phylum Chordata because they both have a notochord. △408.

Physical Chemistry, study of the physical changes associated with chemical reactions and the relationship between physical properties and chemical composition. The main branches are thermodynamics, concerned with the changes of energy in a physical system; chemical kinetics, concerned with rates of reaction; and molecular and atomic structure. Other topics included are electrochemistry, thermochemistry, and some aspects of nuclear physics, radiation physics, and combustion chemistry. △1550.

Physical Therapy. *See* Physiotherapy.

Physical Units, units used in measuring physical quantities. In specifying a unit it is necessary to define an instance of that physical quantity and a way in which it can be compared in making a measurement. For example, the kilogram unit of mass is defined as the mass of a specified block of platinum. Other masses are measured by comparing them, directly or indirectly, with this by weighing. Units are of two types: base units, which like the kilogram have fundamental definitions, and derived units which are defined in terms of these base units. Various systems of units exist, founded on certain base units. They include Imperial units (foot, pound, second), CGS units (centimeter, gram, second), and MKS units (meter, kilogram, second). For all scientific purposes SI units have been adopted (Système International d'Unites), which has seven base units: meter (length), kilogram (mass), second (time), ampere (electric current), kelvin (temperature), candela (luminous intensity), and mole (amount of substance). Derived units are expressed in terms of these: for example the newton (force) is $1kg\ m\ s^{-2}$, and the pascal (pressure) is $1kg\ m^{-1}s^{-2}$.

Physics, study and understanding of natural phenomena in terms of energy and matter. The scientific knowledge thus acquired is put to use by the technologist and engineer. The forms of energy studied include heat, light, mechanical, electrical, sound, and nuclear. The properties of matter itself and the interaction of these different energy forms with matter are also part of physics. It was thought that the properties of matter could be described completely by Newton's laws of motion and gravitation. Although large-scale systems are adequately explained so, classical physics must be replaced by quantum theory (1900) to describe the properties of atoms, etc, and by relativity (1905, 1915) to describe gravitational and very high velocity events. △1480–1548.

Physiocrats, school of 18th-century French economists, led by François Quesnay, that attempted to discover basic economic laws and to combat the mercantilists. Their contributions include the *Tableau économique*, which treated the French economy as a system of flows and clearly showed that money spent initially generated successive multiple spending rounds, and the expansion of the idea of wealth to include the "surplus" produced by the land (as opposed to the mercantilists' concept of wealth as silver and gold). *See also* Mercantilism.

Physiognomy, the outward appearance of anything in so far as it can be taken as an indication of its inner character, especially when considering a person's face as an indicator of individual character. A once popular theory of human personality, this idea has largely been discredited by modern psychology. *See also* Constitutional Types; Phrenology.

Physiology, branch of biology concerned with physical and chemical functions necessary to maintain life. Vast in scope, it includes the study of single cells as well as multicellular organisms. *See also* Biochemistry.

Physiotherapy, also known as physical therapy, the use of varied techniques, including heat, water, diathermy, ultrasound, massage, and exercise, to treat diseases and disorders of the musculoskeletal system in an attempt to relieve pain and to restore use of the affected parts. The work is usually performed by a physical therapist under direction of a specialist physician.

Phytohormone. *See* Plant Hormone.

Phyx. △996.

Pi (π), symbol used for the ratio of the circumference of any circle to its diameter; its value is irrational, 3.14159 . . .; 22/7 is a reasonable approximation. △1462.

Piacenza, city in N Italy, 40mi (64km) SE of Milan; capital of Piacenza prov. It was the terminus of Aemilian Way 187 BC; 12th-century member of Lombard League; given to Farnese family 1545 by Pope Paul III; joined kingdom of Italy 1860; site of 12th–13th century Lombard Romanesque cathedral, uncompleted 16th-century Farnese palace. Industries: chemicals, machinery, food products. Founded 218 BC by Romans. Pop. 102,785.

Piaget, Jean (1896–), Swiss psychologist. Since 1929 he has been the director of the Institut Jean-Jacques Rousseau in Geneva. He has spent many years developing and writing about a comprehensive theory of the intellectual development of children. His theory describes a number of stages of thinking that children go through as they grow from early infancy to adulthood. Largely ignored in the United States prior to the 1950s, he is now universally recognized as a major figure in contemporary psychology. Major works include *The Origins of Intelligence in Children* (1952) and *Six Psychological Studies* (1968). △778.

Piano, or pianoforte, major keyboard stringed instrument of Western music. The piano ranges 7½ octaves with 88 keys; hammers strike metal strings, one to three for each tone. The grand piano, like the harpsichord, has a horizontal frame, the box-shaped upright piano and smaller spinet have vertical frames. Of three pedals, left (soft) acts to mute, right (damper) lifts pads from strings prolonging vibrations, and center (sustaining) modifies dampening effect in lower register.

The basic tool of composers and conductors, it is a versatile, expressive, and popular solo instrument. It is also used for accompaniment and with all types of orchestras and is prominent in jazz band rhythm sections. Evolving from the harpsichord and clavichord, but with improved dynamic possibilities, the earliest pianos were built by Bartolomeo Christofori in Florence (1709). They were in general use by the late 18th century. Mozart and Haydn were the first major piano composers; Beethoven developed orchestral sonority and variety of color; Schumann, Chopin, and Liszt composed and performed great romantic piano music in the 19th century. △1244.

Piast, first royal Polish dynasty founded *c.* 840 by the legendary peasant Piast. The first historical ruler was Mieszko I (*r.* 960–92). Members of the dynasty led Poland for the next four centuries. The last Piast, Casimir III, was a prosperous and powerful ruler.

Piazzi, Giuseppi (1746–1826), Italian astronomer, known for his discovery of the first known asteroid, Ceres (1801). He also founded the observatory of Palermo and there produced a catalog of 7,646 stars (1814). Piazzi demonstrated that most stars are in motion relative to the sun.

Pica, abnormal craving for unnatural foods, such as chalk or ashes. It occurs both in man and animals, usually those who are suffering from nutritional deficiencies.

Picardy, region and former province in N France, bounded by Strait of Dover, Artois and Flanders (N), Champagne (E), Île-de-France (S), Normandy (SW), and English Channel (W); includes Somme, Oise, and Aisne depts.; capital was Amiens. It was a French province 1477 until French Revolution, when all provinces were replaced by smaller departments; scene of heavy fighting in WWI. Area is predominantly farmlands (wheat, sugar beets, potatoes); major centers are seaports of Boulogne-sur-Mer and Calais. Industries: tourism, fishing, textiles.

Picaresque Novel, novel form relating the adventures of a rogue (Spanish picaro), usually in episodic narrative form. It was partly a reaction against idealistic tales of chivalry and romance and usually covered a cross section of society. The first novel in this genre is the Spanish *Lazarillo de Tormes* (1554).

Picasso, Pablo (Pablo Ruiz y Picasso) (1881–1973), Spanish artist. He was a founder of the abstract movement in 20th-century art. In 1900 Picasso went to Paris and there executed the works of his Blue Period (1900–05), a term that referred to both the color and mood of his work. During this time he painted mostly outcasts of society, emphasizing in subject the isolation depicted in style ("The Old Guitarist," 1903). He moved toward a more vigorous style in 1905. "Les Demoiselles d'Avignon" (1906–07) was his first work, dubbed Cubist by critics who stressed the angular, boxlike structure style. "Ambroise Vollard" (1909–10) was a further developmer of the style, marked by greater balance, refinemen and subtlety. By 1910 Cubism was a strongly estal lished style with many practitioners, includin Georges Braque, who worked closely with Picassc Together they developed the technique of pasting cu materials onto canvas, which became known as co lage ("Still Life," 1911–12). Further development c the collage effect, utilizing only the painted surface was evidenced in "Three Musicians," a masterpiec of collage Cubism. Picasso's simultaneously deve oped Neoclassic style ("Mother and Child," 1921–22 merged with the cubist in "Three Dancers" (1925 and was extended in "Guernica" (1937), which de picts the agonies and horrors of war in a powerfu manner. △1296, 1318.

Piccard, Auguste (1884–1962), Swiss physicis who first studied the stratosphere by means of balloo ascents in airtight gondolas, reaching a then recor altitude of 55,577ft (16,951m) in 1932.

Piccolo, woodwind musical instrument of the flut family, but half its size, and pitched one octave highe It is played the same way, by blowing across th mouth hole and fingering the keys. It has a bright penetrating tone and is used in symphony orchestras △1244

Pickerel, freshwater sport and commercial fish foun in E United States. Related to the pike, it has a shove shaped bill and elongated body. Length: 12–24i (30.5–61cm). Species include the grass pickerel *Esc americanus* and the chain pickerel, *E. niger.* Famil Esocidae.

Pickerel Frog, true frog native to S Canada and E United States in streams, bogs, and meadows. It has distinctive rows of dark, rectangular spots on its back and an orange undersurface on hind legs. Its skir secretion is lethal to other frogs and irritating to hu mans. Length: to 3.5in (9cm). Family Ranidae; species *Rana palustris. See also* Frog.

Pickering, Timothy (1745–1829), US military anc political figure, b. Salem, Mass. A member of Massa chusetts' committee of correspondence (1774–75) during the Revolutionary War he served as George Washington's adjutant-general (1777–80) and as quartermaster general (1780–85). He served as post master general (1791–95); secretary of war (1795), ir which post he founded the military academy at West Point; and as secretary of state (1795–1800). He late served Massachusetts as a US senator (1803–12) and representative (1813–17). He was a leader of the Fed eralists.

Pickering, William Henry (1858–1938), US astron omer, b. Boston. He is known for his discovery of Phoebe, the 9th satellite of Saturn (1899). With his brother Edward C. Pickering, he established the Arequipa Observatory in Peru (1891). He then erected the Flagstaff, Ariz., observatory (1894) for the noted astronomer Percival Lowell.

Pickett, George Edward (1825–75), Confederate Civil War general, commander of a Virginia division in the battle of Gettysburg (July 1863), b. Richmond, Va. He is famous as the leader of "Pickett's Charge," perhaps the best-known attack in US military history. More than 60% of his men were killed or wounded in the assault against fortified Union artillery and infantry positions.

Pickford, Mary (1893–), US silent film star, b. Gladys Smith in Canada. On stage from the age of five, she became the Cinderella heroine of many D. W. Griffith films, such as *Rags* (1915) and *Poor Little Rich Girl* (1917). A co-founder of United Artists Films (1919), she demanded and received enormous salaries but was constrained by her image to play child roles and retired early.

Pickling. △396.

Pick's Disease. △764.

Pico della Mirandola, Giovanni, Conte (1463–94), Italian humanist philosopher and scholar who, along with Marsilio Ficino, was an exponent of Renaissance Platonism. Wealthy and well-educated in canon law and Aristotelian philosophy, he exalted the dignity of man and found elements of truth in all the schools and thinkers he studied.

Pico Rivera, city in S California, SE of Los Angeles. Industries: chemicals, automobiles, furniture, toys. Formed by union of Pico and Rivera communities; inc. 1958. Pop. (1970) 54,170.

Pictography, system of using pictures to communi-ate ideas, often used with ideographs. These drawings became very stylized, but it is not considered writing because it represents the object, not the word or the object. △870.

Pictorial Perspective. △1060.

Picts, ancient people of Scotland. First mentioned (AD 297) by Eumenius as invaders of Roman Britain, they had a united kingdom extending between Caithness and Fife by the 7th century and adopted Christianity. In 843, Kenneth I of Dalriada united the Pict lands with his own kingdom and formed Scotland.

Piddock. △478.

Pidgin, a simplified form of a language, usually containing no more than 1,500 words, used for communication between people who do not speak the same language. Most pidgins in use today are based on English, French, Spanish, or Portuguese, with a certain number of native words added. By far the most widely spoken pidgin is the Pidgin English of Papua New Guinea, which is one of the official languages of the country. △866.

Piedmont Plateau, elevated area on the Atlantic coast of the United States, E of the Blue Ridge and Appalachian mts, extending from New York to Alabama; its relatively fertile soil supports diversified farming and livestock raising. Area: approx. 80,000sq mi (207,200sq km).

Pieplant. *See* Rhubarb.

Pierce, Franklin (1804–69), 14th president of the United States (1853–57), b. Hillsborough, N.H. He graduated from Bowdoin College in 1824, and was admitted to the bar in 1827. In 1834 he married Jane Appleton; they had three sons. The son of a Jacksonian Democrat who was twice governor, Franklin Pierce became a member of the New Hampshire legislature in 1829. After serving in both houses of Congress, he retired (at 36) to a successful practice in Concord, N.H.

Known for his pro-slavery views and for his support of the Compromise of 1850, Pierce was acceptable to the southern Democrats in 1852. He was nominated for the presidency on the 49th ballot and went on to win the election.

As president in the turbulent years before the Civil War, Pierce tried to mediate the differences between North and South. The Gadsden Purchase was made during his administration. His support of the Kansas-Nebraska Act (1854) lost him most northern support, and the Ostend Manifesto (1854) further eroded his popularity; he was not renominated by the Democrats in 1856.

Career: New Hampshire legislature, 1829–33; US House of Representatives, 1833–37; US Senate, 1837–42; president, 1853–57. *See also* Compromise of 1850; Gadsden Purchase; Kansas-Nebraska Act;

Piero della Francesca (Piero de' Franceschi) (*c.* 1429–92), Italian painter. An early group of his frescoes in the Este Palace (1450) have been lost. His early work was influenced by Sienese, Florentine, and Umbrian painting. Two other outstanding early works are the "Flagellation," which demonstrates his spatial organization, and "Baptism of Christ" (*c.* 1450–55). His well-known works include his series of frescoes, the "Legend of the True Cross," in the choir of S. Francesco in Arezzo (completed *c.* 1459) and "Madonna del Parto" for his mother's tomb. △844.

Pierre, capital city of South Dakota, in central South Dakota, on Missouri River opposite Fort Pierre; seat of Hughes co. Originally Aricara Indian capital, it developed as trade area 1822–55, steamboat head for Black Hills gold market 1876–85, and railroad trading and shipping center 1880; made state capital 1889. It is site of capitol (1910), Soldiers and Sailors Memorial Building. Its economy is based on state government and agriculture (grain, cattle). Inc. 1883. Pop. (1970) 9,699.

Piers Plowman (*c.* 1362–92), poem attributed to William Langland. Three different versions survive of this moral allegory on the theme "How may I save my soul?" In a dream the poet meets representatives of medieval humanity, personifications of vices and virtues, and finally Piers Plowman, a Christlike figure.

Pietermaritzburg, city in the Republic of South Africa, 40mi (64km) W of Durban, on the Umsunduzi River; became capital of Natal 1843 when the province was annexed to Great Britain; site of Fort Napier (1843), Natal University (1909), teachers' college, technical institute, Voortrekker Museum (1912), Natal museum (1903), art gallery, botanical gardens. Industries: metal, furniture, shoes, tiles, rubber, bricks. Founded 1838 by Boers. Pop. 112,666.

Pietists, religious group that began as a movement within the Lutheran Church in Germany. Led by Philipp Jacob Spener and August Hermann Francke, the Pietists devoted themselves to the "practice of piety." Pietism, which was strongest during the first half of the 18th century, influenced other Protestant sects, such as the Moravian Brethren and Methodism.

Piezoelectricity, electric charge produced by certain asymmetric crystals when they are subjected to pressure. A crystal of quartz or Rochelle salt will produce positive and negative charges on opposing faces when subjected to pressure; the signs of the charges are reversed when the pressure is changed to tension. This property is used in crystal oscillators and pick-ups for record players. △1532.

Pigeon, also often called dove, any of a large family (Columbidae) of wild and domestic birds found throughout temperate and tropical parts of the world, but concentrated in southern Asia and the Australian region. Many have long been domesticated, used for food, and some for carrying messages. Generally less than 18in (46cm) long, pigeons have small heads, short necks, plump bodies, and scaly legs and feet. Loosely but thickly plumaged, they may be brown, gray, white, blue, green, yellow, or orange. They usually feed on seeds, fruits, grain, sometimes on insects, and drink in a unique way by sticking their short slender bill into water and sucking water up. Both sexes typically build a flimsy stick nest in a tree or on the ground, on a ledge, or in a hole, and both incubate the white eggs until the young, or squabs, hatch, at which time they are fed pigeon's milk, a cheesy substance secreted by crop of both sexes. Among well-known pigeons are rock pigeon, ground dove, mourning dove, carrier pigeon, and homing pigeon.

Pigeon Hawk, small brownish or grayish falcon. Species *Falco columbarius. See also* Merlin.

Piggyback Plant, widespreading house plant native to North America. It has long-stemmed, hairy leaves. New plants grow in the leaf bases. Care: bright indirect light, moist soil (equal parts loam, peat moss, sand). Propagation is by leaves with plantlets. Height: to 8in (20cm). Family Saxifragaceae; species *Tolmiea menziesii.*

Pigment, colored insoluble substance used to impart color to an object and incorporated for this purpose into paints, printing inks, plastics, cosmetics, floor coverings, etc. They generally function by absorbing light, though some modern luminescent pigments emit colored light. White pigments include titanium and zinc oxides; black pigments are usually based on carbon black. Colored pigments may be either organic or inorganic compounds. △1554, 1560.

Pigmentation, in anatomy, the coloration of tissues by pigments. In humans, the pigmented areas are skin, hair, and iris of the eye, with the pigments melanin and carotene, combined with the body's hemoglobin, giving the color. △686.

Pigou, Arthur Cecil (1877–1959), English economist, best known for defending the position of classical economists in the face of the Keynesian revolution in the 1930s. According to the classical economists, supply creates its own demand. However, according to Keynes, effective aggregate demand is the immediate determinant of current output (supply). The Pigou effect in economics is concerned with showing that an unregulated economy has a "natural" tendency to gravitate toward full employment. Economists still debate the accuracy of Pigou's position.

Pigweed. *See* Goosefoot.

Pika, short-haired relative of rabbits that cures hay and stores it underground for winter use. The 12 species live in cold regions of Asia and W North America. Most are gray. Length: under 8in (203mm). Genus *Ochotona.* △608.

Pike, Zebulon Montgomery (1779–1813), US explorer, b. Lamberton, N.J. He explored widely in the newly purchased Louisiana Territory, seeking the source of the Mississippi River (1805–06). He later led expeditions to Colorado and New Mexico (1806–07), where he discovered Pikes Peak. He wrote *Account of the Expeditions to the Sources of the Mississippi and Through the Western Parts of Louisiana* (1810), which proved a valuable source of information.

Pike, freshwater fish found in E North America and parts of Europe and Asia. A popular sport and com-

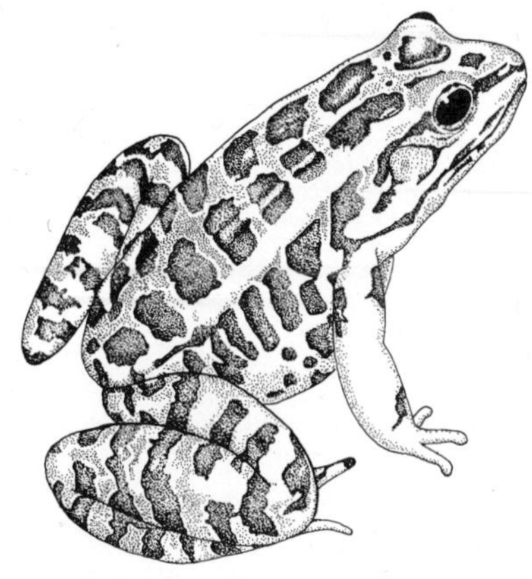

Pickerel frog

Franklin Pierce

Zebulon Pike

Pike

mercial fish, it has a shovel-shaped bill, elongated body, and mottled coloration. It is a long-living fish (40–50 years). Length: to 54in (137.2cm); weight: to 46lb (20.9kg). Family Esocidae, species northern pike *Esox lucius*, Amur pike *Esox reichteri*. △616.

Pike-Perch, freshwater food and game fish of North America, closely related to the walleye and sauger. A dark olive and brass mottled fish, it has an elongated body and large head and mouth. Length: to 3ft (91.4cm); weight: to 25lb (11.3kg). Family Percidae; species *Stizostedion vitreum*.

Pikes Peak, isolated mountain peak in E central Colorado, in the front range of the Rocky Mt system, 10mi (16km) W of Colorado Springs; tourist area, noted for its view. Discovered 1806 by Zebulon Pike, for whom it is named. Height: 14,110ft (4,304m).

Pikesville, residential town in central Maryland; NW suburb of Baltimore. Pop. (1970) 25,395.

Pilate, Pontius, Roman governor of Judea when Jesus Christ was crucified. Pilate was made procurator of Judea, Samaria, and Idumea in AD 26 and earned a reputation for arrogance and cruelty. He may have died in 39. The New Testament Gospels tell of Pilate's role in condemning Jesus (Matthew 27; Mark 15; Luke 23; John 18–19).

Pilchard, marine, schooling, herringlike food fish found along European and Australian coasts. The young are sometimes called sardines. Length: less than 18in (45.7cm). Family Clupeidae, Species *Sardinia pilchardus*. △386.

Pilcomayo, river in S central South America; rises in E Andes Mts in W central Bolivia; flows SE to form Argentina-Paraguay border; empties into the Paraguay River at Port Asunción. Chief tributary is Pilaya River in Bolivia. Length: approx. 700mi (1,127km).

Pile Driver, a machine for driving postlike foundation members (piles) into the ground. △1612, 1758.

Piles. *See* Hemorrhoids.

Pileworm. *See* Shipworm.

Pilgrimage of Grace (1536), uprising of English Roman Catholics protesting against the enclosure movement and dissolution of the monasteries following the abolition of papal supremacy in England. After a small rising in Lincoln had failed, Robert Aske, the leader, and his followers occupied York and then marched to Doncaster with 35,000 men. The duke of Norfolk, King Henry VIII's emissary, held talks with Aske, and he dispersed his men. Further minor outbreaks were suppressed, and Aske was executed (1537).

Pilgrimages. △1086.

Pilgrims, group of colonists who were the first settlers of New England. Most were English separatists who withdrew from the Anglican Church and migrated to Holland. Economic difficulties forced a group of Pilgrims under William Bradford and William Brewster to obtain a land patent from the Virginia Company of London to emigrate to Virginia. The colonists, on the *Mayflower*, landed instead in Massachusetts (1620), establishing the Plymouth Colony. *See also* Mayflower Compact; Plymouth Colony. △1216.

Pilgrim's Progress, The (1678), allegory by John Bunyan recounting the perilous and adventurous journey of Christian from the doomed City of Destruction to the Celestial City. Full of allegorical characters and situations, the book also includes a sequel relating the same journey made by Christiana, Christian's wife, and her children. While sustaining its moral, Puritan standpoint, the book is remarkable for its simple style and has greatly influenced English prose.

Pillars of Hercules, in Greek mythology, two promontories in the Mediterranean. They were called Calpe and Abyla in ancient times. They are usually identified as Gibraltar in Europe and Mt Acha (Mt Hacho) in Africa. According to some legends they were joined together until Hercules tore them apart in order to reach Cadiz.

Pillow Lava, lava extruded under water that commonly takes the form of a distorted globular mass, the so-called pillow shape. It apparently results from the rapid chilling of the outer skin, thus making a more or less spherical balloon that grows and flattens under its own weight. *See also* Lava. △228.

Pilon, Germain (*c.*1537–90), French sculptor. △1146.

Pilot Fish, marine fish found in warm seas, often around sharks and ships. A blue fish with 5–7 dark side bar markings and a white tail, it feeds on food and parasites near sharks. Length: to 2ft (61cm). Family Carangidae; species *Naucrates ductor*.

Pilot Whale, or blackfish, small, black, toothed whale distributed in nonpolar seas. They are trained to perform in captivity. Length: to 28ft (8.5m). Genus *Globicephala*. *See also* Dolphin. △552.

Pilsudski, Józef (1867–1935), Polish general and statesman. He joined the Young Poles; the Russians imprisoned him in Siberia for five years (1887–92). He became a leader of the Polish Socialist party in 1892, was arrested but escaped to England (1902) and formed a secret, private army of 10,000 anti-Russian Poles to fight for independence from Russia. He fought on the side of Austria against the Russians (1914–16); the Germans interned him when he refused to fight further because of their interference. After the war he was hailed as a national hero when he proclaimed the Polish Republic in 1919. With French help he defended Warsaw from the Russians in 1920. From 1926 until his death he was dictator of Poland.

Piltdown Man, name given to fossil skull found in Sussex, England (1909–15), believed for years to be the "missing link" between apes and men. In 1953 modern tests conclusively exposed it as a fake. △648.

Pima, a tribe of North American Indians speaking the Uto-Aztekan tongue, and closely related to the Papago. They occupied the Gila and Salt river valleys in S Arizona, where some 8,000 still reside today. They are the descendents of the ancient Hohokam people.

Pimento. *See* Allspice.

Pimento, a tropical evergreen tree *(Pimento diocia)* of the myrtle family (Myrtaceae), native to the West Indies and Central America. The nearly ripe berries are dried in the sun to furnish the aromatic and pungent spice allspice used in baking. The tree grows to 30ft (9m).

Pi Meson (Pion) Particle. △1484.

Pimpernel, or shepherd's clock, small, trailing annual plant of the Old World and naturalized in England and North America. The scarlet, white, or blue flowers are born at the leaf axils and close during cloudy weather and at night. Family Primulaceae; species *Anagallis arvensis*.

Pinch Effect. *See* Fusion Reactor.

Pincherle, Alberto (1907–). *See* Moravia, Alberto.

Pinching Bug. *See* Stag Beetle.

Pinchot, Gifford (1865–1946), US conservationist and public official, b. Simsbury, Conn. He developed a systematic forestry program (1892), served on numerous conservation commissions, and became chief of Department of Agriculture's Forestry Division (1898–1910). In 1905 he became the first chief forester. He was dismissed (1910) by President Taft after a controversy with secretary of the interior Richard Ballinger. Elected governor of Pennsylvania (1923; 1931), he was a reformer whose books include *A Primer of Forestry* (1899), *The Fight for Conservation* (1909), *Breaking New Ground* (1947). *See also* Ballinger-Pinchot Controversy.

Pinckney, Charles (1757–1824), US statesman, b. Charleston, S.C. He was a member of the Continental Congress (1784–87) and played a major role at the Constitutional Convention (1785–87) suggesting a number of provisions that became part of the Constitution. He later served as South Carolina's governor (1789–92, 1796–98) and as a Democrat in the US Senate (1798–1801). As minister to Spain (1801–05), at the time of the Louisiana Purchase, he failed in his attempts to acquire Florida for the United States. He served again as governor (1806–08), and in the House of Representatives (1819–21).

Pinckney, Charles Cotesworth (1746–1825) American patriot and political figure, b. Charleston, S.C. The brother of Thomas Pinckney, Charles was a member of the first provincial congress (1775) and served as a Continental officer and aide to Gen. George Washington during the Revolution. As a delegate to the Constitutional Convention (1787), he supported the ratification of the Constitution. He was appointed minister to France in 1796 but was not recognized by the French government. He returned home (1797) after negotiations with France were terminated during the scandalous XYZ Affair. He ran unsuccessfully as the Federalist candidate for vice president in 1800 and for president in 1804 and 1808.

Pinckney, Thomas (1750–1828), US soldier and diplomat, b. Charleston, S.C. A Revolutionary War veteran, he served as South Carolina governor (1787–89) and minister to Great Britain (1792–96). He was as a commissioner to Spain (1794–95); he negotiated Pinckney's Treaty, which marked the southern and western boundary lines between the United States and Spain's New World territories. It also opened up the Mississippi River to US boats. He was the Federalist vice-presidential candidate (1796) and served in the US House of Representatives (1796–1801). During the War of 1812, he was a major general.

Pincushion Cactus, cactus native to W United States, Mexico, and Cuba. It has round or oval globular stems, large brilliantly colored flowers, and bright edible berries. Diameter: 0.5in–2ft (1–61cm). Family Cactaceae; genus *Coryphantha*. *See also* Cactus.

Pindar (*c.*522–440 BC), Greek lyric poet. Few of his poems exist in complete form—among them the *Triumphal Odes*, written in honor of the Panhellenic games. Noble by birth, he sometimes revealed his aristocratic attitudes in his poems. His style seemed unorganized, as he rushed through his work in order to develop all of his ideas. He used a variety of meters and wrote all forms of choral lyrics, in colorful language. Much respected by his peers, he was later imitated by Horace, Dryden, and Swift. △998.

Pine, evergreen trees mostly native to cooler temperate regions of the Northern Hemisphere; several grow in warm climates. They have scalelike deciduous leaves or evergreen needlelike clusters. The flowers are catkinlike stalks or pine cones. Many are valued for soft wood, oils, and resins. Family Pinaceae; genus *Pinus*. △442, 592.

Pineal Body, small organ attached to the lower surface of the brain, the function of which is unknown. In humans, the pineal gland degenerates in childhood and is represented only by fibrous tissue in the adult. In some lizards it forms a "third eye" during embryonic stages. Evidence suggests that the pineal may be an endocrine gland.

Pineapple, common name for a tropical herbaceous perennial and its fruit, native to South America and cultivated commercially first in 1850 in the Azores. Grown also in the United States, Cuba, Mexico, Southeast Asia, South Africa, and Australia, the plant has a short, stout stem bearing stiff fleshy leaves and grows to 2–4ft (0.6–1.2m). The fruit is eaten fresh or canned or made into juice. Family Bromeliaceae; species *Ananas comosus*.

Pine Bluff, commercial city in SE central Arkansas 43mi (69km) SE of Little Rock; seat of Jefferson co. Industries: cotton, textiles, lumber products, chemicals. Founded 1818 as Mount Marie, renamed 1832; inc. 1839. Pop. (1970) 57,389.

Pinel, Philippe (1745–1826), French physician. He was an important pioneer in the treatment of the mentally disturbed. Pinel released patients from imprisonment, developed case histories to try to treat patients individually, and attempted to talk and reason with patients—the early beginnings of modern psychotherapies. △762.

Pine Nut, the edible seed obtained from any of several species of low-growing pines called piñon pines (eg *Pinus edulis*, *P. parryana*) of W North America. It was collected by American Indians as a valuable food resource and is now used in confectionery.

Pine Snake, common, harmless snake found in pine barrens and dry areas of the United States. It is black and white or brown with a faded pattern. Length: to 5.5ft (168cm). Family Colubridae; species *Pituophis melanoleucus*. *See also* Bull Snake.

Ping-Pong. *See* Table Tennis.

Pink, common name for the several genera of the pink family, especially the genus *Dianthus* of over 300 species, found chiefly in the Mediterranean region. Primarily short herbaceous perennials, many are hardy evergreens with showy flowers. The stems are often woody at the base, leaves are simple and usually opposite, and the radially symmetrical flowers are usually bisexual. The Deptford pink, maiden pink, Cheddar pink, and proliferous pink grow wild in Great Britain. A few other species, including clove pink and garden pink, have been naturalized in the United states. The florists' carnation is a modification of the clove pink. Family Caryophyllaceae. *See also* Carnation. △444.

Pinkerton, Allan (1819–84), US detective, b. Scotland. Immigrating to the United States (1842), he became a detective on the Chicago Police Force (1850–51) and established his own agency, Pinkerton's National Detective Agency. He organized and headed a federal intelligence service (1861–62). He gained fame for his work in the Admas Express robbery cases (1859–60) and for suppressing the "Molly Maguires," a group of rebellious coal miners in the 1870s. His detective agency still exists. △918.

Pinkney, William (1764–1822), US senator and diplomat, b. Annapolis, Md. He was a delegate to the convention that ratified the Constitution (1788) and was in the state legislature (1788–92). From 1796 through 1811 he spent most of his time in England working without much success on claims under Jay's Treaty (1795), which attempted to settle territorial and maritime disputes, and the Monroe-Pinkney Treaty, which called for a halt to British impressment of US sailors. Pinkney served in James Monroe's cabinet (1811–13), and was minister to Russia. He was instrumental in the Senate's passage of the Missouri Compromise (1820).

Pinnipedia, meat-eating aquatic mammals formerly classified as carnivores. Comprised of eared seals (Family Otariidae), including fur seals and sea lions; earless, true, or hair seals (Family Phocidae); and the walrus (Family Odobenidae). △550.

Pinochle, card game for two to four players with a 48-card deck made up of two each of nine through ace from each suit. With 3 players, each receives 15 cards, with the remaining 3 turned face down on the table. Players, in turn, then bid for the three cards. The bidding usually starts at 300 points. The cards rank ace, 10, king, queen, jack, and 9. Points are awarded according to runs (a sequence from ace to jack), marriages (king and queen of a suit), four of any rank (except 10s and 9s), and the jack of diamonds and queen of spades (a pinochle). After each player lays the cards he is going to declare as points face up on the table, the bidder "buries" three cards from his hand. Tricks are then collected, and the bidder, through the points he originally declared and those he wins during the course of the game, must at least reach the amount he bid.

Pinocytosis, the taking up of fluid by living cells. Rather than passing through the cell membrane as individual molecules, a droplet becomes bound or absorbed on the membrane which forms a pocket and pinches off to form a vesicle in the cytoplasm.

Piñon, or Mexican stone pine, evergreen tree native to Mexico and SW United States. It has large, edible seeds (pine nuts). Height: to 25ft (7.6m). Family Pinaceae; species *Pinus cembroides.*

Pinter, Harold (1930–), English playwright. He was an actor under the name of David Baron and played repertory. His first play, *The Room* (1957), was followed by such other plays as *The Birthday Party* (1958), *The Caretaker* (1960), *The Homecoming* (1965), *Old Times* (1970), and *No Man's Land* (1975). Most of his plays juxtaposed farcical dialogue with an evocation of terror, called by critics the "comedy of menace." He also wrote extensively for radio and television as well as for films.

Pinworm, or seatworm, a tiny worm, which upon infection by ingestion of fecally contaminated material, dwells in the small intestine. Itching in the anal region is a common symptom. Worms can occasionally lodge in the appendix causing symptoms similar to acute appendicitis. Pinworms can be treated with piperazine.

Pion, elementary particle (symbol π) that is a meson. There are three types, forming a nuclear multiplet (triplet). The charged pions, π^+ and π^-, have equal mass, about 280 times the electron mass, and are antiparticles of each other; the neutral π°, of slightly lower mass, is its own antiparticle. All have zero spin. Charged pions decay into muons and muon neutrinos; the π° decays into photons. Virtual pions are thought to be exchanged between nucleons bound together by strong interaction. *See also* Hadron. △1484.

Pioneer. △82.

Pipefish, marine fish found in the shallow warm and temperate waters of the Atlantic and Pacific. Closely related to the seahorse, it has a pencillike body covered with bony rings. Its mouth is at the end of a long snout. The male incubates the young in a brood pouch. Length: to 23in (58.4cm). Family Syngnathidae; species include *Syngnathus fuscus.* △516.

Pipeline, a system of pipes connected to pumps and valves for the conveyance of liquids or gases, usually underground. △1642.

Pipestone, or **Catlinite,** a pink stone carved by Plains Indians into ceremonial pipes. The name catlinite is from George Catlin (the US artist famous for his paintings of Indians). The stone, found at the Pipestone National Monument in SW Minnesota, is reserved for the Indians who quarry it under special permits.

Pipit, two small North American sparrowlike songbirds that frequent wetlands and meadows, often near large animals, feeding on insects. They have a straight beak, short tail, elongated hind claw, and are protectively colored. Nesting on the ground, the male feeds the female while she incubates the blotched whitish eggs. Family Motacillidae; genus *Anthus.*

Pipsissewa, evergreen shrub native to E North America and N central Eurasia. It has pink or white flowers and jagged leaves. Height: 6–12in (15–30cm). Family Ericaceae; species *Chimpaphila umbellata.*

Piraeus, seaport city in E central Greece, on Saronic Gulf; capital of Piraeus dept. and chief port of Athens. City was besieged by Sulla 86 BC; modern development began after Greece achieved independence (19th century). The ancient Long Walls connected it with Athens; preceded Salamis as Athens' naval and maritime headquarters (480 BC). Industries: shipbuilding, chemicals, textiles. Planned *c.* 490 BC by Themistocles, city was built *c.* 450 BC by Hippodamus of Miletus. Pop. 186,223. △994.

Pirandello, Luigi (1867–1936), Italian author of naturalistic plays, novels, and short stories. His work, expressing his philosophy of disillusionment and uncertainty, was widely translated. He won the Nobel Prize for literature in 1934. His plays include *Six Characters in Search of an Author* (1921), *Henry IV* (1922), and *As You Desire Me* (1930). His novels include *The Late Mattia Pascal* (1923) and *The Young and the Old* (1928).

Piranha, or **Piraya,** vicious, freshwater bony fish found in tropical rivers of South America. It has blunt, powerful jaws, and sharp teeth. It usually travels and attacks in schools. Length: to 2ft (61cm). Family Serrasalmidae; genera *Serrasalmus, Rooseveltiella, Pygocentrus.* △514, 618.

Pirarucu, tropical fish native to rivers of South America. A valuable food fish, it has a greenish, pointed head and reddish broad tail. Length: to 8ft (2.4m); weight: 200lb (90kg). Family Osteoglossidae; species *Arapaima gigas.*

Piraya. *See* Piranha.

Pisa, city in central Italy, 12mi (19km) NNE of Leghorn, on the Arno River; capital of Pisa prov. A member of Etruscan confederation, it attained Roman citizenship 89 BC; prospered as maritime republic end of 11th century; defeated by Genoa 1284; sold to Florence 1406; scene of council of Pisa (1409) electing Pope Alexander V; birthplace of Galileo; site of famous Leaning Tower, 11th–12th-century cathedral, Palazzo di Medici, university (1343). Industries: textiles, glass, tourism, machine tools. Pop. 102,717.

Pisano, Nicola or **Niccolò** (1220–84), Italian sculptor and architect. He founded a new school combining Gothic and classical architectural elements, and is best known for designing four pulpits, including the marble pulpit for the Pisa baptistery (*c.* 1260). He also designed the great fountain of Perugia and was assisted by his son Giovanni Pisano (*c.* 1245–*c.* 1314), also a sculptor.

Pisces, or the Fishes, inconspicuous equatorial constellation situated on the ecliptic between Aquarius and Aries; the 12th and last sign of the zodiac. Lacking any stars brighter than the fourth magnitude, it contains a distant spiral galaxy M74 (NGC 628) only visible telescopically. The astrological sign for the period Feb. 19–Mar. 20. △132, 826.

Pisgah, Mount (Nebo, or Jabal an-Naba), peak in N Jordan, in the Abarim Mountains; traditional site where Moses viewed the Promised Land before his death. Height: 2,644ft (806m).

Pissarro, Camille (1830–1903), French painter. An artist after the Impressionist style, he was variously influenced by Paul Cézanne, Claude Monet, Hilaire

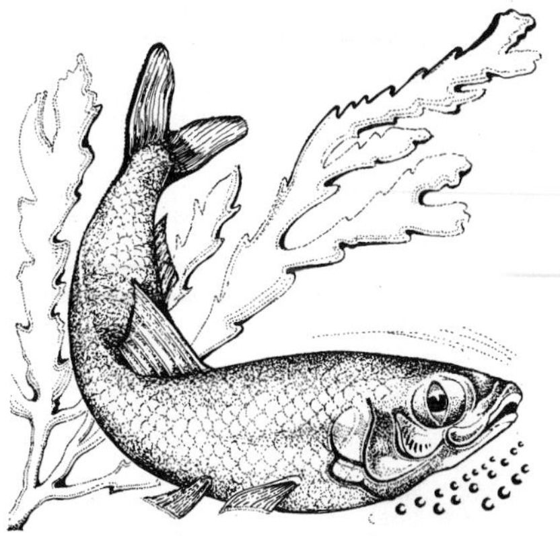

Pilchard

Thomas Pinckney

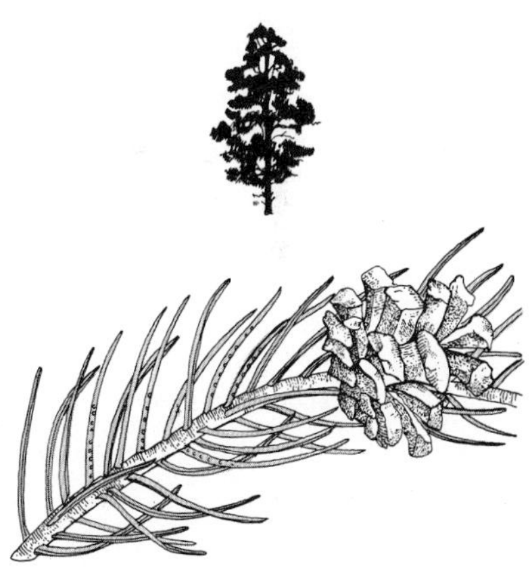

Pine

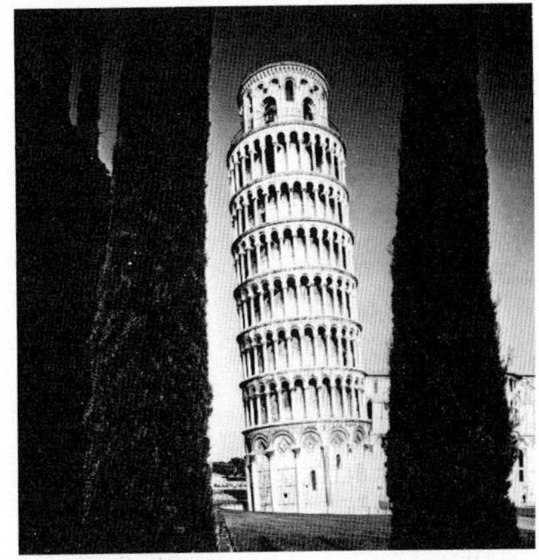

Pisa, Italy

Degas, and Georges Seurat, all close friends of his, along with Vincent van Gogh. After the Franco-Prussian war, he was influential in developing the Impressionist movement in France; he was the only member of the Impressionist group to show in all eight of their exhibitions. His works include "Entrance of the Village of Voisino" (1872) and "Avenue de l'Opéra" (1898). △1254.

Pistachio, deciduous tree native to the Mediterranean region and E Asia. It is grown commercially for the edible greenish seed of its wrinkled red fruit. Height: to 20ft (6m). Family Anacardiaceae; species *Pistacia vera.*

Pistol. △1728, 1730.

Piston, Engine, a solid, sliding piece that moves back and forth in a cylindrical chamber and which is impelled by fluid or gas pressure. There are usually metal rings (piston rings) that fit into grooves in the piston walls to assure snug fit. △1632.

Pitcairn Island, island and British possession in central S Pacific Ocean, SE of the Tuamotu group. Its residents are descendants of the mutineers from the British ship *Bounty* (1790); when discovered in 1831, the original mutineers were moved to Tahiti, and to Norfolk Island 1856; some descendants later returned to Pitcairn. Exports: oranges, pineapples. Area: under 2sq mi (5sq km). Pop. 91.

Pitch, subjective quality of sound that determines its position in a musical scale; measured in terms of frequency, it also depends on loudness and timbre. Increasing the intensity of a note decreases the pitch of a low note but increases the pitch of a high note. △1498, 1500.

Pitcher, Molly (*c.* 1744–1832), American Revolutionary War heroine, b. Mary Ludwig Hays McCauley, near Trenton, N.J. She earned her nickname in the Battle of Monmouth (1778) where she brought water to the troops. Often confused with Margaret Corbin, another heroine, who fought alongside her husband, an artillery gunner.

Pitcher Plant, insect-eating bog plant of North America. The pitcher-shaped leaves, veined with red and green, are lined with bristles. Trapped insects decompose and are absorbed as nutrients by plant cells. The flower is usually red. Height: 8–24in (20–61cm). Species include yellow-flowered *Sarracenia flava.* Family Sarraceniaceae. △444.

Pith, a central strand of parenchymous tissue that occurs in the stems of most vascular plants. It is usually surrounded by vascular tissue and is believed to function chiefly in storage. The term is also used for the soft core at the center of the heartwood of logs, consisting of the dried remains of the pith.

Pithecanthropus, name given to primitive extinct species of man known first from skeletal remains discovered in Java and then from further finds at Choukoutien near Peking. Pithecanthropines lived about half a million years ago, walked erect, made and used crude stone tools, and were possibly capable of speech. Their cranial capacity was about halfway between apes and men; modern man may be descended from them. *See also* Australopithecus; Java Man; Peking Man. △650–52.

Pitot Tube, a device for determining pressure in a moving fluid. It is a manometer with one open end facing upstream and the other open end out of the stream. The different pressures at the two ends cause the liquid in the tube to shift position within the two arms of the tube.

Pitt, William, 1st Earl of Chatham (1708–78), English political figure, known as the Great Commoner. In Parliament from 1735 he became noted for his brilliant oratory and his opposition to the foreign policies of prime ministers Walpole and Carteret and King George II. Pitt sought to shift Britain's emphasis from support of Hanover and Austria to acquisition of colonies abroad and advancement of commercial interests. As paymaster general of the armed forces (1746–55), he won great esteem by his honesty, unusual in the holders of that office. The crisis of the Seven Years War (1756–63) made him effective head of the government, first as secretary of state (1756–57). Widespread criticism of his dismissal from that post (1757) brought about his reappointment as head of the government in coalition with the Duke of Newcastle.

His ministry was a brilliant one, preserving and consolidating Britain's old empire and gaining a new one. Pitt subsidized the forces of Frederick the Great, managed military supply problems efficiently, chose commanders shrewdly, expanded the British navy and harassed the French along their coasts and in Africa and the West Indies, placed his main efforts on successful attempts to conquer Canada and India, and mobilized public opinion behind his policies. He resigned in 1761 when George III refused to declare war on Spain, and he opposed the Treaty of Paris (1763) ending the Seven Years War as inadequate. After the war he spoke out against the prosecution (1763) of John Wilkes and the imposition of the Stamp Act (1765) on the American colonies. The ministry he nominally headed from 1766 to 1768 was a confused and divided one, partly as a result of his physical illnesses (which had plagued him all his life) and periods of mental illness. Created Earl Chatham in 1766, he retired from the House of Commons to the House of Lords in 1768. There he periodically made speeches against repression of the American colonies and in favor of any peace settlement with them short of one granting them independence. He collapsed in Parliament after the last of these speeches and died a month later in the arms of his son William. △1216.

Pitt, William, the Younger (1759–1806), British prime minister (1783–1801, 1804–06); son of William Pitt, the Elder. Entering Parliament (1781), he became chancellor of the exchequer (1782) and prime minister (1783). His financial policy, influenced by Adam Smith's theories, aimed at reducing the national debt. He consolidated colonial power in India (1784) and Canada (1791). Forming coalitions against France (1793–1798), he resigned (1801) when George III refused to accept the Catholic Emancipation Bill in the Union with Ireland Act (1800). He returned as prime minister (1804) and formed (1805) a third coalition of powers against Napoleon. Already ill, his death was accelerated by news of defeat at Austerlitz (1805).

Pitta, bright multicolored bird living in the dark jungles of Africa, S Asia, Malaysia, the Philippines, New Guinea, and Australia. Plump birds, they have large heads, short rounded wings, short square tails, and long legs. Some are migratory. Most feed on termites, other insects, and worms and build large, globular nests with side entrances in the fork of a bush or low tree for their glossy white or buff eggs (2–6). The blue-winged pitta *(Pitta brachyura)* has black mask, white throat, green back, red abdomen, and brown undersides with blue patches on its rump and wings. Length: 7in (17.5cm). Family Pittidae.

Pittsburgh, industrial city and port of entry in SW Pennsylvania, at confluence of Allegheny and Monongahela rivers; seat of Allegheny co; 2nd-largest city in Pennsylvania. Fort Duquesne was erected on site by French *c.* 1750s; it was captured by British 1758 and renamed Fort Pitt; village developed around the fort by 1760, and grew rapidly as a steel manufacturing center (19th century). Pittsburgh is site of Carnegie Institute (1895), Mellon Institute (1913), Carnegie-Mellon University (1900), University of Pittsburgh (1787), Duquesne University (1878), Chatham College (1869), Three Rivers Stadium (1970); home of Pittsburgh Pirates (baseball) and Steelers (football); birthplace of Stephen Foster. Dr. Jonas Salk developed poliomyelitis vaccine at University of Pittsburgh 1958. Industries: steel, glass, machinery, petroleum products, paper goods, electrical equipment, printing, publishing, railroad shops, coal mining, oil, gas, mine safety equipment. Inc. 1794 as borough, 1816 as city. Pop. (1970) 520,117.

Pittsfield, city in SW Massachusetts, 40mi (64km) WNW of Springfield; seat of Berkshire co; site of Berkshire Community College (1960); city library contains works and pictures of Herman Melville who lived here 1850–63; resort area. Industries: transformers, paper, textiles. Inc. as town 1761, as city 1889. Pop. (1970) 57,020.

Pituitary Gland, endocrine gland, sometimes considered the master gland. About the size of a small cherry, the pituitary is connected to the lower surface of the brain by a stalk, the infundibulum. It is composed of three parts: an anterior lobe, a connecting pars intermedia, and a posterior lobe, each of which has its own functions. The anterior lobe, the most active part, secretes at least six hormones: thyroid-stimulating hormone (TSH); adrenocorticotropic hormone (ACTH) that stimulates adrenal secretion; follicle stimulating hormone (FSH) that stimulates ovarian function in females and testicular function in males; luteinizing hormone (LH) that stimulates ovulation in females and testosterone secretion in males; luteotropic hormone (LTH) that functions during pregnancy and the postpartum period; and growth hormone, sometimes called somatotropin, that accelerates body growth. The poorly understood intermediate lobe secretes hormones that affect pigmentation. The posterior pituitary secretes vasopressin, which promotes water retention, and oxytocin which functions in lactation. △690.

Pit Viper, poisonous snake, including the rattlesnake, copperhead, moccasin, lancehead, and bushmaster, found chiefly in the New World, Europe, and Asia. They are characterized by a heat-sensitive pit on each side of the head, used for detecting warm-blooded prey in the dark. The bushmaster is the largest. There are 100 species. Family Crotalidae. *See also* Viper. △522, 600.

Pius IX, Roman Catholic pope (1846–78). △1250

Pius XI (1857–1939), Roman Catholic pope (1922–39), b. Achille Ambrogio Ratti. He founded the Catholic Action movement, supervised the program for world relief, supported missionary work, and improved the Vatican library. In 1929 he signed the Lateran Treaty with Mussolini creating the State of the Vatican City. He recognized Franco's government in 1938, after denouncing Hitler in 1937.

Pius XII (1876–1958), Roman Catholic pope (1939–58), b. Eugenio Pacelli. He served as secretary of state to Pope Pius XI. As pope, he took a neutral position during World War II. He renewed the Catholic Action movement to fight Communism and encouraged Marian devotion. He recognized the need for modernization, and the first Vatican City bank was established during his papacy.

Pixii, Hippolyte. △1536.

Pizarro, Francisco (*c.* 1471–1541), leader of the Spanish conquest of Peru; arrived in the New World in 1502. Of modest origins, Pizarro became a prosperous landholder in Panama City before receiving a commission from the Crown for the conquest of Peru. At the end of 1530, Pizarro set sail for the western coast of South America, and arrived at a time when the Inca empire already was disintegrating. The Inca ruler Atahualpa was captured in 1532; the stronghold of Cuzco fell in 1534. The conquest was completed by 1535. Civil war among the conquerors resulted in the death of Pizarro's partner and rival, Diego Almagro; Francisco Pizarro, in turn, was assassinated by Almagro's son. △1124.

PK. *See* Psychokinesis.

PKU. *See* Phenylketonuria.

Placenta, vascular organ in mammals (except monotremes and marsupials) that connects the fetus to the uterus of the mother and serves as an organ of nutrition, respiration, and excretion for the fetus. In humans, the placenta has three parts: the fetal part, derived from the chorion membrane surrounding the fetus; the maternal part, which is really the decidua basalis layer of the uterine lining; and the intervillous space between these two plates, containing enormous numbers of tiny blood vessel branches and projections through which oxygen and food are carried from the mother to the embryo and wastes are carried from the embryo to the mother to be excreted. The placenta is discharged from the mother's body as the afterbirth, immediately after birth of the baby. △702, 704.

Placental Mammals, mammals whose young develop to an advanced stage attached to a temporary life-support organ—the placenta—inside the mother's uterus. All mammals except the monotremes and marsupials are placentals. △540–44.

Placer Mining, methods of surface mining employed to obtain valuable minerals (especially gold, platinum, and tin ore) from secondary gravel deposits (placer deposits). Generally, dredging or hydraulic techniques are used. The site is either flooded in order to operate dredging equipment, or, in the case of terraced placer deposits, sluicing with jets of water is customary. *See also* Dredging; Hydraulic Mining.

Placoderms. △566.

Placodus. △572.

Placoid Fish, fish, including sharks, rays, and sawfish, with platelike scales that are actually dermal teeth. Placoid scales are the bony part of cartilaginous fish, tip of scale is dentine layered with enamel and lower part is bone anchored to skin. Dermal teeth are modified into large spines in rays and into teeth on snout of the sawfish. △510.

Plages. *See* Flocculi.

Plagioclase, type of feldspar, itself the most abundant group of minerals on Earth. Plagioclases show an oblique cleavage, as opposed to orthoclase or microcline. These feldspars are composed of varying proportions of sodium- and calcium-aluminum silicate.

Plague, an acute infectious disease of man and rodents caused by the bacillus *Pasteurella pestis.* In man it occurs in three forms: bubonic plague, most common and characterized by buboes; pneumonic plague, in which the lungs are infected; and septicemic plague, in which the bloodstream is invaded. Treatment is administration of vaccines, bed rest, fluids, and sulfa drugs.

Plaice, or European flounder, marine flatfish found along the W European coast. An important food fish, its eye side is brown or gray with orange spots. Length: to 4ft (122cm); weight: 26lb (11.8kg). Family Pleuronectidae; species *Pleuronectes platessa.*

Plainfield, city in NE New Jersey, near Watchung Mts 5mi (8km) SSW of Elizabeth; site of Friend's Meeting House (1788), Martine House (1717), and Nathaniel Drake's House (1746). Industries: starch, chemicals, printing, tools, housewares. Founded 1684 by Friends; inc. 1869. Pop. (1970) 46,862.

Plainsong, or **Plain Chant,** religious vocal music sung without accompaniment and with voices in unison, particularly that of the Roman Catholic Church. It includes Gregorian Chant as well as Ambrosian and Roman chants and those of other Mediterranean cultures. △1100.

Plainview, urban area of SE New York, on Long Island, 30mi (48km) E of New York City; residential with industrial parks housing many light industries. Founded as Manetto Hill on land purchased from Indians 1697. Pop. (1970) 32,195.

Planaria, marine and freshwater flatworm identified by triangular head with two light-sensitive eyespots; flat, taillike body; and extendable pharynx for sucking in food. Reproduction is hermaphroditic or by asexual splitting, or regeneration. Length: 1in (2.54cm). Phylum Platyhelminthes; class Turbellaria; species include *Dugesia* and *Polycelis.*

Planck, Max Karl Ernst Ludwig (1858–1947), German theoretical physicist, professor at Kiel and later in Berlin, where he studied the characteristics of the radiation emitted by black bodies. In 1900 he came to the conclusion that the frequency distribution of the radiation could only be accounted for if the radiation was emitted in quanta, rather than continuously. An explanation of radiant heat energy distribution given off from a heated surface was proved by Planck's radiation law (1900). Planck's constant (1900) indicates wave and particle behavior on the atomic scale. His equation, relating the energy of a quantum to the frequency, is the basis of the quantum theory. He was awarded the 1918 Nobel Prize for his work. *See also* Black body; Quantum Theory. △1480, 1526.

Planck's Constant, universal constant (symbol h) of value 6.626×10^{-34} joule second, equal to the energy of a quantum of electromagnetic radiation (photon) divided by the radiation frequency. It appears in formulas describing physical quantities that can only assume certain discrete values. *See also* Quantum Theory.

Plane, flat surface such that the straight line joining any two points on it lies entirely within the surface. Its general equation in three-dimensional Cartesian coordinates takes the form $ax + by + cz + d = 0$ where a,b,c,d are constants.

Plane, Inclined. △1652.

Planer, a machine for cutting metal. △1606.

Planet, a celestial body that revolves in an orbit around the Sun or some other star. The nine planets revolving around the Sun are: Mercury, Venus, Earth, Mars (the terrestrial planets), Jupiter, Saturn, Uranus, Neptune (the giant planets), and Pluto. Between the two groups numerous small bodies, called minor planets or asteroids, are found. △50.

Planetary Nebula, type of celestial object consisting of a shell or ring of highly ionized gas surrounding a very hot central star. Such objects, which superficially resemble planets when viewed through a telescope of low magnification, appear to be stars departing from the red giant stage, which have thrown off their atmospheres (thus producing the gaseous rings) and are evolving into white dwarfs. △106.

Plane Tree, common name for an attractive tree native to Greece and Asia and later introduced into Europe and America. This large tree with widely spreading branches has five-lobed, palmate leaves and tiny unisexual flowers borne in thick groups containing male or female flowers. With its peeling brownish bark, this shade tree resembles the sycamore. Family Platanaceae; species *Platanus orientalis. See also* Sycamore.

Plane Trigonometry, branch of mathematics that deals with the sides and angles of plane triangles and their measurements and relations. *See also* Trigonometry. △1464.

Plankton, drifting mass of plants and animals at the surface of marine and fresh waters. Ranging from tiny algal cells to shrimp, this "meadow of the sea" is an important food source for fish and whales. △624, 626.

Plankton Net. △236.

Plant, living organism, diverse in size, form, activity, and habitat, generally able to manufacture its own food. Over 500,000 plants have been classified. They vary from the short-lived, single-celled bacteria to the slow-growing oaks and redwoods. Sizes vary from a few millimeters to giant forest trees.

Fundamental differences between plants and animals are mode of nutrition, scheme of growth, cell wall composition, and locomotion. Plants depend on inorganic food materials from soil, water, and air to manufacture their own food. Some non-green plants, such as fungi, are parasites, existing on other organisms.

Botantists have named 11 divisions of plants and include 9 small primitive groups under thallophytes. Thallophytes are fungi, bacteria, algae, and lichens. Bryophytes have a more highly developed reproduction system and include mosses and liverworts. Tracheophytes, or vascular plants, have strong roots, a water-conducting system, and green tissue. They include the club mosses, horsetails, ferns, conifers, and flowering plants. △424–56.

Plantain, plant with a rosette of basal leaves and spikes of tiny, greenish flowers that grows in temperate regions. Family Plantaginaceae; genus *Plantago.* Or, tropical banana plant believed native to SE Asia and now cultivated throughout tropics. It has fleshy stems, bright green leaves, and green fruit that is larger and starchier than a banana and eaten cooked. Height: to 33ft (10m). Family Musaceae; species *Musa paradisiaca. See also* Banana.

Plantain Lily. *See* Hosta.

Plantation System, system of slave-labor agriculture used in the South before the Civil War. Large plantations were usually broken up into separate farms, each with an overseer. The principal plantation crops were cotton, rice, tobacco, and sugar cane. Less than one-third of all white southerners were involved with the plantation system. △1276.

Plantation Walking Horse. *See* Tennessee Walking Horse.

Plant Breeding, controlled reproduction of agricultural and horticultural plants by the practical application of genetic theory. Plant breeding has resulted in new varieties characterized by greater productivity, uniformity, adaptability for growth, food value, disease resistance, flower size, and variety of color and form. △366.

Plant Exploration, search for new plant products such as beverages, fibers, lumber, oils, medicines, narcotics, and organic insecticides. In the late 1800s, for example, the insecticide pyrethrum, made from powdered, dried flower heads of chrysanthemums, was found to kill insects without being toxic to warm-blooded animals. △322.

Plant Food, fertilizer or manure containing chemical elements needed to increase fertility of soil or other planting medium. These elements, nitrogen, phosphorus, and potassium, can be supplied by inorganic (mineral, synthetic) or organic (animal, vegetable) fertilizers. These are usually in dry form, or natural, such as animal manure. △316.

Plant Hormone, or phytohormone, organic chemical produced in plant cells and functioning at various sites to affect plant growth, leaf and fruit drop, healing, cambial growth, and possibly flowering. Hormones are transported away from the stem tip. Hormones include abscisin (leaf fall); auxins (growth); cytokinins (leaf and bud growth); gibberellins (growth); florigen (thought to stimulate flowering); and vitamin B_1 (root growth). △430.

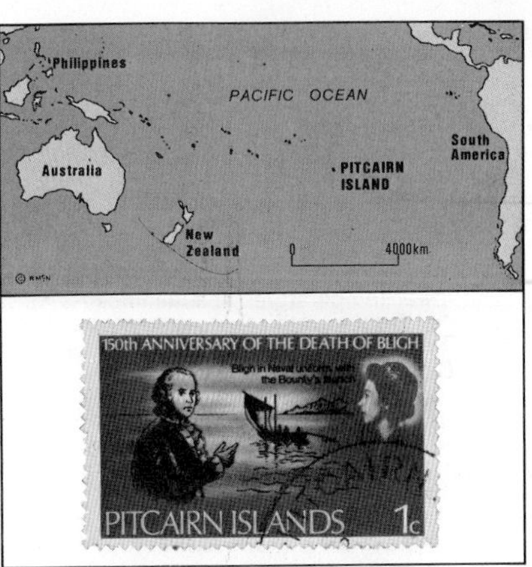
Philippines
PACIFIC OCEAN
South America
Australia
PITCAIRN ISLAND
New Zealand
0
4000km
150th ANNIVERSARY OF THE DEATH OF BLIGH
PITCAIRN ISLANDS
1c

Pitcairn Island

Pitta

Pittsburgh

Max Planck

Plant Louse. *See* Aphid.

Plant Pigment, organic compound present in plant cells and tissues that colors the plant. The most common is green chlorophyll, existing in all higher plants. Carotenoids color plants yellow to tomato red. Located in chloroplasts and chromoplasts, there are more than 60 varieties of these durable pigments. They are a function of photosynthesis and a source of vitamin A. Anthocyanins, responsible for pink, red, blue, and purple, are found in the cell sap. The shorter days and lower temperatures of autumn cause these pigments to combine with other substances and produce the brilliant foliage colors of deciduous trees. *See also* Chlorophyll.

Plant Response, spontaneous or induced reaction of a plant to internal or external stimuli. Spontaneous movements result from internal stimuli, for example, nutation, the circular movement of a plant tip in twining plants. Induced movements, resulting from external stimuli, include tropism and nastic movement that occur as cell turgor changes or growth increases. A tropism is a plant response to stimuli direction and includes geotropism, phototropism, and stereotropism. Nastic movements are responses independent of stimuli direction and include flowers opening or closing and leaves rapidly folding or dropping. Growth responses include photoperiodism, flowering in relation to light intensity, increased growth with higher temperatures, and growth resulting from hormone stimuli. △430.

Plaque, a film of heavy mucus on a tooth that serves as a breeding place for potentially harmful bacteria. It is part of preventive dentistry to remove these deposits by a regimen of hygiene as they are believed to cause pyorrhea. △756.

Plasma, highly ionized state of matter in which substances consist almost entirely of electrons and atomic nuclei. This state, often described as the fourth state of matter, occurs at enormous temperatures, as in the interior of stars and in fusion reactors. *See also* Fusion, Nuclear; Fusion Reactor.

Plasma, Blood, the fluid portion of the blood. It contains an immense number of ions, inorganic and organic molecules such as immunoglobulins, and hormones and their carriers. It will clot upon standing. *See also* Blood. △688.

Plasma Expanders, substances used to temporarily expand the volume of plasma in the body in order to restore blood flow in disorders such as thrombosis or critical blood loss. The substance most often used is a glucose compound called dextran.

Plasmodium, genus of parasitic protozoa that causes malaria. It infects the red blood cells of mammals, birds, and reptiles throughout the world, being transmitted by the bite of a female *Anopheles* mosquito. Four species cause human malaria, passing from mosquito to man as sporozoites in the mosquito's saliva. Once in the red blood cells, they divide, forming up to 24 daughter parasites, then destroy the red blood cells. Entering the plasma, they infect new cells. *See also* Malaria.

Plaster, mixture of slaked lime (calcium hydroxide), sand, and water, often with hair or fibers added as a binder, that is applied wet to interior walls and ceilings to form a smooth hard surface for papering or painting when dry. △1610.

Plaster of Paris, or gypsum cement, powdered form of calcium sulphate hemihydrate obtained by heating gypsum to 262.4°F (128°C). After the addition of water it sets and hardens and is used as a plaster for a wide range of purposes.

Plastic Films. Vinyls, fluoroplastics, and cellulose acetates are films. Vinyl made by a calendering (rolling) process can be sewn as well as heat or electronically sealed. It is used for clothing, shower curtains, in packaging, and as a laminate for paper. Fluoroplastics films can be bonded to metal and are used in printed circuitry, as insulation for flat cable, and for industrial and biological packaging. Cellulose acetate films can be printed and are used in engineering drafting.

Plasticizers. △1612.

Plastic Laminates, several layers of plastic bonded together to produce a rigid, easily machined product. Phenolic resin binders are used to produce high-pressure laminates. These are resistant to humidity and have high mechanical strength. Low-pressure, or contact, laminates, formed by molding reinforcing materials and liquid resins, have great tensile strength and are used in ships, bridges, and auto bodies.

Plastics, synthetic materials composed of organic molecules in predetermined complex combinations. The weight and structure of the molecule determine the physical and chemical properties of a given compound. Plastics are synthesized from such common materials as cellulose from cotton or wood pulp; organic acid from coal tar; casein from skim milk; as well as from petroleum, corn, potatoes, peanuts, and soybeans. The plastics industry began in the 1860s with the development of celluloid by John Wesley Hyatt. Since then many types of plastics have been invented, based on Hermann Staudinger's work on polymerization. △1560, 1618, 1666.

Plastic Surgery, branch of medicine that involves the use of surgical techniques to correct disabling or disfiguring conditions that may be congenital or the result of injury. It usually involves superficial parts of the body. △752, 804.

Plata, Río de la, river in SE South America, formed by the confluence of the Paraná and Uruguay rivers; serves as the major channel into the interior of SE South America; chief ports are Buenos Aires and Montevideo. Discovered 1516 by Juan Diaz de Solis, it was explored 1520 by Ferdinand Magellan, and 1526–30 by Sebastian Cabot. Length: approx. 170mi (274km).

Plataea, ancient city in E central Greece, on Mt Cithaeron; it allied with Athens at Marathon 490 BC; scene of Persian defeat by Greek forces under Pausanias 479 BC, which assured Grecian independence; twice beseiged (429–427, 373 BC) by Thebes and destroyed; rebuilt by Alexander the Great.

Plateau. △260.

Platelet, a light-gray, round or egg-shaped structure found in all mammalian blood. Chemical compounds in platelets, known as factors and cofactors, are essential to the coagulation of the blood. The normal platelet count is 250,000 to 400,000 per cubic millimeter of blood. △688.

Plateresque, ornate architectural style that predominated in Spain between the Gothic and Renaissance styles. The first of two stages lasted from 1480 to 1540. It was used primarily in civic buildings, such as Seville town hall, and was marked by a change from Gothic rib vaulting to round arches and domical vaulting and from flying buttresses to wall buttresses. In churches, such as Granada cathedral, the clerestory was usually no longer used. The second stage of this style lasted from 1540–70. The elements of ornamentation showed the influence of the Italian Renaissance style and tended to be heavy and geometric in design.

Plate Tectonics, a theory proposed in 1960 by H.H. Hess to explain the mechanism of continental drift. Using the evidence of the mid-ocean ridges and deep trenches, he suggested that magma rises by convection from the deep Earth and spreads along the ocean floor and cools. At the same time a heavier layer under the continental crust, the lithosphere, is also being spread apart by the rising magma. The plates of lithosphere push against each other at a rate of more than 2.4in (6cm) per year and one plate is forced to bend down into the deep mantle, or asthenosphere, where it becomes liquid magma again. When one edge of the top crust pushes against another, it wrinkles, forming new mountains like the Andes. △170, 252.

Platform Tennis, a sport played by two sets of partners on a court raised off the ground and enclosed by wire-fence screens. A large-faced, short-handled paddle made of perforated plywood is used along with a sponge rubber ball. The overall dimensions of the court are the same as for a badminton court, and the playing rules are similar to lawn tennis except that only one serve is allowed and the ball may be played off the wire screens. The game originated in Scarsdale, N.Y., in 1928.

Plath, Sylvia (1932–63), US poet, b. Boston. Her intensely personal verse includes *The Colossus and Other Poems* (1960) and *Ariel* (1968). She committed suicide, and the latter volume contains poems written near the end of her life. She also wrote a novel, *The Bell Jar* (1963; under the name Victoria Lucas). She was married to the poet Ted Hughes.

Plating, the electrical, chemical, or mechanical process of applying a metal covering to the surface of an object. When gilding is practiced, base metals are dipped into a chemical salt solution to deposit mercury, then rubbed with gold and mercury amalgam. The mercury is then removed by firing. Mechanical plating involves rolling on gold or silver plate. In electroplating, the layer of metal is deposited by electrolysis.

Platinum, precious metallic element (symbol Pt) of the third transition series, discovered (1735) by Antonio de Ulloa. Chief source is from certain ores of nickel. It is used in jewelry and in resistance wire, thermocouples, electrodes, and other laboratory apparatus. It is chemically unreactive; it does not react with oxygen at normal temperatures nor with common acids. Properties: at. no. 78; at. wt. 195.09; sp gr 21.45; melt. pt. 3,217°F (1,754°C); boil. pt. 6,882°F (3,808°C); most common isotope Pt^{195} (33.8%). *See also* Transition Elements. △1552–54.

Plato (427–347 BC) Greek philosopher. Spending eight years as Socrates' disciple, he founded his Academy of philosophy near Athens, in 387, and taught there until his death. His works are well-preserved, including more than 25 dialogues and some letters. Believing the human mind can attain absolute truth, Plato's is a spiritualistic view of life. His works include *The Republic, Theaetetus, Timaeus, Phaedo,* and *Gorgias.* △852, 858.

Platt Amendment, legislation designed to regulate United States-Cuba relations. Attached to the Army Appropriation Bill (1901), it denied Cuba the right to make treaties with foreign powers other than the United States or to incur public debts. It permitted US intervention to maintain order and provided the United States with a naval base in Cuba. In 1903 the amendment became part of the Cuban-American Treaty, later nullified (1934).

Platte (Little Platte), river in Iowa and Missouri; rises in S Iowa, flows S to the Missouri River in NW Mo. 15mi (24km) NW of Kansas City, Kan. Length: approx. 300mi (483km).

Platte, unnavigable river in central Nebraska; rises at the confluence of the North and South Platte rivers; flows E into the Missouri River just S of Omaha; used for irrigation and hydroelectricity. Length: approx. 310mi (500km).

Platt National Park, park in S Oklahoma. Situated in the Arbuckle Mts, it features numerous cold mineral and freshwater springs including bromide waters. Area: 912acres (369hectares). Est. 1906.

Plattsburgh, city in NE New York, on Lake Champlain; seat of Clinton co; site of State University of New York at Plattsburgh (1889), Clinton Community College (1966), US Air Force Base (1956); scene of naval battle in which British defeated Americans (Oct. 11, 1776), and naval battle of War of 1812 during which Americans defeated British (Sept. 11, 1814). Industries: pulp and paper making, tourism. Settled 1767; inc. 1902. Pop. (1970) 18,715.

Platybelodon. △574.

Platyhelminthes, or flatworms, most primitive phylum of worms, characterized by bilateral symmetry; they have one gut opening, no coelom or blood system, an excretory system of flame cells, and three cell layers. Flatworms have a definite head, central nervous system, and dorsal and ventral surfaces. Reproduction is sexual and asexual. The 15,000 species include flukes, tapeworms, and planaria. △472.

Plautus, comic dramatist of ancient Rome who probably flourished in the late 3rd and early 2nd centuries BC. According to Jerome, Plautus was born at Sarsina in Umbria and died in 200 BC. Cicero dates his death in 184 BC. Perhaps involved in the theater from an early age, he may have been an actor. Aulus Gellius' record of Plautus' life is historically questionable. Manuscripts containing 21 of his plays have survived, including his *Pseudolus, Truculentus,* and *Amphitruo*.

Player, Gary (Jim) (1935–), South African golfer. He won the Masters twice (1961, 1975), the US Open (1965), two PGAs (1962, 1972), and three British Opens (1959, 1968, 1974).

Pleasure Principle, in psychoanalytic theory, idea that the id (biological urges) is satisfied only by bodily pleasures such as food and sex. This idea is often contrasted with the "reality principle," the idea that the ego (conscious thought) must cope with the everyday problems of the real world. How well the individual copes with the demands of the id within the context of reality is one indicator of mental health.

Pleasure Ridge Park, residential community in N central Kentucky. Pop. (1970) 28,566.

Plebeians, or **Plebs,** term for the main body of Roman citizens other than the patricians, or privileged class. They were originally forbidden to hold political or religious office and prohibited from marriage with atricians. By 287 BC they had obtained political quality after a long, fierce struggle. △1014.

lebiscite, from the Latin *plebis citum* (decree of the ommon people), election in which a decision on an sue is made by a simple "yes" or "no" vote. △904.

lecoptera. △492.

léiade, group of seven 16th-century French poets onsard, du Bellay, Baif, Belleau, Jodelle, Tyard, and orat). Under the leadership of Pierre de Ronsard, ey championed the dignity of the French language gainst the academic tradition of Latin and Greek and dvocated linguistic and stylistic reforms. Strict rules ere evolved for literary composition, and the alexan-rine verse form was revived. △1172.

leiades (M45), spectacular open star cluster in the onstellation Taurus, easily visible with the naked eye. he cluster is enveloped in nebulosity, which causes ome distortion of the stellar images as viewed from arth. Brightest star Eta Tauri (Alcyone); distance 500 ght-years. △104, 116, 126.

leistocene Epoch, geological time period begin-ing about 2,000,000 years ago, during which man nd most forms of familiar mammalian life evolved. pisodes of climatic cooling in this epoch led to wide-pread glaciation in the Northern Hemisphere—the e Ages. The present Holocene epoch succeeded ne Pleistocene around 10,000 BC. △648.

lekhanov, Georgi Valentinovich (1857–1918), ussian Marxist and revolutionary leader. At first a opulist, he emigrated to Switzerland in 1880 and ecame converted to Marxism. In 1883 he founded he "Liberation of Labor" group. A major theoretician f the Russian Social Democratic Labor party, orga-ized in 1898, he greatly influenced V. I. Lenin, with hom he worked until he joined the Mensheviks in 903. After the February revolution in 1917 he re-urned to Russia and formed an anti-Bolshevik party, ut died shortly after the October revolution. △1286.

lesiosaur, extinct marine reptile of Jurassic to retaceous times. It had a stout body propelled by owerful paddlelike limbs. Some were long-necked vith small heads; others short-necked with large eads. Length: 15–40ft (4.5–12m). △570, 572.

lessy v. Ferguson (1896), US Supreme Court deci-ion following the Civil Rights Cases of 1883. Plessy eld that a state law requiring separation of races on ublic transportation facilities did not violate the ourteenth Amendment. The court adhered to a doc-rine of "separate but equal" facilities and reasoned hat the 14th Amendment was not intended to abolish ll distinctions based on race. Thus, state-enforced egregation was acceptable until Plessy was over-uled in *Brown* v. *Board of Education of Topeka* in 954. *See also* Brown v. Board of Education of opeka (1954); Civil Rights Cases (1883).

leurisy, painful inflammation of the pleura, a mem-rane lining of the chest cavity, caused by infection in he lung. Treatment is directed toward the cause; pain s controlled with analgesics.

lexiglass. *See* Lucite.

Pliny the Elder (*c.* 23–79), Roman naturalist, full ame Gaius Plinius Secundus. His *Natural History* is n encyclopedic work dealing with the nature of the niverse, anthropology, geography, mineralogy, bot-ny and zoology, medicine, and a history of the fine rts. He died while investigating the eruption of 'esuvius. △1780.

Pliny the Younger (61/62–113), Roman writer and olitical figure, full name Gaius Plinius Caecilius Secundus, the adopted son of Pliny the Elder. He held many important posts in Rome, including consul 100). He died in Pontuo-Bithynia where he was serv-ng as proconsul. His letters, written for publication, re a valuable source for information on contempo-rary Roman life. △1028.

Pliocene Epoch. *See* Tertiary Period.

Pliohippus, pony-sized fossil horse that lived during Pliocene Epoch (12,000,000 years ago). The first one-toed horse, it is the immediate forerunner of *Equus,* modern horse. Side toes were reduced to splints, and teeth were high-crowned for grazing.

Plique à Jour. △1608.

Ploiesti (Ptoiesh), city in SE central Romania, 35mi 56km) N of Bucharest; capital of Prahova co; pros-pered as largest oil-producing center in SE Europe in 19th century. As a result of a cooperation pact Romania signed with Axis powers (1940) supplying Germany with Romanian oil, the city was heavily bombed by Allied powers. Industries: oil refining, petrochemicals. Founded 1596. Pop. 162,937.

Plotinus (205–270), Roman Neo-Platonist philosopher. Greatly influenced by his teacher, Ammonius Saccas, he opened a school in Rome. His theories were basically Platonic with elements of other Greek philosophies. Although he opposed Christianity, his teachings have affected Christian thought. His pupil, Porphyry, compiled the six *Enneads* of Plotinus. *See also* Neo-Platonism.

Plovdiv, city in central Bulgaria, on the Maritsa River, on main route between Europe and Asia Minor; capital of Plovdiv prov. Seized by the Turks in 1364, it remained under Turkish rule for 500 years; center of leading tobacco area; railroad junction. Industries: rice, fruit, wine, tobacco, lead, zinc. Pop. 236,627.

Plover, 38 species of wading shorebirds, many of which migrate long distances over open seas from arctic breeding areas to Southern Hemisphere wintering areas. They have large heads, plump bodies with concealing coloration, and short legs. Speckled, pear-shaped eggs (4) are laid in a depression. Length: 11in (28cm). Family Charadriidae. *See also* Golden Plover. △384.

Plow, agricultural machine used to cut, lift, turn, and partially pulverize soil in preparation for planting. Almost as old as agriculture itself, the plow is one of the most important inventions in farming. Originally single-shared implements drawn by humans, oxen, or horses, modern multiple-shared plows, pulled by tractors, turn over 10-ft (3-m) swaths. *See also* Farm Machinery. △310.

Plum, small fruit tree mostly native to Asia and naturalized in Europe and North America. The Japanese plum *(Prunus salicina)* is native to China; 12 species are native to North America. They have alternate simple leaves, white flowers, and edible, smooth-skinned, oval fruit of purple, red, blue, or green. In the United States plums dried to make prunes are grown mostly on the West Coast. Height: to 30ft (9.1m). Family Rosaceae. △338.

Plume, Solar. △82.

Pluralism, socio-political theory advocating the participation of all groups in a society in the decision-making process. A pluralist society is one made up of a number of different interests whose views, theoretically, are ultimately synthesized into one policy. Pluralism is considered a hallmark of a democratic society. △900.

Plutarch (*c.* 46–120 AD), Greek author, born in Chaeronea. Known as a biographer and Academic philosopher, Plutarch was the last important writer of ancient Greece. Of his many works, approximately one-third survive today. The best known are Plutarch's *Lives,* biographies of soldiers and statesmen. The work presents the lives in pairs, first a Greek, then a Roman, and concludes with a comparison. Plutarch's style is pleasant, though his thoughts are not profound.

Pluto, ninth planet from the Sun, discovered in 1930 by C.W. Tombaugh. Mean distance from the Sun, 3,658,000,000mi (5,900,000,000km); estimated mass, 0.10 times that of Earth; estimated diameter, approx. 3,725mi (5,998km); rotation period, 6.3 days; period of sidereal revolution, 247.7 years; estimated surface temperature, about −382°F (−230° C). *See also* Solar System. △88, 154.

Pluto, Latin name for the Greek god Hades, sovereign of the lower world and lord of the shades of the dead. He was brother of Zeus and husband of Persephone, and of hard and inexorable character who dwelt beneath the secret places of the Earth in a gloomy palace in barren fields. Pluto was considered also to be the giver of wealth in that he possessed all that sprang from the Earth.

Pluton. △176.

Plutonium, radioactive metallic element (symbol Pu) of the actinide group, first made in 1940 by Seaborg, McMillan, Kennedy, and Wahl by deuteron bombardment of uranium. It is found in small amounts in uranium ores. Pu^{239} (half-life 24,360yrs) is made in large quantities in breeder reactors. It is a fissionable material used in nuclear reactors and nuclear weapons. The element is a strong alpha emitter and is absorbed in bone, making it a dangerous radiological hazard. Properties: at. no. 94; sp gr 9.84; melt. pt. 1,186°F (641°C); boil. pt. 6,021°F (3,329°C); most stable iso-

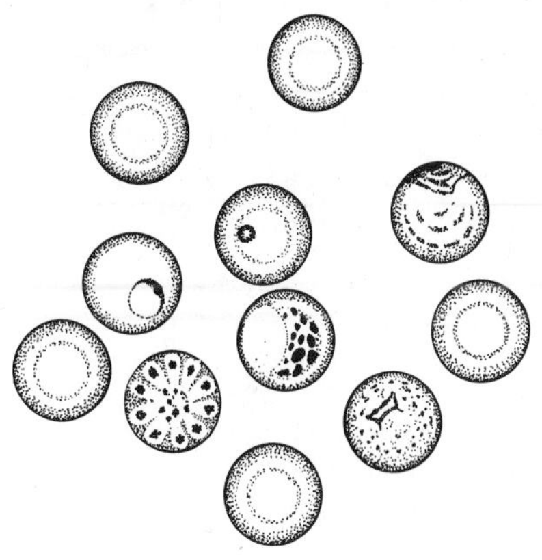

Plasmodium

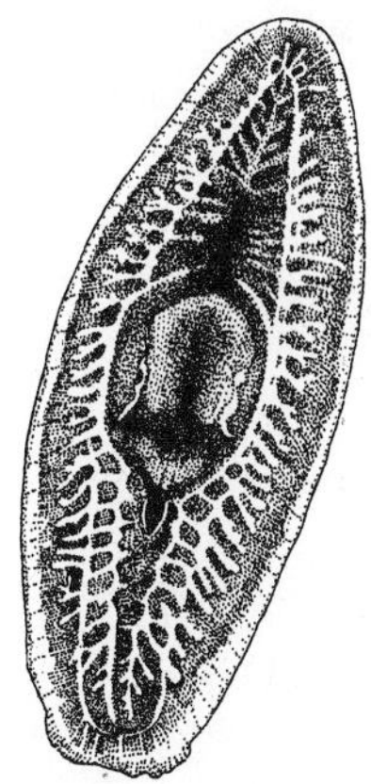

Platyhelminthes

Plovdiv, Bulgaria

Plover

tope Pu^{244} (half-life 8×10^7 yr). *See also* Transuranium elements. △1552, 1554, 1638.

Plymouth, major port in SW England, in Devon, one of the Three Towns with Plymouth (E), Stonehouse (central), and Devonport (W). On the peninsula between Plym and Tamar estuaries, it is England's 2nd-most important naval base. The *Mayflower* set sail for America from here in 1620. Pop. 239,314.

Plymouth, town in SE Massachusetts, on Plymouth Bay, 18mi (29km) SE of Brockton; seat of Plymouth co. In 1620 Pilgrims established the first permanent white settlement in New England here; Mayflower Compact was drawn up to govern colony; site of Plymouth Rock, replica of the original *Mayflower,* 80-ft (24-m) granite monument to National Forefathers (1889), several 17th-century houses, and Cole's Hill and Burial Hill, containing graves of many of the first settlers. Industries: tourism, cranberry packing, fisheries, rope, twine. Pop. (1970) 18,606.

Plymouth Colony, settlement on the coast of Massachusetts (1620). About 100 Pilgrims and other colonists from the *Mayflower* landed near Cape Cod after poor weather diverted the ship from Virginia. Government by majority rule was established by the Mayflower Compact since no royal charter existed: this form lasted until 1636, when a government and series of laws were established by the Great Fundamentals. The hardships of the first winter killed nearly half the settlers, but, under the leadership of Gov. William Bradford and the aid of friendly Indians, the colony grew slowly. Prior to 1623 all property was held in common, but a system of private property proved more acceptable. The colony received a new land patent called the Plymouth Patent (1630) from the Council for New England. It was merged with the Massachusetts Bay Colony and Maine (1691) under royal rule. *See also* Mayflower Compact; Pilgrims; Plymouth Patent. △1216.

Plymouth Patent, land grant obtained by Pilgrims. It was issued in 1621 in their behalf by the Council of New England and was finally received in 1630. The Pilgrims' original patent from the Virginia Company of London was invalid because the *Mayflower* had been diverted from Virginia to Massachusetts due to poor weather. *See also* Council for New England. △1216.

Plymouth Rock Chicken, chicken breed, the most important variety being the White Plymouth Rock. *See also* White Plymouth Rock.

Plywood, a panel made of three or more layers of wood glued together with the grain of plies at right angles to each other. Thin panels are made only of veneer. Thicker panels are comprised of sawed lumber at the center surrounded by veneer. Interior plywood is used in dry locations; exterior plywood employs water-resistant glues.

Plzeň (Pilsen), city in W Czechoslovakia, 52mi (84km) WSW of Prague; famous for its Pilsner beer. Industries: heavy machinery, automobiles, locomotives, armaments, brewing. Founded 1290 by King Wenceslaus II. Pop. 146,000.

Pneumatic Drill. △1486.

Pneumoconiosis, an occupational disease affecting the lungs, caused by inhalation of irritants such as carbon particles inhaled by coal workers.

Pneumonia, an inflammation of the tissue of the lungs as a result of infection, caused by a number of organisms. Mycoplasmal pneumonia is more severe and attacks adults. Symptoms are high fever, chest pain, coughing, and bloody sputum. Treatment is with antibiotics. △714.

PNS. *See* Peripheral Nervous System.

Po, longest river in Italy; rises in Cottian Alps of NW Italy, flows generally E through the Piedmonte; empties into the Adriatic through several mouths. Po valley is important industrial and agricultural region; the river is a major source of irrigation; navigable for 345mi (555km) to Pavia. Length: 405mi (652km).

Pocahontas (1595–1617), daughter of Indian chief Powhatan and wife of Jamestown settler John Rolfe. Famous for saving life of Jamestown leader John Smith, she converted to Christianity before her marriage to Rolfe. She bore one son in England, Thomas Rolfe. *See also* Powhatan; Rolfe, John; Smith, John. △1216.

Pocatello, city in SE Idaho; seat of Bannock co; site of Idaho State University (1901); Fort Hall Indian Reservation is nearby. Industries: chemicals, flour, fertilizer, dairy products, railroad shops. Settled 1882; inc. as village 1889, as city 1892. Pop. (1970) 40,036.

Pochard, diving duck that lives in fresh water. Males typically pursue females with mock brutality. Included are the red-crested pochard *(Netta rufina)* of Europe and the prized sporting North American canvasback. *See also* Canvasback Duck; Duck.

Pocket Billards. *See* Billiards.

Pocket Gopher, any of about 30 species of thickset rodents found in North and Central America. Short-tailed, they have external fur-lined cheek pouches. They make extensive burrows, eating underground portions of plants. Length: 5–18in (13–45cm). Family Geomyidae. *See also* Gopher.

Pocono Mountains, range of the Appalachian system in NE Pennsylvania reaching to Delaware River on New York and New Jersey lines. A year-round vacation area. Height: approx. 2,000 ft (610m).

Podgorny, Nikolai (1903–), Soviet chief of state. A member of the Communist party from 1930 and the Central Committee from 1960, he became Soviet president in 1965. He was a major figure in the "collective leadership" following the fall of Khrushchev and favored "liberalization." △1342.

Podzol, light-colored, infertile soil, poor in lime and iron, found in cool, humid regions, such as coniferous forests. The name comes from the Russian world for "ash soil." *See also* Pedalfer; Pedocal; Soil. △312.

Poe, Edgar Allan (1809–49), US poet and short-story writer, b. Boston. Orphaned in 1811, he was raised in Richmond, Va., by a wealthy merchant, John Allan. He briefly attended the University of Virginia (1826), enlisted in the army, was appointed to West Point, and then, after a final breach with Allan, went to New York City, where a volume of poetry, his third, was published (1831). To support himself he began to write short stories and held several editorial jobs. During 1835–37 he edited the *Southern Literary Messenger* in Richmond, but he began drinking and lost the job. Subsequently, he was editor of *Burton's Gentleman's Magazine* (1839–40) and *Graham's Magazine* (1841–42) in Philadelphia and of the *Evening Mirror* and *Broadway Journal* (1845–46) in New York. He gained repute for his literary criticism, as well as for his numerous short stories. His stories include "The Fall of the House of Usher" (1839), "The Murders in the Rue Morgue" (1841), "The Gold Bug" (1843), "The Tell-Tale Heart" (1843), "The Pit and the Pendulum" (1843), and "The Purloined Letter" (1844), tales of mystery and horror. Although plagued by alcoholism before his death, he produced his finest verse, including "The Raven" (1845), "To Helen" (1848), and "Annabel Lee" (1849). He is regarded as the creator of the modern detective story and greatly influenced other writers. △1374.

Poetry, art form using words for sound and rhythm as well as for speech communication so as to express a poet's feelings or imagination. Good poetry is characterized by succinct, allusive, often figurative language and by pleasing rhythm, often enhanced by metrical patterns and rhyme. The earliest of the literary arts, poetry probably evolved from emotional expressions connected with song and dance. Poetry can be classified by its style—lyric, narrative, dramatic, etc—by its form—sonnet, epic, ballad, ode, free verse, etc—by historic period—Greek, Latin, medieval, Renaissance, Romantic, Victorian, etc. *See also* Versification. △1240, 1420.

Poikilothermal Animal, cold-blooded organism, incapable of regulating its body temperature independently of environmental temperature. △522.

Poincaré, Jules Henri (1854–1912), French mathematician. Appointed professor at the University of Paris he worked on celestial mechanics, winning an award from the king of Sweden for his contribution to the three-body problem. He later worked on the theory of electromagnetic waves and was one of the first to grasp the significance of Einstein's theory of relativity.

Poincaré, Raymond (1860–1934), French statesman; prime minister in 1912, 1922–24, and 1926–29; and president of the republic from 1913–1920. He struggled, through skillful diplomatic peace-making and strengthening of alliances, to prevent World War I, and proved a selfless and determined leader in the ensuing conflict. After the war he helped settle the problem of German reparation and managed to stabilize France politically and financially.

Poinciana, evergreen trees native to E Africa ar Madagascar. They have feathery, oblong leaves ar red, orange, or yellow flowers. *Poinciana regia* ha orchidlike yellow-striped, scarlet flowers. Height: 40ft (12m). Family Leguminoseae.

Poinsettia, showy houseplant native to Mexico wit tapering leaves and tiny yellow flowers centered leaflike red, white, or pink bracts. It is a favorite Chris mas plant. Care: bright light, soil (equal parts loan peat moss, sand) kept dry between waterings. Propa gation is by tip cuttings. Height: 2ft (61cm). Fami Euphorbiaceae; species *Euphorbia pulcherrima.*

Pointer, type of sporting dog used to find birds, poir accurately, and hold until the hunter flushes an shoots. It then retrieves on command. The idea pointer stands on game with high head and tail and steady on shot and when birds take flight. Pointin breeds include the pointer, setter, Brittany spanie Weimaraner, Vizsla, and wirehaired pointing griffor

Pointer, gun dog (sporting group) developed abou 1650 in England, Spain, and Portugal, and the firs breed to stand game. The pointer's wide head has substantial muzzle. Hanging ears are set at eye leve A solid, strong body is set on muscular, powerful legs and the tail tapers to a fine point and is carrie straight. Colored liver, lemon, black, or orange com bined with white, the coat is short, dense, and smooth Average size: 25–28in (63.5–71cm) high at shoulde 55–75lb (25–34kg). *See also* Sporting Dog.

Point Four Program, plan to share US scientific an technological knowledge with developing nations. was first proposed by President Truman in the fourt section of his 1949 inaugural address, whence cam the name. The plan was to be funded by the Unite States, the United Nations, and the recipient coun tries.

Pointillism, a branch of Impressionist painting, als called Pointillisme, Divisionism, or Neo-impression ism. Color is applied in carefully spaced detache specks which merge in the beholder's eye and pro duce intermediary tints more luminous than those ob tainable from premixed pigments. Forms are discerr ible only from a distance. Its inventor and chie exponent was French painter Georges Seurat (1859 91); his masterpiece was "Sunday Afternoon on the Grande-Jatte." Paul Signac (1863–1935), anothe leading Pointillist, originated its color system. △ 1292.

Poisoning, the adverse effects of substances, eithe natural or synthetic, introduced into the body or pro duced as side-products of the organism itself. Phar maceuticals can have poisonous side-effects. Indus trial and pesticidal products include highly toxi chemicals. Environmental poison hazards exist in air water, and food. Bacterial, plant, and animal toxin comprise some of the most lethal substances known Levels of sensitivity and treatments vary, dependin on whether acute or chronic poisoning is involved. △ 712, 1560.

Poison Ivy, Poison Oak, and **Poison Sumac,** sev eral plants that cause a severe, itchy rash on contact all members of the sumac family. Poison ivy *(Rhu radicans)* is a North American creeping shrub, iden tified by its toothed leaves of three leaflets. It ha greenish flowers and white berries. Poison oak *(Rhu diversiloba),* a climbing shrub of NW North Americ also has toothed, three-part leaves and whitish fruit Poison sumac *(Rhus vermix)* is a shrub native to E North America. It has long, featherlike leaves an whitish fruit and grows to 20ft (6m).

Poitier, Sidney (1927–), US actor, b. Miami, Fla The first black to win an Academy Award (for *Lilies o the Field,* 1964), he also starred in *The Blackboar Jungle* (1956), among many other films.

Poitiers, city in W central France, 100mi (161km ESE of Nantes; capital of Vienne dept. The old Gallic settlement of Limonum, it was captured by Romans and made part of Aquitania 56 BC; scene of Charles Martel's defeat of invading Saracens 732; site o University (founded 1432 by Charles VII), Romar amphitheaters and baths. Industries: farming trading, wheat, wine, livestock. Pop. 70,681. △1066 1096.

Poitou, region and former province in W France; now contains depts. of Vienne, Deux-Sèvres, and Vendée bounded by Brittany (NW), Anjou and Samurois (N) Touraine (NE), Marche (E), Limousin (SE), Angoumois and Aunis (S), Atlantic Ocean (W); capital was Poitiers Part of duchy of Aquitania, it was taken by Englanc and held 1152–1204, 1356–69; made part of French rown lands 1416; it was a French province until 790, when France was broken up into present de- artments. A level area between two uplands, chief ndustries are cattle, wheat, and dairying.

oker, one of the most popular card games, played vith a standard deck. There are many variations of the ame, using two or more players. The variations nostly played are five- and seven-card stud and draw. n the five-card game, each player receives one card ace down and the others, one at a time, face up. After each card is dealt, bets are made. In seven-card, the rst, second, and seventh are dealt face down and the thers face up. Draw consists of each player getting ve concealed cards, three of which may be ex- hanged for new cards after the initial bets have been nade. In all forms of poker, except when wild cards re employed, the order of ranking is as follows: traight or royal flush (a five-card sequence in one suit —ace, king, queen, jack, ten), four of a kind, full house three of a kind plus a pair), flush (five of one suit), traight (a five-card sequence regardless of suit), three f a kind, two pairs, one pair, highest card.

okeweed, any of about 150 species of plants of the amily Phytolaccaceae, most of which are native to ropical America. Included are herbs, shrubs, trees, nd vines, all with toothed, alternate leaves, stalked lusters of petalless flowers, and either dry or fleshy ruit. The most common species, *Phytolacca mericana,* is a weed with white flowers, reddish ber- ies and red-veined leaves. Its poisonous root resem- les a horseradish. It is found in wet or sandy parts of North America. The berries are used to color wine, andy, and cloth.

Poland (Polska), independent communist nation in N central Europe. The state has moderated its posi- ion to cope with workers' grievances concerning vages, housing, and food supplies.

Land and economy. Located in NE Europe, Po- and is bounded N by the Baltic Sea, S by Carpathian Mts and Czechoslovakia, W by East Germany, and E by the USSR. With the exception of the S ranges, it is mainly lowlands with a continental climate. Over 20% of the labor force is engaged in agriculture, and Po- and is a leader in growing rye, oats, potatoes, and sugar beets. Its generally poor soil makes food im- ports necessary. Private farmers cultivate nearly 80% of the land; state farms make up the remainder. Since WWII the industrial base has been expanded and now employs 60% of the work force. Poland is a major coal producer and has begun to develop artificial fer- tilizers and petrochemicals.

People. Since WWII, 96% of the population has been ethnically Polish. Before the war, the 35,000,- 000 people occupied 150,000sq mi (388,500sq km) and included Ukrainians, Germans, Jews, and Belorussians. About half the pre-war area was an- nexed to the USSR, and the minorities either fled or were killed. The Jews were exterminated during the 1943–44 Nazi occupation. More than 90% of the Poles are Roman Catholic. Education is free and com- pulsory. Literacy is about 98%.

Government. A 1952 constitution set up an elected parliament which, in turn, elects a Council of State and Council of Ministers. The Polish communist party decrees policy.

History. The shaping of the modern Polish state began in the 9th and 10th centuries as the Piast dy- nasty gained power and introduced Christianity. United to Lithuania by marriage in 1386 and formally in 1569, Poland was one of Europe's most powerful medieval states. After a golden age in the 16th cen- tury, Poland was weakened by independent nobles, attacks by the Turks, and encroachment by its neigh- bors. Poland disappeared through three partitions (1772,1793,1795) that divided its lands among Prussia, Russia, and Austria. During WWI, it was in- vaded by German armies, declared its independence in 1918, and was recognized by the 1919 Treaty of Versailles. Its coalition governments were patterned on the French, with ultra-conservative, nationalistic, and army regimes dominant. In a brief 1939 coalition of Germany and Russia, Poland was invaded and di- vided and remained under foreign domination until the end of WWII. The United States recognized the Polish government-in-exile; however, the Soviets backed a left-wing rival group. The communists won a 1947 election, conducted without supervision and criticized by noncommunist powers. Industry was na- tionalized, estates abolished, schools secularized, and some churchmen jailed. In 1956, Poland moved to a more moderate brand of communism. Many collec- tive farms were abolished, more emphasis was placed on housing and consumer goods. Better relations with the West were symbolized by the ratification (1972) of a treaty with West Germany establishing diplomatic relations and recognizing the Oder-Neisse Line as Po- land's W frontier.

PROFILE

Official name: Polish People's Republic
Area: 120,724sq mi (311,380sq km)
Population: 33,800,000
Density: 280per sq mi (108per sq km)
Chief cities: Warsaw (capital); Lódž; Kraców
Government: Communist
Religion: Roman Catholic
Language: Polish
Monetary unit: Zloty
Gross national product: $60,800,000,000
Industries: petroleum products, transport equipment, chemicals, machinery, motor vehicles, aircraft, aluminum
Agriculture: rye, oats, potatoes, sugar beets, wheat, tobacco, cattle, hogs, sheep, barley, flax
Minerals: coal, zinc, sulphur, salt, oil, natural gas
Trading partners: USSR, E Europe

Poland, Partitions of, divisions of Poland (1772, 1793, 1795) that led to the elimination of the state in the 18th century. The first partition (1772) was proposed by Russia and agreed to by Austria and Prussia. Polish territory was reduced by one-fourth. Poland lost all of its part of Prussia except Danzig and Toruń(to Prussia); Red Russia, Galicia, and western Poldolia and part of Krakó W (to Austria); and White Russia and everything east of the Dvina and Dnepr rivers (to Russia). Consent from the Sejm in 1773 was obtained by bribery. The second partition in 1793 reduced Poland's size by another two-thirds. Danzig and Toruń as well as Great Poland went to Prussia; Russia took most of Lithuania and Western Ukraine. What remained became a Russian puppet state. The third partition in 1795 eliminated Poland as Austria, Prussia, and Russia shared the spoils.

Poland China Swine, a US breed of pigs that originated in 1860 in Ohio from a number of different local breeds improved by the importation of Chinese stock. They are large, compact, white-marked black swine. △376.

Polar Bear, large white bear that lives on Arctic coasts and ice floes. They spend most of their time at sea on drifting ice floes, often swimming for many miles. On land, they can briefly outrun a reindeer. Only pregnant females seem to hibernate during winter. Polar bears prey chiefly on seals and fish. Their chief enemies are Eskimo hunters. Length: 7.5ft (2.3m); weight: to 900lb (405kg). Species *Thalarctos maritimus. See also* Bear. △610.

Polar Exploration, efforts to discover and learn about the Arctic and Antarctic regions of the Earth. Early exploration was stimulated by search for the Northwest Passage. The North Pole was reached (1909) by Admiral Robert Peary. Airplanes and submarines have allowed systematic exploration of the Arctic ice cap. Whalers and sealers touched upon Antarctica, but permanent bases were established only after World War II. Internationalization of the continent was set forth in a treaty in 1959.

Polaris, or Alpha Ursae Minoris, brightest star in the constellation Ursa Minor, and also the star that is currently marking the Earth's north celestial pole. Located at the end of the Little Dipper's handle, Polaris is a triple star system; the main component, a classical Cepheid variable, is associated with a faint companion, and is itself a spectroscopic binary. Characteristics: apparent mag. +2.0; absolute mag. −4.5 (main component); spectral type F8 (main component); distance 650 light-years. △130.

Polarization of Light, suppression of certain directions of vibration of the electric and magnetic fields of a light wave so that the wave form is no longer symmetrical about the direction of propagation. In plane-polarized light the electric vibrations are confined to one direction only, the magnetic vibrations occurring at right angles. Plane-polarized light can be produced by reflection, as from a sheet of glass or a water surface, or by passing light through certain crystals, such as quartz, tourmaline, or calcite. △1520.

Polaroid Camera. △1784.

Polar Solution, solution in which the solvent molecules have substantial dipole moments, such as water. Hydrogen bonding and solvent-solute complexes form, encouraging the association of solvent and solute molecules in preferred orientations in solution. *See also* Aqueous Solution.

Polar Wander, Magnetic, the fluctuation of the latitude and longitude of the magnetic poles in a regular pattern (diurnal change) or erratically during magnetic storms and disturbance. The latter changes are

Edgar Allan Poe

Poinsettia

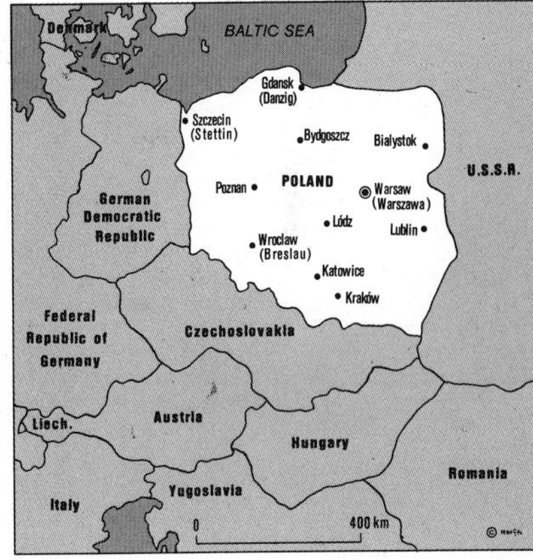
Denmark
BALTIC SEA
Gdansk (Danzig)
Szczecin (Stettin)
Bydgoszcz
Bialystok
U.S.S.R.
German Democratic Republic
Poznan
POLAND
Warsaw (Warszawa)
Lódz
Lublin
Wroclaw (Breslau)
Katowice
Kraków
Federal Republic of Germany
Czechoslovakia
Austria
Liech.
Hungary
Italy
Yugoslavia
Romania
0
400 km
Poland

Polar bear

temporary. *See also* Magnetic Poles; Magnetic Storm. △168, 172.

Polar Wander, Apparent, the change in position of the Earth's rotational and magnetic poles. Magnetized magma shows that the magnetic poles have reversed numerous times in recent geologic ages and tropical fossils found in Antarctica indicate the movement of the rotational poles. But whether this movement reflects polar wandering or continental drift remains a question.

Pole, de la, English noble family descended from **Sir William de la Pole** (died 1366), a rich Hull merchant and baron of the exchequer (1339). His son **Michael** (1330–89), created 1st earl of Suffolk (1385), was chancellor to Richard II but died in exile. Michael's grandson **William** (1396–1450), created duke of Suffolk (1447), was also exiled, after faithfully serving Henry VI. William's son **John** (1442–91) married Elizabeth, sister to Edward IV, and their sons **John** (1464–87), **Edmund** (1472–1513), and **Richard** (died 1525) unsuccessfully claimed the English throne. The line ended with Richard's death at the Battle of Pavia.

Pole, Reginald (1500–58), English Roman Catholic churchman. He opposed King Henry VIII's plan to divorce Catherine of Aragon and wrote a treatise condemning Henry's policy of rejecting the authority of the pope. Pope Paul III made Pole a cardinal. During the reign of Queen Mary, a Catholic, Pole was made archbishop of Canterbury to succeed Thomas Cranmer.

Polecat, small, carnivorous, nocturnal mammal native to wooded areas of Eurasia and N Africa. It has a slender body, long bushy tail, anal scent glands, and brown to black fur commercially known as fitch. Polecats eat small animals, birds, and eggs. American skunks are sometimes called polecats. Length: 18in (45.7cm). Family Mustelidae; species *Mustela putorius*. *See also* Ferret; Weasel.

Poles, Celestial. △130.

Poles, Magnetic. *See* Magnetic Poles.

Polignac, Auguste-Jules-Armand-Marie, Prince de (1780–1847), French statesman. An émigré during the French Revolution, he was later imprisoned by Napoleon I for royalist plots. He served as ambassador to England (1823–29) under Louis XVIII and Charles X. As prime minister and minister of foreign affairs (1829–30), his extreme royalist and clerical policies inspired the July Revolution of 1830. Imprisoned (1830) and later banished (1836), he spent his remaining years in England.

Polio, or infantile paralysis, viral disease of the central nervous system. It frequently attacks young children, although adults are also afflicted. Symptoms vary from mild fever, headache, and nausea to paralysis. Treatment is symptomatic: use of moist heat with physical therapy is effective in stimulating muscles; antibiotics and sulfa help to control secondary infections; a mechanical apparatus called an "iron lung" is used when nerve cells in respiratory centers are destroyed. Vaccines are now available to provide protection against the polio virus. △722.

Polish, the national language of Poland, spoken by virtually all of the country's 34,000,000 people. It is one of the Slavic languages and thus part of the Indo-European family. Polish is written in the Roman (Latin) alphabet, but with a large number of diacritical marks to represent the various Slavic vowels and consonants.

Polish Corridor, established in 1919 by the Treaty of Versailles, a narrow belt of land along the Vistula River to allow Poland access to the Baltic Sea. The city of Danzig was to be a free city, linked to Poland. This settlement was the source of much dispute with Germany. △1334.

Politburo (political bureau), ruling body of the Soviet Communist party and generally, of other Communist parties. Formerly called the presidium, it consists of 11–12 full members and 6–9 alternates, chosen by the party's central committee. In theory, the governmental and party structures are separate entities. In practice, they are so interrelated because of overlapping membership that the politburo virtually runs the country. *See also* Communist Party of the Soviet Union.

Political Party, group organized for the purpose of electing candidates to office and promoting a particular set of political principles. The British two-party system was used as a model for the United States, despite the admonition against parties, or "factions," in the *Federalist Papers* (1789). A two- or multi-party system, in which the party or parties in power represent a majority of plurality of voters, is a feature of democratic societies. △902, 904.

Political Science, study of governments. The study includes analysis of governments at the state and local as well as the national and international levels. In addition to the structure and functions of governments, political science also looks at the relationship of citizens with a government. △898–906.

Politics. △900.

Polk, James Knox (1795–1849), 11th president of the United States (1845–49), b. Mecklenburg co, N.C. As a child he moved to Tennessee with his family. He graduated (1818) from the University of North Carolina and began (1820) to practice law in Columbia, Tenn. In 1824 he married Sarah Childress.

Polk was an ardent Jacksonian Democrat. He entered the US House of Representatives in 1825 and was House leader while Andrew Jackson was president and speaker under President Van Buren. He was governor of Tennessee for one term, and in 1844 he was the compromise candidate of the Democrats for president. He defeated the Whig candidate, Henry Clay, in a close election. Polk's one-term presidency was remarkably productive. He reduced the tariff, restored the Independent Treasury System, settled the Oregon boundary dispute with Great Britain, and admitted Texas and California as states. Relations with Mexico over Texas resulted in the Mexican War. Although the war was unpopular in the North, it was conducted with dispatch and efficiency; its successful completion secured the entire Southwest for the United States. Polk's poor health prevented his running for a second term.

Career: Tennessee legislature, 1823–25; US House of Representatives, 1825–39; governor of Tennessee, 1839–41; president, 1845–49. *See also* Mexican War.

Polk, Leonidas Lafayette (1806–64), US military officer and clergyman, b. Raleigh, N.C. A cousin of Pres. James K. Polk, he graduated from West Point (1827) and was ordained an Episcopal minister (1831). He was made missionary bishop of the Southwest (1838) and became interested in educating slaves. Later, he helped found at Sewanee, Tennessee, the University of the South (1860). He served as a Confederate major general in the Civil War, fighting at Shiloh, Corinth, and against Sherman in Georgia. He was mortally wounded at Pine Mountain.

Polk Doctrine (1848), elaboration of Monroe Doctrine by Pres. James K. Polk. In his first annual message to Congress, he asserted that "people on this continent have the right to decide their own destiny," signaling a halt to European interference and colonization in North America and approving the concept of manifest destiny.

Pollack, or **Pollock,** also coalfish, marine food fish of the cod group found in large schools on both sides of the North Atlantic. Colored green with yellow or gray, it has a jutting lower jaw. Length: to 3.5ft (106.7cm); weight: 35lb (15.9kg). Family Gadidae, species include *Pollachius pollachius* and *Pollachius virens*. △386.

Pollaiuolo, Antonio del (*c.*1429–1498), Italian painter, sculptor, engraver, and goldsmith. His work is similiar in style to that of his brother Piero, making it difficult to distinguish between the two. One of the best known artists in Florence, he was influential in promoting vitality and motion in Florentine art. His works include three compositions on the "Labors of Hercules" (*c.*1460) and "Martyrdom of St Sebastian" (1475). △1138.

Pollen, yellow, powderlike male sex cells of a plant. Pollen grains are produced in the anther chambers on the stamen and have thick walls with a pattern of spines, plates, or ridges, according to species. These markings are the basis of pollen analysis (palynology) used to identify fossil plants and sediments. △424.

Pollination, transfer of pollen from the stamen to the stigma on a flower. Self-pollination occurs on one flower and cross-pollination between two flowers. Cross-pollination is more common and results in diverse genetic combinations and greater plant vigor. Pollination occurs mainly by wind (anemophily) and insects (entomophily). Wind-pollinated flowers are usually small and clustered with a large quantity of small, light, dry pollen grains. Insect-pollinated flowers are brightly colored, strongly scented, contain nectar, and produce heavy, sticky pollen. These flowers are incapable of self-pollination. △324, 456.

Pollock, Jackson (Paul Jackson) (1912–56), U painter, b. Cody, Wyo. His work was influential in mak ing the United States a force in international art. On of the most important members of the Abstract Ex pressionist movement, he is one of the most impo tant 20th-century artists. His early works includ "Male and Female" (1942). He introduced his "drip ping" technique in the 1940s and '50s in a numbe of masterpieces: "Cathedral" (1947), "Number I (1948), and "Lavender Mist" (1950). His later work returned to earlier circular forms. △1320, 1372.

Poll Tax, practice of requiring voters to pay a tax t vote. In the past, the practice was used in the Sout to prohibit blacks from voting. It was declared uncon stitutional in national elections in 1964 and in stat elections in 1966.

Pollution. *See* Air Pollution; Waste Disposal, Nu clear; Water Pollution. △292–98.

Pollux, in Greek mythology, son of Zeus and Leda brother of Helen and twin brother of Castor, whose father was Tyndareus, king of Sparta. The twins were inseparable adventurers. They fought the boar on the Calydonian hunt and rescued Helen from her kidnap per, Theseus. When Castor was slain in a battle ove possession of a herd of oxen, the inconsolable Pollux offered his life instead. Zeus rewarded him by permit ting each of the twins alternate days on Earth and ir the underworld.

Pollux, or **Beta Geminorum,** the brightest star ir the constellation Gemini; a red giant. Characteristics apparent mag. 1.15; absolute mag. 0.7; spectral type KO; distance 35 light-years.

Polo, Marco (*c.*1254–1324), first European travele to cross the length of Asia. As a boy he went with his father, Nicolo, and uncle, Maffeo, on a trading mission (1275) that took them to Kublai Khan, Mongol ruler of China. Returning to Venice from the Chinese coast in 1295, Polo became involved in a war with Genoa and was taken prisoner, during which time he narrated an account of his travels. He was released in 1299 after less than a year in prison. He died in Venice. △1110.

Polo, game played on horseback by two teams of four persons each on an outdoor field. The game is also played indoors by two teams of three persons each. A match consists of six or eight periods (chukkers) that are 7.5 minutes long with a 3-minute time-out between periods to change horses. The outdoor field is 200 by 300 yards (182 by 273m) with 2 goal posts 8 feet (2.4m) wide and about 10 feet (3m) high. Players wear a protective helmet and use a flexible-stemmed mallet 48 to 52 inches (122–132cm) in length. The ball used is made of rubber and inflated, weighing 6–6.5 ounces (170–184 grams). No substitutions are allowed except for injury, and penalties (carrying the ball, dangerous riding, or illegal use of the mallet), which result in automatic goals, free hits, and disqualification, are meted out by an umpire, also on horseback. Play begins by the umpire throwing the ball in a marked-off center court between the two lines of opposing players (this same procedure occurs after every goal). Players are ranked by handicap (descending from 10), based upon the goals they are expected to score in a game.

History. Polo is considered a rich man's sport. The game is believed to have originated in Persia. It then spread to Turkey, India, Tibet, China, and Japan. It was revived in India in the 19th century, where it became popular with British army officers. After being introduced in England in 1869, it was imported to the United States by James Gordon Bennett, a US newspaper publisher. Polo is now played in colleges, as well as on an international basis. Matches for US teams are sanctioned by the US Polo Association.

Polonium, rare radioactive metallic element (symbol Po) of group VIA of the periodic table, discovered in 1898 by Mme. Curie. It is found in trace amounts in uranium ores and may also be synthesized. Properties: at. no. 84; sp gr 9.40; melt. pt. 489°F (254°C); boil. pt. 1,764°F (962°C); most stable isotope Po^{209} (half-life 103yrs). △1554.

Poltava, city in Ukrainian SSR, USSR, on the Vorskla River, 180mi (290km) ESE of Kiev; capital of Poltava oblast. It was ceded by Lithuania to the Tartars in 1430; it was a 17th-century Cossack stronghold. On July 8, 1709, the Russians, under Peter the Great, defeated the Swedes, under Charles XII, marking Russia's emergence as a major European power; it was occupied by Germans 1941–43; site of teachers' and agricultural colleges, regional historical museum, Shevchenko monument. Industries: sugar, wheat, bacon packing, flour milling, sunflower oil extraction, bakery products, machinery works, leather goods, canned foods, textiles, railroad shops. Pop. 220,000.

Polyandry, conjugal situation involving one woman who has marital relations with several men. The men in question are frequently brothers (adelphic, or fraternal, polyandry). *See also* Polygamy.

Polybius (*c.* 200–*c.* 120 BC), Greek historian and politician, b. Megalopolis. A leader in the Achaean League, he was deported to Rome (167) where he obtained the patronage of Paullus and Scipio. He served as Roman ambassador to Spain, Achaea, and Africa and wrote his universal history (40 vols. of which only the first five are wholly extant) describing the rise of Rome in the Mediterranean world from 220 to 146 BC. A work of detailed scholarship, it includes didactic essays on the lessons of history.

Polychlorinated Biphenyl (PCB), several stable mixtures—liquid, resinous, or crystalline—of organic compounds made via the reaction of chlorine with biphenyl. These are used as lubricants, heat-transfer fluids, and fluids in transformers. They are also used to impregnate condensers and capacitators and to give flexibility to protective coatings for wood, concrete, and metal. PCBs are toxic, and their resistance to decomposition in streams and soils poses a threat to wildlife.

Polycythemia, any condition characterized by an abnormal increase of red blood cells, resulting in a danger of clot formation in the circulatory system. Symptoms are headache, dizziness, an enlarged spleen, and reddening of the face.

Polyester, one of a class of organic substances composed of large molecules arranged in a chain or a network and formed from many smaller molecules through the establishment of ester linkages. They are usually prepared from equal amounts of glycols and dibasic acids. Dacron, Fortrel, and Mylar are products made from the long-chain polyester composed of ethylene glycol and terephthalic acid. Polyester fibers are highly elastic and low in moisture absorption. They are resistant to chemicals and may be washed in alkaline solutions or dry-cleaned. They are made into woven and knitted fabrics used in apparel, rugs, draperies, bed linens, ropes, conveyor belts, and tire cords. △1618, 1620, 1644.

Polyethylene, a polymer of ethylene, a partially crystalline lightweight thermoplastic, with high resistance to chemicals, low moisture absorption, and good insulating properties. Polyethylenes vary from soft to hard and from flexible to rigid, depending on manufacturing conditions and the type of catalyst used. Used mainly in packaging, pipes, molded products, and electrical insulation. △1560, 1618, 1644.

Polygamy, conjugal union where more than one spouse is permitted. It is used only to describe those situations where these unions are legal and more often denotes polygyny (several wives) than polyandry (several husbands). *See also* Polyandry. △794.

Polygon, plane geometric figure having three or more sides intersecting at three or more points (vertices). They are named according to the number of sides or vertices: triangle (three-sided), quadrilateral (four-sided), hexagon (six-sided). A regular polygon is equilateral and equiangular. △1466.

Polygraph. *See* Lie Detector. △918.

Polyhedron. △1466.

Polymer, substance formed by the union of from two to several thousand simple molecules (monomers) to form a large molecular structure. Polymers are formed in three ways: addition, as in the formation of polyethylene from ethylene (C_2H_4); condensation (the elimination of a water molecule between monomer units) as in the formation of phenol-formaldehyde resins; or by copolymerization (the union of two or more different monomers), as in copolymers of polyvinyl acetate. Some polymers, such as cellulose, occur in nature, others form the basis of the plastics and synthetic resin industry. △1506, 1570, 1574.

Polymerization, chemical combination of several molecules to form straight-chain and/or cross-linked giant molecules called polymers. Reaction can proceed either by simple addition, such as the polymerization of styrene, or by the elimination of a small molecule such as H_2O, as in terylene manufacture from phthalic acid and ethylene glycol. Nature synthesizes natural polymers, such as proteins and nucleic acids, by the latter mechanism. △1506.

Polymorphism, any variation among members of a biological species. Such difference in structure or function may be genetically determined or due to differing environments. The most common variations involve color and body proportions, blood groups and other chemical factors, and behavior. Polymorphism is common in many plant and animal species and is frequently found to be of adaptive advantage.

Polynesia, E subdivision of Oceania and general term for islands in the central Pacific Ocean; Micronesia and Melanesia lie to W; includes Hawaiian Islands, Phoenix Islands, Tokelau Islands, Samoa group, Cook Islands, French Polynesia as well as many other groups; islands are chiefly of coral or volcanic formation; inhabitants share a similar cultural and linguistic background.

Polynesians, group of people found in the Pacific Ocean area bounded by Hawaii, New Zealand, and Easter Island. They are typically of medium height, stocky build, and light-to-medium skin tone. They are predominantly Caucasoid, similar to the Melanesians and Micronesians, and probably entered the Pacific area through Southeast Asia. △1260.

Polynomial, a sum of terms that are powers of a variable: for example $5x^4 - 3x^3 + 2x^2 + x + 5$ is a polynomial of the fourth degree. In general a polynomial has the form $a_0x^n + a_1x^{n-1} + a_2x^{n-2} + \ldots\ldots\ldots a_{n-2}x^2 + a_{n-1}x + a_n$, although certain powers of x and the constant term a_n may be missing. The values a_n, a_{n-1}, etc, are the coefficients of the polynomial.

Polynucleotides. △1574.

Polyolefin Plastics, a polymer of olefin, a paraffin-based synthetic fiber composed mainly of polyethylene or polypropylene. Several trademarked fibers are polyolefins: Herculon and Vectra are best known. Fiber strength varies with type; the stronger is equal to nylon. They have high resistance to most chemicals and can be dry-cleaned. Used in hosiery, underclothes, upholstery, rugs, and automobile seat covers.

Polypeptide, chain of three or more amino acids linked by peptide bonds. *See* Peptide.

Polyphemus Moth, large American moth whose yellowish-brown wings are banded with pink and have transparent eyespots centered on each wing. Family Saturniidae; species *Antheraea polyphemus.*

Polyphony, music characterized by the interweaving of two or more relatively independent melodic lines (ie, counterpoint). It is often contrasted with homophony and monody. The great age of polyphonic music was the 16th century, culminating in the music of J. S. Bach and Handel.

Polypropylene, a polymer of propylene, resembling polyethylene and used chiefly in making fibers, films, and molded products. *See* Polyethylene; Polyolefin Plastics. △1644.

Polysaccharides. △1574.

Polystyrene, a synthetic organic polymer, composed of long-chain molecules prepared so that many aromatic hydrocarbon styrene molecules become linked. A strong thermoplastic resin results that is acid- and alkaline-resistant, nonabsorbent, and an excellent electrical insulator. Rubber latex may be added to polystyrene to increase its resistance to impact. It is used in housings for refrigerators and air conditioners. △1560, 1618, 1644.

Polytheism, belief in or worship of many gods. Such gods usually have specific attributes or functions. For example, Neptune is the Roman god of the sea, represented with trident. *See also* Ancestor Worship; Animism; Monotheism.

Polytrichum. △436.

Polyurethane, any of various polymers used chiefly in making flexible foams (as in upholstery and mattresses), rigid foams (as in cores for airplane wings), elastomers and resins (for adhesives and coatings). In textiles, the synthetic fiber Spandex is 85% polyurethane. △1644.

Polyvinyl Acetate, a colorless resin polymer used as an ingredient of latex paint and in lacquers, cements, adhesives, and polyvinyl alcohol. It is thermoplastic, flammable, and dissolves in benzene.

Polyvinyl Chloride (PVC), light rubbery thermoplastic polymer of vinyl chloride prepared by catalytic polymerization using a peroxide catalyst. It is availa-

Polecat

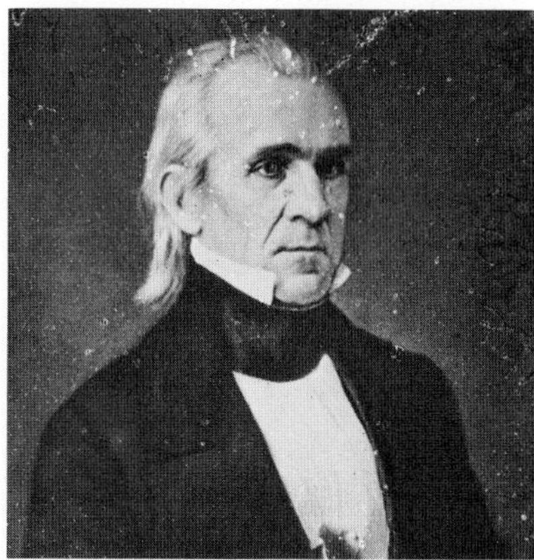

James K. Polk

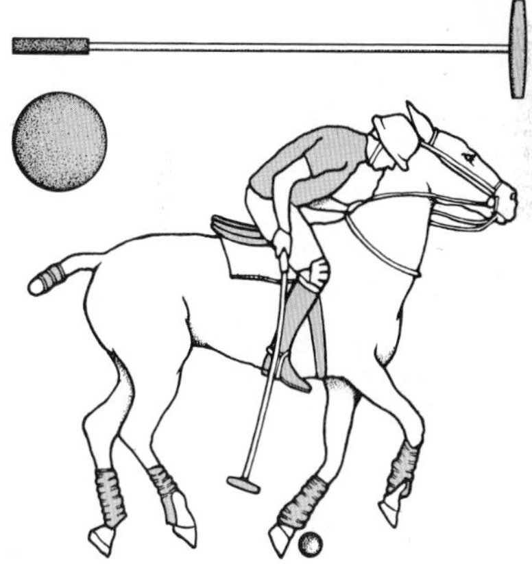

Polo

Polynesia

ble as a powder or in granules and is used in wire insulation, pipes, hoses, moldings, rainwear, and a host of other applications. △1560.

Pomace Fly. *See* Fruit Fly.

Pombal, Sebastião José de Carvalho e Melo, marquês de (1699–1782), Portuguese statesman. He was chief minister to King Joseph after 1756 and was virtual ruler of the country. He greatly increased royal power at the expense of the old nobility, the Inquisition, and the Jesuits, whom he expelled in 1759. His economic policies, both at home and in the colonies (particularly in Brazil), enriched the country. He ruled autocratically and strong opposition to him arose. He was ousted when Maria I became queen. △1180.

Pome, fleshy fruit formed from the flower receptacle or base. Because it is not developed from the carpel, it is a false fruit. Familiar examples are the apple, pear, and quince. *See also* Flower; Fruit.

Pomegranate, deciduous, spiny shrub or small tree native to W Asia and North Africa. It has shiny, oval leaves and showy, orange-red flowers. The round fruit has a red, leathery rind and numerous seeds coated with edible pulp. Family Punicaceae; species *Punica granatum*. △340.

Pomerania (Pomorze), region in N central Europe, running along Baltic Sea from W of Stralsund, East Germany, to Vistula River in Poland, including Rügen Island; passed to Prussia 1815; after WWI it was German state. The USSR occupied Pomerania March–April 1945, when the Potsdam Conference assigned area E of Oder River to Poland. △1074.

Pomeranian, small spitz-type dog (toy group) descended from the sled dogs of Iceland and Lapland. Its wedge-shaped head; small, erect ears; and bright eyes give it a foxlike expression. The short body is set on straight, medium-length legs; the tail turns over the back. Its double coat has a short and thick undercoat and a long, coarse outer coat that stands straight out. Coat may be any color, with sable or black shadings; or sable, black, and tan. Average size: 6in (15.5cm) high at shoulder; 3–7lb (1.5–3kg). *See also* Toy Dog.

Pomology. △338.

Pomona, city in S California, 25mi (40km) E of Los Angeles; site of California State Polytechnic University (1956) and Los Angeles County Fair. Industries: canning, shipping, missile components, paper products. Inc. 1888. Pop. (1970) 87,384.

Pompadour, Jeanne Antoinette Poisson Le Normant d'Etioles, Marquise de (1721–64), influential mistress and confidante of Louis XV. Well-educated as a rich man's prospective wife, she rose to prominence in Parisian society, attracting, and becoming the mistress of, the king. A great patron of the arts, she included among her friends the encyclopedist Voltaire. She urged the rearrangement of alliances, which caused the crushing French defeat of the Seven Years' War.

Pompano, marine and sport fish found worldwide in tropical and temperate waters. It is a blunt-headed and deep-bodied fish. Length: 18in (46cm); weight: 2lb (9kg). Species include the common or Florida *Trachinotus carolinus* and the round pompano *T. falcatus*. Family Carangidae.

Pompano Beach, resort city in SE Florida, 32mi (51km) N of Miami. Inc. 1927. Pop. (1970) 39,012.

Pompeii, ancient city in S Italy, at foot of Mt Vesuvius, 14mi (23km) SE of Naples. A Roman settlement 80 BC, it was destroyed AD 79 by eruption of Mt Vesuvius; ruins were first discovered 1748; excavations began 1763; remains include the forum, temples, baths, theaters, and many homes. Settled by Oscans 5th or 6th century BC. △1016.

Pompey, Gnaeus, called Pompeius Magnus (106–48 BC), Roman general. He fought for Sulla and campaigned in Sicily, Africa, and Spain, and with Crassus ended the Servile War. He was named consul illegally and, enjoying vast power, crushed the pirates and fought brilliantly against Mithradates VI, establishing Roman organization of the East. In Rome he formed the first triumvirate with Crassus and Caesar, his fierce rival and father-in-law. As consul he ruled Spain and sided with the senate against Caesar. He met Caesar with a great army in civil war in Greece where he was utterly defeated at Pharsala (48). Fleeing to Egypt he was stabbed by a soldier of his army. *See also* Spartacus. △1018.

Pompidou, Georges (1911–1974), French prime minister (1962–68) and president of the Republic from 1969 to his death. A teacher until 1944, Pompidou served with de Gaulle's postwar government, becoming a close aide. After some years as a banker, he helped formulate the constitution of the Fifth Republic, arranged a cease-fire in Algeria, and was appointed prime minister in 1962. He helped settle the student worker riots of 1968 and was elected president when de Gaulle resigned. He concentrated on the economy and foreign relations. △1356.

Ponca City, city in N Oklahoma, on Arkansas River; site of pioneer museum and statue by Bryant Baker commemorating pioneer women. Industries: grain storage, oil wells, dairy products. Founded 1893 when Cherokee Strip was opened; inc. 1899. Pop. (1970) 25,940.

Ponce, seaport city in S Puerto Rico, 140mi (225km) SW of San Juan; Puerto Rico's chief Caribbean port; site of Catholic University of Puerto Rico (1948), 18th-century fort, cathedral; trade and distribution center. Exports: sugar. Industries: cement, oil refining, paper products, rum distilling, tourism. Founded 1692, one of the oldest cities in the Americas. Pop. (1970) 156,498.

Ponce de León, Juan (1460?–1521), Spanish explorer. He served in the Moorish wars and was with Columbus on second voyage (1493). He was governor of Puerto Rico (1510–12) and founder of San Juan. Searching for the legendary Fountain of Youth, he explored the coasts of Florida (1513).

Pond Skater. *See* Water Strider.

Pondweed, any of some 60 species of a large family of aquatic perennial seed plants; found mostly in temperate zone regions in freshwater lakes and ponds, but also in brackish and salt water. Pondweeds survive the winter by using food stored in underground stems and tubers. They usually have emergent spikelike flowers and submerged or floating leaves arranged alternately along stem. Common species are leafy pondweed *(Potamogedon foliosus)*, found in North America, with thin leaves; and crisp pondweed *(P. crispus)*, introduced into North America from Europe, with crinkled broader leaves. Many ducks feed almost exclusively on pondweed. Family Potamogedonaceae. △618.

Pontchartrain, Lake, large shallow lake in SE Louisiana, just N of New Orleans; Lake Borgne connects it with the Mississippi River, also connected to Gulf of Mexico; spanned N–S by 10-mi (16-km) bridge; site of Fontainebleau State Park and other resort areas. Area: 630sq mi (1,632sq km). Depth: 10–16ft (3–5m).

Pontiac (died 1769), American Indian chieftain, leader of the Chippewa, Potawatomi, and Ottawa tribes. He helped the French against the British in the French and Indian War (1754–63) and toward the end of it organized the "Conspiracy of Pontiac," an alliance with the French to drive the British and American colonists from west of the Allegheny Mountains. Peace with the British was made in 1766.

Pontiac, city in SE Michigan, on Clinton River, 25mi (40km) NW of Detroit; seat of Oakland co; site of St Mary's Seminary College. Industries: trucks, taxicabs, oil seals, varnishes. Founded 1818; inc. as village 1837, as city 1861. Pop. (1970) 85,279.

Pontiac's Rebellion (1763–66), American Indian war. The campaign, coordinated by Pontiac, the chief of the Ottawa Indians, was to recapture territory lost to the British by the French, who were allied with the Indians, in the French and Indian War. The Indians attacked and took nearly all the English forts between Pennsylvania and Lake Superior. They were finally defeated near Detroit; Pontiac signed a peace treaty (1766) with the British.

Pontius Pilate. *See* Pilate, Pontius.

Pontoon Bridge, a floating bridge. △1756.

Pontus, an ancient country in NE Asia Minor. It gained its independence from Persia (4th century BC) and reached the height of its power under Mithradates the Great who conquered Asia Minor, gained control of the Crimea, and threatened Rome. After his defeat by Pompey (65 BC), the size and power of the country diminished. In 47 BC Pontus was made a Roman province.

Pony, small horse. Usually gentle with children, it is used as a child's mount and for show and work in harness and heavy harness. Types include Shetland, Welsh, Welsh Cob, Highland, Dale and Fell, Dartmoor, Exmoor, New Forest, and Hackney. Height under 58in (147cm) at shoulder; weight: 500–900lb (227–408kg). An American breed, Pony of the Americas, is a western type; height: 46–54in (117–137cm) at shoulder. *See also* Hackney; Shetland Pony; Welsh Pony.

Pony Express, a relay mail service between St Joseph, Mo., and Sacramento, Calif. (1860–61). Established by the freight-carrying company of Russell, Majors, and Waddell, it involved using riders who changed their horses about every 10 miles (16km). It took the pony express about eight days to carry the 20-lb (9kg) mail bags the 2,000 miles (3,220km) between the two cities, a saving of about two weeks over the stagecoach. The express was soon replaced by the telegraph.

Poodle, water retriever breed of dog believed to have originated in Germany in the 15th–16th centuries, but now considered the national dog of France. This elegant, popular dog has a rounded skull and long, straight body; small feet; and high-set, docked tail carried up. The profuse, harsh-textured coat is a solid color—blue, gray, silver, brown, apricot, or cream. The coat is clipped (originally to facilitate swimming) in either puppy, English saddle, or Continental styles. Sizes—three varieties: standard, over 15in (38cm) high at shoulder, and miniature, over 10 and to 15in (25.5–38cm), both in nonsporting group; toy, 10in or less (25.5cm) in toy group.

Pool. *See* Billiards.

Poole, port city in S England, in Dorset, 5mi (8km) W of Bournemouth. On Poole Harbour; resort and naval supply base. Industries: shipbuilding, pottery. Pop. 106,697.

Poona (Pune), city in W India, 80mi (129km) ESE of Bombay; capital of Poona district and division. City served as capital of Maratha confederacy (18th century) until 1817, when it came under British control, used as British military station; site of temple of Parvati, headquarters of southern command and National Defense Academy, Poona University (1948). Industries: metal works, pharmaceuticals, textiles, paper, ammunition. Pop. 732,731.

Poor Laws, English legislation designed to alleviate poverty and prevent begging and vagrancy and requiring individual parishes to provide for the local poor. It distinguished between the genuinely poor, such as the old and sick, and the able-bodied, for whom workhouses were provided. The first poor laws were passed in 1601.

Poorwill, W North American goatsucker with unusual hibernating habits. It lowers its body temperature, lapses into a state of torpor, and hibernates in a rock niche. Species *Phalaenoptilus nuttalli*. *See also* Goatsucker.

Pop Art, an art form that emerged in the mid-1950s inspired by the mass media, consumer sphere, industrial products, science fiction, and movies. Some pop artists saw the world critically; others simply reproduced or enlarged it. English pop art was formulated by the Independence Group. Jasper Johns and Robert Rauschenberg continued the trend in New York, using abstract techniques to depict everyday objects. Roy Lichtenstein and Andy Warhol used commercial techniques. △1372.

Pope, Alexander (1688–1744), English poet, b. London. Small, deformed, and self-taught, he achieved mastery over classical poetic forms, showing early metrical skills in *Pastorals* (1709). He also wrote lyric and elegiac poetry and published fine translations of Homer (1720 and 1726) and *Imitations of Horace* (1733). His great talent was for satire, notably in *The Dunciad* and *An Epistle to Dr. Arbuthnot*. △1184.

Pope, John (1822–92), Union Civil War general, b. Louisville, Ky. After victories in the West, Pope came East to command at the Second Battle of Bull Run (Aug. 18–30, 1862). Badly defeated, he was removed from command.

Pope, head of the Roman Catholic Church. Originally the title was used for all bishops and priests, but in the 11th century St Gregory VII decreed that in the Roman Catholic Church, "pope" would refer only to the bishop of Rome. Sucession is accomplished by the Conclave, a meeting of the college of cardinals that is sequestered in the Vatican 15 to 18 days after a pope's death. Each day the cardinals cast ballots for one of their number in the Sistine Chapel. If the required two-thirds plus one vote has not been attained, the ballots are mixed with wet straw and burned. The resulting black smoke demonstrates to the crowd waiting outside that the new pope has not yet been chosen. When a pope is elected, the ballots are burned with dry straw and the smoke is white. If the election is accepted by the cardinal chosen, he is declared pope and resides in the Vatican, Rome. He is recognized by his followers as the successor of St Peter, head of Christ's apostles. △1072, 1086.

Poplar, deciduous, softwood trees native to cool to temperate regions of the Northern Hemisphere. The oval leaves grow on stalks and flowers are borne in catkins. Some species are called cottonwoods because of the cottonlike fluff on their seeds. Height: to 90ft (27m). Family Salicaceae; genus *Populus.*

Popper, (Sir) Karl Raimund (1902–), British philosopher of natural and social sciences, b. Austria. He was not a logical positivist but was in close contact with the Vienna Circle and had a considerable influence on Rudolph Carnap. His writings include *The Open Society and Its Enemies* (1945) and *The Poverty of Historicism* (1961). △858.

Poppy, common name for plants of the poppy family, especially of the genus *Papaver* of about 100 species of annual and perennial erect herbs, most native to central and S Europe, but also found in the Orient, Great Britain, and Iceland. The plants contain a milky juice, are long-stalked, and have showy blooms. The opium poppy of Greece and the Orient is grown for medical and illicit purposes. Family Papaveraceae. △444.

Popular Front, in USSR. △1310.

Population, in sociology, either the total number of persons living in a specified area—neighborhood, town, county, state, country—or the group of people sharing certain traits, as in "the female population" or the "adolescent population." Also used as a synonym for the adjective "demographic," as in "population studies," or "population statistics." *See also* Demography.

Population, Statistical, the entire group in which a statistician is interested. Statistics representing the entire population would be the collection of every possible observation for the specific variable of interest. △936.

Population I and II Regions. △104.

Populism, socio-political movement arising out of the agrarian economies of the southern and western United States and rooted in a basic distrust of the Eastern industrial establishment. First espoused in the 1870s, the movement coalesced around the Populist party, formed in 1891, which advocated free coinage of silver, abolition of national banks, tariff reform, and a graduated income tax, among other measures. These measures were later adopted into law by Democratic administrations and the Populist party disbanded. △1286.

Populist Party, or **People's Party,** US third party movement organized in the early 1890s by farmers, workers, and small businessmen of the West and South to protest falling prices, poor credit and marketing facilities, and crop failures. Party members advocated free silver to counteract existing inflation, abolition of national banks, and public ownership of transportation, communications, and banking systems. James B. Weaver ran as the Populist candidate for president in 1892 and, although unsuccessful, received considerable support. After 1896, when the Populists backed Democratic party candidate William Jennings Bryan, the Populists gradually disappeared as an organized political party.

Poquelin, Jean Baptiste. *See* Molière.

Porbeagle Shark. △516.

Porcelain, white, vitreous, nonporous, translucent ceramic that gives a clear note when struck. The term is derived from the Italian *porcellus,* meaning little pig and was used by the Portuguese to describe Chinese ceramics that curved and glistened like the upper surface of a pig's back. Porcelain was first developed by the Chinese (7th or 8th century) and made of kaolin (well-decayed feldspar) and petuntse (powdered feldspar or partially decomposed granite). This true, or hard paste, ceramic ware is fired at 1400°C. Meissen ware (early 18th century) was the first successful European attempt to imitate this hard paste porcelain, referred to as "china." Other kinds are English soft paste, composed of clay and powdered glass or frit, fired at a comparatively low temperature, lead glazed, and refired; and English bone china, a soft paste, modified with the addition of calcined bone. *See also* Ceramics; Pottery. △1048.

Porcupine, river in Alaska and Canada; rises in the mountains of N Yukon Territory, Canada; flows NE and turns W to Yukon River at Fort Yukon, Alaska. Discovered 1842 by John Bell. Length: 448mi (721km).

Porcupine, short-legged, mostly nocturnal plant-eating rodent with long quills on its back for defense. Old World porcupines (family Hystricidae) are heavy, have brown to black fur with white-banded quills, and live on the ground. New World porcupines (family Erethizontidae) are smaller with yellow to white quills and can climb trees. A South American porcupine, *Coendou prehensilis,* can hang by its tail. Weight: to 60lb (27kg). △546.

Porcupine Fish, or **Balloon Fish,** tropical marine puffer fish found worldwide. A whitish and brown fish with sharp erectile spines, it can gulp air and swell to a sphere. Length: to 3ft (91.4cm). Among the 15 species is *Diodon hystrix.* Family Diodontidae.

Pore, Skin. △686.

Pore-bearers. *See* Porifera.

Porgy, commercial and sport marine fish found in tropical and temperate waters. It is a deep-bodied, blunt-headed fish with powerful teeth. Length: to 2ft (61cm). Among the 100 species are the northern *Stenotomus chrysops* and Holbrook's *Diplodus holbrooki.* Family Sparidae.

Porgy and Bess (1935), 3-act opera by George Gershwin, English libretto by Ira Gershwin and Du Bose Heyward, from Dorothy and Du Bose Heyward's play *Porgy.* Its premiere was held in Boston, with an all-black cast. The plot concerns a tragedy in a Carolina coastal town. Crown (bass) kills Robbins (baritone) and escapes. Sportin' Life (tenor) tries to get Crown's lady friend Bess (soprano) to go with him to New York, but she goes to live with the crippled Porgy (baritone). Porgy kills Crown and goes to jail; Sportin' Life lures Bess to New York. When Porgy is released he goes to find Bess. △1256.

Porifera, or pore-bearers, also called parazoa, animal phylum containing sponges. They are many celled, nonmobile animals representing an evolutionary dead end. *See also* Sponge. △466, 506.

Pork. △376, 380.

Pork Barrel Legislation, bills authorizing public works projects, generally river-and-harbor, highway, or hospital construction for a particular locale, regardless of need.

Porphyria, an often genetic disease of man and some animals, characterized by abnormalities of porphyrin metabolism and subsequent excretion of porphyrins in the urine as well as extreme sensitivity to light. There is no specific treatment, but therapy can alleviate the symptoms.

Porphyry, textural term applied to rocks that contain large crystals (phenocrysts) in a fine-textured igneous matrix. They are found in both intrusive and extrusive rocks. Different varieties are named after the phenocrysts.

Porpoise, small, toothed whale with blunt beakless snout, inhabiting most oceans. The best known porpoise is the common, or harbor, porpoise of Northern Hemisphere. Its body is black above and white below. Length: 5ft (1.5m). Family Phocaenidae; species *Phocaena phocaena. See also* Whale. △540, 552.

Portage, city in SW Michigan, 8mi (13km) S of Kalamazoo. Industries: pharmaceuticals, paper products, mobile homes. Inc. 1963. Pop. (1970) 33,590.

Portage des Sioux, Treaties of (1815), set of agreements between the United States and Indian tribes that had been previously allied with the British. About 2,000 Indians were involved. The treaties were successful in ending most hostilities in the Old Northwest, opening the area for settlement.

Portal Vein. △694.

Port Arthur, city in SE Texas, 17mi (27km) SE of Beaumont, on Sabine Lake; connected to Gulf of Mexico by canal system; port of entry; industrial, shipping, and recreational center. Exports: oil, petrochemicals, lumber, grain. Industries: oil, livestock, rice, foundries, rubber. Founded 1895; inc. 1898. Pop. (1970) 57,371.

Pompeii, Italy: Temple of Apollo

Pony

ALEXAN
POPE

Alexander Pope

Porcupine

Port-au-Prince, capital city of Haiti, on SE shore of Gulf of Gonâve; served as capital of Saint-Domingue 1770; site of University of Haiti (1944), technical institute (1962). Exports: coffee, sugar, sisal, bananas, rum. Industries: sugar, rum, cottonseed oil, textiles, flour. Founded 1749 by French as L'Hôpital. Pop. 386,250.

Port Chester, village in SE New York, on Long Island Sound. Industries: bakery products, battery cells, candy, hardware. Founded 1650 as Sawpits; name changed 1837; inc. 1868. Pop. (1970) 25,803.

Port Elizabeth, port city in S Republic of South Africa, on Algoa Bay and Indian Ocean; developed after completion of railroad line to Kimberly 1873; site of Fort Frederich (1799), art gallery, museum, Snake Park, University of Port Elizabeth (1964). Industries: automobiles, tires, chemicals, glass, soap, candy, shoes, woodworking, fishing, electrical engineering, timber processing, tanning. Founded 1799 by British settlers. Pop. 381,227.

Porter, Cole (1893–1964), US composer and lyricist of musical comedies, b. Peru, Ind. His plays include *The Gay Divorcee* (1932), with the song "Night and Day"; *Anything Goes* (1934), with the song "You're the Top"; *Jubilee* (1935) with "Begin the Beguine"; and *Rosalie* (1937) with "In the Still of the Night." After a fall in 1937, he continued to compose even though he was confined to a wheelchair. *Kiss Me Kate* (1948) and *Silk Stockings* (1955) were two of his later works.

Porter, Katherine Anne (1894–), US author, b. Indian Creek, Tex. She is primarily noted for her carefully wrought short stories and novellas. *Flowering Judas,* her first short-story collection, appeared in 1930 and won her immediate acclaim. Subsequent works include *Pale Horse, Pale Rider* (1939—three novellas), *The Leaning Tower and Other Stories* (1944), and her only long novel, *Ship of Fools* (1962), for which she won a Pulitzer Prize and a National Book Award in 1963.

Porter, William Sydney *See* Henry, O.

Port Harcourt, city in S Nigeria, on Bonny arm of Niger River delta system approx. 275mi (443km) ESE of Lagos; shipping center and terminus of railroad from interior. Exports: coal, tin, palm products, peanuts, cacao, cigarettes. Est. 1912. Pop. 208,237.

Port Huron, city in SE Michigan, at Lake Huron end of St Clair River; seat of St Clair co; site of St Clair Community College (1923). Industries: salt, fishing equipment, boats, marine hardware, paper. Settled 1686; inc. as village 1849, as city 1857. Pop. (1970) 35,794.

Portland, city and port of entry in SW Maine, on Casco Bay; seat of Cumberland co; largest city in Maine. Settled 1632 by George Cleeve and Richard Tucker, city grew, as Falmouth, into commercial area under Massachusetts Bay Colony (17th century); served as state capital 1820–32; birthplace of Henry Wadsworth Longfellow, and home of Robert E. Peary. It is site of lighthouse (1791), University of Maine at Portland-Gorham, Westbrook College (1831). Industries: shipyards, canneries, fishing, chemicals, lumber, paper, textiles, tourism. Inc. 1786 as town and renamed; inc. 1832 as city. Pop. (1970) 65,116.

Portland, city and port of entry in NW Oregon, on Willamette River; seat of Multnomah co; largest city in Oregon. Settled 1845, it was named for Portland, Maine; it developed as major port for lumber and grain (1850), and as supply station for California gold miners (1860s and '70s), and Alaskan Gold Rush (1897–1900). Portland is the site of Lewis and Clark College (1867), University of Portland (1901), Reed College (1904), Concordia College (1905). Industries: shipyards, lumber, wood products, textiles, metals, machinery. Inc. 1851. Pop. (1970) 380,555.

Portland Cement. *See* Cement, Portland.

Port Louis, capital and seaport city in NW Mauritius in Indian Ocean. Founded in 1736 by Bertrand François Mahé de la Bourdonnais, governor of French colony on the island, to be used as a base of operations against British in India; seized by Great Britain in 1810. It is the site of Citadel (1838) and the Mauritius Institute (1880). Industries: sugar processing, storing and shipping, cigarettes, rum, food products. Pop. 138,150.

Port Moresby, capital city of Papua New Guinea, on Coral Sea, on SE shore of New Guinea island; excellent sheltered harbor; site of Allied base in WWII. Exports: minerals, rubber, and coffee. Discovered 1873; settled 1888; became capital 1946. Pop. 56,206.

Porto (Oporto), port city in NW Portugal, on the Douro River 2mi (3km) from its mouth on the Atlantic Ocean; capital of Porto district and 2nd-largest city in Portugal. An ancient Roman settlement, it was founded *c.* 138 BC; the port was occupied by the Visigoths 540–716 and the Moors 716–997, from whom Alfonso I of Portugal captured it. Porto grew as wine center in 17th century; scene of the unsuccessful "tipplers revolt" against the wine monopoly 1757. City revolted against French rule 1808 during the Peninsular War, and withstood the siege of Don Miguel 1832–33 during the Miguelist Wars; 12th- and 14th-century structures survive, with 18th-century baroque tower, Torre dos Clérigos; site of university (1911). Harbor of Porto is Leixões. Industries: port wine, olives, fruits, cork, chemicals, textiles, canning, fishing. Pop. 310,437.

Pôrto Alegre, city in SE Brazil, on Guaíba River; capital of Rio Grande do Sul state. Chief river port in S Brazil, it is a large commercial center. Industries: meat packing, agriculture, brewing. Founded 1742 by colonists from the Azores, later settled by German and Italian immigrants. Pop. 932,801.

Port of Spain, capital city of Trinidad and Tobago, on Gulf of Paria; former capital of West Indies Federation (1958–62); industrial and commercial center, major Caribbean shipping hub; site of botanical gardens. Tourism is main industry. Pop. 67,867.

Porto-Novo, capital city and port in Benin (Dahomey), W. Africa; settled in 16th century by Portuguese traders; used as a shipping point for African slaves to America; administrative, trade, and shipping center. Founded 16th century. Pop. 87,000.

Port Royal Colony, settlement in Nova Scotia. Founded (1605) as a French trading post, it was partially abandoned (1607) and what remained was destroyed by the English (1613), who later occupied the area with a fort and settlement. In Queen Anne's War (1710) the English took Port Royal, and it became Annapolis Royal. It served as the capital of Nova Scotia until 1749. In 1940 a national park was created on the original site of Port Royal.

Ports. △1760.

Port Said (Būr Said), city in NE Egypt, at entrance to Suez Canal, on a narrow peninsula between Lake Manzala and Mediterranean Sea. In 1956 French and British paratroops landed here during Suez Campaign and occupied city for seven weeks; in Arab-Israeli Wars the Israelis attacked the city; harbor was closed to shipping 1967–1974. Industries: fishing, salt, canal workshops. Founded 1859 by builders of Suez Canal. Pop. 313,000.

Portsmouth, port city in S England, in Hampshire, on Spithead Channel; Britain's chief naval base since the reign of Henry VII. It comprises Landport, Portsea, Cosham, and the resort of Southsea. Nelson's flagship, *H.M.S. Victory,* stands here in dry dock; birthplace of Charles Dickens. Pop. 196,976.

Portsmouth, seaport city in SE New Hampshire, on Atlantic Ocean at mouth of Piscataqua River. Oldest city in state, it was important shipbuilding center during Revolutionary War and War of 1812; scene of 1773 "tea party" held in Market Square protesting British tax; site of North Church (1712), Meserve-Webster House (1760, home of British stamp master), and Portsmouth Naval Base. In 1905 the Treaty of Portsmouth was signed here, ending Russo-Japanese War. Industries: tourism, plastics, buttons, machine tools. Settled 1624, inc. 1653. Pop. (1970) 25,717.

Portsmouth, city in S Ohio, on Ohio River at mouth of Scioto River; seat of Scioto co; site of 1810 House, Mound Park with ancient Indian burial grounds; Wayne National Forest is nearby. Industries: steel, chemicals, bricks, shoes, paper boxes. Founded 1803; inc. as town 1814, as city 1851. Pop. (1970) 27,633.

Portsmouth, city in SE Virginia, on Elizabeth River opposite Norfolk; comprises port of Hampton Roads, together with Norfolk and Newport News; site of large naval facilities including Norfolk Navy Yard (est. 1801) where the *Merrimack* was converted to the ironclad *Virginia* (1861–62), Portsmouth Naval Hospital (est. 1830), and Frederick College (1958); transportation, shipping, and commercial center. Industries: shipyards, chemicals, fertilizer, railroad equipment and shops, tools, plastics. Founded 1752; chartered as city 1858. Pop. (1970) 110,963.

Portsmouth Peace Conference (1905), peace negotiations to settle the Russo-Japanese War. The meeting brought Russia and Japan together with Pres. Theodore Roosevelt acting as mediator in Portsmouth, N.H. It established Japan as the dominant Far Eastern power. Japan gained territory in Manchuria and influence in Korea, plus the South Manchurian Railway, but won no indemnity to repair its impoverished treasury. For his efforts at Portsmouth, Roosevelt received the 1906 Nobel Peace Prize.

Port Sudan (Bur Sudan), city in NE Sudan, on Red Sea; chief port of entry of Sudan; rich cotton growing region. Exports: peanuts, hides, gum, cotton, oilseed. Founded during construction of railroad in 1905, linking Nile River with Red Sea. Pop. 100,700.

Portugal, independent nation in SW Europe, on the Iberian Peninsula. Internal politics were unstable in the mid-1970s as Portugal shifted away from right-wing government and tried to deal with the dislocations caused by the loss of its overseas territories.

Land and economy. A mountainous agricultural country located on one-sixth of the Iberian Peninsula it is bordered by Spain N and E and the Atlantic Ocean S and W and includes the Azores and Madeira islands. The Tagus River divides the country into two topographical regions. The N part of the mainland is covered with mountains, has a heavy rainfall and a moderate climate. To the S are rolling plains with less rainfall and a warmer climate. Long sandy beaches mark its 500-mi (805-km) coastline. Forests cover 19% of the land. About 40% of the land is arable; wheat is the most valuable crop, followed by olives. Port wine is a principal export, and Portugal leads the world in cork production. A large part of the economy comes from tourism and money earned by Portuguese workers abroad. Portuguese overseas possessions now consist only of Macao and enclave at the mouth of the Canton River in China.

People. Although the Romans put their stamp on Portugal with their language, institutions, and culture, ethnically the country reflects invasion by the Goths, Arabs, and Berbers, then settlers from N Europe, Jews who came in the Middle Ages, and slaves from Africa. Before WWII, a poor economy led unskilled workers to emigrate to the United States and Africa. The population is relatively homogeneous with no significant minorities. The principal religion is Roman Catholicism. Literacy is estimated at 65%.

Government. Portugal is a republic, with elected bicameral legislature and advisory Corporative Chamber.

History. An independent state since the 12th century, Portugal's modern history began in 1140. Before that time it had been ruled by Romans, Visigoths, and Moors. Galician, Leonese, and Castilian kings revolted and established the nation of Portugal in 997. Between 1130–39, Alfonso Henriques, son of the Count of Portugal, defeated the small kingdoms, then the Moors, and became Portugal's first king in 1150. Portuguese exploration started about 1336 when navigators reached the Canary Islands. Prince Henry the Navigator encouraged overseas expansion, which led to the 15th–16th century voyages of Vasco da Gama, Bartolomeu Dias, and Pedro Cabal, who claimed vast territories and brought wealth to the Portuguese kingdom. Conflict with neighboring Spain was a constant problem, and Spain ruled Portugal 1580–1640. Independence was reestablished under the Braganzas, who ruled, with interruptions, until 1910, when Manuel II abdicated, and a republic was established. Political instability characterized the next two decades. Antônio de Olivera Salazar took an increasingly prominent role in the government from 1928 and in 1932 gained control as premier. He maintained domestic stability but also repressed all opposition. He retired in 1968, and in 1974 a military junta seized the government. In the next two years Portugal's vast overseas empire disintegrated as colonies gained independence (including Angola and Mozambique) and governmental control moved to leftist civilians. In April 1976 elections brought moderate, democratic leaders to power.

PROFILE

Official name: Republic of Portugal
Area: (continental Portugal) 35,553sq mi (92,082sq km); Azores, 905sq mi (2,344sq km); Madeira 308sq mi. (798sq km)
Population: (continental Portugal) 8,800,000, Azores, 336,100; Madeira, 268,700
Density: (continental Portugal) 247.5per sq mi (95.5per sq km)
Chief cities: Lisbon (capital); Oporto
Government: Republic
Religion: Roman Catholic
Language: Portuguese
Monetary unit: Escudo
Gross national product: $12,200,000,000
Per capita income: $1,308

Industries: canned fish and seafood, olive oil, wine, textiles, ships, forests, sisal cordage, forest products, paper, glassware, petrochemicals
Agriculture: wheat, olives, citrus fruits, fish, forests, almonds
Minerals: wolfram, pyrites
Trading partners: European Economic Community, United States

Portuguese, the national language of both Portugal and Brazil, spoken by about 10,000,000 people in the former and 100,000,000 in the latter. A Romance language, it is closely related to Spanish, but its pronunciation is softer and contains more nasal sounds.

Portuguese Guinea. *See* Guinea-Bissau, Republic of.

Portuguese Man of War, colonial coelenterate found in marine subtropical and tropical waters, recognized by its bright blue gas float and long, trailing tentacles with poisonous stingers. The tentacles are actually a cluster of several kinds of modified medusae and polyps. Length: 60ft (18.3m). Class Hydrozoa, phylum Cnidaria, species *Physalia.* △470, 626.

Portulaca, common name for the purslane family of annual or perennial flowering plants and small shrubs in the United States. They have cylindrical leaves. There are over 500 species. Also, low-growing annual plant *(Portulaca grandiflora)* with red, yellow, or white flowers that open only in sunshine.

Poseidon, in Greek mythology, the god of all waters, Earth-shaker, brother of Zeus. Poseidon controlled the monsters of the deep and sired by gods and mortals the Laestrygonians, Orion, Polyphemus, and Procrustes. Zeus called upon him to bring the Flood when he was displeased with men. He is the Roman Neptune.

Poseidon of Artemisium. △1002.

Positive Ion. *See* Ion.

Positive Number. *See* Number, Natural.

Positivism, philosophic doctrine initially associated with Auguste Comte's notion that the most creative and highest stage of knowledge, the positive, is based on pure fact gained by direct experience. Positivism also is used synonymously with a form of scientific empiricism that tends to regard non-observational terms and theories with skepticism, and unites meaning with verification. *See also* Comte, Auguste. △ 858.

Positron, positively charged antiparticle of the electron (symbol e^+) postulated as the first antiparticle by P. Dirac (1928) and observed (1933) in cosmic rays. It is also emitted from certain radioactive nuclei. It can only exist a brief period before annihilating with an electron. When gamma rays interact with matter, electron-positron pairs can be produced. *See also* Annihilation; Lepton. △1484.

Post, Wiley (1900–35), US aviation pioneer, b. near Grand Saline, Tex. He began his career as a barnstormer, racer, and parachutist at county fairs in the 1920s. After winning the Bendix Trophy race (1930), he and his navigator then set an around-the-world flight record of 8 days, 15 hours, and 51 minutes (1931). On a solo flight, he beat this record by 21 hours (1933). He and cowboy humorist Will Rogers were killed in a plane crash in Alaska.

Postal Service, US, independent agency within the executive branch of the federal government, responsible for mail delivery. The Postal Service is directed by the postmaster general and the deputy postmaster general, both of whom are appointed by, and sit on, the Board of Governors. The nine governors are appointed by the president with the approval of the Senate. The service handles 90,000,000,000 pieces of mail annually and employs approximately 700,000 people.

Post-impressionism, term invented by English critic Roger Fry to denote the movement associated with Paul Gauguin, Vincent van Gogh, and Paul Cézanne. It is generally used for art trends from the mid-1880s to the early 1900s. It stressed subjective and emotional content and was later referred to as Expressionism.

Post-partum Depression, series of depressive symptoms that occasionally appear in mothers shortly after the birth of a child. Some authorities stress psychological causes, others emphasize endocrine and other chemical changes engendered by the termination of pregnancy. △704.

Postulate, statement or proposition that is to be assumed to be true without proof and that forms a framework for the derivation of theorems. The term as now used is synonymous with "axiom." Euclid drew a distinction between postulates, which dealt with geometric properties, and axioms, which were more general statements about equality and inequality. △ 1462.

Posture. △698.

Potash. △1554.

Potassium, common metallic element (symbol K) of the alkali-metal group, first isolated in 1807 by Sir Humphry Davy. Chief ores are sylvite (chloride), carnallite, and polyhalite. The metal is used as a heat-transfer medium but has few other commercial uses. Chemically it resembles sodium, being rather more reactive. The natural element contains a radioisotope K^{40} (half-life 1.4×10^9yrs), which is used in radioactive dating of rocks. Properties: at. no. 19; at. wt. 39.102; sp gr 0.86; melt. pt. 153.77°F (67.70°C); boil pt 1,425°F (774°C); most common isotope K^{39} (93.1%). *See also* Alkali Element; Dating, Radioactive. △1552, 1566.

Potassium-Argon Dating, a method of assessing geological age up to about ten million years. *See also* Dating, Radioactive.

Potassium Carbonate, a commercially produced white solid (K_2CO_3), usually produced by electrolysis of potassium chloride, followed by treatment of the resulting potassium hydroxide with carbon dioxide. It is used in the manufacture of glass and textile dyes and in cleaning and electroplating metals.

Potassium Chloride, a potassium salt (KCl) extracted from lake brines as well as from minerals (sylvite, kainite, carnallite). Colorless or white, with a specific gravity of 1.9, it is used as a fertilizer and as a raw material in the production of potassium hydroxide and potassium carbonate.

Potassium Feldspar. △1558.

Potassium Hydroxide, a commercially produced white solid (KOH) prepared by electrolysis of potassium chloride. It is an alkaline substance used for making soaps and detergents.

Potassium Nitrate (KNO_3), (1) a naturally occurring (nitre) mineral which is a source of nitrogen. It appears as a white crust on rocks, in caves, and in some soils in hot, dry areas. (2) A synthetically produced transparent solid salt prepared by the reaction of sodium nitrate and potassium chloride or by the reaction of nitric acid and potassium hydroxide. Potassium nitrate is used as a fertilizer, in the manufacture of explosives, and as a food preservative.

Potassium Permanganate, purple soluble crystalline salt (formula $KMnO_4$) obtained from pyrolusite (manganese dioxide) and potassium hydroxide. It is used as an oxidizing agent, disinfectant, dye, and in the preparation of other chemicals. Properties: sp gr 2.70; decomposes at 464°F (240°C).

Potato, also white potato, Irish potato; herb native to Central and South America and introduced to Europe by the Spaniards in the 16th century. Best grown in a moist, cool climate, it has oval leaves and violet, pink, or white flowers, which produce a greenish berry fruit. The potato itself is a tuber (underground modified stem). The leaves and green potatoes contain the alkaloid solanine and are poisonous if eaten raw. Family Solanaceae; species *Solanum tuberosa.* △324.

Potato Beetle. *See* Colorado Potato Beetle.

Potato Famine. △1314.

Potawatomi, American Indians of the Algonquian linguistic family. Originally united with the Ottawa and the Ojibwa, these semi-sedentary hunter-farmers were driven by the Sioux southeast from Wisconsin, migrating as far as Indiana before the whites drove them west. They were eventually settled on reservations in Oklahoma, Kansas, Michigan, and Wisconsin, where they now number about 1,300.

Pot-de-fer. △1732.

Potemkin, Grigori Aleksandrovich (1739–91), Russian statesman. Involved in the coup that brought Catherine II to power (1762), he became her lover and favorite in 1771 and remained until his death the

Cole Porter

ATLANTIC OCEAN
France
Andorra
Porto
Coimbra
PORTUGAL
Spain
Lisbon (Lisboa)
MEDITERRANEAN SEA
Algeria
Morocco
0
400 km

Portugal

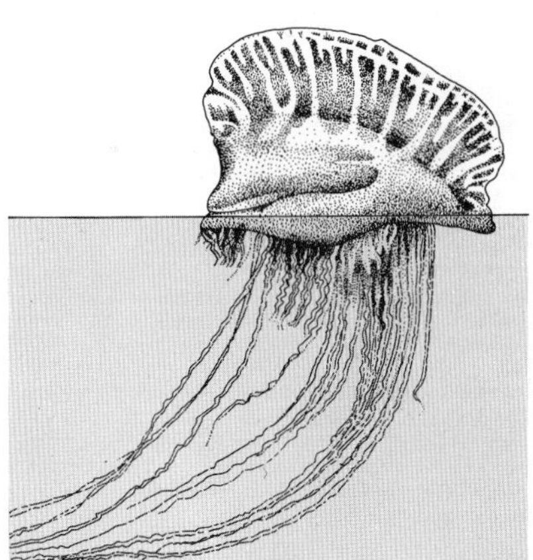

Portuguese man-of-war

Portulaca

most powerful man in Russia. Governor general of "New Russia" (Ukraine), he engineered the colonization of the Ukrainian steppes and the conquest of the Crimea. He became a field marshal in 1784 and was commander in chief during the second Turkish War (1787–91).

Potential Energy, in mechanics, energy that can be transformed into kinetic energy. For example, a swing at the top of its motion has a potential energy equal to its kinetic energy at the bottom of its path. A body of mass m and height h in the Earth's gravitational field g has a potential energy of mgh. *See also* Kinetic Energy. △1486, 1502.

Potentiometer, a special type of rheostat that measures an unknown voltage or potential difference by balancing it by a known potential difference. The simplest form is a resistor with two fixed terminals and a third terminal connected to a variable contact arm. Potentiometers are used as volume controls in audio equipment.

Pothole, in geology, term used for many formations with pot shapes but most commonly denoting a circular, bowl-shaped hollow formed in a rocky stream bed by the grinding action of sand and stones whirled around by eddies or the force of the stream. They are usually found in rapids or at the foot of a waterfall. △258.

Pothos, or devil's ivy, trailing house plant native to the South Pacific islands. It has waxy, heart-shaped leaves marked with yellow or white. Care: bright indirect light, soil (1 part loam, 2 parts peat moss, 1 part sand) kept dry between waterings. Propagation is by stem cuttings. Family Araceae; species *Scindapsus aureus.*

Potlatch, custom from the North West American Coast in which members of Indian tribes gain prestige by using up large amounts of goods in competitive feasts. These feasts are officially gift exchanges, redistributing wealth given for spiritual reasons but they actually involve a great deal of rivalry.

Potomac, river in SE United States; rises in West Virginia at the confluence of the North Branch and South Branch rivers, flows E and SE to Chesapeake Bay, forming natural boundaries of Maryland-West Virginia, Virginia-Maryland, and Virginia-District of Columbia; navigable for large ships to Washington, D.C.; site of many historic landmarks including Mount Vernon. Length: 285mi (459km).

Potsdam, city in central East Germany, on an island in the Havel River, 17mi (27km) SW of West Berlin; capital of Potsdam district. Residence of Frederick William of Brandenburg (1660), who opened city to French refugees by Edict of Potsdam (1685); scene of Peace of Potsdam (1805), which strengthened alliance between Russia and Prussia against France, and Potsdam Conference (July 17–Aug. 2, 1945) which determined administration of Germany after WWII; site of New Palace (1763–69), Town Palace (1745), park Sans Souci (1745–47), Garrison Church (1731–35); center of East German movie industry. Industries: food processing, textiles, pharmaceuticals, electrical equipment. Founded *c.* 10th century. Pop. 111,288.

Potsdam Conference (1945), meeting to settle European problems following World War II. The principal participants included Pres. Harry S. Truman of the United States, Prime Minister Winston Churchill of Britain, and later Prime Minister Clement P. Attlee, and Premier Joseph Stalin of the USSR. Held in Potsdam, Germany, the conference established the Council of Foreign Ministers to prepare draft treaties and to make proposals for settling territorial issues. The occupation of Germany was planned. An "unconditional surrender" ultimatum was issued to Japan.

Potsherd, pottery fragment, one of the archeologist's chief aids in dating sites and tracing cultural contacts after the invention of pottery in Neolithic times. Potsherds are useful because they are often found in large numbers and because potters' conservatism supplies the basis for typological dating.

Potter, Beatrix (1866–1943), English author who created Peter Rabbit, Jemima Puddle-Duck, Squirrel Nutkin, and other animal characters. In the 1890s she began to send illustrated animal stories to a friend's sick child. She published *Peter Rabbit* in 1902. *The Tailor of Gloucester* followed in 1903. Wry humor, simple prose, close observation of nature, and illustrations in the best English watercolor tradition contribute to the books' charm.

Pottery, in its widest sense includes all objects shaped of clay and hardened by fire or dried in the sun. The term is from the French *poterie,* related to the Latin *potare* (to drink). Pottery is dependent on two properties of clay, its plasticity and its durability after firing. It can be divided into three categories according to the degree of hardness and special constitution: earthenware, the ordinary pottery dating back to primitive times, baked at 700°C (1292°F) or lower; stoneware, fired at up to 1,150°C (2102°F), more vitrified or close-grained and nonporous, and produced more commonly in the Far East than in Europe until modern times; and porcelain, fired at 1,400°C (2552°F), a Chinese invention, and the most refined ceramic material, known as hard paste because of its homogeneous composition.

Clay is dug from the Earth's surface and prepared by beating and kneading with the hands, feet, or mallets. A potter's wheel, dating back to ancient times, rotated by feet and later by power, leaves the potter free use of his hands for manipulating the clay. After the object is formed and dried, it is fired in a kiln; glaze is applied, and it is refired. A glaze is a thin layer of glass applied to prevent seepage of liquids and impart a pleasing finish. Different glazes include alkaline, lead, feldspathic, and salt. *See also* Ceramics. △964, 1000, 1064.

Potto, slow-moving squirrel-sized primitive African primate with big eyes and pointed face. The common potto has short tail, and golden, or Calabar, potto is nearly tailless. Species: common *Perodicticus potto,* golden *Arctocebus calabarensis.* △554.

Pottstown, borough in SE Pennsylvania, on the Schuylkill River; site of state's first ironworks (1715) and The Hill School (est. 1851). Industries: fabricated steel, rubber tires and tubes, iron castings, clothing. Settled *c.* 1700; inc. 1815. Pop. (1970) 25,355.

Poughkeepsie, city and river port in SE New York, on E bank of Hudson River; seat of Dutchess co; made temporary capital of state 1777; site of Vassar College (1861), Marist College (1946), Dutchess Community College (1957). Industries: ball bearings, chemicals, clothing, dairy machinery. Founded 1687; inc. as village 1799, as city 1854. Pop. (1970) 32,029.

Poulenc, Francis (1899–1963), French composer. Many of his works are characterized by a light, witty style with simple melodies. Later works are more serious, many with a religious theme, eg, the opera *Les Dialogues des Carmélites* (1957). He is regarded as the most significant 20th-century French composer of songs.

Poultry, domesticated birds raised as a source of meat and eggs. In the United States, important poultry species include chickens and turkeys. In other parts of the world, guinea fowl, pheasant, pigeons, quail, and others are raised for food. △308, 382–84.

Pound, Ezra (Loomis) (1885–1972), US poet and critic, b. Hailey, Idaho. He published *A Lume Spento,* his first volume of poetry, in Venice in 1908; and then settled in London. In England from 1908 to 1920 he wrote *Exultations* (1909) and *Personae* (1909), which made him noted as a poet, and *The Spirit of Romance* (1910), a collection of critical articles. Emphasizing direct and precise language in poetry, he became a leader of the Imagist and Vorticist movements in the years around World War I and the dominant influence in Anglo-American poetry. Distressed by World War I, he began to emphasize the interconnections of the arts and society, beginning his complex epic *The Cantos* in 1915.

He developed an admiration for Fascist dictator Benito Mussolini and during World War II broadcast against the US war effort. Arrested in 1945, he was taken to the United States, found unfit to stand trial by reason of insanity, and confined to a hospital in Washington, D.C. In 1958 the charges against him were dropped, and he returned to Italy. *See also* Cantos, The. △1374.

Pound, Roscoe (1870–1964), US jurist and educator, b. Lincoln, Nebr. He was considered the most profound legal philosopher of his generation. Dean of the University of Nebraska Law School (1903–07), he also taught at Northwestern (1907–09) and the University of Chicago (1909–10), and was dean of Harvard Law School (1916–36). He is especially noted for his belief that laws should be compatible with popular attitudes and mores and adaptable to social and economic changes. His works include *Law and Morals* (1924) and *Outlines and Lectures on Jurisprudence* (1914).

Pound, the unit of force in the English foot-slug-second system of units. One pound is the force that would give a mass of one slug an acceleration of one foot per second per second.

Poussin, Nicolas (1594–1665), French painter of religious and mythological scenes and classical landscapes. His mature works evoked the spirit of the French classic ideal as no other paintings of that period did. His early works include "Victory of Joshua over the Amorites" (1625–26), executed in a Mannerist style, and "The Martyrdom of St Erasmus" (1628–29), in a Baroque style. His mature works include "The Eucharist" (1647) and "The Ashes of Phocion" (1648). After 1653 he enjoyed international prestige. △1166.

Poverty, Culture of, idea developed by social scientists in the 1960s that the poor have certain common beliefs and attitudes. △914.

Poverty Line, an imaginary concept, an attempt to measure the annual income that a person or family would need to maintain itself at the lowest acceptable level in a society. At any income level below the poverty line the individual or family would be unable to purchase goods and services adequate to maintain a socially acceptable standard of living. In 1975, the US poverty line for a four-person urban family was set at over $5,000 a year.

Powderly, Terence Vincent (1849–1924), US labor and political leader, b. Carbondale, Pa. A machinist (1869–77), he became head of the Knights of Labor (1883–93), advocating reforms such as trust regulation, worker ownership of public utilities, and abolition of child labor. Under Pres. William McKinley, he was commissioner general of immigration (1897–1902) and later served as head of the Division of Information of the Bureau of Immigration (1907–21).

Powder Metallurgy, the manufacture of metal powders and their use in producing metal parts. Powder particles are compressed to the desired shape and then sintered. Use of powders is more economical than molten metal in making such items as small gears. Melting may also prove impractical when a metal has a very high melting temperature or when an alloy of unfusable materials is involved. Powder metallurgy is also used for porous end products.

Powell, Frank. △1484.

Powell, Lewis Franklin, Jr., (1907–), US jurist and lawyer, b. Suffolk, Va. He is noted for his role on the Richmond, Va., Board of Education (1952–61) where he helped to achieve peaceful integration. He also served as president of the American Bar Association (1964–65) and president of the ABA Foundation (1969–71). He was nominated an associate justice of the US Supreme Court by Pres. Richard M. Nixon and confirmed in 1971.

Powell v. Alabama (1932), US Supreme Court decision declaring that an accused's right to counsel was fundamental to a fair trial. This holding was limited in *Betts* v. *Brady* in 1942 but reinstated in *Gideon* v. *Wainwright* in 1963. *See also* Gideon v. Wainwright (1963).

Power, rate of doing work. An engine that can lift 550lbs (247.5kg) through a height of one foot in one second is rated at one horsepower. The unit of electrical power is the watt; 746 watts equal one horsepower. Power multiplied by the time of operation gives the total energy consumed.

Power (of a number), the result of multiplying a number or variable by itself a specified number of times. Thus a^2 ($= a \times a$) is the second power of a; a^3 is the third power; a^4 the fourth, etc. The superscript, 2, 3, 4, etc. is the exponent. △1456.

Power, Electrical. △1648–50.

Power Elite, phrase coined by sociologist C. Wright Mills for the loose network of powerful individuals who exert a decisive influence over US society. Mills identified these people as government, corporate, and military executives who share complementary ideas and policies and make key government and social decisions. △890, 1360.

Power Plant, any installation that generates electricity. Such installations are typically hydroelectric, thermal or fossil fuel, or nuclear power plants. In each case potential or unusable energy is converted into easily used electricity. Power plants consist of reservoirs in which fuel is stored, an energy release mechanism (dam, boiler, reactor), turbines, generators, transformers, and a transmission or electrical distribution system. *See also* Hydroelectric Power Plant. △1628–1630.

Powers, Francis Gary, U-2 pilot. *See* U-2 Incident.

Powhatan, or **Wahunsonacock** (1550–1618), chief of Indian tribes in vicinity of Jamestown settlement. Powhatan was not friendly to the colonists until the marriage of his daughter Pocahontas to John Rolfe.

Powhatan, a major Algonkian-speaking confederacy of North American Indians formerly occupying the region from the Potomac River south to Albemarle Sound, in Virginia. They were famous in early American history for their role in the development of the eastern Atlantic area, and the position of two major personages—Powhatan and his daughter Pocahontas. From 9,000 individuals in 30 tribal groups, they have declined in numbers to about 2,000 today.

Poza Rica de Hidalgo, municipality in Mexico, 120mi (193km) S of Tampico. Industries: oil, livestock. Pop. 121,341.

Poznán, city in W Poland, on the Warta River, approx. 170mi (274km) W of Warsaw. One of the oldest cities of Poland, it became first Polish episcopal see (10th century), was a member of the Hanseatic League, and the central power of the Polish state, growing in prosperity until it passed to Prussia 1793; part of Grand Duchy of Warsaw 1807; passed back to Prussia 1815; ceded to Poland 1919; site of a Gothic cathedral, annual international spring fair, university (1919). Industries: metal, chemicals, textiles, food processing, marketing. Pop. 469,000.

PPLO, or pleuropneumonia-like organism, smallest organisms capable of growth and reproduction outside of living host cells. At about 0.25μm (1μm = 1/25,400 of an inch) in diameter, they are smaller than bacteria, but larger than viruses. This group is now classified under the genus *Mycoplasma;* the original name derived from the first such organism isolated which caused pleuropneumonia. Although widespread in humans, only one known disease is caused by mycoplasma—primary atypical pneumonia.

Prado, Madrid, the Spanish National Museum of Fine Art. Founded in 1818, it is an example of Spanish Neoclassical architecture. The major part of its collection derives from the royal collection of the Hapsburg and Bourbon kings of Spain. Almost all the important works of Velázquez and a full representation of El Greco and Goya are contained there. Bosch, Titian, Tintoretto, Veronese, Rubens, van Dyke, and Brueghel are also well represented.

Praesepe, a galactic or open cluster of several hundred stars in the constellation Cancer. It is visible to the unaided eye as a small bright hazy patch. First distinguished as a group of stars by Galileo. The name Praesepe means "cradle" and has been used since early Greek times. An alternative name, Beehive, is of more recent origin. △116.

Praetor, powerful Roman magistrate. △1014.

Praetorian Guards, bodyguard of the Roman emperors from Augustus to Constantine I. They were first selected by Augustus in 27 BC from the *cohort praetoria* that had guarded generals of the republic. Numbering from 9,000 to 16,000 men, they attended the emperor's family and enjoyed special privileges.

Pragmatic Sanction, solemn ordinance or decree by a head of state relating to matters of prime importance and having the force of law. Charles VI, Holy Roman emperor, decreed in 1713 that if he died without male heirs, his eldest daughter would inherit the Hapsburg dominions. This pragmatic sanction was initially agreed to by the major powers, but Prussia disputed it in 1740 when Charles died. The ensuing War of the Austrian Succession decided the issue in favor of Maria Theresa, Charles' daughter.

Pragmatism, development of British Empiricism, associated with the US philosophers C.S. Peirce and William James. Stemming from the Greek *pragma,* things done, pragmatism is both a doctrine of meaning and a definition of truth. The meaning of a symbol is understood in terms of the rational conduct inspired, and a proposition is true when its consequences prove useful and practical. What works best is true. *See also* James, William; Peirce, Charles S. △858.

Prague (Praha), capital of Czechoslovakia, on Vitava River, 160mi (256km) NW of Vienna, Austria. Its location on a strategic trade route and establishment of Charles University (1348) caused rapid growth. It became the capital in 1918 when Czechoslovakia was created. In 1945 the people drove out the Germans who had occupied it since 1939; Russians then took possession; site of Stavovske Theater (where Mozart's "Don Giovanni" was first performed), Old Synagogue (13th century), and 17th-century palace, Waldstein, all in Old Town part of Prague. Industries: automobiles, printing, publishing, airplanes. Founded AD 722. Pop. 1,078,096.

Praguerie (1440), revolt against Charles VII of France. Leaders of the revolt included several feudal lords, who felt that Charles had reduced their influence over the royal government. Among those who participated were the Comte de Dunois; Charles I, duc de Bourbon; Jean II, duc d'Alençon; and Philip the Good of Burgundy. The rebels were quickly defeated.

Praia, seaport town on S shore of São Tiago Island, Cape Verde. It has served as the capital of the archipelago and seat of the governor general and his palace since 1770; site of meteorological observatory; cable station, important link between South America, Europe, and W Africa. Exports: castor oil, sugar cane, oranges, coffee. Industries: straw hats, fish processing, distilling. Pop. 45,079.

Prairie. △584.

Prairie Chicken, chicken-sized, pale brown grouse of W United States. It has brown and black, stiffly pointed neck feathers that stand up when the male inflates orange neck air sacs during courtship displays. Groups of males shuffle about with necks erect and bills pointed down until mating. The female incubates the eggs (12) in a small scraped area and cares for the young. Species *Tympanuchus cupido. See also* Grouse; Heath Hen.

Prairie Dog, squirrellike rodent of North America named for its barking cry. Short-tailed plant and insect eaters, they have grizzled brown to buff fur. Active by day, they live in communal burrows that are connected to form colonies. Length: 12in (30cm). Genus *Cynomys. See also* Ground Squirrel.

Prairie Falcon, common falcon generally found in dry inland areas. Species *Falco mexicanus. See also* Falcon.

Prairie School of Architecture, US school of architecture created by Frank Lloyd Wright at the turn of 20th century. It is typified by low spreading houses set in gardens and terraces, with projecting roofs and wide merging rooms. *See also* Wright, Frank Lloyd.

Prairie Village, city in NE Kansas; residential suburb in greater Kansas City area. Inc. 1951. Pop. (1970) 28,138.

Praseodymium, metallic element (symbol Pr) of the Lanthanide group, first identified spectroscopically (1879) by Lecoq de Boisbaudran. Chief ores are monazite (phosphate) and bastnasite (fluorocarbonate). Praseodymium is used in carbon-arc lamps. Its salts are used in colored glasses. Properties: at. no. 59; at. wt. 140.9077; sp gr 6.773(α), 6.64 (β); melt. pt. 1,708°F (931°C); boil. pt. 5,814°F (3,212°C); most common isotope Pr^{141}(100%). *See also* Lanthanide Elements. △1552–54.

Pratincole, any of about seven species of Old World birds, related to shorebirds. All are brown with white rumps, to about 8in (20cm) long, with forked tails and long, pointed wings. They feed on insects near rivers and nest colonially on the ground. The black-winged pratincole *(Glareola pratincola),* native to the Middle East, is sometimes called the locust bird in its winter home in Africa. Family Glareolidae.

Praxiteles (*fl.* 370–330 BC), Greek sculptor. His graceful style encompassed the 4th-century Greek ideal. One of the most widely imitated of Greek sculptors, he is the author of "Hermes Holding the Infant Dionysos," a work found in Olympia in 1877 and now in the museum there. It may possibly be the original work, but it is more likely a good Roman copy. His most famous work is "Aphrodite (Venus) of Cnidus," a sensuous work that created a new ideal model. The best of several extant copies is at the Vatican museum. △1002.

Praying Mantis. *See* Mantis.

Precambrian Era, the oldest and longest major division of Earth history, lasting from the beginning of the Earth over 4,000,000,000 years ago to the beginnings of a good fossil record 570,000,000 years ago. Precambrian fossils are extremely rare because the earliest life forms are presumed not to have had hard parts suitable for preservation. Also, Precambrian rocks have been greatly changed and deformed. Nonetheless, primitive bacteria and blue-green algae have been identified from deposits 3,300,000,000 years old and later Precambrian localities have

Potto

Ezra Pound

Poznań, Poland

Prague, Czechoslovakia

yielded some questionable finds of more advanced organisms such as jellyfish, worms, and arthropods. △276.

Precession, slow revolution of the Earth's axis of rotation about the poles of the ecliptic. It is caused by lunar and solar perturbations acting on the Earth's equatorial bulge and causes a westward motion of the stars that takes 25,800 years to complete. △826.

Precipitate, formation of an insoluble solid in solution either by direct reaction or by varying the solution composition to diminish the solubility of the dissolved compound. This technique is used for the separation and identification of compounds in chemical processes. △1562, 1568.

Precipitation, all forms of water particles, whether liquid or solid, that fall from the atmosphere to the ground. Distinguished from cloud, fog, dew, and frost, in that it must fall and reach the ground, precipitation includes rain, drizzle, snow, snow and ice pellets and crystals, and hail. Measured by rain and snow gauges, the amount of precipitation is expressed in inches (or mm) of liquid water depth. Precipitation occurs with the condensation of water vapor in clouds into water droplets that coalesce into drops as large as 0.25in. (6mm) in diameter or form from melting ice crystals in the clouds. Drizzle consists of fine droplets, and snow of masses of six-sided ice crystals or prisms. Sleet is produced by freezing of raindrops into small ice pellets, and hail by the freezing of concentric layers of ice in cumulonimbus clouds, with lumps measuring from 0.2 up to 2in. (0.5 to 5cm) in diameter. Ice storms result when rain falls on frozen ground or other objects like trees and wires, freezing into a heavy glaze. Fog is like a cloud in that water vapor condenses, in this case at or near the ground. Dew is water condensed on grass and other objects near the ground when temperatures fall below the dewpoint, and frost forms when the dewpoint is below freezing. △216.

Precipitator. *See* Electrostatic Cleaner.

Precognition, knowledge that some future event will occur that is obtained through extrasensory means rather than through any known process of rational inference; one form of extrasensory perception, or ESP. *See also* Clairvoyance; Parapsychology. △824.

Pre-Columbian Art and Architecture, the art and architecture of Mexico, Central America, and the Andean region of South America before the arrival of Europeans. △970.

Predestination, theological concept whereby certain souls are guaranteed salvation before birth by the grace of an omniscient God. A basic belief (in some form) of Muslims, Roman Catholics, and Jews, predestination took on renewed significance with the Calvinists, who believed that God from eternity had blessed certain souls and damned others, the difference to be seen in the individual's works. △812, 1152.

Predmostians. △652.

Prednisone, or deltacortisone, synthetic steroid, administered orally, sometimes used to treat leukemia or Hodgkins disease. *See also* Steroid.

Pre-established Harmony, theory advocated by the 17th-century German philosopher Gottfried Leibniz, intended to obviate metaphysical inconveniences of interaction and occasionalism. Monads, Leibniz's centers of force and consciousness, do not influence each other, so the universe is rational and designed in accordance with law. *See also* Monad; Occasionalism.

Prefabrication, the assembly of buildings or their components at locations other than their final position. Prefabrication methods are used for kitchen cabinets and appliances, wall and floor panels, roof trusses, window-wall elements, and total buildings. Custom fabrication is used when the design calls for several identical components in a single structure, such as might be used in hospitals, apartment buildings, and schools. General prefabrication is designed for a wide range of building types, such as residential roof trusses, warehouse frames, and bowling alleys.

Pregnancy, the period of time from conception until birth. In the human it is generally divided into three 3-month periods called trimesters. In the first trimester the fetus grows from a small ball of cells to about 3in (7.6cm) in length, during which time all the vital organs, such as the heart, lungs, skeleton, and brain develop. In the second trimester the fetus grows to about 14in (36cm), and movements are first felt about midway. In the third trimester the fetus gains full body weight. △702.

Pregnancy Tests, methods of determining whether or not a developing embryo or fetus is present in the uterus. Pregnancy is suggested or confirmed by the following: elevation of basal body temperature (taken on first waking in the morning) continuing after the first missed period; absence of the "fern" pattern on microscopic examination of cervical mucus; failure to induce menstruation by administering progesterone or neostigmine; finding of high levels of the hormone human chorionic gonadotropin (HCG) in the urine. Tests for HCG are now so refined that an accurate diagnosis of pregnancy can be made by this method on the first day after the missed period. △702.

Prehistoric Art. △950, 1586–90.

Prejudice, a preconceived feeling or attitude, most often unfriendly. A prejudiced person resists change in his view of ideas or people he does not like, and he may use discrimination or violence against them. Prejudice may grow out of individual conflicts or be taught by society. *See also* Apartheid; Discrimination. △894, 896.

Premature Birth, birth of a human less than 36 weeks after conception. 85% of liveborn premature babies survive, those of higher weight having the greater potential for life. Multiple births are frequently premature; poor maternal health and nutrition are also major factors.

Premier, title used by the chief executive in many governments. △902.

Premyslid, Bohemian dynasty established in the 10th century by Premysl. The conversion of Bohemia to Christianity was completed at this time by German priests. Under Bratislav I (1034–55) a stable period ensued. Problems of succession and tribute exacted by the Holy Roman Empire contributed to the decline of the Premyslids, and the dynasty ended with the death of Wenceslaus in 1306.

Prendergast, Maurice Brazil (1861–1924), US painter, b. Roxbury, Mass. One of the most advanced artists of his time, he exhibited with The Eight in their famous show of 1908. His works include "Seashore" (1910), "Promenade" (1914–15), and the watercolors "The Balloon" and "Cape Ann."

Preparedness Movement (1915–16), campaign for greater defense strength. It marked the end of the controversy over the US policy of neutrality in World War I. Among the organizations that brought the issue to public attention was the National Security League. Prominent people including Theodore Roosevelt and Henry Cabot Lodge urged the end of unarmed neutrality. After the *Lusitania* incident (1915), a powerful crusade by military interests verged on becoming a partisan political issue, forcing President Wilson to reverse his position and campaign for preparedness as a national security necessity.

Preposition, the part of speech that shows the relation between its object and some other word in the sentence. The preposition, its object, and the modifiers of the object become a prepositional phrase.

Pre-Raphaelite Brotherhood, formulated in 1848 by Dante Gabriel Rossetti, John Everett Millais, and William Holman Hunt, three young English painters. Reacting against the inflated forms and sentiments that they found in the followers of Raphael, they preferred the sincerity they saw in the Florentine and Sienese who predated him. They tried to bring a new moral and literary seriousness to painting and to study nature directly. △1252.

Presbyterianism, a Protestant faith emphasizing a form of church government with a ranking of elders and ministers. John Calvin did not found but laid the foundation of the Presbyterian faith. John Knox established the church in Scotland where it remains dominant. Today it is one of the largest Protestant groups in the world.

Prescriptive Linguistics, investigation of the problems of language, as it is influenced by reasoning and behavior consistency. Prescriptivism holds that moral principles have more to do with reasoning and with consistency of behavior than with emotion and persuasion.

Preservation, Chemical. *See* Food Preservative.

Presidential Government, system of government in which the center of authority resides in the president, who is the chief executive officer. The US Constitution bestows on the president both defined and implied powers which give him a vast amount of influence over both foreign and domestic policy. In most presidential governments, the chief executive is popularly elected to a specific term of office. △902.

Presidential Powers, authority vested in a president as chief executive to carry out the laws of the land. In the United States, these include the powers of commander-in-chief of the armed forces; the appointment of executive agency heads, of ambassadors, and of Supreme Court justices; veto power over legislation; and the power to make treaties with senatorial consent. The influence of office further invests the president with the political power to ensure favorable action on his legislative program. A system of checks and balances allows the legislative and judicial branches to curb presidential excesses. *See also* Presidential Government; President of the United States.

Presidential Range, mountain chain of the White Mt system in N New Hampshire; culminates at Mt Washington, 6,288ft (1,918m).

Presidential Succession, procedure for filling a presidential vacancy occurring before the end of the prescribed term. The procedure was first outlined in the US Constitution and later amplified in the Presidential Succession Act of 1947. The vice president is first in line to succeed under the Constitution, followed by the speaker of the House of Representatives, the president pro tempore of the Senate, and the secretary of state according to the 1947 act. Amendment XXV to the Constitution, adopted Feb. 10, 1967, covers such emergencies as an incapacitating illness of the president. Under the amendment, the vice president's office is protected from vacancy and the method by which he takes the president's place, should the president be unable to discharge his duties, is specified.

President of the United States, US chief executive officer, as defined in Article II of the Constitution; elected by eligible voters through the Electoral College for a term of four years. No president may serve more than two terms under the provisions of Amendment XXII. The president must be a natural-born citizen and at least 35 years of age.

The Constitution specifies that presidential powers include those of commander-in-chief of the armed forces; the appointment of Supreme Court justices, ambassadors, and other officials; and the authority to grant pardons, make treaties with foreign countries with the advice and consent of two-thirds of the Senate; and veto legislation. The president is required to report to the Congress from time to time on the state of the union; to preserve, protect, and defend the Constitution; and to "faithfully execute" the laws. Presidential power is limited by the system of checks and balances.

Following is a chronological list of the US presidents and their terms of office.

Presidents of the United States

George Washington (1789–97)
John Adams (1797–1801)
Thomas Jefferson (1801–09)
James Madison (1809–17)
James Monroe (1817–25)
John Quincy Adams (1825–29)
Andrew Jackson (1829–37)
Martin Van Buren (1837–41)
William Henry Harrison (1841)
John Tyler (1841–45)
James Knox Polk (1845–49)
Zachary Taylor (1849–50)
Millard Fillmore (1850–53)
Franklin Pierce (1853–57)
James Buchanan (1857–61)
Abraham Lincoln (1861–65)
Andrew Johnson (1865–69)
Ulysses Simpson Grant (1869–77)
Rutherford Birchard Hayes (1877–81)
James Abram Garfield (1881)
Chester Alan Arthur (1881–85)
Grover Cleveland (1885–89, 1893–97)
Benjamin Harrison (1889–93)
William McKinley (1897–1901)
Theodore Roosevelt (1901–09)
William Howard Taft (1909–13)
(Thomas) Woodrow Wilson (1913–21)
Warren Gamaliel Harding (1921–23)
(John) Calvin Coolidge (1923–29)
Herbert Clark Hoover (1929–33)
Franklin Delano Roosevelt (1933–45)
Harry S Truman (1945–53)
Dwight David Eisenhower (1953–61)
John Fitzgerald Kennedy (1961–63)
Lyndon Baines Johnson (1963–69)
Richard Milhous Nixon (1969–74)
Gerald Rudolph Ford (1974–77)
James Earl Carter, Jr. (1977–)

See also Presidential Powers. △902, 1218.

President Pro Tempore of the Senate, US Senator elected by his colleagues to preside over the Senate in the absence of the vice president or when the vice president has assumed the presidency.

Presley, Elvis (1935–), US singer and movie actor, b. Tupelo, Miss. He first recorded in 1953; after the release of his first major hit "Heartbreak Hotel" (1956) he experienced instant success. He attracted followers from country and western, rock 'n' roll, and rhythm and blues musical styles. His unique manner of performing, complete with his famed pelvic gyrations, made him a teenage idol. He later became a movie actor. △1366.

Pressburg, Treaty of (1805), peace treaty between Emperor Francis II and Napoleon I. △1226.

Press Tools. △1606.

Pressure. △1496, 1502–04, 1514.

Pressure Gauge, an instrument used to measure fluid pressure. Liquid-column gauges, such as manometers or pitot tubes, use shifts of liquid positions in U-shaped tubes to measure pressure. Mechanical gauges, such as Bourdon tubes or Bellows-element gauges, utilize elasticity of metals to measure pressure. △1656.

Pressure Groups, special-interest groups seeking to bring the weight of public and/or private opinion to bear on legislative action or the awarding of government contracts. △900, 904.

Pressure-tube Reactor. △1638.

Pressurized-Water Reactor. *See* Fission Reactor.

Prester John, also John the Elder, legendary Christian king in either Asia or Africa. Supposedly descended from one of the Magi, he became the subject of much speculation during the European crusades—he was reported to have severely defeated the Persians. Several explorers joined the search for this possible ruler of either Mongolia or Ethiopia. △974.

Preston, city in NW England, on the River Ribble; administrative center for Lancashire; market town and port. Industries: engineering, textiles, paper, chemicals. Pop. 97,365.

Prestressed Concrete, a type of strong concrete used in bridges and large, roofed structures. While it is settling, tightly drawn steel wires are extended through it, which, after bonding, are cut, releasing tension and compressing the concrete. △1612, 1758.

Pretoria, city in Republic of South Africa, on the Limpopo River 34mi (54km) N of Johannesburg; administrative capital of Republic of South Africa (since 1910) and capital of the Transvaal (since 1860). It was the scene of the imprisonment of Winston Churchill (1899) during the Boer War and of the signing of the Peace of Vereeniging (1902) ending the war; site of the National Cultural History Museum, National Zoological Gardens, several cathedrals, and universities of Pretoria (1930) and South Africa (1873). Founded 1855 by Marthinus Pretorius. Industries: iron, steel, diamonds, food processing. Pop. 543,950.

Pretorius, Marthinus Wessels (1819–1901), Boer political leader. He helped form the Transvaal and was president both of the Transvaal and the Orange Free State (1859–63), which he tried to unite. An early proponent of Boer solidarity, he later became an important figure in their resistance to British rule.

Preventive Medicine, branch of medicine concentrating on attempts to prevent disease through the use of immunization, public health measures, and other means. △738.

Priam, in Greek mythology, the king of Troy at the time of the war with Greece. He had been installed as king in his youth by Hercules, but by the time of the ten-years' war had become a very old man. He lived to see his sons Hector and Paris and his daughter Polyxena killed by the enemy.

Pribilof Islands, group of four volcanic islands in SE Bering Sea, Alaska, 230mi (368km) N of Aleutian Islands. Discovered 1786 by Russian navigator, Gerasim Pribilof, it was purchased by the United States from Russia as part of Alaska purchase 1867. St Paul and St George, the larger islands, are breeding places for blue and white foxes and Alaska fur seals. Since 1911, when extinction of seals was threatened, the United States has administered a strict code of standards for commercial hunting of these animals. Pop. 642.

Price, (Mary) Leontyne (1927–) US soprano, b. Laurel, Miss. She studied at the Juilliard School of Music in New York, initiated a successful concert career in 1954, and made a triumphant debut at the Metropolitan Opera in 1961 in Verdi's *Il Trovatore.* She has since appeared in many of the world's leading opera houses.

Price Fixing, formal or informal arrangement among a group of sellers to set one price for the item they produce, thus avoiding competition and instead enhancing profits. Price fixing without government sanction is usually illegal.

Price-Support Programs, governmental programs that put a floor under the prices of agricultural products. For most products the support price is higher than the market price of the product, and the government, in effect, buys the surplus created by excess production. If a large surplus builds up in government storage it may be sold to the poor or abroad, and government then limits acreage in later years.

Price Theory, in economics, deals with the way prices are determined, including both the demand and the supply components. Price theory involves the study of the individual units within the economy, both the way the individual consumer seeks to maximize his utility position and the theory of the individual firm or business enterprise and its decisions in its attempts to maximize profits.

Prichard, industrial city in SW Alabama, 3mi (5km) W of Mobile. Industries: cotton processing, chemicals. Settled 1900; inc. 1925. Pop. (1970) 41,578.

Prickly Pear, cactus, characterized by flat or cylindrical joints, native to North and South America. The jointed pads have tufts of bristles and the edible fruit is red and pulpy. Its showy yellow blossoms and interesting shape make it a popular house plant. Family Cactaceae; genus *Opuntia. See also* Cactus; Opuntia.

Pride's Purge (1648), expulsion of 140 moderate members of the English House of Commons. It was carried out by Col. Thomas Pride's regiment, on the orders of the republican army council, in preparation for the trial of King Charles I. △1156.

Priestley, J(ohn) B(oynton) (1894–), English author and playwright. His best known novel, *The Good Companions* (1929), is about a wandering music-hall troupe. He also wrote the nostalgic *Lost Empires* (1965) about the music-hall world, as well as several other novels. His nonfiction work includes *Literature and Western Man* (1960). His writing for the theater began with *Dangerous Corner* (1932), a satire on middle-class life, and includes *An Inspector Calls* (1945), another satire; *Time and the Conways* (1937), a science-fiction play; *Johnson Over Jordan* (1939), a modern morality play; and *The Glass Cage* (1957).

Priestly, Joseph (1733–1804), English chemist. A Unitarian minister, his involvement in science grew from his interest in the gases produced by fermentation in a local brewery. He studied the properties of carbon dioxide (then called "fixed air") and invented carbonated drinks. Although an advocate of the phlogiston theory, he discovered oxygen (which he called "dephlogisticated air") and a number of other gases, including ammonia and the oxides of nitrogen. Because of his support for the French Revolution his house was burned by an angry mob and he emigrated to the US, where he renewed a friendship with Benjamin Franklin. *See also* Phlogiston Theory.

Primal Therapy. △774.

Primary Focus. *See* Focus.

Primates, order of mammals including monkeys, apes, and humans. Primates, native to most tropical and subtropical regions, are primarily herbivorous, day-active, tree-dwelling animals. Their hands and feet, usually with flat nails instead of claws, are adapted for grasping. Most species have opposable thumbs, and all but man have opposable big toes. They have a poor sense of smell, good hearing, and acute stereoscopic color vision. The outstanding feature of primates, especially man, is the large, complex brain and high intelligence. Primate characteristics are least pronounced in the relatively primitive *prosimians* (including tree shrews, lemurs, bush babies, lorises, and tarsiers) and are most pronounced in the more numerous and advanced *anthropoids* (monkeys, apes, and humans). △554, 558.

Prefabrication

Maurice Prendergast: Central Park *(detail)*

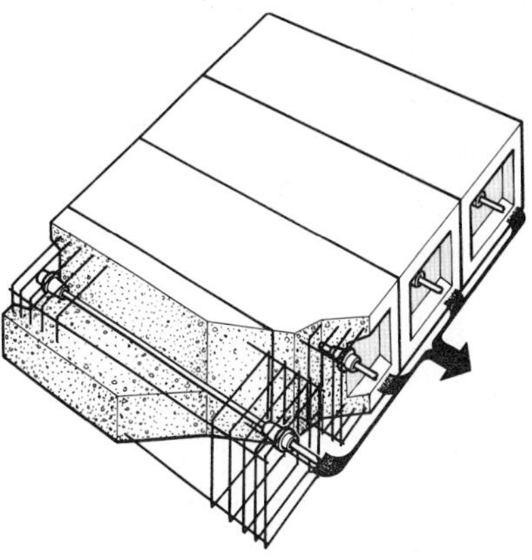

Prestressed concrete

Leontyne Price

Primaticcio, Francesco (1504–70), Italian painter. △1150.

Prime Meridian, meridian adopted as the zero of longitude on a planet, the prime meridian on Earth passing through Greenwich, England.

Prime Minister, chief minister and executive of a country. △902.

Prime Number. *See* Number, Prime.

Primer, Paint, a coat of paint, varnish, or sealer applied to a surface on which a second coating will be applied to ensure complete protection and covering to the surface. Primers are particularly important when the surface to be covered is porous, as cinder block; when the surface is a darker color than the finishing coat; or when the surface is extremely smooth and hard, as in some metals. △1812.

Prime Rate, rate of interest that the large commercial banks charge their prime customers for business loans. A few large banks exert the most influence in setting the prime rate; other commercial banks generally follow their lead.

Primitivism, in art, a style sometimes practiced by highly skilled but untrained, nonacademic artists. The style features everyday subjects, great elaboration of detail, flat colors, unrealistic perspective, and often landscape. Leading primitivistic painters include Henri Rousseau in France and the Americans Grandma Moses, Morris Hirschfield, Israel Litwak, and Joseph Pickett.

Primo de Rivera, José Antonio (1903–36), Spanish political leader. He was the son of Miguel Primo de Rivera, military dictator of Spain from 1923 to 1930. He founded the Falange, the fascistic party of the Nationalists and a weekly newspaper, *El Fascio,* both in 1933. In 1936, Primo de Rivera was executed by the Loyalist government after being convicted on charges of trying to overthrow the republic. He became a martyr to the Nationalist cause.

Primo de Rivera, Miguel (1870–1930), Spanish general and political leader. After a distinguished military career, he staged a coup in 1923 with the full support of King Alfonso XIII. He dissolved the Cortes, rescinded the constitution, and ruled over a military dictatorship. In 1925 he instituted a civilian regime but continued as sole dictator. He ended the war in Morocco but faced varied opposition at home, especially from the Catalans. He was forced from office in 1930 and died in exile.

Primogeniture, under feudalism, the law or practice that entitled the eldest son to inherit his father's estate, necessary if fiefs were to remain intact. In most parts of France and Germany, partition of properties held in fief, known as *parage,* was more common, but in England, primogeniture became the prevailing custom by the 12th century. Although under the feudal system direct inheritance of real property was inconsistent with the concept of fiefs and vassalage, the vassal's son did have the right to apply to his father's lord for the privilege of assuming his father's lands and obligations under a new contract of vassalage. *See also* Feudalism.

Primordial Fireball, in cosmology, hypothetical object of enormous density and temperature that, according to the big-bang theory, existed prior to the explosion with which the universe originally came into existence. The entire mass and energy of the universe was originally contained in this object, which consisted of interacting atomic nuclei, became unstable and exploded at the zero point of cosmic time (2×10^{10} years ago). Energy radiation, chiefly in the form of photons, then dominated the expanding universe, the temperature decreasing until gravitation commenced to bind particles together and form matter. *See also* Big-Bang Theory of Universe. △126, 406.

Primrose, herbaceous perennial plant that grows in the cooler climates of Europe, Asia, Ethiopia, Java, and the United States. It has a tuft of leaves rising from the rootstock and clustered flowers of pale yellow to deep crimson. There are about 500 species. Family Primulaceae; genus *Primula.* △456, 594.

Prince Albert National Park, region in central Saskatchewan, Canada; sanctuary for moose, elk, deer, caribou, and bear. Park has hundreds of lakes, an internationally known golf course, and hotel, motel, and camping facilities. Area: 1,496sq mi (3,875sq km). Est. 1927.

Prince Edward Island, province of E Canada, in the S part of the Gulf of St Lawrence, an arm of the Atlantic Ocean.

Land and economy. High cliffs rise along the coast, but the land is low and rolling. Fertile soils and a temperate climate are favorable to agriculture, which has long been the province's chief source of income. Fishing is important. Manufacturing is limited to a few small plants.

People and education. Because of its small size, Prince Edward Island is the most densely populated province in Canada. English, Irish, and French stocks are predominant. The University of Prince Edward Island is at Charlottetown.

History. The island was discovered by Jacques Cartier in 1534. Known as Île St Jean (St John's Island), it was a French fishing station until it was captured by the British in 1745. Retaken by the French, it finally passed to the British by treaty in 1763. The name was changed to Prince Edward Island in 1798. As the forest was cleared, agriculture broadened the economic base, which had been founded on fishing.

PROFILE

Admitted to Confederation: July 1, 1873; rank, 7th
National Parliament Representatives: Senate, 4; House of Commons, 4
Population: 119,000; rank, 10th
Capital: Charlottetown
Chief Cities: Charlottetown; Summerside
Provincial Legislature: Legislative Assembly, 32
Area: 2,184sq mi (5,657sq km); rank, 10th
Elevation: Highest, 450ft (137m); lowest, sea level
Industries (major products): prefabricated homes, boats
Agriculture (major products): potatoes, dairy products, oats, barley
Fisheries: lobster, oysters, codfish, herring, haddock
Floral Emblem: lady's slipper

Princess Stephanie Bird of Paradise. △538.

Princeton, borough in W central New Jersey, on Millstone River; scene of British defeat by US forces (1777) during American Revolution, Continental Congress (1783), and headquarters of Lord Cornwallis in home of Richard Stockton. Educational facilities include Princeton University (1746) and St Joseph's College (1938). Founded 1696 by Quakers; inc. 1813. Pop. (1970) 12,311.

Princeton University, university in Princeton, N.J. A member of the Ivy League, its areas of specialized study include engineering, architecture, and public and international affairs. Chartered 1746; opened 1747; known as the College of New Jersey until 1896.

Principia Mathematica, three-volume work (1910–13) that resulted from an 11-year collaboration between A.N. Whitehead and Bertrand Russell. △854.

Printed Circuit, electrical device. The wiring and some components consist of a thin coat of electrically conductive material on an insulating base in a pattern. Printed circuits replaced conventional wiring in radios, television sets, and computers for a time after World War II. But in the 1970s smaller and more compact circuits replaced the printed circuits, rendering them obsolete.

Printing. △1770–80.

Printmaking, process in graphics of making impressions from wood blocks, plates, stones, or silk. There are four main groups of graphic techniques. The first is the relief method, in which the parts of the wood block or metal plate that are to be printed are left in relief, and the remainder is cut away. Ink is rolled over and adheres to the raised portions. A print may be made by hand; a press is unnecessary. Some examples are woodcuts, wood engravings, linocuts, and metal cuts. The second is the intaglio method. Here the surface does not print; ink is held in the engraved furrows. Damp paper is pressed by a copper plate press into these cuts and picks up the ink from them. Examples are line engravings, drypoints, etchings, and aquatints. The third method is the surface or planographic method (lithography), in which greased areas on a slab of limestone or a metal plate reject printing ink. In the fourth method, the stencil, color is brushed through a hole in a protecting sheet onto the surface below. Examples are silkscreens and serigraphs.

Pripyat (Pripet or **Pinsk) Marshes,** marshlands in S Belorussian SSR and NW Ukrainian SSR, USSR; extending along Pripyat River 300mi (483km) E and W and 140mi (225km) N and S; largest tract of swamp in Europe, formerly in E Poland. Heavily wooded, largely uninhabited, nearly impassable area forms a natural defense barrier; site of battlefield during WWI, bypassed during WWII. Drainage of area was begun 1870 to reclaim land for cultivation and pasturage.

Prism, piece of transparent glass, plastic, quartz, etc, usually with a rectangular base and triangular ends, in which a light beam is refracted and is also split into its component colors by dispersion. Prisms are thus used to produce spectra in spectrometers. A light ray inside a prism can undergo total internal reflection from one of the sides so that a prism can also be used for inverting an image, as in binoculars, or changing the direction of a beam, as in a periscope. △1516.

Prism (in geometry), solid figure having two identical ends that are polygons in parallel planes, the other faces being parallelograms equal in number to the number of sides of one of the bases. △1466.

Privet, deciduous shrub native to Europe and N Africa. It is frequently planted in England and the United States as a hedge. It has smooth, lance-shaped leaves and loose clusters of tiny, white flowers that appear in June and July. It bears small black berries. Species include the common, or European, privet *(Ligustrum vulgare)* and the hardier California privet *(L. ovalifolium)* popular in the United States. Height: to 15ft (4.6m). Family Oleaceae.

Probability, number representing the likelihood of a given occurrence. The probability of a specified event is the number of ways that event may occur divided by the total possible number of outcomes. For instance, in one throw of a six-sided die there are six possible outcomes, and three of these results in an even number: the probability of throwing an even number is thus $3/6 = \frac{1}{2}$. This assumes that each possibility is equally "likely." A less circular idea of probability utilizes the concept of a limit. If the die were thrown a large number of times the number of even numbers resulting divided by the total number of throws would tend to the value ½. Probability theory is concerned with the analysis of random events of this type. △1474–76.

Probate Court. *See* Surrogate Court.

Proboscis Monkey, large monkey of Borneo with protruding nose that is upturned in young monkeys and long and pendulous in older males. They are gregarious, day-active leaf and fruit eaters and swim and dive freely. Species *Nasalis larvatus. See also* Monkey. △620.

Probus, Marcus Aurelius (died 282), Roman emperor (276–82). △1030.

Procaine, trade name Novocain, synthetic compound used as a local anesthetic. Blocking the conducting capabilities of nerve tissues, it is usually injected subcutaneously in small doses. Its most frequent use is in dental medicine, but it may be used as a spinal anesthetic or applied topically. An allergic reaction may be a side effect.

Proclamation of Amnesty and Reconstruction (May 1865), declaration by President Andrew Johnson providing for restoration of the Confederate states to the Union. Under the plan, pardons were granted to Southerners who took an oath to support the United States. Elected government was restored in former Confederate states after state constitutional conventions repealed ordinances of secession and abolished slavery. Johnson's plan was negated by congressional action. *See also* Reconstruction.

Proclamation of Rebellion, document issued by George III in August 1775. It declared the American colonies to be in state of rebellion and required that every effort must be made to "suppress such rebellion and to bring the traitors to justice."

Proclamation of 1763, British document designed to establish government in territories acquired in the French and Indian wars. Written by Lord Shelburne, head of the Board of Trade, and modified by his successor, the Earl of Hillsborough, it attempted to formulate a policy that would not antagonize the Indians. The provisions forbade American settlement west of the line formed by the Appalachians and ordered all settlers to vacate the area, which was to be reserved for the Indians. Three new provinces were established—Quebec, East Florida, and West Florida. Quebec was to be governed by British law.

Procrustes, in Greek mythology, a brigand in Attica. He tortured travelers that he captured by placing them on a bed and stretching them to fit it if they were too short, or cutting off their limbs if they were too long. Theseus had him killed by his own methods. He is also known as Damastes.

Proctology, branch of medicine dealing with the diagnosis and treatment of diseases of the rectum and lower intestine.

Procyon, or **Alpha Canis Minoris,** the brightest star in the constellation Canis Minor. Procyon A has a faint companion, Procyon B (white dwarf). Characteristics: apparent mag. 0.34 (A), 10.8 (B); absolute mag. 2.8 (A), 13.1 (B); spectral type F5 (A), wF (B); distance 11.4 light-years.

Producer Gas, a mixture of gases, flammable (eg carbon monoxide and hydrogen) and nonflammable (eg nitrogen and carbon dioxide) made by partial combustion of carbonaceous substances (such as coal) in air and steam. It has a lower heating value than other fuels, but can be manufactured with simple equipment. Producer gas is used as a fuel in large industrial furnaces.

Production, in industry. △938.

Progesterone, steroid hormone secreted mainly by the corpus luteum of the mammalian ovary. Its principal function is to prepare and maintain the uterus for pregnancy. *See also* Hormones; Steroid. △700.

Program, Computer, detailed, explicit set of directions for accomplishing some computation or manipulation of data by a computer. The program must be stated in a language suitable for use by the computer input compiler, assembler, or translation input device, or directly in machine language. Computer programming is an activity by human beings that begins with an understanding of the problem, follows with coding the request for solution of the problem in appropriate computer language, entering, and running tests until satisfactory results are achieved from the computer. △1672–74.

Programmed Instruction. *See* Teaching Machine.

Programmed Learning, method of instruction in which the learner proceeds through a series of highly structured materials at his own pace. Items in the materials both instruct and test the learner, providing immediate feedback about learning progress. The method is largely based on B.F. Skinner's research on operant conditioning. *See also* Operant Conditioning.

Program Music, music without words, intended to describe and represent events, people, or a story. Significant examples of program music are Beethoven's "Pastoral" *Symphony No. 6* (about an outing in the country) and Berlioz's *Symphonie Fantastique*. Program music reached great popularity in the late 19th century in such works as Moussorgsky's *Pictures at an Exhibition* and the tone poems of Richard Strauss.

Progression. *See* Arithmetic Progression. △1456.

Progressive Education, movement in 20th-century US education, commonly associated with the philosophy of John Dewey. Educators such as William Heard Kilpatrick applied Dewey's ideas, with additions and distortions, to schooling. Efforts to democratize the classroom, to consider children's needs, and to have them "learn by doing," led in some cases to what critics termed laxness.

Progressive Party, third party movement that split off from the Republicans in 1912, also called the Bull Moose Party. Under the leadership of Theodore Roosevelt, who praised the strength and vigor of the bull moose, the party advocated direct government and promoted advanced social and industrial legislation. Progressives also favored the establishment of a federal labor department in the cabinet and liberal extension of credit to farmers. Support for Progressive party presidential candidate Roosevelt seriously split the Republican vote in 1912, insuring the election of Democratic candidate Woodrow Wilson. However, by 1914, the Progressives were suffering setbacks, and in 1916, the party joined with the Republicans to endorse the nomination of Charles Evans Hughes.

Progressivism, US reform movement. In the early 20th century the Progressives favored such measures as governmental regulation of big business, the establishment of child labor laws, female suffrage, and the institution of such political reforms as the direct primary, the referendum, and the power of recall. The movement, mostly middle class and urban in nature, reached its peak in 1912 with the formation of the Progressive party, which nominated Theodore Roosevelt for president and polled 30% of the popular vote. After 1916 the movement gradually went into decline, but the party attempted revivals in 1924 with Robert LaFollette and in 1948 with Henry A. Wallace.

Prohibition, era in which the manufacture and sale of alcoholic beverages was illegal. It was enacted through the 18th Amendment to the Constitution (1919) and was later repealed by the 21st Amendment (1933). Although the regulation of liquor had previously been under the jurisdiction of the states, the amendment made national previous state and local legislation and engendered widespread conflict between rural and urban groups. The refusal of most citizens to obey the Volstead Act, which enforced the 18th Amendment, led to the condoning of lawlessness, invasion of personal rights by federal agents, corruption of government officials and local police, paralysis of the courts, and the growth of organized crime financed by immense bootlegging profits. △1324.

Project Head Start, US program to help disadvantaged children that originated as a community action program under the Economic Opportunity Act of 1964. Centers were set up around the country to help improve the health, adjustment, and school readiness of young children in poor or otherwise deprived areas.

Projective Geometry, a branch of geometry dealing with the properties of geometric configurations that are unaltered by projective transformation and in which the notion of length does not appear.

Projective Techniques, in psychology, personality tests that require the subject to respond to ambiguous stimuli that can be interpreted in many different ways. Often used are the Rorschach Technique and the Thematic Apperception Test (TAT). The results of such tests are interpreted rather than scored. It is assumed that such instruments reveal the subject's innermost feelings and attitudes, and they are often used to aid in the diagnosis of mental disorders. *See also* Figure-Drawing Test; House-Tree-Person Technique.

Project Mohole. *See* Deep-sea Drilling Project.

Prokofiev, Sergei (1891–1953), Soviet composer and pianist. He used a post-Romantic style featuring melody, biting dissonances, and orchestral brilliance. His most popular works are the ballets *Romeo and Juliet* (1940) and *Cinderella* (1944); the "Classical" *Symphony No. 1* (1917); *Peter and the Wolf* (1936), an orchestral suite for children; and the suite from the opera *The Love for Three Oranges* (1925). He also composed a great deal of piano music, nine piano sonatas, seven symphonies, five piano concertos, chamber music, film music, and an opera, *War and Peace* (1952), based on Tolstoy's novel.

Prolactin, also known as luteotropic hormone, synthesized in the anterior pituitary gland and stimulates milk production by the mammary gland. △690.

Proletariat, term used to describe the working class. It was popularized by Karl Marx in his *Communist Manifesto* (1848). According to Marx, the exploited laboring class must seize power from the capitalists as the first step toward establishing a classless society. △902.

Proline, white crystalline amino acid found in proteins. *See* Amino Acid. △1570.

Promethea Moth, large moth of the giant silkworm family. Males are dark brown or black; females are much lighter. The caterpillar has a yellow head and blue body with rows of mostly black tubercles. Length: 2–3in (5–7.5cm). Family Saturniidae; species *Callosamia promethea*.

Prometheus, in Greek mythology, the fire-giver. His brother Epimetheus (afterthought) created the animals that turn their faces to Earth. Prometheus (forethought) created man who gazes at the stars, provided him with reason, and brought fire down from the Sun for his comfort. For his devotion to humanity Zeus had him chained to a rock in the Caucasus where an eagle consumed his liver for eternity. △834.

Promethium, radioactive metallic element (symbol Pm) of the Lanthanide group, made (1941) by particle bombardment of neodymium and praseodymium. The element does not occur in the Earth's crust. Properties: at. no. 61; melt. pt. (approx) 1,976°F (1,080°C); boil. pt. (approx) 4,460°F (2,460°C); most stable isotope Pm^{145} (half-life 17.7yr). *See also* Lanthanide Elements.

Prominence, Solar, gaseous jet or cloud of hydrogen or helium that erupts from the Sun's surface and can extend a quarter of a million miles above it. Prominences present beautiful filamentous archlike or ribbonlike structures best seen at the Sun's limb during a total solar eclipse. △96.

Malpeque, Prince Edward Island

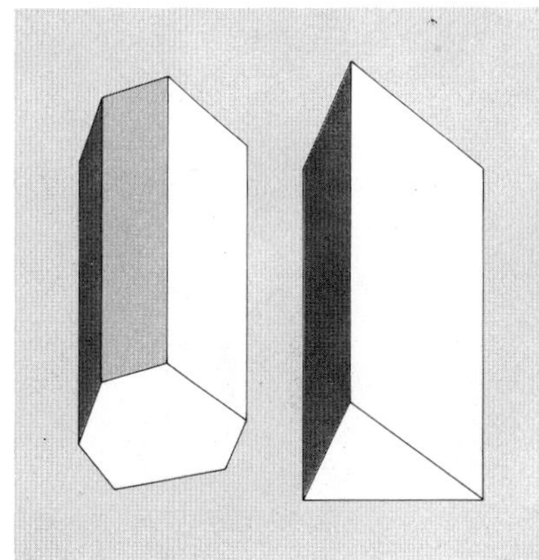

Prism

Proboscis monkey

Sergei Prokofiev

Pronghorn Antelope, North American ruminant native to desert and grasslands of SW Canada, W United States, and N Mexico. Both sexes have horns, shedding the outer sheath annually. Not a true antelope, its upper parts are reddish-brown to tan with black markings on face and neck. Erectile white rump hairs form a conspicuous white patch. It runs 40mi (64km) per hour. It is the only survivor of New World family Antilocapridae. Length: to 4.5ft (1.5m). Species *Antilocapra americana.*

Pronoun, the part of speech used to replace a noun. The noun replaced becomes the antecedent. Classifications: personal, relative, intensive, reflexive, interrogative, indefinite, and demonstrative.

Propaganda, use of words or familiar symbols to communicate ideas and information to a great number of people quickly and efficiently. △904, 1128.

Propane, colorless flammable gas (formula C_3H_8), the third member of the alkane series of hydrocarbons. It occurs in natural gas, from which it is obtained; it is also obtained during petroleum refining. It is used (as bottled gas) as a fuel, as a solvent, and in the preparation of many chemicals. Properties: melt. pt. −310°F (−189.9°C); boil. pt. −44.5°F (−42.5°C).

Propellant, Rocket, material that undergoes chemical, nuclear, or thermoelectric reactions to propel a rocket. △142, 1722.

Proper Motion, very small continuous change of a star's position on the celestial sphere, thus indicating the star's movement relative to the Sun. The largest annual proper motion is about 10 seconds of arc (Barnard's star) but for most stars it is negligible. △38.

Property, Laws of. △910.

Prophesy, Fortune telling and Divination. △822.

Proportion, mathematical relation of equality between two ratios, having the form $a/b = c/d$. A continued proportion is a group of three or more quantities, each bearing the same ratio to its successor, as in 1:3:9:27:81. △1446.

Proportional Representation, legislative representation based on percentage of either the electoral vote or the population. For example, in Europe political parties are awarded seats according to their percentage of the vote, an arrangement conducive to multi-party systems. In the US House of Representatives, each state is represented according to its percentage of the total population, an arrangement favorable to the larger states. △902.

Proprioception. *See* Kinesthetic Sense.

Proserpina, Latin equivalent to Persephone. She was also identified by some with Libitina, who became the goddess of funerals. Whenever anyone died, a piece of money had to be brought to her temple.

Prosody, systematic study of the principles of verse structure, especially meter. *See also* Meter; Versification.

Prospecting, Electrical. △168.

Prosser, Gabriel (*c.* 1775–1800), US black insurrectionist. He planned an unsuccessful slave revolt in Virginia in 1800 and was hanged for it.

Prostaglandins, derivatives of fatty acids, synthesized by the prostate and present in low levels in blood and various tissues. Biological effects include lowering of blood pressure and the stimulation of contraction in a variety of smooth-muscle tissues, such as the uterus.

Prostate Gland, a gland in the male reproductive tract surrounding the urethra. It secretes specific chemicals that mix with sperm cells and secretions of other accessory glands to make up the sperm-containing fluid, semen, that is released at ejaculation. △700.

Prostatitis, inflammation of the prostate gland caused by bacteria or their toxins. Chronic prostatitis sometimes occurs in men over 50, following an acute inflammation. △728.

Prosthesis, manufactured substitute for a missing organ or part, originally an arm or leg. Until the 17th century artificial limbs were either wooden or solid metal, but innovations in metallurgy and engineering design have enabled lighter, jointed limbs to be made. Methods of attachment, too, have greatly improved. More recent prosthetic devices include artificial heart valves made of silicones that have now given excellent service for many years. △752.

Prosthodontics, the dental specialty that deals with the replacement of missing teeth and surrounding tissue with artificial substitutes. The proper fitting of such devices requires a precise knowledge of occlusion and jaw movements and the skills necessary for preparation, impression making, placement, and follow-up care.

Protactinium, rare radioactive metallic element (symbol Pa) of the actinide group, first isolated 1917 by three independent groups. Chief source is pitchblende. Properties: at. no. 91; at. wt. 231.0359; sp gr 15.37; melt. pt. 2,012°F (1,100°C); boil. pt. 7,232°F (4,033°C); most stable isotope Pa^{231} (half-life 3.25×10^4 yrs. *See also* Actinide Elements.

Protectionism, policy of restricting foreign imports through a system of high tariffs and quotas, thus stimulating the domestic economy and "protecting" domestic manufacturers from foreign competition. Protectionist ideology was the basis of United States economic policy since its formulation by Alexander Hamilton in the late 18th century, but was disputed by the South in the decades preceding the Civil War.

Protective Coloration, natural camouflage or warning colors that organisms have to blend in with their surrounding environment or to warn off predators. Tigers and some moths have permanent protective coloring. Chameleons and some flatfish can change color to match the background. Warning colors of an animal usually mean it is poisonous or distasteful to most predators. Predators learn to recognize and avoid these distinctive warning colorations. *See also* Mimicry. △420, 480.

Protectorate, period of English government (1653–59). The Protectorate was established when Oliver Cromwell dissolved the Rump Parliament and instituted the nominated Parliament. When it proved ineffective the army presented and Cromwell accepted a constitutional document, the Instrument of Government. Cromwell became lord protector of the commonwealth of England, Scotland, Ireland, ruling with one house of Parliament and a council. The Protectorate was actually a military dictatorship. Following Cromwell's death the Rump Parliament was recalled and Charles II was returned to the throne (1660). △1156.

Protein, organic compound containing many amino acids linked together. Living cells use about 20 amino acids, but as proteins have thousands of amino acids in each molecule the number of possible proteins is very large. The order of amino acids in proteins is controlled by the genes in the cell's DNA. The most important proteins are the enzymes, which determine all the chemical reactions in the cell. Other proteins are used in structures such as the cell walls and internal membranes. Basic proteins are associated with DNA in the cell nucleus. Tough, flexible proteins include cartilage and keratin, which is used in hair, nails, and horn. *See also* Amino Acid; Enzymes; Peptide. △1560, 1570, 1572–74.

Protestant Episcopal Church, US branch of the Anglican Communion, formally organized in Philadelphia in 1789. It is self-governing, with the laity having a large role in administration duties. A presiding Bishop is elected by the General Convention. The Apostles' Creed and the Nicene Creed are accepted. Membership is approximately 3,200,000. *See also* Apostles' Creed, The; Nicene Creed, The.

Protestant Ethic, social theory devised by Max Weber (1864–1920) that explains the origins and development of capitalism in terms of the Calvinist doctrine of predestination. Calvinists in the 17th century interpreted worldly success as a sign of spiritual salvation. Therefore they worked hard and lived frugally in order to accumulate the symbols of salvation and convince themselves and others of their membership in the elect. This syndrome created a pattern of behavior that fostered the growth of capitalism and individual achievement. △924, 1290.

Protestantism, system of Christian faith and practices first developed in the 16th century. It differs from Roman Catholicism mainly in the question of papal authority. The Protestant church is understood as a fellowship of believers, with Scripture as the source of faith. It began as a number of independent reform attempts, therefore there are many different churches within the Protestant tradition: Lutheran; Calvinist; Anglican or Episcopal; and "free church" are the four main forms of Protestantism. They are usually understood as complementary rather than in opposition in their search for Christian truths. A large body of conservatives, known as fundamentalists, developed in reaction to 18th-century liberalism.

Generally, preaching is stressed as primary before sacramental practices. The Word is the focal point of faith and of Christian living. Asceticism is largely rejected, while personal morality is stressed. Justification is through faith alone. In 1948, the World Council of Churches, open to all denominations, was formed in the effort to unite in an ecumenical movement. *See also* individual Protestant churches. △1152–54, 1264.

Proteus, in Greek mythology, a sea god, son of Poseidon and Amphitrite. He is depicted as a little old man of the sea. Proteus possessed the gift of prophecy and the ability to alter his form at will. In an instant he could become fire, flood, or a wild beast.

Prothrombin, precursor of the blood enzyme thrombin; converted into thrombin by thromboplastin. *See also* Blood Clotting.

Protista, large group of unicellular and simple multicellular organisms including protozoa, algae, bacteria, and fungi. Used to overcome the difficulty of distinguishing simple plants from simple animals, the term also may include organisms with many nuclei within one cell wall (coenocytes).

Protoceratops, horned ornithischian dinosaur of Cretaceous times from Central Asia. It had a frill of bone on the back of its skull but, unlike later forms, its nose was hornless. Fossilized nests of eggs of this reptile have been found. Length: 6ft (1.8m). *See also* Triceratops. △572.

Protochordates. △508.

Protocols of the Elders of Zion, a forged document that describes a Jewish plot for world domination, published in Russia in 1905 by Serge Nilus. Supported by semiofficial, right-wing circles, it contributed to the atmosphere of anti-Semitism.

Protogeometric Pottery. △1000.

Proton, stable elementary particle (symbol p) with a positive charge that is equal in magnitude to that of the electron. It forms the nucleus of the lightest isotope of hydrogen and with the neutron is a constituent of the nuclei of all other elements. It also occurs in primary cosmic rays. It is a baryon with spin ½ and a mass 1836.12 times that of the electron. Beams of high-velocity protons, produced by particle accelerators, are used to study nuclear reactions. *See also* Atomic Number. △1480, 1484.

Protonation, the addition of a proton (an elementary particle identical with the nucleus of the hydrogen atom). *See* Proton.

Protoplanets. △48.

Protoplasm, semifluid, essential living matter within all plant and animal cells. *See* Cell.

Protozoa, phylum of one-celled animals found throughout the world in marine or fresh water and as parasites. First seen in 1674 by van Leeuwenhoek, these microscopic animals have the ability to move (by cilia or psoudopodia) and have nucleus, cytoplasm, and cell wall; some contain chlorophyll. They are transparent, green, iridescent, blue, rose, or yellow. Reproduction is by fission or encystment. Length: 2/25000in (2/1000mm) to 0.2in (5mm). The 30,000–80,000 species are divided into four classes—Flagellata, Rhizopoda, Ciliophora, and Sporozoa. △466.

Protura Proturans. △492.

Proust, Marcel, (1871–1922), French novelist. The son of a doctor, he studied law at the Sorbonne, and deliberately infiltrated the Parisian social élite. Proust was interested in philosophy and translated some works of John Ruskin. He suffered from asthma and nervous disorders and in 1908 withdrew into his corklined bedroom. Here he wrote the seven-part novel cycle *A la recherche du temps perdu (Remembrance of Things Past),* published between 1913–1927. The first volume, *Swann's Way,* was published at his own expense, since his eccentricities and his reputation for dilettantism prevented him from finding a publisher. The second volume (*Within a Budding Grove,* 1918), however, won the Prix Goncourt. With his health failing, Proust raced to complete his work; the last three books were published posthumously.

Provençal, Romance language spoken in SE France, in the historic region of Provence. With most of its speakers fluent in French, it has no official status in the country and is gradually dying out.

Provence, region and former province in SE France; it included present depts. of Var, Vaucluse, and Bouches du Rhône, and parts of Alpes-de-Haute-Provence and Alpes-Maritimes; capital was Aix-en-Provence. Coastal area was settled 600 BC by Greeks; Romans set up colonies 2nd century BC; passed to Louis XI of France 1481; it was a province of France until the French Revolution, when France was divided into departments. Region includes French Riviera, famous vacation spot; valley of Rhône produces many crops; cattle are raised in Camargue; scenery, historic remains, and old towns attract many tourists.

Proverbs (of Solomon), biblical book of the Old Testament, probably the oldest existing example of Hebrew Wisdom literature. Poetic, as is the Song of Solomon, Proverbs deals with practical piety. It makes no mention of Israel's history, instead, God's revelation is seen more in patterns of nature than historical events.

Providence, capital city and port of entry in NE Rhode Island, on Providence Bay; largest city of Rhode Island; seat of Providence co. Founded 1636 by Roger Williams, the city developed as refuge for religious dissenters from Massachusetts; joined Providence Plantations 1644; prospered as trading port with West Indies and as textile center 18th century. In 1772, the city's men captured and burned Britain's ship *Gaspee*; on May 4, 1776, city was scene of signing of Rhode Island Independence Act; made capital of Rhode Island 1900. Landmarks include Stephen Hopkins House (1755), John Brown House (1786), First Baptist meetinghouse (1775); site of Brown University (1764), Bryant College (1863), Rhode Island School of Design (1877), Rhode Island College (1854), Pembroke College (1891), Providence College (1917). Industries: jewelry, electrical equipment, silverware, machine tools, rubber goods. Inc. 1832. Pop. (1970) 179,116.

Provo, city in N central Utah, 38mi (61km) SSE of Salt Lake City, on Provo River; seat of Utah co; site of Brigham Young University (1875); distribution, manufacturing, processing center. Industries: steel, farming, fruit, electronic equipment, mining, tourism. Founded 1849 by Mormons; inc. 1851. Pop. (1970) 53,131.

Prud'hon, Pierre-Paul (1758–1823), French painter. His work served to link the 18th-century Neoclassic style with 19th-century Romanticism. In 1794 he executed a fine series of portraits, which includes "Madame Anthony and Her Children." His best works were produced after 1799 and include "Justice and Divine Vengeance Pursuing Crime."

Prune, variety of plum that can be dried without fermentation at the pit. It is grown in Europe, especially Yugoslavia, and Australia, Chile, South Africa, and United States. The flesh of the fruit easily separates from the pit. Family Rosaceae; species *Prunus domestica*. *See also* Plum.

Pruning, the removal of branches, stems, or buds from a tree or shrub. Pruning is usually done to improve the appearance of ornamental trees and shrubs and the productivity of fruit trees and berry bushes. Fruit trees are usually pruned in the winter or early spring, as are hydrangeas, rose of sharon, and other flowering shrubs that bloom on new wood. Lilac, forsythia, and other spring-blooming shrubs—all of which bloom on old wood—are usually pruned after they have bloomed in order to avoid removing flower buds.

Prussia, former German state, occupying most of N and central Germany; capital was Berlin. Conquered by Teutonic Knights 13th century, it was a secular hereditary duchy under Hohenzollern dynasty of Brandenburg (1525); independent of Poland (1660). Region became strong German military state, especially under Frederick the Great (1740–86); it was expanded to include Rhineland territories (1720), Silesia (1742–63), Poland (1772–95), Saxony (1815), Lauenburg and Schleswig (1865). Region was under Chancellor Otto von Bismarck through three wars, with Denmark (1864), Austria (1866), and France (1870–71). William I of Prussia was proclaimed emperor of Germany 1871, giving Prussia great power in the new German Empire. Prussia became a republic 1918 and joined the Weimar Republic (Germany) as one of its states. Formally abolished by the Allied Control Council, March 1, 1947, Prussian territories were divided between Soviet Union and Poland. △ 1074, 1250.

Przewalski's horse, or **Mongolian Wild Horse,** only surviving species of original wild horse. Once common on Eurasian plains, it is now found only in Mongolia and Sinkiang. It is a small and stocky horse with an erect black mane and no forelock. Its red-brown coat is marked with a darker line on the back and shoulders and leg stripes. Height: 47.2–57.5in (120–146cm) at shoulder; weight: 441–661lb (200–300 kg). Family Equidae; species *Equus caballus przewalski*.

Psalms or **Psalter,** book of the Old Testament, consists of 150 poetic pieces in the form of poems, songs, hymns, or laments; divided into five books; most are dated between *c.* 537BC and *c.* 100BC, and vary in tone and subject.

Psaltery, medieval stringed musical instrument similar to the dulcimer or zither. Several strings on a frame with a shallow sounding board are plucked with fingers or with a plectrum. Originally used in Hebrew services, it was used to accompany the singer of Psalms. It was depicted in classic art as a variant of the kithara or lyre. △1060.

Pseudanthemen Theory. △424.

Pseudo-Isidorian Decretals. *See* False Decretals.

Pseudomorphism. △242.

Pseudoscorpion. △490.

PSI. *See* Extrasensory Perception.

Psilophytales, an order of simple dichotomously branched plants of the Paleozoic Era. They were native to Europe and Canada. This order includes the oldest known land plants with vascular structure. △ 562, 568.

Psi Particles, two elementary particles (mesons), discovered 1974, each with an anomalously long lifetime. *See also* Quark.

Psittacosis, or parrot fever, usually a disease affecting the respiratory system of birds. Probably caused by bacteria, it is transmissible to man through handling of infected birds, bites from them, or dust surrounding them. In birds, there is diarrhea and breathing difficulty; in man, headache and vomiting. Treatment is administration of antibiotics.

Pskov, city in NW Russian SFSR, USSR, on the Velikaya River near the SE shore of Lake Pskov, 155mi (250km) SW of Leningrad; capital of Pskov oblast. Historically important, Pskov dates from the 8th century; originally an outpost of Novgorod, Pskov gained independence in the 13th century and was annexed to Moscow 1510; it was a medieval commercial center; in WWII, it was occupied by the Germans 1941–44 and suffered extensive damage; site of teachers' college, 12th–16th-century Kremlin, 17th-century cathedral containing the tombs of the Pskov princes, many churches, monasteries, and art museums. Industries: flax processing, agricultural machinery, railroad shops, linen, rope, tanning, distilling, flour milling, footwear. Pop. 127,000.

Psocid. △492.

Psocoptera. △492.

Psoriasis, chronic disorder of the skin in which there are patches, plaques, or papules. The red or brown lesions are slightly elevated and usually covered with white scales. They frequently appear on chest, knees, elbows, and scalp. Cause is unknown and there is no specific treatment, though sunlight helps.

Psyche, in Greek mythology, a beautiful mortal loved by Eros (Cupid). Psyche is the Greek word for butterfly and for soul. Apuleius, a writer of the 2nd century AD, tells how the Pythian oracle warned her she would love no mortal, how she wed Cupid, lost him, and how they were reunited. The allegory suggests the freeing of the soul after purification through suffering.

Psychiatry, branch of medicine specializing in analyzing, diagnosing, and treating behavior disorders and mental illnesses. A psychiatrist must first earn an M.D. degree and then take special training in psychology. Methods of treatment range from talking out problems in psychotherapy to more specifically medical measures such as drug therapy. *See also* Abnormal Psychology; Psychoanalysis. △760.

Psychic Surgery. △748.

Psychoanalysis, method for treating behavior disorders and a theory that attempts to explain both normal and abnormal behavior. Sigmund Freud pioneered in treating psychoneurotic patients by such

Pronghorn antelope

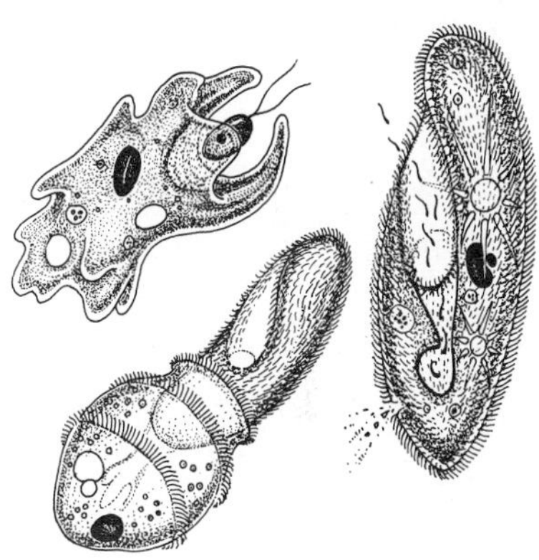

Protozoa

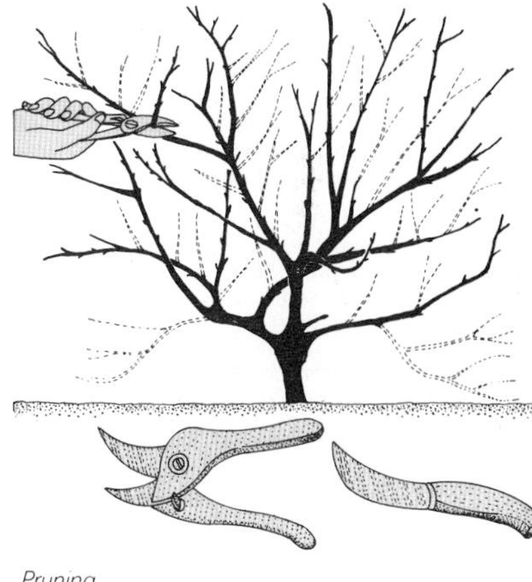

Pruning

Pskov, USSR

methods as encouraging free association and interpreting dreams. Traditional psychoanalysis requires a patient to spend three or more sessions a week with the analyst for a period of years. Freud also proposed theories of personality development, which, despite challenges, remain major influences on psychology, psychiatry, and other fields such as literature. *See also* Freud, Sigmund; Psychiatry. △774.

Psychobiology, field, closely related to physiological psychology, that studies anatomical and biochemical structures and processes as they affect behavior.

Psychodrama. △774.

Psychogenic Disorders, mental disturbances believed to have an underlying psychological origin. Neurotic and functional psychotic disorders are usually thought of as psychogenic.

Psychokinesis (PK), in parapsychology, a change in an object or physical system that is supposedly directly caused by the mind or will rather than by any known physical energy or instrument, for example, influencing the fall of dice by the will alone. *See also* Parapsychology; Telekinesis. △824.

Psycholinguistics, study of language, its patterns, its forms, and the way it is acquired and used. The development of language is studied by observing young children as they learn to speak. It is not known if certain linguistic potentials are innate or learned, and it has not been determined whether other species can learn abstract communication. David Premack's experiments with "Sarah" have shown that this chimpanzee is capable of understanding the concept of words.

Psychological Novel, type of novel whose main emphasis is on characterization and motivation rather than on plot or setting. In a psychological novel internal action explains and develops external action. The term was first applied to certain 19th-century novels, such as those by George Eliot. Its chief use, however, is to describe 20th-century novels influenced by Freudianism. James Joyce's *Ulysses* (1922) is an outstanding example.

Psychology, biosocial science that studies the behavior of humans and other animals. Psychology draws on the biological sciences to study, for example, the structure and functions of the brain, to find out how the eye, ear, and other sense organs work, and to assess the effects of drugs. Psychology is also a social science because it focuses on how humans interact, react, and adjust to other individuals and groups. The stress is on human behavior, but experiments with other animals provide useful information. *See also* individual fields in psychology. △662–80, 776–24.

Psychoneurotic Disorder, relatively mild personality disturbance marked primarily by persistent anxiety that is either experienced directly or controlled through psychological defense mechanisms. Orientation to reality is not impaired and the personality does not show gross disorganization. While all neurotic disorders have the underlying pattern of anxiety and defense, the symptoms vary widely, depending primarily on how the anxiety is handled. Psychoneurotic disorders include anxiety reaction, phobic reaction, obsessive-compulsive reaction, dissociative reaction, conversion reaction, and depressive reaction. △766.

Psychopharmacology, study of how drugs affect behavior. Drugs are classified according to their chemical structure and effect, for example: sedative hypnotics like barbiturates and alcohol, stimulants like amphetamines, opiate narcotics like heroin, and psychedelics and hallucinogens like LSD. Psychologists are particularly concerned with the effect of drugs on behavior, tolerance levels, physical dependence, and drug treatment of mental illness.

Psychophysics, measurement of stimuli and the sensations they produce. Beginning with the 19th-century experimentalists Ernst Weber and Gustav Fechner, specialists in this field have studied the relation between intensity of stimulus (sound, for example) and intensity of sensation (hearing, in this case).

Psychosomatic Disorders, physical by products of psychological disturbances. Continued stress, whether caused by internal or external conditions, will often lead to a physical disturbance, eg, changes in respiration, circulation, digestion, sweat-gland activity, and other hormone regulated activities. Any of these body mechanisms may become the target of a psychosomatic disturbance. For example, continued erosion of the gastric mucosa resulting from stress will lead to gastric ulcers; continued blood-pressure elevation will produce hypertension and greatly increase the risk of heart disease or stroke. A psychosomatic basis has been discovered in some varieties of asthma and dermatitis. △768.

Psychosurgery, any surgical procedure practiced on the central nervous system that is intended to alter behavior; performed upon animals for experimental purposes or upon humans to treat mental illness. △770.

Psychotherapy, techniques (verbal, social, interpersonal, and expressive) used to modify behavior or psychological disturbance. Psychoanalysis (Freudian psychotherapy) emphasizes discovery of the unconscious determinants of behavior and personal-historical antecedents of personality. Humanistic psychotherapists reject the more mechanistic aspects of Freudian therapy in favor of a more optimistic, interpersonal, and integrated approach. Behavior therapy seeks to modify behavior through the application of principles of learning. Other varieties include group therapy; psychodrama; play, music and art therapy; and encounter therapy. △774.

Psychotic Disorders, severe mental disturbances in which there is a profound loss of ability or a basic incapacity adequately to test reality. Psychotic disorders may be of organic or psychogenic origin and are expressed through a wide variety of syndromes, including schizophrenic and paranoid reactions. Delusions and hallucinations are often, though not necessarily, present. Other symptoms often observed are confusion in orientation to time, place, or person; poor judgment; communication disturbance; and social withdrawal. *See also* Brain Disorders; Paranoid Personality; Schizophrenia. △760, 764.

Ptah, in Egyptian mythology, the god of craftsmen and creator of the universe, depicted as a standing, mummified man. He was thought to have created the world. The center of his worship was at Memphis. △832.

Ptarmigan, northern or alpine grouse. Pairs are seasonally monogamous and the male engages in courtship displays and takes a vigorous role in defending the nest and rearing young. The N Eurasian rock ptarmigan *(Lagopus mutus)* has three protective color phases: white in winter, brown in spring and summer, gray in autumn; length: 14in (35cm). The white-tailed ptarmigan *(Lagopus leucurus)* is found in N New World; length: 12in (30cm). *See also* Grouse.

PT Boat, US Navy term for patrol torpedo boat. *See* Torpedo Boat. △1740.

Pteranodon, short-tailed, toothless Cretaceous pterosaur of United States and Europe. A long, bony crest at back of skull balanced its three-foot (0.9m) beak. Its wing span 25ft (7.6m) allowed for gliding rather than active flight as it soared over ancient seas in search of fish. △572.

Pteridophyte, obsolete name for any of a group of spore-bearing plants. At one time, pteridophytes included club moss, horsetails, and ferns, and several fossil groups. These plants have similar life cycles but in other respects are quite distinct. △424, 438.

Pterodactyl. *See* Pterosaur.

Pterosaur, extinct reptile characterized by flying membranes, supported by single, elongated finger on each side. Worldwide in distribution during Jurassic and Cretaceous times, early forms had teeth and tails; later forms were tailless and had toothless beaks. They ranged from sparrow to goose-sized with a wing span to 50ft (15m). △570, 572.

Ptolemaeus. △60.

Ptolemaic System, an arrangement of celestial bodies and their motions, formulated by Ptolemy about AD140, in which the Earth was considered the center of the universe. The stars were thought to be fixed to a sphere, with another sphere, the prime mover, outside. The prime mover provided the force operating the whole system as well as the daily rotation of the heavens. Gradually the Ptolemaic system was superseded by the heliocentric system, from the 16th century onward. △38.

Ptolemy, the name of a 14-member Greek dynasty that ruled Egypt for 300 years (323–30 BC). **Ptolemy I,** one of Alexander the Great's best generals, obtained Egypt upon the latter's death in 323 BC. After struggling for years to maintain his position, he assumed the title of king (305) and built Alexandria into a cultural and commercial center. His son **Ptolemy II** succeeded him and during his reign (285–246) Egypt attained its greatest height. Under **Ptolemy III** (246–221), Egyptian fleets gained control of the eastern Mediterranean. **Ptolemy IV** (221–205) began his reign by murdering his mother and brother to preserve his throne. Weakened by the king's continued decadence, the administration disintegrated, and soon after Ptolemy's death (205) the kings of Syria and Macedonia seized all of Egypt's provinces. The ministers of the infant king **Ptolemy V** appealed to Rome for help and from about 200 BC on the power of the dynasty was superseded by the influence of Rome. The rest of the Ptolemy line ruled ineffectually down to the time of Cleopatra (30 BC), after which Egypt became a Roman province.

Ptolemy, anglicized form of Claudius Ptolemaeus (fl 2nd century AD), Greek scientist, whose influence on scientific thought, especially astronomy, extended well into the 17th century, b. in Ptolemais Hermii, Egypt. Active in Alexandria, he wrote several books on geography, geometry, and optics, but his most famous work is the *Almagest*, a treatise on the motions of the heavenly bodies according to the Ptolemaic system. △38, 128.

Ptomaine Poisoning. *See* Food Poisoning.

Puberty, the period of development climaxed by maturation of sexual organs in both sexes such that reproduction is possible. Secondary sexual characteristics start to become evident. It occurs in males at about 14 years, and 12 in females. △790.

Puberty Rites, rites that are symbolic representations of an adolescent reaching maturity. With boys they occur between the ages of nine and twenty whereas with girls they usually accompany the first menstruation. The rites initiate young people into the society of adults and often involve, in the case of boys, an ordeal (such as scarification among the Nuer) and, with girls, purification. *See also* Rites of Passage. △790.

Pubis. △682.

Public Broadcasting, noncommercial TV system that relies on business grants, foundation grants, and contributions from the public rather than on advertising revenue. Because public TV stations are not dependent on ratings to obtain revenue, they do not have to attract huge audiences and can cater to the needs of their local communities. Programming usually emphasizes cultural and educational fare, from symphonies to "Sesame Street." There are 200 public TV stations in the United States, linked together by the Public Broadcasting Service (PBS).

Public Broadcasting Act, US federal law (1975), allocating more than $500,000,000 for funding of public television over a five-year period. The act requires that for each $1 of federal money, $2.50 of nonfederal money be raised.

Public Health, branch of medicine that attempts to protect and improve the health of people in a community. It is involved with disease control, such as mass vaccination programs, and with establishing and maintaining health standards for housing, food, water, waste disposal, and air quality. △736.

Public Health Service (PHS), service of the US Department of Health, Education, and Welfare. It works to promote the highest level of national health possible and to coordinate major health plans and services with other nations. Among its operating agencies are the Food and Drug Administration, the National Institutes of Health, Health Resources Administration, Health Services Administration, and Center for Disease Control. Established in 1798, it is directed by the assistant secretary of health.

Public Opinion Poll, canvassing of a scientifically selected sample of the population to ascertain attitudes and behavior and to forecast election results. Polling techniques have evolved from the 19th-century method of random selection of names from telephone directories to the computerized methods, based on census data and employing professional pollsters, used today.

Public Utility, firm that possesses a natural monopoly in a given market area. A *natural monopoly* is a firm that offers essential service and can lower its cost by expanding output out to the limits of market demand. Consequently, other firms cannot efficiently compete with it. Natural monopolies become public utilities when they are regulated. The gas, electric, telegraph, and telephone industries are the best known federal- and state-regulated utilities.

Public Works Administration (PWA), New Deal

agency to stimulate the economy by providing employment in public projects. It was established by the National Industrial Recovery Act (1933). The PWA under Sec. of the Interior Harold Ickes (1933–39) built roads, dams, schools, bridges, housing developments, hospitals, sewage systems, and power plants. Under President Franklin D. Roosevelt's 1939 reorganization, the PWA became part of the Federal Works Agency.

Puccini, Giacomo (1858–1924), Italian composer of operas, some of which are among the most popular ever composed. His operas include *Manon Lescaut* (1893), *La Bohème* (1896), *Tosca* (1900), *Madame Butterfly* (1904), *The Girl of the Golden West* (1910), and *Turandot* (left incomplete at his death and first performed posthumously, 1926). △1246, 1256.

Pudu, genus of South American deer that is almost tailless and has short, spikelike antlers. Rivaling musk deer and muntjacs in its small size, it measures only 15in (38cm) at the shoulder. Adults are a rich brown to gray. Family Cervidae. *See also* Deer.

Puebla (Puebla de Zaragoza), city in E central Mexico, 75mi (121km) SE of Mexico City; capital of Puebla prov. The area was occupied by US forces (1847) during Mexican War; scene of French defeat by Mexicans (1862), later occupied by French (1863). Puebla is the site of many old buildings including a cathedral (1552–1649), theater (1790), university (1537). Industries: pottery, glass, soap, leather products, textiles. Founded *c.*1535 as Puebla de los Angeles; renamed *c.*1870 for Gen. Ignacio Zaragoza. Pop. 383,879.

Pueblo, industrial and commercial city in SE central Colorado, 40mi (64km) SSE of Colorado Springs. Industries: steel, iron, aluminum, concrete products, auto parts, beer, lumber. Founded by gold miners 1858; inc. 1873. Pop. (1970) 97,453.

Pueblo, a generic name for the several North American Indian tribes inhabiting the mesa and Rio Grande region of Arizona and New Mexico. These include four language families: the Queres, Tewa (or Tanoan), Shoshonean, and Zuni. Their mud-and-stone architecture is famous throughout the Southwest, and the seven-story structure at Zuni gave rise to the legendary "Seven Cities of Cibola" eagerly sought by the Spaniards.

Pueblo Incident (1968), seizure of a US navy ship, the *Pueblo,* and its 83-member crew by North Korea, while the ship was on an intelligence mission off the North Korean coast. The crew was imprisoned for 11 months until US negotiators signed a confession and apology for intruding into North Korean waters. The US disavowed the confession.

Puerperal Fever, an infection occurring in women after childbirth. It is caused by streptococci entering the body through lack of aseptic techniques. With modern hospital methods, the fever has become a rarity.

Puerto Rico, an autonomous commonwealth in union with the United States; it comprises the smallest and easternmost island of Greater Antilles; includes Vieques, Mona, Culebra. Puerto Rico is located in the N part of the tropical zone and dominates the principal entrance from the Atlantic Ocean to the Caribbean Sea. The land is mountainous, highest peak at Cerro de Punta 4,389ft (1,339m), surrounded by broken coastal plain. Only 1/3 of Puerto Rico's land area is arable; the economy is supported mostly by the production of sugar and sugar products; tobacco, coffee, pineapples, cabbages, corn, tomatoes are also grown. Industries include cement, canning, cigars, dairying, molasses, refrigerators. The 20th century has seen a great increase in the middle class as opposed to the distinct minority of wealthy upper class and majority of poor class of the past. Most of the people are Roman Catholic or Christian and engage in Spanish customs, modified by US influences. Puerto Rico has public school systems and universities for higher education. Social progress is demonstrated by the fact that six Puerto Rican cities, including the capital San Juan, have women mayors.

The government is modeled after the United States; the head of executive branch is a governor, elected for a 4-year term. The United States handles all foreign affairs. The island was discovered by Christopher Columbus in 1493; colonization began with Ponce de León, who was made governor 1510. In 1515 sugar cane was introduced; and by 1518 the first black slaves were brought to Puerto Rico. The Spanish concentrated on the exploitation of gold, by 1570 approx. four million dollars' worth of gold was mined but the resources were exhausted. In 1804 island ports were opened for foreign trade; economic development brought with it the desire for autonomy of native Puerto Ricans. In 1873 slavery and forced labor were abolished; 1898 Spain ceded Puerto Rico to the United States, following the Spanish-American War. Since 1898 the United States has aided development of Puerto Rico, in education, economy, transportation, and communication. In 1917 the Jones Act secured local elections of legislature and US citizenship for all Puerto Ricans. In 1932 the name Porto Rico was officially changed to Puerto Rico.

PROFILE

Official Name: Puerto Rico
Area: 3,435sq mi (8,897sq km)
Population: 2,900,033
Chief Cities: San Juan 444,952, Ponce 156,498, Mayaguez 69,485
Religion: Roman Catholic
Language: Spanish, English
Monetary Unit: US dollar

Puff Adder, widely distributed African and Arabian viper that hunts large rodents in open country. Its skin pattern varies, but it usually has yellow, crescentic markings on brown. Its bite is often fatal to man. Up to 70 live young are born at one time. Length: to 4ft (1.2m). Family Viperidae; species *Bitis arietans. See also* Hognose Snake; Viper. △586.

Puffball, any of a large family of mushrooms (Lycoperdaceae) whose spore masses become powdery at maturity and are expelled in "puffs" when the case is pressed. True puffballs are stemless and mostly edible; false ones have stems and are inedible.

Puffbird, tropical New World dull-colored bird with a large head and loose, puffy plumage. It appears unwary, stupid, seldom fleeing and always perching in the same place, where it catches insects on the wing. It nests in an earth bank. Family Bucconidae.

Puffer, or **Blowfish,** also swellfish, marine fish found in warm and temperate seas. When taken from the water it swallows air and inflates its body. Colors are dusky brown and green with band markings. Smaller, sharp-nosed varieties are often kept in home aquariums. Length: to 36in (91.4cm). Family Tetraodontidae; among the 100 species are the northern *Sphaeroides maculatus.* △514.

Puffin, awkward looking, migratory seabird found in N Northern Hemisphere. The Atlantic puffin *(Fratercula arctica)* has a short neck, long reddish bill, and reddish legs and feet; length: 10in (25cm). A single white, sometimes spotted, egg is laid in a crude nest on an oceanic cliff.

Pug, small dog (toy group) first popular in Holland; probably originated in China and brought West by Dutch East India Company traders. It has a large, round head; blunt, square muzzle; deep face wrinkles; and a well-defined black face mask. Small, thin ears are folded forward or fold over and back. A wide-chested, short body is set on strong, straight, medium-length legs. The tail is tightly curled over the hip. Colored silver, apricot, or fawn with black, the coat is short and soft. Average size: 11in (28cm) high at shoulder; 14–18lb (6.5–8kg). *See also* Toy Dog.

Pugachev, Emelyan Ivanovich (*c.*1742–75), Cossack leader. He led a massive popular revolt against Catherine II that spread along the Ural River and across the Volga basin. In 1773 he proclaimed himself Peter III, promising freedom from serfdom, taxes, and military service, and the elimination of landlords and officials. He was defeated in late 1774, brought to Moscow for trial, and executed.

Puget Sound, arm of the Pacific Ocean in NW Washington, connected with the ocean by Juan de Fuca Strait through Admiralty Inlet; Bremerton, on W shore opposite Seattle, is site of a large navy yard. Explored and named 1792 by Capt. George Vancouver. Area: approx. 561sq mi (1,453sq km).

Pujo Committee (1913), a House of Representatives subcommittee to investigate financial practices. Headed by Rep. Arsene Pujo of Louisiana, the group reported that the concentration of money and credit was an increasingly common practice. The committee reported that these "money trusts" had virtually destroyed competition. The committee recommended reforms, some of which were incorporated into the Federal Reserve System, Clayton Act, and the Esch-Cummins bill, but federal laws had little effect in preventing consolidation of capital. *See also* Esch-Cummins Bill; Federal Reserve System.

Pulaski, Casimir (1748?–79), Polish nobleman, patriot, and soldier. He participated in the founding of the Confederation of Bar (1768), and in the subsequent unsuccessful revolt against Russian control of

Ptarmigan

Pterosaur

Pudu

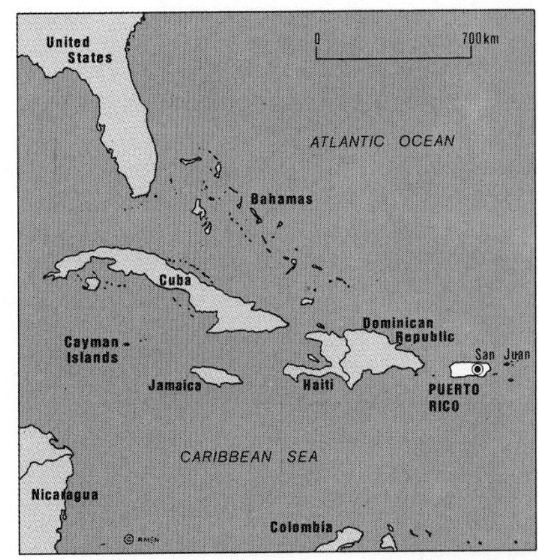
United States
0
700km
ATLANTIC OCEAN
Bahamas
Cuba
Dominican Republic
Cayman Islands
San Juan
Jamaica
Haiti
PUERTO RICO
CARIBBEAN SEA
Nicaragua
Colombia
Puerto Rico

Poland. He fled first to Turkey and then to France, where Benjamin Franklin persuaded him to join the American colonists' revolt (1777). He was appointed brigadier general by the Continental Congress. He was mortally wounded at the siege of Savannah, Georgia (1779).

Puli, Hungarian shepherd dog (working group). Breed is at least 1,000 years old. A vigorous dog, it has a medium-sized, slightly domed head with medium-long muzzle and large nose; V-shaped hanging ears; medium-length, straight-backed body; strong legs; and tail curved over the back. The unusual long, double coat mats into feltlike cords; color must be solid to be acceptable to kennel clubs. Average size: 17–19in (43–48cm) high at shoulder; 25–35lb (11.5–16kg). The puli is considered a good guard and watch dog. *See also* Working Dog.

Pulitzer, Joseph (1847–1911), US journalist, b. Hungary. He emigrated in 1864 and served in the Union Army. He pioneered sensational journalism and founded the Pulitzer prizes. He bought (1878) the St Louis *Post,* merging it with the *Dispatch.* In 1883 he bought the *New York World* and made it the nation's biggest daily by crusading powerfully for oppressed workers and against alleged big business and government corruption, using the "yellow-press" techniques that William Randolph Hearst copied successfully. Part of Pulitzer's $2 million bequest to found Columbia University's School of Journalism finances the annual Pulitzer prizes.

Pulitzer Prizes, annual awards presented for outstanding achievement in journalism, letters, and music. The prizes are paid for by the income of a trust fund of the estate of Joseph Pulitzer (1847–1911) to the trustees of Columbia University. There are eight awards in journalism including best cartoon, best news photograph, and outstanding editorial writing. There are prizes for fiction, drama, history, biography, poetry, and musical composition. Four scholarships are also awarded. Journalism awards are $1,000 each and the letters and music awards are $500 respectively.

Pulleys and Hoists, commonly known as block and tackle, used to gain a mechanical advantage in lifting or moving heavy loads. The system consists of a combination of a flexible material, such as rope or chain, and a wheel (pulley), which changes the direction of motion and the applied force. The mechanical advantage in an ideal system, discounting friction, is determined by counting the number of lines leading to the movable pulley. △1654, 1662.

Pullman, George Mortimer (1831–97), US industrialist and inventor of railroad sleeping car, b. Brocton, N.Y. He was president of Pullman Palace Car Co. and started a paternalistic model town for employees.

Pullman Strike (June–July 1894), US labor struggle. When the manufacturers of Pullman railroad cars in Chicago cut wages, the frustrated workers were joined by the American Railway Union led by Eugene V. Debs. A strike and a boycott of Pullman cars were called. It crippled railroad traffic in 27 states. For the first time in US labor history a court injunction against strikers was issued on July 2. There were outbreaks of violence. Federal troops, sent by Pres. Grover Cleveland, arrived on July 4, to "protect the mail trains." Debs was arrested and jailed on July 17, and the strike ended without a settlement.

Pulmonary Artery. △692.

Pulmonary Embolism, chronic and sometimes fatal obstruction of a pulmonary blood vessel by a massive traveling clot. It generally leads to symptoms of shock, acute high blood pressure in the pulmonary arteries, and eventual failure of the right ventricle of the heart. *See also* Embolism.

Pulmonary Vein. △692.

Pulp Mill. △1624.

Pulsar, rapidly rotating star of extreme density that, although only between about 1.4–3 times as massive as the Sun, has been compressed by gravitational collapse to only a few miles across. Pulsars emit regularly spaced radio pulses and in some cases X-ray and visible pulses; they were first detected in 1967. The magnetic field and force of gravity are also extreme by terrestrial standards. Pulsars are now identified with neutron stars, postulated in the 1930s as dying stars that would be too massive to become stable white dwarfs and that would collapse further with tremendous release of energy. In the ensuing supernova explosion much of the star's mass is blown off to leave a tiny compressed body composed of tightly packed neutrons formed from proton-electron interactions. *See also* Black Hole; Crab Nebula. △106–08.

Pulsating Star, variable star whose luminosity is intrinsically altered as a result of periodic expansions and contractions arising from changes in the star's atmosphere. Most pulsating stars are relatively short-period variables, including the classical Cepheids and the RR Lyrae variables. *See also* Variable Star. △112.

Pulse, a regularly recurrent wave of distention in arteries that results from the flow of blood injected into the arterial system at each contraction of the heart's ventricles. The pulse is usually taken at the wrist, over the radial artery. It may be observed at any point where an artery appears near the surface of the body. Women usually have a higher (78–82 per minute) pulse rate than men (70–72). Abnormalities in pulse rate may indicate disorders of the circulatory system and the heart. △330.

Puma, or mountain lion, cougar, panther, catamount, large New World cat found in mountains, forests, swamps, and jungles of W United States, S Florida, and Central and South America. It has a small round head, erect ears, and heavy tail. It is tawny with dark brown on ears, nose, and tail; underparts are white. The gestation period is 88–97days and 1–6 young are born. Length: body—42–54in (107–137cm); tail —30–36in (76–91cm); weight: 80–200lb (36–91kg). Family Felidae; species *Felis concolor* or *Felis cougar.*

Pumice, rhyolitic lava blown to a low density rock froth by the sudden discharge of gases during a volcanic action. When ground and pressed into cakes it is used as a light abrasive.

Pump, a mechanical device for raising, compressing, propelling, or transferring fluids. The volute centrifugal pump, with rotating blades that are immersed in the liquid to increase its pressure through centrifugal force, is most common for general use.

Pumpkin, or squash, trailing annual vine from warm regions of Old World and United States. The orange, hard-rind garden pumpkin used for pies and Jack-o-lanterns is usually a *Cucurbita pepo* variety. Summer squash *(C. pepo melopepo),* picked when immature, have soft white or yellow flesh. Winter squash *(C. bita maxima* and *moschata),* harvested when ripe, have solid yellow flesh. Family Cucurbitaceae. *See also* Gourd. △334, 446.

Pumpkinseed, or common sunfish, freshwater fish found in E North America. A colorful, iridescent fish, it is identified by a bright red spot on the rear of the gill cover. The male builds a nest in sand and guards the eggs and young. Length: to 9in (22.9cm). Family Centrarchidae; species *Lepomis gibbosus.*

Pun, play on words, usually humorous, exploiting the fact that words sounding alike may mean different things. Although they are often considered a low form of humor, Shakespeare makes frequent and effective use of puns. Hamlet puns on "fret," exclaiming "Call me what instrument you will, though you can fret me, you cannot play upon me," where "fret" may mean to "vex," or the ridges on the neck of a guitar.

Punic Wars, three wars (264–261, 218–201, 149–146 BC) during which Rome, dominant in Italy, wrested from Carthage control of NW Africa and the W Mediterranean. At first Rome negotiated with Carthage, the undisputed commercial power of the area, to protect Italian coastal communities from Punic (Carthaginian) attack. Then two rival Sicilian factions called upon the two powers to settle a dispute and, as the Straits of Messana (Messina) separating Italy from Sicily were of great value to both, their armies met in Sicily. The Carthaginians occupied Messana (264 BC), and the Romans soon drove them from their garrison, precipitating the First Punic War.

After inital successes at Segesta and Agrigentum, the Romans sought to expel Punic forces from Sicily entirely. They built a fleet and won naval victories at Mylae (260) and Cape Ecnomus (256), after which they sent an expeditionary force into Africa under Regulus. It was routed by the Spartan mercenary general Xanthippus (255). The Romans captured Panormus (Palermo) in 254 and Lucius Metellus held it against Punic assault, but they could not take Lilybaeum, the Punic stronghold defended with guerrilla strategy by Hamilcar Barca. The Roman fleet was wrecked and had to be rebuilt. Under Catulus it won the final naval battle of the war near the Aegates islands. Carthage was forced to pay a huge indemnity and evacuate Sicily, then Corsica and Sardinia.

Carthage achieved control of Spain (237–219) through campaigns led by Hamilcar and his sons Hannibal and Hasdrubal. When Hannibal took Rome's ally Saguntum in 219, Rome declared the Second Punic War (218–201). Hannibal marched over the Alps into Italy with select troops and an elephant corps. The Roman armies in Spain led by the brothers Gnaeus and Publius Scipio cut off his supply lines and won Roman dominance at sea. Hannibal destroyed Roman armies at Trebia (218), Trasimene (217), and Cannae (216) but, lacking reinforcements and faced with united Italian opposition, could not take Rome. Hasdrubal was defeated in Spain (215) and in Italy (207). Fabian Cunctator exhausted Hannibal's army with his policy of avoiding pitched battle. Scipio Africanus Major pushed the Punic army from Spain and attacked Africa. Hannibal was recalled to defend Carthage and was defeated at Zama (202) by Scipio and the Numidian king Masinissa.

Carthage became a dependent of Rome. Roman senator Cato the Elder insisted upon the total destruction of Carthage. Rome declared the Third Punic War (149–146), using the Punic resistance to Numidian aggression as an excuse. As described by Polybius, Carthage died without surrender, building by building razed at the command of Scipio Africanus Minor. Her survivors became slaves and her lands the Roman province of Africa. *See also* Carthage. △1012.

Punishment, Criminal. △922.

Punjab, state in N India; Chandigarh is the capital. Formed 1956 with the partitioning of the former Punjab prov. of British India between Pakistan and India, it is largely an irrigated agricultural area. Products: wheat, cotton, millet, barley, cotton, sugar. Industries: animal husbandry, textiles, cloth weaving, woolens, cement, machine tools, steel, farming equipment. Area: 19,495sq mi (50,492sq km). Pop. 13,472,972. △962.

Punjabi, the major spoken language of Pakistan and also one of the constitutional languages of India. It is spoken by about 50,000,000 of Pakistan's 70,000,-000 people, and by about 15,000,000 more in NW India. Punjabi is one of the Indic languages and thus part of the Indo-European family.

Punkie. *See* Midge.

Pupa, quiescent, nonfeeding developmental stage of insects that undergo complete metamorphosis, such as the fly, butterfly, and beetle. It occurs between the larval and adult stage. See also Chrysalis; Cocoon. △ 494, 498.

Pupfish. △604.

Pupil, in Anatomy. △674.

Puppet Theater, theater for puppet shows. They existed as far back as the 5th century BC in Greece, China, and Java, and reached peak popularity in 18th-century Europe. They also flourished in the Puritan period in England when other forms of theater were prohibited. They are often used for religious allegory or satire as well as entertainment. A 20th-century example is *Kukla, Fran, and Ollie.*

Purcell, Henry (1659–95), English composer and organist. Purcell's incidental music for the plays *The Fairy Queen* and *King Arthur* and his opera *Dido and Aeneas* (1689) made him the greatest English composer of the Baroque period. He also composed anthems, instrumental music, and secular songs. *See also* Baroque Music. △1174, 1196.

Pure Democracy. *See* Direct Democracy.

Pure Food and Drug Act (1906), US legislation to regulate food preparation. It required accurate labeling of canned or packaged food and drugs and forbade interstate commerce of adulterated or fraudulently labeled food and drugs. It authorized the Department of Agriculture to enforce the act.

Purim, an ancient Jewish celebration of thanksgiving, which usually takes place in March, commemorating the deliverance of the Jews of Persia from Haman's plot to destroy them. The story appears in the Book of Esther in the Old Testament, which is read on this day in a synagogue service. Charity is stressed on this occasion.

Puritanism, religious reform movement that developed within the Church of England during the late 16th century. The movement found its origin in the writings and thinking of early reformers, such as Thomas Cranmer, and was influenced by contemporary reformers, such as John Calvin. Through church reform, Puritans sought to purify the church of any remaining Roman Catholic influence. Faithful to the Bible, Puritanism provided the format for worship services, which included preaching, prayers, and psalms.

Making their pattern of religious reform the life style of the society, Puritans influenced all aspects of life. They were responsible for the founding of the North American colonies. *See also* Calvin, John; Cranmer, Thomas. △1156.

Purple Heart Urchin. △504.

Purple Martin, gregarious swallow of North America and the West Indies. Males are glossy blue-black; females are duller. They lay their eggs (4–6) in tree cavities. Length: 8in (20cm). Family Hirundinidae; species *Progne subis*. *See also* Swallow.

Purple Sun Star. △504.

Purpura, or wide-mouthed dye shell, gastropod mollusk found in all seas. Having a dull gray-green or brown shell with pink inside, the animal's body secretes a deep purple fluid used for dye. Length: 3in (76.2mm). Family Thaisidae; species *Purpura lapillus*.

Purpura, hemorrhage in the skin usually associated with bleeding in tissues and body cavities, as a result of failure of homeostasis. *See also* Homeostasis.

Purse Seining. △386.

Purslane. *See* Portulaca.

Pus, yellowish-white fluid matter produced by inflammation of body tissue due to microorganisms. It consists of a mass of degenerating leukocytes and tissue debris in a fluid called liquor puris.

Pusan, seaport city in SE South Korea, 200mi (322km) SSE of Seoul; capital of Kyŏngsang prov.; under Japanese domination 1910–45; during Korean War, it was the only port through which the UN army could be supplied; in September 1950, UN troops broke out from this area. Industries: shipbuilding, textiles, metallurgy. Pop. 1,880,710.

Pushkin, Aleksandr (1799–1837), Russian Romantic poet and novelist. His first major work, *Ruslan and Lyudmila,* was published in 1820. In exile for his political views he wrote *The Prisoner of the Caucasus* (1822) and the historical drama *Boris Godunov* (1831). Later, under the protection of Tsar Nicholas I, he completed his masterpiece *Eugene Onegin* (1833) and "The Bronze Horseman" (1833), "The Queen of Spades" (1834), and *The Captain's Daughter* (1836). He was mortally wounded in a duel. △1240.

Pushyamitra. △986.

Pussy Willow, deciduous shrub or small tree native to E North America. It has long, oval leaves with bluish-green undersides. The large, silvery, fuzzy female catkins appear before the leaves in late winter or early spring. Height: to 20ft (6m). Family Salicaceae; species *Salix discolor*.

Putrefaction, decomposition of organic matter, especially proteins, by fungi, bacteria, and oxidation. It results in foul-smelling products. Putrefaction of meat yields hydrogen sulfide, ammonia, and mercaptans.

Putumayo (Içá), river in NW South America; rises in SW part of Colombia, on slope of Andes; flows SE forming a large part of Colombia–Peru border; flows into Brazil, where it is known as the Içá, then into Amazon River. Length: 1,000mi (1610km).

Puyallop, tribe of about 170 native Americans of coastal Washington. Speaking a Salishan tongue of the Algonquian-Wakashan family, the Puyallop were living near present-day Tacoma when the whites came. Giving up their lands in the Treaty of Medicine Creek in 1854, they were assigned a reservation on Puget Sound.

Puzzle Box. *See* Trial-and-Error Learning.

PVC. *See* Polyvinyl Chloride.

PVC Plastics. △1612.

PWA. *See* Public Works Administration.

Pycknic. △814.

Pygmalion, in Greek mythology, a misogynistic sculptor who carved an ivory woman of surpassing beauty. He fell in love with it and offered to build a golden altar to Aphrodite if the statue were brought to life. The name of their son, Paphos, was given to a city sacred to the love goddess.

Pygmy, anthropological term denoting groups whose males average less than 59in (150cm) in height. African Pygmies, or Negrillos, inhabit three areas of central Africa and Zaire; Asian Pygmies, or Negritos, are found in the Philippines, Malaysia, and elsewhere. Pygmies are generally hunters and gatherers with few crafts. Most Pygmy populations are declining rapidly and they seem likely to become extinct fairly soon. △ 660.

Pynchon, Thomas (1937–), US author, b. Glen Cove, N.Y. A novelist, his works are complex narratives encompassing numerous characters and subplots. His books include *V.* (1963), *The Crying of Lot 49* (1966), and *Gravity's Rainbow* (1973).

P'Yŏngyang, industrial city in W North Korea, on the Taedong River; capital of North Korea with provincial status. An ancient city, it served as the capital under the Choson (300–200 BC), Koguryo (*c.* 77 BC–AD 668), and Koryo (10th–12th centuries) kingdoms; made capital of North Korea 1948; during Korean War (1950–53), P'Yŏngyang was taken by UN forces but later fell to communists (1950); site of ancient city walls and tombs, university (1946). Industries: cement, iron and steel, chemicals, rubber, textiles, railroad workshops. Founded *c.* 1122 BC. Pop. 1,346,000.

Pyorrhea or **Periodontitis,** inflammatory condition of the gums and associated tissues that surround and support the teeth. It is thought to be caused by local irritants and bacterial plaques. If untreated it destroys the gums and leads to loss of teeth.

Pyracantha, or firethorn, thorny evergreen shrub native from SE Europe to China and easily grown in subtropical and temperate regions. It has toothed, leathery leaves, white flowers, and red, orange, or yellow berries. Varieties of *Pyracantha coccinea* are popular in the United States. Family Rosaceae.

Pyramid, in architecture, huge monument with a square or rectangular base and, usually, triangular sides rising to an apex. In the 4th through 6th dynasties in Egypt pyramids reached their greatest size and significance. The three 4th-dynasty pyramids at Giza are the best known. That built by Khufu is the largest: 756ft (231m) on a side and 481ft (147m) tall. In the New World, the largest pyramid is at Teotihuacán, northeast of Mexico City. The Temple of the Sun, a truncated, terraced structure, was about 1,450ft (442m) wide at the base and 216ft (66m) high. △ 958, 1118.

Pyramid, in geometry, solid figure having a polygon as one of its faces (base), the other faces being triangles with a common vertex. Its volume is one-third of the base area times the vertical height. △1466.

Pyrenees, mountain range in S France and N Spain; extends in almost straight E-W line from Mediterranean (Cape Creuse) to Bay of Biscay (Cape Higuer) for 258mi (415km). There are few passes through this very compact, high range. Hannibal crossed Pyrenees 218 BC; Charles Martel forced Muslim invaders to retreat beyond Pyrenees at Battle of Tours, AD 732. Range contains deposits of marble, gypsum, oil. Cattle grazing is important industry. Rainfall increases toward W part of range where farming is carried on. Highest peak is Pico de Aneto, 11,168ft (3,406m).

Pyrenees, Peace of the (1659), treaty ending conflict between France and Spain. France received extensive territory in Flanders and the Franco-Spanish border was established at the Pyrenees. A marriage was arranged between Louis XIV and Marie Therese, daughter of Philip IV of Spain. If Marie Therese renounced her claim to the Spanish throne, she was to receive a payment. When the payment was not made the War of Devolution resulted.

Pyrethrum, popular name for the painted daisy (*Chrysanthemum coccineum)* and for several other species of *Chrysanthemum* and *Matricaria*. It is also the name for the insecticide made from the dried flower heads of the Dalmatian chrysanthemum (*C. cinerariaefolium*).

Pyridine, a compound (C_5H_5N) of the heterocyclic series characterized by a six-membered ring structure composed of five carbon atoms and one nitrogen atom. It occurs in bone oil and coal tar and is synthetically produced from acetaldehyde and ammonia. Pyridine is used as a solvent and converted to sulfapyridine (a drug used to combat bacterial and viral infection), pyribenzamine and pyrilamine (antihistamines), piperidine (a product used in processing rubber), and various water repellants, bactericides, and herbicides. △1560.

Pyridoxine, vitamin of the B complex involved in the metabolism of amino acids. *See* Vitamin.

Joseph Pulitzer

Puppet theater (Sicilian)

Aleksandr Pushkin (left)

Pygmy women

Pyrimidine, a colorless liquid ($C_4H_4N_2$) of the heterocyclic series characterized by a ring structure composed of four carbon atoms and two nitrogen atoms. It may be prepared from uracil, a dihydroxy pyrimidine compound, by chemical reactions that remove two oxygen atoms. Cytosine, uracil, thiamine, sulfadiazine, sulfamerazine, and sulfamethazine are well-known pyrimidine compounds.

Pyrite, the most common and widespread sulfide mineral (FeC_2), occurring in all types of rocks and veins. Often called "fool's gold" because of its deceptive color, it is used chiefly to produce sulfuric acid. Crystallizes as cubes, pyritohedra, and octahedra, often twinned; also as granules and globular masses. Opaque, metallic, and brittle; hardness 6.5; sp gr 5.-01. △240.

Pyrolysis, chemical decomposition of a complex substance into simpler ones by the action of heat alone. Garbage and coal may be pyrolyzed to produce valuable fuels and chemicals.

Pyrometallurgy, chemical metallurgy dependent upon roasting or smelting. Roasting involves heating ore in air without fusion. It transforms sulfide ores into oxides. Smelting involves blast furnaces to reduce iron, tin, copper, and lead ores.

Pyrometer, a thermometer for use at extremely high temperatures, above the melting points of ordinary thermometers. The optical pyrometer consists essentially of a small telescope, a rheostat, and a filament. When the telescope is aimed at a furnace or other hot object, the filament appears dark against the background. As electric current is increased slowly using the rheostat, the filament grows brighter until it matches the intensity of the furnace. △1508, 1656.

Pyrosis. *See* Heartburn.

Pyroxene, any of a group of numerous single-chain silicates. They include many important rock-forming minerals. Diagnostic features are prismatic crystal form with interfacial angles of 87° and 93° and good cleavage parallel to these faces. Enstatite, augite, jadeite, and wollastonite are well-known pyroxenes. △240.

Pyrrhus (319–272 BC), king of Epirus (295–272). He greatly expanded his kingdom into Illyria, Macedon and Thessaly and aiding Tarentum he defeated the Romans at Heraclea (280) and Asculum (279) but sustained grievous losses (hence "Pyrrhic victory"). After building a magnificent Hellenized capital at Ambracia, he was killed by a street mob in Argos.

Pyruvic Acid. △1572.

Pythagorean Theorem, geometric theorem stating that in a right-angled triangle the square of the hypotenuse is equal to the sum of the squares of the other two sides. The theorem is named after Pythagoras of Samos (*c.* 580–*c.* 500 BC). △1462.

Python, any of about 20 species of constricting snakes found in tropical regions of Asia, Africa, and Australia. They are distinguished from boas by certain features of skull, geographic distribution, and hatching young from eggs. True pythons *(Python)* of Africa and Asia include several giant species, such as the reticulated python, to 25ft (7.6m). Most are terrestrial, but some are arboreal, and one is a burrower. Family Boidae. *See also* Boa. △522, 598.

Qaddafi, Muammar al- (1938–), Libyan political leader. An army officer, he led a coup against the monarchy of Idris I (1969), naming himself Libya's commander-in-chief and chairman of the Revolutionary Command Council. A militant Arab nationalist, he helped support the Palestinian guerrillas and sought to unite Libya with other Arab countries.

Qatar, State of, nation in Asia occupying a peninsula extending N into the Persian Gulf from the Saudi Arabian mainland. The peninsula, running almost due N–S, is about 125mi (201km) long and 55mi (89km) wide. From the coast the terrain rises sharply to a low, barren plateau. The climate is hot with high humidity along the coast. Rainfall is meager and vegetation scarce. The economy is based almost entirely on petroleum production; the income is used to aid the general welfare. In 1975 the government completed the nationalization of the major independent oil companies. A new three-year industrial plan was introduced to diversify the economy and reduce dependency upon the oil industry. The majority of the people are Arabs, living in villages along the coast. About 50% are indigenous Qataris, with a large minority of Palestinian refugees. Most of the people are Muslims.

Although the country is a monarchy ruled by an emir, the Basic Law of 1970 (similar to a bill of rights) provides for a Council of Ministers and an Advisory Council, all elected for a term of three years. With the move toward constitutional monarchy, an independent judiciary system was installed. A general maritime treaty in 1868 allowed Great Britain to gain predominance in the area. The treaty of 1916 gave Britain control over Qatar's defense and foreign affairs. Oil discoveries in the 1940s stimulated the economy. Qatar became an independent state in 1971, joining the United Nations and the Arab League the same year.

PROFILE

Official name: State of Qatar
Area: 4,400sq mi (11,400sq km)
Population: 160,000
Density: 36.4per sq mi (14per sq km)
Chief cities: Doha, capital; Dukhan
Government: Monarchy
Religion: Muslim (official)
Language: Arabic (official)
Monetary unit: Riyal
Gross national product: $511,000,000
Per capita income: $5,938
Minerals (major): petroleum, natural gas
Trading partners (major): Great Britain

Qattara Depression, desert basin in NW Egypt, in Libyan Desert. Impassable by armies and vehicles, it was S end of British defense at Al-Alamein 1942; stopped Rommel's invasion. Contains lowest point in Africa, 436ft (133m) below sea level. Area: approx. 7,000sq mi (18,130sq km).

Q Fever, mild systemic disease, resembling typhus, caused by the microorganism *Rickettsia burneti.* Commonly accompanied by atypical pneumonia, it is widespread in ruminants and can be transmitted to man in raw milk or by contact.

Qingdao. *See* Tsingtao.

Qinghai. *See* Tsinghai.

Qiqihaer. *See* Tsitsihar.

Qom, city in W central Iran, 75mi (121km) SSW of Tehran; site of many mosques; burial place of Fatima (816), sister of Imam Riza; since 17th century noted pilgrimage place of Shiite Muslims. Industries: textiles, pottery, glass, shoes. Pop. 110,000.

Quadrant (graph), one of the four sections into which a plane is divided by rectangular axes. The four quadrants are called the first, second, third, and fourth, traveling counterclockwise from the first, which contains all points having positive x and y coordinates. △40, 1442, 1464.

Quadratic Equation, mathematical equation in which the highest exponent of the variable is 2; an equation of the second degree. Quadratic equations have the form $a x^2 + b x + c = 0$, where a, b, and c are constants. In general a quadratic equation has two solutions (roots) given by the formula

$$x = \frac{-b \pm \sqrt{b^2-4ac}}{2a}$$

Quadratic Function, mathematical function the value of which depends on the square of the independent variable, x, and is thus given by a quadratic polynomial, as in $f(x) = 4x^2 + 17$ or $f(x) = x^2 + 3x + 2$.

Quaestor, Roman financial magistrate. During the republic the two quaestors were responsible for the treasury. When plebeians were admitted to the office their number rose to four (421 BC) and under Caesar to 40, many being stationed outside Rome and holding military power. The office declined during the empire. △1014.

Quagga, extinct zebra once common in South Africa. Exterminated by the Boers by 1870s, its brown coat was marked with black and cream stripes on head and neck; underparts were white. Family Equidae; species *Equus quagga quagga. See also* Zebra.

Quail, any of a group of Old World chickenlike game birds. The European quail *(Coturnix coturnix),* a small short-tailed bird with white throat and mottled brownish plumage, is found throughout Eurasia and Africa. The Australian quail *(Synoicus ypsilophrus)* is a stocky, sedentary, brownish bird. Mainly ground birds they scrape for fruits and seeds and nest on the ground. New World quails (subfamily Odontophorinae), found from temperate North America to S Brazil, are frequently called bobwhite.

Quakers, members of the Society of Friends. They regard George Fox as their founder. Puritan in spirit they suffered persecutions in England and encountered difficulties in the American colonies. Through voluntary suffering, they bear witness to God. The purpose of life is to worship God, and fellowship of spirit is the group form of worship. They approach God directly, with no need to distinguish a clergy.

Qualitative Analysis. △1568.

Qualities, Primary and Secondary, distinction between primary and secondary qualities, first asserted by Galileo and affirmed by John Locke. Objects exhibit inherent (primary) characteristics—extension motion, rest, and number or so-called "mathematical" qualities; sensible (secondary) characteristics are only apparent and may vary—for example, color or texture.

Quantrill, William Clarke (1837–65), guerrilla leader during the American Civil War, b. Canal Dover, Ohio. Commander of a band that terrorized and murdered Union sympathizers in Missouri and Kansas. Quantrill was declared an outlaw by the North in 1862. Mustered into the Confederate Army that same year and given the rank of captain, Quantrill continued his raids in the border states until 1865, when he was killed by federal forces in Kentucky.

Quantum, or **Quanta.** *See* Quantum Theory.

Quantum Mechanics. *See* Quantum Theory.

Quantum Numbers, any of a set of numbers corresponding to the discrete values of a quantized physical property. Quantum numbers are either integers (1, 2, 3, etc) or half integers (1/2, 3/2, 5/2, etc). For example, an electron in a hydrogen atom can have energies n^2E_0, where n, the principal quantum number, can take values of 1, 2, 3, etc, and E_0 is the lowest energy level ($n = 1$). Similarly the charge of a particle can be thought of as quantized in units of electron charge, so a proton has a charge of $+1$. An elementary particle is defined uniquely by its mass and quantum numbers. △1480, 1550, 1552.

Quantum Theory, theory, proposed by Max Planck (1900), based on the fact that certain physical properties can only assume discrete values; that is, they are quantized. For example, an oscillator cannot gain or lose energy continuously but only in discrete amounts, termed quanta (sing. quantum). A quantum has energy $h\nu$, where h is Planck's constant and ν is the frequency. The quantum of electromagnetic radiation is the photon. Planck used quantum theory to explain black-body radiation, Einstein used it to explain the photoelectric effect (1905), and Bohr applied it to atomic spectra (1913). The older quantum theory has developed into quantum mechanics—a mathematical formalism applied to the behavior of atoms, molecules, and elementary particles. Quantum electrodynamics is an extension of these satisfying relativistic effects, especially those concerning charged particles. △1480, 1526, 1550.

Qu'Appelle River, river in S Saskatchewan, Canada, rises NW of Moose Jaw, flows E through Buffalo Pound Lake and Fishing Lakes across Manitoba border into Assiniboine River; excellent source of whitefish. Length: 270mi (435km).

Quark, particle postulated as a constituent of the hadron group of elementary particles. Baryons consist of three quarks, antibaryons of three antiquarks, and mesons of a quark and an antiquark, all tightly bound together. Originally three kinds of quarks, with fractional charges (+2/3 or −1/3 that of the electron) and slightly different masses, were suggested. The discovery in 1974 of the long-lived psi (or J) particles and their decay products, the chi particles, indicates four or possibly twelve quarks. *See also* Subparticles, Elementary. △1468, 1484.

Quarrying, methods employed in obtaining dimension (cut) stone or other types of nonmetallic rock from shallow, open-pit mines. Dimension stone for building (sandstone, granite, marble) is obtained by separating large blocks from the parent mass by hand, explosives, or machine. Crushed stone for road building is obtained by drilling and blasting. It is then crushed, screened, and sized.

Quarter Horse, or cow pony, light horse breed developed in 18th-century North America to race on quarter-mile track. Now used for racing and working cattle, it is a sturdy horse capable of short bursts of speed. It has a short head; short, muscular back and loin; and short legs. Colors are chestnut, sorrel, bay, or dun. Height: to 60in (152cm) at shoulder; weight: 1,000–1,200lb (450–540kg).

Quartz, silicate mineral, silicon dioxide (SiO_2). Most surface rocks contain quartz. It occurs in two basic forms: (1) well-formed, transparent, hexagonal system, short to long prismatic crystals variously hued (gem varieties include smoky quartz, amethyst, and citrine), and (2) cryptocrystalline varieties of microscopically small crystals divided into two types—chalcedony (agate, onyx, sardonyx, carnelian, and chrysoprase are gem varieties) and the more opaque chert (of which aventurine and jasper are the best-known gem stones). △242–44.

Quartz Clock. △1658.

Quartzite, metamorphic rock, usually produced from sandstone, in which the quartz grains have recrystallized. Fracturing through these grains rather than between them, quartzite is a hard and massive rock. Its color is usually white, light gray, yellow, or buff, but it can be colored green, blue, purple, or black by various minerals. *See also* Metamorphic Rocks.  △ 242.

Quasar or **Quasi-stellar Object,** astronomical object, first observed in the 1960s, that appears to be a massive, highly compressed, extremely powerful source of radio and light waves, characterized by very large red shifts. If the red shift is due to the Doppler effect, quasars must be very remote, thus occurring early in the universe's history, and be receding at velocities close to that of light. Alternatively gravitational red shifts might be involved. The cause of the prodigious energy output is unknown but could result from gravitational collapse, as of a galaxy, or from a gigantic thermonuclear explosion in an unstable object. △124.

Quasimodo, Salvatore (1901–68), Italian poet and translator. His early poetry, such as *Acque e terra* (1930), is hermetic in style. He was imprisoned for antifascist activities during World War II, and his poetry increased in sensitivity, as in *The Promised Land* (1957) and *Debit and Credit* (trans. 1972). Awarded the Nobel Prize (1959).

Quasi-stellar Object. *See* Quasar.

Quaternary Period, the most recent period of the Cenozoic Era, beginning about 2 million years ago and extending through the present. It marks the beginnings of man. It is divided into the Pleistocene or Glacial Epoch, characterized by a periodic succession of four great ice ages, and the Holocene or Recent Epoch, starting some 10,000 years ago. △276, 576.

Quatrain, four-line stanza with a particular rhyme scheme. Quatrains frequently follow the pattern of four iambic pentameters rhyming *abab;* ie, the first and third lines rhyme and the second and fourth lines rhyme. An example is this first quatrain from Thomas Gray's "Elegy Written in a Country Churchyard":

The curfew tolls the knell of parting day,
The lowing herd winds slowly o'er the lea,
The ploughman homeward plods his weary way,
And leaves the world to darkness and to me.

Quatre Bras, village in central Belgium, 20mi (32km) SSE of Brussels; scene of battle June 16, 1815, in which British under Arthur Wellington defeated French under Marshal Michel Ney.

Quebec, province in E Canada, largest in area and 2nd in population among the 10 provinces.

Land and economy. A broken wilderness covers most of the N, reaching along the E shore of Hudson Bay to Hudson Strait. This land is rich in minerals. The St Lawrence River in the extreme S, flowing from the Great Lakes to the Atlantic Ocean, has been vital in Quebec's history and economy. In its valley and to the S lie the agricultural lands. The Appalachian Mts of E North America extend into the far SE. Quebec's wealth in natural resources, especially timber and minerals, has sustained its economy at a high level. Manufacturing is centered in the cities along the St Lawrence and in the S; Montreal is a major port. Tourism makes an important year-round contribution to the province's income.

People. Quebec was the seat of the French colonial empire in North America in the 18th century, and the French heritage remains dominant. More than 80% of the population is of French descent, and French is the official language of the province. The remainder of the population is chiefly of English ancestry.

Education. There are seven major institutions of higher education: Laval University, the University of Montreal, the University of Sherbrooke, McGill University, Sir George Williams University, Bishop's University, and Concordia University.

History. The Frenchman Jacques Cartier found the E coast in 1534 and later sailed up the St Lawrence. The first permanent settlement in the area was Quebec city, founded on the St Lawrence by Samuel de Champlain in 1608. Montreal was est. in 1642. From the expanding colony, the French pushed trading and military posts to the W. Quebec city fell to the British in 1759 during the Seven Years' War, Montreal surrendered in 1760, and in 1763 the entire area was ceded by treaty to Great Britain, and became a British colony. In 1791, Canada was divided into Lower and Upper Canada, Quebec being known as Lower Canada, but in 1841 the parts were united as the province of Canada. With the establishment of the Dominion of Canada in 1867, Quebec became a province under that name. In the mid-20th century French-speaking elements intensified their demands for recognition of their cultural heritage, including independence for Quebec. In 1976 the province hosted the summer Olympic Games, primarily in Montreal.

PROFILE

Admitted to Confederation: July 1, 1867; one of the four provinces that were joined to form the Dominion of Canada.
National Parliament Representatives: Senate, 24; House of Commons, 74
Population: 6,013,000; rank, 2nd
Capital: Quebec
Chief cities: Montreal; Laval; Quebec

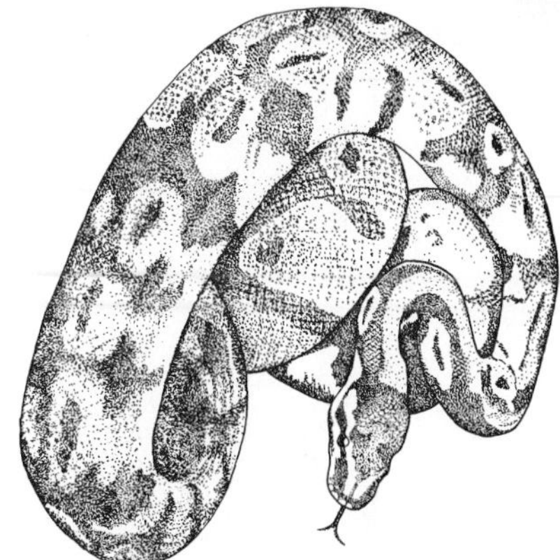
Python

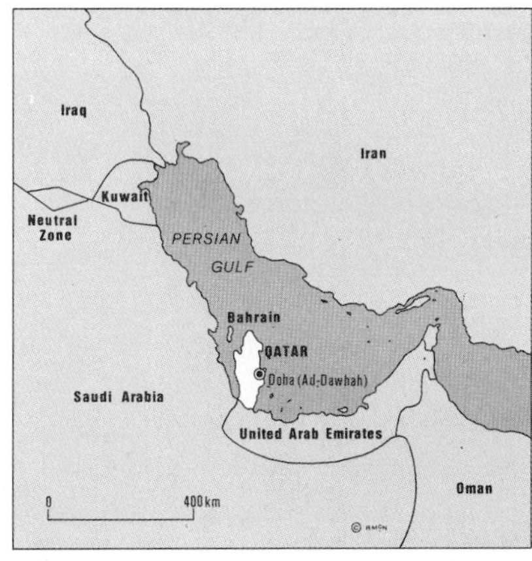
Iraq
Iran
Kuwait
Neutral Zone
PERSIAN GULF
Bahrain
QATAR
Doha (Ad-Dawhah)
Saudi Arabia
United Arab Emirates
Oman
0
400km
Qatar

Salvatore Quasimodo

Quebec: fishing village

Provincial legislature: Provincial Assembly, 110
Area: 594,860sq mi (1,540,687sq km); rank, 1st
Elevation: Highest, 4,160ft (1,269m), Mt Jacques Cartier; lowest, sea level
Industries (major products): pulp and paper, aluminum, petroleum products, electrical equipment, railroad equipment, textiles, clothing, shoes, food products
Agriculture (major products): dairy products, hay, oats, potatoes, cattle, maple sugar and sugar, sugar beets
Minerals (major): iron, copper, asbestos
Floral emblem: madonna lily

Quebec, port city in S Quebec province, Canada, 150mi (242km) NE of Montreal at the confluence of the St Lawrence and St Charles rivers; capital of Quebec prov. and Canada's oldest city. French is the official language as a majority of the population is of French heritage; 98% is Roman Catholic. The city is divided into two sections: Lower Town, built on the waterfront, and Upper Town on Cape Diamond. The site of Quebec, an Indian town of Stadacona, was visited by Jacques Cartier in 1535 and 1541. Samuel de Champlain est. a French trading post 1608 and became its first governor; it was captured by British forces 1629 and held until 1632, when it was returned to France. Quebec served as capital of New France 1663–1763 and rapidly grew as the center of French fur trade. The famous battle on the Plains of Abraham (1759) resulted in a British victory against the French, forcing Quebec to surrender and ultimately to become a British colony (1763). During the American Revolution, Quebec withstood an American siege led by Benedict Arnold and Richard Montgomery (1775). It served as capital of Lower Canada and seat of governor general 1791–1841, when Upper and Lower Canada united; it was twice capital of the United Provinces of Canada (1851–55, 1859–67); scene of Quebec Conference (1943 and 1944). Quebec is the site of Hôtel-Dieu du Précieux-Sang (1639) one of the oldest hospitals in North America, Kent House (1636), Ursuline Convent (1639), Basilica of Notre Dame (1647), Quebec Seminary (1663), Château Frontenac, Laval University (1852), University of Quebec (1969), General Hospital (1692), Citadel (1823), Chapel of Notre Dame des Victoires (1688). Exports: petroleum products, grain, paper and pulp, asbestos. Industries: shipbuilding, tourism, bricks, pulp and paper, leather, textiles, clothing, machinery, canned food, beverages, tobacco, cigars, cigarettes, chemicals. Pop. 182,418.

Quebec Act (1774), act by British Parliament setting up civil government for Canada. A council appointed by the crown was the legislative authority, subject to royal veto. Parliament retained all powers of taxation except for local taxes. Religious tolerance and civil rights were granted to Roman Catholics. Quebec's boundary was extended south to the Ohio River, thus cutting off western claims of Massachusetts, Virginia, and Connecticut. The latter two provisions greatly disturbed the colonists.

Quechua, the most widely spoken of all the American Indian languages, with about 5,000,000 speakers in Peru, 1,500,000 in Bolivia, and 500,000 in Ecuador. Originally the language of the great Inca Empire, it is related to Aymara, the two forming the Quechumaran family.

Queen Anne Style, originally applied to architecture and furniture produced in England between 1702 and 1714 but often extended to include red brick houses and their decoration built *c.* 1660–1720. It is also applied to graceful yet solidly built furniture with modern upholstery.

Queen Anne's War (1702–13), North American extension of the War of Spanish Succession. It involved Indian raids in the southern colonies and French and Indian raids in New England. Deerfield, Mass., was destroyed (1704). Expeditions against French Canada were partially successful, with the English capturing Port Royal and Acadia. The war ended with the Treaty of Utrecht (1713), in which France ceded Acadia, Newfoundland, and Hudson Bay to England.

Queen Charlotte Islands, archipelago off W British Columbia, Canada; separated from mainland by Hecate Strait. Chief islands are Graham, Moresby, Louise, and Lyell; inhabitants are mostly Haida Indians. Industries: mining, timber, fishing. Area: 3,705sq mi (9,596sq km). Pop. 2,222.

Queen Conch. △482.

Queen Elizabeth Islands, formerly Parry Islands; northernmost part of Arctic Archipelago, in Northwest Territories, Canada; includes Ellesmere Island (largest), the Sverdrup and Parry groups, along with many smaller islands. Islands extend to within 500mi (805km) of North Pole; oil drilling is underway. Area: 160,000sq mi (414,400sq km).

Queens, largest borough of New York City, New York, on W end of Long Island; coextensive with Queens co; connected with mainland by Hell Gate Bridge (between Bronx and Astoria) and Triboro Bridge, and with Manhattan by Queensboro and Triboro bridges; also connected by railroad tunnels beneath East River. Mainly residential area, it manufactures consumer products for the area; site of New York World's Fairs 1939–40 and 1964–65 in Flushing Meadows Park; LaGuardia and Kennedy International airports; Queens College (1937) in Flushing, and St John's University (1870) in Jamaica. Industries: baking products, clothing, hosiery, pianos, paint, silk. First settled by Dutch 1635; chartered as borough 1898. Area: 108sq mi (280sq km). Pop. (1970) 1,973,708.

Queensberry, John Sholto Douglas, 8th Marquess of (1844–1900), British sportsman credited with drafting (1865) the rules that govern modern boxing. The rules, standardized in 1889, called for 3-minute rounds with a 1-minute rest period in between and the use of gloves. John Graham Chambers, who helped draft the rules, is sometimes credited as their sole originator.

Queensland, state in NE Australia, bounded by the Coral Sea and Pacific Ocean (NE and E) and the Gulf of Carpentaria and Torres Strait (NW); Brisbane is the capital city. An agricultural state, chief crop is sugar cane; largest cattle-producing state. Major industries: dairying, food processing, mining of copper, coal, lead, zinc. First visited by Capt. James Cook 1770, settled 1824–43 as a penal colony; became Commonwealth state 1901. Area: 667,000sq mi (1,727,530sq km). Pop. 1,799,200.

Quemoy (Chinmen, or Chin-men), island group off SE China, on Formosa Strait, 150mi (242km) W of Taiwan; comprised of Quemoy and Little Quemoy islands and 12 islets. Quemoy Island has been garrisoned by Taiwan since Communist takeover 1949; fishing and agricultural area. Crops: sweet potatoes, peanuts, barley, wheat, vegetables, rice. Pop. 61,305.

Quenching. *See* **Heat treatment**.

Quercy, region and former co of SW France, now occupied by Lot and Tarn-et-Garonne depts. Of Gallo-Roman origin, it was held by English 1360–1440; made part of French crownlands 1472 when it was included in Guienne prov. Region is composed of arid limestone plateaus and fertile river valleys. Industries: sheep, Rocamadour cheese.

Querétaro, state in central Mexico; capital is Querétaro; N terrain is mountainous, plains and valleys are in S. Spanish conquered area 1531 from Chichimec Indians; it was made separate Mexican state 1824. Industries: sugar cane, cotton, tobacco, livestock; mining of opals, silver, iron, copper. Area: 4,544sq mi (11,769sq km). Pop. 464,226.

Querétaro, city in central Mexico, 160mi (258km) NW of Mexico City. Formerly an Aztec city, it was taken 1531 by Spanish; scene of 1867 execution of Emperor Maximilian; revolution against Spain was planned here 1810; site of several colonial landmarks, university, 16th-century cathedral. Industries: cotton, agricultural equipment, tourism, opal mining. Pop. 140,379.

Quesnay, François (1694–1774), leader of the 18th-century French Physiocrats, who invented an economic table for France, which demonstrated the circular flow of economic activity throughout the society. *See also* Physiocrats.

Quetzal, inactive, tree-perching Central American forest bird. The male is bright green above and crimson below with 3-ft (91-cm) tail feathers, once used as authority symbols by the Maya. The duller-colored female nests in a tree hole, laying light blue eggs (2) that are incubated by both parents. Species *Pharomachrus mocinno.*

Quetzalcoatl, in ancient Mexican mythology, the ruler god of the Toltec empire. The Aztecs worshiped him as the bringer of maize and of civilization. He was depicted as a plumed serpent. Montezuma, the Aztec ruler, believed that Hernán Cortés was the god returning to fulfill a prophecy, easing the way for the Spanish conquest.

Quezon, Manuel Luis (1878–1944), Filipino political figure. He was an early leader in the fight for Philippine independence. In 1909 he went to Washington, D.C., as a resident commissioner for the Philippines to the US Congress. When the United States refused to specify a time for Philippine independence in the Jones Act (1916), Quezon resigned and returned to the Philippines, where he led the Nationalist party. In 1935 he was elected first president of the Commonwealth of the Philippines. His term saw improvements and reforms in housing, the military, and government organization. After the Japanese occupation in 1942, he served the Pacific War Council in the United States.

Quezon City, capital city of the Republic of the Philippines, on Luzon island, adjacent to Manila (SW). The 2nd-largest city of the Philippines, it is mainly a residential section, with textile mills and the University of the Philippines; made capital 1948. Pop. 754,452.

Quiché, Mayan Indian group located in the highlands of W Guatemala. Archeological remains show large pre-conquest population centers and an advanced civilization; the *Popul Vuh,* an account of the Quiché myth of creation, is another important source of knowledge about the Quiché.

Quicksand, smooth grains of sand which do not adhere to each other, and are saturated with upward flowing water. It is a soft, shifting mass, yielding easily to pressure. Objects resting on its surface are usually sucked down and engulfed. Where the density of the suspension is exceeded by the object (as in the case of a human body), the object cannot sink below the surface, although struggling may lead to loss of balance and drowning.

Quietism, heretical doctrine of religious spirituality and mysticism, identified with Miguel de Molinos, a 17th-century Spanish priest. The meaning of Quietism is that perfection consists of complete passivity of the soul and the suppression of individual effort, so that divine love and action may reign freely; therefore, the soul, which has undergone mystical death, can will only what God wills. Although his teachings were begun within the Roman Catholic Church, Molinos' teachings were condemned and he was sentenced to prison by Pope Innocent XI in 1687.

Quilmes, city in E Argentina, 9mi (14km) SE of Buenos Aires; site of British landing 1806, capturing Buenos Aires for a short time. Industries: brewing, tourism, textiles, rope, tiles. Founded 1665. Pop. 317,783.

Quince, shrub or small tree native to Asia. It is popular for its greenish-yellow, hard fruit used in preserves. Height: 20ft (6.1m). Family Rosaceae; species *Cydonia oblonga.* △338.

Quincy, Josiah (1772–1864), US politician, b. Braintree, Mass. He was a Federalist and member of the state senate (1804), member of the US House of Representatives (1805–13) and minority leader. Opponent of the Embargo and Nonintercourse acts and of the War of 1812, he was dropped by the Federalist party for his oppositions. He was elected to the Massachusetts house of representatives (1821), elected mayor of Boston (1823), and made president of Harvard University (1829–45).

Quincy, city in W Illinois, on bluffs overlooking Mississippi River; seat of Adams co; named for John Quincy Adams, 6th US president; site of Quincy College (1860), Indian Mounds Park, Parker Memorial Park; scene of Oct. 13, 1858, Lincoln-Douglas debate. Industries: pumps, drills, flour, poultry, farm equipment. Founded 1822; chartered 1840. Pop. (1970) 45,288.

Quincy, city in Massachusetts, on Boston Bay; S suburb of Boston; birthplace of presidents John Adams and John Quincy Adams, whose homes are National Historic sites, and of John Hancock; site of Quincy Junior College (1958), Eastern Nazarene College (1900), First Parish Church (1828). Industries: shipbuilding, packaging machinery, soaps, television tubes. Founded 1625 as trading post; separated from Braintree 1792; inc. as city 1888. Pop. (1970) 87,966.

Quine, Willard Van Orman (1908–), US philosopher and mathematical logician. His work focused on language as a logical system. He was greatly influenced by Rudolph Carnap. Having changed his philosophical position many times during his career, his importance lies mainly in the valuable discussion he provoked. His writings include *A System of Logistic* (1934), *Mathematical Logic* (1940), *Word and Object* (1960), and *Philosophy of Logic* (1969).

Quinine, drug derived from cinchona bark, used principally to treat malaria, if modern drugs are unavailable, and provide relief from chronic leg cramps. It is toxic if taken in large doses. △744, 1560.

Quintana Roo, state in SE Mexico, on Caribbean Sea; occupies most of the Yucatán Peninsula; flat plain area with dense forests; climate is hot and humid; inhabited mostly by Indians. Products: lumber, chicle, sponge, coconuts, turtle fishing. Area: 16,228sq mi (42,031sq km). Pop. 91,044.

Quipu. △1118.

Quirinus, in Roman mythology, a major deity, husband of Hora. His festival was held Feb. 17.

Quisling, Vidkun (1887–1945), Norwegian fascist. He was minister of defense (1931–32) and then left the Agrarian party to found the fascist National Union party. In 1940 he collaborated with Germany in the invasion of Norway; he was made premier in 1942. The Norwegians opposed his attempt to nazify church and school, but he stayed in power until Norway's liberation when he was arrested, convicted of high treason, and shot.

Quito, capital city of Ecuador, in N central part of country, 114mi (184km) from Pacific coast almost on Equator. Site was originally settled by Quito Indians and captured by Incas (1487); taken by Spain in 1534; liberated 1822 by Antonio José de Sucre. Located at foot of Pichincha volcano it has suffered many earthquakes. A cultural and political center with little industry, it is the site of Central University of Ecuador (1787), the oldest art school in Latin America, Catholic University (1946), and an observatory. Industries: textiles, handcrafts. Pop. 528,100.

Qumran. *See* Khirbat Qumran.

Quoits, a game played by two or more persons, similar to horseshoe pitching. The metal, circular quoits, with one rounded and one flat surface, are thrown at a peg in the ground 1 inch (2.54cm) high. The pitching distance for men is 30 feet (9.1m) and the distance for women is 20 feet (6.1m). Points are scored similar to horseshoe pitching, except that only 21 points are needed to win. *See also* Horseshoe Pitching.

Quotient. *See* Division.

Quebec City

Manuel Luis Quezon

Ra. *See* Re.

Rabat, capital city of Morocco, in N Morocco, on Atlantic coast, approx. 55mi (89km) NE of Casablanca. Settlement dates from Phoenician times, but fortified city was founded in 12th century; French protectorate est. 1912; became independent 1956; site of 180-ft (55-m) Hassane Tower (12th century), and University of Rabat. Industries: hand-woven rugs, textiles, food processing. Pop. 325,000.

Rabbi, meaning "my master," since the Middle Ages, the individual responsible for religious education, guidance, and services in the synagogue. His position is based on his learning, but entails no special privileges. His duties include interpreting Jewish law and guiding the spiritual lives of people.

Rabbit, long-eared, herbivorous, prolific mammal of the family Leporidae, including the European common rabbit and the American cottontail. Although usage varies, most so-called rabbits typically are smaller than hares (Lepus), have shorter ears, run without leaping, and their young are born furless, blind, and helpless. The common rabbit *(Oryctolagus cuniculus)* of S Europe and Africa has been introduced in many other regions—notably Australia. It has thick, soft, grayish-brown fur. The wide variety of domesticated rabbits are of this species. Length: 14–18in (35–45cm); weight 3–5lb (1.4–2.3kg). *See also* Cottontail; Hare. △546.

Rabbit Fish. *See* Chimaera.

Rabelais, François (*c.*1494–*c* 1553), French humanist and satirist. He left convent life to study medicine and was appointed hospital physician at Lyons in 1532. He traveled widely in Italy. His life work (*Pantagruel* 1532; *Gargantua* 1534; *Tiers Livre* 1546; *Quart Livre* 1548, 1552) is a series of vivid, hedonistic, satirical digressions. Condemned by theologians and the Sorbonne, his works were widely popular and gained him the protection of important patrons. *See also* Gargantua, *La vie tres horrifique du grand.*

Rabi, Isidor Isaac (1898–), US physicist, b. Austria, who was awarded a 1944 Nobel Prize for his invention of a magnetic resonance method of observing atomic spectra. This invention, in addition to shedding light on atomic and molecular structures, helped determine the nucleus shape of an atom. He also worked on the development of microwave radar.

Rabies, or hydrophobia, acute contagious viral infection of the central nervous system. It occurs in all warmblooded animals, especially canines, mustelids, and bats, and is transmissible to man through the bite of an affected animal. △722, 734.

Rabin, Itzhak (1922–), Israeli statesman. After a distinguished military career, he served as ambassador to the US (1968–73) and minister of labor (1974). Following Golda Meir's resignation, he became (1974) Israel's first native-born premier.

Rabinowitz, Solomon. *See* Aleichem, Shalom.

Raccoon, stout-bodied, omnivorous, mostly nocturnal mammal of North and Central American wooded areas near water. They have a black masklike marking across their eyes and a long, black-banded tail. They have agile and sensitive front paws and typically dip food and other objects in water. Their footprints look human. The seven species include the North American *Procyon lotor.* Length: 16–24in (40–61cm); weight: 10–30lb (4.5–13.6kg). Family Procyonidae.

Race, biological classification of the human species according to hereditary (genetic) differences. The term "geographical race" denotes large groupings of man that contain many "local races," varying in numerical strength from a few hundred to many million. Different racial characteristics arise through genetic mutation, selective breeding, and adaptation to a particular environment. Many aspects of anthropological taxonomy are still confused and debatable. *See also* Australoid Race; Caucasoid Race; Mongoloid Race; Negroid Race. △658–60.

Racematization, transformation of an optically active substance into a mixture of equal quantities of two mirror-image crystals (enantiomorphs), usually by heat or the action of acids or bases. Individually each enantiomorph rotates the plane of polarized light through a characteristic angle, but an equal quantity of each will cancel each other's rotatory effect.

Racer, any of several species of slender snakes ranging from S Canada to Guatemala. They are broad-headed, large-eyed, and varied in color. The E United States species is black. Length: to 5ft (1.5m). Family Colubridae; species include *Coluber constrictor constrictor* △522.

Racerunner, active, slim, long-tailed lizard dis-

Raccoon

Racer

tributed throughout the Americas. There are 12 species in the United States, chiefly in the southwest. They are generally dark-colored with light, longitudinal stripes. Some forms develop from unfertilized eggs. Length: to 16in (41cm). Family Teiidae; genus *Cnemidophorus.*

Rachel, in the Bible, daughter of Laban, Jacob's second wife, and the mother of Joseph and Benjamin. Having labored seven years for Rachel's hand, Jacob was tricked by her father into marrying Leah, her older sister. He worked seven more years to marry Rachel.

Rachmaninoff, Sergei (1873–1943), Russian composer and pianist. He composed in a basically conservative, post-Romantic style modeled after Tchaikovsky and was one of the foremost pianists of the 20th century. His *Piano Concerto No. 2* (1901), *Rhapsody on a Theme of Paganini* (1934), and second symphony are among his most popular works. He also composed songs, preludes and etudes for piano, four piano concertos, and other works. △1246.

Racial Discrimination, denial of rights, privileges, and opportunities to an individual or group because of race. In the United States, such action has been outlawed in the public sector by a series of constitutional amendments (eg the 15th Amendment), judicial decisions (eg *Brown* v. *Board of Education of Topeka,* 1954), and legislative acts beginning with the Civil Rights Act of 1866 and culminating in the Civil Rights Acts of 1964 and 1968. The constitutions of other governments, including that of the Soviet Union, also contain prohibitions against racial discrimination. *See also* Civil Rights and Liberties; Racism. △894–96.

Racialism. △894.

Racine, Jean Baptiste (1639–99), French classical dramatist who perfected disciplined 17th-century tragedy. A theatrical rival of Corneille and Molière, he was encouraged by Louis XIV. Racine wrote *Andromaque* (1667), *Iphigénie* (1674), *Phèdre* (1677), *Esther* (1689), and *Athalie* (1691), the last two in retirement. △1172.

Racine, city and port of entry in SE Wisconsin, 25mi (40km) S of Milwaukee, on Lake Michigan and mouth of Root River; seat of Racine co. Industrial growth was spurred by establishment of threshing machine plant (1842), harbor improvements (*c.* 1844), and the introduction of railroad to the area (1855). Industries: farm machinery, floor wax, electrical equipment, printing, clothing, automobile parts. Settled 1834; inc. 1848. Pop (1970) 95,162.

Racism, doctrine advocating the superiority of one race over any and all others. Racism has, from time to time, been the avowed policy of governments and, as such, the root cause of slavery and discriminatory legislation, such as in the United States before the Civil War, in Nazi Germany during the 1930s, and in several African nations. It has been perpetrated by both white and black administrations. *See also* Civil Rights and Liberties; Racial Discrimination. △896.

Rackets, game played by two or four persons on a court. The court is 60 by 30 feet (18.3 by 9.2m) and is surrounded by three walls 30 feet (9.2m) high and a back wall 15 feet (4.6m) high. Each player uses a gut-strung racket 30 inches (76.2cm) long that has a circular head 7–8 inches (17.8–20.3cm) in diameter and that weighs 8–10 ounces (226–283 grams). The ball with a diameter of 1 inch (2.5cm) is tightly wound cloth and twine and covered by leather. A service line is painted on the front wall at a height of 9 feet, 7.5 inches (2.9m) and a fixed wooden board *(telltale),* also on the front wall, extends 27 inches (68.6cm) up from the floor. These are the markers that determine when a ball is in play. The serve must be put in play above the service line and must then land behind a short line, marked 24 feet (7.3m) from the back wall. Games are played to 15 points. Rackets originated in debtors' prison in England in the 18th century. The game soon spread to the wealthier classes. It was introduced to the United States, where it is governed by the Racquet and Tennis Club (1890), from Canada.

Radar, a contraction of RA(dio) D(etecting) A(nd) R(anging), a method of detecting the position, velocity, and other characteristics of a distant object by analyzing the high frequency radio waves reflected from its surface. The technique was developed simultaneously (*c.* 1935–40) in several countries. Current fields in which radar is used include navigation, meteorology, astronomy, defense systems, and geographical studies. △1802.

Radar Astronomy. *See* Astronomy, Radar.

Radar Telescope. *See* Telescope, Radio.

Radcliffe-Brown, Alfred Reginald (1881–1955), English social anthropologist who was influential in making social anthropology a comparative study of stable and fluctuating systems. He conducted pioneering work in the study and classification of primitive societies. His works include *The Social Organization of Australian Tribes* (1931) and *Structure and Function in Primitive Society* (1952).

Radetzky, Joseph. △1248.

Radhakrishnan, (Sir) Sarvepalli (1888–1975), Indian political figure and author. As writer and teacher, he attempted to spread Indian thought in the West and teach Indians the worth of the individual and the value of a casteless society. His works include *East and West in Religion* (1933) and *Religion in a Changing World* (1967). He was Indian delegate to UNESCO (1946–52) and ambassador to the Soviet Union (1949–52). He became president of India in 1962 and served until 1967.

Radian, unit of plane angle given as the angle subtended at the center of a circle by an arc of length equal to that of the radius of the circle. Thus 2π radians is equal to 360°; one radian is equal to 57.296°.

Radiation, a process of energy transfer by electromagnetic waves propagating through space and other media, as distinguished from conduction and convention. Principal components of solar radiation include waves in radio frequencies, microwaves, long-wave (infrared) radiation, visible light or radiation, and short-wave (ultraviolet) radiation, as well as X and gamma rays of even shorter wavelengths. *See also* Heat Transfer; Solar Constant. △212.

Radiation, Heat, the energy given off by a body in the form of electromagnetic waves. Heat energy is simply a measure of the vibrations of atoms and electrons within a body. But vibrating electrons also give off electromagnetic waves continuously; thus all objects, even ice, radiate heat. △1508.

Radiation, Nuclear, particles or electromagnetic radiation emitted spontaneously and at high energies from atomic nuclei. It can result from radioactive decay to yield alpha particles (helium nuclei), beta particles (electrons), gamma rays, and, more rarely, positrons (antielectrons). It can also result from spontaneous fission of the nucleus, with ejection of neutrons or gamma rays. Spontaneous fission occurs in some heavy atoms without the supply of energy. △1482.

Radiation Biology, study of the effects of ionizing radiations (X rays and radioactive radiation) on living organisms. All forms of life are destroyed by large doses of radiation, the main effect being on cell division and therefore it is the parts of the body that replace themselves most frequently that are the most susceptible. It is for this reason that cancer cells can be destroyed by radiation. Whether or not radiation causes cancer or destroys reoplastic tumors depends on careful control of the dosage.

Radiation Sickness, illness resulting from exposing the body to ionizing radiation (X rays or gamma rays). Diarrhea, vomiting, fever, and hemorrhage are symptoms. Sickness may occur immediately or be delayed. Severity depends upon the degree of radiation. Treatment is effective in mild cases.

Radiation Therapy, the use of X-ray and gamma-ray radiation to treat disease; often used alone or in combination with surgery to eradicate malignant tumors. △750.

Radical, root of a number or quantity, such as its square root or cube root. The radical sign ($\sqrt{\ }$) is qualified, except for a square root, by a superscript number that indicates a particular radical, as with $\sqrt[3]{\ }$ (cube root).

Radical, single atom or group of atoms in which all the atomic valences are not satisfied by chemical bonding. Thus, removal of a hydrogen atom from methane, CH_4, gives the methyl radical CH_3. The term is usually taken to mean a free radical, that is, one existing free for a short time in a reaction. Free radicals are highly reactive: they can be produced by ultraviolet light, pyrolysis, electron impact, and other means, and play an important part in the mechanisms of many chemical reactions.

Radical Republicans, US Republican congressmen and other political figures who proposed and implemented a punitive plan for Reconstruction of the South at the end of the Civil War. Their opposition to Pres. Andrew Johnson led to his impeachment in 1868, although the Radicals failed in their efforts to remove him from office. *See also* Reconstruction.

Radio, the use of electromagnetic waves in the radio frequency range to transmit or receive electric signals through the intervening space without wires. Guglielmo Marconi first realized the potential of these waves as a wireless communications system, and in 1901 transmitted the letter *S* across the Atlantic Ocean. The development in 1904 of the vacuum electron tube by Sir John A. Fleming made possible the transmission of speech and music. Lee de Forest in 1906 invented a three-element tube that could both detect and amplify radio waves. The invention by Edwin H. Armstrong of the circuit for the regenerative receiver made possible long-range radio reception. △1548, 1794.

Radioactive Isotope. *See* Isotope. △1550, 1554.

Radioactive Waste Disposal, the process involved in rendering still-radioactive "hot" nuclear material safe. In the case of nuclear fuel when the reaction producing energy becomes too loaded with impurities to be efficient, the "spent" fuel is still radioactive. Cooling and reprocessing are necessary to remove still-useful material. Long-lived isotopes are buried in deep mines until they are no longer radioactive. Some such isotopes may remain radioactive for thousands of years.

Radioactivity, spontaneous disintegration of the nuclei of radioactive isotopes (radioisotopes) with, in most cases, the emission of alpha particles (helium nuclei) or beta particles (electrons) often accompanied by gamma rays. These two processes of radioactive decay, alpha decay and beta decay, cause the radioisotope to be transformed into a chemically different atom. Alpha decay results in the nucleus losing two protons and two neutrons; beta decay occurs when a neutron changes into a proton, an electron (beta particle) being emitted in the process. Thus the atomic number changes in both cases and an isotope of another element is produced, which might also be radioactive. The stability of different isotopes varies widely. It is impossible to predict when a nucleus will disintegrate but in a large collection of atoms there is a characteristic time (half-life) after which one-half of them can be expected to have decayed. This time varies from about ten billion years to ten billionths of a second. The activity of any radioactive sample decreases exponentially with time, never completely disappearing. *See also* Dating, Radioactive; Isotope. △1480, 1554, 1568.

Radio Astronomy. *See* Astronomy, Radio.

Radio Beacon. △1752.

Radiocarbon Dating, or carbon-14 dating, method of determining age of dead organic matter (such as wood, cotton). Living matter assimilates a certain amount of radioactive carbon-14, which comes from the CO_2 in the air. This balances its amount disintegrating in the tissues. After death only the decay process remains and measurement of the amount of carbon-14 gives an indication of age. △276.

Radio Direction Finding (RDF). △1802.

Radio Galaxy, galaxy emitting strong electromagnetic radiation of radio-frequency wavelengths. These emissions seem to be produced by the high-speed motion of subatomic particles in strong magnetic fields. They probably result from explosions occurring in the nuclei of the galaxies concerned. Some radio galaxies correspond to visual sources, such as Cygnus A, which is a distant double galaxy. Radio galaxies are frequently double and many are of immense dimensions. One, 3C236, appears to be the largest galaxy known, being 18,000,000 light years across. *See also* Radio Source. △124.

Radiography, production on photographic material of the interior of opaque bodies by irradiating with X rays. Industrial X ray photographs can show assembly faults, metal defects, etc. In medicine and dentistry they are invaluable for diagnosing bone damage, tooth decay, and internal disease. The images normally only show bones, some tissue structure, and air spaces. Using very sensitive modern techniques, cross-sectional areas of the body can now be obtained showing organs, blood vessels, and diseased parts. △750.

Radioisotope Tracer, radioactive isotope of an element used to trace the course of that element through a biological system. As the stable isotope and radioisotope behave identically from a chemical point of view, the radioisotope will follow exactly the same path as the stable isotope, but its presence in the cells and tissues of the organism can be monitored by the radiation it emits. Compounds labeled with radioisotopes are used in research and diagnosis. △750.

Radiolaria, order of marine, planktonic, ameboid protozoans characterized by a spherical body and silica skeleton. The skeletons, which are the main components of ocean bottom ooze and flint, are patterned according to species. Shapes include long spines, latticed spheres, polyps, and basket-, bell-, and helmet-like shapes; 5,000 species including *Actipylina, Peripylaria, Hexacontium.* Class Rhizopoda. △506.

Radiology, branch of medicine dealing with the use of X rays and other forms of radiation to diagnose and treat disease. △750.

Radiometer. △1526.

Radio Source, discrete astronomical source of radio waves, detected by radio telescope. Radio sources include the Sun, supernova remnants and pulsars, quasars, and certain nebulae and galaxies, many of which have been identified optically. The strongest sources are the Andromeda Galaxy, Perseus, Taurus A, Puppis A, Virgo A, Centaurus A, Cygnus A, and Cassiopeia A. △96, 124.

Radio Telephone. △1752.

Radio Telescope. *See* Telescope, Radio.

Radish, annual garden vegetable developed from a wild plant native to cooler regions of Asia. Its leaves are long, deeply lobed, and prickly. The fleshy root, red, white, or black, is eaten raw. Red radishes are small and globular; white radishes are long and cylindrical. They mature in 24–45 days; winter crops take 60 days. Family Cruciferae; species *Raphanus sativus.*

Radishchev, Aleksandr Nikolaevich (1749–1802), Russian liberal writer. △1178.

Radium, radioactive metallic element (symbol Ra) of the alkaline-Earth group, first isolated as radium salts (1898) by Pierre and Marie Curie. The metal was isolated by Mme. Curie in 1911. It is present in uranium minerals. The metal is used in research, luminous paints, and medical radiotherapy. It has 13 isotopes that emit alpha, beta, and gamma radiation: radon is a decay product. Properties: at. no. 88; at. wt. 226.0254; sp gr 5 (approx.); melt. pt. 1,292°F (700°C); boil. pt. 2,084°F (1,140°C); most stable isotope Ra^{226} (half-life 1,600 yr). *See also* Alkaline-Earth Elements. △1552.

Radius, distance, or line segment, from the center to any point on the circumference of a circle or the surface of a sphere. △1464.

Radius, Atomic. *See* Atomic Radius.

Radon, radioactive nonmetallic gaseous element (symbol Rn) of the noble-gas group, first discovered in 1900. Rn^{222} (half-life 3.8 days) is a decay product of radium. Thorium decays to Rn^{220} (half-life 54.5s) and actinium gives Rn^{219} (half-life 3.92s). The isotopes, which are alpha emitters, are present in the Earth's atmosphere in trace amounts. Chemically, the element is known to form fluorides. Properties: at. no. 86; density 9.73 g dm^{-3}; melt. pt. −95.8°F (−71°C); boil. pt. −79.24°F (−61.8°C); most stable isotope Rn^{222} (half-life 3.823 days). *See also* Noble Gases. △1558.

Raeder, Erich (1876–1960), German admiral. In 1928 he became chief of the navy department and during 1935–43 he was supreme commander of German naval forces. He was sentenced to life and imprisoned in 1945 by the Nuremberg war crimes tribunal but was released from prison in 1955 because of ill health.

Rafters. △1610.

Ragnarok, in Scandinavian mythology, the end of the world of gods and men. Chaos and tempests will prevail before Ragnarok. Afterward the Earth will rise again.

Ragweed, wind-pollinated plant that is the chief cause of hay fever in late summer and early fall. The common ragweed *(Ambrosia artemisiifolia)* is widespread in N United States and produces large amounts of pollen from branching greenish, tassellike flowers, height: 1–8ft (0.3–2.4m). The giant ragweed *(A. trifida)* is most common on E and SE United States coasts; height: 1.5–20ft (0.45–6m). Family Compositae.

Ragwort, ragged-leaved plants, including golden ragwort or golden groundsel *(Senecio aureus),* a biennial or perennial that bears flat-topped clusters of yellow flower heads; height: to 4ft (1.2m). Family Compositae. *See also* Groundsel. △446.

Rahman, Mujibur. *See* Mujibur Rahman.

Rahu, in Hindu mythology and religion, the mischievous four-armed deity who causes eclipses and the fall of meteors, and who presages trouble and sickness. Rahu is especially worshiped by the Dosadhs and Dhangars of India who show their devotion by walking on a path of hot coals. △838.

Rahway, city in NE New Jersey, on Rahway River 5mi (8km) SSW of Elizabeth; scene of skirmishes here in 1777 that routed the British; burial place of Abraham Clark, signer of Declaration of Independence. Industries: chemicals, pharmaceuticals, soap, automobile parts. Settled 1720; inc. 1858. Pop. (1970) 29,114.

Rail, slender, long-legged, drab-colored marsh bird that is well camouflaged in its dense swampland home. They are shy, generally nocturnal, and often emit melodious calls. They lay marked white or buff-colored eggs (8–15) in a reed-and-grass ground nest. Length: 4–18in (10–46cm). Family Rallidae.

Rail Gauge. △1708.

Railroad. △1676, 1706–10.

Railroad Transportation Act of 1920. *See* Esch-Cummins Act.

Railroad Worm. *See* Apple Maggot.

Railway Labor Act (1926), early labor legislation in the United States, attempted to provide mediation and arbitration services and support use of collective bargaining in order to avoid interruption of rail service. The act has been amended to include airlines and airline unions.

Rain, water drops that fall from the Earth's atmosphere to its surface, as opposed to fog or dew. △216.

Rainbow, a bright band in a circular arc with colors of the spectrum arranged from red inside to blue outside, usually formed opposite to the sun or other light source in sheets of water droplets from which the light is refracted and reflected. △1516.

Rainey, Ma (1886–1939), US blues singer known as the "Mother of the Blues," b. Gertrude Malissa Nix Pridgett in Columbus, Ga. She discovered and encouraged Bessie Smith and was one of the earliest blues singers to record. △1366.

Rain Forest. △596–603.

Rainier III (1923–), in full, Rainier Louis Henri Maxence Bertrand de Grimaldi, prince of Monaco. He succeeded his grandfather Louis II in 1949. He became an international celebrity when he married Grace Kelly, a US film actress, in 1956. They have three children, ensuring the survival of the royal family and hence Monaco's independence from France.

Rainier, Mount (Mount Tacoma), peak in W central Washington, in Mt Rainier National Park (est. 1899); greatest single peak glacier system in the United States radiates from the summit of this ancient volcano. Highest point in the Cascade Range, 14,410ft (4,395m). Discovered and named 1792 by Capt. Vancouver; first scaled 1870.

Rain Tree, or saman, tree native to tropical regions in the West Indies and Central America. It is grown in other tropical areas as a shade tree. The leaflets fold up at night or if rain is imminent. Height: to 80ft (24m). Family Leguminosae; genus *Samanea.*

Raisin, dried, sweet grapes, usually seedless, for eating. *See* Grape.

Rákóczy, name of a noble Hungarian family, princes of Transylvania. During the 16th and 17th centuries these noble Magyars were closely linked with the fortunes of Hungary. **Sigismund** (1544–1608) supported István Bocskay against the Jesuits. **George I** (1591–1648), prince of Transylvania (1631–48), a staunch Protestant, allied himself with Sweden and France to invade Austria in 1644 to protect Protestant rights. **George II** (1621–60) allied with the Swedes and invaded Poland to secure the throne but was forced to retreat. The Turks deposed him. **Francis II** (1676–1735), a Protestant, headed revolt against

Sergei Rachmaninoff

Jean Baptiste Racine

Ragweed

Rail

Austria in Hungary and held power over Hungary and Transylvania before he was defeated by the Austrians (1708) and driven into exile.

Raleigh, (Sir) Walter (1552?–1618), English soldier, political figure, and author. Finding favor at court with Queen Elizabeth I, he was knighted (1585). His captains explored the coast from Florida to North Carolina (1584), and he sent settlers (1585) to Roanoke Island, N.C., but no permanent settlement was made. In 1587 he obtained a patent to take possession of unknown lands in North America, to be named "Virginia." He is credited with the introduction to England from North America of the potato plant and tobacco. Supplanted as the Queen's favorite by the Earl of Essex, he was expelled from court (1592). After the accession of James I he was found guilty of conspiracy and imprisoned (1603–16). While in prison he wrote his *History of the World* (1614). In 1617 he led an unsuccessful expedition to the Orinoco River in search of gold, was arrested on his return, and was executed under terms of his original sentence. △1216.

Raleigh, capital city of North Carolina, in E central part of state, 50mi (81km) S of Virginia border; seat of Wake co; occupied during Civil War by Gen. William Sherman and Union forces (April 1865); birthplace of Pres. Andrew Johnson (1808); site of St Mary's Junior College (1842), Pearce College (1857), Shaw University (1865), St Augustine's College (1867), North Carolina State University at Raleigh (1887), Meredith College (1891); market center for cotton and tobacco trade. Industries: food processing, textiles, electrical equipment. Founded as state capital 1788; inc. 1792. Pop. (1970) 121,577.

Raleigh Safety Bicycle. △1688.

Ram, The. *See* Aries.

Rama, figure in Hindu mythology, specifically the great epic tale the *Ramayana*. He is the perfect Hindu, devoted and chivalrous husband, obedient to sacred law, courageous, patient, and possessed of a great sense of duty. He was considered in the folk legends to be an incarnation of the god Vishnu and his name became synonymous with God.

Ramadan, the 9th month of the Muslim year, set aside for fasting. One of the Five Pillars of Islam, the basic duties of Muslims, is to fast during Ramadan. The month begins with the sighting of the new moon. For 29 days thereafter the faithful do not eat or drink between sunrise and sunset. Since this is a month in a lunar calendar, it comes at a different time each year in the Western calendar. *See also* Islam. △846.

Raman, (Sir) Chandrasekhara Venkata (1888–1970), Indian physicist who greatly influenced and contributed to the growth of science, and to research facilities in his country. He was awarded a 1930 Nobel Prize for his discovery of the Raman Effect. He indicated that in conjunction with the diffusion of light through a transparent material, there are some changes in the wavelength of the light.

Ramapithecus. △648.

Ramat Gan, city in W Israel, 2mi (3km) E of Tel Aviv-Jaffa; site of Bar Ilan University (1953), and Israel's largest sports stadium. Industries: diamond processing, tourism, food processing. Founded 1921. Pop. 115,500.

Ramayana, along with the *Mahabharata*, one of India's two great epic poems. Consisting of seven books and 24,000 couplets in Sanskrit, it was probably written sometime between 500 and 300 BC. Valmiki was the author. It relates the adventures of Rama, his wife Sita, his brother Lakshmana, and others amid royal intrigues and battles.

Rambouillet, Catherine de Vivonne de Savelli (1558–1665), French social figure. She held a famed literary salon in her home, Hôtel de Rambouillet. Notable figures who frequented her salon included Pierre Corneille, Cardinal Richelieu, and Jean Louis Guez de Balzac. Her salon had a profound influence on 17th-century literature.

Rameau, Jean Philippe (1683–1764), French composer and music theorist. His *Treatise on Harmony* (1722) was an important contribution to musicology. He composed harpsichord suites and many operas such as *Les Indes Gallantes* (1735) and *Castor et Pollux* (1737). △1174, 1196.

Ramesses or **Rameses,** the name of 12 kings of the XIXth and XXth dynasties of ancient Egypt. **Ramesses I** (*r.* 1315–1314 BC) succeeded Horemheb but died soon after. **Ramesses II** (grandson of Ramesses I) (*r.* 1292–1225), conducted war against the Hittites in Palestine and Syria, built many luxurious temples, including the temple at Abu Simbel, and is believed to be the Pharaoh of the Hebrew oppression. **Ramesses III** (*r.c.*1198–1166), second king of the XXth dynasty and husband of Tiy, defended Egypt from the attacks of Libya and Syria, but the great wealth of the nobility and the vast accumulation of slaves led to the dynasty's decline, with the priesthood becoming its center of power. The dynasty ended with **Ramesses XII** (*r.* 1118–1090 BC). △972.

Ramla, town in central Israel, 12mi (19km) SE of Tel Aviv-Jaffa; capital of central district; served as capital of ancient Palestine; taken by Israeli forces in 1948 war and settled by Jewish immigrants; site of Great Mosque (12th century) and Square Tower (1318); farming area. Founded *c.* 716 by Arabs. Pop. 30,800.

Ramon y Cajal, Santiago (1852–1934), Spanish histologist. He shared the 1906 Nobel Prize in physiology or medicine with Camillo Golgi for work on the structure of the nervous system. Ramon y Cajal established the neuron theory, which stated that the nervous system is made up entirely of special nerve cells, or neurons, and described their processes.

Ramsay, (Sir) William (1852–1916), British chemist. Working with Lord Rayleigh he discovered argon in air and later discovered helium, neon, and krypton spectroscopically. For this work he was awarded a Nobel Prize in 1904 and was knighted in 1902. He was also interested in radioactivity and showed that helium is produced by radioactive decay.

Rancho Cordova, residential town in N central California. Pop. (1970) 30,451.

Rand, Ayn (1905–), US author, b. St Petersburg (now Leningrad), Russia. She emigrated to the US in 1926 and was naturalized in 1931. Her first novel, *We the Living*, appeared in 1936. Other works include *Anthem* (1938), *The Fountainhead* (1943), and *Atlas Shrugged* (1957). The last two are massive narratives that serve as vehicles for her philosophy of objectivism. Objectivism touts the self-fulfillment of the individual in a capitalist society. Rand scorns weakness and altruism and regards selfishness as a virtue. The heroes of her novels, such as the architect in *The Fountainhead*, are independent, strong-willed people. Rand is the editor of a newsletter for followers of objectivism.

Randolph, A(sa) Philip (1889–), US labor leader and civil rights activist, b. Crescent City, Fla. Randolph was editor of the radical black journal *The Messenger* until 1925, when he founded the Brotherhood of Sleeping Car Porters. He organized the 1941 March on Washington that prompted President Roosevelt to issue a fair employment practices executive order, and helped organize the 1963 March on Washington. He resigned as president of the Brotherhood in 1968 to devote his time to the A. Philip Randolph Institute, a civil rights organization established in 1964.

Randolph, Edmund (1753–1813), US lawyer and statesman, b. near Williamsburg, Va. Randolph was an active participant in the American Revolution and served his state in a number of high political offices. As a delegate to the Federal Convention of 1787, Randolph proposed the Virginia Plan, foreshadowing the stronger federal government subsequently adopted. He was appointed attorney general by George Washington and fulfilled Jefferson's term as secretary of state (1794–95). Randolph later served as senior counsel for Aaron Burr in the famous treason trial of 1807.

Random Error Curve. △1474.

Ranger Probe. △54.

Rangoon, capital and largest city of Burma, on Rangoon River, approx. 21mi (34km) N of Andaman Sea; one of SE Asia's largest seaports. Rangoon was won by Burma 1755; occupied by Britain 1824–26 and taken in Second Anglo-Burmese Wars 1852; occupied by Japan during WWII; site of airport, railhead, university (1920), technical university (1963), extensive parks and gardens; city proper is dominated by the massive 368-ft (112-m) Buddhist shrine, Shwe Dagon Pagoda (588BC). Industries: rice, lead, zinc ore, timber, oil refining, cotton, tobacco. Pop. 1,733,000.

Rank, Occupational. △926.

Rankin, Jeanette (1880–1973), US social reformer, b. Missoula, Mont. Active in the woman suffrage movement, she helped achieve votes for women in Montana (1914). She became the first woman to serve in the US Congress when she was elected to the House of Representatives (1917). That year she voted against the declaration of war on Germany, which cost her her seat. Reelected in 1940, she cast the only vote in the House against entry into World War II (1941).

Rankine, William John Macquorn (1820–72), Scottish engineer and physicist. He became professor of engineering at Glasgow, using his training in physics to acquaint engineers with the fundamentals of thermodynamics. His *Manual of the Steam Engine* (1859) introduced a practical notation system into engineering thermodynamics, and he devised the absolute temperature scale based on the degree Fahrenheit, which is known as the Rankine scale. He also determined the Rankine cycle, which functions as a model for steam-power installation performance.

Rann of Kutch. *See* Kutch, Rann of.

Ransom, John Crowe (1888–1974), US poet and critic, b. Pulaski, Tenn. He taught at Vanderbilt University and Kenyon College and edited (1939–58) the *Kenyon Review*, in which he expounded the New Criticism, which emphasized the close analysis of the text of a poem. Most of his poetry appeared in *Chills and Fever* (1924) and *Two Gentlemen in Bonds* (1926). *See also* New Criticism.

Rantoul, town in E Illinois, ENE of Champaign; site of Chanute Air Force Base (1917); agricultural area. Crops: soybeans, wheat, corn, oats. Founded 1848; inc. 1869. Pop. (1970) 25,562.

Raoult's Law, a statement that the changes in certain properties of a liquid that occur when a substance is dissolved in it are proportional to the number of molecules of solute present for a given quantity of solvent molecules. Discovered by François-Marie Raoult in 1886, it has been fundamental to many theories of solution.

Rape of Lucrece, The (1594), narrative poem by William Shakespeare, written in rhyme royal. It is based on Ovid's tale of Lucrece, wife of Collatinus. Revered as the most chaste woman in Rome, she is raped by Sextus Tarquinius, the king's son.

Raphael, biblical archangel who, with Michael, Gabriel, and Uriel, serves as a messenger of God, healing and relieving the suffering and sick.

Raphael (Raffaello Sanzio) (1483–1520), Italian painter. The major artist of the High Renaissance, he was influential in establishing the standards of that style. Raphael merged the poetic and the dramatic, the rich and the solid to achieve a personal and unique power evidenced even in his early work "Madonna del Granduca" (*c.*1505). While Michelangelo worked on the Sistine Chapel, Raphael executed a series of frescoes on the walls and ceiling of the Stanza della Segnatura in the Vatican Palace, a commission he received from Julius II. His frescoes depicted the four areas of learning, and "School of Athens" (1510–11) is considered his masterpiece. The epitome of the classical spirit of the High Renaissance, it is not unlike Michelangelo's "Last Supper" in spirit and scope. His subsequent works did not approach the magnitude of "School of Athens." "Galatea" (1513), a fresco, is sensuous in comparison to the earlier, more somber, and idealistic work, although both are in the classical tradition. Raphael was an extremely talented portrait painter, merging 15th-century realism with the human ideal of the High Renaissance. "Pope Leo X" (*c.*1518) is typical of his powerful style. △1140.

Rapid City, city in SW South Dakota, 140mi (225km) WSW of Pierre; seat of Pennington co; site of South Dakota School of Mines and Technology (1885), Ellsworth Air Force Base; trading and shipping center. Industries: mining, cement, lumber, brick, tile, jewelry, livestock, dairy products, tourism. Founded 1876; inc. 1878. Pop. (1970) 43,836.

Rapid Eye Movement. *See* REM.

Rapp, George (1755–1847), German-American religious leader, b. Germany. He brought his followers, the Rappists, members of his authoritarian sect, to the United States in 1803. He founded New Harmony, Ind., in 1815 and Economy, Penn., in 1825. After his death the sect declined, ending in 1903.

Rappahannock, river in Virginia; rises in the Blue Ridge Mts, N Virginia; flows SE to Chesapeake Bay, just S of Potomac River mouth; scene of many Civil War battles. Length: 212mi (341km).

Rare Earths. *See* Lanthanide Elements.

Ras al Khaymah, sheikdom in E Arabia and a member state of the United Arab Emirates on the Persian Gulf; part of Sharjah sheikdom until 1921; joined United Arab Emirates 1972; oil producing area. Area: 650sq mi (1,684sq km). Pop. 31,480.

Rasbora, freshwater fish found in SE Asia. A minnow popular with home aquarists, it has distinctive black markings according to species. Length: to 2in (5.1cm). Species include the Harlequin *Rasbora heteromorpha*, pygmy rasbora *R. maculate*. Family Cyprinidae.

Rash, pimples, hives, or wheals on the skin. It may accompany fever, measles, chicken pox, small pox, and scarlet fever. It also occurs as a reaction to some drugs and other substances to which the body is sensitive. Most rashes do not leave scars after drying. △724.

Rashid al-Din. △1112.

Rashomon (In the Woods) (1951), Japanese film. △1370.

Raspberry, bramble fruit grown in polar and temperate regions of North America, Europe, and Asia. The black, purple, or red fruit is eaten fresh or preserved. Canes, rising from perennial roots, bear fruit the second year. Family Rosaceae; genus *Rubus*. △360.

Rasputin, Grigori Efimovich (1871?–1916), Russian peasant mystic who exercised great influence at the court of Nicholas II. Arriving in St Petersburg in 1904, he impressed the royal family with his ability to cure the tsarevich Alexis' hemophilia. In 1911 he created a major scandal through his frivolous appointments. During World War I he virtually ruled Russia. He was assassinated in 1916 by a group of conservative noblemen. △1286.

Rat, any of over 500 groups of small rodents found worldwide in almost all habitats. Most are herbivores and inoffensive. But the best known are the black rat *(Rattus rattus)* and brown rat *(Rattus Norvegicus)*, both of the family Muridae. They are prolific, aggressive, and eat practically anything and carry many deadly diseases and destroy or contaminate property and food. Both are of Asiatic origin, but now live everywhere man does. Black rats are dark gray, under 8in (20cm) long, weigh under 12oz (350g), and have long tails and big ears. Brown rats are slightly heavier and longer with shorter tails and smaller ears. Most lab rats are albino strains of brown rats. △546.

Ratel, or honey badger, solitary, aggressive, burrowing mammal of the weasel family, native to Africa and S Asia. It has a heavy body with light back and dark underparts. Omnivorous, it also is fond of honey and sometimes forms an association with a honey guide bird to locate wild bees' nests and share the spoils. Length: to 30in (76cm). Family Mustelidae; species *Mellivora capensis*.

Ratfish. *See* Chimaera.

Rat Flea. △429.

Ratio, quotient of two numbers or of two quantities of the same kind, such as two prices, both in dollars, or of two lengths, both in meters, that indicates their relative magnitude. Ratios, as of the numbers 3 and 4, can be written as a fraction (3/4) or with a colon (3:4). △1446.

Rationalism, philosophical theory that knowledge is primarily gained by intellectual and deductive means, as opposed to sensory and inductive means. Rationalism holds the primacy of reason, before experience, as the preferred criterion of truth. Rationalism is associated with Descartes, Leibniz, Spinoza, and Malebranche, the eminent 17th-century rationalists. △856, 858, 1184.

Rational Number. *See* Number, Rational.

Rat Islands, group of islands in the W Aleutians, off SW Alaska; comprised of Kiska, Amchitka, Semisopochnoi, Rat, and smaller islets; scene of WWII conflicts.

Ratite Birds, large, usually flightless birds with flat breastbones rather than the keellike prominences found in most flying birds. Ratites include the ostrich, rhea, cassowary, emu, kiwi, the unusual flying tinamou, and extinct forms such as the moa and elephant bird. *See also* individual birds. △526.

Rat Snake, any of some 50 species of terrestrial and arboreal snakes, distributed widely in North America and Europe. Common in North America are the black and yellow rat snakes, fox snakes, and corn snakes. The four-lined and Aesculapian snakes are European. Length: to 5ft (1.5m). Family Colubridae; genus *Elaphe*.

Rattan, climbing palm native to the East Indies and Africa. Its stems grow to 500ft (152m) by climbing over other trees and plants. They are used for making ropes, furniture, and mats. Family Palmaceae; species *Calamus*.

Rattlesnake, any of about 30 species of New World pit vipers characterized by a tail rattle of bony, loosely connected segments, found from Canada to South America, mostly in arid regions. A few are banded but most are blotched with dark diamonds, hexagons, or spots on lighter background. They feed mostly on rodents and bear their young live. The genus *Sistrurus* includes the massasauga and pygmy rattler. *Crotalus* includes all others. Common North American species are timber *(Crotalus horridus)*, prairie *(C. viridis)*, eastern diamondback *(C. adamanteus)*, and western diamondback *(C. atrox)* rattlesnakes. The South American cascabel *(C. durissus)* has the most potent venom. Length: 1–8ft (30cm–2.5m). Family Viperidae. *See also* Pit Viper; Snake. △520–22, 584.

Rauschenberg, Robert (1925–), US painter and graphic artist, b. Port Arthur, Texas. He gained recognition in 1953 with his collages and assemblages. These works combined techniques, including dripped paint and collage ("Rebus," 1955). From 1955 he composed works that juxtaposed common objects such as stuffed birds, buckets, and hats with abstract expressionist painting ("Monogram," 1961). Rauschenberg's work is considered a link between abstract expressionism and pop art. △1318.

Rauwolfia, drug derived from a shrub native to India. Its compounds are used to treat hypertension, anxiety, and psychoses. *See also* Reserpine. △744.

Ravel, Maurice (1875–1937), French composer and pianist. Influenced by Franz Liszt and Claude Debussy, Ravel developed a style featuring exotic harmonies and orchestral brilliance. His piano piece *Jeux d'Eau* (1901) influenced Debussy and the Impressionist movement in music. He composed relatively few works, a number of which are very popular, eg, *Rhapsodie Espagnole* (1907), *La Valse* (1920), and *Bolero* (1928). His other important works include the ballet *Daphnis et Chloé* (1912), two piano concertos, sonatas, songs, and piano music.

Raven, large crow found in deserts, forests, and mountainous areas of the Northern Hemisphere. They have long conical bills, shaggy throat feathers, wedge-shaped tails, and black plumage with a purple sheen. They eat any plant or animal matter and build twig, stick, and bark cliff or tree nests for their greenish eggs (5–7). The common raven *(Corvus corax)* lives in central North America; the white-necked raven *(Corvus cryptoleucus)* lives in the SW United States and Mexico. Length: to 27in (68cm). Family Corvidae.

Ravenna, city in N Italy, 45mi (72km) ESE of Bologna; capital of Ravenna prov. A Roman naval base 1st century BC, it was capital of W Roman Empire AD 5th century; became capital of Byzantine Empire in Italy 6th century; independent republic 13th century; under papal dominion 16th–19th centuries; passed to Italy 1860; site of outstanding Roman and Byzantine architectural remains, including 5th–8th-century churches. Industries: petroleum, furniture, cement, fertilizer, sugar. Pop. 130,137.

Rawalpindi, city in NE Pakistan, approx. 160mi (258km) NNW of Lahore; industrial center. Great Britain signed treaty here Aug. 8, 1919, recognizing independence of Afghanistan. Industries: iron foundries, oil refining, machine shops. Pop. 455,100.

Rawlings, Marjorie Kinnan (1896–1953), US author, b. Washington, D.C. After working as a newspaper reporter, she published her first book, *South Moon Under* (1933). *The Yearling* (1938) won the Pulitzer Prize for fiction in 1939. *Cross Creek Cookery* (1942) is an autobiographical work about her southern friends; all of her works are set in the backwoods of Florida.

Ray, Man (1890–1976), US photographer and painter, b. Philadelphia. In 1917 he founded the New York Dada movement with Marcel Duchamp and Picabia. His early works utilized an airbrush technique. In the 1920s he began making his "Rayographs," in which he placed objects on light-sensitive photograph paper and exposed and developed them (Manikin).

Ray, flat-bodied, bottom-dwelling elasmobranch

Chandrasekhara Raman

Raphael: Madonna of the Chair

Maurice Ravel

Raven

found throughout tropical and subtropical marine waters. Its color ranges from mottled black or brown to purple and white. Gills are located underneath enlarged winglike pectoral fins; many rays also have a tail spine. Young are born alive. There are several families including butterfly, eagle, manta, cownosed, electric, and sting rays. Order Raiiformes (also called Batoidei). *See also* Devilfish; Guitar Fish; Sawfish; Sting Ray; Torpedo Ray. △510.

Rayburn, Samuel Taliaferro (1882–1961), US political leader, b. Roane co, Tenn. Beginning his political career in the Texas state legislature (1907–12), he was elected to the US House of Representatives (1913) and served until his death. He helped Pres. Franklin D. Roosevelt get his New Deal laws passed in the House (1931–37). He was elected speaker of the house (1940), and held that position, except for 4 years, as long as he was in the House, twice as long as any predecessor. He was noted for his knowledge of House rules and his parliamentary skill.

Rayleigh, John William Strutt (Lord) (1842–1919), English physicist, professor at Cambridge and later at the Royal Institution of London. His work was chiefly concerned with various forms of wave motion: the scattering of light, black-body radiation, sound waves, and water and earthquake waves. For his discovery of the inert atmospheric gas argon (with William Ramsay), he was awarded a 1904 Nobel Prize.

Raymond Berengar V, count of Barcelona. *See* Alfonso II (1152–96).

Raynaud's Disease, disorder in which spasms of the arteries to the fingers cause fingertips to become pale and then blue when exposed to cold. It occurs mainly in women.

Rayon, a fine, smooth, man-made textile fiber produced from solutions of modified cellulose of softwood pulp or cotton linters. Cellulose is extruded through spinnerets and solidified in chemicals or in warm air. Viscose rayon, the most common, is spun-dried and has strength approaching that of nylon. The more costly cuprammonium rayon, known as Bemberg, resembles silk. △1618, 1806.

Rayonnant Style. △1104.

Raytown, city in W central Missouri; SE suburb of Kansas City; served as first stop on Sante Fe Trail out of Independence, Mo. Inc. 1950. Pop. (1970) 33,-632.

Razor-billed Auk, or razorbill, chunky seabird of cold Northern Hemisphere coastlines that resembles a small penguin. It is black and white with a white-ringed narrow bill and dives for food. Nesting in large colonies, it lays a single conical egg on bare oceanic cliffs. Length: 17in (43cm). Species *Alca torda*.

Razor Clam. △478.

R Coronae Stars. △114.

Re or **Ra,** in Egyptian religion, the Sun god and lord of the dead, whose center of worship was at Heliopolis. In some traditions he is identified with Osiris or sometimes as the creator of men. In the myths, Re sailed his sun boat across the sky by day and through the underworld by night. He is depicted as a falcon-headed man with a solar disc on his head. △834, 972.

REA. *See* Rural Electrification Administration.

Reactant. *See* Chemical Reaction.

Reaction, Chemical. *See* Chemical Reaction.

Reaction Propulsion, propulsion utilizing Newton's Third Law of Motion: For every action there is an equal and opposite reaction. Both rocket and jet engines build up internal pressure from gases or plasmas that are allowed to escape in one direction, creating an unbalanced force in the other direction. △142, 1722.

Reactor, Fission. *See* Fission Reactor.

Reactor, Fusion. *See* Fusion Reactor.

Reading, county town of Berkshire, S central England, at confluence of Thames and Kennet rivers; railroad and industrial center; seat of University of Reading. Industries: engineering, brewing. Pop. 132,-023.

Reading, city in SE Pennsylvania, on Schuylkill River; seat of Berks co; military base during French and Indian War; cannons were made here during Revolution and Civil War; site of Albright College (1856), Albernia College (1958), and the Pagoda, a Japanese-style observatory on Mt Penn; a rich agricultural region in Pennsylvania Dutch country. Industries: textiles, clothing, leather goods, iron and steel products, batteries. Founded 1748 by Thomas Penn; inc. as borough 1783, as city 1847. Pop. (1970) 87,643.

Reading Disability, learning disability in which the child falls significantly below grade level in reading or reading related skills. Reading impairment may be caused by such factors as developmental lag, low motivation, undetected visual defects, and occasionally neurological disorders.

Reagan, Ronald (1911–), US actor and political leader, b. Tampico, Ill. He began his career as a radio sportscaster and columnist, later becoming an actor in movies and on television. He began his political career as a liberal Democrat but then supported Republican Dwight D. Eisenhower in the 1952 elections. He formally became a Republican (1962) and was California's governor (1966–74). He later led a conservative challenge to President Ford's nomination (1976).

Reagent, substance that takes part in a chemical reaction. The term is often understood to mean a common laboratory reagent, that is, a substance used in routine qualitative or quantitative analytical tests. △1568.

Realism, doctrine that universal concepts and tangibles exist outside the mind, that is, independently of human perception—the opposite of idealism. The term is also applied to the literary effort, best exemplified by Gustave Flaubert, to depict life as it is, without idealizing or romanticizing any of its aspects. Flaubert's realism was extended by the naturalist school, of whom Theodore Dreiser and Emile Zola were chief exponents, to espouse a totally objective inquiry into the social order. Realism was also a 19th-century movement in painting and architecture. Reacting against the subjectivity of Romanticism, realistic artists insisted on portraying everyday matters of ordinary people, including their baser aspects. Gustave Courbet was the first major realist painter. △852, 1252.

Real Number. *See* Number, Real.

Real Wages, are computed by dividing money wages by the Consumer Price Index. If money wages have doubled while prices have remained constant, then real wages have also doubled. However, if prices have risen faster than money wages, then the real wage has decreased. *See also* Consumer Price Index.

Reaper, implement that cuts grain. △310.

Rebekah, in the Bible, daughter of Bethuel, sister of Laban, wife of Isaac, and mother of twins Esau and Jacob. Jacob was her favorite and she helped him win, through deception, Isaac's blessing from the elder Esau.

Rebellion of 1837, uprising in opposition to the power of the Family Compacts and the Church of England in Canada, and French-Canadian desire for cultural autonomy, touched off two years of armed rebellion led by William Lyon Mackenzie and Louis Papineau. The rebellion was poorly organized and militarily unsuccessful but the revolt led to the Durham Report (1839) and Act of Union (1841). *See also* Durham Report; Family Compacts.

Receiver, in communications. △1794.

Receptor, any of several kinds of neurons specialized to transform physical energy into the electrochemical impulses of the nervous system. For example, the rods and cones of the retina are receptors that transform light energy into impulses sent to the brain. △664.

Recession, phase of the business cycle associated with a declining economy. It is associated with increasing unemployment, contracting business activity, and decreasing consumer purchasing power. A recession may have a number of causes and is generally associated with pessimistic business attitudes. Government expansionary policy, such as government spending or tax cuts, may be used to stimulate the economy during a recession. If the recession is not checked, the economy may head into a depression. *See also* Business Cycles.

Recessive Gene, any pair of hereditary genes that remains latent. *See also* Dominance; Heredity. △416.

Rechabites, an ancient sect of Jews, first developed in Sumeria. They stressed strict ritual observances. They did not drink wine, cultivate fields, or build houses. After a move to Judah, they were known as "sons of the water drinkers."

Recife (Pernambuco), city in NE Brazil; capital of Pernambuco state. Located partly on an island and connected to mainland by numerous bridges, it is an excellent port and shipping center. Founded 1548 by Portuguese fishermen. Pop. 1,078,819.

Reciprocal, number or quantity equal to one divided by a specified number or quantity: the reciprocal of 2 is ½; the reciprocal of ½ is 2. The product of a number and its reciprocal is one: $2 \times \frac{1}{2} = 1$.

Reconstruction (1865–77), period in US history after the Civil War. Conflict arose almost immediately between the conflicting policies of President Andrew Johnson and Congress concerning plans and authority for reestablishing the 11 Confederate states within the Union. By overriding presidential vetoes and by limiting the president's powers, Congress, led by Radical Republicans, prevailed. When Johnson attempted to challenge congressional authority, he was impeached (1868), but not convicted. Under the congressional plan, the South was divided into five military districts. The rights of newly-freed blacks were protected by civil rights acts and constitutional amendments. By 1870, all the Southern states had been readmitted to the Union. State governments were, however, controlled by Radical Republicans and their black and Scalawag allies. With the aid of the Ku Klux Klan, white Southerners, many of whom were reenfranchised by the General Amnesty Act (1872), recaptured the state governments. Reconstruction ended in 1877 when the last Federal troops were withdrawn from the South. *See also* Civil Rights Act of 1866 and 1870; Freedmen's Bureau; Ku Klux Klan. △1278.

Recorder, simple woodwind musical instrument dating from 15th- to 18th-century Europe. Easy to play, it has a whistle-shaped mouthpiece and an end-blown straight tube with eight finger holes. It is made in four sizes: bass, tenor, treble (alto), and descant (soprano), each ranging two octaves. Revived by Arnold Dolmetsch in England (1926), it is popular with amateur musicians. △1244.

Recording, Magnetic. *See* Magnetic Recording.

Recording, Sound. *See* Sound Recording and Reproduction.

Rectangle, four-sided geometric figure (quadrilateral) the interior angles of which are right angles and each pair of opposite sides is of equal length and is parallel. It is a special case of a parallelogram.

Rectangular Coordinate System, Cartesian coordinate system in which the axes are at right angles to each other. *See also* Cartesian Coordinate System.

Rectifier, device for converting an alternating current into a direct current. It consists of an electron tube or semiconductor that presents a high resistance to a current flowing in one direction and a low resistance to current flowing in the opposite direction. *See also* Semiconductor. △1530,1546-48.

Rectus Femoris. △684.

Red (Yuan), formerly Koi: a chief river of Vietnam; rises in S China, flows SE across northern Vietnam, passing Hanoi, to Gulf of Tonkin. Important transportation link between China and Vietnam; forms wide fertile delta E of Hanoi (rice-growing region); receives Clear and Black rivers NW of Hanoi. Length: approx. 500mi (805km).

Red Abalone. △482.

Red Admiral Butterfly, anglewing butterfly common in North America and Europe. Its dark front wings are crossed by a broad, bright orange band. The caterpillars feed on elms, nettles, and other plants. Species *Vanessa atalanta*.

Red Algae, a group of typically reddish mostly marine algae (division Rhodophyta) especially numerous in tropical and subtropical seas. Some, including dulse and Irish moss, are common on Northern coasts. The reddish color is caused by a red pigment that conceals the green chlorophyll. Some red algae are single-celled, but most are many-celled plants growing in tentaclelike strands forming shrublike masses. △432.

Red-Bellied Snake, species of small, secretive snake of open woods and bogs of E and central United

States. It is usually brown or gray with four narrow dark stripes, a plain red belly, and three pale spots on neck. Length: to 10in (25cm). Family Colubridae; species *Storeria occipitomaculata*.

Red Blood Cell. *See* Erythrocyte.

Redbud. *See* Judas Tree.

Red Bug. *See* Chigger.

Red Clay, a component of the benthic division of the ocean, occurring with oozes or alone below depths of 16,400ft (5,000m), and consisting of ultrafine organic particles, wind-blown volcanic ash, and meteoric material. Its red-brown color is due to the ferric iron and manganese compounds in it.

Red Colobus. △598.

Red Cross, founded 1863, international organization that seeks to lessen human suffering, particularly through disaster relief, neutral aid to war victims, and services to members of the armed forces. The Red Cross was created as a result of the urging of Jean Henri Dunant, a Swiss citizen, who had been shocked by the suffering of the wounded after the battle of Solferino in 1859. Composed of over 100 independent national societies with central headquarters in Switzerland and staffed largely by volunteers, the Red Cross' name comes from its symbol, a red cross on a white field, which reverses the colors of the Swiss flag.

Red-figure Painting. △1000.

Red Guard. △1348.

Red Hake. *See* Ling.

Redheaded Woodpecker, black and white woodpecker with a crimson head found in North America. An insect eater, it hunts like a flycatcher. Species *Melanerpes erythrocephalus. See also* Woodpecker.

Redlands, city in S California, 8mi (13km) ESE of San Bernardino; site of University of Redlands (1907) and Norton Air Force Base. Industries: aircraft, furniture, electrical vehicles, truck farms. Inc. 1888. Pop. (1970) 36,355.

Redondo Beach, suburban city in S California, 17mi (27km) SE of Los Angeles; supports tourism and light manufacturing. Inc. 1892. Pop. (1970) 57,425.

Redox. *See* Oxidation-Reduction.

Redpoll, seed-eating finch found in colder parts of the Northern Hemisphere. They have pointed conical bills, short forked tails, and brownish plumage with a red patch on the crown. Length: 5in (12.5cm). Genus *Acanthis*.

Red River, river in S United States; rises in highlands of E New Mexico; flows E across Texas panhandle, forms natural boundary between Texas and Oklahoma, turns S in SW Arkansas to Louisiana and empties into the Atchafalaya River (to Gulf of Mexico) and Old River (to the Mississippi River); used for irrigation, hydroelectricity, and industrial traffic. Length: 1,222mi(1,967km).

Red River of the North, river in United States and Canada; rises in North Dakota at the confluence of the Bois de Sioux and Otter Tail rivers; flows N between Minnesota and North Dakota, empties into Lake Winnipeg, Manitoba, Canada; used for irrigation. Length: approx. 310mi (500km).

Red River Rebellion (1869–70), uprising in Manitoba, Canada. After the cession of Hudson's Bay Co. lands to Canada (1869), settlers in Manitoba rebelled against the imposition of federal Canadian law. Their leader, Louis Riel, led the seizure of Fort Garry, resulting in the Manitoba Act of 1870.

Red Sea, narrow arm of the Indian Ocean, between NE Africa and the Arabian Peninsula; connected with the Mediterranean Sea by the Gulf of Suez and Suez Canal. Known in biblical times as the passageway for the Israelite exodus from Egypt, it was an ancient trade route whose importance declined with the discovery of an all-water route around Africa (1498). Its importance greatly increased (1869) with building of Suez Canal, but with the closing of Suez Canal (1967–75) during Arab-Israeli conflicts, building of vessels too large for the canal, and initiation of pipelines, the Red Sea's importance as a trade route diminished. Area: 170,000sq mi (440,300sq km).

Red Shift, shift in the spectral lines of a star, galaxy, or other celestial object toward the red end of the visible spectrum, relative to their positions in an equivalent spectrum produced on Earth. Although sometimes a gravitational effect, it is usually due to the Doppler effect and results from a recessional velocity of the object (a star approaching the Sun has a blue shift). The red shift of galaxies is evidence for the expansion of the universe. *See also* Quasar. △122, 126, 1522.

Red Snapper, tropical marine food fish found from West Indies to Florida. Bright scarlet, it has sharp teeth and a flattened snout. Length: 2–3ft (61–91cm). Family Lutjanidae; species *Lutjanus campechanus*. △392.

Red Spider, or spider mite, red vegetarian mite found worldwide. A serious plant pest, it spins webs, revealing its presence. Length: 0.01–0.03in (0.03–0.8mm). Family Tetranychidae. *See also* Mite.

Redstart, two unrelated warblers. The American flycatching redstart (*Setophaga ruticila*) is a wood warbler. The male is black and orange above and white underneath; length: 5 in (12.5cm). The European redstart (*Phoenicurus phoenicurus*) is slightly larger and the male is grayish with a rust-red breast and tail. *See also* Warbler.

Red Tide, marine phenomenon occurring in subtropical water in which sea water turns red and fish are killed. It is caused by an overabundance of plantlike flagellate protozoans called dinoflagellates. Their pigment causes the water to appear reddish and they produce a toxin that kills fish. One species is *Gonyaulax catanella*.

Reduction Reaction, chemical process in which a specified substance loses oxygen. The term has been extended to include reaction with hydrogen and, more generally, to any reaction involving gain of electrons or other decrease in oxidation number. For instance, the change from a ferric to a ferrous compound is reduction of the ferric compound. *See also* Oxidation-Reduction. △1554, 1566.

Redwood City, city in W California, 18mi (29km) SE of San Francisco; seat of San Mateo co; noted since 1900 for its chrysanthemum industry. Industries: food-processing, electronic equipment, chemicals, cement, plastics. Inc. 1868. Pop. (1970) 55,686.

Redwood National Park, park in NW California. It features coast redwood forests containing virgin groves of ancient trees, including the world's tallest, 367ft (112m). Seals, sea lions, and birds live on offshore islands. The park includes 40mi (64km) of beach. Area: 56,201acres (22,761hectares). Est. 1968.

Red Worm. △474.

Reed, Stanley Forman (1884–), US jurist and lawyer, b. Mason co, Ky. A Kentucky state legislator (1912–16), he was appointed by Pres. Herbert Hoover and served as general counsel for both the Federal Farm Board (1929–32) and the Reconstruction Finance Corporation (1932–35). He was then made US solicitor general (1935–38). He was associate justice of the US Supreme Court (1938–57), appointed by Pres. Franklin D. Roosevelt.

Reed, Walter (1851–1902), US military surgeon, b. Belroi, Va. He headed the commission of physicians sent to Cuba that established that yellow fever was transmitted by the *Aedes aegypti* mosquito. Later he proved that the disease was caused by a virus carried by the mosquito.

Reed, aquatic grass native to wetlands throughout the world. The common reed *(Phragmites communis)* has broad leaves, feathery flower cluster, and stiff smooth stems. Dry reed stems are used for thatching, construction, and musical pipes. Height: to 10ft (3m). Family Gramineae. *See also* Grass. △454.

Reedbuck, light, graceful antelope native to Africa, south of the Sahara, usually near water. Brown to gray, its bushy tail is erect when disturbed. Male has short horns, curved forward at tips. Length: to 4.5ft (1.4m). Family Bovidae; genus *Redunca*.

Reed Instruments, instruments producing tones when air current vibrates a fiber or metal tongue. The accordion, where wind flows in both directions, uses a free reed. In a clarinet or reed organ pipe, where air passes in one direction, a beating reed vibrates against a hole at the end of the tube. The oboe has a double-reed mouthpiece, the two tongues vibrating against each other when blown. △1244.

Reed Switch. △1538.

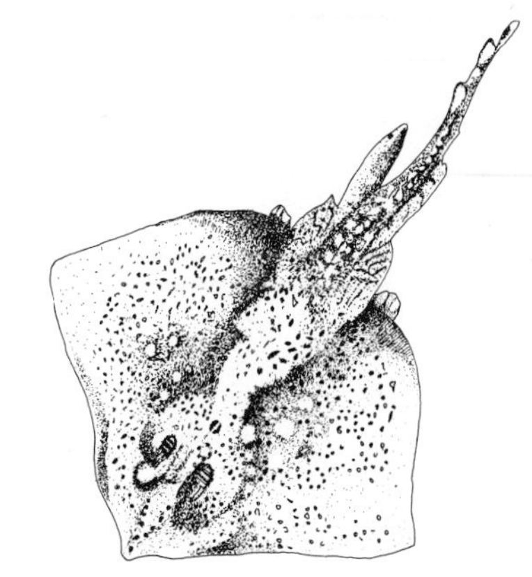

Ray

Sam Rayburn

Redpoll

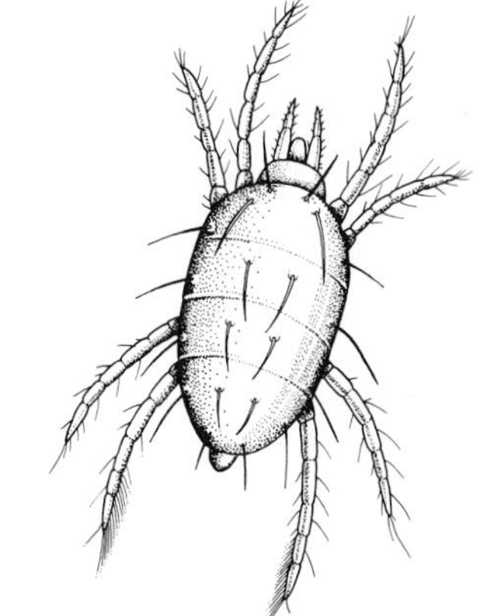

Red spider

Reef. *See* Coral Reef.

Reference Frame. *See* Frame of Reference.

Reference Group, in sociology, any social group that an individual sees as the standard against which to judge his own actions. A reference group may be a family, a peer group, or a social class. A person need not be a member of the group he uses as his reference group. △892.

Refinery, Oil. △1644.

Refining, Ore, the process employed in removing impurities or changing the composition of various ores to obtain the desired metal in reasonably pure form. Employed are pyrometallurgy, or smelting and distillation methods; electrometallurgy, for example, electrolytic refining in which the pure metal forms on one electrode; and hydrometallurgy, or extraction from aqueous solution. *See also* Ore.

Reflection, change in direction of part of a wave motion when a wave, such as a light wave, encounters a surface separating two different media, such as air and metal, and is thrown back into the original medium. The remaining part passes into the second medium. The incident wave, reflected wave, and the line perpendicular to the surface at the point of incidence (the normal) all lie in the same plane. The incident and reflected waves make equal angles with the normal. △1518–20.

Reflector. *See* Telescope, Optical.

Reflex, simple type of unlearned and involuntary behavior, for example, the patellar or "knee-jerk" reflex that occurs when the bent knee is struck by an object. At least two neurons (receptor and effector) must be involved in the reflex arc, although one or more intervening neurons (interneurons) are often present. Additional nerve impulses travel from the arc to the brain via the central nervous system; they inform the individual that the involuntary reflex is occurring. △664.

Reformation, major change within Western Christianity that developed between the 14th and 17th centuries. A large segment of Christianity separated from the Roman Catholic Church. Several intellectuals guided the change. The papacy became the focus of the critics' attack. Apostolic succession, as interpreted by Rome, was seriously questioned and threatened by the reformers. Martin Luther's dispute over the sale of indulgences is claimed as the clear beginning of the reform movement. The worldliness of the papacy was criticized. Ulrich Zwingli's reforms were more radical than those of Luther. John Calvin developed the doctrine of predestination and the concept of the elect. Individual churches eventually developed around the teachings of the reformers. Scripture was the basis of these changes as well as the doctrine of the priesthood of believers and concepts of faith and grace. *See also* Calvin, John; Luther, Martin; Zwingli, Ulrich. △1152.

Reformation, Catholic, internal 16th-century reform movement of the Roman Catholic Church. In part a response to the Protestant Reformation, this reform involved a strengthening and purification of church organization and tradition, as well as an ambitious reclamation of certain former Catholic territories. Greatly aided by the Jesuits, this renewed vigor spread throughout Europe and America.

Reform Bills, a series of 19th-century British electoral measures making parliamentary democracy more representative. Prime Minister Grey's 1832 bill, hotly contested by the House of Lords, abolished obsolete constituencies, redistributed seats in favor of the new industrial population centers, and extended the franchise to the industrial middle class. Benjamin Disraeli's 1867 bill, by lowering property qualifications, enfranchised the urban working class, which almost doubled the electorate. William Gladstone's 1884 bill added 2,000,000 new voters to the list by enfranchising most agricultural workers and miners. The franchise was not extended to women until the 20th century.

Reform Judaism, one of the three divisions that has developed within modern Judaism. It is also called Progressive or Liberal Judaism. It originated in 19th-century Germany. Israel Jacobson, one of the founders, made changes in rituals and used the vernacular for some prayers. Its main tenet stresses the progressive nature of revelation. Customs that had no contemporary meaning were changed or discarded. In 1929 the World Union for Progressive Judaism was founded, uniting world reform congregations.

Refraction, change in direction of a wave, such as a light wave, when it crosses the boundary between one medium and another transparent medium, such as air and glass, and undergoes a change in velocity. The incident wave, refracted wave, and the line perpendicular to the surface at the point of incidence (the normal) all lie in the same plane. The incident and refracted waves make an angle of incidence, *i*, and an angle of refraction, *r*, respectively, with the normal. The new direction of motion is such that the ratio of the sines of these angles, sin *i*/sin *r*, always has the same value for two particular media. This constant value is the index of refraction for the two media. △1518, 1522.

Refractor. *See* Telescope, Optical.

Refractory, any nonmetallic material having high compressive strength at furnace temperatures with low thermal conductivity and a low coefficient of expansion (such as insulating bricks). Most important of the refractory materials are magnesite and dolomite used in open-hearth steel furnaces and portland cement kilns. High-melting oxides, carbides, nitrides, and sulfides are refractories used in nuclear power plants.

Refrigeration, process by which the temperature in a given area is lowered. The use of ice or dry ice (solid carbon dioxide), which absorb heat while melting, is still common. Refrigerants include Freon, methyl chloride, or ammonia. △396, 1820.

Regal moth, large American moth with a wingspread up to 6in (15cm). Its olive-gray front wings are marked with reddish veins and yellow spots; its orange-red hind wings have yellow markings. The caterpillars are known as hickory horned devils because of prominent hornlike appendages. Length: 4–5in (10–12.5cm). Species *Citheronia regalise.*

Regency Period (1811–20), the period of British history when because of King George III's mental incapacity his powers were transferred to his son George, Prince of Wales, as prince regent. Various limitations on the regent's powers were removed in 1812.

Regeneration. △472, 486.

Regensburg, city in SE West Germany, at confluence of Danube and Regen rivers, 65mi (105km) NE of Munich. City flourished as trade center with Near East and India during the 13th century; seat of imperial diet 1663–1806; annexed to Bavaria 1810; became free port 1853. Notable buildings include Gothic cathedral (13th–16th century), remains of Porta Praetoria (179), Schottenkirche St Jakob (12th century), St Emmeram (7th century). Industries: machines, precision instruments, printing, pottery, wood products, chemicals. Pop. 126,642.

Reger, Max (1873–1916), German composer, conductor, and pianist. He admired the music of Johann Sebastian Bach and advocated a return to contrapuntal forms. △1246.

Reggio Calabria (Reggio di Calabria), seaport city in S Italy, 7mi (11km) SE of Messina; capital of Reggio di Calabria prov. and former capital of Calabria region. Founded by Greek colonists 8th century BC, it was allied with Rome 270 BC; conquered by Normans 1060; site of Greek and Roman remains, museum housing fine archaeological collection. Exports: fruit, silk, wine, olive oil, figs. Industries: tourism, perfumes, fisheries, pharmaceuticals, fruit canning. Pop. 164,-819.

Regina, capital and largest city in Saskatchewan, Canada, 355mi (572km) W of Winnipeg. Canadian Pacific Transcontinental Railway and the Transcontinental Highway pass through Regina, making it a very important trade and cooperative business center for the provinces. Originally called Pile O' Bones, for buffalo bones found there. Founded 1882. Pop. 137,-759.

Regulus, or Alpha Leonis, bluish main-sequence star in the constellation Leo. Characteristics: apparent mag. 1.33, absolute mag. 1.0, spectral type B7; distance 85 light-years.

Rehnquist, William Hubbs (1924–), US jurist and lawyer, b. Milwaukee. A law clerk to Supreme Court Justice Jackson (1952–53), he practiced law 1953–69. A political conservative who supported Richard M. Nixon, he was chosen by President Nixon to direct the Office of Legal Counsel of the Department of Justice (1968–71). In 1971, Nixon appointed him an associate justice of the US Supreme Court. Despite opposition from the liberal sector of the Senate, he took his seat in 1972.

Rehovot, town in central Israel, 4mi (6km) SW of Ramla; site of Weizmann Institute of Science (1944). Industries: chemicals, plastics, citrus fruits. Founded 1890. Pop. 36,600.

Reich, Wilhelm. △818.

Reichstag Fire (1933), conflagration that destroyed part of the German Reichstag (lower house of parliament) building. Hitler used the subsequent trial of a Dutchman who set the fire to indict Communist party leaders and discredit the party. △1334.

Reign of Terror (1793–94), stage of the French Revolution. It involved a military dictatorship, directed by a Committee of Public Safety in which Maximilien Robespierre wielded the greatest power. It was established to preserve the Revolution in a period of emergency. The committee sought to reorganize the military, crush counterrevolution, and stabilize the economy. The committee's tactics were harsh. There were many executions for treason and economic problems worsened. In 1794 the National Convention overthrew Robespierre, and the Reign of Terror ended. △1224.

Reims (Rheims), city in NE France, on Vesle River, 83mi (134km) ENE of Paris; port on Aisne-Marne Canal; important town of Roman Gaul. Clovis I was baptized and crowned king of all Franks in cathedral by St Remi, bishop of Rheims (AD 496). Present cathedral is monument of French Gothic architecture; scene of crowning of Charles VII with Joan of Arc at his side (1429). In WWI much of cathedral was destroyed, including outstanding stained glass window. Its restoration 1927–38 was aided by funds from Rockefeller Foundation. City was scene of signing of German unconditional surrender May 7, 1945. Pope Paul III founded university here 1547; birthplace of Jean Baptiste Colbert, French statesman (1619), and St John Baptist de la Salle, founder of the Christian Brothers (1651). Industries: grapes, woolens, glass, baked goods. Pop. 152,967. △1094.

Reincarnation, transmigration, rebirth, or metempsychosis, the passage of the soul through successive bodies. This view of life as being cyclical has appeared in primitive speculations about the fate of the soul after death. In the 6th century BC it was taught as religious-philosophical doctrine in both Greece and India. This belief appears in Hinduism, Buddhism, Jainism, and Sikhism.

Reindeer. *See* Caribou.

Reindeer Moss, a gray tufted, much-branched lichen *(Cladonia rangiferina)* that grows erect on the soil. Large patches of reindeer moss are an important food for caribou and reindeer and are sometimes eaten by people. *See also* Lichen.

Reinforced Concrete, a type of strong concrete used widely in bridge construction. It is hardened onto embedded steel (in the form of rods, bars, or mesh), which adds tensile strength. Reinforced concrete can sustain heavy stresses over considerable spans. △1612–14, 1758.

Reinforcement, in psychology, any event that follows a behavioral response that makes that response more or less likely to happen again. Positive reinforcement is roughly synonymous with "reward," while negative reinforcement is "punishment." The effect of reinforcements on behavior is a fundamental concern of learning theory and operant conditioning. *See also* Operant Conditioning. △768.

Reinhardt, Ad (Adolf) (1913–67), US painter whose works during the 1940s were composed of rectilinear patterns with sharply contrasting abstract shapes. Later he progressively lowered the intensity of color. His last and best-known works are composed of large black rectangles sometimes merged with deep purples and greens.

Reinhardt, Max (1873–1943), Austrian director and stage manager. Renowned as a master of symbolism and poetry in the theater, he directed the Deutsches Theater (1905–20, 1924–32). His world tours included the plays of Shakespeare, Molière, and Shaw, and he directed the yearly performance of *Everyman* in Salzburg.

Relapsing Fever, infectious disease caused by spirochetes and transmitted by tick and lice bites. It is characterized by fever, headache, muscle pain, and vomiting. An attack ends after nine days and then ecurs after a few days. Treatment is antibiotics, bed est, and fluid diet.

Relative Molecular Mass. *See* Molecular Weight.

Relativity Tests, observable phenomena that are outside the scope of Newtonian mechanics but can be explained by, and used to test, relativity theory. They nclude the small discrepancy between the actual orbit of Mercury and that predicted by Newton's theory; the apparent displacements of the positions of tars through the bending of their light rays; the effect of a gravitational field on the wavelength of light emitted by atoms. This proved difficult to detect with certainty, but was verified in 1960 by comparing the toms at the top and bottom of a water tower, the wavelength difference being measured by means of he Mössbauer effect.

Relativity Theory, theory, proposed by Albert Einstein, based on the postulate that the motion of one body can be defined only with respect to that of a econd body and that no absolute meaning can be given to the statement that a body is at rest. This led o the concept of a four-dimensional space-time continuum in which the three space dimensions and time are treated on an equal footing. The special theory, put forward in 1905, is limited to the description of events as they appear to observers in a state of uniform relative motion. The need for it arose from the egative result of the Michelson-Morley experiment 1887), which showed that there was no difference between the velocity of light as measured in the direction of the Earth's motion and its velocity at right ngles to this direction. The more important consequences of the theory are: (1) that the velocity of light s absolute, that is, not relative to the velocity of the bserver; (2) that the mass of a body increases with its elocity; (3) that mass (*m*) and energy (*E*) are equivalent, that is, $E = mc^2$, where c is the velocity of light this shows that when mass is converted to energy, a mall mass gives rise to large energy); (4) the Lorentz-itzgerald contraction, that is, bodies contract as their elocity increases; and (5) time dilation. The general heory of relativity, completed in 1915, is applicable o observers not in uniform relative motion and leads o the concept of gravitation. The presence of matter n space causes space to "curve," forming gravitational fields, thus gravitation becomes a property of pace itself. Later modifications of the geometry of elativity have attempted to combine a representation of the gravitational and electromagnetic fields to form unified field theory. △1524.

Religion, particular system of beliefs and resulting ractices stimulated by some awareness of a supreme being or power. Throughout the historical development of all cultures, some religious system is present. Many stress the individual nature of religion as a personal experience, while others emphasize its social imension. It necessarily develops according to man's elf-understanding in relation to the infinite. It should e seen as a dynamic, rather than a static, process. nstitutional organization shapes religious life into pecific forms. Distinctions are made between authorarian and humanitarian forms and denominations re viewed as different paths to the Divine. The paraoxical nature of religion is evident; some deny the ecessity of faith and its universality, while it is also een as basic to man's nature. Feeling is generally een as essential to religion as well as knowledge and esponse in actions. The religious needs of man are enerally formalized and given direction through enominations. Individual religious bodies are innuerable, and united only in their search for truth. One main division is between Christian and non-Christian eligions. Christianity, Judaism, and Islam are generlly regarded as the most influential religions in the world today. The ecumenical movement is developng within varied religions. It recognizes the common round of religious drives and experiences, and strives to unify men as religious beings. Agnosticism nd theism are frequently studied as religions. *See lso* individual religions. △842.

Religion, Primitive, religions of poor small-scale soieties without literary cultures. Christianity and other advanced" religions are difficult to distinguish from primitive" religions. Few other generalizations can e made, since primitive religions are numerous and how tremendous variety. They tend to take the place f science and philosophy in explaining life and the atural world; through ritual and other practices atempts are made to affect this world. Similarly, primive religions often back up their culture's morality. henomena such as shamanism and totemism are asects of such religions rather than types of primitive eligion. *See also* Animism; Monotheism; Polytheism; haman; Taboo; Totem. △842, 850.

Religion, Wars of (1562–98), series of religious conflicts in France. At stake was freedom of worship for French Protestants. There was also a struggle among the French nobility for power and influence with the French king. The conflicts, also known as the Huguenot Wars, were ended following the Edict of Nantes giving freedom of worship to the Protestants and the Treaty of Vervins (1598). In 1685 Louis XIV revoked the edict.

REM, or rapid eye movement sleep; occupies about 20% of a usual night's sleep, and is a recurring 20-minute period every 90 minutes. Dreaming is believed to occur during REM sleep. △668, 824.

Remainder, in Mathematics. △1446.

Remarque, Erich Maria (1898–1970), German novelist. A wounded veteran of WWI, he later settled in Switzerland in the 1930s as his books were banned in Germany. His novels, including *All Quiet on the Western Front* (1929), *The Road Back* (1931), and *Flotsam* (1941), treat the themes of war and postwar adjustment. *See also* All Quiet on the Western Front.

Rembrandt (Harmenszoon van Rijn) (1606–69), Dutch painter and graphic artist. His early career, the Leyden period (1625–31), during which he executed small, realistic works, was influenced by the work of Caravaggio. Typical of this period is "Tobit and Anna with the Kid" (1626). By 1636 he was in the midst of his High Baroque style ("The Blinding of Samson," 1636). He had also become a popular and wealthy painter of portraits. After 1650 his style shows a new emotional depth and subtle lyricism. "Jacob Blessing the Sons of Joseph" (1656) is typical of this period. In his later works Rembrandt often alludes in mood or composition to works of the Northern Renaissance, as in "The Polish Rider" (*c.*1656), which likens to Albrecht Dürer's "Knight, Death and Devil." "The Return of the Prodigal Son" (1665) is one of Rembrandt's most subtle and expressively emotional religious works. It is evidence of his lifelong sympathy with the downtrodden and the poor. Rembrandt is an important graphic artist whose talent rivals that of Dürer. He was a master of the etching and its wide tonal range not available through techniques in woodcutting or engraving. "Christ Preaching" is a typical print. △1168.

Remington, Frederic (1861–1909), US painter and sculptor, b. Canton, N.Y. For health reasons he moved to the West and began painting scenes of western life. His romantic depictions of cowboys and Indians became immensely popular. His works include "The Scout, Friends or Enemies" (1908) and the bronze "Bronco Buster." His style is detailed and realistic. The Remington Art Memorial, Ogdensburg, N.Y., houses a notable collection.

Remora, or sharksucker, marine fish found worldwide in tropical and temperate seas. Gray, reddish, or brown, it has a ridged sucking disc on top of its head that it uses to cling to sharks, turtles, rays, whales, and boats. Length: 7–36in (18–91cm). The eight species include *Echeneis naucrates* and the whalesucker *Remilegia australis*. Family Echeneidae.

Remote Surveillance. △1796.

Renaissance. △1130.

Renaissance Architecture, architectural style that began in Italy in the 15th century and spread throughout Europe until the advent of Mannerism and the Baroque in the 16th and 17th centuries. Revolting against Gothic architecture, this rebirth of Roman motifs was readily adapted in Italy, where Roman ruins were prevalent and Gothic styles least firmly entrenched. Brunelleschi and Alberti studied actual Roman ruins; Michelozzi, Bramante, and others used the classical orders of architecture and structural elements. In France the style was first employed by Lescot, commissioned by Francis I to work on the Louvre (1546). In England and other European countries classical forms were integrated with medieval motifs. △ 1134, 1138, 1140–46.

Renaissance Art, usually refers to Italian art from 1400–1600 and its spread to the rest of Europe by the early 16th century. The artistic movement is characterized by a revival of interest in classical antiquity, with its ethical and aesthetic values, a new humanistic outlook, and a new interest in naturalism and science. The scientific studies in anatomy, optics, and perspective led to a new realism in painting and sculpture. The new criteria of beauty included harmony, defined as a resolution of complex and conflicting elements, and proportion. Italian Renaissance is grouped into several schools. The Florentines include Giotto, the first artist to apply the new humanism and the rediscovery of the human body to painting; Masaccio, in-

Regensburg, West Germany

Reggio Calabria, Italy

Reims, France

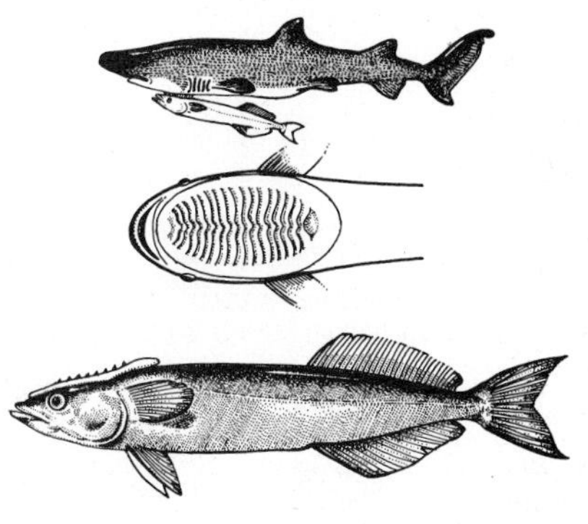

Remora

terested in perspective; Uccello; Mantegna; Botticelli, with his classical subject matter; Verrocchio; Leonardo da Vinci; and Michelangelo. The main architects were Ghiberti and Brunelleschi. The Venetian school, including Bellini, Titian, and Tintoretto, stressed light and color and introduced landscape backgrounds. △1134–46.

Renaissance Music, music composed in Europe from roughly 1400 to 1600. This music was mainly vocal polyphony, ie, works sung by an unaccompanied chorus divided into four to six separate parts. Composers produced many masses and motets in this style, often for religious occasions. Nonreligious music at this time was mainly in the form of songs—Italian and English madrigals. French chansons, German lieder—and some instrumental music composed for organ, clavier, lute, or for small ensembles of musicians. Masters who composed during this period include Ockeghem, Palestrina, Lasso, Byrd, and Gabrieli. *See also* Madrigal; Motet; Polyphony. △1132.

Renaissance Theater. △1148.

Renal Calculi. *See* Kidney Stones.

Renault, Mary (1905–), pseud. of Mary Challens, English author best known for her fictional works depicting ancient times. *The Last of the Wine* (1956) and *The King Must Die* (1958) have been critically praised for their sound scholarship and authenticity. Works set in a contemporary scene include *Return to Night* (1947), *The Purposes of Love* (1939), and *Kind are Her Answers* (1940).

Renin, polypeptide hormone produced by the kidney in response to lowered blood pressure. It activates angiotensin, a powerful vasoconstrictor, which then increases blood pressure.

Rennes, city in NW France, at junction of Ille and Vilaine rivers, 193mi (311km) WSW of Paris. During Middle Ages it served as capital of Brittany; partially destroyed by fire 1720; site of Palais de Justice (1618–54), and cathedral of St Pierre (1787–1844). Industries: leather, printing, linen, cotton yarns. Founded as old Gallic town. Pop. 180,943.

Reno, city in W Nevada, on Truckee River; seat of Washoe co. Founded 1858, it was known as Lake's Crossing; it was renamed Reno after Civil War Gen. Jesse Lee Reno; it grew with coming of Central Pacific Railroad (1868). It is known nationwide for its free port privileges, legalized gambling, and quick divorces; site of University of Nevada (1874), Mackay School of Mines (1907), and annual rodeo, state fair, and national air race. Industries: tourism, mining, agriculture, meat packing, flour milling, beverages, sheet metals. Inc. 1903. Pop. (1970) 72,863.

Renoir, Jean (1894–), French filmmaker and actor, son of the painter Auguste Renoir. Internationally famed for lyric response to nature and humanity and for subtlety of style, Renoir's foremost films include *Nana* (1926), *Madame Bovary* (1934), *La Grand Illusion* (1937), *La Règle du Jeu* (1939), *French Cancan* (1955), and *C'est la Revolution* (1967).

Renoir, Pierre Auguste (1841–1919), French painter and sculptor. His "Lise" was accepted by the 1865 Salon, Paris, although "Diana," after the style of Edouard Manet, was rejected in 1867. "Odalisque" (1870) showed influences of Delacroix. He exhibited in the first Impressionist show (1874) and also in that group's second and seventh exhibitions. One of the finest works of 1874 was "La Loge." At this point he was developing a personal style that culminated in "Le Moulin de la Galette" (1876), a work both sensuous and ethereal. "Les Parapluies" (1882–83) was an attempt to discipline the Impressionist style. In the 1890s he moved to a warmer style, primarily painting women and domestic scenes. His female nudes were soft and of epic proportions. Works of this period include "Young Girls at the Piano" (1892). After 1912 arthritis forced him to paint with a brush strapped to his arm. △1254.

Renton, city and port of entry in W Washington, on Lake Washington and Cedar River; SE suburb of Seattle; site of Longacres Racetrack. Industries: clay works (est. 1901), iron foundry (est. 1905), and Boeing aircraft complex (est. during WWII). Inc. 1901. Pop. (1970) 26,648.

Report on Manufactures (1791), report made by Sec. of Treasury Alexander Hamilton. It was the first systematic attempt to promote the development of manufacturing. It proposed import tariffs to protect industries and bounties to new industries. Agrarian opposition prevented the implementation of its principal features.

Representative, member of US House of Representatives. Chosen for a two-year term, a representative must be a US citizen for at least seven years, 25 or older, and, with some exceptions, must reside in the district represented. Responsible to his constituency, a representative must answer also to his party.

Representative Government, system where representatives are authorized to act on behalf of the citizenry. △900–02, 1280.

Repression, defense mechanism in which an idea or an impulse is excluded or banished from consciousness. Though repression is a form of motivated forgetting, the process is automatic and unconscious. Freud viewed repression as the most fundamental defense mechanism.

Reproduction. △456, 462, 466, 530, 700–06.

Reproduction, Asexual. △466.

Reproduction, Sexual. △462.

Reproduction in Plants. △456.

Reproductive System, the organs of a plant or animal necessary to the reproductive processes. *See* Urogenital System.

Reptile, vertebrates, including turtles, crocodilians, lizards, snakes, and tuatara, distributed worldwide. Majority are found in warm areas. The first true land vertebrates, they lay shelled, fluid-filled, yolky eggs on land. Some species carry eggs in the body and bear live young. Body temperatures are dependent on external environment. The skin is dry and covered with scales or embedded with bony plates. The first reptiles appeared during the Carboniferous Period and 23 orders flourished during the Mesozoic Era. There are now four living orders of about 6,000 species. *See also* Vertebrate. △520–24, 570.

Republic, state where sovereignty is vested in the people (either actually or theoretically) rather than in a king or prince. A republic may be a pure democracy, representative democracy, aristocracy, or dictatorship. Modern usage, however, limits republic to a sovereign state ruled by representatives of a broad electorate, thus a form of democratic representative government. △902, 1014, 1288.

Republicanism, doctrine that the government should represent and serve the common interests of all members and not the special interests of an elite. Originating in the time of the Roman Empire, the concept declined during the Dark Ages but was then revived in the Italian city-states under men such as Marsilius of Padua (*c.* 1270–1342), who espoused popular sovereignty. The provinces in the Netherlands set up a republic after gaining their independence from Spain, as did Switzerland after gaining independence from Austria. France formed a republic in 1792. The United States established an effective republic and this became a popular form of government. Many countries with differing political systems call themselves republics; the USSR is a totalitarian republic, while Great Britain has a democratic republic.

Republican Party, US political party, also known as the G.O.P., or Grand Old Party. It was organized in 1854 as an amalgamation of Whigs and Free Soilers with businessmen, workers, and professional people who formerly had called themselves Independent Democrats, Know-Nothings, Barnburners, and Abolitionists. John C. Fremont was the party's first presidential candidate in 1856. Its first successful candidate was Abraham Lincoln, elected in 1860. The party was particularly strong in the period from the Civil War to 1932. After 1932, Dwight Eisenhower (1952, 1956) and Richard Nixon (1968, 1972) each won election victories but both had to work with largely Democratic Congresses. △1276, 1358.

Republican River, river in Nebraska and Kansas; rises at the confluence of the North Fork Republican and Arikanee rivers, SW Nebraska; flows NE and E through S Nebraska, SE into Kansas to join Smoky Hill River at Junction City and form the Kansas River; subjects of flood control projects; used for irrigation. Length: 422mi (679km).

Republic of California (1846). *See* Bear Flag Revolt.

Reserpine, derivative of rauwolfia used to treat hypertension by acting as a sedative or reducing cardiac output. Its side effects include serious depression. Also known under the trademark Serpasil. △744, 770.

Reservoir, a storage place for water to be used b man. Water may be impounded during periods c higher flows to prevent floods, then released durin times of lower flows. Beginning early in man's histor in southern Asia and northern Africa, the use of rese voirs spread to Europe and then worldwide. They ar usually formed by dams, but sometimes pipelines ar used to carry water from rivers to depressions. Sed mentation causes most reservoirs to become useles after several decades; few last more than 100 years Reservoirs serve a number of functions: water supply irrigation, power generation, flood control, and recre ation. The world's largest reservoirs include Lake Vic toria in Uganda, artificially raised by the Owen Fall Dam; Aswan on the Nile in Egypt; Bratsk on the Ar gara in the Soviet Union; the Kariba on the Zambe in Zambia-Rhodesia; and the Akosombo-Main on th Volta in Ghana. △1614.

Resin, or rosin, viscous substance secreted by var ous plants or trees. It is impermeable to water an when present in large amounts (pine), it makes th wood resistant to rot and weather. Oleoresin secrete by conifers is distilled to produce turpentine, an rosin, a yellow-to-black material, remains after oil c turpentine has been distilled.

Resistance, Aerodynamic. △1718.

Resistor, electrical or electronic circuit componer that has a specified resistance. For electronic circuit resistors usually consist of finely ground carbon part cles mixed with a ceramic, enclosed in an insulate tube. The value of the resistance is denoted by a se of colored rings on the outside of the tube. Resis ances for high currents consist of a coil of insulate wire. △1544,1548.

Resonance, Wave, phenomenon in which a me chanical or acoustic system, set into forced vibration by the application of an external vibration, respond with maximum amplitude. It occurs when the fre quency of the applied force becomes equal to th natural vibrational frequency of the system. The larg vibrations can cause damage to the system.

Resonances, Particle, extremely short-lived ele mentary particles that are produced in high-energ nuclear reactions occurring in particle accelerato and decay in a time (10^{-23} second) characteristic c hadrons. Over 150 have been detected, all since th 1960s. A resonance can be considered as a marke increase in the probability of interaction between tw energetic colliding particles, occurring when the com bined energy of the particles attains a particular er ergy, the resonance energy.

Resource Allocation. *See* Allocation.

Respiration, transfer of gases, usually oxygen an carbon dioxide, between living things and their env ronment. In simple, single-celled organisms this ex change occurs directly through the cell wall. In highe animal forms, lungs or gills have evolved to transpo the gases in and out of the body. Plants use opening (stomata) in their leaves. △692.

Respiration, Cellular, processes used by a cell t release energy for metabolism. This involves the ox dation, or breakdown, of fuel compounds within th cell and the release of simpler compounds, such a carbon dioxide. △484.

Respiratory System, that system of the body cor cerned with external respiration, the process whereb air travels from outside to the lungs. The respirator tract begins with the nose and mouth, through whic air enters the body. The air then passes through th pharynx; into the larynx, or voice box; and into th trachea. The trachea at its lower end branches int two bronchi, each of which leads to a lung, where th exchange of gases between air and blood takes place Exhaled air leaves through the same pathway. △692

Rest Mass, mass of an elementary particle, etc when it is at rest. By the theory of relativity, motio will increase a body's mass although this is only nc ticeable at velocities approaching that of light. Suc velocities are reached in particle accelerators.

Retention, Memory. △670.

Reticulated Puffers. △516.

Reticuloendothelial System, body system mad up of reticular tissue, a specialized type of connectiv tissue that lines and supports the spleen, lymp nodes, and some other organs. Reticular tissue als contains cells that have macrophage action, destroy ing worn-out red blood cells in the spleen or invadin organisms in the lymph nodes.

Retina, inner layer of the wall of the eye, composed mainly of different kinds of neurons (nerve cells), some of which are the actual visual receptors of the eye. These receptor cells are stimulated by light. Some, known as cones, respond primarily to the spectrum of visible colors; others, known as rods, respond mainly to shades of gray and to movement. The rods and cones connect with sensory neurons that in turn connect with the optic nerve that carries the visual stimuli to the brain. △674.

Retinal Detachment, separation of the layers of the retina, after which the outermost layer, the pigment epithelium, remains attached to the choroid. Occurring in older people, it results in blurred vision. The retina is restored to its position by draining fluid and applying heat or cold to the eye's wall.

Retrievers, sporting dog breeds originally used only as water dogs to kill or cripple downed game and return it to the hunter. Today, they are also used to locate game. They have water-repelling coats, good swimming and scenting abilities, and tender mouths. Retrievers were developed in early 19th-century England. Breeds include curly-coated and wavy or flat-coated retrievers, Labrador and golden retrievers, Irish water spaniel, American water spaniel, and poodle.

Retz or **Rais, Jean François Paul de Gondi, Cardinal de** (1614–79), French cardinal. Born of an aristocratic French family, he gained the support of the Parisian bourgeoisie for the Fronde (1648–49), an unsuccessful rebellion against the young Louis XIV. He became a cardinal (1651) and was archbishop of Paris (1654–62) and then retired, spending his later years writing his memoirs.

Reuben, in Genesis, oldest son of Jacob and Leah. He saved his brother Joseph's life, offered his sons to Jacob as pledges for the safe return of his brother Benjamin, and had intercourse with his father's concubine.

Réunion, island constituting an overseas territory of France, in the Indian Ocean 425mi (684km) E of Malagasy Republic; member of the Mascarene group; Saint-Denis is the capital. First visited by Portuguese 16th century, it was claimed (1638) for France, which later colonized it; occupied by British 1810–15; made an overseas territory 1946. Exports: rum, sugar. Industries: agriculture, sugar mills, rum and alcohol distilling, canning. Area: 970sq mi (2,512sq km). Pop. 455,200.

Reuther, Walter (1907–70), US labor leader, b. Wheeling, W. Va. He helped organize the United Automobile Workers of America (UAW) in the 1930s. In 1946 he became UAW president and in 1952, president of the Congress of Industrial Organizations (CIO). A social activist, he led the UAW out of the American Federation of Labor (AFL-CIO) in 1968 in a dispute over union goals.

Revelation, last book of the New Testament, written by the apostle John. Often called the Apocalypse, this book shows great imagery in its treatment of God's relation to all and concentrates on depicting the end of all creation.

Revenue Act. *See* Sugar Act.

Revere, Paul (1735–1818), American patriot, skilled craftsman, silversmith, engraver, and printer, b. Boston. He is best known for his ride (April 18, 1775) warning Massachusetts colonists that British troops were marching toward Lexington and Concord to seize militia supplies. He was an express rider for the Boston Committee of Safety, a leader of the Boston Tea Party (1773), and a lieutenant colonel during the Revolutionary War. He was immortalized in a Longfellow poem.

Revere, city in E Massachusetts; N suburb of Boston; birthplace of Horatio Alger 1834; Revere Beach is popular resort area. Industries: printing, tourism. Founded 1630 as Rumney Marsh; name changed in honor of Paul Revere 1871; inc. as city 1914. Pop. (1970) 43,159.

Revolution, orbital motion of a planet or satellite around its primary. A single revolution is the planet's or satellite's "year" and its length is determined according to any of several different methods. *See also* Geologic Time. △40.

Revolution, the overthrow of the established government by its citizens, a large-scale, successful revolt. A revolution is not always violent (for example, the English Revolution of 1688) nor is it simply the overthrow of one government by another, as in a coup d'état, since the mass of citizenry is not involved. The American, French, and Russian revolutions are classic examples of revolution, but the term is also extended to mean vast changes in ways of doing things and of thinking about them (for example, the Industrial Revolution, the Scientific Revolution).

Revolutionary War, American. *See* American Revolution.

Revolutions of 1848. △1248.

Revolver. △1728.

Rex Cat, domestic cat, coat type recently developed. Each hair is waved and guard hairs are short, giving the coat a marcelled effect. These curly-coated cats are often called "poodle" cats. The type can be transferred to any breed, color, or type of cat. It is a mutation.

Reyes, Alfonso (1889–1959), Mexican writer. A critic, scholar, and poet, he was especially concerned with Latin America's place in the literary world. He advocated a middle ground that was neither provincial nor foreign-oriented, and believed Latin American writers should tackle basic human themes. His poems brought the rhythms of English verse into Castilian and are noted for their beautiful descriptions of nature. Among his best books of poetry are *Pause* (1926) and *The Gulf of Mexico* (1935). He wrote over 100 volumes of prose.

Reykjavík, seaport and capital city of Iceland, on SW coast of the island; major port between Europe and North America; Episcopal see 1796; made seat of Danish administration 1801; became capital of Iceland 1918; served as British and US air base during WWII; site of University of Reykjavík (1911), House of the Althing, National Museum, National Library, a statue of Leif Ericson given by United States on the 1000th anniversary of the Althing (parliament); commercial and fishing center. Industries: food processing, textiles, metallurgy, fishing, printing, shipyards. Founded *c.* 870. Pop. 81,684.

Reymont, Ladislaus (*c.* 1867–1925), Polish novelist. His concern with social themes is evident in his first novel, *The Promised Land* (1899), and the four-volume novel of peasant life, *Chlopi* (1902–09), a comprehensive panorama of rural life. In 1924 he was awarded the Nobel Prize for literature.

Reynolds, (Sir) Joshua (1723–92), English portrait painter and writer. The first president of the Royal Academy of Arts, he was an important artist in linking English painting with that of Europe. His fashionable portraits include the famous "Nelly O'Brien." His classic manner of the late 1760s evolved into a more relaxed, naturalistic style in the 1780s ("Mrs. Thomas Meyrick," *c.* 1782).

Reza Shah Pahlavi (1877–1944), shah of Iran (1925–41). He led a coup d'état in 1921, served as prime minister (1923–25), and after Ahmed Shah was deposed in 1926, became shah. He reduced the power of the tribal chieftains, reorganized government administration, improved finances, and encouraged industrialization. In 1941 he abdicated in favor of his son Mohammed Reza Pahlavi.

Rhaetian Alps (Ratioche Alpen), range of mountains along Italian-Swiss border and Austrian-Swiss border, but primarily in Grisons canton, Switzerland; division of Central Alps. They extend from Splügen Pass (WSW) between Lepontine and Rhaetian alps to Otztal Alps (ENE) and Lechtal Alps (NE). Highest peak is Piz Bernina, 13,304ft (4,058m).

Rhaeto-Romanic, term used to refer to three Romance dialects spoken in SE Switzerland and NE Italy. One of them, Romansch, spoken in the Swiss canton of Graubünden by about 50,000 people, is one of the official languages of the country. The other two are Friulian, with about 500,000 speakers in Friulia, and Ladin, with about 10,000 speakers in Alto Adige.

Rhamphorhynchus. △572.

Rh Disease, anemic disease of fetuses and of newborn infants due to Rh-factor incompatibility between mother and developing embryo. It is marked by destruction of mature red blood cells, presence of many immature red cells, and jaundice. It develops after the first pregnancy; severity varies and increases with each successive pregnancy. Exchange transfusions in which compatible blood is substituted in the newborn now save most afflicted infants. There is also a vaccine that prevents formation of Rh antibodies in the Rh negative mother. *See also* Rh Factor. △702.

Jean Renoir (right)

Paul Revere

Reykjavik, Iceland

Joshua Reynolds

Rhea, large, brownish, flightless, fast-running South American bird resembling a small ostrich. It feeds mostly on plant matter. Males engage in noisy courtship displays, after which several females lay a total of 12–30 eggs in a single concealed ground-scraped nest prepared by the male. Height: to 5ft (1.5m). Species *Rhea americana.* △526, 588.

Rhea, satellite of Saturn. △86.

Rhee, Syngman (1875–1965), president of the Republic of Korea (South Korea) (1948–60). Imprisoned (1898–1904) for his work to free Korea from Japanese rule, he spent more than 30 years in exile (1912–45). Elected South Korea's first president (1948), he was a dictatorial leader purging all opposition and outlawing the Progressive party. Bloody rioting after his reelection in 1960 caused his resignation and retirement to Hawaii. *See also* Korean War.

Rhenium, metallic element (symbol Re) of the third transition series, discovered in 1925. It is found in molybdenite (MoS_2), from which it is obtained as a by-product. It is used in thermocouples and in certain alloys and is also a useful catalyst. Properties: at. no. 75; at. wt. 186.2; sp gr 21.02; melt. pt. 5,756°F (3,180°C); boil. pt. 10,160°F (est.) (5,627°C); most common isotope Re^{103}(100%). *See also* Transition Elements. △1552–54.

Rhesus, medium-sized, yellow-brown macaque monkey of India. Short tailed, it has a large head with bare face, big ears, and closely spaced, deep-set eyes. Omnivorous, day-active, and gregarious, they occupy a wide range of habitats—from densely forested to treeless and from tropical lowlands to temperate uplands. Used in scientific work, the rhesus gave the first two letters of its name to the Rh blood factor. Height: 2ft (61cm). Species *Macaca rhesus. See also* Monkey. △558.

Rhetoric, the art of presenting facts and ideas in clear, convincing, and attractive language. It is designed to instruct, to move, or to delight and requires an understanding of the effect of words and their arrangements as well as an imaginative approach. At one time the Sophists used rhetoric "to make great matters small and small things great," and it became associated with oratorical emptiness, but the basic rhetorical principles are still valid.

Rheumatic Fever, inflammatory disease caused by streptococcal infection and characterized by fever and swelling and pain in the joints. It is associated with inflammation of the heart and often results in rheumatic heart disease. Most frequent in children of ages 5–15, it also affects adults. Treatment is by antibiotics and cortisone. Prevention entails immediate treatment of streptococcal infections.

Rheumatism, general term for disorders characterized by stiffness and pain in the joints or muscles, such as bursitis and rheumatoid arthritis.

Rh Factor, any of a group of antigens (substances that stimulate antibody production) found on the surface of red blood cells, so called because first discovered in the rhesus monkey. Rh-negative blood lacks Rh factor, and Rh-positive blood contains it; it is present in about 85% of the population. Rh incompatibility (Rh-negative mother and Rh-positive fetus) is a major cause of a serious condition in infants, hemolytic disease of the newborn (anemia). It occurs in the Rh-positive fetus of an Rh-negative mother who has previously borne an Rh-positive child and has thus developed antibodies (has become sensitized) against Rh factor at the time of delivery. △702.

Rhine, Joseph B(anks) (1895–), US psychologist, b. Waterloo, Pa. He was a pioneer in the study of extrasensory perception and psychic phenomena. He brought these events under objective, scientific scrutiny and coined the term "parapsychology" for the area of psychology that would study them. In 1937 he founded the *Journal of Parapsychology.* Among his major publications are *New World of the Mind* (1953) and *Parapsychology: Frontier Science of the Mind* (1957, coauthor). △824.

Rhine (Rhein, Rhin, or Rijn), river in W Europe, rises in SE Switzerland in the Swiss Alps and forms a natural boundary between Switzerland, Austria, and Liechtenstein on the W; flows NW, and forms the boundary between Switzerland and Germany. Along its route it connects with numerous other rivers; after joining with the Sieg, Wupper, Ruhr, and Lippe rivers, it flows to the Netherlands and the North Sea. The Rhine has played a prominent part in German history and trade. Length: 820mi (1,320km).

Rhineland, region in W West Germany, along W bank of Rhine River; includes Rhineland Palatinate, Rhenish Hesse, SW Hesse, and W Baden. The Treaty of Versailles (1919) provided for Allied occupation and demilitarization of the area; the last occupational troops were removed in 1930, five years early, but by 1936 Hitler had formed the Siegfried Line, a German defense system, which caused League of Nations' censorship of Germany. This defense was infiltrated by Allies during WWII. Area: 9,000sq mi (23,310sq km).

Rhinencephalon. △680.

Rhinoceros, massive, horned and hoofed, herbivorous mammal native to Africa and Asia. Depending on the species, they have either one or two horns on the snout. They have thick skins and poor eyesight. Mostly solitary grazers or browsers, they rest during the heat of the day and like to wallow in muddy pools. When alarmed they may charge. Now rare except in protected areas, rhinos were hunted heavily for their horns. Weight: 1–3.5ton. Family Rhinocerotidae.

Rhinoceros Beetle, mostly tropical and subtropical plant-eating scarab beetle named for rhinoceroslike horns on males of some species. Length: to 7.5in (19cm). Subfamily Dyanstinae.

Rhizopoda, class of protozoa found in fresh and salt water, damp soil, and animal digestive tracts. They move and capture food by pseudopodia—extensions of protoplasm. They include amoebas, foraminifera, radiolaria, and heliozoa.

Rhode Island, state in the NE United States, on the Atlantic Ocean in the New England region. It is the smallest and second most densely populated of the states.

Land and Economy. The land is level or gently rolling. Narragansett Bay, which contains many islands, cuts deeply into the E section. There are no rivers of importance, but nearly 300 lakes and ponds. Manufacturing, centered in the larger cities, is the economy's mainstay. Fish and shellfish are harvested in coastal waters. Tourism is a valuable source of income.

People. About 87% of the population lives in urban areas. The 1970 census listed 35 places of more than 5,000 population in the state's small area. The first settlers were mostly English, but immigrants from many European countries arrived in the 19th century to work in the factories.

Education. There are 13 institutions of higher education. The University of Rhode Island is state-supported.

History. The first white settlers came in 1636, led by Roger Williams, who had been banished from Massachusetts for his liberal religious and political views. The town he founded at Providence joined later settlements in 1644 to form the colony of Providence Plantations, but in 1663 the charter was revoked by Charles II of England and the area, including some islands that had been governed separately, became the Colony of Rhode Island and Providence Plantations. This remains the official name of the state. Wars with the Indians shook the colony in the late 17th century. Rhode Island was one of the first colonies to show a spirit of revolt against the British Crown. A British revenue cutter was burned by colonists in 1772, and on May 4, 1776, two months before the national Declaration of Independence, the General Assembly declared Rhode Island free of Great Britain. A French fleet aiding the Americans was based at Newport during the Revolution. In the 19th century, the state became a center of the textile industry, but by 1940 most of these enterprises had moved to southern states.

PROFILE

Admitted to the Union: May 29, 1790; 13th of the 13 original states to ratify the US Constitution
US Congressmen: Senate, 2; House of Representatives, 2
Population: 949,723 (1970); rank, 39th
Capital: Providence, 179,116 (1970)
Chief cities: Providence; Warwick, 83,694; Pawtucket, 76,984
State legislature: Senate, 50; House of Representatives, 100
Area: 1,214sq mi (3,144sq km); rank, 50th
Elevation: Highest, 812ft (247m), Jerimoth Hill; lowest, sea level
Industries (major products): jewelry, silverware, metal products, machinery, rubber, plastics, apparel
Agriculture (major products): poultry, dairy products
Minerals (major): stone, sand, gravel
State nickname: Little Rhody, Ocean State
State motto: Hope
State bird: Rhode Island red (chicken)
State flower: violet
State tree: red maple

Rhode Island (formerly Aquidneck Island), island in S Rhode Island, largest island of Narragansett Bay; Newport, Portsmouth, and Middletown located on it. First settled at Portsmouth 1638 as Aquidneck; name changed 1644. Length: 15mi (24km); width: 5mi (8km).

Rhode Island Red, chicken breed raised for its brown-shelled eggs. They have yellow skin and a single comb. Weight: 8.5lb (3.9kg) cock; 6.5lb (3kg) hen.

Rhodes, Cecil John (1853–1902), English capitalist, imperialist, and statesman of Africa. He went to Africa for his health in 1870, where he started a diamond mine. He greatly increased his mining operations and became a firm believer in British colonial expansion. He formed the British South Africa Company in 1889 and with it controlled the large areas of SE Africa later called Rhodesia. Legislator and prime minister (1890–96) of the Cape Colony, he helped exclude black Africans from the democratic process, but his attempt to gain control of Boer Transvaal through the Jameson Raid of 1895 destroyed his political ambitions. He subsequently concentrated on the development of railroads and Rhodesia. He willed his vast fortune to various public works, including noted scholarships for education. △1268.

Rhodes (Rodhos), island in SE Aegean Sea, Greece, in the Dodecanese islands; mountainous interior, fertile coastal areas, fine climate. Colonized by Dorians *c.* 1000 BC; conquered at different times by Persia, Sparta, Athens, Caria, Alexander the Great; part of Byzantine Empire (1204); taken by Turks 1522; ceded to Italy 1923; annexed to Greece 1947. Chief city and capital of Dodecanese dept. is Rhodes. Industries: shipbuilding, sponge diving, fishing, tourism. Area: 540sq mi (1,399sq km). Pop. 68,873.

Rhodesia, independent nation in S central Africa. The predominantly black African population is ruled by a white minority government. Rhodesia unilaterally declared its independence from Britain in 1965, an act denounced internationally.

Land and Economy. A high inland plateau country in S central Africa, its neighbors are Zambia (N), Mozambique (E), Republic of South Africa (S), and Botswana (W). Crossing the country NE to SW is a 4,000–5,000-ft (1,220–1,525-m) high plateau with land sloping to the Zambesi River. Victoria Falls, 335 ft (102m) high and 5,580ft (1,702m) wide, were discovered by David Livingstone in 1855. Temperature is subtropical. US and British economic sanctions against Rhodesia have seriously affected foreign investment in a country with an average annual white wage of $4,722 compared to $440 for Africans. Before sanctions, economic development was at a high level. Rich farmland and minerals have been the economic mainstays, with tobacco a leading export crop.

People. Rhodesia's population includes two groupings: a combination of mostly British Europeans (whites), Asians, and coloreds totaling about 300,000; and an overwhelming number of Bantu Africans descended from two tribes, Mashona and Matebele, offshoots of the Zulus. Shona and Ndebele are the principal language groups; English is the official tongue. A large proportion of Africans are Christians. Less than 30% of the Africans are literate.

Government. The new constitution provides for a president selected by the Executive Council. Parliament contains a minority of Africans.

History. Exploration of ruins at Zimbabwe has revealed an impressive trading culture between the 9th and 13th centuries. Portuguese traders came in the 16th century, and the hinterlands were explored 300 years later by missionaries and traders. Meanwhile, waves of equatorial Bantus came to the region. In 1888, Cecil Rhodes received tribal permission to seek minerals and started the British South Africa Co. Britain took over the company in 1923 and granted the people internal self-government. A 1961 constitution extended privileges, with voting restricted to keep whites in power. When Prime Minister Ian Smith announced independence in 1965, Britain called it illegal, and imposed economic sanctions. A 1970 constitution continued to block full African representation. Black nationalist pressures led Prime Minister Smith to agree in 1976 to majority rule.

PROFILE

Official name: Rhodesia
Area: 150,803sq mi (390,580sq km)
Population: 6,300,000
Density: 41per sq mi (16per sq km)
Chief cities: Salisbury (capital); Bulawayo
Government: Republic
Religion: Christian (major)

Monetary unit: Rhodesian dollar
Gross national product: $2,493,000,000
Per capita income: $406
Industries: chemical products, clothing
Agriculture: tobacco, sugar, tea, cotton, corn, millet, cattle, sorghum
Minerals: asbestos, copper, iron, coal, chrome
Trading partners: South Africa

Rhodesian Ridgeback, South African hunting dog (hound group) bred by Boers and introduced to Rhodesia in 1877; also called African lion hound. It has a long, flat, broad head with a long, deep muzzle; high-set, medium-sized ears close to the head; a powerful body with slightly arched loin; long, heavy legs; and a long, tapered tail. The short, dense, light- to red-wheaten coat has a characteristic ridge of hair on the back. Average size: 25–27in (63.5–68.5cm) high at shoulder; 65–75lb (29.5–34kg). *See also* Hounds.

Rhodium, metallic element (symbol Rh) of the second transition series, discovered (1803) by W. H. Wollaston. It occurs associated with platinum; chief source is as a by-product of nickel smelting. It is used in hard platinum alloys. Properties: at. no. 45; at. wt. 102.9055; sp gr 12.41; melt. pt. 3,571°F (1,966°C); boil. pt. 6,709°F (3,709°C); most common isotope Rh^{103} (100%). *See also* Transition Elements. △1552–54.

Rhododendron, a large genus of shrubs and small trees that prefer the acid soil of cool temperate regions in North America, Europe, and Asia. Primarily evergreen, they have leathery leaves and bell-shaped white, pink, or purple flowers. Many species are used in landscaping. Family Ericaceae. *See also* Azalea; Heath.

Rhodopsin, or visual purple, visual pigment present in the rod cells of the retina of the eye. It absorbs light, producing a nerve impulse that is perceived as vision.

Rhomboid (muscle). △684.

Rhône River, river that rises in Rhône Glacier in Bernese Oberland of Switzerland, flows W through narrow valley to Lake Geneva; from SW end of lake it crosses French border through opening in Jura Mts; continues S through Lyons, Avignon, and Tarascon to Arles, where it branches into Grand Rhône and Petit Rhône. They join the Mediterranean at Marseilles. It is linked with other rivers by extensive canal system; navigable for about 300mi (483km) of its 505mi (813km).

Rhubarb, or pieplant, perennial herbaceous plants native to Asia and cultivated worldwide in cool climates for its large, edible leaf stalks. It has large poisonous leaves and small white or red flowers. The stalks are used in pies, compotes, and preserves; the roots in medicine. *Rheum rhaponticum* is the common cultivated plant found in gardens. Height: to 8ft (2.5m). Family Polygonaceae.

Rhyme, identity or similarity of final sounds in two or more words, such as *keep/deep; baking/shaking.* Rhyme is used in poetry to reinforce meter and to organize related lines into a stanza. End rhymes, the most common, establish verse lines. Internal or Leonine rhymes emphasize rhythmic structures. Rhymes are also classified as male (one-syllable); female (two-syllable); triple (three-syllable); quadruple (four-syllable).

Rhythm, in music, one of the prime elements, referring to how long musical notes last (duration), how fast one note follows another (tempo), and the pattern of sounds formed by changes in duration and tempo. Rhythm in Western cultures is normally metrical, that is notes follow one another in a regular pattern at some specified rate. In Oriental and primitive music rhythms may be more free; there is more improvisation and rhythm is not related to some fundamental pattern.

Rhythm, in poetry, tempo or flow of speech sounds and silences that is essential to poetry. A poem may have rhymed or unrhymed lines; it may be composed according to strict metrical form or in free verse, but it must offer sounds and silences that fill equal or balancing time periods, recurring with pleasing regularity. In true poetry, rhythm is organic; that is, the tempo of the lines follows the rhythm of the feeling intended to be conveyed. *See also* Meter.

Rhythm and Blues. △1366.

Rhythm Method, a technique for preventing pregnancy by abstaining from sexual intercourse at the time during the monthly menstrual cycle that ovulation is presumed to take place.

Rialto, city in S California, 4mi (6km) W of San Bernardino; site of citrus fruit orchards and vineyards. Inc. 1911. Pop. (1970) 28,370.

Rib, curved bones arranged in pairs that form part of the front and side support of the chest. In man there are 12 pairs. The first seven pairs, known as true ribs, are joined by costal cartilage to the sternum; the next three, called false ribs, to the costal cartilage of the seventh pair; the last two, called floating ribs, are not attached to the sternum. The head of each rib joins with a thoracic vertebra in the back. The shafts (main curved part of the bone) of adjacent ribs are joined by intercostal muscles that act to change chest capacity during breathing. △682.

Ribbentrop, Joachim von (1893–1946), German diplomat. A wealthy merchant, he joined the Nazi party in 1932 and became part of Adolf Hitler's inner circle as a foreign affairs adviser. During 1936–38 he was minister to England and during 1938–45 foreign minister. He was tried as a war criminal at the Nuremberg trials, convicted, and executed.

Ribbon Fish, also Seyth or deal fish, marine fish found in cold deep waters. It is identified by its long, thin body and plumelike dorsal fin extending along the entire length of the body. Length: 8ft (243.8cm). Species include *Trachipterus arcticus* and the Pacific northwest king of the salmon fish *Trachipterus altivelus.* Family Trachipteridae.

Ribbon Snake. *See* Garter Snake.

Ribbonworm. *See* Nemertea.

Riboflavin, vitamin of the B complex, lack of which impairs growth and causes skin disorders. *See* Vitamin.

Ribonucleic Acid (RNA), nucleic acid that controls the synthesis of proteins in the cell and in some viruses is the genetic material. The molecule consists of a single strand of nucleotides, each containing the sugar ribose, phosphoric acid, and one of four bases: adenine, guanine, cytosine, or thymine. Messenger RNA carries the information for protein synthesis from DNA in the nucleus to the ribosomes in the cytoplasm. Each amino acid to be formed is specified by a sequence of three bases in messenger RNA. Transfer RNA brings the amino acids to their correct position on the messenger RNA. △1570–74.

Ribosome, a ribonucleoprotein particle in cells, the site of protein synthesis in the cells.

Ricardo, David (1772–1823), English economist. His book *Principles of Economics and Taxation* (1817) made an important contribution to the field of international trade. According to Ricardo, two principles, absolute and comparative advantage, mean that the best policy a nation can pursue is free international trade. According to Ricardo's theory, a nation should erect no trade barriers (eg, tariffs or quotas). Basically, Ricardo posits that people should spend their working time doing the things they do best. In fact, Ricardo would say that if a nation is not "best" at anything, it should devote its energies to the tasks at which it is "least bad." If this is done, total world production will be maximized.

Ricci, Matteo (1552–1610), Italian missionary. A Jesuit, he served in India before going to China (1583). He was the first of the Jesuit missionaries to gain access to the Ming emperors' court (1600). A talented linguist and scientist, he was able to introduce Western science and knowledge to the Chinese court. He translated Western works into Chinese and presented the court with its first maps of the world.

Rice, Elmer (1892–1967), US dramatist, b. Elmer Reizenstein in New York City. He wrote the cinematic *On Trial* (1914), an expressionist satire on regimentation, *The Adding Machine* (1923), the Pulitzer Prize winner *Street Scene* (1929); also other polemics: *Counsellor-at-Law* (1931), *We, the People* (1933), and the anti-Nazi *Flight to the West* (1940). His fantasy *Dream Girl* (1945) was a popular romantic comedy.

Rice, annual cereal grass cultivated since 3000 BC on tropical and temperate submerged lowlands throughout the world. It has long, flattened leaves and flowers that produce the starchy, seedlike grains, usually milled to remove the husk and bran. When only the husk is removed, it is called brown rice and is more nourishing. Rice is used in brewing, distilling, and for flour; bran as animal food; hulls as fuel and fertilizer; and straw as feed, mats, and brooms. Height: to 4ft (1.2m). Family Gramineae; species *Oryza sativa. See also* Grass. △326.

Rhine River

Providence, Rhode Island

Rhode Island red

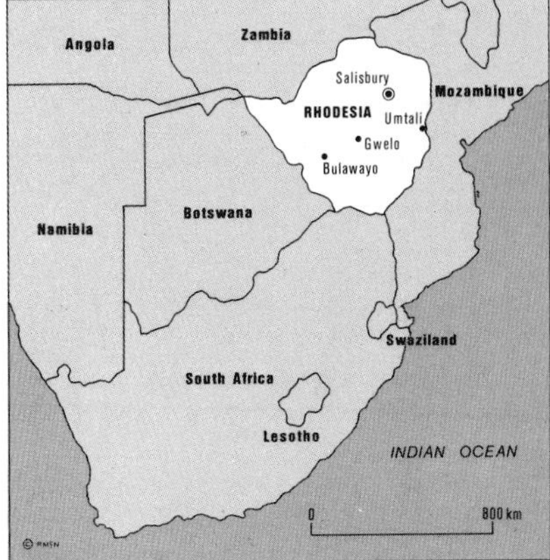
Angola
Zambia
Salisbury
RHODESIA
Umtali
Gwelo
Bulawayo
Mozambique
Namibia
Botswana
Swaziland
South Africa
Lesotho
INDIAN OCEAN
0
800 km
Rhodesia

Richard I (1157–99), king of England, son of Henry II and Eleanor of Aquitaine, known as Richard Coeur de Lion, Richard the Lion-hearted. Richard fought against his father (1173–74; 1188–89) and succeeded Henry in 1189. Although popular, Richard spent little time in England, the country being governed by regents, including his brother, John. Richard joined the Third Crusade (1189) and took Cyprus and Acre (1191) but failed to gain Jerusalem. On his return, he was captured (1192) and held for ransom in Austria. The ransom raised, he returned to England (1194), was again crowned, but spent the rest of his life in France.

Richard II (1367–1400), king of England (1377–99), son of Edward the Black Prince. He married Anne of Bohemia (1382) and Isabella of France (1396). He succeeded his grandfather Edward III. His uncle, John of Gaunt, controlled the government, but Richard met and put down the Peasants Revolt (1381), and Gaunt soon retired to Europe. In 1386 the duke of Gloucester led other lords to confront the king and called for the dismissal of his closest counselors. The king opposed them but his army was defeated at Radcot Bridge (1387) and in 1388 Gloucester, and four other lords, forced the dismissal or execution of Richard's advisers and assumed control of the government. Richard regained authority (1389) and banished or executed the opposition lords. On John of Gaunt's death (1399), Richard confiscated his Lancastrian estates and Gaunt's heir, Henry, duke of Hereford, raised an army against him. Richard was imprisoned and Hereford was crowned as Henry IV in 1399. Richard either starved himself to death or was murdered in 1400.

Richard III (1452–85), king of England (1483–85), brother of Edward IV. He was made duke of Gloucester (1461) at Edward's coronation. Suspected of complicity in the murders of Henry VI and his own brother; he assumed protectorship of the young Edward V on Edward IV's death (1483). He put Edward and his brother, the duke of York, in the Tower of London and crowned himself king. His old supporter, the duke of Buckingham, led a revolt in favor of Henry Tudor, but was executed. Henry landed in Wales (1485) and killed Richard, the last Yorkist king, at Bosworth. His death ended the Wars of the Roses.

Richard, Earl of Cornwall (1209–72), brother of Henry III of England. He recovered Gascony (1225–26) and returned to force Henry to grant him lands and the title earl of Cornwall. He then married Isabella, daughter of the earl of Pembroke (1231) and sided with the barons against the crown. After leading a crusade (1240–41), he married the queen's sister (1243) and supported Henry in the Barons' War (1263–67). Captured at Lewes (1264), he was freed after the battle of Evesham (1265). He had himself crowned Holy Roman emperor (1257) but he was only a titular ruler.

Richard, Maurice (1921–), Canadian ice hockey player, b. Joseph Henri Maurice Richard. Known as the "Rocket" for his great speed, he played forward for the Montreal Canadiens (1942–60) in the National Hockey League and scored 544 goals.

Richard II (*c.*1595), 5-act historical play by William Shakespeare. His historical source was Raphael Holinshed's *Chronicles* (1587). The structure of the play is like Marlowe's *Edward II* (*c.*1593). Richard II, weak and self-indulgent, yields his throne to his powerful cousin Henry Bolingbroke, who becomes Henry IV. Richard is imprisoned, then murdered.

Richard III (*c.*1594), 5-act history play by William Shakespeare. For his hunchbacked royal criminal, Shakespeare draws on many sources—morality plays, the tragedies of Seneca and Niccolò Machiavelli's *The Prince*, and Thomas More's *History of Richard III*. Misshapen Richard, duke of Gloucester, murders his brother, the duke of Clarence. When his other brother, King Edward IV, dies, Richard has Edward's two young sons imprisoned and killed and takes the crown for himself. He is defeated in battle at Bosworth field and killed by the future King Henry VII.

Richardson, Elliot Lee (1920–), US political leader, b. Boston. He served under Pres. Richard M. Nixon as undersecretary of state (1969–70), secretary of health, education, and welfare (1970–73), secretary of defense (1973), and attorney general (1973). He resigned the last post to protest the firing of Special Watergate Prosecutor Archibald Cox (1973). President Ford made him ambassador to Great Britain (1975), and he later served as secretary of commerce (1975–77).

Richardson, Henry Hobson (1838–86), US architect, b. St James Parish, La., who studied in Paris and practiced in Boston. His major innovation was the revival of the European Romanesque style, seen in such buildings as Trinity Church, Boston (1862–77), and Austin Hall, Harvard University (1881). This style was greatly influential in urban development of the late 19th century.

Richardson, Samuel (1689–1761), English novelist and printer. His novels include *Pamela* (4 vols., 1740–41), *Clarissa Harlowe* (1747–48), and *Sir Charles Grandison* (1753–54). He contributed to the development of the psychological novel. *See also* Pamela. △1188.

Richardson, city in NE Texas; N suburb of Dallas; mainly residential area with few light industries. Founded 1873; inc. 1925. Pop. (1970) 48,582.

Richelieu, Armand Jean du Plessis, Cardinal Duc de (1585–1642), French statesman. Bishop of Luçon at 21 (1606), he was sent to the States-General (the legislative assembly) in 1614. He became a cardinal (1622) and was advisor to the exiled Marie de' Medici, Louis XIII's mother. He helped make peace between the two, becoming prime minister 1624–42. He established an ever-increasing royal power that lasted until the French Revolution. In foreign affairs, Richelieu turned the Swedes and Protestant Germans against the Hapsburgs, and in a series of French victories advanced the French cause in the Thirty Years War. Author and wealthy literary patron, he established the Académie Française (1635). He is buried in the chapel of the Sorbonne, which he built. △1154.

Richfield, city in SE central Minnesota, 7mi (11km) S of Minneapolis. Industries: metal products. Settled 1851; inc. 1964. Pop. (1970) 47,231.

Richland, city in S Washington, at junction of Columbia and Yakima rivers; residential area for employees of the Atomic Energy Commission's Hanford Works, est. 1943 for production of plutonium for atomic bombs; site of research laboratories; farm and ranching area. Inc. 1958. Pop. (1970) 26,290.

Richler, Mordecai (1931–), Canadian novelist. Although Richler has lived primarily in England since 1951, he writes about Canadians and about the Jewish ghetto in Montreal where he grew up. His funny, satirical, intense novels include *The Apprenticeship of Duddy Kravitz* (1959), *Cocksure* (1968), and *St Urban's Horseman* (1969).

Richmond, city in W California, 9mi (14km) NNW of Oakland. Industries: oil refineries, chemicals, electronic equipment, port. Founded 1823 as part of a Spanish ranch; inc. 1905. Pop. (1970) 79,043.

Richmond, city in E Indiana, SE of Muncie; midwest center of American Quakers; seat of Wayne co; site of Earlham College (1847), a Quaker institution. Industries: automobile parts, furniture, modular homes. Founded 1806; inc. 1840. Pop. (1970) 43,999.

Richmond, capital city and port of entry in E central Virginia, on James River; seat of Henrico co. Built on site of Fort Charles (1645), city developed as trading center; it was made capital of Commonwealth of Virginia 1779, of state 1785; scene of 2nd and 3rd Virginia Conventions (1775). It was made capital of Confederacy July 1861, and fell to Union forces in 1865. It is site of Hollywood Cemetery (1847) containing tombs of James Monroe, John Tyler, Jefferson Davis; St John's Church (1741), state capitol (1785), Richmond National Battlefield Park, Robert E. Lee's house (1844), Commonwealth University (1804), University of Richmond (1832), Virginia Union University (1865). Industries: metal items, tobacco and tobacco processing, textiles, clothing, chemicals, foodstuffs, paper and paper products, machinery, printing, publishing. Settled 1637; inc. 1782 as town, 1842 as city. Pop. (1970) 249,430.

Richter, C(harles) F(rancis) (1900–), US geophysicist and seismologist, b. Butler co, Ohio. With Beno Gutenberg he developed a scale to measure earthquake intensity at any distance from the recording station. That scale now bears his name. △174.

Richter Scale. △174.

Richthofen, Manfred, Baron von (1892–1918), German World War I flying ace. As an aviator in World War I, he shot down 80 enemy aircraft. His combat group was called "Richthofen's Circus," and he was known as the "Red Baron." He was killed in action.

Rickenbacker, Edward Vernon (1890–1973), US aviator, b. Columbus, Ohio. As a member of the famous World War I "Hat-in-the-Ring" air squadron, he shot down 26 German planes, earning the Congressional Medal of Honor. He was involved in several automobile and airline company ventures and became president of Eastern Airlines (1938). He inspected US Pacific bases during World War II and was shot down on one tour, surviving 23 days in a raft (1942). He returned to Eastern afterward, retiring in 1963. His books include *Fighting the Flying Circus* (1919) and *Seven Came Through* (1943).

Rickets, nutritional disorder characterized by deformities of the skeleton. It is caused by lack of calcium and phosphorus in the blood due to insufficient vitamin D in the diet or inadequate exposure to sunlight. △696.

Rickettsial Disease, a number of illnesses of vertebrate animals, caused by various rickettsiae, a group of microorganisms, usually carried by fleas, lice, and ticks. Typhus, Rocky Mountain spotted fever, and Q Fever can be transmitted to man. Dogs are afflicted with canine rickettsiosis, in which they have fever and nervous system disorders. It is often fatal.

Rickey, (Wesley) Branch (1881–1965), US baseball executive, b. Lucasville, Ohio. In 1947, as president and general manager of the Brooklyn Dodgers he broke baseball's "color barrier" by signing Jackie Robinson. He created the minor league farm system in the 1930s and forced the expansion of the major leagues by threatening to start a third major league in 1960. He also had been a player. In 1967 he was elected to the Baseball Hall of Fame.

Rickover, Hyman George (1900–), US naval officer, b. Russia. Immigrating to the United States (1906), he graduated from the US Naval Academy at Annapolis (1922). He is called the "father of the nuclear submarine" for his work on the first such vessel *The Nautilus*, launched in 1954. He began serving on the US Atomic Energy Commission (1947) and set up the Navy's nuclear power schools. He is also known as an outspoken critic of US education standards, which he considers to be too lax. He wrote *Education and Freedom* (1959) and *American Education; A National Failure* (1963). Rickover became a full admiral in 1973.

Rickshaw. △1704.

Ridgewood, village in NE New Jersey, 5mi (8km) NNE of Paterson; scene of British and colonial encampments during Revolutionary War. Inc. 1876 Pop. (1970) 27,547.

Ridgway, Matthew Bunker (1895–), US military officer, b. Fort Monroe, Va. He graduated from the US Military Academy at West Point (1917). He served in the War Department (1939–42) before he became commander of the 82nd Airborne Division in World War II (1942). He was given command of the Eighth Army in Korea and in 1951 he replaced Douglas MacArthur as commander of the UN forces there. In 1952 he was made US commander in Europe and he was army chief of staff (1953–55).

Riel, Louis (1844–85), Canadian political leader. In 1869 he led the Métis (people of mixed French and Indian descent) against the transfer of the western territories from the Hudson Bay Company to Canada, and established and headed a provisional government in the West. In 1870 Manitoba became a province, and in 1873 Riel was elected to the House of Commons. He never took his seat, and in 1875 he was exiled for five years. He settled in Montana and became a US citizen in 1883. He returned to Canada in 1884 and in 1885 led a Métis uprising. The rebellion was suppressed, and Riel was tried and hanged for treason.

Riemann, Georg Friedrich Bernhard (1826–66), German mathematician. He became professor at Göttingen in 1859 but his life was dogged with ill-health and he died of tuberculosis at the age of 40. He is remembered for his contributions to differential and non-Euclidean geometry, which were later used in the general theory of relativity. △1462.

Riemenschneider, Tilman (*c.*1460–1531), German sculptor. He was a major force in the lower Franconian school. One of his finest and best-known works is the Mary Altar (*c.*1505–10). His work in the late German Gothic style is marked by a combination of vigor, emotion, and restraint, typified in "The Madonna and Child" (1493). △1136.

Riesman, David (1909–), US sociologist, b. Philadelphia. After practicing law for several years, Riesman turned to sociology. He is best known for coauthoring *The Lonely Crowd* (1950). He has done research in the sociology of education and wrote *The Academic Revolution* (1968, with Christopher

Jencks) and *Academic Values and Mass Education* (1970).

Rif (Er Rif), range of Atlas Mts, in NE Morocco, NW Africa; extends from Ceuta to Melilla along Mediterranean coast. It was inhabited by independent Berber tribes until 1925–26, when they were conquered by French and Spanish forces. Highest point is Tidighin, 8,056ft (2,457m).

Rifle. △1728, 1730.

Riflebird. △538.

Rift Valley (Great Rift Valley), geological depression extending from Jordan in SW Asia to Mozambique in SE Africa. Volcanic eruptions caused chain of geological faults, resulting in the Dead Sea, Gulf of Aqaba, Red Sea, lakes in S Ethiopia, and lakes Albert, Edward, Kivu, Tanganyika, and Nyasa.

Riga, capital city of the Latvian republic, NW USSR, at the S extremity of the Gulf of Riga, on the Western Dvina River 9mi (14km) above its mouth. City joined the Hanseatic League in 1282; it was burned 1558 during the Livonian War; it came under Polish domination in 1581; in 1621, Gustavus Adolphus of Sweden took Riga and instituted self-government; it was ceded to Peter the Great of Russia 1710; the port was closed 1915 and evacuated by the Russians; in 1917 it came under Germans. Latvia's independence was declared at Riga in November 1918; from 1920–40, Riga was capital of Vidzeme in independent Latvia; in WWII, it was taken by the Germans (1941) and retaken by the USSR (1944); site of the Latvian State University (1919), agricultural and art academies, teachers' college, conservatory, 16th-century castle, Renaissance parliament building, national opera house. Industries: electric machinery, telephone and radio equipment, superphosphates, glass, wood products, paper, textiles, rubber and leather goods. Exports: timber, paper, linseed oil, dairy products. Founded 1201 by Bishop of Livonia. Pop. 733,000.

Rigel, or Beta Orionis, the brightest star in the constellation Orion; a bluish-white supergiant. Characteristics: apparent mag. +0.08; absolute mag. −7.0; spectral type B8; distance 600 light-years. △102, 134.

Rigging. △1678.

Rights of Man and of the Citizen, Declaration of the, proclamation of human liberties of the French Revolution (1789). It was adopted by the newly formed National Assembly to express the new spirit of liberty and equality in France. It was inspired by the US Declaration of Independence. Longer than its US counterpart, it further established the duty of each man to further personally his own political views. Drafted by Abbé Sieyès, it guaranteed rights of "liberty, property, security, and resistance to oppression," as well as freedom of speech and press.

Right to Privacy. △816, 918.

Right Whale, small-to-large whalebone whale with a huge head and stocky body. Slow and unsinkable when killed, right whales were the mainstay of the whaling industry and, thus, are near extinction. Length: 45–60ft (14–18m). Family Balaenidae. *See also* Whale. △552.

Rig Veda, one of the four sacred books of the Hindu religion, consisting of a collection of 1,017 prayers and hymns contained in 10 chapters. The hymns are generally directed to the gods of the forces of nature such as Indra, Agni, and Varuna. △962.

Riis, Jacob August (1849–1914), US journalist, author, and social activist, b. Ribe, Denmark. Riis decried the conditions of New York City's slums in newspaper articles and in books such as *How the Other Half Lives* (1890). He campaigned for child labor laws, housing codes, and other urban reforms. As a result of his efforts, many tenements were razed and replaced by modern building complexes.

Rijeka (Fiume), city in NW Yugoslavia, on Adriatic Sea and Gulf of Quarnero; largest seaport in Yugoslavia; site of Roman triumphal arch, naval base. Settled by Romans, it was held at various times by Franks, Croatian dukes, Austria-Hungary. Long disputed between Italy and Yugoslavia, it was annexed to Italy 1924, then to Yugoslavia 1947. Industries: shipbuilding, oil refining, engineering. Exports: ores, timber, cotton, tobacco, grain. Pop. 132,933.

Rijswijk (Ryswick), city in NW Netherlands; suburb of The Hague; Treaty of Ryswick was signed here Sept. 20, 1697, ending the War of the Grand Alliance; site of 14th-century church. Pop. 50,172.

Riley, James Whitcomb (1849–1916), US poet and journalist, b. Greenfield, Ind. After working at odd jobs, he became a newspaperman. During 1877–85, he was affiliated with the Indianapolis *Journal.* Many of his poems, which were sentimental and often in Indiana (Hoosier) dialect, first appeared there under the name "Benj. F. Johnson, of Boone." His verse was collected in *The Old Swimmin' Hole* and *'Leven More Poems* (1883) and other books. One of his best-known poems is "Little Orphant Annie" (1905).

Rilke, Rainer Maria (1875–1926), Austrian lyrical poet and translator. His first cycle of poems, *The Book of the Hours* (1905), was inspired by his visits to Russia. *New Poems* (1907–08) showed the influence of the French sculptor Auguste Rodin, whose secretary Rilke had been (1905–06). *Sonnets to Orpheus* (1923) demonstrated the poet's new affirmation of life. He also translated the works of several French authors.

Rimbaud, Arthur (1854–91), French poet. After an unhappy childhood, he lived with the poet Verlaine. They separated (1873) when Verlaine shot him. His prose-poem *A Season in Hell* (1873) appeared soon after, recording his disillusionment with life and art. He traveled in Europe and Africa, working as a gunrunner and merchant, and returned to France in 1891. Verlaine published a collection of Rimbaud's early poetry, *Les Illuminations,* in 1886.

Rimini, city in N Italy, 27mi (43km) ESE of Forlí, on the Adriatic. Founded by Umbrians, it was taken by Rome 286 BC; independent commune 12th century; passed to papal states 1509; site of Roman ruins including triumphal arch and bridge, the Malatesta temple (renovated 15th century). Industries: tourism, food products, wineries, textiles, pharmaceuticals, shipyards. Pop. 114,467.

Rimski-Korsakov, Nikolai (1844–1908), Russian composer and influential musical figure of the late 19th century. He was the leader of the "Russian Five," who were dedicated to promoting Russian nationalism in music. A master of orchestral color, he also taught and influenced Igor Stravinsky. He composed many operas including *The Snow Maiden* (1881) and *Le Coq d'Or* (1907). His most popular works are the orchestral pieces *Scheherazade* (1888), *Capriccio Espagnol* (1886), and the "Flight of the Bumblebee" from the opera *Tsar Saltan* (1900). △1246, 1364.

Rinehart, Mary Roberts (1876–1958), US novelist, b. Pittsburgh. She gained fame first as a mystery novelist and later as a correspondent in World War I. Her works include *The Circular Staircase* (1908), *The Man in Lower Ten* (1909), *The Amazing Adventures of Letitia Carberry* (1911), *Kings, Queens, and Pawns* (1915), and *The Altar of Freedom* (1917). She also wrote plays, including *The Breaking Point* (1923).

Ring Cyclotron. △1484.

Ring Eclipse. *See* Eclipse. △98.

Ringed Snake. *See* Grass Snake.

Ring Nebula in Lyra. △106.

Ring of the Nibelung, The (1848–74), cycle of four operas by Richard Wagner. Called a tetralogy by the composer—the first drama being a prelude to the other three—the entire cycle took more than 26 years to compose. The Ring was first performed as a whole in Bayreuth (1876), in Wagner's own theater. Based on ancient Scandinavian, Germanic, and Icelandic sagas, the four operas include *Das Rheingold* (first performance 1869), *Die Walküre* (1870), *Siegfried* (1876), and *Die Götterdammerung* (1876). Throughout, each principal character is identified by a *leitmotiv,* an individual theme. △1100.

Ring-tailed Cat. *See* Cacomistle.

Ring-tailed Monkey. *See* Capuchin.

Ringworm, an infection of the skin, hair, or nails caused by fungi and named for its growth pattern. It is a red eruption on the skin that spreads at the edges as it heals in the center, forming a ring of inflammation. If on the scalp, it is accompanied by burning, itching, and loss of hair. △724.

Rio de Janeiro, city in SE Brazil, on Guanabara Bay; capital of Guanabara state. Former capital of the country, it was settled by the Portuguese, later colonized by French, who were driven out by Mem de Sá, governor of Portuguese colony of Brazil; by 18th century it

James Whitcomb Riley

Rainer Maria Rilke

Arthur Rimbaud

Nikolai Rimski-Korsakov

had grown as the export center of all gold mined in the hinterlands. The 2nd-largest city in the country, it is the cultural hub of Brazil; contains a major port and scenic harbor; import-export and tourist center. Festive Mardi Gras is celebrated on Shrove Tuesday, the day before Lent begins. Founded 1504. Pop. 4,296,-782.

Rio Grande, river in S United States and N Mexico; rises in the San Juan Mts of SW Colorado; flows generally S through New Mexico, forming the border between New Mexico, Texas, and Mexico, continues to run between the border cities of Texas and Mexico, and empties into the Gulf of Mexico just E of Brownsville, Tex. Used for irrigation, hydroelectricity; subject of flood control projects; made international boundary in 1848 by the Treaty of Guadalupe Hidalgo. Length: approx. 1,885mi (3,035km).

Rio Muni, mainland province in Equatorial Guinea, bordered N by Cameroon, E and S by Gabon, and W by Atlantic Ocean; has mostly mountainous interior with fertile coastal lowland. Industries: lumbering, subsistence farming. Area: 10,040sq mi (26,004sq km). Pop. 203,000.

Rio Negro, river in South America; rises in E Colombia; flows E to Venezuela, S along Colombia-Venezuela boundary, into Brazil and the Amazon River. Length: approx. 1,400mi (2,254km).

Ripley, George (1802–80), US editor and social reformer, b. Greenfield, Mass. Both a Unitarian minister and a transcendentalist, he was founder and editor of the *Dial* (1840–44). He established, at West Roxbury, Mass., Brook Farm (1841–46), an experimental community. It was based on an agrarian-handicraft economy in which goods belonged to the community but private property and inheritance were not completely abolished. After the Brook Farm experiment ended in financial failure, he was literary critic of the *New York Tribune* (1849–1880) and helped found *Harpers New Monthly* magazine (1850). *See also* Brook Farm.

Rising Expectations, sociological theory stating that revolutions are most probable when political, economic, and social conditions begin to improve. Such improvements cause a rise in individual expectations, often creating an intolerable and frustrating disparity between aspirations and achievements. *See also* J-Curve. △1360.

Risorgimento, 19th-century Italian national unification movement culminating in the 1861 establishment of the kingdom of Italy. After Napoleon's defeat (1815), the Austrians regained control of Italy and initially were opposed by the Carbonari and Giuseppe Mazzini's Young Italy group. With the failed liberal and republican revolutions of 1848, the Piedmontese house of Savoy led the unification, ousting Austria (1859) and uniting most of Italy by 1861. The Risorgimento was completed with annexation of Venetia (1866) and papal Rome (1870). △1250.

Risso's Dolphin. *See* Grampus.

Rites of Passage, rites carried out at times of life crises. Such rites accompany an individual's passage from one social status to another and can be divided into three types or stages: rites of separation, marginal rites, and rites of aggregation. Rites of passage (such as marriage, initiation, or funerals) are characterized by ceremonials. *See also* Birth Rites. △830, 880.

Rittenhouse, David (1732–96), American astronomer, b. near Germantown, Pa. He constructed the first apparatus in the colonies for displaying planetary motions. He also built an observatory and transit telescope in the colonies. In 1785 he invented the collimating telescope. He was president of the Council of Safety (1777), Pennsylvania's first treasurer (1777–89), and first director of US Mint (1792–95). He was elected to the Royal Society (1795).

Ritual. △828–30.

River, natural stream of water of considerable volume and velocity, and larger than a brook or creek. By erosion of the underlying earth and/or rock, the water's flow becomes permanent or seasonal. △258.

Rivera, Diego (1886–1957), Mexican painter. Influenced by Cubism in his early work, he painted many oils, watercolors, and portraits. He is primarily known as a muralist. Characteristic of his style are carefully drawn, simplified, flat geometric forms in expressive colors. His murals at the Ministry of Education's Court of Labor in Mexico City reach three stories high and deal with Mexico's activities in industry, agriculture, and the arts. Often, he used symbolism and allegory in his murals to show Mexico's triumph over repression and his hope for a Marxist future.

Riverboat. △1676.

River Capture. △262.

River Engineering. △1762, 1764.

River Erosion. △262.

Rivers, Larry (1923–), US painter, b. New York City. His early works included naturalistic paintings of figures. After a period of abstract expressionism in the 1950s, he returned to a realistic portrayal of the human figure in a style that was a forerunner of pop art.

Riverside, city in S California, 10mi (16km) SSW of San Bernardino; seat of Riverside co; noted for its orange industry since 1873; site of University of California at Riverside (1907). Founded 1870; inc. 1883. Pop. (1970) 140,089.

Riveting. △1604.

Riviera, region in SE France and NW Italy, on Mediterranean Sea, extending 230mi (370km) from La Spezia, Italy and Hyères, France. Scenery and mild climate make it leading resort area of W Europe. Crops: olives, grapes, citrus fruits. Leading cities include Nice, Cannes, Menton, Antibes, and Monte Carlo, Monaco.

Riyadh (Ar-Riyad), city in E central Saudi Arabia, approx. 240mi (386km) inland from Persian Gulf; capital of Saudi Arabia; center of desert trade and travel; focal point of Wahabi movement; site of Riyadh University (1957), royal palace, several mosques. Chief industry is oil production. Pop. 225,000.

RNA. *See* Ribonucleic Acid.

Roach. *See* Cockroach.

Road Building. △1748.

Roanoke, formerly Big Lick; city in Virginia, 148mi (238km) SW of Richmond, on Roanoke River; area developed around Shenandoah Railroad (June 18, 1882); site of National Business College (1886), Virginia Southern College (1933), Virginia Western Community College (1966); industrial and railroad center. Industries: railroad cars, electrical equipment, rayon fabric, clothing, foundry products, tourism. Founded 1740; inc. 1884. Pop. (1970) 92,115.

Roanoke Island Colony, two settlement attempts made by Sir Walter Raleigh on an island off North Carolina. First settlers returned to England (1585–86), the second colony was found deserted (1591); those lost included Virginia Dare, first English child born in America. *See also* Raleigh, (Sir) Walter. △1216.

Roanoke River, river in S Virginia, formed by confluence of rivers in W Va., and flows SE across Blue Ridge Mts to Albemarle Sound in NE North Carolina. Flood control and hydroelectric projects are used on the river. Length: 410mi (660km).

Robalo. *See* Snook.

Robber Fly, gray to black fly to 1 in (25mm) or more in length, found worldwide. It is predaceous on other insects, often attacking those as large or larger than itself. Family Asilidae. *See also* Diptera.

Robbia, Luca della (1400?–82), Italian Florentine sculptor. He worked in bronze and marble, but his fame resulted chiefly from his numerous, glazed, terra-cotta half-length Madonnas, represented against a blue background. He was commissioned to execute many religious sculptures, such as his "Singing Gallery" in the Cathedral of Florence.

Robbins, Jerome (1918–), US choreographer, b. Jerome Rabinowitz in New York City. While associate artistic director for the New York City Ballet (1949–63), he formed and directed his own company, Ballets U.S.A. (1958). He choreographed *West Side Story* (1957) and *Fiddler on the Roof* (1964) and continues to create works for the New York City Ballet. △1368.

Robert, Earl of Gloucester. *See* Gloucester, Robert, Earl of.

Robert I (865?–923), king of the Franks. The brother of Eudes, he ruled the western Franks, at first accepting the succession of Carolingian Charles III the Simple when Eudes died (898). After fighting the Normans for several years in northern France, Robe[rt] gained considerable support and in 922 drov[e] Charles from the throne. Charles gathered an arm[y] and killed Robert in battle the following year. Robert's grandson, Hugh Capet, founded the Capetian dy[nasty].

Robert II (?970–1031), king of France (996–1031). He succeeded his father, Hugh Capet, in 996. H[e] repudiated his wife in 989 and became interested i[n] a relative, Bertha, wife of Eudes I, Count of Blois. The[y] were married after Eudes's death, and Robert wa[s] excommunicated (998). Separated (1001), he remar[ried], fathering four sons. He conquered Burgund[y] (1015) adding it to the French crown.

Robert I, or **Robert the Bruce** (1274–1329), king o[f] Scotland (1306–29). He swore fealty to Edward I o[f] England (1296) but joined the Scottish revolt agains[t] him in 1297. He murdered the Scottish nationalis[t] leader, John Comyn (1306), and was crowned king o[f] Scotland, but, defeated at Methven (1306) by th[e] English, he fled to Ireland. Returning (1307), he de[feated] the English at Loudon Hill and Bannockbur[n] (1314). After a short truce (1323–27), England recog[nized] Scotland's independence in the Treaty o[f] Northampton (1328).

Robert I Guiscard (*c.* 1015–85), also called Robe[rt] de Hauteville, Norman conqueror of southern Italy. He led invasions against Arabs and Byzantines in th[e] Mediterranean islands and southern Italy and estab[lished] his dominion in Calabria. By allying himself t[o] Pope Nicholas II and extending Norman power int[o] Sicily, he laid foundations for the future kingdom o[f] Sicily and French claims there.

Robert II (1054?–1134), also Robert Curthose, duk[e] of Normandy. He was the eldest son of William th[e] Conqueror. He was deprived of the English throne b[y] his brother, King William II; he became duke of Nor[mandy] (1087–1134). After a short war with Willian[m] (1089–94), Robert went on a crusade (1096–99). I[n] his absence William died, and his brother Henry be[came] King Henry I of England. After initial peace Henry invaded Normandy (1106) and took Rober[t] prisoner for life.

Roberts, Joseph Jenkins (1809–76), Liberia[n] statesman, b. Petersburg, Va. He migrated to Liberi[a] in 1829 where he became a merchant and aide t[o] Gov. Thomas H. Buchanan. When Buchanan died i[n] 1842, Roberts was first appointed his replacement and later (1847) elected Liberia's first president.

Robertson, Oscar (1938–), US basketball playe[r], b. Charlotte, Tenn. He was a three time All-America[n] at the University of Cincinnati (1958–60). He playe[d] for Cincinnati (1960–70) and Milwaukee (1970–74) in the National Basketball Association and set a rec[ord] for assists. He scored 28,620 career points.

Robeson, Paul (1898–1976), US actor and bas[s] singer, b. Princeton, N.J. Following graduation fro[m] Rutgers (1919) and Columbia University Law Scho[ol] (1923) he began acting with the Provincetown Play[ers]. He played the title role in Eugene O'Neill's *Em[peror] Jones* and Othello in Shakespeare's tragedy. H[e] was also a concert singer, best known for his renditio[ns] of spirituals. He won the Stalin Peace Prize in 1952 and his association with Communism led to ostracism in the United States. He lived abroad 1958–63.

Robespierre, Maximilien François Marie Isidor[e] de (1758–94), one of the leaders of the French Revo[lution]. He was elected to the newly formed Nationa[l] Assembly in 1789. There he helped form the ne[w] constitution, allied himself with the Jacobins, an[d] gained the support of the Parisian people, wh[o] named him an incorruptible patriot. He became in[volved] with the Paris commune, urged the executio[n] of King Louis XVI, and was elected to the Committe[e] of Public Safety in 1793. Here he supported the Reig[n] of Terror, in which thousands were executed, an[d] tried to establish a worship of Reason. Partly in re[venge] for his past executions, he was himself guillo[tined] in the Thermidorean Reaction of July 1794. △1224.

Robin, thrush found throughout most of North Ame[r]ica. It has a reddish breast, black and white stripe[d] throat, and blackish head; length: 10in (25cm). Spe[cies] *Turdus migratorius.* The European robin *(Er[i]thacus rubecula)* is a warbler and has a yellowish-re[d] breast; length: 6in (15cm). The American robin build[s] a cup-shaped nest; the European robin nests in tre[e] holes and other cavities. Family Turdidae.

Robin Hood, legendary English folk hero generall[y] portrayed as a benevolent outlaw of Sherwood Fores[t] whose traditional adversary was the Sheriff of Notting[ham]

ham. Many attempts have been made to establish his authenticity, the most popular placing him in Richard I's reign (1189–99). Another attempt sets him in the 13th century as an ex-follower of Simon de Montfort. His exploits have been chronicled in books and films.

Robinson, Edwin Arlington (1869–1935), US poet. b. Head Tide, Me. When a child his family moved to Gardiner, Me., which became the Tilbury Town of his poetry. His first volume of poetry, *The Children of the Night*, was published in 1897. In 1904 Pres. Theodore Roosevelt appointed him to a clerkship in the N.Y. Custom House. Upon publication of *The Town down the River* (1910), Robinson left this job and gained financial security with *The Man against the Sky* (1916) and *The Three Taverns* (1920). In simple, realistic, but intellectual verse, Robinson analyzed people and the motivations that moved them to succeed or fail. He was awarded the Pulitzer Prize in 1921, 1924, and 1927.

Robinson, Frank (1935–), US baseball player, b. Beaumont, Tex. He became major league baseball's first black manager (Cleveland Indians, 1975). As a player he had hit over 500 home runs in a career that began in 1956 with the Cincinnati Reds.

Robinson, Jack Roosevelt ("Jackie") (1919–1972), US baseball player, b. Cairo, Ga. Signed by the Brooklyn Dodgers in 1947 after a year in the International League, he was the first black to play in the major leagues. He had a batting average of .311 during his career (1947–56). In 1962 he became the first black elected to the Baseball Hall of Fame.

Robinson, Ray Charles. *See* Charles, Ray.

Robinson, Sugar Ray (1921–), US boxer, b. Walker Smith in Detroit. He held the world's welterweight title (1946–51) and the middleweight title (1951–52; 1955–57; 1958–60). He was elected to the Boxing Hall of Fame in 1967.

Robinson Crusoe (1719), novel by Daniel Defoe. It purports to tell the true story of a man shipwrecked on a desert island. With industry and ingenuity this man salvages materials from the ship, builds homes, sows crops, makes clothes, and domesticates animals. He also rescues and befriends Friday, a savage, before they are themselves rescued. △1184.

Robinson-Patman Act (1936), US legislation amending section 2 of the 1914 Clayton Act, which made certain kinds of price discrimination illegal. However, the courts had difficulty interpreting the intent of section 2. Thus the 1936 amendment tries to clarify what Congress means by "illegal price discrimination." However, the clarification itself has been difficult to interpret. Critics of the Robinson-Patman Act say it has been used to protect inefficient small competitors while failing to preserve market (price) competition.

Robot, an instrumented mechanism used in science or industry to take the place of a human being. It may resemble a human and perform in a human way the tasks set it. But frequently it does not and the line separating a robot from other automated machinery is not always distinct. Sophisticated, individualized machines are most likely to be classed "robots." The word was first used in *R.U.R.*, a play (1921) by Karel Capek. △1670.

Rob Roy (1671–1734), Scots freebooter, whose reputation is enhanced in Sir Walter Scott's novel *Rob Roy* (1818). A Macgregor, he assumed the name of Campbell and held territory between the Montrose and Argyll estates. He took advantage of their rivalry and the Jacobite Rebellion (1715) to further his cattle-stealing and brigandage. Sentenced to transportation (1727), he was finally pardoned.

Rochambeau, Jean Baptiste Donatien de Vimeur, Comte de (1725–1807), French military commander. He served in the French cavalry in his youth and was promoted to brigadier of infantry (1761) after the Minorca expedition. After several conflicts he led a French force in the American Revolution, aiding the Marquis de Lafayette and George Washington in the defeat of Lord Cornwallis at Yorktown. He was made governor of Picardy as a reward. He also fought during the French Revolution, but resigned in 1792.

Roche, Kevin (1922–), US architect, b. Dublin, Ireland. Following studies in Ireland, England, and Chicago, Ill., he joined Saarinen, Saarinen and Associates (1950), and completed such projects as the General Motors Technical Center (Warren, Mich. 1951–57), Dulles International Airport Terminal (Washington, D.C., 1961–62), and the CBS Headquarters Building (New York, 1962). In his later work, such as the Knights of Columbus Building (New Haven, Ct., 1968–71), function is subordinate to the form of basic geometric shapes.

Rochester, city in SE Minnesota, 70mi (113km) SSE of St Paul; seat of Olmsted co, site of Mayo Clinic, founded by Dr. W. W. Mayo and his sons Drs. William J. and Charles H. Mayo in 1889; and Rochester Junior College (1915). Industries: hospital supplies, data processing machines, dairy products. Settled 1854; inc. 1858. Pop. (1970) 53,766.

Rochester, city and port of entry in W New York, 70mi (113km) ENE of Buffalo on Lake Ontario and Genesee River; seat of Monroe co. First permanent settlement was made 1812; industrial growth was spurred by Erie Canal through Rochester (1823); a center of abolitionist movement during Civil War; specialized industries developed between 1850–1900, including Eastman Kodak (est. 1888). Landmarks are St Luke's Episcopal Church (1824), Rochester Institute of Technology (1829), University of Rochester (1850). Industries: cameras, photographic films and supplies, office equipment, food processing, clothing. Inc. 1817 as village, 1834 as city. Pop. (1970) 296,233.

Rock, solid material that comprises the Earth's crust. Although solid, it is not necessarily hard, as clay or volcanic ash are also considered to be rock. It can be composed of a single mineral or can be a compound of several. Rocks are classified by origin into three major groups: (1) Igneous rocks are those formed by the cooling and solidification of molten material from the earth's interior. Volcanic lava and granite are igneous rocks. (2) Sedimentary rocks are formed from older rock that has been transported from its original position by water, glacier, or the atmosphere, and consolidated again into rock. Limestone and sandstone are sedimentary rocks. (3) Metamorphic rocks originate from igneous or sedimentary rocks, but have been changed in texture or mineral content or both by extreme pressure and heat deep within the earth. Marble, derived from limestone, is a metamorphic rock. △242, 246–48, 270–74.

Rock Cycle. △246, 272–274.

Rockefeller, John Davison (1839–1937), US industrialist and philanthropist, b. Richford, N.Y. In 1863, following the drilling of the first US oil well, Rockefeller, with Samuel Andrews and Maurice B. Clark, started an oil refining business. Two years later his brother, William, established a second refinery, and the two firms were consolidated into a joint stock company (1870), Standard Oil of Ohio. With mergers, rebates, and other devices the Standard Oil trust was organized (1882). It soon controlled over 90% of the oil business. In 1892 the Ohio Supreme Court declared the trust in violation of the Sherman Antitrust Act and it was dissolved. It was replaced by a holding company, Standard Oil of New Jersey, and in 1911 the US Supreme Court declared this illegal. When he retired he devoted his attention to charitable corporations, to which his donations amounted to about $500,000,000. His philanthropic work includes the endowment of the University of Chicago (1892), the Rockefeller Institute for Medical Research (1901), and the Rockefeller Foundation (1913). His grandsons included Nelson Rockefeller. △1278.

Rockefeller, Nelson Aldrich (1908–), US vice president and New York governor, b. Bar Harbor, Me. A member of the wealthy Rockefeller family, he held a number of appointive government posts before being elected governor in 1958 as a Republican. He was re-elected three times (1962, 1966, 1970) before resigning in 1973. In 1974, President Gerald Ford picked him to fill the vacant office of vice president. He was an unsuccessful contender for the Republican presidential nomination in 1960, 1964, and 1968. In 1975 he announced that he would not run for election as vice president in 1976.

Rock Engraving. △950, 1214.

Rocket, missile or craft powered by a rocket engine. First mentioned in accounts of 13th-century battles involving Chinese, Mongols, and Arabs. Major applications are military (projectiles and ballistic missiles) and scientific (spacecraft and satellite launchers). Developers of modern rockets include Konstantin Tsiolkovsky (USSR), Hermann Oberth (Germany), and Robert Goddard (United States). △142, 1722.

Rocket Engine, reaction engine carrying its own supply of both fuel and oxidizer, as distinguished from the jet engine, which obtains oxidizer from the surrounding atmosphere. Chemical rocket engines are powered by solid or liquid propellants that are burned

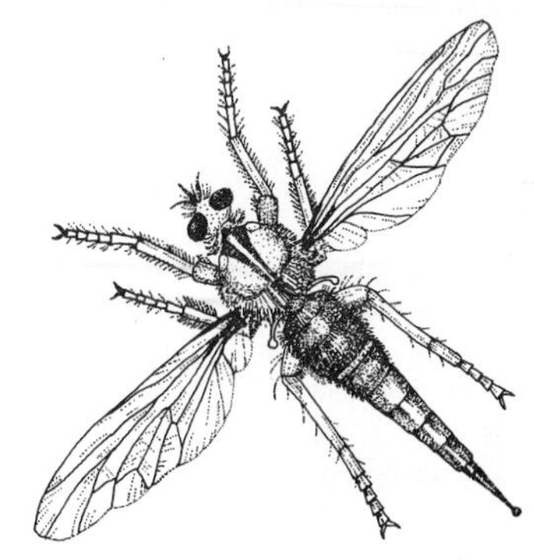

Robber fly

Maximilien Robespierre

Robin

John D. Rockefeller

in a combustion chamber and expelled at supersonic velocities from the exhaust nozzle. Nuclear engines heat fuel by radiation from reactor cores. Ion engines use thermoelectric power to expel ions rather than gases. △1722.

Rockfish. *See* Scorpion Fish.

Rockford, city in N Illinois, on Rock River near Wisconsin line; seat of Winnebago co; 2nd-largest city in state; site of Rockford College (1847), Rock Valley College (1964), and noteworthy clock museum. Industries: machine tools, air conditioning and heating equipment, textiles, hardware. Founded 1834 on Black Hawk War battlefield; inc. 1839. Pop. (1970) 147,370.

Rock Hill, city in N South Carolina, 64mi (103km) N of Columbia; site of Winthrop College (1886). Industries: agriculture, textiles, wood products, hosiery, truck bodies. Settled 1852; inc. 1870. Pop. (1970) 33,846.

Rock Island, city in NW Illinois, W of Chicago, on Mississippi and Rock rivers; seat of Rock Island co; with Davenport, East Moline, and Moline it comprises Quad Cities; site of US Rock Island Arsenal on the island in Mississippi for which the city is named (1862); fortified by British in War of 1812 and United States in 1816. Industries: farm equipment, aluminum, rubber footwear. Settled 1826; inc. 1841. Pop. (1970) 50,166.

Rock Music, form of US popular music, which developed in the 1960s out of the "rock 'n' roll" of the 1950s. It features a steady "beat," intense vocals about love, accompaniment by guitars, and a small group of musicians rather than a whole band. It achieved great popularity, especially with young people, when the English singing group The Beatles began to be heard in 1963. △1366.

Rockne, Knute (Kenneth) (1888–1931), US football coach, b. Norway. Known as a brilliant strategist, he scored a sensational upset with Notre Dame teammate Gus Dorais over highly favored Army by employing the legal but unused forward pass for the first time (1913). As Notre Dame head coach (1918–31), he established the school as a power house. His 105–12–5 record included five undefeated, untied seasons.

Rock River, river in S Wisconsin and N Illinois, rises in SE Wisconsin, flows S and SW across NW Illinois to Mississippi River near Rock Island. Statue of Black Hawk by Lorado Taft stands on bluff above river near Oregon, Ill. Length: 285mi (459km).

Rockville, city in W central Maryland; seat of Montgomery co; site of junior college and scientific research laboratories. Inc. 1860. Pop. (1970) 41,564.

Rockville Centre, residential village in SE New York, on Long Island, 19mi (31km) ESE of New York City. Hempstead Lake State Park adjoins village; site of Molloy Catholic College for Women (1955). Inc. 1893. Pop. (1970) 27,444.

Rockweed, or wrack, coarse brown seaweeds (especially *Fucus* or *Ascophyllum*) growing on rocks, attached by rootlike holdfasts. *See also* Brown Algae. △432.

Rockwell Hardness Test, a method of measuring the hardness of a metal or alloy using an apparatus with a diamond-pointed cone. The cone is pressed into the metal to a standard depth. Resistance to penetration is automatically indicated by a calibrated dial.

Rocky Mount, city in NE North Carolina; site of North Carolina Wesleyan College (1956). Industries: cottonseed oil, textiles, lumber, fertilizer, packing plants. Founded 1818; inc. as town 1867, as city 1907. Pop. (1970) 34,284.

Rocky Mountain National Park, park in central Colorado, noted for its outstanding scenery. Trail Ridge Road features sightseeing on the Continental Divide. More than 107 peaks have heights in excess of 11,000ft (3,355m). The park abounds in wildlife and wildflowers. Area: 262,191acres (106,187hectares). Est. 1915.

Rocky Mountains, major mountain system in W North America, extends from Mexico to the Bering Strait, N of Arctic Circle. They form the Continental Divide, which separates rivers draining to the Atlantic and Arctic oceans from those draining to the Pacific Ocean; geologically formed as a series of pulses over millions of years. Highest point is Mt Elbert in Colorado, 14,431ft (4,401m). Length: approx. 3,000mi (4,830km).

Rocky Mountain Sheep. *See* Bighorn Sheep.

Rocky Mountain Spotted Fever, an infectious disease caused by a rickettsia and transmitted by a wood tick that lives on cattle, sheep, and rodents in addition to man. Symptoms are similar to typhus with rose-colored spots on the body.

Rococo, originally a demeaning expression for 18th-century decorative art but now used objectively by art historians. The style is colorful, fragile, pastoral, with trivial subject matter. It developed in four phases: late Louis XIV; Regency; early-middle Louis XV, the style Pompadour; and late Louis XV. Antoine Lepautre's chapel at Versailles and the paintings of Jean Watteau and François Boucher are examples. △1190.

Rodchenko, Aleksandr (1891–1956), Russian painter, sculptor, and designer. Influenced by K. S. Malevich, he turned from the futurist style of his early works to a completely abstract style, in which he used a ruler and compass to create geometric forms. In his later work, he used metals and wood in abstract three-dimensional compositions, such as mobiles, and he became a leading artist in the constructivist movement. △1320.

Rodent, any member of the vast mammalian order Rodentia, characterized by a pair of gnawing incisor teeth in both the upper and lower jaws. Numbering close to 2,000 species, rodents live all over the world. They may live underground (moles), on the ground (mice), in trees (squirrels), or in water (beavers). Most rodents are small and lightweight, but one species, the South American capybara, weighs up to 110lb (50kg).

The distinctive incisor teeth continue to grow as long as the animal lives. Because the soft inner layer is ground down faster than the hard outer layer, rodent incisors are chisel-shaped and sharpened by use. Most rodents are herbivorous, but some are omnivorous. Some, like chinchillas, are valuable for their fur. Some, like guinea pigs, are important scientific tools. Some rats and mice are pests that carry disease and destroy property. Because there are so many of them, rodents are a major factor in the ecology of the world. △546.

Rodeo, a sport that features calf roping, steer wrestling, bronco riding, and Brahma bull riding. Other events may include bulldogging, bareback riding, quarterhorse cutting, team roping, barrel racing, and greased-pig chasing. Most popular is saddle-bronco riding. In this event a rider carries a rope rein in his hand and uses it to get the animal to buck. Minimum time aboard the horse to qualify for prize money is eight seconds. The rodeo developed in the cattle-raising industry in the W United States in the early 1880s. The Rodeo Cowboys Association controls events for men, and the women's aspect of the sport is governed by the Girls' Rodeo Association. △1410.

Rodgers, Richard (Charles) (1902–), US composer of Broadway musicals, b. New York City. He teamed first with Lorenz Hart and then with Oscar Hammerstein II in a long series of successful musicals including: *Oklahoma!* (1943), *Carousel* (1945), *South Pacific* (1949), *The King and I* (1951), and *Sound of Music* (1959).

Rodin, Auguste (1840–1917), French sculptor and painter. In his early decorative style, he painted landscapes, made reliefs of mythological figures, and sculpted busts and small figurines. He visited Rome, where he was influenced by Michelangelo's work. His first major work, "The Age of Bronze" (1876) was so realistic that he was accused of having cast it from a living figure. Many of Rodin's most famous sculptures, such as "The Thinker" (1880) and "The Kiss" (1886), are taken from his huge "Gates of Hell" design, a maze of twisted, tortured figures. Characteristic of his Romantic style was his interest in movement and his use of modeling to express the intensity of the subject's personality.

Rods and Cones, in Anatomy. △674.

Roe Deer, small agile Eurasian deer frequently found among dense human populations. It has short, erect antlers. The gestation period is almost one year, with the fertilized egg dormant for over four months. Height: to 31in (79cm) at shoulder. Family Cervidae; species *Capreolus capreolus*. *See also* Deer.

Roemer, Olaus. △1522.

Roentgen or Röntgen, Wilhelm Konrad (1845–1923), German physicist. In 1895, while at Würzburg, he discovered X rays, which led to modern physics and medical diagnostic practices. He was awarded the first Nobel Prize for physics (in 1901), and X radiation is also known as Röntgen radiation. His work was also concerned with specific heats of gases, fluid capillary action, and elasticity.

Roentgen, unit (symbol R) used to measure the X rays or gamma rays to which a body is exposed (exposure dose). One roentgen causes sufficient ionization to produce a total electric charge of 2.58×10^{-4} coulomb on all the positive (or negative) ions in one kilogram of air, all the electrons released being stopped. Named for Wilhelm K. Roentgen, discoverer of X rays.

Roethke, Theodore (1908–63), US poet, b. Saginaw, Mich. His first book of verse appeared in 1941. He taught English and published other collections of poetry, including *The Waking: Poems 1933–53*, (1953), for which he won both a Pulitzer Prize and National Book Award.

Roger II (1095–1154), son of Roger I Guiscard and count (1101–30) and king (1130–54) of Sicily. Acknowledged as duke of Calabria (1122) and Apulia (1127), he thus united Norman holdings in Italy and Sicily. In 1130 anti-Pope Anacletus II crowned him king of Sicily; and after 1139, with recognition from Pope Innocent II, he aquired the lands that for seven centuries would constitute the kingdoms of Sicily and Naples (the two Sicilies).

Rogers, Carl R(ansom) (1902–), US psychologist and psychotherapist, b. Oak Park, Ill. He was the founder of client-centered psychotherapy. He has been a leader in making psychologists more aware of the individual's subjective point of view, both in personality theory and in clinical treatment and counseling. His emphasis on the capacity of individuals to self-actualize their own potentials and solve their own problems has made him a pivotal figure in the modern humanistic movement in psychology. His major publications include *Client Centered Therapy* (1951) and *On Becoming a Person* (1961). △774.

Rogers, Will(iam Penn Adair) (1879–1935), US humorist, b. Oologah, Okla. Remembered for his trick roping and his good-natured social criticisms, he worked in vaudeville, films, and radio, and wrote several books and a syndicated newspaper column. He died in an airplane crash in Alaska.

Rogue River, river in SW Oregon; rises in Cascade Range, N of Crater Lake; flows S and W across Coast Range to Pacific Ocean at Gold Beach. Length: 200mi (322km).

Role, in social science, the way a person usually behaves in a given situation. One individual may take several roles. Feminists point out that a woman may be expected to be housekeeper, cook, mother, counselor, and sex object. Acquiring some roles is central to the process of socialization. From families, friends, teachers, and other sources most people learn roles that are considered appropriate for the society they live in. *See also* Internalization; Role Conflict; Role Model; Socialization; Status. △790, 888, 892.

Role Acquisition. *See* Internalization; Role; Socialization.

Role Conflict, in social science, problems that develop when a person's roles clash with each other or when some of his values are incompatible with one of his roles. A politician may find that some of his constituents want him to play the role of guardian of the budget while others expect him to be a spender for public works. If forced to choose one role at the expense of the other, he may face an internal conflict.

Role Model, in social science, a person whom others copy when they are acquiring their attitudes and ways of behaving. A girl may take her mother as a model, or she may learn a role by observing and emulating a singer or a writer or a business executive. *See also* Role. △790.

Rolfe, John (1585–1622), English colonist. He was the first colonist to cultivate tobacco in the Jamestown Colony. He married Pocahontas (1614), and went to England where she died. He returned to Virginia as member of the colony council (1617). *See also* Jamestown Colony; Pocahontas.

Rolland, Romain (1866–1944), French novelist, biographer, and dramatist. Although chiefly remembered for his novel *Jean Christophe* (10 vols., 1904–12) he wrote many biographies including *Beethoven* (1903), *Tolstoy* (1911), and *Mahatma Gandhi* (1926). He was awarded the Nobel Prize in literature for 1915.

Roller Skating, recreation and sport. It consists of

gliding on a smooth surface on skates with wheels that are cushioned by ball bearings. The sport first gained popularity in the early 20th century and, aside from a recreational use, has several competitive forms. Much like its counterpart, ice skating, there are events in figure and dance skating, speed skating, and roller derby (a team sport) and roller hockey. Except for speed skating, which uses oval outdoor tracks, most skating is an indoor activity. As a competitive sport it is most popular with adults. Children generally skate outdoors on steel skates that are attached to the shoe. The sport is popular in many countries, and in the United States there are over 4,000 rinks. Roller skating was first proposed as an Olympic event in 1907, but the request has continuously been rejected.

Rolling, Metal, the most widely used method of shaping metal, hot or cold. It consists of passing the material between revolving rolls. Hot rolling is most common and involves reducing the heated metal to thinner and thinner cross-section (as from ingot to sheet). Cold rolling is used on relatively soft metals to develop new mechanical properties.

Roman Art, the art of ancient Rome. Prior to 400 BC Roman art was largely Etruscan art in the form of tomb decorations. After that Roman art became a welding of Etruscan with Greek influences. Roman painting was largely decorative, consisting of large murals embellishing buildings. In sculpture, the Romans excelled in portrait busts. In architecture the Romans made many notable contributions, most conspicuously the invention of the dome, first exemplified in AD 124 in the erection of the Pantheon in Rome—perhaps the parent of all later domes. △ 1022–24.

Roman Catholic Church, Christian denomination claiming the pope in Rome as the visible head and authority in church affairs. Christ is the invisible head of the church, with the members composing its body. It is founded in tradition, claiming to be one, holy, catholic, and apostolic. The apostle Peter is considered the first pope. The pope, imperfect himself, cannot lead the church into doctrinal error. This is the doctrine of papal infallibility. The pope governs the church through the Roman Curia. It is a hierarchical system of government; the clergy, consisting of bishops, priests, and deacons, are clearly distinguished from other Catholics, the laity. There are seven sacraments that convey grace. There are devotions to the saints, such as novenas. The Mass is the central act of worship in the church, and the focus of its liturgical life. Weekly attendance is required of all members. Religious education is of primary importance. Missionary activity has continued throughout the world. *See also* Pope. △1086, 1154.

Romance Languages, the languages that evolved out of Latin, the language of the Roman Empire. The major Romance languages are Italian, French, Spanish, Portuguese, and Romanian. Others include Catalan, Provençal, and Rhaeto-Romanic. The Romance languages are related to the Germanic, Slavic, Iranian, Indic, and other languages, all of them belonging to the Indo-European family. △866.

Roman de la Rose, an Old French romance of the 13th-century written by Guillaume de Lorris and Jean de Meun. Guillaume began the poem *c.*1230 as an allegory of the progress of a courtly lover. The main narrative, in which the hero dreams of a beautiful garden where he falls in love with a rosebud he sees reflected in a pool, breaks off after 4,000 lines. When Jean continued it *c.* 1275, more than a generation later, he mocked the values of the first half and instead saw love as a means of continuing the species. △1100.

Roman Empire. *See* Rome, Ancient.

Romanesque Architecture, architectural style found throughout Western Europe *c.* 1000 and consisting of a variety of closely related regional styles. Northern Romanesque churches are characterized by the round arch; staggered apse at the east end; radiating chapels along the sides; square bays in the nave, transept, and chancel; vaulted ceilings; and buttressed walls. Regional differences vary the western facade of these churches. Two towers plus a tower over the crossing are found in England and Normandy, a screen facade with no tower is characteristic of southern France, and many towers on both east and west facades can be seen in Germany. △1080–82.

Romanesque Art. △1080–82.

Romania, independent nation in SE Europe. A socialist republic, it has developed economic and political policies increasingly independent of the USSR.

Land and economy. A Balkan state in SE Europe, its S border is the lower course of the Danube River. It extends on either side of the Carpathian and Transylvanian alps which, together with the Balkan Mts, serve as natural barriers. It is bounded by the Black Sea (E), USSR (N and E), Bulgaria (S), Yugoslavia (SW), and Hungary (NW). There are three principal seasons: a severe winter, a brief spring, and a hot summer. Patterned on the centralized and nationalized communist system, Romania, with abundant natural resources, has developed an industrialized economy that accounts for half of its gross national product (GNP). About 40% of the labor force is in agriculture, and farms and forests contribute 29% of the GNP. State farms and cooperatives maintain 96.4% of the arable land.

People. A Roman colony in the first and second centuries, Romanians trace their lineage back to French, Spanish, and Italian ancestry and consider themselves of Latin origin in contrast to their Magyar and Slavic neighbors. Both the Romanian language and culture contain some Slavic and German elements. Principal minorities are Hungarians, Germans, and Jews. The 28% minority population before WWII was decreased by USSR annexation of several provinces and by postwar expulsion of Germans. Religious choice follows ethnic lines; 80% belongs to the Romanian Orthodox Church. Literacy is over 90%.

Government. Governed by a centralized executive appointed by the legislative branch, power lies in the leadership of the Romanian Communist party.

History. From 400 BC, when it was colonized by the Dacians, Romania had a turbulent history. The principalities of Walachia and Moldavia emerged in the Middle Ages, and the Ottoman Empire exerted considerable influence from the 15th century. From 1829–56 the principalities were under Russian protection; independence was assumed gradually. Carol I became king in 1866, and Romania proclaimed itself independent in 1881. Fighting with the Allies in WWI, Romania gained new territory after the war and became an ally of France and a member of the Little and Balkan ententes. In the 1930s the anti-Semitic, anti-Soviet Fascist Iron Guard brought Romania into WWII on the Axis side. Romania's surrender in 1944 was followed by Russian occupation in 1945 and the establishment of a Communist regime. The king abdicated in 1947 when a Romanian People's Republic was declared. Gheorghe Gheorgiu-Dej, the long-time head of the Communist party, died in 1965. He was succeeded by Nicolae Ceausescu, who broadened Romania's contacts with the West and cautiously liberalized the government.

PROFILE

Official name: Socialist Republic of Romania
Area: 91,700sq mi (237,503sq km)
Population: 21,210,000
Density: 231per sq mi (89per sq km)
Chief cities: Bucharest (capital); Cluj
Government: Communist
Religion: Romanian Orthodox (major)
Language: Romanian
Monetary unit: Leu
Gross national product: $31,000,000,000
Per capita income: $1,450
Industries: iron and steel, machinery, oil products, chemicals, building materials, footwear, food processing, textiles
Agriculture: forests, corn, wheat, sugar beets, grapes, fruits, sheep, hogs, cattle
Minerals: oil, natural gas, coal, salt, bauxite, manganese, lead, zinc, gold, silver
Trading partners: USSR, W Europe, Czechoslovakia

Romanian, the official language of Romania, spoken by about 18,000,000 people, or about 90% of the country's population. It is a Romance language, having descended from the Latin that was introduced into the area when it was conquered by the Romans in the second century AD. Originally written in Cyrillic characters, Romanian has used the Latin (Roman) alphabet since 1860.

Roman Law, legal system developed by the ancient Romans. The law of twelve tables (450 BC) applied only to Rome proper. In the 3rd century BC *jus gentium* was added. This was the law applied in dealing with a foreigner, which embodied the highly developed commercial law of the Greek city-states. After the establishment of the Roman Empire, law was enacted by imperial edicts, senate legislation, and judicial officers, growing in complexity and confusion until the codification of Justinian (*c.* 529–34) made Roman law the source of legal knowledge for centuries. It became the basis of Germanic law, and during the Renaissance it spread throughout the world as modern civil law, influencing development of English common law. *Jus gentium* became the basis for commercial law. *See also* Civil Law; Commercial Law; Law; Twelve Tables. △908.

Rocky Mountain National Park

Auguste Rodin: sculpture

Will Rogers and son

Poland
Union of Soviet Socialist Republics
Czechoslovakia
Hungary
Iași
Cluj
ROMANIA
Galati
Timișoara
Ploiești
Constanța
Bucharest
(București)
BLACK SEA
Yugoslavia
Bulgaria
Albania
Turkey
Greece
IONIAN SEA
0
400km

Romania

Roman Mythology. The Romans did not develop a true hierarchical pantheon of gods even as they acquired the deities of their conquered enemies, but rather paid homage to a catalog of powers. With formal rites and sacrifice, they paid or withheld payment to each of their heavenly protectors as occasion demanded. The legends of the Greeks, which strongly influenced Roman mythology as early as the 8th century BC, involved gods of more capricious nature.

Roman Numeral, any of the letters, or their variants, used originally in the counting system of the Romans. Numbers are formed, by simple rules, from combinations of the letters I (one), V (five), X (ten), L (50), C (100), D (500), and M (1000). Zero was an unknown notion, as were multiplication and division. *See also* Numeral. △1448.

Romano, Giulio. △1142.

Romanov, House of, the Russian imperial family from 1613 until the March 1917 revolution. The first tsar, **Michael** (1596–1645), was elected by a general assembly at the end of the Time of Troubles. Male primogeniture operated until **Peter the Great** (1672–1725) established the principle of a choice of successor by the ruling monarch (1722). **Paul I** (1754–1801), however, restored the earlier system (1797). **Nicholas II** (1868–1918), the last tsar, abdicated (1917) and was executed after the Bolshevik seizure of power. △1178, 1286.

Romans, New Testament epistle written by apostle Paul in Corinth *c.*56. He had never been to Rome when he wrote his letter to discuss difficulties existing between Jewish and Gentile members of the Roman church. It shows his pastoral concern for the young churches and states that Christ offers a new life for man.

Romansch. *See* Rhaeto-Romanic.

Romanticism in Architecture, architectural movement of the late 18th and 19th centuries of many different tendencies, united by a common reaction against the supposed artificiality and irrationality of the Baroque. It includes the archeologically inspired Neoclassicism of the late 18th century, as well as the Gothic revival, the revival of medieval forms, and the picturesque cultivation of rustic motifs.

Romanticism in Art, the chief movement in painting and sculpture in the 19th century. As in literature and music, Romanticism stressed the importance of the senses, the emotions, and nature over rationalism and classical forms. Thus, emotional and spiritual themes were emphasized, while subject matter was often drawn from simpler, even everyday ways of living, rather than from religious history or myth. These romantic trends are perhaps best exemplified by landscape painting of the period. Romantic elements are present in the arts of all periods, but reached their height in the 19th century in the works of such artists as Turner, Constable, Whistler, Gericault, Delacroix, Corot, and Friedrich. △1228, 1242.

Romanticism in Literature. △1222.

Romanticism in Music, music composed from roughly 1820 to 1920. Romanticism in music refers to preferences for subjectivity, fantasy, emotionality, and theatricality over the formal or intellectual aspects of music, sometimes at the expense of sound musical structure. Early Romanticism (*c.* 1820–50) began with the late works of Beethoven and Schubert, followed by Weber, Berlioz, Mendelssohn, Schumann, Chopin, and Rossini. Here the forms of the Classical Period were predominant, but with greater emotional intensity. Middle Romanticism (*c.* 1850–90) is represented by Liszt, Franck, Wagner, Bruckner, Smetana, Verdi, Brahms, Tchaikovsky, Dvorak, and Mussorgsky. Here the symphonic poem emerged as a distinct form and nationalistic trends were very evident as serious composers adopted styles of music from their native folk music. Late Romanticism (*c.* 1890–1920) is represented by Elgar, Mahler, Rachmaninoff, R. Strauss, Nielsen, Sibelius, Reger, Holst, and Vaughan-Williams. They enlarged the symphony orchestra and wrote Romantic music more complex than their predecessors'. Romanticism has continued into contemporary music in the works of such composers as Barber and Shostakovitch. *See also* the above composers; Classical Music. △1246.

Romany, the language of the gypsies. It is an Indic language, related to Sanskrit and Hindi, and is known to have originated in India. The gypsies are thought to have begun their migration westward about AD 1000.

Rome (Roma), capital city of Italy, in central Italy, on both sides of the Tiber River; capital of Latium region and Roma prov. Hill settlements combined to form one city 8th century BC; it was traditionally founded by Romulus 735 BC, and was an Etruscan city-kingdom to 6th century BC. The Roman Republic was founded *c.* 500 BC; by the 3rd century BC, Rome ruled most of Italy and began overseas expansion. Julius Caesar ruled 46–44 BC; Roman Empire was founded 30 BC with defeat of Marc Antony by Octavian, who reigned as the emperor Augustus 27 BC–AD 14. Rome was capital of Roman Empire until 330 AD, when Constantinople was named capital. Rome was the medieval spiritual center of Western World; capital of Papal States, which were annexed to France by Napoleon 1809; inc. into Kingdom of Italy 1870; liberated by Allied troops June 4, 1944. It is site of Vatican City, the autonomous papal see housing fine museums and libraries. Roman remains include the Colosseum, catacombs, Forum; five basilicas, including St Peter's and St John Lateran; notable churches, many palaces, including the Farnese (16th century), and villas; site of University of Rome (1303); scene of 1960 Summer Olympics. Industries: tourism, motion pictures, fashion, metallurgy. Pop. 2,798,872. △1010–1030, 1140. *See also* Rome, Ancient; Romulus and Remus.

Rome, city in NW Georgia, 55mi (89km) NW of Atlanta; grain and livestock region. Occupied by Union troops 1864. Founded 1835; inc. 1847. Pop. (1970) 30,759.

Rome, city in central New York, on Mohawk River; seat of Oneida co. Fort Stanwix, on site of present city, was important defense point for colonials during American Revolution. Industries: copper, brass, machine tools, cables, paint. Founded 1786 as Lynchville on Fort Stanwix site; inc. as village of Rome 1819, as city 1870. Pop. (1970) 50,148.

Rome, Ancient. The earliest Roman settlement was built in the 8th century BC according to legend by Romulus and Remus in 753, on the Palatine, the central hill of the seven hills of Rome on the east bank of the Tiber. The Tiber separated the Etruscans from the Latins (of the plain of Latium) and the Sabines and Samnites to the north. The Etruscans affected Rome's culture through the influence of the two Etruscan kings of Rome, Tarquinius Priscus and Tarquinius Superbus. By 500 BC the Romans had rid themselves of Etruscan rule and developed a stable republic that was to endure for four centuries. It was at first governed by patricians, the upper class elite, with two consuls elected by and representing the plebeians, or main body of the population. The plebeians fought a long, bitter struggle for political equality, which they gained by the 3rd century BC. They elected powerful tribunes who came to hold the right of veto over the resolutions of the senate, which enacted legislation and determined policy. The first major code of law, known as the Twelve Tables, was set down in writing by plebeian demand c.450 BC and became the basis of later legislation. The plebeians convened in three comitia, assemblies that gained power from the patricians. Magistrates designated quaestors, aediles, praetors, and censors took up the increasingly complicated business of running the burgeoning state.

The Romans developed their superb military organization as they extended their influence over Italy beginning in the 4th century BC. The Gauls invaded from the north and sacked Rome in 390. The city, rebuilt, recovered gradually and forged its supremacy over its neighbors in Latium and Etruria, dissolving the Latin League. They defeated the warlike Samnites in the drawn-out Samnite Wars, absorbed the Sabines, and made alliances with other peoples. Pushing south, they occupied Greek colonial territories and waged a mutually costly war with Pyrrhus, king of Epirus, who later withdrew to Greece.

Rome thereby retained control of central and S Italy and looked to the Mediterranean for further expansion, coming into fierce conflict with Carthage, the greatest naval and commercial power of the area. Their armies met in Sicily in dispute over the strategically valuable Straits of Messina, beginning the long Punic Wars (264–146 BC). The greater manpower, wealth, perseverance, and discipline of the Roman armies, the loyalty of the Italian peoples to Rome, and the failure of the Carthaginian supply line were all factors in the crushing defeat of Carthage. At the insistence of the influential senator Cato the Elder, Carthage was razed. Rome was the dominant power in Spain, the Mediterranean islands, and N Africa.

The Romans then focused their expansion on the East. They defeated Philip V and Perseus in the Macedonian Wars (215–168 BC), took much of Syria from Antiochus III and Magnesia (189 BC), and dissolved the Achaean League. After subjugating Bithynia, Galatia, Pergamum, and Rhodes, they established their supremacy over Egypt (168 BC). This rapid and gross expansion had dire consequences for Rome. The senate grew corrupt administering the vast wealth of the new provinces and dependent peoples to its own advantage, suppressing the introduction of social reforms supported by Tiberius and Gaius Gracchus. Slave revolts (134–132 and 104–101 BC) were brutally put down. Marius, the leader of the *populares,* defeated Jugurtha (106), the Cimbri, and the Teutones (102), and took the Roman army for the first time into Transalpine Gaul. He and his followers were slaughtered by Sulla who gained support of the optimates and equites. The Social War, led by the Marsi, forced the Romans to grant citizenship to all Italian allies south of the Po (87). The Third Servile War (73–71), led by the gladiator Spartacus, was ruthlessly ended by Crassus and Pompey. Sulla marched in civil war against Rome and established himself as dictator. He introduced constitutional reforms to revive the dying republic and then retired. His former legates, the ambitious general Pompey and the wealthy Crassus, elected consuls, reversed his reforms. Pompey vanquished the Mediterranean pirates, ended the Mithradatic Wars (63), and added Pontus, Syria, and Phoenicia to the empire.

Crassus and Pompey formed an uneasy coalition called the First Triumvirate (60) with the illustrious patrician and popular leader Julius Caesar. While Caesar campaigned brilliantly in the Gallic Wars (58–51), Crassus died (53) and Pompey's hatred of Caesar came to a head. He took up the senate's opposition to Caesar and Caesar, crossing the Rubicon, entered into civil war with Pompey's army, defeating him at Pharsala (48). Caesar was acknowledged dictator of Rome and set about to secure and consolidate the empire and promote liberal legislation at home. His administration ended abruptly with his assassination (44). At the time of Caesar's death Rome was experiencing a period of advanced cultural achievement in arts and letters as exemplified by the works of Cicero. Further civil war followed as Caesar's heir Octavian formed a Second Triumvirate (43) with Antony and Lepidus and defeated the forces of the conspirators Brutus and Cassius at Philippi (42). At Actium (31) Octavian destroyed the armies of Antony and Cleopatra, annexed Egypt, and restored a long-lasting peace (Pax Romana) to Rome as Augustus, imperator. △1012.

Romeo and Juliet (*c.*1596), 5-act tragedy by William Shakespeare, from a poem by Arthur Brooke (1562). It has been the most often and successfully produced of all Shakespeare's plays and has been filmed more often than any other Shakespeare play, from a silent version in 1916 to a 1968 production. In Verona, Italy, the Montague and Capulet families bear an "ancient grudge." Juliet, a Capulet, and Romeo, a Montague, fall in love and are secretly married in defiance of their parents' opposition. When the two lovers die the families make a belated peace.

Rommel, Erwin (1891–1944), German military commander. He rose in the German army during Adolf Hitler's regime and led troops in Austria, Czechoslovakia, Poland, and France in early World War II. In 1942 as commander of the Afrika Korps, a tank corps, he drove the British back almost to Alexandria, Egypt. Known as "the desert fox," he was defeated by the British in November 1942 at El Alamein. In 1944, disenchanted with Hitler's military leadership, he joined an unsuccessful plot to kill him. He was arrested and forced to take poison. △1338.

Romulo, Carlos Pena (1901–), Filipino military and political figure. In 1941 he won the Pulitzer Prize in journalism for his reports on the Pacific military situation before World War II. After the Japanese attack on the Philippines in late 1941, he became an aide-de-camp to Gen. Douglas MacArthur. His "Voice of Freedom" radio broadcasts were famous. He joined the Philippine government in exile in the United States as secretary of information. Returning to the Philippines in 1945, he served variously as president of the United Nations General Assembly (1949–50) ambassador to the United States (1952), president of the University of the Philippines (1962–65), and secretary of education (from 1965).

Romulus and Remus, legendary founders of Rome According to a myth of the late 4th century BC, Rhea Silvia, daughter of Numitor, the king of Alba Longa bore twins by the god Mars. Amulius, Numitor's brother, deposed him and threw the twins into the Tiber. They were rescued and suckled by a wolf and reared by a shepherd. They grew strong and killed Amulius, restoring Numitor to his throne. In 753 BC they founded the settlement on the Palatine hill that became Rome. Romulus walled it and Remus was slain for leaping the wall after a quarrel. Romulus led the rape of the Sabines to obtain wives for his settlement of fugitives. After a long reign he disappeared in a thunderstorm and came to be revered as the god Quirinus. △1012.

Roncesvalles, Battle of (778). △1066.

Rondeau, French medieval verse form, popularized by Guillaume de Machaut in the 14th century. It consisted of four stanzas, the second and third usually containing a refrain echoed from the first line of the first stanza. Rondeaux were sung to music composed for several voices.

Ronsard, Pierre de (1524–85), French poet. In 1549 he formed the Pléiade, a literary group that aimed to reform French verse on classical principles. His *Odes* (1550) and *Amours* (1552) brought him fame and royal patronage, and he wrote several patriotic political poems. After 1574 he retired from public life, but his late *Sonnets pour Hélène* (1578) contained some of his finest work. *See also* Pléiade. △1172.

Roofing. △1610.

Rook, Old World crowlike bird that nests in colonies near the tops of trees. Family Corvidae; species *Corvus frugilegus.*

Roosevelt, Anna Eleanor (1884–1962), US reformer and humanitarian, b. New York City. She was the niece of Theodore Roosevelt and a distant cousin of Franklin Delano Roosevelt, whom she married (1905). She worked for social causes both before and after her marriage. She raised a large family and helped her polio-stricken husband regain his vigor. After she became first lady (1933) she was active in the National Association for the Advancement of Colored People and other social reform organizations, wrote a newspaper column, was a lecturer, and was assistant director of the Office of Civilian Defense (1941–42). She visited battlefronts in World War II and after the war, became the US ambassador to the United Nations (1945, 1949–52, 1961–62). Her books include *This is My Story* (1937) and *This I Remember* (1949).

Roosevelt, Franklin Delano (1882–1945), 32nd president of the United States (1933–45), b. Hyde Park, N.Y. He graduated from Harvard University (1904), attended the Columbia University Law School, and was admitted to the New York bar. In 1905 he married a distant cousin, Eleanor Roosevelt; they had six children.

A distant relative of Theodore Roosevelt, Franklin Roosevelt became a Democrat early in life. He gained notice as an insurgent member of the New York legislature and was chosen by Woodrow Wilson as assistant secretary of the navy. In 1920 he was the unsuccessful Democratic vice-presidential nominee.

In August 1921, Roosevelt was stricken with poliomyelitis, which left him unable to walk. With his wife's encouragement, however, he soon resumed an active political life and was elected (1928) governor of New York. In 1932 he was the Democratic candidate for president and won by a wide margin.

Roosevelt took office at the depths of the Great Depression. He immediately instituted a program, known as the New Deal, that included a wide variety of measures aimed at bringing about an economic recovery. Collectively, the New Deal programs had the effect of revolutionizing US economic, political, and social life. Vigorously denounced by Republicans and conservatives in general, Roosevelt nevertheless was reelected by a landslide in 1936. Roosevelt's second term saw some lessening of public support. His attempt to "pack" the Supreme Court by adding new members was defeated. Although the Republicans had shown some resurgence of strength, Roosevelt decided to run for an unprecedented third term in 1940. He was easily reelected.

Roosevelt's remaining years in office were almost totally concerned with US involvement in World War II. Even before the United States entered the war, Roosevelt had forged strong alliances with the Allies, particularly through the lend-lease program. Once the United States was at war, Roosevelt commanded the most massive war effort in history. He attended a number of conferences where the strategy of the war was determined and where the postwar world was planned. In 1944, Roosevelt ran for a fourth term although clearly in poor health. He won the election but died shortly after inauguration. He was succeeded by Harry S. Truman.

Career: New York legislature, 1910–13; assistant secretary of the navy, 1913–20; governor of New York, 1929–33; president, 1933–45. *See also* New Deal; World War II. △1324.

Roosevelt, Theodore (1858–1919), 26th president of the United States (1901–09), b. New York City. He graduated from Harvard University in 1880. He married Alice Lee (1880) and Edith Carow (1886) and had six children. After deciding against becoming a lawyer, Roosevelt settled into the vocations of author, rancher, and politician. He wrote books and journalism, bought a ranch in Dakota, and was elected as a Republican to the New York legislature.

He quickly won a reputation as a reformer and was appointed to the US Civil Service Commission by Benjamin Harrison; he was reappointed by Grover Cleveland. In 1895 a reform mayor named him president of the New York City police board. In 1897, President McKinley made him assistant secretary of the navy. During the Spanish-American War, Roosevelt organized and fought with the Rough Riders regiment and returned from Cuba a great war hero.

He was chosen in 1898 to run for governor of New York largely because he was a hero. Once elected, however, he alienated Republican regulars by his independence. Partly to remove him from the governor's chair, the Republicans named him (1900) vice-presidential candidate to run with President McKinley in his successful bid for a second term.

When McKinley was assassinated on Sept. 14, 1901, Roosevelt became president. Conservative Republican fears of "that damned cowboy" (as they called him) were soon realized. He forced coal mine owners to negotiate with striking miners; he energetically enforced the Sherman Antitrust Act; and he pushed through land reclamation and conservation laws. In 1904 he ran for and won a full term. Roosevelt's foreign policy was one of increasing US influence, particularly in Latin America. The Panama Canal was begun, and the Monroe Doctrine was strengthened. In 1906 he won the Nobel Peace Prize for helping to end the Russo-Japanese War.

Roosevelt virtually hand-picked his successor, William Howard Taft. By 1912, however, he had become disenchanted with the conservative drift of the Republicans. After failing to win the nomination away from Taft, he organized his own Progressive, or Bull Moose, party. He polled more votes in the election than Taft but Democrat Woodrow Wilson won.

Career: New York legislature, 1882–84; US Civil Service Commission, 1889–95; president, New York City police board, 1895–97; assistant secretary of the navy, 1897–98; governor of New York, 1899–1901; vice president, 1901; president, 1901–09.

Roosevelt Corollary, proposal by Pres. Theodore Roosevelt (1904) to amend the Monroe Doctrine. It altered the doctrine by stating that the United States had a right to intervene in W Hemisphere countries when forced to do so by "flagrant cases of wrongdoing." This was an example of Roosevelt's "big stick" diplomacy.

Root, Elihu (1845–1937), US lawyer and statesman, b. Clinton, N.Y. The leader of the American bar, Root became secretary of war immediately following the end of the war with Spain; he supervised the affairs of Cuba and of the newly acquired territories of the Philippines and Puerto Rico. Root was appointed secretary of state in 1905; he was awarded the Nobel Peace Prize in 1912 for his contribution to peace in the Western hemisphere. Root also served in the US Senate (1909–15) and as president of Andrew Carnegie's philanthropic trusts.

Root, underground portion of a vascular plant that serves as an anchor and absorbs water and nutrients. The primary root develops from the lower end of the plant embryo. Some plants have taproots with smaller lateral branches (dandelion). Others develop fibrous roots with lateral branches equalling the main root in growth (grasses). Adventitious roots are produced from the above-ground portion of the stem (mangrove) and provide additional support and absorption of water and minerals. Some plants have large taproots that store nutrients (beet, parsnip, carrot). △444, 452.

Root Canal. △756.

Roque. *See* Croquet.

Rorqual, five species of whalebone whales distributed worldwide. Gregarious, they travel in groups of several hundred. Genus *Balaenoptera. See also* Finback Whale, Whale.

Rorschach Technique, in psychology, a projective technique used to assess personality characteristics. The individual is presented with a series of ambiguous ink blots, which he then interprets. The technique is often used to aid in the diagnosis of mental disorders. *See also* Projective Techniques. △814.

Rosario, city in E central Argentina, on the Paraná River, 90 mi (145km) S of Santa Fe; export and import hub. Exports: grain, hay, meat, hides, cattle, wool, sugar. Industries: grain, flour mills, tanneries, distilleries. Founded 1725. Pop. 591,428.

Rome: Tivoli villa

Eleanor Roosevelt

CBS
BLUE
CBS

Franklin D. Roosevelt

Theodore Roosevelt

Rosas, Juan Manuel de (1793–1877), Argentine caudillo and governor of Buenos Aires province (1829–32, 1835–52), one of the most important political figures of post-independence Latin America. A rancher, Rosas organized the local militia; by 1835, his rivals in exile or dead, he had become a virtual dictator. Rosas controlled access to markets by controlling Buenos Aires; he survived blockades imposed by the French and the English. It was not until 1851, when Justo José de Urquiza rose in revolt, that the era of Rosas was ended. Rosas went into exile in England.

Rose, wild or cultivated flowering shrubs. The majority are native to Asia, several to America, and a few to Europe and NW Africa. Growing mostly in temperate regions of the Northern Hemisphere, some species are found at high elevations in the tropics and even above the Arctic Circle.

Roses are divided into groups according to type or use: hybrid tea, floribunda, grandiflora, climbing, polyantha, hybrid perpetual, tea, old, and special purpose. The stems are thorny and erect, climbing, or trailing. The leaves have leaflets in pairs with the odd one at the tip. Flowers appear singly or in loose clusters and colors range from white to yellow, pink, crimson, and maroon. About nine species have been involved in the breeding of today's many garden roses. Prized for their fragrant blossoms, roses are also used in medicines, cosmetics, and, a regional favorite, rose-hip jelly. Rose hips are considered an excellent source of vitamin C. There are about 200 species. Family Rosaceae; genus *Rosa*. △324.

Rosebay. *See* Willow Herb.

Rose Beetle, or rose chafer, small, long-legged, tan scarab beetle ranging from New England to Virginia and west to Texas. It feeds on fruit and foliage of grapes, peaches, roses, and other fruit. Species *Macrodactylus subspinosus*.

Rosefish, or ocean perch, marine food fish found in the North Atlantic and usually fished by trawlers at 300–700ft (91–213m). It is bright red or rose. Family Scorpaenidae; species *Sebastes marinus*.

Rose Mallow. *See* Hibiscus.

Rosemary, common name for *Rosmarinis officinalis*, a perennial evergreen undershrub of the mint family with aromatic lance-shaped leaves used in seasoning and yielding an oil used in medicine. Its flowers are pale blue. △358, 446.

Rosemead, city in S California, E of Alhambra. Founded 1867; inc. 1959. Pop. (1970) 40,972.

Rosenberg Case (1951–53), US espionage case. A New York couple, Julius and Ethel Rosenberg, were found guilty of passing atomic bomb secrets to Soviet agents. The couple were executed for the crime. Their trial gained international attention because many felt the couple were the victims of Cold War hysteria. The couple's two sons campaigned to vindicate their parents.

Rose of Sharon, hardy shrub, *Hibiscus syriacus*, native to China. It can be grown farther north than many hibiscus plants. The flowers are red, purple, rose, or white. Height: to 15ft (4.6m). Family Malvaceae. *See also* Hibiscus.

Roseola Infantum, an infectious disease of young children, probably caused by a virus. It is characterized by high fever, followed by a mild rash on the trunk and neck.

Roses, Wars of the (1455–85), English civil wars fought for the possession of the crown and taking their name from the badges of the House of Lancaster (red rose) and the House of York (white rose). By 1455 the incompetence of the Lancastrian Henry VI had led to widespread civil disorder. Henry's interests were promoted by his wife, Margaret of Anjou, who was determined to protect the right of their son Edward (*b.* 1453). Richard, duke of York, and a small group of lords attempted to gain control of the government but were strongly resisted. York was killed in 1460, but his son Edward IV claimed the throne and defeated Henry VI at Towton in 1461. In 1470, Edward's closest ally, the earl of Warwick, deserted him for the Lancastrians. Briefly deposed, Edward regained his throne and defeated his enemies in 1471. Henry VI and his son were killed. After Edward IV died in 1483, his brother usurped the throne as Richard III and Edward's sons were murdered. Their deaths allowed Henry Tudor to rally the Lancastrian faction and Richard was overcome at Bosworth in 1485 by Henry who as Henry VII, married Edward IV's daughter Elizabeth in 1486, thus uniting the two warring factions. The wars illustrated the weakness of the English kings because of their dependence on the armed retinues of the nobility and marked the transition from feudalism to a stronger monarchy. *See also* Henry VI; Henry VII; Richard III.

Rosetta Stone, a slab of black basalt that was the key to deciphering Egyptian hieroglyphics. It was erected in 195 BC to honor Ptolemy Epiphanes. The stone was discovered in Rosetta, Egypt, in 1799 by an officer in Napoleon's army. It bears an inscription in three languages: Greek, hieroglyphics, and demotic or common characters. Using the Greek inscription as a basis, English physicist Thomas Young in 1818 and Jean François Champollion in 1822 were able to decipher the hieroglyphic inscription. The stone is now in the British Museum.

Rosette Nebula. △102.

Roseville, city in SE Michigan; residential suburb 13mi (21km) NE of Detroit. Founded 1918; inc. 1926. Pop. (1970) 60,529.

Roseville, town in SE Minnesota; N suburb of St Paul. Industries: steel products, printing, computers. Inc. 1948. Pop. (1970) 34,518.

Rosewall, Kenneth R. "Ken" (1934–), Australian tennis player. His major victories included the US (1956, 1970), Australian (1953; 1955; 1971–72), and French (1953, 1968) singles championships.

Rosewood, any of several kinds of ornamental wood derived from various kinds of New World and Old World tropical trees. The most important are Honduras rosewood, *Dalbergia stevensoni*, and Brazilian rosewood, *D. nigra*. It varies from deep, ruddy brown to purplish and has a black grain, hard to polish because of high resin content. Once much in demand by cabinetmakers, it is now scarce.

Rosh. *See* Asher ben Yehiel.

Rosh Hashanah, meaning New Year, begins the Jewish year with the Ten Days of Penitence. The festival ends with the Day of Atonement, the 10th day. It does not commemorate a particular event but is a day of reflection and prayer. Man must realize his sins and unite in God. It is celebrated as a day of judgment for man and Israel as a nation.

Rosin, or colophony, yellowish amorphous resin obtained as a residue from the distillation of turpentine. Chief constituent is abietic acid; used in varnishes, soldering fluxes, linoleum, and printing inks. Properties: sp gr 1.08; melt. pt. 212–308°F (100–153°C).

Ross, Barney (1909–1967), US boxer, b. Barnet Rosofsky in New York City. He was the world's welterweight champion (1934; 1935–38). He entered the US Marine Corps in 1942 and was wounded at Guadalcanal. Ross was elected to the Boxing Hall of Fame in 1956.

Ross, Betsy (1752–1836), US seamstress, said to have made the first American flag with stars and stripes, b. Philadelphia as Elizabeth Griscom. According to the account of her grandson William Canby, Gen. George Washington and a committee came to her with a rough drawing of a flag and commissioned her to make it, which she did. Congress then adopted the stars and stripes design as the official flag of the United States. The story is disputed, but Betsy Ross remains a folk hero.

Ross, (Sir) James Clark (1800–62), British naval officer and explorer; participated in six Arctic expeditions in search of a northwest passage linking the Atlantic and Pacific Oceans (1818–33). During the last Arctic expedition, Ross discovered the magnetic north pole (June 1831). Ross later commanded an Antarctic expedition (1839–43), which earned him a knighthood and awards from the Geographical Societies of London and Paris.

Ross Dependency, area of Antarctica, includes Ross Island, coasts along Ross Sea, and nearby islands. Under jurisdiction of New Zealand by act of British Parliament. Area: 175,000sq mi (453,250sq km).

Rossellini, Roberto (1906–), Italian filmmaker. His concern for emotional realism is revealed in his major films *Open City* (1945), *Paisan* (1946), *L'Amore* (1948), *Stromboli* (1949), and *La Paura* (1954). He also made historical dramas for television. △1370.

Rossetti, Christina (1830–94), English poet, a sister of Dante Gabriel Rossetti. She specialized in religious poetry and verses for children. Her works, showing mastery of the sonnet and short lyric, include *Goblin Market and Other Poems* (1862), *The Prince's Progress* (1866), and *A Pageant and Other Poems* (1881). △1240.

Rossetti, Dante Gabriel (1828–82), English poet and painter. He was a founding member, with John Everett Millais and Holman Hunt, of the Pre-Raphaelite Brotherhood. Although his poem *The Blessed Damozel* was first published when he was 19, recognition as a poet came long after his paintings had won acclaim. Apart from a volume of translations (1861), no collection of poems appeared until 1870, when one he had buried in his wife's grave in 1862 was dug up and published with others. This sonnet sequence was *The House of Life*. A further volume, which completed the sequence, appeared in 1881. *See also* Pre-Raphaelite Brotherhood. △1240.

Rossini, Gioacchino (1792–1868), Italian operatic composer. He produced 38 operas before the age of 37, after which he never composed another. His operas include *The Italian Girl in Algiers* (1813), *The Thieving Magpie* (1817), *The Journey to Reims* (1823), *Semiramide* (1823), and his masterpiece, the still popular comic opera *The Barber of Seville* (1816); other works include the overture to the opera *William Tell* (1829). △1246, 1256.

Rosso, Fiorentino (Giovanni Battista di Jacopó di Gaspare) (1494–1540), Italian painter. △1150.

Ross Sea, extension of S Pacific Ocean, in Antarctica, between Edward VII Peninsula and Victoria Land. Discovered 1841 by Capt. James C. Ross.

Rostand, Edmond (1868–1918), French dramatist. His early verse dramas include *Les Romanesques* (1894), *La Princesse Lointaine* (1895), and *La Samaritaine* (1897). His best-known work is *Cyrano de Bergerac* (1897), a tragicomedy about unrequited love. *L'Aiglon* (1900) about Napoleon II, and *Chantecler* (1910), a barnyard fable, are also well known.

Rostock, seaport city in N East Germany, on Warnov River, near Baltic Sea, 41mi (66km) WSW of Stralsund; capital of Rostock district; powerful Baltic member of the Hanseatic League (14th century); seat of university (1419); birthplace of Gebhard von Blücher, Prussian general; site of Church of St Mary (13th century), town hall (15th century), tower (16th century). Industries: shipyards, petroleum storage, farm machinery, fishing, watches, chemicals, food processing, diesel engines, furniture. Founded 1189; chartered 1218. Pop. 198,396.

Roswell, city in SE New Mexico; seat of Chavez co; site of New Mexico Military Institute (1891) and Walker Air Force Base (1941). Artesian wells irrigate the cotton and alfalfa lands. Industries: livestock, fruit, cotton, tourism. Founded 1869 as a trading post; inc. 1903. Pop. (1970) 33,908.

Rotation, turning of a celestial body about its axis. In the solar system the Sun and all the planets, except for Uranus and Venus, rotate from west to east (that is, in a counterclockwise direction).

Rotation, Optical. *See* Optical Rotation.

Rotation of Crops, *See* Crop Rotation.

Roth, Phillip (1933–), US author, b. Newark. A novelist and short story writer, he often draws on his Jewish background to produce amusing works. He won the National Book Award (1960) for *Goodbye, Columbus* (1959), a work comprised of a novella and five short stories. His novels include *Letting Go* (1962) and *Portnoy's Complaint* (1969).

Rothko, Mark (1903–70), US painter, b. Latvia. His early style was realistic. He was briefly influenced by Surrealism and then became increasingly abstract in style. His abstract expressionistic paintings are characterized by two or three vertically arranged rectangular shapes with somewhat blurred outlines painted parallel to each other on a colored background. Depending on the relationship between the colors of the rectangles and their background, the shapes seem either to advance or recede. Most of Rothko's canvases are quite large.

Rothschild, Nathan Mayer (1777–1836), member of the German banking family who established the British house. Designated his father's representative in commercially active Manchester, in 1798, Nathan transferred his operation to London in 1805, where he was instrumental in financing British obligations incurred during the Napoleonic Wars. His success guaranteed close cooperation with the government after peace was concluded and generated an even greater expansion of the family's financial interests.

Rothschild Family, commercial and banking dynasty founded in 19th century Germany by **Meyer Amschel Rothschild** (1743–1812). The five sons of Meyer Amschel established branches in the financial centers of London, Frankfurt, Paris, and Naples. Profits earned during the Napoleonic Wars were invested throughout Europe. Control over the vast empire passed to capable male heirs and came to include branches influential in the sciences and politics as well as finance.

Rotifer, microscopic metazoan found in fresh water. Although they resemble ciliate protozoans, they are many-celled with a general body structure similar to simple worms. Elongated to round, they are identified by a crown of cilia around the mouth. Reproduction is sexual. Class Rotifera; species include *Philodina* and *Conochilus.* △506.

Rotor, Helicopter, engine-driven rotary wing. △1720.

Rotterdam, major seaport and industrial city in W Netherlands, on New Meuse River, 15mi (24km) from North Sea; site of 15th-century church, 18th-century stock exchange. Heart of city was demolished by German bombing, May 14, 1940. Exports: coal, dairy and vegetable products. Industries: chemicals, textiles, paper, ship, rail, and automobile manufacturing, brewing, oil refining, machinery. Chartered 1328. Pop. 686,586.

Rotterdam, town in E New York, NW of Schenectady. Settled 1670, inc. 1821. Pop. (1970) 25,214.

Rottweiler, German cattle dog (working group) descended from dogs brought over the Alps by Romans, 1,900 years ago. It has a medium-length head that is broad between the ears; strong, muscular jaws; hanging ears set high; a short-backed, strong body; muscular, medium-length legs; and high-set short or docked tail. The short, coarse, flat coat is black with brown markings. Average size: 23–27in (58–68.5cm) high at shoulder, 75–90lb (34–41kg). *See also* Working Dog.

Rouault, Georges (1871–1958), French painter and printmaker. His early training was in stained glass. He also painted naturalistic landscapes and pictures with religious and mythological themes. Influenced by Fauvism, his style became less realistic. He used dark reds and blues to paint corrupt judges and prostitutes. He then turned to printmaking for a decade and then back again to painting. This time, his style evolved to the point where he used heavy black lines to delineate his expressionistic clowns and prostitutes who were painted in thick, primary colors.

Rouen, seaport in France, on Seine River, 70mi (113km) NW of Paris; capital of Seine-Maritime dept. An archepiscopal see since 5th century, by 10th century it was capital of Normandy and one of Europe's leading cities; scene of Joan of Arc's trial and burning (1431); site of Cathedral of Notre Dame (12th–15th centuries) with its Tour de Beurre (butter tower), 14th-century Gothic church of St Ouen, and 14th-century Tour de la Gros Horloge (clock tower). Industries: textiles, flour, foundries, perfumes, leather goods. Pop. 120,741.

Roulette, gambling game, popular in casinos. The game consists of a ball, and a wheel with its outer area marked off into 38 squares. The numbers on these squares alternately range in red and black from 1 to 36, with a 0 and double 0 marked in green. Near the wheel is a table with an arrangement of squares corresponding to the wheel. There are many types of bets that may be made, with the odds varying according to the number and/or color selected. After the bets are made, the wheel is spun and the ball tossed into it; its final resting place indicates the winning bets.

Roundworm. *See* Nematode.

Rousseau, Henri (1844–1910), French primitive painter. He received no formal training and taught himself to paint by copying works from the Louvre. His style is characterized by a strong sense of pattern and color combined with the use of imaginative, exotic jungle themes showing tropical plants and beasts. Pablo Picasso viewed Rousseau's directness of expression as an important contribution to 20th-century art.

Rousseau, Jean Jacques (1712–78), French philosopher and author. One of the most original prophets of modernity, he went to Paris in 1741 and was associated with Denis Diderot and the Encyclopedists. Although often living in the provinces or in Switzerland, Rousseau remained in contact with Parisian intellectuals thereafter. In his celebrated *Discourses on the Sciences and Arts* (1750) and in *On Equality* (1754) he argued that man's natural goodness is perverted by artificial and inequitable societies. *The New Héloise* (1761) celebrated love in a new romantic style. In *The Social Contract* (1762) he envisioned a liberated society that would conform with a kind of humanistic, individualized education, also outlined in *Émile* (1762). His *Confessions* (1781–88) convey the impression of a passionate and often persecuted human spirit. *See also* Social Contract. △1184.

Rousseau, (Pierre-Etienne-) Théodore (1812–67), French painter. A member of the Barbizon school, he painted romantic landscapes of mountain scenes with rushing water. His style was influenced by Claude Lorrain and by 17th-century Dutch landscapes. In his later works, a single tree often dominates the landscape, and a great deal of attention is given to the sky. *See also* Barbizon School.

Rove Beetle, small, slender, generally beneficial beetle found chiefly near decaying plant and animal matter. They have short wing covers. Family Staphylinidae.

Rowing, a sport that includes events for eights, fours, and pairs. A coxswain steers the shell for eights by means of tiller ropes attached to a rudder; he also directs the crew. Each crew member uses both hands on one oar. The oars are alternately attached to riggings on opposite sides of the shell. The shell for eights is between 55 and 60 feet (16.8–18.3m) long and 2 feet wide (0.6m). Rowing has been included in the Olympic Games since 1900. The sport has been popular in England since 1829, when the first Oxford and Cambridge crew races were held. In the United States, the first intercollegiate event matched Harvard and Yale in 1852.

Royal Canadian Mounted Police, federal police of Canada. Organized in 1873 as the Northwest Mounted Police to protect western settlements, railroads, and liquor revenues. The Mounties opened their first post at Emerson (1874). Active in the Riel rebellion (1884–85), Yukon gold rush, and both world wars, they enforce all federal laws in Canada and provide police manpower to most provinces.

Royal Fern, or flowering fern, common, widely distributed bush fern of wetlands. It has large leaves rising from a heavy rootstock that forms a mat. The cylindrical pinnae on frond ends are densely covered with sporangia and look like flowers. Height: to 6ft (1.8m). Family Osmundaceae; species *Osmunda regalis. See also* Fern. △438.

Royal Oak, city in SE Michigan; residential suburb 13mi (21km) NW of Detroit. Industries: tools, paints, mattresses. Settled 1820; inc. as village 1891, as city 1921. Pop. (1970) 85,499.

Royal Palm, ornamental palm native to the Caribbean islands and Central America. It has a tall, light-colored trunk and feather-shaped leaves. Species include *Roystonea elata,* the Florida royal palm, to 70ft (21m); *R. oleracea,* the cabbage palm or palmiste, to 120ft (37m); and *R. regia,* the Cuban royal palm, to 70ft (21m). Family Palmaceae.

Royal Waterlily, aquatic plant with floating leaves and fragrant white flowers that turn pink and then red on the second day. Leaf diameter: to 6ft (1.8m). Family Nymphaeaceae; species *Victoria regia.*

RR Lyrae Variable, or cluster variable, intrinsic regular short-period variable star of the Cepheid type, usually completing one cycle of luminosity fluctuations in less than one day. Stars of this type are of Population II, that is, they are old stars commonly found in globular clusters, and appear to be of uniform intrinsic brightness. Like the classic Cepheids, they have been effectively used in distance measurement. △100, 112.

Rubáiyát of Omar Khayyám, collection of quatrains written by an 11th-century Persian poet and scholar and translated into English by Edward Fitzgerald in 1859. The verses exalt the sensual, pleasure-seeking life. The epicurean philosophy of the poems made them extremely popular in the Victorian age.

Rub al-Khali (Ar-Rab' al Khalil), vast desert of S Arabian Peninsula, in SW Saudi Arabia and N Oman; translation of Arabic name is "empty quarter." Length: 750mi (1,208km). Width: 400mi (644km). Area: 250,000sq mi (647,500sq km).

Rubber, elastic solid obtained from the latex of the rubber tree *(Hevea brasiliensis).* Natural rubber consists of a polymer of cis-isoprene and is widely used for

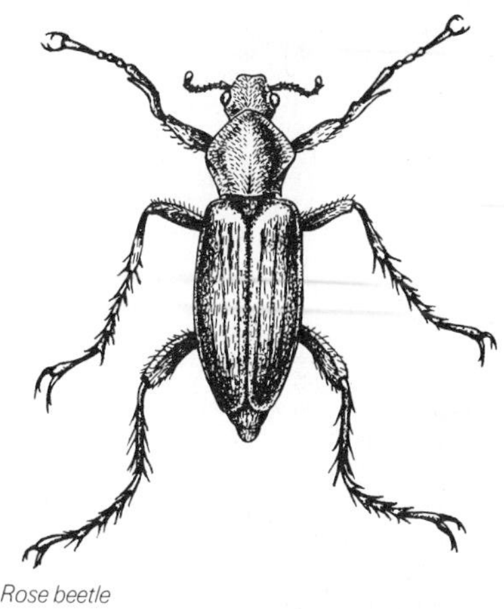

Rose beetle

Gioacchino Rossini

Rotterdam, Netherlands

Jean Jacques Rousseau

tires and other applications, especially after vulcanization. Synthetic rubbers are polymers tailored to excel in specific properties for specific purposes; none has the overall advantages of natural rubber. They include styrene-butadiene rubber (SBR), neoprene, nitrile rubber, and the newer stereo-regular rubbers based on synthetic cis-polyisoprene. △1560, 1574, 1618.

Rubber Plant, evergreen fig native to India and Malaysia. Tree-sized in the tropics, it is grown as a pot plant in temperate regions. Once cultivated for its white latex to make India rubber, it has large, glossy, leathery leaves and a stout, buttressed trunk. Size: to 100ft (30.5m). It begins as an epiphyte (air plant) and later anchors to the ground; fruits are egg-shaped. Height: to 100ft (30.5m) Family Moraceae; species *Ficus elastica.*

Rubber Tree, any of several South American trees whose exudations can be made into rubber; especially *Hevea brasiliensis* (family Euphorbiaceae), a tall softwood tree native to Brazil. The milky exudate, called latex, is obtained from the inner bark by tapping, and then coagulated chemically or by smoking over fires.

Rubella. *See* German Measles.

Rubeola. *See* Measles.

Rubens, Peter Paul (1577–1640), Flemish painter and engraver. During a stay in Italy (1600–08), he painted religious works, in which he paid much attention to careful drawing and decorative detail. He was greatly influenced in his style by the works of Italian High Renaissance masters. Monumental muscular figures in action are characteristic of his heroic, Mannerist style. When he returned to Antwerp (1608), he established a workshop that became highly successful, producing huge portraits and allegorical series for the wealthy and nobility of western Europe. Rubens' best-known works are his many decorative series for churches and palaces, dating from 1620 to 1630. He crowded his Baroque canvases with dynamic bodies and used light and color to give a dramatic sense of action. His 21 paintings of "The Life of Marie de Médicis" (Louvre) are from this period. His later landscapes show a softening of colors. △1162.

Rubenstein, Ida (1885–1960), Russian dancer. △1368.

Rubidium, metallic element (symbol Rb) of the alkali-metal group, discovered (1861) by R.W. Bunsen and G. R. Kirchoff. Lepidolite contains small amounts of rubidium salts and is the chief source. The element has few commercial uses: small amounts are used in photoelectric cells. Chemically it resembles sodium, but is more reactive. Natural rubidium contains 27.85% of the radioisotope Rb^{87} (half-life 6×10^{10}yr). Properties: at. no. 37; at. wt. 85.468, sp gr 1.532; melt. pt. 102°F (38.89°C); boil. pt. 1270°F (688°C); most common isotope Rb^{85} (72.15%). *See also* Alkali Elements.

Rubinstein, Artur (1886–), US pianist, b. Poland. He studied in Germany, made his debut there at the age of 12, and first performed in the United States in 1906. He moved permanently to the United States in 1937. He enjoyed the longest active concert career of any musician—more than three-quarters of a century—touring the world many times. He was especially known for his interpretations of Spanish composers, and of Chopin and other Romantic composers.

Ruby, a transparent red gemstone variety of corundum with high refraction, found mainly in Burma. Brilliant when cut and polished, the ruby lacks fire. Turns green when heated, but regains color. Deep red rubies are valued more highly than diamonds. *See also* Corundum. △244.

Ruby Copper. *See* Cuprite.

Rudder, Aircraft. △1718.

Ruddy Duck, North American stiff-tailed duck with a black and white head and, in the male, brownish-red upper plumage. It typically holds its tail at a jaunty angle while swimming. Length: 15in (8cm). Species *Oxyura jamaicensis. See also* Duck.

Rudolf I (1218–91), German king (1273–91). The first Hapsburg monarch, his election as king ended the period (1250–73) during which there was no accepted German king or Holy Roman emperor. Rudolf laid the foundations of the Hapsburg dominions by obtaining in 1278 Austria, Styria, and Carniola from Bohemia. Although he was conciliatory toward the papacy, he was never crowned Holy Roman emperor by the pope.

Rudolf II (1552–1612), Holy Roman emperor (1576–1612), king of Bohemia (1575–1611), and of Hungary (1572–1608). He was the son and successor of Holy Roman Emperor Maximilian II. Opposed to the Protestant Reformation, his attempt to force Catholicism on Hungary led to a revolt (1604) that his brother Matthias ended. Matthias soon forced Rudolf to cede rule of Hungary, Austria, Moravia (1608), and Bohemia (1611) to him.

Rudolf or **Rudolph, Archduke** (1858–89), only son of Austrian Emperor Francis-Joseph. Patron of the arts. Married Princess Stephanie of Belgium (1881). According to official reports, committed suicide at Mayerling with his companion Baroness Marie Vetsera (June 1889). All information about their deaths was suppressed.

Rudolf, Lake, lake in NW Kenya, in Great Rift Valley; N part is between Ethiopia and SE Sudan; serves as focus for interior drainage; has no outlet; is becoming increasingly saline. Area: approx. 2,500sq mi (6,475sq km).

Rue, evergreen plants or shrubs native to warm regions of S Europe and SW Asia. They have aromatic leaves used in medicine or as flavoring. Family Rutaceae; genus *Ruta.*

Ruffin, Edmund (1794–1865), US agronomist and slavery apologist, b. Prince George County, Va. Ruffin pioneered the use of fertilizers, crop rotation, drainage, and improved methods of plowing to eliminate soil depletion. He was even more famous for the articles he wrote in defense of slavery and secession. He was given the honor of firing the first shot on Ft. Sumter, which began the Civil War. When the Confederacy collapsed, Ruffin committed suicide.

Ruffini Corpuscles. △678.

Rugby, game, also called rugby football, played with a ball by 2 teams of 15 persons each on a field. The field cannot exceed 110 yards (100m) in length or 75 yards (68m) in width. At each end of the 110-yard field is a 25-yard (22.9m) deep in-goal area and a goal post (about the size used in football). The ball is similar to the one used in football, except that it is rounder and larger. A game is divided into two 40-minute periods and may end in a tie. No substitutions are allowed. In the case of a serious injury, the team must play short-handed.

In 15-man rugby (eight forwards, seven backs), the scoring consists of grounding the ball over the opponent's goal line (a try, worth four points), a conversion (kicking the ball between the goal posts) after the try, worth two points; and a penalty goal, dropped goal, and goal from a fair catch, worth three points each. The ball may be kicked, carried, or passed (sideward and to the rear). Tackling is allowed, but not blocking. Professional rugby uses 13-man teams and two substitutes. A try is worth three points, a conversion after the try two points, penalty goals two points, and a dropped goal one point.

History. The sport originated in England in 1823 on the playing fields of Rugby School. Amateur play was organized in 1871 when the English Rugby Union was formed to standardize the game. Professional play was begun in 1895 and now includes unions (leagues) in England, Wales, Scotland, and Ireland. The sport is also popular in France, New Zealand, Australia, and South Africa. In the United States, the game is played by clubs and colleges.

Rugs and Carpets, Oriental, floor coverings of felt, tapestry, a shuttle-woven material, or most frequently a pile fabric, produced by hand and originating in the Indo-European area centering around Persia (Iran). Carpets are named for the town or tribe from which they originate. One of the principal centers for rug weaving is Persia, known for the great court carpets of the 16th century. Some Persian centers are Kerman, Shiraz, Hamadan, Kashan, and Tabriz. Turkey and Asia Minor are also rug-weaving centers, known for carpets of broad spacious designs, rich in harmonious colors, with simpler patterns than the Persians. The Caucasus, another center, is known for simple designs with a coarse weave, eg., Shirvan, Kazak, and the dragon carpets of Kuba. Turcoman carpets are made by nomadic tribes and have dark red coloring and geometric octagon designs in rows and columns. Oriental rugs are also made in Afghanistan, India, Chinese Turkestan, and Tibet. △1058, 1064.

Ruhr, river in West Germany; rises in hills of N central West Germany and flows NW and W to join Rhine River at Duisburg; the Ruhr valley, an industrial mining district, contains large coal deposits. Area along river was occupied by French and Belgian troops 1923–25 because of Germany's default on reparations; strategically important in WWII. Length: 146m (234km).

Ruisdael or **Ruysdael, Jacob Isaacsz van** (c 1628–82), Dutch painter. △1168.

Rukeyser, Muriel (1913–), US author, b. New York City. A poet, her verse expresses intense feeling. Her books include *U.S. I* (1938), *A Turning Win* (1939), *Wake Island* (1942), *Waterlily Fire* (1962) and *The Speed of Darkness* (1968).

Rumelia, name used by the Turks for possessions in the Balkans, including parts of Salonika, Kosovo, Janina, Scutari, and Bosnia-Herzegovina, the ancient provinces of Thrace and Macedonia. During the darkest period of its history (1396–1878), the province was ruled from Sophia under a feudal system of agr cultural taxation. Boys between 10 and 12 years of age were abducted as "janissaries" for the Turkish Army. After the first Russo-Turkish War in 1877, the Congress of Berlin proclaimed Eastern Rumelia an autonomous province of the Turkish Empire. Eastern Rumelia revolted against Turkey in 1885 and was reunited with Bulgaria despite Russian protests.

Rumford, Benjamin Thomson, Count (1753–1814), American-British scientist and administrator, b. Woburn, Mass. A loyalist, he moved to England during the American Revolution. He later went into service of the elector of Bavaria as an administrator, for which in 1791 he was made a count of the Holy Roman Empire. In science, he devised a photometer and a calorimeter; improved home cooking and heating apparatuses; and helped to demolish the phlogiston theory by showing that heat is a form of motion. He measured the equivalence of mechanical energy and heat. In 1799 he returned to England and founded the Royal Institution. △1492.

Ruminant, cud-chewing, even-toed, hooved mammals, including camels, chevrotain, deer, giraffes, antelope, cattle, sheep, and goats. All have four-chambered stomachs except camel and chevrotain. △548.

Rummy, two-to-six-player card game with a standard deck. In the three-or-four hand game, several cards are dealt to each player, and one card is turned up on the table. Players, in order, then either select the most recent discarded card or select a new card from the deck. The first person to meld—set his cards on the table—wins. A player may meld 7 cards of the same suit in sequence, three or four cards in a sequence, or three or four of the same rank. The cards usually rank from king down to ace. One of the popular variations is knock rummy, where a player, except for sequences of three or four cards of the same rank, must total fewer points in his hand than any other player in the game. Aces count one point, picture cards are 10, and all others their face value. *See also* Gin Rummy.

Runic Writing. △870.

Runnymede, meadow in S England, on S bank of Thames River at Egham, Surrey, W of London. It was either here or on a nearby island in the Thames that King John granted the Magna Carta in 1215. The meadow was given to the British nation in 1929. Today it also has a memorial to President John F Kennedy.

Runyon, Damon (1884–1946), US author, b. Manhattan, Kan. A newspaper columnist, he also wrote stories about colorful New York City characters. His inventive colloquialisms were known as "Runyonese." His book *Guys and Dolls* (1932) was made into a musical (1950).

Rupert (1352–1410), German king. Elector palatine (1398), he succeeded Emperor Wenceslaus as king of Germany (1400). Rupert was defeated in Italy while attempting to recover Milan and receive the imperial crown (1401–02). His title was recognized by Pope Boniface IX (1403). Rupert supported the Roman popes during the Great Schism, but was constantly at war within his domain.

Rural Electrification Administration (REA) (1935), agency set up by executive order of President Franklin D. Roosevelt to provide electricity for rural areas. The REA was financed by the Reconstruction Finance Corporation and employed Work Project Administration labor. Despite government encouragement, large power companies refused to extend electricity to unprofitable rural areas. Publicly-owned plants received priority.

Rurik (died 879), semi-legendary leader of the Varangians who ruled as prince of Novgorod after 862 from which the beginning of the Russian state dated. His successor Oleg founded the Kievan state. △1176.

Rush, Benjamin (1745?–1813), US physician, reformer, and signer of the Declaration of Independence, b. Byberry, Pa. He practiced medicine in Philadelphia and was professor of chemistry at the College of Philadelphia (1769–89). In 1789 he became professor of medicine in the University of Pennsylvania, a post he held until his death. As a member of the Continental Congress (1776–77), he signed the Declaration of Independence. An avid reformer, Rush established the first US free medical dispensary (1786), worked for the abolition of slavery and capital punishment, and advocated a modern prison system and education for women. He was the author of *Medical Inquiries and Observations upon the Diseases of the Mind* (1812), the first American treatise on mental illness. He was treasurer of the US Mint (1797–1813).

Rush, tufted, perennial bog plant found in temperate regions. It has long, narrow leaves and small flowers crowded into dense clusters. Among 350 species is *Juncus conglomeratus* of Europe and N Africa. It has dense, brown flowers and ridged stems; height: 1–5ft (30–152cm). *Juncus effusus,* or soft rush, has smooth stems. Family Juncaceae.

Rusk, (David) Dean (1909–), US political leader and diplomat, b. Cherokee County, Ga. After World War II military service, he worked in the State Department on United Nations Affairs (1949) and as assistant secretary of state for Eastern affairs (1950–51). He was involved in the decision to enter the Korean War. As secretary of state under Presidents Kennedy and Johnson (1961–69), he was active in the formulation of policy in the Vietnam War.

Ruskin, John (1819–1900), English art and social critic. His strict religious upbringing combined with appreciation of European painting and architecture imbued his art criticism with ethical and social concerns. He revolutionized art criticism with *Modern Painters* (5 vols., 1843–60), which, most significantly, defended the paintings of J.M.W. Turner. *The Seven Lamps of Architecture* (1849) and *The Stones of Venice* (3 vols., 1851–53) are important studies of architecture. *Sesame and Lilies* (1865) discussed the role of women in society, and *Unto This Last* (4 essays, 1860–62) attacked laissez-faire economics and Victorian business ethics. △1258.

Russell, English noble family. The Russells first became prominent among the nobility in the 16th century. **John Russell** (1486?–1555), lord keeper of the privy seal to Henry VIII and Edward VI, was made 1st earl of Bedford in 1550. His successors were influential in government, and in 1694 the fourth earl was created first duke of Bedford. The family seat is at Woburn, Bedfordshire. The two most notable members of the family, both outside the main line of succession, were **Lord John Russell** (1792–1878), later 1st earl Russell, who played an important part in 19th-century parliamentary reform, and the philosopher **Lord Bertrand Russell** (1872–1970). *See also* Russell, Bertrand; Russell, John.

Russell, Bertrand Arthur William (1872–1970), British philosopher and mathematician. He wrote numerous books on various topics including mathematical logic, the theory of knowledge, and social issues. His philosophy was of logical contructionism, which he first applied to mathematics. He demonstrated that mathematics could be explained by the rules of formal logic. Later he applied this technique to other concepts. His most famous work, *Principia Mathematica* (3 vols., 1910–13), was written in collaboration with his teacher, Alfred North Whitehead. A pacifist except during World War II, Russell organized demonstrations against nuclear weapons and the Vietnam War. He was imprisoned twice for his activities on behalf of peace and nuclear disarmament. He won the Nobel Prize in literature (1950). *See also* Principia Mathematica. △854, 858.

Russell, John Russell, 1st Earl (1792–1878), English statesman. He was the son of the 6th duke of Bedford and made an important contribution to the development of British politics in the 19th century. A Whig, he was associated with the major reform issues of the day, such as Roman Catholic emancipation (1829), parliamentary and municipal reform (1832), and the repeal of the Corn Laws (1846). He led the Whigs in opposition to Sir Robert Peel and was prime minister during 1846–52 and 1865–66. He became an earl in 1861.

Russell, Lillian (1861–1922), US singer, b. Helen Louise Leonard in Clinton, Iowa. The star of the operettas *La Cigale* (1891) and *The American Beauty* (1897), she appeared in many Weber & Fields music hall productions, in which she introduced "When Chloe Sings a Song" (1899) and "Come Down, Ma Evenin' Star" (1902). She was known for her love of jewelry, and her affair with "Diamond Jim" Brady has become a legend.

Russell, Rosalind (1912–76), US film actress, b. Waterbury, Conn. She is best known for her career-woman roles in sophisticated comedies of the 1930s and 1940s. Her major films include *Night Must Fall* (1937), *The Women* (1939), *His Girl Friday* (1940), *My Sister Eileen* (1942), *Picnic* (1955), *Auntie Mame* (1958), and *Gypsy* (1962).

Russell, William Felton "Bill" (1934–), US basketball player, b. Monroe, La. Known as a defensive center, he led the University of San Francisco to two national championships (1955–56). He played on the winning US Olympic team (1956), and for the Boston Celtics in the National Basketball Association (1956–69), where he led the team to 11 championships. He also coached Boston (1967–69) and Seattle, which he joined in 1974.

Russian, the official language of the Soviet Union, the mother tongue of about 150,000,000 people there, or about 60% of the population, and spoken as a second language by about 40,000,000 more. It is the most important of the Slavic languages, which form a subdivision of the Indo-European family. Russian is written in the Cyrillic alphabet, a combination of Latin, Greek, and other characters that was developed in the ninth century.

Russian Architecture, architectural style that began as a regional variety of Byzantine architecture in the 10th century with the Christianization of Russia. Important centers of architectural activity developed at Kiev, Novgorod, and Pskov. Early churches were built of wood, but beginning with the construction of the Cathedral of Sancta Sophia, Kiev (1018–37), stone was used. Early churches also used the characteristic Byzantine design of the inscribed cross and five domes, but in later structures domes, apses, and aisles proliferated. The distinctive onion-shaped dome was introduced in the 12th century at the Cathedral of Sancta Sophia, Novgorod. Although the Byzantine influence remained strong, during the 15th century Russia was subject to a series of western European trends. During the reign of Ivan the Great (1462–1505), Italian architects built the Kremlin in a Renaissance style. Peter the Great and, later, Catherine brought Rococo and Neoclassical principles to the building of St Petersburg. In the 19th century a revival of medieval Russian architecture occurred.

Russian Blue Cat, or American Blue, short-haired domestic cat breed. Of unknown origin, this quiet, fine-boned cat has a longish face, almond-shaped, emerald green eyes, and large, pointed ears. The coat is medium to dark blue with silver.

Russian Orthodox Church. △1178.

Russian Revolution (1917), the overthrow of the Russian monarchy and Bolshevik seizure of power. Misconduct of the war, loss of confidence in the regime, and riots in the capital forced Nicholas II to abdicate in March (February Old Style) 1917. A Provisional Government was formed by liberals in the Duma (legislative assembly), but had to contend with the growing influence of the soviets (workers' and soldiers' councils). The new government was characterized by vacillation, postponing crucial issues until the constituent assembly met. The decision to continue the war and failure to introduce land reform caused popular support to shift to the Supreme Soviet. In July the Bolsheviks tried to seize control, but lacked the support of the Soviet. V.I. Lenin, who had arrived in April, had to flee to Finland. In September the socialist Prime Minister Kerensky summoned troops under General Kornilov to Petrograd to suppress opposition, but changed his mind and called for its defense. After the "Kornilov Affair" the Bolsheviks gained a majority in urban soviets, and in October Lenin returned in disguise. On November 7 (October 25) Bolshevik troops stormed the Winter Palace and captured the government. In January 1918 they disbanded the constituent assembly, and in July executed the royal family. △1286, 1310.

Russian Soviet Federated Socialist Republic (Rossijskaja Sovetskaja Federativnaja), largest constituent republic of the USSR, commonly abbreviated RSFSR, bordered by seas of the Arctic Ocean (N); seas of the Pacific (E); China, Mongolia, and Kazakh (S); Azerbaijan and Georgia (SW); and Ukraine, Belorussia, Baltic republics, and Finland (W). The main cities are Moscow (capital), Leningrad, Gorky, Novosibirsk, Kuibyshev, Sverdlovsk. Republic contains the E European lowland, the Urals, W Sibe-

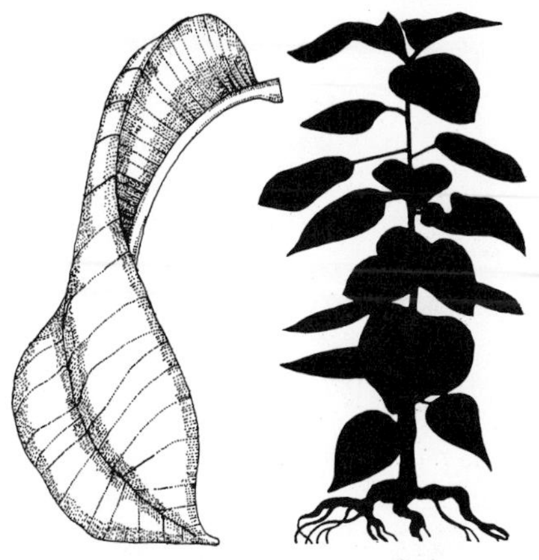

Rubber plant

Artur Rubinstein

Lillian Russell

Russian blue cat

rian Plain, Central Siberian Plateau drained by the Volga, Ob, Jenisej, Lena, and Amur rivers. It was a major portion of the tsarist empire and the first part to come under Soviet control (1917); joined Ukrainian and Belorussian republics and Transcaucasian federated republic to form the USSR 1922. Industries: machinery, chemicals, textiles, leather goods, fish, lumber products, wheat, flax, sugar beet, livestock, coal, iron ore, copper, nickel, lead, manganese, zinc, platinum, oil. Area: 6,592,812sq mi (17,075,383sq km). Pop. 130,090,000.

Russo-Japanese War (1904–05), military conflict between Russia and Japan. Rivalry over Manchuria and Korea caused Japan to break off relations with Russia in February 1904. Declarations of war followed a few days later. In May, Japan crossed the Yalu River from Korea into Manchuria, while its naval forces seized Dairen and besieged Port Arthur, which fell in January 1905. In March 1905 the Japanese captured Mukden, and on May 27 the Japanese annihilated Russia's Baltic fleet, its last hope, at Tsushima. Following US Pres. Theodore Roosevelt's initiative, both parties signed the Treaty of Portsmouth (N.H.) on Sept. 15, 1905. Having proved itself equal to Western forces, Japan required Russia to recognize Japan's "paramount interest" in Korea, recognize Chinese sovereignty in Manchuria, and cede the Kwantung Peninsula and the South Manchurian Railway as far north as Changchow to Japan. Although Japan received no indemnity, it was also given the southern half of Sakhalin by the Russians under the treaty. The Russian defeat was a primary cause of the Russian Revolution of 1905 and established Japan as a world power. △1272.

Rust, in botany, any of many fungal plant diseases characterized by "rusty" reddish-brown or orange blisters and streaks on affected leaves and stems. Rusts stunt plant growth and often kill infected plants. Rust fungi, also called rusts, are particularly serious pests of wheat.

Rutabaga, or Swede turnip, garden vegetable best grown in cool weather. It has large lobed leaves and yellow flowers. The globular, edible root is purplish with yellow flesh. Family Cruciferae; species *Brassica napobrassica*.

Ruth, Babe (1895–1948), US baseball player, b. George Herman Ruth in Baltimore. The all-time home run hitter (714) until surpassed by Hank Aaron in 1974, he played for three teams: Boston Red Sox (1914–19), New York Yankees (1920–34), and Boston Braves (1935). He began his career as a pitcher and established a World Series record of 29 2/3 consecutive scoreless innings that lasted until 1961, when it was broken by Whitey Ford. His personality and awesome home run power helped to save baseball following the 1919 Black Sox scandal. In 1936, he was elected to the Baseball Hall of Fame.

Ruth, biblical book that recounts the story of Ruth, a Moabite woman and mother of Obed, father of Jesse who sired David. A hagiographical book, its main purpose is to give an account of David's ancestors, following Ruth through her marriage to Naomi's son, Mahlon; his death; her decision to stay with Naomi; her marriage to Naomi's husband, Boaz; and Obed's birth.

Ruthenia, now constitutes Transcarpathian oblast, Ukrainian SSR, USSR; capital is Uzhgorod; formerly an autonomous region, the name is Latin word for Russia. During Middle Ages it referred to the Ukraine. After 1918 the term applied only to the easternmost province of Czechoslovakia. Present day Transcarpathian oblast is made up of land ceded to USSR by Czechoslovakia in 1945. Economy is largely agricultural; much of area is heavily forested. Industries: mining, lumbering, furniture, cartons, wood chemicals. Area: 4,981sq mi (12,901sq km). Pop. 1,057,000.

Ruthenium, metallic element (symbol Ru) of the second transition series, first isolated in 1844. It is found associated with platinum. Ruthenium is alloyed with other platinum metals for electrical contacts and is also used as a catalyst. Properties: at. no. 44; at. wt. 101.07; sp gr 12.41; melt. pt. 4190°F (2310°C); boil. pt. 7,052°F (3,900°C); most common isotope Ru^{102} (31.61%). *See also* Transition Elements.

Rutherford, Ernest, 1st Baron (1871–1937), English physicist, b. New Zealand. Leaving New Zealand in 1895, he went to Cambridge to work with J.J. Thomson. After a period at McGill University he returned to Manchester and then to Cambridge, where he succeeded Thomson at the Cavendish Laboratory. His work was the study of radioactivity and atomic structure. He discovered alpha, beta, and gamma radiation, correctly identifying each. He was the first to show that the atom had a nucleus and he carried out the first nuclear reactions. He also identified and named the proton. In 1908 he was awarded a Nobel Prize and in 1931 was created a baron. Although his work led to release of atomic energy, he never believed that the nucleus would provide a source of usable energy. △1480–82.

Rutherfordium. See Element 104.

Rutile, an oxide mineral, titanium dioxide (TiO_2). Found in igneous and metamorphic rocks and quartz veins. Tetragonal system long prismatic and needle-like crystals; also granular masses. Black to red-brown; metallic luster; brittle. Hardness 6–6.5; sp gr 4.2. Used as a gemstone.

Rutledge, John (1739–1800), US political figure and chief justice of the US Supreme Court (1795), b. Charleston, S.C. He was a delegate to the Stamp Act Congress (1765) and two Continental Congresses (1774–76, 1782–83). He was a member of the committee to draft a state constitution (1776) and both president (1776–78) and governor (1779–82) of South Carolina. He played a key role at the federal Constitutional Convention (1787). He was an associate justice on the US Supreme Court (1778–91) and resigned to become chief justice of the South Carolina supreme court (1791–95). He was nominated to be chief justice (1795) but the Senate refused to confirm the appointment because of his adamant criticism of Jay's Treaty.

Rutledge, Wiley Blount, Jr. (1894–1949), US jurist and lawyer, b. Cloverport, Ky. A law professor at Washington University (1926–31) and dean of its law school (1931–35), he was also dean of the University of Iowa law school (1935–39). A US Appeals Court judge (1939–43) and a staunch liberal, he was appointed, by Franklin Delano Roosevelt, associate justice of the US Supreme Court, serving 1943–49. He was noted for his dissents favoring civil liberties, and cast the deciding votes in important cases such as *West Virginia State Board of Education* v. *Barnette* (1942).

Ruwenzori, mountains in central Africa, on the Uganda-Zaire border between lakes Albert and Edward; discovered 1889 by Henry Stanley. Range includes snow-capped peaks; highest is Mt Margherita, 16,763ft (5,113m). Length of range: 75mi (121km); width: 40mi (64km).

Ruysdael. *See* Ruisdael.

Rwanda, republic in E central Africa, between Tanzania and the Democratic Republic of the Congo, bordered by Burundi (S), Uganda (N), Tanzania (E), and Zaire (W). It is one of the most densely populated countries in Africa. The land is mountainous, rugged, with plateaus and deep valleys. The volcanic Virunga Mts (NW) separate the Congo Basin from the Nile Basin; a savanna zone (E) ranges from arid flat lands to low scrublands and bamboo forests; Lake Kivu, country's largest lake, comprises part of the Rwanda-Zaire border. The great abundance of cattle feeding on the thin soil has sped up the erosion process, limiting present and future cultivation for the land; therefore, most of the farming is done on a subsistence level. The major crops include: (subsistence) bananas, beans, peas, sweet potatoes; (cash) coffee, tea, pyrethrum, rice, cotton. Rwanda has put approx. 30,000 families on paysannats (farming communities), to expand the tea crop and ease the economic importance of coffee. With no railroad, and inadequate roads, the social and economic development has been hampered greatly. Industries include textiles, chemicals, tourism, and food processing.

There are 3 major ethnic groups in Rwanda. The Tutsi or Watutsi make up approx. 4% of the population; they are characteristically tall, and have played the role of dominant caste in Rwanda history. The Hutu or Bahutu account for 85% of the population and are mostly farmers, formerly employed by Tutsi landowners. The pygmoid Twa or Batwa are hunters and potters, and make up approx. 1% of total population.

History. The area of Rwanda was first inhabited by the Twa, later the Hutu; the Tutsi were last to come to Rwanda. In the late 19th century Rwanda became part of German East Africa; after WWI administered by Belgium as League of Nations mandate of Rwanda-Urundi, and later a United Nations trust territory. The Belgians governed Rwanda through the Tutsi established supremacy. After two Hutu rebellions, 1928 and 1959, Belgium supported the Hutu provisional government (1960), and in 1961, Rwanda was declared a republic. According to 1962 constitution, the president is elected for a four-year term by universal adult suffrage; the legislative power is in the hands of the 47 member National Assembly. Rwanda is a member of the United Nations and the Organization of African Unity.

PROFILE

Official name: Republic of Rwanda
Area: 10,169sq mi (26,338sq km)
Population: 4,200,000
Chief cities: Kigali (capital); Butare; Nyanza
Religion: Christianity; tribal
Language: Kinyarwanda, French (both official)
Monetary unit: Rwanda franc

Ryazan, (R'azan), city in Ryazan oblast, W central USSR, 120mi (193km) SE of Moscow on Oka River; annexed by Moscow 1521 and held until it became a city 1778; site of Archangel Cathedral (begun late 15th century), Assumption Cathedral (1693–99), and a kremlin wall (1208). Industries: agricultural machinery, radios, machine tools, oil refining. Pop. 357,000.

Rybinsk, formerly Shcherbakov; city in Russian SFSR, USSR, on the Volga River at its efflux from the Rybinsk Reservoir. First mentioned in 1504, it was chartered 1777. It became an important trading and transshipment center after 1703 founding of St Petersburg and construction of Volga-Neva canal systems; site of mid-19th-century cathedral and regional museum. Industries: shipyards, agriculture, matches, machinery, linen, aircraft motors, fish canneries, flour, lumber. Pop. 218,000.

Rye, hardy cereal grass originating in SW Asia and naturalized worldwide. It grows where many other cereals cannot. It has flower spikelets that develop one-seeded grains. It is used for bread flour, animal feed and pasture, and in alcoholic beverages. Height: to 6ft (1.8m). Family Gramineae; species *Secale cereale*. △326.

Ryukyu Islands (Nansei-shoto), Japanese archipelago in W Pacific Ocean, extends approx. 600mi (966km) between Kyushu and Formosa; separates the East China Sea (W) from the Pacific Ocean (E). Island groups include Amami, Okinawa, and Sakishima. Volcanic and coral formations, they have been inhabited since early times; invaded by China 7th century, and by Satsuma of Japan in 17th century; tribute of both countries until relinquished by China to Japan in 1879. After WWII they were administered by the United States; restored to Japan 1971. Agriculture and fishing are chief occupations. Area: approx. 850sq. mi (2,202sq km). Pop. 945,111.

Ryun, James Ronald (1947–), US athlete, b. Wichita, Kan. He ran the first sub 4-minute mile in high school history with a time of 3 minutes, 58.3 seconds (1965). While a student at the University of Kansas (1967), he lowered the world's mile record to 3 minutes, 51.1 seconds and also held the 880-yard record.

S

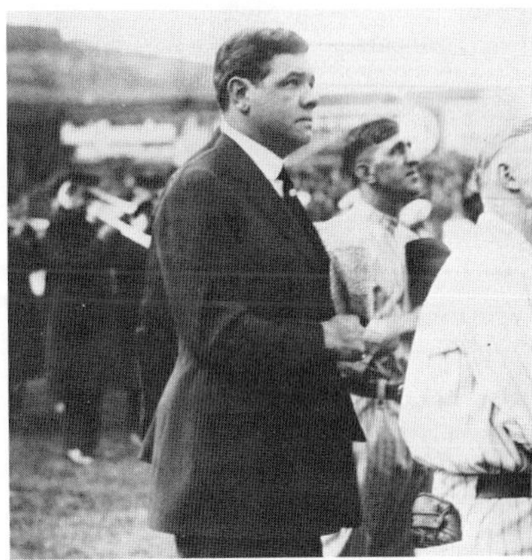

Babe Ruth

Saadiah, Ben Joseph (892–942), a prolific writer and Jewish scholar, b. Egypt. He became well known for his involvement in the controversy with Aaron ben Neir in Babylonia over the Jewish calendar. At this time, he produced many works against heretical thought. He also translated the Old Testament into Arabic. The academy of Sura (Baghdad) was under his leadership (928–35).

Saarbrücken, city in W West Germany, on Saar River, 39mi (62km) SE of Trier; capital of Saarland; seat of counts of Nassau-Saarbrücken 1381–1793; annexed to France 1793–1815, to Prussia 1815; capital of Saar Territory 1919–35, 1945–57; returned to Germany 1935; scene of heavy fighting during WWII; seat of university (1948). Notable buildings include Gothic Castle Church (15th century), city hall (1750), the Ludwigskirche, a baroque church, (1762–75). Industries: coal mining, iron, steel, precision instruments, machinery, printing, beer, cement, sugar. Founded 999; chartered 1321. Pop. 127,989.

Saarinen, (Gottlieb) Eliel (1873–1950), Finnish-American architect, resident in US after 1923. His work had a significant impact on modern US architecture, especially the design of skyscrapers and churches. In Finland, his best-known work is the Helsinki railroad station (1904–14). He was president of Cranbrook Academy of Art (1932–48) and designed several buildings for institutions in Bloomfield Hills, Mich. Also important are his Tabernacle Church of Christ in Columbus, Ind. (1940–42) and Christ Lutheran Church in Minneapolis (1949–50). He collaborated with his son Eero in later years.

Saarland, formerly Saar or Saar Territory; state in SW West Germany; capital is Saarbrücken. Annexed to France 1797; divided between Bavaria and Prussia by Treaty of Paris (1815); made autonomous territory by Treaty of Versailles (1919); restored to Germany by plebiscite 1935; after WWII autonomous under French economic protection; became a German state 1957. Industries: coal and coke mining, iron, steel, glass, chemicals, textiles. Area: 991sq mi (2,567sq km). Pop. 1,127,000.

Sabbath, the seventh day (Saturday), observed as a day of rest by Jews. It is observed to mark God's day of rest after the creation. The Sabbath has become the principal day of worship and work is not permissible. In Christian churches this day of worship and rest was changed to the first day (Sunday) in observance of the Resurrection.

Saber Tooth, extinct cat having long upper canines, for stabbing and slicing thick-skinned prey, often Mastodons. They were worldwide in distribution from Oligocene to Pleistocene epochs. *Smilodon*, last of the North American saber tooths, had 9-inch (23-cm) sabers. Height: 40in (102cm). *See also* Felidae. △576.

Sabin, Albert Bruce (1906–), US virologist, b. Bialystock, Russia. Sabin developed a live virus oral vaccine against poliomyelitis, in contrast to Jonas Salk's inactivated virus vaccine, and began testing Sabin vaccine in 1957.

Sabine River, river in Texas and Louisiana; rises at confluence of many headstreams, NE Texas; flows SE to form Texas-Louisiana border, empties through Sabine Lake and Sabine Pass into the Gulf of Mexico. Length: approx. 360mi (577km).

Sabines, or **Sabini,** people of ancient central Italy inhabiting the Sabine Hills NE of Rome. They were intensely religious and politically diffuse. The legend of Romulus' rape of the Sabine women may have been recounted to explain the Sabine part of the early Roman population. After sporadic fighting they were gradually Romanized while the Romans adopted a number of their customs, including burial rituals.

Sable, marten native of forested areas of N Europe and Siberia. It has been hunted almost to extinction for its thick, soft, durable fur that is dark brown to black, sometimes flecked with white. Now protected in N USSR, they have long bushy tails. Length: 1–2ft (30–60cm). Family Mustelidae; species *Mustela zibellina*.

Sable Antelope, large, heavy antelope native to Africa, south of the Sahara. Both sexes have long, stout horns, curving backward, that are used for defense. Color is brown to black or roan gray. Height: to 6.5ft (165cm) at shoulder; weight: to 616lb (280kg). Family Bovidae; genus *Hippotragus*.

Sac. *See* Sauk.

Sacagawea (1787?–?1812), American Indian interpreter for the Lewis and Clark Expedition (1804–06), b. Idaho. She was born a Shoshone but was captured and sold as a slave to French trapper Toussaint Charbonneau, who later married her. They joined Lewis and Clark, and she became their guide taking them to the Pacific Ocean, befriending the Indians they met on the way. Monuments to her are found in Oregon, Montana, Idaho, and North Dakota.

Saccharide, organic compound based on sugar molecules. Monosaccharides include glucose and fructose, found in fruit and honey. Two sugar molecules join together to make a disaccharide, such as cane sugar. Polysaccharides have more than two sugar molecules. *See also* Carbohydrate. △1570.

Saccharin. *See* Sweetener, Artificial.

Sacco and Vanzetti Case, controversial robbery-murder trial taken up as a cause by intellectuals, radicals and liberals in the 1920s. At the height of the Red Scare (April 1920), two men robbed and killed a paymaster and his guard in South Braintree, Mass. Italian immigrant anarchists Nicola Sacco and Bartolomeo Vanzetti were convicted and executed for the crime. Their supporters claimed the verdict was a reflection of anti-Italian, anti-radical bigotry. There is continued belief in Vanzetti's innocence, although a 1961 ballistics test suggested the fatal bullet came from Sacco's gun. △1326.

Sacculus and Utriculus Canals. △676.

Sachs, Nelly (1891–1970), German-Jewish poet. Having escaped from Nazi Germany, her early stories and later poetic works, including *In the Houses of Death* (1946) and *Later Poems* (1965), bore witness to the sufferings of her people. Her later works included *O the Chimneys: Selected Poems* (1967) and *Seeker and Other Poems* (1970). She shared the Nobel Prize for literature in 1966 with S.Y. Agnon.

Sackville-West, Victoria Mary (1892–1962), English poet and novelist. Wife of Harold Nicolson and with him a member of the Bloomsbury Group. Her best-known novels are *The Edwardians* (1930) and *All Passion Spent* (1931). Her interest in her ancestors and in her family home at Knole dominated her work. *See also* Bloomsbury Group.

Sacral Bone. *See* Sacrum.

Sacramento, capital city and port in central Califor-

Ernest Rutherford

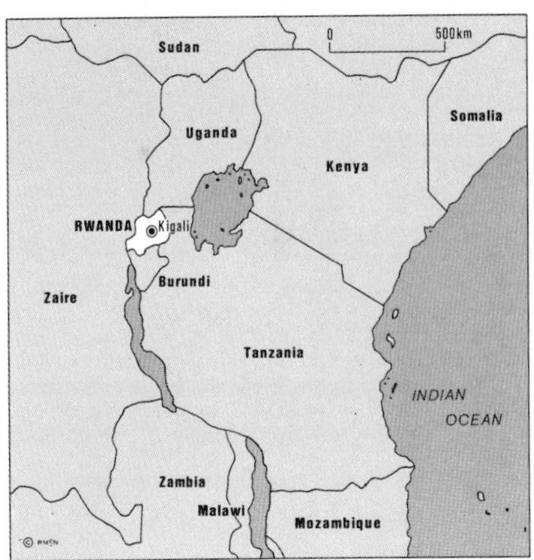
Sudan
0
500km
Somalia
Uganda
Kenya
RWANDA
Kigali
Burundi
Zaire
Tanzania
INDIAN
OCEAN
Zambia
Malawi
Mozambique

Rwanda

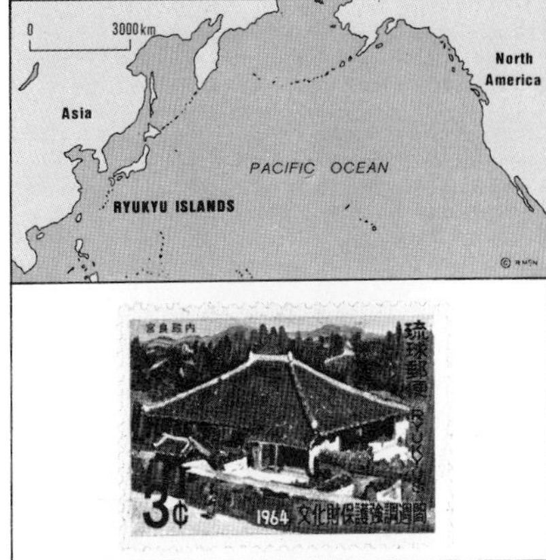
0
3000km
North
America
Asia
PACIFIC OCEAN
RYUKYU ISLANDS
3¢
1964

Ryukyu Islands

nia, 72mi (116km) NE of San Francisco; seat of Sacramento co. Originally a Mexican land grant to John A. Sutter, the city grew around site of fort built 1840, and was called New Helvetia; it experienced a population and prosperity boom after discovery of gold near Sutter's mill (1848); made state capital 1854, W terminus of Pony Express 1860, and W terminus of first transcontinental railroad 1863. It is site of Sacramento City College (1916), California State at Sacramento (1947), American River College (1955), Sutter's Fort; nearby are Mather and McClellan Air Force bases. Industries: food processing, jet fuels, soap, machinery, bricks. Settled 1839; inc. 1850 as town, 1863 as city. Pop. (1970) 257,105.

Sacramento, Battle of (1847), battle during the Mexican War. Col. Alexander W. Doniphan, on a march from Santa Fe to Chihuahua, Mexico, defeated a Mexican force, with 600 Mexican and 12 American casualties.

Sacramento Mountains, range in S New Mexico and W Texas between Pecos and Rio Grande rivers; site of Lincoln National Forest and Mescalero Indian Reservation. Highest peak, Sierra Blanca, 12,003ft (3,661m).

Sacramento River, longest river in California; rises NW near Mt Shasta; flows SW to Suisan Bay, arm of San Francisco Bay, where it joins San Joaquin River at a large delta. Waters have been inc. into Central Valley Project for irrigation of the San Joaquin Valley; navigable by small steamers for approx. 260mi (419km) of its 320mi (515km).

Sacred Baboon. *See* Hamadryas.

Sacrifice, offering or destruction of precious objects, food and drink, flowers and incense, animals and humans for religious purposes. Sacrifices are important in many religions. They are made in the hope of winning divine favor, atoning for guilt, or for some other mystical purpose. △830.

Sacroiliac Suture, immovable joint, or seam, that joins the sacrum and the ilium part of the hip bone to form the pelvis. *See also* Pelvis; Sacrum.

Sacrum, or sacral bone, region of the vertebral column, formed by the fusion of five vertebrae. The sacrum and the two hipbones form the pelvic girdle for the attachment of the legs to the body. △682.

Sadat, Anwar al- (1918–), Egyptian political leader. He succeeded Gamal Abdel Nasser as president of Egypt (1970). In 1973 he led Egypt into war against Israel, demanding the return of Egyptian land occupied by Israel after the Arab-Israeli war of 1967. Sadat later demonstrated his willingness to consider a negotiated peace settlement by his support of the 1974 troop disengagement accord. △1380.

Sadducees, a sect of Judaism, developed around 200 BC. The members were wealthy priests and aristocrats. They stressed a literal interpretation of written law, and rejected oral law. They were often in opposition to the Pharisees. Sadducees were based on the temple cult with the priest as central. They rejected the soul's immortality and the existence of angels. The sect disappeared with the destruction of the Temple, AD 70.

Sade, Marquis de (1740–1814), popular name of Donatien Alphonse François, Comte de Sade; French novelist. He spent over 30 years in prison for sexual offenses and produced several works dealing with sexual pathology, including *Justine* (1791) and *Aline et Valcour* (1795). He was eventually committed to the insane asylum at Charenton. The brilliance of his work has only recently been acknowledged. *See also* Sadism.

Sadism, taking pleasure in hurting or abusing others physically or psychologically. Sadism is frequently connected with deviant sexual behavior in which beating or abuse of the other is a necessary part of sexual arousal or gratification. The sadist often takes pleasure in dominating others or in watching them suffer. As a characteristic it may be linked with *masochism* and a person may alternate between these two forms of aggression. The term is derived from the Marquis de Sade, whose writing included examples of cruelty and sexual abuse.

Safad (Zefat), town in N Israel, 7mi (11km) NNW of the Sea of Galilee; fortified by invading Crusaders (11th century) who devastated Jewish community; by 16th century the Jewish population was reinstated, and Safad grew to be a center of Jewish learning and mysticism, and one of Palestine's four holy cities; scene of conflict between the Arabs and the Israelis during 1948 war of independence; popular health and tourist resort. Pop. 13,100.

Safflower, annual plant with large, orange flower heads that yield a dyestuff. The seeds yield an oil low in saturated fats that is used in cooking, paints, and cosmetics. Family Compositae; species *Carthamus tinctorius.*

Saffron, bulbous perennial crocus native to Asia Minor and cultivated in Europe. It has purple or white flower blooms in autumn. Family Iridaceae; species *Crocus sativus.* Or, the golden, dried stigmas of this plant used as flavoring or dye. Or, the color this dye produces.

Saga, prose tale usually written in Old Norse or Gaelic between the 7th and 14th centuries. Old Norse sagas were generally written in Iceland by anonymous Norwegian expatriates during the 12th and 13th centuries and fall into several types. The "fornaldar sagas," the oldest form, deal with heroic, often mythological figures from Scandinavian and Germanic traditions. The best known of these is *Ragnar Lothbok.* "Family sagas" trace the genealogy of Icelandic families, and "Kings' sagas" (after *c.*1220) are histories similar to Latin chronicles, eg, Snorri Sturluson's *Heimskringla.* Some 13th-century sagas are translations of French romances.

Irish sagas, written in Gaelic, derive from an oral tradition going back to the 6th century or earlier. The oldest extant manuscript is the *Wurzburg Codex* (*c.* 700). They are perhaps the most pagan of any form of Medieval literature and are characterized by a hero of both human and divine descent, the intervention of supernatural and magic forces in men's affairs, taboos, and personal quarrels between brothers or near kinsmen. These sagas provided many of the story lines for Arthurian romances in other languages, although the characters and social milieu are different. *See also* Arthurian Romance; Fenian Cycle.

Sagan, Françoise (1935–), pseud. of Françoise Quoirez, French novelist and playwright. Her works portray the tragic disillusionment of the young and innocent, as in *Bonjour Tristesse* (1954). This theme was developed in *A Certain Smile* (1956) and *Those Without Shadows* (1957). Later works included *Chamade* (1970) and *The Heart Keeper* (1974).

Sage, common name for a number of plants of the mint family, principally *Salvia officinalis,* an aromatic perennial herb used for seasoning. Scarlet sage, common name for *Salvia splendens,* is grown for its showy flowers. Blue sage *(S. pitchere)* is a perennial native to the prairies of central United States. △358, 446.

Sagebrush, aromatic shrubs common in arid areas of W North America. The big sagebrush, *Artemisia tridentata,* has small, silvery-green leaves and bears clusters of tiny white flower heads; height: to 12ft (3.6m). Family Compositae.

Sage Grouse, or sage hen, largest North American grouse. The male fans its long slender tail as background for its inflated orange neck air sacs while it bows, dances, and utters groaning sounds during courtship displays. The female builds the nest, incubates the eggs (7) and cares for the young. Length: to 30in (76cm). Species *Centrocercus urophasianus. See also* Grouse.

Saginaw, city in E Michigan, on Saginaw River, 80mi (129km) NW of Detroit; seat of Saginaw co. Industries: automobile parts, graphite, paper products, mobile homes. Settled 1816 as fur trading post; inc. as city 1857. Pop. (1970) 91,849.

Sagittarius, or the Archer, southern constellation situated on the ecliptic between Scorpius and Capricornus; the ninth sign of the zodiac. Rich in stellar clusters, this constellation also contains much interstellar matter obscuring the central region of the Milky Way Galaxy and is only penetrable with radio telescopes. Two interesting features of Sagittarius are the Lagoon and Trifid nebulae. Brightest star Epsilon Sagittarii (Kaus Australis). The astrological sign for the period Nov. 22–Dec. 21. △136, 826.

Sago Palm, or fern palm, a feather-leaved palm tree native to swampy areas of Malaya and Polynesia. Its thick trunk contains a starch used in foodstuffs. The sago palm flowers once after 15 years of age and then dies when the fruit ripens. Height 4–30ft (1.2–9.1m). Species include *Metroxylon sagus* and *M. rumphii.* Family Palmaceae. Some cycads are called sago palms, but they are not true palms.

Saguaro, large cactus native to Arizona, California, and Mexico. It has 5–6 branches. White, night-blooming flowers appear when the plant is 50–75 years old. Its edible fruit is red. Height: to 40ft (12m). Family Cactaceae; species *Carnegiea gigantea. See also* Cactus.

Sahara, desert in N Africa; extends from Atlantic Ocean to the Red Sea and from the Atlas Mts to the S Sudan region. It is the world's largest desert with an area of more than 3,500,000sq mi (9,065,000sq km). Terrain varies from rocky plateaus and gravel-covered plains (N) to low plateaus and broad plains (S); contains many oases. Region is rich in minerals, especially oil, natural gas, and iron ore. △266.

Sahel, semi-arid region of Africa, bordered by Sahara (N), Senegal (W), savannas (S), and Ethiopia (E); extends through Mauritania, Mali, Upper Volta, Niger, N Nigeria, and Sudan. Normally a land of very little rainfall, a serious drought from late 1960s to mid-70s caused starvation of many.

Saiga, Eurasian antelope, found only in S Russia and central Asia. Sheeplike with "swollen" nose, ending in a piglike snout, it is brown in summer, white in winter. Males carry short, ridged, slightly curved horns. Length: to 5.5ft (1.7m); height: to 32in (81cm). Family Bovidae; species *Saiga.* △584.

Saigon (Ho Chih Minh City), port city in Vietnam, at Saigon River mouth; trade center; former capital of South Vietnam (chosen 1954 by Geneva Convention); site of University of Saigon (1954), Van Hanh University. An ancient Khmer settlement, it passed to Annamese *c.* 17th century; it was captured 1859 by French and ceded to them 1862; capital of Union of Indochina 1887–1902; military headquarters for US and South Vietnamese forces during Vietnam War. In 1968 the city was attacked by Communist forces; severely damaged in Vietnam War; taken by North Vietnamese forces May 1975. Pop. 1,761,335.

Sailboat, boat propelled by sails utilizing the power of the wind. Most important of all vessels until the late 19th century, when they were replaced by steam-driven craft, sailboats are now used for recreational purposes. Most are small and designed for coastal and inland waters. Timber hulls are decreasing in number, being supplanted by fiberglass, metal, and ferrocement constructions. Catboats, sloops, and cutters are single-masted vessels; yawls and ketches are two-masted. △1678.

Sail-fin Leaf Fish. △516.

Sail-finned Sturgeon Fish. △510.

Sailfish, marine billfish found worldwide in tropical seas. A popular sport fish, it is identified by a large, saillike dorsal fin and sword-shaped upper jaw. Length: to 11ft (3.4m); weight: 221lb (99kg). Species include *Istiophorus platypterus* and the smaller Atlantic *I. Americanus.* Family Istiophoridae.

Sailing. *See* Yachting.

Sailor-by-the-Wind. △470.

Saint, an individual who has manifested exceptional love of God and holiness in life. In some Christian writings all believers are called saints, but the title is usually reserved for men and women of the most outstanding merit, such as St Peter and other Apostles, St Augustine and other theologians, St Agnes and other martyrs. The Roman Catholic Church has a process by which additional saints can be named—Joan of Arc was canonized in 1920. Many shrines have been built to honor saints, and Catholics pray to saints to intercede with God for them. *See also* Beatification.

Saint Augustine, resort city in NE Florida, on a peninsula between the Matanzas and San Sebastian rivers; separated from the Atlantic Ocean by Anastasia Island. The oldest city in the United States, founded by Pedro Menéndez de Avilés in 1565, it is a port of entry and a shrimping and shipping center. Inc. 1824. Pop. (1970) 12,352.

Saint Bartholomew's Day Massacre, the slaying of French Protestants, called Huguenots, which began in Paris on Saint Bartholomew's Day, Aug. 24, 1572. Catherine de Médicis, mother of Charles IX, plotted to assassinate Admiral Gaspard de Coligny, a Huguenot who advocated war with Spain. When the assassination attempt failed and her involvement was about to be discovered, Catherine convinced Charles to order the death of Huguenot leaders, many of whom were in Paris for the wedding of Henry of Navarre (later Henry IV). The ensuing bloodbath—3,000 deaths in Paris alone—was justified by Charles' claim of a Huguenot plot against the crown. The massacre horrified Protestant countries and solidified Protestant opposition to the crown within France. △1154.

Saint Bernard, Swiss mountain and rescue dog (working group). A dog of excellent scenting abilities, it has a massive head with forehead wrinkles; short, deep muzzle; hanging lips; high-set, triangular, drop ears; broad, straight body; long, muscular legs; and long, heavy tail. The white and red dense coat may be short-haired (smooth with bushy tail) or long-haired (medium-long, slightly wavy). Average size: 25–29in (63–74cm) at shoulder; 140–170lb (63–76kg). First brought to Hospice of Great St Bernard Pass in 1660–70, this dog has worked with monks to find people lost in the snow. *See also* Working Dog.

Saint Bernard Passes, two alpine passes in Switzerland; link Valais, Switzerland with Valle d'Aosta, Italy; referred to as Great St Bernard and Little St Bernard passes. The passes were used as invasion routes by Gauls, Romans, Charlemagne, Emperor Henry IV, Frederick Barbarossa, and Napoleon I; site of two hospices, ruined temple of Jupiter, scientific institute, hotel, library, church, Great St Bernard Tunnel (opened 1964). Height: 8,098ft (2,470m).

Saint Boniface, industrial city in SE Manitoba, Canada, on Red River. Industries: oil refining, meat packing, metal works, grain mills. A Roman Catholic center for NW Canada; mission was est. 1818. Pop. 46,661.

Saint Catharines, city in S Ontario, Canada; seat of Lincoln co, on Welland Canal. Industries: shipbuilding and repair, automotive parts, food processing, fruit trade center. Inc. 1876. Pop. 109,636.

Saint Charles, city in E Missouri, on Missouri River 20mi (32km) NW of St Louis; seat of St Charles co. First permanent settlement on Missouri River, it served as state capital 1821–26; site of Lindenwood College (1827). Industries: shoes, metal, farm produce. Founded by French traders 1769; inc. as city 1849. Pop. (1970) 31,834.

Saint Christopher. *See* Saint Kitts-Nevis.

Saint Clair Shores, city in SE Michigan, on Lake St Clair, 13mi (21km) NE of Detroit; pleasure boating center. Inc. as village 1925, as city 1950. Pop. (1970) 88,093.

Saint Cloud, city in central Minnesota, on Mississippi River, 58mi (93km) NW of Minneapolis; seat of Stearns co; site of St Cloud College (1866). Industries: granite quarrying (since 1868), optical instruments, metal working, railroad shops. Founded 1851; inc. as city 1889. Pop. (1970) 39,691.

Saint Croix Island (Santa Cruz), largest of US Virgin Islands, in the West Indies; Christiansted, on NE coast, is chief town; agricultural and tourist center. Discovered 1493 by Christopher Columbus, it was taken at various times by Dutch, English, Spanish, and French; purchased by Denmark 18th century; sold to United States 1917. Industries: rum, sugar, livestock. Area: 84sq mi (218sq km). Pop. 31,892.

Saint Croix River, river on boundary of SE Maine and SW New Brunswick, Canada; rises in Chiputneticoo Lakes; flows SE to Passamaquoddy Bay; used for power and transporting logs downstream. St Croix Island in the river is site of a national monument commemorating the French settlement est. 1604 by Samuel de Champlain and colonist Pierre du Gua, Sieur de Monts. Length: 129mi (208km).

St. Denis, Ruth (1877–1968), US modern dancer, b. Newark, N.J. She founded and taught at Denishawn (1914–31) with husband, Ted Shawn. Influenced by Asian culture, her teaching emphasized beauty, idolized woman, and encouraged dance as a form of religious worship.

Saint-Denis, city in N France, 7mi (11km) NNE of Paris. City grew up around abbey (AD 626) built on site of St Denis' tomb (patron saint of France). It was rebuilt in 18th century. Much-copied basilica of St Denis (1136–47) is outstanding example of a Gothic cathedral; contains tombs of Louis XVI, Marie Antoinette, and other French rulers. Industries: metals, chemicals, glass, paper, soap. Pop. 99,268.

Saint Elmo's Fire, an electrical discharge illuminating the tops of tall objects, also called a corposant. It usually occurs during a storm when the atmosphere becomes charged strongly enough to create a discharge between the air and an object. Early sailors named this phenomenon after their patron saint.

Saint-Etienne, city in E central France, 32mi (51km) SW of Lyons on Furens River; capital of Loire dept. Textile and silk industries were est. here 11th century; in 16th century firearms were produced; in 1815 city had its first steel plant and in 1827 terminus of first French railroad was built here; site of arms museum, 17th-century Church of St Louis and Notre Dame. Industries: textiles, small arms, ammunition, alloy steels. Pop. 213,468.

Saint-Exupéry, Antoine de (1900–44), French novelist and aviator. His experiences as a pilot formed the material for his novels, which explore the themes of duty, love, and human fraternity. His novels include *Southern Mail* (1929), *Night Flight* (1931), and *Flight to Arras* (1942). His children's book *The Little Prince* (1943), later made into a film, emphasized that the simple things in life are the best. He was killed in action.

Saint Francis River, river in SE Missouri and E Arkansas; rises in hills of SE Mo.; flows S to Mississippi River near Helena, Ark.; forms part of Missouri-Arkansas boundary. Wappapello Dam (1941) near Poplar Bluff, Mo. forms reservoir and recreation area. Navigable for 125mi (201km) of its 470mi (757km).

Saint-Gaudens, Augustus (1848–1907), US sculptor, b. Ireland. An influential neoclassical sculptor, he received numerous commissions for decorative and monumental sculptures, including Lincoln (Lincoln Park, Chicago) and General Sherman (New York City).

Saint George's (St George), port town on SW coast of Grenada, in the West Indies; capital of Grenada; beautiful harbor; site of St George's church, Fort George; was capital of former British colony of Windward Islands. Industries: rum and sugar processing. Exports: cacao, nutmeg, mace. Founded 1650 as French settlement. Pop. 8,644.

Saint-Germain, Treaty of (1919), World War I peace agreement between the Allies and the Republic of Austria. Signed in Saint-Germain-en-Laye, France, it was concerned with the status of Austria. It established boundaries for the new republic, which was reduced by the loss of a great deal of territory, and declared the Austro-Hungarian monarchy dissolved. It further stated that Austria refrain from entering into political or economic union with Germany, without agreement by the League of Nations, the covenant of which was included in the treaty.

Saint Germain-en-Laye, town in N central France, on Seine River; suburb of W Paris. Once a royal residence, in 12th century Louis VI built a château here that was scene of many treaty signings, the last one in 1919 between allied powers and Austria; birthplace of Charles IX, Margaret of Valois, Henry II, Louis XIV, and Claude Debussy; site of terrace of St Germain, famous European promenade; 16th-century Renaissance château (royal residence of Francis I to Louis XIV) is now a national museum of antiquities; resort area. Pop. 38,808.

Saint Helena, island in S Atlantic Ocean, 1,200mi (1,932km) W of Africa; capital is Jamestown. Discovered 1502 by Portuguese navigator João da Nova Castella, it was annexed by Dutch 1633; annexed by British East India Co. 1659 and made a British crown colony 1834; place of exile of Napoleon I in 1815; his home is maintained as a memorial. St Helena, Ascension Island, and Tristan da Cunha comprise the British dependency of St Helena. Industries: hemp, vegetables, sweet potatoes, livestock. Area: 47sq mi (122sq km). Pop. 4,829.

Saint Helena Redwood. △632.

Saint John, Henry, Viscount Bolingbroke (1678–1751), English political figure and philosopher. He was an influential Tory during Queen Anne's reign, rising to prominence under the patronage of Robert Harley and Abigail Masham. He became Viscount Bolingbroke (1712) but sacrificed his career in an attempt to prevent the Hanoverian succession to the British throne. His secret negotiations with the Stuart pretender were discovered, and he fled the country (1714). He was pardoned for his contacts with the Stuarts in 1723. In his latter years he enjoyed a reputation as a political theorist. His *The Idea of the Patriot King* (1749), advocating benevolent despotism, influenced George III.

Saint John, port city in S New Brunswick, Canada, on N shore of Bay of Fundy, at mouth of St John River; seat of St John co; first Canadian city to be inc. (1785). Industries: shipping, shipbuilding and repair. Pop. 87,910.

Saint John River, river in NE United States and SE Canada; rises in NW Maine; flows NE into Canada, then SE to St John, New Brunswick, emptying into the

Anwar al-Sadat

Sailfish

Saint Bernard

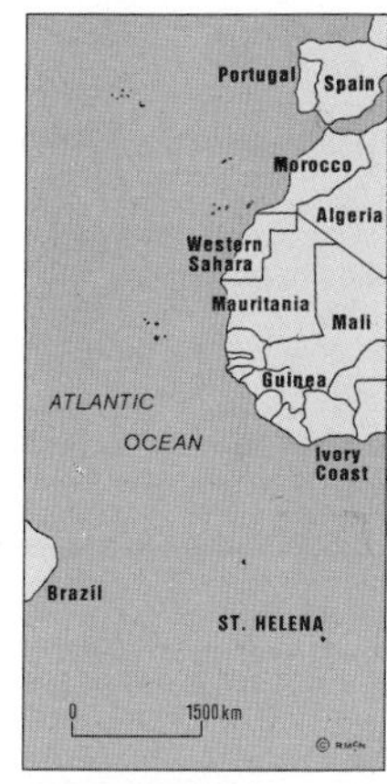
Portugal
Spain
Morocco
Algeria
Western Sahara
Mauritania
Mali
Guinea
ATLANTIC
OCEAN
Ivory Coast
Brazil
ST. HELENA
0
1500km

St. Helena Island

Bay of Fundy; Reversing Falls, located at the river's mouth, are caused by the strong tides of the Bay of Fundy; used for lumber transportation and hydroelectricity. Discovered 1604. Length: 418mi (673km).

Saint John's, capital city and principal port of Newfoundland, Canada, on SE coast; site of Queens College, and Memorial University of Newfoundland. Industries: fishing and fish processing, shipping and shipbuilding, textiles, iron works. Colonized 1583 by British. Pop. 86,290.

Saint Johns River, river in E Florida; rises in E central Florida 28mi (45km) W of Melbourne; flows N to Jacksonville, turns E and enters Atlantic Ocean 28mi (45km) downstream. Lower section is part of Intracoastal Waterway; navigable for 170mi (274km) of its 285mi (459km).

Saint Joseph, city in NW Missouri, on Missouri River, 46mi (74km) NNW of Kansas City; seat of Buchanan co; served as E terminus of Pony Express (1860); site of Missouri Western College (1915), Pony Express Stables (now a museum), and house where Jesse James was killed; railroad center; livestock and grain market. Industries: electrical products, meat packing, flour milling, wire rope. Founded 1826; inc. 1851. Pop. (1970) 72,691.

Saint Joseph River, river in Michigan and Indiana; rises in S Michigan; flows S and W into Indiana, and turns NW to empty into Lake Michigan at St Joseph, Michigan. Length: 210mi (338km).

Saint Kitts-Nevis (Saint Christopher-Nevis), independent state of Leeward Islands, British West Indies; includes islands of St Kitts, Nevis, and Sombrero; Basseterre is capital, on St Kitts; chief town of Nevis is Charlestown; agricultural processing and tourism are important on both Nevis and St Kitts; islands are volcanic, mountainous, and scenic. Discovered 1493 by Christopher Columbus, the islands were settled 1623 by British (under Thomas Warner) at St Kitts, 1628 at Nevis, to be followed shortly after by French settlers. Anglo-French disputes over possession were settled in British favor 1783 by terms of the Treaty of Paris; the islands were part of colony of Leewards 1871–1956; belonged to the West Indies Federation 1958–62; became self-governing (associated with Great Britain) 1967 with Anguilla, which seceded from state 1971. Nevis is site of thermal baths and birthplace of Alexander Hamilton. Exports: cotton, yams, molasses, sugar, coconuts. Area: 118sq mi (306sq km). Pop. 52,020.

Saint Laurent, Louis Stephen (1882–1973), Canadian prime minister (1948–57). A bilingual lawyer, he was minister of justice and attorney general (1941–46). As prime minister he effected court reform and was a moving force in the formation of the North Atlantic Treaty Organization. He led the Liberal party after 1948, succeeding Mackenzie King.

St. Laurent, Yves (1936–), French fashion designer. He popularized trousers for women for all occasions. He is also associated with fur and leather, the "little girl look," the trapeze dress, the shortened skirts of the 1960s, the "chic beatnik" look, metallic and transparent fabrics, and geometric shapes and prints. He also designs clothes for men.

Saint Lawrence, Gulf of, broad, deep, gulf in Atlantic Ocean between Newfoundland and the E coast of mainland Canada (coastal Quebec, NE coastal New Brunswick, and Nova Scotia); joins NE Atlantic Ocean through Cabot Strait (SE) and Strait of Belle Isle (NE); door of the St Lawrence Seaway; contains many islands.

Saint Lawrence River, a principal river of North America, in SE Ontario and S Quebec provinces, Canada; flows from NE end of Lake Ontario, about 760mi (1,224km) to the Gulf of St Lawrence on SE Canadian shore. Length from W end of Lake Superior to the river mouth is over 2,000mi (3,220km), and has been entirely navigable since the completion of the St Lawrence Seaway (1959). River forms boundary between New York and Ontario for approx. 120mi (193km) (this section includes the Thousand Islands); supports extensive lumbering and many hydroelectric power stations.

Saint Lawrence Seaway, deep international waterway in Canada and United States, on the St Lawrence River between Montreal and Lake Ontario, Quebec and New York; connects Great Lakes with Atlantic Ocean. Authorized by Canada 1951, and by the United States 1954, it was planned to break the congestion caused by an outdated canal system along the rapids section of the St Lawrence River. Constructed 1955–59, the seaway has seven locks, and a large hydroelectric power project was built in the international rapids section between Ogdensburg, N.Y. and Cornwall, Ontario. The busiest period for this waterway system, which can now accommodate deep draft vessels, is May-October. The navigation and hydroelectric power project has spurred industrial and agricultural development. Length: 2,342mi (3,771km).

Saint Lô, town in NW France, 34mi (55km) W of Caen. An old Gallo-Roman town, it was fortified by Charlemagne in 8th century; scene of 16th-century massacre of Huguenots. Normandy invasion July 7, 1944, by Allies almost destroyed town. Industries: wood products, plaster, clothing. Pop. 18,615.

Saint-Louis, port city in Senegal, W Africa, on an island in the Senegal River; oldest French settlement in Africa; site of railroad junction, research institute, airport. Industries: meat processing, hides, exporting. Founded 1658 as trade base. Pop. 75,000.

Saint Louis, port city in E Missouri, on Mississippi River; largest city in Missouri. City site was chosen by Pierre LaClède, who est. post here 1764. By terms of secret treaty of Fontainebleau (1762) city was transferred to Spain (1770–1800) and made seat of Upper Louisiana government; it was returned briefly to France 1800; ceded to the United States in Louisiana Purchase 1803; became seat of government for District of Louisiana and capital of Territory of Missouri 1812–21; served as Union supply and hospital center during the Civil War. It was site of Louisiana Purchase Exposition (1904), first international aviation meet (1910), sponsorship of Charles A. Lindbergh's *Spirit of St Louis* transatlantic flight (1927). Landmarks include Jefferson National Expansion Memorial, a national historic site (est. 1935), Missouri Botanical Gardens (1858), Wainwright Building (1891), Busch Memorial Stadium (1966); professional sports teams include baseball's and football's Cardinals and ice hockey's Blues; site of Washington University (1853), St Louis University (1818), University of Missouri at St Louis (1960). Industries: automobiles, brewing, chemicals, aircraft, space capsules, food processing, iron, lead, zinc, copper, aluminum, magnesium. Inc. 1809 as town, 1822 as city. Pop. (1970) 622,236.

Saint Louis Park, city in SE Minnesota, 6mi (10km) WSW of Minneapolis. Industries: sports equipment, hydraulic pumps, metal, plastics. Settled 1853; inc. 1886. Pop. (1970) 48,922.

Saint Lucia, island in Windward Islands, British West Indies, between Atlantic Ocean (E) and Caribbean Sea (W); Castries is capital. A volcanic, mountainous, forested island it was first inhabited by Carib Indians; discovered 1502 by Christopher Columbus; first colonized 17th century by British; later settled by French; island was point of Anglo-French contention until British gained control 1803; member of Federation of West Indies 1958; part of British Windwards colony until 1959; Caribbean Common Market member; in 1967 it became one of six associate states of West Indies, with internal self-government. Bananas are main export. Area: 238sq mi (616sq km). Pop. 101,000.

Saint Malo, seaport in NW France, on English Channel. Town became part of France 1491; during 17th–19th centuries privateers operated from this port; birthplace of Jacques Cartier; site of 15th-century city gates and château (now a museum). In 1966 a power station harnessing tidal power was opened. Industries: tourism, yachting, cod drying. Founded 9th century by refugees from Norman raids on Saint-Servan. Pop. 42,297.

Saint Martin (Sint Maarten), island of NW Leeward Islands in West Indies, between Atlantic Ocean (NE) and Caribbean (SW). It has been politically divided since 1648: N is a dependency of French dept. of Guadeloupe; S (Sint Maarten) is administered by Netherlands Antilles. Principal towns are Marigot (N) and Philipsburg (S). Products: cotton, sugar cane, fruit, cattle, salt. Pop. (combined sections) 10,583.

Saint Michel, residential city in Canada; N suburb of Montreal. Pop. 71,446.

Saint Moritz (Sankt Moritz), village in E Switzerland, on the Imr River, 28mi (45km) SSE of Chur; scene of Olympic games 1928 and 1948; famous tourist resort, noted for curative mineral springs; site of Romanesque church, Engadine historical museum, Leganti museum. Chief industry is tourism. Pop. 5,699.

Saint Paul, capital city and port of entry in E Minnesota, on Mississippi River just E of Minneapolis, its twin city; seat of Ramsey co. Included in Louisiana Purchase (1803), fur-trading post est. 1838; it was named after Father Galtier's St Paul's Church 1841; made territorial capital 1849, state capital 1858. It is site of Hamline University (1854), College of St Thomas (1855), Bethel College (1871), Concordia College (1893), College of St Catherine (1906), capitol (1904), Cathedral of St Paul (1906–15), Indian Mounds Park. Industries: steel, iron, automobiles, machinery, chemicals, paper, tapes, computers, food products. Inc. 1854. Pop. (1970) 309,828.

Saint Petersburg, residential city in W central Florida peninsula, on Tampa Bay; known as Sunshine City. Yachting and fishing resort; site of Sunshine Skyway Bridge, 15mi (24km) long. Industries: concrete, aluminum products. Settled 1888; inc. 1892. Pop. (1970) 216,232.

Saint Pierre and Miquelon, group of nine small islands, 10mi (16km) SW of Newfoundland in Gulf of St Lawrence. Capital is St Pierre on St Pierre Island; French territory. Area: 93sq mi (241sq km). Pop. 5,600.

Saint Quentin, city in N France, on Somme River, 25mi (40km) NW of Laon. Originally a Roman town, during Middle Ages it was site of pilgrimage to tomb of St Quentin, believed to have been persecuted here 284–305 by Emperor Diocletian; became part of French crownlands 1191; scene of many battles due to its strategic location; site of Musée Lécuyer with a collection of pastels by Maurice Quentin de la Tour (born here), 15th-century town hall, and the large Gothic church, Collegiale Saint-Quentin (13th–15th centuries). Industries: textiles, furniture, rubber, food products. Pop. 64,196.

Saint-Saëns, Camille (1835–1921), French composer, pianist, organist, and conductor. △1246.

Saint-Simon, Claude Henri de Rouvroy, Comte de (1760–1825), French political reformer, one of the founders of socialism. As a young man he fought in the American Revolution and supported the French Revolution. In *Memoire sur la science de l'homme* (1813) and other writings (*L'industrie*, for example, written in collaboration with Auguste Comte), Saint-Simon proposed a productive industrialized state directed by scientist-businessmen. Although his writings were largely ignored during his lifetime, they influenced both later socialists and Marxists and advocates of the modern capitalist state. △1326.

Saint Thomas Island, second-largest island of US Virgin Islands, West Indies. Of volcanic origin, the island has a hilly terrain and many coastal inlets including St Thomas Harbor. Charlotte Amalie, capital of US Virgin Islands, is on S shore. Discovered and named by Christopher Columbus 1493, island was first settled by Dutch. Industries: rum, tourism. Area: 28sq mi (72sq km). Pop. 31,867.

Saint-Tropez, town of French Riviera, in SE France, on bay of St Tropez. From 15th–17th centuries it was an independent republic; beach resort and fishing village. Pop. 5,689.

Saint Vincent, island state in Windward Islands, British West Indies. State includes St Vincent Island and N Grenadines; Kingtown is capital of the volcanic, mountainous state. Soufriére volcano is highest point, 4,048ft (1,234m); its 1920 eruption destroyed much of island. Island was reputedly discovered by Christopher Columbus 1498; settled by British 1762; captured by French 1779; regained 1783 by British who had most of native Caribs deported 1797; part of British colony of Windward Islands 1880–1958; West Indies Federation member 1858–62; became self-governing 1969 (associated with Great Britain); member of Caribbean Common Market. Industries: bananas, copra, arrowroot, cotton, tourism. Area: (Saint Vincent I.) 140sq mi (363sq km); (N Grenadines) 10sq mi (26sq km). Pop. 89,129.

Saint Vincent, Cape, SW extremity of Portugal and continental Europe, 60mi (97km) W of Faro; scene of 1797 battle in which British, under command of Commodore Horatio Nelson, defeated Spanish naval forces; contains 15th-century ruins of Prince Henry the Navigator's town.

St Vitus Dance. *See* Chorea.

Saipan, island in Mariana Islands, W Pacific Ocean member of US Trust Territory of the Pacific Islands. A Spanish possession 1565–1899, it came under Germany 1899; mandated to Japan 1919 and used as a naval and air base in WWII; taken by the United States 1944. Products: tropical fruits, sugar cane, coffee mineral deposits have been found. Chief city is Chalan Kanoa; chief port is Tanapag Harbor; Trust Territory government seat is Capital Hill. Area: 70sq mi (181sq km). Pop. 10,458.

Sakai, industrial city in S Honshu, Japan, on Osaka Bay approx. 6mi (10km) S of Osaka, in Osaka industrial belt. An important port 15th–17th centuries, since the harbor silted up its port business has declined; site of Emperor Nitoku's tomb. Industries: machinery, automobiles, chemicals, dyes, fertilizer, iron, steel, textiles. Pop. 594,367.

Sakhalin Island, island off the E coast of Siberian Russian SFSR, USSR, between Tatar Strait and Sea of Japan and Sea of Okhotsk, extending from Cape Yelizaveta to Cape Crillon, separated from Hokkaido, Japan by La Pérouse Strait, containing two parallel mountain ranges. Main urban centers are Aleksandrovsk, Okha, Uglegorsk, Kholmsk, Korsakov, Dolinsk, Yuzhno-Sakhalinsk. Chinese in ancient times, it was first visited by Japanese *c.* 1630; explored by Japanese in late 18th century; disputed between Japan and Russia 1853–75; settled by Russians 1853; came under Russian control 1875 when ceded by Japan in exchange for Kuril Island; occupied by Japanese 1905; returned to USSR 1946 after Allied defeat of Japan. Industries: grains, vegetables, coal, paper, pulp, fish canning, oil. Area: 8,597sq mi (4,066sq km). Pop. 600,000.

Sakharov, Andrei Dimitrievich (1921–), Soviet physicist and social critic. His work in nuclear fusion was instrumental in the development of the Soviet hydrogen bomb. He received international recognition as a scientist and was a member of the American Academy of Arts and Sciences. An outspoken defender of civil liberties, he created the Human Rights Committee in 1970 and received the Eleanor Roosevelt Peace Award (1973) and the Cino del Duca Prize (1974). He believed in the possible unification of East and West through democratic socialism and received the Nobel Peace prize in 1975.

Saki. *See* Munro, Hector Hugh.

Saki, dark, slender monkey of tropical South American forests. They have long bushy tails and are day-active, tree-dwelling omnivores. Weight: 1.5–3.7lb (0.7–1.7kg). Genera *Pithecia* and *Chiropotes*. *See also* Monkey.

Sakti, in Hinduism, the female consort of male deities. Its origin is the story of the inactive god Shiva's ineffectiveness without his wife Sakti's pure activity. △836.

Saladin (*c.* 1137–1193), sultan of Egypt and Syria. As a lieutenant of Nur-ad-din, he suppressed the Fatimite dynasty of Egypt, became vizier, and then proclaimed himself sultan in 1174. After conquering most of Syria, he launched a campaign to drive the Christians from Palestine. His capture of Jerusalem in 1187 brought on the arrival of an army of the third Crusade led by Richard I of England and Philip II of France. After three years of fighting, the Muslims retained most of the territory but conceded to the Christians the right to enter Jerusalem. △1084.

Salads. △336.

Salamanca, city in central Mexico, 17mi (27km) S of Guanajuato, on the Lerma River; rail junction. Products: corn, wheat, sugar cane, alfalfa, cotton. Industries: chemicals, oil refining, cotton goods, flour milling, handicrafts. Pop. 103,740.

Salamanca, city in W Spain, on Tormes River; capital of Salamanca prov.; conquered by Hannibal 220 BC; city was partially destroyed by French during Peninsular War 1808–13; served as capital for the insurgents during Spanish civil war 1937–38. It is the site of a 15th-century university founded by Alfonso X, containing several precious manuscripts, 12th-century Gothic cathedral, 17th-century Plaza Mayor, Roman bridge. Industries: food processing, chemicals. Area: (prov.) 829sq mi (2147sq km). Pop. (city) 125,220; (prov.) 371,607.

Salamander, amphibian found worldwide, except in Australia and polar regions. The 280 species are characterized by slimy, elongated bodies, long tails, and short legs. Most lay eggs, but some give birth to live young. Fertilization is usually internal. The male deposits spermatophore into the female's cloaca. She lays eggs on moist land or in water. Those laid in water hatch into aquatic larvae with gills. Order Caudata (Urodela). *See also* Amphibia. △518.

Salamis, island in E Greece, in Saronic Gulf; scene of Persian War naval battle during which Greek forces, under Themistocles, defeated Persian fleet 480 BC; site of naval base. Industries: wheat, olive oil, wine, fisheries. Area: 37sq mi (96sq km). Pop. 20,645.

Salamis, ruined ancient city that was the main city of ancient Cyprus △994.

"Salary Grab" Act (1873), designation for salary increases voted by the US Congress to its own members, the president, and the Supreme Court justices. Public indignation forced repeal (1874) of the increase granted congressmen.

Salazar, António de Oliveira (1889–1970), Portuguese dictator. He was a professor of political theory with right-wing, pro-Roman Catholic Church leanings. He was briefly finance minister in the right-wing government that came into power in 1926. He was called back to office in 1928 and succeeded in stabilizing Portugal's financial situation. He became premier in 1932 and thereafter ruled as virtual dictator. He supported the Nationalists in the Spanish Civil War, and although sympathetic to the Axis powers in World War II, managed to keep Portugal neutral. He presided over Portugal's economic revival after the war but fought a futile battle to save the Portuguese colonies in Africa. He suffered a stroke in 1968 and died two years later.

Salem, city in NE Massachusetts, on Massachusetts Bay, 14mi (22km) NE of Boston; seat of Essex co; scene of witchcraft trials (1692) during which 20 people were put to death; site of Massachusetts State College at Salem (1854), House of Seven Gables (1668), Nathaniel Hawthorne's birthplace (*c.* 1750), Peabody Museum, Witch House (1642), home of Jonathan Corwin, a judge at witchcraft trials. Industries: leather, precision machines. Founded 1626 as Naumkeag; name changed in 1630; inc. as city 1836. Pop. (1970) 40,556.

Salem, capital city of Oregon, 44mi (71km) S of Portland on Willamette River; seat of Marion co; site of Willamette University (1842), and Salem Technical Vocational Community College (1954). Industries: meatpacking, lumber, canneries, paper, linen, woolens. Founded 1840 by Methodist Episcopal missionaries as a mission station and manual training school for Indians; made territorial capital 1851 and chartered 1857; continued as capital when Oregon joined Union in 1859. Pop. (1970) 68,296.

Salerno, seaport city in S Italy, 29mi (47km) SE of Naples, on the Gulf of Salerno; capital of Salerno prov. Founded by Romans 197 BC, it was conquered by the Normans 1076; sacked by the Swabian Hohenstaufens 1194; became part of Italy 1860; scene of heavy fighting September 1943. First European medical school was founded here 9th century, closed 1817; site of cathedral of San Matteo (founded 845), said to contain tomb of St Matthew and Pope Gregory VII. Industries: textiles, machinery, cement, macaroni, flour, lumber. Pop. 148,127.

Salic Law, rule of succession denying the right of women to inherit royal titles or offices and eliminating royal succession through the female line. In the later Middle Ages the practice was called the Salic Law because it was mistakenly supposed to have been outlined in the *Lex Salica* (*c.* 510), the law of the Salian Franks under Clovis I. Actually, the rule was first applied after the death of Louis X in France (1316), when Philip V took the throne in preference to Louis' daughter Joanna.

Salina, city in central Kansas, on Smoky Hill River; seat of Saline co; site of Kansas Wesleyan University (1886), Marymount College (1922), and a military school. Industries: aircraft, meat packing, flour milling. Founded 1858 by antislavery settlers; inc. 1870. Pop. (1970) 37,714.

Salinas, city in W California, 47mi (76km) SSE of San Jose; seat of Monterey co; birthplace of John Steinbeck. Industries: shipping and processing center; fruits, dairy goods, jams, jellies. Founded 1856; inc. 1874. Pop. (1970) 58,896.

Salinas River, river in W California; rises in Santa Lucia Mts; flows NW past King City and Salinas to Monterey Bay; its irrigated valley is one of the chief US lettuce-producing regions. Length: 150mi (241km).

Salinger, J(erome) D(avid) (1919–), US author, b. New York City. He began publishing stories in magazines. His first book, a novel, was *Catcher in the Rye* (1951). Subsequent works include *Nine Stories* (1953), *Franny and Zooey* (1961), two novellas, and *Raise High the Roof Beam, Carpenters* and *Seymour: An Introduction* (1963), two stories. *See also* Catcher in the Rye.

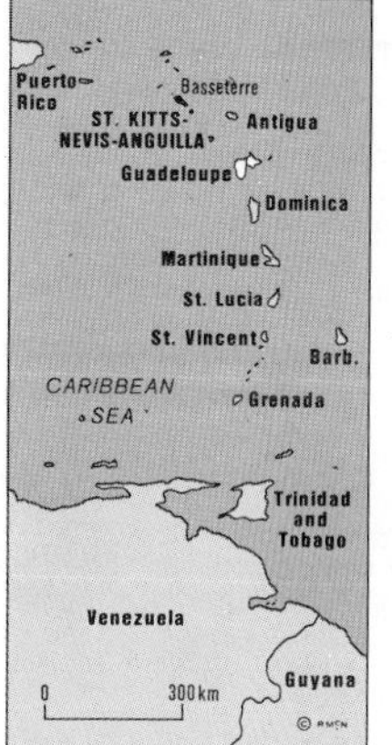
Puerto Rico
Basseterre
ST. KITTS-
NEVIS-ANGUILLA
Antigua
Guadeloupe
Dominica
Martinique
St. Lucia
St. Vincent
Barb.
CARIBBEAN SEA
Grenada
Trinidad and Tobago
Venezuela
0
300km
Guyana
St. Kitts-Nevis-Anguilla: British West Indies

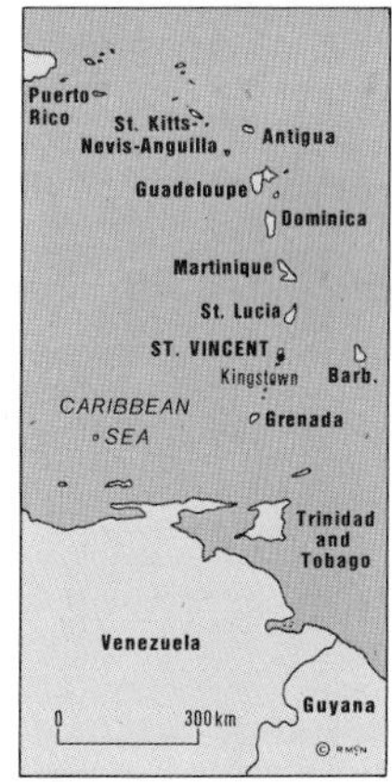
Puerto Rico
St. Kitts-
Nevis-Anguilla
Antigua
Guadeloupe
Dominica
Martinique
St. Lucia
ST. VINCENT
Kingstown
Barb.
CARIBBEAN SEA
Grenada
Trinidad and Tobago
Venezuela
0
300km
Guyana
St. Vincent, British West Indies

Andrei Sakharov

Salamander

Salisbury, Robert Arthur Talbot Gascoyne-Cecil, 3rd Marquess of (1830–1903), English statesman and diplomat. A conservative, he placed great faith in the efficacy of aristocratic and paternalist government. He distrusted reform of Parliament throughout his political career (1853–1902). He was prime minister three times (1885–86, 1886–92, and 1895–1902) and also foreign secretary. His eminence in foreign affairs was established by his leadership of the Congress of Berlin (1878). After the Boer War he retired (1902) and was succeeded by Arthur Balfour, his nephew.

Salisbury, Robert Cecil, 1st Earl of (1563–1612), English statesman. The son of Elizabeth I's secretary of state, Lord Burghley, he succeeded his father in office (1596) and continued as chief minister until his death, assuming the office of treasurer as well in 1608. His financial acumen secured James I an independence that influenced his dealings with Parliament. He was made an earl in 1605.

Salisbury (New Sarum), county town of Wiltshire, S England; a market town, 10mi (16km) S of Stonehenge. Its great 13th-century Early English cathedral has the highest spire in England, 404ft (123m) and was added to original cathedral about 1330. Its library contains one of the four original copies of the Magna Carta. Some of the building materials for this edifice were brought from the razed cathedral at Old Sarum. Town was founded 1220 as site of cathedral. Pop. 35,271.

Salisbury, capital city of Rhodesia, in NE part of the country; also capital of South Mashonaland prov.; commercial, industrial, transportation center. The city was named for former British Prime Minister R.A. Salisbury and served as capital of Federation of Rhodesia and Nyasaland 1953–63; site of University of Rhodesia, (1957), two cathedrals, national museum, library, Rhodes National Gallery. Products: maize, cotton, tobacco, citrus fruits. Industries: gold mining, textiles, steel, processed foods, clothing, tobacco, chemicals, furniture. Founded 1890 as fort by the Pioneer Column. Pop. 435,000.

Salish, a tribe of North American Indians formerly occupying an area in W Montana; they later moved to the Flathead Lake region. They gave their name to one of the major language families of the American Indians. Today approximately 3,000 Salish-speaking Indians occupy several reservations in Washington, Oregon, and Idaho.

Salivary Glands, three pairs of glands located on either side of the mouth that form and secrete saliva. The parotid gland, just below and in front of the ear, is the largest of the salivary glands and the one that becomes enlarged in mumps; the submaxillary is found near the lower jaw angle; and the sublingual under the side of the tongue. △694, 740.

Salk, Jonas Edward (1914–), US medical researcher, b. New York City. He developed the first vaccine against poliomyelitis in 1952, using inactivated polio virus as an immunizing agent. Mass tests of the vaccine began in 1954, and mass immunization programs followed. △722.

Sallust or **Gaius Sallustius Crispus** (86–*c.* 34 BC), Roman historian. △1028.

Salmon, marine and freshwater fish of the N Hemisphere. A popular sport and commercial fish, it is silvery and spotted until spawning season when it turns black or red. The Pacific salmon *(Oncorhynchus)* hatches, spawns, and dies in freshwater, but spends its adult life in the ocean. Pacific species include the pink, sockeye, chinook, dog, silver, and masu varieties. The Atlantic salmon *(Salmo salar)* is actually an ocean-run trout. A marine fish, it spawns in rivers on both sides of the Atlantic and then returns to the sea. It does not die after spawning like the Pacific salmon. Weight: to 80lb (36kg). Family Salmonidae. △390.

Salmonellosis, group of diseases caused by bacteria of the *Salmonella* genus. Some species, attacking animals, cause abortion, others cause blood poisoning and intestinal inflammation to man as well. Other species are a cause of human food poisoning. △422.

Salmon Fly. *See* Stonefly.

Salome, two women in the Bible. The first was the daughter of Herod Philip and Herodias. Although not mentioned by name, she is supposed to be the woman who danced for the head of the executed John the Baptist (Mark 6:16–28). The second was a witness to the Crucifixion and brought offerings to Christ's tomb (Matt. 27:56).

Salonika (Thessaloníki), seaport city in NE Greece, on Gulf of Salonika; 2nd-largest city in Greece and capital of Thessaloníki dept. City served as capital of Macedon 146 BC; site where Paul delivered his two epistles to the Thessalonians; scene of massacre of insurrectionists AD 390 by Theodosius. City was under Ottoman Turks 1430–1912, when it was taken by Greece during Balkan Wars; scene of mass liquidation of Jewish population by Germans during WWII; site of White Tower (15th century), triumphal arch of Constantine, and several Byzantine churches. Exports: grain, livestock, tobacco, manganese, chrome, livestock. Industries: textiles, wine, beer, soap, machinery, flour, cement, explosives. Founded *c.* 315 BC by Cassander, King of Macedon. Pop. 339,496.

Salt, chemical compound formed, along with water, when an acid and a base react together. Salts are typically high melting crystalline compounds that tend to be soluble in water. They are formed of ions held together by electrostatic forces and in solution they conduct electricity. Sodium chloride—common table salt—is a typical example. △240, 280, 1554–1558, 1562.

SALT Agreements, arms control agreements worked out at Strategic Arms Limitations Talks and signed May 26, 1972, by US Pres. Richard Nixon and Soviet General Secretary Leonid Brezhnev. The SALT agreements limited anti-ballistic missile systems and offensive missile launchers. Talks continued concerning offensive strategic weapons. △1344, 1390.

Salt Dome, body of salt that has intruded into a sedimentary rock overlay. The flow of the relatively plastic salt into a dome may be the result of a difference in density between the salt and the overlying rock. This process is not completely understood, however. △178.

Saltillo, city in NE Mexico, on plateau of Sierra Madre Oriental; taken by US forces during Mexican War; site of rail junction, resort, university, cathedral; mining center, for silver, gold, copper, lead, zinc, iron. Industries: textiles, flour, shoes, clothing, kitchen utensils, handicrafts. Founded late 16th century. Pop. 191,879.

Salt Lake City, capital city in N central Utah, 13mi (21km) E of Great Salt Lake on Jordan River; largest city of Utah; seat of Salt Lake co. Founded 1847 by the Mormon Community under Brigham Young, city developed as trading and supply point for westward travelers to California; it was made capital of Provisional State of Deseret 1849, Territory of Utah 1850, state of Utah 1896. Landmarks include Mormon Temple (1853–93), Brigham Young's House (1877) and Museum (1897), Fort Douglas (1862); site of University of Utah (1850), Westminster College (1875), Stevens Henager College (1907); world headquarters of Mormon Church. Industries: food processing, missiles, rocket engines, tourism, oil refining, printing, publishing; zinc, gold, silver, lead, and copper mining. Inc. 1851. Pop. (1970) 175,885.

Salt Marsh. △620.

Saluda River, river that rises in Blue Ridge of NW South Carolina, flows SE through Lake Murray; near Columbia it joins the Broad River to form the Congaree River. The Saluda Dam (1930) furnishes hydroelectric power to area. Length: 200mi (322km).

Saluki, royal coursing dog of Egypt (hound group) and perhaps the oldest domesticated breed dog. Known 7000–6000 BC; brought to England in 1840; also called Persian greyhound. A graceful dog of strong constitution and remarkable vision, it has a long, narrow head; long, hanging ears; deep but narrow-chested body with broad back and slightly arched loin; long legs and tail. The smooth, silky coat is feathered on legs, ears, and tail (no feathering in smooth variety). Colors include white, golden, red, black, and tan. Average size: 23–28in (58–71cm) high at shoulder; 45–60lb (20–27kg). *See also* Hounds.

Salvador (Bahia), seaport city in E central Brazil, 750mi (1,207km) N of Rio de Janeiro; capital of Bahia state. Settled by the Portuguese as Bahia, it was the first formally established colony in Brazil; slave market in 17th and 18th centuries; capital of Brazil until 1763. Industries: exporting, food and tobacco processing, textiles. Founded 1549 by order of King John III of Portugal. Pop. 1,000,647.

Salvation Army, Christian organization formed after a military pattern, with a general as head. Founded in 1865 by William Booth, a Methodist minister and his wife, it concentrates on evangelistic and social work. The Salvation Army in the United States began in 1880. With the Bible as the guide for life, constant conversion programs are enacted. Members must give complete obedience, denying one's self. International headquarters are in London.

Salween (Nujiang), river in SE Asia; rises in Tibetan Plateau, E Tibet; flows SE through Yunnan prov. cutting deep gorges through the rough terrain almost parallel to Mekong, Yangtze, and Irrawaddy rivers; continues into Shan and Karen states of Burma to empty into the Gulf of Martaban, near Moulmein. Along its course, it forms many rapids and is only navigable for 75mi (121km) upstream, limiting its commercial importance as an E-W transportation route. Length: approx. 1,750mi (2,818km).

Salyut. △144.

Salzburg, city in Austria, on the Salzach River 71mi (114km) ESE of Munich, West Germany; site of two archepiscopal palaces, a 17th-century cathedral, and several notable churches and houses; ruled by prince-archbishops for over 1,000 years; birthplace of Mozart; music center. Founded late 7th century. Pop. 127,500.

Saman. *See* Rain Tree.

Samarium, metallic element (symbol Sm) of the Lanthanide group, first identified spectroscopically in 1879 by Lecoq de Boisbaudran. Chief ores are monazite (phosphate) and bastänite (fluorocarbonate). The element is used in pyrophoric alloys and carbon-arc lamps; some samarium alloys are used in making powerful permanent magnets. Properties: at. no. 62; at. wt. 150.35; sp gr 7.5 (α), 7.4 (β); melt. pt. 1962°F (1072°C); boil. pt. 3200°F (1778°C); most common isotope Sm^{152} (26.72%). *See also* Lanthanide Elements. △1552–54.

Samarkand, formerly Maracanda; city in Uzbek SSR, USSR, on W spur of Alai Mts, 180mi (290km) SW of Tashkent, near Zerayshan River; capital of Samarkand oblast. One of the oldest cities in the USSR, it was destroyed by Alexander the Great 329 BC; important 7th-century point on the "Silk Route" from China to Europe, it was again destroyed 1221 by Genghis Khan; it was made capital of Tamerlane's empire 1370; almost uninhabited by 1700, the Russians took it 1868 and it was inc. in the Uzbek SSR 1924; site of Tamerlane's mausoleum (1404), 14th–15th-century mosque and mausoleum of Shakh Zinda, Uzbek State University, institute of tropical medicine, regional museum, agricultural, medical, and teachers' colleges. Industries: cotton, silk, clothing, shoes, wine, tea, food canning, motor vehicle parts, leather. Pop. 267,000.

Samnium, ancient state in S Italy; confederation of Caraceni, Pentri, Caudini and Hirpini; Samnites were enemies of Rome, with whom they fought the three Samnite Wars; they were conquered by Rome *c.* 290 BC. The Samnites were probably of Sabine origin and spoke Oscan.

Samoa. *See* American Samoa; Western Samoa.

Sámos, island in SE Greece; member of the Sporades Islands in Aegean Sea; forms department of Greece with Ikaria and other islands. Developed into maritime power and cultural center under Polycrates 6th century BC, it was a member of Delian League, allied with Athens during Peloponnesian War; held by Ottoman Turks 1475–1912, when it was annexed to Greece; occupied by Axis powers during WWII; home of Aesop, Anacreon, and Rhuecus; birthplace of Pythagoras and Conon; site of Temple of Hera. Industries: shipbuilding, tobacco, silk, wine, fruits, currants, grapes. Area: 184sq mi (477sq km). Pop. 41,124.

Samothrace, island in NE Greece, in NE Aegean Sea; An independent community under Roman protection 2nd century BC, it was occupied by Ottoman Turks 1456–1912, when annexed to Greece. Excavations have unearthed the famous Winged Victory of Samothrace (*c.* 200 BC), ruins of the Sanctuary of the Great Gods, a stoa, and much pottery. Industries: grains, olive oil, honey, sponges. Area: 69sq mi (179sq km). Pop. 3,830.

Samoyed, ancient sled and guard dog (working group) bred in northern Asia. A dog with a smiling expression, it has a broad, wedge-shaped head; thick, erect, triangular ears; dark, almond-shaped eyes; deep-chested, medium-length body with slightly arched loin; moderately long, sturdy legs with large feet; and long tail curved over the back or side. The white, biscuit, or cream double coat stands straight out. Average size: 19–23.5in (48–60cm) high at shoulder; 35–65lb (16–29kg). *See also* Working Dog.

Samoyeds, Uralic-speaking people, who inhabit N

Soviet Union and consist of a number of groups including the Nentsy, Yenisy, Tavgis, and Selkups. They practice fishing, hunting, pastoralism (reindeer and horses) and trapping, but their traditionally nomadic lifestyle has been modified by the implementation of Soviet collective farming.

Samson, biblical Israelite judge and hero. His Philistine wife was given to another man by his father and Samson, in reprisal, ruined Philistine crops. After he killed 1,000 Philistines with the jawbone of an ass, his mistress Delilah discovered his great strength came from his long hair. She had his hair cut and gave him to the Philistines. Though weak and blind, he destroyed a building, killing himself and his captors. △840.

Samsun, city and port in Turkey, on Black Sea, 200mi (322km) NW of Ankara; capital of Samsun prov. Captured by Romans 1st century BC, it became part of Byzantine Empire during Middle Ages. In 14th century it fell to Ottoman Turks. In 1919, Kemal Atatürk landed at Samsun to organize a nationalist movement against Greece; an equestrian statue commemorates his landing. City now serves as Turkey's most important Black Sea port. Industries: cigarettes, textiles. Founded 562 BC by Greek colonists. Pop. 107,510.

Samuel I and II, two books of the Old Testament describing the transition of Israel from a collection of tribes under separate chiefs to a single nation under a king through the stories of the prophet Samuel and of Saul and David, Israel's first two kings. The song of Hannah, Samuel's prayer, and God's prophecy to David are the most important passages.

Samuelson, Paul Anthony (1915–), US economist, b. Gary, Ind. He was noted for his work in macroeconomics and mathematical economics. His best-known work is *Economics: An Introductory Analysis,* a widely used text. Other works include *Foundations of Economic Analysis* (1947). In 1970 he received the Nobel Prize for economics.

Samurai, warrior class of feudal Japan. Beginning its rise to importance in the 12th century, the samurai (or *bushi*) class was firmly fixed at the top of the social order of the Tokugawa era (1603–1867). Samurai alone were privileged to bear arms, usually wearing two swords, and received a pension from their daimyo (feudal lords), to whom they pledged allegiance. Samurai intermarried in their own caste, and their children were samurai from birth, although only the heir received a pension. Samurai followed Bushido, a special code of conduct. Many modern military men had samurai origins, and events such as the Satsuma Rebellion (1877) had their roots in samurai feudalism. △1210, 1272.

Sana (San'a), capital city of Yemen Arab Republic, 40mi (64km) from Hodeida; largest city in S Arabia; agricultural and trade center; Islamic cultural center, site of Muslim University, the Great Mosque (built on site of 6th-century church). Walled city was settled in pre-Islamic times; first became Yemen's capital 4th century; ruled by Ethiopians during Middle Ages; occupied by Ottoman Turks in 17th century, after which it became seat of Rassite dynasty until second Turkish occupation 1872–1918. Modern kingdom of Yemen began 1904 with revolt against Ottoman Turks; independence was achieved in 1918; became capital of Yemen Arab Republic 1962. Industries: leather, jewelry work, vineyards, coffee, raisins. Pop. 125,093.

San Andreas Fault, a right-lateral, strike-slip fault that forms the boundary between the North American plate and the North Pacific plate and separates SW California from the rest of North America. Over the past 60,000,000 years the total movement along the fault has amounted to more than 345mi (555km). The fault is a center for earthquakes; the great San Francisco quake of 1906 occurred along it. △250.

San Angelo, city in W Texas, 180mi (290km) NW of Austin, at confluence of North and Middle Concho rivers; seat of Tom Green co; site of San Angelo State College (1928), Goodfellow Air Force Base, livestock and trading center. Industries: wool, mohair, dairy products, oil, gas, farming, food processing. Settled 1867; inc. 1888. Pop. (1970) 63,884.

San Antonio, city in S central Texas, 74mi (118km) SW of Austin on San Antonio River; seat of Bexar co. Founded 1793 with inc. of Villa de Bejar, San Fernando de Bejar, and mission San Antonio de Valero (later the Alamo); scene of Mexico-Texas struggles at the Alamo (1836). A military center, it is site of Lackland, Randolph, Brooks, and Kelly Air Force bases, Fort Sam Houston, Alamo (1718), Spanish governor's palace (1749), HemisFair Plaza (1968), Trinity University (1869), St Mary's University (1852), Incarnate Word College (1881). Industries: food products, aircraft, building materials, chemicals, wood products, livestock, tourism. Inc. 1837. Pop. (1970) 654,153.

San Bernardino, city in S California, 55mi (89km) E of Los Angeles; seat of San Bernardino co. A Spanish settlement, it was explored in 1772 and named in 1810; Mormons emigrated from 1850. Industries: missiles, steel and iron products, cement, foodstuffs. Founded 1851; inc. 1854. Pop. (1970) 104,783.

San Bernardino Mountains, range in S California; extends about 60mi (97km) NW-SE between San Gabriel and San Jacinto Mts. Highest peak is San Gorgonio, 11,502ft (3,508m).

San Bruno, city in W California, S of San Francisco; site of Federal archives center, marine corps reserve base, and a naval engineering command. Inc. 1914. Pop. (1970) 36,254.

San Carlos, city in W California, 17mi (27km) SE of San Francisco. Industries: electronic equipment, communication products. Inc. 1925. Pop. (1970) 25,924.

Sancho II (1208–48), king of Portugal (1223–48), son and successor of Alfonso II. He allied himself with the nobles at the expense of the Roman Catholic Church, and Pope Innocent IV had him deposed (1245) in favor of his brother, who was crowned as Alfonso III after Sancho's death.

San Cristóbal, city in W Venezuela, at SW end of Cordillera Mérida in Andean uplands; capital of Tachira state; trade center. Industries: coffee, cacao, cotton, sugar, grains, cattle, cement, iron, coal, asphalt mining. Founded 1561. Pop. 156,618.

Sancti-Spiritus, city in W central Cuba, 45mi (72km) SE of Santa Clara on Yayabo River; taken by Fidel Castro 1958; site of 16th-century bridge over Yayabo River, 16th-century church, theater (1839). Industries: processing center for sugar, tobacco, cattle. Founded 1516. Pop. 146,450.

Sand, George (1804–76), pseud. of Amandine Aurore Lucie Dupin, French novelist. After an unhappy marriage to Baron Dudevant, she returned to Paris from her native Nohant. She became famous for her affairs with Alfred de Musset and Frédéric Chopin. Her novels from this period, including *Lélia* (1833) and *Mauprat* (1837), examine women's right to independence. *Le Meunier d'Angibault* (1845) reflects her socialist and republican interests, while her last novels, such as *Francis the Waif* (1847–48), are pastoral studies. △1238.

Sandalwood, tree whose fragrant, reddish wood is used for carved boxes and screens or burned as incense. Many are semiparasitic on roots of other plants. The evergreen *Santalum album* is native to S Asia. Its oval leaves are hairy, and the flowers turn from straw-color to blood red. Height: to 40ft (12m). Family Santalaceae.

Sandburg, Carl (1878–1967), US poet, biographer, and folklorist, b. Galesburg, Ill. The son of Swedish immigrants, he left school at 13 to become a laborer. After serving in the Spanish-American War, he put himself through college, graduating in 1902. He went to work as a newspaper reporter in Milwaukee. In 1908 he married Lillian Steichen, sister of photographer Edward Steichen. He moved to Chicago in 1913 and began contributing to Harriet Monroe's *Poetry* magazine. His first volume of poetry, *Chicago Poems,* appeared in 1915. It contains his most famous poem, "Chicago." Other volumes of poetry include *Cornhuskers* (1918), *Smoke and Steel* (1920), *Good Morning, America* (1928), *The People, Yes* (1936), *Honey and Salt* (1963). He won the Pulitzer Prize for poetry in 1951 for his *Complete Poems* (1950). His poetry, inspired by Walt Whitman, vigorously draws on American history and idiom. He won the 1940 Pulitzer Prize for history for his six volume biography of Abraham Lincoln (1926–39). A novel, *Remembrance Rock* appeared in 1948. *The American Songbag* (1927) and *New American Songbag* (1950) are collections of folk ballads and songs. *Rootabaga Stories* (1922) was the first of several collections of children's stories. △1420.

Sand Casting. △1606.

Sand Crab. *See* Ghost Crab.

Sanddab. *See* Flounder.

Sand Dollar, marine echinoderm with round, flattened body covered with short spines; a fused skeleton; and five radiating double rows of respiratory tube

Salt Lake City, Utah

Samoyed

Carl Sandburg

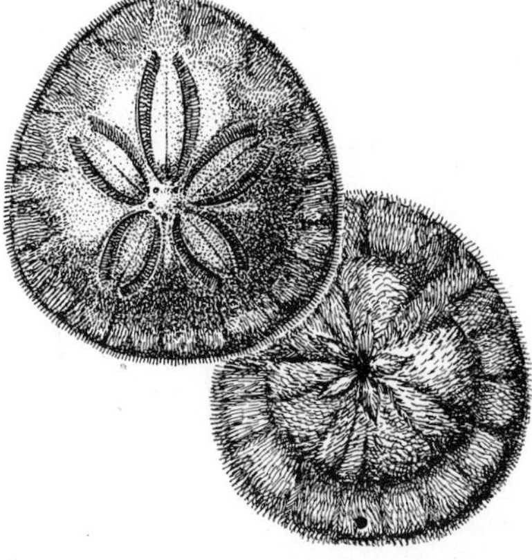
Sand dollar

feet on both sides. Class Echinoidea; species *Echinarachnius parma*.

Sand Grouse, terrestrial bird of central and S Eurasia and Africa that lives in large flocks in open arid areas, feeding on seeds and vegetable shoots, and sometimes resting in shallow sand depressions. They look like grouse but are related to pigeons and, like pigeons, drink with their bills held in the water at water holes at dusk and dawn. They lay elongated, smudged eggs (2–3) in a grass-lined sand depression. The female incubates the eggs during the day, the male at night. Length: 9–16in (23–41cm). Family Pteroclidae.

San Diego, city in S California; seat of San Diego co; important medical center and port of entry for S California, Arizona, New Mexico, lower California; site of four universities and two colleges, large naval and marine bases, zoological park. Industries: aerospace, electronics, shipbuilding. Mission San Diego de Alcalá was founded 1769 by Júnipero Serra; inc. 1850. Pop. (1970) 697,027.

Sand Painting, practiced by the Indians of the Southwest and regarded as the vital core of a powerful magic performance designed to heal. The sand picture is believed to absorb the illness from the sick man sitting in its center.

Sandpiper, shorebird that breeds in cold regions and migrates long distances to winter in warm areas, settling in grass or low bushes near water. They feed on invertebrates, nest in colonies, and lay pointed eggs (4) in a grass-lined ground hole nest. Length: 6–12in (15–30cm). Family Scolopacidae.

Sand Spit. △268.

Sandstone, sedimentary rock composed of sand grains cemented in such materials as silica, iron oxide, or carbonate of lime. Its hardness depends on the character of the cementing material. Its color may be gray, red, buff, brown, or green. *See also* Sedimentary Rocks. △248, 254, 272.

Sandstorm, a strong wind carrying with it dense clouds of desert sand more coarse-grained than the particles in dust storms. *See also* Dust Storm. △216.

Sandusky, port city in N central Ohio, on Sandusky Bay of Lake Erie; seat of Erie co; major coal shipping port, also ships sand, gravel, salt. Industries: fishing, tourism, wine production (from grapes grown in surrounding agricultural region), rubber goods, glue. Founded 1816 as Portland; renamed 1818; inc. 1824. Pop. (1970) 32,674.

Sandworm. *See* Nereis.

Sanford, Edward Terry (1865–1930), US jurist and lawyer, b. Knoxville, Tenn. He was an assistant attorney-general (1907–08) and US District Court judge (1909–23). He became an associate justice of the US Supreme Court (1923–30), appointed by Pres. Warren G. Harding. He wrote the opinion in the *Gitlow* v. *New York* (1925) freedom of expression case.

San Francisco, city and port of entry in W California, on S tip of a peninsula bounded by Pacific Ocean (W) and San Francisco Bay (E), connected by Golden Gate Strait (N); seat of and coextensive with San Francisco co. Founded 1776 as Yerba Buena by Spanish who est. a presidio and mission, it continued under Spanish control until July 9, 1846, when it was taken for the United States by Com. John D. Sloat. Growth was spurred by California gold rush (1848), development of its harbor for foreign trade and fishing (1860s), pony express (1860), and coming of transcontinental railroad (1869). Devastated by San Andreas earthquake and fire (April 1906), it was quickly rebuilt and prospered from opening of Panama Canal (1914). During WWII, city served as embarkation point for Pacific campaigns; scene of drafting of UN Charter (1945), and signing of Japanese Peace Treaty (1951). Landmarks include Chinatown, Fisherman's Wharf, Coit Memorial Tower, Nob Hill, Telegraph Hill, Russian Hill, Treasure Island, Golden Gate Bridge (1937), cable cars, Market Street, Latin Quarter, Presidio of San Francisco (1776), Mission Dolores (1782), Golden Gate Park; site of University of San Francisco (1855), University of California Medical Center (1864), Heald Engineering College (1863), San Francisco State College (1899), City College of San Francisco (1935); many military installations. Industries: tourism, shipbuilding, food processing, oil refining, chemicals, aircraft, fishing, publishing. Inc. 1850. Pop. (1970) 715,674.

San Francisco Bay, inlet of Pacific Ocean on W central coast of California, entered through the Golden Gate, a strait between two peninsulas. San Francisco is on S peninsula and is connected to N peninsula by Golden Gate Bridge (1933–37). Bay was discovered 1579 by Francis Drake. Length: 60mi (97km). Width: 3–12mi (4.8–19km).

San Francisco Conference on International Organization (1945), meeting that drafted the charter forming the United Nations. Delegates representing 50 nations met in San Francisco, beginning on April 25. With World War II ending, the Allies wanted to safeguard peace in the future. The UN charter, which provided the structure of the organization, was signed on June 26.

San Gabriel, city in S California, 8mi (13km) ENE of Los Angeles; has annual three-day festival celebrating the 1771 founding of San Gabriel Mission. Toy manufacture is main industry. Inc. 1913. Pop. (1970) 29,-336.

Sangallo, Guilcaro da. △1138.

Sanger, Margaret Higgins (1883–1966), US social reformer, b. Corning, N.Y. As a public health nurse, she became convinced of the necessity of birth control, especially for the poor. Her crusade for birth control, which began in 1912, was unpopular at first, and she was jailed for sending birth control information through the mail. She established the first birth control clinic in the United States (1916) in Brooklyn, N.Y., and founded the American Birth Control League (1921), which grew into the Planned Parenthood Federation of America (1942). She was the first president of International Planned Parenthood (1953).

Sangre de Cristo Mountains, part of the Rocky Mts, stretching from central Colorado to N central New Mexico; culminates at Blanca Peak, 14,317ft (4,367m). Length: 220mi (354km).

Sanhedrin, the council or court of Judaism, prominent during the period of the Second Temple, before its destruction in 70 AD. There is little information on its development and function. It served as a legislative body on both religious and political issues. It was in essence a rabbinical court, whose authority was accepted by the Jews. It disappeared in the 5th century.

Sanitary Engineering, a branch of civil engineering dealing with problems of water supply and treatment, waste disposal and reclamation of useful waste, pollution control, food and housing sanitation, insect and vermin control, and industrial hygiene. △1614, 1768.

San Jacinto, Battle of (April 1836), engagement on the San Jacinto River, Tex. Led by Sam Houston, the Texans defeated 1,200 Mexicans and captured General Santa Anna.

San José, capital city of Costa Rica, in central Costa Rica, 70mi (113km) E of Puntarenas on the Inter-American Highway; largest city and nation's economic, political, and commercial center; capital of San José prov. Founded *c.* 1736 as Villa Nueva, after Costa Rica declared independence 1821, it developed as the center of liberal faction and was the rival of Cartago; San José succeeded Cartago as capital of Costa Rica 1823. The city soon became the center of a lucrative coffee trade; site of two conferences for the Organization of American States (OAS) 1960. Notable buildings include the National Palace (1855), Municipal Palace (1937), National Museum, National Library, National Theater, cathedral, and the University of Costa Rica (1844). Products: coffee, sugar cane, cacao, vegetables, fruit, tobacco. Industries: livestock, food processing, wine, beer, chocolate, leather goods, textiles, furniture. Pop. 198,523.

San Jose, city in W California, 40mi (64km) SE of San Francisco; seat of Santa Clara co; California's capital 1849–52; site of Rosicrucian Park, Kelley Park, Alum Rock Park, and California State University at San Jose. Industries: fruit orchards, wineries, food-processing, atomic-power equipment. Founded 1777; inc. 1850. Pop. (1970) 445,779.

San Jose Scale, conelike scale insect introduced to California about 1880 from the Orient. Now spread across the United States, they suck juices from trees and shrubs, often destroying the plants. Length: 0.1in (2.5mm). Family Diaspididae; species *Quadraspidiotus perniciosus*. *See also* Scale Insect. △496.

San Juan, capital and largest city of Puerto Rico, on NE coast; made up of Old San Juan, built on an island and connected to the mainland by bridges. Major seaport, governmental and commercial center of Puerto Rico; under US administration since 1898. It prospered as a West Indian Port during 18th and 19th centuries; site of El Morro castle (1539), San Cristobal castle (1631), governors' official residence (1529), San Jose Church (*c.*1523), Casa Blanca (1523), Cathedral of San Juan Bautista, containing tomb of Ponce de Leon, University of Puerto Rico, school of tropical medicine, and several other institutions of higher learning; US air base. Exports: (mainly to United States) sugar, tobacco, fruit. Industries: tourism, cigars, clothing, publishing, sugar refining, rum distilling, jewelry, furniture, pharmaceuticals, plastics. Discovered 1508 by Ponce de Leon who settled 1509 at nearby Caparra; the settlement moved to present site of San Juan 1521. Pop. (1970) 444,952.

San Juan Hill, Battle of (July 1898), decisive battle in the Spanish American War. It was a US victory of the 1st US Volunteer Cavalry organized by Col. "Teddy" Roosevelt. His Rough Riders lacked military form, but their enthusiastic charge won the battle and the strategic hill overlooking Santiago and controlling the Spanish harbor below.

San Juan Islands, archipelago of 172 islands off NW Washington, E of Vancouver Island between Haro and Rosario Straits; comprises the co of San Juan. Discovered 1790 by Spanish explorers, it was subject of US-British boundary dispute decided in 1872. San Juan, Orcas, and Lopez islands are largest. A national park has been est. on San Juan Island (1966), dedicated to peaceful relationship between the United States, Canada, and Britain. Pop. 3,856.

San Leandro, city in W California, 15mi (24km) SE of Oakland. Industries: paper products, foodstuffs, transportation equipment, flowers. Founded by José Joaquin Estudillo 1837; inc. 1872. Pop. (1970) 68,-698.

Sanlúcar de Barrameda, seaport in SW Spain, at the mouth of the Guadalquivir River 18mi (29km) NW of Cadiz; departure point for voyages of Christopher Columbus (1498) and Ferdinand Magellan (1519). It is the site of palace of duke of Montpensier, medieval castle, St George Hospital, 14th-century church. Industries: flour, wine, salt, fisheries. Pop. 41,072.

San Luis Obispo, city in S California, 80mi (129km) NW of Santa Barbara; seat of San Luis Obispo co. Originally a Spanish possession, it became part of United States in 1846. Industries: electronic equipment, foodstuffs, furniture, dairy products. Inc. 1856. Pop. (1970) 28,036.

San Luis Potosi, state in central Mexico, primarily on Mexico's northern plateau; capital is San Luis Potosi. It is the chief mining state of Mexico; some mines have yielded silver, gold, copper, zinc, and bismuth since 18th century. Arid conditions result in little farming. Pánuco River Valley produces coffee, tobacco, sugar, and fiber plants. Area: 24,266sq mi (62,849sq km). Pop. 1,257,028.

San Marino, republic of Europe, in Apennines, 11mi (18km) SSW of Rimini, Italy; capital is San Marino. The world's smallest republic, it is totally surrounded by Italy, and claims to be the oldest existing European state; receives a subsidy from Italy in return for concessions such as not raising tobacco and not having a radio station. Government includes 60-member grand council elected for 5 years; every 6 months they elect 2 regents who, along with a 10-member council of state, are the executive branch. Women were given suffrage in 1960, and the right to hold public office in 1973; site of 19th-century Basilica Santo Marino, 10th-century church. Industries: tourism, postage stamps (mainly for collectors), agriculture. Republic founded 4th century by St Marinus. Area: 24sq mi (62sq km). Pop. 18,320.

PROFILE

Official name: San Marino
Area: 24sq mi (62sq km)
Population: 18,320
Density: 763 per sq mi (255 per sq km)
Chief cities: San Marino, capital; Serravalle
Government: Grand Council, 60; executive council of state, 10
Religion: Roman Catholic
Language: Italian
Unit of currency: Lira
Industries (major products): wine, ceramics, building stone, postage stamps.
Agriculture (major products): grapes, grain, corn.

San Martín, José de (1778–1850), South American independence leader, served as an officer in the Spanish army prior to joining the rebel forces in Argentina in 1812. His reputation as a brilliant military strategist was well-established by 1817, the year he took his army across the Andes into Chile. He combined forces with Bernardo O'Higgins to defeat the royalists. San Martín sailed for Peru in 1820 and entered Lima in victory in 1821. He assumed power in Peru, but in

1822 voluntarily withdrew in favor of Bolívar and left for Europe. △1234.

San Mateo, city in NW California, on the SW shore of San Francisco Bay; a Mexican possession 1822–1846. Introduction of railroad (1863) and influx of San Francisco earthquake victims (1906) led to population boom and prosperity. Founded 1863, inc. 1894. Pop. (1970) 78,991.

San Rafael, city in W California, 13mi (21km) NW of San Francisco; seat of Marin co; site of Mission San Rafael Arcángel (1817). Industries: electrical equipment, metal, plastic, wood products. Inc. 1913. Pop. (1970) 38,977.

San Salvador, capital and largest city of El Salvador, in central part of country; trade and communications center. City has suffered from many earthquakes; served as capital of a federation of Central American states 1831–39. Industries: soap, sugar, beer, textiles, cigars. Founded 1524 by Jorge de Alvarado. Pop. 358,913.

San Sebastián, seaport city in N Spain, on Bay of Biscay 48mi (77km) E of Bilbao; capital of Guipuzcoa prov. Noted for its beautiful scenery and beaches, it is a popular resort area and former royal residence. Industries: metalworking, chemicals, fisheries, cement, tobacco, brewing. First mentioned 1014; inc. late 12th century. Area: (prov.) 771sq mi (1,997sq km). Pop. (city) 165,829; (prov.) 631,003.

Sansevieria, or snake plant, genus of house plant native to tropical Africa with erect, sword-shaped leaves that are green with various markings. Shorter types grow in spreading rosettes. Care: any light, soil (equal parts loam, peat moss, sand) kept dry between waterings. Propagation by suckers of leaf cuttings. Height: 18–30in (46–76cm). Family Agavaceae.

Sanskrit, the ancient classical language of India, the sacred language of the Hindu religion, and the forerunner of the modern Indic languages. Like Latin and Greek, it is an Indo-European language, and was brought to India from the north about 1500 BC. Only a handful of people are able to speak it today but it has nevertheless been designated one of the constitutional languages of India.

Sanskrit Literature. The Sanskrit language was brought to India by the Aryans, immigrants who entered from the northwest in the second millennium BC. After 1000 BC the language spread throughout India. The two main periods in Sanskrit literature are the Vedic (*c.* 1500–*c.* 200BC) and the overlapping Classical (*c.* 500 BC–*c.* AD1000). The Vedic period produced the Vedas, the earliest works in Sanskrit literature and among the most important. They are sacred hymns praising the Aryan gods and containing the liturgy for ritual sacrifices. The foremost collection of Vedas is the *Rigveda.* Later Vedic literature included the *Brahmanas,* which explain the significance of the sacrifices, and the *Upanisads* (Upanishads), which discuss the essence of the universe. The early Classical period contributed India's two great national epics, the *Mahabharata* and the *Ramayana.* They are significant both as literature and Hindu sacred works. Later Classical epics called the *Puranas* have become the main source of modern Hindu mythology. *See also* Brahmanas; Mahabharata.

Sansovino, Jacopo. △1138.

Santa Ana, city in W El Salvador; capital of Santa Ana dept.; 2nd-largest city of country. Industries: coffee, sugar refining. Pop. 104,962.

Santa Ana, city in S California, 20mi (32km) E of Long Beach; seat of Orange co; hub of the Anaheim-Santa Ana-Garden Grove metropolitan area, containing governmental, industrial, medical, and commercial establishments. Industries: electrical equipment, aircraft and nuclear parts, sporting goods, perfume, soft drinks. Founded 1869; inc. 1886. Pop. (1970) 156,601.

Santa Anna, Antonio López de (1794–1876), an enigmatic figure who weaved in and out of the political life of Mexico from 1822 to 1855. Santa Anna seemed at times to be a federalist, at other times a centralist; he identified himself with both liberal and conservative ideologies. He was unable to crush the movement for the independence of Texas and was defeated by General Winfield Scott in the war with the United States (1846–48). He led revolts against the governments of Iturbide, Guerrero, and Bustamante. Santa Anna was president of Mexico on several occasions, each time removed from office but recalled to lead it again.

Santa Barbara, city in S California, 80mi (128km) NW of Los Angeles; seat of Santa Barbara co; site of Spanish Mission (1786), and Santa Ynez Mts, encompassing the Los Padres National Forest. Industries: oil, aerospace research, orchids. Founded 1782; inc. 1850. Pop. (1970) 70,215.

Santa Catalina Island, resort island, off the coast of S California, member of the Santa Barbara group; picturesque, resort island with many coves and beaches. Discovered 1543 by Juan Rodriguez Cabrillo. Area: 70sq mi (181sq km).

Santa Clara, city in W California, 5mi (8km) NW of San Jose; location of University of Santa Clara (1851). Franciscans' Santa Clara de Asís Mission (1777) was the original settlement. Industries: fiberglass, chemicals, paper products, truck farming. Inc. 1852. Pop. (1970) 87,717.

Santa Croce. △1104.

Santa Cruz, city in W California, at the N end of Monterey Bay; seat of Santa Cruz co; site of replica of a mission founded 1791. Industries: tourism, food-processing, electronic equipment, fishing. Founded 1791; inc. 1876. Pop. (1970) 32,076.

Santa Cruz de Tenerife, port city in Spain, on NW coast of Tenerife Island, in the Canary Islands; capital of Tenerife prov. One of two provinces comprising the Canary Islands, it has an excellent harbor; site of San Cristobal castle, Concepcion parochial church, and many institutions of higher learning. Exports: onions, wine, vegetables, tobacco, sugar cane, bananas. Industries: tourism, wine, pottery, oil refining. Area: (prov.) 1,239sq mi (3,209sq km). Pop. (city) 151,361; (prov.) 590,514.

Santa Fe, formerly Santa Fe de Vera Cruz; city in N Argentina, 12mi (19km) WNW of Paraná; capital of Sante Fe prov. Settled by Juan de Garay, it was the center of Jesuit missions and fortification against indians; constitutional seat 1853. Industries: ships, grain, cotton, lumber. Founded 1573. Pop. 208,900.

Santa Fe, city in N New Mexico, 40mi (64km) W of Las Vegas, Nev.; capital of New Mexico and seat of Santa Fe co. As the seat of region's government since its founding *c.* 1609 by Spanish, it is the oldest capital in the United States; became W terminus of Sante Fe Trail (1821); made capital of territory 1851, and of state 1912. It is site of San Miguel Mission Church (1636), Cathedral of St Francis (1869), Palace of the Governors (1610, now a museum), Cristo Rey Church, College of Santa Fe (1947); seat of archbishopric since 1875. Industries: tourism, Indian and Mexican handicrafts. Pop. (1970) 41,167.

Santa Fe Trail, famed wagon trail from Independence, Mo., to Santa Fe, N.M. It was a main trail for western settlement and an important commercial route from about 1820 to 1850, until outdated by the railroad.

Santa Gertrudis. *See* Zebu.

Santa Maria, city in S California, 52mi (84km) NW of Santa Barbara. Industries: oil, agriculture, marine equipment, wire. Est. 1874; originally called Central City, changed to Santa Maria in 1880; inc. 1905. Pop. (1970) 32,749.

Santa Marta, city on the N coast of Colombia; capital of Magdalena dept.; Colombia's oldest city. Built on cliffs, it overlooks a deep bay in the Caribbean and is at the base of Sierra Nevada de Santa Maria; tourist resort and banana shipping center; connected with Bogotá by rail since 1961. Founded 1525. Pop. 129,-223.

Santa Monica, city in S California, 15mi (24km) W of Los Angeles; site of the J. Paul Getty Museum and several state parks. Industries: missiles, aircraft, tourism, chemicals. Inc. 1885. Pop. (1970) 88,289.

Santander, port city in N Spain, on the Bay of Biscay; capital of Santander prov. Linked with Castile during the Middle Ages, it is site of Gothic cathedral with Moorish facade, containing ancient crypts; nearby are caves of Altamira, with prehistoric wall paintings. Industries: shipping, tourism, grain, fishing, livestock. Area: (prov.) 2,042sq mi (5,289sq km). Pop. (city) 149,704; (prov.) 467,138.

Santa Rosa, city in W California, 50mi (80km) NNW of San Francisco; seat of Sonoma co; site of the Church of One Tree (1874) built from one redwood, and the Jack London "Wolf House." Inc. 1868. Pop. (1970) 50,006.

Sandpiper

San Francisco

Margaret Sanger

Fed. Rep. of Ger.
Czech.
Austria
Liech.
Switzerland
France
Hungary
SAN MARINO
Yugoslavia
Italy
Albania
MEDITERRANEAN SEA
Algeria
Tunisia
0
300 km

San Marino

Santayana, George (1863–1952), US philosopher and poet, b. Spain. After emigrating to the United States (1872) he became a professor at Harvard (1889–1912), resigning to settle in Italy. His works tended toward skepticism in the tradition of the Platonic doctrine of Essence. At the same time he admitted a positive knowledge of the realm of universals or "essences." After World War II, he secluded himself from people and events; this withdrawal being paralelled by the moral detachment of his works. A naturalist and materialist, he viewed religion as imaginative but not necessarily significant. His most important works include *The Sense of Beauty* (1896), *The Life of Reason* (1905–06), *Skepticism and Animal Faith* (1923), and *The Last Puritan* (1935).

Santiago, capital of Chile, in central Chile on the Mapocho River; capital of Santiago prov. Founded 1541 by Pedro de Valdivia, it was destroyed by earthquake 1647; President Salvatore Allende died here 1973 during a coup d'état; economic and cultural center of Chile; site of the University of Chile (1843), military academy, presidential palace. Industries: textiles, footwear, foodstuffs, iron and steel foundries. Pop. 2,661,920. △1078.

Santiago de Compostela, city in N central Spain, 32mi (51km) S of La Coruna; major pilgrimage site in Europe. Founded in the 9th century by Alfonso II, who built a chapel on site of St James tomb, the city became the major pilgrimage center in Europe; it was destroyed 997 by the Moors. It is the site of annual festival of St James, cathedral of St James (built 11th–13th centuries on site of original chapel), state university Colegio Fonseca (1525), pontifical university. Industries: tourism, religious articles, livestock, handicrafts, wood carvings, drugs, furniture, tires, leather goods. Pop. 70,893. △1080.

Santiago de Cuba, seaport in E Cuba, on cliff overlooking bay at the E end of Sierra Maestra; 2nd-largest city in Cuba and capital of Oriente prov. City was capital of Cuba 1522–1589; Fidel Castro's campaign against Fulgencio Batista began by attacking military garrison here July 26, 1953; site of historical French and Spanish buildings. Exports: agricultural produce, exotic woods. Founded 1514. Pop. 264,200.

Santiago de los Caballeros, city in N central Dominican Republic, on Rio Yaque del Norte; nation's 2nd-largest city. Industries: tobacco products, honey, beeswax. Founded 1500. Pop. 244,794.

Santo Domingo, name of the Dominican Republic before it became an independent state in 1844. *See* Dominican Republic.

Santo Domingo, capital city and seaport of Dominican Republic, on S coast of Island of Hispaniola, 150mi (241km) E of Port-au-Prince, Haiti. Founded by Bartholomé Columbus in 1496, it is the oldest continuously-settled European-founded community in Western Hemisphere. By 1550 most of the native Indian population had died of disease and warfare; city was almost destroyed by 1930 hurricane. Christopher Columbus' remains are reportedly buried here in the Cathedral of Santa Maria (1514). Industries: sugar, textiles, woodworking. Exports: tobacco, coffee, cacao. Pop. 671,402.

Santos, city in SE Brazil, 45mi (72km) SE of São Paulo on São Vincentes Island; contains largest harbor in Latin America; port is world's largest exporter of coffee and major distributor of other Brazilian products. Founded by Portuguese 1540. Pop. 313,771.

Saône River, river in E France, in Vosges Mts; flows SW past Gray, Chalon-sur-Saône, and Mâcon to join Rhône River at Lyons; connected by canals to Moselle, Marne, Yonne, and Loir rivers. Length: 298mi (480km).

São Paulo, city in SE Brazil, on Tietê River; capital of São Paulo state: was 17th-century base for expeditions into interior seeking slaves and mineral riches. Here Dom Pedro of Portuguese royal house declared Brazil's independence from Portugal in 1822; he later became Emperor Pedro I of Brazil. São Paulo was finance and trading center of coffee industry in the 19th century. Largest city in Brazil and South America, it is the commercial, industrial, and financial hub of Brazil. Industries: car manufacture, metallurgy, chemicals, marketing agricultural products. Founded by Jesuits 1554; inc. 1711. Pop. 5,901,533.

São Tomé and Príncipe, independent W African republic in the Gulf of Guinea, off the W coast of Africa, consisting of the two islands of São Tomé, approx. 150mi (241km) NW of Cape Lopez, Gabon; and Príncipe, about 90mi (145km) NE of São Tomé. The capital of São Tomé is on island of the same name.

Located on the equator, climate is humid with high temperatures and heavy rainfall from September to May of 40–100in (102–254cm). São Tomé island is 30mi (48km) long and 20mi (32km) wide; the highest point is Pico de São Tomé at 6,640ft (2,025m). Príncipe is 10mi (16km) long and 5mi (8km) wide with less rugged surface.

The islands' official language is Portuguese. People are descendants of original Portuguese and Africans with many Portuguese laborers who work on the islands' plantations. Religion is mainly Roman Catholic. Cacao is the chief export. Also grown and exported are coffee, bananas, coconuts, and copra and palm oil from coconuts.

Discovered by Portuguese navigators Pedro Escobar and João de Santarém 1470–71, the islands were officially claimed by Portugal in 1522 (claimed briefly by the Dutch in mid-17th century). Uninhabited at time of discovery, Portuguese came and brought Africans in as slaves. The islands began preparing for independence in 1974 and became independent in July 1975, with Manuel Pinto du Costa as the first president.

PROFILE

Official name: Democratic Republic of São Tomé and Príncipe
Area: 372sq mi (964sq km)
Population: 61,000
Chief city: São Tomé (capital)
Religion: Roman Catholic
Language: Portuguese

Sapodilla. △340.

Sapphire, a transparent to translucent gemstone variety of corundum, varying in color, the most valuable being deep blue. Most sapphires change color with direction of view. Star-sapphires reflect light in a six-pointed star. Brilliant when cut and polished, but lacking fire. *See also* Corundum. △244.

Sappho (late 7th–early 6th century BC) , Greek poetess from Lesbos. Regarded by other poets as the Tenth Muse, she was a noblewoman who ran a girls' school devoted to the study of music and poetry. Her theme was love, and she used nature to express her emotions. Amorous and passionate in style, she wrote love poems, of which large fragments remain, to her students. The Sapphic meter was named for her. △998.

Sapporo, city in W Hokkaido, Japan; capital of Hokkaido prefecture. A growing industrial-commercial city, it has become the business center of Japan's N main island; situated at E foot of a mountain range, the city hosted the 1972 Winter Olympics; site of Hokkaido University. Industries: lumber, food processing, printing, publishing, tourism. Pop. 1,010,123.

Saprophyte, plant that obtains its food from dead or decaying plant and animal tissues. They usually have no chlorophyll and grow in humus. Saprophytes include bacteria, fungi (puffballs, mushrooms, and molds), and flowering plants (Indian pipe). △426.

Sapsucker, North American woodpecker that drills rows of holes in trees to drink the sap. It also eats insects attracted by the flowing sap. They are blackish above with white mottling and yellowish below with a black chest patch. Males have crimson heads and throats. Genus *Sphyrapicus*. *See also* Woodpecker.

Saracens, a term first applied only to the people of NW Arabia and then extended to cover all Arabs and all Muslims. A Saracen invasion of France in the 8th century met defeat, but they were more successful in S Italy and in Sicily which they held from the 9th to the 11th century.

Saragossa, city in NE Spain, on the Ebro River; capital of Zaragoza prov.; traditional capital of Aragon. Originally an Iberian settlement, it was taken by Romans 1st century BC; fell to Visigoths 5th century; captured by Moors 713; taken 1118 by Alfonso I of Aragon. A major industrial and commercial center, it is site of 15th-century arched bridge, cathedral of La Seo (1119), University of Saragossa (1474). Industries: agricultural machinery, chemicals, glass, textiles. Area: (prov.) 6,639sq mi (17,195sq km). Pop. (city) 479,845; (prov.) 760,186.

Sarah, in the Bible, wife and half sister of Abraham and mother of Isaac. Childless, she gave Abraham her maid Hagar, who bore Ishmael. In her old age, Sarah bore Isaac.

Sarajevo, city in SW central Yugoslavia, on Bosna River; capital of Bosnia and Herzegovina; site of university (1946), 15th-century mosque. Founded as Vrh-Bosna citadel, city fell to Turks 1429; passed to Austria-Hungary 1878; inc. into Yugoslavia 1918. City was scene of assassination of Archduke Francis Ferdinand and his wife, June 28, 1914, precipitating WWI. Industries: textiles, steel, tobacco, sugar, beer, carpets, handicrafts, electrical equipment. Founded 1263. Pop. 244,045.

Sarasota, city in W central Florida, on Gulf of Mexico, 51mi (82km) S of Tampa. Winter home of Ringling Brothers Circus; site of Ringling Museum of Art. Settled 1886; inc. 1914. Pop. (1970) 40,237.

Saratoga, city in W California, SW of San Jose; site of James Phelan's Villa Montalvo estate, center for the arts. Tourism and wine making are the main industries. Inc. 1956. Pop. (1970) 27,110.

Saratoga, Battle of, Revolutionary War battle in which British Gen. John Burgoyne's forces were defeated at Saratoga, N.Y. (Oct. 17, 1777). It was a turning point in the war, influencing France to recognize the colonies. Burgoyne's expedition, marching from Canada to Albany, suffered heavy losses. Overwhelmed, he surrendered his entire army to Gen. Horatio Gates.

Saratoga Springs, city in E New York, W of Hudson River in Adirondack foothills, 33mi (53km) N of Albany. A noted health resort since late 18th century, it is site of medicinal springs; site of Saratoga Race Course, where thoroughbred horses have been raced each August since 1850; Congress Park and Casino, former gambling house (1870); Skidmore College (1911); Saratoga Performing Arts center. Industries: tourism, bottled spring water, knit fabrics. Inc. as village 1826, as city 1815. Pop. (1970) 18,845.

Saratov, city in Russian SFSR, USSR, on the Volga River; capital of Saratov oblast. Founded 1590 it moved to the present site in 1674; chartered 1780; developed into a major 19th-century grain trade center; it was successfully defended by Soviet troops in the civil war (1918–19); in 1943 it came under jurisdiction of Russian SFSR government; site of university (1919), institutes for road construction and agricultural mechanization, conservatory, agricultural, medical, and teachers' colleges, archeological and ethnographic museums. Industries: natural gas, chemicals, cotton textiles, leather goods, soap, flour, oilseeds, oil, lumber, shipbuilding, precision instruments. Pop. 758,000.

Sarazen, Gene (1902–), US golfer, b. Gene Saraceni in Harrison, N.Y. He won two US Opens (1922, 1932), a Masters (1935), three Professional Golf Association Championships (1922, 1923, 1933), and the British Open (1932).

Sarcodina, term meaning "living jelly," it is a class of protozoa that includes the amoeba. The original name for this class, it is used alternatively with "Rhizopoda." *See also* Rhizopoda. △466.

Sarcoma, cancerous growth or tumor made up of tissues from muscles and bones or cells embedded in connective tissue. It is usually highly malignant.

Sarcophagi. △1024.

Sardegna. *See* Sardinia.

Sardine, small marine food fish found worldwide. It has a laterally compressed body, large toothless mouth, and oily flesh. Length: to 1ft (30cm). Species include the California *Sardinops Caerulea*, South American *Sardinops sagax*, and the European sardine, or pilchard, *Sardinia pilchardus*. Family Clupeidae.

Sardinia (Sardegna), island in Mediterranean Sea; forms autonomous region of W Italy, with islands of Asinara, Caprera, San Pietro, and La Maddalena; capital city is Cagliari. Major portion of the island is mountainous; Campidano Plain in SW is major agricultural area. Prehistoric civilization existed; island was settled by Phoenicians *c.* 800 BC, Carthaginians *c.* 500 BC; taken by Rome 238 BC; under Vandals AD 5th century; made a Byzantine province 6th–8th centuries; attacked by Saracens 8th-11th centuries; disputed 11th-14th centuries by Pisa and Genoa; given to Aragonese by Pope Boniface VIII 13th century; passed to Spain 15th century, Austria 1713, Savoy 1720 and was included in kingdom of Sardinia. Products: wheat, barley, grapes, olives, livestock. Industries: fishing, processed foods, wine, refined petroleum, paper, cement, textiles. Area: 9,301sq mi (24,090sq km). Highest point is Mt Gennargentu, 6,017ft (1,835m). Pop. 1,488,008.

Sardinia, Kingdom of, the possessions of the House of Savoy from 1720, when they were ceded Sardinia to compensate for the loss of Sicily. It comprised Sardinia, Savoy, Nice, Aosta, Montferrat, Piedmont, and Genoa. Fighting with the Allies against France during the French Revolution, it lost most of its mainland possessions to France from 1798 to 1814 (Napoleon's defeat). Lombardy became part of the kingdom in 1859; most of the Papal States in 1860; the Two Sicilies in 1861—so that from the Risorgimento the kingdom of Sardinia included almost all of modern Italy, and Victor Emmanuel II of Sardinia became king of Italy. △1182.

Sardis, ancient city in Asia Minor, 50mi (80km) E of Smyrna in the Hermus valley; served as capital of ancient Lydia *c.* 650–519 BC; site of first minting of coins (6th century BC); passed to Rome AD 133; one of Seven Churches of Asia Minor; ruined 14th century by Tamerlane. Archeological excavations uncovered the city 1958,; further excavations (1962) revealed temple of Artemis (4th century BC).

Sargasso Sea, the eddy within the North Atlantic gyre, named for the large quantities of floating seaweed *Sargassum* which covers it. Though filled with the seaweed, in reality it is like a great oceanic desert, with the lowest amount of life of any sea water. *See also* Gyre.

Sargassum Fish, marine bony fish found in tropical seas worldwide. A voracious predator, its balloon-shaped body is covered with loose skin camouflaging it as floating seaweed; it also has a "fishing pole" lure on its head. Length: 6in (15.2cm). Family Antennariidae; species *Histrio histrio.*

Sargent, John Singer (1856–1925), US painter, b. Italy. The son of wealthy expatriate parents, he lived and studied abroad. He is best known for his numerous portrait commissions, especially those of society ladies. His infamous portrait of Madame Gautreau (Mme. X) was rejected by his client and also by the French art public because he lowered the neckline of her dress and also exposed her vanity. His later works included Impressionistic watercolors.

Sargon (*fl. c.* 2600 BC), founder of first Semitic dynasty of Akkad in ancient Mesopotamia. His empire lasted over 100 years and stretched from the Persian Gulf to the Mediterranean Sea. △956.

Sargon II (died 705 BC), powerful King of Assyria (721–705), succeeding Shalmaneser V. He conquered Samaria (721), subjugated Babylonia and the other major unconquered states of Syria, and broke the power of Urartu (Armenia). △958, 954, 980, 982.

Sark, island in the English Channel; one of the Channel Islands, E of Guernsey; comprises Great Sark and Little Sark, linked by the Coupée isthmus. Its economy is based on agriculture and tourism. Area: 2sq mi (5sq km). Pop. 590.

Sarmatians, ancient nomadic and pastoral people who in the 5th century BC lived in the area between the Caspian Sea, the Don River, and the Sea of Azov. By the 3d century BC, their territory extended from the Baltic to the Black Sea, from the Vistula River to the Volga. They were overpowered by the Goths from the west and the Huns from Asia in the 4th century AD.

Sarnia, city in SW Ontario; pipeline terminus for oil from Texas and Alberta. Industries: oil refineries, chemical products, lumber. Founded 1807 by French, 1833 by English. Pop. 56,727.

Sarnoff, David (1891–1971), US communications executive, b. Russia. He joined the Marconi Wireless Telegraph Co. (1906) as an office boy and went on to become a radio and television pioneer. As president of Radio Corporation of America (RCA), 1930–49, and then as chairman of the board (1947–70), he was instrumental in the founding of the National Broadcasting Co. and in the change in emphasis from radio to television.

Saroyan, William (1908–), US author, b. Fresno, Calif. He wrote such irreverent short stories as "The Daring Young Man on the Flying Trapeze" (1934). Plays by Saroyan include *My Heart's in the Highlands* and the Pulitzer Prize winner *Time of Your Life* (1939). His autobiography *My Name is Aram* (1940) described his youth as an Armenian-American. He also wrote two memoirs (1961, 1972).

Sarsaparilla, wild perennial plant native to North America. It has greenish flowers. Family Araliaceae; species *Aralia nudicaulis.* Or, several species of *Smilax* (family Liliaceae) cultivated for their roots formerly thought to have medicinal value.

Sarto, Andrea del (1486–1531), Florentine artist known as "the faultless painter" after decorating the Cloisters of the Annunziata in Florence. His work, in which figure and background are closely related, is represented in New York City's Metropolitan Museum by "Holy Family."

Sarton, May (1912–), US author, b. Belgium. She taught at Harvard University and Wellesley College. Collections of poetry include *Encounter in April* (1937), *Inner Landscape* (1939), *The Land of Silence* (1953) and *In Time Like Air* (1957). Novels include *The Single Hound* (1938), *The Bridge of Years* (1946) and *Shadow of a Man* (1950).

Sartorius. △684.

Sartre, Jean-Paul (1905–), French novelist, playwright, and philosopher. He participated in the French Resistance in World War II. The foremost exponent of Existentialism, he was also involved in Marxist politics. For many years he lived with author Simone de Beauvoir. His important works include *Nausea* (1938), *Being and Nothingness* (1943), the trilogy *The Roads to Freedom* (1949), and *Critique of Dialectical Reason* (1964). In 1964 he refused the Nobel Prize for literature. *See also* Existentialism; △856, 1367.

Saskatchewan, province in W central Canada, in the plains region, bordered on the S by the states of Montana and North Dakota.

Land and Economy. The country is gently rolling; the highest elevations are in the SW. The S half is chiefly agricultural land; the N is forested wilderness. Rivers, of which the most important are the North and the South Saskatchewan, cut deep valleys; there are hundreds of lakes. The province has long been a major wheat producer. Oil drilling, tapping of natural gas resources, and uranium mining have developed largely since WWII.

People. Settlement did not begin until the late 19th century, when immigrants came from E Canada, the United States, and Europe. People of English descent form the largest sector of the population, with elements of Germans, Ukrainians, Scandinavians, and French.

Education. The University of Saskatchewan at Saskatoon and the University of Regina are the only institutions of higher education.

History. Henry Kelsey, an agent of the Hudson's Bay Co., fur traders, visited the region in 1690. The first trading post, Fort Lacorne, was built in 1753; the first permanent settlement was Cumberland House, built by the Hudson's Bay Co. in 1774. Slow immigration created farming communities through the 19th century, but the population influx did not begin until after the completion of the transcontinental Canadian Pacific Railroad in 1885. Saskatchewan joined the Confederation on the same day as Alberta in 1905.

PROFILE

Admitted to Confederation: Sept. 1, 1905; rank, 9th
National Parliament Representatives: Senate, 6; House of Commons, 13
Population: 942,000; rank, 6th
Capital: Regina
Chief cities: Regina; Saskatoon; Moose Jaw
Provincial Legislature: Legislative Assembly, 60
Area: 251,700sq mi (651,903sq km); rank, 5th
Elevation: Highest, 4,546ft (1,386m), Cypress Hills; lowest, 699ft (213m), Lake Athabaska
Industries (major products): petroleum products, processed foods
Agriculture (major products): wheat, barley, oats, rye, beef cattle, hogs
Minerals (major): petroleum, natural gas, uranium, potash
Floral emblem: wood lily

Saskatchewan, river in S central Canada; has two tributaries—North and South Saskatchewan rivers. Both rise in E region of the Rocky Mts, continuing E and emptying into Lake Winnipeg, 25mi (40km) E of Prince Albert, Saskatchewan. Discovered 18th century by Sieur de La Vérendrye, it was a well-traveled route for fur trapping companies. Agriculture is prominent around the river's mouth, where irrigation began in 1901. Length: approx. 340mi (547km).

Saskatoon, city in S central Saskatchewan, Canada, on South Saskatchewan River; est. as capital of a temperance society under the direction of the Temperance Colonization Society of Ontario; site of the University of Saskatchewan; commercial and distributing center for surrounding grain farms. Industries: flour, cereal mills, meat packing, dairy products. Founded 1883; inc. 1906. Pop. 125,079.

CHEVROLET
São Paulo, Brazil

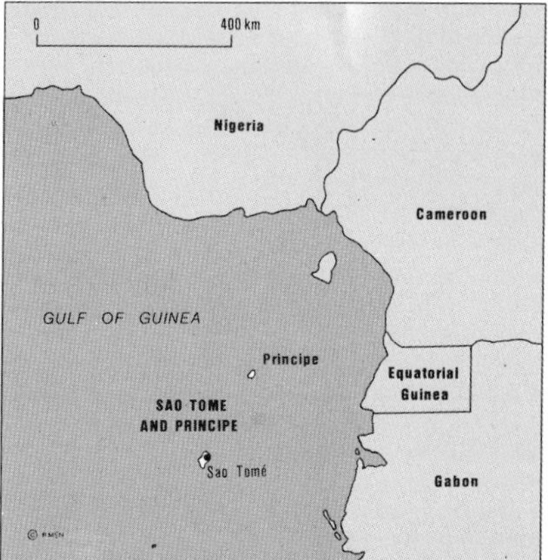
0
400 km
Nigeria
Cameroon
GULF OF GUINEA
Principe
Equatorial Guinea
SAO TOME AND PRINCIPE
Sao Tomé
Gabon
São Tomé and Principe

Jean-Paul Sartre

Saskatchewan, Canada: grain harvest

Sassafras, small E North American tree with furrowed bark, green twigs, yellow flowers, and blue berries. Its leaves have three shapes (3-lobed, 2-lobed, or smooth egg-shape) often on the same branch. An aromatic tea is made from the outer bark of its roots and oil from the roots is used to flavor root beer. Family Lauraceae; species *Sassafras albidum*.

Sassanids, or **Sassanians,** last native dynasty of Persian kings, founded by Ardashir I *c.* AD 226. There were approximately 25 Sassanid rulers, the most important after Ardashir being Shapur II (309–79); Khosrau I (531–79), who invaded Syria; and Khosrau II (590–628), whose conquest of Egypt marks the height of the dynasty's power. The line ended when Persia fell to the Arabs *c.* 641.

Satan, a name for the devil. Originally, Satan simply meant an opponent, and not a particular being. Around the 6th century BC, he appears in the Old Testament as an individual angel, subordinate to God. Gradually, Satan became the source of all evil, responsible for leading man into sin, and thus the tempter opposed to God.

Satellite, Artificial, man-made object orbiting a planet. The first Earth satellite was Sputnik 1, launched Oct. 4, 1957, by the Soviet Union. The main uses of satellites are military reconnaissance, weather studies, communications, and scientific studies. Artificial satellites are distinguished from space probes, which do not orbit planets. *See also* Satellite, Communications; Satellite, Geodetic; Satellite, Weather; Sputnik. △142.

Satellite, Communications, satellite used to beam or reflect electromagnetic signals. Passive satellites such as the aluminized 100-ft (30.5m) high "balloon" (Echo series) serve as reflectors. Active satellites such as Intelsat can handle thousands of telephone circuits or 12 television channels. Synchronous satellites such as Syncom provide 24-hour coverage to large areas. *See also* Synchronous Orbit, Satellite. △1792.

Satellite, Geodetic, satellite whose orbit is studied from widely separated places to provide more accurate maps of oceans and continents. The Geodetic Earth Orbiting Satellite program of 1971 (GEOS) reduced intercontinental distance errors to 10 meters. Laser measurements of vertical Earth movements to forecast incipient earthquakes are also possible.

Satellite, Natural, any of several minor bodies orbiting some of the planets of the solar system. Six planets are known to have satellites, ranging in numbers from one for Earth to 13 presently known for Jupiter. Some satellites appear to be asteroids captured after the solar system was already formed. Others, such as the Moon, may have formed with the planets or coalesced from particles orbiting them. △76, 84, 86, 88.

Satellite, Weather, a satellite studying weather patterns on Earth by photographic, infrared, or other means. Photographic histories of hurricane development and discovery of large-scale coherence in cloud and other weather patterns have had great impact on weather forecasts.

Satinwood Tree, tree native to E India with smooth, hard wood that is valued for furniture and veneer. Height: to 50ft (15m). Family Rutaceae; species *Chloroxylon swietenia*.

Satire, Roman, invented by the poet Gaius Lucilius in the 2nd century BC. Only fragments of his works remain. Satire became agreeably persuasive in Horace's *Satires* and the instructional quality was emphasized even more in the works of Persius. Juvenal was the first great tragic satirist and the satirical romance appeared with the works of Petronius and Apuleius. *See also* Horace; Juvenal; Lucilius, Gaius.

Sato, Eisaku (1901–75), Japanese political figure. In 1947 he became vice-minister of transportation after work with the railway ministry and was finance minister (1958–60). A Liberal-Democratic member of the Diet, he was prime minister (1964–72). His chief foreign policy successes were normalization of relations with South Korea and the signing of a treaty returning Okinawa and the Bonin Islands to Japanese jurisdiction (1969). In 1974 he was awarded the Nobel Prize for peace.

Saturation, condition of a solution when the maximum amount of the dissolved substance, the solute, has been taken into solution at a given temperature. Conditions of supersaturation—excess solute over the limiting condition of the saturated state—can exist for a few seconds, but are unstable. △1562.

Saturation, Color. *See* Color.

Saturn, sixth planet from the sun and second largest in the solar system, encircled by 10 satellites and a system of narrow rings composed of icy or ice covered particles. Mean distance from the Sun, 886,000,000mi (1,427,000,000km); mass and volume, 95.2 and 744 times that of Earth, respectively; equatorial diameter, 75,000mi (120,911km); rotation period, 10hr 14min; period of sidereal revolution, 29.46 years; composition, principally hydrogen, methane, ammonia, and helium. *See also* Solar System. △84–86.

Saturn, in Roman religion, the god of sowing or seed. Saturn's cult partner was the goddess Lua. He is also associated with Ops. His great festival, the Saturnalia, became the most popular of Roman festivals and its influence is still felt throughout the Western world in the celebrations of Christmas and New Year's.

Satyr Butterfly, brown and gray butterfly often having eyespots on wings. Veins of the front wings are typically swollen at wing base. Family Agapetidae; genus *Neonymphia*.

Satyriasis, insatiable sexual appetite in a male. Compulsive sexual activity in which sexual thoughts and behavior completely dominate all else. As in the case of nymphomania, it is the insatiable nature of the need for sexual gratification that defines the syndrome.

Satyricon. *See* Petronius.

Satyrs, in Greek mythology, gods of the woods, fields, and mountains of sensual and lascivious character. They are depicted as goat-bearded and goat-legged, but with the head (though horned) and trunk of a man. In later art their countenance became milder, less animal. They became men with small horns and pointed ears.

Saud (1902–69), king of Saudi Arabia (1953–64). His name in full was Ibn Abd al-Aziz Al Faisal Al Saud. The son and successor of Ibn Saud, he became crown prince (1933). His fiscal mismanagement and personal extravagance caused a severe financial crisis in 1958. Soon after, his brother Faisal took over all administrative powers, formally replacing Saud as king in 1964.

Saudi Arabia, Kingdom of, nation of Arabian Peninsula. The people are Arabic and overwhelmingly Muslim. The country is the birthplace of Islam and site of the holy city of Mecca. As a major oil producer and the foremost Arab leader, Saudi Arabia played a vital role in world economics and politics in the 1970s.

Land and Economy. There are two major geologic regions. The Arabian Shield, in the W, is composed of ancient crystalline rock piled up into mountain chains (7,000–9,000ft; 2,135–2,745m) paralleling the Red Sea. The E region, of sedimentary rock, slopes gently toward the Persian Gulf. The hot, humid Tihamah plain lies between the mountains and coast. The interior is less humid and hot than the coasts. Most of Saudi Arabia is arid; the largest deserts, connected by the Dahna sand belt, are the Rub al-Khali in the S (230,000sq mi; 595,700sq km) and the Great Nafud in the N (26,000sq mi; 67,340sq km). The economy is dominated by oil, exploited from 1938, which furnishes over 90% of revenue. The government has bought control of the Arabian American Oil Company (Aramco), the primary producer. Enormous natural gas deposits occur in conjunction with the oil. Some salt and gypsum are extracted, and clay and limestone are used in cement manufacture. Saudi Arabia falls short of self-sufficiency in food. Dhahran, Jidda, Riyadh, and Medina have international airports. Jidda and Damman are the major ports.

People. The vast majority of the Saudis are descended from indigenous tribes; different Arabic dialects are spoken. About 90% of the people are Sunnite Muslims of the Wahhabi sect; some Shiite Muslims live in the E. Over 50% of the population is nomadic or semi-nomadic; about 25% city-dwellers; the remainder primarily farmers. The family and tribe are the main social units. The population is about 90% illiterate, but extensive education programs have been inaugurated, including expanded opportunities for women.

Government. The constitution is based on Islam's Wahhabi reform movement. The king's power is by the law of Islam and by the Council of Ministers. The principal decisions of the Council are issued as royal decrees. Elections are held only at the municipal level; there are no political parties. Local government is largely in the hands of appointed officials, many of whom are royal relatives. Religious judges preside over the courts, but local administrative officials have certain judicial functions.

History. The area's early history is covered under Arabia. The power of the Saud family, originally rulers of an oasis, grew from 1774 as the Wahhabi movement, which it led, spread in the Nejd. Mecca was occupied (1803), but the Turks then conquered the Nejd (1818). The house of Saud revived, and Ibn Saud recaptured (1902) the ancestral capital of Riyadh. In 1932 he named his kingdom Saudi Arabia. Neutral in World War II, Saudi Arabia was a founding member of the United Nations (1945) and the Arab League. Ibn Saud was succeeded (1953) by his son Saud, deposed in 1964 in favor of his half-brother Faisal. Faisal, assassinated in 1975, was succeeded by his brother Khalid. Saudi Arabia's power has increased as its petroleum has become more valuable, and it has been a leader in Arab opposition to Israel. *See also* Arabia; Arab League.

PROFILE

Official name: Kingdom of Saudi Arabia
Area: 830,000sq mi (2,149,700sq km)
Population: 9,000,000
Density. 11per sq mi (4per sq km)
Chief cities: Riyadh (capital); Jidda; Mecca
Government: Head of state, King Khalid (acceded 1975)
Religion: Islam (official)
Language: Arabic (official)
Monetary unit: Riyal
Gross national product: $10,500,000,000
Per capita income: $1,226
Manufacturing (major products): petroleum products, cement, fertilizers, iron, and steel
Agriculture (major products): dates, vegetables, wheat
Minerals (major): petroleum
Trading partners (major): Japan, Italy, Netherlands, Great Britain

Saugus, town in NE Massachusetts, 8mi (13km) NNE of Boston; site of ironworks (restored 1954), ironmaster's house (1636), and a museum showing development of American iron and steel. Industries: machine shops. Settled 1637; set off from Lynn and inc. 1815. Pop. (1970) 25,110.

Sauk, or **Sac,** an Algonquian-speaking tribe of North American Indians originally occupying the Saginaw Bay region of Michigan. Closely related to the Mesquakie, Potawatomi, and Kickapoo peoples, they are famous for their role in the Black Hawk War of 1832. Approximately 1,200 live on lands in Kansas, Iowa, and Oklahoma today.

Saul, in the Bible, first king of Israel and son of Benjaminite Kish. Anointed by the prophet Samuel to be Israelite leader, he became king after his victory over the Ammonites. His jealousy led to conflicts with Samuel, David, and his son Jonathan. After hearing his defeat and death prophesied, he committed suicide rather than be captured by the Philistines.

Sault Sainte Marie, city in S Ontario, Canada, across St Mary's River from Sault Ste Marie, Michigan; seat of Algoma district. During 17th century it was populated by missionaries, fur traders, and explorers; North-West Fur Co. est. a trading post here in 18th century. City is chief port, close to lakes Huron, Superior, and Michigan. Industries: paper, lumber, steel, iron, farming, chemicals. Founded 1668; inc. 1912. Pop. 78,175.

Sault Sainte Marie Canals (Soo Canals), artificial waterway system on the US-Canadian border, between lakes Huron and Superior at the twin cities of Sault Sainte Marie, N Michigan, and Sault Sainte Marie, S central Ontario. A canal system was needed to bypass the rapids of the St Marys River and connect the vital water routes of the Great Lakes; the Canadian canal was completed in 1799 but was later destroyed by US attacks during the War of 1812; it was rebuilt in 1895. A parallel route on the US side was built 1853–55; this was replaced and enlarged 1881–1919. The US canal is 1.6mi (3km) long with two channels and four locks. Two of the locks, 1,350ft (412m) long and 80ft (24m) wide, are among the largest in the world. The Canadian canal is 1.4mi (2km) long and has one lock. This system, although ice-bound in winter, is one of the world's busiest waterways.

Saurischian, "lizard-hipped" dinosaur, carnivorous as well as herbivorous. Theropoda were meat-eaters, and Sauropoda were plant-eaters. The pelvis was characteristically three-pronged, resembling lizard's. △570, 572.

Sauropoda, saurischian dinosaur that was a swamp-dwelling, semiaquatic giant flourishing worldwide during the Jurassic period until Cretaceous times (65–

136,000,000 years ago). Included were all large, peg-toothed herbivorous types such as Brontosaurus and Diplodocus. △570, 572.

Sausages. △376, 380.

Sava, longest river in Yugoslavia; rises in Julian Alps in NW Slovenia, flows ESE across N Yugoslavia into Danube River at Belgrade; navigable to Sisak. Length: approx. 584mi (940km).

Savanna. △586.

Savannah, city and port of entry in E Georgia, on Savannah River; seat of Chatham co; oldest city in Georgia. Chosen as the seat of colonial government and capital of Georgia Colony 1754, it was captured by British 1778 during American Revolution and held until end of the war; served as state capital 1754–86; grew quickly as cotton center. A Confederate supply depot during Civil War, it was taken by Gen. William Sherman Dec. 21, 1864. Its colonial homes include Pirate's (1754), Herb (1734), Pink (1789), and Wormsloe (1733) houses; birthplace of Juliette Gordon Low; site of Armstrong State College (1935), Savannah State College (1890). Industries: paper, petroleum products, paint, wallboard, refined sugar, food processing, shipbuilding and repair, wood products. Founded 1733 by Gen. James Oglethorpe; inc. 1789. Pop. (1970) 118,349.

Savannah River, river in E Georgia and NW South Carolina; formed by confluence of Tugaloo and Seneca rivers in South Carolina; flows SE forming major part of boundary between Georgia and South Carolina; empties into Atlantic Ocean at Savannah; site of Hartwell and Clark Hill Dams, part of Savannah River Basin development plan. Length: 314mi (505km).

Savigny, Friedrich Karl Von (1779–1861), German jurist and legal historian. He founded the historical school of jurisprudence, which opposed the trend toward legal codification. He was a law professor at the University of Berlin (1810–42) and Prussian minister for legislation (1842–48). His major works included a study of Roman law during the Middle Ages. △908.

Savings and Loan Association, financial intermediary that issues shares or ownership certificates to its depositors. Commercial banks, on the other hand, ordinarily deal in demand deposits or time deposits, which are payable to the depositors within a specified time period. Though savings and loan shares are not payable within any specified time period, they ordinarily are redeemed at the buyer's request.

Savonarola, Girolamo (1452–98), Italian religious reformer. He abandoned medicine to become a monk, when convinced of the sinfulness of the world. Sent to Florence (1482) he was first enchanted and then horrified by Florentine culture. When he returned to Florence (1490) it was as a famous pulpit orator. As prior of St Marks, he was led by visions in a crusade against corruption, and after the collapse of Medici rule (1494) Savonarola became virtual dictator of the city. Consequent to the civil disturbances that ensued, he was executed. Florence, apparently, could only be persuaded to rid itself momentarily of "vanities," against which Savonarola had preached.

Savory, common name for hardy aromatic herbs of the mint family with leaves used, green or dried, for flavoring. Summer savory *(Satureia hortensis)* is an annual. Winter Savory *(S. montana)* is a perennial. △358.

Savoy, royal European dynasty and ruling house of Italy from 1861–1946. Descended from Humbert the Whitehanded (died *c.* 1048), the first count of Savoy, they were dukes from 1416, kings of Sicily from 1720, and kings of Italy from the Risorgimento (1861) through World War II (until 1946). It was under the house of Savoy that Italian unification was achieved (1860–70) and Benito Mussolini's Fascists ruled Italy (1922–43).

Savoy, historic region between Italy and France. Historically important for its control of western Alpine passes, it was part of the first Burgundian kingdom, the kingdom of Arles, and, in the 11th century, the Holy Roman Empire (as a county). In 1416 it became a duchy and then greatly expanded into France, Switzerland, and Italy. Savoy became part of France permanently in 1860, while its rulers became kings of Italy.

Sawback. *See* Map Turtle.

Sawfish, flat-bodied elasmobranch found in tropical marine and brackish waters. Actually a ray, its dark gray or black-brown body has a long saw-toothed sword attached to its nose. It uses it to dig up the ocean bottom and to club prey. Length: to 16ft (5m). Family Prisidae; species W Atlantic common *Pristis pectinotus; See also* Ray. △510.

Sawfly, primitive, plant-feeding wasp that lacks a thread waist. Its larvae are caterpillarlike, with 8 abdominal legs. The females have a two-bladed, sawlike ovipositor for laying eggs in plant tissue. Found worldwide, they rarely exceed 0.8in (20mm) in length. Family Tenthredinidae. *See also* Hymenoptera.

Saxe, Hermann Maurice de (1696–1750), marshal of France, a career military officer and son of Augustus II, elector of Saxony and king of Poland. Saxe joined the French army *c.*1713 and in 1720 was appointed camp marshal to the Duke of Orleans. He was made commander of the French forces as a reward for his defense of Alsace in 1743. A brilliant strategist, Saxe wrote a monograph on the art of war, *Mes Rêveries.*

Saxe-Weimar, former duchy in central Germany; became separate entity 1547 when Ernestine lands were divided into duchies of Weimar, Gotha, Coburg, Eisenach, and Altenburg. In 1741 it became Saxe-Weimar-Eisenach duchy and developed into a European cultural center under Duke Charles Augustus, patron of Johann Wolfgang Von Goethe. In 1920 the duchy was inc. into German state of Thuringia.

Saxifrage, perennial plants native to temperate and mountainous regions of Europe and North America. Leaves are massed at the base and the small flowers are white, pink, purple, or yellow. Height: to 2ft (61cm). Family Saxifragaceae; genus *Saxifraga.*

Saxo Gramaticus (*c.*1150–1220), Danish historian. He wrote *Danish History,* a history of the Danish kingdom to 1186, probably under the patronage of Archbishop Absalon of Lund. Written in 16 books, the first part of which is based almost entirely upon legend, the history is valued for its later volumes.

Saxons, ancient Germanic people. Originating in N Europe, they extended south and west, eventually colonizing Britain (*c.*450). There they amalgamated with the Angles to form the Anglo-Saxon civilization. The continental Saxons warred with the Franks and were finally subjugated by Charlemagne in the early 9th century. Their lands became part of what is now modern Germany.

Saxony, former German state; since WWII it has been part of East Germany. Est. late 9th century by the Duchy of Saxony, it was one of five primary duchies of medieval Germany and included almost all land between Elbe and Saale rivers (E), Rhine (W), and Franconia and Thuringia (E). By 1435 its area had shifted from NW to E central Germany; in 1815 over half of Saxony was ceded to Prussia and, with several Prussian districts, it became the province of Saxony, which included Wittenburg and Thuringia, plus territories between Elbe River and Harz Mts. In 1945 state of Anhalt was added to form Saxony Anhalt state; in 1952 East Germany reorganized its land into smaller administrative units and eliminated Saxony-Anhalt. Industries: agriculture, mining, chemicals, textiles.

Saxophone, wind musical instrument with single-reed, curved conical pipe of metal and holes with keys. Invented by Adolphe Sax in Paris (1840), it is made in seven sizes, soprano to bass, pitched alternately Eb and Bb, with alto and tenor most common. It was used symphonically by Bizet, Debussy, Ravel, Richard Strauss, and Prokofiev. Associated with dance halls after World War I, the hybrid saxophone with its rich, voicelike timbre was accepted in the late 1920s by jazz musicians. △1500.

Sayers, Dorothy (1863–1957), English novelist and playwright. Her first novels were detective stories featuring Lord Peter Wimsey, including *Whose Body?* (1923) and *Strong Poison* (1930). Her plays are religious dramas, such as *The Zeal of Thy House* (1937) and a sequence of radio plays *The Man Born to be King* (1941). She also wrote critical essays on medieval literature.

Sayreville, borough in central New Jersey, on Raritan Bay inlet 5mi (8km) ESE of New Brunswick. Industries: chemicals, plastics, ceramics. Inc. 1919. Pop. (1970) 32,508.

Scab, in botany, any of various plant diseases whose symptoms include scabby scaly spots on fruit and twigs or velvety spots on leaves. Scabby fruit is often stunted or deformed. Scab diseases are serious pests of apples, pears, pecans, peaches, cucumbers, and potatoes.

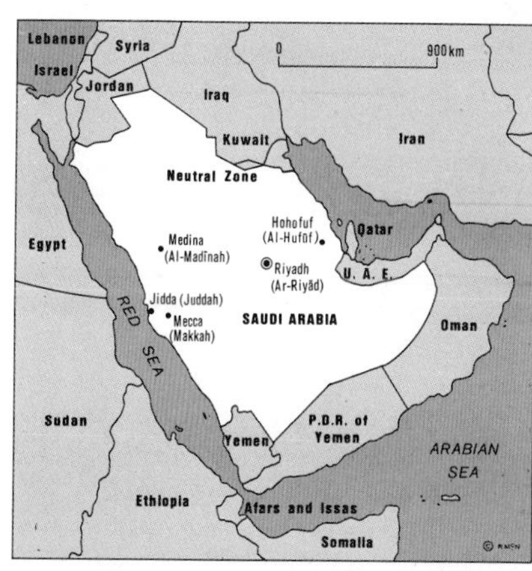

Lebanon
Syria
Israel
Jordan
Iraq
Kuwait
Iran
0
900km
Neutral Zone
Egypt
Medina
(Al-Madinah)
Hohofuf
(Al-Hufūf)
Qatar
Riyadh
(Ar-Riyād)
U. A. E.
RED SEA
Jidda (Juddah)
Mecca
(Makkah)
SAUDI ARABIA
Oman
Sudan
Yemen
P.D.R. of
Yemen
ARABIAN
SEA
Ethiopia
Afars and Issas
Somalia

Saudi Arabia

Mecca, Saudi Arabia

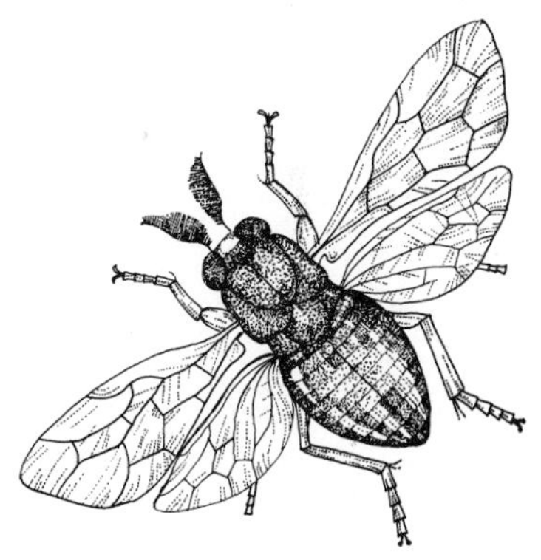

Sawfly

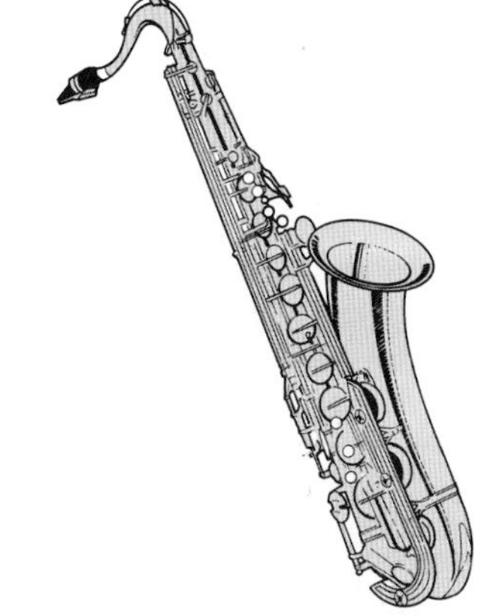

Saxophone

Scabies, inflammation of the skin brought about by a female mite, *Sarcoptes scabei*, burrowing in the skin to lay eggs. It can be seen as a dark wavy line on the skin.

Scafell Pike, mountain in NW England, in Cumbria; highest peak in England, 3,210ft (979m). Neighboring Scafell (Sca Fell) is the second-highest, 3,162ft (964m).

Scalar, quantity that has only a magnitude, as contrasted with a vector. Mass, energy, and speed are scalars, while weight, force, and velocity are vectors. *See also* Vector.

Scaldic Poetry, courtly verse written in Old Norse and popular in Norway from the 10th to the 13th century. It is characterized by elaborate verse forms combining alliteration, rhyme, stanzas, etc. In the pre-Christian period of the 10th and 11th centuries, the subjects were primarily mythological and political; Christian subjects enter in during the last two centuries of its prominence as a form. Scaldic poets include Egill Skalla-Grímsson (*c.* 910–990) and Sighvatr Thórtharson (*c.* 995–1045). *See also* Alliteration.

Scale, flat plates that form the outer covering of most fishes and many reptiles and which cover a few mammals (scaly anteater) and occur on certain body parts of other animals. Scales often overlap one another like shingles and protect softer inner body parts. In bony fishes, the scales are bony disks developed from under the skin; in sharks they are enamel and bone; in reptiles they are usually hardened and horny folded skin. The term is also used for the small flaky leaves that cover plant buds.

Scale Insect, small insect destructive to plants found worldwide. All are covered by a waxy or scalelike covering secreted by the insect. They feed by sucking plant juices. Length: to 1in (25mm). Family Coccidae. *See also* Cochineal, Lac Insect, San Jose Scale. △496.

Scales, The. *See* Libra.

Scalesia. △614.

Scallop, edible bivalve mollusk. Generally the bottom valve is convex with the upper valve almost flat. The shell's surface is ribbed and scalloped. Most possess well-developed eyes that fringe the fleshy mantle. Width: 1–8in (2.5–20cm). Family Pectinidae. *See also* Bivalve, Mollusk. △478.

Scalpel. △752.

Scaly Anteater. *See* Pangolin.

Scanderbeg, or **Skanderbeg** (1403–68), national hero of Albania. His real name was George Castriota; his Turkish name was Iskender Bey. A Serb, he was abducted by Turks at age seven, and became a favorite army commander of Sultan Murad II. In 1443 he renounced Islam, married the daughter of an Albanian chieftan, and drove the Turks out of Albania. For 20 years he maintained the area's independence against every force. His empire collapsed immediately after his death, however, and the Turks took control.

Scandinavia, region of N Europe, consisting of kingdoms of Sweden, Norway, and Denmark; culturally and historically Finland and Iceland are often considered part of this area. It is bordered by the Gulf of Bothnia, the Baltic Sea, the Kattegat and Skagerrak straits, North Sea, and Atlantic and Arctic oceans. Mountainous in W with swift-flowing streams, its coastline has many fjords; land in E and S is gently sloped and has many lakes. Approx. 25% of peninsula lies in Arctic Circle where tundra predominates. S Sweden contains best farmlands; there is much forested land and mineral wealth, and coastal waters supply abundant fish. Largest cities are: Stockholm and Göteborg, Sweden; Oslo, Norway; and Helsinki, Finland. Area of peninsula: 300,000sq mi (777,000sq km). △1068.

Scandium, metallic element (symbol Sc) of group IIIB of the periodic table predicted (as ekaboron) by Mendeleev and discovered in 1879 by Lars Nilson. It is found in thortveitite and, in small amounts, in many other minerals. It is a soft metal with few commercial uses. Chemically it resembles the lanthanides. Properties: at. no. 21; at. wt. 44.9559; sp gr 2.99 (25°C); melt. pt. 2802°F (1539°C); boil. pt. 5130°F (2832°C); most common isotope Sc^{45} (100%). △1554.

Scansion, analysis of the meter of a poem by breaking down each line into metrical feet. Each foot consists of a group of two or three syllables, one of which is stressed, or long. Metrical feet are scanned as: iambs (one short, one long ᴗ—); trochees (one long, one short —ᴗ); anapests (two shorts, one long ᴗᴗ—); dactyls (one long, two shorts —ᴗᴗ); spondees (two longs — —); pyrrhics (two shorts ᴗᴗ). *See also* Meter; Rhythm.

Scapa Flow, landlocked anchorage in Scotland, S of Pomona (Mainland) in the Orkney Islands. The main entrance is from Pentland Firth(S). In both world wars the British fleet was stationed at Scapa Flow; here the German fleet was scuttled 1918, and the battleship *Royal Oak* sunk 1939. Length: 15mi (24km). Width: 8mi (13km).

Scapegoat, in ancient Israel, a goat used in the ritual on the Day of Atonement. The high priest touched the goat and confessed the sins of the community. The animal was then driven from the village, symbolically bearing the sins of the people. Later, as the ritual developed, the scapegoat was pushed to his death from a cliff. The term has come to mean one blamed unfairly for others' misfortunes. △894, 896.

Scaphopods. △480.

Scapula, or shoulder blade, a large, roughly triangular, flat bone, that serves to hold the upper arm bone, or humerus, in place. It allows for the attachment of muscles that function in arm movement. The scapula joins with the clavicle at a point called the acromion process and with the humerus at the glenoid cavity.

Scar, mark left on the skin after a wound or sore heals. No oil glands or elastic tissue exist as in normal skin, thus scars may itch. Severe scars are prone to malignant change. △724.

Scarification. △818.

Scarab Beetle, robust, broad beetle distributed worldwide. Most scarab beetles, including the June bug, Japanese beetle, and rhinoceros beetle, are leaf chafers. A smaller group, including the dung beetle or tumblebug, are scavengers. Family Scarabaeidae.

Scarlatina. *See* Scarlet Fever.

Scarlatti, Alessandro (1660–1725), Italian composer known primarily for his vocal music, which appeared in his 115 operas, 200 masses, and over 700 cantatas and oratorios. △1174, 1196.

Scarlatti, Domenico (1683–1757), Italian composer, son of Alessandro Scarlatti. A harpsichord virtuoso, he settled in Spain and is primarily known for his 545 short pieces for the harpsichord. These pieces advanced keyboard technique and place Scarlatti as the greatest Italian composer of keyboard music of the Baroque period. *See also* Baroque Music. △1196.

Scarlet Fever, or scarlatina, acute contagious disease, usually of children, caused by streptococcal bacteria. It is characterized by body rash, fever, and throat infection. It may be transmitted from person to person by direct contact or through use of the same utensils.

Scattering, Light, deflection of light waves from the main direction of a beam by fine particles of solid, liquid, or gaseous matter. The effects observed depend on the size of the particles, smaller particles causing diffraction while larger particles produce diffraction and reflection. *See also* Diffraction, Reflection.

Scève, Maurice (*c.* 1510–*c.* 1564), French poet. △1172.

Schecter Poultry Corporation v. United States (1935), US Supreme Court decision invalidating Pres. Franklin Roosevelt's National Recovery Administration (NRA). The court declared that the NRA codes could not be applied to a firm not engaged in interstate commerce. This limited view of the commerce clause was short lived, and *NLRB* v. *Jones and Laughlin* subsequently insured success for Roosevelt's New Deal programs. *See also* National Labor Relations Board v. Jones and Laughlin Steel Company (1937); National Recovery Administration.

Scheel, Walter (1919–), West German political figure. As head of the Free Democratic party (1968–74), he formed a coalition government (1969) with the Social Democrats and served as foreign minister in the cabinet of Willy Brandt. When Brandt resigned in 1974, Scheel was briefly chancellor. The same year he was elected president of West Germany.

Scheele, Karl Wilhelm (1742–86), Swedish chemist. An apothecary, his interest in chemistry led to an investigation of combustion and the discovery of oxygen. Publication of this discovery was delayed and the credit went to Joseph Priestley. He made other important discoveries, including chlorine, glycerine, and a number of organic acids.

Scheelite, a molybdate mineral, calcium tungstate-molybdate [Ca (WO_4,MoO_4)]. An important ore of tungsten. In metamorphic deposits and in pegmatites. Tetragonal system bipyramidal crystals; also massive and granular aggregates. In various tints with adamantine luster; brittle. Hardness 4.5–6; sp gr 5. Fluoresces under ultraviolet light.

Schefflera, or umbrella tree, genus of slow-growing ornamental tree native to the South Pacific islands. It has shiny, round leaves of up to 16 oval leaflets on branches rising from a single stem. Care: bright light, soil (equal parts loam, peat moss, sand) kept dry between waterings. Propagation is by seeds. Height: to 6 ft (1.8m).

Scheherazade, one-act ballet choreographed by Michel Fokine; music by Nikolai Rimski-Korsakov. △1368.

Schelde (Sheldt or **Escaut),** river rises in N France, flows N and NE through W Belgium to Antwerp, then NW into North Sea through 2 estuaries (East and West Schelde) in the Netherlands. It is a master stream for a dense network of canals in N France and Belgium; navigable for most of its 270mi (435km).

Scheler, Max (1874–1928), German phenomenologist and social philosopher. Influenced by Franz Brentano and some of Edmund Husserl's disciples, he made important contributions to the phenomenological movement. His works include *Formalism in Ethics and Non-Formal Ethics of Values* (2 vols., 1913–16), *On the Eternal in Man* (1921), and *Man's Place in Nature* (1928).

Schelling, Friedrich von (1775–1854), German philosopher. When a professor at Würzburg (1803–06) he broke with both Hegel and J. G. Fichte. Profoundly romantic, his philosophy of nature *(Naturphilosophie)* links nature and spirit together as real and ideal poles of one essential reality. Ultimately, he asserts, pantheism merges into total mysticism. Clearest accounts of his philosophy appear in *First Sketch of a System of "Naturphilosophie"* (1799) and *Introduction* (1799).

Schenectady, industrial city in E New York, 13mi (20km) NW of Albany on Mohawk River; seat of Schenectady co. In 1661, Arent Van Curler bought the land from Mohawk Indians; it was scene of Indian raid 1690; industrial growth was spurred by completion of Erie Canal (1825) and railroads (1830s); locomotive works (1848) and General Electric plant (1892) still remain as major Schenectady employers; site of Union College and University (1795). Industries: electrical materials, locomotives, chemicals, aerospace, plastics. Inc. 1798. Pop. (1970) 77,958.

Schenk v. United States (1919), landmark US Supreme Court case in which Justice Holmes emerged as the court's spokesman in free speech matters. He stated the "clear and present danger" test defining the limits of 1st Amendment protection. The court ruled that no speech was protected if illegal action was the likely result of such speech. The test adopted has been the subject of continuous debate and the subsequent cases of *Gitlow* v. *New York* and *Whitney* v. *California* refined it.

Schiaparelli, Giovanni Virginio (1835–1910), Italian astronomer. He is best known for his observations of Mars' controversial "canals" (1877). △62.

Schick Test, a test of immunity to diphtheria, devised by the Hungarian-born US pediatrician Béla Schick, in which lack of immunity is demonstrated by the appearance of an area of inflammation at the site of injection of a minute amount of diphtheria toxin.

Schiller, Johann Christoph Friedrich von (1759–1805), influential German dramatist, historian, and democratic philosopher. He wrote blank verse *Sturm und Drang* plays: *Don Carlos* (1787), a trilogy on Wallenstein (1799), *Mary Stuart* (1800), *Maid of Orleans* (1810), and *William Tell* (1804). Beethoven's *9th Symphony* uses his "Hymn to Joy."

Schipperke, Flemish watchdog (nonsporting group) bred several hundred years ago; name means Little Captain, from use on canal boats. Its foxlike face bears a questioning expression. Small, triangular ears are erect. The short, thickset body is set on medium-length legs. Tail is docked. Its abundant harsh coat is short on the ears, legs, and body and longer on the ruffed neck and the back of the hind legs; color is solid black. Average size: 13in (33cm) high at shoulder; 14–18lb (6.3–8kg). *See also* Non-sporting Dog.

Schism, in religion, a division within a church or a break away from a church. In the history of the Christian Church the name is particularly applied to the Great Eastern Schism, the separation of the Roman and Eastern Churches that began in the 9th century, and the Great Western Schism, the period when there were two or three rival popes (1378–1417).

Schist, large group of metamorphic rocks characterized by a preponderance of platy minerals that cause the rocks to split leaving a wavy, uneven surface. They are named for their predominant mineral, eg mica schist. Most probably metamorphose from mud or clay, with slates, shales, and phylites the intermediate products. *See also* Metamorphic Rocks. △248, 252.

Schistosomiasis, or **Snail Fever,** a visceral venous infestation of the human body by certain blood flukes occurring mainly in the tropics. Next to malaria, it is man's most serious parasitic infection. Symptoms are inflammation, cough, fever, skin eruption, and swelling of the liver. It is contracted by working or swimming in water contaminated with miniature stages of the parasite released by snails. Chemotherapy is used to kill adult flukes. △732.

Schizoid Personality, personality pattern disturbance marked by avoidance of close relations with others, inability to express hostility directly, and autistic thinking. The schizoid person appears shy, aloof, and detached, and may be described as introverted and withdrawn. This pattern is often observed early in life and later experience does little to alter it. △766.

Schizophrenia, functional psychotic disorder marked primarily by disturbances of cognitive functioning, particularly thinking. Bleuler, who introduced term in 1911 viewed it as a "splitting of the personality" (from reality), a tendency of thinking to become wish-fulfilling, idiosyncratic, and dominated by fantasy. Currently term is used to describe a diverse assortment of clinical entities. Subtypes include: simple, hebephrenic, catatonic, paranoid, undifferentiated, schizo-affective, and childhood. *See also* Bleuler, Paul Eugen; Psychotic Disorders. △760, 764.

Schleiden, Matthias Jakob (1804–81), German botanist. With Theodor Schwann he established the cell theory for plants, which recognizes that all parts of a plant organism are composed of cells. His landmark paper discussing the cell theory, "Contributions to Phytogenesis," was published in 1838.

Schlesinger, Arthur Meier, Jr. (1917–), US historian, b. Columbus, Ohio. He served with the Office of Strategic Services (1942–45) during World War II. He published his Pulitzer Prize-winning *Age of Jackson* (1945). A co-founder of Americans for Democratic Action, he served as special assistant for Latin American affairs for President Kennedy (1961–64). He won another Pulitzer Prize for *A Thousand Days* (1965), a biography of the Kennedy administration.

Schleswig-Holstein, state in N West Germany; capital is Kiel. Formerly consisting of duchies of Denmark, by 1815 Holstein became German state; Denmark declared union with Schleswig causing revolt with German Confederation; by 1850 peace was declared. By terms of the Treaty of Gastein (1865) Schleswig was awarded to Prussia, Holstein to Austria, and Lauenburg (lost by Denmark to Prussia and Austria 1864) also to Prussia; settlement led to Austro-Prussian War (1866) and all three areas were annexed to Prussia; N Schleswig went to Denmark 1920; it was constituted as a state 1946. Industries: farming, cattle, shipping, fishing, tourism, textiles, shipbuilding, food processing, oil, clothing, machinery. Pop. 2,561,200. △1250.

Schlick, Moritz (1882–1936), German philosopher and head of the Vienna Circle, a group of logical positivists. Studying physics with Max Planck, he later taught (1922) the philosophy of inductive science at the University of Vienna. Unlike other positivists who emphasized experience as the tool to truth, he did not reject metaphysics as being meaningless. His works include *General Theory of Knowledge* (1925) and *Problems of Ethics* (1939). *See also* Logical Positivism.

Schlieffen, Alfred, Graf von (1833–1913), German military commander. He entered the Prussian (later German) army in 1854. During 1891–1905 he was chief of the German general staff and developed the Schlieffen plan for war on two fronts against France and Russia. △1304.

Schliemann, Heinrich (1822–90), German archeologist and excavator of Troy, Mycenae, and Tiryns. In 1871 he began excavations at his own expense at Hissarlik, Turkey, which he believed to be the site of the Homeric city of Troy. He uncovered four superimposed towns. From 1874 to 1876 he excavated in Greece, and in 1875 in Mycenae. His findings in the various excavations were published respectively as *Trojanische Altertümer* (*Antiquities of Troy*, 1874), *Troja und seine Ruinen* (*Troy and Its Remains*, 1875), and *Mykenä* (*Mycenae*, 1878). *See also* Troy. △1292.

Schmalkaldic League, alliance of German Protestant states formed in 1531. △1152.

Schmeling, Maximilian Adolph Ott Siefried "Max" (1905–), German boxer. He beat Jack Sharkey (1930) on a foul for the world's heavyweight championship in New York City and lost it to Sharkey (1932) in Long Island City, N.Y. He was elected to the Boxing Hall of Fame in 1970.

Schmidt, Helmut (1918–), West German statesman. A member of the SPD (Social Democratic party), he replaced Willy Brandt as chancellor in 1974, receiving the unanimous support of SPD and Free Democratic party Bundestag members. In 1974 he visited Moscow and the United States, where he offered to mediate between the United States and the Common Market countries on economic inflation and increases in the price of Arab oil.

Schmidt-Rottluff, Karl (1884–), German painter. His early woodcuts were Impressionistic in style and then became more abstract, with contrasts of black and white. A member of Die Brücke, he used decorative color in his paintings. △1294.

Schnauzer. *See* Giant Schnauzer; Miniature Schnauzer; Standard Schnauzer.

Scholasticism, attempt to analyze the articles of faith through intellectual processes, with a view to deeper understanding of Christian doctrine. Arising in medieval schools, based on teachings of Augustine and Boethius, Scholastic thought was advanced by Johannes Scotus Erigena in the 9th century and by Anselm in the 11th century. After the important work of Duns Scotus and Aquinas, scholasticism declined rapidly in the face of Ockham's nominalism, which denied the possibility of objective knowledge. △856, 1088.

Schönberg, Arnold (1874–1951), Austrian composer, a seminal figure in 20th-century music. His early works were characterized by a post-Romantic style akin to Richard Wagner, eg, *Verklärte Nacht* (1899). In 1914 he broke from the traditional musical stream and devised his own compositional system called 12-tone music. Though never popular, the 12-tone system has exerted an enormous influence on composing techniques used by many other composers, especially by Schönberg's students such as Alban Berg, Anton von Webern, and Ernst Křenek. Schönberg's works include a violin concerto (1936), five string quartets, and chamber, vocal, and piano music. △1364.

Schongauer, Martin (1450–91), German painter and engraver. △1136.

Schooner, usually a two-masted commercial vessel with bowsprit and fore-and-aft sails rather than square sails. △1678.

Schopenhauer, Arthur (1788–1860), German philosopher. He was overshadowed by G.W.F. Hegel until 1852, when Schopenhauer's system was popularized. His main work, *The World as Will and Idea* (1818), establishes will as the moving force behind the world. A primordial drive to endure, it creates the possibility of its own negation as Nirvana. *On Basis of Morality* (1841) cites compassion as the foundation of ethics. Schopenhauer's fame was established by his caustic and witty essays, *Parerga and Paralipomena* (1851).

Schouten, Willem Cornelis (?1567–1625), Dutch navigator. During one of his voyages (1615–16) he found a new trade route to the East. Sailing around the tip of South America, he named Cape Horn after his birthplace, Hoorn. He then sailed on to visit islands in the SW Pacific. Charged with violation of a Dutch East India Company monopoly, he was arrested and his ship seized in Java.

Schrödinger, Erwin (1887–1961), Austrian theoretical physicist who discovered the basic quantum mechanics equation. He was awarded the 1933 Nobel Prize for the development of his wave equation, which

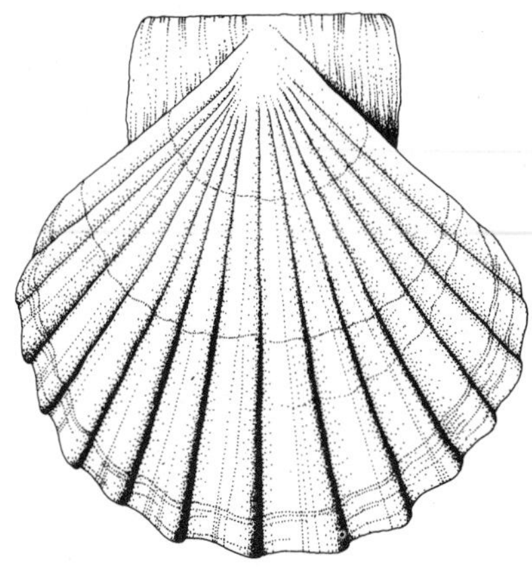
Scallop

Johann Schiller

Schipperke

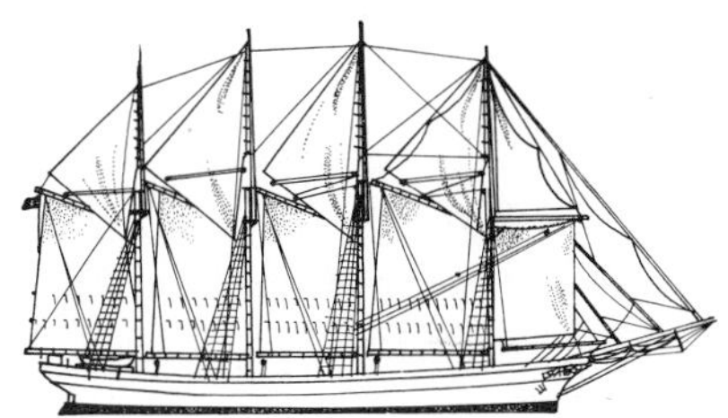
Schooner

is capable of describing electron and small particle behavior. In 1938, he left Austria and became a professor in Dublin. △1480.

Schroter, Johann. △68.

Schubert, Franz (1797–1828), Austrian Romantic composer. A melodic genius, he lived in poverty and was largely unappreciated in his own time. Now his talent, especially as a composer of songs, is recognized. His over 600 songs include those in the cycle *Die Schöne Müllerin* (1823), those in the cycle *Die Winterreise* (1827), "The Erl King" (1815), and "Ave Maria" (1825). Among his other popular works are the "Unfinished" *Symphony No. 8* and the C Major *Symphony No. 9*, piano sonatas, chamber music, masses, and incidental music. *See also* Romanticism in Music. △1246.

Schultz, Alfred. △892.

Schuman, Robert (1886–1963), French political figure. He was noted for his efforts to achieve European economic and political unity. While foreign minister (1950), he successfully proposed the creation of a single authority to control the production of coal and steel in Europe. This agreement was the first of several leading to the formation of the European Economic Community (Common Market) in 1958, which he served, first as president of the assembly, then as assembly member, until his death.

Schumann, Robert (1810–56), German Romantic composer. He married the outstanding pianist Clara Wieck and was a friend to Johannes Brahms, but he spent his last years in madness. He composed many sets of piano pieces, eg, *Kinderscenen, Carnival,* and *Waldscenen.* His best known works include concertos for cello and for piano, four symphonies, chamber music, and about 150 songs. Schumann was also one of the most important music critics of his day. △1246, 1356.

Schumpeter, Joseph (1883–1950), Austrian-American economist. His last book, *History of Economic Policy,* was published posthumously in 1954. He also wrote *Capitalism, Socialism and Democracy* (1942), as well as many other broad-based and diverse books. One of his best-remembered ideas is the "creative gale of destruction." This notion states that real competition for firms comes, not so much from rival firms, but from technological change.

Schuyler, Philip John (1733–1804), US statesman and Revolutionary War general, b. Albany, N.Y. After his membership in the Continental Congress (1775) he was appointed major general and placed in command of northern New York. He organized the Quebec campaign (1775–76). After the fall of Ticonderoga in 1777, Schuyler was replaced by Gen. Horatio Gates. Schuyler was court martialed but was acquitted of neglect of duty charges. He resigned from the army the following year. He became a member of the Continental Congress (1778–98). His daughter, Elizabeth, married Alexander Hamilton.

Schuylkill River, river in SE Pennsylvania, rises in E central Pa., flows SE to Delaware River at Philadelphia. Length: 130mi (209km).

Schwann, Theodor (1810–82), German biologist. With Matthias Jakob Schleiden he established the cell theory. Schwann extended the theory from plants to animals, stating that all living organisms are composed of cells, and that these cells have a life of their own that is subject to the life of the organism as a whole.

Schwann Cells. △664.

Schwarzenberg, (Prince) Karl Philipp von (1771–1820), Austrian soldier. The Austrian army under his command opposed Napoleon's invasion of Russia in 1812; he was made field marshal. Though the Allies were defeated at the battle of Dresden, he led them to victory at Leipzig, the battle of the Nations, in 1813.

Schweitzer, Albert (1875–1965), humanitarian, musician, mission physician, philosopher, and Christian theologian, is perhaps best known for his medical work in Gabon (Africa), where he founded the Lambaréné Hospital in 1913. Although he stayed in Gabon most of his life, he was famous for his work as an organist, as an expert on J.S. Bach, for his theories of Christian history, and for his ethic of "reverence for life." His works included *Kant's Philosophy of Religion* (1899) and *On the Edge of the Primeval Forest* (1922). He received the Nobel Peace prize in 1952.

Schwitters, Kurt (1887–1948), German artist. His early work showed the influence of Vasili Kandinsky and the Dada movement. He is best known for his technique of combining ticket stubs, newspaper pieces, and other scraps into collages. He used the term *"merz"* to label his style and made huge works from trash and scraps, which he called Merz-bau constructions. △1318.

Schwyz, canton in central Switzerland; borders on Lake of Zurich (N) and Lake of Lucerne (SW); capital is Schwyz. One of original Four Forest cantons, it is forested and mountainous. Industries: livestock, fruit, cotton and silk textiles, wood products, tourism. Area: 351sq mi (909sq Km). Pop. 92,072.

Sciatica, neuralgia or neuritis associated with excruciating pain. It is caused by irritation or swelling of the sciatic nerve, which passes from the lower spinal column down the back of thighs and legs. It can be treated with bedrest, sedation, or corrective exercise.

Science, History of. △1160, 1282, 1438–40.

Science Fiction, form of fiction in which the improbable becomes probable, where scientific discovery allows man to supersede preconceived limits, often by the use of mechanical devices still not invented. The first successful science-fiction writer was France's Jules Verne, the first successful English writer was H.G. Wells; and the first American, Edgar Allan Poe. Little science fiction was printed in the 1800s, but the pulp magazines pushed it into prominence in the 1900s. The first magazine to contain only science fiction was *Amazing Stories* (1926), but science fiction did not really come into its own until the mid-1900s. Early pulp stories were criticized as "space operas" where life was cheap and violence and cruelty common. Modern science fiction has taken on a new sophistication, often bringing to the reader a thoughtful message packaged in a plausible well-written story. Among the better-known writers are Isaac Asimov, Ray Bradbury, Arthur C. Clarke, and John Wyndham.

Scientific Method, general logic and procedures common to all the physical and social sciences, which may be outlined as a series of steps: (1) stating a problem or question; (2) forming a hypothesis (possible solution to the problem) based on a theory or rationale; (3) experimentation (gathering empirical data bearing on the hypothesis); (4) interpretation of the data and drawing conclusions; and (5) revising the theory or deriving further hypotheses for testing. Putting the hypothesis in a form that can be empirically tested is one of the chief challenges to the scientist. In addition, all of the sciences try to express their theories and conclusions in some quantitative form and to use standardized testing procedures that other scientists could repeat.

Scilly, Isles of, group of more than 140 islands off SW England; part of Cornwall, 28mi (45km) SW of Land's End. Largest island is St Mary's. The mild climate makes the islands a resort and a center for early spring flowers and vegetables. Pop. 2,428.

Scintillation Counter, instrument containing a crystal that emits scintillations of light when bombarded by radiation. Each light flash, corresponding to a single particle, is converted into an electric pulse by a photomultiplier. The number of pulses, counted electronically, indicates the activity of the source.

Scipio, distinguished Roman family. Lucius Cornelius, consul (259 BC) and censor, won naval victories against Algeria and Corsica. His son Gnaeus Cornelius Scipio Calvus (died 211) attacked Hannibal's supply line in Spain (218) and with his brother Publius defeated Hasdrubal and took Saguntum (212). Publius' son was Scipio Africanus Major whose eldest son adopted the son of Aemilius Paullus, who came to be known as Scipio Africanus Minor. Publius Scipio Nasica Serapio (died *c.* 132 BC) fled Rome after leading the senate riot in which Tiberius Gracchus was killed. His descendant Quintus Caecilius Metellus Pius Scipio (died 46 BC) led troops for Pompey at Pharsala and, fleeing to Africa, was defeated by Caesar.

Scipio, Publius Cornelius (died 211), Roman general, younger brother of Gnaeus and father of Scipio Africanus Major. As consul (218) his attempt to halt Hannibal failed because he was forced to put down a revolt of Gauls in N Italy first. He lost two-thirds of his army fighting Hannibal at Trebia (218). He and his brother were killed in Spain after defeating Hasdrubal (216) near Ibera.

Scipio Africanus Major (Publius Cornelius Scipio) (*c.* 234–183 BC), greatest military genius of the Scipio family and conqueror of Hannibal. Son of Publius Cornelius Scipio, he fought at Cannae and became proconsul of Spain after his father. Supremely self-confident, he pursued an aggressive policy, took Cartagena (209), defeated Hasdrubal, and established Roman rule in Spain. Defying the senate he captured Tunis with a volunteer army and defeated Hannibal's Carthaginians at Zama (202) through brilliant deployment of cavalry. As censor and chief senator (199) he made strong enemies including Cato the Elder. Brought to trial for corruption (on presumably false charges), his influence waned and he retired in anger to Liternum where he died. *See also* Punic Wars.

Scipio Africanus Minor (Publius Cornelius Scipio Aemilianus Africanus Numantius) (*c.* 185–129 BC), Roman general and scholar, second son of Lucius Aemilius Paullus, adopted son of Publius Scipio (eldest son of Scipio Africanus Major). An orator and patron of letters, he improved the army and destroyed Carthage (147) during the Third Punic War. In 134 he devastated Numantia in Spain. He sought to reverse the reforms of Tiberius Gracchus but died suddenly (possibly murdered) during the ensuing crisis. He is celebrated in Cicero's works.

SCLC. *See* Southern Christian Leadership Congress.

Scleroderma, skin disease characterized by thickening and hardening of the tissues beneath the skin. It results in a rigid, hidebound condition.

Scleromochlus. △570.

Sclerosis, degenerative hardening of tissue, especially in the arteries and central nervous system, in which normal tissue is replaced by connective tissue, as in a scar.

Scone, village in central Scotland; Old Scone was the Pictish and Scottish capital where kings of Scotland were crowned 1157–1488. The Coronation stone, or Stone of Scone, was removed to Westminster Abbey by Edward I of England 1296, where it has remained, in spite of an attempt (1950) by Scottish nationalists to return it to Scone.

Scopalamine, derivative of the belladonna plant used to induce sleep when pain is not present and as a sedative during labor in childbirth.

Scopes Trial (1925), court case that culminated the long anti-evolution campaign spearheaded by Fundamentalists. It upheld the constitutionality of a Tennessee law forbidding the teaching of evolutionary theory. The trial involved John Thomas Scopes, a high school biology teacher, and was a forensic battle between defense attorney Clarence Darrow and William Jennings Bryan, who assisted the prosecution. It turned into a national circus and a public humiliation of Bryan, who died a few days after its conclusion.

Scopus, Mount, peak in Israel that has always been important to the defense of Jerusalem. From 1948 to 1967 it was held by the Israelis but was completely surrounded by Arab territory.

Scorpion, variously colored arthropod found in warmer regions worldwide. It has two body parts, two eyes, one pair of pincers, and long slender tail ending in a curved, poisonous stinger. It feeds at night on insects and spiders. It stings in self-defense; some are dangerous. Length: 1.5–7in (4–18cm). Class Arachnida; order Scorpionida. △488.

Scorpion, The. *See* Scorpius.

Scorpion-fish, or rockfish, family of marine fish found in temperate waters at or near rocky bottoms and identified by venomous fin spines capable of inflicting painful and sometimes fatal injury. Young are born alive. Length: 12in (30.5cm). Family Scorpaenidae; species include *Scorpaena scrofa,* lionfish *Pterois volitans,* and ocean perch *Sebastes marinus.* △516.

Scorpion Fly, brown to gray insect limited to the Northern Hemisphere. Its chewing mouthparts are at the end of a long, beaklike structure. The males of some species have abdomens resembling a scorpion's. They are harmless and feed on insects. Length 0.5–1.6in (13–41mm). Order Mecoptera. △492.

Scorpius, or the Scorpion, southern constellation situated on the ecliptic between Libra and Sagittarius, the eighth sign of the zodiac. Usually referred to as Scorpio only for astrological purposes, this constellation contains several open and globular clusters. The Milky Way also passes through it. Brightest star Alpha Scorpii (Antares). The astrological sign for the period Oct. 24–Nov. 21. △134, 826.

Scotland, N part of Great Britain, bounded N and W by the Atlantic Ocean, E by the North Sea, and S by England.

Land and Economy. Scotland has an indented coastline with many lochs and offshore islands; the main island groups are the Inner and Outer Hebrides (W) and the Orkneys and Shetlands (N). High land in the N and W rises from high moorland to Cairngorm Mts and Ben Nevis, 4,406ft (1,344m). The country is drained by fast-flowing rivers providing hydroelectric power and has many lakes (lochs), particularly along Great Glen (Glen More), a fault running SW-NE from Loch Linnhe to the Moray Firth. Low land occurs in central Scotland; it is hilly in S. The principal rivers are the Clyde, Forth, Tay, Tweed, Dee, and Spey. Forestry and lumbering take place in the Highlands, with rough grazing in moorland regions, and stock farming in the hills. The main agricultural crops are cereal and potatoes in river valleys, fruit growing in the E. Scotland's industries are concentrated in the Clyde and Forth river basins and lowlands, and include mining, engineering, shipbuilding, fishing, textiles, chemicals, brewing, and distilling.

People. The population is largely a mixture of Celt, Anglo-Saxon, and Norman, with some Norse influence in the islands and NW. The main religious group is the Church of Scotland (Presbyterian). Less than 2% of the population speaks Gaelic, but national identity is strong.

Government. Scotland is part of Great Britain and sends representatives to Parliament. However, it has its own system of education and its own set of laws, which are based on Roman law. Nationalistic feeling is strong, and plans have been proposed for a regional parliament. The counties of Scotland were regrouped in 1975 into twelve regions, divided into local-government districts.

History. Most of Scotland was united under one king, Kenneth I, in the 9th century. The country first came under English control in 1174 as a result of a treaty obtained by Henry II. In 1292 John de Baliol was crowned king after a struggle among several claimants, and acknowledged Edward I of England as overlord. Edward II of England was defeated at Bannockburn 1314, but over the next century Scotland was torn by civil strife. In 1513 the Scots were badly defeated at Flodden Field. The country was finally united with England in 1603 when James VI succeeded to the English throne as James I.

PROFILE

Official name: Scotland
Area: 30,405sq mi (78,749sq km)
Population: 5,230,152
Density: 171per sq mi (66per sq km)
Chief cities: Glasgow; Edinburgh(capital); Dundee

Scott, David. △1724.

Scott, Sir George Gilbert. △1258.

Scott, James, Duke of Monmouth. *See* Monmouth, James Scott, Duke of.

Scott, Robert Falcon (1868–1912), English antarctic explorer and naval commander. He entered the navy in 1880, and in 1899 was made commander of an expedition into the antarctic. He led another expedition with the intention of reaching the south pole in 1910. Traveling by sled, he and four others came to the pole in January 1912, only to find that Amundsen had been there first. Plagued by fierce weather, sickness, and shortness of supplies, Scott and his men died by March. They were found later that year by a search party.

Scott, (Sir) Walter (1771–1832), Scottish novelist and poet, b. Edinburgh. Scott left Edinburgh University to become a lawyer (1792), but his interest in Border history gave rise to a collection of ballads, *Minstrelsy of the Scottish Border* (3 vols., 1802–03) and *The Lay of the Last Minstrel* (1805). His novels appeared continually from 1808 *(Marmion)* until his death, which was hastened by Scott's efforts to pay off debts following the ruin in 1826 of his partner in a printing business. His other novels included *Lady of the Lake* (1810), *The Heart of Midlothian* (1818), *Ivanhoe* (1819), *Kenilworth* (1821), *Quentin Durward* (1823), and *The Talisman* (1825). △1238.

Scott, Winfield (1786–1866), US military officer, b. Petersburg, Va. He served in the War of 1812, and from 1846–48 in the Mexican War where he led the triumphant march from Vera Cruz to Mexico City which he governed (1847–48). In 1852 he was the Whig candidate for the presidency but lost to Franklin Pierce. Called "Old Fuss and Feathers," he was regarded as the outstanding military figure between George Washington and Robert E. Lee.

Scottish Bluebell. *See* Harebell.

Scottish Deerhound, graceful hunting dog (hound group) dating from at least the 16th century and known as royal dog of Scotland. A keen scenter, it has a long, flat head and pointed muzzle; small, high-set ears, folded back; long neck; deep chest; and well-arched loin; long, broad-boned legs; and long, tapering tail. The 3–4in (8–10cm) long, harsh, and wiry coat is usually dark blue-gray. Average size: 28–32in (71–81cm) high at shoulder; 75–110lb (34–50kg). *See also* Hounds.

Scottish Terrier, ancient Highland breed (terrier group) dating from the 16th century and brought to US in 1883. The Scottie's head is long and slightly domed, with whiskers and dark, piercing eyes set under bushy eyebrows. The short, deep-chested body is set on short, heavy legs. The curved tail is 7in (18cm) long. Coat is short (2in–5cm), hard, and wiry; colors may be steel or iron gray, brindle, grizzle, black, sandy, or wheaten. Average size: 10in (25.5cm) high at shoulder; 19–22lb (8.5–10kg). *See also* Terrier.

Scottsdale, residential city in SW central Arizona, 10mi (16km) E of Phoenix; old western shopping town. Industries: women's clothing, ceramics. Inc. 1951. Pop. (1970) 67,823.

Scouring Rush. *See* Horsetail.

Scranton, city in NE Pennsylvania, on Lackawanna River, 120mi (193km) N of Philadelphia; seat of Lackawanna co. Known as world's major anthracite coal capital until the end of WWII, it is now a city of diversified manufacturing; site of University of Scranton (1888), Lackawanna Junior College (1894), and Marywood College (1915). Industries: textiles, clothing, paints and varnishes, printing supplies. Founded 1788; inc. as borough 1853, as city 1866. Pop. (1970) 103,564.

Screech Owl, common North American owl that is usually brown or gray and has earlike tufts of feathers on its head. Despite its name, it utters a pleasant whistling sound. It is related to the smaller scops owl *(Otus scops)* of Europe, Asia, and Africa. Length: 10in (25cm). Family Strigidae; species *Otus asio. See also* Owl.

Screw. △1438, 1652.

Screw Pine, woody Old World plant native to tropical Asia, Africa, and Indian Ocean and Pacific islands. Not a true pine, its long, narrow, spiny leaves rise from a rosette in a spiral, like threads of a screw. Stilt roots steady the plant in high winds. It bears conelike fruits. Height: to 40ft (12m). Family Pandanaceae. Species include *Pandanus odoratissimus.* △452.

Screwworm, bluegreen fly 0.56 to 0.72in (14–18mm) long. A parasite of warm-blooded animals, the larva enters through wounds in the skin. It is a serious pest of domestic animals in North and South America. Family Calliphoridae, species *Callitroga hominivorax. See also* Diptera.

Scriabin, Alexander (1872–1915), Russian composer and pianist. He composed highly original piano music according to his own principles of harmony, foreshadowing many of the musical developments of the 20th century. His most significant works include nine piano sonatas, five symphonic poems, and numerous short piano pieces. △1364.

Scripps, Edward (1854–1926), US journalist who founded the first United States newspaper chain, b. England. After varied newspaper experience, he founded (1878) with his brothers the Cleveland *Penny Press,* which became the first of 34 newspapers that he bought or founded in 15 states. All were popular, pro-labor newspapers in medium-size cities.

Scripps Institute of Oceanography. △236.

Script. △872.

Scriptures, the books of the Old and New Testaments, often including the Apocrypha; also a text or passage from one of these books of the Bible. The term, as used in the New Testament, refers primarily to sacred Hebraic writings, as in Mark 12:10. *Scripture,* in the singular form, usually refers to the collection of writings thought of as a single book; the plural *Scriptures* refers to the many writings. The term *Scriptures* can also be applied to other sacred writings such as the Koran of the Muslims. *See also* Apocrypha; New Testament, Old Testament.

Scrofula, general name used variously through time in medicine, especially to describe tuberculosis of the bones and lymphatic glands.

Franz Schubert

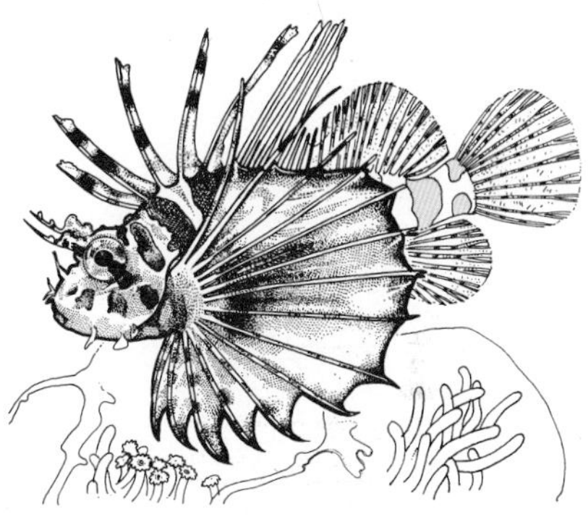

Scorpion

Robert F. Scott

Sir Walter Scott

Scuba Diving, a water sport. It consists of diving with the use of Self-Contained Underwater Breathing Apparatus, known as the aqualung. Other equipment includes a wet suit and rubber fins for the diver's feet. The sport has attracted over 1,000,000 enthusiasts since the design of the modern aqualung by Jacques Yves Cousteau and Emil Gagnan. △238.

Sculpin, bottom-dwelling marine fish found in temperate and cold waters of the North Atlantic. A grayish fish mottled with yellow, it has a large bony head covered with prickles. Its eyes are set high on its head and the pectoral fins are large and fanlike. Length: to 3ft (91.5cm). Family Cottidae. The 300 species include the shorthorn *Myoxocephalus scorpius.*

Sculpture, the art of creating forms and objects in three dimensions or in relief. Works of sculpture may be carved (in marble, stone, wood, ivory, etc) or built up from some flexible or plastic material (plaster, metals, bronze, etc). The history of sculpture basically parallels that of painting. *See also* Painting and related articles on the history of painting.

Scup, or northern porgy, Atlantic marine food and sport fish found in tropical and temperate waters. It is a deep-bodied silver blue fish. Length: to 18in (45.7cm); weight: to 41lb (1.8kg). Family Sparidae; species *Stenotomus chrysops.*

Scurvy, disease caused by a prolonged deficiency of vitamin C. It is characterized by weakness, inflamed gums, loose teeth, and swollen joints and also absorption by tissues of blood from ruptured vessels, which causes anemia. △696.

Scylla and Charybdis, in classical mythology, two monsters of the Sicilian seas. Scylla, a beautiful nymph, daughter of Poseidon, had been changed by the enchantress Circe into a long-necked, six-headed beast who lived in a dark cave in the sea and subsisted on passing dolphins and sailors. Charybdis, another daughter of Poseidon, was a creature out of Homer, who was changed into a violent whirlpool by the thunderbolt of Zeus. She swallowed the waves of the sea and three times each day vomited them forth.

Scythians, an ancient people who ruled an empire in southern Russia from the 7th century BC until defeated by the Sarmatians in the 4th century BC. Of Iranian stock, the Scythians were a nomadic and warlike tribe with a well advanced civilization. They were ferocious warriors, skilled craftsmen, active hunters and fishermen, and good agriculturists.

Sea Anemone, polyp-type coelenterate found in marine tidal pools and along rocky shores. Cylindrical with many tentacles around its mouth and color varying according to species. There is no medusa phase; reproduction is asexual and sexual. Height: 8in (203.2mm). Class Anthozoa; species include *Metridium.* △468.

Sea Bass, marine food fish found in tropical and some temperate waters. It includes white, yellow, and striped bass in the genus *Roccus;* groupers; butterfish; and the black bass *Centropristis striatus.* Many of these species are self-fertilizing. Family Serranidae. *See also* Bass; Grouper; Jewfish. △392.

Seaborg, Glen Theodore (1912–), US physicist, b. Ishpeming, Mich. He became chancellor of the University of California at Berkeley in 1958 and chairman of the US Atomic Energy Commission in 1961. His scientific work was concerned with the transuranic elements and the discovery of the actinide series, for which he was awarded a Nobel prize (jointly with Edwin McMillan) in 1951. In 1942 he was responsible for isolating uranium-233. △1552.

Sea Bream, any of numerous marine, spiny-finned (percoid) fishes, usually of the families Sparidae or Bramidae.

Sea Butterfly. △476.

Sea Cow. *See* Dugong.

Sea Cucumber, marine echinoderm found in rocky areas. A cylindrical animal with a soft, fleshy body, it has branched tentacles around the mouth. Edible species are smoked and dried; the end product is trepang. Species include the cotton-spinner *Holothuria* and the burrowing *Leptopentacta.* Class Holothuroidea. △504, 626.

Sea Dragon, or leafy sea dragon, marine fish found off the coast of Australia. A pipefish, closely related to the seahorse, its reddish-brown body is covered with leafy and spine-like projections, making it resemble floating seaweed. Family Syngnathidae; species *Phycidurus eques* and *Phyllopteryx foliatus.*

Sea Fan, or gorgonian, colonial coelenterate found in coral reefs in tropical marine waters. Colonies are branching but flat; eight-tentacled polyps live in tiny pits along horny branches. Class Anthozoa; subclass Alcyonaria; species *Eunicella verrucosa.*

Sea-floor Spreading, the systematic increase in the Earth's crust occurring along the mid-ocean ridges. Here basaltic magma rises, cools, and is pushed along by new magma eruptions. As the magma cools, it becomes magnetized in the direction of the Earth's current magnetic field. These magnetized strips form identical patterns on either side of the ridges, evidence that new crust is being produced. The spreading has been plotted at rates of 1 to 10 cm (0.4–4in) per year. △170, 228.

Seafood. △392–94.

Sea Goat, The. *See* Capricornus.

Sea Gooseberry. △470.

Sea Gull. *See* Gull.

Sea Hare, marine gastropod found on shore or in shallow offshore waters. It has no shell and in some cases has lost the mantle cavity. Gills are visible externally. It secretes a purple mucus for defense. Class Gastropoda; order Anaspidea; genus *Tethys.*

Sea Islands, chain of more than 100 islands off Atlantic coast of South Carolina, Georgia, and Florida. Notable islands include Port Royal, containing chief city of Beaufort, Paris Island, site of a US Marine Corp. training center, and St Simons, Sea, Jekyll, and Hilton Head islands, all popular resorts.

Seal, large fish-eating aquatic mammal of coastal regions in all oceans, especially colder waters. They have a streamlined body and flippers for limbs. A thick layer of blubber—nearly half the seal's weight—provides insulation, buoyancy, and reserve energy for long periods without food. They return to land to breed; some form breeding colonies of over one million individuals. Skillfull swimmers, they are awkward on land. Fur seals are hunted for their pelts; hair seals, for leather, blubber oil, and meat. Seals range in size from the ringed seal: length 55in (140cm); weight: 200lb (90kg), to the elephant seal: length: 22ft (7m); weight: to 4 tons. Eared seals Family Otariidae. Earless seals Family Phocidae. *See also* Pinnipedia; Sea Lion. △550, 610.

Sealab. △230.

Sea Lamprey. *See* Lamprey.

Sea Lily, crinoid echinoderm found in deep marine waters. Seldom seen, it has many branched arms with ciliated grooves for food collecting radiating from a tiny body disk. Spineless, it attaches itself to the ocean bottom with a stalk. Class Crinoidea. △504.

Sea Lion, eared seal with coarse pelt of little commercial value, found in Southern Hemisphere and N Pacific coastal waters. Largest is the N Pacific Steller's sea lion. Length: over 11ft (3m); weight: over 1ton. Species *Eumetopias Jubata.* The smallest is the gregarious, playful Californian or Japanese sea lion that is the familiar trained seal of circuses and animal shows. Length: 8ft (2.4m); weight: 615lb (277kg). Species *Zalophus californianus. See also* Pinnipedia; Seal. △550.

Sealyham Terrier, dog (terrier group) named for Sealyham Estates, Wales, where the breed was developed 1850–91 to hunt out fox, badger, and otter. The Sealyham's long head is emphasized by whiskers; rounded ears are folded; oval eyes are dark and deep set. The forepart of the body is well let down between the short, strong forelegs. The docked tail is carried up. A hard, wiry top coat is all white. Average size: 10.5in (27cm) high at shoulder; 23–24lb (10–11kg). *See also* Terrier.

Seami Motokiyo (1363–1443) Japanese playwright. He was the principal figure in the development of the No theater. He is the author of most of the No plays that are still performed, many critical works, and the concept of *yugen* (sublime beauty; mysterious power) that is the essence of No.

Sea Mouse, large marine annelid worm with iridescent matted bristles on sides and top of body. Length: to 4in (10cm). The common sea mouse *Aphrodite aculeata* lives in sandy mud on both sides of North Atlantic. Family Aphroditidae. *See also* Annelida. △474, 622.

Seance. △822–24.

Sea Otter, marine otter of the weasel family, originally native to the Pacific coast of N America. Now protected, it was almost exterminated for its valuable dark brown fur. Its hind feet are flattened into flippers and it likes to swim and float on its back within a mile of shore. It eats fish and invertebrates and often uses stones to open hard shells. Length: 40–50in (1–1.2m); weight: 20lb (9kg). Family Mustelidae; species *Enhydra lutris.*

Sea Perch, or surf perch, marine fish found in temperate Pacific waters. Often quite colorful, its young are born alive. Length: 18in (45.7cm). Family Embiotocidae; Species include the rubberlip *Rhacochilus toxotes,* the striped *Embiotoca lateralis,* and a commercial species, white *Phanerodon furcatus.*

Sea Raven, marine fish found in temperate waters. A sculpin identified by its large head with prickles and its ability to gulp air to inflate itself, it varies in color from red and purple to yellow and brown. Length: to 25in (63.5cm); 5lb (2.3kg). Family Cottidae; species *Homotripterus americanus.*

Sea Robin, marine fish found worldwide in tropical and temperate waters. Edible but not popular, it has a bony head, can produce sound, and "walk" on sea bottom with its large pectoral fins. It is red, gray, yellow, or green with dark blotches. Length: to 3ft (91.5cm). Family Triglidae; Among the 85 species are the northern *Prionotus carolinus* and the striped *Prionotus evolons.*

Seaside, city in W California, N of Monterey. Main local industry is tourism. Founded 1887; inc. 1954. Pop. (1970) 35,395.

Sea Slater. △484.

Sea Slug. △482.

Sea Snake, any of about 50 species of colorful, poisonous marine snakes found in coastal waters of Indian, Pacific, and Atlantic oceans. The posterior half of its body is flattened and ends in a paddlelike tip. It has valved nostrils on top of its head. Most bear live young; a few lay eggs on shore. Length: to 4ft (1.2m). Family Hydrophidae. △524.

Seasons, four astronomical and climatic periods of the year based on differential solar heating of the Earth as it makes its annual revolution of the Sun. Due to the parallelism of the Earth's axis of rotation pointed near the Pole Star throughout the year, the Northern Hemisphere receives more solar radiation when its pole is aimed toward the Sun in summer and less in winter when it is aimed away, while the opposite holds for the Southern Hemisphere. The seasons are conventionally initiated at the vernal (spring) and autumnal (fall) equinoxes and the winter and summer solstices. *See also* Equinox; Solstice. △220.

Sea Spider. △490.

Sea Squirt. *See* Tunicate.

Sea Swallow. *See* Tern.

SEATO. *See* Southeast Asia Treaty Organization.

Seattle, city and port of entry in W Washington, between Lake Washington and Puget Sound; seat of King co. Settled during California building boom (1851), it profited as busy port to Orient (1893); it was gateway to Alaska Gold Rush (1897); scene of Alaska-Yukon-Pacific Exposition (1909–10); scene of first labor strike (1919) in US history led by Industrial Workers of the World; site of University of Washington (1861), Seattle University (1900), Seattle Pacific College (1893), 1962 World's Fair—Century 21 Exposition. Industries: aerospace, shipbuilding, precision instruments, building materials, chemicals, lumber, food processing, agriculture, fishing, clothing. Inc. 1869. Pop. (1970) 530,831.

Seatworm. *See* Pinworm.

Sea Urchin, spiny echinoderm found in marine tidal pools along rocky shores. Round with long, radiating often poisonous, moveable spines, it has a mouth on its bottom and anus at the top. Its skeletal plates fuse to form a perforated shell. Class Echinoidea; species include (edible sea urchin) *Echinus* and (purple heart urchin) *Spatangus.* △504.

Sea Walnut, comb jelly or ctenophore, large swarm

live in marine waters. A luminescent animal, it is globular, jellylike, and has eight rows of ciliated plates. Diameter: 0.25in–1ft (0.6–30.5cm). Phylum *Ctenophora.*

Sea Wasps. △470.

Seawater. △222, 280.

Sea Water, Conversion of. △1562.

Seaweed, any of various marine plants, or algae, especially large kinds such as kelp, gulfweed, dulse, rockweed, and sea lettuce. *See also* Algae. △432.

Sebaceous Gland, a skin gland, often occurring along the walls of hair follicles. It secretes sebum, a waxy substance containing fats, proteins, salts, and water, which keeps the hair and skin surface flexible and prevents excessive loss of water from the surface of the body. △686.

Sebastian (1554–78), king of Portugal (1557–78), grandson and successor of John III. His grandmother, Catherine of Austria, and his uncle, Cardinal Henry, acted as regents until he came of age in 1568. Highly religious, he became obsessed with leading a crusade against the Muslims in Morocco. He spent vast sums on the project and led a large expedition there in 1578. He was defeated (and the Portuguese army destroyed) at the battle of Alcazarquivir. Sebastian himself was killed in the battle, but reports of his survival led to the cult known as Sebastianism and to the appearance of several impostors. He was succeeded by Cardinal Henry.

Seborrhea, disease of the sebaceous glands, characterized by an increased and altered secretion of fatty matter that results in oily or scaly skin. It may cause baldness and dandruff.

SEC. *See* Securities and Exchange Commission.

Secession, formal separation from an organized body. The best-known secession in history occurred in 1860–61 when 11 states (South Carolina, Mississippi, Florida, Alabama, Georgia, Louisiana, Texas, Virginia, Arkansas, Tennessee, and North Carolina) seceded from the United States and formed the Confederate States of America. △1276.

Second, fundamental unit of time (symbol s) defined as the time of 9,192,631,770 periods of the electromagnetic radiation corresponding to a transition in the cesium-133 atom. *See also* Physical Units.

Secondary School. *See* High School.

Second Empire (1852–70), French government under Napoleon III. On Dec. 2, 1851, Louis Napoleon Bonaparte, then president of the Second Republic, staged a coup d'état. Shortly afterward he acquired dictatorial power. The Second Empire was formally established by plebiscite in November 1852. The Senate was no longer elected; the lower house met only briefly and did not choose its president or publish its debates. The press was strictly controlled, and officials took an oath of allegiance to the emperor, who had assumed the title Napoleon III. Under the empire industrial development spread; railways tripled in mileage; overseas trade quadrupled in value (1851–69); and credit and banking grew with formation of the Crédit Mobilier and the Société Générale. Napoleon III bettered relations with Britain, allying with it in the Crimean War (1854–56) and signing a commercial treaty (1860) that moved France toward greater freedom of trade. The rise of Prussia, with its defeat of Austria (1866) and drive toward unification of Germany, caught France unprepared. Popular anti-Prussian sentiment swept the emperor into the disastrous Franco-Prussian War (1870–71). After the French defeat at Sedan (October 1870), a republic was proclaimed, and the emperor fled to England, where he died (1873). *See also* Franco-Prussian War; Napoleon III.

Second Republic (1848–52), government of France. Popular insurrection against the reign of King Louis Philippe brought about his abdication and the establishment of a republic in early 1848. In June, Parisian workers rose against the conservative tendencies of the provisional government. The constitution of 1848 provided for election by universal suffrage of a president and assembly but failed to foresee potential conflicts between them. Louis Napoleon, president of the republic, replaced it with the Second Empire in 1852. *See also* Second Empire.

Second Vatican Council. △1388.

Second World War. *See* World War II.

Secretary Bird, bird of prey found in Africa south of the Sahara. It is pale gray with black markings, has quill-like feathers behind its ears, large wings, and long legs and tail. It feeds on reptiles, birds, and mammals and lays reddish-white eggs (2–3) in a tree nest. Height: 4ft (1.2m). Species *Sagittarius serpentarius.*

Secret Service, United States, law enforcement agency within the Treasury Department. It is charged with the job of stopping all counterfeiting and forging of US money, and with the protection of the president, vice president, president-elect, and presidential candidates and their families. It was founded at the end of the Civil War (1865).

Securities and Exchange Commission (SEC), US federal agency. Its general objective is to provide the fullest possible disclosure to the investing public and to protect the interest of the public and investors against malpractice in the securities and financial markets. This includes stock exchange, investment and holding companies. The 5-man commission, appointed by the president, advises district courts on reorganization proceedings for debtor corporations. The commission is vested with quasi-judicial functions and its decisions may be appealed in the courts. It was established in 1934 by the Securities Exchange Act.

Sedan, town in NE France, on Meuse River, 11mi (18km) ESE of Mézières; became part of French crownlands in 1642; Protestant stronghold in 16th and 17th centuries; in 1870 French were defeated here, and Napoleon III surrendered to Prussian forces; site of heavy fighting WWI; in WWII it was Germany's initial capture in French invasion. Pop. 23,037.

Sedative, any drug used to reduce excitement, induce sleep, or control convulsions. Sedatives are classified as barbiturates and non-barbiturates, the latter including bromides and chloral compounds. An overdose can produce serious side effects or death.

Seder, meaning "order" in Hebrew, is a religious observance held on the first night of Passover in Jewish homes in Israel, and the first two nights outside Israel. The Haggadah is recited. The ancient temple service is commemorated and is based on the Mishnah.

Sedge, grasslike perennial plants widely distributed in temperate, cold, and tropical mountain regions, usually on wet ground or in water. Cultivated only as border plants, they have flat leaves and spikes of flowers. Family Cyperaceae; genus *Carex.*

Sediment, in geology a general term used to describe (1) any material in suspension in air or water; (2) the total load transported by a stream, including materials moved along its bed and those that are in solution as well as sediment in suspension; and (3) any unconsolidated sand and gravel deposit in river valleys and along coastlines. △246–248, 270–272.

Sedimentary Rocks, mineral or organic particles that have been moved by the action of water, wind, or glacial ice (or have been chemically precipitated from solution) to a new location. Following a process of compaction and cementation the particles form strata of sedimentary rock. Those formed by particles of volcanic rock are said to have pyroclastic characteristics; derived from other rocks, they are described as clastic. △248, 270–72.

Sedimentation, any process or processes that deposit rock-formation materials. The materials deposited are continental in origin and the debris of landforms worn down and carried off by wind, water, or ice. Whenever the flow of the transporting medium is interrupted or diverted, the carried material is deposited either on land; in desert, lake, or river bed; or on coasts; or as marine sediments. *See also* Deposition; Erosion; Transportation. △246–48.

Sedition Act (1918), US legislation that extended wartime abrogation of civil liberties. It empowered the federal government to punish "disloyal, profane, scurrilous or abusive" opinions. It was used often against discontented workers and unions in the 1920s. Only 10 of over 1,500 arrests made under the act charged actual sabotage. *See also* Smith Act.

Sedum, genus of succulent perennials that grow in dry areas throughout the world. Clusters of tiny flowers are yellow, pink, or blue. Among the hundreds of species are *Sedum acre,* the yellow stonecrop, with small triangular leaves and yellow, star-shaped flowers; *S. rosea,* or roseroot, to 6–12in (15.2–30.5cm), with greenish yellow flowers; and *S. spectabile,* to 12–18in (30.5–45.7cm), with rose pink blooms. Family Crassulaceae.

Seebeck Effect. If wires of two different metals are

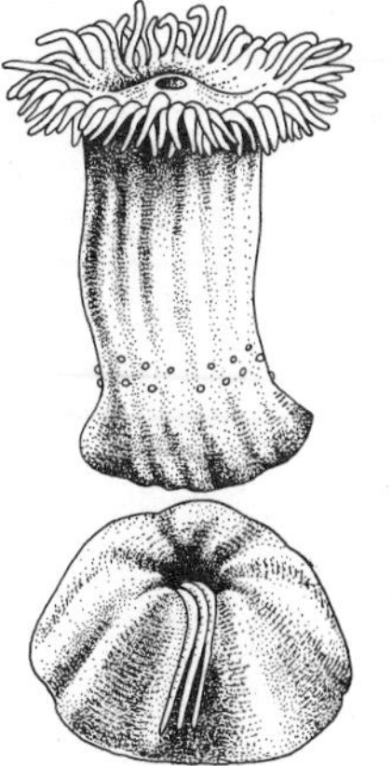

Sea anemone

Sea lion

Sea otter

Secretary bird

joined at their ends to form a circuit, a current will flow around the circuit if the ends are maintained at different temperatures. Named after T. J. Seebeck (1770–1831).

Seed, part of a flowering plant that contains the embryo with its coating and stored food. The seed is formed in the ovary by fertilization of the female gamete by two sperm nuclei. The seed coating may be thin (peanut, garden bean) or hard (Brazil nut). The embryo consists of an axis, two cotyledons, growing shoot, and root. In some seeds, an endosperm develops from nutrients supplied by the parent plant rather than the embryo (corn and cereals). In others, food is stored in the embryo itself (bean). △456.

Seed Fern, extinct group of ferns, thought to be ancestral to gymnosperms. Its fossil history extends from the late Devonian period to the Triassic period. Many had stout trunks bearing crowns of large, feathery leaves; height: to 50ft (15m). Order Cycadofilicales. *See also* Fern; Gymnosperm.

Seed Shrimp. *See* Ostracod.

Seferis, George (1900–71), pseud. of Giorgos Seferiades, outstanding Greek writer and diplomat, b. Turkey. Educated in Paris, he had a distinguished diplomatic career and was Greek ambassador to the United Nations (1956–57) and to Great Britain (1957–62). His writing, especially his lyric poetry, earned him a Nobel Prize for literature in 1963.

Segou, city and port in S Mali, W Africa, on Niger River; part of Bambara kingdom until 1861 when it was captured by a militant Muslim reformer, Al-haji Umar; in 1890 it was occupied by French. Industries: cotton, textiles. Pop. 300,627.

Segovia, Andrés (1893–), Spanish guitarist. After his debut in 1909, through a long career he successfully established the guitar as a concert instrument. He created many new techniques of guitar playing, adapting the instrument to enable him to play complex compositions of serious composers. Many 20th-century composers have created works specifically for him, and he transcribed much early contrapuntal music for solo guitar. He encouraged Julian Bream and taught John Williams.

Segovia, city in Spain, 40mi (64km) NW of Madrid between Eresma and Clamores rivers; capital of Segovia prov. A Roman settlement in 1st century, it was a major textile center in the Middle Ages; taken by Moors in 8th century; captured 1079 by Alfonso VI. It is the site of 2nd-century Roman aqueduct, 16th-century cathedral. Industries: chemicals, rubber, cement, flour, fertilizers. Est. 700 BC. Area: (prov.) 2,683sq mi (6,949sq km). Pop. (city) 41,880; (prov.) 162,770.

Segregation, Racial, separation of blacks and whites in schools, on public transportation, in public institutions and facilities, and in places of employment and residence. △896,1358.

Seine River, river in N central France; rises in Plateau of Langres, flows NW through Paris and empties into English Channel near Le Havre. It is connected to Loire, Rhône, Meuse, Scheldt, Saône, and Somme rivers by canals. The first settlement at Paris was Île de la Cité, an island in the Seine. Other cities on the river are Le Havre, Rouen, and Troyes. The most important river of N France, it is navigable for ocean-going vessels as far as Rouen, and for barges to Nogent-sur-Seine; has been important commercially since Roman times. Navigable for 350mi (564km) of its 482mi (776km).

Seismic Array, the continuous and composite picture accumulated from all the continuous-recording seismographs that are a part of the World Wide Standard Seismograph Network (WWSSN) and the generation of equipment such as Large Aperture Seismic Array (LASA). *See also* Earthquake; Seismology.

Seismic Profile, continuous record of sound waves as bounced off sea-bottom sediments. The sounds become seismic waves and as such are used to determine the thickness and structure of bottom sediments. *See also* Echo Sounder. △174. △228.

Seismic Survey, a method of petroleum exploration involving an underground explosion which sends shock waves through the ground at speeds relative to the transmitting ability of the rock. Calculation of the speed of transmission, taken from readings in many places around the explosion, yeilds a profile of the land's folds and faults, which indicates possible locations of petroleum reservoirs.

Seismic Waves, waves produced by earthquakes. These shock waves go through Earth and emerge on the surface and are recorded. Primary (P) and secondary (S) waves are transmitted by the solid Earth. P waves vibrate in the direction of propagation; S waves vibrate at right angles to the direction of propagation. Only P waves are transmitted through fluid zones. Thus, information about the state of Earth can be gathered by the study of the effect and transmission of the P and S waves. The waves are also affected by differing layers. *See also* Earthquake; Seismology. △174.

Seismograph or **Seismometer,** a device for measuring and recording Earth's crustal movement. The seismographs may be of the pendulum or strain type. The pendulum type is used most frequently to record earthquakes and is an electromagnetic device. A coil on a pendulum is wired to a galvanometer. Motion activates the pendulum in a magnetic field, the coil moves and deflects a beam of light, which is reflected onto a photosensitive paper and recorded. *See also* Seismic Waves. △54, 174, 1440.

Seismology, the study and measurement of the propagation of strain waves. The field began developing in the 1880s and has since been applied to the detection of earthquakes and underground explosions (nuclear and other). The detection involves the separation of events from the ever-present background of seismic noise. Pinpointing sites of events is now very accurate since the development of precise instrumentation and the establishment of the World Wide Standard Seismograph Network (WWSSN). *See also* Earthquake; Seismic Waves. △174.

Sejanus, Lucius Aelius (died 31 AD), Roman political figure. He is best known for his plot to capture power in Rome after the murder of Tiberius' son and heir Drusus (23 AD). Sejanus, the Praetorian prefect, hoped to become regent of an imperial prince in the event of Tiberius' death. His conspiracies came to an end when he was apprehended and executed by the emperor.

Seladang. *See* Gaur.

Selaginella, or spike moss, genus of small-leaved, mosslike plants found worldwide, mostly in the tropics. Two kinds of spores are borne in cones at branch tips. Some grow on trees, others on the ground. The North American rock spike moss *(Selaginella rupestris)* is grayish-green and grows in dense mats on rocks or sand; height: 3in (7.6cm). There are over 700 species. Family Selaginellaceae. *See also* Club Moss. △438.

Selection, in genetics, the probability that one genetic factor or allele will be passed on in favor of another. *See also* Natural Selection. △408.

Selections. *See* Ecologues.

Selective Service Acts, series of laws requiring men to register for military service. The first act, passed during World War I under Pres. Woodrow Wilson, called for registration of men aged 18 to 45 for wartime service. The second, passed in 1940, initiated compulsory military training in peacetime. This act called for registration of men between 21 and 35 years of age and ordered training of 900,000 men in 1941. On Dec. 19, 1941, this ruling was extended to include men aged 20 to 44 years. The Selective Service Act of 1948 was passed to provide manpower for the occupation of Germany and Italy and to support expanding military aid programs. Men 19 to 25 were drafted for 21 months of service; 18-year-olds were permitted to volunteer for 1 year in any of the major services. The draft was ended in 1973.

Selenium, metalloid element (symbol Se) of group VIA of the periodic table, discovered (1817) by J.J. Berzelius. Chief source is as a by-product in the electrolytic refining of copper. The element is photoactive and is extensively used in photocells, solar cells, and xerography. Properties: at. no. 34; at. wt. 78.96; sp gr 4.79 (gray); melt. pt. 423°F (217°C); boil. pt. 1233°F (684°C); most common isotope Se^{80}(49.82%). △1552.

Selenology, study of the Moon's physical and chemical composition and formative processes. Current research reveals that the moon greatly resembles the Earth in physico-chemical makeup. Its surface is composed mainly of volcanic basalts but evidence of considerable chemical differentiation has been found, suggesting that the Moon was formed at a very high temperature along with the other planets of the solar system. △52–60.

Seleucids, a Hellenistic dynasty (312–64 BC) founded in Syria by Seleucus I. The most notable rulers of this dynasty were Seleucus I, Antiochus I, and Antiochus III, who founded new cities and brought prosperity to the Near East through their gifted administrations.

Self-Fulfilling Prophecy, in social psychology, the unconscious tendencies of individuals to make their behaviors or events conform to expected or desired outcomes. For example, a researcher who expects a study to turn out a certain way may (unconsciously) influence the study so that it does turn out that way: this is called "experimenter bias," one form of self-fulfilling prophecy.

Selim I (1467–1520), Ottoman sultan (1512–20) under whom the empire reached its greatest power. A bloody despot, but able administrator, he conquered parts of Persia, all of Syria and Palestine, and Egypt (1514–17). As caliph, he was acknowledged by the holy cities of Arabia as spiritual as well as temporal leader.

Selim III (1761–1808), Ottoman sultan (1789–1807). After ending a war against Russia and Austria in *c.* 1791, he began a program to westernize the state's finances and armed forces. In 1801 Egypt was recovered after being occupied by the French under Napoleon. In 1808 he was strangled during a revolt of the janizaries and conservatives who opposed his reforms.

Seljuk Turks, nomadic tribe which traveled to the Middle East and converted to Islam after the breakup of the Mongolian Empire. In the early 11th century they began long and destructive attacks on the Byzantine Empire. △1056, 1084.

Selkirk, Thomas Douglas, 5th Earl of (1771–1820), Canadian settler leader and financier, b. Scotland. He established settlements in Prince Edward Island and Ontario in 1803. In 1811 he bought a controlling interest in the Hudson's Bay Co. and founded the Red River settlement in Manitoba. Sued by the North West Co. in 1818, he returned to Britain in ill health, leaving a struggling community on the Red River. A friend of Sir Walter Scott, he also wrote widely on the politics and mores of western Canada.

Selkirk, mountain range in SE British Columbia, Canada. An extension of the Rocky Mts, it is traversed by Canadian Pacific Railway; site of portions of Glacier National Park and Mt Revelstok National Park. Highest peak is Mt Sir Sanford, 11,591ft (3,535m). Length: 200mi (322km).

Selma, industrial city in SW central Alabama, 40mi (64km) W of Montgomery, in Dallas co; location of Craig Air Force Base; Confederate arsenal and supply depot in Civil War; scene of civil rights demonstrations in 1965. Industries: cotton and pecans. Settled 1815; inc. 1820; Pop. (1970) 27,379.

Selye, Hans (1907–), Canadian physician, widely known for his pioneer studies of the effects of stress on human and animal physiology. He outlined the "general adaptation syndrome," a series of stages the body undergoes when subjected to stress. His works include *The Stress of Life* (1956) and *Physiology and Pathology of Exposure to Stress* (1960).

Semantic Differential, in psychology, method developed by C.E. Osgood, which uses rating scales and factor analysis in studying connotative (suggestive and emotional) meanings of words.

Semantics, study of words, their meanings and uses and how accurately they reflect reality. Words stand for concepts, and concepts themselves are based on human perceptions of reality that are not necessarily accurate. Thus semantic confusion is possible; people may use the same word to refer to different realities. △864.

Semaphore, device or technique that communicates messages visually. The railroad semaphore consists of a vertical post on which is mounted a single projecting arm. This arm can take three positions, indicating "all clear," "caution," or "stop." The marine semaphore is equipped with two pivoted arms. Letters and numerals are indicated by different placing of these arms. △868, 1790.

Semarang, seaport city in N Java, Indonesia, on Java Sea; capital of Central Java prov. and Semarang residency; occupied by Dutch 1748 and Japanese during WWII; site of Diponegoro University (1957). Exports kapok, rubber, coffee, sugar, tobacco. Industries fishing, shipbuilding, textiles. Pop. 503,153.

Semen, thick, milky-white fluid ejaculated by the

male at orgasm; contains sperms, and the secretions of various accessory sexual glands. Volume is about .085 to .118 ozs. (2.5 to 3.5 ml) and contains about 200 to 300 million sperms per ejaculate. △700.

Semenov, Nikolai Nikolaevich (1896–), Russian chemist. After studying at Leningrad he moved to Moscow State University. In 1956 he shared a Nobel prize with C.N. Hinshelwood for his work on branched chain reactions in combustion processes.

Semicircular Canal. △676.

Semiconductor, substance with electrical conductivity intermediate between that of a conductor and an insulator, whose resistance decreases as its temperature increases. It consists of elements or compounds, such as germanium, silicon, and lead telluride, made up of covalent crystals. At normal temperatures some of the electrons in the atoms have sufficient energy to break free of the covalent bonds and will drift against an imposed field giving rise to n-type conductivity. The vacancies, or holes, left by these electrons behave as if they are positive charges that are free to move about the crystal, giving rise to p-type conductivity. In practical semiconductors impurities are added in controlled amounts during manufacture, the number of valency electrons of the impurity atoms determining whether the majority of the current carriers will be p-type holes or n-type electrons. A semiconductor junction is formed when there is an abrupt change along the length of the crystal from one type of impurity to the other. Such a p-n junction acts as a very efficient rectifier and is the basis of the semiconductor diode. *See also* Transistor. △1506, 1530, 1532, 1546.

Semi-micro Scale. △1568.

Seminole, North American Indian tribe that dates only from about 1725, when the original members separated from the main Creek Indian group under the pressure of wars with whites, and fled into Georgia and Florida, eventually arriving at the Everglades. About 5,000 inhabit Florida and Oklahoma today.

Seminole War (1835–43), second war with Seminole Indians of Florida, who resisted US expansion. A long, bitter conflict resulted between the US Army and the Seminoles, with the United States victorious and the Indians virtually annihilated. The treaty (1842) removed most of the Seminoles to territory west of the Mississippi.

Semipalatinsk, city in Kazakh SSR, USSR, on Irtysh River; capital of Semipalatinsk oblast; site of a teachers' college. Industries: agriculture, livestock, gold mining, lumbering, food processing, meat packing, textiles. Founded 1718 as a Russian frontier post and transferred to present site 1778. Pop. 236,000.

Semipermeable Membrane, membrane that permits the passage of solvent, such as water, but is impermeable to larger dissolved molecules, such as salt and sugar molecules. The property of permeability depends on the molecular diameter of the dissolved substance and the nature of the membrane. Common membranes include thin palladium foil, pig's bladder, cellophane, copper cyanoferrate, and the cell wall, which allows passage of certain molecules and ions into and out of the cell. *See also* Osmosis. △1566.

Semiramis, Greek form of Sammu-ramat, legendary queen of ancient Assyria. Historically she was the wife of Shamshi-Adad V and was queen regent for her son (811–808 BC), but myths have attached to her name that overshadow her historical person. In Assyrian mythology she was daughter of a goddess who abandoned her. Doves nourished her until a kindly shepherd saved her. She eventually became queen by killing her royal husband, and in the myths she is acclaimed as the builder of Babylon.

Semitic Languages, family of languages of peoples native to Asia Minor and N Africa. They have a non-Roman alphabet in which characteristically only the consonants are written, with vowels indicated by marks above or below them, such as Hebrew, Arabic, Aramaic, and Turkish. Egyptian and Abyssinian languages are often distinguished as belonging to the subgroup of Hamitic languages. The words Semitic and Hamitic are derived from the names of Noah's sons, Shem and Ham (Gen. 10). △870.

Semmelweiss, Ignaz (1818–65), Hungarian physician. He was probably the first to recognize the importance of antisepsis in preventing infection. In 1847 he ordered doctors under him at the University of Vienna hospital to wash their hands in strong chemicals before touching a patient—with the immediate result of a dramatic decrease in the incidence of childbed fever.

Senate, Roman, governing body of the Roman republic, first convened during the monarchy as the king's council. By the 2nd century BC it controlled military, religious, financial, domestic, and foreign policy. The senators, chosen for life by the censors, increased to 600 under Sulla, 900 under Caesar, and fell to 600 under Augustus. Patricians had privileges of precedence over plebeian members; all enjoyed freedom of speech during the republic. The Senate met in Rome to debate legislation; resolutions could be vetoed by the tribunes. After Sulla's defeat of Marius (182 BC), the Senate was controlled by generals until Caesar, leading the populares, destroyed Pompey (48 BC). During the empire the Senate's power was reduced to judicial functions and freedom of debate was lost. △1014.

Senate of the United States, upper house of the legislature. It is composed of two senators from each state who are popularly elected and serve six-year terms. Senators are elected in even-numbered years, with about one third of the Senate elected at a time. There are 17 standing committees in the Senate and committee chairmen retain their positions for as long as their party has a majority of the votes. Senate approval by a simple majority is necessary for some presidential appointments and a two-thirds majority for treaties. The vice president serves as the presiding officer and, in his absence, the majority party chooses a "pro-tem" leader. The Senate acts as a court during impeachment proceedings, which are brought by the House. The Senate allows unlimited debate, and the filibuster technique is often employed. △904, 1218.

Sendai, city in NE Honshu, Japan, near shore of Sendai Bay; capital of Miyagi prefecture; seat of the powerful daimyo of Date Masamune 17th–19th centuries. It is chief industrial and commercial center of N Honshu; site of Tokohu Imperial University (1907) and Industrial Art Research Institute (1928). Industries: textiles, yarn, silk, wood products, brewing. Pop. 545,065.

Sendak, Maurice (1928–), US author and illustrator of imaginative books for children, b. Brooklyn, N.Y. His *Where the Wild Things Are* was awarded the Caldecott Medal in 1964. Other books he wrote and illustrated include *Higglety Pigglety Pop!, Or, There Must Be More To Life* (1967) and *In the Night Kitchen* (1970). He has illustrated over 50 books by others, including *Little Bear* (by Else Minarik) and *Bat-Poet* (by Randall Jarrell).

Seneca (the Elder), Lucius Annaeus (*c.* 60 BC–*c.* AD 37), Roman rhetorician and writer. He lived most of his life in his native Spain. His *Controversies* contains model arguments for legal cases while *Persuasions* contains model orations. He also wrote a book on declamations and a history of Rome. △1028.

Seneca (the Younger), Lucius Annaeus (4 BC?–AD 65), Roman philosopher, dramatist, and political figure, the son of Seneca the Elder. Tutor for the young Nero, he was highly influential in the first years of the emperor's reign. A Stoic, he wrote many philosophical essays including *De elementia* on the duty of a ruler to be merciful. His *Dialogue* contained essays on anger, impassivity, divine providence, and other topics. *Quaestiones Naturales* viewed nature from a philosophical perspective. He wrote nine tragedies based on Greek models, the best known of which is *Phaedra*. The tragedies were written to be recited, not performed. Seneca resigned his offices out of alarm and disgust with Nero's excesses. He was compelled by Nero to commit suicide. △1148.

Seneca, the most populous division of the League of the Iroquois; a tribe of North American Indians inhabiting N New York; a few live in Canada. Today, about 850 so-called "Seneca" live in Oklahoma, where they moved in 1832; the main eastern group totals about 7,000 in New York, Ontario, and Pennsylvania.

Seneca Falls Convention (1848), women's rights convention held at Seneca Falls, N.Y. Elizabeth Cady Stanton and Lucretia Mott organized this convention, the first aimed at obtaining equal rights for women. About 300 people attended, and a "Declaration of Sentiments" was issued.

Seneca Lake, lake in W New York, one of the Finger Lakes, joined by Seneca River to Cayuga Lake; part of New York State Barge System. Area: 67sq mi (174sq km).

Senegal, independent republic in W Africa, formerly a French protectorate. Peanuts are the principal crop.
Land and Economy. Located on the bulge of West

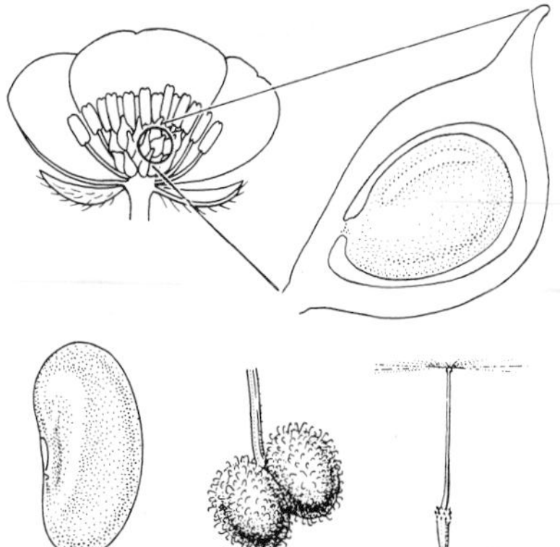

Seed

Andrés Segovia

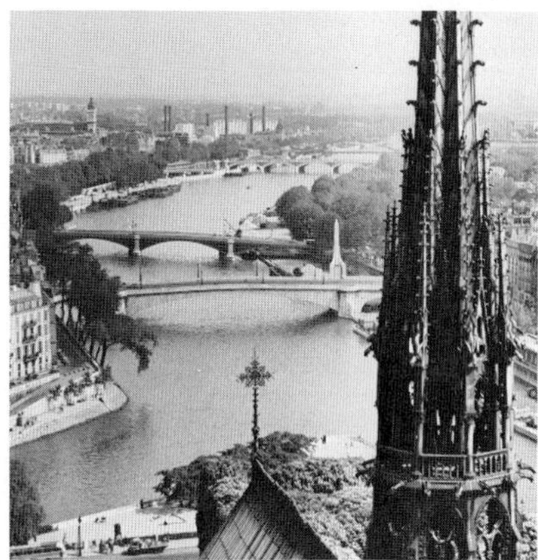

Seine River, Paris

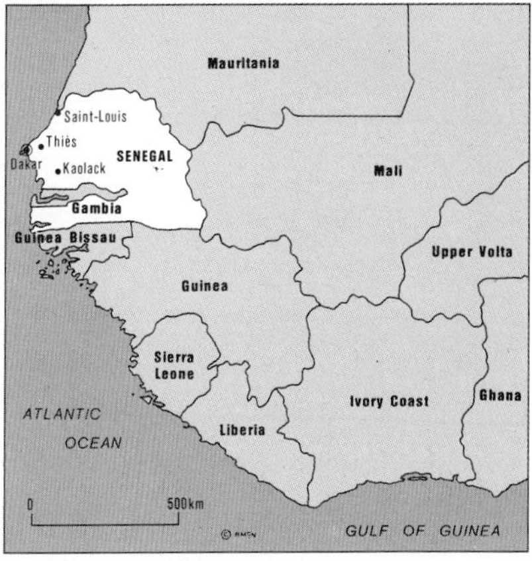
Mauritania
Saint-Louis
Thiès
Dakar
Kaolack
SENEGAL
Mali
Gambia
Guinea Bissau
Upper Volta
Guinea
Sierra Leone
Ivory Coast
Ghana
ATLANTIC
OCEAN
Liberia
0
500km
GULF OF GUINEA

Senegal

Africa, it is bordered by the Atlantic Ocean (W), Mauritania (N), Mali (E), Guinea and Guinea-Bissau (S). Mostly a low altitude country of rolling plains, it includes a SE plateau at the foothills of the Fouta-Djallon Mts. Tropical rain forests cover the SW. Four major rivers, all navigable for large vessels, cross the country—the Senegal, Saloumn, Gambia, and Casamance. The seasons include two hot and two dry periods. Peanuts provide Senegal's main crop, accounting for 80% of export earnings. Attempts to diversify agriculture have added cotton as a cash crop. Commercial fishing is expanding. A high degree of industrialization allows Senegal to process raw materials for export—peanut oil, canned fish, and phosphates, the major mineral resource.

People. Among the chief ethnic groups 35% of the population is Wolof, 17.5% Fulani, 16.5% Serere, 9% Toucouleur, and 9% Diola. Although French is the official language, most tribes have their own tongues. About 80% of the country is Muslim; of the remaining most are animist, with a small percentage of Catholics. Literacy is 5%.

Government. A constitution provides for an executive-presidential system with an elected unicameral legislature. The chief of state is elected by universal adult suffrage, and a prime minister is appointed by the president.

History. Fossils show that Senegal was probably inhabited in prehistoric times. During the 13th and 14th centuries it came under the influence of the Mandingo Empire, and the Djoloff Empire of Senegal was formed. French control over the region started in the 17th century. Senegal became a French protectorate in 1920. By 1956 the franchise had been broadened, and Senegal became a member of the French Community with internal autonomy. An attempt at federation with French Sudan, as the Mali Federation (1959–60) was not successful, and in 1960 Senegal seceded and declared itself a republic. From independence the country was led by Léopold Senghor.

PROFILE

Official name: Republic of Senegal
Area: 76,124sq mi (197,161sq km)
Population: 4,320,000
Density: 57per sq mi (22per sq km)
Chief city: Dakar (capital)
Government: Republic (elected president and appointed prime minister)
Religion: Islam
Language: French (official)
Monetary unit: CFA franc
Gross national product: $1,014,000,000
Per capita income: $252
Industries: canning, chemicals, cement, food processing
Agriculture: peanuts, rice, millet, sorghum
Minerals: phosphates
Trading partners: United States, France

Senegal River, river in Senegal, W Africa; formed by the confluence of the Bafing and Bakarg rivers; rises near the Sierra Leone border; flows N then NW to form Mauritanian-Senegal border; empties into the Atlantic Ocean at St Louis; chief tributary is Falémé River; serves as source of irrigation for rice growing region. Length: approx. 1,015mi (1,634km).

Senghor, Léopold Sédar (1906–), African intellectual and president of Senegal. He studied in France and fought against Germany in World War II. A skillful writer and champion of black African culture, he became involved in the government of Senegal and was elected president of the new republic in 1960. He worked toward greater African unity and the development of W Africa.

Senility, a serious decline in mental and physical abilities in old age. Some old people develop mental disorders marked by such symptoms as lack of attention, forgetfulness, or delusions. Many elderly people do continue to live productive and creative lives, however. △804.

Senna, plants, shrubs, and trees native to warm and tropical regions; some species grow in temperate areas worldwide. They have oblong, featherlike leaves and yellow flowers. Family Leguminosae; genus *Cassia.*

Sennacherib, King of Assyria (704–681 BC), son and successor of Sargon II. His main military campaigns were directed against the Babylonian and Elamite alliance, ending with the capture in 703 then destruction of Babylon in 689 and the defeat of Elam in 691. He led another major campaign against Phoenicia, Palestine, and Philistia in 701. The rest of his reign was spent restoring Nineveh. △980, 978, 958, 954.

Sennett, Mack (1880–1960), US film director, producer, and actor, b. Michael Sinnott in Canada. His many short slapstick comedies enlivened the silent era. His Keystone Studio films brought fame to Charlie Chaplin, Mabel Normand, Charlie Chase, and the Keystone Kops.

Sensation, 19th-century concept describing the elementary or fundamental components of perception. Sensations were viewed as atoms or building blocks that combined to give rise to human impressions of the world. For example the color green might be thought of as being composed of two more elementary sensations, blue and yellow. Sensations were an integral part of structuralist theories and survive today in theories that view perception as a collection of simpler elements. *See also* Perception. △672.

Sensitive Fern, a single species of North American fern, found in damp places, and noted for fragility of its leaves, which wilt when picked and are susceptible to early frosts. Long, coarse, triangular sterile fronds; fertile fronds small and beadlike enclosing sori, to 2ft (61cm) high. Family Polypodiaceae; species *Onoclea sensibilis. See also* Fern.

Sensitivity Training, a group training technique, also referred to as T-group, the purpose of which is to help the individual, through the understanding of group dynamics, to become a more effective communicator, more aware of his own and of other people's feelings. *See also* Group Therapy.

Sensory Adaptation, ability of the perceptual nervous system to adjust or compensate for small changes in the stimulus field. For example, sunlight at dusk has a disproportionate amount of red light, yet most people report that objects appear to be their normal colors, not reddish. Adaptation seems to occur in all of the senses.

Sensory Cortex. △682.

Sensory Deprivation, in psychology, depriving an individual of variation in sensory stimulation. In experiments such deprivation is achieved by confining volunteer subjects to tiny, soundproof rooms and having them wear gloves, goggles, and ear muffs. Studies show that behavior is normally highly dependent on variation in stimulation from the environment, and when stimulation does not vary, the individual will develop (nonpermanent) behavioral abnormalities such as sleeplessness and hallucinations.

Sentence, a complete thought expressed in words. It begins with a capital letter and ends with a period (declarative), a question mark (interrogative), or exclamation point (imperative or exclamatory). Classifications: simple, compound, complex. Parts: subject and predicate for each clause. △780.

Seoul (Soul), capital city of South Korea, in NW South Korea, 40mi (64km) E of its port of Inch'ŏn; capital of Kyonggi prov. As Hansung, it served as the capital of the Yi dynasty (1394–1910); occupied by Japan 1910–45; headquarters of US forces and US military government 1945; made capital of South Korea 1948; occupied by Communist forces 1950–51; sustained heavy damages during Korean War (1950–53); site of Seoul National University (1945); political, economic, cultural center. Industries: textiles, metallurgy, food processing, chemicals, farm equipment. Pop. 5,536,377.

Separation of Powers, a fundamental principle of the US federal and state governments. Fearing the power of a despot, the framers of the Constitution saw the need for separating the powers of government among the legislature, which makes laws; the president, who executes the laws; and the courts, which interpret the laws. The principle was early enunciated in the writings of Locke and Montesquieu. △906.

Separatism. △1128.

Sephardim, the classification of all Jews and their descendants who settled in Spain and Portugal before 1492, when Spanish Jewry was expelled and dispersed. Their language is Ladino or Judeo-Spanish. They now comprise about 17% of the world Jewish population. Today, this category generally includes all Oriental Jews as well.

Sepoy Mutiny. *See* Indian Mutiny.

Seppuku. *See* Hara-kiri.

Septal Region, region of the brain centered about the septum lucidum, a band of tissues that separate the lateral ventricles. *See also* Brain.

September, ninth month of the year. Its name comes from the Latin for seventh because it was the seventh month in the old ten-month calendar. It has 30 days. The birthstone is the sapphire.

Septicemia, generalized bacterial infection in which bacteria, usually staphylococcus, streptococcus, or pneumococcus, multiply in the bloodstream. They may enter from a wound or from an infection within the body.

Septic Tank, a unit for sewage disposal, usually in residences not connected to sewer lines. The compartmented tank is buried in the ground and arranged so that settled sludge contacts waste water flowing through the tank and beyond into a drain field. Bacteria in the sludge decompose solids. △1768.

Septimius Severus, Lucius. *See* Severus, Lucius Septimius.

Septuagint (3rd/2nd century BC), Greek translation of the Hebrew Old Testament, written for the Greek-speaking Jewish community in Egypt. It is the oldest Greek translation of the Bible. The Septuagint contains the entire Jewish Canon plus the Apocrypha. It is divided into four sections: the law, history, poetry, and prophets. The books of the Apocrypha do not form a separate section, but are inserted throughout where suitable. It is still used by the Greek Orthodox Church. *See also* Apocrypha; Old Testament.

Sequoia, two species of mammoth evergreen trees found only in California and S Oregon. They are the giant sequoia or big tree *(Sequoia giganteum)* and the redwood *(Sequoia sempervirens).* The size and scarcity of these trees have made them a natural wonder of the United States. Height: over 300ft (91.5m). Family Pinaceae.

Sequoia National Park, park in E California. It features great groves of giant sequoia trees, the world's largest and among the oldest living things. There is magnificent High Sierra scenery, including Mt Whitney. Area: 386,862acres (156,679hectares). Est. 1890.

Sequoya (1770?–1843), scholar of the Cherokee tribe of American Indians. He invented an alphabet for the Cherokee language so that his people could learn to read and write. He completed his system in 1821 after 12 years' work. With his alphabet he was able to write the history of his people. In 1828 he went to Washington to represent his people to the US government. The sequoia trees are named for him.

Seraphim, heavenly beings described in the Old Testament as having human form but six wings (Isaiah 6:2–6). Though this is the only mention of them in the Bible, the Seraphim became high ranking angels in Jewish and Christian theology.

Serbia (Srbija), largest constituent republic of Yugoslavia, in E Yugoslavia; capital is Belgrade. Mostly mountainous terrain, the fertile NE is drained by the Danube River. Settled by Serbs, it emerged as a state in the 10th century; ruled as a dynasty by Stephen Nemanja (r.1168–96); became chief Slav kingdom under Stephen Dushan (1331–55); taken by Turks 1389 and made part of Ottoman Empire 1459. Serbia rebelled against Turkish rule and was guaranteed autonomy 1829; gained independence 1878, defeated by Bulgaria 1885; gained power and prestige after accession of Peter I (1903). It was drawn into anti-Austrian policy and the First Balkan War (1912); received part of Macedonia after Second Balkan War (1913). Austria declared war on Serbia in 1914, beginning WWI. Defeated by the Central Powers, formed the united kingdom of Serbs, Croats, and Slovenes 1918 (Yugoslavia); region was divided 1929 and made a constituent republic 1946. Industries: agriculture, vineyards, mining. Area: 34,115sq mi (88,358sq km). Pop. 8,436,547. △1232, 1302.

Serbo-Croatian, the principal language of Yugoslavia, spoken by about three-fourths of the country's population, or about 15,000,000 people. It is spoken by two major ethnic groups—the Serbs, who write it in the Cyrillic alphabet, and the Croats, who use the Roman (Latin) alphabet. Serbo-Croatian is a Slavic language.

Serbs, Croats and Slovenes, Kingdom of, a kingdom formed in 1918 following the Allied victory in World War I, which for the first time united all the South Slavs except Bulgaria in a single government, and which became Yugoslavia in 1929. △1302.

Serf, during the Middle Ages in Europe, a peasant bound to his lord's land, part of which he held and developed to provide for his own needs. In the 11th century a peasant voluntarily entered himself and his descendants into serfdom by a symbolic act, similar to fealty and homage for a vassal, consisting of the payment of "head money" and a gesture, such as hanging a bellrope around his neck. By the 13th century, the only serfs were those descended from serfs. Called *villeins* in England, serfs held a social position inferior to that of freemen and superior to that of slaves. *See also* Manorial System. △1090, 1178, 1286.

Serial Learning, in psychology, a technique used to study verbal learning and memory. Items such as words or syllables are presented as an ordered list to be memorized in that order.

Seriema, or cariama, large, cranelike, South American bird with erectile crests above short broad bill. Brownish-crested seriema *(Cariama cristata)* lives in grasslands; grayish Burmeister's seriema *(Chunga burmeisteri)* in woodlands. Both feed on small animals, including reptiles, and lay white or buff-colored eggs.(2).

Series, mathematical expression obtained by adding the terms of a sequence. Thus, the series $1 + 4 + 9 + 16 + \ldots$ is formed from the sequence 1, 4, 9, 16, ... Like sequences, series may be finite or infinite and infinite series may converge or diverge. A series formed from increasing powers of a variable is a power series; convergent power series are used for representing many functions. *See also* Arithmetic, Geometric, and Harmonic Progressions; Exponential Function; Trigonometric Function. △1456.

Serigraphy, or silk-screen printing. A technique in which multiple images are produced by means of a stencil, or mask, glued or painted onto a fine-meshed fabric screen. When certain areas or patterns have been blocked out, paint or ink is applied to the screen and forced onto the surface of the paper by means of a roller or squeegee. Although devised as a commercial reproductive process, it has been used since the 1930s as a fine-arts medium.

Serine, white crystalline amino acid found in proteins. *See* Amino Acid.

Sermon on the Mount, in the New Testament, a dissertation spoken by Jesus to his disciples and others in the hills of Galilee. Delivered early in his ministry, it is recorded in the Gospel of Matthew. Beginning with the Beatitudes, it continues with a discussion of social responsibility, specifically contrasting Jesus' teaching with Jewish legalistic traditions, and a discourse on individual religious observances.

Serpens, or the Serpent, extensive equatorial constellation situated east of Virgo and divided into two parts, Serpens Canada in the east and Serpens Caput in the west, by Ophiuchus, the Serpent-bearer. Serpens Caput contains the bright globular cluster M 5 (NGC 5904), while Serpens Canada includes M 16 (NGC 6611), an open cluster shining through surrounding nebulosity. Brightest star Alpha Serpentis (Unukalhai).

Serpentine, a group of sheet silicate minerals, with a pattern of green mottling like a snake's; hydrous magnesium silicate. Greasy, of varied hues; hardness 2–5; sp gr 2.4. Commonly used in decorative carving, fibrous varieties are used in asbestos cloth.

Serratus Anterior. △684.

Serum, the fluid that remains if whole blood is allowed to clot, and the clot removed; essentially the same composition as plasma, with fibrinogen and clotting factors gone. *See also* Plasma. △688.

Serval, or **Bush Cat,** orange and black spotted doglike cat found in grassy areas of sub-Saharan Africa. It has a narrow head and long legs, neck, and ears. The gestation period is 74 days and 1–3 young are born. Length: body—30–39.4in (70–100cm); tail—13.8–15.7in (35–40cm); weight: 15–25lb (6.8–11.3kg). Family Felidae; species *Felis serval.*

Servetus, Michael (1511–53), Spanish physician and theologian. While studying in France and Germany, he became interested in ideas of the Protestant reformers, but his theological writings were denounced by reformers as well as Rome. He lived under another name in France, practicing medicine. In medical history he is known for discovering that blood is aerated in the lungs before passing into the heart. Forced to flee from France because of his religious beliefs, Servetus was arrested as a heretic and burned by Calvinists in Geneva.

Service, Robert William (1874–1958), Canadian author, b. England. He came to Canada in 1894 and worked for a bank in British Columbia and the Yukon. He wrote rollicking ballads of Canada, such as *Songs of A Sourdough* (1907), which included "The Shooting of Dan McGrew." He also wrote a number of novels including *The Trial of '98: A Northland Romance* (1911) and *The House of Fear* (1927).

Servius Tullius (578–535 BC), sixth king of Rome who, although of Roman or Latin birth, ruled during a period of Etruscan supremacy. He built a temple to the Latin Diana and, according to tradition rejected by modern scholars, built the walls of Rome. He is credited with the Servian Reforms.

Servomechanism, automatic device in which one mechanism is controlled by another mechanism, which has an independent power supply. The device usually forms part of a control system: power steering in a car relies on a servomechanism to provide independent power to turn the wheels in accordance with instructions imparted by the driver through the steering wheel. Some servomechanisms, such as the automatic pilot of an aircraft, incorporate a feedback mechanism that makes the aircraft independent of human control. △1670.

Sesostris, the name of three kings of the XII dynasty of ancient Egypt. Sesostris I, coregent with his father Amenemhet I, became sole ruler *c.*1970 BC. During his reign Nubia was conquered. Sesostris II was also a coregent before succeeding (1906 BC) his father Amenemhet II. Under Sesostris III (reigned *c.*1887–1849), Egypt became very powerful, its southern boundary extending above the 2nd cataract of the Nile.

Sesshu. △1048.

Sessions, Roger (1896–), US composer, b. Brooklyn, N.Y. He has employed a complex, atonal style in numerous works including his *Violin Concerto* (1935), eight symphonies, and choral, chamber, piano, and organ music. *See also* Atonality.

Seth, in the Bible, third son of Adam and Eve, thought by Eve to be recompense from God for the slain Abel. Seth is an ancestor of Christ, according to the New Testament.

Seton, (Saint) Elizabeth Ann (1774–1821), US teacher and organizer of charity, b. New York City. Elizabeth Ann Bayley was the daughter of an Episcopal minister. She married William Seton in 1797 and had five children. Her busband died in 1803; she joined the Roman Catholic Church in 1805 and soon became a leader in church works. She founded a school for girls in Maryland, prepared the way for the US parochial school system, and organized the American Sisters of Charity. Her sainthood was proclaimed in 1975. She was the first US citizen to be canonized.

Seton, Ernest Thompson (1860–1946), US writer and artist, b. England. His wildlife books and paintings were well known standards for childrens' nature study in the early 1900s. Two of the best known are *Wild Animals I Have Known* (1898) and *The Biography of a Grizzly Bear* (1900). In 1902 he organized the Woodcraft Indians, upon which the Boy Scout movement was later patterned.

Seto-naikai. *See* Inland Sea.

Sets, distinct collections of definite objects of perception or thought that can be conceived and considered as a whole. The objects are called the elements or members of the set. The number of members can be finite or infinite or be zero (empty set) or the maximum possible (universal set). Various relations can exist between two sets, A and B: A equals B (written $A = B$) if both sets contain exactly the same members; A is included in or is a subset of B ($A \subset B$) if all members of A are members of B; disjoint sets have no members in common; overlapping sets have one or more common members. Operations on sets produce new sets: the union of A and B ($A \cup B$) contains members of both A and B with no duplicate members; the intersection of A and B ($A \cap B$) contains only those members common to both sets; the complement of A contains all members that do not belong to A. △1458.

Setter, sporting dog used to locate game and stand on point until the hunter arrives. After the shot, it retrieves on command. Setters have a long, more classically shaped head than spaniels, good scenting powers, endurance, and personality. Developed in 16th-century England, types of setters are English, Irish, and Gordon.

Set Theory, theory that attempts to give mathematics a rigidly logical basis, developed by Georg Cantor in the late 19th century and only later recognized as an important branch of mathematics. It is concerned

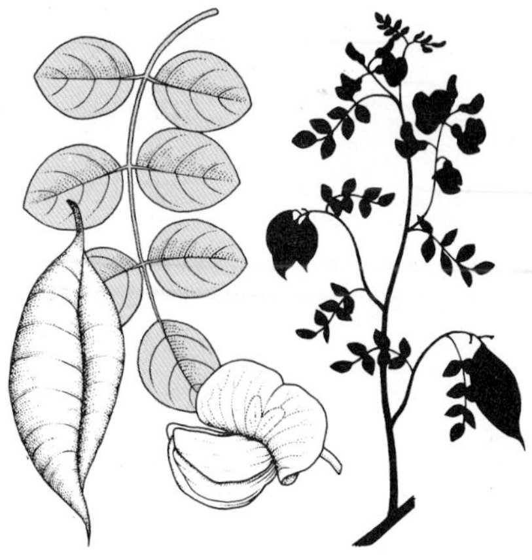

Senna

GENERAL SHERM

Sequoia National Park, California

Seriema

Saint Elizabeth Seton

with the properties of sets, relations between sets, and operations that can be made on sets. Set theory is based on George Boole's work on mathematical logic but manipulates sets of abstract or real objects, finite or infinite in number, rather than logical propositions. △1458.

Settlement, Act of (1701), statute designed to regulate and define the rights of the English monarchy. It provided that, if William III and the future Queen Anne died without heirs, the crown would pass to James I's granddaughter, Sophia of Hanover, or her heirs, if they were Protestants. The act ensured the Protestant Hanoverian succession to the throne and restricted the rights of the crown to appoint foreigners.

Settling Basin, in sanitary engineering, a chamber in a sewage-treatment system. △1768.

Seurat, Georges (1859–91), French painter. A post-Impressionist artist, he was interested in the use of color and atmosphere by the Impressionists and brought order and a sense of brilliantly shimmering light to his pictures by using organized color. He developed a style known as Pointillism, in which he painted forms by using colored dots of a uniform size, as in his masterpiece "A Sunday Afternoon on the Island of La Grande Jatte" (1884–86). He also painted many port scenes at Honfleur. Seurat's style influenced that of other artists, especially Paul Signac and Camille Pissarro. △1254.

Seuss, Dr. (1904–), pseud. of Theodor Seuss Geisel, US writer and illustrator of children's books, b. Springfield, Mass. *And To Think That I Saw It On Mulberry Street* (1937) was the first of his humorous works. In 1957 with *The Cat in the Hat* he initiated the "Beginner Book" series, entertaining books with limited vocabularies designed to help children to learn to read.

Sevan Lake, lake in N Armenian SSR, USSR; largest lake in Caucasus; fed by 30 streams, drained by Razdau River; ice-free in winter; surrounded by high mountains. It is excellent source of fish; part of an extensive hydroelectric system. Area: 540sq mi (1,400sq km).

Sevastopol, formerly Sebastopol; city in Russian SFSR, USSR, on the Black Sea, 190mi (306km) SE of Odessa; site of a late 6th-century Greek colony; in 100 BC it was absorbed into kingdom of Cimmerian Bosporus; site of a 13th-century Tartar settlement; came under Russian control in 1783; site of a naval base since 1784; a commercial port since 1808. It has been the main base of the Russian Black Sea fleet since early 19th century; fell to the Allies in the Crimean War (1855); it fell to the Germans in WWII (1942); recaptured 1944 by Soviet troops; site of institute of physiotherapy, biological marine research station, regional museum, and the Peter-Paul cathedral, a copy of the temple of Theseus at Athens. Industries: shipbuilding, fish processing, tanning, flour milling. Pop. 229,000.

Seven Days' Battles (1862), Civil War engagement that ended the Peninsular Campaign. Although Union Maj. Gen. George McClellan won the final battle at Malvern Hill near Richmond, Va., he retreated afterwards, leaving the field and victory to Gen. Robert E. Lee's Confederate army. △1276.

Seveners. *See* Isma'ilis.

Seven Pines, Battle of (May 31–June 1, 1862), stalemate in the Civil War's Peninsular Campaign. Union Maj. Gen. George McClellan split his army across the Chickahominy River and Confederate Gen. Joseph Johnston attacked the troops nearest Richmond, Va. McClellan then counterattacked across the river. The Union lost 5,000 of its 53,000 men while the Confederates lost 6,000 of their 39,000 men. *See also* Fair Oaks.

Seven-spot Ladybird. △500.

Seventeen-year Locust. *See* Cicada.

Seventh-Day Adventists, Christian denomination whose members expect Christ to return to Earth in person. They also hold the Sabbath on Saturday, the seventh day, and accept the Bible literally as their guide for living. This church was formally organized in 1863. With a worldwide membership of 1,600,000, this is the largest Adventist denomination. *See also* Adventists.

Seven Weeks War. *See* Austro-Prussian War.

Seven Years' War (1756–63), a worldwide conflict growing from the competition between France and England for an overseas empire and between the house of Austria and the kingdom of Prussia for power in Germany. Austria, humiliated by the loss of Silesia to Prussia under the terms of the Treaty of Aix-la-Chapelle (1748), worked toward Russian and French alliances under Prince Kaunitz. He brought about the Diplomatic Revolution, as this reversal of traditional alliances came to be known. He persuaded Louis XV to sign a defensive alliance with Austria (May 1956), and in the following month war broke out between France and England. Frederick II of Prussia, taking the initiative while his enemies were unprepared, invaded Saxony whose wealth he used to finance later campaigns. By January 1757, war was declared on Prussia by most of the German states in the name of the Holy Roman Empire. Austria and Russia signed an agreement to partition Prussia and were joined in alliances with France and Sweden. Frederick responded by invading Bohemia and besieging Prague. When defeated at Kolin (June 1757), he was forced to leave Bohemia. The Anglo-Prussian cause was further harmed by the French victory over the British at Hastenbeck (July 1757) and Russian victories in East Prussia. Frederick, surrounded, responded with military genius. He surprised the French and was victorious at Rossback (November 1757) and defeated the Russians at Zorndorf (August 1758). The English and Hanoverians also began to have more success when William Pitt was put in charge of foreign affairs and pursued the war vigorously on the continent and in the colonies. The tide turned against the Anglo-Prussians when the Russians and Austrians joined forces to defeat them at Kunersdorf (August 1759), and Daun took a Prussian army of 13,000 captive at Maxen (November 1759). The Russians burned Berlin (1760), and in spite of successes at Liegnitz and Jorgan, Prussian losses continued. Frederick lost his English subsidy with the fall of Pitt in 1761. He maintained a defensive position that year, husbanding resources, but was unable to save Schweidnitz from the Austrians or Kolberg from the Russians. He was saved from a critical position by the succession of his admirer Peter III in Russia (January 1762), who immediately made peace and restored all conquests. Sweden made peace the same year. Fighting alone, the Austrians were defeated at Burkersdorf (July 1762). During this same period, the Anglo-French conflict, called the French and Indian Wars in North America, was being decided in favor of the British. The French lost Louisburg in 1758, Quebec in 1759, and Montreal in 1760. In India, the competition between the English and French was decided by British victories at Plassey (1757) and at Pondicherry (1761). Initial French sea superiority was reversed by English naval commander Edward Hawke's victory in Quiberon Bay (1759). Spain's entry into the war in 1761 did little to help France. After long negotiations, the war-weary nations made peace. England, France, and Spain signed the Treaty of Paris (1763), out of which Great Britain emerged as the strongest colonial empire. Austria, Saxony, and Prussia concluded the Treaty of Hubertusburg (1763), restoring the prewar status quo. *See also* French and Indian Wars.

Severnaya Zemlya (Severnaja Zeml'a), archipelago in the Arctic Ocean, Russian SFSR, USSR, N of Taimyr Peninsula, separating Kara and Laptev seas. Main islands are Komsomolets, Pioner, Oktyabrskaya Revolyutsiya, Bolshevik. They were discovered 1913 by Boris Vilkitski. Area: 14,286sq mi (37,001sq km).

Severn River, river in NW Ontario, Canada; rises in Finger Lake area; flows NE through Severn Lake into Hudson Bay; site of Hudson Bay trading post; Fort Severn, at river's mouth, has been in operation since it was rebuilt 1759. Length: 610mi (982 km).

Severn River, one of Britain's chief rivers; rises on Mt Plynlimon, W Wales, flows NE to Shrewsbury, curves SE and then SW to empty into the Bristol Channel. Tributaries include the Vyrnwy, Teme, Stour, Wye, and Upper and Lower Avon rivers; crossed by the Severn Road Bridge. Length: 180mi (290km).

Severus, Lucius Septimius (AD 146–211), Roman emperor (AD 193–211), b. Africa. He was governor of Upper Pannonia. His cohorts murdered Didius Julianus, avenging the death of Pertinax. He defeated and killed Pescennius Niger (194), took Byzantium (196), repulsed Clodius Albinus (197), reoccupied Mesopotamia (198), and invaded Scotland (209). To achieve his military aims, he doubled taxation. He reconstructed the Praetorian Guard with frontier legionnaires. He erected the triple Arch of Septimius Severus and was Papinian's patron. He died in Britain, and Geta and Caracalla succeeded him. △1030.

Sevier, John (1745–1815), US military and political figure, b. New Market, Va. In the American Revolution he led the force that defeated the British at Kings Mountain, N.C. He also led settlers in their battles with the Cherokee Indians. In 1785–88 he was governor of the "State of Franklin," settlement in what is now E Tennessee. He served in the North Carolina senate, was governor of Tennessee (1796–1801; 1803–09), and was a congressman (1789–91; 1811–15).

Sévigné, Marie de Rabutin-Chantal, Marquise de (1626–96), French letter writer. △1172.

Seville (Sevilla), inland port city in SW Spain, on Guadalquivir River, 337mi (543km) SW of Madrid; capital of Sevilla prov. Occupied by Romans 2nd–5th centuries, it was taken by Moors 712; in 1248 Ferdinand III, king of Castile and Leon, conquered Seville; the city prospered in 16th–17th centuries due to trade monopoly between Spanish empire and the New World; prosperity declined in 18th century when powerful mercantile association was transferred to Cadiz (1720), and freedom to trade with America was given to other Spanish ports. It is the site of 15th-century cathedral containing tomb and library of Christopher Columbus and paintings by Goya and El Greco; Giralda tower 1189, crowned by Renaissance bel tower added in 16th century; 14th-century Alcazar Palace. Industries: agricultural machinery, shipbuilding, chemicals, textiles, shipping. Area: (prov.) 5,402sq mi (13,991sq km). Pop. (city) 548,072 (prov.) 1,434,900.

Sewage. *See* Sanitary Engineering; Solid-Waste Disposal. △1614, 1768.

Sewall, Samuel (1652–1730), merchant and magistrate in colonial Massachusetts, b. England. He was the only judge to admit he was in error in sentencing 19 to death for practicing witchcraft in Salem (1692) Considered one of the most distinguished colonia magistrates, Sewall is best-remembered for his diary covering the years 1674–77 and 1685–1729.

Seward, William H. (1801–72), US statesman, b Florida, N.Y. He was an influential senator in 1860 bu lost the Republican nomination for president tc Abraham Lincoln. During the Civil War, he served as Lincoln's secretary of state. After the war, he servec Andrew Johnson in the same capacity and in 1867 purchased Alaska, called at the time "Seward's Folly."

Sewellel, or mountain beaver, small, short-leggec rodent native to humid areas of W North America. No a beaver, it has gray to brown fur and is a burrowing plant-eater. Length: lft (.305m). Family Aplodontia.

Sewing Machine. △1820.

Sex Determination. The sex of an organism is deter mined through the combination of chromosomes There are two types of sex chromosomes, the X type and the Y type. All female eggs have one X chromo some. The sperm may either have the X or the Y. If the sperm that fertilizes the egg has an X chromosome the resulting zygote will be XX, or female. If the egg is fertilized with a Y carrying sperm, the zygote will be XY, or male. △416.

Sex Discrimination, unequal treatment because c sex. This usually involves denial of economic and sc cial opportunities. Efforts to eliminate such discrim nation include women's liberation movements women's political coalitions, consciousness raisin groups, and the establishment of various governmer tal committees on the status of women. The Equa Rights Amendment would prohibit discriminatio based on sex. *See also* Woman Suffrage; Women' Liberation. △896.

Sex Drive, need of an organism for sexual gratifica tion. In lower animals sex drive is primarily controlle by hormones, while in more complex organisms suc as humans psychological factors play a more dom nant role. *See also* Drive.

Sex Hormones, hormones produced mainly in th reproductive organs and controlling reproduction an the development of secondary sex characteristics *See also* Androgens; Estrogens. △790.

Sex Identity, concept of what it means to be male c female. Body structure and other biological facto such as hormones affect the behavior and thus th roles of men and women. But, as psychologists hav pointed out, many of the differences in behavior of th sexes are learned, particularly in childhood and ad lescence. Each culture calls for its boys and girls to ac and dress in a specific way. △782, 790–92.

Sextant, a navigational instrument to establish la tude by determining the angle between the horizo and the Sun or a star. It consists of an arc, marked in degrees, a movable arm with a mirror pivoted at the center, and a telescope mounted to the framework. The telescope is focused on the horizon and the arm moved until the mirror image of Sun or star is reflected in line with the telescope, so that it coincides with the horizon. The angle, which can be read on the arc, and the exact time of day (as registered by a chronometer) allow the latitude to be established by means of printed tables. △1656.

Sexual Reproduction, fusion of the nuclei of two cells. △456, 462, 700–06.

Seychelle Islands, independent republic in the Indian Ocean, 1,000mi (1,610km) off E coast of Africa. The group consists of approx. 85 islands; the largest is Mahe, location of the capital city Victoria. The population is mainly of African, European, Indian, and Chinese descent; and overwhelmingly Roman Catholic. The Seychelles were discovered by Vasco da Gama, 1502; and claimed by France 1756. The British took possesion 1794, and ruled until June 1976, when the Seychelles became an independent republic. The Seychelles became a member of the United Nations 1976. Industry is centered around the exportation of tea, coconuts, and cinnamon, and is heavily dependent on tourism.

PROFILE

Official name: Seychelles
Area: 107sq mi (172sq km)
Population: 54,000
Density: 504per sq mi (195per sq km)
Chief city: Victoria (capital)
Government: President
Language: English (official); Creole

Seymour, Edward, Duke of Somerset. *See* Somerset, Edward Seymour, Duke of.

Seymour, Jane (1509–37), queen of England, the daughter of Sir John Seymour and sister of Thomas Seymour. She was the third wife of Henry VIII, whom she married in 1536. She died in 1537 after the birth of her son, the future Edward VI.

Seymour, Thomas, Baron Seymour of Sudeley, (1508–49), English lord high admiral. He was the brother of Jane Seymour and Edward Seymour, Lord Protector Somerset, and the husband of Henry VIII's widow, Catherine Parr. His ambition to supplant his brother as guardian of Edward VI and his attempt to marry Princess Elizabeth led to his trial and execution for treason in 1549.

Seymouria. △566.

Seyss-Inquart, Artur von (1892–1946), Austrian Nazi leader. He was briefly (1938) chancellor of Austria and governor under the Germans. He signed a document on Mar. 13, 1938, declaring the union of Austria and Germany. As Reich Commissioner in the occupied Netherlands (1940–45), he sent Dutch Jews to slave-labor camps and death. He was later hanged as a war criminal (1946).

Seyth. *See* Ribbon Fish.

Sforza, Italian family that ruled Milan from 1450 to 1535. **Muzio Attendolo** (1369–1424), a *condottiere* (mercenary military leader), founded the family and took the name "Sforza." Thereafter the family's control of Milan was based upon military power. Their first duke of Milan was **Francesco** (1401–66), whose son **Galeazzo Maria** (1444–76) succeeded him and married Louis XI of France's sister-in-law. **Ludovico Sforza** (1451–1508) was driven from the duchy by Louis XII of France in 1499. His son **Francesco Maria** (1492–1535) was restored by Emperor Charles V as duke in 1522; but with Francesco Maria's death the duchy passed to Charles and the Hapsburgs.

Sforza, (Count) Carlo (1873–1952), Italian anti-fascist statesman and foreign minister, from a collateral branch of the Renaissance Sforzas. In protest against Benito Mussolini he was in voluntary exile from 1927–1943. After Mussolini's fall, he returned to Italy, a prominent anti-Fascist and anti-monarchist, to serve the government. He was minister of foreign affairs from 1947 to 1951.

Shad, saltwater food fish of the herring family that swims upriver to spawn. They are prized for their roe. Deep-bodied, they have a notch in the upper jaw for the tip of the lower. The American shad *(Alosa sapidissima)*, formerly only on the Atlantic coast, was introduced on the Pacific coast; the allice and twaite shad are European. Length: to 30in (76cm). Family Clupeidae.

Shadows. △1520.

Shaftesbury, Anthony Ashley Cooper, 1st Earl of (1621–83), English political figure. One of the proprietors of the colony of Carolina, he is chiefly remembered for his opposition to the crown and his friendship with philosopher John Locke. Shaftesbury achieved prominence during the Civil War and Commonwealth as a general and a member of the Council of State. He supported the Restoration (1660), becoming chancellor of the exchequer (1661), and lord chancellor (1672). A leader of the Whigs, he always remained a champion of Parliament, a role that brought him into conflict with the king. He was instrumental in the passage of the Habeas Corpus Act (1679) and supported the duke of Monmouth's claim to the throne.

Shaggy Ink. △428.

Shah Alam. △1202.

Shah Jahan. △1204.

Shahn, Ben (1898–1969), US painter, b. Lithuania. Painting in a colorful and realistic style, he concentrated on social and political subjects.

Shaker Heights, city in N Ohio, 8mi (13km) E of Cleveland. A Shaker community 1822–89, its membership dwindled and settlement was abandoned; land was bought by developers for residential purposes; site of Shaker Museum. Inc. as village 1912, as city 1931. Pop. (1970) 36,306.

Shakers, religious organization, also known as the United Society of Believers in Christ's Second Appearing, or The Millennial Church. In a state of spiritual excitement, their bodies shake. It developed in England from 1747. Numerous US communities were founded from 1776, but by the 1970s few Shakers were still in existence. With a communistic form, the Shakers stress separation from the world. Shakers stress separation of the sexes and complete celibacy.

Shakespeare, William (1564–1616), English playwright and poet. Considered by many to be the greatest playwright of all time, he is the most frequently quoted individual writer in the world. His plays have been presented continuously since their writing. He arrived in London sometime around 1590, when his first plays, the three parts of Henry VI, were written. In 1594 he joined the Lord Chamberlain's (later, King's) Men as an actor and playwright. In 1599 he became a partner in the Globe Theatre; in 1608 of the Blackfriars Theatre. He retired to his birthplace, Stratford-on-Avon, in 1613. His poetry includes the heroic poems *Venus and Adonis* (1593) and *The Rape of Lucrece* (1594), the love poem *The Phoenix and the Turtle* (1601), and the 154 *Sonnets*, first published 1609.

Following is a list of Shakespeare's plays, with the dates of first performances.

Henry VI (Part II	1590
Henry VI (Part III)	1590
Henry VI (Part I)	1590
Titus Andronicus	1593
Richard III	*c.* 1594
The Comedy of Errors	1594
The Taming of the Shrew	*c.* 1594
Love's Labour's Lost	1594
The Two Gentlemen of Verona	1594–95
Richard II	*c.* 1595
A Midsummer Night's Dream	*c.* 1595
Romeo and Juliet	*c.* 1596
King John	1596
The Merchant of Venice	1596
Henry IV (Part I)	1597
Henry IV (Part II)	1597
The Merry Wives of Windsor	*c.* 1597
Much Ado About Nothing	*c.* 1598
Henry V	1598
Julius Caesar	1599
As You Like It	1599
Twelfth Night	1599
Hamlet	1600
Troilus and Cressida	1601
All's Well That Ends Well	1602
Measure for Measure	1604
Othello	1604
King Lear	1605
Macbeth	1605
Antony and Cleopatra	1606
Coriolanus	1607
Timon of Athens	1607
Pericles	*c.* 1607
Cymbeline	1609
The Winter's Tale	1610
The Tempest	1611

William H. Seward

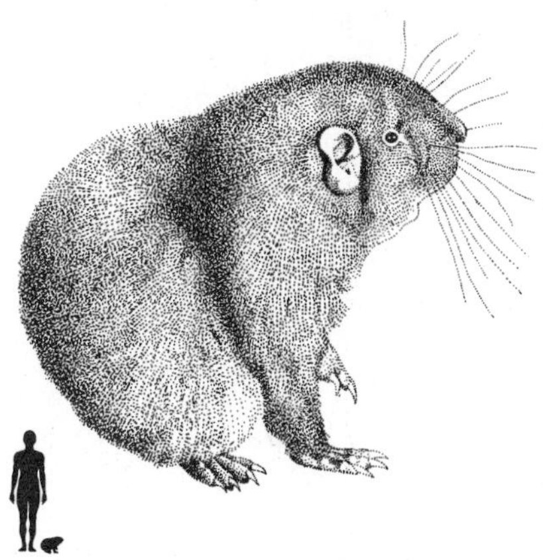
Sewellel

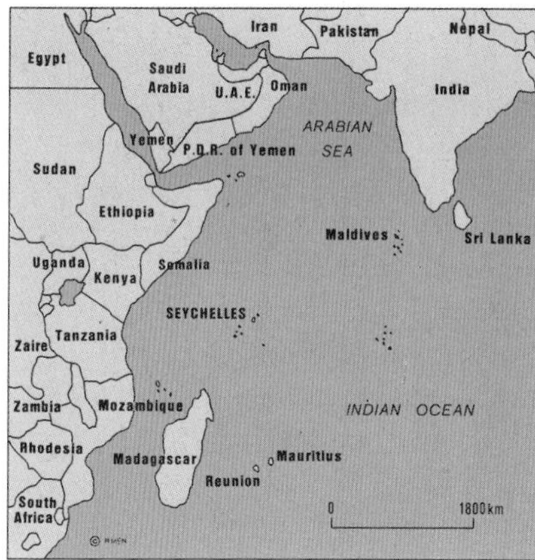
Egypt
Iran
Pakistan
Nepal
Saudi Arabia
U.A.E.
Oman
India
ARABIAN SEA
Yemen
P.D.R. of Yemen
Sudan
Ethiopia
Maldives
Sri Lanka
Uganda
Kenya
Somalia
SEYCHELLES
Zaire
Tanzania
Zambia
Mozambique
INDIAN OCEAN
Rhodesia
Madagascar
Mauritius
Reunion
South Africa
0
1800km
Seychelle Islands

Shad

Henry VIII 1612
Two Noble Kinsmen *c.* 1613
See also individual plays. △1148.

Shalbatana Vallis. △70.

Shale, is a sedimentary rock made from mud or clay. Shales are quite common, comprising over half the world's sedimentary rock, and may contain different materials such as fossils, alumina, carbonaceous matter, and oil. *See also* Sedimentary Rocks. △246, 272.

Shaman, or medicine man, person with magical powers and ability to communicate with the dead and spirits through trances and rituals. By controlling spirits, Shamans ward off evil, heal, and tell the future. *See also* Animism; Sorcery. △842.

Shamba Bolongongo. △1214.

Shamrock, plant with three-part leaves, usually *Trifolium repens* or *T. dubium*, grown for forage. Other plants also called shamrock include *Oxalis acetosella* and *Medicago lupulina*.

Shandong. *See* Shantung.

Shang Dynasty (1766–1122 BC), Chinese dynasty, the earliest dynasty for which accurate records exist. The Shangs, who ruled in the Yellow River Valley, willed to China its complex and sophisticated written language, techniques of flood control and irrigation, and a high level of artistry in bronze works. It eventually grew weak and was overthrown by the Chou Dynasty. △968.

Shanghai (Shang-hai), seaport city in E China, on Hwangpu River, 13mi (21km) from Yangtze delta; largest city in China, most populous in mainland Asia, and a leading world port. City was made a treaty port 1843 and opened to foreign trade; this spurred tremendous economic growth and created concessions held by United States, Great Britain, France, and Japan. By the end of WWII, the entire city was under Chinese control; fell to Communists 1949; industrial, commercial, educational, transportation center. Industries: textiles, steel, chemicals, publishing, food processing, rubber products, farm machinery, shipbuilding, pharmaceuticals. Pop. 11,000,000.

Shannon River, river in Republic of Ireland; rises on Cuilcagh Mt in Cavan and flows S through Loughs Allen, Ree, and Derg to Limerick, then W into Atlantic between Loop Head to N and Kerry Head to S. Length: 230mi (370km).

Shansi (Shanxi), province in NE China; bounded by Yellow River (W and S), Great Wall (N), North China Plain (E); capital is Taiyuan. Ruled 1911–49 by Yen Hsishan, it was occupied by Japanese (1937–45) during Sino-Japanese War; site of Buddhist caves dating from Northern Wei dynasty (386–535). Industries: coal and iron mining, salt, fertilizer, chemicals, machinery, cement, locomotives, lumber, livestock, cotton, grapes, tobacco, grains. Area: approx. 60,656sq mi (157,099sq km). Pop. 18,000,000.

Shantou. *See* Swatow.

Shantung (Shandong), province in NE China; bounded by Hopeh and Honan provs. (W), Honan and Kiangsu provs. (S); the E is a peninsula between the Potlai Gulf (N) and Yellow Sea (E and S); capital is Chi-nan. Strategically located near Manchuria, it was held by Germany 1898–1914, Japan 1919–22, Great Britain 1898–1930; during the Sino-Japanese War, Japan occupied the entire province (1937–45); it was under Communist control 1948; traditional birthplace of Confucius and Mencius; site of China's most sacred Buddhist and Taoist mountain peak, Tai Shan. Industries: agriculture, forest products, fishing, salt. Area: 59,189sq mi (153,299sq km). Pop. 57,000,000.

Shanxi. *See* Shansi.

Shaper, a machine for cutting metal. △1606.

Shaping, in psychology, a procedure used to teach an organism a behavior it would not normally perform; a form of operant conditioning. Approximations to the desired behavior are gradually encouraged by rewards until the organism performs the final behavior; eg, a dog is taught to roll over by first rewarding it when it lies down, then when it also gets up, and finally rewarding only the entire sequence of behaviors when it occurs on command. *See also* Operant Conditioning.

Shapu. △608.

Sharecroppers, type of US tenant farmers. In return for their labor and one-half of their crop they are provided with land, seed, stock, tools, and living facilities. After the Civil War, many former slaves became sharecroppers in the South. △306.

Sharett, Moshe (1894–1965), Israeli political leader, b. Russia. Born Moshe Shertok, he emigrated to Palestine (1906) and he was a member of the Jewish Agency (1933), which represented the Palestinian Jews under the British mandate. He became the agency's political secretary and argued for a Jewish national home before the British government and the United Nations. With the creation of Israel, he became foreign minister (1948–53). He was prime minister of Israel (1954–55).

Sharia. *See* Islamic Law.

Sharks, torpedo-shaped elasmobranch found in subpolar to tropical marine waters. They have well-developed jaws; bony teeth; cartilaginous skeleton; skin denticles; 5–7 gill slits on each side of the head; and a characteristic lobe-shaped tail with longer top lobe. Pit organs are used to detect hydrostatic pressure, sound, chemical composition of water, and possibly the presence of blood. Sharks are carnivorous; at least 10 species are known to attack man. Fertilization is internal, and young are born alive. A few species lay leathery eggs. Sharks first appeared about 240–350,000,000 years ago. There are about 250 living species. Order Selachii. *See also* Chondrichthyes; Dogfish; Hammerhead Shark; Nurse Shark; Tiger Shark; Whale Shark; White Shark. △510, 626.

Sharksucker. *See* Remora.

Sharm al-Sheikh (Sharm ash Shaykh), promontory at S end of Sinai Peninsula, overlooking Strait of Tiran. Captured by Israel from Egypt during 1967 Arab-Israeli War, it has since been surrendered by Israel as result of 1973 war and United Nations negotiations in 1974.

Sharon, Plain of (Plain of Saron), fertile coastal plain in W Israel, extending from Caesarea to Tel-Aviv Jaffa. Area: 500sq mi (1,295sq km).

Sharpsburg, Battle of (Sept. 16–17, 1862), Civil War engagement that ended Confederate Gen. Robert E. Lee's Maryland campaign. More than 24,000 casualties made this the bloodiest day of the war.

Sharp-shinned Hawk, small North American hawk, perhaps the smallest, with short rounded wings and a long tail. Species *Accipiter velox*. *See also* Hawk.

Shatt-al-Arab, channel in SE Iraq, formed by confluence of Tigris and Euphrates rivers; flows SE to Persian Gulf through wide delta containing extensive date palm groves. Navigable for ocean-going vessels as far as Basra, it forms part of Iran-Iraq border. Length: 120mi (193km).

Shaw, George Bernard (1856–1950), renowned English dramatist, essayist, critic, and Fabian socialist, b. Ireland. Influenced by Ibsen, Shaw wrote 50 plays, witty, eloquent, with lengthy prologues, and explicit stage directions, including: *Candida* (1893), *Caesar and Cleopatra* (1900), *Man and Superman* (1903), *Major Barbara* (1905), *Androcles and the Lion* (1912), *Pygmalion* (1912), *Heartbreak House* (1917), *Back to Methuselah* (1921), and *Saint Joan* (1923). He received the Nobel Prize for literature (1925). His complete works, in 30 volumes, were published in 1932.

Shaw, Wilbur (1902–54), US automobile racer, b. Shelbyville, Ind. He was a three-time winner of the Indianapolis 500 (1937, 1939–40) and a two-time winner of the US Automobile Club championship (1937, 1939). He was president of the Indianapolis Speedway from 1945 until his death.

Shawn, Ted (1891–1972), US modern dancer, b. Edwin Meyers Shawn in Kansas City, Mo. Often called the father of American dance, he founded and taught at Denishawn (1915–31) with his wife, Ruth St. Denis. He formed the first all male dance company (1933–40) and founded the Jacob's Pillow Dance Festival (1941), Lee, Mass. △1430.

Shawnee, city in central Oklahoma, on North Canadian River; seat of Pottawatomie co; site of Oklahoma Baptist University (1906) and St Gregory's College (1915). Industries: farming, dairying, oil. Inc. 1894. Pop. (1970) 25,075.

Shawnee, a major Algonquian-speaking tribe of North American Indians who have moved around the United States more than any other tribe. Their early home is recorded as along the Cumberland River in Tennessee, but today most of the 3,000 live in Oklahoma. This includes many Delaware, who are closely related to them. Two famous Shawnee people were Tecumseh and his brother Tenskwatawa, the Shawnee prophet.

Shaxi. *See* Shensi.

Shays Rebellion (1786–87), protest by debt-ridden farmers in western Massachusetts when the legislature adjourned before taking action to halt many farm foreclosures. Daniel Shays, a destitute farmer, led 1,200 insurgents against the state supreme court, sitting in Springfield. Several marches by the rebels were repulsed by government troops, although eventually tax laws were enacted to help the poor.

Shear, or shear stress, a force tending to cause deformation of a material by slipping along a plane parallel to the imposed stress. In nature, the resulting shear is related to the downslope of Earth materials as well as to earthquakes.

Shearing. △376.

Shearwater. *See* Fulmar.

Sheathbill, strong-flying, shore-loving white bird of Antarctica. Pigeon-sized, with short, horny, sheathed bill; spurred, long, wings; and short legs, they feed on seaweed and small crustaceans. Dark-blotched white eggs (2–3) are laid in a rock-or-burrow-sheltered nest. Genus: *Chionis*.

Sheboygan, city and port of entry in E Wisconsin, on Lake Michigan at mouth of Sheboygan River; seat of Sheboygan co; site of North West Co. trading post (1795). Sheboygan Indian Mound Park contains burial mounds dating from 500–750 AD. Industries: dairying, brewing, plastics, sausages, cheese, stainless steel, leather goods. Settled *c.* 1835; inc. 1846 as village, 1853 as city. Pop. (1970) 96,660.

Sheep, common name for eight ruminants of genera *Ovis, Pseudois*, and *Ammotragus*, closely related to goats. Wild species occur in mountains of Europe, Asia, Africa, and North America. One to three young are born after 5–6 months pregnancy. Males are called rams; females, ewes; young, lambs. Sheep were domesticated 7000 years ago in SW Asia. All domestic sheep are *Ovis aries;* no wild specimen survives. Common breeds of domestic sheep are of three types: fine wool, mutton, and fur (karakul). The long fur of wild types has disappeared from domestic breeds that retain only the woolly undercoat. The blue sheep, or bharal *(Pseudois nayaur)*, of W China is the only wild sheep that does not interbreed with domestic sheep. The N African aoudad *(Ammotragus lervia)* is the only wild sheep indigenous to that continent. The genus *Ovis* contains six wild species: bighorn and Dall sheep are North American; argali, Asiatic mouflon, laristan, and European mouflon are Old World species. Family Bovidae. *See also* Wool. △376.

Sheep Liver Fluke, parasitic flatworm that collects in liver bile passages of cattle and sheep. It develops in a host snail—the tailed cercaria escapes, encysts on grass, and is eaten by livestock. Length: 0.75in (19mm). Phylum Platyhelminthes; class Trematoda; species *Fasciola hepatica*. △472.

Sheep Ranching. △308, 370, 376.

Sheepshead, or sea bream, marine food and game fish found in tropical and temperate waters. Deep-bodied, it is greenish yellow with seven dark bars on each side. Length: 2.5ft (76.2cm); weight: 30lb (13.6kg). Family Sparidae; species *Archosargus probatocephalus*.

Sheep Tick, or sheep mite, sheep ked, reddish brown, wingless fly, that is a worldwide external parasite of sheep and goats. It is flat and leathery. Length: 0.25in. (6mm). Family Hippoboscidae; species *Melophagus ovinus*.

Sheffield, industrial city in N England, in South Yorkshire, at confluence of Don and Sheaf rivers. A leading industrial city famous for its special steels and their products, it has been noted since 14th century for manufacture of cutlery; first Bessemer steel plant was built here 1859; seat of University of Sheffield. Pop. 519,703.

Sheldon, William △814.

Shell, Atomic, any of the groupings of orbital electrons around the nucleus of an atom, named K, L, M, etc, outward, each containing a limited number of electrons of a particular energy. *See also* Atom.

Shellac, a purified resin made from the secretions of

the lac insect, *Laccifer lacca*. Shellac is fluid when heated and rigid at room temperature and is used in the production of adhesives, hair sprays, varnishes, and sealers.

Shelley, Mary Wollstonecraft (1797–1851), English novelist, daughter of William Godwin and Mary Wollstonecraft. She went abroad with Percy Bysshe Shelley in 1814, marrying him in 1816. Her works include *Frankenstein* (1818), *The Last Man* (1826), and *Lodore* (1835). *See also* Frankenstein.

Shelley, Percy Bysshe (1792–1822), English author. One of the greatest Romantic lyric poets, he visited Italy and Switzerland and associated with Byron, Keats, and William Godwin, whose daughter he married. His poetry included "Queen Mab" (1813), "Ozymandias" (1818), "Ode to the West Wind" (1819), *Prometheus Unbound* (1820), "Ode to a Skylark" (1820), and "Adonais" (1821). His prose includes *A Philosophical View of Reform* (1819) and *A Defence of Poetry* (1821). He died while sailing off the Italian coast. △1240.

Shellfish, common name for shelled mollusks and crustaceans used as food by man. Shelled mollusks include clams, oysters, and scallops; crustaceans include shrimp, lobsters, crabs, and crayfish. △394, 476–482, 486, 490.

Shells and Shell Collecting, shells, the limy protective cases secreted by various mollusks, have been important to man as tools, decorations, jewelry, and money (cowrie shells in Africa and Pacific islands and wampum of North American Indians). They also have had great economic value—*Murex* was used to make Royal Tyrian purple dye, the basis of Mediterranean trade 3000 years ago, and pearls produced by oysters are sold as precious jewels. Most collectible shells are produced by gastropods. The ideal shell is found alive and then properly cleaned. A famous shell collection is owned by Japan's Emperor Hirohito. The most expensive shell is Glory-of-the-Seas found in the SW Pacific; one of the rarest is Glory-of-India. △482.

Shelton, manufacturing city in SW Connecticut. Industries: hardware, textiles. Settled 1697; inc. 1915. Pop. (1970) 27,165.

Shem, in Genesis, eldest son of Noah. He received the first blessing of Noah after the Flood. He settled land between that of his brothers Ham and Japheth.

Shenandoah National Park, park in N Virginia. It encompasses the most outstanding portion of the Blue Ridge Mts, with Skyline Drive on the crest. There are vistas of historic Shenandoah Valley, hardwood forests, and wildflowers. Area: 193,536acres (78,382hectares). Est. 1926.

Shenandoah Valley, valley in N Virginia, between the Blue Ridge and Allegheny Mts, part of Great Appalachian Valley; scene of much activity during the Civil War; site of Shenandoah National Park and source of Shenandoah River. Explored early 18th century; settled *c.* 1730. Length: 150mi (242km).

Shensi (Shaxi), province in E central China, W of the T'ung-kuan Pass; capital is Sian. The province is divided into four geographical regions: (1) N is a plateau, used for agriculture, with rich coal deposits and some oil production; (2) S is Wei-ho valley, a very fertile and populated region, called "cradle of Chinese civilization;" (3) further S are the Chinling Mts, running E-W for 930mi (1,497km); (4) S of the mountains is Han River valley with mild climate. Province was scene of Muslim rebellion 1860s; seat of Chinese communists 1935–49. Area: 76,000sq mi (196,840sq km). Pop. 21,000,000.

Shepard, Alan Bartlett, Jr. (1923–), US astronaut, b. East Derry, N.H. A naval officer, he was the first American to be launched into space (1961), going 115 miles (185km) above the Earth. He participated in the Apollo 14 flight to the moon in 1971 and was the fifth man to walk on the moon. △142.

Shepherd Dog. *See* German Shepherd.

Shepherd's Clock. *See* Pimpernel.

Sheraton, Thomas (1751–1806), English furniture designer. His furniture style, which is known for its slim legs and simple outlines, had much influence on furniture design. His chair designs show the influence of curving ancient Greek chairs.

Sherbrooke, city in S Quebec, Canada, 93mi (150km) E of Montreal, at the confluence of Magog and St Francis rivers; seat of Sherbrooke co; site of Université de Sherbrooke, and St Peter's cathedral (1844). Industries: textiles, clothing, soft drinks, rubber products, machinery. Inc. 1852. Pop. 80,457.

Sheridan, Philip Henry (1831–88), Union Civil War general, later commanding general of the US Army, b. Albany, N.Y. Known as a fiery leader, he commanded an Army of the Potomac cavalry corps, winning two important victories in the Shenandoah Valley. He forced Confederate Gen. Robert E. Lee's surrender by cutting off his retreat at Appomattox, Va. (1865).

Sheridan, Richard Brinsley (1751–1816), English dramatist b. Dublin. A politician, actor, and partner (1776) in the Drury Lane Theatre, Sheridan excelled in comedies of manners, such as *The Rivals* (1775), *The School for Scandal* (1777), *The Critic* (1779). Sheridan abandoned the theater in 1780 and won fame for oratory as a Whig member of Parliament.

Sherlock Holmes, fictional private detective, a character in works by Arthur Conan Doyle. He first appears in *A Study in Scarlet* (1887). Holmes has many eccentricities and mannerisms, the chief of which are his dressing gown, hypodermic syringe, violin playing, and amazing deductive powers. Dr. Watson acts as his ponderous foil, and Professor Moriarty as a worthy villain-antagonist.

Sherman, John (1823–1900), US public official, b. Lancaster, Ohio. He entered politics as a Whig, but soon joined the new Republican party. He served as US representative (1855–61), senator (1861–77; 1881–97), secretary of the treasury (1877–81), and secretary of state (1897–98). As head of the Senate Finance Committee and then treasury secretary, he helped shape US fiscal policy.

Sherman, William Tecumseh (1820–91), US military officer, b. Lancaster, Ohio. A graduate (1840) of the US Military Academy at West Point, he became brigadier general of volunteers during the Civil War (1861). He took part in the battles of Bull Run, Shiloh, Corinth, and the capture of Vicksburg. His most noted exploit was his march eastward through Georgia, including the "march to the sea" from Atlanta to Savannah (1864). By the end of the war he was General Grant's most dependable general, and Sherman took over from Grant as general and commander of the army in 1869. He retired in 1884. His often-quoted remark "War is hell" was made in 1880. △1276.

Sherman, city in NE Texas, 60mi (97km) N of Dallas; seat of Grayson co; site of Austin College (1849). Industries: oil, food processing, livestock, agriculture, textiles, furniture, flour, electronic equipment, business forms. Settled 1849; inc. 1854 as town, 1895 as city. Pop. (1970) 29,061.

Sherman Anti-Trust Act (1890), US legislation to regulate trusts. It prohibited any industrial combination in restraint of trade or commerce. A critical weakness of the act was its obscure definitions of "trust," "combination," and "restraint," hence it was not vigorously enforced.

Sherman Silver Purchase Act (1890), legislation that obligated the US Treasury to buy the equivalent of the entire US silver production. The silver was to be paid for with treasury notes redeemable for gold or silver. The measure sought to increase the amount of currency in circulation and blunt the movement of free silver. It accomplished neither and because it depleted the gold reserves it was one of the causes of the Panic of 1893. The act was repealed in 1893.

Sherman Tank. △1736.

Sherrington, (Sir) Charles S(cott) (1861–1952), English physiologist. He was a pioneer in the study of how the nervous system works. His book *The Integrative Action of the Nervous System* (1906) helped establish physiological psychology. For his work he received a Nobel Prize in 1932.

Sherwood, Robert Emmett (1896–1955), US writer, b. New Rochelle, N.Y. He wrote comedies and socially significant dramas such as *Waterloo Bridge* (1930), *Reunion in Vienna* (1931), *The Petrified Forest* (1934), the Pulitzer Prize winner *Idiot's Delight* (1936), and *Abe Lincoln in Illinois* (1938). He was a political propagandist in World War II and worked as a speech writer for President Franklin D. Roosevelt. The memoir *Roosevelt and Hopkins* was published in 1948.

Shetland Islands, group of about 100 islands and islets NE of the Orkneys, about 130mi (209km) off N Scotland; administratively the county of Zetland. Main islands are Mainland, Yell, Unst; Lerwick is the chief town. Severe gales hamper agriculture, but Shetland

George Bernard Shaw

Sheathbill

Philip Sheridan

William Sherman

ponies, cattle, and sheep are raised. Patterned "Fair Isle" knitwear is a traditional product.

Shetland Pony, one of the smallest and oldest light horse breeds. Dating from the 6th century in the Shetland Islands of Scotland, it was introduced in the United States in the middle 1800s. A small, hardy horse, it was used for draft or road work and makes an ideal children's mount. It can be any horse color, broken or solid. Height: under 46in (116.8cm) at shoulder; weight: 350lb (158kg).

Shetland Sheepdog, miniature collie (working group) used as guard and farm dog; also called Sheltie. Probably bred from small collies, it has a long, blunted, wedge-shaped head; high-set, small ears held ¾ erect; a moderately long body; medium-length legs; and a long tail. The long, straight double coat is black, blue merle, or sable with white or tan marks; it is short and smooth on face, feet, and ears. Average size: 13–16in (33–41cm) high at shoulder; 15lb (7kg). *See also* Working Dog.

Shi'a, Muslim sect, including about 10% of the followers of Islam. Shiites differ with the majority sect, the Sunnis, about sources of authority in their faith. Sunnis find the source in the Sunna, the customary practice of Mohammed and his close followers. Shiites started as a political party. They find authority in the inspired leadership of a succession of imams starting with Ali, Mohammed's son-in-law. There are two main Shi'a subsects, the Imamis and the Isma'ilis. The largest Shi'a communities are found in Iran, Iraq, Arabia, and India. *See also* Islam.

Shield, a large, low-relief, exposed mass of Precambrian rock, commonly having a very gently convex surface and surrounded by belts of younger rock. Within shields are the Earth's most ancient rocks, more than 2 billion years old, now changed by metamorphism but originally composed of basaltic lava. Shields form the nucleus of continents. Such a region occupies two-thirds of Canada and is known as the Canadian Shield. △1098, 1726.

Shield Bug. △492, 500.

Shihkiachwang (Shijiazhuang, Shihchiachuang), city in China, 160mi (258km) SW of Peking; capital of Hopeh prov. Industries: textiles, fertilizer, pharmaceuticals, iron, steel, machinery, food processing, paper. Pop. 1,500,000.

Shih-Huang-ti (259–210 BC), the first emperor of the Ch'in Dynasty in China (221–207 BC). He centralized rule in ancient China by conquering six feudal states and replacing the feudal system of the Chou Dynasty while king of the northwestern state of Ch'in (246–221 BC). He drove back the Hsiung-Nu and began the Great Wall to keep out nomad tribes. To ensure unity in the new empire he imposed the Ch'in code of law, standardized weights and measures, and created an intelligible written language by standardizing Chinese script. To suppress diversity in customs and thought, he ordered the burning of all but practical books in 212. Defying the decree, 460 scholars were killed. The Shih's son was murdered in retribution for his tyranny, and the Han Dynasty was established in 202. △1038.

Shih Tzu, dog (toy group) bred in imperial court of China as pet of nobility; first brought West about 1930. Name means "lion." It has a broad, round head; square, short muzzle with long moustaches; dark, large eyes; long, drooping ears; long, broad-chested body; short muscular legs; and tail carried curved up over the back. The long, luxurious coat is slightly wavy and may be any color. Average size: 9–10.5in (23–25.4cm) high at shoulder; 12–15lb (5.4–7kg). *See also* Toy Dog.

Shiites. *See* Shi'a.

Shijiazhuang. *See* Shihkiachwang.

Shikoku, smallest of the four main islands of Japan, S of Honshu and E of Kyushu; mostly settled along coast; interior is mountainous and heavily forested. Industries: rice, tea, salt, lumber, fishing, tobacco, copper mining. Area: 7,245sq mi (18,765sq km). Pop. 3,904,014.

Shiloh, ruins of Biblical city in Jordan, on Mt Ephraim, 15mi (24km) W of Jordan River. Ark of the Covenant was kept here until captured by Philistines, and a tabernacle established; modern town called Khirbet Seilun.

Shiloh, Battle of (April 6–7, 1862), battle in the US Civil War, also called "Pittsburg Landing." In this Tennessee engagement Confederate Gen. Albert S. Johnston surprised Union Gen. Ulysses S. Grant's force. On the second day, Grant regained the lost ground and eventually won the battle. Casualties were high: 13,000 Union, 10,000 Confederate. △1276.

Shimonoseki, seaport in SW Honshu, Japan, across Shimonoseki Strait, W door to Inland Sea. A major industrial center and port, it is connected with Kitakyushu (Kyushu Island) by tunnels under the narrow strait; seat of daimyos 10th–19th centuries; scene of attack by European and US ships Sept. 5–8, 1864; treaty ending Sino-Japanese War was signed here 1895; bombed by United States during WWII. Industries: shipbuilding and repair, metal works, machinery, fish canning, textiles, tobacco. Pop. 258,425.

Shin Bone. *See* Tibia.

Shiner, small freshwater minnow often used for bait. Among the 100 species are the spottail *Notropis hudsonius*, the golden *Notemigonus crysoleucas*, and the sailfin *Notropis hypselopterus*. Family Cyprinidae.

Shingles, or herpes zoster, an acute viral infection of the skin and nerves. Groups of small blisters appear along segments of nerves, usually on the back, sometimes preceded by pain in the affected place. △724.

Shinto, the "Way of the Gods," native religion of Japan. It originated as a cult of nature-worship. Confucian and Buddhist influences shaped Shintoism from the 5th century until the 17th-century revival and codification of state Shinto. Shinto is polytheistic and concerned with ceremonial purity, believing that the emperor and the Japanese people are descended from the Gods. Today Shintos number over 60,000,-000. △842.

Ship. △1738, 1740.

Shipbuilding. △1680.

Shipping. △1678–80, 1760.

Shipworm, or teredo, pileworm, wood-boring, elongated clam that burrows with the edge of its tiny shell into ships and wood pilings. The viscera are contained in a wormlike siphon; a limy tube is secreted in burrowed tunnels. Length: 0.25in (6.4mm). Family Teredinidae; species include *Teredo navalis*. △478.

Shiraz, city in SW central Iran, approx. 200mi (322km) SE of Isfahan; capital of Fars prov. Active trade center from 10th century, city served as capital of Persia 1750–59; site of tombs of Hafiz and Sadi, Persian poets; pilgrimage center for Shiite Muslims; seat of Pahlavi University (1945). Nearby are the ruins of Persepolis; industrial and commercial center. Industries: textiles, cement, sugar, fertilizer, wine, carpets, metalworks, petrochemicals, handicrafts. Pop. 280,000.

Shire, earliest draft horse breed. It was developed in England during the 1700s and is a descendant of the Middle Ages' Great Horse. Also called Great Horse, War Horse, and Cart Horse, this heavy-boned horse has a sluggish temperament. Colors are bay, brown, or black with white markings. Height: 64–70in (163–178cm) at shoulder, weight; over 2,000lb (900kg).

Shiva, one of the three great Hindu gods, along with Brahma and Vishnu. A complex god, he represents both reproduction and destruction, although the combining of contradictory qualities is not uncommon in Hinduism. His name means "Auspicious One" in Sanskrit. In paintings and statues he often has three eyes (the third eye provides inward vision and outward destruction), coiled hair, and a serpent and a garland of skulls around his blue neck. In modern Hinduism, Shiva's cult is one of the most popular. △838, 1034.

Shizuoka, city in E Honshu, Japan, approx. 55mi (89km) SW of Tokyo; capital of Shizuoka prefecture; seat of Tokugawa shogunate, founded 1607 by Ieyasu; agricultural trade center for prefecture. Products: textiles, tea, oranges, metals, wood products. Pop. 416,378.

Shock, acute progressive circulatory failure, the result of the heart's inability to pump enough blood through the major organs. It may be caused by injury, burns, hemorrhage or major surgery, or poisoning. It is characterized by weakness, shallow breathing, rapid heartbeat, and low blood pressure. Treatment involves keeping the patient warm and giving oxygen and sedation. △758.

Shock Therapy, treatment in which transient comas or convulsions are induced by electrical, chemical, or other artificial means. Electroconvulsive therapy has been the most popular method. Other procedures include *insulin shock*, in which hypoglycemia and shock are induced by insulin injections, and *anoxic shock*, brought on by the inhalation of gases such as carbon dioxide or nitrogen. Shock therapy is used primarily to treat affective disorders. △770.

Shock Wave, in fluids, a region across which sharp discontinuities in pressure and density occur. Shock waves are brought about by supersonic velocities of a solid or fluid; since the surrounding fluid can propagate disturbances only at the local speed of sound, the moving body "piles up" the disturbances it is causing into a V-shaped "wake" attached to the body. The "sonic boom" of supersonic aircraft is simply the passage of this shock wave past the eardrum. △1496.

Shoebill, tall, strange-looking, storklike wading bird found in papyrus marshes of tropical E Africa. Also known as whale-headed stork, it has a swollen, shoe-shaped bill with a sharp hook; short neck, darkish plumage, and long black legs. It feeds at night on small animals, including lungfish, frogs, and turtles, and lays a single chalky white egg in a reed nest in tall vegetation. Height: to 54in (137cm). Species *Balaeniceps rex*. △618.

Shofar, ancient musical instrument, it is sounded in synagogues on Rosh Hashanah and Yom Kippur. Made from the curved horn of a ram, it produces tones one fifth apart. Joshua's trumpet at Jericho was a shofar.

Shogun ("Barbarian-quelling generalissimo"), military ruler of Japan (1192–1867), conferred upon Yoritomo in 1192, acknowledging him as the supreme military commander in Japan. The Minamoto (1192–1333), Ashikaga (1338–1568), and Tokugawa shogunates (1603–1867) provided the de facto rulers of feudal Japan. Although their authority was in theory purely military, the bakufu ("tent government") exercised control over all aspects of life. Originally based on a system of estates and a code, Japan's particular feudal system evolved, reaching its height during the Tokugawa period, when the combination of the influences of the daimyo (feudal lords) and Confucian ethics provided a stable central government ruling "in the name of the emperor." This period was one of the most active, creative, and prosperous in Japanese history because of its strong and stable government and economy. It ended with the Meiji Restoration. *See also* Ashikaga. △1210, 1272.

Sholokhov, Mikhail (1905–), Soviet novelist. His novels are frequently set in his native Don region and include the epic *The Silent Don* (1928–40); trans. as *And Quiet Flows the Don* and *The Don Flows Home to the Sea*, and the propagandistic *Virgin Soil Upturned* (1932–60). Several of his short stories are collected in *Tales of the Don* (1926). Awarded the Nobel Prize (1965).

Shorebird, birds that live close to water. Most nest in the Arctic and are migratory, making transoceanic trips to winter in warmer areas. They are strong and swift in flight, feeding on fish, shellfish, small worms, and insects, often using a long, specially adapted bill for capturing food. Included are the web-footed gull, tern, skua, jaegar, and skimmer. Others not having webbed feet include the plover, lapwing, sandpiper, snipe, woodcock, curlew, oyster catcher, stilt, sheathbill, auk, puffin, and guillemot. Order Charadriiformes. *See also* Separate entries.

Shorthorn, most widespread beef cattle breed. It is red, red and white, or roan. Developed in Durham, England, there are two types: strictly beef and dual-purpose, used also for milk. Some varieties are hornless or polled. *See also* Beef Cattle; Cattle.

Short Parliament (1640), English parliament ending 11 years of personal rule by Charles I. Its calling was occasioned by his need for money after defeat (1639) in the first of the Scottish Bishops' Wars. It was dissolved after three weeks when its members made redress of political grievances the condition for financial subsidy of the king.

Short Story, brief prose fictional narrative, established as a modern art form by the 19th-century US master Edgar Allan Poe. A short story deals with few characters; aims for unity of effect; often concentrates on mood rather than plot. Two 14th-century works, Geoffrey Chaucer's *Canterbury Tales* and Giovanni Boccaccio's *Decameron* greatly influenced its development. Famous short story writers include Guy de Maupassant, Anton Chekov, Nathaniel Hawthorne, Washington Irving, Bret Harte, and Ernest Hemingway.

Short-tailed Weasel. *See* Ermine.

Short Takeoff and Landing. *See* STOL Aircraft.

Short-Term Memory. *See* Memory.

Short Wave, electromagnetic wave that has a wavelength of less than 80 meters. When a short wave hits certain layers of the ionosphere it is bounced back toward Earth, where it can be picked up and bounced out again. Through repetition of this process a short wave can be transmitted long distances.

Shoshoni, a major Indian tribe, divided into two important subgroups, who have given their name to one of the most prominent American Indian language families; also known as Snake Indians. The total population today is perhaps 50,000 persons, living in Idaho, Wyoming, Nevada, and Utah.

Shostakovich, Dmitri (1906–1975), Soviet composer, b. St. Petersburg, Russia. He composed prolifically in every form and was perhaps the most important modern Russian-born composer after Stravinsky. His style is basically post-Romantic with emphasis on melody. His works include 15 symphonies, 13 string quartets, ballets, concertos, piano music, film music, and vocal works. His opera *Lady Macbeth of Mzensk* (1934) was condemned by the Soviet government but was later revised and accepted as *Katerina Ismailova* (1963). Shostakovitch was the Soviet Union's most honored composer, receiving a number of Lenin and Stalin prizes and the designation Hero of Socialist Labor. △1364.

Shoulder Blade. *See* Scapula.

Shoveler, widely distributed river duck that dabbles, or feeds from the water surface. The male engages in a complex courtship to attract a female. Species *Anas clypeata*. *See also* Duck.

Shreveport, city in NW Louisiana, on Red River; seat of Caddo parish. Founded 1835, it was made capital of Confederacy of Louisiana 1863; developed after the discovery of oil at Caddo Lake 1906. It is site of ruins of Confederate Fort Humbug, annual Louisiana State Fair, Centenary College (1825). Industries: cotton, oil, natural gas, clothing, food products, lumber, chemicals, printing, machinery. Inc. 1839 as town, 1871 as city. Pop. (1970) 182,064.

Shrew, tiny, mouselike insectivore. It is an active, voracious carnivore that eats more than three times its own weight daily. Some have poisonous saliva. The smallest of all mammals, some weigh only 1/15oz (2g). Family Soricidae. See also Insectivore. △546.

Shrewsbury, county town of Salop, W England, on Severn River; market town and rail and road junction; occupies strategic position on border with Wales; site of 11th-century castle, many half-timbered houses of 15th–17th centuries, a famous public school (1552). Industries: engineering, brewing, tanning. Pop. 56,-140.

Shrike, or butcherbird, small bird of prey found worldwide, except in South America and Australia. It dives at prey—insects, small birds, mice—hitting it with its strong hooked bill and then impaling it on a sharp fence post, twig, or thorn. Food is sometimes left impaled for later use. Most, including the North American northern shrike *(Lanius excubitor)* and loggerhead shrike *(Lanius ludovicianus),* are brown or gray above with darker markings on the head, wings, and tail. They lay spotted whitish eggs (3–6) in a bulky cup-shaped twig nest. Family Laniidae.

Shrimp, mostly marine, swimming decapod crustacean including true, sand, and pistol shrimps. Its compressed body has long antennae, stalked eyes, a beak-like prolongation, segmented abdomen with five pairs of swimming legs, and a terminal spine. Large edible shrimp are often called prawns. True prawns include European and American genera *Palaemon* and *Penais*. Length: 2–3in (5–7.6cm); some freshwater shrimp reach 2ft (61cm). *See also* Crustacean; Decapod. △490.

Shrivijaya. △1114.

Shrub, low, woody perennial plant of limited height. Instead of having a main stem, it branches at or slightly above ground level into several equally strong stems. Environment is often a determining factor: species that are shrubs in one climate may be trees in another. △450.

Shuara. *See* Jívaro.

Shute, Nevil (1899–1960), English novelist. His real name was Nevil Shute Norway. He wrote a number of novels whose exciting, fast-moving plots made them immensely popular. Among his books are *An Old Captivity* (1940), *No Highway* (1948), *A Town Like Alice* (1950), *The Far Country* (1952), and *On the Beach* (1957).

Shuvalov, Pëtr Andreevich, Count (1827–89), Russian police official who became head of the political police in 1866 and Alexander II's closest adviser. He was a powerful leader of the reactionary group that opposed liberal reform.

Sial. △166.

Siam, Gulf of, shallow inlet of South China Sea, in Thailand; separates Malay Peninsula from E Thailand, Cambodia, and S Vietnam. Chao Phraya and Tha Chin rivers enter at NW point; Bangkok is the gulf's chief port. Length: 500mi (805km). Width: 350mi (564km).

Siamese Cat, exotic short-haired domestic cat breed of disputed origin. An affectionate pet with a distinctive cry, it has a wedge-shaped head, blue almond-shaped eyes, large ears, long slim body, and long tapered tail. A small- to medium-sized cat, its albino to fawn-colored coat has darker colored points on ears, mask, feet, and tail. Recognized varieties in the United States are seal point, chocolate, blue, and lilac.

Siamese Twins, conjoined, identical twins sometimes sharing organs. Usually fusion is along the trunk or at the head. When both are normal, except for fusion, surgical separation is sometimes possible. When one member is normal, but the other underdeveloped, the weaker one is parasitic and is usually surgically removed.

Sian (Xi'an, or Hsi-an), city in N China, in Wei River Valley; capital of Shensi prov.; early center of Buddhism, Islam, Judaism, and Nestorian Christianity (7th-10th centuries); scene of the "Sian Incident" where Chiang Kai-shek was kidnapped and held until he agreed to form a united front with Communists against Japan (1936); site of Nestorian monument (781), pagodas dating from T'ang dynasty, and city wall constructed during Ming dynasty (1368–1644); seat of Northwestern University (1937), and Northwestern Institute of Technology (1960). Industries: agriculture, textiles, food processing, chemicals, cement, motor vehicles, iron, steel. Pop. 1,900,000.

Siangtan (Xiangtan or Hsiang-t'an), city in SE China, 20mi (32km) SW of Changsha, on Siang River; nearby is Shaoshan, birthplace of Mao-Tse-tung. Industries: food processing, machine tools, textiles, manganese ore, engineering, cement, trucks. Pop. 300,000.

Sibelius, Jean (1865–1957), Finnish composer. He promoted Finnish nationalism in such works as the popular orchestral piece *Finlandia* (1899). Among his best works are *The Swan of Tuonela* (1893), a violin concerto (1903), the *Valse Triste* (1903), and seven symphonies. △1364.

Siberia (Sibir'), vast region in NE Asia, in the USSR, comprising most of the Asiatic part of Russian SFSR, extending from the Ural Mts. to the Pacific Ocean, and from the Arctic Ocean to Kazakhstan and the S border with China and Mongolia. The Tartar Khanate of Siberia was conquered by Russian Cossacks 1581–98; in 1644 Russians reached the Amur River region, but abandoned it to Chinese; it was ceded to Russia 1860; anti-Bolshevik activities led by Admiral Kolchak promoted invasion by Bolsheviks, who made it part of Russian SFSR (1919) and re-established Bolshevik rule; site of large-scale colonization since WWII. Main cities are Novosibirsk, Omsk, Krasnoyarsk, Novokuznetsk, Irkutsk, Barnaul, Kemerovo, Tomsk, Ulan-Ude, Chita. Industries: coal, iron ore, manganese, gold, copper, lead, zinc, tungsten, oil, grains, lumbering, fishing. Area: 5,330,896sq mi (13,807,021sq km). Pop. 35,605,000.

Siberian Husky, endurance sled dog (working group) bred by Chukchi people of northeastern Asia; brought to Alaska in 1910. A gentle, friendly dog, it has a medium-sized, slightly rounded head with medium-length tapered muzzle; high-set, erect, triangular ears; almond-shaped blue, brown, or one of each color, eyes; strong-chested body with lean loin; moderately long legs; and fox brush tail carried in sickle curve. The medium-length double coat is straight and smooth; color ranges from black to white with characteristic head markings. Average size: 21–23.5in (53–60cm) high at shoulder; 40–60lb (18–27kg). *See also* Working Dog.

Shoebill

Dmitri Shostakovich

Siamese cat

Siberian Husky

Sibyl, prophetess in Greek legend and scripture. A famous collection of Sibylline prophecies, the Sibylline Books, were bought by Tarquinius Superbus, the last of the seven kings of Rome, from the Cumaean Sibyl. The books were kept in the temple of Jupiter on the Capitoline Hill.

Sichuan. *See* Szechwan.

Sicilia. *See* Sicily.

Sicilian Vespers (1282), massacre of the French, which began the Sicilian revolt against the Angevin King Charles I of Naples-Sicily. The massacre of 2,000 French began at vespers on Easter Monday at Palermo in response to oppressive French policies and with Peter III of Aragon's support. In the ensuing war the French Angevins fought with the papacy and the Italian Guelphs; the Italian Ghibellines supported the Aragonese.

Sicily, island of Italy in the Mediterranean Sea at the toe of the Italian boot. With nearby islands it forms an autonomous region of Italy. The largest island in the Mediterranean Sea, it has an area of 9,927sq mi (25,711sq km). Once part of the mainland, it is separated from Italy by the narrow Straits of Messina. Mostly mountainous, it has three active volcanoes, Vulcano, 1,637ft (499m), Stromboli, 3,038ft (911m), and Mt Etna, 10,705ft (3,265m). Fertile valleys cover the central plateau. The E coast is famous for its beauty and tourism; the shore is a flat, sandy plain, the least productive portion of the island. Fishing and small farms provide the major occupations in an essentially poor economy. The island's chief cities are Palermo (pop. 661,477), Catania (pop. 413,670), and Messina (pop. 273,526). Sicily was occupied by three peoples—Siculi, Sicani, and Elmyi—when the Greeks came before 413 BC. The modern population of Sicily is 4,867,650, one-third of which lives in the towns on the coast and the fertile slopes of Mt Etna. Most are Roman Catholics. Economic decline increased emigration, and between 1906–10 22% of all Italian emigrants came from Sicily, mostly to the United States.

History. Strategically situated between Europe and Africa, Sicily has frequently been a battlefield. Early settlers came from S Italy and were conquered by Greeks, who were defeated in 415 BC. Invasions by Phoenicia, Carthage, and Rome followed. In AD 535 Sicily became part of the Byzantine Empire. The Normans ruled the islands in the 2nd century until an uprising in 1282. Spain, Savoy, and Austria successively held power until the island passed to the Bourbon kings of Naples in 1738. In 1860, Guiseppe Garibaldi freed Sicily and it joined the newly united Italy (1861).

Sickle Cell Anemia, inheritance of an abnormal hemoglobin, occurring mainly in blacks. The hemoglobin is sensitive to a deficiency of oxygen, and red cells become rigid and sickle-shaped. When oxygen is supplied, the phenomenon is reversed. If anemia becomes chronic, there are bone and kidney changes.

Side-necked Turtle, freshwater turtle characterized by the ability to bend the neck sideways under the shell to hide its head. They are found only on southern continents. There are two families: hidden-necked turtles (Pelomedusidae) of Africa and South American and snake-necked turtles (Chelidae) of Australia and South America. Length: 6–32in (15–81cm). *See also* Matamata; Turtle.

Sidereal Period, time taken for a planet or satellite to complete one orbit around its primary with respect to the fixed stars. Earth's sidereal period is 365.25 days. The sidereal period of rotation of a planet is the interval between successive meridian transits of a given star or celestial point as seen from the planet.

Siderite, carbonate mineral, iron carbonate ($FeCO_3$), found in sedimentary iron ores and as vein deposits with other ores. Hexagonal system rhombohedral crystals or massive or granular. Pearly brown or white; hardness 3.5–4; sp gr 3.8. △92.

Sidewinder, or horned rattlesnake, nocturnal rattlesnake found in deserts of SW United States and Mexico. It has hornlike scales over the eyes and is usually tan with a light pattern. It loops obliquely across the sand, leaving a J-shaped trail. Length: to 30in (76cm). Family Viperidae; species *Crotalus cerastes*. *See also* Rattlesnake. △520.

Sidney, (Sir) Philip (1554–86), English poet and courtier. After leaving Oxford University, he traveled extensively in Europe as a diplomat (1572–75). His major works were *Arcadia*, a combination of pastoral verse and chivalric romance, and *Apologie for Poetry*. Both were published after his death. He died of wounds at the siege of Zutphen while fighting Spain in the Netherlands.

Sidon (Sayda), town in SW Lebanon, 22mi (35km) N of Tyre; site of oil pipeline terminus; most ancient city of Phoenicia, was an important port and trade center; glass-blowing invented here; destroyed in war several times. Industries: oil refineries, textiles, furniture; founded *c.* 2 BC. Pop. 40,000. △956.

Siege, the offensive military operation of surrounding a fortified position, cutting off its supplies, and undermining or destroying its defenses in order to capture it or induce it to surrender. △1732.

Siege Tower. △1018.

Siegfried Line, a system of fortifications built along Germany's western frontier before World War II. In 1944 it provided a brief respite for the retreating German army, preventing a US breakthrough until the spring of 1945.

Siemens-Martin process. *See* Open-Hearth Process. △1594.

Siena, city in central Italy, 33mi (53km) S of Florence; capital of Siena prov. A self-governing commune in 12th century, it was conquered by Charles of Anjou 1270; developed into important art center 13th-14th centuries; ravaged by Black Death 1348; known for its artistic treasures; site of 13th-century Palazzo Pubblico, 11th–14th-century cathedral, 14th-century chapel. Industries: tourism, wine, fertilizer, chemicals. Pop. 65,966.

Sienkiewicz, Henryk (1846–1916), Polish novelist and short-story writer. His war novels include the trilogy *Ogniem i Mieczem* (With Fire and Sword, 1884), *Potop* (The Deluge, 1886), and *Pan Michael* (1888), set in 17th-century Poland. He gained international recognition with *Quo Vadis?* (1896), a story of Nero's Rome. He was awarded the Nobel Prize for literature in 1905.

Sierra Leone, independent nation of West Africa, within the Commonwealth of Nations; bordered by Guinea (N and E), Liberia (S), Atlantic Ocean (W). Mountains in the NE, highest Loma Mansa 6,390ft (1,948m), slope down through a plateau region of savannah to the coastal plains of the SW. Along the coast mangrove swamps and lagoons are the main features. Numerous small rivers flow NE to SW into the Atlantic. The climate is hot throughout the year, and there is a marked seasonal difference in rainfall, with most falling in the summer months. Subsistence farmers produce maize and rice, while cocoa, coffee, palm kernels, and ginger are produced for export. The greatest source of foreign currency comes from the export of diamonds, iron, bauxite, and rutile. Industry refines products such as palm oil, rice, and lumber. The main tribes are the Mende, Temne, Limba, Kuranko, and Susu. Government is by an elected house of representatives, some of its members being hereditary chiefs. First discovered in the 15th century by Portuguese; became a British colony in 1787 when land was sold by local chiefs to the English who later made it a settlement for Africans rescued from slave ships. Independence was granted in 1961.

PROFILE

Official name: Republic of Sierra Leone.
Area: 27,693 sq mi (71,740sq km).
Population: 2,667,000.
Density: 96 per sq mi (37 per sq km).
Chief Cities: Freetown (capital), Bo, Kenema, Makeni.
Government: Head of state, president.
Religion: Animist, Muslim, Christian.
Language: English (official), Krio.
Gross national product: $490,000,000.
Trading partners (major): Great Britain, United States, Japan, Netherlands.

Sierra Madre, mountain range in SE Mexico; extends S into Guatemala; made up of Sierra Madre Occidental, Oriental, and del Sur. The Occidental stretches from N Mexican border to Rio de las Balsas valley; a transportation barrier, it is crossed by a single highway between Mazatlán and Durango. The Oriental extends from Coahuila state to the Isthmus of Tehuantepec. The del Sur extends parallel to the Pacific Ocean, from Guatemala to Rio de las Balsas valley; terrain ranges from hot tropical valleys to permanently snow-covered peaks. Industries: lumber, agriculture, hydroelectric power, silver, copper. Height: 6,000–12,000ft (1,830–3,660m).

Sierra Morena, mountain range in SW Spain, between Guadiana and Guadalquivir rivers, along S border of the Meseta (central plateau), from Portuguese border to the Sierra de Alcaraz. Despenaperros Pass is the main route through the mountains linking Andalusia and Castile. Length: 375mi (604km). Highest peak is Banuelo, approx. 4,339ft (1,323m).

Sierra Nevada, chief mountain range in S Spain, extends E to W in Granada and Almeria prov.; source of iron, lead, copper, zinc, mercury; S slopes are highly agriculturally developed. Contains highest peak in continental Spain, Mt Mulhacen, 11,408ft (3,479m). Length: 60mi (97km).

Sierra Nevada Mountains, mountain system in E California, runs parallel to Coast Ranges; site of Donner Pass, made famous during California Gold Rush of mid-19th century; source of many rivers which are used to irrigate and supply hydroelectricity to surrounding area; famous for their magnificent scenery and popular resort region; contains Yosemite, Sequoia, and Kings Canyon National Parks; culminates at Mt Whitney, 14,494ft (4,421m). Length: 400mi (644km).

Sieyès, Emmanuel Joseph (1748–1836), French political figure. A priest, in his influential pamphlet "What Is the Third Estate?" (1789) he argued that only the Third Estate of the States General truly represented the French nation. His accomplishment in the French Revolution was, he said, that he "remained alive." As a member of the Directory, he conspired to bring Napoleon to power.

Sigismund (1368–1437), Holy Roman emperor (1411–37) and king of Germany (1410–37), Hungary (1387–1437), and Bohemia (1419–37). Crowned king of Hungary in 1387, he was plagued from the outset with much foreign, domestic, and dynastic opposition, suffering a tremendous defeat by the Turks at Nikopol in 1396. Because, as emperor, he was implicated in the execution of John Huss (1415), the Czechs rose against him when he inherited Bohemia in 1419, resulting in 17 years of fighting. He was also active in attempting to end schisms in the Roman Catholic Church.

Sigismund I (1467–1548), king of Poland (1506–48), grand duke of Lithuania (1505–48). During his reign, Polish domains were expanded, he fought successful wars against Russia, and concluded a war with the Teutonic Order in 1525. He also aided the Hungarians against the Turks at the Battle of Mohács in 1526 and at the seige of Vienna in 1529. Lutheranism was introduced in Poland at this time and the diet passed laws initiating serfdom in Poland (1511).

Sigismund II Augustus (1520–72), last of the Jagellon kings of Poland (1548–72), son of Sigismund I, united Lithuania and Ukraine with Poland. Struggles with the nobility and the spread of Protestantism characterized his reign. Married to an Italian princess, he held a brilliant court at Cracow where Renaissance art and poetry flourished.

Sigismund III or **Sigismund Vasa** (1566–1632), son of John III of Sweden, elected king of Poland (1587), king of Sweden (1592–1604). An unstatesmanlike ruler, he fought numerous wars with Sweden to win its throne and intervened in Russia during the Time of Troubles. For his attempts to convert Russia to Catholicism, all Poles were expelled from Moscow. He joined the Holy Roman emperor at the outbreak of the Thirty Years' War.

Sigma Particle. *See* Hyperon.

Signorelli, Luca (*c.*1441–1523), Italian painter. An artist of the Umbrian school and pupil of Piero della Francesca, he was influenced by the sculptural quality of his teacher's figures.

Sigurd, also called Siegfried. A hero of ancient Germanic literature, he was known for his strength and courage. He appears in many stories, most notably, the story of Brunhild.

Sihanouk, Norodom (1922–), Cambodian political figure; king (1941–55); prime minister (1955–60); head of state (1960–70, 1975–76). △1378.

Sikhism, Indian religion that came into being in the 16th and 17th centuries. Combining Hindu and Muslim teachings, Sikh scripture, the *Adi Granth,* stressed the need for a guru's guidance in seeking the One Lord. Sikh means "disciple." Begun by Nanak as a passive way of life, Sikhism later became an activist faith. Today there are some 6,000,000 Sikhs, mainly in the Punjab.

Sikh Wars (1845–46, 1848–49), military conflicts between the Sikhs and the British in India. Overrun by the Moguls, the Sikhs fled to the mountains but returned to form a powerful state at Lahore with Ranjit Singh (1780–1839) as maharaja. By 1824 they controlled most of northern India. The British took Lahore in the first Sikh War, and the Sikhs were completely defeated in the second one.

Sikkim, a tiny, associate state of India in the high Himalayas. Its climate ranges from subtropical to arctic. Known for its Buddhist monasteries, Sikkim's economy is still primitive.

Land and economy. Located in the main chain of the Himalayas, it has perpetual snow above 17,000ft (5,185m). Between 12,000–15,000ft (3,660–4,575m) there are plateaus and summer grazing for cattle. Forests are found from 9,000–12,000ft (2,745–3,660m) and crops such as maize and millet are grown from 4,000–6,000ft (1,220–1,830m). Rice is grown on the lower level. The highest peak is Kanchenjunga, 28,208ft (8,603m). The only town is its capital, Gangtok, and the main river is the Tista. Woolen cloth and cotton are produced by home industry, and there is some primitive copper mining. Monsoons from the Bay of Bengal bring an average annual rainfall of 137in (348cm) in the capital. The area is 2,745sq mi (7,110sq km); the population is 193,020.

People. Sikkim's people are mainly Nepalese with Bhotias, herders in the high altitudes, and Lepchas, pastoral people who were the earliest inhabitants. Buddhism is the state religion. Most of the Nepalese are Hindu. Tibeto-Burmese dialects are the main tongues.

Government. Under a constitution passed by India's parliament, Sikkim is governed by a chief minister appointed by India and a five-member council of ministries. The kingdom's former ruler is the titular head.

History. Sikkim's ruling family claimed it was descended from E Tibetan princes who came to Lhasa in 1641, defeated the Lepchas, and established Buddhist Lamaism as the state religion. British influence started in 1816 when they ousted invading Nepalese Gurkhas, and Sikkim became a British protectorate. When India won independence in 1947, British control over Sikkim declined. In 1950 independent Sikkim became an Indian protectorate. In 1974 it became an associate state of India.

Sikorsky, Igor Ivan (1889–1972), US aeronautical engineer and designer, b. Russia. His first aircraft was a helicopter, which he built in 1909, and he pioneered the multimotored plane (1913). Immigrating to the United States after the Bolshevik Revolution (1917), he established (1923) the Sikorsky Aero Engineering Corporation. Later there were other companies founded by Sikorsky, and a merger with United Aircraft Corporation. Specializing in helicopters, he designed amphibian planes that were used in World War II. He received the National Medal of Science (1967).

Silas, in the New Testament, the man who replaced Barnabas as St Paul's companion in his missionary labors. After considerable travel, he was left with Timothy at Beroea, only to rejoin Paul at Corinth. It is held that he was both Jewish by birth and, like St Paul, a Roman citizen.

Silenus, in Greek mythology, a companion of Dionysus. He was a perpetually drunk, fat old man who followed the god while swaying awkwardly on the back of a donkey. Nevertheless, he was more than tolerated for he knew the past and could fortell the future and had given Dionysus much of his wisdom. King Midas' golden touch was a reward for his considerate care of Silenus after one of the deity's drunken bouts.

Silesia, former province of Czechoslovakia, formed in 1919 from a portion of Austria-Hungary and Upper Silesia. It is also a former Prussian province and is now mostly Polish. In 1927, it was united with Moravia, and by the terms of the Munich Pact of 1938 it was ceded to Germany. At the end of WWII, it returned to Czechoslovakia and in 1960 was made part of the region of Severomoravsky (North Moravia). △1074, 1182.

Silica, silicon dioxide, a compound of silicon and oxygen (SiO_2). Silica is the main constituent of 95% of the Earth's crust. It has three main crystalline varieties: quartz, tridymite, and cristabolite. Silica sand (in the form of portland cement) is used in buildings and roads. It is also used for grinding and polishing glass and stone and in the manufacture of glass, ceramics, and silicone. It is a refractory material and is frequently of gemstone quality.

Silicon, common nonmetallic element (symbol Si) of group IVA of the periodic table, discovered by J.J. Berzelius (1824). It is the second most abundant element in the Earth's crust (25.7% by weight), a common constituent of rocks and minerals. The element is extensively used in transistors and similar devices. Two allotropes exist: a brown amorphous form and a gray crystalline variety. Properties: at. no. 14; at. wt. 28.086; sp gr 2.33 at 25°C; melt. pt. 2570°F (1410°C); boil. pt. 4271°F (2355°C); most common isotope Si^{28} (92.21%). *See also* Silicone. △1506, 1558, 1560.

Silicone, any of a group of polymers lacking carbon. Atoms of silicon and hydrogen alternate in a polysiloxane chain. Silicone is manufactured as a liquid, a resin, or an elastomer and resists decomposition by heat, water, or oxidizing agents. It is used as a liquid to waterproof textiles and paper; as a resin in protective coatings and for laminating glass cloth; and as a elastomer in electrical insulation. △1560, 1600, 1618.

Silicosis, chronic occupational lung disease, caused by prolonged inhalation of silica dust. It affects people employed in such occupations as mining, metal grinding. No treatment exists, but prevention is possible by reducing the amount of dust inhaled.

Silk Moth. △492.

Silk-screen Printing. *See* Serigraphy.

Silkworm, moth caterpillar that feeds chiefly on mulberry leaves. The common domesticated *Bombyx mori* is raised commercially for its silk cocoon. The creamy white caterpillar spins its cocoon from a silk fiber secreted by glands in its body. Length: 3in (7.6cm). Family Bombycidae. △492.

Silky Terrier, small Australian dog (toy group) also called Sidney Silky; bred from Australian and Yorkshire terriers. It has a wedge-shaped head; small, V-shaped, prick ears; long, low-set body; straight, fine-boned legs; and docked tail carried up. The flat, silky, fine coat is 5–6in (12.5–15cm) long and parted from head to tail; there is a topknot on the head. Colors are blue and tan. Average size: 9–10in (23–25.4cm) high at shoulder; 8–10lb (3.6–4.5kg). *See also* Toy Dog.

Sill, sheet-like intrusion of igneous rock that parallels the bedding or other structure of the surrounding rock. Sill rock is normally medium-grained and basic sills (dolerite) are the most common. *See also* Dike. △176, 246

Sillanpää, Frans Eemil (1888–1964), Finnish author. His novels include *Life and Sun* (1916), *Meek Heritage* (1919), and *The Maid Silja* (1931). He was awarded the Nobel Prize for literature in 1939.

Sillitoe, Alan (1928–), English novelist and short-story writer. His angry, blunt accounts of the frustrations of working class life include the novels *Saturday Night and Sunday Morning* (1958) and *The Flame of Life* (1974) and the collection of short stories *The Loneliness of the Long Distance Runner* (1959).

Sills, Beverly (1929–), US coloratura soprano, b. Brooklyn, N.Y. She made her debut in 1946, sang with the San Francisco Opera (1953–55), and from 1955 sang with the New York City Opera. In 1975 she made her long awaited Metropolitan Opera debut.

Silpa Sastras. △1036.

Silone, Ignazio (1900–), pseud. of Secundo Tranquilli, Italian novelist. A socialist, he was hounded by the fascists and wrote much of his work in exile, including *Fontamara* (1933), which describes the impact of fascism on peasants in Abruzzi and *Bread and Wine* (1937). He returned to Italy in 1944 and continued to write extensively.

Silurian Period, the third oldest division of the Paleozoic Era, lasting from 430 to 395,000,000 years ago. Marine invertebrates continue much as in Ordovician times. Fragmentary remains of jawless fishes increase in coastal deposits. The earliest land plants (psilopsids) and first land animals (archaic scorpions) developed. Mountains formed in NW Europe. *See also* Geologic time; Paleozoic Era. △276.

Silver, metallic element (symbol Ag) of the second transition series, known from the earliest times. It occurs native and in argentite (sulfide) and horn silver (chloride). It is also obtained as a by-product in the electrolytic refining of copper. It is the most efficient conductor of heat and electricity known and is used in electrical contacts and printed circuits. Other uses include jewelry and other decorative items, mirrors, and silver salts for photography. The metal does not oxidize in air but quickly tarnishes when exposed to sulfur compounds. Properties: at. no. 47; at. wt. 107.868; sp gr 10.5; melt. pt. 1763°F (961.93°C); boil. pt.

Sidewinder

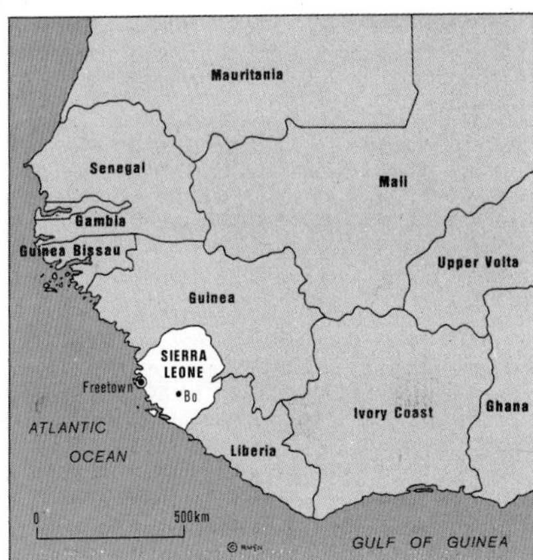
Mauritania
Senegal
Mali
Gambia
Guinea Bissau
Upper Volta
Guinea
SIERRA LEONE
•Bo
Freetown
Ivory Coast
Ghana
ATLANTIC
OCEAN
Liberia
0
500km
GULF OF GUINEA

Sierra Leone

Silky terrier

Beverly Sills

3850°F (2121°C); most common isotope Ag^{107} (51.-82%). *See also* Transition Elements. △1554.

Silverfish, or bristle tail, gray, primitive, wingless insect found worldwide. It lives in cool damp areas, feeding on starches in books, clothes, and wallpaper. Length: 0.5in (13mm). Family Lepismatidae; species *Lepisma saccharina*. △492.

Silver Gar. *See* Garfish.

Silver Spring, community in central Maryland, about 7mi (11km) N of Washington, D.C.; site of Xaverian College (1931); scene of drive toward Washington (July 1864) by Gen. Jubal Early's Confederate raiders, which posed grave threat to the Union government. Chief industry is scientific research. Pop. (1970) 77,-496.

Silverside, or spearing, smelt, small marine fish found in temperate and tropical seas. Not a true smelt, it is identified by broad silvery side bands. Length: 3–20in (7.6–50.8cm). Family Atherinidae. *See also* Grunion.

Silviculture, the study of the relationship of a forest to its environment as well as the effects of such practices as planting, pruning, and harvesting on the forest.

Simenon, Georges (1903–), French novelist from Belgium. A prolific fiction writer, Simenon became famous for the Inspector Maigret series, begun in 1931. He later wrote more ambitious novels, including *The Trial of Bebé Donge* (1942) and *The Stain on the Snow* (1953).

Simeon I (*r.* 893–927), Bulgarian tsar, younger son of Boris I, brilliant administrator and military leader. Waged many battles against Byzantium; advanced to the gates of Constantinople four times 919–24, but was unable to take it for want of a fleet; defeated Magyars; conquered Serbs in 926. Proclaimed himself tsar of Bulgaria and Serbia in 925, and was the strongest ruler in eastern Europe. At his capital at Preslav, advances in education were made.

Simeon II (1937–), Bulgarian child tsar. He succeeded his father Boris III in 1943. The country was ruled by a pro-German regency until the Soviet invasion in 1944. Simeon was ousted by plebiscite in September 1946 and went into exile.

Simferopol, city in Russian SFSR, USSR, 37mi (60km) NE of Sevastopol. It was the site of the ancient Greek settlement of Neapolis and a Scythian capital. This site was occupied after the 16th century by Tartar town of Ak-Mechet; it was seized and destroyed by Russians 1736; refounded and fortified under present name after Russian conquest 1783; occupied by Germans 1941–44; site of agricultural, medical, and teachers' colleges. Industries: fruit, tobacco, canning of fruits and vegetables, flour milling, tanning. Pop. 250,000.

Simile, figure of speech comparing two things. It differs from ordinary comparisons by comparing things usually considered dissimilar although sharing, in most cases, one common characteristic: "fleece as white as snow" is a simile. A simile is most often recognized by its use of "like" or "as." *See also* Metaphor.

Simmel, George (1858–1918), German sociologist and philosopher. He was influential in establishing the field of sociology in Germany. His theories influenced the work of later sociologists, including Lewis Coser and Erving Goffman. Among his best-known works are *Sociology* (1908) and the essays "Conflict," "The Web of Group Affiliations," and "How Is Society Possible?" △888.

Simon, Neil (1927–), US playwright, b. New York. A witty writer of "suburban mentality" comedies, revue sketches, screenplays, and TV shows, his successful plays include: *Come Blow Your Horn* (1960), *Barefoot in the Park* (1963), *The Odd Couple* (1965), the musical *Sweet Charity* (1965), *Promises, Promises* (1968), and *Prisoner of Second Avenue* (1972).

Simon, Pierre, Marquis de Laplace. *See* Laplace, Pierre Simon, Marquis de.

Simple Multiple Proportions, Law of, a law announced in 1804 by the English chemist John Dalton. It states that when two elements combine to form more than one compound, a fixed weight of one element always combines with weights of the other that can be reduced to ratios of small whole numbers. It was a powerful argument for Dalton's atomic theory.

Simpson, O(renthal) J(ames) (1947–), US football player, b. San Francisco. He won the 1968 Heisman Trophy at the University of Southern California as a running back. He joined Buffalo in the National Football League (1969) and set a single season rushing record in 1973 with 2003 yards (1831m). He also appeared in several films.

Simultaneous Equations, set of two or more mathematical equations involving two or more unknowns, for which common solutions are required. For example, in the simultaneous equations $x + 2y = 7$ and $5x + y = 4$, the problem is to find values of x and y that satisfy both equations: this can be done by substituting the value of x from one into the other to give a single equation in y. Simultaneous equations can be solved only if the number of equations equals the number of unknowns. △1452.

Sinai (Sinā') Peninsula, peninsula constituting a governorate of Egypt, bounded by Gulf of Suez and Suez Canal (W), Gulf of Aqaba and the Negev Desert of Israel (E), Mediterranean Sea (N), Red Sea (S); capital is Al-'Arish. A barren plateau region inhabited chiefly by nomads, it is site of Gebel Musas, S mountain group where in tradition Moses received the ten commandments; nearby is St Catherine Monastery (*c.* 250) where the Codex Sinaiticus, early New Testament manuscript, was discovered 1844. The Sinai Peninsula has been the scene of Arab-Israeli conflicts since Oct. 29, 1956, when it was briefly occupied by Israeli forces; during the Six-Day War of 1967, Israel forced Egyptian evacuation of the Sinai June 5, and seized strategically located posts on Gulf of Aqaba; the Suez Canal was closed during the conflict. Egypt successfully recaptured the territory 1973; by January 1974, an agreement was signed calling for Israeli withdrawal from the Sinai, and UN forces were positioned between Egyptian and Israeli troops. This led to the lifting of the oil embargo and reopening of the Suez Canal. On Sept. 4, 1975, delegates from Egypt, Israel, and United States met in Geneva, Switzerland to sign another agreement which included an Israeli withdrawal from Sinai Peninsula, Mitla and Gidi passes, an increased Sinai UN buffer zone, and a 200-man US "early-warning" system in the area; Suez Canal reopened June 5, 1975. Industries: oil, manganese, limestone. Area: 23,442sq mi (60,715sq km). Pop. 140,000.

Sinatra, Frank (1915–), US popular singer and actor, b. Francis Albert Sinatra in Hoboken, N.J. He sang with the bands of Tommy Dorsey and Harry James and became immensely popular with teenagers of the 1940s for such songs as "I'll Never Smile Again." In the 1950s he became a movie star and won an Academy Award for a supporting role in *From Here to Eternity* (1953). Later films included *Guys and Dolls* (1955); *The Manchurian Candidate* (1962); and *The Detective* (1968).

Sinclair, Upton (Beall) (1878–1968), US novelist and social reformer, b. Baltimore. *The Jungle* (1906), a novel about the meatpacking industry, was his greatest success. Following the same pattern, he would concentrate upon a subject and then write a novel on his findings. Such novels include *The Metropolis* (1908), about New York City society, *King Coal* (1917), about the Colorado miners' strikes. He won the Pulitzer Prize in 1942 for *Dragon's Teeth*. A socialist, he ran unsuccessfully from California for the US House of Representatives, the Senate, and the governorship.

Sinderman, Horst (1916–), East German politician and member of the SED (East German Communist Party). He was designated chairman of the council of state by the People's Chamber in 1973, to succeed Willi Stoph.

Sindhi, language of Pakistan and India, spoken by about 7,000,000 people in the province of Sind, S Pakistan, and by about 1,500,000 more across the border in India. It is an Indic language, related to Sanskrit and Hindi.

Sine, ratio of the length of the side opposite to an acute angle to the length of the hypotenuse in a right-angled triangle. The sine of angle A is usually abbreviated to "sin A." *See also* Trigonometric Functions. △1464.

Singapore, island republic in SE Asia, at S end of Malay peninsula, between the Indian Ocean and South China Sea. Its parliamentary form of government is headed by a president and prime minister. Once covered by a tropical rain forest, more than 60% of the land has been cleared to accommodate the rapidly urbanizing economy. Less than 25% of the land is used for agriculture; vegetables, tobacco, fruits, rubber, and coconuts are the chief products. Singapore is the largest importer in SE Asia, one of world's greatest commercial centers and busiest harbors. Principal industries include shipping, shipbuilding, tourism, food processing, steel products. More than 75% of its 2,122,456 inhabitants lives in the capital city of Singapore. Of the total population, 76% is Chinese; the island has one of the highest standard of living in Asia, a high literacy rate, and excellent health facilities. It is the site of University of Singapore (1963) and Nanyang University (1953).

The government, under the constitution of 1966, is a parliamentary democracy. The president, as head of state, with the prime minister, as head of government is responsible to a 65-member unicameral parliament. Singapore was ceded (1819) to British East India Co. by the Sultan of Johore, through the efforts of T. Stanford Raffles, who founded the city of Singapore the same year. It grew, with influx of Chinese and Malay merchants, into a major exporter of rubber and tin; became one of the Straits Settlements (1867-1946). After their abolishment, Singapore joined Christmas Island and Cocos-Keeling islands as a crown colony of Britain (1946); it was made a self-governing state 1959. In 1962, it merged with Malaya, Sarawak and Sabath to form the Federation of Malaya but due to internal and racial strife it involuntarily agreed to separate 1965 and became an independent republic.

PROFILE

Official name: Republic of Singapore
Area: 225sq mi (583sq km)
Density: 9,200per sq mi (3,500per sq km)
Population: 2,110,400
Chief city: Singapore (capital)
Religion: Islam, Christianity, Buddhism, Hinduism
Language: Malay (national), Chinese, Tamil, English (all official)
Monetary unit: Singapore dollar

Singer, Isaac Bashevis (1904–), US novelist and short story writer, b. Poland. In 1935 he emigrated to New York City. Although all his works are written in Yiddish, they have been translated into English. They include *The Family Moskat* (1950), *The Estate* (1969), and *A Crown of Feathers and Other Stories* (1973), for which he won a 1974 National Book Award.

Single-phase Motor. △1542.

Single Tax, form of taxation where the only form of government revenue is a tax on land. Based on the idea that the profit derived from natural resources and the increased value of land should benefit all of society, the theory was popularized by Henry George in his book *Progress and Poverty* (1879). George believed that such a tax would prove sufficient to meet all government costs and eradicate poverty.

Sinhalese, people constituting the largest ethnic group of Sri Lanka (Ceylon). Speaking Sinhala, an Indo-Aryan language, and practicing Theravāda Buddhism, the mainly agriculturalist Sinhalese are divided into two groups: the lowland dwellers, influenced by commercial and social change, and the more traditionalist highlanders around Kandy.

Sinkhole. △256.

Sinn Fein, Irish nationalist movement founded 1899 by Arthur Griffith. Its aim to achieve Irish independence was partially realized with the establishment of the Irish Free State (1921). In 1938, it joined with the Irish Republican Army. △1314.

Sinningia, *See* Gloxinia.

Sino-Japanese War (1894–95), military conflict between China and Japan. Disagreement over Korea and clashes in 1892 and 1894 foreshadowed the Japanese declaration of war against China on Aug. 1, 1894, following a conflict between Japanese and Chinese armies during a Korean revolt. The Japanese seized control over the Korean government. Japan's modernized military had the advantage, and after crippling the Chinese fleet at the mouth of the Yalu River (Sept. 17, 1894), Japanese forces went on to capture Port Arthur and Weiheiwei and the remainder of the Chinese fleet. The war ended with the signing of the Treaty of Shimonoseki (April 17, 1895), by which China ceded territory to Japan and agreed to pay an indemnity. △1270.

Sino-Tibetan Languages, large family of languages which includes Chinese; the Tibeto-Burman languages; the Tai languages; and Miao (Meo) and Yao spoken in S China and Southeast Asia. That these four groups of languages are actually related to each other is still questioned by many linguists.

Sinus, a normal cavity, or opening, in a bone or other organ. The most familiar sinuses are the paranasal sinuses, located in the facial region and lined with epithelium, that normally drain into the nasal cavity.

Sinusitis, acute or chronic disease of the paranasal tissues. Acute sinusitis involving pain and nasal obstruction occurs as an aftermath to a cold, a secondary bacterial infection, improper breathing while swimming, or sudden changes in barometric pressure. Chronic sinusitis causes tendency to colds, obstructed breathing, and loss of the sense of smell.

Sinus Medii or **Central Bay.** △52

Si. *See* Hsi.

Siouan, family of American Indian languages. It includes Sioux (Dakota), spoken mainly in South Dakota; Crow, of Montana; Winnebago, of Wisconsin; Omaha, of Nebraska; and Osage, now spoken mainly in Oklahoma.

Sioux. *See* Dakota Indians.

Sioux City, city in NW Iowa, on Missouri River at confluence of Big Sioux and Floyd rivers; seat of Woodbury co; site of Morningside College (1889), Briar Cliff College (1930), and nearby monument in state park commemorating death (1804) of Sgt. Charles Floyd of Lewis and Clark expedition. Industries: fabricated metals, lumber, tools, grain, meat packing. Inc. 1857. Pop. (1970) 85,925.

Sioux Falls, city in SE South Dakota, 180mi (290km) SE of Pierre, on Big Sioux River; seat of Minnehaha co; largest city in state; site of Augustana College (1860), Sioux Falls College (1860); trading and distribution center. Industries: meat packing, food processing, farm machinery, fertilizer, textiles, granite quarrying, baked goods. Original settlement (1857) abandoned after Sioux Indian attacks; resettled 1865 as military post; inc. 1877 as village, 1883 as city. Pop. (1970) 72,488.

Siqueiros, David Alfaro (1898–74), Mexican painter. He viewed art as a vehicle for social and political expression. Active as a socialist, he did much easel painting but is best known for his murals of revolutionary themes. *The New Democracy,* painted for the Palace of Fine Arts in Mexico City, and *Death to the Invader,* painted in Chile, are examples. He experimented with synthetic lacquer paints and spray painting techniques. His works are realistic and often show struggle and violence.

Siracusa. *See* Syracuse.

Siren, aquatic, tailed amphibian of North America. The adult is neotenic, that is, it reaches sexual maturity while retaining the larval physical form. These eel-like animals have external gills, tiny forelegs, and minute eyes. They have no hind legs. Length: to 36in (91cm). Family Sirenidae. *See also* Amphibia; Salamander. △838.

Sirenia, order of plant-eating aquatic mammals with paddlelike flippers for forelimbs, no hind limbs, and a horizontally flattened tail fin. The four species include the dugong (family Dugongidae) and three manatees (family Trichechidae). Length: 8–13ft (2–4m); weight: to 790lb (356kg). △540.

Sirens, in Greek mythology, sea nymphs that were birds with women's heads. They lived on an island surrounded by rocks onto which they enticed sailors by their songs, devouring their shipwrecked prey. Jason escaped them because the songs of Orpheus were more beautiful, and Odysseus survived by stopping his men's ears with wax and having himself tied to the mast.

Sirius, or **Alpha Canis Majoris,** white main-sequence star in the constellation Canis Major, the brightest star visible from Earth. Also called the Dog Star, Sirius is actually a binary star, situated 8.7 light-years from the Sun. It has an 8th-magnitude white dwarf, Sirius B, as its companion. Characteristics: apparent mag. −1.47 (Sirius A), 8.5 (Sirius B); absolute mag. 0.7 (A), 11.4 (B); spectral type Al (A), DA (B). △134.

Sirsalis Rille. △52

Sisal, or **Sisal Hemp,** fiber plant native to the West Indies and cultivated in Mexico, Java, E Africa, and the Bahamas. Fibers from the leaves are used for rope, insulation, and binder twine; fiber length: 3–5ft (1–1.5m). Family Agavaceae; species *Agave sisalana. See also* Agave.

Sisley, Alfred (1839–99), English painter. He spent most of his life in France, often painting outdoors with Claude Monet. He used an Impressionistic style to show the effects of sunlight on color at various times of the day. His outlines were carefully drawn, and unlike Monet, he did not dissolve his colors or forms. He concentrated on landscapes, especially of the countryside around Paris. △1254.

Sitar, stringed musical instrument of northern India. A smaller, simplified variant of the traditional vina, it has 3 to 7 strings stretched over a metal plate between a drum and a gourd resonator and played tremulously with a plectrum. Ravi Shankar popularized the sitar on world tours (*c.*1960).

Sitatunga. *See* Kudu, Nyala, Sitatunga, and Bushbuck.

Sit-down Strikes, labor technique. It was used by workers at their place of employment and resulted in the virtual occupation of the factory or business. The workers would neither work nor leave until their demands were met. The most dramatic such strike began on Dec. 31, 1936, at General Motors plants in Flint, Mich., and lasted 44 days. The Supreme Court outlawed the practice in *Hague* v. *Congress of Industrial Organizations* (1939).

Sit-in, nonviolent tactic used in civil rights protests. Sit-ins were effectively used in the civil rights movement of the 1960s to protest racial segregation and discrimination. Protestors occupied and refused to leave areas open to the public, such as schools, restaurants, and libraries. Dr. Martin Luther King, Jr., was one of the chief proponents of the policy of "nonviolent coercion." *See also* Integration.

Sitka, city in SE Alaska, on W coast of Baranof Island; first capital of Alaska 1867–1906. Industries: fisheries, tourism. Founded by Russians in 1799 as New Archangel. Pop. (1970) 3,370.

Sitting Bull (c.1831–90), Indian leader, b. Grand River, S.D. He became chief of the northern hunting Sioux (1866) and participated in the peace with the United States that granted the Indians a reservation above the North Platte River (1868). When the terms of the peace were violated, 2,500–4,000 Sioux, Arapahoe, and Cheyenne gathered around him and defied the army. In 1876 this force wiped out the 7th Cavalry detachment led by Col. George Custer at Little Big Horn. He led his men to Canada (1877) and finally surrendered to the Army (1881). He was killed during Indian unrest on the Standing Rock Reservation. △1274.

Situation Ethics, philosophical system that evaluates the morality of a particular action in relation to a specific situation. The emphasis is on the situation rather than on any system of laws or rules. △808.

Sitwell, (Dame) Edith (1887–1964), English poet, sister of Osbert Sitwell. Her anthology *Wheels* (1916) encouraged experimentalism in British verse. Her own verse is witty and inventive. Her purpose was to shock the middle-class public, though her wartime poetry has great compassion. She was a generous patron of younger writers, artists, and musicians.

Sitwell, (Sir) Osbert (1892–1969), English poet and novelist. Brother of the poets Edith and Sacheverell Sitwell, he shared their aristocratic tastes in life and literature. His verse, novels, and criticism are all marked by wit and a graceful style.

Sivatherium. △574.

Six Nations, the League of the Iroquois, after it was joined by the Tuscarora in 1722. The original members were the Cayuga, Oneida, Onondaga, Mohawk, and Seneca.

Sixtus IV, Roman Catholic pope (1471–84), b. Francesco della Rovere (1414). He became a famed preacher and theologian. He was a nepotist and drained the papacy of funds. He erected the Sistine Chapel, and opened the Vatican Library to scholars.

61 Cygni, star situated near the sun in the constellation Cygnus. It is historically important in astronomy since it was the first star to have its distance accurately calculated by parallax measurement (by. F. W. Bessel in 1838). It is a binary star, both components of which are orange. 61 Cygni A has a planetary companion. Characteristics: apparent mag. +5.2 (A), +6.0 (B); absolute mag. +7.5 (A), +8.4 (B); spectral type K5 (A), K7 (B); distance 11.2 light-years.

Sjaelland, largest of islands that form Denmark, bounded N and NW by Kattegat, on W by the Great

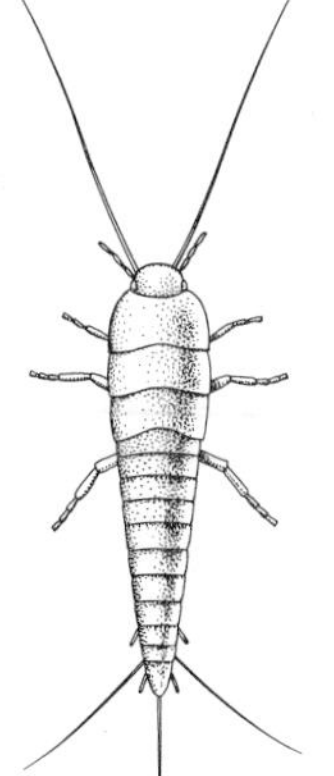

Silverfish

Frank Sinatra

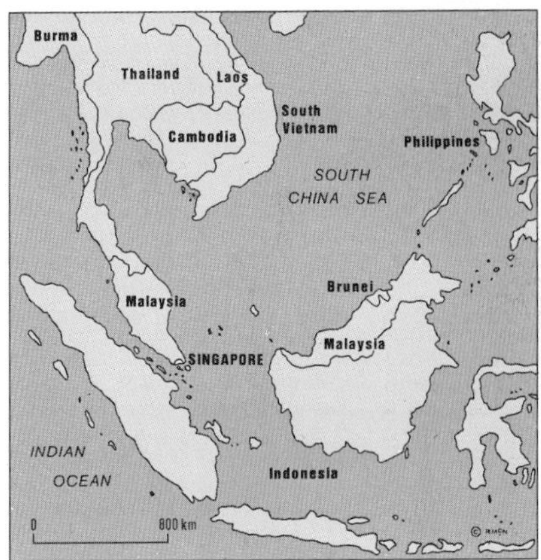
Burma
Thailand
Laos
Cambodia
South Vietnam
Philippines
SOUTH CHINA SEA
Malaysia
Brunei
Malaysia
SINGAPORE
INDIAN OCEAN
Indonesia
0
800 km

Singapore

Sitting Bull

Belt, S by the channel separating it from smaller islands, and E by the Baltic Sea and Øresund. Area: 2,709sq mi (7,016sq km). Pop. 1,855,500.

Skagerrak, strait between Norway and Denmark, connecting North Sea and Baltic Sea by way of Kattegat. Shallow on Danish coast, it deepens as it approaches Norway. Length: 150mi (242km). Width: 85mi (137km).

Skanderbeg. *See* Scanderbeg.

Skate, flat-bodied, bottom-dwelling cartilaginous fish found in most shallow temperate and tropical waters. Brown, white, or gray with spots, it has enlarged pectoral fins attached at the sides of the head, and a short, slender tail, which sometimes has electric organs. Length: 20–96in (50.8–243.8cm). Family Rajidae; species, about 100 including large Pacific *Raja binoculata* and smaller *Raja erinacea*. *See also* Chondrichthyes. △510.

Skeletal System, or **Skeleton,** the bony connective tissue that makes up the general framework of the body. It supports and protects the soft inner organs; serves as a place of attachment for muscles, ligaments, and other structures; provides storage for some minerals; and produces some blood cells. In man the skeleton is divided into two parts: the axial skeleton, or main axis of the body, includes the cranium, or skull; the spinal, or vertebral, column; the sternum, or breastbone; and the ribs. The appendicular skeleton, serving for the attachment of appendages, includes the shoulder girdle and arm bones and the pelvic, or hip, girdle and leg bones. The human skeleton has 206 named bones, with most of them specialized for one or two particular functions. Some of these bones are: the cranium, protecting the brain; the sternum and ribs, protecting the heart and lungs and serving for muscle attachment; and the long arm and leg bones, serving as a framework for muscle attachment and for blood cell formation. △682, 720.

Skelton, John (*c.* 1460–1529), English poet. Originally Henry VIII's tutor and later a Norfolk parson, he used his rollicking "skeltonic" verse to satirize court and clergy, especially Cardinal Wolsey. He could also be sentimental, as in the elegy to *Phyllyp Sparowe*, or Rabelaisian, as when he describes *Elynour Rummyng*.

Skepticism, view that man can never have real knowledge of things. In Greek philosophy, three Skeptic schools emerged: the older school of Pyrrho of Elis (*c.* 300 BC); the Academy of Aenesidemus (1st century BC); and the still later skepticism of Sextus Empiricus (1st half 3rd century BC). Seeds of skepticism reappeared in the 14th-century writings of Duns Scotus and in the 16th-century French Occasionalists.

Skiing, winter sport and recreational activity. It is the national sport of Norway, where skiing began as a competitive sport in the late 19th century. Competition includes four events: jumping, downhill, slalom, and cross-country. In jumping, each participant leaps twice from a specially designed jump slope and scores points on distance and form. Downhill is a straight descent on a sharply twisting course marked off by flags. Most grueling is cross-country, which is over a course from 10 to 50km (6–31mi). Except for jumping, women compete in all events. The first ski club formed in the United States was in 1872. The sport is governed by the Fédération Internationale de Ski, founded in 1924, the same year the first Winter Olympic Games were held at Chamonix, France. As a recreational sport, it has been popular since the 1930s, but it enjoyed a surge in participation in the 1970s.

Skimmer, nocturnal shorebird that frequents warm seas, rivers, and lakes using its knifelike bill to plow the water for food. After courtship, oval, stone-colored blotched eggs (3–5) are laid in deep scrape. Family Rynchopidae.

Skin, continuous, tough, elastic and sensitive covering of the body serving many functions. The skin protects the body from mechanical injury, water loss, and ultraviolet rays. It provides the sensations of touch, warmth, cold, and pain, each perceived at discrete points on the skin surface. It helps regulate body temperature through sweat secretion and reduces moisture loss and keeps itself smooth and pliable with an oily secretion from sebaceous glands.

Structurally the skin consists of two main layers: the outer layer, or epidermis, and the inner layer, called the dermis, corium, or cutis. The epidermis is itself composed of several layers: the stratum corneum, a horny layer made up of closely packed dead cells constantly shed as microscopic scales; the stratum lucidum, a layer of flattened cells best seen on palms and soles; the stratum granulosum, layers of elongated cells; lower layers of stratum germinativum and stratum mucosum, living cell layers which contain pigment and nerve fibrils and which divide to replace outer shed layers. The dermis, or corium, contains dense networks of connective tissue, blood vessels, nerves, glands, and hair follicles. △662, 686, 724.

Skink, any of about 600 species of secretive, agile lizards, mostly small with shiny scales found worldwide, but most numerous in Australia, Asia and Africa. Most are terrestrial; the burrowing species have reduced limbs or are legless. Length: 8–24in (20–61cm). Family Scincidae. *See also* Lizard. △604.

Skinner, B(urrhus) F(redric) (1904–), US psychologist, b. Susquehanna, Pa. He was a pivotal figure in psychological behaviorism. Skinner has made substantial contributions to psychology using rigorous, objective methods. Much of his work has centered on the process of operant conditioning, ie, how behavior is controlled by its consequences or reinforcements. His work led to the development of behavior modification for the treatment of the mentally disturbed and the development of teaching machines in the classroom. Skinner has also expressed concern about the future of mankind in such works as *Walden Two* (1948) and *Beyond Freedom and Dignity* (1971). *See also* Behaviorism; Behavior Modification; Operant Conditioning. △772, 776, 778.

Skinner, Cornelia Otis (1901–), US actress and author, b. Chicago. Her stage debut was in 1921 in her father Otis Skinner's company. Broadway successes included *Major Barbara* (1956) and *The Pleasure of His Company* (1958). Her collections of humorous essays include *Our Hearts Were Young and Gay* (1942, co-authored by Emily Kimbrough), *The Ape in Me* (1959), and *Elegant Wits and Grand Horizontals* (1962). She also wrote the autobiographical *Family Circle* (1948) and a biography of Sarah Bernhardt, *Madame Sarah* (1967).

Skinner Box, device used in psychological studies of operant conditioning, named for B. F. Skinner, its inventor. An animal placed in the box learns to press a lever in order to get food or water (reinforcement). The device allows precise control of learning conditions and measurement of changes occurring in behavior during the learning process. *See also* Behaviorism; Operant Conditioning.

Skin Senses, or cutaneous senses, touch, pain, and temperature (hot and cold). In addition to free nerve endings, other types of receptors seem to be involved although their precise function is unclear. Some receptors are located near hair follicles and "fire" when the hair is moved; others operate in more complex ways. △678.

Skipjack. *See* Click Beetle.

Skipper, day-active insects characterized by darting or skipping flight. They have stouter bodies than butterflies but more slender than moths. There is usually a hooklike extension at the end of each knobbed antenna. Order Lepidoptera; superfamily Hesperioidea. *See also* Lepidoptera. △502.

Skobelev. *See* Fergana.

Skokie, city in NE Illinois, 15mi (24km) N of Chicago; site of Hebrew Theological College (1922). Industries: pharmaceuticals, communications equipment. Founded as Niles Center; inc. 1888, name changed 1940. Pop. (1970) 68,627.

Skopje (Usküp), city in S Yugoslavia, on Vardar River; capital of Macedonia; industrial, transportation, and trade center; site of Macedonian University (1949), Stephen Dušan bridge, mosques of Mustafa Pasha and Sultan Murad (15th century). Medieval Serbian capital (est. 1282), city fell to Turks 1392; inc. into Yugoslavia 1918; severely damaged by 1963 earthquake. Industries: iron, steel, textiles, chemicals, glass, handicrafts. Pop. 312,091.

Skua, dark-colored, swift-flying, sharp-billed shorebird that pirates food from other birds in flight. Skuas nest in colonies, laying spotted, earth-colored eggs (2) on isolated polar islands. Length:24in (61cm). Family Stercorariidae; species *Stercorarius skua*.

Skull, part of the body at the anterior end of the vertebral column. It consists of the cranium, or brain case, which is made up of eight bones; and the facial bones, 14 irregularly shaped bones that support and protect the eyes, nose, and mouth. *See also* Cranium. △682.

Skunk, nocturnal omnivorous mammal native to North, Central, and South America with powerful scent glands used in defense. The size of large house cats, skunks have small heads and slender, thickly-furred bodies with short legs and big bushy tails. They have bold black and white markings. Best known is the striped skunk *(Mephitis mephitis)*—length: 15in (38cm); weight: 10lb (4.5kg). Family Mustelidae.

Skunk Cabbage, evil-smelling perennial plant of E North American and Asian woods and swamps. It has a mottled hood of green or purple enveloping a small, tight, knob-shaped flower cluster and cabbagelike leaves. Height: 1–3ft (30–91cm). Family Araceae; species *Symplocarpus foetidus*. *See also* Arum.

Sky Diving, a sport that consists of jumping from a plane and free-falling before releasing the parachute. △930.

Skye, island off the NW coast of Scotland; largest island in the Inner Hebrides; chief town is Portree. Industries: livestock, tourism. The Cuillin Hills (S) reach 3,309ft (1,009m). Area: 670sq mi (1,735sq km).

Skye Terrier, 400-year-old game breed (terrier group) from Skye Island region, Scotland. Most widely known of the terriers until the end of the 19th century. Once pet of the nobility, the Skye has a long, powerful head with prick or drop ears and brown eyes. The body is long and low, with short legs and long tail. The straight, flat coat is 5.5in (14cm) long and worn parted from head to tail; one overall color of blue black, gray, silver, fawn, or cream is acceptable to kennel clubs. Average size: 10in (25.4cm) high at shoulder; 25lb (11kg). *See also* Terrier.

Skylab, US program of manned orbiting space laboratories. In the mid-1970s three 3-man Skylab crews spent 655 man-days in space. Expanded activities in conjunction with Space Shuttle are planned for the 1980s. *See also* Space Shuttle; Space Station. △142–44.

Skylark, Eurasian bird known for the male's flutelike song and elaborate courtship rite. It is black streaked with dull brown and has white tail feathers. It is an insect and berry eater. Its eggs (3–5) are hatched in a cup-shaped ground nest. Length: 7in (18cm). Species *Alauda arvensis*. *See also* Lark.

Skyros (Skiros), island in Greece, largest of N Sporades group, in Aegean Sea; connected in legend to Theseus, hero of Athens; Rupert Brooke, English poet, is buried here. Industries: wheat, figs, citrus fruits, olive oil, cheese, marble, chromite, iron. Area: 81sq mi (210sq km). Pop. 2,882.

Skyscraper, a very tall building, constructed on a steel skeleton, generally for commercial use. The invention of practical electric elevators and the need for space in central cities spurred construction of taller buildings in the late 19th century. The first were all masonry construction. Next came cage construction —the building's metal framework supported the floors; the masonry walls supported themselves. True skyscraper construction, in which the metal skeleton supported both floors and walls, was introduced in the Home Insurance Building in Chicago (1883). Later skyscrapers have riveted metal skeletons, and the walls merely enclose the internal space. The first design to show concern for environmental impact was that of Rockefeller Center in New York City (1929–40). The tallest skyscraper now in use is Chicago's Sears Tower (110 stories, 1,454ft (443.5m) plus a TV antenna). △1322, 1414.

Slash-and-Burn Agriculture, a primitive agricultural technique that involves the felling and girdling of trees, which are then burned to make land arable. This is a temporary measure, as the land is rarely usable for a second season, and the farmer moves on to new woodland to follow the same procedure. △634.

Slate, a fine-grained homogeneous metamorphic rock, which splits into smooth, thin layers. Formed by the metamorphosis of shale, its regular fissility makes it valuable as a roofing material. The characteristic color is gray-blue. *See also* Metamorphic Rocks. △248.

Slater, Samuel (1768–1835), US textile manufacturer, b. England. Britain, to protect its cotton industry, forbade textile workers to emigrate. Slater traveled secretly to the United States. From memory he recreated complex English textile machinery in a mill in Pawtucket, R.I. (1790). This was the first textile factory in the United States. In 1815 he started wool fabric production.

Slave Coast, name given to a portion of Africa's

Guinean coast that supplied vast numbers of slaves from *c.* 1500–1800. △1212.

Slavery, condition in which persons are held as property by other persons, and the slave is obliged to perform labor or services for the master. Practiced since prehistoric times, the institution probably began with enforced servitude of prisoners of war and then was extended to include countrymen who broke the law. Very common among the classical Greeks and Romans, slavery became fairly rare in the Middle Ages, though more because of economic considerations than any general acceptance that it was immoral. Beginning in the late 15th century, in the New World, slavery provided a supply of much-needed labor. Though native Indians were the first slaves there, trade in African slaves became highly profitable and was carried on with almost unimaginable brutality.

The antislavery movement, which was stimulated by the spread of Enlightenment humanitarian ideals in the 18th century, led to Britain's abolition of slavery in its territories in 1833 and eventually to growing feeling against the institution in the United States. Resistance to abolition, among other things, led to the US Civil War and eventual emancipation. Other countries followed suit, but a 1966 UN report stated that slavery still existed in parts of Asia and Africa. △816, 894, 1016.

Slavic Languages, group of languages spoken in the Soviet Union and E Europe and constituting a major subdivision of the Indo-European family. The Slavic languages spoken today are Russian, Ukrainian, Belorussian, Polish, Czech, Slovak, Bulgarian, Serbo-Croatian, Slovenian, Macedonian, and Sorbian (Lusatian), the last-mentioned spoken in East Germany. Some Slavic languages are written in the Cyrillic alphabet, others in the Roman, depending mainly on whether its speakers are Eastern Orthodox or Roman Catholic. △866.

Slavonia, historic area in N Yugoslavia, between Sava River (S) and Drava and Danube rivers (N and E); now part of constituent republic of Croatia; Croatia and Slavonia were united with Hungary 1102; taken by Turkey 16th century; returned to Hungary 1699; part of Yugoslavia since 1918.

Slavs. △1176.

Sleep and Dreams, relatively new psychological discipline that studies the interrelated phenomena of sleep and dreams. Nobody knows exactly why organisms sleep but one theory suggests that this rest period allows the organism to live longer. Sleep varies from light to deep, with each stage corresponding to specific brain wave patterns. It is also related to the activity of the brain's reticular activating system (RAS). The function of dreaming is also obscure, and some researchers feel that it is merely random brain activity during sleep. Earlier theorists, notably Sigmund Freud, believed that dreams reflected conscious thought, and the concept is a central one in psychoanalysis. Dreaming is often accompanied by rapid eye movements (REM), which can be measured electrically. Some researchers report that depriving an individual of REM sleep produces irritability and even hallucinations. All sleep stages are accompanied by considerable neural activity, suggesting that sleep is not passive. *See also* Sleep Deprivation. △668, 824.

Sleep Deprivation, loss or reduction of sleep over prolonged periods, which leads to personality disorganization and diminishes cognitive abilities through disruption of brain function. Symptoms include confusion, moodiness, irritability, and (in extreme cases) temporary psychotic disturbances involving hallucinations and delusions. Dream deprivation, in which a person is allowed to sleep but prevented from dreaming, results in similar symptoms. Dream loss may therefore be the crucial feature of sleep deprivation.

Sleep Drive, a need for bodily rest combined with inhibition of voluntary activities, a decrease in metabolism, and complete or partial suspension of consciousness. It is controlled by the reticular formation.

Sleeping Beauty (ballet). △1368.

Sleeping Pill, drug prescribed to induce sleep in cases of restlessness or pain. Depending on the cause of insomnia, a sleeping pill may be a sedative, hypnotic drug, powerful analgesic (codeine), or placebo.

Sleeping Sickness, infection with a flagellate protozoan transmitted by the tsetse fly. It is characterized by fever, inflamed lymph nodes, and involvement of brain and spinal cord, leading to profound lethargy. Treatment with drugs is helpful in early stages, but useless later. △732.

Sleepwalking, or somnambulism, thought to be a neurotic dissociative reaction, involving the sleeper's leaving his bed to engage in an activity that releases tension.

Slidell, John (1793–1871), US diplomat, b. New York City. A lawyer, he served in the House of Representatives (1843–45). He was ordered to Mexico by Pres. James K. Polk to negotiate the purchase of upper California, New Mexico, and the Rio Grande boundary, but the Mexican government refused to receive him. He served in the Senate (1853–61). Named commissioner to France from the Confederate states (1861), he was captured on board the *Trent* and finally continued his mission in 1862. He remained in France until 1870. *See also* Trent Affair.

Slider, freshwater turtle common to the New World. Its oval, wrinkled shell is olive with black or brown markings. Males have elongated front claws used in courtship. Pond sliders have red or yellow blotches on sides of head. Length: to 12in (30.5cm). Family Emydidae; genus *Chrysemys. See also* Turtle.

Slide Rule, mechanical calculating device consisting of two rules engraved with logarithmic scales of numbers, one of which slides along the other. Multiplication and division of numbers, and often of their squares, squares roots, and other functions, is thus reduced to mechanical addition and subtraction. △1456.

Slime Eel. *See* Hagfish.

Slime Mold, any of a small group of strange, basically single-celled organisms that are intermediate between the plant and animal kingdoms. During their complex life cycle they pass through several stages, including a flagellated swimming stage; an amebalike stage; and a stage consisting of a slimy mass of protoplasm with many nuclei.

Slipped Disk, or herniated disk, an intervertebral disk in which the center has slipped out from between abutting vertebrae, causing pressure against the spinal cord. Subsequent pain may be in the arms or in the lower back and legs, depending on which disks are displaced. Treatment involves bedrest, analgesic medication, traction, support, physical therapy, and, occasionally, surgical removal of protruded portion. △720.

Slipper Limpet. △476

Sloan, John (1871–1951), US painter, b. Lock Haven, Pa. He worked as a newspaper illustrator in Philadelphia and New York City. He became a member of The Eight (Ashcan school) and painted realistic city scenes of working-class people engaged in their daily activities. Neutral colors prevail in his works.

Sloop, term used to designate a small single-masted sailing vessel with fore and aft sails, and, in the 18th century, a sail-powered warship with 10 to 32 cannon. The term is also used for a small warship, similar to the destroyer, but much slower and often better armed, providing escort for merchant ships.

Sloth, slow-moving herbivorous tropical American mammal. It has long limbs tipped with two or three long claws and spends most of its life in trees. Length: 2ft (61cm); weight: 12lb (5.4kg). Family *Bradypodidae. See also* Edentate. △540, 602.

Sloth Bear, omnivorous, medium-sized bear of Indian and Sri Lankan forests. It has a shaggy black coat with a yellow or white v-shaped marking on its chest. Species *Melursus ursinus.*

Slovak, the second of the two major languages of Czechoslovakia, spoken by about 5,000,000 people in the E third of the country, which is known as Slovakia. It is closely related to Czech and is thought by some to be a dialect of that language. △866.

Slovakia (Slovensko), region of E Czechoslovakia, bounded by Poland (N), USSR (E), Hungary (S), and Austria and Moravia (W). Capital is Bratislava; most of region is crossed by Carpathian Mts. Until 1918 it was primarily under control of Hungary; became part of new country of Czechoslovakia 1918, but retained broad powers of autonomy; occupied by Germany in WWII; occupied by Soviet Union 1968. Mountainous parts of country are rich in minerals; sheep grazing and farming in the valleys are important. Area: 18,923sq mi (49,010sq km).

Slovenes. △1232.

Slovenia, constituent republic of Yugoslavia, in NW part of country, primarily in Karst plateau and Julian

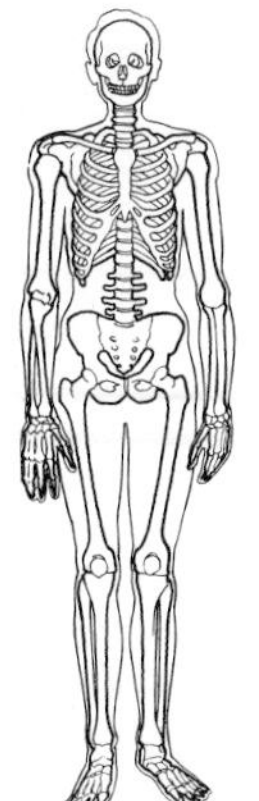

Skeletal system

Skunk

Skyscraper

Slovakia, Czechoslovakia

Alps; bounded by Austria (N), Hungary (NE), Croatia (S), Trieste (SW), and Italy (W); capital is Ljubljana. It was part of kingdom of Austria 1335–1918, when it was included in kingdom of Serbs, Croats, and Slovenes (known as Yugoslavia since 1929). In 1945 it was made a constituent republic of Yugoslavia and added part of Venezia Giulia (formerly part of Italy); most industrialized of all Yugoslav republics. Chief rivers are Sava and Drava. Industries: farming, livestock, iron, steel, textiles, aluminum. Area: 7,819sq mi (20,251sq km). Pop. 1,725,088.

Slug, land gastropod mollusk identified by evolutionary loss of shell and untwisted viscera. It secretes a protective slime also used for locomotion. Length: to 7.9in (201mm). Class Gastropoda; subclass Pulmonata; species include garden *Arion hortensis* and great gray *Limax maximus*.

Slurry. △320.

Sluter, Claus (1340–*c.* 1406), Dutch and Burgundian sculptor. △1136.

Small Intestine, that part of the digestive system that extends—some 23ft (7m) coiled and looped—from the stomach to the large intestine, or colon. Food passes from the stomach through the pyloric sphincter to the duodenum, the first part of the small intestine, then to the jejunum, the second part, and then to the ileum, the third part of the small intestine, from which it passes through the colic valve to the colon. The small intestine secretes intestinal juices that combine with bile from the liver and gall bladder and with pancreatic juice to complete the digestion of foodstuffs. The final products are then absorbed through the thin membranes of fingerlike projections (villi) on the intestinal walls into tiny blood and lymph vessels that carry the nutrients to cells throughout the body. △694, 718.

Smallpox, or variola, highly contagious, often fatal viral disease. Its symptoms are high fever and rash on face and extremities, which becomes papular, then pustular. Pustules become crusted, leaving scars. Death is caused when lungs, heart, and brain are infected. △724, 734.

Smell, or olfaction, a chemical sense, in which the stimulus is a chemical diffused in air. Smell is mediated by olfactory receptors located in a membrane at the top of the nose. When operating properly, olfaction can detect a few molecules per million parts of air. The olfactory cortex is more highly developed in some other species (for example, dogs and cats), than in humans. △680.

Smelt, inshore marine food fish found in temperate and cold waters of N Pacific. It is olive green and silver. Length: to 14in (35.6cm). Family Osmeridae; genus *Osmerus*.

Smetana, Bedrich (1824–84), Czech romantic composer who promoted Czech nationalistic style in operas and orchestral music. His masterpiece is the folk opera *The Bartered Bride* (1866). Also popular is his symphonic poem *The Moldau* (1879). △1246.

Smilodon. △576.

Smith, Adam (1723–90), Scottish economist. He was appointed professor of moral philosophy at Glasgow University (1752). He wrote the economic treatise *An Enquiry into the Nature and Causes of the Wealth of Nations* (1776), after meeting French Physiocrats. He argued that a laissez-faire economy and free trade would stimulate production and thus act in the interests of the public but also recognized the necessity for legal and moral restrictions. △1200.

Smith, Alfred Emanuel (1873–1944), US political leader, b. New York City. A member of New York's Tammany Hall Democratic machine, he held several state offices. He was governor of New York (1919–20, 1923–28), supporting social welfare legislation and public works projects. A candidate for the presidential nomination (1924), he ran in 1928 but lost the election to Herbert Hoover. He published the autobiographical *Up to Now* in 1929, and edited *New Outlook* (1932–34).

Smith, Bessie (1898–1937), US blues singer, b. Chattanooga, Tenn. The most famous of all blues singers, she started recording in 1923, toured with bands as a soloist, and became a highly paid and successful artist. Her many mournful, moving recordings of blues became a part of jazz history. She died from injuries received in an auto accident.

Smith, David (1906–65), US sculptor, b. Decatur, Ind. He is perhaps the most important US sculptor of the 20th century. It was only in 1930–33, however, that he became interested in welded metal sculpture, and he continued to work with metal for the rest of his career. Some of his work has been called "drawing in space" because it seems two-dimensional and linear instead of solid and bulky. Until the 1960s his sculpture was rarely completely abstract, and there were usually suggestions of human figures in it. Later his work became geometric and smooth, as in the "Zig" and "Cubi" series of wholly abstract pieces.

Smith, Ian Douglas (1919–), Rhodesian prime minister. He fought in World War II and then entered Rhodesian politics. He became prime minister in 1964 and declared Rhodesia's independence from Great Britain in 1965. Although he suppressed all dissent to white administration of his overwhelmingly black country, during the mid-1970s Smith made some efforts to negotiate with black leaders. In 1976 he agreed to eventual black majority rule in Rhodesia.

Smith, John (1580–1631), English soldier and colonial leader. He served with the Huguenots in France and against the Turks in eastern Europe. He took a leading part in establishing the Jamestown settlement (1607) and was instrumental in obtaining corn from the Indians, thus saving the colony from destruction during three years of hardship. According to his story, he was rescued from death at the hands of Powhatan by the chief's daughter Pocahontas. He explored the New England coast and gave the region its name. *See also* Jamestown Settlement; Pocahontas.

Smith, Joseph (1805–44), founder of the Church of Jesus Christ of Latter-day Saints, also known as the Mormons, b. Sharon, Vt. From 1820–27 he experienced visions in which the angel Moroni told Smith to establish a church. In 1827, he discovered a set of gold plates whose hieroglyphic inscriptions were later published as The Book of Mormon, and in 1830 he formally founded the Mormon church at Fayette, N.Y. Later he and his followers moved west, finally settling in Nauvoo, Ill. A controversial figure, he was pressured by outside groups, especially concerning Mormon polygamy. In 1844 he was arrested for destroying the presses of a critical local newspaper. He was murdered by a mob and was succeeded by Brigham Young as the Mormons' leader. *See also* Mormon, The Book of; Mormons.

Smith, Margaret. *See* Court, Margaret Smith.

Smith, William (1769–1839), English geologist. A founder of stratigraphic geology, he studied the geological strata of England and Wales and published his findings in a *Geological Atlas of England and Wales* (1815–22). *See also* Stratigraphy. △268, 274.

Smith Act (Alien Registration Act of 1940), legislation requiring the registration of all aliens in the United States. The act also requires an alien to be fingerprinted and to carry a registration card at all times. It is unlawful for aliens to belong to a group or organization advocating the overthrow of the government.

Smith-Connally Anti-Strike Act (1943), US legislation, also known as Labor Disputes Act. It was passed over President Roosevelt's veto. The act authorized the president to seize plants where labor disputes would interfere with the war effort and forbade strikes in plants that had been seized. Unions were required to give 30-day notice before striking an industry engaged in war production. Enforced during World War II in mine and railroad disputes and during Korean War in the steel industry.

Smithson, James (1765–1829), English scientist. A chemist and mineralogist, he traveled widely in Europe, the mineral zinc carbonate (Smithsonite) being named after him. He died without issue and left his fortune to a nephew on the condition that if he died without issue the money should be used to found an establishment for the increase and diffusion of knowledge in Washington, D.C., to be known as the Smithsonian Institution. As the illegitimate son of the duke of Northumberland his bequest may have been an attempt to perpetuate his own name.

Smithsonian Agreement. △1384.

Smithsonian Institution, US independent trust establishment. It was created in 1846 to carry out the will of James Smithson of England who bequeathed (1829) his entire estate to the United States "to found at Washington, under the name of the Smithsonian Institution, an establishment for the increase and diffusion of knowledge among men." The institution is administered by a Board of Regents, composed of the chief justice of the Supreme Court, the vice-president, three members of the Senate, three members of the House of Representatives, and nine citizens appointed by joint resolution of Congress. The institution performs fundamental research, publishes the results of studies, explorations, and investigations, and preserves for study and reference over 65,000,000 items of scientific, cultural, and historic interest. Under it are a number of museums, galleries, parks, cultural centers, and information exchange services.

Smog, a dense atmospheric mixture of fog and smoke or chemical fumes, particularly noted in urban or industrial settings with many sources of air pollution and densest during temperature inversions. *See also* Air Pollution; Inversion. △292.

Smolensk, city in Russian SFSR, USSR, on Dnieper River, 220mi (354km) WSW of Moscow; capital of Smolensk oblast. It was first mentioned 882; early important commercial center; 12th–14th-century capital of Smolensk principality; sacked by Tartars *c.* 1240; taken by Lithuania 1408; ceded to Russia 1686; burned when French invaded Russia 1812; occupied by Germany 1941–43; site of medical and teachers' colleges, cathedral, regional museum, monument to 1812 battle. Industries: linen, textile machines, electrical goods, clothing, flour milling, distilling, brewing, lumber, bricks, glass. Pop. 211,000.

Smollett, Tobias George (1721–71), Scottish novelist and surgeon. His novels include *Roderick Random* (1748), *The Adventures of Peregrine Pickle* (1751), and *Humphrey Clinker* (1770). Smollett also translated Voltaire and edited several periodicals. △1188.

Smut, any of a group of plant diseases caused by parasitic fungi, also called smuts, that attack many flowering plants including corn, wheat, and other cereal grasses. The diseases are named after the sooty black masses of reproductive spores produced by the fungi.

Smuts, Jan Christiaan (1870–1950), South African political leader. A lawyer, he was alarmed by the Jameson Raid of 1895 and entered Boer politics. He was a guerrilla leader during the Boer War (1899–1902) but afterwards worked for the establishment of a unified republic, repressing Boer rebellion during World War I. He helped form the Union of South Africa in 1910, served in various ministries under Louis Botha, and predicted the disastrous failure of the Treaty of Versailles following World War I. A supporter of the League of Nations, he was prime minister from 1919–24 and 1939–48 and helped form the United Nations following World War II. His government was replaced by the anti-British and white supremacist nationalists of D. F. Malan.

Smythson, Robert (*c.* 1536–1614), English architect. △1144.

Snail, gastropod mollusk found in fresh and marine waters and on land. It has coiled protective shell encasing an asymmetric visceral mass; large, fleshy foot and head with tentacles; one or more gills; and radula. Often brightly colored, snails are born with a shell. Many snails are intermediate hosts for parasites such as sheep liver fluke. Height: to 2in (51mm). Class Gastropoda; species include common garden *Helix aspersa*, Roman or edible *Helix pomatia*, pond *Limnea stagnalis*. △476.

Snail Fever. *See* Schistosomiasis.

Snake, any of some 2,700 species of legless, elongated reptiles forming the suborder Serpentes of the order Squamata (which also includes the lizards). There are 10 families. Some are small burrowers, others are large, constricting types. They range in size from 4in (102mm) to over 30ft (9m). There are terrestrial, arboreal, semiaquatic, and aquatic species; one group is entirely marine. Many are poisonous. They have external ear openings, eardrums, or middle ears; sound vibrations are picked up via the ground. Their eyelids are immovable and fused into a transparent protective window. Internal organs are elongated with the left lung reduced or absent. The long, forked, protractile tongue is used to detect odors. Their bodies are scale-covered. Males have paired copulatory organs called hemipenes. Upper and lower jaws are moveable and each half of either jaw can be moved independently of the other, allowing snakes to swallow outsized prey. *See also* Reptile. △520–22.

Snakebird, or anhinga, bird found in freshwater and nearby brush of warm temperate areas. Dark with metallic plumage, it has a straight bill, small head on a long neck, a slender body, long tail, and webbed feet. It swims well and feeds mostly on fish. It lays pale blue eggs (3–5) in a shallow, leaf-lined, cup-shaped stick nest in a bush or tree overhanging water. Length: 35in (90cm). Family Anhingidae.

Snakebite, injection of a poisonous substance (venom) secreted by a snake into the bloodstream, causing damage to blood cells or nervous tissue and often fatal if not treated immediately. Among the venomous snakes are cobras, copperheads, bushmasters, coral snakes, rattlesnakes, mambas, vipers, and water moccasins.

Snakehead, freshwater food fish found in Africa and Asia. An air breather, it wriggles over ground from pond to pond. It has a cylindrical body and flattened head. Length: 6in–3ft (15.2–91.4cm). Family Channidae; species *Channa asiatica*.

Snake-neck Turtle. *See* Side-necked Turtle.

Snake Plant. *See* Sansevieria.

Snake River, river in NW United States; rises in Yellowstone National Park, NW Wyoming; flows SW and N across Idaho; turns N, then W across SE Washington and empties into the Columbia River, near Pasco; site of Hell's Canyon gorge reaching a 7,900-ft (2,410-m) depth; major source of hydroelectricity, and irrigation. Discovered *c.* 1803 by Lewis and Clark. Length: 1,038mi (1,671km).

Snapdragon, any of a genus *(Antirrhinum)* of perennial plants with saclike, two-lipped, purple, red, yellow, or white flowers. The common snapdragon *(A. majus)* is a popular garden plant; height: 0.5–3ft (15–91cm). Family Scrophulariaceae.

Snapper, marine food fish found in tropical waters of the Indo-Pacific and Atlantic. It is usually red or yellow. Length: to 3ft (91cm); weight: 110lb (50kg). The 250 species include red *Lutjanus campechanus*, yellowtail *Ocyurus chrysurus*, and Atlantic gray *L. griseus*. Family Lutjanidae. △392.

Snapping Turtle, large aquatic turtle found in North and South America. It has a large head, broad neck, powerful limbs, and a long saw-toothed tail too bulky to be retracted into its shell. Length: 15in (38cm). Genus *Chelydra*. The much larger related alligator snapper *(Macrochelys temmincki)* of SE United States has a wormlike appendage on its tongue to lure fish. Family Chelydridae. *See also* Turtle.

SNCC. *See* Student Non-violent Coordinating Committee.

Snead, Samuel Jackson "Sam" (1912–), US golfer, b. Hot Springs, Va. Coming out of the West Virginia mountains as an unknown in 1937, he won three PGA titles (1942, 1949, 1951), three Masters (1949, 1952, 1954), and a British Open (1946).

Snipe, migratory, long-billed shorebird, found in swamp grasslands over most of the world. Often valued as game birds, they are mottled black, brown, and buff. Length: 12in (30cm). Family Scolopacidae; Genus *Capella*.

Snodgrass, W(illiam) D(e Witt) (1926–), US poet, b. Wilkinsburg, Pa. A significant figure in the confessional, or autobiographical, school of 20th-century poetry, his works include *Heart's Needle* (1959; Pulitzer Prize 1960) and *After Experience: Poems and Translations* (1968).

Snook, or robalo, marine and freshwater fish found in tropical waters. Large snooks—Atlantic *Centropomus undecimalis*. Length: 56in (142cm); weight: 50lb (22.7kg); freshwater Nile perch *Lates niloticus* (weight: to 200lb, 90kg)—are commercial and sport fish. Small snooks are popular aquarium fish. Family Centropomidae. *See also* Glass Fish.

Snorri Sturluson (1178–1241), Icelandic historian. His *Prose Edda* is a collection of Norse mythology and a discussion of the art of poetry. *Heimskringla*, sagas of the Norwegian king to 1177, mingles history and legend and is an important source for Norwegian history. A lawyer from an aristocratic family, he was politically active, supporting Haakon IV in annexing Iceland to Norway. His son-in-law killed him during political intrigues.

Snow, C(harles) P(ercy) (1905–). English novelist and physicist. He was knighted in 1957 for government work and created baron in 1964. From 1935 he has written a sequence of novels, which included *Strangers and Brothers* (1940), *The Masters* (1951), *The Affair* (1960), *Corridors of Power* (1964), *Last Things* (1970), and *In Their Wisdom* (1974). His nonfiction included *The Two Cultures and the Scientific Revolution* (1959), *Science and Government* (1961), and *Public Affairs* (1971).

Snow, aggregates of frozen water that fall from clouds to Earth's surface, as opposed to frost. *See also* Ice or Snow Crystals. △216.

Snowball, showy shrub widely cultivated in gardens. The snowball or guelder-rose *(Viburnum opulus roseum)* has round-topped, sterile, white or pinkish flower clusters. The Chinese snowball *(Viburnum macrocephalum sterile)* has large balls of white flowers. Family Caprifoliaceae. *See also* Viburnum.

Snowbird. *See* Junco.

Snow Bunting, small, mostly white, seed-eating finch found in circumpolar areas. It builds a cup-shaped nest for its finely spotted eggs (2–6). Species *Plectrophenax nivalis*.

Snowdon, mountain in NW Wales, in Gwynedd. One of its five peaks is the highest in England and Wales, 3,560ft (1,086m). A rack-and-pinion railway climbs it from Llanberis. Much of the area is included in Snowdonia National Park (est. 1951).

Snowdrop, low-growing perennial plant of the Mediterranean region, widely cultivated in gardens worldwide. The green and white, fragrant nodding flowers appear early in spring. The common snowdrop *(Galanthus nivalis)* has long narrow leaves; height: 12in (30cm). Family Amaryllidaceae.

Snowfinch. △608.

Snow Leopard, or ounce, large spotted cat found in central Asian mountains, usually above 8,000ft (2,440m). Not a true leopard, its soft, long fur is whitish to yellow-gray with black spots. The gestation period is 93–103 days and 2–5 young are born. Length: body—47.2–59.1in (120–150cm); tail—35in (89cm); weight: 75–100lb (34–45kg). Family Felidae; species *Uncia uncia*. *See also* Cat. △608.

Snow-on-the-Mountain, annual plant native to W United States. Popular in gardens, it is bushy and has white margins on its upper leaves and small flowers in cuplike clusters. Height: to 2ft (61cm). Family Euphorbiaceae; species *Euphorbia marginata*.

Snowmobile, gasoline-powered racing sled with rubber-cleated tracks and ski runners. In rural areas it is used extensively for transportation in the winter and as a recreational vehicle. As a competitive winter sport, it has been popular since the 1960s and includes a variety of events, classified according to engine displacement (250 cc, 340 cc, 440 cc, and 650 cc). A crude form of the snowmobile was invented in 1928 by Carl Eliason, a Wisconsin woodsman, who attached a 2.5 horsepower outboard motor to a toboggan that had two wooden skis in front. In 1932 he perfected his invention and recorded speeds over 40 miles (64.4km) per hour.

Snowshoe Rabbit, or varying hare, medium-sized hare of N North America with large furry hind feet that act as snowshoes. It is brownish in summer, white in winter. It feeds chiefly on twigs, foliage, and bark. Species *Lepus americanus*. *See also* Hare.

Snowy Owl, white owl that blends with the snowy barren Arctic tundra where it lives. It feeds mainly on lemmings and hares, hunting in daylight during the Arctic summer. Length: to 2ft (61cm). Species *Nyctaea scandiaca*. *See also* Owl.

Soap, substance used to remove dirt and grease, made by the action of alkali on fats. Common soaps are sodium or potassium salts of stearic, oleic, or adipic acids. The molecule has a long chain, one end of which attaches to grease, while the other end dissolves in the water, pulling the grease away into solution. Toilet soaps usually contain colorant and perfume. *See also* Detergent. △1808.

Soap Opera, dramatic serial program, for many years sponsored by companies manufacturing soap and detergents. Soap operas began in the 1930s as 15-minute daytime radio episodes and moved to daytime television in the 1950s, where they were usually extended to 30-minute broadcasts. Soap operas are usually slow-moving episodes of a continuing story with a permanent cast of characters. Often, the story centers around marital problems and other family situations, frequently involving melodramatic events. *As The World Turns* and *The Edge of Night* have continued on US television since 1956.

Soccer, game, also known as association football, played by 2 teams of 11 persons each on a field between 110 and 130 yards (100–118m) long and from 70 to 80 yards (64–73m) wide. Centered at each end of the field is a goal, 8 yards (7.3m) wide by 8 feet (2.4m) high, backed with netting. The round ball is

Bedřich Smetana

Alfred E. Smith

Snapdragon

Snapper

about 28 inches (71cm) in diameter, covered with leather, and inflated. Each team consists of a goalkeeper, two fullbacks, three halfbacks, and five forwards. The object is to advance the ball toward the opponent's goal and between the goal posts by kicking, dribbling, heading, or using any other part of the body other than the arms and hands; the goalkeeper is the only one allowed to use hands. Each goal counts one point. A match consists of two 45-minute periods and may end in a tie. Substitutions are not allowed. The game is controlled by a referee, who is assisted by a linesman, and infractions result in various types of free kicks.

History. Soccer is considered the most popular sport in the world, originating in England in 1863. The sport is governed by the Fédération Internationale de Football Associations, which includes 130 member nations, and sponsors the famed World Cup competition for the Jules Rimet trophy every four years. The game is played on an amateur level throughout the world and professionally in Europe, the United States, and South America. In the United States, where the sport is secondary to US football, interest has increased since the formation of the professional North American Soccer League in 1968. Outside the United States, wagering in soccer pools (choosing a slate of games correctly) is allowed. The sport was first included as an event in the Olympic Games in 1900. △930.

Following is a list of World Cup winners.

WORLD CUP WINNERS

1930	Uruguay
1934	Italy
1938	Italy
1950	Uruguay
1954	W. Germany
1958	Brazil
1962	Brazil
1966	England
1970	Brazil
1974	W. Germany

Social Behaviorism, movement in American sociology emphasizing man's conditioning, learning, and cognition systems in relation to his social roles and structures. Often criticized for neglecting such things as motives, attitudes, and values, it is related to the behaviorism movement in psychology. *See also* Behaviorism. △888.

Social Character, social theory suggesting that each society produces people who share a set of specific personality traits that distinguish that society from all others. According to sociologist Erich Fromm, social character is necessary for the successful functioning of a society and is often acquired at the cost of freedom and will. △888, 892.

Social Contract, concept found in writings of Thomas Hobbes and Jean-Jacques Rousseau that society is based on agreement of the individuals within it. The concept was used to justify struggles for individual rights against oppressive governments in the American and French revolutions.

Social Credit Movement, Canadian political movement. In 1935, William Aberhart won Alberta on a platform of redistribution of income through "social dividends," cash payments to consumers. Social Credit was based on the potential wealth in goods and services of a society. Aberhart's attempts to tax banks and control the money supply were declared unconstitutional and the party polarized into wings stressing monetary reform and populist regionalism. The movement has always been anti-socialist and middle-class. It criticizes federal spending programs and is considered a voice of regional conservatism. Leaders have included W.A.C. Bennett of British Columbia.

Social Darwinism, social concept based on Charles Darwin's theory of natural selection. Popular in the late 19th century, especially among the upper classes, social Darwinism suggested that human social organization was based on the "survival of the fittest" and that certain classes and races dominated because they were biologically superior. The theory has been discredited in the 20th century because it fails to take into consideration gross inequalities of opportunity.

Social Evolution. △876–84.

Socialism, economic system in which the major portion of large-scale productive resources, man-made and natural, are owned by the state or by agencies of the state. While there are various forms of socialism, most socialists agree that public ownership is a necessary component. Socialistic thought is based on the assumption that capitalism is an inefficient way to produce goods and services, and that far greater production is possible under socialism. This production will be divided among the population in a more equitable manner than that characteristic of capitalistic societies, although most socialist writers do not insist on complete equality. △902, 906, 1288, 1326.

Socialist Party, US political group. It was formed by the unification of the Social Democratic party and the Socialist Labor party (1901). The party is dedicated to the state ownership of all public utilities and important industries. Its best known leaders were Eugene V. Debs, its presidential candidate five times, and Norman Thomas, who ran six times.

Socialist Realism, artistic style. Generally recognized as the "official" style of the USSR., it usually takes an idealized, heroic form and is intended to advance the doctrines of the state. It is diametrically opposed to Aestheticism.

Socialist Revolutionary Party, Russian political party established in 1902. It supported radical populism and political terrorism and became the most popular left-wing party before the revolution, when an internal split occurred. A leftist faction did participate in the Bolshevik government until the party was officially suppressed in 1922. △1310.

Socialization, process by which a person learns and internalizes the beliefs, values, and standards of behavior acceptable to his society. Socialization allows the individual to become a functioning member of his group. It is the means by which social continuity and cultural consistency are accomplished. The majority of individuals in any given group must agree on the propriety of certain ways of behaving if that group is to survive. Socialization ensures that agreement. △ 782, 888, 892.

Social Pathology, theory in sociology that applies biological concepts to the analysis of social problems. According to social pathologists, societies can develop abnormally and their problems can be "diagnosed" by comparing them to a "healthy" model. Because of its human orientation, social pathology stresses the importance of adjustment and views such things as alcoholism and poor education as "disease."

Social Perception, in social psychology, the ways in which people's perceptions of others are colored by their past experience, attitudes, and expectations. Some examples include processes of "leveling" (paying attention only to details relevant to one's desires), "sharpening" (emphasizing such details), and "assimilation" (distorting ambiguous information to put it in line with one's expectations). Such processes help individuals maintain their prejudices, stereotypes, and first impressions.

Social Psychology, field that studies individuals interacting with others in groups and with society. Topics include attitudes and how they change, prejudice, rumors, aggression, altruism, group behavior, conformity, and social conflict. Though both have similar subject matter, social psychologists focus more on individuals, sociologists, more on groups. *See also* Sociology. △892.

Social Security Act (1935), US legislation to provide for government-protected social insurance. This act, part of the New Deal of Pres. Franklin D. Roosevelt, required a set amount to be withheld from workers' pay to subsidize old-age and survivors benefits, disability, unemployment insurance, and social welfare. There were grants provided to the states to cover some costs of this system, and a Social Security Board was created to administer it. Historically, benefits and deductions have been raised as prices have increased.

Social War or **Marsic War,** war waged against Rome by her rebellious Italian allies *(socii)*. It began in 91 BC and continued to 87 with the hardest battles fought in 90–89. The Marsian people led the fight to gain Roman citizenship, which had been proposed by Drusus and withheld by the senate. The war was a stalemate and ended only when Rome granted citizenship to Italians S of the Po. △1018.

Society, in sociology any social group that is autonomous and nonspecialized, continues from generation to generation, and is fairly large in population. To be termed a society, members of the social group must also share common attitudes, goals, and basic beliefs, and they must have effective methods for socializing new members and controlling deviants. *See also* Socialization. △878–82, 888–90.

Society Islands, island group in S Pacific Ocean; part of W French Polynesia; comprised of the Windward Islands which include Tahiti, Mooréa, Mehetia, and islets, and the Leeward Islands, including Raiatea, Bora-Bora, Huahine, Maupiti, and several others. Islands contain volcanic mountains and coral formations; they were first sighted 1607 by Portuguese navigator Pedro Fernandes de Queirós; claimed for Great Britain 1767 by Samuel Wallis; claimed for France 1768 by Louis de Bougainville; made a French protectorate in 1843. Islands support tropical fruit industry. Exports: rum, sugar, mother-of-pearl, vanilla. Capital is Papeete, on Tahiti. Area: 621sq mi (1,608sq km). Pop. 81,424.

Sociogram, diagram used by sociologists to illustrate interpersonal relationships and structure in small groups. Circles, representing people, are linked by arrows, representing the reciprocity of relationships. The sociogram provides clues to the way leadership emerges.

Sociohormone. *See* Pheromone.

Sociolinguistics, area of sociology that studies the ways language, spoken and written, changes according to social context. Besides illustrating the influence formal and informal situations have on language, research shows that an individual's class status affects pronunciation of certain vowel and consonant sounds. △866, 890.

Sociology, science that examines society by describing and evaluating its institutions and processes. It attempts to discover the factors and causes that form these institutions and the effects the institutions have on the lives and personalities of those who are required to live under them. △888–96, 1290, 1360.

Sociology of Work. *See* Industrial Sociology.

Sociopathic Personality, personality disturbance marked by inability or unwillingness to conform to accepted social norms. Antisocial behavior does not arouse normal feelings of guilt. Forms of this disturbance include the antisocial reaction, also called the *psychopathic personality,* in which there is a pattern of emotional shallowness, impulsivity, and lack of genuine concern for others and the *dyssocial reaction,* in which concern for others and strong loyalties may exist, but the individual disregards normal social norms or adheres to those of a deviate subculture. Sexual deviations and addictions are other subtypes of the sociopathic personality. △914.

Socrates (469–399 BC), Greek philosopher. Written about by Plato, he spent most of his life in Athens, engaging those he met in profound philosophic discussions. Believing that the highest meaning of life is attained through self-knowledge, he tried to convince his fellow men of the value of self analysis. He was loyal to this "mission," having a "demon" inside that would not let him stray from his pursuit. Found guilty of impiety and corruption of the young, he was condemned to death and poisoned himself. He wrote nothing although his verbal teachings influenced many. △852.

Soda. △1554.

Sodalite, a silicate mineral, sodium aluminum silicate with chlorine, found in alkaline igneous rocks. Cubic system small, dodecahedron crystals; also in masses. Glassy colorless, white, blue, pink; hardness 5.5–6; sp gr 2.2. Sometimes used as gem.

Soddy, Frederick (1877–1956), English chemist who received a Nobel Prize in 1921 for his studies of radioactive substances and his contributions to the isotope theory. With Ernest Rutherford he predicted the formation of helium during radioactive decay, and later, with William Ramsay, detected it spectroscopically. He coined the term isotopes to describe elements that exist in more than one form, have different atomic weights, but are indistinguishable chemically. In 1920 he revealed the value of isotopes in computing geological age.

Sodium, common metallic element (symbol Na) of the alkali-metal group, first isolated in 1807 by Sir Humphry Davy. It occurs in the sea and in many minerals. Chief source is sodium chloride, from which it is extracted by electrolysis. The metal is used as a heat-transfer medium and in making some organic compounds. Its compounds are extensively used commercially. Chemically, sodium is a very reactive electropositive element. Properties: at. no 11; at. wt. 22.9898; sp. gr. 0.971; melt. pt. 208.05°F (97.81°C); boil. pt. 1638°F (892°C); most common isotope Na^{23} (100%). *See also* Alkali elements. △1552, 1556, 1566.

Sodium Chloride (salt). △1506, 1556, 1558, 1562.

Sodium Hydroxide, or caustic soda, white deliquescent crystalline substance (formula NaOH) obtained by the electrolysis of brine or by treating soda ash with a solution of lime in water. It is used in chemical synthesis and as an alkali in the manufacture of rayon, paper, detergents, soap, and aluminum.

Sodium Ion. △1506.

Sodium Salt. △1568.

Sod Worm. *See* Webworm.

Sofia (Sofija), capital city of Bulgaria and of Sofia prov.; in W central Bulgaria, approx. 35mi (56km) from Yugoslav border. Once residence of Constantine the Great, Sofia was ruled by Byzantine Empire 1018–1185, by the second Bulgarian empire (1186–1382), and by the Ottoman Empire (1382–1877). Sofia was taken by Russia 1877 and chosen for capital of Bulgaria in 1879. City contains opera house, museums, 19th-century Church of St George, a university (1888), and several technical schools; it is Bulgaria's most important commercial center. Industries: machinery, textiles, rubber, leather goods, food processing plants. Founded 2nd century. Pop. 950,676.

Softball, a game similar to baseball. It is played by two teams of nine persons each on a field with no set dimensions other than the infield, which measures 60 feet (18.3m) square. The ball is about 12 inches (30.5cm) in diameter, and the rules are close to those of baseball except for the pitching distance (43 feet; 13.1m), the amount of innings (seven), and the pitching delivery (underhand). Softball was originally invented as an indoor game in Chicago in 1887 by Lewis Rober, a Minneapolis fireman, and was known under several different names ("indoor baseball," "kitten ball," "mush ball," "playground ball," "ladies baseball") until 1926. The game began to increase in popularity when it was first moved outdoors in 1930. The first national tournament was held at the Chicago's World's Fair in 1933. The sport is governed by the Amateur Softball Association, founded in 1934.

Soft-coated Wheaten Terrier, sporting dog (terrier group) known for over 200 years in Ireland; brought to US in 1946. Used to hunt small game and guard stock, the soft-coated wheaten has a medium-long head, dark hazel eyes under a strong brow, compact body, moderately long legs, and a docked tail carried up. Its distinctive soft, wavy coat is clear wheaten-colored. Average size: 18–19in (46–48cm) high at shoulder; 35–45lb (16–20.5kg). *See also* Terrier.

Softener, Water, substance added to water to reduce its hardness, that is, its inability to form a lather with soap as a result of the presence of dissolved calcium, magnesium, and iron compounds. Some hardness, mostly due to bicarbonates of these metals, can be removed by boiling; the remaining "permanent" hardness is mostly due to sulfates of the metals and is reduced by adding such compounds as sodium carbonate, trisodium phosphate, or geolites (hydrated silicates of calcium and aluminum) to remove or sequester the metallic ions.

Soft-shelled Turtle, freshwater turtle widely distributed in Old and New Worlds. It has a soft, leathery shell, beak with fleshy lips, and a snorkel-like proboscis. Length: to 30in (76cm). The most common of seven genera is *Trionyx*. Family Trionychidae. *See also* Turtle. △520.

Soil, surface layer of Earth capable of supporting plant life. An aggregation of mineral and organic particles, it consists of undissolved nonliving substances produced by the weathering and breakdown of surface rocks, organic matter, water, and gases, required by plants and subterranean organisms. Soil acts as a reservoir for plant nutrients, absorbing and oxidizing waste products of plant root growth. The chemical composition and physical structure of soil are determined by its original geological material, vegetative cover, and topography. △300.

Soil Conservation and Reclamation, preserving and reconstituting arable soils through programs to prevent soil erosion and nutrient depletion and to improve crop yields. Proper soil management includes crop rotation, green manuring, fertilization, irrigation, drainage, and cultivation techniques, such as strip cropping. Semiarid soils are being reclaimed by laying asphalt moisture barriers below the soil surface to improve water retention and reduce the amount of water needed for irrigation. *See also* Crop Rotation; Irrigation. △300, 364.

Soil Profile, vertical view of horizontal layers, or horizons, of soil from the surface down to the unaltered parent material. This profile is used in classifying soils, with the ideal being one in which soluble substances from the top horizon have leached into the second horizon and the third horizon is the parent material of the surface soil. Bedrock underlies all three.

Soil Testing, process of analyzing the chemical and mineral composition and porosity of soil to determine its ability to support plant life. The principal nutrients needed by plants are nitrogen, potassium, and phosphorus. Soil alkalinity or acidity (pH) can, in some cases, be adjusted chemically or organically to meet a particular crop's needs. △312.

Sol, in Roman mythology, two Sun gods. One was Sol Indiges. The other was Sol Invictus. Emperor Elagabalus tried to make the worship of Sol Invictus the major religion in Rome. △312.

Solar Cell, device to convert sunlight directly to electric power. A solar cell normally consists of a *p*-type silicon crystal coated with an *n*-type silicon crystal. Solar radiation creates a potential difference between the two crystals and current flows between the electrodes connecting them. All wavelengths shorter than one micron can create electrical energy; the cells are about 10% efficient. Several thousand cells may be deployed in panels to provide power of a few hundred watts. △1486, 1636.

Solar Constant, the steady rate at which heat from the Sun is received from just outside the Earth's atmosphere, measuring approximately two gram-calories per square centimeter (perpendicular to the Sun's rays) per minute.

Solar Eclipse. *See* Eclipse, Solar.

Solar Energy, thermal and electromagnetic energy from the Sun. Approximately 35% of the energy reaching the Earth is absorbed; most of this energy is spent evaporating moisture into clouds; some is converted into organic chemical energy by photosynthesis of plants. Man is seeking ways to utilize solar energy in the form of liquid heat storage and generation of electricity through solar photovoltaic cells. The effective use of solar energy is hampered by the diurnal cycle, seasonal and climatic variations, and presently cheaper energy forms. △288, 1636.

Solar Maximum. △94.

Solar Prominence. *See* Prominence, Solar.

Solar System, the celestial group consisting of the Sun and the assemblage of bodies, gas, and dust particles that revolve around it in closed orbits under the influence of its gravitational attraction. The known constituents include the major planets: Mercury, Venus, Earth, Mars, Jupiter, Saturn, Uranus, Neptune, and Pluto, the planetary satellites or moons, thousands of minor planets, or asteroids (mostly between Mars and Jupiter), many comets, meteorites, dust, and gas. △48–50.

Solar Time, system of time reckoning based upon the interval between successive transits of the Sun across the observer's meridian (the solar day). Because of variations in the Earth's orbital velocity and changes in the Sun's apparent position as viewed from the orbiting Earth, solar days vary greatly in length throughout the year. An average or mean solar day has therefore been adopted, giving rise to mean solar time. As measured on the 0° meridian at the Greenwich Observatory, mean solar time takes the form of Greenwich Time or Universal Time.

Solar Wind, particles accelerated by high temperatures of the solar corona to velocities great enough to allow them to escape from the Sun's gravity. The solar wind deflects the tail of the Earth's magnetosphere and the tails of comets away from the Sun. When the solar wind meets the magnetic field of the Earth, a shock wave results.

Solder, alloy of low melting point used to join together metals with higher melting points. Soft solders consist of alloys of tin and lead in varying porportions; brazing solders are alloys of copper and zinc. △1604.

Sole, marine flatfish found in the Atlantic from NW Africa to Norway. This food fish is green-gray or black-brown with dark spots. Length: 23.6in (60cm). Species include common *Solea solea* and hogchocker *Trinectes maculatus*. Family Soleidae. △392.

Solenodon, endangered species of nocturnal insectivores that resemble large shrews; one species occurs in Cuba, the other in Hispaniola. They have long, scaly tails. At least one species has poisonous saliva. Length: 1ft (30cm). Genus *Solenodon*. *See also* Insectivore. △628.

Soccer

Socrates

Sofia, Bulgaria: Alexander II memorial

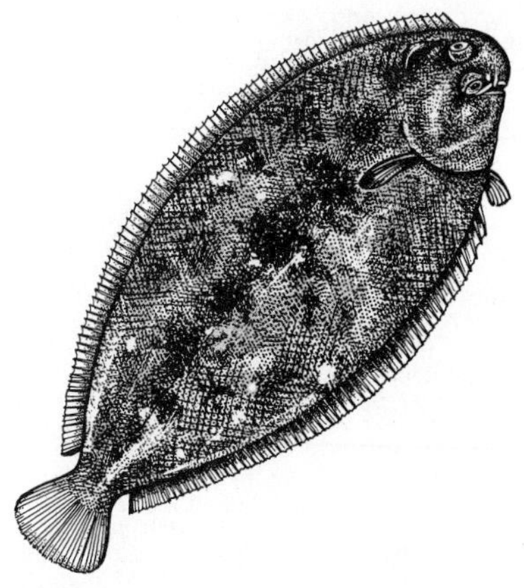

Sole

Solenoid. △1536.

Soleus. △684.

Solid, state of matter in which a substance has a relatively fixed shape and size. The forces between atoms or molecules are strong enough to hold them in definite locations (about which they can vibrate) and to resist change in volume of the material or application of shear stress. *See also* Crystal; Liquid; Gas. △1502–06, 1562.

Solid Geometry. △1466.

Solid South, term used to describe the South's historical allegiance to the Democratic party. This allegiance was strengthened by the Republican party's position against slavery and favoring of a tough Reconstruction policy after the Civil War. Republicans made little headway in the South until Dwight D. Eisenhower's administration (1953–61) and the identification of the Democrats with the civil rights movement. The shift from an agricultural to an industrial economy also played a role in the decline of Democratic strength.

Solid State, state of matter in which the constituent atoms and molecules vibrate about fixed positions. Solid-state electronic devices are based on semiconductors, the term being used to distinguish these devices from electron tubes in which electrons pass through a vacuum or low-pressure gas. *See also* Semiconductor. △1548, 1668.

Solid-State Chemistry, study of the chemical properties of solid chemical compounds. Solid-state chemistry includes investigations into the structure of crystalline compounds and into the mechanism involved in decompositions, oxidations, and other reactions of solids. △1506.

Solid-State Physics, the physics of solid materials. From the study of the structure, binding forces, electrical, magnetic, and thermal properties of solids have come the development of the transistor, semiconductor, maser, laser, solar cell, and the printed circuits used in computers, all technological developments of revolutionary significance. Solid-state physics is a relatively recent branch of physics, involving far more complicated quantum mechanical calculations than the preceding studies of gases and liquids. Among the most eminent solid-state physicists are William Shockley, John Bardeen, and Walter Brattain, developers of the transistor; and Charles Townes, inventor of the maser. All won the Nobel Prize for their inventions.

Solid-Waste Disposal, systems for managing refuse in a healthful and economic way. In urban areas, bulk containers are lifted mechanically into compactor-equipped trucks that transport refuse to a disposal site. Combustible wastes may be burned in an incinerator. Garbage ground into small particles may be discharged into the sewer system. Ocean disposal of refuse is now prohibited in many areas; sanitary land disposal sites create areas that can be used later as parks or golf courses. △1768.

Solingen, city in W West Germany, on Wupper River, 14mi (23km) ESE of Düsseldorf; annexed as part of Prussia 1815; heavily bombed during WWII; world-famous for cutlery made from Solingen steel. Industries: knives, scissors, surgical instruments, razors, chemicals, machine tools, steel castings. Chartered 1374. Pop. 175,167.

Solomon (died *c.* 922 BC), third king of Israel (*c.* 961–922 BC), son of David and Bathsheba. He succeeded David and consolidated the empire. At first he ruled peacefully, made alliances with Egypt and Phoenicia, and showed wisdom. Later he became despotic, heavily taxed the tribes, and brought on the revolt of Jeroboam I. Solomon is regarded as the author of Proverbs, the Song of Solomon, and Wisdom of Solomon. △982.

Solomon Islands, volcanic island group in W Pacific Ocean, E of New Guinea; extends for 900mi (1,449km) and is comprised of the British Solomon Islands Protectorate including Guadalcanal, Malaita, Santa Isabel, Santa Cruz Islands, Shortland Islands, San Cristobal, and others, and to the N, Bougainville, Buka, and Green islands, part of Papua New Guinea. Discovered 1567 by Spaniard Álvaro de Medaña, it was not successfully colonized until the 18th century when German and British traders and missionaries arrived. Germany abandoned the N islands to Britain 1900; after Australian occupation of the N islands in WWI, the League of Nations mandated these (now part of Papua New Guinea) to Australia. Guadalcanal and several other islands were occupied by Japanese in WWII, and were freed by US forces in fierce fighting 1943–44. Inhabitants are mostly Melanesians; subsistence farming is main occupation. Protectorate government is at Honiara, on Guadalcanal. Exports: copra, exotic woods, gold. Area: approx. 15,500sq mi (40,145sq km). Pop. 204,186.

Solomon's Seal, or David's harp, perennial plant native to cool temperate regions of Europe and Asia. It has broad, waxy leaves, white or greenish flowers, and blue or black berries. Height: to 3ft (0.9m). Family Liliaceae; species *Polygonatum multiflorum.*

Solon (*c.* 640–559 BC), Athenian poet and statesman who first gained fame with a poem in 612 BC. In 594 he was made archon and is known for his numerous reforms in law and citizen's rights, including abolishing debt laws, instituting habeas corpus, and freeing some of the slaves. △908, 992.

Solothurn, capital city of Solothurn canton in NNW Switzerland, on the Aare River, 19mi (31km) N of Bern. A former free town of the Holy Roman Empire (1218), it joined the Swiss Confederation 1481; served as the residence of the French ambassadors to the Swiss diet until 1797; site of municipal museum, 18th-century Italian baroque church, 15th-century town hall, 17th-century arsenal, 13th-century clock tower. Products: cattle, cereals. Industries: gas and electrical apparatus, radios, watches, printing, metal goods. Pop. 17,708.

Solstice, either of the two days of the year when the Sun is at its greatest angular distance from the celestial equator, leading to the longest day and shortest night (summer solstice) in one hemisphere of the Earth and the shortest day and longest night (winter solstice) in the other hemisphere. In the northern hemisphere the summer solstice occurs on about June 21 and the winter solstice on about Dec. 22.

Solute, gaseous, liquid, or solid substance that is dissolved and dispersed homogeneously in a solvent to form a solution. Solids, such as calcium bicarbonate, sugars, and starch, dissolve in water. Liquids can dissolve in liquids; for example, ethanol and water are miscible in all quantities at room temperature and gases, such as hydrogen chloride (HCl), are soluble in liquid water. △1562, 1568.

Solution, mixture, homogeneous on a molecular scale, of two or more chemically distinct compounds inseparable by filters. Most common are liquids and solids in liquids, but gases may be dissolved in liquids; and gases, liquids, and solids may also be dissolved in solids. The amount of a substance dissolved in a solvent is called the concentration of a solution and may be expressed in grams per liter, gram equivalents per liter, or as a molar fraction. The ability of one substance to dissolve another depends on the compounds, the temperature, and to a small extent the pressure. An "ideal solution" is one that obeys Raoult's Law: at constant temperature the partial pressure of a component in a liquid mixture is proportional to its mole fraction in the mixture. Heat can be evolved (an exothermic solution) or absorbed (endothermic) when a solution is formed. *See also* Molarity. △1504, 1562, 1568.

Solution, Aqueous, *See* Aqueous Solution.

Solution, Electrolytic. *See* Electrolytic Solution.

Solution, Molal. *See* Molal Solution.

Solvent, substance, especially in liquid form, that dissolves and disperses other substances (solutes) to form a solution. This inert medium may be non-polar, exemplified by hydrocarbons or benzene, as utilized in paints, varnishes, and oils, or polar, such as water or alcohol, which are solvents widely found in nature. △1562, 1568.

Solzhenitsyn, Aleksandr (1918–), Soviet author. Arrested for criticism of Stalin while in the Red Army, he was sentenced to a forced labor camp (1945–53), where he contracted cancer, from which he recovered. Subsequently exiled in Kazakhstan, he was officially rehabilitated in 1957. Now a major spokesman for Soviet dissident intellectuals, his writings include the novels *One Day in the Life of Ivan Denisovich* (1962), *The First Circle* (1964), *Cancer Ward* (1966), *August 1914* (1972), and the nonfiction *The Gulag Archipelago* (1974). He encountered growing opposition from the Soviet regime, was deported to the West (1974), and settled in the United States. He was awarded the Nobel Prize for literature (1970).

Somalia (Somaliya), independent republic in NE Africa, occupies majority of Horn of Africa; bounded by Gulf of Aden (N), Indian Ocean (S and E), and Kenya, Ethiopia, and Afars and Issas (W). Most of the W boundaries, particularly the Ethiopian frontier, are in constant dispute. Somalia's 1,500mi (2,415km) coastline contains no natural harbors and its two rivers, the Shebelle and Juba, are both unnavigable and are used as a source of irrigation. The N section is mountainous with high plateaus; land between the two rivers is low farm country. The climate is tropical and suffers insufficient rainfall, causing disastrous droughts.

The economy is based primarily on livestock and subsistence farming. Chief products are bananas, millet, sesame, sugar, maize, cotton. Main industries include: tuna processing, soap, leather, textiles, and incense; the sea yields fish and resources of salt, limestone, and clay. Somalia is extremely poor, the per capita income is $50 per year; aid from USSR, Italy, United States, Egypt, Communist China, and Britain virtually keeps Somalia from complete economic collapse. Somalis, the principal ethnic group, are a Cushitic people of Middle East origin; most are nomadic or seminomadic Muslims following the Sunni sect of the Shafii. Only 10% is literate; there is no national written language and as a result Somali poetry and classical literature are in danger of being lost.

History. In 1884–86 Britain established a protectorate in N Somalia, while the Italians controlled the S territory. In 1960 the two territories joined to form the independent Somali Democratic Republic. The constitution, confirmed 1961, provides for an election of the deputies for the National Assembly by universal suffrage; the term of service is 5 years. They in turn elect the president, who appoints a premier approved by the assembly.

The Somalis are believed to have arrived in the NW regions *c.* AD 750; by the 10th century Arab influence predominated the coastal areas. The disputes between Ethiopia and Somalia continued through the 13th–16th centuries.

PROFILE

Official name: Somali Democratic Republic
Area: 246,200sq mi (637,658sq km)
Population: 3,000,000
Chief cities: Mogadisho (capital); Hargeisa; Kismayu
Religion: Islam
Language: Somali, English, Italian, Arabic
Monetary unit: Somali shilling

Somaliland, British. *See* British Somaliland.

Somaliland, French. *See* Afars and Issas, French Territory of the.

Somatopsychology, study of how physical problems like disease, disfigurement, or disability affect behavior. Psychologists study and try to help cancer patients, accident victims, the blind, and others with problems of adjustment. This specialty should be distinguished from psychosomatic medicine, which is concerned with illnesses attributed to psychological problems. △814.

Somatotype, or body build, was related to personality by US psychologist William Sheldon. He developed three descriptive categories: the endomorph is round, soft, and smooth-skinned with short arms and legs; the ectomorph is thin-skinned, narrow, and slightly muscled with long arms and legs; and the mesomorph has large bones, very developed muscles, and thick skin. Most people are mixtures of all three but can be rated in each category. Sheldon found that persons rated high in endomorphy tend to be relaxed, sociable, comfort-loving, and tolerant; those high in ectomorphy are often physically inhibited, secretive, and like intellectual activity; and those tending toward mesomorphy are more adventurous, aggressive, and like exercise. Applying his theory to 260 delinquent boys he found the mesomorphic type most disposed to delinquency, but there was not a one-to-one relationship. Sheldon believed this relationship emphasized the genetic influence on behavior; however, behavior influences physique as well. Each may spring from a common environmental cause. △814.

Somerfield-hydrogen Spectrum. △1480.

Somerset, Edward Seymour, Duke of (?1506–52), protector of England, brother of Jane Seymour. Winning Henry VIII's favor, he commanded successfully in Scotland (1544) and at Boulogne (1545). Appointed protector of Edward VI, a minor, on Henry's death (1547), he obtained almost royal powers. His religious reforms, leading to the Act of Uniformity (1549), established Protestantism in England. Deposed from the protectorate (1549), he was subsequently beheaded.

Somerville, city in E Massachusetts, on the Mystic River; site of Old Powder Mill (1703) and Prospect Hill, where Gen. Rufus Putnam raised first flag of

United Colonies (1776). Industries: vehicle bodies, meat packing, clothing. Founded 1630; separated from Charlestown 1842; inc. as city 1872. Pop. (1970) 88,779.

Somme, river that rises in N France, above San Quentin; flows WNW for 150mi (242km) through Amiens and Abbeville to English Channel; scene of heavy fighting July 1–Nov. 18, 1916, between British and Germans; occupied by Germans May–June 1940 and recovered by Allies 1944 in WWII. Length: 152mi (245km).

Somnambulism. *See* Sleepwalking.

Somoza García, Anastasio (1896–1956), central figure in Nicaraguan politics from 1936, when he ousted President Sacasa, until his death. Somoza created both a dictatorial government and a political dynasty; he was succeeded in office by his two sons, Luis and Anastasio.

Sonar, underwater detection and navigation system. The letters stand for SOund, NAvigation, and Radar. The system emits high frequency sound that is reflected by underwater objects. △1802.

Sonata, a composition for one or more instruments (usually including a keyboard instrument) in three movements of fast-slow-fast tempo. A scherzo or minuet is often included before the final movement. Classically, the first movement is in "sonata-allegro form," which involves an exposition of contrasting themes, their development, and a recapitulation. This structure may appear in the later sonata movements as well, and appears in string quartets, symphonies, and concertos. The second movement of a sonata is typically a two- or three-part adagio, and the final movement is presto in rondo form. The term was first used in the 16th century to distinguish an instrumental from a vocal work. Sonatas increased in importance because of increasing emphasis on instrumental music during the baroque era. In the late 17th century the trio sonata emerged as the primary baroque chamber music form. This form was adopted by J.S. Bach and Handel. The outstanding baroque keyboard composer, Domenico Scarlatti, presaged the classical sonata in his explorations of thematic contrast. By the late 18th century, sonatas for groups of instruments became known as string quartets and symphonies, and sonata acquired its modern meaning. The experiments of K.P.E. Bach were particularly influential in this period, culminating in the perfection of the classical form by Haydn, Mozart, and above all Beethoven. In the romantic period the most original development was a striving for thematic unification, most fully realized in Liszt's Sonata in B Minor for piano (1854). Composers of the twentieth century, Paul Hindemith, Stravinsky, Prokofiev, Shostakovich, and Bartok, have introduced dissonant counterpoint and continuing key changes to the sonata.

Song of Solomon, or **Song of Songs,** book of the Old Testament comprised of a series of love poems spoken alternately by a man and a woman. They were perhaps originally written for wedding feasts and edited to their present form in the 3rd century BC.

Sonic Boom, the thunderlike sound produced when the high-pressure shock waves formed at the nose, wing leading edges, and tail of a supersonic aircraft spread out behind the aircraft and strike the ground. *See also* Supersonic Flight. △1496.

Sonnet, lyric poem of 14 lines, generally in iambic pentameter, following a definite rhyme scheme. There are two basic rhyme schemes. The Italian or Petrarchan sonnet follows the scheme abbaabba cdecde. The English or Elizabethan sonnet rhymes abab cdcd efef gg. The sonnet was given its greatest expression in the work of Petrarch, Spenser, Shakespeare, and Milton, among others.

Sons of Liberty, American colonial group. This secret organization began, principally in Connecticut and New York, to protest the Stamp Act (1765); it was dedicated to work for freedom and liberty in the 13 British colonies.

Soo Canals. *See* Sault Sainte Marie Canals.

Soochow (Suzhou, or Su-chow), city in E central China, 55mi (89km) W of Shanghai on Grand Canal; capital of Wu kingdom 5th century BC; famous silk industry developed under Sung dynasty (12th century). It was declared a treaty port 1896; fell to Communist control 1949; noted since 100 BC for its many gardens, temples, and canals. Industries: silk, cotton, embroidery, food processing, chemicals. Pop. 1,500,000.

Soong Family, term used to refer to the talented children of the US-trained missionary, businessman, and industrialist Charles Jones Soong (1866–1918). The children came to be regarded as the first family of modern China. One son, **T. V. Soong** (1894–1971), occupied many high government positions, including minister of foreign affairs (1942–45) and president of the Executive Yuan (1945–47). Three daughters all married famous Chinese leaders. **Ai-ling** (1890–) became Mrs. H. H. Kung; **Ch'ing-ling** (1892–) became Mme. Sun Yat-sen and later held positions under the Communists; and **Mei-ling** (1898–) married Chiang Kai-shek.

Sophists, Greek teachers of the 5th to 4th centuries BC. To train young men of political careers, the Sophists provided what higher education was available in their day. They taught all the known subjects, but emphasized rhetoric as a means of convincing listeners. The Sophists were accused of using rhetoric as a device to win points rather than as a way to expound truth. They tended to teach their students what the students wanted to learn, which was often the way to get ahead rather than the way to truth. A leading Sophist, Protagoras, is a figure in one of Plato's dialogues.

Sophocles (496–406 BC), Greek playwright, born at Colonus. Of 120 plays, only 7 tragedies and part of a satyr play remain. These include *Ajax, Antigone* (441), *Electra, Oedipus Rex* (*c.*428), and *Oedipus at Colonus* (produced 401). His works introduced a third speaking actor, added stage scenery, and increased the chorus from 12 to 15 members. A popular, prominent figure in his day, he was often elected to public offices he had not sought. With Aeschylus and Euripides, he was considered one of the three great tragedians of ancient Greece. *See also* Ajax; Antigone. △998.

Sora, Sora Rail, or Carolina Crake, grayish-brown bird, best known of North American rails. Height: 8in (20cm). Species: *Porzana carolina. See also* Rail.

Sorbs. *See* Wends.

Sorcery, magical manipulation of the natural world for specific ends. Sorcerers often seek the assistance of spirits or try to exercise supernatural powers in carrying out practices designed to cause or cure disease, reveal the future, etc. Anthropologists sometimes distinguish sorcery from witchcraft—witches need inherent spiritual powers whereas sorcerers do not. In many societies, including numerous Amerindian ones, sorcerers enjoy high social status. *See also* Shaman; Witch Doctor.

Sorel, Georges (1847–1922), French social philosopher. Until 1892, Sorel was a civil engineer. Afterward he devoted himself entirely to proclaiming his doctrine of social revolution known as "Syndicalism." Ideologies, for Sorel, were subservient to violent action. His most important work is *Reflections on Violence* (1908). *See also* Syndicalism.

Sorghum, tropical cereal grass native to Africa and cultivated worldwide. Types raised for grain are varieties of *Sorghum vulgare* that has leaves coated with white waxy blooms and panicles that bear up to 3,000 kernels. It is used for meal, oil, starch, dextrose, and alcoholic beverages. Height: 2–8ft (0.6–2.4m). Family Gramineae. △326, 454.

Sorrel, or dock, herbaceous perennial weeds native to temperate regions. They have large basal or stem leaves and small green or brown flowers. Height: to 9ft (2.7m). Family Polygonaceae; genus *Rumex*.

Sorrel Tree, or sourwood, deciduous tree native to E and SE United States. Cultivated varieties are smaller than wild types. It has oval, sour leaves that are red in autumn and small white flowers. Height: 20–80ft (6–24m). Family Ericaceae; species *Oxydendrum arboreum*.

Soul. △850.

Sound, physiological sensation perceived by the ear, caused by an oscillating source, and transmitted through a material medium as a sound (acoustic) wave. The human ear can perceive sounds that have frequencies between 20 hertz and 20,000 hertz; the study of oscillations within this range constitutes the branch of physics known as *acoustics*—infrasonics is concerned with oscillations of lower frequencies and ultrasonics with sounds of higher frequencies.

The velocity *(c)* at which a sound wave travels through a medium depends on the elasticity of the medium *(K)* and its density ρ: $c = \sqrt{K/\rho}$. If the medium is a gas, the sound wave is longitudinal and the velocity of propagation depends on the gas tempera-

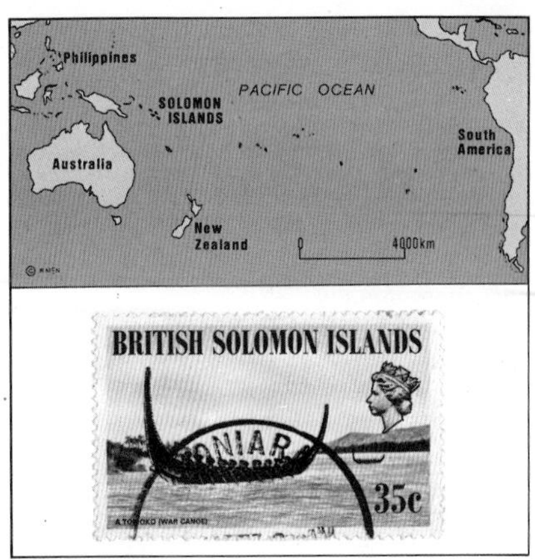

Philippines
SOLOMON ISLANDS
PACIFIC OCEAN
Australia
South America
New Zealand
4000km
BRITISH SOLOMON ISLANDS
35c

Solomon Islands

Aleksandr Solzhenitsyn

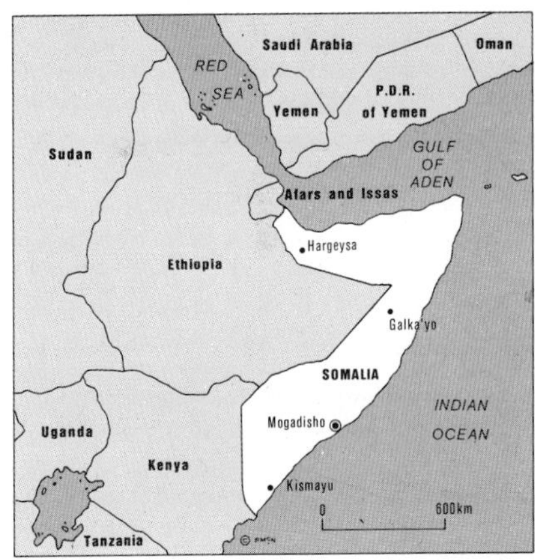

Saudi Arabia
Oman
RED SEA
Yemen
P.D.R. of Yemen
Sudan
GULF OF ADEN
Afars and Issas
Hargeysa
Ethiopia
Galka'yo
SOMALIA
INDIAN OCEAN
Uganda
Mogadisho
Kenya
Kismayu
0
600km
Tanzania

Somalia

Sorrel tree

ture $c_e = c_0\sqrt{1+\alpha\theta}$, where c_0 and c_e are the velocities at 0°C and θ°C and α is the coefficient of expansion of the gas. The velocity of sound in dry air at STP is 331.4 meters per second (740.5mph) and depends on the height above sea level.

Every pure sound is characterized by its intensity, pitch, and timbre. The intensity is the rate of flow of sound energy through unit area perpendicular to the direction of flow. *See also* Noise; Pitch; Sound Sensation. △1498.

Sound, Stereophonic. *See* Stereophonic Sound.

Sounding, any of several techniques used in determining the depth of water. The simplest means of sounding is by dropping a weighted line to the bottom. Acoustical means, using a sonic depth finder, are often used. This underwater device measures the time it takes a sound produced just below the surface to be reflected from the bottom. A transducer converts an electrical pulse into an acoustical pressure wave and, receiving its echo, converts it back to electric energy.

Sound Recording and Reproduction, the storing of sound waves in converted form and their subsequent recovery. Commonly, the sound is first converted into a physical analog, such as vibrations in a microphone diaphragm, which in turn produces electric signals. A tape recorder stores signals by an arrangement of magnetized iron particles on a tape. The sound is recovered when the tape regenerates the voltage pattern, which is then reconverted to sound waves in a loudspeaker. Phonographs store sound as modulations in the spiral groove on a disk. It is reproduced when the groove causes vibrations in a stylus, which are converted to electric signals and back to sound. Optical recording, as in sound tracks, stores sound by exposing the side of a filmstrip to light beams with intensities analogous to the acoustic signals. △1798.

Sound Sensation, physiological sensation perceived by the ear when stimulated by a sound wave within the frequency range 20–20,000 hertz. The sensitivity of the ear depends primarily on the intensity of the sound but also to a lesser extent on its frequency. The intensity of a pure tone that is just audible is known as the threshold of audibility. This varies with frequency but is a minimum at about 3,-500 hertz when the threshold pressure (RMS) is about 0.0008 pascal. At a frequency of 1,000 hertz the maximum intensity that the ear can perceive is 10^{14} times greater than the threshold. Beyond this intensity the sensation becomes one of pain. △1498.

Sound Shielding. *See* Acoustic Shielding.

Sound Transmission. △1794, 1798.

Sound Wave. *See* Sound.

Sourwood. *See* Sorrel Tree.

Sousa, John Philip (1854–1932), US composer and bandmaster, b. Washington, D.C. In 1911 he toured the world with his own band. He composed over 100 marches, including *Semper Fidelis* (1888) and *The Stars and Stripes Forever* (1897).

Sousaphone, largest brass wind musical instrument of the tuba family. It was introduced by John P. Sousa to fortify the bass section of the military band. Its range is 2 octaves below the cornet. The tube coils around the player, with the removable flaring bell directed forward, not upward, as with orchestral tubas.

South Africa (Suid-Afrika), independent nation in extreme southern Africa. It has a government where only whites vote; its goal is to become self-sufficient in an economy with enough resources to achieve that goal.

Land and economy. Situated at the S tip of Africa, it is bordered by Namibia (South West Africa), Botswana, and Rhodesia (N), and by Mozambique and Swaziland (E). It surrounds the independent Kingdom of Lesotho and the territory of Walvis Bay, located on the coast of Namibia. With no important rivers or lakes, water control is essential in this country of narrow coastal regions and interior plateaus. The climate is moderate with an average temperature of about 60 °F (15°C). Until diamonds were discovered in 1867 and gold in 1886, South Africa had been a country of subsistence farmers. Cut off from essential European supplies during WWI and II, it developed its own industries, which now account for 22% of the gross national product. With limitations on the use of nonwhite labor, wages and costs spiraled, and by 1971 import controls were set and the currency devalued. The government's goal is to make South Africa self-sufficient. Minerals are abundant and crop production is high.

People. South Africa's multi-racial society is composed of four groups: whites, descended from Dutch, English, French, and German settlers (17%); Africans, divided into 10 ethnic groups (70%); colored, descended from Cape of Good Hope indigenous people and early European settlers (10%); and Asians, descended from East Indian workers (3%). More than 2,000,000 whites are members of the Dutch Reformed Church. About 50% of the Africans are animist. Literacy is estimated at 100% for whites, 50% for Africans, 75% for coloreds, and 85% for Asians.

Government. A 1961 constitution provides for two houses of Parliament, whose electoral college names the chief of state. A prime minister is leader of the majority party. Only whites, 18 years and over, are allowed to vote.

History. First sighted by the Portuguese in 1486, white settlers came in the 17th century when the Dutch East Indies Co. established a trading station. Dutch, German, and Huguenot refugees from France followed, forming the basis for the modern Afrikaners. British settlement started in 1836, and Afrikan farmers (Boers), eager to escape British political pressure, moved N, defeated the Zulus, and formed the Republic of Transvaal (1852) and the Orange Free State (1854). The discovery of gold brought hordes of European immigrants, which in turn led the Boers into an 1899 unsuccessful war against the British (Boer War). In 1910, the two former republics and British colonies of Cape and Natal formed the Union of South Africa. In 1948 apartheid, the doctrine of the separate development of the races, became official policy. The government has approved the eventual formation of nine Bantu nations. A 1961 referendum approved withdrawal from the British Commonwealth and the establishment of a republic. The increase in black independent nations in Africa from the 1950s led to pressure upon South Africa to change its racial policies, including international censure. Although the government resisted change, there was official contact between government leaders and black African nations in the mid-1970s. *See also* Boer War.

PROFILE

Official name: Republic of South Africa
Area: 471,444sq mi (1,222,011sq km)
Population: 24,700,000
Density: 52 per sq mi (20 per sq km)
Chief cities: Pretoria (administrative capital); Capetown (legislative capital); Johannesburg; Durban
Government: President chosen by the Senate and Assembly. Power rests in the prime minister
Religion: Dutch Reform (major), 50% of Africans are animist
Language: English and Afrikaans (both official)
Monetary unit: Rand
Gross national product: $32,500,000,000
Per capita income: $1,077
Industries: steel, electric motors, textiles, tires, furniture, plastics, automobile assembly, machine tools, fertilizers
Agriculture: corn, sheep, wheat, tobacco, sugar, fruits, peanuts, cattle
Minerals: gold, gem diamonds, antimony, platinum, chrome, copper, uranium, vanadium, vermiculite, manganese, asbestos, coal, iron, lead, zinc
Trading partners: United Kingdom, United States, West Germany, Japan

South African Hake. *See* Stockfish.

South African War (1899–1902). *See* Boer War.

South America, fourth largest continent of the world, entirely in the Western Hemisphere, mostly below the equator. Roughly triangular in shape, it consists of two giant nations, Brazil and Argentina, and eleven smaller ones.

Land. South America's W edge towers above the rest of the continent, which slopes toward the Atlantic Ocean except for the Guiana Highlands (N) and the Brazilian Highlands (central E). The Andes contain the highest peaks of the Americas, with the leader Aconcagua at 22,835ft (6,965m). The driest place in the world is a coastal strip W of the Andes, the Atacama Desert. Major islands are the Falkland, a British crown colony near the continent's S tip, and the Galápagos, a territory of Ecuador 650mi (1,046km) offshore in the Pacific.

Lakes and rivers. Lake Maracaibo in Venezuela is an extension of the Gulf of Venezuela; if classified as a lake, its 5,217sq mi (13,512sq km) make it the largest of South America. Otherwise the largest is Lake Titicaca, on the border between Peru and Bolivia, covering 3,200sq mi (8,288sq km). Lengthy rivers combine to form three major systems that reach the Atlantic. The Amazon ranks, after the Nile, as the second longest river in the world (4,000mi; 6,440km) and largest in the world by volume; flowing S is the Paraguay-Paraná system and NE is the Orinoco.

Climate and vegetation. Except in the mountains and the S, the climate remains generally warm and humid. Much of the N supports tropical rain forest while lowlands in the extreme N and the central region have a cover of tropical grass. The pampas, S of the Tropic of Capricorn, produce temperate grasslands, but vegetation is scarce far SE of the mountains. Pine and other temperate forests grow along the W coast in the S.

Animal life. Mammals include howler and other monkeys, ocelots, pumas, deer, tapirs, peccaries, and coatis. Particular to the Andes are small members of the camel family: llamas, alpacas, and vicuñas, of which only the vicuñas are not domesticated. Colorful birds include large macaws and toucans and tiny hummingbirds. Condors are in the mountains. Dangerous snakes include bushmasters, anacondas, and boa constrictors; piranha fish are in some of the rivers.

People. Some pure-blood Incas (Quechuas) still remain in the Andes, as do some Mapucho (Araucanians) of Chile. But most Indian groups have become mestizos by mixing with the Portuguese in Brazil and the Spaniards in the rest of the continent. Brazil has many blacks, as do the small countries of the N coast. Although many Germans have migrated to Argentina and some, along with Italians, to Chile, people of Spanish and Portuguese descent remain the two main groups and theirs are the dominant languages. Roman Catholicism is the major religion.

Economy. Agriculture occupies most Indians and many of the mestizos, but the land belongs mainly to people of European descent. Valuable ores come from the mountains and the Atacama Desert, with copper, tin, silver, and gemstones being of importance. Venezuela's Maracaibo region yields petroleum. Most countries remain underdeveloped industrially.

History. About 1100, the Incas became the dominant tribe and for 400 years expanded an empire through the central Andes. After Pedro Alvares Cabral discovered Brazil in 1500, the Portuguese gained control there, but the real conquest of South America came with Francisco Pizarro's conquest of the Incas in 1432–33. For nearly 300 years the intruders held the continent. Brazil gained independence peacefully after the Portuguese royal family lived there for a time to escape Napoleon in Europe, and determined generals such as José de San Martín, Simón Bolívar, Antonio José de Sucre, and Bernardo O'Higgins freed much of S, W, and N South America in the 1820s. Political assassinations, overthrows, and territorial conflicts kept nations from cooperating with one another. As a result, South American republics failed to become world powers until nearly the second half of the 20th century, after the formation of the United Nations in 1945 and the OAS (Organization of American States) in 1948 gave them a say in international affairs. Chile tried a communist government for a few years, the first such duly elected regime in the New World, but conservative elements ousted it in 1973. Continent-wide poverty, inflation, political turmoil, and outside propaganda and pressures keep South American lands in the developing-nations category. △1120, 1354.

PROFILE

Area: 6,880,000sq mi (17,819,200sq km).
Largest nations: Brazil, 3,284,426sq mi (8,506,663 sq km); Argentina, 1,072,156sq mi (2,776,884sq km).
Population: 190,038,000.
Density: 27per sq mi (11per sq km).
Most populous nations: Brazil, 93,204,379; Argentina, 23,364,443; Colombia, 19,829,185.
Chief cities: São Paulo, Brazil; Rio de Janeiro, Brazil; Buenos Aires, Argentina.
Manufacturing (major products): petroleum products, chemicals, foodstuffs, drugs, textiles, iron and steel, paper.
Agriculture (major products): wheat, coffee, corn, grapes, sugar cane, cacao, livestock, bananas, cotton.
Minerals (major): petroleum, copper, tin, silver, iron ore, gold, zinc, gemstones.

Southampton, port in S England, at head of Southampton Water on Test and Itchen estuaries; Britain's chief passenger port and a major commercial port; seat of University of Southampton (1952). The Pilgrim Fathers embarked from here at start of their voyage (1620). Industries: shipbuilding, engines, oil refining, food products. Pop. 210,000.

South Australia, state in S central Australia, including Kangaroo and several smaller islands; the terrain includes deserts, mountains, salt lakes, swampland; 66% of the population lives in the capital city, Adelaide; location of Whyalla, home of Australia's largest shipyards, and the Murray River valley, whose grapes produce the finest Australian wine. Industries: mining, metal processing, textiles, food processing. Coastline reputedly visited by the Dutch in 1627; first British settlement 1836; became a state of the Commonwealth 1901. Area: 380,070sq mi (984,381sq km). Pop. 1,164,700.

South Bend, city in N Indiana, 135mi (217km) N of Indianapolis, on St Joseph River; seat of St Joseph co; scene of 1679 camp of French explorer Sieur de La Salle; American Fur Co. post 1820; site of St Joseph County courthouse (1855), now a museum; branch of University of Indiana, Notre Dame University (1842). Industries: automotive parts, paints, plastics, farm machinery. Named South Bend in 1830 for bend of St Joseph River; inc. 1835, chartered (city) 1865. Pop. (1970) 125,580.

South Carolina, state in the SE United States, on the Atlantic Ocean. It was the first state to secede from the Union before the Civil War.

Land and economy. From the seacoast the land rolls gradually up to the Blue Ridge Mt range in the extreme NW. Many rivers flow SE to the Atlantic, including the Pee Dee, the Santee, and the Edisto. The Savannah River forms the SW boundary. The principal lakes are man-made, providing hydroelectric power and flood control. Fertile soils and a mild climate made South Carolina a productive agricultural region from its earliest days. Forests yield an abundant supply of timber. Manufacturing did not become important until the 20th century; it was widely diversified after WWII. The ocean beaches, fine public gardens, and the old-world charm of Charleston attract a lucrative tourist business.

People. The original English settlers were followed by the French Huguenots, Germans, and Swiss. Blacks were brought in to work the plantations, and for many years they were a majority of the population. There are no significant groups of foreign-born residents. About 47% of the people live in urban areas.

Education. There are nearly 50 institutions of higher education.

History. Spaniards and French had short-lived settlements on the coast in the 16th century, but permanent occupation did not begin until the English came a century later. Charles II of Great Britain granted the land to eight proprietors in 1663, and the first settlers arrived in 1670. Charleston (then known as Charles Town) was founded in 1680. Pioneers pushed inland, and in 1729 South Carolina became a royal colony. A plantation society arose; rice, indigo, and cotton were major crops. In the Revolution, the battles of Camden, Kings Mountain, Cowpens, and Eutaw Springs were fought in the area. After joining the Union, South Carolina was a strong defender of states' rights and in 1832 took the extreme step of passing the Order of Nullification, declaring federal tariffs to be null and void in the state. A compromise tariff law settled the dispute, but over the slavery question the state stood firm and was a leader in forming the Confederacy. The first shots of the Civil War were fired on Fort Sumter in Charleston harbor on April 12, 1861. In 1865, a Union army devastated the state and burned Columbia, the capital. Recovery from the catastrophe was long and difficult. Development of the textile industry, aided by the movement of many mills from Northern states, helped to stabilize the economy.

PROFILE

Admitted to Union: May 23, 1788; 8th of the 13 original states to ratify the US Constitution
US Congressmen: Senate, 2; House of Representatives, 6
Population: 2,590,516 (1970); rank, 26th
Capital: Columbia, 113,542 (1970)
Chief cities: Columbia; Charleston, 66,945; Greenville, 61,438; Spartanburg, 44,456
State legislature: Senate, 46; House of Representatives, 124
Area: 31,055sq mi (80,432sq km); rank, 40th
Elevation: Highest, 3,560ft (1,086m), Sassafras Mt; lowest, sea level
Industries: (major products) textiles, lumber, pulp and paper, chemicals, apparel, machinery
Agriculture: (major products) tobacco, cotton, peaches, peanuts, poultry
Minerals (major): clay, cement, limestone, vermiculite
State nickname: Palmetto State
State mottoes: Dum Spiro, Spero (While I breathe, I hope) and Animis opibusque parati (Prepared in soul and resources)
State bird: Carolina wren
State flower: Carolina jessamine
State tree: palmetto

South China Sea, W branch of Pacific Ocean; surrounded by SE China, Indochina, Malay Peninsula, Borneo, Philippines, Taiwan; Formosa Strait connects it to East China Sea: Its chief arms are the Gulf of Tonkin and Gulf of Siam; the Si, Red, Mekong, and Chao Phraya rivers flow into it. Area: approx. 1,000,000sq mi (2,590,000sq km). Depth (max.): 18,000ft (5,490m).

South Dakota, state in the N central United States, in the Plains region.

Land and economy. The land rises gradually from E to W. In the SW are the Badlands, an area of broken terrain, and the Black Hills, a rugged forested region, where the rocky front of Mt Rushmore presents gigantic sculptured portraits of presidents Washington, Jefferson, Lincoln, and Theodore Roosevelt. The Missouri River, flowing from N to S, cuts the state down the middle. Four huge dams have created lakes that supply irrigation and hydroelectric power and control flooding. Fertile farmlands lie generally E of the river; to the W are grasslands for grazing. Rich mineral deposits are found in the Black Hills. Manufacturing is concentrated in the population centers of the E.

People. Settlement did not begin until the 19th century when pioneers from Minnesota, Wisconsin, Illinois, and Iowa occupied the farming country. Some came from Canada and numbers from Sweden, Norway, Germany, the Netherlands, and Russia. After WWI, the influx slowed. A small number of Indians live on reservations. About 45% of the population lives in urban areas.

Education. There are 16 institutions of higher education.

History. French trappers in the 1740s claimed the land for France, from which the United States acquired it in the Louisiana Purchase of 1803. The Lewis and Clark Expedition explored it 1804–05. Fur traders and army garrisons were the only inhabitants until the late 1850s when settlements were made at Sioux Falls, Yankton, and Vermillion. Dakota Territory, which included the present states of North and South Dakota, was formed 1861. Discovery of gold in the Black Hills in 1874 caused a population growth that led to statehood. The last armed conflict between the US Army and the Indians took place at Wounded Knee on Dec. 29, 1890.

PROFILE

Admitted to Union: Nov. 2, 1889, the same day as North Dakota; rank, 39th or 40th
US Congressmen: Senate, 2; House of Representatives, 2
Population: 666,257 (1970); rank 44th
Capital: Pierre, 9,699 (1970)
Chief cities: Sioux Falls, 72,488; Rapid City, 43,836; Aberdeen, 26,476
State legislature: Senate, 35; House of Representatives, 70
Area: 77,047sq mi (199,552sq km); rank, 16th
Elevation: Highest, 7,242ft (2,209m), Harney Peak; lowest, 962ft (293m), Big Stone Lake
Industries: (major products) processed foods, lumber, wood products, farm equipment
Agriculture: (major products) sheep, cattle, hogs, rye, wheat
Minerals (major): gold, beryllium, silver, petroleum, uranium
State nicknames: Coyote State, Sunshine State
State motto: Under God, the People Rule
State bird: ring-necked pheasant
State flower: American pasque
State tree: Black Hills spruce

Southeast Asia, region of Asia, bounded by India (W), China (N), and the Pacific Ocean (E); includes Burma, Thailand, Malaysia, Cambodia, Laos, Vietnam, Philippines, Singapore, and Indonesia. Area: approx. 1,740,000sq mi (4,506,600sq km). *See also* individual countries.

Southeast Asia Treaty Organization (SEATO), alliance formed by the Southeast Asia Collective Defense Treaty (1954) designed to defend member nations against military aggression. Members were Australia, France, Great Britain, New Zealand, Pakistan, Philippines, and United States. SEATO had no military forces, only advisers. SEATO's effectiveness declined and in 1975 members agreed to phase out the alliance.

Southern Ape. *See* Australopithecus.

Southern Christian Leadership Congress (SCLC), an agency for local organizations "seeking full citizenship rights, equality, and the integration of the Negro in all aspects of American life, and subscribing to the Ghandian philosophy of nonviolence." The SCLC's work is mainly directed toward improving civic, religious, economic, and cultural conditions in 16 southern and border states. Members around 247. Founded 1957.

Southern Cross. *See* Crux.

John Philip Sousa

Angola
Zambia
Mozambique
Rhodesia
Namibia
Botswana
Pretoria
Johannesburg
Swaziland
Lesotho
Kimberley
Bloemfontein
Pietermaritzburg
Durban
SOUTH AFRICA
INDIAN OCEAN
East London
(Oos-Londen)
Cape Town
Port Elizabeth
0
800 km

South Africa

Georgetown, South Carolina

Mount Rushmore National Memorial, South Dakota

South Euclid, city in N Ohio, 10mi (16km) E of Cleveland; site of Notre Dame College (1922). Inc. as village 1917, as city 1940. Pop. (1970) 29,579.

Southey, Robert (1774–1843), English poet and biographer. He was related to Samuel Taylor Coleridge by marriage. His long epic poems are *Thalaba the Destroyer* (1801), *Madoc* (1805), *The Curse of Kehama* (1810), and *Roderick the Last of the Goths* (1821). He also wrote numerous biographies, including *The Life of Nelson* (1813), and *History of the Peninsular War* (1823–32). He was made poet laureate in 1813.

Southfield, city in SE Michigan, 15mi (24km) NW of Detroit; site of Duns Scotus College (1930) and Lawrence Institute of Technology (1932). Industries: precision tools, sporting goods. Inc. 1958. Pop. (1970) 69,285.

South Gate, city in S California, 7mi (11km) SSE of Los Angeles. Industries: automobiles, chemicals, furniture, glass. Inc. 1923. Pop. (1970) 56,909.

Southgate, city in SE Michigan, 12mi (19km) S of Detroit. Industries: electronic and automobile parts, construction equipment. Inc. 1958. Pop. (1970) 33,909.

Southington, town in central Connecticut on the Quinnipiac River, 8mi (13km) E of Waterbury. Industries: chemicals, fabricated metals, electrical equipment. Founded 1696; inc. 1779. Pop. (1970) 30,946.

South Island, largest island of New Zealand, SW of North Island, and NE of Stewart Island. Southern Alps mountain range extends length of island, creating many rivers, lakes, and fjords. Principal cities are Christchurch, Dunedin, and Invercargill. Industries: dairying, herding, grain, tourism. Highest peak is Mt Cook, 12,349ft (3,766m). Area: 58,093sq mi (150,461sq km). Pop. 798,681.

South Platte River, river in Colorado and Nebraska; rises at the confluence of many streams in the Rocky Mts, central Colo.; flows SE then NE across Nebraska to join the North Platte River; in SW central Neb. to form the Platte River; used for irrigation and hydroelectricity. Length: 450mi (725km).

South Saint Paul, city in SE Minnesota, on Mississippi River 4mi (6.4km) SSE of St Paul. Industries: meat packing, lubricating oils, sheet metal, wood products. Settled 1853; inc. 1887. Pop. (1970) 25,016.

South San Francisco, city in W California, 9mi (14km) S of San Francisco; in the 19th century grew from cattle ranching and meat packing. Industries: steel, chemicals, processed food. Inc. 1908. Pop. (1970) 46,646.

South Saskatchewan, river in SW Canada; rises in the Rocky Mts; with its tributary, Bow River, it is the longest branch of the Nelson River, 1,205mi (1,940km).

South Sea Bubble, speculation in the shares of the English South Sea Company, ending in financial disaster (1720). This company, founded by Robert Harley (1711), was formed on the assumption of an eventual British trading monopoly in the Pacific Ocean and South America. Although this monopoly failed to materialize, the government, to fund the national debt, encouraged public confidence in the company, persuading investors to exchange state annuities for its stock. Many were ruined, the whole system of chartered companies was discredited, and the House of Commons' inquiry into the scandal revealed corruption and resulted in the chancellor of the exchequer's expulsion.

South Vietnam. *See* Vietnam.

South West Africa. *See* Namibia.

Soutine, Chaim (1894–1943), French painter. He began to make a reputation with his distorted, nightmarish painting in the 1920s. Most sensational of his pictures are those of blood-spattered meat.

Sovereignty, power that permits a nation to govern its own affairs, free from outside interference. △898.

Soviet ("council"), basic political unit in the USSR according to the 1936 constitution. First established after the 1905 revolution, and revived in 1917 as soviets of workers' and soldiers' deputies, they soon came under Bolshevik influence. The Petrograd soviet was instrumental in the overthrow of the Provisional Government in November 1917. △1310.

Sowbug. *See* Wood Louse.

Soybean, hairy, annual plant native to China and Japan. It has oval, three-part leaves and small white or purplish flowers. Grown for food, forage, green manure, and oil, its seed is an important protein source. Height: to 6ft (1.8m). Family Leguminosae; species *Glycine soja*. △330.

Spa. △708.

Spaak, Paul-Henri (1899–1972), Belgian and international statesman. An advocate of European unity, he was premier of Belgium (1938–39; 1946; 1947–49), and foreign minister (1936–38; 1939–45; 1947–49; 1954–57; 1961–66). First president of the UN General Assembly (1946); secretary general of NATO (1957–61).

Space Flight, flight of manned or unmanned vehicles beyond Earth's atmosphere. Dreamed of by ancient Greeks and by Renaissance scientists such as Galileo, Kepler, and Huyghens, it became a reality on Oct. 4, 1957, with the launching of Sputnik 1. Major milestones: first space probe (Explorer 1, discoverer of Van Allen radiation belts, launched Jan. 31, 1958); first lunar probe (Luna 2, Sept. 12, 1959); first manned flight (Yuri Gagarin, April 12, 1961); first close-up pictures of Mars (Mariner 4, 1965); first manned lunar landing (Neil Armstrong, July 20, 1969); first pictures from surface of another planet (Venera 9, Oct. 22, 1975). △142, 1722–24.

Space Photography. △142, 1724.

Space Probe, craft or mission designed to explore regions above one Earth radius (about 4,000mi, or 6,400km) altitude. The first US space probe was Explorer I, launched Jan. 31, 1958; it discovered the inner Van Allen radiation belt. The first lunar probe was Luna 2, launched Sept. 12, 1959. The first planetary probe was Mariner 2, launched Aug. 27, 1962, which flew by Venus. Pioneers 10 and 11 photographed Venus (Oct. 22, 1975); the Viking lander tested the Martian surface for life (1976). △142.

Space Shuttle, reusable rocket and aerodynamic vehicle carrying men and supplies between Earth and a space station. Its development is now a major priority in the United States. A booster stage would launch the shuttle and return to the launch pad to be reused. The shuttle would have rocket power for injection into orbit and for deceleration during reentry, and fold-out wings and tail for flying through the atmosphere. It could orbit a 30-ton payload and land at existing airports.

Space Station, orbiting laboratory in space where men can carry out construction and maintenance of spacecraft and scientific and medical experiments. Early stations included the Russian Soyuz (1971) and the US Skylab (1975). The space station concept was first described by Konstantin Tsiolkovsky in 1895. A basic structure envisioned for the 1990s accommodates 6–12 people, is serviced by a space shuttle, and remains in orbit for up to 10 years. *See also* Skylab; Space Shuttle. △142–44.

Space-Time, treatment, in relativity theory, of the three space dimensions and the dimension of time as forming a four-dimensional space. Hermann Minkowski devised (1907) a presentation of relativity theory by extending three-dimensional geometry to four dimensions. A line drawn in this space represents the whole history of a particle as its path both in space and time (its world line). *See also* Relativity Theory. △1524.

Space Walk. △1724.

Spadefoot Toad, tailless amphibian with a horny space on the inside of each hind foot. They are squat and smooth-skinned. Genus *Scaphiopus* is found from Canada to Mexico and genus *Pelobates* is found in S Europe and N Africa. Family Pelobatidae.

Spain, independent nation in SW Europe, on the Iberian peninsula. After decades of rule by Francisco Franco, Spain entered a new era when King Juan Carlos I took the throne in 1975.

Land and economy. Occupying the major portion of the Iberian peninsula in SW Europe, it is bordered N by France and the Atlantic Ocean; E and S by the Mediterranean, W by Portugal and the Atlantic. Spain also includes the Balearic and Canary islands. The Pyrenees Mts, in which the tiny republic of Andorra is located, form a natural barrier between France and Spain. Except for the Andalusian lowlands, the land mass rises from a narrow coastal plain. The center of the country, a high plateau, is divided by ranges and rivers. Wheat growing and sheep raising are the chief products of this arid plateau, which has only a few fertile valleys. Mainly an agricultural country, 75% of Spain is arid; prosperity has been forestalled by lack of irrigation and mechanization, poor soil, erosion, and an authoritarian system of land tenure. Still the least prosperous nation in W Europe, liberalization toward foreign and private investment has encouraged economic growth since 1960. Tourism is a major source of income.

People. The people are descendants of the succeeding waves of N African and European peoples who invaded and colonized Spain. The most recognizable minority are the Basques, whose unique language is not related to any other tongue. Under Francisco Franco, Roman Catholicism was reinstated as the official religion, although a 1966 organic law guarantees freedom of worship. Over 99% of the population is Roman Catholic. Literacy is 97%. Primary education is compulsory and free.

Government. Spain is a constitutional monarchy. The unicameral assembly can initiate legislation, but the chief of state has veto power and can rule by decree.

History. Its strategic geographical position made Spain a center of invasion and resistance for centuries before it became unified. Phoenicians, Greeks, Carthaginians, and Moors came from the sea and Celts came from the continent. A major influence was the Roman invasion in the 2nd century BC; their language, religion, and law prevailed until the Moors invaded from North Africa in 711 and remained for 700 years. The nation was unified by Isabella and Ferdinand in 1492, the year in which Christopher Columbus discovered the New World. Spain became a major power in the 16th century until its Armada was defeated by England in 1588. Spain's decline in the subsequent centuries invited intervention by other powers, notably France; during the French revolutionary wars Spain was a major battleground. The country also lost its colonies in the Americas, its hold over the Low Countries, and much of its influence in Italy. Efforts to establish a more liberal government were rejected by Ferdinand VII, who returned from exile in 1814. Quarrels over succession to the throne provoked the Carlist Wars in the 19th century. In the Spanish-American War (1898), Spain lost the last of its empire in the Americas and the Pacific. Domestic problems led to the dictatorship in 1923 of Primo de Rivera, who was forced out in 1930. A republic was est. in 1931 and lasted until 1936. Uncompromised disputes between the liberals, the church, landowners, and the working class brought unchecked violence and the 1936–39 Civil War. Following the nationalist victory, Gen. Francisco Franco ruled the devastated nation. His military dictatorship lasted until his death in 1975 when he was succeeded by Prince Juan Carlos as king. *See also* Carlists; Civil War, Spanish.

PROFILE

Official name: Spain (Spanish State)
Area: 194,897sq mi (504,783sq km)
Population: 35,400,000
Density: 181.6per sq mi (70per sq km)
Chief cities: Madrid (capital); Barcelona; Valencia
Government: monarchy
Religion: Roman Catholic (official)
Language: Spanish (official), Catalan, and Basque
Monetary unit: Peseta
Gross national product: $74,600,000,000
Per capita income: $1,850
Industries: machinery, textiles, wine, shoes, paper, automobiles, cork, cement, iron and steel, chemicals, ships, processed foods
Agriculture: wheat, rye, barley, oats, fish, olives, grapes, citrus fruits, onions, almonds, esparto, flax, hemp, tobacco, cotton, rice, sheep
Minerals: lead, iron, copper, zinc, coal, cobalt, mercury, silver, sulfur, phosphates, uranium
Trading partners: United States (major), European Economic Community

Spaniel, sporting dog used to locate and flush game, drop for the hunter's shot, and sometimes retrieve on command. Mentioned as early as 1368, it was called setting spaniel before the gun. Its job then was to locate game and sit while the hunter threw a net over it. Land spaniels include the cocker and toy. Water spaniels are usually retrievers.

Spanish, major world language, spoken in Spain, most of South America (but not in Brazil or Guyana), all of Central America, Mexico, Cuba, the Dominican Republic, Puerto Rico, and a number of other countries. Its total number of speakers is more than 200,000,000. Spanish is a Romance language but its vocabulary contains a number of words of Arabic origin, the result of Spain's being under Moorish domination for many centuries.

Spanish-American War (1898), conflict between

pain and the United States, waged in the Philippines nd Cuba. The destruction of the battleship *Maine* in avana harbor (February 1898) was the immediate ause of US entry; long-range causes included the esire to protect US investments in Cuba and the revailing climate of jingoism. Beginning in April, the var between Spain and the United States essentially nvolved two naval engagements and one encounter n land. Adm. George Dewey annihilated the Spanish eet in Manila Bay (May); Col. Teddy Roosevelt's ough Riders helped achieve the capture of the eights above the port of Santiago de Cuba and laced the Spanish fleet under bombardment, precipiating the decisive naval battle of Santiago, which nded the war. The terms of the Treaty of Paris atified 1899) made Cuba independent; Puerto Rico, uam, and the Philippines were ceded to the United tates, which paid $20,000,000 to Spain. △1234, 278.

panish Bayonet, erect-stemmed plant native to S Jnited States, Mexico, and West Indies. It has long, ointed leaves and large white or purple flowers. leight: 10–25ft (3–7.6m). Family Agavaceae; species *ucca aloifolia.*

panish Cat. *See* Tortoiseshell Cat.

panish Dancer. △476.

panish Inquisition, tribunal founded in 1478 by erdinand II and Isabella I to discover and punish eretics in Spain. It was firmly under royal control, as pposed to the medieval Inquisition, which, regardess of the country in which it operated, was always nder the control of the Roman Catholic Church. The riginal purpose of the Spanish Inquisition was to unish those converted Jews and Muslims who were nsincere in their Christian beliefs. Under the direction f Tomás de Torquemada, however, it soon expanded s jurisdiction to include questioning the beliefs of all Christians (both St Theresa of Ávila and St Ignatius of oyola were brought before the Inquisition). Its exesses are legendary; the auto-da-fé, the ceremony receding the execution of a heretic, became symolic of these excesses. The property of condemned eretics was confiscated, creating suspicion of the notives of the inquisitors. At its height, the Spanish nquisition was established in all of the Spanish colonies, although it never achieved the power there that t did in Spain itself. It was finally abolished in 1834. *See also* Inquisition; Torquemada, Tomás de.

Spanish Literature. Prior to the 15th century Cataan and Galician flourished as literary languages along with Castilian. One of the major early works is the epic oem *Cantar de Mío Cid* (*c.* 1200). French and Italian nfluence predominated until the 16th century when a truly Spanish literature emerged. The late 16th centtury and the 17th century are known as the Golden Age with the work of Miguel de Cervantes, Luis de Góngora, Lope de Vega, and Calderón dominating the era. The 18th century witnessed a decline in Spanish writings. *Costumbrismo,* sketches of Spanish life and customs, flourished in the 19th century, and was incorporated into the realistic novels of Benito Pérez Galdós, Armando Palacio Valdés, and others. In the early 20th century the writers of the Generation of '98 reexamined Spanish traditions and revitalized Spanish culture. Major figures of this group included Pío Baroja y Nessi, Miguel de Unamuno, and Azorín (Jose Martínez Ruiz). Probably the most important Spanish writer of the 20th century was Federico García Lorca.

Spanish Main, term used to refer to the West Indies and the Caribbean coast of Panama, Colombia, and Venezuela during this area's exploration and development.

Spanish Missions, group of 21 Franciscan missions, extending along the California coast; established to convert Indians to Christianity; first built in San Diego (1769) and finished in Sonoma (1823).

Spanish Moss, common name for an epiphytic herbaceous plant, not a true moss. Grown in tropical and subtropical American forests, especially on the live oak of SE United States, the loose gray clumps hang from tree branches. It is used as imitation horsehair stuffing and for insulation. Family Bromeliaceae; species *Tillandsia usneoides.*

Spanish Sahara, region in N Africa, bordered by the Atlantic Ocean (W), Morocco (N), Algeria (NE), and Mauritania (E and S). Spain's last major overseas territory, it was promised self-determination in 1975. Mauritania, Algeria, and Morocco have made claims to it. The capital is El Aaiún, with a population of 24,519. A rocky, sandy desert, it covers 102,703sq mi (266,000sq km). It contains the world's largest phosphate deposits and rich iron ore lodes. The population of 76,425 is composed of approximately 55% nomadic Arabs, Berbers, and black Africans, and 45% Spaniards, most of whom are soldiers. The natives are predominantly Muslim; the official language is Spanish, and the monetary unit is the peseta. The principal trading partner is Spain; the economy consists primarily of goat, camel, and sheep raising, cultivation of date palms and barley, and fisheries.

History. Portuguese sailors reached the N coast in 1434, but there was little European contact until 1884, when Spain made the coast a protectorate; the boundaries were enlarged by Franco-Spanish agreements in 1900, 1904, and 1920. In the early 1970s an independence movement began to develop, and Mauritania, Morocco, and Algeria called upon Spain to relinquish control. In 1976, King Hassan II of Morocco organized a march to take control of the territory; the potential confrontation with Spain was averted when he called off the march.

Spanish Succession, War of the (1701–14), dynastic struggle for the throne of Spain. When it became apparent that Charles II of Spain would die childless, three pretenders—all with dynastic ties to the Spanish royal family—arose: Louis XIV of France; the elector of Bavaria, Joseph Ferdinand; and Holy Roman Emperor Leopold I. England and Holland, fearing both French and Austrian influence in Spain, supported Joseph Ferdinand. In 1698, after lengthy negotiations and a complicated agreement, all sides agreed that Joseph Ferdinand should succeed. His sudden death the following year, however, caused the agreement to disintegrate.

While new negotiations were going on, the dying Charles II named Philip of Anjou, grandson of Louis XIV, as his heir. When he took the throne as Philip V in 1701, most of Europe was plunged into war. Supporting France were Spain, Portugal, Bavaria, and Savoy. The Allies consisted of the imperial forces, England, Holland, and most of the German states. The duke of Marlborough, Prince Eugene of Savoy, commander of the imperial forces, and Louis of Baden were the chief commanders of the Allied forces; the dukes of Vendôme and Villars and the count of Tallard were the French commanders. The war dragged on for a decade and, despite impressive Allied victories at Blenheim, Malplaquet, Ramillies, and in Bavaria, no decisive defeat of the French forces resulted. In 1713, France, Britain, and Holland signed the Treaty of Utrecht, but the Holy Roman emperor continued the war for another year. Finally, in 1714 the war was brought to a close with the Peace of Utrecht. Philip V remained on a badly weakened Spanish throne. *See also* Utrecht, Peace of.

Spanish Town, town in SE central Jamaica, West Indies; large agricultural processing and manufacturing center, on Cobre River. The former capital of Jamaica (1535–1872) it is site of old colonial buildings around central square: St Catherine cathedral (1655), Rodney Memorial, House of Assembly. Industries: sugar milling, rum distilling, food processing. Founded *c.* 1523. Pop. 14,706.

Spanworm. *See* Measuring Worm.

Spark, Muriel (Sarah) (1918–), Scottish novelist. She wrote short stories, plays, verse, and criticism. Her novels include *Memento Mori* (1959), *The Prime of Miss Jean Brodie* (1961), later made into a play and a film, and the *Abbess of Crewe* (1974).

Spark Erosion. △1606.

Spark Plug, Engine, in an internal combustion engine, a device carrying two electrodes separated by an air gap, across which electric current from the ignition discharges, forming a spark. This ignites the fuel. △1632.

Sparrow, two groups of widely distributed seed-eating birds that frequent grasslands and open wooded areas. They have stout, cone-shaped bills; brownish plumage, often streaked with gray; lighter underparts; and medium-sized tails. Old World sparrows, including the house sparrow and tree sparrow, are weaverbirds and nest in rock crevices or holes in trees or buildings, laying speckled white eggs (4–9); Family Ploceidae. New World sparrows, including the song sparrow and field sparrow, are finches and build cup-shaped nests in trees or bushes for white or pale blue eggs (2–3); family Fringillidae. Length: about 6in (15.5cm).

Sparrow Hawk, bird of prey. The American sparrow hawk *(Falco sparverius),* often called the American kestrel, is reddish-brown and eats small animals; length: to 12in (30cm). The slightly larger European sparrow hawk *(Accipter nisus)* feeds on birds.

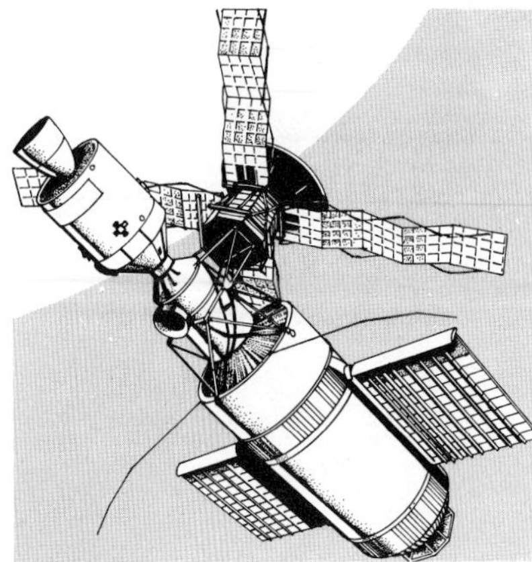

Space station

ATLANTIC OCEAN
France
Bilbao
Andorra
Valladolid
Zaragoza
Barcelona
Portugal
Madrid
SPAIN
Valencia
Murcia
SEA
Seville
Málaga
MEDITERRANEAN
Algeria
Morocco
0
400 km

Spain

Valencia, Spain

Spaniel

Sparta (Spárti), town in SE Peloponnesus, S Greece, on Eurotas River; capital of Laconia department. Just S are ruins of ancient Sparta, a Greek city-state founded by the Dorians *c.* 900 BC in the province of Laconia. The ancient city-state of three classes: the Spartiates (ruling class), perioeci (free inhabitants with no political power), and helots (slaves). After its conquest of Messenia (*c.* 743–724 BC), Sparta flourished as an economic and cultural center. Faced with a massive helot revolt in 7th century BC, Sparta changed into an armed camp with a primitive socio-militaristic government ruled by two kings and later by the gerouisa and ephors; in *c.* 500 BC the Peloponnesian League was formed with Sparta as the most powerful member. After the Persian Wars (500–449 BC), Athens began to rival Sparta, leading to the Peloponnesian War (431–404 BC), which ended in total defeat of Athens. Sparta dominated the Peloponnesus until 371 BC, when it was defeated by Thebes at Leucta, and Messenia was freed. A revival of prosperity occurred under the Romans; Sparta was destroyed by Goths in 395 AD. The modern town was built in 1834. Industries: citrus fruits, olive oil. Pop. 11,981. △992–96.

Spartacus (died 71 BC), Thracian gladiator in Rome who led a slave revolt known as the Third Servile War or Gladiators' War. He won victories at Capua (73) and in S Italy, defeating five Roman armies and entering Cisalpine Gaul. His soldiers devastated the land and moved south toward Sicily where they were eventually defeated by Crassus, who, with Pompey's aid, crucified some 6,000 of the rebels. Spartacus died in battle, his army holding 3,000 Roman prisoners unharmed. △1018.

Spartanburg, city in N South Carolina, 30mi (48km) ENE of Greenville; seat of Spartanburg co; site of Wofford College (1854), Converse College (1889), Spartanburg Junior College (1911); nearby is Cowpens National Battlefield. Industries: agriculture, textiles, clothing, lumber, flour mills, railroad shops, paper products, rubber. Settled *c.* 1785; inc. 1831. Pop. (1970) 44,456.

Sparticists, German political party of the radical left that broke away from the Social Democrats during World War I. Led by Karl Liebknecht and Rosa Luxemburg, the Sparticists refused to sustain the war effort and rejected participation in the post-Versailles republican government. The Sparticists fomented a number of uprisings, including one in Berlin in 1919 that resulted in thousands of casualties. Volunteer armies of ex-servicemen were employed to suppress the movement.

Spathiphyllum, flowering plant native to Colombia, with shiny, lance-shaped leaves pointed at the tips. It has blooms resembling calla lilies. A popular house plant, it is a rapid grower. Family Araceae; species *Spathiphyllum clevelandii.*

Speaker of the House, presiding officer in the US House of Representatives. He is elected from the majority party by the House. His powers include the recognition of members for debate, the appointment of select and conference committees, the referral of bills to committees, and the signing of documents on behalf of the House. The speaker follows the vice president in presidential succession. △1218.

Speaker, Tris(tram E.) (1888–1958), US baseball player, b. Hubbard, Tex. He collected 3,514 hits including 793 two-base hits, a record. He was elected to the Baseball Hall of Fame in 1937.

Spear, in weaponry. △1726.

Speare, Elizabeth George (1908–), US author of books for young people, b. Melrose, Mass. She has received the Newbery Medal twice, first in 1959 for *The Witch of Blackbird Pond* and again in 1962 for *The Bronze Bow.* Other titles include *Calico Captive* (1957) and *Life in Colonial America* (1963).

Spearfish, marine billfish popular as a sport fish. Silvery-blue with long bill, its smaller dorsal fin distinguishes it from sailfish. Length: 6ft (183cm); weight: 60lb (27kg). Species include Pacific shortbill *Tetrapturus angustirostris* and W Atlantic *T. pfleugeri.* Family Istiophoridae.

Spearman, Charles Edward (1863–1945), English psychologist. He was a pioneer in the application of statistical and mathematical methods to the analysis of data. He attempted to analyze human abilities into their components by using a method he helped create called factor analysis. His works include *Psychology Down the Ages* (1937) and *Human Abilities* (published 1950).

Spearmint, common name of *Mentha spicata,* or *M. viridis,* a hardy perennial herb of the mint family with leaves used for flavoring, especially in vinegar, jelly, and beverages. Oil distilled from spearmint is used as a medicine. Its flowers are pale blue and grow in spikes.

Special (Restricted) Theory of Relativity, part of Einstein's theory of relativity that applies only to observers whose relative motion is constant. *See also* Relativity Theory.

Species, group of physically and genetically similar individuals that interbreed under natural conditions. Over 300,000 plant species and more than 1,000,000 animal species have been identified and 15–20,000 new ones are identified every year. Over half the living species are insects and one-third of these are beetles. △408.

Specific Gravity, the ratio of the density of a substance to the density of water. Thus, the specific gravity of gold is 13.2; that is, it is about 13 times heavier than an equal volume of water.

Specific Heat, the heat energy necessary to raise the temperature of a given amount of some substance by one degree. Bodies with high specific heat, such as water, require much more heat energy to raise their temperature than bodies of low specific heat. Thus oceans exert a moderating influence on the Earth's climate by absorbing excess heat from the land during the day and returning it at night. △1502, 1508.

Specific Hunger. When given free choice of a variety of foodstuffs a healthy diet will be selected by the organism. This suggests that there are mechanisms that permit the organism to choose its nutrition according to bodily needs and specific states of tissue deprivation.

Spectacled Bear, small black bear that lives in the Andes. It has white, spectaclelike rings around its eyes and is the only bear in the Southern Hemisphere. Species *Tremarctos ornatus.*

Spectator (1711–12; 1714), English periodical edited and largely written by Richard Steele and Joseph Addison, a successor to the *Tatler.* △1188.

Spectrograph, instrument for producing and recording a spectrum. Light from an incandescent source is formed into a parallel beam in the instrument, falls onto a prism or diffraction grating, and is split into its component wavelengths by dispersion. This emission spectrum is then focused onto a photographic plate. To record an absorption spectrum, light from a source emitting a continuous spectrum is passed through the absorbing medium before entering the instrument. X-ray, ultraviolet, and infrared spectra can also be investigated with suitable dispersing and recording media. △1516.

Spectroscopy. △1282, 1516, 1568.

Spectrum, distribution of the wavelength or frequency components of a wave, as in a visible spectrum which displays rainbow colors ranging from red to violet. It is characteristic of the source of the radiation and is produced by dispersion in a prism or diffraction grating. An emission spectrum, consisting of bright regions on a dark background, is produced when a source is strongly heated or is bombarded by electrons, etc. The positions and brightness of the regions indicate the frequencies present and their intensities. An absorption spectrum, consisting of dark regions on a bright background, is produced when a continuous range of frequencies passes through a medium that absorbs certain frequencies. In a line spectrum, as produced by gas atoms, the light or dark regions are narrow lines. Molecules produce band spectra with wider light or dark bands. △1480, 1516.

Spectrum, Electromagnetic. *See* Electromagnetic Spectrum.

Spectrum, Solar. △94.

Speech, verbal or vocal expression of ideas and feelings, specifically intended to convey meaning. Speech is learned by listening and imitating, by assimilating systematic language patterns. The infant's babbling is the first step toward learning to speak; his progress thereafter depends on the maturing of his speech organs, his ability to hear, his sex, intelligence, and his environment (stimulation, attentive parents, absence of bilingualism, reinforcement of vocalization). △780, 788, 864–66.

Speech Disorders, speech and language defects resulting from such diverse causes as emotional disorder, organic deficiency, faulty speech mechanism and sensory deficiency. Common speech disorder include retarded language development, difficulty i the production of certain sounds, deviations in th intensity or duration of speech sounds, aphasia, an stuttering and halting speech.

Speed, rate of motion. *See* Velocity. △1492.

Speedwell. *See* Veronica.

Speer, Albert (1905–), German architect and Na official, a close associate of Adolf Hitler. Speer dre up the plans for Germany's super-highways and fc the stadium at Nuremberg. By 1943 his authority ove the entire war economy was second only to that c Hermann Goering. Speer was tried in 1946 by th international war crimes tribunal and sentenced to 2 years in Spandau prison. His memoirs, *Inside th Third Reich* (1970), became a best-seller; *Spanda* (1976) is his prison diary.

Speke, John Hanning (1827–1864), British soldie and explorer of Africa. He served in India and afte several African expeditions with Sir Richard Burto discovered Lake Victoria, which he proved to be source of the Nile. △1268.

Speleology, the scientific study of caves and cav systems. Exploration and description of the variou features of caves are the main object. Included, to are the hydrological and geological studies con cerned with the rate of formation of stalagmites an stalactites and the influence of groundwater condi tions on cave formation. A special aspect is the study of the unusual animals that are found in caves. △256

Spemann, Hans (1869–1941), German zoologis and comparative anatomist. He was awarded the 1935 Nobel Prize in physiology or medicine for his discovery of the organizer effect in embryonic devel opment.

Spencer, Herbert (1820–1903), English philoso pher. He generalized evolutionary theory outside the confines of biology. In *First Principles* (1862), *Princi ples of Psychology* (1870–72), and *Sociology* (1876–96), he applied his encyclopedic knowledge to sup port his historicist concept of progress. *See also* Historicism. △1290.

Spender, Stephen (Harold) (1909–), English poet. A prominent poet of the 1930s, his autobiography *World Within World* (1951) is an important account of that period. He served in the Spanish Civil War and was briefly a member of the Communist party. His poetry is often purely subjective and lyrical.

Spengler, Oswald (1880–1936), German philosopher and historian. He expounded a cyclic theory of civilization that quickly established his reputation as a scholar. His *Decline of the West; Outlines of a Morphology of World History* (2 vols., 1918–22) proposed that Western culture was in a period of decline, having passed its creative zenith. Spengler felt that the state needed to have absolute power to reverse this process. After Hitler came into power (1933), however, he went into isolation, since he did not agree with the Nazi belief in Aryan supremacy.

Spenser, Edmund (1552?–99), English poet, b. London. Major works include *The Faerie Queene* (1589, 1596); *The Shepheardes Calender* (1579); elegies, such as *Astrophel* (1586, on Sir Philip Sidney); *Colin Clouts Come Home Againe* (1595), and *Epithalamion* (1595, celebrating his marriage). In 1580 he settled as a colonist in Ireland. He died in distress in London after an Irish uprising had destroyed his home, Kilcolman Castle, and a third part of *The Faerie Queene.* *See also* Spenserian Stanza. △1148.

Spenserian Stanza, poetic form, consisting of nine lines: eight five-foot iambic lines followed by one six-foot iambic line, or alexandrine. It was named after the 16th-century English poet Edmund Spenser, who first used this form in his *The Faerie Queene.* It has been called the stateliest of English measures. It was used in Lord Byron's *Childe Harold's Pilgrimage,* Percy Bysshe Shelley's *Adonais,* and John Keats' *The Eve of St Agnes.*

Spermatozoon, or sperm, male gamete, its function is to fertilize the female ovum. Small and mobile, it consists of a head containing nucleus and chromosomes; midpiece containing mitochondria (energy sources); and flagellum for mobility. △700.

Sperm Whale, largest of the toothed whales. Distinguished by its huge, squarish head with an undershot jaw, it feeds chiefly on squid and cuttlefish, which it hunts in all oceans. Species *Physeter catodon*. *See also* Whale. △552.

Sphenoid Bone. △682.

Sphere, solid geometric figure formed by the locus in space of points equidistant from a given point (the center); surface generated by rotation of a circle about a diameter. The distance from the center to the surface is the radius *(r)*. The volume is $4/3\pi r^3$ and the surface area is $4\pi r^2$. △1454, 1466.

Spherical Triangle, triangle formed by the intersection, on the surface of a sphere, of arcs of three great circles. The sides of spherical triangles are measured in terms of the angles that these arcs subtend at the sphere's center. Spherical trigonometry, the branch of geometry concerned with the properties of such triangles, is used in navigation. △1464.

Spherical Trigonometry, branch of mathematics that deals with the sides, angles, and areas of spherical triangles, that is, portions of the surface of a sphere bounded by three arcs or great circles. *See also* Trigonometry. △1464.

Sphinx Moth. *See* Hawk Moth.

Sphygmomanometer, a device for measuring arterial blood pressure.

Spica, or **Alpha Virginis,** bluish-white star in the constellation Virgo. It is a spectroscopic binary; the main star has a fainter companion of the 3rd magnitude. Characteristics: apparent mag. .98; absolute mag. −3.2; spectral type B1; distance 220 light-years.

Spice Islands, group of small islands within the Moluccas islands in Indonesia. Sparsely populated, they were the center of early spice harvesting. *See also* Moluccas.

Spices. △320, 356, 358.

Spider, land arthropods found worldwide. They have an unsegmented abdomen, attached to the cephalothorax by a slender stalk; eight eyes; and pairs of spinnerets on the abdomen to spin silk for egg cases and webs. Though their prey is killed by a poison injected by chelicerate jaws, only a few are poisonous to humans. Length: 0.1–3.5in (2.5–89mm). Order Araneae; class Arachnida. △488.

Spider Crab, marine crab of the Atlantic and Pacific. It has a spiny, sac-shaped carapace that is pointed in front and long, thin legs. Japanese spider crab *(Macrocheira kaempferi)* is 10ft (3m) across. There are 600 species. Family Majidae. *See also* Crab; Crustacean. △490.

Spider Mite. *See* Red Spider.

Spider Monkey, medium-sized monkey found from S Mexico to SE Brazil. They have long, spidery legs, a fully prehensile tail, and are agile tree dwellers, using the tail as a fifth hand. They are day-active and eat fruits and nuts. Genera *Ateles* and *Brachyteles*. *See also* Monkey.

Spider Plant, house plant native to S Africa with green or green and white arching grasslike leaves. Plantlets and tiny flowers grow on long stems from the plant base. Care: bright indirect light, moist soil (equal parts loam, peat moss, sand). Propagation is by plantlets or root division. Height: to 18in (46cm). Species *Chlorophytum comosum*.

Spiderwort, any of a genus *(Tradescantia)* of New World perennial plants having long, keeled, grasslike leaves and blue, rosy-purple, or white flowers in flat-topped clusters. Family Commelinaceae.

Spike Moss. *See* Selaginella.

Spillane, Mickey (1918–), US author, b. Frank Morrison Spillane in New York City. The author of numerous detective novels featuring Mike Hammer, his tough, often sadistic books include *I, The Jury* (1947), *My Gun Is Quick* (1950), *The Big Kill* (1951), and *The Deep* (1961).

Spin, Nuclear, intrinsic angular momentum of an atomic nucleus, which can be thought of as resulting from rotation about an axis. It is a quantized quantity, assuming certain discrete values. The spin quantum number, from which these are derived, can either be zero, a half integer (for protons and electrons), or an integer (for mesons).

Spina Bifida, a congenital cleft of the vertebral column. It is a result of abnormal development of the neural tube and its linings during early embryonic life.

Spinach, herbaceous annual plant widely cultivated in areas with cool summers. Its dark green leaves contain great food value. Family Chenopodiaceae; species *Spinacia oleracea*. △334.

Spinal Cord, tubular central nerve cord, lying within the vertebral column, or spine. It, along with the brain, makes up the central nervous system, the communication center of the body. It gives off 31 pairs of spinal nerves, each of which has sensory and motor fibers. The spinal cord functions to receive sensory input, interpret the messages, and send messages to the periphery and to the brain. The spinal cord itself, as seen in cross section, is made up of H-shaped gray matter, containing sensory and motor nerve centers, and surrounding white matter, made up of fatty connective sheath around motor nerves, or axons. *See also* Nervous System. △664.

Spinal Fluid. *See* Cerebrospinal fluid.

Spine, the vertebral column, or spinal column; in humans a somewhat S-shaped, flexible column made up of 33 separate bones, known as vertebrae, that forms the backbone and surrounds and protects the spinal cord. The human spinal, or vertebral, column is divided into five sections: the cervical region, or neck section, composed of 7 vertebrae; the thoracic region, or chest, composed of 12 vertebrae; the lumbar region, or small of the back, composed of five vertebrae; the sacral region, or sacrum, composed of five vertebrae; and the coccygeal region, or coccyx, composed of 4 vertebrae. Disk-shaped cartilaginous pads located between vertebrae cushion and absorb shock during movement and reduce wear. *See also* Vertebra. △682.

Spinel, oxide mineral, magnesium aluminum oxide ($MgAl_2O_4$) found in igneous and metamorphic rocks. Cubic system frequently twinned octahedral crystals. Glassy black, red, blue, brown, or white; hardness 7.-5–8; sp gr 3.8. Red spinel from Sri Lanka is a valuable gemstone.

Spinet, keyboard stringed musical instrument. Originally (15th–18th centuries) it was a small, oblong harpsichord with a single keyboard, ranging 3 octaves. In the 19th and 20th centuries, it became a small upright piano, ranging about 7 octaves, with thinner sound than a grand piano, and used as a parlor instrument.

Spingarn, Joel Elias (1875–1939), US educator and literary critic, b. New York City. He was a member of the publishing firm Harcourt, Brace and Co. (1919–32) and an important member of the National Association for the Advancement of Colored People, for which he established the Spingarn medal (1913) awarded annually for outstanding achievement. Works include *The New Criticism* (1911) and *Creative Criticism* (1931).

Spinone Italiano, pointer and gun dog bred in Piedmont region of Italy several centuries ago. This rugged dog has a big, long hound head; large, dropped ears; bushy eyebrows; a pointer's body; and docked tail. The short, hard, rough, weather-resistant coat is solid white or white with yellow or white with light brown patches. Average size: 26in (66cm) high at shoulder; 56lb (25.5kg).

Spinoza, Baruch (1632–77), Dutch philosopher. After his expulsion from the synagogue for "atheism," he worked in seclusion as a lens grinder. Although he was austere and reclusive, his reputation as a philosopher-scientist grew. He refused generous gifts and employment and worked alone on his *Ethica* (Ethics) (1660–66). *The Theological-Political Treatise* (1670) contained the first modern historical interpretation of the Bible. Spinoza declined the chair of philosophy at Heidelberg in order to preserve his independence. Moral autonomy *(Ethics)* and toleration *(Political Treatise)*, were among his central ideas. △854, 858.

Spiny Lizard. *See* Fence Lizard.

Spiny Lobster. △490.

Spiracle, external opening for respiration in various animals. In insects and spiders, it is the opening to a trachea (air tube); in sharks, rays, and some bony fish, water passes through a pair of spiracles during gill respiration; in whales the nasal opening is called a spiracle. △494.

Spiraea, genus of flowering shrubs native to the Northern Hemisphere. They have small lobed leaves and clusters of small white or pink flowers. Many of

Sparrow hawk

Spearfish

Spearmint

Spider monkey

the 75 species are grown as ornamentals. Height: 5ft (1.5m). Family Rosaceae.

Spiral, in Mathematics. △1454, 1456.

Spiral Galaxy, type of regular galaxy in which a condensed nucleus of stars is surrounded by streams of younger stars, gas, and dust spiraling out from opposite sides of it. In normal spirals the nucleus is more or less spherical. Such galaxies are graded in three groups, Sa to Sc, according to increasing openness of their spiral arms. *See also* Barred Spiral Galaxy; Elliptical Galaxy; Galaxy. △118, 122.

Spiral Nebula. △1478.

Spirit Duplicator. △1774.

Spirits. △352.

Spiritualists. △822.

Spirituals, religious folk music, especially that associated with US black culture. The words of spirituals are often based on Biblical stories while the music is often in 4-part harmony with stylistic features peculiar to the spiritual (eg, 5-note melodies). Spirituals are an authentic form of US folk music that have influenced the development of other musical forms such as the blues.

Spirochete, general name applied to group of bacteria that are spiral-rod shaped and capable of flexing and wriggling their bodies as they move about. *See also* Bacteria.

Spitsbergen (Svalbard), island group in the Arctic Ocean, approx. 400mi (644km) N of Norway; Spitsbergen is the chief island. Large coal deposits on Spitsbergen were discovered in the late 19th century, and coal production is now a major industry; copper, asbestos, iron, and other minerals are also mined. The group was discovered in the 12th century by the Vikings, and again in 1596 by Willem Barents. The islands are now occupied by Norway and the USSR. Area: 24,000sq mi (63,158sq km). Pop. 3,654.

Spitteler, Carl Friedrich Georg (1845–1924), pseud. Carl Felix Tandem, Swiss poet. His epics, *Prometheus and Epimetheus* (1881) and *Der Olympische Frühling* (1900), resemble Friedrich Nietzsche's *Zarathustra*, but it is controversial as to who influenced whom. He wrote essays on Nietzsche and a novel *Imago* (1906). He was awarded the Nobel Prize in literature in 1919.

Spittle Bug, or frog hopper, leaping insect found worldwide. Adults are brown to gray. Green to brown nymphs produce frothy masses on plants. Length: 0.5in (13mm). Family Cercopidae. *See also* Homoptera.

Spitz, Mark Andrew (1950–), US swimmer, b. Modesto, Calif. Before retiring from competition (1972), he set US records 35 times and world records 23 times. He won two gold medals at the 1968 Olympics and then an unprecedented seven gold medals at the 1972 Olympics.

Spleen, an important, but nonessential, organ of the circulatory system. It lies in the abdominal cavity to the left of the stomach. The spleen functions to store blood, in an emergency supplying additional blood cells and oxygen. It also destroys, through the action of its macrophages, worn out or damaged red blood cells and produces lymphocytes, a type of white blood cell. △740.

Spleenwort, widely distributed fern with simple or compound fronds. They have crescent-shaped sori and sporangia. The North American ebony spleenwort *(Asplenium playneuron)* has long, stiff, ladderlike, fertile leaves with shorter, less erect sterile leaves; height: to 18in (46cm). Family Aspleniaceae.

Split (Spljet), seaport city in W Yugoslavia, on Dalmatian coast, in Croatia; resort and commercial center; site of palace of Roman emperor Diocletian (295–305), amphitheater, museum, oceanographic institute, teachers' college. City held by Venice 1420–1797; passed to Austria 1797; inc. into Yugoslavia 1918. Industries: shipbuilding, textiles, chemicals, tourism. Pop. 151,875.

Spock, Benjamin McLane (1903–), US pediatrician and author, b. New Haven, Conn. His book *The Common Sense Book of Baby and Child Care* (1946) called for parental warmth and understanding of a child's individual nature, rather than rigid following of feeding and other schedules. The book greatly influenced child care, particularly in the United States. He became a popular and important figure and in the late 1960s was active in anti-Vietnam war protests and in politics.

Spoils System, practice of appointing loyal members of the party in power to public offices. This practice was uncommon in federal government until Pres. Jackson (1829) instituted a "rotation in office." The practice grew, resulting in corruption and inefficiency and led to the Pendleton Act of 1883, which established the civil service.

Spokane, city and port of entry in E Washington, on falls of Spokane River; seat of Spokane co. Originally inhabited by Spokane Indians, a trading post was est. 1810; settlement began *c.* 1871; industry was spurred by arrival of Northern Pacific Railroad (1881). Spokane is the site of Gonzaga University (1887), Whitworth College (1890), Fort Wright College (1907). Industries: lumbering, food processing, metal refining, mining, cement. Inc. 1881 as village, 1891 as city. Pop. (1970) 170,516.

Spondee, metrical foot consisting of two stressed syllables, or two longs. The meter is called spondaic. Spondaic meter is found in Greek poetry in the slow, solemn hymns sung at a "spondee" or drink-offering. In English-language verse spondaic meter is found in this line from John Milton's *Paradise Lost.*

Rocks, caves, lakes, fens, bogs, dens,
and shades of death.

See also Meter.

Sponge, mainly marine animal composed of an outer layer of cells; a middle layer of nonliving, jellylike substance; and an inner layer of collar cells. The body is supported by a skeleton of lime, silica, or spongin. There is no nervous system or cellular coordination. Sponges reproduce sexually and by asexual budding. Length: from 0.04in (1mm)–several feet (1–2 meters). Phylum Porifera; 4,200 species including purse sponge *Grantia* and simple sponge *Leucosolenia*. △466, 506.

Spontaneous Combustion, outbreak of fire without external application of heat. When combustible material, such as hay or coal, is slowly oxidized by bacteria or air, the temperature rises to the ignition point, whereupon it catches fire. △1552, 1564.

Spontaneous Fission. *See* Radiation, Nuclear.

Spontaneous Generation, or abiogenesis, belief, now discredited, that living organisms arise from nonliving matter. It supposedly explained the presence of maggots on decaying meat.

Spoonbill, widely distributed wading bird with long bill that is flat and rounded at the tip. With large wings, long legs, short tails, and white or pinkish plumage, they feed on small plant and animal matter and lay light-colored spotted eggs (3–5) in a stick nest. Length: 3ft (91.5cm). Family Threskiornithidae. △602.

Spoonbill Sturgeon. *See* Paddlefish.

Spore, small reproductive body that detaches from the parent plant to produce new plants. Mostly microscopic, spores are one- or several-celled and produced in large numbers. Some reproduce rapidly, others rest, surviving unfavorable environmental conditions. Although they occur in all plant groups, spores are particularly characteristic of fungi and ferns. △428, 438.

Sporozoa, class of parasitic protozoa characterized by reproduction by sporulation (asexual multiple fission) and absence of special locomotive apparatus for much of their lives. The best example is the plasmodium that causes malaria. △466.

Sporting Dog, dog breeds that hunt by air-scenting. Also called gun or bird dogs, they locate game, flush it, wait for the hunter's shot, and retrieve on command. Breeds in this category are pointer, retriever, setter, spaniel, vizla, Weimaraner, and wirehaired pointing griffon. *See also* Hounds.

Sports, as a term, includes activities in which skill and physical prowess may be demonstrated. Generally, the term is restricted to a contest incorporating a specified set of rules. The types of activities vary greatly, and are classified either by individual or team sports. While individual sports would include those where one person could achieve success without another person's aid, team sports involve those which are designed to succeed due to a coordinated effort of more than one individual. In amateur sports, the major competition is the Olympic Games, held every four years (winter and summer) at a different site. *Se also* specific sports and biographies of sports pe sonalities. △930, 1408.

Spotsylvania, Battle of (May 8–18, 1864), US Civ War engagement, a series of battles in Virginia follow ing the Wilderness Campaign. Union Gen. Ulysses S Grant failed to outflank Confederate Gen. Robert E Lee.

Spotted Cavy. *See* Paca.

Spranger, Bartholomäus. △1150.

Spring, a natural opening for discharge of water fro an underground source. Springs are an important par of the water cycle. They may emerge at points on dr land or in beds of streams or ponds. The compositio of spring water varies with the surrounding soil o rocks. △254.

Springbok, or springbuck, small antelope native to S Africa, it is the national emblem of the Republic o South Africa. Reddish-brown on back grades into dar horizontal band just above white underside. Bot sexes carry short, black, slightly curved horns. Whe alarmed, it raises white fold of hair along back. It onc migrated in herds numbering over 1,000,000, bu now is rare. Length: to 4.5ft (1.4m); weight: to 79l (36kg). Family Bovidae; species *Antidorcas marsupi alis*. △586.

Springer Spaniel. *See* Spaniel.

Springfield, capital city of Illinois, in central Illinois on Sangamon River; seat of Sangamon co. It is noted as the home and area where Abraham Lincoln practiced law 1837–61; made state capital 1839; industrial development started *c.* 1870; site of Lincoln's home, now a national historic site (est. 1971), Lincoln's tomb containing his wife and three of four sons, Lincoln Land Community College (1967), Illinois State Fair. Industries: farm machinery, flour, feed, electronic equipment, tourism. Settled 1818; inc. 1832 as town, 1840 as city. Pop. (1970) 91,753.

Springfield, city in S Massachusetts, on E bank of Connecticut River, 80mi (129km) W of Boston; seat of Hampden co. Burned during King Philip's War (1675), it was scene of Shay's Rebellion (1786–87); station on Underground Railroad; site of Springfield College (1885), American International College (1885), Western New England College (1919), and US Armory (1794–1966; Springfield and Garand rifles were developed here), now an arms museum. Industries: hosiery, matches, firearms, paper, printing. Settled 1636 as Agawam; name changed in 1640; inc. 1641, as city 1852. Pop. (1970) 163,905.

Springfield, city in SW Missouri, approx. 150mi (242km) SSE of Kansas City in resort area of Ozarks; seat of Greene co; site of Drury College (1873), Southwest Missouri State College (1905), Central Bible College (1922), Evangel College (1955); nearby is Mark Twain National Forest. Industries: agriculture, flour, food processing, clothing, furniture, typewriters. Settled 1829; inc. 1855. Pop. (1970) 120,096.

Springfield, city in W central Ohio, on the Mad River 23mi (37km) NE of Dayton; seat of Clark co; scene of 1807 regional peace negotiations between Indian chiefs, including Tecumseh; tablet marks spot of tavern in which meeting was held; site of Wittenberg University (1842). Industries: farm machinery, electric motors, incubators, diesel engines. Founded 1799 by Kentuckians; made seat 1818; inc. as town 1827, as city 1850. Pop. (1970) 81,926.

Springfield, city in W Oregon, 5mi (8km) E of Eugene. Willamette National Forest with recreational facilities is nearby; farming and dairying region. Industries: food processing, chemicals. Inc. 1885. Pop. (1970) 27,047.

Springhaas. *See* Jumping Hare.

Spring Peeper, tree frog native to E and S United States and S Canada. It is brown with a dark, cross-shaped mark on its back. Found on low tree branches or on the ground, its high peeping mating call is a sign of spring in the north. Length: 1.5in (4cm). Family Hylidae; species *Hyla crucifer. See also* Tree Frog.

Springtail, tiny, wingless insect found worldwide. it varies in color and can jump 3–4in (76–102mm), using a leverlike, forked tail under the abdomen that is forced down and backward. Length: 0.19–0.23in (5–6mm). Order Collembola.

Spring Valley, town in SW California; suburb of San Diego; site of Bancroft Ranch House Museum (1856),

National historic landmark; light industries. Pop. (1970) 29,742.

Spruce, evergreen trees, often confused with firs, native to mountainous or cooler temperate regions of the Northern Hemisphere. Pyramid-shaped and dense, they have four-sided needles that fall off easily and pendulous cones. The timber is used in cabinets and some species yield turpentine. Height: to 200 ft (61m); family Pinaceae; genus *Picea*.

Spurge, widely distributed herbs, shrubs, and trees. Some are succulent and others are cactuslike. They exude a milky juice when cut and have small flowers surrounded by large, colorful, flowerlike bracts, as in the poinsettia. Family Euphorbiaceae; genus *Euphorbia*.

Sputnik, the first artificial satellite, launched Oct. 4, 1957, by the Soviet Union. Weighing 184lb (83kg) and equipped with a radio transmitter, it circled the Earth for several months. The launch date of Sputnik is generally agreed to mark the beginning of the Space Age. *See also* Satellite, Artificial. △142.

Squamata. △520.

Squanto (died 1622), American Indian of the Pawtuxet tribe of Massachusetts. He lived in England (1605–14), was sold as a slave in Spain, but was returned to Massachusetts in 1619. He acted as an interpreter for the Pilgrims of Plymouth Colony, helping them make a treaty with Massasoit and teaching them to plant corn and where to fish.

Square, number or quantity resulting when a specified number or quantity is multiplied by itself: the square of 3 is 9; the square of x is x^2. The squares of both positive and negative numbers are positive: $-3^2 = 9$. △1446.

Square, quadrilateral having all its sides equal and all its angles right angles. Its area is the product of adjacent sides. △1462.

Square Root (symbol $\sqrt{\ }$), number or quantity that must be multiplied by itself to give a specified number or quantity. As a number it is usually irrational. The square root of 4 is 2, ie, $\sqrt{4} = 2$; $\sqrt{2} = 1.414213.$ . . . A negative number has imaginary square roots. △1446.

Squash. *See* Pumpkin.

Squash Bug, brown to gray bug found only in the Western Hemisphere. It sucks juices from leaves of pumpkin, squash, and related plants. There is one generation per year. Length: 0.5in (13mm). Family Coreidae; species *Anasa tristis*.

Squash Rackets, game played by two or four persons on a four-walled court. The court is 18.5 feet (5.6m) wide by 32 feet (9.8m) long, and 16 feet (4.9m) high at the front wall. The back wall is usually 9 feet (2.7m) high. Players use a gut-strung racket (27 inches, 68.6cm, long) that is round-headed, and a black, hard-rubber ball that is 1.75 inches (4.4cm) in diameter. The game begins from a designated area behind the floor service line which is 22 feet (6.7m) away from, and parallel to, the front wall. After striking the ball above the *telltale* (a 17-inch, 43.2-cm, horizontal strip) on the front wall, the ball must land in the opposite service court. Volleying (with caroms off the side walls permitted) continues until a point is scored when one of the players fails to return the ball before it strikes the floor twice. A game is 15 points, unless the score is 13-all, in which case the game is played to 15, 16, or 18 points. The game originated in England in the 19th century.

Squat Lobster. △486.

Squawberry. *See* Partridgeberry.

Squid, marine cephalopod mollusk that has a cylindrical body, eight short, suckered tentacles, and two long armlike tentacles surrounding the mouth. They can attain swimming speeds of 30mph (48km/h). Most squid have a horny, internal support called a pen. The giant squid *Architeuthis* of North Atlantic is the largest. There are about 350 species. Length: 2in–60ft (5cm–18m). Order Decapoda; family Teuthoidea. *See also* Cephalopod; Mollusk. △480, 626.

Squint. *See* Strabismus.

Squirrel, large family (Sciuridae) of rodents living almost worldwide. The busy, noisy diurnal tree squirrels of Eurasia and North and South America are the best known. The smallest is the African pygmy; the largest is the Indian giant. They eat nuts, seeds, fruit, insects, and, occasionally, eggs and young birds. Most have glossy fur and bushy tails. Weight: to 6lb (3kg). △592, 598.

Squirrelfish, coral reef fish found worldwide in tropical seas. Bright red, often with white streaks or spots, it has large eyes and sharp spines on gill covers and fins. Length: 1–2ft (30.5–61cm). The 70 species include Atlantic longspine *Holocentrus rufus*. Family Holocentridae.

Squirrel Monkey, small monkey with a long, nonprehensile tail, found from Costa Rica to Paraguay. They are day-active tree dwellers, feed on fruits and flowers, and travel in troops of up to 100. They make lively pets, but do best with one or two other squirrel monkeys as companions. Genus *Saimiri*. *See also* Monkey.

Sri Lanka, Republic of, formerly Ceylon; independent island-state in the Indian Ocean, 20mi (32km) off the SE coast of India. The people are of Indian origin (Sinhalese and Tamil), and the majority is Buddhist.

Land and economy. Sri Lanka, a continuation of the Indian continental shelf, is separated from the mainland by Palk Strait. A mountainous massif dominates the S central island, trailing off to coastal plains to the N, W, and E. The climate is tropical, and 70% of the island is covered by forest and natural grassland. The annual rainfall varies about the island from 40–200in (102—508cm). The economy, primarily agricultural, relies heavily on the export of tea, rubber, and coconuts. Graphite of extremely high quality is the principal mineral export. Industry, once of minor importance, is growing significantly because of government direction of foreign aid funds. The population has more than doubled since 1950, causing serious food and economic problems.

People. The majority of the people is of Indian descent, Sinhalese and Tamil. Sinhalese, Buddhist in belief, account for over 9,000,000 and Tamils, Hindu in belief, account for over 2,500,000. The Tamils divide into two groups: the Ceylonese Tamils, and the Indian Tamils, imported for labor by the British in the late 19th century. Education is universal and the majority of the people are literate.

Government. An independent republic, Sri Lanka is a member of the Commonwealth of Nations. The 1972 constitution established a National State Assembly of 157 members elected every 5 years. The president serves as head of state, while the prime minister heads the cabinet. Local government is invested in provinces and districts. The judicial system consists of a supreme court and many lesser courts. There are four major political parties, often necessitating coalition governments.

History. Sri Lanka has had a recorded history for over 2,000 years. Influenced by its proximity to India, and its position along the E-W trade route, the island fell under European control in the early 16th century. The island was settled in the 5th century BC by the Sinhalese from India and was controlled by their Buddhist kings until the arrival of the Portuguese in 1505. By 1619 the Portuguese governed the entire island only to be driven out by the Dutch, with the help of Sinhalese kings, in 1648. The English gained control in 1796 and continued their dominance until a series of disturbances beginning in 1915 convinced them to grant independence to the people in 1948. The major figure in the early years of independence was S.W.R. Bandaranaike, who was assassinated in 1959. His widow, Sirimavo Bandaranaike, governed 1959–65 and became prime minister again in 1972.

PROFILE

Official name: Republic of Sri Lanka
Area: 25,332sq mi (65,610sq km)
Population: 14,000,000
Density: 552.6per sq mi (213.3per sq km)
Chief cities: Colombo (capital); Jaffna; Kandy; Galle
Government: Republic
Religion: Buddhism
Language: Sinhala (official), English
Monetary unit: Ceylonese rupee
Gross national product: $2,000,000,000
Per capita income: $172
Industries (major products): milled rice, cement, pharmaceuticals, petroleum products
Agriculture (major products): rice, tea, coconuts, rubber
Minerals (major): graphite, salt
Trading partners (major): Great Britain, China, United States, Australia

Srinagar, city in N India, on Jhelum River; capital of Srinagar district and summer capital of Jammu and Kashmir state; site of University of Jammu and Kashmir (1948); summer resort; site of 7th-century Sankaracharya temple, 16th-century fort, many Buddhist remains. Industries: carpets, silk, silver, leather, ply-

Spitsbergen

Spoonbill

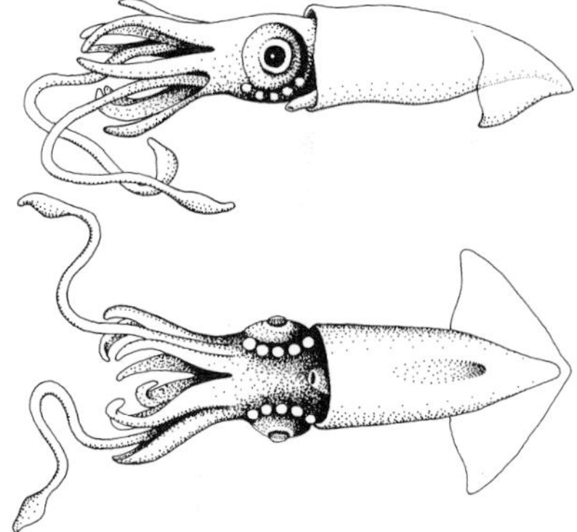
Squid

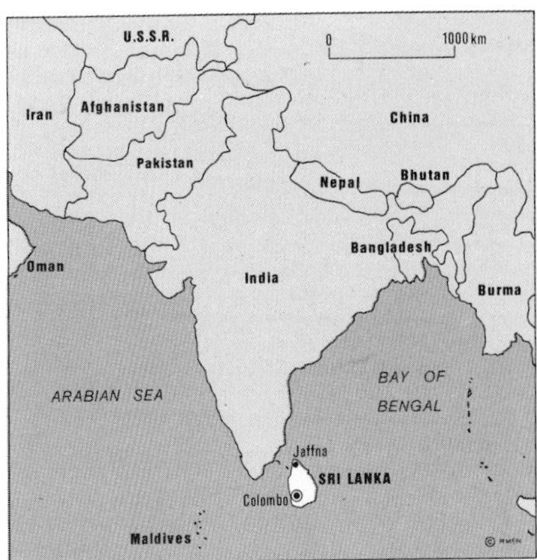
U.S.S.R.
0
1000 km
Iran
Afghanistan
China
Pakistan
Nepal
Bhutan
Bangladesh
Oman
India
Burma
ARABIAN SEA
BAY OF
BENGAL
Jaffna
SRI LANKA
Colombo
Maldives
Sri Lanka

wood, cement, tourism. Founded 6th century. Pop. 327,076.

S.S. (Ger. *Schutzstaffel*), an elite corp of the Nazi party, headed by Heinrich Himmler. It was originally responsible for domestic security, but its powers after 1936 were exceptional throughout German-occupied Europe.

Staël, Germaine, Madame de (1766–1817), French author. Her full name was Anne Louise Germaine Necker, Baronne de Staël-Holstein. The daughter of Jacques Necker, she married the Swedish ambassador to Paris and established a salon that became an intellectual and political center. She did not hesitate to criticize France and Napoleon and was exiled several times. Her novels *Delphine* (1803) and *Corinne* (1807) are considered the first modern feminist psychological novels. She introduced German Romanticism to France in *De l'Allemagne* (1810). *De l'Allemagne* is an account of Germany which introduced the German philosophy and literature of the romantic era to France. Napoleon had it seized and destroyed for being "un-French" and "subversive."

Staffordshire Bull Terrier, fighting dog (terrier group) bred in England in the 19th century. Now an all-purpose dog, the Staffordshire bull has a short, broad head; small drop or half-prick ears; dark eyes; wide-chested body; wide-set well-boned legs; and medium-length, tapered tail. Its smooth, short coat is red, fawn, black, blue, or any of these with white. Average size: 14–16in (35.5–40.5cm) high at shoulder; 28–38lb (12.5–17kg). *See also* Terrier.

Stag Beetle, or pinching bug, large, usually brown or black beetle named for long, antlerlike mandibles present in many species, particularly among males. Family Lucanidae. △500.

Staggers, disease of horses, cattle, and sheep, causing uncoordination, convulsions, and paralysis. Its cause is unknown.

Staghorn Coral. △468.

Staghorn Fern. △438.

Stained Glass, artistic medium. It was used primarily in conjunction with church architecture and was brought to its full flower during the Gothic era, particularly in France. Of Byzantine origin, stained glass is produced in its purest form by impregnating the components of glass with colored dyes and arranging shapes cut from the resultant sheets to form decorative patterns or representational images. These shapes are joined and supported by flexible strips of lead that take the form of dark, emphatic contours as natural light filters through the glass and silhouettes the leading. Details are painted onto the glass surfaces in liquid enamel and fused to the surfaces by heat.

Aside from fragmentary examples, the earliest surviving stained glass is to be found in Augsburg Cathedral, Bavaria, although its precise age is debatable, with speculation ranging from 1050 to 1150 as the date of its installation. At about the latter date, stained-glass windows were created for the French Abbey of Saint-Denis, Paris, and shortly thereafter the great west window of Chartres Cathedral was installed. The Ille de France soon became the art's great center, its influence spreading throughout the northwest of Europe. In modern times, concrete has supplanted the more graceful lead as a support for the glass. △1042, 1094, 1104, 1608.

Stainless Steel. *See* Steel. △1594.

Stalactite, icicle-like formation of calcite, made by the precipitation of calcium carbonate out of ground water that has seeped into limestone caves. Stalagmites are similar formations built up from the floor of the cave. △256, 1562.

Stalagmite. *See* Stalactite.

Stalin, Joseph Vissarionovich (1879–1953), Soviet political leader and dictator, b. Georgia. Born Iosif Vissarionovich Dzhugashvili, he was educated at the Tiflis theological seminary, and expelled in 1898 as a revolutionary. He became a Bolshevik in 1903 and joined the Central Committee in 1913, taking part in terrorist activities. Following the Bolshevik revolution, in October 1917, he served under V.I. Lenin as commissar for nationalities (1921–23), becoming general secretary of the Central Committee in 1922. Following Lenin's death in 1924, Stalin was able to maneuver for supreme power and suppress Lenin's criticism of him. Leon Trotsky was his strongest rival, but Stalin managed to eliminate him and by 1927 he was a virtual dictator. He introduced forced collectivization in 1929. Stalin began a ruthless purge that eliminated possible rivals and resulted in a reign of terror in which millions perished (1936–39). He became premier in 1941, and generalissimo during the war, which he personally supervised. His last years were dominated by his personal eccentricities. After his death, Nikita Khrushchev denounced his tyrannical rule at the 1956 party congress. △1310–12, 1344.

Stalingrad. *See* Volgograd.

Stalingrad, Battle of (1942–43), a decisive conflict in World War II, centering on the Soviet city of Stalingrad. △1338.

Stalino. *See* Donetsk.

Stall, Aircraft. △1626, 1718.

Stamford, city in SW Connecticut, on Long Island Sound and New York border. Industries: electronics, computers, plastics, shipyards. Settled as part of New York 1641; annexed to Connecticut 1662; city inc. within town of Stamford 1893; city and town consolidated 1949. Pop. (1970) 108, 798.

Stamp Act, first direct tax (1765) levied on the colonies by the British Parliament. It was intended to raise revenue to help pay for troops defending the colonies. The act required a tax, in the form of a stamp, affixed to all legal papers, newspaper copies, and other documents. Colonists in secret organizations such as the Sons of Liberty resisted the tax, attacking the stamp distributors and burning stamped paper. The act was repealed in 1766. △1218.

Stamp Act Congress, meeting in opposition to the Stamp Act. Convened in New York City, it was composed of representatives of nine colonies (1765). It resolved that only the colonies could tax themselves and demanded repeal of the Stamp Act. The Declaration of Rights and Grievances was issued as a statement of the colonial position.

Stamping, method of forming metal. A flat blank of metal is stretched over a die and struck with a movable punch until the desired shape is attained. Dies also perforate, bend, and shear when necessary. Stampings are limited to metal ¾in (19mm) or less thick.

Standardbred, light horse breed that includes trotters and pacers. An American breed (once the American Trotter), it was developed about 1849 from several breeds for road driving and racing. More rugged than the thoroughbred, it is smaller, has shorter legs, and is longer bodied. Its speed is attained by extending its legs into rapidly repeated long strides. Colors are bay, brown, chestnut, and black. Height: 60–64in (152–163cm) at shoulder; weight: 900–1300lb (405–591kg).

Standard Deviation, in statistics, a measure of dispersion or deviation of scores from the average or mean of the scores. A small standard deviation indicates that scores cluster around the mean, while a large one indicates that scores are widely dispersed about the mean. The formula for calculating the standard deviation is $\sqrt{\Sigma x^2 \div N}$ where Σ means "the sum of," each x is the deviation of each score from the mean of all scores, and N is the number of scores. *See also* Statistics.

Standard of Living, referring to a country, is measured by the per capita income of the population. It is used to compare the degree of economic development in the various countries. Many economists define an underdeveloped nation as one whose per capita income is less than some percent (25% is sometimes used) of the more developed countries. *See also* Less Developed Countries. △936.

Standard Schnauzer, guard and yard dog (working group) bred in Germany around 15th–16th centuries; oldest of Schnauzer types. It has an elongated, rectangular head with arched eyebrows, moustache, and whiskers. High-set ears are cropped or V-shaped; the compact body has a stiff, straight back. Legs are medium-length and appear heavy because of coat; the high-set tail is docked. The 1.5in (4cm) long coat is hard and wiry; colors are pepper and salt or pure black. Average size: 17–20in (43–51cm) at shoulders; 27–37lb (12–17kg). *See also* Working Dog.

Standard Temperature and Pressure (STP), or normal temperature and pressure (NTP), standard conditions for comparing the volumes of gases, etc. It is a pressure of 760mm of mercury ($1.013/25 \times 10^5$ pascals) and a temperature of 0°C. △1502.

Stanford, Leland (1824–93), US railroad builder and politician, b. Watervliet, N.Y. During the Civil War he was Republican governor of California (1861) and kept it in the Union. He was a founder of the Central Pacific Railroad and president of the Southern Pacific lines. While in the US Senate (1885–93) he secured financial aid for the railroads from state and municipal governments. He founded Stanford University in 1885 and named it for his son Leland.

Stanford-Binet Scales, intelligence tests derived from the first such tests devised by Alfred Binet starting in 1905. The present Stanford-Binet measures IQ beginning at age two and is used primarily to predict likelihood of success in school. *See also* Intelligence Testing.

Stanislas I Leszczyński (1677–1766), Polish nobleman, king of Poland (1704–09, 1733–35). He became king with the support of Charles XII of Sweden, replacing Augustus II, but was forced to relinquish the throne to Augustus after the Swedish defeat at the battle of Poltava (1709). With French help (the result of his daughter's marriage to Louis XV) he regained the throne, but was deposed by Augustus III, who was aided by Russia.

Stanislavsky, Constantin (1863–1938), Russian actor, director, and teacher, b.Constantin Sergeyevich Alekseyev. In 1898 he cofounded the Moscow Art Theatre with Vladimir Nemirovich-Danchenko. One of their first productions was Chekhov's *The Seagull.* Another important production was Gorky's *Lower Depths* in 1902. Stanislavsky's teaching, which came to be called the Method, stressed ensemble acting with each actor identifying with the inner, emotional life of the character.

Stanley, (Sir) Henry Morton (1841–1904), British-US explorer of Africa, b. John Rowlands in Wales. After a miserable childhood, he ran away to the United States, taking the name of a merchant who befriended him. He served in the Confederate army and US Navy. As a journalist, he accompanied an expedition to Abyssinia. Later he was sent by the New York *Herald* to central Africa to find David Livingstone, a missing missionary and explorer, which he did in 1871. A courageous and tenacious explorer, Stanley made several other expeditions into Africa, making vital geographic discoveries and establishing the Congo Free State for Belgium. He authored many successful accounts and served in the British parliament (1895–1900).

Stanley, Thomas, 1st Earl of Derby. *See* Derby, Thomas Stanley, 1st Earl of.

Stanleyville. *See* Kisangani.

Stanton, Edwin McMasters. (1814–69), US statesman, b. Steubenville, Ohio. Best known as Abraham Lincoln's forceful secretary of war during the Civil War, he was especially effective in getting supplies to the Union Army and in stopping corruption in military contracts. As a Radical Republican, he often disagreed with Lincoln and, later, with Andrew Johnson over Reconstruction. Johnson tried to force him to resign, but he stayed in the cabinet until 1868.

Stanton, Elizabeth Cady (1815–1902), US women's rights leader and social reformer, b. Johnstown, N.Y. In 1840, when women were excluded from the world antislavery convention, she joined with Lucretia Mott to fight for equality. In 1848 they organized the first women's rights convention at Seneca Falls, N.Y. In 1851 she joined Susan B. Anthony, and the two worked closely in the struggle for women's rights for 50 years. She edited the feminist journal, *The Revolution* (1868–70). In 1869 she was elected president of the National Women's Suffrage Association, a position she held from 1869–90. She collaborated in the writing of the *History of Women Suffrage* (1881–86). *See also* National Woman Suffrage Association; Seneca Falls Convention.

Stanza, group of verse lines into which a poem is divided. Stanzas are characterized by the number of lines. For example, couplet has two lines; tercet and terza rima, three; quatrain, four; ottava rima, eight. Stanzas can also be characterized by rhyme scheme or meter. Another word for stanza is *stave,* which is closely associated with song.

Staphylococcus, genus of bacteria characterized by gram-positive spherical cells that grow in grapelike clusters. They are facultative anaerobes present normally on the skin and on nasal and other mucous membranes. Some are pathogenic, the basic lesion being an abcess such as in wound infections. They are resistant to most antibiotics and are thus hard to control. *See also* Bacteria.

Star, hot gaseous self-luminous object, such as the Sun, that emits energy principally in the form of heat and light, produced through thermonuclear reactions occurring in its interior. Stars are thought to be formed out of nebular concentrations of interstellar matter, and thereafter follow certain evolutionary patterns governed by their physical characteristics. Their diameters vary considerably, from several hundred million miles for low-density red supergiants to Earth-like dimensions for enormously dense white dwarfs. Stellar temperatures also show wide variations, from about 1,500° K to 80,000° K and stars are grouped into well-defined spectral types and luminosity classes. △100–102, 110–116.

Starch, form of polysaccharide in which carbohydrate is stored in many plants and that is an important source of carbohydrate in the diet of animals. It consists of linked glucose units and exists in two forms: amylose, in which the glucose chains are unbranched, and amylopectin, in which they are branched. It is made commercially from corn, potatoes, etc. and used in the manufacture of adhesives, sizing, and foods. △1570, 1574.

Star Chamber, meeting place of the king's council in Westminster Palace, London. Under the Tudors, the name referred mainly to councilors and legal experts gathered there as a judicial tribunal. Proceeding without a jury, arbitrary in sentencing, and permitting torture, the Star Chamber court became notorious and was abolished (1641).

Star Cluster. △116.

Starfish, marine echinoderm with central disk body and radiating arms (8 to 25). The mouth is on the disk underside, and the stomach can be extruded to take in clams and other echinoderms. Calcareous spines are embedded in the skin. They move by varying water pressure in the water vascular system and tube feet. Class Asteroides; 1,000 species include common *Asterias* and 13-armed *Solaster*. △504, 622.

Stark, Johannes (1874–1957), German physicist. He received a 1919 Nobel Prize for describing the Stark effect (the splitting of the spectral lines of dispersed light when a light source is subjected to a strong electromagnetic field). *See also* Doppler Effect.

Starling, widely distributed aggressive bird that generally roosts in large groups, often in cities. They create a nuisance with their droppings and almost constant chattering, clicking, whistling, and other noises. They have stout bodies, pointed, sometimes notched, wings, and short tails. Most are dark, some are brightly colored. They feed on insects and fruit and build nests in tree cavities or on cliffs for bluish-green or whitish eggs (2–9). Length: 7–13in (18–33cm). Family Sturnidae.

Star Maps. △130–40.

Star of Bethlehem, bulbous house plant native to S Africa. Fragrant, star-shaped, white flowers grow on a central spike rising from slender, arching leaves. Care: direct sunlight, slightly dry soil (equal parts loam, peat moss, sand). Propagation is by offsets or seeds. Height: to 18in (46cm). Family Liliaceae; genus *Ornithogalum*.

Star of David, Magen David, or **Shield of David,** has evolved into a symbol of Judaism. It is a 6-pointed star formed by two equilateral triangles. Its origin is unknown. It was used at one time as an emblem by pagans, Christians, and Muslims alike. The Nazis used it to brand Jews. It is often traced to King David and Jewish warriors used it on their shields.

Star-Spangled Banner, The, US national anthem. The words were written by a young lawyer, Francis Scott Key, while he was detained by the British and forced to witness the bombardment of Fort McHenry in 1814. He was inspired by the sight of the US flag still waving above the fort at dawn. The lyrics were published that same year in a Baltimore newspaper. The tune was taken from "To Anacreon in Heaven," a popular English song. Although long sung by the US Army and Navy, "The Star-Spangled Banner" did not officially become the national anthem until so designated by President Woodrow Wilson in an executive order in 1916.

Following is the text of the first verse of the anthem:

Oh, say can you see by the dawn's early light
What so proudly we hailed at the twilight's last gleaming?
Whose broad stripes and bright stars thru the perilous fight
O'er the ramparts we watched were so gallantly streaming?
And the rockets' red glare, the bombs bursting in air.
Gave proof through the night that our flag was still there.
Oh say, does that star-spangled banner yet wave
O'er the land of the free and the home of the brave?

State, Department of, cabinet-level department within the executive branch. It is charged with developing and maintaining the foreign policy of the United States. Originally, the Continental Congress conducted foreign affairs. It had its origins in 1775 in a committee chaired by Benjamin Franklin. In 1777, a Committee for Foreign Affairs was established, but its real power was limited. The Department of Foreign Affairs (1781) was followed in 1789 by the Department of State, with Thomas Jefferson as its first secretary. The department's responsibilities have expanded, but it is no longer responsible for domestic affairs such as census, issuing patents, and handling territorial affairs. It is primarily concerned with the execution of the US foreign policy to promote long-range US security and well-being through continuous consultations with other nations. It also negotiates treaties and agreements with foreign nations and speaks for the United States in the United Nations and other international organizations and conferences.

State College, residential borough in central Pennsylvania, 22mi (35km) NW of Lewistown; site of Pennsylvania State University (1855). Settled 1859; inc. 1896. Pop. (1970) 33,778.

Staten Island, island in SE New York, in New York Bay, 5mi (8km) SW of Manhattan; separated from Long Island (E) by the Narrows and from New Jersey (W) by narrow Arthur Kill; coextensive with Richmond borough of New York City; connected with Brooklyn by Verrazano-Narrows bridge (1964) and with New York City and Brooklyn by ferries; site of Wagner College (1928), Notre Dame College of Staten Island (1931), US marine and army hospital; Billopp House (1688), Church of St Andrew (1708). Industries: shipbuilding, printing, publishing, oil refining, soap. Settled 1661; inc. with New York City 1898. Area: 64sq mi (166sq km). Pop. (1970) 295,443.

States General. *See* Estates General.

States of Matter. *See* Matter, States of.

State Sovereignty, doctrine of states' authority. Under Article X of the US Constitution, the states possess those powers not delegated to the federal government and not expressly prohibited to the states. △1276.

States' Rights, doctrine that the states have authority in matters not specifically delegated to the federal government. The controversy between federal and state jurisdiction reached a peak with John C. Calhoun's constitutional interpretation that a state could refuse to obey a federal law it deemed unconstitutional. This led to the Nullification Crisis (1832) and ultimately contributed to secession and the Civil War. More recently, it was an issue during the civil rights movement of 1950s and 1960s and in the George C. Wallace presidential campaign of 1968. *See also* Calhoun, John C.

Static Electricity. △1566.

Statics. △1488.

Statistical Mechanics, the study of large-scale properties of matter based on the underlying laws of quantum mechanics in conjunction with the statistical laws of large numbers. Quantum mechanics determines the possible energy states of a substance or system; the large number of molecules in such a system then allows one to use statistics to predict the probability of finding the system in any one of these states. The entropy of the system is related to the number of possible states; a system left to itself will tend to approach the most probable distribution of energy states. *See also* Thermodynamics.

Statistical Population. *See* Population, Statistical.

Statistics, the science that deals with methods for analyzing empirical data, or characteristics of the data itself. Statistics can be descriptive (simply summarizing the data) or inferential (leading to conclusions or inferences about larger populations of which the data are one sample). Inferential statistics are used by all the sciences to lend a greater degree of confidence to one's results, since statistics often allow one to calculate the probability that one's conclusions are in error. *See also* Average; Correlation; Factor Analysis; Fre-

Stained glass

Standard schnauzer

Henry Stanley

Starfish

quency Distribution; Standard Deviation; Validity. △1474.

Statue of Liberty, statue in SE New York, in New York Harbor on Liberty Island, SW of Manhattan Island. A gift from the people of France to the United States in commemoration of the centennial of US independence. Frédéric Auguste Bartholdi conceived the idea and designed it; framework was designed by Gustave Eiffel (creator of Eiffel Tower). Funds were raised by subscription from French people, and the statue was completed in Paris, disassembled, and shipped to the United States. The figure of a woman, it is 151ft (46m) high to top of torch in her uplifted right hand; regally draped, she wears a crown of seven spokes and carries a lawbook inscribed "July 4, 1776." Dedicated by Pres. Grover Cleveland Oct. 28, 1886; national monument since 1924.

Status, Laws of. △910.

Status, in sociology, a person's social position in a hierarchically arranged society in which the position is based on lifestyle, prestige, or some other noneconomic factor. A status group is any community of individuals who share the traits of a particular status. Status can derive from such things as socially enviable possessions (status symbols), valued talents, or friendships with people of high status. △924.

Staunton, city in N central Virginia, 100mi (161km) NW of Richmond; seat of Augusta co; birthplace of President Woodrow Wilson (museum est. 1941); Mary Baldwin College (1842); served as Confederate supply station and temporary headquarters of Gen. Stonewall Jackson during the Civil War; first US city to adopt city manager form of government (1908). Industries: agriculture, livestock, clothing, furniture, machinery, lumber, soft drinks. Founded 1732; inc. 1801 as town, 1871 as city. Pop. (1970) 24,504.

Stavanger, port city in SW Norway, on S bank of mouth of Stavanger Fjord, inlet of the North Sea, capital of Rogaland co. Founded before 10th century, it became bishopric 1125; site of 12th-century church. Industries: shipbuilding, fishing and fish processing. Pop. 82,079.

Stavisky Affair, French financial scandal that led to government crises in 1934. Financier Serge Alexandre Stavisky was found dead shortly after bonds of his credit organization were found to be worthless. Right-wing extremists claimed that the left-wing coalition government was involved in the scandal and hushing up a murder. Riots led to 15 deaths, resignation by two prime ministers, and the establishment of a centrist government under Gaston Doumergue.

Steady-State Theory of Universe, cosmological theory postulating that the universe, though expanding, has the same large-scale structure at all times: it is thus infinitely large, with no beginning and no end. The galaxies are receding, as indicated by their red shift, but matter is being created extremely slowly in the resulting spaces, to form eventually into new galaxies: the average density of galaxies thus remains constant. The theory is incompatible with the existing laws of physics and recent developments in astronomy tend to favor the big-bang theory. △126.

Steam Engine, first machine successfully used in the generation of mechanical power from thermal energy. Pistons driven by high pressure steam move crankshafts providing rotational motion to ships' propulsions, railroad locomotives, and electric generators. The first practical engine was developed by James Watt in 1763, and the origins of the Industrial Revolution can be traced to that time. △1220, 1280, 1584, 1626–28, 1706.

Steam Jacket. △1508.

Steam Turbine *See* Turbine.

Stearate, salt or ester of stearic acid ($C_{17}H_{35}COOH$), the most common fatty acid occurring in natural animal and vegetable fats. Stearates, especially the sodium and potassium salts, are used in soaps, lubricants, cosmetics, food additives, and pharmaceuticals.

Steel, a commercial iron, containing carbon as an essential alloy. Its malleability distinguishes it from cast iron and its freedom of slag from wrought iron. It is the most widely used of all metals. First made in ancient times, it was not until the development of the Bessemer and open-hearth processes in the 19th century, that steel became available for large-scale uses. Carbon steel, used for automobile bodies, machinery, appliances, and ships has only carbon added to iron. Low-alloy steels, with less than 5% of nickel, chromium, and molybdenum or other metals added, are exceptionally strong and are used for structured members of buildings, bridges, and machine parts. High-alloy steels, such as stainless steel, with more than 5% of other metals, are used in tableware and cooking utensils, where lustrous appearance and resistance to rust are required. △1592–94, 1612.

Steele, (Sir) Richard (1672–1729), British essayist and dramatist, b. Dublin. His early works include a moral treatise *The Christian Hero* (1701) and a comedy *The Lying Lover* (1704). He edited and wrote for the periodicals the *Tatler* (1709–11) and the *Spectator* (1711–12) with Joseph Addison. △1188.

Steenbok, Steinbok, or **Grysbok,** three species of small, slender-legged antelopes native to hills of E and S Africa. Colored shades of reddish brown and stippled with white, they are usually solitary. Males carry short, spiked horns. Length: to 34in (85cm); weight: to 30lb (14kg). Family Bovidae; genus *Raphicerus*. *See also* Antelope. △586.

Stegner, Wallace (1909–), US author, b. Lake Mills, Iowa. He taught English at Harvard and Stanford universities and wrote novels, short stories, and historical works. Among his novels are *On a Darkling Plain* (1940), *The Big Rock Candy Mountain* (1943), *The Preacher and the Slave* (1950), *A Shooting Star* (1961), and *Angle of Repose* (1971).

Stegosaurus, plated ornithischian dinosaur of Jurassic times of W United States. It was four-footed with a tiny skull and long tail. Its hallmark was a double row of bony, triangular plates running along its neck, back, and tail that carried long spikes. Length: 20ft (6m); weight: 8ton (7,200kg). △570, 572.

Steichen, Edward (1897–1973), US photographer, considered one of the greatest masters of the medium, b. Luxembourg. He helped Alfred Stieglitz open two photographic galleries in New York. First a portraitist and fashion photographer, he pioneered aerial photography during World War I and commanded naval combat photography during World War II. As director of the photography department of the Museum of Modern Art in New York (1947–62), he organized the famous "Family of Man" exhibition (1955). Many of his expressive images are included in *A Life in Photography* (1963).

Stein, Gertrude (1874–1946), US author and critic, b. Allegheny, Pa. She abandoned the study of medicine to devote her life to literature. She joined her brother in Paris (1903) and established a famous salon where she entertained and became a counselor and confidante of many of the great artists and writers of the time: Cézanne, Picasso, Hemingway, Fitzgerald, and many more.

Her first important book was *Three Lives* (1909). Other important works include *Tender Buttons* (1914), a volume of poems, and *The Making of Americans* (1925), a narrative. Her memoirs, *The Autobiography of Alice B. Toklas* (1933), actually a book by Stein about Stein but presented as the work of her secretary and constant personal companion, attained wide popularity. *See also* Lost Generation.

Steinbeck, John (1902–68), US novelist, b. Salinas, Calif. He gained critical notice in 1935 with the publication of his fourth novel, *Tortilla Flat*. His works are characterized by realistic dialogue and concern for the downtrodden. Among his novels are *Of Mice and Men* (1937), *The Grapes of Wrath* (1939; Pulitzer Prize 1940), *Cannery Row* (1945), *East of Eden* (1952), and *The Winter of Our Discontent* (1961). He was awarded the Nobel Prize for literature in 1962. *See also* Grapes of Wrath, The.

Stellar Cluster. △116.

Stem, main, upward-growing part of a plant that bears leaves, buds, and flowers. The internal structure is composed of vascular tissue arranged in a ring (dicot) or scattered (monocot). Stems usually are erect, but may be climbing (vine) or prostrate (stolon); they can also be succulent (cactus) or modified into underground structures (rhizomes, tubers, corms, bulbs). Stems vary in size from the threadlike stalks of aquatic plants to tree trunks. △430.

Stendhal (1783–1842), pseud. of Marie Henri Beyle, French novelist. After an unhappy childhood, Stendhal sought pleasure in Paris, joined Napoleon's army, and traveled widely in Italy. His literary output ranged from autobiographical studies to a treatise on love, from books on aesthetics through Romanticism into the realism of his two greatest novels, *The Red and the Black* (1831) and *Charterhouse of Parma* (1839). *See also* Charterhouse of Parma. △1238.

Stengel, Casey (1890–1975), US baseball playe and manager, b. Charles Dillon Stengel in Kansas Cit Mo. He was one of the game's greatest personalitie After his playing career (1912–25), Stengel guide the Brooklyn Dodgers (1934–36) and the Bosto Braves (1938–43), but found his great success wit the New York Yankees (1949–60), where he won 1 American League pennants and seven World Serie He last managed the New York Mets (1962–65). H was elected to the Baseball Hall of Fame in 1966.

Stenomylus. △576.

Stentor, freshwater, ciliate protozoan characterize by cone-shaped body with nucleus resembling lon string of beads, clumps of cilia around the mouth, an a stalklike holdfast. Length: to 0.10in (2.5mm). Orde Spirotricha; species include *Stentor polymorphus.* △ 466.

Stephan's Quintet of Galaxies. △126.

Stephen (1097?–1154), king of England. Despite ac knowledging Matilda as heir (1126), Stephen took th English crown on Henry I's death (1135). Harassed b the Scots and Matilda's supporters, Stephen pro voked a revolt (1139) and was temporarily depose (1141). Although he reestablished himself as king, Ste phen could not thereafter control his barons. By th Treaty of Wallingford (1153), he conceded the succes sion to Matilda's son, Henry. *See also* Matilda. △ 1076.

Stephen I, Saint (975?–1038), king of Hungar (997–1038), greatest of Árpád line. Son of Geza, h converted to Christianity during his youth. Stephe married Gisela, sister of Emperor Henry II. He becam duke of Hungary in 997. Pope Sylvester II sent crown for his coronation in 1001 and gave him th title "Apostolic Majesty," which was held by Hur garian sovereigns until the overthrow of the monar chy in 1918. In 1027, Stephen conquered Slovaki Stephen's rule was a period of great prestige for Hu gary, one of consolidation, prosperity, and the sup pression of paganism. With the aid of the clergy, h overcame the powerful tribal chieftains and appro priated their lands; established a centralized gover ment; and brought Hungary into the European com munity. △1074.

Stephen Báthory (1533–86), prince of Transylvani (1571–76), elected king of Poland by the nobility i 1575. Renowned as a soldier, he put down a revolt i Danzig (1577) and defeated Russia's Ivan the Terribl in a war (1579–82). In order to defend his northeast ern frontiers against Moscow and gain access to th sea at Danzig, he brought the Cossacks into his mil tary system, giving them privileges to secure the help in the war with Russia. He also reformed th judicial system.

Stephens, Alexander Hamilton (1812–83), Con federate vice president (1861–65), b. Wilkes co, Ga A brilliant man and leader, Stephens often oppose Confederate Pres. Jefferson Davis, particularly abou the military draft. He worked for peace and was at th Hampton Roads Peace Conference (February 1865) After the war, he wrote *Constitutional View of the Wa Between the States,* a closely reasoned defense of th right of states to secede.

Steppe, the extensive, semiarid plains of norther Asia. The word is a Tartar term that has been adopte by geographers. The plains are covered with lon rough grass and are only partially wooded. The so consists of alluvial deposits. Prairies in the Unite States are similar but not so dry. △584.

Stereographic Mapping. △180.

Stereophonic Sound, a method of reproducin sound so that it gives the illusion of both location an direction. As this depends on a difference in the tim of hearing between the two ears, two separate cha nels are required. In stereophonic phonograph re ords, the groove is modulated in two planes—the la eral and the vertical (groove depth). Depth variation correspond to the difference between the left an right channels of the stereorecording and later modulations correspond to their sum. Two transdu ers in the pick-up cartridge feed two separate ampli ers and two widely spaced loudspeakers. △1794 1798.

Stereoscope, optical binocular device that produce an apparently three-dimensional image by presentin two slightly different plane images, usually phot graphs, to each eye.

Stereotyping, tendency to ascribe to an individu characteristics that are attributed to the group or clas of which the individual is a member. The stereotyped judgment, however, may or may not apply to the individual, and thus stereotyping is an elementary form of prejudice. The most typical stereotypes involve judging people on the basis of characteristics attributed to their sex, race, ethnic group, nationality, age, or religion. *See also* Prejudice. △894–96.

Sterility. △700.

Sterilization, killing of all microorganisms, spores, viruses, or other life forms. Sterile conditions may be created by chemical means, such as DDT, organophosphates affecting toxicological penetration, or chlorine in drinking water; by heat as in the use of steam in some foods and hospital supplies; by cold; or by ionizing radiation which eradicates insects (eg, screw-worm fly) by sexual sterilization.

Sterling Heights, city in SE Michigan, 19mi (39km) N of Detroit. Industries: missile parts, automotive body stampings, chassis assemblies. Inc. 1968. Pop. (1970) 61,365.

Stern, Otto (1888–1969), US physicist, b. Germany. He won the Nobel Prize in physics (1943) for developing the molecular beam as a tool for studying the characteristics of molecules and for his measurement of magnetic moment of the proton.

Sterne, Laurence (1713–68), English novelist. A clergyman, he began as a political and ecclesiastical satirist, but his later works became more sentimental as he catered to public taste and wrote in a sentimental vein. His writings include a novel *The Life and Opinions of Tristram Shandy* (9 vols., 1760–67), *Sermons of Mr. Yorick* (1760), and *A Sentimental Journey through France and Italy* (1768). △1188.

Sternocleidomastoid. △684.

Sternum, or breast bone, the flat, narrow bone in front of the chest between the breasts. It is generally divided into three regions: the manubrium, or upper part; the body; and the xiphoid process, or lower and more flexible cartilaginous part. The top of the manubrium is attached by ligaments to the collarbone on each side, and the body is joined to the ribs by seven pairs of costal cartilages. △682.

Steroid, one of a class of organic compounds characterized by a basic molecular structure of 17 carbon atoms arranged in four rings and bonded to 28 hydrogen atoms. Steroids are widely distributed in animals and plants; the most abundant are the sterols (steroid alcohols), such as cholesterol. Another important group is the steroid hormones, including the corticosteroids, secreted by the adrenal cortex, and the sex hormones. The sex hormones are the estrogens (such as estrone) and progesterone produced by the ovary, and androgens (such as testosterone and androsterone) secreted by the testis. Synthetic steroids are widely used in medicine. △1570.

Stettin. *See* Szczecin.

Steuben, Frederick William, Baron von (1730–94), German and American soldier. Receiving his rigorous military training in Prussia, where he was aide-de-camp to Frederick the Great (1762), he transported these ideas to America, successfully training George Washington's troops before Valley Forge. His treatise on regulations was an official US Army manual until 1812.

Steubenville, city in E Ohio, on the Ohio River; seat of Jefferson co; site of College of Steubenville (1946); Edwin M. Stanton, Lincoln's secretary of war, was born and buried here. Industries: steel, chemicals, dinnerware. Founded 1797 and named for Baron Frederich von Steuben; inc. 1851. Pop. (1970) 30,771.

Stevens, John (1749–1838), US inventor and politician, b. New York City. He began to experiment with steam navigation from 1788 and devoted himself to its development. In 1789 he petitioned the New York legislature for permission to build a steamboat, but Robert Fulton's *Clermont* made a successful voyage before his *Phoenix* was completed. The *Phoenix* did make the first sea voyage by a steamship (1809). His desire to protect his many inventions led to the passage of the first United States patent law (1790). Stevens also built the first steam locomotive in the United States (1825).

Stevens, Thaddeus (1792–1868), US representative from Pennsylvania (1849–53; 1859–68), b. Danville, Vt. He was noted as one of the most radical antislavery persons in Congress and one of the strongest critics of Pres. Andrew Johnson's Reconstruction policy, which stressed leniency toward the Southern states. He helped introduce impeachment proceedings against Johnson.

Stevens, Wallace (1879–1955), US poet, b. Reading, Pa. A lawyer, he was for many years an executive of a Hartford, Conn., insurance company. His first book of poems, *Harmonium*, appeared in 1923. His work is rich in metaphors, and in it he contemplates nature and society. His early poems are often set in the tropics and reflect the lushness of their location. Among his works are *Ideas of Order* (1935), *Owl's Clover* (1936), *The Man with the Blue Guitar and Other Poems* (1937), *Parts of a World* (1942), *Notes Toward a Supreme Fiction* (1942), *Transport to Summer* (1947), and *Collected Poems* (1954; Pulitzer Prize 1955).

Stevenson, Adlai Ewing (1835–1914), US vice president, b. Christian co, Ky. He was a Democratic Congressman from Illinois (1875–77, 1879–81) and as assistant postmaster general during the first Cleveland administration. Stevenson headed the Illinois delegation to the 1892 convention and helped renominate Cleveland; he was rewarded with the vice presidency (1893–97). Stevenson was William Jennings Bryan's running mate in 1900 and a candidate for governor of Illinois in 1908; he won neither contest.

Stevenson, Adlai Ewing (1900–65), US political leader, b. Los Angeles. He practiced law in Chicago before he went into government service during the early New Deal. He was an advisor at the San Francisco conference (1945) that set up the United Nations. After serving as advisor to the US delegation to the United Nations (1946–47), he was elected governor of Illinois (1949). He was the unsuccessful Democratic candidate for president against Dwight D. Eisenhower in 1952 and 1956. In 1961, he was appointed US ambassador to the United Nations. His writings include *A Call to Greatness* (1954) and *Looking Outward: Years of Crisis at the U.N.* (1963).

Stevenson, Robert Louis (1850–94), Scottish novelist, essayist, and poet. He traveled in Europe and the United States, finally settling in Samoa. His essays, many of them about travel, suffer from an artificiality of style, but his novels, including *Treasure Island* (1883), *Dr. Jekyll and Mr. Hyde* (1886), *Kidnapped* (1886), *The Black Arrow* (1888), and *The Master of Ballantrae* (1889), display a keen sense of adventure and are widely read, particularly by children. *A Child's Garden of Verses,* sentimental poems for children, appeared in 1885.

Stewart. *See* Stuart.

Stewart, Potter (1915–), US jurist and lawyer, b. Jackson, Mich. An Ohio attorney, he served as a Cincinnati city councilman (1949–53) and vice-mayor of Cincinnati (1952–53). He was appointed a US Appeals Court judge (1954–58) and in 1958, Pres. Dwight D. Eisenhower appointed him an associate justice of the US Supreme Court. He was confirmed in 1959. Considered a political conservative, he maintained a centrist position on the court. He was the only dissenter in *Engel* v. *Vitale* (1962), the school prayer decision.

Stibnite, a sulfide mineral, antimony trisulfide (Sb_2S_3) found in low-temperature veins and rock impregnations. Orthorhombic system aggregates of prismatic crystals or granular masses. Opaque, sometimes iridescent; gray; hardness 2; sp gr 4.6. Important ore of antimony.

Stick Insect. △492, 496.

Stickleback, small fish found in fresh, brackish, and salt water. Usually brown and green, it is identified by the number of bony plates and spines along its sides and back. It is a popular scientific subject because of its elaborate mating and courtship ritual. The male builds a nest in water plants and, through an elaborate ritual, drives the female into it. He then watches the eggs and cares for the young. Length: 2.5–6.5in (6.4–16.5cm). The 12 or so species include the three-spine *Gasterosteus aculeatus* and the polar nine-spine *Pungitius pungitius.* Family Gasterosteidae. △510, 616.

Stieglitz, Alfred (1864–1946), US photographer, editor, and promoter of modern art, b. Hoboken. He is responsible for establishing photography as a fine art through exhibitions at his New York galleries and through magazines. In 1902 he founded the Photo-Secession Group. His photographs include classic portraits of his wife, Georgia O'Keeffe, studies of Manhattan, and the cloud images known as "equivalents."

Stilbite, a hydrous silicate mineral, hydrous calcium, sodium, aluminum silicate; one of the zeolite group.

Gertrude Stein

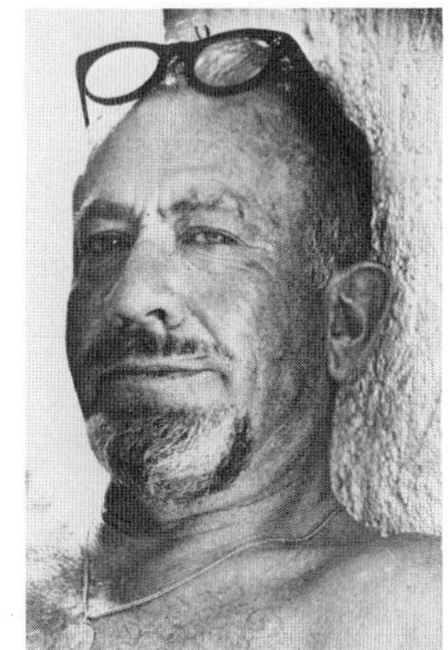

John Steinbeck

Adlai E. Stevenson

Robert Louis Stevenson

Monoclinic system radiating tabular crystals and aggregates. White, yellow, red or brown; hardness 3.-5–4; sp gr 2.1.

Stilicho, Flavius (359?–408), general in the Roman army. Of Vandal origins, he was master of the soldiers and regent for the young emperor, Honorius. In these posts he was the effective ruler of the Western Empire during his lifetime. He was assassinated by court officials jealous of his power.

Still Life, the art of painting pictures of everyday objects, flowers, furniture, etc, as viewed close up. It arose as an independent art in around the 16th century in the works of Caravaggio, for example. The art flourished with Flemish artists of the 17th century. Chardin was the first notable French still-life painter, and still lifes were also an important stage in the development of a number of 20th-century artists and nonrepresentational art, as in the works of Cézanne, Van Gogh, and Picasso.

Stillwater, city in N central Oklahoma; seat of Payne co; site of Oklahoma State University (1891). Industries: meat packing, flour milling, machine shops, gas wells. Founded 1889; inc. 1891 as town, as city 1899. Pop. (1970) 31,126.

Stilt, wading, long-legged marsh bird. It has an elaborate nest defense that includes playing dead and in-flight distraction displays. Pear-shaped, marked olive eggs (4) are laid. Included are whitish pied or black-winged stilt *(Himantopus himantopus)* and the rarer Australasian banded stilt *(Cladorhynchus leucocephaus)*. Length: 14–18in (36–46cm). Family Recurvirostridae.

Stimson, Henry Lewis (1867–1950), US political leader, b. New York City. He was secretary of war under President Taft (1911–13) and an artillery colonel in World War I. Between the world wars, he negotiated the armistice in the civil war in Nicaragua (1927). He was governor general of the Philippines (1927–29), and, as secretary of state under President Hoover (1929–33), he was a delegate to disarmament conferences. His firm attitude toward Adolf Hitler and Benito Mussolini caused Pres. Franklin D. Roosevelt to make him his secretary of war (1940–45).

Stimulant, drug that excites the central nervous system, which results in a mental state associated with heightened alertness and elevation of mood. There are two types: one type affects alertness and has only secondary actions on emotions; the other (called antidepressants) affects the emotions. Stimulants, such as amphetamines, are among the most commonly prescribed drugs; methylxanthines, the ingredients in coffee, tea, and colas that provide stimulation, are the most widely consumed of all drugs. △770.

Stimulus, in psychology, the energy that excites receptors of the nervous system. The term is sometimes applied to the objects that produce or transmit the energy, for example, the light is a *stimulus;* the book or chair that reflects the light is a *stimulus object.* △464.

Stingfish. *See* Stonefish.

Stinging Hydroid. △468.

Stinging Nettle. △446.

Sting Ray, bottom-dwelling elasmobranch found in shallow marine waters. Its flattened, disklike body has winglike fins extending around the head and a long slender tail. Its poison tail spine can inflict serious injury. Width: 1–7ft (30.5cm–2.1m); weight: 1.5–750lb (.7–338kg). There are five genera including the southern *Dasyatis americana.* Family Dasyatidae. *See also* Chondrichthyes; Ray.

Stink Bug, shield-shaped, brown bug with a disagreeable odor found worldwide. Barrel-shaped eggs are laid in clusters on leaves. Subfamilies Acanthosomatinae and Asopinae suck insect juices, while Pentatominae suck plant juices. Length: 1/3in (8mm). Family Pentatomidae. *See also* Harlequin Bug.

Stinkhorn, any of several mushrooms (order Phallales) that are egg-shaped when young. At maturity the stalks grow rapidly and rupture the egg, releasing the spore mass in a sticky, smelly slime. The spores are spread by insects that are attracted by the smell and carry the spores away on their bodies.

Stoat. *See* Ermine.

Stock, certificate of ownership in a corporation. A corporation may issue shares of stock upon its formation. It may also issue additional shares when it needs more capital. The ownership of stock implies sharing in the control of the corporation's operations, and the major stockholder may have prime influence upon the operation of the corporation. Stock is divided into two general classes: common stock and preferred stock.

Stockbreeding. △370–72, 376, 382.

Stockfish, or South African hake, elongated commercial food fish found in cold and temperate marine waters of the S Atlantic. Length: to 4ft (1.2m). Family Merluccidae (or Gadidae); species *Merluccius capensis.*

Stockhausen, Karlheinz (1928–), German avant-garde composer and experimenter in electronic and improvisational music. △1364.

Stockholm, seaport and capital city of Sweden, on Lake Mälaren at the Baltic Sea; strategic location has made Stockholm most important city in Sweden's history. Stockholm's early history was dominated by the German Hanseatic League; in 1520, Christian II of Denmark and Norway proclaimed himself king of Sweden; rule passed to Gustavus I 1523–60, who made Stockholm the center of his kingdom. It became the capital of Sweden 1643; it is now a modern city with wide streets, and several fine buildings and parks; site of Sweden's stock exchange, 13th-century Church of St Nicholas, Stockholm University (1877), technical institute (1827), national museum, royal palace (1754), Nobel Institute, Court Theatre, Riddarholm Church, which contains the tombs of Sweden's monarchs; scene of annual presentation of the Nobel prizes, the first UN Conference of the Human Environment 1972. Industries: textiles, clothing, publishing, food processing, engineering works, rubber, shipbuilding, beer, motor vehicles, porcelain, communications equipment, liquor. Founded *c.* 1250 by Birger Jarl. Pop. 747,490.

Stockholm Bloodbath (1518), a mass execution ordered by Christian II, king of Denmark and Norway, who claimed Sweden's throne. After Sten Sture, the Swedish regent, died in battle, Christian executed 82 people, including nobles, clergy, and merchants, in an effort to eliminate the leaders of Sture's party and any opposition.

Stock Market, or securities market or stock exchange, organized market for the buying and selling of stocks issued by corporations. The stock market allows for the speculative purchase of stock in the hope that the price will increase and thus provide a profit to the investor or provide dividend payment giving a fair rate of return on the investment. Stockbrokers act as the agents for individuals and financial institutions in the purchase and selling of different types of stocks. While the New York Stock Exchange is the best known stock market, accounting for 80% of the volume, there are other smaller US stock exchanges. The stock market is regulated by the Securities and Exchange Commission, which oversees the exchange of stock as well as the operations of the stockbrokers within the United States. △934.

Stockton, Robert Field (1795–1866), US naval officer, b. Princeton, N.J. He served in the War of 1812 and in the war with the Barbary Pirates. In 1821, he negotiated for US rights to Liberia, which was to be used as a colony for freed black slaves. He made his reputation in the Mexican War when he occupied Los Angeles, lost it, and then won it again in 1847. The same year he and Gen. Stephen Kearny quarreled over the right to organize the government of California; Kearny won. Stockton was a senator (1851–53).

Stockton, city in central California, 53mi (85km) E of Oakland; seat of San Joaquin co; supply center during the gold-rush era. Industries: canning, farm machinery, boats. Inc. 1850. Pop. (1970) 109,963.

Stoichiometry, quantitative proportions in which compounds combine or react together. The term also describes the measurement of these proportions and their use in finding formulas, molecular weights, etc.

Stoicism, dominant philosophy of the Hellenistic-Roman period, founded by Zeno of Citium (*c.* 333–262 BC). Chrysippus systematized Zeno's fundamental principles. Stoicism was reworked but remained basically unchanged until it faded after the end of the 3rd century BC. The highest Stoic virtue is to live in harmony with the cosmos. To do this people must live austere and noble lives, above concern for trivial things, and be able to control emotions. The wise man, or sage, puts his own integrity and duty ahead of lesser interests and feelings. △858.

Stoke-on-Trent, industrial city in W central England, on Trent River; covers most of Potteries district; center of pottery industry; comprises the "Five Towns" of Arnold Bennett's novels. Industries: ceramics, bricks, tiles, coal, chemicals, tires. Pop. 265,153.

Stokes, (Sir) George Gabriel (1819–1903), Irish mathematician and physicist. He is remembered for his work with viscous fluids; his law of viscosity, describing the movement of a solid sphere in a fluid; and for his basic notion of vector analysis, Stokes's theorem. He also worked on fluorescence (including the origination of the term); the concept of an ether; and the wave theory of light. He was a pioneer in geodesy. The CGS unit of viscosity is named after him.

Stokowski, Leopold (Antoni Stanislaw) (1882–), US conductor, b. England. He was director of the Cincinnati Symphony (1909–12) and music director and conductor for the Philadelphia Orchestra (1912–36), where his tenure as conductor was particularly brilliant. His interests have been wide ranging, including transcribing Bach's organ works for orchestra, appearing in films (eg, Disney's *Fantasia,* 1940), premiering the works of new composers, and founding new orchestras. In the 1960s, in his eighties, he conducted several operas.

STOL (Short Takeoff and Landing) Aircraft, aircraft with the ability to operate out of extremely small airfields. Present STOL aircraft are capable of taking off and climbing over a 50-foot (15-m) obstacle in less than 500 feet (152.5m). Wings of great lifting ability and powerful engines allow for unusual performance without sacrificing load-carrying capability. *See also* VTOL Aircraft. △1718.

Stolypin, Pëtr Arkadevich (1863–1911), Russian statesman who became minister of the interior and then premier in 1906. △1286.

Stoma. △424, 430.

Stomach, a J-shaped organ, lying to the left and slightly below the diaphragm in man; one of the organs of the digestive system. It is connected at its upper end, or fundus, to the esophagus at the cardiac orifice; at its lower end, or pyloric section, to the small intestine at the pylorus. The stomach itself is lined by three layers of muscle (longitudinal, circular, and oblique) and a mucous layer, the gastric mucosa, that lies in folds (rugae) and contains gastric glands. These glands secrete hydrochloric acid that destroys any food bacteria, dissolves salt in the food, and makes possible the action of pepsin, the active stomach enzyme that digests proteins alone. Gastric gland secretion is controlled by sensory stimuli—the sight, smell, and taste of food—and by hormonal stimuli, chiefly the hormone gastrin. As the food is digested, it is churned by muscular action into a thick liquid state, called chyme, at which point it passes through the pylorus to the small intestine. *See also* Digestive System. △694.

Stone, Edward Durrell (1902–), US architect who achieved recognition for his use of the functional International style in such buildings as the Museum of Modern Art, New York (1937–39), but who later used ornamental veils over his facades, as in the US Embassy in New Delhi (1958) and the Huntington Hartford Museum, New York (1962). His Kennedy Center for the Performing Arts, Washington, D.C. (1971), is distinguished by its functionalism.

Stone, Harlan Fiske (1872–1946), chief justice of the US Supreme Court (1941–46), b. Chesterfield, N.H. He served as dean of Columbia Law School (1910–23), resigning to resume private practice. As US attorney general under Pres. Calvin Coolidge (1924–25), he reorganized the Federal Bureau of Investigation. He was an associate justice of the Supreme Court from 1925 and was appointed Chief Justice by Pres. Franklin D. Roosevelt (1941). Together with Louis Brandeis, Benjamin Cardozo, and Oliver Wendell Holmes, he was a liberal dissenter on social issues, and generally supported New Deal legislation. He supported the protection of individual civil liberties from restrictive state legislation, as in *West Virginia State Board of Education* v. *Barnette* and *Smith* v. *Allwright* (1944), which invalidated all-white political party membership.

Stone, Irving (1903–), US author, b. San Francisco. Beginning with *Lust for Life* (1934), a fictional biography of Vincent Van Gogh, Stone wrote a number of novels based on the lives of historical figures. Other works include *The Agony and the Ecstasy* (1961), about Michelangelo, and *The Greek Treasure* (1974), about Heinrich Schliemann.

Stone, Lucy (1818–93), US feminist, b. near West Brookfield, Mass. A graduate of Oberlin College (1847), she lectured for women's rights and against slavery. With others, she organized the first US women's rights convention (1850). Although she married in 1855, she retained her own name and was known as Mrs. Stone. She organized several organizations for woman suffrage and founded (1870) the *Woman's Journal.*

Stone Age, period in man's evolution lasting over 2,500,000 years, in which he used stone tools and weapons. In this time he progressed from making crude flaked pebble tools to finely worked arrowheads and polished and hafted axes. *See also* Eolithic Age; Mesolithic Age; Neolithic Age; Paleolithic Age. △1586.

Stonechat. △458.

Stonecrop, any member of the genus *Sedum* of the family Crassulaceae, especially creeping sedum *(S. acre),* an evergreen mossy plant of European origin with pungent fleshy leaves and yellow flowers widely used as a ground cover.

Stonefish, or stingfish, deadly marine fish found in tropical Indo-Pacific. Ugly with warty, slime-coated body, its neurotoxic poison is injected by 13 spines. The poison is painful and fatal unless immediately treated with an antidote. Length: 13in (33cm). Family Synancejidae; species *Synanceja verrucosa.* △626.

Stonefly, or salmon fly, soft-bodied insect with long, narrow front wings and chewing mouthparts, found worldwide. The aquatic nymphs have branched gills. Often used as fish bait, adults are brown to black. Length: 0.2–4in(5–102mm). Order Plecoptera.

Stone Fruit. *See* Drupe.

Stonehenge, major prehistoric monument in S England; a group of standing stones on Salisbury Plain, Wiltshire, 3mi (4.8km) W of Amesbury. Erected in the 2nd millennium BC, its four series of stones are circled by a ditch 300ft (91.5m) in diameter. The outermost circle of sandstones, 13.5ft (4.1m) high, are connected by lintels. The next circle is bluestone Menhirs (single standing stones); third ring is horseshoe-shaped. The inner ring is ovoid with an Altar Stone within its confines. NE of circle is a huge upright Heelstone. At one time attributed to the Druids, it is now believed they arrived in Britain much later than the erection of this work, but it is generally agreed that stones served some religious purpose. Latest theory by Gerald Hawkins (1963), a British astronomer, proposes that they were used as an astronomical instrument. Others claim that the Bronze Age culture during which Stonehenge was created was not sophisticated enough to support Hawkins' calculations. This site is one of 40 or 50 such prehistoric "henge" monuments in British Isles. △38, 1444.

Stone, or Umbrella, Pine. △442.

Stony Meteorite, or aerolite, an abundant meteorite type, consisting mostly of silicate minerals, and divided into two groups called chondrites and achondrites. Chondrites are the most common and contain embedded, small spherical bodies called chondrules. Chondrites, mostly with anhydrous silicates, resemble terrestrial volcanic pulp. Those with claylike silicates and carbonaceous material are called carbonaceous chondrites. Achondrites are much rarer, may be secondarily derived from chondrites, and resemble terrestrial igneous rocks low in silica (such as basalt). △92.

Stoph, Willi (1914–), East German politician. He became prime minister of the German Democratic Republic in 1964. He met with West Germany's Willy Brandt in 1970 in an effort to normalize relations between the two countries, and in 1972 a basic treaty was signed in which each state recognized the other's post-war boundaries. In 1974 he was made chairman of the State Council.

Stork, long-legged wading bird living along rivers, lakes, and marshes in temperate and tropical regions. Usually black, white, and gray, they have straight bills, long necks, robust bodies, long broad wings, and partially webbed toes. Diurnal, they feed on small animals and sometimes on carrion. They lay white eggs (3–5) in a platform nest in a tree or on a ledge or rooftop. Length: 3–6ft (0.9–1.8m). Family Ciconiidae. △618.

Storm Petrel, small seabird ranging over the oceans. A strong flyer, even in rough weather, it feeds on plankton. Sooty-colored with a white rump, it has a small hooked bill, narrow sharp wings, long thin legs, and webbed feet. Breeding on oceanic islands and rocky coastlines, it burrows a nest for a single white egg. Length: 12–15in (30–38cm). Family Hydrobatidae.

Story, Joseph (1779–1845), US Supreme Court justice (1811–45) and legal scholar, b. Marblehead, Mass. He served as speaker of the Massachusetts legislature (1810–11) and as a US Congressman (1808–09). He was only 32 when selected to sit on the Supreme Court. His best known opinions were in *Martin* v. *Hunter's Lessee* (1816), his dissent in *Charles River Bridge* v. *Warren Bridge* (1837), and in the *Amistad* case (1841). As Harvard's first Dane Law Professor (1829–45), he introduced a number of legal textbooks and wrote his classic *Commentaries on the Constitution* (1833).

Stoss, Veit. △1106, 1136.

Stowe, Harriet Beecher (1811–96), US author, b. Litchfield, Conn. The daughter of Lyman Beecher, a renowned clergyman, she moved with her family to Cincinnati in 1832. There she taught school and began writing stories of New England. In 1836 she married Calvin E. Stowe. An advocate of the abolition of slavery, she began to write her famous novel about slavery, *Uncle Tom's Cabin,* in 1848. It was serialized in 1851–52 and published in book form in 1852 and brought her to fame. She later wrote a second novel about slavery, *Dred* (1856). Other works, none as popular as her first book, include several novels about New England life, *The Minister's Wooing* (1859) and *Oldtown Folks* (1869). *See also* Uncle Tom's Cabin. △1276.

STP. *See* Standard Temperature and Pressure.

Strabismus, or squint, abnormal condition in which weak or paralyzed eye muscles prevent binocular vision. The eye may be directed inward or outward with a consistent squint if the deviation remains constant. Strabismus may be corrected with glasses or surgery.

Strachey, (Giles) Lytton (1880–1932), English author. His works include the biographies *Eminent Victorians* (1918), *Queen Victoria* (1921), and *Elizabeth and Essex* (1928), and a critical survey *Landmarks in French Literature* (1912).

Strafford, Thomas Wentworth, 1st Earl of (1593–1641), English nobleman, leading advisor of Charles I. Although a loyal monarchist, he opposed Charles's arbitrary conduct of the war against Spain (1626) but was later appointed lord president of the north (1628) and privy councillor (1629). As lord deputy of Ireland (1632–38), he sought to strengthen royal authority and Protestantism and to stimulate agriculture and trade. He was made an earl in 1640. Strafford's advocacy of sovereign power led to conflict with Parliament and his impeachment (1640). He was convicted and executed, Charles reluctantly acquiescing in the hope of appeasing Parliament.

Strain, the change in dimensions of a body subjected to stress. *Longitudinal* strain is the ratio of the change in length of a bar to its original length while being stretched or compressed. *Shearing* strain describes the change in shape of a body whose opposite faces are pushed in different directions. Hooke's law for elastic bodies states that strain is proportional to stress. *See also* Hooke's Law; Stress.

Strain Gauge. △1514.

Strange Particles, elementary particles, all hadrons including the hyperons and kaons, that have an anomalously long lifetime (10^{-10} to 10^{-7} second) compared to that characteristic of most other hadrons (10^{-23} second). The delay is attributed to a property, strangeness, described by a quantum number that is a positive or negative integer for strange particles and zero for other hadrons and must be conserved in particle interactions. *See also* Conservation Law, Nuclear; Hadron.

Strapalptera. △492.

Strasberg, Lee (1901–), US director, b. Austria. With Harold Clurman and Cheryl Crawford he founded the Group Theater (1931), where he directed its first production, *The House of Connelly* (1931), the Pulitzer Prize-winning *Men in White* (1933), and many other plays. With Elia Kazan and Crawford he founded the Actor's Studio (1947) and became its artistic director in 1948. Based on the Stanislavsky System, Strasberg's method of acting placed primary emphasis on "inner truth."

Strasbourg, city in NE France, on Ill River, 2mi (3km) W of confluence with Rhine River; capital of Bas-Rhin dept. Known in Roman times as Argentoratum, it was destroyed by Huns in 5th century; became part of Holy Roman Empire in 923; made a free imperial city 1262; seized by France 1681; site of University of Strasbourg (1621) and 11th-century Cathedral of

Henry L. Stimson

Lucy Stone

Stonehenge

Harriet Beecher Stowe

Notre Dame containing astronomical clock installed 1574. Industries: boatbuilding, oil refining, processed foods. Pop. 249,396.

Strategic Arms Limitation Talks. *See* SALT Agreements.

Stratford, town in SW Connecticut, on Long Island Sound at mouth of Housatonic River; site of Housatonic Community College (1966), American Shakespeare Festival Theater (1955), David Judson House (1723). Industries: aircraft engines, helicopters, asbestos products. Founded and inc. 1639. Pop. (1970) 49,775.

Stratford-upon-Avon, market town in central England, on Avon River; birthplace of William Shakespeare; site of Shakespeare's grave, several places linked with him, and the Memorial Theatre—home of the Royal Shakespeare Company. Pop. 19,449.

Stratification, in geology, the layering in rocks. It occurs in sedimentary rocks and in those igneous rocks formed from lava flows and volcanic fragmental deposits. Layers range in depth and vary in shape. Strata may occur as thin sheets covering many miles or as thick bodies extending only a few feet. Separations between individual layers are called stratification planes. They parallel the strata they bound, being horizontal near flat layers and exhibiting inclination on a sloping surface. In sedimentary rocks, stratification may result from changes during deposition or from pauses in deposition. The sequence may then appear as alternations of coarse and fine particles, a series of color changes, or as similar layers, separated by distinct planes. Folding and faulting are recorded by tilted or broken strata, allowing interpretation of geologic events and the location of mineral deposits, oil fields, and groundwater. *See also* Stratigraphy.

Stratigraphy, branch of geology dealing with stratified or layered rocks. Sediments are layered in the order of deposition by water and hardened. These may then have undergone metamorphosis, folding, faulting, or igneous intrusion. Some igneous rocks are also stratified, particularly those associated with volcanic systems that continue to produce material. *See also* Historical Geology; Paleontology; Superposition, Principle of. △248, 270–72.

Stratosphere, the cloudless shell of gases just above the troposphere in the atmosphere. *See* Atmosphere.

Stratum (pl. strata), distinct layer of sedimentary or igneous rock consisting of material that has been spread out on the Earth's surface. It can be of any thickness but is visibly separated from layers above and below by a change in the kind of material deposited. Sedimentary beds consisting of material transported by ancient rivers and deposited in layers make up a stratum. △270, 272.

Strauss, Johann (the Younger) (1825–99), Austrian composer and conductor known as the "waltz king." He became extremely popular for his more than 400 waltzes, eg, *The Blue Danube, Tales from the Vienna Woods, Wine, Women and Song.* He also composed two popular operettas, *Die Fledermaus* (1874) and *The Gypsy Baron* (1885). △1246.

Strauss, Richard (1864–1949), German composer and conductor. Influenced by Richard Wagner, his music is characterized by Romantic themes and rich orchestral colors. His best known works are a number of symphonic poems, eg, *Don Juan* (1888), *Till Eulenspiegel* (1895), *Also Sprach Zarathustra* (1896), and *Ein Heldenleben* (1898). His operas include *Salome* (1905), *Elektra* (1908), and *Der Rosenkavalier* (1911). He also composed chamber works and songs. △1246, 1256.

Stravinsky, Igor (1882–1971), Russian composer, b. Oranienbaum (now Lomonosov). After studying with Rimsky-Korsakov, he emigrated to Western Europe in 1910 and to the United States in 1939. His early ballets *The Firebird* (1910) and *Petrouchka* (1911) earned him popularity and a reputation as a ballet master. His orchestral masterpiece *Le Sacre du Printemps* (*The Rite of Spring,* 1913) revolutionized orchestral composition and established him as a major composer.

Later works included ballets modeled after Tchaikovsky (eg, *The Fairy's Kiss,* 1928), Neoclassical instrumental and orchestral works (eg, the *Violin Concerto,* 1931) and experiments in serialism and 12-tone music (eg, the ballet *Agon,* 1957). *See also* Neoclassical Music. △1364.

Strawberry, fruit-bearing plant native to northern temperate areas and higher altitudes of tropical South America. Having trifoliate leaves and clusters of white or reddish flowers, the plants send out runners that root and produce new plants. There are two types: June bearers that produce one crop in early summer and everbearers that produce a crop in early summer and another in the fall. Plants that are well cared for can produce good fruit for 5–6 years. The sweet, juicy red fruits are eaten fresh or preserved. Family Rosaceae; genus *Fragaria.* △324, 360.

Streamline, Aircraft. △1718.

Stream-of-Consciousness Novel, type of 20th-century psychological novel that presents the flow of thoughts and images through the minds of its main characters. The stream-of-consciousness novel contains a mass of seemingly disconnected detail that has an underlying pattern. Events that appear trivial are often actually more important than major happenings. James Joyce, William Faulkner, and Virginia Woolf used the stream-of-consciousness technique in their novels.

Streisand, Barbra (1942–), US singer and actress, b. New York City. Her performance on Broadway in *Funny Girl* (1964) made her a superstar. She has performed in concert and made numerous recordings. Her films, mostly lavish productions, include *Funny Girl* (1968), *Hello Dolly!* (1969), *The Owl and the Pussycat* (1970), *What's Up Doc?* (1972), *The Way We Were* (1973), and *Funny Lady* (1974).

Streptococcus, genus of bacteria characterized by gram-positive spherical cells that grow in chains and are generally facultative anaerobes. They occur normally in the mouth, respiratory tract, and intestine of man; some are pathogenic, causing scarlet fever and strep throat; treated with penicillin. *See also* Bacteria.

Streptomycin, antibiotic drug used to treat certain bacterial diseases resistant to penicillin. Its side effects include sensitization and a rash. Its discovery in 1944 by Selman A. Waksman quickly led to the development of other antibiotics.

Stresemann, Gustav (1878–1929), German chancellor (1923) and foreign minister (1923–29), the outstanding statesman of the Weimar Republic. He concluded the Treaty of Locarno in 1925, in one of his many efforts to make a workable settlement with the Allies, for which he shared the Nobel Prize for peace in 1926.

Stress, a tensor quantity describing the internal pressure of a body being stretched, twisted, or squeezed. If any part of the body with cross-sectional area A is subjected to a tensile or compressive force F having components F_n perpendicular to A and F_t tangential to A, then the *normal* stress is F_n/A and the *tangential* (or *shearing*) stress is F_t/A. In a fluid, no shearing stress is possible because the fluid slips sideways—thus all stresses are normal stresses and are denoted by the term "pressure." *See also* Strain.

Stress, a physical and emotional state experienced by the organism when an excessive number of demands are placed upon it. In the human organism its sources may be infections, excessive work load, unfavorable living conditions, emotional strain, and excessive worry. Normally the organism is equipped to cope with a reasonable amount of stress; however, when an accumulation and a prolonged exposure to the above factors are experienced its coping mechanisms undergo physical and/or emotional breakdown. *See also* Psychosomatic Disorders.

Strict Construction, a manner of interpreting the US Constitution. The 10th amendment to the Constitution provides that the powers not specifically granted to the federal government, nor prohibited to the states, belong to the states. "Strict" constructionists take this to mean that the federal government has no rights or powers not expressly granted by the Constitution, thus restricting the authority of the federal government. Conflicts between "strict" and "loose" constructionists have occurred, notably over slavery and civil rights. A "loose" constructionist view allowed the government the flexibility to purchase foreign territory as in the Louisiana Purchase and establishing of the Bank of the United States. During Franklin D. Roosevelt's administration (1933–45), strict constructionists opposed much of his New Deal legislation, deeming it unconstitutional.

Stridulation. △494.

Strike, refusal to work by union members, a method of pressuring an employer to agree to the union's demands. Historically, the union struck first to gain recognition, then to gain wage increases or improvements in other conditions of employment. Since the Wagner Act (1935) strikes for recognition have, for the most part, ceased. Certain types of strikes are forbidden in the United States, and in some situations the government may petition the federal courts for a temporary injunction against a strike. The employer's counterpart weapon to the strike is the lockout.

Strindberg, Johan August (1849–1912), influential Swedish dramatist. A master of language, he wrote over 50 plays in many styles. He is best known abroad for *The Father* (1887) and *Julia* (1888). In his novels and short stories he fictionalized his unhappy life and marriages. △1240.

Stringed Musical Instruments, instruments producing sound by the vibration of strings, usually gut or steel, and tuned by tension. In violins, strings are stroked with a resin-dressed horsehair bow, and sometimes finger-plucked (pizzicato). The strings of harps, lutes, and guitars are strummed or plucked with fingers or a plectrum. In keyboard instruments like the piano, strings are struck with hammers; in the harpsichord, strings are plucked by quills. In both cases keys control the mechanical action. △1244, 1500.

Strip Cropping, practice of planting strips of deep-rooted crops alternately with strips of short-rooted crops to prevent soil erosion. This method is often used on sloping land. *See also* Soil Conservation. △304.

Striped Goby. △516.

Strip Mining, or stripping, method of open-pit mining used for coal. Electric excavator shovels with bucket capacities of 40–100cu yd (30–76cu m) uncover coal beds by removing the overburden in parallel paths and dumping the waste to the side. Smaller shovels follow, removing the coal and making room for more waste. *See also* Open-Pit Mining. △294.

Stroboscope, any of various optic devices capable of making moving, rotating, or vibrating objects appear slowed down or stationary. This effect is achieved by interrupting the observer's continuous view of the moving object.

Stroheim, Erich von (1885–1957), US actor and film director, b. Austria. His films, including *Blind Husbands* (1918), *Foolish Wives* (1921), *Greed* (1923), *The Merry Widow* (1925), and *Queen Kelly* (1928) were noted for realism, sophistication, and imagination. Stroheim's perfectionism limited his output to nine films. After 1930 he worked as an actor.

Stroke, or apoplexy, or cerebrovascular accident, interruption of the flow of blood to the brain. It is caused by blockage or rupture of an artery and results in temporary or permanent paralysis, difficulty in articulating, or loss of muscular coordination. It may occur without symptoms or after a period of headaches and irritability. Treatment includes surgery, drugs to reduce clotting, and physical therapy. △716, 722.

Strong Interaction, Nuclear. *See* Interaction, Nuclear. △1484.

Structural Analysis, the study of rock deformation, faulting, folding, and crumpling of rock strata and the effects of these processes. Structural models simulating Earth materials are used. Structural patterns produced by applied stresses are recorded on models.

Structural Functionalism, theory in sociology that analyzes cultural and social phenomena within the specific and highly refined concepts of "structure" and "function." According to the theory, a *structure* is the character and design observable in a society's stable social relationships and institutions. A *function* is any consequence of either an existence and/or action of things or persons, including intangibles such as attitudes, beliefs, and ideals. *See also* Dysfunction. △1360.

Structuralism, two related theories in sociology. One involves the study of social status systems and status-related duties in order to discover the society's "social morphology," or structure. The other is an interdisciplinary theory that uses anthropology, linguistics, psychology, and folklore to analyze all modes of social behavior—from marriage rites to fashion—in terms of what they communicate about the particular society. Structuralists believe that the patterns of relationships between diverse modes of social behavior form a society's underlying structure. *See also* Status; Structural Functionalism. △1360.

Structural Isomer. *See* Isomers.

Strychnine, lethal poison formerly believed to have

therapeutic value. Symptoms of strychnine poisoning include stiffness and twitching.

Stuart or **Stewart,** Scottish family of Breton origin, the senior branch of which inherited the Scottish crown in 1371 (Robert II) and the English crown in 1603 (James I). The family gained a name for persistent bad luck over several centuries. Seven Stuarts ascended the Scottish throne as minors through sudden deaths. The direct male line died out with James V (1542). His daughter, Mary, Queen of Scots, was succeeded by James VI of Scotland (James I of England). After the execution of James' son Charles I in 1649, Stuarts were excluded from the throne until the restoration of Charles II (1660). They lost the throne with the deposition of James II in 1688. The last male Stuarts of the royal English line were grandsons of James II: Charles (Bonnie Prince Charlie) and Henry, a cardinal. *See also* Charles I and II of England; James I and II of England; James I–VI of Scotland; Mary, Queen of Scots; Robert I of Scotland; Stuart, Charles Edward; Stuart, James Francis Edward.

Stuart, Charles Edward (1720–88), English prince and claimant to the throne, also called "Bonnie Prince Charlie" and the "Young Pretender," b. Italy. A grandson of the deposed James II, he invaded Scotland (1745) to begin the Forty-five, a Jacobite revolt. He was initially victorious at Prestonpans, but the duke of Cumberland annihilated his army at Culloden (1746) and he went into permanent exile in Europe.

Stuart, Don A. *See* Campbell, John Wood, Jr.

Stuart, Gilbert (Charles) (1755–1828), US painter, b. Kingston, R.I. He painted portraits in Europe and eventually settled in Boston. His best known works are his three clearly and precisely rendered portraits of George Washington, for which the subject posed, and his many replicas of these.

Stuart, James Ewell Brown (1833–64), Confederate Civil War general, b. Patrick co, Va. Known as "Jeb" Stuart, he was commander of Robert E. Lee's cavalry at the age of 30. A brilliant leader, he gained fame with his ride around Gen. George McClellan's Army of the Potomac in June 1862. Later exploits included a dash against Gen. John Pope's headquarters and a raid on Manassas Junction, Va., both in August 1862. He was mortally wounded at Yellow Tavern, Va.

Stuart, or **Stewart, James Francis Edward** (1688–1766), also called "The Old Pretender," claimant to the British throne, only son of James II. Brought up in France, he was proclaimed king of England (1701) and tried to take advantage of the 1715 Scottish Jacobite rising, establishing his court at Scone. Forced to flee, he subsequently lived in exile, intriguing in France and Italy.

Stubbs, George (1724–1806), English painter. He began as a portrait painter but gained considerable fame as a painter of animals, especially horses. His book *The Anatomy of the Horse* (1766) is well known. △1186.

Student Non-Violent Coordinating Committee (SNCC), US civil rights organization. Founded in 1960, it led integration and voter registration drives in the South in the early 1960s. After 1966 under the leadership of Stokely Carmichael the group rejected its white members and became more militant. Black Power became the theme of SNCC. In 1969 it was renamed Student National Coordinating Committee.

Students for a Democratic Society (SDS), leftist college student organization. It was involved in radical student protests against US involvement in Vietnam in the 1960s and early 1970s. The small revolutionary group the Weathermen emerged from a declining SDS in 1969.

Stupa, a Buddhist burial mound, found mainly in India, with a domed circular center surrounded by a processional path and a square stone railing. △986, 1038.

Sture Family, Swedish noble family that played a key role in Sweden's fight for independence during the 15th and 16th centuries. Sten Sture the elder (*c.* 1440–1503) was regent in 1470, had to resign in 1497, was regent again in 1501. Svante Sture succeeded him, followed by Sten Sture the younger, who asserted the state's superiority over the church. His refusal to accept Christian II of Denmark as king of Sweden resulted in the Stockholm Bloodbath.

Sturgeon, largest primitive, bony freshwater fish in North America, found in temperate fresh and marine waters of Northern Hemisphere. The source of caviar, this fish has five series of sharp-pointed scales along its sides, fleshy whiskers, and a tapering snoutlike head. Family Acepenseridae; species giant beluga *Huso huso* of E Europe—length: to 14ft (4.3m); weight: 2,200lb (990kg); Atlantic Sturgeon *Acipenser sturio*—length: 11ft (3.3m); weight: 600lb (272kg). *See also* Ganoid Fish, Osteichthyes. △510.

Sturm und Drang. △1222.

Stuttering. △780.

Stuttgart, city in SW West Germany, on Neckar River, 38mi (61km) ESE of Karlsruhe; capital of Baden-Württemberg state; seat of Württemberg royalty 1320–1806; severely damaged during WWII; site of the Solitude Palace (1763–67), New Palace (1746–1807), Rosenstein Palace (1824–29), technical university (1956), agricultural college, academy of fine arts, and a conservatory. Industries: publishing, textiles, chemicals, paper, wine, iron, steel, machinery, footwear, beer, electrical equipment, motor vehicles, musical instruments, tourism. Founded *c.* 950; chartered 1254. Pop. 633,158.

Stuyvesant, Peter (*c.*1610–72), Dutch colonial governor. He became governor of the Caribbean Islands of Curacao, Bonaire, and Aruba (1643) and in 1647 he was named director general of New Netherlands as well. As governor, he ruled in a dictatorial manner, denying freedom to worship and causing discontent among the colonists. He was successful in curbing the sale of liquor to Indians, raising taxes, and improving defense, but the colony did not prosper. In 1650 he negotiated the Treaty of Hartford, which set the boundary between New York and Connecticut, and he ended Swedish influence in Delaware (1655). He ruled until the colony was taken over by the British (1664) and renamed New York.

Sty, infection of an eyelid gland, caused by a staphylococcus organism. It may occur externally, in the margin of the lid, or internally, under the lining of the lid. A small boil or pimple with a central yellow spot erupts, then breaks and discharges its contents.

Styracosaurus. △570.

Styrene. △1560.

Styria, province in central and SE Austria; Graz is capital. Made a duchy 1180; came under Hapsburg domination 1282; S portion passed to Yugoslavia by Treaty of Saint-Germain (1919). Industries: mining, livestock, metals, resorts. Area: 6,324sq mi (16,379sq km). Pop. 1,191,000.

Styron, William (1925–), US novelist, b. Newport News, Va. He achieved considerable success with his first novel, *Lie Down in Darkness* (1951), a story of psychological problems and tangled family relationships. Other novels include *The Long March* (1956), *Set This House on Fire* (1960), and *The Confessions of Nat Turner* (1967), which received a Pulitzer Prize in fiction (1968).

Styx, in Greek mythology, the river between the land of the living and Hades, the land of the dead. Styx, the nymph who personified the river, was the mother of Nike and the daughter of Jethys and Oceanus. The river was considered sacred and oaths taken in her name could not be broken, even by the gods. A poisonous river named the Styx actually flowed through ancient Arcadia.

Subconscious, any of the mental processes that occur just below the level of awareness. Psychoanalysts define it as a zone between the conscious and the unconscious and believe that many important psychological activities occur here. Much of the psychoanalytical method involves bringing into awareness subconscious processes.

Subculture, in sociology, any cultural group bound together by shared attitudes or interests. Subcultures often develop life styles that differ from and conflict with those of the larger society. There are two types of subcultures: *reaction* (juvenile delinquents or motorcycle gangs) and *retreatist* ("hippies" or drug addicts).

Sublimation, in physics, a change from the solid phase directly to the gaseous phase, as seen in dry ice (CO_2). Most substances can sublimate at a certain range of pressure but usually not at atmospheric pressures.

Submarine, seagoing warship capable of traveling both on and under the water, armed principally with torpedoes. *See also* Torpedo. △1684, 1740.

Strawberry

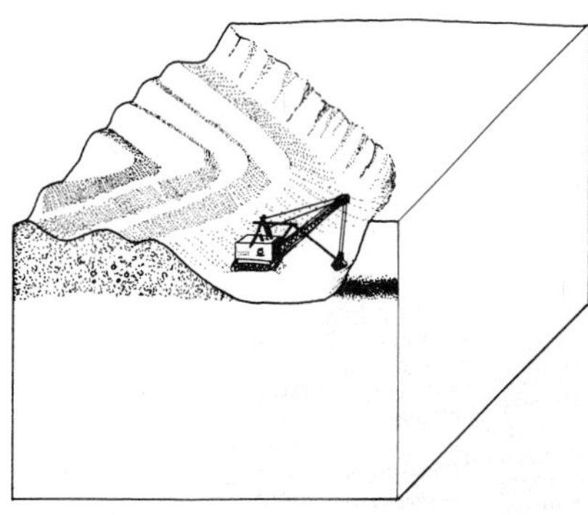
Strip mining

Jeb Stuart

Stupa

Submarine Canyon, a deep (1km or 0.62mi), steep-sided, V-shaped valley that cuts through the continental shelf. Though some line up with large land rivers, others do not. Therefore, it seems likely that they are formed when sediment deposited on the shelf becomes unstable and gravity causes it to slump, forming a turbid muddy bottom current that races downslope onto the deep-sea floor, scouring out the great canyons. △228.

Submersible, Research, small vessel designed for brief periods of undersea exploration. This type of workboat is meant to remain submerged for a few hours or days and life support, power, and navigation systems are limited. Submersibles have been used to collect water and plankton samples, photograph ocean topography, investigate acoustic and electromagnetic properties at various depths. △238.

Subparticles, Elementary, postulated constituents of the hadron group of elementary particles. Experimental evidence indicates that protons are made up of tiny pointlike bodies, termed partons. There is also evidence that the parton is the theoretical quark. Although the four leptons appear to be pointlike particles, the large number of hadrons could be explained by various combinations of three or possibly four or twelve quarks. △1484.

Subsets. *See* Sets.

Subsistence Economy, condition in which economic activity is concentrated within each household; items are produced for consumption by the productive unit, not for sale in a market. In such primitive economies, money and trade are not yet in evidence, and the level of living is usually very low.

Substitution, chemical reaction in which one atom or group of atoms replaces (usually in the same structural position) another group in a molecule or ion. Chemists differentiate electron-rich incoming groups, such as the hydroxyl and halogen ions, from electron-deficient groups, such as the hydroxonium ion (H_3O^+) and the nitro group (NO_2^+), and unstable unpolarized species called radicals.

Subtraction, arithmetical operation signified by −, interpreted as the inverse process of addition. The difference of two numbers, $a - b$, is the number that has to be added to b to give a. a is called the minuend and b the subtrahend. *See also* Arithmetical Operations. △1446.

Subway, an underground mass transportation system using electrified railways in cities and suburbs. △1708.

Succession, orderly change in plant and animal life in a biotic community over a long time period. It is the result of modifications in the community environment. The process ends in establishment of a stable ecosystem (climax community). △580.

Succulent Plant, plant that stores water in its tissues to resist periods of drought. Usually perennial and evergreen, most of the succulent plant body is made up of water storage cells giving it a fleshy appearance. A well-developed cuticle and low rate of daytime transpiration also conserve water. Succulent plants include cactus, milkweed, lily, and stonecrop sedum. △446, 620.

Süchow (Xuzhou or Hsu-chou), city in E central China, 180mi (290km) NW of Nanking; railroad center. Industries: food processing, textiles, flour, machine tools, steel, iron, coal. Pop. 1,500,000.

Sucker, freshwater fish found mainly from N Canada to Gulf of Mexico. A bottom grubber similar to minnows, it has a protrusible sucking mouth. Among the 100 species is the quillback *Carpiodes cyprinus;* length: 26in (66cm); weight: 12lb (5.4kg). Family Catostomidae.

Suckling, (Sir) John (1609–42), English Cavalier poet, author of witty, mocking lyrics. Once described as "the greatest gallant of his time, and the greatest gamester . . . so that no shopkeeper would trust him for 6d." After plotting against Parliament, Suckling fled to Paris, where he reputedly committed suicide. *See also* Cavalier Poets.

Sucre, Antonio José de (1795–1830), South American independence leader, Bolívar's chief of staff, and a key figure in the liberation of Ecuador, Peru, and Bolivia. Sucre commanded the rebel forces during the decisive battle of the independence struggles, Ayacucho (1824). An assembly chose him as the first constitutional president of Bolivia in 1826. He proved a good administrator, but political rivalries forced him to resign in 1829. He reassumed a battlefield command, defeating the Peruvian force that invaded Ecuador in 1829.

Sucre, formerly La Plata, and Chuquisaca; city in S central Bolivia; constitutional capital of Bolivia and capital of Chuquisaca dept. Renamed 1839 for revolutionary leader and first president of Bolivia, Antonio José de Sucre; site of archbishopric, supreme court, University of San Francisco Xavier (1624), oil refinery. Industries: mining. Founded 1538. Pop. 47,800.

Sucrose, disaccharide sugar (formula $C_{12}H_{22}O_{11}$), consisting of linked glucose and fructose units, that occurs in many plants; its principal commercial sources are sugarcane and sugar beet, but it is also obtained from maple trees, date palms, and sorghum. It is widely used for food sweetening and in the manufacture of preserves. △1562.

Suctorida, protozoa having cilia before developing into adults without cilia and with long hollow protoplasmic extensions used to suck in prey. Order Holotricha; class Suctoria; species include *Tokophrya.*

Sudan (As-Sudan), independent nation in N Africa. There are two primary cultural divisions among the people. Agriculture is the most important occupation, with cotton and cottonseed the main crops.

Land and economy. The largest country in Africa, Sudan is bounded on the N by Egypt, W by Libya, Chad, and the Central African Republic, S by Zaïre, Uganda, and Kenya, and E by Ethiopia and the Red Sea. Sudan's diverse geography ranges S to N, through tropical forests, swamplands, tropical grasslands, and arid hills between the Red Sea and the enormous Libyan and Sahara deserts. Flowing through the country for 2,340mi (3,767km) is the White Nile, main artery of the Nile River. In the N, cultivation is dependent on Nile irrigation. The S has enough rainfall for crops or grazing. Cotton and cottonseed are the principal cash crops, accounting for 60% of export earnings. Gum arabic, the 2nd-most important export item, is sold almost exclusively to the United States. Minerals have been found only in small quantities.

People. The integration of Sudan's divided cultural groups is a major problem. In the N two-thirds of the country are Arab-speaking Muslims, including camel-raising nomads and tribes displaced by the Aswan High Dam, who constitute over 70% of the population. In the S are subsistence rural African tribal peoples, mainly animist in religious beliefs, who make up 30% of the population. The literacy rate is 10%–15%.

Government. Officially governed by an elected president and a People's Assembly, the Sudan is actually ruled through a military junta.

History. Until unified by Egypt in 1820, Sudan was a conglomeration of independent states. Egyptian exploitation brought a revolt in 1881, conquest by Anglo-Egyptian forces in 1896, and British domination until 1953, when the British and Egyptians agreed to self-determination. Economic and political problems and a series of military coups and civil governments wracked the parliamentary system. Maj. Gen. Jaafar Muhammed Numeiry was elected president in 1971. He declared a socialist state and gave autonomy to the S.

PROFILE

Official name: Democratic Republic of Sudan
Area: 967,497sq mi (2,505,817sq km)
Population: 18,300,000
Density: 19per sq mi (7.3per sq km)
Chief cities: Khartoum (capital); Omdurman
Government: Military junta
Religion: Islam, Christianity, animist
Language: Arabic (official)
Monetary unit: Pound
Gross national product: $1,875,000,000
Per capita income: $135
Industries: textiles, food processing, vegetable oil, shoes, pharmaceuticals, cement
Agriculture: gum arabic, cotton, peanuts, rice, coffee, sugar cane, tobacco, wheat, dates, cattle, mahogany, forests, camels, sheep
Minerals: chrome, oil, natural gas
Trading partners: United States, Egypt, People's Republic of China, Soviet Union

Sudbury, city in central Ontario, Canada, 38mi (61km) N of Georgian Bay; site of Laurentian University (1960). Canadian Pacific Railroad excavations in 1883 revealed veins of nickel and copper; one of world's richest nickel-producing regions. Industries: nickel, copper, platinum, and palladium mining; lumbering, smelting. Inc. 1892. Pop. 89,898.

Sudden Infant Death Syndrome, or crib death, sudden mysterious, fatal affliction of infants who are unexpectedly found dead in their cribs. It can occu up to about one year after birth. The peak perio seems to be around two months of age. Respirator causes are suspected, with the possible involvemer of a virus. Another theory proposed is an abnorma disruption of breathing at critical points in the slee cycle.

Sudetenland, name given to a strip of territory alon the Sudeten mountains, located in Czechoslovaki but inhabited by Germans. From 1526, under Haps burg rule, Germanic influences permeated througl out Bohemia and Moravia, remaining dominant unt a Czech nationalist movement began in the 19th cer tury. The new independent country of Czechoslovaki was created after World War I, but the German speal ing parts were ceded to Hitler in the Munich pact c 1938. After World War II, Czechoslovakia reclaime Sudetenland and expelled the majority of German △1334.

Suetonius (Gaius Suetonius Tranquillus) (*c.* 69 c.140 AD), Roman author. A lawyer and secretary t Emperor Hadrian, Suetonius is best remembered as biographer. Two collections of his work survive: *D viris illustribus* (*On Famous Men*), biographies of lite ary figures, and *De vita Caesarum* (*The Lives of th Caesars*), biographies of rulers from Julius Caesa through Domitian. His writing was lively and informa tive and had a significant effect on later historiogra phy.

Sueves. △1054.

Suez (As-Suways), city in NE Egypt, at N end of Gu of Suez and S terminus of Suez Canal. A naval an trading station in 16th century, it developed into leac ing port in 1869 after completion of Suez Canal. Cit was occupied by Israelis in 1973 war and suffere damage during fighting; departure point for pilgrim to Mecca. Industries: oil storage and refining, pape fertilizer. Pop. 315,000.

Suez, Gulf of (Suways, Khaty as-), NW extensio of Red Sea; W of Sinai peninsula; connected on N t the Mediterranean Sea by way of the Suez Canal.

Suez Canal, waterway connecting the Mediterra nean with the Red Sea. It was planned and bui (1859–69) by the Suez Canal Company under th leadership of Ferdinand de Lesseps. This sea-leve 105mi (169km) canal has been enlarged to 46ft (14m deep and 196ft (60m) bottom width. Its total cost wa about $136,000,000. After the introduction c steam vessels, its use increased and stockholders i the company realized huge gains. Disraeli purchase (1875) the Egyptian-held stock to make the Britis government the largest stockholder (though neve owning the majority). In 1955 over 120,000,00 tons passed through the canal, much of it petroleum The Suez Canal Company's 99-year concession wa to revert to Egypt in 1968, but the Egyptian goverr ment nationalized it in 1956. Israel, Britain, an France attacked Egypt. The canal was closed fror Oct. 1956 to April 1957, while repairs were bein made, after a United Nation's Task Force entered an stopped the conflict. Egypt gained complete contrc and closed it during the Arab-Israeli War of 1967 an did not open it again until 1975.

Suez Crisis (1956), Middle East conflict. When Grea Britain and the United States announced that the would not provide financing for Egypt's Aswan Dar project, Egyptian Pres. Gamal Abdel Nasser threa ened to nationalize the Suez Canal. Israel, denie canal passage, invaded Egypt, with Britain and Franc giving support. UN intervention ended the crisis, wit Egypt keeping control of the canal. *See also* Arab Israeli Wars.

Suffolk, nonmetropolitan county in E Englanc bounded by the North Sea (E), Stour River (S), an Little Ouse and Waveney rivers (N). County town Ipswich. The land is mainly level, rising to the cha hills of the East Anglian Heights in the SW. The are is principally agricultural, producing grain and suga beets and raising livestock; formerly part of the Angl Saxon kingdom of East Anglia.

Suffolk (sheep). △376.

Suffrage, the constitutional right to vote. The Unite States Constitution, in several amendments, estat lishes suffrage. It guarantees that no citizen shall b denied the vote on account of race, color, previou condition of servitude (14th and 15th Amendments or sex (19th Amendment). In national elections, n citizen shall be subjected to restrictive poll taxe (24th Amendment). The universal voting age is 1 (26th Amendment) and Washington, D.C., residen may vote in presidential elections (23rd Amendment).

Suffragist. *See* Woman Suffrage.

Sufism, communities of Muslim mystics, so named because their ascetic predecessors wore wool (suf). Sufis seek the union with God that is attained through ecstasy. After achieving the cessation of conscious thought, the Sufi attains consciousness of continuous survival in unity with God. Although there have been pantheistic tendencies in Sufism, Sufis are generally faithful to traditional Islamic monotheism. There are numerous orders and suborders within Sufism, including the Dervish. *See also* Dervish.

Sugar, a water-soluble, sweet carbohydrate found in both plants and animals. Sucrose, saccharose, maltose, fructose, and dextrose are among the naturally occurring sugars. △342, 1506, 1570–72.

Sugar Act, or **Revenue Act** (1764), British legislation imposed on the American colonies to gain revenue and halt smuggling of foreign sugar into the colonies. Act reduced duty on foreign molasses, increased duties on refined sugar from England, and imposed duty on Madeira wine. It is considered a minor cause of the Revolution. △1218.

Sugar Beet, variety of beet grown commercially for its high sugar content. It has a thick white root. Species *Beta vulgaris crassa. See also* Beet.

Sugarcane, perennial grass cultivated in tropical and subtropical regions throughout the world. It has clumps of solid stalks with lancelike leaves and regularly spaced joints; each joint bears a single bud. Color varies. The tassel bears hundreds of flowered spikelets. After harvesting, stems are processed in factories, becoming the main source of sugar. Most cultivated canes are *Saccharum officinarum.* Height: to 26ft (8m). Family Gramineae. △342, 454.

Sugar Glider. △544.

Suharto (1921–), Indonesian military and political figure, president (1967–). A lieutenant colonel in a guerrilla army that fought for independence from the Dutch (1945–49), Suharto seized power from President Sukarno in 1966. He was formally elected president in 1968 by the Consultative Congress and was reelected in 1973.

Suicide, act of terminating one's life voluntarily and intentionally. According to the French sociologist Emile Durkheim, there are three types of voluntary death: (1) *altruistic suicide,* which results from an excessive degree of group interaction; (2) *egoistic suicide,* which occurs because the individual is detached and uninvolved; and (3) *anomic suicide,* which occurs because the individual has inadequate self-discipline. About 90% of suicide attempts are by females. Males, however, are three times more successful in completing the act. Suicide rates per 100,000 population vary from less than 2 in Mexico to about 10 in the United States and Great Britain, 15 in France, 20 in Sweden, and 30 in Hungary.

Sui Dynasty (581–618), Chinese dynasty whose two rulers reestablished strong central rule in China following more than 250 years of division and contention. The Grand Canal was completed, military campaigns undertaken, huge palaces constructed, and Chinese prestige restored, all at great human cost leading to revolts and overthrow. △1038.

Suite, set of four or more pieces for orchestra or solo instrument, with movements often consisting of dance rhythms. The suite originated in the Baroque Period of music. Orchestral suites are often derived from operas or ballets (eg, Prokofiev's suite from the opera *The Love for Three Oranges* or Copland's suite from the ballet *Appalachian Spring*).

Suitland, residential town in central Maryland; SE suburb of Washington, D.C. Pop. (1970) 30,355.

Sukarno (1901–70), Indonesian political figure, president (1949–67). After a four-year struggle with the Dutch, he achieved his goal of seeing Indonesia independent in 1949 and became its president. As president he rejected the country's parliamentary system for more authoritarian rule. In 1966 anti-Communist Indonesian military leaders forced a reduction of his powers, and he was deposed in 1967. △1352.

Sukkoth or **Sukkot,** the Jewish festival of tabernacles, which lasts for 7 days. It commemorates the wandering of the Jews in the desert and their salvation through God. A *sukkah,* or simple shelter, is raised in the synagogue and formerly in all Jewish homes, to remind Jews of the temporal nature of possessions. It had been an agricultural event.

Sulawesi (Celebes), island in Indonesia, in the Malay archipelago, separated from Borneo (W) by Makasar Strait; chief city and port is Makasar; with adjacent islands comprises four provinces of Indonesia. Taken from Muslim Malays by Dutch (16th century) for spice trade, it was ruled by Dutch until WWII when occupied by the Japanese; retaken by Dutch at the end of the war; joined Republic of Indonesia 1949: scene of an unsuccessful attempt to form independent government 1957, 1965. Products: rice, yams, maize, cassava, beans, coconuts, coffee, copra, spices, kapok. Industries: handcrafts, asphalt, paper, pearl farming. Area: 72,986sq mi (189,034sq km). Pop. 8,925,000.

Suleiman I or **Suleiman the Magnificent** (1494–1566), Ottoman sultan (1520–66), son and successor of Selim I. He extended his father's conquests in the Balkans and the Mediterranean, captured Belgrade (1521), expelled the Knights Hospitalers from Rhodes (1522), and defeated the Hungarians under Louis II at Mohacs (1526). After the death of John I of Hungary he annexed most of the country. He made an alliance with Francis I of France against the Hapsburgs (1536) and his admiral, Barbarossa, ravaged the coasts of Spain, Italy, and Greece with his Turkish fleet. Suleiman seized Arabian coastal lands but failed to take Tunis and Malta. He died during the siege of Szigetvar (Hungary), and his stepson Selim II succeeded him. △1108.

Sulfa Drug, or sulfonamide, first drugs prescribed to treat bacterial infections. Mostly superseded by modern antibiotics, they are used to treat infections resistant to penicillin or patients allergic to penicillin. Sometimes prescribed as a preventative, they have numerous possible side effects. △746.

Sulfation, preparative method for sulfuric acid esters and salts. Lead sulfate on the plates of lead-acid storage batteries, calcium sulfate on stone are examples of unwanted sulfations. Esters with sulfuric acid and alcohols are used industrially to produce the surfactant, sodium lauryl sulfate.

Sulfonation, preparative method for molecules containing the sulfuric acid group ($-SO_2$) achieved by reacting aromatic hydrocarbons with sulfuric acid or halogen compounds with inorganic sulfates. Sulfonated anthraquinones (wool dyestuffs) and sulfonamides (antibacterial drugs) are prepared by sulfonation.

Sulfur, common nonmetallic element (symbol S), known from ancient times (brimstone). It occurs in iron pyrites (FeS), galena (PbS), cinnabar (HgS), and other minerals; chief source is from native deposits and as a by-product from gas and oil wells. The element is used as a fungicide, a component of gunpowder, and a reagent for vulcanizing rubber. The main use is in the production of sulfuric acid. Sulfur has several allotropic forms, including two crystalline forms (rhombic and monoclinic). Plastic sulfur is a fine powder formed by sublimation. Liquid sulfur also has a variety of allotropic forms depending on the temperature. Chemically sulfur is a reactive element. Properties: at. no. 16; at. wt. 32.064; sp gr 2.07 (rhombic), 1.957 (monoclinic); melt. pt. 235°F (112.9°C); boil. pt. 832°F (444.4°C); most common isotope S^{32} (95.0%). △1568, 1570, 1574.

Sulfur Butterfly, medium-sized, orange or yellow butterfly with wings bordered or otherwise marked with black. The common yellow butterfly of E United States is the cloudless *Callidryas eubule.* White members of this family are called whites. Family Pieridae.

Sulfur Dioxide, colorless gas with choking odor (formula SO_2) obtained by roasting pyrites (FeS_2) or by burning sulfur. It is used in the manufacture of sulfuric acid and other chemicals, in the solvent extraction of lubricating oils, as a bleach, and as a food and drink preservative. Properties: sp gr (liq. 0°C) 1.434; melt. pt. −105°F (−76.2°C); boil. pt. 140°F (60°C).

Sulfuric Acid, corrosive oily liquid manufactured from sulfur dioxide by the contact process and the chamber process. It is used in the manufacture of fertilizers and chemicals, in petroleum refining, and in many other industries. Properties (pure): sp gr 1.84; melt. pt. 50.7°F (10.4°C). △1566.

Sulla, Lucius Cornelius (138–78 BC), Roman general and senate leader. He brought the Jugurthine War with Numidia to an end through diplomacy and opposed Marius to gain control of the Roman forces fighting Mithridates VI. In an unprecedented move he attacked Rome and gained command of the army. He

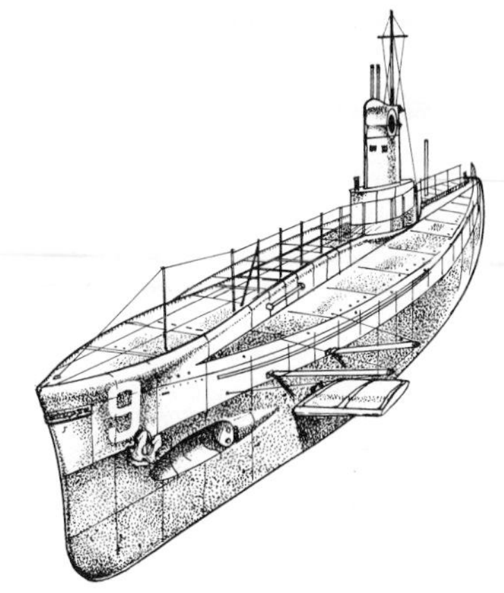

Submarine

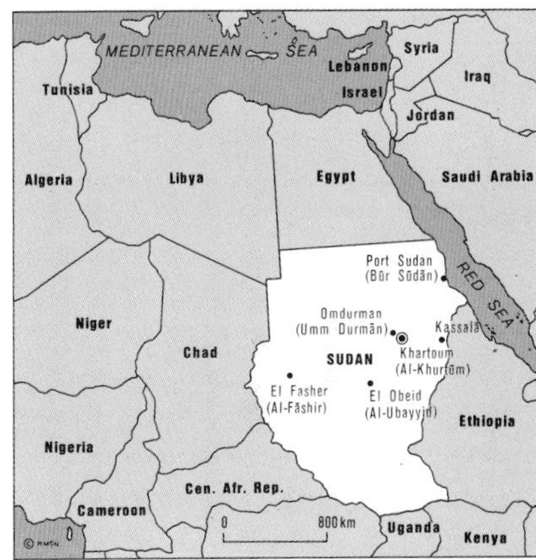
MEDITERRANEAN SEA
Syria
Lebanon
Israel
Iraq
Jordan
Tunisia
Algeria
Libya
Egypt
Saudi Arabia
Port Sudan
(Būr Sūdān)
RED SEA
Omdurman
(Umm Durmān)
Kassala
SUDAN
Khartoum
(Al-Khurṭūm)
Niger
Chad
El Fasher
(Al-Fāshir)
El Obeid
(Al-Ubayyiḍ)
Ethiopia
Nigeria
Cen. Afr. Rep.
Cameroon
0
800km
Uganda
Kenya

Sudan

Sugar cane

Sulawesi

defeated Mithridates, sacked Athens (86), and slaughtered Marius' followers. Proclaimed dictator (82), he instituted political reforms and restored constitutional government before his death. His reforms were soon reversed. △1018.

Sullivan, (Sir) Arthur (1842–1900), English composer. He is best known for composing the music for operettas with W.S. Gilbert. Their works included *H.M.S. Pinafore, The Mikado,* and *The Pirates of Penzance.* Sullivan also composed serious operas, songs, and popular hymns such as "Onward, Christian Soldiers." △1246.

Sullivan, Edward Vincent (1902–74), US radio and TV star, b. New York City. His newspaper column, "Little Ole New York," appeared in *The Daily News* (New York City) 1932–74. He made his radio debut in 1932 and appeared as host of TV's leading variety show "Toast of the Town," later retitled "The Ed Sullivan Show" (1948–70).

Sullivan, John Lawrence "John L." (1858–1918), US boxer, b. Roxbury, Mass. He beat Jake Kilrain (1889) in Richburg, Miss., in the last bare-knuckle heavyweight championship bout. Earlier (1882), he had beaten Paddy Ryan for the title in Mississippi City, Miss. He lost the title (1892) to James J. Corbett, and was elected to the Hall of Fame in 1954.

Sullivan, Louis Henry (1856–1924), US architect, b. Boston. He believed the exterior form of buildings should relate to their function and opposed the classical revival dominating the later 19th century. Most of his successes were executed in partnership with Dankmar Adler (1880–1900). The Wainwright Building in St Louis (1890) and the Transportation Building at the 1893 World's Exhibition in Chicago were outstanding. His Art Nouveau style ornamentation accented function. He wrote *Autobiography of an Idea* (1924).

Sully, Maximilien de Béthune, Duc de (1560–1641), French minister under Henry IV. A Huguenot, he barely escaped the massacre of Protestants on St Bartholomew's Day (1572) and served Henry of Navarre in his struggle for the throne. Once crowned Henry IV, the king entrusted major responsibilities (1597–1610) to Sully. As superintendent of finances he initiated major reforms, encouraged agriculture and trade, and initiated a levy upon officeholders, who, in return, were given their titles to keep or transfer at will.

Sully Prudhomme, René-François-Armand (1839–1907), French poet. A Parnassian poet, his verse includes *Stances et poèmes* (1865), *Les épreuves* (1866), *La Justice* (1878), and *Le Bonheur* (1888). Initially a lyric poet, his work became increasingly formal and impersonal. He was elected to the Académie Française in 1881 and was the first to be awarded the Nobel Prize for literature in 1901.

Sulu Archipelago, volcanic island group in extreme S Philippines, separating Sulu Sea (NW) from Celebes Sea (SE); comprises Sulu prov. The archipelago extends SW from Basilan Island to within 40mi (64km) of the E tip of Borneo, and includes over 400 islands and coral formations, chief of which are Jolo, Tawitawi, Pangutaran, and the Tapul group. Chief occupations are fishing, pearl diving, and cattle. Capital is Jolo. Area: 1,086sq mi (2,813sq km). Pop. 427,386.

Sulu Sea, branch of the W Pacific Ocean amid the SW Philippine Islands; the surrounding islands are Borneo (SW), Palawan (NW), Panay and Negros (NE), and the Sulu Archipelago (SE). The sea itself contains only a few small island clusters, and is used as a fishing ground.

Sumac, shrubs and trees widely distributed in temperate regions. They have long featherlike leaves and red, hairy fruit clusters. Some are grown as ornamentals; some species are poisonous to touch. Height: to 30ft (9m). Family Anacardiaceae; genera *Rhus* and *Toxicodendron. See also* Poison Ivy.

Sumatra (Sumatera), island in W Indonesia, 2nd-largest of the Greater Sunda group after Borneo; chief cities are Palembang, Medan, Padang. The terrain of the W coast is rugged and mountainous, containing the Barisan Mts, rising to Mt Kerintji, 12,500ft (3,813m); E and SE are lowland jungles with many rivers. By the 7th century, India had est. two states in Sumatra, Melayu and Srivijaya, which flourished as centers of trade and Buddhist learning. Island was reached by Portuguese 16th century and Dutch 17th century; Dutch East India Co. had fortresses and trading posts erected 18th century on both coasts. Island was occupied by Japanese 1942–45; made part of Republic of Indonesia 1950. Exports: rubber, tobacco, palm oil, tea, coffee, sisal. Industries: agriculture, mining, oil. Area: 183,000sq mi (473,970sq km). Pop. 19,840,000.

Sumer, S region of ancient Mesopotamia, later the S part of Babylonia, now S central Iraq. An agricultural civilization flourished here during the 3rd and 4th millennia BC. The Sumerians built canals, established an irrigation system, and were skilled in the use of metals (silver, gold, copper) to make pottery, jewelry, and weapons. They invented the cuneiform system of writing. Various kings founded dynasties at Kish, Erech, and Ur. Sargon of Agade brought the region under the Semites (*c.* 2600 BC), who blended their culture with the Sumerians. The final Sumerian civilization at Ur fell to Elam, and when Semitic Babylonia under Hammurabi (*c.* 2000 BC) controlled the land, the Sumerian nation vanished. △956.

Summa Theologica. △1088.

Summer Solstice. *See* Solstice.

Sumner, Charles (1811–74), US senator from Massachusetts (1851–74), b. Boston. An abolitionist, he was assaulted in the Senate in 1856 after denouncing Sen. Andrew Butler of South Carolina in an antislavery speech. Although incapacitated for three years, he retained his Senate seat. He fought for the Radical Republican plan for Reconstruction and was active in the attempt to remove Pres. Andrew Johnson from office (1868). From 1861–71, he was chairman of the Senate foreign relations committee.

Sumner, William Graham (1840–1910), US sociologist and anthropologist, b. Paterson, N.J. One of the founders of sociology in the United States, Sumner was ordained as an Episcopal clergyman but preferred teaching political and social science at Yale (1872–1910). He was an influential proponent of Social Darwinism. His most important works are *Folkways* (1907) and *The Science of Society,* published posthumously in 1927. *Ethnocentrism, folkways, in-group,* and *out-group* are among the many concepts that he introduced. *See also* Social Darwinism.

Sumo Wrestling, a sport, popular in Japan. It pits wrestlers who usually weigh more than 350 pounds (158kg) in a match that is quasi-religious in nature and is fought with much ritual. *See also* Wrestling. △930.

Sumter, Fort, fort in SE Carolina, on S shore of mouth of Charleston harbor, just S of Charleston; Confederate attack on fort (April 12, 1861) marked the beginning of the Civil War. It was est. 1948 as national monument.

Sun, Earth's nearest star and the central body in the solar system, radiating light, heat, and other energy by means of nuclear fusion reactions in its highly compressed high-temperature interior. The less dense cooler (about 6,000°C) gaseous surface (photosphere), which is violently active, is surrounded by the chromosphere and corona of much higher temperature. Magnetic fields in these regions give rise to sunspots, prominences, etc. The Sun is a main-sequence yellow-dwarf star situated in a spiral arm of the Galaxy, about 30,000 light-years from the Galactic center. Characteristics: mass 1.99×10^{30} kg; equatorial diameter 865,000mi (1,392,000km); specific gravity 1.41; mean rotation period 25.38 days; apparent mag. −26.86; absolute mag. +4.7; spectral type G2. △50, 94–98.

Sun Animal. *See* Heliozoa.

Sun Bear, omnivorous, honey-loving, tree-climbing bear found in SE Asia. It has a short-haired black coat with a crescent-shaped yellow mark on its chest and a gray or orange muzzle. It is smallest of all bears. Weight: 100lb (45kg). Family Ursidae, species *Helarctos malayanus.* △600.

Sunbird, tropical nectar-feeding songbird of the Old World, often considered a counterpart of the New World hummingbird. Males are usually brightly colored. After the male's courtship display, the female builds a purselike nest with a spoutlike porch for a single streaked white egg. Length: 3.5–8in (9–20cm). Family Nectariniidae.

Sunburn, an effect on the skin from ultraviolet radiation from the Sun. Redness, swelling, and pain are associated with destruction and coagulation of some of the substances in the cells of the skin, along with enlargement of small vessels beneath the epidermis. In severe cases, blisters and ulcers may form, accompanied by fever. There is a latent period of several hours between exposure and onset of symptoms. Excessive exposure is harmful, hastening the aging process and contributing to the development of keratoses and skin cancer.

Sunday, Billy (1862–1935), US Presbyterian revivalist; full name, William Ashley Sunday, b. Ames, Iowa. After three years in professional baseball, he turned to full-time religious interests in 1886 and became a famous preacher at evangelical mass meetings across the country. Homer A. Rodeheaver led hymn singing at these meetings.

Sunderland, industrial city and seaport in NE England, at mouth of Wear River; shipbuilding center. At nearby Monkwearmouth, incorporated in St Peter's Church, are remains of the great Benedictine abbey (founded 674) where the Venerable Bede studied. Industries: precision engineering, glass, chemicals, coal, pottery. Exports: iron, steel. Pop. 216,892.

Sundew, insectivorous plants native to temperate swamps and bogs. They have hairy, basal leaves that glisten with a dewlike substance to attract, trap, and digest insects. When the hairy projections are touched, the leaves close to trap the insect. These plants are often grown indoors as curiosities. Family Droseraceae; genera *Dionaea* and *Drosera.*

Sundial. △1658.

Sun Dog, or parhelion, also called mock Sun, for two bright and colored spots appearing 22° to each side of the Sun, caused by refraction of the light from ice crystals.

Sunfish, North American freshwater fish. A popular sport fish, similar in appearance to perch, it has a continuous dorsal fin containing spiny and soft rays. It is a nest-building fish. The male guards nest and young. The 300 species range in size from the blue spotted *Enneacanthus gloriosus,* length: 3.5in (8.9cm) to largemouth bass, *Micropterus salmoides* length 32in (81.3cm); weight: 22lb (10kg). Family Centrarchidae. *See also* Bluegill; Pumpkinseed.

Sunflower, coarse annual and perennial plant of North America. The flower heads turn to face the Sun and resemble huge daisies with yellow ray flowers and a center disk of yellow, brown, or purple. The common sunflower *(Helianthus annus)* has 1ft (30.5cm) leaves and flower heads over 1ft (30.5cm) across; height: to 15ft (4.6m). Sunflower seeds are a source of an edible oil and are used as feed for poultry and wild birds. △362.

Sunga Dynasty. △986.

Sungari (Sung-hua), river in NE China; rises in Ch'ang-pai Shan Mts, near North Korean border; flows generally N to Amur River at USSR border; navigable for most of its 1,150mi (1,852km); it is a main trade route in an agricultural area.

Sung Dynasty (960–1279), Chinese dynasty. Divided into the North and South Sung by the Jurchen conquest and establishment of the Chin dynasty in the North, it was a period of refinement and cultural flowering in China. Many of the finest literary, artistic, and cultural treasures of Chinese civilization date from this period including literary essays, prose poems, landscape paintings, and highly valuable ceramics. Southern ports were opened for commerce and relations with South Asia. △1042.

Sunnis, or **Sunnites,** the main body of Muslims, including about 90% of the followers of Islam. This sect finds authority in the entire Sunna, the body of orthodox tradition including teachings outside the Koran. On this point the Sunnis differ from the Shi'a sect, which believes in the inspired leadership of a succession of imams. The Shi'a hold that this succession started with Ali, Mohammed's son-in-law. The Sunnis acknowledge three caliphs before Ali as legitimate rulers. Both Sunnis and Shi'ites believe in the basic Islamic faith: one God, Allah, Mohammed as the Prophet of God, and the Koran as the revealed word of God. *See also* Caliph; Islam; Shi'a.

Sunnyvale, city in W California, 8mi (13km) WNW of San Jose; site of Moffet Field Naval Air Station. Industries: electrical equipment, foodstuffs, paper products, chemicals. Founded 1849; inc. 1912. Pop. (1970) 95,408.

Sunspot, short-lived dark areas, often several thousand miles across, that appear periodically on the Sun's photosphere and participate in its rotation. They have a dark center (the umbra) surrounded by a brighter border (the penumbra). Possessing strong magnetic fields that are caused by localized magnetohydrodynamic disturbances below the surface, they appear dark because they are about 2000°K cooler than the surrounding regions. Sunspots usually appear in groups, and usually follow an 11-year cycle between minima and maxima. △94.

Sunstroke, serious disorder caused by exposure to direct sunlight. It is characterized by extreme elevation of body temperature to 106°–110°F (41°–43°C). The fever exerts a harmful effect on the central nervous system. The usual cause is failure of sweating to remove body heat. Cooling of the body is urgent in sunstroke followed by expert medical care.

Sun Valley, resort area in central Idaho, in a valley of the Sawtooth Mts, just N of Ketchum; originally a ski area developed by Union Pacific Railroad in 1936, it now includes a summer resort. Elevation: 6,000ft (1,830m).

Sun Yat-sen (1866–1925), first president of the Chinese Republic (1911–12) and revolutionary leader of modern China. Sun became convinced after China's defeat by Japan in 1895 that the Manchu dynasty must be overthrown. In exile 1895–1911, he worked through secret societies and with support from overseas Chinese to bring about his aim. His inspiration eventually brought about the revolution of 1911. He joined in founding the Kuomintang (1912) and became its leader and ideologue. △1270, 1328.

Supai. *See* Havasupai.

Superconductivity. △1530, 1536.

Superego, in psychoanalysis, the level of personality that sets standards. The child starts with the unthinking impulses of the id. The ego develops as he learns to deal with reality. Then the superego—roughly, his conscience—develops as he adopts standards determined by his parents' rewards and punishments. *See also* Ego; Id. △786, 812.

Superior, city and port of entry in NW Wisconsin, on Superior Bay; seat of Douglas co. Economic growth was spurred by discovery of iron ore (1880s); site of University of Wisconsin at Superior and one of largest coal and ore docks in United States. Industries: ship yards, grain elevators, oil products, dairying. Inc. 1883. Pop. (1970) 32,237.

Superior, Lake, lake in the United States and Canada; world's largest freshwater lake; bounded by NE Minnesota (W), Ontario, Canada (N and E), and NW Michigan and NW Wisconsin (S); it is connected to Lake Huron and St Lawrence Seaway by Sault Ste Marie Canals. A commercial and recreational fishing source, it is also used for transport of grains and iron ore. It is the highest of the Great Lakes and least polluted. Discovered 1616 by Étienne Brulé, it was settled 1649 at Ashland. Length: 350mi (564km). Width: 160mi (258km). Area: 31,820sq mi (82,414sq km).

Superior Conjunction. *See* Conjunction.

Superior Vena Cava. △688.

Supermultiplet. *See* Multiplet.

Supernova (plural supernovae), star that undergoes a cataclysmic outburst of energy and matter as the result of internal imbalances caused by the exhaustion of its fuel. These imbalances, which may occur in stars beyond a certain critical mass, take the form of accelerated nuclear reactions in the core, enormously increased internal temperatures (up to 5,000,000,000°K), and gravitational collapse. The catastrophic explosion that follows, in which the star blows itself apart, ejecting matter at relativistic speeds, temporarily increases its absolute magnitude to a figure in excess of −14, the brightness of a galaxy. These spectacular but also very rare phenomena usually leave behind a filamentary remnant, such as the Crab Nebula, and the original core may survive as a neutron star or pulsar, or even a black hole. △102.

Superposition, Principle of, geologic principle that the oldest layer in a group of sedimentary strata is the one on the bottom. In the absence of upheavals and folding, or igneous intrusion, the oldest layer of rock and its fossils is the lowest. *See also* Historical Geology. △272, 276.

Supersonic Flight, flight beyond Mach 1, the speed at which sound travels under varying conditions of temperature and pressure. Thus at sea level 760mph (1,223kph) is the critical speed. At high altitude the speed might be 660mph (1,062kph). At these speeds the pressure wave that normally moves away from the airplane is compressed, creating a cone-shaped shock wave. Early attempts to fly through this barrier were unsuccessful. Swept-wing, slender-bodied airplanes fly at supersonic speeds by retarding the formation of the wave. △1716–18, 1744.

Supersonic Velocity, velocity in excess of the local velocity of sound. Its magnitude is usually expressed as a Mach Number (named after Ernst Mach, 1838–1916), which is the ratio of the velocity of a body of fluid to the local velocity of sound. Thus a body traveling at twice the speed of sound has a Mach Number 2. A velocity in excess of Mach 5 is said to be hypersonic. △1498.

Supplementary Angles, two angles whose sum is 180°. Each is the supplement of the other.

Supply and Demand, Law of. The law of supply indicates that other things being equal, as the price of a good increases, suppliers will be willing to produce more and as the price of a good decreases, producers will be willing to produce less. Thus, price and quantity supplied are directly related. The law of demand states the reverse; that is, as prices increase, consumers will demand less, and as prices decrease, consumers will demand more. Thus, price and quantity demanded are inversely related. Through the interaction of supply and demand, an equilibrium position is reached. *See also* Equilibrium. △936.

Suprematism, abstract art movement. Derived from Cubism and launched in Russia in 1913 by the painter Casimir Malevich. △1320.

Supreme Court of Canada, one of two Canadian federal courts. It is generally a court of last resort for both civil and criminal cases. Appeals are brought from superior courts of the provinces where the amount in question exceeds $10,000. Any lesser amount may be granted by the high provincial court, but if refused, the Supreme Court may itself institute appeal. Certain appeals are brought from the Exchequer Court, its companion federal court. In civil cases only, the Supreme Court or superior courts may appeal to the Judicial Committee of the British Privy Council in London. There are nine justices, including a chief justice.

Supreme Court of the United States, US court of last resort. It derives its power from the doctrine of "judicial review" and from its ability to pass on the constitutionality of state and federal legislation and of executive acts. It exercises both original jurisdiction ("in all cases affecting ambassadors, other public ministers, consuls, and those in which a State shall be a party"), and appellate jurisdiction ("both as to law and fact, with such exceptions and under such regulations as Congress shall make," Sect. 2, Art. III, US Constitution). It hears appeals from the courts of appeals, the district courts, and the highest state courts where a federal question is involved. Created by the Judiciary Act of 1789, the Supreme Court consists of justices who are appointed by the president with the advice and consent of the Senate. The number of justices has varied, but since 1869 has remained at nine, including a chief justice. Justices are removeable only by impeachment. The chief justice presides over all sessions and five judges constitute a quorum to hear a case. There must be a majority vote before a decision is made. If a tie exists, the previous decision is upheld.

History. The Supreme Court has heard several hundred cases since it was established, some of which had controversial effects on the country's political and social structure. While some of these decisions were conservative changes, many were quite radical and often openly criticized by the government. Chief Justice John Marshall successfully (*Marbury v. Madison,* 1803) claimed the power to declare acts of Congress unconstitutional. After World War I the Supreme Court's conservative views met opposition by the liberalism of the New Deal Era. After some of Pres. Franklin Roosevelt's most important economic recovery programs were invalidated by the court, he sought to reform the court by filling vacancies with more liberal justices. In 1954 the court issued its landmark desegregation decision, *Brown* v. *Board of Education of Topeka.* This new liberalism continued through Pres. Lyndon Johnson's administration and was most evident in Chief Justice Earl Warren's focusing of the court's attention to civil rights and the enforcement of the Bill of Rights. First Amendment rights of speech, press, assembly, and religious freedom were vigorously enforced. Newspapers were reassured against libel (*New York Times* v. *Sullivan,* 1964), peaceful demonstrators were protected from arrest (*Edwards* v. *South Carolina,* 1963), and civil rights organizations were safeguarded from official harassment (*NAACP* v. *Alabama,* 1958). The provisions of the fair trial rights of federal criminals were extended to the states. The liberalism of all these decisions was openly attacked, and with the election of President Nixon, a change began in the ideological structure of the court

Sumatra

Sunbird

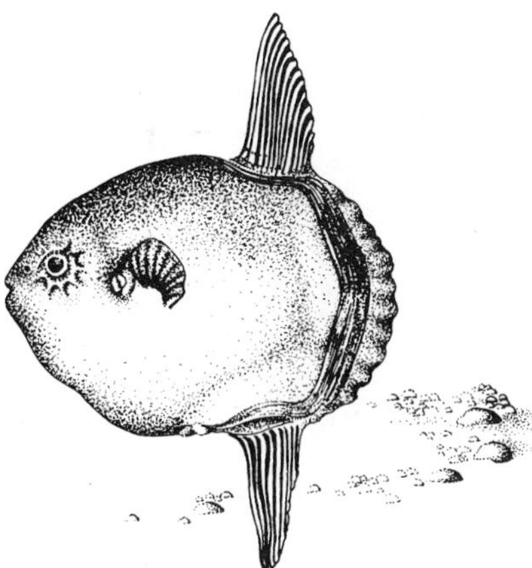

Sunfish

Sunflower

with the appointment of the more conservative Warren Burger as chief justice. Several other vacancies were filled with justices who had criticized previous decisions.

Following is a list of the chief justices of the Supreme Court.

CHIEF JUSTICES OF US SUPREME COURT

	Term
John Jay	1789–95
John Rutledge*	1795
Oliver Ellsworth	1796–1800
John Marshall	1801–35
Roger Brooke Taney	1836–64
Salmon Portland Chase	1864–73
Morrison Remick Waite	1874–88
Melville Weston Fuller	1888–1910
Edward Douglas White	1910–21
William Howard Taft	1921–30
Charles Evans Hughes	1930–41
Harlan Fiske Stone	1941–46
Fred Moore Vinson	1946–53
Earl Warren	1953–69
Warren Earl Burger	1969–

*appointment not confirmed by Senate

Surabaja, seaport city in NE Java, Indonesia, across Surabaja Strait from Madura Island; 2nd-largest city in Indonesia and capital of East Java prov.; occupied by Dutch, and a principal Dutch naval base until WWII, when occupied by Japanese; site of Airlangga University (1954) and naval college; trade center. Exports: rice, sugar cane, spices, tobacco, maize, tapioca, coffee, cocoa, rubber, copra. Pop. 1,273,000.

Surat, city in W India, 150mi (242km) N of Bombay on Tapti River. With the est. of British and Dutch trading posts in the early 17th century, Surat developed into one of India's most populated and busiest port cities; in 1664 it was devastated by a Mahrattas invasion and steadily declined in importance; site of several colleges. Industries: textiles, cotton gins, engineering, rice, paper, soap, gold and silverware, carpets. Pop. 393,915.

Suravarman. △1114.

Surface Tension, the molecular forces associated with the boundary layer of a liquid. Cohesive forces in the liquid tend to resist disruption, so that a pin placed carefully on the surface will "float" even though its density is many times that of the liquid. △1490, 1504.

Surf Perch. *See* Sea Perch.

Surgery, branch of medicine that uses specialized instrumental techniques and manipulations to treat diseases and injuries. △752–54.

Surinam (Suriname), independent nation in NE South America, on the Atlantic Ocean, bordered by Brazil (S), French Guiana (E), and Guyana (W). Surinam is made up of the Guiana Highlands plateau, a flat coastal plain, and a forest inland region which covers 80% of the total land area; its many rivers serve as a source of hydroelectric power. The chief agricultural products are rice, bananas, sugarcane, coffee, coconuts, lumber, and citrus fruits. The economy depends greatly on the export of bauxite, of which it is one of the world's largest producers. The main industries include shrimp freezing, processed foods, paint, plywood, and fruit juices. The people are mostly Indonesian, Creoles, Asian, and Indians; they enjoy complete religious freedom, with denominations of Hindus, Roman Catholics, Muslims, Protestants, and Confucians; education is free. The region was discovered 1499 by Spanish explorer Alfonso de Ojeda. The Dutch founded the first colony in 1616. In 1815 the Congress of Vienna gave the Guyana region to Britain and reaffirmed Dutch control of Surinam. Surinam became officially autonomous 1954, and in 1975, Surinam gained full independence from the Netherlands. The new government, dominated by Creoles, attempted to halt the flight of skilled Surinamese, many of them Hindus. The government is headed by a president, but actual power rests with the premier, who is responsible to a 39-member legislative Council, elected by universal adult suffrage. Surinam became a member of the United Nations in 1975, soon after independence was gained.

PROFILE

Official name: Surinam
Area: 63,037sq mi (163,266sq km)
Population: 375,200
Chief city: Paramaribo
Government: Parliamentary democracy
Religion: Hindu (majority)
Language: Dutch

Surinam Toad, South American aquatic tailless amphibian characterized by the absence of a tongue. It is brown with a flat, square body. The female carries fertilized eggs embedded in the skin on her back; larvae remain until metamorphosed. Length: to 8in (20cm). Family Pipidae; species *Pipa pipa. See also* Frog. △518.

Surmullet. *See* Goatfish.

Surratt, Mary Eugenia (*c.*1817–65), implicated in the assassination of President Abraham Lincoln, b. Waterloo, Md. Mrs. Surratt owned the Washington, D.C., boardinghouse where the plot to abduct Lincoln and the plan to assassinate him were discussed. Judged guilty of a conspiracy with Jefferson Davis and Confederate officials in Canada to murder the president, Mrs. Surratt and three others were condemned to death. She was hanged on July 7, 1865. The case against Mrs. Surratt was the weakest of all; she was not a party to the assassination plans and may not have known about the abduction plot.

Surrealism, influential movement in art and literature, evolved in the mid-1920s from Dadaism. Influenced by psychoanalysis, it represented a reaction against rationalism and advocated creative use of the powers of the unconscious mind. Led by André Breton, who wrote several surrealist manifestos, surrealist writers include Louis Aragon, Paul Eluard, and Benjamin Péret, while painters include Jean Arp, Max Ernst, René Magritte, Yves Tanguy, Salvador Dali, Joan Miró, and Paul Klee. Surrealism in painting took two basic forms, one made up of fanciful, often abstract elements, and the other devoted to the meticulous depiction of dreamlike subject matter. △1318, 1376.

Surrey, nonmetropolitan county of SE England, one of the Home Counties bordering Greater London. County town is Guildford. Important towns are Redhill, Riegate, Epsom and Ewell, Weybridge, and Woking. The region is traversed by the North Downs, across which flow the Wey and Mole rivers. Mainly residential, the county has industries in the N and some dairy farming and market gardening. Pop. 999,-588.

Surrogate Court, or Probate Court, state court with jurisdiction to prove wills and administer estates of decedents, testate or intestate (with or without a will). In some states it supervises guardianship of minors and their estates and protects legally incompetent persons. It is also known as orphans' court.

Surrogate Mother. △784.

Surveying, the accurate measurement of the Earth's surface. Used in establishing land boundaries, the topography of landforms, and major construction and civil engineering work such as dams, bridges, and highways. Measurements are linear or angular, applying principles of geometry and trigonometry. For smaller areas, the land is treated as a horizontal plane. Large areas involve considerations of the Earth's curving shape and are referred to as geodetic surveys. Various surveys, such as topographic, engineering, land, construction, cartographic, and mining require specialized methods and instruments. △180.

Survival of the Fittest, the tendency of the strongest and best adapted of a species to survive and reproduce. *See also* Natural Selection. △418.

Surya, in Hindu mythology, the personification of the Sun, possessed of 12 names and incarnations, among them Indra, Varuna, and Mitra. As Surya he is depicted as a three-eyed, four-armed man of burnished copper, sometimes seated on a lotus or in a chariot drawn by many horses. He is prayed to as a healer and bringer of luck. His festival, the Suryapuja, occurs in the spring. *See also* Indra. △838.

Susa, ruined city in ancient country of Elam, 15mi (24km) SW of modern Dizful, W Iran; served as the winter residence of the Achaemenian kings 7th century–331 BC; scene of the biblical story of Esther and King Ahasuerus. Archeological excavations here unearthed the code of Hammurabi and the stele of Naram-sin.

Su Shih (1036–1101), Chinese poet and prose writer. Also called Su Tung-p'o, he was one of the outstanding writers during the Sung dynasty (960–1279). As a poet he was a master of *tz'u,* the verse form of irregular length that flourished during the Sung. Utilizing the structural freedom of *tz'u,* he wrote vigorously about heroism and beauty.

Suspension, liquid medium in which small solid particles are uniformly disposed. If the particles do not settle out on standing but are unable to pass through a semipermeable membrane the suspension is called a colloid. The particle size in such colloidal suspensions is likely to be in the range 10^{-4} to 10^{-6} millimeters.

Suspension Bridge, a bridge that has its roadway suspended from two or more cables that generally pass over towers and anchor at the ends. △1756–58.

Susquehanna River, river in NE United States, rises in Otsego Lake, central New York; flows S through Pennsylvania to NE corner of Maryland and empties into Chesapeake Bay near Havre de Grace; site of several hydroelectric plants and subject of extensive flood control systems. Length: 444mi (715km).

Sussex, former county of S England, now divided into the nonmetropolitan counties of East Sussex and West Sussex. The area is crossed by the South Downs; its main rivers are the Rother, Duse, and Arun; an agricultural region, with many coastal resorts.

Sussex Spaniel, hunting dog (sporting group) used for upland shooting. Massive and muscular, this determined hunter has a heavy looking head, square muzzle, and hanging lips; thick, large ears are low-set and hanging. The body is round-chested, long, and low; legs are short with large, round feet. Tail is docked and set low. The abundant coat is flat or slightly wavy with feathering on the legs; the characteristic color is rich golden liver. Average size: about 15in (38cm) high at shoulder; 35–45lb (16–20kg). *See also* Sporting Dog.

Sussex Weald. △1592.

Sutherland, Joan (1926–), Australian soprano. She studied at the Sydney Conservatory and made her debut in 1950. She spent a number of years with the Covent Garden Opera in England, establishing a great reputation, before making a spectacular debut at the Metropolitan Opera in 1961 as Lucia in Donizetti's *Lucia Di Lammermoor.* She is highly regarded for both coloratura and dramatic roles.

Sutlej (Langchuhe), tributary of Indus River and longest of the five rivers of the Punjab; rises in SW Tibet, China; flows W through Himalayas and the Punjab plain, joins the Beas River, continues into Pakistan to join Chenab River, forming the Panjnad, which flows to the Indus. Length: approx. 900mi (1,450km).

Sutra, sacred Buddhist text claiming to have been spoken by Buddha himself and recorded by his disciple, Ananda, immediately after Buddha's death in approximately 483 BC. Many Sutras, however, were composed centuries later by unknown authors, and there is disagreement among Buddhists as to their value. *See also* Buddha; Buddhism.

Sutter, Johann Augustus (1803–80), US pioneer, b. Germany. He settled in Sacramento, Calif., in 1839. He acquired a large tract of land and became a prosperous rancher. After gold was found at his mill (1848), he was ruined when miners swarmed over his land.

Suttner, Bertha Felice Sophie, Baroness von (1843–1914), Austrian novelist and free-thinking pacifist. Her best novels include *Lay Down Your Arms* (1889) and *Das Maschinenzeitalter* (1899). Active in the peace movement, she founded the Austrian Society of Friends of Peace (1891) and edited the pacifist journal *Lay Down Your Arms!* (1892–99). She influenced Alfred Nobel to include among his awards the peace prize, which she received in 1905.

Suwannee River, river in SE Georgia and N Florida; rises in Okefenokee Swamp, SE Ga., flows SW across Fla. into Gulf of Mexico at Suwannee Sound. Length: 240mi (386km).

Suzhou. *See* Soochow.

Sverdlovsk, city in Russian SFSR, USSR, in E foothills of the central Urals, on dammed Iset River; capital of Sverdlovsk oblast. Founded as a fortress 1722, it was named Yekaterinburg for Russian empress Catherine I; site of 1918 execution of Tsar Nicholas II and his family; renamed 1924 for Bolshevik revolutionary Yakov Sverdlov; city was placed under direct jurisdiction of Russian SFSR 1943; site of Urals state university (1920), medical, law, mining, forestry, and teachers' colleges, polytechnic school, conservatory, and branch of USSR Academy of Science. Industries: metallurgical and mining equipment, steel, aircraft, ballbearings, railroad cars, radio, television, building materials. Pop. 1,026,000.

Sverdrup Islands. *See* Queen Elizabeth Islands.

vetovid, in Slavic mythology, the principal divinity. e is the god of fertility and the god of war. Among e Baltic Slavs he appeared as Herovit, the god of the my, and as Rugevit with seven faces, and as Porevit th five heads or Triglav with three.

vabia, a duchy in medieval Germany that took its me from the Suevi tribes, its former inhabitants. rkhard, count of Raetia, was recognized as the first ke in 919. The duchy was joined to the imperial own when Emperor Henry IV gave it in 1079 to the use of Hohenstauffen, under whose rule its cities gan to achieve great wealth. In 1331, to defend emselves against aggression by the crown, the cit- s formed an association called the Swabian League, nich lasted intermittently until 1534.

wahili, or Kingwana, a Bantu language of the Niger- rdofanian family of African languages. The most portant, having about 8,000,000 native speakers, s a lingua-franca in most of E Africa to E portion of ongo Basin. Imposed by foreign rulers as the official ngue, it has a large native literature using a form of e Arabic alphabet.

wallow, swift-flying bird with long wings and forked il found worldwide. In some areas, their regular mi- atory habits make them a symbol of spring. Insect aters, they lay 3–5 plain whitish eggs. The barn swal- w *(Hirundo rustica)* builds its mud nest in a tree ole, house, or barn; the cliff swallow *(Petrochelidon yrrhonota)* builds on a cliff. Length: 4.8–6in (12.2– 5.2cm); family Hirundinidae.

wallowtail Butterfly, butterfly found worldwide, at typically has taillike extensions on the hind wings. ost swallowtails are large and black with bright arkings—usually yellow, but often blue, green, or d. The yellow and black giant *Papilio cresphontes* as a wingspread up to 5.5in (14cm). When a swallow- il caterpillar is disturbed, it emits an unpleasant odor om a protrusible organ behind its head. Family Papil- nidae. △502.

wammerdam, Jan (1637–80), Dutch naturalist. is works, including *General History of Insects,* aided e development of the modern study of entymology. e discovered red corpuscles and identified the lym- hatic valves in the human body.

wamp Deer. *See* Marsh Deer.

wamp Lynx. *See* Chaus.

wamp Pink. *See* Grass Pink.

wamp Potato. *See* Arrowhead.

wan, graceful, white waterfowl that nests in N orthern Hemisphere and migrates south for winter. hree species live in the Southern Hemisphere. They ave broad, flat bills, long necks, plump bodies, long gs, webbed feet, and dense plumage over down. hey dip their heads under water to feed on plant atter. Swans form life-long pair bonds, build large rass-and-leaf nests in marshes, and lay white eggs –6). The young are called cygnets. Length: 3.5–6ft .1–1.8m). Family Anatidae; genus *Cygnus.*

wan, The. *See* Cygnus.

wan Flower. *See* Pelican Flower.

wann, Ingo. △824.

wansea (Abertawe), port in South Wales, on wansea Bay, an inlet of Bristol Channel; administra- ve center of West Glamorgan; site of university 920). Industries: metal smelting, tinplate, chemi- als, oil refining. Pop. 172,566.

watow (Shantou, or Shan-t'ou), city in SE China, 70mi (274km) NW of Hong Kong, on Han Shui River elta, on South China Sea. A small fishing village, its conomic growth was spurred when it was declared a eaty port (1869) and opened to foreign traffic; occu- ied by Japan during WWII. Exports: tea, sugar, ranges, tobacco. Industries: fishing, shipbuilding, achine shops. Pop. 400,000.

wazi, Negroid people of S Africa, who are mainly gricultural pastoralists. In their traditionally polyga- ous society power is shared between a hereditary ale ruler and his mother (or a recognized substitute). pproximately half the Swazi continue to practice an- estor worship, witchcraft, and sorcery.

waziland, kingdom in S Africa, bordering the Re- ublic of South Africa and Mozambique. The region an be looked at as 3 topographical zones: high forestland, middle savanna grassland with some farm lands, and low arable land. The economy has flourished since 1950, due to development and diversification in agriculture. The per capita income is approx. $180 a year, which does not indicate the income of Swazis, because most high-level income is in the hands of the white minority. Cattle and dairying are important; industries include food processing, sugar, corn, citrus fruits, cotton, forest products; iron, asbestos, and coal are chief minerals. The construction of a railroad line from Ngwenga to Mozambique has aided economic growth substantially. Most Swazi still practice subsistence farming, but a growing number are working in either skilled or unskilled industrial labor.

Africans comprise approx. 97% of the population, with minorities of Eurafricans and native whites. The majority practices Christianity, the rest adhere to animism. The official language is English, but the Swazi language is SiSwati. There is a university and schools set up by Christian missions; literacy rate is 25%.

History. Independence was granted by the British and Transvaal governments in 1881 and in 1884 a provisional government was created. In 1894 administrative power was given to the South African government; at the end of the South African (Boer) War (1902) rights of power passed to Britain and to the British High Commissioner of South Africa 1906. In 1949 the British denied South Africa's desire to control Swaziland; given self government 1963; independence 1968. Under 1968 constitution, the king is head of state, executive power is exercised by a cabinet and prime minister. The parliament has power to enact all laws except Swazi law and customs. The Swazi law is decided by the Swazi National Council.

Sweat Gland, one of many small tubular, subcutaneous glands that open on the skin surface through pores and release perspiration, water, and some salt to regulate body temperature. △686.

Sweat Shops, exploitive working conditions. Sweatshops were small factories or home industries where laborers, mostly women and children, worked long hours for low wages under unsanitary and cramped conditions. In the United States sweatshops were prevalent during the late 19th century but were later eliminated by federal and state laws.

Sweden (Sverige), independent nation in N Europe, in Scandinavia. One of the most prosperous countries in the world, its government social welfare programs account for one-third of the national budget.

Land and economy. Located in N Europe on the E half of the Scandinavian peninsula, its neighbors are Norway (W) and Finland (NE). Denmark lies across the Kattegat. The border with Norway is mountainous, sloping gently to the S. Half of the country is forested, lakes cover 9%, and 7% of the total is arable. Along the coast are sandy beaches (S), rocky cliffs (N and W), and the fertile central and S plains (Skane) with farmland covering 40%. Two Baltic Sea islands belong to Sweden: Gotland, a fertile 1,160sq mi (3,004sq km) area, and the smaller Oland. The Gulf Stream moderates the climate, although N winters last 6 months or longer. Sweden's high standard of living includes a comprehensive social welfare program. Timber, iron ore, and water power are mainstays of the economy. Sweden is almost self-sufficient in foodstuffs. Industry employs 37% of the work force, agriculture 7%. Although the government controls transportation, water power, communication, and iron ore mining, 93% of the total output is from private enterprise.

People. The most heavily populated Scandinavian country, Sweden now has 650,000 aliens working in its factories. The basic population is a homogeneous mixture with about 35,000 Finns and 10,000 Lapps in the N. Ninety-five percent of the people belong to the Lutheran state church. Education is compulsory and literacy almost 100%.

Government. Sweden is a limited constitutional monarchy; the king is chief of state with very limited powers. Executive power is in the cabinet, which includes the prime minister and the elected parliament (Riksdag).

History. During the Viking era (AD 800), Christianity began to emerge in Sweden, and by 1003 the first Christian king was baptized. During the next 700 years Sweden expanded its influence E to the Black and Caspian seas, trading slaves and furs for gold and silver. Expansion lasted until the 18th century when Russia acquired Sweden's Baltic empire, including Finland. Sweden was joined with Norway 1814–1905 when Norway dissolved the union. Parliamentary government came to Sweden in 1917, universal suffrage in 1921. The Swedish constitution, written in 1809, is the oldest one still in effect in Europe. The king, Charles XVI Gustaf, is mainly a symbol of national unity. During WWI and WWII Sweden remained neutral.

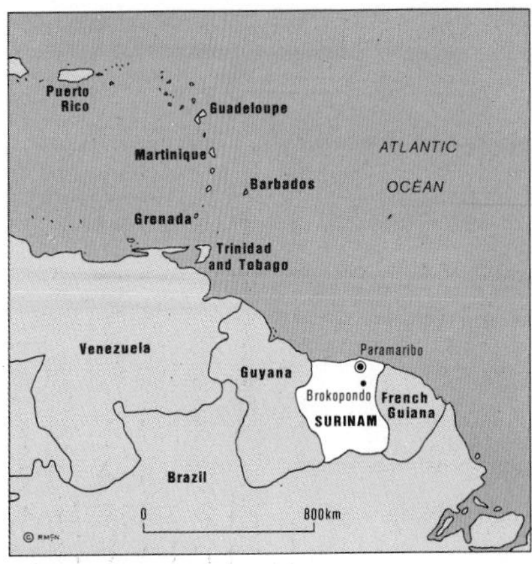

Puerto Rico
Guadeloupe
Martinique
Barbados
ATLANTIC OCEAN
Grenada
Trinidad and Tobago
Venezuela
Guyana
Paramaribo
Brokopondo
SURINAM
French Guiana
Brazil
0
800km

Surinam

Joan Sutherland

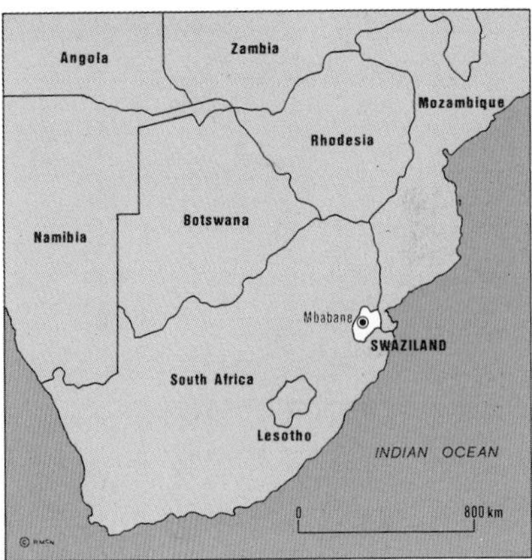

Angola
Zambia
Mozambique
Rhodesia
Botswana
Namibia
Mbabane
SWAZILAND
South Africa
Lesotho
INDIAN OCEAN
0
800 km

Swaziland

NORWEGIAN SEA
Kiruna
Finland
SWEDEN
Norway
Uppsala
Stockholm
Gothenburg (Göteborg)
U.S.S.R.
BALTIC SEA
Denmark
Malmö
Poland
0
400km

Sweden

PROFILE

Official name: Kingdom of Sweden
Area: 173,649sq mi (449,751sq km)
Population: 8,300,000
Density: 48per sq mi (18per sq km)
Chief cities: Stockholm (capital); Göteborg; Malmo
Government: Parliamentary monarchy (limited)
Religion: Lutheran (state church)
Language: Swedish
Monetary unit: Krona
Gross national product: $56,200,000,000
Per capita income: $6,155
Industries: pulp and paper mills, shipbuilding, machinery, automobiles, aircraft, toolmaking, iron and steel
Agriculture: cattle, pigs, forests, oats, sugar beets, potatoes, wheat
Minerals: iron ore
Trading partners: United Kingdom, West Germany

Swedenborg, Emanuel (1688–1772), Swedish philosopher and mystic. Early scientific preoccupations and official duties as inspector of mines were followed by psychical conversion. He professed to have special gifts and divine illumination (1747). In his *Divine Love and Wisdom* he characterized divinity as infinite love. His followers, organized as a sect, were known as Swedenborgians.

Swede Turnip. *See* Rutabaga.

Swedish, the national language of Sweden, spoken by virtually all of the country's 8,000,000 people. Closely related to Norwegian and Danish, it is one of the Germanic languages, and thus part of the Indo-European family.

Swedish Ivy, trailing house plant native to Africa and Australia. It has waxy, scalloped-edged, rounded leaves of green or green edged with white, and fleshy stems. Some species are purplish. Care: bright indirect light, soil (equal parts loam, peat moss, sand) kept barely moist. Propagation is by stem-tip cuttings. Genus *Plectranthus.*

Sweet Alyssum, annual plant native to Europe and used in borders and rock gardens. It has lobed leaves and white or purple flower clusters. Height: 3–6in (7.6–15.2cm). Family Cruciferae; species *Lobularia maritima.*

Sweetener, Artificial, saccharin or cyclamates used to sweeten foods and beverages by people whose sugar intake must be limited, especially diabetics. Saccharin ($C_6H_4SO_2CONH$) is 500 times sweeter than sugar and has no food value. It is used in the form of its soluble sodium salt. Sodium and calcium cyclamate ($C_6H_{11}NHSO_3Na(Ca)$) were used for the same purpose until 1969 when they were banned in the United States owing to a possible cancer risk.

Sweet Flag, or **Calamus,** perennial marsh plant native to the Old World now found in E North America. It has sword-shaped leaves, small green flowers, and a sweet-scented root that yields calamus oil used in liqueurs and perfumes. Height: 1–4ft (30–122cm). Family Araceae; species *Acorus calamus.*

Sweet Gale, or bog myrtle, Scotch gale, fragrant marsh plant found throughout northern temperate wetlands. It has yellowish flowers and bitter leaves used in making medicine. Height: to 6ft (1.8m). Family Myricaceae; species *Myrica gale. See also* Bayberry.

Sweet Gum, deciduous tree native to E North America. In autumn, its maplelike leaves turn brilliant yellow, orange, or red. It has spiny brown seedpods often used for indoor decorations. Height: over 120ft (36.6m). Family Hamamelidaceae; species *Liquidambar styraciflua.*

Sweet Marjoram. *See* Marjoram.

Sweet Pea, tendril-climbing, annual plant native to Italy. It has fragrant, butterfly-shaped flowers of white, pink, rose, lavender, purple, red, or orange. Height: to 6ft (1.8m). Family Leguminosae; species *Lathyrus odoratus.*

Sweet Potato, trailing plant native to South America and cultivated as a vegetable in S United States. Its funnel-shaped flowers are purple. Harvested after the first fall frost, the orange or yellow fleshy, tuberlike root is edible. Family Convolvulaceae; species *Ipomoea batatas.*

Sweet William, common name for a flowering plant of Europe and North America. A smooth plant that reaches about 1ft (30cm) in height, its flowers are pink or white with petals about 0.25in (0.6cm) long. Introduced as a garden plant, sweet william is now a wildflower along roadsides and in waste areas. Family Caryophyllaceae; species *Dianthus barbatus.*

Swellfish. *See* Puffer.

Sweyn I Forkbeard (c. 960–1014), king of Denmark (986–1014), son of Harald Bluetooth. His early attacks on England forced King Ethelred to pay tribute, but after his invasion in 1013 Ethelred fled to Normandy, and Sweyn became king. Sweyn died before the coronation, and his son Canute the Great eventually succeeded him.

Swift, Jonathan (1667–1745), Irish satirist and novelist. He became secretary to Sir William Temple (1689) and was ordained (1694), seeking benefits for Irish clergy. He wrote religious pamphlets and Tory propaganda (*The Examiner* 1710–11). His early works include *A Tale of a Tub* (1704), on religious and scholarly corruption and *The Battle of the Books* (1704), satirizing the controversy over ancient and modern learning. His *Gulliver's Travels* (1726) satirized courts and politicians. Swift had frequent contact with London literary circles until the late 1720s. He wrote numerous works criticizing Britain's treatment of Ireland, including *A Modest Proposal* (1729), which suggested that children be fattened and eaten. His later works were increasingly bitter. △1188.

Swift, any of a family (Apodidae) of fast-flying widely distributed birds. From 3.5 to 9 in (9–23cm) long, they generally have a short, sharply hooked bill, wide mouth, long narrow wings, short weak legs, and darkish plumage. They typically feed on insects that they can catch in flight, and build a nest of plant matter held together with saliva, in a chimney or under a ledge, for their one to six white eggs. Among well known species are the chimney swift; palm swift; common swift. *See also* Chimney Swift.

Swift and Company v. United States, 1905 Supreme Court decision. The court declared that the prosecution of the beef trust by the government was legal. The actual trust was dissolved but its basic structure remained, defying the ruling.

Swimming, recreational activity and competitive sport. Formal competition was first introduced in 1603 in Japan by an imperial edict which ordered interschool competition as an integral part of the curriculum. In 1837 in England, the National Swimming Association was formed, and in 1846 in Sydney, Australia, the first international swimming championships were held. Swimming was first included on a limited basis in the modern Olympic Games in Athens in 1896, and by 1908 the Fédération Internationale de Natation Amateur (FINA), the world governing body, was formed. Recognized distances for men and women include the 100, 200, 400, 800, and 1,500 meters freestyle, the 100 and 200 meters breaststroke, the 100 and 200 meters butterfly, the 100 and 200 meters backstroke, the 4 by 100 meters relay, the 4 by 200 meters relay (for men), the 200 and 400 meters individual medley, and the 4 by 100 meters relay medley.

Swinburne, Algernon Charles (1837–1909), English poet and critic. He became known with *Atalanta and Calydon* (1865), a verse drama, but the pagan and sensual tone of *Poems and Ballads* (1866) brought him widespread notoriety. Rich imagery and stylistic complexity characterize poems such as *The Garden of Proserpine* (1865), *The Triumph of Time* (1865), and *Tristram of Lyonesse* (1882). He was a friend of Rossetti and William Morris but spent the latter part of his life in seclusion. △1240.

Swing. *See* Jazz.

Swiss Chard, annual plant, related to the beet, grown for its spinachlike green or red leaves. The white or red leaf ribs and stems are often cooked separately. Family Chenopodiaceae; species *Beta vulgaris cicla.* △334.

Switzerland (Schweiz, Suisse, Svizzera), independent landlocked nation of W Europe. Noted for its scenery and manufacture of precision instruments, it has historically been a neutral nation.

Land and economy. The most mountainous country in Europe, it is located between West Germany (N), Italy (S), Austria and Lichtenstein (E), and France (W). It is the main watershed for Europe—the Rhine flows into the North Sea, the Inn leads into the Danube, the Rhône runs to the Mediterranean, and the Ticino is a tributary of the Po. Through the S part of the country is the Alpine range, covering 60% of the land. The Jura Mts, SW to NW, cover another 10%. The remaining 30% is lowlands. About 27% of Switzerland is cultivated, 25% is used for grazing, 24% is covered with forests, and the rest is mountains and glacie Dufour Peak, 15,217ft (4,638m) above sea level, the highest point. The country has a temperate mate, varying greatly with altitude. Its highly skill labor force is the backbone of a developed manufa turing economy that imports raw materials and ports finished products, especially watches and pre sion instruments. Tourism, international bankir and insurance comprise important segments of t economy.

People. With so many ethnic groups, the Sw constitution allows for three official languages French, Italian, and German—and four national la guages, the three official ones plus Romansch, relat to Latin and spoken in one canton (state). There a about 800,000 resident foreigners, including 20 of the labor force. With complete freedom of religic 47.8% is Protestant, 49.4% Roman Catholic. Prima education is free and compulsory. Literacy is almc 100%.

Government. A federal state of 22 cantons, legis tive power rests in the elected Federal Assembly (p liament). The constitution provides for initiative a referendum as the final authorities.

History. In 58 BC, Julius Caesar conquered a Cel people, the Helvetians, living in what is now Switz land, and made them part of the Roman Empire. the empire declined, Teutonic tribes from the N a W invaded and settled. Charlemagne and Germ emperors ruled from 800 until 1291, the date Swiss independence when the three forest canto united. They defeated the Austrians (1315) and esta lished a confederation to preserve independence. 1848 the 22 cantons were joined under a consti tion with federal responsibility for trade and defens Many controls were retained by each canton. Perm nent neutrality was internationally accepted, and t Swiss did not participate in WWI or WWII.

PROFILE:

Official name: Swiss Confederation
Area: 15,491sq mi (40,122sq km)
Population: 6,500,000
Density: 419.6per sq mi (162per sq km)
Chief cities: Bern (capital); Geneva; Basel; Zurich
Government: Federal republic
Religion: Protestant and Roman Catholic
Language: German, French, Italian (all official)
Monetary unit: Franc
Gross National Product: $38,800,000,000
Per capita income: $6,346
Industries: watches, precision instruments, che cals, cheese, chocolates, generators, turbines, h droelectric power
Agriculture: cattle, hogs, goats, sheep, hay, livesto feeds, forests
Minerals: salt, limestone, sandstone
Trading partners: European Economic Communi

Sword. △1726.

Swordfish, or broadbill, marine fish found worldwic in temperate and tropical seas. A popular food fish, is silvery-black, dark purple, or blue. Its flattene sword is one-third of its length and used to strike prey. Length: to 15ft (457.5cm); weight: 1,182 (532kg). Family Xiphiidae; species *Xiphias gladius.* 392.

Swordfish, The. *See* Dorado.

Sword of Orion. △104.

Swordtail, freshwater tropical fish found from S Me ico to Guatemala. This popular aquarium fish is ide tified by a long extension of its caudal fin. Young a born alive. Many varieties include red-eyed, red wa tail, and berlin swordtails. Length: to 5in (12.7cm Family Poecilidae; species *Xiphophorus helleri.*

Sycamore, or buttonwood, common names for species of shade tree related to the plane tree, nativ to the United States and grown best in the basin of th lower Ohio and Mississippi rivers. The related Arizor and California sycamores are smaller than the easte species. Introduced into England in the 17th centur the sycamore is also found in W and central Europ Family Platanaceae; species *Platanus occidentali See also* Plane Tree. △450.

Sydenham's Chorea. *See* Chorea.

Sydney, (Sir) Phillip. *See* Sidney, (Sir) Philip.

Sydney, capital city of New South Wales state, Au tralia, on Port Jackson, an inlet on the Pacific Ocea The largest city and center of finance, commerce, i dustry, culture, transportation, and communication Australia; noted for 19th-century buildings, and ob lisk (1819); seat of Roman Catholic and Anglican arc bishops, site of three universities, the National A

Gallery, and an important naval base; world's leading wool-selling market. Industries: automotive parts, textiles, food processing, building materials, chemicals. Founded 1788 as the first British penal colony in Australia. Pop. 2,799,634.

Syllogism, from the Greek *syllogismos* or "a reckoning all together." A construction of argument consisting of at least three propositions: two or more premises and a conclusion. The premises are related in such a way that the conclusion must be valid. △852.

Sylphide, La, two-act ballet choreographed by Felippo Taglioni. △1368.

Sylvester II, Roman Catholic pope (999–1003), b. Gerbert. The first French pope, he stressed learning and encouraged missionary work. He aided in the Christianization of Poland and Hungary and rid the church of simony and the clergy of concubinage.

Symbiosis, relationship between two kinds of organisms that is mutually advantageous. An ectosymbiont is an organism living on its host; an endosymbiont lives within its host. *See also* Mutualism; Parasitism.

Symbolic Logic, also known as modern or mathematical logic. Latest stage in the development of logic, using symbols to represent the forms of sentences expressing propositions. Arising in the 19th century, it is an extension of previous forms of logic. *See also* Logic.

Symbolism, loosely defined art movement in French painting and sculpture. It arose around 1885 as a reaction against the prevailing pragmatism of Gustave Courbet and the Impressionists and strove to give visual expression to spiritual concerns through color and form.

Symbolists, name given to a group of French poets active in the latter part of the 19th century of whom the most famous were Mallarmé, Verlaine, Corbière, Rimbaud, and Laforgue. Influenced by Baudelaire, they had no common technique but shared a desire to transcend reality as portrayed in the realistic novel and to create poetic impressions through suggestion rather than statement.

Symbols, Chemical. *See* Chemical Symbols.

Symmetry, anatomical description of body form or geometrical pattern of a plant or animal. It is used to help classify living things (taxonomy) and to clarify relationships. There are three types of symmetry: spherical, radial, and bilateral. Spherical, like a ball, as found in simple organisms; radial, like a coin, as in a starfish; and bilateral, two similar halves, as in man. △1468.

Symmetry Law, Nuclear, hypothesis that at subatomic levels time reversal would not affect events: there is virtually no distinction between past and future.

Sympathetic Nervous System. *See* Autonomic Nervous System.

Symphony, a work for symphony orchestra, usually having four parts or movements and taking the form of a sonata. The symphony was developed by the Classical composers Haydn and Mozart and reached a pinnacle in the Classical period with the nine symphonies of Beethoven. Significant later composers of symphonies were Schubert, Brahms, and Mahler and, in the 20th century, Vaughan Williams, Sibelius, and Shostakovitch.

Synagogue (Gr. "assembly"), a building constructed for Jewish worship, education, and cultural development. Synagogues serve as communal centers, led by a rabbi. They house the ark and are built facing Jerusalem. They may have developed during the Babylonian exile after 586 BC, and were brought to Israel with the return.

Synapse, space between the axon of one neuron and the receptive area of the next neuron. In a chain of neurons this gap is bridged by a special "transmitter substance," such as acetylcholine, which is produced by structures in the axon endings. *See also* Neuron. △664, 668.

Synchrocyclotron, modification of the cyclotron in which the frequency of the electric field is slowly changed as the particles spiral round the device. This counteracts the increase in particle mass at relativistic velocities and prevents the particles getting out of phase with the field, the radius of the path being proportional to velocity and mass. Energies can reach 700 MeV. *See also* Cyclotron.

Synchronous Orbit, Satellite, circular or near-circular orbit at such a height (22,300mi or 35,900km) that the satellite remains above a single point on the surface. It is used to reflect or actively broadcast television communications to large areas. Spaced correctly, only three synchronous satellites could cover the entire Earth with direct radio or television communications. The first synchronous satellite was Syncom 2 (July 26, 1963). △142.

Synchrotron, field accelerator in which a beam of electrons or protons is focused and guided around a fixed circular path by changing magnetic fields. Millions of revolutions are made. A high-frequency electric field at one point in the path accelerates the particles. Proton energies can reach hundreds of GeV, electron energies tens of GeV. △1484.

Syncline, a downward fold in rocks. The bending of rocks is referred to by geologists as folding. When rock layers fold down into a troughlike form, it is called a syncline. An upward arch-shaped fold is called an anticline. The sides of the fold are called limbs, and the median line between the limbs along or through the crest is known as the axis of the fold. *See also* Geosyncline. △250,252.

Syncope. *See* Fainting.

Syndicalism, theory of revolutionary action associated with French radical Georges Sorel. The syndicalists argued that bourgeois society can only be cured by coordinated violence known as the "myth of the general strike." Trade unions, or "syndicates," are the centers of revolution.

Synesthesia, the experiencing of sensation in one sense modality (eg, visual images) when the actual stimulus is in another modality (eg, sounds). People who report such experiences are called "synesthetes." The Russian composer Scriabin is reported to have experienced colors when he heard music. Thus, he experienced "chromesthesia," the most common form of synesthesia.

Synge, John Millington (1871–1909), Irish dramatist who joined W.B. Yeats and Lady Gregory in the Abbey Theatre. Synge, more dramatist than poet, portrayed peasants critically but with sympathy, in early one-acts *The Shadow of the Glen* (1903) and *Riders to the Sea* (1904) as well as in major dramas *The Well of the Saints* (1905) and *The Playboy of the Western World* (1907). He died leaving *Deirdre of the Sorrows* unfinished.

Synovial Fluid. △682.

Syntax, the phase of grammar dealing with the construction of sentences, clauses, or phrases. The study of syntax examines the effectiveness of the arrangement of words. It also examines how the meaning of a word changes if the words are rearranged. English is said to be a syntactical language. △864.

Syphilis, systemic disease caused by the spirochete *Treponema pallidum.* It is usually transmitted through sexual contact, but sometimes occurs congenitally. The first symptom is a small, hard swelling at the site of inoculation. In the second stage, there are skin lesions or rash. Tertiary symptoms may be incapacitating or fatal, affecting almost any part of the body. Other forms are endemic and non-venereal and include such diseases as yaws and pinta. Laboratory tests can detect syphilis in its earliest stage, when treatment with penicillin can achieve a complete cure. △728.

Syracuse (Siracusa), seaport city in Sicily, Italy, on Ionian Sea; capital of Syracuse province. Founded by Greek colonists 734 BC, it prospered and est. own colonies, triumphing over Carthaginians 480 BC; became a center of Greek culture; defeated Athens 5th century BC; taken by Romans 212 BC; conquered by Byzantines and made capital of Sicily AD 535; siteof 7th-century cathedral built on Greek temple remains, archeological museum, 13th-century castle. Industries: food processing, wine, tourism. Pop. 108,685.

Syracuse, city in central New York, at S end of Onondaga Lake; seat of Onondaga co. Salt springs were discovered here 1654 by Father Simon LeMoyne, French missionary; site of Syracuse University (1870), New York State Upstate Medical Center (1834), Maria Regina College (1934), Le Moyne College (1946), Onondaga Community College (1962), Everson Museum of Art (designed by I.M. Pei), and Lowe Art Center at Syracuse University. Industries: roller bearings, electrical equipment, candles, soda ash, caskets, air-conditioning equipment. Settled 1788; inc. as village

Sweet pea

Belgium
Ger. Dem. Rep.
Poland
Lux.
Federal
Republic of
Germany
Czechoslovakia
France
Basel
Zürich
SWITZERLAND
Berne
Liech.
Austria
Lausanne
Hungary
Genève
Italy
Yugoslavia
ADRIATIC
SEA
0
200 km

Switzerland

Sycamore

Sydney, Australia

1824, as city, including settlements of Salina and Lodi, 1847. Pop. (1970) 197,208.

Syr Darya (Syrdarja or Syr Dar'ya), shallow river flowing through the USSR, formed by the junction of the Naryn and Kara Darya rivers in the Fergana Valley of Uzbek SSR, flowing W past Leninabad in Tadzhik SSR, and N reentering Uzbek SSR at Begovat, into Kazakh SSR below Chinaz, past Chardara, forming the E and N limits of the Kyzyl-Kum desert between Kzyl-Orda and Kazalinsk, to the Aral Sea. It receives the Angren, Chirchik, and Arys rivers. Important for irrigation, it is unnavigable for all of its 1,370mi (2,206km).

Syria (As-Suriyah), independent nation in the Middle East. It is dominated politically by the socialist Baath administration, and its economy has been preoccupied with the continuous Arab-Israeli conflicts.

Land and economy. Situated in the Middle East with Turkey (N), the Mediterranean, Lebanon, and Israel (W), Jordan (S), and Iraq (E), Syria's dominant geographical features are the Anti-Lebanon and Alawite Mts along the coast from Israel to Turkey, the Euphrates River Valley crossing the country from N to SW, the S Jabal al-Druze mountains, and the desert plateau in the SE. Features of the coastline range from cliffs N of Latakia (seaport), to rugged areas between Tripoli and Beirut, to sandy shores near Tyre. The climate is mainly dry. Annual rainfall varies from 50in (127cm) in the mountains to 0.5in (1.3cm) in the desert. Years of drought, a lack of foreign investment, and heavy military expenditures have been drawbacks to the Syrian economy, which is primarily dependent on agriculture and stock-raising. With sufficient arable land for its people, about 65% of the population is dependent on the soil. Cotton is the largest export item, with cereal production second. The most developed industry is textiles. Petroleum reserves in the NE are being exploited.

People. Mostly of Arab stock, there are also minorities of Kurds, living in the N along the Turkish border, and Armenians, mostly urban dwellers. Probably the only indigenous people are the Alawis, a Muslim sect in the province of Latakia. Literacy is rated at 40%.

Government. A 1973 constitution provides for a 186-member People's Council, with most power in the hands of the president.

History. Located where three continents merge, Syria has been a strategic possession since about 2500 BC. Dominated by a series of rulers, it fell into Muslim hands in AD 636, was destroyed by the Mongols in 1400, and was under Turkish rule for 400 years after 1517. It was a French League of Nations mandate after WWI and declared itself a republic in 1941. Full independence came in 1944. For a short time (1958–61), Syria joined Egypt in the United Arab Republic. In 1963 the Socialist Baath party seized power, becoming the only legal party. In the 1967 Israeli-Arab War Syria lost the strategic Golan Heights overlooking Israel.

PROFILE

Official name: Syrian Arab Republic
Area: 71,498sq mi (185,180sq km)
Population: 7,300,000
Density: 102per sq mi (39.4per sq km)
Chief cities: Damascus (capital); Aleppo
Government: Socialist one-party system
Religion: Islam, Christian
Language: Arabic
Monetary unit: Syrian pound
Gross national product: $2,224,000,000
Per capita income: $345
Industries: textiles, flour milling, oil refining, cement, tobacco products, glassware, brassware, soap
Agriculture: cotton, barley, wheat, fruits, vegetables, sugar beets, sheep
Minerals: oil
Trading partners: USSR, People's Republic of China, Lebanon, France, Italy, Japan, United Kingdom

Syrian Desert (Badiyat ash-Sham), arid wasteland in SW Asia, along the E Mediterranean coast; extends N from Arabian Desert in Saudi Arabia, includes W Iraq, E Jordan, and SE Syria. The desert is crossed by oil pipelines and highway from Damascus to Baghdad; site of several oases including Palmyra; Arabian horses are raised on the outskirts of the desert; inhabited by numerous nomadic tribes.

Syrian War, campaigns of 192–189 BC waged between Antiochus III, Seleucid king, and Rome. In an effort to expand his kingdom Antiochus conquered Ptolemaic Syria and Palestine (202–198). Fighting in Thrace he alarmed Rome. He lost three major battles to the Romans (at Thermopylae, Magnesia, and Sipylum), ending Seleucid power in the Mediterranean with the peace of Apamea (188).

Syringa, genus of flowering deciduous shrubs and trees native to Europe and NE Asia.

Syrinx, vocal apparatus of birds located at base of the windpipe. It is well-developed in songbirds with cartilage, membranes, and muscle groups working in pairs, providing a separate voice on each side.

Syrtis Major. △68.

Syrup. △342.

Systems Engineering, application of such methods of analysis as operations research, cybernetics, and information theory to the solution of problems associated with large complex man-made systems in which there is considerable interaction between the component parts of the system. These solutions often involve the use of computers, feedback control systems, and servomechanisms. Originally developed during World War II for military applications, it has broadened into a variety of fields, including telephony, traffic control, and social administration.

Szasz, Thomas S(tephen) (1920–), US psychiatrist, b. Hungary. Concerned with the ethical, moral, and social aspects of treating the mentally disturbed, Szasz has stressed the patient's right to seek or not seek help and hospitalization in such books as *The Myth of Mental Illness* (1961), *Ideology and Insanity* (1970), and *The Manufacture of Madness* (1970).

Szczecin (Stettin), city in NW Poland, on Oder River near its mouth on the Stettiner Haff (bay); capital of Szczecin prov.; a major port and industrial city. Largest city of Pomerania in the 12th century, and a member of the Hanseatic League from 1360, it passed to Sweden 1648 by Peace of Westphalia, then to Prussia at close of Northern War (1720); was returned to Poland by Potsdam Conference 1945. City became an important modern port with the construction of a canal to Berlin (1914); site of technical university (1945) and agricultural college (1954). Industries: shipbuilding, iron works, chemicals, food processing, fishing. Pop. 337,200.

Szechwan (Sichuan), province in SW China; bounded by provs. of Tsinghai, Kansu, and Shensi (N), Hupeh and Hunan (E), Kweichow and Yunnan (S), Tibet (W); completely surrounded by mountains. Capital is Chengtu. Province served as temporary capital of Nationalist China during 2nd Sino-Japanese War (1937–45); seat of Szechwan University. Called the "rice bowl" of China, it is a leading rice producer. Crops: rice, sugar cane, potatoes, fruit, wheat, corn, sugar beets. Industries: forestry, textiles, livestock, salt, oil, natural gas; coal, iron, copper, lead, zinc, asbestos, mercury mining. Area: 220,000sq mi (569,800sq km). Pop. 70,000,000.

Szent-Györgyi von Nagyrapolt, Albert (1893–), US biochemist, b. Hungary. He was awarded the 1937 Nobel Prize in physiology or medicine for his work on biological combustion processes and the isolation of vitamin C. He also studied the biochemistry of muscle, discovering the muscle protein actin that is responsible for muscular contraction when combined with the muscle protein myosin.

Szilard, Leo (1898–1964), US physicist, b. Hungary. His early work established the relation between information transfer and entropy. He devised a means of separating isotopes of artificial radioactive elements; developed the chemostat; and proposed aging, recall, and memory theories. He was also involved in the creation of the first sustained nuclear chain reaction and in the initiation of work on the atom bomb. After WWII he devoted himself to the cause of banning nuclear warfare.

T

aa Matete (Gauguin). △1292.

abasco, state of SE Mexico, on the Gulf of Mexico; ɔunded by Guatemala (SE). First explored by Span- ı 1518, it was taken by Francisco de Montejo 1530; is predominantly a tropical forest plain, with numer- ɹs swamps, lagoons, and rivers; the Grijalva and sumacinta rivers are the main travel routes. Prod- ɪts: hardwood, bananas, cacao, pineapples, rubber, ıicle, fruits, oil. Area: 9,783sq mi (25,338sq km). ɔp. 766,346.

abernacle, the place of worship used by the Jews ɹring their wanderings in Sinai. It is also called Mish- ın, or the dwelling of God. It was a tent constructed ıder instructions from God, rectangular in shape and ɔvered with skins. In it the Ark of the Covenant was ɔntained and hidden by a veil.

abes Dorsalis, or locomotor ataxia, a form of ɘurosyphilis in which the dorsal columns of the spi- ıl cord degenerate, causing intense pain and lack of ıuscular coordination.

able Tennis, table game, also known as Ping Pong ʳademark), played by two or four persons. The table 9 feet (2.7m) long and 5 feet (1.5m) wide and 30 ıches (76.2cm) from the floor. The surface is divided ⁄ a transverse net 6 inches (15.2cm) high, and ılved longitudinally by a light stripe. A hollow, seam- ss, celluloid ball, about 1.5 inches (3.8cm) in diame- r, is hit with wooden paddles that measure, with the ındle, 9.5 inches (24.1cm) long. The surface of the ıddle is covered with either sandpaper or rubber. On e serve, the ball must bounce once before clearing e net on the near surface and then bounce once on e far surface before it is returned. After the serve, e ball may not take more than one bounce on either ırface. If the ball goes foul or fails to be returned ʳoperly, a point is scored. Each player in turn has five ɔnsecutive serves until 21 is reached (games tied at 0–20 continue until a two-point margin is achieved). doubles, the server must deliver the ball into the agonally opposite box. Table tennis, first popular in ıgland, is believed to have originated in the 19th ɘntury.

abloid. △1776.

aboo, or tabu, prohibition of a form of behavior, ɔject, word, etc. In many cultures a thing may be ɘgarded as taboo because it is either unclean or sa- ɘd—there is often a taboo on a totem. Breaking a boo is believed to bring supernatural retribution ıd often brings social ostracism or other punish- ent. The term is of Tongan origin. *See also* Totem.

abor (Tavor), Mount, mountain in N Israel, 5mi km) E of Nazareth; Biblical scene of Christ's transfi- ɹration. Height: 1,929ft (588m).

abriz, city in NW Iran, 38mi (61km) E of Lake Urmia; ıpital of East Azerbaijan prov. An ancient city, it ɘrved as the capital of Armenia under King Tiridates (AD 3rd century). Ghazan Khan developed it as the ief administrative center for his vast Asian empire 295); occupied by Ottomans 1514, 1585–1603, 724–30; held by Russians 1827–28; scene of revo- ɪtion 1946, led by Tudeh regime and supported by ɔviet Union; few historical buildings remain due to ɘvastating earthquakes (858, 1041, 1721); a long- me trade center due to its proximity to Turkey and ɔviet Union; site of university (1946). Industries: car- ɘts, textiles, leather, paint, shoes, soap. Pop. 420,- 00.

abula Rasa (Lat., "blank tablet"), a phrase fre- quently associated with John Locke's claim that prior to experience, the human mind is as empty of ideas as a tablet is of characters before it has been in- scribed. This meaning also suggests the notion that "Nothing is in the intellect which was not first in sense." In effect, there are no innate ideas.

Tachinid Fly, white to black fly, 0.25 to 0.5in (6.25–12.7mm) long, found worldwide. It is an important parasite of harmful insects, and several species have been imported into the United States to control insect pests. Family Tachinidae. *See also* Diptera.

Tachyon, hypothetical particle that travels faster than the speed of light. It might be detectable by the Cerenkov radiation it emits. To satisfy the special theory of relativity it would have to have either real rest mass and imaginary energy and momentum, or imaginary rest mass and real energy and momentum.

Tacitus, Cornelius (*c.* 55–*c.* 117), Roman historian. Often considered the greatest of the Roman historians, he was both an accurate observer of contemporary life and a uniquely effective stylist. His best known works are the *Agricola,* a eulogy on his father-in-law; the *Germania,* a description of the various German tribes; and the *Histories* and the *Annals,* which narrate imperial history from the death of Augustus (AD 14) through AD 96.

Tacitus, Marcus Claudius (200?–276), Roman emperor (275–76). As an elderly senator, he ruled as emperor for six months and then was killed by his own troops at Tyana. △1028.

Tacking, in sailing. △1678.

Tacoma, seaport and city in W Washington, on Commencement Bay and Puget Sound, 26mi (42km) S of Seattle; seat of Pierce co. The city is beautifully situated between water and the Olympic Mts (NW), and Mt Rainier (E) from which the city's Indian name is derived; the area's growth was spurred by the coming of the North Pacific Railway (1887); site of Tacoma Smelter, Point Defiance Park, Fort Nisqually (1833), Washington State Historical Museum, University of Puget Sound (1888), Pacific Lutheran University, Tacoma Community College; industrial and commercial center. Exports: wheat, flour, lumber. Industries: food and forest products, railroad shops, chemicals, explosives, paints, shipbuilding, copper smelting and refining, aluminum reduction. Settled 1852; inc. 1884. Pop. (1970) 154,581.

Taconite, a kind of chert that contains iron, resulting from replacement processes. It is used as an iron ore in some countries. *See* Chert.

Tactics, the maneuver of troops in combat. In the offense, military units are employed in frontal or flanking assaults against specific objectives, and are supported by automatic weapons, tanks, artillery, and aircraft. Forces with defensive missions usually fight from prepared or dug-in positions with mines, obstacles, artillery barrages, and direct fire positioned along the expected approach route of the enemy. Tactical deployments must consider all forces at the disposal of the commander as well as the terrain, weather, and the forces and dispositions of the enemy.

Tadpole, aquatic, fishlike frog or toad larva with finned tail and gills. It lacks lungs and legs. Unlike adults, most tadpoles are vegetarians, feeding on algae and other aquatic plants. During metamorphosis, limbs are grown, the tail is absorbed, and internal

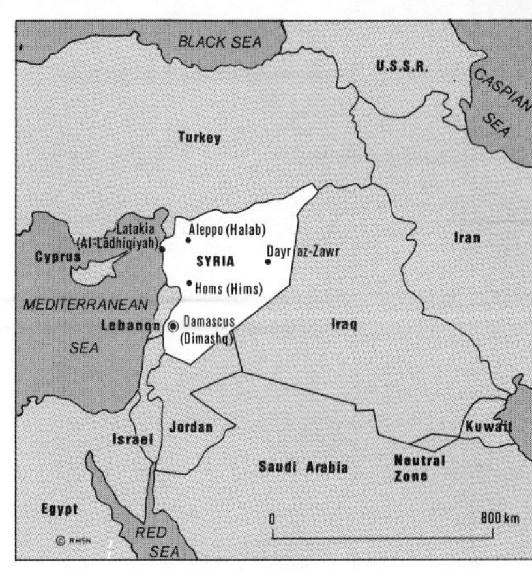
BLACK SEA
U.S.S.R.
CASPIAN SEA
Turkey
Latakia (Al-Lādhiqīyah)
Aleppo (Halab)
Cyprus
SYRIA
Dayr az-Zawr
Homs (Hims)
Iran
MEDITERRANEAN SEA
Lebanon
Damascus (Dimashq)
Iraq
Israel
Jordan
Kuwait
Saudi Arabia
Neutral Zone
Egypt
RED SEA
0
800km
Syria

Syringa

Table tennis

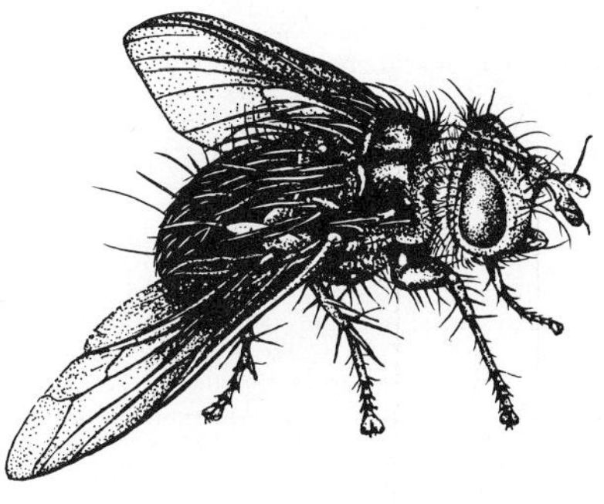
Tachinid fly

lungs take the place of gills. *See also* Frog; Toad. △518.

Tadzhik Soviet Socialist Republic (Tadzikskaja Sovetskaja Socialisticeskaja Respublik, or Tadzhikistan), constituent republic of the USSR, bounded N and W by the Uzbek and Kirghiz republics, S by Afghanistan, and E by China, including the Garno-Badachsanskaja autonomous oblast; contains the Pamir and Trans Abil mountain systems. Main cities are Dusanbe, Leninabad, Ura-T'ube. It was acquired as part of Russian Turkistan 1895; became part of Russian SFSR 1924 and a constituent republic 1929. Crops: cotton, rice, lucerne, fruits, grains, sesame, vegetables, nuts, sugar cane. Minerals: lead, zinc, silver, uranium, arsenic, antimony, bismuth, molybdenum, tungsten, feldspar, coal, petroleum, salt, gold. Exports: cotton, silk, dried fruit, lead-zinc ores. Area: 55,000sq mi (142,000sq km). Pop. 2,900,000.

Taegu, city in S central South Korea, 56mi (90km) NW of Pusan; capital of North Kyŏngsang since 1895 and 3rd-largest city in South Korea; successfully defended by UN troops against Communist invasions during Korean War (1950–53); textile and agricultural center. Pop. 1,082,750.

Taenia. *See* Tenia.

Taft, Alphonso (1810–91), US judge and political leader, b. Townshend, Vt. A superior court judge in Cincinnati (1865–72), he was called to Washington by Pres. Ulysses S. Grant in 1876 to be secretary of war. He served as attorney general (1876–77). He was US minister in Austria-Hungary (1882–84) and St Petersburg (1884–85). His descendants, who include Robert Taft, have been very active in political life.

Taft, Robert Alphonso (1889–1953), US political leader, b. Cincinnati, Ohio. Son of Pres. William Howard Taft, he served in the Ohio state legislature (1920–26, 1930–32) before becoming US senator (1938–53). An isolationist before World War II, he became an active backer of the United Nations after the war. He sponsored the Taft-Hartley Labor Act (1947), which placed some restrictions on organized labor. In 1952 he lost the Republican presidential nomination to Dwight D. Eisenhower.

Taft, William Howard (1857–1930), 27th president of the United States (1909–13) and 10th chief justice of the Supreme Court (1921–30), b. Cincinnati, Ohio. He graduated from Yale University (1878) and Cincinnati Law School (1880). In 1886 he married Helen Herron; they had three children.

A practicing lawyer in Cincinnati, Taft was active in Republican politics from an early age. He served as a state judge and in 1890 Pres. Benjamin Harrison named him solicitor general and later made him a federal judge. He was the first US governor of the Philippines and did much to improve US-Philippine relations.

In 1904, Pres. Theodore Roosevelt named Taft secretary of war. He became one of Roosevelt's closest advisors, and he was Roosevelt's handpicked candidate to succeed him. The Republicans nominated Taft in 1908, and he defeated the Democratic candidate, William Jennings Bryan. In some respects Taft continued Roosevelt's Progressive Republican policies. The antitrust laws continued to be enforced, and, in foreign affairs, Taft continued the activist, adventurous policies of his predecessor. His administration became increasingly more conservative, however, and Taft's relationship with Roosevelt deteriorated. By 1912, Roosevelt was in active opposition and tried to win the Republican nomination away from Taft. After Taft won, Roosevelt ran on his own Progressive, or Bull Moose, ticket. He polled more votes than Taft but the election went to Democrat Woodrow Wilson.

Taft taught law after leaving the White House, and in 1921 President Harding named him chief justice of the United States. While chief justice, he greatly streamlined the operations of the federal judiciary.

Career: US solicitor general, 1890–92; federal circuit judge, 1892–1900; governor of the Philippines, 1900–04; secretary of war, 1904–09; president, 1909–13; chief justice, 1921–30.

Taft-Hartley Act (1947), US labor legislation, also known as the Labor-Management Relations Act. It outlawed the closed shop, a system of hiring only union members; required unions to reveal their financial status; limited union political activity; required union leaders to sign a non-Communist affidavit; and authorized the government to issue 80-day strike injunctions. Other provisions allowed employers to sue unions and established the Federal Mediation and Conciliation Service. It was amended in 1951 to allow union-shop contracts without first polling employees.

Tagalog, the national language of the Philippines. In 1962 it was made the country's official language and given the new name of Pilipino. It is the mother tongue of about 10,000,000 people, living mainly in southern Luzon, but it is estimated that about 20,000,000 more at least understand the language. Tagalog belongs to the Austronesian family of languages.

Taglioni, Filippo (1777–1871), Italian dancer and choreographer. △1368.

Tagore, Rabindranath (1861–1941), Indian poet, philosopher, and social theorist. He received the Nobel Prize for literature in 1913. Written in Bengali, his works reflect his myriad interests. He is most famous in the West for his book of religious verse called *Gitanjali* (1912), but in his own country his poems on love and nature are also popular. He founded an experimental village and a school which eliminated the usual restrictions. He was a dramatist, novelist, painter, and musician as well. △1376.

Tagus (Tajo or Tejo), river in Spain and Portugal; rises in E central Spain; flows to the Atlantic Ocean at Lisbon. The longest river on the Iberian Peninsula, it forms part of Spanish-Portuguese border; above Lisbon the river widens to form a lagoon approx. 7mi (11km) wide; navigable for approx. 100mi (161km). Length: 626mi (1,008km).

Tahiti, island in S Pacific Ocean, in Windward Island group of the Society Islands, French Polynesia. Largest of the French Polynesian islands, Tahiti has long been regarded as an idyllic island paradise. It was discovered by English navigator Samuel Wallis and explored by Capt. James Cook on several visits 1769–77; missionaries were est. in late 18th century; colonized by France 1880; the French painter Paul Gauguin did many of his works here. Tahiti is mountainous and fertile, producing tropical fruits, copra, sugar cane, and vanilla; pearl fishing is an important industry. Majority of inhabitants are Polynesians, and most settlements are situated along the coast. Capital is Papeete. Area: 402sq mi (1,041sq km). Pop. 61,519.

Tahoe, Lake, lake on the N central California-W Nevada border, in the Eldorado National Forest and N Sierra Nevada Mts; drained by the Truckee River. A noted resort and tourist area, it has been cited as one of the most beautiful lakes in the world. Discovered 1844 by John C. Frémont. Area: 193sq mi (500sq km). Max. depth: 1,645ft (504m).

Tahr, gregarious, goatlike ruminant found in the Himalayas, S India, and SE Arabia. Unlike goats, the male is beardless with short horns. Long fur varies from light to dark brown. Length: to 3.5ft (1.1m); weight: to 200lb (90kg). Family Bovidae; genus *Hemitragus*. *See also* Ruminant.

Tai, people of Chinese origins, who inhabit the mainland of Southeast Asia, and who consist of several Tai-speaking groups: the Siamese, Lao, Shan, Lü, Yunnan Tai, and tribal Tai. An agricultural people whose major crop is rice, they practice Theravâda Buddhism, although some animism remains.

Tai Chin (1390–1460), Chinese landscape painter. An important member of the regional Che School, he was known for his precisely rendered subjects and his spontaneous brushwork. He painted the "Fishermen" scroll in the Freer Gallery, Washington, D.C. △1208.

T'ai-chung, or Taichung, city in W central Taiwan; site of Chinese National Palace Museum and Chinese National Central Museum. Industries: agriculture, textiles, food processing, chemicals. Pop. 456,719.

Taiga, a Russian word for the vast, cold, swampy, coniferous-forest region of Siberia; the part that lies between the tundra and the steppe. The term is applied to similar areas in Europe and America.

Taika Reforms. △1046.

Tai Languages, group of languages spoken in Southeast Asia. It includes Thai, of Thailand, Lao, of Laos, Shan, of Burma, plus a number of languages in S China such as Chuang, Puyi (Chungchia), and Tung. Some scholars place the Tai languages in the Sino-Tibetan family, which includes Chinese, but this is disputed by other scholars.

Tailorbird, tropical Asian and African warbler that stitches leaves together, forming a pocket for its nest. Brown spotted eggs (2–6) are laid. Insect-eaters, most species are dull-colored. Length: 5in (12.5cm). Genus *Orthotomus*.

Taimyr Peninsula (Taymyr, Taimir, or Tajmyr), large peninsula in central USSR, on the Kara and Laptev seas, between the Jenisej and Chatanga rive mouths, crossed in the central part by the Taimy River; site of Cape Cel'uskin, Asia's northernmos point, containing the Byrranga Mts and Lake Taimy Length: 700mi (1,127km).

Tainan (T'ainan), city in W central Taiwan, on th Taiwan Strait. Oldest city in Taiwan; held by Dutc 1624–62; served as capital of Taiwan prov. unde Koxinga until the 1885 transfer of government to Ta pei; site of university (1956), temples, shrine of Ko inga. Industries: textiles, aluminum, rubber, plastic iron and steel products, food processing. Settle 1590. Pop. 479,353.

Taine, Hippolyte Adolphe (1828–93), French his torian. His most important philosophical work, *Of Ir telligence* (1870), was deterministic in its outlook. H later turned to the philosophy of history with *Origin of Contemporary France* (1871–94). His influence i still evident in France. He was elected to the Acadé mie Française (1878).

Taipei (T'aipei), capital city of Nationalist China, at end of Taiwan, major trade center for tea in 19t century; in 1885 it replaced T'ainan as the capital c Taiwan prov.; prospered under Japanese rule 1895 1945; became seat of Chinese Nationalist goverr ment 1949; site of National Taiwan University (1928 Industries: wood, paper products, chemicals, fertili ers, food products, machinery, electrical equipmen brewing, printing, railroad shops. Founded 170 Pop. 1,742,626.

Taiping Rebellion (1850–64), an anti-Manchu re volt led by a Hakka fanatic, Hung Hsiu-ch'üan, wh imagined himself to be the son of God and younge brother of Jesus Christ. The fighting laid waste 1 provinces of China and resulted in more than 20 000,000 casualties. The Manchus never recovere their control or ability to govern China with the forme authority. Chinese scholar-statesmen, includin Tseng Kuo-fan and Tso Tsung-t'ang, aided the Mar chus in suppressing the rebels. △1270.

Taira. △1046.

Taishâ. △1272.

T'ai Tsung. △1042.

Taiwan (Formosa), island province of China, 100m (161km) off SE China mainland in the Pacific Ocear seat of the Chinese Nationalist government; provinc includes main island of Taiwan, several islets, and Pe cadores island group; capital is Taipei. The terrain mostly mountainous; climate is semitropical and sub ject to typhoons. Immigration from mainland Chin began 7th century; Portuguese visited the islan 1509 and named it Formosa (beautiful). It was occu pied by Dutch 1624 and seized by Ming dynas 1662; taken by Manchus 1683; made a province c China 1886. It was ceded to Japan 1895 after firs Sino-Japanese War; returned to China 1943 an made seat of government 1949. Area: 13,807sq m (35,760sq km). Pop. 14,810,929. *See also* China Republic of.

Taiyüan (Taiyuan or T'ai-yüan), city in NE China 265mi (427km) SW of Peking, on Fen River; capita of Shansi prov. under Communist control after lon battle in which thousands starved (1948–49); one c richest coal and iron areas in the world; seat of Shan University. Industries: mining, smelting, iron and stee foundries, chemicals, plastics, food processing. Por 2,725,000.

Ta'izz, city in S Yemen, 32mi (52km) E of Mocha served as administrative capital of Yemen (1948–62 marketing center. Pop. 48,000.

Taj Mahal, a Muslim mausoleum, built 1630–48 i Agra, India, by the Mogul emperor Shah Jahan afte the death of his favorite wife. △810.

Takahe. △538.

Talc, a sheet silicate mineral, hydrous magnesiur silicate $[Mg_3Si_4O_{10}(OH)_2]$. Monoclinic system; rare tab ular crystals and as masses. White, green, blue brown. Hardness 1; sp gr 2.6. Used as base for talcur powder and in ceramics.

Tale of Genji, The, Japanese novel combinin fiction and history, relating the amorous adventures c Prince Genji in Japan's feudal court and perceptivel depicts court life. It was written *c.* 1010 by Lad Murasaki Shikibu (*c.* 970–early or mid-11th century The first significant novel written anywhere, it is rate the greatest work of the Heian period (794–1192) an possibly in all Japanese literature. The long, windin arrative is over 1,000 pages in the English transla- on, expertly done by Arthur Waley (6 vols., 1925– 3; 1 vol., 1935). △1048.

allahassee, capital city of Florida, in NW Florida, 60mi (258km) W of Jacksonville; seat of Leon co. It as inhabited by Seminole Indians, settlers from ther southern states, and Spanish missionaries when allahassee was made capital of Florida Territory 824); made state capital 1845; scene of adoption of ecessionist ordinance (1861); 20th-century cultural nd administrative center. It is site of Goodwood 843) and Grove (1830) antebellum houses, Florida tate University (1857). Industries: lumber and lum- er products, food processing, tourism, truck farming. c. 1825. Pop. (1970) 72,586.

allahatchie River, river in Mississippi, rises in NE liss., flows generally S to the Yalobusha River, near reenwood, forming the Yazoo River; its waters, im- ounded by Sardis Dam, form Sardis Lake. Length: 01mi (485km).

allapoosa River, river in NW Georgia and E Ala- ama; rises in NW Ga.; flows SW across Ala. border, en S and W to join Coosa River near Montgomery, a., forming Alabama River. Length: 268mi (431km).

alleyrand-Périgord, Charles Maurice de (1754– 838), French political figure and diplomat. Although member of the Second Estate (the church), he suc- essfully proposed confiscation of church property. In ondon (1791–93) he tried to keep Britain from join- g Austria, Russia, and Prussia in war against the rench revolutionary government. Failing, he re- rned to France after the fall of Maximilien Robes- erre (1794) and was grudgingly admitted to the Di- ectory. He supported Napoleon and was foreign inister (1797–1807), but the two fell out over Napo- on's grandiose European ambitions, and Talleyrand as prominent in the restoration of the Bourbons 814). At the Congress of Vienna (1814–15) he howed superb diplomatic skill, exploiting tensions mong the victors to the benefit of France. His unerr- g political sense led him to support Louis Philippe, hom he served as minister to Britain (1830–34).

allinn (Talin), city and capital of Estonian SSR, SSR, on the Gulf of Finland opposite Helsinki, 00mi (322km) W of Leningrad. It was founded 1219 y Danes on the site of an Estonian settlement; joined anseatic League 1285; sold to Teutonic Knights 346; passed to Sweden 1561; occupied by Russia 710; ceded to Russia by Sweden 1721; developed ommercially in the 19th century; occupied and dam- ged by Germans 1941–44; site of polytechnical and eachers' colleges, conservatory, schools of drama nd applied arts, Danish Toompea castle, 13th-cen- ry episcopal church, 16th-century watch tower, 3th-century Gothic church of St Olai, Hanseatic Black Heads" house. Industries: shipbuilding, cot- n, textiles, plastics, glass, pulp and paper, plywood, rniture, flour, tobacco products. Exports: textiles, aper, timber. Pop. 363,000.

allow Tree, evergreen tree, native to SE China, rown for shade and ornament in the United States. has heart-shaped leaves that turn yellow to red in utumn. The capsule-contained seeds yield a tallow- ke material used in soap and candle making. Height: 40ft (12m). Family Euphorbiaceae; species *Sapium ebiferum.*

almud, 63 books of writings of ancient rabbis, hich were developed in the 5th century AD. They are oncerned with the whole of Jewish life and use para- es and legends. Mishnah, the oral tradition, was re- orded and forms part of the Talmud. The interpreta- on of Mishnah, called Gemara, is included as well. he Talmud includes codes of law as well as legend- y accounts of the Jewish people. The study of the almud is central to Jewish faith. *See also* Mishna.

alon, Jean Baptiste (1625–94), French colonial ader in Canada, first intendant of New France 665–68, 1670–72). Sent to Canada by Jean Col- ert, Talon created the seignorial land system, en- ouraged immigration, established industry, and held e first census in Canada. A tireless, efficient adminis- ator, he developed the political and economic struc- re of French Canada.

alus, the heap of rock waste lying at the bottom of cliff. It is made up of particles, ranging in size from and grains to boulders, that have been loosened om the cliff rock by mechanical weathering. The ac- umulated material is called sliderock and as it contin- es to move within the talus; the movement is known s talus creep.

amarisk, family *(Tamaricacae)* of shrubs and small trees found in temperate to subtropical regions. Deciduous, they have slender branches covered with scalelike leaves and feathery clusters of small, white or pink flowers. Foliage is blue-gray. Height: to 30ft (9.1m).

Tamaulipas, state in NE Mexico. First explored by Spanish 1519, its colonization began 1747; became independent 1824. Region is mountainous with plains and coastal strip; climate is predominantly hot and humid; site of several 18th-century Franciscan missions. Products: petroleum, cotton, sugar cane, corn, citrus fruits, livestock. Industries: chemicals, soap, petroleum by-products, vegetable oil, flour, hides, tourism. Area: 30,734sq mi (79,601sq km). Pop. 1,438,350.

Tambourine. △1244.

Tamerlane, or **Timur** (1336–1405), Oriental conqueror. Descended from Genghis Khan, he controlled a vast empire that extended from the Black Sea to the Indus River and from the Persian Gulf to the Syr Darya River. He made Samarkand, which he took in 1361, his center and personal domain. By defeating the Golden Horde under Toktamysh, Tamerlane inadvertently helped to consolidate Russia. His atrocities have become legendary, and he is the subject of Christopher Marlowe's play *Tamburlaine.* △1108, 1112.

Tamil, language spoken in S India, chiefly in the state of Tamil Nadu on the E coast, by about 40,000,000 people. There are also about 4,000,000 speakers in NE Sri Lanka, about 1,000,000 in Malaysia, and smaller colonies in Singapore, Fiji, Mauritius, and Guyana. Tamil belongs to the Dravidian family of languages.

Taming of the Shrew, The (*c.*1594), 5-act comedy by William Shakespeare. Some sources believe it was based on an anonymous play *The Taming of A Shrew* (1594), although the latter may be simply a pirated version of Shakespeare's work. The main plot concerns the successful efforts of Petrucchio to subdue his fractious wife Katharina. A subplot deals with the courtship of Katharina's sister Bianca by Lucentio. The play has been produced worldwide and provided the basis for the Broadway musical *Kiss Me Kate* (1948). It was filmed in 1908, 1929, and 1967, and *Kiss Me Kate* was made into a film in 1953.

Tampa, port city, W Florida, seat of Hillsborough co, 81mi (130km) SW of Orlando. Developed as major cigar-making center; fishing resort; processing center for citrus and vegetables. Industries: beer, fertilizers, chemicals. Settled as Fort Brooke, 1824; inc. 1855. Pop. (1970) 277,767.

Tampere, city in SW Finland, on Lake Näsijärvi; Finland's 2nd-largest city. In 1918, White Guards of Finland defeated Finnish Bolsheviks (Red Guards) here; site of technological institute (1965), university (1966), and an open-air theater; textile center of N Europe. Industries: footwear, paper, textiles, machinery. Chartered 1775. Pop. 157,697.

Tampico, seaport city in E Mexico, approx. 6mi (10km) from the Gulf of Mexico, on the Panuco River; former site of the Huastec kingdom, which later evolved into the Aztec Empire; settled by Spanish 1532. Oil was discovered *c.* 1900 by US and British geologists; site of episcopal see, state university. Exports: livestock, hides, oil, agricultural products, copper ore. Industries: machinery, lumber, fishing, tourism. Pop. 196,147.

Tanager, small, brightly colored American forest bird that has a downward-curved, cone-shaped bill and short rounded wings. They feed on insects and fruit and build cup- or dome-shaped nests for their eggs (1–5). The male scarlet tanager *(Piranga olivacea)* of E North America has black on its wings and tail; the female is greenish above and yellowish below. Family Thraupidae.

Tananarive (Madag), capital city of Malagasy Republic, on Madagascar Island; became royal residence 1797 for Merina rulers; it was taken by French 1895 and became part of French protectorate; site of University of Madagascar, Collège Rural d'Ambatobe, astronomical observatory. Industries: rice, food processing, textiles, tobacco, leather goods. Pop. 343,670.

Tancred (died 1194), last Norman king (1190–94) of Sicily. Illegitimate son of Duke Roger of Apulia and grandson of King Roger II of Sicily, he had to fight Emperor Henry VI of Germany (married to Roger of Apulia's sister) for the throne. Although Tancred successfully defended his claim, upon his death Henry deposed Tancred's infant heir, William III, and took Naples.

William Howard Taft

Philippines
PACIFIC OCEAN
Australia
TAHITI
South America
New Zealand
0
4000km

Tahiti

Taj Mahal

Charles Maurice de Talleyrand-Périgord

Tancred (1078?–1112), Norman prince. He was one of the leaders of the First Crusade to the Holy Land, participated in the siege of Nicaea and in the battle of Dorylaeum (1097), and helped capture Jerusalem (1099). When Godfrey of Bouillon became king of Jerusalem, he was made prince of Galilee. He drove the Saracens from Syria.

Taney, Roger Brooke (1777–1864), chief justice of the US Supreme Court (1836–64), b. Calvert City, Md. As attorney general (1831), he aided President Jackson in a struggle with the Bank of the United States, advising him in a veto over the recharter of the bank. As secretary of the treasury (1833), he withdrew US funds from the bank, causing a Senate outrage and its refusal to confirm his appointment. He was appointed associate justice (1835) but was never confirmed by the Senate. The next year a Senate Democratic majority confirmed his appointment by President Jackson as chief justice, succeeding John Marshall. A "states' rightist," he nonetheless extended the scope and power of the Supreme Court. He was associated with *Dred Scott* v. *Sanford* (1857), which refused blacks the right of citizenship and gave Congress power to control slavery in the territories. The decision heightened tensions between North and South.

Tanganyika, Lake, navigable lake in E central Africa, between W Tanzania and E Zaire. Area: 12,700sq mi (32,893sq km); depth: 4,710ft (1,437m).

T'ang Chinese, or **T'ang Jen,** people inhabiting the S Chinese provinces of Kwangtung and Kwangsi. Ethnically indistinguishable from the Han Chinese, but speaking a number of different dialects, the T'ang represent refugees from the 12th- and 13th-century Tatar and Mongol invasions in the north.

T'ang Dynasty (618–907), Chinese dynasty that ruled during imperial China's most vigorous and creative age. The capital Ch'ang-an (modern Sian) was a cosmopolitan center of world trade and relations, and Chinese political and cultural institutions were at their height. This was the golden age of Chinese poetry, the period when China had its greatest impact on Korea and Japan, and the age when the civil service examination system came into full vigor. The dynasty was interrupted briefly by the revolt of the tribal military leader An Lu-shan, but recovered and gave renewed thrust to Chinese tradition and institutions. △1042.

Tangaroa. △834.

Tangelo, orange, edible citrus fruit that is a grapefruit-tangerine hybrid. The thick-skinned fruit is grown commercially in SW United States. Family Rutaceae.

Tangent, ratio of the length of the side opposite an acute angle to the length of the side adjacent to the angle in a right-angled triangle. The tangent of angle A is usually abbreviated to "tan A." *See also* Trigonometric Functions. △1464.

Tangerine, or mandarin orange, small, edible citrus fruit native to China. It has a thin skin and easily separated segments. Family Rutaceae; species *Citrus reticulata.*

Tangier (Tanger), seaport in N Morocco, on the Strait of Gibraltar. An ancient Roman port, it was later occupied by Moors; taken by Portuguese 1471; received by England 1662 as part of dowry in marriage of Catherine of Braganza to Charles II; abandoned to Moors 1684. City was est. as an International Zone 1924–56, providing a neutralized seaport which developed into a base for European smuggling; became part of independent Morocco 1956; site of casbah and the old Moorish walled city. Industries: rugs, pottery, shipping, tourism. Pop. 141,714.

T'ang-shan, or **Tangshan,** city in NE China, 100mi (161km) SE of Peking. Much of city was destroyed in an earthquake July 1976. Industries: coal mining, iron, steel, chemicals, petroleum products, textiles. Pop. 1,200,000.

Tanit. △978.

Tank, tracked armored vehicle mounting a single primary weapon, usually a gun, and one or more machine guns. Modern tanks all have an enclosed fully-revolving turret and are heavily armored; main battle tanks presently weigh from 35 to 50 tons and have a crew of 4. Developed in great secrecy by the British during World War I, they were first employed at the Battle of the Somme in 1916. It was not until the Germans concentrated their tanks into armored divisions during early World War II that the tank came into its own as a major weapon system. △1736.

Tanker, a ship that carries bulk liquids, usually petroleum products, as cargo. The crude oil or gasoline is piped into the cargo spaces and transported. No containers are used and the largest tankers (super tankers), more than 1,000 ft (305m) long, can carry 300,000 tons. Propelling machinery is located in the stern with the poop above it; a forecastle and a house are amidships. △1680.

Tannaim, scholars and teachers of the Jewish Oral Law who flourished from AD 10 to 220. Hillel, a *tanna* (scholar), began to spread the Midrash (a homiletical interpretation of the Jewish scriptures) of the Talmud, and Judah I (the last *tanna*) organized and preserved it. Other important teachers were Johanan ben Zaccai, who established the academy at Jamnia, and Akiba ben Joseph, who systematically compiled the Oral Laws and sided with Bar Kokba against Rome.

Tannenberg, Battle of. △1306.

Tanning, process of converting skins and hides into leather. Traditionally, tanning liquids are based on tannin and the process takes one month or more. It is still used for heavy leathers. Light leathers are now tanned in a few hours using chromium salts. *See also* Leather.

Tansy, any of several mostly perennial plants characterized by fernlike aromatic leaves and clusters of yellow, buttonlike flower heads. The poisonous *Tanacetum vulgare,* native to Eurasia, is a common weed in North America; height: to 3ft (91cm). Family Compositae.

Tanta, city in N Egypt, 51mi (82km) N of Cairo on Nile River delta; capital of Gharbiyah governorate; site of three annual festivals for Muslim leader, Ahmad al-Badawi, whose grave is in Tanta. Industries: cotton ginning, shipping. Pop. 253,600.

Tantalum, metallic element (symbol Ta) of the third transition series, first isolated in 1903. Chief ore is columbite-tantalite. It is used in steels and other special alloys. Properties: at. no. 73; at. wt. 180.948; sp gr 16.654; melt. pt. 5,425°F (2,996°C); boil. pt. 9,795°F (5,425°C); most common isotope Ta^{181} (99.988%). *See also* Transition Elements. △1552.

Tanzania, independent nation in E Africa, uniting the formerly separate nations of Tanganyika and Zanzibar. It contains the earliest fossil evidence of mankind. It came under Arab, British, and German domination before independence in 1961.

Land and economy. Tanzania includes Tanganyika and the islands of Zanzibar and Pemba; the mainland is in E Africa, bordering the Indian Ocean. Its neighbors are Kenya and Uganda (N), Rwanda, Burundi, and Zaire (W), Zambia, Malawi, and Mozambique (S). The land is divided into four main regions: the hot coastal plains, the hot, dry central plateau, the moist lake sections, and the temperate highlands. Mt Kilimanjaro, 19,340ft (5,899m) above sea level, is the highest point in Africa. Development has been hampered by a lack of water and the tsetse fly. About 65% of the population lives on the arable land, 10% of the total. Cotton, coffee, and sisal represent 40% of all exports; diamonds are the 4th-largest export.

People. In a population 90% rural, density differs widely, from 3per sq mi (1.2per sq km) in arid regions to 347per sq mi (134per sq km) on Zanzibar. Africans are divided into some 130 ethnic groups, each with its own language. The majority is of Bantu origin. On Zanzibar, Shirazis trace their ancestry back to Persian settlers. Literacy is 15%–20%. Non-Africans constitute 1% of the population.

Government. A single party state, Tanzania operates under an elected president and unicameral National Assembly.

History. Before migrating Bantus replaced the indigenous Bushmen and Hottentots, fossils suggest that E Africa may have been the cradle of mankind. Arabs established trading centers in the 8th century and, with the exception of a Portuguese period in 1506, they remained in control until the British took power in the mid-19th century. Britain was followed by German colonials who brought roads, repression of the natives, and consequent rebellion. German rule ended after WWI. It became a UN trust territory under Britain after WWII. In 1954, Julius K. Nyerere organized the Tanganyika African National Union. Full independence as a republic under the Commonwealth came in 1961; Nyerere was elected president. On April 26, 1964, Zanzibar and Tanganyika united as Tanzania.

PROFILE

Official name: United Republic of Tanzania
Area: 364,882sq mi (945,087sq km)
Population: 14,377,000
Density: 42per sq mi (16per sq km)
Chief cities: Dar es Salaam (capital); Arusha
Government: Single party state with elected pres dent and National Assembly
Religion: Islam (30%), Christian (30%)
Language: Swahili and English (both official)
Monetary unit: Tanzanian shilling
Gross national product: $1,583,000,000
Per capita income: $127
Industries: food processing, clothing, textiles, ce ment, petroleum products, sugar refining, tanning aluminum
Agriculture: cloves, sisal, cotton, coffee, tea, to bacco, cattle
Minerals: diamonds, gold, salt, tin, mica
Trading partners: United Kingdom, European Eco nomic Community, China, Japan, India

Tao-chi (Shis-tao) (1630–*c.*1717), Chinese painte An influential poet, painter, and calligrapher, he wa known for his individuality. He often painted lan scapes in a bold and free style. He became a Buddhis monk. △1208.

T'ao Ch'ien (*c.* 365–427), Chinese poet. He is cor sidered China's greatest poet during the period c political division from AD 221–589. He left a minc official post as a protest against corruption and barel eked out a farming existence with his family. H verse, which has a predominantly Taoist outlook, frequently about nature and wine. His simple sty differed from the ornateness of his contemporaries, s he did not earn full recognition until the 8th centur

Taoism, Chinese philosophy and religion considere next to Confucianism in importance. Taoist philoso phy is traced to a 6th-century BC classic of Lao-tzu, th *Tao tê Ching.* The recurrent theme is the Tao, or path To follow the Tao is to follow the path of the cosmc leading to self-realization. Taoist ethics emphasize pa tience, simplicity, and nature's harmony. As a religior Taoism dates from the time of Chang Tao-ling, wh organized a group of followers in AD 143. It was a stat religion in China for a time, but in modern times mem bership has dwindled. △1040.

Taos, northernmost of the Río Grande Pueblo Ind ans, inhabiting a village erected on both sides of th Taos River in Taos co, N.M., around AD 1700. A though they speak a Tanoan language, their locatio gave them extensive contact with the Plains Indian and greatly influenced their culture. Today about 1 500 people inhabit the village.

Tape Recorder, a device used to record sound o magnetically treated tape and, usually, to play it back Sound is transformed to electric current, and fed to transducer, which converts it into the magnetic varia tions that magnetize the particles on the treated tape △1798.

Tapestry, fabric woven by hand of plain weave wit out shuttle or drawboy, the design being threade into the warp with a bobbin or by hand. The term nov includes many heavy materials that are not true tapes tries, as well as imitation tapestries woven on Jaquar looms. Tapestry design is an ancient art; a few surviv today from 1500 BC Egypt. Brussels was the leadin tapestry center from the 14th to 17th centuries, whe Paris took the lead. Tapestry design has generall followed parallel movements and styles in art. Impo tant tapestry collections in the United States ar found in the Metropolitan Museum in New York an in the Museum of Fine Arts, Boston. △344, 1106.

Tapeworm, parasitic flatworm found in alimentar tract of vertebrate hosts. It has a tiny head, or scolex with hooks and suckers and a long body of segments or proglottids, each having its own reproductive sys tem. Intermediate hosts include cattle, fish, and pigs Infection occurs when improperly cooked, infecte meat is eaten. Length: to 90ft (27m). Phylum Platy helminthes; class Cestoda; species include do *Dipylidium caninum,* pork *Taenia solium,* beef *Taeni saginata.* △472, 710.

Tapies, Antoni (1923–), Spanish painter. △1372

Tapioca. *See* Cassava.

Tapir, nocturnal, plant-eating, hoofed mammal na tive to forests of tropical America, Sumatra, and Ma laya. They have big heads, long, flexible snouts, heav bodies, short legs, and tiny tails. Adult Malayan tapir have a striking half-white, half-black coat; New Worl species are dark brown. Length: 7ft (2.1m); weigh 400lb (180kg). Family Tapiridae.

Tarabulus. *See* Tripoli.

Taranto, city in S Italy, 50mi (81km) SSE of Bari, on Gulf of Taranto. Founded 8th century BC, it was a leading city of Magna Graecia; part of Rome 272 BC; destroyed by Arabs AD 972; Italian fleet was damaged here during harbor bombing WWII; site of national museum, 11th-century cathedral. Industries: agriculture, fishing, steel, chemicals, shipyards. Pop. 216,-565.

Tarantula, large, hairy spider of the Western Hemisphere with a mildly poisonous bite. Its legs grow longer than the body. Body length: to 3.5in (90mm). Family Theraphosidae. *See also* Spider.

Tarascans, Indian group located in Michoacán, Mexico. The Tarascans, who developed a powerful state by 1440, remained neutral during the Spanish conquest of the rival Aztec empire. The Tarascans and the Spanish maintained relatively good relations throughout the colonial period. Lázaro Cárdenas, a former governor of Michoacán, revitalized Tarascan culture during his presidency (1934–40).

Tarawa, atoll in W Pacific Ocean; capital of Gilbert and Ellice Islands, located in N part of the group; trade center for the islands; site of hospital; scene of fierce four-day battle, November 1943, during which the United States freed islands from Japanese occupation. Exports: copra, phosphate rock. Pop. 12,642.

Tarbell, Ida (1857–1944), US journalist, b. Hatch Hollow, Pa. She joined the editorial staff of *McClure's Magazine* in 1894 and wrote a series of articles exposing the oil trust. Her investigations were later published as *A History of the Standard Oil Company* (1904). After resigning from *McClure's,* she joined (1906–15) the staff of *American Magazine.*

Tarbosaurus. △570.

Tariff, tax placed on imports either as a percentage of the value of the item (ad valorem tariff) or per unit (specific duty). Tariffs may be used to discourage the importing of certain types of goods or to adjust for price differentials in order to allow the importing country's products to be competitive. Tariffs are placed on such goods as automobiles in order to prevent foreign competition from gaining an excessive share of the national market. Tariffs may be levied on a specific good, regardless of the country it came from, or may be specifically aimed at discriminating among goods on the basis of country or origin. *See also* Balance of Trade; Trade Barriers. △940, 942, 1276.

Tariff of 1828, US protective tax legislation. It was also called the Tariff of Abominations and represented the height of protectionism before the Civil War. Raw wool was taxed at 50% of its value, while woolen goods were taxed at 45% of their value. The duties on hemp, pig iron, and bar iron were also raised.

Tariff of 1832, US protective tax legislation. It removed some of the "abominations" of the 1828 bill but kept some high duties. It admitted cheap raw wool and flax free, while increasing the duty on woolens. South Carolina at first voted not to pay the duties but finally agreed.

Tarkington, (Newton) Booth (1869–1946), US novelist, b. Indianapolis. He is best known for his depiction of middle-class life in small Midwestern cities. Originally planning to be an illustrator, he turned to writing and produced his first book, *The Gentleman from Indiana,* in 1899. He served a term in the Indiana legislature and won Pulitzer Prizes for *The Magnificent Ambersons* (1918) and *Alice Adams* (1921). Also noted for his novels about childhood, he produced the popular *Penrod* (1914) and *Seventeen* (1916). *See also* Alice Adams.

Taro, large tropical plant native to the Pacific Islands and Southeast Asia and cultivated in other parts of the world for its edible tuberous root. In Hawaii it is eaten as poi. Family Araceae; species *Colocasia esculenta. See also* Arum. △332.

Tarot Cards. △822.

Tarpon, tropical marine game fish. Blue and bright silver, it has a long, deeply forked tail. Its eggs hatch into a bandlike, transparent larval form, and then metamorphose into the juvenile form. Length: to 8ft (244cm); weight: 340lb (154kg). Main species are the small Pacific *Megalops cyprinoides* and the large Atlantic *M. atlanticus.* Family Elopidae.

Tarquinia Madonna (Lippi). △1134.

Tarquinius Priscus (616–578 BC), traditionally the fifth king of Rome. His history is vague. Of Etruscan origin, he is thought to have established the Etruscan culture in Rome. He is attributed with building the Capitoline Triad temple and draining the marshes for the Forum. He is thought to have been murdered as part of an attempt to return the crown to a solely religious function. *See also* Etruscans. △1012.

Tarquinius Superbus (Lat. "Tarquin the Proud") (*r.* 534–510 BC), traditionally the last king of Rome, of Etruscan birth. Largely a legendary figure, he is said to have captured several Latin towns. He was expelled by the senate (509) and the efforts of Lars Porsena and of his own sons to restore him to the throne failed. He fled through Italy, dying at Cumae. △1012, 1014.

Tarragon, perennial plant with 2in (5cm), licorice-flavored leaves used fresh or dried in salads, pickles, etc. Family Compositae; species *Artemisia dracunculus.* △358.

Tarragona, city in Spain, 54mi (87km) SW of Barcelona near the estuary of Francoli River; capital of Tarragona prov. Captured 218 BC from Iberians by Rome's Publius Scipio, it fell to Visigoths AD 469; held by Muslims 714–1085; suffered attacks by French 1640–1811. It is the site of 12th–13th-century cathedral, Roman remains, archeological museum. Exports: wine, olives, almonds. Industries: food processing, distilling, tobacco products. Area: (prov.) 2,426sq mi (6,283sq km). Pop. (city) 78,238; (prov.) 431,961.

Tarsals. △682.

Tarsier, nocturnal tree-dwelling primate of Indonesia resembling a squat, big-eyed rat with long tail and monkeylike hands and feet. Tarsiers have silky grayish-brown coat and can turn their heads 180 degrees. Feeding chiefly on insects, tarsiers represent a stage of evolution intermediate between lemurs and monkeys. Genus *Tarsier. See also* Primates. △554.

Tarsus, city in S Turkey, 23mi (37km) W of Adana on Tarsus River near the Mediterranean Sea. Conquered by Romans 67 BC, it became a leading industrial and cultural center; it was destroyed by Arabs AD 660 and rebuilt by them 780; Ottoman Turks took it in 1515; birthplace of St Paul; agricultural trading center for citrus fruit and cotton grown in area. Copper, chromium, zinc, and coal are mined nearby. Settled by Hittites 14th century BC. Pop. 57,737.

Tartar, Dental, an unsightly encrustation on and between the teeth consisting of caked salivary secretion, food residue, and various calcium and phosphate salts. It is part of good dental hygiene to remove these deposits at regular intervals. △756.

Tartars. *See* Tatars.

Tartrates, salt or ester of tartaric acid. Tartrates, such as potassium bitartrate (cream of tartar) and sodium bitartrate, are used in baking powder in the food industry, as a sequestrant, and in tanning. Antimony potassium tartrate (tartar emetic) is used as an emetic and a mordant.

Tasaday, small group of isolated aboriginal people of the rain forests of S Mindanao in the Philippines, first discovered in 1971. They are food-gathering cave dwellers with a Stone-Age culture, although since their discovery they have adopted hunting and trapping techniques.

Tashkent (Taškent), capital city of the Uzbek SSR, USSR; also capital of Tashkent oblast, in the Tashkent oasis, watered by the Chirchik River, 1,800mi (2,898km) SE of Moscow. It was founded *c.* 7th century; ruled by Arabs until the 11th century; came under Timurid Empire in the 13th century; came under Mongol rule 1361; captured by Russians 1865 and a new city was built around the old one; site of 1966 India-Pakistan conference on Kashmir dispute; severely damaged by 1966 earthquake; site of Central Asian state university and industrial college, medical, agricultural, law, and teachers' colleges, textile and railroad trade schools, Uzbek Academy of Sciences, state library, historical museum, Uzbek academic theater. Industries: cotton, textiles, flour, wine, canned goods, meat, tobacco, radios, porcelain, abrasives, paper, furniture, pottery, chemicals. Pop. 1,385,000.

Tasmania, formerly Van Diemen's Land; island state 150mi (242km) off SE coast of Australia, separated from the mainland by the Bass Strait. Industries: electrochemicals, metal processing, paper, textiles. Discovered by Abel Tasman, Dutch navigator, in 1642; settled 1803 as a penal colony; became an Australian state 1901. Area: 26,383sq mi (68,332sq km). Pop. 392,500.

Roger Brooke Taney

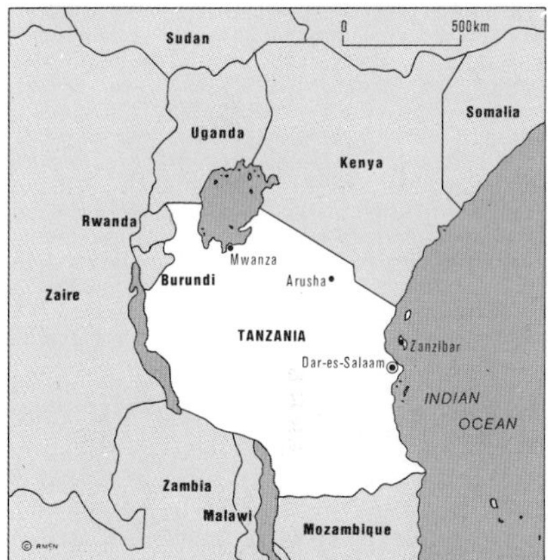

Sudan
0
500km
Somalia
Uganda
Kenya
Rwanda
Mwanza
Burundi
Arusha
Zaire
TANZANIA
Zanzibar
Dar-es-Salaam
INDIAN
OCEAN
Zambia
Malawi
Mozambique

Tanzania

Ida Tarbell

Tashkent oblast, USSR

Tasman Sea, section of the Pacific Ocean between Australia and New Zealand; named for the Dutch explorer Abel Tasman. Sydney, Australia, is the largest port on the sea. Width: approx. 1,200mi (1,932km).

Tasso, Torquato (1544–95), Italian late-Renaissance poet, Bernardo Tasso's son. He had an unhappy childhood, but after writing the epic *Rinaldo* (1562) he joined the Este court at Ferrara. His most famous works are the drama *Aminta* (1573) and the epic *Gerusalemme liberata* (1575). After 1577 he became psychologically disturbed and was confined intermittently in a hospital (1579–86), where he continued writing.

Taste, or gustation, a chemical sense, in which the stimulus is a chemical molecule dissolved in saliva in the mouth; the receptors are specialized cells located in the raised taste buds of the tongue. Taste often represents an interaction between gustation and the sense of smell; for example, food does not taste as palatable when one has a head cold. △680.

TAT. *See* Thematic Apperception Test.

Tatars, or **Tartars,** Turkic-speaking people spread across central Asia. The name "Tatar" has been used loosely for many central Asian nomads, beginning with those of Kipchak in the 1st century AD. By the 15th century the Tatars were generally Muslims, a farming and herding people skilled in leather work, cloth, and ceramic and metal crafts. Their leaders intermarried with Russian aristocracy after 1600. In the 18th century they flourished as middlemen between Russians and central Asian tribesmen. Their feudal social system lasted until the Russian Revolution (1917). The modern Tatar republic is well forested and rich in oil and natural gas in the Soviet Union. The capital, Kazan, is a center of trade and industry, particularly petroleum refining.

Tatlin, Vladimir Evgrafovitch (1885–1953), Russian sculptor. △1320.

Tattooing, coloring or marking the skin for cosmetic or religious purposes. Pigment is inserted under the skin's surface with needles, or scars are made. An ancient and widespread practice, it was most widely cultivated in Polynesia, especially among the Maori. △818.

Tatum, Edward Lawrie (1909–75), US geneticist and biochemist b. Boulder, Colo. He shared the 1958 Nobel Prize in physiology or medicine with George W. Beadle and Joshua Lederberg for his part in the "discovery that genes act by regulating specific chemical processes," a basic principle explaining how genes determine the characteristics of an organism.

Tau Ceti, main-sequence yellow star situated not far from the Sun and located in the constellation Cetus. Characteristics: apparent mag. +3.5; absolute mag. +5.7; spectral type G8; distance 11.9 light-years.

Taunton, city in SE Massachusetts, on Taunton River; seat of Bristol co; birthplace of Isaac Babbitt (1799), US inventor of Babbitt (white) metal. Industries: silverware, jewelry, clothing. Settled 1638; inc. as city 1864. Pop. (1970) 43,756.

Taupo Lake, largest lake in New Zealand, in mountainous central North Island; drained by Waikato River. Area: 234sq mi (606sq km). Depth: 552ft (168m).

Taurus, or the Bull, northern constellation situated on the ecliptic between Aries and Gemini, and lying northwest of Orion; the second sign of the zodiac. It contains the Pleiades and Hyades and the Crab Nebula. Brightest star: Alpha Tauri (Aldebaran). The astrological sign for the period Apr. 20-May 20. △132, 826.

Taurus Mountains (Toros Dağlaii), chain of mountains in S central Turkey, extends 350mi (564km) roughly parallel to Mediterranean coast of S Asia Minor; its NE extension is called Anti-Taurus. Mountains have important deposits of chromium. Highest peak is Ala Dağ, 12,251ft (3,737m).

Taxation, method by which central governments and their subdivisions collect revenue in order to defray the cost of providing services to the population. The different forms of taxation include income taxes, sales taxes, tariffs, property taxes, excise taxes, value-added taxes, and payroll taxes. Most US states have sales taxes, income taxes, and property taxes. Federal government revenues come primarily from individual and corporate income taxes.

Taxco de Alarcén, city in S Mexico; major stopping place between Mexico City and Acapulco during Spanish colonial trade with Philippines; mining center during 18th century; site of colonial church (1717), cobbled streets, fine Spanish architecture. Industries: tourism, gold, silver, silverware. Pop. 64,368.

Taxes, primary revenue sources for governmental units. The federal taxes that produce 95% of 1976 federal tax receipts are income (personal and corporate), social security taxes, and excise taxes. States tend to depend on sales or income taxes rather than vehicle taxes. The primary source of revenue for most municipal governments is the property tax. Taxes are levied on a base (such as income, property, sales) and must include a rate. If the rate is the same for all (such as a 5% sales tax) the tax rate is proportional. If the tax rate is higher as the base increases (such as US income tax) the tax rate is progressive, and if the rate declines as the base increases, the tax is regressive.

Taxonomy, biological classification of plants and animals into groups that reflect natural relationships. Carolus Linnaeus, Swedish botanist, developed the system during the 1750s. △408.

Taylor, Edward (1642?–1729), colonial American poet, b. England. Considered the finest 17th-century colonial poet, in the tradition of the English metaphysical poets, he came to Boston in 1668. Because he requested that none of his works be published, they did not appear until 1939 (*Poetical Works,* Thomas H. Johnson, ed.) after being discovered in the Yale University library, where they had been placed by his grandson.

Taylor, Frederick W. △926.

Taylor, Paul (1930–), US dancer and choreographer, b. Pittsburgh. He danced with the Martha Graham Company (1955–61), appeared with the New York City Ballet (1959–61), and founded the Paul Taylor Dance Company in 1955.

Taylor, Zachary (1784–1850), 12th president of the United States (1849–50), b. Orange co, Va., raised in Kentucky. In 1810 he married Margaret Smith; they had six children. Although his father was a wealthy planter, Zachary Taylor had little formal education. He received a military commission in 1808 and became a career army officer. He fought in the War of 1812, the Black Hawk War, and in the Seminole wars in Florida. In the last, he acquired the nickname "Old Rough and Ready."

In 1845 he was sent to the Texas border to command US troops there. He made a foray into territory in dispute with Mexico, thereby setting off the Mexican War. He took Matamoros, occupied Monterrey, and won the crucial battle of Buena Vista. The end of the war found Taylor a popular hero, and he was nominated for the presidency by the Whigs. He was elected but without a majority of popular votes. As president he advocated the quick admission of California and New Mexico as states and was a moderate on the extension of slavery issue. On July 9, 1850, he died of cholera morbus (acute indigestion) and was succeeded by Vice President Millard Fillmore.

Career: US Army, 1808–49; president, 1849–50. *See also* Mexican War.

Taylor, city in SE Michigan, 20mi (32km) SW of Detroit; named for President Zachary Taylor. Industries: machinery, wood products, sand, gravel, concrete, pipe, glass. Founded as town 1847; inc. as city 1968. Pop. (1970) 70,020.

Tay-Sachs Disease, a rare hereditary disorder (found chiefly in Jewish children) of fat metabolism. It is characterized by an accumulation of gangliosides in the central nervous system, resulting in severe mental deficiency, blindness, and death at about three years of age.

Tbilisi (Tiflis), capital of Georgian SSR, USSR, on the upper Kura River. It was founded *c.* 455 as the capital of the ancient Georgian kingdom; long an important trade center, it was ruled at different times by Persians, Byzantines, Arabs, Mongols, Tatars, and Turks; came under Russian rule 1801; center of 1905 rebellion against Russian government; seat of new administration 1917; made capital of the Transcaucasian Federation 1921; made capital of Georgian SSR 1936; site of Georgian Academy of Sciences (1941), state university (1918), polytechnic, teaching, medical, and art schools, opera, Rustaveli Theater, and botanic gardens. Industries: railroad shops, lathes, oil drills, machinery, electrical goods, ceramics, footwear, clothing, silk and woolen goods, furniture, musical instruments, tobacco, food and wine processing, plastics, chocolate, hydroelectricity. Pop. 889,000.

Tchaikovsky, Pëtr Ilyich (1840–93), Russian Romantic composer whose melodic, emotional works are very popular. His best known works are the three ballets *Swan Lake* (1876), *The Sleeping Beauty* (1890), and *The Nutcracker* (1892); the *Piano Concerto No. 1* (1875); a *Violin Concerto* (1878); the *1812 Overture* (1882); and the orchestral pieces *Romeo and Juliet* (1870) and *Marche Slav* (1876). He wrote six symphonies, of which the Sixth or *Pathétique* (1893) is very popular. His works also included chamber music, songs, and operas. △1246, 1256, 1368.

Tea, family of trees and shrubs with leathery undivided leaves and five-petalled blossoms. Among 500 species is *Camellia thea (Thea sinensis),* the commercial source of tea. Cultivated in moist tropical regions, tea plants, which can reach 30ft (9.1m) height, are kept low by frequent picking of the young shoots for tea leaves; flowers are white. The leaves are dried immediately to produce green tea and are fermented before drying for black tea. Family Theaceae. △354.

Tea Act (1773), legislation by the British Parliament removing export duties on tea. To give relief to financially failing East India Co., the act withdrew duty on tea exported to the colonies and enabled the East India Co. to sell tea directly to the colonies without first going to Britain. Colonial merchants were undersold, and the act led directly to the Boston Tea Party. *See also* Boston Tea Party. △1218.

Teaberry. *See* Wintergreen.

Teach, Edward, English pirate. *See* Blackbeard.

Teaching Machine, device that presents a planned, step-by-step program of instruction. For example, one such machine displays information or a question on a screen. The learner responds by punching a key on a keyboard. The machine at once shows if the response is correct. If the response is right, the student moves on to the next step; if it is wrong, he or she corrects the mistake and then moves ahead. The learner is continually told whether he or she is on the right track. The machine may be simple, displaying a printed program through an opening in a box, or it may use a computer to present material and evaluate answers.

Teak, hardwood tree, native to India, Burma, and the East Indies, valued for its yellowish-brown wood used in furniture and shipbuilding. Height: to 150ft (45.7m). Family Verbenacea; species *Tectona grandis.*

Teal, small, widely distributed river duck that often has bright plumage. The blue-winged teal *(Anas discors)* of North America is a fast, strong flier. They dabble, or feed from the water surface. *See also* Duck.

Teamsters, International Brotherhood of, union chartered by the American Federation of Labor in 1899, adopted present name in 1903. The largest US union, with over 2,000,000 members, the Teamsters have been the target of several government investigations for suspected various illegal activities, (eg financial malpractice, undemocratic procedures, racketeering). The union was expelled from the AFL-CIO in 1957 for unethical practices. In 1964, their then president, James Hoffa, was convicted of jury tampering. Turmoil continued within the union, particularly after the disappearance in 1975 of Hoffa, who was trying to regain power.

Teaneck, residential township in NE New Jersey; site of Luther College of the Bible and Liberal Arts (1948); development was spurred by opening of George Washington Bridge to New York (1931). Inc. 1895. Pop. (1970) 42,355.

Teapot Dome Scandal (1921–24), one of the Harding administration disgraces, it involved fraudulent leases of the naval oil reserves at Teapot Dome and Elk Hills in South Dakota by Secretary of the Interior Albert B. Fall to oilmen Harry Sinclair and Edward Doheny. Fall collected some $409,000 from the two leases. Investigations and litigation, continuing through the decade, ended with Fall's being found guilty of accepting a bribe from Doheny and Doheny and Sinclair's acquittal.

Tears, fluid that moistens the surface of the cornea of the eye, secreted by the lacrimal glands. It is antibacterial in nature, and also improves the optical properties of the eye by forming a thin, smooth film on the cornea and compensating for slight surface imperfections. △740.

Teasdale, Sara (1884–1933), US poet, b. St Louis. She was courted by Vachel Lindsay, married Ernest Filsinger (1914), divorced him (1929), and committed uicide (1933). *The Flame and the Shadow* (1920) is enerally considered her best volume.

echnetium, radioactive metallic element (symbol c) of the second transition series, made in 1937 by . Perrier and E. G. Segrè by bombarding molybenum with deuterons. It was the first element to be ynthesized. No technetium has been found in the arth's crust, although it is present in some stars. roperties: at. no. 43; at. wt. 98.9062 sp gr 11.5; ielt. pt. 3,992°F (2,200°C); most stable isotope Tc^{97} ialf-life 2.6 × 10^{6}yrs). *See also* Transition Elements.

echnological Unemployment. *See* Unemploynent of Labor.

ectonics, study of the Earth's crustal arrangement n large, stable plates that move and the effect of this iovement on the rim of continents, ocean basins, and ne mountain regions that result from crustal movenent compression. Any crustal movement and the esults of it are considered within the area of tectons. *See also* Continental Drift; Deformation; Orogeny. △170, 276.

ecumseh (?1768–1813), Shawnee Indian chief, b. ear Springfield, Ohio. With his brother, The Prophet, ecumseh worked to unite the Western Indians gainst white expansion. After his brother's defeat nd death at Tippecanoe in 1811, Tecumseh joined ne British in the War of 1812. He was killed in action 1813.

eething, the growing in place of milk teeth and the eplacement of the first dentition by the second in hildren and young adults. Twenty deciduous teeth sually appear by the first to second year. Between he ages of 5 and 12 these teeth then drop out and re replaced by permanent teeth. In addition, 12 new iolars (3 on each side of the upper and lower jaw) row in place to yield a complement of 32 adult teeth. *ee also* Tooth.

eflon, a trademarked name for polytetrafluoroethyene, a strong, waxy nonflammable resin. It is a olymer composed of large molecules formed by hemical combinations of small ones into chains. haracterized by a slippery surface and resistance to hemicals, it is used in gaskets, bearings, pipe linings, nd as a protective coating on cooking utensils and ther articles. *See also* Fluorocarbon Plastics.

efnut, in Egyptian mythology, a minor deity, who ersonifies the dew and rain. She was depicted as a voman with the head of a lioness. △834.

egucigalpa, capital city of Honduras, located in the central part of the country and composed of townhips of Tegucigalpa and Comayagüela; site of univerity (1895), teacher training college (1956). Indusies: sugar, textiles, cigarettes. Founded *c.* 1579 as ilver mining center. Pop. 218,510.

ehran, city in N Iran, 65mi (105km) S of Caspian ea; capital of Iran and Tehran prov. City served as apital of Persia 1788; renovation and modernization f the city began in 1797 under Fath Ali Shah and ontinued through reign of Reza Shah Pahlevi (1941); cene of Tehran Conference (Nov. 26–Dec. 2, 1943) etween President Franklin D. Roosevelt, Prime Minster Winston Churchill, and Premier Joseph Stalin. ity contains University of Tehran (1934); National Jniversity (1960); the Gulistan (Rose Garden) Palace 1786) with its marble throne and jeweled peacock hrone; the Shah Mosque, a revolutionary center prior o est. of constitutional government in 1906; Museum f Iranian Ethnology and Museum of Iranian Art, both ousing outstanding collections of cultural artifacts; nd Masjid Sipah-Silar Mosque with its theological ollege; industrial, commercial, and administrative enter. Industries: automobiles, cement, sugar, texles, firearms. Pop. 3,400,000.

ehran Conference (1943), meeting of Allied leadrs Winston Churchill, Joseph Stalin, and Franklin D. Roosevelt in Tehran, Iran, to discuss military and politcal policies in World War II. The leaders agreed to pen a western front in occupied France. The USSR vas assured control of eastern Poland, while agreeing o enter the war against Japan. Discussions were held n the future of Finland and Manchuria, and the postvar independence of Iran was guaranteed.

eilhard de Chardin, Pierre (1881–1955), French Roman Catholic priest and scientist. He joined the Society of Jesus (Jesuits) in 1899, was ordained a riest in 1911, and then began studying paleontology. He worked in China at various times from 1923 to 946 and shared in the discovery of Peking Man. Teilhard is best known for his efforts to produce a ynthesis of scientific views of evolution and Christian faith. His book *The Phenomenon of Man* (finished in 1947 but published after his death), drew world-wide attention from Christians and non-Christians. △1388.

Tektite, generally dark, glassy objects, ranging in diameter from 20 microns to 2mm (microtektites) and larger (to 10cm) believed to be of either lunar origin or formed from splashes of liquefied rock during meteorite impact on Earth. They occur in limited areas, called strewn-fields, on continents and ocean floors. Specimens from Czechoslovakia are called moldavites. △92, 230.

Tel Aviv-Jaffa (Tel Aviv-Yafo), largest city and commercial center in Israel, 34mi (55km) NW of Jerusalem on the Mediterranean Sea. Founded 1909 as a Jewish suburb by the Jewish population of Arab Jaffa, by 1921, Britain had established it as a separate all-Jewish community. During the period of Britain's Palestine mandate (1923–48) and Adolf Hitler's regime in Germany (1933–45), Tel Aviv's immigrant Jewish population grew rapidly, and it became the cultural, administrative, and commercial center of the Jews in Palestine. Not until the close of the 1948–49 Arab-Israeli War was Tel Aviv able to expand physically inland. It served as the seat of the transitional government and legislature (1948–49), when Israel's capital was moved to Jerusalem; incorporated with Jaffa (1950); site of Tel Aviv University (1953), Afro-Asian Institute for Labor Studies and Cooperation, the quadrennial Maccabiah Athletic Games, Temple of Culture (1957), Haaretz Museum, Tel Aviv Museum, Israel Philharmonic Orchestra, Habima Theater (1945), the national theater of Israel; the ministry of defense, headquarters for labor federation, botanical and zoological gardens, and the memorial and library preserved in the home of H.N. Bialik, the national poet. On N end are Tel Quasile excavations, where ruins of Philistine, Hebrew, Persian, Greek, and Roman civilizations have been found. Industries: construction, pharmaceuticals, electrical appliances, publishing, banking, insurance, tourism, textiles, clothing, food processing, chemicals, furniture, soap, cement, paper, plastics, leather, glass, precision instruments. Pop. 362,200.

Telecommunication(s), the science and technology of communicating signals, images, sounds, or writing by wire, cable, radio, or other electromagnetic equipment. Transmission may be digital, in which case the signals are transformed in a coder before being sent, or analogue, in which case the message is sent directly. △1792, 1794.

Telegraph, any communications system that transmits and receives visible or audible signals over a distance. Although most devices are electrically operated and connected by wires or cables, telegraph messages can be sent by radio waves, microwaves, and communication satellites. Pioneering work was performed by many, but credit for the device and code is generally given to Samuel F. B. Morse, who, in 1844, during a demonstration to Congress transmitted the message, "What hath God wrought!" In 1866 the first permanently successful telegraphic cable was laid across the Atlantic Ocean, and in 1874 Thomas A. Edison invented the method to transmit several messages simultaneously over the same wire. △1790.

Teleki, Count Pál (1879–1941), Hungarian statesman and geographer, a member of the counterrevolutionary government that ruled after Béla Kun was deposed in 1920. Count Teleki served as premier 1920, 1926, and 1939–40. When Germany attacked Poland, Hungary refused to allow German troops to cross its territory. When the German-infiltrated army command made a deal to permit German troops to cross Hungary to attack Yugoslavia, Teleki committed suicide as an act of protest.

Telekinesis, in parapsychology, the movement of objects that cannot be explained by any known physical or natural means. *See also* Psychokinesis.

Telemann, Georg Philipp (1681–1767), German composer of numerous Baroque concertos, suites, and sonatas, as well as religious music. △1196.

Telemetry, Spacecraft, system of transmitting data to the ground via electromagmetic waves, normally in digital (on-off) form. Solar cells or chemical batteries provide power for operating high-gain directional antennae on the spacecraft. These beam high-frequency (but low-power) radio waves to large receiving stations on the ground. Data may be transmitted at rates up to 100,000 bits/sec, or stored on tape for later transmission. Voice telemetry was utilized by the Gemini and Apollo astronauts.

Teleostei, superorder of fish, most progressive of

Torquato Tasso

Zachary Taylor

Pëtr Tchaikovsky

Tehran, Iran

bony fish in class Osteichthyes, which contains 30 orders and 20,000 species—the majority of existing fish. Modern teleost families were established during the late Cretaceous Period (65,000,000 years ago). *See also* Osteichthyes. △510.

Telepathy, communication between minds by some means other than known processes, a form of extrasensory perception, or ESP. *See also* Parapsychology. △824.

Telephone, an instrument that communicates speech sounds via wires in an electrical circuit. In 1876 Alexander Graham Bell invented the prototype, which employed a diaphragm of soft iron that vibrated to sound waves. These vibrations caused disturbances in the magnetic field of a nearby bar magnet, causing an electric current of fluctuating intensity in the thin copper wire wrapped around the magnet. This current could be transmitted along wires to a distant identical device which repeated the process in reverse, finally reproducing the audible sound. Later improvements separated the transmitter from the receiver, and replaced the bar magnet with batteries. △1792.

Teleprinter. △1790.

Telescope, Optical, instrument used for producing a magnified image of a distant object, first used in astronomy by Galileo (1609). Two types are employed: the refractor, in which the image is produced by two or more lens systems, and the reflector, in which light is gathered and focused by a concave, usually parabolic, mirror. The image can be recorded photographically or analyzed for its spectrum, etc. Large lenses are difficult to grind accurately and mount and are subject to aberration. These problems are much less severe for mirrors so that large-aperture reflectors are used in many astronomical observatories. *See also* Aberration. △42, 44, 1518.

Telescope, Radio, complex electronic system for detecting, amplifying, and analyzing radio waves from space. One basic design is the large steerable wire-mesh dish, parabolic in shape and based on the precision wartime radar dishes, that reflects radio waves from a small area of the sky onto an antenna. The resulting electrical signal is greatly amplified before analysis. A more sensitive design is the radio interferometer employing arrays of antennas; much smaller radio sources can be detected and larger areas of the sky can be studied at one time. *See also* Astronomy; Radio; Interferometer. △46, 125, 1478.

Telescope, X-Ray, specially designed telescope in which radiation from an astronomical X-ray source can be focused from a double reflecting mirror system, consisting of a paraboloid and a hyperboloid surface, the reflections (specular) occurring at near grazing incidence.

Telestar. △142.

Teletype, the transmission and reception of messages via an electromechanical typewriter and telegraph or telephone wires. In effect, the system employs a receiving typewriter whose keys are operated from the transmitting station. In the United States both simplex and multiplex systems use the Baudot code, which uses various combinations of five equal length pulses to indicate numerals, letters, and punctuation. △1674, 1790.

Teletypewriter Exchange Service (TWX, TELEX), provides subscribers with their own call-up number that connects them to the data-transmission facilities. The line system uses derived direct current circuits and multi-channel carriers. In 1970 Western Union's TELEX service was combined with TWX to form one national service. △1790.

Television, the transmission of scenes, moving or stationary, commonly with accompanying sound, via electromagnetic waves, and the reconversion of those waves into the original scene. Five components are fundamental to television systems: a camera device to record the scene; a transducer to change the light impulses of the scene into corresponding electrical signals; a transmitter; a receiver; and a second transducer to convert the electrical signals back into light impulses, thus reproducing the original scene. An early prototype was patented by Paul Nipkow in Germany in 1884. The development of the electron tube and electronic scanning methods made the marketing of television systems practical in 1945. △1796.

TELEX. *See* Teletypewriter Exchange Service.

Tell el-Amarna, area of ruins and rock tombs on E bank of Nile River, Egypt, 8mi (13km) SE of Mallawi. In 1887, about 400 tablets inscribed in Akkadian cuneiform were found here; they have given much information on ancient Egypt and Middle East. Written by Amenhotep III and Ikhnaton 1411–1354 BC, they are now in British, Berlin, and Cairo museums.

Teller, Edward (1908–), US physicist, b. Hungary. He left Europe because of the Nazis, finally settling in the United States in 1935. He worked on the atom bomb at Los Alamos during World War II. After the war he pioneered the development of the hydrogen bomb.

Teller Resolution, amendment to the US declaration of war against Spain (1898). Proposed by Sen. Henry M. Teller, it stated that the United States was not to "exercise sovereignty, jurisdiction, or control" over Cuba after that island was liberated from Spain.

Tellurium, metalloid element (symbol Te) of group VIA of the periodic table, discovered 1782. It is found native and in calaverite (AuTe); chief source is as a by-product of the electrolytic refining of copper. It is used in some alloys and semiconductor devices. Properties: at. no. 52; at. wt. 127.60; sp. gr. 6.24; melt. pt. 841°F (449.5°C); boil. pt. 1814°F (989.8°C); most common isotope Te^{130} (34.48%).

Temin, Howard M(artin) (1934–), US oncologist, b. Philadelphia. He was awarded part of the 1975 Nobel Prize in physiology or medicine for his studies of the "interaction between tumor viruses and the genetic material of the cell." Temin (independently of colaureate David Baltimore) discovered reverse transcriptase, the enzyme necessary for viral genetic information to be incorporated into an animal cell.

Tempe, city in SW central Arizona, on Salt River, 9mi (14km) E of Phoenix; site of Arizona State University. Industries: electronic equipment, steel, clothing, agriculture. Founded 1872; inc. 1894. Pop. (1970) 63,-550.

Temperament, emotional reactions including characteristic energy level, intensity of reaction moods, mood changes, and threshold of responsiveness. It is presumed that temperament is constitutionally determined, but it is also deeply influenced by life experience. *See also* Personality. △784.

Temperance Movement, campaign in the United States to wipe out the consumption of alcoholic beverages. Beginning in the late 18th century, the temperance crusade reached its peak with the ratification of the 18th Amendment (1919), which brought in the Prohibition Era. The amendment was later repealed (1933) after enforcement proved impossible. Prominent in the movement were Benjamin Rush, Lyman Beecher, Carry Nation, and Frances Willard.

Tempera Painting, artistic medium. It takes its name from the practice of "tempering" powdered pigments with egg yolk diluted in water. Until the late 15th century when it was largely replaced by oil painting, tempera, applied to wooden panels, was the commonest technique used in Western art. Its chief disadvantage is that it turns several shades lighter as it dries, but, unlike oil, it dries at once.

Temperature, a parameter describing the number of energy states available to a substance or system. Observations indicate that two bodies placed in thermal contact exchange heat energy initially but eventually arrive at thermal equilibrium; neither body gains or loses heat. At this point, both bodies are said to have the same temperature; that is, the most probable distribution of energy states of the atoms and molecules composing the bodies has been attained. At high temperatures, the number of energy states available to the atoms and molecules of a system is very large; at lower temperatures, fewer states are available (molecules become locked into position and liquids change to solids). At a sufficiently low temperature, all parts of the system are at their lowest energy levels; this temperature is described as absolute zero. *See also* Absolute Zero. △1502, 1508.

Temperature, Body, in homeothermic animals such as birds and mammals, the body temperature is maintained within narrow limits regardless of the ambient temperature. This is accomplished by muscular activity and normal basal metabolism. In man, the traditional normal temperature is 37°C (98.6°F), which will vary with degree of activity, reaching 40°C (104°F) during exercise, and lower than 37°C during sleep.

Temperature Scales, scales for measuring temperature. The Fahrenheit scale was devised by the German physicist Gabriel Fahrenheit (1686–1736) using two reference points: the freezing point of water (taken to be 32 degrees) and the temperature of the human body (taken to be 96 degrees, although later found t be 98.6 degrees). The Celsius (formerly Centigrade scale was introduced by A. Celsius, an 18th-centur Swedish astronomer. On this scale water freezes a 0°C and boils at 100°C. With the development of the modynamics by Lord Kelvin and the later discover that temperature has a lower bound of −273°C (−459°F), the Absolute (or Kelvin) scale was introducec having a zero point coincident with absolute zero. Th degree Kelvin (or kelvin) represents the same tempe ature difference as the degree Celsius; but both ar 1.8 times as large as the degree Fahrenheit. To trans form from Fahrenheit (F) to Celsius (C), use the fo mula $C=5/9\ (F-32)$. △1508, 1656.

Temperature Sense, one of the skin senses, whic may or may not be distinct from the sense of touch Although specialized thermoreceptors have been pre dicted by various theorists, none has yet been founc Temperature detection seems to be related to othe more subtle sensory impressions, such as the feelin of wetness. △678.

Tempering. *See* Heat Treatment.

Tempest, The (1611), comedy by William Shakes peare. The play recounts how Prospero, the unseate duke of Milan, regains his throne after a tempest ship wrecks his usurpers on the enchanted isle where h lives with his daughter Miranda, the slave Caliban, an the spirit Ariel. Everyone then returns to Naples fo the wedding of Miranda to Ferdinand, the king's sor Shakespeare's last complete work, this romance wa revived in New York City in 1916 and 1945.

Tempesta. △1142.

Templars. △1084, 1098.

Temple, city in central Texas, 35mi (56km) S c Waco; site of Texas Soil Conservation Service, Black land Experiment Station, and Texas branch of Farm ers Home Administration; hospital center. Industries furniture, plastics, footwear, railroad shops, cotton grain, clothing, cottonseed products. Founded 1881 inc. 1882. Pop. (1970) 33,431.

Temple City, city in S California, E of Los Angeles suburban community with small businesses and ligh industries. Founded 1827; inc. 1960. Pop. (1970 31,040.

Temporal Lobes, prominent lobes of the cerebra cortex that, in humans, lie directly below the temples The temporal lobes are directly involved in the inter pretation and generation of language, and injury t them sometimes produces speech disorders. *See als* Brain. △666.

Tenant Farming, system of farming in which renter works the land and pays the land owner rent i cash or a share of the crop. △306.

Ten Commandments, or **Decalogue,** the code c ethical conduct held in Judeo-Christian tradition t have been revealed by God to Moses. Representinc the moral basis of God's Covenant with Israel, they appear in both Exodus 20 and Deuteronomy 5, bu with different phrasing. The first "tablet" (command ments 1–4) exhorts obligation and service to the one God. The second "tablet" (5–10) requires respect fo basic human rights and individual social responsibil ity. Protestant, Catholic, and Jewish traditions eac have slightly different versions of the laws. △844 908.

Tendon, strong, elastic band of connective tissu that connects muscle to bone. △682, 684.

Tendonitis, inflammatory condition of any of th white bands of dense connective tissue that unit muscles with other parts of the body and chiefly trans mit muscle force to bones and joints. Physical traum and hereditary and acquired connective tissue dis eases, especially rheumatoid arthritis, can be causes

Tenebrionid Beetle. △604.

Tenerife Island, island of Spain, in Atlantic Ocear 40mi (64km) WNW of Grand Canary Island; largest o the Canary Islands. Originally inhabited by Guanches it was conquered 15th century by Spain. The island i mountainous and covered with lava layers; site of Picc de Teide, highest peak on the island, approx 12,200ft (3,721m). Industries: tourism, goats, sheep food processing, linen. Crops: bananas, sugar cane almonds, tobacco, cereals. Pop. 500, 381.

Teng Hsiao-p'ing (1904–), Chinese Communis political leader. He rose in the early 1960s to be sec retary general of the Chinese Communist party bu was purged during the late 1960s Cultural Revolution. He reappeared on the Chinese political scene from 1973 to 1976 but was purged again following the death of his supporter, Chou En-lai, in early 1976. After Mao Tse-tung's death later in 1976, Teng emerged again as a principal leader.

Tenia, or **Taenia,** genus of tapeworms including the common beef *(T. saginata)* and pork *(T. solium)* tapeworm that can infest the human intestine as adults. Such an infestation is very debilitating and comes as a result of eating raw or rare beef or pork containing tapeworm larvae. *See also* Tapeworm. △472, 710.

Ten Lost Tribes, the ten tribes composed of descendants from Jacob's sons. Two other tribes formed the southern kingdom of Judah, while the ten tribes formed the northern kingdom, known as Israel. In 722 BC, the Assyrians overcame Israel and the ten tribes wandered into different lands and disappeared. From the Middle Ages onward various explanations developed. Some see them as the Anglo-Saxons, the early Irish settlers, or the American Indians, but they were more likely assimilated into other peoples.

Tennent, Gilbert (1703–64), American religious leader, b. Ireland. A Presbyterian minister and evangelist, he toured the colonies with English revivalist George Whitefield (1739–40) and became prominent in the Great Awakening. When the Presbyterian Church split (1741), he became a leader of the evangelistic New Side. In 1758, he helped reunite the New and Old sides.

Tennessee, state in the SE central United States, between the Appalachian Mts and the Mississippi River.

Land and economy. The Great Smoky Mts of the Appalachian chain, with elevations of more than 6,000ft (1,830m) rise along the E boundary. W of them is the Great Valley of E Tennessee and the Cumberland Plateau. Beyond, the land slopes to the Mississippi River on the W border. The principal river is the Tennessee, which rises in the E, flows S into Alabama, and turns N to flow across the W part of the state. Mountain valleys in the E and the lower lands in the center and W are agricultural regions. Plentiful electric power from the network of the Tennessee Valley Authority, an efficient transportation system, and the state's proximity to major markets have created a diversified manufacturing industry, centered in the E cities and towns, that is unmatched by any Southern state. Industrial research facilities, especially the federal government's nuclear installations at Oak Ridge, which produced material for the first atom bomb and now carry on nuclear studies, are important to the economy.

People. The first settlers were pioneers who crossed the mountains from states on the Atlantic seaboard; their descendants form a major part of the population. Almost 60% live in urban areas.

Education. There are more than 60 institutions of higher education.

History. The region was visited by Spaniards in the 16th century and by English and French a century later. Some forts were built and abandoned; the first permanent settlement was made in the Watauga River Valley in the NE in 1769. Sparsely settled and far removed from theaters of action in the Revolution, the area was little affected by the war. Nashville was founded 1779. North Carolina relinquished its claim to the land in 1784, and dwellers in E Tennessee organized what they called the State of Franklin, which was never recognized by the United States. In 1790, Congress created the Southwest Territory, from which six years later the state of Tennessee was established. As the Civil War approached, Union sentiment was strong in Tennessee, but the state seceded in 1861. Tennesseans served on both sides. More than 400 engagements, including several major battles, were fought in the state. Industrial development began late in the 19th century and was greatly stimulated by WWII.

PROFILE

Admitted to Union: June 1, 1796; rank, 16th
US Congressmen: Senate, 2; House of Representatives, 8
Population: 3,924,164 (1970); rank, 17th
Capital: Nashville, 447,877 (1970)
Chief cities: Memphis, 623,530; Nashville; Knoxville, 174,587; Chattanooga, 119,923
State Legislature: Senate, 33; House of Representatives, 99
Area: 42,244sq mi (109,412sq km); rank, 34th
Elevation: Highest, 6,643ft (2,026m), Clingman's Dome; lowest, 182ft (56m), Mississippi River
Industries: (major products) chemicals, textiles, apparel, electrical machinery, processed foods, forest products
Agriculture: (major products) cattle, dairy products, hogs, tobacco, cotton, soybeans, corn
Minerals (major): zinc, limestone, marble, sandstone, bituminous coal
State nickname: Volunteer State
State motto: Agriculture and Commerce
State bird: mockingbird
State flower: iris
State tree: tulip poplar

Tennessee River, river in Tennessee, N Alabama, and W Kentucky; formed by confluence of Holston and French Broad rivers near Knoxville, Tenn.; flows SW into N Alabama, N across W Tennessee and W Kentucky into Ohio River at Paducah, Ky. Tennessee Valley Authority (1933) has developed the river's water power and transportation facilities along with flood control. Length: 652mi (1,050km). *See also* Tennessee Valley Authority.

Tennessee Valley Authority (TVA), New Deal agency established as part of a long-range regional planning project (1933). An independent public corporation, it was authorized to build dams and power plants to control the Tennessee River and improve the surrounding area. Sen. George Norris of Nebraska proposed the plan that the river be dammed to prevent flooding, produce electricity, and rebuild the eroded farmland. The success of TVA contributed greatly to the Tennessee River Valley's wealth. △1324.

Tennessee Walking, or **Plantation Walking, Horse,** light horse breed developed during the 19th century in Tennessee from several breeds for plantation owners to ride. A comfortable saddle horse with stamina, its three gaits are flat-foot walk, running walk, and canter. It has a plain head and massive body; colors include sorrel, chestnut, black, and golden with white marks on feet and legs. Height: 62in (157.5cm) at shoulder; weight: 1,000–1,200lb (450–540kg).

Tennis, game, played by two or four persons with rackets and a ball. It is played outdoors on a surface of grass, clay, or asphalt and indoors on wood, artificial grass, linoleum, tarmacadam, or carpeting. For singles, the court measures 78 feet by 27 feet (23.8 by 8.2m) and in doubles, 78 feet by 36 feet (11m). The court is divided by a net 3 feet high (.9m). Each half of the court is divided into a service court 21 × 13.5 feet (6.4 × 4.1m) and a backcourt 27 × 18 feet (5.5m). A 4.5 foot (1.4m) alley flanks either side of the court perpendicular to the net; it is used only in doubles play. The ball used is unstitched, felt-covered, inflated rubber about 2.5 inches (6.3cm) in diameter; the oval-headed rackets are usually 27 inches (69cm) long with a strung hitting surface of resilient fiber.

A player serves for an entire game, and is allowed two service tries every time the ball is put into play. The ball is diagonally served from behind the baseline and must bounce into the opposite serving court beyond the net. If the ball fails to enter the opponent's service court on two consecutive services (double fault), a point is awarded the non-server. Also, a foot fault (stepping on or over the baseline on the serve) results in a forfeiture of a point. The players change sides after the first game and then after every two games.

After the serve, the ball may be returned into any area of the opponent's court. Points, which may be won by either the server or the receiver, are scored in a 15, 30, 40, and game procession. In lieu of zero, the term "love" is used. If the game goes to 40–40 (deuce), the first player to win two consecutive points wins. Generally, a game is four points, providing that the margin of victory is at least two points, and every six-game victory constitutes a set. In championship play a match is won by taking two of three sets (women) or three of five sets (men). The game is officiated by an umpire, and sometimes a referee, foot-fault judges, and linesmen.

History. Tennis was invented in Wales in 1873 by Walter C. Wingfield, and has steadily risen to become one of the most popular of international sporting events. The most prestigious tournaments include Wimbledon (Great Britain), Forest Hills (United States), and the singles championships of France and Australia. These four tournaments, for men and women, are now open to professionals and amateurs; if a player captures all four titles in one year, he has won the grand slam. For nations, the most coveted prize is the Davis Cup, originated in 1900. △930.

Tennyson, Alfred, 1st Baron (1809–1892), English poet, poet laureate (1850–1892). His poetry covers the spectrum of lyric, elegiac, dramatic, and epic, taking subject matter from Arthurian legends, classic mythology, and the contemporary crisis in belief. Among his most famous poems are "The Lady of Shalott" (1832), "The Lotus Eaters" (1832), "Locksley Hall" (1842), "Tears, Idle Tears" (1847), "In

Tennessee walking horse

Tennessee: South Holston Lake

Tennessee Valley Authority: Hiwassee Dam, North Carolina

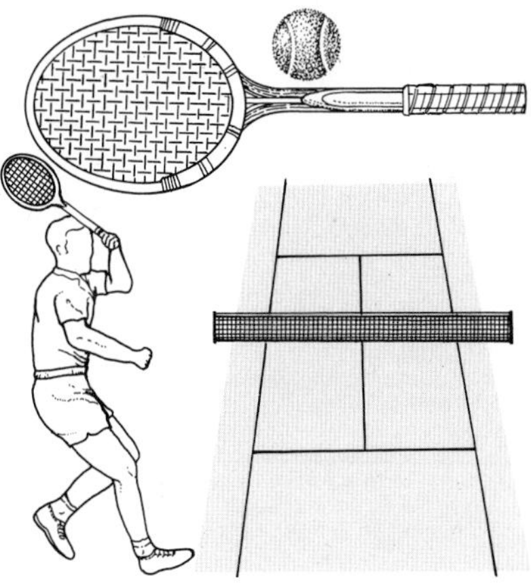

Tennis

Memoriam" (1850), "Maud" (1855), and "Crossing the Bar" (1889). Other works include the cycle *Idylls of the King* (1859–85) and the verse drama *Becket* (1884). △1240.

Tenochtitlán, Aztec capital, founded *c.*1325 on islands in the midst of Lake Texcoco. The initial Aztec settlement grew into a big population and ceremonial center. Gardens within the lake provided produce; aqueducts brought fresh water from Chapultepec. The city was besieged by Cortés in 1521; Mexico City was erected on its ruins. △970, 1118, 1124.

Tenrec, burrowing, insect-eating mammal of Madagascar and the Comoro Islands. The common *Tenrec ecaudatus* is a nocturnal, highly prolific animal with a spiny coat like a hedgehog. It is about the size of a cat. Family Tenrecidae. *See also* Insectivore.

Tensile Strength. △1506.

Tension. △1756.

Ten-Speed Bicycle. △1688.

Tent Caterpillar, medium-sized, hairy, dark-brown moth caterpillar that, in early spring, spins a large communal nest of silk, usually in a tree crotch. Tent caterpillars defoliate many shrubs and trees and are serious pests in North America and Eurasia. The eastern *Malacosoma americanum* of North America has a white stripe down its back with blue and white spots on its sides.

Ten Thousand Immortals. △984.

Tenure, in feudalism, a piece of land, part of a greater estate, granted for a prolonged period by one person to another (the tenant), in exchange for rent, labor, or both. The practice was common in the Frankish empire in France in about the 8th century and was a precursor to the elaborate ownership and land-use systems of feudalism. Unlike some feudal fiefs, the tenure was more directly under the control of the tenant, and was almost always held for life and was hereditary. *See also* Feudalism. △1098.

Tenure of Office Act (1867), US law, passed over the veto of Pres. Andrew Johnson, which prohibited the president from removing any federal officeholder approved by the Senate without the Senate's consent to the removal. Impeachment proceedings were initiated against Johnson (1868) for dismissing Secretary of War Edwin Stanton.

Teosinte, cornlike annual grass native to Mexico and Central America and cultivated in SW United States. It grows in large clumps, branching at the base. Like corn, it has tassels but small ears. Family Gramineae; species *Euchlaena mexicana* or *Zea mexicana*. *See also* Corn.

Teotihuacán, ancient city located NW of Mexico City, arose *c.*100 BC and flourished until 900 AD. Built by an Olmec-based culture, the city, at its peak, covered 8sq mi (21sq km) and supported a population of 50,000. The city was laid out in a grid pattern centered on a thoroughfare named the Street of the Dead —the Pyramid of the Sun and Temple of Quetzalcoatl dominated the E limit; the Pyramid of the Moon the N quadrant. △970.

Tepe Gawra, one of the most important archeological sites in northern Iraq. Excavations have uncovered 26 levels of ancient cities, dating from the 5th to the 2nd millennium BC, and including the civilizations of the Tell Halaf (*c.*5000 BC), Al' Ubaid (*c.*4100–3500 BC), and Jemdet Nasr (3500–3000 BC).

Terbium, metallic element (symbol Tb) of the lanthanide group, first isolated in 1843 by C. G. Mosander. Chief ore is monazite (phosphate). The element is used in semiconductors. Properties: at. no 65; at. wt. 158.9254; sp gr 8.234; melt. pt. 2,480°F (1,360°C); boil. pt. 5,474°F (3,041°C); most common isotope Tb^{159} (100%). *See also* Lanthanide Elements.

Teredo. *See* Shipworm.

Terence, or **Publius Terentius Afer** (*c.* 185–159 BC), after Plautus, the greatest Roman author of comedy. Born in Carthage, he was a slave in Rome, educated and freed by his master, the senator Terentius Lucanus. Befriended by certain noble Romans, he produced 6 plays between 166 and 160 BC. His principal works include *Andria, Phormio,* and *Hecyra.* He was interested primarily in character, and his moralizing mood made him an influential force in the Middle Ages. △1028.

Terman, Lewis M(adison) (1877–1956), US psychologist, b. Johnson co, Ind. He devised the first widely used intelligence test in the United States (an adaptation of tests devised by Alfred Binet). He also performed classic studies of highly intelligent individuals that dispelled many misconceptions about the gifted, such as the notion that more intelligent people are not well adjusted. Major publications include *The Measurement of Intelligence* (1916); *Genetic Studies of Genius* (coauthor, 1925); and *The Gifted Child Grows Up* (coauthor, 1947).

Terminator, boundary between the sunlit and dark sides of a planet or satellite. In the case of a body lacking atmosphere, such as the Moon, the terminator is distinct, although often broken up because of reflections from craters or mountains. Bodies with atmospheres have less well defined terminators owing to the atmospheric scattering that causes twilight. △52.

Termite, or white ant, social insect found worldwide in nests ranging from subterranean to aboveground towers. They have a caste system with a king and queen guarded and tended by soldiers, workers, and nymphs. Usually white and wingless, when the nest becomes crowded, they darken, develop wings, and swarm. They can be distinguished from ants by the lack of a narrow waist. Length: 0.08–0.9in (2–22.9mm); queens: to 4in (102mm).

Tern, or sea swallow, graceful seabird found over most waters of the world, diving for fish and crustaceans. They are white and gray with a blackish head, and have pointed bills, long pointed wings, forked tails, and webbed feet. After long migrations and courtship rituals, they lay eggs (2–3) in a scraped depression in sand. Length: 8–22in (20–56cm). Family Laridae.

Terni, city in central Italy, 49mi (79km) NE of Rome; capital of Terni prov.; nearby waterfalls (including Cascata delle Marmore) furnish hydroelectric power; Roman ruins are nearby; site of medieval churches. Industries: metallurgy, firearms, textiles. Pop. 104,-954.

Terpander (7th century BC), Greek musician and poet, sometimes called the father of Greek classical music. He developed the *nomos,* a hymn to the gods set to flute and lyre music. He also established the first music school in Sparta and is said to have added 3 strings to the lyre. Little of his work remains.

Terpenes, group of unsaturated isomers having the formula $C_{10}H_{16}$. They occur in most essential oils and are colorless liquids. Pinere, the chief ingredient of turpentine, and limonene, found in the essential oils of citrus fruits, are examples. △1570.

Terracing, practice of building terraces into sloping land to prevent soil erosion. Crops are planted on the flat portion of each terrace. In countries where arable land is at a premium, such as Japan, Peru, and Ethiopia, terracing is extensively practiced. It is often avoided in other areas because it involves great labor. △258, 260.

Terra Cotta, fired clay, generally a form made from coarse, porous unglazed clay that assumes a reddish-brown color. Terra cotta figures 5,000 years old have been excavated in Greece. △1588.

Terramycin, trademark for a drug compound with a tetracycline derivative as its base. It may produce mild gastric disturbance. *See also* Tetracycline.

Terrapin, any of various edible North American turtles of the family Emydidae living in fresh or brackish water. The term refers especially to the salt marsh diamondback terrapin *(Malaclemus terrapin)* of the US Atlantic coast.

Terrarium, container enclosing a garden of small plants; or, any small contained garden. Once established, a terrarium maintains itself for years, recycling moisture supplied by transpiration. A terrarium can be any clear glass or plastic container. The bottom is layered with drainage gravel, charcoal, and soil. Suitable woodland plants are mosses, rattlesnake plantain, conifer seedlings, and ferns. These should be dug in early autumn. House plants used should be small and tolerate humid conditions, such as begonias, small orchids, ferns, and inch plant.

Terre Haute, city in W Indiana, on Wabash River, 67mi (108km) WSW of Indianapolis; seat of Vigo co; site of Indiana State University (1865), Rose Polytechnic Institute, St Mary's-of-the-Woods College (1840); birthplace of Eugene Debs and Theodore Dreiser. Industries: food processing, phonograph records, aluminum and steel products. Founded 1811; inc. as town 1832, as city 1853. Pop. (1970) 70,286.

Terrier, dog breeds that dig the earth to rout game. Referred to as early as 1359 and as black and tan dog in the 1500s, they have been used to hunt badgers, foxes, weasels, and rats. On a hunt, they are carried along while hounds trail the quarry. When it is located, terriers are set down to dig it out of its burrow. The separate breeds emerged in 19th-century England. The 22 terriers recognized by the American Kennel Club include Sealyham, Australian, fox, Manchester, Scottish, and Bedlington. Larger types such as the Kerry blue, Airedale, and Irish are used as guard, police, and war dogs.

Terrigenous Deposits, one of the two main groups of marine deposits. They are found near shore and consist of material eroded from the land surface like sand, silt, mud, and intergrading types.

Territorialism, Animal. △536.

Territory, area for mating, nesting, roosting, or feeding, occupied by one or more organisms and defended against others of the same species. It is a spacing mechanism to prevent overcrowding and exhaustion of food supplies. Most vertebrates, some arthropods, such as dragonflies, and even some plants (those secreting repulsive chemicals) are territorial. Marking and defense of territory can involve song and other vocalizations, chemical scents, color displays, and physical aggression. △536.

Terry, (Dame) Ellen Alicia (1848–1928), English actress. Her first stage appearance was at age nine in *A Winter's Tale.* She toured extensively with her sister Kate. In 1907 she toured the United States as a Shakespearean lecturer. In 1908 she published her autobiography and her correspondence with Bernard Shaw. She was made a dame of the British Empire in 1925.

Terry, William Harold ("Bill") (1898–). US baseball player and manager, b. Atlanta. A hitter whose average reached a high point of .401 in 1930, he played for the New York Giants (1923–36) and also managed them (1932–41). He was elected to the Baseball Hall of Fame in 1954.

Tertiary Period, the lower division of the Cenozoic Era, lasting from 65,000,000 to about 3,000,000 years ago. It is divided into four epochs, starting with the Eocene, the earliest part of which is sometimes called the Paleocene, followed by the Oligocene, Miocene, and Pliocene. Early Tertiary times were marked by great mountain-building activity (Rockies, Andes, Alps, and Himalayas) and continental relationships were beginning to resemble those of today. Both marsupial and placental mammals diversified greatly. Archaic forms of carnivores and plant-eaters flourished, along with primitive primates, bats, rodents, and early whales. Later there was a transition to the more modern kinds of mammals. There was also a gradual change from worldwide warm climates to today's climatic zoning. *See also* Cenozoic Era; Geologic Time. △276, 576.

Tertullian (Quintus Septimius Tertullianus) (*c.* 160–*c.*230), one of the Latin Fathers of the Church, b. Carthage. The son of a Roman centurion, he was converted to Christianity *c.*195 and used his training in law and rhetoric to develop a systematic and practical approach to theology and Christian apologetics. His works include *Apologeticus, De Spectaculis,* and *De Anima.* Partly responsible for making Latin the official language of Christian theological writing, he is also remembered for enumerating the Seven Deadly Sins. △1028.

Terza Rima, in Italian poetry, a chain rhyme incorporating stanzas of three lines each (tercets). The second line of each tercet rhymes with the first and third lines of the next. The chain ends with either a couplet or an extra line added to the last tercet. This rhyme scheme first appeared in Dante's *Divine Comedy* (*c.* 1321) and was probably invented by him for that work. It later became popular with both Italian and English poets. *See also* Dante Alighieri; Divine Comedy.

Test Act (1673), English legislation intended to exclude Protestant dissenters and Roman Catholics from public offices. It required all candidates for such offices to profess the established religion of the Church of England. It was made less harsh by the Act of Toleration (1689).

Testis (pl. testes), the male sex gland, a pair located in a pouch, the scrotum, external to the body. The testes are made up of a series of seminiferous tubules in which male sex cells (sperm) are formed and mature, after which they drain into ducts, the epididymis, from which they will be discharged. △700.

estosterone, steroid hormone produced mainly by ie mammalian testis. It is responsible for the growth nd development of male sex organs and male sec- ndary sexual characteristics. *See also* Hormones; teroid.

estudo. △1726.

etanus, infectious disease of the central nervous ystem caused by the toxin secreted by the bacterium *'lostridium tetani*, introduced into the body through skin puncture and not subsequently exposed to oxy- en. The symptoms are extreme stiffness, convul- ons, and painful generalized muscle spasms. Muscle pasms of the jaw are particularly characteristic and esult in difficulty in opening the mouth, which has arned the disease the name "lockjaw." Tetanus has high mortality but is preventable by immunization ith tetanus antitoxin. △722.

ethys, satellite of Saturn. △86.

ethys, Sea of, the hypothetical sea which sepa- ated the Eurasian part from the African part of the upercontinent Pangaea 200,000,000 years ago. It as ancestral to the Mediterranean. The sea is named or the Greek god Oceanus' wife who was the mother f the seas.

et Offensive (1968), in the Vietnam War, a devas- ating military attack by North Vietnamese and Viet ong troops on more than 100 cities and towns in outh Vietnam. It discredited US military reports that aid that victory over North Vietnam was near. △ 378.

eton Range, mountain chain in NW Wyoming and E Idaho, S of Yellowstone National Park; part of ocky Mt system; forms part of Grand Teton National ark and Targhee National Forest. Highest peak is rand Teton, 13,747ft (4,193m).

etrachloride. △1568.

etracyclines, broad-spectrum antibiotics effective gainst anaerobic streptococci and certain bacterial nd rickettsial diseases. Frequently used as a second- noice drug in cases of intolerance to penicillin. Com- on trademarks are Terramycin, Aureomycin.

etrahedrite, a sulfide mineral; copper, iron, an- mony, and arsenic sulfide, found in medium-to-low emperature ore veins. Cubic system well-formed tet- ahedral crystals and also massive. Metallic gray to lack; hardness 3–4.5; sp gr 4.9. Important ore of opper. △1462, 1466.

etrameter, verse line of four metrical feet. Each trameter line is usually broken by a caesura or ause, as is every longer line. The caesura is not ounted in the timing. Tetrameter lines can have a ionotonous effect. *See also* Meter.

etramethylsilane. △1568.

eutonic Knights, Order of the Knights of the Hospi- al of St Mary of the Teutons in Jerusalem. A religious, ilitary order restricted to Germans, and knighthood, o nobles, patterned after the Knights Templar, ormed by German crusaders in 1190. Beginning in ie early 13th century, they took as their mission the hristianization and Germanization of the eastern ontier. During that century, they conquered the hea- ien Slavs of Prussia. By 1329 they held the entire altic region as a papal fief, but their power declined ter defeat at the Battle of Tannenberg by Poles and ithuanians in 1410. The order has kept its identity nd today has headquarters in Vienna, where the nights devote themselves to charitable and nursing ork. △1074, 1084.

eutons, ancient Germanic tribe who migrated in ompany with the neighboring Cimbri from Jutland to France. They were destroyed by Roman general 1arius in 102 BC at the battle of Aquae Sextiae. Some ew may have survived at Miltenberg. Their name ame to mean German after they themselves had dis- ppeared.

ewkesbury Abbey. △1104.

exarkana, city in SW Arkansas, twin city with Tex- rkana, Tex., 137mi (221km) SW of Little Rock; seat f Miller co. Industries: lumber, railroad products, oil ells. Settled 1873. Pop. (1970) 21,682.

exarkana, city in NE Texas, 185mi (298km) NE of allas; twin city with Texarkana, Arkansas. Industries: mber, railroad cars, dairy products, creosote, sand, ravel, tires, mobile homes. Inc. 1874. Pop. (1970) 0,497.

Texas, state in the SW central United States, on the Gulf of Mexico, separated from the republic of Mexico by the Rio Grande. It was an independent republic before joining the Union.

Land and economy. Covering about 12% of the land mass of the 48 coterminous states, Texas exhibits a varied topography. A broad coastal plain lies along the Gulf of Mexico. W and N the land rises to plains and plateaus. Highest elevations are in the far W mountains. Besides the Rio Grande, the principal rivers are the Brazos, the Colorado, the Guadalupe, and the Nueces. There are few natural lakes; throughout the state dams create reservoirs for irrigation and flood control. Irrigation aids the growth of ranching and farming on the plains in the W and N. Manufacturing is largely centered in the populous E and S. Major petroleum deposits and refineries are on or near the Gulf coast, although wells are operated also in the NW. Seaborne transport is a major asset. Houston, linked to the Gulf by a ship canal, is a leading port; others are Beaumont, Port Arthur, Galveston, and Corpus Christi. Networks of railroads and highways cover the state's vast interior. The Manned Spacecraft Center, where the Moon flights were directed, is near Houston.

People. Most Texans were born in the state, descendants of settlers from other states. Among elements of foreign ancestry, Mexicans and Germans are notable. Urbanization, due to the growth of industry, has been rapid; about 80% of the population lives in urban areas.

Education. There are nearly 140 institutions of higher education. The University of Texas system is a state-supported group of academic and professional schools throughout the state.

History. Over Texas have flown the flags of six nations—Spain, France, Mexico, the Republic of Texas, the Confederate States of America, and the United States of America. Spaniards explored the region after 1519 and claimed it. The Sieur de la Salle, descending the Mississippi River in 1682, asserted a French claim by building a fort on Matagorda Bay. The French went no farther, but the Spaniards made a few settlements, and the area became part of Mexico, then a Spanish colony. Mexico won independence in 1821, and in that year Americans began settling Texas in large numbers. They revolted against Mexican rule, and in 1836, after defeating a Mexican army, they established the Republic of Texas, which was recognized by the United States in 1837. It lasted eight years before being admitted to the Union. Texas seceded in 1861 and was an active member of the Confederacy. In later years Texas exerted great political and economic influence in the nation.

PROFILE

Admitted to Union: Dec. 29, 1845; rank, 28th
US Congressmen: Senate, 2; House of Representatives, 24
Population: 11,196,730 (1970); rank, 4th
Capital: Austin, 251,808 (1970)
Chief cities: Houston, 1,232,802; Dallas, 844,401; San Antonio, 654,153
State Legislature: Senate, 31; House of Representatives, 150
Area: 267,338sq mi (692,405sq km); rank, 2nd
Elevation: Highest, 8,751ft (2,672m), Guadalupe Peak; lowest, sea level
Industries (major products): chemicals, refined petroleum, aircraft, aerospace equipment, automobiles, ships and boats, machinery, processed foods
Agriculture (major products): cattle, sheep, poultry, rice, sorghum, fruits, vegetables, nuts, peanuts
Minerals (major): petroleum, natural gas, sulfur, helium, cement, clay
State nickname: Lone Star State
State motto: Friendship
State bird: mockingbird
State flower: bluebonnet
State tree: pecan

Texas City, city in SE Texas, 35mi (56km) SE of Houston, on Galveston Bay; severely damaged by ship explosion and subsequent fires 1947, city was later rebuilt. Industries: chemicals, oil, tin. Exports: phosphate, petroleum, sulfur, chemicals, metal, cotton. Inc. 1912. Pop. (1970) 38,908.

Texas Rangers, mounted law officers organized in 1835 during the Texas Revolution against Mexico. They became a division of the Texas Department of Public Safety in 1935. Stephen Austin, founder of the first Texas colony, hired rangers in 1823, before they were formally organized, to defend the colony from Indian attack. The first Rangers were left to protect small Anglo-American settlements from the Comanche and Apache Indians while the main Texas army was fighting the Mexican army in the south. In the Mexican War (1846–48) they were effective as guerrilla fighters and scouts. Temporarily disbanding in the Reconstruction period, they were organized into

Tenrec

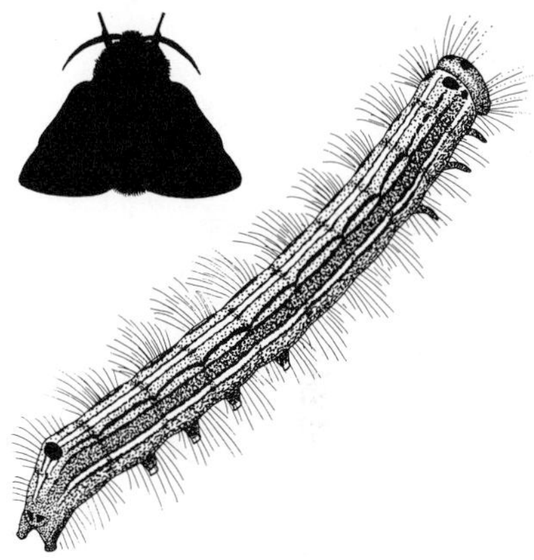
Tent caterpillar

Tern

Texas: Alamo, San Antonio

two battalions in 1874, one to control the frontier range wars, and one to stop banditry and cattle theft along the Rio Grande. This was their period of greatest renown. The fast growth of the cattle business brought about rustling, feuding, shootings, and such lawlessness that the Texas Rangers were in great demand. Their responsibilities decreased and they lost their flamboyancy after the turn of the century.

Texas v. White (1869), US Supreme Court decision affirming Abraham Lincoln's position that the Union was indissoluble and upholding Congress' authority to reconstruct the states. It ruled that, despite secession, Texas had remained a state and that Congress, not the executive, would recognize state governments.

Textbooks. △1778.

Textiles, fabrics produced from natural or synthetic fibers by weaving, knitting, felting, braiding, or netting. They are classified either by the nature of the fiber or of the weave. Fibers include wool, cotton, linen, silk, and synthetics, such as rayon, nylon, and the polyesters. Colored designs are applied to textiles by a variety of methods, ranging from ancient block printing to modern screen printing. △1620.

T-Groups. *See* Sensitivity Training.

Thackeray, William Makepeace (1811–63), English novelist, comic illustrator, and journalist. A prolific writer in several genres, including satiric, historic, and fairy-tale, his works include *Barry Lyndon* (1842), *Vanity Fair* (1848), *Pendennis* (1850), *Henry Esmond* (1852), and *The Virginians* (1859).

Thai, the national language of Thailand, spoken there by about 35,000,000 people, or 85% of the country's population. Closely related to Lao, spoken across the border in Laos, it belongs to the Tai family of languages.

Thailand (Prathet Thai), independent nation in SE Asia. Formerly known as Siam, it is now a constitutional monarchy. Rice is the major crop.

Land and economy. The Kingdom of Thailand is located in the center of SE Asia, bordered by Burma (W and N), Laos (N and E), Cambodia (SE), and Malaysia (S). Its coastline is on the Gulf of Thailand. Thailand is made up of four divisions: central, a fertile region with water from the Chao Phraya River and irrigation canals; NE, a large plateau of poor soil, frequent droughts or floods; N, forested mountains and fertile valleys; and S, a long, narrow rain forest from central Thailand to Malaysia. Monsoons dominate the tropical climate. With a fast-developing economy, Thailand is still dependent on agriculture. Rice is the chief crop and accounts for 20% of foreign earnings. Rubber, corn, and tin, of which it is the world's 4th-largest producer, follow in importance. Tourism is a growing factor in the economy.

People. Composed mainly of Thai stock, the population includes 2,000,000 urban Chinese and about 800,000 Malay-speaking Muslims with minorities of hill tribes and Vietnamese. A rural society population is centered in the fertile valleys. The official language is Thai; English is the second language. Education is compulsory between ages 7 and 14, and literacy is estimated at 70%. Theravada Buddhism is the religion of 90% of the people. Religious freedom is permitted.

Government. A constitutional monarchy functions through a cabinet, unicameral legislative assembly, and centralized administrative system.

History. Historical records indicate that Thais originally ruled a kingdom in what is Yunnan, China, and migrated to Thailand about 1,000 years ago, encouraged by the Mongol invasion of S China. Contact with the West came with the Portuguese in the 16th century. Burmese conquerors in the 18th century were driven out by Rama I, founder of the present Thai ruling family. European colonialism grew stronger, and succeeding rulers modernized Thailand in an attempt to survive as a state. Thailand was occupied by Japan from 1941 until the Allied victory in WWII. The victories of Communist forces elsewhere in SE Asia forced Thailand to modify its pro-Western policies in the mid-1970s. The power of the monarchy is primarily symbolic.

PROFILE

Official name: Kingdom of Thailand
Area: 198,414sq mi (514,000sq km)
Population: 39,787,000
Density: 207per sq mi (80per sq km)
Chief cities: Bangkok (capital); Thon Buri
Government: Constitutional monarchy
Religion: Buddhist
Language: Thai
Monetary unit: Baht
Gross national product: $12,200,000,000
Per capita income: $232
Industries: tapioca, auto assembly, pharmaceuticals, textiles, electric goods
Agriculture: rice, rubber, corn, coconuts, tobacco, pepper, peanuts, beans, cotton, jute
Minerals: tin, iron, manganese, tungsten, antimony
Trading partners: Japan, United States, Malaysia, Singapore, Hong Kong, West Germany, United Kingdom

Thailand, Gulf of. *See* Siam, Gulf of.

Thalamus, forebrain area immediately above the hypothalamus. Sometimes called the sensory-motor receiving area, it obtains impulses from sensory neurons and sends them to other structures in the brain, particularly areas of the cerebral cortex. △666, 678.

Thalassemia, or Cooley's anemia, a genetic condition characterized by a deficiency of hemoglobin in the blood. It is prevalent in Italy, Greece, the Middle East, India, Thailand, and China.

Thales (*c.* 634–546 BC), the first Greek scientist and philosopher of whom we have any knowledge. His parents were Greek and he lived in Miletus in Asia Minor. He made discoveries in geometry, such as that the angles at the base of an isosceles triangle are equal. He predicted the eclipse of the Sun that took place in 585 BC. He founded the Ionian school of natural philosophy, which held that a single elementary matter, water, is the basis of all the transformations of nature. △1438, 1480.

Thallium, metallic element (symbol Tl) of group IIIA of the periodic table, discovered spectroscopically (1861) by Sir William Crookes and isolated by him (1862). It occurs in some rare minerals; chief source is as a by-product from iron pyrites. Thallium is an extremely toxic compound. It is used in infrared detectors and certain specialized glasses. Properties: at. no. 81; at. wt. 204.37; sp gr 11.85; melt. pt. 578°F (303.5°C); boil. pt. 2,655°F (1,457°C); most common isotope Tl^{205} (70.5%).

Thallophyte, subkingdom of nonvascular plants containing more primitive forms of plant life. They have no distinctive roots, stems, or leaves and range in size from one-celled plants to 200-ft (61m) seaweeds. Asexual reproduction is by spores and sexual reproduction is by gamete fusion. Chlorophyll-containing thallophytes are algae, euglenoids, dinoflagellates, and lichens; thallophytes lacking chlorophyll are bacteria, fungi, and slime molds.

Thames, England's chief river. Its four headstreams —Thames, Churn, Coln, and Leach—rise in the Cotswolds, Gloucestershire. It winds E across S England, through London to the North Sea at the Nore. Navigable by barges as far as Lechlade, it is tidal to Teddington. It is crossed by 27 bridges including a new London Bridge. Above London it is mainly a pleasure river with beautiful scenery. Since 1857 the Thames Conservancy has successfully engaged in pollution control.

Thant, U (1909–74), Burmese diplomat, secretary general of the UN (1961–71). From 1947 he represented Burma at the UN. With the death of Dag Hammarskjöld in 1961, he became acting secretary general. He was elected secretary general in 1962 and reelected in 1966. He was involved in settling crises over Soviet missiles in Cuba (1962), civil war in the Congo (Zaire) (1963) and in Cyprus (1964), and the India-Pakistan War (1965). He was less successful in dealing with the Vietnam War, the Middle East, and the India-Pakistan War of 1971. △1350.

Thapsus, an ancient town on the coast of Tunisia about 100 mi (161km) SSE of Carthage. Julius Caesar defeated the Pompeians under Cato the Younger at Thapsus in 46 BC.

Thatching. △1610.

Theater, the art of mimetic representation, has developed among nearly all civilizations throughout known history. Early presentations usually involved honoring gods or mimicking nature. At other times important historical events were reenacted, or ribald and irreverent actions were displayed. Thus, motivations are diverse but are united by a common pleasure; the temporary removal of self-consciousness as feelings merge in a vital, communal flow. Mimetic features can be seen in African tribal dances and in American Indian dance dramas. In Asian theater a combination of poetry, music, and dance called *sangita* prevails. Abstract, symbolic, and fixed in form, it includes the 4th- and 5th-century Sanskrit plays in India, the popular Chinese opera, and the No and Kabuki theater in Japan. Drama, a form of literature written for stage presentation, had its greatest devel opment in Western theater, and after the 19th cer tury grew in the East as well, existing alongside th classical forms. Generally narrative in form, with a interplay of forces resulting in a conflict which is the resolved, Western drama has its roots in ancier Greece, particularly in the works of Aeschylus, Sopho cles, and Euripides, who wrote tragedies, and Aristo phanes and Menander, who wrote comedies. The Ro mans preferred spectacles to drama, and th Christians suppressed it; nevertheless theatrical cont nuity was created from the ancient to the mediev era by traveling mime troops. Medieval drama bega in the church, where sung Latin scripture evolved int mystery, miracle, and morality plays. A rediscovery c classical drama in the Renaissance inspired a grea flowering of the art, most brilliantly displayed in th works of Shakespeare. The late 17th century pro duced the French neoclassical plays of Racine an Molière and English Restoration comedies of mar ners. A romantic reaction to neoclassicism was ex pressed in Germany, the *sturm und drang* movemen later occurring in France and England. Realism emerged in the 19th century, powerfully expressed b Russian dramatists and Norway's Henrik Ibsen. Sym bolism, foreshadowed by Ibsen and expressed in Au gust Strindberg's dream plays, was a reaction to rea ism, as were Oscar Wilde's comedies of manners George Bernard Shaw's uniquely witty and intelligen plays of ideas stand apart from any trend. Naturalism expressed by Sean O'Casey and Eugene O'Neill, is strong 20th-century influence, as is expressionism portraying dehumanization by technology. Federic García Lorca's verse dramas, Bertolt Brecht's epic the ater, and Luigi Pirandello's plays pitting illusio against reality are major 20th-century works. Girau doux elegantly presents an imaginative, rational voic in the French neoclassical tradition. A widesprea sense of the meaninglessness of life followed Worl War II, bringing to the fore the theater of the absur of Samuel Beckett, Eugene Ionesco, and Jean Genê Pessimism has also been expressed in the existentia works of Jean Paul Sartre and Albert Camus, in Harol Pinter's "comedies of menace," and in the more rea istic works of Arthur Miller and Tennessee Williams The theater of cruelty vies to see who can be the mos shockingly outrageous. Boundaries between aud ence and players are being crossed by experimenta groups worldwide. △998, 1100, 1240, 1426.

Theater of the Absurd, a theater form that aban dons traditional devices of drama, including plo meaningful dialogue, and normal characterization, t display the bewilderment and alienation of man. Th roots of this theater form are Surrealism, Dadaism and Existentialism. Playwrights include Eugen Ionesco *(The Bald Soprano,* 1950) and Samuel Beck ett *(Waiting for Godot,* 1952). △1318.

Thebes (Thivai), ancient city in central Egypt (now occupied by Karnak and Luxor) on the Nile; most im portant from 2143 BC until its decline in 10th centur BC; site of noted tomb of Tutankhamen.

Thebes, city in ancient Greece; center of Mycenaea power, destroyed *c.* 1100 BC. Rebuilt, it gained dom nance of the Boeotian League 5th century BC; hostilit to Athens over the Platae district led to alliance wit Persia and later with Sparta in the Peloponnesia Wars. Thebes was victorious (371 BC) in its later clas with Sparta, but was almost destroyed in an uprisin against Alexander the Great (336 BC) and fell to th Romans in 197. It was the seat of the legendary kin Oedipus and the scene of tragedies by Sophocles an Aeschylus. The modern market town of Thebes built on the site of the Theban acropolis. Pop. 15,89 △994.

Thecodonts. △570.

Theism, philosophical and theological systems, de veloped in opposition to atheism. The creed deve oped proposes the existence of one supreme being As the creator of all, he is perfect and merits man worship. Man is allowed freedom of choice, and reve lation is possible.

Thematic Apperception Test (TAT), in psycho ogy, a projective technique used to assess personalit characteristics developed in 1938 by Henry A. Mu ray. The subject is presented with a series of carc with pictures on them, and he or she must make u a story about the characters in each picture. Th method assumes that subjects will reveal their uncor scious feelings and desires in their stories. *See als* Projective Techniques. △814.

Themistocles (*c.* 528–462 BC), Athenian statesman Elected archon in 493, he ostracized many, built u the navy in time to save Athens from Persia, and de vised the battle plan for Salamis. Ousted in 471 fc association with the Persians, he fled to Asia and governed a territory. △994.

Theocracy, government ruled by religious leaders, who believe they possess divine authority. Theocracies were frequent in primitive societies and existed in ancient Egypt and the Orient. The New England Puritan colony (1620–60) was predominately theocratic. △898.

Theodora (?508–48), wife of the Byzantine Emperor Justinian I (*r.* 527–565). △1056.

Theodore Roosevelt National Memorial Park, park in W central North Dakota, in 3 units in the heart of the Badlands, includes bird and animal sanctuaries, museum, camping and picnicking grounds, petrified forest; in memory of President Theodore Roosevelt who owned several ranches in the area. Area: 70,374 acres (28,501hectares). Est. 1947.

Theodoric the Great (454?–526), Ostrogoth king who became king of Italy. Zeno, emperor of the Eastern Roman Empire, encouraged Theodoric to expel Odoacer, the German ruler of Italy. Theodoric defeated Odoacer and established (493) a peaceful reign based on Roman law and administration. Himself an Arian, he tolerated his subjects' Catholicism until an agreement between the churches of Rome and Constantinople (519) raised fears of new persecutions of Arians. *See also* Arianism. △1054.

Theodosius I, the Great (346?–395), Roman emperor (379–95). In 380–82 Theodosius reached a peaceful solution to the problem of the Gothic invasions. The Goths were allowed to settle on the Roman frontier but were made federate allies *(foederati)* of the Roman Empire. In this way Theodosius maintained imperial authority throughout the empire. He is best known, however, for his firm adherence to Christian orthodoxy, which later earned him the title of "the Great."

Theodosius II (401–50), Eastern Roman emperor (408–50). A weak ruler, he was dominated throughout his reign by others, among them his elder sister Pulcheria and his wife Eudocia. During his reign, the fortifications of Constantinople were strengthened, making the city virtually invulnerable to foreign attack. In 438 he published the Theodosian Code, an important legal reference work.

Theology, systematic, scientific investigation of the precepts of a given religion. It is intricately related to philosophical and historical studies. It strives to achieve an understanding of various beliefs. Necessarily, it is concerned with concepts of a divine being, man, and moral law or ethics. It has many branches, such as dogmatic, historical, and systematic theology. △1088

Theophanes the Greek (*fl.* 1378–1405), Byzantine painter. △1060.

Theorbo. △1132.

Theorem, statement or proposition that is to be proved by logical reasoning from given facts and justifiable assumptions. In geometry a proposition is considered as a problem (a construction to be effected) or a theorem (a statement to be proved). Outside geometry two of the more famous theorems are the "binomial theorem" and the "fundamental theorem of algebra."

Theosophy, religious movement founded in the 19th century by H.P. Blavatsky. Using the Upanishads and Sutras as sources, it claims a natural awareness of the Divine. A personal God is denied, and Christ is seen as wholly human. The belief of the transmigration of souls is a central tenet.

Theresa of Avila, Saint (1515–82), Spanish reformer and author of books on the spiritual life. After 19 years as a Carmelite nun, she had a mystical experience of the nearness of God and Christ. Thereafter, she began to found monasteries following an old and more austere Carmelite rule. Her works include *The Way of Perfection,* written to instruct her nuns, and *The Interior Castle,* a book on spiritual experience. Theresa was one of the first two women to be named Doctors of the Church.

Thermal Cracking. *See* Cracking.

Thermal Current or Motion. △1502.

Thermic Lance. △1510.

Thermocline, middle layers of ocean water between surface and deep waters, which are defined by differing densities and temperatures. It is up to 1,000m (3,280ft) thick with a lowest temperature only a few degrees above freezing. The thermocline is important as a stable boundary that tends to prevent interchange between layers.

Thermodynamics, the study of the heat content and interactions of systems. Historically, the laws of thermodynamics were developed from observation of large-scale properties of systems, with no understanding of the underlying atomic structure. It is now possible to calculate those laws from statistical and quantum mechanical principles. Thus the historical subject of thermodynamics is now subsumed in the disciplines of statistical mechanics or quantum thermodynamics. The three laws of thermodynamics follow: the First Law, basically a restatement of the conservation of energy, states that for any substance a quantity called the internal energy can be defined such that the change in the internal energy is the sum of the work done on the system and the heat absorbed by it. The Second Law states that for any substance a quantity called entropy can be defined such that (a) if the system is left alone, its entropy tends to increase, and (b) if the system absorbs heat, its entropy changes by the ratio of the heat absorbed to the temperature. The Third Law states that as the temperature approaches absolute zero, the entropy approaches a constant value independent of all other parameters. *See also* Statistical Mechanics. △1508, 1510.

Thermoelectric Propulsion, any of several rocket propulsion systems combining heat and electrical means to accelerate particles to high velocities. The arc jet engine uses an electric arc to heat liquid hydrogen to 50,000°C; the resulting plasma (separate electrons and protons) is accelerated through a conventional nozzle, or, in the plasma engine, through a magnetic field for greater force. Ion rockets accelerate heavy charged particles such as cesium ions. All thermoelectric rockets produce low but long-lasting thrust—superior for interplanetary space trips.

Thermometer, an instrument for measuring temperature by using those physical liquid, gas, or electrical changes in substances that are dependent on their degree of hotness or coldness. For example, air temperature may be measured by the expansion and contraction of mercury in a glass tube against units of a temperature scale. Common temperature scales are Celsius, Fahrenheit, and Kelvin. *See also* Temperature. △218, 1504, 1508, 1656.

Thermonuclear Bomb. *See* Nuclear Weapon.

Thermonuclear Reaction. *See* Fusion, Nuclear.

Thermoplastic, type of polymer that becomes plastic on being heated and can be repeatedly melted or softened by heat without change of properties. Typical examples are polyethylene, polystyrene, and polyvinyl chloride. *See also* Plastics; Thermosetting Polymer.

Thermopylae (Thermopilai), mountain pass in E central Greece, between Mt Oeta and S Malian Gulf. Strategically located as N entrance to Greece, it was scene of many ancient battles. During Persian Wars, Spartans, under Leonidas, were defeated by Xerxes and Persians (480 BC); also site of Roman victory over Antiochus III of Syria (191 BC), and of German stalemate of Anzacs (1941). △994.

Thermosetting Polymer, type of polymer that loses its plasticity once it has been softened by heat and pressure. Typical examples are the polymers that form a three-dimensional network of cross linkages, such as the phenolic resins, polyesters, epoxy resins, and silicones. *See also* Plastics; Thermoplastic.

Thermostat, device for maintaining a constant temperature, usually by cutting off the heat supply when a predetermined temperature is reached. Most thermostats contain a bimetallic strip that breaks an electrical contact by buckling at a certain temperature. △1538.

Theropoda, saurischian dinosaur that was a biped, sharp-toothed carnivore. During Triassic times (190,000,000 years ago), they were a light, running reptile, eg, Coelophysis. Later, they were several large types, such as the Jurassic Allosaurus and the giant Tyrannosaurus during Cretaceous times. *See also* Saurischian. △570, 572.

Theseus, in Greek mythology, a hero of many adventures. Son of Aethra, a princess of Troezen, by two fathers, Aegeus, king of Athens, and the sea god Poseidon. Theseus killed many villains in his youth, among them Procrustes, who forced his victims to lie on a bed that he used as a measure. Procrustes cut off

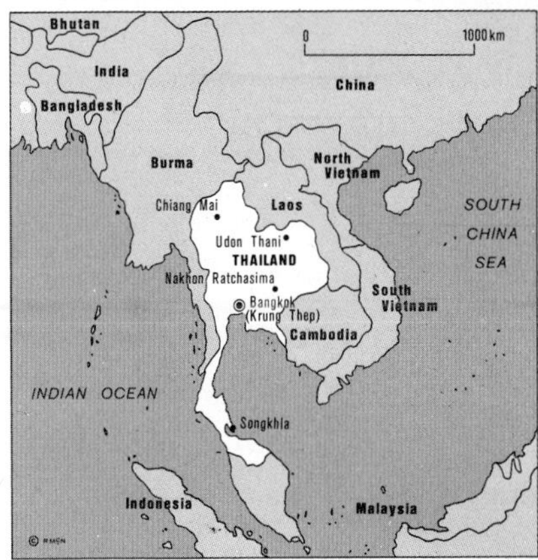
Bhutan
India
Bangladesh
China
0
1000km
Burma
North Vietnam
Chiang Mai
Laos
Udon Thani
THAILAND
Nakhon Ratchasima
Bangkok (Krung Thep)
Cambodia
South Vietnam
SOUTH CHINA SEA
INDIAN OCEAN
Songkhla
Indonesia
Malaysia

Thailand

Thailand: ceremonial dancers

Thames River

Theater: The Glass Menagerie *by Tennessee Williams*

what overlapped or stretched the victim to fit. Theseus slew the Minotaur in the Cretan labyrinth and eventually became king of Attica. △836, 1028.

Thespis (6th century BC), Greek writer, credited with the invention of drama. He was the first to add an actor to performances, which had been dominated by the chorus alone. He is also said to have introduced the use of masks. No work remains.

Thessalonians, First and Second Epistles to, two of Paul's earliest letters, written to the church at Thessalonica. He encourages it and adjacent churches in confirmation of their faith and gives courage through Christ's Second Coming, rectifying their mistaken belief that the day of judgment is at hand.

Thessaloniki. *See* Salonika.

Thessaly (Thessalia), administrative district in N central Greece, almost completely surrounded by mountains. Ancient Thessaly headed the Amphictyonic League (6th century BC); it was subjugated by Philip II of Macedon (344 BC); later under Roman rule, passed to Ottoman Empire 1355; annexed to Greece 1881; site of WWII battle between Germans and troops of Britain and Greece. Crops: grain, cotton, sugar beets. Area: 5,382sq mi (13,939sq km). Pop. 659,243.

Thetis, a daughter of the sea god Nereus, in Greek mythology. She was the mother of the hero Achilles who attempted to make her son immortal to save him from the destiny she perceived for him. At his birth she dipped him in the River Styx, holding him by the heel. Achilles became all but invulnerable. Unfortunately, the Trojan Paris shot him in the heel with a poisoned arrow and he died.

Thiamine, vitamin of the B complex required for carbohydrate metabolism; its deficiency causes the disease beri-beri. *See* Vitamin, Vitamin B_1.

Thiard, Pontus de (1521–1605), French poet. △1172.

Thiers, Adolphe (1797–1877), French statesman and historian. He was a founder of the journal *National,* which attacked King Charles X and helped to precipitate the July Revolution of 1830. Under King Louis Philippe, Thiers held cabinet offices (1832–36) until his aggressive foreign policy led to his dismissal. After the Revolution of 1848, he was elected to the constituent assembly. Although supporting Louis Napoleon for president, Thiers opposed his coup d'etat in 1851 and was exiled. Again elected to the legislature in 1863, he attacked Napoleon III's imperial policies and promoted reforms. After the Franco-Prussian War he was chosen chief executive of the provisional government. He harshly suppressed the 1871 Commune of Paris and became president of the republic until 1873, when he was forced to resign.

Thieu, Nguyen Van (1923–), president of the Republic of Vietnam (1967–75). He participated in the overthrow of President Diem in 1963 and ruled with others until his election as president. In 1968 he declared martial law and suspended most freedoms. He was reelected in 1971 amid dispute. Thieu resigned shortly before the fall of Saigon to the Vietcong and fled to Taiwan.

Thighbone. *See* Femur.

Thinking, mental (ideational or cognitive) activity of the brain, the integration of an external stimulus with the person's response to it. Thinking requires some detachment from the outer world in order to understand, predict, and master that world. Objective thinking reaches its highest level in scientific thinking (investigation). The thinking of the mentally ill is impaired, and the thought processes of autistic children, schizophrenics, and neurotic psychotic people are unique. *See also* Austistic Thinking; Repression; Schizophrenia. △778.

Third International. *See* Communist International.

Third Party Politics, political action by a group challenging the major parties in a two-party system. Third parties usually represent voters who are dissatisfied with the existing parties or who feel their views are not expressed by them. △1358.

Third Reich, the period in German history from 1933–45 when Germany was under the totalitarian dictatorship of Adolf Hitler. The term was used to indicate a closeness with other great periods of German history—the First Reich of the Holy Roman Empire and the Second Reich (1871–1918) founded by Otto von Bismarck.

Third Republic, French government during 1870–1940. It began with the collapse of the Second Empire in the Franco-Prussian War (1870–71), with the bloody uprising of the Paris Commune following soon after (1871). Adolphe Thiers provided the leadership that created republican institutions. Until 1914 the government was marked by bourgeois liberalism and a surge of imperial growth. After 1918 it was beset by economic problems. It collapsed (1940) as it was born, in defeat by Germany. *See also* Franco-Prussian War. △1288.

Third World, name given to less developed nations of Asia, Africa, and Latin America. These nations are outside the larger power blocs and are usually agrarian and lacking advanced technology. They often have unstable governments and a variety of social problems. △732, 1352, 1386.

Thirteen Colonies, name given to the 13 territories that, along with Canada, made up British North America prior to the American Revolution. After the Revolution, the colonies became the first states in the United States. They are New Hampshire, Massachusetts, Connecticut, Rhode Island, New York, New Jersey, Pennsylvania, Delaware, Maryland, Virginia, North Carolina, South Carolina, and Georgia.

Thirty Years War (1618–48), European war. It involved German Protestant princes with France, Sweden, England, and Denmark against the Hapsburgs and Catholic princes of the Holy Roman Empire. Bohemian Protestant princes revolted (1618) against Catholic King Ferdinand (later Emperor Ferdinand II) and the revolt spread throughout Europe. The war left German lands devastated, German population tremendously decreased, the German economy in ruins, the Holy Roman Empire divided, and the Hapsburgs with decreased power. After the war, European religious conflicts decreased; the Peace of Westphalia led to increased religious toleration. *See also* Holy Roman Empire. △1154.

Thistle, plant with thorny leaves and purple, pink, yellow, or white flower heads with prickly bracts. Most thistles belong to the genera *Cirsium, Onopordum,* and *Carduus.* Many, such as the Canada thistle *(Cirsium arvense)* are fast-spreading, troublesome weeds in the United States. Family Compositae. △446.

Thistle Butterfly. *See* Painted Lady Butterfly.

Thomas, Saint, one of the 12 Apostles of Jesus Christ. In the *Gospel of John* he is called Twin (Greek *Didymus*). He has been called "Doubting Thomas" because, after the Resurrection, he at first did not believe he saw the risen Lord (John 20: 24–28). The *Gospel of Thomas* and three other apocryphal works bearing his name were written well after his time.

Thomas, Dylan (1914–53), Welsh poet. His verse is powerfully rhetorical, occasionally willfully obscure, but at its best, as in the poems in *Deaths and Entrances* (1946), both original and simple. His radio play *Under Milk Wood* (1954) makes skillful use of speech rhythms. His obsessive drinking contributed to his early death while on a lecture tour in the United States.

Thomas, Norman Mattoon (1884–1968), US socialist leader, b. Marion, Ohio. A pacifist, he joined the Socialist Party in 1918. In 1926 he became party leader and was its unsuccessful candidate for US president six times (1928–1948). A strong anti-Communist, he campaigned for social welfare measures, civil rights, free speech, and world peace.

Thomas à Kempis (*c.*1380–1471), German theologian. He was born in Germany (family name Hemerken) and entered a monastery in the Netherlands in 1399. There he became a priest and spent most of his life in scholarly work. He was influenced by the "modern devotion," a movement to return to the simple and sincere ways of the early Christians. He is generally believed to be the author of the *Imitation of Christ,* one of the most widely read devotional books, which gives counsel on how to put away worldly interests and follow Christ.

Thomas of Woodstock, Duke of Gloucester. *See* Gloucester, Thomas of Woodstock, Duke of.

Thomism, the philosophy of St Thomas Aquinas, one of the major systems in Scholasticism. Aquinas blended Aristotle's philosophy with Christian theology. Using Aristotle's views of matter and form, Aquinas conceived a hierarchy in which spirit is higher than matter, soul higher than body, and theology above philosophy. He taught that reason, while essential, can reach only so high. There is a point at which faith becomes the final authority. △856, 1088.

Thompson, David (1770–1857), Canadian fur trader and explorer, b. England. He joined the Hudson's Bay Co. (1784), wintered at Calgary (1787), and studied surveying (1789–90). He journeyed to Lake Athabasca (1796), took a 4,000-mile (6,400-km) trip to the Mississippi headwaters (1797–98), and established Kootenae House (1807), the first trading post on the Columbia River. He explored the Columbia to Fort Astoria (1811) and charted the US-Canada boundary (1816–26).

Thompson, river in S British Columbia, Canada; formed by convergence of North Thompson and South Thompson rivers at Kamloops: discovered 1808 by Simon Fraser. Length: 304mi (489km).

Thomson, (Sir) Joseph John (1856–1940), English physicist. His work on the conductivity of gases led him to the discovery of the electron in 1897 and the foundation of the famous atomic research unit at the Cavendish Laboratories in England. He was awarded a Nobel Prize in 1906 for his investigations of electrical conductivity of gases. △1282, 1480.

Thomson, Virgil (1896–), US music critic and composer, b. Kansas City, Mo. He was chief music critic for the New York *Herald Tribune* (1940–57). Many of his works have been based on American folk music. He is best known for the operas *Four Saints in Three Acts* (1928) and *The Mother of Us All* (1947), both with librettos by Gertrude Stein.

Thomson, William, 1st Baron Kelvin. *See* Kelvin, William Thomson, 1st Baron.

Thomson Effect. A potential difference is developed between two points on a metal conductor if the two points are maintained at different temperatures. Named after Sir William Thomson (Lord Kelvin) (1824–1907).

Thon Buri, city in central Thailand, opposite Bangkok on Chao Phraya River; served as capital of Siam (1767–82). Industries: rice processing, sawmills. Pop. 919,000.

Thor, deity common to all the early Germanic peoples, a great warrior represented as a red-bearded, middle-aged man of enormous strength. Thor was an implacable foe of the harmful race of giants, but benevolent toward mankind. He was generally secondary to the god Odin, who in some traditions was his father. In Iceland he was the supreme deity. △1068.

Thorazine. *See* Chlorpromazine.

Thoreau, Henry David (1817–62), US author, b. Concord, Mass. After graduating from Harvard University (1837), he taught school for several years in Concord. There he became friends with Ralph Waldo Emerson and other Transcendentalists. During 1841–43 he lived with Emerson as a handyman and assistant. During this period some of his early prose and poetry appeared in the Transcendentalist journal, *The Dial.*

An ardent individualist, in July 1845, he began to live at Walden Pond, near Concord, in a cabin that he built. He kept a daily journal, recording, among other things, the plant and animal life that he observed and worked on his first book *A Week on the Concord and Merrimack Rivers* (1849). In 1846 he spent one night in jail for refusing to pay a federal poll tax in protest against the Mexican War, which he regarded as a war for the extension of slavery; his famous essay on "Civil Disobedience" (1849) stemming from this incident emphasized his belief that man should live according to his conscience. Thoreau left Walden in September 1847. Subsequently, he worked in his father's pencil factory and at odd jobs. His masterwork, *Walden,* or meditative narrative, appeared in 1854. During the 1850s, he was active in the antislavery movement, helping escaped slaves on their way to Canada, lecturing against slavery, and praising John Brown. He died of tuberculosis. Records of his walking excursions were published in *The Maine Woods* (1864), *Cape Cod* (1865), and *A Yankee in Canada* (1866). His *Poems of Nature* was published in 1895. *See also* Brown, John; Civil Disobedience; Transcendentalism; Walden. △1374.

Thorium, radioactive metallic element (symbol Th) of the actinide group, first discovered in 1828 by J. J. Berzelius. The chief ore is monazite (phosphate). The metal is used in photoelectric and thermionic emitters. Chemically reactive, it burns in air and reacts slowly in water. Properties: at. no. 90; at. wt. 232.-038; sp gr 11.7; melt. pt. 3,182°F (1,750°C); boil. pt. 6,872°F (3,800°C); most stable isotope Th^{232} (1.41×10^{10}yrs). *See also* Actinide Elements.

Thorn Apple, (1) the fruit of the hawthorn. (2) Any

plant of the genus *Datura*, especially Jimson weed *(D. stramomium)*, a very poisonous, tall, coarse, annual weed of tropical Asiatic origin, now naturalized all over the world. It has foul-smelling leaves and large white or violet trumpet-shaped flowers that are succeeded by round prickly fruit. *See also* Hawthorn.

Thorndike, Edward Lee (1874–1949), US psychologist and educator, b. Williamsburg, Mass. He devised the first systematic theory of learning, stressing the importance of the "law of effect" (the principle of reinforcement). He was one of the earliest psychological researchers to do laboratory studies with animals, and he also pioneered in applying psychological knowledge to problems in education and human abilities. Major works include *The Fundamentals of Learning* (1932).

Thorpe, James Francis ("Jim") (1888–1953), US athlete, b. Bright Path near Prague, Okla. A Sac Indian, he won both the pentathlon and decathlon in the 1912 Olympics. A year later, however, he was forced to give up his medals when it was discovered he had played semi-pro baseball. He played professional football with several teams (1915–26) and baseball in the National League with three different teams (1913–19). He was elected to the Football Hall of Fame in 1963. In 1950 an Associated Press Poll ranked him outstanding American athlete of the first half of the 20th century. In 1973 the Amateur Athletic Union voted to restore his Olympic records and medals. He was 1st president of American Professional Football Association later known as the NFL.

Thoth, in Egyptian mythology, the scribe of the gods. In various myths he appears as the record keeper of the dead, patron of the arts and learning, inventor of writing, and as creator of the universe. Thoth is depicted as a man with the head of an ibis or of an ape, bearing pen and ink or the lunar disk and crescent.

Thousand Islands, group of more than 1,800 islands in the St Lawrence River extending about 50mi (81km) along the US-Canada border; about equally divided between both countries; site of two New York state parks and Canada's St Lawrence Islands National Park. The Thousand Island Bridge (1938) connects Collins Landing, New York, with Ivy Lea, Ontario.

Thousand Oaks, city in S California, 30mi (48km) WNW of Los Angeles; original name was Conejo Valley. Industries: aircraft parts, citrus fruits, plastics. Inc. 1964. Pop. (1970) 35,873.

Thrasher, New World songbird related to the mockingbird. The brown thrasher *(Toxostoma rufum)* of E North America is brownish above and pale below with white stripes on its wings. It frequents forest edges and grasslands, feeding on insects and fruit. It builds its nest in thick vines and lays pale blue-green eggs (4–5) marked with reddish spots. Length: 11in (28cm). Several genera are confined to the West Indies, including the trembler *(Cinclocerthia ruficauda)*. Length: 9in (23cm).

Thread Worm. *See* Horsehair Worm.

Threonine, colorless soluble crystalline essential amino acid found in proteins. *See* Amino Acid.

Thresher, agricultural machine used to separate grain from chaff and straw. The first threshers were the feet of humans and animals or flails. Today, the threshing operation is incorporated into the combine. *See also* Combine. △310.

Threshold, in psychology, theoretical point along a physical scale of energy that corresponds to the detection of the stimulus (detection threshold) or the discrimination between stimuli (difference threshold). Thresholds are sometimes called *limens*.

Thrip, slender, sucking insects found worldwide. Varied in color, most are plant feeders and some carry plant diseases. Often found in large numbers, they may be irritating to human skin. Length: 0.02–0.5in (0.5–13mm). Order Thysanoptera.

Thrombin, blood enzyme that converts fibrinogen to fibrin during clot formation. *See also* Blood Clotting.

Thrombophlebitis, inflammation of a vein, coupled with formation of a blood clot that adheres to the wall of the vessel. Treatment is with anticoagulants and application of heat.

Thrombosis, formation or presence of a blood clot in the heart or any blood vessel. Factors involved are injury to the lining of heart or vessels, alterations in normal blood flow, and changes in the coagulability of the blood.

Thrush, family (Turdidae) of small-to-medium-sized perching songbirds, often seen on the ground; found worldwide. Typical thrushes may be brightly colored or black, but most have yellow or orange bills and eye rings. They feed mainly on insects or fruit and build open nests. Included in the family are the robin, hermit thrush, wood thrush, and nightingale.

Thrust, Rocket, the force developed by a rocket engine. It depends on the velocity *(v)* of the exhaust gases, the difference in pressure between the combustion chamber and exit nozzle gases ($P_C - P_e$), the area of the exhaust nozzle (A_e), and the mass of gas expelled per unit time (M): $F = M_V + (P_C - P_e)A_e$. Thus the higher the velocity of the exhaust gases, or the greater their molecular weight, the larger the thrust. △1722.

Thucydides (*c.* 470–*c.* 400 BC), noted ancient historian. After commanding an unsuccessful expedition (424) to Amphipolis in the Peloponnesian War, he went into exile (423–403), during which he wrote his *History of the Peloponnesian War.* △998.

Thugs, members of a secret society in India who would kill in honor of Kali, Hindu goddess of destruction. They strangled their victims. Beginning in 1829 the British stamped out the Thugs through arrests and executions, and by 1848 the menace had ended.

Thule, settlement in NW Greenland, on S shore of Wolstenholme Fjord of Baffin Bay. A large Eskimo population migrated here from Canada 1862–66; its name has been given to an anthropological term describing a pre-European Eskimo culture, also found in other Arctic areas; site of Thule Air Force Base (1952), used for furthering explorations of N Greenland icecap. Founded 1910 by Knud Rasmussen as a Danish trading post. Pop. 600.

Thulium, metallic element (symbol Tm) of the lanthanide group, first discovered in 1879 by P. T. Cleve. Chief ore is monazite (phosphate). The element has few commercial uses. Properties: at. no. 69; at. wt. 168.9342; sp. gr. 9.31 (25°C); melt. pt. 2,813°F (1,545°C); boil. pt. 3,141°F (1,727°C); most stable isotope Tm^{169} (100%). *See also* Lanthanide Elements.

Thunder Bay, city in SW Ontario, Canada, on Thunder Bay, an inlet of Lake Superior; capital of Thunder Bay district; major Canadian port; important transportation center in rich mining region; site of Lakehead University (1965) and Confederation College (1967). Industries: shipyards, oil refineries, grain elevators, paper and pulp mills. Est. 1970 by the merging of Port Arthur and Fort William. Pop. 107,805.

Thunderstorm, or electrical storm, a storm produced by a cumulonimbus cloud, accompanied by lightning, thunder, strong winds, heavy rain, and sometimes hail. Forming with strong updrafts, the thunderhead often builds up to heights of 8 to 10mi (13 to 16km), creating centers of opposite electrical charges within it and with the ground, which are discharged with lightning strokes that produce thunder. As the storm dissipates, columns of precipitation occur with strong downdrafts. *See also* Cloud; Lightning. △214.

Thurber, James (1894–1961), US author, b. Columbus, Ohio. He began his career as a reporter. In 1926 he became regular contributor of essays, short stories, and cartoons to the *New Yorker* magazine. A humorist, his work is ironic and satiric. Collections of his essays and stories include *My Life and Hard Times* (1933), *The Middle Aged Man on the Flying Trapeze* (1935), *My World and Welcome to It* (1942)—which contained the fantasy, "The Secret Life of Walter Mitty"—and *The Thurber Carnival* (1945).

Thurgau, canton in NE Switzerland, bordered (N) by Lake Constance; capital is Frauenfeld. Ruled 1264 by Hapsburgs, it was taken 1460 by Swiss cantons; in 1798 it was invaded by France; joined Swiss Confederation 1803. Products: cereals, fruit, cattle. Chief industry is wine. Area: 388sq mi (1,005 sq km). Pop. 182,835.

Thurmond, (James) Strom (1902–), US senator, b. Edgefield, S.C. He was a state senator (1933–38) and then served as governor of South Carolina (1947–51). In 1948, he was a candidate for president on the States' Rights ticket. A conservative Southerner, he entered the Senate as a Democrat in 1954, but switched to the Republican party in 1964.

Thurstone, Louis Leon (1887–1955), US psychologist, b. Chicago. He was a pioneer in the development

Norman Thomas

Sir J.J. Thomson

James Thorpe

Thrush

of ability tests and statistical methods of analyzing them. Among his publications are *Primary Mental Abilities* (1938) and *Multiple Factor Analysis* (1947).

Thus Spake Zarathustra (1883–85), poetic work of philosophy in aphoristic style by Friedrich Nietzsche. △860.

Thutmose, the royal name of four kings of the XVIIIth dynasty of Egypt (*c.*1525–1398 BC). The most significant achievement of **Thutmose I** was the subjugation of the Nile Valley up to the 3rd cataract. **Thutmose II** married his half-sister Hatshepsut, who in effect ruled Egypt for 22 years. **Thutmose III** reigned for 54 years either alone or with Thutmose II and Hatshepsut, and built his empire to include all of Syria except Phoenicia, extending it from the 3rd cataract to the Euphrates. **Thutmose IV** was the last king of the dynasty, ruling *c.*1406–1398 BC. △972.

Thylacine. △628.

Thyme, common name for *Thymus,* aromatic herbs of the mint family used as ornamental plants and for seasoning. Common thyme and mother-of-thyme, or creeping thyme, have purplish flowers. △358, 446.

Thymus Gland, one of the endocrine, or ductless, glands, located in the upper chest. Sometimes called the gland of childhood, it is large in infancy and atrophies after puberty. Its function was long unknown but it is now thought to be primarily a lymphoid organ, secreting a hormone that acts on lymph tissue and producing antibodies that function in the body's immune mechanism. Disorder of the thymus is often associated with auto-immune diseases. △690.

Thyristor Switch. △1542.

Thyroid Gland, H-shaped endocrine gland lying in the neck region, along the sides of and over the trachea. It secretes the hormone thyroxin, which is essential for the growth and development of the body, regulation of metabolism, and the utilization of some foodstuffs. A lack of thyroxin can produce cretinism in children, myxedema in adolescents and adults. Overactivity of the gland, frequently caused by a goiter, produces weight loss, bulging eyeballs, irritability. *See also* Cretinism; Goiter; Myxedema. △690.

Thyrotropic Hormone, or thyrotropin, glycoprotein produced by the anterior pituitary that stimulates growth and function of the thyroid. △690.

Thyroxin, or thyroid hormone, iodine-containing compound secreted by the thyroid. It regulates the rate of oxygen consumption by stimulation of basic metabolism; required for normal growth and development. △690.

Thysanoptera. △492.

Thysanura. △492.

Tiahuanaco, archeological site located on the S shore of Lake Titicaca in the Bolivian highlands. △ 1120.

Tianjin. *See* Tientsin.

Tiber (Tevere), second-longest river in Italy; rises in Etruscan Apennines; flows S then SW, empties into Tyrrhenian Sea near Ostia; joined to the Arno River by the Chiana Canal; flood-prone; upper Tiber is used to generate electricity. Length: 251mi (404km).

Tiberias (Teverya), lake port town in N Israel, 30mi (48km) E of Haifa on the Sea of Galilee. After the destruction of Jerusalem 2nd century, Tiberius became center of Jewish learning and capital of Jewish Palestine; site of many ancient synagogues and tomb of Maimonides; trade center for rich agricultural community. Industries: tourism, machines. Founded AD 26 by Herod Antipas; named for Roman emperor Tiberius. Pop. 23,900.

Tiberius (42 BC–AD 37), Roman emperor (AD 14–37). He governed Transalpine Gaul and fought well in Germany and Illyricum. He was adopted by Augustus, whose heirs had died, and became emperor at Augustus' death. He pursued Augustan foreign policy and practiced strict economy, leaving Rome great wealth. Harassed by political and family jealousies, he retired from Rome (26), fearing plots upon his life. Unbalanced and unpopular, he commanded numerous executions of suspected conspirators in his last years. △1020.

Tibet (Xizang), Land of the Lamas, a high plateau in central Asia annexed by China in 1951. In 1965 it was declared the Tibetan autonomous region with power in the hands of Peking-backed Chairman Ngapo Ngawang. The capital is Lhasa.

Land and economy. Its 471,700sq mi (1,221,703sq km), with 1,400,000 population, contains the world's highest mountains, the Himalayas, at the S border. This range, part of four great Tibetan mountain systems formed during the glacier period, is still growing. Lakes in one district are said to be remains of an early sea. The average altitude of the country is over 15,000ft (4,575m) and one city, Jiachan, is 15,870ft (4,840m) above sea level. Asia's largest rivers—Yangtze, Mekong, Yellow, Salween, Irrawaddy, Indus, and Brahmaputra—rise in Tibet. Annual rainfall varies from 200in (508cm) on the S side of the Himalayas to 8in (20cm) in the rest of the country. Over 12,000ft (3,660m) the climate is severe, with gale winds and temperatures dropping from 100°F (38°C) at noon to below zero at night; below 12,000ft (3,660m) the climate is pleasant. Trees in the S valleys include spruce, fir, cypress, oak, and walnut. Crops are barley, buckwheat, and medicinal herbs. Sheep, which provide the nomadic N Tibetans with both food and clothing, are raised along with yaks, goats, and horses.

People. With cultural ties to adjacent Chinese provinces and Burma, Tibetans belong to the Mongolian race and are divided into three groups: Bodpo, Khampa, and Amdo. They have few racial differences, share the same language (based on Sanskrit) and the same religion, Lamaism, an offshoot of Buddhism. Before the Communists' rule, highly endowed monasteries were the learning centers; no public schools existed.

Government. In 1964, Peking placed the Panchen Lama on the throne. He remained until 1965, when he was demoted, and Ngapo Ngawang became chairman under Peking's influence. Land reform has been promised. Since 1961, 20,000 Tibetans have fled to India.

History. Religion and history are tied together in Tibet. From Buddhism in the 11th century, Tibet moved to Lamaism in the 15th century, when a successful reformation movement (Yellow Hats) installed the first Dalai Lama as secular and religious chief. Tibet was independent 1913–50. After a Communist invasion in 1950 a pact was signed with the Dalai Lama; however, Tibetans continued to fight Chinese domination. The Chinese invaded again in 1959, and the Dalai Lama fled to India.

Tibetan Terrier, 2,000-year-old breed of dog (nonsporting group) bred in lamaseries of the Lost Valley of Tibet; first brought to West in 1920s. Considered holy and a bringer of luck in Tibet. Not actually a terrier, it has a medium-long head with long furnishings; hanging, V-shaped ears; large, dark eyes; compact body; medium-length legs; and curled tail carried over the back. The double coat is straight or waved, long, fine, and can be any color or colors. Average size: 14–16in (35.5–41cm) high at shoulder; 22–23lb (10–10.3kg). *See also* Nonsporting Dog.

Tibeto-Burman Languages, group of languages spoken in a number of countries of S Asia. It includes Burmese and Tibetan, plus Yi, Lisu, and Lahu, of China; Karen, of Burma; Kachin (or Chingpaw), of Burma and China; Bodo, Garo, Meithei, and Lushei, of E India; and Newari and Murmi, of Nepal. The Tibeto-Burman languages are thought to be part of the Sino-Tibetan family, which includes Chinese.

Tibia, larger of the two lower leg bones. It articulates with the femur, or upper leg bone, at the knee and extends to the ankle, where its lower end forms the projecting ankle bone on the inside of the leg. *See also* Fibula. △682.

Tic Douloureux, or trigeminal neuralgia, a condition of brief, but extremely severe shooting pains along one or more branches of the trigeminal nerve affecting the face. Its cause is unknown and nerve tissue appears unaffected. Surgery and decompression of the nerve roots offer permanent cures.

Ticino River, river in Switzerland and Italy; rises on the slopes of Saint Gotthard Mt; flows SE then S through Ticino canton, joining the Po River in N Italy; scene of Hannibal's victory 218 BC over Scipio in Second Punic War; source of hydroelectricity. Length: 154mi (248km).

Tick, wingless, bloodsucking arthropod found worldwide. It varies in color and is an external parasite on birds, animals, and humans. Several species carry diseases, including relapsing, spotted, and African tick fevers. Their feeding can also cause paralysis. Length: to 1.2in (3cm). Class Arachnida; order Acarina. △484.

Ticonderoga, Fort, formerly Fort Carillon; historic military post in NE New York, strategically located near Lake Champlain. Once on a main water route between Canada and New York City, it was scene of attack by Gen. James Abercromby during French and Indian War (July 1758). Taken by Ethan Allen (May 1775), it became an American base for Canadian invasion; it was occupied by British (July 1777) until Burgoyne's surrender; bought 1820 by New York entrepreneur and restored as museum.

Tidal Flat, an extensive, nearly flat, barren land area that is alternately covered and uncovered by the action of the tide. It consists of mud and sand. A tidal marsh has a covering of salt-tolerant plants and grasses.

Tidal Theory. △48.

Tide, the periodic rise and fall of the surface level of the oceans caused by the gravitational attraction of the Moon and Sun and the opposite force of centrifugal motion. Tides follow the Moon's cycle of 28 days so they arrive at a given spot 50 minutes later each day. When the Sun and Moon are aligned, the greatest tidal range occurs, called spring tides. When they are in quadrature, tidal ranges are lowest and are called neap tides. △226.

Tien Shan, mountain system in central Asia, ranging from Pamir Mts, USSR, through NW China to the border of Mongolia. Highest peak is 24,406ft (7,444m). Length: approx. 1,500mi (2,415km).

Tientsin (Tianjin, or **T'ien-ching),** port city in NE China, 80mi (129km) SE of Peking, at the confluence of Hai River and Grand Canal; 3rd-largest city in China; capital of Hopei prov. Economic and political growth was spurred when it was declared a treaty port 1860, open to foreign traffic, and including agreement with France and Britain to open parts to foreign colonization and military posts; all foreign concessions were abolished by 1946. Suffered severe earthquake damage, July, 1976. Seat of Hopeh University (1960), Nankai University, Tientsin University. Industries: textiles, chemicals, iron, steel, machine shops, flour, food processing, paper, automobiles, tobacco products, fertilizer. Pop. 3,800,000.

Tiepolo, Giovanni Battista (1696–1770), Italian painter. He was a leading artist of the Venetian Rococo. One of his early works is "The Sacrifice of Abraham" (*c.*1715–16) in the Church of Ospedaletto, Venice. He executed ceiling decorations (1720–25) for the vault of the side chapel in the Church of Scalzi, Venice. From 1741 to 1750 he executed his mature works in a classic style. They include "The Miracle of the Holy House of Loreto" (1743–44) and the Cleopatra frescoes (1745–50), a notable group of works in the Labia Palace, Venice. One of his last commissions was the decoration of the Villa Valmarana and "The Apotheosis of the Pisani Family" (1761–62) in the Villa Pisani. △1162.

Tierra del Fuego, archipelago of S Argentina and S Chile, forming the southernmost tip of South America; separated from the mainland by the Strait of Magellan; named by Ferdinand Magellan (1520) from Spanish meaning "Land of Fire." Francis Drake discovered Cape Horn (1578), the southernmost point in the archipelago and Western Hemisphere. Industries: sheep, oil, fishing, timber. Area: 28,434sq mi (73,644sq km). Pop. 15,658.

Tiger, powerful large cat found throughout Asia, mainly in forest areas. Its dark-striped coat is yellow-orange with the chin and underparts white. A non-climbing cat that relies on keen hearing, it feeds on birds, deer, cattle, and reptiles. The gestation period is three months and 1–6 young are born. The largest tiger is the Siberian variety. Length: 13ft (4m); weight: 650lb (292.5kg). The Bengal variety of India may achieve the same weight but is no more than 10ft (3m) long. Other varieties are Indochinese, Sumatran, Javan, Caspian, and south Chinese. Family Felidae; species *Panthera tigris*. *See also* Cat. △628.

Tiger Beetle, active, usually strikingly colored, medium-sized beetle. Adults and larvae prey on other insects. Family Cicindelidae.

Tiger Cat. △544.

Tiger Cowrie. △482.

Tigerfish. △392.

Tiger Moth, stout-bodied, medium-sized moth with bright orange and black wings. Most tiger moth caterpillars, including woolly bears, are covered with long hairs. Family Arctiidae. *See also* Woolly Bear.

Tiger Shark, a large shark found worldwide in inshore and offshore tropical waters. It will enter bays ɪd river mouths. This gray shark is recognized by ɪrtical bars along its sides and its long, lopsided tail. noted scavenger, its young are born alive. Length: ɪ 18ft (5.5m). Family Carcharhinidae; species *Galeo-ɪrdo cuvieri.* See also Chondrichthyes; Sharks.

ɪglath-Pileser II. △980.

ɪgris, river in SW Asia; rises in the Taurus Mts of E ɪrkey; flows SSE through Iraq until it joins the Eu-ɪrates River at Gurna, SE Iraq, to form the Shatt-al-ɪab. Subject to sudden flooding, it is the site of com-ɪex flood-control projects, and the source of large ɪigation systems since ancient times. Length: 180mi (1,990km).

ɪjuana, city in NW Mexico, S of US border, on the ɪacific Coast; developed around the Rancho de Tia ɪana, one of six cattle ranches that merged into a ɪllage 1840. Tijuana gained popularity during US ɪohibition, because of availability of alcoholic bever-ɪges; est. as a free port 1933; site of race track, ɪullfights, casinos. Industries: tourism, food process-ɪg, electronics, textiles. Pop. 354,805.

ɪlburg, city in S Netherlands, near Belgian border, ɪprox. 15mi (24km) NE of Eindhoven; 19th-century ɪxtile manufacturing and research center of Nether-ɪnds. Pop. 152,589.

ɪlden, Samuel Jones (1814–86), US political ɪader, b. New Lebanon, N.Y. A lawyer and reform ɪemocrat, he helped oust the Tweed Ring. From ɪ875–76, he was governor of New York. In 1876, as ɪe Democratic party candidate for president, he won majority of popular votes but lost the election when ɪontested electoral votes were awarded to Republi-ɪan Rutherford B. Hayes by a partisan electoral com-ɪission.

ɪlden, William Tatem, Jr. ("Bill") (1893–1953), ɪS tennis player, b. Philadelphia. He was the greatest ɪayer of his day and won seven US (1920–25; 1929) ɪnd three British singles championships (1920–21; ɪ930). He turned professional in 1931 and won the ɪngles championship twice (1931, 1935). At the age ɪ 52, he won the professional doubles title with Vin-ɪent Richards (1945).

ɪle, thin flat slabs or blocks used structurally or ɪecoratively in building. Traditionally, tiles have been ɪade of glazed or unglazed firing clay, but modern ɪes are also made of plastic, synthetic rubber, glass, ɪsphalt, and asbestos cement. Tiles are used in many ɪays, among them: floors, ceilings, roofs, sound insu-ɪtion, water-shedding surfaces, partitions, walls, ɪove linings, and ornaments.

ɪlefish, or blanquillos, tropical marine fish of some ɪommercial value. Elongated, it is olive green or blue ɪith yellow and rose markings. Length: 2ft (61cm). ɪne 15 species include the Atlantic sand tilefish *Mala-ɪanthus plumieri.* Family Branchiostegidae.

ɪill, nonsorted, nonstratified sediment or drift that is ɪeposited directly from the ice of glaciers. It is a ɪeterogeneous mixture of clay, sand, gravel, and boul-ɪers. Tillite is till that has been converted into solid ɪock.

ɪillich, Paul Johannes Oskar (1886–1965), Ger-ɪan-American theologian and philosopher. He was ɪorn in Germany, was ordained in the Lutheran ɪhurch, and served as a chaplain in World War I. ɪecause he opposed the Nazis, he left Germany for ɪe United States in 1933 and taught at Union Theo-ɪogical Seminary and several universities. He wrote ɪore than 30 books, including *The Courage To Be* ɪ952), *Dynamics of Faith* (1957), and *Systematic ɪheology* (three volumes, 1951–63). In his own words ɪe was a thinker "on the boundary" between theol-ɪgy and philosophy, the church and the rest of the ɪorld, faith and skepticism. By his "method of correla-ɪon" he tried to relate Christian faith to the problems ɪ human living. △1388.

ɪimber, growing trees or their wood, which is used ɪr building construction or carpentry. *See* Lumber; ɪood. △1610–12, 1624.

ɪimbuktu (Tombouctou), town in Mali, W Africa; ɪecame famous throughout Europe as slave and gold ɪarket; destroyed by Moroccan army 1591; seized by ɪrance 1893. Chief industry is salt trade. Settled ɪ000. Pop. 6,600.

ɪime, Measurement of. △1658.

ɪime and Motion Studies, efficiency analyses of ɪbor performances involved in the execution of a ɪven industrial activity. Innovated by Frederick W. Taylor (1856–1915) and Frank B. Gilbreth (1868–1924), the studies involve timing each discrete and overall step for a worker performing a standard task under standard working conditions. The analyses focus on eliminating waste motion and unsafe methods to provide an increase in productivity without creating fatigue. The elemental time standards are used in production scheduling estimates. △926.

Time Division Scrambling (TDS). △868.

Time Zone, any of 24 longitudinal divisions of the Earth established for the purpose of determining local mean solar time. Within each zone the overall local time is standardized and differs from time in a neighboring zone by one hour. Time zones east of the Greenwich (0°) meridian will be so many hours ahead of Greenwich Time, while zones west of it will be so many hours behind. By convention, though zones are meant to be equal, they are usually made to coincide with country or state frontiers for convenience.

Timgad, ruined city in NE Algeria; called the Pompeii of N Africa because of extensive remains that include a forum, theater, capitol, library, triumphal arch, and several baths with mosaic floors. Founded AD 100 by Trajan, as Thamugadi or Thamugadis, city declined in 5th century and was destroyed by native tribes in 7th century. Excavated 1881.

Timisoara (Temesvar), city in W Romania, on the Beja Canal. An ancient Roman settlement, it was ruled by Magyars 896; annexed to Hungary 1010; taken by Turks 1552–1716, liberated by Eugene of Savoy; and passed to Romania 1920; site of 14th–15th-century Hunyadi castle (now a museum), 18th-century town hall, Roman Catholic and Eastern Orthodox cathedrals, university (1945). Industries: engineering works, food processing, tobacco, chemicals, textiles, machinery. Pop. 192,616.

Timor, island in Indonesia, largest member of Lesser Sunda Islands of the Malay archipelago; divided into the Nusa Tenggara Timur prov. of Indonesia (S) and Portuguese Timor territory (N). Portuguese Timor annexed by Indonesia in 1976. Settled by Portuguese *c.* 1520 as trading area; modern boundaries were set by treaties 1859, 1893, 1904; occupied by Japanese WWII. Dutch Timor passed to Indonesia 1949; Portuguese Timor was made a separate colony 1926 and part of Portuguese overseas territory 1951. Industries: fishing, agriculture (tobacco, coffee, sugar, tea). Area: 13,070sq mi (33,851sq km). Pop. 1,450,000.

Timor Sea, branch of the Indian Ocean between Timor Island, S Malay Archipelago, and NW coast of Australia; connects in NE with Arafura Sea. Width: 300mi (483km).

Timothy, First and Second Epistles to, two letters in the New Testament written in the name of Paul, encouraging faith in Christ and demanding Orthodox belief.

Timpani, or kettledrums, principal percussion instruments in the symphony orchestra. Usually paired, they are hemispherical vessels with single skins, tuned by screws and hit with padded mallets. Military kettledrums were played on horseback by Asian nomads and brought to Europe by the Crusaders *c.* 1100. Modern timpani were introduced into orchestras in the 17th century; pedal action for quick retuning was invented in the 19th century. In 17th- and 18th-century scores two timpani were used—one tuned to the tonic pitches and the other to the dominant pitches (1st and 5th notes of the scale). In modern orchestras 3 or more timpani are used with a variety of tuning.

Timur. *See* Tamerlane.

Tin, metallic element (symbol Sn) of group IVA of the periodic table, known from ancient times. Chief ore is cassiterite (oxide). It is used as a protective coating for steel in tin plate, and in solder, pewter, type metal, and similar alloys. Two allotropes exist: the common metallic form (white tin) changes slowly below 13.2°C to a brittle nonmetallic form (gray tin). Properties: at. no. 50; at. wt. 118.69; sp gr 5.75 (gray), 7.31 (white); melt. pt. 449.60°F (231.89°C); boil. pt. 4,118°F (2,270°C); most common isotope Sn^{118} (24.03%). △1596, 1600.

Tinamou, grassland and jungle bird found from Mexico to S South America with a heavy body and camouflaging brown or gray coloration. It has a slender, deeply cleft bill; small weak wings; and a short tail. Glossy pale blue to violet eggs (4–9) are incubated by the male in a leaf-mat nest. Length: 9–15in (23–38cm). Family Tinamidae. △526.

Tibetan terrier

Tierra del Fuego

Tiger

Tiger shark

Tinbergen, Nikolaas (1906–), Dutch ethologist, who shared with K. Lorenz and K. von Frisch the 1973 Nobel Prize in physiology or medicine for his pioneering work in ethology. Tinbergen, cited for his ability to design ingenious experiments, studied how certain stimuli evoke specific responses. *See also* Ethology.

Tinguely, Jean (1925–), Swiss sculptor. His work incorporated motion through small motors. He experimented with motorization and produced progressively more complicated machines, some of which were self-destructive. △1318.

Tinker, Joseph Bert (1880–1948), US baseball player, b. Muscotah, Kans. He was the shortstop on the Chicago Cubs' famed "Tinker-to-Evers-to-Chance" double play comination. He was elected to the Baseball Hall of Fame in 1946. *See also* Chance, Frank Leroy; Evers, John Joseph.

Tin Processing, the extraction of the metal from its principal ore cassiterite (SnO_2). △1596.

Tintoretto, Il, real name **Jacopo Robusti** (1518–94), Italian painter. A major exponent of the Venetian school, he was a leading painter for patrons and Venetian churches. His style had an amazing versatility, and he worked carefully, often utilizing small wax models and candles to study lighting. One of his earliest works is "Apollo and Marsyas" (1545) in the Mannerist style. Other early works include the important "Last Supper" (1547), "Washing of the Feet" (1547), and "St Marcellinus" (1549). His masterpiece, which brought him recognition, is "St Mark Freeing a Slave" (1548), a work marked by vibrant color and vigorous modeling. His important portraits include "Portrait of a Young Man," "Nicola Pruili," "Miracle of St Mark," and the "Marriage at Cana." His later works include "Alvise Cornaro" and "Philosophers." In its final development Tintoretto's style anticipated the Baroque.

Tippecanoe, Battle of (1811), battle on the Tippecanoe River in Illinois in which US forces, under William Henry Harrison, governor of the Indiana Territory, were attacked by the Shawnee under The Prophet, who opposed Harrison's land-grabbing actions. The battle was inconclusive, but it made a hero of Harrison.

Tippoo, or **Tipu Sahib.** △1266.

Tiranë (Tirana), city and capital of Albania; approx. 20mi (32km) inland from the Adriatic Sea, in E central Albania; capital of Tirane prov.; modern manufacturing and trade center (textiles, soap, food processing); location of music and art schools, agricultural and teachers' colleges, national library and university, Etehem Bey mosque, and Scanderbeg Square (government buildings) at the city's center. Founded early 17th century by Turks. Pop. 169,300.

Tires, Automobile. △1696.

Tirpitz, Alfred von (1849–1930), German statesman and admiral. He became secretary of state in 1897 and lord high admiral in 1911. Under him the German navy grew to enormous strength by 1914. His policy of unrestricted submarine warfare against Great Britain led to the sinking of the *Lusitania* (1915).

Tiryns, a prehistoric city in E Peloponnesus, S Greece, just N of Nauplia near Gulf of Argos; port of trade with Crete; flourished as cultural center 1600–1100 BC; fell to ruin *c.* 468 BC with the invasion of Argives. Archeological excavations by Heinrich Schliemann (1884–85) and Wilhelm Dörpfeld uncovered architectural remains of the pre-Homeric period (7th century BC). It is represented as a great state and birthplace of Hercules in *The Illiad.* △966.

Tisza, (Count) Ist ván (1861–1918), Hungarian statesman. He followed his father Kálmán as prime minister of Hungary (1903–05, 1913–17). In that post, he exercised far-reaching authority both in Hungary and in the councils of the dual monarchy in Austria, attempting to prevent war with Serbia in 1914 to avoid larger complications. He was assassinated in 1918.

Tisza (Tisa), river in E Europe, the major tributary of the Danube River; rises at the confluence of the White Tisza and Black Tisza rivers in Carpathian Mts, W Ukrainian republic, USSR; flows W then SW through Hungary; enters NE Yugoslavia to join the Danube above Belgrade; navigable for 450mi (725km) of its 600mi (966km).

Titan, largest of Saturn's satellites. It is comparable in size with Mercury and is believed to support a thin atmosphere, chiefly of methane. Diameter 2980mi (4800km); mean distance from planet 757,640mi (1,220,000km); mean sidereal period 15.95 days. △86, 152.

Titania, satellite of Uranus. △88.

Titanic, British luxury passenger ship, considered unsinkable, that sank (April 14–15, 1912) on its maiden voyage. The disaster occurred after the liner collided with an iceberg in the North Atlantic. Out of the 2,-224 people on board, many of them US and British notables, 1,513 were drowned. The disaster led to the first International Convention for Safety of Life at Sea (1913).

Titanium, common metallic element (symbol Ti) of the first transition series, discovered in 1791 by William Gregor. It is found in many minerals; chief sources are ilmenite (iron titanate) and rutile (oxide). The element is used in steels and other alloys, especially in aircraft and other applications where strength must be combined with lightness. The dioxide (TiO_2) is a white paint pigment. Properties: at. no. 22; at. wt. 47.9; sp gr 4.54; melt. pt. 3,047°F (1,675°C); boil. pt. 6,548°F (3,620°C); most common isotope Ti^{48} (73.-94%). *See also* Transition Elements. △1554.

Titchener, Edward B(radford) (1867–1927), English psychologist. With the German psychologist Wilhelm Wundt, he was a leader of the *structuralism* school of psychology in the late 19th century. He tried to determine the contents (structures) of the mind by means of systematic introspection. Though his theories were replaced by functionalism and behaviorism, he had encouraged US psychology to be more scientific and systematic. His major publication is *Experimental Psychology* (1901–05).

Titian, real name **Tiziano Veceli** (*c.*1477–1576), Venetian painter. Early works that show his vigorous and original style include "St Peter with Donor" (*c.* 1508) and the three frescoes of the "Miracles of St Anthony" (1511) in the Scuola del Santo, Padua. His livelier color erupts in the portraits "Ariosto" (1512) and "Gypsy Madonna" (*c.*1510) and in the St Mark Altarpiece. Two of his most famous works of grandeur are the "Three Ages of Man" (1515) and "Sacred and Profane Love" (1512–15). Titian began a series of mythological pieces for the Duke of Ferrara in 1516, which include "Worship of Venus" (1518–19), "Bacchanal" (1519–22), and "Bacchus and Ariadne" (1523). After 1530 his canvases are marked by bright, shining color, as in the famous "Venus of Urbino" (1538–39). His works of the 1550s are marked by reduced color—"Martyrdom of St Lawrence" (*c.* 1567) and "Rape of Europa" (*c.*1560). After 1560 his colors are once again brighter and his works livelier, as in "The Adoration of the Magi" and the "Annunciation" (*c.*1565). His final works incorporate a new warmth and pathos ("Pieta," 1576). △1142.

Titicaca, lake on Peru-Bolivia border, drains S through Desaguadero River into Lake Poopó; highest large navigable lake in the world. Altitude: 12,500ft (3,813m). Length: 110mi (177km). Depth: 900ft (270m).

Titmouse, small, stubby-bodied and large-headed bird of open woodlands and wooded parks of the Northern Hemisphere and Africa. Active, they move abruptly but agilely, and often hang in awkward positions, feeding on insects. Most true titmice nest in self-drilled holes or abandoned woodpecker holes. Family Paridae; genus *Parus.* The long-tailed titmice and bush tits of Eurasia and W North America are larger and build closed, often hanging, nests. Subfamily Aegithalinae. The penduline tits of Eurasia and Africa build some of the most complicated nests in the bird world. Subfamily Remizinae. Most titmice lay large clutches of freckled white eggs.

Tito, original name Josip Broz (1892–), effective head of the Yugoslav state from 1943, premier from 1945, and president 1953. As a Croatian soldier in the Austro-Hungarian army in World War I, he was captured by the czar's troops (1915) but released by the Communists after the Revolution (1917). Returning home he helped organize the Yugoslav Communist party, and as one of its key members served jail terms after it was outlawed (1929–34)). In World War II he led the partisan resistance forces in Croatia (Draža Mihajlović led the Chetnik guerrillas in Serbia), becoming so powerful that he was able to set up a Communist government in 1945 that achieved international recognition. Russian efforts to control Yugoslavia soon led to a split between Tito and Stalin, who expelled the nation from the Communist bloc in 1948. Tito then became the first independent Communist leader and an important figure to many Third World powers. His rule was marked by strict controls and intolerance of opposition, but in later years he limited the powers of the secret police and encouraged some economic and political freedom. △134 1352.

Titration, method used in analytical chemistry to d termine the concentration of a solution by volumet means. A solution of known concentration is added measured amounts from a buret to the liquid of u known concentration until the reaction is comple (as shown by an indicator). The volume removed fro the buret enables the unknown concentration to calculated. △1568.

Tituila. *See* American Samoa.

Titus (40?–81), Roman emperor (79–81), elder s of Vespasian. He campaigned in Britain and Germa and captured and destroyed Jerusalem in the Jewi war (AD 70). He was briefly (AD 79) coruler with Vesp sian, then sole emperor. As emperor he stopp prosecutions for treason, built lavish baths, a gained great popularity. He died childless and h brother, Emperor Domitian, erected the Arch of Titu His death remains mysterious.

Titus Andronicus (1593), early work attributed Shakespeare, but possibly a collaboration. The pl tells the bloody tale of Titus Andronicus' revenge Tamora, queen of the Goths, for her brutal murde and maimings of his children.

Titus Quinctius. *See* Cincinnatus, Lucius.

Titusville, city in E Florida, on Indian River, 35 (56km) E of Orlando. Inc. 1886. Pop. (1970) 30,51

Tlalnepantla, city in Mexico, 9mi (14km) N of Me ico City; originally inhabited by Otomi Indians; co quered by Aztecs; site of 1583 colonial church, San Cecilia pyramids, noted Aztec monuments. Industrie tin, mercury, cement. Pop. 373,657.

Tlaloc. △838.

Tlalpán, city in central Mexico, S of Mexico Cit residence of early Spanish viceroys; site of Cuicuil pyramid, thought to be oldest man-made structure continent, approx. 10,000 years old; church (153 Industries: textiles, paper. Pop. 115,528.

Tlaquepaque, city in W central Mexico; site of ra road junction. Products: sugarcane, tobacco, cor peanuts, wheat, vegetables. Chief industry is touris Pop. 108,119.

Tlaxcala, city in central Mexico, between Mexi City and Veracruz; capital of Tlaxcala State; ancie capital of Tlaxcalan kingdom, conquered 1519 Hernán Cortes; site of oldest Christian church in t Americas (1521), Ocolan sanctuary and shrine. Pr ducts: wheat, corn, beans, livestock. Industries: shoe rayon, cotton. Pop. 21,424.

Tlaxcaltec, Nahua-speaking Indian group, becam allies of the Spaniards during the conquest of th Aztec empire and provided aid for other campaigns Mexico. △1124.

TNT (Trinitrotoluene), a nitrogen compour ($C_7H_5N_3O_6$) used as an explosive. It is a pale yello crystalline powder, easily soluble in benzene, toluen and acetone and has a specific gravity of 1.65. TN melts at 178°F (82°C), but does not explode belo 464°F (240°C), allowing it to be melted in stea heated vessels and poured into casings. It is the insensitive to shock and requires a detonator to e plode. It is used extensively in munitions and nonmi tary demolition. △1810.

Toad, tailless amphibian found worldwide except Antarctica. It is short and fat with a hopping gait ar has no teeth in its upper jaw. Parotid glands behir eyes secrete an irritating substance. Toads are diffe entiated from frogs by being toothless and having rougher, bumpier skin and a rounder body wi shorter legs. Length: 1–7in (2.5–18cm). Well-know toads are Fowler's toad, American toad, and gree toad. Family Bufonidae. *See also* Amphibia; Frog. 518.

Toadfish, marine bottom-dwelling fish found in ter perate and tropical seas. Capable of living out of wat for a short time, it has a large mouth and head and tapered body. Colors are green, yellow, or brown wi dark blotches. Dorsal fin spines are venomou Length: to 15in (38cm). Among 40 species is th oyster toadfish *Opsanus tau.* Family Batrachoidida △516.

Tobacco, herb native to the Americas but cultivate throughout the world. It has large leaves with no sta and white, pink, or red star-shaped flowers. Heigh

2-9ft (0.6-2.7m). *Nicotiana tabacum* is the principal cultivated species. American Indians smoked the leaves of tobacco and used them medicinally well before the arrival of Europeans in the New World. These plants were more potent than modern blends and often produced unconsciousness in the smoker. Seeds were brought to Europe in 1556-57 by Jean Andre Thevet. Settlers in Virginia obtained seeds from the Spanish colonies (1612) and soon tobacco was the major crop of the Virginia colony and America's first export. Leaves are prepared for smoking by curing (drying) and then aging. Family Solanaceae (nightshade family). △430.

Tobago. *See* Trinidad and Tobago.

Tobit, book in the Roman Catholic and Eastern Orthodox Christian Old Testament, regarded by Protestants and Jews as part of the Apocrypha. A travel narrative of Tobit's son, Tobias, the story involves Tobias' recovery of his family's wealth and Tobit's recovery of his sight through the efforts of the disguised angel, Raphael. *See also* Apocrypha; Old Testament.

Tobogganing, sport in which participants coast down snowy hillsides on a flat-bottomed vehicle made of hard wood. The toboggan is usually 8 feet (2.4m) long and 3 feet (0.9m) wide, and curled at the front end. It is controlled by shifting weight and by trailing one's feet. *See also* Bobsledding.

Tobruk (Tubruq), port town in NE Libya, on the Mediterranean Sea; disputed during WWII, it was taken alternately by British and Germans (1940-42); located on coastal road. Chief industry is trade. Pop. 28,000.

Toennies, Ferdinand. △888.

Togo, Heihachiro. △1272.

Togo, independent nation of West Africa; bordered by Ghana (W), Upper Volta (N), Benin (E), and Gulf of Guinea (S). The Togo Hills running centrally from the NE to the SW, highest point Pic Baumann 3,234ft (986m), divide the country into two regions. To the SE rivers flow directly into the Gulf of Guinea, whereas to the NW they drain N and W into the Volta River system. Temperatures are high throughout the year, and rainfall has a pronounced seasonal variation with by far the most falling during the summer; precipitation also declines inland and vegetation changes from coastal mangrove swamps to savannah and then to more arid grasslands. Subsistence farmers grow maize, millet, and cassava; cash crops are cocoa, coffee, palm nuts, and peanuts; livestock is most important in the N. Phosphate is the principal mineral, and marble is quarried. Industry is of small scale and devoted to processing agricultural products. The population is made up of about 30 ethnic groups, many of which are not indigenous to Togo. Since a coup in 1967 the constitution has been abolished, power lies in the hands of the leader of the one political party. A former UN Trust Territory administered by France; became a republic within French Union in 1956; becoming fully independent in 1960.

PROFILE

Official name: Republic of Togo
Area: 21,617sq mi (56,000sq km)
Population: 1,953,778
Density: 91per sq mi (35per sq km)
Chief cities: Lomé (capital); Sokodé; Palimé
Government: Head of state, Maj.-Gen. Gnassingbe, president
Religion: Animist, Christian, Muslim
Language: French (official), tribal
Gross national product: (1970) $270,000,000
Trading partners: (major): France, Netherlands, West Germany, Great Britain

Tōhaku. △1048.

Tojo, Hideki (1885-1948), Japanese general and political figure. As prime minister (1941-44) during World War II, he approved the Pearl Harbor attack and was responsible for all aspects of the war effort. He resigned in July 1944 when Japan lost Saipan. He was tried for war crimes by the Allies after the defeat of Japan, was found guilty and was hanged.

Token Economics. △772.

Tokugawa, Japanese family holding the title of shogun and maintaining effective control of Japan (1603-1867). Under their shogunate, centralized feudalism was based on an intricate system of allegiances of "autonomous" daimyo (feudal lords) to the Tokugawa family, who owned much of the country's wealth and a quarter of the farmland in strategic locations. The period of their rule is notable for its intense isolationism, improvements in farming, increase in domestic trade, and advances in overall literacy. The regime weakened in the 19th century and fell because of internal and external pressures in 1867, resulting in the Meiji Restoration. *See also* Meiji Restoration. △1048, 1210, 1272.

Tokyo (Tokio), largest city in Japan, at the head of Tokyo Bay, E Honshu; capital of Tokyo prefecture; administrative, cultural, commercial, and industrial center of Japan. Founded in the 12th century as Yedo (or Edo), the village became increasingly important after it was fortified 1457; it became capital of the powerful Tokugawa shogunate under Ieyaso (1603). The city grew rapidly in the 18th and 19th centuries, and as the Japanese Reformation reestablished imperial power, it was made capital of Japan 1868 (replacing Kyoto) and renamed Tokyo ("eastern capital"). Most of Tokyo was destroyed by earthquake and fire 1923; however, the city was reconstructed as a modern metropolis; it was further modernized after extensive US bombings destroyed most of Tokyo 1944-45; the Imperial Palace and surrounding gardens, however, as well as many temples and shrines, remained intact. Tokyo is now the center of a massive industrial-commercial belt extending along the W shore of Tokyo Bay, and including Kawasaki and Yokohama, the latter serving as seaport for Tokyo and vicinity. Modern Tokyo contains over 150 colleges, universities, and specialized schools, including the University of Tokyo (1877), Kieo-Gijuku University (1867), Rikkyo University (1883), Waseda University (1882), Tokyo Women's Medical College (1900); art museums include the Imperial Museum and the Museum of Arms; Asakusa entertainment district is the center of Tokyo's night life, and Ginza Street is a famous shopping area. The city is governed by a popularly elected governor and assembly, with separate assemblies administering local matters of the city's 23 wards. Industries: metals, machinery, electronic and transit equipment, chemicals, textiles, shipbuilding, automobiles, consumer products, tourism. Pop. 8,787,249.

Tokyo Bay, arm of the W Pacific Ocean, on SE coast of Honshu, Japan; forms a large harbor for Tokyo, Yokohama, and Yokosuka; with Osaka Bay, it is one of the two principal port areas of Japan. Length: approx. 30mi (48km). Width: approx. 10-20 mi (16-32km).

Tolbert, William Richard, Jr. (1913-), Liberian political leader. He served in the treasury and legislature before he became vice president in 1951 and president in 1971. He was also leader of the Baptist World Alliance for Africa (1965-70).

Tolbutamide, trademark Orinase, drug used in the treatment of certain types of diabetes. It acts to stimulate release of insulin from the pancreas.

Toledo, city in Spain, on Tagus River, 40mi (64km) SSW of Madrid; capital of Toledo prov. One of Spain's most historically and architecturally important cities, it was captured by Romans 192 BC; a Visigoth king made Toledo his capital 6th century AD; taken 712 by Arabs, in 1085 it was reconquered by Alfonso VI. It is the site of a cathedral (begun 1226), Santo Cristo de la Cruz (Gothic chapel), Trânsito (14th-century synagogue), 13th-century school of scholars and translators, 7th-century wall, Aleaga (a Moorish citadel), former home of El Greco, now a museum containing his paintings. Industries: silk products, metal work, surgical equipment, shell castings. Area: (prov.) 5,934sq mi (15,370sq km). Pop. (city) 44,382; (prov.) 468,925.

Toledo, port city in NW Ohio, on Maumee River as it enters Lake Erie; seat of Lucas co; formed 1833 by union of two villages, Port Lawrence and Vistula. Port Lawrence was est. 1817 next to Fort Industry, built by Gen. Anthony Wayne 1794 after Battle of Fallen Timbers. In 1835, Toledo was awarded to Ohio by Congress after a boundary dispute with Michigan, in the so-called Toledo War (bloodless); site of University of Toledo (1872) and Mary Manse College (1873). Industries: glass, machine tools, oil refining, plastics, cosmetics, tools, dies. Inc. 1837 as Toledo, named for Spanish city. Pop. (1970) 383,818.

Toleration, Act of (1689), English legislation permitting freedom of religious practice to Protestant dissenters, subject to their taking oaths of allegiance to William and Mary. It modified the Test Act, but it did not remove Protestants' political and social disabilities, nor did it extend to Roman Catholics. *See also* Test Act.

Tolkien, J(ohn) R(onald) R(euel) (1892-1973), English philology scholar who achieved fame with his imaginative epic trilogy, *The Lord of The Rings* (3 vols., 1954-55). Both his prose style and fantastic

Tintoretto

Toad

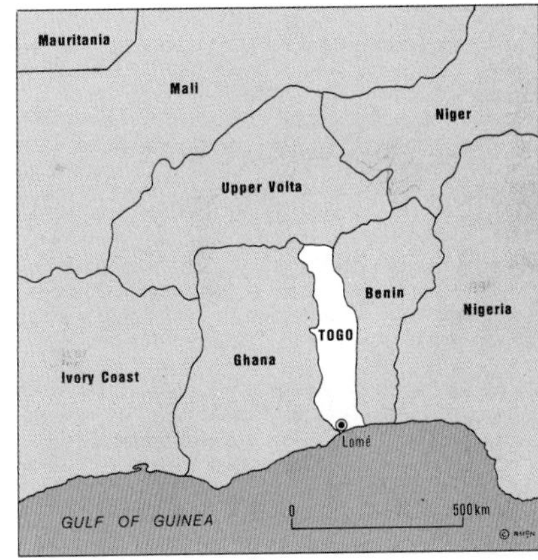
Mauritania
Mali
Niger
Upper Volta
Benin
Nigeria
TOGO
Ghana
Ivory Coast
Lomé
GULF OF GUINEA
0
500km
Togo

Tokyo: Imperial Palace

world are reminiscent of Norse sagas and Anglo-Saxon poetry, which he taught at Oxford University. The trilogy is introduced by *The Hobbit* (1937).

Tolman, Edward C(hace) (1886–1959), US psychologist, b. West Newton, Mass. He was a leading learning theorist. He devised a theory called "purposive behaviorism" involving trial-and-error, goal-directed behavior, and cognitive processes in *Purposive Behavior in Animals and Men* (1932).

Tolpuddle Martyrs, name given to six British farm laborers sentenced (1834) to seven years' transportation to Australia for trade union activities in Tolpuddle. The tremendous popular reaction in their favor defeated the government's intention of creating an example to prevent further working-class discontent. Their sentences were remitted in 1836. △1326.

Tolstoy, (Count) Leo (1828–1910), Russian novelist and philosopher. While serving in the army, he began the autobiographical trilogy *Childhood, Boyhood, and Youth* (1852–57). After taking part in the defense of Sevastopol (1855), he lived on his estate, Yasnaya Polyana, and in St Petersburg, marrying in 1862. After writing *War and Peace* (1865–69) and *Anna Karenina* (1875–77), he underwent a spiritual crisis, as recorded in *Confession* (1879). Later works, including *The Death of Ivan Ilyich* (1886), *The Kreutzer Sonata* (1889), and *Resurrection* (1899–1900), advocate nonviolence and a simple life and reflect his rejection of Orthodox Christianity. Estranged from his wife, he died after fleeing from his home. *See also* Anna Karenina; War and Peace. △1238.

Toltec, the Aztec name from their city of Tollán. A major prehistoric culture in Hidalgo, Mexico, dating from about AD 900–1200. A wide-ranging people, their influence extended from the later capital at Tula to Chichén Itzá in Yucatán, and ultimately as far south as Guatemala. △970.

Toluca, city in central Mexico, at the foot of Nevado de Toluca, 35mi (56km) SW of Mexico City; site of airfield, state museum, El Calvario shrine. Industries: tile, handcrafts, silver, gold, copper, textiles, cigars, brushes, livestock. Pop. 108,602.

Tomato, herb native to the Americas. Not used as food until the 18th century, it was believed poisonous and was grown as an ornamental. The plant was cultivated in Europe as early as 1544 and introduced to the American colonies in 1710. Leaves are deeply toothed or lobed and yellow flowers produce the familiar green fruit which turns reddish-orange as it ripens. Species: *Lycopersicum esculentum*. The small cherry tomato is a variety *(cerasiforme)*. *L. pimpinellifolium*, the currant tomato, is native to Peru and Ecuador and produces a very small fruit. Family Solanaceae. △430.

Tombaugh, Clyde William (1906–), US astronomer, b. Streator, Ill. Working at the Lowell Observatory, Flagstaff, Arizona, he made the discovery of Pluto, the outermost planet of the solar system, in 1930.

Tombstone, city in SE Arizona, about 69mi (110km) SE of Tucson. Primarily a residential town, its legendary past makes it a popular tourist attraction; features Boot Hill, the OK Corral (scene of the Earp and Clanton gunfight) and annual 3-day Helldorado. Inc. 1881. Pop. (1970) 1,241.

Tom Sawyer, The Adventures of (1876), autobiographical novel by Mark Twain about the adventures of a young boy (Tom) in and out of his hometown of St Petersburg, Mo., where he lives with his Aunt Polly, friend Huckleberry Finn, and sweetheart Becky Thatcher. Tom and Huck witness a murder in a cemetery and later run away. Thought to be dead, they return to their own funeral and are taken for corpses. Tom reveals the identity of the murderer (Injun Joe), and later Tom and Becky get lost in a cave where Injun Joe is hiding. After their escape Huck and Becky return to find the treasure that Injun Joe buried. One of Twain's best loved and finest novels, it is a combination of well-told adventure and social comment. *See also* Huckleberry Finn, The Adventures of.

Tomsk, city in Russian SFSR, USSR, on the Tom River, 125mi (201km) NE of Novosibirsk; capital of Tomsk oblast. It was founded 1604 by Boris Godunov; became an important trading post; leading 19th-century Siberian city; bypassed by the Trans-Siberian Railroad, it lost leadership after 1900; site of university (1888), polytechnic institute (1900), medical and teachers' colleges, electro-technical and rail transportation schools, library, and botanic gardens. Industries: electric motors, ball bearings, rubber goods, pencils, matches, light bulbs, flour, tobacco, alcohol, meat, vegetable oil. Pop. 339,000.

Tom Thumb (1838–83), US midget, made famous by P.T. Barnum, b. Charles S. Stratton in Bridgeport, Conn. Brought to New York in 1842, he was billed as Gen. Tom Thumb. He later married Lavinia Warren, a dwarf under Barnum's employ. They toured Europe and also met President Lincoln.

Tone, Theobald Wolfe (1768–98), Irish revolutionary leader. Tone, wanting the Irish to ignore religious differences and combine for political independence, founded the United Irishmen (1791) and promoted the Catholic Relief Act (1793). After visiting America (1795), Tone masterminded the abortive French invasion of Ireland (1796). Captured in 1798, he committed suicide.

Tone Languages, languages that use the pitch of the voice as a major device in giving meaning or indicating grammatical relationships. For example, in Efik language of Nigeria, "akpa" spoken with a rising tone means "first," with a descending tone means "he dies"; in Dinka in Sudan "pany" in a high tone means "wall," in a low tone "walls." Many Oriental and African tongues are tonal.

Tonga, independent republic in SW Pacific Ocean; officially, Kingdom of Tonga; an archipelago comprised of approx. 150 islands which are divided into three groups: Tongatapu, Vavau, and Haapai, traditionally known as Friendly Islands. N islands are of volcanic origin, S islands are mostly coral formations. The archipelago was discovered 1616 by Dutch; English missions were est. in 1797, and British power gradually increased until the islands became a British protectorate (1900) under King George Tupou II, insuring British control over foreign affairs and trade while the islands remained self-governing; the group became completely independent in 1970. The government is composed of a legislative assembly, a prime minister with a cabinet and a privy council, as well as a king. Native inhabitants are Polynesian; subsistence farming and fishing are chief occupations. At age 16, male Tongans have a legal right to 8acres (3.2hectares) of land, to be used for farming, but overcrowding on some of the islands has made it impossible for all Tongans to take advantage of this right. Chief exports: copra, bananas. Area, 270sq mi (699sq km); Pop. 92,000.

Tongue, muscular organ that helps move food in the mouth, helps move it to the back for swallowing, and functions in speech. The tongue contains the taste buds, groups of cells that distinguish the four basic tastes: bitter, tasted on the sides and back of the tongue and the palate; sweet and salty, tasted on the tip and front of the tongue; and sour, tasted mainly on the sides of the tongue. △680.

Tongus Worm. △506.

Tonkin (Tongking), large area of Vietnam; a former French protectorate. △1378.

Tonkin Gulf, Resolution of (1964), US Congressional resolution authorizing the president to take military action to defend US forces and US allies in South Vietnam. It was passed at the urging of President Lyndon B. Johnson after US destroyers in the Gulf of Tonkin allegedly were attacked by North Vietnamese torpedo boats. The resolution was later used by Presidents Johnson and Nixon to justify escalation of US military activities in Southeast Asia. It was repealed in 1970.

Tonsil, mass of lymphatic tissue located at the back of the throat, on either side of the opening of the nasopharynx. It has a pitted surface that frequently becomes infected (tonsillitis). Chronic cases are often treated by surgical removal of the tonsils (tonsillectomy), often along with the adenoids. △740.

Tonsillectomy, surgical removal of the palatine tonsils, which are masses of lymphoid tissue lying in the area around the soft palate and the base of the tongue and between the arches of the passages leading to the pharynx.

Tonsillitis, acute or chronic inflammation of the tonsils, often caused by streptococcus infection. Tissues surrounding the tonsils frequently form pus during acute attacks, causing white specks or coating with white exudate. △714.

Tools. △1602.

Tooth, hard, bonelike, structure located on the jaws or other bones of the oral cavity in vertebrates. Teeth are used mainly for seizing and tearing food and for defense. All true teeth are typically made of three layers. Mammalian teeth have (1) an outer layer of enamel, a hard dense substance over the crown of the tooth, (2) a middle layer of dentine, similar in composition to bone and nourished by (3) the innermost pulp, which contains cells, blood vessels, and a nerve. The root of the tooth below the gum line is covered with cementum, which is not quite as hard as dentine. Many vertebrates other than mammals have rootless teeth; a substance called vitodentine, not quite as hard as enamel, covers the dentine layer. Mammals typically have incisors, canines, premolars, and molars; most other vertebrates have teeth that generally resemble each other. △682, 756.

Toothache, any pain associated with malfunctioning of the teeth and their surrounding tissues. The major cause is tooth decay, or caries, but disease of the gums, nerve irritations, or infections can also be involved. Treatment varies but cleaning and filling of cavities is a standard procedure.

Tooth Shell, or tusk shell, any of several hundred marine species of mollusk having a tubular, toothlike shell that is open at both ends. It burrows into sand with a three-lobed conical foot at the wider end. It has small filaments to gather tiny organisms for food. Sexes are separate and fertilization is external. Length: 0.5–5in (13–127mm). Class Scaphopoda. *See also* Mollusk. △480.

Topaz, an orthosilicate mineral, aluminum fluosilicate ($A1_2SiO_4(F,OH)_2$). Found in pegmatites. Orthorhombic system columnar prisms and granular masses. Transparent; glassy; colorless, white, blue, or yellow; hardness 8; sp gr 3.5. Some large crystals are of gem quality. Some gem varieties of quartz are sometimes misnamed "topaz." △240, 244.

Topeka, capital city of Kansas, in NE Kansas, 55mi (89km) W of Kansas City; seat of Shawnee co. Situated on the Kansas River, Topeka is set in the midst of fertile farm region. The city was founded by antislavery settlers in 1854 and became the state capital in 1861. It is celebrated in song as the center of the Atchison, Topeka, and Santa Fe Railroad; site of Menninger Clinic, renowned for its psychiatric research and treatment programs, the state capitol, the Episcopal cathedral, Forbes Air Force Base, Washburn University of Topeka (1865). Industries: marketing, shipping, and processing of cattle, wheat, and other farm products. Inc. 1857. Pop. (1970) 125,011.

Topkapi. △1108.

Topographic Mapping, representation of the surface of the Earth in relief, using contour lines drawn through points of equal elevation. Intervals are arbitrary. Most topographic maps are made from aerial photographs. Special plotting instruments allow the cartographer to follow a "floating" dot along an elevation, producing contour lines in sequence. △180.

Topography, study of surfaces and their mapping, using fixed points as bases for the calculation. The result of topographic mapping is a relief map or a plan for construction. The terrain of a region is explored using surveyors' instruments or aerial photogrammetry (plotting elevations from photographs). *See also* Surveying. △180.

Topology, basic branch of mathematics concerned with those properties of geometric figures that remain unchanged after a continuous deforming transformation, as by squeezing, stretching, or twisting (but not tearing or breaking). The number of boundaries of a surface is such a property. All plane closed curves are topologically equivalent to a circle; a cube, cylinder, and cone are topologically equivalent to a sphere. These figures can be considered sets of points, each point of one set being transformable into one point in another set. They are also treated as a regular combination of simpler figures. △1470.

Top Shell. △482.

Torah, meaning "to teach" in Hebrew is strictly the first five books of the Old Testament, which are Genesis, Exodus, Leviticus, Numbers, and Deuteronomy. These books are also called the Pentateuch. Moses is generally claimed as the author, having received inspiration from God on Mt Sinai. It is kept in the ark in synagogues and read during Sabbath services. Torah may also indicate the entire Jewish Bible and all laws and customs of Judaism. △848.

Tordesillas, Treaty of. △1124.

Tornado, also called cyclone or twister, a funnel-shaped, violently rotating storm column hanging from a cumulonimbus cloud from which it forms, with a center often several hundred yards in diameter in which devastating winds range from 100 to 300mi (160 to 483km) per hour. Tornadoes occur in deep low pressure areas, associated with fronts or other instabilities, on any continent and in the United States most frequently between the Rockies and Appalachians. △214.

Torne (Torneträsk), river in extreme N Sweden; rises from Torneträsk Lake near the Norwegian border; flows SSE to Pajala, from which point it forms the border of Sweden and Finland before emptying into the Gulf of Bothnia. Length: 354mi (570km).

Toronto, commercial port city in SE Ontario, Canada, 360mi (580km) W of Montreal on Toronto Bay at NW end of Lake Ontario; capital of Ontario prov.; seat of York co; 2nd-largest city in Canada. First visited 1615 by French explorer Étienne Brulé, it was the site of a French fur-trading post, Fort Rouillé, which was burned 1759 to prevent British capture. In 1787, British Loyalists purchased the land from the Indians, and York was founded 1793; by 1797, it replaced Niagara-on-the-Lake as capital of Upper Canada. During the War of 1812 it was besieged twice by US troops, which was used as an excuse for British invasion of Washington 1814; site of separatist uprising 1837; served as capital of Canada 1849–51, 1855–59; made provincial capital 1867; the Municipality of Metropolitan Toronto was est. 1953. Toronto is the site of Exhibition Park hosting the annual Canadian National Exposition (since 1912), Art Gallery of Ontario, Royal Conservatory of Music, Royal Ontario Museum, Casa Loma castle (1911), Ontario Science Center (1919); among its many educational facilities are University of Toronto (1827), Victoria College (1836), Knox College (1844), University of Trinity College (1852); seat of Anglican and Roman Catholic archbishops, and home of hockey's Toronto Maple Leafs and football's Toronto Argonauts. Exports: grain, livestock, meat. Industries: electrical equipment, brewing, printing, publishing, iron and steel products, sugar refining, distilling, flour, meat packing, farm machinery. Inc. 1834. Pop. 698,634.

Torpedo, self-propelled underwater missile used by submarines, small surface warships, and aircraft to destroy enemy vessels. Modern torpedoes may be launched by rocket boosters and often have internal electronic equipment for guiding the missile to the target. △1684.

Torpedo Boat, small, inexpensive, fast coastal naval craft armed with torpedoes and, recently, with anti-ship guided missiles. Torpedo boats are generally used to defend or attack coastal shipping and installations, and to conduct hit-and-run attacks against larger warships. △1740.

Torpedo Ray, or electric ray, flat-bodied elasmobranch found in all tropical and temperate marine waters from shallow depths to 3000ft (915m). Usually shades of brown above and whitish below, it has winglike fins at the sides of the head and a well-developed tail and tail fin. Electric glands next to the head can produce up to 200 volts. Length: 5ft (1.5m); weight: 160–200lb (72–90kg). There are 11 genera with 36 species including the Atlantic *Torpedo nobiliana*. Family Torpedinidae. *See also* Chondrichthyes; Ray.

Torquay, noted seaside resort and yachting center in SW England; now part of district of Torbay. Pop. 108,888.

Torque, the vector quantity describing the rotational force about an axis. A force F applied at a distance r from an axis of rotation produces a torque $T + r \times F$.

Torquemada, Tomás de (1420–98), Spanish churchman and grand inquisitor. He was a Dominican priest and was confessor to Ferdinand II and Isabella I. In 1483 they named him head of the Spanish Inquisition. He became noted for the severity of his judgments and the harshness of his punishments; he is generally held responsible for most of the excesses of the early Spanish Inquisition. He was chiefly responsible for the expulsion of the Jews from Spain in 1492. Toward the end of his career, his power was somewhat restricted by the pope, but he remained grand inquisitor until his death. *See also* Spanish Inquisition.

Torrance, city in S California, 15mi (24km) SSW of Los Angeles. Industries: aircraft, electronic equipment, oil, chemical, aluminum products. Founded 1912; inc. 1921. Pop. (1970) 134,584.

Torreón, city in NE Mexico, on the Nazas River. Industries: mining, cotton, flour, steel, iron, textiles. Pop. 257,045.

Torrey, John (1796–1873), US botanist and chemist, b. New York City. He conducted major studies of North American plant life and amassed one of the most valuable botanical libraries and herbariums of his time. His works include *Flora of the Northern and Middle Sections of the United States* (1824) and *Flora of the State of New York* (1843), which he wrote after being appointed state botanist (1836).

Torricelli, Evangelista (1608–47), Italian physicist, who served as assistant and secretary to Galileo during the latter's last three months of life. He is credited with the first man-made vacuum (the Torricellian vacuum), and he invented the first barometer. He also constructed a primitive microscope and made some improvements on the telescope. His work in geometry eventually contributed to the development of integral calculus. △1656.

Torrid Zone, a belt of the Earth between the tropics over which the Sun is vertical at some period of the year.

Torrington, industrial city in NW Connecticut, 18mi (29km) NNW of Waterbury. Industries: hardware, machinery. Settled 1735; inc. 1923. Pop. (1970) 31,952.

Torsion, in mechanics, the strain in a material subjected to a simple twist. In a rod or shaft, such as an automobile drive shaft, the torsion angle of twist is inversely proportional to the fourth power of the rod diameter and the shear modulus of the material. △476.

Tort, a form of law that settles the rights of monetary damages for injuries in both civil and private cases. Usually, parties involved are private persons or business corporations. Injuries caused from actions such as bursting dams, spoiled food, dangerous structures, or swindling usually constitute a tort case. △910.

Tortoise, any turtle that is terrestrial in habit. The main genera are *Testudo* and *Geochelone* with many species in Europe, Africa, Asia, and South America, and *Gopherus* with three species in North America. There are also species of pond turtle (Emydidae) that have become mainly terrestrial (eg, the North American box turtle *Terrapene carolina*). △522.

Tortoiseshell Butterfly, widespread group of medium-sized anglewing butterflies with wings having tortoiseshell-like markings of black, brown, and white. Genus *Nymphalis*.

Tortoiseshell Cat, also Spanish cat, chintz and white, old variety of domestic cat characterized by patched long- or short-haired coat of black, and light and dark red. The addition of cream is calico. This color is sex-linked and most cats of this breed are female; the males are sterile.

Tortoiseshell Turtle. *See* Hawksbill.

Tortuga (Île de la Tortue), island in the West Indies, off N coast of Haiti. In 17th century, it was used by pirates and buccaneers as a base for attacks on European fleets; administered by Haitian government. Area: approx. 70sq mi (181sq km). Pop. 10,000.

Tory Party, British political party, *c.*1680–1815, chiefly representing the interests and opinions of the country gentry and Anglican clergy. Originally applied derisively to James II's supporters, "Tory" became a general term for those opposed to religious toleration, parliamentary reform, and foreign wars. After 1815 new political alignments caused the term "Conservative" generally to replace "Tory."

Toscanini, Arturo (1867–1957), Italian conductor. He was music director of opera houses in Milan (La Scala) and Bayreuth and of the Salzburg Festivals. During his tenure at La Scala he raised that opera house to one of the world's finest. He conducted the Metropolitan Opera (1907–21), the New York Philharmonic Orchestra (1928–33), and the NBC Symphony (1937–54), which was created specifically for him. Famed for his temperamental and dictatorial ways, he strove throughout his career to bring perfection to operatic and symphonic performances.

Total Eclipse. *See* Eclipse.

Totalitarianism. △902.

Totem, plant, animal, or thing with a special relationship to a clan, tribe, or people. Totems are found in many cultures. A group identifies with its totem, which plays a large part in ritual and ceremony. The group often believes the totem to be its ancestor. *See also* Taboo.

Leo Tolstoy

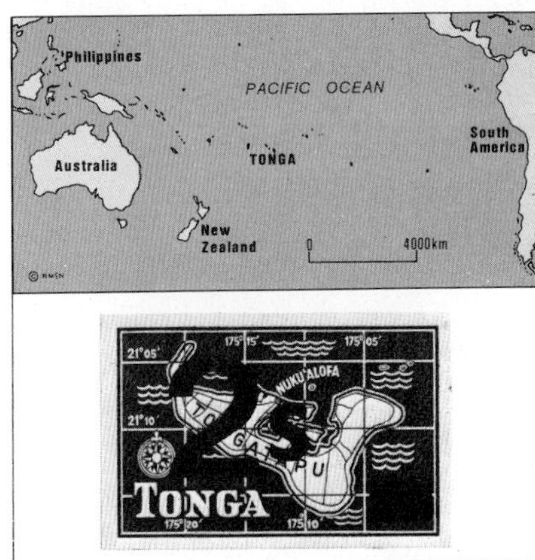
Philippines
PACIFIC OCEAN
Australia
TONGA
South America
New Zealand
4000km
TONGA

Tonga

Toronto

Arturo Toscanini

Totem Pole, thick carved painted pole erected by the Indians of the Pacific Northwest. A totem pole portrays real and mythical animals and objects, which reveal the lineage of the household that erected it. △842.

Toucan, colorful, gregarious forest bird found from Mexico to Argentina and known for its enormous, swollen, and colorful bill. They have red, yellow, blue, black, or orange plumage, often in vivid patterns, and feed on fruit and berries. They nest in tree holes, laying glossy white eggs (1–4) that are incubated by both parents. Length: 1–2ft (30.5–61cm). Family Ramphastidae.

Touch, the principal skin sense, occurs when the skin is mechanically deformed (moved). In addition to free nerve endings, the skin also has special basket cell receptors, which are particularly prevalent around bases of hairs. Touch probably interacts with the kinesthetic sense to produce sensations about body position; the sense of touch may persist even when a limb has been amputated. △678.

Toulon, seaport city in SE France, on Mediterranean Sea, 30mi (48km) ESE of Marseilles. A Roman naval station in 3rd century, it passed to France 1481; scene of Napoleon's victory over English, Spanish, and French royalists 1793; French fleet was scuttled here after German occupation 1942, site of French naval base, church of Ste Marie Majeure (17th–18th centuries). Industries: tourism, shipbuilding, cork, furniture, chemicals. Pop. 174,746.

Toulouse, city in S France, on Garonne River, 133mi (214km) ESE of Bordeaux; capital of Haute-Garonne dept.; canals connect city to Mediterranean Sea and Atlantic Ocean. Capital of Visigoths 5th century, it was captured by Clovis 508; became part of French crown lands 1271; scene of Protestant massacre 1562; site of University of Toulouse (1230), Romanesque Basilica (11th–12th centuries), 16th-century Assezat mansion; center of French aeronautic industry. Industries: paper, knit goods, fertilizer, ammunition. Founded *c.* 4th century BC. Pop. 370,796.

Toulouse-Lautrec, Henri de (1864–1901), French painter, graphic artist, and designer of posters. A childhood accident in which he broke both legs left him permanently deformed. He led a night life, frequenting Paris music halls, and spent his later days in an asylum, where he died of alcoholism. Nonetheless, his vision of the decadent life gave strength to his work; his depictions of bars and circuses reflect both the superficial gaiety and the underlying pathos. His fine work, influenced by both Degas and Gauguin, retains a biting and satiric quality, which is evident in his famous "Moulin Rouge," where he includes himself in the picture, a tiny and certainly unromanticized figure. He was immensely productive, executing numerous paintings and lithographs, which received little attention at the time.

Touraco, or **Turaco,** inquisitive, agile, cuckoolike bird of SE Africa known for its special feather pigments. Forest-dwelling turacos, with red wings due to the copper-containing turacin pigment, are typified by the white-crested touraco *(Tauraco leucolophus)* that is green with red wings and white cheeks and crest; length: 14in (35cm). Bushland-dwelling touracos are typified by the gray plantain-eater *(Crinifer zonurus)* which is brown and white with a greenish-yellow bill. They build fragile, twig-and-stick nests for whitish or green-tinted eggs (2). Family Musophagidae.

Touraine, historical region of NW central France, bounded anciently by Le Maine (N), Orléanais (NE), Berry (SE), Marche (S), Poitou (SW), Saumurois (W), Anjou (NW); capital was Tours. Region now includes most of Indre-et-Loire and parts of Loir-et-Cher and Indre depts. Known for 15th- and 16th-century chateaux, it was made part of French crownlands 1204; called "Garden of France" for its fertile valleys, vineyards, and orchards; birthplace of Descartes, Rabelais, and Balzac.

Touré, Sékou (1922–), African nationalist and president of Guinea. He entered politics as a champion of the labor movement. He helped form black African labor unions and was often chosen as Guinea's territorial representative in the 1950s. He became president of independent Guinea in 1958 and, often in conflict with his African neighbors, severely repressed opposition.

Tourmaline, a silicate mineral, sodium aluminum borosilicate, found in igneous and metamorphic rocks. Hexagonal system; glassy; opaque to transparent; black, red, green, brown, and blue. Hardness 7; sp gr 3.1. Some crystals prized as gems. △244.

Tournai Cathedral. △1094.

Tours, city in NW central France, on Loire River, 129mi (208km) SW of Paris; capital of Indre-et-Loire dept.; scene of battle in which Charles Martel defeated Saracens (AD 732); seat of French government during siege of Paris (1870); birthplace of Honoré de Balzac (1799); site of 18th-century bridge over Loire, 13th–16th-century Cathedral of St Gatien, 17th–18th-century Archbishop's Palace. Industries: tourism, food processing, metals, pharmaceuticals. Pop. 128,120.

Toussaint L'Ouverture, François Dominique (*c.* 1744–1803), Haitian independence leader. The educated son of slave parents, Toussaint became an officer in the French colonial army. He joined the Spanish army when the Spaniards occupied the island in 1793, but withdrew his support in 1794 and emerged as master of the northern part of the colony. By 1800 Toussaint had defeated his rival André Rigaud and controlled all of Hispaniola. In 1802, Napoleon sent troops commanded by Charles Leclerc to re-establish French authority; this they failed to do, but Toussaint was betrayed, captured, and taken to France, where he died in prison.

Tower of London, fortress on the north bank of the Thames River in London. △1082.

Towhee, drab-colored North American sparrow. The chewink *(Pipilo erythrophthalmus)* male has black, white, and rust plumage. The green-tailed towhee *(Chlorura chlorura)* of the W United States has a green tail and reddish crown. Family Fringillidae.

Townes, Charles Hard (1915–), US physicist, b. Greenwill, S.C.. He invented the maser, for which he shared a Nobel Prize in 1964 with Alexander Prokhorov and Nikolai Basov. The Michelson-Morley experiment was accurately confirmed with the aid of masers. *See also* Maser.

Townshend Acts (1767), a series of taxes levied on the American colonies by the British Parliament. Proposed by Chancellor of the Exchequer Charles Townshend, they were designed to provide revenue to defray the cost of colonial government. They taxed such imports as glass, paper, lead, tea, and paint. The acts were opposed by the colonists—"Taxation without representation is tyranny" was the popular phrase. The adverse colonial reaction caused repeal of all duties except that on tea (1770).

Toxemia, poisoned condition of the blood due to circulation in it of bacterial, chemical, or hormonal toxins. Toxemia is often the name applied to a condition occurring in late pregnancy marked by high blood pressure, kidney failure, and convulsions. △702.

Toxin, a poisonous substance, usually referring to a product of certain plants, animals, or bacteria, such as the organisms that cause diphtheria and tetanus. The controlled use of bacterial toxins as immunologic agents has been effective in providing protection against those and other diseases. Antibodies produced against diluted toxins are effective immediately against later invasion of bacteria.

Toxoid, a bacterial toxin that has lost its virulence but can still stimulate the production of antibodies against a disease. *See also* Toxin.

Toxoplasmosis, infection occurring in all warm-blooded animals, including man, of microorganisms of the genus *Toxoplasma.* Symptoms resemble the common cold in adult humans, but can be very damaging to the central nervous system or the eyes of infants.

Toy Dog, dog breeds of small size. Toy dogs range from the tiny Chihuahua and Maltese to the large Pekingese and pug. Most toy breeds are dwarfed from larger types, although the Maltese is not. Often pets of nobility, objects of barter, and royal gifts, they were popular since ancient Greece. Also called pillow, sleeve, lap, comforter, and under the table dogs, they remain popular pets. Weight: 1–18lb (0.5–8kg).

Toy Manchester Terrier. *See* Manchester Terrier.

Toynbee, Arnold Joseph (1889–1975), English historian. Educated at Winchester and Balliol College, Oxford, he taught at Oxford and the University of London. He worked for the government during both world wars and was a member of the British delegation to the Paris Peace Conference (1919). His masterpiece, *A Study of History* (12 vols., 1934–61), emphasized the need to examine whole civilizations rather than individual nations.

Toy Poodle. *See* Poodle.

Trace Fossils. △560.

Tracer, Radioisotope. *See* Radioisotope Tracer.

Trachea, tube that extends from the larynx to about the middle of the breastbone. It is lined with cilia that prevent dirt and other substances from entering the lungs. At its lower end, the trachea splits into two branches, the bronchi, one of which then passes into each lung. △692.

Tracheitis. △714.

Tracheophyte. *See* Vascular Plant.

Tracheotomy, procedure in which an incision is made through the skin into the trachea (windpipe) to enable breathing or give oxygen.

Trachodon, or anatosaurus, large, amphibious, ornithopod dinosaur abundant during late Cretaceous times in North America. The front ends of its upper and lower jaws were toothless and flattened like a duck bill. Farther back in the jaws were hundreds of shearing teeth for chopping vegetation. When swimming, it used its webbed feet and powerful, flattened tail. Unlike many other duck-billed dinosaurs, it had no head crest. Length: 35ft (10.6m). *See also* Ornithopoda. △570.

Trachoma, chronic, contagious rickettsial conjunctivitis characterized by inflammatory granulations on the conjunctival surfaces. In early stages, it responds to sulfonamide treatment. It is a major cause of blindness in Africa and Asia. *See also* Conjunctivitis.

Track and Field, general name for various athletic events. They include competition in foot racing, jumping, hurdling, throwing, and vaulting. Generally, at a track and field meet, the field events (throwing and vaulting) are held within the infield area of the oval track. The field events include the running hop-step-and-jump, the broad jump, the pole vault, the shot put, the discus throw, the hammer throw, the javelin throw, and the high jump. The track events include running races from 60 yards (54.6m) to 10,000 meters, hurdle races from 120 yards (109.2m) to 440 yards (400m), relay races from 400 meters to 4 miles (6.4km), and walking races of 20,000 and 50,000 meters. A combination of both track and field events includes the decathlon (10 events held over a 2-day period) and the pentathlon (5 events in the same day). Scoring for team events is on a point basis. When two teams compete, the scoring is five points for first place, three points for second place, and one point for third place. With more than two teams, the points may range from ten for first place to one for sixth place.

History. Track and field events were held at the original Olympic Games in Greece in 776 BC. The competition was revived in England in the 12th century, and in 1864, Oxford defeated Cambridge in the first college meet. In the United States, the first organized meet was held in 1876. The sport played a major role in the successful resumption of the Olympic Games at Athens in 1896.

Tracking, Automatic, following a moving object, usually by radio or radar, with automatically steerable antennae. △1752, 1802.

Traction, exertion of a pulling force on a part of the skeleton to ensure proper alignment of a fractured bone. The force may be exerted by an elastic device, by pins in the bone, or by rods or wires that can be lengthened or stretched by turning screws.

Tractor, four-wheeled or tracked, self-powered machine designed to pull or push heavy implements over rough terrain. It is commonly used in agriculture, construction, and industry. The tractor replaced draft animals in every phase of modern agriculture. *See also* Farm Machinery. △310.

Tracy, Spencer (1900–67), US film actor, b. Milwaukee, Wis. He was noted first for gangster roles and then for crusty, honorable characters. His nearly 80 films, 9 with Katharine Hepburn (including *Without Love,* 1945, and *The Desk Set,* 1956), are acclaimed for wit and intelligence. His other major films include *Captains Courageous* (1937), *Boys' Town* (1938), for both of which he received Academy Awards, and *The Last Hurrah* (1958).

Trade and Navigation Acts, series of laws that England imposed on its colonies to ensure that trade profits would be kept in England. The acts required that all goods to and from the colonies must be on English ships manned by an English crew (1651); that bounties be placed on colonial goods (1673); and that the admiralty courts enforce the acts (1696).

Trade Barriers, methods a country uses to discourage the importing of goods. Trade barriers include tariffs as well as quotas or absolute bans against importing of certain types of goods. Customs regulations may be so complicated as to constitute an informal trade barrier. Trade barriers are used to protect special interest situations or the perceived national interest of the country. △940.

Tradescantia. △454.

Trade Unionism. *See* Labor Movement in the United States.

Trade Winds, or trades, part of the general atmospheric circulation, blowing toward the equator as northeasterlies in the Northern Hemisphere and southeasterlies in the Southern Hemisphere. *See also* Easterlies.

Trafalgar, Battle of (1805), naval engagement in the Napoleonic Wars fought off Cape Trafalgar, Spain. Nelson, the British admiral, divided his 27 ships into two squadrons and broke the Franco-Spanish line of 33 ships under Admiral de Villeneuve. Though Nelson, on board the *Victory,* was killed, the defeat established British naval supremacy in the 19th century. △1226.

Traffic Control, Air. △1752.

Traffic Engineering, a branch of highway engineering dealing with the planning and design of streets and highways as well as the safe and economical controls of traffic. △1750.

Tragedy, one of the two types of drama. It differs from comedy in its seriousness of style. The story revolves around a central character who struggles to overcome obstacles but is eventually overtaken by disaster. The first tragedies originated in Greece in honor of the god Dionysus in the 5th century BC. *See also* Theater.

Trailing Arbutus, perennial, spreading plant native to central and E United States. This evergreen has thick oval leaves and small, fragrant, pink flowers. Family Ericaceae; species *Epigaea repens.*

Trail of Tears, forced migration of Indians (1829–43) to new reservations west of the Mississippi and Missouri rivers. Bands of Shawnee, Delaware, Wyandot, Cherokee, Seminole, and others were involved and thousands died on the journey from disease, lack of food, or abuse.

Trajan (52?–117), Roman emperor (AD 98–117), adopted son of Nerva, b. Spain. He won military distinction in victories over the Germans (98–99), Dacians (101–06), Parthians (114–16), and Persians and pushed the frontiers of the Roman Empire to their farthest limit. He restored the Appian Way, built a theater, an aqueduct, the Forum of Trajan with noted triumphal column, and partly drained the Pontine Marshes. He died in Cilicia and his ward, Hadrian, succeeded him. △1020.

Trajectory, the path of a projectile. On Earth, and in the absence of air resistance, all trajectories would be portions of an ellipse whose focus was at the Earth's center of mass. Since this is 4,000mi (6,440km) deep, the trajectories are virtually indistinguishable from parabolas, whose foci are located at infinity.

Tranquilizers, currently the drugs most important in the treatment of mental illness. Tranquilizers work on the central nervous system to produce relaxation and calm, which in turn often reduces the intensity of many tension-related symptoms. *Minor tranquilizers* are relatively mild, do not produce sedation, and have few side effects. *Major tranquilizers,* which are used to treat psychotic disorders, can calm even those persons who are markedly agitated, but may produce a host of disturbing side effects including drowsiness, tremor, visual difficulties, dry mouth, skin rashes, and jaundice. △770.

Tranquilli, Secundo. *See* Silone, Ignazio.

Transcaucasia (Transcaucasian Federation or **Transcaucasian Soviet Federated Socialist Republic),** former federated union of the USSR; now the three Soviet Socialist republics of Armenia, Azerbaijan, and Georgia. It was first formed 1917 after the Russian Revolution; soon divided into the above-mentioned separate republics; in 1919–21 Turkish nationalists fought with Bolsheviks for control of this region; in 1922 it was reformed and in 1923 it entered USSR; in 1936 it separated again into three autonomous republics. *See also* Armenia.

Transcendentalism, in literature, philosophic movement prominent in New England from the 1830s to 1860s. A romantic and mystical philosophy, its fundamental basis was the unity of nature and God. Its thought was derived in part from German Romanticism. Transcendentalism encouraged self-expression and individualism. Its proponents included Ralph Waldo Emerson, the movement's chief spokesman; Henry David Thoreau; Jones Very and Christopher Pearse Cranch, poets; Margaret Fuller; Bronson Alcott, and other intellectuals. The transcendentalists published *The Dial* (1840–44), a quarterly magazine expressing their ideas. Many of them participated in the cooperative community, Brook Farm. *See also* Brook Farm; Dial, The. △1374.

Transcendental Meditation (TM), a popular type of meditation taught by Maharishi Mahesh Yogi and practiced twice a day for brief periods, in which the meditator uses his mantra as a vehicle to "transcend," allowing mental activity to decrease. Scientific studies have indicated that TM decreases oxygen consumption and heart rate and increases skin resistance and alpha brain waves, yielding a relaxed mental state differing from sleep or hypnosis. △820.

Transducer, device for converting any nonelectrical signal, such as sound or light, into an electrical signal or vice versa. Examples are microphones, loudspeakers, phonograph pickups, and various measuring instruments used in acoustics. If the transducer derives energy from sources other than the signal itself, it is called an active transducer; if it does not it is passive. The output signal is always a function of the input signal (usually linear).

Transfer Ellipse, or orbit, path followed by a spacecraft while changing from one orbital path to another. The Hohmann, or tangential, ellipse is tangent to the arrival and departure orbits and uses the least energy. Transfer ellipses intersecting the arrival and departure orbits at higher angles use more energy but may be advantageous in other ways.

Transfer Lettering. △1774.

Transfer Payments, payments made by governments, business firms, or individuals to other individuals, businesses, or governments for which nothing is given in exchange. These payments shift purchasing power to the receiving unit and alter the distribution of earned income. Transfer payments include unemployment compensation, veteran's benefits, and social security payments.

Transformer, device for converting alternating current at one voltage to another voltage at the same frequency. It consists of two coils of wire coupled together magnetically. The input current is fed to one coil (the primary), the output being taken from the other coil (the secondary). If core losses are ignored, the ratio of the input voltage to the output voltage is equal to the ratio of the number of turns in the primary coil to the number of turns in the secondary coil. △1540.

Transform Fault, a special class of strike-slip fault characteristic of mid-ocean ridges. Because of the transform faults, the Mid-Atlantic Ridge does not run in a straight line but in offset steps. Some geologists think the four major structures of the Earth's crust are mountains, deep-sea trenches, mid-ocean ridges, and strike-slip faults and that they form continuous networks. △170.

Transfusion, Blood, administration of blood, or a blood component such as plasma, directly into a blood vessel. △752.

Trans-Siberian Railroad, major rail line of Asiatic USSR, linking European Russia with the Pacific coast, running between Chelyabinsk and Vladivostok. Built 1892–1905, it first ran generally E through Orm, Novosibirsk, Krasnoyarsk, Irkutsk, Chita, and through Manchuria (Chinese Eastern RR) to Vladivostok; during WWI a Russian line was completed between Chita and Vladivostok, along the Amur and Ussuri rivers. This railroad opened Siberia to settlement and industrialization. Length: 4,600mi (7,406km). △1286.

Transient Situational Character Disorders, temporary disruption of personality as a consequence of a real external stress. The disturbed behavior occurs when the individual attempts to cope with an overwhelming situation. Temporary adjustment reactions during infancy, adulthood, and old age are also included in this category.

Transistor, semiconductor device capable of amplification. It consists of two p-n semiconductor junctions forming either a p-n-p or n-p-n structure. In a p-n-p

Toucan

Henri de Toulouse-Lautrec: painting

Trachodon

Spencer Tracy in Old Man and the Sea

transistor, the thin central n-region is called the base, one p-region the emitter and the other the collector. The signal to be amplified is fed into the base, a negative voltage being applied to the emitter and a positive voltage to the collector. By suitable design the collector current can be over 100 times as great as the base current. Transistors are very versatile devices that have now replaced electron tubes for most purposes. *See also* Semiconductor. △1546–48, 1552, 1794.

Transition Elements, metallic elements with chemical properties resembling those of their horizontal neighbors in the periodic table. They have incomplete inner electron shells, and are characterized by variable valences, the formation of colored ions, and a tendency to form stable coordination complexes. They include elements with atomic numbers between 21 (scandium) and 30 (zinc), 39 (yttrium) and 48 (cadmium), 57 (lanthanum) and 80 (mercury), and 89 (actinium) and 103 (lawrencium). The lanthanides and actinides are sometimes called inner transition elements. *See also* Periodic Table. △1554.

Transjordan Region, region presently composing the Kingdom of Jordan, in Asia Minor, bounded by Syria (N), Israel (W), Saudi Arabia (S and W), and Iraq (NW). Called Transjordan from early 1900s to 1949, the region passed from a part of the British League of Nations mandate of Palestine (1920) to an independent constitutional state (May 1923). By treaty with Great Britain (1928), British financial assistance to Transjordan continued, accompanied by presence of British military forces in the country; region officially became Hashemite Kingdom of Jordan 1949, when national forces took from Palestine the areas W of the Jordan River which had been named Arab territories by the United Nations. *See also* Jordan.

Transkei, independent nation in S Africa, bounded by Lesotho, the Republic of South Africa, and the Indian Ocean; capital is Umtata. Formerly a self-governing Bantu territory, Transkei became independent on Oct. 26, 1976, the first tribal homeland of the Republic of South Africa to gain independence. Chief Botha Sigcau was named president by the National Independence party, and Chief Matanzima, the party's leader, became prime minister. Area: 16,329sq mi (42,292sq km). Pop. 2,200,000.

Translation Motion. △1502.

Translocation, movement of food materials in solution through plant tissues from one part of a plant to another.

Transmission, Automobile, the device (a gear and shaft or driving chain) for transmitting power from the engine to the live axle. Speed is variable in discrete steps, with gears or chains providing fixed speed ratios. Three general types are in current use: the sliding gear transmission requiring manual operation; the "hydramatic," which combines an automatic clutch with a semi-automatic transmission and allows two or three forward speeds; and the torque-converter, a hydraulic mechanism using engine power, that engages planetary gear trains. △1696.

Transmitter. △1794.

Transmutation, in physics, formation of one isotope from another by radioactive decay or by bombardment with energetic particles.

Transplant, Organ. *See* Organ Transplant. △752.

Transport, in chemistry, movement of measurable entities such as molecules, ions, isotopes, electrical charges, mass, momentum, or energy through or across a medium due to the natural or applied non-uniform conditions existing within it. Transport properties include viscosity, diffusivity, and thermal conductivity. Active transport, in biochemistry, denotes movement of a substance against a concentration gradient.

Transportation, conveyance of passengers and goods from one place to another. △1676–1722.

Transportation, in geology, the movement of particulate matter from a source to an area of deposition. Any movement of material with wind, water, ice, or gravity as the transporting medium falls into this category. Wind, ice, and gravity are mechanical media, whereas water is both a mechanical mover and a solvating medium. *See also* Deposition; Hydrology; Sedimentation. △258.

Transportation, United States Department of (DOT), cabinet-level department within the executive branch. It was established in 1966 to administer transportation programs of the federal government. It also works to develop fast, safe, efficient, low-cost, and convenient transportation. DOT is directed by the secretary who is a cabinet member and appointed by the president.

Transsexualism, act of changing one's sex or the desire to do so. A sex change might be accomplished partially through hormone treatment or through surgery. For a true hermaphrodite, a person born with both male and female characteristics, choice of sex is literally possible. The condition is quite rare, however. Psychological desire to change sex may be exhibited through transvestism. △766.

Transubstantiation, Christian doctrine, defined at the Lateran Council in 1215 as *de fide,* stating that there is a change in substance of the eucharistic elements after the consecration: The substance of bread and wine changes to Christ's actual body and blood. The doctrine is opposed by that of consubstantiation. *See also* Consubstantiation; Eucharist.

Transuranium Elements, radioactive elements with atomic numbers in excess of that of uranium (at. no. 92). They are the actinides neptunium, plutonium, americium, curium, berkelium, californium, einsteinium, fermium, mendelevium, nobelium, and lawrencium and the transactinides with atomic numbers 104 and 105. None except neptunium and plutonium occur naturally, and those two only occur in minute amounts as decay products of uranium. *See also* Periodic Table. △1552.

Transvaal, province in NE Republic of South Africa, between Limpopo and Vaal rivers. Inhabited by Bantu-speaking black Africans in the early 19th century, it was taken by Boers mid-1830s; the Sand River Convention (1852) recognized the right of Boer self-administration. South African Republic was formed 1856, and Boer leader Martin Pretorius became the first president (1857). Internal problems led to Britain's annexing of the South African Republic 1877; scene of Boers' revolt against British 1880, when it was again proclaimed a republic; Britain granted the republic internal self-government 1881. The discovery of gold (1886) attracted many foreigners, but the Boers imposed heavy taxation and denied political rights to newcomers; at the close of the Boer War (1902), the treaty of Vereeniging made Transvaal a crown colony of the British Empire; it became a founding province of the Union of South Africa 1910. It is the site of University of Pretoria, University of the Witwatersrand, Kruger National Park. Major cities include Pretoria (the capital), Johannesburg, Brakpan. Products: livestock, tobacco, cotton, wheat, citrus fruits. Industries: gold, diamonds, uranium, asbestos, chromium, platinum, explosives, mining equipment, iron, steel. Area: 110,450sq mi (286,066sq km). Pop. 7,394,961.

Transverse Wave, type of wave, such as an electromagnetic wave, in which vibrations of the component electric and magnetic fields or of the particles of the transmitting medium occur at right angles to the direction of wave motion. *See also* Wave.

Transvestism, sexual deviation in which the person identifies with and dresses like the opposite sex. Since sexual arousal or gratification is usually dependent upon the individual's wearing garments of the opposite sex, transvestism can be thought of as a mixture of homosexuality and fetishism. △766.

Transylvania, region in central Romania, surrounded by the Carpathian Mts; belonged to Roman Dacia; became Hungarian in 1003; ruled by Austria 1711–1866; reunited with Hungary 1866; after WWI became part of Romania. Transylvania is rich in iron, lead, gold, copper, manganese, salt, sulfur. Industries: chemicals, textiles, livestock. Area: 21,192sq mi (54,887sq km) Pop. 2,500,000.

Transylvania Company, association formed in 1774–75 to explore and colonize much of Kentucky and Tennessee. Cherokee Indians deeded to the company land around the Ohio, Kentucky, and Cumberland rivers. The territory was proposed as a 14th state but was ignored by the Continental Congress.

Traoré, Moussa (1936–), military commander and statesman of Mali. He became president through a coup in 1968, and added the office of premier in 1969.

Trapdoor Spider, light brown to black spider found worldwide. It digs a tubelike burrow, lined with silk, having a hinged lid covering the entrance. When the spider feels vibrations of passing prey, it rushes out and stuffs the captured prey down its burrow. Length: 0.3–1.2in (8–31mm). Family Ctenizidae. *See also* Spider.

Trapezoid, four-sided plane figure with one pair of opposite sides parallel. The area of a trapezoid is one half the sum of its parallel sides times the perpendicular distance between them.

Trapezius. △684.

Trappists, popular name for the Cistercians of the Strict Observance, religious order centered in La Trappe Abbey, France, until moving to Citeaux in 1892. Splitting into three congregations as they spread worldwide, Trappists were united by papal decree in 1893. Maintaining silence, vegetarianism, and rising for Night Office, manual labor is compulsory for the monks.

Trasimene, Lake, large shallow lake in Umbria, central Italy, site of the battle (217 BC) in which Hannibal defeated the army of the Roman consul Flaminius by ambush, destroying nearly two legions. Also called Lake of Perugia.

Traumatic Neurosis, neurotic disturbance caused by a severe emotional shock such as a close brush with death or an extreme frustration. Symptoms include moodiness, difficulty in concentrating, sleep disturbances (frightening dreams), loss of appetite, and irritability. In acute traumatic neurosis the symptoms may be severe but usually begin to disappear spontaneously in the weeks following the trauma. In chronic traumatic neurosis the symptoms linger indefinitely, recurring from time to time in extreme form (eg, the combat veteran who is awakened many years later by nightmares of battle).

Travelers' Tree, palmlike plant native to Madagascar. The trunk is topped with bananalike leaves. Each cup-shaped leaf base holds a quart of water produced by the plant. This is considered a refreshing drink. It has large clusters of white blossoms and blue seeds. Family Strelitziaceae; species *Ravenala madagascariensis.* Height: to 90ft (28m).

Traveling Wave, wave that continuously carries electrical energy, light energy, etc, away from a source. *See also* Wave.

Travis, William Barret (1809–36), US military officer, b. Edgefield co, S.C. Trained as a lawyer, he moved to Texas in 1831 and soon became a leader in the fight for Texas independence from Mexico. When the Alamo was besieged by General Santa Anna's army (1836), Travis, the commander, was killed in its defense.

Trawling, method of catching bottom-dwelling fish such as cod, and spawning herring, to the depths of 1,968ft (600m). A large net, attached to towboards and pulling cables, is towed by the fishing vessel. This method is generally used only in continental shelf areas. Trawling can be used in deeper waters with an echolocater for finding schools and indicating specific depths. △386, 392.

Treacle. △1504.

Treasury, Department of, US cabinet-level department within the executive branch. It is composed of numerous bureaus and divisions that have four basic functions: formulating and recommending financial, tax, and fiscal policies; serving as financial agent for the government; law enforcement; and manufacturing coins and currency. The department is directed by the secretary, who is a cabinet member and a major advisor to the president concerning domestic and international financial policy and tax policy. The Treasury Department was established in 1789.

Treat, Robert (1622?–1710), US soldier and colonial governor, b. England. He arrived in Milford, Conn., in 1639 where he was active in civil and military affairs. From 1667–72 he lived in New Jersey and founded Newark (1666). In 1672 he returned to Connecticut and led troops in King Philip's War (1675–76). He was elected governor of Connecticut in 1683. He opposed the plan for the establishment of the Dominion of New England under Gov. Edmund Andros in 1686 and took part in hiding the charter in the Charter Oak. When Andros was ousted in 1689, Treat resumed the governorship and served until 1698.

Treaty of Paris (1783), agreement between the United States and Great Britain that ended the Revolutionary War. Negotiated by John Adams, Benjamin Franklin, John Jay, and Henry Laurens, the treaty granted the United States independence. Boundary lines were set with the Great Lakes (N), the Mississippi River (W), and the 31st parallel with the Apalachicola and St Mary's rivers (S). Debts were to be recovered, and the restoration of property to Loyalists was recommended. Both countries were granted navigation rights on the Mississippi River. Many of the issues remained controversial and were settled by later treaties.

Treaty of Paris (1898), US agreement with Spain ending the Spanish-American War. Spain was to yield Cuba, cede Puerto Rico and one of the Landrone Islands, and the United States would occupy the Philippines, for which it paid Spain $20,000,000.

Trebbia River (Fiume Trebbia), river in N Italy; rises in Ligurian Apennines; flows N and joins Po River near Piacenza; scene of defeat of Romans by Hannibal 218 BC, and of Russo-Austrian victory over French 1799. Length: approx. 70mi (113km).

Trebizond, Empire of, a Byzantine kingdom located on the Black Sea. It was founded in 1204 by Alexius I (*c.*1180–1222), a member of the Comnenus family. Despite the onslaughts of the Seljuks and the armies of Nicaea and Constantinople, it maintained its autonomy and flourished as a cultural and commercial center. Finally, in 1461 Mohammed II conquered Trebizond and made it part of the Ottoman Empire.

Trebuchet. △1732.

Tree, woody, perennial plant with one main stem or trunk and smaller branches. The trunk increases in diameter each year and leaves are evergreen or deciduous. Trees range in size to the 385ft (117m) redwoods. The giant sequoias live 2,500–3,000 years. △368, 450.

Tree Creeper, or brown creeper, brownish agile bird that scurries up and down trees in cooler areas of the Northern Hemisphere. It uses its long, slightly downcurved bill to probe for insects under bark, bracing itself with its long, spine-tipped, stiff tail. Its eggs (5–8) are laid in a shapeless twig and moss nest behind loose bark. Length: 5in (13cm). Species *Certhia familiaris.*

Tree Cricket, slender, whitish or pale green cricket found worldwide. It lays its eggs in tree or shrub twigs, often causing severe damage. Length: 0.5in (13mm). Family Gryllidae; subfamily Oecanthinae. *See also* Cricket.

Tree Fern, large or small treelike fern. There are 1,500 species. Order Cyatheales. Or, true tree fern growing in tropics of the world, particularly moist mountainous areas. The 80-ft (24-m) trunks are crowned with large fronds, bearing spore cases on lower surfaces. There are 600 species. Family Cyatheaceae; genus *Cyathea. See also* Fern. △438, 596.

Tree Frog, frog found worldwide, to 15,000ft (4,575m) above sea level. Most live in trees and have enlarged sucking disks on their toes and long, thin hind legs. Some are non-climbing swamp dwellers. Of 500 species, those common in the United States are the spring peeper, green tree frog, cricket frog, and chorus frog. Family Hylidae. △518.

Tree of Heaven. *See* Ailanthus.

Tree of Tule, evergreen Mexican bald cypress *(Taxodium mucronatum)* in the churchyard of Tule near Oaxaca, Mexico. It is thought to be the world's oldest living tree. A huge tree for the species, it has a height of 140ft (42.7m) and a diameter of 25ft (7.6m). It may actually be three trees grown together. Age estimates range from 1,500 to 4,000 years old.

Tree Shrew, small mammal ranging from India through SE Asia to Indonesia. It looks like a long-snouted, whiskerless squirrel but is classified as a primitive primate. Tree dwellers, they are dark olive in color and feed on insects and fruit. Family Tupaiidae. *See also* Primates. △554.

Tree Snake. △524.

Trench, Oceanic, a deep V-shaped depression of the sea floor. In plate tectonic theory they are the places where one plate is being pushed down under the other. The movement causes deep earthquakes. They are the deepest (6mi or 9.7km) and longest (15,000mi or 24,150km) formations on Earth and are found on the borders of the Pacific, North and South Atlantic, and Indian oceans. △170.

Trench Fever, infectious disease caused by a rickettsia transmitted by body lice, characterized by fever and pain in muscles, bones, and joints.

Trench Mouth, infection of the respiratory tract and mouth by a bacillus often in association with a spirochete *(Borrelia vincenti),* producing destructive ulceration of the mucous membranes of the cheeks, gums, and throat.

Trent, Council of (1545–63), ecumenical council of the Roman Catholic Church, convened by Pope Paul III to correct the abuses and defects that had spurred the Protestant Reformation and at the same time to examine church doctrine and to reform certain practices. The council was held in three meetings; 1545–47 under Paul III, 1551–52 under Julius III, and 1562–63 under Pius IV. The causes for the long delays between sessions were disagreement on location, general disinterest of intervening popes, and the political changes in Germany. Major decrees issued by the council involved clerical discipline, education, and obligations; doctrinal revision concentrated on redefining and reexamining teachings, particularly justification, the Mass, the sacraments, and indulgences. These were formulated and published in the Catechism of the Council of Trent, written so explicitly that it is still the basis to understanding the modern Roman Catholic Church.

Trent Affair (1861), diplomatic incident between Britain and the United States. Early in the Civil War Union officers seized two Confederate commissioners (James M. Mason and John Slidell) from the British ship *Trent.* Britain claimed its neutrality was violated and demanded their immediate release. President Lincoln, wishing to avoid war with Britain, released the men.

Trenton, capital city of New Jersey, in W New Jersey, on Delaware River; seat of Mercer co. It was scene of American Revolutionary battle in which Gen. George Washington crossed the Delaware River to capture Hessian troops (Dec. 25–26, 1776); made state capital 1790. Trenton is the site of monument (1893) commemorating Washington's victory, old barracks (1758, now a museum), capitol (1792), William Trent House (1719), Trenton State College (1855), Rider College (1865). Industries: automobile parts, plastics, metal products, rubber goods, steel cables, textiles. Settled 1679 by Friends; inc. 1745 as town and borough; 1792 as city. Pop. (1970) 104,-638.

Trephination. △752, 762, 770.

Treponema, a genus of anaerobic, gram-negative spirochetes. Several species are pathogenic in man: *T. pallidum,* causing syphillis, and *T. pertenue,* which causes yaws, an ulcerative skin infection. They are sensitive to penicillin.

Trevelyan, (Sir) George Otto (1838–1928), English historian and statesman. A Liberal member of parliament (1865–97), he spent most of his life in government service. His *The American Revolution* (6 vol., 1899–1914) helped bring about a more sympathetic view of the Revolution among the English. *The Life and Letters of Lord Macauley* (2 vols., 1876) is his finest work.

Trevino, Lee (B.) (1939–), US golfer, b. Dallas. He emerged from obscurity in 1967 and went on to win the US Open (1968, 1971) and the British Open (1971, 1972).

Trial, the judicial examination of the facts surrounding a case of civil or criminal nature. A jury may or may not be present. △912.

Trial-and-Error Learning, in psychology, the process of trying out different solutions to a problem until one works. Original work was done by E. L. Thorndike early in this century using cats as subjects and "puzzle boxes" as problems. The animal could escape from the box by correctly manipulating a latch. Once it had escaped (through trial and error), the cat would know how to escape when next placed in the box. Modern psychology generally subsumes this form of learning under operant conditioning. *See also* Operant Conditioning.

Triangle, plane figure bounded by three straight lines. The sum of the interior angles totals 180°. The area is measured by either (1) half the product of one of the sides and the perpendicular onto it from the opposite vertex (½ x base x height), or (2) half the product of two of the sides and the sine of the angle between them. △1462, 1464.

Triangle Trade, system of trade between New England and Middle Colonies, the West Indies, and African ports. The trade, partly in evasion of British laws, dealt in molasses, rum, and slaves. Imported molasses was made into rum in the colonies; rum was traded for

Transkei

Transylvania: ceremonial vest

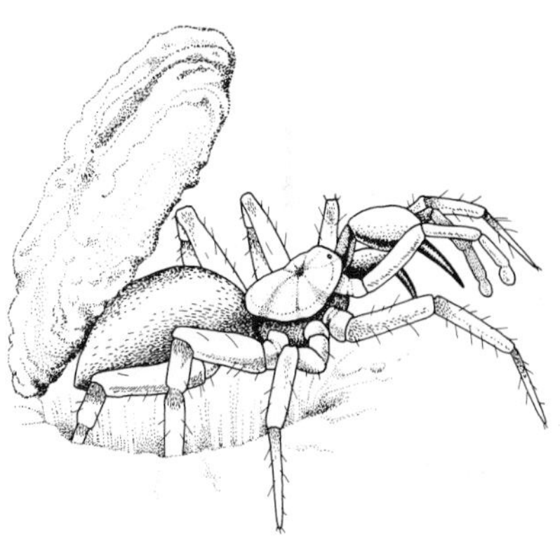

Trap-door spider

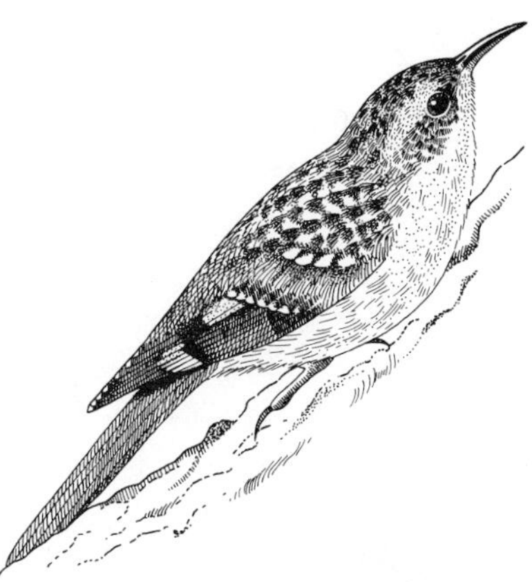

Tree creeper

slaves in Africa, slaves were traded for molasses in the West Indies. △1200.

Triangulation. △180.

Triangulum, or the Triangle, inconspicuous northern constellation situated between Andromeda and Aries. It contains the spiral galaxy M 33 (NGC 598), a member of the Local Group located 2,350,000 light-years from the Milky Way system. △132.

Triangulum Australe, or the Southern Triangle, southern circumpolar constellation situated south of Norma. The three brightest stars Alpha, Beta, and Gamma (all above the third magnitude) form the conspicuous triangular figure. △134.

Triassic Period, the oldest division of the Mesozoic Era, lasting from 225 to 195,000,000 years ago. Following upon a wave of extinctions at the close of the Permian, many new kinds of animals developed. On land lived the first dinosaurs. Mammallike reptiles were common and by the end of the period the first true mammals existed. In the seas lived the first ichthyosaurs, placodonts, and nothosaurs. Also, the first frogs, turtles, crocodilians, and lizards appeared. Although plant life consisted mainly of primitive gymnosperms, the first flowering plants are recorded. The Appalachian Mountains were formed. *See also* Geologic Time; Mesozoic Era. △276.

Tribal Culture. △880–82.

Tribunes, ten senior Roman officers of the legions elected, often from the plebeian class, to protect plebeians from abuse by magistrates. The tribuneship was reformed by Tiberius Gracchus, repressed by Sulla, and restored by Pompey. It declined during the empire. △1014.

Tribute Money. △1134.

Triceps. △684.

Triceratops, large, horned ornithischian dinosaur of late Cretaceous age of W North America. The 8-ft (2.4m) skull carried two 40-in (102-cm) horns above its eyes and a smaller horn at tip of its snout. Length: 20–25ft (6.1–7.6m); height: 8ft (2.4m); weight: 10ton. △572.

Trichinosis, disease of rats, swine, bears, cats, dogs, and humans, caused by infection with the larvae of a parasitic nematode worm *(Trichinella spiralis)*. Most human cases originate from eating raw or improperly cooked pork. Symptoms include abdominal pain, vomiting, swelling, and delirium, and permanent heart and eye damage is possible. In its early stages it may be cured by intestinal washing. Thiabendazole is becoming a widely adopted drug treatment.

Trichoptera. △492.

Trier, city in W West Germany, on Moselle River, near Luxembourg border. Capital of Treveri people of ancient Gaul, it was conquered by Julius Caesar; became part of France 1801 and served as capital of French department of Sarre; awarded to Prussia by Congress of Vienna (1814–15). Notable buildings include 13th-century Gothic cathedral containing coat said to belong to Jesus Christ, Roman amphitheater, imperial palace; seat of Theological Seminary (1773). Industries: leather goods, steel, textiles, wine, beer, cigars. Founded *c.* 15 BC. Pop. 104,093.

Trieste, seaport city in NE Italy, on Gulf of Trieste, 70mi (113km) ENE of Venice; capital of Friuli-Venezia-Giulia region and Trieste prov.; commercial and industrial center. A Roman colony under Julius Caesar, it placed itself under protection of duke of Austria 1382; was made free port 1719 and Austrian crown land 1867; ceded to Italy 1919; occupied by Yugoslavia 1945; Yugoslavia and Italy agreed to territorial compromise 1954, and Trieste was returned to Italy; site of 15th–17th-century cathedral, 14th–17th-century castle. Industries: shipyards, steel, petroleum, textiles. Pop. 279,376.

Triffin, Robert (1911–), US economist, creator of the Triffin Plan for reform of the international monetary system. He made contributions in the areas of international trade and price theory. His most noted book is *Monopolistic Competition and General Equilibrium Theory* (1940).

Trifid Nebula (M20; NGC 6514), emission nebula situated in the constellation Sagittarius. Lanes of dark interstellar matter, superficially resembling a tripod, are situated in space in front of this nebula, against whose shining background they are rendered visible. △104.

Triggerfish, tropical marine fish found in shallow water and identified by an erectile first dorsal fin spine. Its leathery-skinned, compressed body is often beautifully marked and colored. Length: to 17in (43cm). Species include the common *Balistes carolinensis* and the queen *B. vetula*. Family Balistidae. △516.

Triglyceride. *See* Lipid. △1570.

Trigonometric Functions, the six ratios of the sides of a right triangle containing a given acute angle—they are the sine, cosine, tangent, cotangent, secant, and cosecant of the angle. These functions can be extended to cover angles of any size by the use of a system of rectangular coordinates. Thus the sine of an angle increases to 1 from 0–90°, decreases to zero from 90–180°, decreases to −1 from 180–270°, and increases again to 0 from 270–360°. Many relationships exist between different trigonometric functions, including the identities $\sin^2 A + \cos^2 A = 1$; $1 + \tan^2 A = \sec^2 A$; and $1 + \cot^2 A = \operatorname{cosec}^2 A$. Trigonometric functions of numbers can also be defined. Thus, the function $\sin x$ is the sine of an angle of x radians.

Trigonometry, use of trigonometric functions of angles in finding the unknown angles or sides of triangles when other angles and/or sides are known. The unknown values are obtained by using simple formulae and tables of sines, cosines, tangents, and other functions of angles. Trigonometry is extensively used in building, surveying, navigation, etc. △1464.

Trilobite, any of an extinct group of arthropods found fossilized in marine deposits, ranging in age from Cambrian through Permian times. The body shape is mostly oval, tapering toward the rear. The name refers to the division of the body into three distinct longitudinal segments, consisting of a central axis and two pleural lobes. The head bears eyes on top and a mouth beneath. Transverse divisions show segmentation and bear pairs of jointed limbs. Trilobites were mostly bottom-crawling, shallow-water forms and ranged in adult size from .25in (6mm) to 30in (76cm). Mostly only the hard parts, consisting of mineral-impregnated portions of the chitinous covering, are found as fossils. △560, 564.

Trilophodon. △574.

Trinidad and Tobago, island republic in West Indies, formed by southernmost two islands of West Indies, separated from Venezuela's NE coast by Gulf of Paris and Serpent's Mouth channel; Trinidad and Tobago islands are separated from each other by Dragon's Mouth channel. Port of Spain is capital. Islands joined politically in 1888 and were members of West Indies Federation 1958–62. They joined to become an independent nation 1962. Trinidad was discovered 1498 by Christopher Columbus and taken in 1797 by British. Tobago was settled 1616 by English, who had to struggle with hostile Carib aboriginals. Sugar, petroleum, and tourism are major industries. Almost half of the people are of black African descent with East Indians making up one-third; remainder are European, Middle Eastern, and Chinese. English is official language, but a French patois is also used. Since 1960 government secondary schools have been free. The University of the West Indies has schools of agriculture and engineering in Trinidad. Trinidad and Tobago became a republic, Aug. 1, 1976; Sir Ellis Clarke became the first president, replacing Queen Elizabeth as head of state.

PROFILE

Official name: Trinidad and Tobago
Area: Trinidad: 1,980sq mi (5,128sq km) Tobago: 116sq mi (300sq km)
Population: 945,210
Chief cities: Port of Spain (capital), San Fernando, Scarborough
Government: Republic
Religion: Hinduism, Roman Catholicism, Islam
Language: English (official)
Monetary unit: Pound sterling
Industries: (major products) sugar, cocoa, petroleum products, asphalt, chemicals, copra, coffee, bananas, citrus fruit, angostura bitters, tourism

Trinity River, river in NW California, rises in NE Trinity co; flows SW then NW into the Klamath River, near Eureka; gold has been extracted from the river since gold rush era of mid-19th century. Length: 130mi (209km).

Trinity, The, a central doctrine of Christianity, holding that God is three persons, the Father, the Son, and the Holy Spirit (or Holy Ghost). There is only one God, but he exists as "three in one and one in three." Theologians say that the nature of the Trinity is a mystery that cannot be comprehended by humans although they can apprehend some of its meanings. The doctrine of the Trinity was stated in early Christian creeds to counter beliefs such as Gnosticism, which denied that Christ was wholly human during his life on Earth. God the Son was a man, but he is also "of one substance with the Father;" God made man through the power of the Holy Spirit. *See also* Gnosticism.

Triode. △1546–48.

Triolet, poetic form originated by the French in the 13th century. The triolet is comprised of eight lines with two rhymes. The first two lines are repeated as the seventh and eighth lines, and the first line is repeated as the fourth. Triolets were introduced into English-language verse in the 17th century.

Triple Alliance, War of the, also known as the Paraguayan War, a conflict between Paraguay on one side and Argentina-Brazil-Uruguay on the other (1865–70). Long-standing territorial disputes and Brazilian intervention in the Uruguayan civil war prompted Francisco Solano López of Paraguay to declare war on Brazil in 1865; by May of the same year, the conflict involved four countries. The war devastated Paraguay; 300,000 Paraguayan lives and 55,000sq mi (142,450sq km) of Paraguayan territory were lost.

Triple Entente (1907), fused together earlier Anglo-French and Franco-Russian military agreements to offset the Triple Alliance (1882) of Germany, Austria-Hungary, and Italy. It destroyed the unity of the six great powers by placing them into two rival alliances that would become the power blocs of World War I.

Triple Point, the temperature and pressure at which all three phases (solid, liquid, gas) of a substance can coexist. For water, the triple point occurs at 0°C, and at less than 1% of atmospheric pressure.

Tripoli (Tarabulus ESH Sham), seaport city in Lebanon; captured in 638 by Muslim Arabs, it adopted both the Arabic language and Islam religion; taken 1109 by Raymond de Saint-Gilles, count of Toulouse, who built the castle of Sanjil on its site; the medieval town and modern city grew around the castle; destroyed 1289 by the sultans of Egypt. In 1909 Tripoli's port was enlarged, and a railroad was built connecting it to N Syria and surrounding regions; prospered as terminal of petroleum pipeline. Industries: oil refining, soap, silk, oranges, wool, skins, spinning, tobacco, lemons. Pop. 127,611.

Tripoli (Tarabulus Al-Gharb), city in NW Libya, on Mediterranean Sea, 400mi (644km) W of Benghazi; capital of Libya; captured by Romans 1st century BC, Vandals AD 5th century, Arabs 7th century; developed as important terminus for trans-Saharan caravan routes. Taken 1510 by Spain, it was ruled 1528–51 by the Knights of St John; captured 1553 by Ottoman Turks; seat of Karamanli dynasty 1711–1835; served as base for Barbary pirates, leading to Tripolitan War 1801–05 with the United States. In 1911 Tripoli was taken by Italy and made capital of the Italian colony of Libya; captured 1943 by British; site of 19th-century Gurgi mosque, 1736 Karamanli mosque, remains of Roman walls. Industries: tobacco, textiles, woven goods, processed foods. Founded 7th century BC by Phoenicians. Pop. 162,200.

Tripolitan War (1801–05), conflict between Tripoli and the United States. For several years Tripoli and other Barbary states on the north coast of Africa had interfered with US commerce in the Mediterranean, capturing ships and demanding tribute. In 1801, Tripoli declared war on the United States. After several land and sea battles, Tripoli agreed to leave US ships alone and the United States ransomed all prisoners.

Tristan da Cunha Island, island in S Atlantic Ocean about midway between S Africa and South America. The only inhabitable island of five volcanic islands called Tristan da Cunha Islands, it was discovered 1506 by Portuguese; annexed by Great Britain 1816. In 1938 these islands were made part of dependency of St Helena. In 1961 island of Tristan da Cunha suffered a volcanic eruption that caused evacuation; the islanders returned in 1963. Area: 38sq mi (98sq km). Pop. 271.

Trist Mission (1847–48), US peace effort in the Mexican War. Nicholas Trist was a peace commissioner sent to join Gen. Winfield Scott's US troops in the Mexican War. After the first series of negotiations had broken down, President Polk recalled him. Trist, however, stayed on in Mexico and successfully negotiated the treaty ending the war. *See also* Guadalupe Hidalgo, Treaty of.

Tritium, radioactive isotope of hydrogen, the nucleus of which consists of one proton and two neutrons. Only one atom in 10^{17} of natural hydrogen is tritium. Tritiated compounds are used in radioactive tracing. Properties: mass no. 3; atomic mass 3.016; half-life 12.5 years.

Triton, large gastropod mollusk found in tropical marine waters near coral reefs. Its shell is used as a religious and martial musical instrument in Shinto temples in Japan. Length: to 16in (40.6cm). Family Cymatiidae; species include brown and pink *Charonia tritonis.*

Triton, in Greek mythology, a sea god, son of Poseidon and Amphitrite. He was half man, half fish, with a scaled body, sharp teeth and claws, and a forked fishtail. He had power over the waves and possessed the gift of prophecy. Triton blowing his conch seems to have been the personification of the roar of the wild sea.

Triton, satellite of Neptune. △52, 154.

Triton's Trumpet. △482.

Triumvirate. △1018.

Trivandrum, seaport city in SW India, on Arabian Sea; capital of Kerala state; served as capital of Travancore kingdom 1745; site of university (1937) and 18th-century fort housing palaces and temples. Industries: tires, tile, plywood, titanium products, textiles. Pop. 359,580.

Trobriand Islanders, aboriginal inhabitants of the Trobriand Islands. The subject of a famous study by Bronislaw Malinowski, their society is divided into totemic clans. Ceremonial gift exchanges *(kula),* following intricate rules, take place regularly, and each village is headed by a chief and a gardener, who has high social status as a magician.

Trochee, metrical foot consisting of a stressed syllable followed by an unstressed syllable, or a long followed by a short, as in the word *happy.* The meter is called trochaic. Trochaic meter is popular in children's verses ("Mary Had a Little Lamb") and in meter expression of the supernatural, as in William Shakespeare's

Double, double, toil and trouble
Fire burn and cauldron bubble.

See also Meter.

Trogon, fragile, brilliantly colored bird of dark tropical forests in America, S Africa, India, Malay, and the Philippines. About 12in (30.5cm) long, they perch motionless and feed on fruits. Both parents incubate the whitish eggs (3–5) in a dead tree limb nest. Family Trogonidae.

Troilus and Cressida (1602), comical satire by William Shakespeare. It bitterly illustrates human failings through the faithless actions of Cressida, who transfers her love from Troilus to the Greek Diomedes during the siege of Troy.

Trois Rivières (Three Rivers), city in S Quebec Canada, on N bank of St Lawrence River, 75mi (120km) NE of Montreal; site of ruins of Les Forges St Maurice, Canada's first iron foundries (1723–1833), University of Quebec (1969), Seminaire of St Joseph (1663). Industries: iron, textiles, shoes, pulp and paper, shipbuilding. Founded by Samuel de Champlain 1634; inc. 1857. Pop. 55,240.

Trojan Asteroids, minor planets, named after Homeric heroes of the *Iliad,* comprising two groups situated in the orbit of Jupiter, one behind the planet and the other ahead of it. In these positions (Lagrangian points), the asteroids are equidistant from both Jupiter and the Sun and are trapped by gravitational forces. △78.

Trojan War, war between the Greeks and Trojans. The war, which lasted 10 years, began when Paris, son of King Priam of Troy, kidnapped Helen, wife of King Menelaus of Sparta. When the Trojans refused to return her, the Greeks formed an army, led by Agamemnon, that included Greek leaders Achilles, Patroclus, Diomedes, Odysseus, Nestor, the two Ajaxes, and Philoctetes. After nine years of fighting the Greeks pretended to sail for home, leaving behind a large hollow, wooden horse in which they concealed some warriors. Sinon persuaded the Trojans to bring the horse within the fortified city walls of Troy, despite the warnings of Cassandra and Laocoön. That night the Greeks returned and when the concealed warriors opened the city gates, Troy was destroyed. Homer wrote about the events of the war in the epic the *Iliad.* Through excavations done at Troy, historians believe that the legend does reflect a real war (*c.* 1200 BC) between the Greeks and the people of Troas, possibly over the control of the Dardanelles and Black Sea trade.

Troll, in Scandinavian mythology, a grotesque supernatural forest dweller of evil nature but somewhat limited intelligence. They are generally outwitted by their intended victims.

Trolley, an electric-powered street vehicle. Developed by Leo Daft, a US inventor, the trolley was named for its small carriage, or trolley, that ran on two overhead wires, gathering electrical power. Trolleys were popular in several European countries as well as the United States in the late 19th to early 20th centuries, but were then replaced by buses. They had the advantages of quiet operation, avoidance of fumes, and faster acceleration, but had more restricted routes than buses. △1700.

Trollope, Anthony (1815–82), widely traveled English novelist. A prolific author, Trollope satirized the upper-middle class in books such as *Barchester Towers* (1857). Later works, including *The Way We Live Now* (1875), are more harshly critical of society. △1238.

Trombone, brass wind musical instrument with cylindrical bore, cupped mouthpiece, and flaring bell. It is played with a slide, except for a variant with three valves. The tenor and bass trombones range 2½ octaves. The tone is solemn and mellow, often ribald in glissando flourishes. The trombone has been used since the late 15th century in symphonic and martial music, later in jazz.

Trondheim, city in central Norway, on S shore of Trondheim Fjord; capital of St Trøndelag co; site of many old structures, including an 11th-century cathedral and royal palace; an active seaport. Exports: wood and metal products. Industries: brewing, food processing, shipbuilding, hardware. Founded 997 by Olaf Trygvesson. Pop. 127,699.

Troodos, Mount. *See* Olympus, Mount.

Tropical Fish, small fish from the Amazon River Basin and SE Asia kept in captivity by hobbyists in home aquariums. They live in fresh and marine tropical and subtropical waters, generally at temperatures of 75–78°F (23.9–25.6°C). Hundreds of varieties include the guppy, mollie, swordtail, platy, betta, gourami, tetra, and danie. Exotic types include clown triggerfish, brilliant rasbora, regal angelfish, and yellowtail wrasse. The paradise fish, considered to be earliest tropical aquarium fish, was imported to Paris in 1868. The hobby of keeping tropical fish became popular in the United States during the 1930s. More species became available after World War II.

Tropical Medicine. △732.

Tropical Pawpaw. *See* Papaya.

Tropical Year, or solar year, time necessary for the Sun to complete a single one of its apparent journeys along the ecliptic, starting and ending at the First Point of Aries (the vernal equinox). Owing to the westward precession of the equinoxes, the tropical year is about 20 minutes shorter than the sidereal year.

Tropic Bird, black-marked, whitish seabird that flies over warm Atlantic, Pacific, and Indian ocean waters diving for food. They have long, bright bills and long, streamerlike central tail feathers. A single whitish, spotted egg is laid in a hole or crevice and incubated by both parents. Length: to 20in (50cm). Genus *Phaethon;* family Phaethonidae.

Tropic of Cancer, the northernmost parallel of latitude, 23.5° north of the equator, reached by the Sun directly overhead, separating the torrid and north temperate zones. *See also* Solstice.

Tropic of Capricorn, the southernmost parallel of latitude, 23.5° south of the equator, reached by the Sun directly overhead, separating the torrid and south temperate zones. *See also* Solstice.

Tropism, growth or movement of a plant, animal, or part in response to external stimuli, including light, gravity, or temperature. For example, some plants bend toward light; some animals move to warmer areas.

Troposphere, the shell of gases in the atmosphere nearest the Earth. *See also* Atmosphere.

Trotsky, Leon (1879–1940), Russian communist leader, born Leib Davydovich Bronstein. Joining the Social Democratic party, he became a Menshevik

Triceratops

Trieste, Italy

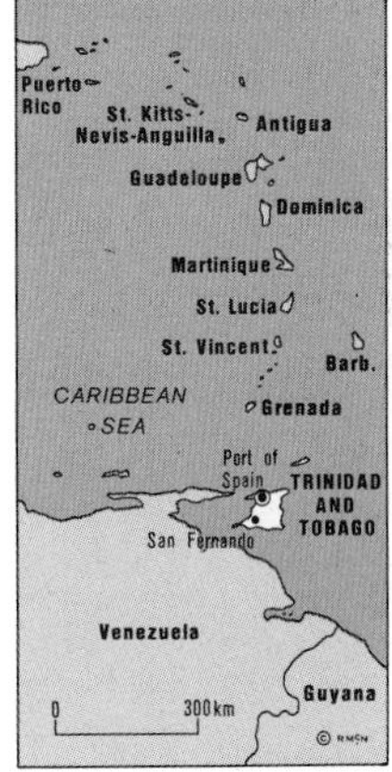

Puerto Rico
St. Kitts-Nevis-Anguilla
Antigua
Guadeloupe
Dominica
Martinique
St. Lucia
St. Vincent
Barb.
CARIBBEAN SEA
Grenada
Port of Spain
TRINIDAD AND TOBAGO
San Fernando
Venezuela
Guyana
0
300km

Trinidad and Tobago

Tropic bird

(1903). Chairman of the St Petersburg Soviet, he was prominent in the 1905 revolution, after which he escaped abroad. Returning to Russia for the March 1917 revolution, he became a Bolshevik. As head of the Petrograd Soviet he organized the seizure of power. As commissar for foreign affairs (1917–18), he was at Brest-Litovsk, but resigned after the treaty was concluded. As commissar for war (1918–25) he created and led the Red army in the civil war. After V.I. Lenin's death he was outmaneuvered by Joseph Stalin and expelled from the party in 1927 and from the country in 1929 as a leader of the left opposition. He was murdered in Mexico by Stalin's agents in 1940. Fiercely independent, he was a brilliant polemicist and fiery speaker. △1310–12.

Trotskyism, revisionist interpretation of Marxism formulated by Leon Trotsky. Trotsky's principal contribution to Marxist theory was his concept of "permanent revolution." Trotsky rejected the idea that parliamentary democracy and capitalism had to precede the formation of a socialist state. Revolution could begin, he argued, in a pre-capitalist society but could not be completed unless there was a chain reaction in industrialized countries. △1310–12.

Trout, freshwater sport fish of North America and Europe. Also a good food fish, it is commonly propagated in hatcheries. Trout move upstream to spawn. Those that migrate to ocean between spawnings are called steelheads. Length: to 40.5in (103cm); weight: 37lb (17kg). Types include: the high mountain golden *Salvelinus aguakonita* of W North America, marked by vertical side bars; rainbow trout *Salmo gairdneri* marked by a longitudinal red stripe; brook trout, or char, *Salvelinus fontinalis* of E North America; large European brown trout *Salmo trutta;* and cutthroat *Salmo clarki* of W North America. Family Salmonidae. △390.

Troy, or **Ilium,** ancient city in northwest Asia Minor. Its legend is a frequent theme in Greek literature. The extensive ruins excavated by Heinrich Schliemann in the 1870s have shown at least 10 cities built on the same site, the second and richest dating from the 22nd century BC. The Troy depicted by Homer in his *Iliad* and *Odyssey* was the seventh in chronological order. From the beginning Troy was the seat of a powerful ruler and an important point on the trade route between Europe and Asia. Tradition says Homer's Troy was destroyed by Agamemnon in 1183 BC, but the date is now thought to be in the 14th century. Afterward no major Greek city existed on the site. △1292.

Troy, city in SE Michigan, SE of Pontiac. Industries: electronic and automotive parts. Settled 1821; inc. 1955. Pop. (1970) 39,419.

Troy, city in E New York, on E bank of Hudson River, 8mi (13km) NE of Albany; seat of Rensselaer co. Henry Hudson first explored area in 1609; site of Rennselaer Polytechnic Institute (1824), Russell Sage College (1916), and Hudson Valley Community College (1953). Industries: men's clothing, automobile parts, steel, paper. First settled 1780s; inc. as village 1794, as city 1816. Pop. (1970) 62,918.

Troyes, Nicolas de, 16th-century French poet. Of his work only the second part of a manuscript collection of short tales survived, and most of them were borrowed from Boccaccio.

Troyes, city of NE France, 92mi (148km) SE of Paris, on Seine River; Capital of Aube dept. and site of the annual champagne fairs 11th–12th centuries; scene of signing of Treaty of Troyes (1420) between Charles VI and Henry V of England; Joan of Arc expelled English from here in 1429; site of Cathedral of Sts Peter and Paul (13th–16th centuries) and Church of St Urban (1262). Industries: hosiery, needles, flour, automobile parts, tires. Founded in pre-Roman times. Pop. 74,-898.

Troyes, Treaty of (1420), truce in the Hundred Years War, between Charles VI of France, Henry V of England, and Philip of Burgundy. It stipulated marriage between Henry and Charles' daughter and stipulated that Henry would be recognized as the heir to the French throne. *See also* Hundred Years War.

Truck, any motor vehicle designed to carry freight or goods. They are powered by gas, diesel, or gasoline engines. Gottlieb Daimler of Germany built the first truck in 1896. Trucks can be either straight, with all the axles on a single frame, or articulated, as in the different types of tractor-trailer combinations. Trucks do the majority of short-distance hauling and also carry a substantial part of long-distance cargoes in most countries. △1702.

Trudeau, Pierre Elliott (1919–), Canadian political figure. A student of economics and political science, he became a labor and civil liberties lawyer (1943). He was elected a Liberal member of Parliament in 1965, serving as parliamentary secretary to Prime Minister Lester Pearson until he was appointed minister of justice and attorney general in 1967. He succeeded Pearson as party leader and as prime minister in 1968. He promoted economic and diplomatic independence for Canada, recognizing the People's Republic of China in 1970. In 1970 he had to temporarily impose martial law to combat French separatist terrorism. The Liberal party lost its majority in 1970, but Trudeau continued to govern with the aid of the small New Democratic party. In 1974 he was reelected prime minister with Liberal support alone.

Truffaut, François (1932–), French filmmaker. His films are distinguished by sensitivity, charm, and a lyric, intensely personal style. Among his major works are *The 400 Blows* (1959), *Shoot the Piano Player* (1960), *Jules and Jim* (1961), *Stolen Kisses* (1968), *The Wild Child* (1971), *Day for Night* (1973), and *The Story of Adele H.* (1975).

Truffle, any of several fungi (family Tuberaceae) that grow underground, mostly among tree roots, and are highly prized edible delicacies. Truffles range in size from pea to potato and in color from black to white. Found in Europe, North Africa, and North America, they are hunted by trained pigs and dogs that can smell them underground. △428.

Trujillo Molina, Rafael Leonidas (1891–1961), dominant figure of the Dominican Republic from 1930 until his death. Initially installed as chief executive by revolutionary coup, Trujillo was several times reelected. As president or maker-of-presidents, Trujillo—together with his family and friends—controlled the nation's institutions for more than a generation.

Truk Islands, island group in E Caroline Islands, W Pacific Ocean; part of US Trust Territory of the Pacific Islands; comprised of about 55 islands and islets, mainly of volcanic origin, surrounded by a reef with navigable passes into natural harbors; inner harbor was site of important Japanese naval base during WWII. Products: fish, copra. Area: 39sq mi (101sq km). Pop. 29,208.

Truman, Harry S. (1884–1972), 33rd president of the United States (1945–53), b. Lamar, Mo. In 1919 he married Elizabeth Wallace; they had one daughter. Unable to attend college, Truman worked at a number of jobs before entering politics. He also commanded an artillery battery in World War I. In 1922, with the support of the Kansas City Democratic machine, he was elected judge (actually, an administrator) of Jackson co; in 1926 he was elected president judge, or chief executive, of the county. In 1935 he went to the US Senate as an ardent New Dealer.

In the Senate, Truman was forced to live down his reputation as a machine politician. He was reelected in 1940, despite strong efforts to unseat him. During World War II, he headed a committee to stop waste in government spending. His success at that task—and his acceptability to all factions of the party—made him Roosevelt's choice for his vice-presidential running mate in 1944. The ticket won easily. Truman was vice president for less than three months; on April 12, 1945, Roosevelt died, and Truman became president. Although ill-prepared, he took quick control of the reins of power. He ordered the bombing of Japanese cities with the atomic bomb, thereby bringing World War II to a victorious end.

The end of the war also saw the end of the alliance with the Soviet Union. The Cold War began, and Truman countered Soviet moves in Europe with such instruments as the Marshall Plan, the Truman Doctrine, the Berlin airlift, and the North Atlantic Treaty Organization. His domestic program, which he named the Fair Deal, was an enlargement of the New Deal programs.

In 1948, Truman was opposed for election by Governor Thomas E. Dewey of New York, who was widely expected to win, and by two splinter tickets of the Democratic party. Despite the opposition, Truman won in one of the great political upsets in US history. Truman's second term was beset by the issue of Communist infiltration of government, particularly by charges leveled by Sen. Joseph McCarthy. His administration was blamed for the "loss" of China to communism. His last years in office were chiefly occupied with waging the Korean War. He chose not to run for reelection in 1952.

Career: judge, Jackson co, Mo., 1922–24; president judge, Jackson co, Mo., 1926–34; US Senate, 1935–45; vice president, 1945; president, 1945–53.

See also Berlin Airlift; Cold War; Korean War; Marshall Plan; Truman Doctrine. △1358.

Truman Doctrine (1947), declaration of US foreign policy by Pres. Harry Truman. It stated that the United States would act to prevent the overthrow of democratic institutions by totalitarian governments anywhere in the world. Although the statement was universal in scope, Truman specifically was referring to the protection of Greece and Turkey against Soviet expansion. The doctrine became the primary statement of US policy in the Cold War.

Trumbull, John (1750–1831), US author, b. Westbury, Conn. A poet and essayist, he wrote *The Progress of Dulness* (1773), a long satirical poem, and *M'Fingal* (1782), an anti-British satire. After the American Revolution, he practiced law and was a member of the Connecticut Wits. *See also* Connecticut Wits. △1192.

Trumbull, John (1756–1843), US painter, b. Lebanon, Conn. His work, mainly portraits and historical subjects, was influenced by Copley and Hogarth. His father and brothers were active patriots in the American Revolution. In 1786 he began a long series of scenes from the American Revolution, as well as portraits of major figures of the Revolution ("Alexander Hamilton," 1792).

Trumbull, Jonathan (1740–1809), US congressman, b. Lebanon, Conn. He sat in the first Congress; was speaker of the second (1791–93); and became a US senator (1795–96). He was Connecticut's governor (1797–1809).

Trumpet, loud, brilliant, brass wind musical instrument of primitive origin. It was used by the Romans for military fanfare. Long-tubed medieval trumpets were folded (*c.*1500), and trumpets were still played only by lip in Bach's time. Piston valves were added (*c.*1820). The common soprano (B*b*) trumpet has a 2½-octave range. △1500.

Trumpeter Swan, swan with a loud, buglelike call found in Canada and NW United States. Once close to extinction, it is now protected by law and no longer endangered. It is one of the heaviest flying birds in North America. Weight: to 40lb (18kg). Species *Cygnus buccinator. See also* Swan.

Trunkfish, or boxfish, boxlike marine fish found in temperate and tropical seas. It is identified by its fused scales and eye spines. Length: to 24in (61cm). Among 30 species is the common West Indian *Lactophrys trigonus* and smooth *L. triqueter,* which releases a poisonous mucous for killing other fish. Family Ostraciontidae. △514.

Truss Bridge, a bridge supported mainly by trusses, straight pieces of metal or timber, forming a series of triangles lying on a single plane. Individual pieces intersect at truss joints where they are connected by bolts, rivets, or welds. Trusses were first used during the Italian Renaissance for constructing covered bridges. Many beautiful covered truss bridges, built in the early history of North America, are still standing. △1758.

Trusteeship, in labor organizations, refers to a situation in which the national body assumes control of the assets and obligations of the local unions. Sometimes misused by national unions, trusteeship is intended to protect local members from dishonest or inept officers. Trusteeship must follow the rules set forth by the Labor Management Reporting and Disclosure Act of 1959.

Trusts, combinations of companies that handed their stock over to be administered by a central controlling board. Later the term came to refer to business combinations in restraint of trade. In the United States, trusts were started about 1880 to prevent falling prices, which were affecting most businesses. By the early 20th century, trusts had been outlawed through legislation and court action.

Truth, Sojourner (1797?–1883), US abolitionist, b. Ulster co, N.Y. She was freed from slavery in 1827, by the New York Emancipation Act. She took the name Sojourner Truth and traveled, lecturing on emancipation and other social issues. Although illiterate, she spoke forcefully and effectively, winning many converts to her causes. Pres. Abraham Lincoln chose her to be counselor to the freedmen in Washington.

Truth-in-Lending Act (1968), law, officially called the Consumer Credit Protection Act, which required lenders, including retailers, to give consumers written information on what they pay in interest and other charges on loans and credit purchases.

Truth Serum, a misnomer for a sedative/hypnotic drug such as sodium amobarbitol used to facilitate uestioning. It is neither a serum, nor does it insure uth.

rypanosome, animallike flagellate protozoan that parasitic in the blood of vertebrates. An elongated ell, with long, undulating membrane and flagellum ong one side, it is harbored by African game, carried y tsetse fly, and injected into blood of humans caus-g sleeping sickness. Length: 1/1250in (1/50mm). lass Mastigophora; species *Trypanosoma brucei.* △66.

rypanosomiasis, a whole array of debilitating dis-ases in man and domestic animals, caused by several pecies of parasitic flagellate protozoans of the genus *rypanosoma.* The vector is usually a fly or other in-ect. Examples are human sleeping sickness and hagas' disease, and nagana and surra in cattle and orses. △466, 732.

rypsin, proteolytic enzyme present in pancreatic ice. It breaks down proteins into short peptides to d in absorption during digestion. △694.

ryptophan, colorless crystalline essential amino cid found in proteins. *See* Amino Acid.

setse Fly, brown fly, with a wasplike body, 0.24 to .72in (6–18mm) long, found south of the Tropic of ancer in Africa. It is blood-sucking and transmits Afri-an sleeping sickness. Family Muscidae, species *Glos-na spp. See also* Diptera.

shombe, Moise Kapenda (1919–69), Congolese ilitary leader, secessionist, and politician. He be-ame involved in the government of Katanga (re-amed Shaba) and formed a separate nation when the est of the Congo became independent in 1960. After ostilities with the United Nations, he fled to Europe, ut returned as premier of a united Congo (now Zaire) 1964. He was dismissed (1965), banished for trea-on, kidnapped, and imprisoned in Algeria (1967), here he died.

sinan (Jinan or Chi-nan), city in E China, 225mi 62km) S of Peking, near Yellow River; capital of hantung prov. An ancient walled city dating from hou dynasty (1122–256 BC), it has been provincial apital since Ming dynasty (1368–1644); scene of attle during Communist takeover 1948 causing eavy loss of Nationalist forces. Industries: textiles, egetable oils, chemicals, machine shops, food proc-ssing, paper, trucks, agricultural machinery, flour, on, steel. Pop. 1,500,000.

sin Dynasty, Chinese dynasty, also known as Chin ynasty. Established in 265 by Tsin Wu Ti (the Mar-al Emperor) and known in history as the West Tsin ynasty, it was destroyed in 316 by the Hsiung-nu or uns, and survivors fled S of the Yangtze to establish e East Tsin Dynasty (317–419), one of the Six ynasties in S China. The migration of thousands of igh-ranking northern officials to the S aided in devel-pment of traditional Chinese style and institutions ere.

singhai (Qinghai), province in W central China, ounded by Sinkiang Uighur (N and NE), Kansu (E), zechwan (SE), Tibet (S and SW), Tibet and Sinkiang ighur (W); capital is Hsi-ning. Originally part of Tibet, was annexed to Mongols 14th century; passed to hina's control 1724; fell 1949 to Communists, who stablished numerous autonomous districts; site of singhai Lake, a salt lake giving its name to the prov-nce; it is the largest lake in China. Industries: coal, oil, on ore, salt, borax, potash, Tsinghai horses, grain, otatoes. Area: 250,000sq mi (647,500sq km). Pop. ,000,000.

singtao (Qingdao, or Ching-tao), seaport city in E China, S Shangtang Peninsula, on Yellow Sea; oc-upied by Japanese 1914–22, 1938–45; served as S naval base 1945–49; fell to Communists 1949. ndustries: textiles, flour, cotton seed oil, food proc-ssing, tobacco, paper, machine shops, railroad cars, hemicals. Pop. 1,900,000.

siolkovskii, Konstantin Eduardovich (1857–935), Soviet aerospace scientist. He showed early enius in physics. After 1882 he turned his attention o aeronautics, improving dirigibles and airfoils. In 898 he developed his theory of mass ratio, indicat-ng the possibility of space flight with liquid fuel and ooster rockets. He was made a member of the Rus-ian Academy of Sciences (1919). △138–44.

sitsihar (Qiqihaer, or Ch'i-Ch'i-ha-erh), port city n NE China, 170mi (274km) NW of Harbin, on Nen iver; former capital of Hokiang and Heilungkiang rovs. Industries: locomotives, paper, cement, food rocessing. Founded 1691. Pop. 1,500,000.

Tsunami, a shallow (3m or 9.8ft), long, sea wave caused by a submarine earthquake, subsidence, or volcanic eruption. Tsunamis spread radially from their source in ever-widening circles. Though rarely detected at sea, in shallow water they build up in force and height, crashing on shore and causing enormous damage. Tsunamis are also called seismic sea waves, but "tidal waves" is erroneous. △174, 226.

Tuatara, nocturnal lizardlike reptile of New Zealand, only survivor of the primitive order Rhynchocephalia. It is brownish-yellow with a unique vestigial third eye on the top of its head, possibly functional in the young, and has a short crest along neck and back. Length: to 2.5ft (76cm). Species *Sphenodon punctatus. See also* Reptile. △614.

Tuba, large brass wind musical instrument in the lowest register. It has a conical bore like the French horn and an oblong shape and cupped mouthpiece like the trumpet. It is held vertically with the bell upward and played with four to five valves. It is made in tenor, bass, and double bass sizes for symphony orchestras. There are also Wagnerian tubas, sousaphones, and other variants in military bands.

Tubal Ligation, a method of sterilizing the female, in which the fallopian tubes leading from the ovaries are tied off with a ligature, preventing the migration of ova to the uterus.

Tube, Electron. *See* Electron Tube.

Tube, X-ray. *See* X-ray Tube.

Tuber, short, swollen, fleshy part of an underground stem, such as a potato. New plants develop from the buds, or eyes, growing in the axils of the scale leaves. Tubers are propagated by cutting them into sections containing at least one eye and planting these sections. △332.

Tuberculosis, an infectious disease, usually involving the lungs, caused by several species of bacillus of the genus *Mycobacterium.* In man, the agent is usually the primate or bovine variety. Pulmonary tuberculosis constitutes over 90% of cases, but other parts of the body may also become tuberculous. Individual susceptibility and severity vary. Fatigue, weight loss, persistent coughing, and hemorrhaging from the lungs are progressive symptoms. Modern methods of early detection and chemotherapy have effectively reduced the former high incidence of this disease in densely populated areas. △714.

Tuberose, Mexican perennial bulb plant frequently grown in S United States. The white sweet-scented flowers are so fragrant they should be mixed with other flowers in bouquets and gardens. Height: to 3ft (91.5cm). Family Agavaceae; species *Polianthes tuberosa.*

Tubman, Harriet (*c.* 1820–1913), US abolitionist, b. Dorchester co, Md. A slave, she escaped (1849) through the Underground Railroad; she then became a "conductor" on the Underground Railroad and was able to lead over 300 slaves to freedom. She worked closely with leading abolitionists, including Ralph Waldo Emerson, Wendell Phillips, and John Brown, and aided the Union during the Civil War.

Tucana, or the Toucan, faint southern constellation containing the Small Magellanic Cloud and the globular cluster 47 Tucanae (NGC 104). There is also a smaller globular, NGC 362. △136.

Tucker, Sophie (1884–1966), US entertainer, b. Sophie Kalish in Russia. On stage in *The Ziegfeld Follies* (1909), *Leave It To Me* (1938), and *High Kickers* (1941), her 60-year career also included vaudeville, nightclub, film, radio, and TV performances. The "Last of the Red-hot Mamas" had as her theme song "Some of These Days."

Tucson, city in SE Arizona, 103mi (166km) SE of Phoenix on Santa Cruz River; seat of Pima co. Originally an Indian settlement, it was settled 1776 as the Spanish walled Presidio de San Augustín de Tuguison; transferred to the United States as part of Gadsden Purchase (1853); served as territorial capital 1867–77; prospered with coming of Southern Pacific Railroad (1880). Landmarks include "Old Adobe" (1868), Colossal Cave, Fort Lowell, San Xavier Mission (1783–97), annual rodeo, University of Arizona (1885). Industries: aircraft parts, missiles, dairy products, meat packing, cotton, mining, electronics, tourism. Inc. 1877. Pop. (1970) 262,933.

Tucumán (San Miguel de Tucumán), city in N Argentina, 665mi (1,071km) NW of Buenos Aires; capital of Tucumán prov.; site of first congress (1816)

Troyes, France

Harry S. Truman

John Trumbull: Declaration of Independence

Harriet Tubman

declaring Argentine independence. Industries: agriculture, lumber, sugar. Founded 1565. Pop. 271,-546.

Tudor, royal family that ruled England 1485–1603. The dynasty was founded by Owen Tudor (1400?–61), a Welsh squire, who married Henry V's widow Catherine of Valois. Owen's son Edmund (1430?–56) married Margaret Beaufort, heiress of John of Gaunt. Their son Henry (1457–1509) defeated Richard III at Bosworth (1485) and became Henry VII. Through his marriage (1486) to Edward IV's daughter Elizabeth, Henry united the houses of York and Lancaster. He was succeeded by his son, Henry VIII (1491–1547), who reigned 1509–47; and grandchildren, Edward VI, Mary I, and Elizabeth I. On Elizabeth's death (1603) James VI of Scotland, a Stuart and great-great-grandson of Henry VII, ascended the throne.

Tudor Architecture, English architectural style of the first half of the 16th century, from the time of Henry VII to Mary I. △1106.

Tuei. *See* Isleta.

Tuff, sedimentary rock made up of particles of igneous rock from volcanic eruptions. The particles vary in size from fine to coarse, and may be either stratified or heterogeneous in their arrangement.

Tu Fu (712–70), Chinese poet. Writing during the T'ang dynasty (618–906), China's literary golden age, he is considered one of his nation's greatest poets. His personal life was troubled, but his verse is polished and powerful with an intricate style rich in nuances. His 1405 poems cover such topics as war, corruption, and patriotism.

Tugboat, a small, powerful vessel used primarily for berthing large ships and towing or pushing barges. Some ocean-going tugboats are employed in salvage. First used in the 18th century in Scotland, where they were powered by a steam engine and a paddle wheel, tugboats are now driven by diesel engines. △1680.

Tugwell, Rexford Guy (1891–), US economist and political leader, b. Sinclairville, N.Y. A professor of economics, he wrote numerous books, including *The Economic Basis of Public Interest* (1922) and *Industry's Coming of Age* (1927), critical of laissez-faire economics. In 1933 he became an advisor to Pres. Franklin Roosevelt, and a member of the "brain trust." His views on planning helped shape early New Deal policies. He served as assistant secretary of agriculture (1934–37), where he was responsible for the Resettlement Administration (1935–36). He was also governor of Puerto Rico (1941–46).

Tui. *See* Parson Bird.

Tularemia, an acute infectious disease resembling plague but less severe, caused by the bacterium *Pasteurella tularensis.* It occurs primarily in wild birds and mammals. Human infection is rare and was first reported in the United States in 1914. Rabbits and hares seem to be the chief agents in transmitting the disease to man; a deerfly can also pass the infection. There are two forms in man: an ulcerative, glandular kind and a less common typhoidlike manifestation. The fatality rate is under 5%. Antibiotic treatment is effective.

Tulip, hardy bulb plants native to Europe, Asia, and North Africa. They have long, pointed leaves growing from the base and elongated cup-shaped flowers that can be almost any color or combination of colors. The bulbs are planted in mid-autumn or spring, depending on climate. They can be planted in pots indoors and forced in winter. The name tulip is derived from the Turkish word for turban. They have been cultivated and hybridized worldwide since the Middle Ages and now vary widely in physical characteristics and blooming times. Family Liliaceae; genus *Tulipa.*

Tulip Tree, or tulip poplar, deciduous tree of North America. It has tulip-shaped, greenish-yellow flowers and long, conelike fruit. Height: 100–200ft (30.5–61m). Family Magnoliaceae; genus *Liriodendron.*

Tull, Jethro (1674–1741), English agriculturist. He invented the agricultural drill (1701), which sowed seeds in drills, or rows, and widely replaced the usual method of sowing by hand. He was also responsible for introducing the practice of pulverizing (breaking down) the soil between rows.

Tulsa, port city in NE Oklahoma, on Arkansas River, seat of Tulsa co. Settled 1830s by Creek Indians, it developed with coming of Atlantic and Pacific Railroad (1882); with discovery of oil (1901), it became booming business center for oil industry; connected to Gulf of Mexico by McClelland-Kerr Waterway (1971). It is site of University of Tulsa (1894), Oral Roberts University, Philbrook Art Center (1938), Old Council Tree, first post office (1879). Industries: oil refining and research, petroleum products, oil field equipment, mining, machinery, aerospace. Inc. 1898. Pop. (1970) 330,350.

Tumblebug. *See* Dung Beetle.

Tumbleweed, plant that breaks off near the ground in autumn and is rolled by the wind. The common western tumbleweed is usually white-stemmed and has pale flowers crowded into the leaf axils. Height: 6–20in (15–51cm). Species include *Amaranthus albus* and *A. graecizans.* Family Amaranthaceae.

Tumen (Tyumen), city in Russian SFSR, USSR, on the Tura River, 180mi (290km) E of Sverdlovsk; capital of Tumen oblast. Founded in 1585, it was the first-settled Russian town E of the Urals. Industries: matches, plywood, shipbuilding, tanning, sheepskins, felt boots, meat, flour, woolen milling. Pop. 1,407,-000.

Tumor, any uncontrolled, abnormal proliferation of new tissue from pre-existing cells that has no useful function in terms of the body as a whole. Tumors fall into several types and are diagnosed as benign or malignant. △712, 722.

Tuna, mackerellike marine fish found in tropical, temperate, and cold seas. An important commercial fish, it has a blue-black and silvery streamlined body with a large, sharply divided tail. Length: to 14ft (4.3m); weight: 1,800lb (810kg). Types of tuna include bluefin, yellowfin, big eye, skipjack, and bonito. Family Scombridae. △392, 626.

Tundra, a Lapp term for the treeless, level or gently undulating plain characteristic of arctic and subarctic regions. The tundra is marshy with dark mucky soil that supports mosses, lichens, and low shrubs. It has a permanently frozen subsoil known as permafrost. △312, 612.

Tung Ch'i-ch'ang (1555–1637), Chinese painter, writer, and government official. △1208.

Tungsten, or wolfram, metallic element (symbol W) of the third transition series, first identified in 1779 and isolated in 1783. Chief ores are wolframite and scheelite. Tungsten has the highest melting point of all metals and is used for filaments in electric light bulbs, electron tubes, etc. It is also used in high-speed steels and other special alloys. The sulfide is used as a lubricant. Chemically, tungsten is fairly unreactive: it oxidizes at high temperatures. Properties: at. no. 74; at. wt. 183.85; sp. gr. 19.3; melt. pt. 6,170°F (3,410°C); boil. pt. 10,701°F (5,921°C); most common isotope W^{184} (30.64%). *See also* Transition Elements. △1506, 1554, 1556.

Tungus, Uralic-Altaic-speaking, Mongoloid people who inhabit E Siberia. Consisting of two main groups, the Evenki and Lamuts, they practice reindeer herding, fishing, and agriculture. Introduction of Russian Orthodoxy resulted in the decline of traditional shamanism.

Tungusic Languages, group of remote languages spoken in the Soviet Union and China, forming part of the Altaic family. A northern branch consists of Evenki (or Tungus) and Even, both spoken in central and E Siberia, while the southern branch consists of Nanai, spoken near the city of Khabarovsk, and Sibo, spoken in northwestern China. Manchu, the language of the Manchus but now nearly extinct, is also a Tungusic language.

Tunicate, or sea squirt, marine, immobile, vase-shaped animal found worldwide. They are solitary or live in colonies. Adults reveal their chordate nature only by numerous gill slits that filter seawater. The tadpole-shaped larvae have well-developed tails, notochords, and nerve cords. Some barrel-shaped tunicates are free-swimming and others are neotenic, retaining their larval shape into maturity. Length: 3/16–11.75in (5mm–30cm). There are 2,000 species. Phylum Chordata; subdivision Urochordata. *See also* Chordate. △508.

Tunis, city in NE Tunisia, N Africa, on Lake of Tunis with canal access to Gulf of Tunis (arm of Mediterranean). A leading industrial and trade center near site of ancient Carthage, the city is divided into Tunisian and European sections; site of museums, Zitouna Mosque (732), medieval walls, University of Tunis (1960). Area was settled by Romans 2nd century BC–AD 5th century; conquered by Muslims 7th century, after which it developed to become 9th-century capital of Tunisia; capital under Hafsid dynasty 13th–16th centuries; occupied by Turks, Spanish, French un independence was recognized 1956. Industries: r workshops, lead smelting, textiles, carpets, olive o chemicals. Pop. 468,997.

Tunisia, independent nation in N Africa. The site ancient Carthage, and many Roman ruins, it is an ag cultural country. Its geographical position makes politically and economically important.

Land and economy. Between Algeria (W) ar Libya (E) on the N coast of Africa, Tunisia exten 1,000mi (1,600km) along the Mediterranean Se The N section, source of most agricultural productio is fertile. Livestock grazing and olive groves are in th coastal plains. The S region borders the Sahara Dese and supports grazing and semi-nomadic tribes. Th economy of Tunisia is divided into three sections state, cooperative, and private. Agriculture is th mainstay of the economy, with livestock second. Mi eral deposits are not large, although Tunisia h enough petroleum to meet domestic needs. Touris has become the largest foreign exchange earner. Fo eign investment has been encouraged.

People. Descended from the Phoenician traders the 12th century BC Tunisians now consist of abo 35% Arabs and 65% Berbers. Arabic is the offici and national language; 1% speak Berber. Most of th population is Sunni Muslim with some Andalusia Moors and Jews in the cities. Europeans constitu 1% of the population, the majority being French.

Government. The country is a republic wit elected president and elected unicameral Nation Assembly.

History. Carthage, the most noted of the Phoer cian trading cities, was established in Tunisia. Later, was a Roman possession; Arabs came in the 7th ce tury when it became an Islamic cultural center. Turkish invasion occurred in 1574; in 1881 Franc occupied the land, making it a protectorate. Tunisia drive for nationalism started after WWI when a const tutional party was formed. In 1934, Habib Bourguib became its leader. Guerrilla warfare persuade France to offer internal autonomy followed by an er to the protectorate in 1956. Clashes continued b tween the two countries, and on July 25, 1957, th Tunisian Constituent Assembly voted to establish republic. Bourguiba was elected president under th banner of the Destoruian Socialist party. Tunisia is member of the Arab League, but favors negotiatior to settle Arab-Israeli disputes.

PROFILE

Official name: Republic of Tunisia
Area: 63,170sq mi (163,610sq km)
Population: 5,700,000
Density: 90per sq mi (35per sq km)
Chief cities: Tunis (capital); Sfax
Government: Republic
Religion: Islam
Language: Arabic (official and national)
Monetary unit: Dinar
Gross national product: $3,600,000,000
Per capita income: $459
Industries: processed foods, wineries, petroleu products, olive oil processing, textiles, clothin construction materials, leather
Agriculture: cereals, wheat, grains, dates, olives, c rus fruits, almonds, figs, cattle, forests, grapes
Minerals: phosphates, iron ore, oil, lead, zinc
Trading partners: France, United States, Italy, We Germany

Tunnel. △1754.

Tunney, Gene (1898–), US boxer, b. James J seph Tunney in New York City. He was the US ligh heavyweight champion (1922–23) who upset Jac Dempsey (1926) for the world's heavyweight char pionship. He successfully defended his crown again Dempsey (1927) in Chicago in the "Battle of the Lor Count," and retired as champion (1928). He wa elected to the Boxing Hall of Fame in 1955.

Tupelo, city in NE Mississippi, 57mi (92km) NNW Columbus; seat of Lee co; scene of Battle of Tupe (July 14, 1864) in which Confederates were defeate by Union forces; now a National Battlefield (es 1929). Industries: power tools, fertilizer, furnitur clothing. Founded 1859; inc. 1870. Pop. (1970) 20 471.

Tupelo, or black gum, deciduous tree of moist fores in North America. Its fine-textured wood is used f furniture, mallets, etc. It has lustrous leaves, minut greenish-white flowers, and dark blue fruit cluste relished by birds. Height: to 100ft (30.5m). Specie include the sour gum *(Nyssa sylvatica)* and wat tupelo or cotton gum *(N. aquatica).* Family Cor aceae.

Turbellaria. △472.

Turbidity Current, a density current in water, air, or other fluid caused by different amounts of matter in suspension. In the ocean, when sediment along the continental shelves breaks off and rushes downslope, the resulting turbidity current carves out submarine canyons and deposits distinctively bedded layers on the ocean floor. △224, 228.

Turbine, rotary engine that converts the energy of a moving stream of water, steam, or gas into mechanical energy. The basic element in a turbine is a wheel or rotor with blades or buckets arranged on its circumference such that moving water or gas exerts tangential force, which turns the wheel. This mechanical energy is transferred through a drive shaft to operate a machine. △1628–34, 1510, 1698.

Turbojet Engine, aircraft propulsion unit that produces power through the reaction of expanding gases. Air taken in at the front through a compressor is forced into a combustion chamber, mixed with fuel, and burned, producing a rush of expanding gas that propels the aircraft in a reaction to the rapid outflow. To maintain the cycle the expanding gas also drives a turbine connected to the air compressor. △1626, 1718, 1744.

Turbot, NE Atlantic marine flatfish. A food fish, it has a deep, thick body, short tail shaft, and bony hooks on scales. Colors are marbled gray or brown. Length: 40in (102cm). Family Scopthalmidae (or Pleuronectidae); species *Scophthalmus maximus.* △392.

Turene, Henri de La Tour d'Auvergne, vicomte de (1611–75), French general. He distinguished himself against the Germans in the Thirty Years' War (1618–48) and in the wars of Louis XIV. He was involved in the Fronde (1649–51) but supported the future Louis XIV against the forces of the Prince de Condé and Spain. Killed in battle against the Germans, he was buried with the kings of France.

Turgenev, Ivan (Sergeevich) (1818–83), Russian novelist, playwright, and short-story writer. He was at his most prolific between 1850–60. The play *A Month in the Country,* which would strongly influence Chekhov, appeared in 1850. *A Sportsman's Sketches,* short stories, was published in 1852. Three novels also appeared: *Rudin* (1855), *A Nest of Gentlefolk* (1859), and *On the Eve* (1860). His works received official disapproval because they spoke out against social and political evils. After the appearance of his greatest novel *Fathers and Sons,* about nihilism, he left Russia. Well-known short stories include "First Love" (1870), "A Lear of the Steppe" (1870), and "Torrents of Spring" (1871). △1240

Turgot, Anne Robert Jacques (1727–81), French philosopher, economist, administrator. Chief administrator for Limoges and controller-general of finance (1774–76), he wrote *Reflections on the Formation and Distribution of Riches* (1766). He was considered a physiocrat (agriculture was the ultimate source of real wealth) and a philosophe. He contributed to the French *Encyclopédie* and labored unsuccessfully to set France's fiscal house in order. *See also* Philosophes; Physiocrats.

Turin (Torino), city in NW Italy, 78mi (126km) NW of Genoa, on the Po River; capital of Piedmont region and of Turin province. Founded by the Taurini, it became Roman military colony, and a Lombard duchy 590–636; it was a free commune 12th and 13th centuries; capital of kingdom of Sardinia 1720–1861; 19th-century center of Risorgimento; site of 15th-century cathedral, Palazzo Madama (begun 13th century), university (1404); important center of industry, commerce, and transportation. Industries: automobiles, airplanes, rubber, paper, leather, fashion. Pop. 1,190,-688.

Turkey (Türkiye), independent nation in Asia Minor and Europe. Located in a geographically vital position, it became a republic in 1923 under nationalist leader Kemal Ataturk.

Land and economy. Situated in two continents, Asia and Europe, Turkey is bordered by Greece and Bulgaria (N), the USSR and Iran (E), Iraq and Syria (S). The strategically important Turkish straits (the Bosporus, Sea of Marmara, and the Dardanelles) connect the Black Sea and the Mediterranean Sea. The mild, narrow coastal plain supports a variety of crops ranging from tea to cotton. The central inland Anatolian plateau's W section grows wheat; the E portion is mountainous with severe winters. The SW is treeless, with some mountains 10,000ft (3,050m) above sea level, with little population. The Tigris and Euphrates rivers rise in the E and flow S to the Persian Gulf. In 1973 a suspension bridge linked Europe and Asia across the Bosporus. With an agricultural economy, Turkey's main crops are cotton, tobacco, and grains; about 65% of the working population is engaged in farming or allied fields. About half of the economy is made up of government-owned or controlled enterprises. Opium production was halted in 1971 and resumed, for medical purposes, in 1974.

People. Turkey's population, 99% Sunni Muslim, lives principally on the Anatolian peninsula in Asia, the rest in the European portion. Once a country of small villages, the urban centers have drawn villagers, and most cities now have communities of squatter homes surrounding them. There is no officially recognized religion and no legal discrimination against the minority groups of Greeks, Armenians, and Jews. The largest ethnic minority, the Kurds, lives in the remote areas of the E and SE in primitive conditions. Public elementary school is free and compulsory. Literacy is 55%.

Government. A 1961 constitution provides for a bicameral legislature and a president. The premier is chosen from the majority party.

History. In classical times a center of Greek civilization, the region of modern Turkey was subsequently under the Roman, Byzantine, and Ottoman empires. When the 600-year-old rule of the Ottoman Empire collapsed after fighting as one of Germany's allies in WWI, nationalism grew and the trappings of the old empire were abolished. Under the leadership of Kemal Ataturk, Turkey became a republic in 1923, with Ataturk its first president. Turning away from imperial traditions it became westernized with social and economic reforms that were the basis of modern Turkey. Turkey joined the Allies near the end of WWII and under the Truman Doctrine received US military and economic aid. In 1950 the Ataturk party was defeated, and the Democratic party was in power until a 1960 coup d'etat. A return to civil government came the following year. Tension with neighboring Greece has been a constant factor in foreign affairs. In 1974 this led to a Turkish invasion of Cyprus, justified by allegations of mistreatment of the Turkish minority. *See also* Byzantine Empire; Ottoman Empire.

PROFILE

Official name: Republic of Turkey
Area: 301,381sq mi (780,577sq km)
Population: 39,900,000
Density: 132per sq mi (51per sq km)
Chief cities: Ankara (capital); Istanbul; Izmir
Government: Republic
Religion: Islam
Language: Turkish
Monetary unit: Lira
Gross national product: $19,000,000,000
Per capital income: $576
Industries: olive oil, yarn (silk and wool), opium, steel, foundry products, footwear, furniture, cement, paper, glassware, appliances
Agriculture: tobacco, cereals, cotton, olives, sheep, cattle, fruits, nuts, sugar beets, opium, forests
Minerals: antimony, borate, copper, chrome, manganese, lead, zinc, coal, iron, oil, silver, mercury, asbestos
Trading partners: European Economic Community, United States

Turkey, North American game bird now widely domesticated throughout the world. These birds support a food industry, particularly in the United States where turkeys have long been traditional fare for Thanksgiving. A Mexican race with white-tipped tails has been bred into many varieties and is raised commercially. The common wild turkey *(Meleagris gallopavo),* once abundant in Canada, United States, and Mexican highlands, was overhunted and is now protected by wildlife management measures. The male, or gobbler, is often bearded. He travels in small groups, feeds on forest floor vegetable matter, and, at mating time, displays his feathers and utters courtship noises. The smaller female builds a well concealed nest for the buffy spotted eggs (12–20). Length: 50in (127cm). The ocellated turkey *(Agriocharis ocellata)* of lowland Mexico and adjacent Central American areas has a yellow knob between its eyes, bright metallicky plumage, and a bare, blue, pimple-covered head and neck. Family Meleagrididae. △384.

Turkeyfish. *See* Lionfish.

Turkic Languages, group of languages forming a branch of the Altaic family. Its most important member is Turkish; most of the rest are spoken in the Soviet Union. These include Azerbaijani, Turkmen, Kazakh, Kirgiz, Tatar, Bashkir, Uzbek, Uigur, and a number of others. Azerbaijani and Turkmen are also spoken in Iran.

Turkish Architecture. △1108.

Tunis, Tunisia

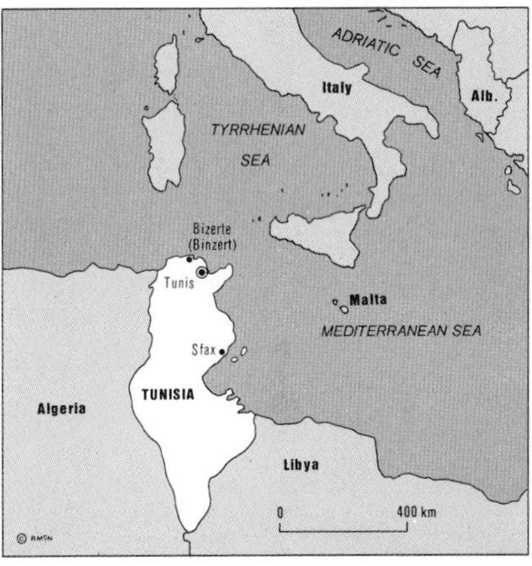
ADRIATIC SEA
Italy
Alb.
TYRRHENIAN SEA
Bizerte (Binzert)
Tunis
Malta
MEDITERRANEAN SEA
Sfax
TUNISIA
Algeria
Libya
0
400 km
Tunisia

Ankara, Turkey: Old Fortress

0
800 km
Romania
U.S.S.R.
Yugoslavia
Bulgaria
BLACK SEA
Istanbul
Bursa
Ankara
Erzurum
Iran
Greece
TURKEY
Izmir
Adana
Gaziantep
Cyprus
Syria
Iraq
MEDITERRANEAN SEA
Lebanon
Israel
Libya
Egypt
Jordan
Saudi Arabia
Turkey

Turkmen Soviet Socialist Republic (Turkmenskaja Sovetskaja Socialisticeskaja Republik, Turkmenia, Turkmenistan), constituent republic of the USSR, in central Asia; bounded by the Caspian Sea (W), Kazakh and Uzbek republics (N and NE), and Afghanistan and Iran (S), containing the four oblasts of Aschabad, Cardzov, Mary, and Tasauz. Main cities are Aschabad (capital), Krasnovodsk, Mary, Nebit-Dag. The area has been inhabited by Turki tribes since the 10th century; after their 1881 defeat, the region became part of Russian Turkistan; organized as a Soviet Republic 1924, it became a constituent republic of the USSR 1925. Industries: sheep, camels, cotton, guayule, sesame, millet, sweet potatoes, dates, sugar cane, grapes, melons, petroleum, ozocerite, iodine, bromine, salt, sulphur, lignite, potash. Exports: cotton, fruit, silk, karakul, petroleum. Pop. 2,158,000.

Turku, seaport city in SW Finland, at mouth of Aurajoki River on Baltic Sea; capital of Turku ja Pori prov.; site of Finnish university (1917) and Swedish university (1918). Industries: steel, textiles, clothing, shipyards. Founded 1157. Pop. 153,300.

Turner, Frederick Jackson (1861–1932), US historian, b. Portage, Wisc. He gained instant acclaim with his treatise *The Significance of the Frontier in American History* (1893). Growing up in frontier territory, he recognized the influence of the constantly moving frontier on American life. His later works were further developments of his original premise, such as *Rise of the New West* (1906), *The Frontier in American History* (1920), and *The Significance of Sections in American History* (1932) for which he won a Pulitzer Prize (1933).

Turner, J(oseph) M(allord) W(illiam) (1775–1851), English painter. By 1790 he was exhibiting his watercolors at the Royal Academy; although he remained a watercolorist, after 1795 he grew increasingly interested in oil painting. Turner's mature style is evidenced in works such as "Death of Nelson" (1806–08) and "London Seen from Greenwich" (1809). After 1820 he grew increasingly preoccupied with light and intense color. His late works emphasized conflict and turmoil ("Rain, Steam, Speed" 1844) and anticipated the Impressionist style. △1242.

Turner, Nat (1800–31), US slave, b. Southampton co, Va., who instigated the "Southampton Insurrection." He said he heard a voice in 1828 saying "the last shall be first." He took this experience plus the solar eclipse of February 1831 as a sign to begin the insurrection in which 85 whites were killed. He was tried, convicted, and hanged.

Turnip, garden vegetable best grown in cool weather. The edible leaves are large and toothed with thick midribs. A biennial, it bears yellow flowers the second year. The edible white, fleshy root is white to purplish-red on the outside; diameter: 3–6in (7.6–15.2cm). It matures in 30–60 days. Height: to 20in (50.8cm). Family Cruciferae; species *Brassica rapa.*

Turnstone, Arctic-nesting, migratory shore bird that uses its curved bill to turn over pebbles in search of food. The vividly marked ruddy turnstone *(Arenaria interpres)* ranges widely in winter; length: 9in (23cm). The larger black turnstone *(Arenaria melanocephala)* favors Pacific North America. Grayish-green spotted eggs (4) are laid in a ground nest.

Turpentine, or gum turpentine, sticky liquid obtained from coniferous trees; it contains rosin and a volatile oil. The volatile oil is obtained by distillation of the gum and is used as a paint thinner, solvent, and in varnishes and lacquers. *See also* Rosin. △1570.

Turquoise, a phosphate mineral, hydrous basic copper aluminum phosphate found in veins of aluminum-rich rocks in deserts. Occurs as tiny crystals and dense masses, crusts, and veins. Blue; hardness 5–6; sp gr 2.7. Popular gemstone. △244.

Turret Lathe. *See* Lathe. △1606.

Turtle, reptile found on land or in marine and fresh waters. On the evolutionary scale, turtles have the most ancient lineage, preceding even the dinosaurs. They have a bony, horn-covered, boxlike shell that encloses shoulder and hip girdles and all internal organs. The head, neck, limbs, and tail project through openings in the shell. Horny jaws, resembling those of birds, replace teeth. All lay eggs on land. Terrestrial turtles are frequently called tortoises and some edible species of brackish waters are called terrapins. Marine turtles usually have smaller, lighter shells. Some species are carnivorous, others are herbivorous. There are two major subgroups, the hidden-necked or cryptodires and the side-necked or pleurodires. Length: 2in–7ft (5cm–2m). There are 300 species in 12 families. Order Chelonia. *See also* Reptile; Soft-shelled Turtle. △520–22.

Turtle Dove, European dove with a white-edged tail and soft, purring voice. Species *Streptopelia turtur. See also* Dove.

Tuscaloosa, commercial and industrial city in W central Alabama, 50mi (81km) SW of Birmingham; seat of Tuscaloosa co.; site of University of Alabama. Railroad and manufacturing center. Industries: cottonseed oil and products, chemicals, paper products. Settled 1816; inc. 1819. Pop. (1970) 65,773.

Tuscan Order, in Architecture. △1022.

Tuscany (Toscana), region in central Italy, on the Tyrrhenian Sea, comprised of the provs. of Massa-Carrara, Lucca, Pistoia, Pisa, Siena, Arezzo, Florence, Grosseto, Leghorn; capital is Florence; chiefly mountainous with fertile areas, particularly in the Arno River Valley. Products: cereal, olives, olive oil, wine, livestock; rich in minerals including lead, zinc, mercury, copper, lignite, marble. Industries: chemicals, metals, textiles, tourism, shipbuilding, handcrafts. Area: 8,876sq mi (22,989sq km). Pop. 3,434,618.

Tuscarora War (1711–13), series of expeditions by colonists from North Carolina, South Carolina, and Virginia against the Tuscarora Indians, who had attacked North Carolina settlers because of encroachments on Indian land. Defeated in 1713, the Tuscaroras moved to western Pennsylvania and became the sixth nation of the Iroquois Confederation.

Tuskegee Institute, nonsectarian private college in Tuskegee, Ala. Founded as a vocational school for blacks (1881), it became a college in 1927. Booker T. Washington was the principal until his death in 1915. It was here that George Washington Carver conducted his agricultural experiments.

Tusk Shell. *See* Tooth Shell.

Tussock Moth, moth whose caterpillar is typically covered with tussocks (tufts) of long hairs. Females of many species, including the gypsy moth, are virtually wingless. Caterpillars of the gypsy moth and some other tussock moths are serious pests of deciduous trees. Family Lymantriidae. *See also* Moths.

Tutankhamen (died *c.* 1340 BC), one of the last kings of the XVIII dynasty of Egypt, whose ascent to the throne was a result of his marriage to the daughter of Akhenaton at the age of 10. During his short, unimpressive reign of 8 years, the god Amon was restored and the capital was moved from Akhetaten back to Thebes. The discovery of his tomb in 1922, still containing most of its royal burial equipment, has made him one of the best known Egyptian pharaohs. △972.

Tutuola, Amos (1920–), African writer. He tells the traditional tales of the Yoruba people of his native Nigeria. A visionary whose world is a mixture of fantasy and reality, Tutuola has been criticized for not advocating political reform. *The Palm Wine Drinkard* (1952), *My Life in the Bush of Ghosts* (1954), and *Ajaiyi and His Inherited Poverty* (1967) are among his best works.

TVA. *See* Tennessee Valley Authority.

TV Wave, or Signal, high-energy radio wave or signal, of microwave frequency, carrying both video and audio information for TV broadcasts. *See also* Electromagnetic Spectrum.

Twain, Mark (1835–1910), pseud. of Samuel Langhorne Clemens, US journalist, lecturer, and author, b. Florida, Mo. The first US author of world rank to write authentically colloquial novels employing a genuine American idiom. His work, which began as pure humor and developed to bitter satire, was marked by an egalitarian attitude and a strong desire for social justice. "The Celebrated Jumping Frog of Calaveras County" (1865), a short story, brought Twain fame. His reputation was furthered by the travel books *Innocents Abroad* (1869), followed by *Roughing It* (1872).

In 1872 Twain settled in Hartford, Conn., whence he made many successful lecture tours around the United States and the world. He collaborated with Charles Dudley Warner on *The Gilded Age* (1873). *Mark Twain's Sketches, Old and New* (1875) was followed by three of his finest and best-known works, all utilizing material from his boyhood: *The Adventures of Tom Sawyer* (novel, 1876), *Life on the Mississippi* (nonfiction, 1883), and *The Adventures of Huckleberry Finn* (novel, 1885). He published another travel book, *A Tramp Abroad* (1880), and two historical novels, *The Prince and the Pauper* (1882) and *A Connecticut Yankee in King Arthur's Court* (1889), a social satire. Saddened and embittered by personal and financial losses, Twain later wrote such pessimistic works as *The Man That Corrupted Hadleyburg and Other Stories and Sketches* (1900), *What Is Man?* (1905), and *The Mysterious Stranger* (1916). Twain's works revolutionized the language of American fiction and had a great influence on many later American writers. △1374.

'Twas the Night Before Christmas (1823), poem by Clement Moore about Santa Claus. It was first published in the Troy (N.Y.) *Sentinel* as "A Visit from St Nicholas."

Tweed, William Marcy (1823–78), US politician, b. New York City. As leader of Tammany, the New York City Democratic political machine, he controlled party nominations. He and his cohorts, known as the Tweed Ring, stole government funds in the 1860s. Finally arrested in 1871, he was sentenced to one year in prison. He was rearrested on other charges, escaped to Spain, but was extradited and jailed.

Twelfth Night (1601), romantic comedy by William Shakespeare. Confusion results when Viola and Sebastian, identical twins, are shipwrecked off the coast of Illyria, and Viola dons male garb to serve as page to Duke Orsino. Mistaken identities complicate the many love interests in this oft-revived and delightful work.

Twelvers. *See* Imamis.

Twelve Tables, basis for Roman law, codified under Theodosius II of Rome (*c.* 450 BC). It was written on tablets, probably of wood, by a committee of decimvirs in response to a plebeian demand for political equality and written law. Compiled from laws of Solon and other Greeks, as well as unwritten Roman laws and customs, only fragments are known today. *See also* Roman Law. △908.

Twelve Tribes of Israel, according to the Bible, the groups of Hebrews descended from Jacob and bearing the names of his sons Reuben, Simeon, Judah, Issachar, Zebulun, Gad, Asher, Benjamin, Dan, and Naphtali. The tribes of Manasseh and Ephraim were named for the sons of Jacob's son, Joseph. The descendants of Jacob's son Levi, the Levites, not counted among the twelve, were devoted to the service of God and acquired no territory in Canaan, but lived among the others. According to the modern critical view, it is unlikely that these tribes all descended from Jacob. *See also* Jacob; Levi. △982.

Twilight, the periods of incomplete darkness following sunset (dusk) and preceding sunrise (dawn), ending or beginning respectively when the Sun is below the horizon by an angle of 6° (civil twilight), 12° (nautical twilight), and 18° (astronomical twilight).

Twilight Poets, The. *See* Crepuscolari.

Twinberry. *See* Partridgeberry.

Twin Falls, city in S Idaho, on Snake River; seat of Twin Falls co. Named for falls divided by Snake River into two channels, which drop 200ft (61m), then reunite. Nearby is Craters of Moon National Monument. Industries: sugar beets, dairy products, livestock. Inc. 1905. Pop. (1970) 21,914.

Twinflower. *See* Linnaea.

Twins, The. *See* Gemini.

Twister. *See* Tornado.

Two Gentlemen of Verona (1592), Shakespearean comedy. Two friends travel to Milan, where they compete for the favors of Silvia, the duke's daughter. Proteus' sweetheart Julia arrives in male garb, and becomes his page. Proteus repents and weds Julia, while Valentine plans to marry Silvia.

Two Noble Kingsmen, The (*c.* 1613), 5-act play ascribed to William Shakespeare and John Fletcher. Many scholars attribute the parts of the play that are not obviously written by Fletcher to Shakespeare; others argue that Philip Massinger was Fletcher's collaborator.

Two-Party System, political system with two parties. In the United States and most English-speaking countries, the two political parties compete for power. A two-party system tends to provide greater stability and usually guarantees one party sufficient strength to govern. △1396.

Two Sicilies, Kingdom of the, state uniting S Italy

with the island of Sicily from the 15th to the 19th centuries. In the 11th century the two areas were united by the Normans and again divided in 1282 between the French Angevins and the Spanish Aragonese. In 1442, Alfonso V of Aragon reunited the two areas and became self-styled king of the Two Sicilies, and in 1816 Ferdinand IV of Naples (Ferdinand III of Sicily) officially merged the kingdoms and became Ferdinand I of the Two Sicilies. In 1861 the kingdom was conquered by and incorporated into the new kingdom of Italy. △1182.

Two-way Radio. △1752.

Two Years before the Mast (1840), book by Richard Henry Dana recounting his adventures aboard the brig *Pilgrim* from Boston around Cape Horn to California and back.

Tylenol. *See* Acetaminophen.

Tyler, John (1790–1862), 10th president of the United States (1841–45), b. Charles City co, Va. He graduated from William and Mary College in 1807. In 1813 he married Letitia Christian; after her death he married (1844) Julia Gardiner. He had 14 children. Tyler was admitted to the bar in 1809, the same year his father became governor of Virginia. Two years later he entered the Virginia legislature.

In 1817 he went to the US House of Representatives as a states' rights Democrat. After a term as governor he went to the US Senate (1827). There he formed an uneasy alliance with Andrew Jackson, whom he supported for president. Later, however, he split with Jackson over fiscal policies and joined the new Whig party. In 1836 he resigned from the Senate over a matter of principle.

In 1840 the Whigs chose Tyler as running mate for William Henry Harrison. Harrison died soon after inauguration, and Tyler became the first vice president to succeed to the presidency. Cool to many Whig policies, Tyler was not able to accomplish much during his tenure; the annexation of Texas was a notable exception. In 1844 the Whigs nominated Henry Clay rather than Tyler.

Career: Virginia House of Burgesses, 1811–16, 1823–25; US House of Representatives, 1817–21; governor of Virginia, 1825–27; US Senate, 1827–36; vice president, 1841; president, 1841–45.

Tyler, Wat (died 1381), English rebel. He was the leader of the Peasants' Revolt (1381), a protest against harsh taxation and low wages. Rebels seized Canterbury and, choosing Tyler as their leader, marched to London, plundering John of Gaunt's palace and capturing the Tower of London. Richard II agreed to several demands made by the rebels. When Tyler presented further demands, he was wounded and subsequently beheaded by the lord mayor of London. After his death the rebellion soon ended.

Tyler, city in NE Texas, 85mi (137km) ESE of Dallas; seat of Smith co; site of Butler College, Texas College (1894), Tyler Junior College (1926); scene of Texas Rose Festival. Industries: oil refining, cotton processing, oil, gas, prefabricated homes, agriculture, roses, lumber. Settled 1840; named for President John Tyler; inc. 1846 as town, 1907 as city. Pop. (1970) 57,700.

Tylor, (Sir) Edward Burnett (1832–1917), English anthropologist, often called the founder of cultural anthropology. His observations of travels in the United States and Mexico were published in *Anahuac: or, Mexico and the Mexicans, Ancient and Modern* (1861). His most important work was *Primitive Culture* (1871). △874, 876.

Tylosaurus. △572.

Tyndale, William (1494?–1536), English Bible translator, pamphleteer, and Protestant martyr. After disputes with ecclesiastical authorities, Tyndale fled in 1524 to Germany, where he issued an English Pentateuch and New Testament. Copies introduced into England were destroyed. Their author was captured at Antwerp and strangled. All his work is noted for its sound scholarship.

Tyndall, John (1820–93), Irish physicist who showed that the blue color of the sky is due to dust scattering the Sun's rays. He also studied the magnetic properties of crystals, and light diffusion by dust and large molecules, an effect which bears his name. By 1881, he helped eliminate the idea of spontaneous generation, by showing that germ-free air does not cause food decay.

Type and Typesetting. △1770–72.

Typewriter. △1822.

Typhoid Fever, an acute, sometimes epidemic communicable disease marked by fever, chills, prostration, enlargement of the spleen, inflammation of the intestinal tract, and the eruption of pink spots. The bacillus *Salmonella typhosa* is transmitted by contaminated water, milk, and food. Inspection of water supplies, pasteurization of milk, typhoid inoculations, and treatment with chloromycetin have greatly reduced the incidence of this disease. △718.

Typhoon, the name given in the Pacific to a hurricane, a violent tropical cyclone. *See also* Hurricane. △214, 216.

Typhus, or typhus fever, three forms of acute, infectious diseases caused by rickettsial bodies: (1) epidemic human body louse-borne typhus, with mortality of up to 70%. Vaccinations and antibiotic treatment are now very effective against this form. (2) Brill-Zinsser disease, a recrudescent milder form of the same disease. (3) Tropical and semitropical endemic typhus transmitted by the rat flea.

Tyrannosaurus, giant bipedal, carnivorous dinosaur that lived during Late Cretaceous times in W North America and Mongolia. Its four-foot (1.2m) head was armed with a series of daggerlike teeth, some being 6in (15cm) long. The hind legs were enormous, but front legs were so tiny they may have been useless. Length: 45ft (14m); height: 18ft (5.5m). *See also* Theropoda. △572.

Tyrant Flycatcher. *See* Kingbird.

Tyrant Kingfish. *See* Kingbird.

Tyre (Sūr), town in SW Lebanon, 22mi (35km) S of Sayda. A flourishing city, it was a maritime power by 1100 BC, and Tyre merchants established colonies in Mediterranean areas, including Sicily, Sardinia, France, and Spain; became part of the Roman Empire 64 BC; fell to Crusaders; was destroyed 1291; Roman sites remain. Industries: finance, manufacture, commerce. Founded 1400 BC by Phoenicians. Pop. 35,000.

Tyrosine, white crystalline amino acid found in proteins. *See* Amino Acid.

Tyrrhenian Sea, part of the Mediterranean Sea, W of Italian mainland, E of Corsica and Sardinia, N of Sicily; site of several small island groups, including Luscan, Lipari, Pontine islands; chief ports are Naples and Palermo. Width: 60–300mi (97–483km). Length: approx. 475mi (765km).

Tyrrhenum Patera. △74.

Tzu Hsi (1835–1908), the famous empress dowager of the Ch'ing Dynasty, known as the "Old Buddha." She was the real power in China from 1862 to 1908, first as co-regent and then as regent. As imperial concubine she learned the politics of the Manchu court and became one of the most powerful and feared women in Chinese history, an obstinate opponent of the West and modernization. △1270.

J. M. W. Turner: Crossing the Stream *(detail)*

Mark Twain

SPOILS

William Marcy (Boss) Tweed by Thomas Nast

John Tyler

U

UAW. *See* United Automobile Workers.

Ubangi. *See* Oubangi.

U-Boat. △1684.

Uccello, Paolo (1397–1475), Italian painter. Primarily a decorative painter, he strongly influenced the minor Florentine masters. His strongest period was 1436–60, during which he executed "John Hawkwood," a fresco monument commissioned in 1436; "Flood" (*c.* 1450); and the "Battle of San Romano," one of his most famous works. These panels (*c.* 1455) were commissioned for the Medici Palace and are primarily decorative. One of Uccello's last works was the predella of the altarpiece in Urbino for the Corpus Domini Society (1465–69).

Udall, Morris King (1922–), US political leader, b. St Johns, Ariz. After a short career as a professional basketball player (1948–49) and county attorney (1953–54), he turned to politics and, as a Democrat, was elected to the US House of Representatives (1961) to finish the unexpired term of his brother Stewart. A progressive, Morris attempted to secure his party's presidential nomination in 1976.

Ufa, city in Russian SFSR, USSR, at Ufa River mouth, 715mi (1,114km) E of Moscow; capital of the Bashkir Autonomous SSR; site of aviation, medical, agricultural, and teachers' colleges, research institutes, revolutionary, regional, and art museums, famous old cathedral, Baskir State University (1957), Palace of Labor and Art, monument to Lenin. Industries: airplanes, mining machinery, cables, typewriters, clothing, shoes, leather goods, flour, meat, dairy products, cotton milling, clay, gypsum, limestone, lumber and veneer. Pop. 773,000.

Uganda, independent nation in E central Africa. Once a British protectorate, it is now ruled by a military dictator.

Land and economy. Mostly a plateau 3,000–6,000ft (915–1,830m) above sea level, Uganda sits on the Equator in E central Africa, bordered on the E by Kenya, the S by Tanzania and Rwanda, W by Zaire, and N by Sudan. Lake Victoria, source of the White Nile, is the most important lake. Margherita, in the Ruwenzori range, is the highest peak, 16,763ft (5,113m). Three major national parks preserve Uganda's wildlife. Altitude variations affect the rainfall, which is sparse in the arid N; the SW and W receive about 50in (127cm) annually. Seasonal changes are mild, including two dry spells a year. Coffee and cotton provide 70% of total exports with agriculture, fishing, and forestry accounting for half of the country's gross domestic product. Principal mineral exports are copper and tin. Textile, steel, and chemical plants have been built, but manufacturing accounts for only 10% of gross domestic production. Uganda's third five-year development program, completed in 1976, aimed at increasing production, with emphasis on Ugandan private enterprise.

People. Four racial groups are represented: Bantu (the most numerous), Nilotic, Nilo-Hamitic, and Sudanic. The bulk of population, dependent on agriculture, lives in the fertile area S of Lake Kyoga. Nearly half the population is Christian (Roman Catholic predominating), 6% is Muslim, and the remainder are followers of tribal beliefs. Until 1972, when Asians holding British passports (Indians and Pakistanis) were expelled, Uganda had 74,000 Asians, mainly small businessmen. Literacy is estimated at 25%.

Government. The country's government is highly centralized, with legislative power and appointments in the hands of the president.

History. When British explorer Capt. John Speke reached Uganda in 1862, he found politically developed African kingdoms. Traders and missionaries followed, and in 1888 the Imperial East Africa Co. made E Africa a British sphere; in 1894 it became a British protectorate. The process leading to independence commenced in 1955, when Africans were granted some representation in the legislature. Full internal self-government came in 1962, and Uganda became fully independent on Oct. 9, 1962. Gen. Idi Amin Dada took power in a 1971 military coup, dissolved parliament, and set up a new government.

PROFILE

Official name: Republic of Uganda
Area: 91,134sq mi (236,037sq km)
Density: 123per sq mi (47per sq km)
Chief city: Kampala (capital)
Government: Military dictatorship
Religion: Christian (major)
Language: English (official)
Monetary unit: Uganda shilling
Gross national product: $1,715,000,000
Per capita income: $161
Industries: textiles, steel, chemicals
Agriculture: coffee, cotton, tea, maize, peanuts, sisal, oil seeds, tobacco, sugar, millet, sweet potatoes
Minerals: copper, tin
Trading partners: United States, United Kingdom, Kenya, Japan, India, West Germany

Ugarit, ancient city in W Syria dating as far back as the Neolithic period. It developed as a great commercial center from its trade with Mesopotamia and later from its alliance with Egypt (2nd millennium BC). Its period of highest prosperity occurred during the 15th and 14th cent. BC.

U Geminorum Stars. △114.

Uglifruit. △338.

Uinta Mountains, mountain range in NE Utah and SW Wyoming, part of the Rocky Mt system; culminates at Kings Peak, the highest point in Utah, 13,528ft (4,126m).

Uintatherium, archaic, hoofed mammal of Eocene North America. The size of a modern African rhinoceros, it was the giant of its day. Its 2.5-ft (0.75-m) skull bore three pairs of bony outgrowths, one pair above the nose, another before the eyes, and a third toward the rear. Males had tusks. *See also* Dinocerata.

Ujjain, city in W central India, on Sipra River 200mi (322km) E of Ahmadabad. One of the seven holy cities of India, it is a pilgrimage center for thousands of Hindus each year; served as the capital of the Avanti kingdom 6th–4th centuries BC; center of Malwa kingdom 120–395, of Sanskrit learning, and Maratha dynasty of Sindhia (18th century); site of Vikram University (1957) and many notable temples and mosques. Pop. 159,024.

Ukrainian, language spoken in the Ukrainian SSR of the Soviet Union by about 35,000,000 people. Like Russian and Belorussian, it belongs to the eastern branch of the Slavic languages.

Ukrainian Soviet Socialist Republic (Ukrainskaja Sovetskaja Socialističeskaja Respublika), constituent republic of the SW European USSR; borders on Poland (NW), Czechoslovakia, Hungary, Romania, and the Moldavian SSR (SW), Black Sea and Sea of Azov (S), Russian SFSR (E and NE), and Belorussian SSR (N); capital is Kiev; Dnieper is main river. It is the 2nd-largest constituent republic of the USSR. A land primarily of fertile steppes, its climate is greatly modified by Black Sea. In the 7th century the Khazars (an ancient Turkish people) held much of the Ukraine; a Varangian dynasty from Scandinavia freed the land from Khazar control 9th century and established a stronghold at Kiev, uniting with the people to form Kievan Russia, a leading Russian principality until 13th century, when Mongols of Golden Horde conquered it. In 1392, Grand Duke of Lithuania seized the Ukraine; in 1569 it came under Polish rule. A Cossack rebellion freed the Ukraine, but the region was unable to stand alone; protection of Muscovy was sought and in 1654 a treaty was signed. Supposedly the Ukraine was internally independent, but this was never accomplished. Conflicts finally resulted in loss of all independence; it became part of Russia 1793. In January 1918 it proclaimed itself an independent country. Four years of war followed and in 1922 USSR reconquered it and made it one of the original constituent republics; it was lost and re-won by USSR in WWII. Industries: iron, steel, tractors, cement, glass, fertilizer, paper, sugar refining. The W Ukraine is mainly agricultural, but there are large petroleum and natural gas fields. Area: 233,089sq mi (603,700sq km). Pop. 47,136,000.

Ulan Bator (Ulaanbaatar), capital city of Mongolian People's Republic; on Tola River; seat of Living Buddhas from mid-17th century–1924, when the last spiritual leader died; center of Mongolian autonomy movement, proclaimed here 1911; occupied by Soviets 1924 during Russian Civil War; industrial development was spurred during Russian influence; site of country's only university (1942); political, cultural, and economic center. Industries: textiles, leather, paper, alcohol, food processing, glassware. Pop. 262,000.

Ulbricht, Walter, (1893–1973), East German Communist party leader and head of the German Democratic Republic. Returning from the Soviet Union in 1945 he played a major role in the establishment of the new Socialist state. As first secretary of the party 1960–71 and chairman of the State Council from 1960 to his death, he effectively crushed opposition to his rigid Stalinist principles.

Ulcers, sores or lesions in the mucosal lining of the gastrointestinal system, frequently caused by abnormally large secretion of gastric juices over a prolonged period. This psychophysiological disorder is often precipitated by emotional stress. Symptoms of ulcers include stomach pains (particularly after eating), nausea, and (in untreated cases) hemorrhaging. △718, 768.

Ulna, one of the two forearm bones, extending from the elbow to the wrist. At the head of the ulna, a projection, the olecranon process, fits into a cavity in the humerus, or upper arm bone; at its lower end, there is a small prominence felt on the small-finger side of the wrist. △682.

Ulster, region of NE Ireland, consisting of nine counties. Six form Northern Ireland; Cavan, Donegal, and Monaghan are part of the Republic of Ireland. "Ulster" also refers to Northern Ireland as a political unit of the United Kingdom. *See also* Ireland, Northern.

Ultrasonic Machining. △1606.

Ultrasonics, study of sound with frequencies beyond the range of human hearing, ie, with frequencies in excess of 20,000 hertz. There is no theoretical upper limit, but a practical limit of 5 megahertz is set by existing means of generation. Generation may be mechanical (as in the Galton whistle), by the magetostrictive effect, or by piezoelectric generators. pplications of ultrasonics include: agitation of liquids o form emulsions, detection of flaws in metals (the ltrasonic wave passed through a metal specimen is eflected by a hairline crack), cleaning small objects y vibrating them ultrasonically in a solvent, echo ounding in deep water, soldering aluminum, and the ocation of a fetus or tumor.

Jltraviolet Astronomy. *See* Astronomy, Ultravio-et.

lltraviolet Wave, type of electromagnetic wave in-ermediate in energy between light and X-rays. Wave-ength range: 400 nanometers (10^{-9} meter) to about 0 nanometers. *See also* Electromagnetic Spectrum. \1554.

llysses (1922), stream-of-consciousness novel by ames Joyce set in Dublin and relating in intimate etail the events of a day (June 16, 1904) in the life f Leopold Bloom, a Jewish Dubliner. The characters, pisodes, and time scheme are enriched by their par-llels with those in Homer's *Odyssey.*

Jmayyads, or Ommiads, Islamic dynasty of 14 ca-phs (AD 661–750), the first of whom was Muawiyah. he Umayyad claim to the caliphate originated when member of their clan, Uthman, became Mo-ammed's son-in-law and the 3rd caliphate. When the ast of the dynasty, Marwan II, was overthrown by the bbassids, one member escaped to Spain and ounded the caliphate of Cordoba (756). This 11-nember dynasty developed a brilliant civilization ex-ending over most of Spain and lasting until it was verthrown by the Berbers in 1031. △1062.

Jmberto I (Eng. Humbert) (1844–1900), king of Italy 1878–1900). Son and successor of Victor Emmanuel and father of Victor Emmanuel III, he followed na-onalistic and imperialistic policies and led Italy into ne Triple Alliance (1882) with Germany and Austria. le encouraged Italy's entry into the armaments race nd its unsuccessful colonial ventures in Africa. In 900 an anarchist killed him in the third attempt on is life.

Jmberto II (1904–), prince of Savoy and last king f Italy (1946). The son of Victor Emmanuel III, upon is father's abdication in May 1946, he became king f Italy but went into exile in Portugal after a national ote of June 1946 determined that Italy should enceforth be a republic.

Jmbilical Cord, long, thick cord that connects the eveloping fetus with the placenta, the hormone-ecreting structure through which the fetus receives ood and oxygen from the mother's bloodstream and ives off waste products. The umbilical cord contains wo large arteries and one vein. At birth, the cord is lamped and cut from the placenta; the part of the ord remaining on the baby's abdomen dries and falls ff, leaving the scar, known as naval, or belly button. \702–04.

Jmbra. △1520.

Jmbrella Bird, large tropical American bird with a etractile, black umbrellalike crest and long, often ubular-shaped, feathered wattle on the throat. The ypical ornate umbrella bird *(Cephalopterus ornatus),* ound from Costa Rica to Brazil, lives high in trees, eeds on fruits, and emits loud piping sounds. During ourtship, males display their crests and emit deep ounds.

Jmbrella Thorn. △586.

Jmbrella Tree, deciduous tree of North America. It as clusters of long leaves at the ends of the branches, arge, white or creamy, foul-smelling flowers, and red-ish fruit. Height: 40ft (12m). Family Magnoliaceae; pecies *Magnolia tripetala.* △450.

Jmbriel, satellite of Uranus. △88.

Jmeå, port city in N Sweden, on Gulf of Bothnia at ne mouth of the Ume River; seat of Västerbotten co. ndustries: wood products, lumber, machinery. Pop. 4,530.

JN. *See* United Nations.

Jn-American Affairs Committee, House (HUAC), ommittee established (1938) to investigate subver-ion. It focused particularly on un-American propa-anda activities and worked to formulate legislation gainst them. The committee, whose first chairman vas Martin Dies, was granted permanent status in 945. The committee began investigating Nazi, Fas-ist, and Communist organizations, but later turned its attention to organized labor, civil rights organizations, and liberal programs. In the early 1950s it investigated alleged Communists, especially in the film industry. The committee was criticized for demagoguery and is still considered controversial. In 1960s the name was changed to the House Internal Security Committee.

Unamuno, Miguel de (1864–1936), Spanish philosopher and writer. Twice exiled for his provocative political attitude, he is thought to have inspired many modern thinkers. *The Tragic Sense of Life in Men and Peoples* (1913) is concerned with the tragedy of life manifested in the conflict between faith and reason and in some respects anticipated modern existentialism. Other works include *Mist—a Tragi-comic Novel* (1914) and *The Life of Don Quixote and Sancho* (1905).

Uncas (*c.*1588–*c.*1683), American Indian, chief of the Mohegan Indians. Born in to the Pequot tribe, as a subchief he rebelled and formed the Mohegan tribe. He sought British support and allied with the British during the Pequot War of 1637. Since he was constantly at war with the Narragansett Indians and other tribes, some of which were British allies, Uncas was eventually distrusted by the British.

Uncertainty Principle, principle put forward by Werner Heisenberg (1927) that simultaneous measurement of the position and momentum of a particle, such as an electron, disturbs the system so that there is always an uncertainty in the result. △1480.

Uncial Writing. *See* Calligraphy.

Uncle Remus. *See* Harris, Joel Chandler.

Uncle Sam, symbol of the US government. Samuel Wilson (1766–1854), Revolutionary War soldier, supplied meat to the US Army in War of 1812. It was stamped "US," and people said it stood for "Uncle Sam" Wilson.

Uncle Tom's Cabin, or Life Among the Lowly (1852), antislavery novel by Harriet Beecher Stowe. One of the most widely circulated books in literary history, it deals with the trials of Tom, a Christian Negro slave who is sold several times and finally ends up in the hands of a brutal plantation owner, Simon Legree, who has him flogged to death. The novel awakened many people in the North to the horrors of slavery; in the South it was regarded as an inaccurate account of that institution. △1276.

Unconformity, in geology, the relation of adjacent rocks or strata showing a distinct break, indicating erosion or nondeposition. Types of unconformity are nonconformity (large intrusion of unstratified material), angular unconformity (two strata at an angle to each other), disconformity (two strata separated by an eroded surface), paraconformity (parallel strata so undifferentiated that they appear to be a single layer). △270.

Unconscious, in psychoanalysis, a term for impulses, ideas, or memories that are generally below the level of awareness but that may affect behavior. Some primitive drives never reach the conscious level. Some thoughts or memories are repressed—pushed below the conscious level—because they seem wrong or threatening. *See also* Id; Repression.

Underground Railroad, network established to help escaping slaves. Beginning about 1804, a group of whites and blacks in the North worked to help fugitive slaves escape from the South. "Conductors" picked up slaves on the plantations and led them north where they passed through a series of hiding places ("stations") until they escaped to safety, often in Canada. One of the most famous conductors was Harriet Tubman.

Underwater Habitats. △230.

Underwater Sound. Sound travels in water some 4.5 times faster than it does in air. The velocity of sound in water depends on its density and temperature—in seawater at 15°C it is 1,510 meters per second (compared to 331.4 m/s in air). Devices based on the transmission of sound under water are used to locate submerged objects or to measure depth. The principle is to transmit a sound or ultrasonic wave from a ship on the surface and to measure the time for its reflection to return. *See also* Sonar.

Underwing Moth, noctuid moth with brightly banded underwings and gray or brown front wings with wavy markings. Genus *Catocalla.*

Paolo Uccello: Portrait of a Lady

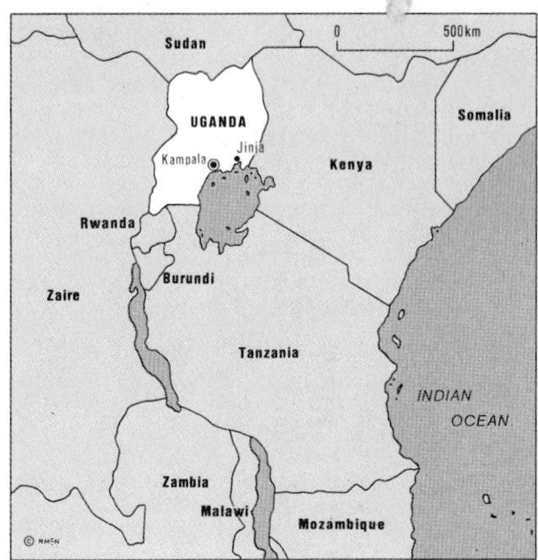
Sudan
0
500km
UGANDA
Kampala
Jinja
Kenya
Somalia
Rwanda
Burundi
Zaire
Tanzania
INDIAN
OCEAN
Zambia
Malawi
Mozambique

Uganda

Ukrainian Soviet Socialist Republic

Umbrella tree

Undset, Sigrid (1882–1949), Norwegian novelist. She became famous with the trilogy *Kristin Lavransdatter* (1920–22), set in medieval Norway. Her other novels, also concerned with woman's role in society, include *The Faithful Wife* (1936), *Madam Dorothea* (1939), and *Return to the Future* (1942). She was awarded the Nobel Prize for literature in 1928.

Unemployment Insurance, financial protection for a worker against job loss, an attempt to solve part of the income insecurity problem of the worker in an industrial society. When a worker in covered employment is discharged for economic reasons (but not for misconduct), a portion of his lost wages is paid to him, under the provisions of the Social Security Act, from funds supplied by employers through federal and state payroll taxes. The payments continue until he finds a new job, returns to his old job, or collects for a maximum number of weeks.

Unemployment of Labor, inability of workers who are ready, able, and willing to work to find employment. Unemployment is usually expressed as a percentage of the labor force.

Cyclical unemployment exists when the level of aggregate demand in the economy is less than that required to maintain full employment. People are laid off, and their jobs simply disappear.

Structural unemployment exists when jobs are available and workers are seeking jobs, but they cannot fill the jobs that are open for some reason (they lack proper training, live too far away, etc.).

Technological unemployment exists when workers are replaced by machines faster than they can find alternative employment.

Seasonal unemployment occurs when workers are unable to find jobs at certain seasons of the year. Such workers are usually engaged in construction or agriculture.

Underemployment is inefficient use of labor, eg, an employer may keep unneeded workers on the payroll when demand falls in order to have experienced help available when demand increases.

UNESCO. *See* United Nations Educational, Scientific, and Cultural Organization.

Unfair Labor Practices, for unions, are forbidden by the Taft-Hartley Act (1947). Similar practices by employers have been forbidden since the Wagner Act (1935). The purpose of the labor law is to promote peaceful industrial relations, and the unfair practices were held by Congress to discourage successful industrial practices. The lists of banned activities given by the two laws are very similar, and either party can refer a claimed violation to the National Labor Relations Board.

Ungulate, mammals characterized by having hoofed feet. Most ungulates, including cattle, sheep, hogs, and deer, are members of the order *Artiodactyla*. The order *Perissodactyla* consists of horses, tapirs, and rhinoceroses, while the orders *Proboscidea* and *Hyracoidea* contain only elephants and hyraxes, respectively.

UNICEF. *See* United Nations Children's Fund.

Unicorn, mythical animal used as a symbol of purity in the Middle Ages. It resembled a horse or goat with a single horn in the middle of its forehead. The wild and fierce beast could be tamed at a virgin's touch. The ground horn of the unicorn was supposed to have had great salutary properties. △832.

Unicorn, The. *See* Monoceros.

Unicorn Plant. *See* Martynia.

Unified Field Theory, attempt to extend general relativity theory to give a simultaneous representation of both gravitational and electromagnetic fields. A more comprehensive theory would also include the strong and weak interactions. Although some success has been achieved in unifying the electromagnetic and weak interactions, the general problem is still unsolved. *See also* Relativity Theory.

Union, township in NE New Jersey, 5mi (8km) WNW of Elizabeth; site of Newark State College 1855. Industries: paint, lacquer, steel, metal goods, truck farms. Settled *c.* 1749 as Connecticut Farms by colonists from Connecticut. Pop. (1970) 52,878.

Union, Act of (1707), act uniting the kingdoms of England and Scotland under one British Parliament at Westminster, with England and Scotland each retaining its own legal system and national church. By union Scotland hoped to achieve economic equality with England, while England acted to prevent a possible Scottish alliance with France and Roman Catholic succession to the English throne.

Union City, city in NE New Jersey, on Hudson River 3mi (5km) N of and adjoining Jersey City; Lincoln Tunnel links Union City with New York City. Industries: embroidery, perfume, incandescent lamps. Formed 1925 by merging West Hoboken and Union Hill. Pop. (1970) 58,537.

Union of Soviet Socialist Republics, or Soviet Union, independent nation spanning Europe and Asia, the largest country in the world in area. It is largely self-sufficient in its economy and resources and is governed by a Communist regime.

Land and economy. A federation of 15 union republics, based on socialist ownership of the means of production, the USSR covers one-sixth of the Earth's surface, making it the largest country in the world. Mostly above 50° N latitude, it stretches across Europe and Asia from the Baltic Sea across the Eurasian land mass to the Bering Strait where it is within 3mi (5km) of an island off the coast of Alaska. Its W neighbors are Norway, Finland, Poland, Czechoslovakia, Hungary, and Romania. Bordering it to the S are Turkey, Iran, Afghanistan, China, Mongolia, and North Korea. The European portion, from the Polish border to the Ural Mts, is a broad plain crossed by two major rivers, the Dneiper, leading to the Black Sea, and the Volga, which empties into the Caspian Sea, the world's largest lake in surface area. The low Urals divide European and Asiatic Russia. To the E are enormous Siberian lowlands and the deserts of central Asia; beyond them are the Siberian highlands and the Far Eastern mountains. Along the shores of the Black and Caspian seas is a small subtropical zone. Long, cold winters and short summers mark much of the USSR's climate. N tundra areas record −90°F (−64 °C). S of the tundra is a vast forest belt, and S of the forest are the prairies (steppes), where the soil is fertile with plentiful rainfall. The steppes, 12% of the total area, contain 66% of the USSR's arable land. Agriculture is organized into collective farms and state farms where members share in the income after state obligations have been met. Since 1966, farm wages have been guaranteed, and peasants are allowed to grow crops for sale on land they use but do not own. These plots account for 33% of gross agricultural production. Operating under a series of 5-year plans, the totally nationalized USSR has become the world's 2nd-largest industrial power. Major problems center about planning and management, increased productivity, efficiency, and modernization. Budget revenues are derived from profits of state enterprises and a levy on all transactions of consumer goods and services. Direct income tax brings in 10% of the total revenue.

People. The indigenous Russians came from two areas. The N primitive forest tribes who fished, used the fur-bearing animals, and cultivated the land are the Slavs, now 70% of the population. Indigenous peoples in the S were nomads, living on horseback and in tents and fighting other tribes. Modern ethnic groups are divided into the following units: Indo-European, 36 groups; Caucasian, 40; Semitic, 6; Finno-Ugrian, 16; Nenets, 1; Turkic, 48; Mongo, 3; Tungis-Manchurian, 6; Palaeo-Asiatic, 9; and far E ancient tribes, 4. The first Russian census in 1897 listed 129,-800,000 persons. The current population of over 240,000,000 has been affected by large-scale emigration to the United States in 1900–09, increases from areas acquired since 1939, deaths from famine, the high mortality rates in the 1930s and 1940s, and 7,000,000 killed during WWII. In 1897 about 76% of the people could neither read nor write. Literacy is currently estimated at over 98% for those between the ages of 9–49. Soviet schools, planned to serve the needs of the state, aim for 10 years of compulsory education. Admission to universities is highly competitive, based on political background and academic records. Efforts to suppress religion have been sporadic, but persecution of Jews has resulted in widespread protests in Western countries. Some churches, mosques, and synagogues have been allowed a limited function, although anti-religious programs continue.

Government. Power rests in the leaders of the Communist party. Government is patterned on Western democracies, but without checks or balances and little separation of powers. Under the 1932 constitution, the Communist party makes state policy.

History. Annals date the first Russian state in the area of Kiev in the 9th century when the Rus, early Norse pirates and later caravan traders, were asked to mediate the disputes of indigenous tribes. Rus descendants brought Christianity, absentee-landed aristocracy, rich merchants, and lucrative trade. Mongols conquered the country in the 13th century; it had freed itself by 1480. Ivan the Terrible (1533–84) reigned during a period of military and financial reform. Peter the Great (1682–1725) expanded the empire. Catherine the Great (1762–96) established local legislation, courts, and charters perpetuating the ruling class. The serfs were emancipated in 1861 under Alexander II. This action set the stage for the future political development of Russia. Over the next years the tsars attempted repressive actions, but it was too late. Revolution was in the air, and in 1917 Tsar Nicholas II was forced to abdicate. The succeeding provisional governments were overthrown in November 1917 by the Bolshevik wing of the Russian Social Democratic Labor party. V. I. Lenin was named head of the new Communist government. Land was declared the property of the state; factories, banks, and railroads were nationalized. Joseph Stalin emerged as party leader after Lenin's death in 1924. His rivals, including Leon Trotsky, were executed, and military, political, and cultural leaders were purged in the 1930s. The United States recognized the Soviet Union in 1933. In 1939, Germany and Russia invaded Poland and divided its territory. The Soviets annexed a portion of Finland in March 1940. In June 1940 they added Estonia, Latvia, and Lithuania, and in July they took two provinces of Romania. Adolf Hitler's brief 1940 collaboration with the Soviets ended on June 22, 1941, when Germany attacked the USSR. In four years of fighting, the Germans advanced as far as Moscow, causing enormous USSR casualties and devastation to the E portion of Russia before being defeated in 1945. After Stalin's death (1953), Nikita S. Khrushchev was installed as first secretary of the Communist party and in 1958 as chairman of the Council of Ministers. Stalin was denounced as a despot, political prisoners were rehabilitated, and limited contact with outside countries was encouraged. Party opposition brought Khrushchev's downfall in 1964, when Leonid I. Brezhnev was named first secretary of the party and Aleksei N. Kosygin became chairman of the Council of Ministers. Although the USSR is ruled by collective leadership, Brezhnev stood first among equals. △1176–78, 1286, 1310–12, 1344.

PROFILE

Official name: Union of Soviet Socialist Republics
Area: 8,649,512sq mi (22,402,236sq km)
Population: 241,748,000
Density: 29per sq mi (11.4per sq km)
Chief cities: Moscow (capital); Leningrad; Kiev; Tashkent; Gorky
Government: Communist
Religion: Russian Orthodox, Christian, Georgian Orthodox
Language: Russian
Monetary unit: Ruble
Gross national product: $710,000,000,000
Per capita income: $2,000
Industries (major products): chemicals, machines, steel, iron, motor vehicles, railway cars and engines, oil refining, machine tools, tractors, clocks, glass, cameras, cement, textiles, paper, aluminum, electronics, carpets, processed foods, rubber, fertilizer
Agriculture (major products): timber, cattle, hogs, sheep, fish, grains and cereals, sugar beets, potatoes, flax, cotton, tea, tobacco, rice, fruits
Minerals (major): coal, oil, manganese, iron ore, potassium phosphates, salt, copper, zinc, mercury, sulphur, barite, molybdenum, lead, gypsum, chromium
Trading partners: Romania, Bulgaria, Poland, Hungary, Czechoslovakia, East Germany, European countries, Japan

Unitarianism, religious movement first significant in Europe during the early Protestant Reformation. It has no formal creed and strives to be universal. It holds that God is one person and denies the trinity. Members prefer to be called "liberal Christians," distinguishing their ways from those of intolerant Christians. Rejecting any missionary work, the heart and mind must lead men into the fellowship. The first Unitarian churches in the American colonies were established in the late 18th century.

Unitary Government, government in which power is concentrated in a single source and in which local governments act only as administrative agents of the central government. It is the opposite of a federal government in which power is shared with the states.

Unitas, John Constantine "Johnny" (1933–), US football player, b. Pittsburgh. A quarterback in the National Football League, he played for Baltimore (1956–72) and San Diego (1973). In 1970 the Associated Press named him Player of the Decade.

Unit Costs. △938.

United Arab Emirates, formerly the Trucial States, union of seven emirates (Dubai, Ajman, Abu Dhabi, Ras alKhaimah, Fujairah, Sharjah, and Umm a

Qaiwain); bordered by Persian Gulf (N), Qatar (NW), Saudi Arabia (W and S), Oman (E). The terrain is flat, consisting mainly of sand and salt flat desert; only in the E does the land rise to any height. The traditional nomad existence is in decline as wealth from oil production attracts people to the towns of the Gulf. Agriculture is limited to the mountain region, oases, and areas where irrigation is provided; main crops are dates and vegetables. Oil production is the economic mainstay of the Union, first produced in 1962 from Abu Dhabi, now also comes from Dubai and offshore sites. Government is carried on by the Supreme Council which is made up of the royal families of the emirates; this elects a president. From the 19th century to 1971 Britain was responsible for the area's defense and foreign relations of the Trucial States; the United Arab Emirates was formed when Britain withdrew.

PROFILE

Official name: United Arab Emirates
Area: 32,278sq mi (83,600sq km).
Population: 300,000
Density: 9per sq mi (3.5per sq km)
Chief cities: Abu Dhabi (capital); Dubai
Government: head of state, Sheikh Zayed bin Sultan al Nahayan, president
Religion: Islam
Language: Arabic
Trading partners (major): Japan, Great Britain, United States

United Arab Republic, political union of Egypt and Syria formed in 1958 with its capital at Cairo and Egypt's Gamal Abdel Nasser as its president. A military coup dissolved the union in 1961 with Syria declaring its independence.

United Automobile Workers (UAW), second largest US union, began as part of the AFL, joined the CIO in 1936, and was successful in organizing the automobile industry through the use of the sit-down strike. Under the leadership of Walter Reuther (1946–70) the union expanded to areas outside the automotive industry. In 1968 the UAW withdrew from the AFL-CIO, and became independent. During 1969–72 the UAW joined the Teamsters in the Alliance for Labor Action.

United Colonies of New England. *See* New England Confederation.

United Empire Loyalists, Canadian organization comprised of descendants of American Loyalists who fled to Canada during the American Revolution. They settled mostly in the Maritime Provinces and Ontario. The organization was formally chartered in 1897 and 1914 and has been a pro-British, conservative force in Canadian politics.

United Irishmen. △1312.

United Kingdom of Great Britain and Northern Ireland. *See* Great Britain.

United Nations (UN), formed in 1945, organization of nations to work together in the cause of international security and peace. Its headquarters are in New York City. As a successor to the League of Nations, it has proved a more durable medium of international cooperation. The principal UN organs are the General Assembly, the Security Council, the Secretariat, the Trusteeship Council, the Economic and Social Council, and the International Court of Justice. The United Nations provides a forum in which some 150 nations can discuss problems with the hope of peaceful solutions. It has helped find remedies to many international disputes and armed conflicts among its member nations.

The UN Charter was signed in San Francisco on June 16, 1945, by 50 countries. Membership expanded as former colonies gained independence in the decades following World War II. Its first major action came in June 1950 when it voted to help South Korea following an invasion by North Korea and 15 members contributed to a UN force. In its "Uniting for Peace" resolution of November 1950, the General Assembly attempted to develop the power it had already exercised. The resolution stipulated that the General Assembly could hold an emergency session to settle emergency matters that the Security Council was unable to settle because of its members' individual veto power. This new function of the assembly was put to the test in 1956 with the Israeli invasion of Egypt and the subsequent intervention of British and French forces. The assembly met and established the UN Emergency Force, which ultimately provided for the withdrawal of British, French, and Israeli forces. UN teams have also played a peace-keeping role in India and Cyprus. In successive Arab-Israeli conflicts the assembly has applied enough pressure on both sides to force a cease-fire until negotiations began. Since the 1960s, when UN forces intervened in the Congo, controversial collective security actions have been avoided, partly because the rise of Afro-Asian, Latin American, and Arab member states has complicated the patterns of power, although it was present in the Congo. The range of the Third World's strength was exhibited in 1975 when it successfully forced the passing of a resolution stipulating that Zionism is a form of racism, a resolution directed against Israel. The resolution caused much controversy and was vigorously opposed by the United States. △1382.

UNITED NATIONS MEMBERS

Afghanistan
Albania
Algeria
Argentina
Australia
Austria
Bahamas
Bahrain
Bangladesh
Barbados
Belgium
Belorussian SSR
Benin (Dahomey)
Bhutan
Bolivia
Botswana
Brazil
Bulgaria
Burma
Burundi (Urundi)
Cameroon
Canada
Cape Verde
Central African Republic
Chad
Chile
China, People's Republic of
Colombia
Comeros (Comoro Is.)
Congo
Costa Rica
Cuba
Cyprus
Czechoslavakia
Denmark
Dominican Republic
Ecuador
Egypt (UAR)
El Salvador
Equatorial Guinea
Ethiopia
Fiji
Finland
France
Gabon
Gambia
German Democratic Republic
Germany, Federal Republic of
Ghana
Greece
Grenada
Guatemala
Guinea
Guinea-Bissau
Guyana
Haiti
Honduras
Hungary
Iceland
India
Indonesia
Iran
Iraq
Ireland
Israel
Italy
Ivory Coast
Jamaica
Japan
Jordan
Kenya
Khmer Republic (Cambodia)
Kuwait
Laos
Lebanon
Lesotho
Liberia
Libya
Luxembourg
Malagasy Republic
Malawi
Malaysia
Maldives
Mali
Malta
Mauritania
Mauritius
Mexico
Mongolia
Morocco
Mozambique
Nepal
Netherlands
New Zealand
Nicaragua
Niger
Nigeria
Norway
Oman (Muscat and Oman)
Pakistan
Panama
Papua New Guinea
Paraguay
Peru
Philippines
Poland
Portugal
Qatar
Romania
Rwanda
São Tomé and Príncipe
Saudi Arabia
Sengal
Seychelles
Sierra Leone
Singapore
Somalia
South Africa
Soviet Union (USSR)
Spain
Sri Lanka (Ceylon)
Sudan
Surinam
Swaziland
Sweden
Syria
Tanzania
Thailand
Togo
Trinidad and Tobago
Tunisia
Turkey
Uganda
Ukrainian SSR
United Arab Emirates
United Kingdom
United States
Upper Volta
Uruguay
Venezuela
Western Samoa
Yemen
Yemen, Democratic People's Republic
Yugoslavia
Zaire
Zambia

United Nations Children's Fund (UNICEF), organization created by the UN General Assembly (1946) to contribute to the welfare of the world's children through voluntary contributions by governments and individuals. UNICEF is not financed through the UN budget. Its programs include provisions of food, medical care, and disease control. In 1965, UNICEF received the Nobel Peace Prize for its work. UNICEF personnel are members of the UN Secretariat.

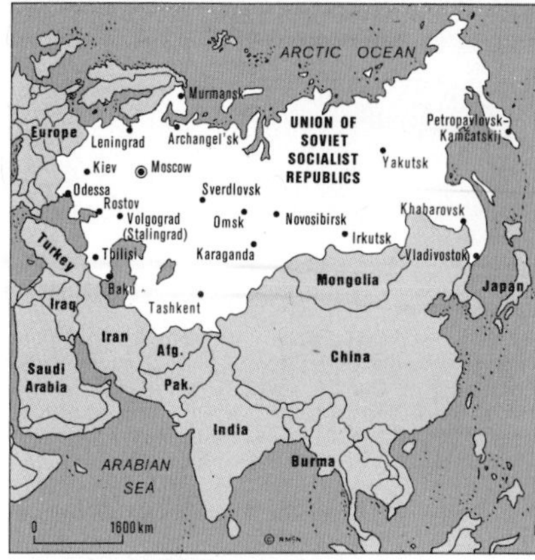
ARCTIC OCEAN
Murmansk
UNION OF SOVIET SOCIALIST REPUBLICS
Petropavlovsk-Kamčatskij
Europe
Leningrad
Archangel'sk
Kiev
Moscow
Yakutsk
Odessa
Sverdlovsk
Rostov
Volgograd (Stalingrad)
Omsk
Novosibirsk
Khabarovsk
Irkutsk
Turkey
Tbilisi
Karaganda
Vladivostok
Baku
Mongolia
Japan
Iraq
Tashkent
Iran
Afg.
China
Saudi Arabia
Pak.
India
ARABIAN SEA
Burma
0
1600km
Union of Soviet Socialist Republics

USSR: Moscow

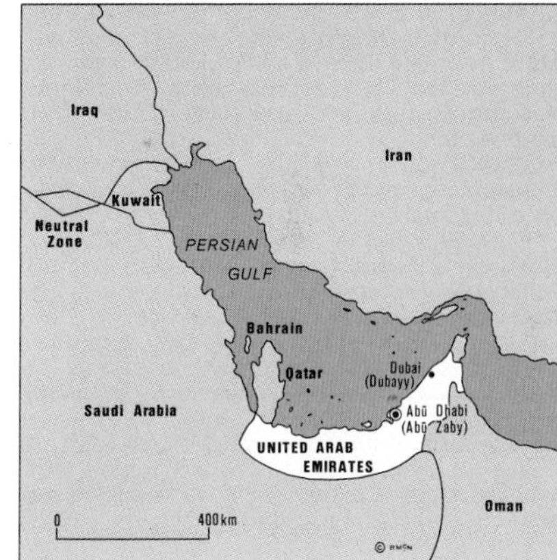
Iraq
Iran
Kuwait
Neutral Zone
PERSIAN GULF
Bahrain
Qatar
Dubai (Dubayy)
Saudi Arabia
Abū Dhabi (Abū Zaby)
UNITED ARAB EMIRATES
Oman
0
400km
United Arab Emirates

United Nations headquarters

United Nations Conference (1945). *See* San Francisco Conference on International Organization.

United Nations Educational, Scientific and Cultural Organization (UNESCO), organization created in 1946 to work in education, the natural sciences, cultural activities, social sciences, and mass communication. Its goal is to promote better understanding of these areas among people throughout the world. Its membership is open to UN member states.

United States, nation in North America. Its official name is the United States of America. It comprises 50 states, of which 48 and the District of Columbia constitute a mass bounded E by the Atlantic Ocean, W by the Pacific, N by Canada, and S by Mexico and the Gulf of Mexico. The state of Alaska, separated from the 48 coterminous states by Canada, is at the NW tip of the continent. The state of Hawaii, an island chain in the Pacific, lies about 2,000mi (3,220km) SW of the mainland. The United States also has sovereignty or jurisdiction over outlying lands, which include the unincorporated territories of Guam and American Samoa, which are islands in the Pacific, and of the US Virgin Islands in the West Indies, and a number of small Pacific islands. Under the United Nations, the United States administers the Trust Territory of the Pacific Islands, which embraces three archipelagoes. Puerto Rico, in the West Indies, is a free commonwealth associated with the United States. The Canal Zone in Panama, through which runs the Panama Canal, is controlled by the US under a treaty with Panama.

Land and economy. The central part is generally a plain, rolling or level, about 1,500mi (2,415km) long and wide, drained by the Mississippi River system, which includes the Missouri and Ohio rivers and scores of tributaries. This is rich agricultural land and also contains valuable mineral deposits. The five Great Lakes, important waterways, lie in the N, forming part of the boundary with Canada. Mountain systems enclose the plain. In the E, behind a narrow level strip along the Atlantic coast, the many parallel ranges of the Appalachian Mts run roughly N to S, reaching a height of 6,600ft (2,013m). W of the plains the ranges of the Rocky Mts run N to S, with 45 peaks over 14,000ft (4,270m). Beyond the Rockies a high plateau, much of it desert land, stretches W to the Sierra Nevada and Cascade ranges, whose altitudes exceed 14,000ft (4,270m) in places. Fertile valleys lie farther W and the low coastal ranges rise along the Pacific shore. The country's vast area and varied climate and terrain permit diversified economic activity in many sections. A transportation complex, based on a national highway network, air freight, railroads, and river and Great Lakes traffic, moves goods and produce rapidly over great distances, and is vital to the economy. Many ports on both coasts handle world commerce, and ports on the Great Lakes have access to the Atlantic through the St Lawrence Seaway. Heavy industry is centered largely in the NE and the Great Lakes region, and in Texas and California. Light industries flourish in most cities and towns. The chief grain lands are in the central plain; cattle ranges are extensive in the W and SW. Truck crops are grown and dairying is carried on in nearly every state. Forests, especially in the NW, support a major timber industry. Coal is mined principally in the Appalachian region and the largest producing petroleum fields are in Louisiana and Texas along the coast of the Gulf of Mexico, but deposits of both fuels are worked in several sections of the country. Metal mining is mostly in E and W mountains. The nation's business and financial structure is broadly based in the large cities.

People. The population is descended largely from European immigrants. The native Indians diminished rapidly as white settlement advanced and live mostly in the SW and W. The earliest pioneers along the Atlantic coast were chiefly from the British Isles. An early mass influx to the country was of blacks from Africa, transported to work the plantations of the S. In the 19th century a tide of immigration began bringing more than 40,000,000 persons into the country up to 1960. Germans, Irish, Italians, and Russians predominated, but every European country was represented. These immigrants spread over the land; their contributions invigorated the nation's life and accelerated its economic growth. Intermarriage produced a population of diverse blood. Nearly 75% of Americans live in urban areas. In the 1970 census, the urban population classification was less than 50% in only seven states. The densest population occurs in the NE. The national density is about 57 persons per square mile (22 per sq km).

Education. There are more than 2,000 institutions of higher education. Every state supports a university, and most of these have many branches. More numerous are privately endowed institutions and those of religious denominations. Enrollments are enormous; the City University of New York has more than 270,000 students and the State University of New York more than 160,000. Some private institutions trace their origins to the 17th century; Harvard University was founded in 1636 and the College of William and Mary in 1693. There are many schools for vocational training. Government and private foundations carry on research, especially in the sciences.

History. The first permanent settlement by Europeans in what is now the United States was made by the Spanish at St Augustine, Fla., in 1565. The English founded Jamestown, Va., in 1607 and Plymouth, Mass., in 1620. The Dutch established New Amsterdam (New York) in 1623. This was taken by the English in 1664 and the spreading communities along the Atlantic coast and inland became British colonies. Having fought off a threat from the French in Canada, the colonists rebelled against British rule in the American Revolution (1775–83), declaring their independence on July 4, 1776. The new nation operated as a confederation of 13 states until 1787, when the national Constitution was drawn up, creating the framework in which the government has continued to function. George Washington was elected the first president in 1788. A federal enclave called the District of Columbia was created in Maryland and Virginia, and the city of Washington was built as the national capital, which was occupied in 1800. Settlements pushed westward into the Mississippi River basin. The Louisiana Purchase from France in 1803 doubled US territory. New states were formed and admitted to the Union. Texas, which had won its independence from Mexico, was annexed in 1845, and after victory in the Mexican War (1846–48), California and what is now New Mexico, Arizona, and Nevada were added to the Union. Old quarrels over slavery and states' rights caused the secession of 11 Southern states in 1861. The four-year Civil War that followed devastated the South but preserved the Union and abolished slavery. The nation expanded quickly. Alaska was purchased from Russia in 1867. Two years later the transcontinental railroad linked the Pacific coast with the E. Hawaii was annexed in 1898, and the Philippine Islands were ceded to the United States by Spain after the Spanish-American War in that year. (The Philippines became independent in 1946.) Booming industry and technology spurred the rise of cities and transformed the face and life of the country, especially after the invention of the automobile in the early 20th century. In 1917 the nation joined the Allies in WWI. About 2,000,000 US soldiers were sent to France. After the Allied victory, President Woodrow Wilson played a major role in the peace conferences. The war stimulated US prosperity until the worldwide Great Depression of the 1930s. The Japanese attack on Pearl Harbor, Hawaii, on Dec. 7, 1941, drew the country into WWII. Wartime demands helped to restore the economy. For four years the United States fought a global war against Japan in the Pacific area and against Nazi Germany in Europe, putting 16,000,000 men and women into uniform. After the war, the possession of nuclear bombs thrust the nation into a position of world power and responsibility. New York City was chosen as headquarters of the United Nations. Anti-communist wars were fought in Korea 1950–53 and in Vietnam in the 1960s. Alaska became the 49th state on Jan. 3, 1959, and Hawaii became the 50th on Aug. 21, 1959. The United States won the lead in space exploration, and on July 20, 1969, an American was the first man to walk on the moon. △1124, 1216–18, 1274–78, 1358, 1392–1430.

PROFILE

Official name: United States of America
Population (including outlying areas): 207,678,247 (1970)
Area (including all areas under US jurisdiction): 3,628,150sq mi (9,396,909sq km)
Capital: Washington, District of Columbia, 756,710 (1970)
Chief cities: New York, 7,895,563; Chicago, 3,369,359; Los Angeles, 2,816,061; Philadelphia, 1,950,098
Government: Federal republic
Head of State and Chief Executive: President
Legislature: Congress (Senate, 100 members; House of Representatives, 435 members)
Elevations: highest, 20,320ft (6,198m), Mount McKinley, Alaska; lowest, 282ft (86m) below sea level, Death Valley, Calif.
Industries (major products): motor vehicles, aircraft, industrial machinery, electrical equipment and appliances, chemicals, petroleum products, fabricated metals, railroad equipment, processed foods
Agriculture (major products): wheat, corn, rye, barley, oats, soybeans, cattle, dairy products, cotton, tobacco, hogs
Minerals (major): coal, petroleum, natural gas, iron ore, copper, cement, stone, uranium ore
National motto: In God We Trust
National flag: The Stars and Stripes, 7 red, 6 white horizontal stripes; a blue field in the upper left corner containing 50 white 5-pointed stars, one for each state
National anthem: "The Star-Spangled Banner"

United States Air Force Academy, US educational institution. It offers a four-year educational curriculum for Air Force cadets that includes a baccalaureate level education in airmanship, related sciences, and the humanities. It was founded in 1955 and established in Colorado Springs, Colo., in 1958. Graduates normally enter the Air Force as second lieutenants.

United States Military Academy, US educational institution. Formally opened in 1802 and located in West Point, N.Y., the academy is a four-year institution in which Army cadets receive a general education, theoretical and practical training as junior officers. Upon course completion the cadets receive a commission as a second lieutenant in the Army and a bachelor of science degree.

United States Naval Academy, US educational institution. It offers a four-year program of academic, military, and professional instruction for the training and education of young people for the naval service. Eighty percent of each class enrolls in engineering, science, or mathematics, the other 20% choose their majors in fields of the humanities or social sciences. Completion of the program normally leads to a commission in the US Navy or the US Marine Corps. It was established in 1845 at Annapolis, Md.

United States v. E.C. Knight Co. (1895), US Supreme Court case holding that the manufacturing process was not a part of "commerce" and therefore could not be regulated by the federal government under the Sherman Antitrust Act. This limited view of the commerce power was abandoned with *U.S.* v. *Darby* and *Heart of Atlanta Motel* v. *U.S. See also* Heart of Atlanta Motel v. United States (1964); United States v. Darby (1941).

Units, Measurement. △1444, 1450.

Universal Lexicon. △1780.

Universal Set, or **Universe,** mathematical set of all the objects that are admissible to that set, such as the set of the seven days of the week or of all the colors of the rainbow. *See also* Sets. △1458.

Universe, aggregate of all matter, energy, and space, consisting of vast cold empty regions with a distribution of high-temperature stars and other objects grouped in galaxies. On a large scale the universe is considered uniform: it is identical in every part. It is also known to be expanding at a uniform rate, the galaxies all receding from each other. The origin, evolution, and future characteristics of the universe are considered in several cosmological theories. Recent developments in astronomy imply a finite universe, as postulated in the big-bang theory. *See also* Cosmology; Red Shift. △126, 156, 1478.

University City, city in E Missouri, 8mi (13km) WNW of St Louis. Inc. 1906. Pop. (1970) 46,309.

Unknown, variable with values that are to be found by solving a given equation. △1452.

Unterwalden, canton in Switzerland; divided into Nidwalden and Obwalden, half cantons. In 1921 it united with Schwyg and Uri cantons to form league that became the center of the Swiss Confederation. The land is mountainous, forested, and pastoral, with orchards and meadow lands for livestock. Industries: dairying, woodworking, cement, glassworks. Area: 296sq mi (767sq km). Pop. 55,323.

Upanishads, Hindu texts of uncertain authorship, dating from approximately 900 BC. The term Upanishads means "to sit nearby devotedly." Of more than 100 *Upanishads* there are about 10 principal ones. Containing philosophical speculations of many centuries of Indian sages, there is a heterogeneity of thought. The content suggests oral instruction rather than methodical exposition. The metaphysical doctrine of Brahman-Atman, the ultimate unity of design, is a central theme. *See also* Hinduism. △962.

Updike, John (1932–), US author, b. Shillington, Pa. He joined the staff of *The New Yorker* magazine in 1955 but later left to concentrate on his own writing. His works include *The Same Door* (1959), a collection of short stories, and the novels *The Poorhouse Fair* (1959), *Rabbit, Run* (1961), *Centaur* (1962), *Couples* (1968), *Rabbit Redux* (1971), and *Marry Me* (1976).

Upland, city in S California, 34mi (55km) E of Los

Angeles. Industries: processing of citrus fruits, paint, auto parts, feed products. Inc. 1906. Pop. (1970) 32,-551.

Upland Plover, short-billed, pleasant-voiced, slender, gray-streaked North American shorebird that has left the shore to breed in pastures of Virginia and northern areas. It often perches on fences. Length: 12in (30cm). Family Charadriidae; species *Bartramia longicauda*.

Upper Arlington, city in central Ohio, 8mi (13km) NNW of Columbus. Inc. 1918. Pop. (1970) 38,630.

Upper Canada, the name for the province of Ontario (1791–1841). The name was changed to Canada West (1841–67) and to Ontario after the formation of the Confederation of Canada (1867).

Upper Class, the highest social position in the hierarchically stratified society. Members of the upper class possess in the greatest quantity whatever characteristics society most values: wealth, power, or status. *See also* Hierarchy; Status; Stratification.

Upper Volta (Haute-Volta), landlocked nation in W Africa. It is bounded on the N by Mali and Niger and to the S by the coastal nations of Ivory Coast, Ghana, Togo, and Benin. More than 90% of the people are self-sustaining farmers. A plateau, ranging from 1,000ft (305m) in the N to 650ft (198m) in the S, occupies most of the country. Although three rivers, the Black Volta, the Red Volta, and the White Volta, flow through the country, the land is generally dry and infertile. Over 90% of the population is engaged in agriculture or raising livestock. Irrigation projects, developing the Black and White voltas, promise brighter agricultural prospects for the future. Much of the population is concentrated in the S and center of the country with 95% living in rural villages. Most of the people are Voltaic or Mande with scattered ethnic minorities. About 75% practice animistic religions; most of the rest are Muslim. Although French is the official language, Moré is the most commonly spoken.

The constitution calls for a president; a unicameral National Assembly, with elections every five years under universal suffrage; a Supreme Court and lesser courts. However, in 1974 Pres. Sangoule Lamizana suspended the constitution, dissolved the assembly, and named a mostly military cabinet to work with him as head of state. Explored by the French in the late 19th century, Upper Volta, after much colonial manipulation, became a French Overseas Territory in 1947. Becoming autonomous in 1958, it gained its independence in 1960, and formed a bilateral agreement with France in 1961. A border dispute with Mali was resolved in 1975, and in that same year it joined with 14 other African states to form ECOWAS (Economic Community of West African States), a common-market type relationship.

PROFILE

Official name: Republic of Upper Volta
Area: 105,792sq mi (274,000sq km)
Population: 5,485,981
Density: 55.7per sq mi (21.5per sq km)
Chief cities: Ouagadougou, capital; Bobo-Dioulasso
Government: Republic
Language: French (official)
Monetary unit: CFA franc
Gross national product: $450,000,000
Per capita income: $79
Manufacturing (major products): bicycles, motorcycles
Agriculture (major products): cotton, rice, peanuts
Minerals (major): manganese
Trading partners (major): France, Ivory Coast, Japan

Uppsala (Upsale), city in W Sweden, 40mi (64km) NNW of Stockholm, on Fyrisan River; capital of Uppsala co; pagan capital of Sweden 6th century; site of University of Uppsala (1477), Royal Society of Sciences, Gustav Werner Institute, Victoria Museum, Linnaean Museum, 13th-century Gothic church, and cathedral of Uppsala. Industries: printing, food processing, metal goods, footwear, clothing. Pop. 101,696.

Upside-down Catfish △516.

Upwelling, the process that brings water of greater density and lower temperature up to the surface water of the ocean. Upwelling is especially characteristic of the western side of continents where winds blow parallel to the coast and the water carried away by the surface current is replaced by the bottom water. △224.

Ur, ancient Babylonian city and birthplace of Abraham. Settled in the 4th millennium BC, it prospered during its First Dynasty (*c.* 3000–2600 BC), and during its Third Dynasty, it became the richest city in Mesopotamia. A century later it was destroyed by the Elamites only to be rebuilt and destroyed again by the Babylonians. After Babylonia came under the control of Persia, the city was abandoned (3rd cent. BC). △956–58.

Uralic Languages, family of languages spoken in parts of N and E Europe and the Soviet Union. Its two branches are the Finno-Ugric languages, which include Finnish and Hungarian, and the Samoyed languages, though the former accounts for 99.9% of the 20 million Uralic speakers. Some scholars believe that the Uralic languages are related to the Altaic languages (constituting a Ural-Altaic family), but this remains to be proven conclusively.

Ural Mountains, mountain system in USSR, extends N-S from the Kara Sea to the W Kirgiz Steppe region; densely forested and rich in minerals, including iron ore, copper, chrome, gold, platinum, coal, potassium, and phosphates. Highest peak: Mt Narodnaya 6,214ft (1,895m). Length: approx. 1,640mi (2,640km).

Uraninite, an oxide mineral, uranium oxide (UO_2), found in pegmatites and medium-temperature veins. Cubic system as cubes, octahedrons, and dodecahedrons; when botryoidal (like a bunch of grapes) with radiating structure, called pitchblende. Greasy or dull black; hardness 5–6; sp gr 6.4–9.7. Pitchblende is major source of uranium.

Uranium, radioactive metallic element (symbol U) of the actinide group, identified (1789) by M.H. Klaproth. It occurs in several minerals, the chief ores being pitchblende (oxide), autunite, and tobernite. The element is important because of its use in fission reactors and bombs. The naturally occurring element contains U^{238} (99.28%), U^{235} (0.71%), and U^{234} (0.-0058%). U^{235} (half-life 7.1×10^8 yrs) is fissionable and will sustain a neutron chain reaction. Fuels used in reactors are enriched with this isotope by gaseous diffusion, using the volatile hexafluoride, or by a centrifuge. In breeder reactors the isotope U^{238} is converted into Pu^{239} by neutron capture. Chemically uranium is a very reactive metal; it oxidizes in air and reacts with cold water. Properties: at. no. 92; at. wt. 238.029; sp. gr. 18.95; melt. pt. 2,070°F (1,132.3°C); boil. pt. 6,904°F (3,818°C); most stable isotope U^{238} (half-life 4.51×10^9 yrs. △1482, 1638, 1502.

Uranium-Thorium-Lead Dating, a method of assessing geological age up to many millions of years. *See also* Dating, Radioactive.

Uranus, seventh planet from the Sun, discovered in 1781 by William Herschel, encircled by 5 satellites. Impermanent clouds can be seen in its atmosphere, which is gaseous and consists of hydrogen, helium, and methane. Its axis is tilted 98° from the perpendicular position. Mean distance from the Sun, 1,783,000,000mi (2,871,000,000km); mass, 14.6 times that of Earth; diameter, 32,375mi (51,800km); rotation period, 10hr 48min; period of sidereal revolution, 84 years. *See also* Solar System. △88, 154.

Uranus, in Greek mythology, the starry sky, husband and son of Gaea, the broad-bosomed Earth. Together they proceeded to people the Earth. Uranus sired the race of Titans and the Cyclopes and three grotesque monsters. Uranus, in horror, buried these last beneath the ground, incurring the vengeance of Gaea who caused her son Cronus to mutilate his father.

Urban II, Roman Catholic pope (1088–99) △1084.

Urban VI, Roman Catholic pope (1378–89), b. Bartolomeo Prignano (c. 1318). The college of cardinals declared his election invalid and appointed an antipope, Clement VII, beginning the Great Schism. His papacy was marked by confusion and financial losses in the papal states. Assumed insane, he is thought to have murdered five cardinals.

Urbana, city in E central Illinois, E of Springfield; seat of Champaign co; site of University of Illinois (1867). Industries: foundries, machine shops, scientific instruments, railroad shops. Founded 1824, inc. 1833, as city 1860. Pop. (1970) 32,800.

Urban Planning, systematic development of new urban areas or altering existing ones to improve quality of life for their inhabitants. Federally assisted urban renewal programs, to clear cities of slums and blighted areas, have had some success, but increasingly complex problems of crime, air pollution, urban sprawl, and municipal bankruptcy have highlighted the need for an integrated approach to city planning. The 1965 Housing Act urged formation of metropolitan and regional agencies for this purpose.

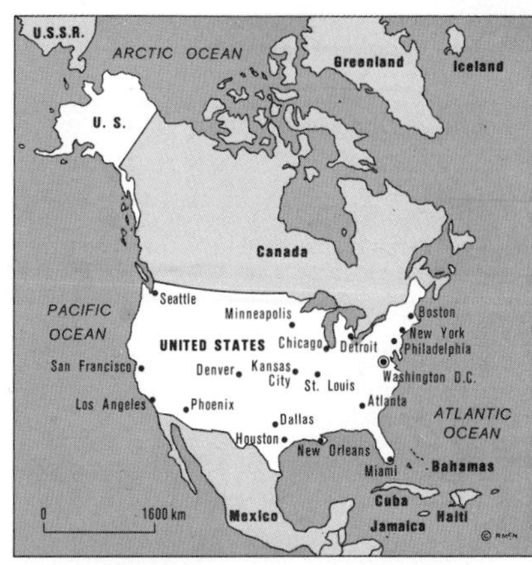
U.S.S.R.
ARCTIC OCEAN
Greenland
Iceland
U. S.
Canada
PACIFIC OCEAN
Seattle
Minneapolis
UNITED STATES
Chicago
Detroit
Boston
New York
Philadelphia
Washington D.C.
San Francisco
Denver
Kansas City
St. Louis
Los Angeles
Phoenix
Dallas
Atlanta
ATLANTIC OCEAN
Houston
New Orleans
Miami
Bahamas
Cuba
Haiti
Jamaica
Mexico
0
1600 km

United States

Capitol Building, Washington, D.C.

UNITED STATES

For additional information in the Alphapedia, see individual articles on states, cities, and points of interest. There are biographies of presidents, vice presidents, chief justices of the Supreme Court, and major figures in the history, government, politics, and arts of America. See also general articles such as President of the United States, Supreme Court of the United States, individual political parties, wars, battles, and legislative acts.

For related coverage in the Colorpedia, see the following pages:

Urban Sociology, sociological study of cities and urban areas. Like its counterpart, rural sociology, it seeks to understand the interplay between a unique environment-type and the social structures within it. Urban sociology examines the effects that such things as high population density, limited space, and heterogeneity have on social organization.

Urdu, the official language of Pakistan, the mother tongue of only about 5 million people there, but used as second language by as much as two-thirds of the population. It is also spoken in India by most of the country's Muslims. Urdu is quite similar to Hindi, the chief difference being that it is written in the Arabic script. Its vocabulary contains many Arabic and Persian borrowings that are absent in Hindi.

Urea, a nitrogen-containing compound in the urine, blood, and lymph, an end product of protein metabolism. △1560.

Uremia, toxic condition due to the accumulation of nitrogenous substances in the blood that are normally eliminated in the urine. It is marked by headaches, vomiting, coma, and convulsions.

Ureter, a long narrow duct that connects the kidney to the urinary bladder, transporting urine from the kidney to the bladder where it is stored until voided. △694.

Urethra, duct through which urine is discharged from the body. Urine is produced in the kidney, stored in the bladder until pressure in the bladder triggers specific neural responses that cause urine, under voluntary control, to be released through the urethra. In males the urethra is also the tube through which semen is ejaculated out of the body through the penis. △694, 700.

Urethritis, inflammation of the urethra, most frequently found in males, due to bacterial or viral infection or to mechanical obstruction. Antibiotics or surgical procedures are used for treatment. △728.

Urey, Harold Clayton (1893–), U.S. chemist, b. Walkerton, Ind. He became professor at Columbia University and in the same year (1934) was awarded a Nobel prize for his isolation of deuterium. Thereafter he worked on isotope separation at the universities of Chicago and California. Concerned that his work on isotopes had aided the construction of nuclear weapons, he turned in later years to geophysics.

Uri, canton in central Switzerland; an alpine region; capital is Altdorf; contains glaciers, forests, pastures. In 853 it became a fief of the Fraumunster convent at Zurich; after 1098 it was part of the Holy Roman imperial bailiwick of Zurich; in 1231 it was made dependency of Emperor Frederick II; joined the league of cantons 1291, forming center of the Swiss Confederation; Uri rejected the Reformation and joined the Catholic Sonderbund 1845; scene of the William Tell legend. Hydroelectricity has made some industry possible, but agriculture is dominant. Area: 415sq mi (1,075sq km). Pop. 34,091.

Uric Acid, an end product of protein metabolism found in urine, blood, and lymph and also as a salt (urate) in calculi such as kidney stones. Excess amount of uric acid in the blood causes gout, with urate deposits around joints.

Urinalysis, examination of the appearance and condition of the urine both grossly and microscopically, and study of its chemical constituents to detect a wide variety of diseases or conditions and to follow the results of treatment. △728.

Urinary Bladder. *See* Bladder, Urinary.

Uris, Leon Marcus (1924–), US author, b. Baltimore. He is noted for his historical novels, the most noted of which was *Exodus* (1958), which dealt with the establishment of the state of Israel. It, along with other of his works, has been made into a movie. Among his other books are *Battle Cry* (1953), *Mila 18* (1960), *Armageddon* (1964), and *Trinity* (1976).

Urodela. △518.

Urogenital System, a major system of the body, containing the urinary system and the genital organs, which are part of the reproductive system. The urinary system, the body's excretory system, consists of kidneys, which lie on upper back part of the abdominal cavity on each side; ureters, 10-in (25-cm) tubes that run from kidneys to the bladder; the urinary bladder, lying in the pelvic cavity and storing urine; and the urethra, from which urine passes from the body. In males, the reproductive system includes paired testes that produce sperm cells and hormones and are located in an external pouch, the scrotum; accessory glands; and the penis, the organ through which urine passes and sperm is ejaculated. In females, the reproductive system consists of paired ovaries, found on each side of the pelvic cavity; Fallopian tubes, or oviducts, which connect ovaries to the uterus; the uterus, or womb, located in the pelvic cavity between the bladder and rectum; the cervix, or lower part of the uterus, which opens into the vagina, the opening for intercourse and childbirth. In females, the urethra and vaginal openings are separate but lying close to each other. *See also* articles on various organs. △700, 728.

Urology, that branch of medicine that deals with the diagnosis and treatment of diseases of the urinary tract in women and of the urinary and genital organs in men. △728, 754.

Ursa Major, the Great Bear, the Big Dipper, conspicuous northern circumpolar constellation lying south of Draco and on the opposite side of the north celestial pole from Ursa Minor. Its seven brightest stars form the familiar bowl-and-handle shape, and include the multiple star Mizar, the second star from the end of the handle, and Merak and Dubhe, the last two stars in the bowl, known as the Pointers because they directly indicate Polaris. The constellation, which is known by several other names, including Charles's Wain and the Plow, contains two galaxies M 81 (NGC 3031) and M 82 (NGC 3034) and a planetary nebula, the Owl Nebula (M 97; NGC 3587). Brightest star Alpha Ursae Majoris (Dubhe). △38, 110, 130.

Ursa Minor, the Little Bear, the Little Dipper, northern circumpolar constellation in which the north celestial pole is located, marked by Polaris, the brightest star in the group. △130.

Ursula, Saint, virgin and martyr. Legends about her date from around 1000. A Latin inscription found in Cologne, Germany, probably dating from the 4th century, tells of virgins martyred there. Who they were is not known, but tradition made Ursula their leader and many stories grew. One is that she and her companions were British and were killed by the Huns. The number of martyrs has been set at 11 and at 11,000. △1052.

Ursulines, oldest religious order of women in the Roman Catholic Church, named for its patron, St Ursula, and founded by St Angela Merici at Brescia in 1535. The order grew, especially in France and Canada, until interrupted by the French Revolution. Increasing in size again in the 19th century, federations of Roman, Canadian, and German convents were formed.

Uruapan, city in SW Mexico, 60mi (96km) SW of Morelia; manufacturing center for gourd lacquerware crafted by Tarascan Indians. Industries: glassware, woodwork, handcrafts. Founded 1540. Pop. 104,-475.

Uruguay, independent nation in Latin America. It is a small republic with state ownership of major utilities and some industry; it has been fighting inflation to maintain its high standard of living and social welfare programs.

Land and economy. Located on the E coast of South America, bounded by Argentina and Brazil, it is the smallest country on the continent. With sufficient water and a temperate climate its prairie grasses have made livestock the most significant economic product. Chief crops from the N agricultural areas are wheat and flax. Wool export, which together with meat makes up 35%–40% of exports, declined after a drop in world market price. Social welfare programs have added to budget deficits and inflation, and in recent years guerrilla action by leftist Tupamaros has discouraged foreign investment.

People. Uruguay is the only South American country with no uninhabited areas; more than 33% of the people live in Montevideo. Spanish, both in language and culture, predominates, although 25% of the population is Italian. Literacy is 95%. The principal church is Roman Catholic. Church and state are completely separated. Primary education is compulsory, and college is free.

Government. Under a 1966 constitution the president is elected for a five-year term, and the bicameral General Assembly is popularly elected. Suffrage is universal.

History. Struggles with Spain and Portugal, and then with Brazil and Argentina, marked its history until independence was achieved in 1828. Civil wars and foreign intervention plagued the country until the end of the 19th century. Since then Uruguay has been known for its stability as a democracy whose pattern of political and social reform was set by President José Batlle y Ordonez in 1903. With the exception of a 1933 coup d'etat and a 1973 military council to wipe out the Tupamaros, it has remained a democracy.

PROFILE

Official name: Eastern Republic of Uruguay
Area: 68,536sq mi (177,508sq km)
Population: 3,100,000
Density: 45per sq mi (17per sq km)
Chief city: Montevideo (capital)
Government: Socialist Republic (now under military control)
Religion: Roman Catholic
Language: Spanish
Monetary unit: Peso
Gross national product: $2,585,000,000
Per capita income: $865
Industries: meat products, wool, hides, construction materials, chemicals, wine
Agriculture: wheat, corn, rice, cattle, sheep, forests, citrus fruits, oats
Trading partners: Western European countries, Argentina, Brazil, United States

Uruguay (Uruguai), river SE South America; rises in S Brazil, and forms part of boundary between Rio Grande do Sul and Santa Catarina states; flows SW to form boundary between Argentina and S Brazil, and Argentina and Uruguay, empties into Rio de la Plata. Important source of hydroelectricity for Argentina and Uruguay. Length: approx. 870mi. (1,401km).

Urumchi (Wulumuqi, or Wu-lu-mu-chi), city in W China, 300mi (483km) E of Kuldja, in Dzungarian basin; capital of Sinkiang Uigur autonomous region; site of Sinkiang University; on caravan routes from USSR, Lanchow, and Kashgar. Industries: printing, tanning, coal, tin, silver, food processing, farm tools. Pop. 500,000.

Üsküdar, city in NW Turkey, opposite Istanbul across the Bosporus channel; commercial and residential suburb of Istanbul; site of mosques and other early structures. Pop. 133,883.

Usumbura. *See* Bujumbura.

Usury, lending of money at an unusually high or unlawful rate of interest. △1126.

Utah, state in the W United States, in the Rocky Mt region. Its SE corner touches Colorado, New Mexico, and Arizona, the only contact of four states in the country.

Land and economy. About 90% of the land is desert or mountains; about 66% is owned by the US government. The Wasatch Range of the Rocky Mts crosses the state from N to S. To the W of this range is a basin of desert land. Great Salt Lake, a saline body of water 72mi (116km) long and 30mi (48km) wide, is in the NE part of the basin. E of the Wasatch Range the Uinta Mts, with 11 peaks over 13,000ft (3,965m), run E and W. Much of the S and E portions of the state are desert plateaus cut by canyons. Agriculture is largely confined to the valleys on the W front of the Wasatch. Irrigation projects have aided production. Manufacturing is concentrated in the area of Ogden-Salt Lake City-Provo. Mining is carried on in many parts of the state. Utah's scenery, especially in the national parks in the S, attracts an important tourist trade.

People. First settlement was by pioneers from other states, whose descendants form the bulk of the population. About 80% live in urban areas.

Education. The University of Utah and Utah State University are state-supported. Brigham Young University is a Mormon church institution.

History. In 1776 two Franciscan friars seeking a way to California crossed the region, which was Mexican territory until ceded to the United States in 1848. The first settlement came in 1847, when Brigham Young led a party of the Church of Jesus Christ of Latter-day Saints (known as Mormons) to the valley between the Wasatch and Great Salt Lake. Through irrigation they created good farmland. Immigrants from Eastern states and Europe established new communities. In 1849 the Mormons organized the State of Deseret and sought admission to the Union, but Congress instead created the Territory of Utah. The transcontinental railroad was completed in 1869 at Promontory Point. A long conflict with federal authorities ended in 1890, when the Mormons agreed to abandon their practice of polygamy. The church's influence is strong in the state; more than 70% of the population is Mormon.

PROFILE

Admitted to Union: Jan. 4, 1896; rank, 45th
US Congressmen: Senate, 2; House of Representatives, 2

'opulation: 1,059,273 (1970); rank, 36th
:apital: Salt Lake City, 175,885 (1970)
:hief cities: Salt Lake City; Ogden, 69,478; Provo, 53,131; Bountiful, 27,751
;tate legislature: Senate, 29; House of Representatives, 75
\rea: 84,916sq mi (219,932sq km); rank, 11th
:levation: Highest, 13,528ft (4,126m) Kings Peak; lowest, 2,000ft (610m), Beaverdam Creek
ndustries: (major products) missiles, rocket engines, aircraft navigation systems, fabricated steel, food products
\griculture: sheep, turkeys, apricots, cherries, barley, sugar beets, winter wheat
/linerals (major): copper, gold, silver, lead, petroleum, uranium
;tate nickname: Beehive State
;tate motto: Industry
;tate bird: California gull
;tate flower: sego lily
;tate tree: blue spruce

Jterus, or **Womb,** a pear-shaped, hollow muscular ›rgan located in the pelvis between the bladder and ectum in women and in which the fetus is carried and levelops. Its upper, wider part, called the body, fun-ius, or corpus, is connected to an ovary on each side ›y a Fallopian tube and held in place by broad liga-nents. Its lower part, called the neck, or cervix, opens nto the vagina through which sperm may enter to ertilize an egg and through which menstruation oc-urs. The lining of the uterus—the endometrium—is hed monthly between puberty and menopause in nenstruation when pregnancy does not occur. During ›regnancy the uterus gradually increases in size to ccommodate the developing fetus and returns to al-nost pre-pregnancy size after childbirth. △700, 702.

Jtica, city in central New York, on the Mohawk River nd New York Barge Canal; seat of Oneida co; origi-ally settled 1773 on site of Old Fort Schuyler; site of Jtica College of Syracuse University (1946), Mohawk /alley Community College (1946), Munson-Williams-'roctor Institute (Art Museum). Industries: tools, fire-rms, textiles, electronic and aviation equipment. Inc. s village 1798, as city 1832. Pop. (1970) 91,611.

Jtilitarianism, social and ethical doctrine as-ociated with James Mill (1773–1836) and Jeremy 3entham (1749–1832), which asserts that the right ct produces the greatest happiness for the greatest umber. △858, 860.

Jto-Aztecan Languages, family of American Indian anguages spoken in SW United States and in Mexico. t includes Papago, Pima, and Hopi, of Arizona; Ute, f Utah and Colorado; Comanche, of Oklahoma; and ;hoshone and Kiowa, spoken in a number of western tates. In Mexico there are Nahuatl (the language of he Aztecs), Tarahumara, and Mayo.

Jtopia, book by Sir Thomas More, published in Latin 1 1516, with the first English edition in 1551. It de-cribes "the best state" found on "the new isle, called Jtopia." △1130.

Jtopianism, a system of political ideas which advo-ates an ideal state. Among the political theorists who dvocated an utopian society were Charles Fourier (1772–1837), Robert Owen (1771–1858), and Karl Marx (1818–83). Marx believed in the overthrow of capitalism and the distribution of goods according to individual needs. Utopian ideals have been the theme of many books. In Sir Thomas More's *Utopia* (1516), a traveler discovers a perfect political, economic, and social state. Other works on Utopianism include *New Atlantis* (1624–29) by Sir Francis Bacon, *Looking Backward* (1888) by Edward Bellamy, and *A Modern Utopia* (1905) by H. G. Wells. Because Utopianism is a reaction to social needs, many of its principles are today called socialistic.

Utrecht, city in central Netherlands, on the Oude Rijn River, approx. 20mi (32km) SSE of Amsterdam; capital of Utrecht prov.; a trade center since medieval times; scene of signing of Union of Utrecht (1579), and Treaty of Utrecht, terminating War of the Spanish Succession (1713); site of university (1636), 15th-century cathedral. Industries: steel, machinery, textiles, electrical equipment, food processing. Chartered 1122. Pop. 278,966.

Utrecht, Peace of, series of treaties (1713–14) concluding the War of the Spanish Succession. It had the effect of ending French expansion and beginning British expansion. Louis XIV confirmed renunciation of claims to French throne of Louis' grandson, Philip V of Spain. France surrendered the Spanish Netherlands, Milan, Naples, and Sardinia to Austria. The treaties also confirmed succession to the British and French thrones. Spain ceded Gibraltar and Minorca to Great Britain, which also was granted sole rights of slave traffic with Spanish America. The right bank of the Rhine was restored to the Holy Roman Empire, and France turned Newfoundland, Nova Scotia, the Hudson's Bay territory, and St Kitts over to Britain. Commercial treaties were also included.

Utrillo, Maurice (1883–1955), French painter. He is known for his scenes of Paris, especially of Montmartre. The son of artist Suzanne Valadon, he began to paint in order to control his alcoholic tendencies. His best works are from his so-called White Period (1908–14) and include "L'Impasse Cottin" (*c.* 1910), "Rue Norvins" (1912), and "Place du Tertre" (1911–12). In 1923 he designed the sets and costumes for Sergei Diaghilev's ballet, *Barabau.*

U-2 Incident (1960), international incident precipitated by the downing of a US plane in the USSR. The plane, a U-2 on a photographic reconnaissance mission over the Soviet Union, was shot down and its pilot, Francis Gary Powers, captured. The United States at first claimed the mission was a meteorological one, but US-USSR diplomatic relations were strained when Powers confessed to being a spy. Soviet Premier Khrushchev embarrassed the United States by demanding an apology and canceling a visit scheduled by Pres. Dwight D. Eisenhower to the USSR. Powers was later freed in exchange for the release of a Soviet spy by the United States.

Uxmal, Maya ceremonial and administrative center located on Mexico's Yucatán peninsula. Two pyramids and a grouping of four rectangular buildings called the Nunnery dominated the 160-acre (65-hectares) site. Uxmal flourished AD 600–900 but was abandoned *c.* 1450.

Leon Uris

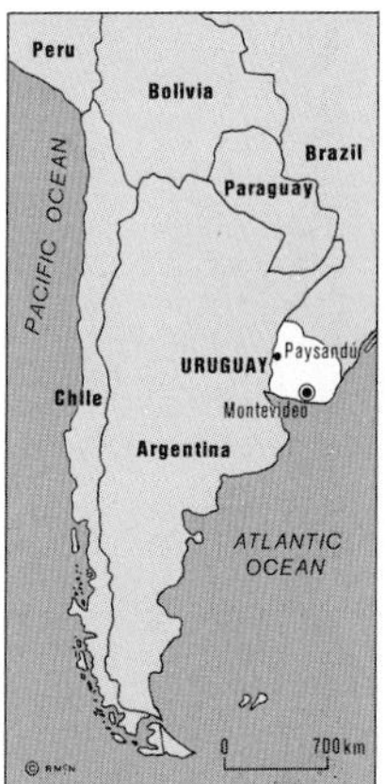
Peru
Bolivia
Brazil
Paraguay
PACIFIC OCEAN
URUGUAY
Paysandú
Chile
Montevideo
Argentina
ATLANTIC OCEAN
0
700km

Uruguay

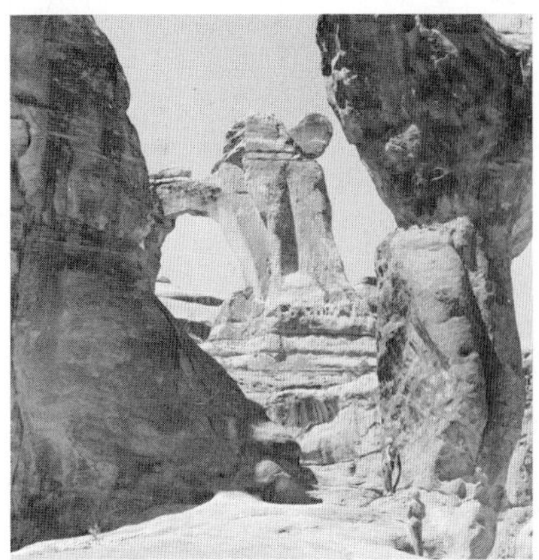

Arches National Park, Utah

V

VA. *See* Veterans Administration.

Vaal River, river in Republic of South Africa; rises in SE Transvaal, flows W forming border of Transvaal and Orange Free State; empties into Orange River. Length: 720mi (1,159km).

Vaccination, injection of a vaccine in order to produce immunity against a disease. The term most often refers specifically to vaccination against smallpox, in which vaccine is scratched into the skin producing a typical "pox" and leaving a small scar. Vaccines are also injected or administered orally. *See also* Vaccine. △722, 738, 1186.

Vaccine, agent used to produce immunity against various diseases without producing serious or fatal symptoms of the disease. The agent may be a live virus but low in virulence or a dead one still able to induce production of antibodies. First of the vaccines to come into general use was the smallpox vaccine, developed in the 19th century. Vaccines against poliomyelitis, influenza, yellow fever, rabies, measles, and other bacterial, viral, and rickettsial diseases are available. *See also* Toxin. △738.

Vacuole, membrane-bound cavity within cell plasma, believed to discharge excess water or wastes. △412.

Vacuum, a state of very low pressure. Interstellar space is an extremely good vacuum, with an average density of about 1 hydrogen atom/cc. Many items of everyday life contain vacuums: electric light bulbs, television picture tubes. △1514.

Vacuum Cleaner. △1818.

Vacuum Flask. △1508.

Vacuum Pump, a device that removes air from an enclosure. The rotary oil pump uses an eccentric cylinder rotating in an enclosed space connected to the vessel to be evacuated. At one point in its cycle, air is compressed in an opening and forces a valve to open, thus reducing the air pressure in the vessel.

Vaduz, capital city of Liechtenstein, on the right bank of the Upper Rhine River, approx. 50mi (80km) SE of Zurich, Switzerland. Destroyed in war between Switzerland and the Holy Roman Empire, it was rebuilt in early 16th century; became a possession of the Liechtenstein family 1712; site of Castle of Vaduz, National Library, Post Office, Postal Museum, art gallery. Chief industry is tourism. Pop. 3,921.

Vagina. △700.

Vaginitis, acute infectious inflammation of the vagina caused by a protozoan *Trichonomas vaginalis* and transmitted during sexual intercourse. The male manifestation is usually a mild urethritis.

Valais (Wallis), canton in S Switzerland; extends from Bernese to Pennine Alps; includes upper Rhone valley, Matterhorn, Dufourspitze, Dom, and Weisshorn peaks; capital is Sion. Taken by Romans 57 BC, it passed to Rudolf III of Burgundy in 999, who was made the bishop of Sion, lord of Valais; it was later divided and Lower Valais passed to duke of Savoy; in 1475 Sion defeated the duke of Savoy and Lower Valais was ruled by Upper Valais until 1798, when Valais was made a canton of the Helvetic Republic; became independent 1802; joined the Swiss Confederation 1815. Industries: hydroelectricity, metal products, chemicals, livestock, agriculture, wine. Area: 2,020sq mi (5,232sq km). Pop. 206,563.

Valdez, town in S Alaska, at the head of the Valdez Arm inside Prince William Sound; S terminus of oil pipeline originating in Prudhoe Bay; site of salmon spawning grounds and an ice-free port. Inc. 1901. Pop. (1970) 1,005.

Valdosta, city in S Georgia, approx. 15mi (24km) N of Florida border in Lowndes co. Industries: livestock, feed, textiles, tobacco. Settled 1859. Pop. (1970) 32,303.

Valence, tendency of atoms to join together forming chemical bonds. Valence is also a measure of the "combining power" of a particular element, equal to the number of (single) chemical bonds one atom can form. Thus hydrogen has a valence of 1, carbon 4, and sulfur 2, as seen in compounds such as CH_4, CS_2, and H_2S. Covalence refers to formation of covalent bonds: coordinate valence to coordinate bonds. Many transition elements have two or more different valences. *See also* Oxidation State. △1556.

Valence Electron, electron in an atom that is transferred or shared in the formation of a chemical bond. The valence electrons of a nontransition metal are those in the outermost shell (furthest from the nucleus), and in forming compounds the atom tends to attain the stable configuration of a noble gas. Transition metals use both the outer shell and the partially filled penultimate shell in chemical bonding. △1556.

Valence Orbital, one of the outer atomic orbitals of an atom, containing the electrons that participate in chemical bonding. In producing ionic bonds electrons are lost or gained by valence orbitals. Covalent bonding involves sharing of electrons between atoms, a process often visualized as overlap of valence orbitals with formation of molecular orbitals. △1556.

Valencia, city in E Spain, on the Guadalquivir River, 188mi (303km) ESE of Madrid; capital of Valencia prov. Originally inhabited by Romans, it passed to Visigoths AD 413; conquered by the Moors and made capital of an independent Moorish kingdom 11th century; reconquered 1238 by James of Aragon; served as capital for loyalist government during Spanish civil war 1936–39. It is the site of 15th-century Gothic cathedral, 14th–17th-century Church of San Nicolas, botanical gardens, bullring; processing and distribution center for surrounding region; El Grao serves as the city's port. Industries: shipyards, electrical equipment, chemicals, textiles, machinery. Founded 138 BC by Roman consul Decimus Junius Brutus. Area: (prov.) 4,156sq mi (10,764sq km). Pop. (city) 653,690; (prov.) 1,767,327.

Valencia, city in N Venezuela, 80mi (128km) W of Caracas; capital of Carabobo state. A major industrial and transport center, city was capital of Venezuela 1812 and 1830; scene of Venezuela's proclamation of independence from Greater Colombia 1830. Industries: auto parts, textiles, paper, cement, soap, dairy products, furniture, feed, lumber, food processing. Founded 1555. Pop. 232,035.

Valentine, Saint. The Roman Martyrology lists two saints of this name: Valentine of Rome and Valentine of Terni. Both are said to have been martyred about 269, and both have their feast day on February 14. In the late Middle Ages a custom developed of sending love notes on this date, probably because it was thought to mark the beginning of the mating season for birds.

Valentino, Rudolph (1895–1926), US silent film star, b. Italy. A prototype of the Latin lover, he enhanced many films with sleek, exotic magnetism including *The Sheik* (1921), *The Young Rajah* (1922 *Cobra* (1925), and *Son of the Sheik* (1926). Vale tino's early death caused widespread hysteria amon his fans. △1362.

Valerian, Publius Licinius (died *c.* 269), Roma emperor (253–60). In 257 he revived the persecu tion of the Christians that had begun under Emper Decius. Christians were required to perform publ acts of worship to the state gods, and penalties wer ordered for those who refused. The persecutio ended when Valerian was captured by the Persians i 260 while attempting to halt their invasion of Syri and Armenia.

Valéry, Paul Ambroise (1871–1945), French poe and critic. Influenced by Mallarmé, his poems, inclu ing *La Jeune Parque* (1917) and *Les Charmes* (1922 are characterized by lyricism and abstract thought. H criticism includes *La Soirée avec Monsieur Test* (1906) and the five volumes of essays *Varieté* (1924 44). He was elected to the French Academy (1925

Valhalla, in Norse mythology, the hall where chose slain warriors live blissfully. The god Odin is the lead of Valhalla and he will lead these warriors to battl against the giants at the time of Ragnarok. △840.

Validity, in statistics and psychometrics, the exter to which a test or method measures what it is su posed to measure. A test's validity may be determine by seeing how well the test predicts some other me sure or criterion that is known to be valid. *See als* Statistics. △854.

Valine, white crystalline essential amino acid foun in proteins. *See* Amino Acid.

Valinomycin. △1570.

Valium, trademark for diazepam, a sedative dru used in the treatment of anxiety and as an anticonvu sant in epilepsy. Habituation is possible. △770.

Valkyries, in Norse mythology, maidens sent b Odin to choose slain warriors for Valhalla.

Valla, Lorenzo. △1130.

Valladolid, city in NW central Spain, on the Pisuerg River, 98mi (157km) NNW of Madrid; capital of Va ladolid prov. Liberated by Castilian kings in 10th ce tury, it was scene of marriage of Ferdinand and Is bella (1469); site of 12th-century university an Romanesque cathedral, church of Santa Ana contai ing paintings by Goya, art museum, monument t Christopher Columbus (who died here 1506), 15t century home of Cervantes. Industries: chemical flour, grain, metal works, textiles, liqueurs, piano gloves. First mentioned 1074. Area: (prov.) 3,166s mi (8,200sq km). Pop. (city) 236,341; (prov.) 412 572.

Vallejo, city in central California, 20mi (32km) N Oakland; originally constructed on land of Ge Mariano G. Vallejo to be the state capital; tempora capital 1852–1853; site of California Maritime Aca emy (1929), Solano College (1945), Mare Island Na Yard (1854); important port and agricultural tra center. Founded by Admiral David Farragut *c.* 185 inc. 1866. Pop. (1970) 71,710.

Valletta, seaport and capital of Malta, located on N coast of the island; site of Cathedral of San Giovan (1576) and Royal University of Malta (1769); heav damaged during WWII; tourist area. Port was bu and named after Jean Parisot de La Valette, grand master of Knights of Malta. Pop. 15,547.

Valley, an elongate, gently sloping depression of the Earth's surface, commonly situated between mountains or hills. It often contains a stream or river that receives the drainage from the surrounding heights. A U-shaped valley was probably formed by a glacier, a V-shaped one by a stream. The term may also be applied to a broad generally flat area that is drained by a large river, like the Mississippi Valley. △252, 258.

Valley Forge, campsite 21mi (34km) north of Philadelphia where American soldiers under George Washington withstood the winter of 1777–78, living in log huts they built, with little food or clothing. The morale of the Americans reached its lowest point here.

Valley Stream, village in SE New York, on Long Island. Kennedy International Airport is W of village. Inc. 1925. Pop. (1970) 40,413.

Valois Dynasty, royal house of France (1328–1589). Valois kings survived challenges in the Hundred Years War (1337–1453) by England and by Burgundian and Armagnac rivals and consolidated royal strength over feudal lords. They established the crown's sole right to tax and to wage war and extended parlements throughout France. Louis XI (*r.* 1461–83) is considered the founder of French royal absolutism. After the death of Henry III (1589), the crown passed to the house of Bourbon.

Valparaíso, city in central Chile; capital of Valparaíso prov. Founded 1536, it was site of treaty signed 1884 by which Bolivia surrendered coastal region with nitrate deposits to Chile; heavily damaged by earthquakes 1906, 1971; principal seaport of Chile; cultural center; site of Chilean Naval Academy, technical university, Catholic university. Industries: chemicals, textiles, sugar, metal products. Pop. 238,557.

Valparaiso, city in NW Indiana, S of Lake Michigan; seat of Porter co; site of Valparaiso University (1859) and Valparaiso Technical Institute (1934). Industries: electrical lighting equipment, bearings, paint, varnish, magnets. Settled 1836; inc. 1856; chartered as city 1865. Pop. (1970) 20,020.

Value Added, in economics, value added to the product at each stage of production. A value-added tax taxes products at each stage based upon the value each stage adds to the total value of the product.

Valve, Engine, a device to control admission and rejection of intake and exhaust gases to the engine cylinder. △1632.

Valves (heart). △688.

Vampire, in legend, a corpse that lives at night and sucks the blood of the living to sustain itself. The victim in turn becomes a vampire. The monster can be killed by driving a wooden stake through its heart. Bram Stoker's *Dracula* (1897) drew on the legend of the vampire to produce a masterwork of horror.

Vampire Bat, small brown bat inhabiting tropical and subtropical America. It feeds only on fresh blood sucked from resting animals. Length: 3in (7.6cm). Family Desmodontidae. *See also* Bat.

Vanadinite, lead chlorovanadate [$Pb_5(VO_4)_3Cl$] found in upper zone of lead ore deposits. Hexagonal system prisms and needlelike masses. Resinous orange to brown; hardness 2.7–3; sp gr 7. Commercial source of vanadium.

Vanadium, metallic element (symbol V) of the first transition series, discovered in 1801. Chief ores are carnotite, patronite, and vanadinite. The metal is used in special steels and vanadium pentoxide is an important catalyst. Chemically it reacts with oxygen and other nonmetals at high temperature. Properties: at. no. 23; at. wt. 50.9414; sp. gr. 6.11 (18.7°C); melt. pt. 3,288°F (1,890°C); boil. pt. 6,116°F (3,380°C); most common isotope V^{51} (99.76%). *See also* Transition Elements. △1554.

Van Allen, James Alfred (1914–), US physicist, b. Mount Pleasant, Iowa. During World War II, he invented a radio proximity fuse. After the war he supervised experiments with German V-2 rockets, leading to research with space satellites and his discovery of the two zones of radiation encircling the Earth (commonly known as the Van Allen radiation belts).

Van Allen Radiation Belts, two belts of intense ionizing radiation that surround the Earth in the upper atmosphere, named for their discovery (1953) by US physicist James A. Van Allen. The belts contain particles carrying energies of from approximately 20,000 electron volts to several million electron volts. The inner belt, of protons, centers about 2,000mi (3,220km) above the equator; the outer belt, of electrons, centers at about 11,000mi (17,710km). △96, 168.

Vanbrugh, John (1664–1726), English architect. He was also a dramatist and soldier, who worked with and was influenced by Christopher Wren. His greatest achievement was the design of Blenheim, the monumental palace given to the duke of Marlborough.

Van Buren, Martin (1782–1862), 8th president of the United States (1837–41), b. Kinderhook, N.Y. In 1807 he married Hannah Hoes; they had four sons. He was admitted to the bar in 1803 and soon entered politics, rising to become an important Democratic leader in New York State. After 1824 he was a close political associate of Andrew Jackson, and Jackson chose him as his running mate in 1832. After four years as vice president the Democrats chose Van Buren as their presidential candidate in 1836.

After winning the presidency in a landslide, Van Buren attempted to continue the Jacksonian policies. The Panic of 1837, however, was blamed on his administration, and his effectiveness suffered. The Independent Treasury System was inaugurated during his term. He was defeated for reelection in 1840 by the Whig candidate, William Henry Harrison. He made two later attempts at the presidency: in 1844 on the Democratic ticket again and in 1848 as head of the Free-Soil party.

Career: New York State Senate, 1813–20, New York attorney general, 1815–19; US Senate, 1821–28; governor of New York, 1829; secretary of state, 1829–31; vice president, 1833–37; president, 1837–41. *See also* Free Soil Party.

Vancouver, George (1757–98), English navigator and explorer. First sailing on exploratory expeditions under Captain James Cook, he was made commander of his own expedition in 1791 and ordered to survey the NW coast of North America and search for a passage from the Pacific to Hudson Bay. He made a detailed survey and found no northern passage to the east, returning by going around Cape Horn in 1794. His journals were published as *A Voyage of Discovery to the North Pacific Ocean and Round the World* (3 vols., 1798).

Vancouver, seaport city in S British Columbia, on S shore of Burrard Inlet; 3rd-largest city in Canada; industrial center of British Columbia, and major port on the Pacific Ocean. First explored 1792 by Capt. George Vancouver aboard the *Discovery;* the first European settlement was est. 1865 as Granville; devastated by forest fire 1886; developed rapidly after completion of transcontinental railroad 1887, Panama Canal 1914. It is the site of annual Vancouver Festival of the Arts (since 1958), Stanley Park, University of British Columbia (1890), Anglican Theological College of British Columbia (1912), Saint Paul's College (1926), Union College of British Columbia (1927), Saint Mark's College (1956), Saint Andrew's Hall (1957), Carey Hall (1960), Simon Fraser University (1963). Exports: forest products, grain, fish and fish products. Industries: lumber, plywood, pulp and paper, shingles, tourism, food processing, chemicals, fishing, shipyards, meat packing. Founded 1881; inc. 1886 as Vancouver. Pop. 422,278.

Vancouver, port city in SW Washington, 8mi (13km) N of Portland, Oregon, on Columbia River; seat of Clark co; important fur center in 19th century; site of Vancouver Barracks (est. 1848, now seat of Oregon Military District), Ulysses S. Grant's house (1852–53) while he was stationed here. Industries: shipyards, lumber, grain elevators, fruit, furniture, wood products. Founded 1824 as Hudson's Bay Co. Post; inc. 1857. Pop. (1970) 42,493.

Vancouver Island, island off SW British Columbia, Canada, in the Pacific Ocean; largest island off W North America; known for its fine harbors, especially Nootka Sound, on inlet on the W coast discovered by Capt. James Cook 1778. Disputed by Spain and Great Britain, the island was chartered 1792 by Capt. George Vancouver; made a British crown colony 1849; became part of British Columbia 1866; site of Pacific Rim National Park and Strathcoma Provincial Park. Industries: lumbering, wood, fishing, tourism, mining. Area: 12,408sq mi (32,137sq km). Pop. 360,000.

Vanda, genus of orchids native from China to N Australia and popular with orchid fanciers. They have leathery leaves and sprays of small flowers. There are many varieties including *V. sanderiana* with 5in

Vaduz, Liechtenstein

Rudolph Valentino

Martin Van Buren

Vancouver, British Columbia

(12.7cm) pink and yellow flowers; *V. tricolor* with fragrant yellow and brown-spotted flowers; and *V. coerulea*, one of the few blue orchids. Height: to 3ft (0.9m). Family Orchidaceae.

Vandals, an ancient Germanic people. About AD 170 they migrated from the Baltic shore to the Hungarian plain. Moving westward, they crossed the Rhine in 406 and continued on to Spain. In North Africa, under the leadership of Gaiseric, they set up their own kingdom. They sacked Rome in 455. △1054.

Van de Graaff Generator, or electrostatic generator, high-voltage source, used as the voltage supply for a type of electrostatic accelerator (the Van de Graaff accelerator). Positive (or negative) charges, sprayed from a set of high-voltage points onto a moving belt, are conveyed into a large hollow metal sphere to which the charges are carried by a second set of points. As charge accumulates on the outside, the voltage of the sphere increases to many millions of volts. △1530.

Vanderbilt, Cornelius (1794–1877), US railroad owner and financier, b. Staten Island, N.Y. Beginning as a boy running a ferry service, he established a steamboat company (1829). He soon won control of most ferries in the New York City area and by 1846 was a millionaire. During the California gold rush (1849), he ran a shipping line between New York and San Francisco, crossing Nicaragua by land. He entered the transoceanic transportation business (1854), but then turned to railroads (1857). During the Civil War he built up a railroad empire by gaining control of existing railroads and in 1873, connected New York and Chicago by rail. His New York Central System had over 4,000 miles (6,440km) of track at the time of his death. △1278.

Van der Waals Forces, weak forces of attraction occurring between atoms and molecules. They result from interactions between dipole moments of adjacent molecules or, if there is no dipole moment, from mutual electrostatic interactions of the electrons and nuclei. Van der Waals forces, so called because they are responsible for the pressure correction term in the Van der Waals equation for an imperfect gas, are much weaker than chemical bonds and fall off sharply with increasing distance. They are the forces holding the molecules together in molecular crystals. △1506.

Van DeVanter, Willis (1859–1941), US jurist and lawyer. A Wyoming railroad attorney, assistant US attorney general (1897–1903), and US circuit court judge (1903–10), he was an associate justice of the US Supreme Court (1911–37). An ultra-conservative staunchly opposed to social welfare legislation, and New Deal measures, he wrote few opinions in his 26 years on the court.

Van Dieman's Land. △1260.

Vandyke, or **Van Dyck, Anthony** (1599–1641), Flemish painter. Best known for his elegant portraits of aristocrats, he also painted religious scenes and was an excellent etcher. He worked in Rubens' studio before traveling abroad, first to England in 1620. In Italy, 1621–27, he painted many portraits of the Genoese nobility. Charles I of England appointed him court painter and knighted him in 1632. His many portraits profoundly influenced 17th- and 18th-century portraiture and can be seen in most major museums.

Van Eyck, Hubert (*c.*1370–*c.*1426), Flemish painter. The only documentation of his artistic existence is an inscription on the Ghent Altarpiece, which he probably executed with his brother Jan. Two other panels are thought to be his: the "Annunciation" (New York City, Metropolitan Museum of Art) and "The Marys at the Tomb" (Rotterdam, Boymans-Van Beumingen Museum). It is probable that he collaborated with Jan on "The Last Judgment" (New York City, Metropolitan Museum of Art). △1136.

Van Eyck, Jan (c.1380–1441), Flemish painter. Often called the father of Flemish painting, he is considered one of the truly original painters of all time. Under his influence oil painting realized a new importance in the north. His earliest signed and dated work is the Ghent Altarpiece, a collaboration with his brother Hubert. "Leal Souvenir" (1432), a three-quarter profile of a head (probably a portrait of Gilles Binchois) established a style of portrait painting that was to remain standard for centuries. Other portraits that evidence his growing interest in light and shadow are "Incehall Madonna" and "Portrait of a Man in a Red Turban" (both 1433). His mastery of light is further developed in the masterpiece "The Arnolfini Marriage" (1434). "Portrait of a Goldsmith" shows softer shadowing. His last dated work is "Portrait of Margaret Van Eyck" (1439). △1136.

Vanga. △538.

Van Gogh, Vincent Willem (1853–1890), Dutch painter and draftsman. He was one of the first to discover the expressive value of color and, as such, was one of the first Expressionists. He did not begin to paint seriously until the 1880s, having clerked in an art gallery and attempted to serve as a self-styled missionary to the poor. His early masterpieces of expressionist flavor include "The Potato Eaters" (1885) and "Shoes with Laces" (1886). In 1887 he met the Impressionists and gradually began to adopt their style and subject matter. His most productive years were 1888 and 1889, when he began to find his own style, producing more than 200 works, including "L'Arlesienne," "The Postman Roulin," "Orchard in Blossom," and "View of Arles with Irises." In 1888 he began to suffer mental conflicts, and until the end of his life he was intermittently hospitalized. It was in an argument with Paul Gauguin in 1888 that van Gogh cut off his own ear. In 1890, while a patient in the hospital of St Remy, he shot himself. △1294

Vanguard. △1722.

Vanilla, climbing orchid found from Mexico to South America. The vines grow to 50ft (15.2m) and bear greenish-yellow flowers that produce long seed pods. The unripened seeds are the source of the vanillin of commerce, prepared by a fermenting process.

Vapor, a gas. The term is sometimes used to refer to a gas in equilibrium with its liquid phase. The pressure at which this occurs is called the vapor pressure. Vapor pressures always increase with temperature—when the vapor pressure equals the surrounding pressure, the substance boils. △1504.

Varanasi (Banaras), formerly Benares; city in N central India, 400mi (644km) WNW of Calcutta on the Ganges River. Considered the holiest city to the Hindus, it is a pilgrimage center with approx. 1,500 shrines, temples, and mosques; Buddha is reputed to have preached his first sermon nearby *c.* 7th century BC; most of the religious buildings date only from *c.* 17th century following Muslim invasion and destruction; site of Benares Hindu University (1916), Golden Temple, Mosque of Aurangzeb, Durga Kund temple housing numerous sacred monkeys. Industries: silk brocade, brassware. Pop. 637,612.

Varangians, Danish and Swedish raiders who invaded eastern Europe during the 9th and 10th centuries while Vikings raided western Europe. They opened routes that crossed Russia. One leader, Rurik, who settled at Novgorod in 862, is the legendary founder of Russia. In the 10th and 11th centuries, Varangians served as mercenaries to Constantinople's emperors and as soldiers to Slavic princes. They eventually merged with the Slavs. △1176.

Varèse, Edgard (1885–1965), French composer. △1364.

Variable, in statistics, item that may change or vary in the course of a particular discussion, unlike a *constant,* which maintains a given value throughout a particular discussion. An example of a variable would be the grade given to each student in a class of 25, which would change from student to student. The constant in this case would be the number of students in the class.

Variable Resistor. △1542.

Variable Star, star that shows regular or irregular fluctuations in brightness. Regular variables include the eclipsing variables and the pulsating stars of the Cepheid or RR Lyrae type. Irregular variables include the novae and the flare stars. Many stars of the red giant or red supergiant class, such as Alpha Orionis (Betelgeuse) or Mira Ceti, show long-period, semi-regular, or totally irregular variability. Except for eclipsing stars, variables are intrinsic, that is, their fluctuations are due to internal disturbances. △112–14.

Variation, a difference, arising either from heredity or environment, between two members of a species. The difference may be one that is passed on to successive generations, and therefore could be relatively permanent. *See also* Adaptation. △418, 420.

Varicella. *See* Chicken Pox.

Varicose Veins, veins that are torturous and distended with blood. They can occur anywhere in the body, but are usually found in the legs. Treatments include wearing elastic-type stockings and surgical stripping of the affected veins. △716.

Variola. *See* Smallpox.

Variscite, a phosphate mineral, hydrous aluminum iron phosphate found with aluminum-rich rocks near surface. Orthorhombic system. Glassy white to green; hardness 3.5–4.5; sp gr 2.5. Used in jewelry, it resembles turquoise, but is greener.

Varna, seaport city of E Bulgaria, on Black Sea, 182mi (293km) NE of Plovdiv; important port while under Turkish rule (1391); taken by Russia 1828; returned to Turkey 1829 by the Peace of Adrianople; ceded to Bulgaria 1878; during Crimean War (1854), it was the major naval base of British and French forces. Industries: textiles, flour, wine, furniture, ceramics, diesel engines, shipbuilding. Founded 580 BC. Pop. 206,297.

Varnish, a liquid preparation that dries by evaporation, forming a hard lustrous coating. Varnish is transparent unless pigments have been added, and serves for decoration and protection. It may be composed of natural or synthetic resins and a base of various oils or spirits.

Varro, Marcus Terentius Reatinus (116–27 BC), Roman scholar and author. △1780.

Varve, term applied to a layer of sediment deposited in a single year in a body of still water. Specifically a varve consists of two layers of sediment, a coarse layer deposited in the summer and a fine layer deposited in the winter in glacial meltwater lakes. Varves have been used to date the age of Pleistocene glacial deposits. △276.

Varying Hare. *See* Snowshoe Rabbit.

Vasa Dynasty (1523–1654), royal dynasty of Sweden. It was established after Gustav Eriksson, a relative of the Stures, revolted against Denmark in 1520, ending the union. He was elected king in 1523 and made Sweden into a national state, stabilized state finances, and confiscated property belonging to the Roman Catholic Church, thus leading to the Reformation in Sweden. The dynasty ended when Christina, daughter of Gustav II, abdicated in 1654.

Vasarely, Victor de (1908–), French painter. △1372.

Vasari, Giorgio (1511–74), Italian painter, architect, and art historiographer. He painted in the Mannerist style and was widely respected in his time, although he is now known mainly for his contributions as a sculptor. His history of Italian art (1550) is an important source of biographical and theoretical information.

Vascular Plant, or tracheophyte, plant with vessels or ducts to carry water and food materials within it. All higher plants—ferns, conifers, and flowering plants—have a vascular system (xylem and phloem). This system exists in roots, stems, and leaves, providing mechanical support and acting as a passageway from the soil. △430, 452.

Vasectomy, a method of sterilizing the male, in which the ductus (vas) deferens, through which the sperm pass to the ejaculatory duct of the testis, is totally or partially removed. △706.

Vasoconstrictor, a chemical compound causing constriction of blood vessels. Decongestants with hydrochlorides act as vasoconstrictors on nasal mucosa.

Vasodilator, compound that opens up blood vessels to permit freer flow of blood. Most frequently used are nitrite preparations to treat angina pectoris.

Vasopressin, or antidiuretic hormone, polypeptide product of the posterior pituitary. It acts on the kidneys to stimulate water and sodium retention; it also constricts blood vessels.

Vassal, in Western European feudalism, a free man who bound himself to another (the lord) by an oath of fealty for mutual protection and maintenance. In exchange for certain obligations, such as military service and loyalty, he would receive direct maintenance in the lord's household or a benefice or fief to work himself. The practice of vassalage is Roman in origin, but became prevalent in the 7th and 8th centuries in France as a result of political upheaval and economic instability. Vassalage became one of the main institutions of feudalism. *See also* Fealty; Feudalism.

Vastus Lateralis. △684.

Vastus Medialis. △684.

Vatican City, an enclave in Italy, 109acres (44hectares), within Rome. It is the smallest sovereign state in the world and is the official home of the pope and the center of the Roman Catholic Church with its own newspaper, railroad system, passports, and stamps.

People. Its population of 648 is mostly Italian and Swiss with citizenship given only to persons who either hold office or are employed in the Vatican, including apostolic delegates and the spiritual staff of the pope. Seventy countries send diplomatic representatives to the Holy See. Italian is the main language; official acts are written in Italian.

Government. Vatican City is governed by a combination of canon law, apostolic constitutions, and laws decreed by the pope.

History. Once a boggy swamp and a charioteers' burial ground, it was made a garden area by AD 59. Popes held sovereignty over mid-Italy (Papal States) until 1861 when conquests shifted much of the papal dominion to the Kingdom of Sardinia; the pope's sovereignty was confined to Rome. In a 1929 treaty, the Holy See and the Italian government agreed to full independence for the Vatican, gave the church special status, and provided compensation for lands taken.

Vatican Council, First (1869–70), 20th ecumenical council of the Roman Catholic Church. Convened by Pope Pius IX to deal with certain contemporary problems, such as rising liberalism and rationalism, the Council is perhaps best remembered for its declaration of papal infallibility, causing widespread protest and minor secessions from the Church. It was cut short by the interference of Italian troops.

Vatican Council, Second, also **Vatican II** (1962–65), 21st ecumenical council of the Roman Catholic Church under Popes John XXIII and Paul VI. Designed to reform and revitalize the Church, the Council redefined the duties of bishops, the relationship of the Catholic to other churches, and the nature of the priesthood and the mass. It condemned anti-Semitism while calling for Christian reunion.

Vaud, canton in W Switzerland; Lausanne is the capital; conquered by Bern and forced to accept the Reformation; independent canton of Leman (1798); joined Switzerland 1803; agricultural area. Area: 1,240sq mi (3,212sq km). Pop. 511,851.

Vaughan Williams, Ralph (1872–1958), English composer. △1364.

VD. *See* Venereal Disease.

Veal. △378.

Veblen, Thorstein Bunde (1857–1929), US economist b. Manitowoc co, Wis. He originated the institutionalist school of economics, studying the economy as a whole while emphasizing institutions and their role in the economic system. His two most famous books are *The Theory of Leisure Class* (1899) and the *Theory of Business Enterprise* (1904).

Vector, quantity that has both a magnitude and a direction, as contrasted with a scalar. For example, to specify the velocity of a body, one must give its speed (how fast it is moving) and the direction in which it is moving. Similarly, a force has both magnitude and direction. Mass is a scalar, but weight (the force of gravity on a body) has a magnitude that depends on the body's mass and position in relation to the Earth's center and a direction corresponding to the direction of the Earth's gravitational field at that position. In mathematics, the concept of a vector is generalized to any number of dimensions, and vectors are treated as special cases of tensors. *See also* Scalar.

Vector, in disease, any agent that carries an infectious agent from one host to another. It may be an insect such as a mosquito or flea, or an inanimate object. It also may serve as an intermediate host for the infectious agent.

Vector Analysis, study of the mathematical properties of vectors. Vectors can be added by the parallelogram law: the result of adding two vectors is the diagonal of a parallelogram formed with the two vectors as adjacent sides. Multiplication of a vector by a scalar *a* gives a vector with the same direction but its magnitude multiplied by *a*. Two vectors can also be multiplied, and this may occur in two ways. The scalar, or dot, product of vectors **a** and **b** (written **a.b**) is a scalar given by $ab \cos \theta$, θ being the angle between the vectors and *a* and *b* being their magnitudes (note that symbols for vectors are usually printed in boldface type). For example, work is the scalar product of force and distance. The vector, or cross product, (written **a** − **b**) is a vector given by $ab \sin \theta$, directed at right angles to the plane of **a** and **b.** The force on a moving charged particle in a magnetic field is the vector product of field strength and current. Rules also exist for differentiation and integration of vectors. △1488.

Vedas, ancient sacred books of the Hindus. There are four Vedas: the *Rigveda,* containing priestly tradition originally brought to India by the Aryans; the *Atharvaveda;* the *Samaveda;* and the *Yajurveda.* Each of the four Vedas contains: *Samhitas* or basic verses; *Brahamanas,* rituals and explanations of rituals; and *Upanishads,* philosophical commentaries. The Vedas were composed over a long period, starting around *c.*1500–900 BC. *See also* Hinduism. △848.

V-E Day (May 8, 1945), the day World War II ended in Europe. The Germans surrendered unconditionally to the United States, England, France, and the USSR.

Veery, thrush of E North America with a reddish-brown back and spotted chest. Species *Turdus fuscescens. See also* Thrush.

Vega, or Alpha Lyrae, white main-sequence star in the constellation of Lyra. Characteristics: apparent mag. 0.03, absolute mag. 0.3; spectral type A0; distance 26 light-years. △110.

Vegetable. △330–36.

Vegetative Reproduction, or vegetative propagation, form of asexual reproduction in higher plants where a piece (leaf, root, stem) of a multicellular organism gives rise to an entire organism. It may occur naturally, as strawberries reproducing by runners, or artificially, as a house plant cutting yielding a new plant. △456.

Vein, blood vessel that carries blood to the heart. The pulmonary vein carries oxygenated blood to the lungs, but all other veins carry deoxygenated, usually dark purplish, blood from the capillaries back to the heart. The vein walls are thinner than arterial walls, lie closer to the surface, and are not so elastic since blood moves sluggishly, not pulsating. *See also* Artery. △688.

Velázquez, Diego Rodríguez de Silva y (1599–1660), Spanish painter. He is the most representative of the Baroque 17th-century painters. His early genre works (1617–22) include "The Old Cook" and "The Water Carrier of Seville." In 1623 he became court painter to Philip IV, and throughout his career painted many royal portraits. He also executed many portraits of dwarfs and jesters in a sensitive and compassionate manner. "Don Sebastian de Morra" is typical of these psychological portraits. One of his finest works is the portrait of Pope Innocent X (*c.*1650), considered to be one of the greatest portraits in existence. His later works began to merge reality and illusion and include "The Hilanderas" (*c.*1644–48) and "Las Meninas." Velázquez influenced many generations of artists and is still considered one of the finest of all portrait painters. △1124, 1164.

Veldelinus. △56.

Velocino Bicycle. △1688.

Velocity, rate of change of a body's position. Average velocity $\bar{\mathbf{v}}$ of a body moving from position $\mathbf{x}_1$ to $\mathbf{x}_2$ in a time t is $\bar{\mathbf{v}} = (\mathbf{x}_2 - \mathbf{x}_1)/t$. The instantaneous velocity $\bar{\mathbf{v}}$ of the body is the value approached by $\bar{\mathbf{v}}$ as t becomes small. As a vector, velocity has a direction associated with it; the magnitude of the velocity is called the speed and has no associated direction. △1486, 1492–94.

Velvet Ant. △502.

Velvet Worm. *See* Peripatus.

Vendetta, private family blood feud, characteristic of the Italian Middle Ages and persisting in modern southern Italy. The obligation of kin to avenge wrong done to a relative, the vendetta usually occurs in circumstances in which the family is the only social unit able to ensure security and the state is considered unable or, because of either its insufficient development or perceived disinterest, unwilling to perform equitable justice.

Veneers, thin layers of wood of uniform thickness (usually 1/40–5/16in (0.6–8mm). Most are cut in a lathe by rotating a log against a knife; that used for furniture is cut sheet by sheet from a log section. Logs intended for veneers are softened first in hot water or steam. After production, veneer is dried in a kiln. In addition to furniture, veneers are used for plywood and containers.

Cornelius Vanderbilt

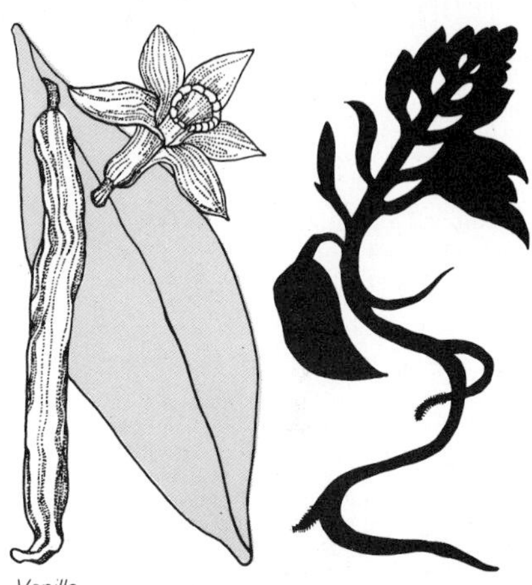

Vanilla

Vatican City

Diego Velazquez: Old Lady Cooking Eggs

Venera. △64.

Venereal Disease, any of several unrelated diseases transmitted essentially by sexual intercourse. Most widespread are syphilis and gonorrhea. Chancroid, lymphogranuloma venereum, and granuloma inguinale are less common. △728.

Venetian School, Italian school of painting during the Renaissance. Centered in Venice, its art was notable for sumptuousness and radiance of color, a legacy from Byzantine art. Its adherents included the Bellinis, Titian, Giorgione, Guardi, and Tintoretto. △1142.

Venezia. *See* Venice.

Veneziano, Domenico. △1134.

Venezuela, independent nation in N Latin America. Its petroleum beds make Venezuela the world's fifth-largest oil producer and one of the wealthiest Latin American countries.

Land and economy. Geographically, the country is divided into four regions: the Orinoco River basin, the Andes Mts, Guyana Highlands, plains E and S of the Orinoco, and the N coastal zone bordering Lake Maracaibo, deep enough for ocean-going vessels. The Guyanan Highlands contain Angel Falls, the highest waterfall in the world. Venezuela includes 72 islands, the largest of which is Margarita, a center for pearl trade. Although 26% of the gross national product and 80% of the country's revenue comes from petroleum, foreign investors have been discouraged by government restrictions. Reversion of oil assets to the Venezuelan government will start in 1983. Next to oil, iron ore is the chief export, followed by coffee, cocoa, steel products, sugar, fish, and fruit. Agrarian reform has increased cultivated acreage and resettled 100,000 families on their own land. In Latin America, Venezuela ranks fourth in hydroelectric production. Tourism increases annually.

People. A country shifting from rural to urban, with a population descended from Spanish colonials and Indians, Venezuela also has post-WWII immigrants from Italy, Portugal, and Spain. Spanish is the official language, Roman Catholicism the dominant religion. Literacy is estimated at 80%. Education is free.

Government. The constitution adopted in 1961 guarantees freedom of religion and a strong central government elected by direct, universal suffrage. Voting is mandatory for all citizens over 18 years of age, and elections are supervised by a federal commission.

History. Christopher Columbus sighted Venezuela in 1498. It was under Spanish domination until 1810 when Simón Bolívar, Venezuela's native son and national hero, led a revolution for independence. Both in the 19th and 20th centuries it had an unstable history under dictators; Romulo Betancourt was the first elected president to serve his full term (1959–65). Since then regular elections have been held.

PROFILE

Official name: Republic of Venezuela
Area: 352,143sq mi (912,050sq km)
Population: 10,398,907
Density: 34per sq mi (13per sq km)
Chief cities: Caracas (capital); Maracaibo
Government: Democracy
Religion: Roman Catholic
Language: Spanish (official)
Monetary unit: Bolivar
Gross national product: $16,120,000,000
Per capita income: $1,357
Industries: petrochemicals, iron, paper products, canned fish, steel, textiles, tires, shoes, dairy products
Agriculture: coffee, cocoa, citrus fruits, sugar cane, rice, tobacco, bananas, cotton, corn, cattle
Minerals: petroleum, gold, copper, coal, salt, nickel, manganese, asbestos
Trading partners: United States, Federal Republic of Germany, Japan

Venezuelan Boundary Dispute, boundary controversy between Great Britain and Venezuela. The British Guiana-Venezuela boundary had been in dispute since the British took control of Guiana from the Dutch (1814). The conflict widened when gold was discovered in the area. The United States became involved (1895) when Secretary of State Richard Olney declared that the United States was allowed, by the Monroe Doctrine, to intervene in the settling of such conflicts in the Americas. The British agreed to the United States' suggestion that an independent commission determine the boundary. The boundary was decided in favor of Britain's claims (1899).

Venice (Venezia), city in NE Italy, 162mi (261km) E of Milan; capital of Venezia prov. and Veneto region. Built on 118 islands, it is separated by narrow canals in Lagoon of Venice; joined to mainland by bridge. Settled 5th century, it was a vassal of the Byzantine Empire through 10th century; its merchants traded in parts of E Mediterranean; defeated Genoa 1380. City reached its zenith 15th century; gradually declined and was ceded to Austria 1797; inc. by Napoleon 1805; united with Italy 1866. Venice is site of the Rialto Bridge (1588–91), cathedral of St Mark (begun 830), the Palace of the Doges (14th–15th century), the Academy of Fine Arts, numerous churches, palaces, and public gardens; gondolas and other boats are used for transportation. Industries: glass, tourism, shipbuilding, textiles. Pop. 367,832.

Venizelos, Eleutherios (1864–1936), a Greek statesman. In 1910 he became prime minister and expanded Greek territories during Balkan Wars and World War I. He clashed with Constantine in support of the Allies and resigned (1915). He was recalled and again dismissed but in 1917 took over the government under Alexander, and Greece entered the war on the Allied side. He negotiated for Greek interests at the Versailles peace conference but was voted out of office in 1920. From 1928–35 he was in and out of office as prime minister.

Venn Diagram, diagrammatical representation of the relations and operations between mathematical sets or logical statements (premises or conclusions). The sets or statements are drawn as geometrical figures, usually circles. In set theory, relations, such as subset of a set, are shown by the relative positions of the circles. Operations, such as union or intersection, are indicated by shaded and nonshaded areas. A similar use of the circles is made in logic. *See also* Euler Diagram. △854, 1458.

Venom, Snake, toxic substance produced in the poison glands of snakes and injected into their victims through ducts in their fangs. Most venoms are dangerous and can be lethal unless counteracted by immune serum. Three types of toxin are present in venoms, the preponderance of each depending on the type of snake. Cobras produce neurotoxins that paralyze the nerve centers controlling breathing, the rattlesnake produces both hemolysins (toxins that dissolve the red blood cells) and hemotoxins (toxins that cause hemorrhage by perforating the blood vessels). Some venoms also contain substances that coagulate the blood; others contain anticoagulants. △520.

Ventricle, either of the two bottom chambers of the 4-chambered heart. *See* Heart.

Ventura, city in SW California, 23mi (37km) SE of Santa Barbara; seat of Ventura co; site of San Buenaventura mission founded in 1782. Official name of the city is San Buenaventura. Industries: food packing, oil products, clothing, electronic research. Inc. 1866. Pop. (1970) 57,964.

Venules. △662.

Venus, second planet from the Sun and almost as large as Earth. It has no satellite. Its dense atmosphere is largely carbon dioxide. Mean distance from the Sun, 67,200,000mi (108,190,000km); mass and volume, 0.82 and 0.88 times that of Earth respectively; diameter, 7,500mi (12,100km); rotation period, about 243 days; sidereal period of revolution, 224.70 days; surface temperature, approx. 900°F (485°C). *See also* Solar System. △64, 150.

Venus, in Roman mythology, goddess of spring and fruitfulness. Later identified with the Greek Aphrodite, her name became synonymous with beauty and charm.

Venus's Flower Basket, sponge found in deep marine waters. Its long cylindrical skeleton is formed from separate silica spicules plus a latticed framework of silica. Length: 10in (25cm). Phylum Porifera; species *Euplectella aspergillum.* △506.

Venus of Willendorf. *See* Willendorf, Venus of.

Veracruz, port city in E Mexico, on the Gulf of Mexico; first Spanish colonial post in Mexico (1519); captured by US forces 1847 during Mexican War; occupied again by the United States (1914) during dispute which resulted in the resignation of Mexico's president, Victariano Huerta; site of railroad terminus, 18th-century parish church, bronze statue of former governor Manuel Gutierrez Tamora, colonial fortress of Santiago. Industries: textiles, tiles, shoes, chocolate. Pop. 242,351.

Verb, the part of speech indicating what action or state of being is described. The tense of the verb indicates the time of the action. Classifications: regular or irregular, transitive or intransitive, or linking.

Verbal Learning, area of study in experimental psychology concerned with how humans learn and remember information. *See also* Associationism; Memory. △778.

Verbena, genus of annual and perennial plants native to the Western Hemisphere. Some species are popular garden plants and have pink, white, or purplish flowers. Family Verbenaceae.

Vercingetorix (died 46 BC), leader of the Gauls who united the diverse Gallic tribes against Caesar's Roman armies in 52 BC. A brilliant strategist, he retreated before Caesar's forces, burning towns to destroy a source of supply for the Romans. He halted at the fortress of Alesia where Caesar encircled him, destroyed his Gallic reinforcements, and captured him. Vercingetorix was displayed in Caesar's triumph (46) and then executed. △1008.

Verdi, Giuseppe (1813–1901), Italian composer considered one of the greatest of operatic composers. His operas *Rigoletto* (1851), *Aïda* (1871), *La Traviata* (1853), and *Il Trovatore* (1852) are among the most frequently performed in all the operatic literature. He composed three operas based on Shakespeare: *Macbeth* (1847), and two masterpieces of his old age, *Otello* (1887) and *Falstaff* (1893). His *Requiem Mass* (1874) is also highly regarded. △1246, 1256.

Verdigris River, river in SE Kansas and NE Oklahoma; rises in E central Kansas; flows S across Oklahoma border to the Arkansas River, near Muskogee; used for irrigation. Length: 351mi (565km).

Verdin, titmouse found in the SW United States and N Mexico. It has a yellow head and throat, brownish-gray upperparts, and whitish underparts. It builds a globular nest with a tubular side entrance on a bush branch for its greenish eggs (15). Length: 4.5in (11.4cm). Family Paridae; species *Auriparus flaviceps.*

Verdun, city in S Quebec, Canada, on the St Lawrence River, on S shore of Montreal island; suburb of Montreal; site of Jean-Jacques Olier College (1951). Pop. 74,520.

Verdun, Battle of (Feb.-Sept., 1916), World War I battle at Verdun, an important fortress in NE France. The battle there was longest and bloodiest of World War I, with over 1,000,000 killed. A strong German offensive under Crown Prince Frederick William began on February 21. A British offensive relieved the pressure on Verdun and by December, France had recovered most of lost territory. Over 2,000,000 men fought at Verdun. △1304.

Verdun, Treaty of (843), treaty that partitioned Charlemagne's empire among his three grandsons, the sons of Emperor Louis I. It marked the end of political unity in Western Europe. Charles II (the Bald) received the western portion (France); Louis the German the eastern portion (Germany); and Lothair I the central portion (Low Countries, part of Germany and France, much of Italy). Lothair remained Holy Roman emperor.

Vergil, or **Virgil,** or **Publius Vergilius Maro,** (70–19 BC), Roman poet and the author of the *Aeneid,* the *Eclogues,* and the *Georgics.* Devoting his life solely to his poetry and related studies, he was nevertheless well informed about the current events of his age and was the friend of such men as Octavian and Gallus. Although Epicurean themes appear in his poetry, this trend is replaced by a stoic and neo-Pythagorean attitude. *See also* Aeneid; Eclogues. △1028.

Verlaine, Paul (1844–96), French poet. His early poetry, *Poèmes Saturniens* (1866) and *Fêtes galantes* (1869), shows the influence of Baudelaire. An intense relationship with Rimbaud broke up his marriage, and he was eventually imprisoned for shooting Rimbaud. While in jail (1874–76), he wrote *Romance sans paroles* (1874). Returning to Catholicism, his later poetry, such as *Sagesse* (1881) and *Jadis et naguère* (1884), deals with the conflict between the spiritual and the carnal.

Vermeer, Jan (1632–75), Dutch painter. Little is known of his life. His work seems to fall into three stages of style and development. The first (1655–60) is marked by a style close to early Italian Baroque and includes "The Procuress," "A Girl Asleep," and "Christ at the House of Mary and Martha." "Little Street in Delft," with its soft coloring, is typical of this period. His middle period marks his classic phase, in which his works often depict a single figure, marked by precise detail and naturalistic lighting. Works from this period include "Woman with a Red Hat" and "Head of a Young Girl." The third period is one in which Vermeer's style began to fail. His late works, of inferior quality, include "Allegory of the New Testament." In all, fewer than 40 works can be attributed to this great master, and only two can be authentically dated. △1168.

Vermiform Appendix. *See* Appendix.

Vermifuge, or **Anthelminthic,** agent that expels worms or parasites from the intestine. Some are toxic and diagnosis of specific parasite should be definite.

Vermont, state in the NE United States, in the New England region.

Land and economy. The N-S ranges of the Green Mts occupy most of the state. A plain lies along Lake Champlain, which forms most of the W boundary. The Connecticut River, along the E border, is the only river important to the state; it is legally in New Hampshire. Dairy farms are found along Lake Champlain and in mountain valleys through the state. Machine tool manufacturing is centered in Springfield. Marble quarries are operated around Rutland, and granite is extracted in the Barre region. Year-round sports facilities have made tourism a major source of income.

People. Vermont was settled by pioneers from other New England states. In the 19th century, numbers of Irish came to build railroads, and Italians, Scots, and Welsh to work the quarries. There is a strong French-Canadian element in the population. Only about 30% of the inhabitants live in urban areas.

Education. There are about 20 institutions of higher education. The University of Vermont and State Agricultural College are state-supported.

History. In 1609 the Frenchman Samuel de Champlain discovered the lake that bears his name, but the first permanent settlement was made in 1724 at Fort Drummer in the Connecticut Valley. After the French and Indian Wars ended in 1763, pioneers spread across the region. Land grant disputes with the colonies of New Hampshire and New York persisted for years. At the start of the Revolution, the Green Mountain Boys, an independent force led by Ethan Allen and Seth Warner, took Fort Ticonderoga and Crown Point on Lake Champlain. In 1777, Vermont declared its independence as the republic of New Connecticut and preserved this unrecognized status until its admission to the Union (1791); it was the first state outside the original 13 to be admitted. In the War of 1812, a fleet of small vessels built at Vergennes defeated the British on Lake Champlain. In the Civil War, Confederate agents operating from Canada robbed banks in St Albans in a raid in October 1864.

PROFILE

Admitted to Union: March 4, 1791; rank, 14th
US Congressmen: Senate, 2; House of Representatives, 1
Population: 444,732 (1970); rank, 48th
Capital: Montpelier, 8,609 (1970)
Chief cities: Burlington, 38,633; Rutland, 19,293; Bennington, 14,586
State legislature: Senate, 30; House of Representatives, 150
Area: 9,609sq mi (24,887sq km); rank, 43rd
Elevation: Highest, 4,393ft (1,340m), Mt Mansfield; lowest, 95ft (28.9m), Lake Champlain
Industries (major products): machine tools, stone products, lumber, furniture
Agriculture (major products): dairy products, maple syrup and sugar, apples
Minerals (major): marble, granite, limestone, asbestos
State nickname: Green Mountain State
State motto: Freedom and Unity
State bird: hermit thrush
State flower: red clover
State tree: sugar maple

Vernal Equinox, equinox occurring when the Sun crosses the celestial equator, moving toward the northern hemisphere, on about March 21. The crossing point on the equator is the First Point of Aries, now actually situated in the constellation Pisces, which is the zero for the celestial coordinate right ascension. *See also* Equinox.

Verne, Jules (1828–1905), French adventure story writer. His early work was published in the magazine *Musée des Familles.* Verne's stories are characterized by fantastic settings and imaginary scientific voyages, and did much to establish science-fiction writing. They include *Journey to the Center of the Earth* (1864), *Twenty Thousand Leagues Under the Sea* (1870), and *Around the World in Eighty Days* (1873). *See also* Around the World in Eighty Days. △1722.

Vernier, Pierre (1580–1637) French mathematician. He spent the greater part of his life in the service of the king of Spain in the Low Countries and is remembered for his secondary scale subdividing a primary scale and thus providing a means (vernier scale) of making accurate measurements. △1464.

Vernier Rocket, small rocket used not for propulsion but for "fine-tuning" of a rocket's orbit. Types of vernier rockets include retrorockets, to slow craft; and attitude control jets, to correct orientation in space.

Vernon, town in N Connecticut, 12mi (19km) NE of Hartford. Industries: electronic components, silk screens, textiles, envelopes, paper boxes. Separated from E Windsor 1726; inc. 1808. Pop. (1970) 27,-237.

Verona, city in NE Italy, 92mi (147km) E of Milan, on the Adige River; capital of Verona prov. Captured by Rome 89 BC, it was a free commune by 12th century; prospered under della Scala family 13th–14th centuries; annexed to Milan 1387, to Venice 1405–1797; held by Austria 1797–1866, when it joined Italy. Verona is site of Roman amphitheater (AD 1st century), church of St Zeno Maggiore (9th–15th centuries), Gothic tombs of the Scaligeri family. Industries: agriculture, textiles, chemicals, paper, printing, wine. Pop. 254,862.

Veronese (Caliari), Paulo (1528–88), Venetian painter and decorator. His earliest dated work is "Christ Among the Doctors" (1548). His mature works include the well-known frescoes at Maser, his largest villa decoration. In 1562 and 1563 he executed a number of large banquet scenes, including "Marriage at Cana," the "Family of Darius before Alexander," and "Cuccina Family Presented to the Virgin," often considered his finest work. A later work is the series for the ceiling of Sala del Collegio, containing the famous allegorical "industry." △1142.

Veronica, or speedwell, widely distributed genus of annual and perennial plants with small white, blue, or violet flowers, usually in clusters. Height: 3in–5ft (7.6–153cm). Family Scrophulariaceae; genus *Veronica. See also* Figwort.

Verrazano, Giovanni da (1480?–1527), explorer in the service of France, b. Florence, Italy. He explored the Atlantic Coast of North America (1524), discovering the Hudson River and Manhattan Island. He may have been hanged as a pirate by the Spanish.

Verrocchio, Andrea del (1435–88), Florentine sculptor, goldsmith, and painter, b. Andrea di Michele di Francesco di Cioni. He is believed to have been a pupil of Donatello. Although an emphasis on surface finish and elaborate detail prevented his works from achieving the power and monumentality, his finest works are imbued with an easy, rhythmic elegance. Among his sculptural works are the tombs of Piero and Giovanni de Medici in San Lorenzo and a "David" (1476) and "A Boy with a Dolphin" (*c.* 1480), both in Florence. △1138.

Versailles, city in N France, 10mi (16km) WSW of Paris; capital of Yvelines dept.; designed around palace built for Louis XIV, 1665–83. It served as the royal residence until 1793 when it was made a national historic museum. Set in a 20-acre (8-hectare) park, the palace contains king's and queen's apartments, famous Hall of Mirrors, museum of French history; magnificent formal French gardens, Swiss Lake, fountains, Grand Canal, and several outlying buildings complete this magnificent estate. It served as German headquarters during Franco-Prussian War (1870–71); scene of signing of Treaty of Versailles, June 28, 1919, ending WWI. City is also site of Cathedral of St Louis (1743–54). Industries: tourism, metalworks, footwear, brandy. Pop. 90,829. △1170.

Versailles, Treaty of (1919), treaty formally ending World War I. The leading figures at the conference were US Pres. Woodrow Wilson, Britian's David Lloyd George, France's Georges Clemenceau, and Italy's Emanuele Orlando. It represented a compromise between Wilson's Fourteen Points and the demands of Britain, France, Italy, and the other Allies for reparations from Germany. It permanently demilitarized and created a triple defense alliance against Germany. It made the former German colonies mandates of the League of Nations; gave Poland a Baltic corridor and Yugoslavia, the Port of Fiume; and created the League of Nations. The Treaty was never ratified by the United States. High reparations levied against Germany in the Treaty contradicted Wilson's program and the newly created League depended on its members' voluntary military support for effectiveness. Based largely on his anti-treaty stand, Warren G. Harding won the 1920 presidential election and made a separate peace with Germany 1921. *See also* Fourteen Points. △1306–08, 1336.

Versification, literally the art or practice of compos-

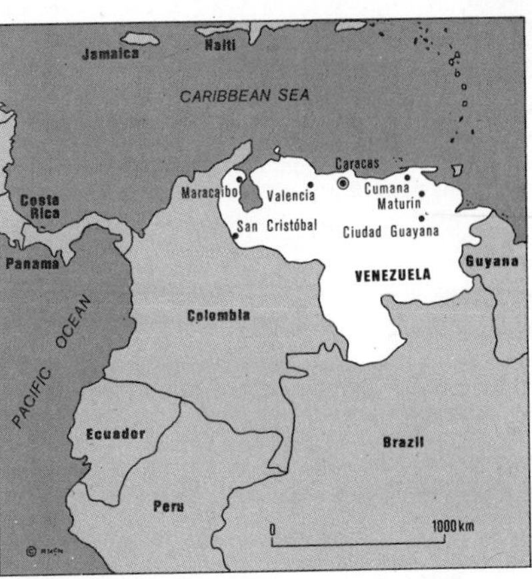
Jamaica
Haiti
CARIBBEAN SEA
Caracas
Maracaibo
Valencia
Cumana
Maturin
Costa Rica
San Cristóbal
Ciudad Guayana
Panama
Guyana
VENEZUELA
Colombia
PACIFIC OCEAN
Ecuador
Brazil
Peru
0
1000km
Venezuela

Venice, Italy: St. Mark's Cathedral

Bennington Battle Monument, Vermont

Versailles, France

ing metrical lines. The terms *verse* and *poetry* are often used interchangeably. When distinctions are made, however, verse is characterized by structure and form, poetry by intensity of feeling and imaginative power. Versification applies particularly to the application of such technical aspects as rhythm, meter, stanzaic pattern, number of syllables in each line, and the distribution of vowels and consonants. The study of versification, especially in its metrical structure, is called prosody. *See also* Meter; Poetry.

Vertebra, one of the small bones making up the vertebral column, also known as the spinal column, or spine. Each vertebra is composed of three parts: a large solid body from the top of which winglike transverse processes project to either side. Behind the body is an opening (vertebral formaen) through which the spinal cord passes, roofed by the spinous and auricular processes of the vertebrae. *See also* Spine. △682.

Vertebrate, animals that have individual disks of bone or cartilage called vertebra surrounding or replacing the embryonic notochord to form a jointed backbone. The head-end of the chordate nerve tube is enlarged into a brain, and the attendent sense organs of smell, taste, sight, hearing, and balance are correspondingly complex. The principal division is between the aquatic, fishlike forms (several extinct and living classes) and the partially (amphibians) and wholly (reptiles, birds, mammals) land-adapted forms.

Four-legged vertebrates are called tetrapods and those with fluid-filled embryonic membranes that permit development on land, amniotes. Birds and mammals are the only vertebrates with circulatory, respiratory, and excretory systems allowing for constant high body temperatures and levels of activity. Their brains and behavior are correspondingly the most complex. Phylum Chordata; subphylum Vertebrata. *See also* Amphibia; Bird; Chordate; Fish; Mammal; Reptile. △508–554, 612.

Vertigo, condition characterized by dizziness and nausea, attributable to disruption of the functions of equilibrium organs. Vertigo may be produced by rapid body rotation, several diseases, or brain disorder.

Verwoerd, Hendrik Frensch (1901–66), South African prime minister. He studied in Germany and later wrote anti-foreign editorials in South Africa. A nationalist, he held a number of government offices and became prime minister in 1958. An ardent segregationist, he led South Africa out of the British Commonwealth (1961) and was later assassinated.

Vesey Slave Plot (1822), attempted slave insurrection. It was led by Denmark Vesey, a freed black slave who had become influential in the Charleston, S.C., area. Under cover of church meetings, Vesey, a preacher, met with his followers and planned an uprising. The plot was revealed by an informer and the conspirators were all caught. Vesey and about 35 others were hanged, although he maintained his innocence.

Vespasian (AD 9–79), Roman emperor (69–79). He commanded in Germany (42) and Britain (43), was made consul (51), served as governor of Judea under Nero, and conducted the war against the Jews (66). His soldiers proclaimed him emperor when Nero died. He improved Rome's financial state, built the temple of Pax and the Colosseum, and romanized Britain with Agricola (78–79). His son Titus acted as coruler with him in 71. △1020.

Vespid Wasp. △492, 502.

Vespucci, Amerigo (1451–1512), Italian navigator and explorer. His name was given to America by Martin Waldseemuller, who translated Vespucci's account of his voyages. After service under the Medici, Vespucci made several expeditions along coast of Central and South America (1497–1503) in the service of Spain. He developed a method for computing nearly exact longitude.

Vesta, in Roman religion, goddess of the hearth, identified with the Greek goddess Hestia and associated with the primitive fire deities Cacus and Caca. Vesta was assured of a prominent place in both family and state worship. As goddess of the hearth fire, she was the patron deity of bakers. Her shrine was in the Forum. △78.

Vestal Virgins, in ancient Rome, the priestesses of the cult of Vesta who tended the sacred fire and officiated at ceremonies in the goddess' honor. The Vestals remained in the service of the temple for 30 years under vows of absolute chastity and were punished severely for breaking those vows. They did, however, enjoy great prestige in the social order of Rome.

Vestigial Organ, organ or part of an organ in a plant or animal that is useless and undersized. It was functional at some time in the past and serves as evidence for evolution.

Vesuvio. *See* Vesuvius, Mount.

Vesuvius, Mount (Vesuvio), active volcano in S Italy, on the Bay of Naples; villages and vineyards are located on lower fertile slopes; site of numerous eruptions of varying intensity, especially AD 79 when Pompeii and Herculaneum were destroyed; height changes with each eruption; site of seismological observatory. Height: 4,203ft (1,282m).

Vetch, annual and perennial plants native to temperate and warm areas of the world. Most are tendril climbers and many are grown for food, green manure, or forage. Family Leguminosae; genus *Vicia*. *See also* Bean.

Veterans Administration (VA), independent federal agency. It administers laws covering a wide range of benefits for former members and dependents and beneficiaries of deceased former members of the US armed forces. The VA also provides benefits to members of the armed forces and to dependent children of seriously disabled veterans. Some of the benefits include health care, insurance, pensions, rehabilitation, and education. The VA was established in 1930, consolidating several agencies.

Veterinary Medicine, medical science of prevention, diagnosis, and treatment of animal diseases and disorders. It was practiced by the Babylonians and Egyptians 4,000 years ago. Late in the 18th century, schools of veterinary medicine were established in Europe. Public health aspects have focused on zoonoses, diseases transmitted to humans by vertebrate animals. △370.

Veto, presidential power to reject legislation. If the president vetoes a bill, it is returned to Congress, where a two-thirds vote of each house is needed to override the veto. The president may also stop legislation by a "pocket veto." If he refuses either to sign or veto a piece of legislation, it will take effect after 10 days of congressional session. If the Congress adjourns before the end of the 10-day period, the legislation is dead.

Viborg, town in N Denmark, on Lake Viborg; capital of Viborg co; pagan religious center in pre-Christian era; site of cathedral (1130). Industries: textiles, brewing, tobacco, machinery. Pop. 25,468.

Viburnum, genus of flowering shrubs and trees native to North America and Eurasia. All have small, fleshy fruits containing single flat seeds. Flowers are small, fragrant, and clustered. Many are cultivated as ornamentals. Well-known species are wayfaring tree, hobblebush, black haw, arrowwood, highbush cranberry, and snowball. There are 200 species. Family Caprifoliaceae.

Vicenza, industrial city in NE Italy, 40mi (64km) W of Venice; capital of Vicenza province; seat of a Lombard duchy. Est. as free commune and member of Lombard League 12th century, it was taken by Venice 1404; held by Austria 1797–1866, until united with Italy; site of the Loggia del Capitanio, Teatro Olimpico (1580–83), Palazzo Chiericato, designed by Andrea Palladio (1508–80). Industries: machinery, chemicals, food processing, printing, agriculture. Pop. 111,-211.

Vice President of the United States, second-highest federal official. He is first in line to succeed to the presidency and does so in the event of death, resignation, physical disability, or removal by impeachment of the president. Although not a member, he presides over the Senate and may vote in the case of a tie, although he cannot participate in debates or committees. He participates in cabinet meetings and is a member of the National Security Council. He is elected on the same ticket as the president to serve a four-year term. He is dependent on the president for extraconstitutional responsibilities and, traditionally, is chosen to balance the ticket and for party appeasement or reward. If the office becomes vacant, the president, with the consent of Congress, chooses another vice president.

VICE PRESIDENTS OF THE UNITED STATES

John Adams (1789–97)
Thomas Jefferson (1797–1801)
Aaron Burr (1801–05)
George Clinton (1805–12)
Elbridge Gerry (1813–14)
Daniel Tompkins (1817–25)
John C. Calhoun (1825–32)
Martin Van Buren (1833–37)
Richard M. Johnson (1837–41)
John Tyler (1841)
George M. Dallas (1845–49)
Millard Fillmore (1849–50)
William R. King (1853)
John C. Breckinridge (1857–61)
Hannibal Hamlin (1861–65)
Andrew Johnson (1865)
Schuyler Colfax (1869–73)
Henry Wilson (1873–75)
William A. Wheeler (1877–81)
Chester A. Arthur (1881)
Thomas A. Hendricks (1885)
Levi P. Morton (1889–93)
Adlai E. Stevenson (1893–97)
Garret A. Hobart (1897–1899)
Theodore Roosevelt (1901)
Charles W. Fairbanks (1905–09)
James S. Sherman (1909–12)
Thomas R. Marshall (1913–21)
Calvin Coolidge (1921–23)
Charles G. Dawes (1925–29)
Charles Curtis (1929–33)
John N. Garner (1933–41)
Henry A. Wallace (1941–45)
Harry S. Truman (1945)
Alben W. Barkley (1949–53)
Richard M. Nixon (1953–61)
Lyndon B. Johnson (1961–63)
Hubert H. Humphrey (1965–69)
Spiro T. Agnew (1969–73)
Gerald R. Ford (1973–74)
Nelson A. Rockefeller (1974–77)
Walter F. Mondale (1977–)

Viceroy Butterfly, large butterfly that has orange brown wings with black veins and borders, noted fo its mimicry of the monarch butterfly. The viceroy car be distinguished from the monarch by its smaller size and a transverse black band on its hind wings. Specie *Limenitis archippus*. *See also* Monarch Butterfly. △502.

Vichy Government (1940–44), collaborationis government of France during World War II from it surrender to Germany to its liberation (1940–44) Under the 1940 armistice agreement, Vichy became the capital of unoccupied France, with Marshal Henr Pétain as premier. Vichy adherents included tradi tional anti-republicans still longing for pre-Revolution ary France and advocates of modern totalitarianism Despite the efforts of Pétain and his even more pro German vice-premier, Pierre Laval, to soften the effects of German occupation, most Frenchmen as sociated Vichy with capitulation to Germany and agreement to forced labor and payment of occupation costs. After 1942, German troops occupied all o France, leaving the government isolated from the ma jority, who supported the Free French movement o Charles de Gaulle or remained aloof from affairs o government.

Vicksburg, port city in W Mississippi, on the Missis sippi and Yazoo rivers; seat of Warren co; made US possession 1798; Rev. Newitt Vick est. mission 1812 scene of Vicksburg Campaign during Civil War, that resulted in complete Union control of Mississipp River. It is site of many antebellum homes, Vicksburg National Military Park (est. 1899), National Cemetery (est. 1865), US Water Experiment Station; headquar ters of US Mississippi River Commission. Industries lumber and lumber products, tourism, chemicals, fer tilizer, food products. Laid out 1819; inc. 1825. Pop (1970) 25,478.

Vicksburg, Siege of (1863), final act of Union Gen Ulysses S. Grant's long Western campaign. As the fal of Vicksburg (Miss.) would give the Union control o the Mississippi River, Confederate troops and civilians suffered greatly to hold this post but had to surrende on July 4. △1276.

Vico, Giovanni Battista (1668–1744), Italian histor ian and philosopher. Although he attended Jesui school and the University of Naples, he educated him self in the library of a family that he tutored. He was appointed royal historiographer for the new Kingdom of Naples (1735). *New Science* (1725, 1730, 1744) his monumental work, included the idea that histor had three stages: the age of the gods, the age o heroes, and the age of men. His ideas still exercise great influence on modern historians.

Victor Emmanuel I (1759–1824), duke of Savoy and king of Sardinia (1802–21). △1250.

Victor Emmanuel II (1820–78), king of Sardinia Piedmont (1849–61) and first king of united Italy (1861–78). Son and successor of Charles Albert, early in his reign he suppressed the republican left and from 1852 had Camillo Cavour lead his government to Italy's initial consolidation (1861). He also encouraged Giuseppe Garibaldi in the conquest of Sicily and Naples (later part of united Italy). He acquired Venetia in 1866 and Rome in 1870.

Victor Emmanuel III (1869–1947), king of Italy (1900–46), and father of Italy's last monarch, Umberto II. His failure to oppose Benito Mussolini's Fascists in 1922 immediately precipitated Mussolini's seizure of power, and the king became a figurehead. Following Italian military losses, in 1943 he had Mussolini arrested; but with Italy still in difficulty in 1946, he abdicated and a plebiscite established the Italian Republic.

Victoria (1819–1901), queen of Great Britain and Ireland (1837–1901), empress of India (1876–1901). She was the daughter of George III's fourth son, Edward, duke of Kent, and Victoria of Saxe-Coburg. She succeeded William IV to the throne and demonstrated her political acuity by engineering the return as prime minister of Lord Melbourne, her friend and advisor (1839). She married her first cousin, Prince Albert of Saxe-Coburg-Gotha (1840), and had nine children. Pro-Germanic and influenced by Albert in state affairs, she supported the more conservative ministers such as Melbourne and Benjamin Disraeli (who had her crowned empress of India) and particularly disliked William Gladstone's policy for Irish Home Rule. She founded the Victoria Cross (1857) during the Crimean War. She took an active part in state affairs, apart from a period of three years after Albert's death (1861–64), and her reign heightened respect for the monarchy. △1262.

Victoria, city in British Columbia, Canada, on SE Vancouver Island; capital, largest city, and chief port of British Columbia; developed during 1858 gold rush as supply base for gold miners; site of the University of Victoria (1902), Royal Roads College (1942), Dominican Astrophysical Observatory; Pacific headquarters of Canadian navy; resort area. Industries: lumber, shipbuilding, fish processing, deep-sea fishing. Founded 1843; became capital 1868. Pop. 60,897.

Victoria, city in S Texas, 125mi (201km) NE of Houston, on Guadalupe River; site of Victoria College (1925), Annunciation College (1959). Industries: aluminum, chemicals, ranching, farming, oil, gas. Settled 1824; inc. 1839. Pop. (1970) 41,349.

Victoria, Lake (Victoria Nyanza), lake in E central Africa; S half is in Tanzania and N half is in Uganda: Indented coastline of 2,000mi (3,200km) provides numerous gulfs and harbors for coastal towns. Lake is the chief reservoir of the Nile River; rainfall is its major water source. The second largest freshwater lake in the world, it supports much of the area's fishing industry. Depth: 265ft (81m). Area: 26,828sq mi (69,485sq km).

Victoria Crowned Pigeon. △538.

Victoria de Durango. *See* Durango.

Victory (Michelangelo). △1150.

Victory (Nike) of Samothrace (Winged Victory), heroic marble statue. △1002.

Vicuña, graceful, even-toed, hoofed South American mammal found in grasslands of Andes Mountains. It resembles the llama and its silky coat is tawny brown with a yellowish bib under the neck. Its lower incisors, like those of rodents, have enamel on only one side and are constantly growing. The gestation period is 11 months with one young born. It can run 30mph (48kph) at high elevations. Height: 34in (86cm) at shoulder. Family Camelidae; species *Lama vicugna.* △548.

Videotape, a magnetic tape that records television signals. As the FM signals are directed through the heads of a videotape recorder, iron particles on the tape are magnetized. The signals are recovered in the reverse process when the tape passes through a reproducing head, and are then demodulated to produce the output signal. Videotape can be erased and reused. △1800.

Vienna (Wien), capital city of Austria, on the Danube River; occupied by the French during Napoleonic Wars (1805–09); after the defeat of Napoleon I, representatives of European powers met for the Congress of Vienna (1814–15). Vienna became the cultural and social center of 19th-century Europe under Emperor Francis Joseph I; suffered economic and political collapse following the defeat of Central Powers in WWI. Chancellor Engelbert Dollfuss established a dictatorship in 1933; in 1938 Hitler's armies invaded Vienna; occupied by joint Soviet-Western forces 1945–55, when Vienna became the free capital of the Second Austrian Republic. City contains St Stephen's Cathedral, the Hofburg (former residence of the Hapsburgs), Capuchin Church, the Winter Palace, Parliament, the State Opera House, Burgtheater, Museum of Art History, the Natural History Museum; also largest central European airport, and headquarters of the International Atomic Energy Agency since 1957; scene of US-USSR disarmament talks of 1970–71. Vienna has been home of composers Mozart, Beethoven, Brahms, and Schubert. Industries: petroleum, metallurgy, chemicals, textiles, furniture, clothing, leather. Settled by Celts; made Roman military station 1st century BC. Pop. 1,603,000.

Vienna, Congress of (1815), assembly of European leaders who reorganized Europe after the defeat of Napoleon. The essential provisions of the treaty lasted for almost a century. With elaborate care and mutual distrust, the four victors—England, Russia, Prussia, and Austria—(plus France) balanced power and territory in Europe, often at the expense of people whose territories were affected. France lost little except the Rhineland to Prussia; Austria received northern Italy; Poland was divided between Russia and Prussia. △1230.

Vientiane, administrative capital of Laos, in N central Laos, on the Mekong River; served as capital of Lao kingdom 1707–1827, when it was destroyed by the Siamese; passed to French 1893 and in 1899 became capital of French protectorate; site of canals, several pagodas, architectural museum, teachers' college, royal palace, railroad, international airport. Industries: textiles, hides, forest products. Pop. 150,000.

Vietcong, members of the National Liberation Front of South Vietnam. Formed in 1960 in South Vietnam by Le Duan, a Communist general from North Vietnam, its purpose was to arm and train the people of South Vietnam to overthrow the Diem regime and to eventually unite North and South Vietnam. *See also* Vietnam War.

Vietminh, League for the Independence of Vietnam, founded by Ho Chi Minh in 1941. They fought against the Japanese during World War II and proclaimed the Democratic Republic of Vietnam (North Vietnam) in Hanoi under Ho Chi Minh in 1945. They defeated the French at Dienbienphu in 1954 after eight years of warfare. They refused to accept the Diem regime of South Vietnam and began an insurgency that became the Vietnam War. *See also* Vietnam War. △1378.

Vietnam, independent nation in SE Asia. Under Chinese and then French influence for centuries, it was divided into two countries (North and South) in 1954 and was reunited in 1975 after the victory of the Communist forces in the S, assisted by the N.

Land and economy. Located in the Indochinese peninsula, Vietnam is bounded N by China, W by Laos and Cambodia, E and S by the Gulf of Thailand, Gulf of Tonkin, and the South China Sea. The country stretches N and S 1,000mi (1,600km); E and W it ranges from 330mi (531km) to 40mi (64km) at the center. Most of the N portion is a thick, mountainous jungle. In the heavily populated and cultivated Red River delta rice is the main crop. The climate is monsoonal with frequent floods. The S portion of Vietnam is dominated by a flat, marshy, muddy coast—the Mekong River system. Year-round tropical climate and rich soil yield abundant rice harvests. The provinces N and E are tropical rain forests and the rugged Annamite Mts. Industry and agriculture were stalled during the war years.

People. The heritage of more than 1,000 years of vassalage to the Chinese exists in language, art, importance of the family, knowledge, and age—the Confucian ethic. It is estimated that N Vietnam has 80%–90% ethnic Vietnamese and many Chinese, principally in the delta region. The S portion, once heavily rural, has several ethnic minorities: Chinese businessmen living in the delta section; Montagnard tribesmen, 30 tribes of farmers and hunters; and Khmers (Cambodians), farmers with a different language and culture. While scientific socialism is the official creed, Buddhist faith is tolerated, especially among the older generation. Approximately 10% of the people are Roman Catholic. Science and vocational training are emphasized in the government-controlled school system. Chinese and Russian are taught and literacy is estimated at 95% in the N, 65% in the S. Vietnamese is the official language.

Government. The government is Communist, with a Provisional Revolutionary Government in control in the S.

History. Originally dwellers in China's Yellow River valley, the Vietnamese were driven S and inhabited the Red River delta. They were under Chinese rule from the 2nd century BC to 939, when they revolted

Amerigo Vespucci

Vicuña

Vienna: State Opera House

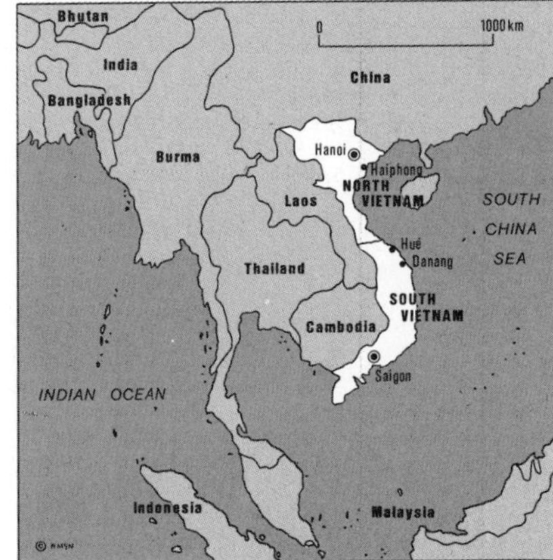
Bhutan
India
Bangladesh
0
1000km
China
Burma
Hanoi
Haiphong
NORTH VIETNAM
Laos
SOUTH CHINA SEA
Hué
Danang
Thailand
SOUTH VIETNAM
Cambodia
Saigon
INDIAN OCEAN
Indonesia
Malaysia

Vietnam

and founded their own empire. They remained independent until the mid-19th century when the French took control over Indochina—Vietnam, Laos, and Cambodia. Inspired by the success of the Chinese freedom drive under Sun Yat-sen, a nationalist movement in 1930 staged an uprising against the French. The same year Ho Chi Minh organized the Indochinese Communist party. Japan occupied all of Vietnam during WWII, and in 1945, with the war over, a Communist-led revolt in Hanoi proclaimed the Democratic Republic of Vietnam. Ho Chi Minh led the Communists in an eight-year guerrilla war against the French, who were defeated in 1954. Vietnam was divided at the 17th parallel into two countries, Communist N and nationalist S. Vague references to free elections and unification were mentioned in the cease-fire agreement. Ngo Dinh Diem, prime minister in the S, faced a ruined economy, refugee problems, and religious and political factions. The Communists established agrarian reform, rebuilt industries, and embarked on a campaign to overthrow the S. In 1961 the United States sent military advisors and the US role gradually escalated. The South Vietnamese government, backed by the United States, was unable to defeat the insurgent guerrillas, backed by North Vietnam. US air strikes against North Vietnam began in 1964 and US troops eventually numbered about 550,000. Strong US opposition to the war influenced the withdrawal of troops from 1969, when peace talks began. A cease-fire agreement was signed in Paris in 1973. Military pressure against South Vietnam continued, however, and in 1975 the Saigon regime collapsed and the country fell to the Communists. *See also* Vietnam War.

PROFILE

Official name: Democratic Republic of Vietnam
Area: 128,408sq mi (332,577sq km)
Population: 41,500,000
Density: 323per sq mi (125per sq km)
Chief cities: Hanoi (capital); Saigon; Danang; Haiphong; Hue
Government: Communist Republic
Religion: Taoism, Buddhism, Roman Catholicism
Language: Vietnamese
Monetary unit: Dong
Gross national product: $4,900,000,000
Industries: shellac, processed food, textiles, rubber products
Agriculture: rice, rubber, fish, forests, pepper, cattle, corn, tea, coffee, maize, sweet potatoes, tobacco, sugar cane, poultry
Minerals: coal, zinc, tin
Trading partners: USSR, People's Republic of China, Japan

Vietnamese, the national language of Vietnam, spoken by about 35,000,000 people there, or nearly 90% of the country's population. It is known to be related to a minor language of Vietnam called Muong, but its relationship to any of the other major languages of Asia is as yet uncertain.

Vietnam War, military conflict between South Vietnamese government forces aided by the United States, and Communist insurgents (Vietcong) supported by North Vietnam. It was initially a civil war aimed at reunification of Vietnam following its partition in 1954 into North (Communist) and South (non-Communist). In the early 1960s the United States became militarily involved; by 1969 there were some 550,000 US troops in South Vietnam. North Vietnam received aid from the USSR and China. Despite US armed forces, the South Vietnamese were unable to defeat the Vietcong and North Vietnamese. By the late 1960s pressure developed in the United States for the withdrawal of US troops. Efforts toward negotiated peace were begun in 1969 and a peace treaty was signed in January 1973 by South Vietnam, the United States, North Vietnam, and the National Liberation Front (the Communist provisional revolutionary government in South Vietnam). It provided for an end to hostilities and for the withdrawal of US forces. Fighting between South Vietnamese and Communists continued, however, and in May 1975 the South Vietnamese government fell to the Communists. △1378.

Vigée-Lebrun, Marie Anne-Elisabeth (1755–1842), French painter. A protégé of Marie Antoinette, she was strongly influenced by Rubens and occasionally worked in the style of David. One of the most successful portraitists of her time, she maintained one of the great French salons and is best known as a painter of women and children.

Vigeland, Adolf Gustav (1869–1943), Norwegian sculptor. A pupil of Auguste Rodin, he worked in a monumental, highly emotive style that combined realism with romanticism. He is known best for his unfinished magnum opus, an immense "Park of Sculpture" in Oslo, Norway.

Vigo, seaport city in NW Spain, on the Vigo Bay, 17mi (27km) S of Pontevedra, near the Portuguese border; divided into new and old sections. Attacked by Francis Drake 1585 and 1589, it was scene of naval battle 1702 between British-Dutch fleet and Spanish galleons carrying gold cargo from the New World; some of the gold sank and is believed to be still at the bottom of the bay; site of ancient palaces. Industries: fishing, fish processing, boats, granite, brandy, tools, soap, machinery. Pop. 197,144.

Viking Mission, exploration of Mars by two US spacecraft landing in the summer of 1976. The mission included experiments to search for evidence of life. △70, 148.

Vikings, Scandinavian pirates. Also called Jarangionsor Norsemen. They conducted raids against areas of Europe and the British Isles during the 10th and 11th centuries. They colonized some of these areas and exerted a great deal of influence on the history of Europe by encouraging the growth of feudalism. They were skilled seafarers and shipbuilders. Their religion was mythological, and their literature grew from heroic legends combined with mythology. △1068.

Villa, Francisco "Pancho" (1877–1923), Mexican revolutionary leader, b. Doroteo Arango. He spent his early life as an outlaw before joining Francisco Madero's revolutionary forces (1910). Later he joined Venustiano Carranza's forces when Carranza ousted Madero. Villa broke with Carranza to ally with Emiliano Zapata, and was defeated (1915). After the United States recognized Carranza's government, Villa murdered US citizens in northern Mexico and New Mexico in retaliation. Although Pres. Woodrow Wilson sent troops against him, Villa continued harassment until 1920. *See also* Carranza, Venustiano; Mexican Border Campaign.

Villa Concepción. *See* Concepción.

Villanovan Culture. △1010.

Villa Park, town in NE Illinois, W of Chicago. Industries: farming, fertilizer, beverages. Inc. 1914. Pop. (1970) 25,891.

Villon, François (1431–after 1463), considered the greatest French poet of the Middle Ages, also known as François de Montcorbier or François des Loges. He took the name of his tutor and guardian Guillaume de Villon, and received a degree from the Sorbonne in 1452 after a colorful and riotous student life. He associated himself both with the nobility and the criminal element of Paris, and featured prostitutes and thieves in his poetry. After several brawls and thefts, he was sentenced to be hanged in 1462 or 1463 for the murder of a priest during a street fight. The sentence was commuted, and he disappeared while in exile. His most famous works are *Ballade des Pendus* (Ballad of the Hanged) and a lyric beginning "Where are the snows of yesteryear," which popularized the theme of the loss of things past.

Villon, Jacques (1875–1963), pseud. of Gaston Duchamp, French painter. His abstract pictures are based on landscape motifs. He was an early adherent of Cubism. His brothers were the artists Marcel Duchamp and Raymond Duchamp-Villon.

Viña del Mar, city in Chile, near Valparaíso on the Pacific Ocean; seaside resort; site of summer palace of Chilean presidents. Industries: tourism, textiles, paints. Pop. 138,457.

Vincennes, port city in SW Indiana, on Wabash River; seat of Knox co. Fortified by French 1732, it was occupied by British 1763; Americans under George Rogers Clark captured it during American Revolution (1779); capital of Indiana Territory 1800–13; site of Pres. William Harrison's home "Grouseland" and Vincennes University (1804). Industries: agriculture, batteries, glass, wool, paper, seed. Oldest setlement in state, founded 1702; inc. 1856. Pop. (1970) 19,867.

Vincent de Paul, Saint (1581–1660), French priest called the Universal Patron of Works of Charity. As a young man he was captured by Barbary pirates and spent two years as a slave in Tunis. After escaping back to France, he began a mission to the peasantry, founding the Congregation of the Mission (or Lazarists). Showing great organizing ability, he later helped found the Daughters of Charity to minister to the sick, the old, and orphans.

Vincent of Beacurais. △1780.

Vinci, Leonardo da. *See* Leonardo da Vinci.

Vindhya, mountain range in India; extends ENE across India to divide the Deccan plateau from the Ganges River basin; historically, it has been used as the dividing line between N and S India. Sandstone extracted from the mountains was used to build the Buddhist stupas at Sanchi (400 BC–AD 11th century), Jain and Brahman temples at Khajraho (11th century), palaces of Gwalior (15th century). Length: 700mi (1,127km).

Vineland, city in SW New Jersey, 11mi (18km) ENE of Bridgeton; site of Vineland Training School (1888) and Cumberland County College (1964). Industries: glassware, chemicals, clothing. Inc. 1952. Pop. (1970) 47,399.

Vinland (Wineland), area in North America, believed to have been the coast of New England or Newfoundland. In AD 1000 as Leif Eriksson sailed from Norway to Greenland, his ship was blown off course to the S and W. He came to a land first sighted in 985 by Bjarni Herjulfsson, where wild grapes and grain grew. Most scholars accept as fact that the Vikings discovered America. Stories of Vinland voyages are told in Old Norse Sagas. △1068.

Vinson, Frederick Moore (1890–1953), US public official and chief justice of US Supreme Court (1946–53), b. Louisa, Ky. He served as congressman (1924–29, 1931–38); associate justice of the US Court of Appeals (1938–42); chief judge of the US Emergency Court Appeals (1942–43). He was also director of the Office of Economic Stabilization (1943–45). Pres. Harry S. Truman named him secretary of treasury (1945–46). Appointed chief justice of the Supreme Court (1946), he was a strong supporter of civil rights but believed in broad powers for the government. This was evident in his dissenting opinion in *Youngstown Sheet and Tube* v. *Sawyer* (1952).

Vinyl Chloride, gas with an etherlike odor (formula CH_2CHCl) manufactured by the chlorination of ethylene. It polymerizes to form polyvinyl chloride (PVC) and is widely used in this form. Properties: sp. gr. (liq. 20°C) 0.9121; melt. pt. −255.4°F (−159.7°C); boil. pt. 7°F (−13.9°C).

Vinyl Plastics, any of several substances (resinous, fibrous, or rubbery) composed of large molecules made by polymerization of vinyl compounds, used in plastic film, upholstery, floor tile, toys, buttons, and fibers. These contain the hydrocarbon vinyl group. The molecules of a single vinyl compound can be made to polymerize; those of two different compounds can also be linked, forming a copolymer. *See also* Polystyrene; Polyvinyl Acetate. △1618.

Vio, Giacomo de. *See* Cajetan.

Viola, stringed musical instrument of the violin family, somewhat larger and tuned a fifth lower. It is held horizontally like the violin and played with a horsehair bow, sometimes pizzicato (finger-plucked). The music, written in alto clef, is warm and mellow. The viola is prominent as a solo instrument, in chamber music, and in the string sections of symphony orchestras. △1244.

Violet, any of about 850 species of herbs, shrubs, and small trees of the family Violaceae, worldwide in distribution. All cultivated species are of the genus *Viola*. More than 500 species of wild violets have been described; they may be annual or perennial with 5-petaled flowers that grow singly on stalks; usually blue, violet, lilac, yellow, or white. In North America the most common species are the blue, or meadow, violet *(V. papilionacea)* and the bird's foot violet *(V. pedata)*. △594.

Violet Sea Snail. △482.

Violin, most important stringed musical instrument played by bow. It is a major component of Western chamber and symphony orchestras, ranking with the piano in virtuoso performances. Derived from ancient Asian fiddles and medieval viols it was developed in Italy by the Amati family (*c.*1575–1680), Stradivari (*c.*1644–1737), and Guarneri (1698–1744). Corelli and Vivaldi (*c.*1700) furthered its performance techniques for their concerti grossi, leading to great violin compositions by Bach, Handel, Haydn, Mozart, Beethoven, and Paganini. The violin, blending well in ensemble, offers a variety of tone colors and dynamics. The body is assembled from curved wooden panels, glued with protruding edges, convex front and back, narrow waist, f-holes, unfretted neck with scroll holding pegs for four strings, which are tuned in fifths and stretched over a bridge. The violin, with a range of 3 to 4 octaves, is held horizontally and played with a horsehair bow, sometimes pizzicato (finger-plucked).

See also Stringed Musical Instruments. △1132, 1244.

Violincello. *See* Cello.

Viol Instruments. △1132.

Viollet-le-Duc, Eugene. △1258.

Viper, or adder, poisonous snake characterized by a pair of long, hollow, venom-injecting fangs in the front of the upper jaw that can be folded back when not in use. There are 150 species. Family Viperidae. Or, true viper of Eurasia and Africa, differing from pit viper in lacking heat-sensitive organs. Also, the common European adder *(Vipera berus)* of Europe and E Asia. Its color varies and it has a dark, zigzag band along its back. It is an aggressive, live-bearing snake. Length: to 24in (61cm). Subfamily Viperinae. *See also* Pit Viper. △522.

Virchow, Rudolf (1821–1902), German pathologist. His finding and succinct statement that "all cells arise from cells" completed the formulation of the cell theory and repudiated spontaneous generation theories. Virchow also studied the nature of disease on a cellular level, establishing the field of cellular pathology.

Vireo, small, American songbird found in forest treetops, city parks, tropical coastline shrubs, and other habitats. They have bristled forehead feathers, slightly down-curved bills, and green, gray, or yellow plumage. They feed on insects and larvae and lay spotted white eggs (3–5) in a complicated cup-shaped nest slung from a tree fork. Family Vireonidae.

Virgil. *See* Vergil.

Virginia, state in E United States, on the Atlantic Ocean, midway between Maine and Florida.

Land and economy. From the coast, the land rises gently to the Blue Ridge Mts. Beyond the Blue Ridge, the Shenandoah Valley is a rich farming region. In the far W, the rugged Allegheny Mts lie along the state boundary. Chesapeake Bay, a large arm of the Atlantic, cuts into the E section; into it flows the James, the York, and the Rappahannock rivers. The Potomac River forms much of the state's N boundary. The rich farmland that long sustained the economy is E of the mountains. Industry is mostly concentrated in the Richmond-Petersburg and the Norfolk areas. Norfolk is a major port. The state's historical shrines are prime attractions for the important tourist industry.

People. Early settlers were English; in the early 18th century numbers of Scots-Irish and Germans arrived, but immigration decreased after 1800. About 63% of the population lives in urban areas.

Education. There are about 70 institutions of higher education. The College of William and Mary, founded in 1693, is the 2nd-oldest in the United States. The state-supported University of Virginia was founded by Thomas Jefferson in 1819.

History. The first permanent settlement in the New World was made at Jamestown in 1607. The General Assembly of 1619 was the first representative local government in America. Virginia became a royal colony in 1624 and developed an aristocratic plantation society in the E, with vast holdings in tobacco acreage. The W was settled by immigrants from overseas and from other colonies in the early 18th century. Virginia's leaders, including Thomas Jefferson, Patrick Henry, and Richard Henry Lee, were foremost in the drive for independence from Great Britain. Jefferson was the principal author of the Declaration of Independence, and George Washington, a Virginian, was commander-in-chief of the Continental army in the Revolution. Lord Cornwallis surrendered his British troops at Yorktown on Oct. 19, 1781. Four of the first five presidents of the United States were Virginians; in all, eight presidents were born in the state. Virginia was one of the last states to join the Confederacy in the Civil War, but Richmond became the Confederate capital. The state was the principal battleground of the war. Gen. Robert E. Lee, the Confederate commander, surrendered his army at Appomattox Court House on April 9, 1865. Social and economic recovery was slow after the war.

PROFILE

Admitted to the Union: June 25, 1788; 10th of the 13 original states to ratify the US Constitution
US Congressmen: Senate, 2; House of Representatives, 10
Population: 4,648,494 (1970); rank, 14th
Capital: Richmond, 249,431 (1970)
Chief cities: Norfolk, 307,951; Richmond; Arlington, 174,284
State legislature: Senate, 40; House of Delegates, 100
Area: 40,817sq mi (105,716sq km); rank, 36th
Elevation: highest, 5,729ft (1,747m), Mt Rogers; lowest, sea level
Industries (major products): chemicals, tobacco products, food products, textiles, apparel, lumber, furniture
Agriculture (major products): tobacco, peanuts, apples, poultry, hogs
Minerals (major): bituminous coal, zinc, limestone
State nickname: Old Dominion
State motto: Sic Semper Tyrannis (Ever Thus to Tyrants)
State bird: cardinal
State flower: American dogwood
State tree: American dogwood

Virginia Beach, city in SE Virginia, on Atlantic Ocean, 18mi (29km) E of Norfolk; site of Cape Henry memorial cross (commemorating first landing of English colonists, 1607, who later founded Jamestown), oldest brick house in the United States built by Adam Thoroughgood 1636; noted tourist center with several recreational facilities and beaches; military complex. Industries: tourism, Guernsey cows, truck farms. Inc. 1906; consolidated with Princess Anne co 1963. Pop. (1970) 172,106.

Virginia City, village in W Nevada, 16mi (26km) SSE of Reno; seat of Storey co. Settled when Comstock Lode was discovered 1859, it grew rapidly into an elegant town with population of 25,000, until the gold and silver ran out *c.* 1886. Now a ghost town with a flourishing tourist business. Pop. (1970) 300.

Virginia Convention (1861), attempt to avoid civil war. *See* Washington Peace Convention.

Virginia Creeper, or woodbine, American ivy, tendril-climbing vine native to North America, but usually found only in eastern areas. It has leaves divided into five parts, green flower clusters, and blue-black inedible berries. Family Vitaceae; species *Parthenocissus quinquefolia.*

Virginia Deer. *See* White-tailed Deer.

Virginia Plan (1787), a program offered at the Philadelphia Constitutional Convention. Proposed by the Virginia delegation, it consisted of 15 resolutions concerning a structure of government for the union. Among its features were: a bicameral national legislature in which the lower house would be elected by the people and the upper house by the lower chamber, an executive to be chosen by the legislature, and a judiciary with a Supreme Court and lower courts elected by the legislature. The plan favored the large states because representation was based on population and wealth. Some features of this plan were included in the Constitution.

Virginia Resolves, declarations by the House of Burgesses (1765) that the Stamp Act was illegal and void, and that only Virginia and not Parliament could tax Virginia.

Virgin Islands, a group of some 100 islands in the Lesser Antilles between the Caribbean Sea and the Atlantic Ocean. A group of 68, the W cluster known as the Virgin Islands of the United States, is a US possession, administered by the US Department of the Interior. The NE group, about 36 islands, is a British colony, called the British Virgin Islands.

The chain of islands is essentially mountain peaks, rising from the Atlantic Ocean; terrain is difficult for agriculture. Because of the mild climate, Old World architecture, and beautiful bays, the islands have become a popular tourist spot over the past 2 decades; tourism is a major contributor to the economy. Some islands such as the US-held St Croix and St Thomas are used for agriculture and livestock, with sugar cane and rum as major products. The Virgin Islands National Park includes most of St John, the third largest of the US islands.

After the last of the islands' native Indian population was eliminated by the Spaniards in the 16th century, immigration brought many nationalities. The slave trade, begun in 1673, brought much of the present population, which today is predominantly black and poor. About 20% of the population is white. Discovered in 1493 by Christopher Columbus, the islands had only sporadic settlements until the Dutch West India Co. came to St Thomas in 1672. The British islands were bought in 1566 from the Dutch, while the US islands were bought in 1917 from Denmark for $25,000,000, because of their strategic position near the Panama Canal. Denmark had claimed St John in 1683 and bought St Croix in 1733 from France, making the group a Danish Royal colony in 1754. The slave trade figures largely in the history of the islands, until violent slave revolts on St John in 1733 and one on St Croix in 1848. The islands were the world's largest slave trading center until the prac-

Viola

Viper

Flat Top Manor, Blue Ridge Parkway, Virginia

Trunk Bay, Virgin Islands

tice was outlawed in 1792 by Denmark. Residents of the US-held islands were made US citizens in 1927, and these islands are administered by a governor appointed by the US president. There is an 11-man elected Senate with a US district judge as chief judicial authority. The governor of the British islands is appointed by the British Crown, with an executive council and a legislature.

PROFILE

Official name: Virgin Islands of the United States; British Virgin Islands
Area: 133sq mi (344sq km) (US); 59sq mi (153sq km) (British)
Population: 62,468 (US); 10,484 (British)
Chief cities: Charlotte Amalie; Christiansted; Roadtown
Religion: Roman Catholic
Language: English
Monetary unit: US dollar, British pound

Virgin Islands National Park, park in St John, Virgin Islands. This is a park of lush green hills, quiet coves, and white sandy beaches covering 75% of St John Island. There are early Carib indian relics, remains of a Danish colonial sugar plantation, and an underwater swimming trail. Area: 14,419acres (5,840hectares). Est. 1956.

Virgin Mary. *See* Mary, Saint.

Virgo, or the Virgin, equatorial constellation situated on the ecliptic between Leo and Libra; the sixth sign of the zodiac. An extensive star group, Virgo lies south of Coma, located in a part of the sky where galaxies and galaxy clusters are very numerous. Brightest star Alpha Virginis (Spica). The astrological sign for the period Aug. 23–Sept. 22. △826.

Virology, the study of viruses. Unknown until 1892, viruses were first discovered by a Russian bacteriologist, D. Ivonovski, who found that the causative agent of tobacco mosaic disease could pass through a porcelain filter impermeable to bacteria. The introduction of the electron microscope in 1940 made it possible to view viruses. *See also* Virus.

Virus, a submicroscopic infectious organism, first discovered when infectious material that had been passed through a fine porcelain filter, which held back bacteria, was still infective (filterable agent). They vary in size from 10 to 300nm (1 nm = 1 billionth of a meter), and contain only genetic material, in the form of deoxyribonucleic acid (DNA) or ribonucleic acid (RNA) enclosed in a protein coat, the capsid. Viruses can grow and reproduce only when they enter another cell, such as a bacterium or animal cell, because they lack energy-producing and protein-synthesizing machinery. When they enter a cell, the host's metabolism is subverted so that viral reproduction is favored. Pathogenesis is the result of cell death or altered metabolism as the virus multiplies. Control of viruses is difficult because harsh measures are required to kill them. The body, however, has devised some protective measures, such as production of interferon and of antibodies directed against specific viruses. One attack of certain viral diseases confers lifetime immunity. Some of the more common virus diseases are: poliomyelitis; influenza virus, causing flu symptoms; rubella virus, causative agent of German measles; ECHO-28 and RS viruses, which cause the common cold; and herpes simplex, which causes cold sores. Where the specific agent can be isolated, vaccines can be developed, but some viruses, such as influenza, change so rapidly that vaccines become ineffective. △422, 710, 1574.

Visalia, city in S central California, 38mi (61km) SE of Fresno; seat of Tulare co; just E of Sequoia and Kings Canyon national parks. Industries: agriculture, electronic equipment. Founded 1852; inc. 1874. Pop. (1970) 27,268.

Visconti, Italian family that ruled Milan from the 13th century until 1447. Ottone Visconti (1207?–95), appointed (1262) archbishop of Milan by Pope Urban IV, used his position to become the first Visconti lord of Milan. Ghibellines (imperial partisans), the Visconti established their hegemony over Lombardy in the 14th century, and in 1339 they took the hereditary title of duke. From the mid-14th century Visconti-Milanese expansionism met allied resistance from other Italian states such as Florence, Venice, the Papal States, and Savoy. Visconti lordship of Milan passed to the Sforza family after the death of Filippo Maria Visconti in 1447.

Viscosity, the internal friction of a liquid or gas. In the flow of a liquid through a pipe, the central portion moves the fastest and the layers next to the pipe move minimally. Thus layers of the fluid are sliding over one another; the more viscous the liquid, the slower it will flow. Viscosity is large for liquids, small for gases. In liquids, it increases rapidly with decreasing temperature. △1504.

Vishnu, in Hindu mythology, one of the supreme triad of Brahma, Siva, and Vishnu. He reigns in heaven with his wife Lakshmi as the most important solar deity. Vishnu is depicted as a young man with four hands holding a shell, wheel, club, and lotus and bearing bow and sword. He was worshiped as a preserver and restorer, as Vishnu, and in his other incarnations, Rama, Krishna, and Radha. △838, 1034.

Visigoths, or **West Goths,** an ancient Germanic people. In the 2nd century AD they migrated from their original home on the Baltic to the shores of the Black Sea. There they separated into two groups, divided by the Dniester River: the Visigoths (West Goths) and the Ostrogoths (East Goths). At the end of the 4th century, they began attacking the frontiers of the Roman Empire. The Gothic invasions remained one of the most serious problems of the empire for many years. △1030, 1052–54.

Vision, sense concerned with the transformation of light energy into the experience of seeing. Light from an object enters the eye through the transparent cornea, passes through the pupil (the size of which is regulated by the iris), is refracted by the lens, and forms an image on the interior of the eye, a special receptor surface called the retina. The retina is composed of two types of cells: rods, found in the periphery, and cone cells, highly concentrated toward the center (fovea) of the retina. Rods operate in dim illumination and are excellent light detectors; cones function best under brighter illumination and are responsible for color vision and the best acuity (pattern vision).

Receptors connect with bipolar and ganglion cells that in turn form the optic nerve. Before they reach the brain the two optic nerves cross (optic chiasma). The optic nerves synapse at the lateral geniculate body, which in turn sends fibers to the optic cortex, located within the occipital lobes. Vision is not yet explainable in purely anatomical terms, and thus many visual phenomena, eg, visual illusions, are studied by psychologists. △674.

Visions of Eternity (Blake). △1228.

VISTA. *See* Volunteers in Service to America.

Vistula (Wista), longest river in Poland; rises in Carpathian Mts, SW Poland, flows NE past Krakow, turns NW through Warsaw then flows NW through Toruń, turning N to mouth of the Bay of Danzig at Gdańsk. The major waterway of Poland, it connects a large area through its tributary system, which includes the Bug, San, Wisloka, Dunajec, Bzura, and Pilica rivers; canal systems connect it to still other important rivers; logging is done along lower course. Length: 675mi (1087km).

Visual Purple. *See* Rhodopsin.

Vitamin, organic substance required in small amounts by living organisms for healthy life and growth. Higher animals cannot synthesize vitamins, which must then form part of their diet. Deficiency of a particular vitamin results in a specific vitamin deficiency disease. Vitamins of the B complex and vitamin C are water-soluble. The B complex vitamins are obtained from yeast, liver, etc, and function as coenzymes in metabolic reactions. They include thiamine (B_1), nicotinic acid, riboflavin (B_2), pantothenic acid, pyridoxine (B_6), biotin, and folic acid. Certain other substances, such as choline, may also be considered as belonging to the B complex. Vitamin C (ascorbic acid) is present in certain fruits and green vegetables; lack of it results in scurvy. All the remaining vitamins are fat-soluble. Deficiency of vitamin A (retinal), which occurs in fish-liver oils, causes night blindness; lack of vitamin D, obtained from fish-liver oils, results in rickets in children. The naturally occurring form is produced by the action of sunlight on the skin. Deficiency of vitamin E (tocopherol) may affect fertility, and vitamin K is required for normal blood clotting. *See also* articles on individual vitamins. △696, 1570, 1572.

Vitamin A, a fat-soluble vitamin found in fish liver and other animal livers, butter, cheese, and vegetables and occurring in two forms: retinol (vitamin A_1) and dehydroretinol (vitamin A_2). Deficiency results in night blindness and various skin disorders.

Vitamin B_1 (thiamine), one of the B complex vitamins; found in green vegetables, corn, beans, liver, egg yolk, and brown rice. Deficiency affects the nervous system, circulation, and gastrointestinal tract and produces such symptoms as sluggish elimination, neuritis, rapid pulse, fluid accumulation, and difficulty in breathing.

Vitamin B_2 (riboflavin), a member of the vitamin B complex group, essential to human nutrition and found in liver, milk, grass, kidneys, eggs, malt, and certain algae. Deficiency causes lesions on the tongue, lips, and face as well as ocular symptoms. Also called vitamin G.

Vitamin B_6, a group of vitamins belonging to the vitamin B complex group and including pyridoxine, pyridoxal, and pyridoxamine. They are found in most foods, particularly in meats, liver, vegetables, cereals, and egg yolk, and are important in the metabolism of amino acids, among other metabolic processes. Deficiency of pyridoxine affects the nervous system, resulting in seizures, irritability, and gastrointestinal symptoms, treated by administration of its hydrochloride salt, which is also used in other conditions such as morning sickness.

Vitamin B_{12} (cyanocobalamin), a vitamin of the B complex group, needed for DNA synthesis and for maturation of red blood cells. It is found especially in liver and eggs and can be produced from cultures of *Streptomyces griseus*, also the source of the antibiotic streptomycin. Deficiency causes pernicious anemia, for which the treatment is administration of the vitamin.

Vitamin B Complex, a large group of water-soluble vitamins that includes riboflavin, thiamine, niacin, nicotinamide, vitamin B_6, cyanocobalamin, biotin, pantothenic acid, folic acid, inositol, and possibly para-aminobenzoic acid and choline. *See also* Vitamin B_1; Vitamin B_2; Vitamin B_6; Vitamin B_{12}; Vitamin H.

Vitamin C (ascorbic acid), a substance found in citrus fruits, strawberries, tomatoes, and other fruits and vegetables and essential to normal metabolism. A deficiency causes the nutritional disorder called scurvy.

Vitamin D, any of several similar compounds related chemically to steroids and essential for normal growth of bone and teeth. They include ergocalciferol and cholecalciferol (vitamin D_2 and D_3) and are found in fish-liver oil and eggs; they can also be made by irradiating ergosterol, a sterol. Deficiency causes such bone diseases as rickets and osteoporosis (thinning of bone).

Vitamin E (alphatocopherol), a vitamin found in beef liver, wheat-germ oil, cereals, and egg yolk and important in reproduction, normal development of muscle, protection of red blood cells, and many other biological processes.

Vitamin G. *See* Vitamin B_2.

Vitamin H (biotin), a B complex vitamin widely distributed in living tissue. Deficiency in experimental animals causes limb paralysis and baldness, as well as graying of fur.

Vitamin K, any of a group of vitamins found in spinach, cabbage, egg yolk, and other sources and important in blood coagulation. The group includes vitamin K_1 (phylloquinone), vitamin K_2 (farnoquinone), and vitamin K_3 (menadione). Vitamins K_1 and K_2 are used to treat hemorrhage, and vitamin K_3, as a vitamin supplement. Deficiency of vitamin K results in prolongation of the clotting time, with subsequent bleeding.

Viticulture, worldwide cultivation of grapes. Most commercially grown grapes in the United States are raised in California and the Finger Lakes region in New York. *See also* Grape. △346.

Vivaldi, Antonio (1680–1743), Italian composer who standardized the three-movement concerto grosso and influenced Johann Sebastian Bach. He composed many concertos, eg, *The Four Seasons* (1725). △1196.

Vizsla, pointer and retriever breed of dog (sporting group) with innate hunting ability; also called Hungarian pointer. The breed existed 1,000 years ago on Hungarian plains. Its lean, muscular head tapers to a square muzzle. Rounded, silky ears are low-set and hanging. The body is well-proportioned. Tail is docked by 1/3. Colored rusty gold or dark sandy yellow, the coat is short, smooth, and dense. Average size: 22–24in (56–61cm) high at shoulder; 40–60lb (18–27kg). *See also* Sporting Dog.

V-J Day (Sept. 2, 1945), the day World War II ended in the Pacific. Japan surrendered on the USS *Missouri* in Tokyo Bay. △1328.

Vladimir, city in Russian SFSR, USSR, on N bank of Klyazma River, 110mi (176km) E of Moscow; capital of Vladimir oblast. One of Russia's oldest cities, it served as capital of Grand Duchy of Vladimir-Suzdal 1157–1238; scene of crowning of grand dukes of Moscow in 14th century; site of Assumption cathedral (1158–61), Demetrius Cathedral (1193–97), and Golden Gate (city gate) erected 1164. Industries: chemicals, cotton textiles, plastics, tractors, machine tools. Founded early 12th century by Vladimir II of Kiev. Pop. 234,000.

Vladimir I (956?–1015), Russian ruler and Orthodox saint. In 979, Vladimir's army of Viking mercenaries conquered Polotsk and Kiev. After murdering his brother, he became grand duke of Kiev (980), conquering parts of Poland (981) and Lithuania (983). After his conversion to Christianity in *c.* 989, he became the first Christian to rule in Russia. He worked to end heathen practices and built cathedrals and schools on the Byzantine model. He married the sister of Basil II of Constantinople.

Vladivostok, seaport city in Russian SFSR, USSR, at S tip of peninsula extending between two bays of Sea of Japan; capital of Primorski Krai (since 1888); a naval base since 1872, it was used as major supply depot by Allies in WWI. They occupied city from 1917–22 following Russian Revolution. During WWII it was major receiving port for lend-lease supplies from the United States; site of Far Eastern University (reopened 1956), Far Eastern branch of Soviet Academy of Sciences, merchant marine college, and an engineering college. Harbor kept open in winter by ice breakers; known as Golden Horn Harbor, it is a base for whaling and fishing fleets. Industries: fish canning, shipbuilding, woodworking, chemicals, food processing. Founded 1860 as a military post. Pop. 442,000.

Vlaminck, Maurice de (1876–1958), French painter. Largely self-taught, he was an early Fauvist. Influenced by Vincent van Gogh, African sculpture, and Paul Cézanne (in that order), he repudiated intellectualism and invested his landscapes with a raw vehemence that was shocking in its time, eg, "Village in the Snow" (Philadelphia Museum of Art). He was also an accomplished novelist, a musician, and an athlete. *See also* Fauvism.

Vltava, longest river in Czechoslovakia; rises in Bohemian Forest of SW Czechoslovakia, flows SE and N to Elbe River at Melnik; supports hydroelectric plants. Length: 267mi (430km).

Vocal Cords. *See* Larynx.

Vocational Aptitude Test. *See* Aptitude Test.

Vocational Education, instruction in an industrial or commercial skill, obtained in trade schools, apprenticeship programs, on-the-job training, some colleges, or through correspondence schools. Such programs answer the great demand for skilled workers inspired by the Industrial Revolution, which lessened the opportunity for informal apprenticeships.

Voice Box. *See* Larynx.

Vojvodina (Voivodina), autonomous province in NE Yugoslavia; bordered by Hungary (N) and Romania (E); Novi Sad is capital; densely populated, fertile agricultural plain: From 1849–60 it was independent crownland of Vojvodina; ceded to Yugoslavia 1920; made autonomous 1946. Industries: fruit, cattle, food processing. Area: 8,301sq mi (21,500sq km). Pop. 1,950,268.

Volcanism. *See* Plutonism.

Volcano, a vent from which molten igneous matter (lava), solid rock debris, and gases are erupted. The term also is applied to the pileup of rock around the vent. Central-vent volcanoes, where the material erupts from a single pipe, are of two main types, shield and composite. Fissure volcanoes extrude material along an extensive fracture, building up plains and plateaus. △176, 252.

Volga, river in E European, USSR; longest river in Europe and USSR's principal waterway; rises in the Valdai Hills, flows E past Rzev and Kalinin through Rybinsk Reservoir, to Kazan' where it turns S and continues past Uljanovsk making a hairpin bend at Kuibyshev, SW to Volgograd, and SE to Caspian Sea through a wide delta below Astrachan, connected with Baltic Sea by Volga-Baltic Waterway, with Moscow by Moscow Canal, and with Black and Azov seas by Volga-Don Canal. Many dams and hydroelectric plants have been built on the river since 1937; most of river is open from March to mid-December. During May and June it is subject to great floods. Low water in late summer brings on the problem of shoals and sandbars that impede navigation. Its waters carry over half of all river freight in USSR, and are used to irrigate the steppes of the lower Volga region. Navigable for almost all of its 2,293mi (3,692km).

Volga-Baltic Waterway, canal and river system in N European USSR; links Volga River with Baltic Sea and Leningrad industrial area. System was started 1709 to connect St Petersburg with interior; course includes Neva River, canal along S shore of Lake Ladoga, Svir River (partially canalized), canal along S shore of Lake Onega, the Vytegra, Beloye canal, Korzha canal, W and S shores of Beloye Ozero (canalized), Sheksna River through Rybinsk Reservoir to Volga River. Major reconstruction was done in 1960s. Length: 701mi (1,129km).

Volgograd, formerly Stalingrad; seaport in Russian SFSR, USSR, on the Volga River and E terminus of Volga-Don Canal; capital of Volgograd oblast: Cossack rebels took city 1670, and Yemelyan Pugachev captured it 1774; during Russian civil war it was defended by Soviet forces under Joseph Stalin, Kliment Voroshilov, and Semyon Budenny; it was taken by Anton Denikin and the White (anti-bolshevik) troops; scene of bitter fighting in WWII that destroyed most of city; house-to-house fighting between German troops and Red Army ultimately turned in favor of USSR. A major rail and heavy industry center, city contains one of the world's largest hydroelectric stations. Industries: oil refining, shipbuilding, iron, steel, aluminum, flour milling, chemicals, cables, oil field equipment. Founded 1589 as defense point on Volga River and called Tsaritsyn. Pop. 818,000.

Volleyball, a sport played indoors or outdoors. The court is 60ft (18.3m) long and 30ft (9.2m) wide. The court is divided by an upright net, the top of which stands 8 feet (2.4m) from the ground. An inflated rubber or leather ball, about 27 inches (68.6cm) in circumference, is used. Each team has six players, three forwards and three backs, who cover an equal area of the court. The ball, which must be served from behind the back lines of the court, is batted with the open hand or fist (only one attempt is allowed). After clearing the top of the net, it may go into any part of the court. Each team has a maximum of three volley passes (from player to player) before returning the ball to the attacking team; the play continues until the ball is batted out of bounds, into the net, or hits the ground. Players may use any part of their body to hit the ball, but may not catch or hold it. A point is scored only by the team serving, and if the serving team wins the point, it maintains possession of the ball; 15 points are needed to win. If the teams are tied at 14, the first team to score two consecutive points wins. Volleyball was originated in 1895 at Holyoke, Mass., by William G. Morgan.

Volstead Act (1920), US legislation that gave Congress and the states power to enforce the 18th Amendment, prohibiting the manufacture and sale of alcoholic beverages. Insufficient money and labor for enforcement plus general flaunting of the law led to bootlegging and other criminal activities, creating a lawless atmosphere. *See also* Prohibition.

Volsungs, in Scandinavian mythology, a family especially favored by Odin. The founder of the family was Odin's son Sigi; Sigi's grandson was Volsung, a noted warrior. Volsung's son Sigmund won many victories with a sword earned from Odin. Sigmund's son was the hero Siegfried.

Volt, unit of electric potential equal to the difference of potential between two points on a conducting wire carrying a constant current of one ampere when the power dissipated between these points is one watt. The volt is also the unit of electromotive force. △1532, 1536, 1542–44.

Volta, (Count) Alessandro (1745–1827), Italian physicist who invented the first electric battery (Voltaic pile). He also invented a charge-accumulating machine, the electrophorous, which serves as the basis of modern electrical condensers, and other devices concerned with static electricity. His investigations into electricity led him to correctly interpret Luigi Galvani's experiments with muscle, showing that the metal electrodes and not the tissue generated the current. The unit of electromotive force was named the "volt" in his honor.

Voltaic Cells. *See* Cells, Electrochemical.

Volta River, main river in Ghana; formed 38mi (61km) NW of Yeji, by the confluence of the Black

Vistula River, Poland

Vizsla

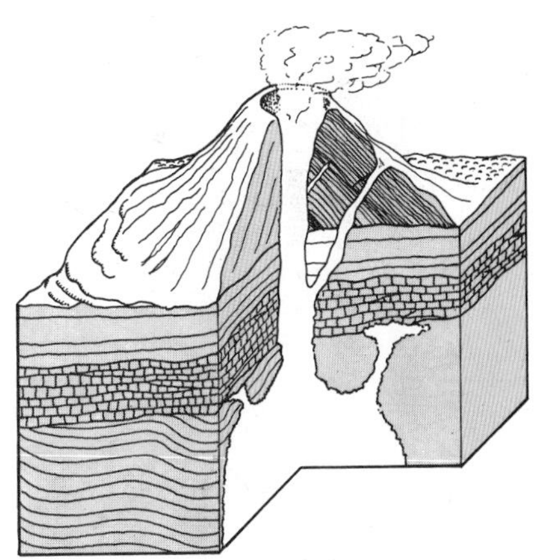

Volcano

Alessandro Volta

Volta and White Volta rivers; flows SE to Gulf of Guinea at Ada. Length: approx. 300mi (483km).

Voltaire (1694–1778), French philosopher, historian, and poet, b. François Marie Arouet, Paris. Voltaire is known for his penetrating wit and brilliant style. He left Paris after publication of *Philosophical Letters* (1734). After a stay in Prussia (1750–53) he settled at Ferney (1758), where he added to his literary reputation based on *The Henriade* (1723), *Zaire* (1732), *Mérope* (1743), *Candide* (1759) by conducting a vigorous philosophical campaign in favor of the Enlightenment and against superstition, obscurantism, and metaphysics. His ethical position, expressed in *Essay on Morals* (1756), was founded on toleration and practical humanitarianism as opposed to dogmatic theology. *See also* Candide; Enlightenment, The. △1180, 1184.

Voltmeter, instrument for measuring voltage. The most common type consists of an ammeter with a high resistance connected in series to it and the scale calibrated in volts. An electrostatic voltmeter is essentially a quadrant electrometer. △1532.

Voluntary Muscle. △662.

Volunteers in Service to America (VISTA), a federal program under ACTION. It is comprised of volunteers working on projects to eliminate poverty and poverty-related human, social, and environmental problems in the United States and its territories. Volunteers serve for up to two years providing such services as day care, health and legal aid, education, and city planning. It was established in 1964.

Volvox, a genus of tiny single-celled organisms propelled by a whiplike flagella. *Volvox* forms hollow, spherical colonies, barely visible to the eye. The lashing of the flagellae of the colony's members makes the whole colony turn slowly about a definite axis.

Von Braun, Wernher (1912–), US engineer, b. Germany. He is known for his role in many aspects of rocketry and space exploration. In 1929 he began experiments with liquid-fuel rockets, and he was instrumental in the development of the German V-2 rocket. In 1945 he was brought to the United States and directed the Redstone rocket program, which launched the first US satellite, Explorer I (1958). In 1970 Von Braun became deputy associate administrator of the National Aeronautics and Space Administration (NASA). He left this post in 1972 to become a business executive. △1722.

Von Herkomer, Hubert. △1252.

Vonnegut, Kurt, Jr. (1922–) US author, b. Indianapolis. Vonnegut's novels and stories protesting the horrors of the 20th century in a black humor vein are particularly popular with college students. Among his novels are *Player Piano* (1951), *Slaughterhouse Five* (1969), and *Breakfast of Champions* (1973).

Voodoo, or vodun, religious and magical beliefs and practices found among blacks in the Caribbean, the US South, and Brazil. Voodoo includes elements of West African cults and a supernatural pantheon borrowed largely from Catholicism. Magic, propitiatory rites, and trance play an important role in voodoo. *See also* Obeah.

Vorasilvograd. *See* Lugansk.

Voronezh (Voronez), city and river port in W central Russian USSR, on the Voronezh River, 165mi (266km) NE of Kharkov; capital of the Voronezh oblast. It became a shipbuilding center under Peter I in his campaign against the Turks at Azov (1695–96). During WWII city was almost totally destroyed; most of it has been rebuilt, including the 18th-century Potemkin Palace and Nikolsk church; site of university transferred here from Tartu (1918). Industries: locomotives, machinery, synthetic rubber, oil, food processing, television sets. Founded 1586 as a frontier fortress. Pop. 660,000.

Voroshilovgrad, city in E Ukrainian SSR, USSR, at confluence of Lugan and Olkhov rivers; capital of Voroshilovgrad oblast. Industries: mining equipment, textiles, food products, locomotives. Founded 1795. Pop. 382,000.

Vorster, Balthazar Johannes (1915–), South African statesman and Nationalist. He served in the legislature and cabinet and succeeded H. F. Verwoerd as prime minister in 1966. Although a strict segregationist, he allowed a softening of apartheid policies and met with black African leaders.

Vortex, the eddy or whirlpool observed in fluid motion. Vortices can not occur in ideal (nonviscous) fluid motion, but they are important in the study of real fluids. In particular, the vortices occurring behind air foils are of great interest in aerodynamic design. In the study of turbulence, a major result is the observation that energy is dissipated most efficiently in the smaller vortices.

Vorticism. △1296.

Voting, process employed to choose candidates for public office or to decide controversial issues. Early forms were by voice or sign, but the written ballot became popular to eliminate the possibility of intimidation and corruption. Absentee voting, or casting a ballot by mail or in advance of the election, originated during the US Civil War for the benefit of military personnel. △904, 1398.

Voting Rights Act (1965), US legislation authorizing federal authorities to check registration and voting procedures in order to protect rights of black voters in parts of Alabama, Mississippi, and Louisiana. Within a year after its passage, the number of blacks registered in five Deep South states had increased by almost 50%.

Voussoirs. △1082.

Voyageurs National Park, park in N Minnesota.
features beautiful northern lakes and interesting gla
cial and geological phenomena. Area: 219,431acre
(88,869hectares). Est. 1971.

VTOL (Vertical Take Off and Landing) Aircraft
experimental airplane designed to perform vertica
take-offs and landings but to maintain flight speed an
payload capabilities superior to those of a helicopte
There are designs that permit rotation of the wing an
engines from vertical for take-off, to horizontal fo
high-speed cruising. Another design allows for th
diversion downward of the exhaust of fixed jet en
gines. A third style has two separate systems of thrus
for upward and forward movement. *See also* STO
Aircraft. △1718.

V2 Rocket, large liquid-fueled rocket developed b
the Germans during World War II, the first ballisti
missile used in war. The bullet-shaped rocket, 42
(12.8m) in length and 5ft (1.5m) in diameter, travele
at over 2,000mph (3,200kph). There was no defens
against the V2 when it was first fired against Englan
in Sept. 1944. The name was an abbreviation for *Ve*
geltungswaffe zwei, German for "Revenge Weapo
Two." △1734.

Vuillard, Jean-Edouard (1868–1940), Frenc
painter, printmaker, and decorator. Drawing on a var
ety of influences—notably Paul Gauguin, Pierre Puvi
de Chavannes, Japanese prints, and his close frien
Pierre Bonnard—he developed a distinctive intimis
style characterized by simplicity, restraint, calm, an
rich surfaces. He specialized in interiors and stree
scenes.

Vulcan, in Roman religion, the god of fire, particu
larly in its destructive aspects, such as conflagration
and volcanoes. He was also the god of the thunderbo
and of the Sun. Vulcan finally became the deity wh
was associated with life-giving warmth. His chief fest
val, the Volcania, was celebrated on August 23. It i
probable that in ancient times human sacrifices wer
offered to Vulcan.

Vulcanization, chemical process discovered i
1839, of heating sulfur or its compounds with natura
or synthetic rubber to improve its durability and resi
ience. Thin articles, such as balloons or gloves, can b
dipped into sulfur chloride; automobile tires, bein
thicker, take longer. △1618.

Vulture, large, keen-sighted, strong-flying bird tha
feeds on carrion. New World vultures, related t
storks and cormorants, are found throughout th
Americas and include the condor, turkey buzzard, an
king vulture. Family Cathartidae. Old World vultures
related to eagles, are found in Africa, Europe, an
Asia and include the griffon vulture. Family Accip
tridae. Most vultures lay white or pale eggs (1–3) in
cave, tree hollow, or cliff ledge nest.

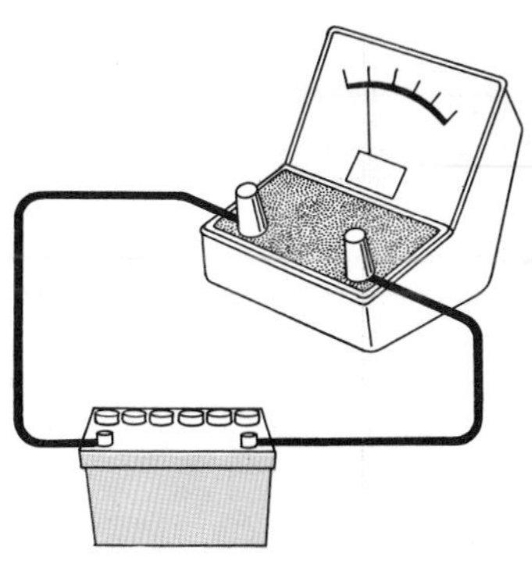

Voltmeter

Waal, river of SW Netherlands, the large S branch of the Rhine River. Formed at fork in lower Rhine near Millingen, the Waal flows WSW across S Netherlands and branches to form the Merwede, Nieuwe, and Oude Mass rivers, before entering North Sea. Length: 52mi (84km).

Waals, Johannes Diderik van der (1837–1923), Dutch physicist who received a Nobel Prize in 1910 for his work involving mathematical equations that described the liquid and gaseous matter states. This research enabled scientists to study temperatures near absolute zero. He introduced into the ideal gas laws two constants (attraction and size), and he derived a more accurate formula, named the van der Waals equation. In tribute to his studies, the weak forces between atoms or molecules are known as van der Waals forces.

Wabanaki. *See* Abnaki.

Wabash, river in Ohio, Indiana, and Illinois; rises in Grand Lake, W Ohio; flows W and SW across Indiana, forms the Indiana-Illinois border before emptying into the Ohio River in SW Indiana; used for irrigation, hydroelectricity, and industrial traffic. Length: 475mi (765km).

Wabash Rate Case *(Wabash, St Louis and Pacific Railway Co.* v. *Illinois)* (1886), US Supreme Court decision. The Court said that a state could not regulate the portion of railroad rates within its borders, reinforcing the right of Congress to regulate interstate commerce.

Wace, Robert (*c.* 1100–1175), Norman poet and chronicler. His works include saints' lives, the *Roman de Rou,* and the *Roman de Brut,* which is based on written and oral accounts of the King Arthur legends.

Waco, city in central Texas, 82mi (144km) S of Fort Worth, on Brazos River; seat of McLennan co; transportation and agricultural center; site of Baylor University (1845), Paul Quinn College (1881), McLennan Community College (1966). Industries: aircraft parts, cotton, grain, tires, furniture, clothing, cottonseed oil products, glass. Settled 1849 on former Waco Indian colony; inc. 1856. Pop. (1970) 95,326.

Waddell, Rube (1876–1914), US baseball player, b. George Edward Waddell in Bradford, Pa. A noted left-hand pitcher at the turn of the century, Waddell won 191 games. He was elected to the Baseball Hall of Fame in 1946.

Wade, Benjamin Franklin (1800–78), US senator and jurist, b. Feeding Hills, Mass. After a successful career in Ohio as a state senator and circuit judge, he became a US senator on the Whig ticket (1851–69). A staunch abolitionist, he opposed the Fugitive Slave Law and the Kansas-Nebraska Act. He denounced President Lincoln's reconstruction plans as too conservative and along with Henry Davis drew up the Wade-Davis Bill (1864), which put the reconstruction plans in the hands of Congress. However, Lincoln vetoed the bill. As president pro tempore of the Senate, Wade would have succeeded to the presidency if Andrew Johnson had been convicted of impeachment charges. In 1869 retired to Ohio to practice law.

Wade-Davis Bill (1864), act passed by the US Congress to outline the reconstruction process in the South after the Civil War. It stipulated that the government of a seceded state be reorganized only after a majority of white male citizens—exclusive of Confederate officeholders—had sworn allegiance to the United States. President Lincoln vetoed the measure.

Wadi. △266.

Wading Birds, large number of birds with long legs and at least partially webbed toes. They readily adapt to life of wading through temperate and tropical rivers, lakes, swamps, and lagoons. Includes stork, egret, flamingo, heron, bittern, ibis, and spoonbill. Orders Ciconiformes and Phoenicopteriformes. *See also* individual birds. △618.

Wage and Price Controls, government-imposed regulation of the rate of price and wage increases. The legislative and executive branches of the government may freeze wages and prices or create more moderate controls in order to achieve a particular goal, such as stemming inflation. Most economists feel that wage and price controls have, based on historical evidence, been relatively ineffective. Wage and price controls are usually only a last resort after fiscal and monetary policies have failed.

Wagler's Pit Viper. △524.

Wagner, Honus (1874–1955), US baseball player, b. John Peter Wagner in Carnegie, Pa. A shortstop and hitter, Wagner won eight batting titles while playing for the Pittsburgh Pirates (1900–17) and compiled 3,430 hits. He was elected to the Baseball Hall of Fame in 1936.

Wagner, Richard (1813–83), German composer of operas, b. Leipzig. His wife Cosima was the daughter of Franz Liszt, who sponsored him. His operas are characterized by continuously flowing melody and the use of leitmotivs. His masterpiece is the tetralogy *The Ring of the Nibelungen,* based on legends from German mythology and consisting of the operas *Das Rheingold* (1854), *Die Walküre* (1856), *Siegfried* (1871), and *Das Götterdämmerung* (*The Twilight of the Gods,* 1874).

He also composed *The Flying Dutchman* (1841), *Tannhäuser* (1845), *Lohengrin* (1848), *Tristan und Isolde* (1859), and *Parsifal* (1882). He composed only one comic opera, *Die Meistersinger von Nürnberg* (1867). All of his operas were immensely successful and subsequently influenced many other composers including Arnold Schoenberg, Richard Strauss, and Gustav Mahler. △1246, 1256.

Wagner, Robert Ferdinand (1877–1953), US political leader, b. Germany. Growing up as a poor immigrant in New York City, he worked in the state legislature (1904–18) to improve workers' conditions. He served on the state supreme court (1919–26). In the US Senate (1926–49), he fought for New Deal legislation, particularly labor bills, helping to establish the National Recovery Administration and social security. He sponsored bills establishing the National Labor Relations Board (1935) and the US Housing Authority (1937).

Wagner Act (1935), US legislation; first modern labor law to be declared constitutional. It represented a positive change in government policy toward labor. The Wagner Act requires that the employer recognize the union, that he bargain collectively with it, and that he do nothing to interfere with employees' rights to join it. The Wagner Act was counterbalanced in 1947 by the Taft-Hartley Act, which restrained the power of organized labor. *See also* Taft-Hartley Act.

Wagner-Steagall Act (1937), US legislation designed to ease the housing shortage. The law established the US Housing Authority (USHA) under the Department of the Interior and gave it power to provide state agencies involved in slum clearing and public housing with long-term, low-interest loans.

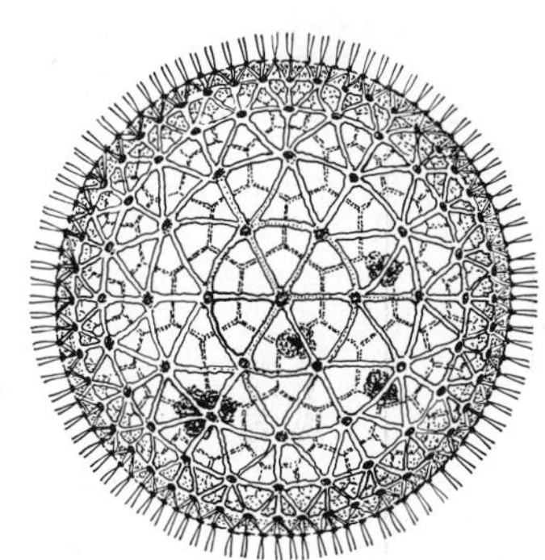

Volvox

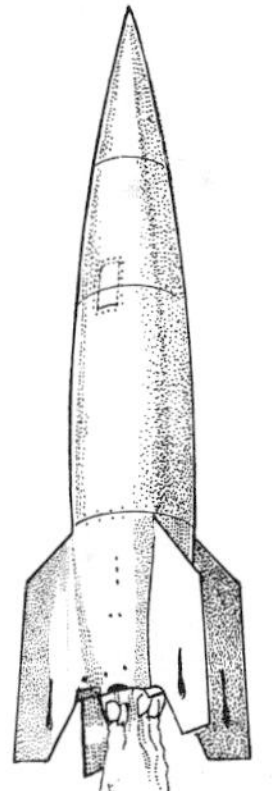

V-2 rocket

Richard Wagner

Wagon. △1686.

Wah. *See* Panda.

Wahhabis, an Islamic sect named after its founder Abd-al-Wahhab (*c.*1703–1791), who opposed all practices, both religious and material, not sanctioned by the Koran. Growing rapidly as a nationalist religious movement, the sect eventually made conquests throughout all of Arabia. Despite two serious setbacks (1818, 1889), the Wahabi movement led by ibn-Saud was able to unify all of its ancestral domains in Arabia under the name Saudia Arabia (1932).

Wahoo, mackerel-type fish found worldwide in tropical marine waters. It is fast-moving with an elongated body. Weight: to 120lb (54kg). Family Scombridae; species *Acanthocybium solanedri.*

Wahusonacook. *See* Powhatan.

Waikato, longest river in New Zealand, in central and NW North Island; rises from Lake Taupo in central mountains; flows NNW into Tasman Sea; provides hydroelectric power for most of North Island; river basin is dairy farming area. Length: 264mi (425km).

Wailing Wall, or Western Wall, a sacred place in Jerusalem for all Jews. It is a remnant of the wall that surrounded Herod's temple and is a place of many pilgrimages to this day. Jews mourn the destruction of their temple at the wall. △844.

Waite, Morrison (1816–88), chief justice of the US Supreme Court (1874–88), b. Lyme, Conn. He gained national prominence as counsel for the United States in the Alabama Claims case (1871–72). Appointed chief justice by President Grant, his major task was interpreting the constitutional amendments that were adopted after the Civil War. He also interpreted the "due process" clause of the 14th Amendment as a means to limit state power. He ruled on the Granger cases (1877), which stipulated that only businesses "clothed with a public interest" were subject to economic regulation by the state, and on the Civil Rights Cases (1883), which stipulated that those who operate inns and places of amusement are agents of the state and discrimination by such people would be considered discrimination by the state.

Waka, a Japanese poetry form consisting of 31 syllables arranged in three 7-syllable and two 5-syllable lines. In the 8th century it became the dominant form; it remained popular, and still is. Contemporary practitioners have been criticized for not saying enough. *Waka* is also called the "Japanese poem."

Wakamatsu. *See* Kitakyushu.

Wakayama, port city in S Honshu, Japan, on Kii Channel, approx. 35mi (56km) SW of Osaka; capital of Wakayama prefecture; forested agricultural region. In feudal times, city was seat of Tokugawa daimyo; site of 16th-century castle of Hideyoshi; suffered earthquake and tidal wave Dec. 21, 1946. Industries: textiles, lumber, laquerware, shipping. Pop. 365,-267.

Wakefield, town in NE Massachusetts, 10mi (16km) N of Boston. Industries: footwear, window screens, iron pipe, plastics. Settled 1639; inc. 1812. Pop. (1970) 25,402.

Wake Island, small coral island in W central Pacific Ocean, N of the Marshall Islands and W of Marianas Islands. Sandy and low, the island is actually three islets that form a lagoon; claimed by the United States 1900; site of commercial air base est. 1935; US marine outpost was taken by Japanese 1941; retaken by US forces 1945; US naval base on island remains active. Area: 3sq mi (8sq km).

Waksman, Selman Abraham (1888–1973), US microbiologist, b. Russia. He was awarded the 1952 Nobel Prize in physiology and medicine for his work on antibiotics, a word he coined. He developed screening techniques to search for antibiotics and in 1944 discovered streptomycin. *See also* Antibiotics; Streptomycin.

Walcott, Jersey Joe (1914–), US boxer, b. Arnold Raymond Cream in Merchantville, N.J. He beat Ezzard Charles (1951) for the heavyweight title in Pittsburgh and lost it (1952) to Rocky Marciano in Philadelphia. Walcott was elected to the Boxing Hall of Fame in 1969.

Wald, George (1906–), US biologist, b. New York City. He shared the 1967 Nobel Prize in physiology and medicine for being "one of the world's greatest authorities on the biochemistry of perception." He studied visual pigments and the effect of light on these pigments. He became an outspoken critic of US policy in Vietnam and lectured against the war throughout the country.

Waldemar IV Atterdag (*c.*1320–75), king of Denmark (1340–75). The disordered kingdom was restored by Waldemar who managed, after years of war and political negotiations, to unite the kingdom by 1361. To reestablish Denmark's control of Baltic trade, he conquered the Swedish island of Gotland. In violation of a treaty with Sweden, he conquered Skane (S Sweden) to gain control of the fishing industry. By conquering their town of Visby he challenged the Hanseatic League, but after trying to restrict them, he made peace in 1370. He married his daughter Margaret, age 6, to the son of Norway's king, hoping to unite the two kingdoms. He was energetic, a skillful politician and unscrupulous.

Walden (1854), narrative by Henry David Thoreau. It is a chronicle of and series of reflections upon his life at Walden Pond near Concord, Mass. In 1845 Thoreau cleared a plot of land belonging to Ralph Waldo Emerson and built a cabin where he lived from July 1845 until September 1847. It was his idea to live simply in order to develop his mind and body. The narrative, derived from journals that he kept during his residence, describes his activities, and reveals his philosophical convictions. The principal tenet of his thought was that each individual should adhere to his inner beliefs regardless of social pressure. His philosophy combined Transcendentalism with his own particular brand of individualism. *See also* Transcendentalism. △1374.

Waldenses, small Christian sect founded in the 12th century by Peter Valdes of Lyons. After translating the Bible into French and preaching without authorization, he and his followers were excommunicated and many were executed as heretics. They relied on the Bible and rejected the structure of the Roman Catholic Church. Contact was later made with the Reformation churches, and John Calvin trained some preachers. Waldensians strive to maintain pure Christianity.

Waldheim, Kurt (1918–), Austrian diplomat, secretary-general of the United Nations. He headed Austria's first UN delegation in 1958 and was its permanent representative (1964–68). Waldheim served as foreign minister (1968–70). Unanimously elected as U Thant's successor, he took office as secretary-general in 1972. △1382.

Wales (Cymru), principality of Great Britain, occupying a broad peninsula in the W of central Britain, bounded by the Irish Sea (N), St George's Channel (W), Bristol Channel (S), and the English counties of Cheshire, Salop, Hereford and Worcester, and Gloucestershire (E).

Land and economy. An upland region, highest in the NW, Wales contains the highest mountain in England and Wales, Snowdon, 3,560ft (1,086m). Lowland areas are confined to the border regions and coastal plains and are widest in the S; principal rivers are Severn, Dee, Wye, Usk Conway, and Teifi. Wrexham is the center of the small N Wales coalfield and industrial region, but S Wales has a major coalfield, heavy industry (iron and steel, engineering, chemicals, metallurgical industries, oil refining), and the main concentration of population. The rest of Wales is mainly agricultural, and tourism is important.

People. The people are of Brythonic Celtic stock. The main religious groups belong to Methodist and other nonconformist churches. About 21% of the population speaks Welsh, and national identity and culture are strong. Plans have been developed to establish a regional parliament and some measure of self-government.

Government. Wales sends representatives to Parliament. In 1974 the old Welsh counties were reorganized into eight new counties.

History. The Celtic inhabitants of Britain were little affected by the Roman invasion. The Anglo-Saxons, however, pushed them W and S into what are now Wales and Cornwall. Celtic inhabitants in Wales were temporarily united under one king, Hywel Dda, in the 10th century. With the Norman Conquest (1066), Wales was increasingly threatened by invasion, but the inhabitants managed to resist full conquest until 1282, when Edward I took over the country. A successful but short-lived rebellion was led by Owen Glendower in the 15th century. With the accession of Henry VII, the first Tudor king, Wales began to be assimilated into the political structure of England. The Act of Union (1536) established English law in Wales and made English the official language.

PROFILE

Official name: Wales
Area: 8,016sq mi (20,764sq km)
Population: 2,723,596
Density: 344per sq mi (132per sq km)
Chief cities: Cardiff (capital); Swansea; Newport
Languages: English, Welsh (official)

Walker, Mickey (1901–), US boxer, b. Edward Patrick Walker in Elizabeth, N.J. Known as "The Toy Bulldog," he was the world's welterweight champion (1922–26) and the middleweight champion (1926–31). He gave up the middleweight crown to fight in the heavyweight division (1931) and retired (1935) to study art. Walker was elected to the Boxing Hall of Fame in 1955.

Walking Fern, North American evergreen fern found in limy soil. Its long, narrow, five-pointed, arching leaves radiate from the rootstock. When leaf tips touch the ground new plants sprout, hence, its name. Height: to 14in (36cm). Family Aspleniaceae; species *Camptosorus rhizophyllus.*

Walking Stick, or Stick Insect, wingless insect that feeds on leaves found worldwide. These slow moving insects rely on their resemblance to twigs and the ability to squirt a foul-tasting liquid from their thorax to escape predators. Tropical species are the largest. Length: to 13in (32.5cm). Family Phasmatidae. *See also* Leaf Insect, Orthoptera. △492.

Walkowitz, Abraham (1880–1965), US painter, b. Siberia. Chiefly a painter of city life and its surroundings and of figures in landscapes, he was a pupil of Henri Laurens and a participant in the historically significant Armory Show (1913). His style was derived from Cézanne.

Wallace, Alfred Russel (1823–1913), English naturalist and evolutionist. Independent of, but simultaneously with, Charles Darwin, he developed a theory of natural selection. Wallace, who was largely self-taught, conducted several expeditions, including explorative trips to the Amazon and the Malay Archipelago, where the idea of natural selection began to occur to him.

In 1855 Wallace published his article "On the Law Which Has Regulated the Introduction of New Species" and sent his ideas to Darwin. The two men presented their theories to the Linnaean Society in 1858; Wallace's paper was "On the Tendency of Varieties to depart Indefinitely from the Original Type." He later published *Contributions to the Theory of Natural Selection* (1870), which, with Darwin's *Origin of Species,* comprised the fundamental explanation and understanding of the theory of evolution through natural selection. △408, 582.

Wallace, George Corley (1919–), US political leader, b. Clio, Ala. A lawyer and judge (1953–59), he was elected Democratic governor of Alabama in 1962. He attempted unsuccessfully to block federal efforts to integrate Alabama public schools (1962–66). He was succeeded (1966) as governor by his first wife, Lurleen Wallace. He ran for president in 1968 as a third-party candidate for the American Independent party, receiving 13% of the popular vote. He was reelected governor in 1970 and 1974. In 1972, while campaigning for the Democratic presidential nomination, he was shot in an assassination attempt in Maryland. The shot left him paralyzed from the waist down. He campaigned unsuccessfully for the Democratic presidential nomination in 1976.

Wallace, Henry Agard (1888–1965), US vice president (1941–45) and agriculturalist, b. Adair co, Iowa. He was editor of *Wallace's Farmer,* and later *Iowa Homestead* and *Wallace's Farmer* magazines (1924–33). He was secretary of agriculture from 1933–40, administering the farm price support program. As vice president under Pres. Franklin D. Roosevelt he worked to promote goodwill in Latin America. He also served as head of the Board of Economic Warfare (1942–43). From 1945–46 he was secretary of commerce under Pres. Harry Truman. In 1948 he was the unsuccessful Progressive party candidate for president.

Wallace, Irving (1916–), US author, b. Chicago. He wrote articles and stories for magazines before publishing *The Fabulous Originals* (1955), a nonfiction work. His novels, all popular successes, include *The Chapman Report* (1960), *The Prize* (1962), and *The Fan Club* (1974).

Wallace, Lew(is) (1827–1905), US author, b. Brookville, Ind., best known for his popular, romantic novel *Ben-Hur* (1880). After serving as an officer in both the Mexican and Civil wars, Wallace published *The Fair God* (1873), a story of the Spanish conquest of Mexico, followed by *Ben-Hur,* a story about the Roman Empire and the rise of Christianity, which brought him success. Other works include *The Boyhood of Christ* (1888) and *The Wooing of Malkaton* (1898).

Wallachia, historic region in Romania; former principality between Danube River and Transylvanian Alps; capital and largest city is Bucharest. Principality was est. *c.* 1290 by Rudolf the Black, vassal of Hungary; it secured temporary independence 1330–69; fell to Turks 1387, and remained under Turkish rule until 19th century. In 1829 the Treaty of Adrianpole made Wallachia and Moldavia protectorates of Russia. In 1861 the union of Wallachia and Moldavia formed the nation of Romania; site of Ploesti oil fields, much fought over during WWII. Products: cereals, leguminous plants, fruit, livestock. Industries: oil, handicrafts. Area: 29,575sq mi (76,599sq km).

Wallaroo. △590.

Walla Walla, city in SE Washington, at confluence of Walla Walla River and Mill Creek; seat of Walla Walla co; site of Whitman College (1859), Walla Walla College (1892), Whitman Mission National Historical Site (est. 1940). Industries: food processing, pulp and paper milling, insecticides, chemicals, farm tools. Founded 1856 around US Army fort; inc. 1862. Pop. (1970) 23,619.

Wallenstein, Albrecht Eusebius Wenzel von (1583–1634), German general. He sided with the Holy Roman Empire when the Thirty Years War broke out in 1618. He eventually became the commander of the imperial armies, but his ambition led Emperor Ferdinand II to order his capture, and he was murdered by his own officers.

Waller, Fats (1904–43), US jazz and blues pianist and composer, b. Thomas Waller in New York City. Early in his career he accompanied the singers Florence Mills and Bessie Smith. He became famous with popular recordings beginning in 1934, displaying his happy, exuberant piano style with humorous vocal renditions. He composed many songs including "Honeysuckle Rose" (1929), "Ain't Misbehavin" (1929), and "Lonesome Me" (1932). △1366.

Walleye, or Walleyed Pike, freshwater game fish of E North America, particularly Lake Erie. Closely related to the sauger and pikeperch, it is mottled greenish-brown with large opaque eyes. Length: to 3ft (91cm); weight: 10–15lb (4.5–6.8kg). Family Percidae; species *Stizostedion vitreum.*

Wallingford, town in S Connecticut, 12mi (19km) N of New Haven; site of a branch of Oneida Community (1851–80), Choate and Putnam preparatory schools; birthplace of Lyman Hall, signer of Declaration of Independence. Industries: silverware, chemicals, hardware, electronic components. Settled 1667; inc. 1670. Pop. (1970) 35,714.

Walloons, term for the French-speaking people who live in the southern provinces of Belgium. The French-speaking south was the industrialized area of Belgium and, therefore, dominated the agricultural, Flemish-speaking north. Because of the rapid economic growth in the 20th century by the north, Walloon dominance has been challenged, and there have been nationalistic conflicts especially over the language to be used in certain regions.

Wallpaper, paper wall coverings that first appeared in Europe in the 16th century as replacements for more expensive cloth wall hangings. Initially the outlines were block printed and the color filled in by brush. By the 18th century paper was glued into a continuous roll before printing. The first large wallpaper factory was started by Jean Papillon in France in 1688, but by the 18th century England was the main producer of wallpaper. By the 19th century wallpaper was being mass produced on roll paper.

Walnut, deciduous tree native to North America, Europe, and Asia. They have smoother bark than hickory trees, to which they are related, and are grown for timber, ornament, and nut production. Height: to 150ft (45.7m). Family Juglandaceae; genus *Juglans.*

Walnut Creek, city in W California, 10mi (16km) N of entrance to Morecambe Bay; site of naval weapons station. Industries: canned foods, walnuts, agriculture. Inc. 1914. Pop. (1970) 39,844.

Walpole, Horace, 4th Earl of Orford (1717–97), English novelist and publisher. A member of Parliament, he wrote and published *The Castle of Otranto* (1764), a supernatural romance, and *Mysterious Mother* (1768), a verse tragedy. His noted letters, some 2,700 in all (1732–97), were published posthumously. △1222.

Walpole, (Sir) Hugh (1884–1941), English novelist and critic, b. New Zealand. His novels include *Mr. Perrin and Mr. Traill* (1911), *Fortitude* (1913), *The Dark Forest* (1916), and the tetralogy *The Herries Chronicles* (1930–33). His prose style is colorful and descriptive but of uneven quality.

Walpole, Robert, 1st Earl of Orford (1676–1745), English statesman. He was a Whig member of Parliament (1701–42), led parliamentary opposition to the Tories, and became chancellor of the exchequer and prime minister (1715). Although he resigned (1717) after developing the first sinking fund, he restored order after the South Sea Bubble (1720). He returned as prime minister (1721–42) and was the first prime minister to develop cabinet government. He transferred power from the House of Lords to the Commons and with royal support strove to unify the cabinet (1733). His financial policies encouraged trade, but he was forced to resign (1742) due to opposition to his noninterventionist foreign policy.

Walras, Léon (1834–1910), French economist. He invented the technique of general equilibrium analysis. Much of economic analysis is devoted to studying equilibrium in one particular market (eg, the supply and demand conditions for wheat). But Walras, through general equilibrium analysis, was concerned with the interrelations among and between all markets. Walras' methodology, consequently, is quite mathematical in approach and abstract in structure.

Walrus, Arctic seal with long tusks resembling a droopy moustache. It feeds on mollusks. It uses its tusks to haul itself onto ice floes and shelves. Its bark resembles a dog's bark or an elephant's trumpeting. Some populations have been hunted almost to extinction by Eskimos. Length: to 12ft (3.7m); weight: to 2,800lb (1,260kg). Species: *Odobenus rosmarus. See also* Pinnipedia; Seal. △550.

Walsall, industrial city in W central England, in Black Country 10mi (16km) NNW of Birmingham. Industries: leather goods, engineering, aircraft parts. Pop. 184,606.

Walsingham, (Sir) Francis (1530?–90), English statesman, secretary of state (1573–90). He was employed on diplomatic missions to France (1570–73; 1581), the Netherlands (1578), and Scotland (1583). Through his efficient espionage system he revealed the Babington plot (1586) and plans for the Spanish Armada (1587). He received little reward from Elizabeth I and died in debt.

Waltham, city in E Massachusetts, on Charles River; site of one of first power looms in United States, designed and built by Francis Cabot Lowell (1813); for the first time all operations of making cotton cloth could be carried on in one building. City was home of Waltham Watch Co. (1854–1950); library has rare collection of these watches; site of Bentley College (1917), and Brandeis University (1947). Industries: electronic components, clothing, paint, varnish. Founded 1636; separated from Watertown 1738; inc. as city 1884. Pop. (1970) 61,582.

Walton, George, (1741–1804), American lawyer and a signer of the Declaration of Independence, b. near Farmville, Va. He was one of Georgia's delegates to the Continental Congress (1776–81) after being captured and released by the British. He was later that state's governor (1779–80, 1789) and a US senator (1795–96).

Walton, Izaak (1593–1683), English biographer and author. His lives of Donne (1640), Sir Henry Wotton (1651), Richard Hooker (1665), George Herbert (1670), and Bishop Sanderson (1678) are the first truly biographical works in English literature. His most famous work, however, is *The Compleat Angler* (1653).

Walton, (Sir) William (1902–), English composer. Using a largely conservative, post-Romantic style, Walton has composed in practically every medium. His best known works are a *Violin Concerto* (1939) and an oratorio *Belshazzar's Feast* (1931).

Walvis Bay (Walvisbaai), inlet port and surrounding territory on W coast of Namibia (South West Africa); annexed by Britain 1878, inc. into Cape Colony 1884, now an enclave of South Africa: site of airfield, radio station, railroad terminus. Industries: whaling, fishing, fish processing. Exports: chilled meats. First visited 1487 by Batholomeu Diaz. Area: 43sq mi (1124sq km) Pop. 17,877.

Wampum, or wampumpeag, beads used by American Indians as ornaments and as a medium of exchange in early colonial trade. Wampum beads were usually made from clam shells and were colored blue

Kurt Waldheim

George Wallace

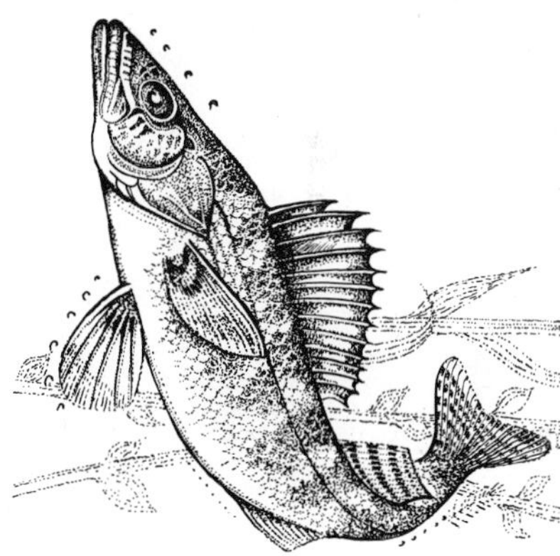

Walleye

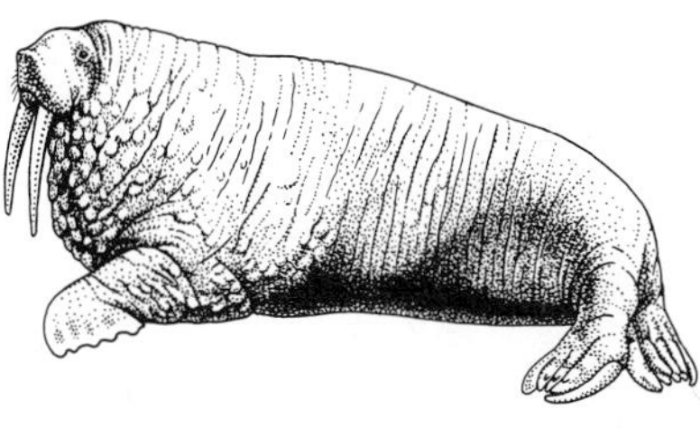

Walrus

and white. They could also be made up into necklaces or belts. △870.

Wandering Jew, either of two closely related tropical American trailing plants. The white-flowered *Tradescantia fluminensis* normally has bright green leaves. Some varieties have variegated, yellow, or white leaves. The reddish-flowered *Zebrina pendula* has purple-striped, white leaves with reddish-purple undersides. One variety has metallic, green leaves striped with white, green, and red. Family Commelinaceae. △454.

Wanderoo, or lion-tailed macaque, a black monkey of India that has a lionlike ruff of gray fur around its face and a tuft at the tip of its tail. Species *Macaca Silenus.* The purple-faced langur *(Presbytis senex)* of E Asia is also called a wanderoo. *See also* Langur; Macaque.

Waner, Lloyd James (1906–), US baseball player, b. Harrah, Okla. He gained his fame playing in the Pittsburgh Pirates' outfield with his brother Paul in the 1930s. He had a lifetime batting average of .316 and was elected to the Baseball Hall of Fame in 1967.

Waner, Paul Glee (1903–1965), US baseball player, b. Harrah, Okla. An outstanding hitter, he compiled 3,152 hits. He is the older brother of Lloyd Waner. He was elected to the Baseball Hall of Fame in 1952.

Wang Mang (33 BC–AD 23), Chinese emperor. A usurper, he attempted the overthrow of the Han Dynasty and proclaimed a Hsin or New Dynasty in AD 8, attempting to carry through a series of drastic changes in the Chinese government and administration. His program led to confusion and anarchy, and the Han was restored by Liu Hsiu. Wang's rule divides Early Han from Later Han China.

Wang Pi (226–249), early Neo-Taoist commentator on the *Lao tzu, Chuang tzu,* and *I Ching.* Making no positive assertions about reality, his most significant idea was his concept of Tao (li) as a "transcendental absolute," which is above all forms and yet unites all things. Wang Pi, along with other Neo-Taoists, kept the true spirit of Taoism alive. *See also* I Ching; Taoism.

Wang Shin-min (1592–1680), Chinese landscape painter. △1208.

Wang Wei (699–759), early Chinese painter and poet of the T'ang dynasty. △1044.

Wankel Engine, the most widely used rotary engine. The rotor is an equal-sided triangular piece that rotates in an orbit within a specially constructed casing. Crescent-shaped combustion chambers are created by the rotor that increase and decrease in size as the rotor turns. Sparks ignite the fuel charge from a carburetor at the appropriate time in each chamber. △1626, 1690.

Wapiti, or **American Elk,** large deer of North America, second only to the moose in size. It is grayish-brown with a yellowish rump. Length: to 7.5ft (2.3m); weight to 770lb (347kg). Its impressive antlers measure over 5ft (1.5m) across. Extensively hunted in the past for their meat and teeth, their range is now greatly restricted. They are commonly seen in groups of 25 or more in national parks. Family Cervidae; species *Cervus canadensis.* △592.

War and Peace (1862–69), novel by Leo Tolstoy. It takes place before, during, and after Napoleon's invasion of Russia. It is both a historical novel, describing the Russian campaign against Napoleon, and a family chronicle examining the lives of several families, centering on the Rostovs. The scope of the work makes it a prose epic.

Warbler, two groups of birds, one of the Old World (Family Sylviidae) and one of New World wood warblers (Family Parulidae). Old World warblers are generally small and related to the thrushes. Excellent songsters, they include the small, brownish grass warblers *(Cisticola);* true warblers *(Sylvia)* of Eurasia and Africa; small, grayish-green leaf warblers; Australian tree warblers *(Gerygone* and *Acanthiza);* and Australian and SW Pacific species. Wood warblers are brightly colored insect-eaters and include the yellow warbler and American redstart. *See also* Wood Warbler. △534.

Warburg, Otto (1883–1970), German biochemist who was awarded the 1931 Nobel Prize in physiology or medicine for his discovery of a respiratory enzyme. He made significant contributions to the understanding of the mechanisms of cellular respiration and energy transfer and of photosynthesis.

War Crimes, conduct that transgresses national or international law in the waging of war, usually relating to treatment of neutrals, prisoners of war, and genocide. After World War II, international military courts were established; high-ranking Germans and Japanese were tried and convicted as war criminals.

Ward, Artemus (1834–67), pseud. of Charles Farrar Browne, popular 19th-century humorist, b. Waterford, Maine. Browne created the character of Artemus Ward to comment on a variety of subjects in books and letters. Browne's lectures as Ward brought him fame.

Ward, Douglas Turner (1930–), US playwright, actor, director, b. Burnside, La. Co-founder of the Negro Ensemble Company, he was an advocate of black-oriented theater. Among his plays are the one-acts *Happy Ending, Day of Absence* (1965); also *The Reckoning* (1969), and *Brotherhood* (1970).

Ward, Lester Frank (1841–1913), US sociologist, b. Joliet, Ill. Educated in botany, Ward worked for the federal government in several positions until 1906. In the mid-1880s he began writing books and articles popularizing sociology, including *Dynamic Sociology* (1883). He served as the first president of the American Sociological Association (1906).

War Hawks, name given to a group of Democratic-Republicans who urged expansionism and nationalism. Mainly from the western frontier, this group's continued outcry against British maritime practices helped start the War of 1812 with Britain. Among its leaders were Henry Clay and John C. Calhoun.

Warhol, Andy (1930–), US painter, printmaker, and filmmaker, b. Philadelphia. A leader of the pop art movement of the early 1960s, he is the creator of many of that style's most familiar images: soup cans, packing cartons, faces of film stars, and the like. His style derives from his early career as a commercial illustrator and depends for its distinctive effects on photomechanical techniques and the repeated presentation, with varying degrees of alteration, of single images in series. To a greater extent than any other "serious" artist, he has obliterated the dividing line between the fine arts and the visual data of daily life as recorded by the mass media. △1372.

Wari. *See* Huari.

War Labor Dispute Act. *See* Smith-Connally Anti-Strike Act (1943).

Warlords, regional military leaders in China. From 1912 to 1927, China was torn by the contention for power among the warlords, whose struggles prevented growth and consolidation of national power and left China weak and unable to resist the pressures of imperial Japan. The warlords were backed by different European powers and Japan.

Warner, Charles Dudley (1829–1900), US essayist and novelist, b. Plainfield, Mass. He is best remembered for his collaboration with Mark Twain on *The Gilded Age* (1873). A popular writer in his own time, Warner wrote essays, travel books, biographies, literary criticism, and a trilogy of novels.

Warner, Pop (1871–1954), US football coach, b. Glenn Scobey Warner in Springville, N.Y. He is credited with introducing the double-wing formation, the practice of numbering plays, and dummy scrimmaging. He was a coach at several universities (1895–1938).

Warner, W(illiam) Lloyd (1898–1970), US social anthropologist, b. Redlands, Calif. Using the methods of anthropological fieldwork, Warner and a team of researchers studied Newburyport, Mass., and produced the Yankee City series of books in the 1940s and 50s, which received attention for their concept of class. Among his other books are *A Black Civilization* (1937) and *Social Class in America* (1949).

Warner Robins, city in central Georgia, S of Macon. Industries: livestock, fruit, nuts, aircraft parts. Inc. 1943. Pop. (1970) 33,491.

War of 1812 (1812–15), conflict between the United States and Great Britain. Since the beginning of the French Revolutionary wars in 1793, both France and Great Britain had made depredations on US merchant ships. British impressment of US sailors to serve on British warships was especially galling to the United States, and anti-British sentiments increased. In addition, southern and western politicians looked upon war with Britain as offering a chance to expand US territory into Canada and into Spanish Florida, which was under the protection of Britain. War was also looked upon as a way of ending British support of western Indian tribes, who were a constant threat to the American settlements in the West. New England, which was economically dependent on trade with Great Britain, was less enthusiastic about the war. The War Hawks—as the followers of John C. Calhoun and Henry Clay were called—prevailed, and on June 18, 1812, Congress declared war on Great Britain. Early efforts by the US forces to take Canada from the British were met with resounding defeats, pointing out to Pres. James Madison the serious weakness of the US army and the ineptitude of its generals. The small US navy, on the other hand, made a better showing for itself, particularly the triumphs of the U.S.S. *Constitution.* US privateers, under government commissions, won impressive prizes of British merchant ships.

By 1813, however, the large and powerful British navy had reasserted itself and had established an efficient blockade of the US coast. That blockade further hurt New England economic interests and aggravated that region's opposition to "Mr. Madison's War." In 1813, however, Commodore Oliver Perry won an impressive naval victory over the British in Lake Erie in September. That in turn led to a land victory by Gen. William Henry Harrison at the Battle of the Thames in Canada. In July 1814 both sides suffered large casualties in the Battle of Lundy's Lake, Ontario.

A more efficient US command was also beginning to be felt in the South. In March 1814, Gen. Andrew Jackson won an impressive victory over the British and their Indian allies at the Battle of Horseshoe Bend in Alabama. In August 1814 a British force landed at Bladensburg, Md., and after a victory there, marched almost unopposed on Washington, D.C. In the most humiliating defeat of the war, the Americans quickly evacuated the capital, with President Madison and the cabinet sent fleeing into the countryside. The British entered and burned the city.

The limited US successes of 1814, however, permitted truce negotiations to begin at Ghent, Belgium, in August 1814. In both nations, organized antiwar groups were becoming more powerful. British shipping interests, continuing to be hurt by the US privateers, pressured the British government to end the war. In New England war opponents, meeting at Hartford, Conn., openly discussed secession from the nation. The Hartford Convention, which they issued, was more moderate in tone but still expressly opposed the war. On Dec. 24, 1814, the negotiators at Ghent reached a truce, but the most spectacular battle of the war was still to take place. On January 8, 1815, before news of the truce had reached the United States, Gen. Andrew Jackson won a resounding victory in the Battle of New Orleans. It was victory that did much to rescue US pride in a war that otherwise had given the Americans more humiliations than victories.

Neither the war nor the Treaty of Ghent settled any of the problems that had originally led to hostilities. Perhaps its only accomplishment, from the US point of view, was that it gave the American people a sense of nationhood and convinced them that the new nation was ready to take its place alongside the major powers of Europe. *See also* Ghent, Treaty of; Hartford Convention; Lake Erie, Battle of.

War Powers, Presidential, Constitutional powers given to the president as supreme military commander. They include the power to appoint armed forces officers with consent of Senate. Congress alone is empowered to declare war, but presidents have carried out military actions without congressional approval or a formal declaration of war, as in ordering troops into Mexico, Korea, and Vietnam.

Warranty, guarantee given by a seller to a buyer that unless the item sold performs in some specified manner some specific action will be taken by the seller to remedy the fault. A warranty may be either express (stated orally or in writing) or implied (obligations imposed by law), and it is subject to the same rules as other contracts. *See also* Contract.

Warren, Earl (1891–1974), US jurist and chief justice of the US Supreme Court (1953–69), b. Los Angeles. He was governor of California (1943–53) and was the unsuccessful Republican candidate for vice president with Thomas E. Dewey (1948). Appointed by Pres. Dwight D. Eisenhower (1953) as chief justice of the Supreme Court, he began the "Warren Revolution" that lasted until his retirement (1969). He was less concerned with legal exactitude and more with social justice, and during his tenure brought about many social and political changes. Some of the Warren Court's noteworthy cases made segregation in the public schools unconstitutional, *Brown* v. *Board of Education of Topeka* (1954); established "one-man, one-vote" districts for apportionment in state legislatures, *Reynolds* v. *Simms* (1964); prohibited prayers in public schools, *Engel* v. *Vitale* (1962); made it obligatory that a suspect be informed of his rights, be provided with free state counsel, and given the right to remain silent, *Miranda* v. *Arizona* (1966). *See also* Supreme Court of the United States; Warren Commission.

Warren, Robert Penn (1905–), US poet and novelist, b. Guthrie, Ky. A graduate of Vanderbilt University (1925), he was a member there of the Fugitives, a literary group that included several notable poets. In his works, he concentrates on Southern themes and characters that are usually related to actual incidents. In *All The King's Men* (1946), for example, the central character resembled Louisiana's Huey Long. The book brought him the Pulitzer Prize for literature (1947). He won the prize again (1958) for poetry for his book *Promises*. He taught literature at Yale University (1950–56, 1961–73) until his retirement.

Warren, city in SE Michigan, adjacent to Detroit on N, 8mi (13km) W of Lake St Clair; site of Detroit Tank Arsenal and General Motors Technical center. Industries: steel, electrical equipment, tools and dies, plastic molding. Inc. as village 1893, as city 1955. Pop. (1970) 179,260.

Warren, city in NE Ohio, 13mi (21km) NW of Youngstown; seat of Trumbull co; fertile farming area; site of Trumbull branch of Kent State University. Industries: steel, electrical equipment, automobile and truck parts, appliance wiring. Founded 1797; inc. as village 1834, as city 1869. Pop. (1970) 63,494.

Warren Commission, US committee to investigate the assassination of Pres. John F. Kennedy. Established in 1963 under the leadership of US Supreme Court Chief Justice Earl Warren, it reported its findings in 1964. The published results were highly criticized by many politicians and citizens. The report concluded that Lee Harvey Oswald acted alone when he shot Kennedy and that there was no conspiracy. In 1976, a second investigation was conducted by a committee headed by Sen. Frank Church.

Warrington, industrial town in NW England, on Mersey River. Industries: wire, metal goods, chemicals, soap, brewing, distilling, tanning. Pop. 68,262.

Warsaw (Warszawa), capital city of Poland, in E Poland on the Vistula River; city constitutes separate province, and is capital of Warsaw prov., which surrounds it. The largest city in Poland, its first settlements date from the 11th century. Founded 1300, it quickly became a trade center, and was made capital of Poland 1596; taken by Russia 1813; scene of Polish insurrection 1830–31; occupied by Germans WWI and WWII; returned to Poland following WWII. The Warsaw Pact (Warsaw Treaty Organization) was signed here 1955 joining E European nations in communist bloc; site of Gothic cathedral, medieval castle (Zamek), national theater and museum, University of Warsaw. Industries: heavy machinery, automobiles, chemicals, pharmaceuticals, textiles, food processing. Pop. 1,308,000.

Warsaw, Grand Duchy of, French dependency, created in 1807 by Napoleon I out of the land Prussia had received in the 2nd and 3rd partitions of Poland. Napoleon modeled its constitution on the French one and appointed a grandson of Augustus III as duke. Polish soldiers who fought with Napoleon's army hoped for independence. After Napoleon's defeat in 1815, however, about one-fourth of the area became the Grand Duchy of Poznán under Prussian control, while the rest became Congress Poland.

Warsaw Pact. △1346.

Warsaw Uprising. On Aug. 1, 1944, the Polish underground of Warsaw attacked the German occupation troops in the city to ensure the postwar authority of the government in exile. The breakthrough of Allied armies in France and the rapid approach of Soviet forces to the outskirts of Warsaw encouraged the resistance soldiers, but the Soviets halted their advance. The unaided Poles fought valiantly for 62 days before they were defeated. The German reprisals were savage, and the city was entirely destroyed.

Wars of the Roses. *See* Roses, Wars of the.

Wart, raised and well-defined small growth on the outermost surface of the skin, caused by a virus. It is usually painless unless in pressure areas. Warts are considered contagious and are treated locally by chemical and electrical freezing. They often disappear spontaneously even without treatment.

Wart Hog, wild, tusked hog native to forested areas of S and E Africa. It has brownish-black skin with a crest of thin hair along the back and a long thin tail tipped by long hair. The warts, between the eyes and the tusks, on the cheeks are prominent only on the male. Height: 2–2.5ft (61–76cm) at shoulder; weight: 200lb (90kg). Family Suidae; species *Phacochoerus aethopicus*.

Warwick, Richard Neville, Earl of (1428–71), English statesman and soldier. Known as "the kingmaker," in the Wars of the Roses he helped the Yorkists to victory at St Albans (1455) and captured Henry VI at Northampton (1460). Warwick was the real ruler of England (1461–64) in the first part of the reign of Edward IV, but, losing power, he sided with the Lancastrians and routed Edward (1470), subsequently placing Henry VI on the throne. He was killed by Edward's forces at Barnet. *See also* Roses, Wars of the.

Warwick, city in central Rhode Island, 10mi (16km) S of Providence, on Pawtuxet River and Narragansett Bay. Originally called Shawomet, for the Indian tribe from whom the land was purchased, city was renamed for Earl of Warwick; site of Rocky Point, one of oldest seaside resorts in New England. Industries: tourism, aluminum, clothing, electronic equipment. Founded 1643 by Samuel Gorton; inc. 1644 as town, 1931 as city. Pop. (1970) 83,694.

Warwickshire, county in central England; Warwick is county town; site of Shakespeare Memorial Theatre at Stratford-upon-Avon, Warwick Castle, Mereyale and Stoneleigh abbeys. Industries: diversified agriculture, mining, motor vehicles, textiles. Area: 973sq mi (2,520sq mi). Pop. 2,079,799.

Wasatch Range, mountain chain extending from central Utah to SE Idaho; part of Rocky Mt system; rich in mineral deposits. Highest point is Mt Timpanogos, 12,008ft (3,662m).

Wash, The, shallow inlet of the North Sea in NE England, between Lincolnshire and Norfolk. The Witham, Welland, Nene, and Great Ouse rivers empty into it. Two deep-water channels lead to Boston and King's Lynn. Area: 22mi (35km) long by 15mi (24km) wide.

Washing Machine. △1818.

Washington, Booker Taliaferro (1856–1915), noted US educator, b. near Hale's Ford, Va. He worked his way through Hampton Institute and started teaching there in 1879. In 1881 he organized a black normal school that later became Tuskegee Institute, and he headed the school until his death. Washington became an advocate of black vocational education and gradual adjustment rather than political agitation for civil rights. △1406.

Washington, George (1732–99), 1st president of the United States, called the "Father of His Country," b. Westmoreland co, Va. In 1759 he married Martha Dandridge Custis, a widow; they had no children. Washington was born into a wealthy planter family. He became a surveyor and charted lands in western Virginia. In 1752, upon the death of his half-brother Lawrence, he inherited large estates, including Mount Vernon. That same year he became an officer in the Virginia militia. He fought in the last of the French and Indian Wars, and by the time he ended (1759) his career in the militia, he had achieved the rank of colonel and the reputation of an astute military commander.

Washington entered (1759) the Virginia House of Burgesses, where he served until 1774, when he went as a delegate to the Continental Congress. The Congress chose Washington as commander in chief of the Continental forces in the American Revolution. Against overwhelming odds, Washington was able finally to triumph over the British and in 1781 General Cornwallis surrendered to him and the independence of the new nation was assured. In 1783, Washington retired to Mount Vernon, but in 1787 he was called back to the Federal Constitutional Convention, over which he presided. After the new Constitution was adopted and ratified, Washington was elected the country's first president.

Washington's personal prestige and dignity were of incalculable benefit to the new nation. He attempted to govern in a nonpartisan manner and chose for his cabinet men of the various political groups. Soon, however, the factions coalesced into two: the Federalists under the leadership of Alexander Hamilton and the Republicans under Thomas Jefferson. Unanimously reelected, Washington in his second term followed a more conservative, Federalist line, as Hamilton became his most influential adviser. In 1797 Washington retired once more to Mount Vernon, where he died two years later, universally honored as the symbol of the new nation.

Andy Warhol

Earl Warren

Booker T. Washington

George Washington

Career: Virginia State Militia, 1752–59; Virginia House of Burgesses, 1759–74; Delegate, Continental Congress, 1774–75; commander in chief, Continental forces, 1775–83; presiding delegate, Federal Constitutional Convention, 1787; president, 1789–97.

See also American Revolution; Continental Congress; Washington's Farewell Address. △1218.

Washington, state in the NW United States, on the Pacific Ocean and bordered on the N by the province of British Columbia, Canada.

Land and Economy. Puget Sound, an arm of the Pacific, extends about 125mi (201km) into the NW part of the state. It contains hundreds of islands, and its broken shoreline provides many harbors. W of the sound, the Olympic Mts dominate the Olympic Peninsula. The densely forested Cascade Range splits the state from N to S, with an average elevation of 8,000ft (2,440m). E of the Cascades, the land is largely a plateau, farming and grazing country. The Columbia River enters from Canada in the NE and flows S, turning W to form much of the state's S boundary. A number of dams on the river have created huge lakes that provide hydroelectric power and irrigation for vast areas. The Hanford plant in the SE produces nuclear fuels and power. Manufacturing is centered principally in the cities along Puget Sound. Seattle is a major port for communications with Alaska and the Pacific area.

People. Washington was settled by pioneers from other states. Canadians, Norwegians, and Swedes were the chief foreign-born elements. About 72% of the population lives in urban areas, principally in the W.

Education. There are more than 40 institutions of higher education.

History. Bruno Heceta, a Spanish navigator, discovered the mouth of the Columbia River in 1775; he laid claim to the area, and in 1791 a Spanish settlement on the coast survived for a short time. US fur traders established a post at Spokane in 1810 and at the Columbia's mouth the next year. Missionaries came to the site of Walla Walla in 1843. The region's boundary with Canada was fixed by treaty with Great Britain in 1846, and in 1848 Oregon Territory was organized, including the present states of Oregon and Washington. Washington Territory was created separately in 1848. Its natural resources in timber, furs, and fisheries spurred development. The railroad reached the area in 1883, and a few years later Seattle became the supply center for gold-seekers flocking to Alaska. WWI brought a boom to the state, especially in shipbuilding, and before and after WWII huge aircraft plants were established.

PROFILE

Admitted to Union: Nov. 11, 1889; rank, 42nd
US Congressmen: Senate, 2; House of Representatives, 7
Population: 3,409,169 (1970); rank, 22nd
Capital: Olympia, 23,111 (1970)
Chief cities: Seattle, 530,831; Spokane, 170,516; Tacoma, 154,581
State legislature: Senate, 49; House of Representatives, 98
Area: 68,192sq mi (176,617sq km); rank, 20th
Elevation: highest, 14,410ft (4,395m), Mt Ranier; lowest, sea level
Industries (major products): aircraft, pulp and paper, aluminum, lumber, metal products, chemicals
Agriculture (major products): wheat, dairy products, pears, apples, cattle, potatoes, sheep, blueberries, apricots
Minerals (major): sand and gravel, zinc, lead
State nickname: Evergreen State
State motto: Alki (By and By)
State bird: willow goldfinch
State flower: coast rhododendron
State tree: western hemlock

Washington, capital city of the United States, on E bank of Potomac River between Maryland and Virginia; coextensive with the District of Columbia; legislative, judicial, and administrative center of the United States. It was chosen 1790 by Pres. George Washington as site of seat of government and was planned by Major Pierre L'Enfant, French engineer. During the War of 1812, it was occupied by the British and almost totally burned. Landmarks include the White House (1792), Capitol (1793), Washington Monument (1848), Lincoln Memorial (1922), Jefferson Memorial (1943), National Archives (1935), Smithsonian Institution (1846), Library of Congress (1897), Pentagon (1943), Supreme Court, Senate, House of Representatives, National Gallery of Art, Constitution Hall, John F. Kennedy Center for the Performing Arts (1971), National Symphony Orchestra, National Shrine of the Immaculate Conception, National Science Foundation, National Aeronautics and Space Administration, numerous embassies, military installations, and professional trade, labor, and professional organization headquarters. Educational facilities include Georgetown University (1789), George Washington University (1821), Catholic University (1887), Howard University (1867), American University (1893). Inc. 1802. Pop. (1970) 756,510.

Washington, Treaty of (1871), agreement between the United States and Great Britain to submit outstanding disputes to an international arbitration commission. The disputes involved included the Alabama claims, the rights of US fishermen in Canadian waters, and the boundary between British Columbia and the state of Washington. *See also* Alabama Claims.

Washington Armament Conference (1921–22), meeting of several nations to discuss disarmament. It convened in Washington, D.C., in the hope that efforts to limit arms might prevent war. Nine treaties resulted from this conference, including the Four-Power Pacific Treaty and the Nine-Power Treaty on China. Among the nations participating were Great Britain, France, Japan, Italy, and the United States.

Washington Peace Convention (1861), effort to avert the Civil War. This convention was called by the Virginia Assembly and met in Washington, D.C. Former Pres. John Tyler chaired the meeting, at which northern, southern, and border states were represented. Its proposals were rejected.

Washington's Farewell Address (1796), speech, dated September 17, but never delivered orally, in which Pres. George Washington gave his reasons for declining a third term. He also warned against the geographical divisions encouraged by the party system and advised the nation to steer clear of permanent alliances with foreign nations. It was written with the help of John Jay and Alexander Hamilton.

Wasp, or **Hornet,** member of the families Vespidae and Sphecidae, with representatives found worldwide. These families have both social and solitary members. Some of the most common in North America are the yellowjacket, paper wasp, and mud dauber wasp. The European hornet, *Vespa crabro,* has become established in the United States. The adults feed on nectar and the larvae are fed insects. They can give a venomous sting, and do so repeatedly. See also Hymenoptera; Mud Dauber Wasp. △498.

Wassermann Test, a test for syphilis devised by the German bacteriologist August von Wassermann, in which a specific reaction (the Wassermann reaction) occurring in a mixture of beef heart extract, animal serum, and washed red blood cells, and the patient's serum indicates the presence of the disease.

Waste Disposal, Nuclear. Fission reactors and their fuel preparation plants produce waste residues containing highly radioactive substances. After uranium, plutonium, and any other useful fission products have been removed some long-lived radioactive products remain, such as cesium-137 and strontium-90. These wastes have to be disposed of so that they will not contaminate the earth, seas, or atmosphere. International regulations exist for disposing of the wastes, separate regulations applying to liquids, gases, and solids. In general, disposal consists of burying the materials under controlled conditions in underground tanks, in disused mines, and in the sea. △1482.

Waste Land, The, (1922) poem by T.S. Eliot. In 434 lines it sums up the disillusionment and moral disgust of the post-World War I generation with the barrenness and corruption of modern civilization. Influenced by the French Symbolist movement, in it Eliot used dense literary and mythological allusions and a difficult structure, as well as providing his own set of explanatory notes. Originally a controversial work, it quickly became an accepted and honored part of modern literature.

Water, odorless colorless liquid that covers about 70% of the Earth's surface and is the most widely used solvent. It is a compound of hydrogen and oxygen (H_2O) with the two H-O links of the molecule forming an angle of 105°. This asymmetry results in polar properties and a force of attraction (hydrogen bond) between opposite ends of neighboring molecules. These forces maintain the substance as a liquid, in spite of its low molecular weight, and account for its unusual property of having its maximum density at 4 °C. Properties: sp gr (4°C) 1.0000; melt. pt. 32°F (0° C); boil. pt. 212°F (100°C). △1504,1562,1568.

Water Bearer, The. *See* Aquarius.

Water Beetle, aquatic beetle, especially predaceous diving beetle (Family Dytiscidae); water scavenger beetle (Family Hydrophilidae); or whirligig beetle (Family Gyrinidae). *See also* Diving Beetle, Water Scavenger Beetle, Whirligig Beetle. △500.

Water Boatman, aquatic insect, gray to black, found worldwide. It is oval and flat with fringed, oarlike hind legs. It feeds on algae and microorganisms in ponds and streams and is an important fish food. Length: 0.23–0.43in (6–11mm). Family Corixidae. *See also* Hemiptera.

Waterbuck, Kob, or **Lechwe,** large, gregarious, coarse-haired antelope, native to Africa, south of the Sahara, and the Nile Valley. Some species are yellowish, others almost black, many have white markings. Long, ringed horns in males slope backwards, then curve forward at the tip. Length: 4.5–7ft (1.4–2.1m); height: 44–58in (112–147cm) high at shoulder. Family Bovidae; genus *Kobus. See also* Antelope. △586.

Water Buffalo, or **Carabao,** large ox, widely domesticated from Egypt to the Philippines and in Hungary and S Europe; it is wild or feral in N India and Burma. Ash gray to black, with long narrow face, it has stiff, scanty hair and large, splayed hooves. Flat-fronted, ringed horns are widest of any bovid, up to 77in (195.6cm) across. Mainly a draft animal, it is also used for milk; its meat is of poor quality. Length: to 10ft (3m); height: to 6ft (1.8m); weight: to 1,760lb (800kg). Family Bovidae; species *Bubalus bubalis.* △548.

Waterbug, Giant, aquatic bug found worldwide. It preys on other insects, tadpoles, snails, and small fish. It is a strong flier, often attracted to lights. Length: to 4in (102mm). Family Belostomatidae. *See also* Hemiptera.

Waterbury, industrial city in S Connecticut, 18mi (29km) NNW of New Haven; brass center of United States. Industries: clocks, electronics. Settled 1677; inc. 1853. Pop. (1970) 108,033.

Water Cannon. △1496.

Water Chestnut, floating, aquatic weed found in Europe and SE United States. It has diamond-shaped leaves and edible, spiny chestnutlike fruit. Its rapid growth tends to clog streams. Family Hydrocaryaceae; species *Trapa natans.* The water chestnut of Chinese cookery is the tuber of a Chinese sedge, *Eleocharis tuberosus.* △336.

Watercolor, painting technique. In this method finely ground pigments, combined with water-soluble gums, are moistened to produce a transparent stain that is applied in washes to plain or tinted paper. The medium is an ancient one, traceable in its essentials to the papyrus paintings of early Egyptian art and the paintings, on silk or rice paper, of China and Japan.

Although used by Dürer in the late 15th century, and later by such 17th-century artists as Rembrandt and Claude Lorrain (who restricted their efforts to monochrome), its full coloristic range was not exploited in the West until the early 19th century, when it became the principal technique for English topographical painting. Still later, in the hands of such artists as J. R. Cozens, John Sell Cotman, Thomas Girtin, and J. M. W. Turner, it established the English as the great virtuosi of the form. In America, the most notable exponents of the medium were Winslow Homer and John Marin. In its pure form, watercolor painting abjures the use of opaque body colors and scratched-out highlights. △1416.

Water Cycle. △254, 1766.

Wateree, river in central South Carolina; rises in North Carolina as Catawba River and enters South Carolina as Wateree River; flows to the Congaree River to form Santee River; used for hydroelectricity. Length: 395mi (636km).

Waterfall. △258, 260.

Water Fern. △438.

Water Flea, tiny branchiopod crustacean, including freshwater *Daphnia,* commonly used as fish food in aquariums. The head projects from a bivalve carapace. Its long projecting antennae are used for swimming. Order Cladocera. *See also* Arthropod; Crustacean. △486, 490.

Waterford, town in Republic of Ireland, near mouth of Suir River; county town of County Waterford; noted for Waterford cut glass. Industries: beer, paper. Pop. 31,692.

Waterfowl, birds, including ducks, geese, swans, and South American screamers, found throughout most of the world. Large flocks migrate, often in "V"-

haped formations, from cool nesting spots to warm winter homes. All have short bills, short legs, and dense plumage underlaid by down. They engage in a complex courtship and lay large numbers of eggs. Order Anseriformes. *See also* Duck; Goose; Swan. △532.

Watergate Affair (1972–74), US political scandal involving the Nixon administration. It was precipitated by an attempted burglary on Democratic party's national offices, by persons working for President Nixon's reelection committee. The administration's efforts to cover up the connection provoked Senate and Justice Department investigations and ultimately implicated the president. Impeachment proceedings against him were begun (1973). In August 1974, after being forced by a Supreme Court ruling to relinquish tape recordings that attested to his involvement in the coverup, Nixon resigned. Although Nixon was pardoned by his successor, Gerald Ford, other administration members were prosecuted and convicted. △1396, 1422–24.

Water Hyacinth, plant of the Pickerelweed family native to tropical America and considered weeds in Florida. They have swollen, floating petioles and spikes of violet flowers. Species *Eichhornia crassipes.*

Waterlily, aquatic plant widely distributed in temperate and tropical regions. They have thick perennial rootstocks and showy flowers of white, pink, red, blue, or yellow. Family Nymphaceae; genera *Nymphaea, Nuphar,* and *Nelumbo.*

Waterloo, town in SE Ontario, Canada; industrial and arts center; site of Waterloo Lutheran College (1910), University of Waterloo (1959). Industries: metal products, furniture, distilleries, plastics, mushrooms. Settled by Mennonites from Pennsylvania 1800–05. Pop. 37,245.

Waterloo, city in NE Iowa, on Cedar River 52mi (84km) NW of Cedar Rapids; seat of Black Hawk co; scene of annual National Dairy Cattle Congress. Industries: tractors, meat packing, dairying. Founded 1845 as Prairie Rapids Crossing; renamed 1851; inc. 1868. Pop. (1970) 75,533.

Waterloo, Battle of (1815), last battle of the Napoleonic Wars. The French under Napoleon and Marshal Ney hoped to defeat the Allies by preventing the Prussians under General von Blücher from joining Arthur Wellesley, future duke of Wellington, and the British. The Prussians were defeated at Ligny, but the British drove back the French at Quatre Bras and took up position near Waterloo, now in Belgium. On June 18, Napoleon delayed his attack on the British until midday. By the evening the Prussians had arrived, and Napoleon was finally routed. *See also* Wellington, Duke of. △1226.

Water Louse. △490.

Watermelon, trailing annual vine native to tropical Africa and Asia and cultivated in warm areas of the United States. Its fruit has a hard, greenish rind, sweet, red, juicy flesh, and many seeds. Family Cucurbitaceae; species *Citrullus vulgaris. See also* Gourd.

Water Mint. △444.

Water Mite, bright red to green aquatic mite found worldwide. The larva is parasitic on aquatic insects and most nymphs and adults are predators. Length: 0.25in (6mm). Order Acari; suborder Prostigmata. *See also* Mite.

Water Moccasin, or cottonmouth, venomous semiaquatic pit viper of SE United States, closely related to the copperheads. It is olive, black, or brown with indistinct bands and a paler belly. It vibrates its tail and holds its white mouth open when excited. Length: to 4ft (1.2m). Family Viperidae; species *Ancistrodon piscivorus.*

Water Monster. *See* Hydra.

Water of Crystallization, definite molecular proportion of water that is chemically combined with certain substances in the crystalline state. Much of this water will be lost on heating to about 100°C but some, the water of constitution, will be retained to a much higher temperature. Cupric sulfate ($CuSO_4 \cdot 5H_2O$), for example, loses four molecules of water at 100°C, becoming $CuSO_4 \cdot H_2O$.

Water on the Knee. △720.

Water Pollution, Oil, the effect of an oil spill from a tanker, an undersea well, or a coastal refinery. It does much damage to sea birds, estuarine ecosystems, and the plankton in the waters which are a major source of global oxygen. There is ongoing research in the areas of prevention and removal of spills. △298.

Water Pollution, Sewage, the result of domestic wastewater discharged directly into waterways. Sewage encompasses all kitchen, body, laundry, and household cleaning wastes. All these waters are rich in nitrogen compounds and bacteria. The result is the spread of waterborne disease and the degradation of the receiving waters. △296, 1768.

Water Pollution, Thermal, results from the use of water as a cooling agent in some industrial processes. Increased temperature reduces the capacity of water to carry oxygen. This interferes with organisms living in the water. Thermal pollution becomes a problem when small bodies of water are affected. This is often a problem in nuclear power plant location. △296.

Water Polo, a swimming sport that employs features of basketball, hockey, football, and soccer. It is played by 2 teams of 7 persons each in a pool 57–90ft (17.4–27.5m) long and a maximum of 60ft (18.3m) wide. At each end of the pool is a net-enclosed goal, which one of the players defends. Only one hand may be used to advance the leather-covered ball, which is about 27 inches (68.6cm) in circumference, and the ball must be kept on the surface. It is a rough game where players may be held under water. The game as played in the United States uses six-man teams, a larger pool, and a smaller ball, which is allowed to be carried under water, resulting in much rougher play. The game originated in England in 1870, and was introduced in the United States in 1897. It has been an Olympic Games event since 1900.

Water Power, mechanical power derived from the fall or rush of water striking water-wheel paddles or buckets. It has been used over the years as a means of powering grain and sawmills and some factories. At present, water power is used to turn large electric turbine generators. Large, deep reservoirs, such as Grand Coulee and Hoover dams, are established as sources of potential energy for generating power for millions of users. △1220, 1486, 1634.

Water Purification. △1766–68.

Water Quality Improvement Act (1970), US legislation that tightened control on thermal pollution from nuclear power plants by requiring applicants seeking permission to operate such plants to prove that they would meet state water quality standards. The act also specified penalties for oil pollution and called for control of sewage from watercraft and pollution stemming from acid mine drainage.

Water Scavenger Beetle, oval, dark-colored, aquatic beetle that eats decaying plant and animal matter. It is distinguished from the predaceous diving beetle by its club-shaped antennae. Length: to 2in (5cm). Family Hydrophilidae. *See also* Diving Beetle.

Water Scorpion, brown aquatic bug found worldwide. It has long, slender breathing tubes, grasping front legs, and will bite humans if disturbed. Width: 1–1.5in (25–38mm). Family Nepidae. *See also* Hemiptera.

Watershed, originally a term signifying the line, ridge, or summit of high ground separating two drainage basins. Watershed lines were often used as boundary lines. Watershed has come to mean the region drained by a stream, lake, or other body of water.

Water Skiing, water sport that began in France in the 1920s, in which a person rides on skis on the surface of the water while being towed by a motor-driven boat. Competition skiing usually includes three events—slalom, jumping, and trick riding. Skis must be 4 feet (1.2m) long and 4–8 inches (10.2–20.3cm) wide. In the slalom, skiers are towed through a series of staggered buoys and must ski outside each of them. In jumping, the skiers must ski over an inclined wooden ramp 6 feet (1.8m) high and 20–22 feet (6.1–6.7m) long. Trick riding has no set pattern, and the skiers choose their own intricate routines.

Water Snake, any of numerous races of about 50 species of harmless, semiaquatic snakes found on all continents except South America. Most are heavy-bodied and brown with blotches, streaks, or cross-bands. Length: to 4.5ft (1.4m). Family Colubridae.

Water Softener. *See* Softener, Water.

Water Spider. △488.

Gig Harbor, Washington

Washington Monument, Washington, D.C.

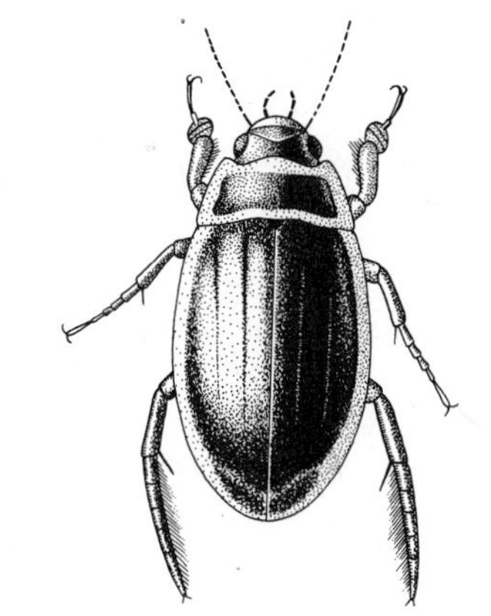

Water beetle

Waterbuck

Water Strider, or pond skater, dark-brown to black aquatic insect found worldwide. Traveling in groups, it has long legs used to glide on the surface of calm waters. Members of the genus *Halobates* are often found far out at sea. Length: 0.3–1in (8–25mm). Family Gerridae. *See also* Hemiptera.

Water Table, the surface between an upper level, the zone of aeration, and a lower level, the zone of saturation. In the zone of aeration the open spaces are filled mainly with air. In the zone of saturation, a subsurface level, the openings are filled with water. The water table is a subdued imitation of the ground surface. △254.

Waterton Lakes National Park, park in SW Alberta, Canada, on the US border. Park adjoins Glacier National Park in NW Montana; together they form the Waterton-Glacier International Peace Park (est. 1932 by Canadian Parliament and US Congress). The parks are connected by the Chief Mt International Highway and the Continental Divide; terrain is mountainous with numerous lakes, glaciers, hiking trails, birds, and wild flowers. *See also* Glacier National Park.

Watertown, city in N New York, on Black River; seat of Jefferson co. Falls of river drop 112ft (34m) in city; used to supply electric power to area; site of Jefferson Community College (1963). Industries: paper, automobile parts, rubber and plastic products, snow plows. Settled 1800; inc. as village 1815, as city 1869. Pop. (1970) 30,787.

Water Treatment, the removal of undesirable elements from a water supply. Unpleasant tastes and odors are removed by aeration. Bacteria are destroyed by the addition of chlorine (the taste of chlorine is then removed with sodium sulfite). Hardness is reduced with lime or by using zeolite as a water softener. Other organic and mineral matter is removed with alum. Fluoride is added to the water supply of many communities to reduce dental caries. △1766.

Water Turkey. *See* Snakebird.

Water Vapor, water in its gaseous state, composing up to 3% by weight of the atmosphere, determining the humidity and forming clouds as it condenses. Most of the atmosphere's water vapor is found in the troposphere, half of it below an altitude of 1.25mi (2km). Water vapor absorbs infrared (long-wave) radiation strongly, holding such radiation in the atmosphere in the greenhouse effect, and plays a vital role in the transfer of energy and the Earth's heat balance. △212.

Waterwheel. △314.

Watson, James Dewey, (1928–), US geneticist and biophysicist, b. Chicago. He is known for his role in the discovery of the molecular structure of DNA (deoxyribonucleic acid), the substance that is the basis of heredity. He shared the Nobel Prize in physiology and medicine in 1962 for his work. Watson later helped break the genetic code of the DNA base sequences and found the RNA (ribonucleic acid) messenger that transfers the DNA code to the cell's protein-forming structures. Writings include *The Double Helix* (1968). △414.

Watson, John B(roadus) (1878–1958), US psychologist, b. Greenville, S.C. He was the founder of behaviorism in the United States. In the early 1900s he rejected mentalism and introspection and advocated a purely objective psychology that would be concerned solely with observable behavior. His work did much to make psychological research more objective and rigorous, and his point of view continues today in the work of B.F. Skinner. Among his major works are *Behaviorism* (1925); and *Psychological Care of the Infant and Child* (1928). *See also* Behaviorism.

Watt, the unit of power in the metric meter-kilogram-second (mks) system of units. A machine consuming one joule of energy per second has a power output of one watt. One horsepower corresponds to 746 watts.

Watt, James (1736–1819), Scottish inventor. In 1765 he invented a separate condensing vessel for the steam engine. Until this time the cylinder itself was used as a condenser. Watt's invention proved to be very efficient; it used about one third the amount of steam needed in previous steam engines. From 1775–1800 he had a partnership with Matthew Boulton in the Soho Engineering Works. Their company produced steam engines on a large scale—almost 500 engines before 1800. Among Watt's other inventions were the pressure gauge (1790) and the double-action piston (1782). He coined the term *horsepower*. The units *watt* and *kilowatt* were named after him. △1186, 1582–84.

Watteau, Jean Antoine (1684–1721), French painter of Flemish parentage. Generally considered the preeminent French master before the Revolution, he started his career as a theatrical designer. His earliest influence was the Flemish painter David Teniers. The Flemish influence showed in pictures whose simple realism contrasted markedly with his more contrived, idealized works. Under the influence of Rubens, Titian, and Paolo Veronese, he invested his pictures with the pearlescent flesh tones and vibrant colors of those masters. His art is of historical importance because it freed French painting from its reliance on academic concepts derived from Italy, giving impetus to a Parisian style that was to prevail in France until the onset of neoclassicism. △1190.

Watts, Isaac (1674–1748), English clergyman and author. He is now remembered for his *Divine Songs for Children* (1715) and his hymns, notably "When I Survey the Wondrous Cross" and "O God Our Help in Ages Past." Watts is considered the creator of the modern English hymn. He also published several religious and educational treatises.

Waugh, Evelyn (Arthur St John) (1903–66), English novelist. His novels, usually considered satiric, include *Decline and Fall* (1928), *Vile Bodies* (1930), *Brideshead Revisited* (1945), *The Loved One* (1948), and a trilogy about World War II: *Men at Arms* (1952), *Officers and Gentlemen* (1955), and *Unconditional Surrender* (1961).

Waukegan, port city in NE Illinois, 40mi (64km) N of Chicago. Industries: outboard motors, wire, steel, gypsum, asbestos, building materials. Founded as Little Fort on old Indian village site 1835; inc. 1849, as city 1859. Pop. (1970) 65,269.

Waukesha, city in SE Wisconsin, on Fox River; seat of Waukesha co; site of Cutler Park, containing three ancient Indian mounds; health resort, noted for mineral water 1870–early 1900s; seat of Carroll College. Industries: electronic equipment, aluminum, internal combustion engines. Settled 1835; inc. 1896. Pop. (1970) 40,274.

Wausau, city in central Wisconsin, on Wisconsin River; seat of Marathon co; site of University of Wisconsin at Wausau. Industries: dairying, insurance, woodworking, paper, machinery, tourism. Founded 1839; inc. 1872 as Big Bull Falls. Pop. (1970) 32,806.

Wauwatosa, city in SE Wisconsin; W suburb of Milwaukee, on Menominee River. Industries: chemicals, metal, concrete, lumber. Settled 1835; inc. 1897. Pop. (1970) 58,676.

Wave, in oceanography, a moving disturbance traveling on or through water but which does not move the water itself. Wind causes waves by frictional drag. Waves not under pressure of strong winds are called swells. Waves begin to break on shore or "feel bottom" when they reach a depth shallower than one half the wave's length. When the water depth is 1 1/3 times the wave height, the wave front is so steep that the top falls over and the wave breaks. The wave activity between the line of breakers and the shore is called the surf or swash. As the water moves up the beach, it loses its energy and then flows back into the water; the backward flow is called the backwash. △226.

Wave, in physics, vibrating disturbance, either continuous or transient, by which energy is transmitted through a medium at a velocity dependent on the type of wave and on the medium. Electromagnetic waves, such as light, consist of varying magnetic and electric fields vibrating at right angles to each other and to the direction of motion; they are transverse waves. Sound waves are transmitted by the vibrations of the particles of the medium itself, the vibrations being in the direction of wave motion; they are longitudinal waves. Thus sound waves, unlike electromagnetic waves, cannot travel through a vacuum and cannot undergo polarization. Both types of waves can be reflected, refracted, and can give rise to interference phenomena. A wave is characterized by its wavelength or frequency, the velocity of wave motion being the product of wavelength and frequency. The velocity of electromagnetic waves greatly exceeds that of sound. △1516, 1520.

Wave Amplitude, peak (maximum or minimum) value of a periodically varying quantity, such as an alternating current or voltage or an electromagnetic wave.

Wave Diffraction. *See* Diffraction. △1526.

Wave Dispersion, variation of the index of refraction of a medium with wavelength. It occurs with all electromagnetic waves but is most obvious at optical wavelengths, causing light to be separated into its component colors. This can be achieved by passing a light beam through a refracting medium, such as a glass prism. As every spectral color has a different wavelength, each color present in the light is refracted by a different amount, red (high wavelength) being bent less than violet (low wavelength), and the emergent beam is colored. Dispersion is used to produce spectra but causes chromatic aberration in lens images.

Wave Erosion. △268.

Wave Frequency (symbol ν or f), number of complete oscillations or wave cycles in unit time of a vibrating system; measured in hertz. For a wave it is given by wave velocity divided by wavelength. By quantum theory the frequency of electromagnetic radiation is proportional to the energy of the component photons. The characteristics of electromagnetic radiation depend on the frequency. △1516.

Wave Front, contour, which may be plane, spherical, etc, and which is usually at right angles to the direction of wave motion, on which every point is vibrating in step (that is, in phase). Each point is a source of secondary wavelets, the forward vibration limits of which give the wave front position a short time later.

Wave Interference, phenomenon in which two waves of the same wavelength and in step (in phase) at their source interact at a point, having traveled along different paths. The amplitude of the overlapping waves is the sum of the individual amplitudes; two maxima or two minima will reinforce each other and the amplitude is doubled; a maximum and a minimum cancel, producing zero amplitude. With two light waves, such as two identical laser beams, an interference pattern of light and dark bands or rings can be seen on a screen in the overlap region. △1520, 1522, 1526.

Wavelength (symbol λ), distance between two similar and successive points, that is, points having the same phase, of an electromagnetic wave, sound wave, etc, as between two successive points of maximum displacement. It is equal to the wave velocity divided by the wave frequency. △1516, 1794.

Wavell, Archibald Percival Wavell, 1st Earl of (1883–1950), British field marshal. He fought in South Africa, France, and Palestine. As commander in chief for the Middle East (1939), he defeated the Italians in North and East Africa (1940–41) but was forced back by the Germans under Field Marshal Rommel (1941). He subsequently commanded forces in Southeast Asia but lost Malaya, Singapore, and Burma to the Japanese (1941–42). He became viceroy and governor-general of India (1943–47).

Wave Mechanics. △1556.

Waverley (1814), first novel of Sir Walter Scott. △1238.

Wax, solid non-greasy insoluble substances of low melting point. They are of three kinds: Animal and vegetable waxes are simple lipids consisting of esters of the higher fatty acids with monohydric alcohols; examples are beeswax and spermaceti (animal) and carnauba and candelilla (vegetable). Mineral waxes, such as paraffin and montan, are esters of the higher hydrocarbons. Synthetic waxes are of diverse origin and include polyethylenes and chloronaphthalenes. They are all used in the manufacture of polishes, cosmetics, candles, etc. △1506, 1560, 1570.

Waxwing. *See* Cedar Waxwing.

Wayne, Anthony (1745–96), US general, b. Waynesboro, Pa. Called "Mad Anthony" because of his daring, he served under George Washington in the Revolutionary War campaigns around New York and Pennsylvania and in 1779 he led the successful night attack on Stony Point, N.Y. In 1781–83 he fought in the South. In the West after the war he defeated the Ohio Indians in the Battle of Fallen Timbers (1794) and signed the Treaty of Greenville, the first treaty in which Indian title to US lands was recognized.

Wayne, John (1907–), US film star, one of the most successful in film history. He debuted in *Salute* (1929), was a Western player of the 1930s, and became a major Hollywood star in the 1940s. He won a

Best Actor Academy Award for *True Grit* (1969), one of the many Western films he is identified with.

Wayne, town in SE Michigan, on South Branch of River Rouge; named for Gen. "Mad Anthony" Wayne. Industries: automobile and aircraft parts, agriculture. Founded 1824; inc. as village 1869, as city 1960. Pop. (1970) 21,854.

WCTU. *See* Woman's Christian Temperence Union.

Weakfish, or aqueteague, common sea trout, commercial and game marine fish found in tropical and temperate waters. Dark gray and blue with black spots, soft mouth with a fishing hook easily tearing it. Weight: to 16lb (7.3kg). Family Sciaenidae; species *Cynoscion regalis.*

Weak Interaction. *See* Interaction, Nuclear. △1484.

Weaponry. △1726, 1728, 1730, 1746.

Weasel, small, carnivorous, mostly ground-dwelling mammal native to Eurasia, N Africa, and North and South America. Most have small heads, long necks, slender bodies, and short legs. Reddish-brown with light underparts, some turn all white in winter. They are fierce predators and often attack much larger animals. Although they destroy domestic poultry, weasels are one of the most effective forms of rodent control. The dwarf weasel is the smallest, the wolverine the largest. Length: 6–40in (15–102cm). Family Mustelidae; genus *Mustela.*

Weather, the state of the atmosphere in a given locality or over a broad area, particularly as it affects human activities. Weather refers to short-term states of minutes or hours as opposed to long-term climatic conditions. Weather involves such elements as atmospheric temperature, pressure, humidity, precipitation, cloudiness, brightness, visibility, and wind. Many of these are shown on weather maps and are accurately measured by weathermen, or meteorologists, by means of instruments on satellites, balloons, or at radar and weather stations. *See also* Climate; Meteorology; Weather Map; Weather Modification; Weather Observations. △214–218.

Weather Forecasting, prediction of features and effects of the weather, such as temperature, precipitation, storms and fair weather, travel and sea conditions, by means of data from many observations gathered from weather stations and using a variety of computational and mapping techniques. △218.

Weather Maps, charts made up by meteorologists of weather elements and conditions over wide areas, such as the whole United States or Europe, to assist them in their forecasts and to inform the public. Made up for surface or upper-level atmospheric conditions, such maps often show wind speed and direction, isotherms (lines of constant temperature), isobars (lines of constant pressure) depicting high- and low-pressure areas, ridges, and troughs, various kinds of fronts and the cyclones and anticyclones associated with them, and types of precipitation expected. *See also* Weather; Weather Forecasting. △218.

Weather Modification, changing of natural weather conditions or systems by man, still on a largely experimental basis. Greater knowledge of precipitation has led to many cloud-seeding experiments to increase or decrease rain or snow in local areas. Overseeding of hail-spawning clouds and of thunderstorms has been attempted but reduction in hail or lightning suppression is difficult to measure. Attempts to reduce the severity of hurricanes by seeding the walls around the center have yielded controversial results. Cold fogs can be dissipated somewhat by seeding, however, and warm fogs by heating. Techniques for weather modification are still in their infancy. *See also* Cloud Seeding; Weather.

Weather Observations, furnishing the data required for weather description, analysis, and prediction from thousands of weather stations and instruments around the globe, such as ships and aircraft, balloons, and weather satellites. Weather stations measure and record weather conditions in their vicinity and survey with radar up to 100 to 200 mi. (161 to 320 km). Upper-air conditions are obtained from radiosonde balloons reporting instrument readings, from high-flying aircraft, and from stratospheric balloons operating for long periods at heights up to 20mi. (32km). Weather satellites, in polar orbits covering the whole Earth rotating under them, or observing the development of conditions from stationary orbits above the equator, obtain day and night observations in visible and infrared wavelengths. They provide pictures of cloud cover and storm disturbances as well as data on vertical temperature and moisture profiles of the atmosphere, making more accurate long-term weather forecasts possible. △218.

Weaver, James Baird (1833–1912), US political leader, b. Dayton, Ohio. A Union Army hero in the Civil War, he received the post of federal assessor of internal revenue in Iowa after the war (1867–73). Initially a Republican, he joined the Greenback party and served in the House of Representatives (1879–81; 1885–89). He was the Greenback's presidential candidate (1880) and that of the Populist party (1892), when he polled over 1,000,000 votes.

Weaver, John (1673–1760), English dancer. One of the most prominent figures in the English School of dance and ballet, he was famous for his role as the clown in the English pantomime. He was the first producer of pantomime ballet. His first production was *The Tavern Bilkers,* played at the Drury Lane Theater in 1702. △1194.

Weaverbird, short-billed, arboreal, and ground-dwelling birds known for their sophisticated nesting habits. Some build "play" nests, some let foster parents raise their young, and some weave complex nests. The family includes the common house sparrow and other Old World sparrows; African weavers, the destructive red-billed quelea of tropical Africa; and African widow birds whose ornamented males are polygamous. The sociable weaver *(Philetarius socius)* of Africa builds an apartment-house nest. With a group, it erects a canopy high in an isolated grassland tree, weaves straw and grass into retort-shaped chambers for each pair, and constructs vertical tunnels from the egg chambers. Family Ploceidae. △586.

Weaving, fabric art, performed by interlacing two or more sets of yarn at right angles. △1622.

Web △488.

Webb, Sidney (1859–1947), and **Beatrice** (1858–1943), English socialists. The Webbs were cofounders and participants in the Fabian Society of England (1884). Their position was that socialism was the "best" form of political and economic system for society to adopt. Consequently, their efforts were devoted to trying to "educate" people toward preferring socialism to capitalism. *See also* Fabian Society. △1326.

Webb-Kenyon Interstate Liquor Act (1913), US legislation passed over President Taft's veto, it prohibited the shipment of intoxicating liquors to any state, territory, or district where they were to be used to violate local laws. It marked a major success for national prohibitionists. *See also* Anti-Saloon League; Prohibition.

Webb-Pomerene Act (1918), US legislation repealing the anti-trust laws for export associations. It enabled US firms to be more competitive in foreign markets against foreign cartels.

Weber, Ernst (1795–1878), German physiologist. He was a pioneer in the study of sensation and perception. He laid the foundations for the branch of psychology called "psychophysics," influenced other thinkers such as Gustav Fechner, and encouraged psychology to be more scientific and methodical.

Weber, Karl Maria von (1786–1826), German composer, conductor, and pianist. He influenced Wagner and helped establish a German national style in his operas *Der Freischütz* (1820) and *Euryanthe* (1823). He also composed piano and chamber music, concertos, and the popular *Invitation to the Dance* (1819). △1246, 1256.

Weber, Max (1864–1920), German sociologist. He made vital contributions to research in the sociology of religion, the nature of authority, the rationalization of modern life, and the methodology of the social sciences. Disagreeing with the Marxist stress on economics, he emphasized the plurality and interdependence of causative factors in social action, particularly the role of values, ideologies, and individual leaders. He advanced the concept of "ideal types," generalized models of social situations as an analytical tool and insisted that the social sciences should be empirical, based on comparative social history, and free of value judgments. In political sociology he delineated traditional, charismatic, and legal-rational types of leadership. Much of his work was only published in article form in his lifetime, to be collected in book form (such as *Economy and Society,* 1922) after his death. In his most important work, *The Protestant Ethic and the Spirit of Capitalism* (1904–05), he presented the influential and controversial thesis that the asceticism fostered by Calvinism in turn fostered the

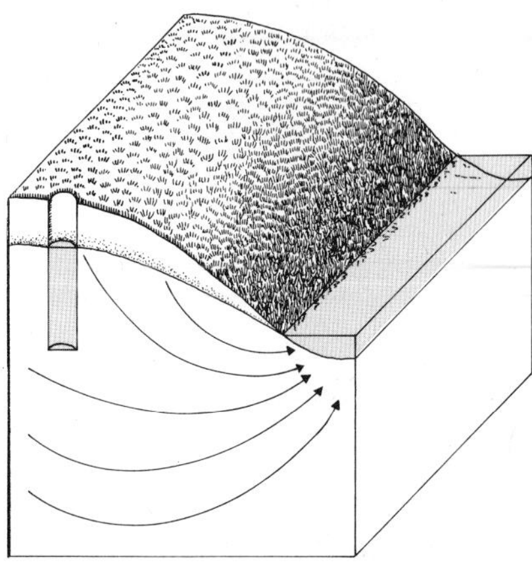

Water table

James Watson

Jean Watteau: Love Disarmed

Weasel

rise of capitalism. He helped to draft the German constitution of 1920.

Weber, Max (1881–1961), US painter, b. Russia. He was one of the first American artists to recognize the importance of the onset of the modern movement. Early in his career he embraced Fauvist and Cubist devices and theories, but he soon turned to a less radical style derived from Cézanne, a style he later employed to produce colorful, expressionistic, rather fluidly painted scenes of New York Jewish life. △890, 1290.

Weber, river in N Utah, rises in Uinta Mts, flows N and NW to join Ogden River at Ogden; together they flow into Great Salt Lake; source of irrigation. Length: 100mi (161km).

Webern, Anton von (1883–1945), Austrian composer, a student of Arnold Schoenberg. He adopted the 12-tone system and though his music contains relatively few works, which have never been generally popular, he influenced many other composers. △1364.

Webster, Daniel (1782–1852), US statesman and orator, b. Salisbury, N.H. He was, with John C. Calhoun and Henry Clay, one of the three great political leaders of the mid-19th century. He served in the US House of Representatives (1813–17; 1823–27) where he made his name as an orator. In the Senate (1827–41; 1845–50) and as secretary of state (1841–43; 1850–52), he was influential in maintaining the Union and in dealing with foreign countries. His great disappointment was never becoming president. He negotiated the Webster-Ashburton Treaty (1842) and supported the Compromise of 1850. *See also* Webster-Ashburton Treaty. △1396.

Webster, Noah (1758–1843), US lexicographer and author. In 1783 he published his *American Spelling Book* (popularly known as the "Blue-backed Speller"), which became a standard textbook in American schools. In 1828 he completed his monumental *American Dictionary of the English Language,* containing 70,000 words, the largest English dictionary published up to that time.

Webster-Ashburton Treaty (1842), agreement that settled the disputed northeastern boundary between Maine and New Brunswick, named after US Sec. of State Daniel Webster and Britain's Lord Ashburton. It gave the United States about 7,000sq mi (18,130sq km) of the territory in dispute. The United States paid $150,000 to both Maine and Massachusetts to settle their claims, and Britain retained military routes between Quebec and New Brunswick. The United States received rights of navigation on the St John River, and free navigation on the St Lawrence, Detroit, and St Clair rivers. The New York and Vermont boundaries were established along with that between Lake Superior and Lake of the Woods.

Webster Groves, city in E Missouri, 8mi (13km) W of St Louis; site of Webster College (1915) and Eden Theological Seminary (1850). Founded 1854; inc. 1896. Pop. (1970) 27,455.

Webster-Hayne Debate (1830), debate in the US Senate on the issue of the preservation of the Union. The question of restricting the sale of public land in the West opened debate on the issue of states' rights. Robert Hayne of South Carolina stated the case against federal interference and consolidation of the federal government. Daniel Webster of Massachusetts defended the federal union, saying, "Liberty and Union, now and forever, one and inseparable!"

Webworm, or sod worm, various caterpillars found worldwide in meadows and lawns feeding on grass stems, crowns, and roots. They live on webs at the base of grass. The white to yellow-brown adult moth flies in the evening; length: 0.3–0.5in (7.6–12.7mm). Family Pyralidae.

Wechsler, David (1896–), US psychologist, b. Romania. He developed several widely used intelligence tests—the Wechsler Adult Intelligence Scale (or WAIS, originated in 1939 as the Wechsler-Bellevue) and the Wechsler Intelligence Scale for Children (or WISC, originated in 1949). Among his publications are *The Measurements of Adult Intelligence* (1944) and *Wechsler Preschool and Primary Scale of Intelligence* (1967).

Wechsler Intelligence Scales, widely used intelligence tests devised by psychiatrist David Wechsler. They include the WAIS (Wechsler Adult Intelligence Scale), WISC (Wechsler Intelligence Scale for Children), and WPPSI (Wechsler Preschool and Primary Scale of Intelligence). Each test consists of 11 subtests that reveal the subject's strengths and weaknesses. *See also* Intelligence Testing.

Wedgwood, Josiah (1730–95), English potter. A member of the fourth of nine generations of potters in his family, he was responsible for making a major industry of his craft. The developer of a creamy white earthenware (Queen's Ware) that largely supplanted porcelain throughout Europe, he also invented Jasper ware, for which he is best known.

Weed, Thurlow (1797–1882), US journalist and politician, b. Cairo, N.Y. He was an influential writer and became editor of the Rochester *Telegraph* (1822), purchasing the paper three years later. He was powerful in three parties, the Anti-Masons, Whigs, and Republicans. He never held office himself but helped nominate and elect presidents. During the Civil War (1861), he represented the Union cause on diplomatic missions in England and France.

Weed, uncultivated or unwanted plant usually found on wasteland and along roadsides. It produces many seeds, enabling it to colonize rapidly, crowding out other plants. Annual or perennial weeds are a threat to commercial crops because they compete for water and sunlight and harbor pests and diseases that can spread to the crop plants. Common weeds include dodder, poison ivy, poison oak, goldenrod, chickweed, and narrow- and broad-leaved plantain. Edible weeds include purslane and dandelion. △446.

Weeping Willow. *See* Willow.

Weevil, beetle that is an agricultural pest, especially the numerous snout beetles with long, down-curved beaks for boring into plants. There are several thousand weevil species, each typically specialized for feeding on particular parts of particular plants. Family Curculionidae. △498.

Wegener, Alfred Lothar (1880–1930), German geologist, meteorologist, and arctic explorer. In *The Origin of Continents and Oceans* (1915) he set forth his theory of continental drift. He is also noted for his expeditions to Greenland. On one of these he died.

Wegner, Abraham Gottlob. △172.

Wei, river in China; originates in W Kansu prov., flows E to join Yellow River at its E bend. The fertile river valley has supported great populations since 1st millennium BC. Length: 537mi (865km).

Weight, the force on a body due to gravity. A body's weight *W* is the product of its mass and the acceleration due to gravity at that point. Mass remains constant, but weight depends on position on the Earth's surface, decreasing with increasing altitude. *See also* Gravity; Mass.

Weightlessness, the condition of a body in space, when motion is controlled by inertia and the force of gravity is neutralized. Zero gravity is the term used to describe the weightless state. Other than in space flight, weightlessness may be felt in a free-falling elevator or in an airplane flying in unpowered flight along a curved trajectory like that of an artillery shell. Spacecraft pilots have weightlessness problems (called hypogravics) such as decreased circulation of blood, less water retention in tissues and bloodstreams, and loss of muscle tone. Several protective mechanisms have been developed to combat the problems of weightlessness and others are being studied.

Weight Lifting, as a competitive sport, is popular in Europe, Egypt, Japan, Turkey, and the United States. Competitions are conducted according to weight classes that range from bantamweight to super heavyweight. In a weight-lifting meet, each participant uses three standard lifts: two-hand press, clean-and-jerk, and snatch. The man who lifts the greatest combined total of weights wins. Weight lifting was introduced at the Olympic Games in 1896, but did not become a regular event until 1920.

Weights and Measures, a system of basic measurements applied in the areas of mass, volume, length, and area and now extended to temperature, luminosity, pressure, and electric current. Uniformity and unit standards are fundamental. Uniformity requires accurate reliable standards of mass and length. A standard is the physical embodiment of a unit. The system may be evolutionary, growing out of custom, or planned, such as the modern Système International (SI) used by scientists throughout the world. The base units of this system are: length, meter; mass, kilogram; time, second; electric current, ampere; thermodynamic temperature, degrees Kelvin; light intensity, candela. In the United States, the decimal system is the basis of currency, but the metric system introduced in France for other measurements in the early 19th century was rejected in favor of the English system, which used the yard (3 feet) and the avoirdupois pound (7,000 grains), for example. Standards have been fixed throughout all the US since the mid-19th century, having been established by the Office of Standard Weights and Measures, which in 1901 became the National Bureau of Standards (NBS). Within the NBS, the Institute for Basic Standards provides the basis of a consistent system of physical measurements and coordinates that system with those of other nations. △1450.

US WEIGHTS AND MEASURES

Linear Measure
12 inches=1 foot
3 feet=1 yard
5½ yards=1 rod
40 rods=1 furlong
8 furlongs=1 statute mile

Area Measure
144 square inches=1 square foot
9 square feet=1 square yard
30¼ square yards=1 square rod
160 square rods=1 acre
640 acres=1 square mile
1 mile square=1 section of land
6 miles square=1 township

Cubic Measure
1728 cubic inches=1 cubic foot
27 cubic feet=1 cubic yard

Liquid Measure
4 gills=1 pint
2 pints=1 quart
4 quarts=1 gallon

Dry Measure
2 pints=1 quart
8 quarts=1 peck
4 pecks=1 bushel

Avoirdupois Weight
27 11/32 grains=1 dram
16 drams=1 ounce
16 ounces=1 pound
100 pounds=1 hundredweight
20 hundredweights=1 ton

Troy Weight
24 grains=1 pennyweight
20 pennyweights=1 ounce troy
12 ounces troy=1 pound troy

Apothecaries' Weight
20 grains=1 scruple
3 scruples=1 dram apothecaries
8 drams apothecaries=1 ounce apothecaries
12 ounces apothecaries=1 pound apothecaries

Apothecaries' Fluid Measure
60 minims=1 fluid dram
8 fluid drams=1 fluid ounce
16 fluid ounces=1 pint
2 pints=1 quart
4 quarts=1 gallon

METRIC WEIGHTS AND MEASURES

Linear Measure
10 millimeters=1 centimeter
10 centimeters=1 decimeter
10 decimeters=1 meter
10 meters=1 dekameter
10 dekameters=1 hectometer
10 hectometers=1 kilometer

Area Measure
100 sq. millimeters=1 sq. centimeter
10,000 sq. centimeters=1 sq. meter
100 sq. meters=1 are
100 ares=1 hectare
100 hectares=1 sq. kilometer

Volume Measure
1000 milliliters=1 liter
100 liters=1 hectoliter
10 hectoliters=1 kiloliter

Cubic Measure
1000 cubic millimeters=1 cubic centimeter
1000 cubic centimeters=1 cubic decimeter
1000 cubic decimeters=1 cubic meter

Weight
1000 milligrams=1 gram
1000 grams=1 kilogram
1000 kilograms=1 metric ton

CONVERSION TABLES

Linear Measure
1 inch=2.5400 centimeters
1 foot=0.3048 meters
1 mile=1.6093 kilometers
1 centimeter=0.3937 inch
1 meter=39.37 inches
3.2808 feet
1 kilometer=0.6214 mile

Area Measure
1 square inch=6.4516 square centimeters
1 square foot=0.0929 square meter
1 square mile=2.5900 square kilometers
1 acre=0.4047 hectare
1 square centimeter=0.1550 square inch
1 square meter=10.7639 square feet
1 hectare=2.4711 acres
1 square kilometer=0.3861 square mile
Cubic Measure
1 cubic inch=16.3871 cubic centimeters
1 cubic yard=0.7646 cubic meter
1 cubic centimeter=0.06102 cubic inch
1 cubic meter=1.3080 cubic yards
Liquid Measure
1 ounce=29.5727 milliliters
1 quart=0.9463 liter
1 milliliter=0.0338 fl. ounce
1 liter=1.0567 quarts
Dry Measure
1 pint=0.5506 liter
1 peck=8.8095 liters
1 liter=1.8162 pints
1 dekaliter=1.1351 pecks
Avoirdupois Weight
1 grain=64.7989 milligrams
1 avoirdupois ounce=28.3495 grams
1 avoirdupois pound=0.4536 kilogram
1 milligram=0.0154 grain
1 gram=0.0353 avoirdupois ounce
1 kilogram=2.2046 avoirdupois pounds
Mariner's Measure
6 feet=1 fathom
1012.7 fathoms=1 nautical mile
3 nautical miles=1 marine league
1 nautical mile per hour=1 knot (measure of speed)

Weil, Simone (1909–43), French philosopher. She became a teacher and also wrote for Socialist and Communist journals. In ill health, she began to study Bible and Hindu teachings, and became a Roman Catholic. She wrote *Waiting for God* (1951) and *Oppression and Liberty* (1958).

Weill, Kurt (1900–50) German composer noted for his satirical operas *The Rise and Fall of the City of Mahagonny* (1927) and *The Threepenny Opera* (1928) done in collaboration with Bertolt Brecht and for the music for a number of Broadway shows.

Weil's Disease. *See* Leptospirosis.

Weimar, city in central East Germany, 13mi (21km) E of Erfurt. City was capital of duchy of Saxe-Weimar 1547–1918; Weimar Republic was est. 1919 by German National Assembly, and abolished by its Chancellor, Adolf Hitler 1933 to establish his dictatorship; cultural center, home of Goethe and Schiller in late 18th century; site of Goethe National Museum, Liszt Museum, Weimar Castle. Industries: farm tools, building materials, chemicals, furniture. Founded 975; chartered 1348. Pop. 63,689.

Weimaraner, hunting dog (sporting group) originally used on big game by nobles of Weimar court; brought to US in 1929. A dog of speed and endurance, it has a long, aristocratic head; light amber, gray, or blue-gray eyes; slightly folded, high-set, lobular ears; medium-length body; straight forelegs and well-angulated hind legs; webbed feet; and tail docked to 6in (15cm). The short, sleek coat is mouse or silver-gray. Average size: 23–27in (58.5–68.5cm) high at shoulder; 55–85lb (25–38.5kg). *See also* Sporting Dog.

Weimar Republic (1919–33), the German federal republic set up after World War I, with a constitution that provided for a democratically elected president and a Reichstag of deputies. Forced by the Allies to agree to the humiliating demands of the Versailles Treaty and financially crippled by demands for reparations that could not be met, the Weimar governments were convulsed by a succession of economic and political crises, which facilitated the rise of extremist groups such as the Nazis. It was abolished by the Nazis in 1933. △1308, 1334.

Weir, Julian Alden (1852–1919), US painter and etcher, b. West Point, N.Y. An Impressionist, he was the founder of "The Ten," a group of like-minded artists including George Wesley Bellows and John Henry Twachtman.

Weirton, city in NW West Virginia, 26mi (42km) N of Wheeling, on Ohio River; site of blast furnace (1790s) that supplied cannon balls for Oliver Hazard Perry's fleet (1813). Industries: coal mining, steel manufacturing, chemicals, cement, tin plating. Settled 1790s; inc. 1947. Pop. (1970) 27,131.

Weismann, August (1834–1914), German biologist. His book discussing the germ plasm theory, *The Continuity of the Germ Plasm* (1885), proposed the immortality of the germ line cells as opposed to body cells and was influential in the development of modern genetic study.

Weissmuller, Johnny (1905–), US swimmer and actor, b. Windbar, Pa. He won gold medals at the 1924 and 1928 Olympics. He later went on to play Tarzan in a number of Hollywood films and appeared in numerous roles on television.

Weizmann, Chaim (1874–1952), the first president of the State of Israel, was a Zionist leader as well as a noted chemist. He believed Zionism must be political, practical, and cultural. During World War I he had a large role in persuading the British government to agree to the establishment of a Jewish national home in Palestine. From 1920–29 and 1935–46, he served as president of the World Zionist Organization. He was president of Israel from 1949 until his death in 1952. He strove for cooperation with the Arabs.

Weld, Theodore Dwight (1803–95), US abolitionist, b. Hampton, Conn. In 1833 he helped to organize the American Anti-Slavery Society. Trained as a minister, he organized anti-slavery debates that led to his dismissal from the seminary (1834). From the students, he chose a group that he had trained, by 1836, as agents for the American Anti-Slavery Society. In the 1840s he retired from public life, his voice ruined by constant preaching. He taught in Massachusetts and New Jersey and continued to concern himself with social reform issues.

Welding, a technique for joining metallic parts by applying heat or pressure. A number of processes have been developed to accommodate the physical properties of the materials involved and the use to which they are applied. Arc welding, which employs a continuous supply of electric current, is most important for joining steel. Fusion welding involves generating sufficient heat either by electricity or gas to create and maintain a pool of molten metal. Resistance, or spot, welding, a process in which the heat is generated at the interface by the electrical resistance of the joint, requires little time and uses low-voltage, high-current power. Spot welds are made at regular intervals on sheet metal that has an overlap. *See also* Brazing. △1542, 1604.

Welfare Economics, branch of economics dealing with the maximizing of the total utility or welfare of the society through the economic system, which became a separate discipline with A.C. Pigou's *The Economics of Welfare* (1920). Welfare economics also includes the study of optimizing resource allocations and the distribution of goods and services in order to achieve the maximum level of satisfaction for the sum of all members of society. △936.

Welfare State, nation in which the government assumes the responsibility for the welfare of its citizens. Several European countries are welfare states. Beginning with some of the legislation of the New Deal of Pres. Franklin D. Roosevelt, the United States has had many of the features of a welfare state, such as social security and unemployment insurance. Public medical care, care of the aged and handicapped, retirement benefits, and income redistribution are other characteristics of the welfare state. △936.

Welkom, planned city in Republic of South Africa; commercial center for nearby mines. Founded 1947. Pop. 137,400.

Welland, town in S Ontario, Canada, on the Welland Canal; capital of Welland co. Industries: textiles, fertilizer, wine, iron, stainless steel. Inc. 1917. Pop. 44,-222.

Welland Ship Canal, canal in S Ontario, Canada; first built with 25 locks, 1824–33; rebuilt with 8 locks for shipping, 1912–32; connects Port Colborne on Lake Erie to Port Weller on Lake Ontario. Length: 27.6mi (44.4km).

Weller, Thomas Huckle (1915–), US bacteriologist and virologist, b. Ann Arbor, Mich. He shared the 1954 Nobel Prize in physiology or medicine with John F. Enders and Frederick C. Robbins for the discovery of the ability of the poliomyelitis virus to grow in cultures of various types of tissue, a finding that made possible the development of a polio vaccine.

Daniel Webster

Noah Webster

Webworm

Weimaraner

Welles, (George) Orson (1915–), US actor, director, and filmmaker, b. Kenosha, Wis. He is best known for his brilliant first film *Citizen Kane* (1941), a fictional life of Hearst that revolutionized cinematographic technique. Welles' clash with the studio system limited his directing and forced him to work in Europe. His other notable films include *The Magnificent Ambersons* (1942), *Journey into Fear*, and *Touch of Evil* (1958). He also acted extensively. △1370.

Wellesley, town in E Massachusetts, 12mi (19km) WSW of Boston; site of Wellesley College (1870), Babson Institute (1919), and its Coleman Map Building containing relief map of the United States which took 17 years to complete. Settled 1660; inc. 1881. Pop. (1970) 28,051.

Wellington, Arthur Wellesley, Duke of (1769–1852), British general and statesman, b. Dublin. He entered the army in 1787 and fought in India (1796–1805), became Irish secretary (1807), commanded (1809) allied forces in the Peninsular War, and drove the French back over the Pyrenees (1814). Created duke (1814), he represented Britain at the Congress of Vienna (1814–15) and, with the Prussian general von Blücher, defeated Napoleon and the French at Waterloo (1815). He became Tory cabinet minister (1818) and prime minister (1828–30). He supported the Catholic Emancipation Act (1829), but opposed the Reform Bill (1831–32). He joined Robert Peel's cabinet (1834–35, 1841–46), and retired as chief warden of the cinque ports (1851). *See also* Waterloo, Battle of. △1226.

Wellington, capital of New Zealand, on S end of North Island, on an inlet of Pacific Ocean near Cook Strait; cultural, governmental, and educational center of New Zealand. Wellington has an excellent harbor with floating docks for ship repair and has been a rail center since the 1870s, growing into a busy commercial and industrial hub of New Zealand. City is surrounded by picturesque suburbs, and is site of National Art Gallery (1936), Dominion Museum, Victoria University of Wellington (1962), Parliament building, and government offices. Industries: textiles, machinery, food processing. Founded 1840; became capital 1865. Pop. 135,242.

Well Logging. △1642.

Wells, H(erbert) G(eorge) (1866–1946), English author. He is best known for his science fiction, such as the novels *The Time Machine* (1895), *The Invisible Man* (1897), and and *War of the Worlds* (1898). Other novels include *Love and Mr. Lewisham* (1900) and *Tono-Bungay* (1909). He enthusiastically believed in the value of scientific progress, supported various causes, including Fabian socialism, and used fiction as a vehicle for his ideas. His nonfiction includes *The Outline Of History* (1919–1930).

Wells Fargo, an American express company. It was established in 1852 by Henry Wells and William Fargo to serve the banking and shipping needs of California miners. The company owned the Pony Express, and in 1866 it operated the largest stagecoach network in America. By 1888, Wells Fargo had a transcontinental rail route. In 1918 it merged with the American Railway Express Company and today operates an armored car service in the eastern United States.

Welsh Pony, light horse breed known since Saxon times in Wales. Usually a mount for older children, it has the physique of a miniature coach horse with good head and neck, short muscular body, and great endurance. Color can be gray, roan, black, bay, brown, and chestnut. Height: 40–56in (102–142cm) high at shoulder; weight: 500lb (225kg).

Welsh Springer Spaniel, water and gun dog (sporting group) found in Wales and western England for several hundred years; able to withstand temperature extremes. This medium-sized dog has a slightly domed head with a square muzzle. The small ears are low-set and hanging; body is strong and muscular; legs medium-length; tail short and low-set. The flat, thick, silky coat is dark red and white. A good guard and gentle with children, it must be trained young. Average size: 17in (43cm) high at shoulder; 30–40lb (13.5–18kg). *See also* Sporting Dog.

Welsh Terrier, sporting dog (terrier group) brought to US in 1888. An old breed also called Old English terrier, the Welsh's flat, long head appears rectangular because of chin whiskers. V-shaped ears are set high and carried forward; dark hazel eyes are small and wide-set. The short, straight body is set on straight, muscular legs; the tail is carried up. Hard, wiry, and abundant, the coat is black and tan or black grizzle, and tan. Average size: 15in (38cm) high at shoulder; 20lb (9kg). *See also* Terrier.

Welty, Eudora (1909–), US author, b. Jackson, Miss. A short-story writer and novelist, many of her works are set in her native Mississippi. Among these are *Delta Wedding* (1946), about a modern plantation family, and *The Ponder Heart* (1954), which deals with small-town life. Collections of her stories include *A Curtain of Green* (1941) and *The Golden Apples* (1949).

Welwitschia. △440.

Wenceslaus (1361–1419), Holy Roman emperor (1378–1400) and king of Bohemia (1378–1419), as Wenceslaus IV. His reign was characterized by wars, conspiracies, and periods of anarchy. He was deposed as emperor in 1400 by a group of rebellious princes, and his powers as Bohemian king were undermined by the challenges of his brother Sigismund. △1074.

Wen Cheng-ming (1470–1559), Chinese painter of the Ming dynasty. An exponent of *wen-jen hua* (painting of the literati), he was a pupil of Shen Chou and an innovative figure whose combinations of dry brush and wet washes influenced many successors. △1208.

Wends, or Sorbs, group of Slavonic tribes who by the Middle Ages had settled in Germany between the Elbe and Oder rivers. Over the centuries their strength was gradually diminished as the Germans either exterminated or Christianized them, although they produced a wealth of national literature at the end of the 19th century.

Wentle Trap. △482.

Werewolf, in legend, a person who can turn himself into a wolf. Throughout the world people believe in the ability possessed by some to change themselves into various animals. In Africa the fierce leopard is object of the metamorphosis, in Haiti, it is a birdlike beast. The ability to change is termed lycanthropy.

Werfel, Franz (1890–1945), Austrian dramatist, novelist, and poet. His religious, historical, and modernist dramas include *The Trojan Women* (1915), *Paulus among the Jews* (1926), and *Jacobowsky and the Colonel* (1943). *The Forty Days of Musa Dagh* (1933), *Embezzled Heaven* (1939), *The Song of Bernadette* (1941), and *Star of the Unborn* (1946) are among Werfel's most famous novels. His popular expressionist poetry, found in *The Friend of the World* (1911) and *Each Other* (1915), expressed his love for mankind.

Wergeland, Henrik (Arnold) (1808–45), Norwegian poet. Regarded as Norway's national poet, he advocated cultural independence from Denmark. His poetry includes *Creation, Man, and Messiah* (1830), *The Jew* (1842), and *Jan van Huysum's Flowerpiece* (1840).

Werner, Abraham Gottlob (1750–1817), German geologist. He was the first to classify minerals systematically. His theory of the Earth's origins, called neptunism, posited that the Earth was originally a vast ocean from which solid rocks were precipitated to form land.

Werner, Alfred (1866–1916), German-Swiss chemist. After working with Pierre Berthelot in Paris he returned to a professorship at Zurich. In 1913 he was awarded a Nobel Prize for his coordination theory of valency.

Wertheimer, Max (1880–1943), German psychologist. He was one of the founders of the Gestalt psychology movement. His early work was on visual perception. Later he attempted to apply Gestalt principles to thinking and educational problems in such works as *Productive Thinking* (published 1945). *See also* Gestalt Psychology.

Weser, river in West Germany; formed by the junction of the Fulda and Werra rivers at Münden; flows NW to North Sea through a vast estuary near Bremerhaven. Length: 273mi (439km).

Wesley, John (1703–91), English theologian and evangelist who founded Methodism. With his brother Charles, Wesley founded the "Holy Club" at Oxford. The brothers, both clergymen, went to Georgia (1735) where the "first rudiments of the Methodist societies" were formed. There he experienced a conversion, and soon after he was preaching in the fields an extremely emotional personal sense of Christ's saving grace. In *Notes on the New Testament* Wesley's Evangelical Arminianism is clearly indicated. Methodism, as his religious views were called, spread remarkably after his return to England. His *Journal* (1739) records the great extent of his itinerant preaching, which often brought Christianity and organization to many who had not known either before.

Wessex, Anglo-Saxon kingdom, possibly settled by the Saxon Cerdic in 495. During Ceawlin's reign (560–93) it extended from the English Channel to the Thames River, between Berkshire and Devon. Resisting attack by the Danes (865), Alfred of Wessex became king (886) of all England not under Danish rule.

West, Benjamin (1738–1820), US painter. He spent most of his working life abroad, first in Italy and then in England, where he became historical painter to George III and, in 1792, president of the Royal Academy, succeeding Sir Joshua Reynolds. He was the first native-born American artist to achieve recognition in Europe. He supported himself as a portraitist while working on vast historical canvases, notable chiefly for his depictions of figures in modern dress instead of in the ancient costumes favored by the neoclassicists. △1192.

West, Jerry (1938–), US basketball player, b. Cheylan, W. Va. He was a gold medalist with the US Olympic team (1960) and became one of the best guards in the history of the National Basketball Association, playing with the Los Angeles Lakers, whose coach he became in 1976.

West, Morris Langlo (1916–), Australian novelist. He became a teacher, later served as secretary to William Morris Hughes, the former prime minister, and finally turned to writing as a career with the publication of *Gallows on the Sand* (1956). West, an award-winning novelist, wrote such international best-sellers as *The Devil's Advocate* (1959), *Shoes of the Fisherman* (1963), *The Ambassador* (1965), and *Tower of Babel* (1968).

West, Nathanael (1903–40), US author, b. Nathan Weinstein in New York City. He wrote only four novels, which gained critical acclaim after his death. They are: *The Dream Life of Balso Snell* (1931); *Miss Lonelyhearts* (1933), a grimly comic story about the writer of a column for the lovelorn; *A Cool Million* (1934); and *The Day of the Locust* (1939), a macabre, surrealistic story about false dreams and failed lives in Hollywood, where West spent his last years as a scriptwriter.

West, (Dame) Rebecca (1892–), pseud. of Cicely Fairfield, English novelist and social and literary critic, b. Ireland. Her novels include *The Thinking Reed* (1936), *The Fountain Overflows* (1956), and *The Birds Fall Down* (1966). Her criticism includes *The Strange Necessity* (1928) and *The Count and the Castle* (1957). Her political writings include *Black Lamb and Grey Falcon* (1942), *The Meaning of Treason* (1947), and *A Train of Powder* (1955).

West Allis, city in SE Wisconsin; W suburb of Milwaukee; site of headquarters of Allis-Chalmers Manufacturing Co., producers of industrial and farm machinery; it gave its name to city 1902; scene of annual Wisconsin State Fair (est. 1892). Industries: electronic equipment, heavy machinery, generators. Settled 1827 as Honey Creek; inc. 1906. Pop. (1970) 71,649.

West Bromwich, urban district in W central England, 5mi (8km) NW of Birmingham. Industries: coal mining, metal goods, chemicals, electrical products. Pop. 166,626.

West Covina, city in S California, W of Los Angeles. Crops: citrus fruits, walnuts. Inc. 1923. Pop. (1970) 68,034.

Westerlies, any broad currents or persistent patterns of winds from the west, such as the circumpolar and middle-latitude westerlies, reflecting the dominant west-to-east motion of the atmosphere centered over the middle latitudes of both hemispheres. *See also* Easterlies.

Westerly, town in extreme S Rhode Island on Pawcatuck River and Block Island Sound; connected to Connecticut by bridge; site of many old buildings, US Coast Guard station, and a lighthouse. Industries: tourism, plastics, textiles, furniture. First settled in 1648; inc. 1669; involved in Connecticut border dispute until 1728. Pop. (1970) 17,248.

Western Front. △1306.

Western Reserve, strip of land along Lake Erie in NE Ohio claimed by Connecticut. Most of the original 13 states had claims to western lands that were relinquished. When Connecticut ceded its lands to the federal government (1786), it retained this tract of 4,000,000 acres (1,618,800 hectares), and in 1792 awarded some of it to citizens whose property had been burned during the American Revolution. The remaining land was bought by the Connecticut Land Company (1795), which established a settlement at Cleveland. It was incorporated into the Ohio Territory (1800), under the provisions of the Northwest Ordinance (1787).

Westerns, type of popular fiction indigenous to the United States. First appearing in 19th-century dime novels and popular magazines, Westerns are adventure stories about the American West and have as principal characters cowboys, Indians, historical persons, frontiersmen, lawmen, and bandits. Owen Wister's *The Virginian* (1902) was the first Western to achieve literary fame. Westerns became very popular in films and on television in the 20th century.

Western Samoa, independent state in the island group of Samoa; includes Savaii, Apolima, and Manona islands. The chief islands are summits of an underwater volcanic range. The climate is tropical and wet; the islands yield yams, taro, bananas, breadfruit, papayas, coconut palms, pigs, poultry. The main industries include food processing, construction materials, furniture, tourism.

The people are overwhelmingly of Polynesian ancestry; society is organized around the family, each is headed by a chief called a Matai. Some Samoans have converted to Christianity, many keep their traditional belief of animism. Communication, trade, and W influence in education has brought about social change; New Zealand est. an agricultural school and teacher's college in Western Samoa.

The constitution of Western Samoa provides for a head of state, who appoints a cabinet and prime minister from the legislative assembly. Some offices are filled by members of royal families, representatives for the remainder are elected by universal suffrage. In 1976, after 14 years of independence, Western Samoa became a UN member. It is a member of the South Pacific Commission and the Commonwealth of Nations.

Area, 1,133sq mi (2,937sq km); pop., 148,565.

Western Wall. *See* Wailing Wall.

Western White Pine. △442.

Westfield, city in SW Massachusetts, on Westfield River; site of Westfield State College (1839). Industries: bicycles, school furniture, boilers, textile machinery. Founded as Woronoke (1660); name changed 1669; inc. as city 1920. Pop. (1970) 31,433.

Westfield, town in NE New Jersey, 7mi (11km) W of Elizabeth. Settled as part of Elizabeth prior to 1700; inc. 1903. Pop. (1970) 33,720.

West Goths. *See* Visigoths.

West Hartford, town in central Connecticut; suburb of Hartford; site of St Joseph's College (1925), University of Hartford (1877), American School for Deaf (1817); birthplace of Noah Webster (1758). Industries: tobacco shipping, tools and dies, aircraft accessories, plastics. Settled 1679; inc. 1854. Pop. (1970) 68,031.

West Haven, suburban residential town in S Connecticut, across West River from New Haven. Industries: aircraft products, velvets, beer. Inc. 1921. Pop. (1970) 52,851.

West Highland Terrier, hunting dog (terrier group) bred in Scotland and dating from the time of King James I. Also called Westie and Highlander, this hardy dog has a broad head tapering to a large nose; small, pointed, erect ears; dark eyes under heavy eyebrows; compact, deep-chested body; short legs; and short tail carried up. Bred white to distinguish it from game, the Westie's double coat features a straight, hard outer coat. Average size: 11in (28cm) high at shoulder; 13–20lb (6–9kg). *See also* Terrier.

West Indies Associated States, composed of the Leeward and Windward islands, formed in 1967. Full internal power rests with the islands' independent governments; Britain has authority only with regard to defense and foreign affairs.

West Indies Federation, single nation composed of Britain's Antillean colonies, inaugurated in 1958 with its capital in Trinidad. Political rivalries and ambitions led to the collapse of the federation in 1962.

Westinghouse, George (1846–1914), US inventor, b. Central Bridge, N.Y. During the Civil War he served in the Union navy and became interested in mechanical inventions. His first invention was a railroad "frog," a track junction device. In 1868 he invented the air brake, which made high speed rail travel safe and which is still standard equipment. He formed the Westinghouse Electric Co., a firm holding more than 400 patents dealing with rail transportation. △1708.

West Irian. *See* Irian Barat.

West Jersey, colonial proprietorship located in southwestern New Jersey. It was formed after the English seizure of New Netherland (1664), and was originally granted to Lord John Berkeley. The first English settlement was at Fenwick (1675). Besides the Dutch, Swedes, and Puritans, West Jersey also attracted Quakers because Berkeley allowed "freedom of conscience." Acquired by the Quakers (1674), with William Penn becoming part owner (1684), the land was reunited with East Jersey (1702) as royal province. *See also* East Jersey.

Westland, city in SE Michigan, 20mi (32km) W of Detroit. Pop. (1970) 86,749.

West Memphis, city in E Arkansas, 8mi (13km) W of Memphis, Tenn. Founded 1910; inc. 1927. Pop. (1970) 26,070.

West Mifflin, borough in SW Pennsylvania; suburb of Pittsburgh on Monongahela River. Industries: steel, coal, automobile bodies, cans. Founded 1788 and named for Thomas Mifflin, state's first governor; inc. 1944. Pop. (1970) 28,070.

Westminster, borough of Greater London, England, comprising the City of Westminster, Paddington, and St Marylebone. The City is the seat of Great Britain's government and contains many historic buildings, such as the Houses of Parliament, Buckingham Palace, and Westminster Abbey. Pop. 300,332.

Westminster, city in S California, SE of Long Beach; near Los Alanitos Naval Air Base. Settled 1870 as a religious commune for Presbyterians; inc. 1957. Pop. (1970) 59,874.

Westminster, Statute of (1931), act of the British Parliament implementing decisions reached at sessions of the Imperial Conference. It gave legislative independence to dominions of the British Empire and declared them autonomous dominions of the Commonwealth of Nations bound together by common allegiance to the British throne.

Westminster Abbey, Anglican cathedral in London. Originally a Benedictine monastery, Elizabeth I rededicated it to St Peter (1560). The present Gothic structure dates mainly from the 13th century. Henry VII's chapel (begun 1503) and Nicholas Hawksmoor's western towers (1722–40) are notable additions. British monarchs are crowned and buried here. In the Poet's Corner (south transept) great poets are buried. △1094.

West New York, city in NE New Jersey, on Hudson River 4mi (6.4km) N of Jersey City. Industries: textiles, leather, rubber goods, silk, toys. Settled 1790; inc. 1898. Pop. (1970) 40,627.

Weston, Edward (1886–1958), US photographer, b. Highland Park, Ill. Weston began his enduring portrait of the Western landscape in 1906. He cofounded the *f*/64 group whose sharp, carefully composed images greatly influenced photographic aesthetics. His celebrated photographs of sand dunes, nudes, plants, and other natural forms are rated among the classic works in the medium.

West Orange, town in NE New Jersey, 5mi (8km) NW of Newark; "Glenmont," home of Thomas Alva Edison after 1887 (made a national monument 1961), is in nearby Llewellyn Park. Industries: electrical appliances, truck farming. Separated from Orange 1862; inc. 1900. Pop. (1970) 43,715.

West Palm Beach, winter resort city in SE Florida, on Lake Worth, 65mi (105km) N of Miami. Industries: computers, commercial fisheries. Settled 1893; inc. 1894. Pop. (1970) 57,375.

Westphalia, an area lying roughly between the valleys of the Rhine and Weser rivers, now part of West Germany. Originally belonging to Saxony, it was first separated in 1180. It was ruled as a duchy by the Elector of Cologne until 1803, was later conquered by Napoleon, and after the Congress of Vienna in 1815 was given to Prussia. The Ruhr region was occupied by the French after World War I and after heavy destruction in World War II it was in the British zone of occupation until 1946.

Wellington, New Zealand

Franz Werfel

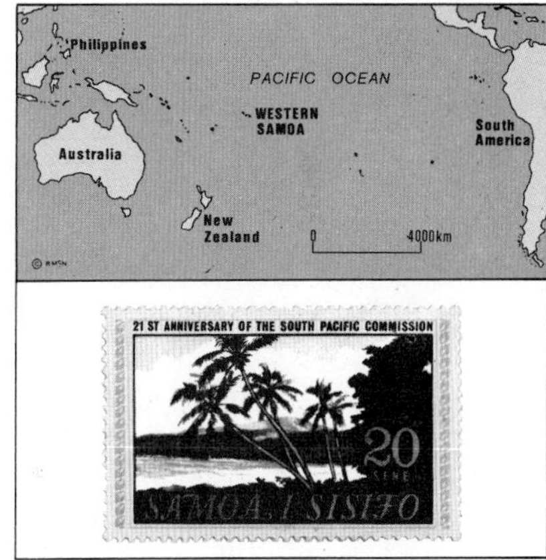
Philippines
PACIFIC OCEAN
WESTERN SAMOA
Australia
South America
New Zealand
0
4000km
21 ST ANNIVERSARY OF THE SOUTH PACIFIC COMMISSION
20
SAMOA I SISIFO

Western Samoa

George Westinghouse

Westphalia, Peace of. △1154.

West Point, US military post in SE New York, on W bank of Hudson River, just SE of Storm King and Crow's Nest Mts, approx. 50mi (81km) NW of New York City. First occupied and fortified 1778 by colonists as military post during Revolution, it was site of Benedict Arnold's surrender plot (1780); seat of US Military Academy since 1802; the West Point Museum, Cadet Chapel, and Old Cadet Chapel are noteworthy buildings on post grounds. Area: 3,500acres (1,417hectares).

Westport, town in SW Connecticut, on Long Island Sound at the mouth of the Saugatuck River; scene of Great Swamp Fight that ended the Pequot Indian War, 1637. Industries: hardware, tacks, tourism, soap, twine. Settled 1645; inc. 1835. Pop. (1970) 27,414.

West River. *See* Hsi.

West Side Story, musical play with lyrics by Stephen Sondheim, music by Leonard Bernstein, book by Arthur Laurents, and choreography by Jerome Robbins, first produced on Broadway in 1959. It transferred Shakespeare's *Romeo and Juliet* story to the setting of modern New York City street gangs. It featured highly praised dance sequences as well as singing and was made into a successful film in 1961.

West Virginia, state in the E United States in the Appalachian Mt region.

Land and Economy. The Allegheny Mt ranges run NE-SW in much of the E half of the state. The W portion is a plateau dropping gradually to the Ohio River, which marks the W boundary. The state's mineral resources supply the manufacturing industries and are the mainstay of the economy. Industries are located principally in the cities along the Ohio River, which is a valuable transportation artery. Agriculture is a minor element in the state.

People. The early settlers came from states to the E. Most were of English, Scots-Irish, and German descent. Later, immigrants from Poland, Hungary, and other central European countries came to work the mines. Less than 40% of the population lives in urban areas.

Education. There are 25 institutions of higher education. West Virginia University, West Virginia State College, and West Virginia Institute of Technology are state-supported.

History. Pioneers from Virginia pushed across the mountains into the region in the late 18th century. Settlement expanded in the early 19th century, especially along the Ohio River. The area was part of the state of Virginia, but political and economic tensions arose between the new settlements and the older society to the E. When Virginia seceded in 1861, a convention of westerners who supported the Union repudiated the act. Later that year they formed a new state named Kanawha, which was admitted to the Union two years later as West Virginia. In later years, the state's fortune depended on the varying prosperity of the coal mining industry.

PROFILE

Admitted to Union: June 20, 1863; rank, 35th
US Congressmen: Senate, 2; House of Representatives, 4
Population: 1,744,237 (1970); rank, 34th
Capital: Charleston, 71,505 (1970)
Chief cities: Huntington, 74,315; Charleston; Wheeling, 48,188; Parkersburg, 44,208
State legislature: Senate, 34; House of Delegates, 100
Area: 24,181sq mi (62,629sq km); rank, 41st
Elevation: highest, 4,862ft (1,483m), Spruce Knob; lowest, 240ft (73m), Potomac River
Industries (major products): chemicals, synthetic fibers, plastics, steel, fabricated metals, glass, pottery
Agriculture (major products): poultry, dairy products, apples
Minerals (major): bituminous coal, natural gas, petroleum, salt, stone
State nickname: Mountain State
State motto: Montani Semper Liberi (Mountaineers Are Always Free)
State bird: cardinal
State flower: rhododendron maximum
State tree: sugar maple

Westwerks. △1080.

Wethersfield, town in central Connecticut, on Connecticut River; adjoins Hartford (N). The oldest permanent settlement in state, it has many preserved buildings; the Webb House was scene of 1781 meeting between George Washington and Comte de Rochambeau to coordinate French aid to American forces. Industries: oil burners, bakery goods, tools, electrical components. Founded 1634 by settlers from Watertown, Mass.; inc. 1637. Pop. (1970) 26,662.

Wetland, marshy ground in an intertidal zone that has prolific vegetation. Coastal wetlands are said to produce more living matter per acre than any other part of the world. Protective laws have recently been passed to stop their destruction for they have come to be recognized as an important part of the oceanic food cycle. △618.

Weyden, Rogier van der (*c.*1400–64), Flemish painter. Among the greatest of the northern European artists of his era, he is believed to have entered the workshop of Robert Campin in 1427 and to have left as an accredited master five years later. Appointed official painter of Brussels in 1435, he spent most of his career there, but in 1450 he traveled to Italy, where his style was influenced somewhat by Renaissance art. In its maturity his style was characterized by clear, subtly modulated colors; great refinement and sensitivity. He influenced the work of Dirk Bouts and Hans Memling. △1136.

Weyl, Herman (1885–1955), US mathematician, b. Germany. After holding professorships at Zurich and Göttingen he moved to Princeton University in 1933 with the advent of the Nazis. His work on geometry and relativity led to a unified field theory in which the electromagnetic and gravitational fields appear as geometric properties of space-time. His *Group Theory and Quantum Mechanics* (1928) helped form the modern views of quantum theory.

Whale, aquatic, generally social mammal inhabiting all oceans and some fresh waters. They have fishlike bodies with paddle-shaped flippers for forelimbs and no external hind limbs. Easily distinguished from large fish by horizontally flattened tail fins, they have no distinct neck or external ears, and nose openings (blowholes) are on top of the head. A few bristles remain of the characteristic mammalian hair and beneath the thick smooth skin is a layer of insulating blubber.

Ranging in size from porpoises to blue whales, they are highly vocal, using sound signals for communication and for sonarlike navigation. Most have teeth and eat chiefly fish. Many large whales with no teeth have a filter of baleen (whalebone) which strains plankton from the water. Length: 4ft (1.25m) to 100ft (30m); weight: to 150 tons. Order Cetacea. △552.

Whalebone, or baleen, plates of elastic horny material making up the food-catching filter in the mouth of baleen whales. It was once used for making corset stays. △552.

Whale Shark, largest shark, found worldwide in tropical waters. Brownish to dark gray with white or yellow spots and stripes, this docile, egg-laying fish often travels at water surface in schools. Length: 30ft (9m). Family Rhincodontidae, species *Rhincodon typus*. *See also* Chondrichthyes; Sharks.

Whaling, begun during the Middle Ages, this industry grew rapidly during the 18th and 19th centuries, when it was dominated by American whalers. The modern whaling era began in the 1850s with the development of harpoons with explosive heads and reached a peak after 1925, when ocean-going factory ships were sent to the Antarctic. During the next 50 years, most larger whale species, including the blue whale, were hunted to near extinction and whalers turned to smaller species. International regulation of the industry is weak, and the outlook for many species of whales is bleak. △634.

Wharton, Edith (Newbold Jones) (1862–1937), US novelist, b. New York City. Of wealthy and socially prominent parents, she married Edward Wharton, a Boston banker in 1885; they were divorced in 1913. Her first novel, *The House of Mirth* (1905) brought her success, which continued with such outstanding works as *Ethan Frome* (1911), *The Custom of the Country* (1913), and *The Age of Innocence* (1920). The latter novel won the Pulitzer Prize in 1921. Although she often wrote of the folly and sterility of New York society, she did not limit herself to that milieu. Her work ranged from the mountain villages of New England to the battlefields of World War I.

Wheat, cereal grass originating in the Middle East. Cultivated there since 7000 BC, it is now cultivated worldwide. It has long, slender leaves, hollow stems, and flowering heads. *Triticum vulgane* is the large-grained variety used for bread; *T. durum* for pasta; and *T. compactum* for cake and pastry flour. Winter wheat is sown in the fall; spring wheat may be planted in spring or fall, depending on the area's climate. It is also used for malt, dextrose, and alcohol. Family Gramineae. △326, 454.

Wheat Jointworm, black, antlike, chalcid wasp 0.08 to 0.12in (2–3mm) long, that attacks the stems of wheat. It is found in most of the wheat-growing regions of North America. Family Eurytomidae, species *Harmolita tritici*. *See also* Hymenoptera.

Wheaton, city in NE Illinois, W of Chicago; seat of Du Page co; site of Wheaton College (1853); headquarters of Theosophical Society of America; farming region. Settled by Jesse and Warren Wheaton 1837; inc. 1859. Pop. (1970) 31,138.

Wheaton, residential city in central Maryland; SW suburb of Baltimore. Pop. (1970) 66,247.

Wheat Ridge, city in N central Colorado; suburb of Denver. Pop. (1970) 29,795.

Wheel, Potter's. △1882.

Wheel and Axle, a simple machine based on the principle that a small force applied to the rim of a wheel will exert a much larger force on an object attached to the axle. The mechanical advantage, or multiplication factor for the applied force, is the ratio of the diameter of the wheel to that of the axle. △1488.

Wheelchair Games, an athletic competition for permanently disabled persons, mostly performed in wheelchairs. The competition includes many track and field events in addition to bowling, basketball, table tennis, archery, swimming, weightlifting, and other specialty events, such as wheelchair slalom. The competition grew out of the many rehabilitation programs initiated for permanently injured veterans returning from World War II. The first National Wheelchair Games were held in 1957, and have since grown to include competition on an international scale where representative countries compete for gold, silver, and bronze medals. In the United States, the National Wheelchair Athletic Association supervises all events.

Wheeler-Howard Act. *See* Indian Reorganization Act (1934).

Wheeling, city and port of entry in N West Virginia, on Ohio River; seat of Ohio co. Settlement developed around Fort Henry (1774); scene of one of last American Revolution battles (Sept. 11–13, 1782); prospered as W terminus of National Road (1818) and Baltimore and Ohio Railroad (1852); site of Wheeling Conventions (1861–62); served as state capital 1863–70, 1875–85; site of Wheeling College (1954). Industries: steel, iron, nails, coal and natural gas mining, tobacco, plastics, textiles. Settled 1769; inc. 1836. Pop. (1970) 48,188.

Wheel-lock Mechanism. △1728.

Whelk, marine gastropod mollusk found along marine shores. It has a large coiled shell, smooth rim and notch at lower end. Length: 5–7in (127–177.8mm). Family Fasciolariidae; species include Japanese gourmet delicacy *Buccimum tenuissimum* and dog whelk *Nucella*. △476, 622.

Whigs, one of two major US political parties from 1834 to 1852. Formed out of the Federalist party when John Quincy Adams and Henry Clay joined forces against Andrew Jackson it was a coalition party drawing strength from eastern capitalists, western farmers and southern plantation owners. Its principal leaders were Clay and Daniel Webster. The party elected two presidents, William Henry Harrison (1840) and Zachary Taylor (1848). The issue of slavery generated such bitter dispute that the party disintegrated. △1396.

Whinchat. △528.

Whippet, sporting dog (hound group) bred in England for racing and rabbit coursing. An elegant pet that is capable of running at speeds of 35mph (56.5km); it has a long, lean head and tapered muzzle; small ears thrown back and folded; a long-backed body with arched loin; long, powerful legs; and a long, tapering tail carried low. The close, smooth coat may be any color. Average size: 19–22in (48–56cm) high at shoulder; 20lb (9kg). *See also* Hound.

Whippet Bicycle. △1688.

Whipple, George Hoyt (1878–76), US pathologist b. Ashland, N.H.. He shared the 1934 Nobel Prize in physiology or medicine with George R. Minot and William P. Murphy for his work on anemia and its treatment with liver extract. *See also* Anemia.

Whippoorwill, brownish-colored migratory goatsucker that winters in Central America and breeds in N North America. It is known for its repetitive and distinctive "whip-poor-will" call. Species *Caprimulgus vociferus*. *See also* Goatsucker.

Whip Scorpion. △490.

Whipsnake. *See* Coachwhip Snake.

Whirligig Beetle, medium-sized, dark-colored water beetle often seen resting or gyrating on the surface of a still pool. They prey on small insects. Family Gyrinidae.

Whirlpool, circular motion of a fluid. Whirlpools in rivers occur in regions where waterfalls or sharp breaks in topographic continuity make steady flow impossible. *See also* Vortex.

Whirlpool Galaxy. △122.

Whiskers, in Ceramics. △1608.

Whiskey. △352.

Whiskey Rebellion (1794), revolt by backwoods farmers in Pennsylvania's western counties. They refused to pay a federal excise tax for the manufacture of whiskey, which they made with surplus grain. US troops put down the riot, but the public reaction damaged the image of the Federalist party, which was responsible for the tax.

Whiskey Ring, group of US public officials and liquor distillers who defrauded the US government of liquor taxes after the Civil War. In 1875, Treasury Department agents broke up the ring and arrested the persons involved. President Grant's secretary, Orville Babcock, was indicted in the scandal but acquitted.

Whisk Fern. △438.

Whist, card game for two sets of partners, played with a standard deck. After the full deck has been distributed, the dealer turns over his last card to indicate trump. Cards rank from ace through 2. The highest card or trump wins the trick. Six tricks make a book, and each trick over the book counts one point. It requires seven points to win in the US game.

Whistler, James Abbott McNeill (1834–1903), US painter and etcher, b. Lowell, Mass. Influenced early in his career by Courbet and Velázquez and later by Japanese woodblock prints, he worked for several years in Paris, then moved to London in 1859, where he soon became known for his dandified, eccentric ways. His painting style combined subtle tonal relationships with a judicious arrangement of forms, and his pictures are characterized by their serenity, as seen in his best-known work, a portrait of his mother (Paris, Louvre). An accomplished and prolific etcher, he produced some 400 plates. △1416.

White, Byron Raymond (1917–), US jurist and lawyer, b. Fort Collins, Colo. A college and professional football player, known as "Whizzer White," he studied at Yale Law School while playing with the Detroit Lions (1940–41). Also a Rhodes scholar, he served as a law clerk for Chief Justice Vinson (1946–47), practiced law (1947–61), and served as US deputy attorney general (1961–62). In 1962 he was appointed an associate justice of the US Supreme Court by John F. Kennedy. On the Court, he has maintained a moderate position.

White, Edward Douglass (1845–1921), chief justice of the US Supreme Court (1910–21), b. Lafourche Parish, La. He served in the Confederate army (1861–63), and as state senator (1874–78) before being appointed judge of the state supreme court (1879–80). He served as US senator from Louisiana (1891–94) and was appointed associate justice of the US Supreme Court (1894) by President Cleveland. Appointed chief justice by President Taft, he was considered a conservative, and is best known for his "rule of reason" interpretation of the Sherman Antitrust Act, which dissolved Standard Oil Co. and the American Tobacco Co. (1911). He is also responsible for the decision upholding the constitutionality of the Adamson Act (1910), which set an eight-hour day for railroad workers. △1724.

White, E(lwyn) B(rooks) (1899–), US essayist and author, b. Mt. Vernon, N.Y. On the staff of *The New Yorker* (1926–1937), he wrote the "Talk of the Town" column. His humorous books for adults include *Is Sex Necessary?* (with James Thurber, 1929) and *One Man's Meat* (1942). His books for children, *Stuart Little* (1945), *Charlotte's Web* (1952) and *The Trumpet of the Swan* (1970) have become classics.

White, Leslie. △884.

White, Patrick (1912–), Australian writer. His first novel, *The Happy Valley*, appeared in 1939. Many of his novels are set in the Australian outback. His later works, *The Tree of Man* (1955), *Voss* (1957), *Riders in the Chariot* (1961), *The Eye of the Storm* (1974), and *The Cockatoos* (1975), won universal praise. In 1973 he was awarded the Nobel Prize in literature. He was also a successful dramatist.

White, Walter (1893–1955), US civil rights activist and author, b. Atlanta. As secretary of the NAACP (1918–55), he campaigned for desegregation, voting rights, and antilynching legislation. His books include *Rope and Faggot* (1929), *A Rising Wind* (1945), and the autobiography *A Man Called White* (1948).

White, William A(lanson) (1870–1937), US psychiatrist, b. Brooklyn, N.Y. He was superintendant of St Elizabeth's Hospital in Washington, D.C., from 1903 to 1937. He was a pioneer in the establishment of psychiatric training and research, and he helped psychoanalytic theory to gain acceptance in the United States. Among his works are *Essays on Psychopathology* (1925); *Insanity and the Criminal Law* (1923); and *Crimes and Criminals* (1933).

White Ant. *See* Termite.

White Ash. △450.

Whitebait, tropical marine fish found near Australia and New Zealand. Elongated, the scaleless fish has its dorsal fin set far back. Term whitebait is also applied to young of several types of European herring. Length: to 4in (10.2cm). Family Galaxiidae; species *Galaxias attentuatus*.

White Blood Cell. *See* Leukocyte.

White Cells. △740.

White Dwarf Star, very faint hot star of planetary dimensions but with a mass comparable to that of the Sun. The results of gravitational collapse in stars not massive enough to have become supernovae, white dwarfs represent the last stage in the evolution of stars like the Sun, which, having exhausted their fuel, contract under their own weight to become over a million times denser than water. With time white dwarfs cool down to become cold dark globes. They are found on the bottom left of the Hertzsprung-Russell diagram. △100, 102.

White-eye, or spectacle bird, greenish bird of Old World tropical forests with a prominent ring of white feathers around the eye. It has short, rounded wings; squarish tail; straight, pointed bill; and brush-tipped, extensible tongue for feeding on nectar. It also eats insects and fruit. Bluish, greenish, or whitish eggs (3–5) are laid in a grass, spider webbing, and bark basket nest hung in a tree or bush fork. Length: 4–5in (10–12.7cm). Family Zosteropidae.

Whitefield, George (1714–70), English evangelist. An Anglican priest, he preached in the American colonies 1739–41 and figured predominantly in the Great Awakening. In London, he emerged as leader of Calvinistic Methodists (1741), breaking with John Wesley. He made several more trips to the colonies (1744–69). On his last trip he converted his Savannah, Ga., orphanage into Bethesda College (1769).

Whitefish, or cisco, freshwater food fish of the Northern Hemisphere, to Arctic waters. It is colored a dull silver. Length: to 59in (150cm); weight: 63lb (29kg). Species include least cisco or lake herring *Coregonus artedii*. Family Salmonidae. △390.

Whitehall, city in central Ohio; 7mi (11km) E of Columbus. Industries: water coolers, packaged meat. Inc. 1948. Pop. (1970) 25,263.

Whitehead, Alfred North (1861–1947), British philosopher and mathematician. He attempted to combine his interests in mathematics, morals, and aesthetics into a comprehensive metaphysical system of scientific cosmology. This system is presented in "An Essay on Cosmology" in his *Process and Reality* (1929). His *Principia Mathematica* (3 vols., written in collaboration with Bertrand Russell, 1910–13) has had a notable influence on contemporary philosophy. Other works include *Adventures of Ideas* (1933), *Essays in Science and Philosophy* (1947). △854.

Whitehorse, town in Yukon, Canada, 52mi (84km) N of British Columbia border, on the Yukon River; capital of Yukon Territory; developed as trading town during the Klondike gold rush (1897–98); headquarters for the Royal Canadian Mounted Police and Air

West Virginia: John Brown's Fort, Harper's Ferry

Edith Wharton

Whirligig beetle

James Whistler

Force, and N terminus of the Alaska Highway and the White Pass and Yukon Railway. Industries: tourism, copper mining, hunting, fur trapping. Pop. 11,084.

White House, executive mansion and official residence of the US president. On an 18-acre (7.3-hectare) site chosen by George Washington, it was designed by James Hoban, made of Virginia freestone. Its cornerstone was laid in 1792. John Adams was the first president to live there (1800). Restored after being burned by the British in 1814, its name became official when Pres. Theodore Roosevelt had it engraved on his stationery. It contains the offices of the president and his staff, and is used for official entertaining and state occasions.

White Leghorn, chicken breed widely raised for egg production. A small chicken, it has yellow skin, a single comb, and lays white-shelled eggs. Weight: 6lb (2.7kg) cock; 4.5lb (2kg) hen.

White Mountains, part of Appalachian Range in N New Hampshire and SW Maine; consists of two main groups, Presidential Range and Franconia Mts, divided by Crawford Notch. White Mountain National Forest includes much of these ranges. Highest peak is Mt Washington, 6,288ft (1,918m).

White Nile, river in NE Africa; converges with the Blue Nile at Khartoum to form the Nile River; rises in Lake Victoria, flows E with the Sobat River, N through Sudan to Khartoum. Length: 2,172mi (3,497km).

White Plains, city in SE New York, between Bronx and Mamaroneck rivers. New York's provincial congress met here in 1776 to ratify Declaration of Independence; scene of American defeat at Battle of White Plains, Oct. 28, 1776, now a national battlefield site; site of College of White Plains (1923) and Elijah Miller House (George Washington's headquarters). The county seat, it contains government offices, many major corporate offices and large retail stores, and a few light industries. Settled 1683; inc. as village 1866, as city 1916. Pop. (1970) 50,346.

White Plymouth Rock, important meat-producing chicken breed. They have yellow skin, a single comb, and brown-shelled eggs. Weight: 9.5lb (4.3kg) cock; 7.5lb (3.4kg) hen.

White Potato. *See* Potato.

White River, rises in Boston Mts, NW Arkansas, flows N to SW Missouri, SE across Arkansas to the Mississippi River. Series of dams on river have been built from 1957–65 to provide hydroelectric power. River is navigable for approx. 260mi (419km) of its 690mi (1,111km) length.

White Sands National Monument, area in S New Mexico, in Tularosa Basin between San Andres Mts (W) and Sacramento Mts (E); includes great expanse of white gypsum sand drifting into dunes. Plant and animal life show great adaptation to environment. Est. 1933. Area: 146,535 acres (59,347hectares).

White Sea, large inlet of Barents Sea on N coast of Russian SFSR, USSR, between the Kola Peninsula (W) and Kanin Peninsula (E). Mezen, Northern Dvina, and Onega rivers empty into it. Its chief port is Arkhangelsk, which is kept open by ice breakers from November to May. Herring, cod fishing, and sealing are carried on. White Sea is connected to Baltic Sea by canals. Area: 34,700sq mi (89,873sq km).

White Shark, or man eater, great white shark, aggressive, dangerous shark found worldwide in tropical and subtropical marine waters. Known to attack and eat man, it is grayish above and dirty white below. Its teeth are broad and triangular with sawtoothed edges. Length: to 40ft (12.2m); weight: to 7,000lb (3,180kg). Family Isuridae (also called Lamnidae); species *Carcharodon carcharias. See also* Chondrichthyes; Sharks.

White-tailed Deer, or Virginia deer, common deer found from S Canada to N South America. Its antlers have one main beam with minor branches. Full-size antlers are usually attained by the fourth year. These deer do not congregate in herds. They mate in November and December. The gestation period is seven months and two fawns are born. It is a popular game animal. Height: to 3.5ft (1.1m) high at shoulder. Family Cervidae; species *Odocoileus virginianus. See also* Deer.

White Volta, (Volta Blanche) river in W Africa; rises in Upper Volta and flows SW then S into Lake Volta, in Ghana. Length: 550mi (885km).

Whitgift, John (1530–1604). English archbishop of Canterbury. Vice-chancellor of Cambridge University (1570), he helped to revise the university statutes. In 1571 he was appointed dean of Lincoln; in 1577 he became bishop of Worcester and in 1583 archbishop of Canterbury. His vigorous persecution of Puritans enjoyed the approval of Queen Elizabeth.

Whiting, several unrelated food fish. The European whiting *Merlangius merlangus* is a haddocklike cod found in shallow E Atlantic waters from the polar cap to the coast of Spain; length: 23.6–27.6in (60–70cm). The silver hake *(Merluccius bilinearis)* is found along the Atlantic coast of the United States; length: 2.5ft (76.2cm); weight: 5lb (2.3kg). The kingfish *(Menticirrhus saxatilis)* is a dusky silver with dark side bars; length: 17in (43.2cm); weight: 3lb (1.4kg). △392.

Whitman, Walt(er) (1819–92), US poet and essayist, recognized as the poetic spokesman of the American spirit, b. Huntington, N.Y. In 1855 he published *Leaves of Grass,* a collection of poems, the radical form and content of which brought critical disdain and left the poet with a life-long unsavory reputation. Whitman frequently revised and augmented *Leaves of Grass* over the next 35 years.

In 1865, while employed as a government clerk, he published *Drum-Taps,* reissued in 1866 with *Sequel to Drum-Taps;* both included in a later edition of *Leaves of Grass.* A collection of essays, *Democratic Vistas* (1871), was incorporated with more poems in *Two Rivulets* (1876) and published with *Leaves of Grass.* Publicity over an 1881 edition of his poems brought Whitman his first financial success, and only at the time of his death was he beginning to be recognized as an important world poet, whose work had a vital influence on contemporaries and succeeding generations alike. △1374, 1420.

Whitney, Eli (1765–1825), US inventor, b. Westborough, Mass. He went to Georgia as a teacher and became interested in the cotton industry, which was then limited by the slow, hard work of removing the seeds by hand. Whitney invented a machine to do this task after great difficulties, including manufacturing his own tools (1793). His cotton gin was stolen and patented by others, and although his claims were upheld in 1807, he was denied permission to renew his patent (1812). He received a government contract for firearms (1798) and developed a system in which interchangeable parts were manufactured and assembled by workers with little skill. His factory, in New Haven, Conn., was an early example of mass production △1400.

Whitney, Mount, peak in E California, in the Sierra Nevada at the E edge of Sequoia National Park. Connected to Death Valley by highway. Named for US geologist Josiah D. Whitney who surveyed it in 1864. Second-highest US peak (Mt McKinley in Alaska is first), 14,494ft (4,421m).

Whittier, John Greenleaf (1807–92), US poet and editor, b. Haverhill, Mass. A Quaker, he early became involved in the abolitionist movement and much of his verse is antislavery in theme. He also wrote sentimentally of New England rural life. From 1829 he worked as an editor on various publications to support himself. His works include *Poems Written During the Progress of the Abolition Question* (1838), *Lays of My Home and Other Poems* (1843), *Voices of Freedom* (1846), *Songs of Labor* (1850), and *Among the Hills and Other Poems* (1869). Among his best-known poems are "Maud Muller," regrets for a lost love; "The Barefoot Boy" and "Snowbound," recollections of a rural boyhood; and "Barbara Frietchie," a Civil War poem. △1420.

Whittier, city in S California, 12mi (19km) ESE of Los Angeles; hometown of President Richard M. Nixon. Industries: automobile and aircraft parts, oil and steel products. Founded 1887 by Quakers; inc. 1898. Pop. (1970) 72,863.

WHO. *See* World Health Organization.

Wholesale Price Index (WPI), a measure of changes in prices at the wholesale or primary market level. It is compiled by the US Bureau of Labor Statistics.

Wholesaling, marketing activity that buys and sells in relatively large quantities. Generally the wholesaler buys directly from the manufacturer and sells to retailers, to other manufacturers, to institutional and commercial users, but not normally to the ultimate consumer. *See also* Marketing.

Whooping Cough, or pertussis, an acute, highly contagious childhood respiratory disease. It is caused by the bacterium *Bordetella pertussis* and marked by spasms of coughing, followed by a long-drawn intak of air, or "whoop," frequently ending with vomitinc Severe manifestations can last up to 6 weeks an serious complications used to be common. Now, im munization vaccinations are routinely administered t infants.

Whooping Crane, North American bird with shril buglelike call. Once close to extinction, it became th object of successful intensive preservation efforts. nests in marshes of W Canada and migrates to winte in S United States. It has large wingspan and blac and white plumage. Height: to 5ft (1.5m). Specie *Grus americana. See also* Crane. △526, 630.

Whorf, Benjamin Lee (1897–1941), US structura linguist, b. Winthrop, Mass. He formed the Whorf hy pothesis (also called Sapir-Whorf hypothesis). The hy pothesis states "that the structure of language influ ences thought processes and our perception of th world around us."

Wichita, city in S central Kansas, 177mi (285km) SV of Kansas City, at the confluence of Arkansas an Little Arkansas rivers; seat of Sedgwick co; largest cit in Kansas. Est. 1864 as trading post by James Mea and Jesse Chisholm; it developed with coming of Chis holm Trail and railroad (1872); industrial growth wa spurred by discovery of oil (1915) and by develop ment of aircraft industry (1920). It is site of Wichit State University (1892), Friends University (1898) Sacred Heart College (1933), Century II, modern cor vention and cultural complex. Industries: railroa shops, aircraft, oil refining, grain, meat packing. Inc 1871 as village, 1886 as city. Pop. (1970) 276,554

Wichita Falls, city in N Texas, 105mi (169km) NV of Fort Worth, on Wichita River; seat of Wichita co site of Wichita Falls Junior College (1922). Industries oil refining, oil-field equipment, textiles, cottonsee and dairy products, electronic components, farm ma chinery, flour milling, clothing. Settled 1876; inc 1889. Pop. (1970) 96,265.

Widgeon, river duck with brownish plumage. The feed from the surface and engage in complex cour ship displays. Included are the North America *Mareca americana* and European *Mareca penelope See also* Duck.

Wieland, Christoph Martin (1733–1813), Germa novelist and poet. His works reveal his pronounce sensuality, and Greece was for him the only lan where man could lead a healthy life. His works includ prose translations of 22 plays by Shakespeare, th novels *Agathon* (1766), *Peregrinus Proteus* (1791) *Aristipp* (4 vols., 1800–01), and *Der goldene Spiege* (1772), a verse idyll *Musarion* (1768), and *Obero* (1780). He later went to Weimar as a tutor to th duke, and there he edited the influential *Der teutsch Merkur* (1773–1810).

Wieniawski, Henri (1835–80), Polish violinist an Romantic composer. He was a child prodigy and be came renowned for his violin virtuosity. Today he i chiefly remembered for his two violin concertos.

Wiesbaden, city in central West Germany, on Rhin River, 20mi (32km) W of Frankfurt am Main; capita of Hesse state. Made free imperial city *c.* 1242, it wa capital of duchy of Nassau 1806–66; headquarters o Rhineland Commission 1918–29; taken by Allies du ing WWII (March 1945). City contains mineral spring known since Roman times. Industries: tourism, meta goods, concrete, chemicals, plastics, wine, printing Pop. 250,122.

Wigglesworth, Michael (1631–1705), colonia American poet, b. England. He came to Massachu setts Bay Colony with his parents in 1638. He was minister and physician. His crude but forceful poetr set forth Puritan theology. His most popular work wa *The Day of Doom* (1662).

Wight, Isle of, island county in S England, separate from Hampshire by the Solent and Spithead, a popu lar holiday resort area. Area: 147sq mi (381sq km) Chief town is Newport. Pop. 109,284.

Wigwam, hut used by Indians from the Great Lake eastward. Designs vary from semicircular to conica but most wigwams have arched tops and are cor structed of hides, bark, etc, spread over a pole frame

Wilberforce, William (1759–1833), English socia reformer. He served as a member of Parliament fo more than 40 years. In 1784, Wilberforce was cor verted to Evangelical Christianity, and he won recog nition for his opposition to the slave trade. He was a officer of the anti-slavery society, but died a mont before the Emancipation Bill was passed. The tract

Practical View (1797) was immensely popular, and with Hannah More, he worked for the "reformation of manners."

Wilbur, Richard (1921–), US poet, b. New York City. He taught English at Wesleyan University from 1957. His collections of poetry include *Things of This World* (1956), which gained him both the Pulitzer Prize and National Book Award in 1957.

Wild Boar, tusked, cloven-hoofed mammal of the hog family that lives wild in forested areas of Eurasia and Africa. Favorite game animals, wild boars are dangerous when attacked. Now rare in Europe, they were introduced into North America during the 16th century and still roam SE United States. Length: to 5ft (153cm); weight: to 450lb (203kg). Family Suidae; species *Sus scrofa.*

Wildcat Strikes, work stoppages called while a contract is in force, normally without consulting the union leaders, which may result in legal action. Because there is today less suspicion between labor and management and grievance procedures are more efficient, wildcat strikes are less common than in the early days of the labor movement. *See also* Strike.

Wild Coffee. *See* Lemonwood.

Wildebeest. *See* Gnu.

Wilder, Laura Ingals (1867–1957), US author of the "Little House" series of books for children, b. Lake Pepin, Wis. The story of her own childhood, growing up, and marriage in pioneer America is the subject of these famous books. *The Little House in the Big Woods* appeared in 1932 and was followed by seven other titles. The series was reissued in 1953 with fine illustrations by Garth Williams.

Wilder, Thornton Niven (1897–1975), US author and playwright, b. Madison, Wis. Expressing his ideas in a simple, realistic style, he won Pulitzer Prizes for his novel *The Bridge of San Luis Rey* (1928) and the plays *Our Town* (1938) and *Skin of Our Teeth* (1942). His *The Matchmaker* became the popular musical *Hello Dolly.* In 1968 *The Eighth Day* won the National Book Award. △1240.

Wilderness, Battle of the (May 1864), US Civil War battle. The opening of Union Gen. Ulysses S. Grant's Richmond Campaign, this was a full-scale battle, complete with trench warfare between Grant's 100,000 men and Robert E. Lee's 60,000 Confederates. Grant lost about 18,000 men; Lee lost close to 8,000.

Wilderness Preservation Act (1964), legislation establishing a National Wilderness Preservation System and Primitive Areas System of more than 14,000,000 acres (5,665,800 hectares) to retain areas "where the Earth and its community of life are untrammeled by man." These areas are open to the public for recreation and study.

Wilderness Road, road through the Appalachian Mountains. Marked out in 1775 by Daniel Boone, it served as an emigrant route from the east coast through the Cumberland Gap to Ohio. It was commissioned by Richard Henderson.

Wild Rice, annual grass native to wetlands of North America. Its stems are crowned with large, open flower clusters. The 1-in (2.5-cm), rodlike grains are dark brown or black. It was an important food for North American Indians. Height: to 10ft (3m). Family Gramineae; species *Zizania aquatica.*

Wilfrid, or **Wilfred, Saint** (634–709), Anglo-Saxon bishop. In his youth he was sent from England to Rome and Lyons to study. Returning to Northumbria, he was named bishop of York, and in that post he improved services and built notable churches. Because he objected to a plan to divide his see of York, Wilfrid was exiled for six years, although he appealed his case to Rome and won a favorable decision. During this time he converted the South Saxons and built a monastery at Selsey. Later he was bishop of Hexham.

Wilhelm I. △1250.

Wiligelmus. △1082.

Wilkes, Charles (1798–1877), US explorer and admiral, b. New York City. He is credited with discovering the Antarctic continent in 1840; Wilkes Land is named for him. In the Civil War he precipitated the Trent Affair by stopping a British ship and removing two Confederate diplomats. *See also* Trent Affair.

Wilkes, John (1727–97), English political figure and journalist. Elected to Parliament (1757), he opposed Lord Bute's ministry, attacking it in his journal, *The North Briton.* An issue (1763) of this publication carrying a vitriolic article on the king's speech brought about Wilkes' arrest on a general warrant. Subsequent proceedings led to the outlawing of such a warrant, but Wilkes was dismissed from Parliament for his "obscene" *Essay on Woman* (1764). Reelected (1768), he was expelled several times but enjoyed sufficient popularity to regain his seat (1774–90). After 1774, having secured a measure of press freedom, he ceased to be politically important.

Wilkes Barre, city in E Pennsylvania, on Susquehanna River 18mi (29km) SW of Scranton; seat of Luzerne co. The city was burned in 1778 by Indians and British as a result of nearby Wyoming Valley Massacre and again in 1784 during the Yankee-Pennamite Wars; site of Wilkes College (1933), King's College (1946), Luzerne County Community College (1966), and Swetland Homestead (early 1800s); much of city was damaged during flooding of Susquehanna, June 1972. Industries: pencils, clothing, footwear, tobacco products, radios. Settled 1769; named for John Wilkes and Isaac Barre, colonial supporters in Parliament during Revolutionary War; inc. as borough 1806, as city 1871. Pop. (1970) 58,856.

Wilkins, Maurice Hugh Frederick (1916–), English biophysicist. He shared the 1962 Nobel Prize in physiology or medicine with James D. Watson and Francis Crick for his X-ray diffraction studies that helped to determine the molecular structure of DNA (deoxyribonucleic acid) the basic hereditary material of most cells. *See also* Deoxyribonucleic Acid.

Wilkins, Roy (1901–), US civil rights leader, b. St Louis. He was managing editor of the black weekly, Kansas City *Call* (1923–31), before joining the staff of the National Association for the Advancement of Colored People (NAACP). Rising in the organization, he was executive secretary (1955–65) and executive director (1965–77). He was an opponent of violent tactics, but worked vigorously for black rights.

Wilkinsburg, borough in SW Pennsylvania, 7mi (11km) E of Pittsburgh. Industries: machine tools, bricks. Founded 1780; inc. as borough 1887. Pop. (1970) 26,780.

Wilkinson, James (1757–1825), US general, b. Calvert co, Md. He served in the American Revolution but was forced to resign his commission in 1778 because of his part in the Conway cabal. In 1784 he moved to Kentucky and joined a conspiracy with the Spanish governor of Louisiana to gain trade monopolies for himself and to give Kentucky to Spain. When Indian warfare broke out in Ohio, Wilkinson returned to active service under Anthony Wayne, and upon Wayne's death became ranking officer of the US army (1796). In 1803, Wilkinson officiated at the transfer of Louisiana to US ownership and was Louisiana's governor (1805–06). He then conspired with Aaron Burr to take a large segment of the West to form Burr's own republic. When Burr was brought to trial, Wilkinson was the chief prosecution witness. In 1813 he commanded American forces in Canada and was honorably discharged from the army in 1815.

Willamette River, river in Oregon; rises in Cascade Range, flows N past Eugene, Salem, and Portland to Columbia River NW of Portland; its valley is the most densely populated part of Oregon. Since 1938 a federal project has built dams to provide hydroelectric power, control floods, and improve navigation. River is navigable for most of its 300mi (483km).

Willard, Frances Elizabeth Caroline (1839–98), US social reformer, b. Churchville, N.Y. She left the education field to work for the temperance cause, serving as president of the National Woman's Christian Temperance Union (1879–98). Combining interest in woman suffrage with her temperance work, she was also president of National Council of Women (1888). She organized the WCTU into separate, activist departments involving more women than any other 19th-century organization. She was influential in the Prohibition party. She wrote *Women and Temperance* (1883) and *Glimpses of Fifty Years* (1889).

Willard, Jess (1881–1968), US boxer, b. Pottawatomie County, Kans. He won the world's heavyweight championship from Jack Johnson (1915) in Havana, Cuba, and lost the title to Jack Dempsey (1919) in Toledo, Ohio.

Willemstad, town on Curacao Island; capital of Netherland Antilles, island group N of Venezuela in Caribbean Sea. A major oil refining and shipping center for Venezuelan oil, city also ships coffee from its fine

Walt Whitman

Eli Whitney

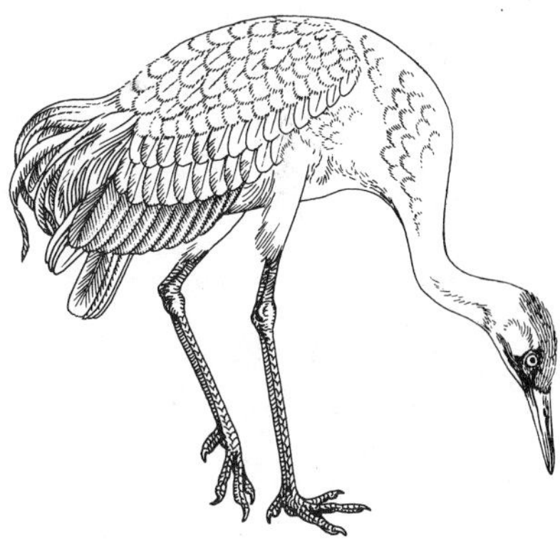

Whooping crane

Thornton Wilder

harbor; tourism is an important industry. Founded 1634. Pop. 43,547.

Willendorf, Venus of, statuette in the Vienna (Austria) Museum of Natural History. Representing a female fertility figure in a highly stylized form, it is quite rotund. Found at Willendorf, Austria, it is one of the earliest known works of Paleolithic art. △950.

Will Hay. △84.

William I (1797–1888), German emperor and king of Prussia. He was a symbol of reaction in the Revolution of 1848 and succeeded his brother as king of Prussia in 1861. His belief in the divine right of kings led to constitutional conflict, but Chancellor Bismarck's aggressively expansionist policy largely distracted liberal opposition and resulted in the annexation of many new territories. William's glory was at its peak in 1871 when he was proclaimed German emperor at the palace of Versailles. △1076.

William II (1859–1941), German emperor and king of Prussia. Succeeding his father, Frederick III, in 1888, he believed in the absolute powers of the monarchy and attempted to rule on his own initiative, which led to Chancellor Bismarck's resignation in 1890. William made many serious errors of judgment, especially in the area of foreign policy, causing Germany's isolation from former allies and causing him to be blamed by some critics as a cause of World War I. In 1918, with Germany on the brink of collapse, he was forced to abdicate and flee to the Netherlands, where he lived in retirement until his death.

William I, or **William the Conqueror** (1027–87), king of England (1066–87) and duke of Normandy. The illegitimate son of Robert I of Normandy, he was unwillingly accepted as Robert's heir, succeeding to the dukedom of Normandy in 1035. Supported initially by Henry I, king of France, he consolidated his position in Normandy against hostile neighbors throughout the 1050s and expanded his territory in 1060. Having apparently been designated Edward the Confessor's successor as king of England, William secured the agreement of Harold, Earl of Wessex to his accession. Harold's assumption of kingship was the direct cause of William's invasion of England and the ensuing Battle of Hastings (1066). Ruthlessly crushing internal resistance and defeating the invading Danes, he completed his conquest by 1070. He established stable government through astute land distribution and by instituting feudalism in England. One of the greatest achievements of his reign was the compilation of the *Domesday Book* (1086). △1076.

William II (1056–1100), king of England (1087–1100), second surviving son of William I. Known as Rufus because of his ruddy complexion, he was of a brutal, warlike temperament, and his rule in England, although stable, was repressive. He ruthlessly quelled two baronial revolts, humbled the Welsh and Scots, and secured Normandy from his elder brother Robert.

William III (1650–1702), king of England, Scotland, and Ireland (1689–1702) and prince of Orange, b. the Netherlands. Born eight days after the death of his father, William II, Prince of Orange, he was prevented from succeeding him as stadholder of Holland until 1672. He commanded the Dutch forces against France, also forming a coalition including England. He married Mary, daughter of the duke of York (later James II of England) in 1677 and concluded the treaty of Nijmegen with France in 1678. Following the Glorious Revolution (1688), he superseded James II (1689), ruling jointly with Mary until her death (1694). He defeated James at the Battle of the Boyne in Ireland (1690), partially reduced Scotland, and carried on a second war with France, also forming the Grand Alliances with European powers. *See also* Glorious Revolution.

William IV (1765–1837), king of Great Britain and Ireland (1830–37) and of Hanover (1830–37). The third son of George III, he at first pursued a naval career, obtaining the rank of rear admiral (1790). He became duke of Clarence (1789) and took as mistress the actress Dorothea Jordan, by whom he had several children before breaking with her (1811). He succeeded his brother George IV as king (1830). His political attitudes were reactionary but did not prevent the passage of the 1832 Reform Act.

William I (1772–1843), king of the Netherlands and grand duke of Luxembourg (1815–40). He commanded the Dutch in the French wars (1793–95). Son of the last stadholder, William V, Prince of Orange, he was first king of the Kingdom of the Netherlands. He granted a fairly liberal constitution, but could not truly unite Belgium and Holland and finally signed treaty of separation (1839). He abdicated (1840) in favor of his son William.

William II (1792–1849), king of the Netherlands and grand duke of Luxembourg (1840–49). Succeeded his father, William I. He fought against France in the Napoleonic Wars and against the Belgian rebels (1830). At first opposed to reforms, he secured a liberal constitution in 1848, despite a conservative states general.

William III (1817–90), king of the Netherlands and grand duke of Luxembourg (1849–90), son of William II. He reluctantly appointed Jan Thorbecke to head the government and accepted his liberal reforms, such as extension of suffrage. He abolished slavery in Dutch West Indies (1862). With his death the male line of Orange ended, and his daughter Wilhelmina succeeded him.

William I, known as **William the Silent** (1533–84), prince of Orange and founder of Dutch Republic. Emperor Charles V appointed him stadholder of northern Holland provinces in 1555. The political and religious persecution of the Dutch by Philip II, Charles' successor in Spain, turned William against Spain, and he opposed the king (1559–67). He fled to Germany (1567). William and his brothers led "War of Liberation" (1568–76) and suffered several defeats but managed to unite the provinces in their resistance. He was first stadholder (1579–84); office made hereditary (1581). He was assassinated by Balthasar Gérard before final victory. △1154.

William II (1626–50), prince of Orange, stadholder of the Netherlands (1647–50). He succeeded his father, Frederick Henry, and married Mary, daughter of Charles I of England. William unwillingly made peace with Spain (1648) and negotiated treaty with France (1650). He came into conflict with leaders of the states general and imprisoned some of them (1650), thus weakening the state-rights movement. He was succeeded by his son, William III of England.

William of Occam. *See* Occam, or Ockham, William.

Williams, Daniel Hale (1856–1931), US surgeon, b. Hollidaysburg, Pa. He performed the first successful heart operation in 1893. He founded Provident Hospital in Chicago, which provided medical training for blacks, and the National Medical Association and was a charter member of the American College of Surgeons.

Williams, George Washington (1849–91), US historian, b. Bedford Springs, Pa. His two-volume *History of the Negro Race in America* (1883) is a classic reference of primary sources. His other books include a history of the governments of Sierra Leone and Liberia and a *History of the Negro Troops in the War of the Rebellion* (1877). He was US minister to Haiti (1885–86).

Williams, Roger (1603–83), advocate of religious freedom and founder of Rhode Island, b. London. After a short term as a chaplain in England, he went to Boston (1631). As a minister at Salem, he had a conflict with the Massachusetts Bay Colony civil authorities, when he stated that a man's conscience was not under state control and that the king had no legal right to Indian land. Banished from the colony (1635), he founded Providence (1636) after buying land from Indians. Williams obtained a patent for Rhode Island, allowing full religious freedom (1644). He served the colony as a civil leader in several posts for many years.

Williams, Tennessee (Thomas Lanier) (1911–), US playwright, b. Columbus, Miss. His first Broadway play, *The Glass Menagerie* (1945) was awarded the New York Drama Critic's Circle Award. He received the Pulitzer Prize for *A Streetcar Named Desire* (1947) and *Cat on a Hot Tin Roof* (1955). Among his other works were *The Rose Tattoo* (1951), *Camino Real* (1953), *Sweet Bird of Youth* (1959), and *The Night of the Iguana* (1961). He also wrote poetry, short stories and a novel, and several of his works became motion pictures. Many of his plays were set in the South, where he grew up. △1426.

Williams, Theodore Samuel ("Ted") (1918–), US baseball player, b. San Diego. During his career, he won six batting titles and hit 521 home runs. He played for the Boston Red Sox (1939–42; 1946–60) and was elected to the Baseball Hall of Fame in 1966.

Williams, William Carlos (1883–1963), US author, b. Rutherford, N.J. A practicing physician, he produced numerous poems. He is regarded as the founder of the Objectivist school of poetry. Williams' poems deal with everyday life. His works include *Paterson* (5 vols., 1946–58), a long poem set in Paterson, N.J., and *Pictures from Breughel* (1963; Pulitzer Prize 1964). He also wrote short stories, plays, novels, and the nonfiction work *In the American Grain* (1925).

Williamsburg, historic town in E Virginia, 50mi (80km) SE of Richmond; seat of James co. Settled 1633, it was made state capital 1699–1780, when seat of government moved to Richmond. Williamsburg is visited annually by thousands of tourists and was made part of Colonial National Historic Park (est. 1936). Included in its landmarks are College of William and Mary (1693), Capitol, Public Gaol (1704), Magazine and Guardhouse (1715), Raleigh Tavern, Governor's Palace (1720), Bruton Parish Church (1715), Brush-Everard House (1717), Courthouse (1770). Inc. 1722. Pop. (1970) 9,069.

Williamsport, city in central Pennsylvania, on the Susquehanna River; seat of Lycoming co; site of Lycoming College (1812), Williamsport Area Community College (1920), and national headquarters of Little League Baseball. Industries: paper and lumber products, textiles, chemicals, aircraft engines, valves, wire rope. Settled 1772; chartered as borough 1806; inc. as city 1866. Pop. (1970) 37,918.

William Tell, in Swiss legend, a hero who for his rebellious spirit was forced by the Austrian baliff of Uri to shoot an arrow through an apple on his son's head. Tell later shot the bailiff, signaling a general uprising that led to the beginning of the Swiss Confederation in the early 14th century.

Willkie, Wendell, (1892–1944), US lawyer and political leader, b. Elwood, Ind. Becoming president (1933) of a large utilities company, he fought government intervention in business under Pres. Franklin D. Roosevelt, together with projects like the Tennessee Valley Authority (1933). Although formerly a Democrat, he ran against Roosevelt as the Republican (1940) nominee. During World War II, he toured the world in support of Roosevelt's foreign policy. In his book *One World* (1943) he advocated the formation of a post-war world organization.

Willow, deciduous shrubs and trees native to cool or mountainous temperate regions. They have long, pointed leaves and flowers borne on catkins. Familiar species include the weeping willow *(Salix babylonica)* with drooping branches and pussy willow *(Salix discolor)* with fuzzy catkins. Family Salicaceae.

Willow Herb, or **Rosebay,** perennial plants (genus *Epilobium*) with willowlike leaves. Giant willowherb, or fireweed, *(E. angustifolium)* bears spiky terminal clusters of purple flowers; height: to 8ft (2.4m). Family Onagraceae.

Wills, Helen Newington *See* Moody, Helen Newington Wills.

Wilmette, residential town in NE Illinois, on Lake Michigan, N of Chicago; site of Mallinckrodt College (1918), and a Bahai temple. Pop. (1970) 32,134.

Wilmington, city in N Delaware at junction of Delaware and Christina rivers and Brandywine Creek; seat of New Castle co; largest city in Delaware, with shipyards, railroad shops, chemical and manufacturing plants, including DuPont; site of numerous historical buildings, including Fort Christina, built 1638 by Swedes, now a state park; and 3 junior colleges. Settled 1638; inc. 1832. Pop. (1970) 80,386.

Wilmington, seaport city in SE North Carolina, on Cape Fear River; seat of New Hanover co; scene of resistance to Stamp Act (1765); occupied by Lord Cornwallis before British march on Yorktown; served as port of entry for blockade runners during Civil War; site of Wilmington College (1947), Cornwallis' house (1771), and Greenfield Park, noted for its gardens. Industries: clothing, fertilizer, textiles, paper. Settled *c.* 1730; inc. as town 1740, as city 1866. Pop. (1970) 46,169.

Wilmot Proviso (1846), an attempt to prohibit slavery in territory acquired from Mexico. It was made in the form of an amendment to an appropriations bill by Rep. David Wilmot of Pennsylvania. The proviso passed the House but was defeated twice in the Senate.

Wilson, Charles Thomson Rees (1869–1959), English physicist who won, with A.H. Compton, the Nobel Prize for physics in 1927, for his invention of the Wilson cloud chamber. This device is used in the study of radioactivity, X rays and cosmic rays. He also devised a way of protecting barrage balloons from lightning and published his theory of thunderstorm electricity.

Wilson, Edmund (1895–1972), US author, b. Red Bank, N.J. Primarily a social and literary critic, he was managing editor of *Vanity Fair* (1920–21) and literary editor of *The New Republic* (1926–31). His work examines the social and political implications of literature. His books include *Axel's Castle* (1931), on the Symbolists; *To the Finland Station* (1940), on European revolutionary traditions; and *Patriotic Gore* (1962), on the literature of the American Civil War.

Wilson, (James) Harold (1916–), British prime minister (1964–70, 1974–76). A Labourite, he held several academic and government posts before entering Parliament (1945). He was president of the Board of Trade (1947–51). He was Labour party leader from 1963–76 and became prime minister after the elections of 1964 and 1974. He supported Britain's membership in the European Economic Community. He resigned as prime minister in 1976 but remained in Parliament.

Wilson, J(ohn) T(uzo) (1908–), Canadian geophysicist and geologist. He determined global patterns of faulting and the structure of the continents. His investigations have influenced theories of continental drift, sea-floor spreading, and convection currents within the Earth. *See also* Continental Drift.

Wilson, Richard (1714–82), Welsh landscape painter. △1192.

Wilson, Woodrow (Thomas Woodrow Wilson) (1856–1924), 28th president of the United States (1913–21), b. Staunton, Va. He graduated from the College of New Jersey (Princeton) in 1879, studied law at the University of Virginia, and was admitted (1882) to the Georgia bar. He married Ellen Axson in 1885, and they had three daughters; in 1915 he married Edith Bolling Galt.

Wilson taught at Bryn Mawr, Wesleyan, and Princeton before becoming president of Princeton in 1902. After a successful tenure there he ran (1910) as a Democrat for the governorship of New Jersey. He won, and his success in that office brought him nationwide attention. In 1912 he was nominated for president. The Republicans were split that year; William Howard Taft and Theodore Roosevelt were both running. As a result, Wilson won but with a minority of the popular vote.

As president, Wilson put through a decrease in the tariff and the Clayton Antitrust Act (1914). The Federal Reserve System (1913) and the Federal Trade Commission (1914) were both instituted during his first term. He waged an aggressive policy toward Latin America; Marines were landed in Mexico, Cuba, the Dominican Republic, and Haiti. Wilson ran for reelection in 1916 and won a narrow victory. Even before Wilson's reelection, World War I was occupying more and more of his attention. US sentiment was decidedly anti-German, but Wilson attempted a neutral stance. Relations deteriorated, however, and war was declared on April 6, 1917.

Wilson assumed wide powers, and he successfully converted the nation to a war footing. In 1918, near the successful end of the war, he issued his Fourteen Points, which were to form the basis for the peace. After an armistice was signed (November 1918), Wilson sailed to Europe to attend the peace conference. He used his enormous prestige to good advantage in drawing up the Treaty of Versailles. At home, isolationists marshalled strong opposition to the League of Nations. Wilson's last years in office were spent in an unsuccessful campaign to win public approval for the League. His health deteriorated, and he suffered a stroke, from which he never fully recovered.

Career: president, Princeton University, 1902–10; governor of New Jersey, 1911–13; president, 1913–21.

See also Fourteen Points; League of Nations; Versailles, Treaty of. △1308.

Wilson, city of E North Carolina; seat of Wilson co; site of Atlantic Christian College (1902). Industries: tobacco, agricultural implements, clothing, fertilizer. Settled 1847; inc. 1849. Pop. (1970) 29,347.

Wilson-Gorman Act (1894), US tax legislation. It began as a reform act in the House, but the Senate changed its purpose. Duties were lowered to 4% with lumber, wool, and copper added to the free list.

Wilt, any of a group of plant diseases characterized by yellowing and wilting of leaves and young stems, often followed by death of the plant. Wilt diseases are caused by bacteria or fungi that grow in the sapwood and plug water-conducting tissues or disrupt the plant's water balance in some other way.

Winchester, city in N Virginia, in Shenandoah Valley, 70mi (112km) WNW of Alexandria. George Washington began his career here as a surveyor (1748); site of Washington's office and the Old Presbyterian church (1790, now an armory), Shenandoah College and Conservatory of Music (1875). Founded 1744; inc. as town 1779, as city 1874. Pop. (1970) 14,463.

Winckelmann, Johann (Ioachim) (1717–68), German archeologist and art historian whose writings helped to popularize ancient art, especially that of Greece, and stimulated the neoclassical revival of the late 18th century. An influential work is *Geschichte der Kunst des Alterthums* ("History of the Art of the Ancients," 1764).

Windaus, Adolf (1876–1959), German chemist. In 1907 he synthesized histamine and in 1928 was awarded a Nobel Prize for his work on steroid structure and the photochemistry of vitamin D.

Wind Cave National Park, park in SW South Dakota. This park features limestone caverns in the Black Hills, decorated by attractive boxwork and calcite crystal formations. Animal life includes elk, pronghorn, prairie dog towns, bison, and black-footed ferret. Area: 28,059acres (11,364hectares). Est. 1903.

Windhoek, capital and largest city of Namibia, W Africa; administrative, economic, communications headquarters. City originally served as headquarters of Nana Chief; in 1892 it was made capital of German colony; captured during WWI by South African troops; site of railroad terminus; world's major trade center for karakul sheep skins; city contains three German medieval-style castles. Industries: clothing, meat and bone meal processing. Pop. 61,260.

Windisch-Graetz, Prince Alfred Candidus Ferdinand zu (1787–1862), Austrian general. △1248.

Windpipe. *See* Trachea.

Wind Power, mechanical power extracted from climatic air currents by windmills. The sails of the windmill are at an angle to the wind and provision is made to keep the sails always facing the wind. Windmills have been used in the past as water pumping devices and for grinding grain. Modern windmills are looked upon as a means of electric power generation for home use. △288, 1634, 1648.

Winds, air in natural horizontal motion at any speeds relative to the surface of the Earth. Air currents in motion vertical to the surface are usually called updrafts or downdrafts. Winds are named for the direction from which they come relative to the Earth; a west wind blows from west to east, a northeasterly gale from northeast to southwest. Wind direction is indicated by wind or weather vanes, wind speed by anemometers, and wind force by the Beaufort wind scale. Steady, periodic winds around the Earth are named, like the doldrums, the trade winds, and the polar easterlies. Monsoons are seasonal winds in Asia as well as Europe and other regions, caused by excess temperatures and pressures over continents in winter and deficits in summer compared with oceans. Foehns (föhns) are warm, dry winds produced by adiabatic compression as they descend the lee of mountains, yielding arid conditions. Foehns are found in the Alps, are called Chinooks in the Rockies, and occur in nearly all mountainous areas. Siroccos are hot, humid Mediterranean winds often bringing rain and fog to continental Europe. *See also* Doldrums; Easterlies; Trade Winds; Westerlies. △214, 266.

Windsor, name by which the British royal family has been known since 1917. Queen Victoria's descendants in the male line originally belonged to the German house of Saxe-Coburg-Gotha, family of her husband, Prince Albert. During World War I, however, this German connection proved embarrassing. In a proclamation in 1917, George V decreed that British subjects descended from Victoria in the male line take the surname "of Windsor." In 1952, Elizabeth II modified this decree to the effect that all her descendants, in both lines, should take the surname Windsor or Windsor-Mountbatten.

Windsor, city in SE Ontario, Canada, on the Detroit River; seat of Essex co; industrial and transportation center, served by the Canadian National and Canadian Pacific railroads; port of entry; site of Assumption College (1857), Holy Names College (1934), University of Windsor (1963). Industries: automobiles, pharmaceuticals, chemicals, salt. Settled 1749 by French. Pop. 199,784.

Windsor (New Windsor), town in S central England, on Thames River. Windsor Castle has been the chief residence of English monarchs since William the

Roger Williams

Pussy willow

Willow herb

Woodrow Wilson

Conqueror. The castle contains the magnificent St George's Chapel, with several royal tombs. Windsor town hall was built by Sir Christopher Wren. Pop. 16,447.

Wind Tunnel, chamber in which aircraft components and scale models are tested by being exposed to mechanically produced wind. The first wind tunnel, built in 1871, used a steam-driven fan. Modern tunnels can reproduce conditions of temperature and pressure that aircraft may encounter and can generate winds far into the hypersonic range. △1496.

Windward Islands, S group of Lesser Antilles in West Indies, between Caribbean Sea (W) and Atlantic Ocean (E); chain extends from Leeward Islands (N) to NE coast of Venezuela, and includes French Martinique, Grenada, and the British Windwards (Dominica, St Lucia, and St Vincent). Barbados, Trinidad, and Tobago are not included in group. Group is mountainous, of volcanic origin; tropical agricultural center; Rouseau and Kingstown are chief towns; aboriginal Carib inhabitants were forced out with British and French settlements (17th century). English and French disputed possession until Congress of Vienna (1815) fixed ownership with Britain. Industries: bananas, spices, limes, cacao, tourism. Area: approx. 700sq mi (1,813sq km). Pop. 2,149,750.

Windward Passage, strait in West Indies, between Cuba (W) and Haiti (E); approx. 50mi (81km) wide from Cape Maisi, Cuba, to Cape du Mole, Haiti; links the Caribbean Sea (S) with the Atlantic Ocean (N). It is a direct shipping route between the United States and the Panama Canal.

Wine and Winemaking. △344–48.

Wing, specialized, feathered forelimb structure used by birds for flight. The basal and central parts are supported by an upper arm bone and two forearm bones, respectively, with the outer forearm bone bearing long flight feathers. Three fused and modified hand bones support flight quills. *See also* Bird; Flight, Bird. △528.

Wing, Aircraft, an airfoil whose major function is to provide lift. It does this by exploiting the difference in pressure above and below the wing as it moves through the air. *See also* Airfoil. △1718, 1744.

Winged Victory. *See* Victory of Samothrace.

Winnebago Lake, lake in E Wisconsin. Fox River flows through it. Wisconsin's largest lake, it is part of water route connecting Great Lakes and Mississippi River. Fond du Lac and Oshkosh are on lake. Recreation site. Area: 215sq mi (557sq km).

Winnipeg, city in Manitoba, Canada, at the junction of Assiniboine and Red rivers; capital of Manitoba prov. City developed in 1880s around the Canadian Pacific Railway; site of University of Winnipeg (1871), University of Manitoba (1877), and Winnipeg Grain Exchange, one of the world's largest. In 1812 the Red River settlement was founded by the Hudson's Bay Co.; the Canadian government took ownership 1870 when the province was est., and Winnipeg was made capital. Industries: cotton, furniture, meat packing, flour, stockyards, food processing. Inc. 1873. Pop. 243,208.

Winnipesaukee, Lake, lake in central New Hampshire; largest lake in the state; summer resort and tourist region. Area: 71sq mi (184sq km).

Winona, city and riverport in SE Minnesota, on the Mississippi River 40mi (64km) E of Rochester; seat of Winona co; site of Winona State College (1858), College of St Teresa (1907), St Mary's College (1912). Industries: flour, cosmetics, pharmaceuticals, fertilizers. Settled 1851; inc. 1857. Pop. (1970) 26,438.

Winston-Salem, city in central North Carolina, 68mi (109km) NNE of Charlotte; seat of Forsyth co. Salem was settled 1766 by Moravians; in 1849 land, later called Winston, was purchased from Moravians for seat of newly est. Forsyth co; the two communities united 1913. City contains Brothers House (1769), Miksch Tobacco Shop (1771), Salem Tavern (1784), Salem Academy (1772), Wake-Forest University (1834), Winston-Salem State University (1892), Salem College (1772). Industries: tobacco, brewing, clothing, textiles, electrical equipment. Salem inc. 1856; Winston inc. 1859. Pop. (1970) 32,913.

Winter Cherry. *See* Chinese Lantern Plant.

Wintergreen, or checkerberry, teaberry, creeping, woody, evergreen shrub native to E North America. It has oval leaves, white or pinkish flowers, and red fruit. An aromatic oil made from its leaves is used as a flavoring. Family Ericaceae; species *Gaultheria procumbens.*

Winter Park, resort city in central Florida, 5mi (8km) NE of Orlando; site of Rollins College. Founded 1858; inc. 1882. Pop. (1970) 21,895.

Winter Solstice. *See* Solstice.

Winter's Tale, The (1611), Shakespearean romance. Leontes, king of Sicily, imprisons his wife Hermione for an imagined indiscretion with his friend Polixenes, and banishes their newborn daughter. All are reunited when his daughter is wooed by Polixenes' son, her true identity is discovered, and Hermione, believed dead, emerges from hiding.

Winterthur, city in N Switzerland, 12mi (19km) NE of Zurich; made a free city (1415) under Holy Roman Empire and bought by Zurich (1467); site of 15th- and 17th-century castles, Gothic church (*c.* 13th–16th centuries), fine art museum. Industries: machinery, diesel engines, locomotives, textiles. Pop. 92,722.

Winthrop, John (1588–1649), Puritan colonist and theocratic governor of the Massachusetts Bay Colony. Originally a London lawyer, as governor he led 700 colonists first to Salem (1630) and later to Charlestown and Boston. He served as governor for 12 years (1630–34; 1637–40; 1642–44; 1646–49). He served as president of the New England Confederation and wrote "History of New England 1630–49." *See also* Massachusetts Bay Colony; New England Confederation.

Winthrop, John (1606–76), colonial governor of Connecticut. Son of John Winthrop, the governor of the Massachusetts Bay Colony, he settled Ipswich, Mass. (1633) and built Fort Saybrook on the Connecticut River (1634). He served as governor (1657–76). He obtained a liberal charter (1662), uniting Connecticut and New Haven and giving the colonists the same rights as Englishmen.

Winthrop, town in E Massachusetts, 4mi (6.4km) ENE of Boston, on a peninsula in Boston Bay. Named for colonial Gov. John Winthrop whose home is preserved here; resort and yachting center. Founded 1635; separated from N Chelsea and inc. 1852. Pop. (1970) 20,335.

Wirehaired Pointing Griffon, pointer and water retriever breed of dog (sporting group) developed in Holland and France at the end of the 19th century; brought to US about 1900. It has a long head and square muzzle; high-set ears hanging flat; and large yellow or light brown eyes. A short-backed body is low-set on very straight forelegs and well-developed hind legs. Its unique coat is harsh, bristly, and unkempt; colors are steel gray, gray-white, dirty white with chestnut, or chestnut. Average size: 21.5–23.5in (54.5–59.5cm) high at shoulder; 45–60lb (20.5–27kg). *See also* Sporting Dog.

Wiretapping. △868.

Wireworm, long, cylindrical larva of a click beetle. Wireworms are distinctly segmented and usually brown or yellow. Most live in the soil and some cause serious damage to roots of cultivated crops. Family Elateridae. *See also* Click Beetle.

Wiring. △1648–50.

Wirt, William (1772–1834), US lawyer and author, b. Bladensburg, Md. In 1803 he published his first and best work *Letters of a British Spy,* and (1807) was prosecution counsel in the treason trial of Aaron Burr. As US attorney general (1817–29) under presidents Madison, Monroe, and John Quincy Adams, he argued some of the precedent-setting cases in US constitutional history. He initiated the tradition of publishing the opinions of the attorney general. In 1832 Wirt ran for the presidency on the Anti-Masonic party ticket.

Wisconsin, state in the N central United States, in the Great Lakes region, bordered on the E by Lake Michigan and on the N partly by Lake Superior.

Land and Economy. The land is a rolling plain that slopes down from the high ground in the N. The Mississippi River flows along the W boundary; many small rivers are within the state, and there are more than 8,000 lakes. Fertile pasturelands through most of the state support the dairy herds that make Wisconsin the nation's leader in production of milk and dairy products. Manufacturing is chiefly in the cities along Lake Michigan, which gives a water outlet to markets. Milwaukee, Racine, Sheboygan, and Green Bay have developed harbors. In the far NW, Superior is part of the Lake Superior port of Duluth, Minn., center of iron ore shipping.

People. Early settlers came from E states, especially New England. They were followed by New England immigrants, chiefly Germans, Norwegians, and Swedes. Milwaukee became a center of German culture in the nation. About 65% of the population lives in urban areas.

Education. There are about 60 institutions of higher education. The University of Wisconsin is state-supported.

History. Jean Nicolet landed at Green Bay in 1634 and claimed the region for France. French fur trappers were active there through the 18th century. The area was ceded in 1763 to Great Britain, which yielded it to the United States in 1783. Settlement began slowly with exploitation of the lead deposits in the SW. Land was obtained by treaties with the Indians, and the Territory of Wisconsin was created on July 3, 1836. After admission to the Union, the new state was a leader in wheat growing. This declined after 1870, and dairying dominated the economy. In the 20th century, Wisconsin was known for its progressive state governments, which pioneered in many liberal political measures.

PROFILE

Admitted to Union: May 29, 1848; rank, 30th
US Congressmen: Senate, 2; House of Representatives, 9
Population: 4,417,933 (1970); rank, 16th
Capital: Madison, 172,007 (1970)
Chief cities: Milwaukee, 717,372; Madison; Racine, 95,162; Green Bay, 87,809
State legislature: Senate, 33; Assembly, 99
Area: 56,154sq mi (145,439sq km); rank, 26th
Elevation: Highest, 1,952ft (595m), Timms Hill; lowest, 581ft (177m), Lake Michigan
Industries (major products): machinery, food products, beer, motor vehicle parts and equipment, steel, metal products, paper
Agriculture (major products): dairy products, hay, corn, hogs, poultry
Minerals (major): zinc, lime, cement, stone, lead
State nickname: Badger State
State motto: Forward
State bird: robin
State flower: butterfly violet
State tree: sugar maple

Wisconsin River, rises in lake district of NE Wisconsin; flows S through central Wisconsin, turns W and empties into the Mississippi River near Prairie du Chien. Connected to Lake Michigan by canal and Fox River. Hydroelectric projects are on river. Due to shifting sandbars it is navigable for only 200mi (322km) of its 430mi (692km).

Wisdom of Solomon, biblical book of the Old Testament Apocrypha. The first nine chapters deal with the moral and intellectual aspects of the doctrine of Wisdom, the remaining 10 chapters with the doctrine's place in history.

Wise, Isaac Mayer (1819–1900), US rabbi, founder of Reform Judaism in the United States, b. Bohemia. He moved to New York City in 1846 and later to Ohio, serving as rabbi in both places. He tried to unify Reform Jews and in 1873 founded the Union of American Hebrew Congregations. In 1889 he helped develop the Rabbinic Council of Reform Judaism.

Wise, Stephen Samuel (1874–1949), US rabbi of Reform Judaism and leader of the Zionist movement, b. Hungary. In 1907 he founded the Free Synagogue in New York to create a pulpit free of restraints, stressing democracy. He was a founder of the Zionist Organization of America and of the American Jewish Congress. In 1922 he founded the Jewish Institute of Religion in New York. He vigorously opposed excessive dogmatism in Judaism.

Wister, Owen (1860–1938), US author, b. Philadelphia. He wrote novels, humor, nature studies, poetry, and biographies of three presidents. His novel *The Virginian* (1902) was a great popular success and did much to shape the romantic conception of the cowboy West.

Wisteria, genus of hardy woody vines native to North America, Japan, and China. They have showy, fragrant flower clusters of purplish, white, pink, or blue. Family Leguminosae.

Witchcraft, Primitive. *See* Sorcery.

Witch Doctor, person regarded as supernaturally powerful, especially in Africa. Witch doctors fight or control evil spirits and heal the sick, using herbs and rituals. They wield considerable social power. *See also* Shaman; Sorcery.

Vitch Hazel, shrub and small tree of temperate re-ions that blooms in late autumn or early spring. The ommon witch hazel (Hamamelis *virginiana*) has yel-ow flowers and is native to E North America. Family lamamelidaceae.

Vithdrawal, in drug addiction. △730.

Vitherite, a carbonate mineral, barium carbonate 3aCO$_3$), found in low-temperature lead and fluorite re veins. Orthorhombic system twinned, pseudohex-gonal twinned crystals, and in crusts and granular. ilassy white, yellow, or gray; hardness 3–3.5; sp gr .5.

Vitmer, Lightner (1867–1956), US clinical psy-hologist, b. Philadelphia. He was the founder of the rst psychological clinic in the United States and nany throughout the country. He helped create the rofession of clinical psychology, devised tests for iagnosing mental disorders, and founded the *Jour-al of Clinical Psychology* in 1907.

Vitt, Jan de (1625–72), Dutch statesman. As bur-omaster of Dort, opposed the House of Orange. irand pensionary from 1653 until his murder in 672, he led the Dutch in two wars against England nd one against France.

Vittelsbach, German family that ruled Bavaria from 180 to 1918 and was one of the dynasties which haped the history of Germany. In 1255 the duchy of 3avaria was divided between the dukes of Bavaria at Aunich and the counts of the Rhenish Palatinate at leidelberg. The resulting struggle for power among he different branches of the family eliminated the ossibility of a strong unified Bavaria until 1806, vhen Maximilian I became sole ruler.

Vittenberg, town in central East Germany, on Elbe River. In 1502, Frederick III founded university here hat became center of Protestant Reformation during enure of Martin Luther and Philip Melanchthon. In 517 Martin Luther nailed his 95 theses to the door f Schlosskirche (castle church), which still stands, nd in 1520 he burned papal bull outside Elster Gate; own passed to Prussia 1815. Industries: machinery, hemicals, rubber products. Founded late 12th cen-ury; chartered 1293. Pop. 47,151.

Vittfogel, Karl. △882, 884.

Vittgenstein, Ludwig (1889–1951), Austrian phi-osopher. A colleague of Bertrand Russell, he was ac-vely involved in the Vienna Circle. In *Tractatus logi-o-philosophicus* (1921), he analyzed the problem of anguage and its limits which later influenced the rise f logical positivism and linguistic analysis. *Philosoph-cal Investigations* (1953) and *Remarks on the Foun-lations of Mathematics* (1956) were published post-umously. *See also* Linguistic Analysis; Logical ositivism. △854, 858.

Vitwatersrand, the Rand region in Republic of iouth Africa, developed in 1880s as one of the rich-st gold mining regions in the world; site of cities of ohannesburg, Benoni, Boksburg Springs, Germiston. ndustries: gold mining, diamond cutting, food proc-ssing, steel milling, metallurgy, machines, cement, hemicals. Width: approx. 23mi (37km); Length: i2mi (100km).

Voburn, city in NE Massachusetts; birthplace of hor-iculturist Loammi Baldwin (1745), for whom the Bald-vin apple is named; Charles Goodyear first vulcanized ubber here in 1839; birthplace of inventor Benjamin Rumford (1753), his home is a museum. Industries: eather, chemicals, greenhouses. Founded 1640 as art of Charlestown; inc. as township 1642, as city 888. Pop. (1970) 37,406.

Vodehouse, (Sir) P(elham) G(renville) (1881–975), English novelist. In 1910 he began a series of umorous novels and short stories set in the upper-lass world of the Edwardian period and the 1920s nd created the characters Bertie Wooster and eeves. His novels include *Carry on Jeeves* (1925), *The Code of the Woosters* (1938), and *A Pelican at 3landings* (1969). He became an American citizen 1955) and was knighted (1975).

Vöhler, Friedrich (1800–82), German chemist who irst isolated aluminum and beryllium and discovered alcium carbide. His synthesis of urea demolished the italism of G.E. Stahl and laid the foundation for mod-ern organic chemistry.

Volcott, Oliver, (1726–97), a signer of the Declara-ion of Independence. Serving in the Continental Con-jress (1775–78; 1780–84), he was later lieutenant governor (1787–96), and then governor of Connecti-cut (1796–97).

Wolf, Hugo. △1246.

Wolf, wild dogs originally native to most of North America and Eurasia. Packs of wolves do kill large mammals, but a large part of the wolf's omnivorous diet consists of rodents and other small animals. Attacks on humans are rare. The gray or timber wolf *(Canis lupus)* is the largest member of the dog family and an ancestor of domestic dogs. It resembles a large malamute—length: 4ft (1.2m); weight: 115lb (53kg). It is usually gray but the Arctic wolf is mostly white. It is now restricted to thinly populated, mostly northern regions of Europe and North America. The red wolf *(Canis niger)* of S United States is smaller, more slender, and tawny-gray in color. *See also* Canidae. △592, 612.

Wolfe, James (1727–59), British military officer. He fought in North America during the French and Indian Wars. At Louisbourg (1758), he was given command of the expedition against Quebec. He took 5,000 men down the St Lawrence River where they scaled the heights to the Plains of Abraham, taking the city from Marquis Montcalm and his French forces. Both Wolfe and Montcalm died in this decisive battle that cost France its holdings in Canada.

Wolfe, Thomas (1900–38), US author, b. Asheville, N.C. A graduate of the University of North Carolina (1920), he went to Harvard University to study the writing of plays, but finally realized that his talent was for writing novels. During 1924–30 he taught intermittently at New York University, alternating his teaching with long trips to Europe. His first novel, *Look Homeward, Angel,* a massive fictionalized autobiography, was published in 1929. With it began Wolfe's productive collaboration with Maxwell Perkins, his editor, who also helped cut the voluminous manuscript for *Of Time and the River* (1935).

Subsequent works, all intense and basically autobiographical, include *The Web and the Rock* (1939) and *You Can't Go Home Again* (1940). Both were published after Wolfe's untimely death from complications following pneumonia. Wolfe also wrote *A Portrait of Bascom Hawke* (1932), a short novel, and *From Death to Morning* (1935), a collection of short stories.

Wolff, Christian von (1679–1754), Polish academic philosopher. While professor of mathematics at Halle, Wolff, always a prolific author, acquired a great reputation as a systematizer and popularizer of the thought of W. G. Leibnitz. In the *Radical Thoughts* (1712) Leibnitz's metaphysics was as much distorted as it was simplified. The Wolffian system, known for its rigid and narrow rationalism, was satirized by Voltaire in *Candide.*

Wolfhound. *See* Irish Wolfhound.

Wolfram. *See* Tungsten.

Wolframite, a tungstate mineral, iron-manganese tungstate [(Fe,Mn)WO_4], found in high- and medium-temperature quartz veins and in pegmatites. Monoclinic system black bladed crystals embedded in white quartz, or prismatic crystals, or massive granular groups. Black to brown; hardness 4–4.5; sp gr 7.3. Important ore of tungsten.

Wolfram von Eschenbach (*c.* 1170–*c.* 1220), German lyric poet and romance writer, b. Eschenbach, Bavaria. Associated with the court of Landgrave Herrman of Thuringia, he probably knew Walther von der Vogelweide and Hartman von Aue. His works include the romances *Parzival, Willehalm,* and *Titurel,* and eight or nine lyric poems. He became a major character, much romanticized, in Wagner's *Tannhäuser. See also* Parzival.

Wolf-Rayet star, type of very hot blue star of spectral type W, having a temperature of around 80,000 °K, which puts them among the hottest stars known. Wolf-Rayet stars, named after the two 19th-century astronomers who first analyzed them systematically, are short-lived phenomena that show several bright emission lines in their spectra due chiefly to neutral and singly ionized helium. △100.

Wolf Spider, common, worldwide spider that is gray to brown and lives under debris or in burrows. The female attaches the egg sac to her spinnerets and, when the eggs hatch, she carries the young spiders on her back. Length: 0.2–1.5in (5–38mm). Family Lycosidae. The hairy European wolf spider *(Lycosas tarentula)* was formerly thought to be a poisonous tarantula; length: 1in (25mm). *See also* Spider.

John Winthrop

Madison, Wisconsin

Wisteria

Witch hazel

Wolgemut, Michael (1434–1519), German painter and designer of woodcuts. He was a pioneer in the use of woodcuts in book illustration. One of the most influential artists of his era, he was responsible for the acceptance of the pure, untinted woodcut as a legitimate, self-sufficient medium. Even more important, it was in his workshop that young Albrecht Dürer was trained as a painter and graphic artist.

Wollaston, William Hyde (1766–1828), English scientist. He developed a method of working platinum, which made him wealthy; discovered palladium and rhodium; and invented a goniometer, the camera lucida, and the double-image prism that bears his name. He observed dark lines in the solar spectrum but failed to understand them and he was a member of the 1819 Royal Commission that delayed metrication in Britain.

Wollongong, city in New South Wales, Australia, 40mi (64km) S of Sydney; major seaport and urban center. Industries: steel, textiles, dairying, brickmaking. Settled 1815. Pop. 160,630.

Wollstonecraft, Mary (1759–97), English author. Family misfortunes, the loss of her best friend, and an unsettled existence marred much of her life. She visited revolutionary France, had an unhappy love affair there, and returned to England, marrying William Godwin (1797) and giving birth to a daughter, the future Mary Shelley. Her *Vindication of the Rights of Women* (1792) is an early feminist work.

Wolseley, Garnet Joseph Wolseley, 1st Viscount (1833–1913), British military commander. In a career in which he was eventually elevated to commander in chief of the British Army (1895–99), he saw action during the Crimean War, the Indian Mutiny, and the Anglo-French conflict against China. He quelled rebellion in Canada (1871) and held high commands in Cyprus and Africa. Made field marshal in 1894, he is best known for his army reforms, upon which the modern British military system is founded.

Wolsey, Thomas (1475?–1530), English cardinal and statesman. He served as papal legate (1518–30) and lord chancellor of England (1515–29). Of humble birth, he was an ambitious man who rose quickly in church affairs, becoming Henry VII's chaplain and then dean of Lincoln (1509). Appointed a privy councillor (1511) by Henry VIII, he soon virtually controlled English politics. He became archbishop of York and was granted the two bishoprics of Lincoln and Tournai (1514). He aimed to secure international prestige in Europe for both his country and himself. Eventually he incurred the jealousy of the nobility, and his failure to obtain Henry VIII's divorce from Catherine of Aragon finally brought his ruin. △1128.

Wolverhampton, industrial city in W central England, in Black Country. Industries: automobiles, tires, rayon, chemicals, hardware, tools. Pop. 268,847.

Wolverine, solitary, ferocious mammal native to pine forests of North America and Eurasia. The largest member of the weasel family, it has brown fur with lighter back and side bands, bushy tail, and large feet. Sometimes called glutton, it eats small animals, birds, berries, and carrion, and often attacks animals much larger than itself. Length: to 40in (1m); weight: to 60lb (27.5kg). Family Mustelidae; species *Gulo gulo.*

Woman's Christian Temperance Union (WCTU), organization formed to oppose the manufacture and use of alcoholic beverages. It was founded in Cleveland, Ohio, in 1874. Its object is to educate the public against the abuses of liquor and it became an important woman's pressure group devoted to many types of social reform. Frances Willard, president of WCTU (1879–98), made it an international society in 1883.

Woman Suffrage, the right of women to vote. The movement to obtain this right for women in the United States got its start at the Seneca Falls Convention for women's rights (1848). In 1869, disappointed over the failure to include women in the 15th Amendment, which enfranchised blacks, Susan B. Anthony and Elizabeth Cady Stanton formed the National Woman Suffrage Association to work for passage of another amendment for women. Also in 1869, Lucy Stone formed the National American Woman Suffrage Association, which united with the Anthony-Cady group in 1890. While some states, notably Wyoming in 1869, granted women the vote, national suffrage was not achieved until the passage of the Constitution's Amendment XIX in 1920. *See also* Constitution of the United States; National Woman Suffrage Association; Seneca Falls Convention. △904.

Womb. *See* Uterus.

Wombat. △544.

Women's Liberation Movement, resurgent feminist movement that developed in the United States in the 1960s. Under the leadership of the National Organization for Women (NOW) and other groups, the movement fought for abortion reform, equal employment opportunity, equal pay for women, child care facilities, and, in general, for an end to social, economic, and political discrimination on the basis of sex. Pursuant to its goals, the movement supported the Equal Rights Amendment to the US Constitution. *See also* National Organization for Women. △904.

Women's Rights Convention (1848). *See* Seneca Falls Convention.

Women's Rights Movement, international movement since the early 19th century for the dignity and equality of women. Originally concentrating on women's suffrage (attained in America in 1920), the movement has since worked for equality of employment opportunity and pay, freedom from unjust social, political, and theological expectations, and an awakening of physical, intellectual, and emotional awareness for the female majority of the world's population.

Wonsan, seaport city in SE North Korea, on Sea of Japan; capital of Kangwŏn prov.; made a treaty port 1883; served as Japanese naval base during WWII. Industries: engineering, fishing and fish processing, oil refining, food processing, textiles. Pop. 300,000.

Wood, Grant (1892–1942), US painter, b. Anamosa, Iowa. In a meticulously detailed style, he depicted simple, prosaic aspects of American life and the midwestern landscape, often investing his pictures with mildly satiric overtones, as in his well-known canvas, *American Gothic,* in the Chicago Art Institute.

Wood, the hard substance that forms the trunks of trees, used by man for construction material and fuel. Wood consists of fine cellular tubes, arranged vertically within the trunk, which carry water and minerals from roots to leaves; this accounts for the markings or grain found in all wood. The rings are reflections of growth. In the central portion of the trunk (called the heartwood), the ducts become plugged with resins. Heartwood is usually darker than sapwood. Woods are classified as hardwood, from deciduous trees, or softwood, from conifers. Hardwoods have long, continuous ducts, lacking in softwoods. Most lumber is softwood; hardwood is used mainly for furniture and flooring. △364.

Wood Betony, or lousewort, hardy perennial with dense whorls of small purple flowers. Height: to 3ft (1m). Family Scrophulariaceae; species *Stachys officinalis.*

Woodbine. *See* Virginia Creeper.

Woodchuck, or groundhog, marmot found from Alaska to the Gulf States, having grizzled black-brown hair. Using sharp front teeth and short strong legs, it digs burrows usually having more than one entrance. The woodchuck eats plants, often becoming a garden pest. It feeds heavily in autumn before hibernating. Length: 2ft (61cm); Weight: to 14lb (6.3kg). Species *Marmota monax. See also* Marmot.

Woodcock, shorebird that nests in cool parts of the Northern Hemisphere and winters in warm areas. Both the European *Scolopax rusticola* and American *Philohela minor* are reddish-brown. They insert their long flexible bills into swampy ground to clasp worms. Males make noises with their feathers during elaborate courtship flights. Buff-colored eggs (4) are laid in a grass-lined ground depression. Weight: 0.5lb (225g); Length: 12in (30cm).

Woodcut, oldest printmaking technique. Its simple principle has been in use at least since the 5th century, when relief designs on wooden blocks were used to print fabrics in Asia. The technique did not reach Europe until the early 15th century, when paper came into widespread use there, particularly in Germany. In their simplest form, woodcut prints are produced by tracing a design on a flat wooden surface and cutting away those parts of the wood that are not to be inked. Ink then is applied to the remaining lines and masses and transferred to paper to produce a reverse image. The woodcuts of Albrecht Dürer are unsurpassed in the West. The use of color was perfected by Japanese artists in the 18th century. △1144.

Wood Duck, North American perching duck with a long green, purple, and white crest. It perches in forest trees and nests well above the ground. Length: 18in (46cm). Species *Aix sponsa. See also* Duck.

Wooden, John (1910–), US basketball coach, Martinsville, Ind. While at UCLA (1948–75) he wo ten national championships (1964–65; 1967–7 1975) and a record 88 consecutive victories (1971 74).

Wood Engraving, printmaking technique. This me dium evolved from the woodcut; a design is achieve by pushing a sharp chisel (burin) against the grain c a polished hardwood surface to produce myriad fir incisions, often while the surface is being rotated facilitate curved contours. Characterized by the der sity and richness of its effects, the medium was e ploited most successfully in the 15th century by A brecht Dürer.

Wood Frog, true frog found in moist, wooded area of Canada and NE United States, sometimes far fro water. It has a dark patch extending backward from i eyes. Length: to 3in (7.6cm). Family Ranidae; specie *Rana sylvatica.*

Woodland, city in N central California, 15mi (24kn WNW of Sacramento; seat of Yolo co; site of man historical homes and a state historical farm. Center c mobile home manufacture; area produces vegetable Inc. 1871. Pop. (1970) 20,677.

Woodlands. △592–597.

Woodlawn, residential town in N Maryland; W su urb of Baltimore; includes community of Woodmoo Pop. (1970) 28,811.

Wood Louse, or **Sowbug,** terrestrial and semi-terres trial crustacean found worldwide under logs an stones and in houses. It has an oval, segmented bod and gills, greatly reduced, for breathing air. The pil bug can roll its body into a tight ball. Length: 0.75i (20mm). Suborder Oniscoidea. *See also* Crustacear

Wood Nymph, any of several striking butterflie whose caterpillars are brightly colored. Some feed o grape leaves. Family Satyridae.

Wood Parasol. △428.

Woodpecker, tree-climbing birds found worldwide except in Madagascar and Australia. Emitting a drum ming noise as they drill into trees, they have stron chisel-shaped beaks, long protrusible tongues, ofte equipped with harpoonlike tips for extracting insec larvae, and stiff tail with a spiny end used as a brac when they climb and walk on trees. They have black red, white, yellow, brown, or green plumage an some are crested. They lay white eggs (2–8) on woo chips in a tree hole nest. Family Picidae. △534.

Woodruff, Hale (1900–), US painter, b. Cairo, Il After studying at the Herron Institute of Indianapoli and in Paris he became an art instructor at Atlant University. His paintings depict landscapes and th conditions of blacks in Georgia.

Woods, Lake of the, resort lake in Manitoba an Ontario, Canada and N Minnesota, United States Area: 1,695sq mi (4,390sq km).

Wood Sorrel. *See* Oxalis.

Wood Thrush, North American song bird with red dish-brown upperparts and white breast marked wit darker spots. It builds an open cup-shaped nest wit a core of mud for its whitish or bluish eggs. Length 8in (20cm). Species *Hylocichla mustelina. See als* Thrush.

Wood Warbler, any of a family (Parulidae) of smal generally colorful birds of the New World with song considered less pleasant than those of Old World wa blers. They feed on insects and sometimes fruit. Mos females build open cup-shaped nests in a tree o bush; some build roofed, side-entranced nests fo marked whitish eggs (2–5) that they incubate alone Males help feed the young.

Woodward, Robert Burns (1917–), US chemis b. Boston, Mass. He became professor at Harvard i 1950 and was awarded a Nobel Prize in 1965 in rec ognition of his synthesis of a number of complex o ganic substances including quinine, cholesterol, cort sone, strychnine, lysergic acid, reserpine, chlorophyl and tetracycline.

Woodwind Instruments, in the modern symphon orchestra, instruments that are played by blowin over mouth holes (flute, piccolo) or by vibrations of a elastic reed (clarinet, English horn, oboe, bassoor saxophone). These are contrasted with brass instru ments. *See also* Orchestra. △1244.

Woodworking Machinery, fixed power tools used to cut, work and join lumber. Use of machinery speeds output and reduces costs. Automated machines permit continuous operation. Included are circular bench saws and radial-arm saws for general cutting such as sawing planks and for ripping, edging and crosscutting; band saws; surface planers for smoothing and reducing timber; mortising machines for making joints; molding cutters for making trim and molding; and sanders for finishing planed surfaces.

Woodworking Tools, implements used by carpenters to cut, work, and join lumber. Hand tools of ancient vintage include planes for smoothing rough surfaces and reducing wood to size; saws for cutting wood; chisels for removing surplus wood or cutting special shapes; and hammers, screwdrivers, awls, gimlets, and pliers. Tri-squares test right angles; bevels test all other angles. Modern powered hand tools include electric drills, saws, and routers. △1602.

Woodworth, Robert S(essions) (1869–1962), US psychologist, b. Belchertown, Mass. He was a professor at Columbia University (1903–42). He helped turn US psychology away from the structuralism of Wilhelm Wundt and E.B. Titchener toward a consideration of cause and effect in mental processes, which came to be known as the functionalist school of US psychology. Among his publications are the textbook *Psychology* (1921, 5th ed. 1947); and *Experimental Psychology* (1938).

Wool, soft, curly fibers chiefly obtained from fleece of domesticated sheep, although vicuña, alpaca, goats, and other animals also yield wool. Used extensively in textile manufacturing, it differs from hair, by having scales that cover numerous small fibers that interlock at base. Curl permits resilience. High tensile strength allows wool fabrics to retain shape. *See also* Lanolin. △376.

Woolen Act (1699), English legislation that forbade colonial US wool cloth to be sold outside of place of weaving, protecting English weavers from colonial exports.

Woolf, Virginia (1882–1941), English novelist and critic, daughter of Leslie Stephen, and a member of the Bloomsbury Group. She founded the Hogarth Press (1917) with her husband Leonard. Her novels include *Night and Day* (1919), *Jacob's Room* (1922), *Mrs. Dalloway* (1925), *To the Lighthouse* (1927), *Orlando* (1928), *The Waves* (1931), and *The Years* (1937). They display her experimentation with fictional forms, particularly the stream-of-consciousness technique. *See also* Bloomsbury Group.

Woollcott, Alexander Humphreys (1887–1943), US journalist, b. Phalanx, N.J. He became a reporter for the *New York Times* (1909) and was made drama critic (1914). He wrote criticism for three other New York newspapers (1922–28), was a regular contributor to the *New Yorker* magazine, and conducted a radio interview program (1929–43). He inspired the George S. Kaufman and Moss Hart play *The Man Who Came to Dinner,* in which he played the part of Sheridan Whiteside.

Woolly Bear, tiger moth caterpillar whose body is densely covered with long hairs. The North American banded *Isia isabella* is black in front and behind with a rusty-colored middle band of variable width. Unusually wide rusty bands are said to presage a warm winter and unusually narrow ones, a cold winter.

Woonsocket, city in N Rhode Island, 13mi (21km) NNW of Providence, on Blackstone River. Site was bought from Nipuc Indians 1662; heavy European and Canadian immigration occurred during 19th century due to increased industrial growth. Industries: textiles, electronic components, machine tools, paper, chemicals, clothing. Settled 1666 by John and Richard Arnold; inc. 1871 as town, 1888 as city. Pop. (1970) 46,820.

Worcester, city in central Massachusetts, 37mi (60km) W of Boston on Blackstone River; seat of Worcester co. Industrial development was spurred by canal system down Blackstone River to Providence, R.I. (1828); site of College of the Holy Cross (1843), Worcester Polytechnic Institute (1865), Clark University (1887). Industries: machinery, metal goods, chemicals, pharmaceuticals, electrical equipment, plastics. Settled 1673; inc. 1722 as town, 1848 as city. Pop. (1970) 176,572.

Worden, Alfred. △1724.

Wordsworth, William (1770–1850), English poet. He spent much of his youth exploring the countryside around Cumberland. He visited France twice (1790–92), sympathizing with the revolutionaries. With his sister Dorothy, to whom he was very close, he settled in Dorsetshire and became friends with Samuel Coleridge, with whom he wrote *Lyrical Ballads* (1798). Disillusioned with politics, Wordsworth explored the correlation between nature and the development of the human mind in poems such as "The Ruined Cottage" (1797), "Tintern Abbey" (1798), "The Prelude" (1805, 1850), "Intimations of Immortality" (1807), and "Resolution and Independence" (1807). △1240.

Work, in physics, the energy expended in moving a body against an opposing force. If the opposing force is the body's weight mg, the work done in raising it a height h is mgh. This work has been transferred to the body in the form of potential energy; if the body falls, the kinetic energy at the bottom will equal the work done in raising it. △1486.

Work, in Sociology. △924–28.

Working Dog, dog breeds used primarily to perform certain tasks. Included are dogs used as draft animals (Bernese mountain dog), shepherds (Belgian sheepdogs, Briard, collie), cattle drivers (Old English sheepdog), sled dogs (Alaskan malamute), police dogs (boxer, German shepherd), war dogs (Irish terrier), guard dogs (bull mastiff, Kuvasz), Seeing Eye dogs (various breeds), and Alpine rescue dogs (Saint Bernard). Members of the group vary widely in description, but most are large and sturdily built.

Works Progress Administration (WPA) (1935), New Deal agency to aid the unemployed. Under Harry Hopkins, the WPA spent billions of dollars and provided work for millions of people. Among its projects were schools, parks, airports, bridges, dams, and sewers. It cleared slums, planted forests, and electrified rural areas. It also employed out-of-work writers, artists, and musicians. After 1939 it was called the Works Projects Administration until it was disbanded in 1943.

World Bank. *See* International Bank for Reconstruction and Development.

World Council of Churches, an ecumenical association formed in 1948 in Amsterdam. It is comprised of Protestant and Orthodox Eastern Churches. The Roman Catholic Church and Russian Orthodox Church are not represented. Unity and renewal of Christianity are central concerns. △1388.

World Court, established by the League of Nations (1920) as the Permanent Court of International Justice and as the International Court of Justice by the United Nations in 1945. While the extent of its jurisdiction has been disputed, the World Court has added to the importance, impartiality, and frequency of use of arbitration in international disputes.

World Food Resources. △302.

World Health Organization (WHO), United Nations agency dealing with health problems in the world. It collects and shares information in medical and scientific areas and promotes the establishment of international standards for drugs and vaccines. It officially became a UN agency in 1948. △734.

World's Columbian Exposition (1893), international fair in Chicago celebrating the 400th anniversary of America's discovery. Its "White City," an assemblage of some 150 buildings designed by noted artists, led to a trend which imitated Classical and Renaissance architecture.

World Trade. △940–43, 1384–87.

World War I (1914–18), primarily European conflict of unprecedented size and brutality, often called the Great War. With the first large-scale use of poison gas, machine guns, aircraft, and other modern devices of war, it led to at least 13,000,000 military deaths and twice that number of wounded. Some of its causes can be found in the Franco-Prussian War (1870–71), when the Prussians and Austrians inflicted a humiliating defeat on France and took Alsace-Lorraine, outraging French nationalists. The Franco-Prussian War itself was an early expression of the rising European nationalism and desire for expansion that accompanied the industrial revolution and the rise of popular government. Territorial conflicts, traditional boundary disputes, the decline of the Ottoman Empire: all came to a head with the assassination of Austrian Archduke Francis Ferdinand by a Serbian nationalist on June 28, 1914, in Sarajevo, Yugoslavia. War broke out on July 28, 1914, and by the end of 1915 the Central Powers of Austria-Hungary, Germany, Bulgaria, and the Ottoman Empire were fighting against the Allied Powers of Great Britain, Russia, Italy, France, Bel-

Wolverine

Woodchuck

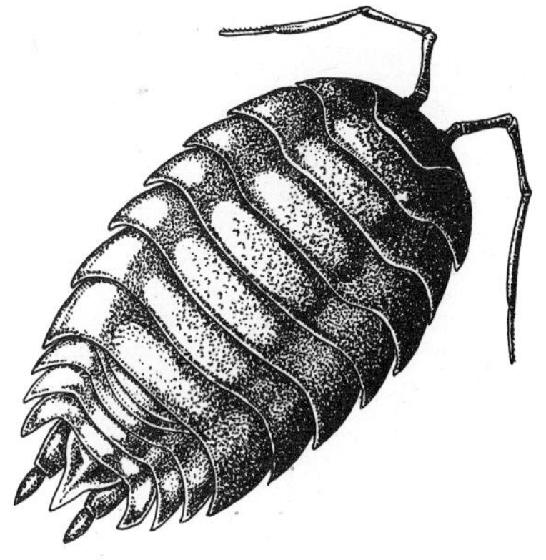

Wood louse

Woodpecker

gium, Serbia, Montenegro, and Japan. In April 1917, the United States was prompted by the sinking of the *Lusitania* to join the Allies, intending, as President Woodrow Wilson said, "to make the world safe for democracy."

The actual fighting of World War I began with the rapid German invasion of France through Belgium in early August 1914. This offensive was stemmed by the battles of the Marne, the Aisne, Ypres, and the Yser, so that by November the Western Front had settled into miserable trench warfare that would consume three long years and millions of lives without an appreciable shift in boundaries.

In the East, the Germans defeated a Russian invasion in August-September 1914, and by late 1915 they and the Austro-Hungarians had occupied most of Poland. The Russian forces, under General Brusilov, were hampered by increasing political conflicts, and after a final great offensive in 1916 were effectively crippled by the Russian Revolution. By March 1918, a peace had been made at Brest-Litovsk, allowing the Germans to concentrate their forces in a new offensive on the Western Front.

Meanwhile, extensive fighting on the Italian Front since May 1915 had resulted in a near Austro-Italian stalemate. The introduction of efficient German troops in the Battle of Caporetto (October-November 1917) resulted in a Central Powers victory, which was offset by the severe Austrian defeat in the Battle of Vittorio Venete almost a year later. An armistice was signed for the Italian Front on Nov. 4, 1918.

In addition to several minor campaigns in Africa and Asia, as well as an extensive naval war, there was considerable fighting of varied outcome between the British and the Turks in Egypt and the Near East, and Russia and the Turks in the Caucasus. The ultimate Allied victory resulted in an armistice on Oct. 31, 1918. The Balkan Campaign, which drew Romania and then Greece to the Allies, involved similar indecisive victories on both sides and resulted in eventual Austrian surrender on Nov. 3, 1918.

The last major campaign of the Western Front came in early 1918, when the truce with the Russians gave the Germans a sudden numerical superiority in the West. Seeking a victory in France before large-scale US involvement, they began the great Somme offensive in March and rapidly advanced 40 miles (64km) under General Ludendorff. This German victory inspired Allied centralization of command under General Foch, and the resulting efficiency, bolstered by a rapid influx of US troops under Gen. John Pershing, led to final defeat of the exhausted German war machine and the signing of an armistice on Nov. 11, 1918.

The Allies quickly occupied the German Rhineland, and peace talks began. The end result was that Germany was forced in 1919 to accept the humiliating terms of the Treaty of Versailles, which limited the German army to 100,000, blamed Germany for the war itself, ceded West Prussia to Poland and Alsace-Lorraine to France, and subjected Germany to other military, economic, and political restrictions and minor losses of land. Other treaties took lands from Austria, Hungary, and Bulgaria, outlawed Austro-German union *(Anschluss)*, and imposed such harsh conditions on Turkey that a new treaty was drawn up in 1923. The rigid peace conditions of World War I were a contributing factor to World War II, but the ghastly toll and methods of World War I also created a temporary aversion to war and aided the formation of the League of Nations. *See also* League of Nations; Versailles, Treaty of. △1304–06.

World War II (1939–45), largest conflict in human history, arose from the industrial and nationalistic expansion of the 19th and 20th centuries, and eventually engulfed every occupied continent on the globe. The toll in human life was staggering, with roughly 40,000,000 to 60,000,000 dead, of which at least 20,000,000 were Russians and at least 6,000,000 were Jews executed in Nazi concentration camps.

The causes of the war can be traced in part to the peace terms of World War I. Deprived of valuable territory, demoralized, economically shattered by the war, and forced into the Treaty of Versailles, post-war Germany struggled for survival before the revolutionary leadership of Adolf Hitler. Simultaneously, Japan had completed a rapid transition into a world industrial power and began to feel a pressing need for expanded markets and new sources of raw materials. In addition, the rise of popular government, the extreme economic insecurity of post-war Europe in the Great Depression, and continuing nationalism led to a global rise in demagogic totalitarianism that posed a grave threat to the Communist and democratic nations.

In 1931–32, Japan occupied Manchuria and went on to invade China, then torn by civil war. Adolf Hitler meanwhile engineered a startling rise to power, and after his appointment as chancellor in 1933 he actively rebuilt Germany's economy and armed forces and strengthened the Nazi party for the creation of a new German empire. Allied with fascist Italy and Japan as the Axis powers, Germany suddenly annexed Austria in 1938. Italy, under Benito Mussolini, dissatisfied with the results of World War I, had conquered Ethiopia in 1935 and in 1939 followed the German occupation of Czechoslovakia with the annexation of Albania. The former Allied powers, still weary from World War I, followed a policy of conciliation, seeking appeasement of the expanding fascist powers. The United States held stubornly to its policy of isolation. Yet, with the German invasion of Poland on Sept. 1, 1939, the Allies could no longer deny German intentions; France and the British Commonwealth (except Ireland) declared war on Germany two days later.

The German *Blitzkrieg*, a new style of warfare heavily reliant on armor and aircraft, soon overwhelmed Poland, which was divided with the USSR. The USSR defeated Finland, and in the spring of 1940 the Germans pushed Allied forces from France and Belgium and might have crushed British resistance except for the successful evacuation of British troops at Dunkirk. The French Vichy government of Marshal Pétain was established after a truce with Germany, but British victory in the aerial Battle of Britain prevented German advances on the British Isles, which rallied under Prime Minister Winston Churchill. Meanwhile, the Italians had begun the North African campaign, and by summer of 1941 Germany had overrun Denmark, Norway, Greece, Crete, and Yugoslavia and gained Romania, Hungary, Finland, and Bulgaria as allies in the invasion of the Soviet Union. The Axis powers made rapid advances there and were halted by the Russian winter of 1941–42.

During this time the United States, though providing increasing financial support to Britain, refused to build up its armed forces or threaten active intervention in the European war. Recently recovered from the Great Depression under Pres. Franklin D. Roosevelt, the US answer to Japanese imperialism was restricted US-Japanese trade. Japan responded with the sudden aerial bombardment of Pearl Harbor on Dec. 7, 1941, hoping to so cripple the US Navy as to successfully secure valuable colonies in the Pacific. The United States, the Netherlands, and the British Commonwealth (except Ireland), declared war on Japan the next day, and were followed by China on December 9.

Seriously impaired by the Japanese attack, the inadequate US forces were a small obstacle to Japan's conquest of the Philippines, Indonesia, Malaya, Burma, and various islands of the Pacific. In the summer of 1942 the US Navy stemmed this conquest at Coral Sea and Midway, and Allied troops engaged the Japanese in New Guinea and Guadalcanal. Under Gen. Douglas MacArthur the Allies gradually forced the Japanese from New Guinea, the Solomon and Mariana islands, Okinawa, Iwo Jima, the Philippines, Burma, and other territories, and began intensive bombing of Japan. The Japanese, although unable to withstand the Allied armies, refused surrender, and in a controversial effort to end the war the United States, under the new Pres. Harry S. Truman, dropped an atomic bomb on Hiroshima on Aug. 6, 1945. Three days later Nagasaki was leveled by another blast and the Japanese surrendered (Aug. 14–Sept. 2, 1945).

Four days after the Pearl Harbor disaster, the United States found itself at war in Europe. In 1942 German Field Marshal Rommel (the "Desert Fox") was rapidly conquering North Africa, but the spectacular German offensive in Russia gradually ground to a halt. The Axis powers, greatly outnumbered and lured on by early success, had overextended themselves. Britain's General Montgomery defeated Rommel at El Alamein, and by the summer of 1943, Lt. Gen. Dwight Eisenhower's combined British, American, and Free French had retaken North Africa. In the USSR, following the Battle of Stalingrad and worn out by the Russian winter, the Germans began to retreat before Joseph Stalin's forces in 1943.

The Allies took Sicily in July and August, 1943, and invaded Italy (which surrendered that September). They then turned their attention to France, and invaded the coast of Normandy, with Eisenhower as supreme commander, on June 6, 1944 (D-Day). The Allied forces, led by such men as Omar Bradley, Montgomery, and George Patton, rapidly retook France and entered Germany. The Russians were making tremendous advances in the east, and by May 2, 1945 had taken Berlin. Hitler had committed suicide on April 30. Corresponding Allied victories to the west and south brought an end to the European war on May 9, 1945.

Although treaties with the former Axis powers were concluded in the early 1950s, the world retained a permanent political instability emerging from the vast ramifications of World War II. The war had brought the United States and the USSR to positions of supreme power, positions in part determined by the Yalta and Potsdam conferences. The development and use of the atomic bomb revolutionized modern concepts of warfare. Japan and the Western part of a divided Germany, deprived of military concerns, became flourishing economic powers, partly through US aid, and strong allies against the Soviet Union. World desire for peace led to the founding of the United Nations. *See also* Potsdam Conference; United Nations; Yalta Conference. △1336–40.

Worming, the chemical removal of any of a variety of parasitic worms or their larvae from the lungs, liver, intestines, stomach, or bloodstream of a variety of animals, principally swine, cattle, horses, sheep, dogs, and cats. Worms include roundworms, flukes, spiny-headed worms, screwworms, and tapeworms.

Worms, port city in W West Germany, on Rhine River, 10mi (16km) NNW of Manheim. Made a free imperial city early 13th century, it joined Rhenish Confederation 1255; scene of Diet of Worms (1521), where Martin Luther appeared before Charles V to defend his position on Protestantism; the Edict of Worms (1521) proclaimed Luther a heretic. City was awarded to France 1801; passed to Hess-Darmstadt state 1815; occupied by French 1918–30; taken by Allies 1945; it is setting of epic poem "Nibelungenlied." Industries: leather, machinery, chemicals, paints, ceramics. Pop. 77,642.

Worms, invertebrate animals characterized by elongated shape; many are parasitic. Phyla Platyhelminthes (flatworm), Nemertea (ribbon-worm), Nematoda (roundworm), Acanthocephala (spiny-headed worm), Annelida (segmented worm), Sipunculoida (acorn worm), and Chaetognatha (arrow worm). △472, 474.

Worms, Concordat of (1122), arrangement between Holy Roman Emperor Henry V and Pope Calixtus II which decided the question of investiture for members of the clergy. New church officials were to be elected by the clergy, with the emperor settling electoral disputes. Afterwards the emperor would endow the officials with their due worldly possessions and duties and the church would follow suit with religious concerns.

Worms, Diet of (1521), conference of the Holy Roman Empire, held in Worms, Germany and presided over by Emperor Charles V. Martin Luther was summoned and appeared before the Diet to explain his position and beliefs. Luther refused to renounce his writings, and the Edict of Worms (May 25, 1521) declared him an outlaw. △1152.

Worm Snake, harmless snake found in E and central United States. It is brown or purple with a pink belly. Secretive, it lives under moist logs and eats earthworms and insects. Length: to 11in (28cm). Family Colubridae; species *Carphophis amoenus.*

Wormwood, aromatic bitter shrub and herb, including the common wormwood *(Artemisia absinthium)*, a European shrub that yields a bitter, dark green oil used to make absinthe. Family Compositae.

Worship, specific acts of devotion that are believed to be owed to Divine Beings. Forms vary according to differing concepts of God and man, and of their roles. △848.

Worthing, seaside resort in S England; site of prehistoric and Roman ruins; grows greenhouse products. Pop. 88,210.

Wouk, Herman (1915–), US author, b. New York City. A radio scriptwriter before turning to writing novels, his works include *The Caine Mutiny* (1951), for which he won a Pulitzer Prize (1952), *Marjorie Morningstar* (1955), *Youngblood Hawke* (1962), *Don't Stop the Carnival* (1965), and *The Winds of War* (1971).

Wounded Knee, Massacre at (1890), last engagement between Indians and whites. It took place at Wounded Knee Creek, S. Dak., where over 200 Sioux were cut down by the US 7th cavalry.

Wozzeck. △1256.

WPA. *See* Works Progress Administration.

WPI. *See* Wholesale Price Index.

Wrack. *See* Rowing.

Wracks. △622.

Wrangel, (Baron) Pětr N(ikolaevich) (1878–1928), Russian military commander. A field commander in World War I, he joined the White Army and elped capture Volgograd from the Communists in 919. He led the Whites after 1920, seeking an alli-nce with Poland, but was defeated in the Ukraine. He elped evacuate 150,000 refugees from Russia be-ore emigrating to Belgium.

Vrangel (Vrangel'a), island of the USSR, in the Arc-c Ocean between the East Siberian Sea and the huckchi Sea. Off NE USSR, it is separated from main-and by 83-mi (134-km) wide Long Strait; discovered y Thomas Long, US whaling captain, in 1867. Since 924, USSR has controlled island and has a small ermanent settlement. Cold winters, and summers arely above freezing make it a breeding ground for olar bears, polar foxes, seals, and lemmings. Area: ,000sq mi (5180sq km).

Vrasse, brilliantly colored, inshore tropical marine sh. Many are popular aquarium species. They have rotrusible mouths and sleep on their sides. Many emove parasites from larger fish. Length: 3in–10ft 7.6–305cm). Among 600 species are the yellowtail *oris gaimardi* and the rainbow *Labroides dimidiatus.* amily Labridae.

Vren, Sir Christopher (1632–1723), English archi-ect, mathematician, and professor of astronomy. Vren became an architect after the great London fire f 1666. He is best known for his London churches nd St Paul's Cathedral. The churches show a consid-rable and ingenious variety of styles, and St Paul's, vith its magnificent dome, is a triumph of structural omplexity. Among his other buildings are Chelsea ospital and Greenwich Hospital, the latter showing Vren's fullest use of the Baroque. △1192.

Vren, small, insect-eating song birds of Europe, Asia, nd most of the New World. Both sexes sing all year ong, sometimes in a duet. During courtship, many nales build false nests that are near but more ex-osed than the true domed nest that has a long side ntrance tunnel. The eggs (2–10) range from white to rown, depending on species. Groups often share ousekeeping chores and the young help feed the econd-generation young. The typical insectivorous vinter wren *(Troglodytes troglodytes)* has a slender ill, rounded wings, perky tail, and dark brownish plu-nage; length: to 4in (10cm). Many species, including vood wrens *(Henicorhina)* of Mexican and South merican forests, have white facial lines. Family Tro-lodytidae.

Vrestling, sport that matches two unarmed oppo-ents in a contest where the object is to try to secure fall by means of body grips, strength, and adroitness. he most common styles include Greco-Roman, most opular in continental Europe, which permits no trip-ing or holds below the waist, and free-style, which ermits tackling, leg holds, tripping, and other rough eatures, and is most popular in the United States and ngland. Other forms include sumo wrestling, popular n Japan; yagli, a Turkish form in which the contest-nts smear themselves with grease to make the holds ifficult; sambo, a Russian form of jacket wrestling imilar to judo; and Cumberland-and-Westmoreland, n ancient style of wrestling that continues in England nd has the competitors start with their arms clasped ehind each other's backs. Amateur wrestling, con-ucted in free-style and Greco-Roman, is classified by veight and conducted on a mat. A match consists of hree periods of three minutes each, with points warded for falls (pinning both shoulders to the mat) nd other maneuvers. Professional wrestling uses the ee-style method, but has been lightly regarded since is no more than planned entertainment.

History. Competitive wrestling has its origins in ncient Greece, where it was regarded as the most mportant event after discus throwing, in the Olympic ames. Greco-Roman style wrestling was first in-luded in the modern Olympics in 1896, was removed s an event in 1900, and reinstated in 1904 when ee-style was also included. In the United States the port is governed by the Amateur Athletic Union and he National Collegiate Athletic Association. *See also* umo Wrestling.

Vright, Frank Lloyd (1869–1959), US architect, b. ichland Center, Wis., noted for his great originality. lis first independent designs were for domestic ouses, which he built with low, horizontal lines in his o-called prairie style; the Robie house, Chicago 1909) is the most famous. He attempted to bring new nechanical methods and materials into architectural esign, and to create open planning and free-flowing nternal space. Notable buildings include the Larkin)ffice Building, Buffalo (1904), Taliesin, at Spring Green, Wis. (1911, twice rebuilt), the Imperial Hotel, okyo (1916), and the Solomon R. Guggenheim Mu-eum, New York City (1945–59). △1298, 1322.

Vright, James (1927–), US poet, b. Martins Ferry, Ohio. His first book of verse, *The Green Wall,* appeared in 1957. Subsequent works include *The Branch Will Not Break* (1963) and *Collected Poems* (1971), which won him a Pulitzer Prize for poetry in 1972.

Wright, Richard (1908–60), US author, b. near Natchez, Miss. A short story writer and novelist, he was the first black American to gain international ac-claim as a writer. His works, which deal with racial prejudice in the United States, are realistic and brutal. They include *Native Son* (1940); *Black Boy* (1945), an account of the author's boyhood in the South; and *Twelve Million Black Voices* (1941), a folk history of blacks in America. After World War II Wright resided in Paris.

Wright, Wilbur (1867–1912), b. Millville, Ind., and **Orville** (1871–1948), b. Dayton, Ohio, aviation pio-neers. Their first joint venture was a weekly newspa-per. They entered bicycle manufacturing in the 1890s, studied aeronautical literature, and experi-mented with gliders to learn wing control and lateral balancing. The rolling sand dunes and fairly constant winds at Kitty Hawk, N.C. allowed them to test gliders (1900–01). Orville made the first piloted flight in a power-driven plane at Kitty Hawk (1903). Their work was neither believed nor publicized until a reporter, D. Bruce Salley, witnessed their 1000-foot (305-meter) flight (1908). French public recognition preceded US Army's acceptance of their plane (1909). Their success where others had failed us-ually is attributed to their working as a unit. △1676, 1752.

Writing, History of. △870–72.

Wroclaw, formerly Breslau; industrial city in SW Po-land, on the Oder River, approx. 150mi (242km) NW of Krakow; capital of Wroclaw province. Settlement became episcopal see 1000; it was destroyed by Mongols 1241; rebuilt by Germans and passed to Bo-hemia 1335; came under Hapsburgs 1526, and under Prussia 1742; grew as a trade center in 19th century; became part of Poland by Potsdam Confer-ence 1945; site of 13th-century cathedral and churches, Gothic structures, university (1702). Indus-tries: railroad cars and repairs, heavy machinery, food processing, textiles, chemicals. Pop. 523,100.

Wrought Iron, a commercial form of smelted iron (the other is cast iron) containing less than 0.3% car-bon with 1 or 2% slag mixed with it. △1584, 1756.

Wuhan (Wu-han), city in central China, at conflu-ence of Han and Yangtze rivers; capital of Hupeh prov.; a municipality inc. (1950) the former cities of Hankow, Hanyang, Wuchang; scene of first uprising (1911) from which the Chinese Republic evolved; site of Hupeh and Wuhan universities. Industries: iron, steel, railroad shops, textiles, food processing, paper, glass, metallurgy. Pop. 4,250,000.

Wundt, Wilhelm (1832–1920), German psycholo-gist. He established the first psychological laboratory in 1879 at Leipzig. Known as "the father of experi-mental psychology," Wundt did much to convince early psychologists that the mind could be studied with objective, scientific methods. His major publica-tion is *Physiological Psychology* (1880).

Wuppertal, city in W West Germany, on Wupper River, 16mi (26km) ENE of Düsseldorf. As center of ball bearing and chemical production, city was heavily bombed by Allies during WWII. Industries: textiles, pharmaceuticals, paper, chemicals. Formed 1929 by inc. of Barmen, Elberfeld, Vohwinkel, and several vil-lages. Pop. 413,042.

Württemberg, former state in SW West Germany, between Bavaria and Baden states; capital was Stutt-gart. States of Baden and Württemberg divided into three states 1945: Baden, Württemberg-Baden, and Württemberg-Hohenzollern. All were inc. into Baden-Württemberg State 1951.

Würzburg, city in central West Germany, on Main River, 60mi (97km) ESE of Frankfurt am Main; made an episcopal see by St Boniface 741; secularized by Treaty of Lunéville 1801; annexed to Bavaria 1803; made an electorate and grand duchy under Ferdinand III of Tuscany (1805); returned to Bavaria 1815; seat of University of Würzburg (1582) whose professors have included Rudolf Virchow, and Wilhelm Roent-gen (who discovered the X-ray, 1895). Notable build-ings include Marienberg Castle (1201), Romanesque cathedral (11th–13th centuries). Industries: printing, machine tools, chemicals, textiles, brewing. Pop. 120,145.

World War II: signing of Japanese surrender

Frank Lloyd Wright

Wilbur and Orville Wright

Würzburg, West Germany

Würzburg School, a group of psychologists headed by Oswald Külpe (1862–1915) at the University of Würzburg, Germany, who developed a psychological method called "systematic experimental introspection." They concluded that thought can proceed without sensory input. This was an outgrowth of Wilhelm Wundt's studies that saw psychology as the introspective analysis of the contents of immediate experience.

Wu Tao-tzu (*c.* 700–*c.* 760), Chinese painter of the T'ang dynasty. One of the most revered artists China has produced, he is celebrated as the earliest Chinese figure painter and the inventor of various styles and techniques, including a method of printing designs on silk. His works are known only through copies. His style would seem to have been characterized by monumentality, naturalism, and profound religiosity. △1044.

Wu Tse-t'ien. △1042.

Wyandotte, city in SE Michigan, on Detroit River; site of first US Bessemer steel plant (1864). Industries: chemicals, automobile parts, hardware, detergents. Founded 1818 on site of Wyandotte Indian Village; inc. as city 1867. Pop. (1970) 41,061.

Wyatt, (Sir) Thomas (1503–42), English poet. A courtier, he was sent on many diplomatic missions and imprisoned several times in the Tower of London on charges ranging from immorality to treason. He was a friend and possibly a lover of Anne Boleyn. He introduced the sonnet form into English versification, and 96 of his poems appear in the anthology Tottel's *Miscellany* (1557). He also translated Plutarch and wrote and translated satirical verse. *See also* Sonnet.

Wycliffe, John (?1320–84), English theologian and religious reformer. A cleric, student, and teacher at Oxford (1356–82), he obtained his doctorate in theology in 1372. He came to reject the doctrine of transubstantiation and attacked the formation and hierarchical system of the Roman Catholic Church. He came under the patronage of John of Gaunt and during the 1380s initiated the first English translation of the Bible. He was declared a heretic after his death.

Wyeth, Andrew (Newell) (1917–), US painter, b. Chadds Ford, Pa. He is known for his meticulously detailed portraits, landscapes, and the artifacts of rural and coastal American life. His best known painting is "Christina's World" (1948) in the Museum of Modern Art, New York City. He was trained by his father, the illustrator N.C. Wyeth. His son, James, is also a noted painter. △1416.

Wylie, Philip Gordon (1902–71), US author, b. Beverly, Mass. Primarily a short-story writer and novelist, his works often became vehicles for criticism of American society and culture. His novels include *An April Afternoon* (1938), *Opus 21* (1949), and *Triumph* (1963). A noted work of nonfiction is *Generation of Vipers* (1942), a much discussed, bold essay on American customs and beliefs.

Wynn, Early (1920–), US baseball player, b. Hartford, Ala. A pitcher with three American League teams (1939–44; 1946–63), he recorded 300 victories and was elected to the Baseball Hall of Fame in 1972.

Wyoming, state in the NW United States, in the Rocky Mt region.

Land and Economy. The E half of the state is part of the Great Plains, rising to the ranges of the Rocky Mts, which occupy most of the W. High plateaus lie among the ranges. Rivers include the Belle Fourche, Cheyenne, and North Platte, flowing E; the Big Horn and Powder, flowing N; the Snake, flowing NW, and the Green, flowing S. Dams have made reservoirs on many streams. Much of the open country is grazing land. Hay, wheat, barley, and oats are the crops grown, principally under irrigation. Mineral resources supply the greater part of income. Petroleum is mined and refined. Vast reserves of coal and other minerals exist. Wyoming is one of the least industrialized states.

People. Wyoming is sparsely populated, with a density of only 3.4 persons per sq mi (1.3 per sq km). About 60% of the people lives in urban areas.

Education. There are 8 institutions of higher education. The University of Wyoming is state-supported.

History. In the early 19th century US trappers roamed the region, which had been visited by Frenchmen a century before. For 15 years after 1825, the trappers met annually at a rendezvous at Henry's Fork of the Green River in SW Wyoming. Wagon trains bringing supplies to these gatherings were accompanied by scientists and missionaries. Beginning in the 1840s, thousands of immigrants to California and Oregon followed the Oregon Trail through S Wyoming, obtaining supplies at Fort Laramie in the SE and Fort Bridger in the SW, the only posts in the area. Hostile Indians were a threat to settlement until the 1870s. The Union Pacific Railroad was built through S Wyoming in 1867; the cities of Cheyenne, Laramie, Rawlins, and Rock Springs arose along its route. Wyoming Territory was created by Congress in 1868. Later in the 19th century, enmity between cattlemen and sheep ranchers occasionly broke into violence. In the development of nuclear weapons after WWII the state profited from exploitation of uranium deposits. A missile launching site was located near Cheyenne.

PROFILE

Admitted to Union: July 10, 1890; rank, 44th
US Congressmen: Senate, 2; House of Representatives, 1
Population: 332,416 (1970); rank, 49th
Capital: Cheyenne, 40,914 (1970)
Chief cities: Cheyenne; Casper, 39,361; Laramie, 23,143
State legislature: Senate, 30; House of Representatives, 62
Area: 97,914sq mi (253,597sq km); rank, 9th
Elevation: highest, 13,804ft (4,210m), Gannett Peak; lowest, 3,100ft (946m), Belle Fourche River
Industries (major products): refined petroleum, petroleum products, processed foods
Agriculture (major products): cattle, sheep, dairy products
Minerals (major): petroleum, natural gas, coal, uranium, iron ore
State nickname: Equality State
State motto: Equal Rights
State bird: western meadowlark
State flower: Indian paintbrush
State tree: cottonwood

Wyoming, city in W Michigan, on Grand River. Industries: automobile and aircraft parts, home appliances, aluminum. Settled 1832; inc. 1959. Pop. (1970) 56,560.

Wyszynski, Cardinal Stefan (1901–), Polish Roman Catholic cardinal. As Polish archbishop of Gniezno and Warsaw, the cardinal protested to Communist authorities against accusations launched against the church during the trial of Bishop Kaczmarek, bishop of Kielce. The cardinal was imprisoned from 1953–56.

Wythe, George, (1726–1806), American patriot and judge and a signer of the Declaration of Independence, b. Elizabeth City co, Va. A legal educator, he taught Thomas Jefferson. He was the first professor of law in the United States at the College of William and Mary (1779–90).

Fort Laramie National Historic Site, Wyoming

Xanthine, a yellow substance found in plants, in most body tissues and fluids, and in urinary tract stones and which can be oxidized to form uric acid. It is a muscle stimulant, particularly of cardiac muscle, and its synthetic derivatives are used to dilate blood vessels and bronchi and as diuretics.

Xanthoma, skin condition causing a disturbance in cholesterol metabolism. Related to liver disease, it is marked by flat, raised, yellowish patches or nodules on eyelids, neck, or back.

Xavier, Francis (1506–52), first Jesuit missionary, called "Apostle of the Indies," a Roman Catholic saint. He helped Ignatius Loyola found the Jesuit order in 1534. Ordained in 1537, he served at Rome until 1540. King John III of Portugal asked him to go to Goa as a missionary, and he spent the rest of his life in the Orient—in Goa and the SW coast of India (1542–45), Malacca and the Moluccas (1545–46), Ceylon (1547), Japan (1549–51). He died while returning to Goa to organize the missionary effort in China. △1264.

Xenacanthus. △566.

Xenia, city in SW Ohio, 15mi (24km) ESE of Dayton; seat of Greene co; scene of a tornado that on April 3, 1974, destroyed approx. half of the city. Industries: rope, twine, paint, furniture, monuments, rubber goods. Founded 1803; inc. 1814, as city 1834. Pop. (1970) 25,373.

Xenon, gaseous nonmetallic element (symbol Xe) of the noble-gas group, first discovered (1898) by William Ramsay and M. W. Travers. Xenon is present in the Earth's atmosphere (0.000008% by volume) and is obtained by fractionation of liquid air. It is used in discharge lamps. The element forms several compounds including XeF_2, XeF_4, XeF_6, $XePtF_6$, and XeO_3. Properties: at. no. 54; at. wt. 131.30; density 5.887 g dm^{-3}; melt. pt. −169.42°F (−111.9°C); boil pt. −160.78°F (−107.1°C); most common isotope Xe^{132} (26.89%). *See also* Noble Gases. △1558.

Xenophobia, irrational fear of strangers or foreigners. It is often expressed in hatred for the outsider or in stereotyped ideas about persons who are "different."

Xenophon, (430?–?354 BC), Greek historian, essayist, and general. He marched in Cyrus' expedition against Artaxerxes of Persia (401) and rose to leadership in the Greek army. His works include the *Anabasis* (on Cyrus' march), the *Memorabilia* (on Socrates' teachings), and the *Hellenica*. *See also* Anabasis, Hellenica. △994, 998.

Xerophyte, plant able to survive under dry conditions or in areas subject to drought. These plants have a reduced leaf area, thick stems, wax coating to reduce evaporation, and, on desert-living species, spines instead of leaves. Cactus and stonecrop sedum are examples. Cacti make good house plants. △604.

Xerxes, son of Darius, king of Persia (486–465 BC) He carried on his father's punishment of the Greeks, setting out with a large force in 480. He was at first successful, overcoming the Spartans at Thermopylae, but the defeat at Salamis ended the campaign, and he returned to his harem, leaving Mardonius in charge. Xerxes' forces were driven out of Asia Minor by 467, and he was assassinated by a soldier two years later. △984.

Xiamen. *See* Amoy.

Xi'an. *See* Sian.

Xingu, river in N Brazil; rises in the Serra do Roncador mountains in central Mato Grosso State; flows N into Amazon River at its delta, below Pôrto de Moz. It is only navigable in its lower course for 100mi (160km). Length: 1,230mi (1,980km).

Xining. *See* Hsining.

Xi Particle. *See* Hyperon.

Xochimilco, federal district in central Mexico, 10mi (16km) S of Mexico City on Lake Xochimilco; site of Floating Gardens originally built by Aztecs, canals, 16th-century church. Chief industry is tourism. Pop. 117,083.

X-ray Astronomy. *See* Astronomy, X-ray.

X-ray Diffractometer, instrument used in the analysis of the atomic arrangement that determines the crystal structure of minerals. X rays, when passing through the symmetrically arranged atoms of a crystal are deflected in a regular pattern, with the atoms acting as a diffraction grating. Photos of these patterns permit deductions of interatomic dimensions, spacing, and bonding arrangements within crystals. *See also* Crystallography. △1504–06.

X-ray Goniometer. △1506.

X-ray Photograph. *See* Radiography; X rays.

X rays, electromagnetic radiation, first observed by W. K. Roentgen (1895), produced by bombarding a target substance, such as tungsten, with a beam of energetic electrons in an evacuated tube. X rays lie between ultraviolet and gamma rays in the electromagnetic spectrum, the wavelength range being about 10^{-8} to 10^{-11} meters. Typically, they have a continuous range of energies (the bremsstrahlung) with more intense sharp peaks at characteristic energies, resulting from electron transitions in the atom. They blacken photographic film and cause ionization along their path.

X rays, in medicine, short-wavelength rays of the electromagnetic spectrum directed toward the body to permit visualization of internal body structures or to destroy diseased or unwanted tissue. Passed through the body onto a photographic plate, X rays reveal such abnormalities as fractures, tumors, foreign bodies, and enlargement of organs. The capacity of X rays to break up cells makes them useful in the treatment of such diseases as cancer. △718–20, 738, 750.

X-ray Telescope. *See* Telescope, X-ray.

X-ray Tube, evacuated tube used to provide a source of X rays for medical or other purposes. It consists of an electron gun producing a stream of electrons that strike an anode, part of which is made of a heavy metal such as tungsten. The tungsten emits X rays when it is bombarded by the stream of high-energy electrons.

Xylem, woody vascular tissue of a plant. It usually consists of elongated vessels, tracheids, fibers, and parenchyma. This water-conducting tissue also gives support to stems, leaves, and roots. Xylem cells are thickened with lignin. *See also* Phloem. △430.

Jackson Lake, Wyoming

George Wythe

Xenophon

Xylophone, melodic percussion instrument similar to the marimba. It has hardwood bars (metal in metallophone) tuned to a 3-octave chromatic scale, framed over cylindrical metal resonators, and played with mallets. A European folk instrument (16th century), it was revived by Gusikov *c.* 1830. It is used not only for novelty, but also in major works by Saint-Saens, Shostakovich, de Falla, Khatchaturian, and Stravinsky.

XYZ Affair (1797–98), incident that strained US relations with France. Pres. John Adams sent three representatives, Charles Pinckney, John Marshall, and Elbridge Gerry, to negotiate a treaty with France to end French interference with US commerce. Three French agents, known as X, Y, and Z, demanded that loans and a $240,000 bribe be given to France before discussion could begin. The Americans refused. The revelation of the bribe attempt caused an uproar and the US representatives returned home.

Yachting, a boating sport and recreation. It includes any vessel that employs sail, power, or a combination of power and sail (auxiliary yachts). Sailing yachts, which are usually fore and aft rigged, vary from 20 feet (6.1m) to over 100 feet (30.5m) and include cutters, schooners, ketches, sloops, and yawls, as well as other types. Those fitted with diesel or gasoline engines are usually classified as cruising yachts. Yachts are capable of speeds up to 25 miles (40km) per hour, although the average speed is 10 knots. Although most yachts are used for vacationing and cruising, the sport has been a competitive attraction since 1851 when the Royal Yacht Squadron, formed at Cowes, England, in 1812, offered a silver cup as a prize for a race of 60 miles (97km) around the Isle of Wight. The race was won by the schooner yacht, *America,* owned by the members of the New York Yacht Club (organized 1844), and has since been known as the America's Cup, most prized of all international tournaments. Through 1976, the United States had never lost this trophy. Other famous ocean yacht sailing races include the Newport (R. I.) to Bermuda Race, the Trans-Pacific Race, and the Chicago Yacht Club to Mackinac Island Race.

Yahweh, a personal name for God used in Judaism. It was revealed by God to Moses. It is formed by four Hebrew consonants, YHWH, called the Tetragrammaton. It was replaced after the 3rd century BC, by Adonai, as it was considered too sacred to speak. Its origin is unknown as is its original pronunciation and meaning. Its usage came to be reserved for the high priest.

Yak, large, powerful, long-haired black ox, native to N India and Tibet, with domesticated races throughout central Asia. It inhabits barren heights to 20,000ft (6,000m). Domesticated races are smaller and varied in color. Its horns curve up and forward. Sure-footed beasts of burden, they are also used for meat and milk. Height: to 6.5ft (2m) at shoulders; weight: to 1,200lbs (540kg). Family Bovidae; species *Bos grunniens. See also* Cattle. △608.

Yakohi. △1036.

Yakshi. △1036.

Yale University, university in New Haven, Conn. It is among the Ivy League schools and operates several colleges of study including divinity, law, medicine, art, theater, and architecture. Its different locations were Killingworth (now Clinton) 1702 and Saybrook (now Old Saybrook) 1717. Chartered in 1701 in Branford, Conn.; current charter 1745.

Yalta Conference (1945), meeting between US Pres. Franklin D. Roosevelt, Prime Minister Winston Churchill of Britain, and Premier Joseph Stalin of the USSR. It took place at Yalta in the Crimea. They met to plan the final attacks on Germany, its postwar occupation and control, and the punishment of war crimes. A conference to establish what became the United Nations was called to meet at San Francisco. Eastern Poland was awarded to Russia. In return for Far East concessions, Russia agreed to join the war against Japan within three months of Germany's defeat. △1342.

Yalu, river in NE China and North Korea; rises in the Ch'ang-pai Shan Mts; flows SW to Korea Bay near Tan-tung; commercially important for production of hydroelectricity at Sunpung Dam and transportation of lumber; site of Communist invasion of North Korea during Korean War. Length: 501mi (807km).

Yam, herbaceous vines native to warm and tropical regions. The large, tuberous roots are sometimes edible and often confused with the sweet potato. Family Dioscoreaceae; genus *Dioscorea.*

Yama, in Indian mythology, lord, guide, and judge of the dead, also a deified hero worshiped as the first mortal man. He and his sister, Yami, are children of Vivasvat, the Sun. △840.

Yamasaki, Minoru (1912–), US architect, b. Seattle. He designed Lambert-St Louis Municipal Airport terminal (1951), noted for its concrete vaults. Other major works include the American consulate in Kobe, Japan (1954); the McGregor Memorial Community Conference Center (1958) and the Reynolds Metal Company (1969), both in Detroit; the US science pavilion at the Seattle Exposition (1962); the Plaza Hotel, Los Angeles (1966); and the Eastern Airlines Terminal, Boston (1968). He was a chief designer of the World Trade Center in New York City (1962–72).

Yamasee War (1715–16), waged by Yamasee Indians angered over land seizures by South Carolina settlers. Indians were driven south into Florida and west to Alabama, opening the way to the settling of Georgia.

Yamato, term meaning "Great Peace" applied to the Japanese state *c.* 400–800. Society then was based on a hierarchy of tribal groups. △1046.

Yamato-e Style. △1048.

Yangtze (Chang, or Ch'ang), river in E central China; the longest and most economically important waterway in the country. Rising in the Kunlun Mts in NE Tibet, it flows E through the central Chinese provinces to the East China Sea at Shanghai. In its upper course it is known as the Kinsha River; navigation is difficult at Yangtze Gorges, between Ichang and Fengkich; along with its main tributaries, the Yalung, Min, Kialing, Wu, Yü, Han, and Siang, it traverses one of the world's most populated areas, providing fertile land and hydroelectricity. Length: approx. 3,434mi (5,529km).

Yantai. *See* Chefoo.

Yantra. △1204.

Yaoundé (Yaunde), capital city of Cameroon, W Africa, 125mi (201km) E of Atlantic coast, on Gulf of Guinea; educational center, site of university (1962). Industries: soap, tile, dairy products, tobacco, coffee, rubber, timber. Founded 1888, became capital 1922. Pop. 178,000.

Yap Islands, island group in W Caroline Islands, W Pacific Ocean, approx. 800mi (1,288km) E of the Philippines; became member of US Trust Territory of the Pacific Islands in 1947. Yap Island is largest of the group, followed by three other large islands and about ten smaller ones. Area: 85sq mi (220sq km). Pop. 7,247.

Yaqui, Indian group concentrated in the Mexican state of Sonora. The Yaqui fiercely resisted Spanish attempts at conquest and colonization and fought guerrilla campaigns against the Mexican authorities until 1918.

Yard. *See* Weights and Measures.

Yardang. △266.

Yaroslavl (Jaroslavl'), city in W central USSR, on Volga River, 160mi (258km) NE of Moscow; capital of Yaroslavl oblast. In 1218 the city was capital of Yaroslavl principality absorbed by Moscow in 1463. From March-July 1612 it served as Russia's capital; site of 12th-century monastery, 17th-century church of St John Chrysostom, and Volkov theater (1911). Industries: linen (since 18th century), diesel engines, construction equipment, oil refining. Founded 1010 by Yaroslavl the Great. Pop. 517,000.

Yarrow, hardy Northern Hemisphere perennial plant. The common yarrow or milfoil *(Achillea millefolium)* has fernlike leaves and flat clusters of white or pink flower heads. Height: to 3ft (91cm). Family Compositae.

Yawl, a two-masted sailboat with the mainmast higher than the mizzenmast, rigged with one or more jib sails, a mainsail, and a mizzen. Unlike the ketch, the yawl has the mizzenmast astern the rudder post. Dinghys and light sailing vessels rigged with lugsails are often referred to as yawls.

Yaws, or frambesia, contagious skin disease found worldwide in the humid tropics. It is caused by a spirochete *(Treponema pertenue)* indistinguishable from the organism causing syphilis. Yaws, however, is not venereal, but is passed along by flies and by direct skin contact with the open raspberry-red sores characteristic of this infection. Unlike syphilis, secondary and tertiary symptoms are not typical, although they can develop.

Yayoi Culture. △1046.

Yazoo Controversy, dispute over land near the Yazoo River. The land, 35,000,000 acres (14,164,500 hectares) in Alabama and Mississippi, was sold by the Georgia legislature to land companies (1795). The next year the legislature rescinded the sale.

Yeast, any of a group of single-celled microscopic fungi (class Ascomycetes) that grow wild all over the world in the soil and in organic matter. Yeasts are also produced commercially for use in baking, brewing, wine making, and nutrition. Yeast feeding on sugar can convert it into carbon dioxide (which makes bread rise) and alcohol (which makes wine and beer potent). Yeast is also a rich source of B-complex vitamins. Yeasts reproduce asexually and, like other fungi, must obtain food from their environment. Yeast spores can remain dormant for many years. △328, 426.

Yeats, William Butler (1865–1939), Irish poet, b. Dublin. A founder-member of the Rhymers Club in London (1891), his verse became increasingly austere as he developed a complex symbolism to commemorate public events and private friendships. With his friend Lady Gregory he helped to found the Abbey

Theatre in Dublin (1904), for which he wrote plays. He was also involved in Irish nationalist politics and was a skeptical adherent of spiritualism. He married Georgie Hyde-Lees in 1917 and served as a senator of the Irish Free State (1922–28). He received the Nobel Prize for literature in 1923. Among his many memorable poems are "Easter, 1916," "The Second Coming," and "Sailing to Byzantium." *See also* Abbey Theatre; Gregory, Lady Augusta; Irish Literary Renaissance. △ 1240.

Yellow-Dog Contract, employer anti-union weapon widely used before 1932. The employer would require that the employee, as a condition of employment, sign a contract in which he agreed not to take part in any union activity, including organizing or striking. The yellow-dog contract was banned by the Norris-LaGuardia Act (1932).

Yellow Fever, acute infectious disease marked by sudden onset of headaches, high fever, jaundice, and bloody vomiting. It is caused by a virus transmitted by several species of mosquito, especially in tropical and subtropical regions. Monkeys are also vulnerable. Live-virus vaccines are highly effective. △732.

Yellowhammer, or yellow bunting, small Old World finch known for its pair formation ceremony when males and females drop and pick up small inanimate objects before mating. Species *Emberiza calandra.*

Yellow Jack, tropical marine food fish of the Indo-Pacific. A golden fish, it is marked with 8–12 dark bands. Length: to 3ft (91cm). Family Carangidae; species *Caranx bartholomaei.*

Yellowknife, largest town and capital of Northwest Territories, Canada, on NW shore of Great Slave Lake at mouth of Yellowknife River. Founded 1935 when gold and silver were discovered; site of airport and Royal Canadian Mounted Police post. Pop. 5,867.

Yellow (Hwang-Ho), river in N central and E China; rises in Amne Machin Shan; flows across Inner Mongolia, E through gorges along N Honan border. Lower course across Great Plains has shifted often, vitally affecting 35,000,000acres (14,175,000hectares) of rich farmland; construction for dam and reservoir system was begun 1955. Length: 2,903mi (4,673km).

Yellow Sea, branch of the Pacific Ocean, N of East China Sea between China's mainland and Korea; the Strait of Chihli connects it to the Chihli and Liaotung gulfs; the Yellow, Huai, Liao, and Yalu rivers empty into it. Depth (max.): 250ft (76m). Area: 180,000sq mi (446,200sq km).

Yellowstaining Mushroom. △428.

Yellowstone National Park, park in Wyoming, Montana, and Idaho. It is the largest and the oldest of the national parks. It features the world's largest geyser area, with about 3,000 geysers and hot springs. The park is famous for its beautiful scenery, petrified forests, lava formations, and Old Faithful geyser. Bears, bison, moose, elk, and mountain sheep are found. Area: 2,221,772acres (899,818hectares). Est. 1872.

Yellowstone River, river that rises in NW Wyoming; flows N through Yellowstone National Park, across the Montana border, and ENE into the Missouri River near the North Dakota line; after it drains Yellowstone Lake in NW Wyoming it drops 109ft (33m) at the Upper Falls, then another drop of 308ft (94m) at Lower Falls to enter the Grand Canyon of the Yellowstone. River has been used for irrigation since 1860. Length of river: 671mi (1,080km).

Yellowtail, or California yellowtail, popular marine game fish found in the Sea of Cortez off S California coast. A solid-bodied fish with big eyes and scimitar-shaped tail, it is yellow, green, and silver. Weight: to 40lb (18kg). Family Carangidae; species *Seriola dorsalis.*

Yellowthroat, small New World warbler, especially *Geothlypis trichas* that has a brownish back, yellow throat, and, in the male, a black facial mask. The yellow-throated warbler *(Dendroica dominica)* is a wood warbler.

Yemen, People's Democratic Republic of, formerly Southern Yemen, republic on the SE end of the Arabian Peninsula, E of the Yemen Arab Republic; it includes the islands of Kamaran, Perim, Socotra; the capital is Aden. Rising from a coastal plain to mountains and highland plateaus (average height 6,500ft/1,983m), the area is generally arid and hot.

Agriculture forms the economic base, heavily relying on foreign aid. Crops include: cotton (main cash crop), tobacco, coffee, millet, grains, and dates. The petroleum refinery (at Little Aden) is the major industry, accounting for about 75% of all exports; other industries include: fishing, textiles, handcrafts, shipbuilding, furniture. The people are mostly Arabs, with some mixed African and European influences. There are some nomadic tribes in the N, however Yemenites along the S coast are much more settled and less tribe-oriented.

There is a three-man Presidential Council under the 1970 constitution, with a 101-member supreme People's Council. The only legal political party is the National Liberation Front. Southern Yemen flourished under the Minaean, Sabaean, and Himyarite empires, and was part of a larger entity called Al-Yemen. It came under Muslim influence in the 600s, and the Ottoman Empire and the imams of Yemen in the 16th century. British occupation began in 1839; by 1914, through the purchase of islands, area mainlands, and treaty agreements with local rulers, a British protectorate was est., leading eventually to the Federation of South Arabia. Terrorist campaigns against British control began in the 1960s, and the National Liberation Front forced the federation's collapse; Southern Yemen became independent November 1967. A new constitution was received 1970, and the name was changed to People's Democratic Republic of Yemen.

PROFILE

Official name: People's Democratic Republic of Yemen
Area: 112,075sq mi (290,274sq km)
Population: 1,436,000
Chief cities: Aden (capital); Mukalla
Religion: Islam
Language: Arabic

Yemen Arab Republic, republic at the SW tip of the Arabian Peninsula; earliest seat of Arab culture. The nation consists of the Tihamah, a narrow coastal lowland area, and interior highlands.

Most of the population works in agriculture; chief crops include coffee (shipped worldwide from the Port of Mocha) and gat, a shrub whose leaves yield a narcotic. Much of the farming is at a subsistence level; handcrafts play a major part in the economy. Yemenites are a settled population, unlike their nomadic neighbors, chiefly Arabs, with some Arab-African mixing in the Tihamah; literacy is estimated at about 5%.

An absolute monarchy until 1962, Yemen now is governed by an Army Council, which seized power in 1974. A 1970 constitution est. a presidency and councils. The cradle of three major early civilizations, the Minaeans, Sabaeans, and Himyarites, the area was invaded by Romans in 1st century BC; after subsequent Ethiopian conquests and the rise of Christianity and Judaism, Islam arrived in the 7th century. Following the breakup of the Muslim caliphs the Rassite Dynasty took power, evolving a political structure that survived until 1962, when a republic was proclaimed. From 1958–61 Yemen was joined in the nominal United Arab States alliance with Egypt and Syria. For a time the area saw an international struggle, as Egypt supported republic forces while Saudi Arabia and Jordan supported the royalists.

PROFILE

Official name: Yemen Arab Republic
Area: 75,290sq mi (195,001sq km)
Population: 6,500,000
Chief cities: Sana; Hodeida; Taizz
Religion: Muslim
Language: Arabic
Monetary unit: Riyal

Yen, C. K. (Yen Chia-kan) (1905–), Chinese political leader. He became president of the Republic of China at the death of Chiang Kai-shek in 1975. He had served as a key economic minister in bringing about Taiwan's rapid industrial and commercial progress.

Yenan (Yan'an, or Yen-an), town in N central China, on Yen River, 160mi (258km) NNE of Sian. Known as the center of Chinese Communist party (1936–48) during its struggle with the Nationalist forces for control of China and terminus of the Red Eighth Route Army's "Long March," it was captured by Nationalists March 19, 1947; fell to Communists April 22, 1949; site of revolutionary museum, former homes of Mao Tse-tung and Chou En-lai, pagoda built during Sung dynasty (960–1279). Pop. 45,000.

Yenisei (Jenisej), chief river in central Siberia, USSR; formed by confluence of Bolshoi Yenisei and Maly Yenisei; flows W and N through Sayan Mts past Minusinsk into Yenisei Gulf on Kara Sea (arm of Arctic Ocean). Chief tributaries are the Angara, Stony, Tunguska, and Lower Tunguska rivers; connected to Ob River by canals. River is frozen during winter months; ice melting on upper part of river before that on lower river causes severe flooding as water backs up. A

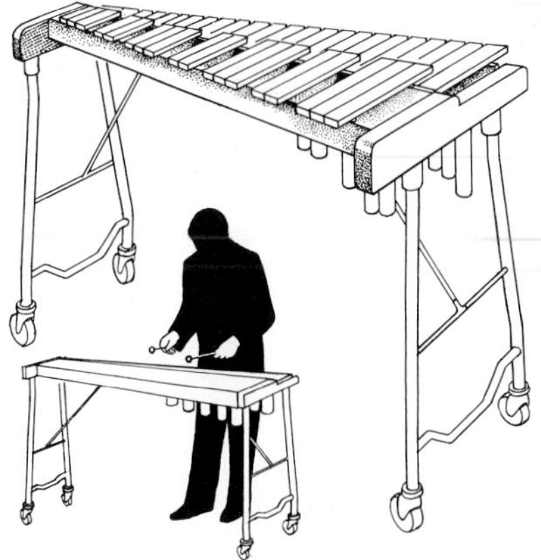
Xylophone

Yangtze River

Yaroslavl, USSR

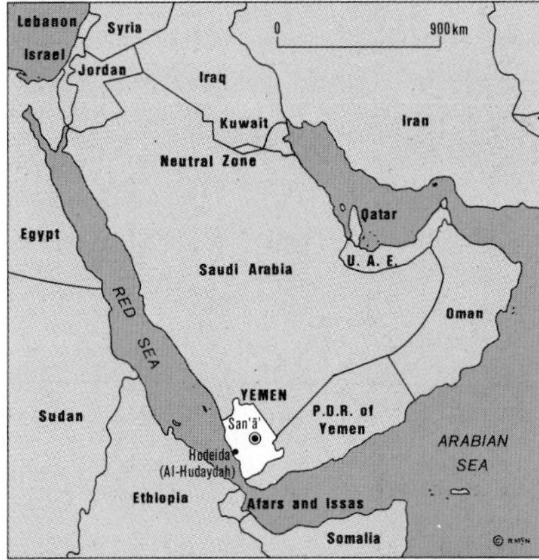
Lebanon
Syria
Israel
Jordan
0
900km
Iraq
Kuwait
Iran
Neutral Zone
Egypt
Qatar
Saudi Arabia
U. A. E.
Oman
RED SEA
YEMEN
San'a'
Sudan
P.D.R. of Yemen
ARABIAN SEA
Hodeida
(Al-Hudaydah)
Ethiopia
Afars and Issas
Somalia
Yemen

large hydroelectric station has been built at Krasnoyarsk. River supports fishing for sturgeon and salmon; lumber, grain and construction materials are shipped. Length: 2,566mi (4,131km).

Yerba Maté. *See* Maté.

Yerevan (Jerevan), capital of Armenian SSR, SE European USSR, on Razdan River. In 7th century city was capital of Armenia (under Persian control); site of crossroads of caravan routes between India and Transcaucasia. At different times Persia and Turkey held Yerevan; it was taken by Russia 1827; became capital of Armenian SSR 1920; site of Yerevan State University (1920), Armenian Academy of Sciences (1943), 16th-century Turkish fortress. Industries: chemicals, plastics, synthetic rubber, cables, electrical equipment. Founded AD 7th century. Pop. 767,000.

Yerkes, Robert M(earns) (1876–1956), US biologist and psychologist, b. Breadysville, Pa. He pioneered in the comparative study of apes, the development of methods to test the abilities of animals and humans, and was director of the Yerkes Laboratories of Primate Biology at Yale University (1919–41). Among his many publications are *The Mind of a Gorilla* (1927) and *Chimpanzees: A Laboratory Colony* (1943).

Yerushalayim. *See* Jerusalem.

Yevtushenko, Yevgeny Aleksandrovich (1933–), Soviet poet. An outspoken writer frequently criticized by Soviet authorities, much of his work remains unpublished in the Soviet Union. His verse includes *Zima Junction* (1956), *Babi Yar* (1961), *Precocious Autobiography* (1963), and *Stolen Apples* (1971).

Yew, evergreen shrubs and trees native to temperate regions of the Northern Hemisphere. They have stiff, narrow, dark green needles, often with pale undersides, and red, berrylike fruits. Height: to 60ft (18.3m). Family Taxaceae; genus *Taxus*.

Yggdrasill, in Norse mythology, a giant ash tree supporting the world. It had three roots; one extending into the underworld, the second, into the land of the giants, and the third, into the home of the gods. △834, 838.

Yiddish, language spoken for centuries by Jews living in central and E Europe and in other countries of the world (including the United States) to which Jews had migrated. It is basically a variety of German, with many Hebrew and Slavic words added, and written in the Hebrew alphabet. More than half of all Yiddish speakers perished during World War II and the number of speakers today is steadily declining.

Yin-yang, in Chinese philosophy, two cosmic energy modes comprising the Tao or the eternal dynamic way of the universe. A recurrent theme in Taoist and Confucian texts, heaven is yang, or the active, bright, male principle, and Earth is yin, or the passive, dark, female principle. All the things of nature and society are composed of different combinations of the two principles. The trigrams of the *I Ching* embody yin and yang. *See also* I Ching. △1040.

Ymir, in Teutonic mythology, the father of all the giants. Bor married one of Ymir's daughters, Bestla. With her he fathered three gods, Odin, Vili, and Ve. These sons killed Ymir and formed the Earth with his inert body. The flesh of Ymir became the land and his blood formed the seas.

Yoga (Sanskrit for "union"), term used for a number of Hindu disciplines to aid the soul's merging with God. Based on the Yoga-sutras of Patañjali (written around the time of Christ), the practice of yoga generally involves moral restraints, meditation, and the awakening of physical energy centers through specific postures *(asanas)* or exercises. Devoted to freeing the soul or self from earthly cares, these ancient practices have become popular in the West as a means of relaxation, self-control, and enlightenment. △698.

Yogurt. △374.

Yokohama, seaport and industrial city in SE Honshu, Japan, on W shore of Tokyo Bay, approx. 18mi (29km) SSW of Tokyo; capital of Kanagawa prefecture. It is main port for Tokyo, Kawasaki, Yokohama industrial region; grew from a small fishing village to a major port after being visited 1854 by Comm. Matthew C. Perry; it was opened to foreign trade 1859; site of Yokohama Municipal University and Yokohama National University (both 1949). Industries: steel, automobiles, oil refining, silk textiles, machinery, chemicals, shipbuilding, fish canning, electronic equipment. Pop. 2,279,483.

Yom Kippur, the Day of Atonement in Judaism. It is the last of the Ten Days of Penitence that begin the new year. On this solemn day set aside for prayer and fasting, man is called to account for his sins and reconcile himself with God and man. It is described as the Sabbath of Sabbaths.

Yonkers, city in SE New York, on Hudson River, adjoining greater New York City. Land was originally purchased from Indians in 1639 by Dutch West India Co.; site of St Joseph's College and Seminary (1839), Elizabeth Seton College (1961), Philipse Manor (17th century), and Hudson River Museum. Industries: elevators (since 1852), chemicals, cables, telephone parts, art supplies. Inc. as village 1855, as city 1872. Pop. (1970) 204,370.

Yoritomo. △1046, 1210.

York, Richard Plantagenet, 3rd Duke of (1411–60), contender for the English throne during the Wars of the Roses, father of Edward IV and Richard III. Succeeding his uncle, Edward, as duke of York (1415), he became Edward III's heir by primogeniture (1425). Loyal to Henry VI, he protected the realm during the king's illness (1453–54), but conflicted with the jealous Edmund Beaufort, duke of Somerset, and Margaret of Anjou. Rivalry flared into war (1455). After some initial successes, York was killed in battle at Wakefield (1460).

York, House of, branch of the Plantagenet family—an English royal family—descended from Edmund of Langley, 1st duke of York (1341–1402), fourth surviving son of Edward III. The duke of York's hereditary claim to the English throne was strengthened when it became linked to that of the descendants of Lionel, duke of Clarence, Edmund's elder brother. Upon the deposition of Richard II (1399), the crown reverted to the House of Lancaster, in the person of Henry IV. Minor demonstrations of disloyalty by the Yorkists followed, becoming more marked under Henry VI, and culminating in the outbreak of the Wars of the Roses (1455), after which Henry Tudor ascended the throne as Henry VII (1485).

York, city in N England, at confluence of Ouse and Foss rivers; rail center, makes confectionery and other products. As Eboracum, city was the chief Roman military base and has been an ecclesiastical center of N England since the 7th century; site of York Minster cathedral (1154); 8th-century educational center. Pop. 104,513. △1104.

York, city in S Pennsylvania, 23mi (37km) S of Harrisburg; seat of York co; scene of the Continental Congress 1777–78; occupied briefly by Confederates 1863; rich farm region in Pennsylvania Dutch country; site of York College of Pennsylvania (1941); Friends Meeting house (1765); and several colonial houses. Industries: refrigerators, stoves, roofing materials, paper products. Founded 1741; inc. as borough 1787, as city 1887. Pop. (1970) 50,335.

Yorkshire, former county of N England, now divided into the nonmetropolitan counties of Cleveland, North Yorkshire, West Yorkshire, South Yorkshire, and Humberside. The region is bounded by the North Sea (E), Tees River (N), the Pennines (W), and the Humber (SE); famous for its coal, iron, steel, wool, and textiles from such industrial centers as Middlesbrough, Bradford, Leeds, and Sheffield.

Yorkshire Terrier, long-haired dog (toy group) bred in Lancashire and Yorkshire, England, about 1860 as Scotch terrier; brought to US 1880. Its small head with short muzzle is carried high. Small, V-shaped ears are erect. The compact body has a short, straight back. Straight legs are hidden under the coat. The docked tail is carried high. The straight, fine, silky coat is floor length; colors are blue and tan. Average size: 9in (23cm) high at shoulder; 4–7lb (2–3kg). *See also* Toy Dog.

Yorktown Campaign (1781), final military campaign of the American Revolution. British Gen. Lord Cornwallis had fortified the Virginia community of Yorktown to protect entry to the York River. Gen. George Washington, with the help of French soldiers and the French fleet, laid siege to the town and, in October after less than two weeks, forced Cornwallis to capitulate (Oct. 19, 1781). △1218.

Yoruba, Negroid people of SW Nigeria. They are mainly agriculturalists, crops include yams, maize, and cocoa. Many Yoruba live in towns built around the palace of an *oba*, or chief, and commute to their outlying farms. Religions include Christianity and Islam; traditional deities are also still worshiped.

Yosemite National Park, park in central California. It is a mountainous, glacial area of outstanding beauty. It features the nation's highest waterfall, Yosemite Valley, and other breathtaking gorges. There are three groves of giant redwood trees. Area: 761,320acres (308,335hectares). Est. 1890.

Young, Brigham (1801–77), US religious leader, b. Whittingham, Vt. An early convert (1832) to the Church of Jesus Christ of Latter-Day Saints, Young took over the leadership when Joseph Smith, the church founder, was killed by a mob (1844) in Illinois. A strong leader, Young held the group together through persecutions and led them in their great westward migration (1846–47). In Utah he directed the settlement that became Salt Lake City. He was governor of Utah territory (1850–57), but was replaced when the Morman practice of polygamy brought them into conflict with the federal government. As head of the Mormon church he remained the effective ruler in Utah until his death.

Young, (Denton True) "Cy" (1867–1955), US baseball player, b. Gilmore, Ohio. The game's top pitcher with 511 victories, Young played for five teams (1890–1911) and was elected to the Baseball Hall of Fame in 1937.

Young, Thomas (1773–1829), English physicist and physician who did pioneer work in the accommodation of the eye and who detailed the cause of astigmatism. In 1803 he showed the wave nature of light and computed the visible light wavelength. He also helped present the Young-Helmholtz three-color theory; explained that double refraction was due to the transverse state of light waves; and worked with elastic substances. △1282.

Young, Whitney, Jr. (1921–71), US black leader, b. Lincoln Ridge, Ky. A leader in the civil rights movement, he advocated improvement in economic opportunities, housing, and welfare. He was executive director of the National Urban League (1961–71). His books include *To Be Equal* (1964).

Younger Brothers, American outlaws, three brothers, James (d. 1902), Robert (d. 1889), and Cole (1844–1916) Younger. As members of the outlaw gang of Jesse James, they were arrested during an attempted bank robbery in Northfield, Minn. (1876). Sentenced to life imprisonment, Robert died in prison (1889), Cole and James were paroled 1901; James committed suicide, and Cole joined a Wild West show.

Young Men's Christian Association (YMCA), Christian community organization with programs that seek the improvement of conditions and opportunities for young men of all races and economic backgrounds. The YMCA stresses physical training and fitness and tries to develop cultural, intellectual, social, and vocational interests. First organized in London in 1844 by Sir George Williams, the association spread to North America by 1851.

Youngstown, city in NE Ohio, on Mahoning River 43mi (69km) E of Akron; seat of Mahoning co. One of the largest US steel producing centers, it is the site of Youngstown University (1908), First Presbyterian Church (1799), and the modern gothic St Columba's Cathedral (1958). Industries: iron, steel, office equipment, electric light bulbs, plastics, paper products. Founded 1797 when John Young bought area from Western Reserve Land Co.; inc. as town 1848; chartered as city 1867. Pop. (1970) 139,788.

Youngstown Sheet and Tube Company v. Sawyer (1952), noted US Supreme Court decision holding that President Truman had exceeded his powers in nationalizing a steel company to avert a strike that would have affected the Korean War effort. The court held that other avenues were open to keep the company operating and that an executive order was improper.

Young Women's Christian Association (YWCA), organization dedicated to the welfare and needs of women and girls, whose programs offer growth in their spiritual, intellectual, social, vocational, and physical development. It was first organized in London in 1855 by Lady Kinnaird, and officially became the YWCA 1877. The organization spread to North America where a New York City prayer group, started by Mrs. Marshall O. Roberts (1858), is considered the first US YWCA.

Youth Culture, the way of life of a loosely defined group, often those 18 to 30. △792.

Ypres, Battle of. △1306.

Ypsilanti, city in SE Michigan, on Huron River; site of Eastern Michigan University (1849) and Cleary College (1883). Industries: automobile parts, paper, ladders. Settled 1825; inc. as village 1832, as city 1858. Pop. (1970) 29,538.

Ytterbium, metallic element (symbol Yb) of the lanthanide group, first isolated in 1878 along with lutetium. Chief ore is monazite (phosphate). The element has few commercial uses. Properties: at. no. 70; at. wt. 173.04; sp gr 6.965 (δ), 6.54 (β); melt. pt. 1,515°F (824°C); boil. pt. 2,179°F (1,193°C); most common isotope Yb^{174} (31.84%). *See also* Lanthanide Elements. △1554.

Yttrium, metallic element (symbol Y) of group IIIB of the periodic table, first isolated in 1828 by Friedrich Wohler. It is found associated with the lanthanides in monazite (phosphate) and bastnasite (fluorocarbonate) and resembles the lanthanides in its chemistry. The element has few commercial uses. Properties: at. no. 39; at. wt. 88.9059; sp gr 4.469; melt. pt. 2,773 °F (1,523°C); boil pt. 6,039°F (3,337°C); most common isotope Y^{89} (100%). △1552.

Yüan Dynasty (1264–1368), Chinese dynasty, the period of Mongol rule in China by the descendants of Genghis Khan. Kublai Khan, known as the Chinese Emperor Shih-tsu, was able to conquer all of China and eliminate the last Sung Dynasty pretender in 1279. Mongol rulers sent expeditions to attempt to conquer Japan and to SE Asia and brought China into contact with areas of Europe and the Middle East. The Yüan period became the golden age of Chinese drama. △1042. 1112.

Yüan Shih-k'ai (1859–1916), Chinese military officer of the Manchu Dynasty. △1270.

Yucatán, peninsula consisting of SE Mexico, British Honduras, and N Guatemala, separates the Gulf of Mexico from the Caribbean Sea; includes Campeche and Yucatán states, and the territory of Quintana Roo, Mexico. The terrain is mostly low-lying limestone region, with beautiful beaches along the coast, and dense tropical forests chiefly in Guatemala and British Honduras. The peninsula was the seat of the ancient Maya civilization; site of several ruined cities, temples, and pyramids. Area: approx. 70,000sq mi (181,300sq km).

Yucatán, state in SE Mexico, on N end of Yucatán Peninsula; seat of ancient Maya civilization; conquered 1546 by Francisco de Montejo. Terrain is flat plains, sparse hills, and forest lands. Products: lumber, tobacco, tropical fruit, honey, corn, sugar. Industries: fishing, tourism, sisal hemp, shoes, bags, hats. Area: approx. 14,900sq mi (38,600sq km). Pop. 774,011.

Yucca, stemless or trunked plants native to S United States, Mexico, and West Indies. The flowers grow in clusters and are usually white, but may be tinged with yellow or purple. Some of the trees take on grotesque shapes. Height: to 40ft (12m). Family Agavaceae; genus *Yucca. See also* Joshua Tree; Spanish Bayonet.

Yucca Moth, small white moth that has a symbiotic relationship with the yucca plant. Yucca plant flowers are pollinated exclusively by yucca moths and the moth larvae feed only on yucca plant seeds. Genus *Tegeticula.* △604.

Yudenich, Nikolai A. △1310.

Yugoslavia (Jugoslavija), independent nation in SE Europe. With historical ethnic and religious differences among its various regions, the country has been held together under Marshal Tito since the end of WWII.

Land and economy. Located in SE Europe, it is bordered by Italy and the Adriatic Sea (W), Austria, Hungary, and Romania (N), Bulgaria (E), and Greece and Albania (S). Politically it is divided into the republics of Bosnia and Herzegovina, Croatia, Macedonia, Montenegro, Serbia, Slovenia, and the autonomous regions of Vojvodina and Kossovo. Geographically, it is divided into two regions. Agricultural plains, low hills, and a few mountain ranges outline the area from Zagreb in the NW to Nis in the SE, including about 35% of the country. Minerals, timber, and sheep raising are in the mountainous section, which covers the remaining 65% of the country. The Danube River, the major water route between central and E Europe, flows through Yugoslavia. In the interior the climate is moderate; summers are hot, winters mild, and it is rainy along the Adriatic. Wars and drought have hindered the economy; most industry is socialized and managed by workers' councils. Private farms are restricted to 25acres (10hectares). Tourism is a major factor in the economy. In 1965, Yugoslavia attempted to increase production by shifting its centrally controlled economy to a decentralized system.

People. Great diversity marks the Yugoslav population. The main nationality groups are: Serbs 42%; Croats 23%; Slovenes 8%; Macedonians, Albanians, and Bosnian Muslims 6% each; Montenegrins 3%; Hungarians 2%; and Turks 1%. Religious preferences are based mainly on ethnic divisions. Seven million Serbs, Montenegrins, and Macedonians belong to the Eastern Orthodox Church, while 5,000,000 Croats, Slovenes, and Hungarians belong to the Roman Catholic Church. Three languages are officially approved—Slovenian, Macedonian, and Serbo-Croatian. Education is free and compulsory to age 14. Literacy is 80%.

Government. A socialist federal republic, it is governed by an elected Federal Assembly, which elects the president of the republic and the president of the assembly, as well as the Federal Executive Assembly.

History. Yugoslavia's history has been characterized by ethnic and religious crises. Centuries as an Ottoman Empire vassal were followed by territorial expansion after the 1913 Balkan Wars and the 1914 Sarejevo assassination of Austrian Archduke Ferdinand, which precipitated WWI. A monarchy was established in 1918. Serb and Croat nationalist demands erupted in 1928 when a Croatian leader was assassinated, and King Alexander established a royal dictatorship in 1929. At the start of WWII, pro-Allied Serb elements staged a coup d'etat and replaced Prince Paul, who had become regent in 1934, with King Peter. The Axis powers then invaded Yugoslavia, and the government went into exile. Yugoslav resistance forces were divided between those loyal to the monarchy and those allied with the National Liberation Army led by Tito (Partisans). At the close of WWII the Partisans were in power. A 1945 constitution made Yugoslavia a republic, and Marshal Tito became head of the government. Initially a Soviet satellite, Yugoslavia broke with Joseph Stalin and the USSR in 1948 and subsequently followed an independent policy that brought increased contacts with the West. During the mid-1970s, domestic policy was often concerned with the anticipated problem of succession to Marshal Tito.

PROFILE

Official name: Socialist Federal Republic of Yugoslavia
Area: 98,766sq mi (255,804sq km)
Population: 20,504,516
Density: 214per sq mi (83per sq km)
Chief cities: Belgrade (capital); Zagreb; Skopje
Government: Federated republic
Religion: Eastern Orthodox and Roman Catholic
Language: Slovenian, Macedonian, Serbo-Croatian; all government recognized
Monetary unit: Dinar
Gross national product: $18,400,000,000
Per capita income: $859
Industries: wood products, iron, steel, processed foods, chemicals, machinery, textiles
Agriculture: maize, wheat, barley, rye, tobacco, oats, hops, fruits, sugar beets, fish, cattle, potatoes
Minerals: coal, iron, copper, chrome, antimony, manganese, lead, mercury, salt, bauxite
Trading partners: West Germany, Italy, United Kingdom, USSR, Czechoslovakia

Yukawa, Hidelei. △1484.

Yukon River, third-longest river in North America; rises at the confluence of the Lewes and Pelly rivers in SW Yukon Territory, Canada; flows NW across the border into Alaska, then SW across central Alaska to the Bering Sea S of Norton Sound. Lower course of river was first explored by Russians in 1836–37; upper course by Robert Campbell 1843. Navigable for three months of year up to Whitehorse, Alaska, *c.* 1,775mi (2,858km) of its 2,000mi (3,220km).

Yukon Territory, territory of extreme NW Canada, bordered on the W and SW by the state of Alaska, and on the N by the Arctic Ocean.

Land and economy. The highest peaks in Canada are in the St Elias Mts in the SW. Most of the region is a rough plateau, broken by mountains and deep river valleys. The Yukon River, which flows W into Alaska, and its tributaries form the principal river system and are a potential source of great hydroelectric power. Most of the S and central portions are forested, but transportation problems have hampered exploitation of the timber. The famous gold deposits are worked with heavy equipment, and other minerals are mined. Arable land lies in some river valleys, but its use has been limited to farming for local use.

People and education. The population consists largely of immigrants from Canada and the United

Yorkshire terrier

Brigham Young

Thomas Young

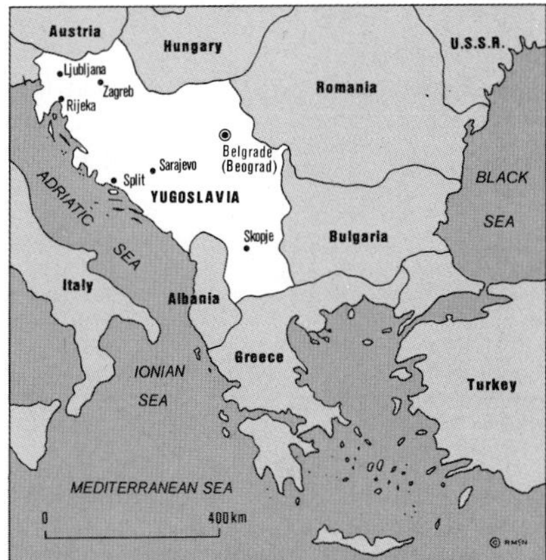
Austria
Hungary
U.S.S.R.
Ljubljana
Zagreb
Rijeka
Romania
Belgrade (Beograd)
Sarajevo
Split
YUGOSLAVIA
ADRIATIC SEA
BLACK SEA
Skopje
Bulgaria
Italy
Albania
Greece
IONIAN SEA
Turkey
MEDITERRANEAN SEA
0
400km

Yugoslavia

States, concentrated around Whitehorse, the capital. A few Indians are scattered about the territory. The territorial government directs the education of children. There are no institutions of higher education.

History. Fur traders of the Hudson's Bay Co. and surveyors explored the region, then part of the Northwest Territories, after 1840. Small strikes of gold were discovered beginning in 1873 and in 1896 a rich find occurred on a tributary of the Klondike River. Prospectors stampeded to the territory, swelling its population to more than 22,000 by 1901. More than $100,000,000 in gold was taken from the diggings in 10 years. The gold rush subsided; by 1921 the population was just over 4,000 and in 1941 it was only 4,914. Defense needs in WWII stimulated the territory. The Alaska Highway to S Canada and the United States, a chain of airfields, and a pipeline to carry oil from the Northwest Territories to a refinery constructed at Whitehorse were built. The pipeline and the refinery were closed after the war but the highway and the airfields were kept in operation.

PROFILE

Created territory: 1898
National Parliament representatives: Senate, 0; House of Commons, 1
Population: 16,000
Chief city: Whitehorse (capital)
Provincial legislature: Territorial Council, 12
Area: 207,076sq mi (536,327sq km)
Elevation: highest, 19,850ft (6,054m), Mt Logan; lowest, sea level
Economy: mining (gold, silver, lead, zinc), furs
Floral emblem: fireweed

Yuma, city in SW Arizona, on Colorado River, 20mi (32km) N of Mexican border. Industries: shipping of fruits and vegetables, gold mining. Settled 1854; inc. 1871. Pop. (1970) 29,007.

Yunnan, province in S China, bounded by Tibet autonomous region and Szechwan prov. (N), Laos and Vietnam (S), Kweichow prov. and Kwangsi autonomous region (E), Burma (W); capital is Kunming. Beseiged by Kublai Khan 1253; became part of China 1659; scene of Muslim revolt 1855–72; fell to Communists 1950. Crops: rice, corn, sweet potatoes, wheat, soybeans, tea, sugar cane, tobacco, cotton. Industries: livestock, lumber, tin, iron, coal, copper, zinc, gold, mercury, silver, antimony, sulfur. Area: 168,417sq mi (436,200sq km). Pop. 23,000,000.

Z

Zabrze, formerly Hindenburg; city in S Poland, W of Katowice, in Katowice mining district. Founded 1300, it grew rapidly in 19th century as a mining center; named Hindenburg after German occupation 1915; passed to Poland 1945. Industries: coal mining, iron founding, chemicals. Pop. 197,200.

Zafrullah Khan, Muhammad (1893–), Pakistani statesman and diplomat. He was a member of the Punjab Legislative Council 1926–35; and president of the All-India Muslim League 1931–32. In 1939 he acted as leader of the Indian delegation to the League of Nations. He led the Pakistani delegation to the United Nations (1947–54). He was a member of the International Court of Justice (1954–61) and again became Pakistan's UN representative (1961–64) and served as president of the UN General Assembly 1962–63. He once more became a member of the International Court of Justice 1964 and served as its president, 1970.

Zagreb, city in NW Yugoslavia, on Sava River; 2nd-largest city in Yugoslavia, and capital of Croatia; industrial and trade center; site of St Stephen's Cathedral, Yugoslav Academy of Arts and Sciences (1861), nuclear energy institute, university (1669), botanical gardens. The ancient Roman town of Andautonia, it was chief city of Croatia and Slavonia late 13th century; became center of nationalist (Yugoslav) movement in 19th century. Industries: textiles, chemicals, leather goods, machinery. Pop. 566,084.

Zagros, mountain range in S and SW Iran; extends from Soviet-Turkish border to the Persian Gulf; topography varies from rugged peaks (N), to ridges and valleys (central), to lowland marshes and rock (S). The nomadic Kurds inhabit the Zagros, graze their sheep and goats in central and lower parts; one of world's most productive oil fields is located in W foothills. Sabalan is the highest peak, 14,921ft (4,551m). Length: approx. 1,000mi (1,610km).

Zaharias, Babe Didrikson. *See* Didrikson, (Mildred) Babe.

Zaibatsu, great industrial combines of modern Japan. Aided by subsidies and favorable tax laws, several family-controlled banking and industrial firms, such as Mitsui, Sumitomo and Mitsubishi, became economically and politically very powerful.

Zaire, independent nation in W central Africa. Formerly known as the Belgian Congo and, after independence, as the Democratic Republic of the Congo, it changed its name to Zaire ("river") in 1971.

Land and economy. With only a narrow strip of land offering access to the sea, Zaire is located on the equator in W central Africa bounded W by the People's Republic of the Congo, N by the Central African Republic and Sudan; E by Uganda, Rwanda, Burundi, and Tanzania; S by Angola and Zambia. The central area is a large, low, rain forest plateau surrounded by mountains (W), plateaus (S and SW), and grasslands (NW). High ranges, the Mts of the Moon, cover the E section, including Mt Margherita, 16,763ft (5,113m) above sea level. One of the longest rivers in the world, the Zaire (Congo) rises near the Zambian border. It is one of the most economically developed countries in Africa. Most of the agricultural revenue comes from large European-owned plantations. Zairians are mainly subsistence farmers (80%). Industrial diamonds are a principal export item, along with copper, tin, and several rare metals. Offshore petroleum is being explored.

People. The Zairian population is divided into three groups: Pygmies, believed to be the first inhabitants of the Zaire River basin; Negroid people, classified as either Bantu, Sudanese, or Nilotics; and Hamites. About 200 languages are spoken, with 4 dominant sets: Lingala, Kingwana, Kikongo, and Tshiluba. French is the official language. Literacy is estimated at 35%. Regional religions—monotheism, animism, vitalism, ancestor worship, and witchcraft—are practiced by about half the population; the other half is Christian.

Government. The government is a strong, centralized presidential form, with both the president and unicameral National Assembly elected by universal suffrage.

History. The country was settled in the 9th and 10th centuries by Bantus from Nigeria. The Portuguese navigator Diego Cao explored the mouth of the Zaire in 1482; Belgian influence came in 1877 when Henry Morton Stanley penetrated the region for Belgium, whose undisputed control over the region lasted until 1907. Opposition to colonial domination grew, culminating in riots and then independence in 1960. Patrice Lumumba, elected first premier, formed a coalition government, put down attempted secession of Katanga prov., and was himself removed. Leftist uprisings precipitated several government changes before 1970 when it stabilized under Mobutu Sese Seko. Under his leadership Zaire took a more active role in world and African affairs.

PROFILE

Official name: Republic of Zaire
Area: 905,063sq mi (2,344,113sq km)
Population: 16,585,944
Density: 27per sq mi (10per sq km)
Chief cities: Kinshasa (capital); Luluabourg; Lubumbashi
Government: Republic
Religion: Christian and tribal (evenly divided)
Language: French (official)
Monetary unit: Zaire
Gross national product: $3,129,000,000
Per capita income: $147
Industries: palm oil, processed foods, clothing, textiles, soap
Agriculture: forests, bananas, coffee, rubber, rice, sugar cane, mangoes, plantain
Minerals: copper, cobalt, diamonds, cadmium, gold, silver, tin, zinc, iron, tungsten, manganese, uranium
Trading partners: Belgium (major), United States

Zaire River. *See* Congo (Zaire).

Zama, name of one or more ancient towns on the N coast of Africa (in modern Tunisia), traditionally the site of the last battle of the Second Punic War in which the Roman general Scipio Africanus Major defeated Hannibal of Carthage in 202 BC.

Zambezi, river in S central Africa; rises in NW Zambia and flows E through Angola and along the Zambia-Rhodesia border; empties into the Mozambique Channel in the Indian Ocean. Because navigable stretches are separated by rapids, it is used for local transportation only; has great hydroelectric potential. River was first explored by David Livingstone 1851–53. Length: 1,700mi (2,737km).

Zambia, independent nation in S Africa. Formerly the British colony of Northern Rhodesia, it was the first British territory to become a republic immediately after independence. Its economy is dependent on copper.

Land and economy. A land-locked plateau crossed by streams flowing into two of Africa's greatest rivers, the Zaire (Congo) and the Zambesi, Zambia is bordered by Zaire and Tanzania (N); Malawi and Mozambique (E); Rhodesia, Botswana, and Namibia (S); and Angola (W). Victoria Falls, on the Zambesi River, is twice as wide and more than twice the height of Niagara Falls. The climate is subtropical with rainfall 25–30in (63–76cm) annually. Copper is the mainstay of Zambian economy and accounts for 50% of the gross national product, 90% of the value of exports, and 60% of government revenue. In 1970 the government acquired a 51% interest in copper mines and other major industries.

People. Although copper mining has brought many rural Zambians into the N copper belt, the majority remain subsistence farmers. Ninety-nine percent of the population is African and Bantu, divided into some 70 tribes speaking 8 tongues. English is the official language. Animism is the dominant religion with a Christian minority. Literacy is rated between 15%–20%.

Government. The republic is headed by a strong president and unicameral National Assembly, both elected by universal suffrage. Tribal interests are represented by the House of Chiefs, an advisory body.

History. It is probable that immigrants into Zambia came about 2,000 years ago, displaced the Stone Age hunters and were themselves absorbed by waves of Bantu-speaking immigrants. European missionaries and traders came in the 19th century. David Livingstone saw Victoria Falls in 1855, and in 1888 Cecil

Rhodes obtained mineral concessions and led the way for British commercial interests, proclaiming both Northern and Southern Rhodesia as British spheres of influence. Northern Rhodesia became a British protectorate in 1924 and remained one until 1953 when it became part of the Federation of Rhodesia and Nyasaland with Southern Rhodesia and Nyasaland (now Malawi). After years of nationalist turmoil directed against white domination, a 1962 election allowed Northern Rhodesia to secede. On Oct. 24, 1964, it became the Republic of Zambia.

PROFILE

Official name: Republic of Zambia
Area: 290,585sq mi (752,615sq km)
Population: 4,396,000
Density: 16per sq mi (6per sq km)
Chief city: Lusaka
Government: Republic
Religion: Animist (major)
Language: English (official)
Monetary unit: Kwacha
Gross national product: $2,425,000
Per capita income: $503
Industries: copper, tobacco
Agriculture: cattle, forests
Minerals: copper, zinc, cobalt, gold, vanadium, manganese, coal
Trading partners: United Kingdom, Japan, West Germany, Italy, United States

Zanesville, city in central Ohio, on Muskingum River 50mi (81km) E of Columbus; seat of Muskingum co; served as state capital 1810–1812; birthplace of novelist Zane Grey (1875). Industries: batteries, radiators, cement, farm machinery. Founded 1797 by Ebenezer Zane; inc. as village 1814, as city 1850. Pop. (1970) 33,045.

Zanzibar, major island of Tanzania, E Africa, in the Indian Ocean. The first inhabitants date to *c.* AD 1000; under Arab domination until *c.* 1505 when controlled by Portuguese; taken by Arabs from Oman 1698; made a British protectorate 1890; inc. into German East Africa 1895; gained self-government 1963; became part of Tanzania 1964. Island economy is based mainly on agriculture; Zanzibar is the largest producer of cloves in the world. Industries: copra, spices, coconuts, cacao, fishing. Area: 641sq mi (1,660sq km). Pop. 190,494.

Zanzibar, city in Tanzania, on the coast of Zanzibar Island, 45mi (72km) N of Dar es Salaam; center of East African trade. Capital was transferred here in 1832; political and commercial importance has declined with the rise of competing ports. Industries: cloves, citrus fruits, chilies, copra, mangrove bark, clove oil, soap, coconut oil, handcrafts. Pop. 57,923.

Zapata, Emiliano (*c.* 1879–1919), leader of the Mexican Revolution, champion of agrarian reform in his native Morelos. Of middle-class background, Zapata steadfastly demanded that successive revolutionary governments abide by his Plan of Ayala, issued in 1911, which called for dividing the sugar plantations of Morelos and restoring the land to the Indians. He allied himself with Villa in capturing Mexico City in 1914, but soon retreated to his stronghold in the south. Led into a trap by forces loyal to Carranza, Zapata was captured and executed.

Zápolya, John (1487–1540), governor of Transylvania (1511–26), regent for Louis II (1516–26); elected king of Hungary in 1526. He was supported by the Turks in his struggle against Holy Roman Emperor Ferdinand I of Germany, who also claimed to be king of Hungary, a dispute settled by the Treaty of Nagyvarad in 1526. Zápolya was king of Hungary 1526–40, but was subservient to the Ottoman Empire.

Zapopan, city in W Mexico, approx. 10mi (16km) W of Guadalajara; trade center for agricultural products; site of 17th-century church. Products: fertilizer, flour, textiles. Pop. 182,934.

Zaporozhye (Zaporožje), city in Ukrainian republic, USSR, on W bank of Dnieper River, 45mi (72km) S of Dnepropetrovsk; originally settled 16th century as a Cossack stronghold; the historic site on islands downstream from present-day city has been almost obliterated by the construction of a dam and large hydroelectric plant (1927–32). The new city dates from 1930s as an industrial site. Industries: steel, coke, aluminum, magnesium, chemicals, soap, farm machinery. Old city was founded 1770 on site of Cossack camp and called Aleksandrovsk until 1921. Pop. 658,000.

Zapotec, Indian group inhabiting a section of the Mexican state of Oaxaca. The Zapotec built great preconquest urban centers at Mitla and Monte Albán. They sought contact with the Spaniards in order to preserve their independence from the rival Mixes and Aztecs; their numbers were drastically reduced as a result of Spanish labor demands. Benito Juárez, president of Mexico, was a full-blooded Zapotec. △970.

Zaragoza (Saragossa), city in NE Spain, on Ebro River, approx. 170mi (274km) NE of Madrid; capital of Zaragoza prov.; commercial and industrial center; site of Gothic cathedrals and churches. City was taken by Rome 1st century BC, by Moors early 8th century; taken by Alfonso I of Aragon and made capital of Aragon 1118. Industries: heavy machinery, building materials, textiles. Area: (prov.) 6,639sq mi (17,195sq km). Pop. (city) 479,845; (prov.) 760,186.

Zarathustra. *See* Zoroaster.

Zealots, a sect of Jewish extremists originating as early as the 2nd century BC. Driven by their religious fanaticism and intense hatred for foreign paganism, this faction organized into a political party during the reign of Herod the Great (37–4 BC). For nearly a century, they conducted acts of violence in opposition to Roman rule, ultimately prompting a revolt in which Jerusalem was destroyed (AD 70).

Zebra, common equine of African plains. More like an ass than a horse, it has long ears, short stiff mane, tufted tail, narrow hooves, and white coat striped with black, patterned according to species. Gestation period is 345–390 days; one colt is born. Varieties of true zebra are mountain, cape, cape mountain, Hartmann's, and plains. Height: 46–55in (118–140cm) at shoulder; weight: 600lb (270kg). Family Equidae; subgenus *Hippotigris;* species *Equus zebra.* Grevy's zebra is larger and has larger ears. Height: 55.1–63in (140–160cm) at shoulder. Family Equidae; subgenus *Dolichohippus;* species *Equus grevyi.* △548.

Zebra Fish. *See* Lionfish.

Zebu, or Brahman cattle, numerous domestic varieties of a single species of ox, native to India, used extensively in Asia and Africa, and recently introduced in the New World. △372, 628.

Zechariah, biblical author and 11th of the 12 minor prophets. He was Haggai's contemporary and shared his concern for rebuilding the Temple in Jerusalem.

Zedler, Johann Heinrich. △1780.

Zeeman, Pieter (1865–1943), Dutch physicist. He shared a Nobel Prize in 1902 with his teacher Hendrik Lorentz for their discovery (1896) of the Zeeman effect, the splitting of spectral lines when a light source is placed in a strong magnetic field. He also detected the magnetic fields at the surface of the Sun.

Zelea-Codreanu, Corneliu. *See* Codreanu, Corneliu Zelea-.

Zemstvos (1864–1917), locally elected assemblies in Russia. △1286.

Zen, a Japanese school of Buddhism initially developed in China. Instead of doctrines and scriptures, mind-to-mind instruction from master to disciple is emphasized in order to achieve *satori,* or awakening of the Buddha-nature inherent in everyone. There are two major Zen sects. One called Rinzai, introduced to Japan from China in 1191, emphasizes sudden shock and meditation on paradoxical statements. The other, the Soto sect, also transmitted from China (in 1227), prefers the method of quiet sitting. In its secondary emphasis on mental tranquillity, fearlessness, and spontaneity, Zen has had a great influence on Japanese culture. Zen priests inspired art, literature, the tea ceremony, and the No play. Over the last several decades, a number of Zen groups have formed in the United States and several European countries. △820, 846.

Zener Cards. △824.

Zenger, John Peter (1697–1746), American printer and journalist, b. Germany. Editor of the *New York Weekly Journal* (1733) he attacked Gov. William Cosby and was jailed for libel (1734). He was later tried by a jury and acquitted. His case established the truth of statements made as a defense for libel and made Zenger a symbol of freedom of the press. He was public printer of New York (1737) and New Jersey (1738).

Zenithal. △180.

Zenobia, (*fl.* 3rd century AD), queen of Palmyra, a part of the Roman Empire in the East. After the death (267) of her husband Odenathus, she secured power

Niger
0
800km
Chad
Nigeria
Sudan
Central African Republic
Ethiopia
Cameroon
Equat. Gui.
Gabon
Congo
Kisangani (Stanleyville)
Uganda
Kenya
Rwanda
ZAIRE
Burundi
Kinshasa (Léopoldville)
Kananga (Luluabourg)
Mbuji-Mayi (Bakwanga)
Tanzania
ATLANTIC OCEAN
Angola
Likasi (Jadotville)
Lubumbashi (Élisabethville)
Malawi
Zambia

Zaire

Zambezi River

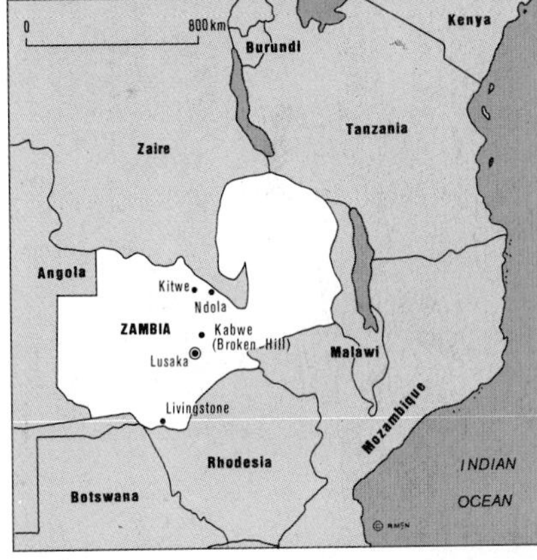
0
800km
Kenya
Burundi
Tanzania
Zaire
Angola
Kitwe
Ndola
ZAMBIA
Kabwe (Broken Hill)
Lusaka
Malawi
Mozambique
Livingstone
Rhodesia
Botswana
INDIAN OCEAN

Zambia

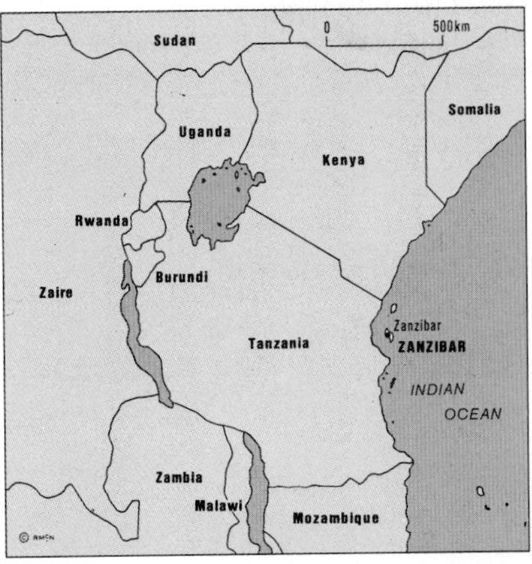
Sudan
0
500km
Somalia
Uganda
Kenya
Rwanda
Zaire
Burundi
Zanzibar
ZANZIBAR
Tanzania
INDIAN OCEAN
Zambia
Malawi
Mozambique

Zanzibar

for herself in the name of her young son Vaballathus. Under her leadership, in 271 Palmyra broke off from the Roman Empire and became an independent state. She was defeated (272) by Aurelian, taken to Rome, but later pardoned.

Zephaniah, biblical author and ninth of the 12 minor prophets. He condemned Israel's religious and political corruption and stressed the certainty of God's judgment against Israel.

Zephyr Lily. *See* Atamasco Lily.

Zeppelin, Ferdinand, Count von (1838–1917), German army officer and designer-builder of large-scale rigid dirigible balloons. △1712.

Zero, integer, denoted by 0, that symbolizes the concept of emptiness, absence of something. It can be added to or subtracted from a number, etc, so as to leave the number unchanged: $x + 0 = x$; $x - 0 = x$; also $x \times 0 = 0$; $0 \div x = 0$; $x^0 = 1$. △1448.

Zero Gravity or **Zero g,** the condition of experiencing no net gravitational force. It may be attained by airplane pilots for a few minutes during free fall, or by astronauts in satellites or lunar probes. Physiological accompaniments include some muscle wastage and lower blood pressure, but no major harmful effects have yet been noted. △144, 1724.

Zero Population Growth, social movement that urges families to have no more than two children, thereby maintaining the present population. The movement was initiated by Paul R. Ehrlich, an American biologist, whose book *The Population Bomb* (rev. ed. 1971) stated that overpopulation was causing a depletion of food supplies.

Zeus, in the mythology of the Greeks, the sky god, lord of the wind, clouds, rain, and thunder. Later he was the supreme deity, omnipresent, omniscient, omnipotent. Zeus ruled from Mt Olympus, where he dwelt with all the gods, and consorted with gods and men as he pleased. He was depicted as a mature, strong man with stern features and thick hair and beard, bearing the sceptre in one hand and in the other, the thunderbolt. The centers of his worship were at Dodona, Mount Lycaeus in Arcadia, and the temples at Olympia and Athens, though he was honored throughout the country. △832.

Zhengzhou (Chengchow), city in N China, 10mi (16km) S of Yellow River; capital of Honan prov.; railroad junction. Industries: cotton, food processing, agricultural tools, thermal power. Pop. 1,500,000.

Zhuangaerpendi. *See* Dzungar.

Zhukov, Georgi K(onstantinovich) (1894–1974), Soviet military commander and political figure. A draftee in World War I, he joined the Communists in 1918 as a cavalry commander. He studied in Germany and commanded successfully in Manchuria (1938). In World War II he led the defense of Moscow (1941), broke the German sieges of Stalingrad and Leningrad, and led the final assault on Berlin (1945). He became defense minister in 1955, helping to modernize the Soviet armed forces. He was a member of the Presidium (1957) and received the Order of Lenin (1971). △1338.

Ziggurat, a temple in Babylonian and Assyrian architecture, constructed as a truncated pyramid in diminishing tiers, usually square or rectangular. The shrine at the top was reached by a series of ramps. Ziggurats date from 3000 to 600 BC. △956–58.

Zimbabwe, ruined city in SE Rhodesia, near Fort Victoria. Name means "houses of stone" and refers to the large, well preserved buildings. Ruins were discovered in 1868 and indicate the first inhabitants may have lived during Iron Age. Construction of stone monuments began in 1450; most noted are the famous Elliptical Building, Conical tower, and Acropolis. △1116.

Zimmerman Note (1917), cable intercepted by British intelligence from German Foreign Minister. It stated Germany's intent to wage unrestricted submarine warfare and proposed that Mexico be offered three US states if it allied herself with Germany. Because it violated the *Sussex* Pledge, President Wilson severed diplomatic relations with Germany, which led to US entry into World War I.

Zinc, metallic element (symbol Zn) of group IIB of the periodic table, known from early times. Chief ores are zinc blende (sulfide), smithsonite (carbonate), and calamine (silicate). The element is used in many alloys, including brass, bronze, nickel, silver, and soft solder. It is also used in galvanizing iron and in producing zinc compounds. Properties: at. no. 30; at. wt. 65.38; sp gr 7.133 (25°C); melt. pt. 787.2°F (419.58 °C); boil. pt. 1,665°F (907°C); most common isotope Zn^{64} (48.89%). △1566.

Zinc Oxide, white powder used in ointments as a mild antiseptic, astringent, and protectant against drying in cases of eczema and other skin conditions.

Zinnia, genus of chiefly annual plants native to North and South America. Most garden zinnias are varieties of *Z. elegans,* that has flower heads of all colors but blue and green. Height: to 3ft (91cm); flower diameter: to 6in (15cm). Family Compositae.

Zinoviev, Grigori E(vseevich) (1883–1936), Soviet political leader. He was a close collaborator of V.I. Lenin in exile (1908–17) and supported a coalition government after the 1917 revolution. His support of pluralistic government led to his arrest during Stalin's purge trials (1934) and execution (1936). △1310.

Zion (Sion), height in E part of Jerusalem, Israel; center of Jewish spiritual life; site of Temple of David; referred to in Bible as the City of David.

Zionism, a movement within Judaism which advocates the return to the land of Israel (Zion). It is based on the conception of the coming of the Messiah connected with the land of the fathers, Israel. In 1897, Theodor Herzl developed the movement into an organized body. Zionism gained momentum in the 19th century as the Jews developed a sense of nationalism and as actual movement to Israel began. Practical, political, and cultural Zionism developed. Herzl believed that only through public law would Zionist aims be achieved. Conflicts developed within the leadership and outside the movement. Hebrew was revived as a modern, daily language and in 1948 when the state of Israel was founded, Hebrew became its official language. Zionism continues as an effective movement, combating anti-Semitism and improving conditions of Jewish life. △1380.

Zion National Park, park in SW Utah. It is famous for its scenic trails, canyons, colorful cliffs, and mesas. There is evidence of past volcanic activity. The outstanding feature is a deep, many colored gorge cut by the Virgin River. Area: 147,034acres (59,549hectares). Est. 1909.

Zipper. △1816.

Zircon, an orthosilicate mineral, zirconium silicate ($ZrSiO_4$) found in igneous rocks and metamorphosed limestones and in sand and gravel. Tetragonal system prismatic crystals. Brilliant, colorless or of varied hues; hardness 7.5; sp gr 4.6. Used widely as a gemstone because of its high refractive index.

Zirconium, metallic element (symbol Zr) of the second transition series, first discovered (1789) by M. H. Klaproth. Chief source is the gemstone zircon (silicate). It has a number of minor commercial uses. Chemically it is similar to titanium. Properties: at. no. 40; at. wt. 91.22; sp gr 6.506; melt pt. 3,366°F (1,852°C); boil. pt. 7,911°F (4,377°C); most common isotope Zr^{90} (51.46%). *See also* Transition Elements.

Zither, stringed musical instrument from ancient China via the Near East to medieval Europe. It is still popular for folk music in Austria, Bavaria, and the rural United States. The flat wooden sound box holds 30 to 40 strings, the five nearest stretched over a fretted board for melody, and plucked with fingers or a plectrum. *See also* Psaltery.

Zodiac, region of the sky extending either side of the ecliptic and containing the 12 constellations through which the Sun appears to move. Ancient astrologers divided it into 12 equal signs or houses, roughly coincident with these constellations. But owing to the Earth's precession, the constellations have now shifted eastward and lag behind the signs. △128, 826.

Zodiacal Light, a faint, cone-shaped sky glow extending upward on the ecliptic from the horizon in the west after sunset and in the east before sunrise, probably caused by scattering of sunlight from dust particles in the plane of the solar system. Observations transmitted from Earth satellites have shown that this light does not vary as previously believed.

Zog I, original name **Ahmed Bey Zogu** (1895–1961), king of Albania (1928–39). Son of a Muslim chieftain, he was prominent in the struggle for independence, 1912–14, supporting William of Wied. Zogu was premier 1922–24. When Albania was proclaimed a republic in 1925, Zogu was elected president. In 1928 he was proclaimed king. As head of state, he consistently championed modernization and reforms. His rule became autocratic, however, and he was ineffectual in resisting the Fascist takeover in 1939.

Zoisite, an orthosilicate mineral, hydrous calcium aluminum silicate, found in metamorphic rocks. Orthorhombic system prismatic crystals and masses. Glassy, transparent gray, white, brown, green, or pink; hardness 6–6.5; sp gr 3.2. A vivid blue variety, tanzanite, of Tanzania is a gemstone.

Zola, Émile (1840–1902), French novelist. A leader of the naturalist school, his novels include *L'Assommoir* (1877), *Nana* (1880), *Germinal* (1885), and *Le Docteur Pascal* (1893), which were published under the collective title of *Les Rougon-Macquart.* He was tried for writing a letter *J'accuse* (1898), in support of Alfred Dreyfus, and fled to a short exile in England. △1238.

Zone Refining, method of purifying crystals, especially for use in semiconductor devices. The material is placed in a long tube and passed through a furnace in which hot and cold zones alternate. As the rod moves through the furnace, impurities remain in the molten state while melting and recrystallization of the material takes place; the impurities are thus transferred to one end of the tube.

Zones, Oceanic. △202, 230–234.

Zoning, municipal land-use regulations that divide property in areas for residential, industrial, commercial, or recreational use. Such regulations were first enacted in New York City to restrict the size and height of buildings (1916). The right to zone land was given to the cities by the states.

Zoogeography, or animal geography, study of the geographic distribution of animals. Formerly, the approach of this science was descriptive. Presently, it utilizes various data, including isotope dating and ocean-bottom core sampling. △578.

Zoological Garden, or zoo, public or private institution in which living animals are kept and exhibited. Organized zoos, sometimes called menageries or aquariums, open to the general public, have been operating for over 400 years in Europe. Currently, nonprofit organizations or zoological societies run most zoos in a scientific manner. Some outstanding examples are the zoological societies of San Diego, New York, Philadelphia, London, Antwerp, and Munich. Most zoos are run for public recreation as well as for scientific and educational purposes. Worldwide representations of animal groups and rarities are frequently displayed. Present emphasis is on exhibiting animals in natural settings. Conservation programs are undertaken by some zoological societies, as is the breeding of rare species. △638.

Zoology, study of animals. When combined with botany, it comprises the science of biology. Various subdivisions of zoological study include: taxonomy, classification of animals; zoogeography, distribution of animals; ecology, relationship of animals to each other and to their environment; paleontology, fossils; anthropology, man; evolution, origin of species and changes through history; anatomy, structure of body and its organs; morphology, functions of structure; embryology, development from conception to birth; genetics, heredity; physiology, function; pathology, abnormal function and structure; and psychology, behavior. △458.

Zoonosis, an infection or infestation of lower animals that can be transmitted to man. Examples include some parasites such as fleas or canine tapeworms, and bacteria such as *Bacillis anthracis,* a primary cause of disease of sheep and cows.

Zoospores. △432.

Zoraptera. △492.

Zoroaster, or **Zarathustra** (*c.* 628–*c.* 551 BC), Persian religious figure, founder of Zoroastrianism. Zoroaster is believed to have been born in western Persia. Persian religion at the time was a polytheism in a state of decadence; it was run by a hereditary priesthood and numerous animal sacrifices were required. Zoroaster, after a series of revelations, preached a new religion in which a single Wise Lord, Ahura Mazda, was recognized as the creator of the universe. Pitted against Ahura Mazda was Ahriman and the forces of evil. Unable to convert the petty chieftains of his native area, Zoroaster traveled to the east, where in Chorasmia (now in Khorasan province in northeastern Iran) he converted the royal family, including King Vishtaspa. By the time of Zoroaster's death, his new religion had spread to a large part of Persia. Parts of the Avesta, the holy scripture of Zoroastrianism, are believed to have been written by Zoroaster himself.

Zoroastrianism, religion originated by Zoroaster in the 6th century BC, which became the state religion of Persia in the period from 229–652. Viewing the world as divided between the spirits of good and evil, Zoroastrians worship Ahura Mazda as the Supreme Deity. Islam's conquest in the 7th century led to the decline and near disappearance of the religion in Persia. Today the Parsis of India comprise most of the 125,000 followers of Zoroastrianism. *See also* Ahura Mazda; Parsi; Zoroaster.

Zuccarelli, Francesco (1702–88), Italian painter of the Venetian School. He was the leading landscapist of Venice in his time. Very popular with English patrons, he spent many years in London and became a charter member of the Royal Academy. Influenced by Marco Ricci, his brilliantly atmospheric landscapes in turn influenced several British painters, notably Richard Wilson. *See also* Venetian School.

Zucchini, variety of summer squash. A bushy annual plant, it produces a cucumber-shaped, dark green fruit with a smooth rind. Family Cucurbitaceae.

Zuider Zee (Zuyder Zee), former landlocked inlet of the North Sea on the N coast of the Netherlands. Since the completion of the dike of IJsselmeer (1932), this area is divided between the saline Wadden Zee and freshwater IJsselmeer Lake. *See also* IJsselmeer.

Zulu, Negroid people of South Africa, living mainly in Natal. They are closely related to the Swazi and the Xhosa. Traditionally agriculturalists, concentrating on grain production but also possessing large herds of cattle, which perform the function of status symbols, the Zulus have a patriarchal, polygynous society with a strong militaristic tradition. Unified under their leader Shaka in the 19th century, they fiercely resisted the encroachments of white colonialists. Today many Zulu males work as migrant laborers in the mines of South Africa or on white-owned farms. The predominant religion is now Christianity, although traditional ancestor worship, sorcery, and fetishism are still common. △828, 880.

Zululand, an historical region of NE Natal province, E Republic of South Africa; site of intense battles between native Zulu tribes and British and Boers in late 19th century; region now comprised of native reserves (Kwazulu). Sugarcane is economic staple. Area: 10,362sq mi (26,838sq km). Pop. 570,160. △1268.

Zuñi, major tribe of Pueblo Indians speaking an individual tongue, occupying a village area in McKinley and Valencia counties, New Mexico. They were the first Indian village visited by Coronado on his famed *entrada* in 1541 in search of the Seven Cities of Cíbola. Noted for their fine jewelry making, about 5,100 people live today in the village area.

Zürich, capital city of Zurich canton in Switzerland, on Limmat River, at NW end of Lake Zurich, in the foothills of the Alps; largest city in Switzerland. Conquered by Romans 58 BC, it passed to Alemanni, Franks, Swabia after 5th century; became free imperial city 1218; joined Swiss Confederation 1351; starting point of Swiss Reformation 16th century; site of Swiss National Museum, 11th- and 13th-century Protestant cathedrals, 13th-century St Peter's Church, University of Zurich, Federal Institute of Technology. Industries: automobiles, banking, travel, machinery, paper, trade, textiles, publishing, beer, chemicals. Pop. 422,640.

Zwingli, Ulrich or **Huldreich** (1484–1531), Swiss theologian. Ordained in 1506, he studied the New Testament in Erasmus' editions. He preached reformed doctrine in Zurich and made that city a center of the Reformation. More radical than Luther, he saw communion as symbolic and commemorative. The *First Helvetic Confession* (1536), compiled by his followers, was based on his opinions. Zwingli died as a chaplain in battle with Roman Catholics at Kappel. △1152.

Zygomatic Bone. △682.

Zygote, cell formed by fusion of male and female gametes. The fertilized egg contains a diploid number of chromosomes, half contributed by the sperm, half by the ovum. △700.

Émile Zola

Zuider Zee, Holland

BIBLIOGRAPHY

This bibliography of approximately 1,500 citations is divided into the seven sections that comprise the *Colorpedia:* The Universe; The Earth; Life on Earth; Man; History and Culture; Man and Science; Man and Machines.

Each section of the bibliography begins with a short list of periodicals that cover events in the field. The sections are subdivided into major subject categories. Within each of these categories, citations are listed alphabetically by author. When appropriate, titles of general interest appear under more than one heading.

THE UNIVERSE

Periodicals that report on events and developments concerning "The Universe" include *Aviation Week, Natural History, Physics Today, Science, Scientific American, Sky and Telescope, Smithsonian,* and *Space World.*

General Astronomy

Alter, Dinsmore, et al., *Pictorial Astronomy,* rev. ed. (New York, 1974).

Asimov, Isaac, *Of Matters Great and Small* (New York, 1975).

Baker, Robert A., and Laurence W. Fredrick, *An Introduction to Astronomy,* 7th ed. (Princeton, N.J., 1967).

Branley, Franklyn M., *Astronomy* (New York, 1975).

Burbidge, Geoffrey (ed.), *Annual Review of Astronomy and Astrophysics,* Vol. 13 (Palo Alto, Calif., 1975).

Calder, Nigel, *Violent Universe: An Eyewitness Account of the New Astronomy* (New York, 1970).

Culver, Roger B., *An Introduction to Experimental Astronomy* (San Francisco, 1974).

Englis, S.J., *Planets, Stars, and Galaxies: An Introduction to Astronomy,* 3rd ed. (New York, 1972).

Fanning, Anthony E., *Planets, Stars, and Galaxies: Descriptive Astronomy for Beginners* (New York, 1966).

Gingerich, Owen, *New Frontiers in Astronomy: Readings from Scientific American* (San Francisco, 1975).

Glasstone, Samuel, *Source Book on the Space Sciences* (New York, 1965).

Hoyle, Fred, *Frontiers of Astronomy* (New York, 1955).

Jastrow, R., and M.H. Thompson, *Astronomy: Fundamentals and Frontiers* (New York, 1972).

McGraw-Hill Encyclopedia of Science and Technology, "Astronomy" (New York, 1970).

Scientific American Editors, *The New Astronomy* (New York, 1956).

Shapley, Harlow (ed.), *Source Book in Astronomy, 1900–1950* (Cambridge, Mass., 1960).

Weigert, Arnold, and Helmut Zimmerman, *A Concise Encyclopedia of Astronomy* (New York, 1968).

Wyatt, Stanley P., and James B. Kaler, *Principles of Astronomy: A Short Version* (Boston, 1974).

History of Astronomy

Asimov, Isaac, *The Universe: From Flat Earth to Quasar,* rev. ed. (New York, 1971).

Berry, Arthur, *A Short History of Astronomy* (New York, 1961).

De Santillana, Giorgio, *The Crime of Galileo* (Chicago, 1955).

Dreyer, John L., *History of Astronomy from Thales to Kepler* (New York, 1933).

Hey, J.S., *The Evolution of Radio Astronomy* (New York, 1973).

Ley, Willy, *Watchers of the Skies: An Informal History of Astronomy from Babylon to the Space Age* (New York, 1963).

Moore, Patrick, *Suns, Myths and Men,* rev. ed. (New York, 1969).

———, *Watchers of the Stars: The Scientific Revolution* (New York, 1974).

Telescopes

Howard, Neale E., *Standard Handbook for Telescope Making* (New York, 1959).

———, *The Telescope Handbook and Star Atlas* (New York, 1967; rev. ed., 1975).

McGraw-Hill Encyclopedia of Science and Technology, "Astronomical Instruments" (New York, 1970).

Page, Thornton, and Lou W. Page (eds.), *Telescopes: How to Make and Use Them* (New York, 1966).

The Universe

Eddington, Arthur S., *The Expanding Universe* (Cambridge, Eng., 1946).

Gamow, George, *The Creation of the Universe* (New York, 1952; rev. ed., 1961).

Lovell, Bernard A., *The Explosion of Science: The Physical Universe* (London, 1967).

———, *Our Present Knowledge of the Universe* (Cambridge, Mass., 1967).

———, *Man's Relation to the Universe* (San Francisco, 1975).

Hoyle, Fred, *The Nature of the Universe,* rev. ed. (New York, 1960).

———, *Astronomy and Cosmology* (San Francisco, 1975).

Menzel, Donald Howard, *A Field Guide to the Stars and Planets, Including the Moon, Satellites, Comets, and Other Features of the Universe* (Boston, 1964).

Moore, Patrick, *The Concise Atlas of the Universe* (New York, 1974).

National Geographic Society, *The Amazing Universe* (Washington, D.C., 1975).

Scientific American Editors, *The Universe* (New York, 1957).

Smart, W.M., *The Riddle of the Universe* (New York, 1968).

The Solar System—General

Asimov, Isaac, *The Solar System* (Chicago, 1974).

Berlage, H.P., *The Origin of the Solar System* (New York, 1968).

Butler, S.T., and Robert Raymond, *The Family of the Sun* (New York, 1975).

Cousins, F.W., *The Solar System* (New York, 1972).

Page, Thornton, and Lou W. Page, *The Origin of the Solar System: Genesis of the Sun and Planets, and Life on Other Worlds* (New York, 1966).

Scientific American Editors, *The Solar System,* Vol. 233 (3), Sept., 1975 (New York, 1975).

Smithsonian Institution, *Man and Cosmos: Nine Guggenheim Lectures on the Solar System* (New York, 1975).

Whipple, Fred L., *Earth, Moon and Planets,* 3rd ed. (Cambridge, Mass., 1968).

Planets, Moons, and Non-Stellar Objects

Alexander, A.F. O'Donel, *The Planet Saturn* (London, 1962).

———, *The Planet Uranus* (London, 1965).

Baum, R., *The Planets: Some Myths and Realities* (New York, 1973).

Bonestell, Chesley, and Arthur C. Clarke, *Beyond Jupiter: The Worlds of Tomorrow* (Boston, 1972).

de Callatay, Vincent, and Audouin Dollfus, *Atlas of the Planets* (Toronto and Buffalo, 1974).

Elvius, A. (ed.), *From Plasma to Planet (Nobel Symposium 21)* (New York, 1972).

Gehrels, T. (ed.), *Jupiter: The Giant Planet* (Tucson, Ariz., 1976).

Hartmann, William K., *Moons and Planets* (Belmont, Calif., 1972).

Jackson, Joseph H., III, *Pictorial Guide to the Planets,* rev. ed. (New York, 1973).

Kaula, W.M., *An Introduction to Planetary Physics: The Terrestrial Planets* (New York, 1968).

Ley, Willy, *The Gas Giants: The Largest Planets* (New York, 1969).

Lowell, Laurel, *Pluto* (St. Paul, Minn., 1973).

McGraw-Hill Encyclopedia of Science and Technology Yearbook 1975, "Comets" (New York, 1975).

Mutch, Thomas A., *Geology of the Moon: A Stratigraphic View* (Princeton, N.J., 1970).

NASA, *Mars as Viewed by Mariner 9* (Washington, D.C., 1974).

Nourse, Alan, *Nine Planets,* rev. ed. (New York, 1970).

Page, Thornton, and Lou W. Page, *Neighbors of the Earth* (New York, 1965).

Sulentic, Jack W., and William C. Tifft, *The Revised New General Catalogue of Non-Stellar Astronomical Objects* (Tucson, Ariz., 1973).

Taylor, Stuart Ross, *Lunar Science: A Post-Apollo View* (Elmsford, N.Y., 1975).

The Sun

Asimov, Isaac, *The Sun* (Chicago, 1972).

Baxter, W.M., *The Sun and the Amateur Astronomer* (N. Pomfret, Vt., 1973).

Brandt, John C., *Introduction to the Solar Wind* (San Francisco, 1970).

Gamow, George, *The Birth and Death of the Sun* (New York, 1949).

———, *A Star Called the Sun* (New York, 1964).

McGraw-Hill Encyclopedia of Science and Technology, "Sun" (New York, 1970).

Menzel, Donald, *Our Sun,* rev. ed. (Cambridge, Mass., 1959).

Moore, Patrick, *The Sun* (New York, 1968).

Stars and Space

Allen, Richard H., *Star Names: Their Lore and Meaning* (New York, 1963).

Asimov, Isaac, *The Stars in Their Courses* (New York, 1971).

Bok, Bart, and Priscilla Bok, *The Milky Way,* 4th ed. (Cambridge, Mass., 1974).

Bova, Ben, *In Quest of Quasars: An Introduction to Stars and Starlike Objects* (New York, 1970).

Burbidge, Geoffrey R., and Margaret Burbidge, *Quasi-Stellar Objects* (San Francisco, 1967).

Goldsmith, Donald, and Donald Levy, *From the Black Hole to the Infinite Universe* (San Francisco, 1974).

Gordon, M.A., and L.E. Snyder (eds.), *Molecules in the Galactic Environment* (New York, 1972).

Levitt, I.M., *Beyond the Known Universe: From Dwarf Stars to Quasars* (New York, 1974).

Hoyle, Fred, *Galaxies, Nuclei, and Quasars* (New York, 1965).

Jastrow, Robert, *Red Giants and White Dwarfs: Man's Descent from the Stars,* rev. ed. (New York, 1970).

McGraw-Hill Encyclopedia of Science and Technology Yearbook 1972, "Energy Sources in Galaxies and Quasars" (New York, 1972).

McGraw-Hill Encyclopedia of Science and Technology, "Star" (New York, 1970).

Moore, Patrick, *The New Guide to the Stars* (New York, 1976).

Murchie, Guy, *Music of the Spheres,* 2 vols. (Boston, 1961; rev. ed., New York, 1961).

Nature Editors, *Pulsating Stars,* 2 vols. (New York, 1961 and 70).

Page, Thornton, and Lou W. Page (eds.), *Beyond the Milky Way* (New York, 1969).

Page, Thornton, and Lou W. Page, *The Evolution of Stars* (New York, 1967).

Peltier, Leslie C., *Guideposts to the Stars: Exploring the Skies Through the Year* (New York, 1972).

Shapley, Harlow, *Galaxies,* rev. ed. (Cambridge, Mass., 1974).

Sutton, Richard M., *Physics of Space* (New York, 1965).

Whitney, Charles A., *Whitney's Star Finder: A Field Guide to the Heavens* (New York, 1974).

Space Exploration

Armstrong, Neil, et al., *First on the Moon: The Astronauts' Own Story* (Waltham, Mass., 1970).

Branley, Franklyn M., *Experiements in the Principles of Space Travel* (New York, 1973).

Cooper, Henry S., Jr., *Apollo on the Moon* (New York, 1969).

Davies, Merton, and Bruce Murray, *The View from Space: Photographic Exploration of the Planets* (New York, 1971).

Fimmel, Richard O., et al., *Pioneer Odyssey: Encounter with a Giant* (Washington, D.C., 1974).

Gagarin, Yuri, and Vladimir Lebedev, *Survival in Space* (New York, 1969).

Herron, Matt, and Jeanine Herron, *Voyage of Aquarius* (New York, 1975).

Lovell, Bernard A., *The Exploration of Outer Space* (New York, 1962).

McGraw-Hill Encyclopedia of Science and Technology Yearbook 1975, "Skylab" (New York, 1975).

Moore, Patrick, *The Next Fifty Years in Space* (New York, 1976).

Murray, Bruce C., and Eric Burgess, *Flight to Mercury* (New York, 1976).

Rickert, Russell K., *Astronomy and Space Exploration* (Reading, Mass., 1974).

Sharpe, Mitchell R., *Living in Space: The Astronaut and His Environment* (New York, 1969).

Von Braun, Werner, and Frederick Ordway, *The Rockets' Red Glare* (New York, 1976).

Extraterrestrial Life

Sagan, Carl, *Cosmic Connection: An Extraterrestrial Perspective* (New York, 1973).

———, (ed.), *Communication with Extraterrestrial Intelligence* (Cambridge, Mass., 1973).

Shklovsky, I.S., and Carl Sagan, *Intelligent Life in the Universe* (San Francisco, 1969).

Sullivan, Walter, *We Are Not Alone: The Search for Intelligent Life on Other Worlds,* rev. ed. (New York, 1966).

THE EARTH

Periodicals that report on events and developments concerning "The Earth" include *Environment, Geological Magazine, National Geographic, Natural History, Oceans, Popular Science, Science, Scientific American, Sea Frontiers,* and *Smithsonian.*

Face of the Land—Geography

Costello, David F., *The Mountain World* (New York, 1975).

Hammond, Inc., *Earth and Space,* rev. ed. (Maplewood, N.J., 1970).

Leveson, David, *A Sense of the Earth* (New York, 1972).

McGraw-Hill Encyclopedia of Science and Technology Yearbook 1974, "Geomorphology" (New York, 1974).

Man's Domain: A Thematic Atlas of the World Mapping Man's Relationship with his Environment, 3rd ed. (New York, 1975).

Robinson, Arthur H., and Randall D. Sale, *Elements of Cartography,* 3rd ed. (New York, 1969).

Shimer, John A., *This Sculptured Earth: The Landscape of America* (New York, 1959).

United States Military Academy, *Atlas of Land Forms,* 2nd ed. (New York, 1974).

The Structure of the Earth—Geology

American Geological Institute, *Dictionary of Geological Terms,* rev. ed. (New York, 1976).

Bascom, Willard, *A Hole in the Bottom of the Sea: The Story of the Mohole Project* (New York, 1961).

Bates, Robert L., and Walter C. Sweet, *Geology: An Introduction,* 2nd ed. (Indianapolis, Ind., 1973).

Bloom, A.L., *The Surface of the Earth* (Englewood Cliffs, N.J., 1969).

Cargo, D.N., and B.F. Mallory, *Man and His Geologic Environment* (Reading, Mass., 1974).

Challinor, John, *A Dictionary of Geology,* 4th ed. (New York, 1974).

Compton, Robert R., *Manual of Field Geology* (New York, 1961).

Donath, Fred A., *Annual Review of Earth and Planetary Sciences,* Vol. 3 (Palo Alto, Calif., 1975).

Fenton, Carroll Lane, and Mildred Adams Fenton, *Giants of Geology* (Garden City, N.Y., 1952).

Folsom, Franklin, *Exploring American Caves: Their History, Geology, Lore and Location* (New York, 1962).

Harbaugh, John W., and G. Bonham-Carter, *Computer Simulation in Geology* (New York, 1970).

Hills, E. Sherbon, *Elements of Structural Geology,* 2nd ed. (New York, 1972).

Krauskopf, Konrad B., *The Third Planet: An Invitation to Geology* (San Francisco, 1974).

McGraw-Hill Encyclopedia of Science and Technology Yearbook 1973, "Gravitational Constant" (New York, 1973).

Reader's Digest, *Marvels and Mysteries of the World Around Us* (Pleasantville, N.Y., 1972).

Moore, Ruth E., *The Earth We Live On: The Story of Geological Discovery,* 2nd ed. (New York, 1971).

Shepard, Francis Parker, *The Earth Beneath the Sea,* rev. ed. (Baltimore, 1967).

Young, Keith, *Geology: The Paradox of Earth and Man* (Boston, 1975).

The History of the Earth

Ager, Derek V., *The Nature of the Stratigraphic Record* (New York, 1975).

Clark, Thomas Henry, and Colin W. Stearn, *Geological Evolution of North America,* 2nd ed. (New York, 1968).

Dott, Robert H., and Roger L. Batten, *Evolution of the Earth* (New York, 1971).

Eicher, D.L., *Geologic Time* (Englewood Cliffs, N.J., 1968).

Faul, Henry, *Ages of Rocks, Planets and Stars* (New York, 1966).

Hurley, Patrick M., *How Old is the Earth?* (New York, 1959).

Kay, Marshall, and E.H. Colbert (eds.), *Stratigraphy and Life History* (New York, 1965).

Read, H.H., *Geology: An Introduction to Earth-History* (New York, 1949).

Vita-Finzi, Claudio, *Recent Earth History* (New York, 1975).

The New Geology—Drifting Continents

Anderson, Alan H., Jr., *Drifting Continents* (New York, 1971).

Calder, Nigel, *The Restless Earth: A Report on the New Geology* (New York, 1973).

Colbert, Edwin, *Wandering Lands and Animals* (New York, 1973).

Royal Society of London, *Geodynamics Today* (London, 1975).

Scientific American Editors, *Continents Adrift* (San Francisco, 1972).

Sullivan, Walter, *Continents in Motion* (New York, 1974).
Wyllie, Peter J., *The Way the Earth Works: An Introduction to the New Global Geology and Its Revolutionary Development* (New York, 1976).

Water on the Earth

Bardach, John, *Downstream: A Natural History of the River* (New York, 1966).
Barton, Robert, *Atlas of the Sea* (New York, 1974).
Bellamy, David, *The Life-Giving Sea* (New York, 1975).
Carson, Rachel, *The Sea Around Us* (New York, 1951; rev. ed., 1961).
Coker, R.E., *Streams, Lakes and Ponds* (New York, 1954).
Cousteau, Jacques, *Guide to the Sea* (New York, 1975).
———, and Phillipe Diolé, *Three Adventures: Galapagos, Titicaca, the Blue Holes* (New York, 1973).
Davis, Stanley, S.N., and Roger J.M. DeWiest, *Hydrogeology* (New York, 1966).
Freuchen, Peter, and David Loth, *Peter Freuchen's Book of the Seven Seas* (New York, 1957).
Geraghty, James J., et al., *Water Atlas of the United States,* 3rd ed. (Port Washington, N.Y., 1973).
Hill, M.N. (ed.), *The Sea: Ideas and Observations in the Study of the Seas,* 4 vols. (New York, 1962–71).
Huxley, Anthony (ed.), *Standard Encyclopedia of the World's Oceans and Islands* (New York, 1962).
Law of the Sea Institute, *Law of the Sea* (Cambridge, Mass., 1974).
Long, Edward J. (ed.), *Ocean Sciences* (New York, 1964).
McGraw-Hill Encyclopedia of Science and Technology Yearbook 1971, "Mariculture" (New York, 1971).
——— *Yearbook 1976,* "Permafrost" (New York, 1976).
Maury, Matthew F., *Physical Geography of the Sea and Its Meteorology* (Cambridge, Mass., 1963).
National Research Council, Study Panel on Assessing Potential Ocean Pollutants, *Assessing Potential Ocean Pollutants* (Washington, D.C., 1975).
Schultz, Gwen, *Glaciers and the Ice Age* (New York, 1963).
Scientific American Editors, *Oceanography* (San Francisco, 1971).
Shephard, Francis P., and Robert F. Dill, *Submarine Canyons and Other Sea Valleys* (New York, 1971).
UNESCO, et al., *Equalant I and Equalant II: Ocean-graphic Atlas, Vol. 1, Physical Oceanography* (Paris, 1973; New York, 1975).
Wertenbaker, W., *The Floor of the Sea* (Boston, 1974).
Zimmerman, J.D., *Irrigation* (New York, 1966).

Earthquakes and Volcanoes

Macdonald, Gordon Andrew, *Volcanoes* (Englewood Cliffs, N.J., 1972).
McGraw-Hill Encyclopedia of Science and Technology Yearbook 1975, "Earthquake Prediction" (New York, 1975).
Richter, Charles Francis, *Elementary Seismology* (San Francisco, 1958).

Atmosphere and Weather

Baldwin, John L. (maps), *Weather Atlas of the United States* (Detroit, 1975).
Kraus, E.B., *Atmosphere-Ocean Interactions* (New York, 1972).
McGraw-Hill Encyclopedia of Science and Technology Yearbook 1973, "Man's Impact on Climate" (New York, 1973).
——— *Yearbook 1976,* "Ozone in the Atmosphere" (New York, 1976).
Riley, Denis, and Lewis Spolton, *World Weather and Climate* (Cambridge, Mass., 1974).
Ruffner, James A., and Frank E. Bair (eds.), *The Weather Almanac* (Detroit, 1974).

Mineral Resources

Barger, H., and S.H. Schurr, *The Mining Industries, 1899–1939* (New York, 1975).
Bidwell, P.W., *Raw Materials* (Westport, Conn., 1974).
Fenton, Carroll Lane, and Mildred Adams Fenton, *Riches from the Earth,* rev. ed. (New York, 1970).
———, and ———, *A Rock Book* (New York, 1970).
Hurlbut, C.S., *Dana's Manual of Mineralogy,* 18th ed. (New York, 1971).
International Workshop on Environmental Problems of the Extractive Industries, 1973, *Extraction of Minerals and Energy: Today's Dilemmas* (Ann Arbor, Mich., 1974).
McDivitt, J.F., and G. Manners, *Minerals and Man: An Exploration of the World of Minerals and Metals,* rev. and enl. ed. (Baltimore, 1974).
National Research Council, *Mineral Resources and the Environment* (Washington, D.C., 1975).
Parson, Ruben A., *Conserving American Resources,* 3rd ed. (Englewood Cliffs, N.J., 1972).
Roberts, Willard L., et al., *Encyclopedia of Minerals* (New York, 1974).
Rowe, John, *The Hard-Rock Men* (New York, 1974).
Shaub, Benjamin M., *Treasures from the Earth: The World of Rocks and Minerals* (New York, 1975).
Shinkankas, J., *Prospecting for Gemstones and Minerals* (New York, 1975).
Vanders, Iris, and Paul F. Kerr, *Mineral Recognition* (New York, 1967).

Energy Resources

Fong, P.P., *Physical Science, Energy and Our Environment* (New York, 1976).
Hammond, A.C., et al., *Energy for the Future* (Washington, D.C., 1973).
Landes, Kenneth K., *Petroleum Geology of the United States* (New York, 1970).
Maddox, John, *Beyond the Energy Crisis* (New York, 1975).
Odum, Howard T., *Environmental Power and Society* (New York, 1971).
Titratsoo, E.N., *Oilfields of the World* (New York, 1973).
Tompkins, Dorothy Campbell, *Strip-Mining for Coal* (Berkeley, Calif., 1973).
Udall, Stewart, et al., *The Energy Balloon* (New York, 1974).

Preserving the Earth

Becht, J.E., and L.D. Belzung, *World Resource Management* (Englewood Cliffs, N.J., 1975).
Brower, David, *Only a Little Planet* (New York, 1975).
Calder, Nigel (ed.), *Nature in the Round: A Guide to Environmental Science* (New York, 1974).
Caudill, Harry M., *My Land is Dying* (New York, 1973).
Commoner, Barry, *The Closing Circle* (New York, 1971).
Ehrlich, P.R., and A.H. Ehrlich, *The End of Affluence* (New York, 1974).
Giddings, J. Calvin, *Chemistry, Man, and Environmental Change* (New York, 1973).
Harte, John, and Robert M. Socolow (eds.), *Patient Earth* (New York, 1972).
McGraw-Hill Encyclopedia of Science and Technology Yearbook 1972, "Solid-Waste Management" (New York, 1972).
Meier, R.L., *Planning for an Urban World: The Design of Resource Conserving Cities* (Cambridge, Mass., 1974).
Owen, O.S., *Natural Resources Conservation,* 2nd ed. (New York, 1975).
Pinchot, Gifford, *The Fight for Conservation* (New York, 1910; repr., Seattle, 1969).
Rienow, Robert, and Leona Train Rienow, *Moment in the Sun: A Report on the Deteriorating Quality of the American Environment* (New York, 1967).
Sondheimer, E., and John B. Simeon (eds.), *Chemical Ecology* (New York, 1970).
Smith, Frank E., *Conservation in the United States,* 5 vols. (New York, 1971).
Smith, G.H. (ed.), *Conservation of Natural Resources,* 4th ed. (New York, 1971).

Agriculture

Barnard, C.S., and J.S. Nix, *Farm Planning and Control* (New York, 1973).
Boshoff, W.H., *Using Field Machinery* (New York, 1968).
Brewbaker, James L., *Agricultural Genetics* (Englewood Cliffs, N.J., 1964).
Brown, Lester R., *Seeds of Change: The Green Revolution and Development in the 1970's* (New York, 1970).
Castle, Emery, et al., *Farm Business Management: The Decision Making Process,* 2nd ed. (New York, 1972).
Crawford, Patricia, *Homesteading: A Practical Guide to Living off the Land* (New York, 1975).
Fassell, G.E., *Farming Techniques from Prehistoric to Modern Times* (New York, 1966).
Evenson, R.E., and Y. Kisley, *Agricultural Research and Productivity* (New Haven, Conn., 1975).
Foth, Henry D., and Z.M. Turk, *Fundamentals of Soil Science,* 5th ed. (New York, 1972).
Grigg, D.B., *The Agricultural Systems of the World* (New York, 1974).
Gunther, F.A., and L.R. Jeppson, *Modern Insecticides and World Food Production* (New York, 1960).
Higham, Charles, *Earliest Farmers and the First Cities* (New York, 1972).
Kains, M.G., *Five Acres and Independence* (New York, 1940; repr. 1973).
Kepner, Robert A., et al., *Principles of Farm Machinery* (Westport, Conn., 1972).
Pollution and the Use of Chemicals in Agriculture (Ann Arbor, 1974).

Food and Famine

Aykroyd, W.R., *The Conquest of Famine* (New York, 1975).
Borgstrom, G., *The Hungry Planet: the Modern World at the Edge of Famine* (New York, 1966; rev. ed., 1972).
Brown, Lester, and Gail W. Finsterbush, *Man and His Environment: Food* (New York, 1972).
Castro, Josue de, *The Geography of Hunger* (Boston, 1952).
DeKruif, Paul, *Hunger Fighters* (New York, 1967).
Heiser, Charles B., Jr., *Seed to Civilization: The Story of Man's Food* (San Francisco, 1973).
Hunter, Beatrice Trum, *Consumer Beware! Your Food and What's Being Done to It* (New York, 1971).
Johnson, Arnold H., and Martin S. Peterson, *Encyclopedia of Food Technology* (Westport, Conn., 1974).
Tannahill, Reay, *Food in History* (New York, 1973).
Trager, James, *The Foodbook* (New York, 1970).
World Atlas of Food (New York, 1974).

Food Plants

Allard, Robert W., *Principles of Plant Breeding* (New York, 1960).
Edlin, H.L., *Plants and Man* (New York, 1969).
Faust, Joan Lee, *The New York Times Book of Vegetable Gardening* (New York, 1975).
Fenton, Carroll L., and Hermine B. Kitchen, *Plants We Live On: The Story of Grains and Vegetables,* rev. ed. (New York, 1971).
Gibbons, Euell, *Stalking the Wild Asparagus* (New York, 1970).
Harrison, S.G., et al., *Oxford Book of Food Plants* (New York, 1969).
Hedrick, V.P. (ed.), *Sturtevant's Edible Plants of the World* (New York, 1972).
Hvass, Else, *Plants That Feed Us* (New York, 1970).
———, *Plants That Serve Us* (New York, 1970).
Hyams, Edward, *Plants in the Service of Man* (Philadelphia, 1972).
Knutsen, Karl, *Wild Plants You Can Eat* (New York, 1975).
Krutch, Joseph W., *Herbal* (Boston, 1975).
Lehner, Ernst, and Johanna Lehner, *Folklore and Odysseys of Food and Medicinal Plants* (New York, 1973).
Leighton, Ann, *Early American Gardens: For Meate or Medicine* (Boston, 1970).
Leonard, Warren H., and John H. Martin, *Cereal Crops* (New York, 1963).
Matz, Samuel A., *Cereal Science* (Westport, Conn., 1969).
Muenscher, Walter C., and M.A. Rice, *Garden Spice and Wild Pot-Herbs* (Ithaca, N.Y., 1955).
Popenole, Wilson, *Manual of Tropical and Subtropical Fruits* (New York, 1974).
Purseglove, J.W., *Tropical Crops,* 3 vols. (New York, 1969–1972).
Stavis, B., *Making Green Revolution* (Ithaca, N.Y., 1974).
Western, J., *Diseases of Plant Crops* (New York, 1972).

Plant Products

Baron, Stanley W., *Brewed in America: A History of Beer and Ale in the United States* (New York, 1962).
Beadle, Leigh, *Brew It Yourself,* rev. ed. (New York, 1973).
Bramah, Edward, *Tea and Coffee: A Modern View of 300 Years of Tradition* (London, 1972).
Densmore, Frances, *How Indians Use Wild Plants for Food, Medicine and Crafts* (New York, 1974).
Lichine, Alexis, *Alexis Lichine's New Encyclopedia of Wines and Spirits,* 2nd ed. (New York, 1974).
Johnson, Hugh, *Wine,* rev. ed. (New York, 1975).
Porter, John, *All About Beer* (New York, 1975).
Schapira, Joel, et al., *The Book of Coffee and Tea: A Guide to the Appreciation of Fine Coffees, Teas and Herbal Beverages* (New York, 1975).
Simon, Andre L., *Wines of the World,* rev. ed. (New York, 1972).

Domesticated Animals and Their Products

Campbell, John R., and John F. Lasley, *The Science of Animals that Serve Mankind,* 2nd ed. (New York, 1975).
Cole, H.H., and Magnar Ronning, *Animal Agriculture: The Biology of Domestic Animals and Their Use by Man* (San Francisco, 1974).
Hyams, Edward, *Animals in the Service of Man* (Philadelphia, 1972).
Misch, Robert J., *Quick Guide to Cheese* (New York, 1973).
Neumann, A.L., and R.R. Snapp, *Beef Cattle,* 6th ed. (New York, 1969).
Norris, P.E., *Everything You Want to Know About Milk, Cheese and Eggs* (New York, 1973).
Radke, Don, *Cheese-Making at Home: The Complete Illustrated Guide* (New York, 1974).
Rice, J.E., and H.E. Botsford, *Practical Poultry Management,* 6th ed. (New York, 1956).
Rouse, John E., *Cattle of North America,* 3 vols. (Norman, Okla., 1973).
———, *World Cattle,* 2 vols. (Norman, Okla., 1970).
Zeuner, Friedrich, *A History of Domesticated Animals* (New York, 1963).

Forestry

Duerr, William A., *Fundamentals of Forestry Economics* (New York, 1960).
Edlin, H.L., *Trees and Man* (New York, 1976).
McGraw-Hill Encyclopedia of Science and Technology Yearbook 1974, "Wood" (New York, 1974).
Minckler, L.S., *Woodland Ecology* (Syracuse, 1975).
Peattie, Donald C. (ed.), *Natural History of Trees of Eastern and Central North America* (Boston, 1966).
Schenck, C.A., *The Birth of Forestry in America* (Santa Cruz, Calif., 1974).

Fisheries

Browning, Robert, *Fisheries of the North Pacific: History, Species, Gear, Processes* (Edmonds, Alaska, 1974).
Cushing, D.H., *Fisheries Resources of the Sea and Their Management* (Oxford, Eng., 1975).
———, *Marine Ecology and Fisheries* (Cambridge, Eng., 1975).
Firth, Frank E., *Encyclopedia of Marine Resources* (New York, 1969).
Hickling, C.F., *The Farming of Fish* (New York, 1968).

LIFE ON EARTH

Periodicals that report on events and developments concerning "Life on Earth" include *Audubon, Bioscience, Conservationist, Environment, National Geographic, National Wildlife, Natural History, Science, Scientific American, Smithsonian*

General

Asimov, Isaac, *A Short History of Biology* (New York, 1964).
Dubos, René, *Dreams of Reason: Science and Utopias* (New York, 1961).
———, *Man Adapting* (New Haven, 1965).
Gardner, Eldon J., *History of Biology,* 3rd ed. (New York, 1972).
Gray, Peter, *Encyclopedia of the Biological Sciences* (New York, 1970).
Monod, Jacques, *Chance and Necessity: An Essay on the Natural Philosophy of Modern Biology* (New York, 1971).
von Frisch, Karl, *Man and the Living World* (New York, 1963).

Evolution

Alvin, K.L., et. al. (eds.), *Studies on Fossil Plants* (New York, 1968).
Ardrey, Robert, *African Genesis* (New York, 1961).
Asimov, Isaac, *The Wellsprings of Life* (New York, 1962).
Bates, Marston, *Man in Nature,* 2nd ed. (Englewood Cliffs, N.J., 1964).
Beerbower, James R., *Search for the Past: An Introduction to Paleontology,* 2nd ed. (Englewood Cliffs, N.J., 1968).
Blum, Harold F., *Time's Arrow and Evolution* (Princeton, N.J., 1965).
Clarke, W.E., *Fossil Evidence for Human Evolution: An Introduction to the Study of Paleoanthropology,* 2nd ed. (Chicago, 1964).
———, *Antecedents of Man: An Introduction to the Evolution of the Primates* (New York, 1971).
Darwin, Charles, *On the Origin of Species* (London, 1859; repr. Cambridge, Mass., 1975).
Dunbar, Carl O., and Karl M. Waage, *Historical Geology,* 3rd ed. (New York, 1969).
Eiseley, Loren, *The Immense Journey* (New York, 1957).
———, *Darwin's Century; Evolution and the Men Who Discovered It* (Garden City, N.Y., 1958).
Fenton, Carroll L., and Mildred A. Fenton, *Fossil Book* (New York, 1959).
Greene, John C., *The Death of Adam: Evolution and Its Impact on Western Thought* (Ames, Iowa, 1959).
Hamblin, Dora J., et al., *Life Before Man* (New York, 1972).
Howard, Robert W., *The Dawnseekers: The First History of American Paleontology* (New York, 1975).
Huxley, Julian, *Evolution in Action* (New York, 1953).
Krutch, Joseph W., *The Great Chain of Life* (Boston, 1957).
Kurten, Bjorn, *Age of Dinosaurs* (New York, 1968).
———, *Age of Mammals* (New York, 1972).
Leakey, L.S., P.V. Tobias, and M.D. Leakey (eds.), *Olduvai Gorge,* 3 vols (Cambridge, Eng., 1965; repr. New York, 1972).

Levi-Setti, Riccardo, *Trilobites: A Photographic Atlas* (Chicago, 1975).
Ley, Willy, *Exotic Zoology,* rev. ed. (New York, 1959).
MacFall, Russell P., and Jay Wollin, *Fossils for Amateurs* (Princeton, N.J., 1972).
McGraw-Hill Encyclopedia of Science and Technology Yearbook 1971, "Origin of Life" (New York, 1971).
Matthew, William D., *Climate and Evolution* (New York, 1974).
Moore, Ruth, *Man, Time and Fossils,* rev. ed. (New York, 1961).
———, *Evolution,* rev. ed. (New York, 1969).
Romer, Alfred S., *The Vertebrate Story,* rev. ed. (Chicago, 1959).
———, *The Procession of Life* (New York, 1972).
Silverberg, Robert, *Forgotten by Time: A Book of Living Fossils* (New York, 1966).
Vanderpool, Harold Y., *Darwin and Darwinism* (Indianapolis, 1973).

Genetics and Cell Biology
Ashton, Beryl G., *Genes, Chromosomes, and Evolution* (Boston, 1969).
Beadle, George W., and Muriel Beadle, *Language of Life: An Introduction to the Science of Genetics* (New York, 1966).
Bodmer, W.F., and L.L. Cavalli-Sforza, *Genetics, Evolution and Man* (San Francisco, 1976).
Borek, Ernst, *Atoms Within Us* (New York, 1961).
———, *The Sculpture of Life* (New York, 1973).
———, *Code of Life* (New York, 1975).
Dagley, S., and D.E. Nicholson, *An Introduction to Metabolic Pathways* (New York, 1970).
Dobzhansky, Theodosius, *Genetics of the Evolutionary Process* (New York, 1971).
Evans, A., *Glossary of Molecular Biology* (New York, 1975).
Fraenkel-Conrat, Heinz, and Robert R. Wagner, (eds.), *Comprehensive Virology, Volume I: Descriptive Catalogue of Viruses* (New York, 1974).
Gardner, E.J., *Principles of Genetics,* 5th ed. (New York, 1975).
———, and Thomas R. Mertens, *Genetics Laboratory Investigations,* 6th ed. (Minneapolis, 1975).
Hayes, W., *Genetics of Bacteria and Their Viruses: Studies in Basic Genetics and Molecular Biology,* 2nd ed. (New York, 1976).
King, Robert C., *A Dictionary of Genetics,* 2nd rev. ed. (New York, 1974).
Kuspira, John, and George W. Walker, *Genetics: Questions and Problems* (New York, 1973).
Olby, Robert, *The Path to the Double Helix* (Seattle, 1974).
Srb, Adrian M. (ed.), *Genes, Enzymes and Populations* (New York, 1973).
Wallace, Bruce, *Chromosomes, Giant Molecules and Evolution* (New York, 1966).
Watson, James D., *Molecular Biology of the Gene,* 2nd ed. (New York, 1970).

The Microscopic World
Curtis, Helena, *Marvelous Animals: An Introduction to the Protozoa* (New York, 1968).
Hegner, Robert, *Big Fleas Have Little Fleas or, Who's Who Among the Protozoa* (New York, 1968).
Jahn, L., *How to Know the Protozoa* (Dubuque, Iowa, 1949).
Monod, Jacques, and E. Borek, (eds.), *Of Microbes and Life* (New York, 1971).
Rosebury, Theodor, *Life on Man* (New York, 1969).
———, *Microbes and Morals* (New York, 1976).
Vickerman, Keith, and F.E. Cox, *Protozoa* (Boston, 1967).
Wyss, O., and C.E. Eklund, *Microorganisms and Man* (New York, 1971).

Plants
Alexopoulos, Constantine J., and Harold C. Bold, *Algae and Fungi* (New York, 1967).
Anderson, Bernice H., and Arthur H. Holmgren, *A Beginner's Guide to Mountain Flowers* (Logan, Utah, 1968).
Barber, Peter, and C.E. Lucas-Phillips, *The Trees Around Us* (Chicago, 1975).
Bell, P.R., and C.L. Woodcock, *The Diversity of Green Plants,* 2nd ed. (Reading, Mass., 1972).
Bews, John W., *The World's Grasses: Their Differentiation, Distribution, Economics and Ecology* (New York, 1973).
Birdseye, Clarence, and Eleanor Birdseye, *Growing Woodland Plants* (New York, 1972).
Bland, John, *Forests of Lilliput: The Realm of Mosses and Lichens* (Englewood Cliffs, N.J., 1971).
Bloom, Adrian, *Conifers for Your Garden* (New York, 1975).
Charles, Vera K., *Introduction to Mushroom Hunting* (New York, 1974).
Cobb, Boughton, *Field Guide to the Ferns and Their Related Families* (Boston, 1975).
Conard, Henry S., *How to Know the Mosses and Liverworts,* rev. ed. (Dubuque, Iowa, 1956).
Dallimore, W., and A.B. Jackson, *Handbook of Coniferae and Ginkgoaceae,* 4th ed. (New York, 1966).
Darnell, A.W., *Unfamiliar Flowers for Your Garden* (New York, 1975).
Davis, Bette, *The World of Mosses* (New York, 1975).
Dietz, Marjorie J., *10,000 Garden Questions Answered by 20 Experts,* 3rd ed. (New York, 1974).
Durand, Herbert, *Fieldbook of Common Ferns,* rev. ed. (New York, 1949).
Eyre, S.R., *Vegetation and Soils: A World Picture,* 2nd ed. (Chicago, 1968).
Fernald, Merritt L., and Alfred C. Kinsey, *Edible Wild Plants of Eastern North America* (New York, 1958).
Funder, Sigurd, *Practical Mycology: Manual for Identification of Fungi,* 3rd rev. ed. (New York, 1968).
Galston, Arthur W., *The Life of the Green Plant* (Englewood Cliffs, N.J., 1961; 2nd ed., 1964).
Grimm, W.C., *Recognizing Flowering Wild Plants* (New York, 1974).
Heywood, Vernon H., *Plant Taxonomy* (New York, 1967).
Hitchcock, A.S., *Manual of Grasses of the United States,* 2 vols. (Washington, D.C., 1935; 2nd rev. ed., 1950)
McIlvaine, Charles, and Robert MacAdam, *One Thousand American Fungi* (New York, 1973).
Mertens, Thomas, and Forrest F. Stevenson, *Plant Life Cycles* (New York, 1975).
Meunscher, Walter C., *Poisonous Plants of the United States,* rev. ed. (New York, 1975).
Mohlenbrock, Robert H., *Flowering Plants: Lilies to Orchids* (Carbondale, Ill., 1970).
O'Brien, Terence P., and Margaret E. McCully, *Plant Structure and Development* (New York, 1969).
Perry, Frances (ed.), *Flowers of the World* (New York, 1972).
Peterson, R.T., *Field Guide to Wildflowers* (New York, 1968).
Petrides, G., *Guide to Trees and Shrubs* (New York, 1972).
Salisbury, F., *Flowering Process* (New York, 1963).
Taylor, Norman, *One Thousand and One Questions Answered About Flowers* (New York, 1963).
Whitehead, Stanley B., *The Observer's Book of Flowering Trees and Shrubs* (New York, 1972).

Animals—Anatomy, Behavior, Distribution
Ardrey, Robert, *Territorial Imperative* (New York, 1966).
Barker, Will, *Familiar Animals of America* (New York, 1956).
Barnett, Samuel A., *Instinct and Intelligence: Behavior in Animals and Men* (Englewood Cliffs, N.J., 1967).
Caras, Roger, *The Private Lives of Animals* (New York, 1974).
———, *Venomous Animals of the World* (Englewood Cliffs, N.J., 1974).
Darlington, Philip J., *Zoogeography: The Geographic Distribution of Animals* (New York, 1957).
Eisner, Thomas, et al. (eds.), *Animal Behavior: Readings from Scientific American* (San Francisco, 1975).
Grzimek, Bernhard (ed.), *Grzimek's Animal Life Encyclopedia* (New York, 1972).
Hanson, Earl D., *Animal Diversity,* 3rd ed. (Englewood Cliffs, N.J., 1972).
Michelmore, Susan, *Sexual Reproduction* (New York, 1964).
Milne, Lorus, et al., *The Secret Life of Animals: Pioneering Discoveries in Animal Behavior* (New York, 1975).
Murie, Olaus J., *A Field Guide to Animal Tracks,* 2nd ed. (Boston, 1975).
Romer, Alfred S., *The Vertebrate Story,* 4th ed. (Chicago, 1959).
Tinbergen, Nikolaas, *Curious Naturalists* (New York, 1968).
von Frisch, Karl, *Animal Architecture* (New York, 1974).

Simple Animals
Bartsch, Paul, *Mollusks* (New York, 1968).
Bush, Eric W., *Flowers of the Sea* (New York, 1970).
Buchsbaum, Ralph, *Animals Without Backbones,* 2nd ed. (Chicago, 1972).
Coe, Wesley R., *Starfishes, Serpent Stars, Sea Urchins, and Sea Cucumbers of the Northeast* (New York, 1972).
Lenhoff, Howard M., and W. Farnsworth Loomis (eds.), *Biology of the Hydra and Some Other Coelenterates* (Coral Gables, Fla., 1961).
Nichols, David, and John Cooke, *Oxford Book of Invertebrates* (New York, 1971).
Pimentel, Richard A., *Invertebrate Identification Manual* (New York, 1967).
Solem, Alan, *The Shell Makers: Introducing Mollusks* (New York, 1974).
Stix, Hugh, Marguerite Stix, and R. Tucker Abbott, *The Shell: Five Hundred Years of Inspired Design* (New York, 1973).
Straughan, Robert P., *Keeping Live Corals and Invertebrates* (New York, 1975).
———, *The Marine Collector's Guide* (New York 1975).
Wagner, R.J.L., and R.T. Abbott, *Van Nostrand's Standard Catalogue of Shells* (Princeton, N.J., 1967).
Webb, Walter F., *Handbook for Shell Collectors,* 16th rev. ed. (Wellesley Hills, Mass., 1948).
Wells, M., *Lower Animals* (New York, 1968).

Insects and their Relatives
Anderson, Margaret J., *Exploring the Insect World* (New York, 1974).
Clausen, Lucy W., *Insect Fact and Folklore* (New York, 1962).
Dickens, Michael, and Eric Storey, *The World of Butterflies* (New York, 1975).
Emsley, Michael G., *Butterfly Magic* (New York, 1975).
Fabre, J. Henri, *Life of the Spider* (New York, 1913; repr. 1971)
Farb, Peter, *Insects* (New York, 1962).
Kaston, B.J., *How to Know the Spiders* (Dubuque, Iowa, 1972).
Klots, Alexander, *Living Insects of the World* (New York, 1975).
Lutz, Frank E., *Field Book of Insects of U.S. and Canada,* rev. ed. (New York, 1948).
Price, Peter W., *Insect Ecology* (New York, 1975).
Sharp, David, *Insects,* 2 vols. (New York, 1970).
Smart, Paul, *The International Butterfly Book* (New York, 1975).
Tweedie, Michael, *Atlas of Insects* (New York, 1974).
von Frisch, Karl, *The Dancing Bees: An Account of the Life and Senses of the Honey Bee* (New York, 1955).
Watson, Alan, and Paul E.S. Whalley, *The Dictionary of Butterflies and Moths in Color* (New York, 1975).
Wilson, Edward O., *The Insect Societies* (Cambridge, Mass., 1971).

Fish
Axelrod, Herbert R., *Fresh Water Fishes* (Neptune, N.J., 1974).
The Complete Aquarists' Guide to Freshwater Tropical Fishes (New York, 1970).
Cooper, Allan, *Fishes of the World* (New York, 1972).
Cousteau, Jacques, *Life and Death in a Coral Sea* (New York, 1971).
Greenwood, P.H., and J.R. Norman, *A History of Fishes,* 3rd ed. (New York, 1975).
Herold, Earl, *Living Fishes of the World* (New York, 1975).
Innes, William T., *Exotic Aquarium Fishes* (New York, 1935; 19th ed., Philadelphia, 1956).
Julian, T.W., *The Dell Encyclopedia of Tropical Fish* (New York, 1974).
Lindberg, G.U., *Fishes of the World: A Key to Families and a Checklist* (New York, 1974).
Madsen, J.M., *Aquarium Fishes in Color* (New York, 1975).
Marshall, Norman B., *The Life of Fishes* (Cleveland, 1966).
Ulrich, Heinz, *America's Best Lake, Stream and River Fishing* (New York, 1962).
Walden, Howard T., *Familiar Freshwater Fishes of America* (New York, 1964).
Walker, Braz, *Oddball Fishes and Other Strange Creatures of the Deep* (New York, 1975).
———, *Sharks and Loaches* (Neptune, N.J., 1974).
Wheeler, Alwyne, *Fishes of the World: An Illustrated Dictionary* (New York, 1975).

Amphibians and Reptiles
Breen, John F., *Encyclopedia of Amphibians and Reptiles* (Neptune, N.J., 1974).
Cochran, Doris, *Living Amphibians of the World* (New York, 1966).
Conant, Roger, *A Field Guide to Reptiles and Amphibians of Eastern and Central North America,* 2nd ed. (Boston, 1975).
Morris, Percy, *An Introduction to the Reptiles and Amphibians of the United States* (New York, 1974).
Pope, Clifford H., *Reptile World* (New York, 1955).
Schmidt, Karl P., and Robert F. Inger, *Living Reptiles of the World* (New York, 1975).
Stebbins, Robert C., *A Field Guide to the Western Reptiles and Amphibians* (Boston, 1966).
Stidworthy, John, *Snakes of the World* (New York, 1974).

Birds
American Ornithologists Union, *Check-List of North American Birds,* 5th ed. (Baltimore, 1957).
Audubon, John J., *Audubon and His Journals,* 2 vols., Maria Audubon (ed.) (New York, 1897; repr. 1960).
Baird, Spencer F., et al., *Birds of North America* (Philadelphia, 1860; repr. New York, 1974).
Bent, Arthur C., *Life Histories of North American Birds,* 20 vols. (Washington, D.C., 1919–67).
Booth, Ernest S., *Field Record for Birds* (Anacortes, Wisc., 1960).
Bruun, Bertel, *The Dell Encyclopedia of Birds* (New York, 1974).
Campbell, Bruce, and Richard T. Holmes (eds.), *The Dictionary of Birds in Color* (New York, 1974).
Chapman, Frank M., *Handbook of Birds of Eastern North America,* 2nd ed. (New York, 1940).
Delacour, Jean, *The Waterfowl of the World,* 4 vols. (New York, 1974).
Dennis, John V., *A Complete Guide to Bird Feeding* (New York, 1975).
Dorst, Jean, *The Migration of Birds* (Boston, 1962).
———, *The Life of Birds* (New York, 1974).
Elman, Robert, and Walter Osborne, *The Atlantic Flyway* (New York, 1973).
Hall, Henry M., *A Gathering of Shore Birds* (Greenwich, Conn., 1960).
Kaufman, John, *Wings, Sun and Stars: The Story of Migration* (New York, 1969).
Krutch, Joseph W., and Paul S. Eriksson (eds.), *Treasury of Birdlore* (New York, 1969).
Merne, Oscar J., *Ducks, Geese, and Swans* (New York, 1974).
Peterson, Roger T., *Field Guide to Western Birds* (Boston, 1972).
Pettingill, Olin Sewall, Jr., *The Bird Watcher's America* (New York, 1965).
Porter, Eliot, *Birds of North America* (New York, 1972).
Robbins, Chandler S., et al., *A Guide to Field Identification: Birds of North America* (New York, 1966).
Saunders, Aretas, *A Guide to Bird Songs* (New York, 1959).
Scott, Peter M. (ed.), *The World Atlas of Birds* (New York, 1974).
Thomas, Gilliard E., *Living Birds of the World* (New York, 1975).

Mammals
Anderson, Sydney, and J.K. Jones, Jr. (eds.), *Recent Mammals of the World: A Synopsis of Families* (New York, 1967).
Bueler, Lois E., *Wild Dogs of the World* (New York, 1973).
Cousteau, Jacques, *Whale: Mighty Monarch of the Sea* (New York, 1972).
———, and Philippe Diolé, *Dolphins and Freedom* (New York, 1975).
Fichter, George S., *Cats* (Racine, Wisc., 1967).
Graham, Alistair D., and Peter Beard, *The Eyelids of Morning* (Greenwich, Conn., 1973).
Hahn, Emily, *On the Side of Apes* (New York, 1971).
Hanney, Peter W., *Rodents: Their Lives and Habits* (New York, 1975).
Leakey, Louis S.B., et al., *Adam or Ape* (Morristown, N.J., 1971).
Leen, Nina and Alvin Novick, *World of Bats* (New York, 1970).
McGraw-Hill Encyclopedia of Science and Technology Yearbook 1975, "Mammalian Fertilization" (New York, 1975).
McNulty, Faith, *The Great Whales* (New York, 1974).
Mochi, Ugo, and T. Donald Carter, *Hoofed Mammals of the World* (New York, 1971).
Morcombe, Michael, *Australian Marsupials and Other Native Animals* (New York, 1974).
Morris, Desmond, *Human Zoo* (New York, 1970).
Osman, William C., *Evolutionary Biology of the Primates* (New York, 1972).
Sanderson, Ivan, *Living Mammals of the World* (New York, 1975).
Schaller, George B., *Mountain Gorilla: Ecology and Behavior* (Chicago, 1963).
Scheffer, Victor B., *Year of the Whale* (New York, 1969).
Simonds, Paul E., *The Social Primates* (New York, 1974).
Simons, Elwyn L., *Primate Evolution: An Introduction to Man's Place in Nature* (New York, 1972).
van Lawick-Goodall, Jane, *My Friends the Wild Chimpanzees* (Washington, D.C., 1967).
Walker, Ernest P., et al., *Mammals of the World,* 2 vols., 3rd ed. (Baltimore, 1975).

Ecology—General
Colinvaux, P.A., *Introduction to Ecology* (New York, 1972).
Curry-Lindahl, Kai, *Conservation for Survival: An Ecological Strategy* (New York, 1972).
Darlington, P.J., *Zoogeography: The Geographical Distribution of Animals* (New York, 1957).
Ehrenfeld, David, *Conserving Life on Earth* (New York, 1972).
Ehrlich, Paul, *Man and the Ecosphere* (San Francisco, 1971).

Faith, W.L., and A.A. Atkisson, *Air Pollution,* 2nd ed. (New York, 1972).
Huth, Hans, *Nature and the American: Three Centuries of Changing Attitudes* (Lincoln, Neb., 1972).
Marine, Gene, *America the Raped* (New York, 1969).

Habitats
Arnold, Augusta, *Sea Beach at Ebbtide* (New York, 1968).
Arnov, Boris, Jr., *Homes Beneath the Sea: An Introduction to Ocean Ecology* (Boston, 1969).
Bellamy, David, and Michael Boorer, *Green Worlds: Plants, Forests and Forest Life* (New York, 1976).
Beston, Henry, *The Outermost House, A Year of Life on the Great Beach of Cape Cod* (New York, 1928).
Carson, Rachel, *Under the Sea Wind: A Naturalist's Picture of Ocean Life* (New York, 1952).
Chapman, Valentine S., *Salt Marshes and Salt Deserts of the World* (London, 1960).
Costello, David, *Prairie World* (New York, 1969).
———, *The Desert World* (New York, 1972).
———, *The Mountain World* (New York, 1972).
David, Millard, *The Near Woods* (New York, 1975).
Humphrey, Robert R., *The Desert Grassland* (Tucson, Ariz., 1968).
Jaeger, Edmund C., *The North American Deserts* (Palo Alto, Calif., 1957).
Krutch, Joseph W., *Voice of the Desert* (New York, 1955).
———, *Desert Year* (New York, 1963).
Mandahl-Barth, G., *Woodland Life,* 2nd ed. (New York, 1974).
Meggers, Betty J. (ed.), *Tropical Forest Ecosystems in Africa and South America: A Comparative Review* (New York, 1973).
Muir, John, *Gentle Wilderness: The Sierra Nevada* (San Francisco, 1967).
———, *The Wilderness World of John Muir* (Boston, 1976).
Neal, Ernest G., *Woodland Ecology,* 2nd ed. (Cambridge, Mass., 1960).
Reid, George K., *Ecology of Inland Waters and Estuaries* (New York, 1961).
Richards, Paul W., *The Tropical Rain Forest* (Cambridge, Eng., 1952).
Ricketts, Edward F., and Jack Calvin, *Between Pacific Tides,* 4th ed. (Palo Alto, Calif., 1968).
Russell, Richard J., *River Plains and Sea Coasts* (Berkeley, Calif., 1967).
Spurr, Stephen H., and Burton V. Barnes, *Forest Ecology,* 2nd ed. (New York, 1973).
Straughan, Robert P., *Exploring the Reef,* rev. ed. (New York, 1973).
Teal, John, and Mildred Teal, *Life and Death of the Salt Marsh* (New York, 1969).
Weaver, John E., *North American Prairie* (Lincoln, Neb., 1954).
Zottoli, Robert, *Introduction to Marine Environments* (St. Louis, 1973).
Zwinger, Ann H., and Beatrice E. Willard, *Land Above the Trees: A Guide to American Alpine Tundra* (New York, 1972).

Animal Conservation
Bridges, William, *A Gathering of Animals* (New York, 1974).
Burton, Jane, *Animals of the African Year* (New York, 1972).
Carr, Archie, *Land and Wildlife of Africa,* rev. ed. (New York, 1967).
Crandall, Lee S., *Management of Wild Mammals in Captivity* (Chicago, 1964).
———, *Zoo Man's Notebook* (Chicago, 1966).
Durrell, Gerald, *Birds, Beasts and Relatives* (New York, 1969).
———, *A Bevy of Beasts* (New York, 1973).
Ehrlich, Paul, *The Population Bomb,* rev. ed. (River City, Mass., 1975).
Fitter, Richard, *Vanishing Wild Animals of the World* (New York, 1969).
Greenway, James C., Jr., *Extinct and Vanishing Birds of the World,* (New York, 1958).
Jordan, Emil L., *Animal Atlas of the World* (New York, 1969).
Moorehead, Alan, *No Room in the Ark* (New York, 1960).
Pennant, Thomas, *Arctic Zoology* (New York, 1974).
Schaller, George B., *Serengeti: A Kingdom of Predators* (New York, 1972).
———, *Golden Shadows, Flying Hooves* (New York, 1973).
Summers, Gerald, *An African Bestiary* (New York, 1974).
Whitehead, Peter J., *Wildlife of the South Seas* (New York, 1967).

MAN

Periodicals that report on the human body, health, and human behavior include *American Anthropologist, American Psychologist, Family Health, Human Behavior, Foreign Affairs, National Geographic, Natural History, New Scientist, Parents' Magazine, Psychology Today, Science, Scientific American,* and *Smithsonian.*

The Human Body—Structure, Function, and Health
Anthony, Catherine P., *Structure & Function of the Body,* 4th ed. (St. Louis, 1972).
Asimov, Isaac, *Human Body and Operation* (New York, 1964).
Boyd, William, *An Introduction to the Study of Disease,* 6th ed. (Philadelphia, 1971).
Brecher, E.M., *Licit and Illicit Drugs* (New York, 1972).
Castiglioni, Arturo, *A History of Medicine* (New York, 1941; repr. 1973).
Clark, Duncan, and Brian W. MacMahon, *Preventive Medicine* (Boston, 1967).
Clark, Randolph L., and Russell W. Cumley (eds.), *The Book of Health,* 3rd ed. (New York, 1973).
Colquhoun, W.P., *Biological Rhythms and Human Performance* (New York, 1971).
De Coursey, Russell M., *The Human Organism,* 4th rev. ed. (New York, 1974).
De Kruif, Paul, *Microbe Hunters* (New York, 1926).
———, *Men Against Death* (New York, 1934).
Dubos, René, *Mirage of Health* (New York, 1971).
Ferguson, L. Kraeer, and John H. Kerr, *Explain It To Me, Doctor* (Philadelphia, 1971).
Fielder, Mildred, *Plant Medicine and Folklore* (New York, 1975).
Grinspoon, Lester, *Marijuana Reconsidered* (New York, 1972).
Fishbein, Morris (ed.), *Modern Family Health Guide,* rev. ed. (New York, 1968).
Hamburger, Jean, *The Power and the Frailty: The Future of Medicine and the Future of Man* (New York, 1973).
Holvey, David N. (ed.), *The Merck Manual of Diagnosis and Therapy,* 12th ed. (Rahway, N.J., 1972).
Jacob, Stanley W., and Clarice A. Francone, *Structure and Function in Man,* 3rd ed. (Philadelphia, 1974).
Jarvis, D.C., *Folk Medicine: A Vermont Doctor's Guide to Good Health* (New York, 1958).
Lasagna, Louis, *Doctor's Dilemmas* (New York, 1962).
Luria, Salvador E., *Life: The Unfinished Experiment* (New York, 1973).
———, *Thirty-six Lectures in Biology* (Cambridge, Mass., 1975).
McGraw-Hill Encyclopedia of Science and Technology Yearbook 1971, "Organ Culture" (New York, 1971).
——— *Yearbook 1972,* "Pathology of Heavy Metals" (New York, 1972).
——— *Yearbook 1973,* "Biorheology;" "Health-care Delivery Systems" (New York, 1973).
——— *Yearbook 1974,* "Internal Prostheses" (New York, 1974).
——— *Yearbook 1976,* "Cryobiology;" "Genetic Engineering" (New York, 1976).
Memmler, Ruth L., and Ruth B. Rada, *Human Body in Health and Disease,* 3rd ed. (Philadelphia, 1970).
Miller, Benjamin F., and John J. Burt, *Good Health,* 3rd ed. (Philadelphia, 1972).
Mitchell, Helen S., et al., *Cooper's Nutrition in Health and Disease,* 15th ed. (Philadelphia, 1968).
Netter, Frank H. (illus.), *The CIBA Collection of Medical Illustrations,* 6 vols. (Summit, N.J., 1974).
Robinson, Corinne H., *Basic Nutrition and Diet Therapy,* 3rd ed. (New York, 1975).
Rosebury, Theodor, *Life on Man* (New York, 1969).
Rothenberg, Robert E. (ed.), *What Every Patient Wants to Know* (New York, 1975).
Singer, Charles, *Short History of Anatomy and Physiology: From the Greeks to Harvey* (New York, 1957).
———, and Ashworth E. Underwood, *Short History of Medicine,* 2nd ed. (New York, 1962).
Stonehouse, Bernard, *The Way Your Body Works* (New York, 1974).
Swain, Tony, *Plants in the Development of Modern Medicine* (Cambridge, Mass., 1972).
Vroman, Leo, *Blood* (New York, 1967).
Waterman, A.J., *Chordate Structure and Function* (New York, 1971).
Wilcocks, C., *Medical Advance, Public Health and Social Evolution* (New York, 1966).

Anthropology
Ardrey, Robert, *The Social Contract* (New York, 1970).
Beals, Ralph, and Harry Hoijer, *An Introduction to Anthropology,* 3rd ed. (New York, 1965).
Benedict, Ruth, *Patterns of Culture* (Boston, 1934).
Brace, C. Loring, *Stages of Human Evolution* (Englewood Cliffs, N.J., 1967).
Bronowski, Jacob, *The Ascent of Man* (Boston, 1974).
Childe, V. Gordon, *A Short Introduction to Archaeology* (London, 1956).
Clark, Grahame, *World Prehistory—An Outline,* 2nd ed. (New York, 1969).
Clark, John G., and Stuart Piggott, *Prehistoric Societies* (New York, 1965).
Clark, Robin, and Geoffrey Hindley, *The Challenge of the Primitives* (New York, 1975).
Clifton, J.A., *Introduction to Cultural Anthropology* (Boston, 1968).
Debzhansky, Theodosius, *Mankind Evolving: The Evolution of the Human Species* (New Haven, Conn., 1962).
Dubos, René, *Man Adapting* (New Haven, Conn., 1965).
———, *So Human an Animal* (New York, 1968).
Garn, Stanley, *Human Races,* 2nd ed. (Springfield, Ill., 1965).
Goodall, Vanne (ed.), *The Quest for Man* (New York, 1975).
Greenway, John, *The Primitive Reader: An Anthology of Myths, Tales, Songs, Riddles, and Proverbs of Aboriginal Peoples Around the World* (Hatboro, Pa., 1965).
Hammond, Peter B. (ed.), *Physical Anthropology and Archaeology: Selected Readings* (New York, 1964).
Hegeman, Elizabeth, and Leonard Kooperman (eds.), *Anthropology and Community Action* (New York, 1974).
Huxley, Julian S., and H.B.D. Kettlewell, *Charles Darwin and His World* (New York, 1965).
Leakey, Louis S., *Adam's Ancestors: The Evolution of Man and His Culture,* 4th ed. (New York, 1960).
Lewis, I.M. (ed.), *History and Social Anthropology* (New York, 1968).
McGraw-Hill Encyclopedia of Science and Technology Yearbook 1976, "Genetic Engineering" (New York, 1976).
Malinowski, Bronislaw, *Crime and Custom in Savage Society* (New York, 1926).
Maple, T., and D.W. Matheson, *Aggression, Hostility and Violence: Nature or Nurture?* (New York, 1973).
Mead, Margaret, *Cooperation and Competition Among Primitive Peoples* (New York, 1937).
Montagu, Ashley, *An Introduction to Physical Anthropology,* 3rd ed. (Springfield, Ill., 1960).
Pelto, Pertti J., *The Study of Anthropology* (Columbus, Ohio, 1965).
Sills, David L. (ed.), *International Encyclopedia of the Social Sciences* (New York, 1968).
Wallace, Anthony F.C., *Religion: An Anthropological View* (New York, 1966).

Sociology
Akers, Ronald, and Edward Sagarin (eds.), *Crime Prevention and Social Control* (New York, 1974).
Applebaum, Ronald, et al., *Speech Communication: Basic Anthology* (New York, 1974).
Bernal, J.D., *Science in History,* 4 vols. (Cambridge, Mass., 1970).
Boas, George, *History of Ideas: An Introduction* (New York, 1969).
Bodmer, Frederick, *Loom of Language,* Lancelot Hogben (ed.) (London, 1944).
Caldwell, Robert G., *Criminology,* 2nd ed. (New York, 1965).
Carpenter, Edmund, and Marshall McLuhan (eds.), *Explorations in Communication: An Anthology* (Boston, 1960).
Chase, Stuart, and Marian T. Chase, *Power of Words* (New York, 1954).
Cherry, Colin, *On Human Communication: A Review, a Survey and a Criticism,* 2nd ed. (Cambridge, Mass., 1966).
Clark, Ronald W., *Scientific Breakthrough: The Impact of Modern Invention* (New York, 1974).
Clark, Kenneth B., *Dark Ghetto: Dilemmas of Social Power* (New York, 1965).
Coser, L.A., *Masters of Sociological Thought* (New York, 1971).
Cox, Fred M., et al. (eds.), *Strategies of Community Organization: A Book of Readings,* 2nd ed. (Itasca, Ill., 1974).
Drucker, Peter, *Technology, Management and Society* (New York, 1970).
Encyclopedia of Sociology (Guilford, Conn., 1974).
Genovese, Eugene D., *The Political Economy of Slavery* (New York, 1965).
Hawley, A.H., *Urban Society: An Ecological Approach* (New York, 1971).
Hawley, Willis D., and Frederick M. Wirt, *The Search for Community Power,* 2nd ed. (Englewood Cliffs, N.J., 1974).
Hood, Roger, and Richard Sparks, *Key Issues in Criminology* (New York, 1970).
Inkeles, Alex, *What Is Sociology? An Introduction to the Discipline and Profession* (Englewood Cliffs, N.J., 1964).
Jespersen, Otto, *Language, Its Nature, Development and Origin* (London, 1922; repr. New York, 1964).
Jones, J., *Prejudice and Racism* (Reading, Mass., 1972).
Kranzberg, Melvin, *Technology and Culture* (New York, 1975).
Lynd, Robert S., and Helen M. Lynd, *Middletown* (New York, 1959).
McGraw-Hill Encyclopedia of Science and Technology Yearbook 1971, "Social System Dynamics" (New York, 1971).
MacKay, Charles, *Extraordinary Popular Delusions and The Madness of Crowds* (New York, 1932).
McKee, James B., *Introduction to Sociology,* 2nd ed. (New York, 1974).
McLean, R.J., *Education for Crime Prevention and Control* (Springfield, Ill., 1975).
McLuhan, Marshall, and Quentin Fiore, *The Medium Is the Message* (New York, 1967).
———, *War and Peace in the Global Village* (New York, 1968).
Mannheim, H., *Comparative Criminology* (Boston, 1965).
Montagu, Ashley (ed.), *Studies and Essays in the History of Science and Learning* (New York, 1975).
Pei, Mario, *The Story of Language,* rev. ed. (Philadelphia, 1965).
———, *Voices of Man* (New York, 1962; repr., 1972).
Piel, Gerald, *The Acceleration of History* (New York, 1972).
Rose, Caroline B., *Sociology: The Study of Man in Society* (Columbus, Ohio, 1965).
Rose, Jerry D., *Introduction to Sociology* (Chicago, 1974).
Sanders, Irwin, *Community: An Introduction to a Social System,* 2nd ed. (New York, 1966).
Sapir, Edward, *Language: An Introduction to the Study of Speech* (New York, 1921; repr., 1955).
Sartre, Jean Paul, *Anti-Semite and Jew* (New York, 1965).
Schramm, Wilbur, and D.F. Robert (eds.), *The Process and Effects of Mass Communication,* rev. ed. (Urbana, Ill., 1971).
Sills, David L. (ed.), *International Encyclopedia of the Social Sciences* (New York, 1968).
Warner, Aaron W. (ed.), *Environment of Change* (New York, 1969).
Work in America: Report of a Special Task Force to the Secretary of Health, Education, and Welfare (Cambridge, Mass., 1972).

Psychology
Arieti, Silvano (ed.), *American Handbook of Psychiatry,* 3 vols. (New York, 1966).
Bardwick, J.M., *Psychology of Women: A Study of Bio-cultural Conflicts* (New York, 1971).
Bruner, Jerome S., et al., *A Study of Thinking* (New York, 1956).
Campbell, Keith, *Body and Mind* (New York, 1970).
Chester, Phyllis, *Women and Madness* (New York, 1973).
Chomsky, Noam, *Language and Mind* (New York, 1972).
Edmund, Simeon, *Miracles of the Mind: An Introduction to Parapsychology* (Springfield, Ill., 1965).
Encyclopedia of Psychology (Guilford, Conn., 1973).
Engle, T.L., and Louis Snellgrove, *Psychology: Its Principles and Applications,* 6th ed. (New York, 1973).
Erikson, Erik H., *Childhood and Society,* 2nd ed. (New York, 1963).
Foulkes, David, *The Psychology of Sleep* (New York, 1966).
Freud, Sigmund, *The Basic Writings of Sigmund Freud,* A.A. Brill (ed.) (New York, 1938).
Goldenson, Robert M., *The Encyclopedia of Human Behavior: Psychology, Psychiatry, and Mental Health* (New York, 1970).
Hall, Calvin S., *A Primer of Freudian Psychology* (New York, 1954).
Hendin, David, *Death as a Fact of Life* (New York, 1973).
Hilgard, Ernest R., and Richard C. Atkinson, *Introduction to Psychology,* 5th ed. (New York, 1971).
Hollander, E.P., *Principles and Methods of Social Psychology,* 2nd ed. (New York, 1971).
Isaacson, R.L., et al., *A Primer of Physiological Psychology* (New York, 1971).
Jersild, A., *Child Psychology,* 6th ed. (Englewood Cliffs, N.J., 1968).
Johnson, Wendell, *People in Quandries: The Semantics of Personal Adjustment* (New York, 1946).
Jones, Ernest, *The Life and Works of Sigmund Freud,* 3 vols. (New York, 1953, 1957).
Katchadourian, H.A., and D.T. Lunde, *Fundamentals of Human Sexuality* (New York, 1972).
Kleitman, Nathaniel, *Sleep and Wakefulness,* rev. ed. (Chicago, 1963).
Kübler-Ross, Elisabeth, *On Death and Dying* (New York, 1970).
———, *Death—The Final Stage of Life* (Englewood Cliffs, N.J., 1975).

Lennard, H.L., et al., *Mystification and Drug Abuse* (San Francisco, 1971).
Lindzey, Gardner, and E. Aronson (eds.), *Handbook of Social Psychology* (Reading, Mass., 1968).
Lorenz, Konrad, *Evolution and Modification of Behavior* (Chicago, 1965).
———, *Studies in Animal and Human Behavior,* 2 vols. (Cambridge, Mass., 1971).
McGraw-Hill Encyclopedia of Science and Technology Yearbook 1976, "Behavior Modification" (New York, 1976).
Miller, George A., *Language and Communication* (New York, 1951).
Neugarten, Bernice L. (ed.), *Middle Age and Aging* (Chicago, 1968).
Piaget, Jean, and Barbel Inhelder, *Psychology of the Child* (New York, 1969).
Rhine, Joseph B., and J.G. Pratt, *Parapsychology* (Springfield, Ill., 1957).
Rogers, Carl R., *Becoming Partners: Marriage and Its Alternatives* (New York, 1972).
Schmeidler, Gertrude R., *Extrasensory Perception* (Chicago, 1969).
Seward, G., and R.E. Williamson, *Sex Roles in a Changing Society* (New York, 1970).
Sheridan, M.D., *Children's Developmental Progress from Birth to Five Years: The 5 Year Sequence* (Atlantic Highlands, N.J., 1973).
Shneidman, Edwin S., et al., *The Psychology of Suicide* (New York, 1970).
Skinner, B. F., *Verbal Behavior* (Englewood Cliffs, N.J., 1957).
———, *Beyond Freedom and Dignity* (New York, 1971).
Szasz, Thomas, *Law, Liberty, and Psychiatry* (New York, 1963).
Tinbergen, Nikolaas, *Study of Instinct* (New York, 1969).
Turner, Merle B., *Realism and The Explanation of Behavior* (Englewood Cliffs, N.J., 1971).
Wrightsman, Lawrence S., and Fillmore H. Sanford, *Psychology: A Scientific Study of Human Behavior,* 4th ed. (Belmont, Calif., 1975).
Wyburn, G.M., et al. (eds.), *Human Senses and Perception* (Toronto, 1964).

Philosophy

Cassirer, Ernst, *Language and Myth,* tr. ed. (New York, 1946).
Cohen, Morris R., and Ernest Nagel, *Introduction to Logic* (New York, 1934; repr., 1962).
Copleston, Frederick, *History of Philosophy,* 8 vols. (London, 1947).
Durant, Will, *Story of Philosophy,* rev. ed. (New York, 1961).
Edwards, Paul (ed.), *The Encyclopedia of Philosophy* (New York, 1967).
Jaspers, Karl, *The Great Philosophers,* 2 vols. (New York, 1966).
Maritain, Jacques, *Moral Philosophy* (New York, 1964).
Munitz, Milton, *Modern Introduction to Ethics* (Glencoe, Ill., 1958).
Urmson, J.B. (ed.), *The Concise Encyclopedia of Western Philosophy and Philosophers* (New York, 1960).
Whitehead, Alfred N., *Adventure of Ideas* (New York, 1933).

Religion and Mythology

Bouquet, Alan C., *The Christian Faith and the Non-Christian Religions* (New York, 1958).
Brandon, S.G.F. (ed.), *A Dictionary of Comparative Religion* (New York, 1970).
Brown, W. Norman, *Man in the Universe: Some Continuities in Indian Thought* (Berkeley, Calif., 1966).
Catholic University of America, *New Catholic Encyclopedia,* 15 vols. (New York, 1967).
Comstock, W. Richard, *Religion and Man: Study of Religion and Primitive Religion* (New York, 1972).
Conze, Edward, *Buddhism: Its Essence and Development* (New York, 1951).
Dumoulin, Heinrich, *A History of Zen Buddhism* (New York, 1963).
Encyclopedia Judaica (Jerusalem, 1972).
Finegan, Jack, *Archeology of World Religions,* 3 vols. (Princeton, N.J., 1952).
Frazer, James G., *The Golden Bough: A Study in Magic and Religion,* 12 vols., 3rd ed. (New York, 1966).
Gibbs, H.A.R., et al. (eds.), *Shorter Encyclopedia of Islam* (Ithaca, N.Y., 1953).
Hamilton, Edith, *Mythology* (New York, 1961).
Hemingway, Patricia D., *Transcendental Meditation Primer* (New York, 1975).
Huber, Jack, *Through an Eastern Window* (New York, 1975).
Kaufmann, Walter A., *Critique of Religion and Philosophy* (New York, 1972).
Kitigawa, Joseph M., *Religions of the East* (Philadelphia, 1960).
Kramer, Samuel N. (ed.), *Mythologies of the Ancient World* (New York, 1961).
Larue, Gerald A., *Ancient Myth and Modern Man* (Englewood Cliffs, N.J., 1975).
Latourette, Kenneth S., *A History of Christianity* (New York, 1953).
Leach, Maria (ed.), *Funk & Wagnalls Standard Dictionary of Folklore, Mythology, and Legend* (New York, 1949).
Levi-Strauss, Claude, *An Introduction to a Science of Mythology,* 2 vols. (New York, 1969–73).
Lewis, John, *Religions of the World Made Simple,* rev. ed. (New York, 1958).
Luquet, G.H., et al., *Larousse Encyclopedia of Mythology* (New York, 1959).
O'Dea, Thomas F., et al., *Religion and Man: Judaism, Christianity and Islam* (New York, 1972).
Pye, Michael, *Comparative Religion* (New York, 1973).
Radhakrishnan, Sarvepalli, *Eastern Religions and Western Thought,* 2nd ed. (New York, 1940).
Silver, Daniel Jeremy, *A History of Judaism* (New York, 1974).
Smith, Huston, *Religions of Man* (New York, 1958).
White, John (ed.), *What is Meditation?* (New York, 1974).

The Occult

Ashby, Robert H., *The Guidebook for the Study of Psychical Research* (New York, 1972).
Cavendish, Richard (ed.), *Encyclopedia of the Unexplained: Magic, Occultism and Parapsychology* (New York, 1974).
MacNiece, L., *Astrology* (Garden City, N.Y., 1964).
Murray, Margaret, *The God of the Witches* (New York, 1953).
Newell, Venetia, *Encyclopedia of Witchcraft and Magic* (New York, 1974).
Oesterreich, Traugott K., *Possession, Demoniacal and Other,* 2nd ed. (New York, 1966).
Robbins, Russell H., *Encyclopedia of Witchcraft and Demonology* (New York, 1959).
Salter, W.H., *The Society for Psychic Research: An Outline of Its History,* rev. ed. (London, 1970).

Political Science

Burns, James M., et al., *Government by the People,* 9th ed. (Englewood Cliffs, N.J., 1975).
Campbell, Colin, and William Christian, *Political Parties and Ideologies in Canada: Liberals, Conservatives, Socialists* (Toronto, 1974).
Cox, Archibald, et al., *Civil Rights, the Constitution and the Courts* (Cambridge, Mass., 1967).
Douglas, William O., *Democracy and Finance* (New Haven, Conn., 1940).
Fowler, R.B., and J.R. Orenstein, *Contemporary Issues in Political Theory* (New York, 1977).
Heilbroner, Robert L., *Between Capitalism and Socialism* (New York, 1970).
Johnson, S.A., *Essentials of Comparative Government* (New York, 1973).
Neustadt, Richard E., *Presidential Power: The Politics of Leadership* (New York, 1976).
Pross, A. Paul (ed.), *Pressure Group Behavior in Canadian Politics* (Toronto, 1975).
Sabine, George H., *A History of Political Theory,* 3rd ed. (New York, 1961).
Sills, David L. (ed.), *International Encyclopedia of the Social Sciences* (New York, 1968).
Sorauf, Francis J., *Political Science: An Informal Overview* (Columbus, Ohio, 1965).
Van Loon, Richard J., and Michael G. Whittington, *The Canadian Political System: Environment, Structure, and Process* (Toronto, 1971).

Economics

Aliber, Robert Z., *International Money Game,* 2nd ed. (New York, 1975).
Asch, Peter, *Economic Theory and the Antitrust Dilemma* (New York, 1970).
Bell, John F., *History of Economic Thought,* 2nd ed. (New York, 1967).
Bergsten, Fred, and Lawrence Krause (eds.), *World Politics and International Economics* (Washington, D.C., 1975).
Berle, Adolf A., *American Economic Republic* (New York, 1965).
Bladen, V.W., *From Adam Smith to Maynard Keynes: The Heritage of Political Economy* (Toronto, 1974).
Calder, Nigel, *Technopolis* (New York, 1970).
Galbraith, John M., *Economic Development* (Cambridge, Mass., 1964).
Johnson, Harry G. (ed.), *Trade Strategy for Rich and Poor Nations* (Toronto, 1971).
———, *On Economics and Society* (Chicago, 1975).
Keynes, John Maynard, *The General Theory of Employment, Interest, and Money* (New York, 1936).
Kuznets, Simon, *Economic Growth of Nations: Total Output and Production Structure* (Cambridge, Mass., 1971).
Lekachman, Robert, *Inflation: The Permanent Problem of Boom and Bust* (New York, 1973).
Martin, Richard S., and R.G. Miller, *Economics and Its Significance* (Columbus, Ohio, 1965).
Marx, Karl, *Capital, The Communist Manifesto, and Other Writings* (New York, 1932).
Meade, James E., H.H. Leisner, and S.J. Wells, *Case Studies in European Economic Union: The Mechanics of Integration* (New York, 1962).
Mumford, Lewis, *Myth of the Machine,* 2 vols. (New York, 1970).
Samuelson, Paul A., *Economics,* 9th ed. (New York, 1973).
Schumpeter, Joseph A., *Ten Great Economists from Marx to Keynes* (New York, 1951).
Sills, David L. (ed.), *International Encyclopedia of the Social Sciences* (New York, 1968).
Smith, Adam, *An Inquiry into the Nature and Causes of the Wealth of Nations* (London, 1776; repr. Baltimore, 1970).
Soule, George, *Ideas of the Great Economists* (New York, 1955).

History and Culture

Periodicals that report on events and developments concerning History and Culture include *American Heritage, Archeology, Architectural Record, Dance Magazine, Foreign Affairs, History Today, Musical Quarterly, National Geographic, Opera News, Scientific American,* and *Smithsonian.*

World History and Culture and International Affairs

Axline, W. Andrew, and James A. Stegenga, *The Global Community: A Brief Introduction to International Relations* (New York, 1972).
Briggs, Asa (ed.), *The Nineteenth Century* (New York, 1970).
Bruun, Geoffrey, and Dwight E. Lee, *Second World War and After* (Boston, 1964).
Buchan, Alastair, *Change Without War: The Shifting of World Power* (London, 1974).
Carr, Edward H., *International Relations Between the Two World Wars 1919–1939* (New York, 1947).
Churchill Winston Spencer, *The Second World War,* 6 vols. (Boston, 1948–53).
———, *History of the English Speaking Peoples,* 4 vols. (New York, 1956–58).
Clark, Kenneth, *Civilisation: A Personal View* (New York, 1969).
Edmonds, Sir James, *A Short History of World War I* (Fair Lawn, N.J., 1951).
Einstein, Alfred, *A Short History of Music,* rev. ed. (New York, 1954).
Ewen, David, *The New Encyclopedia of the Opera* (New York, 1971).
Falls, Cyril B., *A Hundred Years of War* (London, 1953).
———, *The Great War* (New York, 1959).
Feis, Herbert, *Churchill, Roosevelt, Stalin* (Princeton, N.J., 1957).
Fuller, John F.C., *The Second World War, 1939–45* (New York, 1949).
Gardner, Helen, *Art Through the Ages,* 6th rev. ed. , H. de la Croix and R.G. Tansey (eds.) (New York, 1975).
Geiger, Theodore, *Conflicted Relationship: The West and the Transformation of Asia, Africa and Latin America* (New York, 1967).
Guggenheim, Peggy (ed.), *Art of This Century* (New York, 1942).
Janson, Horst, and Joseph Kerman, *History of Art and Music* (New York, 1968).
Jessup, Phillip C., *Birth of Nations* (New York, 1974).
Kraus, Richard, *History of the Dance: In Art and Education* (Englewood Cliffs, N.J., 1969).
Lach, Donald F., and Edmund S. Wehrle, *International Politics in East Asia Since World War Two* (New York, 1975).
Madsen, Roy, *The Impact of Films: The Living Image* (New York, 1973).
Millon, Henry A., *Key Monuments of the History of Architecture* (Englewood Cliffs, N.J., 1964).
Moholy-Nagy, Laszlo, *Painting, Photography and Film* (Cambridge, Mass., 1969).
Nathan, George J., *Encyclopedia of the Theatre* (Cranbury, N.J., 1970).
New Cambridge Modern History, 13 vols. (New York, 1957–70).
Nicoll, Allardyce, *Film and Theatre* (New York, 1936; repr. 1972).
Nussbaum, Frederich L., *The Triumph of Science and Reason 1660–1685* (New York, 1953).
Parry, John H., (ed.), *Establishment of the European Hegemony: 1415–1715. Trade and Exploration in the Age of the Renaissance* (New York, 1963).
———, *European Reconnaissance* (New York, 1968).
———, *Trade and Dominion: European Overseas Empires in the Eighteenth Century* (New York, 1972).
Pledge, H.T., *Science Since 1500: A Short History of Mathematics, Physics, Chemistry and Biology* (London, 1939).
Potter, Elmer B., and Chester. W. Nimitz (eds.), *Sea Power: A Naval History* (Englewood Cliffs, N.J., 1960).
Rostow, Eugene V., *Law, Power and The Pursuit of Peace* (Lincoln, Neb., 1968).
Sachs, Curt, *Rise of Music in the Ancient World* (New York, 1943).
———, *World History of the Dance* (New York, 1963).
Scholl, S., and S. White, *Music and the Culture of Man* (New York, 1970).
Singer, Charles (ed.), *Studies in the History and Method of Science* (New York, 1975).
Steinberg, Leo, *Other Criteria: Confrontations with Twentieth Century Art* (New York, 1972).
Stoessinger, John G., *Might of Nations: World Politics in Our Time,* 3rd ed. (New York, 1969).
Thorndike, Lynn, *A History of Magic and Experimental Science,* 8 vols. (New York, 1923–58).
Toynbee, Arnold J., *A Study of History,* 12 vols. (New York, 1935–61).
Trevor-Roper, Hugh (ed.), *The Age of Expansion: Europe and the World 1559–1660* (New York, 1968).
Ulich, Robert (ed.), *Three Thousand Years of Educational Wisdom: Selections from Great Documents,* 2nd enl. ed. (Cambridge, Mass. 1954).
———, *Education in Western Culture* (New York, 1965).
Ward, Barbara, *Space Ship Earth* (New York, 1966).
Watterson, Joseph, *Architecture: A Short History,* rev. ed. (New York, 1968).
Weber, Eugen, *The Western Tradition: From the Renaissance to the Present,* 3rd ed. (Indianapolis, 1972).
Wolf, Eric R., *Peasant Wars of the Twentieth Century* (New York, 1969).
Worner, Karl H., *The History of Music: A Book for Study and Reference,* 5th ed. (New York, 1973).
Wright, Edward A., and Lenthiel H. Downs, *Primer for Playgoers,* 2nd ed. (Englewood Cliffs, N.J., 1969).

The Ancient World; Prehistory to the Middle Ages

Bacon, Edward, *Archaeology: Discoveries in the 1960's* (New York, 1971).
Barr, Stringfellow, *Mask of Love* (Philadelphia, 1966).
Bibby, Geoffrey, *Looking for Dilmun* (New York, 1970).
Bloch, Raymond, *Etruscans* (New York, 1958).
Bury, John B., *Invasion of Europe by the Barbarians* (New York, 1963).
Caldwell, W.E., and M.F. Gyles, *Ancient World,* 3rd ed. (New York, 1966).
Cambridge Ancient History, 12 vols., 2nd ed. (Cambridge, Eng., 1924–66).
Cary, Max, and H.H. Scullard, *A History of Rome,* 3rd ed. (New York, 1975).
Ceram, C.W., *Gods, Graves and Scholars,* 2nd ed. (New York, 1972).
Chadwick, Nora K., *Celt and Saxon* (New York, 1963).
Childe, V. Gordon, *New Light on the Most Ancient East,* 4th ed. (New York, 1969).
Clark, Grahame, *World Prehistory—An Outline,* 2nd ed. (New York, 1969).
Clemoes, Peter (ed.), *Anglo Saxon England,* 2 vols. (New York, 1973).
Cochrane, Charles N., *Christianity and Classical Culture: A Study of Thought and Action from Augustus to Augustine* (New York, 1957).
Cottrell, Leonard, *Anvil of Civilization* (New York, 1957).
Cowell, F.R., *Life in Ancient Rome* (New York, 1975).
De Graft-Johnson, John C., *African Glory: The Story of Vanished Negro Civilizations* (New York, 1955).
Durant, Will, *Life of Greece* (New York, 1939).
Evans, Arthur, *Palace of Minos,* 4 vols. (New York, 1921).
Fagan, Brian M., *In the Beginning: An Introduction to Archaeology,* 2nd ed. (Boston, 1975).
Ferguson, John, *The Heritage of Hellenism* (New York, 1973).
Finley, Moses I., *Early Greece: The Bronze and Archaic Ages* (New York, 1970).
Fiore, Silvestro, *Voices from the Clay: The Development of Assyro-Babylonian Literature* (Norman, Okla., 1965).
Grabar, André, *The Golden Age of Justinian* (New York, 1967).
Green, Peter, *Ancient Greece: An Illustrated History* (New York, 1973).
Hadas, Moses, *History of Rome from Its Origins to 529 AD, As Told by the Roman Historians* (New York, 1956).
———, *Hellenistic Culture* (New York, 1972).
Hamilton, Edith, *Echo of Greece* (New York, 1957).
———, *The Roman Way* (New York, 1932; repr. 1973).
Hapgood, Charles H., *Maps of the Ancient Sea Kings: Evidence of Advanced Civilization in the Ice Age* (Philadelphia, 1966).

Hawkes, Jacquetta (ed.), *World of the Past,* 2 vols. (New York, 1963).
Hood, Sinclair, *Home of the Heroes: The Aegean Before the Greeks* (New York, 1967).
———, *Minoans* (New York, 1971).
Jones, Gwyn, *History of the Vikings* (New York, 1968).
Kagan, Donald, *Botsford and Robinson's Hellenic History,* 5th ed. (New York, 1969).
Larousse Encyclopedia of Archaeology (New York, 1972).
Leroi-Gourhan, André, *Treasures of Prehistoric Art* (New York, 1967).
Lewis, Naphthali, and Meyer Reinhold (eds.), *Roman Civilization,* 2 vols. (New York, 1951–55).
Mead, Robert D., *Hellas and Rome: The Story of Graeco-Roman Civilization* (New York, 1972).
Oppenheim, A. Leo, *Ancient Mesopotamia* (Chicago, 1964).
Pallottino, Massimo, *The Etruscans,* rev. ed. by David Ridgway (Bloomington, Ind., 1975).
Piggott, Stuart, *Ancient Europe: From the Beginnings of Agriculture to the Classical Antiquity* (Chicago, 1966).
Rees, Alwyn, and Brinley Reed, *Celtic Heritage: Ancient Tradition in Ireland and Wales* (Levittown, N.Y., 1975).
Robinson, Cyril E., *Hellas: A Short History of Ancient Greece* (Boston, 1955).
Roebuck, Carl (ed.), *Muses at Work: Arts, Crafts and Professions in Ancient Greece and Rome* (Cambridge, Mass., 1969).
Rostovtzeff, Mikhail, *Social and Economic History of the Hellenistic World,* 3 vols. (New York, 1941).
Saggs, H.W., *Greatness That Was Babylon: A Survey of the Ancient Civilization of the Tigris-Euphrates Valley* (New York, 1969).
Seaholm, Charles H., *The Kelts and the Vikings* (New York, 1974).
Shinnie, Margaret, *Ancient African Kingdoms* (New York, 1965).
Whitehouse, David, and Ruth Whitehouse, *Archaeological Atlas of the World* (San Francisco, 1975).
Wunderlich, Hans G., *The Secret of Crete* (New York, 1974).

Europe: From the Middle Ages to Modern Times

Ashley, Maurice, *A History of Europe 1648–1815* (Englewood Cliffs, N.J., 1973).
Baron, Salo, *A Social and Religious History of the Jews,* 15 vols., 2nd ed. (New York, 1952–76).
Barrett, William, *Irrational Man* (New York, 1958).
Bautier, Robert-Henri, *Economic Development of Medieval Europe* (New York, 1971).
Berenson, Bernard, *The Italian Painters of the Renaissance,* 2 vols. rev. ed. (London, 1930: repr. New York, 1952).
Billington, James H., *Icon and the Axe: An Interpretive History of Russian Culture* (New York, 1966).
Blum, Jerome, et al., *The European World: A History,* 2nd ed. (Boston, 1970).
Bowen, James, *A History of Western Education,* 2 vols. (New York, 1972, 1975).
Burke, Peter (ed.), *Economy and Society in Early Modern Europe* (New York, 1972).
Bush, M.L., *Renaissance, Reformation and The Outer World 1450–1660* (New York, 1969).
Cantor, Norman F., *Perspectives on the European Past: Conversations with Historians* (New York, 1971).
———, *The Meaning of the Middle Ages: A Sociological and Cultural History* (New York, 1973).
Castelot, André, *Napoleon* (New York, 1971).
Cobban, Alfred (ed.), *The Eighteenth Century: Europe in the Age of Enlightment* (New York, 1969).
Chambers, Frank P., *This Age of Conflict: The Western World 1914 to the Present,* 3rd ed. (New York, 1962).
Cherniavsky, Michael (ed.), *Structure of Russian History* (New York, 1970).
Clough, Shepard B., et al., *European History in a World Perspective,* 2 vols., 3rd ed. (Indianapolis, 1975).
Coulton, George G., *The Medieval Village, Manor and Monastery* (Cambridge, Eng., 1925; repr. New York, 1960).
Courthion, Pierre, *Impressionism,* (New York, 1971).
Craig, Gordon A., *Europe Since 1815,* 3rd ed. (New York, 1971).
———, *Europe Since 1914,* 3rd ed. (New York, 1972).
Davies, K.G., *The North Atlantic World in the 17th Century* (Minneapolis, 1974).
Demolen, Richard L., et al., *One Thousand Years: Western Europe in the Middle Ages* (Boston, 1974).
Elton, G.R., *Reformation Europe 1517–1559* (New York, 1968).
Ergang, Robert, *Europe from the Renaissance to Waterloo,* 3rd ed. (Indianapolis, 1967).
Finkelstein, Louis, *The Jews.* Vol. 1, *History;* Vol. 2, *Religion and Culture;* Vol 3, *Role in Civilization,* 4th ed. (New York, 1970).
Fuller, J.F.C., *A Military History of the Western World,* 3 vols. (New York, 1969).
Gay, Peter, and Robert Webb, *Modern Europe* (New York, 1973).
Gottschalk, Louis, and Donald F. Lach, *Toward the French Revolution: Europe and America in the 18th Century World* (New York, 1973).
Hale, J.R., *Renaissance Europe: Individual and Society 1480–1520* (New York, 1972).
Harcave, Sidney, *Russia: A History,* 6th ed. (Philadelphia, 1968).
Hatton, Ragnhild N., *Europe in the Age of Louis Fourteen* (New York, 1969).
Hay, Denys, *Medieval Centuries,* 2nd ed. (New York, 1964).
Held, Julius, and Donald Posner, *Seventeenth and Eighteenth Century Art: Baroque and Rococo* (New York, 1972).
Herold, J. Christopher, *Age of Napoleon* (New York, 1963).
Hill, Christopher, *Intellectual Origins of the English Revolution* (Oxford, Eng., 1965).
———, *Reformation to Industrial Revolution: A Social and Economic History of Britain, 1530–1780* (London, 1967).
———, *The World Turned Upside Down: Radical Ideas During the English Revolution* (London, 1972).
———, *Change and Continuity in Seventeenth Century England* (Cambridge, Mass., 1975).
Hoetzsch, Otto, *Evolution of Russia* (New York, 1966).
Holborn, Hajo, *A History of Modern Germany,* 3 vols. (New York, 1959–69).
Holt, Elizabeth G. (ed.), *From Classicists to the Impressionists: A Documentary History of Art and Architecture in the 19th Century* (New York, 1966).
Horizon Editors, *Horizon Book of the Arts of Russia* (New York, 1970).
Horton, Rod W., and Vincent F. Hopper, *Backgrounds of European Literature,* 2nd ed. (Englewood Cliffs, N.J., 1975).
Hubert, Jean, *Europe of the Invasions* (New York, 1969).
Hussey, Maurice (ed.), *Chaucer's World: A Pictorial Companion* (New York, 1967).
Kunstler, Gustav (ed.), *Romanesque Art in Europe* (New York, 1973).
Mattingly, Garrett, *Renaissance Diplomacy* (New York, 1970).
Nowell, Charles E., *Great Discoveries and The First Colonial Empires* (Ithaca, N.Y., 1954).
Oliva, L. Jay (ed.), *Russia and the West: From Peter to Khrushchev* (Indianapolis, 1965).
Postan, M.M., *The Medieval Economy and Society: An Economic History of Britain, 1100–1500* (Berkeley, Calif., 1973).
Power, Eileen, *Medieval People,* 10th ed. (New York, 1963).
Robertson, William, *Progress of Society in Europe: A Historical Outline from the Subversion of the Roman Empire to the Beginning of the 16th Century* (Chicago, 1972).
Rubin, William S., *Dada, Surrealism and Their Heritage* (New York, 1968).
Shirer, William L., *The Rise and Fall of the Third Reich* (New York, 1960).
Sitwell, Sacheverell, *Gothic Europe* (New York, 1969).
Spector, Ivar, *Introduction to Russian History and Culture,* 5th ed. (New York, 1969).
Syme, Ronald, *Colonial Elites: Rome, Spain and the Americas* (New York, 1958).
Trevelyan, George M., *English Social History: A Survey of Six Centuries, Chaucer to Queen Victoria* (London, 1942).
Tuchman, Barbara, *The Guns of August* (New York, 1962).
———, *The Proud Tower* (New York, 1966).
Vernadsky, George, *History of Russia,* rev. ed. (New Haven, Conn., 1961).
Wedgewood, Cecily V., *Thirty Years War* (New York, 1962).
Zarnecki, George, *Art of the Medieval World: Architecture, Sculpture, Painting —The Sacred Arts* (Englewood Cliffs, N.J., 1975).

Africa and the Middle East

Bascom, William R., and Melville J. Herskovits (eds.), *Continuity and Change in African Cultures* (Chicago, 1958).
Brand, Charles M. (ed.), *Icon and Minaret: Sources of Byzantine and Islamic Civilization* (Englewood Cliffs, N.J., 1969).
Davidson, Basil, *The African Past: Chronicles from Antiquity to Modern Times* (Boston, 1964).
Gailey, Harry A., *A History of Africa,* 2 vols. (New York, 1970–72).
Gaskin, L.J.P., *A Bibliography of African Art* (London, 1965).
Gibbs, Hamilton A., and Harold Bowen, *Islamic Society and the West: A Study of the Impact of Western Civilization on Moslem Culture in the Near East,* 2 vols. (New York, 1950–57).
Gibbs, J.L., Jr. (ed.), *Peoples of Africa* (New York, 1956).
Greenberg, Joseph H., *The Languages of Africa* (Bloomington, Ind., 1963).
Hanes, W.A., *Geography of Modern Africa,* 2nd ed. (New York, 1975).
Hartwig, G.W., and W.M. O'Barr, *The Student Africanist's Handbook* (New York, 1975).
Hatch, J.C., *Africa Emergent* (Chicago, 1974).
Hitti, Philip K., *History of the Arabs,* 8th ed. (New York, 1966).
———, *Makers of Arab History* (New York, 1968).
Hughes, Langston, ed., *An African Treasury: Articles, Essays, Stories, Poems by Black Africans* (New York, 1960).
Jackson, John G., *Introduction to African Civilization* (New York, 1970).
Laqueur, Walter, *A History of Zionism* (New York, 1972).
Lenczowski, George, *The Middle East in World Affairs* (Ithaca, N.Y., 1962).
Leuzinger, Elsy, *Art of the World: Africa* (New York, 1960).
Mintz, S.W. (ed.), *Slavery, Colonialism, and Racism* (New York, 1975).
Moorehead, Alan, *The White Nile* (New York, 1960).
———, *The Blue Nile* (New York, 1962).
Murdock, George P., *Africa: Its People and Their Cultural History* (New York, 1959).
Ottenberg, Simon, and Phoebe Ottenberg (eds.), *Culture and Societies of Africa* (New York, 1960).
Patai, Raphael, *Golden River to Golden Road: Society, Culture, and Change in the Middle East* (Philadelphia, 1962).
Payne, Pierre, *The Holy Sword: The Story of Islam from Muhammad to the Present* (New York, 1959).
Rubin, L. and B. Weinstein, *Introduction to African Politics* (New York, 1974).
Trimingham, John S., *A History of Islam in West Africa* (New York, 1962).
———, *A History of Islam in East Africa* (New York, 1964).
Whiteley, Wilfred H., *A Selection of African Prose,* 2 vols. (London, 1964).

Asia and Oceania

Beasley, W.G., *The Modern History of Japan* (New York, 1974).
Benedict, Ruth, *Chrysanthemum and Sword: Patterns of Japanese Culture* (New York, 1967).
Buttinger, Joseph, *Vietnam: A Dragon Embattled,* 2 vols. (New York, 1967).
Dardess, John, *Conquerors and Confucians: Aspects of Political Change in Late Yuan China* (New York, 1973).
Eberhard, Wolfram, *A History of China,* 3rd rev. ed. (Berkeley, Calif., 1969).
Freeman, Otis W., *The Geography of the Pacific* (New York, 1951).
Grattan, Clinton H., *The Southwest Pacific to 1900* (Ann Arbor, Mich., 1963).
———, *The Southwest Pacific since 1900* (Ann Arbor, Mich., 1963).
Greenwood, Gordon (ed.), *Australia: A Social and Political History,* 3rd ed. (Sydney, 1964).
Hall, David G.E., *A History of Southeast Asia,* 2nd ed. (New York, 1964).
Harrison, John A., *China Since 1800* (New York, 1967).
Hsu, Immanuel C., *Readings in Modern Chinese History* (New York, 1971).
Latourette, Kenneth S., *The Chinese: Their History and Culture,* 4th rev. ed. (New York, 1964).
Levenson, Joseph R., and Franz Schurmann, *China, An Interpretive History, From the Beginnings to the Fall of Man* (Berkeley, Calif., 1969).
McVey, Ruth T. (ed.), *Indonesia* (New Haven, Conn., 1963).
Quale, G. Robina, *Eastern Civilizations,* 2nd ed. (Englewood Cliffs, N.J., 1975).
Reischauer, Edwin O., *Japan: The Story of a Nation,* rev. ed. (New York, 1974).
———, and John K. Fairbank, *A History of East Asian Civilization,* 2 vols. (Boston, 1960–65).
Riesenberg, Felix, *The Pacific Ocean* (New York, 1940).
Rowe, David N., *Modern China: A Brief History* (New York, 1959).
Smith, Bradley, *Japan: A History in Art* (New York, 1971).
———, and Wan-go Weng, *China: A History in Art* (New York, 1973).
Smith, Vincent A., *Early History of India,* 4th ed. (New York, 1957).
Sullivan, Michael, *Arts of China: A Short History* (Berkeley, Calif., 1975).
Tung, Wu, *Unearthing China's Past* (Boston, 1973).
Watson, William, *China: Before the Han Dynasty* (New York, 1966).
Yutang, Lin, *Imperial Peking: Seven Centuries of China* (Lawrence, Mass., 1961).

Latin America

Busey, J.L., *Latin American Political Guide,* 16th ed. (Manitou Springs, Colo., 1975).
Collier, S.D.W., *From Cortés to Castro* (New York, 1974).
Dockstader, Frederick J., *Indian Art in Middle America* (New York, 1964).
Helms, Mary W., *Middle America: A Cultural History* (Englewood Cliffs, N.J., 1975).
Herring, Hubert H., *History of Latin America,* 3d ed. (New York, 1968).
James, Preston E., *Latin America,* 4th ed., (New York, 1970).
Keen, Benjamin (ed.), *Latin American Civilization,* 2 vols., 3rd ed. (Boston, 1974).
Savoy, Gene, *On the Trail of the Feathered Serpent* (Indianapolis, 1974).
Smith, Bradley, *Mexico: A History in Art* (New York, 1971).
Steward, Julian H. (ed.), *Handbook of South American Indians,* 6 vols. (Washington, D.C., 1946–50).
———, and Louis C. Faron, *Native Peoples of South America* (New York, 1959).
Stuart, G.H., and J.L. Tignes, *Latin America and the United States,* 6th ed. (Englewood Cliffs, N.J., 1975).
Williams, F., *Latin American Culture* (New York, 1975).
Worcester, Donald E., and Wendell G. Schaeffer, *Growth and Culture of Latin America,* 2 vols. (New York, 1971).

United States and Canada: History and Society

Adams, A.J., and Joan M. Burke, *Civil Rights: A Current Guide to People, Organizations, and Events,* 2d ed., (New York, 1974).
Ahlstrom, Sidney E., *Religious History of the American People,* 2 vols. (New York, 1975).
American Heritage and *Business Week* Editors, *American Heritage History of American Business and Industry* (New York, 1972).
Arendt, Hannah, *Crises of the Republic* (New York, 1972).
Bailey, Thomas A., *A Diplomatic History of the American People,* 7th ed. (New York, 1964).
Bailyn, Bernard, *Origins of American Politics* (New York, 1970).
Bain, George S., *Growth of White-Collar Unionism* (New York, 1970).
Bancroft, George, *History of the United States: From the Discovery of the Continents,* 6 vols. (Boston, 1876; repr. 1890).
Barker, L.J., and T.W. Barber (eds.), *Civil Liberties and the Constitution,* 2nd ed. (Englewood Cliffs, N.J., 1975).
Barnes, Harry E., *Society in Transition,* 2nd ed. (New York, 1952).
Beck, Carlton E., et al., *Education for Relevance: The Schools and Social Change* (Boston, 1968).
Berman, Ronald, *America in the Sixties: An Intellectual History* (New York, 1968).
Billington, Ray Allen, *America's Frontier Heritage* (New York, 1967).
Binkley, Wilfred E., *American Political Parties,* 4th rev. ed. (New York, 1963).
Bok, Derek C., and John T. Dunlop, *Labor and the American Community* (New York, 1970).
Boorstin, Daniel J., *American Civilization* (New York, 1972).
———, *The Americans,* 3 vols. (New York, 1958, 1965, 1973).
Capitman, William G., *Panic in the Boardroom: New Social Realities Share Old Corporate Structures* (New York, 1973).
Catton, Bruce, *The Centennial History of the Civil War,* 3 vols. (New York, 1965).
Chan, J.H.M., *Vietnam, A Comprehensive Bibliography* (Metuchen, N.J., 1973).
Chapelle, Howard I., *The History of American Sailing Ships* (New York, 1935).
Ceram, C.W., *The First American: A Story of North American Archaeology* (New York, 1971).
Cohen, I. Bernard, *Some Early Tools of American Science* (Cambridge, Mass., 1967).
Cohen, Sol, *Education in the United States: A Documentary History,* 4 vols. (New York, 1974).
Colbourn, H. Trevor, *Colonial Experience: Readings in Early American History* (Boston, 1966).
Commager, Henry S. (ed.), *Immigration and American History* (Minneapolis, 1961).
———, and Richard B. Morris (eds.), *The Spirit of 'Seventy-Six: The Story of the American Revolution as Told by the Participants* (New York, 1975).
Creighton, Donald, *Canada's First Century, 1867–1967* (Toronto, 1970).
Crow, Duncan, *The Victorian Woman* (New York, 1972).
Devine, Donald J., *The Political Culture of the United States: Influence of Member Values on Regime Maintenance* (Boston, 1972).
Dictionary of American Biography, 20 vols. with Supplements (New York, 1928ff.).

Driver, Harold E., *Indians of North America* (Chicago, 1961).
Dukes, Paul, *Emergence of the Super-Powers: A Short Comparative History of the USA and the USSR* (New York, 1970).
Dulles, Foster R., *Labor in America: A History* 3rd ed. (New York, 1966).
Esposito, Vincent J. (ed.), *The West Point Atlas of American Wars* (New York, 1959).
Galambos, Louis, and Barbara B. Spence, *The Public Image of Big Business in America 1880–1940: A Study in Social Change* (Baltimore, 1975).
Galbraith, John K., *Affluent Society,* 2nd ed. (New York, 1969).
Gans, Herbert J., *Popular Culture and High Culture* (New York, 1975).
Gardner, Paul, *Nice Guys Finish Last: Sport and American Life* (New York, 1975).
Genovese, Eugene D., *The Political Economy of Slavery* (New York, 1965).
———, *Roll, Jordan, Roll: The World the Slaves Made* (New York, 1974).
Goodman, Jack (ed.), *While You Were Gone: A Report on Wartime Life in the United States* (New York, 1974).
Green, Constance M., *Rise of Urban America* (New York, 1965).
Gumbert, Edgar B., Jr., and Joel H. Spring, *The Super School and the Super State: American Education in the Twentieth Century 1918–1970* (New York, 1974).
Gutek, Gerald L., *Historical Introduction to American Education* (New York, 1970).
Handlin, Oscar, *American People in the 20th Century* (Cambridge, Mass., 1954).
Hansen, Marcus L., *The Immigrant in American History,* Arthur Schlesinger (ed.) (Cambridge, Mass., 1940).
Head, Sydney W., *Broadcasting in America,* 2nd ed. (Boston, 1972).
Hofstadter, Richard, *American Political Tradition* (New York, 1973).
Jacobs, Jane, *Economy of Cities* (New York, 1969).
Johnson, Arthur H. (ed.), *The American Economy: An Historical Introduction to the Problems of the 1970's* (New York, 1974).
Joseph, Alvin M., Jr., *Indian Heritage of America* (New York, 1968).
Julian, Joseph, *This Was Radio: A Personal Memoir* (New York, 1975).
Katz, W.L., *Minorities in American History* (New York, 1975).
Kirkland, Edwin C., *History of American Economic Life,* 4th ed. (New York, 1969).
Laird, Charlton, *Language in America* (Englewood Cliffs, N.J., 1972).
Lebergott, Stanley, *The American Economy: Income, Wealth and Want* (Princeton, N.J., 1975).
Lester, Richard A., *As Unions Mature: An Analysis of the Evolution of American Unionism* (Princeton, N.J., 1958).
Lord, Walter, *The Good Years: From Nineteen Hundred to the First World War* (New York, 1960).
Loth, David G., *Public Plunder: A History of Graft in America* (New York, 1938).
Madsen, David, *Early National Education 1776–1830* (New York, 1974).
Martineau, Harriet, *Society in America* (London, 1834; repr. New York, 1966).
Morison, Samuel Eliot, *The Two-Ocean War* (New York, 1963).
———, *The Oxford History of the American People* (New York, 1965).
———, *The European Discovery of America,* 2 vols. (New York, 1971, 1974).
Morris, Richard B., *The Making of a Nation,* new ed. (New York, 1974).
Mortimer, J.E., *Trade Unions and Technological Change* (New York, 1971).
Morton, W.L., *The Canadian Identity,* 2nd ed. (Madison, Wisc., 1972).
Moyers, Bill, *Listening to America* (New York, 1971).
Myrdal, Gunnar, *An American Dilemma: The Negro Problem and Modern Democracy* (New York, 1944, rev. 1962).
Nevins, Allan, *Ordeal of the Union,* 8 vols. (New York, 1947–65).
Nichols, Roy (ed.), *Battles and Leaders of the Civil War,* 4 vols. (New York, 1957).
Ostrander, Gilman M., *American Civilization in the First Machine Age 1890–1940* (New York, 1970).
Parrington, Vernon L., *Main Currents in American Thought,* 3 vols. (New York, 1927–31).
Ploski, H.A., and Ernest Kaiser (eds.), *Afro USA: A Reference Work on the Black Experience* (New York, 1971).
Raffaele, J.A., *System and Unsystem: How American Society Works* (New York, 1974).
Ridgway, Matthew B., *The Korean War* (Garden City, N.Y., 1967).
Rose, Peter I. (ed.), *Slavery and Its Aftermath* (New York, 1970).
Rosenberg, Harold, *Discovering the Present: Three Decades in Art, Culture and Politics* (Chicago, 1973).
Sage, G.H., *Sport and American Society: Selected Readings,* 2nd ed. (Reading, Mass., 1974).
Santayana, George, *Character and Opinion in the United States* (New York, 1920).
Scheer, G.F., and H.F. Rankin, *Rebels and Redcoats,* (New York, 1972).
Schlesinger, Arthur M., Jr., and Morton White (eds.), *Paths of American Thought* (Boston, 1970).
Sexton, Patricia, and Brendan Sexton, *Blue Collars and Hard Hats: The Working Class and the Future of American Politics* (New York, 1971).
Smith, James W., and A.L. Jamison (eds.), *Religion in American Life,* 4 vols. (Princeton, N.J., 1961).
Smith, Page, *As a City Upon a Hill* (New York, 1966).
Sochen, J., *Movers and Shakers: American Women Thinkers and Activists, 1900–1970* (New York, 1973).
Spencer, Robert F., et al., *The Native American: Ethnology and Background of the North American Indian,* 2nd ed. (New York, 1977).
Steinberg, Alfred, *The Bosses* (New York, 1972).
Stover, John F., *American Railroads* (Chicago, 1961).
Susman, Warren (ed.), *Culture and Commitment* (New York, 1973).
Taft, Robert, *Photography and The American Science: A Social History 1839–1899* (New York, 1938).
Tesconi, Charles A., *Schooling in America: A Social Philisophical Perspective* (Boston, 1975).
Time-Life Books Editors, *This Fabulous Century,* 8 vols. (New York, 1970).
Toffler, Alvin, *The Culture Consumers* (New York, 1973).
Tyler, Parker, *Magic and Myth of the Movies* (New York, 1970).
Ward, Christopher, *The War of the Revolution,* 2 vols. (New York, 1952).
Weisberger, Bernard A., Michael Harwood, et al. (eds.), *The American Heritage History of the American People* (New York, 1971).
Willey, Gordon R., *An Introduction to American Archeology,* Vol. 1, *North and Middle America* (Englewood Cliffs, N.J., 1966).
Woodward, C. Vann, *The Strange Career of Jim Crow* (New York, 1974).

United States and Canada: Arts and Letters
Blum, Daniel, *Pictorial History of the American Theatre 1860–1970,* 3rd enl. ed. (New York, 1969).
Britannica Encyclopedia of American Art (New York, 1975).
Burchard, John, and Albert Bush-Brown, *The Architecture of America: A Social and Cultural History* (Boston, 1961).
Cambridge History of American Literature (New York, 1943).
Condit, Carl W., *American Building Art,* 2 vols. (New York, 1960–61).
Craven, Wayne, *Sculpture in America* (New York, 1968).
Dockstader, Frederick J., *Indian Art in America* (New York, 1966).
Hart, James D., *The Popular Book: A History of America's Literary Taste* (Berkeley, Calif., 1950).
Hitchcock, H. Wiley, *Music in the United States: A Historical Introduction* (Englewood Cliffs, N.J., 1969).
Hornung, Clarence P., *Treasury of American Design,* 2 vols. (New York, 1972).
Kilbourn, Elizabeth, *Great Canadian Painting* (Toronto, 1966).
Klinck, Carl F., et al. (eds.), *Literary History of Canada* (Toronto, 1965).
Kouwenhoven, John A., *Arts in Modern American Civilization* (New York, 1967).
McLanathan, Richard, *American Tradition in the Arts* (New York, 1968).
Mumford, Lewis, *The Brown Decades: A Study of the Arts in America 1865–1895,* 3rd rev. ed (New York, 1971).
Nye, Russel, *Unembarrassed Muse: The Popular Arts in America* (New York, 1970).
Rossi, Paul A., and David C. Hunt, *The Art of the Old West* (New York, 1971).
Spiller, Robert E., *Literary History of the United States: Bibliography* (New York, 1974).
Tebbel, John, *A History of Book Publishing in the United States,* 2 vols. (New York, 1972).
Tougas, Gérard, *History of French-Canadian Literature* (Toronto, 1966).
Ulanov, Barry, *Two Worlds of American Art* (New York, 1965).
———, *A History of Jazz in America* (New York, 1972).

MAN AND SCIENCE

Periodicals that report on events and developments concerning "Man and Science" include *Bulletin of Atomic Scientists, Chemistry, National Geographic, Natural History, New Scientist, Physics Today, Radio and Electronics, Science, Science and Public Affairs, Scientific American, Sea Frontiers,* and *Smithsonian.*

General
Bronowski, Jacob, *Science and Human Values,* rev. and enl. ed. (New York, 1972).
Bragg, Gordon M., *Principles of Experimentation and Measurement* (Englewood Cliffs, N.J., 1974).
Clifford, William K., *The Common Sense of the Exact Sciences* (New York, 1955).
Cohen, I. Bernard, *Science, Servant of Man: A Layman's Primer for the Age of Science* (Boston, 1948).
Heisenberg, Werner, *Physics and Philosophy: The Revolution in Modern Science* (New York, 1958).
Hogben, Lancelot, *Science for the Citizen,* 4th ed. (New York, 1957).
McGraw-Hill Encyclopedia of Science and Technology Yearbook 1972, "Science in Art" (New York, 1972).
Needham, Joseph, *Science and Civilization in China,* 4 vols. (New York, 1954–70).
Newman, James R., *Science and Sensibility,* 2 vols. (New York, 1961).
Shubnikov, A.V., *Symmetry in Science and Art* (New York, 1974).

History of Science
Bronowski, Jacob, *The Ascent of Man* (Boston, 1973).
Cohen, I. Bernard, *Science and American Society in the First Century of the Republic* (Columbus, Ohio, 1961).
Crombie, Alistair C., *Robert Grosseteste and the Origins of Experimental Science* (New York, 1955).
Dampier, William C., *History of Science,* 4th ed. rev. (New York, 1949).
Holton, Gerald, *Thematic Origins of Scientific Thought: Kepler to Einstein* (Cambridge, Mass., 1973).
Sarton, George, *A History of Science,* 2 vols. (Cambridge, Mass., 1959).

Mathematics—History
Baron, M.E., *Origins of the Infinitesimal Calculus* (New York, 1969).
Bell, Eric T., *Mathematics, Queen and Servant of Science* (New York, 1951).
———, *Men of Mathematics* (New York, 1961).
Bochner, Salomon, *The Role of Mathematics in the Rise of Science* (Princeton, N.J., 1966).
Boyer, Carl B., *A History of Mathematics* (New York, 1968).
Bunt, L.N.H., et al., *The Historical Roots of Elementary Mathematics* (Englewood Cliffs, N.J., 1976).
Caruccio, Ettore, *Mathematics and Logic in History and Contemporary Thought* (London, 1964).
Durbin, John R., *Mathematics: The Spirit and Evolution* (New York, 1973).
Gillings, Richard J., *Mathematics in the Time of the Pharoahs* (Cambridge, Mass., 1972).
Gittleman, Arthur, *History of Mathematics* (Columbus, Ohio, 1975).
Gow, James, *Short History of Greek Mathematics* (New York, 1968).
Klein, Jacob, *Greek Mathematical Thought and the Origin of Algebra* (Cambridge, Mass., 1968).
Kline, Morris, *Mathematics in Western Culture* (New York, 1955).
———, *Mathematical Thought from Ancient to Modern Times* (New York, 1972).
Morgan, Bryan, *Man and Discoveries in Mathematics* (London, 1972).
Resnikoff, H.L., and R.O. Wells, *Mathematics in Civilization: Geometry and Calculation as Keystones of Culture* (New York, 1973).
Struik, Dirk J., *Concise History of Mathematics,* 3rd rev. ed. (New York, 1967).
Todhunter, Isaac, *History of the Mathematical Theory of Probability* (New York, 1949).
Turnbull, Herbert W., *Great Mathematicians* (New York, 1961).
Wilder, Raymond L., *Evolution of Mathematical Concepts: An Elementary Study* (New York, 1968).

Basic Mathematics
Dantzig, Tobias, *Number, the Language of Science,* 4th rev. ed. (New York, 1954).
Dowdy, Shirley M., *Mathematics: Art and Science* (New York, 1971).
Gardner, Martin, *The Scientific American Book of Mathematical Puzzles and Diversions* (New York, 1959).
Geerts, W., *Working with a Slide Rule* (New York, 1969).
Green, J.A., *Sets and Groups* (Boston, 1971).
Hogben, Lancelot, *The Wonderful World of Mathematics* (Garden City, N.Y., 1968).
James, Glenn, and Robert C. James, *Mathematics Dictionary,* 3rd ed. (New York, 1968).
Kleene, Stephen Cole, *Mathematical Logic* (New York, 1967).
Newman. James R. (ed.), *The World of Mathematics,* 4 vols. (New York, 1956).
Ore, Oystein, *Number Theory and its History* (New York, 1948).
Polya, G., *How to Solve It* (Princeton, N.J., 1971).
Pettofrezzo, Anthony J., and Donald W. Hight, *Elementary Mathematics: Number Systems and Algebra* (Glenview, Ill., 1970).
Stephenson, Geoffrey, *Matrices, Sets and Groups* (New York, 1966).
Whitehead, Alfred North, *An Introduction to Mathematics* (New York, 1958).
Wilder, Raymond L., *Evolution of Mathematical Concepts: An Elementary Study* (New York, 1968).

Algebra, Geometry, and Trigonometry
Adler, Irving, *New Look at Geometry* (New York, 1966).
Ballard, William R., *Geometry* (Philadelphia, 1970).
Braverman, Harvey, *Precalculus Mathematics: Algebra, Trigonometry, Analytic Geometry* (Baltimore, 1975).
Cohn, P.M., *Solid Geometry* (Boston, 1968).
Coolidge, Julian L., *Treatise on Algebraic Plane Curves* (New York, 1959).
Davis, E.A., and J. Pedersen, *Essentials of Trigonometry,* 2nd ed. (New York, 1973).
Forman, William, and Lester L. Gavurin, *Elements of Arithmetic, Algebra and Geometry* (New York, 1972).
Fulton, William, *Algebraic Curves: An Introduction to Algebraic Geometry* (New York, 1969).
Greenberg, Marvin J., *Euclidean and Non-Euclidean Geometries* (San Francisco, 1974).
Hemmerling, Edwin M., *Elementary Mathematics: Arithmetic, Algebra and Geometry* (New York, 1965).
McHale, T.J., and P.T. Witzke, *Basic Trigonometry* (Reading, Mass., 1971).
Rees, Paul K., *Algebra, Trigonometry and Analytic Geometry* (New York, 1967).
Yale, Paul B., *Geometry and Symmetry* (San Francisco, 1968).

Calculus
Boyce, William E., and Richard C. DiPrima, *Introduction to Differential Equations* (New York, 1970).
Buck, R. Creighton, *Advanced Calculus,* 2nd ed. (New York, 1965).
Ferrar, William L., *Calculus for Beginners* (New York, 1967).
Hart, William L., *Brief Calculus* (New York, 1974).

Topology
Brown, R., *Elements of Modern Topology* (New York, 1968).
Gemignani, Michael C., *Elementary Topology,* 2nd ed. (Reading, Mass., 1972).
Thomeier, S. (ed.), *Topology and Its Applications* (New York, 1975).

Probability and Statistics
Bashaw, W.L., *Mathematics for Statistics* (New York, 1969).
Bass, Jean, *Elements of Probability Theory* (New York, 1966).
Blum, Julius R., and Judah I. Rosenblatt, *Probability and Statistics* (Philadelphia, 1972).
Chao, Lincoln, *Statistics: Methods and Analyses,* 2nd ed. (New York, 1974).
Ehrenberg, A.S., *Data Reduction: Analyzing and Interpreting Statistical Data* (New York, 1975).
Godambe, V.P., and D.A. Sprott, *Foundations of Statistical Inference* (New York, 1972).
Hoel, Paul Gerhard, *Introduction to Mathematical Statistics,* 3rd ed. (New York, 1962).

Physics—History
Amaldi, Ginestra, *Nature of Matter: Physical Theory from Thales to Fermi* (Chicago, 1966).
Gamow, George, *Biography of Physics* (New York, 1961).
Jacob. M.C., *The Newtonians and the English Revolution, 1689–1720* (Ithaca, N.Y., 1976).
Lanczos, Cornelius, *Space Through the Ages* (New York, 1970).
Ronchi, Vaso, *Nature of Light: An Historical Survey* (Cambridge, Mass., 1970).
Trigg, G.L., *Landmark Experiments in Twentieth Century Physics* (New York, 1975).

Physics—General
Asimov, Isaac, *Understanding Physics: Light, Magnetism and Electricity* (New York, 1969).
———, *Understanding Physics: Motion, Sound and Heat* (New York, 1969).
Besancon, Robert M. (ed.), *The Encyclopedia of Physics,* 2nd ed. (New York, 1974).
Bridgman, Percy W., *The Logic of Modern Physics* (New York, 1958).

———, *The Nature of Physical Theory* (New York, 1936).
———, *Physics of High Pressure* (London, 1931).
Born, Max, *The Restless Universe*, 2nd ed. (New York, 1951).
Gray, H.J., and Alan Isaacs (eds.), *A New Dictionary of Physics*, 2nd ed. (New York, 1975).
Gamow, George, *One, Two, Three Infinity* (New York, 1971).
Inglish, Stuart J., *Physics: An Ebb and Flow of Ideas* (New York, 1970).
Kittel, Charles, *Introduction to Solid State Physics*, 3rd ed. (New York, 1966).
McGraw-Hill Encyclopedia of Science and Technology Yearbook 1972, "Surface Physics" (New York, 1972).
Magie, William F., *Source Book in Physics*, rev. ed. (Cambridge, Mass., 1963).
Pierce, John R., *Almost All About Waves* (Cambridge, Mass., 1974).
Sears, Francis M., Robert W. Brehme, and M.W. Zemansky, *University Physics Part 1, Mechanics, Heat and Sound*, 4th ed. (Reading, Mass., 1970).
———, *University Physics Part 2, Electricity and Magnetism, Light, and Atomic Physics*, 4th ed. (Reading, Mass., 1970).
Weast, Robert C. (ed.), *Handbook of Chemistry and Physics: A Ready Reference Book of Chemical and Physical Data*, 56th ed. (Cleveland, 1975).

The Structure of Matter
Asimov, Isaac, *Understanding Physics: The Electron, Proton and Neutron* (New York, 1969).
Barnaby, Frank, *Man and the Atom: The Uses of Nuclear Energy* (New York, 1972).
Bernstein, Jeremy, *Elementary Particles and Their Currents* (San Francisco, 1968).
Bitter, Francis, *Currents, Fields and Particles* (Cambridge, Mass., 1956).
Brown, B., *General Properties of Matter* (New York, 1969).
Burcham, W.E., *Nuclear Physics: An Introduction*, rev. ed. (New York, 1973).
Fano, U., and L. Fano, *Physics of Atoms and Molecules: An Introduction to the Structure of Matter* (Chicago, 1972).
Flowers, B.H., and E. Mendoza, *Properties of Matter* (New York, 1970).
Goodstein, David L., *States of Matter* (Englewood Cliffs, N.J., 1975).
Segre, Emilio (ed.), *Annual Review of Nuclear Science* (Palo Alto, Calif., 1975).
Semat, Henry, and J. Albright, *Introduction to Atomic and Nuclear Physics*, 5th ed. (New York, 1972).
Solomon, J., *Structure of Matter* (New York, 1974).
Stearns, Robert L., *Basic Concepts of Nuclear Physics* (New York, 1968).

Energy and Motion
Angrist, Stanley W., and Loren G. Hepler, *Order and Chaos: Laws of Energy and Entropy* (New York, 1967).
Bondi, Herman, *Relativity and Common Sense* (New York, 1964).
Holman, Jack P., *Thermodynamics* (New York, 1974).
Huang, T.C., *Engineering Mechanics: Vol. 1 Statistics: Vol. 2 Dynamics* (Reading, Mass., 1967).
Meriam, J.L., *Dynamics*, 2nd ed. (New York, 1971).
———, *Statics*, 2nd ed. (New York, 1975).
Overman, Michael, *Understanding Energy* (New York, 1975).
Shames, Irving H., *Introduction to Statics* (Englewood Cliffs, N.J., 1970).
Stearns, Robert L., *Focus on Physics-Mechanics One: Statics, Dynamics and Kinematics* (New York, 1970).
Sussman, M.V., *Elementary General Thermodynamics* (Reading, Mass., 1972).
Theobald, D.W., *The Concept of Energy* (New York, 1966).

Relativity
Eddington, Arthur S., *Space, Time and Gravitation: An Outline of the General Relativity Theory* (New York, 1959).
Gardner, Martin, *Relativity for the Million* (New York, 1962).
Resnick, Robert, *Introduction to Special Relativity* (New York, 1968).
———, *Basic Concepts in Relativity and Early Quantum Theory* (New York, 1972).
Russell, Bertrand, *The ABC of Relativity*, rev. ed. (London, 1958).
Sears, Francis W., and Robert W. Brehme, *Introduction to the Theory of Relativity* (Reading, Mass., 1968).

Electricity and Magnetism
Adler, Richard B., et al., *Introduction to Semiconductor Physics* (New York, 1964).
Benjamin, Park, *A History of Electricity* (New York, 1975).
Bleaney, B.I., and B. Bleaney, *Electricity and Magnetism*, 2nd ed. (New York, 1965).
Brookes, A.M., *Advanced Electric Circuits* (London, 1966).
———, *Basic Electric Circuits*, 2nd ed. (New York, 1975).
Cowan, Eugene, *Basic Electromagnetism* (New York, 1968).
Cullity, Bernard D., *Introduction to Magnetic Materials* (Reading, Mass., 1972).
Duffin, W.J., *Electricity and Magnetism*, 2nd ed. (New York, 1973).
Gebert, Kenneth L., et al., *Transformers*, 2nd ed. (Chicago, 1974).
Gray, Paul E., and Campbell L. Searle, *Electronic Principles: Physics, Models and Circuits* (New York, 1969).
Hammond, P., *Applied Electromagnetism* (New York, 1972).
Harris, D.J., and P.N. Robson, *The Physical Basis of Electronics*, rev. ed. (New York, 1974).
Hauser, Walter, *Introduction to Principles of Electromagnetism* (Reading, Mass., 1971).
Howatson, A.M., *Principles of Applied Electricity* (New York, 1973).
Leach, Donald P., *Basic Electric Circuits* (New York, 1969).
Lloyd, Tom C., *Electric Motors and Their Applications* (New York, 1969).
Mandl, Matthew, *Basics of Electricity and Electronics* (Englewood Cliffs, N.J., 1975).
Meyer, Herbert W., *History of Electricity and Magnetism* (Cambridge, Mass., 1972).
Smith, Robert A., *Semiconductors* (Cambridge, Eng., 1959).
Wagner, D., *Introduction to the Theory of Magnetism* (New York, 1972).

Heat, Light, Sound
Allen, L., *Essentials of Lasers* (New York, 1969).
Becker, R., *Theory of Heat*, 2nd ed. (New York, 1967).
Born, M., and E. Wolf, *Principles of Optics*, 5th ed. (New York, 1975).
Burnham, Robert W., et al., *Color: A Guide to Basic Facts and Concepts* (New York, 1963).
Carroll, John M., *Story of the Laser*, rev. ed. (New York, 1970).
Clerc, L., *Fundamentals: Light, Image, Optics* (Englewood Cliffs, N.J., 1974).
Evans, Ralph Merrill, *An Introduction to Color* (New York, 1948).
Goethe, Johann W., *Theory of Colours* (Cambridge, Mass., 1970).
Hall, J.A., *The Measurement of Temperature* (New York, 1966).
Kock, Winston E., *Sound Waves and Light Waves* (New York, 1965).
Levarie, Siegmund, and Ernst Levy, *Tone: A Study in Musical Acoustics* (Kent, Ohio, 1968).
Morse, Philip M., and K.V. Ingard, *Theoretical Acoustics* (New York, 1968).
Siegman, A.E., *Introduction to Lasers and Masers* (New York, 1971).
Tannenbaum, Beulah, and Myra Stillman, *Understanding Sound* (New York, 1972).
Zemansky, M.W., *Heat and Thermodynamics: An Intermediate Textbook*, 5th ed. (New York, 1968).

Chemistry—History
Asimov, Isaac, *Short History of Chemistry* (New York, 1965).
Burland, Collie A., *The Arts of the Alchemists* (New York, 1968).
Farber, Eduard, *Great Chemists* (New York, 1961).
———, *Evolution of Chemistry: A History of Its Ideas, Methods and Materials*, 2nd ed. (New York, 1969).
Partington, James R., *History of Chemistry*, 4 vols. (New York, 1961–64).
Weeks, Mary E., *Discovery of the Elements*, 7th ed. (Easton, Pa., 1968).

Basic Chemistry
Ahrland, S., et al., *The Chemistry of the Actinides* (New York, 1975).
Asimov, Isaac, *Search for the Elements* (New York, 1962).
———, *World of Nitrogen*, rev. ed. (New York, 1962).
———, *World of Carbon*, rev. ed. (New York, 1966).
———, *Asimov on Chemistry* (New York, 1974).
Bell, R.P., *Acids and Bases*, 2nd ed. (New York, 1972).
Bennett, H. (ed.), *Concise Chemical and Technical Dictionary*, 3rd enl. ed. (New York, 1974).
Clark, George L., and G.G. Hawley (eds.), *Encyclopedia of Chemistry*, 2nd ed. (New York, 1966).
Cockett, A.H., et al., *The Chemistry of Monatomic Gases* (New York, 1975).
Ebsworth, E.A., et al., *The Chemistry of Oxygen* (New York, 1975).
Geffner, Saul L., *Fundamental Concepts of Modern Chemistry* (New York, 1968).
Handbook of Chemistry and Physics, pub. annually (Cleveland, 1913ff.).
Holden, Alan, *Bonds Between Atoms* (New York, 1971).
Johnson, Ronald C., *Introductory Descriptive Chemistry: Selected Nonmetals, Their Properties and Behavior* (New York, 1967).
Ledbetter, Elaine W., and Jay A. Young, *Oxidation-Reduction Reactions* (Reading, Mass., 1974).
McGraw-Hill Encyclopedia of Science and Technology Yearbook 1973, "Plutonium-244" (New York, 1973).
———, *Yearbook 1976*, "Vander Waals Forces" (New York, 1976).
Masterton, William L., and Emil J. Slowinski, *Chemical Principles*, 3rd ed. (Philadelphia, 1973).
Moeller, T., *The Chemistry of the Lanthanides* (New York, 1975).
Nicholls, D., *The Chemistry of Iron, Cobalt and Nickel* (New York, 1975).
Pauling, Linus, *General Chemistry*, 3rd ed. (San Francisco, 1970).
Pimentel, George C., and Richard D. Sprattley, *Chemical Bonding Clarified Through Quantum Mechanics* (San Francisco, 1969).
Sisler, Harry H., *Electronic Structure, Properties, and the Periodic Law*, 2nd ed. (New York, 1973).
Smith, E. Brian, *Basic Chemical Thermodynamics* (New York, 1973).
Welcher, Frank J., *Chemical Solutions* (New York, 1966).
Williamson, Arthur G., *An Introduction to Non-Electrolyte Solutions* (New York, 1967).

Electrochemistry
Baizer, M.M. (ed.), *Organic Electrochemistry: An Introduction and a Guide* (New York, 1973).
Bockris, J., et al., *An Introduction to Electro-chemical Science* (London, 1974).
———, and B.E. Conway (eds.), *Modern Aspects of Electrochemistry* (New York, 1971).
———, and Amulya K. Reddy, *Modern Electrochemistry: An Introduction to an Interdisciplinary Area*, 2 vols. (New York, 1973).
Frey, A.J., and G. Dryhurst, *Organic Electrochemistry* (New York, 1972).
Lyons, Ernest H., Jr., *Introduction to Electrochemistry* (Indianapolis, 1967).
Ruben, Samuel, *The Founders of Electrochemistry* (Philadelphia, 1975).
Yeager, Ernest, and Lavin J. Salkind (eds.), *Techniques of Electrochemistry* (New York, 1972).

Chemical Analysis
Connors, K.A., *Reaction Mechanisms in Organic Analytical Chemistry* (New York, 1972).
Ettre, Leslie S., and Albert Zlatikis (eds.), *Practice of Gas Chromatography* (New York, 1967).
Grunwald, Ernest, and Louis J. Kirschenbaum, *Introduction to Quantitative Chemical Analysis* (Englewood Cliffs, N.J., 1972).
Gouw, T.H. (ed.), *Guide to Modern Methods of Instrumental Analysis* (New York, 1972).
Peters, D.G., et al., *A Brief Introduction to Modern Chemical Analysis* (Philadelphia, 1976).
McGraw-Hill Encyclopedia of Science and Technology Yearbook 1971, "Computer-assisted Analytical Chemistry" (New York, 1971).
Skoog, D.A., and D.M. West, *Analytic Chemistry*, 2nd ed. (New York, 1974).

Physical Chemistry
Eyring, H., *Annual Review of Physical Chemistry* (Palo Alto, Calif., 1975).
Moore, Walter J., *Physical Chemistry*, 4th ed. (Englewood Cliffs, N.J., 1972).

Inorganic Chemistry
Basolo, Fred, and Ralph G. Pearson, *Mechanisms of Inorganic Reactions*, 2nd ed. (New York, 1967).
Cotton, F. Albert, and Geoffrey Wilkinson, *Basic Inorganic Chemistry* (New York, 1975).
Durrant, Philip J., and Beryl Durrant, *Introduction to Advanced Inorganic Chemistry*, 2nd ed. (New York, 1970).
Lippard, Stephen J. (ed.), *Progress in Inorganic Chemistry* (New York, 1959ff.).

Organic Chemistry
Barker, Robert, *Organic Chemistry of Biological Compounds* (Englewood Cliffs, N.J., 1971).
Lenz, Robert W., *Organic Chemistry of Synthetic High Polymers* (New York, 1967).
Morrison, Robert T., and Robert N. Boyd, *Organic Chemistry*, 3rd ed. (Boston, 1973).
Odian, George, *Principles of Polymerization* (New York, 1969).
Saunders, K.J., *Organic Polymer Chemistry* (New York, 1973).
Schultz, Jerold, *Polymer Materials Science* (Englewood Cliffs, N.J., 1974).
Streitwieser, A., and C.H. Heathcock, *Introduction to Organic Chemistry* (New York, 1976).
Tobolsky, Arthur, and Herman F. Mark, *Polymer Science and Materials* (New York, 1971).
Weiss, F.T., *Determination of Organic Compounds: Methods and Procedures* (New York, 1970).

Biochemistry—History
Florkin, M., and E.H. Stotz, *History of Biochemistry*, Vol. 1 (New York, 1972).
Leicester, Henry M., *Development of Biochemical Concepts from Ancient to Modern* (Cambridge, Mass., 1974).
Needham, Joseph (ed.), *The Chemistry of Life: Eight Lectures on the History of Biochemistry* (Cambridge, Eng., 1970).

The Chemistry of Life
Baldwin, E., *Introduction to Comparative Biochemistry*, 4th ed. (New York, 1975).
Bohinski, R.C., *Modern Concepts in Biochemistry*, 2nd ed. (Boston, 1976).
Dagley, S., and Donald E. Nicholson, *Introduction to Metabolic Pathways* (New York, 1970).
Farago, Peter, and John Lagnado, *Life in Action: Biochemistry Explained* (New York, 1972).
Fruton, Joseph S., *Molecules and Life: Historical Essays on the Interplay of Chemistry and Biology* (New York, 1972).
Gutfreund, Herbert, *Enzymes: Physical Principles* (New York, 1972).
Holum, J.R., *Elements of General and Biological Chemistry: An Introduction to the Molecular Basis of Life*, 3rd ed. (New York, 1972).
Johnson, A.R., and J.B. Davenport (eds.), *Biochemistry and Methodology of Lipids* (New York, 1971).
McGilvery, Robert W., *Biochemical Concepts* (Philadelphia, 1975).
Nicolau, Claude (ed.), *Experimental Methods in Biophysical Chemistry* (New York, 1973).
Orton, James M., and Otto W. Neuhaus, *Human Biochemistry* (St. Louis, 1975).
Plummer, David T., *An Introduction to Practical Biochemistry* (New York, 1971).
Singer, Thomas P. (ed.), *Biological Oxidations* (New York, 1968).
Snell, Esmond E., *Annual Review of Biochemistry*, Vol. 44 (Palo Alto, Calif., 1975).
Stenesh, J., *Dictionary of Biochemistry* (New York, 1975).
Walton, Alan G., and John Blackwell, *Biopolymers* (New York, 1973).
Watson, James D., *Molecular Biology of the Gene*, 2nd ed. (New York, 1970).
Williams, Roger J., *Encyclopedia of Biochemistry* (New York, 1967).

MAN AND MACHINES

Periodicals that report on events and developments concerning "Man and Machines" include *Bulletin of Atomic Scientists, ChemTech, Datamation, Electronics, Environmental Science and Technology, Industry Week, Natural History, New Scientist, Popular Science, Science, Scientific American*, and *Smithsonian*.

History of Technology
Asimov, Isaac, *Science Past—Science Future* (New York, 1975).
Daumas, Maurice (ed.), *A History of Technology and Invention* (New York, 1969).
DeCamp, L. Sprague, *Ancient Engineers* (New York, 1974).
Derry, Thomas K., and Trevor I. Williams, *Short History of Technology from Earliest Times to A.D. 1900* (New York, 1961).
Hodges, Henry, *Technology in the Ancient World* (New York, 1970).
Klemm, Friedrich, *A History of Western Technology* (Cambridge, Mass., 1964).
Kranzberg, Melvin, *Technology and Culture* (New York, 1975).
Leighton, Albert C., *Transport and Communication in Early Medieval Europe A.D. 500–1100* (New York, 1972).
Singer, Charles, et al. (eds.), *A History of Technology*, 5 vols. (New York, 1954–58).

Machines and Technology
Ayres, Robert U., *Technological Forecasting and Long-Range Planning* (New York, 1969).
Banham, Reyner, *Theory and Design in the First Machine Age*, 2nd ed. (New York, 1967).
Bateson, Robert, *Introduction to Control System Technology* (Columbus, Ohio, 1973).
Beckett, Edmund, *A Treatise on Clocks* (New York, 1974).
Burstall, Aubrey F., *Simple Working Models of Historic Machines* (Cambridge, Mass., 1975).
Considine, Douglas M. (ed.), *Chemical and*

Process Technology Encyclopedia (New York, 1974).
Crouse, William H., *Small Engines: Operation and Maintenance* (New York, 1974).
Deutschman, A.D., et al., *Machine Design* (New York, 1975).
Ellul, Jacques, *The Technological Society* (New York, 1964).
Gabor, Dennis, *Innovations: Scientific, Technological and Social* (New York, 1970).
Hartsuch, Paul J., *Think Metric Now: A Step-by-Step Guide to Understanding and Applying the Metric System* (Chicago, 1974).
Kirk, R.E., and D.F. Othmer, *Encyclopedia of Chemical Technology,* 2nd ed., 22 vols. (New York, 1963–72).
Kuo, Benjamin C., *Automatic Control Systems,* 3rd ed. (Englewood Cliffs, N.J., 1975).
Lodewijk, T., et al. (eds.), *The Way Things Work: An Illustrated Encyclopedia of Technology* (New York, 1973).
McGraw-Hill Encyclopedia of Science and Technology Yearbook 1971, "Nondestructive Testing" (New York, 1971).
———, *Yearbook 1974,* "Technology Assessment" (New York, 1974).
Obert, Edward F., *Internal Combustion Engines,* 3rd ed. (New York, 1968).
Prenting, Theodore O., and Nicholas Thomopoulos, *Humanism and Technology in Assembly Line Systems* (Rochelle Park, N.Y., 1974).
Purvis, Jud, *All About Small Gas Engines* (South Holland, Ill., 1963).
Somers, G.G., et al., *Adjusting to Technological Change* (Westport, Conn., 1974).
Teich, Albert H. (ed.), *Technology and Man's Future* (New York, 1972).
The Way Things Work—An Encyclopedia of Modern Technology, 2 vols. (New York, 1967, 1971).
Willsberger, Johann, *Clocks and Watches* (New York, 1975).

Producing Energy
Capes, Edward C., et al. (eds.), *Coal Processing* (New York, 1975).
Commoner, Barry, et al. (eds.), *Alternative Technologies for Power and Production* (New York, 1975).
———, *Human Welfare: The End Use of Power* (New York, 1975).
———, *The Social Costs of Power Production* (New York, 1975).
Gordon, R.L., *U.S. Coal and the Electric Power Industries* (Baltimore, 1975).
Healy, Timothy J., *Energy, Electric Power, and Man* (San Francisco, 1974).
Kosow, Irving, *Electric Machinery and Transformers* (Englewood Cliffs, N.J., 1972).
McGraw-Hill Encyclopedia of Science and Technology Yearbook 1973, "Management of Waste Heat" (New York, 1973).
———, *Yearbook 1976,* "Nuclear Reactor Safety" (New York, 1976).
National Academy of Engineering, Task Force on Energy, *U.S. Energy Prospects: An Engineering Viewpoint* (Washington, D.C., 1974).
Portola Institute, *Energy Primer: Solar, Wind, and Biofuels* (Menlo Park, Calif., 1974).
Seale, Robert L., and Raymond Sierka (eds.), *Energy Needs and the Environment* (Tucson, Ariz., 1973).
Shuttlesworth, D.E., and L. Williams, *Disappearing Energy* (New York, 1974).
Van Krevelen, Dirk W., *Coal,* 2nd ed. (New York, 1962).
Van Wylen, G., and R.E. Sonntag, *Fundamentals of Classical Thermodynamics,* 2nd ed. (New York, 1972).
Wills, J.G., *Nuclear Power Plant Technology* (New York, 1967).

Transportation
American Heritage Editors, *The American Heritage History of Flight* (New York, 1962).
Angelucci, Enzo, *Airplanes: From the Dawn of Flight to the Present Day* (New York, 1973).
Baker, R.G., *The Highway Risk Problem: Policy Issues in Highway Safety* (New York, 1971).
Buel, Ronald A., *Dead End: The Automobile in Mass Transportation* (Baltimore, 1973).
Burgess, Robert, *Ships Beneath the Sea: A History of Subs and Submersibles* (New York, 1975).
Carpenter, Reginald, *Modern Ships* (New York, 1970).
Creighton, Roger L., *Urban Transportation Planning* (Urbana, Ill., 1970).
Elkin, B., *Dynamics of Atmospheric Flight* (New York, 1972).
Emmons, Frederick, *The Atlantic Liners, 1925–70* (New York, 1973).
———, *Pacific Liners,* 1927–72 (New York, 1974).
Evenson, A.E., *The Complete Handbook of Automotive Engines and Systems* (Blue Ridge Summit, Penna., 1974).
Gentle, Ernest, J., and Lawrence W. Reithmaier (eds.), *Aviation and Space Dictionary,* 5th ed. (Fallbrook, Calif., 1974).
Gibbs, Anthony, *Passion for Cars* (New York, 1974).
Green, William (comp.), *The Observer's Book of Aircraft* (New York, 1975).
———, and Gordon Swanborough (comp.), *The Observer's World Airlines and Airliners Directory* (New York, 1975).
Hastings, Paul, *Railroads: An International History* (New York, 1972).
Kelly, Charles J., Jr., *Sky's the Limit: The History of the Airlines* (New York, 1963).
Kuethe, A.M., and Chuen-Yen Chow, *Foundations of Aerodynamics: Bases of Aeronautical Design* (New York, 1976).
Landström, Björn, *The Ship: An Illustrated History* (New York, 1961).
Miller, John A., *Fares Please: A Popular History of Trolleys, Horsecars, Streetcars, Buses, Elevateds and Subways* (New York, 1960).
Nicholson, T.R., *Passenger Cars 1863–1904* (New York, 1970).
Nock, O.S., and Clifford Meadway, *Dawn of the World's Railways 1800–1850* (New York, 1972).
Paquette, Radnor J., et al., *Transportation Engineering: Planning and Design* (New York, 1972).
Phillips-Birt, Douglas, *A History of Seamanship* (New York, 1971).
Profile Publications Limited, *Aircraft in Profile Series* (vols. 1–6, 1968–70); *Locomotives in Profile Series* (1972) (New York); *Cars in Profile Series* (1974).
Stein, Ralph, *The World of the Automobile* (New York, 1973).
Strakosch, G.R., *Vertical Transportation: Elevators and Escalators* (New York, 1967).
Taylor, John W.R. (ed.), *Janes' Pocket Book of Commercial Transport Aircraft* (New York, 1973).
———, and Gordon Swanborough, *Civil Aircraft of the World* (New York, 1974).
Toland, John, *The Great Dirigibles: Their Triumphs and Disasters,* rev. ed. (New York, 1972).
Von Braun, Wernher, and Frederick I. Ordway, *A History of Rocketry and Space Travel,* rev. ed. (New York, 1969).

Weapons
Blackman, Raymond V., *World's Warships,* 3rd ed. (New York, 1963).
Breyer, Siegfried, *Battleships and Battle Cruisers, 1905–1970* (New York, 1973).
Bruce, J.M., *War Planes of the First World War,* 5 vols. (New York, 1965–72).
Chant, Christopher, et al., *The Encyclopedia of Air Warfare* (New York, 1975).
Cookson, John, and Judith Nottingham, *Survey of Chemical and Biological Warfare* (New York, 1969).
Dupuy, Trevor N., and Gay M. Hammerman (eds.), *A Documentary History of Arms Control and Disarmament* (New York, 1973).
Foss, Christopher, *Artillery of the World* (New York, 1974).
Guilmartin, J.F., Jr., *Gunpowder and Galleys* (New York, 1975).
Jablonski, Edward, *Airwar,* 2 vols. (New York, 1971).
Kahn, Herman, *On Thermonuclear War* (Princeton, N.J., 1960).
Klass, Philip J., *Secret Sentries in Space* (New York, 1971).
Krivinyi, N., *World Military Aviation* (New York, 1974).
McGregory, Malcom, *Armoured Fighting Vehicles* (New York, 1974).
Pollard, Hugh B., *The History of Firearms* (New York, 1974).
Quick, John, *Dictionary of Weapons and Military Terms* (New York, 1973).
Rogers, H.B., *A History of Artillery* (Secaucus, N.J., 1974).
Saxtorph, Niels M., *Warriors and Weapons of Early Times* (New York, 1972).
Smith, W.H.B., *Small Arms of the World: A Basic Manual of Small Arms,* 10th rev. and updated ed. (Harrisburg, Penna., 1973).
Taylor, John W. (ed.), *Combat Aircraft of the World: From 1909 to the Present* (New York, 1969).
Warner, Oliver, et al., *The Encyclopedia of Sea Warfare* (New York, 1975).

Engineering
Bodman, S.W., *Industrial Practice of Chemical Process Engineering* (Cambridge, Mass., 1968).
Braun, Per, *Port Engineering* (Houston, Tex., 1973).
Coulson, J.M., and J.F. Richardson, *Chemical Engineering,* 2 vols., 2nd rev. ed. (New York, 1968).
Fair, Gordon M., et al., *Elements of Water Supply and Waste Water Disposal,* 2nd ed. (New York, 1971).
Fink, Donald G. (ed.), *Electronics Engineers' Handbook* (New York, 1975).
Fintel, Mark (ed.), *Handbook of Concrete Engineering* (New York, 1974).
McGraw-Hill Encyclopedia of Science and Technology Yearbook 1972, "Risk Evaluation in Engineering" (New York, 1972).
———, "Fire Engineering"; "Sensors for Industrial Automation" (New York, 1975).
Overman, Michael, *Water: Solutions to a Problem of Supply and Demand* (New York, 1969).
Russell, T.W.F., and M.M. Denn, *Introduction to Chemical Engineering Analysis* (New York, 1972).
Schwab. G.O., R.K. Frevert, et al. (eds.), *Elementary Soil and Water Engineering,* 2nd ed. (New York, 1971).
Zillys, Robert G. (ed.), *Handbook of Environmental Engineering* (New York, 1975).

Building
Ambrose, J.E., *Building Structures Primer* (New York, 1967).
Ayers, C., *Specifications: For Architecture, Engineering, and Construction* (New York, 1975).
Beaver, Patrick, *A History of Tunnels* (Secaucus, N.J., 1973).
Bowyer, Jack, *A History of Building* (New York, 1973).
Browne, Dan, *The Housebuilding Book* (New York, 1974).
Burton, Anthony, *The Canal Builders* (New York, 1972).
Crawley, S.W., and R.M. Dillon, *Steel Buildings: Analysis and Design* (New York, 1970).
Day, David A., *Construction Equipment Guide* (New York, 1973).
Harris, C.M. (ed.), *Dictionary of Architecture and Construction* (New York, 1975).
Hornbostel, Caleb, and William J. Hornung, *Materials and Methods for Contemporary Construction* (Englewood Cliffs, N.J., 1974).
Horonjeff, Robert, *Planning and Design of Airports,* 2nd ed. (New York, 1975).
Mason, Peter, *Bridges and Roads* (New York, 1962).
Merritt, Frederick A., *Building Construction Handbook,* 3rd ed. (New York, 1975).
O'Connor, C., *Design of Bridge Superstructures* (New York, 1971).
Parker, H., *Simplified Design of Structural Steel,* 3rd ed. (New York, 1965).
———, *Simplified Engineering for Architects and Builders,* 4th ed. (New York, 1967).
———, *Simplified Design of Reinforced Concrete,* 3rd ed. (New York, 1968).
Sandstrom, G.E., *Man the Builder* (New York, 1970).
Scott, John D., *A Dictionary of Building,* 2nd ed. (Baltimore, 1974).
Shirley-Smith, H., *Worlds Great Bridges,* rev. ed. (New York, 1965).
Siegel, C., *Structure and Form in Modern Architecture* (Huntington, N.Y., 1975).
Smith, Norman, *A History of Dams* (Secaucus, N.J., 1972).
Smith, Ronald C., *Principles and Practices of Heavy Construction* (Englewood Cliffs, N.J., 1967).
Watson, Donald A., *Construction Materials and Processes* (New York, 1972).

Electronics—General
Anderson, L.W., and W.W. Beeman, *Electronic Circuits and Modern Electronics* (New York, 1973).
Einbinder, J. (ed.), *Designing with Linear Integrated Circuits* (New York, 1969).
———, *Semiconductor Memories* (New York, 1971).
Feldzamen, A.N., and Faye Henle, *The Calculator Handbook* (New York, 1973).
IEEE Electrical and Electronics Dictionary (New York, 1972).
Lurch, E.N., *Fundamentals of Electronics,* 2nd ed. (New York, 1971).
Robbins, Michael S., *Electronic Clocks and Watches* (Indianapolis, 1975).

Communication
Augerbauer, George J., *Electronics for Modern Communication* (Englewood Cliffs, N.J., 1974).
Bawden, L., *The Oxford Companion to Film* (New York, 1976).
Beesley, M.J., *Lasers and Their Applications* (New York, 1971).
Bower, R., *Television and the Public* (New York, 1973).
Buxton, Frank, and Bill Owen, *The Big Broadcast: Radio's Golden Age 1920–1950,* rev. ed. (New York, 1972).
Carter, Thomas F., and L.C. Goodrich, *Invention of Printing in China and Its Spread Westward,* 2nd ed. (New York, 1955).
Coke, Van Deren (ed.), *One Hundred Years of Photographic History* (Albuquerque, N.M., 1975).
Diringer, David, *The Alphabet: A Key to the History of Mankind,* 2 vols. (New York, 1948).
Gattegno, Caleb, *Towards a Visual Culture: Educating Through Television* (New York, 1969).
Greenfield, Howard, *Books: From Writer to Reader* (New York, 1976).
Kent, Allen, *Information Analysis and Retrieval* (New York, 1971).
McGraw-Hill Encyclopedia of Science and Technology Yearbook 1973, "The Wired World" (New York, 1973).
———, *Yearbook 1974,* "Optical Communications" (New York, 1974).
McLuhan, Marshall, *Gutenberg Galaxy: The Making of Typographic Man* (New York, 1969).
———, *Understanding Media: The Extensions of Man* (New York, 1973).
Mickelson, Sig, *Electric Mirror: Politics in an Age of Television* (New York, 1972).
Mueller, G.E., and E.R. Spangler, *Communication Satellites* (New York, 1964).
Ogg, Oscar, *Twenty-six Letters,* rev. ed. (New York, 1971).
Pope, Maurice, *The Story of Archaeological Decipherment: From Egyptian Hieroglyphs to Linear B* (New York, 1975).
Stambler, Irwin, *Revolution in Light Lasers and Holography* (New York, 1972).

Computers
Arms, W.Y., et al., *A Practical Approach to Computing* (New York, 1976).
Cardenas, A.F., et al. (eds.), *Computer Science* (New York, 1972).
Chapin, Ned, *Fundamentals of Computer Use* (San Francisco, 1975).
Computer Security Research Group, *Computer Security Handbook* (New York, 1973).
Feldzamen, A., *Intelligent Man's Easy Guide to Computers* (New York, 1971).
Goldstine, Herman M., *The Computer from Pascal to Von Neumann* (Princeton, N.J., 1972).
Katzan, Harry, Jr., *Introduction to Computer Science* (New York, 1975).
Lynch, Robert E., and John R. Rice, *Computers, Their Impact and Use* (New York, 1975).
McGraw-Hill Encyclopedia of Science and Technology Yearbook 1973, "Computer-assisted Education" (New York, 1973).
Orr, W.D. (ed.), *Conversational Computers* (New York, 1968).
Overman, Michael, *Understanding the Computer* (New York, 1975).
Paschkis, V., and F.L. Ryder, *Direct Analog Computers* (New York, 1968).
Siegel, P., *Understanding Digital Computers* 2nd ed. (New York, 1971).
Spencer, Donald, *The Story of Computers* (Ormond Beach, Fla., 1975).
———, *Computer Science Mathematics* (Columbus, Ohio, 1976).

Industry and Materials
Arnold, Lionel K., *Introduction to Plastics* (Ames, Iowa, 1968).
Balsam, M.S., and Edward Sagarin (eds.), *Cosmetics: Science and Technology,* 2nd ed., 3 vols. (New York, 1972–74).
Begeman, M.L., and B.H. Amstead, *Manufacturing Processes,* 6th ed. (New York, 1969).
Carriere, Gerardus, *Lexicon of Detergents, Cosmetics and Toiletries* (New York, 1966).
Conrad, John W., *Ceramic Formulas: A Guide to Clay, Glaze, Enamel, Glass and Their Colors* (New York, 1973).
Cottier-Angeli, Fiorella, *Ceramics* (New York, 1974).
Duck, E.W., *Plastics and Rubbers* (New York, 1972).
Hudson, Kenneth, *Industrial Archaeology: An Introduction,* 2nd rev. ed. (London, 1966).
Mark, H.F., et al. (eds.), *Encyclopedia of Polymer Science and Technology,* 16 vols. (New York, 1964–72).
Moncrieff, R.W., *Man Made Fibres,* 6th ed. (New York, 1975).
Norton, Frederick H., *Elements of Ceramics,* 2nd ed. (Reading, Mass., 1974).
Peet, Louise J., et al., *Household Equipment,* 7th ed. (New York, 1975).
Reeves, W.A., et al., *Fire Resistant Textiles Handbook* (Westport, Conn., 1974).
Sax, N. Irving, *Dangerous Properties of Industrial Materials,* 4th ed. (New York, 1975).
Schlenker, B.R., *Introduction to Materials Sciences* (New York, 1969).
Swann, Philip D., *Extraction of Useful Chemical Derivatives from Coal* (New York, 1975).
Waddams, Austen L., *Chemicals from Petroleum: An Introductory Survey,* 2nd ed. (New York, 1969).
Wernick, Simon, *Surface Treatment and Finishing of Aluminum and Its Alloys,* 2 vols., 4th ed. (New York, 1972).
Wilcox, Donald J., *New Design in Ceramics* (New York, 1975).

PICTURE CREDITS

Credits are listed in this manner: [1] page numbers appear first, in bold type; [2] illustration numbers appear next, in brackets; [3] photographers' names appear next, followed where applicable by the names of the agencies representing them.

Credits for photographs in the *Time Chart* read left to right across each two-page section.

COLORPEDIA

The Universe
32–3 Hale Observatories. **35** Photri. **36** McDonnell-Douglas Corporation. **37** Photri. **38–9** [Key] Patrick Moore Collection. **40–1** [8] Patrick Moore Collection. **42–3** [6] Hale Observatories, Mount Wilson and Palomar, [7] Hale Observatories, Mount Wilson and Palomar. **44–5** [Key] Patrick Moore Collection; [1] Novosti Press Agency; [2] Australian Information Service; [3] Lick Observatory; [4A] Hale Observatories, Mount Wilson and Palomar; [5] Patrick Moore Collection; [6] US Naval Observatory. **46–7** [Key] Bell Laboratories; [2] J. Arthur Dixon/by courtesy of Sir Bernard Lovell; [3] P. Daly; [4] Hale Observatories, Mount Wilson and Palomar; [5] Lund Observatory; [7] US Naval Observatory. **52–3** [Key] Georgetown University Observatory; [4A] Ronan Picture Library; [4B] Patrick Moore Collection; [6] Picturepoint; [7] H. R. Hatfield; [8, 9] NASA; [10] Hale Observatories, Mount Wilson and Palomar; [11, 12] NASA; [13] H. Brinton. **54–5** [Key] Royal Astronomical Society; [11, 12, 13, 14, 15, 16A–E] NASA. **56–7** [7A] Lick Observatory; [8] Royal Astronomical Society. **58–9** [Key] Fairchild Space and Defence Systems. **60–1** [Key] Novosti Press Agency; [1, 2, 3, 4, 5, 6, 7, 8] NASA. **62–3** [Key] Patrick Moore Collection; [4] NASA/Courtesy of Dr John Guest; [8, 9, 10, 11, 12] NASA. **64–5** [4] H. R. Hatfield; [5, 9, 10, 11A, 11B, 12] NASA. **66–7** [1A, 3] NASA. **68–9** [Key] NASA; [5A–D] C. F. Capen. **70–1** [Key, 4, 8] NASA; [9] Photri; [10] NASA. **74–5** All photographs NASA. **76–7** [2, 3A–C, 4A–C] NASA; [6] Photri; [7] NASA. **78–9** [1] Max Wolf/Royal Astronomical Society; [2] F. C. Acfield. **80–1** [5] G. P. Kuiper; [6] Lowell Observatory, Arizona. **82–3** [Key] H. E. Dall; [1, 2, 3, 4, 5] NASA. **84–5** [Key] US Naval Observatory; [7] Patrick Moore Collection; [8] H. R. Hatfield; [11] Hale Observatories, Mount Wilson and Palomar. **86–7** [4] G. P. Kuiper; [6A, B] G. P. Kuiper; [7] G. P. Kuiper. **88–9** [4] G. P. Kuiper; [7] G. P. Kuiper; [9A, B] Patrick Moore Collection. **90–1** [Key] Source unknown; [5] Hale Observatories, Mount Wilson and Palomar; [6] E. E. Barnard/Royal Astronomical Society; [7] E. M. Lindsay/Royal Astronomical Society; [8] Hale Observatories, Mount Wilson and Palomar; [9] Royal Greenwich Observatory. **92–3** [Key] Butler/Royal Astronomical Society; [4] D. McLean/Royal Astronomical Society/Kitt Peak Observatory; [5] T. J. C. A. Moseley; [7] Patrick Moore Collection; [8] Source unknown; [9] Institute of Meteorites, New Mexico; [10] Source unknown; [11] Novosti Press Agency; [12] Source unknown; [13] Source unknown. **94–5** [Key] Royal Greenwich Observatory, Herstmonceaux; [2B] P. Daly; [6] Hale Observatories, Mount Wilson and Palomar; [7] Hale Observatories, Mount Wilson and Palomar. **96–7** [Key] W. M Baxter; [2A, B, C] Roberts/Royal Astronomical Society; [4] Patrick Moore Collection; [5] NASA; [6] NASA. **98–9** [2] NASA; [4] H. Brinton; [5] NASA; [6] A. Kung; [7, 8, 9] NASA. **100–1** [1] P. Gill; [2] J. McBain/Patrick Moore Collection; [4] H. R. Hatfield; [5] H. R. Hatfield. **102–3** [1, 4] Hale Observatories, Mount Wilson and Palomar. **104–5** [Key] H. R. Hatfield; [3, 4] Hale Observatories, Mount Wilson and Palomar; [5B] Source unknown; [6B, 7, 8] Hale Observatories, Mount Wilson and Palomar. **106–7** [Key] Hale Observatories, Mount Wilson and Palomar; [1] US Naval Observatory; [2, 3, 4, 5, 6] Hale Observatories, Mount Wilson and Palomar. **108–9** [Key] Hale Observatories, Mount Wilson and Palomar; [3A, B] Royal Astronomical Society. **110–1** [Key A, B, 6B, 15B] H. R. Hatfield. **112–13** [Key] Mount Stromlo Observatory, Australia; [2] Patrick Moore Collection; [3, 4] Hale Observatories, Mount Wilson and Palomar. **114–15** [1] K. G. Malin-Smith; [7] Hale Observatories, Mount Wilson and Palomar; [8] Source unknown; [9] Hale Observatories, Mount Wilson and Palomar; [10] T. J. C. A. Moseley; [11] Patrick Moore Collection. **116–17** [2] US Naval Observatory; [3] K. G. Malin-Smith; [4] H. R. Hatfield; [5] K. G. Malin-Smith; [7] Royal Astronomical Society; [8] Hale Observatories, Mount Wilson and Palomar; [9] US Naval Observatory; [10] Hale Observatories, Mount Wilson and Palomar. **118–19** [Key, 3] Carnegie Institute, Washington/Hale Observatories, Mount Wilson and Palomar; [4, 6] Hale Observatories, Mount Wilson and Palomar; [7] US Naval Observatory; [8] Lund Observatory. **120–1** [1] Carnegie Institute, Washington/Hale Observatories, Mount Wilson and Palomar; [2] US Naval Observatory; [3, 4] Hale Observatories, Mount Wilson and Palomar; [5] Mount Stromlo Observatory, Australia; [6] Royal Astronomical Society; [7] Radcliffe Observatory. **122–3** [Key] Hale Observatories, Mount Wilson and Palomar; [2] Lick Observatory; [3, 4, 5, 6, 7, 8] Hale Observatories, Mount Wilson and Palomar; [9] Lick Observatory; [10, 12] Hale Observatories, Mount Wilson and Palomar; [13, 14, 15] US Naval Observatory; [16] Hale Observatories, Mount Wilson and Palomar. **124–5** [1, 2] Hale Observatories, Mount Wilson and Palomar; [3] US Naval Observatory; [4, 5] Hale Observatories, Mount Wilson and Palomar; [6A, B] Royal Greenwich Observatory; [7, 8] Source unknown. **126–7** [Key, 2, 3] Hale Observatories, Mount Wilson and Palomar; [4] US Naval Observatory; [5] Hale Observatories, Mount Wilson and Palomar. **128–9** [4, 5A–F, 6A] Photoresources; [6B] Snark International; [7] Source unknown. **142–3** [1, 2] Patrick Moore Collection; [3] NASA; [4, 5, 6] Novosti Press Agency; [7, 8] NASA; [9, 10, 11] Photri; [12] NASA; [13] Novosti Press Agency; [14] NASA; [15, 16, 17] Photri; [18] Novosti Press Agency. **144–5** [Key] Patrick Moore Collection. **146–7** [Key] NASA; [1] by permission of Mme Malthete Melies/Copyright S.P.A.D.E.M. Paris 1976; [2] Royal Astronomical Society. **148–9** [Key] NASA; [1] Photri. **152–3** [Key] Patrick Moore Collection. **156–7** [Key] Hale Observatories, Mount Wilson and Palomar.
Color photographs credited above to Hale Observatories are copyright by the California Institute of Technology and the Carnegie Institute of Washington.

The Earth
160–1 Peter J. Kaplan. **162–3** Jon Gardey/Robert Harding Associates. **164** Leonard McCombe/T.L.P.A. © Time Inc. 1976/Colorific. **165** Mats Wibe Lund. **170–1** [Key] Scripps Institute of Oceanography. **172–3** [3] Trans Antarctic Expedition; [6] C. E. Abranson. **174–5** [1] Bill Ray Life © Time Inc. 1976; [9] Wide World Photos. **176–7** [5] Picturepoint; [8] Mats Wibe Lund; [9] C. E. Abranson; [10] Heather Angel. **178–9** [6] David Strickland. **180–1** [Key] Photri. **182–3** [1] Jon Levy; [2, 3] NASA. **190–1** [1, 2, 3, 4, 5, 6A, 6B] NASA/Sachem. **192–3** [1, 2, 3, 4, 5, 6] NASA. **198–9** [1, 2, 3, 4, 5, 6] NASA. **202–3** [1, 2, 3, 4, 5, 6] NASA; [7] Jon Levy; [8] NASA. **206–7** [1, 2, 3, 4, 5, 6, 7, 8] NASA. **210–1** [1, 2, 3, 4, 5, 6] NASA; [7] Jon Levy; [8] NASA. **214–5** [Key] Barnabys Picture Library. **216–7** [Key] Jon Levy; [2A] Ken Pilsbury; [2B] Martyn Bramwell; [2C] Ken Pilsbury; [7] Bettman Archive, **218–9** [Key] NBC; [1] C. E. Abranson; [6] Jon Levy/NASA; [7] The Controller HMSO: The Director General of the Meteorological Office, photographs taken at East Hill Dunstable by W. G. Harper. **220–1** [2A] Janine Wiedel/Robert Harding Associates; [5B] Spectrum Colour Library; [6A] F. Jackson/Robert Harding Associates. **222–3** [2] ZEFA; [8] Martyn Bramwell. **224–5** [16] Robert Cundy/Robert Harding Associates; [4] Dr J. Wilson; [6A] Robert Harding Associates/Alan Durand; [6B] ZEFA. **226–7** [2] Picturepoint; [5] Bill Ray: Life © Time Inc. 1976/Colorific; [8A–B] Tony Stone Associates. **228–9** [Key] Institute of Oceanographic Sciences; [4] Dr Kempe/British Museum [Natural History]; [7A] C. E. Abranson. **236–7** [Key] Courtesy National Oceanic and Atmospheric Administration National Marine Fisheries Service; [1] C. E. Abranson; [6A–B, 7] O.S.F./Bruce Coleman Ltd. **238–9** [7] Vickers Oceanics Ltd. **240–1** [Key, 2, 3, 4, 5, 6, 7, 8] C. E. Abranson; [12] Institute of Geological Sciences. **242–3** [Key] Spectrum Colour Library; [1A–C] C. E. Abranson; [7, 8, 9, 10] Basil Booth; [11, 12, 13] C. E. Abranson; [14A–C] Basil Booth. **242–3** [Key] Ron Boardman; [2] Courtesy of De Beers Consolidated Mines Ltd.; [6A] Institute of Geological Sciences; [6B] C. E. Abranson; [6C] Basil Booth; [6D, 7A] Institute of Geological Sciences; [7B] Basil Booth; [8A] Institute of Geological Sciences; [8B] C. E. Abranson; [9A–B, 10A–B, 11A–B, 12A] Institute of Geological Sciences; [12B] C. E. Abranson; [13A–B, 14A–B, 15A–B, 16A–B, 17A–B, 18A–B] Institute of Geological Sciences. **244–5** [6, 7A–D] Basil Booth. **246–7** [3, 4, 5A] Basil Booth; [5B–D] C. E. Abranson; [5E–F] Basil Booth. **252–3** [7] Picturepoint; [8] Australian Tourist Commission. **254–5** [6] Spectrum Colour Library. **256–7** [3] Dr A. C. Waltham; [4] Ardea Photographics; [5] C. E. Abranson; [6] C. J. Ott/Bruce Coleman Ltd.; [7] C. E. Abranson. **260–1** [Key] David Strickland; [4, 5] P. Morris; [6] Picturepoint. **262–3** [Key] Spectrum Colour Library; [3] Picturepoint; [4] Barnabys Picture Library; [5] Picturepoint; [6, 7] Barnabys Picture Library. **264–5** [3] Barnabys Picture Library. **266–7** [Key] Chris Bryan/Robert Harding Associates; [6] C. Walker/Natural Science Photos; [7A–B] Paul Brierley; [12] Picturepoint. **268–9** [2] Picturepoint; [6] G. R. Roberts. **270–1** [Key, 2] Picturepoint; [5] Isobel Bennett/Natural Science Photos. **274–5** [6] D. Dixon. **276–7** [4] F. Jackson/Robert Harding Associates; [6] C. E. Abranson; [7] A. J. Deane/Bruce Coleman Ltd. **278–9** [Key, 4, 5, 6] C. E. Abranson; [7, 8] Basil Booth. **280–1** [Key] M. F. Woods & Associates; [3] W. Bockhaus/ZEFA; [4] Spectrum Colour Library; [6] C. E. Abranson; [7] Weir Group Ltd. **282–3** [Key] Institute of Geological Sciences; [5] Photri; [6] Picturepoint. **284–5** [Key] C. E. Abranson. **286–7** [5] Barnabys Picture Library; [7] C. E. Abranson; [8] Basil Booth. **288–9** [3] J. Nuyton/Robert Harding Associates; [7] Henry Monroe/DPI. **290–1** [Key] George Hall/Susan Griggs Picture Agency; [2A–B] Joy Mfg. Co., Exxon; [3] Picturepoint; [5] John G. Ross/Susan Griggs Picture Agency. **292–3** [5] Wide World Photos. **294–5** [Key] Spectrum Colour Library; [3] Source unknown. **296–7** [6A–B] Picturepoint. **300–1** [Key] Daily Telegraph Colour Library; [2] Fairey Surveys; [3] KLM Aerocarts. **302–3** [8] Picturepoint. **304–5** [1, 5] Picturepoint; [7] Museum of English Rural Life, University of Reading; [8] Aerofilms; [9] Picturepoint. **306–7** [2] Picturepoint; [4] Adam Woolfitt/Susan Griggs Picture Agency; [5] Picturepoint. **308–9** [Key] International Harvester. **310–1** [1] Photri; [6] David Strickland. **314–5** [Key] Spectrum Colour Library; [1] J. Edwards/Robert Harding Associates; [2] Leonard Freed/Magnum; [3] Ronald Sheridan; [4A] C. E. Abranson; [4C] Photri. **316–7** [Key] Shell Photographic Library; [5] New Zealand High Commission. **318–9** [Key] Fisons Agricultural Division; [6] Tropical Products Institute [Crown Copyright]; [8A] Glasshouse Crops Research Institute; [8B] Ministry of Agriculture & Fisheries; [8E] National Vegetable

Research Station. **320–1** [Key] Farmers Weekly/Philip Felkin; [4] Basil Booth. **322–3** [Key] Plant Breeding Institute Trumpington, Cambs. **326–7** [Key] ZEFA. **328–9** [Key] Ron Boardman; [4] Robert Harding Associates/Tim Megarry; [5] Picturepoint. **330–1** [Key] American Soybean Association. **332–3** [Key] Potato Marketing Board. **338–9** [1] Bruce Coleman Ltd./John Markham; [2] E. W. Tattersall. **340–1** [1A] William MacQuitty; [1B] Picturepoint. **342–3** [5] British Sugar Corporation; [8] Source unknown; [9] Photri. **344–5** [Key] Scala/Napoli Museo Nazionale; [1] Mansell Collection; [2] Source unknown; [3A] Michael Holford; [3B] Michael Holford/British Museum; [4] Michael Holford; [5] Photographie Giraudon/Musée de Cluny; [7] Photographie Giraudon/Musée Conde Chantilly. **346–7** [Key] John Bulmer [3A–D, 4A] Pierre Mackiewicz. **348–9** [Key] Source unknown. **350–1** [Key] Michael Holford; [2] Fisons Photo Studio; [3A] Spectrum Colour Library; [3B] Brewers Association. **352–3** [Key] Source unknown; [2, 3, 4] International Distillers and Vintners; [5] Streets Financial Ltd./Highland Distilleries; [8] C. E. Abranson. **354–5** [Key] ZEFA; [1] Mary Evans Picture Library; [2] C. E. Abranson; [4] Spectrum Colour Library; [7] C. E. Abranson/Museum of Mankind. **356–7** [2] Robert Harding Associates/Jon Gardey. **360–1** [3] Bill Holden; **363–4** [Key] C. E. Abranson; [2] David Strickland; [3B] C. E. Abranson; [6] David Strickland. **364–5** [Key] Bruce Thomas/Nancy Palmer; [8] Barnabys Picture Library; [10] Picturepoint. **366–7** [1, 2] Hilliers Nurseries, Winchester. **368–9** [Key] Robert Harding Associates/Jeffrey Craig [Key] A–Z Botanical Collection. **370–1** [Key] Ron Boardman; [4] Spectrum Colour Library; [7] Picturepoint; [8] Camera Press. **372–3** [Key, 2] C. E. Abranson, [3] Spectrum Colour Library. **374–5** [Key] Museum of English Rural Life; [3] Mr Pampa; [4] Oxfam/Nick Fogden; [5] Daily Telegraph Colour Library; [6] Express Dairies. **376–7** [2] David Strickland; [3] University of Connecticut; [4] New Zealand Consulate; [6] 4-H Clubs of America; [7] G. Riethmeier/ZEFA; [8] David Strickland. **378–9** [7A–B] David Strickland. **382–3** [Key] Photri. **384–5** [Key] Mansell Collection. **386–7** [Key] Harry Barrett/Fishing News; [9A–B] Michael Francis Wood & Associates. **388–9** [Key] Photri; [1] Photo Fratelli Fabbri Editori; [5] Marine Harvest Ltd.; [6] Michael Francis Wood & Associates. **390–1** [Key A] Photri; [Key B] Frank W. Lane/R. Thompson; [3] Frank W. Lane/F. W. Lane. **392–3** [Key] Keystone. **396–7** [Key] David Strickland; [1] C. E. Abranson/National Maritime Museum; [2] John Massey-Stewart; [3] Spectrum Colour Library; [4] David Strickland; [5] Mansell Collection; [6] H. J. Heinz & Co. Ltd.; [7] David Strickland. **398–9** [4] Texas Meat Brokerage Inc., Burlingame, California; [7] Courtaulds Ltd.; [8] B. P. Proteins/British Petroleum Ltd.; [9] Mansell Collection.

Life on Earth
400–1 Warren Garst/Tom Stack and Associates. **402–3** Eric Hosking. **404–5** O.S.F./Bruce Coleman Ltd. **406–7** [2] Institute of Molecular Evolution. **408–9** [2] Jane Burton/Bruce Coleman Ltd. **412–3** [2] Gene Cox/Bruce Coleman Ltd; [3] Gene Cox. **414–5** [Key] M. H. F. Wilkins; [6] Gene Cox. **416–7** [5] Mansell Collection. **422–3** [6, 7, 8] C. James Webb. **426–7** [5, 11] Heather Angel; **428–9** [1] Heather Angel; [3, 5, 6] Dr D. A. Reid; [8] Brian Hawkes. **434–5** [2, 3] Heather Angel; [4A] Eric Hosking; [4B] R & C Foord/N.H.P.A. **436–7** [3] Heather Angel. **438–9** [5] A–Z Botanical Collection; [8, 10] Heather Angel; [11] P. H. Ward/Natural Science Photos. **440–1** [4] Laboratory of Tree-Ring Research, University of Arizona; [9A] A–Z Botanical Collection. **442–3** [4] Bruce Coleman/Bruce Coleman Ltd; [5] W. F. Davidson; [6] Arne Schmitz/Bruce Coleman Ltd; [10] Claude Nardin/Jacana; [11] F. H. C. Birch/Sonia Halliday. **452–3** [9] Ron Boardman. **462–3** [5D] P. H. Ward/Natural Science Photos; [6] Francisco Erize/Bruce Coleman Ltd. **466–7** [7] Ronan Picture Library. **468–9** [1] O.S.F./Bruce Coleman Ltd; [2] Allan Power/Bruce Coleman Ltd; [4] Jane Burton/Bruce Coleman Ltd; [6] Allan Power/Bruce Coleman Ltd. **472–3** [8] Gene Cox/Bruce Coleman Ltd; [10] K. S. Seymour. **474–5** [3] Oxford Scientific Films; [4, 5] Heather Angel; [7] ZEFA; [8] Heather Angel; [9] Australian News & Information Bureau; [10] Dr J. D. George/British Museum [Natural History]. **476–7** [4] Oxford Scientific Films; [5] Jane Burton/Bruce Coleman Ltd; [7A] S. C. Bisserot/Bruce Coleman Ltd; [8, 9] Heather Angel; [10] Bruce Coleman/Bruce Coleman Ltd; [11] Isobel Bennett/Natural Science Photos. **478–9** [6] Dr D. P. Wilson. **480–1** [3] J. L. Mason/Ardea Photographics; [7A–B] Dr D. P. Wilson. **486–7** [2] Heather Angel; [4, 5] O.S.F./Bruce Coleman Ltd.; [9A–B] Jane Burton/Bruce Coleman Ltd. **488–9** [3] P. H. Ward/Natural Science Photos; [4, 5] A. Bannister/N.H.P.A.; [6, 8] P. H. Ward/Natural Science Photos. **504–5** [3] Dr D. P. Wilson; [4] Heather Angel. **508–9** [5, 6] Dr D. P. Wilson; [11, 13] Heather Angel. **512–3** [2] Jane Burton/Bruce Coleman Ltd; [3] Dr D. P. Wilson. **522–3** [4] P. Kirkpatrick/Frank W. Lane; [8] N. Myers/Bruce Coleman Ltd. **536–7** [2] L. Lee Rue III/Bruce Coleman Ltd; [4] Nina Leen/Life © Time Inc. 1976/Colorific. **550–1** [1] J. Whitman/Ardea Photographics; [6] Jeff Foott/Bruce Coleman Ltd. **558–9** [4] Ron Boardman. **560–1** [6A–C] W. R. Hamilton/Imitor. **562–3** [Key] Institute of Geological Sciences; [1B] Oxford Scientific Films; [5] A. C. Waltham; [9A] W. R. Hamilton/Imitor; [9B] C2M/Natural Science Photos. **564–5** [5] Heather Angel; [6] Peder Aspen; [9] Heather Angel; [13] W. F. Davidson. **566–7** [5] James Allan. **578–9** [2] Mary Evans Picture Library. **580–1** [1] A. J. Sutcliffe/Natural Science Photos; [2] C. J. Pruett/Natural Science Photos; [3] M. Stanley Price/Natural Science Photos; [4] Dick Brown/Natural Science Photos; [5] A. Leutscher/Natural Science Photos; [6] P. H. Ward/Natural Science Photos. **586–7** [4] Lyn Cawley. **588–9** [1] Francisco Erize/Bruce Coleman Ltd. **590–1** [4] J. A. Grant/Natural Science Photos; [5] N. McFarland/Natural Science Photos. **596–7** [2] Hans & Judy Beste/Ardea Photographics; [4] John Brownlie/Bruce Coleman Ltd. **598–9** [4] P. H. Ward/Natural Science Photos. **604–5** [Key] Picturepoint; [2] P. Morris/Ardea Photographics; [4] C. Banks/Natural Science Photos; [9] Jane Burton/Bruce Coleman Ltd. **612–3** [3] Brian Hawkes. **616–7** [3] Picturepoint. **620–1** [Key] R. Scott/Institute of Terrestrial Ecology; [2C] Eric Hosking; [3A] P. Morris/Ardea Photographics; [6A] Ivan Polunin/N.H.P.A. **622–3** [1A] Heather Angel; [1B] Dr D. P. Wilson; [1C] Joyce Pope; [4] Isobel Bennett/Natural Science Photos; [5] P. Scoones/Photo Aquatics. **624–5** [Key] Dr D. P. Wilson; [3] Peter David/Seaphot; [4] Hans Dossenbach/Natural Science Photos. **626–7** [2] Christian Petron/Seaphot; [3] Seaphot; [4] Christian Petron/Seaphot; [5] Allan Power/Bruce Coleman Ltd. **628–9** [1] David Strickland; [6] Bill Eppridge/Life © Time Inc. 1976/Colorific; [8] Douglas Botting; [10] M. Stanley Price/Natural Science Photos. **632–3** [Key] Kim Sayer. **634–5** [4] Hans Reinhard/Bruce Coleman Ltd. **636–7** [Key] Joe Rychetnik/Transworld; [1] Horst Munzig/Susan Griggs Picture Agency; [2] Rex Graham Reserve, Mildenhall; [3] L. Lee Rue IV/Bruce Coleman Ltd; [4] Robert Schroeder/Bruce Coleman Ltd; [7] Nigel Sitwell. **638–9** [Key] Zoological Society of London; [1] New York Zoological Society; [3] Spectrum Colour Library; [6] Zoological Society of London; [7] Spectrum Colour Library; [8] New York Botanical Garden; [9] Spectrum Colour Library.

Man
640–1 US Olympic Committee. **642–3** Okamura/T.L.P.A. © Time Inc. 1976/Colorific. **644** W. Braun/ZEFA. **645** Farrell Greham/Susan Griggs Picture Agency. **650–1** [2] Aubrey Singer/BBC/Robert Harding Associates; [4] British Museum [Natural History]. **654–5** [Key] Mark Edwards. **662–3** [Key] Photri; [2] Daily Telegraph Colour Library; [3] Ron Boardman; [4] Gene Cox; [5] C. James Webb; [6] Ron Boardman. **670–1** [Key] Photri. **672–3** [1] Courtesy of Bell Telephone Laboratories. **678–9** [Key] Mike Busselle; [6] ZEFA. **696–7** [6A] Westminster Medical School; [6B–C] Dept. of Human Nutrition, London School of Hygiene & Tropical Medicine; [6D] Peter Hansell/Westminster Medical School; [6E–F] Dept. of Human Nutrition, London School of Hygiene & Tropical Medicine; [7] No credit; [8] David Strickland; [9] Ralph Morse © Time Magazine 1975/Colorific. **706–7** [Key] Mansell Collection; [5, 6] Transworld. **708–9** [Key, 1, 2, 4, 5] Mary Evans Picture Library; [6] Mansell Collection; [7] Mary Evans Picture Library; [8] Mansell Collection. **710–11** [Key] Radio Times Hulton Picture Library; [1] Chris Steele-Perkins; [3] Keystone Press; [4A–D] C. James Webb; [4E] Ron Boardman; [4F] C. James Webb. **712–3** [Key] Glaxo; [3A–B] Prof. Werner Wright; [5] Institute of Dermatology; [7] Barnes Engineering. **714–5** [4A] Picturepoint; [4B] Sally & Richard Greenhill; [4C–D] C. James Webb. **716–7** [7] T. Clegg/Dept. of Photography/University of Newcastle upon Tyne. **718–9** [2A–B] Dr Tonkin/Endoscopy Unit, Westminster Hospital; [3, 7] C. James Webb. **720–1** [Key A, B, 2, 7] C. James Webb. **722–3** [1A–C] Transport & Road Research Laboratory; [2] Dr Stepanek/ZEFA; [4] Mike Hardy/Marshall Cavendish Picture Library; [6] C. Henneghein/Bruce Coleman Ltd; [7] Mary Evans Picture Library. **724–5** [2] Picturepoint; [4] Institute of Dermatology; [9] Chris Steele-Perkins; [11] Institute of Dermatology; [12] Picturepoint. **726–7** [Key] Leicester Museum & Art Galleries; [3] Syndication International; [4] Prof. Orsi/University of Geneva Medical School; [8] Mike Ricketts. **728–9** [3] Picturepoint; [5E] C. James Webb. **730–1** [Key] Western Americana. **732–3** [3] C. James Webb; [8] Picturepoint; [10] C. James Webb. **734–5** [7] WHO/UNICEF; [8, 9] Picturepoint. **736–7** [Key] Mary Evans Picture Library; [2] Photri; [3] The New Haven Register; [4] Meat & Livestock Commission; [5] Barnabys Picture Library; [6] Bill Holden; [7] Kim Sayer; [9] Picturepoint; [10] Keystone Press; [11] Kim Sayer. **738–9** [2] Spectrum Colour Library; [3] The Wellcome Foundation Ltd; [5] David Strickland; [7A–B] Ken Moreman; [9] David Strickland. **742–3** [2, 4] Graeme French; [5] Mary Evans Picture Library; [6] H. Schumacher/EFA; [9] Picturepoint. **744–5** [Key] Kim Sayer; [4] Photri; [5] Kim Sayer; [7] Vautier-Decool. **746–7** [Key] D. K. Miller; [2A–B] Mansell Collection; [2C] Popperfoto; [3] Bristol-Myers Co.; [5] Popperfoto; [6] Picturepoint; [7] Keystone Press; [8] Kim Sayer. **748–9** [Key] WHO; [1] Photri; [2] Marcus Brooke/Colorific; [4] Courtesy of Thomas Y. Crowell Inc.; [5, 6] Source unknown; [7] Graeme French. **750–1** [Key] Ronan Picture Library; [4] Dept. of Medical Photography/Barts Hospital; [5, 7] E.M.I. **752–3** [4] Robert Hunt Library/Imperial War Museum; [6] Daily Telegraph Colour Library. **756–7** All photographs supplied by Peter Hurst. **758–9** [Key] Kim Sayer. **760–1** [Key] Robert Hunt Library. **762–3** [Key] Mansell Collection; [1] Museum of Archaeology & Ethnology, Cambridge University; [2] Mansell Collection; [3] Scala; [4] Mansell Collection; [5] Mary Evans Picture Library; [6] Mansell Collection; [8A] International Society for Educational Information, Tokyo. **764–5** [Key] National Gallery of Art, Washington/Rosenwald Collection. **766–7** [Key] Mansell Collection. **768–9** [Key] Chris Steele-Perkins; [1B] Stern Archive; [3] Mary Evans Picture Library. **770–1** [Key] Ronan Picture Library/E. P. Goldschmidt & Co. Ltd; [6] Popperfoto. **772–3** [1] Mansell Collection; [5] Alfred A. Knopf. **776–7** [Key] Kim Sayer. **780–1** [Key] Kim Sayer. **782–3** [Key, 1] Kim Sayer; [2, 5, 6, 7] David Strickland. **784–5** [Key] Spectrum Colour Library; [5] Rex Features; [6] David Strickland. **786–7** [Key] Kim Sayer. **790–1** [Key] David Hurn/Magnum; [4] DPI; [5] Rex Features; [6] Ray Green; [7] F. Paul/ZEFA. **792–3** [Key] Mansell Collection; [1] Colin Maher; [2] Kobal Collection; [3] Osterreichische Galerie/Fotostudio Otto; [4] Angelo Hornak/V & A; [5] Picturepoint; [6] Wide World Photos; [7, 8]. **794–5** [Key] Syd Greenberg/DPI; [1] Mary Evans Picture Library; [2] Keystone Press; [3] National Gallery; [5] Popperfoto; [6] Wide World Photos; [7] Popperfoto; [8] UPI. **796–7** [Key] Picturepoint; [1B, 2B] Richard R.

Collins/DPI. **798–9** [Key] Phoebe Dunn/DPI; [1B] Al Kaplan/DPI; [2B] Lida Moser/DPI. **800–1** [Key] Werner Neumeuster; [1B] John V. Dunigan/DPI; [2B] Bea Goodwyn/DPI. **804–5** [Key] Popperfoto; [5] Staat Museen Preussischer Kulturbesitz Gemaldegalerie. **806–7** [Key] Associated Press; [3] Photoresources; [4] Mansell Collection; [5] P. Thiele/ZEFA; [6, 7A, 7B] No credit. **808–9** [Key, 1] Popperfoto; [2, 3, 4] Camera Press; [5] Transworld; [6] Camera Press. **810–1** [Key] David Strickland; [1] Cooper Bridgeman; [2] Graeme French; [3] Mansell Collection; [4] Picturepoint; [5] Mary Evans Picture Library; [6] Spectrum Colour Library; [7] Scala; [8] Cooper Bridgeman/National Gallery, Scotland; [9] Mary Evans Picture Library. **812–3** [1] The Cavalry Club; [2] Mary Evans Picture Library; [3] Giraudon/Louvre; [4] A. F. Kersting; [6] David Hughes/Bruce Coleman Ltd; [7] Mary Evans Picture Library; [8] Source unknown. **814–5** [1A–C] Zentralbibliothek, Zurich. **816–7** [Key] Imperial War Museum; [1] Robert Hunt Library; [2] United Society for the Propagation of the Gospel/Weidenfeld & Nicolson; [3] Photri; [4, 5] Picturepoint; Collection; [2] Sally & Richard Greenhill; [3] Keystone Press; [4] Photri; [6] Popperfoto; [7] Mansell Collection; [8] Popperfoto; [9] Wide World Photos.˙ **906–7** [2] Dev O'Neill; [5] National Park Service; [7] Peter Arnold/Gerhard E. Gscheidle; [10, 11] Wide World Photos; [15] US Department of Transportation. **908–9** [Key] Spectrum Colour Library; [2] Marshall Cavendish Picture Library/Bodleian Library, Oxford; [3, 5, 6, 7] Mary Evans Picture Picture Library. **910–1** [2] Spectrum Colour Library; [4] Bill Eppridge/Life Magazine © Time Inc. 1976 Colorific; [5] Popperfoto; [6] Keystone Press; [7] Picturepoint. **912–3** [2] Mary Evans Picture Library; [3] Camera Press. **914–5** [Key] Bodleian Library, Oxford; [4] Tony Ray Jones/Magnum; [5] Wide World Photos. **916–7** [2] Popperfoto; [3] John Frost Newspaper Collection; [4] Popperfoto; [5A] Norris McNamara/Nancy Palmer; [6] US Department of Justice; [7, 8] Camera Press; [9] Popperfoto. **918–9** [Key] Western Americana; [1] Mary Evans Picture Library; [2] Jacques Penry, Inventor; [3] Mansell Collection: [4] Keystone Press; [5] Daily Telegraph Colour Library; [6] Camera Press; [7] David Strickland/courtesy Security Express. **922–3** [Key, 10] Sean McConville; [12] Bettmann Archive; [13] State of New York. [6] Cooper Bridgeman; [7] John Webb/Trustees of the Tate Gallery. **818–9** [1A, B] Mary Evans Picture Library; [1C] Popperfoto; [3] J. Bitsch/ZEFA; [5] The Frick Collection; [6] O. Luz/ZEFA; [7] R. Scutt & C. Gotch from *Skin Deep*/Japanese Tatoo Club; [9] Elmer E. Green/Menninger Foundation. **820–1** [Key] Monitor; [6] V. Wentzel/ZEFA; [7] SRM Foundation of Great Britain; [8] TM®. **822–3** [Key] Ronan Picture Library; [1] Picturepoint; [2, 4, 5, 6] Mary Evans Picture Library; [7] Popperfoto; [8] Psychic News; [9] David Strickland. **824–5** [1] Ronan Picture Library; [2] Foundation for the Research of Man; [3B, 5B] Janet Mitchell; [6A–C] Paraphysical Laboratory, Downton, Wiltshire; [8] Ben Martin/Colorific. **826–7** [2] Source unknown. **828–9** [Key] Popperfoto; [2] R. M. Bloomfield/Ardea Photographics; [3] David Strickland; [4] F. Walther/ZEFA; [5] Ron Boardman; [6] Sonia Halliday; [8] Keystone Press; [9] Picturepoint. **830–1** [Key] Spectrum Colour Library; [2] John Moss/Colorific; [3] M. Block; [4] Sybil Sassoon/Robert Harding Associates; [6] Mirella Ricciardi/Bruce Coleman Ltd. **832–3** [Key] Source unknown; [3] Angelo Hornak; [4] Josephine Powell; [6] Photoresources; [7] Michael Holford; [8] Werner Forman Archive. **834–5** [Key] Giraudon, Musée Condé, Chantilly; [1] Statens Museum fur Kunst; [2] John Freeman & Co.; [3] Giraudon; [4] Museum of Fine Arts, Boston; [5] Photoresources; [6] Michael Holford/British Museum; [7, 8] Axel Poignant; [9] Photorescourses; [10] Michael Holford/British Museum; [11] Scala. **836–7** [Key] Giraudon/Musée Condé, Chantilly; [1, 2] Photoresources; [3] Mansell Collection; [4] Werner Forman Archive; [5] Photoresources; [6, 7] Angelo Hornak/British Museum; [8] Werner Forman Archive; [9] National Gallery. **838–9** [Key] Giraudon/Musée Condé, Chantilly; [1] Michael Holford/British Museum; [2] Photoresources/Louvre; [3] The Granger Collection; [4] The Bettman Archive; [5] Source unknown; [6] Michael Holford/Bardo Museum; [7] Michael Holford/V & A; [8] Michael Holford/British Museum; [9] Ann & Bury Peerless/Baroda Museum. **840–1** [1] Michael Holford/British Museum; [2] Merseyside County Museum; [3] Michael Holford; [4] Trevor Wood/Ranworth Church Council/Norwich Castle Museum; [5] Freiburg Augustine Museum; [6, 7] Michael Holford; [9] John Webb/Trustees of the Tate Gallery. **842–3** [Key] Michael Holford/British Museum; [1] Bodleian Library, Oxford; [2] Isobel Bennett/Natural Science Photos; [3] William MacQuitty; [4] Source unknown; [5] Cooper Bridgeman; [6] Photri; [7] Topkapi Museum. **844–5** [Key] Scala; [1] Van Phillipps/ZEFA; [2, 3] Angelo Hornak; [4] Transworld; [5] Source unknown; [6] National Gallery; [7] Scala. **846–7** [Key] Photoresources/British Museum; [1, 2] Middle East Archives; [3] Michael Holford; [5] Ann & Bury Peerless; [6] Werner Forman Archive; [7] Photoresources; [9] William MacQuitty. **848–9** [Key] Middle East Archives; [1] Hamlyn Group Picture Library; [2] National Gallery; [3] Ann & Bury Peerless; [4] Michael Holford; [5, 6] Werner Forman Archive; [7] Michael Holford. **850–1** [Key] Mansell Collection; [1] Angelo Hornak/V & A; [2] Photri; [3] Phillip Daly; [4] Camera Press; [5] Mike Peters; [6, 7] Camera Press. **852–3** [Key] Mansell Collection; [2, 8] Mary Evans Picture Library. **854–5** [Key] Mary Evans Picture Library; [2] Popperfoto. **856–7** [Key] Scala; [1] Bodleian Library; [3] Mary Evans Picture Library; [6] Cooper Bridgeman; [7, 8A] Mary Evans Picture Library; [8B] Popperfoto. **860–1** [Key] Mary Evans Picture Library; [1A] Giraudon/Louvre; [1B] Bodleian Library, Oxford; [3] Popperfoto; [4, 5] Mary Evans Picture Library; [6] Mansell Collection; [7] Mary Evans Picture Library. **862–3** All photographs from Paul Ekman & Wallace V. Freisens *Unmasking the Face.* **864–5** [Key] Popperfoto; [3A–C] Copyright © 1973 Ziff-Davis Publishing Company. Reprinted by permission of *Psychology Today* magazine. **870–1** [2] Michael Holford. **872–3** [Key, 1] Trustees of the British Museum; [2] The British Library; [3] Ronald Sheridan; [4, 5B] Photoresources; [6] Trustees of the British Museum; [7] Bodleian Library, Oxford; [8] Trustees of the British Museum; [9] Bodleian Library, Oxford; [10A] Michael Holford/British Museum; [10B] Source unknown/photo Geoff Goode; [10C] Bodleian Library, Oxford; [10D] Michael Holford/Musée Jacquemart-André; [11] No credit. **874–5** [Key] Mary Evans Picture Library; [2] Werner Forman Archive; [3] Radio Times Hulton Picture Library; [4, 5] Mary Evans Picture Library; [7] John Moss/Colorific. **876–7** [Key] Bob Van Doren/Courtesy CRM/Random House; [1] Clem Haagner/Ardea Photographics; [2] Picturepoint; [3] Ronald Sheridan. **878–9** [1A] Camera Press; [1B] Picturepoint; [2] Peter Fraenkel; [3] Russell Ryman. **880–1** [Key] Camera Press; [2] Spectrum Colour Library; [3] P. Conklin/Colorific; [4, 5] Tony Morrison; [7] Jeffrey Craig/Robert Harding Associates; [8] Peter Ibbotson/Robert Harding Associates; [9] Ron Boardman. **882–3** [Key] Prof. C. Haimandorf. **884–5** [Key] David Moore/Colorific; [2] Karl Wittfogel; [3] Picturepoint; [4] Institute of Archaeology; [7] Radio Times Hulton Picture Library; [8] Werner Forman Archive. **886–7** [Key] Mansell Collection; [2] Ronan Picture Library; [3] Mary Evans Picture Library; [4] Radio Times Hulton Picture Library; [5] Mansell Collection; [6] Picturepoint; [7] Mansell Collection; [8] Werner Forman Archive; [9] Mary Evans Picture Library. **888–9** [Key] Popperfoto; [4] Punch Publications Ltd; [7] Kim Sayer. **890–1** [1] Popperfoto; [2] Wide World Photos; [3] Spectrum Colour Library; [4] Keystone Press; [5] Spectrum Colour Library; [6] Alfredo Zennaro; [7] David Strickland. **892–3** [2] Mrs Alfred Schutz; [3] Punch Publications Ltd; **894–5** [Key] Popperfoto; [1] R & M Borland/Bruce Coleman Ltd; [2] Ray Green; [3, 4, 5] Mansell Collection; [6] Associated Press; [7] Towers of London/National Film Archive; [8] Marc Riboud/Magnum. **896–7** [Key] Camera Press; [1] Bettmann Archive; [4, 5] Wide World Photos; [6] Popperfoto. **898–9** [Key] Picturepoint; [5] Mary Evans Picture Library; [6] Camera Press; [7, 8] Mary Evans Picture Library; [9] Bill Angove/Colorific. **900–1** [1, 6] Popperfoto. **902–3** [Key] Barnabys Picture Library; [6A, 8] Popperfoto. **904–5** [Key] Mansell Collection **926–7** [2] Spectrum Colour Library; [3] Volvo Concessionaries Ltd. **930–1** [Key] Little League Baseball; [1] Picturepoint; [2, 3, 4] Spectrum Colour Library; [5] Colorsport; [6] Picturepoint; [7] Source unknown; [8] Colorsport; [9] Spectrum Colour Library; [10] Picturepoint. **934–5** [Key] Camera Press. **936–7** [Key] Picturepoint; [6] DPI; [8] Wide World Photos. **940–1** [Key] A. Clifton/Colorific; [2] Picturepoint. **942–3** [6] Spectrum Colour Library; [7] C.O.I.

History and Culture

944–5 Photographed by European Art Color. **946** [1] Keystone Press Agency; [2] Novosti Press Agency. **947** Trustees of the National Gallery. **948** Hubert Josse. **949** Bodleian Library, Oxford. **950–1** [1] Colorphoto Hans Hinz, Basle; [2] Achille B. Weider, Zurich; [3, 4] Photoresources; [5] Picturepoint; [6] D. F. E. Russell/Robert Harding Associates; [7] Published by permission of the Danish National Museum; [9] Federico Arborio Mella. **952–3** [3] Jon Gardey/Robert Harding Associates; [6] Picturepoint; [12] C. M. Dixon. **954–5** [Key, 2, 3, 4, 6, 7] P. Hulin; [8] Staatliche Museen, Berlin. **956–7** [Key] Ronald Sheridan; [1] P. Hulin; [4] Ronald Sheridan; [5A–B] Michael Holford/British Museum; [6] Photoresources/British Museum; [8] Photoresources/Istanbul Archaeological Museum. **958–9** [Key, 1B] P. Hulin; [2] Source unknown; [3] Photoresources/British Museum; [4] P. Hulin; [6] Mansell Collection; [7] Giraudon/Louvre; [8] Lauros Giraudon/Louvre. **960–1** [Key] Michael Holford; [2] Werner Forman Archive; [3A] Museum of Fine Arts, Boston, Harvard Boston Expedition Fund; [3B, 5] Ronald Sheridan; [6] Roger Wood; [7, 8] Ronald Sheridan; **962–3** [Key] All pictures Ann and Bury Peerless; [2] J. Allan Cash; [3] Ann and Bury Peerless; [6] J. Powell/Karachi Museum; [7] Source unknown; [8] Ann and Bury Peerless. **964–5** [Key] Ronald Sheridan; [5] Leonard Von Matt; [6, 7] Ronald Sheridan; [9] Patricia W. Ehresmann. **966–7** [Key] Ronald Sheridan; [3] Mrs Alan Wace; [6, 7] Photoresources; [8] Hirmer Fotoarchiv, Munich/National Museum, Athens. **968–9** [Key] William MacQuitty; [1] Paolo Koch; [2, 3, 4, 5, 7] William MacQuitty; [8] William MacQuitty/Shanghai Museum. **970–1** [Key] Instituto Nacional de Antropologia E Historia, Mexico/Norman Hammond; [1, 2, 3] Norman Hammond; [4] Tony Morrison; [5] G. Bushnell; [7] Tatiana Proskouriakoff/Peabody Museum; [8] Norman Hammond. **972–3** [Key] Barnabys Picture Library; [1] Werner Forman Archive/Charles Edwin Wilbour Fund, Brooklyn Museum; [2A, 2B, 4] Ronald Sheridan; [5] Michael Holford; [6] Erich Lessing/Magnum; [7] Werner Forman Archive/Cairo Museum. **974–5** [Key A, B] Source unknown; [2, 3, 4] Werner Forman Archive; [5] Roger Wood; [6] Alan Hutchinson; [7] Werner Forman Archive. **976–7** [Key] P. Hulin; [1] Hirmer Fotoarchiv, Munich; [2] Richard Ashworth/Robert Harding Associates; [3A] Ronald Sheridan; [3B] Werner Forman Archive/Schimmel Collection, New York; [4] Ronald Sheridan; [5] Richard Ashworth/Robert Harding Associates; [6] P. Hulin; [7] Mansell Collection; [8] Photoresources. **978–9** [Key] Hirmer Fotoarchiv, Munich/Baghdad Museum; [1] Ronald Sheridan; [2] Trustees of the British Museum; [4] Ronald Sheridan; [5] Michael Holford/British Museum; [6] Photoresources; [7] Michael Holford; [8] Source unknown. **980–1** [Key] Staatliche Museen, Berlin; [2] Ronald Sheridan; [3] Michael Holford/British Museum; [4] Mansell Collection; [5] Ronald Sheridan; [6, 7] P. Hulin; [8] Michael Holford/British Museum; [9] P. Hulin. **982–3** [Key] Ronald Sheridan; [2] Camera Press; [3] Ronald Sheridan; [4] C. M. Dixon; [6] Scala; [7] Photoresources/British Museum; [8] Source unknown. **984–5** [Key, 2, 3] William MacQuitty; [4] Ray Gardner/Trustees of the British Museum; [5, 8, 9] William MacQuitty. **986–7** [Key] India Office Library and Records/John F. Freeman; [2, 3A, B, 4] Ann and Bury Peerless; [5A–B] Trustees of the British Museum/Ray

Gardner; [7, 8] Ann and Bury Peerless. **988–9** [Key] Ann and Bury Peerless; [1] A. F. Kersting; [3, 4] Ann and Bury Peerless; [5] Source unknown; [6] Musée Louis Finot, Hanoi; [7] Bill and Claire Leimbach/Robert Harding Associates; [8] Museum of Fine Arts, Boston/Ross Collection. **990–1** [Key, 2, 3, 4] Anne Ross; [5, 6] National Museum of Ireland; [7] Photoresources; [8] Anne Ross/Musée de Chatillon-sur-Seine; [9] Photoresources; [10] National Museum of Ireland; [11] Anne Ross. **992–3** [Key] Trustees of the British Museum; [3] Erich Lessing/Magnum; [5] Michael Holford; [6] Metropolitan Museum of Art, New York, Purchase 1947, Joseph Pulitzer Bequest. **994–5** [Key] Metropolitan Museum of Art, New York/Rogers Fund 1906; [1] Photoresources/Acropolis Museum, Athens; [6] Photoresources/National Museum, Athens; [7] Ronald Sheridan; [8] Mauro Pucciarelli. **996–7** [Key] Ronald Sheridan; [1] Edwin Smith; [3] Published by permission of the Danish National Museum; [4] Michael Holford; [5] Photoresources; [6] Wadsworth Atheneum, Hartford, Connecticut; [7] Michael Holford; [8] Metropolitan Museum of Art, New York/Rogers Fund 1914. **998–9** [Key] Trustees of the British Museum/Ray Gardner; [1] Michael Holford/British Museum; [2] Staatliche Museen, Berlin; [3, 4] Dimitrios Harissiadis; [5] Hirmer Fotoarchiv, Munich; [7] Scala. **1000–1** [Key] Ronald Sheridan; [2] Roger Wood; [3] Michael Holford; [4] Hirmer Fotoarchiv, Munich; [5] Trustees of the British Museum; [6, 7] Photoresources; [8] Photoresources/Delphi Museum. **1002–3** [Key] Russell Ash; [2] Ronald Sheridan; [4] Joseph Ziolo/Olympia Museo; [5] Photoresources; [6] Photoresources/Vatican Museum; [7] Joseph Ziolo. **1004–5** [Key] Trustees of the British Museum/Ray Gardner; [1] Michael Holford; [2] Photoresources/National Museum, Naples; [5] Photoresources/British Museum; [6] Bodleian Library, Oxford. **1006–7** [Key] Ronan Picture Library/Royal Astronomical Society; [1, 3] Ronan Picture Library; [5] Michael Holford/Ann Mowlem; [7] Michael Holford/National Maritime Museum. **1008–9** [Key, 2, 3] Anne Ross; [4A–B] C. M. Dixon; [5, 6A–B, 7, 8, 9] Anne Ross. **1010–1** [Key, 2] Photoresources; [4, 5] Michael Holford; [6, 8] Leonard von Matt. **1012–3** [Key] Photoresources; [2] Source unknown; [3] Vatican Library/Octopus Books; [4] Aquileia Museum Rome/Fototeca Unione; [5] K. E. Lowther; [6A–B] Trustees of the British Museum/Ray Gardner. **1014–5** [Key] Mansell Collection; [2] K. E. Lowther; [4] Sonia Halliday/F. H. C. Birch; [5] Scala; [6] C. M. Dixon; [7] Mansell Collection. **1016–7** [Key, 1, 2, 3, 4] Scala; [5] Scala/National Museum, Naples; [6] Scala; [7] C. M. Dixon; [8] Mansell Collection; [9] Photoresources. **1018–9** [Key] Mansell Collection; [1] Trustees of the British Museum/Ray Gardner; [2] Scala; [3] Trustees of the British Museum/Ray Gardner; [4] Mansell Collection; [5] Scala; [8] Giraudon; [9] Roger-Viollet. **1020–1** [Key] Photoresources; [2] Angelo Hornak; [3] Scala; [4] Angelo Hornak; [6, 7] Photoresources; [8] Michael Holford/Gerry Clyde; [9] Mansell Collection. **1022–3** [Key] Trustees of the British Museum; [1] Mansell Collection; [2] Scala/Vatican Museum; [3] Lauros Giraudon; [4] Russell Ash; [5] Scala; [7, 8] Photoresources. **1024–5** [Key] C. M. Dixon; [2] Scala; [3] Picturepoint; [4] C. M. Dixon; [5] Picturepoint; [6] C. M. Dixon/British Museum; [7] Trustees of the British Museum/Ray Gardner; [8] Michael Holford. **1026–7** [Key] Scala; [2] Ronald Sheridan; [3] C. M. Dixon; [4] Ronald Sheridan; [5, 6, 7] Scala. **1028–9** [Key] Scala; [1] Bodleian Library, Oxford; [2] Photoresources; [3] Michael Holford/British Museum; [4] Sotheby's; [5] Snark International; [6] Scala/Biblioteca Vaticana; [7] Photoresources; [8] Scala. **1030–1** [Key] Scala; [1] Giraudon/Louvre; [2] Ronald Sheridan; [3A] Mansell Collection; [3B] C. M. Dixon/Louvre; [5] Trustees of the British Museum/Ray Gardner; [6] Photoresources; [7] Angelo Hornak, **1032–3** [Key] Ronan Picture Library; [2, 3] Mansell Collection; [4] Ronan Picture Library; [7] Mansell Collection; [9] Ronan Picture Library. **1034–5** [Key] Hamlyn Group Picture Library; [1, 2, 3, 4] Ann and Bury Peerless; [5] Trustees of the British Museum/Ray Gardner; [6] Peter Fraenkel; [8] Mansell Collection; [9] Oriental Art Archives, University of Michigan. **1036–7** [Key, 1] from *The Art of Indian Asia* by Heinrich Zimmer/Gunvor Moitessier; [3] Ann and Bury Peerless; [4] Trustees of the British Museum; [5] Michael Holford/Musée Guimet, Paris; [6] Victoria and Albert Museum/Carltograph; [7, 8, 9] Michael Holford/Victoria and Albert Museum; [10] Ann and Bury Peerless. **1038–9** [Key, 1] William MacQuitty; [3] Mary Evans Picture Library; [4, 5, 6, 7] William MacQuitty; [8] Robert Harding Associates; [9, 10] William MacQuitty. **1040–1** [Key] British Museum/Hamlyn Group Picture Library; [1] Royal Ontario Museum, Toronto/Hamlyn Group Picture Library; [2] Howard Sochurek/T.L.P.A. © Time Inc. 1976/Colorific; [3] Source unknown; [4] William MacQuitty; [5] Metropolitan Museum of Art, New York/Munsey Bequest, 1924; [6] Victoria and Albert Museum/Godfrey New Photographics; [7] Sally and Richard Greenhill; [8] Bildarchiv Foto Marburg. **1042–3** [1] Trustees of the British Museum; [2] Victoria and Albert Museum; [3] Robert Harding Associates/Witty, Times Newspapers Ltd; [4, 6] William MacQuitty; [8] Source unknown; [9] William MacQuitty; [10] Mansell Collection. **1044–5** [Key] National Palace Museum, Taiwan; [1, 2] Trustees of the British Museum; [3] After "Ma-Wang-Tui Hao Han Mu"; [4, 5] Trustees of the British Museum; [5] [6] National Palace Museum, Taiwan; [7] Reproduced by permission of the Syndics of the Fitzwilliam Museum, Cambridge; [8] National Palace Museum, Taiwan; [9] Werner Forman Archive, Palace Museum, Peking. **1046–7** [Key] Bradley Smith; [2] International Society for Educational Information; [3] Ministry of Foreign Affairs, Japan; [4] International Society for Educational Information; [5] Ministry of Foreign Affairs, Japan; [6] International Society of Educational Information; [7] Ministry of Foreign Affairs, Japan; [8] Bradley Smith. **1048–9** [Key] Sakamoto/Joseph P. Ziolo; [1, 2] K. Ogawa/Joseph P. Ziolo; [3, 4, 5, 6, 7] Sakamoto/Joseph P. Ziolo; [8A–B] Zauhopress/Joseph P. Ziolo/Musée D'Atami; [9] Victoria and Albert Museum; [10] Michael Holford. **1050–1** [Key] Anne Ross; [2, 3] Trinity College, Dublin/The Green Studio; [4A, B, 5A, B] National Museum of Ireland; [6, 7] C. M. Dixon. **1052–3** [Key] Bodleian Library, Oxford; [2] Kunsthistorisches Museum, Vienna; [3] Michael Holford; [5] Bavaria Verlag; [6] Joseph P. Ziolo; [7] National Museum of Ireland; [8] Scala; [10] Burgerbibliothek, Bern. **1054–5** [4A] Lauros Giraudon; [4B] Photoresources; [4C] Ashmolean Museum, Oxford; [5] C. M. Dixon; [6] Snark International; [7] Scala; [8] C. M. Dixon. **1056–7** [5A–B] Trustees of the British Museum/Ray Gardner; [6] C. M. Dixon; [10] With courtesy of the Trustees, National Gallery, London. **1058–9** [Key] Ronald Sheridan; [1] Spencer Collection, The New York Public Library, Astor Lenox and Tilden Foundations/Hamlyn Group Picture Library; [2] Edinburgh University Library; [3] Ronald Sheridan; [4] Camera Press; [5] Ronald Sheridan; [6] Gerry Clyde/Michael Holford; [7] Photoresources. **1060–1** [Key] Osvaldo Bohm/Biblioteca Marciana; [1] E. J. W. Hawkins; [2] C. M. Dixon; [3] Hirmer Fotoarchiv, Munich/Bibliotheque Nationale; [4] Sonia Halliday; [5] Mansell Collection; [6A–B] Scala; [7, 8] Sonia Halliday; [9] Hirmer Fotoarchiv, Munich; [10] Hirmer Fotoarchiv, Munich/Victoria and Albert Museum. **1062–3** [Key] Snark International; [1] Edinburgh University Library; [3] Dr Georg Gerster/John Hillelson Agency; [5] Madame Solange Ory; [6] C. M. Dixon; [7] Radio Times Hulton Picture Library; [8] Tunisian National Tourist Office. **1064–5** [Key] Roloff Beny, Rome; [2] Victoria and Albert Museum; [3] The Pierpont Morgan Library; [4] Victoria and Albert Museum; [5] Peter Fraenkel; [6] Courtesy of the Smithsonian Institution, Freer Gallery of Art, Washington, DC; [7] Ronald Sheridan; [8] Werner Forman Archive; [9] The Metropolitan Museum of Art, New York. **1066–7** [Key, 1] Mansell Collection; [2] Giraudon/Louvre; [4] Snark International; [5] Trustees of the British Museum; [6, 7] Snark International. **1068–9** [Key] Photoresources; [2A] Crown Copyright, reproduced with permission of the Controller, Her Majesty's Stationery Office; [4] National Museum of Iceland/Leifur Porsteinson; [7] Forhistorisk Museum, Denmark; [8] Spectrum Colour Library; [9] Werner Forman Archive. **1070–1** [Key] Bodleian Library, Oxford; [2A–D] Trustees of the British Museum/Ray Gardner; [3] Scala; [4] Ronald Sheridan. **1072–3** [Key] Roger Viollet; [3] Photo Meyer, Vienna; [4] Magnum/Erich Lessing; [5] Hatle Werbung; [6] Vatican Library; [8] Corpus Christi College, Cambridge; [9] The Granger Collection; [10] Bavaria Verlag. **1074–5** [1] Bildarchiv der Osterreichische Nationalbibliothek; [2] Source unknown; [3] Bavaria Verlag; [4] Bildarchiv Foto Marburg; [5] Bavaria Verlag. **1076–7** [Key] British Tourist Authority; [1] Michael Holford; [2] Public Record Office; [6] Aerofilms; [7] Trustees of the British Museum; [8] Perfecta Publications Ltd. **1078–9** [Key] Michael Holford; [1, 2, 3] Ampliaciones Y Reproducciones Mas; [4] Ampliaciones Y Reproducciones Mas/Barcelona University; [5, 7] Ampliaciones Y Reproducciones Mas; [8] Camera Press; [9] Ampliaciones Y Reproducciones Mas. **1080–1** [1] Bildarchiv Foto Marburg; [2] Edistudio; [4] Roger Viollet; [5] Mansell Collection; [6A–B] Photo Zodiaque; [7] Giraudon; [8] Michael Holford. **1082–3** [Key] Photo Zodiaque; [1] A. F. Kersting; [4] Trustees of the British Museum; [5] Corpus Christi College, Cambridge; [6] Photo Zodiaque; [7] Architectural Association; [8] Photo Zodiaque; [9] French Tourist Office. **1084–5** [Key] Aerofilms; [1] Snark International; [7] A. F. Kersting; [8] Michael Holford; [9] Corpus Christi College, Cambridge; [10] Michael Holford. **1086–7** [2, 3] Bodleian Library, Oxford; [5] Mansell Collection; [6] Giraudon; [8] Bildarchiv Foto Marburg; [9] Scala; [10] Ronald Sheridan. **1088–9** [Key] Mansell Collection; [1] Scala; [2] Trustees of the British Museum; [3] Scala/Vatican; [4] Bodleian Library, Oxford; [5, 6] Scala; [7, 8] Bodleian Library, Oxford; [9] Ronan Picture Library. **1090–1** [2] Roger Viollet; [3] Mauro Pucciarelli, Rome; [5] Scala. **1092–3** [1, 2, 3, 5, 6, 8, 9] C. Wilson; [10] Source unknown; [11] Sonia Halliday/Winchester Cathedral Library. **1094–5** [1] Source unknown; [2, 3] C. Wilson; [4] Source unknown; [5, 6] C. Wilson; [8] A. F. Kersting; [9] Howard C. Moore/Woodmansterne Ltd. **1096–7** [Key] Giraudon/Reims Cathedral; [4] A. F. Kersting; [5] Giraudon; [6] Snark International; [7] Bodleian Library, Oxford; [8] Snark International; [9] Bayerische Staatbibliothek, Munich; [10] Lauros Giraudon/Louvre. **1098–9** [1] Giraudon/Musée Condé, Chantilly; [2] Trustees of the British Museum; [4] Source unknown; [5] British Tourist Authority; [6] Aerofilms; [7] Bavaria Verlag; [8] Snark International. **1100–1** [Key] Larousse Archives; [1] Giraudon/Musée Condé, Chantilly; [2] Mansell Collection; [3] Mary Evans Picture Library; [4] Giraudon/Musée Condé, Chantilly; [5] Mary Evans Picture Library; [6] Scala; [7] Michael Holford/British Museum; [8] Scala; [9] Bibliotheque Nationale. **1102–3** [Key] Trustees of the British Museum/Ray Gardner; [4] Cooper Bridgeman/Bodleian Library, Oxford; [6] Museo Del'Opera Di Santa Croce, Florence; [7] Photographie Giraudon; [8] Scala. **1104–5** [1, 2] C. Wilson; [3] Georgina Russell; [4, 5] Giraudon; [7] Georgina Russell; [8, 9, 11] Scala. **1106–7** [1] Giraudon/Musée Condé, Chantilly; [2] Christopher Wilson; [3] Michael Holford; [4] Georgina Russell; [5] Lauros Giraudon/Cluny, Paris; [6] Bavaria Verlag; [7] Brian Knox/Statni Ustav Pamatkove Pece A Ochrany Prirody Y Praze; [8] Trustees of the British Museum/Weidenfeld and Nicolson Archives; [9, 11] Christopher Wilson. **1108–9** [Key] Sonia Halliday; [2] Sybil Sassoon/Robert Harding Associates; [3, 5] Sonia Halliday; [6] Mansell Collection; [7] Ronald Sheridan; [9] Sonia Halliday. **1110–1** [Key] Mary Evans Picture Library; [1] Royal Geographical Society; [2] Bodleian Library, Oxford; [4, 5] Mansell Collection; [7] Cooper Bridgeman Library; [8] National Maritime Museum. **1112–3** [Key, 3] Radio Times Hulton Picture Library; [4] Source unknown; [5] Edinburgh University Library; [6] Trustees of the British Museum; [7] Sybil Sassoon/Robert Harding Associates; [8] Edinburgh University Library. **114–5** [Key] Source unknown; [2] Anthony Hutt/Robert Harding Associates; [4] Sybil Sassoon/Robert Harding Associates; [5] Source unknown; [6, 7] A. Christie. **116–7** [Key] Michael Holford/British

Museum/Museum of Mankind; [3] Bibliotheque Nationale; [4] Werner Forman Archive; [5] Source unknown. **1118–9** [Key] Instituto Nacionale de Antropologia e Historia, Mexico; [1, 3, 4, 5, 6, 7] Norman Hammond. **1120–1** [Key] Marion Morrison; [1] Roger Perry; [2] Norman Hammond; [4, 5, 6, 7, 8, 9] Tony Morrison; [10] Faculty of Archaeology & Anthropology, Cambridge. **1122–3** [Key] Mansell Collection; [1] Royal Geographical Society; [2] Pierpont Morgan Library; [3] Mansell Collection; [5] Royal Geographical Society; [7] Bruno Barbey/John Hillelson Agency; [8] Royal Geographical Society. **1124–5** [Key] C. M. Dixon; [2] Ampliacones Y Reproducciones Mas; [4] Mansell Collection; [5] Ronald Sheridan; [7] John Judkyn Memorial/Photo Derek Balmer/Orbis; [8] Foto Salmer. **1126–7** [Key] Source unknown; [2] Trustees of the British Museum/John R. Freeman; [3] Lincoln Central Library, Local Collection reproduced by permission of the Lincolnshire Library Service; [4] Michael Holford; [5] Snark International/Louvre; [6] Scala [7] Bayer Staatsgemaldesammlungen, Munich/Kunst Dias Blauel; [8] Mansell Collection; [9] Reproduced by courtesy of Professor Charles Wilson, author of *The Dutch Republic*/ Weidenfeld and Nicolson Archives. **1128–9** [3] Mansell Collection; [4] Crown Copyright Reserved; [6] By permission of the Governors of Christ Church College, Oxford; [7] Mary Evans Picture Library; [8] Historia Foto. **1130–1** [Key] Mansell Collection; [1] Source unknown; [3] Scala; [5] Metropolitan Museum of Art, New York/Maria De Witt Jesup Fund, 1964; [6A] British Library/Ray Gardner; [6B] Cooper Bridgeman/Louvre; [8] Trustees of the British Museum/John R. Freeman. **1132–3** [Key] Bettmann Archive; [1] Picturepoint; [3] Larousse Archives; [4] Fotomas Index [J. R. Freeman]; [6] Bayerische Staatsbibliothek. **1134–5** [Key] Mansell Collection; [1] Michael Holford; [2, 3] Scala; [4] André Held/Joseph P. Ziolo; [5, 7, 8, 9] Scala. **1136–7** [Key] Trustees of the British Museum; [1] Lauros Giraudon; [2] Giraudon; [3] Trustees of the National Gallery; [4] Germanischen National Museum; [5] Giraudon/Louvre; [6] Kohnklijk Museum Voor Schone Kunsten/Musée Royal des Beaux-Arts; [7] A. E. Kersting. **1138–9** [Key] Mansell Collection; [1] Scala/Museo Del Bargello; [2, 3, 4, 5] Scala; [7] Mansell Collection; [8] Scala. **1140–1** [1] Scala; [2] Scala/Uffizi; [3] Scala; [4] C. M. Dixon; [5] Cooper Bridgeman/Louvre; [6] Victoria and Albert Museum; [7] Scala; [8] Museum of Fine Arts, Budapest. **1142–3** [Key] Mansell Collection; [1] Scala/Prado Museum, Madrid; [2, 4] Scala; [5] Staatliche Kunstammlungen, Dresden/Gerhard Reinhold, Leipzig-Moelkau; [6] The Isabella Stewart Gardner Museum, Boston; [7, 8] Scala. **1144–5** [Key] Trustees of the British Museum; [1] Verlag Joachim Blauel/Alte Pinakothek, Munich; [2] Erwin Bohm; [3] Crown Copyright Reserved; [4] Cooper Bridgeman/Colmar; [5] The Metropolitan Museum of Art, Rogers Fund 1912; [6] Cooper Bridgeman/Prado Museum, Madrid; [7] ZEFA; [8] Bavaria Verlag. **1146–7** [Key] Photographie Bulloz/Louvre; [1] Musée Jacquemart-André; [2] Bildarchiv Preussischer Kulturbesitz; [3] Giraudon/Brussels, Musée Royaux des Beaux-Arts; [4] Jean Roubier; [5] Michael Holford; [7] Giraudon. **1148–9** [1] G. Mandel/Ziolo; [2, 3] Trustees of the British Museum; [6] Devonshire Collection, Chatsworth. Reproduced by Permission of the Trustees of the Chatsworth Settlement/Courtauld Institute; [7] National Portrait Gallery; [8] Trustees of the British Museum. **1150–1** [Key] Scala; [1] Giraudon/Fontainebleau Chateau; [2] Mauro Pucciarelli; [3, 4, 5] Scala; [6] Der Museumsabteilung Der Bayer; [7, 8] Photo Meyer, Vienna. **1152–3** [Key] Lauros Giraudon/Heidelberg Kurpfalzisches Museum; [1] Mary Evans Picture Library; [2] Stadt und Universitatbibliothek, Bern; [3] Trustees of the British Museum/Ray Gardner; [4] Mary Evans Picture Library; [6] Lauros Giraudon/Munich Alte Pinakothek; [7] Spectrum Colour Library; [8] Hereford Cathedral Library/Clive Friend; [8] Trustees of the British Museum/John R. Freeman. **1154–5** [Key] Michael Holford/Prado Museum, Madrid; [2] Mary Evans Picture Library; [3] C. M. Dixon; [4] Musée Cantonel des Beaux Arts/André Held; [6] J. E. Bulloz; [7A] Michael Holford; [8] Mary Evans Picture Library; [9] Trustees of the National Gallery. **1156–7** [Key] Radio Times Hulton Picture Library; [1] British Library; [3] Trustees of the National Gallery; [4] John R. Freeman; [6] Mary Evans Picture Library; [9] Cooper Bridgeman. **1158–9** [Key] Trustees of the British Museum; [3] John R. Freeman; [4] Cooper Bridgeman/Kunsthistorisches Museum, Vienna; [7] Rijksmuseum, Amsterdam; [10] Mansell Collection; [11] Governor & Co of the Bank of England. **1160–1** [Key] Ronan Picture Library; [1] Ronan Picture Library/E. P. Goldsmith & Co Ltd; [2] National Maritime Museum; [3] Ronan Picture Library; [5] Mansell Collection; [6] Ronan Picture Library; [7] Ronan Picture Library/E. P. Goldsmith & Co Ltd; [9] Ronan Picture Library. **1162–3** [Key] Fratelli Alinari; [1, 2] Scala; [3] Bavaria Verlag; [4, 5] A. F. Kersting; [6] Trustees of the National Gallery. **1164–5** [Key] Mansell Collection; [1] Museo del Prado; [2] G. A. Mather/Robert Harding Associates; [3] Copyright The Frick Collection, New York; [4] Scala; [5] Mauro Pucciarelli; [6] Giraudon/Louvre; [7] E. Kornreich/Robert Harding Associates. **1166–7** [Key] Courtauld Institute; [1] Lauros Giraudon; [2] Lauros Giraudon/Louvre; [3] Trustees of the National Gallery; [4] Giraudon/Louvre; [5] Michael Holford; [6] P. Trela/Joseph P. Ziolo. **1168–9** [Key] Trustees of the British Museum/John R. Freeman; [1] Frans Hals Museum, Haarlem; [2] Trustees of the National Gallery; [3] Reproduced by permission of the Trustees of the Wallace Collection/John R. Freeman; [4] Crown Copyright Reserved; [5] The Cleveland Museum of Art, Purchase John L. Severance Fund; [7] By courtesy of the Provost, Worcester College, Oxford; [8] Rijksmuseum, Amsterdam. **1170–1** [1] Giraudon/Louvre. [3] Snark International. **1172–3** [Key] Snark International; [1] Giraudon; [2, 3A] Snark International; [3B] Giraudon; [4] Mansell Collection; [5] Snark International; [6, 7] Giraudon; [8] British Library/Ray Gardner; [9] Lauros Giraudon/Chateau de Versailles. **1174–5** [Key] Tiroler Landesmuseum Ferdinandeum/Anton Demanega; [2] Mander & Mitchenson Theatre Collection; [4] Permission of the Glyndebourne Festival Opera/Guy Gravett; [6] Mander & Mitchenson Theatre Collection; [7] Giraudon/Musée Condé, Chantilly; [8] Trustees of the National Portrait Gallery; [9] By kind permission of Viscount Fitzharris/Hamlyn Picture Library; [10] Mander & Mitchenson Theatre Collection; [11] Barenreiter-Verlag. **1176–7** [3] Novosti Press Agency; [5] Historical Research Unit; [7, 8] Novosti Press Agency; [9] Michael Holford. **1178–9** [Key] Novosti Press Agency; [4] Victor Kennett; [6] Novosti Press Agency; [9] Victor Kennett; [10] Historical Research Unit. **1180–1** [Key] Ullstein Bilderdienst; [3] National Army Museum; [4] Archivfür Kunst und Geschikte; [5] Bavaria Verlag; [6] Ampliaciones Y Reproducciones Mas/Madrid Museo Municipal. **1182–3** [Key] Cooper Bridgeman; [4] Mansell Collection; [6] Henry E. Huntington Library & Art Gallery; [7] Cooper Bridgeman/Victoria Art Gallery, Bath. **1184–5** [Key, 1] Source unknown; [2] Trustees of the National Portrait Gallery; [3] Bibliotheque Nationale, Paris; [4] Mansell Collection; [5] Germanisches National Museum, Nuremburg; [6] Mansell Collection; [7] Lauros Giraudon; [8A] J. E. Bulloz. **1186–7** [Key] Radio Times Hulton Picture Library; [1] National Maritime Museum; [2] By kind permission of the President & Council of the Royal College of Surgeons of England; [3] Rijksmuseum Van Naturerlijke Historie; [4] Akademie der Wissenschaften der DDR/George Rainbird Ltd; [5] Trustees of the British Museum/Ray Gardner; [6A] India Office Library; [6B] Trustees of the British Museum/Ray Gardner; [7] Source unknown; [8] By permission of the Royal College of Physicians of London; [9] Radio Times Hulton Picture Library. **1188–9** [Key] Crown Copyright Reserved; [1] Snark International; [2] By permission of Mrs Barbara Edwards/Carter Nash Cameron; [3] By courtesy of the Feoffes of Chetham's Library, Manchester; [4] Snark International; [5A–B] British Library/Ray Gardner; [6] Mansell Collection; [7] Trustees of the Tate Gallery/John Webb. **1190–1** [Key] F. Lugt Collection, Holland; [1] Lauros Giraudon/Chateau de Versailles; [2] Giraudon/Louvre; [3] Michael Holford; [4] Bavaria Verlag; [5] Reproduced by permission of the Trustees of the Wallace Collection/John R. Freeman; [6] Telarci Giraudon/Louvre. **1192–3** [Key] Angelo Hornak; [1] Metropolitan Museum of Art, Gift of Henry G. Marquand 1889; [2] Iveagh Bequest, London; [3] Victoria & Albert Museum; [4] Angelo Hornak; [5] Trustees of the Croome Estate/Don J. Adams; [6] Angelo Hornak; [7] National Gallery; [8] Angelo Hornak; [9] Yale University Art Gallery. **1194–5** [Key] Giraudon; [1, 2] British Museum/John R. Freeman; [3] Victoria & Albert Museum; [4] Mansell Collection; [5] Reproduced by permission of the Trustees of the Wallace Collection/John R. Freeman; [6] Angelo Hornak/V & A; [7] Victoria & Albert Museum; [8] British Museum/John R. Freeman. **1196–7** [Key] Mansell Collection; [1] Scala; [2] Germanisches National Museum; [3, 4] Bildarchiv Preussischer Kulturbesitz, Berlin; [5] Ullstein Bilderdienst. **1198–9** [Key] Royal Academy of Arts; [1] Reproduced by permission of the Trustees of the Wallace Collection/John R. Freeman; [2] Cooper Bridgeman/Towneley Hall Museum & Art Gallery, Burnley; [4] Trustees of the Tate Gallery/John Webb; [5] New York Historical Society; [6] Giraudon/Musée Royaux des Beaux-Arts; [7] Lauros Giraudon/Louvre. **1200–1** [2] Lauros Giraudon/Musée de la Marine, Paris; [4] Radio Times Hulton Picture Library; [5] Angelo Hornak/V & A; [6] Trustees of the British Museum/John R. Freeman; [7] Ampliaciones Y Reproducciones Mas, Barcelona; [8] Mansell Collection. **1202–3** [Key] India Office Library & Records; [1, 3, 4] Ann and Bury Peerless; [5, 7, 8, 9, 10] India Office Library & Records. **1204–5** [Key] Michael Holford/V & A; [1] Ann and Bury Peerless; [2] Victoria & Albert Museum; [3] By kind permission of Air India; [4] Michael Holford; [5] India Office Library & Records/Ann and Bury Peerless; [6] By kind permission of Air India; [7] Michael Holford/V & A; [8] Victoria & Albert Museum. **1206–7** [Key] William MacQuitty; [2] Trustees of the British Museum; [3, 4] William MacQuitty; [5] Radio Times Hulton Picture Library; [7] Trustees of the British Museum; [8] Cooper Bridgeman/National Maritime Museum. **1208–9** [Key] Museum of Fine Arts, Boston; [1] Percival David Foundation; [2] Courtesy of the Smithsonian Institution, Freer Gallery of Art, Washington DC; [3] Nelson Gallery-Atkins Museum, Kansas City, Missouri (Nelson Fund); [4] National Palace Museum, Taiwan; [5] Trustees of the British Museum; [6] William MacQuitty; [7] Aubrey Singer, BBC/Robert Harding Associates; [8, 9] Trustees of the British Museum. **1210–1** [Key] International Society for Educational Information, Tokyo; [1] Bradley Smith; [3] International Society for Educational Information, Tokyo; [4, 5] Bradley Smith; [6] Weidenfeld & Nicolson; [7] International Society of Educational Information, Tokyo; [8] Orion Press. **1212–3** [Key] Werner Forman Archive; [2, 3, 4] Mansell Collection; [6] Mary Evans Picture Library; [7] Mansell Collection. **1214–5** [Key] Trustees of the British Museum; [1] D. E. F. Russell/Robert Harding Associates; [2] John Picton; [3] Prof. Thurston-Shaw; [4] John Picton; [5] Trustees of the British Museum/Museum of Mankind/Angelo Hornak; [6, 7] Trustees of the British Museum/Museum of Mankind; [8] Photograph copyright 1976 by the Barnes Foundation; [9] Archivoe Studio; [10] From *Nuba Personal Art* by James C. Faris/Duckworth, 1972. **1216–7** [6] By kind permission of the City of Bristol Archives/David Strickland; [7] Mansell Collection; [8] Bettmann Archive; [9] Bettmann Archive/Smithsonian Institution. **1218–9** [3] Mary Evans Picture Library; [4] Metropolitan Museum of Art, New York, Gift of Mrs Russell Sage, 1910; [6] Copyright Yale University Art Gallery; [7] Mansell Collection. **1220–1** [2] Ronan Picture Library; [5] A. F. Kersting; [6] Ronan Picture Library; [7] Derby Borough Councils & Art Gallery; [8] Josiah Wedgwood & Co; [9] Cooper Bridgeman/Lord Mountbatten. **1222–3** [Key] The British Library; [1] Angelo Hornak; [2] Bavaria Verlag; [3] John R. Freeman; [4] Trustees of the Tate Gallery/John Webb; [5] Trustees of the British Museum/John R. Freeman; [6] Giraudon; [7] Archiv fur Kunst und Geschichte, Berlin; [8]

Mansell Collection; [9] Crown Copyright Reserved. **1224–5** [Key] The Granger Collection; [4] Roger Viollet; [5] Giraudon/B. N. Estempes, Paris; [7] Giraudon/Chateau Versailles; [8] Reunion des Musées Nationale. **1226–7** [Key] Roger Viollet; [2] Cooper Bridgeman/Coram Foundation; [3] Giraudon/Chateau Versailles, [5] Garanger Giraudon/Musée de l'Armée, Prague; [7] Angelo Hornak/V & A; [8] National Army Museum. **1228–9** [Key] Trustees of the British Museum; [1] Courtesy of the Detroit Institute of Arts, Gift of Mr & Mrs Bert L. Smokler & Mr & Mrs Lawrence A. Fleischman; [2] Courtesy of Birmingham City Museum & Art Gallery; [3] Museo del Prado; [4] Kunst Dias Blauel/Stadelsches Kunstinstitut; [5] Telarci Giraudon/Louvre; [6] Lauros Giraudon/Louvre; [7] Telarci Giraudon/Louvre. **1230–1** [Key] John R. Freeman; [2] Der Museen Der Stadt, Vienna; [3] Crown Copyright Reserved; [4] Der Museen Der Stadt, Vienna; [5] Trustees of the National Portrait Gallery; [6] Lauros Giraudon/Louvre. **1232–3** [Key] Turkish Tourist & Information Office; [1] J. E. Bulloz; [3A–B] Bildarchiv Der Osterreichische Nationalbibliothek; [4] William Allan; [5] National Army Museum; [6] Radio Times Hulton Picture Library; [7] Bildarchiv Der Osterreichische Nationalbibliothek. **1234–5** [Key] Bettmann Archive; [2] National Archives; [3] Mansell Collection; [4] Douglas Botting; [5] Mike Andrews; [6, 7, 8] Bettmann Archive. **1236–7** [Key] Mary Evans Picture Library; [4] Mansell Collection; [8] By permission of the Science Museum, London; [9A] By permission of Stanley Gibbons Ltd/Angelo Hornak; [10] Mansell Collection. **1238–9** [Key] Mansell Collection; [1] Trustees of the Tate Gallery/John Webb; [2] J. Whitaker/Sphere Books; [3] Angelo Hornak/Scolar Press; [4A] John Frost Newspaper Collection/Angelo Hornak; [4B] Radio Times Hulton Picture Library; [5] Lauros Giraudon © S.P.A.D.E.M., Paris, 1976; [6] Roger Viollet; [7] Sally Chappell/V & A; [8] Giraudon/Louvre; [9] Society of Cultural Relations with the USSR. **1240–1** [Key] University College, Oxford/Angelo Hornak; [1] Trustees of the British Museum; [2] John Massey Stewart; [3] Roger Viollet; [4] Scala; [5] Snark International; [6] Mander & Mitchenson Theatre Collection; [7] Society for Cultural Relations with the USSR; [8] Mander & Mitchenson Theatre Collection; [9] Radio Times Hulton Picture Library. **1242–3** [Key] Ashmolean Museum, Oxford; [1] Whitworth Art Gallery, University of Manchester; [2] Cooper Bridgeman/V & A; [3] Ralph Kleinhempel, Hamburg; [4] Cooper Bridgeman/Staatliche Kunstammlungen, Dresden; [5] Gulbenkian Museum, Lisbon; [6] Trustees of the Tate Gallery; [7] Laing Art Gallery, Newcastle upon Tyne; [8] Trustees of the Tate Gallery. **1246–7** [2] Spectrum Colour Library; [3] K. M. Andrew; [4] Novosti Press Agency; [5, 6, 7, 8] Bildarchiv Preussischer Kulturbesitz, Staatsbibliothek, Berlin; [9] Mary Evans Picture Library. **1248–9** [Key] Mansell Collection; [3] Roger Viollet/Bibliotheque Nationale; [4] Ullstein Bilderdienst; [5] Scala; [7] Snark International. **1250–1** [Key] Mansell Collection; [1] Bildarchiv Preussischer Kulturbesitz, Staatsbibliothek, Berlin; [3] John R. Freeman; [4] Out of copyright; [5] Mauro Pucciarelli; [6] Instituto per la Storia del Risorgimento, Rome. **1252–3** [Key] Helmut Gernsheim Collection; [1] Angelo Hornak/Wellington Museum; [2] Lauros Giraudon/Musée Fabre, Montpellier/© A.D.A.G.P. Paris, 1976; [3] Giraudon/Louvre; [4] Trustees of the Tate Gallery/John Webb; [5] Cooper Bridgeman/Sir Colin Anderson; [6] Trustees of the Tate Gallery; [7] Courtesy of Jefferson Memorial College, Thomas Jefferson University; [8] Walters Art Gallery, Baltimore; [9] Royal Academy of Arts, London; [10] Trustees of the Tate Gallery/John Webb. **1254–5** [Key] J. E. Bulloz; [1] Giraudon/Musée Marmottan, Paris/© S.P.A.D.E.M. Paris, 1976; [2] Museum of Fine Arts, Boston, Arthur Gordon Thompkins Residuary Fund/© S.P.A.D.E.M. Paris, 1976; [3, 4] Service de Documentation Photographique de la Reunion des Musées Nationauk/Musée Jeu de Paume/© S.P.A.D.E.M., Paris, 1976; [5] Service de Documentation Photographique de la Reunion des Musées Nationaux/Musée Jeu de Paume; [6] K. X. Rousseu; [7] Service de Documentation Photographique de la Reunion des Musées Nationaux/Musée Jeu de Paume; [8] Service de Documentation Photographique de la Reunion des Musées Nationaux/Musée Jeu de Paume/© S.P.A.D.E.M., Paris, 1976; [9] Giraudon/Musée Jeu de Paume/© S.P.A.D.E.M., Paris, 1976; [10] Philadelphia Museum of Art/John G. Johnson Collection. **1256–7** [Key] Brenda Houston Rogers; [1] Osterreichische Nationalbibliothek; [2] Roger Viollet; [3] Novosti/National Russian Museum; [4] Mander & Mitchenson Theatre Collection; [5] Brenda Houston Rogers; [7] Gunter Englert; [8] UPI; [9] Stuart Robinson. **1258–9** [Key] J. E. Bulloz; [1] Royal Academy of Arts; [2] A. F. Kersting; [4] From *Entretiens sur L'Architecture,* 1863; [5] From the *Pelican History of Art* by B. Abbott; [7] Mauro Pucciarelli; [8] The Museum of London; [9] Mauro Pucciarelli; [10] James Austin. **1260–1** [Key] Geoff Goode/Trustees of the British Museum/Museum of Mankind; [2] Mansell Collection; [3] Trustees of the National Portrait Gallery; [4] Mary Evans Picture Library; [5] Trustees of the National Portrait Gallery; [8] Radio Times Hulton Picture Library; [9] Rijksmuseum, Amsterdam; [10] British Museum/Photo © Aldus Books, London. **1262–3** [Key] Kim Sayer; [3] Mary Evans Picture Library; [5] Mansell Collection; [6] Bildarchiv Preussischer Kulturbesitz, Berlin. **1264–5** [Key] Werner Forman Archive/Anspach Collection, NY; [2] Romano Cagnoni; [3] Charles Perry Weimer; [5A–B] Anthony Atmore; [6] Popperfoto; [7] Ann and Bury Peerless. **1266–7** [Key] Punch Publications Ltd; [2] National Army Museum; [3] Rick Strange/Robert Harding Associates; [4] National Army Museum; [5] Mansell Collection; [6] National Army Museum; [7] Trustees of the National Portrait Gallery; [8] India Office Library & Records; [9] National Army Museum. **1268–9** [Key] Source unknown; [2] Mary Evans Picture Library; [3] Radio Times Hulton Picture Library; [4] Sybil Sassoon/Robert Harding Associates; [5] Radio Times Hulton Picture Library; [6] From *Tribal Innovators* by I. Schapera; [7] Angelo Hornak/From *Life, Scenery & Customs of Sierra Leone & Gambia* by T. E. Poole; [8] Radio Times Hulton Picture Library. **1270–1** [Key] Roger Viollet; [3] Radio Times Hulton Picture Library; [4] Library Archives of Weidenfeld & Nicolson; [8] V & A/Weidenfeld & Nicolson; [9] Mansell Collection. **1272–3** [Key] Newcastle upon Tyne Public Libraries; [1] Radio Times Hulton Picture Library; [3] International Society for Education Information, Tokyo; [4] Novosti Press Agency; [5] International Society for Educational Information, Tokyo; [6] Bradley Smith; [8] International Society for Educational Information, Tokyo; **1274–5** All pictures from Western Americana. **1276–7** [5] American History Picture Library; [9] Mansell Collection. **1278–9** [1] Mansell Collection; [2] Western Americana; [3] Brown Brothers; [4] Nick Polus-Carson Pirie Scott & Co.; [7] Brown Brothers. **1280–1** [Key] Culver Pictures; [1] Royal Geographical Society; [2] Bradley Smith; [3, 4] National Maritime Museum; [6, 7] Radio Times Hulton Picture Library. **1282–3** [Key] Cavendish Laboratory/University of Cambridge; [1] The Royal Institution/Cooper Bridgeman; [2] Ronan Picture Library; [3] C. E. Abranson; [4] Mansell Collection; [5] The Royal Institution of Great Britain; [6] Ronan Picture Library; [7] Mansell Collection; [8] Popperfoto; [9] Mansell Collection; [10] Bavaria Verlag. **1284–5** [Key] By kind permission of Marks & Spencer Ltd; [2, 4] Radio Times Hulton Picture Library; [5] Angelo Hornak; [6] Mansell Collection. **1286–7** [Key] Novosti Press Agency; [1, 2] Radio Times Hulton Picture Library; [3] John R. Freeman; [4] Novosti Press Agency; [5] Courtesy of Cultural Relations with the USSR; [6] Novosti Press Agency; [8] Radio Times Hulton Picture Library; [9, 10] Novosti Press Agency. **1288–9** [Key] Mansell Collection; [1] Punch Publications Ltd; [3] From the John Gorman Collection; [4] Radio Times Hulton Picture Library; [5] Giraudon; [6] British Red Cross Society; [7] Radio Times Hulton Picture Library. **1290–1** [Key] Mansell Collection; [2] Manchester Public Libraries; [3A–B] Radio Times Hulton Picture Library; [3C] Mansell Collection; [5A] Giraudon; [5B] Angelo Hornak/V & A. **1292–3** [Key] Geoff Goode/By permission of The Society of Antiquaries of London; [1] Geoff Goode; [2] Picturepoint; [3] Smithsonian Institution National Anthropological Archives; [4] Mansell Collection; [5] Radio Times Hulton Picture Library; [6] Dr M. H. Day/property of the Government of Tanzania; [7] Times Newspapers; [8] Marion Morrison. **1294–5** [Key] Cooper Bridgeman/Rasmus Meyer Collection, Bildegalerie, Bergen; [1] Hans Hinz, Kunst Museum, Basle; [2] Trustees of Tate Gallery/© A.D.A.G.P., Paris, 1976; [3] Harry N. Abrams Inc/The Hermitage, Leningrad/© S.P.A.D.E.M. Paris, 1976; [4] Trustees of the Tate Gallery/© S.P.A.D.E.M. 1976/John Webb; [5] Hans Hinz, Basle; [6] Hans Hinz, Basle/© S.P.A.D.E.M., Paris, 1976; [7] Kunstammlung Nordhein Westfalen/© S.P.A.D.E.M., Paris, 1976; [8] By courtesy of Marlborough Fine Art (London) Ltd. **1296–7** [Key] Trustees of the Tate Gallery/© A.D.A.G.P., Paris, 1976; [1] Collection Alex Maguy/© A.D.A.G.P., Paris, 1976; [2] Giraudon/Kunst Museum, Basle; [3] Charles Uht/By permission of Nelson A. Rockefeller/© S.P.A.D.E.M., Paris, 1976; [4] Collection, the Museum of Modern Art, New York, Bequest of Alma Erickson Levene/© A.D.A.G.P., Paris, 1976; [5] Philadelphia Museum of Art, The A. E. Gallatin Collection/Alfred J. Wyatt/© S.P.A.D.E.M., Paris, 1976; [6] Musée Leger/© S.P.A.D.E.M., Paris, 1976; [7] Collection, the Museum of Modern Art, New York. Acquired through the Lillie P. Bliss Bequest/©S.P.A.D.E.M., Paris, 1976; [8] Private collection, Milan; [9] Collection, the Museum of Modern Art, New York. Acquired through the Lillie P. Bliss Bequest. **1298–9** [Key] Architectural Association; [1] A. F. Kersting; [2] Christabel Valkenberg; [3, 4A–B] Architectural Association; [5] Bill Engdahl/Hedrich Blessing; [6B] Architectural Association. **1300–1** [Key] Ronan Picture Library; [1] Mary Evans Picture Library; [3] Ullstein Bilderdienst; [5] Ostereichisches Nationalbibliothek; [6] Source unknown; [7] Snark International; [8] Radio Times Hulton Picture Library. **1302–3** [Key] Source unknown; [1] Bildarchiv Preussicher Kulturbesitz Staatsbibliothek, Berlin; [2] Cyril & Methodius National Library, Sofia, Bulgaria; [3] Mansell Collection; [4] Archiv Für Kunst und Geschichte; [6] IBA, Zurich; [8] Radio Times Hulton Picture Library. **1304–5** [Key] Roger Viollet; [1] Radio Times Hulton Picture Library; [2] Ullstein Bilderdienst; [7] Source unknown; [8] Ullstein Bilderdienst. **1306–7** [Key] Imperial War Museum; [5] UPI; [7] Robert Hunt Library; [10] Camera Press. **1308–9** [Key, 2] Roger Viollet; [5] Novosti Press Agency; [8] Mansell Collection; [9] Ullstein Bilderdienst. **1310–1** [Key 1] Novosti Press Agency; [2] Mansell Collection; [3] Bettmann Archive; [4, 5] Novosti Press Agency; [6] Radio Times Hulton Picture Library; [7] Novosti Press Agency; [8] Snark International; [9] Geoff Goode/Courtesy The School of Slavonic Studies; [11] Radio Times Hulton Picture Library. **1312–3** [Key] Camera Press; [1, 2, 4] Radio Times Hulton Picture Library; [5] Popperfoto; [8] Radio Times Hulton Picture Library; [9] Life © Time Inc. 1976/Colorific; [10] Radio Times Hulton Picture Library; [11] Robert Hunt Library. **1314–5** [1, 4A–C, 5] Radio Times Hulton Picture Library; [8] Camera Press. **1316–7** [Key] Kobal Collection; [1, 3, 4, 5] Museum of Modern Art; [6] Kobal Collection; [7] The Granger Collection; [8] Kobal Collection. **1318–9** [Key] D. Bellon/Images et Textes/© A.D.A.G.P., Paris, 1976; [1] Gimpel Fils, London/© A.D.A.G.P., Paris, 1976; [2] Kunstammlung Nordhein Westfalen/© S.P.A.D.E.M., Paris, 1976; [3] Collection of the Museum of Modern Art, New York, Purchase; [4] Harry N. Abrams Inc/Permission of Nelson A. Rockefeller; [5] Collection of the Museum of Modern Art, New York. Acquired through an Anonymous Fund, The Mr & Mrs Joseph Slifka & Armand G. Erpf Funds, and by gift from the artist/© A.D.A.G.P., Paris, 1976; [6] Museum Boymans-Van Bernigen Rotterdam/© A.D.A.G.P., Paris, 1976; [7] Arts Council of Great Britain/© S.P.A.D.E.M., Paris, 1976; [8] Collection of the Museum of Modern Art, New York. The A. Conger Goodyear Fund; [9] National Museum, Moderna Museet, Stockholm. **1320–1** [Key] Collection of the Museum of Modern Art, New York. Gift of Mr & Mrs David M.

Solinger; [1] Kunstammlung Nordhein Westfalen, Dusseldorf/© A.D.A.G.P., Paris, 1976; [2] Stedelijk Museum, Amsterdam; [3] Angelo Hornak; [4] Haags Gemeentemuseum; [5] Trustees of the Tate Gallery; [6] Colourphoto Hans Hinz, Basle/Kunstmuseum, Basle/© A.D.A.G.P., Paris, 1976; [7] By kind permission of Henry Moore/Trustees of the Tate Gallery/John Webb; [8] Metropolitan Museum of Art, New York, George A. Heard Fund, 1957. **1322–3** [Key] James Austin; [1] Angelo Hornak; [2] Cadbury Brown/Architectural Association; [4] Roger Whitehouse/Architectural Association; [6] James Stirling/Architectural Association; [7] Adrian Atkinson/Architectural Association; [8] Geoffrey Munro/Architectural Association; [9] James Stirling/Architectural Association. **1324–5** [Key] Bettmann Archive; [4] Woolf, Laing, Christie & Partners; [5] Bettmann Archive; [6] Radio Times Hulton Picture Library; [7] Picturepoint; [9] Bettmann Archive. **1326–7** [Key] Library of Congress; [1] Mansell Collection; [2, 3] Radio Times Hulton Picture Library; [4, 5] Roger Viollet; [6] Solidarity House; [8] Radio Times Hulton Picture Library; [9] Maurice Rickards. **1328–9** [Key] Camera Press; [1] Source unknown; [3] Radio Times Hulton Picture Library; [4] Keystone Press; [5] Camera Press; [7] Keystone Press; [9] Wide World Photos. **1330–1** [Key, 1] Radio Times Hulton Picture Library; [2] National Army Museum; [3] Popperfoto; [4] Camera Press; [5] Mansell Collection; [6] Geoslides; [7] National Army Museum; [8] Robert Hunt Library; [10] Keystone Press. **1332–3** [Key] Daily Mirror; [2] Trustees of the National Portrait Gallery; [3] Radio Times Hulton Picture Library; [5] Keystone Press; [6] Camera Press; [7] Royal Commonwealth Institute; [8] Associated Press. **1334–5** [Key] International Bilder-Agentur [2, 3, 5] Ullstein Bilderdienst; [5] Wide World Photos; [6] International Bilder-Agentur [8] Snark International. **1336–7** [Key, 1] Keystone Press; [2] Robert Hunt Library/Associated Press; [4] Archiv Für Kunst und Geschichte; [7] Robert Hunt Library; [8] Cartoon by David Low by arrangement with the Trustees of the London *Evening Standard;* [9] Robert Hunt Library. **1338–9** [2A–B] Robert Hunt Library; [2C] Imperial War Museum; [4, 6, 8] Robert Hunt Library. **1340–1** [Key] UPI; [1] Radio Times Hulton Picture Library; [2] Library of Congress; [3] Imperial War Museum; [4] Fox Photos; [5, 6] Roger Viollet; [7] Angelo Hornak/Imperial War Museum; [8] Novosti Press Agency; [9] US Army; [10] Snark International; [11] IBA, Zurich; [12] Snark International. **1342–3** [Key] Novosti Press Agency; [1] Robert Hunt Library/Imperial War Museum; [2] Radio Times Hulton Picture Library; [3] IBA, Zurich; [4] Associated Press; [6] Keystone Press Agency; [7] IBA, Zurich; [8, 9] Popperfoto. **1344–5** [Key] Novosti Press Agency; [1, 2] Popperfoto; [3] John F. Freeman; [5] Popperfoto; [8] Colorsport. **1346–7** [Key] Camera Press; [2] Popperfoto; [3] Camera Press; [4] Associated Press; [5] Popperfoto; [6] Ginette Laborde, Paris; [7] Picturepoint. **1348–9** [Key] Eastfoto; [1] Henri Cartier Bresson/John Hillelson Agency; [2] Eastfoto; [4] Camera Press; [6A] Sally and Richard Greenhill; [6B, 7] Camera Press; [9] Magnum Distribution. **1350–1** [Key] Popperfoto; [2] Camera Press; [4] Popperfoto; [5, 6] Camera Press; [7] Australian News & Information Bureau. **1352–3** [Key] Source unknown; [1] UPI; [2, 3] Camera Press; [4] Associated Press; [5] Popperfoto; [7] Camera Press; [8] Keystone Press; [9] United Nations; [10] Agency for Public Information/Errol Harvey. **1354–5** [Key] General Secretariat, Organization of American States; [1] National Palace of Mexico; [2] Radio Times Hulton Picture Library; [3] Camera Press; [4] Robert Cundy/Robert Harding Associates; [5] Associated Press; [7] G. A. Mather/Robert Harding Associates; [8] Romano Cagnoni; [9] Douglas Botting; [10] Associated Press. **1356–7** [Key] Associated Press; [1] Roger Viollet; [2] Popperfoto; [4A–B] Roger Viollet; [6, 7] Associated Press; [9] Camera Press; [10] Associated Press. **1358–9** [Key] Robert Kubic-DPI; [2A–D] Camera Press; [2E] Wide World Photos; [2F] Camera Press; [2G] Wide World Photos; [3] BP North America; [4] Associated Press. **1360–1** [Key] Margaret Murray; [2] Phoebe Dunn/DPI; [3] Kibbutz Representatives; [4] Scottish New Towns Development Board; [6] Keystone Press; [7] Ted Lau, Fortune © Time Inc 1976/Colorific; [8] Columbia University, Harvard University; [9, 10] Camera Press. **1362–3** [Key] Copyright unknown; [1, 2] Museum of Modern Art; [3, 4, 5] Kobal Collection; [6] Museum of Modern Art; [7, 8, 9] Kobal Collection. **1364–5** [Key] Universal [Edition] London Ltd; [3A] EMI; [3B] Photo Macdomnic, by courtesy of EMI; [4] Osterreiches Nationalbibliothek; [9] Copyright unknown; [10] James Klosty/Edition Peters. **1366–7** [Key] Max Jones; [2] American History Picture Library; [3, 4] Max Jones; [5] Redferns/pic by Herman Leonard (Charles Stewart Collection); [6] Max Jones; [7] Redferns/Stephen Morley; [8] Redferns/David Redfern; [9] CBS Records/photograph by Don Hunstein; [10] Jill Furmanovsky/Hipgnosis. **1368–9** [Key] Mander & Mitchenson Theatre Collection; [2] Angelo Hornak/V & A; [3] Frank Sharman; [4] Musée des Arts Decoratifs, Paris; [5] Mander & Mitchenson Theatre Collection; [6] Fred Fehl; [7] Anthony Crickmay. **1370–1** [Key] Museum of Modern Art; [1] Robert J. Flaherty/B.F.I.; [2] Anycon Co/B.F.I.; [3] Ian Cameron; [4] Societé du Cinema du Pantheon/B.F.I.; [5] RKO General Inc/B.F.I.; [6] Contemporary Films/B.F.I.; [7] Toho International/B.F.I.; [8] Aktiebolaget Svensk Filmindustri/B.F.I.; [9] Rizzoli Films SPA/B.F.I.; [10] Museum of Modern Art. **1372–3** [Key] Leo Castelli, New York; [1] Tubingen Kunsthalle, Germany; [2] Kasmin Ltd; [3] Galerie Reckermann, Cologne/Germot Langer; [4] Museum of Modern Art, New York. Gift of D. & J. de Menil; [5] Waddington Galleries; [6] Nigel Greenwood/Douglas Thompson; [7] Denise Rene Gallery, Paris; [8] Trustees of the Tate Gallery/John Webb. **1374–5** [Key] Mansell Collection; [1, 2] Trustees of the British Museum/Ray Gardner; [3] Library of Congress; [4] Culver Pictures; [5] Sheila Orme/The National Trust; [6] SEFA; [7] Topix; [8] Henri Cartier Bresson/John Hillelson Agency; [9] Helen Breaker, Paris; [10] Alskog Inc; [11] Eva Sereny/Sygma/John Hillelson Agency; [12] Photo Baker, London; [13] Ian Whyles/Robert Harding Associates. **1376–7** [Key] UN; [1] Viking Press; [2] Culver Pictures; [3] Harcourt, Brace, Jovanovich; [5, 7] The Granger Collection; [9] UPI; [10] © 1977 Jill Krementz; [11] Henri Cartier-Bresson/Magnum. **1378–9** [Key] Romano Cagnoni; [2] Popperfoto; [3, 4, 5, 9] Camera Press; [10] Popperfoto. **1380–1** [Key] Institute of Contemporary History/Weiner Library/Geoff Goode; [3] Central Zionist Archives; [4] Central Press; [5] Camera Press. **1382–3** [Key] United Nations; [1, 2] Associated Press; [4A–D] United Nations; [6] Camera Press; [7] Keystone Press; [8] Camera Press; [9] F. Botte-FAO. **1384–5** [Key] Terry Kirk/Financial Times; [3] Régis Bossu/Copyright SYGMA/Magnum. **1386–7** [Key] Camera Press; [3] Bruno Barbey/Magnum; [4] Paolo Koch; [5] C. Gascoigne/Robert Harding Associates; [6] Picturepoint; [7] Margaret Murray/Ikon Productions; [8] Peter Fraenkel **1388–9** [Key] Popperfoto; [1] World Council of Churches; [2, 4] Camera Press; [5] Associated Press; [6] Shostal; [7] Camera Press; [8] Associated Press; [9] Chris Steele-Perkins. **1390–1** [Key, 2] Associated Press; [3] Elliot Erwitt/Magnum; [4, 5, 6] Associated Press; [7] Neal Boenzi/The New York Times/John Hillelson Agency; [9] Camera Press; [10] UPI. **1392–3** [Key] Tony Linck; [2] The Granger Collection; [3] American Museum of Natural History; [8] Michael Heron; [5] Washington University Gallery of Art, St. Louis; [6, 7] Museum of the American Indian; [8] Michael Heron. **1394–5** [Key, 2] The Granger Collection; [3] Museum of the City of New York; [4] Martin Adler Levick/Black Star; [5] Yoram Kahana/Peter Arnold Photo Archives; [6] The Granger Collection; [7] Vic Cox/Peter Arnold Photo Archives; [8] State of Washington, Department of Emergency Services. **1396–7** [Key] New York Public Library; [2, 3] The Granger Collection; [4] Dartmouth College; [5] Maryland Historical Society; [6] Library of Congress; [7] Brown Brothers; [8] UPI; [9] B. W. Owen/Black Star. **1398–9** [Key] Hanson Carroll/Peter Arnold Photo Archives; [2, 3] Library of Congress; [4] League of Women Voters; [5] City of Chicago; [6] Burton Berinsky; [7] League of Women Voters. **1400–1** [Key] Rhode Island Department of Economic Development; [1] The New York Historical Society; [3] Yale University Art Gallery, Gift of George Hoadley; [4] Culver Pictures, Inc.; [5] The J. Clarence Davies Collection, Museum of the City of New York; [6] The Granger Collection; [7] Museum of Fine Arts, Boston. **1402–3** [Key] National Portrait Gallery, Smithsonian Institution; [1] Library of Congress; [2] The Harry T. Peters Collection, Museum of the City of New York; [3] International Museum of Photography, at the George Eastman House; [5] Wide World Photos; [6] Franklin D. Roosevelt Library; [7] American Iron and Steel Institute; [8] Burton McNeely/The Image Bank; [9] The Coca Cola Company. **1404–5** [Key] John Lewis Stage/The Image Bank; [2] New Mexico Department of Development; [3] Rhode Island Department of Economic Development; [4] Museum of Fine Arts, Boston; [5] New York Public Library; [6] Burk Uzzle/Magnum Photos; [7] Culver Pictures, Inc.; [8] Ed Drews/Photo Researchers, Inc.; [9] Gianni Tortoli/Photo Researchers, Inc. **1406–7** [Key] Museum of the City of New York; [1] New York Public Library, Rare Book Room; [2] The Granger Collection; [4] The Butler Institute of American Art; [5] Columbia University; [6] UPI; [8] Susan McCartney/Photo Researchers, Inc.; [9] James H. Karales/Peter Arnold Photo Archives; [10] Burton Berinsky. **1408–9** [Key] UPI; [1] National Collection of Fine Arts, Smithsonian Institution; [2] New York Public Library; [3] Houston Astrodome; [4, 5] UPI; [6] Tennis Hall of Fame; [7] Whitney Museum of Art; [8] Lewis Portnoy/Spectra-Action; [9] UPI; [10] J. DiMaggio-J. Kalish/Peter Arnold Photo Archives. **1410–1** [Key] Abby Aldrich Rockefeller Folk Art Collection, Williamsburg, Va.; [1] Historical Society of Pennsylvania; [2] The Granger Collection; [3] Museum of Fine Arts, Boston; [4] © Walt Disney Productions; [5] Gene Daniels/Black Star; [6] Diane F. Downs/Peter Arnold Photo Archives; [8] Clyde H. Smith/Peter Arnold Photo Archives; [9] Constantine Manos/Magnum. **1412–3** [Key] Toledo Museum of Art; [1] New Mexico Department of Development; [2] Virginia State Travel Service; [3] Connecticut Department of Commerce; [4] Library of Congress; [5] Virginia State Travel Service; [6] University of Virginia Library; [7] Norvell/Historic Foundation of Charleston; [8] Michigan Department of State Archives; [9] The New York Historical Society; [10] Connecticut Department of Commerce; [11] Boston Public Library; [12] David R. Phillips. **1414–5** [Key] Pennsoil Corporation; [1] New York Public Library; [2] Elliott Erwitt/Magnum Photos; [3A] Hedrich-Blessing; [3B] David R. Phillips; [4A] Culver Pictures, Inc.; [4B] Bill Engdahl/Hedrich-Blessing; [4C] University of Pittsburgh; [5] Philadelphia Savings Fund Society; [6] Rockefeller Center; [8] Alcoa; [9] John Hancock Life Insurance Company. **1416–7** [Key] Museum of Fine Arts, Boston; [1] The Brooklyn Museum; [2] New York Public Library; [3] National Collection of Fine Arts, Smithsonian Institution; [4] The Layton Art Collection, Milwaukee Art Center, Gift of Frederick Layton, 1888; [5] The New York Historical Society; [6] Chester Dale Collection/National Portrait Gallery, Smithsonian Institution; [7] Los Angeles County Museum of Art; [8] The Metropolitan Museum of Art, The Alfred Stieglitz Collection, 1949; [9] Inland Steel; [10] Museum of Fine Arts, Houston, Gift of Mrs. William Stamps Farrish **1418–9** [Key] Museum of Fine Arts, Boston; [1] W. S. Keller/National Park Service; [2] The New York Historical Society; [3] Smithsonian Institution; [4] Minute Man National Historical Park; [5] Chicago Historical Society; [6] The New York Historical Society; [7, 8, 9, 10, 11] Whitney Museum of American Art. **1420–1** [Key] The Granger Collection; [1, 2] New York Public Library, Rare Book Room; [3] The Granger Collection; [4] National Portrait Gallery, Smithsonian Institution; [5] American Antiquarian Society; [6] Burt Glinn/Magnum; [7] Joanna T. Steichen; [8] UPI; [9] Burt Glinn/Magnum; [10] The Granger Collection; [11] UPI. **1422–3** [Key] The Granger

Collection; [1] The New York Historical Society; [2] National Gallery of Art; [3] Culver Pictures, Inc.; [4] Library of Congress; [5] New York Public Library; [6] Collection of Joseph Pulitzer, Jr.; [7] New York Public Library; [8] Time-Life Picture Agency; [10] *Washington Post.* **1424–5** [Key] Wide World Photos; [1] RCA News; [2] New York Public Library; [3] The Granger Collection; [4, 6] NBC; [7, 8] CBS; [9] Childrens' Television Workshop. **1426–7** [Key] UPI; [1] The New York Historical Society; [2] New York Public Library, Lincoln Center for the Performing Arts; [3] Culver Pictures, Inc.; [4, 5, 6] New York Public Library, Lincoln Center for the Performing Arts; [7] © Jill Krementz; [8] New York Public Library, Lincoln Center for the Performing Arts; [9] Wide World Photos; [10] Martha Swope. **1428–9** [Key] The Granger Collection; [1] Historical Society of Pennsylvania; [2] National Portrait Gallery, Smithsonian Institution; [3] UPI; [4] New York Public Library; [5] Culver Pictures, Inc.; [6] The Granger Collection; [7] Dave Repp/Black Star; [8] Martha Swope; [9] Wide World Photos; [10] Fletcher Drake/Wolf Trap Farm Park. **1430–1** [Key] New York Public Library, Lincoln Center for the Performing Arts [1] Historical Society of York County; [2] Abby Aldrich Rockefeller Folk Art Collection, Williamsburg, Va.; [3] Museum of Fine Arts, Boston; [4] Harvard Theatre Collection; [5] Wide World Photos; [6, 7] New York Public Library, Lincoln Center for the Performing Arts; [8] Randy Masser; [9] Martha Swope; [10] Vinnie Fish.

Man and Science
1432–3 Francis Laping. **1434–5** Adam Woolfitt/Susan Griggs Picture Agency. **1436** Fritz Goro/T.L.P.A. © Times Inc 1976/Colorific. **1437** Paul Brierley. **1438–9** [3A–B, 5] Spectrum Colour Library; [6] Michael Holford; [7] Ronan Picture Library. **1440–1** [4A] Ronan Picture Library. **1442–3** [Key] Ronan Picture Library/ Royal Astronomical Society; [1A] Trustees of the British Museum; [1B] Ronan Picture Library/E. P. Goldschmidt & Co Ltd; [1C] Ronan Picture Library; [5A] Ronan Picture Library/Royal Astronomical Society; [5B, 6A–B] Ronan Picture Library. **1444–5** [Key] Paul Brierley; [1] Mary Evans Picture Library; [2] Anthony Howarth/Susan Griggs Picture Agency; [5] Ken Lambert/Bruce Coleman Ltd; [7] Cooper Bridgeman Library; [8] David Levin. **1446–7** [Key] Hans Schmid/ZEFA; [4] Gerry Cranham; [8] Barnabys Picture Library; [9] David Levin. **1448–9** [Key] Sally & Richard Greenhill; [2] David Levin; [4] Mansell Collection; [6A] David Levin; [9A] Roosevelt Raceway; [9B] IBM. **1450–1** [Key, 1A, B] Dr D. E. H. Jones; [1C, 2] Paul Brierley; [4] Fritz Goro/T.L.P.A. © Time Inc 1976/Colorific; [6] Dr D. E. H. Jones; [7] Photri. **1452–3** [Key] Spectrum Colour Library; [3, 7] David Levin. **1454–5** [Key, 5] Dr D. E. H. Jones. **1456–7** [Key] Paul Brierley; [2] Spectrum Colour Library; [5, 6A, B, 7] David Levin. **1458–9** [Key] Pictor; [1A] David Levin; [8A] Barnabys Picture Library. **1460–1** [Key] The Royal Institution; [1, 3] Dr D. E. H. Jones; [4B] Spectrum Colour Library; [5] Dr D. E. H. Jones; [6B] ZEFA. **1462–3** [Key, 7] Dr D. E. H. Jones. **1464–5** [Key] Art & Antiques Weekly; [8A] David Levin; [8B] Brian Coates/Bruce Coleman Ltd. **1466–7** [Key] Institute of Electrical & Electronics Engineers Inc; [5, 7, 8] Dr D. E. H. Jones; [10] William MacQuitty. **1468–9** [Key] R. K. Pilsbury/Bruce Coleman Ltd; [4] Ron Boardman; [5] Escher Foundation, The Hague; [6A] David Strickland; [8A] Spectrum Colour Library. **1470–1** [Key] Dr D. E. H. Jones; [7] Dieter Buslau/Construction News. **1472–3** [Key A, B] National Gallery. **1474–5** [Key] Paul Brierley/S.T.L. Research; [7] Barnabys Picture Library. **1476–7** [Key] David Levin; [5] David Strickland. **1478–9** [Key] Photri; [2] CERN; [3] Dr A. M. Field, Virus Reference Laboratory, Colindale; [4] Spectrum Colour Library; [5] Scala; [6] Spectrum Colour Library; [7] Photri. **1480–1** [1] C. M. Dixon; [2] Ron Boardman; [5] Ronan Picture Library; [6] Solvay & Cie; [7] Popperfoto; [9] Bettmann Archive. **1482–3** [Key] Photri; [1, 2] Spectrum Colour Library; [3, 4A] Ronan Picture Library; [4B] Cavendish Laboratory/Cambridge University; [7] Science Museum; [8] UK Atomic Energy Authority. **1484–5** [1] F. Rust/ZEFA; [2] David Levin; [3] International Society for Educational Information, Tokyo; [4] American History Picture Library; [6E, 8] Photri. **1486–7** [Key, 1] Photri; [2] David Levin; [3, 5] Photri; [6] David Levin; [7] ZEFA. **1488–9** [Key] John Walmsley; [3] Spectrum Colour Library; [5D] London Transport Executive; [6] David Strickland. **1490–1** [3] Photri; [5D] David Levin. **1492–3** [Key] Spectrum Colour Library; [3] Popperfoto; [4, 6] Camera Press; [7] Ronan Picture Library. **1494–5** [Key] Adam Woolfitt/Susan Griggs Picture Agency; [2, 3A] Spectrum Colour Library; [4] Photri; [5] Spectrum Colour Library; [9] Institution of Civil Engineers. **1496–7** [Key] Hawker Siddeley Aviation; [1B] Spectrum Colour Library; [4] Picturepoint; [6] Spectrum Colour Library. **1498–9** [2] Lyn Cawley. **1500–1** [5, 6] David Strickland; [7] Fabbri. **1502–3** [Key, 2] Picturepoint; [4B] Camera Press; [7] Photri. **1504–5** [2] Shell Photographic Library; [5] Picturepoint; [6] CERN; [7] Graeme French; [8, 9] David Levin. **1506–7** [Key] Ron Boardman; [4] *Construction News;* [5] K. Helbig/ZEFA; [6] Picturepoint; [8] Gerry Cranham. **1508–9** [Key] Mansell Collection; [8] B.O.C. Ltd. **1510–1** [1, 2] Photri; [3] Paul Brierley. **1512–3** [2A] Air Products & Chemicals Inc; [4A, B] Paul Brierley; [5A] CERN. **1514–5** [Key] De Beers Industrial Diamond Division; [1A] Picturepoint; [1B] Paul Brierley/Daly Instruments; [2] Paul Brierley/British Aluminium Co; [3] Ford Motor Co; [4A–B] Joseph Lucas Ltd, [5] Paul Brierley/RCA; [6] Paul Brierley/Southampton University; [7] Photri. **1516–7** [Key] Ronan Picture Library; [1] Spectrum Colour Library. **1520–1** [3] Bob Croxford; [6, 8A–B, 9] David Strickland. **1522–3** [Key] Horst Munzig/Susan Griggs Picture Agency; [3] Victor Englebert/Susan Griggs Picture Agency; [4] Paul Brierley. **1524–5** [Key] Library of Congress; [5] Photri. **1526–7** [Key] Science Museum; [5, 7] Spectrum Colour Library; [8] Picturepoint; [10] Courtesy of the GPO. **1528–9** [Key] Paul Brierley; [7A] Paul Brierley/Welding Institute; [7B–C] William Vandivert. **1532–3** [9] Central Electricity Generating Board. **1534–5** [Key] The Royal Institution; [5] Mansell Collection. **1536–7** [Key] UPI; [5] Spectrum Colour Library. **1538–9** [1] Imperial War Museum; [10] Cubestore Ltd. **1540–1** [4E] Otis Elevators Ltd; [7] Paul Brierley/Lintrol/Imperial College. **1542–3** [Key] W. Canning & Co Ltd; [1] Paul Brierley; [2, 5] A.S.E.A.; [8] Monitor. **1544–5** [2A] David Levin; [2B] Paul Brierley/UKAEA Culham Lab; [6A] David Levin; [6B] Central Electricity Generating Board; [8] Spectrum Colour Library. **1546–7** [8A] David Levin; [9A] Marshall Cavendish/Kim Sayer; [10A–B] Paul Brierley. **1548–9** [Key] Mullard Valves Ltd; [5A–B] David Levin. **1550–1** [Key] Paul Brierley; [2] Chris Steele-Perkins/Science Museum. **1552–3** [6] UK Atomic Energy Authority; [7] Paul Brierley/STL Research. **1554–5** [Key] Cooper Bridgeman; [2] Picturepoint; [3] David Levin; [4] Picturepoint; [5] National Gallery; [6] Michael Holford; [9] Mary Evans Picture Library. **1556–7** [1] Popperfoto; [7] Shell Photographic Library; [8] Photri; [9A–B] Kim Sayer. **1558–9** [Key] David Strickland; [4] ZEFA; [6] Dr J. Holloway/Leicester University/Courtesy Argonne National Laboratory, Argonne, Illinois, USA; [12] Source unknown. **1560–1** [Key] David Strickland; [3] Radio Times Hulton Picture Library; [4] Spectrum Colour Library; [7] A. F. Kersting; [8] Citroen. **1562–3** [Key] Picturepoint; [3] Spectrum Colour Library. **1564–5** [Key] Paul Brierley. **1566–7** [Key] Mansell Collection; [1] Ronan Picture Library; [3] Vitatron UK Ltd. **1568–9** [Key, 1, 2] Paul Brierley. **1572–3** [Key] Colorsport; [4] P. H. Ward/Natural Science Photos. **1574–5** [Key] Dr Robert Horne; [4A–C] Sir John Kendrew; [5] Dr Audrey Glavert; [8] Daily Telegraph Colour Library.

Man and Machines
1576–7 Peter J. Kaplan. **1579** Jan Eyerman/T.L.P.A. © Time Inc 1976/Colorific. **1580** Lautman Photography. **1581** ASEA. **1582–3** [4] Paul Brierley; [6] Dead Sea Works; [7] Spectrum Colour Library; [8] Ronan Picture Library. **1584–5** [Key] Ironbridge Gorge Museum Trust. **1586–7** [3] Mark Boulton/Bruce Coleman Ltd; [4] Barnabys Picture Library. **1588–9** [2, 3] Michael Holford; [6A–B] Basil Booth. **1590–1** [Key] Jen and Des Bartlett/Bruce Coleman Ltd; [8] Photoresources; [9] Sybil Sassoon/Robert Harding Associates. **1592–3** [Key] Aerofilms; [5, 6] Mansell Collection. **1594–5** [Key, 5] ASEA. **1596–7** [Key] Picturepoint; [1A] Photoresources; [1B] Paul Brierley; [2] Michael Holford/British Museum; [3] AEC Ltd/Tin Research Institute; [5] Copper Development Association; [6] Mullard Valves Ltd; [7] Kim Sayer/By permission of the Gardening Centre Ltd, Syon Park; [8] Wilmot Breeden Ltd; [9] UKAEA. **1598–9** [2] Radio Times Hulton Picture Library; [11] R. Sheridan/ZEFA. **1600–1** [Key] Spectrum Colour Library; [1, 2] Photri; [3] Cambridge Instruments Co; [4] Michael Francis Wood & Associates; [5] Paul Brierley; [6] Hans Gunter Möuer; [7] F. James. **1602–3** [Key] Mansell Collection; [1] The Stanley Works; [4] Trinity College Chapel, Oxford/Leslie Harris; [6] Kim Sayer; [7] Photri; [8] The Stanley Works; [9] Richard Cooke. **1604–5** [2] Picturepoint; [4, 5] David Strickland. **1606–7** [Key] British Steel Corporation. **1608–9** [Key] Paul Brierley; [3] Trustees of the British Museum; [6] Paul Brierley; [7] UKAEA; [8] David Levin. **1610–11** [6A–B] Timber Research and Development Association. **1612–3** [Key] Angelo Hornak. **1616–7** [2] ZEFA. **1618–9** [4] Royal National Lifeboat Institute; [7] GPG Holdings; [9] C. E. Abranson. **1620–1** [Key] Courtaulds Ltd; [2] Bruce Coleman/Bruce Coleman Ltd; [3] Jane Burton/Bruce Coleman Ltd; [5] Asbestos & Rubber Co Ltd; [6] MB Copyright; [7] Photri **1622–3** [3, 5, 6] Courtaulds Ltd; [8] A–Z Botanical Collection. **1624–5** [Key] Ronan Picture Library; [1] Ronald Sheridan; [3A] ZEFA; [4] Geoff Goode/By Permission of the National Postal Museum. **1626–7** [Key] Basil Smith. **1628–9** [3] Times Newspapers; [4] Ronan Picture Library. **1630–1** [Key, 5] Central Electricity Generating Board. **1634–5** [Key] Barnabys Picture Library. **1636–7** [Key, 1] ZEFA; [3] Daily Telegraph Colour Library. **1638–9** [7, 8] UKAEA. **1640–1** [4] National Coal Board; [5] National Smokeless Fuel Ltd; [6] National Coal Board. **1644–5** [Key] R. Halin/ZEFA. **1646–7** [5] William MacQuitty. **1648–9** [Key] Fabian Acker; [1] Picturepoint; [5] Fabian Acker. **1652–3** [Key] Spectrum Colour Library; [2] Picturepoint; [8] Architectural Association; [9] Spectrum Colour Library. **1654–5** [4] Phil Sheldon/ZEFA. **1658–9** [Key] Mary Evans Picture Library; [7] SSIH [UK] Ltd (Omega Division). **1660–1** [Key] ASEA [2] The Science Museum; [4] British Leyland; [5A–C] Ford Motor Co; [6] Paul Brierley; [7] ASEA. **1662–3** [Key] Ronan Picture Library; [5] Popperfoto; [7] Lancer Boss Ltd. **1664–5** [Key] Mansell Collection; [1] E. Webber/ZEFA; [2] F. Park/ZEFA; [3] H. Helbig/ZEFA; [5] Picturepoint. **1666–7** [1] Spectrum Colour Library; [2B] By permission of the German Embassy; [3A] ZEFA; [4B–C] Rolair Systems [UK] Ltd; [5A 6B] Hydranautics Inc. **1668–9** [Key] Toshiba/Michael Turner Associates; [2] Spectrum Colour Library; [4A–B] David Levin; [6A–B] Paul Brierley; [7A] Eagle International. **1670–1** [6] Queen Mary College. **1672–3** [1] Chris Steele-Perkins/Courtesy of the Science Museum; [2] Spectrum Colour Library; [5] IBM. **1674–5** [Key] Lloyds Bank Ltd; [1] IBM; [2] Honeywell Ltd; [7] ASEA; [8] David Strickland. **1676–7** [Key] Textron's Bell Aerospace Division, Buffalo, NY. **1684–5** [Key] Mansell Collection; [2] Popperfoto; [3] Robert Hunt Library; [4, 8] Photri. **1688–9** [Key] Mansell Collection. **1700–1** [Key] Mansell Collection; [2] Fotolink; [3] GMC Truck and Coach; [4] London Transport Executive; [6] UN; [7] P. Phillips/ZEFA; [8] Fotolink. **1704–5** [4] Ann Keatley/National Academy of Sciences, Washington; [5] Spectrum Colour Library. **1710–1** [2] British Railways Board. **1712–3** [7] Radio Times Hulton Picture Library; [8] Times Newspapers. **1720–1** [3] Crown Copyright 1973; [5] Smithsonian Institution; [8] Picturepoint. **1722–3** [Key, 2] Patrick Moore Collection; [4A] Novosti Press Agency; [4B–C, 8A–B] NASA. **1724–5** [Key, 2, 3, 4, 5, 6, 7, 8, 9, 10, 11] NASA. **1730–1** [3] Popperfoto; [5A] Robert Hunt Library; [7] General Electric Aircraft Equipment Division. **1732–3** [Key] Crown Copyright, Reproduced by permission of the Department of

the Environment; [1] Michael Holford/British Museum; [5] Permission of the Governing Body of Christ Church, Oxford; [7A] National Portrait Gallery. **1734–5** [Key] John Massey Stewart; [5, 7, 8] Photri; [10] Robin Adshead. **1736–7** [1] Imperial War Museum; [5] Popperfoto; [7] US Army. **1746–7** [Key] Robert Hunt Library/Imperial War Museum; [2] Robert Hunt Library; [7, 8] Photri. **1750–1** [Key] Associated Press; [1] Freeman Fox & Partners. **1754–5** [Key] Sir Robert McAlpine; [6] Chesapeake Bay Bridge & Tunnel District. **1756–7** [2] Mary Evans Picture Library; [3] Loren McIntyre. **1758–9** [Key] Douglas Pike; [2] Bill Stirling/Robert Harding Associates; [3, 4] Construction News; [5] US Department of Transportation; [7] City of Chicago; [8] Port Authority of New York and New Jersey. **1760–1** [Key] J. Allan Cash. **1762–3** [Key] Spectrum Colour Library; [7] ZEFA; [9] KLM Aerocarto. **1764–5** [Key] J. Allan Cash; [8] Paul Almasy. **1768–9** [Key] Mansell Collection; [3] Boyd Body Co.; [4A] Picturepoint; [4B] Spectrum Colour Library; [5] Redland Purle Ltd. **1770–1** [2, 3] Mansell Collection; [4] The Granger Collection; [6B, 8, 9] Mansell Collection; [10] Linotype U.K. **1772–3** [Key] G. Sommer/ZEFA; [3E] David Strickland; [4] Picturepoint. **1774–5** [4] Rank Xerox Ltd. **1776–7** [Key] Monitor; [2] Picturepoint; [3] Jerry Watcher; [6] IBM. **1778–9** [Key, 1] Kim Sayer; [2] © 1977 Jill Krementz; [3] Peter Arnold; [4A–F] Kim Sayer; [6] Gerfried Brutzer. **1780–1** [Key] Kim Sayer; [1, 2, 3] David Levin; [4A–I] Graeme French. **1782–3** [Key] Dupont [UK] Ltd; [1] John Crossley & Sons Ltd; [2A] IBM; [2B] Honeywell; [4A] Angelo Hornak; [5] British Airways. **1786–7** [Key] Chris Steele-Perkins; [1A–B, 2A–C] Guy Rycart; [7A–C] David Strickland. **1788–9** [7] EMI. **1790–1** [Key] By courtesy of the Post Office; [1] Ronan Picture Library; [2] David Strickland; [5] Chris Steele-Perkins/The Science Museum **1792–3** [Key] J. Allen Cash. **1794–5** [Key] The Science Museum; [1] Mansell Collection; [2A] Chris Steele-Perkins; [3] Radio Times Hulton Picture Library; [6A] BBC; [6B] P. Freytag/ZEFA; [6C] David Levin. **1798–9** [Key] EMI; [6] Sotheby's; [7] Toshiba/Michael Turner Associates. **1800–1** [1, 3A] Ampex [Great Britain] Ltd; [3B] David Levin; [5] Ampex [Great Britain] Ltd; [7] RCA. **1802–3** [Key] Radio Times Hulton Picture Library. **1804–5** [Key] ICI Ltd; [1] Aerofilms Ltd; [3] ZEFA; [5] Centre File Ltd. **1806–7** [1B] Picturepoint. **1808–9** [1] Picturepoint; [2] Unilever Ltd; [7] Picturepoint. **1810–1** [Key] Popperfoto; [3] Photri; [7] Pains Wessex Ltd/Michael Turner Associates. **1812–3** [Key] Ronan Picture Library; [2] Graham Nash; [3] Bill Holden; [4] Photoresources/Metropolitan Museum of Art; [5] Michael Holford; [8] Basil Booth; [9] David Levin; [11] Toshiba/Michael Turner Associates. **1814–5** [Key] Picturepoint; [3A] French Government Tourist Office; [3B] Spectrum Colour Library; [4] Max Factor Ltd; [5A] Educational Products Ltd/Max Factor Ltd; [6] Times Newspapers; [7B–C] Educational Products Ltd/Max Factor Ltd.

Time Chart

1825 American Museum of Natural History. **1828–9** Photoresources; Werner Forman Archive; Aerofilms; Museum of the American Indian, Heye Foundation; Michael Holford/British Museum; Picturepoint/Iraq Museum; A. F. Kersting. **1830–1** Ronald Sheridan; C. M. Dixon; Werner Forman Archive; Barnabys Picture Library; Werner Forman Archive; American Museum of Natural History. **1832–3** Michael Holford; Michael Holford/British Museum; Mexican National Tourist Council; Sonia Halliday/Hittite Museum, Ankara; Mansell Collection; Photoresources/British Museum. **1834–5** American Museum of Natural History; Metropolitan Museum of Art, New York. Rogers Fund 1914; Camera Press; Photoresources/The Hermitage, Leningrad; Ronald Sheridan; Photoresources. **1836–7** Mansell Collection; Richard Davis/DPI; Michael Holford; Mansell Collection; Ronald Sheridan; Ann and Bury Peerless. **1838–9** Michael Holford; Michael Holford; Roger Wood; Werner Forman Archive; Mexican National Tourist Council. **1840–1** American Museum of Natural History; Ray Gardner/Trustees of British Museum; Mansell Collection; Robert Harding Associates; Michael Holford; K. Ogana/J. Ziolo. **1842–3** Werner Forman Archive; Mansell Collection; Richard Davis/DPI; Ronan Picture Library. **1844–5** Michael Holford; Christopher Wilson; Radio Times Hulton Picture Library; Mexican National Tourist Council. **1846–7** Bodleian Library, Oxford; American Museum of Natural History; Scala; Mansell Collection; Mansell Collection; Mary Evans Picture Library; Mansell Collection; Ray Gardner/Trustees of the British Museum. **1848–9** Mansell Collection; Mary Evans Picture Library; Michael Holford/V & A; Mansell Collection; Mansell Collection; Mansell Collection; New York Public Library. **1850–1** Mansell Collection; Sonia Halliday/Topkapi Palace Museum, Istanbul; Mary Evans Picture Library; Mansell Collection; Michael Holford; Mansell Collection. **1852–3** Mary Evans Picture Library; New York Public Library; Cooper Bridgeman/Rijksmuseum, Amsterdam; Cooper Bridgeman; A. F. Kersting. **1854–5** Giraudon; Mansell Collection; New York Public Library; Mansell Collection; Michael Holford; Camera Press; Mansell Collection; Mansell Collection. **1856–7** Mrs Barbara Edwards/Carter Nash Cameron; Michael Holford/V & A; Mansell Collection; New York Public Library; Mansell Collection; Mansell Collection; Ronan Picture Library. **1858–9** Michael Holford; Michael Holford/Louvre; Giraudon. **1860–1** New York Public Library; Mansell Collection; Cooper Bridgeman; Mansell Collection; Mansell Collection. **1862–3** Mansell Collection; Cooper Bridgeman; Cooper Bridgeman; Mansell Collection; New York Public Library. **1864–5** Ronan Picture Library; Mansell Collection; Ronan Picture Library; Robert Hunt Library; Mansell Collection; Bildarchiv Preussischer Kulturbesitz. **1866–7** Mansell Collection; Mansell Collection; Bildarchiv Foto Marburg. **1868–9** Mansell Collection; Mansell Collection; Imperial War Museum; Mansell Collection; Mansell Collection. **1870–1** Radio Times Hulton Picture Library; Popperfoto; Maurice Rickards; Robert Hunt Library; Novosti Press Agency; Novosti Press Agency; Camera Press. **1872–3** Camera Press; Camera Press; Camera Press; Keystone Press; Camera Press; Camera Press; Camera Press; Camera Press; Camera Press.

ALPHAPEDIA

1881 [1] Library of Congress. **1883** [1, 2, 3] Library of Congress. **1885** [1] UPI; [4] French Embassy Press and Information Division. **1889** [4] US Navy. **1891** [3] Alabama Development Office; [4] BP North America. **1893** [3] Atheneum; [4] Alberta Government Photographic Services. **1895** [2] Library of Congress. **1899** [1] Library of Congress. **1903** [4] UPI. **1905** [2] Joel Gordon; [3] Library of Congress. **1907** [2] The Granger Collection. **1911** [3] Library of Congress. **1913** [1] State of Maryland. **1915** [3] Library of Congress. **1919** [4] UPI. **1921** [1] State of Arkansas; [4] The Granger Collection. **1923** [1] The Granger Collection; [4] UPI. **1927** [1] MGM. **1939** [2] New York City Ballet; [4] Bob Adelman. **1945** [2] Library of Congress; [4] US Information Agency. **1947** [1] The Granger Collection; [2] Library of Congress. **1953** [4] Library of Congress. **1955** [4] Library of Congress. **1957** [4] UN. **1959** [4] Library of Congress. **1963** [1] Israeli Tourist Board. **1965** [3, 4] The Granger Collection **1967** [2] The Granger Collection; [4] Library of Congress. **1969** [2] Library of Congress. **1973** [2] Columbia University. **1975** [3] McGraw Hill. **1977** [1, 2] Library of Congress. **1979** [1] State of Massachusetts **1981** [3] Library of Congress. **1983** [4] The Granger Collection. **1987** [3] Novosti Press Agency. **1989** [1] British Columbia. **1991** [1] New York Convention and Visitors Bureau; [2] Library of Congress. **1993** [2] Library of Congress; [3] The Granger Collection. **1995** [4] The Granger Collection. **1997** [1, 2] Library of Congress. **1999** [3] US Navy. **2003** [1] Egyptian Government Tourist Office; [2, 3] Library of Congress; [4] California Division of Highways. **2005** [4] UN. **2007** [4] Canadian Government Travel Bureau. **2013** [2] Library of Congress; [4] UPI. **2015** [3] Library of Congress. **2017** [4] Wide World Photos. **2019** [1, 2] Library of Congress. **2021** [1] UPI. **2031** [4] The Granger Collection. **2033** [2] The Granger Collection. **2037** [3] UPI; [4] Chicago Convention and Tourism Bureau. **2043** [2] The Granger Collection. **2047** [3] State of Colorado. **2049** [1, 4] Library of Congress. **2051** [2, 4] Library of Congress. **2053** [1] The Granger Collection. **2057** [1] Library of Congress. **2059** [4] State of Colorado. **2061** [2] International Harvester; [4] Library of Congress. **2069** [1] Wide World Photos. **2071** [1, 2, 3, 4] New York Public Library. **2073** [1, 2, 3, 4] New York Public Library. **2075** [1, 2, 3, 4] New York Public Library. **2077** [3] The Granger Collection; [4] Library of Congress. **2083** [4] Musée Fabré, Montpellier. **2087** [2] Library of Congress. **2089** [1] CBS. **2091** [2] State of Kentucky. **2093** [1] Library of Congress. **2097** [2] City of Chicago. **2101** [1, 3, 4] Library of Congress. **2103** [2, 4] Library of Congress. **2105** [3] Scripps Institution of Oceanography. **2107** [1] The Granger Collection; [2] Library of Congress; [3] Wide World Photos. **2109** [4] Library of Congress. **2111** [4] © Foto Georg Gerster/Photo Researchers. **2113** [4] Library of Congress. **2115** [1] Library of Congress; [4] The Granger Collection. **2117** [1] Library of Congress; [4] Royal Library, Copenhagen. **2119** [3] Walt Disney Productions; [4] National Portrait Gallery, London. **2121** [2] Library of Congress. **2125** [3] Library of Congress; [4] Ray Lustig. **2127** [4] US Army. **2129** [3] Library of Congress. **2131** [1] US Information Agency. **2135** [2] Library of Congress; [4] Kodak. **2137** [2, 4] Library of Congress. **2141** [3] Library of Congress. **2147** [1] CBS Records; [4] Library of Congress. **2151** [2] UPI. **2153** [3] UPI; [4] State of New York. **2155** [3] Library of Congress. **2161** [1, 4] UPI. **2163** [4] The Granger Collection. **2167** [2] Library of Congress. **2169** [3] Library of Congress. **2173** [2, 3] Library of Congress. **2175** [2, 4] Library of Congress. **2179** [1] State of Florida. **2181** [3, 4] Library of Congress. **2183** [4] Library of Congress. **2187** [1] UPI; [2] Library of Congress; [4] Pictorial Parade. **2189** [1, 2] The Granger Collection; [3] Wide World Photos. **2191** [1] Library of Congress. **2193** [3] Library of Congress. **2195** [1, 2, 4] Library of Congress. **2197** [1] Library of Congress. **2199** [4] UPI. **2201** [1, 2, 4] Library of Congress. **2203** [4] Library of Congress. **2205** [4] Library of Congress. **2207** [2] Pictorial Parade. **2209** [2, 3] Library of Congress. **2213** [2] Library of Congress. **2217** [1, 3] Library of Congress. **2219** [1] Library of Congress. **2221** [4] Library of Congress. **2223** [1] State of Connecticut; [2] National Portrait Gallery, London. **2225** [2] Clair Burket/National Park Service; [4] UN. **2227** [1, 2] New York Public Library. **2229** [3, 4] Library of Congress. **2237** [2, 3] Library of Congress. **2239** [1] Library of Congress; [2] UN; [3, 4] Library of Congress. **2241** [3] Library of Congress. **2243** [2] Library of Congress; [3] The Granger Collection. **2245** [3, 4] Library of Congress. **2247** [1] Library of Congress; [2] UPI. **2249** [4] Library of Congress. **2251** [3] National Portrait Gallery, London; [4] Library of Congress. **2253** [1, 3] Library of Congress. **2255** [4] Library of Congress. **2257** [3] Library of Congress; [4] Wide World Photos. **2259** [2, 3, 4] Library of Congress. **2263** [1, 2] Library of Congress. **2265** [3] Library of Congress; [4] New York Public Library. **2267** [3, 4] Library of Congress. **2269** [3] Library of Congress. **2271** [1] UPI. **2277** [2] State of Idaho; [4] City of Chicago. **2281** [3] Photo Researchers. **2283** [3] UN; [4] Wide World Photos. **2287** [1] UPI; [3] State of Florida. **2289** [1] Wide World Photos. **2291** [4] Library of Congress. **2293** [4] Israeli Tourist Board. **2297** [1] Library of Congress; [4] State of Florida. **2299** [2, 3] Library of Congress. **2301** [3, 4] Library of Congress. **2305** [2] UPI; [4] New York Public Library. **2307** [1] UPI; [2, 3] Library of Congress. **2309** [3] Library of Congress. **2313** [3] UPI. **2315** [1] Library of Congress; [2] Warner Bros.; [4] Library of Congress. **2317** [1] Library of Congress; [2] State of Kentucky; [4] Library of Congress. **2319** [2] New York Sets; [3] UPI. **2321** [2] UPI. **2325** [1] UN; [4] G. Weiss/DPI. **2331** [1, 2] Library of Congress. **2333** [2] Library of Congress. **2339** [2]

Library of Congress. **2345** [1] US Information Agency; [2] Library of Congress. **2347** [3, 4] Library of Congress. **2349** [2] Library of Congress. **2351** [4] Library of Congress. **2353** [3] Library of Congress. **2355** [2] Library of Congress. **2357** [4] State of Louisiana. **2359** [1, 2] Library of Congress. **2363** [3] US Army; [4] Library of Congress. **2365** [4] Library of Congress. **2367** [2] Library of Congress. **2369** [2] UPI; [3] Maine Department of Commerce and Industry. **2375** [3] The Granger Collection. **2377** [3] Library of Congress. **2379** [1] Library of Congress. **2381** [1, 2] Library of Congress; [3] US Army; [4] Bob Willis. **2383** [1] State of Massachusetts. **2385** [1] Library of Congress. **2387** [4] Library of Congress. **2389** [3] Wide World Photos. **2391** [1, 2] Library of Congress. **2395** [3] Mexican National Tourist Council. **2397** [3] Michigan Tourist Council. **2399** [3] Collection of Duncan Schiedt; [4] National Portrait Gallery, London. **2401** [2] State of Minnesota. **2403** [1] Louisiana Tourist Development Commission; [2] State of Missouri; [4] Library of Congress. **2407** [4] Library of Congress. **2409** [1] UPI; [2] Grant M. Haist/Photo Researchers; [4] Canada Tourist Council. **2411** [3] Library of Congress. **2413** [1, 2] Library of Congress. **2415** [1] Library of Congress; [2] UPI. **2417** [3, 4] Library of Congress. **2423** [4] Library of Congress. **2425** [4] Josephus Daniels/Photo Researchers. **2429** [4] Robert E. Smallman/DPI. **2431** [1] State of New Jersey; [2] State of New Mexico; [3] National Portrait Gallery, London; [4] State of New York. **2435** [2] State of New York. **2439** [1] Wide World Photos; [2] Library of Congress; [3, 4] Wide World Photos. **2441** [1, 2] Wide World Photos. **2443** [2] State of North Carolina; [3] State of North Dakota. **2445** [4] Jerry Frank/DPI. **2447** [3] National Accelerator Laboratory. **2449** [3] New York Public Library; [4] Wide World Photos. **2451** [4] Library of Congress. **2453** [1] State of Ohio; [3] State of Oklahoma. **2455** [3] Library of Congress; [4] Canada Tourist Council. **2457** [1] Princeton University; [4] State of Oregon. **2461** [2] Deutsches Museum, Munich. **2465** [2] Library of Congress. **2469** [4] French Government Tourist Office. **2473** [2] US Army. **2477** [1] Library of Congress; [2] State of Pennsylvania. **2479** [2, 3] Library of Congress; [4] US Army. **2487** [2, 3] Library of Congress. **2489** [2] Library of Congress. **2495** [1] Library of Congress. **2497** [2] Library of Congress. **2503** [2] Library of Congress. **2505** [4] Library of Congress. **2507** [1] Canada Tourist Council. **2513** [1] Library of Congress. **2515** [4] Canada Tourist Council. **2517** [1] Canada Tourist Council; [2] Library of Congress. **2523** [2] Library of Congress. **2527** [2] Library of Congress; [4] Royal Academy of Art, London. **2529** [2] UPI. **2531** [1] Library of Congress. **2533** [4] Library of Congress. **2535** [1] National Park Service; [2] Musée Rodin, Paris; [3] Library of Congress. **2537** [2, 3, 4] Library of Congress. **2541** [2, 3] Library of Congress. **2545** [1] UPI. **2547** [3] UPI. **2549** [3] Library of Congress. **2551** [3] Library of Congress. **2555** [2] UPI. **2563** [2] Wide World Photos; [3] Alfonso Preindl/DPI. **2565** [2] National Park Service; [4] UPI. **2567** [1] Library of Congress. **2569** [3, 4] Library of Congress. **2575** [2] UPI; [4] Library of Congress. **2579** [2] Library of Congress. **2583** [2] Farrar, Straus and Giroux, Inc. **2585** [1] Library of Congress; [3] Bruce Roberts/Photo Researchers; [4] State of South Dakota. **2595** [1, 2, 3] Library of Congress; [4] National Portrait Gallery, London. **2597** [1, 2, 4] Library of Congress. **2599** [3] Library of Congress. **2611** [1] Library of Congress. **2613** [1, 3] Library of Congress. **2615** [1] Uffizi Gallery, Florence; [2] Library of Congress. **2617** [1] State of Tennessee; [2] Tennessee Valley Authority. **2619** [4] Library of Congress. **2623** [1] New York Public Library; [3] Library of Congress. **2631** [2] Musée Toulouse-Lautrec, Albi. **2637** [2] Harry S. Truman Library; [4] The Granger Collection. **2639** [4] Turkish Information Office. **2641** [1] Tate Gallery, London; [2, 3, 4] Library of Congress. **2643** [1] Collection of Jules Bach, Metropolitan Museum of Art. **2645** [4] State of New York. **2647** [2] Werner Stoy/DPI. **2649** [1] Trinity. **2651** [2, 3,] Library of Congress; [4] Canada Tourist Council. **2653** [1] Library of Congress; [4] National Gallery of Scotland, Edinburgh. **2655** [3] State of Vermont. **2659** [3] Blue Ridge Parkway; [4] National Park Service. **2663** [4] Louvre, Paris. **2665** [1, 2] Library of Congress. **2667** [1, 2, 3, 4] Library of Congress. **2669** [1] State of Washington; [2] Werner Stoy/DPI. **2673** [1, 2] Library of Congress. **2675** [4] Library of Congress. **2677** [2, 4] Library of Congress. **2679** [1] Library of Congress; [2] The Granger Collection; [4] Library of Congress. **2681** [1, 4] Library of Congress. **2683** [1] Library of Congress; [2] State of Wisconsin. **2687** [1, 2, 3] Library of Congress. **2689** [1, 2] Wyoming Travel Division; [3] Library of Congress. **2693** [2] Library of Congress; [3] British Museum, London.

ART CREDITS

Art Editors
Angela Downing; George Glaze; James Marks; Mel Peterson; Ruth Prentice; Bob Scott

Visualizers
David Aston; Javed Badar; Allison Blythe; Angela Braithwaite; Alan Brown; Michael Burke; Alistair Campbell; Terry Collins; Mary Ellis; Judith Escreet; Albert Jackson; Barry Jackson; Ted Kindsey; Kevin Maddison; Erika Mathlow; Paul Mundon; Peter Nielson; Patrick O'Callaghan; John Ridgeway; Peter Saag; Malcolme Smythe; John Stanyon; John Stewart; Justin Todd; Linda Wheeler

Artists
Stephen Adams; Geoffrey Alger; Terry Allen; Jeremy Alsford; Frederick Andenson; John Arnold; Peter Arnold; David Ashby; Michael Badrock; William Baker; John Barber; Norman Barber; Arthur Barvoso; John Batchelor; John Bavosi; David Baxter; Stephen Bernette; John Blagovitch; Michael Blore; Christopher Blow; Roger Bourne; Alistair Bowtell; Robert Brett; Gordon Briggs; Linda Broad; Lee Brooks; Rupert Brown; Marilyn Bruce; Anthony Bryant; Paul Buckle; Sergio Burelli; Dino Bussetti; Patricia Casey; Giovanni Casselli; Nigel Chapman; Chensie Chen; David Chisholm; David Cockcroft; Michael Codd; Michael Cole; Gerry Collins; Peter Connelly; Roy Coombs; David Cox; Patrick Cox; Brian Cracker; Gordon Cramp; Gino D'Achille; Terrence Daley; John Davies; Gordon C. Davis; David Day; Graham Dean; Brian Delf; Kevin Diaper; Madeleine Dinkel; Hugh Dixon; Paul Draper; David Dupe; Howard Dyke; Jennifer Eachus; Bill Easter; Peter Edwards; Michael Ellis; Jennifer Embleton; Ronald Embleton; Ian Evans; Ann Evens; Lyn Evens; Peter Fitzjohn; Eugene Flurey; Alexander Forbes; David Carl Forbes; Chris Fosey; John Francis; Linda Francis; Sally Frend; Brian Froud; Gay Galfworthy; Ian Garrard; Jean George; Victoria Goaman; David Godfrey; Miriam Golochoy; Anthea Gray; Harold Green; Penelope Greensmith; Vanna Haggerty; Nicholas Hall; Horgrave Hans; David Hardy; Douglas Harker; Richard Hartwell; Jill Havergale; Peter Hayman; Ron Haywood; Peter Henville; Trevor Hill; Garry Hinks; Peter Hutton; Faith Jacques; Robin Jacques; Lancelot Jones; Anthony Joyce; Pierre Junod; Patrick Kaley; Sarah Kensington; Don Kidman; Harold King; Martin Lambourne; Ivan Lapper; Gordon Lawson; Malcolm Lee-Andrews; Peter Levaffeur; Richard Lewington; Brian Lewis; Ken Lewis; Richard Lewis; Kenneth Lilly; Michael Little; David Lock; Garry Long; John Vernon Lord; Vanessa Luff; John Mac; Lesley MacIntyre; Thomas McArthur; Michael McGuinness; Ed McKenzie; Alan Male; Ben Manchipp; Neville Mardell; Olive Marony; Bob Martin; Gordon Miles; Sean Milne; Peter Mortar; Robert Morton; Trevor Muse; Anthony Nelthorpe; Michael Neugebauer; William Nickless; Eric Norman; Peter North; Michael O'Rourke; Richard Orr; Nigel Osborne; Patrick Oxenham; John Painter; David Palmer; Geoffrey Parr; Allan Penny; David Penny; Charles Pickard; John Pinder; Maurice Pledger; Judith Legh Pope; Michael Pope; Andrew Popkiewicz; Brian Price-Thomas; Josephine Rankin; Collin Rattray; Charles Raymond; Alan Rees; Ellsie Rigley; John Ringnall; Christine Robbins; Ellie Robertson; James Robins; John Ronayne; Collin Rose; Peter Sarson; Michael Saunders; Ann Savage; Dennis Scott; Edward Scott-Jones; Rodney Shackell; Chris Simmonds; Gwendolyn Simson; Cathleen Smith; Lesley Smith; Stanley Smith; Michael Soundels; Wolf Spoel; Ronald Steiner; Ralph Stobart; Celia Stothard; Peter Sumpter; Rod Sutterby; Allan Suttie; Tony Swift; Michael Terry; John Thirsk; Eric Thomas; George Thompson; Kenneth Thompson; David Thorpe; Harry Titcombe; Peter Town; Michael Trangenza; Joyce Tuhill; Glenn Tutssel; Carol Vaucher; Edward Wade; Geoffrey Wadsley; Mary Waldron; Michael Walker; Dick Ward; Brian Watson; David Watson; Peter Weavers; David Wilkinson; Ted Williams; John Wilson; Roy Wiltshire; Terrence Wingworth; Anne Winterbotham; Albany Wiseman; Vanessa Wiseman; John Wood; Michael Woods; Owen Woods; Sidney Woods; Raymond Woodward; Harold Wright; Julia Wright

Studios
Add Make-up; Alard Design; Anyart; Arka Graphics; Artec; Art Liaison; Art Workshop; Bateson Graphics; Broadway Artists; Dateline Graphics; David Cox Associates; David Levin Photographic; Eric Jewel Associates; Flag Research Center; George Miller Associates; Gilcrist Studios; Hatton Studio; Jackson Day; Kirchoff-Wohlberg, Inc.; Libragraphics; Lock Pettersen Ltd; Mitchell Beazley Studio; Negs Photographic; Paul Hemus Associates; Product Support Graphics; Q.E.D. [Campbell Kindsley]; Rendart Graphic Color, Inc.; Stobart and Sutterby; Studio Briggs; Technical Graphics; The Diagram Group; Tri Art; Typographics; Venner Artists

Agents
Artist Partners; Freelance Presentations; Garden Studio; Linden Artists; N. E. Middletons; Portman Artists; Saxon Artists; Thompson Artists

Flags of the world: 1

In the modern world the flag is a symbol of national or communal identity, but before the rise of modern nation states or even of empires it was more likely to have been a personal symbol of a king, a noble, or a warlord. The aim of the flag has always been the same: to be an immediately recognizable focal point for people with common military, political, and even religious allegiances. It can inspire feelings of cohesiveness and pride in the abstract as well as provide a physical rallying point in the turmoil of battle.

The ancestral roots of the modern flag lie in the standards of the armies and rulers of the ancient Middle Eastern civilizations. In Egypt the rallying symbol was likely to be an object of cultural or religious significance set on top of a pole. Later, these objects were decorated with or replaced by streamers. Eventually the streamers gave way to the flag: a piece of light fabric bearing the same emblem on both sides.

The earliest flags probably appeared in China and India. The first ruler of the Chou dynasty in China (*c.* 1030 BC) was preceded in public by a white flag, and this soon came to be closely identified with kingship in its own right. It was an offense even to lay hands on the bearer of the flag; for it to fall in battle signified defeat. It has been recorded that the early kings of India carried flags on chariots and elephants.

Flags from Asia

From China and India cloth flags apparently spread into Burma, Siam, and Southeast Asia, and to the Middle East. The modern flags of Asia vary greatly in appearance but, even so, their graphic form effectively demonstrates some of the methods by which visual symbols promote a sense of unity.

An immediately obvious factor is the use of religious or dynastic emblems. The Sun, for example, is a central feature of the Japanese national flag; it represents the Japanese religious belief that the emperor is a direct descendant of the Holy Sun and therefore of prime importance to the nation's welfare. In the Taiwan flag the Sun also appears, but there it is a political symbol of the founding Kuomintang party.

Both Sun and Moon form part of the Nepalese flag (the only national flag that is not rectangular). Originally the Sun represented the Royal House, and the moon stands for the Rana family, which ruled the country until 1951.

As might be expected, the basic color red signifies the political affinities of the Asian communist countries, although each interprets the color in its own way. The Chinese People's Republic, for example, shows five stars, representing party and workers. Cultural links can survive political change, however, and this is shown by the appearance of the Chinese Yang and Yin symbol (good and evil) on the flag of South Korea.

Internal divisions also receive attention in some national flags. The 14 smaller stars on the Burmese flag underline the existence in that country of various ethnic groups and the need for living in harmony. Perhaps it is significant that the flag of Cyprus ignores its two communities, the Greeks and Turks, who also use the flags of Greece and Turkey as their own symbols.

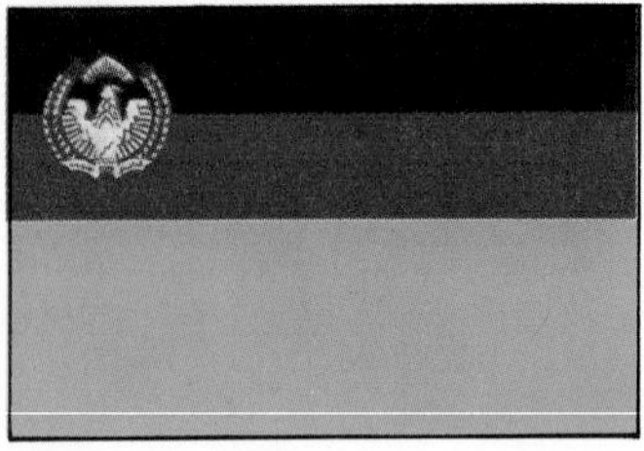
Afghanistan

Bahrein

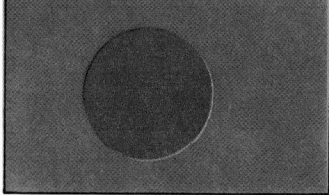

Bangladesh

Bhutan

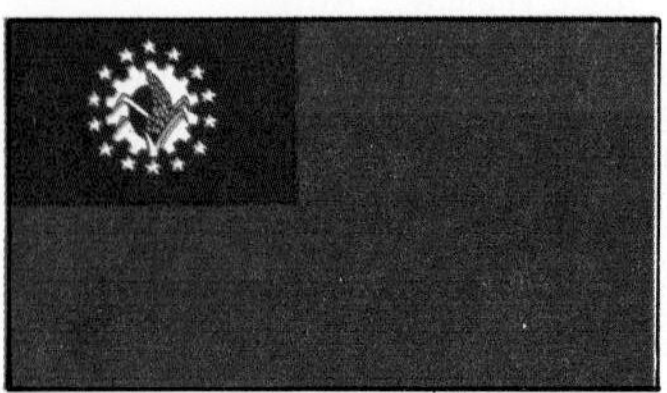
Burma

Cambodia

China, People's Republic

Cyprus

India

Indonesia

Iran

Iraq

Israel

Japan

Jordan

Korea, North

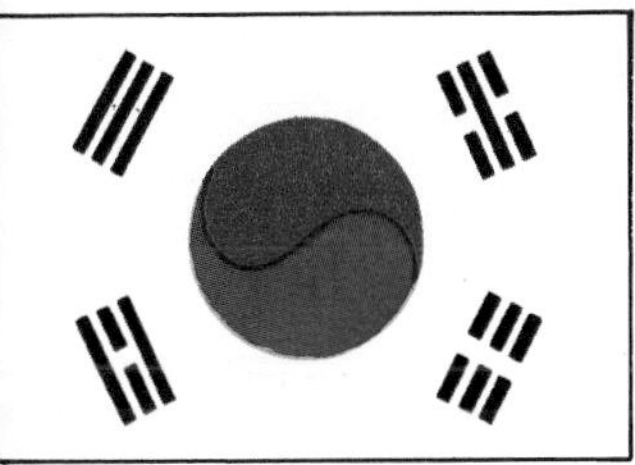
Korea, South

Kuwait

Laos

Lebanon

Malaysia

Maldives

Mongolia

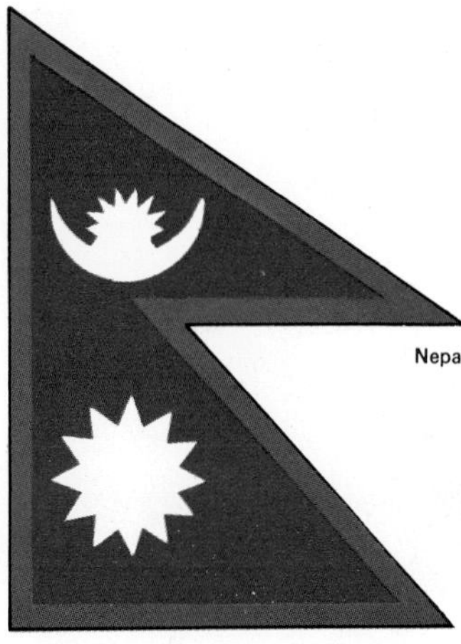
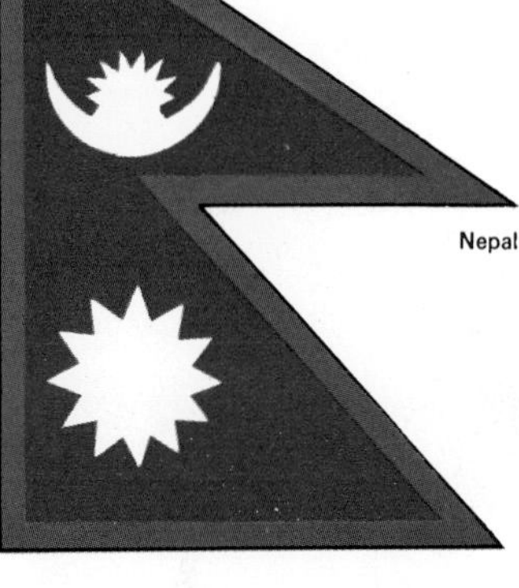
Nepal

Oman

Pakistan

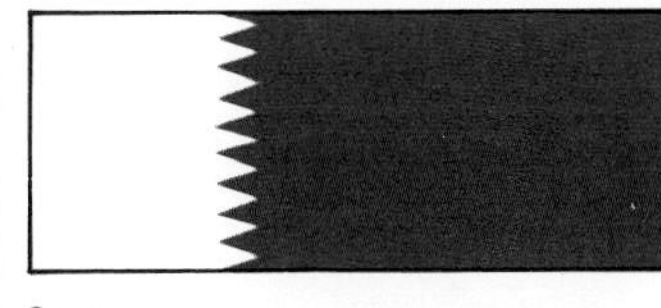
Qatar

Saudi Arabia

Singapore

Sri Lanka

Syria

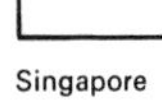

Taiwan

Thailand

Turkey

Vietnam

Yemen

Yemen, People's Democratic Republic

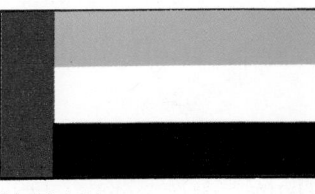
United Arab Emirates

Flags of the world: 2

The Americas

The country that wields the greatest power in the New World—the United States—also possesses the national flag with the longest and most complicated history. There have been no fewer than 28 different designs to date. The first (1775) was an adaptation of the British Red Ensign; instead of the red background the flag carried 13 red and white stripes to signify the 13 original states and the Union as a whole. With independence, the British Ensign was dropped from the corner and replaced by 13 white stars on a blue field. The arrangement of the stars varied greatly over the years. In 1818, Congress decided to add a star for each new state: to date there are 50 such stars. It was not until 1912 that a standard pattern was established for the details.

Canada's first true national flag was introduced in 1965 to replace the British Red Ensign. The maple leaf, however, has always been Canada's national symbol and is instantly recognizable.

Farther south, it is possible to discern signs of common colonial backgrounds. Venezuela, Colombia, and Ecuador were all Spanish possessions. Their separation from Spain is similarly celebrated in their tricolor flags. In each case yellow represents the independent state's separation by the sea (blue) from Spain (red).

The complicated Brazilian flag is one of the few in the world to carry a message in words (*Ordem e Progresso*—"Order and Progress").

Argentina

Bahamas

Barbados

Belize (not fully independent)

Bolivia

ORDEM E PROGRESSO
Brazil

Canada

Chile

Colombia

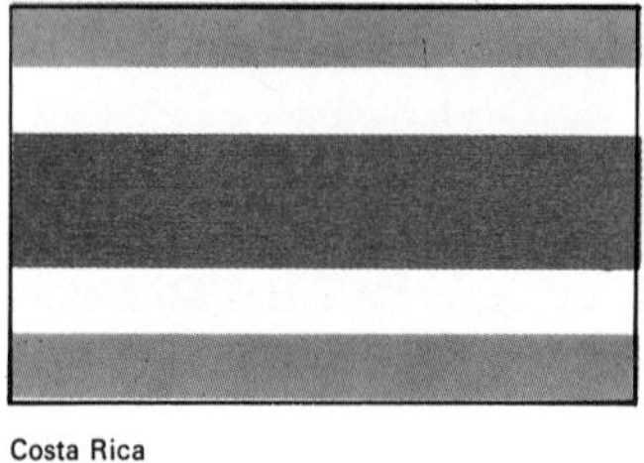
Costa Rica

Cuba

Dominican Republic

Ecuador

El Salvador

Grenada

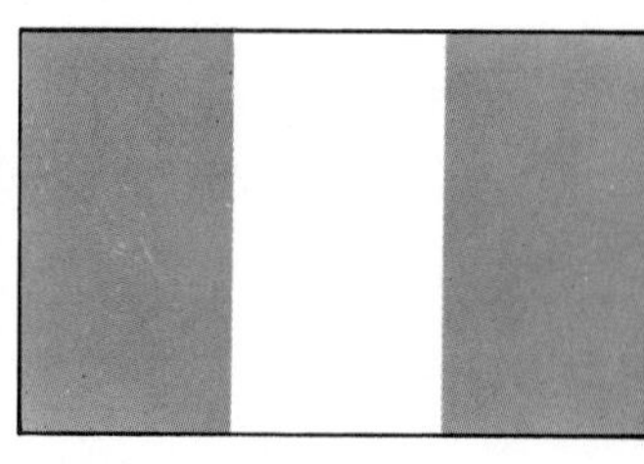
Guatemala

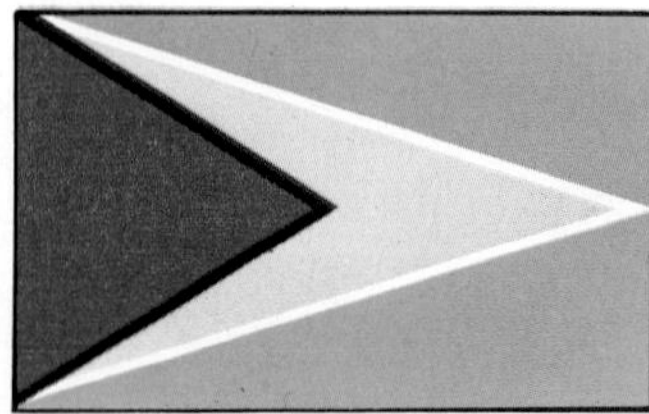
Guyana

Haiti

Honduras

Jamaica

Mexico

Netherlands Antilles (not fully independent)

Nicaragua

Panama

Paraguay

Peru

Surinam

Trinidad and Tobago

United States

Uruguay

Venezuela

Australasia and Oceania

Geographical and historical symbols are curiously mingled in some flags. Both the Australian and New Zealand flags take as their basis the British Blue Ensign, which is associated with imperial days. But they also carry a representation of the Southern Cross. This is a salient feature of the night sky in these latitudes and therefore implies geographical position. The stars in the New Zealand flag are of different sizes, and their positioning is not symmetrical.

The Australian flag was chosen after a public competition in which 30,000 different designs were presented. The seven points of the largest star stand for the six states and the Northern Territory.

Since gaining full independence from Australia in September 1975, Papua New Guinea has continued to use the flag it adopted in 1971.

The flag of Western Samoa similarly shows the Southern Cross, which denotes that country's association with New Zealand. The historical and geographical mix occurs even more specifically in the flag of Nauru. It also features a star that has nothing to do with the Southern Cross but represents the island itself, and its positioning represents the island's actual proximity to the Equator (the yellow line). The 12 points of the star stand for the original 12 tribes that inhabited the island. The influence of the Christian missionaries is recalled by the red cross of the Tongan flag. The red signifies the blood shed by Christ on Calvary.

Australia

Fiji

Nauru

New Zealand

Papua New Guinea

Philippines

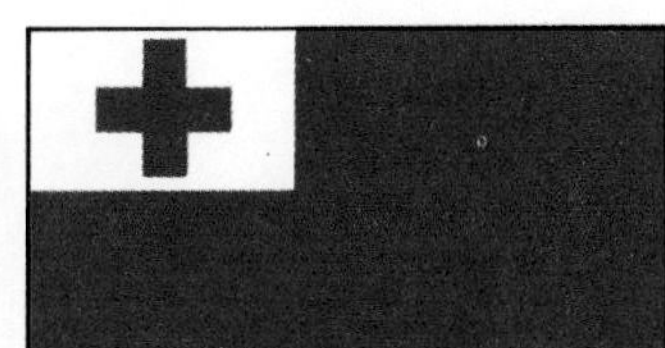
Tonga

Western Samoa

Flags of the world: 3

Africa

The flags of Africa are visible proof that the "wind of change" predicted in the 1950s has blown across the continent. Most of the flags were raised for the first time during the period 1957 to 1975 as the various colonies achieved independence. In general, they are the youngest flags in the world.

Traces of colonialism survive in many African flags. Some are obvious—such as the British Union Flag incorporated in the flag of South Africa, which also carries those of the Orange Free State (with the Dutch tricolor in the corner) and the Transvaal (again based on the Dutch flag).

Other colonial influences are more subtle. Most countries that were once French, for example, seem to have adopted the vertical tricolor; those with a British background have assumed tricolors with horizontal stripes.

One of the latter countries is Ghana, the first black state to become independent (1957) after World War II. Its flag provided a model for those of many later independent nations. Its colors—the pan-African colors of red, yellow, and green first used in 1894 by Abyssinia (present-day Ethiopia), the oldest independent African state—were to become synonymous with African aspirations. Red represents the battle for independence, yellow represents the mineral wealth, and green signifies forest and agricultural resources.

The Ghanaian flag, like many belonging to the emergent African nations, also carries a star that stands for freedom. It may have been inspired by the United States flag, which was the first national flag to use stars.

There is absolutely no doubt, however, of the inspirational source of the Liberian flag. It was a group of former Americans who brought about the founding of Liberia (1822), the first black republic in Africa. The number of stripes on the flag commemorates the number of signatories to the Liberian Declaration of Independence.

During the colonial period, Africa was divided up by the European powers in a rather arbitrary way; frontiers frequently cut tribes in half or grouped together others who might have little in common. In short, the new African leaders have inherited countries that in many cases have no historical unity. It is clear that they have looked to their flags for help in changing this. Not only do the flags reflect the bubbling vitality of the new nations; some also seek to recall the African heritage of their peoples. The flag of Kenya is a case in point. The crossed spears and shield were deliberately placed on it to remind the people of others who, much earlier, sought to defend their homelands.

Africa also has a number of Muslim countries. One of these, Egypt, spearheaded the struggle for Arab liberation. Its flag, with its pan-Arab colors of red, white, and black, also provided a model for other Arab countries in the Middle East. Since 1972, Egypt, Libya, and Syria have used the same flag.

Arab states in Africa, such as Morocco, Tunisia, and Algeria, have settled for the traditional simplicities of Islam; a one-color ground with just a star or star and crescent (symbols of peace and life). This simplicity is a reflection of Islamic distrust of idolatrous images.

Algeria

Angola

Benin

Botswana

Burundi

Cameroon

Cape Verde

Central African Republic

Chad

Comoro Islands

Congo-Brazzaville

Egypt

Equatorial Guinea

Ethiopia

Gabon

Gambia

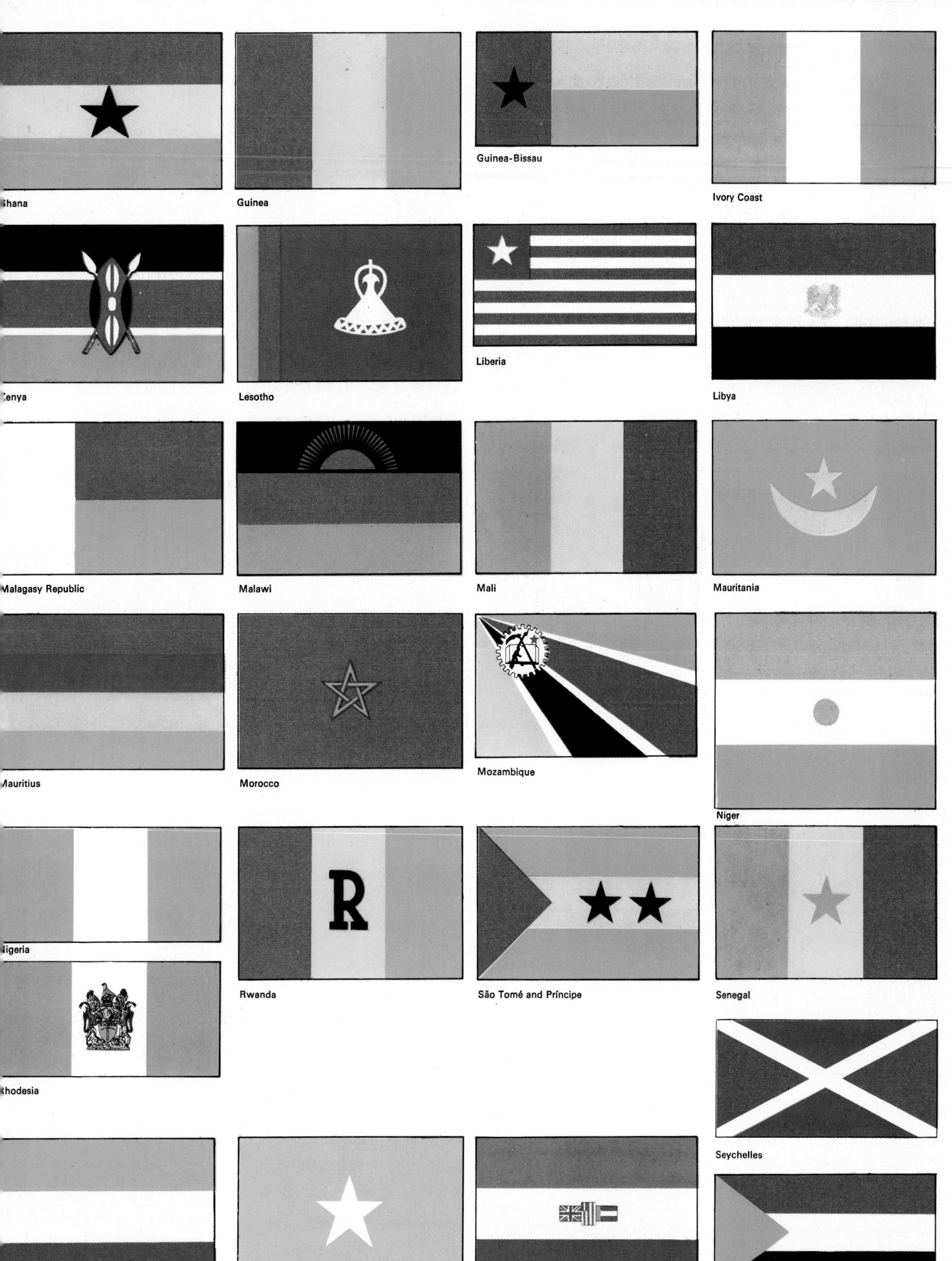

hana
Guinea
Guinea-Bissau
Ivory Coast
enya
Lesotho
Liberia
Libya
Malagasy Republic
Malawi
Mali
Mauritania
auritius
Morocco
Mozambique
Niger
igeria
Rwanda
São Tomé and Príncipe
Senegal
hodesia
Seychelles
ierra Leone
Somalia
South Africa
Sudan

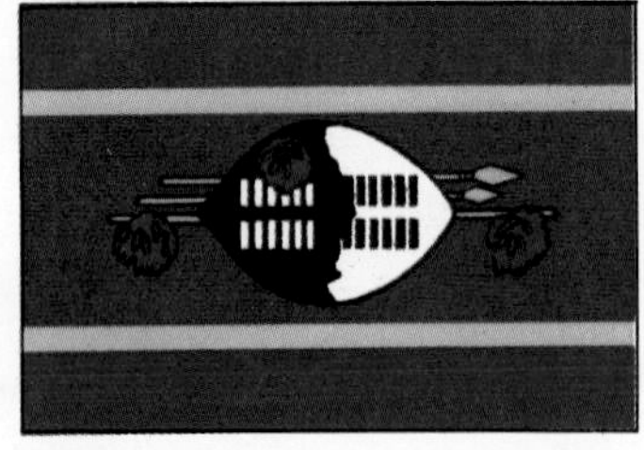

Swaziland

Tanzania

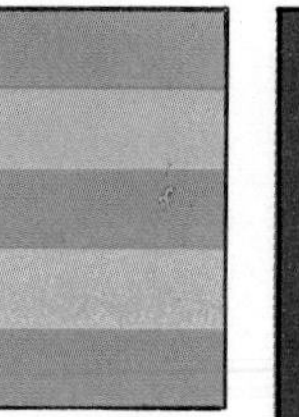

Togo

Tunisia

Uganda

Upper Volta

Zaïre

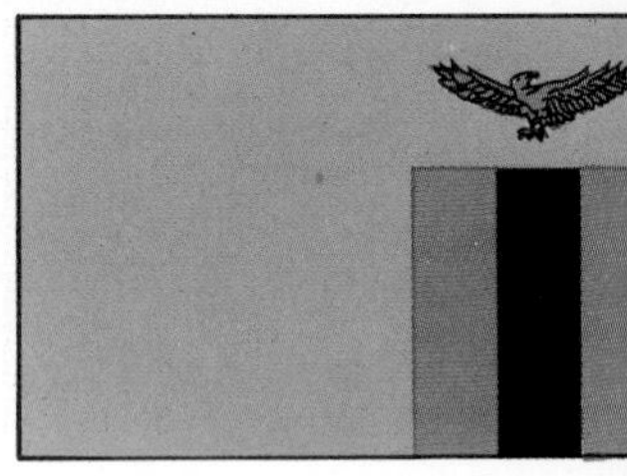

Zambia

Flags of the world: 4

Europe

Flags were probably introduced into Europe as a result of the Crusaders' contact with the Saracens. The Christian symbol of the cross, adopted by the Crusaders nearly 900 years ago, has since been profoundly influential in the history of flags. Similarly, the flags of Egypt, Libya, and Syria use a symbol that dates from the Crusades—the eagle of Saladin (1137–93), the Saracen leader.

One of the first European flags was that of Denmark, which according to legend appeared from the sky in 1219. It is also interesting for another reason: like many European banners it has a cross motif, and the same cross is found in different forms in the other Scandinavian flags. This is because Denmark once ruled these countries; the crosses represent an ancient affiliation.

The British Union Flag is a concise history of the United Kingdom; it successively combined the crosses of England, Scotland, and Ireland. In 1606 the English cross of St George was combined with the saltire of St Andrew of Scotland, to form the first Union Jack. In 1800 the red saltire of St Patrick was added to the flag, and the flag of the United Kingdom has remained the same to this day.

Striped flags also have a long history. The tricolor—in red, white, and blue—first became a symbol of liberty when it was taken up by the Netherlands in the long fight against Spanish domination during the sixteenth century. It is thought to have been first employed in 1579 (the red was originally orange). The idea received even greater acceptance after the French Revolution adopted the tricolor, this time in a vertical form. The flag of Italy is also a tricolor, but with green instead of blue, and its roots may be dated back to 1796, although the present Italian flag dates from 1946.

The French and American revolutions introduced great changes in the concept of a flag. With the ensuing growth of nationalism in the nineteenth century, flags became potent political symbols, acting as a focus for nationalist movements.

The history of Germany's flags is exceptionally complex. Since the unification of German states in 1871, the German national flag has been changed four times, until the current black-red-gold design was adopted by both German republics in 1949. The German Democratic Republic added its state arms to distinguish between the two flags in 1959.

Since 1785, red and gold have been official Spanish colors, although their heraldic source dates back into the thirteenth century. Portugal's flag includes an armillary sphere, a navigational instrument symbolic of the Portuguese voyages of exploration in the fifteenth and sixteenth centuries.

The simple vertical bicolor of the Maltese flag is believed by some to date back to 1090, when the Normans took Malta from the Muslims, although this is in some doubt. In the top left corner of the flag there is the George Cross, which Britain awarded to the island for its bravery during World War II.

The spartan appearance of the flag of the USSR with its famous hammer and sickle has not followed the spread of communist government. Most European communist regimes have striped flags.

Albania

Andorra

Austria

Belgium

Bulgaria

Czechoslovakia

Denmark

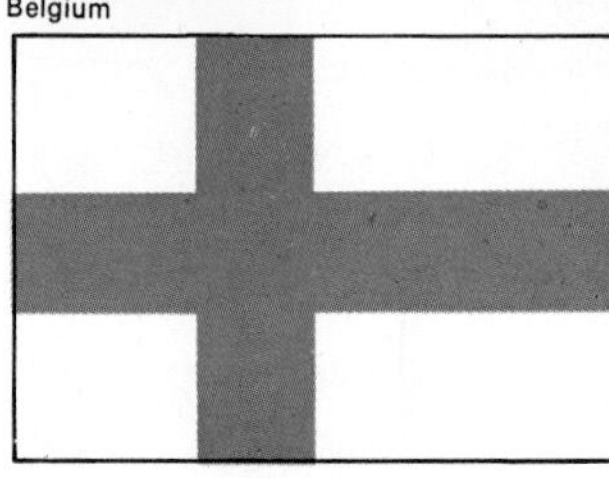

Finland

France

German Democratic Republic

Germany, Federal Republic of

Greece

Hungary

Iceland

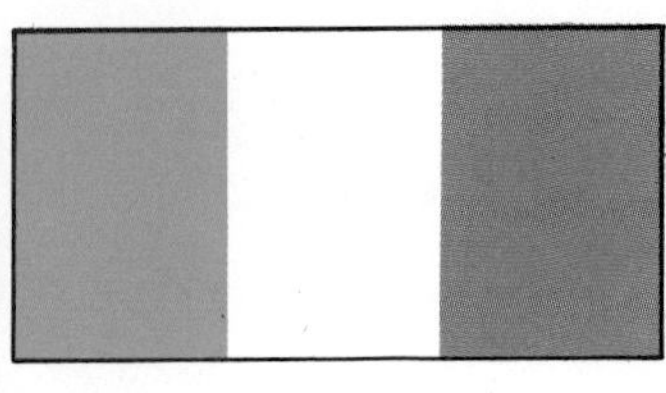
Ireland

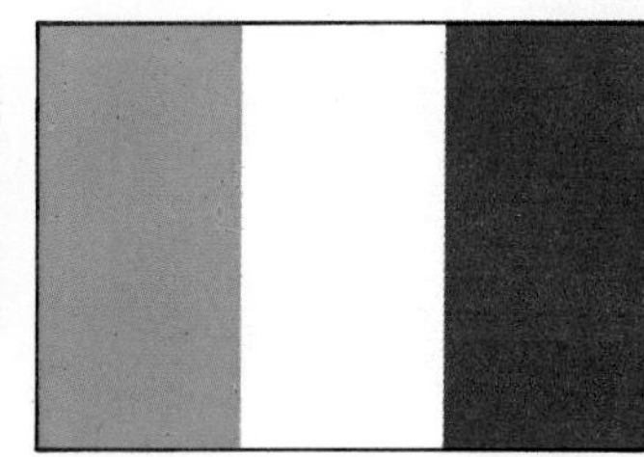
Italy

Liechtenstein

Luxembourg

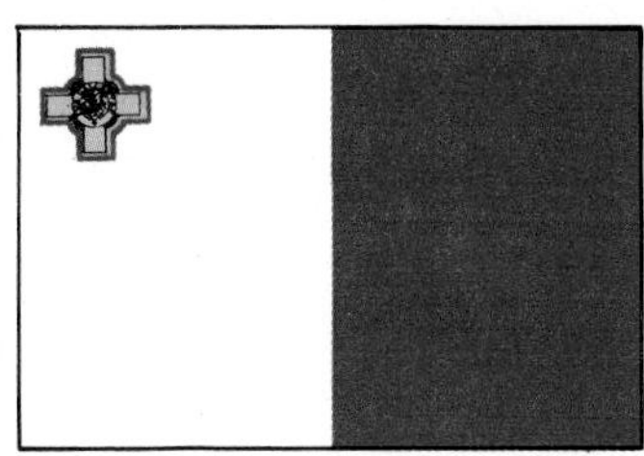
Malta

Monaco

Netherlands

Norway

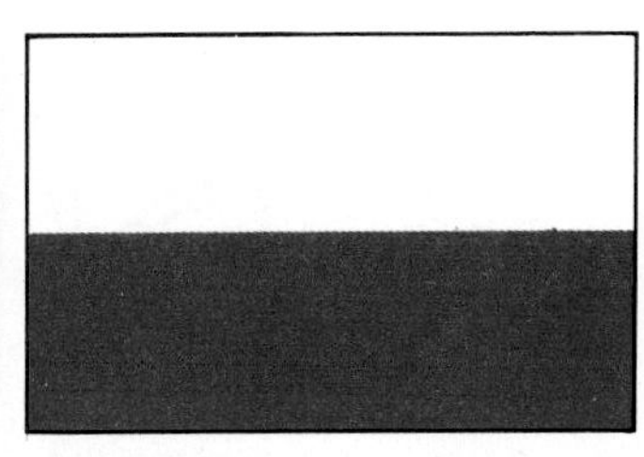
Poland

Portugal

Romania

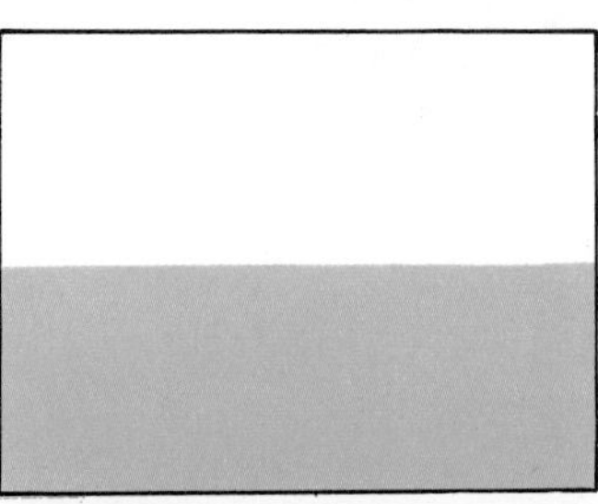
San Marino

Spain

Sweden

Switzerland

USSR

Yugoslavia

United Kingdom

Vatican

CAVRVS·CHORVS·VEL·IAPIX·SIVE·ARGESTES
CIRCIVS VEL·TRESIIAS
FAVONIVS·ZEPHIRVS
EVROPA
LIBIA INTERIOR
AFFRICA
ETHIOPIA·INTERIOR
AFRICVS·VEL·LIBS
LIBONOTVS·EVROAVSTER

ATLAS

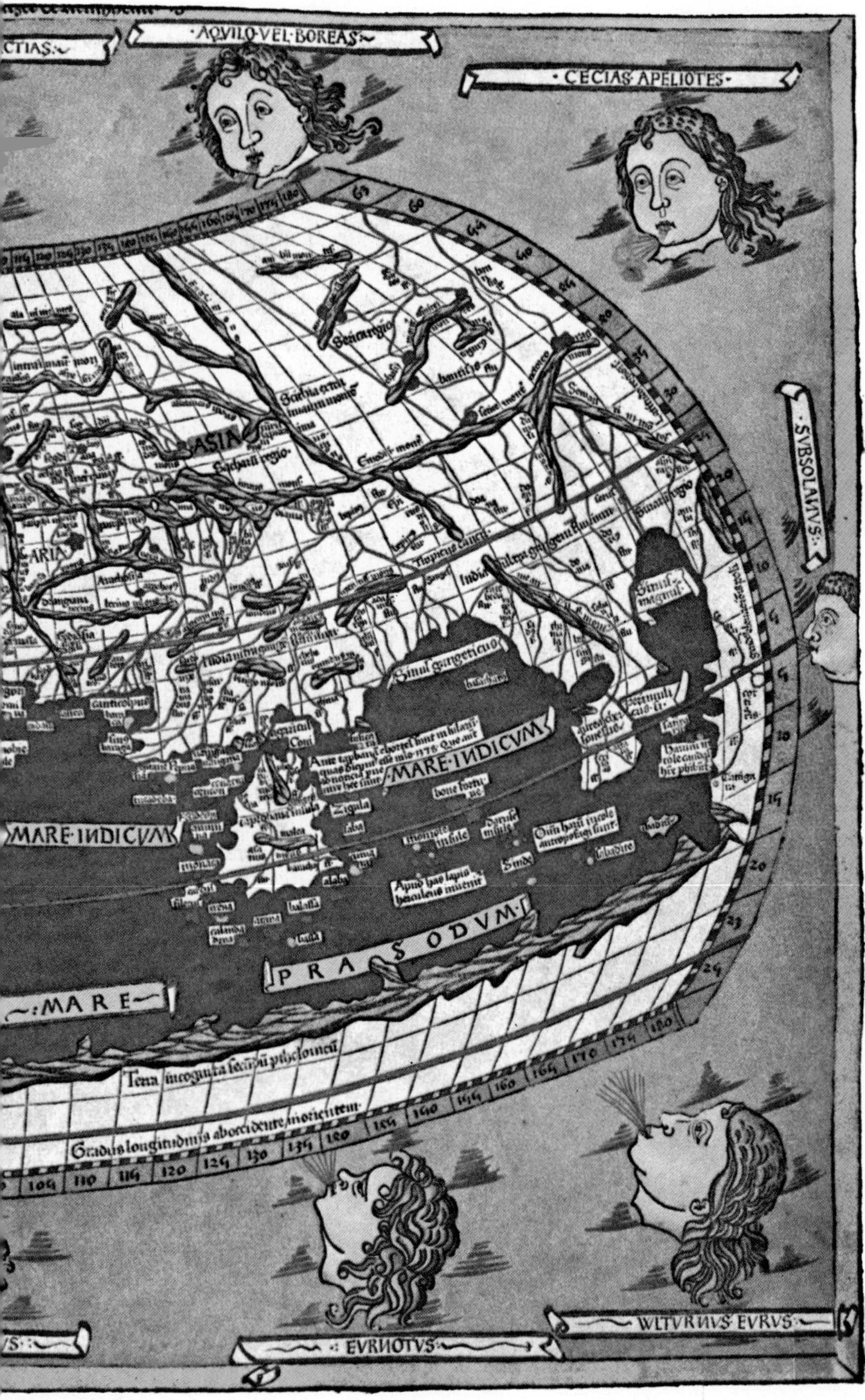

AQVILO·VEL·BOREAS
CECIAS·APELIOTES
SVBSOLANVS
ASIA
MARE·INDICVM
MARE·INDICVM
PRASODVM
MARE
Terra incognita secundum ptholomeum
Gradus longitudinis ab occidente in orientem
EVRNOTVS
VLTVRNVS·EVRVS

MAP SYMBOLS

Inhabited Localities

The symbol represents the number of inhabitants within the locality

At scales 1:4 000 000 to 1:9 000 000

- 0—10,000
- 10,000—25,000
- 25,000—100,000
- 100,000—250,000
- 250,000—1,000,000
- >1,000,000

At 1:16 000 000 scale

- 0—50,000
- 50,000—100,000
- 100,000—250,000
- 250,000—1,000,000
- >1,000,000

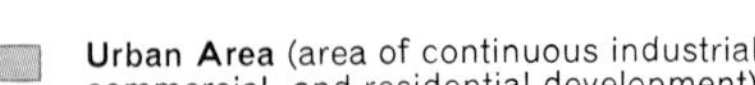
Urban Area (area of continuous industrial, commercial, and residential development)

The size of type indicates the relative economic and political importance of the locality

Écommoy	Lisieux	Rouen
Trouville	Orléans	PARIS
Jabrin °	Oasis	

Capitals of Political Units

BUDAPEST	Independent Nation
Cayenne	Dependency (Colony, protectorate, etc.)
Lasa	State, Province, etc.

Alternate Names

MOSKVA 'MOSCOW	English or second official language names are shown in reduced size lettering
Basel Bâle	
Volgograd (Stalingrad)	Historical or other alternates in the local language are shown in parentheses

Political Boundaries

International (First-order political unit)

- Demarcated and Undemarcated
- Disputed de jure
- Indefinite or Undefined
- Demarcation Line (used in Korea and Vietnam)

Internal

	State, Province, etc. (Second-order political unit)
MURCIA	Historical Region (No boundaries indicated)
PANTELLERIA (Italy)	Administering Country

Transportation

- Primary Road
- Secondary Road
- Minor Road, Trail
- Railway
- Canal du Midi — Navigable Canal
- Bridge
- Tunnel
- Ferry

Miscellaneous Cultural Features

KRUGER NATIONAL PARK
National Park or Monument

HOOVER DAM — Dam

Hydrographic Features

- Shoreline
- Undefined Shoreline
- Amur — River, Stream
- Intermittent Stream
- Rapids, Falls
- Irrigation or Drainage Canal
- Reef
- The Everglades — Swamp
- VATNAJÖKULL — Glacier
- L. Victoria — Lake, Reservoir

Tuz Gölü

- Salt Lake
- Intermittent Lake, Reservoir
- Dry Lake Bed
- (395) — Lake Surface Elevation

Topographic Features

Mt. Kenya △ 5199	Elevation Above Sea Level
76 ▽	Elevation Below Sea Level
Mount Cook ▲ 3764	Highest Elevation in Country
Khyber Pass 1067	Mountain Pass
133 ▼	Lowest Elevation in Country

Elevations are given in metres

The Highest and Lowest Elevation in a continent are underlined

- Sand Area
- Lava
- Salt Flat

A N D E S BODELE	Mountain Range, Plateau, Valley, etc.
KAMČATKA CABO DE HORNOS	Peninsula, Cape, Point, etc.
BAFFIN ISLAND ÎLE D'OUESSANT	Island

ATLAS: CONTENTS

World Political

ARCTIC OCEAN
GREENLAND (Den.)
Beaufort Sea
Baffin Bay
VICTORIA ISLAND
BAFFIN ISLAND
U.S.S.R.
UNITED STATES
Yellowknife
Godthåb
Reykjavik
Hudson Bay
Bering Sea
Gulf of Alaska
CANADA
ALEUTIAN ISLANDS
Winnipeg
IRELAND
NEWFOUNDLAND
Seattle
Montréal
Toronto
NORTH AMERICA
DETROIT
CHICAGO
NEW YORK
Washington
APPALACHIAN MOUNTAINS
ATLANTIC OCEAN
PORTUGAL
PACIFIC
SAN FRANCISCO
UNITED STATES
Denver
St. Louis
LOS ANGELES
Phoenix
Mississippi
Atlanta
AÇORES AZORES (Port.)
ARQUIPÉLAGO DA MADEIRA (Port.)
Casablanca
MOROCCO
BERMUDA (U.K.)
MIDWAY ISLANDS (U.S.)
OCEAN
Houston
New Orleans
ISLAS CANARIAS CANARY ISLANDS (Sp.)
Gulf of Mexico
Miami
BAHAMAS
Monterrey
Tropic of Cancer
WESTERN SAHARA
HAWAIIAN ISLANDS (U.S.)
Honolulu
MEXICO
La Habana
Guadalajara
CUBA
CIUDAD DE MÉXICO
BELIZE (U.K.)
Caribbean Sea
HAITI
DOMINICAN REPUBLIC
JAMAICA
PUERTO RICO (U.S.)
MAURITANIA
GUADELOUPE (Fr.)
GUATEMALA
HONDURAS
CAPE VERDE
SENEGAL
MARTINIQUE (Fr.)
EL SALVADOR
NICARAGUA
GAMBIA
TRINIDAD AND TOBAGO
GUINEA-BISSAU
CLIPPERTON (Fr. Poly.)
Caracas
Panamá
COSTA RICA
GUINEA
PANAMA
VENEZUELA
SIERRA LEONE
GUYANA
Bogotá
SURINAM
FRENCH GUIANA
LIBERIA
COLOMBIA
Equator
Quito
CANTON AND ENDERBURY (U.K.—U.S.)
ARCHIPIÉLAGO DE COLÓN GALAPAGOS ISLANDS (Ec.)
ECUADOR
Belém
Manaus
Amazon
Fortaleza
BRAZIL
PERU
TOKELAU ISLANDS (N.Z.)
ÎLES MARQUISES
Recife
WALLIS AND FUTUNA (Fr.)
W. SAMOA
AM. SAMOA
Lima
SOUTH AMERICA
Salvador
ATLANTIC OCEAN
FIJI
POLYNESIA
La Paz
BOLIVIA
Brasília
NIUE (N.Z.)
COOK ISLANDS (N.Z.)
FRENCH POLYNESIA
TONGA
Tropic of Capricorn
PARAGUAY
SÃO PAULO
RIO DE JANEIRO
PITCAIRN (U.K.)
Antofagasta
ISLA DE PASCUA EASTER ISLAND (Chile)
Asunción
CHILE
Pôrto Alegre
International Date Line
Córdoba
URUGUAY
Santiago
BUENOS AIRES
Montevideo
Co. Aconcagua 6959
ARGENTINA
PACIFIC
OCEAN
CHATHAM ISLAND (N.Z.)
FALKLAND ISLANDS (U.K.)
Punta Arenas
CABO DE HORNOS CAPE HORN
SOUTH GEORGIA (Falk. Is.)
SOUTH ORKNEY ISLANDS (B.A.T.)
Antarctic Circle
Bellingshausen Sea
Weddell Sea
Ross Sea
Vinson Massif 5140
ANTAR

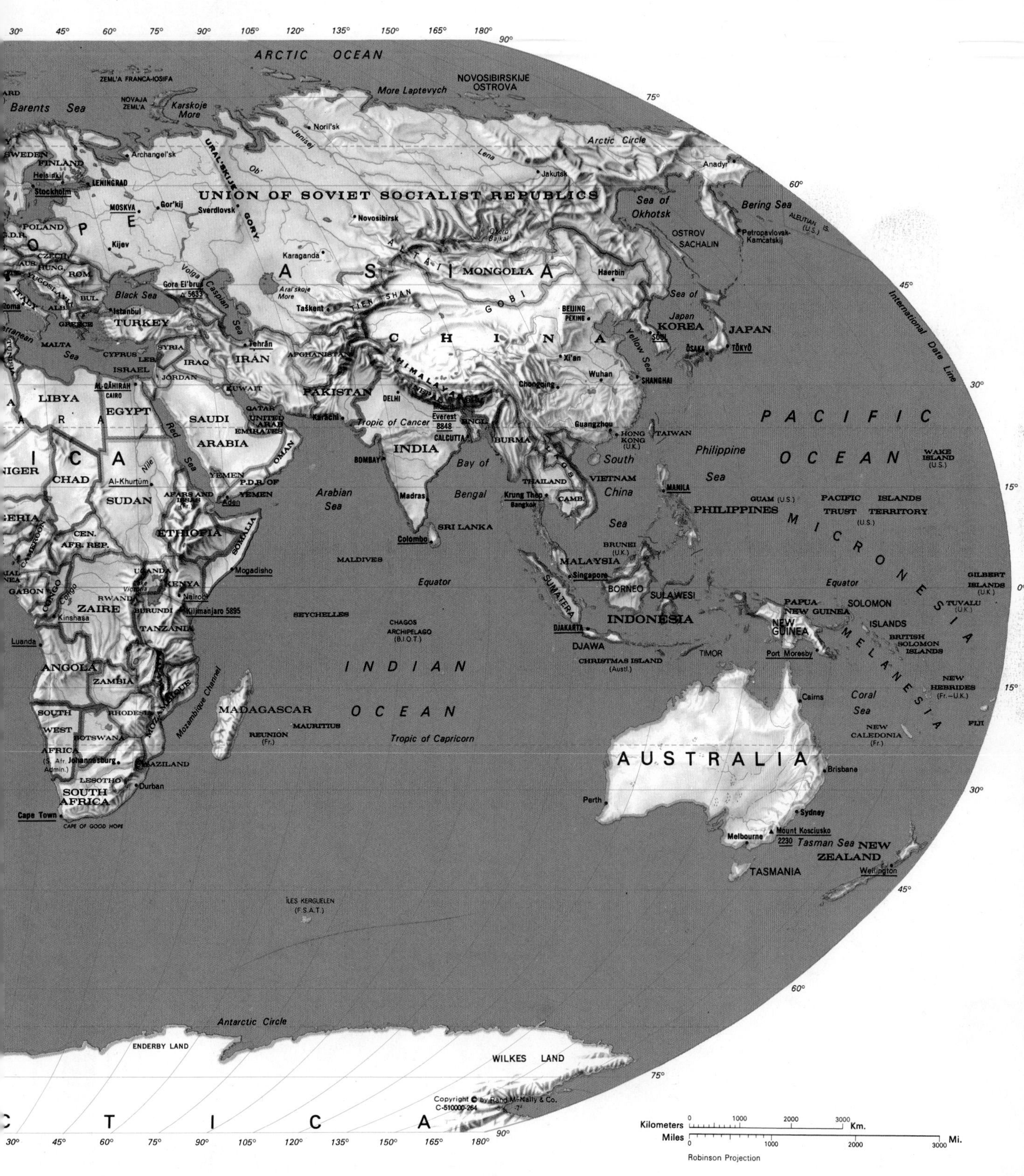
ARCTIC OCEAN
NOVOSIBIRSKIJE OSTROVA
More Laptevych
Barents Sea
Karskoje More
UNION OF SOVIET SOCIALIST REPUBLICS
Sea of Okhotsk
Bering Sea
MONGOLIA
CHINA
KOREA
JAPAN
Sea of Japan
Yellow Sea
TURKEY
IRAN
IRAQ
AFGHANISTAN
PAKISTAN
INDIA
Black Sea
Caspian Sea
LIBYA
EGYPT
SAUDI ARABIA
SUDAN
CHAD
ETHIOPIA
ZAIRE
ANGOLA
ZAMBIA
MADAGASCAR
SOUTH AFRICA
Arabian Sea
Bay of Bengal
South China Sea
Philippine Sea
PHILIPPINES
PACIFIC OCEAN
INDIAN OCEAN
INDONESIA
AUSTRALIA
NEW ZEALAND
TASMANIA
Tasman Sea
Coral Sea
MICRONESIA
MELANESIA
Tropic of Cancer
Tropic of Capricorn
Equator
Arctic Circle
Antarctic Circle
International Date Line
ENDERBY LAND
WILKES LAND
Copyright © by Rand McNally & Co.
C-510000-264
Kilometers 0 1000 2000 3000 Km.
Miles 0 1000 2000 3000 Mi.
Robinson Projection

Arctic Region

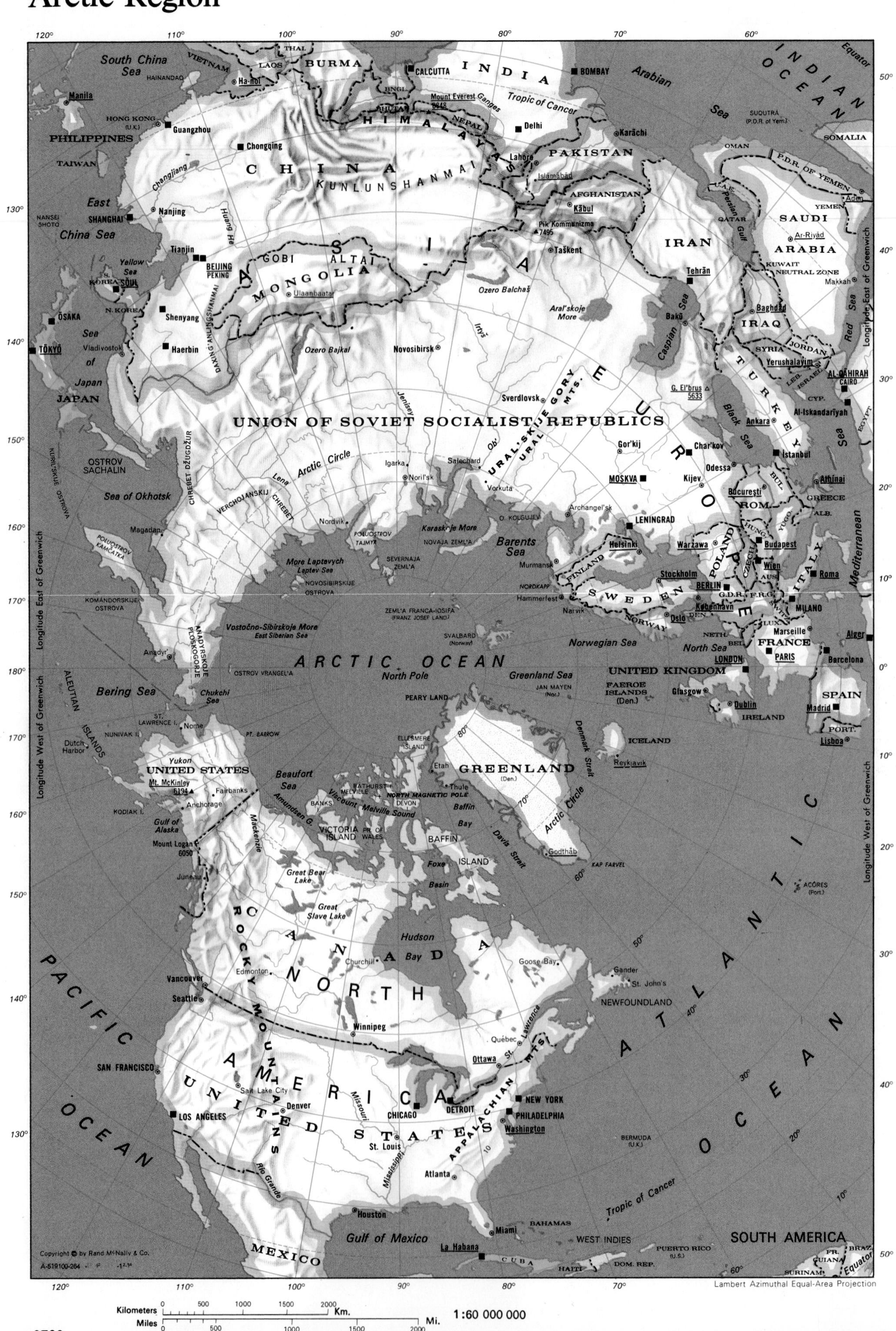
ARCTIC OCEAN
North Pole
UNION OF SOVIET SOCIALIST REPUBLICS
CHINA
INDIA
MONGOLIA
ASIA
EUROPE
NORTH AMERICA
CANADA
UNITED STATES
GREENLAND
ATLANTIC OCEAN
PACIFIC OCEAN
INDIAN OCEAN
Arctic Circle
Tropic of Cancer
Lambert Azimuthal Equal-Area Projection
1:60 000 000
Kilometers 0 500 1000 1500 2000 Km.
Miles 0 500 1000 1500 2000 Mi.

Antarctic Region

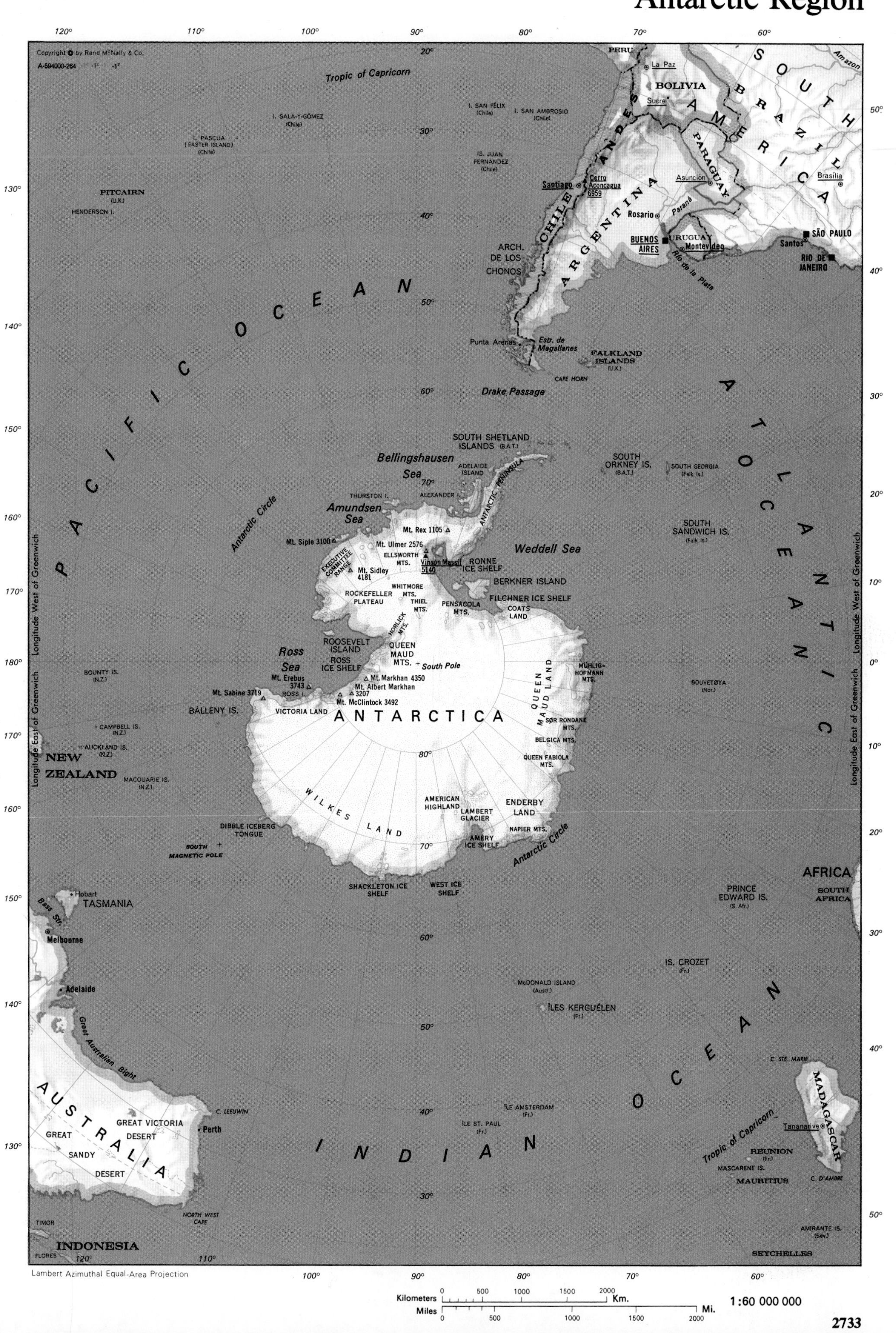

Copyright © by Rand McNally & Co.
A-594000-264
Tropic of Capricorn
PACIFIC OCEAN
ATLANTIC OCEAN
INDIAN OCEAN
SOUTH AMERICA
BOLIVIA
La Paz
Sucre
BRAZIL
PARAGUAY
Asunción
Brasília
ARGENTINA
ANDES
CHILE
Santiago
Cerro Aconcagua 6959
Rosario
Paraná
BUENOS AIRES
URUGUAY
Montevideo
Río de la Plata
SÃO PAULO
Santos
RIO DE JANEIRO
PERU
Amazon
I. SAN FÉLIX (Chile)
I. SAN AMBROSIO (Chile)
I. SALA-Y-GÓMEZ (Chile)
I. PASCUA (EASTER ISLAND) (Chile)
IS. JUAN FERNANDEZ (Chile)
PITCAIRN (U.K.)
HENDERSON I.
ARCH. DE LOS CHONOS
Punta Arenas
Estr. de Magallanes
FALKLAND ISLANDS (U.K.)
CAPE HORN
Drake Passage
SOUTH SHETLAND ISLANDS (B.A.T.)
SOUTH ORKNEY IS. (B.A.T.)
SOUTH GEORGIA (Falk. Is.)
SOUTH SANDWICH IS. (Falk. Is.)
Bellingshausen Sea
ADELAIDE ISLAND
ANTARCTIC PENINSULA
THURSTON I.
ALEXANDER I.
Amundsen Sea
Antarctic Circle
Mt. Rex 1105
Mt. Siple 3100
Mt. Ulmer 2576
ELLSWORTH MTS.
Vinson Massif 5140
EXECUTIVE COMMITTEE RANGE
Mt. Sidley 4181
RONNE ICE SHELF
Weddell Sea
BERKNER ISLAND
FILCHNER ICE SHELF
WHITMORE MTS.
ROCKEFELLER PLATEAU
THIEL MTS.
PENSACOLA MTS.
COATS LAND
HORLICK MTS.
ROOSEVELT ISLAND
Ross Sea
ROSS ICE SHELF
QUEEN MAUD MTS.
South Pole
Mt. Erebus 3743
ROSS I.
Mt. Markhan 4350
Mt. Albert Markhan
3207
Mt. McClintock 3492
Mt. Sabine 3719
BALLENY IS.
VICTORIA LAND
ANTARCTICA
QUEEN MAUD LAND
MÜHLIG-HOFMANN MTS.
SØR RONDANE MTS.
BELGICA MTS.
QUEEN FABIOLA MTS.
BOUVETØYA (Nor.)
BOUNTY IS. (N.Z.)
CAMPBELL IS. (N.Z.)
AUCKLAND IS. (N.Z.)
NEW ZEALAND
MACQUARIE IS. (N.Z.)
WILKES LAND
AMERICAN HIGHLAND
LAMBERT GLACIER
ENDERBY LAND
NAPIER MTS.
AMERY ICE SHELF
DIBBLE ICEBERG TONGUE
SOUTH MAGNETIC POLE
SHACKLETON ICE SHELF
WEST ICE SHELF
AFRICA
SOUTH AFRICA
PRINCE EDWARD IS. (S. Afr.)
Hobart
TASMANIA
Bass Str.
Melbourne
Adelaide
IS. CROZET (Fr.)
McDONALD ISLAND (Austl.)
ÎLES KERGUÉLEN (Fr.)
Great Australian Bight
AUSTRALIA
GREAT VICTORIA DESERT
GREAT SANDY DESERT
C. LEEUWIN
Perth
ÎLE AMSTERDAM (Fr.)
ÎLE ST. PAUL (Fr.)
C. STE. MARIE
MADAGASCAR
Tananarive
REUNION (Fr.)
MASCARENE IS.
MAURITIUS
C. D'AMBRE
NORTH WEST CAPE
TIMOR
INDONESIA
FLORES
AMIRANTE IS. (Sey.)
SEYCHELLES
Longitude West of Greenwich
Longitude East of Greenwich
Lambert Azimuthal Equal-Area Projection
Kilometers 0 500 1000 1500 2000 Km.
Miles 0 500 1000 1500 2000 Mi.
1:60 000 000

Canada

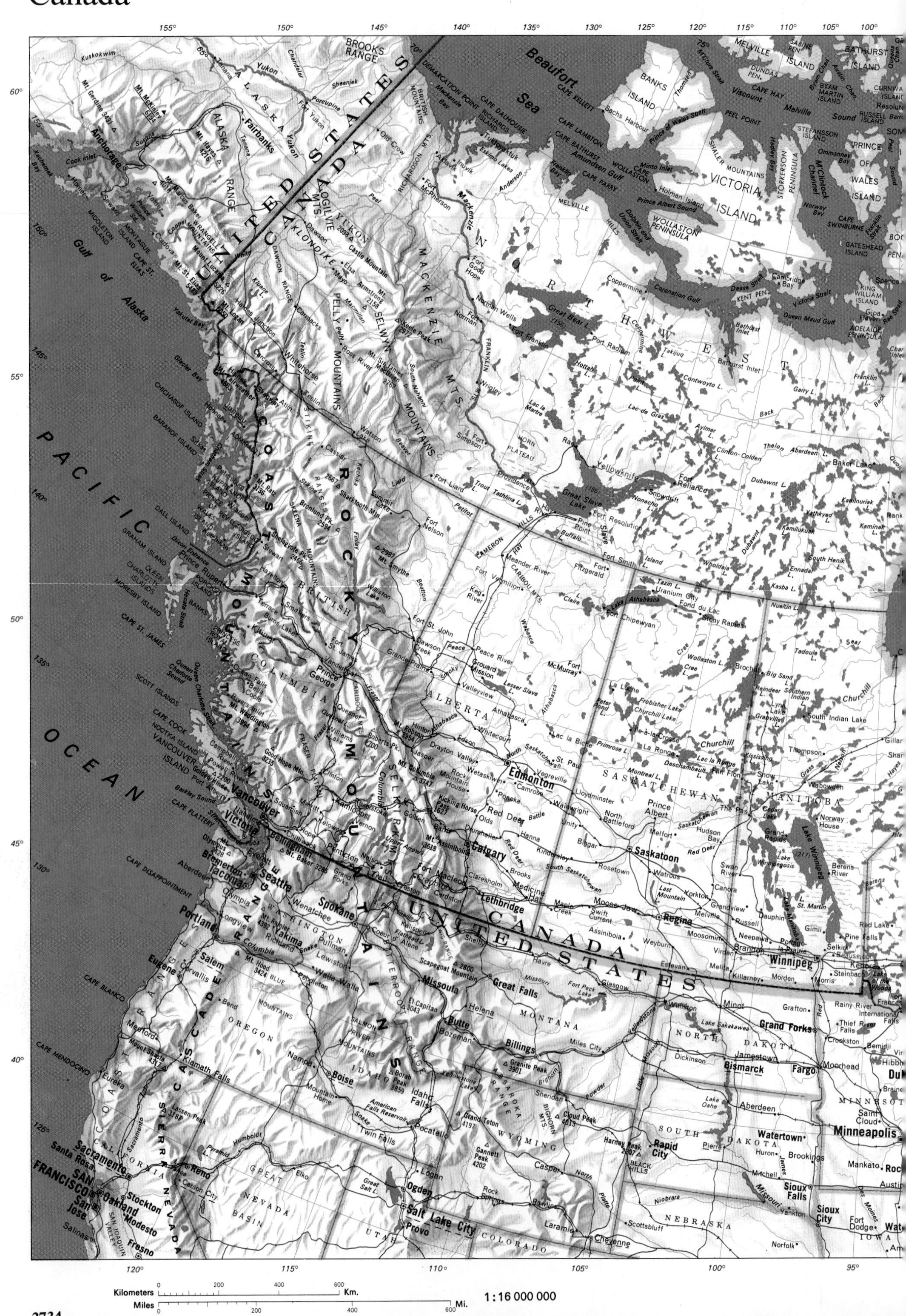

GREENLAND
(Denmark)
Baffin
Bay
Davis
Strait
Labrador
Sea
ATLANTIC
OCEAN
ATLANTIC
OCEAN
Hudson
Bay
James
Bay
Foxe
Basin
Ungava
Bay
BAFFIN
ISLAND
SOUTHAMPTON
ISLAND
PÉNINSULE
D'UNGAVA
LABRADOR
QUÉBEC
NEWFOUNDLAND
ONTARIO
MICHIGAN
NEW
BRUNSWICK
NOVA
SCOTIA
PRINCE EDWARD
ISLAND
CAPE BRETON ISLAND
ST. PIERRE
AND MIQUELON
(Fr.)
APPALACHIAN MTS.
MONTS NOTRE DAME
Gulf of St. Lawrence
All islands within Hudson Bay, James Bay,
and Ungava Bay lie within Northwest Territories
Arctic Circle
St. John's
Halifax
Sydney
Moncton
Charlottetown
Saint John
Fredericton
Québec
MONTREAL
Ottawa
Hull
TORONTO
Hamilton
Kingston
Sudbury
Sault Ste. Marie
Thunder Bay
Timmins
Chicoutimi
Sherbrooke
Trois-Rivières
Sept-Îles
Corner Brook
Goose Bay
Schefferville
Labrador City
Godthåb
Bangor
Portland
BOSTON
Providence
Hartford
New Haven
NEW YORK
PHILADELPHIA
Albany
Syracuse
Rochester
Buffalo
Utica
Binghamton
Erie
Cleveland
Toledo
DETROIT
Flint
Lansing
Grand Rapids
Milwaukee
CHICAGO
South Bend
Green Bay
Copyright © by Rand McNally & Co.

Lambert Conformal Conic Projection

United States

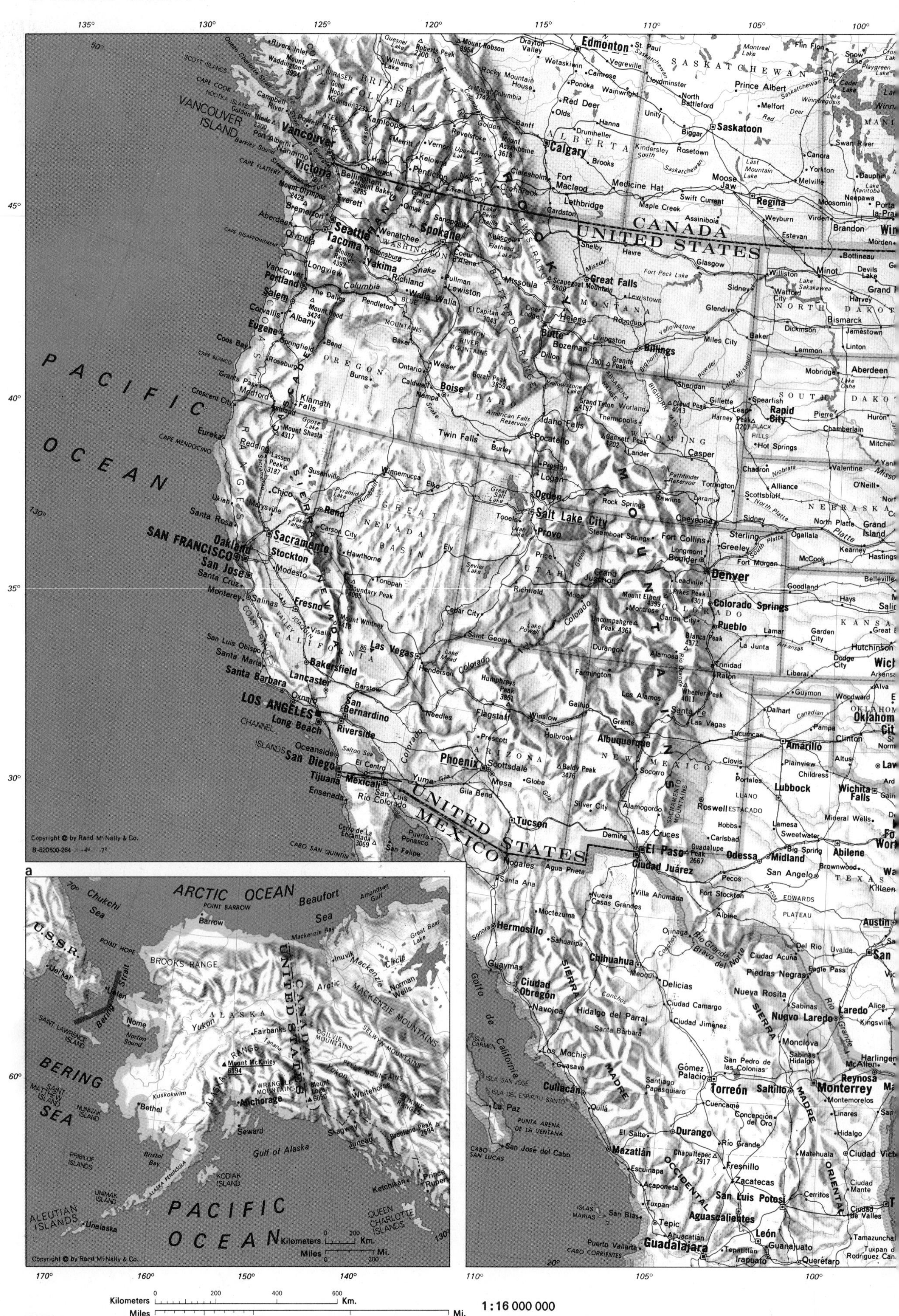

135°
130°
125°
120°
115°
110°
105°
100°
45°
40°
35°
30°
PACIFIC OCEAN
CANADA
UNITED STATES
MEXICO
SASKATCHEWAN
ALBERTA
BRITISH COLUMBIA
WASHINGTON
OREGON
IDAHO
MONTANA
WYOMING
NEVADA
UTAH
COLORADO
ARIZONA
NEW MEXICO
CALIFORNIA
NORTH DAKOTA
SOUTH DAKOTA
NEBRASKA
KANSAS
OKLAHOMA
TEXAS
ROCKY MOUNTAINS
GREAT BASIN
SIERRA NEVADA
CASCADE RANGE
COAST RANGES
SIERRA MADRE OCCIDENTAL
SIERRA MADRE ORIENTAL
Golfo de California
VANCOUVER ISLAND
Edmonton
Calgary
Saskatoon
Regina
Vancouver
Victoria
Seattle
Tacoma
Spokane
Portland
Salem
Eugene
Boise
Great Falls
Helena
Butte
Billings
Salt Lake City
Ogden
Provo
Reno
Sacramento
SAN FRANCISCO
Oakland
San Jose
Stockton
Fresno
Bakersfield
LOS ANGELES
Long Beach
San Bernardino
Riverside
San Diego
Tijuana
Mexicali
Las Vegas
Phoenix
Tucson
Albuquerque
Santa Fe
El Paso
Ciudad Juárez
Denver
Colorado Springs
Pueblo
Cheyenne
Casper
Rapid City
Amarillo
Lubbock
Odessa
Midland
Abilene
San Angelo
Hermosillo
Chihuahua
Torreón
Saltillo
Monterrey
Nuevo Laredo
Laredo
Durango
Mazatlán
Culiacán
Zacatecas
San Luis Potosí
Aguascalientes
Guadalajara
León
Copyright © by Rand McNally & Co.
a
ARCTIC OCEAN
Beaufort Sea
Chukchi Sea
BERING SEA
U.S.S.R.
ALASKA
BROOKS RANGE
ALASKA RANGE
MACKENZIE MOUNTAINS
Mount McKinley 6194
Barrow
Nome
Fairbanks
Anchorage
Juneau
Whitehorse
Gulf of Alaska
ALEUTIAN ISLANDS
PACIFIC OCEAN
170°
160°
150°
140°
Kilometers 0 200 400 600 Km.
Miles 0 200 400 600 Mi.
1:16 000 000

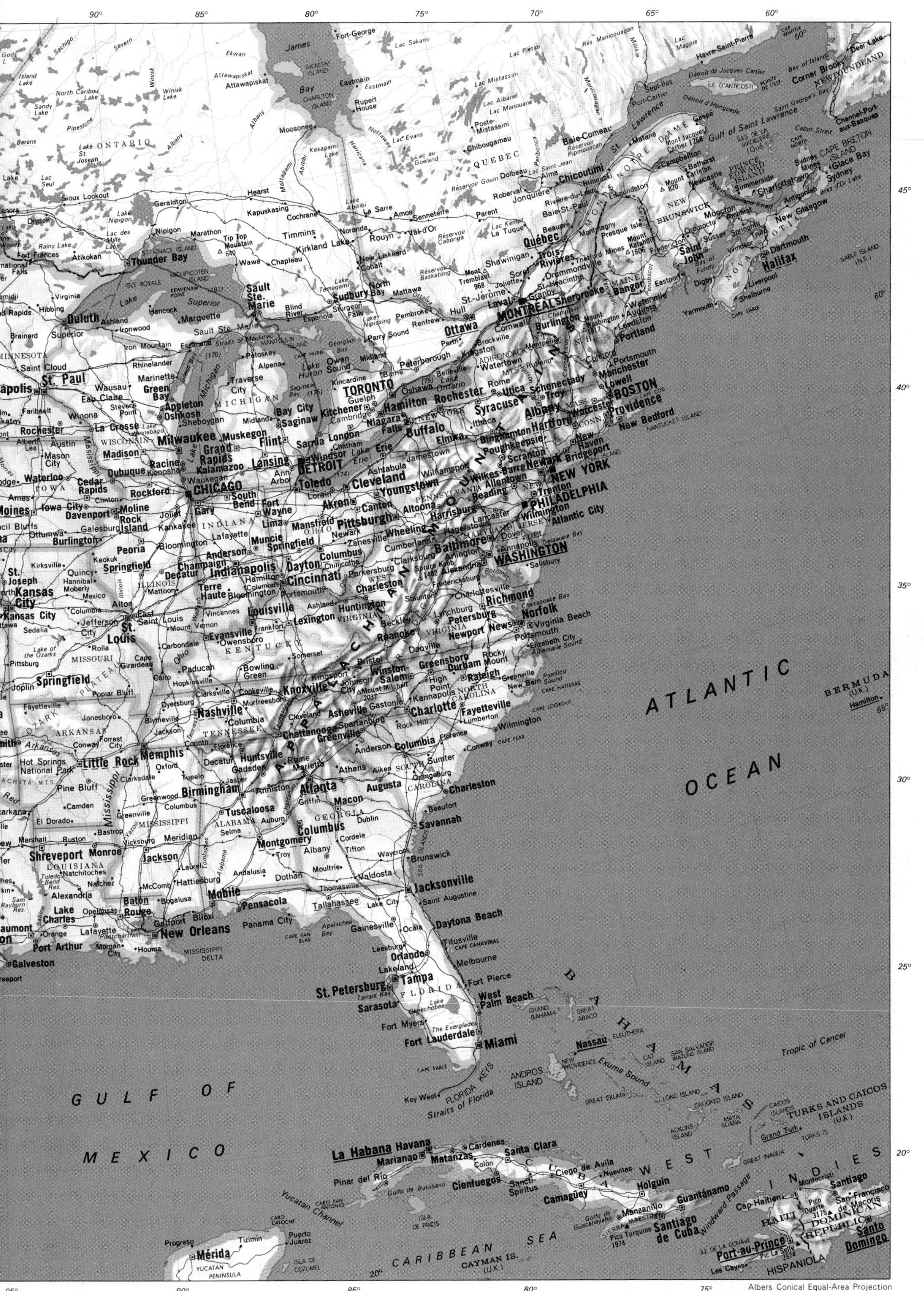

ATLANTIC
OCEAN
GULF OF
MEXICO
CARIBBEAN SEA
WEST INDIES
BAHAMAS
APPALACHIAN MOUNTAINS
Tropic of Cancer
Straits of Florida
Yucatan Channel
Windward Passage
Gulf of Saint Lawrence
St. Lawrence
James Bay
ONTARIO
QUEBEC
NEW BRUNSWICK
NOVA SCOTIA
PRINCE EDWARD ISLAND
NEWFOUNDLAND
MAINE
MINNESOTA
WISCONSIN
MICHIGAN
IOWA
ILLINOIS
INDIANA
OHIO
PENNSYLVANIA
NEW YORK
MISSOURI
KENTUCKY
WEST VIRGINIA
VIRGINIA
TENNESSEE
NORTH CAROLINA
SOUTH CAROLINA
ARKANSAS
MISSISSIPPI
ALABAMA
GEORGIA
LOUISIANA
FLORIDA
CUBA
HAITI
DOMINICAN REPUBLIC
HISPANIOLA
YUCATAN PENINSULA
BERMUDA (U.K.)
Hamilton
CAYMAN IS. (U.K.)
TURKS AND CAICOS ISLANDS (U.K.)
Grand Turk
Lake Superior
Lake Michigan
Lake Huron
Lake Erie
Lake Ontario
Lake Okeechobee
The Everglades
MISSISSIPPI DELTA
Thunder Bay
Duluth
Sault Ste. Marie
Sudbury
North Bay
Ottawa
MONTREAL
Québec
Trois Rivières
Sherbrooke
Chicoutimi
Baie-Comeau
Halifax
Saint John
Charlottetown
Sydney
Corner Brook
TORONTO
Hamilton
Rochester
Buffalo
Syracuse
Albany
BOSTON
Providence
Hartford
NEW YORK
PHILADELPHIA
Baltimore
WASHINGTON
Richmond
Norfolk
Pittsburgh
Cleveland
Toledo
DETROIT
Lansing
Flint
Grand Rapids
Milwaukee
CHICAGO
Madison
St. Paul
Rockford
Peoria
Springfield
Indianapolis
Columbus
Dayton
Cincinnati
Louisville
Lexington
St. Louis
Kansas City
Springfield
Memphis
Nashville
Knoxville
Chattanooga
Little Rock
Charlotte
Greensboro
Raleigh
Columbia
Charleston
Savannah
Atlanta
Birmingham
Montgomery
Jackson
Shreveport
Baton Rouge
New Orleans
Mobile
Pensacola
Tallahassee
Jacksonville
Orlando
Tampa
St. Petersburg
Miami
Fort Lauderdale
West Palm Beach
Key West
Nassau
La Habana Havana
Matanzas
Santa Clara
Cienfuegos
Camagüey
Holguín
Santiago de Cuba
Guantánamo
Port-au-Prince
Santo Domingo
Santiago
Mérida
Progreso
CAPE HATTERAS
CAPE COD
CAPE SABLE
CAPE CANAVERAL
ANDROS ISLAND
GRAND BAHAMA
ISLA DE PINOS

Albers Conical Equal-Area Projection

Alaska

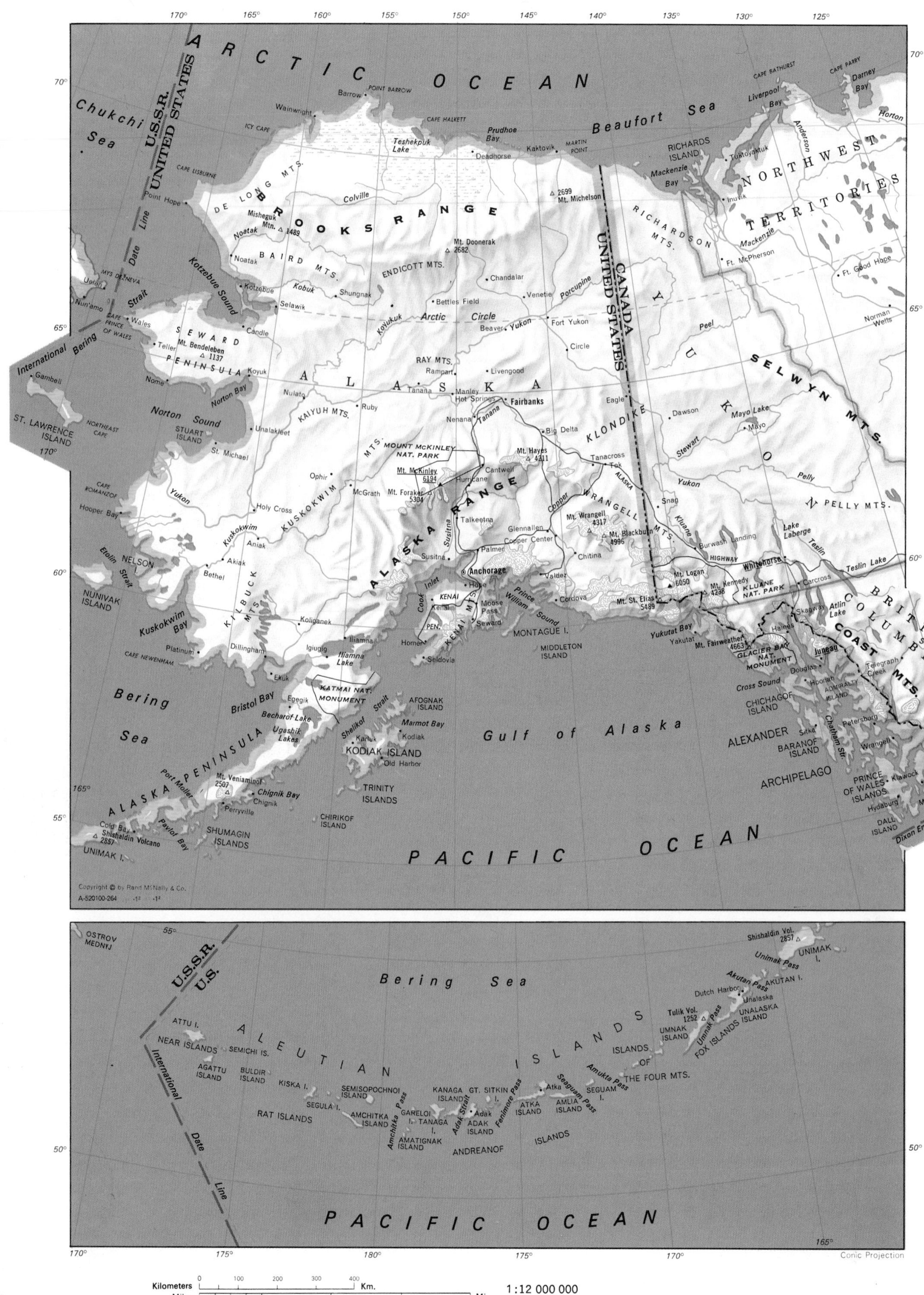

ARCTIC OCEAN
Chukchi Sea
Beaufort Sea
U.S.S.R.
UNITED STATES
International Date Line
Bering Strait
Barrow
POINT BARROW
Wainwright
CAPE HALKETT
ICY CAPE
Prudhoe Bay
Teshekpuk Lake
Deadhorse
Kaktovik
MARTIN POINT
CAPE LISBURNE
Point Hope
DE LONG MTS.
BROOKS RANGE
Colville
Misheguk Mtn. 1489
Noatak
BAIRD MTS.
Mt. Doonerak 2682
ENDICOTT MTS.
2699 Mt. Michelson
Chandalar
Venetie
Porcupine
Kotzebue Sound
Kotzebue
Kobuk
Shungnak
Selawik
Bettles Field
Koyukuk
Arctic Circle
Beaver
Yukon
Fort Yukon
Circle
Wales
CAPE PRINCE OF WALES
Candle
Teller
SEWARD PENINSULA
Mt. Bendeleben 1137
Koyuk
Nome
Norton Bay
Norton Sound
Gambell
ST. LAWRENCE ISLAND
NORTHEAST CAPE
STUART ISLAND
St. Michael
Unalakleet
Nulato
Ruby
KAIYUH MTS.
RAY MTS.
Rampart
Livengood
ALASKA
Tanana
Manley Hot Springs
Fairbanks
Nenana
Eagle
Big Delta
KLONDIKE
MOUNT McKINLEY NAT. PARK
Mt. Hayes 4211
Tanacross
Tok
Mt. McKinley 6194
Cantwell
Mt. Foraker 5304
Hurricane
ALASKA RANGE
McGrath
Ophir
KUSKOKWIM MTS.
Holy Cross
Yukon
Hooper Bay
CAPE ROMANZOF
Kuskokwim
Aniak
Akiak
Bethel
NELSON I.
Etolin Strait
NUNIVAK ISLAND
KILBUCK MTS.
Kuskokwim Bay
Platinum
CAPE NEWENHAM
Dillingham
Koliganek
Talkeetna
Susitna
Glennallen
Copper Center
Copper
WRANGELL MTS.
Mt. Wrangell 4317
Mt. Blackburn 4996
Chitina
Palmer
Anchorage
Valdez
Cordova
Cook Inlet
KENAI PEN.
Kenai
Hope
Moose Pass
Seward
Homer
Seldovia
Prince William Sound
MONTAGUE I.
MIDDLETON ISLAND
Mt. St. Elias 5489
Mt. Logan 6050
Mt. Kennedy 4238
KLUANE NAT. PARK
Yukutat Bay
Yakutat
Mt. Fairweather 4663
GLACIER BAY NAT. MONUMENT
Iliamna
Iliamna Lake
Igiugig
Ekuk
Bristol Bay
Egegik
KATMAI NAT. MONUMENT
Becharof Lake
Ugashik Lakes
Shelikof Strait
AFOGNAK ISLAND
Marmot Bay
Kodiak
Karluk
KODIAK ISLAND
Old Harbor
TRINITY ISLANDS
CHIRIKOF ISLAND
Bering Sea
Gulf of Alaska
ALASKA PENINSULA
Port Moller
Mt. Veniaminof 2507
Chignik Bay
Chignik
Perryville
Cold Bay
Shishaldin Volcano 2857
Pavlof Bay
SHUMAGIN ISLANDS
UNIMAK I.
PACIFIC OCEAN
CANADA
UNITED STATES
RICHARDSON MTS.
RICHARDS ISLAND
Mackenzie Bay
Tuktoyaktuk
Inuvik
Ft. McPherson
Mackenzie
NORTHWEST TERRITORIES
Liverpool Bay
CAPE BATHURST
CAPE PARRY
Darnley Bay
Horton
Anderson
Ft. Good Hope
Norman Wells
Peel
YUKON
SELWYN MTS.
Dawson
Mayo Lake
Mayo
Stewart
Pelly
PELLY MTS.
Snag
Kluane
Burwash Landing
ALASKA HIGHWAY
Whitehorse
Lake Laberge
Teslin
Teslin Lake
Carcross
Skagway
Atlin Lake
Haines
Juneau
BRITISH COLUMBIA
COAST MTS.
Telegraph Creek
Douglas
Hoonah
ADMIRALTY ISLAND
Cross Sound
CHICHAGOF ISLAND
Sitka
BARANOF ISLAND
Chatham Str.
Petersburg
Wrangell
ALEXANDER ARCHIPELAGO
PRINCE OF WALES ISLANDS
Klawock
Hydaburg
DALL ISLAND
Dixon Entrance
Copyright © by Rand McNally & Co.
A-520100-264
OSTROV MEDNYJ
U.S.S.R.
U.S.
Bering Sea
ATTU I.
NEAR ISLANDS
SEMICHI IS.
AGATTU ISLAND
BULDIR ISLAND
KISKA I.
SEGULA I.
RAT ISLANDS
ALEUTIAN ISLANDS
SEMISOPOCHNOI ISLAND
AMCHITKA ISLAND
Amchitka Pass
GARELOI I.
TANAGA I.
AMATIGNAK ISLAND
KANAGA ISLAND
GT. SITKIN I.
Adak Strait
Adak
ADAK ISLAND
ANDREANOF ISLANDS
Fenimore Pass
ATKA ISLAND
Atka
AMLIA ISLAND
Seaguam Pass
SEGUAM I.
Amukta Pass
ISLANDS OF THE FOUR MTS.
UMNAK ISLAND
Tulik Vol. 1252
Umnak Pass
FOX ISLANDS
UNALASKA ISLAND
Unalaska
Dutch Harbor
Akutan Pass
AKUTAN I.
Unimak Pass
UNIMAK I.
Shishaldin Vol. 2857
PACIFIC OCEAN
Conic Projection
Kilometers 0 100 200 300 400 Km.
Miles 0 50 100 200 300 400 Mi.
1:12 000 000

Maine and the Gaspé Region

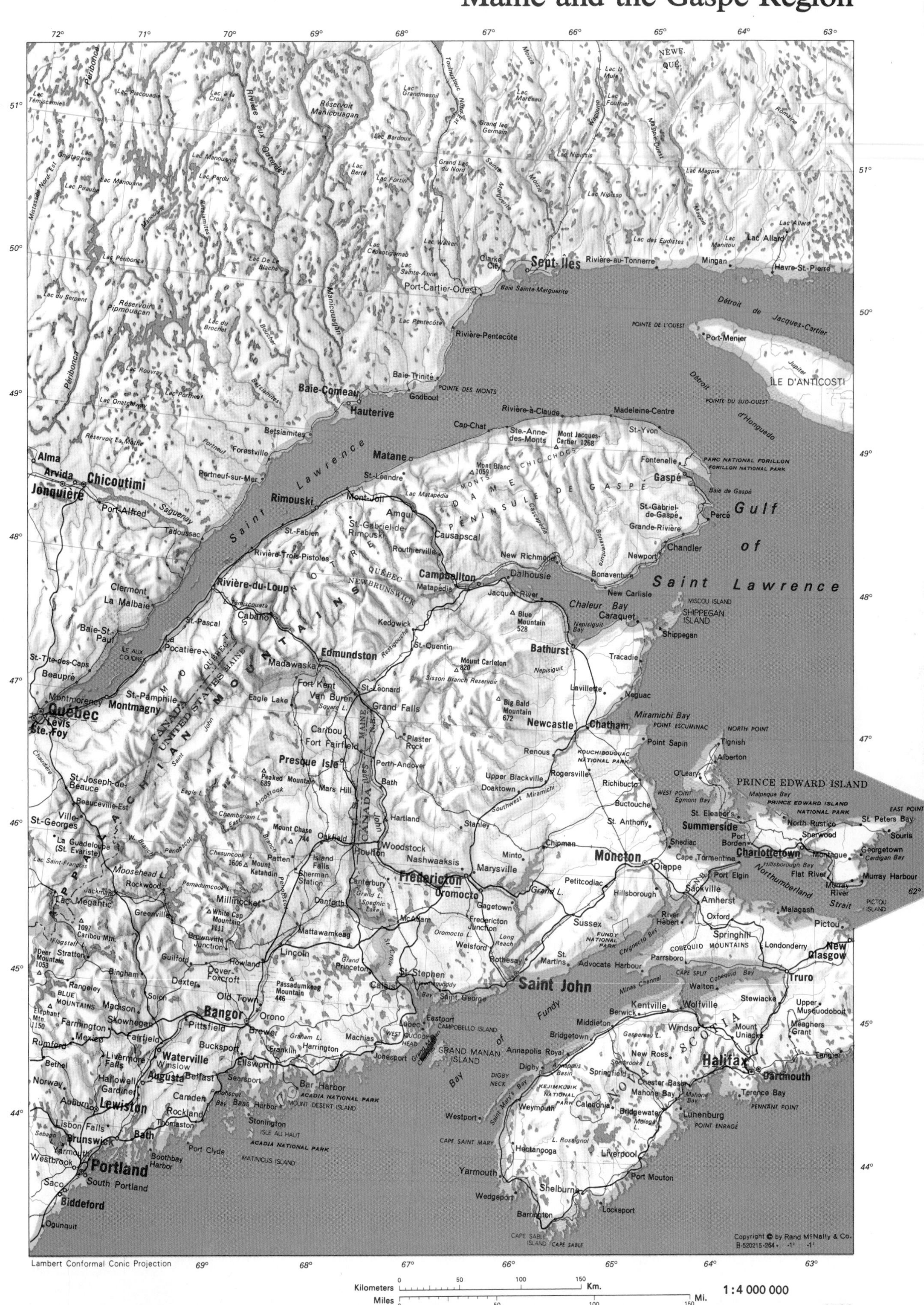
Gulf of Saint Lawrence
Saint Lawrence
Sept-Îles
Baie-Comeau
Hauterive
Matane
Rimouski
Chicoutimi
Jonquière
Québec
Gaspé
Campbellton
Edmundston
Bathurst
Newcastle
Chatham
Moncton
Fredericton
Saint John
Bay of Fundy
Halifax
Dartmouth
Charlottetown
PRINCE EDWARD ISLAND
ÎLE D'ANTICOSTI
Bangor
Portland
Lewiston
Augusta
Waterville
Presque Isle
NOTRE DAME MOUNTAINS
APPALACHIAN MOUNTAINS
PÉNINSULE DE GASPÉ
NOVA SCOTIA
Copyright © by Rand McNally & Co.
B-520215-264

Lambert Conformal Conic Projection

Kilometers 0 50 100 150 Km.

Miles 0 50 100 150 Mi.

1:4 000 000

Northeastern United States

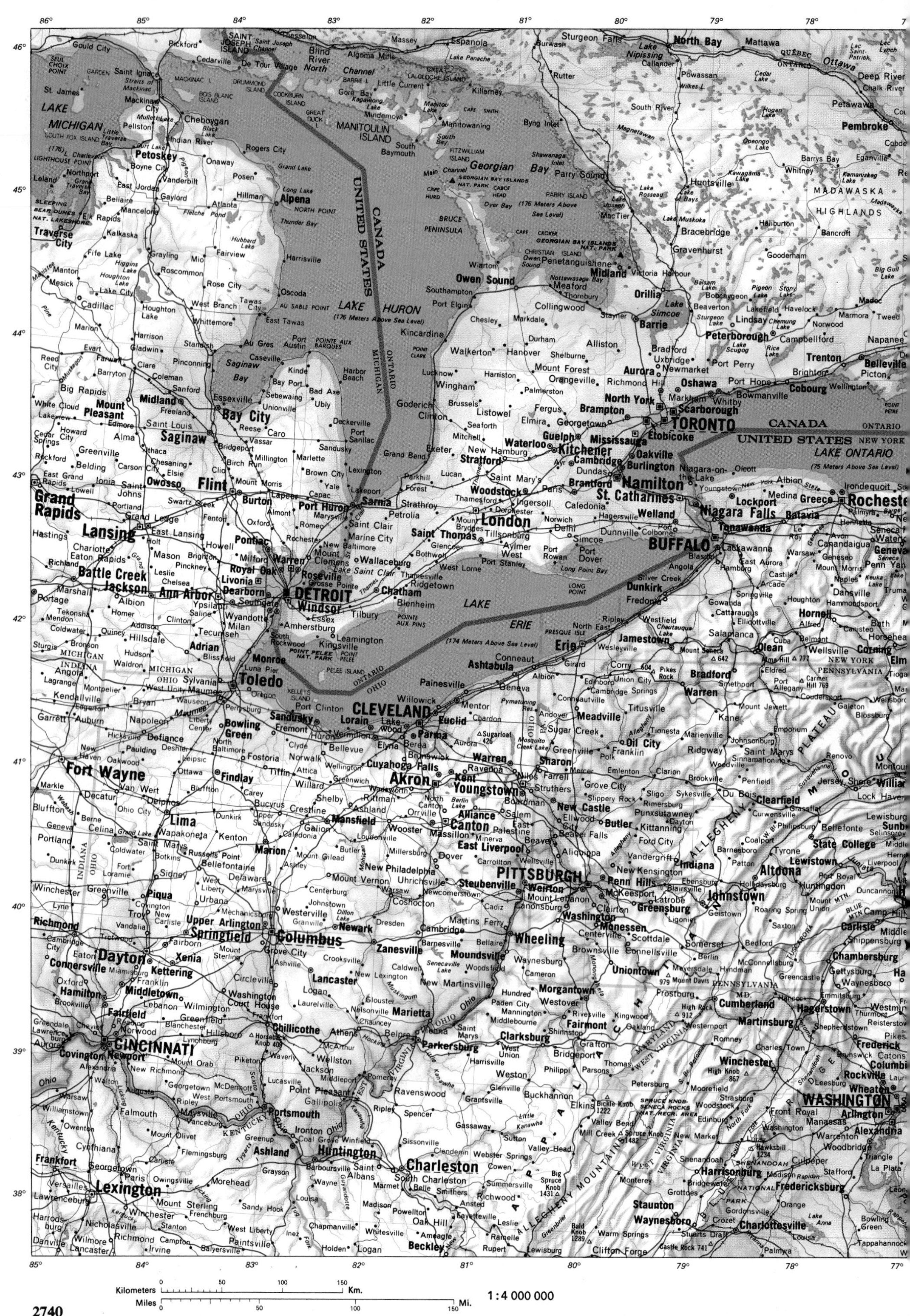

86°
85°
84°
83°
82°
81°
80°
79°
78°
46°
45°
44°
43°
42°
41°
40°
39°
38°
LAKE MICHIGAN
LAKE HURON
(176 Meters Above Sea Level)
Georgian Bay
(176 Meters Above Sea Level)
Saginaw Bay
LAKE ERIE
(174 Meters Above Sea Level)
LAKE ONTARIO
(75 Meters Above Sea Level)
North Channel
MANITOULIN ISLAND
BRUCE PENINSULA
Lake Nipissing
Lake Simcoe
CANADA
UNITED STATES
MICHIGAN
ONTARIO
OHIO
INDIANA
KENTUCKY
PENNSYLVANIA
NEW YORK
WEST VIRGINIA
MARYLAND
VIRGINIA
QUÉBEC
MADAWASKA HIGHLANDS
ALLEGHENY PLATEAU
ALLEGHENY MOUNTAINS
APPALACHIAN MOUNTAINS
BLUE RIDGE
Sault Ste. Marie
Mackinaw City
Cheboygan
Petoskey
Alpena
Traverse City
Cadillac
Bay City
Midland
Saginaw
Flint
Grand Rapids
Lansing
Battle Creek
Jackson
Ann Arbor
Pontiac
Warren
Detroit
Dearborn
Livonia
Royal Oak
Windsor
Sarnia
Port Huron
London
Kitchener
Waterloo
Guelph
Hamilton
Burlington
Oakville
Mississauga
Brampton
North York
Scarborough
Toronto
Etobicoke
Oshawa
Barrie
Orillia
Owen Sound
Peterborough
Pembroke
North Bay
Sudbury
St. Catharines
Niagara Falls
Buffalo
Rochester
Lockport
Erie
Jamestown
Toledo
Sandusky
Lorain
Cleveland
Euclid
Parma
Akron
Canton
Youngstown
Warren
Mansfield
Findlay
Lima
Fort Wayne
Marion
Columbus
Newark
Springfield
Dayton
Kettering
Middletown
Hamilton
Cincinnati
Covington
Newport
Zanesville
Wheeling
Steubenville
Pittsburgh
Johnstown
Altoona
State College
Clarksburg
Morgantown
Parkersburg
Marietta
Huntington
Ashland
Charleston
Lexington
Frankfort
Portsmouth
Chillicothe
Athens
Beckley
Staunton
Harrisonburg
Charlottesville
Winchester
Hagerstown
Frederick
Cumberland
Washington
Alexandria
Arlington
Fredericksburg
Chambersburg

Kilometers 0 50 100 150 Km.
Miles 0 50 100 150 Mi.
1:4 000 000

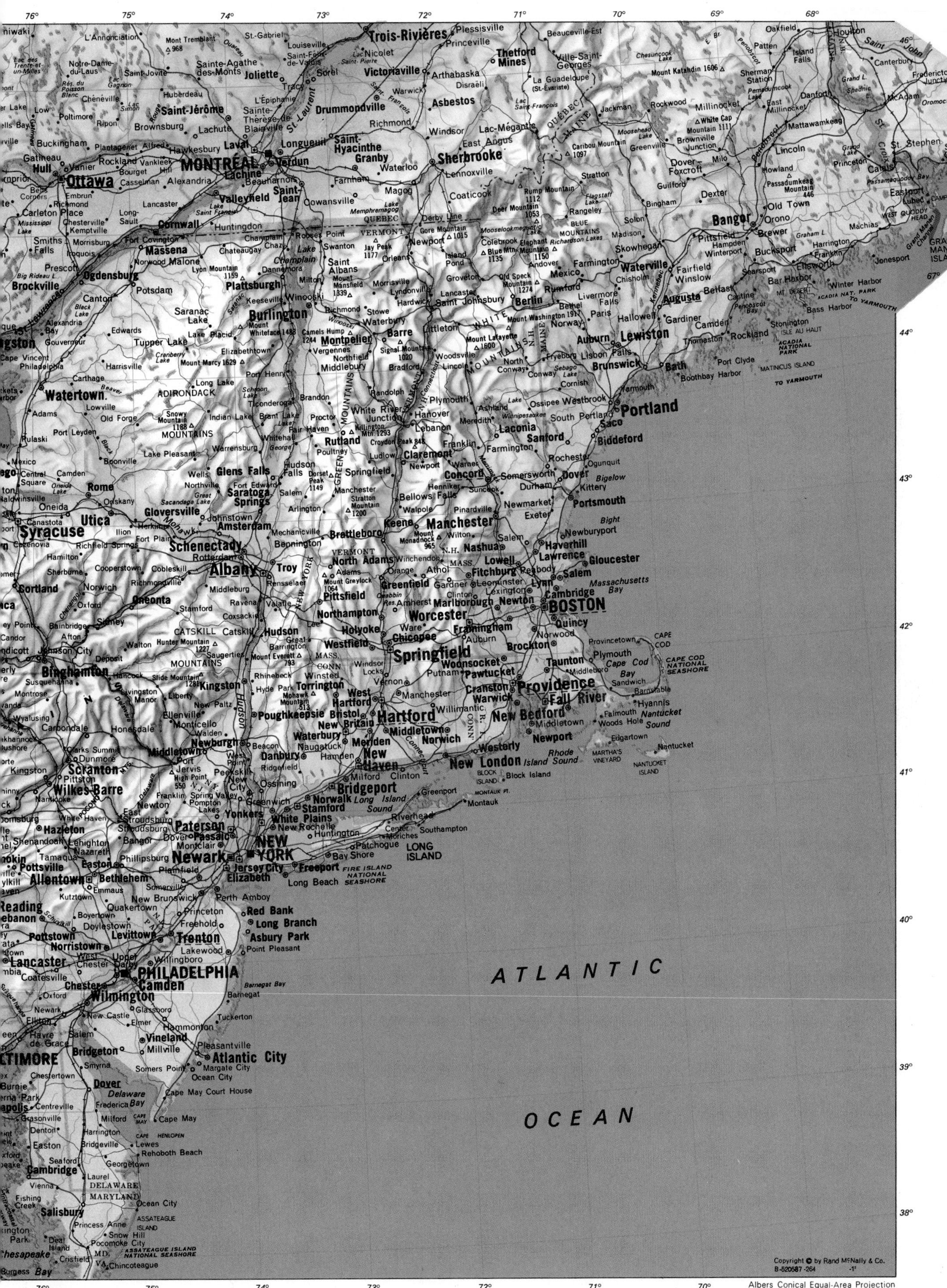

76°
75°
74°
73°
72°
71°
70°
69°
68°
Trois-Rivières
Plessisville
Beauceville-Est
Oakfield
Houlton
Patten
Island Falls
Saint John
Canterbury
Fredericton Junction
McAdam
Oromocto L.
L'Annonciation
Mont Tremblant 968
St-Gabriel
Louiseville
Nicolet
Princeville
Thetford Mines
Ville-Saint-Georges
Chesuncook Lake
Mount Katahdin 1606
Sherman Station
Notre-Dame-du-Laus
Sainte-Agathe-des-Monts
Joliette
Sorel
Victoriaville
Arthabaska
Disraëli
La Guadeloupe (St-Évariste)
Hubberdeau
Chénéville
L'Épiphanie
Drummondville
Warwick
Asbestos
Saint-Jérôme
Sainte-Thérèse-de-Blainville
St. Laurent
Richmond
Jackman
Rockwood
Millinocket
East Millinocket
Danforth
Poltimore
Ripon
Brownsburg
Lachute
Windsor
Lac-Mégantic
QUÉBEC
MAINE
White Cap Mountain 1111
Mattawamkeag
Buckingham
Plantagenet
Alfred
Hawkesbury
Laval
Longueuil
Saint-Hyacinthe
Granby
Sherbrooke
East Angus
Moosehead Lake
Brownville Junction
Gatineau
Hull
Vanier
Rockland
Vankleek Hill
MONTREAL
Verdun
Lachine
Waterloo
Lennoxville
Caribou Mountain 1097
Greenville
Lincoln
St. Stephen
Saint George
Ottawa
Bourget
Casselman
Alexandria
Beauharnois
Saint-Jean
Farnham
Magog
Stratton
Dover-Foxcroft
Milo
Princeton
Calais
Howland
Passadumkeag Mountain 446
Eastport
Lubec
CAMPOBELLO ISLAND
45°
Embrun
Lancaster
Valleyfield
Cowansville
Coaticook
Rump Mountain 1112
Flagstaff Lake
Guilford
Dexter
Old Town
Carleton Place
Richmond
Long-Sault
Lake St. Francis
Memphremagog
QUEBEC
Derby Line
Deer Mountain 1053
Rangeley
Bingham
Orono
Bangor
Chesterville
Kemptville
Cornwall
Huntingdon
VERMONT
Gore Mountain 1015
Mooselookmeguntic Lake
BLUE MOUNTAINS
Solon
Machias
WEST QUODDY HEAD
Smiths Falls
Morrisburg
Fort Covington
Champlain
Rouses Point
Swanton
Newport
Colebrook
Elephant Mountain 1150
Richardson Lakes
Madison
Pittsfield
Hampden
Brewer
Harrington
GRAND MANAN ISLAND
Iroquois
Massena
Chateaugay
Chazy
Lake Champlain
Jay Peak 1177
Orleans
Blue Mtn. 1135
Skowhegan
Winterport
Bucksport
Franklin
Jonesport
Prescott
Norwood
Malone
Saint Albans
Island Pond
Andover
Farmington
Waterville
Fairfield
Ellsworth
Ogdensburg
Lyon Mountain 1159
Dannemora
Mount Mansfield 1339
Morrisville
Groveton
Old Speck Mountain 1274
Mexico
Chisholm
Winslow
Searsport
Bar Harbor
Winter Harbor
67°
Brockville
Potsdam
Plattsburgh
Milton
Winooski
Lyndonville
Lancaster
Rumford
Livermore Falls
Augusta
Belfast
MT. DESERT
ACADIA NAT. PARK
Canton
Keeseville
Hardwick
Saint Johnsbury
Berlin
Castine
Bass Harbor
TO YARMOUTH
Burlington
Richmond
Stowe
Waterbury
Bethel
Paris
Hallowell
Gardiner
Saranac Lake
Mount Whiteface 1483
Camels Hump 1244
Montpelier
Barre
Littleton
WHITE
Mount Washington 1917
Norway
Lewiston
Camden
Stonington
ISLE AU HAUT
Edwards
Lake Placid
Signal Mountain 1020
Mount Lafayette 1600
Auburn
Rockland
Thomaston
ACADIA NATIONAL PARK
44°
Gouverneur
Tupper Lake
Elizabethtown
Vergennes
Northfield
Woodsville
MOUNTAINS
Fryeburg
Lisbon Falls
Brunswick
Cape Vincent
Philadelphia
Harrisville
Mount Marcy 1629
Middlebury
Bradford
Lincoln
North Conway
Bath
Port Clyde
MATINICUS ISLAND
Carthage
Port Henry
Conway
Sebago Lake
Boothbay Harbor
Watertown
ADIRONDACK
Long Lake
Schroon Lake
Brandon
Randolph
Plymouth
Cornish
Yarmouth
Ticonderoga
White River Junction
Hanover
Ashland
Ossipee
Westbrook
Portland
Adams
Lowville
Old Forge
Snowy Mountain 1188
Indian Lake
Brant Lake
Proctor
Lebanon
Meredith
Winnipesaukee
South Portland
Saco
Port Leyden
MOUNTAINS
Whitehall
Fair Haven
Killington Mtn. 1293
Laconia
Sanford
Biddeford
Pulaski
Warrensburg
Lake George
Rutland
Croydon Peak 845
Franklin
Farmington
Lake Pleasant
Poultney
Claremont
Rochester
Ogunquit
Boonville
Wells
Glens Falls
Hudson Falls
Springfield
Newport
Warner
Concord
Somersworth
Dover
Bigelow
Kittery
Central Square
Camden
Rome
Northville
Fort Edward
Dorset Peak 1149
Manchester
Henniker
Suncook
Durham
Portsmouth
43°
Oneida
Oriskany
Saratoga Springs
Sacandaga Lake
Salem
Stratton Mountain 1200
Bellows Falls
Pinardville
Newmarket
Exeter
Gloversville
Johnstown
Arlington
Walpole
Bight
Canastota
Utica
Amsterdam
Mohawk
Keene
Manchester
Syracuse
Ilion
Herkimer
Fort Plain
Mechanicville
Brattleboro
Mount Monadnock 965
Wilton
Salem
Newburyport
Cazenovia
Richfield Springs
Schenectady
Bennington
Nashua
Haverhill
Hamilton
Rotterdam
VERMONT
Winchendon
N.H.
MASS.
Lowell
Lawrence
Gloucester
Sherburne
Cooperstown
Cobleskill
Albany
Troy
North Adams
Orange
Athol
Fitchburg
Peabody
Salem
Cortland
Norwich
Richmondville
Rensselaer
Adams
Mount Greylock 1064
Greenfield
Gardner
Leominster
Lexington
Lynn
Cambridge
Massachusetts Bay
Middleburg
Oneonta
NEW YORK
Pittsfield
Quabbin Res.
Amherst
Marlborough
Clinton
Newton
BOSTON
Oxford
Stamford
Ravena
Valatie
Coxsackie
Northampton
Worcester
Quincy
Bainbridge
Sidney
CATSKILL
Catskill
Hudson
Holyoke
Ware
Framingham
Norwood
Provincetown
CAPE COD
42°
Afton
Walton
Hunter Mountain 1227
Great Barrington
Westfield
Chicopee
Auburn
Brockton
Johnson City
Deposit
Saugerties
MOUNTAINS
Mount Everett 793
MASS.
CONN.
Springfield
Woonsocket
Taunton
Plymouth
Cape Cod Bay
CAPE COD NATIONAL SEASHORE
Binghamton
Hancock
Slide Mountain 1281
Rhinebeck
Winsted
Windsor Locks
Putnam
Pawtucket
Middleboro
Susquehanna
Kingston
Hyde Park
Torrington
Vernon
Cranston
Providence
Sandwich
Montrose
Livingston Manor
Liberty
New Paltz
Mohawk Mountain 513
Bristol
West Hartford
Manchester
Warwick
Fall River
Barnstable
Hyannis
Ellenville
Poughkeepsie
New Britain
Hartford
Willimantic
New Bedford
Falmouth
Nantucket Sound
Carbondale
Honesdale
Monticello
Walden
Middletown
Woods Hole
Middletown
Newport
Waterbury
Naugatuck
Meriden
Middletown
Norwich
Edgartown
Clarks Summit
Dunmore
Newburgh
Beacon
Danbury
Hamden
New Haven
Westerly
Rhode Island Sound
MARTHA'S VINEYARD
Nantucket
NANTUCKET ISLAND
Kingston
Scranton
Port Jervis
High Point 550
Peekskill
Ridgefield
New London
BLOCK ISLAND
Block Island
41°
Pittston
Wilkes-Barre
Ossining
Milford
Clinton
Nanticoke
Franklin
Spring Valley
Pompton Lakes
New City
Bridgeport
Greenport
MONTAUK PT.
Montauk
Newton
Greenwich
Norwalk
Long Island Sound
White Haven
East Stroudsburg
Stroudsburg
Yonkers
Stamford
Riverhead
Hazleton
Paterson
White Plains
New Rochelle
Center Moriches
Southampton
Shenandoah
Lehighton
Bangor
Dover
Passaic
Huntington
Nazareth
Montclair
NEW YORK
Patchogue
LONG ISLAND
Pottsville
Easton
Phillipsburg
Newark
Jersey City
Freeport
Bay Shore
Allentown
Bethlehem
Plainfield
Elizabeth
Long Beach
FIRE ISLAND NATIONAL SEASHORE
Emmaus
Somerville
Kutztown
New Brunswick
Perth Amboy
Reading
Quakertown
Princeton
Red Bank
Lebanon
Boyertown
Doylestown
Freehold
Long Branch
40°
Pottstown
Levittown
Trenton
Asbury Park
Norristown
Lakewood
Point Pleasant
Lancaster
West Chester
Upper Darby
Willingboro
Coatesville
PHILADELPHIA
Camden
ATLANTIC
Barnegat Bay
Chester
Wilmington
Barnegat
Oxford
Newark
New Castle
Glassboro
Elkton
Elmer
Hammonton
Tuckerton
Havre de Grace
Salem
Vineland
Pleasantville
BALTIMORE
Bridgeton
Millville
Atlantic City
Smyrna
Somers Point
Margate City
Ocean City
39°
Chestertown
Dover
Delaware Bay
Cape May Court House
Centreville
Frederica
Milford
CAPE MAY
Cape May
OCEAN
Harrington
CAPE HENLOPEN
Lewes
Bridgeville
Rehoboth Beach
Easton
Seaford
Georgetown
Cambridge
Laurel
Vienna
DELAWARE
MARYLAND
Fishing Creek
Ocean City
Salisbury
ASSATEAGUE ISLAND
38°
Princess Anne
Snow Hill
Deal Island
Pocomoke City
ASSATEAGUE ISLAND NATIONAL SEASHORE
Crisfield
MD.
VA.
Chincoteague
Chesapeake Bay

76° 75° 74° 73° 72° 71° 70°

Albers Conical Equal-Area Projection

Great Lakes Region

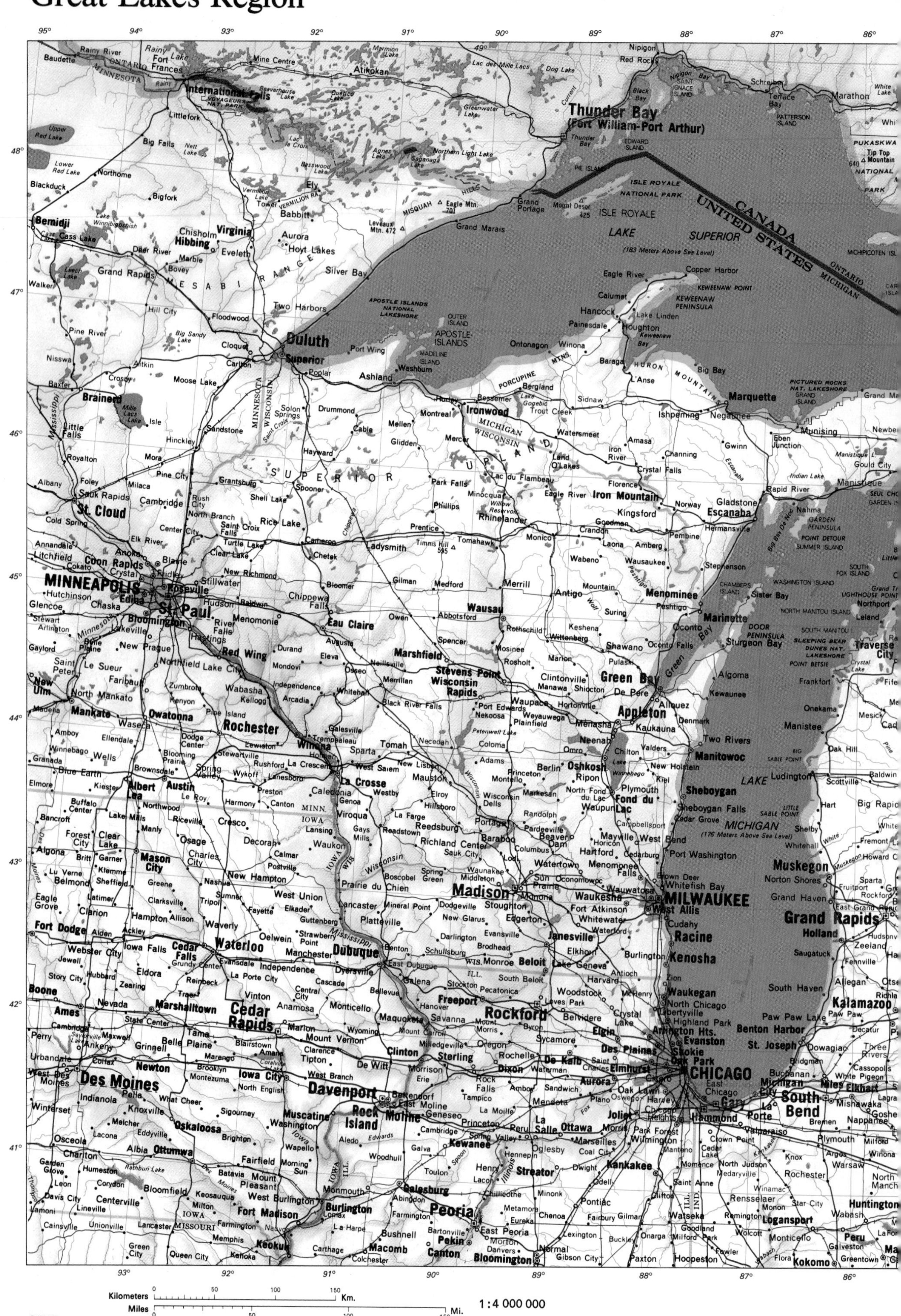

LAKE SUPERIOR
(183 Meters Above Sea Level)
LAKE MICHIGAN
(176 Meters Above Sea Level)
CANADA
UNITED STATES
ONTARIO
MINNESOTA
WISCONSIN
MICHIGAN
IOWA
ILL.
IND.
MISSOURI
MINNEAPOLIS
St. Paul
Duluth
Thunder Bay
(Fort William-Port Arthur)
MILWAUKEE
CHICAGO
Madison
Green Bay
Rochester
Des Moines
Cedar Rapids
Davenport
Peoria
Rockford
Grand Rapids
South Bend
ISLE ROYALE NATIONAL PARK
APOSTLE ISLANDS NATIONAL LAKESHORE
PICTURED ROCKS NAT. LAKESHORE
SLEEPING BEAR DUNES NAT. LAKESHORE
VOYAGEURS NAT. PARK
PUKASKWA NATIONAL PARK
MESABI RANGE
SUPERIOR UPLAND
Kilometers 0 50 100 150 Km.
Miles 0 50 100 150 Mi.
1:4 000 000

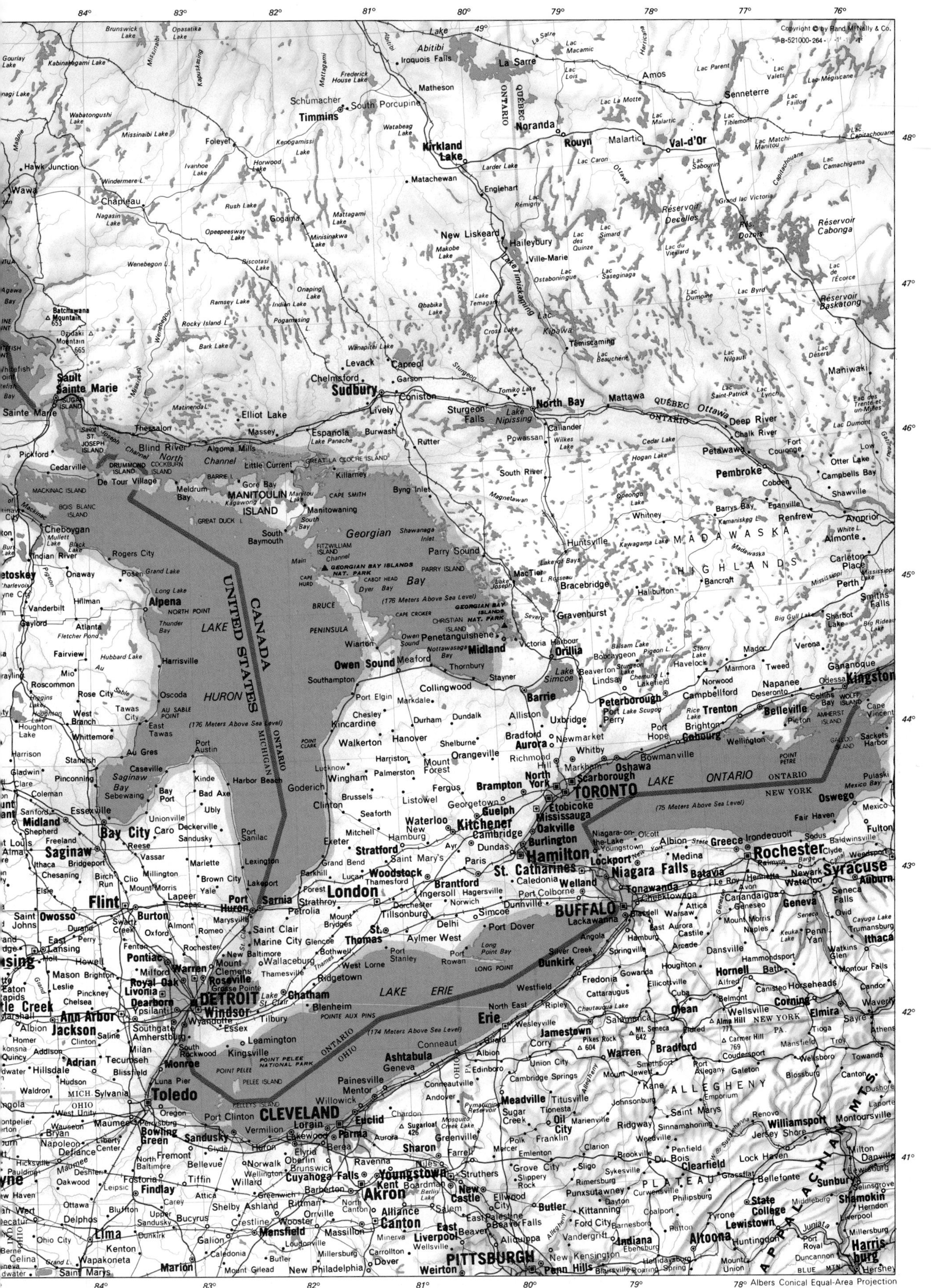
Copyright © by Rand McNally & Co.
B-521000-264-
84°
83°
82°
81°
80°
79°
78°
77°
76°
48°
47°
46°
45°
44°
43°
42°
41°
Brunswick Lake
Opasatika Lake
Lake Abitibi
49°
Iroquois Falls
La Sarre
Lac Macamic
Gourlay Lake
Kabinakagami Lake
Frederick House Lake
Matheson
ONTARIO
QUEBEC
Amos
Lac Parent
Senneterre
Schumacher
South Porcupine
Timmins
Noranda
Rouyn
Malartic
Val-d'Or
Wabatongushi Lake
Missinaibi Lake
Foleyet
Kenogamissi Lake
Kirkland Lake
Lac Caron
Hawk Junction
Horwood Lake
Ivanhoe Lake
Larder Lake
Windermere L.
Matachewan
Wawa
Englehart
Chapleau
Rush Lake
Nagasin Lake
Gogama
Mattagami Lake
Réservoir Decelles
Réservoir Cabonga
Opeepeesway Lake
Minisinakwa Lake
New Liskeard
Haileybury
Ville-Marie
Lac des Quinze
Lac Simard
Wenebegon L.
Biscotasi Lake
Onaping Lake
Ostaboningue
Lac Saseginaga
Lac Dumoine
Lac Byrd
Réservoir Baskatong
Batchawana Mountain 653
Ramsey Lake
Indian Lake
Obabika Lake
Lake Temagami
Lake Timiskaming
Lac Kipawa
Rocky Island L.
Pogamasing L.
Cross Lake
Témiscaming
Ogidaki Mountain 665
Bark Lake
Wanapitei Lake
Lac Beauchêne
Lac Nilgaut
Levack
Capreol
Maniwaki
Sault Sainte Marie
Chelmsford
Garson
Sudbury
Coniston
Tomiko Lake
North Bay
Mattawa
QUÉBEC
Ottawa
ONTARIO
Deep River
Sainte Marie
Sugar Island
Matinenda L.
Elliot Lake
Lively
Sturgeon Falls
Lake Nipissing
Callander
Thessalon
Massey
Espanola
Burwash
Chalk River
Lac Dumont
St. Joseph Island
Blind River
Algoma Mills
Lake Panache
Rutter
Powassan
Wilkes Lake
Cedar Lake
Fort Coulonge
Low
Pickford
North Channel
Little Current
Great La Cloche Island
Killarney
Hogan Lake
Petawawa
Otter Lake
Cedarville
Drummond Island
Cockburn Island
Barrie I.
South River
Pembroke
Campbells Bay
De Tour Village
Gore Bay
Manitoulin Island
Byng Inlet
Cobden
Shawville
Mackinac Island
Meldrum Bay
Kagawong L.
Manitou Lake
Cape Smith
Magnetawan
Opeongo Lake
Bois Blanc Island
Manitowaning
Barrys Bay
Eganville
Cheboygan
Great Duck I.
South Bay
Whitney
Kamaniskeg L.
Renfrew
Arnprior
Mullett Lake
Black Lake
South Baymouth
Georgian
Shawanaga Inlet
Madawaska
White L.
Almonte
Indian River
Rogers City
Fitzwilliam Island
Main Channel
Parry Sound
Huntsville
Kawagama Lake
Highlands
Carleton Place
Petoskey
Onaway
Posen
Grand Lake
Georgian Bay Islands Nat. Park
Parry Island
Lake of Bays
Bancroft
Cape Hurd
Cabot Head
Bay
MacTier
L. Rosseau
Perth
Long Lake
Dyer Bay
Lake Joseph
Bracebridge
Haliburton
Smiths Falls
Vanderbilt
Alpena
North Point
(176 Meters Above Sea Level)
Bruce
Cape Croker
Georgian Bay Islands Nat. Park
Gravenhurst
Big Gull Lake
Sharbot Lake
Gaylord
Atlanta
Thunder Bay
Lake
Peninsula
Christian Island
Severn
Fletcher Pond
Canada
United States
Wiarton
Owen Sound
Penetanguishene
Midland
Nottawasaga Bay
Victoria Harbour
Orillia
Balsam Lake
Stony Lake
Madoc
Verona
Fairview
Hubbard Lake
Harrisville
Owen Sound
Meaford
Thornbury
Bobcaygeon
Pigeon L.
Havelock
Tweed
Gananoque
Mio
Au Sable
Southampton
Stayner
Lake Simcoe
Beaverton
Sturgeon Lake
Lindsay
Chemung L.
Lakefield
Marmora
Kingston
Roscommon
Collingwood
Norwood
Napanee
Odessa
Rose City
Oscoda
Huron
Port Elgin
Markdale
Barrie
Peterborough
Campbellford
Deseronto
Collins Bay
Wolfe Island
Tawas City
Au Sable Point
Chesley
Durham
Dundalk
Alliston
Uxbridge
Port Perry
Lake Scugog
Rice Lake
Trenton
Belleville
Amherst Island
Cape Vincent
West Branch
East Tawas
(176 Meters Above Sea Level)
Kincardine
Hanover
Bradford
Newmarket
Brighton
Cobourg
Picton
Houghton Lake
Whittemore
Ontario
Michigan
Point Clark
Walkerton
Shelburne
Aurora
Whitby
Port Hope
Wellington
Galloo Island
Sackets Harbor
Harrison
Au Gres
Port Austin
Harriston
Mount Forest
Orangeville
Richmond Hill
Markham
Oshawa
Bowmanville
Point Petre
Pulaski
Gladwin
Standish
Caseville
Lucknow
Wingham
Palmerston
North York
Scarborough
Lake Ontario
Ontario
Mexico Bay
Clare
Pinconning
Saginaw Bay
Kinde
Harbor Beach
Goderich
Fergus
Brampton
Toronto
New York
Oswego
Coleman
Sebewaing
Bay Port
Bad Axe
Brussels
Listowel
Georgetown
Etobicoke
(75 Meters Above Sea Level)
Mexico
Sanford
Midland
Essexville
Unionville
Ubly
Clinton
Seaforth
Guelph
Mississauga
Fair Haven
Fulton
Shepherd
Bay City
Caro
Deckerville
Sandusky
Port Sanilac
Mitchell
Waterloo
New Hamburg
Kitchener
Cambridge
Oakville
Burlington
Niagara-on-the-Lake
Olcott
Albion
Greece
Irondequoit
Sodus
Baldwinsville
St. Louis
Freeland
Reese
Exeter
Stratford
Ayr
Dundas
Hamilton
Youngstown
Medina
Rochester
Clyde
Weedsport
Alma
Saginaw
Vassar
Marlette
Lexington
Saint Mary's
Paris
St. Catharines
Lockport
Niagara Falls
Batavia
Newark
Syracuse
Ithaca
Bridgeport
Millington
Grand Bend
Woodstock
Caledonia
Welland
Le Roy
Henrietta
Avon
Waterloo
Auburn
Chesaning
Birch Run
Clio
Brown City
Parkhill
Lucan
Thamesford
Brantford
Hagersville
Port Colborne
Tonawanda
Cheektowaga
Canandaigua
Geneva
Seneca Falls
Elsie
Mount Morris
Yale
Lakeport
Forest
London
Ingersoll
Norwich
Dunnville
Buffalo
Lackawanna
Attica
Geneseo
Ovid
Flint
Lapeer
Capac
Port Huron
Sarnia
Strathroy
Dorchester
Tillsonburg
Simcoe
Blasdell
Warsaw
Mount Morris
Cayuga Lake
Trumansburg
Saint Johns
Owosso
Burton
Swartz Creek
Almont
Marysville
Saint Clair
Petrolia
Mount Brydges
Delhi
Port Dover
East Aurora
Castile
Seneca
Keuka Lake
Penn Yan
Durand
Perry
Oxford
Romeo
Marine City
Glencoe
St. Thomas
Aylmer West
Long Point Bay
Angola
Hamburg
Arcade
Nunda
Naples
Dansville
Watkins Glen
East Lansing
Fenton
Holly
Rochester
New Baltimore
Bothwell
Port Stanley
Port Rowan
Silver Creek
Springville
Hammondsport
Howell
Pontiac
Mount Clemens
Wallaceburg
Thames
West Lorne
Long Point
Dunkirk
Houghton
Hornell
Bath
Montour Falls
Mason
Brighton
Milford
Warren
Roseville
Thamesville
Ridgetown
Fredonia
Gowanda
Alfred
Canisteo
Horseheads
Leslie
Pinckney
Royal Oak
Grosse Pointe
Chatham
Lake Erie
Westfield
Cattaraugus
Ellicottville
Cuba
Belmont
Corning
Candor
Eaton Rapids
Livonia
Dearborn
Lake St. Clair
Blenheim
North East
Ripley
Chautauqua Lake
Olean
Wellsville
Elmira
Waverly
Battle Creek
Chelsea
Ann Arbor
Ypsilanti
Detroit
Windsor
Tilbury
Pointe aux Pins
Erie
Wesleyville
Salamanca
Mt. Seneca 642
Eldred
Alma Hill 777
New York
Pa.
Tioga
Sayre
Marshall
Albion
Jackson
Saline
Southgate
Wyandotte
Essex
(174 Meters Above Sea Level)
Jamestown
Carmer Hill 769
Mansfield
Troy
Athens
Homer
Clinton
Amherstburg
Milan
Leamington
Ontario
Ohio
Conneaut
Girard
Corry
Pikes Rock 604
Bradford
Coudersport
Quincy
Addison
Adrian
Tecumseh
Monroe
South Rockwood
Kingsville
Point Pelee National Park
Ashtabula
Geneva
Albion
Union City
Warren
Smethport
Port Allegany
Galeton
Wellsboro
Towanda
Coldwater
Hillsdale
Blissfield
Point Pelee
Edinboro
Mount Jewett
Blossburg
Canton
Hudson
Luna Pier
Pelee Island
Painesville
Mentor
Conneautville
Cambridge Springs
Kane
Allegheny
Emporium
Dushore
Waldron
Mich.
Ohio
Sylvania
Toledo
Oregon
Pelee Island
Willowick
Andover
Meadville
Titusville
Johnsonburg
Saint Marys
Laporte
Angola
West Unity
Port Clinton
Cleveland
Euclid
Chardon
Pymatuning Reservoir
Sugar Creek
Tionesta
Oil City
Renovo
Montoursville
Montpelier
Bryan
Wauseon
Maumee
Perrysburg
Bowling Green
Vermilion
Lorain
Lakewood
Parma
Aurora
Sugarloaf 426
Mosquito Creek Lake
Greenville
Marienville
Ridgway
Sinnamahoning
Williamsport
Jersey Shore
Auburn
Napoleon
Defiance
Liberty Center
Sandusky
Clyde
Huron
Elyria
Oberlin
Berea
Sharon
Farrell
Polk
Franklin
Clarion
Weedville
Penfield
Milton
Danville
Hicksville
Paulding
Fremont
North Baltimore
Bellevue
Norwalk
Brunswick
Ravenna
Niles
Youngstown
Mercer
Emlenton
Brookville
Du Bois
Clearfield
Lock Haven
Lewisburg
Oakwood
Deshler
Fostoria
Tiffin
Willard
Wellington
Cuyahoga Falls
Kent
Boardman
Struthers
Grove City
Sligo
Sykesville
Bellefonte
Sunbury
Selinsgrove
New Haven
Leipsic
Findlay
Attica
Greenwich
Barberton
Akron
Berlin Lake
New Castle
Ellwood City
Slippery Rock
Rimersburg
Punxsutawney
Curwensville
Plateau
Philipsburg
Shamokin
Herndon
Van Wert
Ottawa
Bluffton
Carey
Upper Sandusky
Bucyrus
Shelby
Ashland
Rittman
Orrville
North Canton
Alliance
Salem
Butler
Dayton
Kittanning
Coalport
State College
Middleburg
Decatur
Delphos
Lima
Crestline
Wooster
Canton
East Palestine
Beaver Falls
Ford City
Barnesboro
Tyrone
Lewistown
Liverpool
Ohio
Ohio City
Dunkirk
Galion
Mansfield
Massillon
Minerva
East Liverpool
Wellsville
Beaver
Aliquippa
Vandergrift
Indiana
Ebensburg
Patton
Altoona
Juniata
Millersburg
Berne
Celina
Wapakoneta
Kenton
Caledonia
Loudonville
Millersburg
Carrollton
Dover
Pittsburgh
New Kensington
Huntingdon
Port Royal
Duncannon
Harrisburg
Bridgewater
Grand L.
Saint Marys
Marion
Mount Gilead
Butler
New Philadelphia
Weirton
Penn Hills
Blairsville
Roaring Spring
Hollidaysburg
Mount Union
Blue Mtn.
Hershey
Appalachian Mts.
84°
83°
82°
81°
80°
79°
78° Albers Conical Equal-Area Projection

Southeastern United States

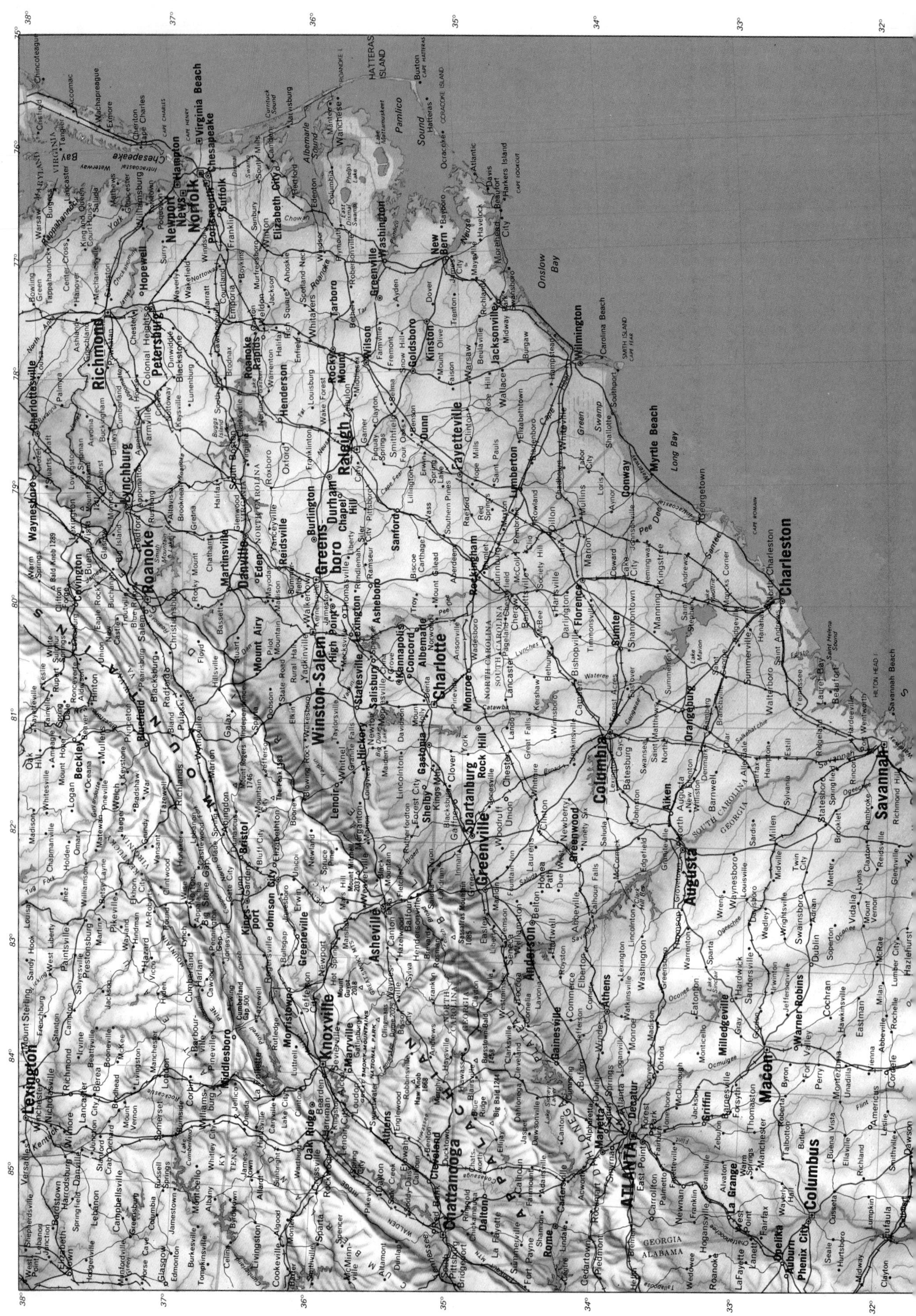

Richmond
Petersburg
Norfolk
Portsmouth
Chesapeake
Virginia Beach
Suffolk
Newport News
Hampton
Hopewell
Lynchburg
Roanoke
Danville
Charlottesville
Winston-Salem
Greensboro
High Point
Durham
Raleigh
Chapel Hill
Rocky Mount
Wilson
Goldsboro
Greenville
Fayetteville
Wilmington
Jacksonville
New Bern
Charlotte
Gastonia
Asheville
Hickory
Spartanburg
Greenville
Anderson
Rock Hill
Columbia
Sumter
Florence
Myrtle Beach
Conway
Charleston
Savannah
Augusta
Aiken
Orangeburg
Macon
Columbus
Athens
Atlanta
Marietta
Decatur
Gainesville
Rome
Dalton
Chattanooga
Knoxville
Oak Ridge
Bristol
Johnson City
Kingsport
Morristown
Lexington
Middlesboro
Beckley
Bluefield
Albemarle Sound
Pamlico Sound
Onslow Bay
Long Bay
Chesapeake Bay
Hatteras Island
Cape Hatteras
Cape Lookout
Cape Fear
Cape Charles
Cape Henry
Ocracoke Island
Smith Island
Hilton Head I.
Great Smoky Mountains National Park
Blue Ridge
Mount Mitchell 2037
Mount Rogers 1746
NORTH CAROLINA
SOUTH CAROLINA
VIRGINIA
GEORGIA
ALABAMA
38°
37°
36°
35°
34°
33°
32°
76°
77°
78°
79°
80°
81°
82°
83°
84°
85°

ATLANTIC
OCEAN
GULF OF
MEXICO
UNITED STATES
BAHAMAS
Jacksonville
St. Augustine
Daytona Beach
Orlando
Titusville
CAPE CANAVERAL
Merritt Island
Cocoa
Cocoa Beach
Melbourne
Vero Beach
Fort Pierce
West Palm Beach
Delray Beach
Pompano Beach
Fort Lauderdale
Hollywood
Miami Beach
MIAMI
Hialeah
Coral Gables
Key West
Tampa
St. Petersburg
Clearwater
Sarasota
Bradenton
Fort Myers
Naples
Lakeland
Ocala
Gainesville
Tallahassee
Valdosta
Waycross
Brunswick
Thomasville
Moultrie
Lake Okeechobee
The Everglades
Big Cypress Swamp
Okefenokee Swamp
Florida Bay
FLORIDA KEYS
Straits of Florida
Nassau
NEW PROVIDENCE
ANDROS ISLAND
GRAND BAHAMA
GREAT ABACO
LITTLE ABACO ISLAND
ELEUTHERA
BERRY ISLANDS
BIMINI ISLANDS
Freeport
West End
Northwest Providence Channel
Northeast Providence Channel
Copyright © by Rand McNally & Co.
Albers Conical Equal-Area Projection
Kilometers
Miles
1:4 000 000

Mississippi Valley

CHICAGO
INDIANAPOLIS
ST. LOUIS
KANSAS CITY
Louisville
Nashville
Fort Wayne
Springfield
Peoria
Des Moines
Omaha
Evansville
Terre Haute
Springfield
Topeka
St. Joseph
Joplin
Lafayette
Kokomo
Muncie
Anderson
Decatur
Champaign
Bloomington
Jefferson City
Columbia
Davenport
Rock Island
Moline
Jacksonville
Quincy
Hannibal
Paducah
Owensboro
Bowling Green
Clarksville
Murfreesboro
Cape Girardeau
Carbondale
Mount Vernon
Sedalia
Lawrence
Independence
Lake of the Ozarks
OZARK PLATEAU
SALEM UPLAND
SPRINGFIELD PLATEAU
BOSTON MOUNTAINS
IOWA
MISSOURI
ILL.
IND.
OHIO
KANSAS
OKLAHOMA
ARKANSAS
TENN.
KY.
Mississippi
Missouri
Illinois
Ohio
Wabash
Des Moines
96°
95°
94°
93°
92°
91°
90°
89°
88°
87°
86°
85°
41°
40°
39°
38°
37°
36°

Memphis
Little Rock
Chattanooga
Huntsville
Birmingham
Tuscaloosa
Montgomery
Jackson
Shreveport
Monroe
Vicksburg
Meridian
Mobile
Pensacola
Baton Rouge
NEW ORLEANS
Alexandria
Lafayette
Beaumont
Port Arthur
HOUSTON
Galveston
Texarkana
Pine Bluff
Hot Springs National Park
Gulfport
Biloxi
Hattiesburg
Natchez
Columbus
Tupelo
Corinth
Gadsden
Anniston
Dothan
Panama City
GULF OF MEXICO
MISSISSIPPI DELTA
Chandeleur Sound
Atchafalaya Bay
Mississippi
35°
34°
33°
32°
31°
30°
29°
95°
94°
93°
92°
91°
90°
89°
88°
87°
Copyright © by Rand McNally & Co.
B-521292-264
Albers Conical Equal-Area Projection
Kilometers 0 50 100 150 Km.
Miles 0 50 100 150 Mi.
1:4 000 000

Southern Great Plains

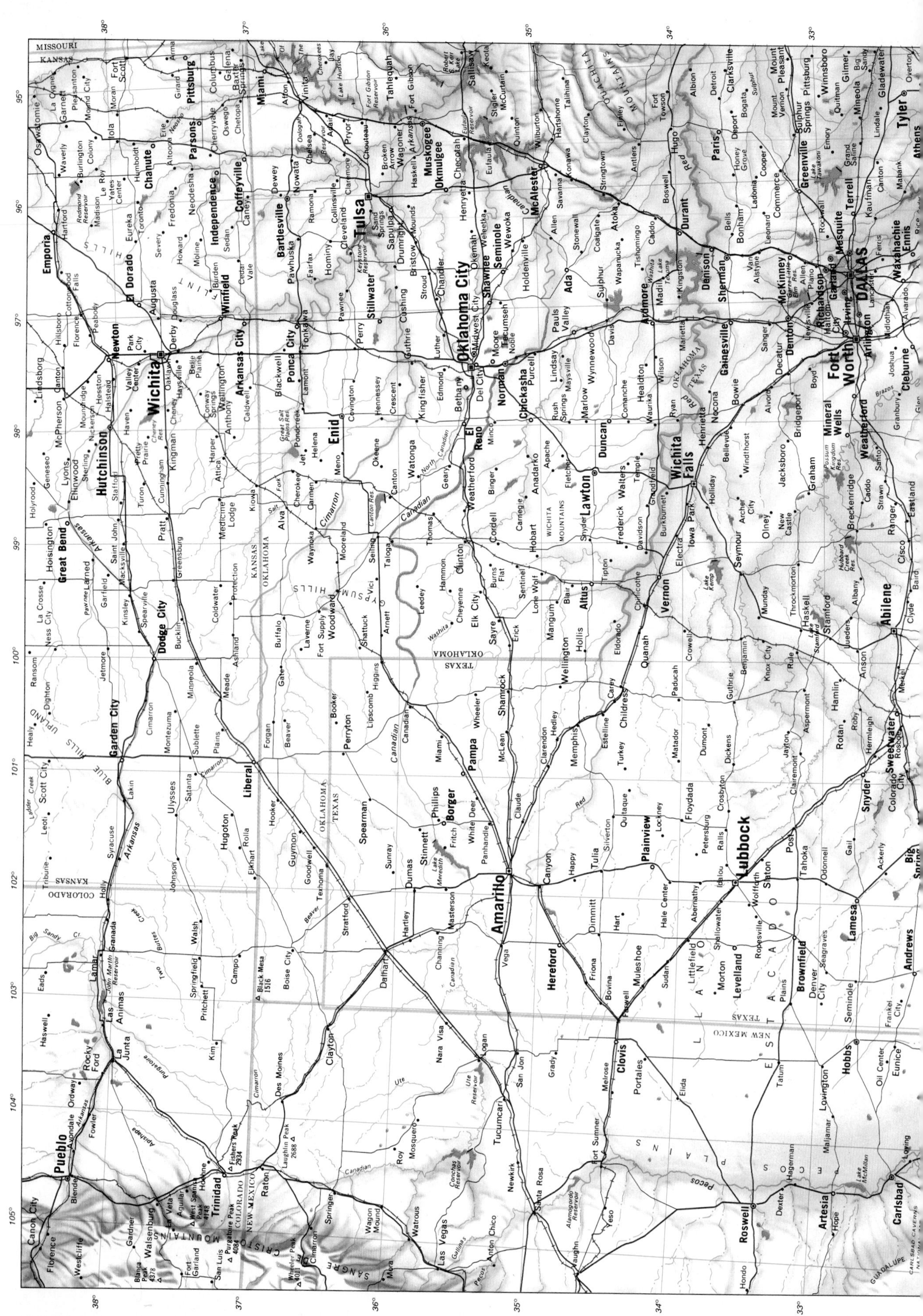

MISSOURI
KANSAS
COLORADO
OKLAHOMA
TEXAS
NEW MEXICO
Emporia
El Dorado
Winfield
Arkansas City
Wichita
Newton
Hutchinson
Great Bend
Dodge City
Garden City
Liberal
Pratt
Chanute
Parsons
Pittsburg
Independence
Coffeyville
Bartlesville
Miami
Tulsa
Muskogee
Okmulgee
McAlester
Stillwater
Enid
Ponca City
Oklahoma City
Norman
Shawnee
Seminole
Ada
Chickasha
Lawton
Duncan
Ardmore
Durant
El Reno
Altus
Woodward
Guymon
Amarillo
Pampa
Borger
Plainview
Lubbock
Childress
Vernon
Wichita Falls
Denison
Sherman
Paris
Greenville
McKinney
Denton
Gainesville
Fort Worth
DALLAS
Arlington
Mesquite
Terrell
Tyler
Abilene
Sweetwater
Snyder
Lamesa
Brownfield
Levelland
Hereford
Clovis
Portales
Hobbs
Roswell
Artesia
Carlsbad
Tucumcari
Clayton
Raton
Trinidad
Pueblo
Lamar
La Junta
Las Vegas
Santa Rosa
SANGRE DE CRISTO MOUNTAINS
OUACHITA MOUNTAINS
WICHITA MOUNTAINS
GYPSUM HILLS
FLINT HILLS
LLANO ESTACADO
Canadian
Cimarron
Arkansas
Red
Pecos

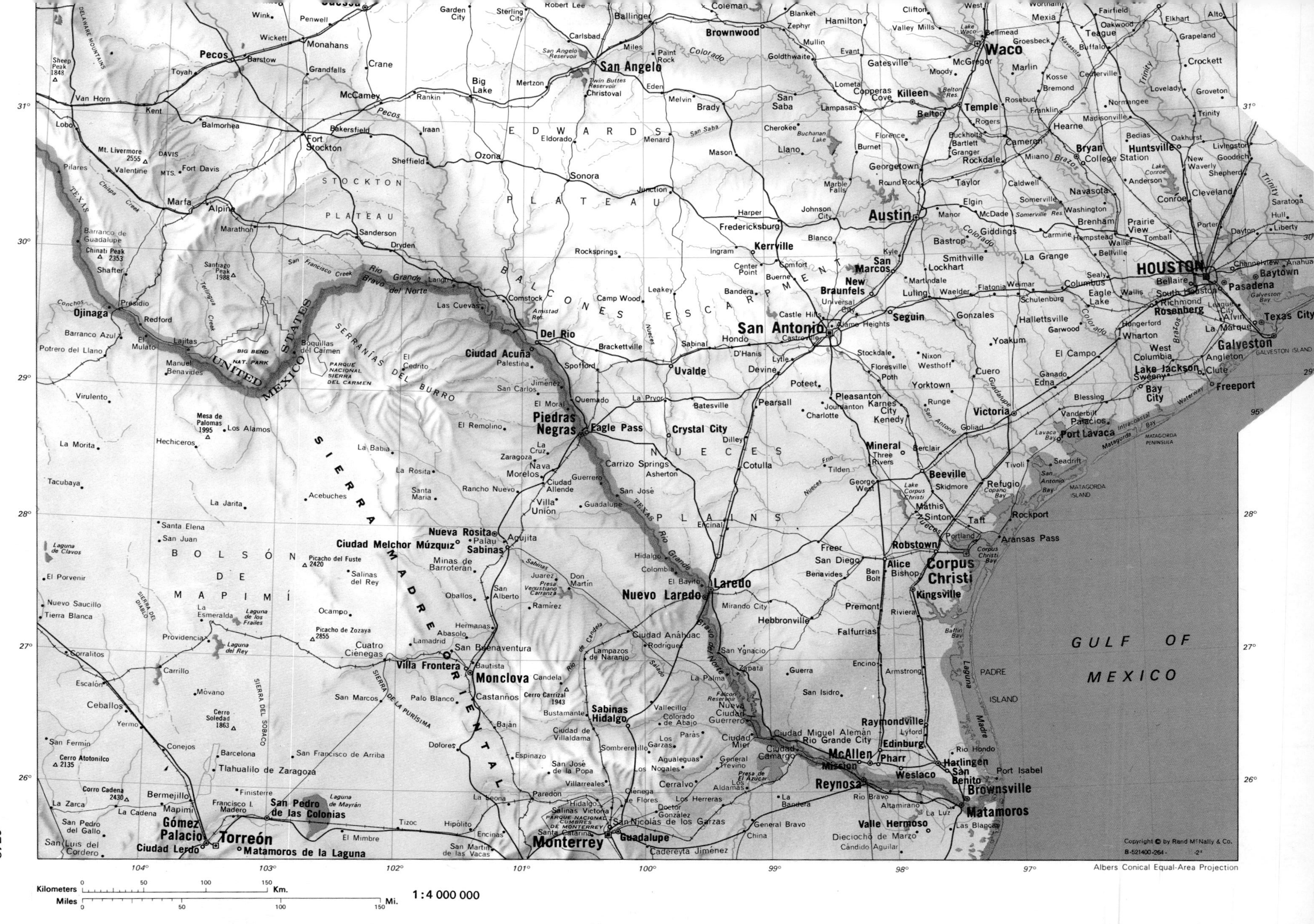

GULF OF MEXICO
SIERRA MADRE ORIENTAL
EDWARDS PLATEAU
BALCONES ESCARPMENT
NUECES PLAINS
STOCKTON PLATEAU
BOLSÓN DE MAPIMÍ
SERRANÍAS DEL BURRO
UNITED STATES
MEXICO
TEXAS
Rio Grande
Bravo del Norte
PADRE ISLAND
Laguna Madre
HOUSTON
San Antonio
Austin
Corpus Christi
Laredo
Nuevo Laredo
Monterrey
Torreón
Brownsville
Matamoros
Galveston
Waco
San Angelo
Del Rio
Ciudad Acuña
Eagle Pass
Piedras Negras
Monclova
Ojinaga
Victoria
McAllen
Reynosa
Gómez Palacio
Ciudad Lerdo
Kilometers
Miles
1:4 000 000
Albers Conical Equal-Area Projection
Copyright © by Rand McNally & Co.
B-521400-264-2

Northern Great Plains

Winnipeg
Portage-la-Prairie
Brandon
Kenora
Lake of the Woods
CANADA
UNITED STATES
MANITOBA
NORTH DAKOTA
SOUTH DAKOTA
MINNESOTA
MONTANA
WYOMING
SASKATCHEWAN
Grand Forks
Fargo
Moorhead
Bemidji
Brainerd
St. Cloud
Fergus Falls
Willmar
New Ulm
Mankato
Worthington
Fairmont
Devils Lake
Jamestown
Bismarck
Mandan
Minot
Williston
Dickinson
Aberdeen
Watertown
Brookings
Huron
Mitchell
Pierre
Rapid City
Miles City
Glendive
Wolf Point
Lake Sakakawea
Oahe Reservoir
Fort Peck Reservoir
RED RIVER VALLEY
COTEAU DES PRAIRIES
COTEAU DU MISSOURI
WILLISTON BASIN
SOURIS PLAIN
BLACK HILLS
BADLANDS NATIONAL MONUMENT
THEODORE ROOSEVELT NAT. MEM. PARK (NORTH UNIT)
THEODORE ROOSEVELT NAT. MEM. PARK (SOUTH UNIT)
Missouri
Yellowstone
Red

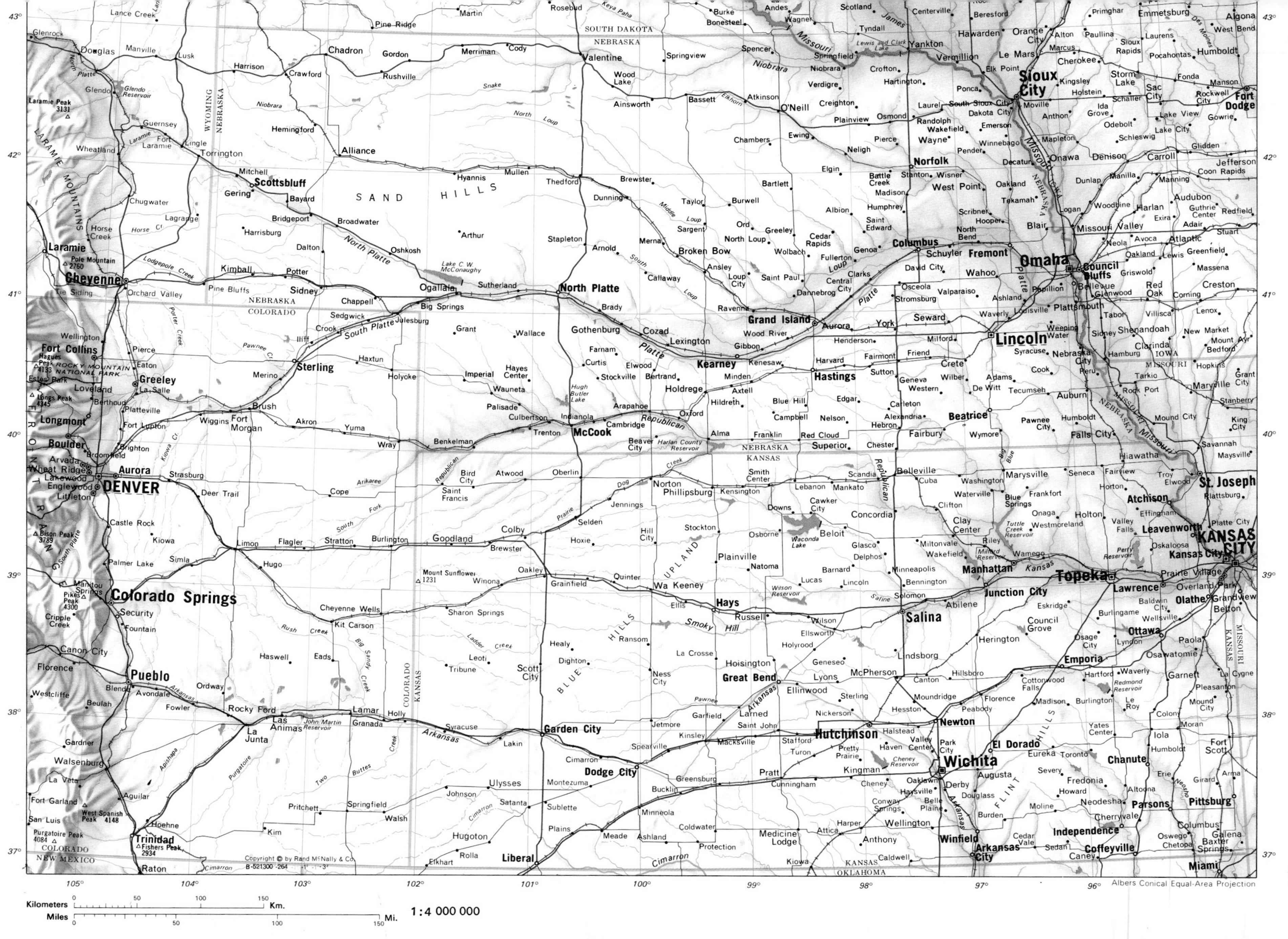

SOUTH DAKOTA
NEBRASKA
WYOMING
COLORADO
KANSAS
IOWA
MISSOURI
OKLAHOMA
NEW MEXICO
SAND HILLS
LARAMIE MOUNTAINS
FRONT RANGE
ROCKY MOUNTAIN NATIONAL PARK
UPLAND
SMOKY HILL
BLUE HILLS
FLINT HILLS
Missouri
North Platte
South Platte
Platte
Republican
Arkansas
Niobrara
Kansas
Cimarron
DENVER
Aurora
Boulder
Longmont
Fort Collins
Greeley
Colorado Springs
Pueblo
Trinidad
Laramie
Cheyenne
Scottsbluff
Alliance
Chadron
Valentine
North Platte
McCook
Kearney
Grand Island
Hastings
Lincoln
Omaha
Council Bluffs
Sioux City
Norfolk
Columbus
Fremont
Beatrice
Sterling
Goodland
Colby
Hays
Salina
Junction City
Manhattan
Topeka
Lawrence
KANSAS CITY
St. Joseph
Atchison
Leavenworth
Emporia
Ottawa
Newton
Hutchinson
Wichita
El Dorado
Great Bend
Garden City
Dodge City
Liberal
Winfield
Arkansas City
Independence
Coffeyville
Parsons
Pittsburg
Chanute
Miami
Laramie Peak 3131
Pole Mountain 2760
Longs Peak 4345
Pikes Peak 4300
Mount Sunflower 1231
West Spanish Peak 4148
Fishers Peak 2934
Copyright © by Rand McNally & Co.
B-521300 -264
105°
104°
103°
102°
101°
100°
99°
98°
97°
96°
43°
42°
41°
40°
39°
38°
37°
Albers Conical Equal-Area Projection
Kilometers
Km.
Miles
Mi.
1:4 000 000

Southern Rocky Mountains

DENVER
Aurora
Englewood
Colorado Springs
Pueblo
Boulder
Longmont
Greeley
Fort Collins
Cheyenne
Laramie
Casper
ROCKY
MOUNTAINS
FRONT
PARK
RANGE
SAWATCH
SANGRE DE CRISTO
WYOMING
COLORADO
UTAH
IDAHO
NEVADA
Rawlins
Rock Springs
Green River
Grand Junction
Glenwood Springs
Salt Lake City
Ogden
Provo
Logan
Pocatello
Idaho Falls
Twin Falls
Mountain Home
Great Salt Lake
Utah Lake
GREAT SALT LAKE DESERT
Bonneville Salt Flats
SNAKE RIVER PLAIN
WIND RIVER RANGE
UINTA MOUNTAINS
WYOMING RANGES
RUBY MOUNTAINS
DINOSAUR NATIONAL MONUMENT
FLAMING GORGE NATIONAL RECREATION AREA
GRAND TETON NATIONAL PARK
ARCHES NATIONAL PARK
CANYONLANDS NATIONAL PARK
CAPITOL REEF NATIONAL PARK
COLORADO NATIONAL MONUMENT
CRATERS OF THE MOON NATIONAL MONUMENT
ROCKY MOUNTAIN NATIONAL PARK
Pikes Peak 4300
Longs Peak 4345
Kings Peak 4123
Grand Teton 4196
Gannett Peak 4202

ROCKY MOUNTAINS
SANGRE DE CRISTO MTS.
Santa Fe
Albuquerque
Los Alamos
Rio Grande
SAN ANDRES MOUNTAINS
SACRAMENTO MOUNTAINS
WHITE SANDS NATIONAL MONUMENT
Alamogordo
Las Cruces
El Paso
Ciudad Juárez
DIABLO PLATEAU
Rio Grande
Bravo del Norte
NEW MEXICO
TEXAS
UNITED STATES
MEXICO
BLACK RANGE
PLAINS OF SAN AGUSTIN
Socorro
Grants
Gallup
ZUNI MOUNTAINS
Farmington
SAN JUAN BASIN
CHACO CANYON NATIONAL MONUMENT
NEW MEXICO
ARIZONA
PETRIFIED FOREST NATIONAL PARK
CANYON DE CHELLY NATIONAL MONUMENT
BLACK MESA
MONUMENT VALLEY
HOPI BUTTES
PAINTED DESERT
PLATEAU
WUPATKI NATIONAL MONUMENT
Flagstaff
Humphreys Peak 3851
SAN FRANCISCO PEAKS
GRAND CANYON NATIONAL PARK
GRAND CANYON
KAIBAB PLATEAU
MARBLE CANYON
GLEN CANYON DAM
COCONINO PLATEAU
MOGOLLON RIM
MAZATZAL MOUNTAINS
Phoenix
Scottsdale
Mesa
Chandler
Tucson
SAGUARO NATIONAL MONUMENT
CHIRICAHUA NATIONAL MONUMENT
GALIURO MOUNTAINS
Nogales
Douglas
Agua Prieta
Bisbee
Cananea
ORGAN PIPE CACTUS NATIONAL MONUMENT
GILA BEND MOUNTAINS
SONORA DESERT
HUALAPAI MOUNTAINS
LAKE MEAD NATIONAL RECREATION AREA
Las Vegas
Lake Mead
Yuma
San Luis Río Colorado
DESIERTO DE ALTAR
Golfo de California
Puerto Peñasco
UTAH
ARIZONA
NEVADA
CALIFORNIA
Colorado
Albers Conical Equal-Area Projection
1:4 000 000
Kilometers 0 50 100 150 Km.
Miles 0 50 100 150 Mi.
Copyright © by Rand McNally & Co.

Northwestern United States

125° 124° 123° 122° 121° 120° 119° 118° 117° 116°
49° 48° 47° 46° 45° 44° 43° 42° 41°
CANADA
UNITED STATES
BRITISH COLUMBIA
WASHINGTON
OREGON
IDAHO
CALIFORNIA
NEVADA
PACIFIC OCEAN
VANCOUVER ISLAND
Vancouver
Victoria
Nanaimo
Port Alberni
Burnaby
Port Coquitlam
Chilliwack
Penticton
Nelson
Trail
Cranbrook
Bellingham
Mount Vernon
Everett
SEATTLE
Tacoma
Olympia
Bremerton
Aberdeen
Hoquiam
Port Angeles
Wenatchee
Ellensburg
Yakima
Richland
Pasco
Kennewick
Walla Walla
Spokane
Coeur d'Alene
Moses Lake
Pullman
Moscow
Lewiston
Longview
Astoria
Vancouver
PORTLAND
Oregon City
Salem
Albany
Corvallis
Eugene
Springfield
Bend
The Dalles
Pendleton
La Grande
Baker
Ontario
Boise
Nampa
Caldwell
Roseburg
Coos Bay
Grants Pass
Medford
Ashland
Klamath Falls
Burns
Lakeview
Eureka
Crescent City
Yreka
Weed
Mount Shasta
Dunsmuir
Winnemucca
McDermitt
HARNEY BASIN
GREAT SANDY DESERT
COLUMBIA BASIN
BLUE MOUNTAINS
CASCADE RANGE
COAST RANGES
KLAMATH MOUNTAINS
OLYMPIC NATIONAL PARK
MOUNT RAINIER NAT. PARK
NORTH CASCADES NAT. PARK
Mount Rainier 4392
Mount Saint Helens 2950
Mount Adams 3742
Mount Hood 3424
Mount Jefferson 3199
Mount Shasta 4317
Columbia
Snake
Willamette
Deschutes
Strait of Juan de Fuca
Strait of Georgia
Puget Sound

Kilometers 0 50 100 150 Km.

Miles 0 50 100 150 Mi.

1:4 000 000

114°
113°
112°
111°
110°
109°
108°
107°
106°
49°
48°
47°
46°
45°
44°
43°
42°
41°
CANADA
UNITED STATES
BRITISH COLUMBIA
ALBERTA
SASKATCHEWAN
MONTANA
Pincher Creek
Raymond
Magrath
Stirling
Foremost
Manyberries
Pakowki Lake
Consul
Frontier
Orkney
Masefield
Rockglen
Cardston
Milk River
Coutts
Govenlock
Sweetgrass
Opheim
Scobey
Peerless
Mount Darrah 2755
Mount Cleveland 3190
Waterton-Glacier International Peace Park
Sunburst
Sweetgrass Hills
Fresno Reservoir
Cut Bank
Shelby
Rudyard
Chester
Havre
Chinook
Harlem
Saco
Hinsdale
Malta
Glasgow
Nashua
Wolf Point
Williston Basin
Browning
East Glacier Park
Two Medicine
Hungry Horse
Whitefish
Columbia Falls
Evergreen
Kalispell
Hungry Horse Reservoir
Valier
Conrad
Tiber Res.
Box Elder
Big Sandy
Bearpaw Mts.
Little Rocky Mts.
Hays
Fort Peck Lake
Somers
Flathead Lake
Swan Peak 2831
Rocky Mountain 2863
Silvertip Mountain 2707
Dutton
Choteau
Fairfield
Fort Benton
Teton
Marias
Missouri
Piney Buttes
Circle
Polson
Hot Springs
Ronan
Augusta
Great Falls
Black Eagle
Ulm
Belt
Highwood Baldy 2324
Winifred
Jordan
Big Sheep Mountain 1105
Denton
Judith Peak 1959
Musselshell
Saint Ignatius
Cascade
Stockett
Geyser
Stanford
Lewistown
Winnett
Scapegoat Mountain 2805
Seeley Lake
Squaw Peak 2437
Wolf Creek
Little Belt Mountains
Big Baldy Mountain 2797
Moore
Greathouse Pk. 2646
Flatwillow Creek
Big Porcupine Cr.
Lincoln
Orchard Homes
Missoula
Blackfoot
Big Belt Mountains
Judith Gap
Melstone
Miles City
Lolo
Lolo Pass 1596
Sliderock Mountain 2384
Drummond
MacDonald Pass 1939
East Helena
Helena
Canyon Ferry Lake
White Sulphur Springs
Harlowton
Roundup
Hysham
Forsyth
Yellowstone
Stevensville
Philipsburg
Deer Lodge
Mount Edith 2897
Townsend
Crow Peak 2869
Musselshell
Ryegate
Bull Mountains
Custer
Hamilton
Anaconda
Mount Haggin 3233
Boulder
Butte
Crazy Mts.
Crazy Pk. 3423
Bighorn
Tongue
El Capitan 3043
Silver Bow Park
Floral Park
Whitehall
Three Forks
Big Timber
Clyde Park
Billings Heights
Billings
Ballantine
Hardin
Crow Agency
Lame Deer
Ashland
Trapper Peak 3096
Anaconda Range
Belgrade
Bozeman
Livingston
Columbus
Laurel
Joliet
Busby
Lost Trail Pass 2138
Twin Bridges
Granite Peak 3228
Madison Range
Absarokee
Pryor Cr.
Wisdom
Waugh Mountain 2707
Tweedy Mountain 3400
Sheridan
Mount Blackmore 3095
Tumble Mountain 3452
Mount Wood 3859
Bridger
Bighorn Lake
Lodge Grass
Tongue River Res.
Virginia City
Ennis
Granite Peak 3901
Red Lodge
Salmon
Dillon
Bear Tooth Pass 3337
Bighorn Canyon Nat. Recr. Area
Montana
Wyoming
Ranchester
Sheridan
Gardiner
Mount McGuire 3073
Ruby Range
Koch Peak 3440
Beartooth Range
Lovell
Hunt Mountain 3097
Granite Pass 2753
Clearmont
Powder
Yellowstone National Park
Beaverhead Mountains
Hogback Mountain 3225
Mount Holmes 3150
Powell
Taylor Mountain 3036
Lemhi
Hebgen Lake
West Yellowstone
Trout Peak 3732
Cody
Big Horn
Lima
Cloud Peak 4013
Buffalo
Twin Peaks 3152
Big Creek Peak 3459
Garfield Mountain 3341
Mount Jefferson 3108
Yellowstone Lake
Greybull
Challis
Centennial Mts.
Manderson
Powder River Pass 2946
Scott Peak 3473
Mount Sheridan 3142
Fortress Mountain 3684
Shoshone Lake
Meeteetse
Bighorn Mountains
Lost River Range
Diamond Peak 3718
Dubois
Needle Mountain 3690
Worland
Ten Sleep
Borah Peak 3859
Ashton
Francs Peak 4009
Basin
Kaycee
Saint Anthony
Sugar City
Rexburg
Grand Teton Nat. Park
Jackson Lake
Togwotee Pass 2909
Pinnacle Buttes 3510
Mount Crosby 3794
Owl Creek Mountains
Hamilton Dome
Thermopolis
Leatherman Peak 3727
Hyndman Peak 3660
Roberts
Rigby
Driggs
Grand Teton 4197
Dubois
Copper Mountain 2521
Linch
Edgerton
Midwest
Ketchum
Sun Valley
Arco
Ucon
Idaho Falls
Jackson
Doubletop Peak 3574
Downs Mountain 4069
Boysen Res.
Smokey Dome 3077
Hailey
Big Southern Butte 2304
Shelley
Elkhorn Peaks 3060
Gannett Peak 4207
Pavillion
Shoshoni
Craters of the Moon National Monument
Palisades Res.
Wind River Range
Riverton
Casper
Mountain View
Snake River Plain
Blackfoot
Grays Lake
Etna
Fort Washakie
Hudson
Lander
Rattlesnake Hills
Richfield
Chubbuck
Blackfoot Reservoir
Daniel
Pinedale
Garfield Peak 2513
Shoshone
Aberdeen
Pocatello
Mount McDougall 3281
Afton
Wind River Peak 4021
Granite Mts
Sweetwater
Wendell
American Falls Reservoir
American Falls
Jerome
Lake Walcott
Rupert
Lava Hot Springs
Soda Springs
McCammon
Idaho
Wyoming
Wyoming Peak 3463
Atlantic Peak 3807
Jeffrey City
Pathfinder Reservoir
Twin Falls
Kimberly
Heyburn
Burley
Rockland
Grace
Meade Peak 3035
Georgetown
Big Piney
South Pass 2301
Continental Peak 2570
Downey
Montpelier
Sublett Range
Oakley
Cache Peak 3151
Malad City
Paris
La Barge
Fontenelle Res.
Eden
Seminoe Reservoir
Monument Peak 2457
Wasatch Range
Bear Lake
Cokeville
Steamboat Mountain 2647
Great Divide Basin
Hanna
Idaho
Utah
Preston
Lewiston
Laketown
Rawlins
Sinclair
Smithfield
Logan
Kemmerer
South Superior
Wamsutter
Elk Mountain 3400
Garland
Tremonton
Providence
Hyrum
Diamondville
Randolph
Granger
Blacks Fork
Rock Springs
Green River
Medicine Bow Mts.
Saratoga
Grouse Creek
Great Salt Lake Desert
Brigham City
Perry
Fort Bridger
Lyman
Flaming Gorge National Recreation Area
Flaming Gorge Res.
Encampment
Bridger Peak 3354
Plain City
North Ogden
Huntsville
Great Salt Lake (1278)
Antelope Peak 2679
Montello
Desert Peak 2129
Ogden
Roy
Layton
Evanston
Wyoming
Colorado
Baggs
Elkhead Mts.
Fremont Island
Antelope Island
Morgan
Farmington
Coalville
Wyoming
Utah
Manila
Dutch John
Pilot Peak 3266
Copyright © by Rand McNally & Co.
B-520597-264
Albers Conical Equal-Area Projection

California, Nevada and Hawaii

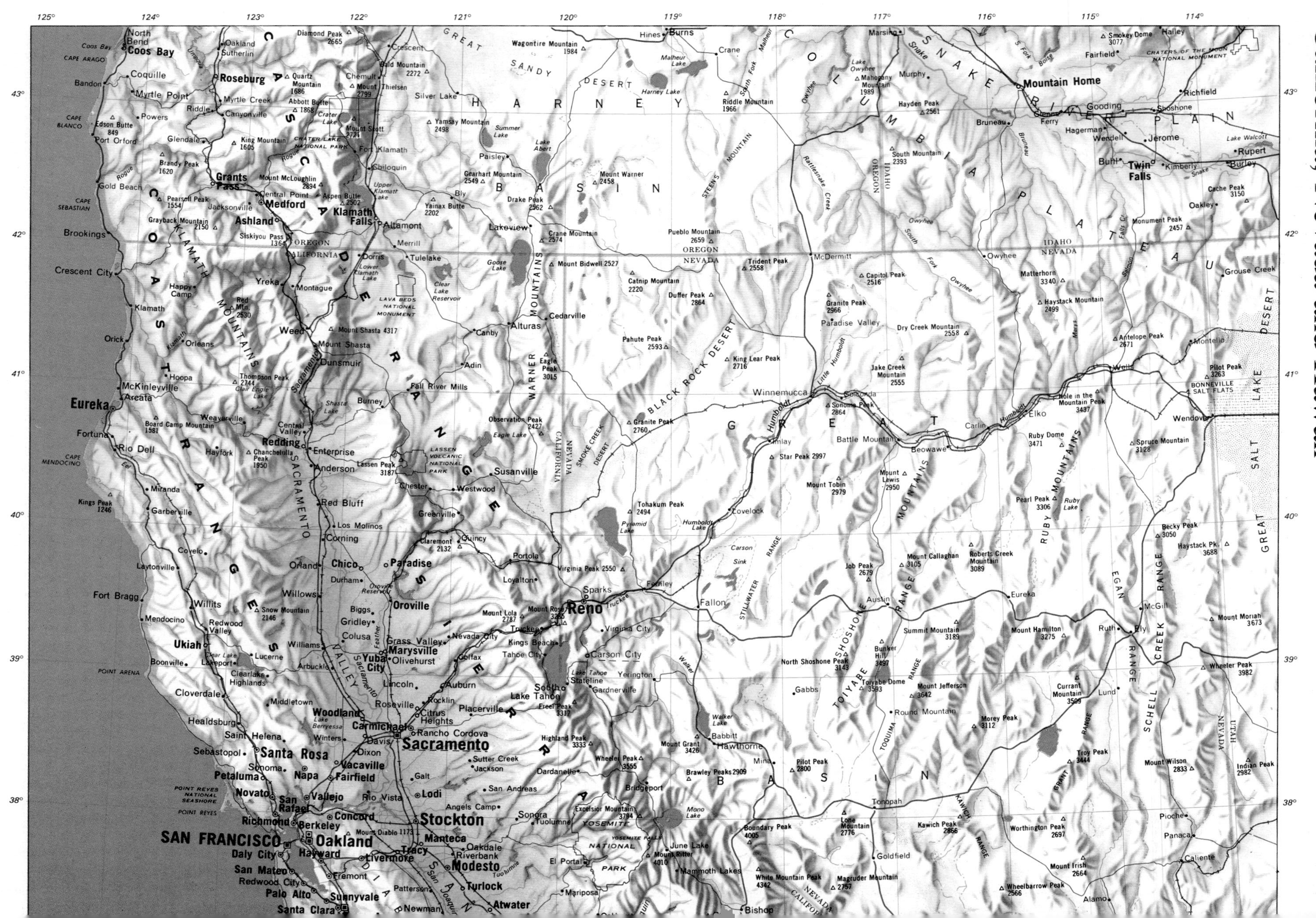

SNAKE RIVER PLAIN
COLUMBIA PLATEAU
GREAT BASIN
GREAT SALT LAKE DESERT
BLACK ROCK DESERT
SMOKE CREEK DESERT
GREAT SANDY DESERT
HARNEY BASIN
CASCADE RANGE
COAST RANGES
SIERRA NEVADA
KLAMATH MOUNTAINS
SACRAMENTO VALLEY
SAN JOAQUIN
STEENS MOUNTAIN
WARNER MOUNTAINS
RUBY MOUNTAINS
EGAN RANGE
SCHELL CREEK RANGE
TOIYABE RANGE
SHOSHONE MOUNTAINS
STILLWATER RANGE
KAWICH RANGE
IDAHO
OREGON
NEVADA
CALIFORNIA
UTAH
LASSEN VOLCANIC NATIONAL PARK
YOSEMITE NATIONAL PARK
CRATER LAKE NATIONAL PARK
LAVA BEDS NATIONAL MONUMENT
POINT REYES NATIONAL SEASHORE
CRATERS OF THE MOON NATIONAL MONUMENT
BONNEVILLE SALT FLATS
SAN FRANCISCO
Oakland
Sacramento
Stockton
Modesto
Reno
Carson City
Sparks
Eureka
Redding
Chico
Medford
Klamath Falls
Ashland
Grants Pass
Roseburg
Coos Bay
Twin Falls
Mountain Home
Burns
Winnemucca
Elko
Ely
Tonopah
Santa Rosa
Crescent City
Lake Tahoe
Mono Lake
Pyramid Lake
Goose Lake
Mount Shasta 4317
Lassen Peak 3187
43°
42°
41°
40°
39°
38°
114°
115°
116°
117°
118°
119°
120°
121°
122°
123°
124°
125°

PACIFIC OCEAN
PACIFIC OCEAN
Albers Conical Equal-Area Projection
1:4 000 000
Kilometers
Km.
Miles
Mi.
Copyright © by Rand McNally & Co.
B-520566-264
Copyright © by Rand McNally & Co.
B-520512-264
a
Las Vegas
Lake Mead
Fresno
Bakersfield
Santa Barbara
LOS ANGELES
Long Beach
Pasadena
San Bernardino
Riverside
SAN DIEGO
Tijuana
Mexicali
Ensenada
Salinas
Monterey
San Luis Obispo
Lompoc
Ventura
Oxnard
Santa Monica
Lancaster
Barstow
Victorville
Needles
Yuma
El Centro
Brawley
Calexico
Visalia
Tulare
Hanford
Porterville
Delano
Santa Maria
Oceanside
Escondido
Palm Springs
Indio
Salton Sea
MOJAVE DESERT
DEATH VALLEY
SIERRA NEVADA
COAST RANGES
CHANNEL ISLANDS
SAN CLEMENTE ISLAND
SAN NICOLAS ISLAND
SANTA CATALINA ISLAND
SAN JOAQUIN VALLEY
COLORADO DESERT
IMPERIAL VALLEY
DESIERTO DE ALTAR
Golfo de California
SIERRA DE JUÁREZ
SIERRA SAN PEDRO MÁRTIR
ARIZONA
NEVADA
CALIFORNIA
U.S.
MEXICO
Colorado
NIIHAU
KAUAI
OAHU
MOLOKAI
LANAI
MAUI
KAHOOLAWE
HAWAII
Honolulu
Hilo
Lihue
Kailua
Kaneohe
Kauai Channel
Kaulakahi Channel
Kaiwi Channel
Alenuihaha Channel
Mauna Kea
Mauna Loa
HAWAII VOLCANOES NATIONAL PARK
HALEAKALA NAT. PARK
36°
35°
34°
33°
32°
31°
22°
21°
20°
19°
116°
155°
156°
157°
158°
159°
160°

Mexico

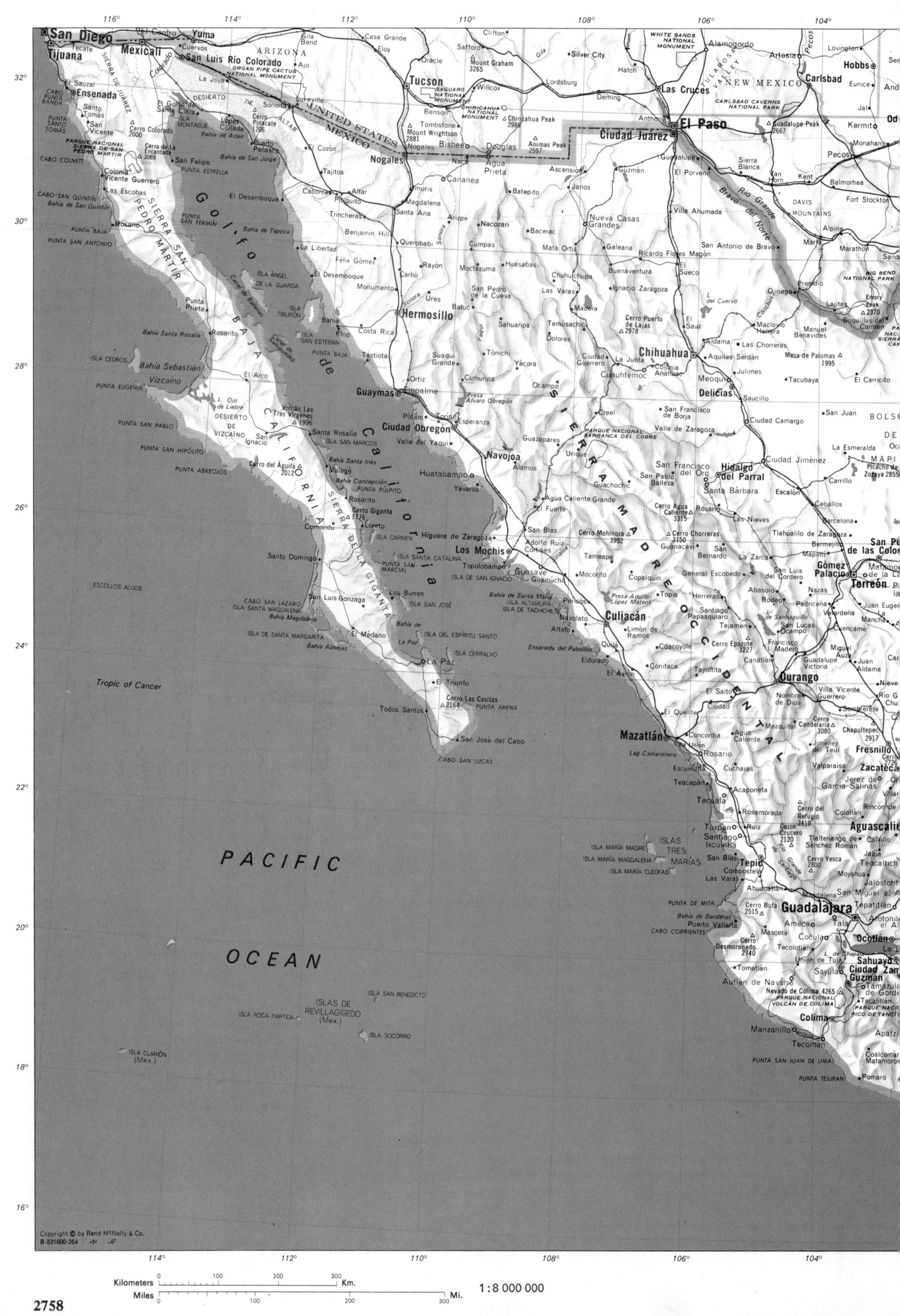

116°
114°
112°
110°
108°
106°
104°
32°
30°
28°
26°
24°
22°
20°
18°
16°
San Diego
Tijuana
Mexicali
Yuma
San Luis Río Colorado
Ensenada
ARIZONA
NEW MEXICO
Tucson
Nogales
Las Cruces
El Paso
Ciudad Juárez
Carlsbad
Hobbs
Pecos
UNITED STATES
MEXICO
ORGAN PIPE CACTUS NATIONAL MONUMENT
SAGUARO NATIONAL MONUMENT
CHIRICAHUA NATIONAL MONUMENT
WHITE SANDS NATIONAL MONUMENT
CARLSBAD CAVERNS NATIONAL PARK
BIG BEND NATIONAL PARK
DESIERTO DE ALTAR
SIERRA DE JUÁREZ
SIERRA SAN PEDRO MÁRTIR
Golfo de California
BAJA CALIFORNIA
SIERRA DE LA GIGANTA
SIERRA MADRE OCCIDENTAL
Río Grande del Norte
Hermosillo
Guaymas
Ciudad Obregón
Navojoa
Los Mochis
Culiacán
Mazatlán
Chihuahua
Delicias
Hidalgo del Parral
Durango
Torreón
Gómez Palacio
Fresnillo
Zacatecas
Aguascalientes
Tepic
Guadalajara
Colima
Manzanillo
Ciudad Guzmán
Ocotlán
La Paz
Santa Rosalía
Bahía Sebastián Vizcaíno
ISLA CEDROS
DESIERTO DE VIZCAÍNO
Bahía Magdalena
ISLA SANTA MARGARITA
ISLA TIBURÓN
ISLA ÁNGEL DE LA GUARDA
ISLA DEL ESPÍRITU SANTO
ISLA CERRALVO
San José del Cabo
CABO SAN LUCAS
Todos Santos
ISLAS TRES MARÍAS
ISLA MARÍA MADRE
ISLA MARÍA MAGDALENA
ISLA MARÍA CLEOFAS
Puerto Vallarta
CABO CORRIENTES
Nevado de Colima 4265
Tropic of Cancer
PACIFIC OCEAN
ISLAS DE REVILLAGIGEDO (Mex.)
ISLA SAN BENEDICTO
ISLA ROCA PARTIDA
ISLA SOCORRO
ISLA CLARIÓN (Mex.)
ESCOLLOS ALIJOS
Copyright © by Rand McNally & Co.
B-531600-264 -1¹¹ -4¹
114°
112°
110°
108°
106°
104°
Kilometers 0 100 200 300 Km.
Miles 0 100 200 300 Mi.
1:8 000 000

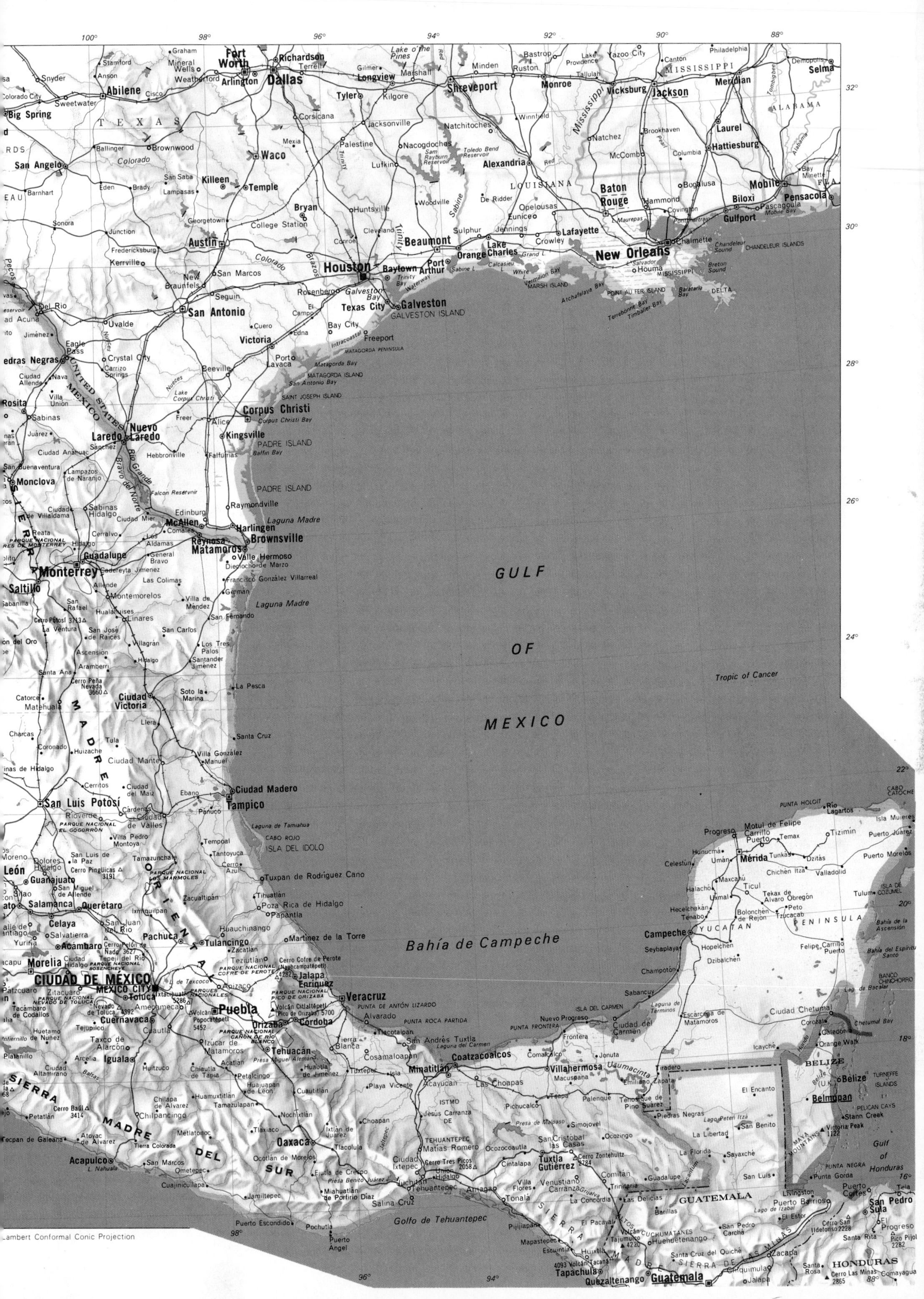

100°
98°
96°
94°
92°
90°
88°
32°
30°
28°
26°
24°
22°
20°
18°
16°
GULF
OF
MEXICO
Bahía de Campeche
Tropic of Cancer
Golfo de Tehuantepec
Gulf of Honduras
TEXAS
LOUISIANA
MISSISSIPPI
ALABAMA
UNITED STATES
MEXICO
BELIZE
GUATEMALA
HONDURAS
YUCATAN PENINSULA
SIERRA MADRE ORIENTAL
SIERRA MADRE DEL SUR
ISTMO DE TEHUANTEPEC
MAYA MOUNTAINS
Fort Worth
Dallas
Richardson
Arlington
Abilene
Big Spring
Sweetwater
Snyder
San Angelo
Waco
Killeen
Temple
Bryan
College Station
Austin
San Marcos
New Braunfels
San Antonio
Seguin
Del Rio
Uvalde
Eagle Pass
Houston
Baytown
Galveston
Texas City
Freeport
Victoria
Port Lavaca
Corpus Christi
Kingsville
Alice
Beeville
Laredo
Nuevo Laredo
McAllen
Harlingen
Brownsville
Tyler
Longview
Marshall
Kilgore
Corsicana
Jacksonville
Palestine
Nacogdoches
Lufkin
Huntsville
Beaumont
Port Arthur
Orange
Lake Charles
Shreveport
Monroe
Ruston
Alexandria
Lafayette
Baton Rouge
New Orleans
Houma
Vicksburg
Jackson
Meridian
Laurel
Hattiesburg
Natchez
McComb
Bogalusa
Biloxi
Gulfport
Pascagoula
Mobile
Pensacola
Selma
Demopolis
Toledo Bend Reservoir
Sam Rayburn Reservoir
Lake Pontchartrain
Galveston Bay
GALVESTON ISLAND
MATAGORDA ISLAND
PADRE ISLAND
Laguna Madre
Falcon Reservoir
CHANDELEUR ISLANDS
MISSISSIPPI DELTA
Monclova
Piedras Negras
Sabinas
Monterrey
Saltillo
Guadalupe
Reynosa
Matamoros
Linares
Ciudad Victoria
Ciudad Mante
Ciudad Madero
Tampico
San Luis Potosí
León
Guanajuato
Salamanca
Querétaro
Celaya
Morelia
CIUDAD DE MÉXICO
MEXICO CITY
Toluca
Pachuca
Tulancingo
Puebla
Cuernavaca
Orizaba
Córdoba
Jalapa Enríquez
Veracruz
Tehuacán
Iguala
Acapulco
Oaxaca
Salina Cruz
Tehuantepec
Coatzacoalcos
Minatitlán
Villahermosa
Tuxtla Gutiérrez
San Cristóbal las Casas
Tapachula
Campeche
Mérida
Progreso
Ciudad del Carmen
Ciudad Chetumal
Belize
Belmopan
Quezaltenango
Guatemala
San Pedro Sula
Tuxpan de Rodríguez Cano
Poza Rica de Hidalgo
Lambert Conformal Conic Projection

Central America and the Caribbean

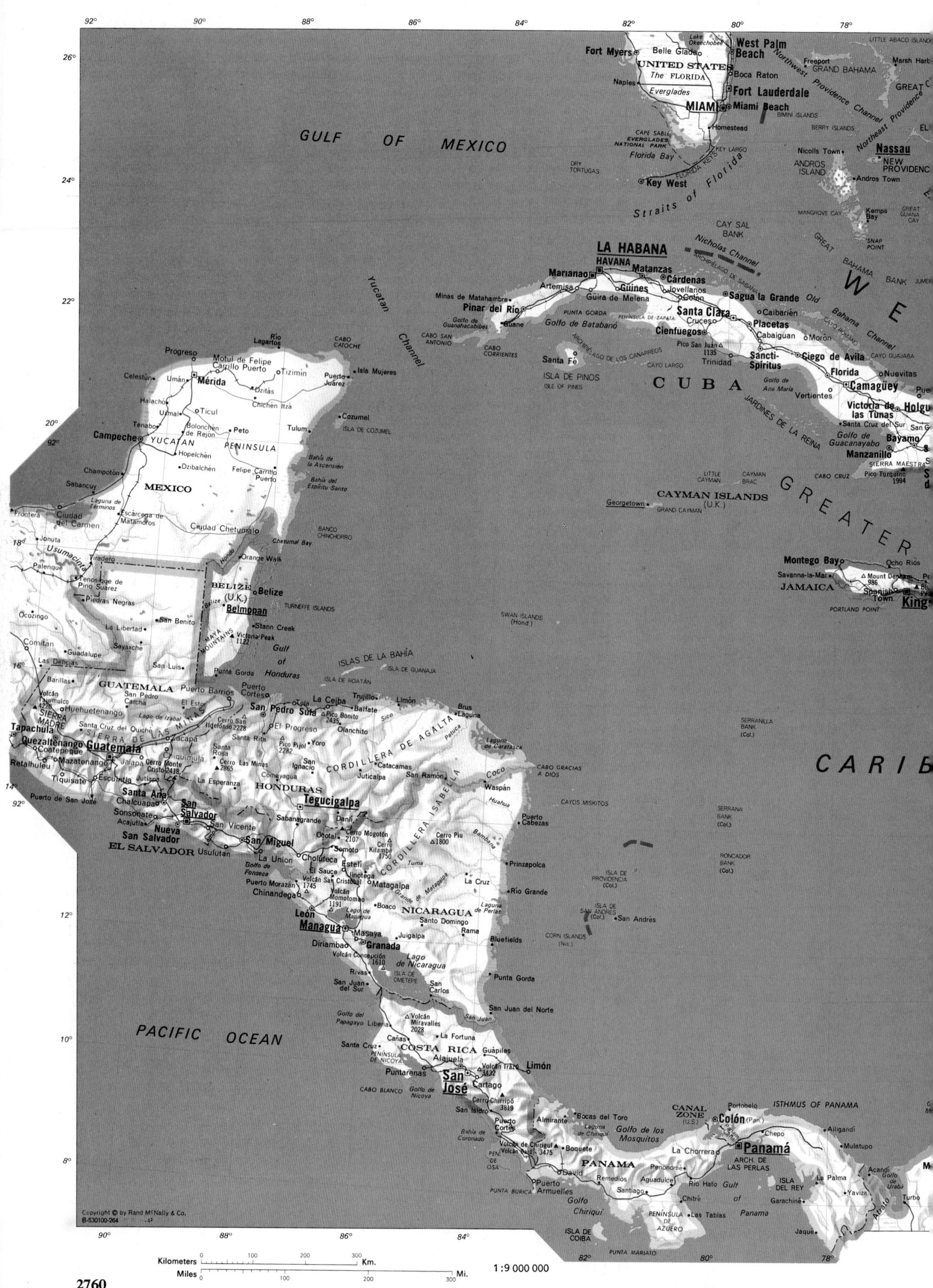

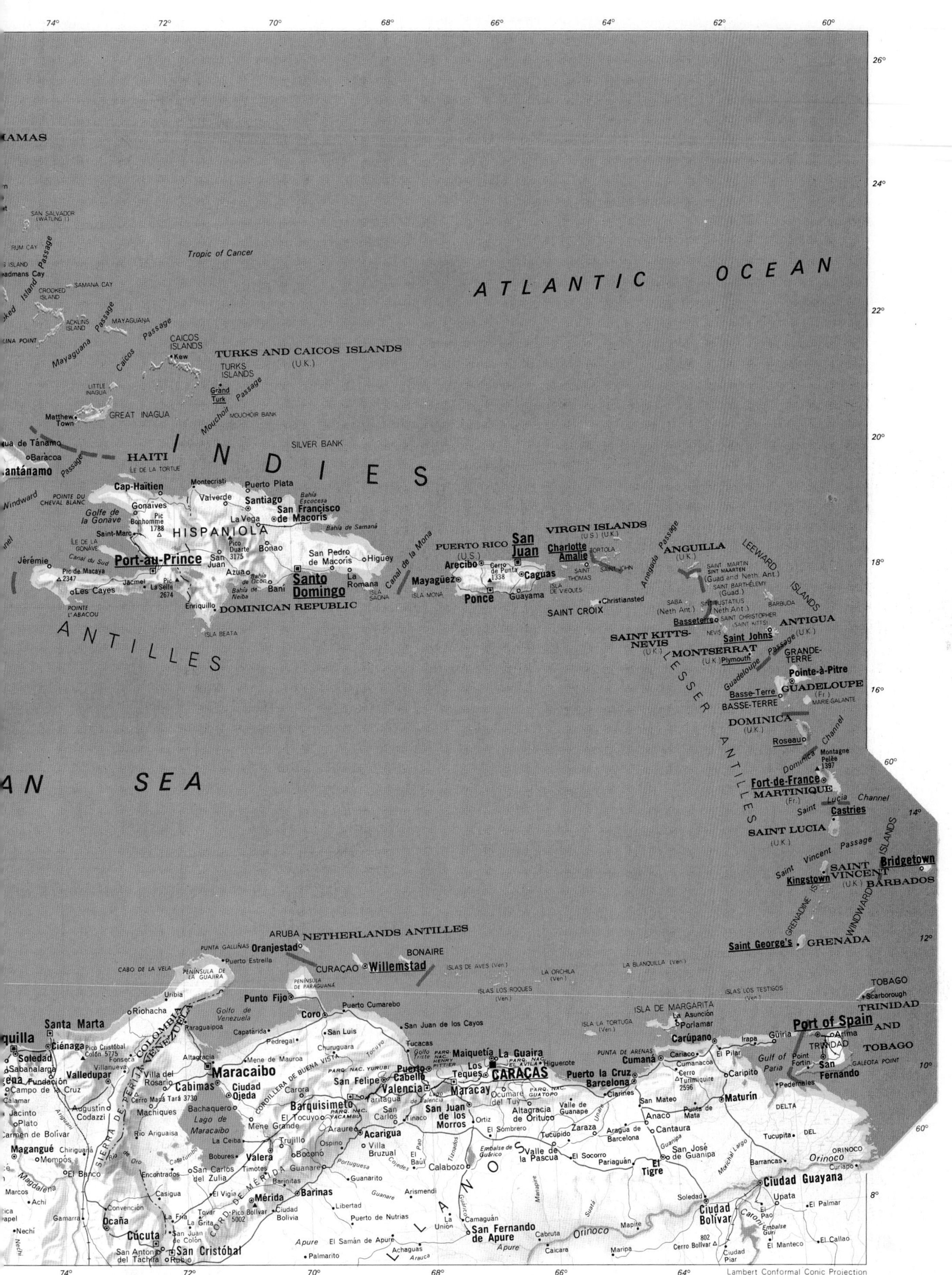

74°
72°
70°
68°
66°
64°
62°
60°
26°
24°
22°
20°
18°
16°
14°
12°
10°
8°
ATLANTIC OCEAN
Tropic of Cancer
SAN SALVADOR (WATLING I.)
RUM CAY
SAMANA CAY
CROOKED ISLAND
Crooked Island Passage
ACKLINS ISLAND
MAYAGUANA
Mayaguana Passage
Caicos Passage
CAICOS ISLANDS
Kew
TURKS AND CAICOS ISLANDS
(U.K.)
TURKS ISLANDS
Grand Turk
Turks Passage
Mouchoir Passage
MOUCHOIR BANK
LITTLE INAGUA
GREAT INAGUA
Matthew Town
SILVER BANK
Baracoa
HAITI
ÎLE DE LA TORTUE
Windward Passage
INDIES
ANTILLES
Cap-Haïtien
Montecristi
Puerto Plata
Valverde
Santiago
POINTE DU CHEVAL BLANC
Gonaïves
Golfe de la Gonâve
Pic Bonhomme 1788
Bahía Escocesa
San Francisco de Macorís
Bahía de Samaná
La Vega
HISPANIOLA
Saint-Marc
ÎLE DE LA GONÂVE
Pico Duarte 3175
Bonao
Jérémie
Canal du Sud
Port-au-Prince
San Juan
Pic de Macaya 2347
Azua
San Pedro de Macorís
Higüey
Jacmel
Pic La Selle 2674
Bahía de Ocoa
Baní
Santo Domingo
La Romana
Les Cayes
Bahía de Neiba
ISLA SAONA
POINTE L'ABACOU
Enriquillo
DOMINICAN REPUBLIC
ISLA BEATA
Canal de la Mona
ISLA MONA
PUERTO RICO
(U.S.)
San Juan
Arecibo
Cerro de Punta 1338
Mayagüez
Caguas
Ponce
Guayama
ISLA DE VIEQUES
VIRGIN ISLANDS
(U.S.) (U.K.)
Charlotte Amalie
TORTOLA
SAINT THOMAS
SAINT JOHN
Christiansted
SAINT CROIX
Anegada Passage
ANGUILLA
(U.K.)
LEEWARD ISLANDS
SAINT MARTIN
SINT MAARTEN
(Guad and Neth. Ant.)
SAINT BARTHÉLEMY
(Guad.)
SABA
(Neth Ant.)
SINT EUSTATIUS
(Neth Ant.)
BARBUDA
Basseterre
SAINT CHRISTOPHER (SAINT KITTS)
NEVIS
ANTIGUA
SAINT KITTS-NEVIS
(U.K.)
Saint Johns
(U.K.)
MONTSERRAT
(U.K.) Plymouth
Guadeloupe Passage
GRANDE-TERRE
Pointe-à-Pitre
LESSER ANTILLES
Basse-Terre
GUADELOUPE
(Fr.)
BASSE-TERRE
MARIE-GALANTE
DOMINICA
(U.K.)
Roseau
Dominica Channel
Montagne Pelée 1397
Fort-de-France
MARTINIQUE
(Fr.)
Saint Lucia Channel
Castries
SAINT LUCIA
(U.K.)
Saint Vincent Passage
SAINT VINCENT
(U.K.)
Kingstown
Bridgetown
BARBADOS
WINDWARD ISLANDS
GRENADINE IS.
Saint George's
GRENADA
SEA
ARUBA
NETHERLANDS ANTILLES
PUNTA GALLINAS
Oranjestad
BONAIRE
Puerto Estrella
CURAÇAO
Willemstad
CABO DE LA VELA
PENÍNSULA DE LA GUAJIRA
ISLAS DE AVES (Ven.)
LA ORCHILA (Ven.)
LA BLANQUILLA (Ven.)
PENÍNSULA DE PARAGUANÁ
ISLAS LOS ROQUES (Ven.)
ISLAS LOS TESTIGOS (Ven.)
TOBAGO
Scarborough
TRINIDAD AND TOBAGO
Uribia
Punto Fijo
Riohacha
Golfo de Venezuela
Coro
Puerto Cumarebo
ISLA DE MARGARITA
La Asunción
Porlamar
ISLA LA TORTUGA (Ven.)
Santa Marta
COLOMBIA
VENEZUELA
Paraguaipoa
Capatárida
San Luis
San Juan de los Cayos
Port of Spain
Arima
Ciénaga
Pico Cristóbal Colón 5775
Pedregal
Churuguara
Tucacas
Golfo Triste
Maiquetía
La Guaira
Carúpano
Irapa
Güiria
TRINIDAD
Soledad
Fonseca
Altagracia
Mene de Mauroa
PARQ. NAC. HENRY PITTIER
PARQ. NAC. EL ÁVILA
Higuerote
PUNTA DE ARENAS
Cumaná
Cariaco
El Pilar
Gulf of Paria
Point Fortin
San Fernando
GALEOTA POINT
Valledupar
Villanueva
Maracaibo
CORDILLERA DE BUENA VISTA
PARQ. NAC. YURUBÍ
Puerto Cabello
Los Teques
CARACAS
Puerto la Cruz
Cumanacoa
Cerro Turimiquire 2596
Caripito
Fundación
Villa del Rosario
Cabimas
Carora
San Felipe
Valencia
Barcelona
Pedernales
Campo de la Cruz
Cerro Mamá Tará 3730
Ciudad Ojeda
Yaritagua
Maracay
Ocumare del Tuy
PARQ. NAC. GUATOPO
Clarines
Maturín
Barquisimeto
Altagracia de Orituco
Valle de Guanape
San Mateo
DELTA
Agustín Codazzi
Machiques
Bachaquero
El Tocuyo
San Carlos
Tinaco
San Juan de los Morros
Ortiz
Anaco
Punta de Mata
Plato
Lago de Maracaibo
Mene Grande
Araure
Acarigua
El Sombrero
Tucupido
Zaraza
Aragua de Barcelona
Cantaura
Tucupita
Carmen de Bolívar
Río Ariguaisa
La Ceiba
Trujillo
Ospino
Villa Bruzual
San José de Guanipa
ORINOCO
Magangué
Chiriguaná
Boconó
Embalse de Guárico
Valle de la Pascua
El Socorro
Orinoco
Mompós
Bobures
Valera
Portuguesa
El Baúl
Calabozo
Pariaguán
El Tigre
Barrancas
Curiapo
El Banco
San Carlos del Zulia
Timotes
CORD. DE MÉRIDA
Guanare
LLANOS
Encontrados
Barinitas
Guanarito
Ciudad Guayana
Magdalena
Casigua
El Vigía
Mérida
Barinas
Arismendi
Soledad
Upata
El Palmar
Convención
Libertad
Caroní
Achi
Tovar
Pico Bolívar 5002
Ciudad Bolivia
Puerto de Nutrias
Ciudad Bolívar
Pao
Ocaña
La Fría
La Grita
Camaguán
Embalse Guri
Nechí
Cúcuta
San Juan de Colón
La Unión
San Fernando de Apure
Cabruta
Mapire
802 Cerro Bolívar
El Callao
San Antonio del Táchira
San Cristóbal
Rubio
Apure
El Samán de Apure
Achaguas
Caicara
Maripa
Ciudad Piar
El Manteco
Palmarito
Arauca
Lambert Conformal Conic Projection

Northern South America

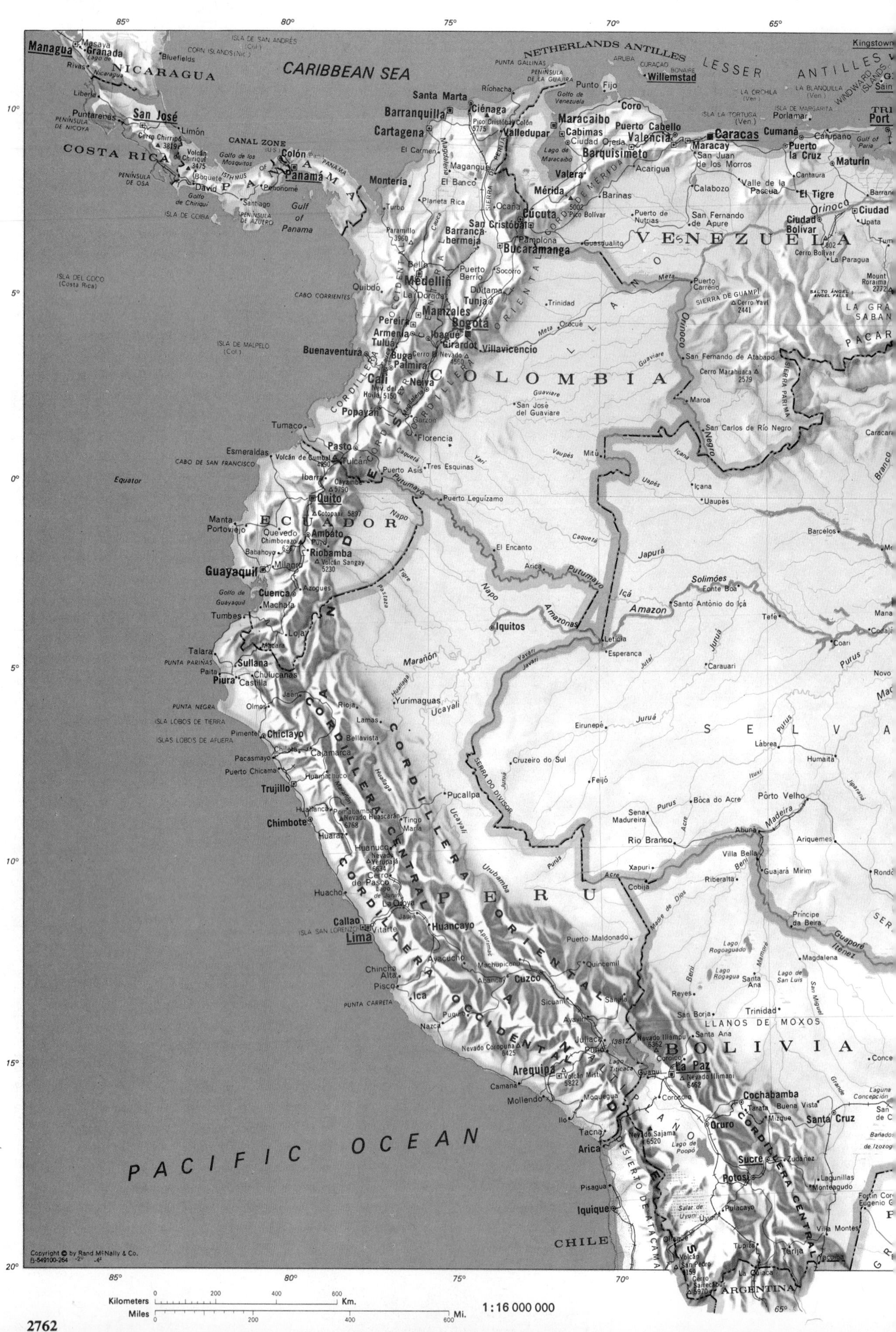

CARIBBEAN SEA
NETHERLANDS ANTILLES
LESSER ANTILLES
Managua
Granada
Masaya
Bluefields
CORN ISLANDS (Nic.)
ISLA DE SAN ANDRÉS (Col.)
NICARAGUA
Rivas
Liberia
Puntarenas
San José
Limón
PENÍNSULA DE NICOYA
COSTA RICA
Cerro Chirripó 3819
Volcán Chiriquí 3475
CANAL ZONE (U.S.)
Colón
Golfo de los Mosquitos
Panamá
PANAMA
Boquete
David
Penonomé
PENÍNSULA DE OSA
Golfo de Chiriquí
ISLA DE COIBA
Santiago
PENÍNSULA DE AZUERO
Gulf of Panama
ARUBA
CURAÇAO
BONAIRE
Willemstad
PUNTA GALLINAS
PENÍNSULA DE LA GUAJIRA
Punto Fijo
Ríohacha
Golfo de Venezuela
Santa Marta
Ciénaga
Barranquilla
Cartagena
Pico Cristóbal Colón 5775
Valledupar
Maracaibo
Cabimas
Ciudad Ojeda
Coro
Puerto Cabello
Valencia
Caracas
Cumaná
Carúpano
Gulf of Paria
Lago de Maracaibo
Barquisimeto
Maracay
San Juan de los Morros
Acarigua
Puerto la Cruz
Maturín
Cantaura
El Carmen
Magangué
El Banco
Montería
Valera
Mérida
Barinas
Calabozo
Valle de la Pascua
El Tigre
Turbo
Planeta Rica
Ocaña
Cúcuta
5002 Pico Bolívar
Puerto de Nutrias
San Fernando de Apure
Orinoco
Ciudad Bolívar
Ciudad Guayana
Upata
San Cristóbal
Barrancabermeja
Paramillo 3960
Pamplona
Bucaramanga
Guasdualito
VENEZUELA
Cerro Bolívar
La Paragua
LA ORCHILA (Ven.)
LA BLANQUILLA (Ven.)
ISLA DE MARGARITA
ISLA LA TORTUGA (Ven.)
Porlamar
Kingstown
ISLA DEL COCO (Costa Rica)
CABO CORRIENTES
Quibdó
Bello
Medellín
Puerto Berrío
Socorro
Duitama
La Dorada
Tunja
Manizales
Pereira
Bogotá
Armenia
Ibagué
Girardot
Villavicencio
Tuluá
Trinidad
Meta
Orocué
Puerto Carreño
SIERRA DE GUAMPÍ
Cerro Yaví 2441
SALTO ÁNGEL (ANGEL FALLS)
Mount Roraima 2772
LA GRAN SABANA
ISLA DE MALPELO (Col.)
Buenaventura
Buga
Palmira
Cali
Neiva
Nevado del Huila 5150
COLOMBIA
Guaviare
San José del Guaviare
San Fernando de Atabapo
Cerro Marahuaca 2579
SIERRA PARIMA
Maroa
Popayán
Garzón
Florencia
San Carlos de Río Negro
Negro
Tumaco
Pasto
Tulcán
Esmeraldas
CABO DE SAN FRANCISCO
Volcán de Cumbal 4890
Mitú
Vaupés
Puerto Asís
Tres Esquinas
Caquetá
Yarí
Içana
Uaupés
Equator
Ibarra
Cayambe 5790
Quito
Putumayo
Puerto Leguízamo
Cotopaxi 5897
Napo
ECUADOR
Manta
Portoviejo
Quevedo
Chimborazo 6267
Ambato
Babahoyo
Riobamba
Volcán Sangay 5230
Milagro
Guayaquil
El Encanto
Japurá
Barcelos
Golfo de Guayaquil
Cuenca
Azogues
Machala
Tumbes
Arica
Solimões
Fonte Boa
Içá
Santo Antônio do Içá
Amazon
Tefé
Amazonas
Iquitos
Leticia
Esperança
Coari
Loja
Talara
PUNTA PARIÑAS
Paita
Sullana
Piura
Chulucanas
Castilla
Marañón
Yavarí
Javari
Jutaí
Juruá
Carauari
Purus
PUNTA NEGRA
Olmos
Jaén
Rioja
Yurimaguas
Ucayali
ISLA LOBOS DE TIERRA
ISLAS LOBOS DE AFUERA
Pimentel
Chiclayo
Lamas
Bellavista
Eirunepé
SELVA
Chilete
Cajamarca
Pacasmayo
Puerto Chicama
Lábrea
Humaitá
Cruzeiro do Sul
SERRA DO DIVISOR
Huallaga
Trujillo
Feijó
Pucallpa
Jiparaná
Sena Madureira
Boca do Acre
Pôrto Velho
Huallanca
Nevado Huascarán 6768
Tingo María
Chimbote
Madeira
Abunã
Rio Branco
Ariquemes
Huaraz
Huánuco
Nevado Yerupajá 6634
Villa Bella
Xapurí
Guajará Mirim
Cerro de Pasco
Urubamba
Beni
Riberalta
Huacho
La Oroya
Cobija
PERU
Jauja
Callao
Lima
ISLA SAN LORENZO
Vitarte
Huancayo
Apurímac
Madre de Dios
Puerto Maldonado
Príncipe da Beira
Guaporé (Iténez)
Lago Rogoaguado
Mamoré
Magdalena
Ayacucho
Quincemil
Machupicchu
Chincha Alta
Abancay
Cuzco
Lago Rogagua
Santa Ana
Lago de San Luis
Pisco
Ica
Reyes
PUNTA CARRETA
Sicuani
Sandia
San Borja
Trinidad
San Miguel
LLANOS DE MOXOS
Nazca
Puquio
Ayaviri
Santa Ana
Nevado Coropuna 6425
Juliaca
Puno
Nevado Illampu 6362
BOLIVIA
Concepción
Lago Titicaca
La Paz
Arequipa
Volcán Misti 5822
Guaqui
Nevado Illimani 6462
Camaná
Mollendo
Moquegua
Corocoro
Cochabamba
Tarata
Buena Vista
Laguna Concepción
Mizque
Santa Cruz
Ilo
Tacna
Nevado Sajama 6520
Oruro
Lago de Poopó
PACIFIC OCEAN
Arica
Bañados de Izozog
Sucre
Zudáñez
Potosí
Lagunillas
Monteagudo
Pisagua
Fortín Coronel Eugenio Garay
Iquique
Salar de Uyuni
Uyuni
Pulacayo
Villa Montes
CHILE
DESIERTO DE ATACAMA
Tupiza
Tarija
Yacuiba
Volcán San Pedro 6159
Cerro Sairecabur 5970
La Quiaca
ARGENTINA
Copyright © by Rand McNally & Co.
B-549100-264 -2°- -4°
85° 80° 75° 70° 65°
10° 5° 0° 5° 10° 15° 20°
Kilometers 0 200 400 600 Km.
Miles 0 200 400 600 Mi.
1:16 000 000

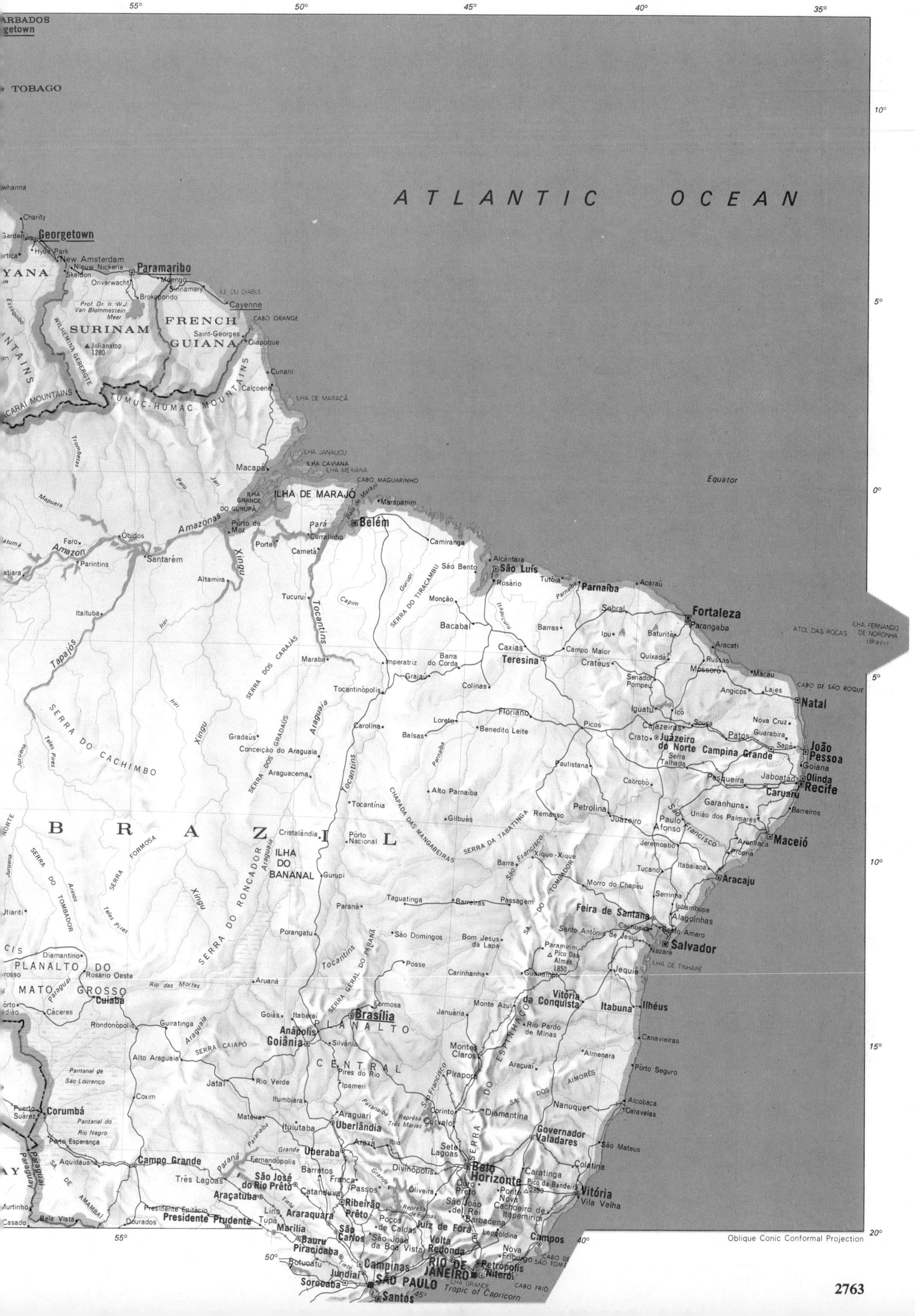

55° 50° 45° 40° 35°

BARBADOS
Georgetown
TOBAGO

10°

ATLANTIC OCEAN

Charity
Georgetown
Hyde Park
New Amsterdam
Nieuw Nickerie
Skeldon
Paramaribo
Onverwacht
Moengo
Brokopondo
Sinnamary
ÎLE DU DIABLE
Cayenne
Prof. Dr. Ir. W.J. Van Blommestein Meer
SURINAM
FRENCH GUIANA
CABO ORANGE
Saint-Georges
Oiapoque
Julianatop 1280
WILHELMINA GEBERGTE
TUMUC-HUMAC MOUNTAINS
ACARAI MOUNTAINS
Cunani
Calçoene
ILHA DE MARACÁ

5°

Trombetas
Macapá
ILHA JANAUCU
ILHA CAVIANA
ILHA MEXIANA
CABO MAGUARINHO
Equator
0°
Paru
Jari
Mapuera
ILHA GRANDE DO GURUPÁ
ILHA DE MARAJÓ
Baía de Marajó
Marapanim
Amazonas
Pôrto de Moz
Pará
Belém
Curralinho
Óbidos
Faro
Amazon
Parintins
Santarém
Portel
Cametá
Camiranga
Alcântara
São Bento
São Luís
Rosário
Tutóia
Parnaíba
Acaraú
Altamira
Xingu
Tucuruí
Tocantins
Capim
Gurupi
SERRA DO TIRACAMBU
Monção
Itapicuru
Fortaleza
Parangaba
Sobral
Itaituba
Iriri
Bacabal
Barras
Ipu
Baturité
Aracati
Tapajós
SERRA DOS CARAJÁS
Marabá
Imperatriz
Barra do Corda
Caxias
Teresina
Campo Maior
Crateús
Quixadá
Russas
Mossoró
Macau
ATOL DAS ROCAS
ILHA FERNANDO DE NORONHA (Brazil)
Grajaú
Colinas
Senador Pompeu
Angicos
Lajes
CABO DE SÃO ROQUE
5°
Tocantinópolis
Natal
SERRA DO CACHIMBO
Iriri
Floriano
Iguatu
Icó
Loreto
Benedito Leite
Picos
Nova Cruz
Guarabira
Carolina
Balsas
Cajazeiras
Sousa
Patos
Sapé
João Pessoa
Gradaús
Conceição do Araguaia
SERRA DOS GRADAÚS
Araguaia
Crato
Juàzeiro do Norte
Campina Grande
Serra Talhada
Goiana
Teles Pires
Juruena
Araguacema
Parnaíba
Paulistana
Pesqueira
Jaboatão
Olinda
Recife
Alto Parnaíba
Cabrobó
Caruaru
Tocantínia
CHAPADA DAS MANGABEIRAS
Garanhuns
Gilbués
Remanso
Petrolina
Juàzeiro
Paulo Afonso
União dos Palmares
Barreiros
BRAZIL
Cristalândia
Pôrto Nacional
SERRA DA TABATINGA
São Francisco
SERRA FORMOSA
ILHA DO BANANAL
Jeremoabo
Arapiraca
Maceió
Própria
SERRA DO RONCADOR
Barra
Xique-Xique
10°
Tucano
Itabaiana
Aracaju
SERRA DO TOMBADOR
Gurupi
Morro do Chapéu
Arinos
Serrinha
Utiariti
Xingu
Taguatinga
Barreiras
Passagem
Paranã
Feira de Santana
Inhambupe
Alagoinhas
Porangatu
São Domingos
Bom Jesus da Lapa
Santo Antônio de Jesus
Cachoeira
Santo Amaro
Salvador
Nazaré
Tocantins
SERRA GERAL DO PARANÁ
Paramirim
Pico Das Almas 1850
ILHA DE TINHARÉ
Diamantino
PLANALTO DO MATO GROSSO
Rosário Oeste
Posse
Carinhanha
Guanambi
Jequié
Paraguai
Rio das Mortes
Aruanã
Cuiabá
Cáceres
Formosa
Brasília
Vitória da Conquista
Itabuna
Ilhéus
Goiás
Itaberaí
Januária
Monte Azul
SERRA DO ESPINHAÇO
Rondonópolis
Guiratinga
Anápolis
PLANALTO CENTRAL
Rio Pardo de Minas
Goiânia
Silvânia
Araguaia
SERRA CAIAPÓ
Montes Claros
Canavieiras
15°
Alto Araguaia
Almenara
Pantanal de São Lourenço
Araçuaí
Pôrto Seguro
Pires do Rio
Jataí
Rio Verde
Ipameri
São Francisco
Pirapora
AIMORÉS
Coxim
Itumbiara
Paranaíba
Represa Três Marias
Alcobaça
Caravelas
Puerto Suárez
Corumbá
Pantanal do Rio Negro
Mateira
Araguari
Corinto
Diamantina
Nanuque
Ituiutaba
Uberlândia
Curvelo
Governador Valadares
Pôrto Esperança
Paraguai
Grande
Uberaba
Araxá
Ibiá
Sete Lagoas
São Mateus
Aquidauana
Campo Grande
Paraná
Fernandópolis
Divinópolis
Belo Horizonte
Caratinga
Colatina
Três Lagoas
SERRA DE AMAMBAÍ
Barretos
São José do Rio Prêto
Franca
Pico da Bandeira 2890
Ouro Prêto
Araçatuba
Catanduva
Passos
Oliveira
Ponte Nova
Vitória
Vila Velha
Tietê
Ribeirão Prêto
São João del Rei
Cachoeiro de Itapemirim
Murtinho
Presidente Epitácio
Represa de Furnas
Barbacena
Bela Vista
Presidente Prudente
Lins
Araraquara
Poços de Caldas
Juiz de Fora
Leopoldina
Casado
Dourados
Tupã
Marília
São Carlos
São João da Boa Vista
Campos
20°
55°
Bauru
Volta Redonda
40°
Oblique Conic Conformal Projection
Piracicaba
Nova Friburgo
CABO DE SÃO TOMÉ
50°
Botucatu
Campinas
RIO DE JANEIRO
Petrópolis
Niterói
Jundiaí
Sorocaba
SÃO PAULO
ILHA GRANDE
CABO FRIO
Santos
45°
Tropic of Capricorn

Southern South America

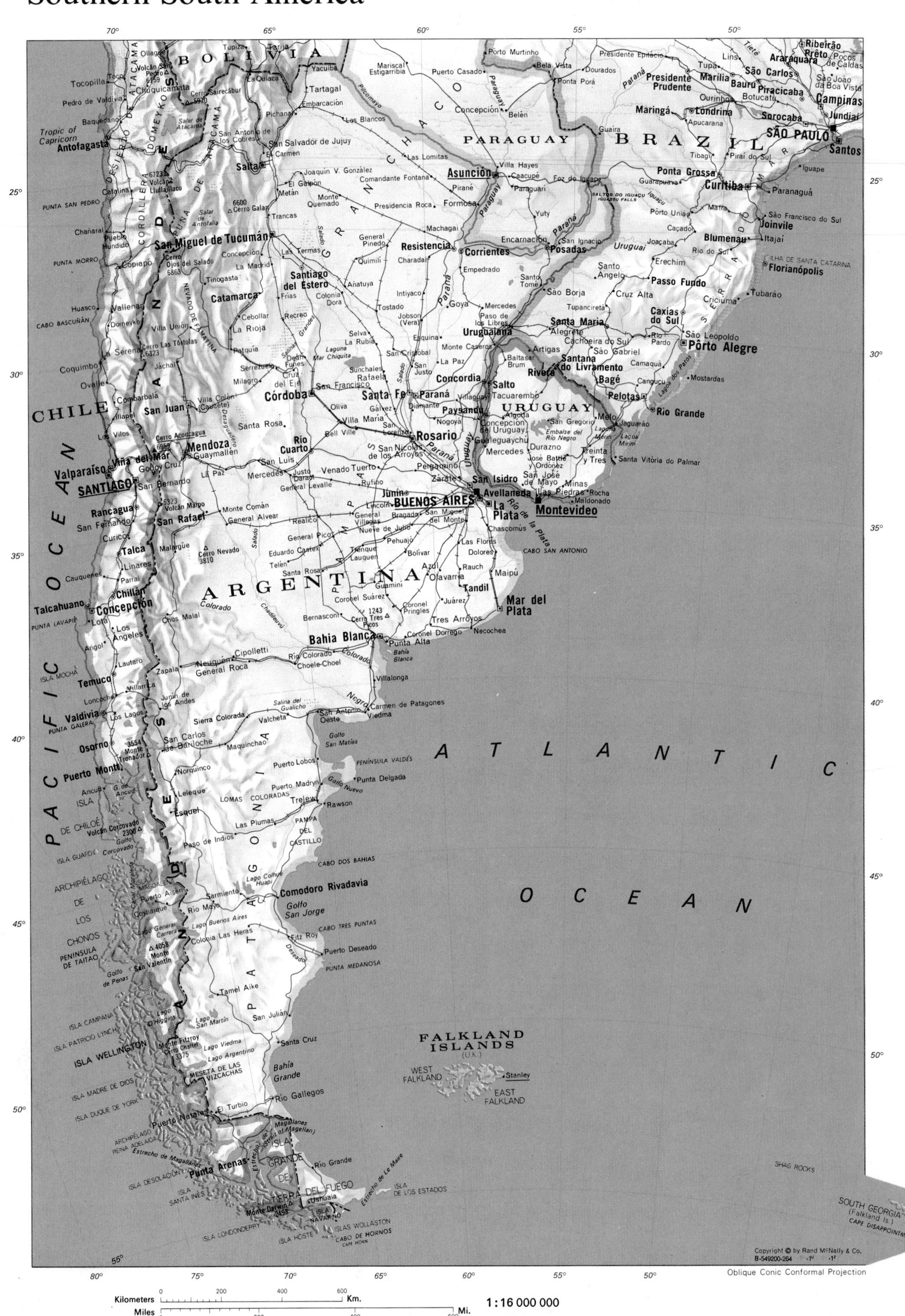

BOLIVIA
PARAGUAY
BRAZIL
CHILE
ARGENTINA
URUGUAY
PACIFIC OCEAN
ATLANTIC OCEAN
FALKLAND ISLANDS (U.K.)
WEST FALKLAND
EAST FALKLAND
Stanley
SOUTH GEORGIA (Falkland Is.)
Asunción
Montevideo
BUENOS AIRES
SANTIAGO
SÃO PAULO
Córdoba
Rosario
Mendoza
Valparaíso
Concepción
Bahia Blanca
Mar del Plata
Comodoro Rivadavia
Rio Gallegos
Punta Arenas
Ushuaia
TIERRA DEL FUEGO
Antofagasta
San Miguel de Tucumán
Pôrto Alegre
Curitiba
Tropic of Capricorn
Copyright © by Rand McNally & Co.
B-549200-264
Oblique Conic Conformal Projection
Kilometers 0 200 400 600 Km.
Miles 0 200 400 600 Mi.
1 : 16 000 000

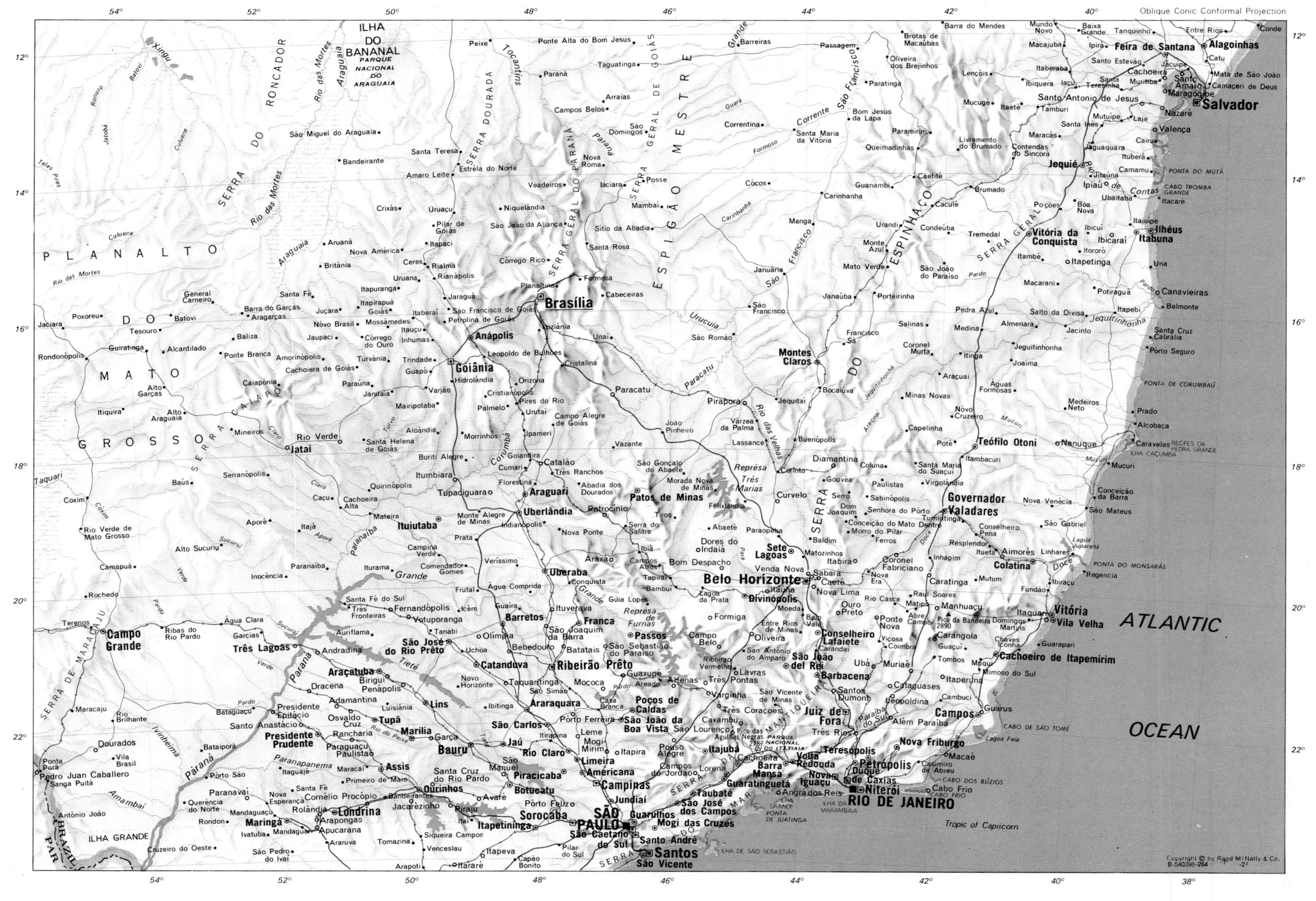

Oblique Conic Conformal Projection
ATLANTIC
OCEAN
Tropic of Capricorn
Salvador
Feira de Santana
Alagoinhas
Ilhéus
Itabuna
Vitória da Conquista
Jequié
Teófilo Otoni
Governador Valadares
Vitória
Vila Velha
Cachoeiro de Itapemirim
Colatina
Montes Claros
Belo Horizonte
Sete Lagoas
Divinópolis
Juiz de Fora
Barbacena
Petrópolis
Niterói
RIO DE JANEIRO
Nova Friburgo
Campos
Volta Redonda
Barra Mansa
Nova Iguaçu
Duque de Caxias
Brasília
Anápolis
Goiânia
Uberlândia
Uberaba
Patos de Minas
Araguari
Franca
Ribeirão Prêto
Campinas
Jundiaí
SÃO PAULO
Santos
São Vicente
Santo André
Mogi das Cruzes
São José dos Campos
Taubaté
Sorocaba
Piracicaba
Limeira
Americana
Araraquara
São Carlos
Rio Claro
Bauru
Marília
Presidente Prudente
Londrina
Maringá
Campo Grande
Três Lagoas
São José do Rio Prêto
Araçatuba
Barretos
Catanduva
Jataí
Rio Verde
ILHA DO BANANAL
PARQUE NACIONAL DO ARAGUAIA
SERRA DO ESPINHAÇO
SERRA GERAL DE GOIÁS
ESPIGÃO MESTRE
SERRA DO RONCADOR
PLANALTO DO MATO GROSSO
SERRA DE MARACAJU
SERRA DO MAR
SERRA DA MANTIQUEIRA
Represa Três Marias
Rio das Velhas
São Francisco
Grande
Paraná
Tocantins
Araguaia
Rio das Mortes
Xingu
ILHA GRANDE
BRAZIL
PAR.
Copyright © by Rand McNally & Co.

Europe

ICELAND
Reykjavík
Akureyri
Hekla 1491
VATNAJÖKULL
Arctic Circle
NORWEGIAN SEA
NORWAY
SWEDEN
FAEROE ISLANDS (Den.)
Tórshavn
SHETLAND ISLANDS
Lerwick
ROCKALL (U.K.)
ORKNEY ISLANDS
HEBRIDES
SCOTLAND
Aberdeen
Dundee
Glasgow
Edinburgh
UNITED KINGDOM
Belfast
ISLE OF MAN
IRELAND
Dublin
Cork
Newcastle
Teesside
Leeds
York
Manchester
Liverpool
Kingston upon Hull
Sheffield
Nottingham
Birmingham
Norwich
Leicester
Coventry
Swansea
Oxford
Cardiff
Bristol
LONDON
Southampton
Portsmouth
Plymouth
ATLANTIC OCEAN
NORTH SEA
DENMARK
København
Odense
Århus
Ålborg
Göteborg
Malmö
Bergen
Stavanger
Oslo
Trondheim
Stockholm
NETHERLANDS
Amsterdam
's-Gravenhage
Rotterdam
Antwerpen
Bruxelles
BELGIUM
LUXEMBOURG
Hamburg
Bremen
Hannover
GERMAN DEMOCRATIC REPUBLIC
BERLIN
Leipzig
Dresden
FEDERAL REPUBLIC OF GERMANY
Essen
Dortmund
Düsseldorf
Köln
Bonn
Frankfurt
Stuttgart
München
Nürnberg
English Channel
Le Havre
Rouen
PARIS
Lille
Reims
Strasbourg
Brest
Rennes
Nantes
Le Mans
Tours
FRANCE
Dijon
Lyon
Genève
Saint-Étienne
Grenoble
Bordeaux
Bay of Biscay
Toulouse
Marseille
Nice
Toulon
MONACO
SWITZERLAND
Zürich
Bern
Basel
Lausanne
AUSTRIA
Wien
Innsbruck
Salzburg
Graz
Praha
CZECHOSLOVAKIA
Brno
POLAND
Gdańsk
Szczecin
Poznań
Wrocław
ITALY
Milano
Torino
Genova
Venezia
Verona
Bologna
Firenze
Livorno
Roma
Napoli
Bari
Taranto
Reggio di Calabria
Palermo
Messina
Catania
SICILIA
CORSE CORSICA (Fr.)
SARDEGNA SARDINIA (It.)
Cagliari
Tyrrhenian Sea
Adriatic Sea
Ionian Sea
YUGOSLAVIA
Zagreb
Ljubljana
Trieste
Rijeka
Split
SAN MARINO
Ancona
PORTUGAL
Porto
Lisboa
SPAIN
Madrid
Barcelona
Valencia
Zaragoza
Bilbao
San Sebastián
Valladolid
Sevilla
Córdoba
Granada
Málaga
Murcia
Alicante
Cartagena
Almería
Cádiz
Gibraltar (U.K.)
La Coruña
Vigo
Oviedo
Gijón
ANDORRA
ISLAS BALEARES BALEARIC ISLANDS
Palma
MALLORCA
MEDITERRANEAN SEA
Tanger
Tétouan
Ceuta (Sp.)
Melilla (Sp.)
MOROCCO
Rabat
Casablanca
Fès
Meknès
Oujda
ALGERIA
Alger
Oran
Constantine
Annaba
ATLAS MOUNTAINS
TUNISIA
Tunis
Sfax
MALTA
Valletta
Copyright © by Rand McNally & Co.
Kilometers 0 200 400 600 Km.
Miles 0 200 400 600 Mi.
1:16 000 000

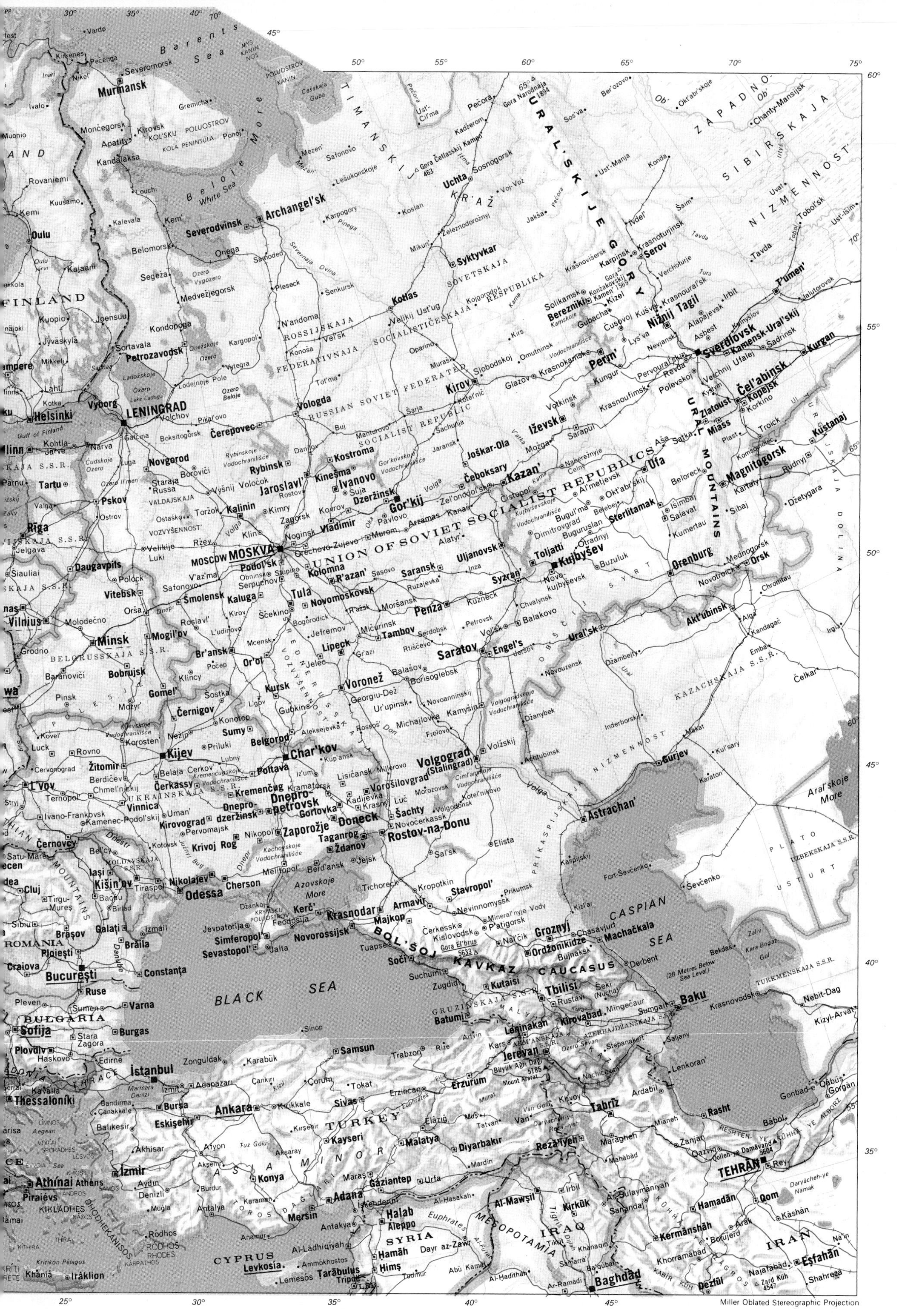
Barents Sea
Beloje More
White Sea
Murmansk
Archangel'sk
Severodvinsk
Kola Peninsula
FINLAND
Helsinki
LENINGRAD
Petrozavodsk
Vyborg
Novgorod
Pskov
Tartu
Riga
Daugavpils
Vilnius
Minsk
Kalinin
Jaroslavl'
Rybinsk
Vologda
Kostroma
Ivanovo
Gor'kij
Vladimir
MOSKVA
MOSCOW
Tula
Kaluga
Smolensk
Vitebsk
Mogil'ov
Gomel'
Br'ansk
Or'ol
Kursk
Voronež
Lipeck
Tambov
R'azan'
Penza
Saratov
Engel's
Volgograd
(Stalingrad)
Kijev
Char'kov
Poltava
Dnepropetrovsk
Doneck
Zaporožje
Rostov-na-Donu
Odessa
Nikolajev
Cherson
Kišin'ov
L'vov
Žitomir
Vinnica
Kirovograd
Krivoj Rog
Černigov
Sumy
Belgorod
Kazan'
Čeboksary
Joškar-Ola
Uljanovsk
Kujbyšev
Toljatti
Syzran'
Orenburg
Ufa
Sterlitamak
Magnitogorsk
Čel'abinsk
Sverdlovsk
Nižnij Tagil
Perm'
Iževsk
Kirov
Syktyvkar
Uchta
Kotlas
Kurgan
Tumen'
Kustanaj
Orsk
Ural'sk
Akt'ubinsk
Gurjev
Astrachan'
Elista
Stavropol'
Krasnodar
Groznyj
Machačkala
Ordžonikidze
Tbilisi
Kutaisi
Batumi
Jerevan
Baku
Kirovabad
Leninakan
Sumgait
Krasnovodsk
Nebit-Dag
Aral'skoje More
CASPIAN SEA
(28 Metres Below Sea Level)
BLACK SEA
Azovskoje More
Simferopol'
Sevastopol'
Kerč'
Novorossijsk
Soči
BOL'ŠOJ KAVKAZ
CAUCASUS
Gora El'brus 5633
UNION OF SOVIET SOCIALIST REPUBLICS
RUSSIAN SOVIET FEDERATED SOCIALIST REPUBLIC
ROSSIJSKAJA SOVETSKAJA FEDERATIVNAJA SOCIALISTIČESKAJA RESPUBLIKA
URAL'SKIJE GORY
URAL MOUNTAINS
TIMANSKIJ KR'AŽ
ZAPADNO-SIBIRSKAJA NIZMENNOST'
PRIKASPIJSKAJA NIZMENNOST'
KAZACHSKAJA S.S.R.
UKRAINSKAJA S.S.R.
BELORUSSKAJA S.S.R.
GRUZINSKAJA S.S.R.
AZERBAJDŽANSKAJA S.S.R.
ARM'ANSKAJA S.S.R.
TURKMENSKAJA S.S.R.
UZBEKSKAJA S.S.R.
PLATO USTURT
ROMANIA
București
Constanța
Brăila
Galați
Cluj
BULGARIA
Sofija
Varna
Burgas
Ruse
Plovdiv
TURKEY
ASIA MINOR
İstanbul
Ankara
Bursa
İzmir
Eskişehir
Konya
Kayseri
Adana
Mersin
Samsun
Trabzon
Erzurum
Malatya
Diyarbakır
Gaziantep
CYPRUS
Levkosía
SYRIA
Halab
Aleppo
Ḥamāh
Ḥimş
IRAQ
MESOPOTAMIA
Al-Mawşil
Kirkūk
Baghdād
IRAN
TEHRĀN
Tabrīz
Rasht
Hamadān
Qom
Eşfahān
Kermānshāh
Reżā'īyeh
Thessaloníki
Athínai
Athens
Iráklion
Miller Oblated Stereographic Projection

Scandinavia

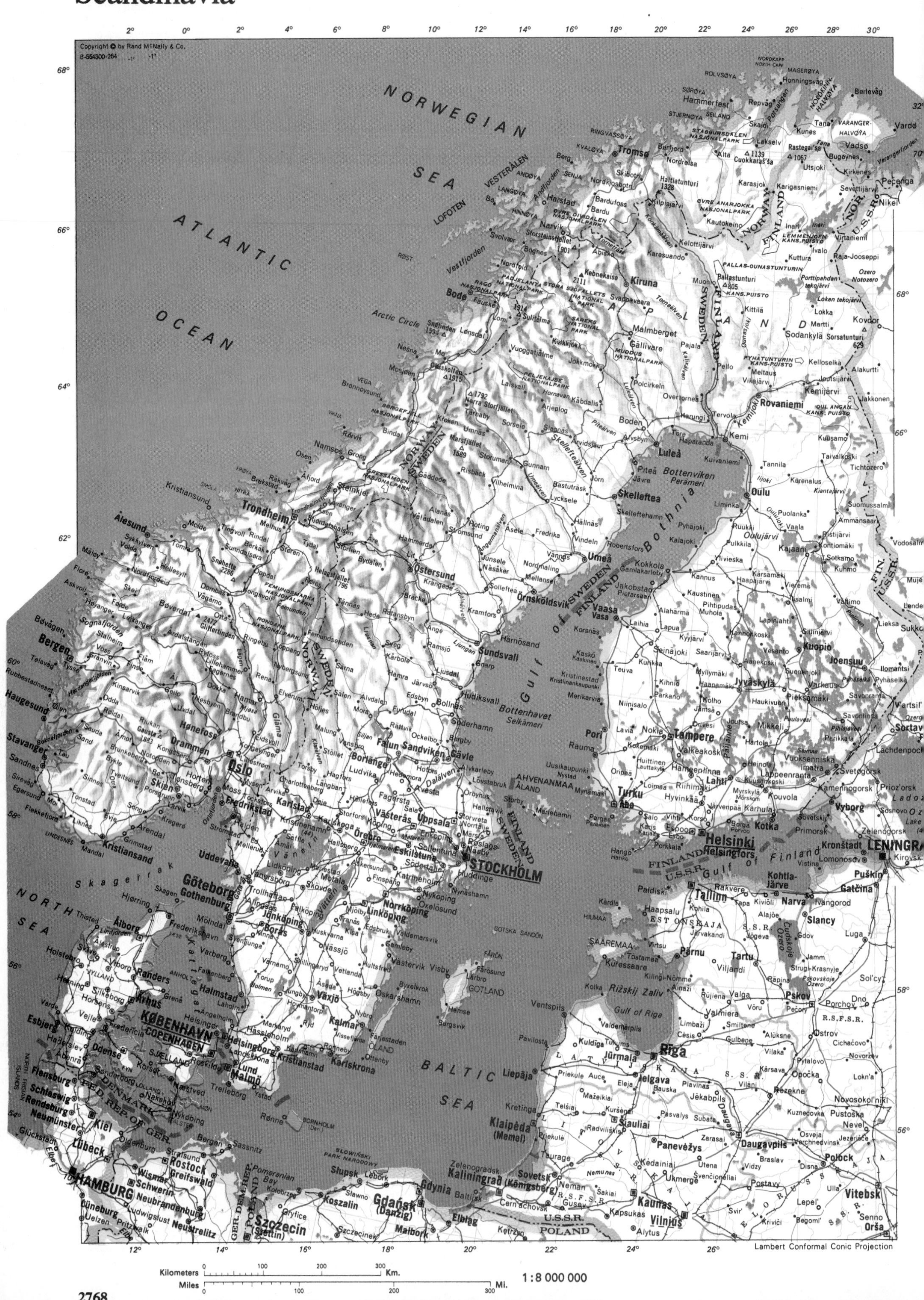

Copyright © by Rand McNally & Co.
NORWEGIAN SEA
ATLANTIC OCEAN
NORTH SEA
BALTIC SEA
Gulf of Bothnia
Bottenviken
Perämeri
Bottenhavet
Selkämeri
Gulf of Finland
Gulf of Riga
Rižskij Zaliv
Skagerrak
Kattegat
Väner
Vättern
LOFOTEN
VESTERÅLEN
GOTLAND
BORNHOLM
ÅHVENANMAA
ÅLAND
SAAREMAA
HIIUMAA
NORWAY
SWEDEN
FINLAND
DENMARK
U.S.S.R.
POLAND
FED. REP. OF GER.
GER. DEM. REP.
LAPLAND
ESTONSKAJA S.S.R.
LATVIJA
R.S.F.S.R.
OSLO
STOCKHOLM
Helsinki
Helsingfors
KØBENHAVN
COPENHAGEN
LENINGRAD
Riga
Bergen
Trondheim
Göteborg
Gothenburg
Malmö
Tampere
Turku
Åbo
Oulu
Tallinn
Kaliningrad (Königsberg)
Gdańsk (Danzig)
Szczecin (Stettin)
HAMBURG
Kiel
Lübeck
Rostock
Vilnius
Kaunas
Vitebsk
Pskov
Narva
Vyborg
Kotka
Kuopio
Joensuu
Jyväskylä
Vaasa
Umeå
Luleå
Skellefteå
Sundsvall
Östersund
Kiruna
Narvik
Tromsø
Hammerfest
Bodø
Stavanger
Kristiansand
Ålesund
Uppsala
Västerås
Örebro
Norrköping
Linköping
Jönköping
Kalmar
Karlskrona
Helsingborg
Ålborg
Århus
Odense
Esbjerg
Liepāja
Klaipėda (Memel)
Šiauliai
Daugavpils
Rovaniemi
Arctic Circle

Lambert Conformal Conic Projection

Kilometers 0 100 200 300 Km.

Miles 0 100 200 300 Mi.

1:8 000 000

British Isles

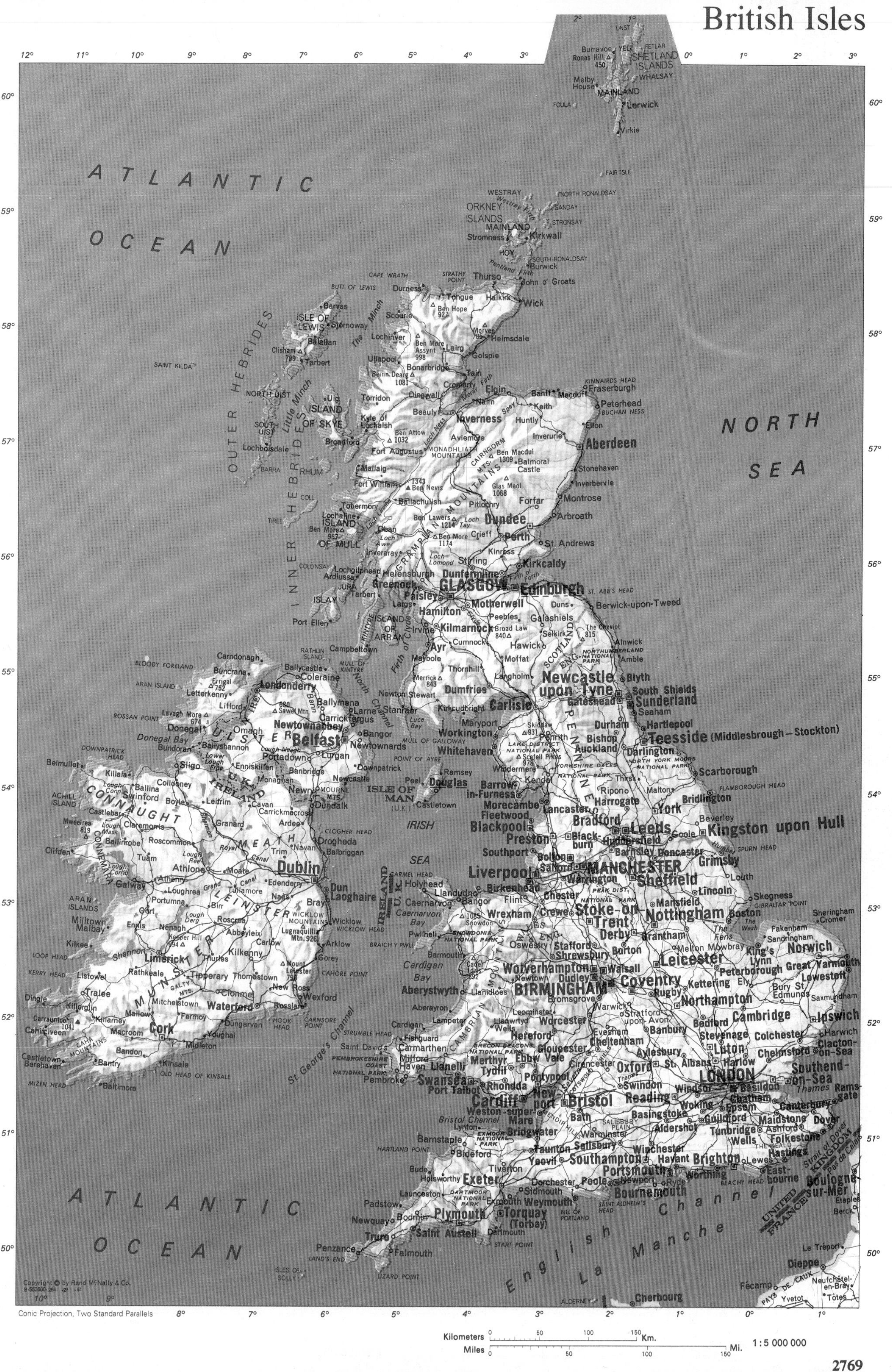

ATLANTIC OCEAN
NORTH SEA
IRISH SEA
English Channel
La Manche
St. George's Channel
North Channel
Bristol Channel
Cardigan Bay
Caernarvon Bay
Donegal Bay
The Minch
Little Minch
Firth of Clyde
Firth of Forth
Moray Firth
Pentland Firth
Strait of Dover
Pas de Calais
SHETLAND ISLANDS
MAINLAND
Lerwick
Virkie
UNST
YELL
FETLAR
WHALSAY
FOULA
FAIR ISLE
Ronas Hill 450
Burravoe
Melby House
ORKNEY ISLANDS
WESTRAY
NORTH RONALDSAY
SANDAY
STRONSAY
SOUTH RONALDSAY
HOY
Stromness
Kirkwall
Burwick
Thurso
John o' Groats
Wick
Halkirk
CAPE WRATH
STRATHY POINT
BUTT OF LEWIS
Durness
Tongue
Ben Hope 927
Helmsdale
Golspie
Lairg
Ben More Assynt 998
Lochinver
Scourie
ISLE OF LEWIS
Barvas
Stornoway
Balallan
Tarbert
Clisham 799
SAINT KILDA
OUTER HEBRIDES
NORTH UIST
SOUTH UIST
Lochboisdale
BARRA
Uig
ISLAND OF SKYE
RHUM
COLL
TIREE
COLONSAY
ISLAY
JURA
INNER HEBRIDES
Ullapool
Beinn Dearg 1081
Bonarbridge
Tain
Cromarty
Dingwall
Torridon
Kyle of Lochalsh
Beauly
Inverness
Nairn
Elgin
Banff
Macduff
Fraserburgh
KINNAIRDS HEAD
Peterhead
BUCHAN NESS
Keith
Huntly
Inverurie
Ellon
Aberdeen
Stonehaven
Inverbervie
Montrose
Arbroath
Forfar
Dundee
St. Andrews
Perth
Kinross
Kirkcaldy
Dunfermline
Edinburgh
GLASGOW
ST. ABB'S HEAD
Berwick-upon-Tweed
Aviemore
Ben Attow 1032
Fort Augustus
Broadford
Mallaig
Fort William
Ben Nevis 1343
MONADHLIATH MOUNTAINS
CAIRNGORM MTS.
Ben Macdui 1309
Balmoral Castle
Glas Maol 1068
GRAMPIAN MOUNTAINS
Pitlochry
Ballachulish
Ben Lawers 1214
Ben More 1174
Crieff
Tobermory
Lochaline
ISLAND OF MULL
Ben More 967
Oban
Inveraray
Loch Lomond
Stirling
Lochgilphead
Ardlussa
Helensburgh
Greenock
Tarbert
Paisley
Largs
Hamilton
Motherwell
Peebles
Galashiels
Duns
Selkirk
Hawick
The Cheviot 815
Kilmarnock
Broad Law 840
Irvine
ISLAND OF ARRAN
KINTYRE
Campbeltown
Port Ellen
RATHLIN ISLAND
MULL OF KINTYRE
Ayr
Cumnock
Maybole
Moffat
Thornhill
Merrick 843
Newton Stewart
Stranraer
Dumfries
Kirkcudbright
Langholm
Carlisle
MULL OF GALLOWAY
Luce Bay
SCOTLAND
ENGLAND
Alnwick
Amble
NORTHUMBERLAND NATIONAL PARK
Newcastle upon Tyne
Blyth
South Shields
Gateshead
Sunderland
Seaham
Durham
Hartlepool
Teesside (Middlesbrough – Stockton)
Bishop Auckland
Darlington
NORTH YORK MOORS NATIONAL PARK
Scarborough
FLAMBOROUGH HEAD
Bridlington
Malton
Thirsk
Ripon
Harrogate
York
Beverley
Kingston upon Hull
Goole
SPURN HEAD
Grimsby
Louth
Maryport
Workington
Whitehaven
Skiddaw 931
Penrith
LAKE DISTRICT NATIONAL PARK
Scafell Pikes 978
Windermere
Kendal
YORKSHIRE DALES NATIONAL PARK
PENNINES
POINT OF AYRE
Ramsey
ISLE OF MAN (U.K.)
Peel
Douglas
Castletown
Barrow-in-Furness
Morecambe
Lancaster
Fleetwood
Blackpool
Preston
Blackburn
Bradford
Leeds
Huddersfield
Barnsley
Doncaster
Southport
Bolton
Salford
MANCHESTER
Liverpool
Birkenhead
Warrington
Sheffield
Lincoln
Skegness
GIBRALTAR POINT
PEAK DIST. NATIONAL PARK
Chester
Flint
Mansfield
Nottingham
Boston
The Wash
Sheringham
Cromer
Fakenham
Sandringham
Norwich
Great Yarmouth
Lowestoft
King's Lynn
The Fens
CARMEL HEAD
Holyhead
Llandudno
Bangor
Caernarvon
Snowdon 1085
SNOWDONIA NATIONAL PARK
Pwllheli
BRAICH Y PWLL
Wrexham
Crewe
Stoke-on-Trent
Derby
Grantham
Melton Mowbray
Leicester
Peterborough
Oswestry
Stafford
Shrewsbury
Burton
Wolverhampton
Walsall
Coventry
Newtown
Dudley
BIRMINGHAM
Rugby
Kettering
Ely
Bury St. Edmunds
Saxmundham
Northampton
Bromsgrove
Warwick
Barmouth
Cader Idris
Aberystwyth
Llanidloes
Aberayron
CAMBRIAN MOUNTAINS
Lampeter
Cardigan
Llandrindod Wells
Leominster
Worcester
Stratford-upon-Avon
Banbury
Bedford
Cambridge
Ipswich
Harwich
Colchester
Stevenage
Luton
Chelmsford
Clacton-on-Sea
Fishguard
STRUMBLE HEAD
Saint David's
PEMBROKESHIRE COAST NATIONAL PARK
Carmarthen
Milford Haven
Pembroke
Llanelli
Swansea
Port Talbot
BRECON BEACONS NATIONAL PARK
Hereford
Merthyr Tydfil
Ebbw Vale
Gloucester
Cheltenham
Evesham
Aylesbury
St. Albans
Harlow
LONDON
Southend-on-Sea
Thames
Basildon
Chatham
Canterbury
Ramsgate
Rhondda
Pontypool
Cardiff
Newport
Bristol
Cirencester
Oxford
Swindon
Reading
Windsor
Woking
Epsom
Maidstone
Dover
Weston-super-Mare
Bath
SALISBURY PLAIN
Basingstoke
Guildford
Aldershot
Tunbridge Wells
Ashford
Folkestone
Hastings
Lynton
EXMOOR NATIONAL PARK
Bridgwater
Warminster
Barnstaple
HARTLAND POINT
Bideford
Taunton
Salisbury
Winchester
Yeovil
Southampton
Havant
Brighton
Lewes
Eastbourne
BEACHY HEAD
Portsmouth
Worthing
Newport
Ryde
Bude
Holsworthy
Exeter
Tiverton
Dorchester
Poole
Bournemouth
SAINT ALDHELM'S HEAD
Sidmouth
Weymouth
BILL OF PORTLAND
Exmouth
Launceston
DARTMOOR NATIONAL PARK
Torquay (Torbay)
Dartmouth
START POINT
Plymouth
Padstow
Newquay
Bodmin
Truro
Saint Austell
Falmouth
Penzance
LAND'S END
ISLES OF SCILLY
LIZARD POINT
ALDERNEY
Cherbourg
UNITED KINGDOM
FRANCE
Boulogne-sur-Mer
Étaples
Berck
Le Tréport
Dieppe
Fécamp
PAYS DE CAUX
Yvetot
Neufchâtel-en-Bray
Tôtes
BLOODY FORELAND
ARAN ISLAND
Carndonagh
Buncrana
Errigal 752
Letterkenny
Londonderry
Coleraine
Ballycastle
Lifford
Ballymena
Bann
Sawel Mtn. 680
Larne
Carrickfergus
Newtownabbey
Bangor
Belfast
Newtownards
Omagh
ULSTER
Lavagh More 674
Donegal
ROSSAN POINT
Ballyshannon
Bundoran
Lower Lough Erne
Enniskillen
Lough Neagh
Portadown
Lurgan
Banbridge
Downpatrick
Monaghan
Newcastle
Newry
MOURNE MTS.
Dundalk
U.K.
IRELAND
DOWNPATRICK HEAD
Belmullet
Killala
Sligo
Collooney
Ballina
Lough Conn
Swinford
Boyle
Leitrim
Cavan
Carrickmacross
ACHILL ISLAND
Castlebar
CONNAUGHT
Claremorris
Granard
Ardee
CLOGHER HEAD
Drogheda
Balbriggan
Mweelrea 819
Lough Mask
Ballinrobe
Roscommon
MEATH
Trim
Navan
Royal Canal
Clifden
CONNEMARA
Tuam
Lough Ree
Athlone
Moate
Dublin
Dun Laoghaire
Lough Corrib
Galway
Athenry
Grand Canal
Tullamore
Edenderry
Naas
Bray
ARAN ISLANDS
Loughrea
Portumna
Birr
LEINSTER
WICKLOW MOUNTAINS
Wicklow
WICKLOW HEAD
Lugnaquillia Mtn. 926
Milltown Malbay
Gort
Lough Derg
Roscrea
Ennis
Nenagh
Abbeyleix
Carlow
Arklow
Kilkee
Shannon
Keeper Hill 694
Kilkenny
Gorey
LOOP HEAD
Limerick
Thurles
Mount Leinster 796
CAHORE POINT
KERRY HEAD
Listowel
Rathkeale
Tipperary
Thomastown
New Ross
Wexford
Tralee
GALTY MTS.
MUNSTER
Dingle
Killorglin
Mitchelstown
Waterford
Rosslare
CARNSORE POINT
Carrauntoohil 1041
Killarney
Mallow
Fermoy
HOOK HEAD
Cahirciveen
Macroom
Cork
Dungarvan
Youghal
MACGILLYCUDDY'S REEKS
CAHA MOUNTAINS
Bandon
Midleton
Castletown Berehaven
Bantry
Kinsale
OLD HEAD OF KINSALE
MIZEN HEAD
Baltimore
Copyright © by Rand McNally & Co.
Conic Projection, Two Standard Parallels
Kilometers 0 50 100 150 Km.
Miles 0 50 100 150 Mi.
1:5 000 000

Central Europe

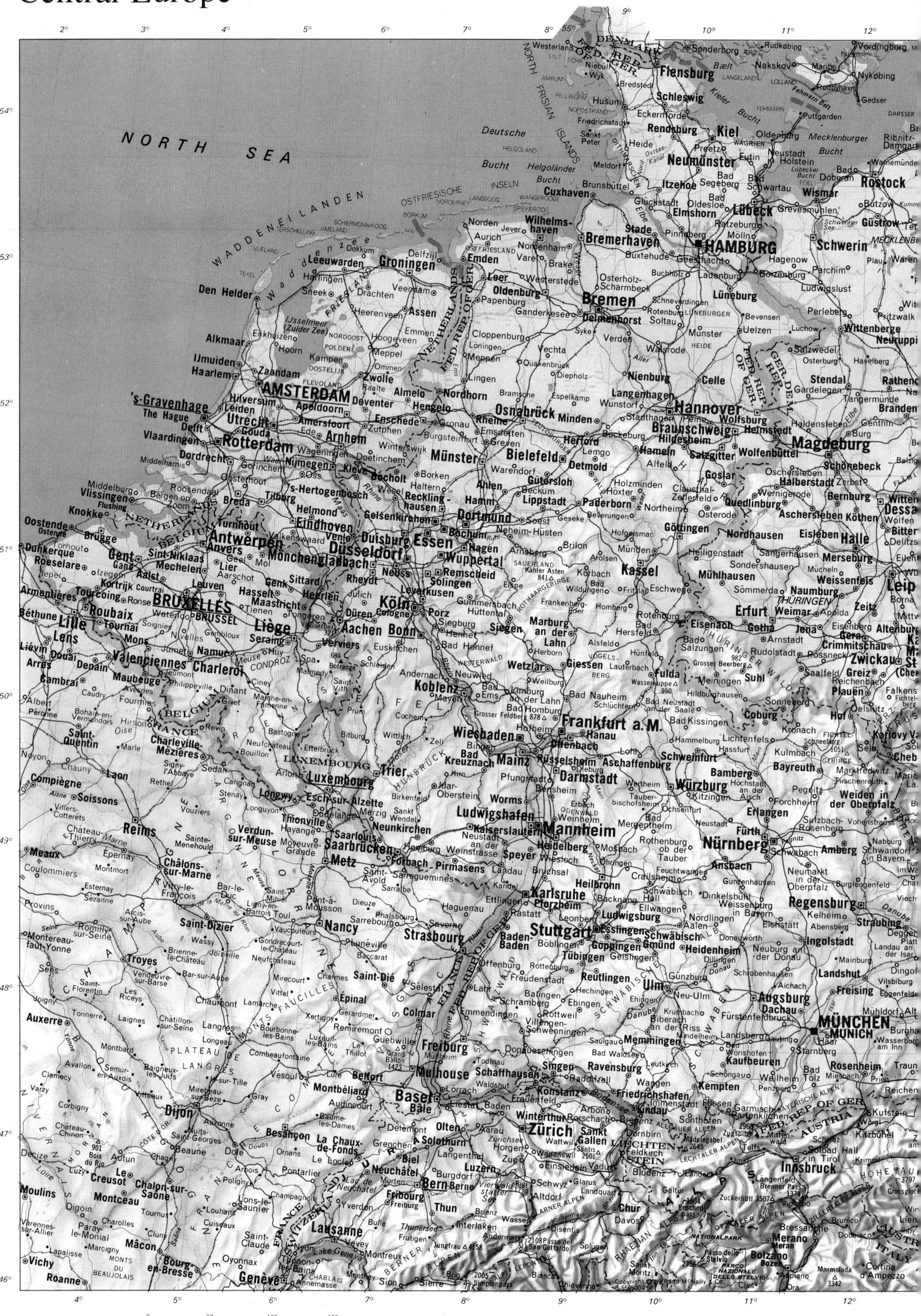

NORTH SEA
WADDENEILANDEN
Waddenzee
NORTH FRISIAN ISLANDS
Deutsche Bucht
Helgoländer Bucht
OSTFRIESISCHE INSELN
DENMARK
FED. REP. OF GER.
NETHERLANDS
BELGIUM
LUXEMBOURG
FRANCE
SWITZERLAND
AUSTRIA
LIECHTENSTEIN
ITALY
GER. DEM. REP.
AMSTERDAM
's-Gravenhage
The Hague
Rotterdam
Utrecht
BRUXELLES
BRUSSEL
Antwerpen
Liège
Lille
Düsseldorf
Köln
Essen
Dortmund
Bremen
HAMBURG
Hannover
Kiel
Lübeck
Rostock
Schwerin
Magdeburg
Halle
Kassel
Frankfurt a.M.
Mainz
Wiesbaden
Koblenz
Bonn
Mannheim
Ludwigshafen
Karlsruhe
Stuttgart
Nürnberg
Würzburg
Regensburg
Augsburg
MÜNCHEN
MUNICH
Ulm
Strasbourg
Metz
Nancy
Reims
Dijon
Besançon
Basel
Zürich
Bern
Genève
Lausanne
Luzern
Innsbruck
Freiburg
Saarbrücken
Trier
Luxembourg
Kilometers
0
50
100
150
Km.
Miles
0
50
100
150
Mi.
1:4 000 000

BALTIC SEA
Gulf of Danzig
Pomeranian Bay
Kaliningrad (Königsberg)
Gdańsk (Danzig)
Gdynia
Sopot
Szczecin (Stettin)
Bydgoszcz
Toruń
Olsztyn (Allenstein)
Białystok
Grodno
Brest
Poznań
BERLIN
WARSZAWA WARSAW
Łódź
Radom
Lublin
Wrocław (Breslau)
Dresden
Częstochowa
Kielce
Katowice
Kraków
PRAHA PRAGUE
Brno
Ostrava
CARPATHIAN MOUNTAINS
Košice
Bratislava
WIEN VIENNA
Linz
Graz
Miskolc
Debrecen
BUDAPEST
Szeged
Pécs
Oradea
Arad
Győr
POLAND
U.S.S.R.
CZECHOSLOVAKIA
HUNGARY
ROMANIA
YUGOSLAVIA
GER. DEM. REP.
WIELKOPOLSKA
MORAVA
Balaton
ojection, Two Standard Parallels

France and the Alps

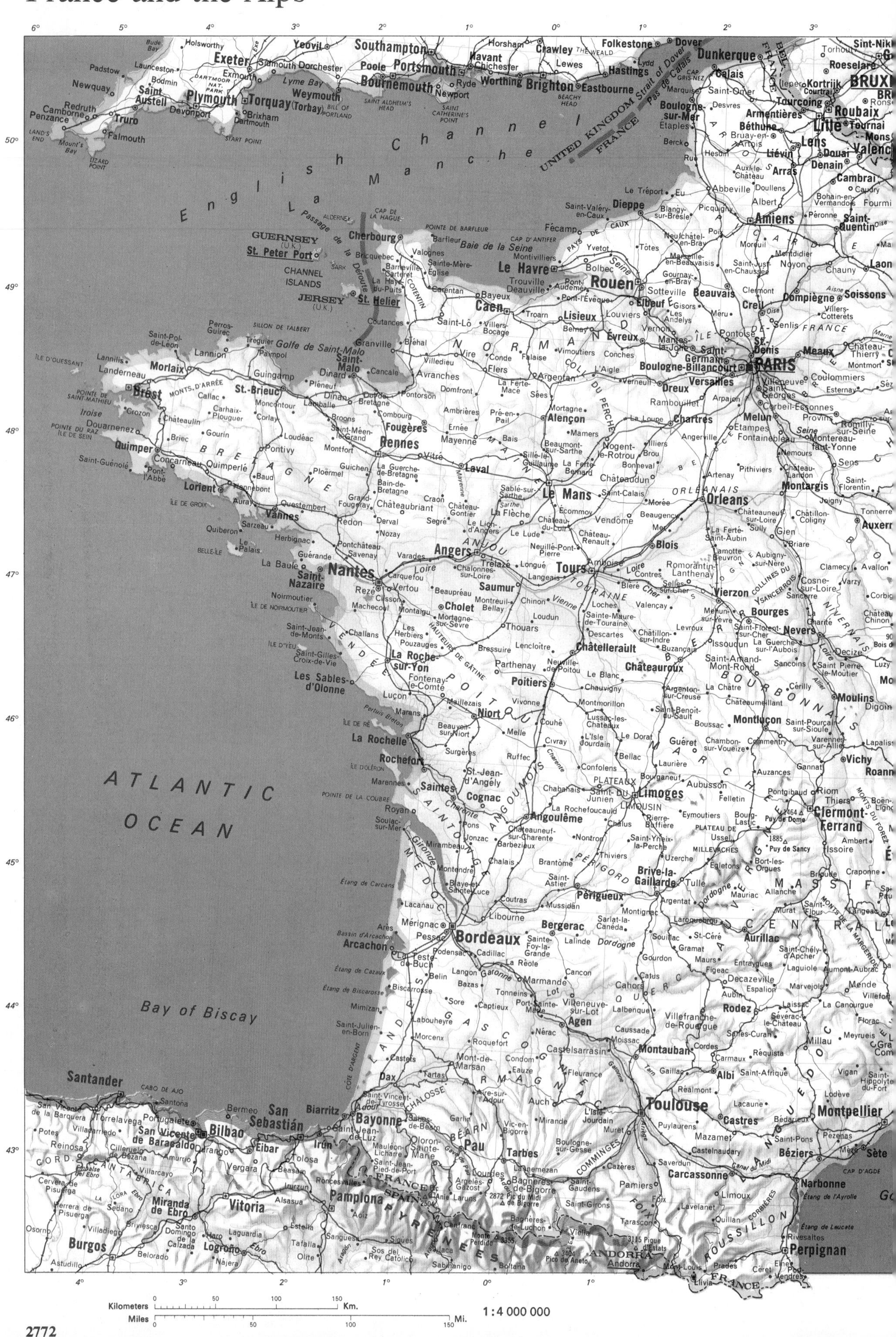
English Channel
La Manche
ATLANTIC OCEAN
Bay of Biscay
CHANNEL ISLANDS
GUERNSEY (U.K.)
St. Peter Port
JERSEY (U.K.)
St. Helier
UNITED KINGDOM
FRANCE
Strait of Dover
Pas de Calais
Southampton
Portsmouth
Bournemouth
Brighton
Plymouth
Exeter
Torquay (Torbay)
Dover
Folkestone
Hastings
Eastbourne
Dunkerque
Calais
Lille
Roubaix
Amiens
Cherbourg
Le Havre
Rouen
Caen
Dieppe
Beauvais
Compiègne
Soissons
Reims
PARIS
Versailles
Boulogne-Billancourt
Saint-Denis
Meaux
Chartres
Orleans
Le Mans
Laval
Rennes
Saint-Malo
St.-Brieuc
Morlaix
Brest
Quimper
Lorient
Vannes
Nantes
Saint-Nazaire
Angers
Tours
Blois
Bourges
Nevers
Vierzon
Saumur
Cholet
Poitiers
Châtellerault
Châteauroux
La Roche-sur-Yon
Les Sables-d'Olonne
Niort
La Rochelle
Rochefort
Saintes
Cognac
Angoulême
Limoges
Clermont-Ferrand
Vichy
Moulins
Montluçon
Périgueux
Brive-la-Gaillarde
Bordeaux
Arcachon
Bergerac
Agen
Montauban
Toulouse
Albi
Castres
Rodez
Aurillac
Montpellier
Béziers
Sète
Narbonne
Carcassonne
Perpignan
Pau
Tarbes
Bayonne
Biarritz
Dax
Lourdes
Andorra
ANDORRA
Santander
Bilbao
San Sebastián
Vitoria
Pamplona
Burgos
Logroño
Irún
BRETAGNE
NORMANDIE
ANJOU
TOURAINE
POITOU
VENDÉE
BERRY
LIMOUSIN
AUVERGNE
MASSIF CENTRAL
GASCOGNE
ARMAGNAC
LANDES
BÉARN
LANGUEDOC
ROUSSILLON
PYRENEES
Loire
Seine
Gironde
Dordogne
Garonne
Kilometers
Km.
Miles
Mi.
1 : 4 000 000

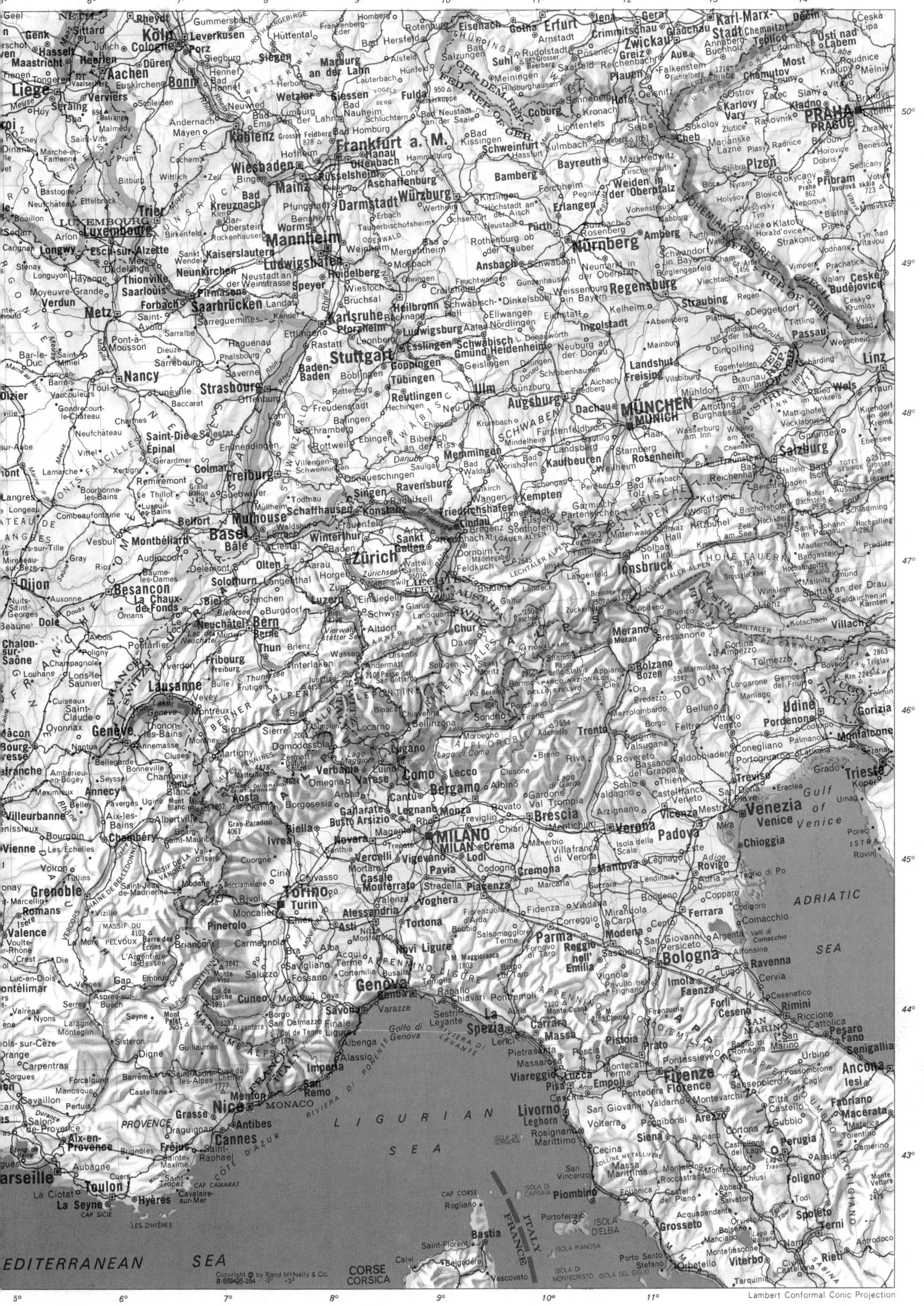

Köln
Cologne
Bonn
Aachen
Liège
Koblenz
Frankfurt a. M.
Wiesbaden
Mainz
Darmstadt
Würzburg
Mannheim
Ludwigshafen
Heidelberg
Saarbrücken
Metz
Nancy
Luxembourg
Karlsruhe
Stuttgart
Strasbourg
Nürnberg
Regensburg
München
MUNICH
Augsburg
Ulm
Erfurt
Zwickau
Karl-Marx-Stadt
Plzeň
PRAHA
PRAGUE
Passau
Linz
Salzburg
Innsbruck
Basel
Bâle
Zürich
Bern
Mulhouse
Dijon
Besançon
Lausanne
Genève
Grenoble
Torino
Turin
MILANO
MILAN
Bergamo
Brescia
Verona
Venezia
Venice
Padova
Trieste
Bologna
Genova
La Spezia
Firenze
Florence
Livorno
Leghorn
Nice
Cannes
Toulon
Marseille
Ancona
Perugia
Gulf of Venice
ADRIATIC SEA
LIGURIAN SEA
MEDITERRANEAN SEA
CORSE
CORSICA
MONACO
SAN MARINO
ALPS
Copyright © by Rand McNally & Co.
Lambert Conformal Conic Projection

Spain and Portugal

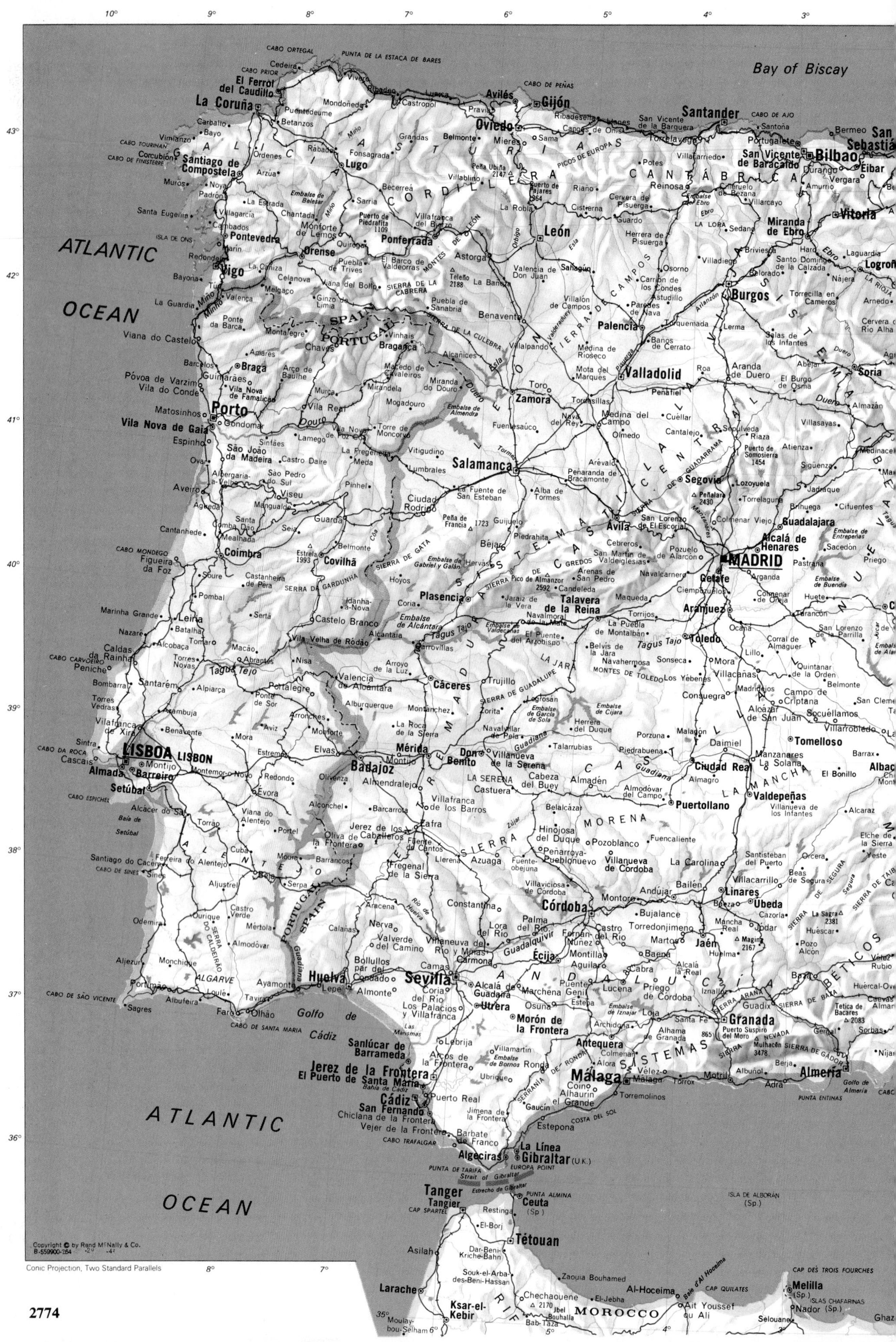

Bay of Biscay
ATLANTIC
OCEAN
ATLANTIC
OCEAN
CABO ORTEGAL
PUNTA DE LA ESTACA DE BARES
CABO DE PEÑAS
CABO DE AJO
CABO TOURIÑAN
CABO DE FINISTERRE
ISLA DE ONS
CABO MONDEGO
CABO CARVOEIRO
CABO DA ROCA
CABO ESPICHEL
CABO DE SINES
CABO DE SÃO VICENTE
CABO DE SANTA MARIA
CABO TRAFALGAR
PUNTA DE TARIFA
EUROPA POINT
PUNTA ALMINA
CAP SPARTEL
PUNTA ENTINAS
CAP DES TROIS FOURCHES
CAP QUILATES
ISLA DE ALBORÁN (Sp.)
ISLAS CHAFARINAS
El Ferrol del Caudillo
La Coruña
Cedeira
Betanzos
Mondoñedo
Ribadeo
Luarca
Avilés
Gijón
Oviedo
Ribadesella
Llanes
San Vicente de la Barquera
Santander
Santoña
Torrelavega
Portugalete
Bermeo
San Sebastián
Bilbao
San Vicente de Baracaldo
Durango
Eibar
Vergara
Vitoria
Miranda de Ebro
Logroño
Carballo
Bayo
Vimianzo
Corcubión
Santiago de Compostela
Arzúa
Lugo
Noya
Muros
Padrón
La Estrada
Villagarcía
Cambados
Pontevedra
Marín
Redondela
Vigo
Bayona
La Guardia
Valença
Monção
Melgaço
Orense
Celanova
Ginzo de Limia
Monforte de Lemos
Chantada
Sarria
Becerreá
Fonsagrada
Grandas
Belmonte
Mieres
Sama
Cangas de Onís
Pola de Siero
Villablino
Peña Ubiña 2147
Puerto de Pajares 1364
La Robla
Riaño
Cistierna
Guardo
Cervera de Pisuerga
Reinosa
Potes
Villarcayo
Villacarriedo
León
Ponferrada
Astorga
Villafranca del Bierzo
Puerto de Piedrafita 1109
Puebla de Trives
El Barco de Valdeorras
Teleño 2188
La Bañeza
Valencia de Don Juan
Sahagún
Herrera de Pisuerga
Osorno
Carrión de los Condes
Villadiego
Briviesca
Haro
Santo Domingo de la Calzada
Nájera
Belorado
Burgos
Torrecilla en Cameros
Arnedo
Cervera del Río Alhama
Astudillo
Paredes de Nava
Palencia
Torquemada
Lerma
Salas de los Infantes
Puebla de Sanabria
Benavente
Villalón de Campos
Villalpando
Medina de Rioseco
Mota del Marqués
Valladolid
Baños de Cerrato
Roa
Aranda de Duero
Peñafiel
El Burgo de Osma
Soria
Almazán
Medinaceli
Sigüenza
Atienza
Riaza
Sepúlveda
Puerto de Somosierra 1454
Cuéllar
Cantalejo
Olmedo
Medina del Campo
Tordesillas
Toro
Zamora
Nava del Rey
Fuentesaúco
Arévalo
Peñaranda de Bracamonte
Segovia
Peñalara 2430
Lozoyuela
Torrelaguna
Jadraque
Brihuega
Cifuentes
Guadalajara
Alcalá de Henares
Sacedón
Pastrana
Priego
Colmenar Viejo
San Lorenzo de El Escorial
Ávila
Cebreros
San Martín de Valdeiglesias
Pozuelo de Alarcón
MADRID
Getafe
Arganda
Navalcarnero
Ciempozuelos
Colmenar de Oreja
Huete
Tarancón
Aranjuez
Ocaña
Toledo
Torrijos
La Puebla de Montalbán
Talavera de la Reina
Maqueda
Arenas de San Pedro
Pico de Almanzor 2592
Candeleda
Jaraíz de la Vera
Navalmoral de la Mata
El Puente del Arzobispo
Belvís de la Jara
Navahermosa
Sonseca
Mora
Villacañas
Madridejos
Consuegra
Los Yébenes
Lillo
Corral de Almaguer
Quintanar de la Orden
Belmonte
Campo de Criptana
Alcázar de San Juan
Socuéllamos
Tomelloso
Villarrobledo
Daimiel
Manzanares
La Solana
Ciudad Real
Almagro
Valdepeñas
Villanueva de los Infantes
Puertollano
Almodóvar del Campo
Piedrabuena
Porzuna
Malagón
Almadén
Salamanca
Vitigudino
Lumbrales
Ciudad Rodrigo
La Fuente de San Esteban
Alba de Tormes
Guijuelo
Piedrahita
Béjar
Peña de Francia 1723
Hervás
Plasencia
Coria
Hoyos
Alcántara
Garrovillas
Arroyo de la Luz
Cáceres
Trujillo
Logrosán
Zorita
Montánchez
Mérida
Don Benito
Villanueva de la Serena
Castuera
Cabeza del Buey
Herrera del Duque
Talarrubias
Navalvillar de Pela
La Roca de la Sierra
Badajoz
Montijo
Almendralejo
Olivenza
Villafranca de los Barros
Zafra
Jerez de los Caballeros
Fregenal de la Sierra
Fuente de Cantos
Llerena
Azuaga
Fuente-obejuna
Peñarroya-Pueblonuevo
Hinojosa del Duque
Pozoblanco
Villanueva de Córdoba
Fuencaliente
La Carolina
Bailén
Linares
Úbeda
Andújar
Montoro
Córdoba
Constantina
Aracena
Nerva
Valverde del Camino
Huelva
Lepe
Ayamonte
Almonte
Bollullos par del Condado
Sevilla
Alcalá de Guadaira
Utrera
Coria del Río
Los Palacios y Villafranca
Carmona
Écija
Marchena
Osuna
Estepa
Lucena
Puente Genil
Montilla
Aguilar
Baena
Priego de Córdoba
Alcalá la Real
Jaén
Martos
Torredonjimeno
Castro del Río
Bujalance
Palma del Río
Lora del Río
Villanueva del Río y Minas
Morón de la Frontera
Lebrija
Sanlúcar de Barrameda
Jerez de la Frontera
El Puerto de Santa María
Cádiz
San Fernando
Chiclana de la Frontera
Vejer de la Frontera
Barbate de Franco
Puerto Real
Arcos de la Frontera
Ubrique
Villamartín
Ronda
Jimena de la Frontera
Gaucín
Estepona
La Línea
Gibraltar (U.K.)
Algeciras
Strait of Gibraltar
Estrecho de Gibraltar
Antequera
Archidona
Loja
Álora
Coín
Alhaurín el Grande
Málaga
Torremolinos
Vélez-Málaga
Torrox
Motril
Alhama de Granada
Santa Fe
Granada
Puerto Suspiro del Moro 865
Mulhacén 3478
Guadix
Baza
Huéscar
Cazorla
Jódar
Mancha Real
Huelma
Sierra Mágina 2167
La Sagra 2381
Pozo Alcón
Orcera
Villacarrillo
Beas de Segura
Santisteban del Puerto
Albuñol
Adra
Berja
Almería
Gérgal
Tabernas
Sorbas
Níjar
Tetica de Bacares 2083
Vélez Rubio
Huércal-Overa
Cuevas de Almanzora
Elche de la Sierra
Yeste
Alcaraz
El Bonillo
Golfo de Almería
Golfo de Cádiz
Las Marismas
Bahía de Cádiz
Viana do Castelo
Ponte da Barca
Ponte de Lima
Montalegre
Chaves
Vinhais
Bragança
Macedo de Cavaleiros
Mirandela
Miranda do Douro
Mogadouro
Torre de Moncorvo
Vila Nova de Foz Côa
Barcelos
Braga
Guimarães
Póvoa de Varzim
Vila do Conde
Vila Nova de Famalicão
Amares
Arco de Baulhe
Murça
Vila Real
Matosinhos
Porto
Vila Nova de Gaia
Gondomar
Espinho
Ovar
São João da Madeira
Lamego
Sinfães
Castro Daire
Meda
Pinhel
Guarda
Aveiro
Águeda
Albergaria-a-Velha
São Pedro do Sul
Viseu
Mangualde
Santa Comba Dão
Seia
Mealhada
Cantanhede
Coimbra
Figueira da Foz
Soure
Pombal
Estrela 1993
Covilhã
Belmonte
Castanheira de Pera
Idanha-a-Nova
Sertã
Castelo Branco
Vila Velha de Ródão
Marinha Grande
Leiria
Batalha
Nazaré
Alcobaça
Tomar
Caldas da Rainha
Peniche
Torres Novas
Abrantes
Nisa
Macão
Bombarral
Santarém
Alpiarça
Torres Vedras
Portalegre
Ponte de Sor
Valencia de Alcántara
Alburquerque
Arronches
Avis
Monforte
Elvas
Estremoz
Vilafranca de Xira
Azambuja
Benavente
Mora
Sintra
Cascais
LISBOA
LISBON
Almada
Montijo
Barreiro
Setúbal
Montemor-o-Novo
Redondo
Évora
Alconchel
Barcarrota
Alcácer do Sal
Baía de Setúbal
Torrão
Viana do Alentejo
Portel
Moura
Barrancos
Cuba
Santiago do Cacém
Sines
Ferreira do Alentejo
Beja
Serpa
Aljustrel
Castro Verde
Mértola
Odemira
Ourique
Almodôvar
Aljezur
Monchique
Portimão
Albufeira
Loulé
Faro
Olhão
Tavira
Sagres
ALGARVE
SERRA DO CALDEIRÃO
ALENTEJO
GALICIA
ASTURIAS
CORDILLERA CANTÁBRICA
PICOS DE EUROPA
MONTES DE LEÓN
SIERRA DE LA CABRERA
SIERRA DE LA CULEBRA
TIERRA DE CAMPOS
SISTEMA IBÉRICO
SISTEMA CENTRAL
SIERRA DE GUADARRAMA
SIERRA DE GREDOS
SIERRA DE GATA
SIERRA DA GARDUNHA
MONTES DE TOLEDO
LA JARA
SIERRA DE GUADALUPE
EXTREMADURA
CASTILLA LA NUEVA
CASTILLA LA VIEJA
LEÓN
LA MANCHA
LA SERENA
SIERRA MORENA
ANDALUCÍA
SISTEMAS BÉTICOS
SIERRA DE SEGURA
SIERRA NEVADA
SIERRA DE GÁDOR
SERRANÍA DE RONDA
SIERRA DE BAZA
SIERRA ARANA
LA RIOJA
LA LORA
COSTA DEL SOL
SPAIN
PORTUGAL
Embalse de Belesar
Embalse de Almendra
Embalse de Gabriel y Galán
Embalse de Alcántara
Embalse de Valdecañas
Embalse de García de Sola
Embalse de Cijara
Embalse de Entrepeñas
Embalse de Buendía
Embalse del Ebro
Embalse de Bornos
Embalse de Iznájar
Miño
Duero
Douro
Esla
Órbigo
Pisuerga
Arlanzón
Ebro
Tormes
Côa
Tagus
Tajo
Tejo
Guadiana
Guadalquivir
Zújar
Río Tinto
Río de Huelva
Tanger
Tangier
Ceuta (Sp.)
Restinga
El-Borj
Tétouan
Asilah
Dar-Beni-Kriche-Bahn
Souk-el-Arba-des-Beni-Hassan
Larache
Ksar-el-Kebir
Moulay-bou-Selham
Chechaouene 2170
Zaouia Bouhamed
El-Jebha
Jbel Bouhalla
Bab-Taza
Al-Hoceima
Baie d'Al Hoceima
Aït Youssef ou Ali
MOROCCO
RIF
Melilla (Sp.)
Nador (Sp.)
Selouane
10°
9°
8°
7°
6°
5°
4°
3°
43°
42°
41°
40°
39°
38°
37°
36°
35°

Conic Projection, Two Standard Parallels

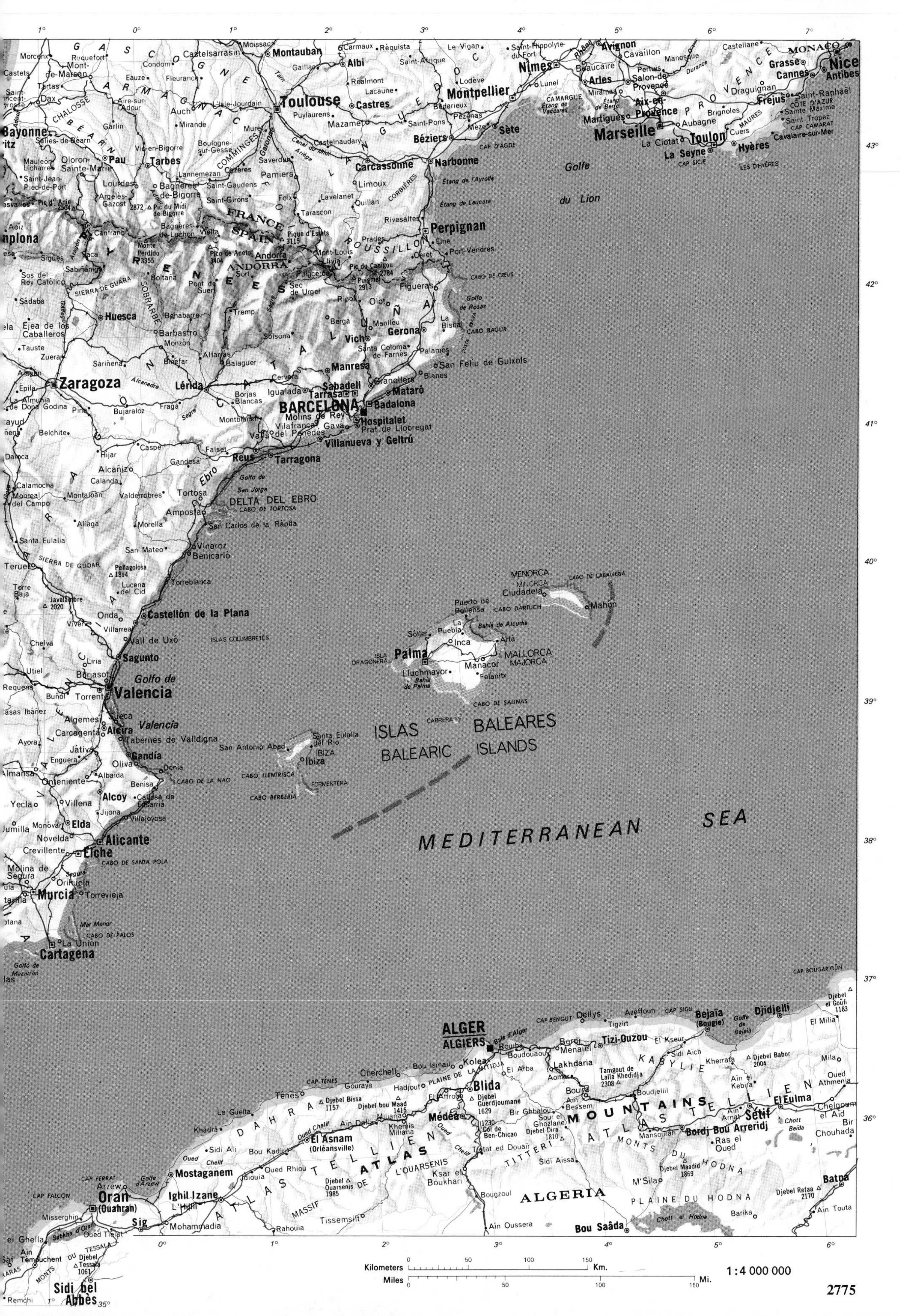

GASCOGNE
ARMAGNAC
BÉARN
CHALOSSE
COMMINGES
LANGUEDOC
ROUSSILLON
PROVENCE
CAMARGUE
CORBIÈRES
PYRENEES
ANDORRA
CATALUÑA
SOBRARBE
SIERRA DE GUARA
SIERRA DE GÚDAR
VALENCIA
FRANCE
SPAIN
Montauban
Toulouse
Albi
Castres
Carcassonne
Narbonne
Béziers
Sète
Montpellier
Nîmes
Avignon
Arles
Aix-en-Provence
Marseille
Toulon
Hyères
La Seyne
La Ciotat
Aubagne
Cannes
Grasse
Nice
Antibes
Fréjus
Saint-Raphaël
Draguignan
MONACO
Perpignan
Pau
Tarbes
Lourdes
Bayonne
Auch
Foix
Pamiers
Limoux
Golfe du Lion
CAP D'AGDE
CAP SICIÉ
CÔTE D'AZUR
LES D'HYÈRES
Huesca
Zaragoza
Lérida
Gerona
Figueras
Vich
Manresa
Sabadell
Tarrasa
Mataró
BARCELONA
Badalona
Hospitalet
Villanueva y Geltrú
Tarragona
Reus
Tortosa
Amposta
DELTA DEL EBRO
CABO DE TORTOSA
Ebro
Golfo de San Jorge
Vinaroz
Benicarló
Teruel
Castellón de la Plana
ISLAS COLUMBRETES
Sagunto
Valencia
Golfo de Valencia
Alcira
Gandía
Denia
CABO DE LA NAO
Alcoy
Elda
Alicante
Elche
CABO DE SANTA POLA
Murcia
Torrevieja
Mar Menor
CABO DE PALOS
Cartagena
Golfo de Mazarrón
Pico de Aneto 3404
Monte Perdido 3355
Pique d'Estats 3115
Pic du Canigou 2784
Puigmal 2913
Peñagolosa 1814
Javalambre 2020
CABO DE CREUS
Golfo de Rosas
CABO BAGUR
San Felíu de Guixols
MENORCA
Ciudadela
Mahón
CABO DE CABALLERÍA
MALLORCA
MAJORCA
Palma
Inca
Manacor
Felanitx
Lluchmayor
Sóller
Bahía de Palma
Bahía de Alcudia
CABO DE SALINAS
ISLA DRAGONERA
CABRERA
ISLAS BALEARES
BALEARIC ISLANDS
IBIZA
Ibiza
San Antonio Abad
Santa Eulalia del Rio
FORMENTERA
CABO BERBERÍA
MEDITERRANEAN SEA
CAP BOUGAR'OUN
ALGER
ALGIERS
Baie d'Alger
Blida
Médéa
Cherchell
Ténès
CAP TÉNÈS
Tizi-Ouzou
Bejaïa (Bougie)
Golfe de Bejaïa
Djidjelli
Dellys
CAP BENGUT
CAP SIGLI
Sétif
El Eulma
Bordj Bou Arreridj
M'Sila
El Asnam (Orléansville)
Mostaganem
Golfe d'Arzew
Arzew
Oran (Ouahran)
CAP FERRAT
CAP FALCON
Sig
Sidi bel Abbès
Bou Saâda
Batna
Chott el Hodna
KABYLIE
DAHRA
TELL ATLAS
ATLAS TELLIEN
MONTS DU HODNA
PLAINE DU HODNA
MASSIF DE L'OUARSENIS
MONTS TITTERI
ALGERIA
Djebel Babor 2004
Djebel Bissa 1157
Djebel Ouarsenis 1985
Djebel Maadid 1869
Djebel Refaa 2170
Tamgout de Lalla Khedidja 2308
Kilometers 0 50 100 150 Km.
Miles 0 50 100 150 Mi.
1:4 000 000

ADRIATIC SEA
LIGURIAN SEA
Gulf of Venice
Venezia
Venice
Milano
Milan
Torino
Turin
Genova
Genoa
Bologna
Firenze
Florence
Trieste
Ljubljana
Zagreb
Sarajevo
Budapest
Wien
Vienna
Bratislava
München
Munich
Zürich
Bern
Berne
Innsbruck
Salzburg
Graz
Linz
Rijeka
Split
Zadar
Dubrovnik
Ancona
Pescara
Perugia
Livorno
Leghorn
Nice
Monaco
Bastia
Corse
Corsica
Isola d'Elba
Padova
Verona
Trento
Bolzano
Parma
Modena
Ravenna
Rimini
Pisa
Siena
Arezzo

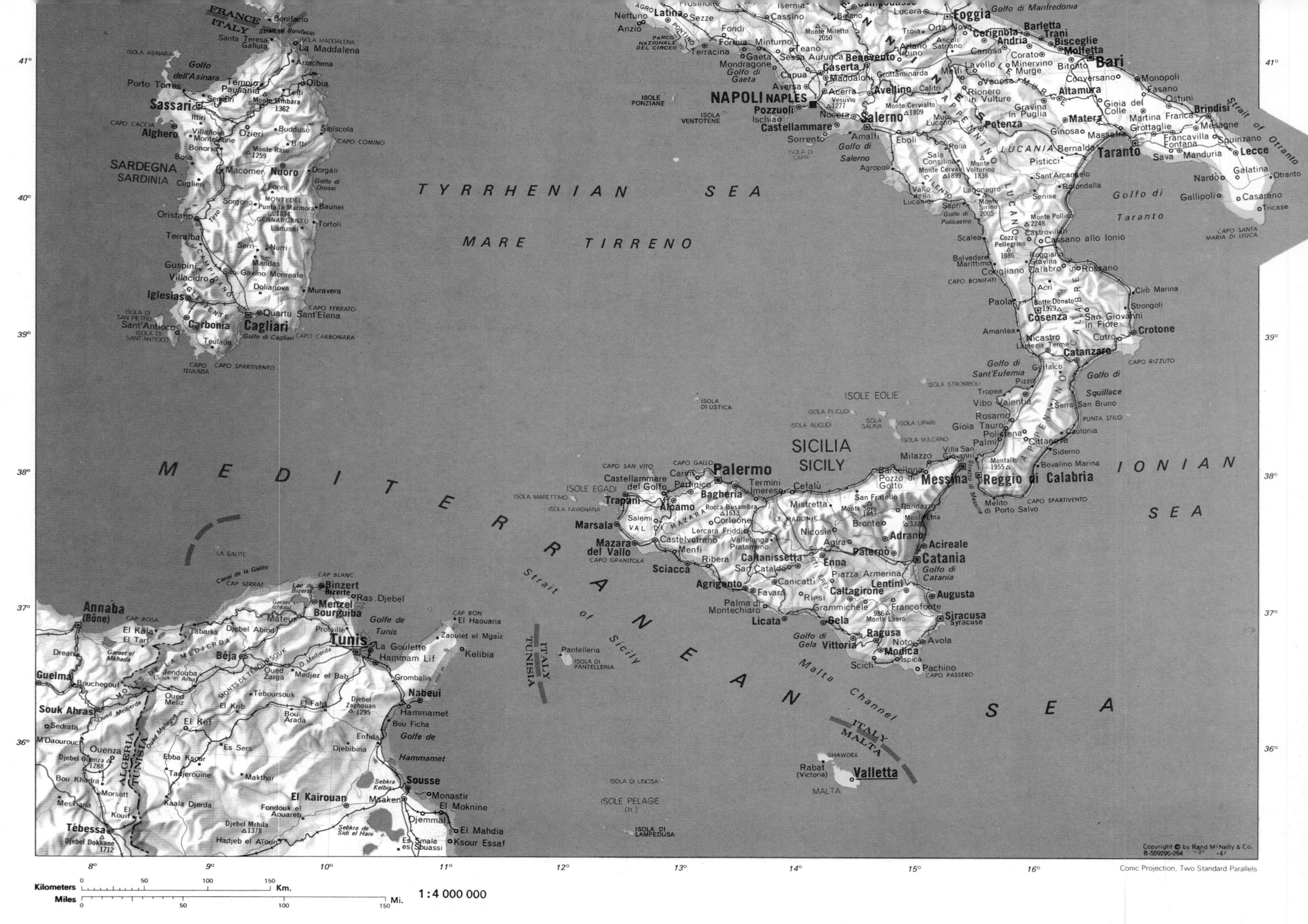
TYRRHENIAN SEA
MARE TIRRENO
IONIAN SEA
MEDITERRANEAN SEA
Strait of Sicily
Malta Channel
Strait of Otranto
Strait of Bonifacio
Golfo di Taranto
Golfo di Manfredonia
Golfo di Squillace
Golfo di Sant'Eufemia
Golfo de Tunis
Golfe de Hammamet
Golfo dell'Asinara
SICILIA
SICILY
SARDEGNA
SARDINIA
ISOLE EOLIE
ISOLE EGADI
ISOLE PELAGIE (It.)
ISOLA DI USTICA
ISOLE PONZIANE
ISOLA DI PANTELLERIA
ISOLA DI LAMPEDUSA
FRANCE
ITALY
ITALY
TUNISIA
ITALY
MALTA
ALGERIA
TUNISIA
MALTA
NAPOLI NAPLES
Foggia
Bari
Taranto
Lecce
Brindisi
Matera
Potenza
Salerno
Caserta
Benevento
Avellino
Cosenza
Catanzaro
Crotone
Reggio di Calabria
Messina
Catania
Siracusa
Ragusa
Palermo
Trapani
Marsala
Agrigento
Caltanissetta
Enna
Cagliari
Sassari
Nuoro
Oristano
Iglesias
Tunis
Binzert
Bizerte
Menzel Bourguiba
Sousse
Nabeul
El Kairouan
Annaba (Bône)
Souk Ahras
Tébessa
Valletta
Rabat (Victoria)
Conic Projection, Two Standard Parallels
Copyright © by Rand McNally & Co.
Kilometers
Miles
1:4 000 000

Southeastern Europe

BLACK SEA
CARPATHIAN MOUNTAINS
WALLACHIA
MOLDAVIA
DOBRUDJA
LUDOGORIE
BANAT
TRANSYLVANIA
HORTOBÁGY
ŠUMADIJA
KOPAONIK
Mouths of the Danube
Iron Gate Reservoir
BUCUREȘTI
BUCHAREST
BUDAPEST
Beograd
Belgrade
Sofija
Sofia
Kišin'ov
Kishinev
Constanța
Varna
Burgas
Ruse
Pleven
Craiova
Ploiești
Brașov
Sibiu
Cluj
Oradea
Timișoara
Arad
Debrecen
Miskolc
Szeged
Novi Sad
Sarajevo
Niš
Galați
Brăila
Iași
Tulcea
Tiraspol'
Bendery
Černovcy
Užgorod
Košice
Pécs
Győr
Danube
Dunav
Prut
Siret
Olt
Tisza
Sava
Drava
HUNGARY
ROMANIA
YUGOSLAVIA
BULGARIA
CZECHOSLOVAKIA
U.S.S.R.
MOLDAVSKAJA S.S.R.
UKRAINSKAJA S.S.R.

ADRIATIC SEA
AEGEAN SEA
IONIAN SEA
MEDITERRANEAN SEA
IONIAN ISLANDS
Strait of Otranto
ITALY
Otranto
Tricase
TURKEY
GREECE
BULGARIA
YUGOSLAVIA
ALBANIA
Marmara Denizi
Sea of Marmara
İSTANBUL
Edirne
Kırklareli
Lüleburgaz
Çorlu
Tekirdağ
Çanakkale
Gelibolu
Bursa
İnegöl
Mustafakemalpaşa
Bandırma
Balıkesir
Edremit
Bergama
Akhisar
Manisa
İzmir
Turgutlu
Salihli
Uşak
Ödemiş
Nazilli
Aydın
Denizli
Söke
Selçuk
Muğla
Milas
Bodrum
Marmaris
Thessaloníki
Salonika
Kavála
Dráma
Xánthi
Komotiní
Alexandroúpolis
Sérrai
Lárisa
Vólos
Lamía
Tríkala
Kateríni
Véroia
Ioánnina
Árta
Agrínion
Pátrai
Kórinthos
Trípolis
Kalámai
Spárti
Návplion
Pírgos
ATHÍNAI
ATHENS
Piraiévs
Khalkís
ÉVVOIA
Thívai
Korçë
Tiranë
Durrës
Elbasan
Berat
Vlorë
Bitola
Ohrid
Titov Veles
Prilep
Kérkira
KÉRKIRA
CORFU
Préveza
Levkás
KEFALLINÍA
ZÁKINTHOS
Mitilíni
LÉSVOS
LESBOS
Khíos
KHÍOS
CHIOS
LÍMNOS
SAMOTHRÁKI
SAMOTHRACE
THÁSOS
SÁMOS
KOS
Ródhos
RÓDHOS
RHODES
KÁRPATHOS
DHODHEKÁNISOS
DODECANESE
KIKLÁDHES
CYCLADES
NÁXOS
PÁROS
TÍNOS
ÁNDROS
MÍLOS
SKÍROS
KÍTHIRA
KRÍTI
CRETE
Iráklion
Khaniá
Réthimnon
Kritikón Pélagos
Sea of Crete
Mirtóön Pélagos
Thrakikón Pélagos
Thermaïkós Kólpos
Saronikós Kólpos
Argolikós Kólpos
Lakonikós Kólpos
Kiparissiakós Kólpos
Korinthiakós Kólpos
Gulf of Corinth
PELOPÓNNISOS
KHALKIDHIKÍ
Kerme Körfezi
Kilometers
Miles
1:4 000 000
Conic Projection, Two Standard Parallels
Copyright © by Rand McNally & Co.

Moscow, Leningrad and the Baltic

BALTIC SEA
Gulf of Finland
Suomenlahti
Finskij Zaliv
Gulf of Riga
Rižskij Zaliv
Rigas Jūras Līcis
Åland Sea
FINLAND
SWEDEN
U.S.S.R.
ESTONIA
LATVIA
LITHUANIA
POLAND
ESTONSKAJA S.S.R.
LATVIJSKAJA S.S.R.
LITOVSKAJA S.S.R.
BELORUSSKAJA S.S.R.
ROSSIJSKAJA S.F.S.R.
BELORUSSIJA
POLESJE
Helsinki
Helsingfors
Espoo
Esbo
Turku
Hango
Hanko
Ekenäs
Porvoo
Borgå
Kotka
Vyborg
Leningrad
Kronštadt
Lomonosov
Puškin
Kolpino
Gatčina
Tallinn
Paldiski
Haapsalu
Pärnu
Narva
Kohtla-Järve
Sillamäe
Tartu
Võru
Valga
Valka
Pskov
Luga
Novgorod
Staraja Russa
Čudskoje Ozero
Peipsi Järv
Hiiumaa
Saaremaa
Kingisepp
Riga
Jūrmala
Jelgava
Ogre
Ventspils
Liepāja
Cēsis
Valmiera
Daugavpils
Rēzekne
Madona
Ludza
Klaipėda
(Memel)
Šiauliai
Panevėžys
Kaunas
Vilnius
Utena
Alytus
Druskininkai
Sovetsk
Tilsit
Kaliningrad
Königsberg
Baltijsk
Pillau
Černjachovsk
Insterburg
Gusev
Gumbinnen
Velikije Luki
Nevel'
Polock
Vitebsk
Orša
Mogil'ov
Minsk
Molodečno
Borisov
Bobrujsk
Gomel'
Grodno
Lida
Baranoviči
Slonim
Pinsk
Brest
Białystok
Olsztyn
Allenstein
Siedlce
Łomża
Suwałki
Augustów
Ostrołęka
Biała Podlaska
Kilometers
Miles
Km.
Mi.
1 : 4 000 000
Copyright © by Rand McNally & Co.

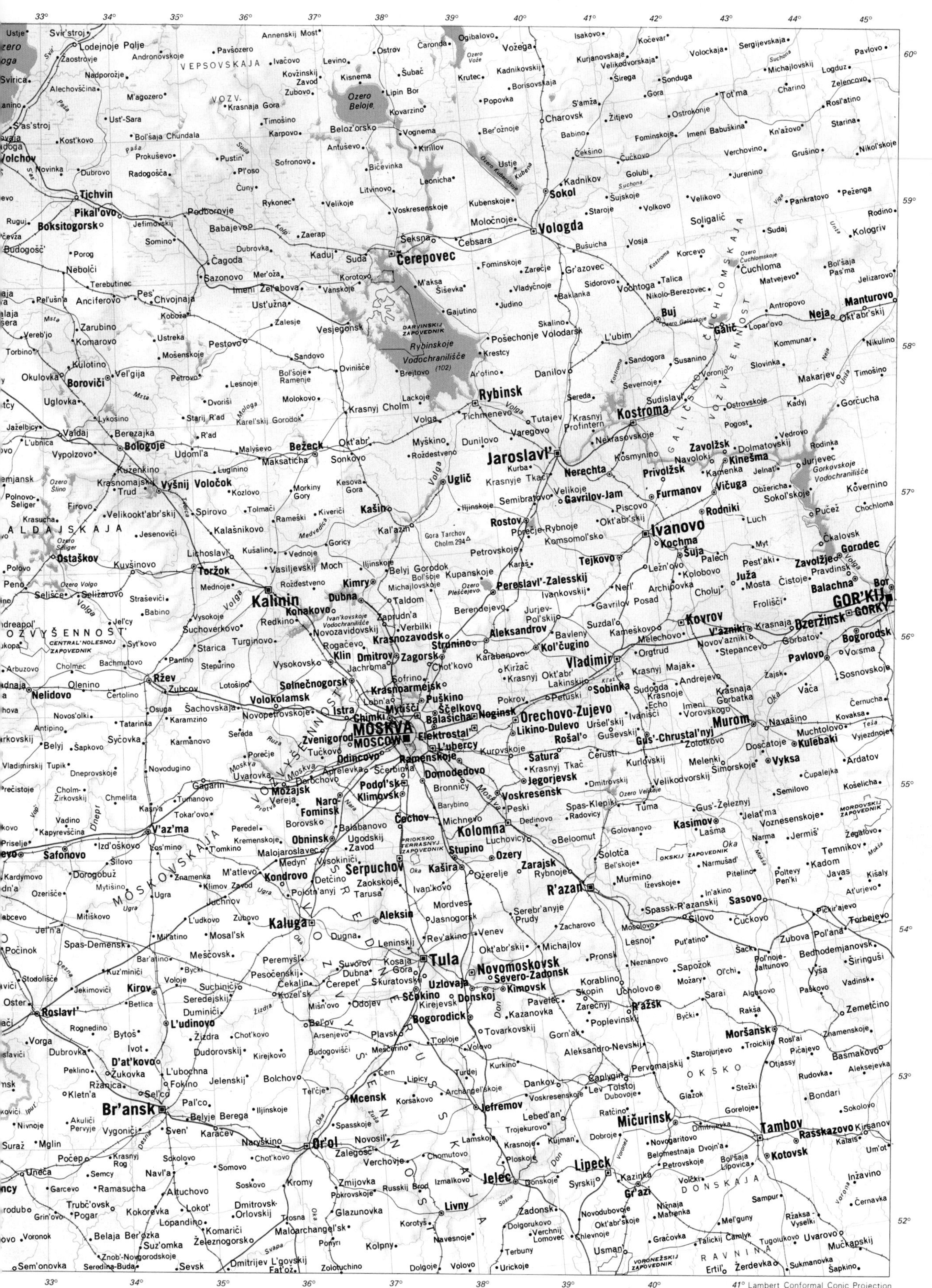
33°
34°
35°
36°
37°
38°
39°
40°
41°
42°
43°
44°
45°
60°
59°
58°
57°
56°
55°
54°
53°
52°
Tichvin
Pikal'ovo
Boksitogorsk
Vologda
Sokol
Čerepovec
Rybinskoje Vodochranilišče
DARVINSKIJ ZAPOVEDNIK
Ozero Beloje
Kirillov
Rybinsk
Jaroslavl'
Kostroma
Galič
Buj
Manturovo
Neja
Ivanovo
Kinešma
Rostov
Uglič
Kašin
Bežeck
Bologoje
Vyšnij Voloček
Boroviči
Valdaj
Ostaškov
Toržok
Kalinin
Konakovo
Dubna
Kimry
Pereslavl'-Zalesskij
Aleksandrov
Vladimir
Kovrov
Dzeržinsk
GOR'KIJ
GORKY
Bogorodsk
Pavlovo
Murom
Vyksa
Kulebaki
Gus'-Chrustal'nyj
Orechovo-Zujevo
Noginsk
Elektrostal'
MOSKVA
MOSCOW
Zvenigorod
Odincovo
Istra
Solnečnogorsk
Volokolamsk
Klin
Dmitrov
Zagorsk
Krasnoarmejsk
Puškino
Mytišči
L'ubercy
Ramenskoje
Podol'sk
Domodedovo
Voskresensk
Jegorjevsk
Kolomna
Mošajsk
Naro-Fominsk
Obninsk
Serpuchov
Kaluga
Tula
Novomoskovsk
Aleksin
Stupino
Kašira
Ozery
R'azan'
Kasimov
Sasovo
Moršansk
Tambov
Rasskazovo
Kotovsk
Mičurinsk
Lipeck
Jelec
Or'ol
Mcensk
Livny
Br'ansk
Roslavl'
Rževs
Nelidovo
Safonovo
V'az'ma
Gagarin
Kirov
L'udinovo
D'at'kovo
Efremov
Bogorodick
Donskoj
Uzlovaja
Ščokino
Kimovsk
Rjažsk
Ržev
Kondrovo
Galičskaja Vozvyšennost'
Čuchloma
Nerechta
Furmanov
Vičuga
Kochma
Šuja
Tejkovo
Sobinka
Kol'čugino
Petuški
Kineshma
Ozero Seliger
Volga
Oka
Moskva
Don
Desna
Sosna
VEPSOVSKAJA VOZV.
VALDAJSKAJA
VOZVYŠENNOST'
MOSKOVSKAJA
SREDNERUSSKAJA VOZVYŠENNOST'
OKSKO DONSKAJA RAVNINA
CENTRAL'NOLESNOJ ZAPOVEDNIK
PRIOKSKO TERRASNYJ ZAPOVEDNIK
OKSKIJ ZAPOVEDNIK
MORDOVSKIJ ZAPOVEDNIK
VORONEŽSKIJ ZAPOVEDNIK
Gorkovskoje Vodochranilišče
Gora Tarchov Cholm 294
Lambert Conformal Conic Projection

Ukraine

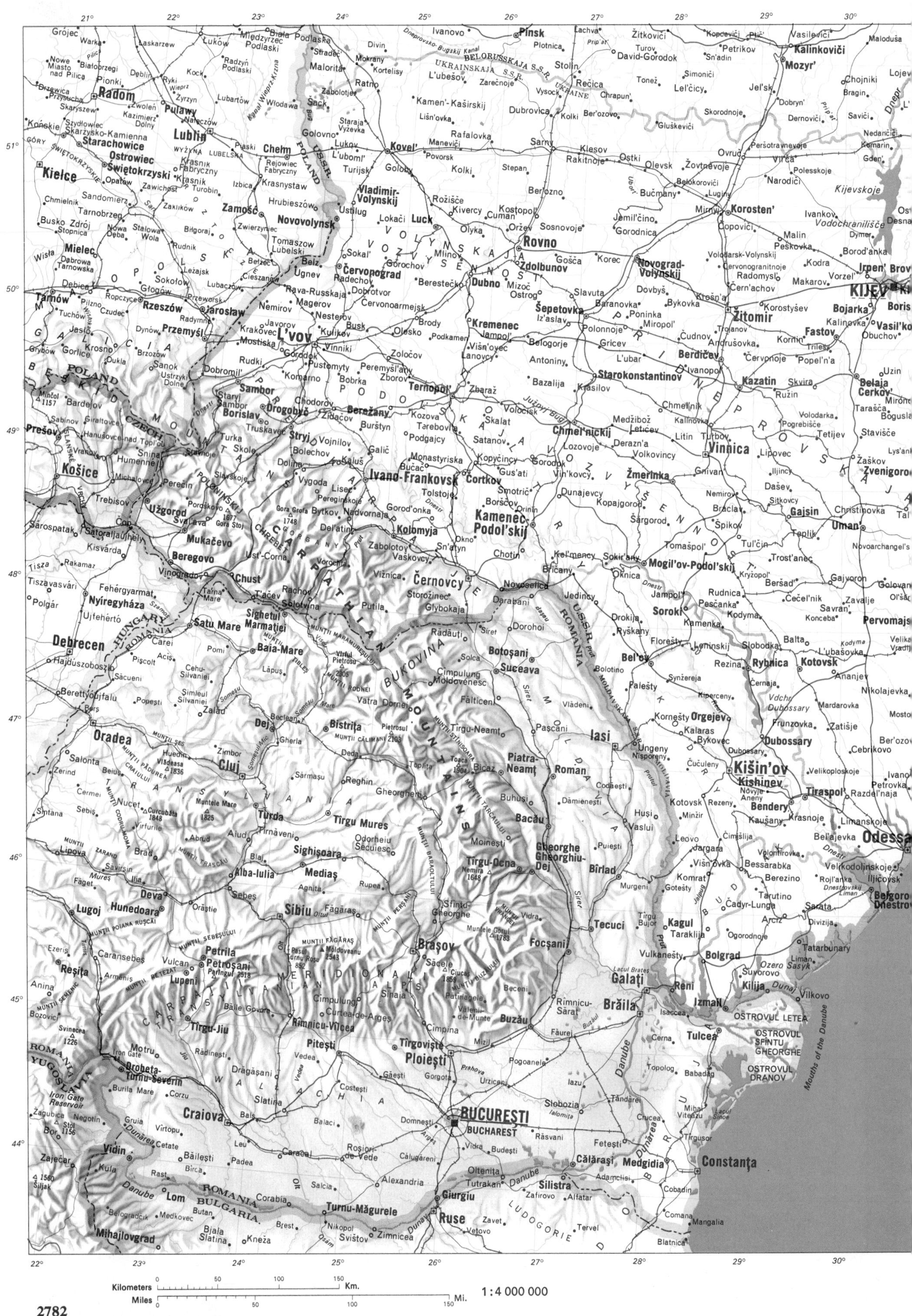

Pinsk
Kalinkoviči
Mozyr'
Radom
Lublin
Kielce
Kovel'
Vladimir-Volynskij
Novovolynsk
Luck
Rovno
Zdolbunov
Novograd-Volynskij
Korosten'
Kijev
Žitomir
Berdičev
Červonograd
Dubno
Šepetovka
Kremenec
L'vov
Rzeszów
Jarosław
Przemyśl
Tarnów
Mielec
Drogobyč
Sambor
Stryj
Ternopol'
Starokonstantinov
Chmel'nickij
Kazatin
Vinnica
Ivano-Frankovsk
Kolomyja
Kamenec-Podol'skij
Černovcy
Mogil'ov-Podol'skij
Užgorod
Mukačevo
Beregovo
Chust
Košice
Prešov
Nyíregyháza
Debrecen
Satu Mare
Baia-Mare
Suceava
Botoşani
Iasi
Bel'cy
Soroki
Kišin'ov
Kishinev
Tiraspol'
Bendery
Odessa
Izmail
Galaţi
Brăila
Constanţa
Tulcea
Oradea
Cluj
Turda
Alba-Iulia
Sibiu
Braşov
Ploieşti
Piteşti
Craiova
Bucureşti
Bucharest
Giurgiu
Ruse
Vidin
Lom
Bacău
Focşani
Tecuci
Bîrlad
CARPATHIAN MOUNTAINS
TRANSYLVANIA
WALACHIA
MOLDAVIA
BUKOVINA
PODOLSKAJA VOZVYŠENNOST'
VOLYNSKAJA VOZVYŠENNOST'
PRIDNEPROVSKAJA VOZVYŠENNOST'
BELORUSSKAJA S.S.R.
UKRAINSKAJA S.S.R.
POLAND
U.S.S.R.
CZECH.
HUNGARY
ROMANIA
YUGOSLAVIA
BULGARIA
Danube
Dnestr
Mouths of the Danube

Kilometers 0 50 100 150 Km.

Miles 0 50 100 150 Mi.

1:4 000 000

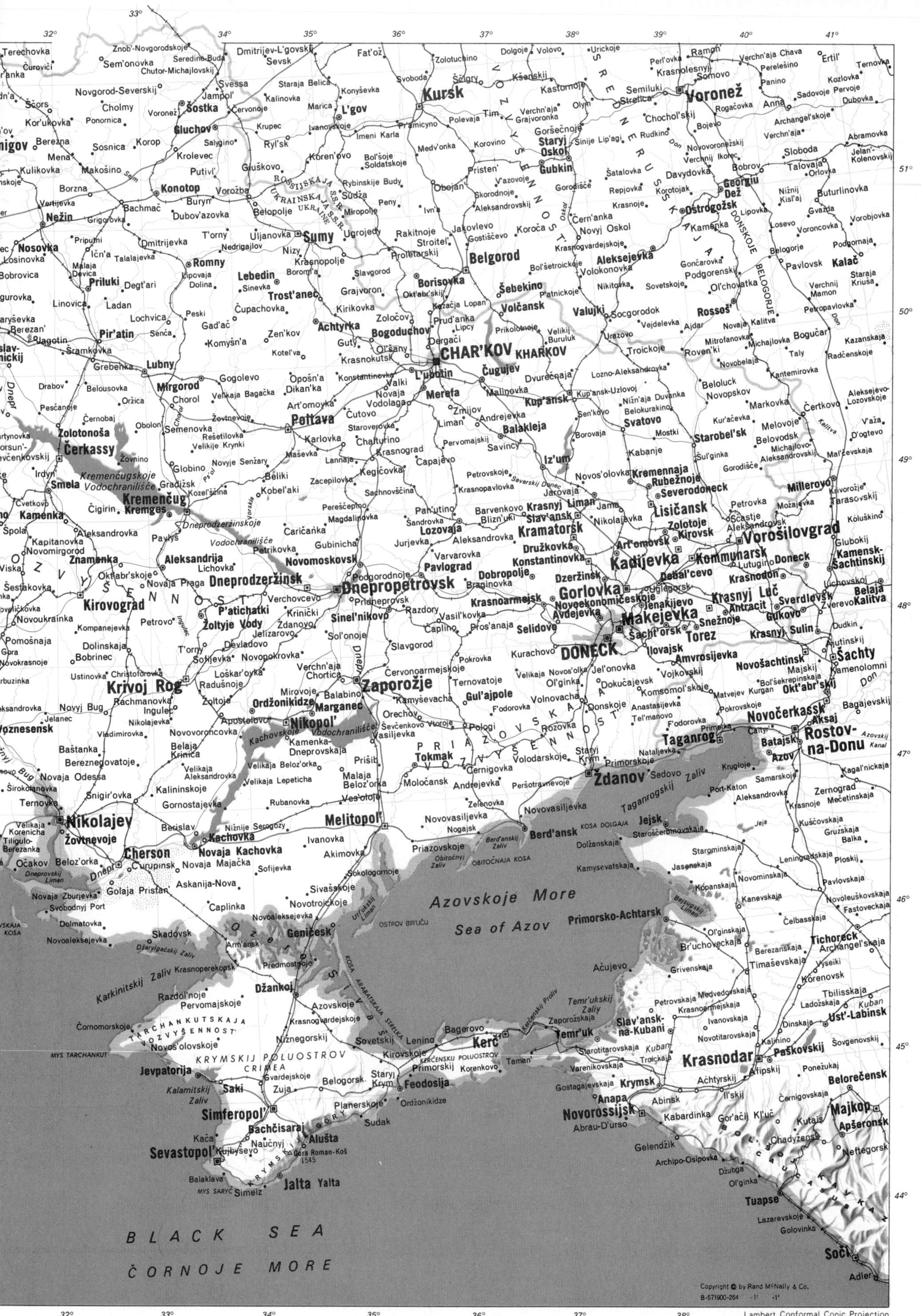

Kursk
Voronež
Sumy
Belgorod
CHAR'KOV
KHARKOV
Poltava
Kremenčug
Čerkassy
Kirovograd
Dnepropetrovsk
Dneprodzeržinsk
Zaporožje
Krivoj Rog
Nikopol'
Nikolajev
Cherson
Melitopol'
DONECK
Gorlovka
Makejevka
Kadijevka
Vorošilovgrad
Kramatorsk
Slav'ansk
Lisičansk
Severodoneck
Taganrog
Ždanov
Berd'ansk
Rostov-na-Donu
Novočerkassk
Šachty
Krasnodar
Novorossijsk
Tuapse
Soči
Majkop
Kerč'
Feodosija
Simferopol'
Sevastopol'
Jalta
Jevpatorija
Džankoj
Konotop
Nežin
Priluki
Lubny
Mirgorod
Romny
Achtyrka
Izjum
Kup'ansk
Lozovaja
Pavlograd
Novomoskovsk
Marganec
Tokmak
Geničesk
Azovskoje More
Sea of Azov
BLACK SEA
ČORNOJE MORE
KRYMSKIJ POLUOSTROV
CRIMEA
Taganrogskij Zaliv
Karkinitskij Zaliv
Kremenčugskoje Vodochranilišče
Kachovskoje Vodochranilišče
ROSSIJSKAJA S.S.R.
UKRAINSKAJA S.S.R.
Dnepr
Don
Kuban
Copyright © by Rand McNally & Co.
B-571900-264
Lambert Conformal Conic Projection
32°
33°
34°
35°
36°
37°
38°
39°
40°
41°
44°
45°
46°
47°
48°
49°
50°
51°

Eastern Soviet Union

BARENTS SEA
Beloje More
White Sea
KOL'SKIJ POLUOSTROV
KOLA PENINSULA
NOVAJA ZEML'A
KARSKOJE MORE
KARA SEA
Pečorskoje More
SEVERNAJA ZEML'A
OSTROV KOMSOMOLEC
OSTROV OKT'ABR'SKOJ REVOL'UCII
OSTROV BOL'ŠEVIK
ARCHIPELAG NORDENŠEL'DA
OSTROVA SERGEJA KIROVA
OSTROVA IZVESTIJ CIK
OSTROVA ARKTIČESKOGO INSTITUTA
POLUOSTROV JAMAL
GYDANSKIJ POLUOSTROV
POLUOSTROV TAJMYR
GORY BYRRANGA
SEVERO SIBIRSKAJA NIZMENNOST'
BOL'SEZEMEL'SKAJA TUNDRA
TIMANSKIJ KRJAŽ
Arctic Circle
URAL MOUNTAINS
ZAPADNO-SIBIRSKAJA NIZMENNOST'
PLATO PUTORANA
SREDNE SIBIRSKOJE PLOSKOGORJE
ROSSIJSKAJA SOVETSKAJA FEDERATIVNAJA SOCIALISTIČESKAJA
RUSSIAN SOVIET FEDERATED SOCIALIST
UNION OF SOVIET SOCIALIST
Vorkuta
Noril'sk
Dudinka
Igarka
Salechard
Nadym
Surgut
Tobol'sk
Perm'
Berezniki
Serov
Nižnij Tagil
Sverdlovsk
Čel'abinsk
Zlatoust
Miass
Kurgan
T'umen
Petropavlovsk
Kustanaj
Omsk
Novosibirsk
Tomsk
Kemerovo
Barnaul
Novokuzneck
Prokopjevsk
Krasnojarsk
Bratsk
Irkutsk
Angarsk
Ulan-Ude
Abakan
Bijsk
Rubcovsk
Semipalatinsk
Ust'-Kamenogorsk
Pavlodar
Celinograd
Karaganda
Temirtau
Alma-Ata
Yining
Kuldja
Balchaš
Ozero Balchaš
KAZACHSKIJ MELKOSOPOČNIK
KAZACHSKAJA S.S.R.
ZAPADNYJ SAJAN
SAYAN MOUNTAINS
VOSTOČNYJ SAJAN
CHINA
XINJIANG WEIWUER ZIZHIQU
MONGOLIA
Ulaanbaatar
Darchan
Ob'
Jenisej
Irtyš
Lake Baykal
1:16 000 000
Copyright © by Rand McNally & Co.
B-570000-264

Kilometers 0 200 400 600 Km.
Miles 0 200 400 600 Mi.

1:16 000 000

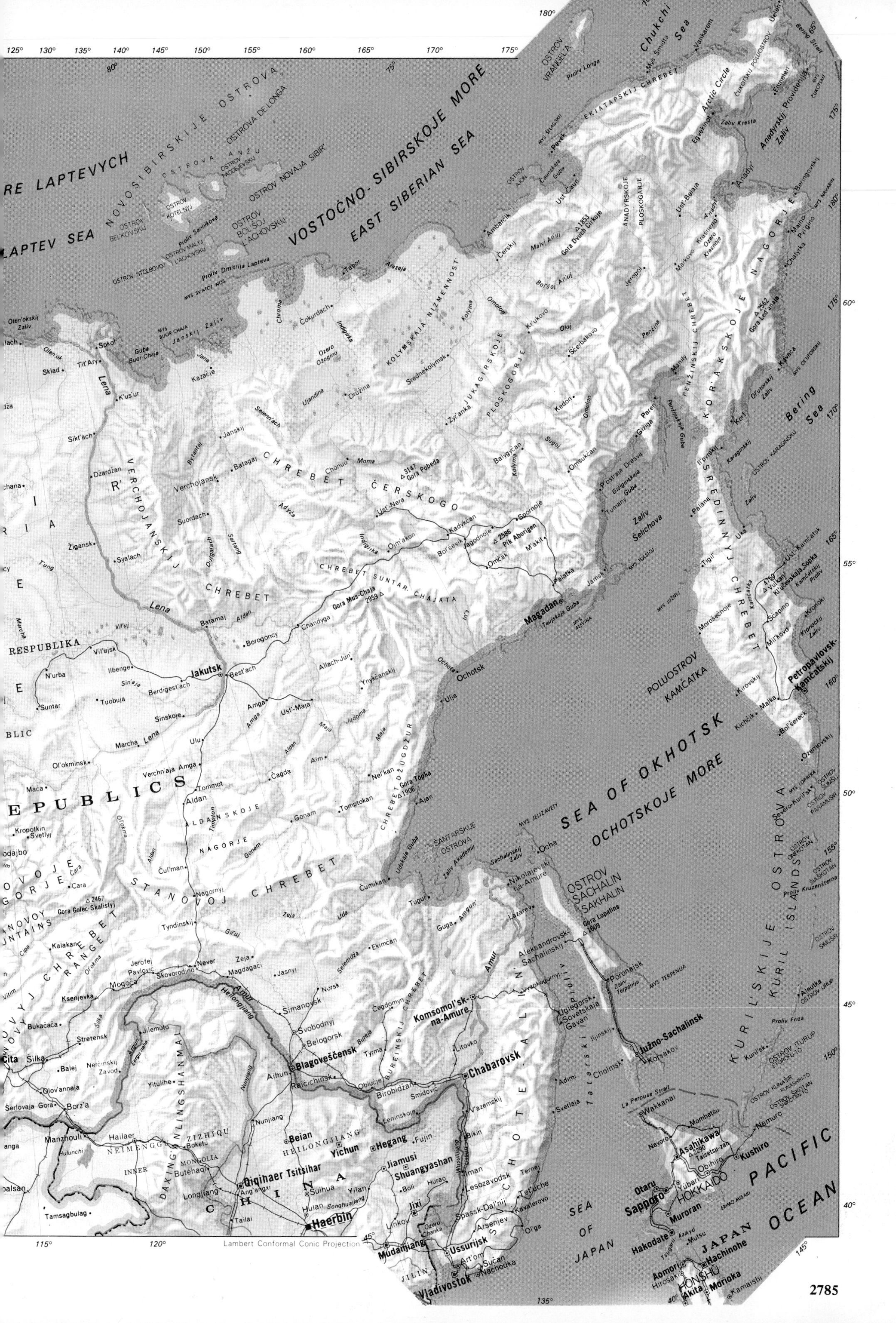

SEA OF OKHOTSK
OCHOTSKOJE MORE
VOSTOČNO-SIBIRSKOJE MORE
EAST SIBERIAN SEA
LAPTEV SEA
Chukchi Sea
Bering Sea
SEA OF JAPAN
PACIFIC OCEAN
POLUOSTROV KAMČATKA
OSTROV SACHALIN
SAKHALIN
HOKKAIDO
HONSHU
JAPAN
CHINA
KURIL'SKIJE OSTROVA
KURIL ISLANDS
CHREBET ČERSKOGO
VERCHOJANSKIJ CHREBET
STANOVOJ CHREBET
KOLYMSKAJA NIZMENNOST
Magadan
Jakutsk
Chabarovsk
Vladivostok
Petropavlovsk-Kamčatskij
Južno-Sachalinsk
Komsomol'sk-na-Amure
Blagoveščensk
Haerbin
Sapporo
Lambert Conformal Conic Projection

Western North Africa

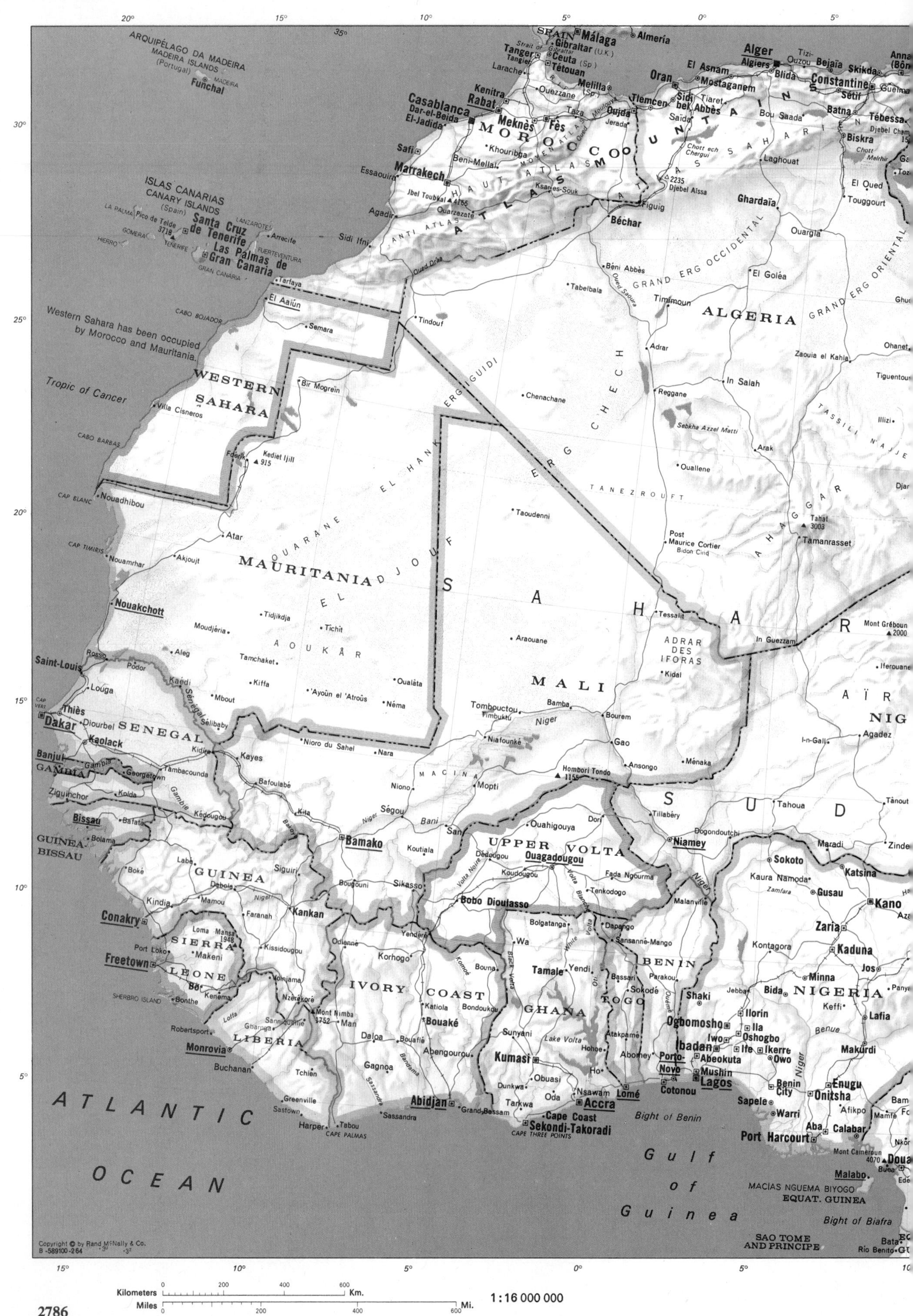

ARQUIPÉLAGO DA MADEIRA
MADEIRA ISLANDS
(Portugal)
Funchal
ISLAS CANARIAS
CANARY ISLANDS
(Spain)
Santa Cruz de Tenerife
Las Palmas de Gran Canaria
Pico de Teide 3718
LANZAROTE
FUERTEVENTURA
GRAN CANARIA
TENERIFE
GOMERA
HIERRO
LA PALMA
Arrecife
SPAIN
Málaga
Almería
Strait of Gibraltar
Gibraltar (U.K.)
Tanger
Tangier
Ceuta (Sp.)
Tétouan
Larache
Kenitra
Rabat
Casablanca
Dar-el-Beida
El-Jadida
Meknès
Fès
Ouezzane
Melilla (Sp.)
Taza
Oujda
Jerada
MOROCCO
Khouribga
Beni-Mellal
Safi
Essaouira
Marrakech
Jbel Toubkal 4165
Ouarzazate
Agadir
Sidi Ifni
HAUT ATLAS
ANTI ATLAS
ATLAS MOUNTAINS
Ksar-es-Souk
Figuig
Béchar
Oued Drâa
Tarfaya
El Aaiún
CABO BOJADOR
Semara
Western Sahara has been occupied by Morocco and Mauritania.
Tropic of Cancer
WESTERN SAHARA
Villa Cisneros
CABO BARBAS
Bir Mogreïn
Kediet Ijill 915
Fdérik
CAP BLANC
Nouadhibou
CAP TIMIRIS
Nouamrhar
Atar
Akjoujt
MAURITANIA
Nouakchott
Tidjikdja
Tichit
Moudjéria
Aleg
Tamchaket
AOUKÂR
Kiffa
'Ayoûn el 'Atroûs
Oualâta
Néma
Rosso
Podor
Kaédi
Saint-Louis
Louga
Mbout
CAP VERT
Thiès
Dakar
Diourbel
SENEGAL
Kaolack
Sélibaby
Kidira
Banjul
GAMBIA
Tambacounda
Georgetown
Kolda
Ziguinchor
Kédougou
Bissau
Bafatá
Bolama
GUINEA-BISSAU
Boké
Labé
GUINEA
Dabola
Mamou
Kindia
Faranah
Siguiri
Kankan
Conakry
Kissidougou
SIERRA LEONE
Port Loko
Makeni
Freetown
Loma Mansa 1948
Bo
Kenema
SHERBRO ISLAND
Bonthe
Voinjama
Nzérékoré
Mont Nimba 1752
Gbarnga
Sanniquellie
Man
LIBERIA
Robertsport
Monrovia
Buchanan
Tchien
Greenville
Sastown
Harper
Tabou
CAPE PALMAS
ATLANTIC OCEAN
Tindouf
ERG IGUIDI
EL HANK
OUARANE
EL DJOUF
SAHARA
Béni Abbès
Tabelbala
Oued Saoura
GRAND ERG OCCIDENTAL
Timimoun
ALGERIA
Adrar
Reggane
Chenachane
ERG CHECH
Sebkha Azzel Matti
TANEZROUFT
Taoudenni
Post Maurice Cortier
Bidon Cinq
Tessalit
Araouane
ADRAR DES IFORAS
Kidal
MALI
Tombouctou
Timbuktu
Bamba
Bourem
Niger
Niafounké
Gao
Ansongo
Ménaka
Hombori Tondo 1155
Nioro du Sahel
Nara
Kayes
Bafoulabé
Kita
Niono
MACINA
Mopti
Ségou
Bani
San
Bamako
Koutiala
Bougouni
Sikasso
Ouahigouya
Dori
UPPER VOLTA
Dédougou
Ouagadougou
Koudougou
Fada Ngourma
Tenkodogo
Bobo Dioulasso
Volta Noire
Volta Blanche
Tillabéry
Niamey
Dogondoutchi
Malanville
Odienné
Korhogo
Yendéré
IVORY COAST
Katiola
Bondoukou
Bouna
Bouaké
Daloa
Bouaflé
Gagnoa
Abengourou
Bandama
Sassandra
Abidjan
Grand-Bassam
Bolgatanga
Wa
Tamale
Yendi
Black Volta
White Volta
Dapango
Sansanné-Mango
GHANA
Lake Volta
Sunyani
Kumasi
Obuasi
Dunkwa
Oda
Tarkwa
Nsawam
Accra
Sekondi-Takoradi
Cape Coast
CAPE THREE POINTS
Hohoe
Ho
Lomé
TOGO
BENIN
Parakou
Bassari
Sokodé
Atakpamé
Abomey
Porto-Novo
Cotonou
Bight of Benin
Gulf of Guinea
Alger
Algiers
Tizi-Ouzou
Bejaïa
Skikda
Annaba (Bône)
Constantine
Sétif
Guelma
El Asnam
Blida
Oran
Mostaganem
Tiaret
Sidi bel Abbès
Tlemcen
Saïda
Bou Saada
Batna
Tébessa
Djebel Chambi
Biskra
Chott ech Chergui
Chott Melrhir
Laghouat
SAHARIAN ATLAS
2235 Djebel Aïssa
Ghardaïa
Touggourt
El Oued
Ouargla
El Goléa
GRAND ERG ORIENTAL
Zaouia el Kahla
In Salah
Ohanet
Tiguentourine
TASSILI N'AJJER
Illizi
Arak
Ouallene
AHAGGAR
Tahat 3003
Tamanrasset
In Guezzam
Mont Gréboun 2000
Iferouane
AÏR
NIGER
Agadez
I-n-Gall
Tahoua
Tânout
SUDAN
Maradi
Zinder
Sokoto
Katsina
Kaura Namoda
Gusau
Zamfara
Kano
Zaria
Kontagora
Kaduna
Jos
Minna
NIGERIA
Bida
Jebba
Shaki
Keffi
Ilorin
Lafia
Ogbomosho
Ila
Oshogbo
Iwo
Ife
Ikerre
Owo
Ibadan
Abeokuta
Mushin
Lagos
Benue
Makurdi
Enugu
Onitsha
Afikpo
Benin City
Sapele
Warri
Aba
Calabar
Port Harcourt
Mamfe
Mont Cameroun 4070
Douala
Malabo
Buea
MACIAS NGUEMA BIYOGO
EQUAT. GUINEA
Bight of Biafra
SAO TOME AND PRINCIPE
Bata
Río Benito
Copyright © by Rand McNally & Co.
B-589100-264
Kilometers 0 200 400 600 Km.
Miles 0 200 400 600 Mi.
1:16 000 000

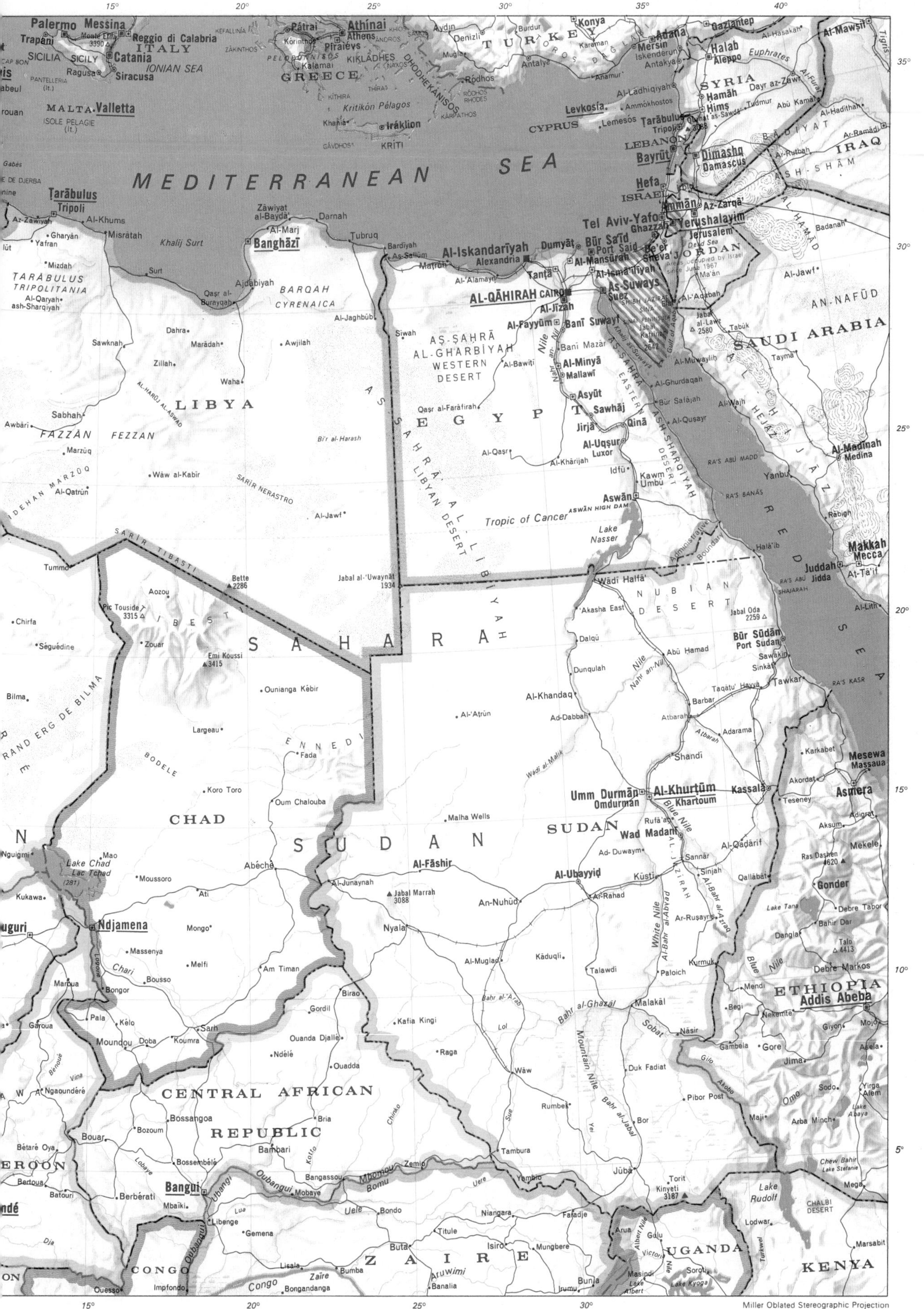

Miller Oblated Stereographic Projection

Southern Africa and Madagascar

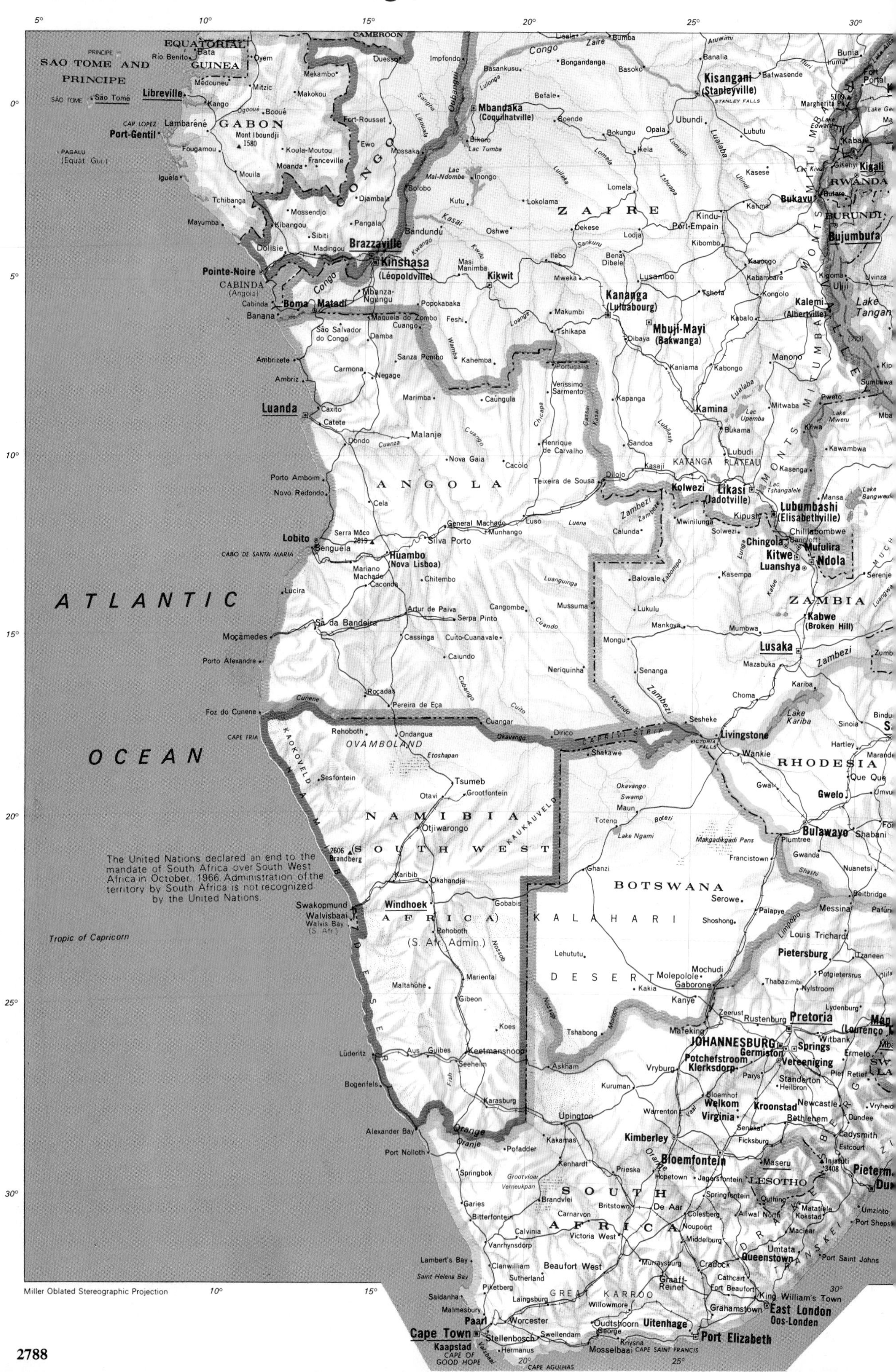

SAO TOME AND PRINCIPE
EQUATORIAL GUINEA
GABON
CONGO
ZAIRE
ANGOLA
ZAMBIA
RHODESIA
BOTSWANA
NAMIBIA (SOUTH WEST AFRICA)
(S. Afr. Admin.)
SOUTH AFRICA
LESOTHO
RWANDA
BURUNDI
CAMEROON
CABINDA (Angola)
ATLANTIC
OCEAN
KALAHARI DESERT
GREAT KARROO
KATANGA PLATEAU
CAPRIVI STRIP
KAOKOVELD
KAUKAUVELD
OVAMBOLAND
NAMIB DESERT
DRAKENSBERG
TRANSKEI
The United Nations declared an end to the mandate of South Africa over South West Africa in October, 1966. Administration of the territory by South Africa is not recognized by the United Nations.
Tropic of Capricorn
Libreville
Port-Gentil
São Tomé
Brazzaville
Kinshasa (Léopoldville)
Pointe-Noire
Luanda
Lobito
Benguela
Huambo (Nova Lisboa)
Sá da Bandeira
Moçâmedes
Kisangani (Stanleyville)
Mbandaka (Coquilhatville)
Kananga (Luluabourg)
Mbuji-Mayi (Bakwanga)
Lubumbashi (Elisabethville)
Likasi (Jadotville)
Kolwezi
Kigali
Bujumbura
Bukavu
Kalemi (Albertville)
Lusaka
Ndola
Kitwe
Chingola
Kabwe (Broken Hill)
Livingstone
Bulawayo
Gwelo
Windhoek
Swakopmund
Walvisbaai
Walvis Bay (S. Afr.)
Lüderitz
Tsumeb
Gaborone
Francistown
Pretoria
JOHANNESBURG
Kimberley
Bloemfontein
Maseru
Cape Town
Kaapstad
CAPE OF GOOD HOPE
Port Elizabeth
East London
Oos-Londen
Durban
Pietermaritzburg
Lake Kariba
Lake Tanganyika
Zambezi
Congo
Kasai
Cuanza
Cunene
Okavango
Orange
Oranje
Vaal
Limpopo
Okavango Swamp
Lake Ngami
Makgadikgadi Pans
2606 Brandberg
2619 Serra Môco
Mont Iboundji 1580
3408 Injasuti
5109 Margherita Pk.
5°
10°
15°
20°
25°
30°
0°
Miller Oblated Stereographic Projection

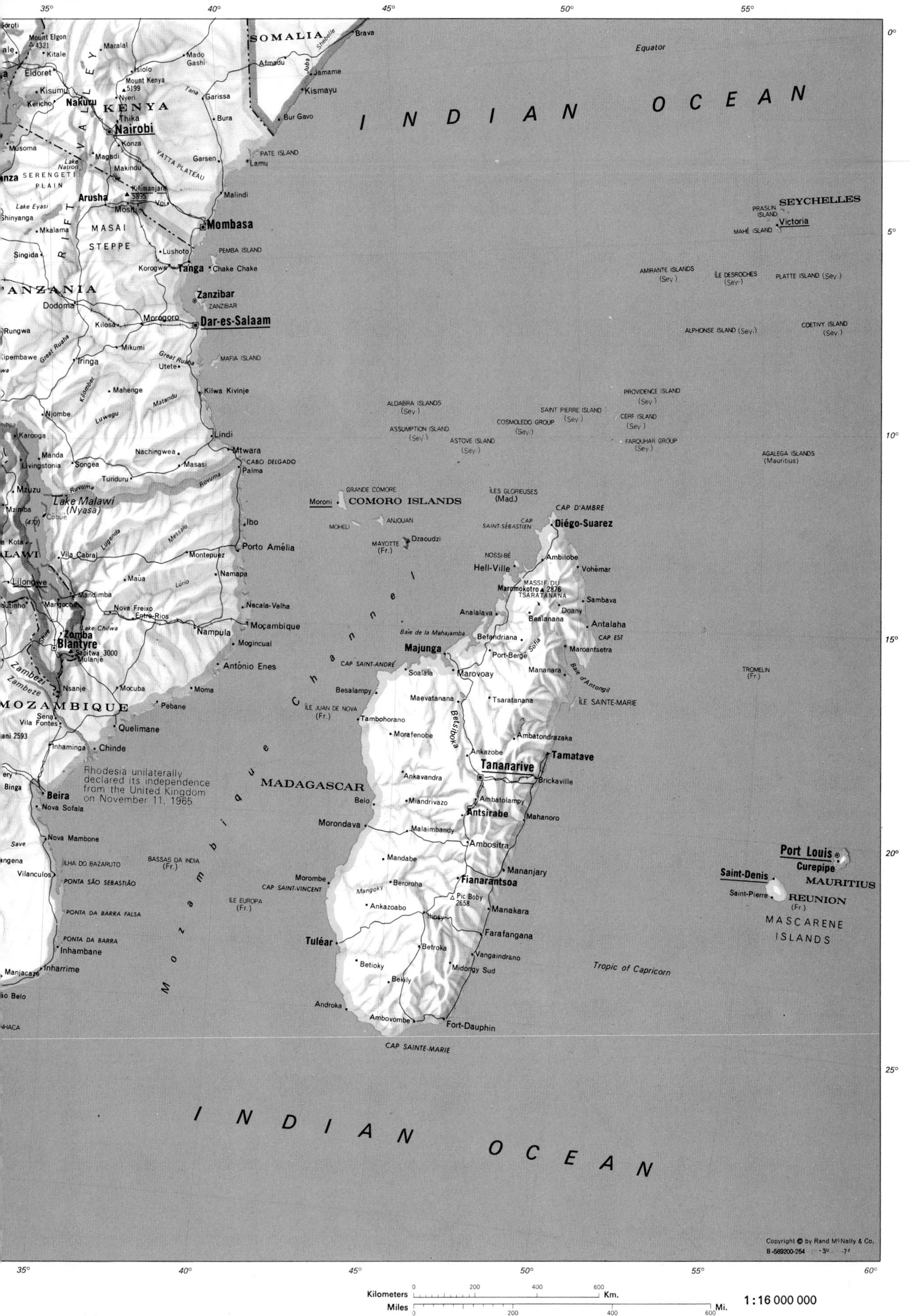

Northeast Africa and Arabia

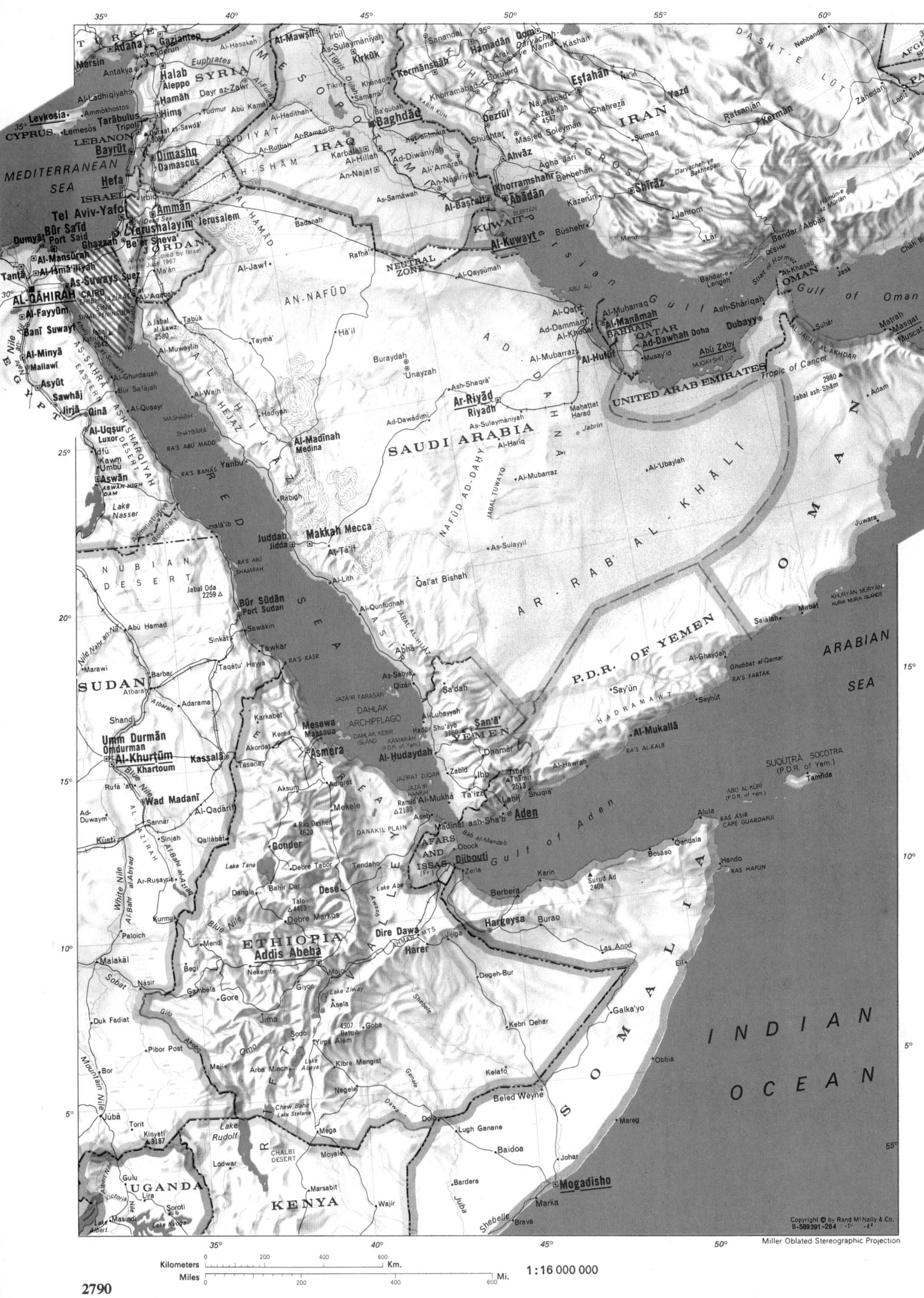

32° 34° 36° 38° 40°

Korkuteli
Antalya
Serik
Akseki
Hadım
Karaman
TOROS DAĞLARI
Tarsus
Adana
Mersin
Osmaniye
Gaziantep
Urfa
Viranşehir
Darbāsīyah
Al-Qāmishlī
Manavgat
Alanya
Ermenak
Mut
Erdemli
Ceyhan
İslâhiye
Nizip
Birecik
Sürüç
Ceylânpınar
Ra's al-'Ayn
Tall Tamir
Antalya Körfezi
Gulf of Antalya
Kumluca
Kazancı
Silifke
İskenderun Körfezi
Dörtyol
Kilis
Oğuzeli
Barak
Jarābulus
Akçakale
TURKEY
Al-Khābūr
Al-Ḥasakah
İskenderun
Kırıkhan
Manbij
SYRIA
Gazipaşa
Anamur
ANAMUR BURNU
İNCEKUM BURNU
RESÜLHINZIR
Reyhanlı
Ḥalab Aleppo
Samandağı
Antakya
Antioch
Maskanah
Ar-Raqqah
Shaddādī
Sabkhat al-Jabbūl
Idlib
RA'S AL-BASĪṬ
Euphrates
Al-Furāt
Aṣ-Ṣuwār
AKR. APOSTÓLOU ANDRÉA
Rizokárpason
CYPRUS
Jisr ash-Shughūr
Ma'arrat an-Nu'mān
AKR. KORMAKÍTI
Kirínia
Al-Lādhiqīyah
Latakia
Al-Ḥaffah
Jabal Tlété
Ouâte Gharbī
867
Dayr az-Zawr
Rawḍah
Buṣayrah
Kólpos Mórfou
Trikomon
Kólpos Ammókhostou
Jablah
Ṣūrān
Al-Kawm
Lefkosía
Nicosia
Ammókhostos
Famagusta
Bāniyās
Ḥamāh
Al-Mayādīn
Pólis
Ólimbos
1951
Lárnax
Larnaca
AKR. PIDÁLION
Ṭarṭūs
As-Sukhnah
Sabkhat al-Burghūth
Ḥimṣ Homs
Néa Páfos
Paphos
Yermasoyia
Lemesós
Limassol
AKR. GÁTAS
Tall Kalakh
Furqlus
Tudmur
Palmyra
Abū Kamāl
Ṭarābulus
Tripoli
Ḥalbā
Shinshār
Al-Qā'im
Al-Hirmil
Qurnat as-Sawdā'
3083
Al-Batrūn
Bsharrī
Al-Qaryatayn
LEBANON
An-Nabk
Beirut Bayrūt
B'abdā
Ba'labakk
Baalbek
Zaḥlah
Wādī Ukash
Al-Quṭayfah
SYRIA
IRAQ
Ṣaydā
Sidon
Dūmā
Dimashq Damascus
Wādī Ḥawrān
MEDITERRANEAN SEA
Qaṭanā
Jabal ash-Shaykh
2814
Ṣūr Tyre
Jwayya
Qiryat Shemona
Dārayyā
Al-Mismiyah
Nahariya
Har Meron
1208
Al-Qunayṭirah
Ar-Rutbah
'Akko Acre
Hefa Haifa
Yam Kinneret
Teverya
As-Suwaydā'
ISRAEL
'Afula
Dar'ā
1801
SYRIA
JORDAN
BĀDIYAT ASH-SHĀM
Tirat Karmel
Hadera
Jenin
Irbid
Ar-Ramtha
Tall Ghīn
Buṣrā ash-Shām
Ṣalkhad
PALESTINE
Ṭūlkarm
Jordan
'Ajlūn
Jarash
Al-Mafraq
Netanya
Nābulus
Jabal 'Anazah
940
Petaḥ Tiqwa
Az-Zarqā
TEL AVIV-YAFO
Lod
Rām Allāh
'Ammān
IRAQ
SAUDI ARABIA
Rishon leZiyyon
Madaba
Reḥovot
Yerushalayim Jerusalem
At-Turayf
Area occupied by Israel since June 1967
Ashqelon
Bayt Laḥm
Buḥayrat al-Burullus
Baltīm
Dumyāṭ
Maṣabb Dumyāṭ
Ghazzah Gaza
Al-Khalīl
Dead Sea
(-396)
Wādī al-Mīrah
AL-ḤAMAD
ISKANDARĪYAH
ALEXANDRIA
Rashīd
Fāriskūr
Būr Sa'īd
Port Said
Khān Yūnis
Maḥaṭṭat al-Qatrānah
Al-Ḥadīthah
Kāf
Al-Jalāmīd
Wādī Ḥāmir
Fuwah
Disūq
Kafr ash-Shaykh
Al-Manzilah
Būr Fu'ad
Sabkhat al-Bardawīl
Rafaḥ
Be'er Sheva'
Al-Karak
ARD AṢ-ṢAWWĀN
Damanhūr
Al-Manṣūrah
Al-Maṭarīyah
Al-'Arīsh
Dimona
AL-ḤARRAH
WĀDĪ AS-SIRḤĀN
Badanah
'Ar'ar
Wādī 'Ar'ar
Ṭanṭā
Al-Maḥallah al-Kubrā
Rummānah
Al-Qanṭarah
HANEGEV
Qeẓiot
EGYPT
Aṭ-Ṭafīlah
Qulbān al-'Isāwīyah
Ziftā
Mīt Ghamr
Al-Ismā'īlīyah
Qanāt as-Suways
Suez Canal
Bi'r Jifjāfah
Mizpe Ramon
Wādī al-Jayb
Shibīn al-Kawm
Minūf
Ashmūn
Az-Zaqāzīq
Banhā
Qalyūb
Al-Buḥayrah al-Murrah al-Kubrā
Great Bitter Lake
Jabal Yu'alliq
1094
Wādī al-'Arīsh
Ash-Shawbak
Al-Jafr
QĀ' AL-JAFR
Imbābah
Al-Jīzah
AL-QĀHIRAH
CAIRO
Ḥulwān
As-Suways
Suez
Būr Tawfīq
An-Nakhl
Al-Kuntillah
Ma'ān
Ra's an-Naqb
JORDAN
SAUDI ARABIA
AL-BUSAYṬAH
Sakākah
Al-Qārah
Al-Jawf
Al-'Ayyāṭ
Birkat Qārūn
Aṣ-Ṣaff
Ibshaway
Sinnūris
Al-Wāsiṭah
Al-Fayyūm
Khalīj as-Suways
Ath-Thamad
Elat
Al-'Aqabah
Jabal Ramm
1754
Al-Mudawwarah
JABAL AT-TUBAYQ
Wādī Fajr
AT-TAWĪL
JABAL AT-TĪH
SHIBH JAZĪRAT SĪNĀ'
SINAI PENINSULA
JABAL AL-'AJMAH
Bi'r Za'farānah
Abū Zanīmah
Ḥaql
Banī Suwayf
Bibā
Al-Fashn
Maghāghah
Wādī 'Arabah
Gulf of Suez
1626
Ra's al-Junaynah
Nuwaybi' al-Muzayyinah
Gulf of Aqaba
Al-Bi'r
AL-'URAYQ
AN-NAFŪD
Banī Mazār
Bahr Yūsuf
Jabal Mūsā
Mount Sinai
2285
2642
Jabal Katrīnah
Dhahab
Jabal al-Lawz
2580
Al-Bid'
AL-HUFRAH
Al-Qalībah
Wādī Nayyāl
Samālūṭ
Al-Minyā
Wādī Hawāshīyah
Wādī aṭ-Ṭarfā
Aṭ-Ṭūr
Nabq
Al-Maqnah
Tabūk
ḤISMĀ
Al-'Assāfīyah
Jubbah
Tallah
Abū Qurqāṣ
Jabal Ṣabrā
1459
Aynūnah
Ash-Sharmah
MADYAN
Qal'at al-Akhḍar
28°
Mallawī
AS-ṢAḤRĀ' ASH-SHARQĪYAH
ARABIAN DESERT
Wādī Qinā
Sharm ash-Shaykh
Madīq Jūbāl
Madīq Tīrān
JAZĪRAT TĪRĀN
JAZĪRAT SANĀFĪR
RA'S MUḤAMMAD
Al-Muwaylīḥ
HARRAT AR-RAHĀ
Qal'at al-Mu'aẓẓam
Wādī al-Akhḍar
Taymā'
Daljā
Dayrūṭ
Al-Qūṣiyah
Manfalūṭ
Abnūb
Wādī al-Asyūṭī
Jamsah
JUZUR TAWĪLAH
JAZĪRAT SHĀKIR
Ad-Dār al-Ḥamrā'
HARRAT AL-'UWAYRIḌ
Asyūṭ
Al-Badārī
Abū Tīj
Ṭimā
Ṭahṭā
Nile
Al-Ghurdaqah
JAZĀ'IR JIFTŪN
Ḍibā
AN-NU'MĀN
Madā'in Ṣāliḥ
Jabal Shā'ib al-Banāt
2187
Akhmīm
Al-Marāghah
Sawhāj
Al-Manshāh
Jirjā
Al-Balyanā
Nahr an-Nīl
Būr Safājah
JAZĪRAT SAFĀJAH
AN-NABQIYAH
AL-'UWAYNḌIYAH
Al-'Ulā
Hafīrat al-'Aydā
Zurayghīt
HARRAT HUTAYM
Dishnā
Qinā
Nag' Ḥammādī
Al-Ballāṣ
Qifṭ
Coptos
Naqādah
Qūṣ
Al-Quṣayr
Al-Wajh
RAYYIKHAH
Wādī al-Jizl
Al-Bi'r al-Jadīd
Ar-Rawḍah
26°
Al-Maḥāriq
Armant
Al-Karnak
Al-Uqṣur
Luxor
Jabal as-Sibā'ī
1477
RED SEA
AL-BAḤR AL-AḤMAR
UMM URUMAH
MASHĀBIH
AL-ḤIJĀZ
Wādī al-Ḥamḍ
Ḥanak
Ash-Shuqaq
Khaybar
HARRAT KHAYBAR
Al-Ḥuwayyiṭ
Al-Khārijah
Aṣfūn al-Maṭā'inah
Al-'Udaysāt
Ad-Dayr
Isnā
SHAYBARA
Ḥadīyah
Abū an-Na'am
Būlāq
Wādī al-Miyāh
Idfū
Ar-Radīsiyah Baḥrī
Jabal Nuqruṣ
1505
Umm Lajj
AL-ḤASSĀNĪ
RA'S ABŪ MADD
HARRAT AL-'UWAYRIḌ
HEJAZ
Bi'r Nāṣif
Bārīs
Salwā Baḥrī
Al-Nasser
Wādī Natash
JAZĪRAT WĀDĪ JIMĀL
RA'S ḤUNKURĀB
Jabal Raḍwā
1814
HARRAT KURAMĀ'
Abyār 'Alī
Al-Madīnah
Medina
Sūq Suwayq
Bimbān
Kawm Umbū
Darāw
Aswān
SADD AL-'ĀLĪ
ASWAN HIGH DAM
Lake Nasser
Jabal Ḥamāṭah
1977
RA'S BARĪDĪ
Yanbu'
Al-Musayjīd
Al-Ḥamrā'
HARRAT RAHAT
Wādī al-'Aqīq
RA'S BANĀS
24°

Lambert Conformal Conic Projection

34° 36° 38° 40°

Kilometers 0 100 200 300 Km.
Miles 0 100 200 300 Mi.

1 : 6 000 000

India

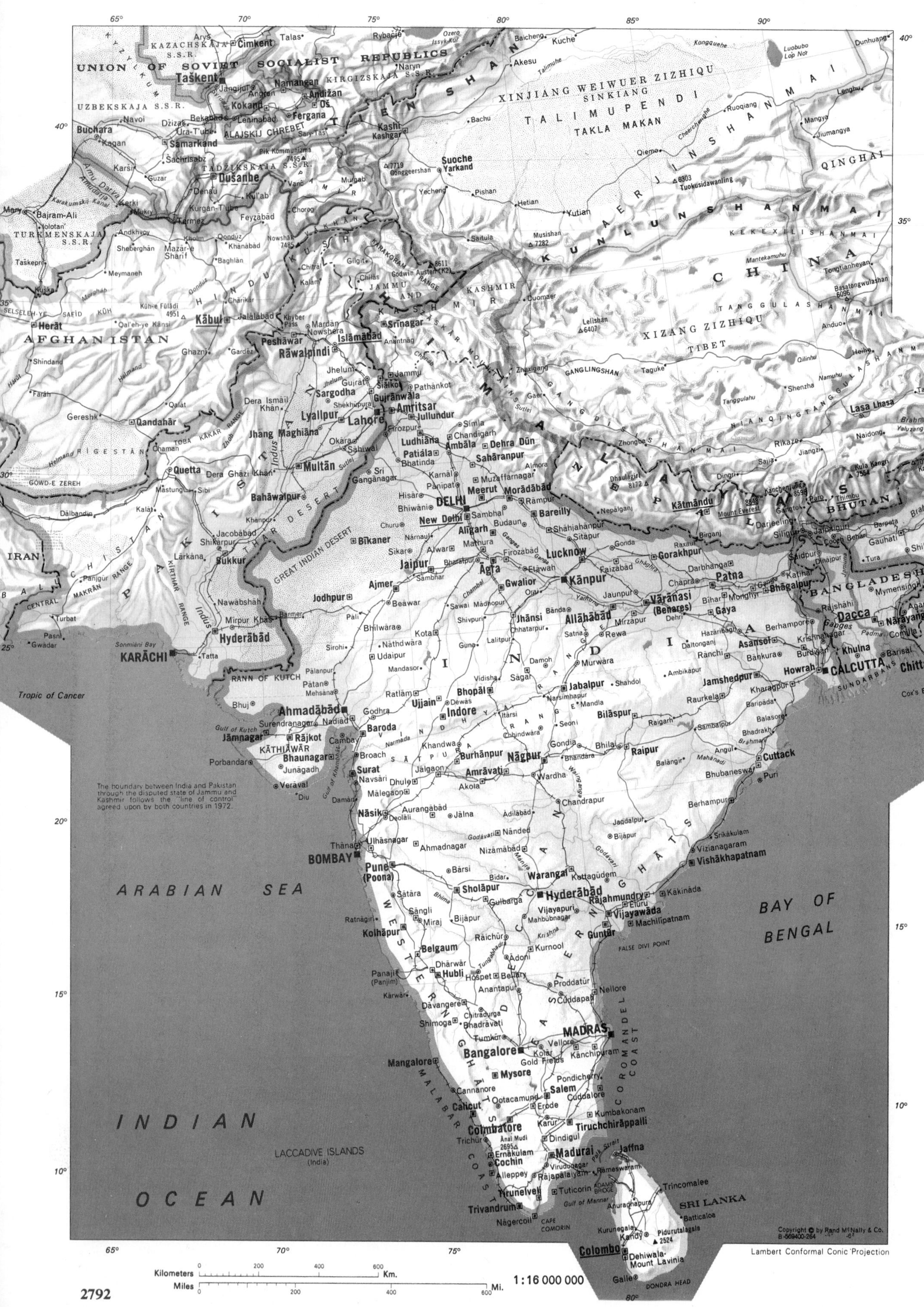

UNION OF SOVIET SOCIALIST REPUBLICS
KAZACHSKAJA S.S.R.
UZBEKSKAJA S.S.R.
KIRGIZSKAJA S.S.R.
TADŽIKSKAJA S.S.R.
TURKMENSKAJA S.S.R.
Taškent
Cimkent
Samarkand
Dušanbe
Buchara
Fergana
Namangan
Andižan
Kokand
Leninabad
Kashi Kashgar
Suoche Yarkand
Hetian
XINJIANG WEIWUER ZIZHIQU
SINKIANG
TALIMUPENDI
TAKLA MAKAN
TIEN SHAN
KUNLUNSHANMAI
ARJINSHANMAI
QINGHAI
CHINA
XIZANG ZIZHIQU
TIBET
TANGGULASHANMAI
NIANQINGTANGGULASHANMAI
Lasa Lhasa
AFGHANISTAN
Kābul
Herāt
Qandahār
HINDU KUSH
KARAKORAM RANGE
Godwin Austen (K2) 8611
JAMMU AND KASHMIR
Srīnagar
PAKISTAN
Islāmābād
Rāwalpindi
Peshāwar
Lahore
Multān
Quetta
Hyderābād
KARĀCHI
IRAN
BALUCHISTAN
THAR DESERT
GREAT INDIAN DESERT
RANN OF KUTCH
Tropic of Cancer
INDIA
DELHI
New Delhi
Amritsar
Jaipur
Āgra
Lucknow
Kānpur
Vārānasi (Benares)
Allāhābād
Patna
NEPAL
Kātmāndu
Mount Everest 8848
BHUTAN
Thimbu
BANGLADESH
Dacca
CALCUTTA
Ahmadābād
Baroda
Surat
Indore
Bhopāl
Jabalpur
Nāgpur
VINDHYA RANGE
SĀTPURA RANGE
BOMBAY
Pune (Poona)
Hyderābād
Vishākhapatnam
DECCAN
WESTERN GHĀTS
EASTERN GHĀTS
Bangalore
Mysore
MADRAS
COROMANDEL COAST
MALABAR COAST
Cochin
Madurai
Trivandrum
CAPE COMORIN
SRI LANKA
Colombo
Jaffna
Trincomalee
ARABIAN SEA
BAY OF BENGAL
INDIAN OCEAN
LACCADIVE ISLANDS (India)
The boundary between India and Pakistan through the disputed state of Jammu and Kashmir follows the "line of control" agreed upon by both countries in 1972.
Copyright © by Rand McNally & Co.
Lambert Conformal Conic Projection
Kilometers 0 200 400 600 Km.
Miles 0 200 400 600 Mi.
1:16 000 000

Southern India and Sri Lanka

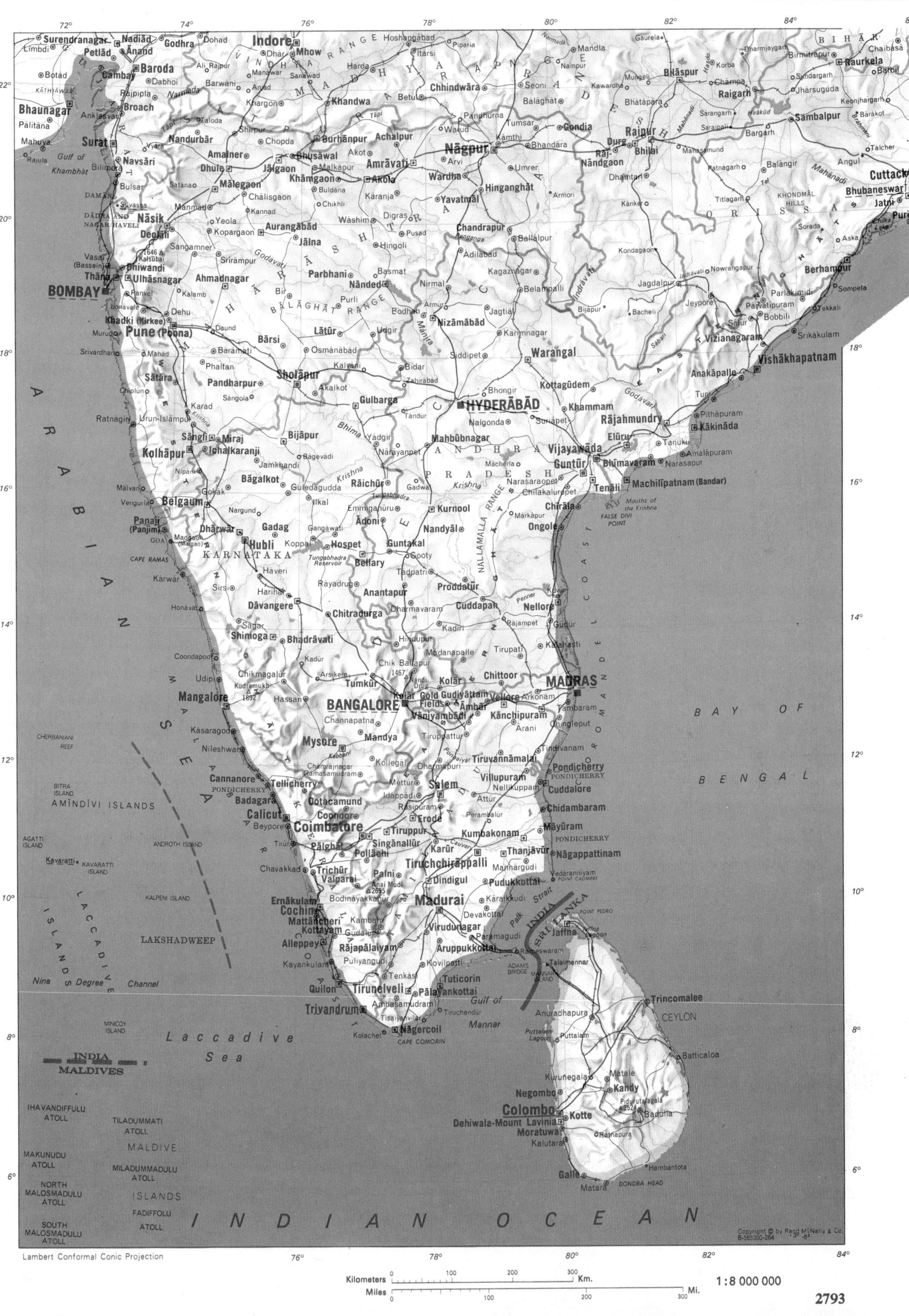

72°
74°
76°
78°
80°
82°
84°
86°
22°
20°
18°
16°
14°
12°
10°
8°
6°
Surendranagar
Limbdi
Nadiād
Petlād
Ānand
Godhra
Dohad
Indore
Mhow
Dhār
Hoshangābād
Itārsi
Piparia
Mandla
Gaurela
Chaibāsa
Birmitrapur
Raurkela
Barbil
Botād
Cambay
Baroda
Dabhoi
Ali Rājpur
Manāwar
Sanāwad
Harda
Chhindwāra
Seoni
Nainpur
Mungeli
Bilāspur
Korba
Chāmpa
Jhārsuguda
Sundargarh
KĀTHIĀWĀR
Rājpipla
Broach
Barwāni
Anjad
Khargon
Khandwa
Betul
Bālāghāt
Kawardha
Bhātapāra
Raigarh
Keonjhargarh
Bhaunagar
Pālitāna
Mahuva
Rājula
Gulf of Khambhāt
Ankleshwar
Surat
Taloda
Shirpur
Tāpi
Pandhurna
Tumsar
Gondia
Rajnāndgaon
Durg
Raipur
Bhilai
Sarangarh
Sambalpur
Bargarh
Bārākot
Talcher
Nandurbār
Vyāra
Chopda
Burhānpur
Achalpur
Wārud
Kāmthi
Bhandāra
Mahāsamund
Navsāri
Bilimora
Amalner
Bhusāwal
Akot
Nāgpur
Arvi
Umrer
Dhamtari
Ratnāgarh
Balāngir
Angul
Cuttack
Dhule
Jalgaon
Malkāpur
Amrāvati
Khāmgaon
Akola
Wardha
Hinganghāt
Bhubaneswar
Jatni
Puri
DAMAN
Bulsār
Satānao
Mālegaon
Buldana
Chikhli
Kāranja
Yavatmāl
Armori
Titlāgarh
KHONDMĀL HILLS
Kānker
Mahānadi
Silvassa
DĀDRA AND NAGAR HAVELI
Chālisgaon
Kannad
Manmād
Nāsik
Yeola
Kopargaon
Deolāli
Aurangābād
Wāshim
Digras
Pusad
Chandrapur
Ballālpur
Sorada
Aska
Chilka Lake
Jālna
Hingoli
Sangamner
Shrīrāmpur
Godāvari
Kondagaon
Vasai (Bassein)
Kalsubai 1646
Bhiwandi
Thāna
Ulhāsnagar
Parbhani
Basmat
Adilābād
Kagaznagar
Indrāvati
Nowrangapur
Berhampur
Ahmadnagar
Nānded
Nirmal
Belampalli
Jagdalpur
Sompeta
BOMBAY
Panvel
Kalamb
Bīr
Purli
BĀLĀGHĀT RANGE
Bodhan
Armūr
Jagtiāl
Bijāpur
Bacheli
Jeypore
Parlākimidi
Pārvatipuram
Tekkali
Bobbili
Khadki (Kirkee)
Dehu
Daund
Nizāmābād
Sālūr
Vizianagaram
Srīkākulam
Murud
Pune (Poona)
Lātūr
Udgir
Karīmnagar
Bārsi
Māñjra
Srivardhan
Mahād
Bārāmati
Osmānābād
Siddipet
Warangal
Vishākhapatnam
Phaltan
Kalyāni
Bīdar
Anakāpalle
Sātāra
Pandharpur
Sholāpur
Zahirābād
Kottagūdem
Tuni
Chiplun
Akalkot
Bhongir
Godāvari
Pithāpuram
Sāngola
Gulbarga
HYDERĀBĀD
Khammam
Kākināda
Karad
Tāndūr
Nalgonda
Suriāpet
Rājahmundry
Ratnāgiri
Urun-Islāmpur
Bhīma
Krishna
Sāngli
Miraj
Bijāpur
Yādgīr
Mahbūbnagar
Elūru
Tanuku
Kolhāpur
Ichalkaranji
Bāgevādi
Nārāyanpet
ANDHRA PRADESH
Vijayawāda
Amalāpuram
Narasāpur
Jamkhandi
Mācherla
Guntūr
Bhīmavaram
Nipāni
Bāgalkot
Rāichūr
Krishna
Machilīpatnam (Bandar)
Tenāli
Narasaraopet
Chilakalūrupet
Mālvan
Gokak
Guledagudda
Gadwāl
Tungabhadra
Vengurla
Belgaum
Ilkal
Chīrāla
Mouths of the Krishna
FALSE DIVI POINT
Nargund
Emmiganūru
Kurnool
Ādoni
Markāpur
Panaji (Panjim)
Dhārwār
Gadag
Gangāwati
Nandyāl
Ongole
GOA
Madgaon (Margao)
Hubli
Koppal
Hospet
Guntakal
Gooty
NALLAMALLA RANGE
KARNATAKA
Tungabhadra Reservoir
Bellary
CAPE RAMAS
Kārwār
Haveri
Tādpatri
Sirsi
Rāyadrug
Anantapur
Proddatūr
Harihar
Penner
Kāvali
Honāvar
Dāvangere
Dharmavaram
Cuddapah
Nellore
Chitradurga
Sāgar
Kadiri
Rājampet
Gūdūr
Shimoga
Bhadrāvati
Hindupur
Tirupati
Kālahasti
Coondapoor
Kadūr
Madanapalle
Udipi
Chikmagalūr
Arsikere
Chik Ballāpur
Chittoor
Kudremukh 1892
1467
Tumkūr
Nandi Drug
Kolār
MADRAS
Mangalore
Hassan
Kolār Gold Fields
Gudiyāttam
Vellore
Arkonam
BANGALORE
Āmbūr
Vāniyambādi
Kānchipuram
Tāmbaram
Chingleput
Channapatna
Arani
Kāsaragod
Mandya
Tiruppattūr
CHERBANIANI REEF
Nileshwar
Mysore
Kabbani
Kollegāl
Tindivanam
Dharmapuri
Tiruvannāmalai
Chāmrājnagar
Ramasamudram
Ponnaiyār
Pondicherry
PONDICHERRY
Cannanore
Tellicherry
Mettūr
Villupuram
Nellikuppam
PONDICHERRY
Idappādi
Salem
Cuddalore
BITRA ISLAND
AMĪNDĪVI ISLANDS
Badagara
Ootacamund
Rāsipuram
Ātūr
Coonoor
Perambalūr
Chidambaram
Calicut
Beypore
Coimbatore
Erode
Tiruppur
Kumbakonam
Māyūram
AGATTI ISLAND
ANDROTH ISLAND
Tirūr
Pālghāt
Singānallūr
Karūr
Cauvery
Thanjāvūr
Nāgappattinam
Pollāchi
Kavaratti
KAVARATTI ISLAND
Chavakkad
Trichūr
Tiruchchirāppalli
Mannārgudi
Vālpārai
Palni
Anai Mudi 2695
Dindigul
Pudukkottai
Vedāranniyam
POINT CALIMERE
KALPENI ISLAND
Ernākulam
Bodinayakkanūr
Madurai
Kāraikkudi
Cochin
Mattancheri
Kottayam
Kambam
Gūdalūr
Devakottai
Virudunagar
Palk Strait
INDIA
SRI LANKA
POINT PEDRO
Jaffna
Jaffna Lagoon
LAKSHADWEEP
Alleppey
Rājapālaiyam
Aruppukkottai
Paramagudi
Rameswaram
Kayankulam
Puliyangudi
Kovilpatti
ADAMS BRIDGE
Talaimannar
MANNAR ISLAND
Nine Degree Channel
Tenkāsi
Tuticorin
Quilon
Tirunelveli
Pālayankottai
Trincomalee
Ambāsamudram
Gulf of Mannar
Trivandrum
Tiruchendūr
Anuradhapura
CEYLON
MINICOY ISLAND
Tisaiyanvilai
Nāgercoil
Kolachel
CAPE COMORIN
Puttalam Lagoon
Puttalam
Laccadive Sea
INDIA
MALDIVES
Batticaloa
Kurunegala
Matale
Kandy
Negombo
Pidurutalagala 2524
Colombo
Kotte
Badulla
IHAVANDIFFULU ATOLL
TILADUMMATI ATOLL
Dehiwala-Mount Lavinia
Moratuwa
Ratnapura
MALDIVE
Kalutara
MAKUNUDU ATOLL
MILADUMMADULU ATOLL
Hambantota
NORTH MALOSMADULU ATOLL
ISLANDS
Galle
Matara
DONDRA HEAD
FADIFFOLU ATOLL
SOUTH MALOSMADULU ATOLL
INDIAN OCEAN
BAY OF BENGAL
ARABIAN SEA
Lambert Conformal Conic Projection
Kilometers 0 100 200 300 Km.
Miles 0 100 200 300 Mi.
1:8 000 000

Northern India and the Himalayas

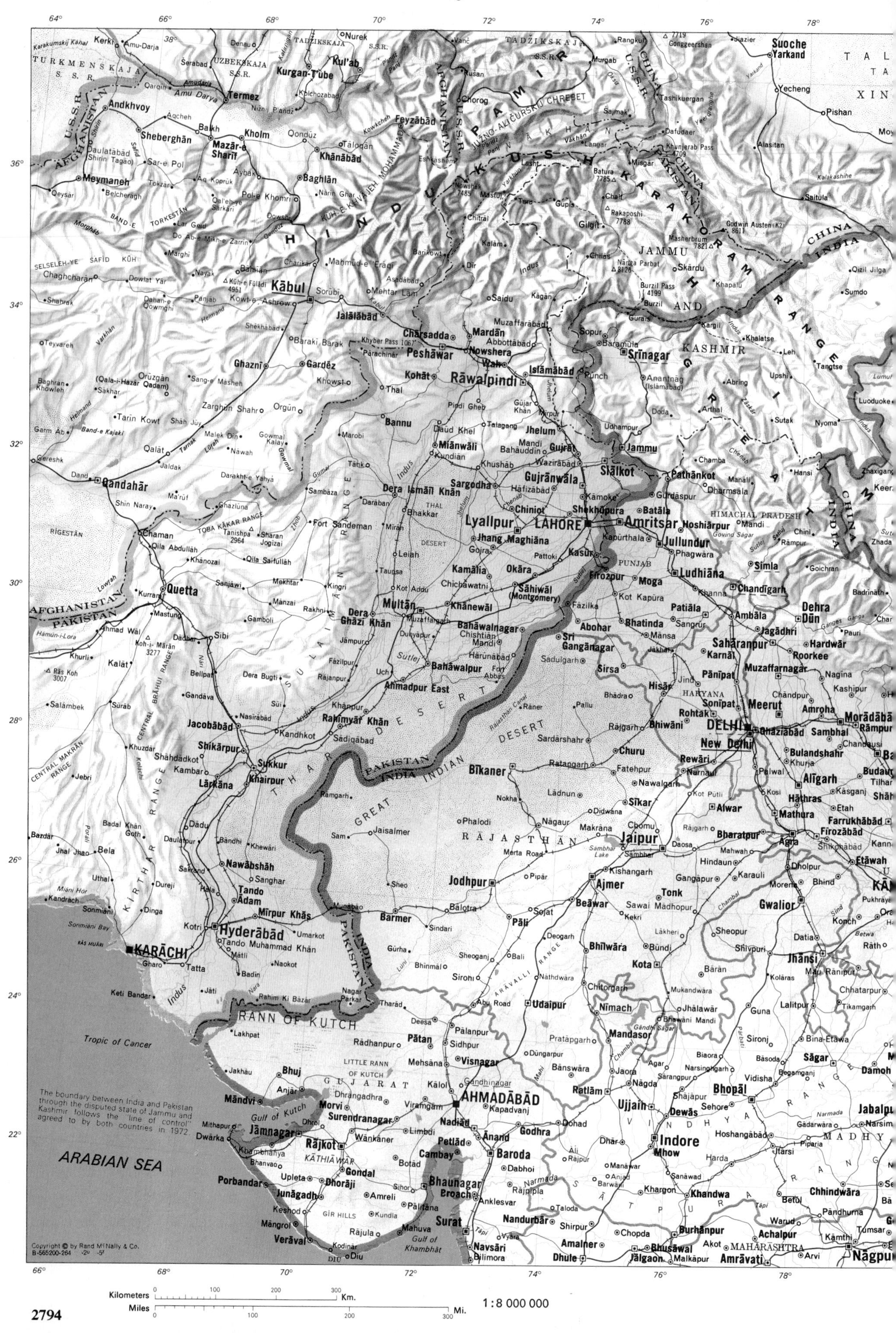

64°
66°
68°
70°
72°
74°
76°
78°
36°
34°
32°
30°
28°
26°
24°
22°
TURKMENSKAJA S.S.R.
UZBEKSKAJA S.S.R.
TADZIKSKAJA S.S.R.
U.S.S.R.
AFGHANISTAN
PAKISTAN
CHINA
INDIA
Kerki
Amu-Darja
Termez
Kurgan-Tube
Kul'ab
Nurek
Andkhvoy
Sheberghān
Mazār-e Sharīf
Kholm
Qonduz
Tāloqān
Khānābād
Feyzābād
Baghlān
Meymaneh
Chorog
PAMIR
HINDU KUSH
KARAKORAM RANGE
Rangkul
Murgab
Tashikuergan
Suoche
Yarkand
Yecheng
Pishan
Gilgit
Batura 7785
Rakaposhi 7788
Godwin Austen (K2) 8611
Masherbrum 7821
Nanga Parbat 8126
Skārdu
JAMMU AND KASHMIR
Chitral
Dir
Kābul
Jalālābād
Sorubi
Bāmiān
Ghaznī
Gardēz
Charsadda
Mardān
Peshāwar
Nowshera
Khyber Pass 1067
Kohāt
Rāwalpindi
Islāmābād
Abbottābād
Muzaffarābād
Srīnagar
Sopur
Bāramula
Anantnāg (Islāmābād)
Leh
Kargil
Jammu
Sialkot
Pathānkot
Gujrānwāla
Gujrāt
Jhelum
Sargodha
Miānwāli
Bannu
Dera Ismāīl Khān
Lyallpur
LAHORE
Amritsar
Batāla
Jullundur
Hoshiārpur
Ludhiāna
Simla
Chandīgarh
HIMACHAL PRADESH
PUNJAB
Firozpur
Moga
Patiāla
Ambāla
Dehra Dūn
Jhang Maghiāna
Okāra
Sāhīwāl (Montgomery)
Multān
Khānewāl
Kamālia
Dera Ghāzi Khān
Bahāwalnagar
Bahāwalpur
Ahmadpur East
Rahīmyār Khān
Sādiqābād
Sri Gangānagar
Bhatinda
Sirsa
Hisār
Rohtak
Bhiwāni
HARYANA
Pānīpat
Karnāl
Saharanpur
Hardwār
Roorkee
Muzaffarnagar
Meerut
Sonīpat
DELHI
New Delhi
Ghāziābād
Morādābād
Rāmpur
Bulandshahr
Alīgarh
Hāthras
Mathura
Āgra
Farrukhābād
Fīrozābād
Etāwah
Kandahār
Chaman
Quetta
Sibi
Kalāt
Jacobābād
Shikārpur
Sukkur
Khairpur
Lārkāna
SULAIMAN RANGE
KIRTHAR RANGE
THAR DESERT
GREAT INDIAN DESERT
RĀJASTHĀN
Bīkaner
Churu
Sīkar
Jaipur
Alwar
Bharatpur
Jaisalmer
Jodhpur
Ajmer
Nāgaur
Beāwar
Tonk
Gwalior
Jhānsi
Nawābshāh
Tando Ādam
Mīrpur Khās
Hyderābād
KARĀCHI
Tatta
Badin
Bhuj
RANN OF KUTCH
Tropic of Cancer
Gulf of Kutch
Māndvi
Jāmnagar
Dwārka
Porbandar
Rājkot
Gondal
Junāgadh
Verāval
KĀTHIĀWĀR
GUJARAT
Morvi
Surendranagar
AHMADĀBĀD
Gāndhinagar
Nadiād
Cambay
Baroda
Bhaunagar
Broach
Surat
Navsāri
Gulf of Khambhāt
Diu
Pālanpur
Pātan
Mehsāna
Udaipur
Chitorgarh
Bhīlwāra
Kota
Būndi
Nīmach
Mandasor
Ratlām
Ujjain
Dewās
Indore
Mhow
Bhopāl
Sāgar
Jabalpur
Hoshangābād
Khandwa
Burhānpur
Bhusāwal
Jalgaon
Dhule
Amalner
Amrāvati
Achalpur
Nāgpur
MAHĀRĀSHTRA
VINDHYA RANGE
SĀTPURA
Narmada
Indus
Sutlej
Chenab
Jhelum
ARABIAN SEA
The boundary between India and Pakistan through the disputed state of Jammu and Kashmir follows the "line of control" agreed to by both countries in 1972.
Copyright © by Rand McNally & Co. B-565200-264
Kilometers 0 100 200 300 Km.
Miles 0 100 200 300 Mi.
1:8 000 000

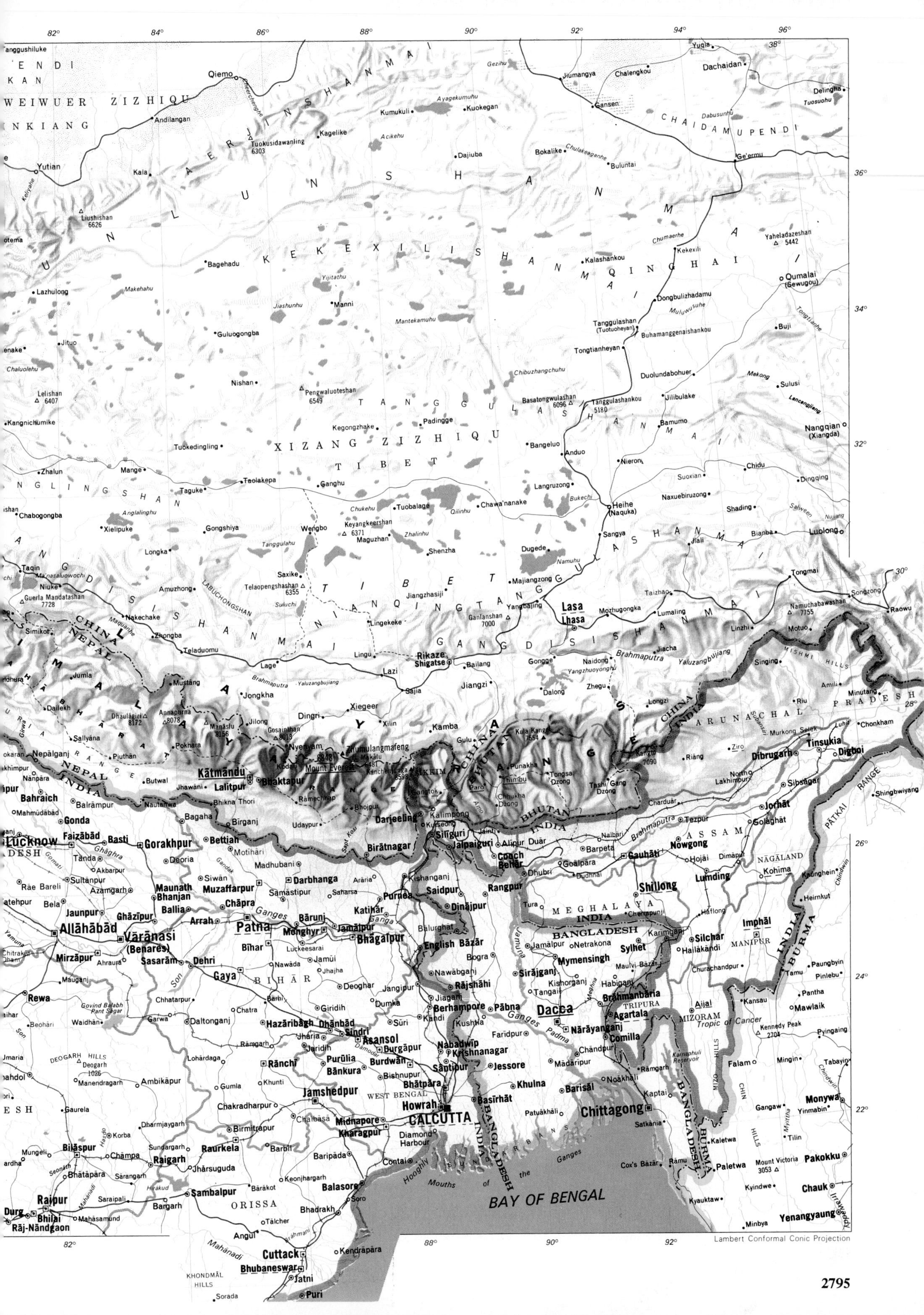
XIZANG ZIZHIQU
TIBET
BAY OF BENGAL
Mouths of the Ganges
Lasa
Lhasa
Kātmāndu
Mount Everest
CALCUTTA
Dacca
Chittagong
Patna
Lucknow
Allāhābād
Vārānasi
(Benares)
Shillong
Imphāl
Tropic of Cancer
Lambert Conformal Conic Projection

China, Japan and Korea

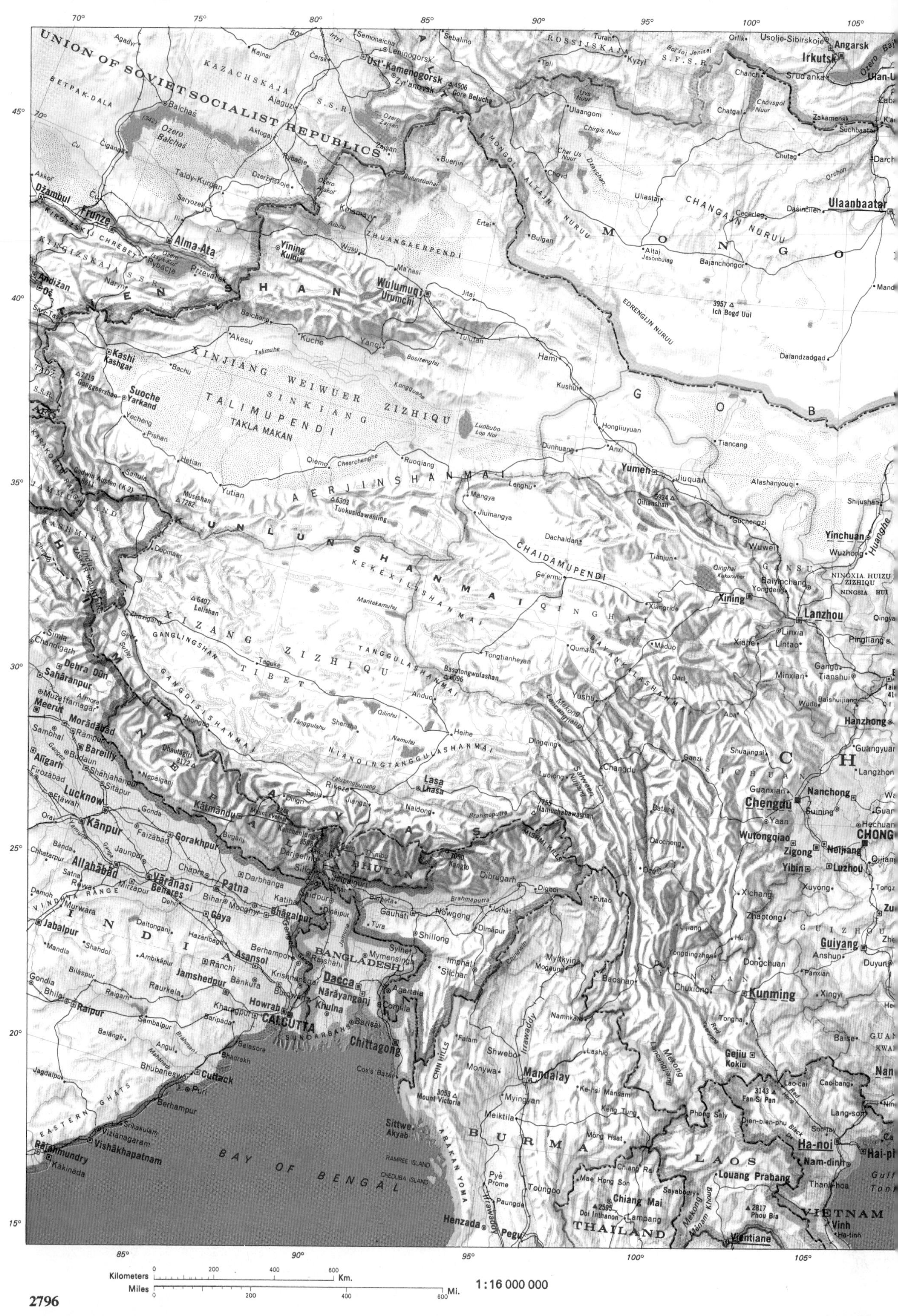

UNION OF SOVIET SOCIALIST REPUBLICS
KAZACHSKAJA S.S.R.
BETPAK-DALA
Ozero Balchaš
Balchaš
Semipalatinsk
Ust'-Kamenogorsk
Leninogorsk
Zyr'anovsk
4506 Gora Belucha
Zajsan
Ozero Zajsan
Ajaguz
Aktogaj
Taldy-Kurgan
Džambul
Frunze
Alma-Ata
Issyk-Kul'
Rybač'e
Prževal'sk
KIRGIZSKAJA S.S.R.
Naryn
Andižan
Oš
TIEN SHAN
Yining Kuldja
Wusu
Kelamayi
ZHUNGAERPENDI
Ma'nasi
Wulumuqi Urumchi
Jitai
Baicheng
Akesu
Kuche
Yanqi
Tulufan
Bositenghu
Hami
Kushui
Kashi Kashgar
Bachu
Suoche Yarkand
Yecheng
Pishan
Hetian
Yutian
Qiemo
Ruoqiang
XINJIANG WEIWUER ZIZHIQU
SINKIANG
TALIMUPENDI
TAKLA MAKAN
Luobubo Lop Nor
AERJINSHANMAI
6303 Tuokusidawanling
KUNLUNSHANMAI
KEKEXILISHANMAI
Mangya
Jiumangya
Dachaidan
CHAIDAMUPENDI
Ge'ermu
QINGHAI
Qinghai Kukunor
Xining
Lanzhou
Yinchuan
Wuwei
Lenghu
Dunhuang
Anxi
Yumen
Jiuquan
5934 Qilianshan
Tianjun
Honglluyuan
Tiancang
Alashanyouqi
Godwin Austen (K2) 8611
JAMMU AND KASHMIR
KARAKORAM RANGE
Musishan 7282
6407 Lelishan
Mantekamuhu
XIZANG ZIZHIQU
TIBET
GANGLINGSHAN
GANGDISISHANMAI
TANGGULASHANMAI
Basitongwulashan 6096
Tongtianheyan
Qumalai
BAYANKALASHANMAI
Maduo
Anduo
Heihe
Shenzha
Namuhu
NIANQINGTANGGULASHANMAI
Lasa Lhasa
Rikaze
Yaluzangbujiang
Naidong
Mount Everest
Kanchenjunga
Dhaulagiri 8172
NEPAL
Kātmāndu
Nepalganj
HIMALAYAS
Namuchabawashan 7755
Changdu
Dingqing
Luolong
Salween Nujiang
Mekong Lancangjiang
Yushu
Ganzi
Batang
Daocheng
SICHUAN
Chengdu
Ya'an
Guanxian
Nanchong
Suining
Neijiang
Zigong
Yibin
Luzhou
Xichang
Wutongqiao
Guiyang
Anshun
GUIZHOU
Kunming
Chuxiong
Dongchuan
Lijiang
Baoshan
YUNNAN
Xiahe
Linxia
Lintao
Pingliang
Tianshui
Minxian
Hanzhong
Guangyuan
Aba
Dari
Shuajingsi
Simla
Chandigarh
Dehra Dūn
Sahāranpur
Meerut
Morādābād
Bareilly
Aligarh
Shāhjahānpur
Lucknow
Kānpur
Gorakhpur
Allahābād
Vārānasi Benares
Patna
Gaya
Bhāgalpur
Darjeeling
Thimbu
BHUTAN
7090 Kangto
Dibrugarh
Brahmaputra
Gauhāti
Shillong
Imphāl
Silchar
BANGLADESH
Dacca
Khulna
Chittagong
CALCUTTA
Howrah
Asansol
Rānchi
Jamshedpur
Raipur
Jabalpur
Cuttack
Puri
Berhampur
Vishākhapatnam
Rājahmundry
Kākināda
INDIA
VINDHYA RANGE
EASTERN GHATS
BAY OF BENGAL
SUNDARBANS
Cox's Bazar
CHIN HILLS
3053 Mount Victoria
Sittwe Akyab
RAMREE ISLAND
CHEDUBA ISLAND
ARAKAN YOMA
BURMA
Mandalay
Myitkyina
Shwebo
Monywa
Meiktila
Lashio
Irrawaddy
Pyè Prome
Toungoo
Henzada
Pegu
THAILAND
Chiang Mai
Chiang Rai
2595 Doi Inthanon
Lampang
LAOS
Louang Prabang
Vientiane
2817 Phou Bia
VIETNAM
Ha-noi
Hai-phong
Nam-dinh
Thanh-hoa
Vinh
Ha-tinh
3143 Fan-Si Pan
Lao-cai
Dien-bien-phu
Lang-son
Gulf of Tonkin
MONGOLIA
CHANGAJN NURUU
MONGOL ALTAJN NURUU
GOBI
Ulaanbaatar
Ulaangom
Uvs Nuur
Chövsgöl Nuur
Chovd
Uliastaj
Altaj
Bajanchongor
3957 Ich Bogd Uul
Dalandzadgad
Irkutsk
Angarsk
Kyzyl
ROSSIJSKAJA S.F.S.R.
Kilometers 0 200 400 600 Km.
Miles 0 200 400 600 Mi.
1:16 000 000

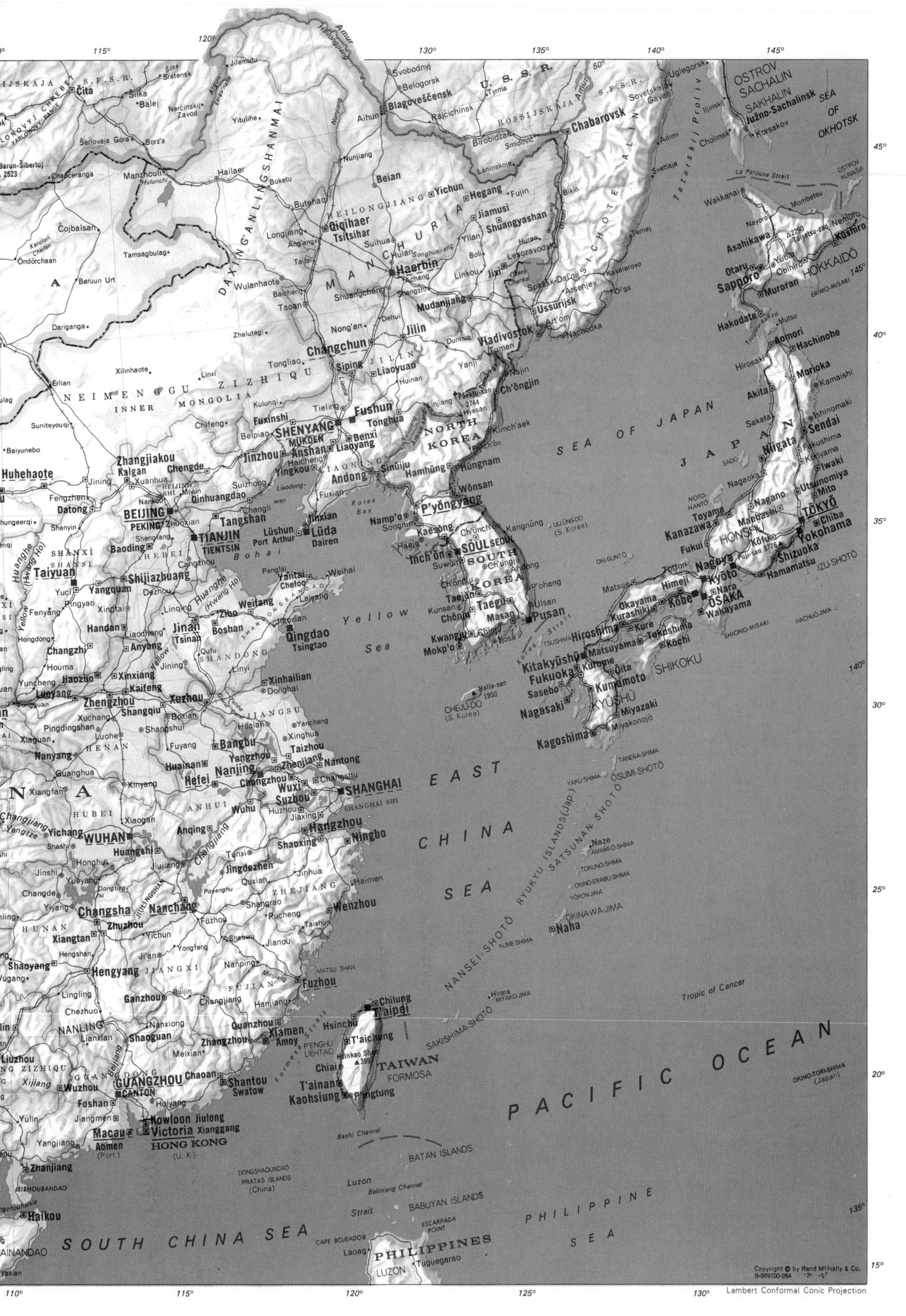

U. S. S. R.
MANCHURIA
HEILONGJIANG
JILIN
DAXINGANLINGSHANMAI
NEIMENGGU ZIZHIQU
INNER MONGOLIA
LIAONING
HEBEI
SHANXI
SHANDONG
JIANGSU
ANHUI
HENAN
HUBEI
HUNAN
JIANGXI
ZHEJIANG
FUJIAN
NORTH KOREA
SOUTH KOREA
JAPAN
HOKKAIDŌ
HONSHU
SHIKOKU
KYŪSHŪ
TAIWAN
FORMOSA
HONG KONG (U. K.)
PHILIPPINES
LUZON
SEA OF JAPAN
SEA OF OKHOTSK
Yellow Sea
Bohai
Korea Bay
EAST CHINA SEA
SOUTH CHINA SEA
PHILIPPINE SEA
PACIFIC OCEAN
Tropic of Cancer
Formosa Strait
Korea Strait
Tatarskij Proliv
La Pérouse Strait
Bashi Channel
Luzon Strait
Balintang Channel
BATAN ISLANDS
BABUYAN ISLANDS
RYUKYU ISLANDS (Jap.)
NANSEI-SHOTŌ
SATSUNAN-SHOTŌ
SAKISHIMA-SHOTŌ
OSUMI-SHOTŌ
IZU-SHOTŌ
CHEJU-DO (S. Korea)
ULLŪNG-DO (S. Korea)
OKINAWA-JIMA
OSTROV SACHALIN
SAKHALIN
DONGSHAQUNDAO
PRATAS ISLANDS (China)
Amur
Heilongjiang
Huanghe (Hwang Ho)
Changjiang (Yangtze)
Chita
Blagoveščensk
Chabarovsk
Južno-Sachalinsk
Vladivostok
Harbin
Qiqihaer
Tsitsihar
Changchun
Jilin
Shenyang
Mukden
Fushun
Anshan
Andong
Lüda
Dairen
Port Arthur
Beijing
Peking
Tianjin
Tientsin
Tangshan
Taiyuan
Shijiazhuang
Jinan
Tsinan
Qingdao
Tsingtao
Zhengzhou
Xuzhou
Nanjing
Hefei
Shanghai
Hangzhou
Ningbo
Wuhan
Changsha
Nanchang
Fuzhou
Xiamen
Amoy
Guangzhou
Canton
Kowloon
Victoria
Macau
Aomen (Port.)
Shantou
Swatow
Haikou
Zhanjiang
Huhehaote
Zhangjiakou
Kalgan
Datong
P'yŏngyang
Sinŭiju
Hamhŭng
Wŏnsan
Ch'ŏngjin
Kaesŏng
Sŏul
Seoul
Inch'ŏn
Taegu
Pusan
Kwangju
Mokp'o
Taipei
Chilung
T'aichung
T'ainan
Kaohsiung
Tōkyō
Yokohama
Ōsaka
Kyōto
Kōbe
Nagoya
Hiroshima
Kitakyūshū
Fukuoka
Nagasaki
Kagoshima
Sapporo
Hakodate
Aomori
Sendai
Niigata
Kanazawa
Naha
Fuji-san 3776
Halla-san 1950
Paektu-san 2744
Copyright © by Rand McNally & Co.
Lambert Conformal Conic Projection

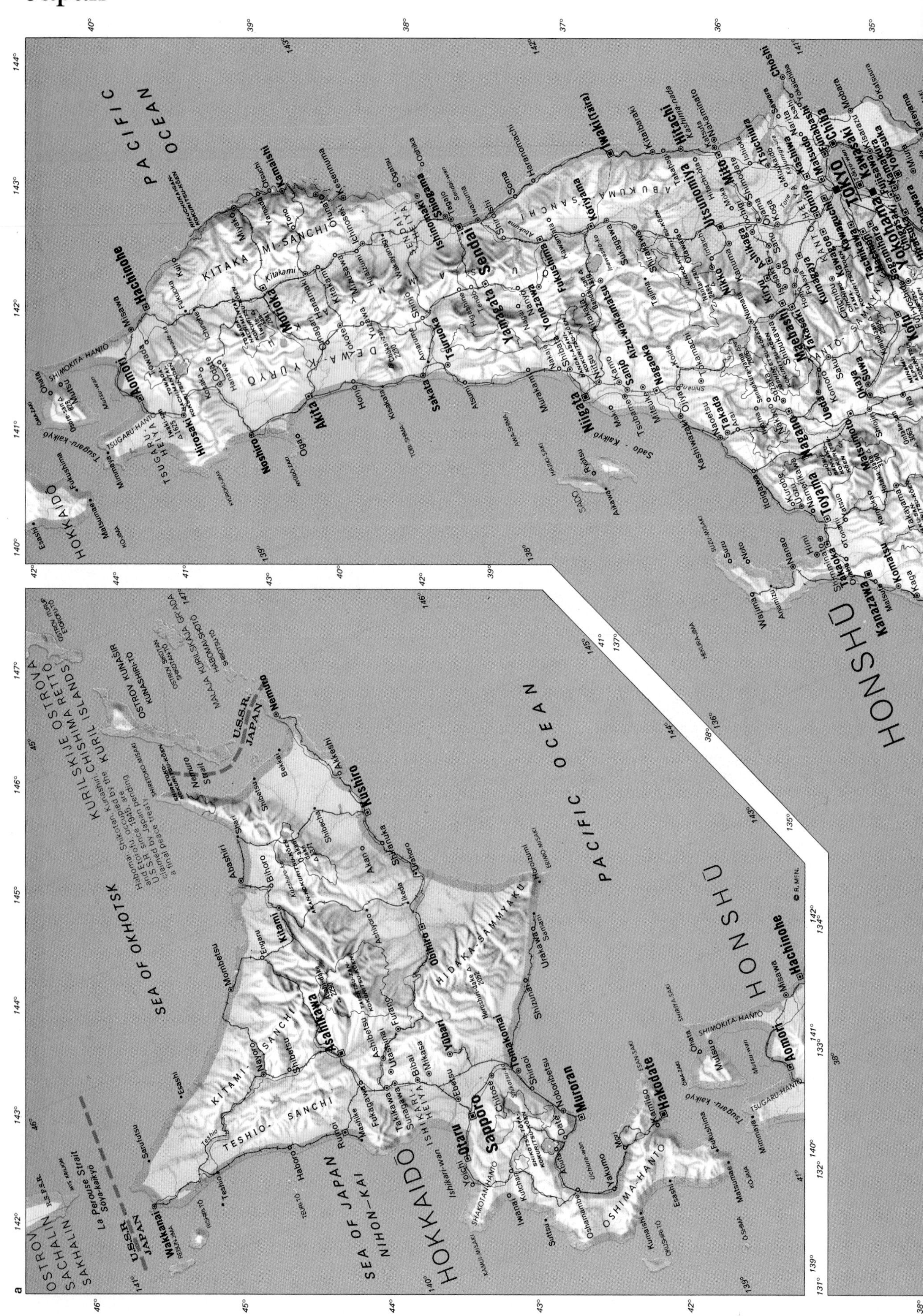
PACIFIC OCEAN
KITAKAMI-SANCHI
DEWA-KYURYO
ABUKUMA-SANCHI
Hachinohe
Aomori
Hirosaki
Akita
Noshiro
Morioka
Kamaishi
Sendai
Yamagata
Sakata
Tsuruoka
Fukushima
Koriyama
Iwaki (Taira)
Niigata
Nagaoka
Sado
Utsunomiya
Mito
Hitachi
Maebashi
Nagano
Toyama
Kanazawa
Takaoka
Matsumoto
Kofu
TOKYO
Yokohama
Kawasaki
Chiba
Choshi
HONSHŪ
SEA OF OKHOTSK
KURILSKIJE OSTROVA
CHISHIMA-RETTO
KURIL ISLANDS
OSTROV SAKHALIN
SAKHALIN
La Perouse Strait
Soya-kaikyo
U.S.S.R.
JAPAN
Wakkanai
SEA OF JAPAN
NIHON-KAI
HOKKAIDŌ
TESHIO-SANCHI
KITAMI-SANCHI
HIDAKA-SAMMYAKU
Asahikawa
Kitami
Abashiri
Kushiro
Nemuro
Obihiro
Sapporo
Otaru
Tomakomai
Muroran
Hakodate
OSHIMA-HANTO
Tsugaru-kaikyo
SHIMOKITA-HANTO

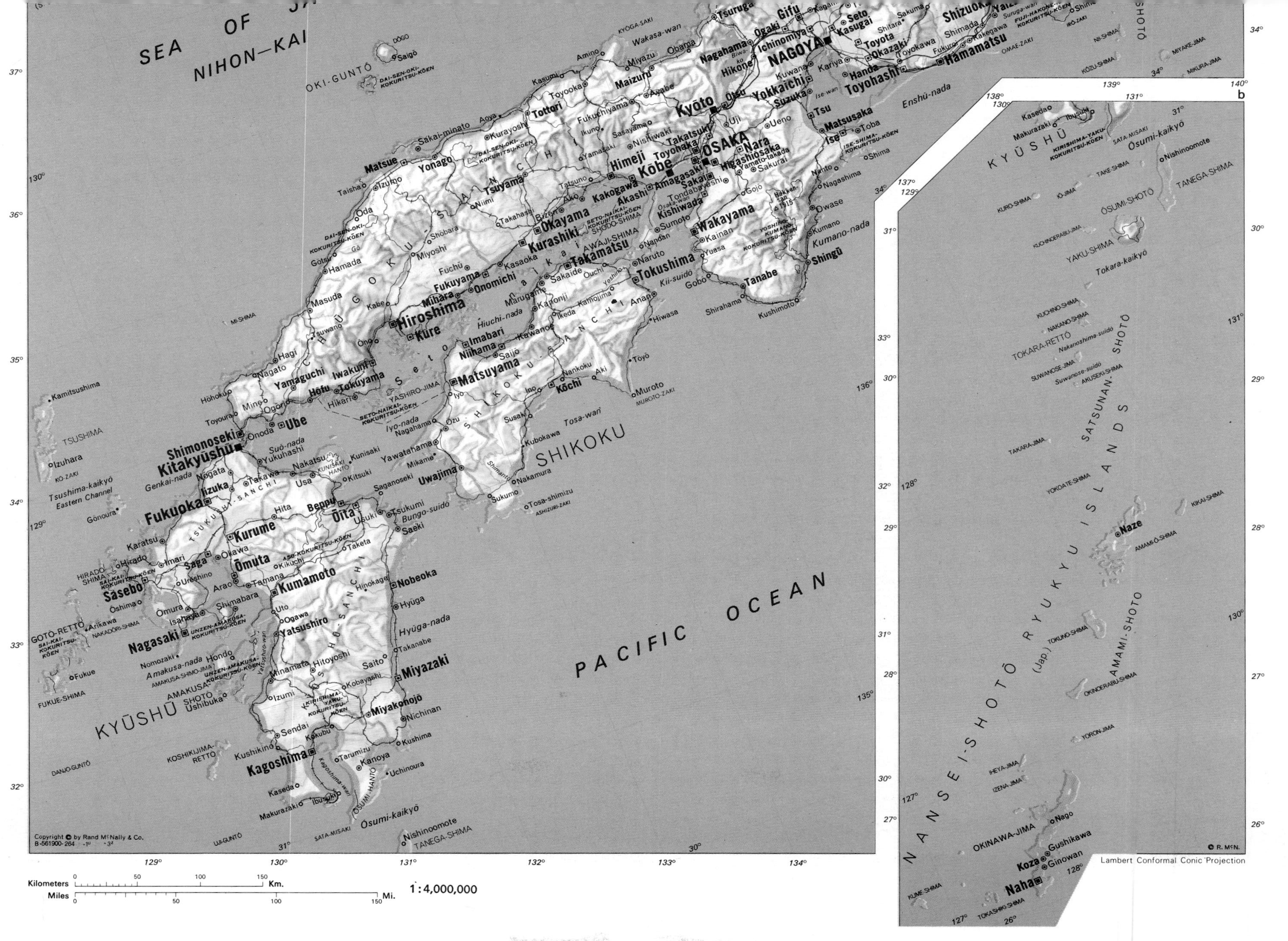

SEA OF
NIHON-KAI
PACIFIC OCEAN
OKI-GUNTŌ
Saigō
DAI-SEN-OKI-KOKURITSU-KŌEN
Tsuruga
Gifu
Seto
Kasugai
Shizuoka
NAGOYA
Ogaki
Ichinomiya
Nagahama
Hikone
Toyota
Okazaki
Toyokawa
Hamamatsu
Toyohashi
Handa
Kariya
Yokkaichi
Suzuka
Tsu
Matsusaka
Ise
Toba
Enshū-nada
Wakasa-wan
Obama
Miyazu
Maizuru
Ayabe
Kyōto
Ōtsu
Uji
ŌSAKA
Nara
Higashiōsaka
Sakai
Kishiwada
Wakayama
Tanabe
Shingū
Kumano-nada
Kii-suidō
Kōbe
Amagasaki
Himeji
Kakogawa
Akashi
Okayama
Kurashiki
Takamatsu
Tokushima
Naruto
Anan
Tottori
Yonago
Matsue
Izumo
Hamada
Tsuyama
Kurayoshi
Fukuyama
Onomichi
Mihara
Hiroshima
Kure
Iwakuni
Tokuyama
Yamaguchi
Hōfu
Ube
Hagi
Shimonoseki
Kitakyūshū
Fukuoka
Kurume
Ōmuta
Kumamoto
Saga
Sasebo
Nagasaki
Ōita
Beppu
Nobeoka
Miyazaki
Miyakonojō
Kagoshima
Sendai
Yatsushiro
Minamata
Imabari
Niihama
Matsuyama
Kōchi
Uwajima
Saijō
SHIKOKU
Tosa-wan
Muroto
Ashizuri-zaki
Hiuchi-nada
Iyo-nada
Suō-nada
Bungo-suidō
Hyūga-nada
Genkai-nada
Tsushima-kaikyō
Eastern Channel
TSUSHIMA
Izuhara
Kamitsushima
GOTŌ-RETTŌ
FUKUE-SHIMA
Fukue
KYŪSHŪ
AMAKUSA-SHOTŌ
KOSHIKIJIMA-RETTŌ
Ōsumi-kaikyō
Nishinoomote
TANEGA-SHIMA
CHŪGOKU-SANCHI
SHIKOKU-SANCHI
KYŪSHŪ-SANCHI
Seto-naikai
Copyright © by Rand McNally & Co.
B-561900-264
Kilometers 0 50 100 150 Km.
Miles 0 50 100 150 Mi.
1:4,000,000
b
KYŪSHŪ
Ōsumi-kaikyō
ŌSUMI-SHOTŌ
YAKU-SHIMA
TANEGA-SHIMA
Tokara-kaikyō
TOKARA-RETTŌ
SATSUNAN-SHOTŌ
NANSEI-SHOTŌ (Jap.)
RYUKYU ISLANDS
AMAMI-SHOTŌ
AMAMI-Ō-SHIMA
Naze
TOKUNO-SHIMA
OKINOERABU-SHIMA
YORON-JIMA
OKINAWA-JIMA
Nago
Gushikawa
Koza
Ginowan
Naha
© R. McN.
Lambert Conformal Conic Projection

Eastern China, Hong Kong and Taiwan

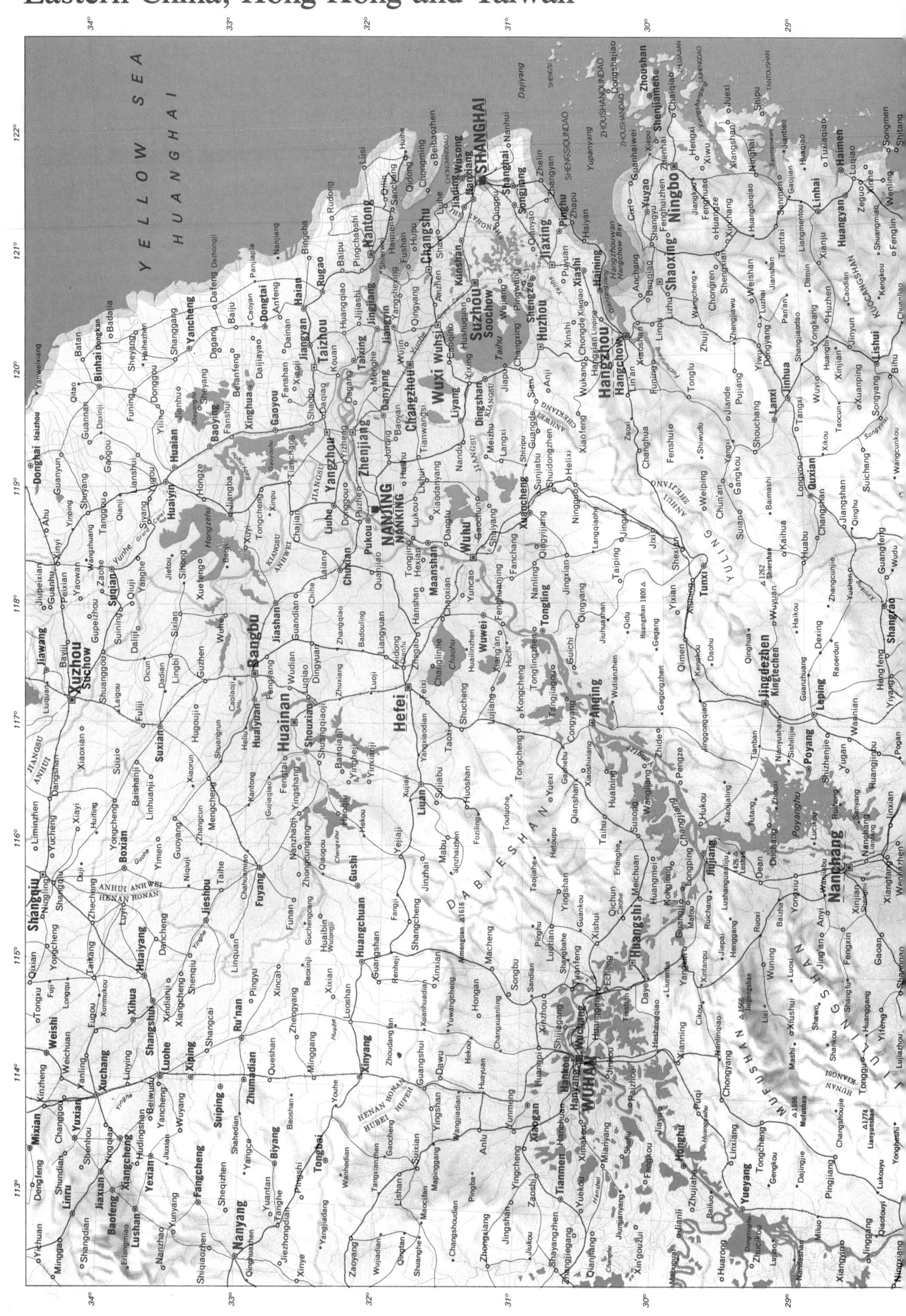

YELLOW SEA
HUANGHAI
SHANGHAI
NANJING
NANKING
WUHAN
Hefei
Hangzhou
Suzhou
Soochow
Wuxi
Changzhou
Zhenjiang
Yangzhou
Wuhu
Anqing
Bangbu
Huainan
Xuzhou
Nanchang
Jingdezhen
Ningbo
Shaoxing
Nantong
Huangshi
DABIESHAN
Poyanghu
Taihu

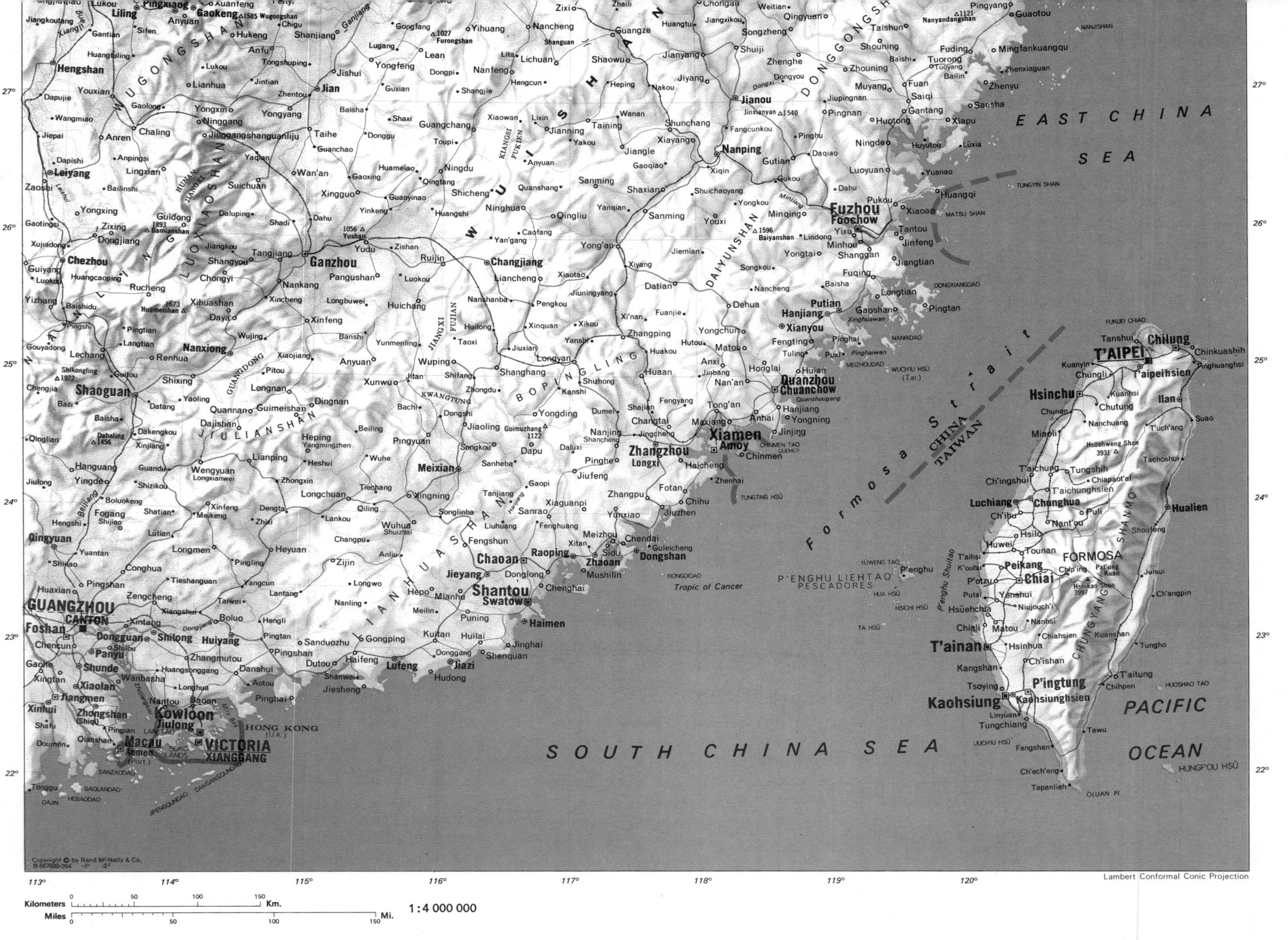

EAST CHINA SEA
SOUTH CHINA SEA
PACIFIC OCEAN
Formosa Strait
CHINA TAIWAN
FORMOSA
T'AIPEI
Kaohsiung
T'ainan
Fuzhou
Foochow
Xiamen
Amoy
Quanzhou
Chuanchow
Zhangzhou
Shantou
Swatow
GUANGZHOU
CANTON
HONG KONG (U.K.)
VICTORIA
Kowloon
Macau
Ganzhou
Hengshan
P'ENGHU LIEHTAO
PESCADORES
Tropic of Cancer
Lambert Conformal Conic Projection
1:4 000 000
Kilometers
Miles
Copyright © by Rand McNally & Co.

Southeast Asia

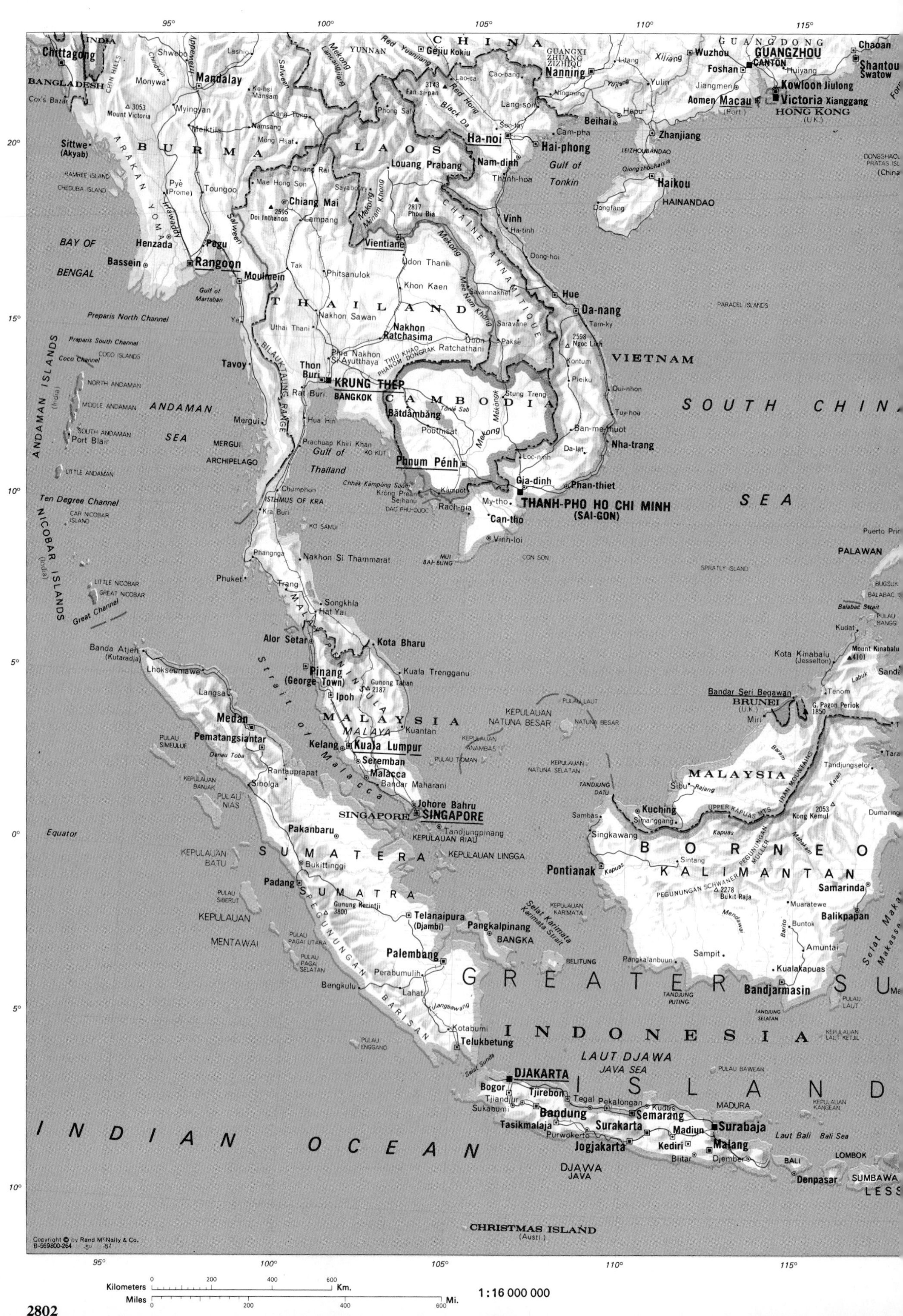
95°
100°
105°
110°
115°
20°
15°
10°
5°
0°
5°
10°
INDIA
Chittagong
BANGLADESH
Cox's Bazar
CHIN HILLS
Shwebo
Chindwin
Irrawaddy
Lashio
Monywa
Mandalay
Ke-hsi Mansam
Salween
Mekong Lancangjiang
YUNNAN
Red Yuanjiang
Gejiu Kokiu
C H I N A
GUANGXI ZHUANG ZIZHIQU
Nanning
Lao-cai
Cao-bang
3143 Fan Si-pan
Black Da
Red Hong
Lang-son
Ningming
Yujiang
Yulin
Xijiang
Wuzhou
GUANGDONG
GUANGZHOU
CANTON
Foshan
Huiyang
Chaoan
Shantou Swatow
Jiangmen
Kowloon Jiulong
Aomen Macau (Port.)
Victoria Xianggang
HONG KONG (U.K.)
Beihai
Hepu
Zhanjiang
LEIZHOUBANDAO
Qiongzhouhaixia
Haikou
HAINANDAO
Dongfang
DONGSHAQUN PRATAS ISL. (China)
3053 Mount Victoria
Myingyan
Meiktila
Keng Tung
Namsang
Mong Hsat
Sittwe (Akyab)
B U R M A
ARAKAN YOMA
RAMREE ISLAND
CHEDUBA ISLAND
Pyè (Prome)
Toungoo
Irrawaddy
Henzada
Pegu
Bassein
Rangoon
Moulmein
Gulf of Martaban
BAY OF BENGAL
Phong Saly
L A O S
Louang Prabang
Ha-noi
Son-tay
Cam-pha
Hai-phong
Nam-dinh
Thanh-hoa
Gulf of Tonkin
Chiang Rai
Mae Hong Son
Sayaboury
Chiang Mai
2595 Doi Inthanon
Lampang
Mekong Menam Khong
2817 Phou Bia
CHAINE ANNAMITIQUE
Vinh
Ha-tinh
Vientiane
Mekong
Dong-hoi
Tak
Phitsanulok
Udon Thani
Khon Kaen
Savannakhet
Mae Nam Khong
Hue
Da-nang
Tam-ky
T H A I L A N D
Nakhon Sawan
Uthai Thani
Nakhon Ratchasima
Saravane
Ubon Ratchathani
Pakse
2598 Ngoc Linh
Kontum
VIETNAM
PARACEL ISLANDS
Preparis North Channel
Preparis South Channel
COCO ISLANDS
Coco Channel
Ye
BILAUKTAUNG RANGE
Tavoy
Phra Nakhon Si Ayutthaya
THIU KHAO PHANOM DONGRAK
Thon Buri
KRUNG THEP
BANGKOK
Rat Buri
C A M B O D I A
Stung Treng
Tonlé Sab
Bătdâmbâng
Pouthisat
Mekong
Mekong
Pleiku
Qui-nhon
Tuy-hoa
Ban-me-thuot
Nha-trang
Da-lat
ANDAMAN ISLANDS (India)
NORTH ANDAMAN
MIDDLE ANDAMAN
SOUTH ANDAMAN
Port Blair
LITTLE ANDAMAN
ANDAMAN SEA
Mergui
MERGUI ARCHIPELAGO
Hua Hin
Prachuap Khiri Khan
KO KUT
Gulf of Thailand
Phnum Pénh
Loc-ninh
Gia-dinh
Phan-thiet
SOUTH CHINA SEA
Chhâk Kâmpóng Saôm
Krŏng Preăh Seihanŭ
Kampot
DAO PHU-QUOC
Rach-gia
My-tho
THANH-PHO HO CHI MINH (SAI-GON)
Can-tho
Vinh-loi
MUI BAI-BUNG
CON SON
Ten Degree Channel
Chumphon
ISTHMUS OF KRA
Kra Buri
KO SAMUI
CAR NICOBAR ISLAND
NICOBAR ISLANDS (India)
LITTLE NICOBAR
GREAT NICOBAR
Great Channel
Phangnga
Nakhon Si Thammarat
Phuket
Trang
Songkhla
Hat Yai
SPRATLY ISLAND
Puerto Princesa
PALAWAN
BUGSUK
BALABAC IS.
Balabac Strait
PULAU BANGGI
Kudat
Alor Setar
Kota Bharu
Banda Atjeh (Kutaradja)
Lhokseumawe
Pinang (George Town)
Kuala Trengganu
Gunong Tahan 2187
Ipoh
Langsa
Strait of Malacca
PENINSULA
M A L A Y S I A
MALAYA
Kuantan
Medan
Pematangsiantar
PULAU SIMEULUE
Danau Toba
Kelang
Kuala Lumpur
Seremban
Malacca
Bandar Maharani
Rantauprapat
Sibolga
KEPULAUAN BANJAK
PULAU NIAS
Johore Bahru
SINGAPORE
SINGAPORE
Tandjungpinang
KEPULAUAN RIAU
KEPULAUAN LINGGA
Pakanbaru
PULAU LAUT
KEPULAUAN NATUNA BESAR
NATUNA BESAR
KEPULAUAN ANAMBAS
PULAU TOMAN
KEPULAUAN NATUNA SELATAN
TANDJUNG DATU
Kota Kinabalu (Jesselton)
Mount Kinabalu 4101
Labuk
Sandakan
Tenom
Bandar Seri Begawan
BRUNEI (U.K.)
G. Pagon Periok 1850
Miri
Baram
IRAN MOUNTAINS
Tandjungselor
Tarakan
MALAYSIA
Rajang
Sibu
Kajan
UPPER KAPUAS MTS.
Kuching
Simanggang
2053 Kong Kemul
Dumaring
Sambas
Singkawang
Kapuas
Mahakam
Equator
KEPULAUAN BATU
S U M A T E R A
Bukittinggi
Padang
S U M A T R A
PULAU SIBERUT
Gunong Kerintji 3800
KEPULAUAN MENTAWAI
Pontianak
Kapuas
Sintang
B O R N E O
K A L I M A N T A N
PEGUNUNGAN SCHWANER
PEGUNUNGAN MULLER
2278 Bukit Raja
Samarinda
Muaratewe
Balikpapan
Mendawai
Barito
Buntok
Amuntai
Selat Makassar
Telanaipura (Djambi)
Pangkalpinang
BANGKA
Selat Karimata
Karimata Strait
KEPULAUAN KARIMATA
PULAU PAGAI UTARA
PULAU PAGAI SELATAN
PEGUNUNGAN
Palembang
Perabumulih
Bengkulu
Lahat
BELITUNG
Sampit
Pangkalanbuun
Kualakapuas
Bandjarmasin
G R E A T E R S U
TANDJUNG PUTING
TANDJUNG SELATAN
PULAU LAUT
BARISAN
Tulangbawang
Kotabumi
Telukbetung
PULAU ENGGANO
I N D O N E S I A
KEPULAUAN LAUT KETJIL
LAUT DJAWA
JAVA SEA
Selat Sunda
DJAKARTA
PULAU BAWEAN
I S L A N D
Bogor
Tjirebon
Tjiandjur
Sukabumi
Tegal
Pekalongan
Kudus
Semarang
MADURA
KEPULAUAN KANGEAN
Bandung
Tasikmalaja
Purwokerto
Surakarta
Madiun
Surabaja
Laut Bali
Bali Sea
Jogjakarta
Kediri
Malang
Blitar
Djember
LOMBOK
BALI
Denpasar
SUMBAWA
LESSER
DJAWA JAVA
I N D I A N O C E A N
CHRISTMAS ISLAND (Austl.)
Copyright © by Rand McNally & Co.
B-569800-264
95°
100°
105°
110°
115°
Kilometers 0 200 400 600 Km.
Miles 0 200 400 600 Mi.
1:16 000 000

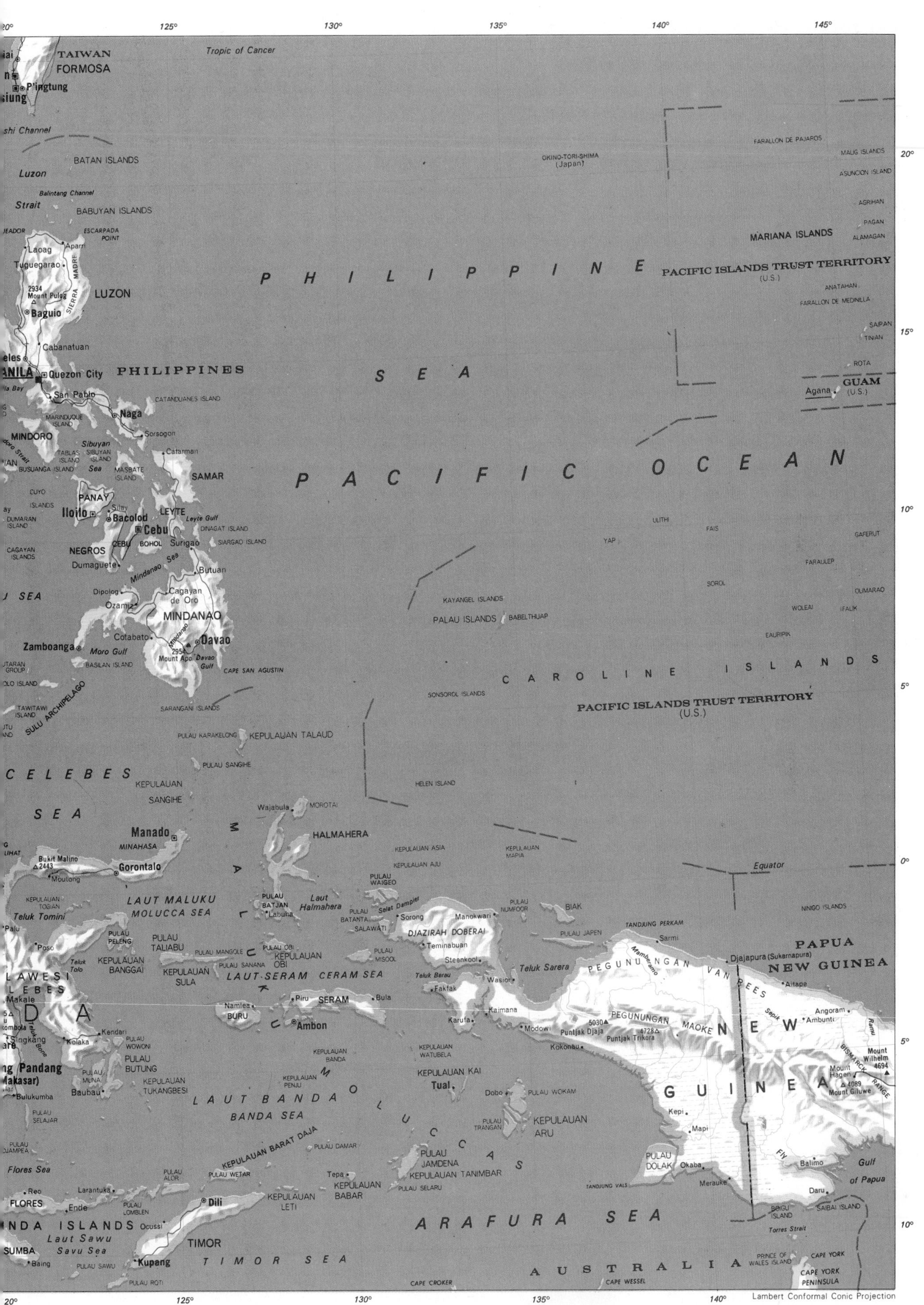
TAIWAN
FORMOSA
P'ingtung
Tropic of Cancer
PHILIPPINE SEA
PACIFIC OCEAN
BATAN ISLANDS
Luzon Strait
Balintang Channel
BABUYAN ISLANDS
ESCARPADA POINT
Laoag
Aparri
Tuguegarao
2934 Mount Pulog
SIERRA MADRE
LUZON
Baguio
Cabanatuan
PHILIPPINES
Quezon City
San Pablo
CATANDUANES ISLAND
Naga
MARINDUQUE ISLAND
MINDORO
Sorsogon
Sibuyan Sea
TABLAS ISLAND
SIBUYAN ISLAND
BUSUANGA ISLAND
MASBATE ISLAND
Catarman
SAMAR
CUYO ISLANDS
PANAY
Iloilo
Bacolod
LEYTE
Leyte Gulf
DUMARAN ISLAND
Cebu
DINAGAT ISLAND
CAGAYAN ISLANDS
NEGROS
CEBU
BOHOL
Surigao
SIARGAO ISLAND
Dumaguete
Mindanao Sea
Butuan
Dipolog
Cagayan de Oro
Ozamiz
MINDANAO
Cotabato
Zamboanga
Moro Gulf
2954 Mount Apo
Davao
Davao Gulf
BASILAN ISLAND
CAPE SAN AGUSTIN
SULU ARCHIPELAGO
TAWITAWI ISLAND
SARANGANI ISLANDS
PULAU KARAKELONG
KEPULAUAN TALAUD
PULAU SANGIHE
CELEBES SEA
KEPULAUAN SANGIHE
Wajabula
MOROTAI
Manado
MINAHASA
HALMAHERA
Bukit Malino 2443
Gorontalo
Moutong
KEPULAUAN TOGIAN
Teluk Tomini
LAUT MALUKU
MOLUCCA SEA
PULAU BATJAN
Labuha
Laut Halmahera
Selat Dampier
PULAU BATANTA
SALAWATI
PULAU WAIGEO
Sorong
Manokwari
DJAZIRAH DOBERAI
Teminabuan
Steenkool
Palu
Poso
PULAU PELENG
PULAU TALIABU
PULAU MANGOLE
PULAU OBI
KEPULAUAN OBI
PULAU MISOOL
Teluk Tolo
KEPULAUAN BANGGAI
KEPULAUAN SULA
PULAU SANANA
LAUT SERAM
CERAM SEA
Teluk Berau
Fakfak
Wasior
Teluk Sarera
Piru
SERAM
Bula
Namlea
BURU
Ambon
Kaimana
Karufa
Makale
Kendari
Kolaka
Singkang
PULAU WOWONI
PULAU BUTUNG
PULAU MUNA
Baubau
KEPULAUAN TUKANGBESI
Bulukumba
PULAU SELAJAR
KEPULAUAN BANDA
KEPULAUAN PENJU
LAUT BANDA
BANDA SEA
KEPULAUAN WATUBELA
KEPULAUAN KAI
Tual
Dobo
PULAU WOKAM
PULAU TRANGAN
KEPULAUAN ARU
KEPULAUAN BARAT DAJA
PULAU DAMAR
PULAU JAMDENA
KEPULAUAN TANIMBAR
PULAU SELARU
Tepa
KEPULAUAN BABAR
KEPULAUAN LETI
Flores Sea
Reo
Larantuka
FLORES
Ende
PULAU ALOR
PULAU WETAR
PULAU LOMBLEN
Dili
Ocussi
Laut Sawu
Savu Sea
SUMBA
Baing
PULAU SAWU
Kupang
TIMOR
TIMOR SEA
PULAU ROTI
ARAFURA SEA
AUSTRALIA
CAPE CROKER
CAPE WESSEL
MOLUCCAS
OKINO-TORI-SHIMA (Japan)
FARALLON DE PAJAROS
MAUG ISLANDS
ASUNCION ISLAND
AGRIHAN
PAGAN
ALAMAGAN
MARIANA ISLANDS
PACIFIC ISLANDS TRUST TERRITORY (U.S.)
ANATAHAN
FARALLON DE MEDINILLA
SAIPAN
TINIAN
ROTA
GUAM (U.S.)
Agana
ULITHI
FAIS
YAP
GAFERUT
FARAULEP
SOROL
OLIMARAO
WOLEAI
IFALIK
EAURIPIK
KAYANGEL ISLANDS
PALAU ISLANDS
BABELTHUAP
CAROLINE ISLANDS
SONSOROL ISLANDS
HELEN ISLAND
KEPULAUAN ASIA
KEPULAUAN AJU
KEPULAUAN MAPIA
Equator
PULAU NUMFOOR
BIAK
NINIGO ISLANDS
TANDJUNG PERKAM
PULAU JAPEN
Sarmi
Mamberamo
Djajapura (Sukarnapura)
PAPUA NEW GUINEA
PEGUNUNGAN VAN REES
Aitape
Sepik
Angoram
Ambunti
Ramu
PEGUNUNGAN MAOKE
5030 Puntjak Djaja
4728 Puntjak Trikora
Modowi
Kokonau
NEW GUINEA
BISMARCK RANGE
Mount Wilhelm 4694
Mount Hagen
4089 Mount Giluwe
Kepi
Mapi
PULAU DOLAK
Okaba
Merauke
TANDJUNG VALS
Fly
Balimo
Gulf of Papua
Daru
BOIGU ISLAND
SAIBAI ISLAND
Torres Strait
PRINCE OF WALES ISLAND
CAPE YORK
CAPE YORK PENINSULA
Lambert Conformal Conic Projection

Indochina

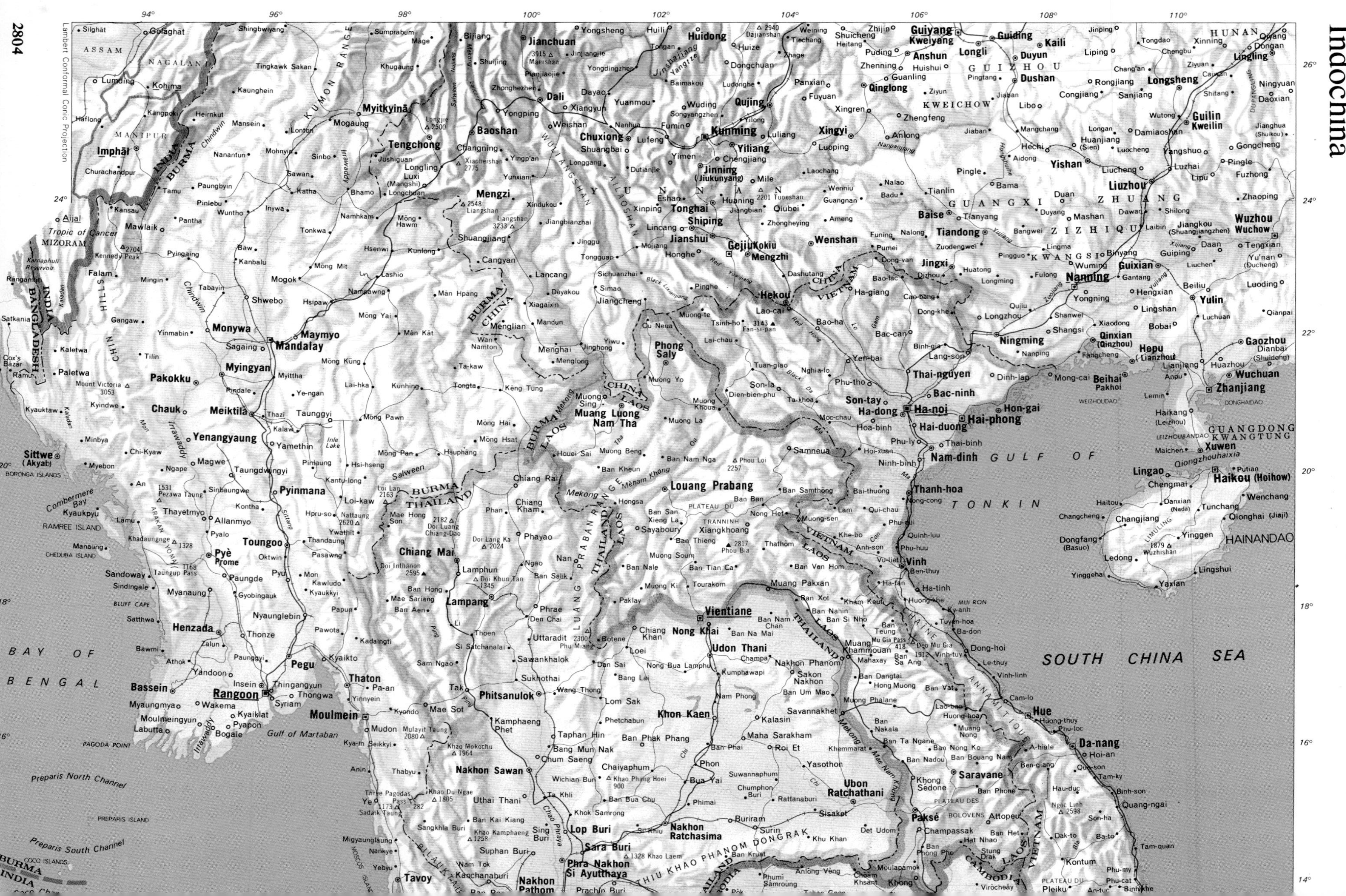

SOUTH CHINA SEA
GULF OF TONKIN
BAY OF BENGAL
Gulf of Martaban
HAINANDAO
GUANGDONG
KWANGTUNG
GUANGXI ZHUANG ZIZHIQU
KWANGSI
GUIZHOU
KWEICHOW
YUNNAN
HUNAN
BURMA
INDIA
BANGLADESH
CHINA
LAOS
THAILAND
VIETNAM
CAMBODIA
Ha-noi
Hai-phong
Hue
Da-nang
Vientiane
Louang Prabang
Mandalay
Rangoon
Moulmein
Kunming
Nanning
Guiyang
Kweiyang
Guilin
Kweilin
Zhanjiang
Haikou (Hoihow)
Chiang Mai
Nakhon Ratchasima
Ubon Ratchathani
Sittwe (Akyab)
Imphāl
Tropic of Cancer
Mekong
Irrawaddy
Salween
Chindwin
Red
Black
Lambert Conformal Conic Projection

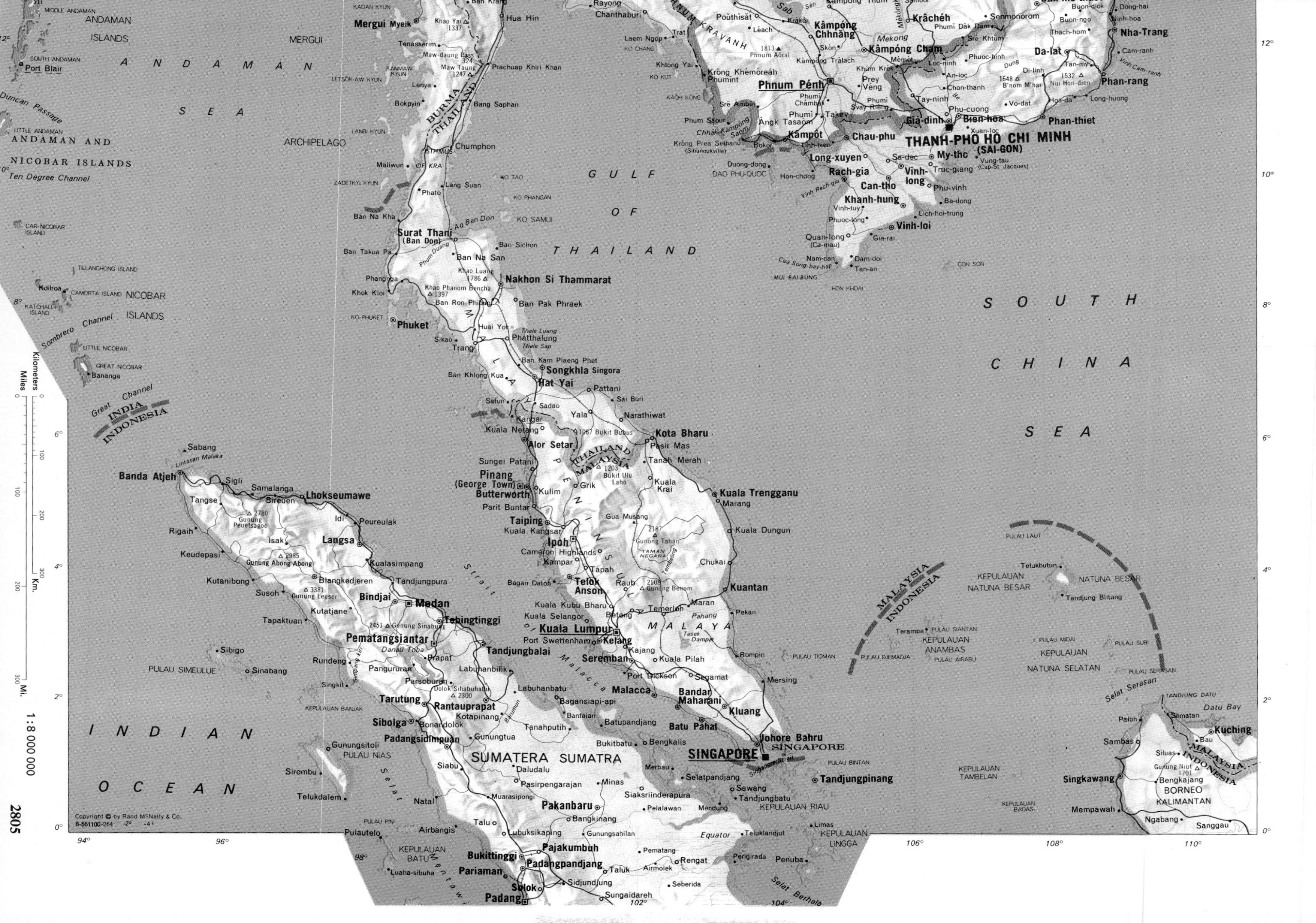
ANDAMAN SEA
GULF OF THAILAND
SOUTH CHINA SEA
INDIAN OCEAN
MERGUI ARCHIPELAGO
ANDAMAN ISLANDS
ANDAMAN AND NICOBAR ISLANDS
NICOBAR ISLANDS
Ten Degree Channel
Duncan Passage
Sombrero Channel
Great Channel
Port Blair
Mergui Myeik
Surat Thani (Ban Don)
Phuket
Nakhon Si Thammarat
Songkhla Singora
Hat Yai
Phnum Penh
THANH-PHO HO CHI MINH (SAI-GON)
Kota Bharu
Kuala Trengganu
Kuantan
Alor Setar
Pinang (George Town)
Butterworth
Taiping
Ipoh
Telok Anson
Kuala Lumpur
Seremban
Malacca
Bandar Maharani
Kluang
Batu Pahat
Johore Bahru
SINGAPORE
Tandjungpinang
MALAYA
Strait of Malacca
Banda Atjeh
Lhokseumawe
Langsa
Medan
Bindjai
Tebingtinggi
Pematangsiantar
Tandjungbalai
Tarutung
Sibolga
Rantauprapat
Padangsidimpuan
SUMATERA SUMATRA
Pakanbaru
Bukittinggi
Padangpandjang
Pariaman
Padang
Solok
Pajakumbuh
KEPULAUAN RIAU
KEPULAUAN LINGGA
KEPULAUAN ANAMBAS
KEPULAUAN NATUNA BESAR
KEPULAUAN NATUNA SELATAN
KEPULAUAN TAMBELAN
Kuching
Singkawang
BORNEO KALIMANTAN
MALAYSIA
INDONESIA
THAILAND
BURMA
INDIA
Equator
Kilometers
Km.
Miles
Mi.
1:8 000 000
Copyright © by Rand McNally & Co.
B-561100-264

Australia

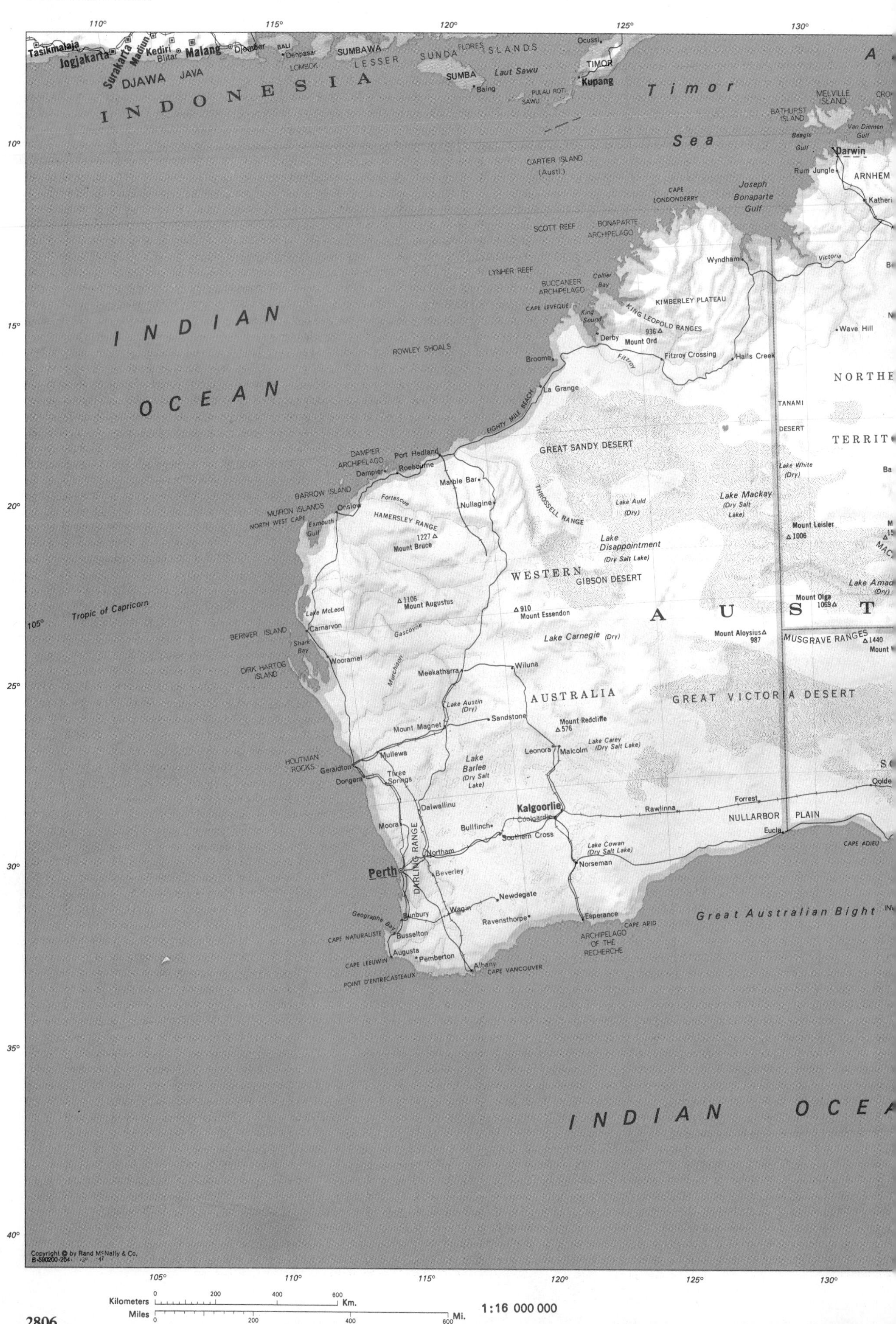

INDONESIA
DJAWA
JAVA
Jogjakarta
Surakarta
Madiun
Kediri
Blitar
Malang
Tasikmalaja
BALI
Denpasar
LOMBOK
SUMBAWA
LESSER SUNDA ISLANDS
FLORES
SUMBA
Baing
Laut Sawu
PULAU ROTI
SAWU
TIMOR
Kupang
Ocussi
Timor Sea
MELVILLE ISLAND
BATHURST ISLAND
Van Diemen Gulf
Beagle Gulf
Darwin
Rum Jungle
ARNHEM
Katherine
CARTIER ISLAND (Austl.)
CAPE LONDONDERRY
Joseph Bonaparte Gulf
SCOTT REEF
BONAPARTE ARCHIPELAGO
Wyndham
Victoria
LYNHER REEF
BUCCANEER ARCHIPELAGO
Collier Bay
KIMBERLEY PLATEAU
CAPE LEVEQUE
King Sound
KING LEOPOLD RANGES
936
Derby
Mount Ord
Wave Hill
INDIAN OCEAN
ROWLEY SHOALS
Broome
Fitzroy
Fitzroy Crossing
Halls Creek
NORTHERN
La Grange
EIGHTY MILE BEACH
TANAMI DESERT
TERRITORY
GREAT SANDY DESERT
DAMPIER ARCHIPELAGO
Port Hedland
Roebourne
Dampier
Lake White (Dry)
Marble Bar
BARROW ISLAND
Fortescue
Nullagine
MUIRON ISLANDS
NORTH WEST CAPE
Onslow
Exmouth Gulf
HAMERSLEY RANGE
1227
Mount Bruce
THROSSELL RANGE
Lake Auld (Dry)
Lake Mackay (Dry Salt Lake)
Mount Leisler
1006
Lake Disappointment (Dry Salt Lake)
WESTERN
GIBSON DESERT
Lake Amadeus (Dry)
105°
Tropic of Capricorn
1106
Mount Augustus
910
Mount Essendon
AUSTRALIA
Mount Olga
1069
Lake McLeod
Carnarvon
BERNIER ISLAND
Gascoyne
Lake Carnegie (Dry)
Mount Aloysius
987
MUSGRAVE RANGES
1440
Shark Bay
Wooramel
DIRK HARTOG ISLAND
Murchison
Meekatharra
Wiluna
Lake Austin (Dry)
GREAT VICTORIA DESERT
Sandstone
Mount Redcliffe
576
Mount Magnet
Lake Carey (Dry Salt Lake)
Leonora
Malcolm
HOUTMAN ROCKS
Mullewa
Lake Barlee (Dry Salt Lake)
Geraldton
Dongara
Three Springs
Forrest
Dalwallinu
Kalgoorlie
Coolgardie
Rawlinna
NULLARBOR PLAIN
Moora
Bullfinch
Southern Cross
Eucla
CAPE ADIEU
DARLING RANGE
Northam
Lake Cowan (Dry Salt Lake)
Norseman
Perth
Beverley
Newdegate
Geographe Bay
Bunbury
Wagin
Ravensthorpe
Esperance
CAPE ARID
Great Australian Bight
CAPE NATURALISTE
Busselton
ARCHIPELAGO OF THE RECHERCHE
Augusta
CAPE LEEUWIN
Pemberton
Albany
CAPE VANCOUVER
POINT D'ENTRECASTEAUX
110°
115°
120°
125°
130°
10°
15°
20°
25°
30°
35°
40°
Kilometers
Miles
Km.
Mi.
0
200
400
600
1:16 000 000

Coral Sea
Solomon Sea
PAPUA NEW GUINEA
NEW GUINEA
BRITISH SOLOMON ISLANDS
Port Moresby
Gulf of Carpentaria
Torres Strait
CAPE YORK PENINSULA
GREAT BARRIER REEF
GREAT DIVIDING RANGE
QUEENSLAND
GREAT ARTESIAN BASIN
NEW SOUTH WALES
VICTORIA
TASMANIA
A.C.T.
Canberra
SYDNEY
Brisbane
MELBOURNE
Adelaide
Hobart
Newcastle
Wollongong
Rockhampton
Townsville
Cairns
Bass Strait
PACIFIC OCEAN
Tasman Sea
Tropic of Capricorn
Lambert Conformal Conic Projection

New Zealand

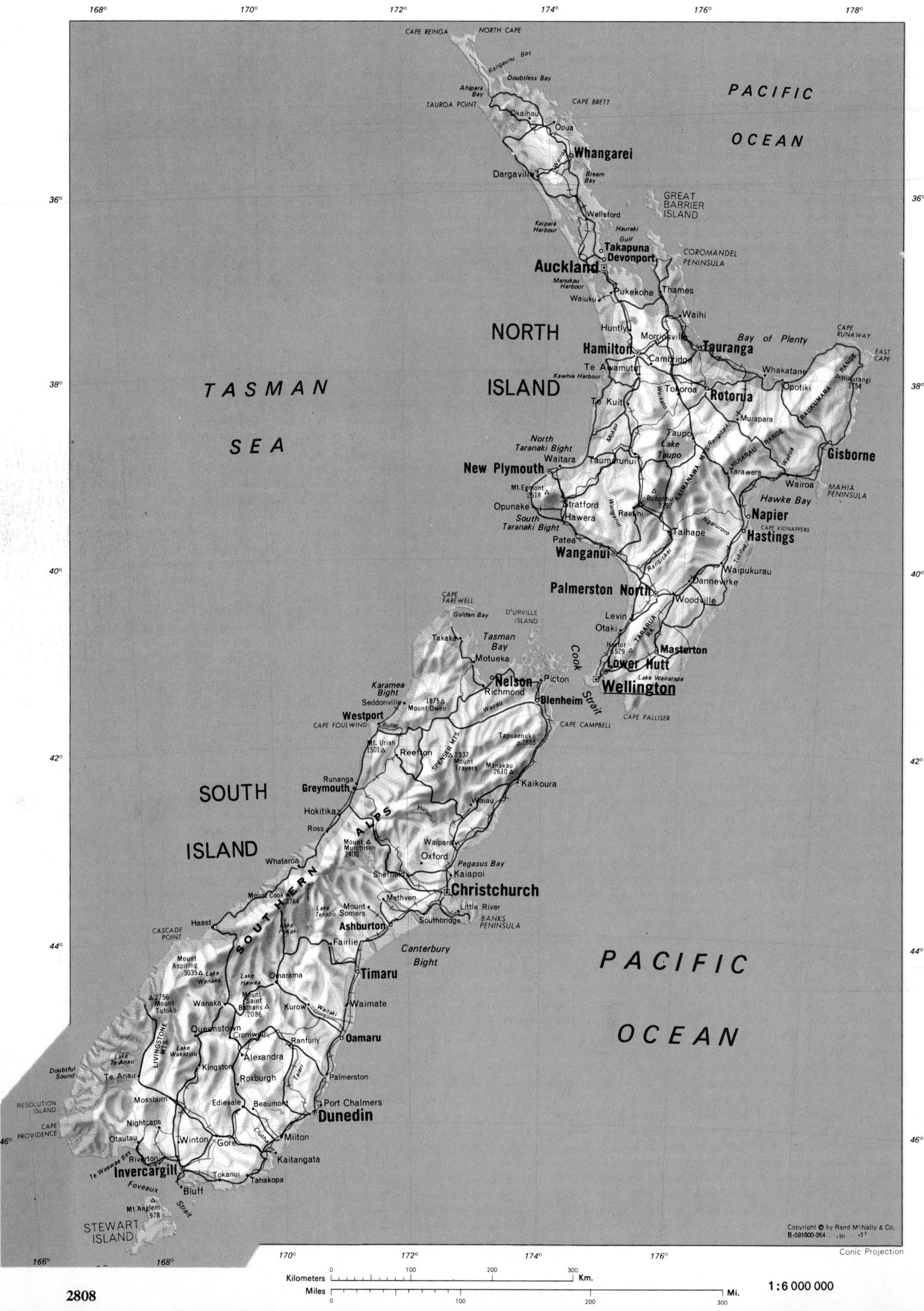

PACIFIC OCEAN
TASMAN SEA
NORTH ISLAND
SOUTH ISLAND
STEWART ISLAND
CAPE REINGA
NORTH CAPE
Doubtless Bay
CAPE BRETT
Whangarei
Dargaville
GREAT BARRIER ISLAND
Wellsford
Hauraki Gulf
Takapuna
Devonport
Auckland
COROMANDEL PENINSULA
Pukekohe
Thames
Waihi
Huntly
Morrinsville
Hamilton
Cambridge
Tauranga
Bay of Plenty
Whakatane
Opotiki
Rotorua
Te Awamutu
Tokoroa
Te Kuiti
Taupo
Lake Taupo
Gisborne
New Plymouth
Waitara
Taumarunui
Stratford
Hawera
Opunake
Patea
Wanganui
Napier
Hastings
Hawke Bay
Wairoa
Taihape
Palmerston North
Dannevirke
Waipukurau
Woodville
Levin
Otaki
Masterton
Lower Hutt
Wellington
Cook Strait
CAPE PALLISER
CAPE FAREWELL
Golden Bay
Tasman Bay
D'URVILLE ISLAND
Takaka
Motueka
Nelson
Richmond
Picton
Blenheim
Westport
CAPE FOULWIND
CAPE CAMPBELL
Reefton
Kaikoura
Greymouth
Runanga
Hokitika
Ross
Whataroa
Waiau
Waipara
Oxford
Pegasus Bay
Kaiapoi
Christchurch
Methven
Little River
Southbridge
BANKS PENINSULA
Ashburton
Fairlie
Canterbury Bight
Timaru
Waimate
Oamaru
Haast
CASCADE POINT
SOUTHERN ALPS
Mount Cook 3764
Mount Aspiring 3035
Wanaka
Omarama
Kurow
Queenstown
Cromwell
Alexandra
Ranfurly
Kingston
Roxburgh
Palmerston
Te Anau
Doubtful Sound
Mossburn
Edievale
Beaumont
Port Chalmers
Dunedin
RESOLUTION ISLAND
CAPE PROVIDENCE
Nightcaps
Otautau
Winton
Gore
Milton
Riverton
Kaitangata
Invercargill
Tokanui
Tahakopa
Bluff
Foveaux Strait
Mt Anglem 978
168° 170° 172° 174° 176° 178°
36° 38° 40° 42° 44° 46°
166°
Copyright © by Rand McNally & Co.
Conic Projection
Kilometers 0 100 200 300 Km.
Miles 0 100 200 300 Mi.
1:6 000 000

ATLAS INDEX

The Index includes in a single alphabetical list some 21,000 names appearing on the maps. Each name is followed by a page reference and the location of the feature on the map in coordinates of latitude and longitude. If a page contains several maps, a lowercase letter identifies the particular map. The page reference for two-page maps is always to the left-hand page.

Most map features are indexed to the largest-scale map on which they appear. Countries, mountain ranges, and other extensive features are generally indexed to the map that shows them in their entirety.

The features indexed are of three types: *point, areal,* and *linear*. For *point* features (for example, cities, mountain peaks, dams), latitude and longitude coordinates give the location of the point on the map. For *areal* features (countries, mountain ranges, etc.), the coordinates generally indicate the approximate center of the feature. For *linear* features (rivers, canals, aqueducts), the coordinates locate a terminating point—for example, the mouth of a river.

NAME FORMS Names in the Index, as on the maps, are generally in the local language and insofar as possible are spelled according to official practice. Most features that extend beyond the boundaries of one country have no single official name, and these are usually named in English. Many conventional English names are cross referenced to the primary map name. All cross references are indicated by the symbol →. A name that appears in a shortened version on the map due to space limitations is given in full in the Index, with the portion that is omitted on the map enclosed in brackets, for example, Acapulco [de Juárez].

TRANSLITERATION For names in languages not written in the Roman alphabet, the locally official transliteration system has been used where one exists. Thus, names in the Soviet Union and Bulgaria have been transliterated according to the systems adopted by the academies of science of these countries. Similarly, the transliteration for mainland Chinese names follows the Pinyin system, which has been officially adopted in mainland China. For languages with no one locally accepted transliteration system, notably Arabic, transliteration in general follows closely a system adopted by the United States Board on Geographic Names.

ALPHABETIZATION Names are alphabetized in the order of the letters of the English alphabet. Spanish *ll* and *ch*, for example, are not treated as distinct letters. Furthermore, diacritical marks are disregarded in alphabetization—German or Scandinavian *ä* or *ö* are treated as *a* or *o*.

The names of physical features may appear inverted, since they are always alphabetized under the proper, not the generic, part of the name, thus: "Gibraltar, Strait of ꓵ." Otherwise every entry, whether consisting of one word or more, is alphabetized as a single continuous entity. "Lakeland," for example, appears after "La Crosse" and before "La Paz." Names beginning with articles (Le Havre, Den Helder, Al-Qāhirah, As-Suways) are not inverted. Names beginning "Mc" are alphabetized as though spelled "Mac," and names beginning "St." and "Sainte" as though spelled "Saint."

In the case of identical names, towns are listed first, then political divisions, then physical features. Entries that are completely identical (including symbols, discussed below) are distinguished by abbreviations of their official country names and are sequenced alphabetically by country name. The many duplicate names in Canada, the United Kingdom, and the United States are further distinguished by abbreviations of the names of their primary subdivisions. (See list of abbreviations below.)

ABBREVIATION AND CAPITALIZATION Abbreviation and styling have been standardized for all languages. A period is used after every abbreviation even when this may not be the local practice. The abbreviation "St." is used only for "Saint." "Sankt" and other forms of the term are spelled out.

All names are written with an initial capital letter except for a few Dutch names, such as 's-Gravenhage. Capitalization of noninitial words in a name generally follows local practice.

SYMBOL The symbols that appear in the Index graphically represent the broad categories of the features named, for example, for mountain (Everest, Mount ∧). Superior numbers following some symbols in the Index indicate finer distinctions, for example, ∧[1] for volcano (Fuji-san ∧[1]). A complete list of the symbols and those with superior numbers is given on page 2810.

LIST OF ABBREVIATIONS

	LOCAL NAME	ENGLISH
Afr.	—	Africa
Ala., U.S.	Alabama	Alabama
Alaska, U.S.	Alaska	Alaska
Alg.	Algérie	Algeria
Alta., Can.	Alberta	Alberta
Ang.	Angola	Angola
Antig.	Antigua	Antigua
Arg.	Argentina	Argentina
Ariz., U.S.	Arizona	Arizona
Ark., U.S.	Arkansas	Arkansas
Ar. Sa.	Al-'Arabīyah as-Sa'ūdīyah	Saudi Arabia
As.	—	Asia
Austl.	Australia	Australia
Ba.	Bahamas	Bahamas
B.C., Can.	British Columbia	British Columbia
Bel.	Belgique België	Belgium
Ber.	Bermuda	Bermuda
Bharat	Bhārat	India
Blg.	Bâlgarija	Bulgaria
Bol.	Bolivia	Bolivia
Bra.	Brasil	Brazil
B.R.D.	Bundesrepublik Deutschland	Federal Republic of Germany
Calif., U.S.	California	California
Can.	Canada	Canada
Cay. Is.	Cayman Islands	Cayman Islands
Česko.	Československo	Czechoslovakia
Col.	Colombia	Colombia
Colo., U.S.	Colorado	Colorado
Comores	Comores	Comoro Islands
Conn., U.S.	Connecticut	Connecticut
C.R.	Costa Rica	Costa Rica
Dan.	Danmark	Denmark
D.C., U.S.	District of Columbia	District of Columbia
D.D.R.	Deutsche Demokratische Republik	German Democratic Republic
Del., U.S.	Delaware	Delaware
Dom.	Dominica	Dominica
Ec.	Ecuador	Ecuador
Eire	Eire	Ireland
Ellás	Ellás	Greece
El Sal.	El Salvador	El Salvador
Eng., U.K.	England	England
Esp.	España	Spain
Eur.	—	Europe
Falk. Is.	Falkland Islands	Falkland Islands (Islas Malvinas)
Fla., U.S.	Florida	Florida
Fr.	France	France
Ga., U.S.	Georgia	Georgia
Gam.	Gambia	Gambia
Gren.	Grenada	Grenada
Guat.	Guatemala	Guatemala
Guinée	Guinée	Guinea
Guy.	Guyana	Guyana
Guy. fr.	Guyane française	French Guiana
H.K.	Hong Kong	Hong Kong
Hond.	Honduras	Honduras
Idaho, U.S.	Idaho	Idaho
Ill., U.S.	Illinois	Illinois
Ind., U.S.	Indiana	Indiana
Indon.	Indonesia	Indonesia
I. of Man	Isle of Man	Isle of Man
Iowa, U.S.	Iowa	Iowa
Īrān	Īrān	Iran
'Irāq	Al-'Irāq	Iraq
It.	Italia	Italy
Jam.	Jamaica	Jamaica
Jugo.	Jugoslavija	Yugoslavia
Kans., U.S.	Kansas	Kansas
Kípros	Kípros Kıbrıs	Cyprus
Ky., U.S.	Kentucky	Kentucky
La., U.S.	Louisiana	Louisiana
Liber.	Liberia	Liberia
Lībiyā	Lībiyā	Libya
Lubnān	Al-Lubnān	Lebanon
Macau	Macau	Macau
Magreb	Al-Magreb	Morocco
Maine, U.S.	Maine	Maine
Mali	Mali	Mali
Malta	Malta	Malta
Man., Can.	Manitoba	Manitoba
Mass., U.S.	Massachusetts	Massachusetts
Md., U.S.	Maryland	Maryland
Méx.	México	Mexico
Mich., U.S.	Michigan	Michigan
Minn., U.S.	Minnesota	Minnesota
Miss., U.S.	Mississippi	Mississippi
Mo., U.S.	Missouri	Missouri
Mont., U.S.	Montana	Montana
Mya.	Myanma	Burma
N.A.	—	North America
N.B., Can.	New Brunswick	New Brunswick
N.C., U.S.	North Carolina	North Carolina
N. Dak., U.S.	North Dakota	North Dakota
Nebr., U.S.	Nebraska	Nebraska
Ned.	Nederland	Netherlands
Nepāl	Nepāl	Nepal
Nev., U.S.	Nevada	Nevada
Newf., Can.	Newfoundland	Newfoundland
N.H., U.S.	New Hampshire	New Hampshire
Nic.	Nicaragua	Nicaragua
Nig.	Nigeria	Nigeria
Nihon	Nihon	Japan
N. Ire., U.K.	Northern Ireland	Northern Ireland
N.J., U.S.	New Jersey	New Jersey
N. Mex., U.S.	New Mexico	New Mexico
Nor.	Norge	Norway
N.S., Can.	Nova Scotia	Nova Scotia
N.W. Ter., Can.	Northwest Territories	Northwest Territories
N.Y., U.S.	New York	New York
N.Z.	New Zealand	New Zealand
Ohio, U.S.	Ohio	Ohio
Okla., U.S.	Oklahoma	Oklahoma
Ont., Can.	Ontario	Ontario
Oreg., U.S.	Oregon	Oregon
Öst.	Österreich	Austria
Pa., U.S.	Pennsylvania	Pennsylvania
Pāk.	Pākistān	Pakistan
Pan.	Panamá	Panama
Para.	Paraguay	Paraguay
Perú	Perú	Peru
Pil.	Pilipinas	Philippines
Port.	Portugal	Portugal
P.R.	Puerto Rico	Puerto Rico
Que., Can.	Québec	Quebec
Rep. Dom.	República Dominicana	Dominican Republic
Réu.	Réunion	Reunion
Rh.	Rhodesia	Rhodesia
R.I., U.S.	Rhode Island	Rhode Island
Rom.	România	Romania
S.A.	—	South America
S. Afr.	South Africa Suid-Afrika	South Africa
Sask., Can.	Saskatchewan	Saskatchewan
S.C., U.S.	South Carolina	South Carolina
Schw.	Schweiz; Suisse; Svizzera	Switzerland
Scot., U.K.	Scotland	Scotland
S. Dak., U.S.	South Dakota	South Dakota
Sén.	Sénégal	Senegal
Sey.	Seychelles	Seychelles
S.L.	Sierra Leone	Sierra Leone
S.S.S.R.	Sojuz Sovetskich Socialističeskich Respublik	Union of Soviet Socialist Republics
Sūd.	As-Sūdān	Sudan
Sve.	Sverige	Sweden
S.W. Afr.	South West Africa	South West Africa
Taehan	Taehan-Min'guk	South Korea
T'aiwan	T'aiwan	Taiwan

Introduction to the Index

LIST OF ABBREVIATIONS CONT'D

	LOCAL NAME	ENGLISH
Tchad	Tchad	Chad
Tenn., U.S.	Tennessee	Tennessee
Tex., U.S.	Texas	Texas
Trin.	Trinidad and Tobago	Trinidad and Tobago
Tun.	Tunisie	Tunisia
Tür.	Türkiye	Turkey
U.K.	United Kingdom	United Kingdom
'Umān	'Umān	Oman
Ur.	Uruguay	Uruguay
U.S.	United States	United States
Utah, U.S.	Utah	Utah
Va., U.S.	Virginia	Virginia
Ven.	Venezuela	Venezuela
Vt., U.S.	Vermont	Vermont
Wales, U.K.	Wales	Wales
Wash., U.S.	Washington	Washington
Wis., U.S.	Wisconsin	Wisconsin
W. Va., U.S.	West Virginia	West Virginia
Wyo., U.S.	Wyoming	Wyoming
Yai.	Yaitopya	Ethiopia
Yukon, Can.	Yukon	Yukon
Zaïre	Zaïre	Zaire
Zam.	Zambia	Zambia
Zhg.	Zhongguo	China

KEY TO SYMBOLS

- ∧ **Mountain**
- ∧[1] Volcano
- ∧[2] Hill
- ⩘ **Mountains**
- ⩘[1] Plateau
- ⩘[2] Hills
-)(**Pass**
- ∨ **Valley, Canyon**
- ⌣ **Plain**
- ⌣[1] Basin
- ⌣[2] Delta
- ≻ **Cape**
- ≻[1] Peninsula
- ≻[2] Spit, Sand Bar
- I **Island**
- I[1] Atoll
- I[2] Rock
- II **Islands**
- II[1] Rocks
- ⊥ **Other Topographic Features**
- ⊥[1] Continent
- ⊥[2] Coast, Beach
- ⊥[3] Isthmus
- ⊥[4] Cliff
- ⊥[5] Cave, Caves
- ⊥[6] Crater
- ⊥[7] Depression
- ⊥[8] Dunes
- ⊥[9] Lava Flow
- ≏ **River**
- ≏[1] River Channel
- ≡ **Canal**
- ≡[1] Aqueduct
- ⅃ **Waterfall, Rapids**
-)(**Strait**
- C **Bay, Gulf**
- C[1] Estuary
- C[2] Fjord
- C[3] Bight
- ⊕ **Lake, Lakes**
- ⊕[1] Reservoir
- ⩩ **Swamp**
- ⍓ **Ice Features, Glacier**
- ⊤ **Other Hydrographic Features**
- ⊤[1] Ocean
- ⊤[2] Sea
- ⊤[3] Anchorage
- ⊤[4] Oasis, Well, Spring
- ✦ **Submarine Features**
- ✦[1] Depression
- ✦[2] Reef, Shoal
- ✦[3] Mountain, Mountains
- ✦[4] Slope, Shelf
- □ **Political Unit**
- □[1] Independent Nation
- □[2] Dependency
- □[3] State, Canton, Republic
- □[4] Province, Region, Oblast
- □[5] Department, District, Prefecture
- □[6] County
- □[7] City, Municipality
- □[8] Miscellaneous
- □[9] Historical
- ♉ **Cultural Institution**
- ♉[1] Religious Institution
- ♉[2] Educational Institution
- ♉[3] Scientific, Industrial Facility
- ⊥ **Historical Site**
- ♠ **Recreational Site**
- ⊠ **Airport**
- ■ **Military Installation**
- ⇾ **Miscellaneous**
- ⇾[1] Region
- ⇾[2] Desert
- ⇾[3] Forest, Moor
- ⇾[4] Reserve, Reservation
- ⇾[5] Transportation
- ⇾[6] Dam
- ⇾[7] Mine, Quarry
- ⇾[8] Neighborhood
- ⇾[9] Shopping Center

Name	Page	Lat °′	Long °′
A			
Aachen	2770	50.47 N	6.05 E
Aalst	2770	50.56 N	4.02 E
Äänekoski	2768	62.36 N	25.44 E
Aarau	2772	47.23 N	8.03 E
Aarschot	2770	50.59 N	4.50 E
Aba, Nig.	2786	5.06 N	7.21 E
Aba, Zhg.	2796	33.06 N	101.59 E
Ābādān	2790	30.20 N	48.16 E
Abaeté	2765	19.09 S	45.27 W
Abajo Peak ∧	2752	37.51 N	109.28 W
Abakan	2784	53.43 N	91.26 E
Abancay	2762	13.35 S	72.55 W
Abashiri	2798a	44.01 N	144.17 E
Abasolo, Méx.	2748	25.57 N	100.24 W
Abasolo, Méx.	2758	25.18 N	104.40 W
Abaya, Lake ⊕	2790	6.20 N	37.55 E
Abaza	2784	52.39 N	90.06 E
Abbadia San Salvatore	2776	42.53 N	11.41 E
Abbeville, Fr.	2772	50.06 N	1.50 E
Abbeville, Ga., U.S.	2744	31.59 N	83.18 W
Abbeville, La., U.S.	2746	29.58 N	92.08 W
Abbeville, Miss., U.S.	2746	34.25 N	89.37 W
Abbeville, S.C., U.S.	2744	34.11 N	82.23 W
Abbotsford	2742	44.57 N	90.19 W
Abbott Butte ∧	2754	42.57 N	122.33 W
'Abd al-Kūrī I	2790	12.12 N	52.15 E
Abe, Lake ⊕	2790	11.06 N	41.50 E
Abéché	2786	13.49 N	20.49 E
Abéjar	2774	41.48 N	2.47 W
Abengourou	2786	6.44 N	3.29 W
Abeokuta	2786	7.10 N	3.26 E
Aberayron	2769	52.15 N	4.15 W
Aberdeen, Scot., U.K.	2769	57.10 N	2.04 W
Aberdeen, Idaho, U.S.	2754	42.57 N	112:50 W
Aberdeen, Md.. U.S.	2740	39.30 N	76.10 W
Aberdeen, Miss., U.S.	2746	33.49 N	88.33 W
Aberdeen, N.C., U.S.	2744	35.08 N	79.26 W
Aberdeen, S. Dak., U.S.	2750	45.28 N	98.29 W
Aberdeen, Wash., U.S.	2754	46.59 N	123.50 W
Aberdeen Lake ⊕	2734	64.27 N	99.00 W
Abernathy	2748	33.50 N	101.51 W
Aberystwyth	2769	52.25 N	4.05 W
Abhā	2790	18.13 N	42.30 E
Abidjan	2786	5.19 N	4.02 W
Abilene, Kans., U.S.	2750	38.55 N	97.13 W
Abilene, Tex., U.S.	2748	32.27 N	99.44 W
Abingdon, Ill., U.S.	2746	40.48 N	90.24 W
Abingdon, Va., U.S.	2744	36.43 N	81.59 W
Abisko	2768	68.20 N	18.51 E
Abitibi ≏	2734	51.03 N	80.55 W
Abitibi, Lake ⊕	2734	48.42 N	79.45 W
Abohar	2794	30.09 N	74.11 E
Abomey	2786	7.11 N	1.59 E
Aborigen, Pik ∧	2784	61.59 N	149.19 E
Abrantes	2774	39.28 N	8.12 W
Absaroka Range ⩘	2736	44.45 N	109.50 W
Absarokee	2754	45.31 N	109.27 W
Abū 'Alī I	2790	27.20 N	49.33 E
Abū Ḥamad	2786	19.32 N	33.19 E
Abū Kamāl	2791	34.27 N	40.55 E
Abukuma-sanchi ⩘	2798	37.30 N	140.45 E
Abū Madd, Ra's ≻	2790	24.50 N	37.07 E
Abunã	2762	9.42 S	65.23 W
Abū Shajarah, Ra's ≻	2786	21.04 N	37.14 E
Abū Ẓaby	2790	24.28 N	54.22 E
Acajutla	2760	13.36 N	89.50 W
Acámbaro	2758	20.02 N	100.44 W
Acaponeta	2758	22.30 N	105.22 W
Acapulco [de Juárez]	2758	16.51 N	99.55 W
Acarai Mountains ∧	2762	1.50 N	57.40 W
Acaraú	2762	2.53 S	40.07 W
Acarigua	2760	9.33 N	69.12 W
Acatlán [de Osorio]	2758	18.12 N	98.03 W
Acayucan	2758	17.57 N	94.55 W
Accomac	2744	37.43 N	75.40 W
Accra	2786	5.33 N	0.13 W
Acebuches	2748	28.15 N	102.43 W
Acerra	2776	40.57 N	14.22 E
Achalpur	2793	21.16 N	77.31 E
Acheng	2796	45.32 N	126.59 E
Achill Island I	2769	54.00 N	10.00 W
Achtubinsk	2766	48.17 N	46.10 E
Achtyrka	2782	50.19 N	34.55 E
Ačinsk	2784	56.17 N	90.30 E
Acireale	2776	37.37 N	15.10 E
Ackerly	2748	32.32 N	101.43 W
Ackerman	2746	33.19 N	89.10 W
Ackley	2742	42.33 N	93.03 W
Acklins Island I	2760	22.25 N	74.00 W
Acomita	2752	35.03 N	107.35 W
Aconcagua, Cerro ∧	2764	32.39 S	70.00 W
Acquapendente	2776	42.44 N	11.52 E
Acqui Terme	2776	44.41 N	8.28 E
Acre ≏	2762	8.45 S	67.22 W
Acri	2776	39.29 N	16.23 E
Acworth	2744	34.04 N	84.41 W
Ada, Minn , U.S.	2750	47.18 N	96.31 W
Ada, Okla., U.S.	2748	34.46 N	96.41 W
Adair, Iowa, U.S.	2750	41.30 N	94.39 W
Adair, Okla., U.S.	2748	36.26 N	95.16 W
Adair, Cape ≻	2734	71.24 N	71.13 W
Adairsville	2744	34.22 N	84.56 W
Ādam	2790	22.24 N	57.32 E
Adamantina	2765	21.42 S	51.04 W
Adamawa ⩘	2786	7.00 N	12.00 E
Adams, Mass., U.S.	2740	42.37 N	73.07 W
Adams, Nebr., U.S.	2750	40.28 N	96.31 W
Adams, N. Dak., U.S.	2750	48.25 N	98.05 W
Adams, N.Y., U.S.	2740	43.49 N	76.01 W
Adams, Tenn., U.S.	2746	36.35 N	87.04 W
Adams, Wis., U.S.	2742	43.58 N	89.49 W
Adams, Mount ∧	2754	46.12 N	121.28 W
Adamsville	2746	35.14 N	88.23 W
Adana	2766	37.01 N	35.18 E
Adapazarı	2766	40.46 N	30.24 E
Adarama	2786	17.05 N	34.54 E
Ad-Dabbah	2786	18.03 N	30.57 E
Ad-Dahnā' ⇾[2]	2790	24.30 N	48.10 E
Ad-Dammām	2790	26.26 N	50.07 E
Ad-Dawādimī	2790	24.28 N	44.18 E
Ad-Dawḥah (Doha)	2790	25.17 N	51.32 E
Addis Ababa → Addis Abeba	2790	9.00 N	38.50 E
Addis Abeba	2790	9.00 N	38.50 E
Addison	2742	41.59 N	84.21 W
Ad-Dīwānīyah	2790	31.59 N	44.56 E
Ad-Duwaym	2786	14.00 N	32.19 E
Adel	2744	31.08 N	83.25 W
Adelaide	2806	34.55 S	138.35 E
Adelaide Peninsula ≻[1]	2734	68.09 N	97.45 W
Aden	2790	12.45 N	45.12 E
Aden, Gulf of C	2790	12.30 N	48.00 E
Adieu, Cape ≻	2806	31.59 S	132.09 E
Adige ≏	2776	45.10 N	12.20 E
Adigrat	2790	14.18 N	39.31 E
Ādilābād	2793	19.40 N	78.32 E
Adimi	2784	47.20 N	138.56 E
Adin	2756	41.12 N	120.57 W
Adirondack Mountains ⩘	2740	44.00 N	74.00 W
Admiralty Inlet C	2734	73.00 N	86.00 W
Ādoni	2793	15.38 N	77.17 E
Adra	2774	36.44 N	3.01 W
Adrano	2776	37.40 N	14.50 E
Adrar	2786	27.54 N	0.17 W
Adria	2776	45.03 N	12.03 E
Adrian, Ga., U.S.	2744	32.32 N	82.35 W
Adrian, Mich., U.S.	2742	41.54 N	84.02 W
Adrian, Minn , U.S.	2750	43.38 N	95.56 W
Adrian, Mo., U.S.	2746	38.24 N	94.21 W
Adriatic Sea ⊤[2]	2766	42.30 N	16.00 E
Adyča ≏	2784	68.13 N	134.41 E
Aegean Sea ⊤[2]	2778	38.30 N	25.00 E
A'erjinshanmai ⩘	2794	37.30 N	86.30 E
Afars and Issas □[2]	2790	11.30 N	43.00 E
Affton	2746	38.33 N	90.20 W
Afghanistan □[1]	2792	33.00 N	65.00 E
Afikpo	2786	5.53 N	7.56 E
Åfjord	2768	63.58 N	10.12 E
Afmadu	2788	0.32 N	42.10 E
Africa ⊥[1]	2730	10.00 N	22.00 E
Afton, N.Y., U.S.	2740	42.14 N	75.32 W
Afton, Okla., U.S.	2748	36.42 N	94.58 W
Afton, Wyo., U.S.	2754	42.44 N	110.56 W
'Afula	2791	32.36 N	35.17 E
Agadez	2786	16.58 N	7.59 E
Agadir	2786	30.26 N	9.36 W
Agalega Islands II	2788	10.24 S	56.37 E
Agalta, Cordillera de ⩘	2760	15.00 N	85.53 W
Agana	2802	13.28 N	144.45 E
Agapa	2784	71.27 N	89.15 E
Agartala	2794	23.49 N	91.16 E
Agen	2772	44.12 N	0.37 E
Āghā Jārī	2790	30.42 N	49.50 E
Agira	2776	37.39 N	14.32 E
Agnone	2776	41.48 N	14.22 E
Āgra	2794	27.11 N	78.01 E
Ágreda	2774	41.51 N	1.56 W
Agrigento	2776	37.18 N	13.35 E
Agrihan I	2802	18.46 N	145.40 E
Agrínion	2778	38.37 N	21.24 E
Agropoli	2776	40.21 N	15.00 E
Agua Caliente	2758	23.20 N	105.20 W
Agua Caliente Grande	2758	26.31 N	108.22 W
Água Clara	2765	20.27 S	52.52 W
Agualeguas	2748	26.18 N	99.34 W
Agua Prieta	2758	31.18 N	109.34 W
Aguascalientes	2758	21.53 N	102.18 W
Águas Formosas	2765	17.05 S	40.57 W
Águeda	2774	40.34 N	8.27 W
Aguila	2752	33.56 N	113.11 W
Aguilar, Esp.	2774	37.31 N	4.39 W
Aguilar, Colo., U.S.	2750	37.24 N	104.46 W
Águilas	2774	37.24 N	1.35 W
Agujita	2748	27.53 N	101.09 W
Agustín Codazzi	2760	10.02 N	73.14 W
Ahaggar ⩘	2786	23.00 N	6.30 E
Ahipara Bay C	2808	35.10 S	173.07 E
Ahmadābād	2794	23.02 N	72.37 E
Ahmadnagar	2793	19.05 N	74.44 E
Ahmadpur East	2794	29.09 N	71.16 E
Ahmar Mountains ⩘	2790	9.15 N	41.00 E
Ahoskie	2744	36.17 N	76.59 W
Ahuacatlán	2758	21.03 N	104.29 W
Ahvāz	2790	31.19 N	48.42 E
Aibihu ⊕	2796	44.55 N	82.55 E
Aichach	2772	48.28 N	11.08 E
Aiea	2757a	21.23 N	157.56 W
Aihun	2796	50.13 N	127.33 E
Aiken	2744	33.34 N	81.43 W
Aim	2784	58.50 N	134.12 E
Aimorés	2765	19.30 S	41.04 W
Ainsworth	2750	42.33 N	99.52 W
Aïr ⩘	2786	18.00 N	8.30 E
Aire-sur-l'Adour	2772	43.42 N	0.16 W
Air Force Island I	2734	67.55 N	74.10 W
Aisne ≏	2772	49.26 N	2.50 E
Aïssa, Djebel ∧	2786	32.51 N	0.30 W
Aitkin	2742	46.32 N	93.43 W
Aix-en-Provence	2772	43.32 N	5.26 E
Aix-la-Chapelle → Aachen	2770	50.47 N	6.05 E
Aix-les-Bains	2772	45.42 N	5.55 E
Aizu-wakamatsu	2798	37.30 N	139.56 E
Ajaccio	2776	41.55 N	8.44 E
Ajaguz	2784	47.56 N	80.23 E
Ajan	2784	56.27 N	138.10 E
Ajan ≏	2784	70.10 N	95.50 E
Ajdābiyah	2786	30.48 N	20.14 E
'Ajlūn	2791	32.20 N	35.45 E
Ajmer	2794	26.27 N	74.38 E
Ajo	2752	32.22 N	112.52 W
Ajo, Cabo de ≻	2774	43.31 N	3.35 W
Ajon, Ostrov I	2784	69.50 N	168.40 E
Ajtos	2778	42.42 N	27.15 E
Aju, Kepulauan II	2802	0.28 N	131.03 E
Ajusco	2756	31.35 N	116.25 W
Akademii, Zaliv C	2784	54.15 N	138.05 E
Akan	2798a	43.06 N	144.10 E
'Akasha East	2786	21.05 N	30.43 E
Akashi	2798	34.38 N	134.59 E
Akçakale	2791	36.41 N	38.56 E
Akesu	2796	41.10 N	80.20 E
Akharnaí	2778	38.05 N	23.44 E
Akhisar	2766	38.55 N	27.51 E
Akimiski Island I	2734	53.00 N	81.20 W
Akita	2798	39.43 N	140.07 E
Akjoujt	2786	19.45 N	14.23 W
'Akko (Acre)	2791	32.55 N	35.05 E
Aklavik	2734	68.12 N	135.00 W
Akō	2798	34.45 N	134.24 E
Akobo ≏	2786	7.47 N	33.01 E
Akola	2793	20.44 N	77.00 E
Akordat	2790	15.35 N	37.54 E
Akpatok Island I	2734	60.25 N	68.00 W
Akron, Colo., U.S.	2750	40.10 N	103.13 W
Akron, Ohio, U.S.	2740	41.05 N	81.31 W
Aksaray	2766	38.23 N	34.03 E
Akşehir	2766	38.21 N	31.25 E
Aksum	2790	14.08 N	38.48 E
Akt'ubinsk	2766	50.17 N	57.10 E

Symbols against index entries represent categories identified in the key on page 2810.

Name	Page	Lat °′	Long °′
Akureyri	2766	65.44 N	18.08 W
Ål	2768	60.38 N	8.34 E
Alabama □[3]	2736	32.50 N	87.00 W
Alabama ≃	2746	31.08 N	87.57 W
Alachua	2744	29.47 N	82.30 W
Alagoinhas	2765	12.07 S	38.26 W
Alagón	2774	41.46 N	1.07 W
Al-'Alamayn	2786	30.49 N	28.57 E
Alamagan I	2802	17.36 N	145.50 E
Al-'Amārah	2790	31.50 N	47.09 E
Alameda	2752	35.11 N	106.37 W
Alamo, Nev., U.S.	2756	37.22 N	115.10 W
Alamo, Tenn., U.S.	2746	35.47 N	89.07 W
Alamogordo	2752	32.54 N	105.57 W
Alamo Heights	2748	29.28 N	98.28 W
Alamosa	2752	37.28 N	105.52 W
Alanäs	2768	64.10 N	15.42 E
Alapajevsk	2766	57.52 N	61.42 E
Al-'Aqabah	2791	29.31 N	35.00 E
Alaşehir	2778	38.21 N	28.32 E
Alashanyouqi	2796	40.02 N	103.33 E
Alaska Peninsula ➤[1]	2738	57.00 N	158.00 W
Alaska Range ⋀	2738	62.30 N	150.00 W
Alassio	2776	44.00 N	8.10 E
Al-'Aṭrūn	2786	18.11 N	26.36 E
Alatyr'	2766	54.51 N	46.36 E
Alazeja ≃	2784	70.51 N	153.34 E
Alba	2776	44.42 N	8.02 E
Albacete	2774	38.59 N	1.51 W
Alba de Tormes	2774	40.49 N	5.31 W
Albaida	2774	38.51 N	0.31 W
Albanel, Lac ⊜	2734	50.55 N	73.12 W
Albania □[1]	2766	41.00 N	20.00 E
Albano Laziale	2776	41.44 N	12.39 E
Albany, Austl.	2806	35.02 S	117.53 E
Albany, Ga., U.S.	2744	31.35 N	84.10 W
Albany, Ky., U.S.	2746	36.42 N	85.08 W
Albany, Minn., U.S.	2742	45.38 N	94.34 W
Albany, Mo., U.S.	2746	40.15 N	94.20 W
Albany, N.Y., U.S.	2740	42.39 N	73.45 W
Albany, Oreg., U.S.	2754	44.38 N	123.06 W
Albany, Tex., U.S.	2748	32.44 N	99.18 W
Albany ≃	2734	52.17 N	81.31 W
Al-Baṣrah	2790	30.30 N	47.47 E
Albatross Bay C	2806	12.45 S	141.43 E
Al-Batrūn	2791	34.15 N	35.39 E
Al-Bawīṭī	2786	28.21 N	28.52 E
Albemarle	2744	35.21 N	80.12 W
Albemarle Sound ꓤ	2744	36.03 N	76.12 W
Albenga	2776	44.03 N	8.13 E
Albergaria-a-Velha	2774	40.42 N	8.29 W
Albert	2772	50.00 N	2.39 E
Albert, Lake ⊜	2788	1.40 N	31.00 E
Alberta □[4]	2734	54.00 N	113.00 W
Albert Lea	2742	43.39 N	93.22 W
Albert Nile ≃	2786	3.36 N	32.02 E
Alberton	2754	47.00 N	114.29 W
Albertville, Fr.	2772	45.41 N	6.23 E
Albertville, Ala., U.S.	2746	34.16 N	86.12 W
Albertville → Kalemi, Zaïre	2788	5.56 S	29.12 E
Albi	2772	43.56 N	2.09 E
Albia	2742	41.02 N	92.48 W
Albino	2776	45.46 N	9.47 E
Albion, Ill., U.S.	2746	38.23 N	88.04 W
Albion, Mich., U.S.	2742	42.15 N	84.45 W
Albion, Nebr., U.S.	2750	41.42 N	98.00 W
Albion, N.Y., U.S.	2740	43.15 N	78.12 W
Albion, Pa., U.S.	2740	41.53 N	80.22 W
Albion, Tex., U.S.	2748	27.45 N	98.05 W
Alborán, Isla de I	2774	35.58 N	3.02 W
Ålborg	2768	57.03 N	9.56 E
Alborz, Reshteh-ye Kūhhā-ye ⋀	2766	36.00 N	53.00 E
Albufeira	2774	37.05 N	8.15 W
Albuñol	2774	36.47 N	3.12 W
Albuquerque	2752	35.05 N	106.40 W
Alburquerque	2774	39.13 N	7.00 W
Albury	2806	36.05 S	146.55 E
Alcácer do Sal	2774	38.22 N	8.30 W
Alcalá de Guadaira	2774	37.20 N	5.50 W
Alcalá de Henares	2774	40.29 N	3.22 W
Alcalá la Real	2774	37.28 N	3.56 W
Alcalde	2752	36.05 N	106.03 W
Alcamo	2776	37.59 N	12.58 E
Alcañices	2774	41.42 N	6.21 W
Alcañiz	2774	41.03 N	0.08 W
Alcântara, Bra.	2762	2.24 S	44.24 W
Alcántara, Esp.	2774	39.43 N	6.53 W
Alcantarilla	2774	37.58 N	1.13 W
Alcaraz	2774	38.40 N	2.29 W
Alcázar de San Juan	2774	39.24 N	3.12 W
Alcira	2774	39.09 N	0.26 W
Alcoa	2744	35.48 N	83.59 W
Alcobaça, Bra.	2765	17.30 S	39.13 W
Alcobaça, Port.	2774	39.33 N	8.59 W
Alconchel	2774	38.31 N	7.04 W
Alcoy	2774	38.42 N	0.28 W
Aldabra Islands I[1]	2788	9.25 S	46.22 E
Aldan	2784	58.37 N	125.24 E
Aldan ≃	2784	63.28 N	129.35 E
Aldanskoje Nagorje ⋀[1]	2784	57.00 N	127.00 E
Alden	2742	42.31 N	93.23 W
Aldershot	2769	51.15 N	0.47 W
Alderson	2744	37.43 N	80.39 W
Aledo	2746	41.12 N	90.45 W
Aleg	2786	17.03 N	13.55 W
Alegrete	2764	29.46 S	55.46 W
Alegros Mountain ▲	2752	34.09 N	108.11 W
Alejsk	2784	52.58 N	82.45 E
Aleksandrija	2782	48.40 N	33.07 E
Aleksandrov	2780	56.24 N	38.43 E
Aleksandrovsk-Sachalinskij	2784	50.54 N	142.10 E
Aleksejevka	2782	50.37 N	38.42 E
Aleksejevsk	2784	57.50 N	108.23 E
Aleksin	2780	54.31 N	37.05 E
Além Paraíba	2765	21.52 S	42.41 W
Alençon	2772	48.26 N	0.05 E
Aléria	2776	42.05 N	9.30 E
Alès	2772	44.08 N	4.05 E
Alessandria	2776	44.54 N	8.37 E
Alessano	2776	39.53 N	18.20 E
Ålesund	2768	62.28 N	6.09 E
Aleutian Islands II	2738	52.00 N	176.00 W
Aleutka	2784	45.57 N	150.10 E
Alevina, Mys ➤	2784	58.50 N	151.20 E
Alexander	2750	47.51 N	103.39 W
Alexander Archipelago II	2738	56.30 N	134.00 W
Alexander Bay	2788	28.40 S	16.30 E
Alexander City	2746	32.56 N	85.57 W
Alexandra	2808	45.15 S	169.24 E
Alexandria, Ky., U.S.	2740	38.58 N	84.23 W
Alexandria, La., U.S.	2746	31.18 N	92.27 W
Alexandria, Minn., U.S.	2750	45.53 N	95.22 W
Alexandria, Nebr., U.S.	2750	40.15 N	97.23 W
Alexandria, S. Dak., U.S.	2750	43.39 N	97.47 W
Alexandria, Tenn., U.S.	2746	36.05 N	86.02 W
Alexandria, Va., U.S.	2740	38.48 N	77.03 W
Alexandria Bay	2740	44.20 N	75.55 W
Alexandroúpolis	2778	40.50 N	25.52 E
Alfaro	2774	42.11 N	1.45 W
Alfarrás	2774	41.49 N	0.35 E
Al-Fāshir	2786	13.38 N	25.21 E
Al-Fayyūm	2786	29.19 N	30.50 E
Alfenas	2765	21.25 S	45.57 W
Alfred	2740	42.15 N	77.47 W
Alga	2766	49.46 N	57.20 E
Algarve □[9]	2774	37.10 N	8.15 W
Algeciras	2774	36.08 N	5.30 W
Algemesí	2774	39.11 N	0.26 W
Alger (Algiers)	2786	36.47 N	3.03 E
Algeria □[1]	2786	28.00 N	3.00 E
Al-Ghayḍah	2790	16.12 N	52.15 E
Alghero	2776	40.34 N	8.19 E
Al-Ghurdaqah	2786	27.14 N	33.50 E
Algiers → Alger	2786	36.47 N	3.03 E
Algoma	2742	44.36 N	87.27 W
Algona	2742	43.04 N	94.14 W
Algood	2746	36.12 N	85.27 W
Algorta	2764	32.25 S	57.23 W
Al-Ḥadīthah	2790	34.07 N	42.23 E
Al-Ḥaffah	2791	35.35 N	36.02 E
Al-Ḥamād ⋍	2790	32.00 N	39.30 E
Alhama de Granada	2774	37.00 N	3.59 W
Al-Ḥarīq	2790	23.37 N	46.31 E
Al-Harūj al-Aswad ⋀[2]	2786	27.00 N	17.10 E
Al-Ḥasakah	2791	36.29 N	40.45 E
Alhaurín el Grande	2774	36.38 N	4.41 W
Al-Ḥawrah	2790	13.49 N	47.37 E
Al-Ḥijāz (Hejaz) ✦[1]	2790	24.30 N	38.30 E
Al-Ḥillah	2790	32.29 N	44.25 E
Al-Hirmil	2791	34.23 N	36.23 E
Al-Ḥudaydah	2790	14.48 N	42.57 E
Al-Hufūf	2790	25.22 N	49.34 E
Aliaga	2774	40.40 N	0.42 W
Alicante	2774	38.21 N	0.29 W
Alice	2748	27.45 N	98.04 W
Alice Springs	2806	23.42 S	133.53 E
Alice Town	2744	25.44 N	79.17 W
Aliceville	2746	33.08 N	88.09 W
Alīgarh	2794	27.54 N	78.05 E
Alingsås	2768	57.56 N	12.31 E
Aliquippa	2740	40.37 N	80.15 W
Al-Iskandarīyah (Alexandria)	2786	31.12 N	29.54 E
Al-Ismā'īlīyah	2786	30.35 N	32.16 E
Aliwal North	2788	30.45 S	26.45 E
Al-Jabal al-Akhḍar ⋀	2790	23.15 N	57.20 E
Al-Jafr	2791	30.18 N	36.13 E
Al-Jaghbūb	2786	29.45 N	24.31 E
Al-Jawf, Ar. Sa.	2790	29.50 N	39.52 E
Al-Jawf, Lībīya	2786	24.11 N	23.19 E
Al-Jazīrah ✦[1]	2786	14.25 N	33.00 E
Aljezur	2774	37.19 N	8.48 W
Al-Jīzah	2786	30.01 N	31.13 E
Al-Junaynah	2786	13.27 N	22.27 E
Aljustrel	2774	37.52 N	8.10 W
Al-Karak	2791	31.11 N	35.42 E
Al-Kawm	2791	35.11 N	38.48 E
Al-Khalīl	2791	31.32 N	35.06 E
Al-Khandaq	2786	18.36 N	30.34 E
Al-Khārijah	2786	25.26 N	30.33 E
Al-Khaṣab	2790	26.12 N	56.15 E
Al-Khubar	2790	26.17 N	50.12 E
Al-Khums	2786	32.39 N	14.16 E
Al-Khurṭūm (Khartoum)	2786	15.36 N	32.32 E
Alkmaar	2770	52.37 N	4.44 E
Al-Kuwayt	2790	29.20 N	47.59 E
Allach-Jun'	2784	61.08 N	138.03 E
Al-Lādhiqīyah (Latakia)	2791	35.31 N	35.47 E
Allāhābād	2794	25.27 N	81.51 E
Allanche	2772	45.14 N	2.56 E
Allardt	2746	36.23 N	84.53 W
Allegan	2742	42.32 N	85.51 W
Allegheny Mountains ⋀	2740	38.30 N	80.00 W
Allegheny Plateau ⋀[1]	2740	41.30 N	78.00 W
Allen, Okla., U.S.	2748	34.53 N	96.25 W
Allen, Tex., U.S.	2748	33.06 N	96.40 W
Allendale	2744	33.06 N	81.18 W
Allentown	2740	40.36 N	75.29 W
Allentsteig	2770	48.42 N	15.20 E
Alleppey	2793	9.29 N	76.19 E
Alliance, Nebr., U.S.	2750	42.06 N	102.52 W
Alliance, Ohio, U.S.	2740	40.55 N	81.06 W
Allison	2742	42.45 N	92.48 W
Al-Līth	2790	20.09 N	40.16 E
Allouez	2742	44.29 N	88.01 W
Al-Luḥayyah	2790	15.42 N	42.42 E
Alma, Qué., Can.	2739	48.33 N	71.39 W
Alma, Ga., U.S.	2744	31.33 N	82.28 W
Alma, Mich., U.S.	2742	43.23 N	84.39 W
Almada	2774	38.41 N	9.09 W
Al-Madīnah (Medina)	2790	24.28 N	39.36 E
Al-Mafraq	2791	32.21 N	36.12 E
Almagro	2774	38.53 N	3.43 W
Al-Manāmah	2790	26.13 N	50.35 E
Almansa	2774	38.52 N	1.05 W
Al-Manṣūrah	2786	31.03 N	31.23 E
Al-Marj	2786	32.30 N	20.54 E
Almas, Pico das ▲	2762	13.33 S	41.56 W
Al-Maṣīrah I	2790	20.25 N	58.50 E
Al-Mawṣil	2790	36.20 N	43.08 E
Al-Mayādīn	2791	35.01 N	40.27 E
Almazán	2774	41.29 N	2.32 W
Almelo	2770	52.21 N	6.39 E
Almenara	2765	16.11 S	40.42 W
Almendralejo	2774	38.41 N	6.24 W
Almería	2774	36.50 N	2.27 W
Al'metjevsk	2766	54.53 N	52.20 E
Al-Minyā	2786	28.06 N	30.45 E
Al-Mismīyah	2791	33.03 N	36.20 E
Almodôvar	2774	37.31 N	8.04 W
Almodóvar del Campo	2774	38.43 N	4.10 W
Almont	2742	42.55 N	83.03 W
Almonte	2774	37.15 N	6.31 W
Almora	2794	29.36 N	79.41 E
Al-Mubarraz, Ar. Sa.	2790	25.55 N	49.36 E
Al-Mubarraz, Ar. Sa.	2790	22.17 N	46.44 E
Al-Muglad	2786	11.02 N	27.44 E
Al-Muḥarraq	2790	26.16 N	50.37 E
Al-Mukallā	2790	14.32 N	49.08 E
Al-Mukhā	2790	13.19 N	43.15 E
Al-Muwayliḥ	2790	27.41 N	35.27 E
Alnwick	2769	55.25 N	1.42 W
Aloândia	2765	17.43 S	49.29 W
Alor, Pulau I	2802	8.15 S	124.45 E
Álora	2774	36.48 N	4.42 W
Alor Setar	2804	6.07 N	100.22 E
Aloysius, Mount ▲	2806	26.00 S	128.34 E
Alpena	2742	45.04 N	83.26 W
Alpharetta	2744	34.04 N	84.18 W
Alphonse Island I	2788	7.00 S	52.45 E
Alpiarça	2774	39.15 N	8.35 W
Alpine, Ariz., U.S.	2752	33.51 N	109.09 W
Alpine, Tex., U.S.	2748	30.22 N	103.40 W
Alps ⋀	2766	46.25 N	10.00 E
Al-Qaḍārif	2786	14.02 N	35.24 E
Al-Qāhirah (Cairo)	2786	30.03 N	31.15 E
Al-Qāmishlī	2791	37.02 N	41.14 E
Al-Qaryah ash-Sharqīyah	2786	30.24 N	13.36 E
Al-Qaryatayn	2791	34.14 N	37.14 E
Al-Qaṣr	2786	25.42 N	28.53 E
Al-Qaṭīf	2790	26.33 N	50.00 E
Al-Qaṭrūn	2786	24.56 N	14.38 E
Al-Qayṣūmah	2790	28.16 N	46.03 E
Al-Qunayṭirah	2791	33.07 N	35.49 E
Al-Qunfudhah	2790	19.08 N	41.05 E
Al-Quṣayr	2786	26.06 N	34.19 E
Al-Quṭayfah	2791	33.44 N	36.36 E
Alsasua	2774	42.54 N	2.10 W
Alsea ≃	2754	44.26 N	124.05 W
Alta	2768	69.55 N	23.12 E
Altagracia de Orituco	2760	9.52 N	66.23 W
Altai ⋀	2796	48.00 N	90.00 E
Altaj (Jesönbulag)	2796	46.25 N	96.20 E
Altamira	2762	3.12 S	52.12 W
Altamirano	2748	25.55 N	97.47 W
Altamont, Oreg., U.S.	2754	42.12 N	121.44 W
Altamont, Tenn., U.S.	2746	35.26 N	85.43 W
Altamura	2776	40.50 N	16.33 E
Altar	2758	30.43 N	111.44 W
Altata	2758	24.38 N	107.55 W
Altavista	2744	37.06 N	79.17 W
Altdorf	2772	46.53 N	8.39 E
Altiplano ⋀[1]	2762	18.00 S	68.00 W
Alto	2748	31.39 N	95.04 W
Alto Araguaia	2765	17.19 S	53.12 W
Alton, Ill., U.S.	2746	38.54 N	90.10 W
Alton, Mo., U.S.	2746	36.42 N	91.24 W
Altoona	2740	40.30 N	78.24 W
Alto Parnaíba	2762	9.06 S	45.57 W
Altötting	2770	48.13 N	12.40 E
Alturas	2756	41.29 N	120.32 W
Altus	2748	34.38 N	99.20 W
Al-'Ubaylah	2790	21.59 N	50.57 E
Al-Ubayyiḍ	2786	13.11 N	30.13 E
'Alula	2790	11.58 N	50.48 E
Al-Uqṣur (Luxor)	2786	25.41 N	32.39 E
Alušta	2782	44.42 N	34.24 E
Alva	2748	36.48 N	98.40 W
Alvarado, Méx.	2758	18.46 N	95.46 W
Alvarado, Tex., U.S.	2748	32.24 N	97.13 W
Alvaton	2744	33.10 N	84.35 W
Älvdalen	2768	61.14 N	14.02 E
Alvin	2748	29.25 N	95.15 W
Älvkarleby	2768	60.34 N	17.27 E
Alvord	2748	33.22 N	97.42 W
Alvord Desert ✦[2]	2754	42.30 N	118.25 W
Älvsbyn	2768	65.39 N	20.59 E
Al-Wajh	2790	26.15 N	36.26 E
Alwar	2794	27.34 N	76.36 E
Alzamaj	2784	55.33 N	98.39 E
Amadeus, Lake ⊜	2806	24.50 S	130.45 E
Amadjuak Lake ⊜	2734	65.00 N	71.00 W
Amagasaki	2798	34.43 N	135.25 E
Amakusa-nada ▼[2]	2798	32.35 N	130.05 E
Amakusa-shotō II	2798	32.20 N	130.15 E
Åmål	2768	59.03 N	12.42 E
Amalfi	2776	40.38 N	14.36 E
Amalner	2794	21.03 N	75.04 E
Amambaí, Serra de ⋀	2762	23.10 S	55.30 W
Amami-Ō-shima I	2799b	28.15 N	129.20 E
Amami-shotō II	2799b	28.16 N	129.21 E
Amana	2742	41.48 N	91.52 W
Amantea	2776	39.08 N	16.05 E
Amares	2774	41.38 N	8.21 W
Amargosa Range ⋀	2756	36.30 N	116.45 W
Amarillo	2748	35.13 N	101.49 W
Amasa	2742	46.14 N	88.27 W
Amazon (Solimões) (Amazonas) ≃	2762	0.05 S	50.00 W
Ambāla	2794	30.20 N	77.05 E
Ambarčik	2784	69.39 N	162.20 E
Ambato	2762	1.15 S	78.37 W
Ambatolampy	2788	19.23 S	47.25 E
Ambatondrazaka	2788	17.50 S	48.25 E
Amberg	2742	45.30 N	88.00 W
Ambérieu-en-Bugey	2772	45.57 N	5.21 W
Ambert	2772	45.33 N	3.45 E
Ambikāpur	2794	23.08 N	83.11 E
Ambilobe	2788	13.12 S	49.04 E
Amble	2769	55.20 N	1.34 E
Amboise	2772	47.25 N	0.59 E
Ambon	2802	3.43 S	128.12 E
Ambositra	2788	20.31 S	47.15 E
Ambovombe	2788	25.11 S	46.05 E
Amboy, Ill., U.S.	2746	41.44 N	89.20 W
Amboy, Minn., U.S.	2742	43.59 N	94.10 W
Ambre, Cap d' ➤	2788	11.57 S	49.17 E
Ambrières	2772	48.24 N	0.38 W
Ambriz	2788	7.50 S	13.06 E
Ambrizete	2788	7.14 S	12.52 E
Āmbūr	2793	12.47 N	78.42 E
Ameagle	2744	37.57 N	81.25 W
Ameca	2758	20.33 N	104.02 W
Amecameca [de Juárez]	2758	19.07 N	98.46 W
Amelia Court House	2744	37.21 N	77.59 W
Americana	2765	22.45 S	47.20 W
American Falls	2754	42.47 N	112.51 W
American Falls Reservoir ⊜[1]	2754	43.00 N	113.00 W
American Fork	2752	40.23 N	111.48 W
American Highland ⋀[1]	2733	72.30 S	78.00 E
American Samoa □[2]	2730	14.20 S	170.00 W
Americus	2744	32.04 N	84.14 W
Amersfoort	2770	52.09 N	5.24 E
Ames	2742	42.02 N	93.37 W
Amfilokhia	2778	38.51 N	21.10 E
Ámfissa	2778	38.31 N	22.24 E
Amga	2784	60.53 N	132.00 E
Amga ≃	2784	62.38 N	134.32 E
Amgun' ≃	2784	52.56 N	139.40 E
Amherst, N.S., Can.	2739	45.49 N	64.14 W
Amherst, Mass., U.S.	2740	42.23 N	72.31 W
Amherst, Va., U.S.	2744	37.35 N	79.03 W
Amherstburg	2740	42.06 N	83.06 W
Amidon	2750	46.29 N	103.19 W
Amiens	2772	49.54 N	2.18 E
Amīndīvi Islands II	2793	11.23 N	72.23 E
Amirante Islands II	2788	6.00 S	53.10 E
Amite	2746	30.44 N	90.30 W
'Ammān	2791	31.57 N	35.56 E
Ämmänsaari	2768	64.53 N	28.55 E
Ammókhostos (Famagusta)	2791	35.07 N	33.57 E
Ammókhostou, Kólpos C	2791	35.15 N	34.10 E
Amory	2746	33.59 N	88.29 W
Åmot	2768	59.35 N	8.00 E
Amphitrite Group II	2802	17.00 N	112.25 E
Amposta	2774	40.43 N	0.35 E
Amqui	2739	49.28 N	67.26 W
Amrāvati	2793	20.56 N	77.45 E
Amritsar	2794	31.35 N	74.53 E
Amroha	2794	28.55 N	78.28 E
Amsterdam, Ned.	2770	52.22 N	4.54 E
Amsterdam, N.Y., U.S.	2740	42.57 N	74.11 W
Amstetten	2770	48.07 N	14.53 E
Am Timan	2786	11.02 N	20.17 E
Amundsen Gulf C	2734	71.00 N	124.00 W
Amundsen Sea ▼[2]	2733	72.30 S	112.00 W
Amuntai	2802	2.26 S	115.15 E
Amur (Heilongjiang) ≃	2784	52.56 N	141.10 E
Amvrosijevka	2782	47.47 N	38.29 E
Anabar ≃	2784	73.08 N	113.36 E
Anaco	2760	9.27 N	64.28 W
Anacoco	2746	31.15 N	93.20 W
Anaconda	2754	46.08 N	112.57 W
Anaconda Range ⋀	2754	45.55 N	113.30 W
Anadarko	2748	35.04 N	98.15 W
Anadyr'	2784	64.45 N	177.29 E
Anadyr' ≃	2784	64.55 N	176.05 E
Anadyrskij Zaliv C	2784	64.00 N	179.00 W
Anadyrskoje Ploskogorje ⋀[1]	2784	67.00 N	172.00 E
Anagni	2776	41.44 N	13.09 E
Anaheim	2756	33.51 N	117.57 W
Anahuac	2748	29.46 N	94.41 W
Ānai Mudi ▲	2793	10.10 N	77.04 E
Anakāpalle	2793	17.41 N	83.01 E
Analalava	2788	14.38 S	47.45 E
Anambas, Kepulauan II	2804	3.00 N	106.00 E
Anamoose	2750	47.53 N	100.15 W
Anamosa	2742	42.07 N	91.17 W
Anamur	2766	36.06 N	32.50 E
Anamur Burnu ➤	2791	36.03 N	32.48 E
Anan	2798	33.55 N	134.39 E
Ānand	2794	22.34 N	72.56 E
Anantapur	2793	14.41 N	77.36 E
Anantnāg (Islāmābād)	2794	33.44 N	75.10 E
Anápolis	2765	16.20 S	48.58 W
Anatahan I	2802	16.22 N	145.40 E
Añatuya	2764	28.30 S	62.50 W
'Anazah, Jabal ▲	2791	32.12 N	39.18 E
Anchorage	2738	61.13 N	149.53 W
Ancona	2776	43.38 N	13.30 E
Ancud	2764	41.52 S	73.50 W
Ancud, Golfo de C	2764	42.00 S	73.00 W
Andalucía □[9]	2774	37.36 N	4.30 W
Andalusia	2746	31.19 N	86.29 W
Andaman Islands II	2804	12.30 N	92.45 E
Andaman Sea ▼[2]	2804	10.00 N	95.00 E
Andermatt	2772	46.38 N	8.36 E
Andernach	2770	50.26 N	7.24 E
Anderson, Calif., U.S.	2756	40.27 N	122.18 W
Anderson, Ind., U.S.	2746	40.10 N	85.41 W
Anderson, Mo., U.S.	2746	36.39 N	94.27 W

Symbols against index entries represent categories identified in the key on page 2810.

Name	Page	Lat °′	Long °′
Anderson, S.C., U.S.	2744	34.31 N	82.39 W
Anderson, Tex., U.S.	2748	30.29 N	95.59 W
Anderson ≛	2734	69.43 N	128.58 W
Andes ⋀	2762	17.00 S	70.00 W
Andkhvoy	2794	36.56 N	65.08 E
Andong, Taehan	2796	36.35 N	128.44 E
Andong, Zhg.	2796	40.08 N	124.20 E
Andorra □1	2766	42.30 N	1.30 E
Andover	2740	41.36 N	80.34 W
Andradina	2765	20.54 S	51.23 W
Andrews, N.C., U.S.	2744	35.12 N	83.49 W
Andrews, S.C., U.S.	2744	33.27 N	79.34 W
Andrews, Tex., U.S.	2748	32.19 N	102.33 W
Andria	2776	41.13 N	16.18 E
Androka	2788	25.02 S	44.05 E
Ándros I	2778	37.45 N	24.42 E
Andros Island I	2760	24.25 N	78.00 W
Andújar	2774	38.03 N	4.04 W
Anduo	2794	32.18 N	91.04 E
Anegada Passage ⩫	2760	18.15 N	63.45 W
Anegam	2752	32.23 N	112.02 W
Ang'angxi	2796	47.09 N	123.48 E
Angara ≛	2784	58.06 N	93.00 E
Angarsk	2784	52.34 N	103.54 E
Ånge	2768	62.31 N	15.37 E
Ángel, Salto (Angel Falls) ⌊	2762	5.57 N	62.30 W
Angeles	2802	15.09 N	120.35 E
Angel Falls → Ángel, Salto ⌊	2762	5.57 N	62.30 W
Ängelholm	2768	56.15 N	12.51 E
Angels Camp	2756	38.04 N	120.32 W
Angers	2772	47.28 N	0.33 W
Angerville	2772	48.19 N	2.00 E
Angicos	2762	5.40 S	36.36 W
Angle Inlet	2750	49.21 N	95.04 W
Angleton	2748	29.10 N	95.26 W
Angmagssalik	2734	65.36 N	37.41 W
Angol	2764	37.48 S	72.43 W
Angola, Ind., U.S.	2746	41.38 N	85.00 W
Angola, N.Y., U.S.	2740	42.38 N	79.02 W
Angola □1	2788	12.30 S	18.30 E
Angoulême	2772	45.39 N	0.09 E
Angra dos Reis	2765	23.00 S	44.18 W
Anguilla □2	2760	18.15 N	63.05 W
Angul	2794	20.51 N	85.06 E
Anhui □4	2796	32.00 N	117.00 E
Animas	2752	31.57 N	108.48 W
Animas Peak Λ	2752	31.35 N	108.47 W
Anjiang	2796	27.11 N	110.04 E
Anjouan I	2788	12.15 S	44.25 E
Ankang	2796	32.31 N	109.19 E
Ankara	2766	39.56 N	32.52 E
Ankavandra	2788	18.46 S	45.18 E
Ankazoabo	2788	22.18 S	44.31 E
Ankazobe	2788	18.21 S	47.07 E
Ankeny	2742	41.44 N	93.36 W
Anna	2746	37.28 N	89.15 W
Annaba (Bône)	2786	36.54 N	7.46 E
An-Nabk	2791	34.01 N	36.44 E
An-Nafūd ✈2	2790	28.30 N	41.00 E
An-Najaf	2790	31.59 N	44.20 E
Annandale	2742	45.16 N	94.08 W
Annapolis	2740	38.59 N	76.30 W
Annapurna Λ	2794	28.34 N	83.50 E
Ann Arbor	2742	42.18 N	83.45 W
An-Nāṣirīyah	2790	31.02 N	46.16 E
Annecy	2772	45.54 N	6.07 E
Annemasse	2772	46.12 N	6.15 E
Anniston	2746	33.40 N	85.50 W
Annonay	2772	45.14 N	4.40 E
An-Nuhūd	2786	12.42 N	28.26 E
Anoka	2742	45.11 N	93.23 W
Anqing	2800	30.31 N	117.02 E
Anshan	2796	41.08 N	122.59 E
Anshun	2804	26.19 N	105.50 E
Ansley	2750	41.18 N	99.23 W
Anson	2748	32.45 N	99.54 W
Ansonville	2744	35.06 N	80.07 W
Ansted	2740	38.08 N	81.06 W
Antakya	2766	36.14 N	36.07 E
Antalaha	2788	14.53 S	50.16 E
Antalya	2766	36.53 N	30.42 E
Antarctica ⚓1	2733	90.00 S	0.00
Antequera	2774	37.01 N	4.33 W
Anthon	2750	42.23 N	95.52 W
Anthony, Fla., U.S.	2744	29.18 N	82.07 W
Anthony, Kans., U.S.	2750	37.09 N	98.02 W
Anthony, Tex., U.S.	2758	32.00 N	106.36 W
Anti Atlas ⋀	2786	30.00 N	8.30 W
Antibes	2772	43.35 N	7.07 E
Antigo	2742	45.09 N	89.09 W
Antigonish	2734	45.35 N	61.55 W
Antigua □1	2760	17.03 N	61.48 W
Antioch → Antakya, Tür.	2766	36.14 N	36.07 E
Antioch, Ill., U.S.	2742	42.29 N	88.06 W
Antlers	2748	34.14 N	95.37 W
Antofagasta	2764	23.39 S	70.24 W
Antofalla, Salar de ⩸	2764	25.40 S	67.45 W
Anton Chico	2748	35.12 N	105.09 W
Antongil, Baie d' C	2788	15.45 S	49.50 E
António Enes	2788	16.14 S	39.54 E
Antônio João	2765	23.15 S	55.31 W
Antonito	2752	37.05 N	106.00 W
Antrodoco	2776	42.25 N	13.05 E
Antsirabe	2788	19.51 S	47.02 E
Antwerpen (Anvers)	2770	51.13 N	4.25 E
Anxi	2796	40.32 N	95.51 E
Anyang	2796	36.06 N	114.21 E
Anžero-Sudžensk	2784	56.07 N	86.00 E
Anzio	2776	41.27 N	12.37 E
Anžu, Ostrova II	2784	75.30 N	143.00 E
Aoiz	2774	42.47 N	1.22 W
Aomori	2798	40.49 N	140.45 E
Aosta	2776	45.44 N	7.20 E
Aoukâr ✈1	2786	18.00 N	9.30 W
Aozou	2786	21.49 N	17.25 E
Apache	2748	34.54 N	98.22 W
Apalachee Bay C	2744	30.00 N	84.13 W
Apalachicola	2744	29.44 N	84.59 W
Apalachicola ≛	2744	29.44 N	84.59 W
Aparri	2802	18.22 N	121.39 E
Apatity	2766	67.34 N	33.18 E
Apatzingán [de la Constitución]	2758	19.05 N	102.21 W
Apeldoorn	2770	52.13 N	5.58 E
Apennines → Appennino ⋀	2776	43.00 N	13.00 E
Apizaco	2758	19.25 N	98.09 W
Apo, Mount Λ	2802	6.59 N	125.16 E
Aporé	2765	18.58 S	52.01 W
Apostle Islands II	2742	46.50 N	90.30 W
Apostle Islands National Lakeshore ✦	2742	46.55 N	91.00 W
Apostólou Andréa, Akrotírion ≻	2791	35.42 N	34.35 E
Appalachia	2744	36.54 N	82.47 W
Appalachian Mountains ⋀	2736	41.00 N	77.00 W
Appennino (Apennines) ⋀	2776	43.00 N	13.00 E
Appiano	2776	46.28 N	11.15 E
Appleton, Minn., U.S.	2750	45.12 N	96.01 W
Appleton, Wis., U.S.	2742	44.16 N	88.25 W
Appomattox	2744	37.21 N	78.50 W
Apurímac ≛	2762	12.17 S	73.56 W
Aqaba, Gulf of C	2790	29.00 N	34.40 E
Aquidauana	2762	20.28 S	55.48 W
Arab	2746	34.19 N	86.29 W
'Arab, Baḥr al- ≛	2786	9.02 N	29.28 E
Arabian Sea ⩱2	2790	15.00 N	65.00 E
Aracaju	2762	10.55 S	37.04 W
Aracati	2762	4.34 S	37.46 W
Araçatuba	2765	21.12 S	50.25 W
Aracena	2774	37.53 N	6.33 W
Araçuaí	2765	16.52 S	42.04 W
Arad	2778	46.11 N	21.20 E
Arafura Sea ⩱2	2802	11.00 S	135.00 E
Arago, Cape ≻	2754	43.18 N	124.25 W
Aragón □9	2774	41.00 N	1.00 W
Araguacema	2762	8.50 S	49.34 W
Araguaia ≛	2765	5.21 S	48.41 W
Araguari	2765	18.38 S	48.11 W
Arak, Alg.	2786	25.18 N	3.45 E
Arāk, Īrān	2790	34.05 N	49.41 E
Arakan Yoma ⋀	2804	19.00 N	94.40 E
Aral'skoje More ⩱2	2766	45.00 N	60.00 E
Aranda de Duero	2774	41.41 N	3.41 W
Arandas	2758	20.42 N	102.21 W
Aran Island I	2769	54.58 N	8.33 W
Aran Islands II	2769	53.07 N	9.43 W
Aranjuez	2774	40.02 N	3.36 W
Aransas Pass	2748	27.54 N	97.09 W
Arapahoe	2750	40.18 N	99.54 W
Arapiraca	2762	9.45 S	36.39 W
Araraquara, Bra.	2765	21.47 S	48.10 W
Araraquara, Bra.	2765	21.08 S	42.22 W
Ararat	2806	37.17 S	142.56 E
Ararat, Mount → Büyük Ağrı Dağı Λ	2766	39.42 N	44.18 E
Araure	2760	9.34 N	69.13 W
Arāvalli Range ⋀	2794	25.00 N	73.30 E
Araxá	2765	19.35 S	46.55 W
Arba Minch	2790	6.02 N	37.40 E
Arbois	2772	46.54 N	5.46 E
Arbon	2772	47.31 N	9.26 E
Arbroath	2769	56.34 N	2.35 W
Arbuckle	2756	39.01 N	122.03 W
Arcachon	2772	44.37 N	1.12 W
Arcade	2740	42.32 N	78.25 W
Arcadia, Fla., U.S.	2744	27.14 N	81.52 W
Arcadia, La., U.S.	2746	32.33 N	92.55 W
Arcadia, Wis., U.S.	2742	44.15 N	91.30 W
Arcata	2756	40.52 N	124.05 W
Archangel → Archangel'sk	2766	64.34 N	40.32 E
Archangel'sk	2766	64.34 N	40.32 E
Archer City	2748	33.36 N	98.38 W
Archidona	2774	37.05 N	4.23 W
Arcis-sur-Aube	2772	48.32 N	4.08 E
Arco	2754	43.38 N	113.18 W
Arco de Baúlhe	2774	41.29 N	7.58 W
Arcola	2746	39.41 N	88.19 W
Arcos de la Frontera	2774	36.45 N	5.48 W
Arctic Bay	2734	73.02 N	85.11 W
Arctic Ocean ⩱1	2732	85.00 N	170.00 E
Ardabīl	2766	38.15 N	48.18 E
Årdalstangen	2768	61.14 N	7.43 E
Ardennes ✈1	2770	50.10 N	5.45 E
Ardlussa	2769	56.02 N	5.47 W
Ardmore, Ala., U.S.	2746	34.59 N	86.52 W
Ardmore, Okla., U.S.	2748	34.10 N	97.08 W
Åre	2768	63.24 N	13.04 E
Arecibo	2760	18.28 N	66.43 W
Arena de la Ventana, Punta ≻	2758	24.04 N	109.52 W
Arenas de San Pedro	2774	40.12 N	5.05 W
Arendal	2768	58.27 N	8.48 E
Arequipa	2762	16.24 S	71.33 W
Arès	2772	44.46 N	1.08 W
Arévalo	2774	41.04 N	4.43 W
Arezzo	2776	43.25 N	11.53 E
Arganda	2774	40.18 N	3.26 W
Arga-Sala ≛	2784	68.30 N	112.12 E
Argelès-Gazost	2772	43.01 N	0.06 E
Argenta	2776	44.37 N	11.50 E
Argentan	2772	48.45 N	0.01 W
Argentat	2772	45.06 N	1.56 E
Argentera Λ	2776	44.10 N	7.18 E
Argentina □1	2764	34.00 S	64.00 W
Argentino, Lago ⊜	2764	50.15 S	72.25 W
Argenton-sur-Creuse	2772	46.35 N	1.31 E
Argonne ✈1	2772	49.30 N	5.00 E
Árgos, Ellás	2778	37.39 N	22.44 E
Argos, Ind., U.S.	2746	41.14 N	86.15 W
Argostólion	2778	38.10 N	20.30 E
Argun' (Eergu'nahe) ≛	2796	53.20 N	121.28 E
Århus	2768	56.09 N	10.13 E
Ariano Irpino	2776	41.09 N	15.05 E
Arica, Chile	2762	18.29 S	70.20 W
Arica, Col.	2762	2.08 S	71.47 W
Arid, Cape ≻	2806	34.00	123.09 E
Arīḥā (Jericho)	2791	31.52 N	35.27 E
Arima	2760	10.38 N	61.17 W
Arinos ≛	2762	10.25 S	58.20 W
Aripuanã ≛	2762	5.07 S	60.24 W
Ariquemes	2762	9.56 S	63.04 W
Arizona □3	2736	34.00 N	112.00 W
Arizpe	2758	30.20 N	110.10 W
Arjeplog	2768	66.00 N	17.58 E
Arjona	2760	10.15 N	75.21 W
Arkadelphia	2746	34.07 N	93.04 W
Arkansas □3	2736	34.50 N	93.40 W
Arkansas ≛	2736	33.48 N	91.04 W
Arkansas City, Ark., U.S.	2746	33.36 N	91.12 W
Arkansas City, Kans., U.S.	2750	37.04 N	97.02 W
Arklow	2769	52.48 N	6.09 W
Arktičeskogo Instituta, Ostrova II	2784	75.20 N	81.55 E
Arles	2772	43.40 N	4.38 E
Arlington, Ga., U.S.	2744	31.27 N	84.44 W
Arlington, Minn., U.S.	2742	44.36 N	94.05 W
Arlington, S. Dak., U.S.	2750	44.22 N	97.08 W
Arlington, Tex., U.S.	2748	32.44 N	97.07 W
Arlington, Vt., U.S.	2740	43.05 N	73.09 W
Arlington, Va., U.S.	2740	38.52 N	77.05 W
Arlington, Wash., U.S.	2754	48.12 N	122.08 W
Arlington Heights	2742	42.05 N	87.59 W
Arlon	2772	49.41 N	5.49 E
Arma	2750	37.33 N	94.42 W
Armançon ≛	2772	47.57 N	3.30 E
Armavir	2766	45.00 N	41.08 E
Armenia	2762	4.31 N	75.41 W
Armentières	2772	50.41 N	2.53 E
Armidale	2806	30.31 S	151.39 E
Armour	2750	43.19 N	98.21 W
Armstrong, Iowa, U.S.	2750	43.24 N	94.29 W
Armstrong, Tex., U.S.	2748	26.55 N	97.47 W
Armstrong, Mount Λ	2734	63.12 N	133.16 W
Armstrong Station	2734	50.18 N	89.02 W
Arnedo	2774	42.13 N	2.06 W
Arnett	2748	36.08 N	99.46 W
Arnhem	2770	51.59 N	5.55 E
Arnhem, Cape ≻	2806	12.21 S	136.21 E
Arnhem Land ✈1	2806	13.10 S	134.30 E
Árnissa	2778	40.48 N	21.50 E
Arno ≛	2776	43.41 N	10.17 E
Arnold, Mo., U.S.	2746	38.26 N	90.23 W
Arnold, Nebr., U.S.	2750	41.26 N	100.12 W
Arona	2776	45.46 N	8.34 E
Arpajon	2772	48.35 N	2.15 E
Ar-Rab' al-Khālī ✈2	2790	20.00 N	51.00 E
Arrah	2794	25.34 N	84.40 E
Ar-Rahad	2786	12.43 N	30.39 E
Ar-Ramādī	2790	33.25 N	43.17 E
Ar-Ramthā	2791	32.34 N	36.00 E
Arran, Island of I	2769	55.35 N	5.15 W
Ar-Raqqah	2791	35.56 N	39.01 E
Arras	2772	50.17 N	2.47 E
Arrecife	2786	28.57 N	13.32 W
Arriaga	2758	16.14 N	93.54 W
Ar-Riyāḍ (Riyadh)	2790	24.38 N	46.43 E
Arronches	2774	39.07 N	7.17 W
Arroyo de la Luz	2774	39.29 N	6.35 W
Arroyo Grande	2756	35.07 N	120.34 W
Ar-Ruṣayriṣ	2786	11.51 N	34.23 E
Ar-Ruṭbah	2791	33.02 N	40.17 E
Arsenjev	2784	44.10 N	133.15 E
Árta, Ellás	2778	39.09 N	20.59 E
Artá, Esp.	2774	39.42 N	3.21 E
Artemisa	2760	22.49 N	82.46 W
Artenay	2772	48.05 N	1.53 E
Artesia, Colo., U.S.	2752	40.15 N	109.01 W
Artesia, N. Mex., U.S.	2748	32.51 N	104.24 W
Arthabaska	2740	46.02 N	71.55 W
Arthur, Ill., U.S.	2746	39.43 N	88.28 W
Arthur, Nebr., U.S.	2750	41.35 N	101.41 W
Arthur, N. Dak., U.S.	2750	47.06 N	97.13 W
Artigas	2764	30.24 S	56.28 W
Art'om	2784	43.22 N	132.13 E
Art'omovsk, S.S.S.R.	2782	48.35 N	38.00 E
Art'omovsk, S.S.S.R.	2784	54.21 N	93.26 E
Artur de Paiva	2788	14.28 S	16.20 E
Artvin	2766	41.11 N	41.49 E
Aru, Kepulauan II	2802	6.00 S	134.30 E
Arua	2786	3.01 N	30.55 E
Aruanã	2765	14.54 S	51.05 W
Aruba I	2760	12.30 N	69.58 W
Aruppukkottai	2793	9.31 N	78.06 E
Arusha	2788	3.22 S	36.41 E
Aruwimi ≛	2788	1.13 N	23.36 E
Arvada	2752	39.50 N	105.05 W
Arvida	2739	48.25 N	71.11 W
Arvidsjaur	2768	65.35 N	19.07 E
Arvika	2768	59.39 N	12.36 E
Arvonia	2744	37.41 N	78.20 W
Arzachena	2776	41.05 N	9.22 E
Arzamas	2766	55.23 N	43.50 E
Arzignano	2776	45.31 N	11.20 E
Arzúa	2774	42.56 N	8.09 W
Asahikawa	2798a	43.46 N	142.22 E
Asansol	2794	23.41 N	86.59 E
Asbest	2766	57.00 N	61.30 E
Asbestos	2740	45.46 N	71.57 W
Asbury Park	2740	40.13 N	74.01 W
Ascensión	2758	24.20 N	99.55 W
Asciano	2776	43.14 N	11.33 E
Ascoli Piceno	2776	42.51 N	13.34 E
Ascoli Satriano	2776	41.12 N	15.34 E
Aseb	2790	13.00 N	42.45 E
Asela	2790	7.59 N	39.08 E
Åsele	2768	64.10 N	17.20 E
Åsen	2768	63.36 N	11.03 E
Asenovgrad	2778	42.01 N	24.52 E
Ashburn	2744	31.43 N	83.39 W
Ashburton	2808	43.55 S	171.45 E
Ashdown	2746	33.41 N	94.08 W
Asheboro	2744	35.42 N	79.49 W
Asheville	2744	35.34 N	82.33 W
Ashford, Eng., U.K.	2769	51.26 N	0.27 W
Ashford, Ala., U.S.	2746	31.11 N	85.14 W
Ash Fork	2752	35.13 N	112.29 W
Ash Grove	2746	37.19 N	93.35 W
Ashibetsu	2798a	43.31 N	142.11 E
Ashikaga	2798	36.20 N	139.27 E
Ashizuri-zaki ≻	2798	32.44 N	133.01 E
Ashland, Ala., U.S.	2746	33.16 N	85.50 W
Ashland, Kans., U.S.	2750	37.11 N	99.46 W
Ashland, Ky., U.S.	2740	38.28 N	82.38 W
Ashland, Mo., U.S.	2746	38.47 N	92.16 W
Ashland, Mont., U.S.	2754	45.35 N	106.16 W
Ashland, Nebr., U.S.	2750	41.03 N	96.22 W
Ashland, N.H., U.S.	2740	43.42 N	71.38 W
Ashland, Ohio, U.S.	2740	40.52 N	82.19 W
Ashland, Oreg., U.S.	2754	42.12 N	122.42 W
Ashland, Va., U.S.	2744	37.45 N	77.29 W
Ashland, Wis., U.S.	2742	46.35 N	90.53 W
Ashland City	2746	36.16 N	87.04 W
Ashley, Ill., U.S.	2746	38.20 N	89.11 W
Ashley, N. Dak., U.S.	2750	46.02 N	99.22 W
Ashley, Ohio, U.S.	2740	40.25 N	82.57 W
Ashqelon	2791	31.40 N	34.35 E
Ash-Shaqrā'	2790	25.15 N	45.15 E
Ash-Shāriqah	2790	25.22 N	55.23 E
Ash-Shawbak	2791	30.32 N	35.34 E
Ashtabula	2740	41.52 N	80.48 W
Ashton, Idaho, U.S.	2754	44.04 N	111.27 W
Ashton, Iowa, U.S.	2750	43.19 N	95.47 W
Ashville, Ala., U.S.	2746	33.50 N	86.15 W
Ashville, Ohio, U.S.	2740	39.43 N	82.57 W
Asia ⚓1	2730	50.00 N	100.00 E
Asia, Kepulauan II	2802	1.03 N	131.18 E
Asia Minor ✈1	2766	39.00 N	32.00 E
Asino	2784	57.00 N	86.09 E
'Asīr ✈1	2790	19.00 N	42.00 E
Askham	2788	26.59 S	20.47 E
Askvoll	2768	61.21 N	5.04 E
Asmera	2790	15.20 N	38.53 E
Aspang Markt	2770	47.33 N	16.06 E
Aspen	2752	39.11 N	106.49 W
Aspen Butte Λ	2754	42.19 N	122.05 W
Aspermont	2748	33.08 N	100.14 W
Aspiring, Mount Λ	2808	44.23 S	168.44 E
Aspres-sur-Buëch	2772	44.31 N	5.45 E
Aṣ-Ṣabyā	2790	17.09 N	42.37 E
✈2 Ṣaḥrā' al-Gharbīyah (western Desert)	2786	27.00 N	27.00 E
Aṣ-Ṣaḥrā' al-Lībīyah (Libyan Desert) ✈2	2786	24.00 N	25.00 E
✈2 Ṣaḥrā' ash-Sharqīyah (eastern Desert)	2786	28.00 N	32.00 E
As-Sallūm	2786	31.34 N	25.09 E
As-Salṭ	2791	32.03 N	35.44 E
As-Samāwah	2790	31.18 N	45.17 E
Assateague Island I	2740	38.05 N	75.10 W
Assen	2770	52.59 N	6.34 E
Assiniboia	2734	49.38 N	105.59 W
Assiniboine, Mount Λ	2734	50.52 N	115.39 W
Assis	2765	22.40 S	50.25 W
Assisi	2776	43.04 N	12.37 E
As-Sulaymānīyah, Ar. Sa.	2790	24.09 N	46.19 E
As-Sulaymānīyah, 'Irāq	2790	35.33 N	45.26 E
As-Sulayyil	2790	20.27 N	45.34 E
Assumption Island I	2788	9.45 S	46.30 E
Aṣ-Ṣuwār	2791	35.30 N	40.39 E
As-Suwaydā'	2791	32.42 N	36.34 E
As-Suways (Suez)	2786	29.58 N	32.33 E
Asti	2776	44.54 N	8.12 E
Astorga	2774	42.27 N	6.03 W
Astoria, Ill., U.S.	2746	40.14 N	90.21 W
Astoria, Oreg., U.S.	2754	46.11 N	123.80 W
Astove Island I	2788	10.06 S	47.45 E
Astrachan'	2766	46.21 N	48.03 E
Astudillo	2774	42.12 N	4.18 W
Asunción	2764	25.16 S	57.40 W
Asuncion Island I	2802	19.40 N	145.24 E
Aswān	2786	24.05 N	32.53 E
Aswān High Dam ✈6	2786	24.05 N	32.53 E
Asyūṭ	2786	27.11 N	31.11 E
Atacama, Desierto de ✈2	2764	22.30 S	69.15 W
Atacama, Puna de ⋀1	2764	25.00 S	68.00 W
Atacama, Salar de ⩸	2764	23.30 S	68.15 W
Atakpamé	2786	7.32 N	1.08 E
Atami	2798	35.05 N	139.04 E
Atar	2786	20.31 N	13.03 W
Atascadero	2756	35.29 N	120.40 W
'Aṭbarah	2786	17.42 N	33.59 E
'Aṭbarah (Atbara) ≛	2786	17.40 N	33.56 E
Atchafalaya Bay C	2746	29.25 N	91.20 W
Atchison	2750	39.34 N	95.07 W
Ateca	2774	41.20 N	1.47 W
Athabasca	2734	54.43 N	113.17 W
Athabasca ≛	2734	58.40 N	110.50 W
Athabasca, Lake ⊜	2734	59.07 N	110.00 W
Athena	2754	45.49 N	118.30 W
Athenry	2769	53.18 N	8.45 W
Athens → Athínai, Ellás	2778	37.58 N	23.43 E
Athens, Ala., U.S.	2746	34.48 N	86.58 W
Athens, Ga., U.S.	2744	33.57 N	83.23 W
Athens, Ohio, U.S.	2740	39.20 N	82.06 W
Athens, Pa., U.S.	2740	41.57 N	76.31 W
Athens, Tenn., U.S.	2744	35.27 N	84.36 W

Symbols against index entries represent categories identified in the key on page 2810.

Name	Page	Lat °′	Long °′
Athens, Tex., U.S.	2748	32.12 N	95.51 W
Athínai (Athens)	2778	37.58 N	23.43 E
Athlone	2769	53.25 N	7.56 W
Athol	2740	42.36 N	72.14 W
Ati	2786	13.13 N	18.20 E
Atienza	2774	41.12 N	2.52 W
Atikokan	2734	48.45 N	91.37 W
Atikonak Lake ⊜	2734	52.40 N	64.30 W
Atkinson	2750	42.32 N	98.59 W
Atlanta, Ga., U.S.	2744	33.45 N	84.23 W
Atlanta, Mich., U.S.	2742	45.00 N	84.09 W
Atlanta, Tex., U.S.	2746	33.07 N	94.10 W
Atlantic, Iowa, U.S.	2750	41.24 N	95.01 W
Atlantic, N.C., U.S.	2744	34.54 N	76.20 W
Atlantic City	2740	39.22 N	74.26 W
Atlantic Ocean ⊤[1]	2730	0.00	25.00 W
Atlantic Peak ∧	2754	42.37 N	109.00 W
Atlas Mountains ⋀	2786	33.00 N	2.00 W
Atlas Saharien ⋀	2786	33.25 N	1.20 E
Atlin	2734	59.35 N	133.42 W
Atmore	2746	31.02 N	87.29 W
Atoka	2748	34.23 N	96.08 W
Atotonilco, Cerro ⋀	2748	26.08 N	104.38 W
Atotonilco el Alto	2758	20.33 N	102.31 W
Atrisco	2752	34.59 N	106.41 W
Aṭ-Ṭafīlah	2791	30.50 N	35.36 E
Aṭ-Ṭā'if	2790	21.16 N	40.24 E
Attalla	2746	34.01 N	86.05 W
Attawapiskat	2734	52.55 N	82.26 W
Attawapiskat ≃	2734	52.57 N	82.18 W
Attica, Ind., U.S.	2746	40.17 N	87.15 W
Attica, Kans., U.S.	2750	37.15 N	98.13 W
Attica, N.Y., U.S.	2740	42.52 N	78.17 W
Attica, Ohio, U.S.	2740	41.04 N	82.53 W
Attow, Ben ∧	2769	57.14 N	5.17 W
Atwater, Calif., U.S.	2756	37.21 N	120.36 W
Atwater, Minn , U.S.	2750	45.08 N	94.47 W
Atwood	2750	39.48 N	101.03 W
Aubagne	2772	43.17 N	5.34 E
Aube ≃	2772	48.34 N	3.43 E
Aubigny-sur-Nère	2772	47.29 N	2.26 E
Aubin	2772	44.32 N	2.14 E
Auburn, Ala., U.S.	2746	32.36 N	85.29 W
Auburn, Calif., U.S.	2756	38.54 N	121.04 W
Auburn, Ind., U.S.	2746	41.22 N	85.04 W
Auburn, Maine, U.S.	2740	44.06 N	70.14 W
Auburn, Nebr., U.S.	2750	40.23 N	95.51 W
Auburn, N.Y., U.S.	2740	42.56 N	76.34 W
Auburn, Wash., U.S.	2754	47.18 N	122.13 W
Aubusson	2772	45.57 N	2.11 E
Auch	2772	43.39 N	0.35 E
Auckland	2808	36.52 S	174.46 E
Audincourt	2772	47.29 N	6.50 E
Audubon	2750	41.43 N	94.55 W
Au Gres	2742	44.03 N	83.42 W
Augusta, It.	2776	37.13 N	15.13 E
Augusta, Ark., U.S.	2746	35.17 N	91.22 W
Augusta, Ga., U.S.	2744	33.29 N	81.57 W
Augusta, Ill., U.S.	2746	40.14 N	90.57 W
Augusta, Kans., U.S.	2750	37.41 N	96.58 W
Augusta, Ky., U.S.	2740	38.46 N	84.00 W
Augusta, Maine, U.S.	2740	44.19 N	69.47 W
Augusta, Mont., U.S.	2754	47.30 N	112.24 W
Augusta, Wis., U.S.	2742	44.41 N	91.07 W
Augustus, Mount ∧	2806	24.20 S	116.50 E
Auld, Lake ⊜	2806	22.32 S	123.44 E
Aumont-Aubrac	2772	44.43 N	3.17 E
Aurangābād	2793	19.53 N	75.20 E
Auray	2772	47.40 N	2.59 W
Auriflama	2765	20.41 S	50.34 W
Aurillac	2772	44.56 N	2.26 E
Aurora, Ont., Can.	2740	44.00 N	79.28 W
Aurora, Colo., U.S.	2752	39.44 N	104.52 W
Aurora, Ill., U.S.	2746	42.46 N	88.19 W
Aurora, Ind., U.S.	2746	39.04 N	84.54 W
Aurora, Minn , U.S.	2742	47.31 N	92.14 W
Aurora, Mo., U.S.	2746	36.58 N	93.43 W
Aurora, Nebr., U.S.	2750	40.52 N	98.00 W
Aurora, Ohio, U.S.	2740	41.19 N	81.21 W
Aus	2788	26.40 S	16.15 E
Au Sable ≃	2742	44.25 N	83.20 W
Au Sable Point ➤	2742	44.20 N	83.20 W
Auschwitz → Oświęcim	2770	50.03 N	19.12 E
Austin, Ind., U.S.	2746	38.45 N	85.48 W
Austin, Minn , U.S.	2742	43.40 N	92.59 W
Austin, Tex., U.S.	2748	30.16 N	97.45 W
Austin, Lake ⊜	2806	27.40 S	118.00 E
Austin Channel
Ʉ	2734	75.35 N	103.25 W
Australia □[1]	2806	25.00 S	135.00 E
Austria □[1]	2766	47.20 N	13.20 E
Autlán de Navarro	2758	19.46 N	104.22 W
Autun	2772	46.57 N	4.18 E
Auxerre	2772	47.48 N	3.34 E
Auxi-le-Château	2772	50.14 N	2.07 E
Auxonne	2772	47.12 N	5.23 E
Auzances	2772	46.02 N	2.30 E
Ava, Ill., U.S.	2746	37.53 N	89.30 W
Ava, Mo., U.S.	2746	36.57 N	92.40 W
Avallon	2772	47.29 N	3.54 E
Avalon	2756	33.49 N	118.16 W
Aveiro	2774	40.38 N	8.39 W
Avellaneda	2764	34.40 S	58.20 W
Avellino	2776	40.54 N	14.47 E
Avenal	2756	36.00 N	120.08 W
Avery Island	2746	29.55 N	91.55 W
Avesnes	2772	50.07 N	3.56 E
Avesta	2768	60.09 N	16.12 E
Avezzano	2776	42.02 N	13.25 E
Aviemore	2769	57.12 N	3.50 W
Avignon	2772	43.57 N	4.49 E
Ávila	2774	40.39 N	4.42 W
Avilés	2774	43.33 N	5.55 W
Aviz	2774	39.03 N	7.53 W
Avoca	2750	41.29 N	95.20 W
Avola	2776	36.54 N	15.09 E
Avon	2740	42.55 N	77.45 W
Avondale, Ariz., U.S.	2752	33.26 N	112.21 W
Avondale, Colo., U.S.	2750	38.14 N	104.21 W
Avon Park	2744	27.36 N	81.31 W
Avranches	2772	48.41 N	1.22 W
Awaji-shima I	2798	34.21 N	134.51 E
Awash ≃	2790	11.45 N	41.05 E
Awbārī	2786	26.35 N	12.46 E
Awe, Loch ⊜	2769	56.15 N	5.15 W
Awjilah	2786	29.09 N	21.15 E
Axtell	2750	40.29 N	99.08 W
Ayacucho	2762	13.07 S	74.13 W
Ayamonte	2774	37.13 N	7.24 W
Ayaviri	2762	14.52 S	70.35 W
Ayden	2744	35.25 N	77.20 W
Aydın	2778	37.51 N	27.51 E
Áyion Óros ➤[1]	2778	40.15 N	24.15 E
Áyios Nikólaos	2778	35.11 N	25.42 E
Aylesbury	2769	51.18 N	0.29 E
Aylmer Lake ⊜	2734	64.05 N	108.30 W
Aynor	2744	34.00 N	79.12 W
Ayora	2774	39.04 N	1.03 W
'Ayoûn el 'Atroûs	2786	16.40 N	9.37 W
Ayr	2769	55.28 N	4.38 W
Ayre, Point of ➤	2769	54.26 N	4.22 W
Ayvalık	2778	39.18 N	26.41 E
Azalea Park	2744	28.32 N	81.15 W
Azambuja	2774	39.04 N	8.52 W
Azare	2786	11.40 N	10.11 E
Azogues	2762	2.44 S	78.50 W
Azov	2782	47.07 N	39.25 E
Azov, Sea of → Azovskoje More ⊤[2]	2782	46.00 N	36.00 E
Azovskoje More ⊤[2]	2782	46.00 N	36.00 E
Aztec	2752	36.49 N	107.59 W
Aztec Peak ∧	2752	33.48 N	110.55 W
Azua	2760	18.27 N	70.44 W
Azuaga	2774	38.16 N	5.41 W
Azuero, Península de ➤[1]	2760	7.40 N	80.30 W
Azul	2764	36.45 S	59.50 W
Aẓ-Ẓahrān (Dhahran)	2790	26.18 N	50.08 E
Az-Zarqā'	2791	32.05 N	36.06 E
Az-Zāwiyah	2786	32.45 N	12.44 E
Azzel Matti, Sebkha ≚	2786	25.55 N	0.56 E
B			
Babaeski	2778	41.26 N	27.06 E
Babahoyo	2762	1.49 S	79.31 W
Babar, Kepulauan II	2802	7.50 S	129.45 E
Babbitt, Minn , U.S.	2742	47.43 N	91.57 W
Babbitt, Nev., U.S.	2756	38.39 N	118.37 W
B'abdā	2791	33.50 N	35.32 E
Babelthuap I	2802	7.30 N	134.36 E
Bābol	2766	36.34 N	52.42 E
Baboquivari Peak ∧	2752	31.46 N	111.35 W
Babuyan Islands II	2802	19.10 N	121.40 E
Bacabal	2762	4.14 S	44.47 W
Bacău	2778	46.34 N	26.55 E
Bacerac	2758	30.18 N	108.50 W
Bachaquero	2760	9.56 N	71.08 W
Bachčisaraj	2782	44.45 N	33.51 E
Bachta	2784	62.28 N	89.00 E
Bachu	2796	39.50 N	78.20 E
Back ≃	2734	67.15 N	95.15 W
Bacolod	2802	10.40 N	122.57 E
Baconton	2744	31.23 N	84.10 W
Badagara	2793	11.36 N	75.35 E
Badajoz	2774	38.53 N	6.58 W
Badalona	2774	41.27 N	2.15 E
Badanah	2790	30.59 N	41.02 E
Bad Aussee	2770	47.36 N	13.47 E
Bad Axe	2742	43.48 N	83.00 W
Baden, Öst.	2770	48.00 N	16.14 E
Baden, Schw.	2772	47.29 N	8.18 E
Badgastein	2770	47.07 N	13.08 E
Bad Ischl	2770	47.43 N	13.37 E
Badlands ⋀	2750	46.45 N	103.30 W
Badlands National Monument ♦	2750	43.47 N	102.15 W
Bad Lauterberg	2770	51.38 N	10.28 E
Baena	2774	37.37 N	4.19 W
Baeza	2774	37.59 N	3.28 W
Bafatá	2786	12.10 N	14.40 W
Baffin Bay C, N.A.	2732	73.00 N	66.00 W
Baffin Bay C, Tex., U.S.	2748	27.15 N	97.33 W
Baffin Island I	2734	68.00 N	70.00 W
Bafwasende	2788	1.05 N	27.16 E
Bāgalkot	2793	16.11 N	75.42 E
Bağarası	2778	37.42 N	27.33 E
Bagdad, Ariz., U.S.	2752	34.34 N	113.11 W
Bagdad → Baghdād, 'Irāq	2790	33.21 N	44.25 E
Bagdarin	2784	54.26 N	113.36 E
Bagé	2764	31.20 S	54.06 W
Baggs	2754	41.02 N	107.39 W
Baghdād	2790	33.21 N	44.25 E
Bagheria	2776	38.05 N	13.30 E
Baghlān	2794	36.13 N	68.46 E
Bagley	2750	47.31 N	95.24 W
Bagnères-de-Bigorre	2772	43.04 N	0.09 E
Bagnères-de-Luchon	2772	42.47 N	0.36 E
Bagnols-sur-Cèze	2772	44.10 N	4.37 E
Baguio	2802	16.25 N	120.36 E
Bahamas □[1]	2760	24.15 N	76.00 W
Bahāwalnagar	2794	29.59 N	73.16 E
Bahāwalpur	2794	29.24 N	71.41 E
Bahía, Islas de la II	2760	16.20 N	86.30 W
Bahía Blanca	2764	38.44 S	62.16 W
Bahía Kino	2758	28.50 N	111.55 W
Bahir Dar	2790	11.35 N	37.28 E
Bahraich	2794	27.36 N	81.36 E
Bahrain □[1]	2790	26.00 N	50.30 E
Baia-Mare	2778	47.40 N	23.35 E
Bai-bung, Mui ➤	2804	8.38 N	104.44 E
Baicheng, Zhg.	2796	45.38 N	122.46 E
Baicheng, Zhg.	2796	41.46 N	81.52 E
Baidoa	2790	3.04 N	43.48 E
Baie-Comeau	2739	49.13 N	68.10 W
Baie-Saint-Paul	2739	47.27 N	70.30 W
Baigneux-les-Juifs	2772	47.36 N	4.38 E
Bailén	2774	38.06 N	3.46 W
Bainbridge, Ga., U.S.	2744	30.54 N	84.34 W
Bainbridge, N.Y., U.S.	2740	42.18 N	75.29 W
Bain-de-Bretagne	2772	47.50 N	1.41 W
Baing	2802	10.14 S	120.34 E
Baird	2748	32.24 N	99.24 W
Bais	2772	48.15 N	0.22 W
Baise	2804	23.57 N	106.26 E
Baishuijiang	2796	33.29 N	106.01 E
Baiyinchang	2796	36.47 N	104.07 E
Baiyunebo	2796	41.58 N	110.02 E
Baja	2770	46.11 N	18.57 E
Baja California ➤[1]	2758	27.30 N	113.00 W
Baján	2748	26.32 N	101.15 W
Bajanchongor	2796	46.10 N	100.45 E
Bajkal, Ozero (Lake Baykal) ⊜	2784	53.00 N	107.40 E
Bajkal'skoje	2784	55.21 N	109.12 E
Bajkit	2784	61.41 N	96.25 E
Baker, La., U.S.	2746	30.35 N	91.10 W
Baker, Mont., U.S.	2750	46.22 N	104.17 W
Baker, Oreg., U.S.	2754	44.47 N	117.50 W
Baker, Mount ∧	2754	48.47 N	121.49 W
Baker Butte ∧	2752	34.27 N	111.22 W
Baker Lake	2734	64.15 N	96.00 W
Bakersfield, Calif., U.S.	2756	35.23 N	119.01 W
Bakersfield, Tex., U.S.	2748	30.53 N	102.12 W
Bakhtegān, Daryācheh-ye ⊜	2790	29.20 N	54.05 E
Bakoye ≃	2786	13.49 N	10.50 W
Baku	2766	40.23 N	49.51 E
Balabac Island I	2802	7.57 N	117.01 E
Balabac Strait Ʉ	2802	7.35 N	117.00 E
Ba'labakk (Baalbek)	2791	34.00 N	36.12 E
Balachna	2780	56.30 N	43.36 E
Balaguer	2774	41.47 N	0.49 E
Balakleja	2782	49.27 N	36.52 E
Balakovo	2766	52.02 N	47.47 E
Balallan	2769	58.05 N	6.35 W
Balāngīr	2793	20.43 N	83.29 E
Balašicha	2780	55.49 N	37.58 E
Balasore	2794	21.30 N	86.56 E
Balašov	2766	51.32 N	43.08 E
Balaton ⊜	2770	46.50 N	17.45 E
Balboa	2760	8.57 N	79.34 W
Balbriggan	2769	53.37 N	6.11 W
Balcones Escarpment ⚍[4]	2748	29.30 N	99.15 W
Bald Knob	2746	35.19 N	91.34 W
Bald Mountain ∧, Colo., U.S.	2752	40.45 N	105.41 W
Bald Mountain ∧, Oreg., U.S.	2754	43.16 N	121.21 W
Baldwin, Mich., U.S.	2742	43.54 N	85.51 W
Baldwin, Wis., U.S.	2742	44.58 N	92.22 W
Baldwin City	2750	38.47 N	95.11 W
Baldwinsville	2740	43.09 N	76.20 W
Baldwyn	2746	34.31 N	88.38 W
Baldy Peak ∧	2752	33.55 N	109.35 W
Baleares, Islas (Balearic Islands) II	2774	39.30 N	3.00 E
Baleine, Rivière à la ≃	2734	58.15 N	67.40 W
Balej	2784	51.36 N	116.38 E
Balfate	2760	15.48 N	86.25 W
Balfour	2744	35.21 N	82.28 W
Bali I	2802	8.20 S	115.00 E
Bali, Laut (Bali Sea) ⊤[2]	2802	7.45 S	115.30 E
Balıkesir	2778	39.39 N	27.53 E
Balikpapan	2802	1.17 S	116.50 E
Balimo	2802	8.03 S	142.56 E
Balintang Channel Ʉ	2802	19.49 N	121.40 E
Bali Sea → Bali, Laut ⊤[2]	2802	7.45 S	115.30 E
Baliza	2765	16.15 S	52.25 W
Balkan Mountains → Stara Planina ⋀	2778	43.15 N	25.00 E
Ballachulish	2769	56.40 N	5.10 W
Ballantine	2754	45.57 N	108.09 W
Ballarat	2806	37.34 S	143.52 E
Ballia	2794	25.45 N	84.10 E
Ballina	2769	54.07 N	9.09 W
Ballinger	2748	31.44 N	99.57 W
Ballinrobe	2769	53.37 N	9.13 W
Ballycastle	2769	55.12 N	6.15 W
Ballymena	2769	54.52 N	6.17 W
Ballyshannon	2769	54.30 N	8.11 W
Balmoral	2769	57.20 N	3.15 W
Balmorhea	2748	30.59 N	103.45 W
Balovale	2788	13.33 S	23.06 E
Balsas	2762	7.31 S	46.02 W
Baltasar Brum	2764	30.44 S	57.19 W
Baltic Sea ⊤[2]	2766	57.00 N	19.00 E
Baltijsk	2780	54.39 N	19.55 E
Baltimore, Eire	2769	51.29 N	9.22 W
Baltimore, Md., U.S.	2740	39.17 N	76.37 W
Baluchistan □[9]	2792	28.00 N	63.00 E
Balygyčan	2784	63.56 N	154.12 E
Bamako	2786	12.39 N	8.00 W
Bambari	2786	5.45 N	20.40 E
Bamberg	2744	33.17 N	81.02 W
Bamenda	2786	5.56 N	10.10 E
Banalia	2788	1.33 N	25.20 E
Banana	2788	6.01 S	12.24 E
Bananal, Ilha do I	2762	11.30 S	50.15 W
Banās, Ra's ➤	2786	23.54 N	35.48 E
Banbridge	2769	54.21 N	6.16 W
Banbury	2769	52.04 N	1.20 W
Bancroft	2742	43.18 N	94.13 W
Bānda	2794	25.29 N	80.20 E
Banda, Kepulauan II	2802	4.35 S	129.55 E
Banda, Laut (Banda Sea) ⊤[2]	2802	5.00 S	128.00 E
Banda Atjeh (Kutarādja)	2804	5.34 N	95.20 E
Bandama ≃	2786	5.10 N	5.00 W
Bandar 'Abbās	2790	27.11 N	56.17 E
Bandar-e Lengeh	2790	26.33 N	54.53 E
Bandar Maharani	2804	2.02 N	102.34 E
Bandar Seri Begawan	2802	4.56 N	114.55 E
Banda Sea → Banda, Laut ⊤[2]	2802	5.00 S	128.00 E
Banded Peak ∧	2752	37.06 N	106.38 W
Bandeira, Pico da ∧	2765	20.26 S	41.47 W
Bandera	2748	29.44 N	99.04 W
Bandırma	2778	40.20 N	27.58 E
Bandjarmasin	2802	3.20 S	114.35 E
Bandon, Eire	2769	51.45 N	8.45 W
Bandon, Oreg., U.S.	2754	43.07 N	124.25 W
Bandundu	2788	3.18 S	17.20 E
Bandung	2802	6.54 S	107.36 E
Banes	2760	20.58 N	75.43 W
Banff, Alta., Can.	2734	51.10 N	115.34 W
Banff, Scot., U.K.	2769	57.40 N	2.33 W
Bangalore	2793	12.59 N	77.35 E
Bangassou	2786	4.50 N	23.07 E
Bangbu	2800	32.58 N	117.24 E
Banggai, Kepulauan II	2802	1.30 S	123.15 E
Banggi, Pulau I	2802	7.17 N	117.12 E
Banghāzī	2786	32.07 N	20.04 E
Bangka I	2802	1.48 N	125.09 E
Bangkok → Krung Thep	2804	13.45 N	100.31 E
Bangladesh □[1]	2792	24.00 N	90.00 E
Bangor, N. Ire., U.K.	2769	54.40 N	5.40 W
Bangor, Wales, U.K.	2769	53.13 N	4.08 W
Bangor, Maine, U.S.	2740	44.49 N	68.47 W
Bangor, Pa., U.S.	2740	40.52 N	75.13 W
Bangs, Mount ∧	2752	36.48 N	113.51 W
Bangui	2786	4.22 N	18.35 E
Bangweulu, Lake ⊜	2788	11.05 S	29.45 E
Baní	2760	18.17 N	70.20 W
Banī Mazār	2786	28.30 N	30.48 E
Banī Suwayf	2786	29.05 N	31.05 E
Bāniyās	2791	35.11 N	35.57 E
Banjak, Kepulauan II	2804	2.10 N	97.15 E
Banja Luka	2776	44.46 N	17.11 E
Banjul	2786	13.28 N	16.39 W
Banks Island I, B.C., Can.	2734	53.25 N	130.10 W
Banks Island I, N.W. Ter., Can.	2734	73.15 N	121.30 W
Banks Lake ⊜[1]	2754	47.45 N	119.15 W
Banks Strait Ʉ	2806	40.40 S	148.07 E
Bānkura	2794	23.15 N	87.04 E
Ban-me-thuot	2804	12.40 N	108.03 E
Bann ≃	2769	55.10 N	6.46 W
Banning	2756	33.56 N	116.52 W
Bannu	2794	32.59 N	70.36 E
Baños de Cerrato	2774	41.55 N	4.28 W
Banská Bystrica	2770	48.44 N	19.07 E
Bantry	2769	51.41 N	9.27 W
Baoding	2796	38.52 N	115.29 E
Baofeng	2800	33.55 N	113.02 E
Baoji	2796	34.22 N	107.14 E
Baoshan	2804	25.09 N	99.09 E
Baotou	2796	40.40 N	109.59 E
Baoying	2800	33.16 N	119.20 E
Ba'qūbah	2790	33.45 N	44.38 E
Baquedano	2764	23.20 S	69.51 W
Baraboo	2742	43.28 N	89.45 W
Baracoa	2760	20.21 N	74.30 W
Baraga	2742	46.47 N	88.30 W
Baram ≃	2802	4.36 N	113.59 E
Baranagar	2794	22.38 N	88.22 E
Baranoviči	2780	53.08 N	26.02 E
Barataria	2746	29.44 N	90.08 W
Barat Daja, Kepulauan II	2802	7.25 S	128.00 E
Barbacena	2765	21.14 S	43.46 W
Barbados □[1]	2760	13.10 N	59.33 W
Barbar	2786	18.01 N	33.59 E
Barbas, Cabo ➤	2786	22.18 N	16.41 W
Barbastro	2774	42.02 N	0.08 E
Barbate de Franco	2774	36.12 N	5.55 W
Barberton	2740	41.01 N	81.36 W
Barbezieux	2772	45.28 N	0.09 W
Barboursville	2740	38.24 N	82.18 W
Barbourville	2744	36.52 N	83.53 W
Barbuda I	2760	17.38 N	61.48 W
Barcaldine	2806	23.33 S	145.17 E
Barcellona Pozzo di Gotto	2776	38.09 N	15.13 E
Barcelona, Esp.	2774	41.23 N	2.11 E
Barcelona, Ven.	2760	10.08 N	64.42 W
Barcelos, Bra.	2762	0.58 S	62.57 W
Barcelos, Port.	2774	41.32 N	8.37 W
Bardera	2790	2.21 N	42.20 E
Bardīyah	2786	31.46 N	25.06 E
Bardstown	2746	37.49 N	85.28 W
Bardufoss	2768	69.04 N	18.30 E
Bareilly	2794	28.21 N	79.25 E
Barents Sea ⊤[2]	2766	69.00 N	40.00 E
Barfleur	2772	49.40 N	1.15 W
Bar Harbor	2740	44.23 N	68.13 W
Bari	2776	41.07 N	16.52 E
Barillas	2760	15.48 N	91.18 W
Barinas	2760	8.38 N	70.12 W
Baripāda	2794	21.56 N	86.43 E
Barisāl	2794	22.42 N	90.22 E
Barkley, Lake ⊜[1]	2746	36.40 N	87.55 W
Barkley Sound Ʉ	2734	48.53 N	125.20 W
Barkly Tableland ⋀[1]	2806	19.00 S	138.00 E
Bar-le-Duc	2772	48.47 N	5.10 E
Barlee, Lake ⊜	2806	29.10 S	119.30 E
Barletta	2776	41.19 N	16.17 E
Barmer	2794	25.45 N	71.23 E
Barmouth	2769	52.43 N	4.03 W
Barnard	2750	39.11 N	98.03 W
Barnaul	2784	53.22 N	83.45 E
Barnegat	2740	39.45 N	74.13 W
Barnesboro	2740	40.40 N	78.47 W

Symbols against index entries represent categories identified in the key on page 2810.

Symbols against index entries represent categories identified in the key on page 2810.

Symbols against index entries represent categories identified in the key on page 2810.

Name	Page	Lat °′	Long °′
Bouaflé	2786	6.59 N	5.45 W
Bouaké	2786	7.41 N	5.02 W
Bouar	2786	5.57 N	15.36 E
Bou Arada	2776	36.20 N	9.38 E
Bou Ficha	2776	36.18 N	10.29 E
Bougainville Reef ✣[2]	2806	15.30 S	147.06 E
Bougouni	2786	11.25 N	7.29 W
Bouillon	2770	49.48 N	5.04 E
Boulder, Colo., U.S.	2752	40.01 N	105.17 W
Boulder, Mont., U.S.	2754	46.14 N	112.07 W
Boulder City	2756	35.59 N	114.50 W
Boulogne-Billancourt	2772	48.50 N	2.15 E
Boulogne-sur-Mer	2772	50.43 N	1.37 E
Bouna	2786	9.16 N	3.00 W
Boundary Peak ∧	2756	37.51 N	118.21 W
Bountiful	2752	40.53 N	111.53 W
Bourbon	2746	38.09 N	91.15 W
Bourbonnais □[9]	2772	46.20 N	3.00 E
Bourbonne-les-Bains	2772	47.57 N	5.45 E
Bourem	2786	16.57 N	0.21 W
Bourganeuf	2772	45.57 N	1.46 E
Bourg-en-Bresse	2772	46.12 N	5.13 E
Bourges	2772	47.05 N	2.24 E
Bourg-Lastic	2772	45.39 N	2.33 E
Bourgogne □[9]	2772	47.00 N	4.30 E
Bourgoin	2772	45.35 N	5.17 E
Bourg-Saint-Andéol	2772	44.22 N	4.39 E
Bourg-Saint-Maurice	2772	45.37 N	6.46 E
Bourke	2806	30.05 S	145.56 E
Bournemouth	2769	50.43 N	1.54 W
Bou Saâda	2786	35.12 N	4.11 E
Bouse	2752	33.56 N	114.00 W
Boussac	2772	46.21 N	2.13 E
Bousso	2786	10.29 N	16.43 E
Bøvågen	2768	60.40 N	4.58 E
Bovalino Marina	2776	38.09 N	16.11 E
Bovec	2776	46.20 N	13.33 E
Bøverdal	2768	61.43 N	8.21 E
Bovey	2742	47.17 N	93.25 W
Bovina	2748	34.31 N	102.53 W
Bowbells	2750	48.48 N	102.15 W
Bowdle	2750	45.27 N	99.39 W
Bowen	2806	20.01 S	148.15 E
Bowie, Ariz., U.S.	2752	32.19 N	109.29 W
Bowie, Md., U.S.	2740	39.00 N	76.47 W
Bowie, Tex., U.S.	2748	33.34 N	97.51 W
Bowling Green, Ky., U.S.	2746	37.00 N	86.27 W
Bowling Green, Mo., U.S.	2746	39.20 N	91.12 W
Bowling Green, Ohio, U.S.	2740	41.22 N	83.39 W
Bowling Green, Va., U.S.	2740	38.03 N	77.21 W
Bowman	2750	46.11 N	103.24 W
Bowman-Haley Reservoir ⊜[1]	2750	46.00 N	103.20 W
Bowmanville	2740	43.55 N	78.41 W
Boxian	2800	33.53 N	115.45 E
Boyce	2746	31.23 N	92.40 W
Boyd	2748	33.05 N	97.34 W
Boykins	2744	36.35 N	77.12 W
Boyle, Eire	2769	53.58 N	8.18 W
Boyle, Miss., U.S.	2746	33.42 N	90.50 W
Boyne City	2742	45.13 N	85.01 W
Boynton Beach	2744	26.32 N	80.03 W
Boysen Reservoir ⊜[1]	2754	43.19 N	108.11 W
Bozburun	2778	36.41 N	28.04 E
Bozeman	2754	45.41 N	111.02 W
Bozoum	2786	6.19 N	16.23 E
Bra	2776	44.42 N	7.51 E
Bracciano	2776	42.06 N	12.10 E
Bracebridge	2740	45.02 N	79.19 W
Bräcke	2768	62.43 N	15.27 E
Brackettville	2748	29.19 N	100.24 W
Bradenton	2744	27.29 N	82.34 W
Bradford, Eng., U.K.	2769	53.48 N	1.45 W
Bradford, Pa., U.S.	2740	41.58 N	78.39 W
Bradford, Vt., U.S.	2740	43.59 N	72.09 W
Bradley, Ark., U.S.	2746	33.06 N	93.39 W
Bradley, S. Dak., U.S.	2750	45.05 N	97.39 W
Bradshaw	2744	37.21 N	81.49 W
Brady, Nebr., U.S.	2750	41.01 N	100.22 W
Brady, Tex., U.S.	2748	31.08 N	99.20 W
Braga	2774	41.33 N	8.26 W
Bragado	2764	35.10 S	60.30 W
Bragança	2774	41.49 N	6.45 W
Brāhmanbāria	2794	23.59 N	91.07 E
Brāhmani ≃	2794	20.39 N	86.46 E
Brahmaputra (Yaluzangbujiang) ≃	2794	24.02 N	90.59 E
Braich y Pwll ≻	2769	52.48 N	4.36 W
Brăila	2778	45.16 N	27.58 E
Brainerd	2742	46.21 N	94.12 W
Brampton	2740	43.41 N	79.46 W
Branchville	2744	33.15 N	80.49 W
Branco ≃	2762	1.24 S	61.51 W
Brandberg ∧	2788	21.10 S	14.33 E
Brandbu	2768	60.28 N	10.30 E
Brandon, Man., Can.	2734	49.50 N	99.57 W
Brandon, Fla., U.S.	2744	27.56 N	82.17 W
Brandon, Vt., U.S.	2740	43.48 N	73.05 W
Brandvlei	2788	30.25 S	20.30 E
Brandy Peak ∧	2754	42.36 N	123.53 W
Branford	2744	29.58 N	82.56 W
Br'ansk	2780	53.15 N	34.22 E
Branson	2746	36.39 N	93.13 W
Brantford	2740	43.08 N	80.16 W
Brant Lake	2740	43.41 N	73.45 W
Brantley	2746	31.35 N	86.22 W
Brantôme	2772	45.22 N	0.39 E
Bras d'Or Lake ⊜	2734	45.52 N	60.50 W
Brasília	2765	15.47 S	47.55 W
Brașov	2778	45.39 N	25.37 E
Bratislava	2770	48.09 N	17.07 E
Bratsk	2784	56.05 N	101.48 E
Bratskoje Vodochranilišče ⊜[1]	2784	56.10 N	102.10 E
Brattleboro	2740	42.51 N	72.34 W
Braunau [am Inn]	2770	48.15 N	13.02 E
Brava	2790	1.05 N	44.02 E
Brava, Costa ≗[2]	2774	41.45 N	3.04 E
Bravo del Norte (Rio Grande) ≃	2736	25.57 N	97.09 W
Brawley	2756	32.59 N	115.31 W
Bray	2769	53.12 N	6.06 W
Bray Island I	2734	69.20 N	76.45 W
Brazil	2746	39.32 N	87.08 W
Brazil □[1]	2762	10.00 S	55.00 W
Brazos ≃	2748	28.53 N	95.23 W
Brazzaville	2788	4.16 S	15.17 E
Brčko	2778	44.53 N	18.48 E
Breaux Bridge	2746	30.16 N	91.54 W
Breckenridge, Colo., U.S.	2752	39.29 N	106.03 W
Breckenridge, Minn., U.S.	2750	46.16 N	96.35 W
Breckenridge, Tex., U.S.	2748	32.45 N	98.54 W
Brecon Beacons National Park ♠	2769	51.52 N	3.25 W
Breda	2770	51.35 N	4.46 E
Bredstedt	2770	54.37 N	8.59 E
Breese	2746	38.36 N	89.32 W
Bregenz	2770	47.30 N	9.46 E
Bréhal	2772	48.54 N	1.31 W
Brekstad	2768	63.41 N	9.41 E
Bremen, Ga., U.S.	2744	33.43 N	85.09 W
Bremen, Ind., U.S.	2746	41.27 N	86.09 W
Bremerton	2754	47.34 N	122.38 W
Bremond	2748	31.10 N	96.41 W
Brenner Pass)(	2770	47.00 N	11.30 E
Breno	2776	45.57 N	10.18 E
Brescia	2776	45.33 N	13.15 E
Breslau → Wrocław	2770	51.06 N	17.00 E
Bressanone	2776	46.43 N	11.39 E
Bressuire	2772	46.51 N	0.30 W
Brest, Fr.	2772	48.24 N	4.29 W
Brest, S.S.S.R.	2780	52.06 N	23.42 E
Breton Sound ꓤ	2746	29.30 N	89.30 W
Brevard	2744	35.09 N	82.44 W
Brewer	2740	44.48 N	68.46 W
Brewster, Kans., U.S.	2750	39.22 N	101.23 W
Brewster, Nebr., U.S.	2750	41.56 N	99.52 W
Brewster, Wash., U.S.	2754	48.06 N	119.47 W
Brewton	2746	31.07 N	87.04 W
Brežice	2776	45.54 N	15.36 E
Bria	2786	6.32 N	21.59 E
Briançon	2772	44.54 N	6.39 E
Briare	2772	47.38 N	2.44 E
Brickaville	2788	18.49 S	49.04 E
Bricquebec	2772	49.28 N	1.38 W
Bridgeport, Ala., U.S.	2746	34.57 N	85.43 W
Bridgeport, Calif., U.S.	2756	38.10 N	119.13 W
Bridgeport, Conn., U.S.	2740	41.11 N	73.11 W
Bridgeport, Ill., U.S.	2746	38.43 N	87.46 W
Bridgeport, Mich., U.S.	2742	43.22 N	83.53 W
Bridgeport, Nebr., U.S.	2750	41.40 N	103.06 W
Bridgeport, Tex., U.S.	2748	33.13 N	97.45 W
Bridgeport, Wash., U.S.	2754	48.00 N	119.40 W
Bridgeport, W. Va., U.S.	2740	39.17 N	80.15 W
Bridger	2754	45.18 N	108.55 W
Bridger Peak ∧	2754	41.12 N	107.02 W
Bridgeton	2740	39.26 N	75.14 W
Bridgetown	2760	13.06 N	59.37 W
Bridgeville	2740	38.45 N	75.36 W
Bridgewater, S. Dak., U.S.	2750	43.33 N	97.30 W
Bridgewater, Va., U.S.	2740	38.18 N	78.59 W
Bridgman	2742	41.57 N	86.33 W
Bridgwater	2769	51.08 N	3.00 W
Bridlington	2769	54.05 N	0.12 W
Brienne-le-Château	2772	48.24 N	4.32 E
Brienz	2772	46.46 N	8.03 E
Brienzer See ⊜	2772	46.43 N	7.57 E
Brig	2772	46.19 N	8.00 E
Brigham City	2752	41.31 N	112.01 W
Brighton, Eng., U.K.	2769	50.50 N	0.08 W
Brighton, Colo., U.S.	2752	39.59 N	104.49 W
Brighton, Iowa, U.S.	2742	41.10 N	91.49 W
Brighton, Mich., U.S.	2742	42.32 N	83.47 W
Brighton, N.Y., U.S.	2740	43.08 N	77.34 W
Brihuega	2774	40.48 N	2.52 W
Brindisi	2776	40.38 N	17.56 E
Brinkley	2746	34.53 N	91.12 W
Brioude	2772	45.18 N	3.23 E
Brisbane	2806	27.28 S	153.02 E
Bristol, Eng., U.K.	2769	51.27 N	2.35 W
Bristol, Conn., U.S.	2740	41.41 N	72.57 W
Bristol, S. Dak., U.S.	2750	45.21 N	97.45 W
Bristol, Tenn., U.S.	2744	36.36 N	82.11 W
Bristol Bay C	2738	58.00 N	159.00 W
Bristow	2748	35.50 N	96.23 W
British Columbia □[4]	2734	54.00 N	125.00 W
British Mountains ⋀	2734	69.00 N	140.20 W
Britstown	2788	30.37 S	23.30 E
Britt	2742	43.06 N	93.48 W
Britton	2750	45.48 N	97.45 W
Brive-la-Gaillarde	2772	45.10 N	1.32 E
Briviesca	2774	42.33 N	3.19 W
Brno	2770	49.12 N	16.37 E
Broach	2793	21.42 N	72.58 E
Broadford	2769	57.14 N	5.54 W
Broad Law ∧	2769	55.30 N	3.22 W
Broadus	2750	45.27 N	105.25 W
Broadwater	2750	41.36 N	102.51 W
Brochet	2734	57.53 N	101.40 W
Brockton	2740	42.05 N	71.01 W
Brockville	2740	44.35 N	75.41 W
Brodeur Peninsula ≻[1]	2734	73.00 N	88.00 W
Brodhead, Ky., U.S.	2744	37.24 N	84.25 W
Brodhead, Wis., U.S.	2742	42.37 N	89.22 W
Brodnax	2744	36.42 N	78.02 W
Broken Bow, Nebr., U.S.	2750	41.24 N	99.38 W
Broken Bow, Okla., U.S.	2746	34.02 N	94.44 W
Broken Hill	2806	31.57 S	141.27 E
Brokopondo	2762	5.03 N	54.59 W
Bromsgrove	2769	52.20 N	2.03 W
Bronlund Peak ∧	2734	57.26 N	126.38 W
Brønnøysund	2768	65.30 N	12.10 E
Bronson	2742	41.52 N	85.12 W
Bronte, It.	2776	37.48 N	14.50 E
Bronte, Tex., U.S.	2748	31.53 N	100.18 W
Brookeland	2746	31.09 N	94.00 W
Brookfield	2746	39.47 N	93.04 W
Brookhaven	2746	31.35 N	90.26 W
Brookings, Oreg., U.S.	2754	42.03 N	124.17 W
Brookings, S. Dak., U.S.	2750	44.19 N	96.48 W
Brooklet	2744	32.23 N	81.40 W
Brooklyn	2742	41.44 N	92.27 W
Brookneal	2744	37.03 N	78.57 W
Brookport	2746	37.08 N	88.38 W
Brooks	2734	50.35 N	111.53 W
Brooks Range ⋀	2738	68.00 N	154.00 W
Brookston	2746	40.36 N	86.52 W
Brooksville, Fla., U.S.	2744	28.33 N	82.23 W
Brooksville, Miss., U.S.	2746	33.14 N	88.35 W
Brookville, Ind., U.S.	2746	39.25 N	85.01 W
Brookville, Pa., U.S.	2740	41.09 N	79.05 W
Broome	2806	17.58 S	122.14 E
Broomfield	2752	39.56 N	105.04 W
Broons	2772	48.19 N	2.16 W
Brou	2772	48.13 N	1.11 E
Brovary	2782	50.31 N	30.46 E
Browerville	2750	46.05 N	94.52 W
Brown City	2742	43.13 N	82.59 W
Brown Deer	2742	43.10 N	87.59 W
Brownfield	2748	33.11 N	102.16 W
Browning	2754	48.34 N	113.01 W
Brownsburg, Qué., Can.	2740	45.41 N	74.25 W
Brownsburg, Ind., U.S.	2746	39.51 N	86.24 W
Brownsdale	2742	43.44 N	92.52 W
Brownstown	2746	38.53 N	86.03 W
Browns Valley	2750	45.36 N	96.50 W
Brownsville, Oreg., U.S.	2754	44.24 N	122.59 W
Brownsville, Tenn., U.S.	2746	35.36 N	89.15 W
Brownsville, Tex., U.S.	2748	25.54 N	97.30 W
Brownville Junction	2740	45.21 N	69.03 W
Brownwood	2748	31.43 N	98.59 W
Broxton	2744	31.38 N	82.53 W
Bruay-en-Artois	2772	50.29 N	2.33 E
Bruce, Mount ∧	2806	22.36 S	118.08 E
Bruce Peninsula ≻[1]	2740	44.50 N	81.20 W
Bruck an der Leitha	2770	47.57 N	16.44 E
Bruck an der Mur	2770	47.25 N	15.16 E
Brugge	2770	51.13 N	3.14 E
Brundidge	2746	31.43 N	85.49 W
Bruneau	2754	42.53 N	115.48 W
Bruneau, East Fork ≃	2754	42.34 N	115.38 W
Brunei □[1]	2802	4.30 N	114.40 E
Brunico	2776	46.48 N	11.56 E
Brunkeberg	2768	59.26 N	8.29 E
Brunswick, Ga., U.S.	2744	31.10 N	81.29 W
Brunswick, Maine, U.S.	2740	43.55 N	69.58 W
Brunswick, Md., U.S.	2740	39.19 N	77.37 W
Brunswick, Mo., U.S.	2746	39.26 N	93.08 W
Brunswick, Ohio, U.S.	2740	41.14 N	81.50 W
Brush	2750	40.15 N	103.37 W
Brussels → Bruxelles	2770	50.50 N	4.20 E
Bruxelles (Brussel)	2770	50.50 N	4.20 E
Bryan, Ohio, U.S.	2740	41.28 N	84.33 W
Bryan, Tex., U.S.	2748	30.40 N	96.22 W
Bryce Canyon National Park ♠	2752	37.29 N	112.12 W
Bryson City	2744	35.26 N	83.27 W
Brzeg	2770	50.52 N	17.27 E
Bsharrī	2791	34.15 N	36.01 E
Būbiyān I	2790	29.47 N	48.10 E
Bucaramanga	2762	7.08 N	73.09 W
Buccaneer Archipelago II	2806	16.17 S	123.20 E
Buchanan, Liber.	2786	5.57 N	10.02 W
Buchanan, Mich., U.S.	2742	41.50 N	86.22 W
Buchanan, Va., U.S.	2744	37.32 N	79.41 W
Buchanan Lake ⊜[1]	2748	30.48 N	98.25 W
Buchan Gulf C	2734	71.47 N	74.16 W
Bucharest → București	2778	44.26 N	26.06 E
Buckatunna	2746	31.27 N	88.32 W
Buckhannon	2740	38.59 N	80.14 W
Buckholts	2748	30.52 N	97.08 W
Buckingham, Qué., Can.	2740	45.35 N	75.25 W
Buckingham, Va., U.S.	2744	37.32 N	78.37 W
Buckley	2746	40.36 N	88.02 W
Bucklin, Kans., U.S.	2750	37.33 N	99.38 W
Bucklin, Mo., U.S.	2746	39.47 N	92.53 W
Bucksport	2740	44.34 N	68.48 W
București	2778	44.26 N	26.06 E
Bucyrus	2740	40.48 N	82.58 W
Budapest	2770	47.30 N	19.05 E
Budaun	2794	28.03 N	79.07 E
Buddusò	2776	40.35 N	9.16 E
Bude, Eng., U.K.	2769	50.50 N	4.33 W
Bude, Miss., U.S.	2746	31.28 N	90.51 W
Buea	2786	4.09 N	9.14 E
Buenaventura	2762	3.53 N	77.04 W
Buena Vista, Bol.	2762	17.27 S	63.40 W
Buena Vista, Colo., U.S.	2752	38.50 N	106.08 W
Buena Vista, Ga., U.S.	2744	32.19 N	84.31 W
Buena Vista, Va., U.S.	2744	37.44 N	79.21 W
Buenópolis	2765	17.54 S	44.11 W
Buenos Aires	2764	34.36 S	58.27 W
Buerjin	2796	47.43 N	86.53 E
Buffalo, Mo., U.S.	2746	37.39 N	93.06 W
Buffalo, N.Y., U.S.	2740	42.54 N	78.53 W
Buffalo, Okla., U.S.	2748	36.50 N	99.38 W
Buffalo, S. Dak., U.S.	2750	45.35 N	103.33 W
Buffalo, Tex., U.S.	2748	31.28 N	96.04 W
Buffalo, Wyo., U.S.	2754	44.21 N	106.42 W
Buffalo Center	2742	43.23 N	93.57 W
Buffalo Lake	2750	44.44 N	94.37 W
Buffalo Lake ⊜	2734	60.10 N	115.30 W
Buford	2744	34.07 N	84.00 W
Bug ≃	2766	52.31 N	21.05 E
Buga	2762	3.54 N	76.17 W
Bugøynes	2768	69.58 N	29.39 E
Bugsuk Island I	2802	8.15 N	117.18 E
Bugul'ma	2766	54.33 N	52.48 E
Buhl	2754	42.36 N	114.46 W
Buj	2780	58.30 N	41.30 E
Bujalance	2774	37.54 N	4.22 W
Bujaraloz	2774	41.30 N	0.09 W
Bujnaksk	2766	42.49 N	47.07 E
Bujumbura	2788	3.23 S	29.22 E
Bukačača	2784	52.59 N	116.55 E
Bukama	2788	9.12 S	25.51 E
Bukavu	2788	2.30 S	28.52 E
Bukittinggi	2804	0.19 S	100.22 E
Bukoba	2788	1.20 S	31.49 E
Bula	2802	3.06 S	130.30 E
Bulandshahr	2794	28.24 N	77.51 E
Bulawayo	2788	20.09 S	28.36 E
Buldan	2778	38.03 N	28.51 E
Bulgan	2796	46.53 N	91.05 E
Bulgaria □[1]	2766	43.00 N	25.00 E
Bulle	2772	46.37 N	7.04 E
Bullfinch	2806	30.59 S	119.06 E
Bull Mountains ⋀	2754	46.05 N	109.00 W
Bullsgap	2744	36.15 N	83.05 W
Bulukumba	2802	5.33 S	120.11 E
Buluntuohai ⊜	2796	47.15 N	87.20 E
Bumba	2788	2.11 N	22.28 E
Bunbury	2806	33.19 S	115.38 E
Buncrana	2769	55.08 N	7.27 W
Bundaberg	2806	24.52 S	152.21 E
Bundoran	2769	54.28 N	8.17 W
Bungo-suidō ꓤ	2798	33.00 N	132.13 E
Bunia	2788	1.34 N	30.15 E
Bunkie	2746	30.57 N	92.11 W
Buñol	2774	39.25 N	0.47 W
Buntok	2802	1.42 S	114.48 E
Buolkalach	2784	72.56 N	119.50 E
Buor-Chaja, Guba C	2784	71.30 N	131.00 E
Buor-Chaja, Mys ≻	2784	71.56 N	132.40 E
Bura	2788	1.06 S	39.57 E
Burao	2790	9.30 N	45.30 E
Buras	2746	29.21 N	89.32 W
Buraydah	2790	26.20 N	43.59 E
Burbank	2756	34.12 N	118.18 W
Burden	2750	37.19 N	96.45 W
Burdur	2766	37.43 N	30.17 E
Burdwān	2794	23.15 N	87.51 E
Bureinskij Chrebet ⋀	2784	50.35 N	133.35 E
Bureja ≃	2784	49.25 N	129.35 E
Burfjord	2768	69.56 N	22.00 E
Burgas	2778	42.30 N	27.28 E
Bur Gavo	2788	1.10 S	41.50 E
Burgaw	2744	34.33 N	77.56 W
Burgdorf	2772	47.04 N	7.37 E
Burgess	2744	37.53 N	76.21 W
Burghūth, Sabkhat al- ⊜	2791	34.58 N	41.06 E
Burgos	2774	42.21 N	3.42 W
Burgundy → Bourgogne □[9]	2772	47.00 N	4.30 E
Burhaniye	2778	39.30 N	26.58 E
Burhānpur	2793	21.18 N	76.14 E
Burjasot	2774	39.31 N	0.25 W
Burkburnett	2748	34.06 N	98.34 W
Burke	2750	43.11 N	99.18 W
Burkesville	2746	36.48 N	85.22 W
Burketown	2806	17.44 S	139.22 E
Burley	2754	42.32 N	113.48 W
Burlingame	2750	38.45 N	95.50 W
Burlington, Ont., Can.	2740	43.19 N	79.47 W
Burlington, Colo., U.S.	2750	39.18 N	102.16 W
Burlington, Iowa, U.S.	2742	40.49 N	91.14 W
Burlington, Kans., U.S.	2750	38.12 N	95.45 W
Burlington, N.C., U.S.	2744	36.04 N	79.26 W
Burlington, Vt., U.S.	2740	44.29 N	73.13 W
Burlington, Wash., U.S.	2754	48.28 N	122.20 W
Burlington, Wis., U.S.	2742	42.41 N	88.17 W
Burma □[1]	2796	22.00 N	98.00 E
Burnet	2748	30.46 N	98.14 W
Burney	2756	40.53 N	121.40 W
Burnie	2806	41.04 S	145.54 E
Burns	2754	43.35 N	119.03 W
Burns Flat	2748	35.21 N	99.10 W
Burnside	2744	36.59 N	84.36 W
Burns Lake	2734	54.14 N	125.46 W
Burnt ≃	2754	44.22 N	117.14 W
Burravoe	2769	60.32 N	1.28 W
Bursa	2778	40.11 N	29.04 E
Būr Sa'īd (Port Said)	2786	31.16 N	32.18 E
Būr Sūdān (Port Sudan)	2786	19.37 N	37.14 E
Burton	2742	43.02 N	83.36 W
Burton upon Trent	2769	52.49 N	1.36 W
Buru I	2802	3.24 S	126.40 E
Burundi □[1]	2788	3.15 S	30.00 E
Burwell	2750	41.47 N	99.08 W
Burwick	2769	58.44 N	2.57 W
Bury Saint Edmunds	2769	52.15 N	0.43 E
Busalla	2776	44.34 N	8.57 E
Buṣayrah	2791	35.09 N	40.26 E
Busby	2754	45.32 N	106.58 W
Būshehr	2790	28.59 N	50.50 E
Bushnell, Fla., U.S.	2744	28.40 N	82.07 W
Bushnell, Ill., U.S.	2746	40.33 N	90.30 W
Buṣrá ash-Shām	2791	32.31 N	36.29 E
Busselton	2806	33.39 S	115.20 E
Bustamante	2748	26.33 N	100.30 W
Busto Arsizio	2776	45.37 N	8.51 E
Busuanga Island I	2802	12.05 N	120.05 E
Buta	2786	2.48 N	24.44 E
Butare	2788	2.36 S	29.44 E
Butehaqi	2796	48.02 N	122.43 E
Butler, Ala., U.S.	2746	32.05 N	88.13 W
Butler, Ga., U.S.	2744	32.34 N	84.14 W
Butler, Mo., U.S.	2746	38.16 N	94.20 W
Butler, Ohio, U.S.	2740	40.35 N	82.26 W
Butte	2754	46.00 N	112.32 W
Butterworth	2804	5.24 N	100.24 E
Butt of Lewis ≻	2769	58.31 N	6.15 W
Buttonwillow	2756	35.24 N	119.28 W

Symbols against index entries represent categories identified in the key on page 2810.

Name	Page	Lat °′	Long °′
Butuan	2802	8.57 N	125.33 E
Butung, Pulau I	2802	5.00 S	122.55 E
Buxton	2744	35.16 N	75.32 W
Büyük Ağrı Dağı (Mount Ararat) ▲	2766	39.42 N	44.18 E
Buzançais	2772	46.53 N	1.25 E
Buzău	2778	45.09 N	26.49 E
Búzi ≃	2788	19.50 S	34.43 E
Buzuluk	2766	52.47 N	52.15 E
Byam Channel ⋃	2734	75.20 N	105.20 W
Byam Martin Island I	2734	75.15 N	104.00 W
Bydgoszcz	2770	53.08 N	18.00 E
Byhalia	2746	34.52 N	89.41 W
Bylas	2752	33.08 N	110.07 W
Bylot Island I	2734	73.13 N	78.34 W
Byrdstown	2746	36.34 N	85.08 W
Byron, Ga., U.S.	2744	32.39 N	83.46 W
Byron, Ill., U.S.	2742	42.08 N	89.15 W
Byrranga, Gory ⛰	2784	75.00 N	104.00 E
Bytantaj ≃	2784	68.46 N	134.20 E
Bytom (Beuthen)	2770	50.22 N	18.54 E
Byxelkrok	2768	57.20 N	17.00 E
C			
Ca ≃	2802	18.46 N	105.47 E
Caacupé	2764	25.23 S	57.09 W
Cabaiguán	2760	22.05 N	79.30 W
Cabanatuan	2802	15.29 N	120.58 E
Cabeza del Buey	2774	38.43 N	5.13 W
Cabimas	2760	10.23 N	71.28 W
Cabinda	2788	5.33 S	12.12 E
Cabinda □[5]	2788	5.00 S	12.30 E
Cabinet Mountains ⛰	2754	48.08 N	115.46 W
Cable	2742	46.13 N	91.17 W
Cabonga, Réservoir ◎[1]	2734	47.20 N	76.35 W
Caborca	2758	30.37 N	112.06 W
Cabot Head ›	2740	45.14 N	81.17 W
Cabot Strait ⋃	2734	47.20 N	59.30 W
Cabra	2774	37.28 N	4.27 W
Cabrobó	2762	8.31 S	39.19 W
Caçador	2764	26.47 S	51.00 W
Čačak	2778	43.53 N	20.21 E
Cáceres, Bra.	2762	16.04 S	57.41 W
Cáceres, Esp.	2774	39.29 N	6.22 W
Cache Peak ▲	2754	42.11 N	113.40 W
Cachimbo, Serra do ⛰	2762	8.30 S	55.50 W
Cachoeira	2765	12.36 S	38.58 W
Cachoeira do Sul	2764	30.02 S	52.54 W
Cachoeiro de Itapemirim	2765	20.51 S	41.06 W
Cacólo	2788	10.07 S	19.17 E
Caconda	2788	13.43 S	15.06 E
Caddo, Okla., U.S.	2748	34.07 N	96.16 W
Caddo, Tex., U.S.	2748	32.38 N	98.40 W
Cadena, Cerro ▲	2748	25.50 N	104.05 W
Cader Idris ▲	2769	52.42 N	3.54 W
Cadillac, Fr.	2772	44.38 N	0.19 W
Cadillac, Mich., U.S.	2742	44.15 N	85.24 W
Cádiz, Esp.	2774	36.32 N	6.18 W
Cadiz, Ohio, U.S.	2740	40.16 N	81.00 W
Cádiz, Golfo de C	2774	36.50 N	7.10 W
Caen	2772	49.11 N	0.21 W
Caernarvon Bay C	2769	53.05 N	4.30 W
Caeté	2765	19.54 S	43.40 W
Cagayan de Oro	2802	8.29 N	124.39 E
Cagayan Islands II	2802	9.40 N	121.16 E
Čagda	2784	58.45 N	130.37 E
Cagli	2776	43.33 N	12.39 E
Cagliari	2776	39.20 N	9.00 E
Caguas	2760	18.14 N	66.02 W
Caha Mountains ⛰	2769	51.45 N	9.45 W
Cahirciveen	2769	51.57 N	10.13 W
Cahore Point ›	2769	52.34 N	6.11 W
Cahors	2772	44.27 N	1.26 E
Caiapó, Serra ⛰	2765	17.00 S	52.00 W
Caibarién	2760	22.31 N	79.28 W
Caicara	2760	7.37 N	66.10 W
Caicos Islands II	2760	21.50 N	71.50 W
Caicos Passage ⋃	2760	22.15 N	72.40 W
Cairngorm Mountains ⛰	2769	57.06 N	3.30 W
Cairns	2806	16.55 S	145.46 E
Cairo, Ga., U.S.	2744	30.53 N	84.12 W
Cairo, Ill., U.S.	2746	37.00 N	89.11 W
Caiundo	2788	15.46 S	17.28 E
Cajamarca	2762	7.10 S	78.31 W
Cajàzeiras	2762	6.54 S	38.34 W
Čakovec	2776	46.23 N	16.26 E
Calabar	2786	4.57 N	8.19 E
Calabozo	2760	8.56 N	67.26 W
Calahorra	2774	42.18 N	1.58 W
Calais, Fr.	2772	50.57 N	1.50 E
Calais, Maine, U.S.	2740	45.11 N	67.17 W
Calamian Group II	2802	12.00 N	120.00 E
Calamocha	2774	40.55 N	1.18 W
Calanda	2774	40.56 N	0.14 W
Călărași	2778	44.11 N	27.20 E
Calatayud	2774	41.21 N	1.38 W
Calcasieu Lake ◎	2746	29.50 N	93.17 W
Calçoene	2762	2.30 N	50.57 W
Calcutta	2794	22.32 N	88.22 E
Caldas da Rainha	2774	39.24 N	9.08 W
Caldwell, Idaho, U.S.	2754	43.40 N	116.41 W
Caldwell, Kans., U.S.	2750	37.02 N	97.37 W
Caldwell, Ohio, U.S.	2740	39.45 N	81.31 W
Caldwell, Tex., U.S.	2748	30.32 N	96.42 W
Caledonia, N.S., Can.	2739	44.22 N	65.02 W
Caledonia, Minn., U.S.	2742	43.38 N	91.29 W
Caledonia, Ohio, U.S.	2740	40.38 N	82.58 W
Calera	2746	33.06 N	86.45 W
Calexico	2756	32.40 N	115.30 W
Calgary	2734	51.03 N	114.05 W
Calhoun, Ala., U.S.	2746	32.03 N	86.33 W
Calhoun, Ga., U.S.	2744	34.30 N	84.57 W
Calhoun, Ky., U.S.	2746	37.32 N	87.16 W
Calhoun, Tenn., U.S.	2744	35.17 N	84.45 W
Calhoun City	2746	33.51 N	89.19 W
Calhoun Falls	2744	34.06 N	82.36 W
Cali	2762	3.27 N	76.31 W
Calicut	2793	11.15 N	75.46 E
Caliente	2756	37.37 N	114.31 W
California	2746	38.38 N	92.34 W
California □[3]	2736	37.30 N	119.30 W
California, Golfo de C	2758	28.00 N	112.00 W
Calion	2746	33.20 N	92.32 W
Calipatria	2756	33.08 N	115.31 W
Calispell Peak ▲	2754	48.26 N	117.30 W
Calitri	2776	40.54 N	15.27 E
Callac	2772	48.24 N	3.26 W
Callahan	2744	30.34 N	81.49 W
Callao	2762	12.02 S	77.05 W
Callaway	2750	41.17 N	99.56 W
Callosa de Ensarriá	2774	38.39 N	0.07 W
Calmar	2742	43.11 N	91.52 W
Caltagirone	2776	37.14 N	14.31 E
Caltanissetta	2776	37.29 N	14.04 E
Calumet	2742	47.14 N	88.27 W
Calunda	2788	12.06 S	23.23 E
Calvary	2744	30.44 N	84.21 W
Calvi	2776	42.34 N	8.45 E
Calvinia	2788	31.25 S	19.45 E
Camacho	2758	24.25 N	102.18 W
Camagüey	2760	21.23 N	77.55 W
Camaná	2762	16.36 S	72.40 W
Camapuã	2765	19.30 S	54.05 W
Camaquã	2764	30.51 S	51.49 W
Camas	2774	37.24 N	6.02 W
Cambados	2774	42.30 N	8.48 W
Cambay	2794	22.18 N	72.37 E
Cambodia □[1]	2802	13.00 N	105.00 E
Cambrai	2772	50.10 N	3.14 E
Cambria	2756	35.34 N	121.05 W
Cambrian Mountains ⛰	2769	52.35 N	3.35 W
Cambridge, Ont., Can.	2740	43.22 N	80.19 W
Cambridge, Eng., U.K.	2769	52.13 N	0.08 E
Cambridge, Idaho, U.S.	2754	44.34 N	116.41 W
Cambridge, Ill., U.S.	2746	41.18 N	90.12 W
Cambridge, Iowa, U.S.	2742	41.54 N	93.32 W
Cambridge, Md., U.S.	2740	38.34 N	76.04 W
Cambridge, Mass., U.S.	2740	42.22 N	71.06 W
Cambridge, Minn., U.S.	2742	45.31 N	93.14 W
Cambridge, Nebr., U.S.	2750	40.17 N	100.10 W
Cambridge, Ohio, U.S.	2740	40.02 N	81.35 W
Cambridge Bay	2734	69.03 N	105.05 W
Cambuci	2765	21.34 S	41.55 W
Camden, Ala., U.S.	2746	31.59 N	87.17 W
Camden, Ark., U.S.	2746	33.35 N	92.50 W
Camden, Maine, U.S.	2740	44.12 N	69.04 W
Camden, N.C., U.S.	2744	36.20 N	76.10 W
Camden, N.Y., U.S.	2740	43.02 N	75.45 W
Camden, S.C., U.S.	2744	34.16 N	80.36 W
Camden, Tenn., U.S.	2746	36.04 N	88.06 W
Camdenton	2746	38.00 N	92.45 W
Cameron, La., U.S.	2746	29.48 N	93.19 W
Cameron, Mo., U.S.	2746	39.44 N	94.14 W
Cameron, Tex., U.S.	2748	30.51 N	96.59 W
Cameron, W. Va., U.S.	2740	39.50 N	80.34 W
Cameron, Wis., U.S.	2742	45.25 N	91.44 W
Cameron Hills ⛰[2]	2734	59.48 N	118.00 W
Cameroon □[1]	2786	6.00 N	12.00 E
Cameroun, Mont ▲	2786	4.12 N	9.11 E
Cametá	2762	2.15 S	49.30 W
Camilla	2744	31.14 N	84.12 W
Camiranga	2762	1.48 S	46.17 W
Camooweal	2806	19.55 S	138.07 E
Camorta Island I	2802	8.10 N	93.30 E
Campana, Isla I	2764	48.25 S	75.20 W
Campbell, Mo., U.S.	2746	36.30 N	90.04 W
Campbell, Nebr., U.S.	2750	40.18 N	98.44 W
Campbell River	2734	50.01 N	125.15 W
Campbellsport	2742	43.36 N	88.17 W
Campbellsville	2746	37.21 N	85.20 W
Campbellton	2739	48.00 N	66.40 W
Campbeltown	2769	55.26 N	5.36 W
Campeche	2758	19.51 N	90.32 W
Campeche, Bahía de C	2758	20.00 N	94.00 W
Cam-pha	2802	21.07 N	107.19 E
Campina Grande	2762	7.13 S	35.53 W
Campinas	2765	22.54 S	47.05 W
Campo Alegre de Goiás	2765	17.39 S	47.45 W
Campobasso	2776	41.34 N	14.39 E
Campo Belo	2765	20.53 S	45.16 W
Campo de Criptana	2774	39.24 N	3.07 W
Campo de la Cruz	2760	10.23 N	74.53 W
Campo Grande	2765	20.27 S	54.37 W
Campo Maior	2762	4.49 S	42.10 W
Campos	2765	21.45 S	41.18 W
Campos do Jordão	2765	22.44 S	45.35 W
Camp Point	2746	40.03 N	91.04 W
Campton	2744	37.44 N	83.33 W
Camp Verde	2752	34.34 N	111.51 W
Camp Wood	2748	29.40 N	100.01 W
Camrose	2734	53.01 N	112.50 W
Canada □[1]	2734	60.00 N	95.00 W
Canadian	2748	35.55 N	100.23 W
Canadian ≃	2736	35.27 N	95.03 W
Çanakkale	2778	40.09 N	26.24 E
Çanakkale Boğazı (Dardanelles) ⋃	2778	40.15 N	26.25 E
Canal Zone □[2]	2760	9.10 N	79.48 W
Canandaigua	2740	42.54 N	77.17 W
Cananea	2758	30.57 N	110.18 W
Canarias, Islas (Canary Islands) II	2786	28.00 N	15.30 W
Canastota	2740	43.10 N	75.45 W
Canaveral, Cape ›	2744	28.27 N	80.32 W
Canavieiras	2765	15.39 S	38.57 W
Canberra	2806	35.17 S	149.08 E
Canby, Calif., U.S.	2756	41.27 N	120.52 W
Canby, Minn., U.S.	2750	44.43 N	96.16 W
Canby, Oreg., U.S.	2754	45.16 N	122.42 W
Cancale	2772	48.41 N	1.51 W
Cancon	2772	44.32 N	0.38 E
Candela	2748	26.50 N	100.40 W
Candeleda	2774	40.09 N	5.14 W
Cándido Aguilar	2758	25.30 N	98.02 W
Cando	2750	48.32 N	99.12 W
Candor	2740	42.14 N	76.21 W
Cañete	2774	40.03 N	1.35 W
Caney	2750	37.01 N	95.56 W
Canfranc	2774	42.43 N	0.31 W
Cangas de Onís	2774	43.21 N	5.07 W
Cangombe	2788	14.24 S	19.59 E
Canguçu	2764	31.24 S	52.41 W
Cangzhou	2796	38.19 N	116.51 E
Caniapiscau ≃	2734	57.40 N	69.30 W
Caniapiscau, Lac ◎	2734	54.10 N	69.55 W
Canicatti	2776	37.21 N	13.51 E
Canisteo	2740	42.16 N	77.36 W
Canistota	2750	43.36 N	97.18 W
Cañitas	2758	23.36 N	102.43 W
Çankırı	2766	40.36 N	33.37 E
Cannanore	2793	11.51 N	75.22 E
Cannelton	2746	37.55 N	86.45 W
Cannes	2772	43.33 N	7.01 E
Cannon Beach	2754	45.55 N	123.57 W
Canon City	2752	38.27 N	105.14 W
Canora	2734	51.37 N	102.26 W
Canosa [di Puglia]	2776	41.13 N	16.04 E
Cantábrica, Cordillera ⛰	2774	43.00 N	5.00 W
Cantalejo	2774	41.15 N	3.55 W
Cantanhede	2774	40.21 N	8.36 W
Cantaura	2760	9.19 N	64.21 W
Canterbury	2769	51.17 N	1.05 E
Canterbury Bight C[3]	2808	44.15 S	171.38 E
Can-tho	2804	10.02 N	105.47 E
Canton, Ga., U.S.	2744	34.14 N	84.29 W
Canton, Ill., U.S.	2746	0.00	0.00
Canton, Minn., U.S.	2742	43.32 N	91.56 W
Canton, Miss., U.S.	2746	32.37 N	90.02 W
Canton, N.C., U.S.	2744	35.32 N	82.50 W
Canton, N.Y., U.S.	2740	44.36 N	75.10 W
Canton, Ohio, U.S.	2740	40.48 N	81.22 W
Canton, Okla., U.S.	2748	36.03 N	98.35 W
Canton, S. Dak., U.S.	2750	43.18 N	96.35 W
Canton, Tex., U.S.	2748	32.33 N	95.52 W
Canton → Guangzhou, Zhg.	2800	23.06 N	113.16 E
Cantonment	2746	30.38 N	87.19 W
Cantù	2776	45.44 N	9.08 E
Canyon	2748	34.59 N	101.55 W
Canyon Ferry Lake ◎[1]	2754	46.33 N	111.37 W
Canyonlands National Park ✦	2752	38.10 N	110.00 W
Canyonville	2754	42.56 N	123.17 W
Cao-bang	2804	22.40 N	106.15 E
Capac	2742	43.01 N	82.56 W
Cape Charles	2744	37.16 N	76.01 W
Cape Coast	2786	5.05 N	1.15 W
Cape Cod National Seashore ✦	2740	41.56 N	70.06 W
Cape Dorset	2734	64.14 N	76.32 W
Cape Girardeau	2746	37.19 N	89.32 W
Cape May	2740	38.56 N	74.55 W
Cape May Court House	2740	39.05 N	74.50 W
Cape Town (Kaapstad)	2788	33.55 S	18.22 E
Cape Verde □[1]	2730	16.00 N	24.00 W
Cape Vincent	2740	44.08 N	76.20 W
Cape York Peninsula ›[1]	2806	14.00 S	142.30 E
Cap-Haïtien	2760	19.45 N	72.15 W
Capim ≃	2762	1.40 S	47.47 W
Capitan	2752	33.35 N	105.35 W
Čapljina	2776	43.07 N	17.42 E
Caprivi Strip □[9]	2788	17.59 S	23.00 E
Captieux	2772	44.18 N	0.16 W
Capua	2776	41.06 N	14.12 E
Caquetá (Japurá) ≃	2762	3.08 S	64.46 W
Čara	2784	56.54 N	118.12 E
Čara ≃	2784	60.22 N	120.50 E
Caracaraí	2762	1.50 N	61.08 W
Caracas	2760	10.30 N	66.56 W
Carajás, Serra dos ⛰	2762	6.00 S	51.20 W
Carangola	2765	20.44 S	42.02 W
Caraquet	2739	47.48 N	64.57 W
Caratasca, Laguna de C	2760	15.20 N	83.50 W
Caratinga	2765	19.47 S	42.08 W
Carauari	2762	4.52 S	66.54 W
Caravaca	2774	38.06 N	1.51 W
Caravelas	2765	17.45 S	39.15 W
Carballo	2774	43.13 N	8.41 W
Carbondale, Colo., U.S.	2752	39.24 N	107.13 W
Carbondale, Ill., U.S.	2746	37.44 N	89.13 W
Carbonear	2734	47.44 N	53.13 W
Carboneras de Guadazaon	2774	39.53 N	1.48 W
Carbon Hill	2746	33.48 N	87.32 W
Carbonia	2776	39.11 N	8.32 E
Carcagente	2774	39.08 N	0.27 W
Carcassonne	2772	43.13 N	2.21 E
Carcross	2734	60.10 N	134.42 W
Cárdenas, Cuba	2760	23.05 N	81.10 W
Cárdenas, Méx.	2758	22.00 N	99.40 W
Cardiff	2769	51.29 N	3.13 W
Cardigan	2769	52.06 N	4.40 W
Cardigan Bay C	2769	52.30 N	4.20 W
Cardston	2734	49.12 N	113.18 W
Carentan	2772	49.18 N	1.14 W
Carey, Ohio, U.S.	2740	40.57 N	83.23 W
Carey, Tex., U.S.	2748	34.28 N	100.20 W
Carey, Lake ◎	2806	29.05 S	122.15 E
Caribbean Sea ⊤[2]	2760	15.00 N	73.00 W
Cariboo Mountains ⛰	2734	53.00 N	121.00 W
Caribou	2739	46.52 N	68.01 W
Caribou Mountains ⛰	2734	59.12 N	115.40 W
Carignan	2772	49.38 N	5.10 E
Cariñena	2774	41.20 N	1.13 W
Carinhanha	2765	14.18 S	43.47 W
Carini	2776	38.08 N	13.11 E
Caripito	2760	10.08 N	63.06 W
Carleton	2750	40.18 N	97.41 W
Carleton, Mount ▲	2739	47.23 N	66.53 W
Carleton Place	2740	45.08 N	76.09 W
Carlin	2756	40.43 N	116.07 W
Carlinville	2746	39.17 N	89.53 W
Carlisle, Eng., U.K.	2769	54.54 N	2.25 W
Carlisle, Ky., U.S.	2740	38.19 N	84.02 W
Carlow	2769	52.50 N	6.55 W
Carlsbad, Calif., U.S.	2756	33.10 N	117.21 W
Carlsbad, N. Mex., U.S.	2748	32.25 N	104.14 W
Carlsbad, Tex., U.S.	2748	31.36 N	100.38 W
Carlsbad Caverns National Park ✦	2748	32.08 N	104.35 W
Carlton	2742	46.40 N	92.25 W
Carlyle	2746	38.37 N	89.22 W
Carlyle Reservoir ◎[1]	2746	38.40 N	89.18 W
Carmacks	2734	62.05 N	136.18 W
Carmagnola	2776	44.51 N	7.43 E
Carmarthen	2769	51.52 N	4.19 W
Carmaux	2772	44.03 N	2.09 E
Carmel, Calif., U.S.	2756	36.33 N	121.55 W
Carmel, N.Y., U.S.	2740	41.26 N	73.41 W
Carmel Head ›	2769	53.24 N	4.34 W
Carmen	2748	36.35 N	98.28 W
Carmen, Isla I	2758	25.55 N	111.10 W
Carmen de Patagones	2764	40.48 S	63.00 W
Carmichael	2756	38.38 N	121.19 W
Carmine	2748	30.09 N	96.41 W
Carmona, Ang.	2788	7.37 S	15.03 E
Carmona, Esp.	2774	37.28 N	5.38 W
Carnarvon, Austl.	2806	24.53 S	113.40 E
Carnarvon, S. Afr.	2788	30.56 S	22.08 E
Carndonagh	2769	55.15 N	7.15 W
Carnegie, Lake ◎	2806	26.10 S	122.30 E
Car Nicobar Island I	2804	9.10 N	92.47 E
Carnsore Point ›	2769	52.10 N	6.22 W
Caro	2742	43.29 N	83.24 W
Carol City	2744	25.56 N	80.16 W
Carolina	2762	7.20 S	47.28 W
Carolina Beach	2744	34.02 N	77.54 W
Caroline Islands II	2802	8.00 N	140.00 E
Carpathian Mountains ⛰	2766	48.00 N	24.00 E
Carpații Meridionali ⛰	2778	45.30 N	24.15 E
Carpentaria, Gulf of C	2806	14.00 S	139.00 E
Carpentras	2772	44.03 N	5.03 E
Carpi	2776	44.47 N	10.53 E
Carpinteria	2756	34.24 N	119.31 W
Carpio	2750	48.27 N	101.43 W
Carquefou	2772	47.18 N	1.30 W
Carrabelle	2744	29.51 N	84.40 W
Carrara	2776	44.05 N	10.06 E
Carrauntoohill ▲	2769	52.00 N	9.45 W
Carreta, Punta ›	2762	14.12 S	76.17 W
Carrickfergus	2769	54.43 N	5.49 W
Carrickmacross	2769	53.58 N	6.43 W
Carrillo	2758	26.54 N	103.55 W
Carrington	2750	47.27 N	99.08 W
Carrión de los Condes	2774	42.20 N	4.36 W
Carrizal, Cerro ▲	2748	26.45 N	100.35 W
Carrizo Springs	2748	28.31 N	99.52 W
Carrizozo	2752	33.38 N	105.53 W
Carroll	2750	42.04 N	94.52 W
Carrollton, Ala., U.S.	2746	33.16 N	88.05 W
Carrollton, Ga., U.S.	2744	33.35 N	85.05 W
Carrollton, Ill., U.S.	2746	39.18 N	90.24 W
Carrollton, Ky., U.S.	2746	38.41 N	85.11 W
Carrollton, Mo., U.S.	2746	39.22 N	93.30 W
Carrollton, Ohio, U.S.	2740	40.34 N	81.05 W
Čarsk	2784	49.35 N	81.05 E
Carson	2750	46.25 N	101.34 W
Carson City, Mich., U.S.	2742	43.11 N	84.51 W
Carson City, Nev., U.S.	2756	39.10 N	119.46 W
Cartagena, Col.	2760	10.25 N	75.32 W
Cartagena, Esp.	2774	37.36 N	0.59 W
Cartago	2760	9.52 N	83.55 W
Cartersville	2744	34.10 N	84.48 W
Carthage, Ill., U.S.	2746	40.25 N	91.08 W
Carthage, Miss., U.S.	2746	32.46 N	89.32 W
Carthage, Mo., U.S.	2746	37.11 N	94.19 W
Carthage, N.C., U.S.	2744	35.21 N	79.25 W
Carthage, S. Dak., U.S.	2750	44.10 N	97.43 W
Carthage, Tex., U.S.	2746	32.09 N	94.20 W
Cartier Island I	2806	12.32 S	123.32 E
Cartwright	2734	53.42 N	57.01 W
Caruaru	2762	8.17 S	35.58 W
Carúpano	2760	10.40 N	63.14 W
Caruthersville	2746	36.11 N	89.39 W
Cary	2744	35.47 N	78.46 W
Casablanca (Dar-el-Beida)	2786	33.39 N	7.35 W
Casacalenda	2776	41.44 N	14.51 E
Casa Grande	2752	32.53 N	111.45 W
Casale Monferrato	2776	45.08 N	8.27 E
Casarano	2776	40.00 N	18.10 E
Casas Ibáñez	2774	39.17 N	1.28 W
Cascade, Idaho, U.S.	2754	44.31 N	116.02 W
Cascade, Iowa, U.S.	2742	42.18 N	91.01 W
Cascade, Mont., U.S.	2754	47.16 N	111.42 W
Cascade Range ⛰	2736	49.00 N	120.00 W
Cascade Reservoir ◎[1]	2754	44.35 N	116.06 W
Cascais	2774	38.42 N	9.25 W
Cascina	2776	43.41 N	10.33 E
Caserta	2776	41.04 N	14.20 E
Caseville	2742	43.56 N	83.16 W
Casigua	2760	8.46 N	72.30 W
Caspe	2774	41.14 N	0.02 W
Casper	2754	42.51 N	106.19 W
Caspian Sea ⊤[2]	2766	42.00 N	50.30 E
Cassai (Kasai) ≃	2788	3.06 S	16.57 E
Cassano allo Ionio	2776	39.47 N	16.20 E
Casselton	2750	46.54 N	97.13 W
Cassiar	2734	59.16 N	129.40 W
Cassinga	2788	15.08 S	16.05 E
Cassino	2776	41.30 N	13.49 E
Cass Lake	2742	47.23 N	94.36 W
Cass Lake ◎	2742	47.25 N	94.32 W
Cassopolis	2742	41.55 N	86.01 W
Cassville	2746	36.41 N	93.52 W
Castanheira de Pêra	2774	40.00 N	8.13 W

Symbols against index entries represent categories identified in the key on page 2810.

Name	Page	Lat°′	Long°′
Castaños	2748	26.47 N	101.25 W
Castel del Piano	2776	42.53 N	11.32 E
Castelfranco Veneto	2776	45.40 N	11.55 E
Castellamare del Golfo	2776	38.01 N	12.53 E
Castellammare [di Stabia]	2776	40.42 N	14.29 E
Castellane	2772	43.51 N	6.31 E
Castellón de la Plana	2774	39.59 N	0.02 W
Castelnaudary	2772	43.19 N	1.57 E
Castelo Branco	2774	39.49 N	7.30 W
Castelsarrasin	2772	44.02 N	1.06 E
Castelvetrano	2776	37.41 N	12.47 E
Castets	2772	43.53 N	1.09 W
Castiglione del Lago	2776	43.07 N	12.03 E
Castile	2740	42.38 N	78.03 W
Castilla	2762	5.12 S	80.38 W
Castilla la Nueva □[9]	2774	40.00 N	3.45 W
Castillo, Pampa del ≚	2764	45.58 S	68.24 W
Castine	2740	44.23 N	68.48 W
Castlebar	2769	53.52 N	9.17 W
Castleberry	2746	31.17 N	87.02 W
Castleblayney	2769	54.07 N	6.44 W
Castle Dale	2752	39.13 N	111.01 W
Castle Hills	2748	29.32 N	98.31 W
Castle Mountain ▲	2734	64.35 N	135.55 W
Castle Peak ▲, Colo., U.S.	2752	39.00 N	106.55 W
Castle Peak ▲, Idaho, U.S.	2754	44.02 N	114.35 W
Castle Rock, Colo., U.S.	2752	39.22 N	104.51 W
Castle Rock, Wash., U.S.	2754	46.17 N	122.54 W
Castle Rock ▲	2754	44.02 N	118.11 W
Castletown	2769	54.04 N	4.40 W
Castletown Berehaven	2769	51.39 N	9.55 W
Castlewood, S. Dak., U.S.	2750	44.43 N	97.02 W
Castlewood, Va., U.S.	2744	36.54 N	82.17 W
Castres	2772	43.36 N	2.15 E
Castries	2760	14.01 N	61.00 W
Castro Daire	2774	40.54 N	7.56 W
Castro del Río	2774	37.41 N	4.28 W
Castropol	2774	43.32 N	7.02 W
Castrovillari	2776	39.49 N	16.13 E
Castroville, Calif., U.S.	2756	36.46 N	121.45 W
Castroville, Tex., U.S.	2748	29.21 N	98.53 W
Castuera	2774	38.43 N	5.33 W
Cataguases	2765	21.24 S	42.41 W
Catahoula Lake ⊜	2746	31.30 N	92.06 W
Catalão	2765	18.10 S	47.57 W
Catalina	2764	25.13 S	69.43 W
Catamarca	2764	28.30 S	65.45 W
Catanduanes Island I	2802	13.45 N	124.15 E
Catanduva	2765	21.08 S	48.58 W
Catania	2776	37.30 N	15.06 E
Catanzaro	2776	38.54 N	16.36 E
Catarman	2802	12.30 N	124.38 E
Catastrophe, Cape ≻	2806	34.59 S	136.00 E
Catete	2788	9.06 S	13.43 E
Cathcart	2788	31.18 S	27.09 E
Cat Island I	2760	24.30 N	75.30 W
Catoche, Cabo ≻	2758	21.36 N	87.07 W
Cato Island I	2806	23.15 S	155.32 E
Catonsville	2740	39.16 N	76.44 W
Catorce	2758	23.42 N	100.54 W
Catskill	2740	42.13 N	73.52 W
Catskill Mountains ⋀	2740	42.10 N	74.30 W
Cattolica	2776	43.58 N	12.44 E
Catus	2772	44.34 N	1.20 E
Cauca ≚	2760	8.54 N	74.28 W
Caucasus			
→ Bol'šoj Kavkaz ⋀	2766	42.30 N	45.00 E
Caudry	2772	50.08 N	3.25 E
Caulonia	2776	38.23 N	16.25 E
Caúngula	2788	8.25 S	18.40 E
Čaunskaja Guba C	2784	69.20 N	170.00 E
Cauquenes	2764	35.58 S	72.21 W
Causapscal	2739	48.22 N	67.14 W
Caussade	2772	44.10 N	1.32 E
Cavalaire-sur-Mer	2772	43.10 N	6.32 E
Cavalier	2750	48.48 N	97.37 W
Cavan	2769	54.00 N	7.21 W
Cave City, Ark., U.S.	2746	35.57 N	91.33 W
Cave City, Ky., U.S.	2746	37.08 N	85.58 W
Caviana, Ilha I	2762	0.10 N	50.10 W
Cawker City	2750	39.30 N	98.26 W
Cawood	2744	36.47 N	83.14 W
Caxambu	2765	21.59 S	44.56 W
Caxias	2762	4.50 S	43.21 W
Caxias do Sul	2764	29.10 S	51.11 W
Caxito	2788	8.33 S	13.36 E
Cayambe ▲[1]	2762	0.02 N	77.59 W
Cayce	2744	33.59 N	81.04 W
Cayenne	2762	4.56 N	52.20 W
Cayman Islands □[2]	2760	19.30 N	80.30 W
Cayuga	2746	39.57 N	87.28 W
Cayuga Heights	2740	42.28 N	76.30 W
Cayuga Lake ⊜	2740	42.45 N	76.45 W
Cazenovia	2740	42.56 N	75.51 W
Cazères	2772	43.13 N	1.05 E
Cazin	2776	44.58 N	15.57 E
Cazorla	2774	37.55 N	3.00 W
Čeboksary	2766	56.09 N	47.15 E
Cebollar	2764	29.06 S	66.34 W
Cebollita Peak ▲	2752	34.43 N	107.51 W
Cebreros	2774	40.27 N	4.28 W
Cebu	2802	10.18 N	123.54 E
Cebu I	2802	10.20 N	123.45 E
Cecerleg	2796	48.55 N	101.09 E
Čechov	2780	55.09 N	37.27 E
Cecina	2776	43.19 N	10.31 E
Cedarburg	2742	43.17 N	87.59 W
Cedar City	2752	37.41 N	113.04 W
Cedar Creek Reservoir ⊜[1]	2748	32.20 N	96.10 W
Cedar Falls	2742	42.32 N	92.27 W
Cedar Grove	2742	43.33 N	87.45 W
Cedar Key	2744	29.08 N	83.02 W
Cedar Lake	2746	41.22 N	87.26 W
Cedar Lake ⊜[1]	2734	53.10 N	100.00 W
Cedar Rapids, Iowa, U.S.	2742	41.59 N	91.40 W
Cedar Rapids, Nebr., U.S.	2750	41.34 N	98.09 W
Cedar Springs	2742	43.13 N	85.33 W
Cedartown	2744	34.01 N	85.15 W
Cedarville, Calif., U.S.	2756	41.32 N	120.10 W
Cedarville, Mich., U.S.	2742	46.00 N	84.22 W
Ceduna	2806	32.07 S	133.40 E
Cefalù	2776	38.02 N	14.01 E
Čegdomyn	2784	51.07 N	133.05 E
Cegléd	2770	47.10 N	19.48 E
Cehegín	2774	38.06 N	1.48 W
Cela	2788	11.25 S	15.07 E
Čel'abinsk	2766	55.10 N	61.24 E
Celano	2776	42.05 N	13.33 E
Celanova	2774	42.09 N	7.58 W
Celaya	2758	20.31 N	100.37 W
Celebes			
→ Sulawesi I	2802	2.00 S	121.00 E
Celebes Sea ⊤[2]	2802	3.00 N	122.00 E
Celina, Ohio, U.S.	2740	40.33 N	84.34 W
Celina, Tenn., U.S.	2746	36.33 N	85.30 W
Celje	2776	46.14 N	15.16 E
Čelkar	2766	47.50 N	59.36 E
Center, Colo., U.S.	2752	37.45 N	106.06 W
Center, N. Dak., U.S.	2750	47.07 N	101.18 W
Center, Tex., U.S.	2746	31.48 N	94.11 W
Centerburg	2740	40.18 N	82.42 W
Center City	2742	45.24 N	92.49 W
Center Cross	2744	37.48 N	76.47 W
Center Moriches	2740	40.48 N	72.48 W
Center Point, Ala., U.S.	2746	33.38 N	86.41 W
Center Point, Tex., U.S.	2748	29.57 N	99.02 W
Centerville, Iowa, U.S.	2742	40.43 N	92.52 W
Centerville, S. Dak., U.S.	2750	43.07 N	96.58 W
Centerville, Tenn., U.S.	2746	35.47 N	87.28 W
Centerville, Tex., U.S.	2748	31.16 N	95.59 W
Cento	2776	44.43 N	11.17 E
Central, Cordillera ⋀, Bol.	2762	18.30 S	64.55 W
Central, Cordillera ⋀, Col.	2762	5.00 N	75.00 W
Central, Cordillera ⋀, Perú	2762	8.00 S	77.00 W
Central, Massif ⋀	2772	45.00 N	3.10 E
Central, Planalto ⋀[1]	2762	18.00 S	47.00 W
Central, Sistema ⋀	2774	40.30 N	5.00 W
Central African Republic			
□[1]	2786	7.00 N	21.00 E
Central City, Iowa, U.S.	2742	42.12 N	91.31 W
Central City, Ky., U.S.	2746	37.18 N	87.07 W
Central City, Nebr., U.S.	2750	41.07 N	98.00 W
Centralia, Ill., U.S.	2746	38.31 N	89.08 W
Centralia, Mo., U.S.	2746	39.13 N	92.08 W
Centralia, Wash., U.S.	2754	46.43 N	122.58 W
Central Makrān Range ⋀	2794	26.40 N	64.30 E
Central Point	2754	42.23 N	122.57 W
Central Valley	2756	40.41 N	122.22 W
Centre	2746	34.09 N	85.40 W
Centreville, Ala., U.S.	2746	32.56 N	87.08 W
Centreville, Md., U.S.	2740	39.03 N	76.04 W
Centreville, Miss., U.S.	2746	31.05 N	91.04 W
Century	2746	30.58 N	87.16 W
Ceram Sea			
→ Seram, Laut ⊤[2]	2802	2.30 S	128.00 E
Čeremchovo	2784	53.09 N	103.05 E
Čerepovec	2780	59.08 N	37.54 E
Céret	2772	42.29 N	2.45 E
Cerf Island I	2788	9.32 S	50.59 E
Cerignola	2776	41.16 N	15.54 E
Cérilly	2772	46.37 N	2.49 E
Čerkassy	2782	49.26 N	32.04 E
Čerkessk	2766	44.14 N	42.04 E
Čern'achovsk (Insterburg)	2780	54.38 N	21.49 E
Černigov	2782	51.30 N	31.18 E
Černogorsk	2784	53.49 N	91.18 E
Černovcy	2782	48.18 N	25.56 E
Černyševskij	2784	63.00 N	112.15 E
Cerrillos	2752	35.26 N	106.08 W
Cerritos	2758	22.26 N	100.17 W
Cerro de Pasco	2762	10.41 S	76.16 W
Čerskij	2784	68.45 N	161.45 E
Čerskogo, Chrebet ⋀	2784	52.00 N	114.00 E
Cervera del Río Alhama	2774	42.01 N	1.57 W
Cervera de Pisuerga	2774	42.52 N	4.30 W
Cervia	2776	44.15 N	12.22 E
Cervione	2776	42.20 N	9.31 E
Červonograd	2782	50.24 N	24.14 E
Cesena	2776	44.08 N	12.15 E
Cesenatico	2776	44.12 N	12.24 E
České Budějovice	2770	48.59 N	14.28 E
Češskaja Guba C	2766	63.30 N	46.30 E
Cessnock	2806	32.50 S	151.21 E
Četlasskij Kamen', Gora			
▲[2]	2766	64.22 N	50.45 E
Ceuta	2786	35.53 N	5.19 W
Ceyhan	2791	37.04 N	35.47 E
Ceylânpınar	2791	36.51 N	40.02 E
Ceylon			
→ Sri Lanka □[1]	2792	7.00 N	81.00 E
Chabanais	2772	45.52 N	0.43 E
Chabarovsk	2784	48.27 N	135.06 E
Chad □[1]	2786	15.00 N	19.00 E
Chad, Lake (Lac Tchad)			
⊜	2786	13.20 N	14.00 E
Chadbourn	2744	34.19 N	78.50 W
Chadileuvú ≚	2764	37.46 S	66.00 W
Chadron	2750	42.50 N	103.02 W
Chaffee	2746	37.11 N	89.40 W
Chagny	2772	46.55 N	4.45 E
Chāh Bahār	2790	25.18 N	60.37 E
Chaidamupendi ≚[1]	2794	37.00 N	95.00 E
Chaîne Annamitique ⋀	2804	17.00 N	106.00 E
Chake Chake	2788	5.15 S	39.46 E
Chalais	2772	45.16 N	0.02 E
Chalbi Desert ◆[2]	2790	3.00 N	37.20 E
Challans	2772	46.51 N	1.53 W
Challis	2754	44.30 N	114.14 W
Chalonnes-sur-Loire	2772	47.21 N	0.46 W
Châlons-sur-Marne	2772	48.57 N	4.22 E
Chalon-sur-Saône	2772	46.47 N	4.51 E
Châlus	2772	45.39 N	0.59 E
Chama	2752	36.54 N	106.35 W
Chaman	2794	30.55 N	66.22 E
Chambal ≚	2794	26.30 N	79.15 E
Chamberlain	2750	43.49 N	99.20 W
Chambers	2752	35.11 N	109.26 W
Chambers Island I	2742	45.11 N	87.12 W
Chambéry	2772	45.34 N	5.56 E
Chambi, Djebel ▲	2786	35.11 N	8.42 E
Chambon-sur-Voueize	2772	46.11 N	2.25 E
Chamonix-Mont-Blanc	2772	45.55 N	6.52 E
Champagne □[9]	2772	49.00 N	4.30 E
Champagnole	2772	46.45 N	5.55 E
Champaign	2746	40.07 N	88.14 W
Champlain	2740	44.59 N	73.27 W
Champlain, Lake ⊜	2736	44.45 N	73.15 W
Chañaral	2764	26.21 S	70.37 W
Chanch	2796	51.30 N	100.40 E
Chandeleur Islands II	2746	29.48 N	88.51 W
Chandeleur Sound ⱶ	2746	29.55 N	89.10 W
Chandīgarh	2794	30.44 N	76.55 E
Chandler, Qué., Can.	2739	48.21 N	64.41 W
Chandler, Ariz., U.S.	2752	33.18 N	111.50 W
Chandler, Okla., U.S.	2748	35.42 N	96.53 W
Chandrapur	2793	19.57 N	79.18 E
Chandyga	2784	62.40 N	135.36 E
Changajn Nuruu ⋀	2796	47.30 N	100.00 E
Changchun	2796	43.53 N	125.19 E
Changde	2796	28.55 N	111.38 E
Changdu	2796	31.11 N	97.15 E
Changhua	2800	24.05 N	120.32 E
Changjiang	2800	25.52 N	116.20 E
Changjiang (Yangtze) ≚	2800	31.48 N	121.10 E
Changli	2796	39.43 N	119.11 E
Changsha	2800	28.11 N	113.01 E
Changshu	2800	31.39 N	120.45 E
Changzhi	2796	36.11 N	113.08 E
Changzhou (Changchow)	2800	31.47 N	119.57 E
Chanka, Ozero (Xingkathu)			
⊜	2784	45.00 N	132.24 E
Channel Islands II, Eur.	2766	49.20 N	2.20 W
Channel Islands II, Calif.,			
U.S.	2756	34.00 N	120.00 W
Channel-Port-aux-Basques	2734	47.34 N	59.09 W
Channelview	2748	29.46 N	95.07 W
Channing, Mich., U.S.	2742	46.09 N	88.05 W
Channing, Tex., U.S.	2748	35.41 N	102.20 W
Chantada	2774	42.37 N	7.46 W
Chantajskoje, Ozero ⊜	2784	68.20 N	91.00 E
Chantrey Inlet C	2734	67.48 N	96.20 W
Chanute	2750	37.41 N	95.27 W
Chaoan	2800	23.41 N	116.38 E
Chapčeranga	2784	49.42 N	112.24 E
Chapel Hill	2744	35.55 N	79.04 W
Chapleau	2734	47.50 N	83.24 W
Chapmanville	2744	37.24 N	79.10 W
Chappell	2750	41.06 N	102.28 W
Chāpra	2794	25.46 N	84.45 E
Chapultepec	2756	31.50 N	116.38 W
Chapultepec ▲	2758	23.27 N	103.04 W
Charadai	2764	27.40 S	59.55 W
Charcas	2758	23.08 N	101.07 W
Chardon	2740	41.35 N	81.12 W
Chari ≚	2786	12.58 N	14.31 E
Chārīkār	2794	35.01 N	69.11 E
Chariton	2742	41.01 N	93.19 W
Charity	2762	7.24 N	58.36 W
Char'kov (Kharkov)	2782	50.00 N	36.15 E
Charleroi	2770	50.25 N	4.26 E
Charles City	2742	43.04 N	92.40 W
Charles Island I	2734	62.40 N	74.15 W
Charleston, Ill., U.S.	2746	39.30 N	88.10 W
Charleston, Miss., U.S.	2746	34.00 N	90.04 W
Charleston, Mo., U.S.	2746	36.55 N	89.21 W
Charleston, S.C., U.S.	2744	32.48 N	79.57 W
Charleston, W. Va., U.S.	2740	38.21 N	81.38 W
Charlestown, Ind., U.S.	2746	38.27 N	85.40 W
Charles Town, W. Va., U.S.	2740	39.17 N	77.52 W
Charleville	2806	26.24 S	146.15 E
Charleville-Mézières	2772	49.46 N	4.43 E
Charlevoix	2742	45.19 N	85.16 W
Charlevoix, Lake ⊜	2742	45.15 N	85.08 W
Charlotte, Mich., U.S.	2742	42.36 N	84.50 W
Charlotte, N.C., U.S.	2744	35.14 N	80.50 W
Charlotte, Tex., U.S.	2748	28.52 N	98.43 W
Charlotte Amalie	2760	18.21 N	64.56 W
Charlottenberg	2768	59.53 N	12.17 E
Charlottesville	2740	38.02	78.29 W
Charlottetown	2739	46.14 N	63.08 W
Charlton Island I	2734	52.00 N	79.30 W
Charmes	2772	48.22 N	6.17 E
Charolles	2772	46.26 N	4.17 E
Chārsadda	2794	34.09 N	71.44 E
Charters Towers	2806	20.05 S	146.16 E
Chartres	2772	48.27 N	1.30 E
Char Us Nuur ⊜	2796	48.00 N	92.10 E
Chasavjurt	2766	43.15 N	46.37 E
Chascomús	2764	35.35 S	58.00 W
Chaska	2742	44.47 N	93.35 W
Chatanbulag	2796	43.11 N	109.10 E
Chatanga	2784	71.58 N	102.30 E
Chatanga ≚	2784	72.55 N	106.00 E
Chatangskij Zaliv C	2784	73.30 N	109.00 E
Châteaubriant	2772	47.43 N	1.23 W
Château-du-Loir	2772	47.42 N	0.25 E
Châteaudun	2772	48.05 N	1.20 E
Chateaugay	2740	44.56 N	74.05 W
Château-Gontier	2772	47.50 N	0.42 W
Château-Landon	2772	48.09 N	2.42 E
Châteaulin	2772	48.12 N	4.05 W
Châteaumeillant	2772	46.34 N	2.12 E
Châteauneuf-sur-Charente	2772	45.36 N	0.03 W
Châteauneuf-sur-Loire	2772	47.52 N	2.14 E
Château-Renault	2772	47.35 N	0.55 E
Châteauroux	2772	46.49 N	1.42 E
Château-Thierry	2772	49.03 N	3.24 E
Châtellerault	2772	46.49 N	0.33 E
Chatgal	2796	50.26 N	100.07 E
Chatham, N.B., Can.	2739	47.02 N	65.28 W
Chatham, Ont., Can.	2740	42.24 N	82.11 W
Chatham, Eng., U.K.	2769	51.23 N	0.32 E
Chatham, Ill., U.S.	2746	39.40 N	89.42 W
Chatham, La., U.S.	2746	32.19 N	92.27 W
Chatham, Va., U.S.	2744	36.50 N	79.24 W
Châtillon	2776	45.45 N	7.37 E
Châtillon-Coligny	2772	47.50 N	2.51 E
Châtillon-sur-Indre	2772	46.59 N	1.11 E
Châtillon-sur-Seine	2772	47.51 N	4.33 E
Chatom	2746	31.28 N	88.16 W
Chatsworth	2744	34.46 N	84.46 W
Chattahoochee	2744	30.42 N	84.51 W
Chattahoochee ≚	2736	30.52 N	84.57 W
Chattanooga	2746	35.03 N	85.19 W
Chattaroy	2744	37.42 N	82.17 W
Chatyrka	2784	62.03 N	175.15 E
Chauk	2804	20.54 N	94.50 E
Chaumont	2772	48.07 N	5.08 E
Chauncey	2740	39.24 N	82.08 W
Chauny	2772	49.37 N	3.13 E
Chau-phu	2804	10.42 N	105.07 E
Chauvigny	2772	46.34 N	0.39 E
Chaves	2774	41.44 N	7.28 W
Chazy	2740	44.53 N	73.26 W
Cheaha Mountain ▲	2746	33.30 N	85.47 W
Cheboygan	2742	45.39 N	84.29 W
Chech, Erg ◆[2]	2786	25.00 N	2.15 W
Checotah	2748	35.28 N	95.31 W
Cheduba Island I	2804	18.48 N	93.38 E
Cheektowaga	2740	42.55 N	78.46 W
Cheerchenghe ≚	2794	39.25 N	88.20 E
Chehalis	2754	46.40 N	122.58 W
Cheju-do I	2796	33.20 N	126.30 E
Chelan	2754	47.51 N	120.01 W
Chełm	2770	51.10 N	23.28 E
Chełmno	2770	53.22 N	18.26 E
Chelmsford	2769	51.44 N	0.28 E
Chelsea, Mich., U.S.	2742	42.19 N	84.01 W
Chelsea, Okla., U.S.	2748	36.32 N	95.26 W
Cheltenham	2769	51.54 N	2.04 W
Chelva	2774	39.45 N	0.59 W
Chemult	2754	43.13 N	121.47 W
Chenāb ≚	2794	29.23 N	71.02 E
Chenachane	2786	26.00 N	4.15 E
Cheney	2750	37.38 N	97.47 W
Cheney Reservoir ⊜[1]	2750	37.45 N	97.50 W
Chengde	2796	40.58 N	117.53 E
Chengdu	2796	30.39 N	104.04 E
Chenoa	2746	40.45 N	88.43 W
Cheraw	2744	34.42 N	79.53 W
Cherbourg	2772	49.39 N	1.39 W
Chergui, Chott ech ⊜	2786	34.21 N	0.30 E
Cheriton	2744	37.17 N	75.58 W
Cherokee, Iowa, U.S.	2750	42.45 N	95.33 W
Cherokee, Okla., U.S.	2748	36.45 N	98.21 W
Cherokee, Tex., U.S.	2748	30.59 N	98.43 W
Cherokees, Lake O' The			
⊜[1]	2748	36.39 N	94.49 W
Cherokee Sound	2744	26.17 N	77.02 W
Cherryvale	2750	37.16 N	95.33 W
Cherson	2782	46.38 N	32.35 E
Chesaning	2742	43.11 N	84.07 W
Chesapeake	2744	36.43 N	76.15 W
Chesapeake Bay C	2736	38.40 N	76.25 W
Chesapeake Beach	2740	38.41 N	76.32 W
Chester, Eng., U.K.	2769	53.12 N	2.54 W
Chester, Calif., U.S.	2756	40.19 N	121.14 W
Chester, Ill., U.S.	2746	37.55 N	89.49 W
Chester, Mont., U.S.	2754	48.31 N	110.58 W
Chester, Nebr., U.S.	2750	40.01 N	97.37 W
Chester, S.C., U.S.	2744	34.43 N	81.12 W
Chester, Va., U.S.	2744	37.21 N	77.27 W
Chesterfield, Eng., U.K.	2769	53.15 N	1.25 W
Chesterfield, S.C., U.S.	2744	34.44 N	80.05 W
Chesterfield, Îles II	2806	19.30 S	158.00 E
Chesterfield Inlet	2734	63.21 N	90.42 W
Chesterfield Inlet C	2734	63.25 N	90.45 W
Chestertown	2740	39.13 N	76.04 W
Cheta ≚	2784	71.54 N	102.06 E
Chetek	2742	45.19 N	91.39 W
Chetopa	2750	37.02 N	95.05 W
Cheval Blanc, Pointe du			
≻	2760	19.41 N	73.27 W
Cheviot	2740	39.11 N	84.35 W
Chew Bahir (Lake Stefanie)			
⊜	2790	4.40 N	36.50 E
Chewelah	2754	48.17 N	117.43 W
Cheyenne	2748	35.37 N	99.40 W
Cheyenne ≚	2736	44.40 N	101.15 W
Cheyenne Wells	2750	38.51 N	102.11 W
Chezhou	2800	25.48 N	112.59 E
Chhatarpur	2794	24.54 N	79.36 E
Chhindwāra	2794	22.04 N	78.56 E
Chiai	2800	23.29 N	120.27 E
Chiang Mai	2804	18.46 N	98.58 E
Chiang Rai	2804	19.54 N	99.50 E
Chiari	2776	45.32 N	9.56 E
Chiavari	2776	44.19 N	9.19 E
Chiavenna	2776	46.19 N	9.24 E
Chiba	2798	35.36 N	140.07 E
Chibougamau	2734	49.55 N	74.22 W
Chibuto	2788	24.44 S	33.33 E
Chicago	2742	41.53 N	87.38 W
Chicago Heights	2746	41.30 N	87.38 W
Chicapa ≚	2788	6.26 S	20.47 E
Chichén Itzá	2758	20.40 N	88.34 W
Chichén Itzá ⊥	2758	20.40 N	88.35 W
Chichester	2769	50.50 N	0.48 W
Chickamauga	2744	34.52 N	85.18 W
Chickasaw	2746	30.46 N	88.05 W
Chickasha	2748	35.02 N	97.58 W
Chiclana de la Frontera	2774	36.25 N	6.08 W
Chiclayo	2762	6.46 S	79.50 W
Chico	2756	39.44 N	121.50 W
Chicoa	2788	15.37 S	32.24 E
Chicopee	2740	42.10 N	72.36 W

Symbols against index entries represent categories identified in the key on page 2810.

Name	Page	Lat°′	Long°′
Chicoutimi	2739	48.26 N	71.04 W
Chidambaram	2793	11.24 N	79.42 E
Chidester	2746	33.42 N	93.01 W
Chidley, Cape ➤	2734	60.23 N	64.26 W
Chiefland	2744	29.29 N	82.52 W
Chieri	2776	45.01 N	7.49 E
Chieti	2776	42.21 N	14.10 E
Chifeng	2796	42.18 N	119.00 E
Chigasaki	2798	35.19 N	139.24 E
Chihuahua	2758	28.38 N	106.05 W
Chilapa de Alvarez	2758	17.36 N	99.10 W
Chilās	2794	35.26 N	74.05 E
Childersburg	2746	33.16 N	86.21 W
Childress	2748	34.25 N	100.13 W
Chile □[1]	2764	30.00 S	71.00 W
Chilete	2762	7.14 S	78.51 W
Chililabombwe (Bancroft)	2788	12.18 S	27.43 E
Chillán	2764	36.36 S	72.07 W
Chillicothe, Ill., U.S.	2746	40.55 N	89.29 W
Chillicothe, Mo., U.S.	2746	39.48 N	93.33 W
Chillicothe, Ohio, U.S.	2740	39.20 N	82.59 W
Chillicothe, Tex., U.S.	2748	34.10 N	99.31 W
Chilliwack	2734	49.10 N	121.57 W
Chiloé, Isla de I	2764	42.30 S	73.55 W
Chilok	2784	51.21 N	110.28 E
Chiloquin	2754	42.35 N	121.52 W
Chilpancingo [de los Bravos]	2758	17.33 N	99.30 W
Chilton	2742	44.02 N	88.10 W
Chilung	2800	25.08 N	121.44 E
Chilwa, Lake ⊜	2788	15.12 S	35.50 E
Chimayo	2752	36.00 N	105.56 W
Chimborazo ∧[1]	2762	1.28 S	78.48 W
Chimbote	2762	9.05 S	78.36 W
Chimki	2780	55.54 N	37.26 E
China	2748	25.42 N	99.14 W
China □[1]	2796	35.00 N	105.00 E
China Grove	2744	35.34 N	80.35 W
Chinati Peak ∧	2748	29.57 N	104.29 W
Chincha Alta	2762	13.27 S	76.08 W
Chincilla de Monte Aragón	2774	38.55 N	1.55 W
Chincoteague	2744	37.56 N	75.23 W
Chinde	2788	18.37 S	36.24 E
Chindwin ≃	2804	21.26 N	95.15 E
Chingola	2788	12.32 S	27.52 E
Chin Hills ⋀[2]	2804	22.30 N	93.30 E
Chiniot	2794	31.43 N	72.59 E
Chinju	2796	35.11 N	128.05 E
Chinko ≃	2786	4.50 N	23.53 E
Chinle	2752	36.09 N	109.33 W
Chinon	2772	47.10 N	0.15 E
Chino Valley	2752	34.45 N	112.27 W
Chioggia	2776	45.13 N	12.17 E
Chipata	2788	13.39 S	32.40 E
Chippewa ≃	2742	44.25 N	92.10 W
Chippewa Falls	2742	44.56 N	91.24 W
Chiquimula	2760	14.48 N	89.33 W
Chīrāla	2793	15.49 N	80.21 E
Chirfa	2786	20.57 N	12.21 E
Chirgis Nuur ⊜	2796	49.12 N	93.24 E
Chiricahua Peak ∧	2752	31.52 N	109.20 W
Chiriquí, Golfo C	2760	8.00 N	82.20 W
Chiriquí, Volcán de (Volcán Barú) ∧[1]	2760	8.49 N	82.32 W
Chirripó, Cerro ∧	2760	9.29 N	83.29 W
Chisholm, Maine, U.S.	2740	44.29 N	70.12 W
Chisholm, Minn , U.S.	2742	47.29 N	92.53 W
Chitembo	2788	13.34 S	16.40 E
Chitipa	2788	9.43 S	33.15 E
Chitradurga	2793	14.14 N	76.24 E
Chitrāl	2794	35.51 N	71.47 E
Chittagong	2794	22.20 N	91.50 E
Chittoor	2793	13.12 N	79.07 E
Chiusi	2776	43.01 N	11.57 E
Chivasso	2776	45.11 N	7.53 E
Chmel'nickij	2782	49.25 N	27.00 E
Choapan	2758	17.20 N	95.57 W
Choctaw	2746	32.13 N	88.06 W
Choele-Choel	2764	39.15 S	65.30 W
Cholet	2772	47.04 N	0.53 W
Cholmsk	2784	47.03 N	142.03 E
Choma	2788	16.48 S	26.59 E
Chomutov	2770	50.28 N	13.26 E
Chon Buri	2804	13.22 N	100.59 E
Ch'ŏngjin	2796	41.47 N	129.50 E
Ch'ŏngju	2796	36.39 N	127.31 E
Chongqing	2796	29.39 N	106.34 E
Chŏnju	2796	35.49 N	127.08 E
Chonos, Archipiélago de los II	2764	45.00 S	74.00 W
Chonuu	2784	66.27 N	143.06 E
Chōshi	2798	35.44 N	140.50 E
Chos Malal	2764	37.20 S	70.15 W
Choteau	2754	47.49 N	112.11 W
Chouteau	2748	36.11 N	95.21 W
Chovd ≃	2796	48.06 N	92.11 E
Chövsgöl Nuur ⊜	2796	51.00 N	100.30 E
Chowchilla	2756	37.07 N	120.16 W
Christanshåb	2734	68.50 N	51.12 W
Christchurch	2808	43.42 S	172.38 E
Christian, Cape ➤	2734	70.31 N	68.18 W
Christian Island I	2740	44.50 N	80.13 W
Christiansburg	2744	37.08 N	80.24 W
Christiansted	2760	17.45 N	64.42 W
Christmas Island □[2]	2802	10.30 S	105.40 E
Christoval	2748	31.12 N	100.30 W
Chroma ≃	2784	71.36 N	144.49 E
Chromtau	2766	50.17 N	58.27 E
Chrzanów	2770	50.09 N	19.24 E
Chu ≃	2802	19.53 N	105.45 E
Chubbuck	2754	42.55 N	112.28 W
Chūgoku-sanchi ⋀	2798	34.58 N	132.57 E
Chukchi Sea ⩨[2]	2732	69.00 N	171.00 W
Chula Vista	2756	32.39 N	117.05 W
Chulucanas	2762	5.06 S	80.10 W
Chumphon	2804	10.32 N	99.13 E
Ch'unch'ŏn	2796	37.52 N	127.43 E
Chunchula	2746	30.55 N	88.12 W
Ch'ungju	2796	36.58 N	127.58 E
Chungking → Chongqing	2796	29.39 N	106.34 E
Chupaderos	2758	23.50 N	102.20 W
Chuquicamata	2764	22.19 S	68.56 W
Chur	2772	46.51 N	9.32 E
Churchill	2734	58.46 N	94.10 W
Churchill ≃, Can.	2734	58.47 N	94.12 W
Churchill ≃, Newf., Can.	2734	53.30 N	60.10 W
Churchill Lake ⊜	2734	55.55 N	108.20 W
Church Point	2746	30.24 N	92.13 W
Churu	2794	28.18 N	74.57 E
Chuska Peak ∧	2752	35.53 N	108.50 W
Chust	2782	48.10 N	23.18 E
Chutag	2796	49.23 N	102.43 E
Chuxian	2800	32.19 N	118.17 E
Chuxiong	2804	25.02 N	101.30 E
Chužir	2784	53.11 N	107.20 E
Chvalynsk	2766	52.30 N	48.07 E
Cibecue	2752	34.03 N	110.29 W
Cicero	2746	41.51 N	87.45 W
Ciechanów	2770	52.53 N	20.38 E
Ciego de Avila	2760	21.51 N	78.46 W
Ciempozuelos	2774	40.10 N	3.37 W
Ciénaga	2760	11.01 N	74.15 W
Ciénega de Flores	2748	25.57 N	100.11 W
Cienfuegos	2760	22.09 N	80.27 W
Cieszyn	2770	49.45 N	18.38 E
Cieza	2774	38.14 N	1.25 W
Cifuentes	2774	40.47 N	2.37 W
Cilleruelo de Bezana	2774	42.58 N	3.51 W
Cimarron, Kans., U.S.	2750	37.48 N	100.21 W
Cimarron, N. Mex., U.S.	2752	36.31 N	104.55 W
Cimarron ≃	2736	36.10 N	96.17 W
Ciml'anskoje Vodochranilišče ⊜[1]	2766	48.00 N	43.00 E
Cincinnati	2740	39.06 N	84.31 W
Çine	2778	37.36 N	28.04 E
Ciney	2770	50.18 N	5.06 E
Cipa ≃	2784	55.23 N	115.55 E
Cipolletti	2764	38.56 S	67.59 W
Circle	2754	47.25 N	105.35 W
Circleville	2740	39.36 N	82.57 W
Cirencester	2769	51.44 N	1.59 W
Ciriè	2776	45.14 N	7.36 E
Cirò Marina	2776	39.22 N	17.08 E
Cisco	2748	32.23 N	98.59 W
Cisne	2746	38.31 N	88.26 W
Cistierna	2774	42.48 N	5.07 W
Čistopol'	2766	55.21 N	50.37 E
Čita	2784	52.03 N	113.30 E
Citra	2744	29.25 N	82.06 W
Citronelle	2746	31.06 N	88.14 W
Citrus Heights	2756	38.42 N	121.17 W
Città di Castello	2776	43.27 N	12.14 E
Ciudad	2758	23.44 N	105.42 W
Ciudad Acuña	2758	29.18 N	100.55 W
Ciudad Altamirano	2758	18.20 N	100.40 W
Ciudad Bolívar	2760	8.08 N	63.33 W
Ciudad Camargo, Méx.	2758	27.40 N	105.10 W
Ciudad Camargo, Méx.	2758	26.19 N	98.50 W
Ciudad Chetumal	2758	18.30 N	88.18 W
Ciudad del Carmen	2758	18.38 N	91.50 W
Ciudad del Maíz	2758	22.24 N	99.36 W
Ciudad de México (Mexico City)	2758	19.24 N	99.09 W
Ciudad de Valles	2758	21.59 N	99.01 W
Ciudadela	2774	40.02 N	3.50 E
Ciudad Guayana	2760	8.22 N	62.40 W
Ciudad Guzmán	2758	19.41 N	103.29 W
Ciudad Hidalgo	2758	19.41 N	100.34 W
Ciudad Ixtepec	2758	16.34 N	95.06 W
Ciudad Jiménez	2758	27.08 N	104.55 W
Ciudad Juárez	2758	31.44 N	106.29 W
Ciudad Lerdo	2748	25.32 N	103.32 W
Ciudad Madero	2758	22.16 N	97.50 W
Ciudad Mante	2758	22.44 N	98.57 W
Ciudad Melchor Múzquiz	2758	27.53 N	101.31 W
Ciudad Miguel Alemán	2748	26.23 N	99.01 W
Ciudad Obregón	2758	27.29 N	109.56 W
Ciudad Ojeda	2760	10.12 N	71.19 W
Ciudad Real	2774	38.59 N	3.56 W
Ciudad Rodrigo	2774	40.36 N	6.32 W
Ciudad Victoria	2758	23.44 N	99.08 W
Civita Castellana	2776	42.17 N	12.25 E
Civitanova Marche	2776	43.18 N	13.44 E
Civitavecchia	2776	42.06 N	11.48 E
Civray	2772	46.09 N	0.18 E
Clackamas ≃	2754	45.22 N	122.36 W
Clacton-on-Sea	2769	51.48 N	1.09 E
Claire, Lake ⊜	2734	58.30 N	112.00 W
Clairemont	2748	33.10 N	100.45 W
Clairton	2740	40.18 N	79.53 W
Clamecy	2772	47.27 N	3.31 E
Clanton	2746	32.50 N	86.38 W
Clanwilliam	2788	32.11 S	18.54 E
Clare	2742	43.49 N	84.46 W
Claremont	2740	43.23 N	72.20 W
Claremore	2748	36.19 N	95.36 W
Claremorris	2769	53.44 N	9.00 W
Clarence	2742	41.53 N	91.04 W
Clarendon	2748	34.56 N	100.53 W
Claresholm	2734	50.02 N	113.35 W
Clarinda	2750	40.44 N	95.02 W
Clarion, Iowa, U.S.	2742	42.44 N	93.44 W
Clarion, Pa., U.S.	2740	41.13 N	79.24 W
Clark	2750	44.53 N	97.44 W
Clarkdale	2752	34.46 N	112.03 W
Clark Fork	2754	48.08 N	116.11 W
Clarksburg	2740	39.17 N	80.21 W
Clarksdale	2746	34.12 N	90.34 W
Clarks Hill	2746	40.15 N	86.43 W
Clarkson	2746	37.30 N	86.13 W
Clarks Summit	2740	41.30 N	75.42 W
Clarksville, Ark., U.S.	2746	35.28 N	93.28 W
Clarksville, Ga., U.S.	2744	34.37 N	83.31 W
Clarksville, Iowa, U.S.	2742	42.47 N	92.40 W
Clarksville, Tenn., U.S.	2746	36.32 N	87.21 W
Clarksville, Tex., U.S.	2748	33.37 N	95.03 W
Clarksville, Va., U.S.	2744	36.37 N	78.34 W
Claude	2748	35.07 N	101.22 W
Clavos, Laguna de ⊜	2748	27.40 N	104.50 W
Claxton	2744	32.10 N	81.55 W
Clay Center	2750	39.23 N	97.08 W
Clayton, Ala., U.S.	2746	31.53 N	85.27 W
Clayton, N. Mex., U.S.	2748	36.27 N	103.11 W
Clayton, N.C., U.S.	2744	35.39 N	78.28 W
Clayton, Okla., U.S.	2748	34.35 N	95.21 W
Clearfield	2740	41.02 N	78.27 W
Clear Lake, Iowa, U.S.	2742	43.08 N	93.23 W
Clear Lake, S. Dak., U.S.	2750	44.45 N	96.41 W
Clear Lake, Wis., U.S.	2742	45.15 N	92.16 W
Clearlake Highlands	2756	38.57 N	122.38 W
Clearmont	2754	44.38 N	106.23 W
Clearwater	2744	27.58 N	82.48 W
Clearwater ≃	2754	46.25 N	117.02 W
Clearwater Mountains ⋀	2754	46.00 N	115.30 W
Cleburne	2748	32.21 N	97.23 W
Cle Elum	2754	47.12 N	120.56 W
Clemson	2744	34.41 N	82.50 W
Clendenin	2740	38.29 N	81.21 W
Clermont, Fr.	2772	49.23 N	2.24 E
Clermont, Fla., U.S.	2744	28.33 N	81.46 W
Clermont-Ferrand	2772	45.47 N	3.05 E
Cles	2776	46.22 N	11.02 E
Cleveland, Ga., U.S.	2744	34.36 N	83.46 W
Cleveland, Miss., U.S.	2746	33.45 N	90.50 W
Cleveland, Ohio, U.S.	2740	41.30 N	81.41 W
Cleveland, Okla., U.S.	2748	36.19 N	96.28 W
Cleveland, Tenn., U.S.	2746	35.10 N	84.53 W
Cleveland, Tex., U.S.	2748	30.21 N	95.05 W
Clewiston	2744	26.45 N	80.56 W
Clifden	2769	53.29 N	10.01 W
Clifton, Ariz., U.S.	2752	33.03 N	109.18 W
Clifton, Ill., U.S.	2746	40.56 N	87.56 W
Clifton, Kans., U.S.	2750	39.34 N	97.17 W
Clifton, Tex., U.S.	2748	31.47 N	97.35 W
Clifton Forge	2744	37.49 N	79.49 W
Clingmans Dome ∧	2736	35.35 N	83.30 W
Clinton, B.C., Can.	2734	51.05 N	121.35 W
Clinton, Ark., U.S.	2746	35.36 N	92.28 W
Clinton, Conn., U.S.	2740	41.17 N	72.32 W
Clinton, Ill., U.S.	2746	40.09 N	88.57 W
Clinton, Iowa, U.S.	2742	41.51 N	90.12 W
Clinton, Ky., U.S.	2746	36.40 N	89.02 W
Clinton, La., U.S.	2746	30.52 N	91.01 W
Clinton, Mass., U.S.	2740	42.25 N	71.41 W
Clinton, Mich., U.S.	2742	42.04 N	83.58 W
Clinton, Miss., U.S.	2746	32.20 N	90.20 W
Clinton, Mo., U.S.	2746	38.22 N	93.46 W
Clinton, N.C., U.S.	2744	35.00 N	78.20 W
Clinton, Okla., U.S.	2748	35.31 N	98.59 W
Clinton, S.C., U.S.	2744	34.29 N	81.53 W
Clinton, Tenn., U.S.	2744	36.06 N	84.08 W
Clinton-Colden Lake ⊜	2734	63.58 N	107.27 W
Clintonville	2742	44.37 N	88.46 W
Clintwood	2744	37.09 N	82.27 W
Clio, Ala., U.S.	2746	31.43 N	85.36 W
Clio, S.C., U.S.	2744	34.35 N	79.33 W
Clogher Head ➤	2769	53.48 N	6.12 W
Cloncurry	2806	20.42 S	140.30 E
Clonmel	2769	52.21 N	7.42 W
Cloquet	2742	46.43 N	92.28 W
Cloud Peak ∧	2754	44.25 N	107.10 W
Clover	2744	35.07 N	81.14 W
Cloverdale, Calif., U.S.	2756	38.48 N	123.01 W
Cloverdale, Ind., U.S.	2746	39.31 N	86.48 W
Cloverport	2746	37.50 N	86.38 W
Clovis, Calif., U.S.	2756	36.49 N	119.42 W
Clovis, N. Mex., U.S.	2748	34.24 N	103.12 W
Cluj	2778	46.47 N	23.36 E
Cluny	2772	46.26 N	4.39 E
Cluses	2772	46.04 N	6.36 E
Clusone	2776	45.53 N	9.57 E
Clute	2748	29.01 N	95.24 W
Clutha ≃	2808	46.21 S	169.48 E
Clyde, N.W. Ter., Can.	2734	70.25 N	68.30 W
Clyde, N.Y., U.S.	2740	43.05 N	76.52 W
Clyde, Ohio, U.S.	2740	41.18 N	82.59 W
Clyde, Tex., U.S.	2748	32.24 N	99.30 W
Clyde ≃	2769	55.56 N	4.29 W
Clyde, Firth of C[1]	2769	55.42 N	5.00 W
Clyde Park	2754	45.53 N	110.36 W
Coachella	2756	33.41 N	116.10 W
Coacoyole	2758	24.31 N	106.34 W
Coahoma	2748	32.18 N	101.18 W
Coahuila	2756	32.12 N	114.59 W
Coalcomán de Matamoros	2758	18.47 N	103.09 W
Coalgate	2748	34.32 N	96.13 W
Coal Grove	2740	38.30 N	82.39 W
Coalinga	2756	36.09 N	120.21 W
Coalport	2740	40.45 N	78.32 W
Coari	2762	4.05 S	63.08 W
Coast Mountains ⋀	2734	55.00 N	129.00 W
Coast Ranges ⋀	2736	41.00 N	123.30 W
Coatesville	2740	39.59 N	75.49 W
Coaticook	2740	45.08 N	71.48 W
Coats Island I	2734	62.30 N	83.00 W
Coats Land ←[1]	2733	77.00 S	28.00 W
Coatzacoalcos	2758	18.09 N	94.25 W
Cobalt	2734	47.24 N	79.41 W
Cobija	2762	11.02 S	68.44 W
Cobourg	2740	43.58 N	78.10 W
Cóbuè	2788	12.04 S	34.50 E
Coburg Island I	2734	76.00 N	79.25 W
Cochabamba	2762	17.24 S	66.09 W
Cochin	2793	9.58 N	76.14 E
Cochran	2744	32.23 N	83.21 W
Cochrane	2734	49.04 N	81.01 W
Coco ≃	2760	15.00 N	83.08 W
Coco, Isla del I	2762	5.32 N	87.04 W
Cocoa	2744	28.21 N	80.44 W
Cocoa Beach	2744	28.19 N	80.36 W
Coco Channel ⩍	2804	13.45 N	93.00 E
Cocodrie Lake ⊜[1]	2746	30.58 N	92.25 W
Coco Islands II	2804	14.05 N	93.18 E
Coconino Plateau ⋀[1]	2752	36.00 N	112.35 W
Côcos	2765	14.10 S	44.33 W
Cocula	2758	20.23 N	103.50 W
Cod, Cape ➤	2740	41.42 N	70.15 W
Codajás	2762	3.50 S	62.05 W
Codigoro	2776	44.49 N	12.08 E
Codogno	2776	45.09 N	9.42 E
Codroipo	2776	45.58 N	12.59 E
Cody, Nebr., U.S.	2750	42.56 N	101.15 W
Cody, Wyo., U.S.	2754	44.32 N	109.03 W
Coen	2806	13.56 S	143.12 E
Coetivy Island I	2788	7.08 S	56.16 E
Coeur d'Alene	2754	47.41 N	116.46 W
Coeur d'Alene ≃	2754	47.28 N	116.48 W
Coeur d'Alene Lake ⊜[1]	2754	47.32 N	116.48 W
Coeur d'Alene Mountains ⋀	2754	47.50 N	116.05 W
Coffeeville	2746	33.59 N	89.40 W
Coffeyville	2750	37.02 N	95.37 W
Coffs Harbour	2806	30.18 S	153.08 E
Cognac	2772	45.42 N	0.20 W
Coiba, Ilha de I	2760	7.23 N	81.48 W
Coimbatore	2793	11.00 N	76.58 E
Coimbra, Bra.	2765	20.52 S	42.48 W
Coimbra, Port.	2774	40.12 N	8.25 W
Coín	2774	36.40 N	4.45 W
Čojbalsan	2796	48.34 N	114.50 E
Cokato	2742	45.05 N	94.11 W
Cokeville	2754	42.05 N	110.57 W
Čokurdach	2784	70.38 N	147.55 E
Colatina	2765	19.32 S	40.37 W
Colby	2750	39.24 N	101.03 W
Colchester	2769	51.54 N	0.54 E
Cold Spring	2742	45.27 N	94.26 W
Coldwater, Kans., U.S.	2750	37.16 N	99.19 W
Coldwater, Mich., U.S.	2742	41.57 N	84.60 W
Coldwater, Ohio, U.S.	2740	40.29 N	84.38 W
Colebrook	2740	44.54 N	71.30 W
Cole Camp	2746	38.28 N	93.12 W
Coleman	2748	31.50 N	99.26 W
Coleraine	2769	55.08 N	6.40 W
Colesberg	2788	30.45 S	25.05 E
Colfax, Calif., U.S.	2756	39.06 N	120.57 W
Colfax, Iowa, U.S.	2742	41.41 N	93.14 W
Colfax, La., U.S.	2746	31.31 N	92.42 W
Colfax, Wash., U.S.	2754	46.53 N	117.22 W
Colhué Huapi, Lago ⊜	2764	45.30 S	68.48 W
Colima	2758	19.14 N	103.43 W
Colinas	2762	14.12 S	48.03 W
Coll I	2769	56.40 N	6.35 W
Collbran	2752	39.14 N	107.57 W
College Place	2754	46.03 N	118.23 W
College Station	2748	30.37 N	96.21 W
Collier Bay C	2806	16.10 S	124.15 E
Collierville	2746	35.03 N	89.40 W
Collingwood	2740	44.29 N	80.13 W
Collins	2746	31.39 N	89.33 W
Collinsville	2748	36.22 N	95.51 W
Collooney	2769	54.11 N	8.29 W
Colman	2750	43.59 N	96.49 W
Colmar	2772	48.05 N	7.22 E
Colmenar	2774	36.54 N	4.20 W
Colmenar de Oreja	2774	40.06 N	3.23 W
Colmenar Viejo	2774	40.40 N	3.46 W
Cologne → Köln	2770	50.56 N	6.59 E
Coloma	2742	44.02 N	89.31 W
Colomb-Béchar → Béchar	2786	31.37 N	2.13 W
Colombia	2748	27.42 N	99.45 W
Colombia □[1]	2762	4.00 N	72.00 W
Colombo	2793	6.56 N	79.51 E
Colón, Cuba	2760	22.43 N	80.54 W
Colón, Pan.	2760	9.22 N	79.54 W
Colón, Archipiélago De (Galapagos Islands) II	2730	0.30 S	90.30 W
Colonet	2756	31.05 N	116.10 W
Colonia Dora	2764	28.40 S	63.00 W
Colonia Las Heras	2764	46.33 S	68.57 W
Colonial Heights	2744	37.15 N	77.25 W
Colonia Progreso	2756	32.35 N	115.37 W
Colonia Vicente Guerrero	2758	30.45 N	116.00 W
Colony	2750	38.04 N	95.22 W
Coloradas, Lomas ⋀[2]	2764	43.15 S	67.20 W
Colorado □[3]	2736	39.30 N	105.30 W
Colorado ≃, Arg.	2764	39.50 S	62.08 W
Colorado ≃, N.A.	2736	31.45 N	114.40 W
Colorado ≃, Tex., U.S.	2748	28.36 N	95.58 W
Colorado City, Ariz., U.S.	2752	36.58 N	112.58 W
Colorado City, Tex., U.S.	2748	32.24 N	100.52 W
Colorado de Abajo	2748	26.28 N	99.54 W
Colorado National Monument ✦	2752	39.04 N	108.25 W
Colorado Plateau ⋀[1]	2752	36.30 N	108.00 W
Colorado Springs	2752	38.50 N	104.49 W
Colotlán	2758	22.06 N	103.16 W
Colquitt	2744	31.10 N	84.44 W
Columbia, Ky., U.S.	2746	37.06 N	85.18 W
Columbia, La., U.S.	2746	32.06 N	92.05 W
Columbia, Miss., U.S.	2746	31.15 N	89.56 W
Columbia, Mo., U.S.	2746	38.57 N	92.20 W
Columbia, N.C., U.S.	2744	35.55 N	76.15 W
Columbia, Pa., U.S.	2740	40.02 N	76.30 W
Columbia, S.C., U.S.	2744	34.00 N	81.03 W
Columbia, Tenn., U.S.	2746	35.37 N	87.02 W
Columbia ≃	2736	46.15 N	124.05 W
Columbia, Mount ∧	2734	52.09 N	117.25 W
Columbia Basin ⩉[1]	2754	46.45 N	119.05 W
Columbia City	2746	41.10 N	85.29 W
Columbia Falls	2754	48.23 N	114.11 W
Columbiana	2746	33.11 N	86.36 W
Columbia Plateau ⋀[1]	2754	44.00 N	117.30 W

Symbols against index entries represent categories identified in the key on page 2810.

Name	Page	Lat °′	Long °′
Columbus, Ga., U.S.	2744	32.29 N	84.59 W
Columbus, Ind., U.S.	2746	39.13 N	85.55 W
Columbus, Kans., U.S.	2750	37.10 N	94.50 W
Columbus, Miss., U.S.	2746	33.30 N	88.25 W
Columbus, Mont., U.S.	2754	45.38 N	109.15 W
Columbus, Nebr., U.S.	2750	41.25 N	97.22 W
Columbus, N. Mex., U.S.	2752	31.50 N	107.38 W
Columbus, N. Dak., U.S.	2750	48.54 N	102.47 W
Columbus, Ohio, U.S.	2740	39.57 N	83.00 W
Columbus, Tex., U.S.	2748	29.42 N	96.33 W
Columbus, Wis., U.S.	2742	43.21 N	89.01 W
Colusa	2756	39.13 N	122.01 W
Colville	2754	48.33 N	117.54 W
Comacchio	2776	44.42 N	12.11 E
Comanche, Okla., U.S.	2748	34.22 N	97.58 W
Comanche, Tex., U.S.	2748	31.54 N	98.36 W
Comandante Fontana	2764	25.20 S	59.41 W
Comayagua	2760	14.25 N	87.37 W
Combarbalá	2764	31.11 S	71.02 W
Combeaufontaine	2772	47.43 N	5.53 E
Combourg	2772	48.25 N	1.45 W
Comer	2744	34.04 N	83.08 W
Comfort	2748	29.58 N	98.49 W
Comilla	2794	23.27 N	91.12 E
Comitán [de Domínguez]	2758	16.15 N	92.08 W
Commentry	2772	46.17 N	2.44 E
Commerce, Ga., U.S.	2744	34.12 N	83.28 W
Commerce, Tex., U.S.	2748	33.15 N	95.54 W
Committee Bay C	2734	68.30 N	86.30 W
Como	2776	45.47 N	9.05 E
Como, Lago di ⊜	2776	46.00 N	9.20 E
Comodoro Rivadavia	2764	45.50 S	67.30 W
Comorin, Cape ❯	2793	8.04 N	77.34 E
Comoro Islands □[1]	2788	12.10 S	44.15 E
Compiègne	2772	49.25 N	2.50 E
Comstock	2748	29.41 N	101.11 W
Čona ≐	2784	62.54 N	111.06 E
Conakry	2786	9.31 N	13.43 W
Concarneau	2772	47.52 N	3.55 W
Conceição do Araguaia	2762	8.15 S	49.17 W
Concepción, Arg.	2764	27.20 S	65.36 W
Concepción, Bol.	2762	16.15 S	62.04 W
Concepción, Chile	2764	36.50 S	73.03 W
Concepción, Para.	2764	23.25 S	57.17 W
Concepción, Laguna ⊜	2762	17.29 S	61.25 W
Concepción, Volcán ▲[1]	2760	11.33 N	85.37 W
Concepcion del Oro	2758	24.38 N	101.25 W
Concepción del Uruguay	2764	32.30 S	58.14 W
Conception, Point ❯	2756	34.27 N	120.27 W
Conches	2772	48.58 N	0.56 E
Conchos ≐	2758	29.32 N	104.25 W
Concord, Calif., U.S.	2756	37.59 N	122.02 W
Concord, N.H., U.S.	2740	43.12 N	71.32 W
Concord, N.C., U.S.	2744	35.25 N	80.35 W
Concordia, Arg.	2764	31.24 S	58.02 W
Concordia, Méx.	2758	23.17 N	106.04 W
Concordia, Kans., U.S.	2750	39.34 N	97.39 W
Condé	2772	48.51 N	0.33 W
Condom	2772	43.58 N	0.22 E
Condon	2754	45.14 N	120.11 W
Conegliano	2776	45.53 N	12.18 E
Conejos	2748	26.14 N	103.53 W
Confolens	2772	46.01 N	0.41 E
Congo □[1]	2788	1.00 S	15.00 E
Congo (Zaire) (Zaïre) ≐	2788	6.04 S	12.24 E
Conitaca	2758	24.10 N	106.43 W
Conn, Lough ⊜	2769	54.04 N	9.20 W
Connaught □[9]	2769	53.45 N	9.00 W
Conneaut	2740	41.57 N	80.34 W
Conneautville	2740	41.36 N	80.18 W
Connecticut □[3]	2736	41.45 N	72.45 W
Connecticut ≐	2740	41.17 N	72.21 W
Connell	2754	46.40 N	118.52 W
Connellsville	2740	40.01 N	79.35 W
Connemara ✦[1]	2769	53.25 N	9.45 W
Connersville	2746	39.39 N	85.08 W
Conrad	2754	48.10 N	111.57 W
Conroe	2748	30.19 N	95.27 W
Conselheiro Lafaiete	2765	20.40 S	43.48 W
Consett	2769	54.51 N	1.49 W
Con Son II	2804	8.43 N	106.36 E
Constance, Lake → Bodensee ⊜	2772	47.35 N	9.25 E
Constanța	2778	44.11 N	28.39 E
Constantina	2774	37.52 N	5.37 W
Constantine	2786	36.22 N	6.37 E
Consuegra	2774	39.28 N	3.36 W
Continental Peak ▲	2754	42.16 N	108.43 W
Contres	2772	47.25 N	1.26 E
Contwoyto Lake ⊜	2734	65.42 N	110.50 W
Conversano	2776	40.58 N	17.08 E
Conway, Ark., U.S.	2746	35.05 N	92.26 W
Conway, Mo., U.S.	2746	37.30 N	92.49 W
Conway, N.H., U.S.	2740	43.59 N	71.07 W
Conway, S.C., U.S.	2744	33.50 N	79.03 W
Conway Springs	2750	37.24 N	97.39 W
Conyers	2744	33.40 N	84.01 W
Cooch Behār	2794	26.19 N	89.26 E
Cook	2750	40.31 N	96.10 W
Cook, Cape ❯	2734	50.08 N	127.55 W
Cook, Mount ▲	2808	43.36 S	170.10 E
Cookeville	2746	36.10 N	85.31 W
Cook Inlet C	2738	60.30 N	152.00 W
Cooks Peak ▲	2752	32.32 N	107.44 W
Cookstown	2769	54.39 N	6.45 W
Cook Strait ꞩ	2808	41.15 S	174.30 E
Cooktown	2806	15.28 S	145.15 E
Coolgardie	2806	30.57 S	121.10 E
Coolidge, Ariz., U.S.	2752	32.59 N	111.31 W
Coolidge, Ga., U.S.	2744	31.01 N	83.52 W
Coolin	2754	48.28 N	116.51 W
Cooma	2806	36.14 S	149.08 E
Coonoor	2793	11.21 N	76.49 E
Coon Rapids, Iowa, U.S.	2750	41.52 N	94.41 W
Coon Rapids, Minn., U.S.	2742	45.09 N	93.18 W
Cooper	2748	33.23 N	95.35 W
Cooperstown, N. Dak., U.S.	2750	47.27 N	98.07 W
Cooperstown, N.Y., U.S.	2740	42.42 N	74.56 W
Coos Bay	2754	43.22 N	124.13 W
Copano Bay C	2748	28.05 N	97.05 W
Copeland	2744	25.57 N	81.22 W
Copenhagen → København	2768	55.40 N	12.35 E
Copiapó	2764	27.22 S	70.20 W
Copparo	2776	44.54 N	11.49 E
Copperas Cove	2748	31.08 N	97.54 W
Copper Harbor	2742	47.27 N	87.53 W
Coppermine	2734	67.50 N	115.05 W
Coppermine ≐	2734	67.49 N	115.04 W
Copper Mountain ▲	2754	43.27 N	107.57 W
Coquille	2754	43.11 N	124.11 W
Coquimbo	2764	29.58 S	71.21 W
Coral Gables	2744	25.45 N	80.16 W
Coral Harbour	2734	64.08 N	83.10 W
Coral Sea ⊤[2]	2806	20.00 S	158.00 E
Corato	2776	41.09 N	16.25 E
Corbeil-Essonnes	2772	48.36 N	2.29 E
Corbigny	2772	47.15 N	3.40 E
Corby	2769	52.29 N	0.40 W
Corcoran	2756	36.06 N	119.33 W
Corcovado, Golfo C	2764	43.30 S	73.20 W
Corcovado, Volcán ▲[1]	2764	43.12 S	72.48 W
Corcubión	2774	42.57 N	9.11 W
Cordele	2744	31.58 N	83.47 W
Cordell	2748	35.17 N	98.59 W
Córdoba, Arg.	2764	31.25 S	64.10 W
Córdoba, Esp.	2774	37.53 N	4.46 W
Córdoba, Méx.	2758	18.53 N	96.56 W
Cordova	2746	33.46 N	87.11 W
Corfu → Kérkira	2778	39.36 N	19.56 E
Coria	2774	39.59 N	6.32 W
Coria del Rio	2774	37.16 N	6.03 W
Corigliano Calabro	2776	39.36 N	16.31 E
Coringa Islets II	2806	16.58 S	149.58 E
Corinth → Kórinthos, Ellás	2778	37.56 N	22.56 E
Corinth, Miss., U.S.	2746	34.56 N	88.31 W
Corinto	2765	18.21 S	44.27 W
Cork	2769	51.54 N	8.28 W
Corlay	2772	48.19 N	3.03 W
Corleone	2776	37.49 N	13.18 E
Corleto Perticara	2776	40.23 N	16.03 E
Çorlu	2778	41.09 N	27.48 E
Cornelia	2744	34.31 N	83.32 W
Corner Brook	2734	48.57 N	57.57 W
Corning, Ark., U.S.	2746	36.24 N	90.35 W
Corning, Calif., U.S.	2756	39.56 N	122.11 W
Corning, Iowa, U.S.	2750	40.59 N	94.44 W
Corning, N.Y., U.S.	2740	42.09 N	77.04 W
Cornish	2740	43.48 N	70.48 W
Corn Islands II	2760	12.15 N	83.00 W
Cornwall	2740	45.02 N	74.44 W
Cornwallis Island I	2734	75.15 N	94.30 W
Coro	2760	11.25 N	69.41 W
Corocoro	2762	17.12 S	68.29 W
Coroico	2762	16.10 S	67.50 W
Coromandel Coast ⩡[2]	2793	14.00 N	80.10 E
Coromandel Peninsula ❯[1]	2808	36.50 S	175.35 E
Corona	2752	34.15 N	105.36 W
Coronado	2756	32.41 N	117.11 W
Coronation Gulf C	2734	68.25 N	110.00 W
Coronel Dorrego	2764	38.45 S	61.17 W
Coronel Fabriciano	2765	19.31 S	42.38 W
Coronel Pringles	2764	38.00 S	61.20 W
Coronel Suárez	2764	37.25 S	61.56 W
Coropuna, Nevado ▲	2762	15.30 S	72.41 W
Corpus Christi	2748	27.48 N	97.24 W
Corpus Christi, Lake ⊜[1]	2748	28.10 N	97.53 W
Corpus Christi Bay C	2748	27.48 N	97.20 W
Corral de Almaguer	2774	39.46 N	3.11 W
Corralitos	2748	26.57 N	104.39 W
Correggio	2776	44.46 N	10.47 E
Corrib, Lough ⊜	2769	53.05 N	9.10 W
Corrientes	2764	27.30 S	58.50 W
Corrientes, Cabo ❯, Col.	2762	5.30 N	77.34 W
Corrientes, Cabo ❯, Méx.	2758	20.25 N	105.42 W
Corrigan	2746	30.59 N	94.50 W
Corry	2740	41.56 N	73.39 W
Corsica	2750	43.25 N	98.24 W
Corsicana	2748	32.06 N	96.28 W
Corte	2776	42.18 N	9.08 E
Cortemilia	2776	44.35 N	8.12 E
Cortez	2752	37.21 N	108.35 W
Cortina d'Ampezzo	2776	46.32 N	12.08 E
Čortkov	2782	49.01 N	25.48 E
Cortland	2740	42.36 N	76.11 W
Çorum	2766	40.33 N	34.58 E
Corumbá	2762	19.01 S	57.39 W
Corvallis	2754	44.34 N	123.16 W
Corydon, Ind., U.S.	2746	38.13 N	86.07 W
Corydon, Iowa, U.S.	2742	40.45 N	93.19 W
Corydon, Ky., U.S.	2746	37.44 N	87.43 W
Cosamaloapan [de Carpio]	2758	18.22 N	95.48 W
Cosenza	2776	39.17 N	16.15 E
Coshocton	2740	40.16 N	81.51 W
Cosmoledo Group II	2788	9.43 S	47.35 E
Cosne-sur-Loire	2772	47.24 N	2.55 E
Costa Mesa	2756	33.39 N	117.55 W
Costa Rica	2758	28.55 N	111.36 W
Costa Rica □[1]	2760	10.00 N	84.10 W
Costiera, Catena ⩕	2776	39.20 N	16.05 E
Costilla	2752	36.59 N	105.32 W
Cotabato	2802	7.13 N	124.15 E
Cotonou	2786	6.21 N	2.26 E
Cotopaxi ▲[1]	2762	0.40 S	78.26 W
Cottage Grove	2754	43.48 N	123.03 W
Cottondale, Ala., U.S.	2746	33.11 N	87.27 W
Cottondale, Fla., U.S.	2746	30.48 N	85.23 W
Cotton Valley	2746	32.49 N	93.25 W
Cottonwood, Ariz., U.S.	2752	34.45 N	112.01 W
Cottonwood, Idaho, U.S.	2754	46.03 N	116.21 W
Cottonwood Falls	2750	38.22 N	96.32 W
Cotulla	2748	28.26 N	99.14 W
Coudersport	2740	41.46 N	78.01 W
Couhé	2772	46.18 N	0.11 E
Coulee City	2754	47.37 N	119.17 W
Coulommiers	2772	48.49 N	3.05 E
Council	2754	44.44 N	116.26 W
Council Bluffs	2750	41.16 N	95.52 W
Council Grove	2750	38.40 N	96.29 W
Country Homes	2754	47.45 N	117.24 W
Courtland	2744	36.43 N	77.04 W
Coushatta	2746	32.00 N	93.21 W
Coutances	2772	49.03 N	1.26 W
Coutras	2772	45.02 N	0.08 W
Covelo	2756	39.48 N	123.15 W
Coventry	2769	52.25 N	1.30 W
Covered Wells	2752	32.10 N	112.08 W
Covilhã	2774	40.17 N	7.30 W
Covington, Ind., U.S.	2746	40.09 N	87.24 W
Covington, Ky., U.S.	2740	39.05 N	84.30 W
Covington, La., U.S.	2746	30.29 N	90.06 W
Covington, Ohio, U.S.	2740	40.07 N	84.21 W
Covington, Okla., U.S.	2748	36.18 N	97.35 W
Covington, Tenn., U.S.	2746	35.34 N	89.38 W
Covington, Va., U.S.	2744	37.47 N	79.59 W
Cowan, Lake ⊜	2806	31.50 S	121.50 E
Cowansville	2740	45.12 N	72.45 W
Coward	2744	33.58 N	79.45 W
Cowen	2740	38.25 N	80.34 W
Coxim	2765	18.30 S	54.45 W
Coxsackie	2740	42.21 N	73.48 W
Cox's Bāzār	2794	21.26 N	91.59 E
Coyhaique	2764	45.34 S	72.04 W
Cozad	2750	40.52 N	99.59 W
Cozumel, Isla de I	2758	20.25 N	86.55 W
Crab Orchard	2744	37.28 N	84.30 W
Cradock	2788	32.08 S	25.36 E
Craig	2752	40.31 N	107.33 W
Craigmont	2754	46.15 N	116.28 W
Craiova	2778	44.19 N	23.48 E
Cranbrook	2734	49.31 N	115.46 W
Crandon	2742	45.34 N	88.54 W
Crane, Ind., U.S.	2746	38.54 N	86.54 W
Crane, Tex., U.S.	2748	31.24 N	102.21 W
Crane Mountain ▲	2754	42.04 N	120.13 W
Cranston	2740	41.47 N	71.26 W
Craon	2772	47.51 N	0.57 W
Craponne	2772	45.20 N	3.51 E
Crater Lake ⊜	2754	42.56 N	122.06 W
Crater Lake National Park ♦	2754	42.49 N	122.08 W
Craters of the Moon National Monument ♦	2754	43.20 N	113.35 W
Cratéus	2762	5.10 S	40.40 W
Crato	2762	7.14 S	39.23 W
Crauford, Cape ❯	2734	73.43 N	84.50 W
Crawford	2750	42.41 N	103.25 W
Crawfordsville	2746	40.02 N	86.54 W
Crawley	2769	51.07 N	0.12 W
Crazy Mountains ⩕	2754	46.08 N	110.20 W
Crazy Woman Creek ≐	2754	44.29 N	106.08 W
Cree ≐	2734	59.00 N	105.47 W
Cree Lake ⊜	2734	57.30 N	106.30 W
Creighton	2750	42.28 N	97.54 W
Creil	2772	49.16 N	2.29 E
Crema	2776	45.22 N	9.41 E
Cremona	2776	45.07 N	10.02 E
Crenshaw	2746	34.30 N	90.12 W
Crépy-en-Valois	2772	49.14 N	2.54 E
Cres	2776	44.58 N	14.25 E
Crescent	2748	35.57 N	97.36 W
Crescent City, Calif., U.S.	2756	41.45 N	124.12 W
Crescent City, Fla., U.S.	2744	29.26 N	81.30 W
Crescent Group II	2802	16.31 N	111.38 E
Cresco	2742	43.22 N	92.07 W
Crestline	2740	40.47 N	82.44 W
Creston	2750	41.04 N	94.22 W
Crestone Peak ▲	2752	37.58 N	105.36 W
Crete	2750	40.38 N	96.58 W
Crete → Kríti I	2778	35.29 N	24.42 E
Crevillente	2774	38.15 N	0.48 W
Crewe, Eng., U.K.	2769	53.05 N	2.27 W
Crewe, Va., U.S.	2744	37.05 N	78.08 W
Criciúma	2764	28.40 S	49.23 W
Crikvenica	2776	45.11 N	14.42 E
Crimea → Krymskij Poluostrov ❯[1]	2782	45.00 N	34.00 E
Cripple Creek	2752	38.45 N	105.11 W
Crisfield	2744	37.59 N	75.51 W
Cristalândia	2762	10.36 S	49.11 W
Cristalina	2765	16.45 S	47.36 W
Cristianópolis	2765	17.13 S	48.45 W
Cristóbal	2760	9.20 N	79.55 W
Cristóbal Colón, Pico ▲	2760	10.50 N	73.45 W
Črnomelj	2776	45.34 N	15.11 E
Crocker	2746	37.57 N	92.16 W
Crockett	2748	31.19 N	95.28 W
Crofton, Ky., U.S.	2746	37.03 N	87.29 W
Crofton, Nebr., U.S.	2750	42.44 N	97.30 W
Croker Island I	2806	11.12 S	132.32 E
Cromarty	2769	57.40 N	4.02 W
Crooked Island I	2760	22.45 N	74.12 W
Crooked Island Passage ꞩ	2760	23.00 N	74.30 W
Crookston	2750	47.47 N	96.37 W
Crosby, Minn., U.S.	2742	46.28 N	93.57 W
Crosby, Miss., U.S.	2746	31.17 N	91.04 W
Crosby, Mount ▲	2754	43.53 N	109.20 W
Crosbyton	2748	33.40 N	101.14 W
Cross City	2744	29.39 N	83.07 W
Crossett	2746	33.08 N	91.58 W
Crossman Peak ▲	2752	34.32 N	114.07 W
Cross Plains	2748	32.08 N	99.11 W
Crossville	2746	35.58 N	85.02 W
Crotone	2776	39.05 N	17.07 E
Crow Agency	2754	45.36 N	107.27 W
Crowell	2748	33.59 N	99.43 W
Crowley	2746	30.13 N	92.22 W
Crown Point, Ind., U.S.	2746	41.25 N	87.22 W
Crown Point, N.Y., U.S.	2740	43.57 N	73.25 W
Crown Prince Frederick Island I	2734	70.02 N	86.50 W
Croydon	2806	18.12 S	142.14 E
Crozet	2740	38.04 N	78.42 W
Crozon	2772	48.15 N	4.29 W
Cruces	2760	22.21 N	80.16 W
Cruz Alta	2764	28.39 S	53.36 W
Cruz del Eje	2764	30.44 S	64.49 W
Cruzeiro do Sul	2762	7.38 S	72.36 W
Crystal	2742	45.00 N	93.25 W
Crystal City, Mo., U.S.	2746	38.13 N	90.23 W
Crystal City, Tex., U.S.	2748	28.41 N	99.50 W
Crystal Falls	2742	46.05 N	88.20 W
Crystal Lake	2742	42.14 N	88.19 W
Crystal Lake ⊜	2742	44.40 N	86.10 W
Crystal River	2744	28.54 N	82.36 W
Crystal Springs	2746	31.59 N	90.21 W
Cuando (Kwando) ≐	2788	18.27 S	23.32 E
Cuangar	2788	17.36 S	18.39 E
Cuango	2788	6.17 S	16.41 E
Cuango (Kwango) ≐	2788	3.14 S	17.23 E
Cuanza ≐	2788	9.19 S	13.08 E
Cuauhtémoc	2758	28.25 N	106.52 W
Cuautla	2758	18.48 N	98.57 W
Cuba, Port.	2774	38.10 N	7.53 W
Cuba, Kans., U.S.	2750	39.48 N	97.27 W
Cuba, Mo., U.S.	2746	38.04 N	91.24 W
Cuba, N. Mex., U.S.	2752	36.01 N	107.04 W
Cuba □[1]	2760	21.30 N	79.00 W
Cubango (Okavango) ≐	2788	18.50 S	22.25 E
Cucharas	2758	22.52 N	105.19 W
Cúcuta	2760	7.54 N	72.31 W
Cudahy	2742	42.57 N	87.52 W
Cuddalore	2793	11.45 N	79.45 E
Cuddapah	2793	14.28 N	78.49 E
Cuddy Mountain ▲	2754	44.46 N	116.47 W
Čudskoje Ozero (Peipsi Järv) ⊜	2780	58.45 N	27.30 E
Cuéllar	2774	41.25 N	4.19 W
Cuenca, Ec.	2762	2.53 S	78.59 W
Cuenca, Esp.	2774	40.04 N	2.08 W
Cuencamé [de Ceniceros]	2758	24.53 N	103.42 W
Cuernavaca	2758	18.55 N	99.15 W
Cuero	2748	29.06 N	97.18 W
Cuers	2772	43.14 N	6.04 E
Cuervos	2758	32.38 N	114.52 W
Cuevas del Almanzora	2774	37.18 N	1.53 W
Cuglieri	2776	40.11 N	8.34 E
Cuiabá	2762	15.35 S	56.05 W
Cuiseaux	2772	46.30 N	5.24 E
Cuito ≐	2788	18.01 S	20.48 E
Cuito-Cuanavale	2788	15.10 S	19.10 E
Čukotskij, Mys ❯	2784	64.14 N	173.10 W
Čukotskij Poluostrov ❯[1]	2784	66.00 N	175.00 W
Culbertson, Mont., U.S.	2750	48.09 N	104.31 W
Culbertson, Nebr., U.S.	2750	40.14 N	100.50 W
Culiacán	2758	24.48 N	107.24 W
Cullman	2746	34.11 N	86.51 W
Čul'man	2784	56.52 N	124.52 E
Culpeper	2740	38.28 N	77.53 W
Čulym	2784	55.06 N	80.58 E
Cumalı	2778	36.42 N	27.27 E
Cumaná	2760	10.28 N	64.10 W
Cumbal, Volcán de ▲[1]	2762	0.57 N	77.52 W
Cumberland, Ky., U.S.	2744	36.59 N	82.59 W
Cumberland, Md., U.S.	2740	39.39 N	78.46 W
Cumberland, Va., U.S.	2744	37.30 N	78.15 W
Cumberland ≐	2744	36.18 N	85.55 W
Cumberland, Lake ⊜[1]	2746	36.57 N	84.55 W
Cumberland Gap)(	2744	36.36 N	83.41 W
Cumberland Islands II	2806	20.40 S	149.09 E
Cumberland Peninsula ❯[1]	2734	66.50 N	64.00 W
Cumberland Plateau ⩕[1]	2744	36.30 N	84.20 W
Cumberland Sound ꞩ	2734	65.10 N	65.30 W
Čumikan	2784	54.42 N	135.19 E
Cumming	2744	34.13 N	84.08 W
Cumnock	2769	55.27 N	4.16 W
Čun'a ≐, S.S.S.R.	2784	61.36 N	96.30 E
Čuna ≐, S.S.S.R.	2784	57.47 N	95.26 E
Cunani	2762	2.52 N	51.06 W
Cunene ≐	2788	17.20 S	11.50 E
Cuneo	2776	44.23 N	7.32 E
Cunnamulla	2806	28.04 S	145.41 E
Cunningham	2750	37.39 N	98.26 W
Curaçao I	2760	12.11 N	69.00 W
Curepipe	2788	20.19 S	57.31 E
Curicó	2764	34.59 S	71.14 W
Curitiba	2764	25.25 S	49.15 W
Curralinho	2762	1.48 S	49.47 W
Curtis	2750	40.38 N	100.31 W
Curvelo	2765	18.45 S	44.25 W
Curwensville	2740	40.58 N	78.32 W
Cushing	2748	35.59 N	96.46 W
Čusovoj	2766	58.17 N	57.49 E
Cusseta	2744	32.18 N	84.47 W
Custer, Mont., U.S.	2754	46.08 N	107.33 W
Custer, S. Dak., U.S.	2750	43.46 N	103.36 W
Cut Bank	2754	48.38 N	112.20 W
Cuthbert	2744	31.46 N	84.48 W
Cutro	2776	39.02 N	16.59 E
Cuttack	2794	20.30 N	85.50 E
Cuyahoga Falls	2740	41.08 N	81.29 W
Cuyo Islands II	2802	11.04 N	120.57 E
Cuzco	2762	13.31 S	71.59 W
Cynthiana	2740	38.23 N	84.18 W
Cyprus □[1]	2791	35.00 N	33.00 E
Czechoslovakia □[1]	2766	49.30 N	17.00 E
Częstochowa	2770	50.49 N	19.06 E

Symbols against index entries represent categories identified in the key on page 2810.

Symbols against index entries represent categories identified in the key on page 2810.

Name	Page	Lat °′	Long °′
Dolisie	2788	4.12 S	12.41 E
Dolo	2790	4.13 N	42.08 E
Dolomites			
→ Dolomiti ⛰	2776	46.25 N	11.50 E
Dolomiti ⛰	2776	46.25 N	11.50 E
Dolores, Arg.	2764	36.19 S	57.40 W
Dolores, Méx.	2748	26.20 N	101.29 W
Dolores, Colo., U.S.	2752	37.28 N	108.30 W
Dolores Hidalgo	2758	21.10 N	100.56 W
Dolphin and Union Strait ≍	2734	69.05 N	114.45 W
Dombås	2768	62.05 N	9.08 E
Domeyko	2764	28.57 S	70.54 W
Domeyko, Cordillera ⛰	2764	24.30 S	69.00 W
Dominica □[1]	2760	15.20 N	61.25 W
Dominica Channel ≍	2760	15.10 N	61.15 W
Dominican Republic □[1]	2760	19.00 N	70.40 W
Dominion, Cape ≻	2734	66.13 N	74.28 W
Domodedovo	2780	55.26 N	37.46 E
Domodossola	2776	46.07 N	8.17 E
Domžale	2776	46.08 N	14.36 E
Don ≃	2766	47.04 N	39.18 E
Donaldson	2746	34.14 N	92.55 W
Donaldsonville	2746	30.06 N	90.59 W
Donau			
→ Danube ≃	2766	45.20 N	29.40 E
Don Benito	2774	38.57 N	5.52 W
Doncaster	2769	53.32 N	1.07 W
Dondo	2788	9.38 S	14.25 E
Donecr	2782	48.00 N	37.48 E
Donegal Bay C	2769	54.30 N	8.30 W
Donga ≃	2786	8.19 N	9.58 E
Dongara	2806	29.15 S	114.56 E
Dongchuan	2804	26.10 N	103.01 E
Dongfang	2796	19.05 N	108.39 E
Dongguan	2800	23.03 N	113.46 E
Donghai (Haizhou)	2800	34.34 N	119.11 E
Donghaidao I	2804	21.02 N	110.25 E
Dong-hoi	2804	17.29 N	106.36 E
Dongshan	2800	23.46 N	117.31 E
Dongshaqundao (Pratas Islands) II	2796	20.42 N	116.43 E
Dongtai	2800	32.51 N	120.20 E
Dongtinghu ⊜	2800	29.20 N	112.54 E
Don Martín	2748	27.32 N	100.37 W
Donskoj	2780	53.58 N	38.20 E
Door Peninsula ≻[1]	2742	44.55 N	87.20 W
Dorchester	2769	50.43 N	2.26 W
Dorchester, Cape ≻	2734	65.29 N	77.30 W
Dordogne □[5]	2772	45.10 N	0.45 E
Dordrecht	2770	51.49 N	4.40 E
Dores do Indaiá	2765	19.27 S	45.36 W
Dorgali	2776	40.17 N	9.35 E
Dori	2786	14.02 N	0.02 W
Dornbirn	2770	47.25 N	9.44 E
Dorris	2756	41.58 N	121.55 W
Dos Bahías, Cabo ≻	2764	44.55 S	65.32 W
Dos Palos	2756	36.59 N	120.37 W
Dothan	2746	31.13 N	85.24 W
Douai	2772	50.22 N	3.04 E
Douala	2786	4.03 N	9.42 E
Douarnenez	2772	48.06 N	4.20 W
Double Springs	2746	34.09 N	87.24 W
Doubletop Peak ▲	2754	43.21 N	110.17 W
Douglas, I. of Man	2769	54.09 N	4.28 W
Douglas, Ariz., U.S.	2752	31.21 N	109.33 W
Douglas, Ga., U.S.	2744	31.31 N	82.51 W
Douglass	2750	37.31 N	97.01 W
Dourados	2765	22.13 S	54.48 W
Dove Creek	2752	37.46 N	108.54 W
Dover, Eng., U.K.	2769	51.08 N	1.19 E
Dover, Del., U.S.	2740	39.10 N	75.32 W
Dover, N.H., U.S.	2740	43.12 N	70.56 W
Dover, N.J., U.S.	2740	40.53 N	74.34 W
Dover, N.C., U.S.	2744	35.13 N	77.26 W
Dover, Ohio, U.S.	2740	40.32 N	81.29 W
Dover, Tenn., U.S.	2746	36.29 N	87.50 W
Dover, Strait of (Pas de Calais) ≍	2769	51.00 N	1.30 E
Dover-Foxcroft	2740	45.11 N	69.13 W
Dowagiac	2742	41.59 N	86.06 W
Downey	2754	42.26 N	112.07 W
Downpatrick	2769	54.20 N	5.43 W
Downpatrick Head ≻	2769	54.20 N	9.20 W
Downs	2750	39.30 N	98.33 W
Downs Mountain ▲	2754	43.18 N	109.40 W
Doylestown	2740	40.19 N	75.08 W
Drâa, Oued ∨	2786	28.43 N	11.09 W
Drachten	2770	53.06 N	6.05 E
Dragoon	2752	32.02 N	110.02 W
Draguignan	2772	43.32 N	6.28 E
Drain	2754	43.40 N	123.19 W
Drake	2750	47.55 N	100.23 W
Drake Peak ▲	2754	42.19 N	120.07 W
Dráma	2778	41.09 N	24.08 E
Drammen	2768	59.44 N	10.15 E
Draper	2752	40.32 N	111.52 W
Drau (Drava) ≃	2766	45.33 N	18.55 E
Drava (Drau) ≃	2766	45.33 N	18.55 E
Drayton	2750	48.38 N	97.11 W
Drayton Valley	2734	53.13 N	114.59 W
Dresden	2740	40.07 N	82.01 W
Dreux	2772	48.44 N	1.22 E
Driggs	2754	43.44 N	111.14 W
Drogheda	2769	53.43 N	6.21 W
Drumheller	2734	51.28 N	112.42 W
Drummond, Mont., U.S.	2754	46.40 N	113.09 W
Drummond, Wis., U.S.	2742	46.20 N	91.15 W
Drummond Island I	2742	46.00 N	83.40 W
Drummondville	2740	45.53 N	72.29 W
Drumright	2748	35.59 N	96.36 W
Družina	2784	68.14 N	145.18 E
Dryden, Ont., Can.	2734	49.47 N	92.50 W
Dryden, Tex., U.S.	2748	30.03 N	102.07 W
Dry Tortugas II	2744	24.38 N	82.55 W
Duarte, Pico ▲	2760	19.00 N	71.00 W
Dubach	2746	32.42 N	92.39 W
Dubai			
→ Dubayy	2790	25.18 N	55.18 E
Dubawnt ≃	2734	64.33 N	100.06 W
Dubawnt Lake ⊜	2734	63.08 N	101.30 W
Dubayy	2790	25.18 N	55.18 E
Dubbo	2806	32.15 S	148.36 E
Dublin (Baile Átha Cliath), Eire	2769	53.20 N	6.15 W
Dublin, Ga., U.S.	2744	32.32 N	82.54 W
Dublin, Tex., U.S.	2748	32.05 N	98.21 W
Dubna	2780	56.44 N	37.10 E
Dubno	2782	50.26 N	25.44 E
Dubois, Idaho, U.S.	2754	44.10 N	112.14 W
Du Bois, Pa., U.S.	2740	41.07 N	78.46 W
Dubois, Wyo., U.S.	2754	43.33 N	109.38 W
Dubossary	2782	47.07 N	29.10 E
Dubrovnik	2776	42.38 N	18.07 E
Dubuque	2742	42.30 N	90.41 W
Duchesne	2752	40.10 N	110.24 W
Duchess	2806	21.22 S	139.52 E
Ducktown	2744	35.03 N	84.23 W
Dudelange	2770	49.28 N	6.05 E
Dudinka	2784	69.25 N	86.15 E
Duero (Douro) ≃	2766	41.08 N	8.40 W
Due West	2744	34.20 N	82.23 W
Dufour Spitze ▲	2776	45.55 N	7.52 E
Dufur	2754	45.27 N	121.08 W
Duga Resa	2776	45.27 N	15.30 E
Duifken Point ≻	2806	12.33 S	141.38 E
Duitama	2762	5.50 N	73.02 W
Duk Fadiat	2786	7.45 N	31.25 E
Dulce	2752	36.56 N	107.00 W
Dulgalach ≃	2784	67.44 N	133.12 E
Duluth, Ga., U.S.	2744	34.00 N	84.09 W
Duluth, Minn., U.S.	2742	46.47 N	92.06 W
Dūmā	2791	33.35 N	36.24 E
Dumaguete	2802	9.18 N	123.18 E
Dumaran Island I	2802	10.33 N	119.51 E
Dumaring	2802	1.36 N	118.12 E
Dumas, Ark., U.S.	2746	33.53 N	91.29 W
Dumas, Tex., U.S.	2748	35.52 N	101.58 W
Dumbarton	2769	55.57 N	4.35 W
Dumfries	2769	55.04 N	3.37 W
Dumyâṭ	2786	31.25 N	31.48 E
Dunaújváros	2770	46.58 N	18.57 E
Duncan, Ariz., U.S.	2752	32.43 N	109.06 W
Duncan, Miss., U.S.	2746	34.03 N	90.45 W
Duncan, Okla., U.S.	2748	34.30 N	97.57 W
Duncannon	2740	40.23 N	77.02 W
Dundalk	2769	54.01 N	6.25 W
Dundas	2740	43.16 N	79.58 W
Dundas Peninsula ≻[1]	2734	74.50 N	111.30 W
Dundee, S. Afr.	2788	28.12 S	30.16 E
Dundee, Scot., U.K.	2769	56.28 N	3.00 W
Dunedin, N.Z.	2808	45.52 S	170.30 E
Dunedin, Fla., U.S.	2744	28.00 N	82.47 W
Dunfermline	2769	56.04 N	3.29 W
Dungarvan	2769	52.05 N	7.37 W
Dunhua	2796	43.21 N	128.13 E
Dunkerque	2772	51.03 N	2.22 E
Dunkirk, Ind., U.S.	2746	40.23 N	85.13 W
Dunkirk, N.Y., U.S.	2740	42.29 N	79.20 W
Dunkirk, Ohio, U.S.	2740	40.48 N	83.39 W
Dunkwa	2786	5.22 N	1.12 W
Dún Laoghaire	2769	53.17 N	6.08 W
Dunlap, Iowa, U.S.	2750	41.51 N	95.36 W
Dunlap, Tenn., U.S.	2746	35.23 N	85.23 W
Dunmore	2740	41.25 N	75.38 W
Dunmore Town	2744	25.30 N	76.39 W
Dunn	2744	35.19 N	78.37 W
Dunnellon	2744	29.03 N	82.28 W
Dunning	2750	41.50 N	100.06 W
Dunnville	2740	42.54 N	79.36 W
Dunqulah	2786	19.10 N	30.29 E
Duns	2769	55.47 N	2.20 W
Dunseith	2750	48.50 N	100.02 W
Dunsmuir	2756	41.13 N	122.16 W
Duntou	2800	29.21 N	119.46 E
Duomaer	2796	34.15 N	79.45 E
Dupree	2750	45.03 N	101.36 W
Duque de Caxias	2765	22.47 S	43.18 W
Duque de York, Isla I	2764	50.37 S	75.25 W
DuQuoin	2746	38.01 N	89.14 W
Durand, Mich., U.S.	2742	42.55 N	83.59 W
Durand, Wis., U.S.	2742	44.38 N	91.58 W
Durango, Esp.	2774	43.10 N	2.37 W
Durango, Méx.	2758	24.02 N	104.40 W
Durango, Colo., U.S.	2752	37.16 N	107.53 W
Durant, Miss., U.S.	2746	33.04 N	89.51 W
Durant, Okla., U.S.	2748	34.00 N	96.23 W
Durazno	2764	33.22 S	56.31 W
Durban	2788	29.55 S	30.56 E
Đurđevac	2776	46.03 N	17.04 E
Durg	2793	21.11 N	81.17 E
Durgāpur	2794	23.29 N	87.20 E
Durham, Eng., U.K.	2769	54.47 N	1.34 W
Durham, Calif., U.S.	2756	39.44 N	121.48 W
Durham, N.H., U.S.	2740	43.08 N	70.56 W
Durham, N.C., U.S.	2744	35.59 N	78.54 W
Durness	2769	58.33 N	4.45 W
Durrës	2778	41.19 N	19.26 E
Dursunbey	2778	39.35 N	28.38 E
Dušekan	2784	60.39 N	109.03 E
Dushan	2804	25.53 N	107.30 E
Dushore	2740	41.31 N	76.24 W
Dutch John	2752	40.55 N	109.24 W
Duyun	2804	26.12 N	107.31 E
Dvuch Cirkoje, Gora ▲	2784	67.35 N	168.07 E
Dwight	2746	41.05 N	88.26 W
Dyer	2746	36.04 N	88.59 W
Dyer, Cape ≻	2734	66.37 N	61.18 W
Dyer Bay C	2740	45.10 N	81.18 W
Dyersburg	2746	36.03 N	89.23 W
Dyersville	2742	42.29 N	91.08 W
Džalinda	2784	53.29 N	123.54 E
Džambejty	2766	50.16 N	52.35 E
Džankoj	2782	45.43 N	34.24 E
Džanybek	2766	49.25 N	46.51 E
Dzaoudzi	2788	12.47 S	45.17 E
Džardžan	2784	68.43 N	124.02 E
Dzavchan ≃	2796	48.54 N	93.23 E
Dzeržinsk	2780	56.15 N	43.24 E
Dzeržinskoje	2784	45.50 N	81.07 E
Džetygara	2766	52.11 N	61.12 E
Dzierżoniów (Reichenbach)	2770	50.44 N	16.39 E
Džugdžur, Chrebet ⛰	2784	58.00 N	136.00 E
E			
Eads	2750	38.29 N	102.47 W
Eagle	2752	39.39 N	106.50 W
Eagle Bend	2750	46.10 N	95.03 W
Eagle Grove	2742	42.40 N	93.54 W
Eagle Lake, Maine, U.S.	2739	47.02 N	68.36 W
Eagle Lake, Tex., U.S.	2748	29.35 N	96.20 W
Eagle Mountain ▲[2]	2742	47.54 N	90.33 W
Eagle Nest Butte ▲	2750	43.27 N	101.39 W
Eagle Pass	2748	28.43 N	100.30 W
Eagle River, Mich., U.S.	2742	47.24 N	88.18 W
Eagle River, Wis., U.S.	2742	45.55 N	89.15 W
Eagle Rock	2744	37.38 N	79.48 W
Earlimart	2756	35.53 N	119.16 W
Earlington	2746	37.16 N	87.30 W
Easley	2744	34.50 N	82.36 W
East Angus	2740	45.29 N	71.40 W
East Aurora	2740	42.46 N	78.37 W
Eastbourne	2769	50.46 N	0.17 E
East Brewton	2746	31.05 N	87.04 W
East Chicago	2746	41.38 N	87.27 W
East China Sea ⊤[2]	2796	30.00 N	126.00 E
Eastern Ghāts ⛰	2793	14.00 N	78.50 E
East Falkland I	2764	51.45 S	58.50 W
East Glacier Park	2754	48.27 N	113.13 W
East Grand Forks	2750	47.56 N	97.01 W
East Grand Rapids	2742	42.56 N	85.35 W
East Helena	2754	46.35 N	111.56 W
East Jordan	2742	45.10 N	85.07 W
Eastland	2748	32.24 N	98.49 W
East Lansing	2742	42.44 N	84.29 W
East Liverpool	2740	40.38 N	80.35 W
East London (Oos-Londen)	2788	33.00 S	27.55 E
Eastmain	2734	52.15 N	78.30 W
Eastmain ≃	2734	52.15 N	78.35 W
Eastman	2744	32.12 N	83.11 W
East Millinocket	2740	45.37 N	68.35 W
East Moline	2746	41.31 N	90.25 W
Easton, Md., U.S.	2740	38.46 N	76.04 W
Easton, Pa., U.S.	2740	40.42 N	75.12 W
Eastover	2744	33.52 N	80.41 W
East Palatka	2744	29.40 N	81.35 W
East Palestine	2740	40.50 N	80.33 W
East Peoria	2746	40.40 N	89.34 W
East Point	2744	33.40 N	84.27 W
Eastport	2740	44.54 N	67.00 W
East Prairie	2746	36.47 N	89.23 W
East Saint Louis	2746	38.38 N	90.08 W
East Stroudsburg	2740	41.00 N	75.11 W
Eaton Rapids	2742	42.36 N	84.39 W
Eatonton	2744	33.20 N	83.23 W
Eau Claire	2742	44.49 N	91.31 W
Eau-Claire, Lac à l' ⊜	2734	56.10 N	74.25 W
Eauripik I[1]	2802	6.42 N	143.03 E
Eauze	2772	43.52 N	0.06 E
Ebano	2758	22.13 N	98.22 W
Ebba Ksour	2776	35.57 N	8.50 E
Ebbw Vale	2769	51.47 N	3.12 W
Eben Junction	2742	46.21 N	86.58 W
Ebensburg	2740	40.29 N	78.44 W
Eberndorf	2770	46.35 N	14.38 E
Ebetsu	2798a	43.07 N	141.34 E
Eboli	2776	40.37 N	15.04 E
Ebolowa	2786	2.54 N	11.09 E
Ebro ≃	2774	40.43 N	0.54 E
Ebro, Delta del ≃[2]	2774	40.43 N	0.54 E
Écija	2774	37.32 N	5.05 W
Eckert	2752	38.51 N	107.58 W
Eclipse Sound ≍	2734	72.38 N	79.00 W
Écommoy	2772	47.50 N	0.16 E
Ecuador □[1]	2762	2.00 S	77.30 W
Ed	2768	58.55 N	11.55 E
Ede	2770	52.03 N	5.40 E
Edéa	2786	3.48 N	10.08 E
Eden, Tex., U.S.	2748	31.13 N	99.51 W
Eden, Wyo., U.S.	2754	42.03 N	109.26 W
Edenderry	2769	53.21 N	7.35 W
Edenton	2744	36.04 N	76.39 W
Edgar	2750	40.22 N	97.58 W
Edgartown	2740	41.23 N	70.31 W
Edgefield	2744	33.47 N	81.56 W
Edgeley	2750	46.22 N	98.43 W
Edgemont	2750	43.18 N	103.50 W
Edgerton, Ohio, U.S.	2740	41.27 N	84.45 W
Edgerton, Wis., U.S.	2742	42.50 N	89.04 W
Edgerton, Wyo., U.S.	2754	43.25 N	106.15 W
Edgewood	2746	38.55 N	88.40 W
Edina	2742	44.55 N	93.20 W
Edinboro	2740	41.52 N	80.08 W
Edinburg, Ind., U.S.	2746	39.21 N	85.58 W
Edinburg, N. Dak., U.S.	2750	48.30 N	97.52 W
Edinburg, Tex., U.S.	2748	26.18 N	98.10 W
Edinburgh	2769	55.57 N	3.13 W
Edirne	2778	41.40 N	26.34 E
Edjeleh	2786	27.38 N	9.50 E
Edmonds	2754	47.48 N	122.22 W
Edmonton, Alta., Can.	2734	53.33 N	113.28 W
Edmonton, Ky., U.S.	2746	36.59 N	85.37 W
Edmore, Mich., U.S.	2742	43.25 N	85.03 W
Edmore, N. Dak., U.S.	2750	48.25 N	98.27 W
Edmundston	2739	47.22 N	68.20 W
Edna	2748	28.59 N	96.39 W
Edremit	2778	39.35 N	27.01 E
Edrengijn Nuruu ⛰	2796	44.15 N	97.45 E
Edsbyn	2768	61.23 N	15.49 E
Edson	2734	53.35 N	116.26 W
Eduardo Castex	2764	35.55 S	64.20 W
Edward, Lake ⊜	2788	0.25 S	29.30 E
Edwards, Miss., U.S.	2746	32.20 N	90.36 W
Edwards, N.Y., U.S.	2740	44.20 N	75.15 W
Edwards Plateau ⛰[1]	2748	31.20 N	101.00 W
Effingham, Ill., U.S.	2746	39.07 N	88.33 W
Effingham, Kans., U.S.	2750	39.31 N	95.24 W
Egede og Rothes Fjord C[2]	2734	66.00 N	38.00 W
Egedesminde	2734	68.42 N	52.45 W
Eger	2770	47.54 N	20.23 E
Egersund	2768	58.27 N	6.00 E
Eggenfelden	2770	48.25 N	12.46 E
Égletons	2772	45.24 N	2.03 E
Egvekinot	2784	66.19 N	179.10 E
Egypt □[1]	2786	27.00 N	30.00 E
Ehrenberg	2752	33.36 N	114.31 W
Eibar	2774	43.11 N	2.28 W
Eidsvoll	2768	60.19 N	11.14 E
Eifel ⛰	2770	50.15 N	6.45 E
Eighty Mile Beach ≛[2]	2806	19.45 S	121.00 E
Eil	2790	8.00 N	49.51 E
Eindhoven	2770	51.26 N	5.28 E
Einsiedeln	2772	47.08 N	8.45 E
Eirunepé	2762	6.40 S	69.52 W
Eisenerz	2770	47.33 N	14.53 E
Eisenstadt	2770	47.51 N	16.32 E
Ejea de los Caballeros	2774	42.08 N	1.08 W
Ekalaka	2750	45.53 N	104.33 W
Ekiatapskij Chrebet ⛰	2784	68.30 N	179.00 E
Ekimčan	2784	53.04 N	132.58 E
Ekwan ≃	2734	53.14 N	82.13 W
El Aaiún	2786	27.09 N	13.12 W
El Asnam	2786	36.10 N	1.20 E
Elat	2791	29.33 N	34.57 E
El Avión	2758	24.08 N	106.59 W
Elâziğ	2766	38.41 N	39.14 E
El Azúcar, Presa de ⊜[1]	2748	26.15 N	99.00 W
Elba	2746	31.25 N	86.04 W
Elba, Isola d' I	2776	42.46 N	10.17 E
El Banco	2760	9.00 N	73.58 W
El Barco de Valdeorras	2774	42.25 N	6.59 W
Elbasan	2778	41.06 N	20.05 E
El Bayito	2748	27.33 N	99.31 W
Elbe (Labe) ≃	2770	53.50 N	9.00 E
Elbert, Mount ▲	2752	39.07 N	106.27 W
Elberton	2744	34.07 N	82.52 W
Elbeuf	2772	49.17 N	1.00 E
Elbing			
→ Elbląg	2770	54.10 N	19.25 E
Elbląg (Elbing)	2770	54.10 N	19.25 E
El Bonillo	2774	38.57 N	2.32 W
Elbow Lake	2750	45.59 N	95.58 W
El'brus, Gora ▲	2766	43.21 N	42.26 E
Elbrus, Mount			
→ El'brus, Gora ▲	2766	43.21 N	42.26 E
El Burgo de Osma	2774	41.35 N	3.04 W
Elburz Mountains			
→ Alborz, Reshteh-ye Kūhhā-ye ⛰	2766	36.00 N	53.00 E
El Cajon	2756	32.48 N	116.58 W
El Campo	2748	29.12 N	96.16 W
El Carmen	2764	24.24 S	65.15 W
El Carmen de Bolívar	2760	9.43 N	75.08 W
El Carrizo	2758	29.58 N	105.16 W
El Centro	2756	32.48 N	115.34 W
Elche	2774	38.15 N	0.42 W
Elche de la Sierra	2774	38.27 N	2.03 W
El Ciprés	2756	31.50 N	116.38 W
El Cozón	2758	31.18 N	112.29 W
Elda	2774	38.29 N	0.47 W
El Descanso	2756	32.12 N	116.55 W
El Desemboque	2758	29.30 N	112.27 W
El Djouf ◆[2]	2786	20.30 N	8.00 W
Eldon	2746	38.21 N	92.35 W
Eldora	2742	42.19 N	93.26 W
Eldorado, Méx.	2758	24.17 N	107.21 W
El Dorado, Ark., U.S.	2746	33.13 N	92.40 W
Eldorado, Ill., U.S.	2746	37.49 N	88.26 W
El Dorado, Kans., U.S.	2750	37.49 N	96.52 W
Eldorado, Okla., U.S.	2748	34.28 N	99.39 W
Eldorado, Tex., U.S.	2748	30.52 N	100.36 W
El Dorado Springs	2746	37.52 N	94.01 W
Eldoret	2788	0.31 N	35.17 E
Eldred	2740	41.57 N	78.23 W
Electra	2748	34.02 N	98.55 W
Elektrostal'	2780	55.47 N	38.28 E
El Encanto	2762	1.37 S	73.14 W
El Estor	2760	15.32 N	89.21 W
Eleuthera I	2760	25.15 N	76.20 W
Eleva	2742	44.35 N	91.28 W
Elevsis	2778	38.02 N	23.32 E
El Fahs	2776	36.22 N	9.55 E
El Ferrol del Caudillo	2774	43.29 N	8.14 W
Elfrida	2752	31.41 N	109.41 W
El Galpón	2764	25.24 S	64.39 W
Elgin, Scot., U.K.	2769	57.39 N	3.20 W
Elgin, Ill., U.S.	2742	42.02 N	88.17 W
Elgin, Nebr., U.S.	2750	41.59 N	98.05 W
Elgin, N. Dak., U.S.	2750	46.24 N	101.51 W
Elgin, Oreg., U.S.	2754	45.34 N	117.55 W
Elgin, Tex., U.S.	2748	30.21 N	97.22 W
El Goléa	2786	30.30 N	2.50 E
El Golfo de Santa Clara	2758	31.34 N	114.19 W
Elgon, Mount ▲	2788	1.08 N	34.33 E
El Hank ≛[4]	2786	24.30 N	7.00 W
El Haouaria	2776	37.03 N	11.02 E
Elida	2748	33.57 N	103.39 W
Élisabethville			
→ Lubumbashi	2788	11.40 S	27.28 E
Elista	2766	46.16 N	44.14 E
Elizabeth, Austl.	2806	34.43 S	138.40 E
Elizabeth, La., U.S.	2746	30.52 N	92.48 W
Elizabeth, N.J., U.S.	2740	40.40 N	74.11 W
Elizabeth City	2744	36.18 N	76.14 W

Symbols against index entries represent categories identified in the key on page 2810.

Symbols against index entries represent categories identified in the key on page 2810.

Symbols against index entries represent categories identified in the key on page 2810.

Name	Page	Lat° ′	Long° ′
Furneaux Group II	2806	40.10 S	148.05 E
Furqlus	2791	34.36 N	37.05 E
Fürstenfeld	2770	47.03 N	16.05 E
Fürstenfeldbruck	2770	48.10 N	11.15 E
Furudal	2768	61.10 N	15.08 E
Fushun	2796	41.52 N	123.53 E
Fuste, Picacho del ▲	2748	27.37 N	102.47 W
Fuxian, Zhg.	2796	39.37 N	122.01 E
Fuxian, Zhg.	2796	36.02 N	109.13 E
Fuxinshi	2796	42.03 N	121.46 E
Fuyang	2800	32.52 N	115.42 E
Fuzhou (Foochow), Zhg.	2800	26.06 N	119.17 E
Fuzhou, Zhg.	2800	28.01 N	116.20 E
G			
Gabbs	2756	38.52 N	117.55 W
Gabès	2786	33.53 N	10.07 E
Gabès, Golfe de C	2786	34.00 N	10.25 E
Gabon □[1]	2788	1.00 S	11.45 E
Gaborone	2788	24.45 S	25.55 E
Gabriel Strait ʎʎ	2734	61.45 N	65.30 W
Gabrovo	2778	42.52 N	25.19 E
Gackle	2750	46.38 N	99.09 W
Gadag	2793	15.25 N	75.37 E
Gäddede	2768	64.30 N	14.09 E
Gadsden	2746	34.02 N	86.02 W
Gaer (Geeryasha)	2794	31.44 N	80.21 E
Gaeta	2776	41.12 N	13.35 E
Gaferut I	2802	9.14 N	145.23 E
Gafsa	2786	34.25 N	8.48 E
Gagliano del Capo	2776	39.50 N	18.22 E
Gagnoa	2786	6.08 N	5.56 W
Gagnon	2734	51.53 N	68.10 W
Gail	2748	32.46 N	101.27 W
Gainesville, Fla., U.S.	2744	29.40 N	82.20 W
Gainesville, Ga., U.S.	2744	34.18 N	83.50 W
Gainesville, Mo., U.S.	2746	36.36 N	92.26 W
Gainesville, Tex., U.S.	2748	33.37 N	97.08 W
Gairdner, Lake ⊜	2806	31.35 S	136.00 E
Gajsin	2782	48.48 N	29.24 E
Galán, Cerro ▲	2764	25.55 S	66.52 W
Galashiels	2769	55.37 N	2.49 W
Galați	2778	45.26 N	28.03 E
Galatina	2776	40.10 N	18.10 E
Galax	2744	36.40 N	80.56 W
Galena, Ill., U.S.	2742	42.25 N	90.26 W
Galena, Kans., U.S.	2750	37.04 N	94.38 W
Galena, Mo., U.S.	2746	36.48 N	93.28 W
Galera, Punta ➤	2764	39.59 S	73.43 W
Galesburg	2746	40.57 N	90.22 W
Galesville	2742	44.05 N	91.21 W
Galeton	2740	41.44 N	77.39 W
Galič	2780	58.23 N	42.21 E
Galicia □[9], Esp.	2774	43.00 N	8.00 W
Galicia □[9], Eur.	2770	49.50 N	21.00 E
Galion	2740	40.44 N	82.47 W
Galiuro Mountains ⩕	2752	32.40 N	110.20 W
Galka'yo	2790	6.49 N	47.23 E
Gallarate	2776	45.40 N	8.47 E
Gallatin, Mo., U.S.	2746	39.55 N	93.58 W
Gallatin, Tenn., U.S.	2746	36.24 N	86.27 W
Gallinas, Punta ➤	2760	12.25 N	71.40 W
Gallipoli	2776	40.03 N	17.58 E
Gallipolis	2740	38.49 N	82.12 W
Gällivare	2768	67.07 N	20.45 E
Galloway, Mull of ➤	2769	54.38 N	4.50 W
Gallup	2752	35.32 N	108.44 W
Galt	2756	38.15 N	121.18 W
Galtür	2770	46.58 N	10.11 E
Galty Mountains ⩕	2769	52.25 N	8.10 W
Galva	2746	41.10 N	90.03 W
Galveston, Ind., U.S.	2746	40.35 N	86.11 W
Galveston, Tex., U.S.	2748	29.18 N	94.48 W
Galveston Bay C	2748	29.36 N	94.57 W
Galveston Island I	2748	29.13 N	94.55 W
Gálvez	2764	32.02 S	61.15 W
Galway	2769	53.16 N	9.03 W
Gamarra	2760	8.20 N	73.45 W
Gambela	2790	8.18 N	34.37 E
Gambia □[1]	2786	13.25 N	16.00 W
Gambia (Gambie) ≃	2786	13.28 N	16.34 W
Gamboa	2760	9.05 N	79.40 W
Gamleby	2768	57.54 N	16.24 E
Ganado, Ariz., U.S.	2752	35.43 N	109.33 W
Ganado, Tex., U.S.	2748	29.02 N	96.31 W
Gananoque	2740	44.20 N	76.10 W
Gander	2734	48.57 N	54.37 W
Gandesa	2774	41.03 N	0.26 E
Gandía	2774	38.58 N	0.11 W
Gangdisishanmai ⩕	2794	29.30 N	87.00 E
Ganges (Ganga) (Padma) ≃	2794	23.22 N	90.32 E
Ganglingshan ⩕	2794	32.00 N	83.00 E
Gangu	2796	34.38 N	105.27 E
Gannat	2772	46.06 N	3.12 E
Gannett Peak ▲	2754	43.11 N	109.39 W
Gansu □[4]	2796	37.00 N	103.00 E
Gantt	2746	31.25 N	86.29 W
Ganzhou	2800	25.54 N	114.55 E
Ganzi	2796	31.40 N	100.01 E
Gao	2786	16.16 N	0.03 W
Gaokeng	2800	27.40 N	113.58 E
Gaoyou	2800	32.47 N	119.27 E
Gaozhou	2804	21.55 N	110.50 E
Gap	2772	44.34 N	6.05 E
Garanhuns	2762	8.54 S	36.29 W
Garberville	2756	40.06 N	123.48 W
Garça	2765	22.14 S	49.37 W
Garda, Lago di ⊜	2776	45.40 N	10.41 E
Garden City, Kans., U.S.	2750	37.58 N	100.53 W
Garden City, Mo., U.S.	2746	38.34 N	94.12 W
Garden City, Tex., U.S.	2748	31.52 N	101.29 W
Garden Grove	2742	40.50 N	93.36 W
Garden Island I	2742	45.49 N	85.30 W
Garden Peninsula ➤[1]	2742	45.45 N	86.35 W
Garden Reach	2794	22.33 N	88.17 E
Gardēz	2794	33.37 N	69.07 E
Gardiner, Maine, U.S.	2740	44.14 N	69.46 W
Gardiner, Mont., U.S.	2754	45.02 N	110.42 W
Gardner, Colo., U.S.	2750	37.47 N	105.10 W
Gardner, Mass., U.S.	2740	42.34 N	71.60 W
Gardnerville	2756	38.56 N	119.45 W
Gardone Val Trompia	2776	45.41 N	10.11 E
Garfield, Kans., U.S.	2750	38.05 N	99.14 W
Garfield, Wash., U.S.	2754	47.01 N	117.09 W
Garfield Peak ▲	2754	42.47 N	107.18 W
Garibaldi	2754	45.34 N	123.55 W
Garies	2788	30.30 S	18.00 E
Garissa	2788	0.28 S	39.38 E
Garland, Tex., U.S.	2748	32.54 N	96.39 W
Garland, Utah, U.S.	2752	41.45 N	112.10 W
Garlin	2772	43.34 N	0.15 W
Garner, Iowa, U.S.	2742	43.06 N	93.36 W
Garner, N.C., U.S.	2744	35.43 N	78.37 W
Garnett	2750	38.17 N	95.14 W
Garonne ≃	2772	45.02 N	0.36 W
Garoua	2786	9.18 N	13.24 E
Garretson	2750	43.43 N	96.30 W
Garrett	2746	41.21 N	85.08 W
Garrison, N. Dak., U.S.	2750	47.40 N	101.25 W
Garrison, Tex., U.S.	2746	31.49 N	94.29 W
Garrovillas	2774	39.43 N	6.33 W
Garry Lake ⊜	2734	66.00 N	100.00 W
Garsen	2788	2.16 S	40.07 E
Gary	2746	41.36 N	87.20 W
Garza-Little Elm Reservoir ⊜[1]	2748	33.08 N	97.00 W
Garzón	2762	2.12 N	75.38 W
Gas City	2746	40.29 N	85.37 W
Gascoyne ≃	2806	24.52 S	113.37 E
Gaspé	2739	48.50 N	64.29 W
Gassaway	2740	38.40 N	80.47 W
Gaston	2744	36.30 N	77.38 W
Gaston, Lake ⊜[1]	2744	36.35 N	78.00 W
Gastonia	2744	35.16 N	81.11 W
Gátas, Akrotírion ➤	2791	34.34 N	33.02 E
Gatčina	2780	59.34 N	30.08 E
Gate	2748	36.51 N	100.04 W
Gate City	2744	36.38 N	82.35 W
Gateshead	2769	54.58 N	1.37 W
Gateshead Island I	2734	70.22 N	100.27 W
Gatesville	2748	31.26 N	97.45 W
Gatlinburg	2744	35.43 N	83.31 W
Gatun Lake ⊜[1]	2760	9.10 N	79.55 W
Gaucín	2774	36.31 N	5.19 W
Gauhāti	2794	26.11 N	91.44 E
Gavá	2774	41.18 N	2.01 E
Gävle	2768	60.40 N	17.10 E
Gavrilov-Jam	2780	57.18 N	39.51 E
Gawler Ranges ⩕	2806	32.30 S	136.00 E
Gaya	2794	24.47 N	85.00 E
Gaylord, Mich., U.S.	2742	45.02 N	84.40 W
Gaylord, Minn., U.S.	2742	44.33 N	94.13 W
Gayndah	2806	25.37 S	151.36 E
Gays Mills	2742	43.19 N	90.51 W
Gaziantep	2766	37.05 N	37.22 E
Gaziantep □[4]	2791	37.00 N	37.20 E
Gbarnga	2786	7.00 N	9.29 W
Gdańsk (Danzig)	2770	54.23 N	18.40 E
Gdynia	2770	54.32 N	18.33 E
Gearhart Mountain ▲	2754	42.30 N	120.53 W
Geary	2748	35.38 N	98.19 W
Geel	2770	51.10 N	5.00 E
Geelong	2806	38.08 S	144.21 E
Ge'ermu	2794	36.23 N	94.50 E
Geiger	2746	32.52 N	88.18 W
Geilo	2768	60.31 N	8.12 E
Geistown	2740	40.17 N	78.52 W
Gejiu (Kokiu)	2804	23.22 N	103.06 E
Gela	2776	37.03 N	14.15 E
Gelibolu	2778	40.24 N	26.40 E
Gembloux	2770	50.34 N	4.41 E
Gemena	2786	3.15 N	19.46 E
Gemlik	2778	40.26 N	29.09 E
Gemona del Friuli	2776	46.16 N	13.09 E
Genale ≃	2790	5.43 N	40.53 E
General Alvear	2764	34.59 S	67.42 W
General Bravo	2758	25.48 N	99.10 W
General Carneiro	2765	15.42 S	52.45 W
General Levalle	2764	34.00 S	63.55 W
General Machado	2788	12.03 S	17.30 E
General Pico	2764	35.38 S	63.46 W
General Pinedo	2764	27.20 S	61.20 W
General Roca	2764	39.02 S	67.33 W
General Treviño	2748	26.14 N	99.29 W
General Villegas	2764	35.02 S	63.02 W
Genesee	2754	46.33 N	116.56 W
Geneseo, Ill., U.S.	2746	41.27 N	90.09 W
Geneseo, Kans., U.S.	2750	38.31 N	98.09 W
Geneseo, N.Y., U.S.	2740	42.48 N	77.49 W
Geneva, Ala., U.S.	2746	31.02 N	85.52 W
Geneva, Ind., U.S.	2746	40.36 N	84.58 W
Geneva, Nebr., U.S.	2750	40.32 N	97.36 W
Geneva, N.Y., U.S.	2740	42.52 N	77.00 W
Geneva, Ohio, U.S.	2740	41.48 N	80.57 W
Geneva, Lake ⊜	2772	46.25 N	6.30 E
Genève	2772	46.12 N	6.09 E
Geničesk	2782	46.11 N	34.48 E
Genk	2770	50.58 N	5.30 E
Genkai-nada ⩐[2]	2798	34.00 N	130.00 E
Genoa, Nebr., U.S.	2750	41.27 N	97.44 W
Genoa, Wis., U.S.	2742	43.35 N	91.13 W
Genova (Genoa)	2776	44.25 N	8.57 E
Genova, Golfo di C	2776	44.10 N	8.55 E
Gent (Gand)	2770	51.03 N	3.43 E
Geographe Bay C	2806	33.35 S	115.15 E
George	2788	33.58 S	22.24 E
George ≃	2734	58.49 N	66.10 W
George, Lake ⊜	2788	0.00 N	30.12 E
Georgetown, Ont., Can.	2740	43.39 N	79.55 W
Georgetown, Cay. Is.	2760	19.18 N	81.23 W
Georgetown, Gam.	2786	13.30 N	14.47 W
Georgetown, Guy.	2762	6.48 N	58.10 W
Georgetown, Del., U.S.	2740	38.42 N	75.23 W
Georgetown, Idaho, U.S.	2754	42.29 N	111.22 W
Georgetown, Ill., U.S.	2746	39.59 N	87.38 W
Georgetown, Ky., U.S.	2740	38.13 N	84.33 W
Georgetown, Ohio, U.S.	2740	38.52 N	83.54 W
Georgetown, S.C., U.S.	2744	33.23 N	79.17 W
Georgetown, Tex., U.S.	2748	30.38 N	97.41 W
George West	2748	28.20 N	98.07 W
Georgia □[3]	2736	32.50 N	83.15 W
Georgiana	2746	31.33 N	86.44 W
Georgian Bay C	2740	45.15 N	80.50 W
Georgina ≃	2806	23.30 S	139.47 E
Georgiu-Dež (Liski)	2782	50.59 N	39.30 E
Geral do Paraná, Serra ⩕[2]	2765	14.45 S	47.30 W
Geraldton, Austl.	2806	28.46 S	114.36 E
Geraldton, Ont., Can.	2734	49.44 N	86.57 W
Gérardmer	2772	48.04 N	6.53 E
Gereshk	2794	31.48 N	64.34 E
Gérgal	2774	37.07 N	2.33 W
Gering	2750	41.50 N	103.40 W
German Democratic Republic (East Germany) □[1]	2766	52.00 N	12.30 E
Germantown	2746	35.05 N	89.49 W
Germany, Federal Republic of (West Germany) □[1]	2766	51.00 N	9.00 E
Germiston	2788	26.15 S	28.05 E
Gerona	2774	41.59 N	2.49 E
Getafe	2774	40.18 N	3.43 W
Gettysburg, Pa., U.S.	2740	39.50 N	77.14 W
Gettysburg, S. Dak., U.S.	2750	45.01 N	99.57 W
Geyser	2754	47.16 N	110.30 W
Ghāghra ≃	2794	25.47 N	84.37 E
Ghana □[1]	2786	8.00 N	2.00 W
Ghanzi	2788	21.38 S	21.45 E
Ghardaïa	2786	32.31 N	3.37 E
Gharyān	2786	32.10 N	13.01 E
Ghāt	2786	24.58 N	10.11 E
Ghawdex I	2776	36.03 N	14.15 E
Ghazāl, Baḩr al- ≃	2786	9.31 N	30.25 E
Ghāziābād	2794	28.40 N	77.26 E
Ghāzīpur	2794	25.35 N	83.34 E
Ghaznī	2794	33.33 N	68.26 E
Ghazzah (Gaza)	2791	31.30 N	34.28 E
Ghedi	2776	45.24 N	10.16 E
Ghent → Gent	2770	51.03 N	3.43 E
Gheorghe Gheorghiu-Dej	2778	46.14 N	26.44 E
Ghīn, Tall ▲	2791	32.39 N	36.43 E
Ghisonáccia	2776	42.00 N	9.25 E
Ghudāmis	2786	30.08 N	9.30 E
Gia-dinh	2804	10.48 N	106.42 E
Gibbon	2750	40.45 N	98.51 W
Gibeon	2788	25.09 S	17.43 E
Gibraltar	2774	36.09 N	5.21 W
Gibraltar □[2]	2766	36.11 N	5.22 W
Gibraltar, Strait of (Estrecho de Gibraltar) ʎʎ	2774	35.57 N	5.36 W
Gibraltar Point ➤	2769	53.05 N	0.19 E
Gibsland	2746	32.33 N	93.03 W
Gibson Desert ✦[2]	2806	24.30 S	126.00 E
Giddings	2748	30.11 N	96.56 W
Gien	2772	47.42 N	2.38 E
Gifford	2744	27.41 N	80.25 W
Gifu	2798	35.25 N	136.45 E
Gijón	2774	43.32 N	5.40 W
Gila ≃	2752	32.43 N	114.33 W
Gila Bend	2752	32.57 N	112.43 W
Gila Bend Mountains ⩕	2752	33.10 N	113.10 W
Gila Mountains ⩕	2752	33.05 N	109.50 W
Gilbert Islands □[2]	2730	4.00 S	175.00 E
Gilbertown	2746	31.53 N	88.19 W
Gilbert Peak ▲	2754	46.30 N	121.25 W
Gilbués	2762	9.50 S	45.21 W
Gilgit	2794	35.55 N	74.18 E
Gillam	2734	56.21 N	94.43 W
Gillespie	2746	39.07 N	89.49 W
Gillett	2746	34.07 N	91.22 W
Gillette	2750	44.18 N	105.30 W
Gilman, Ill., U.S.	2746	40.46 N	87.59 W
Gilman, Wis., U.S.	2742	45.10 N	90.48 W
Gilmer	2748	32.44 N	94.57 W
Gilo ≃	2790	8.10 N	33.15 E
Gilroy	2756	37.00 N	121.43 W
Gil'uj ≃	2784	53.58 N	127.30 E
Giluwe, Mount ▲	2802	6.05 S	143.50 E
Gimli	2734	50.38 N	96.59 W
Ginosa	2776	40.34 N	16.46 E
Gioia del Colle	2776	40.48 N	16.56 E
Gioia Tauro	2776	38.26 N	15.54 E
Girard	2750	37.31 N	94.51 W
Girardot	2762	4.18 N	74.48 W
Girifalco	2776	38.49 N	16.25 E
Gisborne	2808	38.40 S	178.01 E
Gisenyi	2788	1.42 S	29.15 E
Gisors	2772	49.17 N	1.47 E
Giugliano [in Campania]	2776	40.56 N	14.12 E
Giulianova	2776	42.45 N	13.57 E
Giurgiu	2778	43.53 N	25.57 E
Givet	2772	50.08 N	4.50 E
Givors	2772	45.35 N	4.46 E
Giyon	2790	8.30 N	38.00 E
Gižiga	2784	62.03 N	160.30 E
Gižiginskaja Guba C	2784	61.30 N	158.00 E
Gjirokastër	2778	40.05 N	20.10 E
Gjoa Haven	2734	68.38 N	95.57 W
Glace Bay	2734	46.12 N	59.57 W
Glacier Bay National Monument ♦	2738	58.45 N	136.30 W
Glacier Peak ▲	2754	48.07 N	121.07 W
Gladewater	2748	32.33 N	94.56 W
Gladstone, Austl.	2806	23.51 S	151.16 E
Gladstone, Mich., U.S.	2742	45.50 N	87.03 W
Gladstone, Mo., U.S.	2746	39.13 N	94.34 W
Gladwin	2742	43.59 N	84.29 W
Glåma ≃	2768	59.12 N	10.57 E
Glarner Alpen ⩕	2772	46.55 N	9.00 E
Glarus	2772	47.02 N	9.04 E
Glasco	2750	39.22 N	97.50 W
Glasgow, Scot., U.K.	2769	55.53 N	4.15 W
Glasgow, Ky., U.S.	2746	37.00 N	85.55 W
Glasgow, Mo., U.S.	2746	39.14 N	92.50 W
Glasgow, Mont., U.S.	2754	48.12 N	106.38 W
Glasgow, Va., U.S.	2744	37.38 N	79.27 W
Glassboro	2740	49.32 N	99.15 W
Glazov	2766	58.09 N	52.40 E
Gleason	2746	36.13 N	88.37 W
Gleisdorf	2770	47.06 N	15.44 E
Glenburn	2750	48.31 N	101.13 W
Glen Burnie	2740	39.10 N	76.37 W
Glen Canyon	2752	37.05 N	111.41 W
Glen Canyon V	2752	37.10 N	110.50 W
Glen Canyon National Recreation Area ♦	2752	37.00 N	111.20 W
Glencoe, Ont., Can.	2740	42.45 N	81.43 W
Glencoe, Ala., U.S.	2746	33.57 N	85.56 W
Glencoe, Minn., U.S.	2742	44.46 N	94.09 W
Glendale, Ariz., U.S.	2752	33.32 N	112.11 W
Glendale, Calif., U.S.	2756	34.10 N	118.17 W
Glendale, Oreg., U.S.	2754	42.44 N	123.26 W
Glendive	2750	47.06 N	104.43 W
Glen Innes	2806	29.44 S	151.44 E
Glenmora	2746	30.59 N	92.35 W
Glenns Ferry	2754	42.57 N	115.18 W
Glennville	2744	31.56 N	81.56 W
Glen Rose	2748	32.14 N	97.45 W
Glens Falls	2740	43.19 N	73.39 W
Glen Ullin	2750	46.49 N	101.50 W
Glenville	2740	38.56 N	80.50 W
Glenwood, Ark., U.S.	2746	34.20 N	93.33 W
Glenwood, Iowa, U.S.	2750	41.03 N	95.45 W
Glenwood, Minn., U.S.	2750	45.39 N	95.23 W
Glenwood, N. Mex., U.S.	2752	33.19 N	108.53 W
Glenwood, Va., U.S.	2744	36.35 N	79.22 W
Glenwood Springs	2752	39.33 N	107.19 W
Glidden, Iowa, U.S.	2750	42.04 N	94.44 W
Glidden, Wis., U.S.	2742	46.09 N	90.34 W
Glina	2776	45.20 N	16.06 E
Glittertinden ▲	2768	61.39 N	8.33 E
Gliwice (Gleiwitz)	2770	50.17 N	18.40 E
Globe	2752	33.24 N	110.47 W
Gloggnitz	2770	47.40 N	15.57 E
Gloster, La., U.S.	2746	32.12 N	93.49 W
Gloster, Miss., U.S.	2746	31.12 N	91.01 W
Gloucester, Eng., U.K.	2769	51.53 N	2.14 W
Gloucester, Mass., U.S.	2740	42.41 N	70.39 W
Gloucester, Va., U.S.	2744	37.25 N	76.32 W
Glouster	2740	39.30 N	82.05 W
Gloversville	2740	43.03 N	74.20 W
Gluchov	2782	51.41 N	33.53 E
Gmünd	2770	48.47 N	15.00 E
Gmunden	2770	47.55 N	13.48 E
Gnarp	2768	62.03 N	17.16 E
Gniezno	2770	52.31 N	17.37 E
Gnjilane	2778	42.28 N	21.29 E
Goba	2790	7.02 N	40.00 E
Gobabis	2788	22.30 S	18.58 E
Gobi ✦[2]	2796	43.00 N	105.00 E
Godāvari ≃	2793	17.00 N	81.45 E
Goderich	2740	43.45 N	81.43 W
Godhavn	2734	69.15 N	53.33 W
Godhra	2794	22.45 N	73.38 E
Godoy Cruz	2764	32.55 S	68.50 W
Gods Lake ⊜	2734	54.45 N	94.00 W
Godthåb	2734	64.11 N	51.44 W
Godwin Austen (K2) ▲	2794	35.53 N	76.30 E
Goéland, Lac au ⊜	2734	49.47 N	76.48 W
Goélands, Lac aux ⊜	2734	55.27 N	64.17 W
Goiana	2762	7.33 S	34.59 W
Goiânia	2765	16.40 S	49.16 W
Goiás	2765	15.56 S	50.08 W
Gol'čicha	2784	71.43 N	83.36 E
Golconda, Ill., U.S.	2746	37.22 N	88.29 W
Golconda, Nev., U.S.	2756	40.57 N	117.30 W
Gold Beach	2754	42.25 N	124.25 W
Golden	2734	51.18 N	116.58 W
Golden City	2746	37.24 N	94.05 W
Goldendale	2754	45.49 N	120.50 W
Golden Hinde ▲	2734	49.40 N	125.45 W
Golden Meadow	2746	29.23 N	90.16 W
Goldfield	2756	37.42 N	117.14 W
Goldsboro	2744	35.23 N	77.59 W
Goldthwaite	2748	31.27 N	98.34 W
Golec-Skalistyj, Gora ▲	2784	56.24 N	119.12 E
Goliad	2748	28.40 N	97.23 W
Golspie	2769	57.58 N	3.58 W
Gombe ≃	2788	4.38 S	31.40 E
Gomel'	2780	52.25 N	31.00 E
Gomera I	2786	28.06 N	17.08 W
Gómez Palacio	2758	25.34 N	103.30 W
Gonaïves	2760	19.30 N	72.40 W
Gonam	2784	57.21 N	131.12 E
Gonam ≃	2784	57.21 N	131.14 E
Gonâve, Golfe de la C	2760	19.20 N	73.15 W
Gonâve, Île de la I	2760	18.45 N	73.00 W
Gonda	2794	27.08 N	81.56 E
Gondal	2794	21.58 N	70.48 E
Gonder	2790	12.40 N	37.30 E
Gondia	2793	21.27 N	80.12 E
Gondomar	2774	41.09 N	8.32 W
Gondrecourt-le-Château	2772	48.31 N	5.30 E
Gönen	2778	40.06 N	27.39 E
Gonggeershan ▲	2794	38.37 N	75.20 E
Gōnoura	2798	33.45 N	129.41 E
Gonzales, Calif., U.S.	2756	36.31 N	121.32 W
Gonzales, La., U.S.	2746	30.14 N	90.55 W
Gonzales, Tex., U.S.	2748	29.30 N	97.27 W
González Ortega	2756	32.40 N	115.23 W
Goochland	2744	37.41 N	77.53 W
Good Hope, Cape of ➤	2788	34.24 S	18.30 E
Good Hope Mountain ▲	2734	51.09 N	124.10 W

Symbols against index entries represent categories identified in the key on page 2810.

Name	Page	Lat °′	Long °′
Guttenberg	2742	42.47 N	91.06 W
Guyana □[1]	2762	5.00 N	59.00 W
Guymon	2748	36.41 N	101.29 W
Guyot, Mount ∧	2744	35.42 N	83.15 W
Gwādar	2792	25.07 N	62.19 E
Gwai	2788	19.15 S	27.42 E
Gwalior	2794	26.13 N	78.10 E
Gwanda	2788	20.57 S	29.01 E
Gwelo	2788	19.27 S	29.49 E
Gwinn	2742	46.17 N	87.26 W
Gympie	2806	26.11 S	152.40 E
Gyöngyös	2770	47.47 N	19.56 E
Győr	2770	47.42 N	17.38 E
Gypsum Hills ⩕[2]	2748	36.25 N	99.20 W
H			
Haapajärvi	2768	63.45 N	25.20 E
Haapamäki	2768	62.15 N	24.28 E
Haarlem	2770	52.23 N	4.38 E
Haast	2808	43.53 S	169.03 E
Hachijō-jima I	2796	33.05 N	139.48 E
Hachinohe	2798	40.30 N	141.29 E
Hachiōji	2798	35.39 N	139.20 E
Hackberry, Ariz., U.S.	2752	35.22 N	113.44 W
Hackberry, La., U.S.	2746	29.59 N	93.21 W
Ḥadd, Ra's al- ⊁	2790	22.32 N	59.48 E
Hadejia ≃	2786	12.50 N	10.51 E
Hadera	2791	32.26 N	34.55 E
Haderslev	2768	55.15 N	9.30 E
Hadīyah	2790	25.34 N	38.41 E
Hadjeb el Aïoun	2776	35.24 N	9.33 E
Hadley Bay C	2734	72.30 N	107.45 W
Ha-dong	2804	20.58 N	105.46 E
Ḥaḍramawt ✦[1]	2790	15.00 N	50.00 E
Ḥaḍūr Shu'ayb ∧	2790	15.18 N	43.59 E
Haeju	2796	38.02 N	125.42 E
Haerbin	2796	45.45 N	126.41 E
Hafun, Ras ⊁	2790	10.27 N	51.26 E
Hagerman, Idaho, U.S.	2754	42.49 N	114.54 W
Hagerman, N. Mex., U.S.	2748	33.07 N	104.20 W
Hagerstown	2740	39.39 N	77.43 W
Hagfors	2768	60.02 N	13.42 E
Haggin, Mount ∧	2754	46.05 N	113.05 W
Hagi	2798	34.24 N	131.25 E
Haguenau	2772	48.49 N	7.47 E
Hagues Peak ∧	2752	40.29 N	105.38 W
Haian	2800	32.34 N	120.28 E
Haicheng	2796	40.52 N	122.45 E
Haifa → Ḥefa	2791	32.50 N	35.00 E
Haikou	2804	20.06 N	110.21 E
Ḥā'il	2790	27.33 N	41.42 E
Hailaer	2796	49.12 N	119.42 E
Hailey	2754	43.31 N	114.19 W
Haimen, Zhg.	2800	28.41 N	121.27 E
Haimen, Zhg.	2800	23.14 N	116.38 E
Hainandao I	2804	19.00 N	109.30 E
Haines City	2744	28.07 N	81.37 W
Haines Junction	2734	60.45 N	137.30 W
Hainfeld	2770	48.02 N	15.46 E
Haining	2800	30.25 N	120.32 E
Hai-phong	2804	20.52 N	106.41 E
Haiti (Haïti) □[1]	2760	19.00 N	72.25 W
Hakodate	2798a	41.45 N	140.43 E
Ḥalab (Aleppo)	2791	36.12 N	37.10 E
Ḥalā'ib	2786	22.13 N	36.38 E
Ḥalbā	2791	34.33 N	36.05 E
Halden	2768	59.09 N	11.23 E
Hale	2746	39.36 N	93.20 W
Haleakala Crater ⩕[6]	2757a	20.43 N	156.13 W
Hale Center	2748	34.04 N	101.51 W
Haleyville	2746	34.14 N	87.37 W
Halfway, Md., U.S.	2740	39.37 N	77.46 W
Halfway, Oreg., U.S.	2754	44.53 N	117.07 W
Halifax, N.S., Can.	2739	44.39 N	63.36 W
Halifax, N.C., U.S.	2744	36.20 N	77.35 W
Halifax, Va., U.S.	2744	36.46 N	78.56 W
Halifax Bay C	2806	18.50 S	146.30 E
Halkirk	2769	58.30 N	3.30 W
Halla-san ∧	2796	33.22 N	126.32 E
Hällefors	2768	59.47 N	14.30 E
Hallein	2770	47.41 N	13.06 E
Hallettsville	2748	29.27 N	96.56 W
Halliday	2750	47.21 N	102.20 W
Hällnäs	2768	64.19 N	19.38 E
Hallock	2750	48.47 N	96.57 W
Hallowell	2740	44.17 N	69.48 W
Hall Peninsula ⊁[1]	2734	63.30 N	66.00 W
Hallsberg	2768	59.04 N	15.07 E
Halls Creek	2806	18.13 S	127.40 E
Hallstavik	2768	60.03 N	18.36 E
Halmahera I	2802	1.00 N	128.00 E
Halmahera, Laut ⊤[2]	2802	1.00 S	129.00 E
Halmstad	2768	56.39 N	12.50 E
Hälsingborg → Helsingborg	2768	56.03 N	12.42 E
Halstad	2750	47.21 N	96.50 W
Halstead	2750	38.00 N	97.30 W
Haltiatunturi ∧	2766	69.18 N	21.16 E
Haltom City	2748	32.48 N	97.16 W
Hamada	2798	34.53 N	132.05 E
Hamadān	2790	34.48 N	48.30 E
Ḥamāh	2791	35.08 N	36.45 E
Hamamatsu	2798	34.42 N	137.44 E
Hamar	2768	60.48 N	11.06 E
Hamburg, Ark., U.S.	2746	33.14 N	91.48 W
Hamburg, Iowa, U.S.	2750	40.36 N	95.39 W
Hamburg, N.Y., U.S.	2740	42.43 N	78.50 W
Hamden	2740	41.21 N	72.56 W
Hämeenlinna	2768	61.00 N	24.27 E
Hamersley Range ⩕	2806	21.53 S	116.46 E
Hamhŭng	2796	39.54 N	127.32 E
Hami	2796	42.47 N	93.32 E
Hamilton, Ber.	2736	32.17 N	64.46 W
Hamilton, Ont., Can.	2740	43.15 N	79.51 W
Hamilton, N.Z.	2808	37.47 S	175.17 E
Hamilton, Scot., U.K.	2769	55.47 N	4.03 W
Hamilton, Ala., U.S.	2746	34.09 N	88.06 W
Hamilton, Mont., U.S.	2754	46.15 N	114.09 W
Hamilton, N.Y., U.S.	2740	42.50 N	75.33 W
Hamilton, Ohio, U.S.	2740	39.26 N	84.30 W
Hamilton, Tex., U.S.	2748	31.42 N	98.07 W
Hamilton Dome	2754	43.46 N	108.34 W
Hamlet	2744	34.53 N	79.42 W
Hamlin	2748	32.53 N	100.08 W
Hammamet	2776	36.24 N	10.37 E
Hammam Lif	2776	36.44 N	10.20 E
Hammerdal	2768	63.36 N	15.21 E
Hammerfest	2768	70.40 N	23.42 E
Hammon	2748	35.38 N	99.23 W
Hammond, Ind., U.S.	2746	41.36 N	87.30 W
Hammond, La., U.S.	2746	30.30 N	90.28 W
Hammondsport	2740	42.25 N	77.13 W
Hammonton	2740	39.38 N	74.48 W
Hampstead	2744	34.22 N	77.49 W
Hampton, Ark., U.S.	2746	33.32 N	92.28 W
Hampton, Fla., U.S.	2744	29.52 N	82.07 W
Hampton, Iowa, U.S.	2742	42.45 N	93.12 W
Hampton, S.C., U.S.	2744	32.52 N	81.07 W
Hampton, Va., U.S.	2744	37.01 N	76.22 W
Hanahan	2744	32.55 N	80.00 W
Hanamaki	2798	39.23 N	141.07 E
Hanapepe	2757a	21.55 N	159.35 W
Hancock, Md., U.S.	2740	39.42 N	78.11 W
Hancock, Mich., U.S.	2742	47.07 N	88.35 W
Hancock, Minn., U.S.	2750	45.30 N	95.48 W
Hancock, N.Y., U.S.	2740	41.57 N	75.17 W
Handa	2798	34.53 N	136.56 E
Handan	2796	36.37 N	114.29 E
Hando	2790	10.39 N	51.08 E
HaNegev ✦[1]	2791	30.30 N	34.55 E
Hanford	2756	36.20 N	119.39 W
Hangchow → Hangzhou	2800	30.15 N	120.10 E
Hangö (Hanko)	2768	59.50 N	22.57 E
Hangzhou (Hangchow)	2800	30.15 N	120.10 E
Hangzhouwan C	2800	30.20 N	121.00 E
Ḥanīsh, Jazā'ir II	2790	13.45 N	42.45 E
Hanjiang	2800	25.30 N	119.06 E
Hankinson	2750	46.04 N	96.54 W
Hanna, Alta., Can.	2734	51.38 N	111.54 W
Hanna, Wyo., U.S.	2754	41.52 N	106.34 W
Hannaford	2750	47.19 N	98.11 W
Hannah	2750	48.58 N	98.42 W
Hannibal	2746	39.42 N	91.22 W
Hannover	2770	52.24 N	9.44 E
Ha-noi	2804	21.02 N	105.51 E
Hanover, Ill., U.S.	2742	42.15 N	90.17 W
Hanover, N.H., U.S.	2740	43.42 N	72.18 W
Hanover, Pa., U.S.	2740	39.48 N	76.59 W
Hanover, Va., U.S.	2744	37.46 N	77.22 W
Hanzhong	2796	32.59 N	107.11 E
Haparanda	2768	65.50 N	24.10 E
Happy	2748	34.45 N	101.52 W
Happy Camp	2756	41.48 N	123.22 W
Ḥarash, Bi'r al- ⊤[4]	2786	25.30 N	22.12 E
Harbor Beach	2742	43.51 N	82.39 W
Hardangerfjorden C[2]	2768	60.10 N	6.00 E
Hardeeville	2744	32.17 N	81.05 W
Hardin, Ill., U.S.	2746	39.09 N	90.37 W
Hardin, Mont., U.S.	2754	45.44 N	107.37 W
Hardinsburg	2746	37.47 N	86.28 W
Hardwār	2794	29.58 N	78.10 E
Hardwick, Ga., U.S.	2744	33.09 N	83.13 W
Hardwick, Vt., U.S.	2740	44.30 N	72.22 W
Hardy	2746	36.19 N	91.29 W
Harer	2790	9.18 N	42.08 E
Hargeysa	2790	9.30 N	44.03 E
Harkers Island	2744	34.42 N	76.34 W
Harlan, Iowa, U.S.	2750	41.39 N	95.19 W
Harlan, Ky., U.S.	2744	36.51 N	83.19 W
Harlan County Reservoir ⊜[1]	2750	40.04 N	99.16 W
Harlem	2754	48.32 N	108.47 W
Harlingen, Ned.	2770	53.10 N	5.24 E
Harlingen, Tex., U.S.	2748	26.11 N	97.42 W
Harlow	2769	51.47 N	0.08 E
Harlowton	2754	46.26 N	109.50 W
Harmony	2742	43.33 N	92.01 W
Harney Basin ⩕[1]	2754	43.15 N	120.40 W
Harney Peak ∧	2750	44.00 N	103.30 W
Härnösand	2768	62.38 N	17.56 E
Haro	2774	42.35 N	2.51 W
Harper, Liber.	2786	4.25 N	7.43 W
Harper, Kans., U.S.	2750	37.17 N	98.01 W
Harper, Tex., U.S.	2748	30.18 N	99.15 W
Harricana ≃	2734	51.15 N	79.45 W
Harriman	2744	35.56 N	84.33 W
Harrington	2740	38.56 N	75.35 W
Harrisburg, Ill., U.S.	2746	37.44 N	88.33 W
Harrisburg, Nebr., U.S.	2750	41.33 N	103.44 W
Harrisburg, Oreg., U.S.	2754	44.16 N	123.10 W
Harrisburg, Pa., U.S.	2740	40.16 N	76.52 W
Harrison, Ark., U.S.	2746	36.14 N	93.07 W
Harrison, Mich., U.S.	2742	44.01 N	84.48 W
Harrison, Nebr., U.S.	2750	42.41 N	103.53 W
Harrison, Cape ⊁	2734	54.55 N	57.55 W
Harrisonburg	2740	38.27 N	78.52 W
Harrisonville	2746	38.39 N	94.21 W
Harrisville, Mich., U.S.	2742	44.39 N	83.17 W
Harrisville, N.Y., U.S.	2740	44.09 N	75.19 W
Harrisville, W. Va., U.S.	2740	39.13 N	81.03 W
Harrodsburg	2746	37.46 N	84.51 W
Harrogate	2769	54.00 N	1.33 W
Harstad	2768	68.46 N	16.30 E
Hart, Mich., U.S.	2742	43.42 N	86.22 W
Hart, Tex., U.S.	2748	34.23 N	102.07 W
Hartford, Ala., U.S.	2746	31.06 N	85.42 W
Hartford, Conn., U.S.	2740	41.46 N	72.41 W
Hartford, Kans., U.S.	2750	38.18 N	95.58 W
Hartford, Ky., U.S.	2746	37.27 N	86.55 W
Hartford, S. Dak., U.S.	2750	43.37 N	96.57 W
Hartford, Wis., U.S.	2742	43.19 N	88.22 W
Hartford City	2746	40.27 N	85.22 W
Hartington	2750	42.37 N	97.16 W
Hartland Point ⊁	2769	51.02 N	4.31 W
Hartlepool	2769	54.42 N	1.11 W
Hartley, Rh.	2788	18.10 S	30.14 E
Hartley, Iowa, U.S.	2750	43.11 N	95.29 W
Hartley, Tex., U.S.	2748	35.53 N	102.24 W
Hartselle	2746	34.27 N	86.56 W
Hartshorne	2748	34.51 N	95.34 W
Hartsville	2744	34.23 N	80.04 W
Hartville	2746	37.15 N	92.31 W
Hartwell	2744	34.21 N	82.56 W
Hārūt ≃	2792	31.35 N	61.18 E
Harvard, Ill., U.S.	2742	42.25 N	88.37 W
Harvard, Nebr., U.S.	2750	40.37 N	98.06 W
Harvey, Ill., U.S.	2746	41.37 N	87.39 W
Harvey, N. Dak., U.S.	2750	47.47 N	99.56 W
Harwich	2769	51.57 N	1.17 E
Haskell, Okla., U.S.	2748	35.50 N	95.40 W
Haskell, Tex., U.S.	2748	33.10 N	99.44 W
Haskovo	2778	41.56 N	25.33 E
Hasselt	2770	50.56 N	5.20 E
Hässleholm	2768	56.09 N	13.46 E
Hastings, N.Z.	2808	39.38 S	176.51 E
Hastings, Eng., U.K.	2769	50.51 N	0.36 E
Hastings, Mich., U.S.	2742	42.39 N	85.17 W
Hastings, Minn., U.S.	2742	44.44 N	92.51 W
Hastings, Nebr., U.S.	2736	40.35 N	98.23 W
Haswell	2750	38.27 N	103.09 W
Hatch, N. Mex., U.S.	2752	32.40 N	107.09 W
Hatch, Utah, U.S.	2752	37.39 N	112.26 W
Hāthras	2794	27.36 N	78.03 E
Ha-tinh	2804	18.20 N	105.54 E
Hatteras	2744	35.13 N	75.42 W
Hatteras, Cape ⊁	2744	35.13 N	75.32 W
Hattiesburg	2746	31.19 N	89.16 W
Hatton	2750	47.38 N	97.27 W
Hat Yai	2804	7.01 N	100.27 E
Haugesund	2768	59.25 N	5.18 E
Haukivuori	2768	62.01 N	27.13 E
Haut Atlas ⩕	2786	31.30 N	6.00 W
Hauterive	2739	49.12 N	68.16 W
Havana, Fla., U.S.	2744	30.38 N	84.25 W
Havana, Ill., U.S.	2746	40.18 N	90.04 W
Havant	2769	50.51 N	0.29 W
Havasu Lake ⊜[1]	2752	34.30 N	114.20 W
Havelock, Ont., Can.	2740	44.26 N	77.53 W
Havelock, N.C., U.S.	2744	34.53 N	76.54 W
Haven	2750	37.54 N	97.47 W
Haverhill	2740	42.47 N	71.05 W
Havířov	2770	49.47 N	18.27 E
Havre	2754	48.33 N	109.41 W
Havre de Grace	2740	39.33 N	76.06 W
Havre-Saint-Pierre	2739	50.14 N	63.36 W
Hawaii □[3]	2757a	20.00 N	157.45 W
Hawaii I	2757a	19.30 N	155.30 W
Hawaii Volcanoes National Park ♦	2757a	19.23 N	155.17 W
Hawarden	2750	43.00 N	96.29 W
Hawi	2757a	20.14 N	155.50 W
Hawick	2769	55.25 N	2.47 W
Hawke Bay C	2808	39.20 S	177.30 E
Hawkesbury	2740	45.36 N	74.37 W
Hawkinsville	2744	32.17 N	83.28 W
Hawley	2750	46.53 N	96.19 W
Hawthorne, Fla., U.S.	2744	29.36 N	82.05 W
Hawthorne, Nev., U.S.	2756	38.32 N	118.38 W
Haxtun	2750	40.39 N	102.38 W
Hay	2806	34.30 S	144.51 E
Hay ≃, Austl.	2806	25.14 S	138.00 E
Hay ≃, Can.	2734	60.52 N	115.44 W
Hay, Cape ⊁	2734	74.25 N	113.00 W
Hayange	2772	49.20 N	6.03 E
Hayden, Ariz., U.S.	2752	33.00 N	110.47 W
Hayden, Colo., U.S.	2752	40.30 N	107.16 W
Hayes ≃	2734	57.03 N	92.09 W
Hayes Center	2750	40.31 N	101.01 W
Hayesville	2744	35.03 N	83.49 W
Hayfork	2756	40.33 N	123.11 W
Haynesville	2746	32.58 N	93.08 W
Hayrabolu	2778	41.12 N	27.06 E
Hay River	2734	60.51 N	115.40 W
Hays, Kans., U.S.	2750	38.53 N	99.20 W
Hays, Mont., U.S.	2754	48.03 N	108.43 W
Haystack Peak ∧	2752	39.50 N	113.55 W
Haysville	2750	37.34 N	97.21 W
Hayti, Mo., U.S.	2746	36.14 N	89.44 W
Hayti, S. Dak., U.S.	2750	44.40 N	97.12 W
Hayward, Calif., U.S.	2756	37.40 N	122.05 W
Hayward, Wis., U.S.	2742	46.01 N	91.29 W
Hazard	2744	37.15 N	83.12 W
Hazāribāgh	2794	23.59 N	85.21 E
Hazelton, B.C., Can.	2734	55.15 N	127.40 W
Hazelton, N. Dak., U.S.	2750	46.29 N	100.17 W
Hazelwood	2744	35.28 N	83.00 W
Hazen	2750	47.18 N	101.38 W
Hazlehurst, Ga., U.S.	2744	31.52 N	82.36 W
Hazlehurst, Miss., U.S.	2746	31.52 N	90.24 W
Hazleton	2740	40.58 N	75.59 W
Headland	2746	31.21 N	85.20 W
Healdsburg	2756	38.37 N	122.52 W
Healdton	2748	34.14 N	97.29 W
Hearne	2748	30.53 N	96.36 W
Hearst	2734	49.41 N	83.40 W
Heavener	2748	34.53 N	94.36 W
Hebbronville	2748	27.18 N	98.41 W
Hebei □[4]	2796	38.00 N	116.00 E
Heber, Ariz., U.S.	2752	34.26 N	110.36 W
Heber, Utah, U.S.	2752	40.30 N	111.25 W
Heber Springs	2746	35.30 N	92.02 W
Hebrides II	2766	57.00 N	6.30 W
Hebron, Newf., Can.	2734	58.12 N	62.38 W
Hebron, Nebr., U.S.	2750	40.10 N	97.35 W
Hebron, N. Dak., U.S.	2750	46.54 N	102.03 W
Hecate Strait ⋃	2734	53.00 N	131.00 W
Hechi	2804	24.51 N	107.59 E
Hechiceros	2748	28.33 N	103.38 W
Hechuan	2796	30.00 N	106.16 E
Hecla	2750	45.53 N	98.09 W
Hector	2750	44.45 N	94.43 W
Hedemora	2768	60.17 N	15.59 E
Hedley	2748	34.52 N	100.39 W
Heerenveen	2770	52.57 N	5.55 E
Heerlen	2770	50.54 N	5.59 E
Ḥefa (Haifa)	2791	32.50 N	35.00 E
Hefei	2800	31.51 N	117.17 E
Heflin	2746	33.39 N	85.35 W
Hegang	2796	47.24 N	130.17 E
Heidenreichstein	2770	48.52 N	15.07 E
Heihe (Naquka)	2794	31.34 N	92.00 E
Heilbron	2788	27.21 S	27.58 E
Heilongjiang □[4]	2796	48.00 N	128.00 E
Heinola	2768	61.13 N	26.02 E
Hekla ∧[1]	2766	64.00 N	19.39 W
Hekou	2804	22.38 N	103.56 E
Helena, Ark., U.S.	2746	34.32 N	90.35 W
Helena, Mont., U.S.	2754	46.36 N	112.01 W
Helena, Okla., U.S.	2748	36.33 N	98.16 W
Helen Island I	2802	2.58 N	131.49 E
Helensburgh	2769	56.01 N	4.44 W
Hellesylt	2768	62.05 N	6.54 E
Hellín	2774	38.31 N	1.41 W
Hells Canyon ∨	2754	45.20 N	116.45 W
Hell-Ville	2788	13.25 S	48.16 E
Helmand ≃	2794	31.45 N	64.20 E
Helmond	2770	51.29 N	5.40 E
Helmsdale	2769	58.07 N	3.40 W
Helper	2752	39.41 N	110.51 W
Helsingborg	2768	56.03 N	12.42 E
Helsingfors → Helsinki	2768	60.10 N	24.58 E
Helsinki (Helsingfors)	2768	60.10 N	24.58 E
Hemet	2756	33.45 N	116.58 W
Hemingford	2750	42.19 N	103.04 W
Hemingway	2744	33.45 N	79.27 W
Hemphill	2746	31.20 N	93.51 W
Hempstead	2748	30.06 N	96.05 W
Hemse	2768	57.14 N	18.22 E
Henan □[4]	2800	34.00 N	114.00 E
Henderson, Ky., U.S.	2746	37.50 N	87.35 W
Henderson, Nebr., U.S.	2750	40.47 N	97.49 W
Henderson, Nev., U.S.	2756	36.02 N	114.59 W
Henderson, N.C., U.S.	2744	36.20 N	78.25 W
Henderson, Tenn., U.S.	2746	35.27 N	88.38 W
Henderson, Tex., U.S.	2746	32.09 N	94.48 W
Hendersonville, N.C., U.S.	2744	35.19 N	82.28 W
Hendersonville, Tenn., U.S.	2746	36.18 N	86.37 W
Hengelo	2770	52.15 N	6.45 E
Hengshan	2800	27.15 N	112.51 E
Hengyang	2796	26.51 N	112.30 E
Henlopen, Cape ⊁	2740	38.48 N	75.05 W
Hennepin	2746	41.15 N	89.21 W
Hennessey	2748	36.06 N	97.54 W
Henniker	2740	43.11 N	71.49 W
Henning	2750	46.19 N	95.27 W
Henrietta, N.Y., U.S.	2740	43.03 N	77.37 W
Henrietta, Tex., U.S.	2748	33.49 N	98.12 W
Henrietta Maria, Cape ⊁	2734	55.09 N	82.20 W
Henrique de Carvalho	2788	9.39 S	20.24 E
Henry	2746	41.47 N	89.41 W
Henryetta	2748	35.27 N	95.59 W
Henry Kater, Cape ⊁	2734	69.05 N	66.44 W
Hensley	2746	34.30 N	92.12 W
Henzada	2804	17.38 N	95.28 E
Heppner	2754	45.21 N	119.33 W
Hepu (Lianzhou)	2804	21.39 N	109.11 E
Herāt	2792	34.20 N	62.07 E
Herbignac	2772	47.27 N	2.19 W
Herculaneum	2746	38.16 N	90.23 W
Hereford, Eng., U.K.	2769	52.04 N	2.43 W
Hereford, Tex., U.S.	2748	34.49 N	102.24 W
Herington	2750	38.40 N	96.57 W
Herkimer	2740	43.02 N	74.59 W
Hermann	2746	38.42 N	91.27 W
Hermano Peak ∧	2752	37.13 N	108.48 W
Hermansville	2742	45.42 N	87.37 W
Hermanus	2788	34.25 S	19.16 E
Hermiston	2754	45.51 N	119.17 W
Hermitage	2746	37.56 N	93.19 W
Hermleigh	2748	32.38 N	100.46 W
Hermosillo	2758	29.04 N	110.58 W
Hernando	2746	34.49 N	89.59 W
Herndon	2740	40.43 N	76.51 W
Herning	2768	56.08 N	8.59 E
Heron Lake	2750	43.47 N	95.19 W
Herreid	2750	45.50 N	100.04 W
Herrera del Duque	2774	39.10 N	5.03 W
Herrera de Pisuerga	2774	42.36 N	4.20 W
Herrin	2746	37.48 N	89.02 W
Herscher	2746	41.03 N	88.06 W
Hershey	2740	40.17 N	76.39 W
Hertford	2744	36.11 N	76.28 W
Hervás	2774	40.16 N	5.51 W
Hesdin	2772	50.22 N	2.02 E
Hesston	2750	38.08 N	97.26 W
Hetian	2794	37.08 N	79.54 E
Hettinger	2750	46.00 N	102.39 W
Heyburn	2754	42.34 N	113.46 W
Hialeah	2744	25.49 N	80.17 W
Hiawassee	2744	34.58 N	83.46 W
Hiawatha	2750	39.51 N	95.32 W
Hibbing	2742	47.25 N	92.56 W
Hickory, Miss., U.S.	2746	32.19 N	89.01 W
Hickory, N.C., U.S.	2744	35.44 N	81.21 W
Hickory Township	2740	41.15 N	80.27 W
Hicksville	2740	41.18 N	84.46 W
Hico	2748	31.59 N	98.02 W
Hidaka-sammyaku ⩕	2798a	42.35 N	142.45 E
Hidalgo, Méx.	2748	27.47 N	99.52 W
Hidalgo, Méx.	2758	24.15 N	99.26 W
Hidalgo del Parral	2758	26.56 N	105.40 W

Symbols against index entries represent categories identified in the key on page 2810.

Name	Page	Lat°′	Long°′
Hierro ▮	2786	27.45 N	18.00 W
Higashiōsaka	2798	34.39 N	135.35 E
Higgins	2748	36.07 N	100.02 W
Higgins Lake ⊜	2742	44.30 N	84.45 W
Higginsville	2746	39.04 N	93.43 W
Highland	2746	38.44 N	89.41 W
Highland Home	2746	31.57 N	86.19 W
Highland Park	2742	42.11 N	87.48 W
Highmore	2750	44.31 N	99.27 W
High Point	2744	35.58 N	80.01 W
High Rock	2744	26.36 N	76.18 W
High Springs	2744	29.50 N	82.36 W
High Wycombe	2769	51.38 N	0.46 W
Higüey	2760	18.37 N	68.42 W
Híjar	2774	41.10 N	0.27 W
Ḥijāz, Jabal al- ⋀	2790	19.45 N	41.55 E
Hikari	2798	33.58 N	131.56 E
Hikone	2798	35.15 N	136.15 E
Hildreth	2750	40.20 N	99.03 W
Hill City, Kans., U.S.	2750	39.22 N	99.51 W
Hill City, Minn., U.S.	2742	46.59 N	93.36 W
Hillcrest Center	2756	35.23 N	118.57 W
Hilliard	2744	30.41 N	81.55 W
Hill Island Lake ⊜	2734	60.29 N	109.50 W
Hillman	2742	45.04 N	83.54 W
Hillsboro, Ill., U.S.	2746	39.09 N	89.29 W
Hillsboro, Kans., U.S.	2750	38.21 N	97.12 W
Hillsboro, N. Mex., U.S.	2752	32.55 N	107.34 W
Hillsboro, N. Dak., U.S.	2750	47.26 N	97.03 W
Hillsboro, Ohio, U.S.	2740	39.12 N	83.37 W
Hillsboro, Tex., U.S.	2748	32.01 N	97.08 W
Hillsboro, Wis., U.S.	2742	43.39 N	90.21 W
Hillsdale	2742	41.55 N	84.38 W
Hillsville	2744	36.46 N	80.44 W
Hilo	2757a	19.43 N	155.05 W
Hilversum	2770	52.14 N	5.10 E
Himalayas ⋀	2794	28.00 N	84.00 E
Himeji	2798	34.49 N	134.42 E
Ḥimṣ (Homs)	2791	34.44 N	36.43 E
Hinchinbrook Island ▮	2806	18.23 S	146.17 E
Hinckley, Minn., U.S.	2742	46.01 N	92.56 W
Hinckley, Utah, U.S.	2752	39.20 N	112.40 W
Hindman	2744	37.20 N	82.59 W
Hindu Kush ⋀	2794	36.00 N	71.30 E
Hines	2754	43.34 N	119.05 W
Hinesville	2744	31.51 N	81.36 W
Hinganghāt	2793	20.34 N	78.50 E
Hinojosa del Duque	2774	38.30 N	5.09 W
Hinsdale	2754	48.24 N	107.05 W
Hinton, Alta., Can.	2734	53.25 N	117.34 W
Hinton, W. Va., U.S.	2744	37.41 N	80.53 W
Hirado	2798	33.22 N	129.33 E
Hirara	2796	24.48 N	125.17 E
Hiratsuka	2798	35.19 N	139.21 E
Hirosaki	2798	40.35 N	140.28 E
Hiroshima	2798	34.24 N	132.27 E
Hirson	2772	49.55 N	4.05 E
Hisār	2794	29.10 N	75.43 E
Hispaniola ▮	2760	19.00 N	71.00 W
Hita	2798	33.19 N	130.56 E
Hitachi	2798	36.36 N	140.39 E
Hitoyoshi	2798	32.13 N	130.45 E
Hitra ▮	2768	63.33 N	8.45 E
Hjørring	2768	57.28 N	9.59 E
Ho	2786	6.35 N	0.30 E
Hobart, Austl.	2806	42.53 S	147.19 E
Hobart, Okla., U.S.	2748	35.01 N	99.06 W
Hobbs	2748	32.42 N	103.08 W
Hobe Sound	2744	27.04 N	80.08 W
Hodge	2746	32.17 N	92.43 W
Hodgenville	2746	37.34 N	85.44 W
Hódmezővásárhely	2770	46.25 N	20.20 E
Hodna, Chott el ⊜	2774	35.25 N	4.45 E
Hodonín	2770	48.51 N	17.08 E
Hoehne	2750	37.17 N	104.23 W
Hoffman	2750	45.50 N	95.48 W
Hofors	2768	60.33 N	16.17 E
Hōfu	2798	34.03 N	131.34 E
Hogansville	2744	33.11 N	84.55 W
Hohenau an der March	2770	48.36 N	16.55 E
Hohenwald	2746	35.33 N	87.33 W
Hohe Tauern ⋀	2770	47.10 N	12.30 E
Hohoe	2786	7.09 N	0.28 W
Hōhoku	2798	34.17 N	130.57 E
Hoisington	2750	38.31 N	98.47 W
Hokitika	2808	42.43 S	170.58 E
Hokkaidō ▮	2798a	44.00 N	143.00 E
Holbrook	2752	34.54 N	110.10 W
Holden, Utah, U.S.	2752	39.06 N	112.16 W
Holden, W. Va., U.S.	2744	37.50 N	82.04 W
Holdenville	2748	35.05 N	96.24 W
Holdrege	2750	40.26 N	99.22 W
Holguín	2760	20.53 N	76.15 W
Höljes	2768	60.54 N	12.36 E
Hollabrunn	2770	48.34 N	16.05 E
Holladay	2752	40.40 N	111.49 W
Holland	2742	42.47 N	86.07 W
Holland → Netherlands □1	2766	52.15 N	5.30 E
Hollandale	2746	33.10 N	90.58 W
Holliday	2748	33.49 N	98.42 W
Hollis	2748	34.41 N	99.55 W
Hollister	2756	36.51 N	121.24 W
Holly	2750	38.03 N	102.07 W
Holly Hill	2744	29.14 N	81.02 W
Holly Springs	2746	34.41 N	89.26 W
Hollywood	2744	26.00 N	80.09 W
Holman Island	2734	70.43 N	117.43 W
Holmen	2742	43.58 N	91.15 W
Holmes, Mount ▲	2754	44.49 N	110.51 W
Holmes Reefs ✣2	2806	16.27 S	148.00 E
Holstebro	2768	56.21 N	8.38 E
Holstein	2750	42.29 N	95.33 W
Holsteinsborg	2734	66.55 N	53.40 W
Holston, North Fork ≃	2744	36.33 N	82.36 W
Holsworthy	2769	50.49 N	4.21 W
Holt, Ala., U.S.	2746	33.15 N	87.29 W
Holt, Mich., U.S.	2742	42.39 N	84.31 W
Holton	2750	39.28 N	95.44 W
Holtville	2756	32.49 N	115.23 W
Holyhead	2769	53.19 N	4.38 W
Holyoke, Colo., U.S.	2750	40.35 N	102.18 W
Holyoke, Mass., U.S.	2740	42.12 N	72.37 W
Hombori Tondo ▲	2786	15.16 N	1.40 W
Home Bay C	2734	68.45 N	67.10 W
Homedale	2754	43.37 N	116.56 W
Home Hill	2806	19.40 S	147.25 E
Homer, La., U.S.	2746	32.48 N	93.04 W
Homer, Mich., U.S.	2742	42.09 N	84.49 W
Homer, N.Y., U.S.	2740	42.38 N	76.11 W
Homerville	2744	31.02 N	82.45 W
Homestead	2744	25.29 N	80.29 W
Homewood	2746	33.29 N	86.48 W
Hominy	2748	36.25 N	96.24 W
Homosassa	2744	28.47 N	82.37 W
Honaker	2744	37.01 N	81.59 W
Hondo, Nihon	2798	32.27 N	130.12 E
Hondo, N. Mex., U.S.	2752	33.23 N	105.16 W
Hondo, Tex., U.S.	2748	29.21 N	99.09 W
Honduras □1	2760	15.00 N	86.30 W
Honduras, Gulf of C	2760	16.10 N	87.50 W
Honea Path	2744	34.27 N	82.24 W
Hønefoss	2768	60.10 N	10.18 E
Honesdale	2740	41.34 N	75.16 W
Honey Grove	2748	33.35 N	95.55 W
Hon-gai	2804	20.57 N	107.05 E
Hongdong	2796	36.19 N	111.39 E
Honghu	2800	29.48 N	113.27 E
Hong Kong → Victoria	2800	22.17 N	114.09 E
Hong Kong □2	2800	22.15 N	114.10 E
Hongliuyuan	2796	41.04 N	95.26 E
Hongzehu ⊜	2800	33.16 N	118.34 E
Honningsvåg	2768	70.59 N	25.59 E
Honokaa	2757a	20.05 N	155.28 W
Honolulu	2757a	21.19 N	157.52 W
Honomu	2757a	19.52 N	155.07 W
Hood, Mount ▲	2754	45.23 N	121.41 W
Hood Canal C	2754	47.35 N	123.00 W
Hood River	2754	45.43 N	121.31 W
Hoodsport	2754	47.24 N	123.09 W
Hoogeveen	2770	52.43 N	6.29 E
Hooker	2748	36.52 N	101.13 W
Hook Head ≻	2769	52.07 N	6.55 W
Hoopa	2756	41.03 N	123.40 W
Hooper	2750	41.37 N	96.33 W
Hoopeston	2746	40.28 N	87.40 W
Hoorn	2770	52.38 N	5.04 E
Hopatcong	2740	40.56 N	74.39 W
Hope, B.C., Can.	2734	49.23 N	121.26 W
Hope, Ark., U.S.	2746	33.40 N	93.36 W
Hope, N. Mex., U.S.	2748	32.49 N	104.44 W
Hope, Ben ▲	2769	58.24 N	4.36 W
Hope, Point ≻	2738	68.21 N	166.50 W
Hopedale, Newf., Can.	2734	55.28 N	60.13 W
Hopedale, La., U.S.	2746	29.51 N	89.41 W
Hope Mills	2744	34.59 N	78.57 W
Hopetown	2788	29.34 S	24.03 E
Hopewell	2744	37.18 N	77.17 W
Hopkins	2750	40.33 N	94.49 W
Hopkinsville	2746	36.52 N	87.29 W
Hoquiam	2754	46.59 N	123.53 W
Horgen	2772	47.15 N	8.36 E
Horicon	2742	43.27 N	88.38 W
Hormuz, Strait of ꓘ	2790	26.34 N	56.15 E
Horn	2770	48.40 N	15.40 E
Hornell	2740	42.19 N	77.40 W
Hornepayne	2734	49.13 N	84.47 W
Hornos, Cabo de (Cape Horn) ≻	2764	56.00 S	67.16 W
Horn Plateau ⋀1	2734	62.15 N	119.15 W
Horseback Knob ▲2	2740	39.14 N	83.06 W
Horse Cave	2746	37.11 N	85.54 W
Horseheads	2740	42.10 N	76.50 W
Horse Heaven Hills ⋀2	2754	46.10 N	119.45 W
Horsens	2768	55.52 N	9.52 E
Horse Shoe Bend	2754	43.55 N	116.12 W
Horsham	2806	36.43 S	142.13 E
Horten	2768	59.25 N	10.30 E
Hortonville	2742	44.20 N	88.38 W
Hoshiārpur	2794	31.32 N	75.54 E
Hospet	2793	15.16 N	76.24 E
Hospitalet	2774	41.22 N	2.08 E
Hoste, Isla ▮	2764	55.10 S	69.00 W
Hotchkiss	2752	38.48 N	107.43 W
Hotevilla	2752	35.56 N	110.41 W
Hoting	2768	64.07 N	16.10 E
Hot Springs, Mont., U.S.	2754	47.37 N	114.40 W
Hot Springs, N.C., U.S.	2744	35.54 N	82.50 W
Hot Springs, S. Dak., U.S.	2750	43.26 N	103.29 W
Hot Springs National Park	2746	34.30 N	93.03 W
Hot Sulphur Springs	2752	40.04 N	106.06 W
Hottah Lake ⊜	2734	65.04 N	118.29 W
Houghton, Mich., U.S.	2742	47.06 N	88.34 W
Houghton, N.Y., U.S.	2740	42.25 N	78.10 W
Houghton Lake	2742	44.18 N	84.45 W
Houma, La., U.S.	2746	29.36 N	90.43 W
Houma, Zhg.	2796	35.40 N	111.29 E
Houston, Miss., U.S.	2746	33.54 N	89.00 W
Houston, Mo., U.S.	2746	37.22 N	91.58 W
Houston, Tex., U.S.	2748	29.46 N	95.22 W
Houtman Rocks ▮▮1	2806	28.35 S	113.45 E
Hoven	2750	45.15 N	99.47 W
Hovmantorp	2768	56.47 N	15.08 E
Howard, Kans., U.S.	2750	37.28 N	96.16 W
Howard, S. Dak., U.S.	2750	44.01 N	97.32 W
Howard City	2742	43.24 N	85.28 W
Howell	2742	42.36 N	83.55 W
Howland	2740	45.14 N	68.40 W
Howrah	2794	22.35 N	88.20 E
Hoxie	2746	36.03 N	90.58 W
Hoy ▮	2769	58.52 N	3.18 W
Høyanger	2768	61.13 N	6.05 E
Hoyos	2774	40.10 N	6.43 W
Hoyt Lakes	2742	47.31 N	92.08 W
Hradec Králové	2770	50.12 N	15.50 E
Hsinchu	2800	24.48 N	120.58 E
Hsinkao Shan ▲	2800	23.28 N	120.57 E
Huacho	2762	11.07 S	77.37 W
Huachuca City	2752	31.34 N	110.21 W
Hua Hin	2804	12.34 N	99.58 E
Huaian	2800	33.32 N	119.10 E
Huainan	2800	32.40 N	117.00 E
Huaiyang	2800	33.44 N	114.53 E
Huaiyin	2800	33.35 N	119.02 E
Huaiyuan	2800	32.57 N	117.12 E
Hualapai Mountains ⋀	2752	34.50 N	113.55 W
Hualapai Peak ▲	2752	35.04 N	113.54 W
Hualien	2800	23.58 N	121.36 E
Huallaga ≃	2762	5.07 S	75.30 W
Huallanca	2762	8.50 S	77.50 W
Huamachuco	2762	7.50 S	78.05 W
Huambo	2788	12.44 S	15.47 E
Huancayo	2762	12.04 S	75.14 W
Huangchuan	2800	32.09 N	115.03 E
Huanghe ≃	2796	37.32 N	118.19 E
Huangling	2796	35.41 N	109.09 E
Huangshi	2800	30.13 N	115.05 E
Huangyan	2800	28.39 N	121.15 E
Huánuco	2762	9.55 S	76.14 W
Huaraz	2762	9.32 S	77.32 W
Huascarán, Nevado ▲	2762	9.07 S	77.37 W
Huasco	2764	28.28 S	71.14 W
Huatabampo	2758	26.50 N	109.38 W
Huauchinango	2758	20.11 N	98.03 W
Hubbard, Iowa, U.S.	2742	42.18 N	93.18 W
Hubbard, Tex., U.S.	2748	31.51 N	96.48 W
Hubbard Creek Reservoir ⊜1	2748	32.45 N	99.00 W
Hubei □4	2796	31.00 N	112.00 E
Hubli	2793	15.21 N	75.10 E
Huddersfield	2769	53.39 N	1.47 W
Huddinge	2768	59.14 N	17.59 E
Hudiksvall	2768	61.44 N	17.07 E
Hudson, Fla., U.S.	2744	28.22 N	82.42 W
Hudson, Mich., U.S.	2742	41.51 N	84.21 W
Hudson, N.Y., U.S.	2740	42.15 N	73.47 W
Hudson, Wis., U.S.	2742	44.53 N	92.45 W
Hudson, Wyo., U.S.	2754	42.54 N	108.35 W
Hudson ≃	2740	40.42 N	74.02 W
Hudson Bay	2734	52.52 N	102.25 W
Hudson Bay C	2734	60.00 N	86.00 W
Hudson Strait ꓘ	2734	62.30 N	72.00 W
Hudsonville	2742	42.52 N	85.52 W
Hue	2802	16.28 N	107.36 E
Huehuetenango	2760	15.20 N	91.28 W
Huelma	2774	37.39 N	3.27 W
Huelva	2774	37.16 N	6.57 W
Huércal-Overa	2774	37.23 N	1.57 W
Huesca	2774	42.08 N	0.25 W
Hughenden	2806	20.51 S	144.12 E
Hughes	2746	34.57 N	90.28 W
Hugo, Colo., U.S.	2750	39.08 N	103.28 W
Hugo, Okla., U.S.	2748	34.01 N	95.31 W
Hugoton	2750	37.11 N	101.21 W
Huhehaote	2796	40.51 N	111.40 E
Huidong	2804	26.41 N	102.36 E
Huila, Nevado del ▲	2762	3.00 N	76.00 W
Huili	2804	26.43 N	102.10 E
Huinan	2796	42.40 N	126.00 E
Huittinen (Lauttakylä)	2768	61.11 N	22.42 E
Huitzuco [de los Figueroa]	2758	18.18 N	99.21 W
Huixtla	2758	15.09 N	92.28 W
Huiyang (Huizhou)	2800	23.05 N	114.24 E
Hulan	2796	46.00 N	126.38 E
Hulett	2750	44.41 N	104.36 W
Hull	2740	45.26 N	75.43 W
Hultsfred	2768	57.29 N	15.50 E
Hulunchi ⊜	2796	49.01 N	117.32 E
Humaitá	2762	7.31 S	63.02 W
Humansville	2746	37.48 N	93.35 W
Humber ≃	2769	53.40 N	0.10 W
Humboldt, Ariz., U.S.	2752	34.30 N	112.14 W
Humboldt, Iowa, U.S.	2750	42.44 N	94.13 W
Humboldt, Kans., U.S.	2750	37.49 N	95.26 W
Humboldt, Nebr., U.S.	2750	40.10 N	95.57 W
Humboldt, Tenn., U.S.	2746	35.49 N	88.55 W
Humboldt ≃	2736	40.02 N	118.31 W
Humeston	2742	40.52 N	93.30 W
Humphrey, Ark., U.S.	2746	34.25 N	91.42 W
Humphrey, Nebr., U.S.	2750	41.41 N	97.29 W
Hunan □4	2796	28.00 N	111.00 E
Hundred	2740	39.41 N	80.28 W
Hunedoara	2778	45.45 N	22.54 E
Hungary □1	2766	47.00 N	20.00 E
Hŭngnam	2796	39.50 N	127.38 E
Hungry Horse	2754	48.23 N	114.04 W
Hungry Horse Reservoir ⊜1	2754	48.15 N	113.50 W
Hunsrück ⋀	2770	49.50 N	6.40 E
Hunter Island ▮	2806	40.32 S	144.45 E
Huntingburg	2746	38.18 N	86.57 W
Huntingdon, Eng., U.K.	2769	52.20 N	0.12 W
Huntingdon, Pa., U.S.	2740	40.29 N	78.01 W
Huntingdon, Tenn., U.S.	2746	36.00 N	88.26 W
Huntington, Ind., U.S.	2746	40.53 N	85.30 W
Huntington, N.Y., U.S.	2740	40.51 N	73.25 W
Huntington, Oreg., U.S.	2754	44.21 N	117.16 W
Huntington, W. Va., U.S.	2740	38.25 N	82.26 W
Huntington Beach	2756	33.39 N	117.60 W
Hunt Mountain ▲	2754	44.44 N	107.45 W
Huntsville, Ont., Can.	2740	45.20 N	79.13 W
Huntsville, Ala., U.S.	2746	34.44 N	86.35 W
Huntsville, Mo., U.S.	2746	39.26 N	92.33 W
Huntsville, Tenn., U.S.	2744	36.25 N	84.29 W
Huntsville, Tex., U.S.	2748	30.43 N	95.33 W
Huntsville, Utah, U.S.	2752	41.16 N	111.46 W
Hurao	2796	45.46 N	132.59 E
Hurd, Cape ≻	2740	45.13 N	81.44 W
Hurley, Miss., U.S.	2746	30.40 N	88.30 W
Hurley, N. Mex., U.S.	2752	32.42 N	108.08 W
Hurley, Wis., U.S.	2742	46.28 N	90.08 W
Huron, Ohio, U.S.	2740	41.24 N	82.33 W
Huron, S. Dak., U.S.	2750	44.22 N	98.13 W
Huron, Lake ⊜	2736	44.30 N	82.15 W
Huron Mountains ⋀2	2742	46.45 N	87.45 W
Hurricane	2752	37.11 N	113.17 W
Hurtsboro	2746	32.14 N	85.25 W
Húsavík	2766	66.04 N	17.18 W
Huskvarna	2768	57.48 N	14.16 E
Hutchinson, Kans., U.S.	2750	38.05 N	97.56 W
Hutchinson, Minn., U.S.	2742	44.54 N	94.22 W
Hutch Mountain ▲	2752	34.47 N	111.22 W
Hüttental	2770	50.54 N	8.02 E
Huy	2770	50.31 N	5.14 E
Huzhou	2800	30.52 N	120.06 E
Hvannadalshnúkur ▲	2766	64.01 N	16.41 W
Hvar	2776	43.10 N	16.27 E
Hwang Ho → Huanghe ≃	2796	37.32 N	118.19 E
Hyannis, Mass., U.S.	2740	41.39 N	70.17 W
Hyannis, Nebr., U.S.	2750	41.59 N	101.44 W
Hyden	2744	37.10 N	83.22 W
Hyde Park, Guy.	2762	6.30 N	58.16 W
Hyde Park, N.Y., U.S.	2740	41.47 N	73.56 W
Hyderābād, Bhārat	2793	17.23 N	78.28 E
Hyderābād, Pāk.	2794	25.22 N	68.22 E
Hyères	2772	43.07 N	6.07 E
Hyesan	2796	41.23 N	128.12 E
Hyndman	2740	39.49 N	78.44 W
Hyndman Peak ▲	2754	43.50 N	114.10 W
Hysham	2754	46.18 N	107.14 W
Hyūga	2798	32.25 N	131.38 E
Hyūga-nada ⩪2	2798	32.00 N	131.35 E
Hyvinkää	2768	60.38 N	24.52 E
I			
Iași	2778	47.10 N	27.35 E
Ibadan	2786	7.17 N	3.30 E
Ibagué	2762	4.27 N	75.14 W
Ibarra	2762	0.21 N	78.07 W
Ibb	2790	14.01 N	44.10 E
Iberville, Mont d' ▲	2734	58.53 N	63.43 W
Ibiá	2765	19.29 S	46.32 W
Ibiza	2774	38.54 N	1.26 E
Ibiza ▮	2774	39.00 N	1.25 E
Ibo	2788	12.20 S	40.35 E
Iboundji, Mont ▲	2788	1.08 S	11.48 E
Ica	2762	14.04 S	75.42 W
Içana	2762	0.21 N	67.19 W
İçel □4	2791	36.45 N	34.00 E
Iceland □1	2766	65.00 N	18.00 W
Ichalkaranji	2793	16.42 N	74.28 E
Ich Bogd Uul ⋀	2796	44.55 N	100.20 E
Ichinomiya	2798	35.18 N	136.48 E
Icó	2762	6.24 S	38.51 W
Idabel	2746	33.54 N	94.50 W
Ida Grove	2750	42.21 N	95.28 W
Idaho □3	2736	45.00 N	115.00 W
Idaho City	2754	43.50 N	115.50 W
Idaho Falls	2754	43.30 N	112.02 W
Idaho Springs	2752	39.45 N	105.31 W
Idalou	2748	33.40 N	101.41 W
Idanha-a-Nova	2774	39.55 N	7.14 W
Idfū	2786	24.58 N	32.52 E
Idlib	2791	35.55 N	36.38 E
Ieper	2770	50.51 N	2.53 E
Ierápetra	2778	35.00 N	25.45 E
Iesi	2776	43.31 N	13.14 E
Ifalik ▮1	2802	7.15 N	144.27 E
Ife	2786	7.30 N	4.30 E
Iferouâne	2786	19.04 N	8.24 E
Iforas, Adrar des ⋀	2786	20.00 N	2.00 E
Igarka	2784	67.28 N	86.35 E
Iglesias	2776	39.19 N	8.32 E
Igloolik	2734	69.24 N	81.49 W
Iguala	2758	18.21 N	99.32 W
Igualada	2774	41.35 N	1.38 E
Iguape	2764	24.43 S	47.33 W
Iguatu	2762	6.22 S	39.18 W
Iguéla	2788	1.55 S	9.19 E
Iguidi, Erg ⩪8	2786	26.35 N	5.40 W
Ihosy	2788	22.24 S	46.08 E
Iida	2798	35.31 N	137.50 E
Iisalmi	2768	63.34 N	27.11 E
Iizuka	2798	33.38 N	130.41 E
Ijill, Kediet ▲	2786	22.38 N	12.33 W
IJmuiden	2770	52.27 N	4.36 E
IJsselmeer (Zuiderzee) ⩪2	2770	52.45 N	5.25 E
Ika	2784	59.18 N	106.12 E
Ikela	2788	1.11 S	23.16 E
Ikerre	2786	7.31 N	5.14 E
Ila	2786	8.01 N	4.55 E
Ilan	2800	24.45 N	121.44 E
Ilbenge	2784	62.49 N	124.24 E
Île-à-la-Crosse, Lac ⊜	2734	55.40 N	107.45 W
Ilebo	2788	4.19 S	20.35 E
Île-de-France □9	2772	49.00 N	2.20 E
Île Desroches ▮	2788	5.41 S	53.41 E
Ilhéus	2765	14.49 S	39.02 W
Iliff	2750	40.45 N	103.04 W
Ilion	2740	43.01 N	75.02 W
Ilirska Bistrica	2776	45.34 N	14.15 E
Iljinskij	2784	47.58 N	142.12 E
Illampu, Nevado ▲	2762	15.50 S	68.34 W
Illapel	2764	31.38 S	71.10 W
Illescas	2758	23.13 N	102.07 W
Illiers	2772	48.18 N	1.15 E
Illimani, Nevado ▲	2762	16.39 S	67.48 W
Illinois □3	2736	40.00 N	89.00 W
Illinois ≃	2746	38.58 N	90.27 W
Illizi	2786	26.29 N	8.28 E
Il'men', Ozero ⊜	2780	58.17 N	31.20 E

Symbols against index entries represent categories identified in the key on page 2810.

Name	Page	Lat °′	Long °′
Ilo	2762	17.38 S	71.20 W
Iloilo	2802	10.42 N	122.34 E
Ilomantsi	2768	62.40 N	30.55 E
Ilorin	2786	8.30 N	4.32 E
Il'pyrskij	2784	59.56 N	164.10 E
Imabari	2798	34.03 N	133.00 E
Iman	2784	45.55 N	133.43 E
Imatra	2768	61.10 N	28.46 E
Immokalee	2744	26.25 N	81.25 W
Imola	2776	44.21 N	11.42 E
Imperatriz	2762	5.32 S	47.29 W
Imperia	2776	43.53 N	8.03 E
Imperial, Calif., U.S.	2756	32.51 N	115.34 W
Imperial, Nebr., U.S.	2750	40.31 N	101.39 W
Imperial Beach	2756	32.35 N	117.08 W
Impfondo	2788	1.37 N	18.04 E
Imphāl	2794	24.49 N	93.57 E
Imst	2770	47.14 N	10.44 E
Imuris	2758	30.47 N	110.52 W
Ina	2798	35.50 N	137.57 E
In'a ≛	2784	59.23 N	144.54 E
Inari	2768	68.54 N	27.01 E
Inca	2774	39.43 N	2.54 E
İncekum Burnu ᐳ	2791	36.13 N	33.58 E
Inch'ŏn	2796	37.28 N	126.38 E
Independence, Calif., U.S.	2756	36.48 N	118.12 W
Independence, Iowa, U.S.	2742	42.28 N	91.54 W
Independence, Kans., U.S.	2750	37.13 N	95.42 W
Independence, Mo., U.S.	2746	39.05 N	94.24 W
Independence, Va., U.S.	2744	36.37 N	81.09 W
Independence, Wis., U.S.	2742	44.21 N	91.25 W
Inderborskij	2766	48.33 N	51.44 E
India □[1]	2792	20.00 N	77.00 E
Indiana	2740	40.37 N	79.09 W
Indiana □[3]	2736	40.00 N	86.15 W
Indianapolis	2746	39.46 N	86.09 W
Indian Lake	2740	43.47 N	74.16 W
Indian Ocean ∓[1]	2730	10.00 S	70.00 E
Indianola, Iowa, U.S.	2742	41.22 N	93.34 W
Indianola, Miss., U.S.	2746	33.27 N	90.39 W
Indianola, Nebr., U.S.	2750	40.14 N	100.25 W
Indian Peak Λ	2752	38.16 N	113.53 W
Indian River	2742	45.25 N	84.37 W
Indian Springs	2756	36.34 N	115.40 W
Indiantown	2744	27.01 N	80.28 W
Indigirka ≛	2784	70.48 N	148.54 E
Indio	2756	33.43 N	116.13 W
Indispensable Reefs ✢[2]	2806	12.40 S	160.25 E
Indonesia □[1]	2802	5.00 S	120.00 E
Indore	2794	22.43 N	75.50 E
Indus ≛	2794	24.20 N	67.47 E
İnegöl	2778	40.05 N	29.31 E
Inez	2744	37.52 N	82.32 W
I-n-Gall	2786	16.47 N	6.56 E
Ingham	2806	18.39 S	146.10 E
Ingram	2748	30.04 N	99.14 W
In Guezzam	2786	19.32 N	5.42 E
Inhambane	2788	23.51 S	35.29 E
Inhambupe	2762	11.47 S	38.21 W
Inhaminga	2788	18.24 S	35.00 E
Inharrime	2788	24.29 S	35.01 E
Inman	2744	35.03 N	82.05 W
Inn (En) ≛	2770	48.35 N	13.28 E
Innamincka	2806	27.45 S	140.44 E
Inner Hebrides II	2769	57.00 N	6.45 W
Innsbruck	2770	47.16 N	11.24 E
Inongo	2788	1.57 S	18.16 E
Inoucdjouac	2734	58.27 N	78.06 W
Inowrocław	2770	52.48 N	18.15 E
In Salah	2786	27.12 N	2.28 E
Interlaken	2772	46.41 N	7.51 E
International Falls	2742	48.36 N	93.25 W
Inthanon, Doi Λ	2804	18.38 N	98.30 E
Intiyaco	2764	28.40 S	60.05 W
Intracoastal Waterway ☲	2744	33.40 N	79.00 W
Inuvik	2734	68.25 N	133.30 W
Inveraray	2769	56.13 N	5.05 W
Invercargill	2808	46.24 S	168.21 E
Inverell	2806	29.47 S	151.07 E
Inverness, Scot., U.K.	2769	57.27 N	4.15 W
Inverness, Fla., U.S.	2744	28.51 N	82.20 W
Inverness, Miss., U.S.	2746	33.21 N	90.35 W
Inverurie	2769	57.17 N	2.23 W
Investigator Group II	2806	33.45 S	134.30 E
Investigator Strait ⩌	2806	35.25 S	137.10 E
Inyangani Λ	2788	18.20 S	32.50 E
Inyokern	2756	35.39 N	117.49 W
Inza	2766	53.51 N	46.21 E
Ioánnina	2778	39.40 N	20.50 E
Iola	2750	37.55 N	95.24 W
Ione	2754	48.45 N	117.25 W
Ionia	2742	42.59 N	85.04 W
Ionian Islands → Iónioi Nísoi II	2778	38.30 N	20.30 E
Ionian Sea ∓[2]	2766	39.00 N	19.00 E
Iónioi Nísoi II	2778	38.30 N	20.30 E
Iowa □[3]	2736	42.15 N	93.15 W
Iowa ≛	2742	41.10 N	91.02 W
Iowa City	2742	41.40 N	91.32 W
Iowa Falls	2742	42.31 N	93.16 W
Iowa Park	2748	33.57 N	98.40 W
Ipameri	2765	17.43 S	48.09 W
Ipiaú	2765	14.08 S	39.44 W
Ipoh	2804	4.35 N	101.04 E
Ipswich, Austl.	2806	27.36 S	152.46 E
Ipswich, Eng., U.K.	2769	52.04 N	1.10 E
Ipswich, S. Dak., U.S.	2750	45.27 N	99.02 W
Ipu	2762	4.20 S	40.42 W
Iquique	2762	20.13 S	70.10 W
Iquitos	2762	3.50 S	73.15 W
Iraan	2748	30.54 N	101.54 W
Iráklion	2778	35.20 N	25.09 E
Iran □[1]	2766	35.00 N	50.00 E
Iran □[1], As.	2790	32.00 N	53.00 E
Īrānshahr	2790	27.13 N	60.41 E

Name	Page	Lat °′	Long °′
Irapuato	2758	20.41 N	101.28 W
Iraq □[1]	2790	33.00 N	44.00 E
Irbid	2791	32.33 N	35.51 E
Irbīl	2790	36.11 N	44.01 E
Irbit	2766	57.41 N	63.03 E
Ireland □[1]	2766	53.00 N	8.00 W
Irgiz	2766	48.37 N	61.16 E
Iringa	2788	7.46 S	35.42 E
Iriri ≛	2762	3.52 S	52.37 W
Irish Sea ∓[2]	2769	53.30 N	5.20 W
Irkutsk	2784	52.16 N	104.20 E
Irondequoit	2740	43.12 N	77.36 W
Iron Gate V	2778	44.41 N	22.31 E
Iron Mountain	2742	45.49 N	88.04 W
Iron River	2742	46.05 N	88.39 W
Ironton, Mo., U.S.	2746	37.36 N	90.38 W
Ironton, Ohio, U.S.	2740	38.31 N	82.40 W
Ironwood	2742	46.27 N	90.10 W
Irrawaddy ≛	2804	15.50 N	95.06 E
Irumu	2788	1.27 N	29.52 E
Irún	2774	43.21 N	1.47 W
Irurzun	2774	42.55 N	1.50 W
Irvine, Scot., U.K.	2769	55.37 N	4.40 W
Irvine, Ky., U.S.	2744	37.42 N	83.58 W
Irving	2748	32.49 N	96.56 W
Irwinton	2744	32.49 N	83.10 W
Isabella, Cordillera ⩕	2760	13.45 N	85.15 W
Ísafjörður	2766	66.08 N	23.13 W
Isana (Içana) ≛	2762	0.26 N	67.19 W
Ischia	2776	40.44 N	13.57 E
Ise	2798	34.29 N	136.42 E
Isernia	2776	41.36 N	14.14 E
Ise-wan C	2798	34.43 N	136.43 E
Ishikari-wan C	2798a	43.25 N	141.01 E
Ishinomaki	2798	38.25 N	141.18 E
Ishpeming	2742	46.30 N	87.40 W
Isiolo	2788	0.21 N	37.35 E
Isiro	2786	2.47 N	27.37 E
İskenderun	2791	36.37 N	36.07 E
İskenderun Körfezi C	2791	36.30 N	35.40 E
Iskitim	2784	54.38 N	83.18 E
Islāmābād	2794	33.42 N	73.10 E
Island Falls	2740	46.00 N	68.16 W
Island Lake ❂	2734	53.47 N	94.25 W
Island Pond	2740	44.49 N	71.53 W
Isla Vista	2756	34.25 N	119.53 W
Islay I	2769	55.46 N	6.10 W
Isle	2742	46.08 N	93.29 W
Isle of Man □[2]	2769	54.15 N	4.30 W
Isle Royale National Park ♦	2742	48.00 N	89.00 W
Isola della Scala	2776	45.16 N	11.00 E
Ispica	2776	36.46 N	14.55 E
Israel (Yisra'el) □[1]	2791	31.30 N	35.00 E
Issoire	2772	45.33 N	3.15 E
Issoudun	2772	46.57 N	2.00 E
Is-sur-Tille	2772	47.31 N	5.06 E
İstanbul	2778	41.01 N	28.58 E
İstanbul Boğazı (Bosporus) ⩌	2778	41.00 N	29.00 E
Istokpoga, Lake ❂	2744	27.22 N	81.17 W
Itabaiana	2762	10.41 S	37.26 W
Itaberaí	2762	16.02 S	49.48 W
Itabira	2765	19.37 S	43.13 W
Itabuna	2765	14.48 S	39.16 W
Itacoatiara	2762	3.08 S	58.25 W
Itaituba	2762	4.17 S	55.59 W
Itajaí	2764	26.53 S	48.39 W
Itajubá	2765	22.26 S	45.27 W
Italy	2748	32.11 N	96.53 W
Italy □[1]	2766	42.50 N	12.50 E
Itaperuna	2765	21.12 S	41.54 W
Itapetinga	2765	15.15 S	40.15 W
Itapetininga	2765	23.36 S	48.03 W
Itapeva	2765	23.58 S	48.52 W
Itapicuru ≛	2762	2.52 S	44.12 W
Itapira	2765	22.26 S	46.50 W
Itararé	2765	24.07 S	49.20 W
Itārsi	2794	22.37 N	77.46 E
Itasca	2748	32.10 N	97.09 W
Ithaca, Mich., U.S.	2742	43.18 N	84.36 W
Ithaca, N.Y., U.S.	2740	42.27 N	76.30 W
Itta Bena	2746	33.30 N	90.20 W
Ittiri	2776	40.36 N	8.33 E
Ituberá	2765	13.44 S	39.09 W
Ituiutaba	2765	18.58 S	49.28 W
Itumbiara	2765	18.25 S	49.13 W
Ituri ≛	2788	1.40 N	27.01 E
Iturup, Ostrov (Etorofu-tō) I	2784	44.54 N	147.30 E
Ituverava	2765	20.20 S	47.47 W
Ituxi ≛	2762	7.18 S	64.51 W
Iuka	2746	34.49 N	88.11 W
Ivalo	2768	68.42 N	27.30 E
Ivanhoe	2750	44.28 N	96.15 W
Ivanić Grad	2776	45.42 N	16.24 E
Ivano-Frankovsk	2782	48.55 N	24.43 E
Ivanovo	2780	57.00 N	40.59 E
Ivdel'	2766	60.42 N	60.24 E
Ivigtut	2734	61.12 N	48.10 W
Ivory Coast □[1]	2786	8.00 N	5.00 W
Ivrea	2776	45.28 N	7.52 E
Ivujivik	2734	62.24 N	77.55 W
Iwaki (Taira)	2798	37.03 N	140.55 E
Iwakuni	2798	34.09 N	132.11 E
Iwanai	2798a	42.58 N	140.30 E
Iwo	2786	7.38 N	4.11 E
Iyo-nada ∓[2]	2798	33.40 N	132.20 E
Izegem	2770	50.55 N	3.12 E
Iževsk	2766	56.51 N	53.14 E
Izmail	2782	45.21 N	28.50 E
İzmir	2778	38.25 N	27.09 E
İzmit	2766	40.46 N	29.55 E
Iznalloz	2774	37.23 N	3.31 W
Izozog, Bañados de ☷	2762	18.48 S	62.10 W
Izúcar de Matamoros	2758	18.36 N	98.28 W
Izuhara	2798	34.12 N	129.17 E

Name	Page	Lat °′	Long °′
Iz'um	2782	49.12 N	37.19 E
Izumo	2798	35.22 N	132.46 E
Izu-shotō II	2798	34.30 N	139.30 E
Izvestij CIK, Ostrova II	2784	75.55 N	82.30 E
J			
Jabalpur	2794	23.10 N	79.57 E
Jabbūl, Sabkhat al- ❂	2791	36.03 N	37.39 E
Jablah	2791	35.21 N	35.55 E
Jablonec nad Nisou	2770	50.44 N	15.10 E
Jablonovyj Chrebet (Yablonovy Range) ⩕	2784	53.30 N	115.00 E
Jaboatão	2762	8.07 S	35.01 W
∓[4]Īn	2790	23.17 N	48.58 E
Jaca	2774	42.34 N	0.33 W
Jáchal	2764	30.15 S	68.45 W
Jackman	2740	45.38 N	70.16 W
Jacksboro	2748	33.13 N	98.10 W
Jackson, Ala., U.S.	2746	31.31 N	87.53 W
Jackson, Calif., U.S.	2756	38.21 N	120.46 W
Jackson, Ga., U.S.	2744	33.18 N	83.58 W
Jackson, Ky., U.S.	2744	37.33 N	83.23 W
Jackson, Mich., U.S.	2742	42.15 N	84.24 W
Jackson, Minn , U.S.	2750	43.37 N	95.01 W
Jackson, Miss., U.S.	2746	32.18 N	90.12 W
Jackson, Mo., U.S.	2746	37.23 N	89.40 W
Jackson, N.C., U.S.	2744	36.23 N	77.25 W
Jackson, Ohio, U.S.	2740	39.03 N	82.39 W
Jackson, Tenn., U.S.	2746	35.37 N	88.49 W
Jackson, Wyo., U.S.	2754	43.29 N	110.38 W
Jackson Lake ❂[1]	2754	43.55 N	110.40 W
Jacksonville, Ala., U.S.	2746	33.49 N	85.46 W
Jacksonville, Ark., U.S.	2746	34.52 N	92.07 W
Jacksonville, Fla., U.S.	2744	30.20 N	81.40 W
Jacksonville, Ill., U.S.	2746	39.44 N	90.14 W
Jacksonville, N.C., U.S.	2744	34.45 N	77.26 W
Jacksonville, Oreg., U.S.	2754	42.19 N	122.57 W
Jacksonville, Tex., U.S.	2748	31.58 N	95.17 W
Jacobābād	2794	28.17 N	68.26 E
Jacques-Cartier, Détroit de ⩌	2734	50.00 N	63.30 W
Jacques-Cartier, Mont Λ	2739	48.59 N	65.57 W
Jadraque	2774	40.55 N	2.55 W
Jaén, Esp.	2774	37.46 N	3.47 W
Jaén, Perú	2762	5.21 S	78.28 W
Jafr, Qā' al- ⩊[7]	2791	30.17 N	36.20 E
Jagādhri	2794	30.10 N	77.18 E
Jagdalpur	2793	19.04 N	82.02 E
Jagersfontein	2788	29.44 S	25.29 E
Jagodnoje	2784	62.33 N	149.40 E
Jaguarão	2764	32.34 S	53.23 W
Jahrom	2790	28.31 N	53.33 E
Jaipur	2794	26.55 N	75.49 E
Jajce	2776	44.21 N	17.16 E
Jakarta → Djakarta	2802	6.10 S	106.48 E
Jakobshavn	2734	69.13 N	51.06 W
Jakobstad (Pietarsaari)	2768	63.40 N	22.42 E
Jakša	2766	61.48 N	56.49 E
Jakutsk	2784	62.13 N	129.49 E
Jal	2748	32.07 N	103.12 W
Jalālābād	2794	34.26 N	70.28 E
Jalapa	2760	14.38 N	89.59 W
Jalapa Enríquez	2758	19.32 N	96.55 W
Jālgaon	2793	21.01 N	75.34 E
Jālna	2793	19.50 N	75.53 E
Jalostotitlán	2758	21.12 N	102.28 W
Jalpaiguri	2794	26.31 N	88.44 E
Jalta (Yalta)	2782	44.30 N	34.10 E
Jamaica □[1]	2760	18.15 N	77.30 W
Jamaica Channel ⩌	2760	18.00 N	75.30 W
Jamālpur	2794	25.18 N	86.30 E
Jamame	2788	0.04 N	42.46 E
Jambol	2778	42.29 N	26.30 E
Jamdena, Pulau I	2802	7.36 S	131.25 E
James ≛	2736	42.52 N	97.18 W
James Bay C	2734	53.30 N	80.30 W
James City	2744	35.05 N	77.02 W
Jamestown, Ky., U.S.	2746	36.59 N	85.04 W
Jamestown, N.C., U.S.	2744	35.59 N	79.56 W
Jamestown, N. Dak., U.S.	2750	46.54 N	98.42 W
Jamestown, N.Y., U.S.	2740	42.06 N	79.14 W
Jamestown, Tenn., U.S.	2746	36.26 N	84.57 W
Jamiltepec	2758	16.17 N	97.49 W
Jammu	2794	32.42 N	74.52 E
Jammu and Kashmir □[2]	2794	34.00 N	76.00 E
Jāmnagar	2794	22.28 N	70.04 E
Jämsä	2768	61.52 N	25.12 E
Jamshedpur	2794	22.48 N	86.11 E
Jamsk	2784	59.35 N	154.10 E
Jamuna ≛	2794	23.51 N	89.45 E
Jana ≛	2784	71.31 N	136.32 E
Janaucu, Ilha I	2762	0.30 N	50.10 W
Janesville	2742	42.41 N	89.01 W
Janīn	2791	32.28 N	35.18 E
Janskij	2784	68.28 N	134.48 E
Janskij Zaliv C	2784	71.50 N	136.00 E
Januária	2765	15.29 S	44.22 W
Japan □[1]	2796	36.00 N	138.00 E
Japan, Sea of ∓[2]	2796	40.00 N	135.00 E
Japen, Pulau I	2802	1.45 S	136.15 E
Jaqué	2760	7.45 N	78.15 W
Jarābulus	2791	36.49 N	38.01 E
Jaraiz de la Vera	2774	40.04 N	5.45 W
Jarash	2791	32.17 N	35.54 E
Jarcevo	2780	55.04 N	32.41 E
Jari ≛	2762	1.09 S	51.54 W
Jaroslavl'	2780	57.37 N	39.52 E
Jarosław	2770	50.02 N	22.42 E
Jarratt	2744	36.48 N	77.28 W
Järvenpää	2768	60.28 N	25.06 E
Järvsö	2768	61.43 N	16.10 E
Jāsk	2790	25.38 N	57.46 E
Jasnyj	2784	53.17 N	127.59 E
Jasper, Alta., Can.	2734	52.53 N	118.05 W

Name	Page	Lat °′	Long °′
Jasper, Ala., U.S.	2746	33.50 N	87.17 W
Jasper, Ark., U.S.	2746	36.00 N	93.11 W
Jasper, Fla., U.S.	2744	30.31 N	82.57 W
Jasper, Ga., U.S.	2744	34.28 N	84.26 W
Jasper, Ind., U.S.	2746	38.24 N	86.56 W
Jasper, Minn , U.S.	2750	43.51 N	96.24 W
Jasper, Tex., U.S.	2758	30.55 N	94.01 W
Jataí	2765	17.53 S	51.43 W
Játiva	2774	38.59 N	0.31 W
Jatni	2794	20.10 N	85.42 E
Jaú	2765	22.18 S	48.33 W
Jauaperi ≛	2762	1.26 S	61.35 W
Jauja	2762	11.46 S	75.28 W
Jaunpur	2794	25.44 N	82.41 E
Java → Djawa I	2802	7.30 S	110.00 E
Java Sea → Djawa, Laut ∓[2]	2802	5.00 S	110.00 E
Jävre	2768	65.09 N	21.59 E
Jaworzno	2770	50.13 N	19.15 E
Jay	2748	36.25 N	94.48 W
Jayb, Wādī al- V	2791	30.58 N	35.24 E
Jayton	2748	33.15 N	100.34 W
Jaz Mūrīān, Hāmūn-e ❂	2790	27.20 N	58.55 E
Jeanerette	2746	29.55 N	91.40 W
Jebba	2786	9.08 N	4.50 E
Jefferson, Ga., U.S.	2744	34.07 N	83.35 W
Jefferson, Iowa, U.S.	2750	42.01 N	94.23 W
Jefferson, N.C., U.S.	2744	36.26 N	81.28 W
Jefferson, Oreg., U.S.	2754	44.43 N	123.01 W
Jefferson, Tex., U.S.	2746	32.46 N	94.21 W
Jefferson, Mount Λ	2754	44.40 N	121.47 W
Jefferson City, Mo., U.S.	2746	38.34 N	92.10 W
Jefferson City, Tenn., U.S.	2744	36.07 N	83.30 W
Jeffersonville, Ga., U.S.	2744	32.41 N	83.20 W
Jeffersonville, Ind., U.S.	2746	38.17 N	85.44 W
Jeffrey City	2754	42.29 N	107.49 W
Jefremov	2780	53.09 N	38.07 E
Jegorjevsk	2780	55.23 N	39.02 E
Jejsk	2782	46.42 N	38.16 E
Jelec	2780	52.37 N	38.30 E
Jelenia Góra (Hirschberg)	2770	50.55 N	15.46 E
Jelgava	2780	56.39 N	23.42 E
Jelizavety, Mys ᐳ	2784	54.24 N	142.42 E
Jellico	2744	36.35 N	84.08 W
Jeloguj ≛	2784	63.13 N	87.45 E
Jemez Springs	2752	35.46 N	106.42 W
Jena	2746	31.41 N	92.08 W
Jenašimskij Polkan, Gora Λ	2784	59.50 N	92.52 E
Jendouba (Souk el Arba)	2776	36.30 N	8.47 E
Jenisej ≛	2784	71.50 N	82.40 E
Jenisejsk	2784	58.27 N	92.10 E
Jenisejskij Zaliv C	2784	72.30 N	80.00 E
Jenkinsville	2744	34.16 N	81.17 W
Jennings, Fla., U.S.	2744	30.36 N	83.06 W
Jennings, Kans., U.S.	2750	39.41 N	100.18 W
Jennings, La., U.S.	2746	30.13 N	92.39 W
Jequié	2765	13.51 S	40.05 W
Jerada	2786	34.17 N	2.13 W
Jérémie	2760	18.39 N	74.08 W
Jeremoabo	2762	10.04 S	38.21 W
Jerevan	2766	40.11 N	44.30 E
Jerez de García Salinas	2758	22.39 N	103.00 W
Jerez de la Frontera	2774	36.41 N	6.08 W
Jerez de los Caballeros	2774	38.19 N	6.46 W
Jerofej Pavlovič	2784	53.58 N	122.01 E
Jerome	2754	42.43 N	114.31 W
Jeropol	2784	65.15 N	168.40 E
Jersey □[2]	2769	49.15 N	2.10 W
Jersey City	2740	40.44 N	74.02 W
Jersey Shore	2740	41.12 N	77.16 W
Jeršov	2766	51.20 N	48.17 E
Jerusalem → Yerushalayim	2791	31.46 N	35.14 E
Jesenice	2776	46.27 N	14.04 E
Jessore	2794	23.10 N	89.13 E
Jesup	2744	31.36 N	81.53 W
Jesús Carranza	2758	17.26 N	95.02 W
Jet	2748	36.40 N	98.11 W
Jetmore	2750	38.03 N	99.54 W
Jeumont	2772	50.18 N	4.06 E
Jever	2770	53.34 N	7.54 E
Jevpatorija	2782	45.12 N	33.22 E
Jewell	2742	42.20 N	93.39 W
Jhang Maghiāna	2794	31.16 N	72.19 E
Jhānsi	2794	25.26 N	78.35 E
Jhelum	2794	32.56 N	73.44 E
Jhelum ≛	2794	31.12 N	72.08 E
Jiading	2800	31.23 N	121.15 E
Jiamusi	2796	46.50 N	130.21 E
Ji'an	2800	27.07 N	114.58 E
Jianchuan	2804	26.34 N	99.53 E
Jiangmen	2800	22.35 N	113.05 E
Jiangsu □[4]	2796	33.00 N	120.00 E
Jiangxi □[4]	2796	28.00 N	116.00 E
Jiangyan	2800	32.31 N	120.09 E
Jiangyin	2800	31.54 N	120.16 E
Jiangzi	2794	28.57 N	89.35 E
Jianou	2800	27.03 N	118.19 E
Jianshui	2804	23.38 N	102.49 E
Jiaoxian	2796	36.18 N	119.58 E
Jiaozuo	2796	35.15 N	113.18 E
Jiashan	2800	32.47 N	118.00 E
Jiawang	2800	34.27 N	117.27 E
Jiaxian	2800	34.00 N	113.12 E
Jiaxing	2800	30.46 N	120.45 E
Jiazi	2800	22.55 N	116.04 E
Jieshou	2800	33.18 N	115.20 E
Jieyang	2800	23.35 N	116.21 E
Jihlava	2770	49.24 N	15.36 E
Jijiga	2790	9.22 N	42.47 E
Jijona	2774	38.32 N	0.30 W
Jilemutu	2796	52.14 N	120.47 E
Jilin	2796	43.51 N	126.33 E
Jilin □[4]	2796	44.00 N	126.00 E
Jima	2790	7.36 N	36.50 E

Symbols against index entries represent categories identified in the key on page 2810.

Name	Page	Lat °′	Long °′
Jimena de la Frontera	2774	36.26 N	5.27 W
Jinan (Tsinan)	2796	36.40 N	116.57 E
Jingdezhen (Kingtechen)	2800	29.16 N	117.11 E
Jingjiang	2800	32.01 N	120.15 E
Jingxi	2804	23.08 N	106.29 E
Jinhua	2800	29.07 N	119.39 E
Jining, Zhg.	2796	41.06 N	112.58 E
Jining, Zhg.	2796	35.25 N	116.36 E
Jinja	2788	0.26 N	33.12 E
Jinning (Jiukunyang)	2804	24.41 N	102.35 E
Jinshi	2796	29.33 N	111.50 E
Jinxian	2796	39.04 N	121.40 E
Jinzhou	2796	41.07 N	121.08 E
Jiparaná ≈	2762	8.03 S	62.52 W
Jirjā	2786	26.20 N	31.53 E
Jisr ash-Shughūr	2791	35.48 N	36.19 E
Jitai	2796	44.01 N	89.28 E
Jiujiang	2800	29.44 N	115.59 E
Jiulingshan ⋀	2796	28.46 N	114.45 E
Jiumangya	2794	37.40 N	91.50 E
Jiuquan	2796	39.45 N	98.34 E
Jixi	2796	45.17 N	130.59 E
Joaçaba	2764	27.10 S	51.30 W
João Belo	2788	25.02 S	33.34 E
João Pessoa	2762	7.07 S	34.52 W
Joaquín V. González	2764	25.05 S	64.11 W
Jobson (Vera)	2764	29.30 S	60.10 W
Jódar	2774	37.50 N	3.21 W
Jodhpur	2794	26.17 N	73.02 E
Joensuu	2768	62.36 N	29.46 E
Jogjakarta	2802	7.48 S	110.22 E
Johannesburg, S. Afr.	2788	26.15 S	28.00 E
Johannesburg, Calif., U.S.	2756	35.22 N	117.38 W
Johar	2790	2.48 N	45.33 E
John Day	2754	44.25 N	118.57 W
John Martin Reservoir ⊜[1]	2750	38.05 N	103.02 W
John o' Groats	2769	58.38 N	3.05 W
Johnson	2750	37.34 N	101.45 W
Johnsonburg	2740	41.29 N	78.41 W
Johnson City, N.Y., U.S.	2740	42.07 N	75.57 W
Johnson City, Tenn., U.S.	2744	36.19 N	82.21 W
Johnson City, Tex., U.S.	2748	30.17 N	98.25 W
Johnsondale	2756	35.58 N	118.32 W
Johnston	2744	33.50 N	81.48 W
Johnston City	2746	37.49 N	88.56 W
Johnstown, N.Y., U.S.	2740	43.00 N	74.22 W
Johnstown, Ohio, U.S.	2740	40.09 N	82.41 W
Johnstown, Pa., U.S.	2740	40.20 N	78.55 W
Johore Bahru	2804	1.27 N	103.45 E
Joigny	2772	47.59 N	3.24 E
Joinvile	2764	26.18 S	48.50 W
Joinville	2772	48.27 N	5.08 E
Jokkmokk	2768	66.37 N	19.50 E
Joliet, Ill., U.S.	2746	41.32 N	88.05 W
Joliet, Mont., U.S.	2754	45.29 N	108.58 W
Joliette	2740	46.01 N	73.27 W
Jolo Island I	2802	5.58 N	121.06 E
Jonesboro, Ark., U.S.	2746	35.50 N	90.42 W
Jonesboro, Ga., U.S.	2744	33.32 N	84.21 W
Jonesboro, Ill., U.S.	2746	37.27 N	89.16 W
Jonesboro, La., U.S.	2746	32.15 N	92.43 W
Jonesboro, Tenn., U.S.	2744	36.18 N	82.28 W
Jonesport	2740	44.32 N	67.36 W
Jones Sound)(	2734	76.00 N	85.00 W
Jonestown	2746	34.14 N	90.28 W
Jonesville, S.C., U.S.	2744	34.50 N	81.41 W
Jonesville, Va., U.S.	2744	36.41 N	83.07 W
Jönköping	2768	57.47 N	14.11 E
Jonquière	2739	48.24 N	71.15 W
Jonzac	2772	45.27 N	0.26 W
Joplin	2746	37.06 N	94.31 W
Jordan	2754	47.19 N	106.55 W
Jordan □[1]	2791	31.00 N	36.00 E
Jordan ≈	2791	31.46 N	35.33 E
Jorhāt	2794	26.45 N	94.13 E
Jörn	2768	65.04 N	20.02 E
Jos	2786	9.55 N	8.53 E
José Battle y Ordóñez	2764	33.28 S	55.07 W
Joseph	2754	45.21 N	117.14 W
Joseph, Lac ⊜	2734	52.45 N	65.15 W
Joseph Bonaparte Gulf C	2806	14.15 S	128.30 E
Joseph City	2752	34.57 N	110.20 W
Joshua	2748	32.28 N	97.23 W
Joshua Tree	2756	34.08 N	116.19 W
Joshua Tree National Monument ♦	2756	33.55 N	116.00 W
Joškar-Ola	2766	56.38 N	47.52 E
Jourdanton	2748	28.55 N	98.33 W
Joutsijärvi	2768	66.40 N	28.00 E
Jovellanos	2760	22.48 N	81.12 W
Juan Aldama	2758	24.19 N	103.21 W
Juan de Fuca, Strait of)(	2734	48.15 N	124.00 W
Juan de Nova, Île I	2788	17.03 S	42.45 E
Juárez	2764	37.41 S	59.49 W
Juàzeiro	2762	9.25 S	40.30 W
Juàzeiro do Norte	2762	7.12 S	39.20 W
Jūbā	2786	4.51 N	31.37 E
Juba ≈	2790	0.12 N	42.40 E
Juchitán [de Zaragoza]	2758	16.26 N	95.01 W
Juddah (Jidda)	2790	21.30 N	39.12 E
Judenburg	2770	47.10 N	14.40 E
Judoma ≈	2784	59.08 N	135.06 E
Juiz de Fora	2765	21.45 S	43.20 W
Jukagirskoje Ploskogorje ⋀[1]	2784	66.00 N	155.00 E
Jukte	2784	63.23 N	105.41 E
Julesburg	2750	40.59 N	102.16 W
Juliaca	2762	15.30 S	70.08 W
Julian Alps ⋀	2772	46.00 N	14.00 E
Julianatop ▲	2762	3.40 N	56.30 W
Julianehåb	2734	60.43 N	46.01 W
Jullundur	2794	31.19 N	75.34 E
Jumet	2770	50.26 N	4.25 E
Jumilla	2774	38.29 N	1.17 W
Junāgadh	2794	21.31 N	70.28 E
Junction	2748	30.29 N	99.46 W
Junction City, Kans., U.S.	2750	39.02 N	96.50 W
Junction City, Ky., U.S.	2746	37.35 N	84.48 W
Junction City, Oreg., U.S.	2754	44.13 N	123.12 W
Jundiaí	2765	23.11 S	46.52 W
Juneau	2738	58.20 N	134.27 W
June Lake	2756	37.47 N	119.04 W
Jungfrau ▲	2772	46.32 N	7.58 E
Junín	2764	34.35 S	60.58 W
Junín, Lago de ⊜	2762	11.00 S	76.09 W
Junín de los Andes	2764	39.55 S	71.05 W
Junsele	2768	63.41 N	16.54 E
Jupiter	2744	26.56 N	80.06 W
Jura I	2769	56.00 N	5.50 W
Jurga	2784	55.42 N	84.51 E
Jūrmala	2780	56.58 N	23.42 E
Juruá ≈	2762	2.37 S	65.44 W
Juruena ≈	2762	7.20 S	58.03 W
Justo Daract	2764	33.52 S	65.11 W
Jutaí ≈	2762	2.43 S	66.57 W
Jutiapa	2760	14.17 N	89.54 W
Juticalpa	2760	14.42 N	86.15 W
Juwara	2790	18.55 N	57.17 E
Juža	2780	56.35 N	42.01 E
Južno-Sachalinsk	2784	46.58 N	142.42 E
Južnyj, Mys ≻	2784	57.45 N	156.45 E
Južnyj Bug ≈	2766	46.59 N	31.58 E
Jwayyā	2791	33.14 N	35.19 E
Jyväskylä	2768	62.14 N	25.44 E

K

Name	Page	Lat °′	Long °′
K2 → Godwin Austen ▲	2794	33.53 N	76.30 E
Kaala Djerda	2776	35.40 N	8.36 E
Kabale	2788	1.15 S	29.59 E
Kabalo	2788	6.03 S	26.55 E
Kabambare	2788	4.42 S	27.43 E
Kåbdalis	2768	66.10 N	20.00 E
Kabīr Kūh ⋀	2790	33.25 N	46.45 E
Kabompo ≈	2788	14.10 S	23.11 E
Kabongo	2788	7.19 S	25.35 E
Kābul □[4]	2794	34.30 N	69.00 E
Kabwe (Broken Hill)	2788	14.27 S	28.27 E
Kachovskoje Vodochranilišče ⊜[1]	2782	47.25 N	34.10 E
K'achta	2784	50.26 N	106.25 E
Kačug	2784	53.58 N	105.52 E
Kadijevka	2782	48.34 N	38.40 E
Kadoka	2750	43.50 N	101.31 W
Kaduna	2786	10.33 N	7.27 E
Kâduqlī	2786	11.01 N	29.43 E
Kadykčan	2784	63.02 N	146.50 E
Kadžerom	2766	64.41 N	55.54 E
Kaédi	2786	16.09 N	13.30 W
Kaesŏng	2796	37.59 N	126.33 E
Kafia Kingi	2786	9.16 N	24.25 E
Kafue ≈	2788	15.56 S	28.55 E
Kagoshima	2798	31.36 N	130.33 E
Kagul	2782	45.54 N	28.11 E
Kahemba	2788	7.17 S	19.00 E
Kahoka	2746	40.25 N	91.43 W
Kahuku	2757a	21.41 N	157.57 W
Kahului	2757a	20.54 N	156.28 W
Kai, Kepulauan II	2802	5.35 S	132.45 E
Kaibab Plateau ⋀[1]	2752	36.30 N	112.15 W
Kaieteur Fall L	2762	5.10 N	59.35 W
Kaifeng	2796	34.51 N	114.21 E
Kaikoura	2808	42.25 S	173.41 E
Kaili	2804	26.22 N	108.01 E
Kailua	2757a	21.24 N	157.44 W
Kailua Kona	2757a	19.39 N	155.59 W
Kaimana	2802	3.39 S	133.45 E
Kaimanawa Mountains ⋀	2808	39.15 S	175.54 E
Kaitangata	2808	46.18 S	169.51 E
Kajaani	2768	64.14 N	27.41 E
Kakamas	2788	28.45 S	20.33 E
Kakie	2788	24.51 S	23.20 E
Kākināda	2793	16.56 N	82.13 E
Kakogawa	2798	34.46 N	134.51 E
Kalač	2782	50.25 N	41.01 E
Kaladan ≈	2804	20.09 N	92.57 E
Kalahari Desert ✦[2]	2788	24.00 S	21.30 E
Kalajoki	2768	64.15 N	23.57 E
Kalakan	2784	55.08 N	116.45 E
Kalām	2794	35.28 N	72.35 E
Kalama	2754	46.01 N	122.51 W
Kalámai	2778	37.04 N	22.07 E
Kalamazoo	2742	42.17 N	85.32 W
Kalapana	2757a	19.22 N	154.58 W
Kalāt	2794	29.02 N	66.35 E
Kalb, Ra's al- ≻	2790	14.02 N	48.40 E
Kale	2778	37.26 N	28.51 E
Kalemi (Albertville)	2788	5.56 S	29.12 E
Kalevala	2766	65.13 N	31.08 E
Kalgoorlie	2806	30.45 S	121.28 E
Kalima	2788	2.34 S	26.37 E
Kálimnos	2778	36.57 N	26.59 E
Kalinin	2780	56.52 N	35.55 E
Kaliningrad (Königsberg)	2780	54.43 N	20.30 E
Kalinkoviči	2780	52.08 N	29.21 E
Kalispell	2754	48.12 N	114.19 W
Kalisz	2770	51.46 N	18.06 E
Kalkaska	2742	44.44 N	85.11 W
Kalmar	2768	56.40 N	16.22 E
Kaluga	2780	54.31 N	36.16 E
Kama ≈	2766	55.45 N	52.00 E
Kamaishi	2798	39.16 N	141.53 E
Kamakura	2798	35.19 N	139.33 E
Kamālia	2794	30.44 N	72.39 E
Kamarān I	2790	15.21 N	42.34 E
Kamas	2752	40.38 N	111.17 W
Kamčatka ≈	2784	56.15 N	162.30 E
Kamčatka, Poluostrov ≻[1]	2784	56.00 N	160.00 E
Kamčatskij Zaliv C	2784	55.35 N	162.21 E
Kamen', Gora ▲	2784	69.06 N	94.48 E
Kamenec-Podol'skij	2782	48.41 N	26.36 E
Kamenka	2782	49.02 N	32.06 E
Kamen'-na-Obi	2784	53.47 N	81.20 E
Kamensk-Šachtinskij	2782	48.21 N	40.19 E
Kamensk-Ural'skij	2766	56.28 N	61.53 E
Kamiah	2754	46.14 N	116.02 W
Kamienna Góra	2770	50.47 N	16.01 E
Kamilukuak Lake ⊜	2734	62.22 N	101.40 W
Kamina	2788	8.44 S	25.00 E
Kaminak Lake ⊜	2734	62.10 N	95.00 W
Kaminuriak Lake ⊜	2734	63.00 N	95.40 W
Kamitsushima	2798	34.50 N	129.28 E
Kamloops	2734	50.40 N	120.20 W
Kampala	2788	0.19 N	32.25 E
Kampen	2770	52.33 N	5.54 E
Kâmpóng Cham	2804	12.00 N	105.27 E
Kâmpóng Chhnăng	2804	12.15 N	104.40 E
Kâmpóng Saôm, Chhâk C	2804	10.50 N	103.32 E
Kâmpôt	2804	10.37 N	104.11 E
Kamskoje Vodochranilišče ⊜[1]	2766	58.52 N	56.15 E
Kamuela (Waimea)	2757a	20.01 N	155.41 W
Kamyšin	2766	50.06 N	45.24 E
Kamyšlov	2766	56.52 N	62.43 E
Kanab	2752	37.03 N	112.32 W
Kanairiktok ≈	2734	55.05 N	60.20 W
Kananga (Luluabourg)	2788	5.54 S	22.25 E
Kanarraville	2752	37.32 N	113.11 W
Kanaš	2766	55.31 N	47.30 E
Kanazawa	2798	36.34 N	136.39 E
Kānchenjunga ▲	2794	27.42 N	88.08 E
Kānchipuram	2793	12.50 N	79.43 E
Kandagač	2766	49.28 N	57.25 E
Kandalakša	2766	67.09 N	32.21 E
Kane	2740	41.40 N	78.49 W
Kaneohe	2757a	21.25 N	157.48 W
Kangaroo Island I	2806	35.50 S	137.06 E
Kangean, Kepulauan II	2802	6.55 S	115.30 E
Kangnŭng	2796	37.45 N	128.54 E
Kango	2788	0.09 N	10.08 E
Kangto ▲	2794	27.52 N	92.30 E
Kaniama	2788	7.31 S	24.11 E
Kanin, Poluostrov ≻[1]	2766	68.00 N	45.00 E
Kanin Nos, Mys ≻	2766	68.39 N	43.16 E
Kankakee	2746	41.07 N	87.52 W
Kankakee ≈	2746	41.23 N	88.16 W
Kankan	2786	10.23 N	9.18 W
Kannapolis	2744	35.30 N	80.37 W
Kannonkoski	2768	62.58 N	25.15 E
Kannus	2768	63.54 N	23.54 E
Kano	2786	12.00 N	8.30 E
Kanonji	2798	34.07 N	133.39 E
Kanoya	2798	31.23 N	130.51 E
Kānpur	2794	26.28 N	80.21 E
Kansas □[3]	2736	38.45 N	98.15 W
Kansas ≈	2750	39.07 N	94.36 W
Kansas City, Kans., U.S.	2750	39.07 N	94.39 W
Kansas City, Mo., U.S.	2746	39.05 N	94.35 W
Kansk	2784	56.13 N	95.41 E
Kantō-sammyaku ⋀	2798	35.50 N	138.50 E
Kanye	2788	24.59 S	25.19 E
Kaohsiung	2800	22.38 N	120.17 E
Kaohsiunghsien	2800	22.38 N	120.21 E
Kaokoveld ⋀[1]	2788	21.00 S	14.20 E
Kaolack	2786	14.09 N	16.04 W
Kapaa	2757a	22.05 N	159.19 W
Kapanga	2788	8.21 S	22.35 E
Kapfenberg	2770	47.26 N	15.18 E
Kaplan	2746	30.00 N	92.17 W
Kaposvár	2770	46.22 N	17.47 E
Kapuskasing	2734	49.25 N	82.26 W
Kara-Bogaz-Gol, Zaliv C	2766	41.00 N	53.15 W
Karabük	2766	41.12 N	32.37 E
Karacabey	2778	40.13 N	28.21 E
Karacaköy	2778	41.24 N	28.22 E
Karāchi	2794	24.52 N	67.03 E
Karaginskij, Ostrov I	2784	58.50 N	164.00 E
Karaginskij Zaliv C	2784	58.50 N	164.00 E
Karagoš, Gora ▲	2784	51.44 N	89.24 E
Karakelong, Pulau I	2802	4.15 N	126.48 E
Karakoram Range ⋀	2794	35.30 N	77.00 E
Karaman, Tür.	2766	37.11 N	33.14 E
Karaman, Tür.	2778	37.05 N	29.20 E
Karamürsel	2778	40.42 N	29.36 E
Karasburg	2788	28.00 S	18.43 E
Karasjok	2768	69.27 N	25.30 E
Karaton	2766	46.25 N	53.30 E
Karaul	2784	70.06 N	83.08 E
Karbalā'	2790	32.36 N	44.02 E
Kårböle	2768	61.59 N	15.19 E
Karcag	2770	47.19 N	20.56 E
Kardhítsa	2778	39.21 N	21.55 E
Kărdžali	2778	41.39 N	25.22 E
Kargasok	2784	59.07 N	80.53 E
Kargopol'	2766	61.30 N	38.58 E
Karhula	2768	60.31 N	26.57 E
Kariba	2788	16.30 S	28.45 E
Kariba, Lake ⊜[1]	2788	17.00 S	28.00 E
Karibib	2788	21.58 S	15.51 E
Karigasniemi	2768	69.24 N	25.50 E
Karimata, Kepulauan II	2802	1.25 S	109.05 E
Karimata, Selat (Karimata Strait))(	2802	2.05 S	108.40 E
Karin	2790	10.51 N	45.45 E
Karis (Karjaa)	2768	60.05 N	23.40 E
Karkabet	2790	16.13 N	37.30 E
Karlovac	2776	45.29 N	15.34 E
Karlovo	2778	42.38 N	24.48 E
Karlovy Vary	2770	50.11 N	12.52 E
Karlshamn	2768	56.10 N	14.51 E
Karlskoga	2768	59.20 N	14.31 E
Karlskrona	2768	56.10 N	15.35 E
Karlstad, Sve.	2768	59.22 N	13.30 E
Karlstad, Minn , U.S.	2750	48.35 N	96.31 W
Karnak	2746	37.18 N	88.58 W
Karnāl	2794	29.41 N	76.59 E
Karnes City	2748	28.53 N	97.54 W
Karonga	2788	9.56 S	33.56 E
Kárpathos I	2778	35.40 N	27.10 E
Karpenísion	2778	38.55 N	21.40 E
Karpogory	2766	64.00 N	44.24 E
Kars	2766	40.36 N	43.05 E
Kärsämäki	2768	63.58 N	25.46 E
Kartal	2778	40.53 N	29.10 E
Kartaly	2766	53.03 N	60.40 E
Karufa	2802	3.53 S	133.24 E
Karungi	2768	66.03 N	23.57 E
Karūr	2793	10.57 N	78.05 E
Karviná	2770	49.50 N	18.30 E
Kārwār	2793	14.48 N	74.08 E
Kasai (Cassai) ≈	2788	3.06 S	16.57 E
Kasaji	2788	10.22 S	23.27 E
Kasama	2788	10.13 S	31.12 E
Kasanga	2788	8.28 S	31.09 E
Kasba Lake ⊜	2734	60.18 N	102.07 W
Kaseda	2798	31.25 N	130.19 E
Kasempa	2788	13.27 S	25.50 E
Kasenga	2788	10.22 S	28.38 E
Kasese	2788	1.38 S	27.07 E
Kāshān	2790	33.59 N	51.29 E
Kashi (Kashgar)	2796	39.29 N	75.59 E
Kashima-nada ▾[2]	2798	36.15 N	140.45 E
Kashiwa	2798	35.52 N	139.59 E
Kashmir → Jammu and Kashmir □[2]	2794	34.00 N	76.00 E
Kasimov	2780	54.56 N	41.24 E
Kašin	2780	57.21 N	37.37 E
Kaširа	2780	54.51 N	38.10 E
Kaskaskia ≈	2746	37.59 N	89.56 W
Kaskö (Kaskinen)	2768	62.23 N	21.13 E
Kasongo	2788	4.27 S	26.40 E
Kaspijskij	2766	45.22 N	47.24 E
Kasr, Ra's ≻	2786	18.02 N	38.35 E
Kassalā	2786	15.28 N	36.24 E
Kastoría	2778	40.31 N	21.15 E
Kasugai	2798	35.14 N	136.58 E
Kasūr	2794	31.07 N	74.27 E
Katahdin, Mount ▲	2736	45.55 N	68.55 W
Katanga ≈	2784	58.18 N	104.10 E
Katanga Plateau ⋀[1]	2788	10.30 S	25.30 E
Katchall Island I	2804	7.57 N	93.22 E
Kateríni	2778	40.16 N	22.30 E
Katherine	2806	14.28 S	132.16 E
Katihār	2794	25.32 N	87.35 E
Kāthiāwār ≻[1]	2794	22.00 N	71.00 E
Katiola	2786	8.08 N	5.06 W
Katmai National Monument ♦	2738	58.30 N	155.00 W
Kātmāndu	2794	27.43 N	85.19 E
Katowice	2770	50.16 N	19.00 E
Katrīnah, Jabal ▲	2786	28.31 N	33.57 E
Katrineholm	2768	59.00 N	16.12 E
Katsina	2786	13.00 N	7.32 E
Kattegat)(	2768	57.00 N	11.00 E
Kauai I	2757a	22.00 N	159.30 W
Kaufman	2748	32.35 N	96.19 W
Kaukauna	2742	44.17 N	88.17 W
Kaukauveld ⋀	2788	20.00 S	20.30 E
Kaunakakai	2757a	21.06 N	157.01 W
Kaunas	2780	54.54 N	23.54 E
Kaura Namoda	2786	12.35 N	6.35 E
Kaustinen	2768	63.32 N	23.42 E
Kavača	2784	60.16 N	169.51 E
Kavacık	2778	39.40 N	28.30 E
Kavalerovo	2784	44.15 N	135.04 E
Kavála	2778	40.56 N	24.25 E
Kawagoe	2798	35.55 N	139.29 E
Kawaguchi	2798	35.48 N	139.43 E
Kawambwa	2788	9.47 S	29.05 E
Kawanoe	2798	34.01 N	133.34 E
Kawasaki	2798	35.32 N	139.43 E
Kawm Umbū	2786	24.28 N	32.57 E
Kayangel Islands II	2802	8.04 N	134.43 E
Kaycee	2754	43.43 N	106.38 W
Kayes	2786	14.27 N	11.26 W
Kayseri	2766	38.43 N	35.30 E
Kažačinskoje	2784	57.49 N	93.17 E
Kazačje	2784	70.44 N	136.13 E
Kazan'	2766	55.49 N	49.08 E
Kazanlăk	2778	42.38 N	25.21 E
Kazatin	2782	49.43 N	28.50 E
Kāzerūn	2790	29.37 N	51.38 E
Keams Canyon	2752	35.49 N	110.12 W
Kearney	2750	40.42 N	99.05 W
Kearns	2752	40.39 N	111.59 W
Kearny	2752	33.03 N	110.55 W
Kebri Dehar	2790	6.47 N	44.17 E
Kechika ≈	2734	59.36 N	127.05 W
Kecskemét	2770	46.54 N	19.42 E
Kediri	2802	7.49 S	112.01 E
Kedon	2784	64.08 N	159.14 E
Kédougou	2786	12.33 N	12.11 W
Kędzierzyn	2770	50.20 N	18.12 E
Keele Peak ▲	2734	63.26 N	130.19 W
Keelung → Chilung	2800	25.08 N	121.44 E
Keene	2740	42.56 N	72.17 W
Keeper Hill ▲[2]	2769	52.45 N	8.16 W
Keeseville	2740	44.30 N	73.29 W
Keetmanshoop	2788	26.36 S	18.08 E
Kefallinía I	2778	38.15 N	20.35 E
Keffi	2786	8.51 N	7.52 E
Keflavík	2766	64.02 N	22.36 W
Keg River	2734	57.48 N	117.52 W
Ke-hsi Mānsām	2796	21.56 N	97.50 E
Keith	2769	57.32 N	2.57 W
Keizer	2754	44.57 N	123.01 W
Kekexilishanmai ⋀	2794	35.20 N	90.00 E
Kelafo	2790	5.40 N	44.20 E
Kelamayi	2796	45.37 N	84.53 E
Kelang	2804	3.02 N	101.28 E
Kelibia	2776	36.51 N	11.06 E

Symbols against index entries represent categories identified in the key on page 2810.

Symbols against index entries represent categories identified in the key on page 2810.

L

Symbols against index entries represent categories identified in the key on page 2810.

Name	Page	Lat °′	Long °′
La Oroya	2762	11.32 S	75.54 W
Laos □1	2802	18.00 N	105.00 E
Lapalisse	2772	46.15 N	3.38 E
La Palma, Méx.	2748	26.53 N	99.24 W
La Palma, Pan.	2760	8.25 N	78.07 W
La Palma I	2786	28.40 N	17.52 W
La Paragua	2762	6.50 N	63.20 W
La Paz, Arg.	2764	30.45 S	59.38 W
La Paz, Arg.	2764	33.28 S	67.34 W
La Paz, Bol.	2762	16.30 S	68.09 W
La Paz, Méx.	2758	24.10 N	110.18 W
La Paz, Méx.	2758	23.41 N	100.43 W
La Paz, Bahía de C	2758	24.15 N	110.30 W
Lapeer	2742	43.03 N	83.19 W
La Perouse Strait ⁑	2796	45.45 N	142.00 E
La Piedad [Cavadas]	2758	20.21 N	102.00 W
La Pine	2754	43.40 N	121.30 W
Lapinlahti	2768	63.22 N	27.24 E
Lapland ◆1	2766	68.00 N	25.00 E
La Plata, Arg.	2764	34.55 S	57.57 W
La Plata, Md., U.S.	2740	38.32 N	76.59 W
La Plata, Mo., U.S.	2746	40.02 N	92.29 W
La Plata ≃	2752	36.54 N	108.15 W
La Porte, Ind., U.S.	2746	41.36 N	86.43 W
Laporte, Pa., U.S.	2740	41.25 N	76.30 W
La Porte City	2742	42.19 N	92.12 W
Lappeenranta	2768	61.04 N	28.11 E
La Pryor	2748	28.57 N	99.51 W
Laptevych, More (Laptev Sea) ▼2	2784	76.00 N	126.00 E
Lapua	2768	62.57 N	23.00 E
La Puebla	2774	39.46 N	3.01 E
La Puebla de Montalbán	2774	39.52 N	4.21 W
La Quiaca	2764	22.05 S	65.36 W
L'Aquila	2776	42.22 N	13.22 E
Lār	2790	27.41 N	54.17 E
Larache	2786	35.12 N	6.10 W
Laramie ≃	2752	42.12 N	104.32 W
Larantuka	2802	8.21 S	122.59 E
L'Arbresle	2772	45.50 N	4.37 E
Lärbro	2768	57.47 N	18.47 E
Larchwood	2750	43.27 N	96.26 W
Laredo	2748	27.31 N	99.30 W
La Réole	2772	44.35 N	0.02 W
Largeau	2786	17.55 N	19.07 E
L'Argentière-la-Bessée	2772	44.47 N	6.33 E
Largo	2744	27.55 N	82.47 W
Largs	2769	55.48 N	4.52 W
Larimore	2750	47.54 N	97.38 W
La Rioja	2764	29.25 S	66.50 W
Lárisa	2778	39.38 N	22.25 E
Larjak	2784	61.16 N	80.15 E
Lārkāna	2794	27.33 N	68.13 E
Lárnax (Larnaca)	2791	34.55 N	33.38 E
Larne	2769	54.51 N	5.49 W
Larned	2750	38.11 N	99.06 W
La Robla	2774	42.48 N	5.37 W
La Roca de la Sierra	2774	39.07 N	6.41 W
La Rochefoucauld	2772	45.45 N	0.23 E
La Rochelle	2772	46.10 N	1.10 W
La Roche-sur-Yon	2772	46.40 N	1.26 W
La Roda	2774	39.13 N	2.09 W
La Romana	2760	18.25 N	68.58 W
La Ronge	2734	55.06 N	105.17 W
Laroquebrou	2772	44.58 N	2.11 E
Larose	2746	29.35 N	90.23 W
La Rosita	2748	28.24 N	101.43 W
La Rubia	2764	30.05 S	61.50 W
La Rumorosa	2756	32.34 N	116.06 W
Laruns	2772	42.59 N	0.25 W
Larvik	2768	59.04 N	10.00 E
Lasa (Lhasa)	2794	29.40 N	91.09 E
La Sal	2752	38.19 N	109.15 W
La Salle, Colo., U.S.	2752	40.21 N	104.42 W
La Salle, Ill., U.S.	2746	41.20 N	89.06 W
Las Animas	2750	38.04 N	103.13 W
Las Anod	2790	8.26 N	47.24 E
La Sarre	2734	48.48 N	79.12 W
Las Blancas	2748	25.42 N	97.35 W
Las Choapas	2758	17.55 N	94.05 W
Las Colimas	2758	25.21 N	98.40 W
Las Cruces	2752	32.23 N	106.29 W
Las Delicias	2758	15.58 N	91.50 W
La Selle, Pic ▲	2760	18.22 N	72.00 W
La Serena	2764	29.54 S	71.16 W
Las Escobas	2758	30.33 N	115.56 W
La Seyne	2772	43.06 N	5.53 E
Las Flores	2764	36.02 S	59.07 W
Lashio	2804	22.56 N	97.45 E
Laško	2776	46.09 N	15.14 E
Las Lomitas	2764	24.43 S	60.35 W
Las Minas, Cerro ▲	2760	14.33 N	88.39 W
La Solana	2774	38.56 N	3.14 W
Las Palmas de Gran Canaria	2786	28.06 N	15.24 W
La Spezia	2776	44.07 N	9.50 E
Las Piedras	2764	34.44 S	56.13 W
Las Plumas	2764	43.40 S	67.15 W
Lassen Peak ▲1	2756	40.29 N	121.31 W
Lassen Volcanic National Park ◆	2756	40.30 N	121.19 W
Las Termas	2764	27.30 S	64.50 W
Last Mountain Lake ⊜	2734	51.05 N	105.10 W
Las Tórtolas, Cerro ▲	2764	29.56 S	69.54 W
Las Varas	2758	29.29 N	108.01 W
Las Vegas, Nev., U.S.	2756	36.11 N	115.08 W
Las Vegas, N. Mex., U.S.	2752	35.36 N	105.13 W
La Teste-de-Buch	2772	44.38 N	1.09 W
Latimer	2742	42.46 N	93.22 W
Latina	2776	41.28 N	12.52 E
La Tortuga, Isla I	2760	10.56 N	65.20 W
Latrobe	2740	40.19 N	79.23 W
Latta	2744	34.21 N	79.26 W
La Tuque	2734	47.26 N	72.47 W
Lātūr	2793	18.24 N	76.35 E
Lauderdale	2746	32.31 N	88.31 W
Laughlin Peak ▲	2748	36.38 N	104.12 W
Launceston, Austl.	2806	41.26 S	147.08 E
Launceston, Eng., U.K.	2769	50.38 N	4.21 W
La Union, El Sal.	2760	13.20 N	87.51 W
La Unión, Esp.	2774	37.37 N	0.52 W
Laurel, Del., U.S.	2740	38.33 N	75.34 W
Laurel, Md., U.S.	2740	39.06 N	76.51 W
Laurel, Miss., U.S.	2746	31.42 N	89.08 W
Laurel, Mont., U.S.	2754	45.40 N	108.46 W
Laurel, Nebr., U.S.	2750	42.26 N	97.06 W
Laurel Bay	2744	32.27 N	80.48 W
Laurelville	2740	39.28 N	82.44 W
Laurens, Iowa, U.S.	2750	42.51 N	94.51 W
Laurens, S.C., U.S.	2744	34.30 N	82.01 W
Laurière	2772	46.05 N	1.28 E
Laurinburg	2744	34.47 N	79.27 W
Lausanne	2772	46.31 N	6.38 E
Laut, Pulau I	2804	4.43 N	107.59 E
Lautaro	2764	38.31 S	72.27 W
Laut Ketjil, Kepulauan II	2802	4.50 S	115.45 E
Lavaca Bay C	2748	28.35 N	96.35 W
Lavagh More ▲	2769	54.45 N	8.05 W
Lava Hot Springs	2754	42.37 N	112.01 W
Laval, Qué., Can.	2740	45.33 N	73.44 W
Laval, Fr.	2772	48.04 N	0.46 W
Lavapié, Punta ≻	2764	37.09 S	73.35 W
La Vega	2760	19.13 N	70.31 W
Lavello	2776	41.03 N	15.48 E
Laverne	2748	36.43 N	99.54 W
Lavia	2768	61.36 N	22.36 E
Lavonia	2744	34.26 N	83.06 W
La Voulte-sur-Rhône	2772	44.48 N	4.47 E
Lavras	2765	21.14 S	45.00 W
Lawers, Ben ▲	2769	56.33 N	4.15 W
Lawrence, Ind., U.S.	2746	39.50 N	86.02 W
Lawrence, Kans., U.S.	2750	38.58 N	95.14 W
Lawrence, Mass., U.S.	2740	42.42 N	71.09 W
Lawrenceburg, Ind., U.S.	2746	39.06 N	84.51 W
Lawrenceburg, Ky., U.S.	2746	38.02 N	84.54 W
Lawrenceburg, Tenn., U.S.	2746	35.15 N	87.20 W
Lawrenceville, Ill., U.S.	2746	38.44 N	87.41 W
Lawrenceville, Va., U.S.	2744	36.45 N	77.51 W
Lawton	2748	34.37 N	98.25 W
Lawz, Jabal al- ▲	2790	28.40 N	35.18 E
Layton	2752	41.04 N	111.58 W
Laytonville	2756	39.41 N	123.29 W
La Zarca	2758	25.50 N	104.44 W
Lazarev	2784	52.13 N	141.32 E
Lead	2750	44.21 N	103.46 W
Leadbetter Point ≻	2754	46.38 N	124.03 W
Leadville	2752	39.15 N	106.20 W
League City	2748	29.31 N	95.05 W
Leakesville	2746	31.09 N	88.33 W
Leamington	2740	42.03 N	82.36 W
Leary	2744	31.29 N	84.31 W
Leatherman Peak ▲	2754	44.05 N	113.44 W
Leavenworth, Kans., U.S.	2750	39.19 N	94.55 W
Leavenworth, Wash., U.S.	2754	47.36 N	120.40 W
Leawood	2746	37.03 N	94.31 W
Lebanon, Ind., U.S.	2746	40.03 N	86.28 W
Lebanon, Kans., U.S.	2750	39.49 N	98.33 W
Lebanon, Ky., U.S.	2746	37.34 N	85.15 W
Lebanon, Mo., U.S.	2746	37.41 N	92.40 W
Lebanon, Ohio, U.S.	2740	39.26 N	84.13 W
Lebanon, Oreg., U.S.	2754	44.32 N	122.54 W
Lebanon, Pa., U.S.	2740	40.20 N	76.25 W
Lebanon, Tenn., U.S.	2746	36.12 N	86.18 W
Lebanon □1	2791	33.50 N	35.50 E
Lebanon Junction	2746	37.50 N	85.44 W
Lebec	2756	34.50 N	118.52 W
Lebedin	2782	50.36 N	34.30 E
Le Blanc	2772	46.38 N	1.04 E
Lębork	2770	54.33 N	17.44 E
Lebrija	2774	36.55 N	6.04 W
Lecce	2776	40.23 N	18.11 E
Lecco	2776	45.51 N	9.23 E
Le Cheylard	2772	44.45 N	4.25 E
Lecompte	2746	31.05 N	92.24 W
Le Creusot	2772	46.48 N	4.26 E
Led'anaja, Gora ▲	2784	61.53 N	171.09 W
Le Dorat	2772	46.13 N	1.05 E
Lee	2740	42.19 N	73.15 W
Leech Lake ⊜	2742	47.09 N	94.23 W
Leeds, Eng., U.K.	2769	53.50 N	1.35 W
Leeds, N. Dak., U.S.	2750	48.17 N	99.27 W
Leesburg, Ga., U.S.	2744	31.44 N	84.10 W
Leesburg, Va., U.S.	2740	39.07 N	77.34 W
Leesville	2746	31.08 N	93.16 W
Leeuwarden	2770	53.12 N	5.46 E
Leeuwin, Cape ≻	2806	34.22 S	115.08 E
Leeward Islands II	2760	17.00 N	62.00 W
Leghorn → Livorno	2776	43.33 N	10.19 E
Legnago	2776	45.11 N	11.18 E
Legnano	2776	45.36 N	8.54 E
Legnica (Liegnitz)	2770	51.13 N	16.09 E
Le Havre	2772	49.30 N	0.08 E
Lehighton	2740	40.49 N	75.45 W
Lehututu	2788	23.58 S	21.51 E
Leibnitz	2770	46.48 N	15.32 E
Leicester	2769	52.38 N	1.05 W
Leichhardt ≃	2806	17.35 S	139.48 E
Leiden	2770	52.09 N	4.30 E
Leighton Buzzard	2769	51.55 N	0.40 W
Leikanger	2768	61.10 N	6.52 E
Leinster □9	2769	53.05 N	7.00 W
Leinster, Mount ▲	2769	52.37 N	6.44 W
Leipsic	2740	41.06 N	83.59 W
Leiria	2774	39.45 N	8.48 W
Leisler, Mount ▲	2806	23.28 S	129.17 E
Leitchfield	2746	37.29 N	86.18 W
Leitrim	2769	54.00 N	8.04 W
Leiyang	2800	26.24 N	112.51 E
Leizhoubandao ≻1	2804	21.15 N	110.09 E
Leland, Mich., U.S.	2742	45.01 N	85.45 W
Leland, Miss., U.S.	2746	33.24 N	90.54 W
Leleque	2764	42.24 S	71.04 W
Le Lion-d'Angers	2772	47.38 N	0.43 W
Lelishan ▲	2794	33.26 N	81.42 E
Le Locle	2772	47.03 N	6.45 E
Le Lude	2772	47.39 N	0.09 E
Le Maire, Estrecho de ⁑	2764	54.50 S	65.00 W
Le Mans	2772	48.00 N	0.12 E
Le Mars	2750	42.47 N	96.10 W
Leme	2765	22.12 S	47.24 W
Lemesós (Limassol)	2791	34.40 N	33.02 E
Lemhi ≃	2754	45.12 N	113.53 W
Lemhi Range ⩓	2754	44.30 N	113.25 W
Lemmon	2750	45.56 N	102.10 W
Lemmon, Mount ▲	2752	32.26 N	110.47 W
Lemoore	2756	36.18 N	119.47 W
Lena ≃	2784	72.25 N	126.40 E
Lencloître	2772	46.49 N	0.20 E
Lenghu	2796	38.30 N	93.15 E
Leninaran	2766	40.48 N	43.50 E
Leningrad	2780	59.55 N	30.15 E
Leninogorsk	2784	50.27 N	83.32 E
Leninsk-Kuzneckij	2784	54.38 N	86.10 E
Leninskoje	2784	47.56 N	132.38 E
Lenkoran'	2766	38.45 N	48.50 E
Lennoxville	2740	45.22 N	71.51 W
Lenoir	2744	35.55 N	81.32 W
Lenoir City	2744	35.48 N	84.16 W
Lenox	2750	40.53 N	94.34 W
Lens	2772	50.26 N	2.50 E
Lensk	2784	61.00 N	114.50 E
Lentini	2776	37.17 N	15.00 E
Leoben	2770	47.23 N	15.06 E
Leola	2750	45.43 N	98.56 W
Leominster, Eng., U.K.	2769	52.14 N	2.45 W
Leominster, Mass., U.S.	2740	42.32 N	71.45 W
León, Esp.	2774	42.36 N	5.34 W
León, Nic.	2760	12.26 N	86.54 W
Leon, Iowa, U.S.	2742	40.44 N	93.45 W
Leonard	2748	33.23 N	96.15 W
Leonardtown	2740	38.17 N	76.38 W
León [de los Aldamas]	2758	21.07 N	101.40 W
Leonora	2806	28.53 S	121.20 E
Léopold II, Lac → Mai-Ndombe, Lac ⊜	2788	2.00 S	18.20 E
Leopoldina	2765	21.32 S	42.38 W
Léopoldville → Kinshasa	2788	4.18 S	15.18 E
Leoti	2750	38.29 N	101.21 W
Le Palais	2772	47.21 N	3.09 W
Lepe	2774	37.15 N	7.12 W
Leping	2800	28.57 N	117.05 E
L'Épiphanie	2740	45.51 N	73.30 W
Le Puy	2772	45.02 N	3.53 E
Lercara Friddi	2776	37.45 N	13.36 E
Lerici	2776	44.04 N	9.55 E
Lérida	2774	41.37 N	0.37 E
Lerma	2774	42.02 N	3.45 W
Le Roy, Kans., U.S.	2750	38.05 N	95.38 W
Le Roy, Minn., U.S.	2742	43.31 N	92.30 W
Lerwick	2769	60.09 N	1.09 W
Les Andelys	2772	49.15 N	1.25 E
Les Cayes	2760	18.12 N	73.45 W
Les Échelles	2772	45.26 N	5.45 E
Les Herbiers	2772	46.52 N	1.01 W
Leskovac	2778	42.59 N	21.57 E
Leslie, Ark., U.S.	2746	35.50 N	92.34 W
Leslie, Ga., U.S.	2744	31.57 N	84.05 W
Leslie, Mich., U.S.	2742	42.27 N	84.26 W
Leslie, W. Va., U.S.	2740	38.03 N	80.43 W
Lesotho □1	2788	29.30 S	28.30 E
Lesozavodsk	2784	45.28 N	133.27 E
Les Sables-d'Olonne	2772	46.30 N	1.47 W
Lesser Antilles II	2760	15.00 N	61.00 W
Lesser Slave Lake ⊜	2734	55.25 N	115.30 W
Lesser Sunda Islands II	2802	9.00 S	120.00 E
Le Sueur	2742	44.27 N	93.54 W
Lešukonskoje	2766	64.54 N	45.40 E
Lésvos I	2778	39.10 N	26.20 E
Leszno	2770	51.51 N	16.35 E
Lethbridge	2734	49.42 N	112.50 W
Lethem	2762	3.20 N	59.50 W
Le Thillot	2772	47.53 N	6.46 E
Leti, Kepulauan II	2802	8.13 S	127.50 E
Leticia	2762	4.09 S	69.57 W
Le Tréport	2772	50.04 N	1.22 E
Letterkenny	2769	54.57 N	7.44 W
Leuven	2770	50.53 N	4.42 E
Levádhia	2778	38.25 N	22.54 E
Levanger	2766	63.45 N	11.18 E
Levante, Riviera di ✦2	2776	45.15 N	9.30 E
Leveaux Mountain ▲2	2742	47.37 N	90.47 W
Levelland	2748	33.35 N	102.23 W
Leveque, Cape ≻	2806	16.24 S	122.56 E
Levie	2776	41.42 N	9.07 E
Levittown, N.Y., U.S.	2740	40.41 N	73.31 W
Levittown, Pa., U.S.	2740	40.09 N	74.50 W
Levkosía (Nicosia)	2791	35.10 N	33.22 E
Lewes, Eng., U.K.	2769	50.52 N	0.01 E
Lewes, Del., U.S.	2740	38.47 N	75.08 W
Lewis	2750	41.18 N	95.05 W
Lewis ≃	2754	45.51 N	122.48 W
Lewis, Isle of I	2769	58.10 N	6.40 W
Lewisburg, Pa., U.S.	2740	40.58 N	76.53 W
Lewisburg, Tenn., U.S.	2746	35.27 N	86.48 W
Lewisburg, W. Va., U.S.	2744	37.48 N	80.27 W
Lewis Smith Lake ⊜1	2746	34.05 N	87.07 W
Lewiston, Idaho, U.S.	2754	46.25 N	117.01 W
Lewiston, Maine, U.S.	2740	44.06 N	70.13 W
Lewiston, Minn., U.S.	2742	44.00 N	91.49 W
Lewistown, Ill., U.S.	2746	40.24 N	90.09 W
Lewistown, Mont., U.S.	2754	47.04 N	109.26 W
Lewistown, Pa., U.S.	2740	40.36 N	77.31 W
Lewisville	2748	33.03 N	96.60 W
Lexington, Ga., U.S.	2744	33.52 N	83.07 W
Lexington, Ill., U.S.	2746	40.39 N	88.47 W
Lexington, Ky., U.S.	2744	38.03 N	84.30 W
Lexington, Mass., U.S.	2740	42.27 N	71.14 W
Lexington, Mich., U.S.	2742	43.16 N	82.32 W
Lexington, Miss., U.S.	2746	33.07 N	90.03 W
Lexington, Mo., U.S.	2746	39.11 N	93.52 W
Lexington, Nebr., U.S.	2750	40.47 N	99.45 W
Lexington, N.C., U.S.	2744	35.49 N	80.15 W
Lexington, Oreg., U.S.	2754	45.27 N	119.41 W
Lexington, S.C., U.S.	2744	34.00 N	81.14 W
Lexington, Tenn., U.S.	2746	35.39 N	88.24 W
Lexington, Va., U.S.	2744	37.47 N	79.27 W
Lexington Park	2740	38.16 N	76.27 W
Leyte I	2802	10.50 N	124.50 E
Leyte Gulf C	2802	10.50 N	125.25 E
L'gov	2782	51.43 N	35.17 E
Lhokseumawe	2804	5.10 N	97.08 E
Lianxian	2796	24.41 N	112.21 E
Liaocheng	2796	36.30 N	115.59 E
Liaodongwan C	2796	40.30 N	121.30 E
Liaohe ≃	2796	40.40 N	122.09 E
Liaoning □4	2796	41.00 N	123.00 E
Liaotung Gulf of → Liaodongwan C	2796	40.30 N	121.30 E
Liaoyang	2796	41.17 N	123.11 E
Liaoyuan	2796	42.54 N	125.07 E
Liard ≃	2734	61.52 N	121.18 W
Libby	2754	48.23 N	115.33 W
Libenge	2786	3.39 N	18.38 E
Liberal	2750	37.02 N	100.55 W
Liberec	2770	50.46 N	15.03 E
Liberia	2760	10.38 N	85.27 W
Liberia □1	2786	6.00 N	10.00 W
Liberty, Ky., U.S.	2746	37.19 N	84.56 W
Liberty, Mo., U.S.	2746	39.15 N	94.25 W
Liberty, N.C., U.S.	2744	35.51 N	79.34 W
Liberty, S.C., U.S.	2744	34.48 N	82.42 W
Liberty, Tex., U.S.	2748	30.03 N	94.47 W
Liberty Center	2740	41.27 N	84.07 W
Libertyville	2742	42.17 N	87.57 W
Libourne	2772	44.55 N	0.14 W
Libreville	2788	0.23 N	9.27 E
Libya □1	2786	27.00 N	17.00 E
Licata	2776	37.05 N	13.56 E
Lida	2780	53.53 N	25.18 E
Lidgerwood	2750	46.05 N	97.09 W
Lidköping	2768	58.30 N	13.10 E
Lido di Ostia	2776	41.44 N	12.14 E
Liechtenstein □1	2766	47.09 N	9.35 E
Liège	2770	50.38 N	5.34 E
Lieksa	2768	63.19 N	30.01 E
Lienz	2770	46.50 N	12.47 E
Liepāja	2780	56.31 N	21.01 E
Lier	2770	51.08 N	4.34 E
Liestal	2772	47.29 N	7.44 E
Liévin	2772	50.25 N	2.46 E
Liezen	2770	47.35 N	14.15 E
Lifford	2769	54.50 N	7.29 W
Lighthouse Point ≻	2742	45.13 N	85.32 W
Ligny-en-Barrois	2772	48.41 N	5.20 E
Ligonier	2740	40.15 N	79.14 W
Ligurian Sea ▼2	2776	43.30 N	9.00 E
Lihou Reefs ✧2	2806	17.25 S	151.40 E
Lihue	2757a	21.59 N	159.22 W
Lijiang	2796	26.57 N	100.15 E
Likasi (Jadotville)	2788	10.59 S	26.44 E
Likino-Dulevo	2780	55.43 N	38.58 E
Liknes	2768	58.19 N	6.59 E
Likouala ≃	2788	0.50 S	17.11 E
Liling	2800	27.40 N	113.30 E
Lille	2772	50.38 N	3.04 E
Lillehammer	2768	61.08 N	10.30 E
Lillestrøm	2768	59.57 N	11.05 E
Lillington	2744	35.24 N	78.49 W
Lillo	2774	39.43 N	3.18 W
Lilongwe	2788	13.59 S	33.44 E
Lima, Perú	2762	12.03 S	77.03 W
Lima, Ohio, U.S.	2740	40.46 N	84.06 W
Limeira	2765	22.34 S	47.24 W
Limerick	2769	52.40 N	8.38 W
Liminka	2768	64.49 N	25.24 E
Limmen Bight C3	2806	14.45 S	135.40 E
Límnos I	2778	39.54 N	25.21 E
Limoges	2772	45.50 N	1.16 E
Limón, C.R.	2760	10.00 N	83.02 W
Limon, Colo., U.S.	2750	39.16 N	103.41 W
Limousins, Plateau du ⩓1	2772	45.30 N	1.15 E
Limoux	2772	43.04 N	2.14 E
Linares, Chile	2764	35.51 S	71.36 W
Linares, Esp.	2774	38.05 N	3.38 W
Linares, Méx.	2758	24.52 N	99.34 W
Linch	2754	43.37 N	106.12 W
Lincoln, Arg.	2764	34.55 S	61.30 W
Lincoln, Eng., U.K.	2769	53.14 N	0.33 W
Lincoln, Calif., U.S.	2756	38.54 N	121.17 W
Lincoln, Ill., U.S.	2746	40.09 N	89.22 W
Lincoln, Kans., U.S.	2750	39.02 N	98.09 W
Lincoln, Maine, U.S.	2740	45.22 N	68.30 W
Lincoln, Mont., U.S.	2754	46.58 N	112.41 W
Lincoln, Nebr., U.S.	2750	40.48 N	96.42 W
Lincoln, N.H., U.S.	2740	44.03 N	71.40 W
Lincolnton, Ga., U.S.	2744	33.48 N	82.28 W
Lincolnton, N.C., U.S.	2744	35.29 N	81.14 W
Lind	2754	46.58 N	118.37 W
Lindale	2748	32.31 N	95.25 W
Linden, Ala., U.S.	2746	32.18 N	87.47 W
Linden, Tenn., U.S.	2746	35.37 N	87.50 W
Lindesnes ≻	2768	58.00 N	7.02 E
Lindi	2788	10.00 S	39.43 E
Lindsay, Ont., Can.	2740	44.21 N	78.44 W
Lindsay, Calif., U.S.	2756	36.12 N	119.05 W
Lindsay, Okla., U.S.	2748	34.50 N	97.38 W
Lindsborg	2750	38.35 N	97.40 W
Lineville	2742	40.35 N	93.32 W
Lingao	2804	20.00 N	109.40 E
Lingga, Kepulauan II	2802	0.00 S	104.35 E
Lingling	2804	26.11 N	111.29 E
Linh, Ngoc ▲	2804	15.04 N	107.59 E
Linhai	2800	28.51 N	121.07 E
Linjiang	2796	41.49 N	126.54 E

Symbols against index entries represent categories identified in the key on page 2810.

Name	Page	Lat°′	Long°′
Linköping	2768	58.25 N	15.37 E
Linkou	2796	45.15 N	130.16 E
Linn	2746	38.29 N	91.51 W
Linneus	2746	39.53 N	93.11 W
Linqing	2796	36.53 N	115.41 E
Linru	2800	34.11 N	112.49 E
Lins	2765	21.40 S	49.45 W
Lintao	2796	35.27 N	103.46 E
Linton, Ind., U.S.	2746	39.02 N	87.10 W
Linton, N. Dak., U.S.	2750	46.16 N	100.14 W
Linxi	2796	43.30 N	118.00 E
Linxia	2796	35.34 N	103.08 E
Linyi	2796	35.04 N	118.22 E
Linz	2770	48.18 N	14.18 E
Lipari	2776	38.28 N	14.57 E
Lipeck	2780	52.37 N	39.35 E
Lipscomb	2748	36.14 N	100.16 W
Lira	2786	2.15 N	32.54 E
Liria	2774	39.38 N	0.36 W
Lisala	2788	2.09 N	21.31 E
Lisboa (Lisbon)	2774	38.43 N	9.08 W
Lisbon			
→ Lisboa, Port.	2774	38.43 N	9.08 W
Lisbon, N. Dak., U.S.	2750	46.27 N	97.41 W
Lisbon Falls	2740	44.03 N	70.03 W
Lishui	2800	28.27 N	119.54 E
Lisičansk	2782	48.55 N	38.26 E
Lisieux	2772	49.09 N	0.14 E
L'Isle Jourdain	2772	46.14 N	0.41 E
Lisman	2746	32.05 N	88.17 W
Lismore	2806	28.48 S	153.17 E
Listowel	2769	52.27 N	9.29 W
Lit	2768	63.19 N	14.49 E
Litang	2796	23.11 N	109.05 E
Litchfield, Ill., U.S.	2746	39.11 N	89.39 W
Litchfield, Minn., U.S.	2742	45.08 N	94.31 W
Litchville	2750	46.39 N	98.11 W
Litija	2776	46.03 N	14.50 E
Litovko	2784	49.15 N	135.11 E
Little Andaman I	2804	10.45 N	92.30 E
Little Belt Mountains ⋀	2754	46.45 N	110.35 W
Little Bighorn ≃	2754	45.44 N	107.34 W
Little Cayman I	2760	19.41 N	80.03 W
Little Current	2740	45.58 N	81.56 W
Little Falls	2742	45.59 N	94.21 W
Littlefield	2748	33.55 N	102.20 W
Littlefork	2742	48.24 N	93.33 W
Little Minch ⅃⅃	2769	57.35 N	6.45 W
Little Missouri ≃	2736	47.30 N	102.25 W
Little Nicobar I	2804	7.20 N	93.40 E
Little Rock	2746	34.44 N	92.15 W
Little Rock ≃	2750	43.16 N	96.15 W
Little Rocky Mountains ⋀	2754	47.50 N	108.10 W
Little Sable Point ≻	2742	43.38 N	86.32 W
Little Salmon ≃	2754	45.25 N	116.19 W
Littleton, Colo., U.S.	2752	39.37 N	105.01 W
Littleton, N.H., U.S.	2740	44.18 N	71.46 W
Liuan	2800	31.44 N	116.31 E
Liuhe	2800	32.22 N	118.49 E
Liuzhou	2804	24.22 N	109.32 E
Live Oak	2744	30.18 N	82.59 W
Livermore	2756	37.41 N	121.46 W
Livermore Falls	2740	44.28 N	70.11 W
Liverpool, N.S., Can.	2739	44.02 N	64.43 W
Liverpool, Eng., U.K.	2769	53.25 N	2.55 W
Liverpool, Pa., U.S.	2740	40.34 N	77.00 W
Liverpool, Cape ≻	2734	73.38 N	78.06 W
Livingston, Ala., U.S.	2746	32.35 N	88.11 W
Livingston, Ky., U.S.	2744	37.18 N	84.13 W
Livingston, Mont., U.S.	2754	45.40 N	110.34 W
Livingston, Tenn., U.S.	2746	36.23 N	85.19 W
Livingston, Tex., U.S.	2748	30.43 N	94.56 W
Livingstone	2788	17.50 S	25.53 E
Livingstonia	2788	10.36 S	34.07 E
Livingston Manor	2740	41.54 N	74.50 W
Livno	2776	43.50 N	17.01 E
Livny	2780	52.25 N	37.37 E
Livonia	2742	42.25 N	83.23 W
Livorno (Leghorn)	2776	43.33 N	10.19 E
Liyang	2800	31.26 N	119.29 E
Lizard Point ≻	2769	49.56 N	5.13 W
Ljubljana	2776	46.03 N	14.31 E
Ljungby	2768	56.50 N	13.56 E
Ljusdal	2768	61.50 N	16.05 E
Llandudno	2769	53.19 N	3.49 W
Llanelli	2769	51.42 N	4.10 W
Llanes	2774	43.25 N	4.45 W
Llanidloes	2769	52.27 N	3.32 W
Llano	2748	30.45 N	98.41 W
Llanwrtyd Wells	2769	52.07 N	3.38 W
Llera	2758	23.19 N	99.01 W
Llerena	2774	38.14 N	6.01 W
Llivia	2772	42.28 N	1.59 E
Lloydminster	2734	53.17 N	110.00 W
Lluchmayor	2774	39.29 N	2.54 E
Llullaillaco, Volcán ▲[1]	2764	24.43 S	68.33 W
Loa	2752	38.24 N	111.38 W
Loange (Luangue) ≃	2788	4.17 S	20.02 E
Lobaye ≃	2786	3.41 N	18.35 E
Lobito	2788	12.20 S	13.34 E
Lobo	2748	30.52 N	104.48 W
Lobos de Afuera, Islas II	2762	6.57 S	80.42 W
Lobos de Tierra, Isla I	2762	6.27 S	80.52 W
Locarno	2772	46.10 N	8.48 E
Lochaline	2769	56.32 N	5.47 W
Lochboisdale	2769	57.09 N	7.19 W
Loches	2772	47.08 N	1.00 E
Lochgilphead	2769	56.03 N	5.26 W
Lockhart	2748	29.53 N	97.41 W
Lock Haven	2740	41.08 N	77.27 W
Lockney	2748	34.07 N	101.27 W
Lockport, Ill., U.S.	2746	41.36 N	88.03 W
Lockport, N.Y., U.S.	2740	43.10 N	78.42 W
Loc-ninh	2804	11.51 N	106.36 E
Locust Grove	2748	36.12 N	95.10 W
Lod	2791	31.58 N	34.54 E
Lodejnoje Polje	2780	60.44 N	33.30 E
Lodève	2772	43.43 N	3.19 E
Lodge Grass	2754	45.19 N	107.22 W
Lodi, It.	2776	45.19 N	9.30 E
Lodi, Calif., U.S.	2756	38.08 N	121.16 W
Lodi, Wis., U.S.	2742	43.19 N	89.32 W
Lodja	2788	3.29 S	23.26 E
Lodwar	2790	3.07 N	35.36 E
Łódź	2770	51.46 N	19.30 E
Loffa ≃	2786	6.36 N	11.08 W
Logan, Iowa, U.S.	2750	41.39 N	95.47 W
Logan, N. Mex., U.S.	2748	35.22 N	103.25 W
Logan, Ohio, U.S.	2740	39.32 N	82.25 W
Logan, Utah, U.S.	2752	41.44 N	111.50 W
Logan, W. Va., U.S.	2744	37.51 N	81.59 W
Logan, Mount ▲, Yukon, Can.	2734	60.34 N	140.24 W
Logan, Mount ▲, Wash., U.S.	2754	48.32 N	120.57 W
Logansport, Ind., U.S.	2746	40.45 N	86.21 W
Logansport, La., U.S.	2746	31.58 N	93.58 W
Logone ≃	2786	12.06 N	15.02 E
Logroño	2774	42.28 N	2.27 W
Logrosán	2774	39.20 N	5.29 W
Loimaa	2768	60.51 N	23.03 E
Loire ≃	2772	47.16 N	2.11 W
Loja, Ec.	2762	4.00 S	79.13 W
Loja, Esp.	2774	37.10 N	4.09 W
Lokolama	2788	2.34 S	19.53 E
Loks Land I	2734	62.26 N	64.38 W
Lol ≃	2786	9.13 N	28.59 E
Lolo	2754	46.45 N	114.05 W
Loma Mansa ▲	2786	9.13 N	11.07 W
Lomami ≃	2788	0.46 N	24.16 E
Lomax	2746	40.41 N	91.04 W
Lombard	2746	41.53 N	88.01 W
Lomblen, Pulau I	2802	8.25 S	123.30 E
Lombok I	2802	8.45 S	116.30 E
Lomé	2786	6.08 N	1.13 E
Lomela	2788	2.18 S	23.17 E
Lomela ≃	2788	0.14 S	20.42 E
Lometa	2748	31.13 N	98.24 W
Lomond, Loch ⊜	2769	56.08 N	4.38 W
Lomonosov	2780	59.55 N	29.46 E
Lompoc	2756	34.38 N	120.27 W
Łomża	2770	53.11 N	22.05 E
Loncoche	2764	39.22 S	72.38 W
London, Ont., Can.	2740	42.59 N	81.14 W
London, Eng., U.K.	2769	51.30 N	0.10 W
London, Ky., U.S.	2744	37.08 N	84.05 W
London, Ohio, U.S.	2740	39.53 N	83.27 W
Londonderry	2769	55.00 N	7.19 W
Londonderry, Cape ≻	2806	13.45 S	126.55 E
Londonderry, Isla I	2764	55.03 S	70.40 W
Lone Pine	2756	36.36 N	118.04 W
Lone Star	2746	32.56 N	94.43 W
Longa, Proliv ⅃⅃	2784	70.20 N	178.00 E
Longarone	2776	46.16 N	12.18 E
Long Beach, Calif., U.S.	2756	33.46 N	118.11 W
Long Beach, Miss., U.S.	2746	30.22 N	89.07 W
Long Beach, N.Y., U.S.	2740	40.35 N	73.41 W
Long Beach, Wash., U.S.	2754	46.21 N	124.03 W
Longboat Key	2744	27.24 N	82.39 W
Long Branch	2740	40.18 N	74.00 W
Longeau	2772	47.46 N	5.18 E
Long Island I, Ba.	2760	23.10 N	75.10 W
Long Island I, N.Y., U.S.	2740	40.50 N	73.00 W
Long Island Sound ⅃⅃	2740	41.05 N	72.58 W
Longjiang	2796	47.19 N	123.12 E
Long Lake	2740	43.58 N	74.25 W
Long Lake ⊜, Mich., U.S.	2742	45.12 N	83.30 W
Long Lake ⊜, N. Dak., U.S.	2750	46.43 N	100.07 W
Longli	2804	26.26 N	106.58 E
Longmont	2752	40.10 N	105.06 W
Long Point ≻[1]	2740	42.34 N	80.15 W
Long Prairie	2750	45.59 N	94.52 W
Long Range Mountains ⋀	2734	49.20 N	57.30 W
Longreach	2806	23.26 S	144.15 E
Longsheng	2804	25.42 N	110.01 E
Longs Peak ▲	2752	40.15 N	105.37 W
Longué	2772	47.23 N	0.06 W
Longueuil	2740	45.32 N	73.30 W
Longuyon	2772	49.26 N	5.36 E
Longview, N.C., U.S.	2744	35.44 N	81.23 W
Longview, Tex., U.S.	2746	32.30 N	94.44 W
Longview, Wash., U.S.	2754	46.08 N	122.57 W
Longwy	2772	49.31 N	5.46 E
Long-xuyen	2804	10.23 N	105.25 E
Lonigo	2776	45.23 N	11.23 E
Lonoke	2746	34.47 N	91.54 W
Lønsdal	2768	66.44 N	15.28 E
Lons-le-Saunier	2772	46.40 N	5.33 E
Loogootee	2746	38.41 N	86.55 W
Lookout, Cape ≻, N.C., U.S.	2744	34.35 N	76.32 W
Lookout, Cape ≻, Oreg., U.S.	2754	45.20 N	124.00 W
Lookout Mountain ▲	2744	34.25 N	85.40 W
Loop Head ≻	2769	52.34 N	9.56 W
Lopatina, Gora ▲	2784	50.52 N	143.10 E
Lopatka, Mys ≻	2784	50.52 N	156.40 E
Lop Buri	2804	14.48 N	100.37 E
Lopez, Cap ≻	2788	0.37 S	8.43 E
López Collada	2758	31.45 N	113.55 W
Lora del Río	2774	37.39 N	5.32 W
Lorain	2740	41.28 N	82.10 W
Lorca	2774	37.40 N	1.42 W
Lord Howe Island I	2806	31.33 S	159.05 E
Lordsburg	2752	32.21 N	108.43 W
Loreto, Bra.	2762	7.05 S	45.09 W
Loreto, Méx.	2758	22.16 N	101.58 W
Lorient	2772	47.45 N	3.22 W
Loriol[-du-Comtat]	2772	44.45 N	4.49 E
Loris	2744	34.04 N	78.53 W
Lorman	2746	31.49 N	91.03 W
Lorraine □[9]	2772	49.00 N	6.00 E
Los Alamos, Méx.	2748	28.40 N	103.30 W
Los Alamos, N. Mex., U.S.	2752	35.53 N	106.19 W
Los Aldamas	2758	26.03 N	99.11 W
Los Ángeles, Chile	2764	37.28 S	72.21 W
Los Angeles, Calif., U.S.	2756	34.03 N	118.15 W
Los Banos	2756	37.04 N	120.51 W
Los Blancos	2764	23.40 S	62.35 W
Los Garzas	2748	26.23 N	99.46 W
Los Herreras	2748	25.55 N	99.24 W
Los Lagos	2764	39.51 S	72.50 W
Los Lunas	2752	34.48 N	106.44 W
Los Mochis	2758	25.45 N	108.57 W
Los Molinos	2756	40.03 N	122.06 W
Los Palacios y Villafranca	2774	37.10 N	5.56 W
Los Teques	2760	10.21 N	67.02 W
Lost River Range ⋀	2754	44.10 N	113.35 W
Lost Trail Pass)(	2754	45.41 N	113.57 W
Los Vilos	2764	31.55 S	71.31 W
Los Yébenes	2774	39.34 N	3.53 W
Lota	2764	37.05 S	73.10 W
Louang Prabang	2804	19.52 N	102.08 E
Louchi	2766	66.04 N	33.00 E
Loudéac	2772	48.10 N	2.45 W
Loudon	2744	35.44 N	84.20 W
Loudonville	2740	40.38 N	82.14 W
Loudun	2772	47.01 N	0.05 E
Louga	2786	15.37 N	16.13 W
Loughborough	2769	52.47 N	1.11 W
Loughrea	2769	53.12 N	8.34 W
Louhans	2772	46.38 N	5.13 E
Louisa, Ky., U.S.	2744	38.07 N	82.36 W
Louisa, Va., U.S.	2740	38.01 N	78.01 W
Louisburg	2744	36.06 N	78.18 W
Louisiade Archipelago II	2806	11.00 S	153.00 E
Louisiana	2746	39.27 N	91.03 W
Louisiana □[3]	2736	31.15 N	92.15 W
Louis Trichardt	2788	23.01 S	29.43 E
Louisville, Ga., U.S.	2744	33.00 N	82.24 W
Louisville, Ill., U.S.	2746	38.46 N	88.30 W
Louisville, Ky., U.S.	2746	38.16 N	85.45 W
Louisville, Miss., U.S.	2746	33.07 N	89.03 W
Louisville, Nebr., U.S.	2750	41.00 N	96.10 W
Loulé	2774	37.08 N	8.02 W
Loup ≃	2750	41.24 N	97.19 W
Lourdes	2772	43.06 N	0.03 W
Lourenço Marques			
→ Maputo	2788	25.58 S	32.35 E
Louth	2769	53.22 N	0.01 W
Louviers	2772	49.13 N	1.10 E
Loveč	2778	43.08 N	24.43 E
Lovelady	2748	31.08 N	95.27 W
Loveland	2752	40.24 N	105.05 W
Lovell	2754	44.50 N	108.24 W
Lovelock	2756	40.11 N	118.28 W
Lovere	2776	45.49 N	10.04 E
Loves Park	2742	42.19 N	89.03 W
Loving	2748	32.17 N	104.06 W
Lovingston	2744	37.46 N	78.52 W
Lovington	2748	32.57 N	103.21 W
Lövstabruk	2768	60.24 N	17.53 E
Low, Cape ≻	2734	63.07 N	85.18 W
Lowell, Mass., U.S.	2740	42.39 N	71.18 W
Lowell, Mich., U.S.	2742	42.56 N	85.20 W
Lowell, Oreg., U.S.	2754	43.55 N	122.47 W
Lower Hutt	2808	41.13 S	174.55 E
Lowestoft	2769	52.29 N	1.45 E
Lowville	2740	43.47 N	75.29 W
Loyalton	2756	39.41 N	120.14 W
Loznica	2778	44.32 N	19.13 E
Lozovaja	2782	48.54 N	36.20 E
Lozoyuela	2774	40.55 N	3.37 W
Lua ≃	2786	2.46 N	18.26 E
Lualaba ≃	2788	0.26 N	25.20 E
Luanda	2788	8.48 S	13.14 E
Luanguinga ≃	2788	15.11 S	22.56 E
Luangwa (Aruângua) ≃	2788	15.36 S	30.25 E
Luanshya	2788	13.08 S	28.24 E
Luarca	2774	43.32 N	6.32 W
Lubang Island I	2802	13.46 N	120.11 E
Lubbock	2748	33.35 N	101.51 W
Lubec	2740	44.52 N	66.59 W
L'ubercy	2780	55.41 N	37.53 E
Lubilash ≃	2788	6.02 S	23.45 E
Lubin	2770	51.24 N	16.13 E
Lublin	2770	51.15 N	22.35 E
Lubny	2782	50.01 N	33.00 E
Lubudi	2788	6.51 S	21.18 E
Lubumbashi (Élisabethville)	2788	11.40 S	27.28 E
Lubutu	2788	0.44 S	26.35 E
Lucania, Mount ▲	2734	61.01 N	140.28 W
L'uca-Ongokton, Gora ▲	2784	67.52 N	106.24 E
Lucas	2750	39.04 N	98.32 W
Lucasville	2740	38.53 N	82.60 W
Lucca	2776	43.50 N	10.29 E
Luce Bay C	2769	54.47 N	4.50 W
Lucedale	2746	30.55 N	88.35 W
Lucena	2774	37.24 N	4.29 W
Lucena del Cid	2774	40.08 N	0.17 W
Luc-en-Diois	2772	44.37 N	5.27 E
Lucera	2776	41.30 N	15.20 E
Lucerne			
→ Luzern, Schw.	2772	47.03 N	8.18 E
Lucerne, Calif., U.S.	2756	39.06 N	122.48 W
Luchiang	2800	24.04 N	120.26 E
Lucira	2788	13.51 S	12.31 E
Luck	2782	50.44 N	25.20 E
Lucknow	2794	26.51 N	80.55 E
Luçon	2772	46.27 N	1.10 W
Lüda (Dairen)	2796	38.53 N	121.35 E
Lüderitz	2788	26.38 S	15.10 E
Ludhiāna	2794	30.54 N	75.51 E
Ludington	2742	43.57 N	86.27 W
L'udinovo	2780	53.52 N	34.27 E
Ludlow	2740	43.24 N	72.42 W
Ludowici	2744	31.43 N	81.45 W
Ludvika	2768	60.09 N	15.11 E
Lueders	2748	32.48 N	99.37 W
Luena ≃	2788	12.31 S	22.34 E
Lufeng	2800	22.57 N	115.38 E
Lufkin	2758	31.20 N	94.44 W
Luga	2780	58.44 N	29.52 E
Lugano	2772	46.01 N	8.58 E
Lugenda ≃	2788	11.25 S	38.33 E
Lugh Ganane	2790	3.56 N	42.32 E
Lugnaquillia Mountain ▲	2769	52.58 N	6.27 W
Lugo, Esp.	2774	43.00 N	7.34 W
Lugo, It.	2776	44.25 N	11.54 E
Lugoj	2778	45.41 N	21.54 E
Luilaka ≃	2788	0.52 S	20.12 E
Luino	2776	46.00 N	8.44 E
Lukeville	2752	31.53 N	112.49 W
Lukulu	2788	14.25 S	23.12 E
Lula	2746	34.27 N	90.29 W
Luleå	2768	65.34 N	22.10 E
Lüleburgaz	2778	41.24 N	27.21 E
Luling	2748	29.41 N	97.39 W
Lulonga ≃	2788	0.42 N	18.23 E
Lumber City	2744	31.56 N	82.41 W
Lumberton, Miss., U.S.	2746	31.00 N	89.27 W
Lumberton, N.C., U.S.	2744	34.37 N	79.00 W
Lumbrales	2774	40.56 N	6.43 W
Lumding	2794	25.45 N	93.10 E
Luna Pier	2742	41.48 N	83.27 W
Lund, Sve.	2768	55.42 N	13.11 E
Lund, Nev., U.S.	2756	38.52 N	115.00 W
Lundazi	2788	12.19 S	33.13 E
Lunel	2772	43.41 N	4.08 E
Lunenburg, N.S., Can.	2739	44.23 N	64.19 W
Lunenburg, Va., U.S.	2744	36.58 N	78.16 W
Lunéville	2772	48.36 N	6.30 E
Lunga ≃	2788	14.34 S	26.25 E
Luobubo (Lop Nor) ⊜	2796	40.20 N	90.15 E
Luohe	2800	33.35 N	114.01 E
Luolong	2794	30.45 N	96.09 E
Luoyang	2796	34.41 N	112.28 E
Lure	2772	47.41 N	6.30 E
Lurgan	2769	54.28 N	6.20 W
Lúrio ≃	2788	13.35 S	40.32 E
Lusaka	2788	15.25 S	28.17 E
Lusambo	2788	4.58 S	23.27 E
Lushan	2800	33.45 N	112.53 E
Lushnje	2778	40.56 N	19.42 E
Lushoto	2788	4.47 S	38.17 E
Lüshun (Port Arthur)	2796	38.48 N	121.16 E
Luso	2788	11.47 S	19.52 E
Lussac-les-Châteaux	2772	46.24 N	0.44 E
Lūt, Dasht-e ◆[2]	2790	33.00 N	57.00 E
Lutcher	2746	30.02 N	90.42 W
Luther	2748	35.40 N	97.12 W
Luton	2769	51.53 N	0.25 W
Lutong	2802	4.32 N	114.00 E
Luttrell	2744	36.12 N	83.44 W
Luverne, Ala., U.S.	2746	31.43 N	86.16 W
Lu Verne, Iowa, U.S.	2742	42.55 N	94.05 W
Luverne, Minn., U.S.	2750	43.39 N	96.13 W
Luwegu ≃	2788	8.31 S	37.23 E
Luxembourg	2770	49.36 N	6.09 E
Luxembourg □[1]	2766	49.45 N	6.05 E
Luzern	2772	47.03 N	8.18 E
Luzhou	2796	28.54 N	105.27 E
Luzon I	2802	16.00 N	121.00 E
Luzon Strait ⅃⅃	2802	20.30 N	121.00 E
Luzy	2772	46.48 N	3.58 E
L'vov	2782	49.50 N	24.00 E
Lyallpur	2794	31.25 N	73.05 E
Lyck			
→ Ełk	2770	53.50 N	22.22 E
Lycksele	2768	64.36 N	18.40 E
Lydenburg	2788	25.10 S	30.29 E
Lyford	2748	26.24 N	97.48 W
Lyman	2754	41.20 N	110.18 W
Łyna (Lava) ≃	2770	54.37 N	21.14 E
Lynch	2744	36.58 N	82.55 W
Lynchburg, Ohio, U.S.	2740	39.14 N	83.48 W
Lynchburg, Va., U.S.	2744	37.24 N	79.10 W
Lynden	2754	48.57 N	122.27 W
Lyndon	2750	38.36 N	95.41 W
Lyndonville	2740	44.32 N	72.01 W
Lynher Reef ◆[2]	2806	15.27 S	121.55 E
Lynn, Ala., U.S.	2746	34.03 N	87.33 W
Lynn, Ind., U.S.	2746	40.03 N	84.56 W
Lynn, Mass., U.S.	2740	42.28 N	70.57 W
Lynndyl	2752	39.31 N	112.22 W
Lynn Gardens	2744	36.35 N	82.34 W
Lynn Lake	2734	56.51 N	101.03 W
Lynton	2769	51.15 N	3.50 W
Lyon	2772	45.45 N	4.51 E
Lyons, Ga., U.S.	2744	32.12 N	82.19 W
Lyons, Kans., U.S.	2750	38.21 N	98.12 W
Lytle	2748	29.14 N	98.48 W
M			
Ma'ān	2791	30.12 N	35.44 E
Maanshan	2800	31.42 N	118.30 E
Ma'arrat an-Nu'mān	2791	35.38 N	36.40 E
Maastricht	2770	50.52 N	5.43 E
Mabank	2748	32.22 N	96.06 W
Maben	2746	33.33 N	89.05 W
Mača	2784	59.54 N	117.35 E
Macaé	2765	22.23 S	41.47 W
McAlester	2748	34.56 N	95.46 W
McAllen	2748	26.12 N	98.15 W
Macão	2774	39.33 N	8.00 W
Macao			
→ Macau □[2]	2800	22.10 N	113.33 E
Macapá	2762	0.02 N	51.03 W
Macará	2762	4.23 S	79.57 W
Macarani	2765	15.33 S	40.24 W
McArthur	2740	39.15 N	82.29 W
Macau, Bra.	2762	5.07 S	36.38 W
Macau (Aomen), Macau	2800	22.14 N	113.35 E
Macau (Aomen) □[2]	2800	22.10 N	113.33 E

Symbols against index entries represent categories identified in the key on page 2810.

Name	Page	Lat °′	Long °′
McCall	2754	44.55 N	116.06 W
McCamey	2748	31.08 N	102.13 W
McCammon	2754	42.39 N	112.12 W
Macclenny	2744	30.18 N	82.07 W
Macclesfield	2769	53.16 N	2.07 W
McClintock, Mount ∧	2733	80.13 S	157.26 E
McClusky	2750	47.29 N	100.27 W
McColl	2744	34.40 N	79.33 W
McComb	2746	31.14 N	90.27 W
McConnellsburg	2740	39.56 N	77.59 W
McCook	2736	40.12 N	100.38 W
McCormick	2744	33.55 N	82.17 W
McDade	2748	30.17 N	97.15 W
McDavid	2746	30.52 N	87.19 W
McDermitt	2756	41.59 N	117.36 W
McDermott	2740	38.50 N	83.04 W
MacDonald Pass)(	2754	46.34 N	112.18 W
Macdonnell Ranges ⋀	2806	23.45 S	133.20 E
McDonough	2744	33.27 N	84.09 W
McDougall, Mount ∧	2754	42.54 N	110.36 W
Macduff	2769	57.40 N	2.29 W
Macdui, Ben ∧	2769	57.04 N	3.40 W
Macedo de Cavaleiros	2774	41.32 N	6.58 W
Macedonia □[9]	2766	41.00 N	23.00 E
Maceió	2762	9.40 S	35.43 W
Macerata	2776	43.18 N	13.27 E
McFarland	2756	35.41 N	119.14 W
McGehee	2746	33.38 N	91.24 W
McGill	2756	39.23 N	114.47 W
McGregor	2748	31.26 N	97.24 W
Machačkala	2766	42.58 N	47.30 E
Machagai	2764	26.56 S	60.05 W
Machala	2762	3.16 S	79.58 W
Machecoul	2772	47.00 N	1.50 W
McHenry	2742	42.21 N	88.16 W
Machias	2740	44.43 N	67.28 W
Machilīpatnam (Bandar)	2793	16.10 N	81.08 E
Machiques	2760	10.04 N	72.34 W
Machupicchu	2762	13.08 S	72.32 W
Maćias Nguema Biyogo I	2786	3.30 N	8.40 E
Macina ⇾[1]	2786	14.30 N	5.00 W
McIntosh, Ala., U.S.	2746	31.16 N	88.02 W
McIntosh, Minn., U.S.	2750	47.38 N	95.53 W
McIntosh, S. Dak., U.S.	2750	45.55 N	101.21 W
Mackay	2806	21.09 S	149.11 E
Mackay, Lake ⊜	2806	22.30 S	129.00 E
McKee	2744	37.25 N	84.01 W
McKeesport	2740	40.21 N	79.52 W
McKenzie	2746	36.08 N	88.31 W
Mackenzie ≃	2734	69.15 N	134.08 W
McKenzie ≃	2754	44.07 N	123.06 W
Mackenzie Bay C	2734	69.00 N	136.30 W
Mackenzie Mountains ⋀	2734	64.00 N	130.00 W
Mackinac, Straits of ⋃	2742	45.49 N	84.42 W
Mackinac Island	2742	45.51 N	84.37 W
Mackinaw City	2742	45.47 N	84.44 W
McKinley, Mount ∧	2738	63.30 N	151.00 W
McKinleyville	2756	40.57 N	124.06 W
McKinney	2748	33.12 N	96.37 W
Macksville	2750	37.58 N	98.58 W
McLaughlin	2750	45.49 N	100.49 W
McLean, Ill., U.S.	2746	40.19 N	89.10 W
McLean, Tex., U.S.	2748	35.14 N	100.36 W
McLeansboro	2746	38.06 N	88.32 W
Maclear	2788	31.02 S	28.23 E
McLeod, Lake ⊜	2806	24.00 S	113.35 E
McLoughlin, Mount ∧	2754	42.27 N	122.19 W
Macmillan ≃	2734	62.52 N	135.55 W
McMinnville, Oreg., U.S.	2754	45.13 N	123.12 W
McMinnville, Tenn., U.S.	2746	35.41 N	85.46 W
McNary	2752	34.04 N	109.51 W
McNeill	2746	30.40 N	89.38 W
Macomb	2746	40.27 N	90.40 W
Macomer	2776	40.16 N	8.46 E
Mâcon, Fr.	2772	46.18 N	4.50 E
Macon, Ga., U.S.	2744	32.50 N	83.38 W
Macon, Miss., U.S.	2746	33.07 N	88.34 W
Macon, Mo., U.S.	2746	39.44 N	92.28 W
McPherson	2750	38.22 N	97.40 W
McRae	2744	32.04 N	82.53 W
McRoberts	2744	37.12 N	82.40 W
MacTier	2740	45.08 N	79.47 W
McVille	2750	47.46 N	98.11 W
Ma'dabā	2791	31.43 N	35.48 E
Madagascar □[1]	2788	19.00 S	46.00 E
Madawaska	2739	47.21 N	68.20 W
Madawaska Highlands ⋀[1]	2740	45.15 N	77.35 W
Maddaloni	2776	41.02 N	14.23 E
Madden Lake ⊜[1]	2760	9.15 N	79.34 W
Maddock	2750	47.58 N	99.32 W
Madeira I	2786	32.44 N	17.00 W
Madeira ≃	2762	3.22 S	58.45 W
Madeira, Arquipélago da (Madeira Islands) II	2786	32.40 N	16.45 W
Madeleine, Îles de la II	2734	47.30 N	61.45 W
Madelia	2742	44.03 N	94.25 W
Madeline Island I	2742	46.50 N	90.40 W
Madera	2756	36.57 N	120.03 W
Madill	2748	34.06 N	96.46 W
Madīnat ash-Sha'b	2790	12.50 N	44.56 E
Madingou	2788	4.09 S	13.34 E
Madison, Ala., U.S.	2746	34.42 N	86.45 W
Madison, Ga., U.S.	2744	33.36 N	83.28 W
Madison, Ind., U.S.	2746	38.44 N	85.23 W
Madison, Kans., U.S.	2750	38.08 N	96.08 W
Madison, Maine, U.S.	2740	44.48 N	69.53 W
Madison, Minn., U.S.	2750	45.01 N	96.11 W
Madison, Nebr., U.S.	2750	41.50 N	97.27 W
Madison, N.C., U.S.	2744	36.23 N	79.58 W
Madison, S. Dak., U.S.	2750	44.00 N	97.07 W
Madison, W. Va., U.S.	2740	38.04 N	81.49 W
Madison, Wis., U.S.	2742	43.05 N	89.22 W
Madison Range ⋀	2754	45.15 N	111.20 W
Madisonville, Ky., U.S.	2746	37.20 N	87.30 W
Madisonville, Tex., U.S.	2748	30.57 N	95.55 W
Madiun	2802	7.37 S	111.31 E
Madjene	2802	3.33 S	118.57 E
Mado Gashi	2788	0.44 S	39.10 E
Madras, Bhārat	2793	13.05 N	80.17 E
Madras, Oreg., U.S.	2754	44.38 N	121.08 W
Madre, Laguna C, Méx.	2758	25.00 N	97.40 W
Madre, Laguna C, Tex., U.S.	2748	27.00 N	97.35 W
Madre, Sierra ⋀	2802	17.15 N	122.00 E
Madre de Dios ≃	2762	10.59 S	66.08 W
Madre de Dios, Isla I	2764	50.15 S	75.10 W
Madre del Sur, Sierra ⋀	2758	17.00 N	100.00 W
Madre Occidental, Sierra ⋀	2758	25.00 N	105.00 W
Madre Oriental, Sierra ⋀	2758	22.00 N	99.30 W
Madrid	2774	40.24 N	3.41 W
Madridejos	2774	39.28 N	3.32 W
Maduo	2796	34.53 N	98.24 E
Madura I	2802	7.00 S	113.20 E
Madurai	2793	9.56 N	78.07 E
Maebashi	2798	36.23 N	139.04 E
Mae Hong Son	2804	19.16 N	97.56 E
Maeser	2752	40.28 N	109.32 W
Maestra, Sierra ⋀	2760	20.00 N	76.45 W
Maevatanana	2788	16.56 S	46.49 E
Mafeking	2788	25.53 S	25.39 E
Mafia Island I	2788	7.50 S	39.50 E
Mafra	2764	26.07 S	49.49 W
Magadan	2784	59.34 N	150.48 E
Magadi	2788	1.54 S	36.17 E
Magallanes, Estrecho de (Strait of Magellan) ⋃	2764	54.00 S	71.00 W
Magangué	2760	9.14 N	74.45 W
Magazine Mountain ∧	2746	35.10 N	93.38 W
Magdagači	2784	53.27 N	125.48 E
Magdalena, Bol.	2762	13.20 S	64.08 W
Magdalena, Méx.	2758	30.38 N	110.57 W
Magdalena, N. Mex., U.S.	2752	34.07 N	107.14 W
Magdalena ≃	2760	11.06 N	74.51 W
Magdalena, Isla I	2764	44.42 S	73.10 W
Magenta	2776	45.28 N	8.53 E
Maggiore, Lago ⊜	2776	46.00 N	8.40 E
Magione	2776	43.08 N	12.12 E
Magnitogorsk	2766	53.27 N	59.04 E
Magnolia, Ark., U.S.	2746	33.16 N	93.14 W
Magnolia, Miss., U.S.	2746	31.09 N	90.28 W
Magog	2740	45.16 N	72.09 W
Magpie, Lac ⊜	2734	51.00 N	64.41 W
Maguarinho, Cabo ≻	2762	0.18 S	48.22 W
Mahābād	2766	36.45 N	45.43 E
Mahābhārat Range ⋀	2794	27.40 N	84.30 E
Mahajamba, Baie de la C	2788	15.24 S	47.05 E
Mahānadi ≃	2792	20.19 N	86.45 E
Mahanoro	2788	19.54 S	48.48 E
Maḥaṭṭat al-Qaṭrānah	2791	31.15 N	36.03 E
Maḥaṭṭat Ḥaraḍ	2790	24.08 N	49.05 E
Mahbūbnagar	2793	16.44 N	77.59 E
Mahé Island I	2788	4.40 S	55.28 E
Mahenge	2788	8.41 S	36.43 E
Mahnomen	2750	47.19 N	96.01 W
Mahón	2774	39.53 N	4.15 E
Maiden	2744	35.35 N	81.13 W
Maidstone	2769	51.17 N	0.32 E
Maiduguri	2786	11.51 N	13.10 E
Maillezais	2772	46.22 N	0.44 W
Mai-Ndombe, Lac ⊜	2788	2.00 S	18.20 E
Maine □[3]	2736	45.15 N	69.15 W
Mainland I, Scot., U.K.	2769	60.20 N	1.22 W
Mainland I, Scot., U.K.	2769	59.00 N	3.10 W
Maipo, Volcán ∧[1]	2764	34.10 S	69.50 W
Maipú	2764	36.52 S	57.54 W
Maiquetía	2760	10.36 N	66.57 W
Maitland	2806	32.44 S	151.33 E
Maizuru	2798	35.27 N	135.20 E
Maja ≃	2784	54.31 N	134.41 E
Maji	2790	6.11 N	35.38 E
Majkop	2782	44.35 N	40.07 E
Majno-Pyl'gino	2784	62.32 N	177.02 E
Majunga	2788	15.43 S	46.19 E
Makale	2802	3.06 S	119.51 E
Makarska	2776	43.18 N	17.02 E
Makasar → Udjung Pandang, Indon.	2802	5.07 S	119.24 E
Makasar, Indon.	2802	5.07 S	119.24 E
Makasar, Selat (Makassar Strait) ⋃	2802	2.00 S	117.30 E
Makat	2766	47.39 N	53.19 E
Makejevka	2782	48.02 N	37.58 E
Makeni	2786	8.53 N	12.03 W
Makgadikgadi Pans ≚	2788	20.45 S	25.30 E
Makindu	2788	2.17 S	37.49 E
M'akit	2784	61.24 N	152.09 E
Makkah (Mecca)	2790	21.27 N	39.49 E
Maklakovo	2784	58.16 N	92.29 E
Makó	2770	46.13 N	20.29 E
Makokou	2788	0.34 N	12.52 E
Makthar	2776	35.51 N	9.12 E
Makumbi	2788	5.51 S	20.41 E
Makurazaki	2798	31.16 N	130.19 E
Makurdi	2786	7.45 N	8.32 E
Malabar Coast ⊥[2]	2793	10.00 N	76.15 E
Malabo	2786	3.45 N	8.47 E
Malacca	2804	2.11 N	102.16 E
Malacca, Strait of ⋃	2804	2.30 N	101.20 E
Malad City	2754	42.12 N	112.15 W
Málaga	2774	36.43 N	4.25 W
Malagón	2774	39.10 N	3.51 W
Malaimbandy	2788	20.20 S	45.36 E
Malaja Kuril'skaja Gr'ada (Habomai-shotō) II	2798a	43.30 N	146.10 E
Malakāl	2786	9.31 N	31.39 E
Malang	2802	7.59 S	112.37 E
Malanje	2788	9.32 S	16.20 E
Malanville	2786	11.52 N	3.23 E
Malargüe	2764	35.30 S	69.35 W
Malatya	2766	38.21 N	38.19 E
Malawi □[1]	2788	13.30 S	34.00 E
Malay Peninsula ≻[1]	2802	6.00 N	102.00 E
Malaysia □[1]	2802	2.30 N	112.30 E
Malbork	2770	54.02 N	19.01 E
Malcolm	2806	28.56 S	121.30 E
Malden	2746	36.34 N	89.57 W
Maldive Islands II	2793	5.00 N	73.00 E
Maldives □[1]	2793	3.15 N	73.00 E
Maldonado	2764	34.54 S	54.57 W
Mālegaon	2793	20.33 N	74.32 E
Malha Wells	2786	15.08 N	26.12 E
Malheur ≃	2754	44.03 N	116.59 W
Mali □[1]	2786	17.00 N	4.00 W
Malik, Wādī al- V	2786	18.02 N	30.58 E
Malindi	2788	3.13 S	40.07 E
Malino, Bukit ∧	2802	0.45 N	120.47 E
Malka	2784	53.20 N	157.30 E
Malkara	2778	40.53 N	26.54 E
Mallaig	2769	57.00 N	5.50 W
Mallawī	2786	27.44 N	30.50 E
Mallnitz	2770	46.59 N	13.10 E
Mallorca I	2774	39.30 N	3.00 E
Mallow	2769	52.08 N	8.39 W
Malmberget	2768	67.10 N	20.40 E
Malmédy	2770	50.25 N	6.02 E
Malmesbury	2788	33.28 S	18.44 E
Malmö	2768	55.36 N	13.00 E
Malone	2740	44.51 N	74.17 W
Måløy	2768	61.56 N	5.07 E
Malpelo, Isla de I	2762	3.59 N	81.35 W
Malta	2754	48.21 N	107.52 W
Malta □[1]	2766	35.50 N	14.35 E
Maltahöhe	2788	24.50 S	17.00 E
Maluku (Moluccas) II	2802	2.00 S	128.00 E
Maluku, Laut (Molucca Sea) ▼[2]	2802	0.30 S	125.00 E
Malung	2768	60.40 N	13.44 E
Malvern	2746	34.22 N	92.49 W
Malyj An'uj ≃	2784	68.30 N	160.49 E
Malyj L'achovskij, Ostrov I	2784	74.07 N	140.36 E
Malyj Tajmyr, Ostrov I	2784	78.08 N	107.12 E
Mama	2784	58.18 N	112.54 E
Mamberamo ≃	2802	1.26 S	137.53 E
Mamers	2772	48.21 N	0.23 E
Mamfe	2786	5.46 N	9.17 E
Mammoth	2752	32.43 N	110.38 W
Mammoth Cave National Park ♠	2746	37.08 N	86.13 W
Mammoth Lakes	2756	37.38 N	118.58 W
Mammoth Spring	2746	36.30 N	91.33 W
Mamoré ≃	2762	10.23 S	65.23 W
Mamou, Guinée	2786	10.23 N	12.05 W
Mamou, La., U.S.	2746	30.38 N	92.25 W
Man	2786	7.24 N	7.33 W
Mana	2757a	22.02 N	159.46 W
Manacapuru	2762	3.18 S	60.37 W
Manacor	2774	39.34 N	3.12 E
Manado	2802	1.29 N	124.51 E
Managua	2760	12.09 N	86.17 W
Manakara	2788	22.08 S	48.01 E
Mananara	2788	16.10 S	49.46 E
Mananjary	2788	21.13 S	48.20 E
Ma'nasi	2796	44.18 N	86.13 E
Manassas	2740	38.45 N	77.28 W
Manaus	2762	3.08 S	60.01 W
Manawa	2742	44.28 N	88.55 W
Manbij	2791	36.31 N	37.57 E
Mancha Real	2774	37.47 N	3.37 W
Manchester, Eng., U.K.	2769	53.30 N	2.15 W
Manchester, Conn., U.S.	2740	41.47 N	72.31 W
Manchester, Ga., U.S.	2744	32.51 N	84.37 W
Manchester, Iowa, U.S.	2742	42.29 N	91.27 W
Manchester, Ky., U.S.	2744	37.09 N	83.46 W
Manchester, N.H., U.S.	2740	42.59 N	71.28 W
Manchester, Tenn., U.S.	2746	35.29 N	86.05 W
Manchester, Vt., U.S.	2740	43.10 N	73.05 W
Manchuria ⇾[1]	2796	47.00 N	125.00 E
Manciano	2776	42.35 N	11.31 E
Mand ≃	2790	28.11 N	51.17 E
Manda	2788	10.28 S	34.35 E
Mandal	2768	58.02 N	7.27 E
Mandala, Puntjak ∧	2802	4.44 S	140.20 E
Mandalay	2804	22.00 N	96.05 E
Mandalgov'	2796	45.45 N	106.20 E
Mandan	2750	46.50 N	100.54 W
Mandas	2776	39.39 N	9.08 E
Mandasor	2794	24.04 N	75.04 E
Mandeb, Bāb el- ⋃	2790	12.40 N	43.20 E
Manderson	2754	44.16 N	107.58 W
Mandimba	2788	14.21 S	35.39 E
Mandla	2794	22.36 N	80.23 E
Manduria	2776	40.24 N	17.38 E
Māndvi	2794	22.50 N	69.22 E
Mandya	2793	12.33 N	76.54 E
Manerbio	2776	45.21 N	10.08 E
Manfredonia	2776	41.38 N	15.55 E
Mangabeiras, Chapada das ⋀[2]	2762	10.00 S	46.30 W
Mangalore	2793	12.52 N	74.53 E
Mangham	2746	32.19 N	91.47 W
Mangkalihat, Tandjung ≻	2802	1.02 N	118.59 E
Mangoche	2788	14.28 S	35.16 E
Mangoky ≃	2788	23.27 S	45.13 E
Mangole, Pulau I	2802	1.53 S	125.50 E
Mangualde	2774	40.36 N	7.46 W
Mangum	2748	34.53 N	99.30 W
Mangya	2796	37.40 N	90.50 E
Manhattan	2750	39.11 N	96.35 W
Manicoré	2762	5.49 S	61.17 W
Manicouagan ≃	2734	49.11 N	68.13 W
Manila, Pil.	2802	14.35 N	121.00 E
Manila, Utah, U.S.	2752	40.59 N	109.43 W
Manila Bay C	2802	14.30 N	120.45 E
Manilla	2750	41.53 N	95.14 W
Manisa	2778	38.36 N	27.26 E
Manistee	2742	44.15 N	86.19 W
Manistee ≃	2742	44.15 N	86.21 W
Manistique	2742	45.57 N	86.15 W
Manistique Lake ⊜	2742	46.15 N	85.45 W
Manito	2746	40.25 N	89.47 W
Manitoba □[4]	2734	54.00 N	97.00 W
Manitoba, Lake ⊜	2734	51.00 N	98.45 W
Manitoulin Island I	2740	45.45 N	82.30 W
Manitou Springs	2752	38.52 N	104.55 W
Manitowoc	2742	44.06 N	87.40 W
Maniwaki	2740	46.23 N	75.58 W
Manizales	2762	5.05 N	75.32 W
Manjacaze	2788	24.44 S	33.53 E
Mānjra ≃	2793	18.49 N	77.52 E
Mankato, Kans., U.S.	2750	39.47 N	98.12 W
Mankato, Minn., U.S.	2742	44.10 N	94.01 W
Mankoya	2788	14.47 S	24.48 E
Manlléu	2774	42.00 N	2.17 E
Manly	2742	43.17 N	93.12 W
Mannar, Gulf of C	2793	8.30 N	79.00 E
Manning, Iowa, U.S.	2750	41.55 N	95.03 W
Manning, N. Dak., U.S.	2750	47.14 N	102.47 W
Manning, S.C., U.S.	2744	33.42 N	80.13 W
Mannington	2740	39.32 N	80.20 W
Manokwari	2802	0.52 S	134.05 E
Manono	2788	7.18 S	27.25 E
Manor	2748	30.20 N	97.33 W
Manosque	2772	43.50 N	5.47 E
Manresa	2774	41.44 N	1.50 E
Mansa	2788	11.12 S	28.53 E
Mansel Island I	2734	62.00 N	79.50 W
Mansfield, Eng., U.K.	2769	53.09 N	1.11 W
Mansfield, Ark., U.S.	2746	35.04 N	94.13 W
Mansfield, La., U.S.	2746	32.02 N	93.43 W
Mansfield, Ohio, U.S.	2740	40.46 N	82.31 W
Mansfield, Pa., U.S.	2740	41.48 N	77.05 W
Manson	2750	42.32 N	94.32 W
Manta	2762	0.57 S	80.44 W
Manteca	2756	37.48 N	121.13 W
Mantekamuhu ⊜	2794	34.30 N	89.15 E
Manteno	2746	41.14 N	88.12 W
Mantes-la-Jolie	2772	48.59 N	1.43 E
Manti	2752	39.16 N	111.38 W
Manton	2742	44.24 N	85.24 W
Mantova	2776	45.09 N	10.48 E
Manturovo	2780	58.20 N	44.46 E
Manukau Harbour C	2808	37.01 S	174.44 E
Manvel	2750	48.04 N	97.10 W
Many	2746	31.34 N	93.29 W
Manzanares	2774	39.00 N	3.22 W
Manzanillo, Cuba	2760	20.21 N	77.07 W
Manzanillo, Méx.	2758	19.03 N	104.20 W
Manzano Peak ∧	2752	34.35 N	106.26 W
Manzhouli	2796	49.35 N	117.22 E
Mao	2786	14.07 N	15.19 E
Maoke, Pegunungan ⋀	2802	4.00 S	138.00 E
Mapastepec	2758	15.26 N	92.54 W
Mapi	2802	7.07 S	139.23 E
Mapia, Kepulauan II	2802	0.50 N	134.20 E
Mapimí	2758	25.49 N	103.51 W
Mapimí, Bolsón de ⇾[2]	2758	27.30 N	103.15 W
Mapire	2760	7.45 N	64.42 W
Maple Creek	2734	49.55 N	109.27 W
Maplesville	2746	32.47 N	86.52 W
Mapleton, Iowa, U.S.	2750	42.10 N	95.47 W
Mapleton, Oreg., U.S.	2754	44.02 N	123.52 W
Mapuera ≃	2762	1.05 S	57.02 W
Maputo (Lourenço Marques)	2788	25.58 S	32.35 E
Maqueda	2774	40.04 N	4.22 W
Maquela do Zombo	2788	6.03 S	15.07 E
Maquinchao	2764	41.15 S	68.44 W
Maquoketa	2742	42.04 N	90.40 W
Marabá	2762	5.21 S	49.07 W
Maracá, Ilha de I	2762	2.05 N	50.25 W
Maracaibo	2760	10.40 N	71.37 W
Maracaibo, Lago de ⊜	2760	9.50 N	71.30 W
Maracay	2760	10.15 N	67.36 W
Marādah	2786	29.14 N	19.13 E
Maradi	2786	13.29 N	7.06 E
Marāgheh	2766	37.23 N	46.13 E
Maragogipe	2765	12.46 S	38.55 W
Marahuaca, Cerro ∧	2762	3.34 N	65.27 W
Marais des Cygnes ≃	2746	38.02 N	94.14 W
Marajó, Baía de C	2762	1.00 S	48.30 W
Marajó, Ilha de I	2762	1.00 S	49.30 W
Maralal	2788	1.06 N	36.42 E
Marambaia, Ilha da I	2765	23.04 S	43.58 W
Marana	2752	32.27 N	111.13 W
Marandellas	2788	18.10 S	31.36 E
Marañón ≃	2762	4.30 S	73.35 W
Marans	2772	46.19 N	1.00 W
Marapanim	2762	0.42 S	47.42 W
Maraş	2766	37.36 N	36.55 E
Marathon, Ont., Can.	2734	48.40 N	86.25 W
Marathon, Tex., U.S.	2748	30.12 N	103.15 W
Marawī	2790	18.29 N	31.49 E
Marble	2742	47.19 N	93.18 W
Marble Bar	2806	21.11 S	119.44 E
Marble Canyon V	2752	36.30 N	111.50 W
Marble Falls	2748	30.34 N	98.17 W
Marble Hill	2746	37.18 N	89.58 W
Marcaria	2776	45.07 N	10.32 E
Marceline	2746	39.43 N	92.57 W
Marcha	2784	61.49 N	122.20 E
Marcha ≃	2784	63.28 N	118.50 E
Marche-en-Famenne	2770	50.12 N	5.20 E
Marchena	2774	37.20 N	5.24 W
Mar Chiquita, Laguna ⊜	2764	30.42 S	62.36 W
Marcola	2754	44.10 N	122.52 W
Marcus	2750	42.50 N	95.48 W
Marcy, Mount ∧	2740	44.07 N	73.56 W
Mardān	2794	34.12 N	72.02 E
Mar del Plata	2764	38.01 S	57.35 W
Mardin	2766	37.18 N	40.44 E
Mareeba	2806	17.00 S	145.26 E
Mareg	2790	3.47 N	47.18 E
Marengo	2742	41.48 N	92.04 W

Symbols against index entries represent categories identified in the key on page 2810.

Symbols against index entries represent categories identified in the key on page 2810.

Symbols against index entries represent categories identified in the key on page 2810.

Name	Page	Lat °′	Long °′
Monticello, Ind., U.S.	2746	40.45 N	86.46 W
Monticello, Iowa, U.S.	2742	42.15 N	91.12 W
Monticello, Ky., U.S.	2746	36.50 N	84.51 W
Monticello, Miss., U.S.	2746	31.33 N	90.07 W
Monticello, Mo., U.S.	2746	40.07 N	91.43 W
Monticello, N. Mex., U.S.	2752	33.24 N	107.27 W
Monticello, N.Y., U.S.	2740	41.39 N	74.42 W
Monticello, Utah, U.S.	2752	37.52 N	109.21 W
Montichiari	2776	45.25 N	10.23 E
Montignac	2772	45.04 N	1.10 E
Montijo, Esp.	2774	38.55 N	6.37 W
Montijo, Port.	2774	38.42 N	8.58 W
Montilla	2774	37.35 N	4.38 W
Montivilliers	2772	49.33 N	0.12 E
Mont-Louis	2772	42.31 N	2.07 E
Montluçon	2772	46.21 N	2.36 E
Montmagny	2739	46.59 N	70.33 W
Montmorillon	2772	46.26 N	0.52 E
Montmort	2772	48.55 N	3.49 E
Montoro	2774	38.01 N	4.23 W
Montour Falls	2740	42.21 N	76.51 W
Montoursville	2740	41.15 N	76.55 W
Montpelier, Idaho, U.S.	2754	42.19 N	111.18 W
Montpelier, Ind., U.S.	2746	40.33 N	85.17 W
Montpelier, Ohio, U.S.	2740	41.35 N	84.36 W
Montpelier, Vt., U.S.	2740	44.16 N	72.35 W
Montpellier	2772	43.36 N	3.53 E
Montréal, Qué., Can.	2740	45.31 N	73.34 W
Montreal, Wis., U.S.	2742	46.26 N	90.14 W
Montreal Lake ⊜	2734	54.20 N	105.40 W
Montreuil-Bellay	2772	47.08 N	0.09 W
Montreux	2772	46.26 N	6.55 E
Montrose, Scot., U.K.	2769	56.43 N	2.29 W
Montrose, Colo., U.S.	2752	38.29 N	107.53 W
Montrose, Pa., U.S.	2740	41.50 N	75.53 W
Montserrat □2	2760	16.45 N	62.12 W
Monument Peak ∧, Colo., U.S.	2752	39.43 N	107.55 W
Monument Peak ∧, Idaho, U.S.	2754	42.07 N	114.14 W
Monument Valley V	2752	36.50 N	110.20 W
Monywa	2804	22.05 N	95.08 E
Monza	2776	45.35 N	9.16 E
Monzón	2774	41.55 N	0.12 E
Moody	2748	31.19 N	97.21 W
Moora	2806	30.39 S	116.00 E
Moorcroft	2750	44.16 N	104.57 W
Moore, Mont., U.S.	2754	46.59 N	109.42 W
Moore, Okla., U.S.	2748	35.20 N	97.29 W
Moorefield	2740	39.04 N	78.58 W
Mooreland	2748	36.26 N	99.12 W
Mooresville, Ind., U.S.	2746	39.37 N	86.22 W
Mooresville, N.C., U.S.	2744	35.35 N	80.48 W
Moorhead	2750	46.53 N	96.45 W
Mooringsport	2746	32.41 N	93.58 W
Moose Jaw	2734	50.23 N	105.32 W
Moose Lake	2742	46.26 N	92.45 W
Moosomin	2734	50.07 N	101.40 W
Moosonee	2734	51.17 N	80.39 W
Mopti	2786	14.30 N	4.12 W
Moquegua	2762	17.20 S	70.55 W
Mora, Esp.	2774	39.41 N	3.46 W
Mora, Port.	2774	38.56 N	8.10 W
Mora, Sve.	2768	61.00 N	14.33 E
Mora, Minn., U.S.	2742	45.53 N	93.18 W
Mora, N. Mex., U.S.	2752	35.58 N	105.20 W
Morādābād	2794	28.50 N	78.47 E
Morada Nova de Minas	2765	18.37 S	45.22 W
Morafenobe	2788	17.49 S	44.55 E
Moraleda, Canal ⥮	2764	44.30 S	73.30 W
Moran	2750	37.55 N	95.10 W
Mor'arovskij Zaton	2784	56.45 N	84.41 E
Morawhanna	2762	8.17 N	59.44 W
Moray Firth C1	2769	57.50 N	3.30 W
Morden	2734	49.11 N	98.05 W
More, Ben ∧	2769	56.23 N	4.31 W
More Assynt, Ben ∧	2769	58.07 N	4.51 W
Moreau ≃	2750	45.18 N	100.43 W
Morecambe	2769	54.04 N	2.53 W
Moree	2806	29.28 S	149.51 E
Morehead	2740	38.11 N	83.25 W
Morehead City	2744	34.43 N	76.43 W
Morelia	2758	19.42 N	101.07 W
Morella	2774	40.37 N	0.06 W
Morelos	2748	28.25 N	100.53 W
Morenci	2752	33.05 N	109.22 W
Moresby Island I	2734	52.50 N	131.55 W
Moreuil	2772	49.46 N	2.29 E
Mórfou, Kólpos C	2791	35.10 N	32.50 E
Morgan	2752	41.02 N	111.41 W
Morgan City	2746	29.42 N	91.12 W
Morganfield	2746	37.41 N	87.55 W
Morgan Hill	2756	37.08 N	121.39 W
Morganton	2744	35.45 N	81.41 W
Morgantown, Ky., U.S.	2746	37.14 N	86.41 W
Morgantown, W. Va., U.S.	2740	39.38 N	79.57 W
Morghāb (Murgab) ≃	2792	38.18 N	61.12 E
Mori	2798a	42.06 N	140.35 E
Moriarty	2752	34.59 N	106.03 W
Morkoka ≃	2784	65.10 N	115.52 E
Morlaix	2772	48.35 N	3.50 W
Morning Sun	2742	41.05 N	91.15 W
Mornington Island I	2806	16.33 S	139.24 E
Moro	2754	45.29 N	120.44 W
Morocco □1	2786	32.00 N	5.00 W
Morogoro	2788	6.49 S	37.40 E
Moro Gulf C	2802	6.51 N	123.00 E
Morombe	2788	21.45 S	43.22 E
Morón	2760	22.06 N	78.38 W
Morondava	2788	20.17 S	44.17 E
Morón de la Frontera	2774	37.08 N	5.27 W
Moroni, Comores	2788	11.41 S	43.16 E
Moroni, Utah, U.S.	2752	39.32 N	111.35 W
Morošečnoje	2784	56.24 N	156.12 E
Morotai I	2802	2.20 N	128.25 E
Morozovsk	2766	48.22 N	41.50 E
Morrilton	2746	35.09 N	92.45 W
Morrinhos	2765	17.44 S	49.07 W
Morris, Man., Can.	2734	49.21 N	97.22 W
Morris, Ill., U.S.	2746	41.22 N	88.26 W
Morris, Minn., U.S.	2750	45.35 N	95.55 W
Morrisburg	2740	44.54 N	75.11 W
Morrison	2746	41.49 N	89.58 W
Morrisonville	2746	39.25 N	89.27 W
Morristown, Ariz., U.S.	2752	33.51 N	112.37 W
Morristown, S. Dak., U.S.	2750	45.56 N	101.43 W
Morristown, Tenn., U.S.	2744	36.13 N	83.18 W
Morrisville	2740	44.34 N	72.44 W
Morro, Punta ≻	2764	27.07 S	70.57 W
Morro Bay	2756	35.22 N	120.51 W
Morro do Chapéu	2762	11.33 S	41.09 W
Morrow	2746	30.50 N	92.05 W
Moršansk	2780	53.26 N	41.49 E
Mortagne	2772	48.31 N	0.33 E
Mortagne-sur-Sèvre	2772	47.00 N	0.57 W
Mortara	2776	45.15 N	8.44 E
Mortes, Rio das ≃	2762	11.45 S	50.44 W
Morton, Ill., U.S.	2746	40.37 N	89.28 W
Morton, Minn., U.S.	2750	44.33 N	94.59 W
Morton, Tex., U.S.	2748	33.44 N	102.46 W
Morton, Wash., U.S.	2754	46.33 N	122.17 W
Morven ∧	2769	58.13 N	3.42 W
Morvi	2794	22.49 N	70.50 E
Morwell	2806	38.14 S	146.24 E
Moscow → Moskva, S.S.S.R.	2780	55.45 N	37.35 E
Moscow, Idaho, U.S.	2754	46.44 N	117.00 W
Moselle	2746	31.30 N	89.17 W
Moselle (Mosel) ≃	2770	50.22 N	7.36 E
Moses Lake	2754	47.08 N	119.17 W
Moshi	2788	3.21 S	37.20 E
Mosinee	2742	44.47 N	89.43 W
Mosjøen	2768	65.50 N	13.10 E
Moskva (Moscow)	2780	55.45 N	37.35 E
Mosquito Creek Lake ⊜1	2740	41.22 N	80.45 W
Mosquitos, Golfo de los C	2760	9.00 N	81.20 W
Moss	2768	59.26 N	10.42 E
Mossaka	2788	1.13 S	16.48 E
Mosselbaai	2788	34.11 S	22.08 E
Mossendjo	2788	2.57 S	12.44 E
Mossoró	2762	5.11 S	37.20 W
Moss Point	2746	30.25 N	88.29 W
Most	2770	50.32 N	13.39 E
Mostaganem	2786	35.51 N	0.07 E
Mostar	2776	43.20 N	17.49 E
Mostardas	2764	31.06 S	50.57 W
Møsting, Kap ≻	2734	64.00 N	41.00 W
Mota del Marqués	2774	41.38 N	5.10 W
Motala	2768	58.33 N	15.03 E
Motherwell	2769	55.48 N	4.00 W
Motilla del Palancar	2774	39.34 N	1.53 W
Motril	2774	36.45 N	3.31 W
Mott	2750	46.22 N	102.20 W
Motueka	2808	41.07 S	173.00 E
Motygino	2784	58.11 N	94.40 E
Mouchoir Passage ⥮	2760	21.15 N	71.00 W
Moudjéria	2786	17.53 N	12.20 W
Mouila	2788	1.52 S	11.01 E
Moulamein Creek ≃	2806	35.06 S	144.02 E
Moulins	2772	46.34 N	3.20 E
Moulmein	2804	16.30 N	97.38 E
Moulouya, Oued ≃	2786	35.05 N	2.25 W
Moultrie	2744	31.11 N	83.47 W
Mound City, Ill., U.S.	2746	37.05 N	89.10 W
Mound City, Kans., U.S.	2750	38.08 N	94.49 W
Mound City, Mo., U.S.	2746	40.07 N	95.14 W
Moundou	2786	8.34 N	16.05 E
Moundridge	2750	38.12 N	97.31 W
Mounds	2748	35.53 N	96.04 W
Moundsville	2740	39.55 N	80.44 W
Moundville	2746	32.59 N	87.38 W
Mountain	2742	45.11 N	88.28 W
Mountainair	2752	34.31 N	106.15 W
Mountain Brook	2746	33.29 N	86.46 W
Mountain City	2744	36.28 N	81.48 W
Mountain Creek	2746	32.43 N	86.29 W
Mountain Grove	2746	37.08 N	92.16 W
Mountain Home, Ark., U.S.	2746	36.20 N	92.23 W
Mountain Home, Idaho, U.S.	2754	43.08 N	115.41 W
Mountain Nile (Baḥr al-Jabal) ≃	2786	9.30 N	30.30 E
Mountain View, Ark., U.S.	2746	35.52 N	92.07 W
Mountain View, Mo., U.S.	2746	36.59 N	91.42 W
Mountain View, Wyo., U.S.	2754	41.16 N	110.20 W
Mount Airy	2744	36.31 N	80.37 W
Mount Ayr	2750	40.43 N	94.14 W
Mount Carmel, Ill., U.S.	2746	38.25 N	87.46 W
Mount Carmel, Pa., U.S.	2740	40.48 N	76.25 W
Mount Carroll	2742	42.06 N	89.58 W
Mount Clemens	2742	42.36 N	82.53 W
Mount Dora	2744	28.48 N	81.38 W
Mount Enterprise	2746	31.55 N	94.41 W
Mount Gambier	2806	37.50 S	140.46 E
Mount Gilead, N.C., U.S.	2744	35.10 N	79.56 W
Mount Gilead, Ohio, U.S.	2740	40.33 N	82.50 W
Mount Holly	2744	35.18 N	81.01 W
Mount Hope, Austl.	2806	34.07 S	135.23 E
Mount Hope, W. Va., U.S.	2744	37.54 N	81.10 W
Mount Ida	2746	34.34 N	93.38 W
Mount Isa	2806	20.44 S	139.30 E
Mount Lebanon	2740	40.23 N	80.03 W
Mount Magnet	2806	28.04 S	117.49 E
Mount Morris, Ill., U.S.	2742	42.03 N	89.26 W
Mount Morris, Mich., U.S.	2742	43.07 N	83.42 W
Mount Morris, N.Y., U.S.	2740	42.44 N	77.53 W
Mount Olive, Ill., U.S.	2746	39.04 N	89.43 W
Mount Olive, Miss., U.S.	2746	31.46 N	89.39 W
Mount Olive, N.C., U.S.	2744	35.12 N	78.04 W
Mount Olivet	2740	38.32 N	84.02 W
Mount Orab	2740	39.02 N	83.56 W
Mount Pleasant, Iowa, U.S.	2742	40.58 N	91.33 W
Mount Pleasant, Mich., U.S.	2742	43.35 N	84.47 W
Mount Pleasant, Tenn., U.S.	2746	35.32 N	87.13 W
Mount Pleasant, Tex., U.S.	2748	33.09 N	94.58 W
Mount Pleasant, Utah, U.S.	2752	39.33 N	111.27 W
Mount Pulaski	2746	40.01 N	89.17 W
Mount Rainier National Park ✦	2754	46.52 N	121.43 W
Mount Shasta	2756	41.19 N	122.19 W
Mount Sterling, Ill., U.S.	2746	39.59 N	90.45 W
Mount Sterling, Ky., U.S.	2744	38.04 N	83.56 W
Mount Sterling, Ohio, U.S.	2740	39.43 N	83.16 W
Mount Union	2740	40.23 N	77.53 W
Mount Vernon, Ala., U.S.	2746	31.05 N	88.01 W
Mount Vernon, Ga., U.S.	2744	32.11 N	82.36 W
Mount Vernon, Ill., U.S.	2746	38.19 N	88.55 W
Mount Vernon, Ind., U.S.	2746	37.56 N	87.54 W
Mount Vernon, Iowa, U.S.	2746	41.55 N	91.23 W
Mount Vernon, Ky., U.S.	2744	37.21 N	84.20 W
Mount Vernon, Mo., U.S.	2746	37.06 N	93.49 W
Mount Vernon, Ohio, U.S.	2740	40.23 N	82.29 W
Mount Vernon, Oreg., U.S.	2754	44.25 N	119.07 W
Mount Vernon, Tex., U.S.	2748	33.11 N	95.13 W
Mount Vernon, Wash., U.S.	2754	48.25 N	122.20 W
Moura, Bra.	2762	1.27 S	61.38 W
Moura, Port.	2774	38.08 N	7.27 W
Mourne Mountains ∧∧	2769	54.10 N	6.04 W
Moussoro	2786	13.39 N	16.29 E
Moutong	2802	0.28 N	121.13 E
Moville	2750	42.29 N	96.04 W
Moxos, Llanos de ⩸	2762	15.00 S	65.00 W
Moyahua	2758	21.16 N	103.10 W
Moyale	2790	3.32 N	39.03 E
Moyen Atlas ∧∧	2786	33.30 N	5.00 W
Moyeuvre-Grande	2772	49.15 N	6.02 E
Možajsk	2780	55.30 N	36.01 E
Mozambique □1	2788	18.15 S	35.00 E
Mozambique Channel ⥮	2788	19.00 S	41.00 E
Možga	2766	56.23 N	52.17 E
Mozyr'	2782	52.03 N	29.14 E
Mpanda	2788	6.22 S	31.02 E
Mpika	2788	11.54 S	31.26 E
Mrkonjić Grad	2776	44.25 N	17.05 E
Msaken	2776	35.44 N	10.35 E
Mtwara	2788	10.16 S	40.11 E
Muang Luong Nam Tha	2804	20.57 N	101.25 E
Muaratewe	2802	0.57 S	114.53 E
Muchinga Mountains ∧∧	2788	12.00 S	31.45 E
Mudanjiang	2796	44.35 N	129.36 E
Mufulira	2788	12.33 S	28.14 E
Muğla	2778	37.12 N	28.22 E
Mühldorf	2770	48.15 N	12.32 E
Mühlviertel ✦1	2770	48.25 N	14.10 E
Muhola	2768	63.20 N	25.05 E
Muiron Islands II	2806	21.35 S	114.20 E
Mukačevo	2782	48.27 N	22.45 E
Mula	2774	38.03 N	1.30 W
Mulanje	2788	16.02 S	35.30 E
Mulberry	2744	27.54 N	81.59 W
Muleshoe	2748	34.13 N	102.43 W
Mulhacén ∧	2774	37.03 N	3.19 W
Mulhouse	2772	47.45 N	7.20 E
Mull, Island of I	2769	56.27 N	6.00 W
Mullen	2750	42.03 N	101.01 W
Mullens	2744	37.35 N	81.23 W
Muller, Pegunungan ∧∧	2802	0.40 N	113.50 E
Mullewa	2806	28.33 S	115.31 E
Mullin	2748	31.33 N	98.40 W
Mullins	2744	34.12 N	79.15 W
Multān	2794	30.11 N	71.29 E
Mumbwa	2788	14.59 S	27.04 E
Muna, Pulau I	2802	5.00 S	122.30 E
Muncie	2746	40.11 N	85.23 W
Munday	2748	33.27 N	99.38 W
Munfordville	2746	37.16 N	85.54 W
Mungbere	2786	2.38 N	28.30 E
Munhango	2788	12.12 S	18.42 E
Munich → München	2770	48.08 N	11.34 E
Munising	2742	46.25 N	86.40 W
Munsons Corners	2740	42.35 N	76.13 W
Munster □9	2769	52.25 N	8.20 W
Muqayshiṭ I	2790	24.12 N	53.42 E
Muraši	2766	59.24 N	48.55 E
Murat	2772	45.07 N	2.52 E
Murat ≃	2766	38.39 N	39.50 E
Murau	2770	47.07 N	14.10 E
Muravera	2776	39.25 N	9.35 E
Murča	2774	41.24 N	7.27 W
Murchison ≃	2806	26.01 S	117.06 E
Murcia	2774	37.59 N	1.07 W
Murdo	2750	43.53 N	100.43 W
Muret	2772	43.28 N	1.21 E
Murfreesboro, Ark., U.S.	2746	34.04 N	93.41 W
Murfreesboro, N.C., U.S.	2744	36.27 N	77.06 W
Murfreesboro, Tenn., U.S.	2736 2746	35.51 N	86.23 W
Murmansk	2766	68.58 N	33.05 E
Murom	2780	55.34 N	42.02 E
Muroran	2798a	42.18 N	140.59 E
Muros	2774	42.47 N	9.02 W
Muroto	2798	33.18 N	134.09 E
Murphy	2754	43.13 N	116.33 W
Murphysboro	2746	37.46 N	89.20 W
Murray, Ky., U.S.	2746	36.37 N	88.19 W
Murray, Utah, U.S.	2752	40.40 N	111.53 W
Murray River	2739	46.01 N	62.37 W
Murraysburg	2788	31.58 S	23.47 E
Murten	2772	46.56 N	7.07 E
Murukta	2784	67.46 N	102.01 E
Murwāra	2794	23.51 N	80.24 E
Murwillumbah	2806	28.19 S	153.24 E
Mürzzuschlag	2770	47.36 N	15.41 E
Muş	2766	38.44 N	41.30 E
Musay'īd	2790	24.59 N	51.32 E
Muscat and Oman → Oman □1	2792	22.00 N	58.00 E
Muscatine	2742	41.25 N	91.03 W
Mus-Chaja, Gora ∧	2784	62.35 N	140.50 E
Muscle Shoals	2746	34.45 N	87.40 W
Musgrave	2806	14.47 S	143.30 E
Musgrave Ranges ∧∧	2806	26.10 S	131.50 E
Mushin	2786	6.32 N	3.22 E
Musishan ∧	2794	36.03 N	80.07 E
Muskegon	2742	43.14 N	86.16 W
Muskegon ≃	2742	43.14 N	86.20 W
Muskogee	2748	35.45 N	95.22 W
Musoma	2788	1.30 S	33.48 E
Musselshell ≃	2754	47.21 N	107.58 W
Mussidan	2772	45.02 N	0.22 E
Mussuma	2788	14.14 S	21.59 E
Mustafakemalpaşa	2778	40.02 N	28.24 E
Mut	2791	36.39 N	33.27 E
Mutoraj	2784	61.20 N	100.30 E
Mutsu	2798	41.17 N	141.10 E
Mutsu-wan C	2798	41.05 N	140.55 E
Muzaffarnagar	2794	29.28 N	77.41 E
Muzaffarpur	2794	26.07 N	85.24 E
Mwanza	2788	2.31 S	32.54 E
Mweelrea ∧	2769	53.38 N	9.50 W
Mweka	2788	4.51 S	21.34 E
Mweru, Lake ⊜	2788	9.00 S	28.45 E
Mwinilunga	2788	11.44 S	24.26 E
Myingyan	2804	21.28 N	95.23 E
Myitkyinā	2804	25.23 N	97.24 E
Myllymäki	2768	62.32 N	24.17 E
Mymensingh	2794	24.45 N	90.24 E
Mynämäki	2768	60.40 N	22.00 E
Myrskylä (Mörskom)	2768	60.40 N	25.51 E
Myrtle Beach	2744	33.42 N	78.52 W
Myrtle Creek	2754	43.01 N	123.17 W
Myrtle Grove	2746	30.25 N	87.18 W
Myrtle Point	2754	43.04 N	124.08 W
Mysen	2768	59.33 N	11.20 E
Mysore	2793	12.18 N	76.39 E
Mys Šmidta	2784	68.56 N	179.26 W
My-tho	2804	10.21 N	106.21 E
Mytišči	2780	55.55 N	37.46 E
Myton	2752	40.12 N	110.04 W
Mzimba	2788	11.52 S	33.34 E
Mzuzu	2788	11.27 S	33.55 E
N			
Naalehu	2757a	19.04 N	155.35 W
Naas	2769	53.13 N	6.39 W
Nabadwīp	2794	23.25 N	88.22 E
Naberežnyje Čelny	2766	55.42 N	52.19 E
Nabeul	2776	36.27 N	10.44 E
Nābulus	2791	32.13 N	35.16 E
Nacala-Velha	2788	14.32 S	40.37 E
Naches ≃	2754	46.38 N	120.31 W
Nachičevan'	2766	39.13 N	45.24 E
Nachingwea	2788	10.23 S	38.46 E
Nachodka	2784	42.48 N	132.52 E
Naco	2758	31.20 N	109.56 W
Nacogdoches	2746	31.36 N	94.39 W
Nadiād	2794	22.42 N	72.52 E
Nadym ≃	2784	66.12 N	72.00 E
Næstved	2768	55.14 N	11.46 E
Naga	2802	13.37 N	123.11 E
Nagahama	2798	35.23 N	136.16 E
Nagano	2798	36.39 N	138.11 E
Nagaoka	2798	37.27 N	138.51 E
Nāgappattinam	2793	10.46 N	79.50 E
Nagasaki	2798	32.48 N	129.55 E
Nāgaur	2794	27.12 N	73.44 E
Nāgercoil	2793	8.10 N	77.26 E
Nago	2799b	26.35 N	127.59 E
Nagornyj	2784	55.58 N	124.57 E
Nagoya	2798	35.10 N	136.55 E
Nāgpur	2793	21.09 N	79.06 E
Nagykanizsa	2770	46.27 N	17.00 E
Nagykőrös	2770	47.02 N	19.43 E
Naha	2799b	26.13 N	127.40 E
Nahariyya	2791	33.00 N	35.05 E
Nahma	2742	45.50 N	86.40 W
Nahunta	2744	31.12 N	81.59 W
Naidong	2794	29.14 N	31.46 E
Nain, Newf., Can.	2734	56.32 N	61.41 W
Nā'īn, Īrān	2790	32.52 N	53.05 E
Nairn	2769	57.35 N	3.53 W
Nairobi	2788	1.17 S	36.49 E
Najafābād	2790	32.37 N	51.21 E
Nájera	2774	42.25 N	2.44 W
Najin	2796	42.15 N	130.18 E
Nakhon Phanom	2804	17.22 N	104.46 E
Nakhon Ratchasima	2804	14.57 N	102.09 E
Nakhon Sawan	2804	15.42 N	100.06 E
Nakhon Si Thammarat	2804	8.26 N	99.58 E
Nakina	2734	50.10 N	86.42 W
Nakskov	2768	54.50 N	11.09 E
Nakuru	2788	0.17 S	36.04 E
Nal'čik	2766	43.29 N	43.37 E
Nālūt	2786	31.52 N	10.59 E
Namak, Daryācheh-ye ⊜	2790	34.45 N	51.36 E
Namapa	2788	13.43 S	39.50 E
Nambour	2806	26.38 S	152.58 E
Nam Dinh	2804	20.25 N	106.10 E
Namhkam	2804	23.50 N	97.41 E
Namlea	2802	3.18 S	127.06 E
Nampa	2754	43.34 N	116.34 W
Namp'o	2796	38.45 N	125.23 E
Nampula	2788	15.07 S	39.15 E
Namsen ≃	2768	64.27 N	11.28 E
Namsos	2768	64.29 N	11.30 E
Namuchabawashan ∧	2794	29.38 N	95.04 E
Namuhu ⊜	2794	30.42 N	90.30 E
Namur	2770	50.28 N	4.52 E
Nanaimo	2734	49.10 N	123.56 W
Nanao	2798	37.03 N	136.58 E
Nanchang	2800	28.41 N	115.53 E
Nanchong	2796	30.48 N	106.04 E

Symbols against index entries represent categories identified in the key on page 2810.

Name	Page	Lat °′	Long °′
Nancowry Island I	2802	7.58 N	93.33 E
Nancy	2772	48.41 N	6.12 E
Nānded	2793	19.09 N	77.20 E
N'andoma	2766	61.40 N	40.12 E
Nandurbār	2793	21.22 N	74.15 E
Nandyāl	2793	15.29 N	78.29 E
Nanjing (Nanking)	2800	32.03 N	118.47 E
Nanking			
→ Nanjing	2800	32.03 N	118.47 E
Nankoku	2798	33.39 N	133.44 E
Nankou	2796	40.14 N	116.07 E
Nanling ⩘	2796	25.00 N	112.00 E
Nanning	2804	22.48 N	108.20 E
Nanping	2800	26.38 N	118.10 E
Nansei-shotō (Ryukyu Islands) II	2796	26.30 N	128.00 E
Nantes	2772	47.13 N	1.33 W
Nanticoke	2740	41.12 N	76.00 W
Nantong	2800	32.02 N	120.53 E
Nantua	2772	46.09 N	5.37 E
Nantucket	2740	41.17 N	70.06 W
Nantucket Island I	2740	41.16 N	70.03 W
Nantucket Sound Ʉ	2740	41.30 N	70.15 W
Nanuque	2765	17.50 S	40.21 W
Nanxiang	2800	31.17 N	121.18 E
Nanxiong	2800	25.10 N	114.20 E
Nanyang	2800	33.00 N	112.32 E
Náousa	2778	40.37 N	22.05 E
Napa	2756	38.18 N	122.17 W
Napanee	2740	44.15 N	76.57 W
Napier	2808	39.29 S	176.55 E
Naples			
→ Napoli, It.	2776	40.51 N	14.17 E
Naples, Fla., U.S.	2744	26.08 N	81.48 W
Naples, Idaho, U.S.	2754	48.34 N	116.24 W
Naples, N.Y., U.S.	2740	42.37 N	77.25 W
Napo ≃	2762	3.20 S	72.40 W
Napoleon, N. Dak., U.S.	2750	46.30 N	99.46 W
Napoleon, Ohio, U.S.	2740	41.23 N	84.08 W
Napoli (Naples)	2776	40.51 N	14.17 E
Nappanee	2746	41.27 N	86.00 W
Nara, Mali	2786	15.10 N	7.17 W
Nara, Nihon	2798	34.41 N	135.50 E
Naracoorte	2806	36.58 S	140.44 E
Nara Visa	2748	35.37 N	103.06 W
Nārāyanganj	2794	23.37 N	90.30 E
Narbonne	2772	43.11 N	3.00 E
Nardò	2776	40.11 N	18.02 E
Narmada ≃	2794	21.38 N	72.36 E
Nārnaul	2794	28.03 N	76.07 E
Narni	2776	42.31 N	12.31 E
Narodnaja, Gora ∧	2766	65.04 N	60.09 E
Naro-Fominsk	2780	55.23 N	36.43 E
Narsimhapur	2794	22.57 N	79.12 E
Narssag	2734	60.54 N	46.00 W
Naruto	2798	34.11 N	134.37 E
Narva	2780	59.23 N	28.12 E
Narvik	2768	68.26 N	17.25 E
Nashua, Iowa, U.S.	2742	42.57 N	92.32 W
Nashua, Minn , U.S.	2750	46.02 N	96.18 W
Nashua, Mont., U.S.	2754	48.08 N	106.22 W
Nashua, N.H., U.S.	2740	42.46 N	71.27 W
Nashville, Ark., U.S.	2746	33.57 N	93.51 W
Nashville, Ga., U.S.	2744	31.12 N	83.15 W
Nashville, Ill., U.S.	2746	38.21 N	89.23 W
Nashville, Ind., U.S.	2746	39.12 N	86.15 W
Nashville, Tenn., U.S.	2746	36.09 N	86.48 W
Nāsik	2793	19.59 N	73.48 E
Nāsir	2786	8.36 N	33.04 E
Nassau	2760	25.05 N	77.21 W
Nasser, Lake ⊜[1]	2786	22.40 N	32.00 E
Nässjö	2768	57.39 N	14.41 E
Natal	2762	5.47 S	35.13 W
Natanes Plateau ⩘[1]	2752	33.35 N	110.15 W
Natchez	2746	31.34 N	91.23 W
Natchitoches	2746	31.46 N	93.05 W
Nāthdwāra	2794	24.56 N	73.49 E
Natoma	2750	39.11 N	99.01 W
Natron, Lake ⊜	2788	2.25 S	36.00 E
Natuna Besar I	2804	4.00 N	108.15 E
Natuna Besar, Kepulauan II	2804	4.40 N	108.00 E
Natuna Selatan, Kepulauan II	2804	2.45 N	109.00 E
Naturaliste, Cape ≻	2806	33.32 S	115.01 E
Naturita	2752	38.14 N	108.34 W
Naugatuck	2740	41.30 N	73.04 W
Nava del Rey	2774	41.20 N	5.05 W
Navahermosa	2774	39.38 N	4.28 W
Navalcarnero	2774	40.18 N	4.00 W
Navalmoral de la Mata	2774	39.54 N	5.32 W
Navalvillar de Pela	2774	39.06 N	5.28 W
Navan	2769	53.39 N	6.41 W
Navarin, Mys ≻	2784	62.16 N	179.10 E
Navarino, Isla I	2764	55.05 S	67.40 W
Navasota	2748	30.23 N	96.05 W
Navasota ≃	2748	30.20 N	96.09 W
Navojoa	2758	27.06 N	109.26 W
Navolato	2758	24.47 N	107.42 W
Navsāri	2793	20.51 N	72.55 E
Nawābshāh	2794	26.15 N	68.25 E
Náxos I	2778	37.02 N	25.35 E
Nayoro	2798a	44.21 N	142.28 E
Nazaré, Bra.	2765	13.02 S	39.00 W
Nazaré, Port.	2774	39.36 N	9.04 W
Nazareth	2740	40.44 N	75.19 W
Nazca	2762	14.50 S	74.55 W
Naze	2799b	28.23 N	129.30 E
Nazilli	2778	37.55 N	28.21 E
Ndélé	2786	8.24 N	20.39 E
Ndjamena (Fort-Lamy)	2786	12.07 N	15.03 E
Ndola	2788	12.58 S	28.38 E
Neagh, Lough ⊜	2769	54.38 N	6.24 W
Neah Bay	2754	48.22 N	124.37 W
Néa Páfos (Paphos)	2791	34.45 N	32.25 E
Neápolis	2778	36.30 N	23.04 E
Nebit-Dag	2766	39.30 N	54.22 E
Nebraska □[3]	2736	41.30 N	100.00 W
Nebraska City	2750	40.41 N	95.52 W
Necedah	2742	44.02 N	90.05 W
Neche	2750	48.59 N	97.33 W
Neckar ≃	2770	49.31 N	8.26 E
Necochea	2764	38.34 S	58.45 W
Nederland	2746	29.58 N	93.60 W
Needle Mountain ∧	2754	44.05 N	109.37 W
Needles	2756	34.51 N	114.37 W
Neenah	2742	44.11 N	88.28 W
Neepawa	2734	50.13 N	99.29 W
Negage	2788	7.45 S	15.16 E
Negaunee	2742	46.30 N	87.36 W
Negele	2790	5.20 N	39.36 E
Negra, Punta ≻	2762	6.06 S	81.10 W
Negro ≃, Arg.	2764	41.02 S	62.47 W
Negro ≃, S.A.	2762	3.06 S	59.52 W
Negros I	2802	10.00 N	123.00 E
Nehalem ≃	2754	45.40 N	123.56 W
Nehbandān	2790	31.32 N	60.02 E
Neiba, Bahía de C	2760	18.15 N	71.00 W
Neijiang	2796	29.35 N	105.03 E
Neillsville	2742	44.34 N	90.36 W
Neimenggu Zizhiqu (Inner Mongolia) □[4]	2796	43.00 N	115.00 E
Neiva	2762	2.56 N	75.18 W
Neja	2780	58.18 N	43.54 E
Nekemte	2790	9.02 N	36.31 E
Nekoosa	2742	44.19 N	89.54 W
Nelidovo	2780	56.13 N	32.46 E
Neligh	2750	42.08 N	98.02 W
Nel'kan	2784	57.40 N	136.13 E
Nellore	2793	14.26 N	79.58 E
Nelson, B.C., Can.	2734	49.29 N	117.17 W
Nelson, N.Z.	2808	41.17 S	173.17 E
Nelson, Nebr., U.S.	2750	40.12 N	98.04 W
Nelson ≃	2734	57.04 N	92.30 W
Nelsonville	2740	39.27 N	82.14 W
Néma	2786	16.37 N	7.15 W
Nemours	2772	48.16 N	2.42 E
Nemuro	2798a	43.20 N	145.35 E
Nemuro Strait Ʉ	2798a	44.00 N	145.20 E
Nenagh	2769	52.52 N	8.12 W
Neodesha	2750	37.25 N	95.41 W
Neoga	2746	39.19 N	88.27 W
Neola, Iowa, U.S.	2750	41.27 N	95.37 W
Neola, Utah, U.S.	2752	40.26 N	110.02 W
Neosho	2746	36.52 N	94.22 W
Neosho ≃	2750	35.48 N	95.18 W
Nepal (Nepāl) □[1]	2792	28.00 N	84.00 E
Nepālganj	2794	28.03 N	81.37 E
Nephi	2752	39.43 N	111.50 W
Nérac	2772	44.08 N	0.20 E
Nerastro, Sarīr ⇢[2]	2786	24.20 N	20.37 E
Nerčinskij Zavod	2784	51.19 N	119.36 E
Nerechta	2780	57.28 N	40.34 E
Neriquinha	2788	15.58 S	21.42 E
Nerva	2774	37.42 N	6.32 W
Nesbyen	2768	60.34 N	9.09 E
Neskaupstaður	2766	65.10 N	13.43 W
Nesna	2768	66.12 N	13.02 E
Ness, Loch ⊜	2769	57.15 N	4.30 W
Ness City	2750	38.27 N	99.54 W
Netanya	2791	32.20 N	34.51 E
Netherlands □[1]	2766	52.15 N	5.30 E
Netherlands Antilles (Nederlandse Antillen) □[2]	2760	12.15 N	69.00 W
Nettilling Lake ⊜	2734	66.30 N	70.40 W
Nettleton	2746	34.05 N	88.44 W
Nettuno	2776	41.27 N	12.39 E
Neuchâtel	2772	46.59 N	6.56 E
Neuchâtel, Lac de ⊜	2772	46.52 N	6.50 E
Neufchâteau, Bel.	2770	49.50 N	5.26 E
Neufchâteau, Fr.	2772	48.21 N	5.42 E
Neufchâtel-en-Bray	2772	49.44 N	1.27 E
Neuillé-Pont-Pierre	2772	47.33 N	0.33 E
Neunkirchen	2770	47.43 N	16.05 E
Neuquén	2764	39.00 S	68.05 W
Neustadt [an aisch]	2770	49.34 N	10.37 E
Neutral Zone □[2]	2790	29.10 N	45.30 E
Neuville-de-Poitou	2772	46.41 N	0.15 E
Nevada, Iowa, U.S.	2742	42.01 N	93.27 W
Nevada, Mo., U.S.	2746	37.51 N	94.22 W
Nevada □[3]	2736	39.00 N	117.00 W
Nevada, Sierra ⩘, Esp.	2774	37.05 N	3.10 W
Nevada, Sierra ⩘, Calif., U.S.	2756	38.00 N	119.15 W
Nevada City	2756	36.16 N	121.01 W
Nevado, Cerro ∧	2764	35.34 S	68.29 W
Never	2784	53.58 N	124.05 E
Nevers	2772	47.00 N	3.09 E
Nevinnomyssk	2766	44.38 N	41.56 E
Nevis, Ben ∧	2769	56.48 N	5.01 W
Nevjansk	2766	57.32 N	60.13 E
New Albany, Ind., U.S.	2746	38.18 N	85.49 W
New Albany, Miss., U.S.	2746	34.29 N	89.00 W
New Amsterdam	2762	6.17 N	57.36 W
Newark, Del., U.S.	2740	39.41 N	75.45 W
Newark, N.J., U.S.	2740	40.44 N	74.10 W
Newark, N.Y., U.S.	2740	43.03 N	77.06 W
Newark, Ohio, U.S.	2740	40.04 N	82.24 W
New Athens	2746	38.19 N	89.53 W
New Baltimore	2742	42.41 N	82.44 W
New Bedford	2740	41.38 N	70.56 W
Newberg	2754	45.18 N	122.58 W
New Bern	2744	35.07 N	77.03 W
Newberry, Fla., U.S.	2744	29.39 N	82.37 W
Newberry, Mich., U.S.	2742	46.21 N	85.30 W
Newberry, S.C., U.S.	2744	34.17 N	81.37 W
New Boston	2746	33.28 N	94.25 W
New Braunfels	2748	29.42 N	98.08 W
New Britain	2740	41.40 N	72.47 W
New Brunswick	2740	40.29 N	74.27 W
New Brunswick □[4]	2734	46.30 N	66.15 W
Newburgh	2740	41.30 N	74.01 W
Newburyport	2740	42.49 N	70.53 W
New Caledonia □[2]	2730	21.30 S	165.30 E
Newcastle, Austl.	2806	32.56 S	151.46 E
Newcastle, N.B., Can.	2739	47.00 N	65.34 W
Newcastle, S. Afr.	2788	27.49 S	29.55 E
Newcastle, N. Ire., U.K.	2769	54.12 N	5.54 W
New Castle, Del., U.S.	2740	39.40 N	75.34 W
New Castle, Ind., U.S.	2746	39.55 N	85.22 W
New Castle, Pa., U.S.	2740	41.00 N	80.20 W
New Castle, Tex., U.S.	2748	33.12 N	98.44 W
New Castle, Va., U.S.	2744	37.30 N	80.07 W
Newcastle, Wyo., U.S.	2750	43.50 N	104.11 W
Newcastle-under-Lyme	2769	53.00 N	2.14 W
Newcastle upon Tyne	2769	54.59 N	1.35 W
Newcastle Waters	2806	17.24 S	133.24 E
New City	2740	41.09 N	73.59 W
Newcomerstown	2740	40.16 N	81.36 W
Newdegate	2806	33.06 S	119.01 E
New Delhi	2794	28.36 N	77.12 E
Newell	2750	44.43 N	103.25 W
New Ellenton	2744	33.24 N	81.40 W
Newellton	2746	32.10 N	91.14 W
New England	2750	46.32 N	102.52 W
Newfoundland □[4]	2734	52.00 N	56.00 W
Newfoundland I	2734	48.30 N	56.00 W
New Freedom	2740	39.44 N	76.42 W
New Georgia I	2806	8.15 S	157.30 E
New Glarus	2742	42.49 N	89.38 W
New Glasgow	2739	45.35 N	62.39 W
New Guinea I	2802	5.00 S	140.00 E
New Hamburg	2740	43.23 N	80.42 W
New Hampshire □[3]	2736	43.35 N	71.40 W
New Hampton	2742	43.03 N	92.19 W
New Harmony	2746	38.08 N	87.56 W
New Haven, Conn., U.S.	2740	41.18 N	72.56 W
New Haven, Ind., U.S.	2746	41.04 N	85.01 W
New Hebrides □[2]	2730	16.00 S	167.00 E
New Holstein	2742	43.57 N	88.05 W
New Hope	2746	34.32 N	86.24 W
New Iberia	2746	30.00 N	91.49 W
New Jersey □[3]	2736	40.15 N	74.30 W
New Kensington	2740	40.34 N	79.46 W
Newkirk	2748	35.04 N	104.16 W
Newland	2744	36.05 N	81.56 W
New Lexington	2740	39.43 N	82.13 W
New Lisbon	2742	43.53 N	90.10 W
New Liskeard	2734	47.30 N	79.40 W
New London, Conn., U.S.	2740	41.21 N	72.07 W
New London, Minn , U.S.	2750	45.18 N	94.56 W
New London, Mo., U.S.	2746	39.35 N	91.24 W
New Madrid	2746	36.36 N	89.32 W
Newman	2756	37.19 N	121.01 W
Newmarket, Ont., Can.	2740	44.03 N	79.28 W
Newmarket, Eng., U.K.	2769	52.15 N	0.25 E
New Market, Iowa, U.S.	2750	40.44 N	94.54 W
Newmarket, N.H., U.S.	2740	43.05 N	70.56 W
New Market, Va., U.S.	2740	38.39 N	78.40 W
New Martinsville	2740	39.39 N	80.52 W
New Meadows	2754	44.58 N	116.32 W
New Mexico □[3]	2736	34.30 N	106.00 W
Newnan	2744	33.23 N	84.48 W
New Norfolk	2806	42.47 S	147.03 E
New Orleans	2746	29.58 N	90.07 W
New Paltz	2740	41.45 N	74.05 W
New Philadelphia	2740	40.30 N	81.27 W
New Plymouth, N.Z.	2808	39.04 S	174.05 E
New Plymouth, Idaho, U.S.	2754	43.58 N	116.49 W
Newport, Eng., U.K.	2769	50.42 N	1.18 W
Newport, Wales, U.K.	2769	52.01 N	4.51 W
Newport, Ark., U.S.	2746	35.37 N	91.17 W
Newport, Ky., U.S.	2740	39.06 N	84.29 W
Newport, N.H., U.S.	2740	43.21 N	72.09 W
Newport, Oreg., U.S.	2754	44.38 N	124.03 W
Newport, R.I., U.S.	2740	41.13 N	71.18 W
Newport, Tenn., U.S.	2744	35.58 N	83.11 W
Newport, Vt., U.S.	2740	44.57 N	72.12 W
Newport, Wash., U.S.	2754	48.11 N	117.03 W
Newport News	2744	37.04 N	76.28 W
New Port Richey	2744	28.16 N	82.43 W
New Prague	2742	44.32 N	93.34 W
New Providence I	2760	25.25 N	78.35 E
Newquay	2769	50.25 N	5.05 W
New Richmond, Qué., Can.	2739	48.10 N	65.52 W
New Richmond, Ohio, U.S.	2740	38.57 N	84.17 W
New Richmond, Wis., U.S.	2742	45.07 N	92.32 W
New Roads	2746	30.42 N	91.26 W
New Rochelle	2740	40.55 N	73.47 W
New Rockford	2750	47.41 N	99.15 W
New Ross	2769	52.24 N	6.56 W
Newry	2769	54.11 N	6.20 W
New Salem	2750	46.51 N	101.25 W
New Smyrna Beach	2744	29.02 N	80.56 W
Newton, Ala., U.S.	2746	31.20 N	85.36 W
Newton, Ill., U.S.	2746	38.59 N	88.10 W
Newton, Iowa, U.S.	2742	41.42 N	93.03 W
Newton, Kans., U.S.	2750	38.03 N	97.21 W
Newton, Mass., U.S.	2740	42.21 N	71.11 W
Newton, Miss., U.S.	2746	32.19 N	89.10 W
Newton, N.J., U.S.	2740	41.03 N	74.45 W
Newton, N.C., U.S.	2744	35.40 N	81.13 W
Newton, Tex., U.S.	2746	30.51 N	93.46 W
Newton Stewart	2769	54.57 N	4.29 W
New Town	2750	47.59 N	102.30 W
Newtownabbey	2769	54.42 N	5.54 W
Newtownards	2769	54.36 N	5.41 W
New Ulm	2742	44.19 N	94.28 W
New Waverly	2748	30.32 N	95.29 W
New York	2740	40.43 N	74.01 W
New York □[3]	2736	43.00 N	75.00 W
New Zealand □[1]	2808	41.00 S	174.00 E
Nežin	2782	51.03 N	31.54 E
Nezperce	2754	46.14 N	116.14 W
Ngami, Lake ⊜	2788	20.37 S	22.40 E
Ngaoundéré	2786	7.19 N	13.35 E
Nguigmi	2786	14.15 N	13.07 E
Nguru	2786	12.52 N	10.27 E
Nha-trang	2804	12.15 N	109.11 E
Niafounké	2786	15.56 N	4.00 W
Niagara Falls, Ont., Can.	2734	43.06 N	79.04 W
Niagara Falls, N.Y., U.S.	2740	43.06 N	79.02 W
Niagara-on-the-Lake	2740	43.15 N	79.04 W
Niamey	2786	13.31 N	2.07 E
Niangara	2786	3.42 N	27.52 E
Nianqingtanggula-shanmai ⩘	2794	30.00 N	90.00 E
Nias, Pulau I	2804	1.05 N	97.35 E
Nicaragua □[1]	2760	13.00 N	85.00 W
Nicaragua, Lago de ⊜	2760	11.35 N	85.25 W
Nicastro (Lamezia Terme)	2776	38.59 N	16.20 E
Nice	2772	43.42 N	7.15 E
Niceville	2746	30.31 N	86.29 W
Nichinan	2798	31.36 N	131.23 E
Nicholas Channel Ʉ	2760	23.25 N	80.05 W
Nicholasville	2744	37.53 N	84.34 W
Nickerson	2750	38.08 N	98.05 W
Nicobar Islands II	2804	8.00 N	93.30 E
Nicolet	2740	46.13 N	72.37 W
Nicolls Town	2744	25.08 N	78.00 W
Nicosia, It.	2776	37.45 N	14.24 E
Nicosia			
→ Levkosía, Kípros	2791	35.10 N	33.22 E
Nicoya, Golfo de C	2760	9.47 N	84.48 W
Nicoya, Península de ≻[1]	2760	10.00 N	85.25 W
Nieuw Nickerie	2762	5.57 N	56.59 W
Nieves	2758	24.00 N	103.01 W
Niger □[1]	2786	16.00 N	8.00 E
Niger ≃	2786	5.33 N	6.33 E
Nigeria □[1]	2786	10.00 N	8.00 E
Nigríta	2778	40.55 N	23.30 E
Niigata	2798	37.55 N	139.03 E
Niihama	2798	33.58 N	133.16 E
Niihau I	2757a	21.55 N	160.10 W
Niinisalo	2768	61.50 N	22.29 E
Níjar	2774	36.58 N	2.12 W
Nijmegen	2770	51.50 N	5.50 E
Nikkō	2798	36.45 N	139.37 E
Nikolajev	2782	46.58 N	32.00 E
Nikolajevsk-na-Amure	2784	53.08 N	140.44 E
Nikopol'	2782	47.35 N	34.25 E
Nikšić	2778	42.46 N	18.56 E
Nile (Nahr an-Nīl) ≃	2786	30.10 N	31.06 E
Niles, Mich., U.S.	2742	41.50 N	86.15 W
Niles, Ohio, U.S.	2740	41.11 N	80.45 W
Nīmach	2794	24.28 N	74.52 E
Nimba, Mont ∧	2786	7.37 N	8.25 W
Nîmes	2772	43.50 N	4.21 E
Nine Degree Channel Ʉ	2793	9.00 N	73.00 E
Ninety Six	2744	34.11 N	82.01 W
Ningbo	2800	29.52 N	121.31 E
Ningming	2804	22.07 N	107.09 E
Ningxia Huizu Zizhiqu □[4]	2796	37.00 N	106.00 E
Niobrara	2750	42.45 N	98.02 W
Niobrara ≃	2736	42.45 N	98.00 W
Niono	2786	14.15 N	6.00 W
Nioro du Sahel	2786	15.15 N	9.35 W
Niort	2772	46.19 N	0.27 W
Nipigon	2734	49.01 N	88.16 W
Nipigon, Lake ⊜	2734	49.50 N	88.30 W
Nipissing, Lake ⊜	2740	46.17 N	80.00 W
Niš	2778	43.19 N	21.54 E
Nisa	2774	39.31 N	7.39 W
Nishinoomote	2799b	30.44 N	131.00 E
Nisswa	2742	46.31 N	94.17 W
Niterói	2765	22.53 S	43.07 W
Nitra	2770	48.20 N	18.05 E
Nivelles	2770	50.36 N	4.20 E
Nixon	2748	29.16 N	97.46 W
Nizāmābād	2793	18.40 N	78.07 E
Nižn'aja Pojma	2784	56.11 N	97.13 E
Nižn'aja Tunguska ≃	2784	65.48 N	88.04 E
Nižneangarsk	2784	55.47 N	109.33 E
Nižneilimsk	2784	57.11 N	103.16 E
Nižneudinsk	2784	54.54 N	99.03 E
Nižnij Tagil	2766	57.55 N	59.57 E
Nizza Monferrato	2776	44.46 N	8.21 E
Njombe	2788	9.20 S	34.46 E
Nkhota Kota	2788	12.57 S	34.17 E
Nkongsamba	2786	4.57 N	9.56 E
Nobeoka	2798	32.35 N	131.40 E
Noble, Ill., U.S.	2746	38.42 N	88.13 W
Noble, Okla., U.S.	2748	35.08 N	97.24 W
Noblesville	2746	40.03 N	86.01 W
Nocatee	2744	27.09 N	81.53 W
Nocera [Inferiore]	2776	40.44 N	14.38 E
Nochixtlán	2758	17.28 N	97.14 W
Nocona	2748	33.47 N	97.44 W
Nogales, Méx.	2758	31.20 N	110.56 W
Nogales, Ariz., U.S.	2752	31.20 N	110.56 W
Nogent-le-Rotrou	2772	48.19 N	0.50 E
Noginsk	2780	55.51 N	38.27 E
Nogoyá	2764	32.22 S	59.49 W
Noirmoutier	2772	47.00 N	2.14 W
Nokia	2768	61.28 N	23.30 E
Nokomis, Fla., U.S.	2744	27.07 N	82.27 W
Nokomis, Ill., U.S.	2746	39.18 N	89.18 W
Nombre de Dios	2758	23.51 N	104.14 W
Nome	2738	64.30 N	165.24 W
Nonacho Lake ⊜	2734	61.42 N	109.40 W
Nong'an	2796	44.25 N	125.10 E
Nong Khai	2804	17.52 N	102.45 E
Nontron	2772	45.32 N	0.40 E
Noonan	2750	48.54 N	103.01 W
Noordoost Polder ⇢[1]	2770	52.42 N	5.45 E
Nootka Island I	2734	49.32 N	126.42 W
Noranda	2734	48.15 N	79.02 W
Nordenšel'da, Archipelag II	2784	76.45 N	96.00 E
Nordfjordeid	2768	61.54 N	6.00 E
Nordfold	2768	67.46 N	15.12 E
Nordkjosbotn	2768	69.13 N	19.30 E
Nordmaling	2768	63.34 N	19.30 E
Nordreisa	2768	69.46 N	21.03 E
Nordre Strømfjord C[2]	2734	67.50 N	52.00 W

Symbols against index entries represent categories identified in the key on page 2810.

Name	Page	Lat° ′	Long° ′
Nordvik	2784	74.02 N	111.32 E
Norfolk, Nebr., U.S.	2750	42.02 N	97.25 W
Norfolk, Va., U.S.	2744	36.40 N	76.14 W
Noril'sk	2784	69.20 N	88.06 E
Norlina	2744	36.27 N	78.12 W
Normal	2746	40.31 N	88.59 W
Norman	2748	35.13 N	97.26 W
Normandie □[9]	2772	49.00 N	0.05 W
Normangee	2748	31.02 N	96.07 W
Norman Park	2744	31.16 N	83.38 W
Normanton	2806	17.40 S	141.05 E
Norman Wells	2734	65.17 N	126.51 W
Ñorquincó	2764	41.50 S	70.55 W
Norris City	2746	37.59 N	88.20 W
Norristown	2740	40.07 N	75.21 W
Norrköping	2768	58.36 N	16.11 E
Norrtälje	2768	59.46 N	18.42 E
Norseman	2806	32.12 S	121.46 E
Norsk	2784	52.20 N	129.55 E
Norte, Serra do ⋀[1]	2762	11.20 S	59.00 W
North	2744	33.37 N	81.06 W
North, Cape ⊥[2]	2734	47.02 N	60.25 W
North Adams	2740	42.42 N	73.07 W
Northam	2806	31.39 S	116.40 E
North America ⊥[1]	2730	45.00 N	100.00 W
Northampton, Eng., U.K.	2769	52.14 N	0.54 W
Northampton, Mass., U.S.	2740	42.19 N	72.38 W
North Andaman I	2804	13.15 N	92.55 E
North Atlanta	2744	33.51 N	84.21 W
North Augusta	2744	33.30 N	81.58 W
North Baltimore	2740	41.11 N	83.41 W
North Battleford	2734	52.47 N	108.17 W
North Bay	2740	46.19 N	79.28 W
North Bend, Nebr., U.S.	2750	41.28 N	96.47 W
North Bend, Oreg., U.S.	2754	43.24 N	124.14 W
North Branch	2742	45.31 N	92.58 W
North Canton	2740	40.53 N	81.24 W
North Caribou Lake ⊜	2734	52.50 N	90.40 W
North Carolina □[3]	2736	35.30 N	80.00 W
North Cascades National Park ♠	2754	48.30 N	121.00 W
North Channel Ʉ	2740	46.02 N	82.50 W
North Charleston	2744	32.53 N	80.00 W
North Chicago	2742	42.20 N	87.51 W
North Conway	2740	44.03 N	71.08 W
North Dakota □[3]	2736	47.30 N	100.15 W
North East	2740	42.13 N	79.50 W
North English	2742	41.31 N	92.05 W
Northern Territory □[8]	2806	20.00 S	134.00 E
Northfield, Minn., U.S.	2742	44.27 N	93.09 W
Northfield, Vt., U.S.	2740	44.09 N	72.40 W
North Flinders Ranges ⋀	2806	31.00 S	139.00 E
North Fond du Lac	2742	43.38 N	88.28 W
North Frisian II	2770	54.50 N	8.12 E
North Island I	2808	39.00 S	176.00 E
North Judson	2746	41.13 N	86.46 W
North Las Vegas	2756	36.12 N	115.07 W
North Loup	2750	41.30 N	98.46 W
North Manchester	2746	41.00 N	85.46 W
North Manitou Island I	2742	45.06 N	86.01 W
North Mankato	2742	44.10 N	94.00 W
North Miami	2744	25.54 N	80.11 W
North Ogden	2752	41.18 N	112.00 W
Northome	2742	47.52 N	94.17 W
North Platte	2750	41.08 N	100.46 W
North Platte ≃	2736	41.15 N	100.45 W
North Point ≻	2742	45.02 N	83.16 W
North Pole ⊸	2732	90.00 N	0.00
Northport, Ala., U.S.	2746	33.14 N	87.35 W
Northport, Mich., U.S.	2742	45.08 N	85.37 W
North Santiam ≃	2754	44.41 N	123.00 W
North Saskatchewan ≃	2734	53.15 N	105.06 W
North Sea ⊤[2], Eur.	2766	55.20 N	3.00 E
Northumberland National Park ♠	2769	55.15 N	2.20 W
Northumberland Strait Ʉ	2734	46.00 N	63.00 W
North Vernon	2746	39.00 N	85.38 W
North Vietnam → Vietnam □[1]	2802	16.00 N	108.00 E
Northville	2740	43.13 N	74.11 W
North West Cape ≻	2806	21.45 S	114.10 E
North West River	2734	53.32 N	60.08 W
Northwest Territories □[4]	2734	70.00 N	100.00 W
Northwood, Iowa, U.S.	2742	43.27 N	93.13 W
Northwood, N. Dak., U.S.	2750	47.44 N	97.34 W
North York Moors National Park ♠	2769	54.23 N	0.50 W
Norton, Kans., U.S.	2750	39.50 N	99.53 W
Norton, Va., U.S.	2744	36.56 N	82.38 W
Norton Sound Ʉ	2738	63.50 N	164.00 W
Norwalk, Conn., U.S.	2740	41.07 N	73.27 W
Norwalk, Ohio, U.S.	2740	41.15 N	82.37 W
Norway, Maine, U.S.	2740	44.13 N	70.32 W
Norway, Mich., U.S.	2742	45.47 N	87.55 W
Norway □[1]	2766	62.00 N	10.00 E
Norway Bay C	2734	71.08 N	104.35 W
Norway House	2734	53.59 N	97.50 W
Norwegian Sea ⊤[2]	2732	70.00 N	2.00 E
Norwich, Eng., U.K.	2769	52.38 N	1.18 E
Norwich, Conn., U.S.	2740	41.32 N	72.05 W
Norwich, N.Y., U.S.	2740	42.32 N	75.31 W
Norwood, Colo., U.S.	2752	38.08 N	108.20 W
Norwood, Mass., U.S.	2740	42.11 N	71.12 W
Norwood, N.C., U.S.	2744	35.14 N	80.07 W
Norwood, N.Y., U.S.	2740	44.45 N	75.00 W
Norwood, Ohio, U.S.	2740	39.10 N	84.28 W
Noshiro	2798	40.12 N	140.02 E
Nosovka	2782	50.55 N	31.35 E
Nossi-Bé I	2788	13.20 S	48.15 E
Notch Peak ∧	2752	39.08 N	113.24 W
Noto	2776	36.53 N	15.05 E
Notodden	2768	59.34 N	9.17 E
Noto-hantō ≻[1]	2798	37.20 N	137.00 E
Notre Dame, Monts ⋀	2734	48.10 N	68.00 W
Notre Dame Bay C	2734	49.45 N	55.15 W
Nottawasaga Bay C	2740	44.40 N	80.30 W
Nottaway ≃	2734	51.22 N	79.55 W
Nottingham	2769	52.58 N	1.10 W
Nottingham Island I	2734	63.20 N	77.55 W
Nottoway	2744	37.08 N	78.05 W
Nouadhibou	2786	20.54 N	17.04 W
Nouakchott	2786	18.06 N	15.57 W
Nouamrhar	2786	19.22 N	16.31 W
Noupoort	2788	31.10 S	24.57 E
Nouveau-Québec, Cratère du ⊥[6]	2734	61.17 N	73.40 W
Nova América	2765	15.01 S	49.56 W
Nova Cruz	2762	6.28 S	35.26 W
Nova Freixo	2788	14.49 S	36.33 E
Nova Friburgo	2765	22.16 S	42.32 W
Nova Gaia	2788	10.09 S	17.31 E
Nova Gradiška	2776	45.16 N	17.23 E
Nova Iguaçu	2765	22.45 S	43.27 W
Novaja Kachovka	2782	46.45 N	33.23 E
Novaja Sibir', Ostrov I	2784	75.00 N	149.00 E
Nova Lima	2765	19.59 S	43.51 W
Nova Lisboa → Huambo	2788	12.44 S	15.47 E
Nova Mambone	2788	20.59 S	35.01 E
Novara	2776	45.28 N	8.38 E
Nova Scotia □[4]	2734	45.00 N	63.00 W
Nova Sofala	2788	20.09 S	34.42 E
Novato	2756	38.06 N	122.34 W
Novelda	2774	38.23 N	0.46 W
Nové Zámky	2770	47.59 N	18.11 E
Novgorod	2780	58.31 N	31.17 E
Novi Ligure	2776	44.46 N	8.47 E
Novinger	2746	40.19 N	92.42 W
Novi Pazar, Blg.	2778	43.21 N	27.12 E
Novi Pazar, Jugo.	2778	43.08 N	20.31 E
Novi Sad	2778	45.15 N	19.50 E
Novoaltajsk	2784	53.24 N	83.58 E
Novoanninskij	2766	50.32 N	42.41 E
Novo Aripuanã	2762	5.08 S	60.22 W
Novočerkassk	2782	47.25 N	40.06 E
Novograd-Volynskij	2782	50.36 N	27.36 E
Novogrudok	2780	53.36 N	25.50 E
Novokujbyševsk	2766	53.07 N	49.58 E
Novokuzneck	2784	53.45 N	87.06 E
Novo Mesto	2776	45.48 N	15.10 E
Novomoskovsk	2782	48.37 N	35.12 E
Novo Redondo	2788	11.13 S	13.50 E
Novorossijsk	2782	44.45 N	37.45 E
Novorybnoje	2784	72.50 N	105.50 E
Novošachtinsk	2782	47.47 N	39.56 E
Novosibirsk	2784	55.02 N	82.55 E
Novosibirskije Ostrova II	2784	75.00 N	142.00 E
Novosibirskoje Vodochranilišče ⊜[1]	2784	54.35 N	82.35 E
Novotroick	2766	51.12 N	58.20 E
Novouzensk	2766	50.28 N	48.08 E
Novozybkov	2780	52.32 N	31.56 E
Novska	2776	45.21 N	16.59 E
Nowa Sól (Neusalz)	2770	51.48 N	15.44 E
Nowata	2748	36.42 N	95.38 W
Nowgong	2794	26.21 N	92.40 E
Nowshāk ∧	2794	36.26 N	71.50 E
Nowshera	2794	34.01 N	71.59 E
Nowy Sącz	2770	49.38 N	20.42 E
Nowy Targ	2770	49.29 N	20.02 E
Noxapater	2746	33.00 N	89.04 W
Noyon	2772	49.35 N	3.00 E
Nozay	2772	47.34 N	1.38 W
Nsanje	2788	16.55 S	35.12 E
Nsawam	2786	5.50 N	0.20 W
Nuanetsi	2788	21.22 S	30.45 E
Nubian Desert ⊸[2]	2786	20.30 N	33.00 E
Nueces ≃	2748	27.50 N	97.30 W
Nueces Plains ≍	2748	28.30 N	99.15 W
Nueltin Lake ⊜	2734	60.20 N	99.50 W
Nueva Casas Grandes	2758	30.25 N	107.55 W
Nueva Ciudad Guerrero	2748	26.35 N	99.15 W
Nueva Rosita	2758	27.57 N	101.13 W
Nueve de Julio	2764	35.30 S	60.50 W
Nuevitas	2760	21.33 N	77.16 W
Nuevo, Golfo C	2764	42.42 S	64.35 W
Nuevo Laredo	2758	27.30 N	99.31 W
Nuevo Léon	2756	32.20 N	115.12 W
Nuits-Saint-Georges	2772	47.08 N	4.57 E
Nullagine	2806	21.53 S	120.06 E
Nullarbor Plain ≍	2806	31.00 S	129.00 E
Numazu	2798	35.06 N	138.52 E
Numfoor, Pulau I	2802	1.03 S	134.54 E
Nuneaton	2769	52.32 N	1.28 W
Nunivak Island I	2738	60.00 N	166.30 W
Nunjiang	2796	49.10 N	125.11 E
Nunjiang ≃	2796	45.25 N	124.40 E
Nuoro	2776	40.19 N	9.20 E
N'urba	2784	63.17 N	118.20 E
Nurri	2776	39.42 N	9.14 E
Nyala	2786	12.03 N	24.53 E
Nyasa, Lake ⊜	2788	12.00 S	34.30 E
Nybro	2768	56.45 N	15.54 E
Nyeri	2788	0.25 S	36.57 E
Nyíregyháza	2770	47.59 N	21.43 E
Nykøbing	2768	55.55 N	11.41 E
Nyköping	2768	58.45 N	17.00 E
Nylstroom	2788	24.42 S	28.20 E
Nynäshamn	2768	58.54 N	17.57 E
Nyngan	2806	31.34 S	147.11 E
Nyon	2772	46.23 N	6.14 E
Nyons	2772	44.22 N	5.08 E
Nysa	2770	50.29 N	17.20 E
Nyssa	2754	43.53 N	117.00 W
Nzérékoré	2786	7.45 N	8.49 W

O

Name	Page	Lat° ′	Long° ′
Oahe, Lake ⊜[1]	2736	45.30 N	100.25 W
Oahu I	2757a	21.30 N	158.00 W
Oak Creek	2752	40.16 N	106.57 W
Oakdale, Calif., U.S.	2756	37.46 N	120.51 W
Oakdale, La., U.S.	2746	30.49 N	92.40 W
Oakes	2750	46.08 N	98.06 W
Oakfield	2740	46.06 N	68.10 W
Oak Grove	2746	32.52 N	91.23 W
Oak Harbor	2754	48.18 N	122.39 W
Oak Hill, Fla., U.S.	2744	28.52 N	80.51 W
Oak Hill, Mich., U.S.	2742	44.13 N	86.19 W
Oak Hill, W. Va., U.S.	2740	37.59 N	81.09 W
Oakhurst	2756	37.19 N	119.40 W
Oakland, Calif., U.S.	2756	37.47 N	122.13 W
Oakland, Iowa, U.S.	2750	41.19 N	95.23 W
Oakland, Md., U.S.	2740	39.25 N	79.24 W
Oakland, Nebr., U.S.	2750	41.50 N	96.28 W
Oakland, Oreg., U.S.	2754	43.25 N	123.18 W
Oakland City	2746	38.20 N	87.21 W
Oak Lawn, Ill., U.S.	2746	41.43 N	87.45 W
Oaklawn, Kans., U.S.	2750	37.36 N	97.18 W
Oakley, Idaho, U.S.	2754	42.15 N	113.53 W
Oakley, Kans., U.S.	2750	39.08 N	100.51 W
Oak Park	2742	41.53 N	87.48 W
Oakridge, Oreg., U.S.	2754	43.45 N	122.28 W
Oak Ridge, Tenn., U.S.	2744	36.01 N	84.16 W
Oaktown	2746	38.52 N	87.26 W
Oakville	2740	43.27 N	79.41 W
Oakwood, Ohio, U.S.	2740	41.06 N	84.23 W
Oakwood, Tex., U.S.	2748	31.35 N	95.51 W
Oamaru	2808	45.06 S	170.58 E
Oaxaca [de Juárez]	2758	17.03 N	96.43 W
Oban	2769	56.25 N	5.29 W
Obbia	2790	5.20 N	48.38 E
Oberlin, Kans., U.S.	2750	39.49 N	100.32 W
Oberlin, La., U.S.	2746	30.37 N	92.46 W
Oberlin, Ohio, U.S.	2740	41.18 N	82.13 W
Oberwart	2770	47.17 N	16.13 E
Obi, Kepulauan II	2802	1.30 S	127.45 E
Obi, Pulau I	2802	1.30 S	127.45 E
Óbidos	2762	1.55 S	55.31 W
Obihiro	2798a	42.55 N	143.12 E
Obion	2746	36.16 N	89.12 W
Obluč'je	2784	49.03 N	131.04 E
Obninsk	2780	55.05 N	36.37 E
Obock	2790	11.59 N	43.16 E
Obrovac	2776	44.12 N	15.41 E
Observatoire, Caye de l' I	2806	21.25 S	158.50 E
Obuasi	2786	6.14 N	1.39 W
Ocala	2744	29.11 N	82.07 W
Ocaña, Col.	2760	8.15 N	73.20 W
Ocaña, Esp.	2774	39.56 N	3.31 W
Occidental, Cordillera ⋀, Col.	2762	5.00 N	76.00 W
Occidental, Cordillera ⋀, Perú	2762	14.00 S	74.00 W
Oceana	2744	37.42 N	81.38 W
Ocean City, Md., U.S.	2740	38.20 N	75.05 W
Ocean City, N.J., U.S.	2740	39.16 N	74.36 W
Ocean Falls	2734	52.21 N	127.40 W
Oceanside	2756	33.12 N	117.23 W
Ocean Springs	2746	30.25 N	88.50 W
Ocha	2784	53.34 N	142.56 E
Ochlocknee	2744	30.59 N	84.05 W
Ochoco Mountains ⋀	2754	44.30 N	120.35 W
Ochota ≃	2784	59.20 N	143.04 E
Ochotsk	2784	59.23 N	143.18 E
Ockelbo	2768	60.53 N	16.43 E
Oconomowoc	2742	43.07 N	88.30 W
Oconto	2742	44.43 N	87.52 W
Oconto Falls	2742	44.42 N	88.08 W
Ocotal	2760	13.37 N	86.31 W
Ocotlán	2758	20.21 N	102.46 W
Ocracoke	2744	35.07 N	75.58 W
Ocumare del Tuy	2760	10.07 N	66.46 W
Ocussi	2802	9.12 S	124.21 E
Oda	2786	5.55 N	0.59 W
Oda, Jabal ∧	2786	20.21 N	36.39 E
Ōdate	2798	40.16 N	140.34 E
Odawara	2798	35.15 N	139.10 E
Odda	2768	60.04 N	6.33 E
Odebolt	2750	42.19 N	95.15 W
Odell	2746	41.00 N	88.31 W
Odemira	2774	37.36 N	8.38 W
Ödemiş	2778	38.13 N	27.59 E
Odense	2768	55.24 N	10.23 E
Oder (Odra) ≃	2770	53.32 N	14.38 E
Odessa, S.S.S.R.	2782	46.28 N	30.44 E
Odessa, Tex., U.S.	2748	31.51 N	102.22 W
Odessa, Wash., U.S.	2754	47.20 N	118.41 W
Odienné	2786	9.30 N	7.34 W
Odincovo	2780	55.41 N	37.17 E
Odonnell	2748	32.58 N	101.50 W
Odum	2744	31.40 N	82.02 W
Oelwein	2742	42.41 N	91.55 W
Ōgaki	2798	35.21 N	136.37 E
Ogallala	2750	41.08 N	101.43 W
Ogbomosho	2786	8.08 N	4.15 E
Ogden	2736	41.14 N	111.58 W
Ogdensburg	2740	44.42 N	75.29 W
Ogilvie Mountains ⋀	2734	65.00 N	139.30 W
Oglesby	2746	41.18 N	89.04 W
Ogooué ≃	2788	0.49 S	9.00 E
Ogulin	2776	45.16 N	15.14 E
Oğuzeli	2791	36.59 N	37.30 E
Ohanet	2786	28.45 N	8.55 E
Ōhata	2798	41.24 N	141.10 E
O'Higgins, Lago (Lago San Martín) ⊜	2764	49.00 S	72.40 W
Ohio □[3]	2736	40.15 N	82.45 W
Ohio ≃	2736	36.59 N	89.08 W
Ohio City	2740	40.46 N	84.37 W
Oiapoque	2762	3.50 N	51.50 W
Oil Center	2748	32.30 N	103.16 W
Oil City	2740	41.26 N	79.42 W
Oildale	2756	35.25 N	119.01 W
Ōita	2798	33.14 N	131.36 E
Ojai	2756	34.27 N	119.15 W
Ojinaga	2758	29.34 N	104.25 W
Ojm'akon	2784	63.28 N	142.49 E
Ojos del Salado, Cerro ∧	2764	27.06 S	68.32 W
Oka ≃, S.S.S.R.	2780	56.20 N	43.59 E
Oka ≃, S.S.S.R.	2784	55.15 N	102.10 E
Okaba	2802	8.06 S	139.42 E
Okahandja	2788	21.59 S	16.58 E
Okanogan	2754	48.22 N	119.35 W
Okāra	2794	30.49 N	73.27 E
Okavango (Cubango) ≃	2788	18.50 S	22.25 E
Okavango Swamp ≣	2788	18.45 S	22.45 E
Okaya	2798	36.03 N	138.03 E
Okayama	2798	34.39 N	133.55 E
Okazaki	2798	34.57 N	137.10 E
Okeechobee	2744	27.15 N	80.50 W
Okeechobee, Lake ⊜	2744	26.55 N	80.45 W
Okeene	2748	36.07 N	98.19 W
Okefenokee Swamp ≣	2744	30.42 N	82.20 W
Okemah	2748	35.26 N	96.19 W
Okhotsk, Sea of (Ochotskoje More) ⊤[2]	2784	53.00 N	150.00 E
Oki-guntō II	2798	36.15 N	133.15 E
Okinawa-jima I	2799b	26.30 N	128.00 E
Okino-Erabu-shima I	2799b	27.22 N	128.35 E
Okino-Tori-Shima I	2796	20.25 N	136.00 E
Oklahoma □[3]	2736	35.30 N	98.00 W
Oklahoma City	2748	35.28 N	97.32 W
Okmulgee	2748	35.37 N	95.58 W
Okolona	2746	34.00 N	88.45 W
Okt'abr'skij, S.S.S.R.	2766	54.28 N	53.28 E
Okt'abr'skij, S.S.S.R.	2782	47.28 N	40.04 E
Okt'abr'skoj Revol'ucii, Ostrov I	2784	79.30 N	97.00 E
Olancha	2756	36.17 N	118.01 W
Olanchito	2760	15.30 N	86.35 W
Olar	2744	33.11 N	81.11 W
Olathe, Colo., U.S.	2752	38.36 N	107.59 W
Olathe, Kans., U.S.	2750	38.53 N	94.49 W
Olavarría	2764	36.53 S	60.20 W
Olbia	2776	40.55 N	9.29 E
Ol'chon, Ostrov I	2784	53.09 N	107.24 E
Olcott	2740	43.20 N	78.43 W
Old Bahama Channel Ʉ	2760	22.33 N	78.05 W
Old Crow ≃	2734	67.35 N	139.50 W
Old Forge	2740	43.43 N	74.58 W
Old Head of Kinsale ≻	2769	51.36 N	8.32 W
Olds	2734	51.47 N	114.06 W
Old Town	2740	44.56 N	68.39 W
Olean	2740	42.05 N	78.26 W
Ølen	2768	59.36 N	5.48 E
Olenij, Ostrov I	2784	72.25 N	77.45 E
Olen'ok	2784	68.33 N	112.18 E
Olen'ok ≃	2784	73.00 N	119.55 E
Olen'okskij Zaliv C	2784	73.20 N	121.00 E
Oleśnica	2770	51.13 N	17.23 E
Ol'ga	2784	43.45 N	135.18 E
Olga, Mount ∧	2806	25.19 S	130.46 E
Olhão	2774	37.02 N	8.50 W
Olimarao I[1]	2802	7.41 N	145.52 E
Ólimbos ∧, Ellás	2778	40.05 N	22.21 E
Ólimbos ∧, Kípros	2791	34.56 N	32.52 E
Olímpia	2765	20.44 S	48.54 W
Olinda	2762	8.01 S	34.51 W
Olite	2774	42.29 N	1.39 W
Oliva, Arg.	2764	35.05 S	63.35 W
Oliva, Esp.	2774	38.55 N	0.07 W
Oliva de la Frontera	2774	38.16 N	6.55 W
Olive Branch	2746	34.58 N	89.50 W
Olivehurst	2756	39.06 N	121.34 W
Oliveira	2765	20.41 S	44.49 W
Olivenza	2774	38.41 N	7.06 W
Olivia	2750	44.46 N	94.59 W
Olla	2746	31.54 N	92.14 W
Ollagüe	2764	21.14 S	68.16 W
Olmedo	2774	41.23 N	4.41 W
Olmos	2762	5.59 S	79.46 W
Olney, Ill., U.S.	2746	38.44 N	88.05 W
Olney, Tex., U.S.	2748	33.22 N	98.45 W
Oloj ≃	2784	66.29 N	159.29 E
Ol'okma ≃	2784	60.22 N	120.42 E
Ol'okminsk	2784	60.24 N	120.24 E
Olomouc	2770	49.36 N	17.16 E
Oloron-Sainte-Marie	2772	43.12 N	0.36 W
Olot	2774	42.11 N	2.29 E
Olov'annaja	2784	50.56 N	115.35 E
Olsztyn (Allenstein)	2770	53.48 N	20.29 E
Olten	2772	47.21 N	7.54 E
Ol'utorskij, Mys ≻	2784	59.55 N	170.27 E
Ol'utorskij Zaliv C	2784	59.55 N	170.27 E
Olympia	2754	47.03 N	122.53 W
Olympic Mountains ⋀	2754	47.50 N	123.45 W
Olympic National Park ♠	2754	47.48 N	123.30 W
Olympus, Mount → Ólimbos ∧, Ellás	2778	40.05 N	22.21 E
Olympus, Mount ∧, Wash., U.S.	2754	47.48 N	123.43 W
Omagh	2769	54.36 N	7.18 W
Omaha	2750	41.16 N	95.57 W
Omak	2754	48.24 N	119.31 W
Oman □[1]	2790	22.00 N	58.00 E
Oman, Gulf of C	2790	24.30 N	58.30 E
Omar	2744	37.46 N	82.00 W
Omčak	2784	61.38 N	147.55 E
Omegna	2776	45.53 N	8.24 E
Ometepec	2758	16.41 N	98.25 W
Ōmiya	2798	35.54 N	139.38 E
Ommanney Bay C	2734	73.07 N	100.11 W
Ommen	2770	52.32 N	6.25 E
Omo ≃	2790	4.32 N	36.04 E
Omolon ≃	2784	68.42 N	158.36 E
Omro	2742	44.02 N	88.44 W
Omsukčan	2784	62.32 N	155.48 E
Ōmura	2798	32.54 N	129.57 E

Symbols against index entries represent categories identified in the key on page 2810.

Symbols against index entries represent categories identified in the key on page 2810.

Name	Page	Lat °′	Long °′
Paraná, Bra.	2765	12.33 S	47.52 W
Paraná ≃	2764	33.43 S	59.15 W
Paranaguá	2764	25.31 S	48.30 W
Paranaíba	2765	19.40 S	51.11 W
Paranavaí	2765	23.04 S	52.28 W
Parangaba	2762	3.45 S	38.33 W
Parás	2748	26.30 N	99.31 W
Paratinga	2765	12.42 S	43.10 W
Paraúna	2765	17.02 S	50.26 W
Paray-le-Monial	2772	46.27 N	4.07 E
Parbhani	2793	19.16 N	76.47 E
Pardeeville	2742	43.32 N	89.18 W
Pardubice	2770	50.02 N	15.47 E
Parece Vela → Okino-Tori-Shima I	2796	20.25 N	136.00 E
Parecis, Serra dos ⛰	2762	13.00 S	60.00 W
Paredes de Nava	2774	42.09 N	4.41 W
Paredón	2748	25.56 N	100.58 W
Paren'	2784	62.28 N	163.05 E
Parent	2734	47.55 N	74.37 W
Parepare	2802	4.01 S	119.38 E
Pargas (Parainen)	2768	60.18 N	22.18 E
Paria, Gulf of C	2760	10.20 N	62.00 W
Pariaman	2804	0.38 S	100.08 E
Parikkala	2768	61.33 N	29.30 E
Parima, Sierra ⛰	2762	2.30 N	64.00 W
Pariñas, Punta >	2762	4.40 S	81.20 W
Parintins	2762	2.36 S	56.44 W
Paris, Ont., Can.	2740	43.12 N	80.23 W
Paris, Fr.	2772	48.52 N	2.20 E
Paris, Ark., U.S.	2746	35.18 N	93.44 W
Paris, Idaho, U.S.	2754	42.14 N	111.24 W
Paris, Ill., U.S.	2746	39.36 N	87.42 W
Paris, Ky., U.S.	2740	38.13 N	84.14 W
Paris, Maine, U.S.	2740	44.16 N	70.30 W
Paris, Mo., U.S.	2746	39.29 N	92.00 W
Paris, Tenn., U.S.	2746	36.19 N	88.20 W
Paris, Tex., U.S.	2748	33.40 N	95.33 W
Parkano	2768	62.01 N	23.01 E
Park City	2750	37.46 N	97.19 W
Parker, Ariz., U.S.	2752	34.09 N	114.17 W
Parker, S. Dak., U.S.	2750	43.24 N	97.08 W
Parker, Cape >	2734	75.04 N	79.40 W
Parkersburg	2740	39.17 N	81.32 W
Park Falls	2742	45.56 N	90.32 W
Park Forest	2746	41.28 N	87.38 W
Parkhill	2740	43.09 N	81.41 W
Park Range ⛰	2752	40.00 N	106.30 W
Park Rapids	2750	46.55 N	95.04 W
Park River	2750	48.24 N	97.45 W
Parkston	2750	43.24 N	97.59 W
Parma, It.	2776	44.48 N	10.20 E
Parma, Ohio, U.S.	2740	41.22 N	81.43 W
Parma ≃	2776	44.56 N	10.26 E
Parnaíba	2762	2.54 S	41.47 W
Parnaíba ≃	2762	3.00 S	41.50 W
Pärnu	2780	58.24 N	24.32 E
Paro	2794	27.26 N	89.25 E
Parral	2764	36.09 S	71.50 W
Parras de la Fuente	2758	25.25 N	102.11 W
Parry, Cape >	2734	70.08 N	124.24 W
Parry Bay C	2734	68.07 N	82.00 W
Parry Sound	2740	45.21 N	80.02 W
Parshall	2750	47.57 N	102.08 W
Parsons, Kans., U.S.	2750	37.20 N	95.16 W
Parsons, Tenn., U.S.	2746	35.39 N	88.07 W
Parsons, W. Va., U.S.	2740	39.06 N	79.41 W
Parthenay	2772	46.39 N	0.15 W
Partinico	2776	38.03 N	13.07 E
Paru ≃	2762	1.33 S	52.38 W
Parys	2788	27.04 S	27.16 E
Pasadena, Calif., U.S.	2756	34.09 N	118.09 W
Pasadena, Tex., U.S.	2748	29.42 N	95.13 W
Pascagoula	2746	30.23 N	88.31 W
Pasco	2754	46.14 N	119.06 W
Pascua, Isla de (Easter Island) I	2730	27.07 S	109.22 W
Pas de Calais (Strait of Dover) ⋃	2772	51.00 N	1.30 E
P'asina ≃	2784	73.50 N	87.10 E
P'asino, Ozero ⊜	2784	69.45 N	87.45 E
P'asinskij Zaliv C	2784	74.00 N	86.00 E
Paškovskij	2782	45.02 N	39.06 E
Pasni	2792	25.16 N	63.28 E
Paso de Indios	2764	43.50 S	69.06 W
Paso de los Libres	2764	29.45 S	57.05 W
Paso Robles	2756	35.38 N	120.41 W
Passagem	2765	12.11 S	43.14 W
Passaic	2740	40.51 N	74.08 W
Passo Fundo	2764	28.15 S	52.24 W
Passos	2765	20.43 S	46.37 W
Pastaza ≃	2762	4.50 S	76.25 W
Pasto	2762	1.13 N	77.17 W
Pastora Peak ∧	2752	36.47 N	109.10 W
Pastrana	2774	40.25 N	2.55 W
Patagonia	2752	31.33 N	110.45 W
Patagonia ↞¹	2764	44.00 S	68.00 W
Pātan	2794	23.50 N	72.07 E
Pate Island I	2788	2.07 S	41.03 E
Paternò	2776	37.34 N	14.54 E
Paterson	2740	40.55 N	74.10 W
Pathānkot	2794	32.17 N	75.39 E
Pathfinder Reservoir ⊜¹	2754	42.30 N	106.50 W
P'atigorsk	2766	44.03 N	43.04 E
Patna	2794	25.36 N	85.07 E
Patos	2762	7.01 S	37.16 W
Patos, Lagoa dos C	2764	31.06 S	51.15 W
Patos de Minas	2765	18.35 S	46.32 W
Patquía	2764	30.02 S	66.55 W
Pátrai	2778	38.15 N	21.44 E
Patricio Lynch, Isla I	2764	48.35 S	75.30 W
Patrocínio	2765	18.57 S	46.59 W
Patten	2740	46.01 N	68.27 W
Patterson, Calif., U.S.	2756	37.28 N	121.07 W
Patterson, La., U.S.	2746	29.42 N	91.18 W
Patton	2740	40.38 N	78.39 W
Pattonsburg	2746	40.03 N	94.08 W
Patuca ≃	2760	15.50 N	84.18 W
Pátzcuaro	2758	19.31 N	101.36 W
Pau	2772	43.18 N	0.22 W
Paulding	2740	41.08 N	84.35 W
Paulistana	2762	8.09 S	41.09 W
Paulistas	2765	18.25 S	42.52 W
Paullina	2750	42.59 N	95.41 W
Paulo Afonso	2762	9.21 S	38.14 W
Pauls Valley	2748	34.44 N	97.13 W
Paungde	2804	18.29 N	95.30 E
Pavia	2776	45.10 N	9.10 E
Pavillion	2754	43.15 N	108.42 W
Pavlograd	2782	48.32 N	35.53 E
Pavlovo	2780	55.58 N	43.04 E
Pavlovskij Posad	2780	55.47 N	38.40 E
Pavullo nel Frignano	2776	44.20 N	10.50 E
Pawhuska	2748	36.40 N	96.20 W
Pawnee City	2750	40.07 N	96.09 W
Paw Paw	2742	42.13 N	85.53 W
Paw Paw Lake	2742	42.12 N	86.15 W
Pawtucket	2740	41.53 N	71.23 W
Paxton	2746	40.27 N	88.06 W
Payette	2754	44.05 N	116.56 W
Paynesville	2750	45.23 N	94.43 W
Paysandú	2764	32.19 S	58.05 W
Payson, Ariz., U.S.	2752	34.14 N	111.20 W
Payson, Utah, U.S.	2752	40.03 N	111.44 W
Pazardžik	2778	42.12 N	24.20 E
Pazarköy	2778	39.51 N	27.24 E
Pazin	2776	45.14 N	13.56 E
Peabody, Kans., U.S.	2750	38.10 N	97.07 W
Peabody, Mass., U.S.	2740	42.32 N	70.55 W
Peace ≃	2734	59.00 N	111.25 W
Peace River	2734	56.14 N	117.17 W
Peach Springs	2752	35.32 N	113.25 W
Peak District National Park ♠	2769	53.17 N	1.45 W
Peale, Mount ∧	2752	38.26 N	109.14 W
Pearisburg	2744	37.20 N	80.44 W
Pearl	2746	32.18 N	90.12 W
Pearl Harbor C	2757a	21.22 N	157.58 W
Pearl River	2746	30.23 N	89.45 W
Pearsall	2748	28.53 N	99.06 W
Pearson	2744	31.18 N	82.51 W
Pebane	2788	17.10 S	38.08 E
Peć	2778	42.40 N	20.19 E
Pecatonica	2742	42.19 N	89.22 W
Pečenga	2766	69.33 N	31.07 E
Pečora	2766	65.10 N	57.11 E
Pečora ≃	2766	68.13 N	54.15 E
Pecos, N. Mex., U.S.	2752	35.29 N	105.41 W
Pecos, Tex., U.S.	2748	31.25 N	103.30 W
Pecos ≃	2758	29.42 N	101.22 W
Pecos Plains ≚	2748	33.20 N	104.30 W
Pécs	2770	46.05 N	18.13 E
Pedro de Valdivia	2764	22.36 S	69.40 W
Peekskill	2740	41.17 N	73.55 W
Peel	2769	54.13 N	4.40 W
Peel ≃	2734	67.37 N	134.40 W
Peel Point >	2734	73.22 N	114.35 W
Peel Sound ⋃	2734	73.15 N	96.30 W
Pegu	2804	17.20 N	96.29 E
Pehuajó	2764	35.45 S	61.58 W
Peikang	2800	23.35 N	120.19 E
Pekalongan	2802	6.53 S	109.40 E
Pekin	2746	40.35 N	89.40 W
Peking → Beijing	2796	39.55 N	116.25 E
Pelagie, Isole II	2776	35.40 N	12.40 E
Pelée, Montagne ∧	2760	14.48 N	61.10 W
Pelee Island I	2740	41.46 N	82.39 W
Peleng, Pulau I	2802	1.20 S	123.10 E
Pelican Rapids	2750	46.34 N	96.05 W
Pella	2742	41.25 N	92.55 W
Pell City	2746	33.35 N	86.17 W
Pello	2768	66.47 N	24.00 E
Pellston	2742	45.33 N	84.47 W
Pelly ≃	2734	62.47 N	137.19 W
Pelly Mountains ⛰	2734	62.00 N	133.00 W
Pelopónnisos ↞¹	2778	37.30 N	22.00 E
Pelotas	2764	31.46 S	52.20 W
Pematangsiantar	2804	2.57 N	99.03 E
Pemba Island I	2788	7.31 S	39.25 E
Pemberton	2806	34.28 S	116.01 E
Pembina	2750	48.58 N	97.15 W
Pembine	2742	45.38 N	87.59 W
Pembroke, Ont., Can.	2740	45.49 N	77.07 W
Pembroke, Wales, U.K.	2769	51.41 N	4.55 W
Pembroke, Ga., U.S.	2744	32.08 N	81.37 W
Peñafiel	2774	41.36 N	4.07 W
Penápolis	2765	21.24 S	50.04 W
Peñaranda de Bracamonte	2774	40.54 N	5.12 W
Peñarroya-Pueblonuevo	2774	38.18 N	5.16 W
Penas, Golfo de C	2764	47.20 S	75.00 W
Pender	2750	42.07 N	96.43 W
Pendleton	2754	45.40 N	118.47 W
Pend Oreille, Lake ⊜	2754	48.10 N	116.11 W
Penfield	2740	41.13 N	78.34 W
P'enghu Liehtao II	2800	23.30 N	119.30 E
Penglai	2796	37.48 N	120.42 E
Peniche	2774	39.21 N	9.23 W
Penjamo	2758	20.26 N	101.44 W
Penju, Kepulauan II	2802	5.22 S	127.46 E
Penne	2776	42.27 N	13.55 E
Penn Hills	2740	40.28 N	79.53 W
Pennines ⛰	2769	54.10 N	2.05 W
Pennington Gap	2744	36.41 N	83.02 W
Pennsauken	2740	39.58 N	75.04 W
Pennsylvania □³	2736	40.45 N	77.30 W
Penn Yan	2740	42.40 N	77.03 W
Penobscot ≃	2736	44.30 N	68.50 W
Penonomé	2760	8.31 N	80.21 W
Penrith	2769	54.40 N	2.44 W
Pensacola	2746	30.25 N	87.13 W
Pensacola Bay C	2746	30.25 N	87.06 W
Penticton	2734	49.30 N	119.35 W
Pentland Firth ⋃	2769	58.44 N	3.13 W
Penwell	2748	31.44 N	102.35 W
Penza	2766	53.13 N	45.00 E
Penzance	2769	50.07 N	5.33 W
Penžina ≃	2784	62.28 N	165.18 E
Penžinskaja Guba C	2784	61.30 N	163.00 E
Penžinskij Chrebet ⛰	2784	62.30 N	167.00 E
Peoria	2746	40.42 N	89.36 W
Perabumulih	2802	3.27 S	104.15 E
Perdido	2746	31.00 N	87.37 W
Pereira	2762	4.49 N	75.43 W
Pereira de Eça	2788	17.03 S	15.47 E
Perejaslav-Chmel'nickij	2782	50.06 N	31.30 E
Pereslavl'-Zalesskij	2780	56.44 N	38.51 E
Pergamino	2764	33.53 S	60.36 W
Pergine Valsugana	2776	46.04 N	11.14 E
Perham	2750	46.36 N	95.34 W
Péribonca ≃	2734	48.45 N	72.05 W
Périgueux	2772	45.11 N	0.43 E
Perijá, Sierra de ⛰	2760	10.00 N	73.00 W
Perkam, Tandjung >	2802	1.28 S	137.54 E
Perkinston	2746	30.47 N	89.08 W
Perlas, Archipiélago de las II	2760	8.20 N	79.02 W
Perm'	2766	58.00 N	56.15 E
Pernik	2778	42.36 N	23.02 E
Péronne	2772	49.56 N	2.56 E
Perpignan	2772	42.41 N	2.53 E
Perrine	2744	25.36 N	80.21 W
Perros-Guirec	2772	48.49 N	3.27 W
Perry, Fla., U.S.	2744	30.07 N	83.35 W
Perry, Iowa, U.S.	2742	41.50 N	94.06 W
Perry, Mich., U.S.	2742	42.50 N	84.13 W
Perry, Okla., U.S.	2748	36.17 N	97.17 W
Perry, Utah, U.S.	2752	35.18 N	105.22 W
Perry Reservoir ⊜¹	2750	39.20 N	95.30 W
Perrysburg	2740	41.33 N	83.38 W
Perryton	2748	36.24 N	100.48 W
Perryville	2746	37.43 N	89.52 W
Persia → Iran □¹	2792	32.00 N	53.00 E
Persian Gulf C	2790	27.00 N	51.00 E
Perth, Austl.	2806	31.56 S	115.50 E
Perth, Ont., Can.	2740	44.54 N	76.15 W
Perth, Scot., U.K.	2769	56.24 N	3.28 W
Perth Amboy	2740	40.31 N	74.16 W
Peru, Ill., U.S.	2746	40.45 N	86.04 W
Peru, Ind., U.S.	2746	40.45 N	86.04 W
Peru, Nebr., U.S.	2750	40.29 N	95.44 W
Peru (Perú) □¹	2762	10.00 S	76.00 W
Perugia	2776	43.08 N	12.22 E
Perušić	2776	44.39 N	15.23 E
Pervomajsk	2782	48.37 N	38.35 E
Pervoural'sk	2766	56.54 N	59.58 E
Pesaro	2776	43.54 N	12.55 E
Pescara	2776	42.28 N	14.13 E
Pescia	2776	43.54 N	10.41 E
Peshāwar	2794	34.01 N	71.33 E
Peshtigo	2742	45.03 N	87.45 W
Peshtigo ≃	2742	44.58 N	87.40 W
Pesqueira	2762	8.22 S	36.42 W
Pessac	2772	44.48 N	0.38 W
Petah Tiqwa	2791	32.05 N	34.53 E
Petaluma	2756	38.14 N	122.39 W
Petatlán	2758	17.31 N	101.16 W
Petawawa	2740	45.54 N	77.17 W
Peterborough, Austl.	2806	32.58 S	138.50 E
Peterborough, Ont., Can.	2740	44.18 N	78.19 W
Peterborough, Eng., U.K.	2769	52.35 N	0.15 W
Peterhead	2769	57.30 N	1.49 W
Peter Pond Lake ⊜	2734	55.55 N	108.44 W
Petersburg, Ill., U.S.	2746	40.01 N	89.51 W
Petersburg, Ind., U.S.	2746	38.30 N	87.17 W
Petersburg, Tex., U.S.	2748	33.52 N	101.36 W
Petersburg, Va., U.S.	2744	37.13 N	77.24 W
Petersburg, W. Va., U.S.	2740	39.00 N	79.07 W
Petitot ≃	2734	60.14 N	123.29 W
Petitsikapau Lake ⊜	2734	54.45 N	66.25 W
Petlād	2794	22.28 N	72.48 E
Petone	2808	41.13 S	174.52 E
Petoskey	2742	45.22 N	84.57 W
Petra ⊥	2791	30.20 N	35.26 E
Petre, Point >	2740	43.50 N	77.09 W
Petrified Forest National Park ♠	2752	34.55 N	109.49 W
Petrila	2778	45.27 N	23.25 E
Petrinja	2776	45.26 N	16.17 E
Petrolina	2762	9.24 S	40.30 W
Petropavlovsk-Kamčatskij	2784	53.01 N	158.39 E
Petrópolis	2765	22.31 S	43.10 W
Petroșani	2778	45.25 N	23.22 E
Petrovsk	2766	52.19 N	45.23 E
Petrovsk-Zabajkal'skij	2784	51.17 N	108.50 E
Petrozavodsk	2766	61.47 N	34.20 E
Pevek	2784	69.42 N	170.17 E
Pézenas	2772	43.27 N	3.25 E
Phalsbourg	2772	48.46 N	7.16 E
Phangnga	2804	8.28 N	98.32 E
Phanom Dongrak, Thiu Khao ⛰	2804	14.25 N	103.30 E
Phan-rang	2804	11.34 N	108.59 E
Pharr	2748	26.12 N	98.11 W
Phet Buri	2804	13.06 N	99.56 E
Philadelphia, Miss., U.S.	2746	32.46 N	89.07 W
Philadelphia, N.Y., U.S.	2740	44.09 N	75.43 W
Philadelphia, Pa., U.S.	2740	39.57 N	75.07 W
Phil Campbell	2746	34.21 N	87.42 W
Philip	2750	44.02 N	101.40 W
Philippeville	2770	50.12 N	4.32 E
Philippi	2740	39.09 N	80.02 W
Philippines □¹	2802	13.00 N	122.00 E
Philippine Sea ⊤²	2802	15.00 N	135.00 E
Philipsburg	2740	40.53 N	78.05 W
Phillips, Tex., U.S.	2748	35.42 N	101.22 W
Phillips, Wis., U.S.	2742	45.41 N	90.24 W
Phillipsburg, Kans., U.S.	2750	39.45 N	99.19 W
Phillipsburg, N.J., U.S.	2740	40.42 N	75.12 W
Philpots Island I	2734	74.48 N	80.00 W
Phitsanulok	2804	16.49 N	100.15 E
Phnum Pénh	2804	11.33 N	104.55 E
Phoenix	2752	33.27 N	112.05 W
Phong Saly	2804	21.41 N	102.06 E
Phra Nakhon Si Ayutthaya	2804	14.21 N	100.33 E
Phuket	2804	7.54 N	98.24 E
Phu-quoc, Dao I	2804	10.12 N	104.00 E
Piacenza	2776	45.01 N	9.40 E
Piana	2776	42.14 N	8.38 E
Piatra-Neamț	2778	46.56 N	26.22 E
Piazza Armerina	2776	37.23 N	14.22 E
Pibor Post	2786	6.48 N	33.08 E
Picacho	2752	32.43 N	111.30 W
Picardie □⁹	2772	50.00 N	3.30 E
Picayune	2746	30.26 N	89.41 W
Pichanal	2764	23.20 S	64.15 W
Pickens	2746	32.53 N	89.58 W
Pickford	2742	46.10 N	84.22 W
Pickle Crow	2734	51.30 N	90.04 W
Pickwick Lake ⊜¹	2746	34.55 N	88.10 W
Picos	2762	7.05 S	41.28 W
Picquigny	2772	49.57 N	2.09 E
Pictured Rocks National Lakeshore ♠	2742	46.35 N	86.20 W
Pidálion, Akrotírion >	2791	34.56 N	34.05 E
Piedmont, Ala., U.S.	2746	33.55 N	85.37 W
Piedmont, Mo., U.S.	2746	37.09 N	90.42 W
Piedrabuena	2774	39.02 N	4.10 W
Piedrahita	2774	40.28 N	5.19 W
Piedras Negras, Guat.	2760	17.11 N	91.15 W
Piedras Negras, Méx.	2758	28.42 N	100.31 W
Pieksämäki	2768	62.18 N	27.08 E
Pierce, Colo., U.S.	2752	40.38 N	104.45 W
Pierce, Idaho, U.S.	2754	46.29 N	115.48 W
Pierce, Nebr., U.S.	2750	42.12 N	97.32 W
Pierre	2750	44.22 N	100.21 W
Pierre-Buffière	2772	45.42 N	1.21 E
Pierson	2744	29.14 N	81.28 W
Pietermaritzburg	2788	29.37 S	30.16 E
Pietersburg	2788	23.54 S	29.25 E
Pie Town	2752	34.18 N	108.09 W
Pietrasanta	2776	43.57 N	10.14 E
Piet Retief	2788	27.01 S	30.50 E
Pigeon ≃	2742	45.27 N	84.33 W
Piggott	2746	36.23 N	90.11 W
Pihlajavesi ⊜	2768	61.45 N	28.50 E
Pihtipudas	2768	63.23 N	25.34 E
Pijijiapan	2758	15.42 N	93.14 W
Pikal'ovo	2780	59.31 N	34.06 E
Pikes Peak ∧	2752	38.51 N	105.03 W
Pikesville	2740	39.23 N	76.44 W
Piketberg	2788	32.54 S	18.46 E
Piketon	2740	39.04 N	83.01 W
Pikeville	2744	37.29 N	82.31 W
Piła (Schneidemühl)	2770	53.10 N	16.44 E
Pilar do Sul	2765	23.49 S	47.42 W
Pilcomayo ≃	2764	25.21 S	57.42 W
Pīlībhīt	2794	28.38 N	79.48 E
Pilot Grove	2746	38.53 N	92.55 W
Pilot Knob ∧	2746	35.42 N	93.57 W
Pilot Mountain	2744	36.23 N	80.28 W
Pilot Rock	2754	45.29 N	118.50 W
Pima	2752	32.54 N	109.50 W
Pimentel	2762	6.45 S	79.55 W
Pina	2774	41.29 N	0.32 W
Pinang (George Town)	2804	5.24 N	100.19 E
Pinar del Río	2760	22.25 N	83.42 W
Pinardville	2740	42.59 N	71.33 W
Pinckney	2742	42.27 N	83.57 W
Pinckneyville	2746	38.05 N	89.23 W
Pinconning	2742	43.51 N	83.58 W
Píndhos Óros ⛰	2778	39.49 N	21.14 E
Pindus Mountains → Píndhos Óros ⛰	2778	39.49 N	21.14 E
Pine ≃	2742	44.15 N	85.55 W
Pine Bluff	2746	34.13 N	92.01 W
Pine Bluffs	2750	41.11 N	104.04 W
Pine Castle	2744	28.28 N	81.22 W
Pine City	2742	45.50 N	92.59 W
Pinedale	2754	42.52 N	109.52 W
Pine Falls	2734	50.35 N	96.15 W
Pinega ≃	2766	64.08 N	41.54 E
Pine Hill	2746	31.59 N	87.35 W
Pine Island	2742	44.12 N	92.38 W
Pinellas Park	2744	27.51 N	82.43 W
Pine Mountain ∧	2744	36.55 N	83.20 W
Pine Point	2734	61.01 N	114.15 W
Pine Ridge	2750	43.02 N	102.33 W
Pine River	2742	46.43 N	94.24 W
Pinerolo	2776	44.53 N	7.21 E
Pineville, Ky., U.S.	2744	36.46 N	83.42 W
Pineville, La., U.S.	2746	31.19 N	92.26 W
Pineville, Mo., U.S.	2746	36.36 N	94.23 W
Pineville, N.C., U.S.	2744	35.05 N	80.53 W
Pineville, W. Va., U.S.	2744	37.35 N	81.32 W
Piney Buttes ∧	2754	47.30 N	107.00 W
Pingdingshan	2796	33.44 N	113.18 E
Pinghu	2800	30.42 N	121.01 E
Pingliang	2796	35.27 N	107.10 E
P'ingtung	2800	22.40 N	120.29 E
Pingxiang	2800	27.38 N	113.50 E
Pingyao	2796	37.16 N	112.09 E
Pinhel	2774	40.46 N	7.04 W
Pinnacle Buttes ∧	2754	43.44 N	109.57 W
Pinnacles National Monument ♠	2756	36.28 N	121.19 W
Pinos, Isla de (Isle of Pines) I	2760	21.40 N	82.50 W
Pins, Pointe aux >	2740	42.15 N	81.51 W
Pinsk	2780	52.07 N	26.04 E
Pioche	2756	37.56 N	114.27 W
Piombino	2776	42.55 N	10.32 E
Pioner, Ostrov I	2784	79.50 N	92.30 E
Piotrków Trybunalski	2770	51.25 N	19.42 E

Symbols against index entries represent categories identified in the key on page 2810.

Name	Page	Lat°′	Long°′
Pipestone	2750	43.58 N	96.19 W
Pipestone ≃	2734	52.53 N	89.23 W
Pipmoucan, Réservoir ⊜[1]	2739	49.35 N	70.30 W
Piqua	2740	40.09 N	84.15 W
Piracicaba	2765	22.43 S	47.38 W
Piraeus			
→ Piraiévs	2778	37.57 N	23.38 E
Piraí do Sul	2764	24.31 S	49.56 W
Piraiévs (Piraeus)	2778	37.57 N	23.38 E
Piran	2776	45.32 N	13.34 E
Pirané	2764	25.44 S	59.07 W
Pirapora	2765	17.21 S	44.56 W
Pir'atin	2782	50.15 N	32.30 E
Pires do Rio	2765	17.18 S	48.17 W
Pírgos	2778	37.41 N	21.28 E
Piru	2802	3.04 S	128.12 E
Pisa	2776	43.43 N	10.23 E
Pisagua	2762	19.36 S	70.13 W
Pisco	2762	13.42 S	76.13 W
Písek	2770	49.19 N	14.10 E
Pishan	2794	37.37 N	78.18 E
Pisinimo	2752	32.02 N	112.19 W
Pisticci	2776	40.23 N	16.34 E
Pistoia	2776	43.55 N	10.54 E
Pitcairn □[2]	2730	25.04 S	130.06 W
Piteå	2768	65.20 N	21.30 E
Pitești	2778	44.52 N	24.52 E
Pithiviers	2772	48.10 N	2.15 E
Pitiquito	2758	30.42 N	112.02 W
Pitlochry	2769	56.43 N	3.45 W
Pittsboro	2744	35.43 N	79.11 W
Pittsburg, Kans., U.S.	2750	37.25 N	94.42 W
Pittsburg, Tex., U.S.	2748	33.00 N	94.58 W
Pittsburgh	2740	40.26 N	80.00 W
Pittsfield, Ill., U.S.	2746	39.36 N	90.48 W
Pittsfield, Maine, U.S.	2740	44.47 N	69.23 W
Pittsfield, Mass., U.S.	2740	42.27 N	73.15 W
Pittston	2740	41.19 N	75.47 W
Piu, Cerro ∧	2760	13.38 N	84.52 W
Piura	2762	5.12 S	80.36 W
Pizzo	2776	38.44 N	16.10 E
Placentia Bay C	2734	47.15 N	54.30 W
Placerville	2756	38.43 N	120.48 W
Placetas	2760	22.19 N	79.40 W
Plain City	2752	41.18 N	112.06 W
Plainfield, Ind., U.S.	2746	39.42 N	86.24 W
Plainfield, N.J., U.S.	2740	40.37 N	74.26 W
Plainfield, Wis., U.S.	2742	44.13 N	89.30 W
Plains, Kans., U.S.	2750	37.16 N	100.35 W
Plains, Tex., U.S.	2748	33.11 N	102.50 W
Plainview, Nebr., U.S.	2750	42.21 N	97.47 W
Plainview, Tex., U.S.	2748	34.11 N	101.43 W
Plainville	2750	39.14 N	99.18 W
Planada	2756	37.18 N	120.19 W
Planeta Rica	2760	8.25 N	75.36 W
Plankinton	2750	43.43 N	98.29 W
Plano, Ill., U.S.	2746	41.40 N	88.32 W
Plano, Tex., U.S.	2748	33.01 N	96.42 W
Plantation	2744	26.05 N	80.14 W
Plant City	2744	28.01 N	82.08 W
Plaquemine	2746	30.17 N	91.14 W
Plasencia	2774	40.02 N	6.05 W
Plaški	2776	45.05 N	15.22 E
Plast	2766	54.22 N	60.50 E
Plato	2760	9.47 N	74.47 W
Platte	2750	43.23 N	98.51 W
Platte ≃, Nebr., U.S.	2750	41.04 N	95.53 W
Platte City	2746	39.22 N	94.47 W
Platte Island I	2788	5.52 S	55.23 E
Platteville, Colo., U.S.	2752	40.13 N	104.49 W
Platteville, Wis., U.S.	2742	42.44 N	90.29 W
Plattsburg	2746	39.34 N	94.27 W
Plattsburgh	2740	44.42 N	73.28 W
Plattsmouth	2750	41.01 N	95.53 W
Pleasant Hill, Ill., U.S.	2746	39.27 N	90.52 W
Pleasant Hill, Mo., U.S.	2746	38.47 N	94.16 W
Pleasanton	2748	28.58 N	98.29 W
Pleasantville	2740	39.23 N	74.32 W
Pleiku	2804	13.59 N	108.00 E
Pléneuf	2772	48.36 N	2.33 W
Plenty, Bay of C	2808	37.40 S	177.00 E
Plentywood	2750	48.47 N	104.34 W
Pleseck	2766	62.43 N	40.20 E
Plessisville	2740	46.14 N	71.47 W
Pleternica	2776	45.17 N	17.48 E
Plétipi, Lac ⊜	2734	51.44 N	70.06 W
Pleven	2778	43.25 N	24.37 E
Plevna	2750	46.25 N	104.31 W
Pljevlja	2778	43.21 N	19.21 E
Ploče	2776	43.04 N	17.26 E
Płock	2770	52.33 N	19.43 E
Plöckenpass)(	2770	46.36 N	12.58 E
Ploërmel	2772	47.56 N	2.24 W
Ploiești	2778	44.56 N	26.02 E
Plouguenast	2772	48.17 N	2.43 W
Plovdiv	2778	42.09 N	24.45 E
Plummer	2754	47.20 N	116.53 W
Plumtree	2788	20.30 S	27.50 E
Plymouth, Monts.	2760	16.42 N	62.13 W
Plymouth, Eng., U.K.	2769	50.23 N	4.10 W
Plymouth, Ind., U.S.	2746	41.21 N	86.19 W
Plymouth, Mass., U.S.	2740	41.58 N	70.41 W
Plymouth, N.H., U.S.	2740	43.45 N	71.41 W
Plymouth, N.C., U.S.	2744	35.52 N	76.43 W
Plymouth, Wis., U.S.	2742	43.45 N	87.58 W
Plzeň	2770	49.45 N	13.23 E
Pobeda, Gora ∧	2784	65.12 N	146.12 E
Pocahontas, Ark., U.S.	2746	36.16 N	90.58 W
Pocahontas, Iowa, U.S.	2750	42.44 N	94.40 W
Pocatello	2754	42.52 N	112.27 W
Počep	2780	52.56 N	33.27 E
Pochutla	2758	15.44 N	96.28 W
Poções	2765	14.31 S	40.21 W
Pocomoke City	2740	38.05 N	75.34 W
Pocono Mountains ∧∧[2]	2740	41.10 N	75.20 W
Poços de Caldas	2765	21.48 S	46.34 W
Podensac	2772	44.39 N	0.22 W
Podkamennaja Tunguska	2784	61.36 N	90.09 E
Podkamennaja Tunguska ≃	2784	61.36 N	90.18 E
Podol'sk	2780	55.26 N	37.33 E
Podor	2786	16.40 N	14.57 W
Podravska Slatina	2776	45.42 N	17.42 E
Pofadder	2788	29.10 S	19.22 E
Poggibonsi	2776	43.28 N	11.09 E
P'ohang	2796	36.03 N	129.20 E
Point Au Fer Island I	2746	29.15 N	91.15 W
Pointe a la Hache	2746	29.35 N	89.48 W
Pointe-à-Pitre	2760	16.14 N	61.32 W
Pointe-Noire	2788	4.48 S	11.51 E
Point Lake ⊜	2734	65.15 N	113.04 W
Point Pelee National Park ♠	2740	41.57 N	82.30 W
Point Pleasant, N.J., U.S.	2740	40.05 N	74.04 W
Point Pleasant, W. Va., U.S.	2740	38.52 N	82.08 W
Poitiers	2772	46.35 N	0.20 E
Poix	2772	49.47 N	1.59 E
Poland □[1]	2766	52.00 N	19.00 E
Polesje ⊸[1]	2780	52.10 N	28.00 E
Polevskoj	2766	56.26 N	60.11 E
Pólis	2791	35.02 N	32.25 E
Polistena	2776	38.25 N	16.05 E
Polk	2740	41.22 N	79.56 W
Pol'kino	2784	71.10 N	99.13 E
Polkville	2746	32.12 N	89.41 W
Pollāchi	2793	10.40 N	77.01 E
Pollock	2750	45.55 N	100.17 W
Polock	2780	55.31 N	28.46 E
Polson	2754	47.41 N	114.09 W
Poltava	2782	49.35 N	34.34 E
Polynesia II	2730	4.00 S	156.00 W
Pomabamba	2762	8.50 S	77.25 W
Pomaro	2758	18.20 N	103.18 W
Pombal	2774	39.55 N	8.38 W
Pomeranian Bay C	2770	54.00 N	14.15 E
Pomeroy, Ohio, U.S.	2740	39.02 N	82.02 W
Pomeroy, Wash., U.S.	2754	46.28 N	117.36 W
Pomona	2756	34.04 N	117.45 W
Pompano Beach	2744	26.15 N	80.07 W
Pompton Lakes	2740	41.00 N	74.17 W
Ponca	2750	42.34 N	96.43 W
Ponca City	2748	36.42 N	97.05 W
Ponce	2760	18.01 N	66.37 W
Ponce de Leon	2746	30.44 N	85.56 W
Ponchatoula	2746	30.26 N	90.26 W
Pondcreek	2748	36.40 N	97.48 W
Pondicherry	2793	11.56 N	79.53 E
Pond Inlet	2734	72.41 N	78.00 W
Ponferrada	2774	42.33 N	6.35 W
Ponoj	2766	67.05 N	41.07 E
Ponoka	2734	52.42 N	113.35 W
Pons	2772	45.35 N	0.33 W
Ponta Grossa	2764	25.05 S	50.09 W
Pont-à-Mousson	2772	48.54 N	6.04 E
Ponta Porã	2765	22.32 S	55.43 W
Pontarlier	2772	46.54 N	6.22 E
Pontassieve	2776	43.46 N	11.26 E
Pont-Audemer	2772	49.21 N	0.31 E
Pontchartrain, Lake ⊜	2746	30.10 N	90.10 W
Pontchâteau	2772	47.26 N	2.05 W
Pont de Suert	2774	42.24 N	0.45 E
Ponte Branca	2765	16.27 S	52.40 W
Ponte da Barca	2774	41.48 N	8.25 W
Pontedera	2776	43.40 N	10.38 E
Ponte de Sor	2774	39.15 N	8.01 W
Ponte Nova	2765	20.24 S	42.54 W
Pontevedra	2774	42.26 N	8.38 W
Pontgibaud	2772	46.50 N	2.51 E
Pontiac, Ill., U.S.	2746	40.53 N	88.38 W
Pontiac, Mich., U.S.	2742	42.37 N	83.18 W
Pontianak	2802	0.02 S	109.20 E
Pontivy	2772	48.04 N	2.59 W
Pont-l'Abbé	2772	47.52 N	4.13 W
Pontoise	2772	49.03 N	2.06 E
Pontorson	2772	48.33 N	1.31 W
Pontotoc	2746	34.15 N	89.00 W
Pontypool	2769	51.43 N	3.02 W
Poole	2769	50.43 N	1.59 W
Poopó, Lago de ⊜	2762	18.45 S	67.07 W
Popayán	2762	2.27 N	76.36 W
Popigaj ≃	2784	72.54 N	106.36 E
Poplar, Mont., U.S.	2750	48.07 N	105.12 W
Poplar, Wis., U.S.	2742	46.35 N	91.48 W
Poplar Bluff	2746	36.45 N	90.24 W
Poplarville	2746	30.51 N	89.32 W
Popokabaka	2788	5.42 S	16.35 E
Popomanasiu, Mount ∧	2806	9.42 S	160.04 E
Poquoson	2744	37.07 N	76.21 W
Porangatu	2762	13.26 S	49.10 W
Porbandar	2794	21.38 N	69.36 E
Porcher Island I	2734	53.57 N	130.30 W
Porcupine Mountains ∧∧	2746	46.40 N	89.40 W
Pordenone	2776	45.57 N	12.39 E
Poreč	2776	45.13 N	13.37 E
Pori	2768	61.29 N	21.47 E
Porkkala	2768	59.59 N	24.26 E
Porlamar	2760	10.57 N	63.51 W
Poronajsk	2784	49.14 N	143.04 E
Porsgrunn	2768	59.09 N	9.40 E
Portadown	2769	54.26 N	6.27 W
Portage, Mich., U.S.	2742	42.12 N	85.41 W
Portage, Wis., U.S.	2742	43.33 N	89.28 W
Portage-la-Prairie	2734	49.57 N	98.25 W
Portageville	2746	36.26 N	89.42 W
Port Alberni	2734	49.14 N	124.48 W
Portalegre	2774	39.17 N	7.26 W
Portales	2748	34.11 N	103.20 W
Port Allegany	2740	41.49 N	78.17 W
Port Angeles	2754	48.07 N	123.27 W
Port Arthur, Tex., U.S.	2746	29.55 N	93.55 W
Port Arthur			
→ Lüshun, Zhg.	2796	38.48 N	121.16 E
Port Augusta	2806	32.30 S	137.46 E
Port-au-Prince	2760	18.32 N	72.20 W
Port Austin	2742	44.03 N	83.01 W
Port Barre	2746	30.34 N	91.57 W
Port-Bergé	2788	15.33 S	47.40 E
Port Blair	2804	11.40 N	92.45 E
Port Borden	2739	46.15 N	63.42 W
Port-Cartier-Quest	2739	50.01 N	66.52 W
Port Chalmers	2808	45.49 S	170.37 E
Port Charlotte	2744	26.59 N	82.06 W
Port Clinton	2740	41.31 N	82.56 W
Port Colborne	2740	42.53 N	79.14 W
Port Dover	2740	42.47 N	80.12 W
Port Edwards	2742	44.21 N	90.05 W
Portel, Bra.	2762	1.57 S	50.49 W
Portel, Port.	2774	38.18 N	7.42 W
Port Elgin	2740	44.26 N	81.24 W
Port Elizabeth	2730	33.58 S	25.40 E
Port Ellen	2769	55.39 N	6.12 W
Porter	2748	30.06 N	95.14 W
Porterville	2756	36.04 N	119.01 W
Port-Gentil	2788	0.43 S	8.47 E
Port Gibson	2746	31.58 N	90.58 W
Port Harcourt	2786	4.43 N	7.05 E
Port Hedland	2806	20.19 S	118.34 E
Port Henry	2740	44.03 N	73.28 W
Port Hope	2740	43.57 N	78.18 W
Port Hueneme	2756	34.09 N	119.12 W
Port Huron	2742	42.58 N	82.27 W
Portimão	2774	37.08 N	8.32 W
Port Isabel	2748	26.04 N	97.13 W
Port Jervis	2740	41.22 N	74.41 W
Portland, Austl.	2806	38.21 S	141.36 E
Portland, Maine, U.S.	2740	43.39 N	70.17 W
Portland, Mich., U.S.	2742	42.52 N	84.54 W
Portland, Oreg., U.S.	2754	45.33 N	122.36 W
Portland, Tenn., U.S.	2746	36.35 N	86.31 W
Portland, Tex., U.S.	2748	27.53 N	97.20 W
Portland, Bill of ➤	2769	50.31 N	2.27 W
Port Lavaca	2748	28.37 N	96.38 W
Port Leyden	2740	43.35 N	75.21 W
Port Lincoln	2806	34.44 S	135.52 E
Port Loko	2786	8.46 N	12.47 W
Port Louis	2788	20.10 S	57.30 E
Port-Lyautey			
→ Kenitra	2786	34.16 N	6.40 W
Port Macquarie	2806	31.26 S	152.55 E
Port-Menier	2739	49.48 N	64.20 W
Port Moresby	2806	9.30 S	147.10 E
Port Neches	2746	29.59 N	93.58 W
Port Nolloth	2788	29.17 S	16.51 E
Port-Nouveau-Québec	2734	58.32 N	65.54 W
Porto	2774	41.11 N	8.36 W
Pôrto Alegre	2764	30.04 S	51.11 W
Porto Alexandre	2788	15.49 S	11.53 E
Porto Amboim	2788	10.44 S	13.44 E
Porto Amélia	2788	12.58 S	40.30 E
Pôrto de Moz	2762	1.45 S	52.14 W
Pôrto Esperança	2762	19.37 S	57.27 W
Pôrto Esperidião	2762	15.51 S	58.28 W
Portoferraio	2776	42.49 N	10.19 E
Pôrto Ferreira	2765	21.51 S	47.28 W
Port of Spain	2760	10.39 N	61.31 W
Portogruaro	2776	45.47 N	12.50 E
Portola	2756	39.48 N	120.28 W
Pôrto Murtinho	2762	21.42 S	57.52 W
Pôrto Nacional	2762	10.42 S	48.25 W
Porto-Novo	2786	6.29 N	2.37 E
Port Orchard	2754	47.32 N	122.38 W
Port Orford	2754	42.45 N	124.30 W
Porto San Giorgio	2776	43.11 N	13.48 E
Porto Santo Stefano	2776	42.26 N	11.07 E
Pôrto São José	2765	22.43 S	53.10 W
Pôrto Seguro	2765	16.26 S	39.05 W
Porto Torres	2776	40.50 N	8.23 E
Pôrto União	2764	26.15 S	51.05 W
Porto-Vecchio	2776	41.35 N	9.16 E
Pôrto Velho	2762	8.46 S	63.54 W
Portoviejo	2762	1.03 S	80.27 W
Port Pirie	2806	33.11 S	138.01 E
Port Radium	2734	66.05 N	118.02 W
Port Royal	2740	40.32 N	77.23 W
Port-Sainte-Marie	2772	44.15 N	0.24 E
Port Saint Joe	2746	29.49 N	85.18 W
Port Saint Johns	2788	31.38 S	29.33 E
Port Sanilac	2742	43.26 N	82.33 W
Port Shepstone	2788	30.46 S	30.22 E
Portsmouth, Eng., U.K.	2769	50.48 N	1.05 W
Portsmouth, N.H., U.S.	2740	43.04 N	70.46 W
Portsmouth, Ohio, U.S.	2740	38.45 N	82.59 W
Portsmouth, Va., U.S.	2744	36.52 N	76.24 W
Port Sulphur	2746	29.29 N	89.42 W
Port Talbot	2769	51.36 N	3.47 W
Port Townsend	2754	48.07 N	122.46 W
Portugal □[1]	2766	39.30 N	8.00 W
Portugalete	2774	43.19 N	3.01 W
Portugália	2788	7.20 S	20.47 E
Portuguese Guinea			
→ Guinea-Bissau □[1]	2786	12.00 N	15.00 W
Portumna	2769	53.06 N	8.13 W
Port-Vendres	2772	42.31 N	3.07 E
Port Washington	2742	43.23 N	87.53 W
Port Wentworth	2744	32.09 N	81.10 W
Port Wing	2742	46.47 N	91.23 W
Porzuna	2774	39.09 N	4.09 W
Posadas	2764	27.25 S	55.50 W
Poschiavo	2772	46.18 N	10.04 E
Posen	2742	45.16 N	83.42 W
Poso	2802	1.23 S	120.44 E
Posse	2765	14.05 S	46.22 W
Post	2748	33.12 N	101.23 W
Poste-de-la-Baleine	2734	55.17 N	77.45 W
Poste-Mistassini	2734	50.25 N	73.52 W
Post Falls	2754	47.43 N	116.57 W
Post Maurice Cortier (Bidon Cinq)	2786	22.18 N	1.05 E
Postojna	2776	45.47 N	14.13 E
P'ostraja Dresva	2784	61.34 N	156.41 E
Postville	2742	43.05 N	91.34 W
Potchefstroom	2788	26.46 S	27.01 E
Poté	2765	17.49 S	41.49 W
Poteau	2746	35.03 N	94.37 W
Poteet	2748	29.02 N	98.34 W
Potenza	2776	40.38 N	15.49 E
Potes	2774	43.09 N	4.37 W
Potgietersrus	2788	24.15 S	28.55 E
Poth	2748	29.04 N	98.05 W
Potholes Reservoir ⊜[1]	2754	47.01 N	119.19 W
Potiraguá	2765	15.36 S	39.53 W
Potiskum	2786	11.43 N	11.05 E
Potlatch	2754	46.55 N	116.54 W
Potomac ≃	2740	38.00 N	76.18 W
Potosí, Bol.	2762	19.35 S	65.45 W
Potosi, Mo., U.S.	2746	37.56 N	90.47 W
Potrero del Llano	2748	29.12 N	104.28 W
Potsdam	2740	44.40 N	74.59 W
Potts Camp	2746	34.39 N	89.18 W
Pottstown	2740	40.15 N	75.38 W
Pottsville	2740	40.41 N	76.12 W
Poughkeepsie	2740	41.42 N	73.56 W
Poulsbo	2754	47.44 N	122.39 W
Poultney	2740	43.31 N	73.14 W
Pound	2744	37.07 N	82.36 W
Pouso Alegre	2765	22.13 S	45.56 W
Poŭthĭsăt	2804	12.32 N	103.55 E
Pouzauges	2772	46.47 N	0.50 W
Póvoa de Varzim	2774	41.23 N	8.46 W
Povungnituk	2734	60.02 N	77.10 W
Powassan	2740	46.05 N	79.22 W
Poway	2756	32.58 N	117.02 W
Powder ≃, U.S.	2736	46.44 N	105.26 W
Powder ≃, Oreg., U.S.	2754	44.45 N	117.03 W
Powder River Pass)(	2754	44.09 N	107.04 W
Powell	2754	44.45 N	108.46 W
Powell, Lake ⊜[1]	2736	37.25 N	110.45 W
Powell River	2734	49.52 N	124.33 W
Powellton	2740	38.05 N	81.19 W
Powers	2754	42.53 N	124.04 W
Powers Lake	2750	48.34 N	102.39 W
Powhatan	2744	37.29 N	77.55 W
Poxoreu	2765	15.50 S	54.23 W
Poyang	2800	28.59 N	116.40 E
Poyanghu ⊜	2800	29.00 N	116.25 E
Poza Rica de Hidalgo	2758	20.33 N	97.27 W
Poznań	2770	52.25 N	16.55 E
Pozo Alcón	2774	37.42 N	2.56 W
Pozoblanco	2774	38.22 N	4.51 W
Pozuelo de Alarcón	2774	40.26 N	3.49 W
Pozzuoli	2776	40.49 N	14.07 E
Prachuap Khiri Khan	2804	11.48 N	99.47 E
Prague			
→ Praha	2770	50.05 N	14.26 E
Praha (Prague)	2770	50.05 N	14.26 E
Prainha	2762	7.16 S	60.23 W
Prairie City	2754	44.28 N	118.43 W
Prairie du Chien	2742	43.03 N	91.09 W
Prairie View	2748	30.04 N	96.00 W
Prairie Village	2750	39.01 N	94.38 W
Praslin Island I	2788	4.19 S	55.44 E
Prat de Llobregat	2774	41.20 N	2.06 E
Prato	2776	43.53 N	11.06 E
Pratt	2750	37.39 N	98.44 W
Prattville	2746	32.28 N	86.29 W
Pravia	2774	43.29 N	6.07 W
Predazzo	2776	46.19 N	11.36 E
Predlitz [-Turrach]	2770	47.04 N	13.55 E
Pré-en-Pail	2772	48.27 N	0.12 W
Premont	2748	27.22 N	98.08 W
Prentice	2742	45.33 N	90.17 W
Prentiss	2746	31.36 N	89.52 W
Preparis North Channel ‿‿	2804	15.27 N	94.05 E
Preparis South Channel ‿‿	2804	14.40 N	94.00 E
Přerov	2770	49.27 N	17.27 E
Prescott, Ont., Can.	2740	44.43 N	75.31 W
Prescott, Ariz., U.S.	2752	34.33 N	112.28 W
Prescott, Ark., U.S.	2746	33.48 N	93.23 W
Presho	2750	43.54 N	100.04 W
Presidencia Roca	2764	26.08 S	59.36 W
Presidente Epitácio	2765	21.46 S	52.06 W
Presidente Prudente	2765	22.07 S	51.22 W
Presidio	2748	29.33 N	104.23 W
Prešov	2770	49.00 N	21.15 E
Presque Isle	2739	46.41 N	68.01 W
Preston, Eng., U.K.	2769	53.46 N	2.42 W
Preston, Idaho, U.S.	2754	42.06 N	111.53 W
Preston, Minn., U.S.	2742	43.40 N	92.05 W
Prestonsburg	2744	37.40 N	82.46 W
Pretoria	2788	25.45 S	28.10 E
Pretty Prairie	2750	37.47 N	98.01 W
Préveza	2778	38.57 N	20.44 E
Příbram	2770	49.42 N	14.01 E
Price	2752	39.36 N	110.48 W
Prichard	2746	30.44 N	88.07 W
Priego	2774	40.27 N	2.18 W
Priego de Córdoba	2774	37.26 N	4.11 W
Prieska	2788	29.40 S	22.42 E
Priest River	2754	48.11 N	116.55 W
Prievidza	2770	48.47 N	18.37 E
Prijedor	2776	44.59 N	16.43 E
Prikaspijskaja Nizmennost' ≚	2766	48.00 N	52.00 E
Prikumsk	2766	44.46 N	44.09 E
Prilep	2778	41.20 N	21.33 E
Priluki	2782	50.36 N	32.24 E
Primghar	2750	43.05 N	95.38 W
Primorsko-Achtarsk	2782	46.03 N	38.11 E
Primrose Lake ⊜	2734	54.55 N	109.45 W
Prince Albert	2734	53.12 N	105.46 W
Prince Albert Sound ‿‿	2734	70.25 N	115.00 W
Prince Charles Island I	2734	67.50 N	76.00 W

Symbols against index entries represent categories identified in the key on page 2810.

Name	Page	Lat ° ′	Long ° ′
Prince-de-Galles, Cap du ➤	2734	61.36 N	71.30 W
Prince Edward Island □4	2734	46.20 N	63.20 W
Prince Frederick	2740	38.33 N	76.35 W
Prince George	2734	53.55 N	122.45 W
Prince of Wales, Cape ➤	2738	65.40 N	168.05 W
Prince of Wales Island I, Austl.	2806	10.40 S	142.10 E
Prince of Wales Island I, N.W. Ter., Can.	2734	72.40 N	99.00 W
Prince of Wales Island I, Alaska, U.S.	2738	55.47 N	132.50 W
Prince of Wales Strait ⅄	2734	73.00 N	117.00 W
Prince Regent Inlet C	2734	73.00 N	90.30 W
Prince Rupert	2734	54.19 N	130.19 W
Princess Anne	2740	38.12 N	75.41 W
Princess Royal Island I	2734	52.57 N	128.49 W
Princeton, Ill., U.S.	2746	40.45 N	89.45 W
Princeton, Ind., U.S.	2746	38.21 N	87.34 W
Princeton, Ky., U.S.	2746	37.07 N	87.53 W
Princeton, Mo., U.S.	2746	40.24 N	93.35 W
Princeton, N.J., U.S.	2740	40.21 N	74.40 W
Princeton, W. Va., U.S.	2744	37.22 N	81.06 W
Princeton, Wis., U.S.	2742	43.51 N	89.08 W
Princeville	2740	46.10 N	71.53 W
Prince William Sound ⅄	2738	60.40 N	147.00 W
Príncipe I	2788	1.37 N	7.25 E
Príncipe da Beira	2762	12.25 S	64.25 W
Prineville	2754	44.18 N	120.51 W
Prinzapolca	2760	13.20 N	83.35 W
Priština	2778	42.39 N	21.10 E
Pritchett	2750	37.22 N	102.52 W
Privas	2772	44.44 N	4.36 E
Privolžsk	2780	57.23 N	41.17 E
Proctor	2740	43.40 N	73.02 W
Proddatūr	2793	14.44 N	78.33 E
Professor Dr. Ir. W.j. Van Blommestein Meer ⊜1	2762	4.45 N	55.05 W
Progreso	2758	21.17 N	89.40 W
Prokopjevsk	2784	53.53 N	86.45 E
Prokuplje	2778	43.14 N	21.36 E
Propriá	2762	10.13 S	36.51 W
Prospect	2740	40.27 N	83.11 W
Prosser	2754	46.12 N	119.46 W
Prostějov	2770	49.29 N	17.07 E
Protville	2776	36.54 N	10.01 E
Providence, Ky., U.S.	2746	37.24 N	87.39 W
Providence, R.I., U.S.	2740	41.50 N	71.25 W
Providence, Utah, U.S.	2752	41.43 N	111.49 W
Providence Island I	2788	9.14 S	51.02 E
Providencia	2748	27.06 N	103.32 W
Providencia, Isla de I	2760	13.21 N	81.22 W
Providenija	2784	64.23 N	173.18 W
Provincetown	2740	42.03 N	70.11 W
Provins	2772	48.33 N	3.18 E
Provo	2752	40.14 N	111.39 W
Prozor	2776	43.49 N	17.37 E
Prudhoe Bay C	2738	70.20 N	148.20 W
Pruszków	2770	52.11 N	20.48 E
Prut ≃	2778	45.27 N	28.12 E
Pryor	2748	36.19 N	95.19 W
Przemyśl	2770	49.47 N	22.47 E
Pskov	2780	57.50 N	28.20 E
Ptolemaís	2778	40.31 N	21.41 E
Ptuj	2776	46.25 N	15.52 E
Pucallpa	2762	8.20 S	74.30 W
Pucheng	2800	27.55 N	118.31 E
Pudukkottai	2793	10.23 N	78.49 E
Puebla de Sanabria	2774	42.03 N	6.38 W
Puebla de Trives	2774	42.20 N	7.15 W
Puebla [de Zaragoza]	2758	19.03 N	98.12 W
Pueblo	2752	38.16 N	104.37 W
Pueblo Hundido	2764	26.23 S	70.03 W
Puentedeume	2774	43.24 N	8.10 W
Puente-Genil	2774	37.23 N	4.47 W
Puerto Aisén	2764	45.24 S	72.42 W
Puerto Ángel	2758	15.40 N	96.29 W
Puerto Asís	2762	0.30 N	76.31 W
Puerto Barrios	2760	15.43 N	88.36 W
Puerto Berrío	2762	6.29 N	74.24 W
Puerto Cabello	2760	10.28 N	68.01 W
Puerto Cabezas	2760	14.02 N	83.24 W
Puerto Carreño	2762	6.12 N	67.22 W
Puerto Casado	2764	22.20 S	57.55 W
Puerto Chicama	2762	7.42 S	79.27 W
Puerto Cortés	2760	15.48 N	87.56 W
Puerto de Nutrias	2760	8.05 N	69.18 W
Puerto de Pollensa	2774	39.55 N	3.05 E
Puerto Deseado	2764	47.45 S	65.55 W
Puerto Escondido	2758	15.50 N	97.10 W
Puerto Juárez	2758	21.11 N	86.49 W
Puerto la Cruz	2760	10.13 N	64.38 W
Puerto Leguízamo	2762	0.12 S	74.46 W
Puertollano	2774	38.41 N	4.07 W
Puerto Lobos	2764	42.01 S	65.04 W
Puerto Madryn	2764	42.46 S	65.02 W
Puerto Maldonado	2762	12.36 S	69.11 W
Puerto Montt	2764	41.28 S	72.57 W
Puerto Natales	2764	51.44 S	72.31 W
Puerto Padre	2760	21.12 N	76.36 W
Puerto Peñasco	2758	31.20 N	113.33 W
Puerto Plata	2760	19.48 N	70.41 W
Puerto Princesa	2802	9.44 N	118.44 E
Puerto Real	2774	36.32 N	6.11 W
Puerto Rico □2	2760	18.15 N	66.30 W
Puerto Suárez	2762	18.57 S	57.51 W
Puerto Vallarta	2758	20.37 N	105.15 W
Puget Sound ⅄	2754	47.50 N	122.30 W
Puigcerdá	2774	42.26 N	1.56 E
Pukë	2778	42.03 N	19.54 E
Pukekohe	2808	37.12 S	174.55 E
Pukou	2800	32.07 N	118.43 E
Pula	2776	44.52 N	13.50 E
Pulacayo	2762	20.25 S	66.41 W
Pulaski, N.Y., U.S.	2740	43.34 N	76.08 W
Pulaski, Tenn., U.S.	2746	35.12 N	87.02 W
Pulaski, Va., U.S.	2744	37.03 N	80.47 W
Pulaski, Wis., U.S.	2742	44.41 N	88.14 W
Pulkkila	2768	64.16 N	25.52 E
Pullman	2754	46.44 N	117.10 W
Pulog, Mount ▲	2802	16.36 N	120.54 E
Pune (Poona)	2793	18.32 N	73.52 E
Puno	2762	15.50 S	70.02 W
Punta Alta	2764	38.53 S	62.04 W
Punta Arenas	2764	53.09 S	70.55 W
Punta Delgada	2764	42.43 S	63.38 W
Punta Gorda, Belize	2760	16.07 N	88.48 W
Punta Gorda, Fla., U.S.	2744	26.56 N	82.03 W
Puntarenas	2760	9.58 N	84.50 W
Punto Fijo	2760	11.42 N	70.13 W
Punxsutawney	2740	40.57 N	78.59 W
Puolanka	2768	64.52 N	27.40 E
Purcell	2748	35.01 N	97.22 W
Purgatoire Peak ▲	2752	37.04 N	105.13 W
Puri	2794	19.48 N	85.51 E
Purnea	2794	25.47 N	87.31 E
Purūlia	2794	23.20 N	86.22 E
Purus (Purús) ≃	2762	3.42 S	61.28 W
Purvis	2746	31.09 N	89.25 W
Purwakarta	2802	6.34 S	107.26 E
Pusan	2796	35.06 N	129.03 E
Puškin	2780	59.43 N	30.25 E
Puškino	2780	56.01 N	37.51 E
Putao	2796	27.21 N	97.24 E
Putian	2800	25.28 N	119.02 E
Puting, Tandjung ➤	2802	3.31 S	111.46 E
Putorana, Plato ⛰1	2784	69.00 N	95.00 E
Putumayo (Içá) ≃	2762	3.07 S	67.58 W
Puyallup	2754	47.11 N	122.18 W
Puy de Dôme ▲	2772	45.47 N	2.58 E
Puy de Sancy ▲	2772	45.32 N	2.49 E
Puylaurens	2772	43.34 N	2.01 E
Puyo	2762	1.28 S	77.59 W
Pweto	2788	8.28 S	28.54 E
Pwllheli	2769	52.53 N	4.25 W
Pyè (Prome)	2804	18.49 N	95.13 E
Pyhäjoki	2768	64.28 N	24.14 E
Pyhäselkä	2768	62.26 N	29.58 E
Pyinmana	2804	19.44 N	96.13 E
P'yŏngyang	2796	39.01 N	125.45 E
Pyramid Lake ⊜	2756	40.00 N	119.35 W
Pyrenees ⛰	2774	42.40 N	1.00 E
Pyskowice	2770	50.24 N	18.38 E
Q			
Qalāt	2794	32.07 N	66.54 E
Qal'at Bīshah	2790	20.01 N	42.36 E
Qal'eh-ye Kānsī	2792	34.32 N	65.15 E
Qallābāt	2786	12.58 N	36.09 E
Qamar, Ghubbat al- C	2790	16.00 N	52.30 E
Qandahār	2794	31.32 N	65.30 E
Qandala	2790	11.23 N	49.53 E
Qaṣr al-Burayqah	2786	30.25 N	19.34 E
Qaṣr al-Farāfirah	2786	27.03 N	27.58 E
Qaṭanā	2791	33.26 N	36.05 E
Qatar □1	2790	25.00 N	51.10 E
Qazvīn	2766	36.16 N	50.00 E
Qeshm I	2790	26.45 N	55.45 E
Qeẓi'ot	2791	30.53 N	34.27 E
Qiemo	2794	38.08 N	85.32 E
Qijiang	2796	29.02 N	106.39 E
Qilianshan ▲	2796	38.57 N	99.07 E
Qilinhu ⊜	2794	31.50 N	89.00 E
Qinā	2786	26.10 N	32.43 E
Qingdao (Tsingtao)	2796	36.06 N	120.19 E
Qinghai □4	2794	36.00 N	96.00 E
Qinghai ⊜	2796	36.50 N	100.20 E
Qingjiang	2800	28.05 N	115.29 E
Qingyang	2796	36.06 N	107.47 E
Qingyuan, Zhg.	2796	24.35 N	108.45 E
Qingyuan, Zhg.	2800	23.43 N	113.01 E
Qinhuangdao	2796	39.56 N	119.36 E
Qinlingshanmai ⛰	2796	34.00 N	108.00 E
Qinxian (Qinzhou)	2804	21.59 N	108.36 E
Qiongzhou haixia ⅄	2804	20.10 N	110.15 E
Qiqihaer (Tsitsihar)	2796	47.19 N	123.55 E
Qiryat Shemona	2791	33.13 N	35.34 E
Qīzān	2790	16.54 N	42.29 E
Qom	2790	34.39 N	50.54 E
Qondūz	2794	37.45 N	68.51 E
Qondūz ≃	2794	37.00 N	68.16 E
Quakertown	2740	40.26 N	75.21 W
Quanah	2748	34.18 N	99.44 W
Quantico	2740	38.31 N	77.17 W
Quanzhou	2800	24.54 N	118.35 E
Quartu Sant'Elena	2776	39.14 N	9.11 E
Quartz Hill	2756	34.39 N	118.13 W
Quartz Lake ⊜	2734	70.55 N	80.33 W
Quartzsite	2752	33.40 N	114.13 W
Québec	2739	46.49 N	71.14 W
Quebec (Québec) □4, Can.	2734	52.00 N	72.00 W
Québec □4, Can.	2736	52.00 N	72.00 W
Queen Charlotte Islands II	2734	53.00 N	132.00 W
Queen Charlotte Sound ⅄	2734	51.30 N	129.30 W
Queen Charlotte Strait ⅄	2734	50.50 N	127.25 W
Queen City	2746	40.25 N	92.34 W
Queen Maud Gulf C	2734	68.25 N	102.30 W
Queen Maud Land ⟞1	2733	72.30 S	12.00 E
Queens Channel II	2734	76.11 N	96.00 W
Queenstown, N.Z.	2808	45.02 S	168.40 E
Queenstown, S. Afr.	2788	31.52 S	26.52 E
Quelimane	2788	17.53 S	36.51 E
Quemado	2752	34.20 N	108.30 W
Que Que	2788	18.55 S	29.49 E
Querétaro	2758	20.36 N	100.23 W
Querobabi	2758	30.03 N	111.01 W
Quesnel	2734	52.59 N	122.30 W
Quesnel Lake ⊜	2734	52.32 N	121.05 W
Questa	2752	36.42 N	105.36 W
Questembert	2772	47.40 N	2.27 W
Quetta	2794	30.12 N	67.00 E
Quevedo	2762	1.02 S	79.29 W
Quezaltenango	2760	14.50 N	91.31 W
Quezon City	2802	14.38 N	121.00 E
Qufu	2796	35.36 N	117.02 E
Quibdó	2762	5.42 N	76.40 W
Quiberon	2772	47.29 N	3.07 W
Quilá	2758	24.23 N	107.13 W
Quilcene	2754	47.49 N	122.53 W
Quillan	2772	42.52 N	2.11 E
Quilon	2793	8.53 N	76.36 E
Quilpie	2806	26.37 S	144.15 E
Quimilí	2764	27.40 S	62.30 W
Quimper	2772	48.00 N	4.06 W
Quimperlé	2772	47.52 N	3.33 W
Quincemil	2762	13.15 S	70.40 W
Quincy, Calif., U.S.	2756	39.56 N	120.57 W
Quincy, Ill., U.S.	2746	39.56 N	91.23 W
Quincy, Mass., U.S.	2740	42.15 N	71.01 W
Quincy, Mich., U.S.	2742	41.57 N	84.53 W
Quincy, Wash., U.S.	2754	47.14 N	119.51 W
Quintanar de la Orden	2774	39.34 N	3.03 W
Quinter	2750	39.04 N	100.14 W
Quinton	2748	35.07 N	95.22 W
Quiroga	2774	42.29 N	7.16 W
Quitaque	2748	34.22 N	101.04 W
Quitman, Ga., U.S.	2744	30.47 N	83.33 W
Quitman, Miss., U.S.	2746	32.03 N	88.43 W
Quitman, Tex., U.S.	2748	32.48 N	95.27 W
Quito	2762	0.13 S	78.30 W
Quixadá	2762	4.58 S	39.01 W
Qujing	2804	25.32 N	103.41 E
Qulin	2746	36.36 N	90.15 W
Qumalai (Sewugou)	2794	34.35 N	95.27 E
Quoich ≃	2734	64.00 N	93.30 W
Qutdligssat	2734	70.04 N	53.01 W
Quthing	2788	30.30 S	27.36 E
Quxian	2800	28.58 N	118.52 E
R			
Raalte	2770	52.24 N	6.16 E
Rab	2776	44.46 N	14.46 E
Raba	2802	8.27 S	118.46 E
Rábade	2774	43.07 N	7.37 W
Rabat, Magreb	2786	34.02 N	6.51 W
Rabat (Victoria), Malta	2776	36.02 N	14.14 E
Rabat, Malta	2776	35.52 N	14.25 E
Rābigh	2790	22.48 N	39.01 E
Race, Cape ➤	2734	46.40 N	53.10 W
Raceland	2746	29.48 N	90.40 W
Rach-gia	2804	10.01 N	105.05 E
Racibórz (Ratibor)	2770	50.06 N	18.13 E
Racine	2742	42.43 N	87.48 W
Radcliff	2746	37.51 N	85.57 W
Radeče	2776	46.04 N	15.11 E
Radom	2770	51.25 N	21.10 E
Radomsko	2770	51.05 N	19.25 E
Rae	2734	62.50 N	116.03 W
Raeford	2744	34.59 N	79.14 W
Rae Isthmus ⊥3	2734	66.55 N	86.10 W
Rae Strait ⅄	2734	68.45 N	95.00 W
Raetihi	2808	39.26 S	175.17 E
Rafaela	2764	31.17 S	61.30 W
Rafaḥ	2791	31.18 N	34.15 E
Rafḥā'	2790	29.42 N	43.30 E
Rafsanjān	2790	30.24 N	56.01 E
Raga	2786	8.28 N	25.41 E
Ragusa, It.	2776	36.55 N	14.44 E
Ragusa → Dubrovnik, Jugo.	2776	42.38 N	18.07 E
Rahīmyār Khān	2794	28.25 N	70.18 E
Rāichūr	2793	16.12 N	77.22 E
Raigarh	2793	21.54 N	83.24 E
Rainelle	2744	37.58 N	80.47 W
Rainier, Mount ▲	2754	46.52 N	121.46 W
Rainy Lake ⊜	2734	48.42 N	93.10 W
Raipur	2794	21.14 N	81.38 E
Raja, Bukit ▲	2802	0.40 S	112.41 E
Rājahmundry	2793	16.59 N	81.47 E
Raja-Jooseppi	2768	68.28 N	28.21 E
Rājapālaiyam	2793	9.27 N	77.34 E
Rajčichinsk	2784	49.46 N	129.25 E
Rājkot	2794	22.18 N	70.47 E
Rāj-Nāndgaon	2793	21.06 N	81.02 E
Rājshāhi	2794	24.22 N	88.36 E
Råkvåg	2768	63.46 N	10.05 E
Raleigh, Miss., U.S.	2746	32.02 N	89.30 W
Raleigh, N.C., U.S.	2744	35.47 N	78.39 W
Ralls	2748	33.41 N	101.23 W
Rama	2760	12.09 N	84.15 W
Ramah	2752	35.08 N	108.30 W
Rām Allāh	2791	31.54 N	35.12 E
Rambouillet	2772	48.39 N	1.50 E
Ramenskoje	2780	55.34 N	38.14 E
Ramer	2746	32.03 N	86.13 W
Rāmeswaram	2793	9.17 N	79.18 E
Ramírez	2748	25.57 N	97.46 W
Ramla	2791	31.55 N	34.52 E
Ramlo ▲	2790	13.20 N	41.45 E
Ramona, Calif., U.S.	2756	33.08 N	116.52 W
Ramona, Okla., U.S.	2748	36.32 N	95.55 W
Rāmpur	2794	28.49 N	79.02 E
Ramree Island I	2804	19.06 N	93.48 E
Ramseur	2744	35.44 N	79.39 W
Ramsey	2769	54.20 N	4.21 W
Ramsgate	2769	51.20 N	1.25 E
Rancagua	2764	34.10 S	70.45 W
Rancharia	2765	22.15 S	50.55 W
Ranches of Taos	2752	36.22 N	105.37 W
Ranchester	2754	44.54 N	107.16 W
Rānchī	2794	23.21 N	85.20 E
Rancho Cordova	2756	38.36 N	121.17 W
Rancho Nuevo	2748	26.22 N	99.54 W
Randazzo	2776	37.53 N	14.57 E
Randers	2768	56.28 N	10.03 E
Randleman	2744	35.49 N	79.48 W
Randolph, Nebr., U.S.	2750	42.23 N	97.21 W
Randolph, Vt., U.S.	2740	43.55 N	72.40 W
Randolph, Wis., U.S.	2742	43.35 N	89.00 W
Rangeley	2740	44.58 N	70.39 W
Rangely	2752	40.05 N	108.48 W
Ranger	2748	32.28 N	98.41 W
Rangoon	2804	16.47 N	96.10 E
Rangpur	2794	25.45 N	89.15 E
Rankin	2748	31.13 N	101.56 W
Rankin Inlet	2734	62.45 N	92.10 W
Rann of Kutch ≚	2794	24.00 N	70.00 E
Ransom	2750	38.38 N	99.56 W
Rantauprapat	2804	2.06 N	99.50 E
Rantekombola, Bulu ▲	2802	3.21 S	120.01 E
Rantoul	2746	40.19 N	88.09 W
Raoping	2800	23.43 N	117.01 E
Rapallo	2776	44.21 N	9.14 E
Rapid City	2750	44.05 N	103.14 W
Rapid River	2742	45.56 N	86.58 W
Ra's al-'Ayn	2791	36.51 N	40.04 E
Ra's an-Naqb	2791	30.00 N	35.29 E
Ras Dashen ▲	2790	13.10 N	38.26 E
Ras Djebel	2776	37.13 N	10.09 E
Rasht	2766	37.16 N	49.36 E
Raspberry Peak ▲	2746	34.23 N	94.01 W
Rasskazovo	2780	52.40 N	41.53 E
Rätansbyn	2768	62.29 N	14.32 E
Rat Buri	2802	13.32 N	99.49 E
Rathbun Lake ⊜1	2742	40.54 N	93.05 W
Rathkeale	2769	52.32 N	8.56 W
Rathlin Island I	2769	55.18 N	6.13 W
Ratlām	2794	23.19 N	75.04 E
Ratnāgiri	2793	16.59 N	73.18 E
Raton	2748	36.54 N	104.24 W
Rattlesnake Hills ⛰2	2754	42.45 N	107.10 W
Rättvik	2768	60.53 N	15.06 E
Ratz, Mount ▲	2734	57.23 N	132.19 W
Rauch	2764	36.47 S	59.05 W
Rauma	2768	61.08 N	21.30 E
Rauma ≃	2768	62.33 N	7.43 E
Raurkela	2794	22.13 N	84.53 E
Ravena	2740	42.29 N	73.49 W
Ravenna, It.	2776	44.25 N	12.12 E
Ravenna, Nebr., U.S.	2750	41.02 N	98.55 W
Ravenna, Ohio, U.S.	2740	41.09 N	81.15 W
Ravenshoe	2806	17.37 S	145.29 E
Ravensthorpe	2806	33.35 S	120.02 E
Ravenswood	2740	38.57 N	81.46 W
Rāwalpindi	2794	33.36 N	73.04 E
Rawlinna	2806	31.01 S	125.20 E
Rawlins	2754	41.47 N	107.14 W
Rawson	2764	43.18 S	65.06 W
Raxaul	2792	26.59 N	84.51 E
Ray, Ariz., U.S.	2752	33.11 N	111.00 W
Ray, N. Dak., U.S.	2750	48.21 N	103.10 W
Raymond, Miss., U.S.	2746	32.15 N	90.25 W
Raymond, Wash., U.S.	2754	46.41 N	123.44 W
Raymondville	2748	26.29 N	97.47 W
Rayne	2746	30.14 N	92.16 W
Raytown	2746	39.00 N	94.28 W
Rayville	2746	32.28 N	91.45 W
R'azan'	2780	54.38 N	39.44 E
Razgrad	2778	43.32 N	26.31 E
R'ažsk	2780	53.43 N	40.04 E
Reading, Eng., U.K.	2769	51.28 N	0.59 W
Reading, Ohio, U.S.	2740	39.14 N	84.27 W
Reading, Pa., U.S.	2740	40.20 N	75.56 W
Readstown	2742	43.27 N	90.45 W
Realicó	2764	35.02 S	64.16 W
Réalmont	2772	43.47 N	2.12 E
Recanati	2776	43.24 N	13.32 E
Recherche, Archipelago of the II	2806	34.05 S	122.45 E
Rečica	2780	52.22 N	30.25 E
Recife	2762	8.03 S	34.54 W
Recreo	2764	29.20 S	65.04 W
Red (Hong) (Yuanjiang) ≃, As.	2804	20.17 N	106.34 E
Red ≃, N.A.	2736	50.24 N	96.48 W
Red ≃, U.S.	2758	31.00 N	91.48 W
Red ≃, Idaho, U.S.	2754	45.48 N	115.28 W
Red Bank, N.J., U.S.	2740	40.21 N	74.03 W
Red Bank, Tenn., U.S.	2746	35.07 N	85.17 W
Red Bay	2746	34.27 N	88.09 W
Red Bluff	2756	40.11 N	122.15 W
Red Bud	2746	38.13 N	89.59 W
Redcliff	2752	39.31 N	106.22 W
Redcliffe, Mount ▲	2806	28.25 S	121.32 E
Red Cloud	2750	40.05 N	98.32 W
Red Deer	2734	52.16 N	113.48 W
Red Deer ≃, Can.	2734	52.53 N	101.01 W
Red Deer ≃, Can.	2734	50.56 N	109.54 W
Redding	2756	40.35 N	122.24 W
Redfield, Iowa, U.S.	2750	41.35 N	94.12 W
Redfield, S. Dak., U.S.	2750	44.53 N	98.31 W
Redford	2748	29.47 N	104.10 W
Red Lake	2734	51.03 N	93.49 W
Red Lake Falls	2750	47.53 N	96.16 W
Redlands	2756	34.03 N	117.11 W
Red Lion	2740	39.54 N	76.36 W
Red Lodge	2754	45.11 N	109.15 W
Redmond	2754	44.17 N	121.11 W
Redmond Reservoir ⊜1	2750	38.18 N	95.55 W
Red Oak	2750	41.01 N	95.14 W
Redon	2772	47.39 N	2.05 W
Redondela	2774	42.17 N	8.36 W
Redondo	2774	38.39 N	7.33 W
Red Sea ⊽2	2790	20.00 N	38.00 E
Red Springs	2744	34.49 N	79.11 W
Redwing	2742	44.34 N	92.31 W
Redwood City	2756	37.29 N	122.13 W
Redwood Falls	2750	44.32 N	95.07 W
Redwood Valley	2756	39.16 N	123.12 W

Symbols against index entries represent categories identified in the key on page 2810.

Name	Page	Lat °′	Long °′
Ree, Lough ⊜	2769	53.35 N	8.00 W
Reed City	2742	43.53 N	85.31 W
Reeder	2750	46.06 N	102.57 W
Reedley	2756	36.36 N	119.27 W
Reedsburg	2742	43.32 N	90.00 W
Reedsport	2754	43.42 N	124.06 W
Reese	2742	43.27 N	83.42 W
Reform	2746	33.23 N	88.01 W
Refugio	2748	28.18 N	97.17 W
Regencia	2765	19.36 S	39.49 W
Reggane	2786	26.42 N	0.10 E
Reggio di Calabria	2776	38.07 N	15.39 E
Reggio nell'Emilia	2776	44.43 N	10.36 E
Regina	2734	50.25 N	104.39 W
Rehoboth, S.W. Afr.	2788	17.53 S	15.04 E
Rehoboth, S.W. Afr.	2788	23.18 S	17.03 E
Rehoboth Beach	2740	38.43 N	75.05 W
Reḥovot	2791	31.54 N	34.49 E
Reidsville, Ga., U.S.	2744	32.06 N	82.07 W
Reidsville, N.C., U.S.	2744	36.21 N	79.40 W
Reims	2772	49.15 N	4.02 E
Reina Adelaida, Archipiélago II	2764	52.20 S	74.50 W
Reinbeck	2742	42.19 N	92.36 W
Reindeer Lake ⊜	2734	57.15 N	102.40 W
Reinosa	2774	43.00 N	4.08 W
Reisterstown	2740	39.28 N	76.50 W
Remada	2786	32.19 N	10.24 E
Remanso	2762	9.41 S	42.04 W
Remiremont	2772	48.01 N	6.35 E
Rend Lake ⊜[1]	2746	38.05 N	88.58 W
Rendova I	2806	8.32 S	157.20 E
Rendsburg	2770	54.18 N	9.40 E
Renfrew	2740	45.28 N	76.41 W
Renick	2740	38.00 N	80.22 W
Rennell Island I	2806	11.40 S	160.10 E
Rennes	2772	48.05 N	1.41 W
Reno	2756	39.31 N	119.48 W
Renovo	2740	41.20 N	77.38 W
Rensselaer, Ind., U.S.	2746	40.57 N	87.09 W
Rensselaer, N.Y., U.S.	2740	42.39 N	73.44 W
Renville	2750	44.48 N	95.13 W
Reo	2802	8.19 S	120.30 E
Republic	2754	48.39 N	118.44 W
Republican ≃	2736	39.03 N	96.48 W
Repulse Bay	2734	66.32 N	86.15 W
Repvåg	2768	70.45 N	25.41 E
Reserve, La., U.S.	2746	30.04 N	90.34 W
Reserve, N. Mex., U.S.	2752	33.43 N	108.45 W
Resistencia	2764	27.30 S	58.59 W
Reşiţa	2778	45.17 N	21.53 E
Resolute	2734	74.41 N	94.54 W
Resolution Island I	2734	61.30 N	65.00 W
Resülhınzır ➤	2791	36.22 N	35.45 E
Rethel	2772	49.31 N	4.22 E
Réthimnon	2778	35.22 N	24.29 E
Reunion (Réunion) □[2]	2788	21.06 S	55.36 E
Reus	2774	41.09 N	1.07 E
Revda	2766	67.55 N	34.30 E
Revelstoke	2734	50.59 N	118.12 W
Revillagigedo, Islas de II	2758	19.00 N	111.30 W
Revillo	2750	45.01 N	96.34 W
Revin	2772	49.56 N	4.38 E
Rewa	2794	24.32 N	81.18 E
Rexburg	2754	43.49 N	111.47 W
Rey	2766	35.35 N	51.25 E
Rey, Laguna del ⊜	2748	27.02 N	103.25 W
Reyes	2762	14.19 S	67.23 W
Reyes, Point ➤	2756	38.00 N	123.01 W
Reyhanlı	2791	36.18 N	36.32 E
Reykjavík	2766	64.09 N	21.51 W
Reynosa	2758	26.07 N	98.18 W
Reẕā'īyeh	2766	37.33 N	45.04 E
Reẕā'īyeh, Daryācheh-ye ⊜	2766	37.40 N	45.30 E
Rēzekne	2780	56.30 N	27.19 E
Rhaetian Alps ⛰	2776	46.30 N	10.00 E
Rhine (Rhein) (Rhin) ≃	2770	51.52 N	6.02 E
Rhinebeck	2740	41.56 N	73.55 W
Rhinelander	2742	45.38 N	89.25 W
Rho	2776	45.32 N	9.02 E
Rhode Island □[3]	2736	41.40 N	71.30 W
Rhodes → Ródhos	2778	36.26 N	28.13 E
Rhodesia □[1]	2788	20.00 S	30.00 E
Rhodope Mountains ⛰	2778	41.30 N	24.30 E
Rhondda	2769	51.40 N	3.27 W
Rhône ≃	2772	43.20 N	4.50 E
Riau, Kepulauan II	2804	1.00 N	104.30 E
Riaza	2774	41.17 N	3.28 W
Ribadeo	2774	43.32 N	7.02 W
Ribadesella	2774	43.28 N	5.04 W
Ribeirão Prêto	2765	21.10 S	47.48 W
Ribera	2776	37.30 N	13.16 E
Riberalta	2762	10.59 S	66.06 W
Riccione	2776	43.59 N	12.39 E
Rice	2748	32.15 N	96.30 W
Rice Lake	2742	45.30 N	91.44 W
Riceville	2742	43.22 N	92.33 W
Richards Island I	2734	69.20 N	134.30 W
Richardson	2748	32.57 N	96.44 W
Richardson Mountains ⛰	2734	67.15 N	136.30 W
Richardton	2750	46.53 N	102.19 W
Richey	2750	47.39 N	105.04 W
Richfield, Idaho, U.S.	2754	43.03 N	114.09 W
Richfield, Utah, U.S.	2752	38.46 N	112.05 W
Richfield Springs	2740	42.51 N	74.59 W
Rich Hill	2746	38.06 N	94.22 W
Richland, Ga., U.S.	2744	32.06 N	84.39 W
Richland, Mo., U.S.	2746	37.51 N	92.26 W
Richland, Tex., U.S.	2748	31.56 N	96.26 W
Richland, Wash., U.S.	2754	46.17 N	119.18 W
Richland Center	2742	43.20 N	90.23 W
Richlands	2744	37.06 N	81.48 W
Richmond, Austl.	2806	20.44 S	143.08 E
Richmond, Calif., U.S.	2756	37.57 N	122.22 W
Richmond, Ind., U.S.	2746	39.50 N	84.54 W
Richmond, Ky., U.S.	2744	37.45 N	84.18 W
Richmond, Mo., U.S.	2746	39.17 N	93.58 W
Richmond, Tex., U.S.	2748	29.35 N	95.46 W
Richmond, Utah, U.S.	2752	41.55 N	111.48 W
Richmond, Vt., U.S.	2740	44.24 N	72.59 W
Richmond, Va., U.S.	2744	37.30 N	77.28 W
Richmond Hill, Ont., Can.	2740	43.52 N	79.27 W
Richmond Hill, Ga., U.S.	2744	31.56 N	81.18 W
Richmondville	2740	42.38 N	74.34 W
Richwood	2740	38.14 N	80.32 W
Riddle	2754	42.57 N	123.22 W
Riddle Mountain ▲	2754	43.07 N	118.30 W
Ridgecrest	2756	35.38 N	117.36 W
Ridgefield	2740	41.17 N	73.30 W
Ridgeland	2744	32.29 N	80.59 W
Ridgway, Colo., U.S.	2752	38.09 N	107.46 W
Ridgway, Pa., U.S.	2740	41.26 N	78.44 W
Ried im Innkreis	2770	48.13 N	13.30 E
Riesi	2776	37.17 N	14.05 E
Rieti	2776	42.24 N	12.51 E
Rif ⛰	2786	35.00 N	4.00 W
Rift Valley V	2788	3.00 S	29.00 E
Rīga	2780	56.57 N	24.06 E
Rigby	2754	43.40 N	111.55 W
Rīgestān -•-[1]	2794	31.00 N	65.00 E
Riggins	2754	45.25 N	116.19 W
Rigolet	2734	54.20 N	58.35 W
Riihimäki	2768	60.45 N	24.46 E
Rijeka	2776	45.20 N	14.27 E
Rikaze	2794	29.17 N	88.53 E
Riley	2750	39.18 N	96.50 W
Rimersburg	2740	41.02 N	79.30 W
Rimini	2776	44.04 N	12.34 E
Rimouski	2739	48.26 N	68.33 W
Rincon, Ga., U.S.	2744	32.18 N	81.14 W
Rincon, N. Mex., U.S.	2752	32.40 N	107.04 W
Rindal	2768	63.03 N	9.13 E
Ringebu	2768	61.31 N	10.10 E
Ringgold	2746	32.20 N	93.17 W
Riobamba	2762	1.40 S	78.38 W
Río Benito	2786	1.35 N	9.37 E
Rio Branco	2762	9.58 S	67.48 W
Río Bravo, Méx.	2748	28.17 N	100.55 W
Río Bravo, Méx.	2748	25.59 N	98.06 W
Rio Claro	2765	22.24 S	47.33 W
Río Colorado	2764	39.01 S	64.05 W
Río Cuarto	2764	33.08 S	64.20 W
Rio de Janeiro	2765	22.54 S	43.15 W
Rio Dell	2756	40.30 N	124.07 W
Rio do Sul	2764	27.13 S	49.39 W
Río Gallegos	2764	51.37 S	69.10 W
Río Grande, Arg.	2764	53.50 S	67.40 W
Rio Grande, Bra.	2764	32.02 S	52.05 W
Río Grande, Méx.	2758	23.50 N	103.02 W
Rio Grande City	2748	26.23 N	98.49 W
Ríohacha	2760	11.33 N	72.55 W
Rio Hondo	2748	26.14 N	97.35 W
Rioja	2762	6.03 S	77.05 W
Riom	2772	45.54 N	3.07 E
Río Mayo	2764	45.40 S	70.15 W
Río Negro, Embalse del ⊜[1]	2764	32.45 S	56.00 W
Rio Negro, Pantanal do ☲	2762	19.00 S	56.00 W
Rionero in Vulture	2776	40.56 N	15.41 E
Rio Pardo	2764	29.59 S	52.22 W
Rio Pardo de Minas	2762	15.37 S	42.33 W
Rio Verde, Bra.	2765	17.43 S	50.56 W
Ríoverde, Méx.	2758	21.56 N	99.59 W
Rio Vista	2756	38.10 N	121.42 W
Rioz	2772	47.25 N	6.04 E
Ripley, Miss., U.S.	2746	34.44 N	88.57 W
Ripley, N.Y., U.S.	2740	42.16 N	79.43 W
Ripley, Ohio, U.S.	2740	38.45 N	83.51 W
Ripley, Tenn., U.S.	2746	35.45 N	89.32 W
Ripley, W. Va., U.S.	2740	38.49 N	81.43 W
Ripoll	2774	42.12 N	2.12 E
Ripon, Eng., U.K.	2769	54.08 N	1.31 W
Ripon, Wis., U.S.	2742	43.51 N	88.50 W
Rishon leZiyyon	2791	31.58 N	34.48 E
Rising Star	2748	32.06 N	98.58 W
Rison	2746	33.58 N	92.11 W
Rittman	2740	40.58 N	81.47 W
Ritzville	2754	47.08 N	118.23 W
Riva	2776	45.53 N	10.50 E
Rivas	2760	11.26 N	85.51 W
Rivera	2764	30.54 S	55.31 W
Riverbank	2756	37.44 N	120.56 E
River Falls	2742	44.52 N	92.38 W
Riverhead	2740	40.55 N	72.40 W
Riverside	2756	33.59 N	117.22 W
Rivers Inlet	2734	51.41 N	127.15 W
Riverton, Ill., U.S.	2746	39.51 N	89.33 W
Riverton, Wyo., U.S.	2754	43.02 N	108.23 W
Riverton Heights	2754	47.28 N	122.17 W
Rivesaltes	2772	42.46 N	2.52 E
Rivesville	2740	39.32 N	80.07 W
Riviera	2748	27.18 N	97.49 W
Riviera Beach	2744	26.47 N	80.04 W
Rivière-du-Loup	2739	47.50 N	69.32 W
Rivoli	2776	45.04 N	7.31 E
Rize	2766	41.02 N	40.31 E
Rizokárpason	2791	35.36 N	34.23 E
Rižskij Zaliv C	2780	57.30 N	23.35 E
Roa	2774	41.42 N	3.55 W
Roanne	2772	46.02 N	4.04 E
Roanoke, Ala., U.S.	2746	33.09 N	85.22 W
Roanoke, Ind., U.S.	2746	40.58 N	85.22 W
Roanoke, Va., U.S.	2744	37.16 N	79.57 W
Roanoke Rapids	2744	36.28 N	77.40 W
Roaring Spring	2740	40.20 N	78.24 W
Roatán, Isla de I	2760	16.23 N	86.26 W
Robbinsville	2744	35.19 N	83.48 W
Robeline	2746	31.41 N	93.18 W
Robersonville	2744	35.50 N	77.15 W
Roberta	2744	32.43 N	84.01 W
Robert Lee	2748	31.54 N	100.29 W
Roberts	2754	43.43 N	112.08 W
Robertsfors	2768	64.11 N	20.51 E
Roberts Peak ▲	2734	52.57 N	120.32 W
Robertsport	2786	6.45 N	11.22 W
Roberval	2734	48.31 N	72.13 W
Robinson	2746	39.00 N	87.44 W
Roboré	2762	18.20 S	59.45 W
Robson, Mount ▲	2734	53.07 N	119.09 W
Robstown	2748	27.47 N	97.40 W
Roby	2748	32.45 N	100.23 W
Roçadas	2788	16.43 S	15.01 E
Rocas, Atol das I[1]	2762	3.52 S	33.59 W
Roccastrada	2776	43.00 N	11.10 E
Rocha	2764	34.29 S	54.20 W
Rochdale	2769	53.38 N	2.09 W
Rochefort	2772	45.57 N	0.58 W
Rochelle, Ga., U.S.	2744	31.57 N	83.27 W
Rochelle, Ill., U.S.	2746	41.56 N	89.04 W
Rochester, Ind., U.S.	2746	41.04 N	86.13 W
Rochester, Mich., U.S.	2742	42.41 N	83.08 W
Rochester, Minn , U.S.	2742	44.02 N	92.29 W
Rochester, N.H., U.S.	2740	43.18 N	70.59 W
Rochester, N.Y., U.S.	2740	43.10 N	77.36 W
Rockall I	2766	57.35 N	13.48 W
Rock Creek Butte ▲	2754	44.49 N	118.07 W
Rockdale	2748	30.39 N	97.00 W
Rock Falls	2746	41.47 N	89.41 W
Rockford, Ala., U.S.	2746	32.53 N	86.13 W
Rockford, Ill., U.S.	2742	42.17 N	89.06 W
Rockford, Mich., U.S.	2742	43.07 N	85.33 W
Rockhampton	2806	23.23 S	150.31 E
Rock Hill	2744	34.56 N	81.01 W
Rockingham	2744	34.56 N	79.46 W
Rocklake	2750	48.47 N	99.15 W
Rockland, Ont., Can.	2740	45.33 N	75.17 W
Rockland, Idaho, U.S.	2754	42.34 N	112.53 W
Rockland, Maine, U.S.	2740	44.06 N	69.06 W
Rockledge	2744	28.20 N	80.43 W
Rocklin	2756	38.48 N	121.14 W
Rockmart	2744	34.00 N	85.02 W
Rockport, Ky., U.S.	2746	37.20 N	86.59 W
Rock Port, Mo., U.S.	2746	40.25 N	95.31 W
Rockport, Tex., U.S.	2748	28.01 N	97.04 W
Rock Rapids	2750	43.26 N	96.10 W
Rocksprings, Tex., U.S.	2748	30.01 N	100.13 W
Rock Springs, Wyo., U.S.	2754	41.35 N	109.13 W
Rock Valley	2750	43.12 N	96.18 W
Rockville, Ind., U.S.	2746	39.46 N	87.14 W
Rockville, Md., U.S.	2740	39.05 N	77.09 W
Rockwall	2748	32.56 N	96.28 W
Rockwell City	2750	42.24 N	94.38 W
Rockwood	2744	35.52 N	84.41 W
Rocky Ford	2750	38.03 N	103.43 W
Rocky Mount, N.C., U.S.	2744	35.56 N	77.48 W
Rocky Mount, Va., U.S.	2744	37.00 N	79.54 W
Rocky Mountain ▲	2754	47.49 N	112.49 W
Rocky Mountain House	2734	52.22 N	114.55 W
Rocky Mountain National Park ♠	2752	40.19 N	105.42 W
Rocky Mountains ⛰	2736	48.00 N	116.00 W
Rodeo	2752	31.50 N	109.02 W
Rodez	2772	44.21 N	2.35 E
Ródhos (Rhodes)	2778	36.26 N	28.13 E
Ródhos I	2778	36.10 N	28.00 E
Rodniki	2780	57.06 N	41.44 E
Roebourne	2806	20.47 S	117.09 E
Roeselare	2770	50.57 N	3.08 E
Roes Welcome Sound ⵯ	2734	64.00 N	88.00 W
Rogagua, Lago ⊜	2762	13.43 S	66.54 W
Rogers, Ark., U.S.	2746	36.20 N	94.07 W
Rogers, Tex., U.S.	2748	30.56 N	97.14 W
Rogers City	2742	45.25 N	83.49 W
Rogersville, Ala., U.S.	2746	34.50 N	87.17 W
Rogersville, Tenn., U.S.	2744	36.25 N	83.02 W
Roggiano Gravina	2776	39.37 N	16.09 E
Rogliano	2776	42.57 N	9.25 E
Rogue River	2754	42.26 N	123.10 W
Rohtak	2794	28.54 N	76.34 E
Roland	2746	34.54 N	92.30 W
Røldal	2768	59.49 N	6.48 E
Rolette	2750	48.40 N	99.51 W
Rolla, Kans., U.S.	2750	37.07 N	101.38 W
Rolla, Mo., U.S.	2746	37.57 N	91.46 W
Rolla, N. Dak., U.S.	2750	48.52 N	99.37 W
Rolling Fork	2746	32.55 N	90.52 W
Roma (Rome)	2776	41.54 N	12.29 E
Roman	2778	46.55 N	26.56 E
Romania (România) □[1]	2766	46.00 N	25.30 E
Romans[-sur-Isère]	2772	45.03 N	5.03 E
Rome → Roma, It.	2776	41.54 N	12.29 E
Rome, Ga., U.S.	2744	34.16 N	85.11 W
Rome, N.Y., U.S.	2740	43.13 N	75.27 W
Romeo	2742	42.48 N	83.01 W
Romilly-sur-Seine	2772	48.31 N	3.43 E
Romney	2740	39.21 N	78.45 W
Romny	2782	50.45 N	33.30 E
Romorantin-Lanthenay	2772	47.22 N	1.45 E
Ronan	2754	47.32 N	114.06 W
Roncador, Serra do ⛰[1]	2765	12.00 S	52.00 W
Roncesvalles	2774	43.01 N	1.19 W
Ronceverte	2744	37.45 N	80.28 W
Ronda	2774	36.44 N	5.10 W
Rondônia	2762	10.52 S	61.57 W
Rondonópolis	2765	16.28 S	54.38 W
Ronge, Lac la ⊜	2734	55.10 N	105.00 W
Rønne	2768	55.06 N	14.42 E
Ronneby	2768	56.12 N	15.18 E
Ronne Ice Shelf ⛿	2733	78.30 S	61.00 W
Ronse	2770	50.45 N	3.36 E
Roof Butte ▲	2752	36.28 N	109.05 W
Roorkee	2794	29.52 N	77.53 E
Roosendaal	2770	51.32 N	4.28 E
Roosevelt	2752	40.18 N	109.59 W
Roosevelt ≃	2762	7.35 S	60.20 W
Roosevelt Lake ⊜[1]	2752	33.42 N	111.07 W
Ropesville	2748	33.26 N	102.09 W
Roquefort	2772	44.02 N	0.19 W
Roraima, Mount ▲	2762	5.12 N	60.44 W
Røros	2768	62.35 N	11.20 E
Rorschach	2772	47.29 N	9.30 E
Rørvik	2768	64.51 N	11.14 E
Rošal'	2780	55.40 N	39.51 E
Rosamond	2756	34.52 N	118.10 W
Rosamorada	2758	22.08 N	105.12 W
Rosario, Arg.	2764	32.57 S	60.40 W
Rosário, Bra.	2762	2.57 S	44.14 W
Rosario, Méx.	2758	30.01 N	115.40 W
Rosario, Méx.	2758	23.00 N	105.52 W
Rosário Oeste	2762	14.50 S	56.25 W
Rosarito	2756	32.20 N	117.02 W
Rosarno	2776	38.29 N	15.59 E
Rosas, Golfo de C	2774	42.10 N	3.15 E
Roscoe, S. Dak., U.S.	2750	45.27 N	99.20 W
Roscoe, Tex., U.S.	2748	32.27 N	100.32 W
Roscommon, Eire	2769	53.38 N	8.11 W
Roscommon, Mich., U.S.	2742	44.30 N	84.35 W
Roscrea	2769	52.57 N	7.47 W
Roseau, Dom.	2760	15.18 N	61.24 W
Roseau, Minn , U.S.	2750	48.51 N	95.46 W
Rosebud, S. Dak., U.S.	2750	43.14 N	100.51 W
Rosebud, Tex., U.S.	2748	31.04 N	96.59 W
Roseburg	2754	43.13 N	123.20 W
Rose City	2742	44.25 N	84.07 W
Rosedale	2746	33.51 N	91.02 W
Rose Hill	2744	34.50 N	78.02 W
Rosenberg	2748	29.33 N	95.48 W
Rose Peak ▲	2752	33.26 N	109.22 W
Rosetown	2734	51.33 N	108.00 W
Roseville, Calif., U.S.	2756	38.45 N	121.17 W
Roseville, Mich., U.S.	2742	42.30 N	82.56 W
Roseville, Minn , U.S.	2742	45.01 N	93.09 W
Rosholt, S. Dak., U.S.	2750	45.52 N	96.44 W
Rosholt, Wis., U.S.	2742	44.38 N	89.18 W
Rosignano Marittimo	2776	43.24 N	10.28 E
Roskilde	2768	55.39 N	12.05 E
Roslags-Näsby	2768	59.26 N	18.04 E
Roslavl'	2780	53.57 N	32.52 E
Rosman	2744	35.03 N	82.49 W
Rossano	2776	39.35 N	16.39 E
Rossan Point ➤	2769	54.42 N	8.48 W
Rossel Island I	2806	11.21 S	154.09 E
Ross Ice Shelf ⛿	2733	81.30 S	175.00 W
Rossijskaja Sovetskaja Federativnaja Socialist □[3]	2784	60.00 N	100.00 E
Ross Lake National Recreation Area ♠	2754	48.45 N	121.00 W
Rosslare	2769	52.17 N	6.23 W
Rosso	2786	16.30 N	15.49 W
Rossoš'	2782	50.12 N	39.34 E
Ross River	2734	61.59 N	132.27 W
Ross Sea ▾[2]	2733	76.00 S	175.00 W
Rossville	2746	40.23 N	87.40 W
Rostov	2780	57.11 N	39.25 E
Rostov-na-Donu	2782	47.14 N	39.42 E
Roswell	2748	33.24 N	104.32 W
Rota I	2802	14.10 N	145.12 E
Rotan	2748	32.51 N	100.28 W
Rothschild	2742	44.54 N	89.50 W
Roti, Pulau I	2802	10.45 S	123.10 E
Rotondella	2776	40.10 N	16.32 E
Rotorua	2808	38.09 S	176.15 E
Rotterdam, Ned.	2770	51.55 N	4.28 E
Rotterdam, N.Y., U.S.	2740	42.48 N	74.01 W
Roubaix	2772	50.42 N	3.10 E
Rouen	2772	49.26 N	1.05 E
Rough River Reservoir ⊜[1]	2746	37.40 N	86.25 W
Round Mountain	2756	38.43 N	117.04 W
Round Rock	2748	30.31 N	97.41 W
Roundup	2754	46.27 N	108.33 W
Rouses Point	2740	45.00 N	73.22 W
Rouyn	2734	48.15 N	79.01 W
Rovaniemi	2768	66.34 N	25.48 E
Rovato	2776	45.34 N	10.00 E
Rovereto	2776	45.53 N	11.02 E
Rovigo	2776	45.04 N	11.47 E
Rovinj	2776	45.05 N	13.38 E
Rovno	2782	50.37 N	26.15 E
Rowland	2744	34.32 N	79.18 W
Rowley Island I	2734	69.08 N	78.50 W
Rowley Shoals ⊹[2]	2806	17.30 S	119.00 E
Roxboro	2744	36.24 N	78.59 W
Roxie	2746	31.30 N	91.04 W
Roy, N. Mex., U.S.	2748	35.57 N	104.12 W
Roy, Utah, U.S.	2752	41.10 N	112.02 W
Royal Canal ☲	2769	53.21 N	6.15 W
Royale, Isle I	2742	48.00 N	89.00 W
Royal Oak	2742	42.30 N	83.08 W
Royalton	2742	45.50 N	94.18 W
Royan	2772	45.37 N	1.01 W
Royston	2744	34.17 N	83.06 W
Rtiščevo	2766	52.16 N	43.47 E
Rubbestadneset	2768	59.49 N	5.17 E
Rubcovsk	2784	51.33 N	81.10 E
Ruby Range ⛰	2754	45.15 N	112.15 W
Rudnyj	2766	52.57 N	63.07 E
Rudolf, Lake ⊜	2790	3.30 N	36.00 E
Rudyard	2754	48.34 N	110.33 W
Rue	2772	50.16 N	1.40 E
Rufā 'ah	2786	14.46 N	33.22 E
Ruffec	2772	46.02 N	0.42 E
Rufino	2764	34.16 S	62.40 W
Rufus	2754	45.42 N	120.44 W
Rugao	2800	32.25 N	120.36 E
Rugby, Eng., U.K.	2769	52.23 N	1.15 W
Rugby, N. Dak., U.S.	2750	48.22 N	100.00 W
Ruian	2800	27.49 N	120.38 E
Ruidoso	2752	33.20 N	105.40 W
Ruijin	2796	25.50 N	116.00 E
Rukwa, Lake ⊜	2788	8.00 S	32.25 E
Rule	2748	33.11 N	99.54 W
Ruma	2778	45.00 N	19.49 E
Rumbek	2786	6.48 N	29.41 E

Symbols against index entries represent categories identified in the key on page 2810.

Name	Page	Lat °′	Long °′
Rumford	2740	44.33 N	70.33 W
Rumia	2770	54.35 N	18.25 E
Rum Jungle	2806	13.01 S	131.00 E
Rumoi	2798a	43.56 N	141.39 E
Runan	2800	33.01 N	114.22 E
Runanga	2808	42.24 S	171.16 E
Runge	2748	28.54 N	97.43 W
Rungwa	2788	6.57 S	33.31 E
Ruoqiang	2796	38.30 N	88.05 E
Rupert, Idaho, U.S.	2754	42.37 N	113.41 W
Rupert, W. Va., U.S.	2744	37.58 N	80.41 W
Rupert House	2734	51.30 N	78.45 W
Rural Hall	2744	36.15 N	80.18 W
Ruse	2778	43.50 N	25.57 E
Rush City	2742	45.41 N	92.58 W
Rush Springs	2748	34.47 N	97.58 W
Rushville, Ill., U.S.	2746	40.07 N	90.34 W
Rushville, Ind., U.S.	2746	39.37 N	85.27 W
Rushville, Nebr., U.S.	2750	42.43 N	102.28 W
Rusk	2748	31.48 N	95.09 W
Ruskin	2744	27.43 N	82.26 W
Russas	2762	4.56 S	37.58 W
Russell	2750	38.54 N	98.52 W
Russell Island I	2734	73.55 N	98.25 W
Russells Point	2740	40.28 N	83.54 W
Russell Springs	2746	37.03 N	85.05 W
Russellville, Ala., U.S.	2746	34.30 N	87.44 W
Russellville, Ark., U.S.	2746	35.17 N	93.08 W
Russellville, Ky., U.S.	2746	36.51 N	86.53 W
Rüsselsheim	2770	50.00 N	8.25 E
Rustavi	2766	41.33 N	45.02 E
Rustavi, S.S.S.R.	2766	41.33 N	45.02 E
Rustburg	2744	37.17 N	79.06 W
Rustenburg	2788	25.37 S	27.08 E
Ruston	2746	32.32 N	92.38 W
Ruth, Miss., U.S.	2746	31.23 N	90.19 W
Ruth, Nev., U.S.	2756	39.17 N	114.59 W
Rutherfordton	2744	35.22 N	81.57 W
Rutland	2740	43.36 N	72.59 W
Rutledge	2744	36.17 N	83.31 W
Ruukki	2768	64.40 N	25.06 E
Ruvuma (Rovuma) ≃	2788	10.29 S	40.28 E
Ruzajevka	2766	54.04 N	44.57 E
Ružomberok	2770	49.06 N	19.18 E
Rwanda □[1]	2788	2.30 S	30.00 E
Ryan	2748	34.01 N	97.57 W
Rybačje	2784	46.27 N	81.32 E
Rybinsk	2780	58.03 N	38.52 E
Rybinskoje Vodochranilišče ⊜[1]	2780	58.30 N	38.25 E
Rybnica	2782	47.45 N	29.01 E
Rybnik	2770	50.06 N	18.32 E
Ryde	2769	50.44 N	1.10 W
Ryder	2750	47.55 N	101.40 W
Ryegate	2754	46.18 N	109.15 W
Ryfoss	2768	61.09 N	8.49 E
Ryōtsu	2798	38.05 N	138.26 E
Rzeszów	2770	50.03 N	22.00 E
Ržev	2780	56.16 N	34.20 E

S

Name	Page	Lat °′	Long °′
Saarbrücken	2770	49.14 N	6.59 E
Saaremaa I	2780	58.25 N	22.30 E
Saarijärvi	2768	62.43 N	25.16 E
Saarlouis	2770	49.21 N	6.45 E
Sab, Tônlé ⊜	2804	13.00 N	104.00 E
Sabadell	2774	41.33 N	2.06 E
Sabanalarga	2760	10.38 N	74.55 W
Sabang	2802	0.11 N	119.51 E
Sabanilla	2758	25.08 N	101.44 W
Sabará	2765	19.54 S	43.48 W
Sabhah	2786	27.03 N	14.26 E
Sabi (Save) ≃	2788	21.00 S	35.02 E
Sabinal	2748	29.19 N	99.28 W
Sabiñánigo	2774	42.31 N	0.22 W
Sabinas	2758	27.51 N	101.07 W
Sabinas Hidalgo	2758	26.30 N	100.10 W
Sabine ≃	2758	30.00 N	93.45 W
Sabine Bay C	2734	75.35 N	109.30 W
Sable, Cape ≻, N.S., Can.	2734	43.25 N	65.35 W
Sable, Cape ≻, Fla., U.S.	2744	25.12 N	81.05 W
Sable, Îles de I	2806	19.15 S	159.56 E
Sable Island I	2734	43.55 N	59.50 W
Sacajawea Peak ∧	2754	45.15 N	117.17 W
Sac City	2750	42.25 N	95.00 W
Sacedón	2774	40.29 N	2.43 W
Sachalin, Ostrov (Sakhalin) I	2784	51.00 N	143.00 E
Sachalinskij Zaliv C	2784	53.45 N	141.30 E
Sachigo ≃	2734	55.06 N	88.58 W
Sachs Harbour	2734	72.00 N	125.00 W
Šachty	2782	47.42 N	40.13 E
Šachunja	2766	57.40 N	46.37 E
Sackets Harbor	2740	43.57 N	76.07 W
Sackville	2739	45.54 N	64.22 W
Saco, Maine, U.S.	2740	43.29 N	70.28 W
Saco, Mont., U.S.	2754	48.28 N	107.21 W
Sacramento	2756	38.03 N	121.56 W
Sacramento ≃	2756	38.03 N	121.56 W
Sacramento Valley ∨	2756	39.15 N	122.00 W
Sádaba	2774	42.17 N	1.16 W
Sá da Bandeira	2788	14.55 S	13.30 E
Ṣa'dah	2790	16.52 N	43.37 E
Saddle Mountains ⩕	2754	46.50 N	119.55 W
Sado I	2798	38.00 N	138.25 E
Sado-kaikyō ⋃	2798	37.50 N	138.40 E
Šadrinsk	2766	56.05 N	63.38 E
Säffle	2768	59.08 N	12.56 E
Safford	2752	32.50 N	109.43 W
Safi	2786	32.20 N	9.17 W
Safīd Kūh, Selseleh-ye ⩕	2794	34.40 N	65.00 E
Safonovo, S.S.S.R.	2766	65.42 N	47.39 E
Safonovo, S.S.S.R.	2780	55.06 N	33.15 E
Saga	2798	33.15 N	130.18 E
Sagamihara	2798	35.32 N	139.23 E
Sagami-nada C	2798	35.00 N	139.30 E
Sāgar	2794	23.50 N	78.45 E
Saginaw	2742	43.25 N	83.58 W
Saginaw Bay C	2742	43.50 N	83.40 W
Saglouc	2734	62.14 N	75.38 W
Sagres	2774	37.00 N	8.56 W
Saguache	2752	38.05 N	106.08 W
Sagua de Tánamo	2760	20.35 N	75.14 W
Sagua la Grande	2760	22.49 N	80.05 W
Saguaro National Monument ♦	2752	32.12 N	110.38 W
Sagunto	2774	39.41 N	0.16 W
Sahagún	2774	42.22 N	5.02 W
Sahara ◆[2]	2786	26.00 N	13.00 E
Sahāranpur	2794	29.58 N	77.33 E
Sāhīwāl (Montgomery)	2794	30.40 N	73.06 E
Sahuaripa	2758	29.03 N	109.14 W
Sahuarita	2752	31.57 N	110.58 W
Sahuayo	2758	20.04 N	102.43 W
Saibai I	2806	9.24 S	142.40 E
Saïda	2786	34.50 N	0.09 E
Saidpur	2794	25.47 N	88.54 E
Saigō	2798	36.12 N	133.20 E
Sai-gon → Thanh-pho Ho Chi Minh	2804	10.45 N	106.40 E
Saijō	2798	33.55 N	133.11 E
Saimaa ⊜	2768	61.15 N	28.15 E
Saint Abb's Head ≻	2769	55.54 N	2.09 W
Sainte-Agathe	2750	49.34 N	97.10 W
Sainte-Agathe-des-Monts	2740	46.03 N	74.17 W
Saint Albans, Eng., U.K.	2769	51.46 N	0.21 W
Saint Albans, Vt., U.S.	2740	44.49 N	73.05 W
Saint-Amand-Mont-Rond	2772	46.44 N	2.30 E
Saint-Ambroix	2772	44.15 N	4.11 E
Saint-André, Cap ≻	2788	16.11 S	44.27 E
Saint-André-les-Alpes	2772	43.58 N	6.30 E
Saint Andrews, Scot., U.K.	2769	56.20 N	2.48 W
Saint Andrews, S.C., U.S.	2744	32.47 N	80.00 W
Saint Anne	2746	41.01 N	87.43 W
Saint Anthony, Newf., Can.	2734	51.22 N	55.35 W
Saint Anthony, Idaho, U.S.	2754	43.58 N	111.41 W
Saint-Astier	2772	45.09 N	0.32 E
Saint Augustine	2744	29.54 N	81.19 W
Saint-Augustin-Saguenay	2734	51.14 N	58.39 W
Saint Austell	2769	50.20 N	4.48 W
Saint-Avold	2772	49.06 N	6.42 E
Saint-Benoît-du-Sault	2772	46.27 N	1.23 E
Saint-Brieuc	2772	48.31 N	2.47 W
Saint-Calais	2772	47.55 N	0.45 E
Saint Catharines	2740	43.10 N	79.15 W
Saint-Céré	2772	44.52 N	1.53 E
Saint-Chamond	2772	45.28 N	4.30 E
Saint Charles, Ill., U.S.	2746	41.54 N	88.19 W
Saint Charles, Mo., U.S.	2746	38.47 N	90.29 W
Saint-Chély-d'Apcher	2772	44.48 N	3.17 E
Saint Clair, Mich., U.S.	2742	42.49 N	82.30 W
Saint Clair, Mo., U.S.	2746	38.20 N	90.59 W
Saint Clair, Lake ⊜	2742	42.25 N	82.41 W
Saint-Claude	2772	46.23 N	5.52 E
Saint Cloud, Fla., U.S.	2744	28.15 N	81.17 W
Saint Cloud, Minn , U.S.	2742	45.33 N	94.10 W
Saint Croix I	2760	17.45 N	64.45 W
Saint Croix Falls	2742	45.24 N	92.38 W
Saint David's	2769	51.54 N	5.16 W
Saint-Denis, Fr.	2772	48.56 N	2.22 E
Saint-Denis, Réu.	2788	20.52 S	55.28 E
Saint-Dié	2772	48.17 N	6.57 E
Saint-Dizier	2772	48.38 N	4.57 E
Saint Edward	2750	41.34 N	97.52 W
Saint Elias, Mount ∧	2734	60.18 N	140.55 W
Saint-Florentin	2772	48.00 N	3.44 E
Saint-Florent-sur-Cher	2772	46.59 N	2.15 E
Saint-Flour	2772	45.02 N	3.05 E
Sainte-Foy-la-Grande	2772	44.50 N	0.13 E
Saint Francis	2750	39.46 N	101.48 W
Saint Francisville	2746	30.47 N	91.23 W
Saint Francois Mountains ⩕[2]	2746	37.30 N	90.35 W
Saint-Gaudens	2772	43.07 N	0.44 E
Sainte Genevieve	2746	37.59 N	90.03 W
Saint George, Austl.	2806	28.02 S	148.35 E
Saint George, S.C., U.S.	2744	33.11 N	80.35 W
Saint George, Utah, U.S.	2752	37.06 N	113.35 W
Saint George's, Gren.	2760	12.03 N	61.45 W
Saint-Georges, Guy. fr.	2762	3.54 N	51.48 W
Saint George's Bay C	2734	48.20 N	59.00 W
Saint George's Channel ⋃	2769	52.00 N	6.00 W
Saint-Germain	2772	48.54 N	2.05 E
Saint-Gilles-croix-de-Vie	2772	46.42 N	1.57 W
Saint-Girons	2772	42.59 N	1.09 E
Saint Helena	2756	38.30 N	122.28 W
Saint Helena Bay C	2788	32.43 S	18.05 E
Saint Helens	2754	45.52 N	122.48 W
Saint Helens, Mount ∧	2754	46.12 N	122.11 W
Saint-Hippolyte	2772	47.19 N	6.49 E
Saint-Hyacinthe	2740	45.38 N	72.57 W
Saint Ignace Island I	2734	48.48 N	87.55 W
Saint Ignatius	2754	47.19 N	114.06 W
Saint James, Mich., U.S.	2742	45.45 N	85.31 W
Saint James, Minn , U.S.	2750	43.59 N	94.38 W
Saint James, Mo., U.S.	2746	38.00 N	91.37 W
Saint James, N.Y., U.S.	2740	40.53 N	73.09 W
Saint James, Cape ≻	2734	51.56 N	131.01 W
Saint-Jean	2740	45.19 N	73.16 W
Saint-Jean, Lac ⊜	2734	48.35 N	72.05 W
Saint-Jean-d'Angély	2772	45.57 N	0.31 W
Saint-Jean-de-Maurienne	2772	45.17 N	6.21 E
Saint-Jean-de-Monts	2772	46.48 N	2.03 W
Saint-Jean-Pied-de-Port	2772	43.10 N	1.14 W
Saint-Jérôme	2740	45.46 N	74.00 W
Saint John, N.B., Can.	2739	45.16 N	66.03 W
Saint John, Kans., U.S.	2750	38.00 N	98.46 W
Saint John, Wash., U.S.	2754	47.05 N	117.35 W
Saint John I	2760	18.20 N	64.45 W
Saint John ≃	2734	45.15 N	66.04 W
Saint John, Cape ≻	2734	50.00 N	55.32 W
Saint Johns, Antig.	2760	17.06 N	61.51 W
Saint John's, Newf., Can.	2734	47.34 N	52.43 W
Saint Johns, Ariz., U.S.	2752	34.30 N	109.22 W
Saint Johns, Mich., U.S.	2742	43.00 N	84.33 W
Saint Johns ≃	2744	30.24 N	81.24 W
Saint Johnsbury	2740	44.25 N	72.01 W
Saint Joseph, La., U.S.	2746	31.55 N	91.14 W
Saint Joseph, Mich., U.S.	2742	42.06 N	86.29 W
Saint Joseph, Lake ⊜	2734	51.05 N	90.35 W
Saint-Julien-en-Born	2772	44.04 N	1.14 W
Saint-Junien	2772	45.53 N	0.54 E
Saint-Just-en-Chaussée	2772	49.30 N	2.26 E
Saint Kilda I	2769	57.49 N	8.36 W
Saint Kitts-Nevis □[2]	2760	17.20 N	62.45 W
Saint Lawrence ≃	2736	49.30 N	67.00 W
Saint Lawrence, Gulf of C	2734	48.00 N	62.00 W
Saint-Lô	2772	49.07 N	1.05 W
Saint-Louis, Sén.	2786	16.02 N	16.30 W
Saint Louis, Mich., U.S.	2742	43.25 N	84.36 W
Saint Louis, Mo., U.S.	2736	38.38 N	90.11 W
Saint Lucia □[2]	2760	13.53 N	60.58 W
Saint Lucia Channel ⋃	2760	14.15 N	61.00 W
Saint-Malo	2772	48.39 N	2.01 W
Saint-Marcellin	2772	45.09 N	5.19 E
Sainte-Marie, Cap ≻	2788	25.36 S	45.08 E
Sainte-Marie, Île I	2788	16.50 S	49.55 E
Saint Maries	2754	47.19 N	116.35 W
Saint Marks	2744	30.09 N	84.12 W
Saint-Martin (Sint Maarten) I	2760	18.04 N	63.04 W
Saint Martin, Lake ⊜	2734	51.37 N	98.29 W
Saint Martinville	2746	30.07 N	91.50 W
Saint Mary Peak ∧	2806	31.30 S	138.33 E
Saint Marys, Austl.	2806	41.35 S	148.10 E
Saint Mary's, Ont., Can.	2740	43.16 N	81.08 W
Saint Marys, Ga., U.S.	2744	30.44 N	81.33 W
Saint Marys, Ohio, U.S.	2740	40.33 N	84.23 W
Saint Marys, Pa., U.S.	2740	41.26 N	78.34 W
Saint Marys, W. Va., U.S.	2740	39.23 N	81.12 W
Saint Marys ≃	2740	41.05 N	85.08 W
Saint Matthews, Ky., U.S.	2746	38.15 N	85.39 W
Saint Matthews, S.C., U.S.	2744	33.40 N	80.46 W
Sainte-Maure-du-Touraine	2772	47.07 N	0.37 E
Sainte-Maxime	2772	43.18 N	6.38 E
Saint-Méen-le-Grand	2772	48.11 N	2.12 W
Saint Meinrad	2746	38.10 N	86.49 W
Sainte-Menehould	2772	49.05 N	4.54 E
Saint Michaels	2740	38.47 N	76.14 W
Saint-Mihiel	2772	48.54 N	5.33 E
Saint-Moritz → Sankt Moritz	2772	46.30 N	9.50 E
Saint-Nazaire	2772	47.17 N	2.12 W
Saint Neots	2769	52.14 N	0.17 W
Saint-Omer	2772	50.45 N	2.15 E
Saint Paul, Alta., Can.	2734	53.59 N	111.17 W
Saint Paul, Minn , U.S.	2742	44.58 N	93.07 W
Saint Paul, Nebr., U.S.	2750	41.13 N	98.27 W
Saint Pauls	2744	34.48 N	78.58 W
Saint Peter	2742	44.17 N	93.57 W
Saint Petersburg	2744	27.46 N	82.38 W
Saint-Pierre	2788	21.19 S	55.29 E
Saint Pierre and Miquelon □[2]	2734	46.55 N	56.15 W
Saint Pierre Island I	2788	9.19 S	50.43 E
Saint-Pierre-le-Moûtier	2772	46.48 N	3.07 E
Saint-Pol-de-Léon	2772	48.41 N	3.59 W
Saint-Pons	2772	43.29 N	2.46 E
Saint-Pourçain-sur-Sioule	2772	46.19 N	3.17 E
Saint-Quentin	2772	49.51 N	3.17 E
Saint-Raphaël	2772	43.25 N	6.46 E
Saint Regis	2754	47.18 N	115.06 W
Saint-Sébastien, Cap ≻	2788	12.26 S	48.44 E
St. Stephen, N.B., Can.	2740	45.12 N	67.17 W
Saint Stephen, S.C., U.S.	2744	33.24 N	79.55 W
Sainte-Thérèse-de-Blainville	2740	45.39 N	73.49 W
Saint Thomas, Ont., Can.	2740	42.47 N	81.12 W
Saint Thomas, N. Dak., U.S.	2750	48.37 N	97.27 W
Saint Thomas I	2760	18.21 N	64.55 W
Saint Vincent □[2]	2760	13.15 N	61.12 W
Saint-Vincent, Cap ≻	2788	21.57 S	43.16 E
Saint Vincent, Gulf C	2806	35.00 S	138.05 E
Saint Vincent Passage ⋃	2760	13.30 N	61.00 W
Saint-Vith	2770	50.17 N	6.08 E
Saipan I	2802	15.12 N	145.45 E
Sairecábur, Cerro ∧	2762	22.43 S	67.54 W
Saito	2798	32.06 N	131.24 E
Saitula	2794	36.21 N	78.02 E
Sajama, Nevado ∧	2762	18.06 S	68.54 W
Sajia	2794	28.55 N	88.05 E
Sajnšand	2796	44.55 N	110.11 E
Sakai	2798	34.35 N	135.28 E
Sakaide	2798	34.19 N	133.52 E
Sakakawea, Lake ⊜[1]	2750	47.50 N	102.20 W
Sakami, Lac ⊜	2734	53.15 N	76.45 W
Sakata	2798	38.55 N	139.50 E
Saki	2782	45.09 N	33.35 E
Sakishima-guntō II	2796	24.46 N	124.00 E
Sakito	2798	33.02 N	129.32 E
Sala	2768	59.55 N	16.36 E
Sala Consilina	2776	40.24 N	15.36 E
Salado ≃	2764	31.40 S	60.41 W
Ṣalālah	2790	17.00 N	54.06 E
Salamanca, Esp.	2774	40.58 N	5.39 W
Salamanca, Méx.	2758	20.34 N	101.12 W
Salamanca, N.Y., U.S.	2740	42.09 N	78.43 W
Salamis ⊥	2791	35.10 N	33.54 E
Salavat	2766	53.21 N	55.55 E
Salawati I	2802	1.07 S	130.52 E
Saldanha	2788	33.00 S	17.56 E
Sale	2806	38.06 S	147.04 E
Sale Creek	2746	35.23 N	85.07 W
Salem, Bhārat	2793	11.39 N	78.10 E
Salem, Ark., U.S.	2746	36.22 N	91.49 W
Salem, Ill., U.S.	2746	38.38 N	88.57 W
Salem, Ind., U.S.	2746	38.36 N	86.06 W
Salem, Mass., U.S.	2740	42.31 N	70.55 W
Salem, Mo., U.S.	2746	37.39 N	91.32 W
Salem, N.H., U.S.	2740	42.47 N	71.12 W
Salem, N.J., U.S.	2740	39.34 N	75.28 W
Salem, N.Y., U.S.	2740	43.10 N	73.20 W
Salem, Ohio, U.S.	2740	40.54 N	80.52 W
Salem, Oreg., U.S.	2754	44.57 N	123.01 W
Salem, S. Dak., U.S.	2750	43.44 N	97.23 W
Salem, Va., U.S.	2744	37.17 N	80.03 W
Salemi	2776	37.49 N	12.49 E
Salem Upland ⩕[1]	2746	37.25 N	91.30 W
Sälen	2768	61.10 N	13.16 E
Salerno	2776	40.41 N	14.47 E
Salford	2769	53.28 N	2.18 W
Salgótarján	2770	48.07 N	19.48 E
Sali	2776	43.56 N	15.10 E
Salida	2752	38.32 N	106.00 W
Salihli	2778	38.29 N	28.09 E
Salina, Kans., U.S.	2750	38.50 N	97.37 W
Salina, Utah, U.S.	2752	38.58 N	111.51 W
Salina Cruz	2758	16.10 N	95.12 W
Salinas, Bra.	2765	16.10 S	42.17 W
Salinas, Calif., U.S.	2756	36.40 N	121.39 W
Salinas de Hidalgo	2758	22.38 N	101.43 W
Saline	2742	41.59 N	83.37 W
Salisbury, Rh.	2788	17.50 S	31.03 E
Salisbury, Eng., U.K.	2769	51.05 N	1.48 W
Salisbury, Md., U.S.	2740	38.22 N	75.36 W
Salisbury, Mo., U.S.	2746	39.25 N	92.48 W
Salisbury, N.C., U.S.	2744	35.40 N	80.29 W
Salisbury Island I	2734	63.30 N	77.00 W
Salisbury Plain ≚	2769	51.12 N	1.55 W
Salish Mountains ⩕	2754	48.15 N	114.45 W
Saljany	2766	39.34 N	48.58 E
Ṣalkhad	2791	32.29 N	36.43 E
Sallisaw	2748	35.28 N	94.47 W
Salmon	2754	45.11 N	113.54 W
Salmon ≃	2754	45.51 N	116.46 W
Salmon River Mountains ⩕	2754	44.45 N	115.30 W
Salo	2768	60.23 N	23.08 E
Salome	2752	33.47 N	113.37 W
Sal'sk	2766	46.28 N	41.33 E
Salsomaggiore Terme	2776	44.49 N	9.59 E
Salta	2764	24.47 S	65.24 W
Saltillo	2758	25.25 N	101.00 W
Salt Lake City	2752	40.46 N	111.53 W
Salto	2764	31.23 S	57.58 W
Salton Sea ⊜	2756	33.19 N	115.50 W
Saluda, N.C., U.S.	2744	35.14 N	82.21 W
Saluda, S.C., U.S.	2744	34.00 N	81.46 W
Saluda, Va., U.S.	2744	37.36 N	76.36 W
Saluzzo	2776	44.39 N	7.29 E
Salvador	2765	12.59 S	38.31 W
Salvador, Lake ⊜	2746	29.45 N	90.15 W
Salvatierra	2758	20.13 N	100.53 W
Salween (Nujiang) ≃, As.	2794	30.50 N	96.10 E
Salween ≃, As.	2802	16.31 N	97.37 E
Salyersville	2744	37.45 N	83.04 W
Salzburg	2770	47.48 N	13.02 E
Salzgitter	2770	52.10 N	10.25 E
Sama [de Langreo]	2774	43.18 N	5.41 W
Samaná, Bahía de C	2760	19.10 N	69.30 W
Samandağı	2791	36.07 N	35.56 E
Samar I	2802	12.00 N	125.00 E
Samarinda	2802	0.30 S	117.09 E
Sāmarrā'	2790	34.12 N	43.52 E
Sambalpur	2794	21.27 N	83.58 E
Sambas	2804	1.20 N	109.15 E
Sambava	2788	14.16 S	50.10 E
Sambhal	2794	28.35 N	78.33 E
Sāmbhar	2794	26.55 N	75.12 E
Sambor	2782	49.32 N	23.11 E
Samobor	2776	45.48 N	15.43 E
Samoded	2766	63.38 N	40.29 E
Sámos □[5]	2778	37.48 N	26.44 E
Sampit	2802	2.32 S	112.57 E
Sam Rayburn Reservoir ⊜[1]	2746	31.27 N	94.37 W
Samsun	2766	41.17 N	36.20 E
Samtown	2746	31.20 N	92.26 W
Samui, Ko I	2804	9.30 N	100.04 E
Samut Prakan	2804	13.35 N	100.40 E
Samut Sakhon	2804	13.31 N	100.15 E
San	2786	13.18 N	4.54 W
Ṣan'ā'	2790	15.23 N	44.12 E
Sanaga ≃	2786	3.35 N	9.38 E
San Agustin, Cape ≻	2802	6.16 N	126.11 E
San Agustin, Plains of ≚	2752	33.50 N	108.00 W
Sanana, Pulau I	2802	2.12 S	125.55 E
Sanandaj	2790	35.19 N	47.00 E
San Andreas	2756	38.12 N	120.41 W
San Andrés, Isla de I	2760	12.33 N	81.42 W
San Andres Mountains ⩕	2752	32.55 N	106.45 W
San Andrés Tuxtla	2758	18.27 N	95.13 W
San Angelo	2748	31.28 N	100.26 W
San Angelo Reservoir ⊜[1]	2748	31.30 N	100.30 W
San Antonio, N. Mex., U.S.	2752	33.55 N	106.52 W
San Antonio, Tex., U.S.	2748	29.28 N	98.31 W
San Antonio ≃	2748	28.30 N	96.50 W
San Antonio, Cabo ≻, Arg.	2764	36.40 S	56.42 W
San Antonio, Cabo ≻, Cuba	2760	21.52 N	84.57 W
San Antonio Abad	2774	38.58 N	1.18 E
San Antonio Bay C	2748	28.20 N	96.45 W
San Antonio de Bravo	2758	30.10 N	104.42 W
San Antonio de los Cobres	2764	24.15 S	66.20 W
San Antonio Mountain ∧	2752	36.52 N	106.02 W
San Antonio Oeste	2764	40.44 S	64.57 W
San Augustine	2746	31.32 N	94.07 W
San Benedetto del Tronto	2776	42.57 N	13.53 E
San Benito, Guat.	2760	16.55 N	89.54 W
San Benito, Tex., U.S.	2748	26.08 N	97.38 W
San Bernardino	2756	34.06 N	117.17 W

Symbols against index entries represent categories identified in the key on page 2810.

Name	Page	Lat° ′	Long° ′
San Bernardino Mountains ⋀	2756	34.10 N	117.00 W
San Bernardo	2764	33.36 S	70.43 W
San Blas, Méx.	2758	26.05 N	108.46 W
San Blas, Méx.	2758	21.31 N	105.16 W
San Blas, Cape ≻	2744	29.40 N	85.22 W
San Blas, Cape ≻, Fla., U.S.	2746	0.00	0.00
San Borja	2762	14.49 S	66.51 W
San Carlos, Ariz., U.S.	2752	33.21 N	110.27 W
San Carlos, Ven.	2760	9.40 N	68.36 W
San Carlos de Bariloche	2764	41.08 S	71.15 W
San Carlos de la Rápita	2774	40.37 N	0.36 E
San Carlos del Zulia	2760	9.01 N	71.55 W
San Carlos de Río Negro	2762	1.55 N	67.04 W
San Cataldo	2776	37.29 N	14.04 E
Sánchez	2758	27.27 N	99.40 W
San Clemente	2756	33.26 N	117.37 W
San Cristóbal, Arg.	2764	30.20 S	61.15 W
San Cristóbal, Ven.	2760	7.46 N	72.14 W
San Cristóbal las Casas	2758	16.45 N	92.38 W
Sancti-Spíritus	2760	21.56 N	79.27 W
Sand	2768	59.29 N	6.15 E
Sandakan	2802	5.53 N	118.05 E
Sanday I	2769	59.15 N	2.30 W
Sanders	2752	35.13 N	109.20 W
Sanderson	2748	30.09 N	102.24 W
Sandersville	2744	32.59 N	82.48 W
Sand Hills ⋀[2]	2750	41.45 N	102.00 W
Sandia	2762	14.14 S	69.25 W
Sandia Crest ∧	2752	35.13 N	106.27 W
San Diego, Calif., U.S.	2756	32.43 N	117.09 W
San Diego, Tex., U.S.	2748	27.46 N	98.14 W
Sandnes	2768	58.51 N	5.44 E
Sandoa	2788	9.41 S	22.52 E
San Donà di Piave	2776	45.38 N	12.34 E
Sandpoint	2754	48.16 N	116.33 W
Sand Springs	2748	36.09 N	96.07 W
Sandston	2744	37.31 N	77.19 W
Sandstone, Austl.	2806	27.59 S	119.17 E
Sandstone, Minn , U.S.	2742	46.08 N	92.52 W
Sandusky, Mich., U.S.	2742	43.25 N	82.50 W
Sandusky, Ohio, U.S.	2740	41.27 N	82.42 W
Sandviken	2768	60.37 N	16.46 E
Sandwich, Ill., U.S.	2746	41.39 N	88.37 W
Sandwich, Mass., U.S.	2740	41.46 N	70.30 W
Sandy Lake ⊛	2734	53.00 N	93.07 W
Sandy Springs	2744	33.55 N	84.23 W
San Felipe, Méx.	2756	31.00 N	114.52 W
San Felipe, N. Mex., U.S.	2752	35.27 N	106.28 W
San Felipe, Ven.	2760	10.20 N	68.44 W
San Felíu de Guixols	2774	41.47 N	3.02 E
San Fermín	2748	26.20 N	104.49 W
San Fernando, Chile	2764	34.35 S	71.00 W
San Fernando, Esp.	2774	36.28 N	6.12 W
San Fernando, Méx.	2758	24.50 N	98.10 W
San Fernando, Trin.	2760	10.17 N	61.28 W
San Fernando, Calif., U.S.	2756	34.17 N	118.26 W
San Fernando de Apure	2760	7.54 N	67.28 W
San Fernando de Atabapo	2762	4.03 N	67.42 W
Sanford, Fla., U.S.	2744	28.48 N	81.16 W
Sanford, Maine, U.S.	2740	43.26 N	70.46 W
Sanford, Mich., U.S.	2742	43.40 N	84.23 W
Sanford, N.C., U.S.	2744	35.29 N	79.10 W
San Francisco, Arg.	2764	31.27 S	62.05 W
San Francisco, Calif., U.S.	2756	37.48 N	122.24 W
San Francisco, Cabo de ≻	2762	0.40 N	80.05 W
San Francisco de Borja	2758	27.53 N	106.41 W
San Francisco del Oro	2758	26.52 N	105.51 W
San Francisco del Rincón	2758	21.01 N	101.51 W
San Francisco de Macorís	2760	19.18 N	70.15 W
San Francisco Mountains ⋀	2752	33.45 N	109.00 W
San Francisco Peaks ⋀	2752	35.20 N	111.45 W
San Fratello	2776	38.01 N	14.36 E
San Gabriel Mountains ⋀	2756	34.20 N	118.00 W
Sangamon ≃	2746	40.07 N	90.20 W
San Gavino Monreale	2776	39.33 N	8.48 E
Sangay, Volcán ∧[1]	2762	2.00 S	78.20 W
Sanger, Calif., U.S.	2756	36.42 N	119.27 W
Sanger, Tex., U.S.	2748	33.22 N	97.10 W
Sangha ≃	2788	1.13 S	16.49 E
Sangihe, Kepulauan II	2802	3.00 N	125.30 E
Sangihe, Pulau I	2802	3.35 N	125.32 E
San Giovanni in Fiore	2776	39.16 N	16.42 E
San Giovanni in Persiceto	2776	44.38 N	11.11 E
San Giovanni Valdarno	2776	43.34 N	11.32 E
Sāngli	2793	16.52 N	74.34 E
Sangre de Cristo Mountains ⋀	2752	37.30 N	105.15 W
San Gregorio	2764	32.37 S	55.40 W
Sangüesa	2774	42.35 N	1.17 W
San Ignacio	2764	27.15 S	55.30 W
San Isidro, Arg.	2764	34.29 S	58.31 W
San Isidro, Tex., U.S.	2748	26.43 N	98.27 W
San Jacinto, Col.	2760	9.50 N	75.08 W
San Jacinto, Calif., U.S.	2756	33.47 N	116.57 W
Sanjō	2798	37.37 N	138.57 E
San Joaquin Valley ∨	2756	36.50 N	120.10 W
San Jon	2748	35.06 N	103.20 W
San Jorge, Golfo C	2764	46.00 S	66.50 W
San Jorge, Golfo de C	2774	40.53 N	1.00 E
San José, C.R.	2760	9.56 N	84.05 W
San Jose, Calif., U.S.	2756	37.20 N	121.53 W
San Jose, N. Mex., U.S.	2752	35.24 N	105.29 W
San José, Isla I	2758	25.00 N	110.38 W
San José de Chiquitos	2762	17.51 S	60.47 W
San José de Guanipa	2760	8.54 N	64.09 W
San José de la Popa	2748	26.10 N	100.47 W
San José del Cabo	2758	23.03 N	109.41 W
San José del Guaviare	2762	2.35 N	72.38 W
San José de Mayo	2764	34.20 S	56.42 W
San José de Raíces	2758	24.35 N	100.14 W
San Juan, Arg.	2764	31.30 S	68.30 W
San Juan, Méx.	2758	27.47 N	103.57 W
San Juan, P.R.	2760	18.28 N	66.07 W
San Juan ≃	2752	37.18 N	110.28 W
San Juan Basin ≍[1]	2752	36.15 N	108.20 W
San Juan [de la Maguana]	2760	18.48 N	71.14 W
San Juan del Norte	2760	10.56 N	83.42 W
San Juan de los Morros	2760	9.55 N	67.21 W
San Juan del Río	2758	20.23 N	100.00 W
San Juan del Sur	2760	11.15 N	85.52 W
San Juan Island National Historical Park ♦	2754	48.28 N	123.00 W
San Juan Mountains ⋀	2752	37.35 N	107.10 W
San Julián	2764	49.19 S	67.40 W
San Justo	2764	30.47 S	60.35 W
Sankt Gallen, Öst.	2770	47.41 N	14.37 E
Sankt Gallen, Schw.	2772	47.25 N	9.23 E
Sankt Johann im Pongau	2770	47.21 N	13.12 E
Sankt Moritz	2772	46.30 N	9.50 E
Sankt Peter	2770	54.18 N	8.38 E
Sankt Pölten	2770	48.12 N	15.37 E
Sankt Veit an der Glan	2770	46.46 N	14.21 E
Sankt Wendel	2770	49.28 N	7.10 E
Sankuru ≃	2788	4.17 S	20.25 E
San Lorenzo	2764	32.45 S	60.44 W
San Lorenzo, Isla I	2762	12.06 S	77.14 W
San Lorenzo de El Escorial	2774	40.35 N	4.09 W
San Lorenzo de la Parrilla	2774	39.51 N	2.22 W
Sanlúcar de Barrameda	2774	36.47 N	6.21 W
San Lucas, Cabo ≻	2758	22.50 N	109.55 W
San Luis, Arg.	2764	33.20 S	66.20 W
San Luis, Cuba	2760	20.12 N	75.51 W
San Luis, Guat.	2760	16.14 N	89.27 W
San Luis, Colo., U.S.	2752	37.12 N	105.25 W
San Luis, Lago de ⊛	2762	13.45 S	64.00 W
San Luis de la Paz	2758	21.18 N	100.31 W
San Luis Obispo	2756	35.17 N	120.40 W
San Luis Peak ∧	2752	37.59 N	106.56 W
San Luis Potosí	2758	22.09 N	100.59 W
San Luis Río Colorado	2758	32.29 N	114.48 W
San Manuel	2752	32.36 N	110.38 W
San Marcos, Méx.	2758	26.41 N	102.07 W
San Marcos, Méx.	2758	16.48 N	99.21 W
San Marcos, Tex., U.S.	2748	29.53 N	97.57 W
San Marino ☐[1]	2766	43.56 N	12.25 E
San Martín, Cerro ∧[1]	2758	18.19 N	94.48 W
San Martín de Valdeiglesias	2774	40.21 N	4.24 W
San Mateo, Esp.	2774	40.28 N	0.11 E
San Mateo, Calif., U.S.	2756	37.35 N	122.19 W
San Mateo, N. Mex., U.S.	2752	35.20 N	107.39 W
San Matías, Golfo C	2764	41.30 S	64.20 W
San Miguel, El Sal.	2760	13.29 N	88.11 W
San Miguel, Calif., U.S.	2756	35.45 N	120.42 W
San Miguel ≃	2762	13.52 S	63.56 W
San Miguel de Allende	2758	20.55 N	100.45 W
San Miguel del Monte	2764	35.25 S	58.49 W
San Miguel de Tucumán	2764	26.49 S	65.13 W
San Miguel el Alto	2758	21.01 N	102.21 W
Sannār	2786	13.33 N	33.38 E
Sannicandro Garganico	2776	41.50 N	15.34 E
San Nicolás de los Arroyos	2764	33.20 S	60.13 W
San Nicolás de los Garzas	2748	25.45 N	100.18 W
Sannikova, Proliv Ʉ	2784	74.30 N	140.00 E
Sanniquellie	2786	7.22 N	8.43 W
Sanok	2770	49.34 N	22.13 E
San Onofre	2760	9.44 N	75.32 W
San Pablo	2802	14.04 N	121.19 E
San Pablo Balleza	2758	26.57 N	106.21 W
San Pedro, Punta ≻	2764	25.30 S	70.38 W
San Pedro, Volcán ∧[1]	2764	21.53 S	68.25 W
San Pedro Carchá	2760	15.29 N	90.16 W
San Pedro Channel Ʉ	2756	33.35 N	118.25 W
San Pedro de las Colonias	2758	25.45 N	102.59 W
San Pedro del Gallo	2748	25.33 N	104.18 W
San Pedro de Macorís	2760	18.27 N	69.18 W
San Pedro Sula	2760	15.27 N	88.02 W
San Quintín, Cabo ≻	2758	30.21 N	116.00 W
San Rafael, Arg.	2764	34.40 S	68.21 W
San Rafael, Méx.	2758	25.01 N	100.33 W
San Rafael, Calif., U.S.	2756	37.59 N	122.31 W
San Rafael, N. Mex., U.S.	2752	35.06 N	107.53 W
San Remo	2776	43.49 N	7.46 E
San Saba	2748	31.12 N	98.43 W
San Salvador	2760	13.42 N	89.12 W
San Salvador (Watling Island) I	2760	24.00 N	74.30 W
San Salvador de Jujuy	2764	24.10 S	65.20 W
Sansanné-Mango	2786	10.21 N	0.28 E
San Sebastián	2774	43.19 N	1.59 W
Sansepolcro	2776	43.34 N	12.08 E
San Severo	2776	41.41 N	15.23 E
San Simon ≃	2752	32.50 N	109.39 W
Sanski Most	2776	44.46 N	16.40 E
Santa Ana, Bol.	2762	15.31 S	67.30 W
Santa Ana, Bol.	2762	13.45 S	65.35 W
Santa Ana, El Sal.	2760	13.59 N	89.34 W
Santa Ana, Méx.	2758	24.04 N	100.30 W
Santa Ana, Méx.	2758	30.33 N	111.07 W
Santa Ana, Calif., U.S.	2756	33.43 N	117.54 W
Santa Bárbara, Méx.	2758	26.48 N	105.49 W
Santa Barbara, Calif., U.S.	2756	34.25 N	119.42 W
Santa Barbara Channel Ʉ	2756	34.15 N	119.55 W
Santa Catalina Island I	2756	33.23 N	118.26 W
Santa Catarina	2756	31.37 N	115.48 W
Santa Catarina, Ilha de I	2764	27.36 S	48.30 W
Santa Clara, Cuba	2760	22.24 N	79.58 W
Santa Clara, Calif., U.S.	2756	37.21 N	121.57 W
Santa Coloma de Farnés	2774	41.52 N	2.40 E
Santa Comba Dão	2774	40.24 N	8.08 W
Santa Cruz, Arg.	2764	50.00 S	68.32 W
Santa Cruz, Bol.	2762	17.48 S	63.10 W
Santa Cruz, Calif., U.S.	2756	36.58 N	122.01 W
Santa Cruz del Quiché	2760	15.02 N	91.08 W
Santa Cruz de Tenerife	2786	28.27 N	16.14 W
Santa Cruz do Rio Pardo	2765	22.55 S	49.37 W
Santa Cruz Island I	2756	34.01 N	119.45 W
Santa Elena	2748	27.28 N	102.33 W
Santa Eugenia	2774	42.33 N	9.00 W
Santa Eulalia	2774	40.34 N	1.19 W
Santa Eulalia del Río	2774	38.59 N	1.31 E
Santa Fe, Arg.	2764	31.40 S	60.40 W
Santa Fé, Bra.	2765	15.40 S	51.16 W
Santa Fé, Cuba	2760	21.45 N	82.45 W
Santa Fe, Esp.	2774	37.11 N	3.43 W
Santa Fe, N. Mex., U.S.	2752	35.42 N	106.57 W
Santa Fe Baldy ∧	2752	35.50 N	105.46 W
Santa Inés, Isla I	2764	53.40 S	73.00 W
Santa Isabel → Malabo	2786	3.45 N	8.47 E
Santa Isabel I	2806	8.00 S	159.00 E
Santa Maria, Bra.	2764	29.41 S	53.48 W
Santa Maria, Calif., U.S.	2756	34.57 N	120.26 W
Santa Maria, Cabo de ≻	2788	13.25 S	12.32 E
Santa Maria do Suaçuí	2765	18.12 S	42.25 W
Santa Marta	2760	11.15 N	74.13 W
Santa Monica	2756	34.01 N	118.30 W
Santana do Livramento	2764	30.53 S	55.31 W
Santander	2774	43.28 N	3.48 W
Sant' Antioco	2776	39.04 N	8.27 E
Santa Paula	2756	34.21 N	119.04 W
Santaquin	2752	39.59 N	111.47 W
Sant'Arcangelo	2776	40.15 N	16.17 E
Santarém, Bra.	2762	2.26 S	54.42 W
Santarém, Port.	2774	39.14 N	8.41 W
Santa Rita	2760	15.09 N	87.53 W
Santa Rosa, Arg.	2764	32.20 S	65.10 W
Santa Rosa, Arg.	2764	36.40 S	64.15 W
Santa Rosa, Calif., U.S.	2756	38.26 N	122.43 W
Santa Rosa, N. Mex., U.S.	2748	34.57 N	104.41 W
Santa Rosa Beach	2746	30.23 N	86.14 W
Santa Rosa [de Copán]	2760	14.47 N	88.46 W
Šantarskije Ostrova II	2784	55.00 N	137.36 E
Santa Teresa Gallura	2776	41.15 N	9.12 E
Santa Vitória do Palmar	2764	33.31 S	53.21 W
Santhià	2776	45.22 N	8.10 E
Santiago, Chile	2764	33.27 S	70.40 W
Santiago, Pan.	2760	8.05 N	80.59 W
Santiago de Compostela	2774	42.53 N	8.33 W
Santiago de Cuba	2760	20.01 N	75.49 W
Santiago del Estero	2764	27.50 S	64.15 W
Santiago [de los Caballeros]	2760	19.27 N	70.42 W
Santiago do Cacém	2774	38.01 N	8.42 W
Santiago Ixcuintla	2758	21.49 N	105.13 W
Santiago Papasquiaro	2758	25.03 N	105.25 W
Sāntipur	2794	23.15 N	88.26 E
Santisteban del Puerto	2774	38.15 N	3.12 W
Santo	2748	32.36 N	98.13 W
Santo Amaro	2765	12.32 S	38.43 W
Santo Anastácio	2765	21.58 S	51.39 W
Santo André	2765	23.40 S	46.31 W
Santo Ângelo	2764	28.18 S	54.16 W
Santo Antônio de Jesus	2765	12.58 S	39.16 W
Santo Antônio do Içá	2762	3.05 S	67.57 W
Santo Domingo, Nic.	2760	12.16 N	84.59 W
Santo Domingo, Rep. Dom.	2760	18.28 N	69.54 W
Santo Domingo de la Calzada	2774	42.26 N	2.57 W
Santo Domingo Pueblo	2752	35.31 N	106.22 W
Santoña	2774	43.27 N	3.27 W
Santos	2765	23.57 S	46.20 W
Santos Dumont	2765	21.28 S	43.34 W
Santo Tomás	2758	31.33 N	116.24 W
Santo Tomé	2764	28.35 S	56.05 W
San Valentín, Monte ∧	2764	46.40 S	73.25 W
San Vicente, El Sal.	2760	13.38 N	88.48 W
San Vicente, Méx.	2758	31.20 N	116.15 W
San Vicente de Baracaldo	2774	43.18 N	2.59 W
San Vicente de la Barquera	2774	43.26 N	4.24 W
San Ygnacio	2748	27.03 N	99.27 W
Sanza Pombo	2788	7.19 S	15.59 E
São Bento	2762	2.42 S	44.50 W
São Borja	2764	28.39 S	56.00 W
São Caetano do Sul	2765	23.36 S	46.34 W
São Carlos	2765	22.01 S	47.54 W
São Domingos	2765	13.24 S	46.19 W
São Francisco ≃	2762	10.30 S	36.24 W
São Francisco do Sul	2764	26.14 S	48.39 W
São Gabriel	2764	19.01 S	40.32 W
São João da Boa Vista	2765	21.58 S	46.47 W
São João da Madeira	2774	40.54 N	8.30 W
São João del Rei	2765	21.09 S	44.16 W
São Joaquim da Barra	2765	20.35 S	47.53 W
São José do Rio Prêto	2765	20.48 S	49.23 W
São José dos Campos	2765	23.11 S	45.53 W
São Leopoldo	2764	29.46 S	51.09 W
São Lourenço	2765	22.07 S	45.03 W
São Lourenço, Pantanal de ☰	2762	17.30 S	56.30 W
São Luís	2762	2.31 S	44.16 W
São Manuel	2765	22.44 S	48.34 W
São Mateus	2765	18.44 S	39.51 W
São Paulo	2765	23.32 S	46.37 W
São Pedro do Ivaí	2765	23.51 S	51.51 W
São Pedro do Sul	2774	40.45 N	8.04 W
São Romão	2765	16.22 S	45.04 W
São Roque, Cabo de ≻	2762	5.29 S	35.16 W
São Salvador do Congo	2788	6.16 S	14.15 E
São Sebastião, Ponta ≻	2788	22.07 S	35.30 E
São Sebastião do Paraíso	2765	20.55 S	47.00 W
São Tomé	2788	0.20 N	6.44 E
São Tomé I	2788	0.12 N	6.39 E
São Tomé, Cabo de ≻	2765	21.59 S	40.59 W
Sao Tome and Principe ☐[1]	2788	1.00 N	7.00 E
São Vicente	2765	23.58 S	46.23 W
São Vicente, Cabo de ≻	2774	37.01 N	9.00 W
Sapé	2762	7.06 S	35.13 W
Sapele	2786	5.54 N	5.41 E
Sapitwa ∧	2788	15.57 S	35.36 E
Sapporo	2798a	43.03 N	141.21 E
Sapri	2776	40.04 N	15.38 E
Sapulpa	2748	36.00 N	96.06 W
Sarajevo	2778	43.52 N	18.25 E
Saranac Lake	2740	44.20 N	74.08 W
Sarangani Islands II	2802	5.25 N	125.26 E
Saransk	2766	54.11 N	45.11 E
Sarapul	2766	56.28 N	53.48 E
Sarasota	2744	27.20 N	82.34 W
Saratoga, Calif., U.S.	2756	37.16 N	122.02 W
Saratoga, Tex., U.S.	2748	30.17 N	94.31 W
Saratoga, Wyo., U.S.	2754	41.27 N	106.48 W
Saratoga Springs	2740	43.05 N	73.47 W
Saratov	2766	51.34 N	46.02 E
Saravane	2804	15.43 N	106.25 E
Sardalas	2786	25.46 N	10.34 E
Sardegna I	2776	40.00 N	9.00 E
Sardinia → Sardegna I	2776	40.00 N	9.00 E
Sarera, Teluk C	2802	2.30 S	135.20 E
Sargent	2750	41.38 N	99.22 W
Sargents	2752	38.25 N	106.24 W
Sargodha	2794	32.05 N	72.40 E
Sarh	2786	9.09 N	18.23 E
Sariñena	2774	41.48 N	0.10 W
Šarja	2766	58.24 N	45.30 E
Şarköy	2778	40.37 N	27.06 E
Sarles	2750	48.57 N	99.00 W
Sarmi	2802	1.51 S	138.44 E
Sarmiento	2764	45.35 S	69.05 W
Sarmiento, Monte ∧	2764	54.25 S	70.50 W
Särna	2768	61.41 N	13.08 E
Sarnia	2740	42.58 N	82.23 W
Sarria	2774	42.47 N	7.24 W
Sartang ≃	2784	67.44 N	133.12 E
Sarufutsu	2798a	45.16 N	142.12 E
Sasarām	2794	24.57 N	84.02 E
Sasebo	2798	33.10 N	129.43 E
Saskatchewan ☐[4]	2734	54.00 N	105.00 W
Saskatchewan ≃	2734	53.12 N	99.16 W
Saskatoon	2734	52.07 N	106.38 W
Saskylach	2784	71.55 N	114.01 E
Sasovo	2780	54.21 N	41.54 E
Sassandra	2786	4.58 N	6.05 W
Sassandra ≃	2786	4.58 N	6.05 W
Sassari	2776	40.44 N	8.33 E
Sassuolo	2776	44.33 N	10.47 E
Sastown	2786	4.40 N	8.26 W
Sata-misaki ≻	2798	30.59 N	130.40 E
Satanta	2750	37.26 N	100.59 W
Sātāra	2793	17.41 N	73.59 E
Satellite Beach	2744	28.11 N	80.35 W
Satka	2766	55.03 N	59.01 E
Satna	2794	24.35 N	80.50 E
Sātpura Range ⋀	2793	22.00 N	78.00 E
Satsunan-shotō II	2799b	29.00 N	130.00 E
Satu Mare	2778	47.48 N	22.53 E
Šatura	2780	55.34 N	39.32 E
Saucier	2746	30.38 N	89.08 W
Sauda	2768	59.39 N	6.20 E
Saudi Arabia ☐[1]	2790	25.00 N	45.00 E
Saugatuck	2742	42.40 N	86.12 W
Saugerties	2740	42.05 N	73.57 W
Sauk Centre	2750	45.44 N	94.57 W
Sauk City	2742	43.17 N	89.43 W
Sauk Rapids	2742	45.34 N	94.09 W
Saulgau	2770	48.01 N	9.30 E
Sault Sainte Marie, Ont., Can.	2734	46.31 N	84.20 W
Sault Sainte Marie, Mich., U.S.	2742	46.30 N	84.21 W
Saumarez Reef ✢[2]	2806	21.50 S	153.40 E
Sauveterre, Causse ⋀[1]	2772	44.20 N	3.10 E
Sava	2776	40.24 N	17.34 E
Sava ≃	2778	44.50 N	20.26 E
Savage	2754	47.27 N	104.21 W
Savanna, Ill., U.S.	2742	42.05 N	90.08 W
Savanna, Okla., U.S.	2748	34.50 N	95.51 W
Savannah, Ga., U.S.	2744	32.04 N	81.05 W
Savannah, Mo., U.S.	2746	39.56 N	94.50 W
Savannah, Tenn., U.S.	2746	35.14 N	88.14 W
Savannah ≃	2744	32.02 N	80.53 W
Savannah Beach	2744	32.01 N	80.51 W
Savannakhet	2804	16.33 N	104.45 E
Savaştepe	2778	39.22 N	27.40 E
Save (Sabi) ≃	2788	21.00 S	35.02 E
Savigliano	2776	44.38 N	7.40 E
Savona	2776	44.17 N	8.30 E
Savonlinna	2768	61.52 N	28.53 E
Savonranta	2768	62.11 N	29.12 E
Sawai Mādhopur	2794	26.00 N	76.39 E
Sawākin	2786	19.07 N	37.20 E
Sawatch Range ⋀	2752	39.10 N	106.25 W
Sawdā', Qurnat as- ∧	2791	34.18 N	36.07 E
Sawel Mountain ∧	2769	54.49 N	7.02 W
Sawhāj	2786	26.33 N	31.42 E
Sawknah	2786	29.04 N	15.47 E
Sawtooth National Recreation Area ♦	2754	44.00 N	114.55 W
Sawu, Laut (Savu Sea) ⊤[2]	2802	9.40 S	122.00 E
Sawu, Pulau I	2802	10.30 S	121.54 E
Şawwān, Arḍ aṣ- ≍	2791	30.45 N	37.15 E
Sawyer	2750	48.05 N	101.03 W
Saxmundham	2769	52.13 N	1.29 E
Saxton	2740	40.13 N	78.15 W
Sayaboury	2804	19.15 N	101.45 E
Sayan Mountains (Sajany) ⋀	2784	52.45 N	96.00 E
Sayaxché	2760	16.31 N	90.10 W
Şaydā (Sidon)	2791	33.33 N	35.22 E
Sayḥūt	2790	15.12 N	51.14 E
Sayre, Okla., U.S.	2748	35.18 N	99.38 W
Sayre, Pa., U.S.	2740	41.59 N	76.32 W
Sayula	2758	19.52 N	103.37 W
Say'ūn	2790	15.56 N	48.47 E
Scafell Pikes ∧	2769	54.27 N	3.12 W
Scandia	2750	39.48 N	97.47 W
Ščapino	2784	55.19 N	159.25 E
Ščelkovo	2780	55.55 N	38.00 E
Ščerbakovo	2784	65.15 N	160.30 E
Schaffhausen	2772	47.42 N	8.38 E
Schaller	2750	42.30 N	95.18 W
Schefferville	2734	54.48 N	66.50 W

Symbols against index entries represent categories identified in the key on page 2810.

Name	Page	Lat°′	Long°′
Schenectady	2740	42.47 N	73.53 W
Schio	2776	45.43 N	11.21 E
Schladming	2770	47.23 N	13.41 E
Schleiden	2770	50.31 N	6.28 E
Schleswig, B.R.D.	2770	54.31 N	9.33 E
Schleswig, Iowa, U.S.	2750	42.10 N	95.26 W
Schneverdingen	2770	53.07 N	9.47 E
Schongau	2770	47.49 N	10.54 E
Schramberg	2770	48.13 N	8.23 E
Schrobenhausen	2770	48.33 N	11.17 E
Schulenburg	2748	29.41 N	96.54 W
Schuyler	2750	41.27 N	97.04 W
Schuylkill Haven	2740	40.38 N	76.10 W
Schwabach	2770	49.20 N	11.01 E
Schwaben □[9]	2770	48.20 N	10.30 E
Schwäbische Alb ⛰	2770	48.25 N	9.30 E
Schwäbisch Gmünd	2770	48.48 N	9.47 E
Schwäbisch Hall	2770	49.07 N	9.44 E
Schwandorf in Bayern	2770	49.20 N	12.08 E
Schwaner, Pegunungan ⛰	2802	0.40 S	112.40 E
Schwarzwald ⛰	2770	48.00 N	8.15 E
Schwaz	2770	47.20 N	11.42 E
Schwechat	2770	48.08 N	16.29 E
Schweinfurt	2770	50.03 N	10.14 E
Schwyz	2772	47.02 N	8.40 E
Sciacca	2776	37.30 N	13.06 E
Scicli	2776	36.47 N	14.43 E
Scilly, Isles of II	2769	48.57 N	6.15 W
Ščokino	2780	54.01 N	37.31 E
Scooba	2746	32.50 N	88.29 W
Scotland	2750	43.09 N	97.43 W
Scotland Neck	2744	36.02 N	77.32 W
Scotlandville	2746	30.31 N	91.11 W
Scott, Mount ∧	2754	42.56 N	122.01 W
Scott City	2750	38.29 N	100.54 W
Scottdale	2740	40.06 N	79.35 W
Scott Islands II	2734	50.48 N	128.40 W
Scott Mountain ∧	2754	44.11 N	115.47 W
Scott Peak ∧	2754	44.21 N	112.50 W
Scott Reef ⇀[2]	2806	14.00 S	121.50 E
Scottsbluff	2750	41.52 N	103.40 W
Scottsboro	2746	34.40 N	86.02 W
Scottsburg	2746	38.41 N	85.46 W
Scottsdale, Austl.	2806	41.10 S	147.31 E
Scottsdale, Ariz., U.S.	2752	33.30 N	111.56 W
Scottsville	2746	36.45 N	86.11 W
Scottville	2742	43.57 N	86.17 W
Scourie	2769	58.20 N	5.08 W
Scranton	2740	41.24 N	75.40 W
Screven	2744	31.29 N	82.01 W
Scribner	2750	41.40 N	96.40 W
Seadrift	2748	28.30 N	96.47 W
Seaford	2740	38.39 N	75.37 W
Seagraves	2748	32.57 N	102.34 W
Seaham	2769	54.52 N	1.21 W
Sea Islands II	2744	31.20 N	81.20 W
Seal ≃	2734	59.04 N	94.48 W
Seale	2746	32.18 N	85.10 W
Searchlight	2756	35.28 N	114.55 W
Searcy	2746	35.15 N	91.44 W
Searsport	2740	44.28 N	68.56 W
Seaside, Calif., U.S.	2756	36.37 N	121.50 W
Seaside, Oreg., U.S.	2754	46.02 N	123.55 W
Seattle	2754	47.36 N	122.20 W
Šebalino	2784	51.17 N	85.40 E
Sebastian, Cape ≻	2754	42.19 N	124.26 W
Sebastián Vizcaíno, Bahía C	2758	28.00 N	114.30 W
Sebastopol	2756	38.24 N	122.49 W
Sebeka	2750	46.38 N	95.05 W
Šebekino	2782	50.25 N	36.56 E
Sebewaing	2742	43.44 N	83.27 W
Sebree	2746	37.36 N	87.32 W
Sebring	2744	27.30 N	81.26 W
Sedalia	2746	38.42 N	93.14 W
Sedano	2774	42.43 N	3.45 W
Sedgwick	2750	40.56 N	102.31 W
Sedona	2752	34.52 N	111.46 W
Sedro Woolley	2754	48.30 N	122.14 W
Seeheim	2788	26.50 S	17.45 E
Seeley Lake	2754	47.11 N	113.29 W
Segeža	2766	63.44 N	34.19 E
Ségou	2786	13.27 N	6.16 W
Segovia	2774	40.57 N	4.07 W
Séguédine	2786	20.12 N	12.59 E
Seguin	2748	29.34 N	97.58 W
Seia	2774	40.25 N	7.42 W
Seiling	2748	36.09 N	98.56 W
Seinäjoki	2768	62.47 N	22.50 E
Šeki (Nucha), S.S.S.R.	2766	41.12 N	47.12 E
Seki, Tür.	2778	36.24 N	29.13 E
Sekondi-Takoradi	2786	4.59 N	1.43 W
Šelagskij, Mys ≻	2784	70.06 N	170.26 E
Selah	2754	46.39 N	120.32 W
Selajar, Pulau I	2802	6.05 S	120.30 E
Selaru, Pulau I	2802	8.09 S	131.00 E
Selatan, Tandjung ≻	2802	4.10 S	114.38 E
Selb	2770	50.10 N	12.08 E
Selby	2750	45.31 N	100.02 W
Selçuk	2778	37.56 N	27.22 E
Selden	2750	39.33 N	100.34 W
Selemdža ≃	2784	51.42 N	128.53 E
Selenn'ach ≃	2784	67.48 N	144.54 E
Selfridge	2750	46.02 N	100.56 W
Sélibaby	2786	15.10 N	12.11 W
Šelichova, Zaliv C	2784	60.00 N	158.00 E
Selidovo	2782	48.08 N	37.18 E
Seligman	2752	35.20 N	112.53 W
Selinsgrove	2740	40.48 N	76.52 W
Selkirk, Man., Can.	2734	50.09 N	96.52 W
Selkirk, Scot., U.K.	2769	55.33 N	2.50 W
Selkirk Mountains ⛰	2734	51.00 N	117.40 W
Sellersburg	2746	38.24 N	85.45 W
Sells	2752	31.55 N	111.53 W
Selma, Ala., U.S.	2746	32.25 N	87.01 W
Selma, Calif., U.S.	2756	36.34 N	119.37 W
Selma, N.C., U.S.	2744	35.32 N	78.17 W
Selmer	2746	35.11 N	88.36 W
Selva	2764	29.50 S	62.02 W
Selvas ⇀[3]	2762	5.00 S	68.00 W
Selway ≃	2754	46.08 N	115.36 W
Selwyn Mountains ⛰	2734	63.10 N	130.20 W
Semara	2786	26.44 N	14.41 W
Semarang	2802	6.58 S	110.25 E
Seminoe Reservoir ⊜[1]	2754	42.00 N	106.50 W
Seminole, Okla., U.S.	2748	35.14 N	96.41 W
Seminole, Tex., U.S.	2748	32.43 N	102.39 W
Seminole, Lake ⊜[1]	2744	30.46 N	84.50 W
Semipalatinsk	2784	50.28 N	80.13 E
Šemonaicha	2784	50.39 N	81.54 E
Sena	2788	17.27 S	35.00 E
Senador Pompeu	2762	5.35 S	39.22 W
Sena Madureira	2762	9.04 S	68.40 W
Senanga	2788	16.06 S	23.16 E
Senath	2746	36.08 N	90.10 W
Senatobia	2746	34.39 N	89.58 W
Sendai, Nihon	2798	31.49 N	130.18 E
Sendai, Nihon	2798	38.15 N	140.53 E
Seneca, Kans., U.S.	2750	39.50 N	96.04 W
Seneca, S.C., U.S.	2744	34.41 N	82.57 W
Seneca Falls	2740	42.55 N	76.48 W
Seneca Lake ⊜	2740	42.40 N	76.57 W
Senegal (Sénégal) □[1]	2786	14.00 N	14.00 W
Sénégal ≃	2786	15.48 N	16.32 W
Senekal	2788	28.30 S	27.32 E
Senigallia	2776	43.43 N	13.13 E
Senise	2776	40.09 N	16.18 E
Šenkursk	2766	62.08 N	42.53 E
Senneterre	2734	48.23 N	77.15 W
Sennori	2776	40.48 N	8.34 E
Senta	2778	45.56 N	20.04 E
Sentinel	2748	35.09 N	99.10 W
Seo de Urgel	2774	42.21 N	1.28 E
Seoni	2794	22.06 N	79.32 E
Šepetovka	2782	50.11 N	27.04 E
Sepik ≃	2802	3.51 S	144.34 E
Sept-Îles (Seven Islands)	2739	50.12 N	66.23 W
Sepúlveda	2774	41.18 N	3.45 W
Sequim	2754	48.05 N	123.06 W
Sequoia National Park ♦	2756	36.30 N	118.30 W
Seraing	2770	50.36 N	5.29 E
Seram I	2802	3.00 S	129.00 E
Seram, Laut (Ceram Sea) ⊤[2]	2802	2.30 S	128.00 E
Serdobsk	2766	52.28 N	44.13 E
Seremban	2804	2.44 N	101.56 E
Serengeti Plain ≚	2788	2.50 S	35.00 E
Serenje	2788	13.15 S	30.14 E
Sergeja Kirova, Ostrova II	2784	77.12 N	89.30 E
Šerlovaja Gora	2784	50.34 N	116.15 E
Serov	2766	59.29 N	60.31 E
Serowe	2788	22.25 S	26.44 E
Serpa	2774	37.56 N	7.36 W
Serpa Pinto	2788	14.36 S	17.48 E
Serpuchov	2780	54.55 N	37.25 E
Sérrai	2778	41.05 N	23.32 E
Serra San Bruno	2776	38.35 N	16.20 E
Serra Talhada	2762	7.59 S	38.18 W
Serrezuela	2764	30.40 S	65.20 W
Serri	2776	39.41 N	9.09 E
Serrinha	2762	11.39 S	39.00 W
Sertã	2774	39.48 N	8.06 W
Sesfontein	2788	19.07 S	13.39 E
Sesheke	2788	17.19 S	24.18 E
Sessa Aurunca	2776	41.14 N	13.56 E
Sestri Levante	2776	44.16 N	9.24 E
Sete Lagoas	2765	19.27 S	44.14 W
Sétif	2786	36.09 N	5.26 E
Seto	2798	35.14 N	137.06 E
Seto-naikai ⊤[2]	2798	34.20 N	133.30 E
Setúbal	2774	38.32 N	8.54 W
Seul, Lac ⊜	2734	50.20 N	92.30 W
Seul Choix Point ≻	2742	45.56 N	85.52 W
Sevan, Ozero ⊜	2766	40.20 N	45.20 E
Sevastopol'	2782	44.36 N	33.32 E
Ševčenko	2766	43.35 N	51.05 E
Severn ≃, Ont., Can.	2734	56.02 N	87.36 W
Severn ≃, Eng., U.K.	2769	51.35 N	2.40 W
Severnaja Dvina ≃	2766	64.32 N	40.30 E
Severnaja Zeml'a II	2784	79.30 N	98.00 E
Severna Park	2740	39.04 N	76.33 W
Severodvinsk	2766	64.34 N	39.50 E
Severo-Kuril'sk	2784	50.40 N	156.08 E
Severomorsk	2766	69.05 N	33.24 E
Severo-Sibirskaja Nizmennost' ≚	2784	73.00 N	100.00 E
Severo-Zadonsk	2780	54.00 N	38.23 E
Severy	2750	37.37 N	96.14 W
Sevettijärvi	2768	69.26 N	28.38 E
Sevier Lake ⊜	2752	38.55 N	113.09 W
Sevierville	2744	35.52 N	83.34 W
Sevilla	2774	37.23 N	5.59 W
Seville → Sevilla	2774	37.23 N	5.59 W
Seward, Alaska, U.S.	2738	60.06 N	149.26 W
Seward, Nebr., U.S.	2750	40.55 N	97.06 W
Seychelles □[1]	2788	4.53 S	55.40 E
Seyðisfjörður	2766	65.16 N	14.00 W
Seymour, Ind., U.S.	2746	38.58 N	85.53 W
Seymour, Mo., U.S.	2746	37.09 N	92.46 W
Seymour, Tex., U.S.	2748	33.35 N	99.16 W
Sezze	2776	41.30 N	13.03 E
Sfax	2786	34.44 N	10.46 E
's-Gravenhage (The Hague)	2770	52.06 N	4.18 E
Shabani	2788	20.20 S	30.02 E
Shackleton Ice Shelf ⍂	2733	66.00 S	100.00 E
Shaddādī	2791	36.02 N	40.45 E
Shadehill Reservoir ⊜[1]	2750	45.45 N	102.15 W
Shafter, Calif., U.S.	2756	29.49 N	104.18 W
Shafter, Tex., U.S.	2748	29.49 N	104.18 W
Shag Rocks II[1]	2764	53.33 S	42.02 W
Shahdol	2794	23.20 N	81.21 E
Shāhjahānpur	2794	27.53 N	79.55 E
Shahreẕā	2790	32.01 N	51.52 E
Shakawe	2788	18.23 S	21.50 E
Shaki	2786	8.39 N	3.25 E
Shaler Mountains ⛰	2734	72.35 N	110.45 W
Shallotte	2744	33.58 N	78.23 W
Shallowater	2748	33.41 N	101.59 W
Shām, Bādiyat ash- ⇀[2]	2791	32.00 N	40.00 E
Shām, Jabal ash- ∧	2790	23.13 N	57.16 E
Shamattawa	2734	55.52 N	92.05 W
Shamokin	2740	40.47 N	76.34 W
Shamrock	2748	35.13 N	100.15 W
Shandī	2786	16.42 N	33.26 E
Shandong □[4]	2796	36.00 N	118.00 E
Shandongbandao ≻[1]	2796	37.00 N	121.00 E
Shanghai, Zhg.	2800	31.01 N	121.25 E
Shanghai, Zhg.	2800	31.14 N	121.28 E
Shanghai Shih □[7]	2800	31.10 N	121.30 E
Shangqiu	2800	34.27 N	115.42 E
Shangrao	2800	28.26 N	117.58 E
Shangshui	2800	33.39 N	114.39 E
Shangzhi	2796	45.13 N	127.59 E
Shannon	2744	34.20 N	85.04 W
Shannon ≃	2769	52.36 N	9.41 W
Shannontown	2744	33.53 N	80.21 W
Shantou (Swatow)	2800	23.23 N	116.41 E
Shantung Peninsula → Shandongbandao ≻[1]	2796	37.00 N	121.00 E
Shānxī □[4], Zhg.	2796	37.00 N	112.00 E
Shǎnxī □[4], Zhg.	2796	35.00 N	109.00 E
Shanyin	2796	39.35 N	112.58 E
Shaoguan	2800	24.50 N	113.37 E
Shaowu	2800	27.20 N	117.28 E
Shaoxing	2800	30.00 N	120.35 E
Shaoyang	2796	27.06 N	111.25 E
Shark Bay C	2806	25.30 S	113.30 E
Sharktooth Mountain ∧	2734	58.35 N	127.57 W
Sharon	2740	41.14 N	80.31 W
Sharon Springs	2750	38.54 N	101.45 W
Shashi	2796	30.19 N	112.14 E
Shashi ≃	2788	22.14 S	29.20 E
Shasta, Mount ∧[1]	2756	41.20 N	122.20 W
Shasta Lake ⊜[1]	2756	40.50 N	122.25 W
Shattuck	2748	36.16 N	99.53 W
Shaw	2746	33.36 N	90.46 W
Shawano	2742	44.47 N	88.36 W
Shawinigan	2734	46.33 N	72.45 W
Shawnee	2748	35.20 N	96.55 W
Shawneetown	2746	37.42 N	88.08 W
Shaybārā I	2790	25.27 N	36.48 E
Shaykh, Jabal ash- ∧	2791	33.26 N	35.51 E
Shebele (Shebelle) ≃	2790	0.50 N	43.10 E
Sheberghān	2794	36.41 N	65.45 E
Sheboygan	2742	43.46 N	87.36 W
Sheboygan Falls	2742	43.44 N	87.49 W
Sheffield, Eng., U.K.	2769	53.23 N	1.30 W
Sheffield, Ala., U.S.	2746	34.46 N	87.40 W
Sheffield, Iowa, U.S.	2742	42.54 N	93.13 W
Sheffield, Tex., U.S.	2748	30.41 N	101.49 W
Shekhūpura	2794	31.42 N	73.59 E
Shelagyote Peak ∧	2734	55.58 N	127.12 W
Shelbina	2746	39.47 N	92.02 W
Shelburne	2739	43.46 N	65.19 W
Shelby, Mich., U.S.	2742	43.37 N	86.22 W
Shelby, Mont., U.S.	2754	48.30 N	111.51 W
Shelby, N.C., U.S.	2744	35.17 N	81.32 W
Shelby, Ohio, U.S.	2740	40.53 N	82.40 W
Shelbyville, Ill., U.S.	2746	39.24 N	88.48 W
Shelbyville, Ind., U.S.	2746	39.31 N	85.47 W
Shelbyville, Ky., U.S.	2746	38.13 N	85.14 W
Shelbyville, Mo., U.S.	2746	39.48 N	92.02 W
Shelbyville, Tenn., U.S.	2746	35.29 N	86.27 W
Sheldon	2750	43.11 N	95.51 W
Shelley	2754	43.23 N	112.07 W
Shell Lake	2742	45.45 N	91.55 W
Shellman	2744	31.46 N	84.37 W
Shelton	2754	47.13 N	123.06 W
Shenandoah, Iowa, U.S.	2750	40.46 N	95.22 W
Shenandoah, Pa., U.S.	2740	40.49 N	76.12 W
Shenandoah, Va., U.S.	2740	38.29 N	78.37 W
Shengfang	2796	39.04 N	116.42 E
Shengze	2800	30.55 N	120.39 E
Shenjiamen	2800	29.58 N	122.17 E
Shenyang (Mukden)	2796	41.48 N	123.27 E
Shenzha	2794	30.57 N	88.38 E
Shepherd	2742	43.32 N	84.41 W
Shepherdstown	2740	39.26 N	77.48 W
Shepherdsville	2746	37.59 N	85.43 W
Shepparton	2806	36.23 S	145.25 E
Sheppey, Isle of I	2769	51.24 N	0.50 E
Sherbro Island I	2786	7.45 N	12.55 W
Sherbrooke	2740	45.25 N	71.54 W
Sherburne	2740	42.41 N	75.30 W
Sheridan, Ark., U.S.	2746	34.19 N	92.24 W
Sheridan, Ind., U.S.	2746	40.08 N	86.13 W
Sheridan, Mont., U.S.	2754	45.27 N	112.12 W
Sheridan, Oreg., U.S.	2754	45.06 N	123.24 W
Sheridan, Wyo., U.S.	2754	44.48 N	106.58 W
Sheridan, Mount ∧	2754	44.16 N	110.32 W
Sheringham Cromer	2769	52.57 N	1.12 E
Sherman, Miss., U.S.	2746	34.22 N	88.57 W
Sherman, Tex., U.S.	2748	33.38 N	96.36 W
's-Hertogenbosch	2770	51.41 N	5.19 E
Shetland Islands II	2769	60.30 N	1.30 W
Sheyenne	2750	47.39 N	99.07 W
Shibetsu	2798a	43.40 N	145.08 E
Shibotsu-tō I	2798a	43.30 N	146.09 E
Shijiazhuang	2796	38.03 N	114.28 E
Shijushan	2796	39.20 N	106.50 E
Shikārpur	2794	27.57 N	68.38 E
Shikoku I	2798	33.45 N	133.30 E
Shikoku-sanchi ⛰	2798	33.47 N	133.30 E
Shikotsu-ko ⊜	2798a	42.45 N	141.20 E
Shillong	2794	25.34 N	91.53 E
Shilong	2800	23.07 N	113.48 E
Shimizu	2798	35.01 N	138.29 E
Shimoga	2793	13.55 N	75.34 E
Shimonoseki	2798	33.57 N	130.57 E
Shīndand	2792	33.18 N	62.08 E
Shingū	2798	33.44 N	135.59 E
Shinjō	2798	38.46 N	140.18 E
Shinshār	2791	34.36 N	36.44 E
Shinyanga	2788	3.40 S	33.26 E
Shiogama	2798	38.19 N	141.01 E
Shiono-misaki ≻	2796	33.26 N	135.45 E
Shiping	2804	23.47 N	102.30 E
Shipman	2744	37.43 N	78.51 W
Shippensburg	2740	40.03 N	77.31 W
Shiprock	2752	36.47 N	108.41 W
Shīrāz	2790	29.36 N	52.32 E
Shire ≃	2788	17.42 S	35.19 E
Shishaldin Volcano ∧[1]	2738	54.45 N	163.57 W
Shivpuri	2794	25.26 N	77.39 E
Shizuoka	2798	34.58 N	138.23 E
Shkodër	2778	42.05 N	19.30 E
Shōdo-shima I	2798	34.30 N	134.17 E
Sholāpur	2793	17.41 N	75.55 E
Shoshone	2754	42.56 N	114.24 W
Shoshone Lake ⊜	2754	44.22 N	110.43 W
Shoshone Mountains ⛰	2756	39.25 N	117.15 W
Shoshong	2788	22.59 S	26.30 E
Shoshoni	2754	43.14 N	108.07 W
Shouxian	2800	32.35 N	116.47 E
Show Low	2752	34.15 N	110.02 W
Shreveport	2746	32.30 N	93.45 W
Shrewsbury	2769	52.43 N	2.45 W
Shuajingsi	2796	32.00 N	103.05 E
Shuangcheng	2796	45.26 N	126.18 E
Shuangyashan	2796	46.37 N	131.22 E
Shubuta	2746	31.52 N	88.42 W
Shullsburg	2742	42.34 N	90.14 W
Shunde	2800	22.50 N	113.14 E
Shuqrā'	2790	13.21 N	45.42 E
Shuqualak	2746	32.59 N	88.34 W
Shūshtar	2790	32.03 N	48.51 E
Shwebo	2804	22.34 N	95.42 E
Siālkot	2794	32.30 N	74.31 E
Siam,, Gulf of → Thailand, Gulf of C	2804	10.00 N	101.00 E
Siargao Island I	2802	9.53 N	126.02 E
Šiaškotan, Ostrov I	2784	48.49 N	154.06 E
Šiauliai	2780	55.56 N	23.19 E
Sibaj	2766	52.42 N	58.39 E
Šibenik	2776	43.44 N	15.54 E
Siberia → Sibir' ⇀[1]	2784	65.00 N	110.00 E
Siberut, Pulau I	2802	1.20 S	98.55 E
Sibi	2794	29.33 N	67.53 E
Sibir' (Siberia) ⇀[1]	2784	65.00 N	110.00 E
Sibir'akova, Ostrov I	2784	72.50 N	79.00 E
Sibiti	2788	3.41 S	13.21 E
Sibiu	2778	45.48 N	24.09 E
Sibley, Iowa, U.S.	2750	43.24 N	95.45 W
Sibley, La., U.S.	2746	32.33 N	93.18 W
Sibolga	2804	1.45 N	98.48 E
Sibu	2802	2.19 N	111.51 E
Sibutu Island I	2802	4.46 N	119.29 E
Sibuyan Island I	2802	12.25 N	122.34 E
Sibuyan Sea ⊤[2]	2802	12.50 N	122.40 E
Sichote-Alin' ⛰	2784	48.00 N	138.00 E
Sichuan □[4]	2796	31.00 N	105.00 E
Sicilia I	2776	37.30 N	14.00 E
Sicily → Sicilia I	2776	37.30 N	14.00 E
Sicily, Strait of ≍	2776	37.20 N	11.20 E
Sicuani	2762	14.15 S	71.15 W
Siderno	2776	38.16 N	16.18 E
Sidi bel Abbès	2786	35.13 N	0.10 W
Sidi Ifni	2786	29.24 N	10.12 W
Sidmouth	2769	50.41 N	3.15 W
Sidnaw	2742	46.30 N	88.43 W
Sidney, Iowa, U.S.	2746	40.45 N	95.39 W
Sidney, Mont., U.S.	2750	47.43 N	104.09 W
Sidney, Nebr., U.S.	2750	41.09 N	102.59 W
Sidney, N.Y., U.S.	2740	42.19 N	75.24 W
Sidney, Ohio, U.S.	2740	40.17 N	84.09 W
Siedlce	2770	52.11 N	22.16 E
Siegburg	2770	50.47 N	7.12 E
Siegen	2770	50.52 N	8.02 E
Siĕmréab	2804	13.22 N	103.51 E
Siena	2776	43.19 N	11.21 E
Sierra Blanca	2752	31.11 N	105.21 W
Sierra Blanca Peak ∧	2752	33.23 N	105.48 W
Sierra Colorada	2764	40.35 S	67.50 W
Sierra Leone □[1]	2786	8.30 N	11.30 W
Sierra Vista	2752	31.33 N	110.18 W
Sierre	2772	46.18 N	7.32 E
Sighetul Marmației	2778	47.56 N	23.54 E
Sighișoara	2778	46.13 N	24.48 E
Siglufjörður	2766	66.10 N	18.56 W
Sigourney	2742	41.20 N	92.12 W
Sigüenza	2774	41.04 N	2.38 W
Sigües	2774	42.38 N	1.00 W
Siguiri	2786	11.25 N	9.10 W
Sigurd	2752	38.50 N	111.58 W
Siilinjärvi	2768	63.05 N	27.40 E
Sīkar	2794	27.37 N	75.09 E
Sikasso	2786	11.19 N	5.40 W
Sikeston	2746	36.53 N	89.35 W
Sikiá	2778	40.02 N	23.56 E
Síkinos	2778	25.07 N	26.43 E
Šikotan, Ostrov (Shikotan-tō) I	2784	43.47 N	146.45 E
Sikt'ach	2784	69.55 N	125.02 E
Silandro	2776	46.38 N	10.46 E
Silao	2758	20.56 N	101.26 W
Silay	2802	10.48 N	122.58 E
Silba	2776	44.23 N	14.42 E
Silchar	2794	24.49 N	92.48 E
Siler City	2744	35.44 N	79.28 W
Silifke	2791	36.22 N	33.56 E
Silīguri	2794	26.42 N	88.26 E

Symbols against index entries represent categories identified in the key on page 2810.

Name	Page	Lat°′	Long°′
Silistra	2778	44.07 N	27.16 E
Šilka	2784	51.51 N	116.02 E
Šilka ≃	2784	53.22 N	121.32 E
Silkeborg	2768	56.10 N	9.34 E
Sillamäe	2780	59.24 N	27.45 E
Siloam Springs	2746	36.11 N	94.32 W
Silsbee	2746	30.21 N	94.11 W
Silvânia	2762	16.42 S	48.38 W
Silva Porto	2788	12.22 S	16.56 E
Silver Bay	2742	47.17 N	91.16 W
Silver Bell	2752	32.23 N	111.30 W
Silver Bow Park	2754	46.01 N	112.28 W
Silver City	2752	32.46 N	108.17 W
Silver Creek	2740	42.33 N	79.10 W
Silver Lake	2754	43.08 N	120.56 W
Silver Spring	2740	39.02 N	77.03 W
Silverton, Colo., U.S.	2752	37.49 N	107.40 W
Silverton, Oreg., U.S.	2754	45.01 N	122.47 W
Silverton, Tex., U.S.	2748	34.28 N	101.19 W
Silvi	2776	42.34 N	14.05 E
Simanggang	2802	1.12 N	111.32 E
Šimanovsk	2784	52.00 N	127.42 E
Simcoe	2740	42.50 N	80.18 W
Simeulue, Pulau I	2804	2.35 N	96.00 E
Simferopol'	2782	44.57 N	34.06 E
Simi Valley	2756	34.16 N	118.47 W
Simla, Bhārat	2794	31.06 N	77.10 E
Simla, Colo., U.S.	2750	39.09 N	104.05 W
Simmesport	2746	30.59 N	91.49 W
Simojovel [de Allende]	2758	17.12 N	92.38 W
Simplon Pass)(	2772	46.15 N	8.02 E
Simpson Desert ⇝2	2806	25.00 S	137.00 E
Simpson Peninsula ➤1	2734	68.34 N	88.45 W
Simušir, Ostrov I	2784	46.58 N	152.02 E
Sīnā' (Sinai Peninsula), Shib Jazīrat ➤1	2786	29.30 N	34.00 E
Sinai Peninsula → Sīnā', Shibh Jazīrat ➤1	2786	29.30 N	34.00 E
Sin'aja ≃	2784	61.06 N	126.50 E
Sīnāwan	2786	31.02 N	10.36 E
Sincé	2760	9.15 N	75.09 W
Sincelejo	2760	9.18 N	75.24 W
Sinclair	2754	41.47 N	107.07 W
Sindri	2794	23.45 N	86.42 E
Sinel'nikovo	2782	48.20 N	35.31 E
Sines	2774	37.57 N	8.52 W
Sinfães	2774	41.04 N	8.05 W
Singānallūr	2793	11.00 N	77.01 E
Singapore	2804	1.17 N	103.51 E
Singapore □1	2802	1.22 N	103.48 E
Singapore Strait ⅃⅃	2804	1.15 N	104.00 E
Singen [hohentwiel]	2770	47.46 N	8.50 E
Singida	2788	4.49 S	34.45 E
Singkang	2802	4.08 S	120.01 E
Singkawang	2804	0.54 N	109.00 E
Siniscola	2776	40.34 N	9.41 E
Sinj	2776	43.42 N	16.38 E
Sinjah	2786	13.09 N	33.56 E
Sinkāt	2786	18.50 N	36.50 E
Sinnamahoning	2740	41.19 N	78.06 W
Sinnamary	2762	5.23 N	52.57 W
Sinoia	2788	17.22 S	30.12 E
Sinop	2766	42.01 N	35.09 E
Sinskoje	2784	61.08 N	126.48 E
Sintang	2802	0.04 N	111.30 E
Sint-Niklaas	2770	51.10 N	4.08 E
Sinton	2748	29.41 N	95.58 W
Sintra	2774	38.48 N	9.23 W
Sinŭiju	2796	40.05 N	124.24 E
Sion	2772	46.14 N	7.21 E
Sioux City	2750	42.30 N	96.23 W
Sioux Falls	2750	43.32 N	96.44 W
Sioux Lookout	2734	50.06 N	91.55 W
Sioux Rapids	2750	42.53 N	95.09 W
Siping	2796	43.12 N	124.20 E
Siracusa	2776	37.04 N	15.17 E
Sirājganj	2794	24.27 N	89.43 E
Sir Edward Pellew Group II	2806	15.40 S	136.48 E
Siret ≃	2778	45.24 N	28.01 E
Sirevåg	2768	58.30 N	5.47 E
Sir James MacBrien, Mount ⋀	2734	62.07 N	127.41 W
Sirohi	2794	24.53 N	72.52 E
Sirsa	2794	29.32 N	75.01 E
Sisak	2776	45.29 N	16.23 E
Sisseton	2750	45.40 N	97.03 W
Sissonville	2740	38.32 N	81.38 W
Sister Bay	2742	45.11 N	87.07 W
Sisters	2754	44.17 N	121.33 W
Sītāpur	2794	27.34 N	80.41 E
Sittard	2770	51.00 N	5.53 E
Sittwe (Akyab)	2804	20.09 N	92.54 E
Siuslaw ≃	2754	44.01 N	124.08 W
Sivas	2766	39.45 N	37.02 E
Sīwah	2786	29.12 N	25.31 E
Skagen	2768	57.44 N	10.36 E
Skagerrak ⅃⅃	2768	57.45 N	9.00 E
Skagit ≃	2754	48.20 N	122.25 W
Skagway	2738	59.28 N	135.19 W
Skaidi	2768	70.25 N	24.30 E
Skarżysko-Kamienna	2770	51.08 N	20.53 E
Skeena Mountains ⋀	2734	57.00 N	128.30 W
Skegness	2769	53.10 N	0.21 E
Skeldon	2762	5.57 N	57.09 W
Skellefteå	2768	64.46 N	20.57 E
Skelleftehamn	2768	64.41 N	21.14 E
Skibotn	2768	69.24 N	20.16 E
Skiddaw ∧	2769	54.38 N	3.08 W
Skidmore	2748	28.15 N	97.41 W
Skien	2768	59.12 N	9.36 E
Skierniewice	2770	51.58 N	20.08 E
Skikda	2786	36.50 N	6.58 E
Skillingaryd	2768	57.26 N	14.05 E
Sklad	2784	71.55 N	123.33 E
Škofja Loka	2776	46.10 N	14.18 E
Skokie	2742	42.02 N	87.46 W
Sropje	2778	41.59 N	21.26 E
Skövde	2768	58.24 N	13.50 E
Skovorodino	2784	53.59 N	123.55 E
Skowhegan	2740	44.46 N	69.43 W
Skull Valley	2752	34.30 N	112.41 W
Skye, Island of I	2769	57.15 N	6.10 W
Slagnäs	2768	65.34 N	18.05 E
Slancy	2780	59.06 N	28.04 E
Slano	2776	42.47 N	17.54 E
Slater	2746	39.13 N	93.04 W
Slaton	2748	33.26 N	101.39 W
Slav'ansk-na-Kubani	2782	45.15 N	38.08 E
Slave ≃	2734	61.18 N	113.39 W
Slavonia → Slavonija ◆1	2776	45.00 N	18.00 E
Slavonija ◆1	2776	45.00 N	18.00 E
Slavonska Požega	2776	45.20 N	17.41 E
Slavonski Brod	2778	45.10 N	18.01 E
Sleeping Bear Dunes National Lakeshore ♠	2742	44.50 N	86.08 W
Sleepy Eye	2750	44.18 N	94.43 W
Slidell	2746	30.17 N	89.47 W
Sligo, Eire	2769	54.17 N	8.28 W
Sligo, Pa., U.S.	2740	41.07 N	79.29 W
Sliven	2778	42.40 N	26.19 E
Slobodskoj	2766	58.42 N	50.12 E
Slonim	2780	53.06 N	25.19 E
Slovenjgradec	2776	46.31 N	15.05 E
Slovenska Bistrica	2776	46.23 N	15.34 E
Sluck	2780	53.01 N	27.33 E
Sl'ud'anka	2784	51.38 N	103.42 E
Słupsk (Stolp)	2770	54.28 N	17.01 E
Smederevo	2778	44.40 N	20.56 E
Smela	2782	49.14 N	31.53 E
Smethport	2740	41.49 N	78.27 W
Smidovič	2784	48.36 N	133.49 E
Šmidta, Ostrov I	2784	81.08 N	90.48 E
Smith Center	2750	39.47 N	98.47 W
Smithers, B.C., Can.	2734	54.47 N	127.10 W
Smithers, W. Va., U.S.	2740	38.11 N	81.18 W
Smithfield, N.C., U.S.	2744	35.30 N	78.21 W
Smithfield, Utah, U.S.	2752	41.50 N	111.50 W
Smiths Falls	2740	44.54 N	76.01 W
Smithton	2806	40.51 S	145.07 E
Smithville, Ga., U.S.	2744	31.54 N	84.15 W
Smithville, Tenn., U.S.	2746	35.58 N	85.49 W
Smithville, Tex., U.S.	2748	30.00 N	97.09 W
Smokey Dome ∧	2754	43.29 N	114.56 W
Smoky ≃	2734	56.10 N	117.21 W
Smoky Hill ≃	2750	39.03 N	96.48 W
Smolensk	2780	54.47 N	32.03 E
Smyrna, Del., U.S.	2740	39.18 N	75.36 W
Smyrna, Ga., U.S.	2744	33.53 N	84.31 W
Smyrna, Tenn., U.S.	2746	35.59 N	86.31 W
Smythe, Mount ∧	2734	57.54 N	124.53 W
Snake ≃	2754	46.12 N	119.02 W
Snake River Plain ≍	2754	43.00 N	113.00 W
Sneads	2744	30.42 N	84.56 W
Sneek	2770	53.02 N	5.40 E
Snohomish	2754	47.55 N	122.06 W
Snowdon ∧	2769	53.04 N	4.05 W
Snowdonia National Park ♠	2769	53.00 N	3.57 W
Snowdoun	2746	32.15 N	86.18 W
Snowdrift	2734	62.23 N	110.47 W
Snowflake	2752	34.30 N	110.05 W
Snow Hill, Md.. U.S.	2740	38.11 N	75.24 W
Snow Hill, N.C., U.S.	2744	35.27 N	77.40 W
Snow Lake	2734	54.53 N	100.02 W
Snowmass Mountain ∧	2752	39.07 N	107.04 W
Snow Peak ∧	2754	48.35 N	118.29 W
Snyder, Okla., U.S.	2748	34.40 N	98.57 W
Snyder, Tex., U.S.	2748	32.44 N	100.55 W
Soalala	2788	16.06 S	45.20 E
Soap Lake	2754	47.23 N	119.29 W
Sobat ≃	2786	9.22 N	31.33 E
Sobinka	2780	55.59 N	40.01 E
Sobral	2762	3.42 S	40.21 W
Soči	2782	43.35 N	39.45 E
Society Hill	2744	34.31 N	79.51 W
Socorro, Col.	2762	6.29 N	73.16 W
Socorro, N. Mex., U.S.	2752	34.04 N	106.54 W
Socorro, Tex., U.S.	2752	31.39 N	106.18 W
Socuéllamos	2774	39.17 N	2.48 W
Sodankylä	2768	67.29 N	26.32 E
Soda Springs	2754	42.39 N	111.36 W
Söderhamn	2768	61.18 N	17.03 E
Södertälje	2768	59.12 N	17.37 E
Sodo	2790	6.52 N	37.47 E
Sodus	2740	43.14 N	77.04 W
Soest	2770	51.34 N	8.07 E
Sofia → Sofija	2778	42.41 N	23.19 E
Sofia ≃	2788	15.27 S	47.23 E
Sofija (Sofia)	2778	42.41 N	23.19 E
Sognafjorden C2	2768	61.06 N	5.10 E
Søgne	2768	58.05 N	7.49 E
Soignies	2770	50.35 N	4.04 E
Šokal'skogo, Proliv ⅃⅃	2784	79.00 N	100.25 E
Söke	2778	37.45 N	27.24 E
Sokodé	2786	8.59 N	1.08 E
Sokol, S.S.S.R.	2780	59.28 N	40.10 E
Sokol, S.S.S.R.	2784	72.24 N	126.48 E
Sokoto	2786	13.04 N	5.16 E
Sol, Costa del ♟2	2774	36.30 N	4.30 W
Solbad Hall in Tirol	2770	47.17 N	11.31 E
Soledad, Col.	2760	10.55 N	74.46 W
Soledad, Calif., U.S.	2756	36.26 N	121.19 W
Solen	2750	46.23 N	100.48 W
Solihull	2769	52.25 N	1.45 W
Solikamsk	2766	59.39 N	56.47 E
Solingen	2770	51.10 N	7.05 E
Sollefteå	2768	63.10 N	17.16 E
Sollentuna	2768	59.28 N	17.54 E
Sóller	2774	39.46 N	2.42 E
Solnečnogorsk	2780	56.11 N	36.59 E
Sologoncy	2784	66.13 N	114.14 E
Solok	2804	0.48 S	100.39 E
Solomon	2750	38.55 N	97.22 W
Solomon Islands II	2730	8.00 S	159.00 E
Solon	2740	44.57 N	69.52 W
Solon Springs	2742	46.22 N	91.48 W
Solothurn	2772	47.13 N	7.32 E
Solsona	2774	41.59 N	1.31 E
Soltau	2770	52.59 N	9.49 E
Solvang	2756	34.36 N	120.08 W
Solwezi	2788	12.11 S	26.25 E
Soma	2778	39.10 N	27.36 E
Somalia □1	2790	10.00 N	49.00 E
Sombor	2778	45.46 N	19.07 E
Sombrerete	2758	23.38 N	103.39 W
Somers	2754	48.05 N	114.13 W
Somerset, Ky., U.S.	2744	37.05 N	84.36 W
Somerset, Pa., U.S.	2740	40.01 N	79.05 W
Somerset Island I	2734	73.15 N	93.30 W
Somersworth	2740	43.16 N	70.52 W
Somerton	2752	32.36 N	114.43 W
Somerville, N.J., U.S.	2740	40.34 N	74.37 W
Somerville, Tenn., U.S.	2746	35.15 N	89.21 W
Somerville, Tex., U.S.	2748	30.21 N	96.32 W
Sønderborg	2768	54.55 N	9.47 E
Søndre Strømfjord	2734	66.59 N	50.40 W
Sondrio	2776	46.10 N	9.52 E
Songea	2788	10.41 S	35.39 E
Songhuajiang ≃	2796	47.44 N	132.32 E
Songjiang	2800	31.01 N	121.14 E
Songkhla	2804	7.13 N	100.34 E
Songnim	2796	38.44 N	125.38 E
Sonīpat	2794	28.59 N	77.01 E
Son-la	2804	21.13 N	103.54 E
Sonmiāni Bay C	2794	25.15 N	66.30 E
Sonoita	2758	31.51 N	112.50 W
Sonoma	2756	38.17 N	122.28 W
Sonora, Calif., U.S.	2756	37.59 N	120.23 W
Sonora, Tex., U.S.	2748	30.34 N	100.39 W
Sonora Desert ⇝2	2752	33.00 N	114.00 W
Sonseca	2774	39.42 N	3.57 W
Sonsonate	2760	13.43 N	89.44 W
Sonsorol Islands II	2802	5.20 N	132.13 E
Son-tay	2804	21.08 N	105.30 E
Sonthofen	2770	47.31 N	10.17 E
Soochow → Suzhou	2800	31.18 N	120.37 E
Soperton	2744	32.23 N	82.35 W
Sopot	2770	54.28 N	18.34 E
Sopron	2770	47.41 N	16.36 E
Sora	2776	41.43 N	13.37 E
Sorel	2740	46.02 N	73.07 W
Sorgono	2776	40.01 N	9.06 E
Soria	2774	41.46 N	2.28 W
Sorocaba	2765	23.29 S	47.27 W
Soroki	2782	48.09 N	28.17 E
Sorol I1	2802	8.08 N	140.23 E
Sorong	2802	0.53 S	131.15 E
Soroti	2786	1.43 N	33.37 E
Sorrento	2776	40.37 N	14.22 E
Sorsele	2768	65.30 N	17.30 E
Sorsogon	2802	12.58 N	124.00 E
Sort	2774	42.24 N	1.08 E
Sortavala	2766	61.42 N	30.41 E
Sos del Rey Católico	2774	42.30 N	1.13 W
Sosnogorsk	2766	63.37 N	53.51 E
Sosnovo-Oz'orskoje	2784	52.31 N	111.30 E
Sosnowiec	2770	50.18 N	19.08 E
Šoštanj	2776	46.23 N	15.03 E
Šostka	2782	51.52 N	33.30 E
Sos'va	2766	63.40 N	61.55 E
Sotkamo	2768	64.08 N	28.25 E
Soto la Marina	2758	23.46 N	98.13 W
Sŏul (Seoul)	2796	37.33 N	126.58 E
Souris	2739	46.21 N	62.15 W
Souris ≃	2736	49.39 N	99.34 W
Souris Plain ≍	2750	48.15 N	100.15 W
Sousa	2762	6.45 S	38.14 W
Sousse	2774	35.49 N	10.38 E
South Africa □1	2788	30.00 S	26.00 E
South America ♟1	2730	48.00 S	70.00 W
Southampton, Ont., Can.	2740	44.29 N	81.23 W
Southampton, Eng., U.K.	2769	50.55 N	1.25 W
Southampton, N.Y., U.S.	2740	40.53 N	72.24 W
Southampton Island I	2734	64.20 N	84.40 W
South Andaman I	2804	11.45 N	92.45 E
South Aulatsivik Island I	2734	56.45 N	61.30 W
South Baldy ∧	2752	33.59 N	107.11 W
South Baymouth	2740	45.33 N	82.01 W
South Beloit	2742	42.29 N	89.02 W
South Bend, Ind., U.S.	2746	41.41 N	86.15 W
South Bend, Wash., U.S.	2754	46.40 N	123.48 W
South Boston	2744	36.42 N	78.54 W
South Bruny I	2806	43.23 S	147.17 E
South Carolina □3	2736	34.00 N	81.00 W
South Charleston	2740	38.22 N	81.44 W
South China Sea ▾2	2802	10.00 N	113.00 E
South Dakota □3	2736	44.15 N	100.00 W
South East Cape ➤	2806	43.39 S	146.50 E
Southend-on-Sea	2769	51.33 N	0.43 E
Southern Alps ⋀	2808	43.30 S	170.30 E
Southern Cross	2806	31.13 S	119.19 E
Southern Indian Lake ⊜	2734	57.10 N	98.40 W
Southern Pines	2744	35.11 N	79.24 W
South Fox Island I	2742	45.25 N	85.50 W
South Fulton	2746	36.30 N	88.53 W
Southgate	2742	42.12 N	83.13 W
South Georgia I	2764	54.15 S	36.45 W
South Haven	2742	42.24 N	86.16 W
South Henik Lake ⊜	2734	61.30 N	97.30 W
South Hill	2744	36.44 N	78.08 W
South Houston	2748	29.40 N	95.14 W
South Indian Lake	2734	56.46 N	98.57 W
South Island I	2808	43.00 S	171.00 E
South Lake Tahoe	2756	38.57 N	119.57 W
Southlawn	2746	39.45 N	89.37 W
South Manitou Island I	2742	45.01 N	86.07 W
South Mills	2744	36.27 N	76.20 W
South Nahanni ≃	2734	61.03 N	123.20 W
South Orkney Islands II	2733	60.35 S	45.30 W
South Pass)(	2754	42.22 N	108.55 W
South Pittsburg	2746	35.01 N	85.42 W
South Platte ≃	2736	41.07 N	100.42 W
Southport, Eng., U.K.	2769	53.39 N	3.01 W
Southport, N.C., U.S.	2744	33.55 N	78.01 W
South Portland	2740	43.38 N	70.15 W
South Rockwood	2742	42.04 N	83.16 W
South Ronaldsay I	2769	58.46 N	2.50 W
South Saskatchewan ≃	2734	53.15 N	105.05 W
South Shetland Islands II	2733	62.00 S	60.00 W
South Shields	2769	55.00 N	1.25 W
South Sioux City	2750	42.28 N	96.24 W
South Superior	2754	41.46 N	108.58 W
South Tuscon	2752	32.12 N	110.58 W
South Vietnam → Vietnam □1	2802	16.00 N	108.00 E
South West Africa □2	2788	22.00 S	17.00 E
South West Cape ➤	2806	47.17 S	167.28 E
Sovetsk (Tilsit)	2780	55.05 N	21.53 E
Sovetskaja Gavan'	2784	48.58 N	140.18 E
Soviet Union → Union of Soviet Socialist Republics □1	2730	60.00 N	80.00 E
Spa	2770	50.30 N	5.52 E
Spain □1	2766	40.00 N	4.00 W
Spanish Fork	2752	40.07 N	111.39 W
Spanish North Africa □2	2786	35.53 N	5.19 W
Spanish Peak ∧	2754	44.24 N	119.46 W
Spanish Sahara → Western Sahara □2	2786	24.30 N	13.00 W
Spanish Town	2760	18.00 N	76.57 W
Sparks	2756	39.32 N	119.45 W
Sparta → Spárti, Ellás	2778	37.05 N	22.27 E
Sparta, Ga., U.S.	2744	33.17 N	82.58 W
Sparta, Ill., U.S.	2746	38.07 N	89.42 W
Sparta, Mich., U.S.	2742	43.10 N	85.42 W
Sparta, N.C., U.S.	2744	36.30 N	81.07 W
Sparta, Tenn., U.S.	2746	35.56 N	85.29 W
Sparta, Wis., U.S.	2742	43.57 N	90.47 W
Spartanburg	2744	34.57 N	81.55 W
Spartel, Cap ➤	2774	35.48 N	5.56 W
Spárti (Sparta)	2778	37.05 N	22.27 E
Spartivento, Capo ➤	2776	38.53 N	8.50 E
Spassk-Dal'nij	2784	44.37 N	132.48 E
Spearfish	2750	44.30 N	103.52 W
Spearman	2748	36.12 N	101.12 W
Spearville	2750	37.51 N	99.45 W
Speedway	2746	39.47 N	86.15 W
Spence Bay	2734	69.32 N	93.31 W
Spencer, Ind., U.S.	2746	39.17 N	86.46 W
Spencer, Iowa, U.S.	2750	43.09 N	95.09 W
Spencer, Nebr., U.S.	2750	42.53 N	98.42 W
Spencer, N.C., U.S.	2744	35.37 N	80.26 W
Spencer, Tenn., U.S.	2746	35.45 N	85.28 W
Spencer, W. Va., U.S.	2740	38.48 N	81.21 W
Spencer, Wis., U.S.	2742	44.45 N	90.18 W
Spey ≃	2769	57.40 N	3.06 W
Speyer	2770	49.19 N	8.26 E
Spirit Lake	2750	43.26 N	95.06 W
Spittal an der Drau	2770	46.48 N	13.30 E
Spitz	2770	48.22 N	15.25 E
Split	2776	43.31 N	16.27 E
Splügen	2772	46.33 N	9.20 E
Spokane	2754	47.40 N	117.23 W
Spokane, Mount ∧	2754	47.55 N	117.07 W
Spoleto	2776	42.44 N	12.44 E
Spooner	2742	45.50 N	91.53 W
Spornoje	2784	62.20 N	151.03 E
Sprague	2754	47.18 N	117.59 W
Spratly Island I	2802	8.38 N	111.55 E
Springbok	2788	29.43 S	17.55 E
Spring City	2744	35.42 N	84.52 W
Springdale, Newf., Can.	2734	49.30 N	56.04 W
Springdale, Ark., U.S.	2746	36.11 N	94.08 W
Springdale, Wash., U.S.	2754	48.04 N	117.45 W
Spring Dale, W. Va., U.S.	2744	37.53 N	80.48 W
Springer	2748	36.22 N	104.36 W
Springfield, Colo., U.S.	2750	37.24 N	102.37 W
Springfield, Fla., U.S.	2746	30.09 N	85.37 W
Springfield, Ga., U.S.	2744	32.22 N	81.18 W
Springfield, Ill., U.S.	2746	39.47 N	89.40 W
Springfield, Ky., U.S.	2746	37.41 N	85.13 W
Springfield, Mass., U.S.	2740	42.07 N	72.36 W
Springfield, Minn , U.S.	2750	44.14 N	94.59 W
Springfield, Mo., U.S.	2746	37.14 N	93.17 W
Springfield, Ohio, U.S.	2740	39.56 N	83.49 W
Springfield, Oreg., U.S.	2754	44.03 N	123.01 W
Springfield, S. Dak., U.S.	2750	42.49 N	97.54 W
Springfield, Tenn., U.S.	2746	36.31 N	86.52 W
Springfield, Vt., U.S.	2740	43.18 N	72.29 W
Springfield Plateau ⋀1	2746	37.10 N	93.30 W
Springfontein	2788	30.19 S	25.36 E
Spring Garden	2762	6.59 N	58.30 W
Spring Green	2742	43.11 N	90.04 W
Springhill, N.S., Can.	2739	45.39 N	64.03 W
Springhill, La., U.S.	2746	33.00 N	93.28 W
Spring Hill, Tenn., U.S.	2746	35.45 N	86.56 W
Spring Lake	2744	35.10 N	78.58 W
Springs	2788	26.13 S	28.25 E
Spring Valley, Ill., U.S.	2746	41.20 N	89.12 W
Spring Valley, Minn , U.S.	2742	43.41 N	92.23 W
Spring Valley, N.Y., U.S.	2740	41.07 N	74.03 W
Springview	2750	42.49 N	99.45 W
Springville, N.Y., U.S.	2740	42.31 N	78.40 W
Springville, Utah, U.S.	2752	40.10 N	111.37 W
Spruce Knob ∧	2740	38.42 N	79.32 W
Spruce Pine	2744	35.55 N	82.04 W
Squamish	2734	49.42 N	123.09 W
Squinzano	2776	40.26 N	18.03 E
Sredinnyj Chrebet ⋀	2784	56.00 N	158.00 E
Srednekolymsk	2784	67.27 N	153.41 E

Symbols against index entries represent categories identified in the key on page 2810.

Name	Page	Lat°′	Long°′
Srednerusskaja Vozvyšennost' ⛰¹	2780	52.00 N	38.00 E
Srednesibirskoje Ploskogorje ⛰¹	2784	65.00 N	105.00 E
Sremska Mitrovica	2778	44.58 N	19.37 E
Sri Gangānagar	2794	29.55 N	73.53 E
Srīkākulam	2793	18.18 N	83.54 E
Sri Lanka □¹	2792	7.00 N	81.00 E
Srīnagar	2794	34.05 N	74.49 E
Stade	2770	53.36 N	9.28 E
Stadthagen	2770	52.19 N	9.13 E
Stafford, Eng., U.K.	2769	52.48 N	2.07 W
Stafford, Kans., U.S.	2750	37.58 N	98.36 W
Stafford, Tex., U.S.	2748	29.37 N	95.34 W
Stafford, Va., U.S.	2740	38.25 N	77.24 W
Staked Plain → Estacado, Llano ≚	2736	33.30 N	102.40 W
Stalheim	2768	60.50 N	6.40 E
Stallo	2746	32.55 N	89.07 W
Stalowa Wola	2770	50.35 N	22.02 E
Stamford, N.Y., U.S.	2740	42.25 N	74.37 W
Stamford, Tex., U.S.	2748	32.57 N	99.48 W
Stamford, Lake ⊜¹	2748	33.05 N	99.35 W
Stamps	2746	33.22 N	93.30 W
Stanberry	2750	40.13 N	94.35 W
Standerton	2788	26.58 S	29.07 E
Standish	2742	43.59 N	83.57 W
Stanford, Ky., U.S.	2744	37.32 N	84.40 W
Stanford, Mont., U.S.	2754	47.09 N	110.13 W
Stanke Dimitrov	2778	42.16 N	23.07 E
Stanley, Falk. Is.	2764	51.42 S	57.51 W
Stanley, N. Dak., U.S.	2750	48.19 N	102.23 W
Stanley Falls ↳	2788	0.15 N	25.30 E
Stanleyville → Kisangani	2788	0.30 N	25.12 E
Stann Creek	2760	16.58 N	88.13 W
Stanovoj Chrebet ⛰	2784	56.20 N	126.00 E
Stanovoje Nagorje (Stanovoy Mountains) ⛰	2784	56.00 N	114.00 E
Stanton, Ky., U.S.	2744	37.54 N	83.52 W
Stanton, Nebr., U.S.	2750	41.57 N	97.14 W
Stanton, N. Dak., U.S.	2750	47.19 N	101.23 W
Stanton, Tex., U.S.	2748	32.08 N	101.48 W
Stanwood	2754	48.15 N	122.23 W
Staples	2750	46.21 N	94.48 W
Stapleton	2750	41.29 N	100.31 W
Starachowice	2770	51.03 N	21.04 E
Staraja Russa	2780	58.00 N	31.23 E
Stara Planina (Balkan Mountains) ⛰	2778	43.15 N	25.00 E
Stara Zagora	2778	42.25 N	25.38 E
Starbuck	2754	47.31 N	118.08 W
Star City, Ark., U.S.	2746	33.56 N	91.51 W
Star City, Ind., U.S.	2746	40.58 N	86.33 W
Stargard Szczeciński (Stargard in Pommern)	2770	53.20 N	15.02 E
Starke	2744	29.57 N	82.07 W
Starkville	2746	33.28 N	88.48 W
Starnberg	2770	48.00 N	11.20 E
Starobel'sk	2782	49.16 N	38.56 E
Starogard Gdański	2770	53.59 N	18.33 E
Starokonstantinov	2782	49.46 N	27.13 E
Start Point ≻	2769	50.13 N	3.38 W
Staryj Oskol	2782	51.19 N	37.51 E
State Center	2742	42.01 N	93.10 W
State College, Miss., U.S.	2746	33.26 N	88.47 W
State College, Pa., U.S.	2740	40.48 N	77.52 W
Stateline	2756	38.57 N	119.57 W
State Road	2744	36.19 N	80.52 W
Statesboro	2744	32.27 N	81.47 W
Statesville	2744	35.47 N	80.53 W
Staunton, Ill., U.S.	2746	39.01 N	89.47 W
Staunton, Va., U.S.	2740	38.09 N	79.04 W
Stavanger	2768	58.58 N	5.45 E
Stavropol'	2766	45.02 N	41.59 E
Stayton	2754	44.48 N	122.48 W
Steamboat Mountain ∧	2754	41.58 N	108.58 W
Steamboat Springs	2752	40.29 N	106.50 W
Steele	2750	46.51 N	99.55 W
Steelville	2746	37.58 N	91.22 W
Steenkool	2802	2.07 S	133.32 E
Steens Mountain ⛰	2754	42.35 N	118.40 W
Stefansson Island I	2734	73.17 N	106.45 W
Steinbach	2734	49.32 N	96.41 W
Steinkjer	2768	64.01 N	11.30 E
Stellenbosch	2788	33.58 S	18.50 E
Stepanakert	2766	39.49 N	46.44 E
Stephen	2750	48.27 N	96.53 W
Stephens	2746	33.25 N	93.04 W
Stephenson	2742	45.20 N	87.38 W
Stephenville	2748	32.13 N	98.12 W
Sterling, Colo., U.S.	2750	40.37 N	103.13 W
Sterling, Ill., U.S.	2746	41.48 N	89.42 W
Sterling City	2748	31.50 N	100.59 W
Sterlitamak	2766	53.37 N	55.58 E
Steubenville	2740	40.22 N	80.37 W
Stevenage	2769	51.55 N	0.14 W
Stevenson, Ala., U.S.	2746	34.52 N	85.50 W
Stevenson, Wash., U.S.	2754	45.42 N	121.53 W
Stevens Point	2742	44.31 N	89.34 W
Stevensville	2754	46.30 N	114.05 W
Stewart, B.C., Can.	2734	55.56 N	129.59 W
Stewart, Minn , U.S.	2742	44.43 N	94.29 W
Stewart Island I	2808	47.00 S	167.50 E
Stewartville	2742	43.51 N	92.29 W
Steyr	2770	48.03 N	14.25 E
Stickney	2750	43.35 N	98.26 W
Stigliano	2776	40.24 N	16.14 E
Stikine ≃	2734	57.00 N	131.50 W
Stikine Ranges ⛰	2734	58.45 N	130.00 W
Stillwater, Minn , U.S.	2742	45.04 N	92.49 W
Stillwater, Okla., U.S.	2748	36.07 N	97.04 W
Stillwell	2746	35.49 N	94.38 W
Stinnett	2748	35.50 N	101.27 W
Štip	2778	41.44 N	22.12 E
Stirling	2769	56.07 N	3.57 W
Stjørdalshalsen	2768	63.28 N	10.56 E
Stockdale	2748	29.14 N	97.58 W
Stockerau	2770	48.23 N	16.13 E
Stockett	2754	47.21 N	111.10 W
Stockholm	2768	59.20 N	18.03 E
Stockton, Calif., U.S.	2756	37.57 N	121.17 W
Stockton, Ill., U.S.	2742	42.21 N	90.01 W
Stockton, Kans., U.S.	2750	39.26 N	99.16 W
Stockton, Mo., U.S.	2746	37.42 N	93.48 W
Stockton, Utah, U.S.	2752	40.27 N	112.22 W
Stockton Plateau ⛰¹	2748	30.30 N	102.30 W
Stockville	2750	40.32 N	100.23 W
Stœng Trêng	2804	13.31 N	105.58 E
Stoke-on-Trent	2769	53.00 N	2.10 W
Stolbovoj, Ostrov I	2784	74.05 N	136.00 E
Stolp → Słupsk	2770	54.28 N	17.01 E
Ston	2776	42.50 N	17.42 E
Stonefort	2746	37.37 N	88.42 W
Stonehaven	2769	56.38 N	2.13 W
Stonewall	2748	34.39 N	96.31 W
Stonington	2740	44.09 N	68.40 W
Stony Rapids	2734	59.16 N	105.50 W
Storby	2768	60.13 N	19.34 E
Støren	2768	63.02 N	10.18 E
Storfors	2768	59.32 N	14.16 E
Storkerson Peninsula ≻¹	2734	72.30 N	106.30 W
Storlien	2768	63.19 N	12.06 E
Storm Lake	2750	42.39 N	95.13 W
Stornoway	2769	58.12 N	6.23 W
Storuman	2768	65.06 N	17.06 E
Storvreta	2768	59.58 N	17.42 E
Story City	2742	42.11 N	93.36 W
Stoughton	2742	42.55 N	89.13 W
Stowe	2740	44.28 N	72.41 W
Strahan	2806	42.09 S	145.19 E
Strakonice	2770	49.16 N	13.55 E
Stranraer	2769	54.55 N	5.02 W
Strasburg, Colo., U.S.	2750	39.44 N	104.20 W
Strasburg, N. Dak., U.S.	2750	46.08 N	100.10 W
Strasburg, Va., U.S.	2740	38.59 N	78.22 W
Stratford, Ont., Can.	2740	43.22 N	80.57 W
Stratford, Conn., U.S.	2740	41.14 N	73.07 W
Stratford-upon-Avon	2769	52.12 N	1.41 W
Stratton, Colo., U.S.	2750	39.18 N	102.36 W
Stratton, Maine, U.S.	2740	45.08 N	70.26 W
Straubing	2770	48.53 N	12.34 E
Strawberry Point	2742	42.41 N	91.32 W
Strawn	2748	32.33 N	98.30 W
Streator	2746	41.07 N	88.50 W
Stretensk	2784	52.15 N	117.43 E
Stringtown	2748	34.28 N	96.03 W
Stromness	2769	58.57 N	3.18 W
Stromsburg	2750	41.07 N	97.36 W
Strömstad	2768	58.56 N	11.10 E
Strömsund	2768	63.51 N	15.35 E
Strong	2746	33.07 N	92.21 W
Stronsay I	2769	59.08 N	2.38 W
Stroud	2748	35.45 N	96.40 W
Stroudsburg	2740	40.59 N	75.12 W
Strumble Head ≻	2769	52.02 N	5.04 W
Strumica	2778	41.26 N	22.38 E
Strunino	2780	56.23 N	38.34 E
Struthers	2740	41.04 N	80.38 W
Stryj	2782	49.15 N	23.51 E
Stuart, Fla., U.S.	2744	27.12 N	80.15 W
Stuart, Iowa, U.S.	2750	41.30 N	94.19 W
Stuart, Va., U.S.	2744	36.38 N	80.16 W
Stuart, Mount ∧	2754	47.29 N	120.54 W
Stuarts Draft, Va., U.S.	2740		
	2744	38.01 N	79.02 W
Stupino	2780	54.53 N	38.05 E
Sturgeon	2746	39.14 N	92.17 W
Sturgeon Bay	2742	44.50 N	87.23 W
Sturgeon Falls	2740	46.22 N	79.55 W
Sturgis, Mich., U.S.	2742	41.48 N	85.25 W
Sturgis, S. Dak., U.S.	2750	44.25 N	103.31 W
Stuttgart, B.R.D.	2770	48.46 N	9.11 E
Stuttgart, Ark., U.S.	2746	34.30 N	91.33 W
Subiaco	2776	41.55 N	13.06 E
Sublette	2750	37.29 N	100.50 W
Sublett Range ⛰	2754	42.20 N	112.50 W
Subotica	2778	46.06 N	19.39 E
Sučan	2784	43.08 N	133.09 E
Suceava	2778	47.39 N	26.19 E
Süchbaatar	2796	50.17 N	106.10 E
Suchumi	2766	43.01 N	41.02 E
Sucre	2762	19.02 S	65.17 W
Sudan	2748	34.04 N	102.32 W
Sudan □¹	2786	15.00 N	30.00 E
Sudan ✦¹	2786	10.00 N	20.00 E
Sudbury	2734	46.30 N	81.00 W
Sue ≃	2786	7.41 N	28.03 E
Sueca	2774	39.12 N	0.19 W
Suez Canal → Suways, Qanāt as- ☰	2790	29.55 N	32.33 E
Suffolk	2744	36.44 N	76.35 W
Sugar City	2754	43.52 N	111.45 W
Sugar Creek	2740	41.25 N	79.49 W
Sugar Island I	2742	46.25 N	84.12 W
Sugoj ≃	2784	64.15 N	154.29 E
Şuḥār	2790	24.22 N	56.45 E
Suide	2796	37.33 N	110.04 E
Suihua	2796	46.37 N	127.00 E
Suining	2796	30.31 N	105.34 E
Suiping	2800	33.10 N	113.57 E
Suizhong	2796	40.20 N	120.19 E
Šuja	2780	56.50 N	41.23 E
Sukabumi	2802	6.55 S	106.56 E
Sukarno, Pegunungan → Djaja, Puntjak ∧	2802	4.05 S	137.11 E
Sukkertoppen	2734	65.25 N	52.53 W
Sukkur	2794	27.42 N	68.52 E
Sukumo	2798	32.56 N	132.44 E
Sula, Kepulauan II	2802	1.52 S	125.22 E
Sulawesi (Celebes) I	2802	2.00 S	121.00 E
Sullana	2762	4.53 S	80.42 W
Sulligent	2746	33.54 N	88.08 W
Sullivan, Ill., U.S.	2746	39.36 N	88.37 W
Sullivan, Ind., U.S.	2746	39.06 N	87.24 W
Sullivan, Mo., U.S.	2746	38.13 N	91.10 W
Sulmona	2776	42.03 N	13.55 E
Sulphur, La., U.S.	2746	30.14 N	93.23 W
Sulphur, Okla., U.S.	2748	34.31 N	96.58 W
Sulphur Springs	2748	33.08 N	95.36 W
Sulu Archipelago II	2802	6.00 N	121.00 E
Sulu Sea ⌅²	2802	8.00 N	120.00 E
Sulzbach-Rosenberg	2770	49.30 N	11.45 E
Sumatera (Sumatra) I	2802	0.00 S	102.00 E
Sumba I	2802	10.00 S	120.00 E
Sumbawa I	2802	8.40 S	118.00 E
Sumbawanga	2788	7.58 S	31.37 E
Šumen	2778	43.16 N	26.55 E
Sumgait	2766	40.36 N	49.38 E
Summerfield	2744	36.12 N	79.54 W
Summer Island I	2742	45.34 N	86.39 W
Summerside	2739	46.24 N	63.47 W
Summersville	2740	38.17 N	80.51 W
Summerton	2744	33.36 N	80.20 W
Summerville, Ga., U.S.	2744	34.29 N	85.21 W
Summerville, S.C., U.S.	2744	33.01 N	80.11 W
Summit	2746	31.17 N	90.28 W
Summit Lake	2734	54.17 N	122.38 W
Summit Peak ∧	2752	37.21 N	106.42 W
Sumoto	2798	34.21 N	134.54 E
Šumperk	2770	49.58 N	16.58 E
Sumrall	2746	31.25 N	89.33 W
Šumšu, Ostrov I	2784	50.45 N	156.20 E
Sumter	2744	33.55 N	80.20 W
Sumy	2782	50.55 N	34.45 E
Sunagawa	2798a	43.29 N	141.55 E
Sunbright	2744	36.15 N	84.40 W
Sunbury, N.C., U.S.	2744	36.27 N	76.37 W
Sunbury, Pa., U.S.	2740	40.52 N	76.47 W
Sunchales	2764	30.57 S	61.35 W
Sun City	2752	33.36 N	112.17 W
Suncook	2740	43.08 N	71.27 W
Sunda, Selat ⅃⅃	2802	6.00 S	105.45 E
Sundance	2750	44.24 N	104.23 W
Sundarbans ✦¹	2794	22.00 N	89.00 E
Sunderland	2769	54.55 N	1.23 W
Sundsvall	2768	62.23 N	17.18 E
Suniteyouqi	2796	42.32 N	112.58 E
Sunland Park	2752	32.15 N	106.45 W
Sunndalsøra	2768	62.40 N	8.33 E
Sunnyside	2754	46.20 N	120.00 W
Sunnyvale	2756	37.23 N	122.01 W
Sun Prairie	2742	43.11 N	89.13 W
Suntar	2784	62.10 N	117.40 E
Suntar-Chajata, Chrebet ⛰	2784	62.00 N	143.00 E
Sun Valley	2754	43.42 N	114.21 W
Sunyani	2786	7.20 N	2.20 W
Suoche (Yarkand)	2794	38.25 N	77.16 E
Suomussalmi	2766	64.53 N	29.05 E
Suō-nada ⌅²	2798	33.50 N	131.30 E
Suonenjoki	2768	62.37 N	27.08 E
Suordach	2784	66.43 N	132.04 E
Superior, Ariz., U.S.	2752	33.18 N	111.06 W
Superior, Mont., U.S.	2754	47.12 N	114.53 W
Superior, Nebr., U.S.	2750	40.01 N	98.04 W
Superior, Wis., U.S.	2742	46.44 N	92.05 W
Superior, Lake ⊜	2736	48.00 N	88.00 W
Superior Upland ⛰¹	2742	46.00 N	90.30 W
Supetar	2776	43.23 N	16.33 E
Suqian	2800	33.59 N	118.18 E
Suquṭrā (Socotra) I	2790	12.30 N	54.00 E
Şūr (Tyre), Lubnān	2791	33.16 N	35.11 E
Şūr, 'Umān	2790	22.35 N	59.31 E
Surabaja	2802	7.15 S	112.45 E
Surakarta	2802	7.35 S	110.50 E
Şūrān	2791	35.17 N	36.45 E
Surat	2793	21.10 N	72.50 E
Surat Thani (Ban Don)	2804	9.06 N	99.20 E
Surendranagar	2794	22.42 N	71.41 E
Surigao	2802	9.45 N	125.30 E
Surinam □¹	2762	4.00 N	56.00 W
Suring	2742	44.59 N	88.22 W
Sūrmaq	2790	31.03 N	52.48 E
Surry	2744	37.08 N	76.50 W
Surt	2786	31.12 N	16.35 E
Surt, Khalīj C	2786	31.30 N	18.00 E
Surud Ad ∧	2790	10.41 N	47.18 E
Suruga-wan C	2798	34.51 N	138.33 E
Susa	2776	45.08 N	7.03 E
Susanville	2756	40.25 N	120.39 W
Susquehanna	2740	41.57 N	75.36 W
Susquehanna ≃	2740	39.33 N	76.05 W
Sussex	2739	45.43 N	65.31 W
Susurluk	2778	39.54 N	28.10 E
Sutherland, S. Afr.	2788	32.24 S	20.40 E
Sutherland, Nebr., U.S.	2750	41.10 N	101.08 W
Sutherlin	2754	43.25 N	123.19 W
Sutlej (Satluj) (Langchuhe) ≃	2794	29.23 N	71.02 E
Sutter Creek	2756	38.23 N	120.48 W
Sutton, Nebr., U.S.	2750	40.36 N	97.52 W
Sutton, W. Va., U.S.	2740	38.40 N	80.43 W
Suwa	2798	36.02 N	138.08 E
Suwałki	2770	54.07 N	22.56 E
Suways, Qanāt as- ☰	2790	29.55 N	32.33 E
Suwŏn	2796	37.17 N	127.01 E
Suxian	2800	33.38 N	116.58 E
Suzhou (Soochow)	2800	31.18 N	120.37 E
Suzuka	2798	34.51 N	136.35 E
Suzzara	2776	45.00 N	10.45 E
Svalbard and Jan Mayen □²	2732	71.00 N	8.20 W
Svappavaara	2768	67.39 N	21.04 E
Svartenhuk ≻¹	2734	71.55 N	55.00 W
Sv'atoj Nos, Mys ≻	2784	72.52 N	140.42 E
Svatovo	2782	49.23 N	38.13 E
Sveg	2768	62.02 N	14.21 E
Svenljunga	2768	57.30 N	13.07 E
Sverdlovsk	2766	56.51 N	60.36 E
Svetlaja	2784	46.33 N	138.18 E
Svetlyj	2784	58.26 N	115.55 E
Svištov	2778	43.37 N	25.20 E
Svobodnyj	2784	51.24 N	128.08 E
Svolvær	2768	68.14 N	14.34 E
Swainsboro	2744	32.36 N	82.20 W
Swakopmund	2788	22.41 S	14.34 E
Swan Hill	2806	35.21 S	143.34 E
Swan Island II	2760	17.25 N	83.55 W
Swan River	2734	52.06 N	101.16 W
Swansboro	2744	34.36 N	77.07 W
Swansea, Wales, U.K.	2769	51.38 N	3.57 W
Swansea, S.C., U.S.	2744	33.44 N	81.06 W
Swanton	2740	44.55 N	73.07 W
Swartz Creek	2742	42.58 N	83.50 W
Swaziland □¹	2788	26.30 S	31.30 E
Sweden □¹	2766	62.00 N	15.00 E
Sweeny	2748	29.02 N	95.42 W
Sweet Home	2754	44.24 N	122.44 W
Sweetwater, Tenn., U.S.	2744	35.36 N	84.28 W
Sweetwater, Tex., U.S.	2748	32.28 N	100.25 W
Sweetwater ≃	2754	42.31 N	107.02 W
Swellendam	2788	34.02 S	20.26 E
Świdnica (Schweidnitz)	2770	50.51 N	16.29 E
Swift Current	2734	50.17 N	107.50 W
Swinburne, Cape ≻	2734	71.14 N	98.34 W
Swindon	2769	51.34 N	1.47 W
Swinford	2769	53.57 N	8.57 W
Świnoujście (Swinemünde)	2770	53.53 N	14.14 E
Switzerland □¹	2766	47.00 N	8.00 E
Syalach	2784	66.12 N	124.00 E
Sycamore	2742	41.59 N	88.41 W
Sydney, Austl.	2806	33.52 S	151.13 E
Sydney, N.S., Can.	2734	46.09 N	60.11 W
Sydney Mines	2734	46.14 N	60.14 W
Syke	2770	52.54 N	8.49 E
Sykesville	2740	41.03 N	78.49 W
Sykkylven	2768	62.24 N	6.35 E
Syktyvkar	2766	61.40 N	50.46 E
Sylacauga	2746	33.10 N	86.15 W
Sylhet	2794	24.54 N	91.52 E
Sylva	2744	35.23 N	83.13 W
Sylvan Hills	2746	34.51 N	92.12 W
Sylvania, Ga., U.S.	2744	32.45 N	81.38 W
Sylvania, Ohio, U.S.	2740	41.43 N	83.42 W
Sylvester	2744	31.32 N	83.49 W
Sym	2784	60.20 N	88.23 E
Syracuse, Kans., U.S.	2750	37.59 N	101.45 W
Syracuse, Nebr., U.S.	2750	40.39 N	96.11 W
Syracuse, N.Y., U.S.	2740	43.03 N	76.09 W
Syria □¹	2791	35.00 N	38.00 E
Syzran'	2766	53.09 N	48.27 E
Szczecin (Stettin)	2770	53.24 N	14.32 E
Szczecinek (Neustettin)	2770	53.43 N	16.42 E
Szeged	2770	46.15 N	20.09 E
Székesfehérvár	2770	47.12 N	18.25 E
Szentes	2770	46.39 N	20.16 E
Szolnok	2770	47.10 N	20.12 E
Szombathely	2770	47.14 N	16.38 E
T			
Tabarka	2776	36.57 N	8.45 E
Tabasco	2758	32.35 N	114.50 W
Tabatinga, Serra da ⛰²	2762	10.25 S	44.00 W
Tabelbala	2786	29.23 N	3.15 W
Tabernes de Valldigna	2774	39.04 N	0.16 W
Tablas Island I	2802	12.24 N	122.02 E
Tabor, S.S.S.R.	2784	71.16 N	150.12 E
Tabor, Iowa, U.S.	2750	40.54 N	95.40 W
Tabora	2788	5.01 S	32.48 E
Tabor City	2744	34.09 N	78.52 W
Tabou	2786	4.25 N	7.21 W
Tabrīz	2766	38.05 N	46.18 E
Tabūk	2790	28.23 N	36.35 E
Tacámbaro de Codallos	2758	19.14 N	101.28 W
Tachikawa	2798	35.42 N	139.25 E
Tacna, Perú	2762	18.01 S	70.15 W
Tacna, Ariz., U.S.	2752	32.41 N	114.01 W
Tacoma	2754	47.15 N	122.27 W
Tacuarembó	2764	31.44 S	55.59 W
Tacubaya	2758	28.20 N	104.34 W
Tadjerouine	2776	35.54 N	8.34 E
Tadoule Lake ⊜	2734	58.36 N	98.20 W
Taegu	2796	35.52 N	128.35 E
Taejŏn	2796	36.20 N	127.26 E
Tafalla	2774	42.31 N	1.40 W
Taft, Calif., U.S.	2756	35.08 N	119.28 W
Taft, Tex., U.S.	2748	27.57 N	97.46 W
Taganrog	2782	47.12 N	38.56 E
Taglio di Po	2776	45.00 N	12.12 E
Taguatinga	2765	12.25 S	46.26 W
Taguke	2794	32.07 N	84.35 E
Tagula Island I	2806	11.30 S	153.30 E
Tagus (Tejo) (Tajo) ≃	2774	38.40 N	9.24 W
Tahan, Gunong ∧	2804	4.38 N	102.14 E
Tahat ∧	2786	23.18 N	5.47 E
Tahlequah	2748	35.55 N	94.58 W
Tahoe, Lake ⊜	2756	38.58 N	120.00 W
Tahoka	2748	33.10 N	101.48 W
Tahoua	2786	14.54 N	5.16 E
Taibaishan ∧	2796	33.54 N	107.46 E
T'aichung	2800	24.09 N	120.41 E
Taihape	2808	39.40 S	175.48 E
Taihu ⊜	2800	31.15 N	120.10 E
Tailai	2796	46.23 N	123.27 E
Tain	2769	57.48 N	4.04 W
T'ainan	2800	23.00 N	120.11 E
T'aipei	2800	25.03 N	121.30 E
T'aipeihsien	2800	25.00 N	121.27 E
Taiping	2804	4.51 N	100.44 E
Taisetsu-zan ∧	2796	43.30 N	142.57 E

Symbols against index entries represent categories identified in the key on page 2810.

Symbols against index entries represent categories identified in the key on page 2810.

Name	Page	Lat ° ′	Long ° ′
Timişoara	2778	45.45 N	21.13 E
Timmins	2734	48.28 N	81.20 W
Timmonsville	2744	34.08 N	79.57 W
Timor I	2802	8.50 S	126.00 E
Timor Sea ▼[2]	2802	10.00 S	128.00 E
Timpton ≃	2784	58.43 N	127.12 E
Tims Ford Lake ⊜[1]	2746	35.15 N	86.10 W
Tindouf	2786	27.50 N	8.04 W
Tingo María	2762	9.09 S	75.56 W
Tingvoll	2768	62.54 N	8.12 E
Tinharé, Ilha de I	2762	13.30 S	38.58 W
Tinian I	2802	15.00 N	145.38 E
Tinogasta	2764	28.05 S	67.34 W
Tinsukia	2794	27.30 N	95.22 E
Tioga	2740	41.55 N	77.08 W
Tioman, Pulau I	2804	2.48 N	104.10 E
Tionesta	2740	41.30 N	79.27 W
Tipperary	2769	52.29 N	8.10 W
Tipton, Ind., U.S.	2746	40.17 N	86.02 W
Tipton, Iowa, U.S.	2742	41.46 N	91.08 W
Tipton, Mo., U.S.	2746	38.39 N	92.47 W
Tipton, Okla., U.S.	2748	34.30 N	99.08 W
Tipton, Mount ▲	2752	35.32 N	110.12 W
Tip Top Mountain ▲	2734	48.16 N	85.59 W
Tiracambu, Serra do ⋀[1]	2762	3.15 S	46.30 W
Tiranë	2778	41.20 N	19.50 E
Tirano	2776	46.13 N	10.10 E
Tiraspol'	2782	46.51 N	29.38 E
Tirat Karmel	2791	32.46 N	34.58 E
Tire	2778	38.04 N	27.45 E
Tiree I	2769	56.31 N	6.49 W
Tîrgovişte	2778	44.56 N	25.27 E
Tîrgu-Jiu	2778	45.02 N	23.17 E
Tîrgu Mureş	2778	46.33 N	24.33 E
Tîrgu-Ocna	2778	46.15 N	26.37 E
Tírnavos	2778	39.45 N	22.17 E
Tirschenreuth	2770	49.53 N	12.21 E
Tiruchchirāppalli	2793	10.49 N	78.41 E
Tirunelveli	2793	8.44 N	77.42 E
Tiruppur	2793	11.06 N	77.21 E
Tiruvannāmalai	2793	12.13 N	79.04 E
Tishomingo	2748	34.14 N	96.40 W
Tisza ≃	2766	45.15 N	20.17 E
Tit-Ary	2784	71.58 N	127.01 E
Titicaca, Lago ⊜	2762	15.50 S	69.20 W
Titograd	2778	42.26 N	19.14 E
Titovo Užice	2778	43.51 N	19.51 E
Titov Veles	2778	41.41 N	21.48 E
Titule	2786	3.17 N	25.32 E
Titusville	2740	41.38 N	79.41 W
Tiverton	2769	50.55 N	3.29 W
Tivoli, It.	2776	41.58 N	12.48 E
Tivoli, Tex., U.S.	2748	28.27 N	96.53 W
Tizimín	2758	21.10 N	88.10 W
Tizi-Ouzou	2786	36.48 N	4.02 E
Tjirebon	2802	6.44 S	108.34 E
Tlahualilo de Zaragoza	2758	26.07 N	103.27 W
Tlaltenango de Sánchez Román	2758	21.47 N	103.19 W
Tlaxiaco	2758	17.16 N	97.41 W
Tlemcen	2786	34.52 N	1.15 W
Tlêtê Ouâte Gharbī, Jabal ▲	2791	35.20 N	39.13 E
Toba, Danau ⊜	2802	2.35 N	98.50 E
Tobago I	2760	11.15 N	60.40 W
Toba Kākar Range ⋀	2794	31.15 N	68.00 E
Tobarra	2774	38.35 N	1.41 W
Tobermory	2769	56.37 N	6.05 W
Tobruk → Ṭubruq	2786	32.05 N	23.59 E
Tocantínia	2762	9.33 S	48.22 W
Tocantinópolis	2762	6.20 S	47.25 W
Tocantins ≃	2762	1.45 S	49.10 W
Toccoa	2744	34.35 N	83.19 W
Töcksfors	2768	59.30 N	11.50 E
Toco	2764	22.05 S	69.35 W
Tocopilla	2764	22.05 S	70.12 W
Todi	2776	42.47 N	12.24 E
Todos Santos	2758	23.27 N	110.13 W
Todtnau	2770	47.50 N	7.56 E
Togian, Kepulauan II	2802	0.20 S	122.00 E
Togo □[1]	2786	8.00 N	1.10 E
Togwotee Pass)(	2754	43.45 N	110.04 W
Tohopekaliga, Lake ⊜	2744	28.12 N	81.23 W
Toiyabe Range ⋀	2756	39.10 N	117.10 W
Tokara-kaikyō ⋓	2799b	30.10 N	130.10 E
Tokara-rettō II	2799b	29.36 N	129.43 E
Tokat	2766	40.19 N	36.34 E
Tokmak	2782	47.15 N	35.43 E
Tokuno-shima I	2799b	27.45 N	128.58 E
Tokushima	2798	34.04 N	134.34 E
Tokuyama	2798	34.03 N	131.49 E
Tōkyō	2798	35.42 N	139.46 E
Tolbuhin	2778	43.34 N	27.50 E
Toledo, Esp.	2774	39.52 N	4.01 W
Toledo, Ill., U.S.	2746	39.16 N	88.15 W
Toledo, Ohio, U.S.	2740	41.39 N	83.32 W
Toledo, Oreg., U.S.	2754	44.37 N	123.56 W
Toledo Bend Reservoir ⊜[1]	2758	31.30 N	93.45 W
Tolentino	2776	43.12 N	13.17 E
Toljatti	2766	53.31 N	49.26 E
Tol'ka	2784	64.02 N	81.55 E
Tolmezzo	2776	46.24 N	13.01 E
Tolmin	2776	46.11 N	13.44 E
Tolo, Teluk C	2802	2.00 S	122.30 E
Tolono	2746	39.59 N	88.16 W
Tolosa	2774	43.08 N	2.04 W
Tolstoj, Mys ≻	2784	59.10 N	155.12 E
Toluca [de Lerdo]	2758	19.17 N	99.40 W
Tom' ≃	2784	56.50 N	84.27 E
Tomah	2742	43.59 N	90.30 W
Tomahawk	2742	45.28 N	89.44 W
Tomakomai	2798a	42.38 N	141.36 E
Tomar	2774	39.36 N	8.25 W
Tomaszów Mazowiecki	2770	51.32 N	20.01 E
Tomatlán	2758	19.56 N	105.15 W
Tombador, Serra do ⋀[1]	2762	12.00 S	57.40 W
Tomball	2748	30.06 N	95.37 W
Tombigbee ≃	2758	31.04 N	87.58 W
Tombouctou (Timbuktu)	2786	16.46 N	3.01 W
Tombstone	2752	31.43 N	110.04 W
Tomelloso	2774	39.10 N	3.01 W
Tomini, Teluk C	2802	0.20 S	121.00 E
Tommot	2784	58.58 N	126.19 E
Tompkinsville	2746	36.42 N	85.41 W
Tomptokan	2784	57.06 N	133.59 E
Tomra	2768	62.35 N	6.56 E
Tomsk	2784	56.30 N	84.58 E
Toms River	2740	39.58 N	74.12 W
Tonalá	2758	16.04 N	93.45 W
Tonawanda	2740	43.01 N	78.53 W
Tongbai	2800	32.22 N	113.24 E
Tongchuan	2796	35.01 N	109.01 E
Tongeren	2770	50.47 N	5.28 E
Tongguan	2796	34.38 N	110.20 E
Tonghai	2804	24.07 N	102.49 E
Tonghua	2796	41.50 N	125.55 E
Tongliao	2796	43.39 N	122.14 E
Tongling	2800	30.53 N	117.46 E
Tongtianheyan	2794	33.50 N	92.28 E
Tongue	2769	58.28 N	4.25 W
Tongzi	2796	28.08 N	106.49 E
Tonk	2794	26.10 N	75.47 E
Tonkawa	2748	36.41 N	97.18 W
Tonkin, Gulf of C	2804	20.00 N	108.00 E
Tonopah	2756	38.04 N	117.14 W
Tønsberg	2768	59.17 N	10.25 E
Tonstad	2768	58.40 N	6.43 E
Tooele	2752	40.32 N	112.18 W
Toowoomba	2806	27.33 S	151.57 E
Topeka	2750	39.03 N	95.41 W
Topia	2758	25.13 N	106.34 W
Topka, Gora ▲	2784	57.08 N	137.24 E
Toppenish	2754	46.23 N	120.19 W
Tordesillas	2774	41.30 N	5.00 W
Töre	2768	65.54 N	22.39 E
Torez	2782	48.01 N	38.37 E
Torhout	2770	51.04 N	3.06 E
Torino (Turin)	2776	45.03 N	7.40 E
Torit	2786	4.24 N	32.34 E
Torneälven ≃	2766	65.48 N	24.08 E
Torngat Mountains ⋀	2734	59.00 N	64.00 W
Tornillo	2752	31.27 N	106.05 W
Toro	2774	41.31 N	5.24 W
Toronto, Ont., Can.	2740	43.39 N	79.23 W
Toronto, Kans., U.S.	2750	37.48 N	95.57 W
Tororo	2788	0.42 N	34.11 E
Toros Dağları ⋀, Tür.	2766		
	2791	37.00 N	33.00 E
Torquay (Torbay)	2769	50.28 N	3.30 W
Torquemada	2774	42.02 N	4.19 W
Torrance	2756	33.50 N	118.19 W
Torrão	2774	38.18 N	8.13 W
Torre Annunziata	2776	40.45 N	14.27 E
Torre Baja	2774	40.07 N	1.15 W
Torreblanca	2774	40.13 N	0.12 E
Torrecilla en Cameros	2774	42.16 N	2.37 W
Torre de Moncorvo	2774	41.10 N	7.03 W
Torredonjimeno	2774	37.46 N	3.57 W
Torrelaguna	2774	40.50 N	3.32 W
Torrelavega	2774	43.21 N	4.03 W
Torremaggiore	2776	41.41 N	15.17 E
Torremolinos	2774	36.37 N	4.30 W
Torrens, Lake ⊜	2806	31.00 S	137.50 E
Torrente	2774	39.26 N	0.28 W
Torreón	2758	25.33 N	103.26 W
Torres Novas	2774	39.29 N	8.32 W
Torres Strait ⋓	2806	10.25 S	142.10 E
Torres Vedras	2774	39.06 N	9.16 W
Torrevieja	2774	37.59 N	0.41 W
Torridon	2769	57.33 N	5.31 W
Torriglia	2776	44.31 N	9.10 E
Torrijos	2774	39.59 N	4.17 W
Torrington, Conn., U.S.	2740	41.48 N	73.08 W
Torrington, Wyo., U.S.	2750	42.04 N	104.11 W
Torrox	2774	36.46 N	3.58 W
Torsby	2768	60.08 N	13.00 E
Tórshavn	2766	62.01 N	6.46 W
Tortola I	2760	18.26 N	64.37 W
Tortoli	2776	39.55 N	9.39 E
Tortona	2776	44.54 N	8.52 E
Tortosa	2774	40.48 N	0.31 E
Toruń	2770	53.02 N	18.35 E
Toržok	2780	57.03 N	34.58 E
Tosa-shimizu	2798	32.46 N	132.57 E
Tosa-wan C	2798	33.20 N	133.40 E
Tostado	2764	29.15 S	61.45 W
Totana	2774	37.46 N	1.30 W
Toteng	2788	20.22 S	22.58 E
Tot'ma	2780	59.57 N	42.45 E
Tottori	2798	35.30 N	134.14 E
Toubkal, Jbel ▲	2786	31.05 N	7.55 W
Touggourt	2786	33.10 N	6.00 E
Toulon	2746	41.06 N	89.52 W
Toungoo	2804	18.56 N	96.26 E
Tournai	2770	50.36 N	3.23 E
Touside, Pic ▲	2786	21.02 N	16.25 E
Towanda	2740	41.46 N	76.26 W
Tower	2742	47.48 N	92.17 W
Towner	2750	48.21 N	100.25 W
Townsville	2806	19.16 S	146.48 E
Towson	2740	39.24 N	76.36 W
Toyah	2748	31.19 N	103.47 W
Toyama	2798	36.41 N	137.13 E
Toyama-wan C	2798	36.50 N	137.10 E
Toyohashi	2798	34.46 N	137.23 E
Toyonaka	2798	34.47 N	135.28 E
Toyooka	2798	35.32 N	134.50 E
Toyota	2798	35.05 N	137.09 E
Tozeur	2786	33.55 N	8.08 E
Trabzon	2766	41.00 N	39.43 E
Tracy, Qué., Can.	2740	46.01 N	73.09 W
Tracy, Calif., U.S.	2756	37.44 N	121.25 W
Tracy, Minn., U.S.	2750	44.14 N	95.37 W
Traer	2742	42.12 N	92.28 W
Tralee	2769	52.16 N	9.42 W
Tranås	2768	58.03 N	14.59 E
Trancas	2764	26.20 S	65.20 W
Trang	2804	7.33 N	99.36 E
Trangan, Pulau I	2802	6.35 S	134.20 E
Trani	2776	41.17 N	16.26 E
Transylvanian Alps → Carpaţii Meridionali ⋀	2778	45.30 N	24.15 E
Trapani	2776	38.01 N	12.31 E
Trapper Peak ▲	2754	45.54 N	114.18 W
Traun	2770	48.13 N	14.14 E
Traunstein	2770	47.52 N	12.38 E
Traverse City	2742	44.46 N	85.37 W
Travnik	2776	44.14 N	17.40 E
Trecate	2776	45.26 N	8.44 E
Tregosse Islets II	2806	17.41 S	150.43 E
Treinta y Tres	2764	33.14 S	54.23 W
Trelew	2764	43.15 S	65.20 W
Trelleborg	2768	55.22 N	13.10 E
Tremblant, Mont ▲	2740	46.16 N	74.35 W
Tremonton	2752	41.43 N	112.10 W
Tremp	2774	42.10 N	0.54 E
Trempealeau	2742	44.00 N	91.26 W
Trenčín	2770	48.54 N	18.04 E
Trenque Lauquen	2764	35.58 S	62.44 W
Trento	2776	46.04 N	11.08 E
Trenton, Ont., Can.	2740	44.06 N	77.35 W
Trenton, Mo., U.S.	2746	40.05 N	93.37 W
Trenton, Nebr., U.S.	2750	40.11 N	101.01 W
Trenton, N.J., U.S.	2740	40.13 N	74.45 W
Trenton, N.C., U.S.	2744	35.04 N	77.21 W
Trenton, Tenn., U.S.	2746	35.59 N	88.56 W
Tres Arroyos	2764	38.22 S	60.15 W
Três Corações	2765	21.42 S	45.16 W
Tres Esquinas	2762	0.43 N	75.16 W
Três Lagoas	2765	20.48 S	51.43 W
Tres Marías, Islas II	2758	21.25 N	106.28 W
Três Marias, Represa ⊜[1]	2765	18.12 S	45.15 W
Tres Picos, Cerro ▲	2764	38.09 S	61.57 W
Três Pontas	2765	21.22 S	45.31 W
Tres Puntas, Cabo ≻	2764	47.05 S	65.50 W
Três Rios	2765	22.07 S	43.12 W
Treviglio	2776	45.31 N	9.35 E
Treviso	2776	45.40 N	12.15 E
Triangle	2740	38.33 N	77.20 W
Trichūr	2793	10.31 N	76.13 E
Trieben	2770	47.29 N	14.30 E
Trier	2770	49.45 N	6.38 E
Trieste	2776	45.40 N	13.46 E
Tríkala	2778	39.34 N	21.46 E
Tríkomon	2791	35.17 N	33.52 E
Trikora, Puntjak ▲	2802	4.15 S	138.45 E
Trim	2769	53.34 N	6.47 W
Trincat Island I	2802	8.05 N	93.35 E
Trincheras	2758	30.24 N	111.32 W
Třinec	2770	49.41 N	18.40 E
Trinidad, Bol.	2762	14.47 S	64.47 W
Trinidad, Col.	2762	5.25 N	71.40 W
Trinidad, Colo., U.S.	2750	37.10 N	104.31 W
Trinidad, Tex., U.S.	2748	32.09 N	96.06 W
Trinidad I	2760	10.30 N	61.15 W
Trinidad and Tobago □[1]	2760	11.00 N	61.00 W
Trinity	2748	30.57 N	95.22 W
Trinity ≃	2748	29.47 N	94.42 W
Trinity Bay C	2734	48.00 N	53.40 W
Tripoli → Ṭarābulus, Lībiya	2786	32.54 N	13.11 E
Tripoli, Iowa, U.S.	2742	42.48 N	92.16 W
Trípolis	2778	37.31 N	22.21 E
Triton Island I	2802	15.47 N	111.12 E
Trivandrum	2793	8.29 N	76.55 E
Trnava	2770	48.23 N	17.35 E
Trobriand Islands II	2806	8.35 S	151.05 E
Trogir	2776	43.31 N	16.15 E
Troick	2766	54.06 N	61.35 E
Trois-Rivières	2740	46.21 N	72.33 W
Trojan	2778	42.51 N	24.43 E
Trollhättan	2768	58.16 N	12.18 E
Trombetas ≃	2762	1.55 S	55.35 W
Tromelin I	2788	15.52 S	54.25 E
Tromsø	2768	69.40 N	18.58 E
Trona	2756	35.45 N	117.23 W
Tronador, Monte ▲	2764	41.10 S	71.54 W
Trondheim	2768	63.25 N	10.25 E
Trondheimsfjorden C[2]	2768	63.39 N	10.49 E
Tropea	2776	38.41 N	15.54 E
Tropic	2752	37.37 N	112.05 W
Trost'anec	2782	50.28 N	34.59 E
Trotwood	2740	39.48 N	84.18 W
Troup	2748	32.09 N	95.07 W
Trout	2746	31.42 N	92.11 W
Trout Creek	2742	46.28 N	89.01 W
Trout Lake ⊜	2734	60.35 N	121.10 W
Trout Peak ▲	2754	44.36 N	109.32 W
Troutville	2744	37.25 N	79.53 W
Trowbridge	2769	51.20 N	2.13 W
Troy, Ala., U.S.	2746	31.48 N	85.58 W
Troy, Idaho, U.S.	2754	46.44 N	116.46 W
Troy, Kans., U.S.	2750	39.47 N	95.05 W
Troy, Mo., U.S.	2746	38.59 N	90.59 W
Troy, N.C., U.S.	2744	35.22 N	79.53 W
Troy, N.Y., U.S.	2740	42.43 N	73.40 W
Troy, Ohio, U.S.	2740	40.02 N	84.13 W
Troy, Pa., U.S.	2740	41.47 N	76.47 W
Trucial States → United Arab Emirates □[1]	2790	24.00 N	54.00 E
Truckee	2756	39.20 N	120.11 W
Trujillo, Esp.	2774	39.28 N	5.53 W
Trujillo, Hond.	2760	15.55 N	86.00 W
Trujillo, Perú	2762	8.10 S	79.02 W
Trujillo, Ven.	2760	9.22 N	70.26 W
Truman	2750	43.50 N	94.26 W
Trumann	2746	35.41 N	90.31 W
Trumansburg	2740	42.33 N	76.40 W
Trumbull, Mount ▲	2752	36.25 N	113.10 W
Truro, N.S., Can.	2739	45.22 N	63.16 W
Truro, Eng., U.K.	2769	50.16 N	5.03 W
Truth or Consequences (Hot Springs)	2752	33.08 N	107.15 W
Trutnov	2770	50.34 N	15.55 E
Tryon	2744	35.13 N	82.14 W
Tržič	2776	46.22 N	14.19 E
Tsaratanana	2788	16.47 S	47.39 E
Tsaratanana, Massif du ⋀	2788	14.00 S	49.00 E
Tshabong	2788	26.03 S	22.29 E
Tshangalele, Lac ⊜	2788	10.55 S	27.03 E
Tshikapa	2788	6.25 S	20.48 E
Tshofa	2788	5.14 S	25.15 E
Tshuapa ≃	2788	0.14 S	20.42 E
Tsu	2798	34.43 N	136.31 E
Tsuchiura	2798	36.05 N	140.12 E
Tsugaru-kaikyō ⋓	2798	41.35 N	141.00 E
Tsukumi	2798	33.04 N	131.52 E
Tsukushi-sanchi ⋀	2798	33.30 N	130.30 E
Tsumeb	2788	19.13 S	17.42 E
Tsuruga	2798	35.39 N	136.04 E
Tsuruoka	2798	38.44 N	139.50 E
Tsushima II	2798	34.30 N	129.22 E
Tsushima-kaikyō ⋓	2798	34.00 N	129.00 E
Tsuyama	2798	35.03 N	134.00 E
Tual	2802	5.40 S	132.45 E
Tuapse	2782	44.07 N	39.05 E
Tubac	2752	31.37 N	111.03 W
Tuba City	2752	36.08 N	111.14 W
Ṭubruq	2786	32.05 N	23.59 E
Tucano	2762	10.58 S	38.48 W
Tuckerman	2746	35.44 N	91.12 W
Tuckerton	2740	39.36 N	74.20 W
Tucson	2752	32.13 N	110.58 W
Tucumcari	2748	35.10 N	103.44 W
Tucupita	2760	9.04 N	62.03 W
Tucuruí	2762	3.42 S	49.27 W
Tudela	2774	42.05 N	1.36 W
Tudmur (Palmyra)	2791	34.33 N	38.17 E
Tuguegarao	2802	17.37 N	121.44 E
Tugur	2784	53.48 N	136.48 E
Tukangbesi, Kepulauan I	2802	5.40 S	123.50 E
Tuktoyaktuk	2734	69.27 N	133.02 W
Tula, Méx.	2758	23.00 N	99.43 W
Tula, S.S.S.R.	2780	54.12 N	37.37 E
Tulancingo	2758	20.05 N	98.22 W
Tulare, Calif., U.S.	2756	36.13 N	119.21 W
Tulare, S. Dak., U.S.	2750	44.44 N	98.31 W
Tularosa	2752	33.04 N	106.01 W
Tulcán	2762	0.48 N	77.43 W
Tulcea	2778	45.11 N	28.48 E
Tuléar	2788	23.21 S	43.40 E
Tulelake	2756	41.57 N	121.29 W
Tulia	2748	34.32 N	101.46 W
Ṭūlkarm	2791	32.19 N	35.02 E
Tullahoma	2746	35.22 N	86.11 W
Tullamore	2769	53.16 N	7.30 W
Tulsa	2748	36.09 N	95.58 W
Tuluá	2762	4.06 N	76.11 W
Tulufan	2796	42.56 N	89.10 E
Tulun	2784	54.35 N	100.33 E
Tumaco	2762	1.49 N	78.46 W
Tumany	2784	60.56 N	155.56 E
Tumba, Lac ⊜	2788	0.48 S	18.03 E
Tumbes	2762	3.30 S	80.25 W
Tumble Mountain ▲	2754	45.19 N	110.02 W
Tumen	2796	42.58 N	129.49 E
Tumeremo	2762	7.18 N	61.30 W
Tumiritinga	2765	18.58 S	41.38 W
Tumkūr	2793	13.21 N	77.05 E
Tummo	2786	22.40 N	14.10 E
Tumuc-Humac Mountains ⋀	2762	2.20 N	55.00 W
Tumwater	2754	47.01 N	122.54 W
Tunbridge Wells	2769	51.08 N	0.16 E
Tunduru	2788	11.07 S	37.21 E
T'ung ≃	2784	63.46 N	121.35 E
Tungabhadra ≃	2793	15.57 N	78.15 E
Tunica	2746	34.41 N	90.23 W
Tunis	2776	36.48 N	10.11 E
Tunisia □[1]	2786	34.00 N	9.00 E
Tunja	2762	5.31 N	73.22 W
Tunkhannock	2740	41.32 N	75.57 W
Tunxi	2800	29.44 N	118.18 E
Tuobuja	2784	62.00 N	122.02 E
Tuokusidawanling ▲	2794	37.14 N	85.47 E
Tuolumne	2756	37.58 N	120.14 W
Tupã	2765	21.56 S	50.30 W
Tupaciguara	2765	18.35 S	48.42 W
Tupanciretã	2764	29.05 S	53.51 W
Tupelo	2746	34.16 N	88.43 W
Tupiza	2762	21.27 S	65.43 W
Tupper Lake	2740	44.13 N	74.29 W
Tura, Bhārat	2794	25.31 N	90.13 E
Tura, S.S.S.R.	2784	64.17 N	100.15 E
Tura ≃	2766	0.00	0.00
Turan	2784	52.08 N	93.55 E
Turbat	2792	25.59 N	63.04 E
Turbo	2760	8.06 N	76.43 W
Turda	2778	46.34 N	23.47 E
Turgutlu	2778	38.30 N	27.43 E
Turin → Torino	2776	45.03 N	7.40 E
Turkey	2748	34.23 N	100.54 W
Turkey □[1], As., Eur.	2766	39.00 N	35.00 E
Turks and Caicos Islands □[2]	2736	21.45 N	71.35 W
Turku (Åbo)	2768	60.27 N	22.17 E
Turlock	2756	37.30 N	120.51 W
Turneffe Islands II	2760	17.22 N	87.51 W
Turnhout	2770	51.19 N	4.57 E
Turnu-Măgurele	2778	43.45 N	24.53 E
Turon	2750	37.48 N	98.26 W
Turquino, Pico ▲	2760	19.59 N	76.51 W

Symbols against index entries represent categories identified in the key on page 2810.

Name	Page	Lat °′	Long °′
Turrell	2746	35.23 N	90.15 W
Turtle Lake, N. Dak., U.S.	2750	47.31 N	100.53 W
Turtle Lake, Wis., U.S.	2742	45.24 N	92.08 W
Turu ≃	2784	64.38 N	100.00 E
Turuchan ≃	2784	65.56 N	87.42 E
Turuchansk	2784	65.49 N	87.59 E
Tuscaloosa	2746	33.13 N	87.33 W
Tuscola, Ill., U.S.	2746	39.48 N	88.17 W
Tuscola, Tex., U.S.	2748	32.12 N	99.48 W
Tuscumbia	2746	34.44 N	87.42 W
Tuskegee	2746	32.26 N	85.42 W
Tuticorin	2793	8.47 N	78.08 E
Tutóia	2762	2.45 S	42.16 W
Tuttle	2750	47.09 N	100.00 W
Tuttle Creek Reservoir ⊜[1]	2750	39.22 N	96.40 W
Ṭuwayq, Jabal ⋀	2790	23.00 N	46.00 E
Tuxpan	2758	21.57 N	105.18 W
Tuxpan de Rodríguez Cano	2758	20.57 N	97.24 W
Tuxtla Gutiérrez	2758	16.45 N	93.07 W
Túy	2774	42.03 N	8.38 W
Tuy-hoa	2804	13.05 N	109.18 E
Tuz Gölü ⊜	2766	38.45 N	33.25 E
Tuzla	2778	44.32 N	18.41 E
Tveitsund	2768	59.01 N	8.32 E
Tweedy Mountain ∧	2754	45.29 N	112.58 W
Twentynine Palms	2756	34.08 N	116.03 W
Twin Bridges	2754	45.33 N	112.20 W
Twin City	2744	32.35 N	82.10 W
Twin Falls	2754	42.34 N	114.28 W
Twin Peaks ⋀	2754	44.35 N	114.29 W
Twin Valley	2750	47.16 N	96.16 W
Twisp	2754	48.22 N	120.07 W
Two Harbors	2742	47.01 N	91.40 W
Two Medicine ≃	2754	48.29 N	112.14 W
Two Rivers	2742	44.09 N	87.34 W
Tychy	2770	50.09 N	18.59 E
Tyler, Minn., U.S.	2750	44.17 N	96.08 W
Tyler, Tex., U.S.	2748	32.21 N	95.18 W
Tylertown	2746	31.07 N	90.09 W
Tyndall	2750	42.59 N	97.52 W
Tyrma	2784	50.03 N	132.12 E
Tyrone	2740	40.40 N	78.14 W
Tyrrhenian Sea (Mare Tirreno) ▾[2]	2776	40.00 N	12.00 E
Tysse	2768	60.22 N	5.45 E
Tzaneen	2788	23.50 S	30.09 E
U			
Uatumã ≃	2762	2.26 S	57.37 W
Uaupés	2762	0.08 S	67.05 W
Ubá	2765	21.07 S	42.56 W
Ubangi (Oubangui) ≃	2786	1.15 N	17.50 E
Ube	2798	33.56 N	131.15 E
Úbeda	2774	38.01 N	3.22 W
Uberaba	2765	19.45 S	47.55 W
Uberlândia	2765	18.56 S	48.18 W
Ubly	2742	43.43 N	82.56 W
Ubon Ratchathani	2804	15.15 N	104.54 E
Ubundi	2788	0.21 S	25.29 E
Učami	2784	63.50 N	96.29 E
Ucayali ≃	2762	4.30 S	73.30 W
Uchiura-wan C	2798a	42.20 N	140.40 E
Uchta	2766	63.33 N	53.38 E
Ucon	2754	43.36 N	111.58 W
Uda ≃, S.S.S.R.	2784	54.42 N	135.14 E
Uda ≃, S.S.S.R.	2784	56.05 N	99.34 E
Udaipur	2794	24.35 N	73.41 E
Uddevalla	2768	58.21 N	11.55 E
Udine	2776	46.03 N	13.14 E
Udon Thani	2804	17.25 N	102.48 E
Udskaja Guba C	2784	54.50 N	135.45 E
Udža	2784	71.14 N	117.10 E
Ueda	2798	36.24 N	138.16 E
Uele ≃	2790	4.09 N	22.26 E
Uelen	2784	66.10 N	169.48 W
Uelzen	2770	52.58 N	10.33 E
Uere ≃	2786	3.42 N	25.24 E
Ufa	2766	54.44 N	55.56 E
Uganda □[1]	2788	1.00 N	32.00 E
Ugarit ⊥	2791	35.35 N	35.45 E
Uglegorsk	2784	49.02 N	142.03 E
Uglič	2780	57.32 N	38.19 E
Uhrichsville	2740	40.24 N	81.20 W
Uinta Mountains ⋀	2752	40.45 N	110.05 W
Uitenhage	2788	33.40 S	25.28 E
Ujandina ≃	2784	68.23 N	145.50 E
Ujiji	2788	4.55 S	29.41 E
Ujjain	2794	23.11 N	75.46 E
Uka	2784	57.50 N	162.06 E
Ukiah	2754	45.08 N	118.56 W
Ulaanbaatar	2796	47.55 N	106.53 E
Ulaangom	2796	49.58 N	92.02 E
Ulan-Ude	2784	51.50 N	107.37 E
Ulhāsnagar	2793	19.13 N	73.07 E
Uliastaj	2796	47.45 N	96.49 E
Ulindi ≃	2788	1.40 S	25.52 E
Ulithi I[1]	2802	9.58 N	139.40 E
Ulja	2784	58.51 N	141.50 E
Uljanovsk	2766	54.20 N	48.24 E
Ullapool	2769	57.54 N	5.10 W
Ullŭng-do I	2796	37.29 N	130.52 E
Ulm, B.R.D.	2770	48.24 N	10.00 E
Ulm, Mont., U.S.	2754	47.26 N	111.30 W
Ulsan	2796	35.34 N	129.19 E
Ulster □[9]	2769	54.35 N	7.00 W
Ulu	2784	60.19 N	127.24 E
Ulysses	2750	37.35 N	101.22 W
Umag	2776	45.25 N	13.32 E
Uman'	2782	48.44 N	30.14 E
Umanak	2734	70.40 N	52.07 W
Umanak Fjord C[2]	2734	70.55 N	53.00 W
Umeå	2768	63.50 N	20.15 E
Umm Durmān (Omdurman)	2786	15.38 N	32.30 E
Umnäs	2768	65.24 N	16.10 E
Umpqua ≃	2754	43.42 N	124.03 W
Umtali	2788	18.58 S	32.40 E
Umtata	2788	31.35 S	28.47 E
Umvuma	2788	19.19 S	30.35 E
Umzinto	2788	30.22 S	30.33 E
Unadilla	2744	32.16 N	83.44 W
Unalakleet	2738	63.53 N	160.47 W
'Unayzah	2790	26.06 N	43.56 E
Uncompahgre Plateau ⋀[1]	2752	38.30 N	108.25 W
Underwood	2750	47.27 N	101.08 W
Ungava Bay C	2734	59.30 N	67.30 W
União dos Palmares	2762	9.10 S	36.02 W
Unicoi	2744	36.12 N	82.21 W
Unimak Island I	2738	54.50 N	164.00 W
Union, Miss., U.S.	2746	32.34 N	89.14 W
Union, Mo., U.S.	2746	38.27 N	91.00 W
Union, Oreg., U.S.	2754	45.13 N	117.52 W
Union, S.C., U.S.	2744	34.43 N	81.37 W
Union, W. Va., U.S.	2744	37.36 N	80.33 W
Union City, Pa., U.S.	2740	41.54 N	79.51 W
Union City, Tenn., U.S.	2746	36.26 N	89.03 W
Union of Soviet Socialist Republics □[1], As., Eur.	2730	60.00 N	80.00 E
Union Springs	2746	32.09 N	85.49 W
Uniontown, Ala., U.S.	2746	32.22 N	87.31 W
Uniontown, Pa., U.S.	2740	39.54 N	79.44 W
Unionville, Ga., U.S.	2744	31.27 N	83.30 W
Unionville, Mich., U.S.	2742	43.39 N	83.28 W
Unionville, Mo., U.S.	2746	40.29 N	93.01 W
United Arab Emirates □[1]	2790	24.00 N	54.00 E
United Kingdom □[1]	2766	54.00 N	2.00 W
United States □[1]	2736	38.00 N	97.00 W
Unity	2734	52.27 N	109.10 W
Universal City	2748	29.33 N	98.17 W
University	2746	34.21 N	89.32 W
University City	2746	38.39 N	90.19 W
University Park	2752	32.17 N	106.45 W
Upata	2760	8.01 N	62.24 W
Upemba, Lac ⊜	2788	8.36 S	26.26 E
Upernavik	2734	72.47 N	56.10 W
Upham	2750	48.35 N	100.44 W
Upington	2788	28.25 S	21.15 E
Upper Arlington	2740	40.00 N	83.03 W
Upper Arrow Lake ⊜	2734	50.30 N	117.55 W
Upper Red Lake ⊜	2742	48.10 N	94.40 W
Upper Sandusky	2740	40.50 N	83.17 W
Upper Volta □[1]	2786	13.00 N	2.00 W
Uppsala	2768	59.52 N	17.38 E
Upton	2750	44.06 N	104.38 W
Ural ≃	2766	47.00 N	51.48 E
Ural'sk	2766	51.14 N	51.22 E
Ural'skije Gory (Ural Mountains) ⋀	2766	60.00 N	60.00 E
Uranium City	2734	59.34 N	108.36 W
Uravan	2752	38.22 N	108.44 W
Urbana, Ill., U.S.	2746	40.07 N	88.12 W
Urbana, Ohio, U.S.	2740	40.07 N	83.45 W
Urbandale	2742	41.38 N	93.48 W
Urbino	2776	43.43 N	12.38 E
Urfa	2766	37.08 N	38.46 E
Uriah	2746	31.18 N	87.30 W
Urich	2746	38.28 N	94.02 W
Urla	2778	38.18 N	26.46 E
Uruaçu	2765	14.30 S	49.10 W
Uruapan	2756	31.38 N	116.15 W
Uruapan [del Progreso]	2758	19.25 N	102.04 W
Urubamba ≃	2762	10.43 S	73.48 W
Uruguaiana	2764	29.45 S	57.05 W
Uruguay □[1]	2764	33.00 S	56.00 W
Ur'ung-Chaja	2784	72.48 N	113.23 E
Urup, Ostrov I	2784	46.00 N	150.00 E
Ur'upinsk	2766	50.47 N	41.59 E
Uşak	2778	38.41 N	29.25 E
Ushibuka	2798	32.11 N	130.01 E
Ushuaia	2764	54.47 S	68.20 W
Üsküdar	2778	41.01 N	29.01 E
Usolje-Sibirskoje	2784	52.47 N	103.38 E
Ussuri (Wusulijiang) ≃	2796	48.27 N	135.04 E
Ussurijsk	2784	43.48 N	131.59 E
Ust'-Barguzin	2784	53.27 N	108.59 E
Ust'-Belaja	2784	65.30 N	173.20 E
Ust'-Čaun	2784	68.47 N	170.30 E
Ust'-Cil'ma	2766	65.27 N	52.06 E
Ústí nad Labem	2770	50.40 N	14.02 E
Ust'-Kamčatsk	2784	56.15 N	162.30 E
Ust'-Kamenogorsk	2784	49.58 N	82.38 E
Ust'-Kut	2784	56.46 N	105.40 E
Ust'-Labinsk	2782	45.13 N	39.42 E
Ust'-Maja	2784	60.25 N	134.32 E
Ust'-Manja	2766	62.11 N	60.20 E
Ust'-Nera	2784	64.34 N	143.12 E
Ust'urt, Plato ⋀[1]	2766	43.00 N	56.00 E
Ust'-Usa	2766	65.59 N	56.54 E
Utah □[3]	2736	39.30 N	111.30 W
Utah Lake ⊜	2752	40.13 N	111.49 W
Utete	2788	7.59 S	38.47 E
Uthai Thani	2804	15.20 N	100.02 E
Utiariti	2762	13.02 S	58.17 W
Utica, Miss., U.S.	2746	32.07 N	90.37 W
Utica, N.Y., U.S.	2740	43.05 N	75.14 W
Utiel	2774	39.34 N	1.12 W
Utrecht	2770	52.05 N	5.08 E
Utrera	2774	37.11 N	5.47 W
Utsunomiya	2798	36.33 N	139.52 E
Uusikaupunki (Nystad)	2768	60.48 N	21.25 E
Uvalde	2748	29.13 N	99.47 W
Uvdal	2768	60.16 N	8.44 E
Uvinza	2788	5.06 S	30.22 E
Uvs Nuur ⊜	2796	50.20 N	92.45 E
Uwajima	2798	33.13 N	132.34 E
'Uwaynāt, Jabal al- ∧	2786	21.54 N	24.58 E
Uxbridge	2740	44.06 N	79.07 W
Uyuni	2762	20.28 S	66.50 W
Uyuni, Salar de ≚	2762	20.20 S	67.42 W
Užgorod	2782	48.37 N	22.18 E
Uzlovaja	2780	53.59 N	38.10 E
Uzunköprü	2778	41.16 N	26.41 E
Užur	2784	55.20 N	89.50 E
V			
Vaala	2768	64.26 N	26.48 E
Vaasa (Vasa)	2768	63.06 N	21.36 E
Vác	2770	47.47 N	19.08 E
Vacaville	2756	38.21 N	121.59 W
Vach ≃	2784	60.45 N	76.45 E
Vadsø	2768	70.05 N	29.46 E
Vaduz	2770	47.09 N	9.31 E
Váh ≃	2770	47.55 N	18.00 E
Vaiden	2746	33.20 N	89.45 W
Vākhān ≃	2794	37.00 N	72.40 E
Vålådalen	2768	63.10 N	12.57 E
Valcheta	2764	40.40 S	66.10 W
Valdagno	2776	45.39 N	11.18 E
Valdecañas, Embalse de ⊜[1]	2774	39.45 N	5.30 W
Valdemarsvik	2768	58.12 N	16.36 E
Valdepeñas	2774	38.46 N	3.23 W
Valderrobres	2774	40.53 N	0.09 E
Valders	2742	44.09 N	87.53 W
Valdés, Península ≻[1]	2764	42.30 S	64.00 W
Valdivia	2764	39.48 S	73.14 W
Val-d'Or	2734	48.07 N	77.47 W
Valdosta	2744	30.50 N	83.17 W
Vale	2754	43.59 N	117.15 W
Valença, Bra.	2765	13.22 S	39.05 W
Valença, Port.	2774	42.02 N	8.38 W
Valencia, Esp.	2774	39.28 N	0.22 W
Valencia, Ven.	2760	10.11 N	68.00 W
Valencia, Golfo de C	2774	39.50 N	0.30 E
Valencia de Alcántata	2774	39.25 N	7.14 W
Valencia de Don Juan	2774	42.18 N	5.31 W
Valentine, Nebr., U.S.	2750	42.52 N	100.33 W
Valentine, Tex., U.S.	2748	30.34 N	104.29 W
Valenza	2776	45.01 N	8.38 E
Valera	2760	9.19 N	70.37 W
Valga	2780	57.47 N	26.02 E
Valier	2754	48.18 N	112.15 W
Valjevo	2778	44.16 N	19.53 E
Valkeakoski	2768	61.16 N	24.02 E
Valkenswaard	2770	51.21 N	5.28 E
Valladolid	2774	41.39 N	4.43 W
Vall de Uxó	2774	39.49 N	0.14 W
Valle de la Pascua	2760	9.13 N	66.00 W
Valle de Santiago	2758	20.23 N	101.12 W
Valle de Zaragoza	2758	27.28 N	105.49 W
Valledupar	2760	10.29 N	73.15 W
Valle Hermoso	2758	25.39 N	97.52 W
Vallejo	2756	38.07 N	122.14 W
Vallelunga Pratameno	2776	37.41 N	13.50 E
Vallenar	2764	28.35 S	70.46 W
Valletta	2776	35.54 N	14.31 E
Valley Bend	2740	38.46 N	79.56 W
Valley Center	2750	37.50 N	97.22 W
Valley City	2750	46.55 N	97.59 W
Valley Falls	2750	39.21 N	95.28 W
Valleyfield	2740	45.15 N	74.08 W
Valley Head	2740	38.33 N	80.02 W
Valley Mills	2748	31.39 N	97.28 W
Valley Station	2746	38.06 N	85.52 W
Valleyview	2734	55.04 N	117.17 W
Vallo della Lucania	2776	40.14 N	15.17 E
Valls	2774	41.17 N	1.15 E
Valparai	2793	10.22 N	76.58 E
Valparaíso, Chile	2764	33.02 S	71.38 W
Valparaíso, Méx.	2758	22.46 N	103.34 W
Valparaiso, Fla., U.S.	2746	30.29 N	86.30 W
Valparaiso, Ind., U.S.	2746	41.28 N	87.03 W
Valparaiso, Nebr., U.S.	2750	41.05 N	96.50 W
Vals, Tandjung ≻	2802	8.26 S	137.38 E
Valtimo	2768	63.40 N	28.48 E
Valujki	2766	50.13 N	38.08 E
Valverde	2760	19.34 N	71.05 W
Valverde del Camino	2774	37.34 N	6.45 W
Van	2766	38.28 N	43.20 E
Van Alstyne	2748	33.25 N	96.35 W
Vanavara	2784	60.22 N	102.16 E
Van Buren, Ark., U.S.	2746	35.26 N	94.21 W
Van Buren, Maine, U.S.	2739	47.09 N	67.56 W
Van Buren, Mo., U.S.	2746	37.00 N	91.01 W
Vanceburg	2740	38.36 N	83.19 W
Vancouver, B.C., Can.	2734	49.16 N	123.07 W
Vancouver, Wash., U.S.	2754	45.39 N	122.40 W
Vancouver, Cape ≻	2806	35.01 S	118.12 E
Vancouver Island I	2734	49.45 N	126.00 W
Vandalia, Ill., U.S.	2746	38.58 N	89.06 W
Vandalia, Mo., U.S.	2746	39.19 N	91.29 W
Vandalia, Ohio, U.S.	2740	39.53 N	84.12 W
Vanderbilt, Mich., U.S.	2742	45.09 N	84.40 W
Vanderbilt, Tex., U.S.	2748	28.49 N	96.37 W
Vandergrift	2740	40.36 N	79.34 W
Vanderhoof	2734	54.01 N	124.01 W
Vandervoort	2746	34.23 N	94.22 W
Van Diemen Gulf C	2806	11.50 S	132.00 E
Vänersborg	2768	58.22 N	12.19 E
Vangaindrano	2788	23.21 S	47.36 E
Vangunu I	2806	8.38 S	158.00 E
Van Horn	2748	31.03 N	104.50 W
Vanier	2740	45.26 N	75.40 W
Vāniyambādi	2793	12.41 N	78.37 E
Vankarem	2784	67.51 N	175.50 W
Vännäs	2768	63.55 N	19.45 E
Van Rees, Pegunungan ⋀	2802	2.35 S	138.15 E
Vanrhynsdorp	2788	31.36 S	18.44 E
Vansant	2744	37.14 N	82.06 W
Vansbro	2768	60.31 N	14.13 E
Vansittart Island I	2734	65.50 N	84.00 W
Van Wert	2740	40.52 N	84.35 W
Vārānasi (Benares)	2794	25.20 N	83.00 E
Varaždin	2776	46.19 N	16.20 E
Varazze	2776	44.22 N	8.34 E
Varberg	2768	57.06 N	12.15 E
Vardø	2768	70.21 N	31.02 E
Varese	2776	45.48 N	8.48 E
Varginha	2765	21.33 S	45.26 W
Varkaus	2768	62.19 N	27.55 E
Varna	2778	43.13 N	27.55 E
Värnamo	2768	57.11 N	14.02 E
Vass	2744	35.15 N	79.17 W
Vassar	2742	43.22 N	83.35 W
Västerås	2768	59.37 N	16.33 E
Västervik	2768	57.45 N	16.38 E
Vasto	2776	42.07 N	14.42 E
Vas'ugan ≃	2784	59.07 N	80.46 E
Vatican City (Città del Vaticano) □[1]	2776	41.54 N	12.27 E
V'atka ≃	2766	55.36 N	51.30 E
Vatnajökull ⊠	2766	64.25 N	16.50 W
Vaughn	2752	34.36 N	105.13 W
Vaupés (Uapés) ≃	2762	0.02 S	67.16 W
Växjö	2768	56.52 N	14.49 E
Vazante	2765	18.00 S	46.54 W
V'azemskij	2784	47.32 N	134.48 E
V'az'ma	2780	55.13 N	34.18 E
V'azniki	2780	56.15 N	42.10 E
Veblen	2750	45.52 N	97.17 W
Vechta	2770	52.43 N	8.16 E
Veedersburg	2746	40.07 N	87.16 W
Veendam	2770	53.06 N	6.58 E
Vega	2748	35.15 N	102.26 W
Vegreville	2734	53.30 N	112.03 W
Veguita	2752	34.31 N	106.46 W
Vejer de la Frontera	2774	36.15 N	5.58 W
Vejle	2768	55.42 N	9.32 E
Vela Luka	2776	42.58 N	16.43 E
Velenje	2776	46.21 N	15.06 E
Vélez-Málaga	2774	36.47 N	4.06 W
Vélez Rubio	2774	37.39 N	2.04 W
Velike Lašče	2776	45.50 N	14.38 E
Velikije Luki	2780	56.20 N	30.32 E
Velikij Ust'ug	2766	60.48 N	46.18 E
Veliko Târnovo	2778	43.04 N	25.39 E
Vella Lavella I	2806	7.45 S	156.40 E
Velletri	2776	41.41 N	12.47 E
Vellore	2793	12.56 N	79.08 E
Vel'sk	2766	61.05 N	42.05 E
Velva	2750	48.04 N	100.56 W
Venado Tuerto	2764	33.46 S	61.58 W
Venezia (Venice)	2776	45.27 N	12.21 E
Venezuela □[1]	2762	8.00 N	66.00 W
Venezuela, Golfo de C	2760	11.30 N	71.00 W
Venice → Venezia, It.	2776	45.27 N	12.21 E
Venice, Fla., U.S.	2744	27.06 N	82.27 W
Venice, La., U.S.	2746	29.17 N	89.21 W
Venice, Gulf of C	2776	45.15 N	13.00 E
Venlo	2770	51.24 N	6.10 E
Venosa	2776	40.57 N	15.49 E
Ventspils	2780	57.24 N	21.36 E
Ventura	2756	34.17 N	119.18 W
Venus	2744	27.04 N	81.21 W
Venustiano Carranza	2758	16.21 N	92.33 W
Venustiano Carranza, Presa ⊜[1]	2748	27.30 N	100.40 W
Vera	2774	37.15 N	1.52 W
Veracruz	2756	32.25 N	115.05 W
Veracruz [Llave]	2758	19.12 N	96.08 W
Verāval	2794	20.54 N	70.22 E
Verbania	2776	45.56 N	8.33 E
Vercelli	2776	45.19 N	8.25 E
Verchn'aja Amga	2784	59.30 N	126.08 E
Verchneimbatskoje	2784	63.11 N	87.58 E
Verchnij Ufalej	2766	56.04 N	60.14 E
Verchojansk	2784	67.35 N	133.27 E
Verchojanskij Chrebet ⋀	2784	67.00 N	129.00 E
Verchoturje	2766	58.52 N	60.48 E
Verden	2770	52.55 N	9.13 E
Verdigre	2750	42.36 N	98.02 W
Verdun	2740	45.27 N	73.34 W
Vereeniging	2788	26.38 S	27.57 E
Vergara	2774	43.07 N	2.25 W
Vergennes	2740	44.10 N	73.15 W
Verísimo Sarmento	2788	8.10 S	20.39 E
Veríssimo	2765	19.42 S	48.18 W
Vermilion	2740	41.25 N	82.22 W
Vermilion ≃	2746	39.53 N	87.22 W
Vermilion Bay C	2746	29.40 N	92.00 W
Vermilion Bluffs ⍝[4]	2752	40.50 N	108.30 W
Vermilion Lake ⊜	2742	47.53 N	92.25 W
Vermillion	2750	42.47 N	96.56 W
Vermont □[3]	2736	43.50 N	72.45 W
Vernal	2752	40.27 N	109.32 W
Vernon, B.C., Can.	2734	50.16 N	119.16 W
Vernon, Ala., U.S.	2746	33.45 N	88.07 W
Vernon, Conn., U.S.	2740	41.52 N	72.27 W
Vernon, Ind., U.S.	2746	38.59 N	85.36 W
Vernon, Tex., U.S.	2748	34.09 N	99.17 W
Vernon, Utah, U.S.	2752	40.06 N	112.26 W
Vernonia	2754	45.52 N	123.11 W
Vero Beach	2744	27.38 N	80.24 W
Véroia	2778	40.31 N	22.12 E
Verona, It.	2776	45.27 N	11.00 E
Verona, Miss., U.S.	2746	34.12 N	88.43 W
Versailles, Ind., U.S.	2746	39.04 N	85.15 W
Versailles, Ky., U.S.	2746	38.03 N	84.44 W
Versailles, Mo., U.S.	2746	38.26 N	92.51 W
Vert, Cap ≻	2786	14.43 N	17.30 W
Vertientes	2760	21.16 N	78.09 W
Verviers	2770	50.35 N	5.52 E
Vestmannaeyjar	2766	63.26 N	20.12 W
Vesuvio ∧[1]	2776	40.49 N	14.26 E
Vesuvius → Vesuvio ∧[1]	2776	40.49 N	14.26 E
Veszprém	2770	47.06 N	17.55 E
Vetlanda	2768	57.26 N	15.04 E
Vevey	2772	46.28 N	6.51 E
Viadana	2776	44.56 N	10.31 E
Viana del Bollo	2774	42.11 N	7.06 W

Symbols against index entries represent categories identified in the key on page 2810.

Name	Page	Lat °′	Long °′
Viana do Alentejo	2774	38.20 N	8.00 W
Viana do Castelo	2774	41.42 N	8.50 W
Viareggio	2776	43.52 N	10.14 E
Viborg	2768	56.26 N	9.24 E
Vibo Valentia	2776	38.40 N	16.06 E
Viburnum	2746	37.43 N	91.08 W
Vicco	2744	37.13 N	83.04 W
Vicenza	2776	45.33 N	11.33 E
Vich	2774	41.56 N	2.15 E
Vici	2748	36.09 N	99.18 W
Vicksburg	2746	32.14 N	90.56 W
Viçosa	2765	20.45 S	42.53 W
Victoria, B.C., Can.	2734	48.25 N	123.22 W
Victoria (Xianggang), H.K.	2800	22.17 N	114.09 E
Victoria, Sey.	2788	4.38 S	55.27 E
Victoria, Tex., U.S.	2748	28.48 N	97.00 W
Victoria □3	2806	38.00 S	145.00 E
Victoria, Lake ⊜	2788	1.00 S	33.00 E
Victoria, Mount ∧	2804	21.14 N	93.55 E
Victoria de las Tunas	2760	20.58 N	76.57 W
Victoria Falls L	2788	17.55 S	25.51 E
Victoria Harbour	2740	44.45 N	79.46 W
Victoria Island I	2734	71.00 N	114.00 W
Victoria Land ⊹1	2733	75.00 S	163.00 E
Victoria Nile ≃	2786	2.14 N	31.26 E
Victoria Peak ∧	2760	16.47 N	88.36 W
Victoria Strait ≍	2734	69.15 N	100.30 W
Victoriaville	2740	46.03 N	71.57 W
Victoria West	2788	31.25 S	23.04 E
Victorville	2756	34.32 N	117.18 W
Vičuga	2780	57.13 N	41.56 E
Vidalia, Ga., U.S.	2744	32.13 N	82.25 W
Vidalia, La., U.S.	2746	31.34 N	91.26 W
Vidisha	2794	23.32 N	77.49 E
Viechtach	2770	49.05 N	12.53 E
Viedma	2764	40.50 S	63.00 W
Viedma, Lago ⊜	2764	49.40 S	72.30 W
Viella	2774	42.42 N	0.48 E
Vienna			
→ Wien, Öst.	2770	48.13 N	16.20 E
Vienna, Ga., U.S.	2744	32.06 N	83.47 W
Vienna, Ill., U.S.	2746	37.25 N	88.54 W
Vienna, Md.. U.S.	2740	38.29 N	75.49 W
Vienna, Mo., U.S.	2746	38.11 N	91.57 W
Vienna, W. Va., U.S.	2740	39.20 N	81.26 W
Vientiane	2804	17.58 N	102.36 E
Vieremä	2768	63.45 N	27.01 E
Vierwaldstätter See ⊜	2772	47.00 N	8.28 E
Vieste	2776	41.53 N	16.10 E
Vietnam □1	2802	16.00 N	108.00 W
Vigevano	2776	45.19 N	8.51 E
Vignola	2776	44.29 N	11.00 E
Vigo	2774	42.14 N	8.43 W
Vihti	2768	60.25 N	24.20 E
Vijayapuri	2792	16.52 N	79.35 E
Vijayawâda	2793	16.31 N	80.37 E
Vikajärvi	2768	66.37 N	26.12 E
Vila Cabral	2788	13.18 S	35.14 E
Vila Coutinho	2788	14.37 S	34.19 E
Vila do Conde	2774	41.21 N	8.45 W
Vila Fontes	2788	17.50 S	35.21 E
Vilafranca del Panadés	2774	41.21 N	1.42 E
Vila Franca de Xira	2774	38.57 N	8.59 W
Vilanculos	2788	22.01 S	35.19 E
Vila Nova de Famalicão	2774	41.25 N	8.32 W
Vila Nova de Foz Côa	2774	41.05 N	7.12 W
Vila Nova de Gaia	2774	41.08 N	8.37 W
Vila Pery	2788	19.08 S	33.29 E
Vila Real	2774	41.18 N	7.45 W
Vila Velha	2765	20.20 S	40.17 W
Vila Velha de Ródão	2774	39.38 N	7.40 W
Vilhelmina	2768	64.37 N	16.39 E
Vilhena	2762	12.43 S	60.07 W
Vil'kickogo, Proliv ≍	2784	77.55 N	103.00 E
Villa Ahumada	2758	30.37 N	106.31 W
Villa Bella	2762	10.23 S	65.24 W
Villablino	2774	42.56 N	6.19 W
Villa Bruzual	2760	9.20 N	69.06 W
Villacañas	2774	39.38 N	3.20 W
Villacarriedo	2774	43.14 N	3.48 W
Villacarrillo	2774	38.07 N	3.05 W
Villach	2770	46.36 N	13.50 E
Villacidro	2776	39.27 N	8.44 E
Villa Cisneros	2786	23.43 N	15.57 W
Villa Colón (Caucete)	2764	31.40 S	68.20 W
Villa del Rosario	2760	10.19 N	72.19 W
Villa de Méndez	2758	25.07 N	98.34 W
Villadiego	2774	42.31 N	4.00 W
Villafranca del Bierzo	2774	42.36 N	6.48 W
Villafranca de los Barros	2774	38.34 N	6.20 W
Villafranca di Verona	2776	45.21 N	10.50 E
Villa Frontera	2758	26.56 N	101.27 W
Villagarcía	2774	42.36 N	8.45 W
Villaguay	2764	31.55 S	59.00 W
Villa Hayes	2764	25.06 S	57.34 W
Villahermosa	2758	17.59 N	92.55 W
Villa Hidalgo	2756	30.59 N	116.10 W
Villajoyosa	2774	38.30 N	0.14 W
Villalón de Campos	2774	42.06 N	5.02 W
Villalonga	2764	39.55 S	62.40 W
Villalpando	2774	41.52 N	5.24 W
Villa María	2764	32.25 S	63.15 W
Villamartín	2774	36.52 N	5.38 W
Villa Montes	2762	21.15 S	63.30 W
Villanova Monteleone	2776	40.30 N	8.28 E
Villanueva de Córdoba	2774	38.20 N	4.37 W
Villanueva de la Serana	2774	38.58 N	5.48 W
Villanueva de los Infantes	2774	38.44 N	2.59 W
Villanueva del Río y Minas	2774	37.39 N	5.42 W
Villanueva y Geltrú	2774	41.14 N	1.44 E
Villa Pedro Montoya	2758	21.38 N	99.49 W
Villarcayo	2774	42.56 N	3.34 W
Villarreal	2774	39.56 N	0.06 W
Villarrica	2764	39.16 S	72.13 W
Villarrobledo	2774	39.16 N	2.36 W
Villa San Giovanni	2776	38.13 N	15.39 E
Villasayas	2774	41.21 N	2.37 W
Villa Unión	2764	29.24 S	62.47 W
Villavicencio	2762	4.09 N	73.37 W
Villaviciosa de Córdoba	2774	38.05 N	5.01 W
Villena	2774	38.38 N	0.51 W
Ville Platte	2746	30.42 N	92.16 W
Ville-Saint-Georges	2740	46.07 N	70.40 W
Villingen-Schwenningen	2770	48.04 N	8.28 E
Villisca	2750	40.56 N	94.59 W
Villupuram	2793	11.56 N	79.29 E
Vilnius	2780	54.41 N	25.19 E
Vilsbiburg	2770	48.27 N	12.12 E
Vil'uj ≃	2784	64.24 N	126.26 E
Vil'ujsk	2784	63.45 N	121.35 E
Vimianzo	2774	43.07 N	9.02 W
Vina ≃	2786	7.45 N	15.36 E
Viña del Mar	2764	33.02 S	71.34 W
Vinaroz	2774	40.28 N	0.29 E
Vincennes	2746	38.41 N	87.32 W
Vincent	2746	33.23 N	86.25 W
Vindeln	2768	64.12 N	19.44 E
Vindhya Range ⋀	2794	23.00 N	77.00 E
Vineland	2740	39.29 N	75.02 W
Vinh	2804	18.40 N	105.40 E
Vinhais	2774	41.50 N	7.00 W
Vinh-loi	2804	9.17 N	105.44 E
Vinh-long	2804	10.15 N	105.58 E
Vinita	2748	36.39 N	95.09 W
Vinkovci	2778	45.17 N	18.49 E
Vinnica	2782	49.14 N	28.29 E
Vinton	2742	42.10 N	92.01 W
Vipava	2776	45.51 N	13.58 E
Vipiteno	2776	46.54 N	11.26 E
Viranşehir	2791	37.13 N	39.45 E
Virden, Man., Can.	2734	49.51 N	100.55 W
Virden, N. Mex., U.S.	2752	32.42 N	109.00 W
Virginia	2744	36.33 N	78.52 W
Virginia, S. Afr.	2788	28.12 S	26.49 E
Virginia, Ill., U.S.	2746	39.57 N	90.13 W
Virginia, Minn., U.S.	2742	47.31 N	92.32 W
Virginia □3	2736	37.30 N	78.45 W
Virginia Beach	2744	36.51 N	75.58 W
Virginia City, Mont., U.S.	2754	45.18 N	111.56 W
Virginia City, Nev., U.S.	2756	39.19 N	119.39 W
Virgin Islands □2	2760	18.20 N	66.45 W
Virje	2776	46.04 N	16.59 E
Virkie	2769	59.53 N	1.18 W
Viroqua	2742	43.34 N	90.53 W
Virovitica	2776	45.50 N	17.23 E
Virtaniemi	2768	68.53 N	28.27 E
Virudunagar	2793	9.36 N	77.58 E
Vis	2776	43.03 N	16.12 E
Visalia	2756	36.20 N	119.18 W
Visby	2768	57.38 N	18.18 E
Viscount Melville Sound ≍	2734	74.10 N	113.00 W
Viseu	2774	40.39 N	7.55 W
Vishākhapatnam	2793	17.42 N	83.18 E
Visnagar	2794	23.42 N	72.33 E
Vista	2756	33.12 N	117.15 W
Vistula			
→ Wisła ≃	2770	54.22 N	18.55 E
Vitarte	2762	12.02 S	76.54 W
Vitebsk	2780	55.12 N	30.11 E
Viterbo	2776	42.25 N	12.06 E
Vitigudino	2774	41.01 N	6.26 W
Vitim	2784	59.28 N	112.34 E
Vitim ≃	2784	59.26 N	112.34 E
Vitória, Bra.	2765	20.19 S	40.21 W
Vitoria, Esp.	2774	42.51 N	2.40 W
Vitória da Conquista	2765	14.51 S	40.51 W
Vittoria	2776	36.57 N	14.32 E
Vittorio Veneto	2776	45.59 N	12.18 E
Viver	2774	39.55 N	0.36 W
Vivero	2774	43.38 N	7.35 W
Vivian	2746	32.53 N	93.59 W
Vizcachas, Meseta de las ⋀1	2764	50.35 S	71.55 W
Vizianagaram	2793	18.07 N	83.25 E
Vlaardingen	2770	51.54 N	4.21 E
Vladimir	2780	56.10 N	40.25 E
Vladimir-Volynskij	2782	50.51 N	24.20 E
Vladivostok	2784	43.10 N	131.56 E
Vlissingen (Flushing)	2770	51.26 N	3.35 E
Vlorë	2778	40.27 N	19.30 E
Vltava ≃	2770	50.21 N	14.30 E
Vöcklabruck	2770	48.01 N	13.39 E
Vodnjan	2776	44.57 N	13.51 E
Vogelsberg ⋀	2770	50.30 N	9.15 E
Voghera	2776	44.59 N	9.01 E
Vohémar	2788	13.21 S	50.02 E
Vohenstrauss	2770	49.37 N	12.21 E
Voi	2788	3.23 S	38.34 E
Voinjama	2786	8.25 N	9.45 W
Voitsberg	2770	47.03 N	15.10 E
Voj-Vož	2766	62.56 N	54.56 E
Volchov	2780	59.55 N	32.20 E
Volda	2768	62.09 N	6.06 E
Volga ≃	2766	45.55 N	47.52 E
Volgodonsk	2766	47.33 N	42.08 E
Volgograd (Stalingrad)	2766	48.44 N	44.25 E
Volgogradskoje Vodochranilišče ⊜1	2766	49.20 N	45.00 E
Volkovysk	2780	53.10 N	24.28 E
Voločanka	2784	71.00 N	94.28 E
Vologda	2780	59.12 N	39.55 E
Volokolamsk	2780	56.02 N	35.57 E
Vólos	2778	39.21 N	22.56 E
Vol'sk	2766	52.02 N	47.23 E
Volta, Lake ⊜1	2786	7.30 N	0.15 E
Volta Blanche (White Volta) ≃	2786	9.10 N	1.15 W
Volta Noire (Black Volta) ≃	2786	8.41 N	1.33 E
Volta Redonda	2765	22.32 S	44.07 W
Volterra	2776	43.24 N	10.51 E
Volžskij	2766	48.50 N	44.44 E
Vorían Sporádhes II	2778	39.17 N	23.23 E
Voronež	2782	51.40 N	39.10 E
Vorošilovgrad	2782	48.34 N	39.20 E
Voskresensk	2780	55.19 N	38.42 E
Voss	2768	60.39 N	6.26 E
Vostočno-Sibirskoje More (East Siberian Sea) ⊤2	2784	74.00 N	166.00 E
Vostočnyj Sajan ⋀	2784	53.00 N	97.00 E
Votkinsk	2766	57.03 N	53.59 E
Votuporanga	2765	20.24 S	49.59 W
Voyageurs National Park ♠	2742	48.30 N	93.00 W
Voznesensk	2782	47.34 N	31.20 E
Vraca	2778	43.12 N	23.33 E
Vrangel'a, Ostrov I	2784	71.00 N	179.30 W
Vranje	2778	42.33 N	21.54 E
Vrhnika	2776	45.58 N	14.18 E
Vryburg	2788	26.55 S	24.45 E
Vryheid	2788	27.52 S	30.38 E
Vsevoložsk	2780	60.01 N	30.40 E
Vukovar	2778	45.21 N	19.00 E
Vuoggatjålme	2768	66.36 N	16.22 E
Vuoksenniska	2768	61.13 N	28.49 E
Vyborg	2780	60.42 N	28.45 E
Vygozero, Ozero ⊜	2766	63.35 N	34.42 E
Vyška	2780	57.31 N	35.57 E
Vyšnij Voločok	2780	57.35 N	34.34 E
Vysokogornyj	2784	50.09 N	139.09 E
Vytegra	2766	61.00 N	36.24 E
W			
Wa	2786	10.04 N	2.29 W
Wabasca ≃	2734	58.22 N	115.20 W
Wabash	2746	40.48 N	85.49 W
Wabash ≃	2736	37.46 N	88.02 W
Wabasha	2742	44.23 N	92.02 W
Wabeno	2742	45.26 N	88.39 W
Wabowden	2734	54.55 N	98.38 W
Wachapreague	2744	37.36 N	75.41 W
Waco	2748	31.55 N	97.08 W
Waco, Lake ⊜1	2748	31.34 N	97.13 W
Waconda Lake ⊜1	2750	39.30 N	98.35 W
Waddeneilanden II	2770	53.26 N	5.30 E
Waddenzee ⊤2	2770	53.15 N	5.15 E
Waddington, Mount ∧	2734	51.23 N	125.15 W
Wadena	2750	46.26 N	95.08 W
Wädenswil	2772	47.14 N	8.40 E
Wadesboro	2744	34.58 N	80.04 W
Wādī Ḥalfā'	2786	21.56 N	31.20 E
Wadley	2744	32.52 N	82.24 W
Wad Madanī	2786	13.25 N	33.28 E
Wadsworth	2740	41.02 N	81.44 W
Wageningen	2770	51.58 N	5.40 E
Wager Bay C	2734	65.26 N	88.40 W
Wagga Wagga	2806	35.07 S	147.22 E
Wagin	2806	33.18 S	117.21 E
Wagoner	2748	35.58 N	95.22 W
Wagon Mound	2748	36.01 N	104.42 W
Wągrowiec	2770	52.49 N	17.11 E
Wah	2794	33.48 N	72.42 E
Waha	2786	28.16 N	19.54 E
Wahiawa	2757a	21.30 N	158.01 W
Wahoo	2750	41.13 N	96.37 W
Wahpeton	2750	46.16 N	96.36 W
Waialua	2757a	21.34 N	158.08 W
Waianae	2757a	21.27 N	158.11 W
Waidhofen an der Ybbs	2770	47.58 N	14.47 E
Waigeo, Pulau I	2802	0.14 S	130.45 E
Waihi	2808	37.24 S	175.51 E
Waikabubak	2802	9.38 S	119.25 E
Wailuku	2757a	20.53 N	156.30 W
Wainganga ≃	2792	18.50 N	79.55 E
Wainwright	2734	52.49 N	110.52 W
Waipukurau	2808	40.00 S	176.34 E
Waitsburg	2754	46.16 N	118.09 W
Wajir	2790	1.45 N	40.04 E
Wakasa-wan C	2798	35.45 N	135.40 E
Wakayama	2798	34.13 N	135.11 E
Wa Keeney	2750	39.01 N	99.53 W
Wakefield, Nebr., U.S.	2750	42.16 N	96.52 W
Wakefield, Va., U.S.	2744	36.58 N	76.59 W
Wake Forest	2744	35.59 N	78.30 W
Wake Island □2	2730	19.17 N	166.36 E
Wakkanai	2798a	45.25 N	141.40 E
Wałbrzych (Waldenburg)	2770	50.46 N	16.17 E
Walcott, Lake ⊜1	2754	42.40 N	113.23 W
Walden, Colo., U.S.	2752	40.44 N	106.17 W
Walden, N.Y., U.S.	2740	41.34 N	74.11 W
Waldport	2754	44.26 N	124.04 W
Waldron, Ark., U.S.	2746	34.54 N	94.05 W
Waldron, Mich., U.S.	2742	41.44 N	84.25 W
Waldshut	2770	47.37 N	8.13 E
Wales Island I	2734	68.00 N	86.43 W
Walgett	2806	30.01 S	148.07 E
Walhalla, N. Dak., U.S.	2750	48.55 N	97.55 W
Walhalla, S.C., U.S.	2744	34.46 N	83.04 W
Walker	2742	47.06 N	94.35 W
Walkertown	2744	36.10 N	80.10 W
Wall	2750	43.59 N	102.14 W
Wallace, Idaho, U.S.	2754	47.28 N	115.56 W
Wallace, Nebr., U.S.	2750	40.50 N	101.10 W
Wallace, N.C., U.S.	2744	34.44 N	77.59 W
Wallaceburg	2740	42.36 N	82.23 W
Walla Walla	2754	46.08 N	118.20 W
Waller	2748	30.04 N	95.56 W
Wallowa	2754	45.34 N	117.32 W
Walls	2746	34.58 N	90.16 W
Walnut	2746	34.57 N	88.54 W
Walnut Grove	2746	32.36 N	89.28 W
Walnut Ridge	2746	36.04 N	90.57 W
Walpole	2740	43.05 N	72.26 W
Walsall	2769	52.35 N	1.58 W
Walsenburg	2752	37.37 N	104.47 W
Walsh	2750	37.23 N	102.17 W
Walsrode	2770	52.52 N	9.35 E
Walterboro	2744	32.55 N	80.39 W
Walters	2748	34.22 N	98.19 W
Walton, Ky., U.S.	2740	38.52 N	84.37 W
Walton, N.Y., U.S.	2740	42.10 N	75.08 W
Walvisbaai (Walvis Bay)	2788	22.59 S	14.31 E
Wamba ≃	2788	3.56 S	17.12 E
Wamego	2750	39.12 N	96.18 W
Wampsville	2740	43.05 N	75.42 W
Wamsutter	2754	41.40 N	107.58 W
Wanaka	2808	44.42 S	169.09 E
Wanchese	2744	35.51 N	75.38 W
Wanganui	2808	39.56 S	175.03 E
Wanganui ≃	2808	39.56 S	175.00 E
Wangaratta	2806	36.22 S	146.20 E
Wangen [im Allgäu]	2770	47.41 N	9.50 E
Wankie	2788	18.22 S	26.29 E
Wanxian	2796	30.52 N	108.22 E
Wapakoneta	2740	40.34 N	84.12 W
Wapanucka	2748	34.22 N	96.25 W
Wapato	2754	46.27 N	120.25 W
Wapello	2742	41.11 N	91.11 W
War	2744	37.18 N	81.41 W
Warangal	2793	18.00 N	79.35 E
Warden	2754	46.58 N	119.02 W
Wardha	2793	20.45 N	78.37 E
Ware	2740	42.16 N	72.15 W
Warendorf	2770	51.57 N	7.59 E
Warminster, Eng., U.K.	2769	51.13 N	2.12 W
Warminster, Pa., U.S.	2740	40.12 N	75.06 W
Warm Springs, Ga., U.S.	2744	32.54 N	84.41 W
Warm Springs, Oreg., U.S.	2754	44.46 N	121.16 W
Warm Springs, Va., U.S.	2740	38.03 N	79.47 W
Warner	2740	43.17 N	71.49 W
Warner Peak ∧	2754	42.27 N	119.44 W
Warner Robins	2744	32.37 N	83.36 W
Warren, Ark., U.S.	2746	33.37 N	92.04 W
Warren, Ind., U.S.	2742	40.41 N	85.26 W
Warren, Mich., U.S.	2742	42.28 N	83.01 W
Warren, Minn., U.S.	2750	48.12 N	96.46 W
Warren, Ohio, U.S.	2740	41.14 N	80.52 W
Warren, Pa., U.S.	2740	41.51 N	79.08 W
Warren Peaks ⋀	2750	44.29 N	104.28 W
Warrensburg, Mo., U.S.	2746	38.46 N	93.44 W
Warrensburg, N.Y., U.S.	2740	43.30 N	73.46 W
Warrenton, S. Afr.	2788	28.09 S	24.47 E
Warrenton, Ga., U.S.	2744	33.24 N	82.40 W
Warrenton, N.C., U.S.	2744	36.24 N	78.09 W
Warrenton, Oreg., U.S.	2754	46.10 N	123.56 W
Warrenton, Va., U.S.	2740	38.43 N	77.48 W
Warri	2786	5.31 N	5.45 E
Warrina	2806	28.12 S	135.50 E
Warrington	2769	53.24 N	2.37 W
Warrior	2746	33.49 N	86.49 W
Warrnambool	2806	38.23 S	142.29 E
Warroad	2750	48.54 N	95.19 W
Warsaw			
→ Warszawa, Port.	2770	52.15 N	21.00 E
Warsaw, Ind., U.S.	2746	41.14 N	85.51 W
Warsaw, N.C., U.S.	2744	35.00 N	78.05 W
Warsaw, N.Y., U.S.	2740	42.44 N	78.08 W
Warsaw, Ohio, U.S.	2740	40.20 N	82.00 W
Warsaw, Va., U.S.	2744	37.57 N	76.46 W
Warszawa (Warsaw)	2770	52.15 N	21.00 E
Warta ≃	2770	52.35 N	14.39 E
Wartburg	2744	36.06 N	84.36 W
Warthe			
→ Warta ≃	2770	52.35 N	14.39 E
Warwick, Austl.	2806	28.13 S	152.02 E
Warwick, Eng., U.K.	2769	52.17 N	1.34 W
Warwick, R.I., U.S.	2740	41.43 N	71.28 W
Wasatch Plateau ⋀1	2752	39.20 N	111.30 W
Wasatch Range ⋀	2752	41.15 N	111.30 W
Wasco	2756	35.36 N	119.20 W
Waseca	2742	44.05 N	93.30 W
Washburn, N. Dak., U.S.	2750	47.17 N	101.02 W
Washburn, Wis., U.S.	2742	46.41 N	90.52 W
Washington, D.C., U.S.	2740	38.54 N	77.01 W
Washington, Ga., U.S.	2744	33.44 N	82.44 W
Washington, Ind., U.S.	2746	38.40 N	87.10 W
Washington, Iowa, U.S.	2742	41.18 N	91.42 W
Washington, Kans., U.S.	2750	39.49 N	97.03 W
Washington, Mo., U.S.	2746	38.33 N	91.01 W
Washington, N.C., U.S.	2744	35.33 N	77.03 W
Washington, Pa., U.S.	2740	40.10 N	80.15 W
Washington, Tex., U.S.	2748	30.20 N	96.10 W
Washington, Va., U.S.	2740	38.43 N	78.10 W
Washington □3	2736	47.30 N	120.30 W
Washington, Mount ∧	2740	44.15 N	71.15 W
Washington Court House	2740	39.32 N	83.26 W
Washington D.C.			
→ District of Columbia □5	2736	38.54 N	77.01 W
Washington Island I	2742	45.23 N	86.55 W
Wasior	2802	2.43 S	134.30 E
Wassen	2772	46.42 N	8.36 E
Waterbury, Conn., U.S.	2740	41.33 N	73.02 W
Waterbury, Vt., U.S.	2740	44.20 N	72.46 W
Waterford, Eire	2769	52.15 N	7.06 W
Waterford, Wis., U.S.	2742	42.46 N	88.13 W
Waterloo, Bel.	2770	50.43 N	4.23 E
Waterloo, Ont., Can.	2740	43.28 N	80.31 W
Waterloo, Qué., Can.	2740	45.21 N	72.31 W
Waterloo, Ill., U.S.	2746	38.20 N	90.09 W
Waterloo, Iowa, U.S.	2742	42.30 N	92.20 W
Waterloo, N.Y., U.S.	2740	42.54 N	76.52 W
Waterman	2746	41.46 N	88.46 W
Waterproof	2746	31.48 N	91.23 W
Watersmeet	2742	46.13 N	89.11 W
Watertown, N.Y., U.S.	2740	43.59 N	75.55 W
Watertown, S. Dak., U.S.	2750	44.54 N	97.07 W
Watertown, Wis., U.S.	2742	43.12 N	88.43 W
Water Valley	2746	34.09 N	89.38 W
Waterville, Kans., U.S.	2750	39.42 N	96.45 W
Waterville, Maine, U.S.	2740	44.33 N	69.38 W
Waterville, Wash., U.S.	2754	47.39 N	120.04 W
Watford City	2750	47.48 N	103.17 W

Symbols against index entries represent categories identified in the key on page 2810.

mbols against index entries represent categories identified in the key on page 2810.

X

Y

Z

Symbols against index entries represent categories identified in the key on page 2810